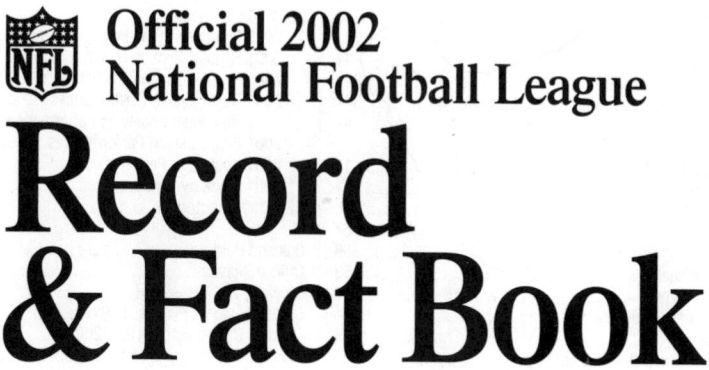

Official 2002
National Football League
Record
& Fact Book

NATIONAL FOOTBALL LEAGUE
280 Park Avenue, New York, N.Y. 10017 (212) 450-2000. NFL Internet Address: http://www.NFL.com

Printed in the United States of America.

A National Football League Book.

Compiled by the NFL Communications Department and Seymour Siwoff, Elias Sports Bureau.

Edited by Randall Liu, NFL Communications Department, and Matt Marini, NFL Publishing Group. Layout by William Tham. Proofread by Joe Velazquez and John Fawaz. Print managing by Dick Falk, Tina Dahl, and Lawson Desrochers. Cover design by Bill Madrid. Typesetting by Jim Gigliotti, Jackie O'Camb, Susan Kaplan, and Samantha Kang.

Statistics by Elias Sports Bureau.

Produced by the Publishing Group of the National Football League, Los Angeles.

Cover photograph of Tom Brady by Allen Kee.

Workman Publishing Co.
708 Broadway, New York, N.Y. 10003
Manufactured in the United States of America.
First printing, July 2002.
10 9 8 7 6 5 4 3 2 1

A National Football League Book
Workman Publishing Co., New York

INDEX

2002 SCHEDULE AND NOTE CALENDAR

(All times local except American Bowl game, which is EDT.)
Nationally televised games indicated by network in parentheses.

Saturday, August 3	American Bowl at Osaka, Japan	
	San Francisco _____ vs. Washington _____	(ESPN) 10:00
Monday, August 5	AFC-NFC Pro Football Hall of Fame Game at Canton, Ohio	
	Houston _____ vs. New York Giants _____	(ABC) 8:00

PRESEASON/FIRST WEEK

Thursday, August 8	New York Jets _____ at Pittsburgh _____	(ESPN) 8:00
Friday, August 9	Cincinnati _____ at Buffalo _____	7:30
	Detroit _____ at Baltimore _____	8:00
	Jacksonville _____ at Atlanta _____	7:30
	Oakland _____ at Dallas _____	8:00
Saturday, August 10	Arizona _____ at San Diego _____	7:00
	Cleveland _____ at Minnesota _____	7:00
	Denver _____ at Chicago (Champaign, Ill.) _____	7:00
	Green Bay _____ at Philadelphia _____	7:30
	Houston _____ at New Orleans _____	7:00
	Indianapolis _____ at Seattle _____	7:00
	Kansas City _____ at San Francisco _____	6:00
	New England _____ at New York Giants _____	8:00
	St. Louis _____ at Tennessee _____	7:00
	Washington _____ at Carolina _____	8:00
Monday, August 12	Miami _____ at Tampa Bay _____	(ESPN) 8:00

PRESEASON/SECOND WEEK

Thursday, August 15	Oakland _____ at Tennessee _____	(ESPN) 7:00
	New Orleans _____ at Miami _____	7:00
	New York Jets _____ at Baltimore _____	8:00
Friday, August 16	Chicago _____ at St. Louis _____	(FOX) 7:00
	Minnesota _____ at Buffalo _____	7:30
	Seattle _____ at San Diego _____	8:00
	Tampa Bay _____ at Jacksonville _____	7:00
Saturday, August 17	Philadelphia _____ at New England _____	(CBS) 8:00
	Cincinnati _____ at Indianapolis _____	7:00
	Dallas _____ at Carolina _____	8:00
	Detroit _____ at Cleveland _____	8:00
	Green Bay _____ at Arizona _____	7:00
	Houston _____ at Kansas City _____	7:30
	New York Giants _____ at Atlanta _____	4:00
Sunday, August 18	Pittsburgh _____ at Washington _____	8:00
Monday, August 19	San Francisco _____ at Denver _____	(ABC) 6:00

PRESEASON/THIRD WEEK

Thursday, August 22	San Diego _____ at St. Louis _____	(CBS) 8:00
Friday, August 23	Baltimore _____ at Philadelphia _____	(FOX) 8:00
	Carolina _____ at New England _____	8:00
	Jacksonville _____ at Chicago (Champaign, Ill.) _____	7:00
	Tennessee _____ at Minnesota _____	7:00
Saturday, August 24	Atlanta _____ at Dallas _____	7:00
	Buffalo _____ at Indianapolis _____	7:00
	Denver _____ at Arizona _____	7:00
	Kansas City _____ at Seattle _____	7:00
	Miami _____ at Houston _____	7:00
	New Orleans _____ at Cincinnati _____	7:30
	New York Giants _____ at New York Jets _____	8:00
	Pittsburgh _____ at Detroit _____	12:30
	San Francisco _____ at Oakland _____	6:00
	Washington _____ at Tampa Bay _____	8:00
Monday, August 26	Cleveland _____ at Green Bay _____	(ABC) 7:00

PRESEASON/FOURTH WEEK

Wednesday, August 28	San Diego _____ at San Francisco _____	6:00
Thursday, August 29	Arizona _____ at Oakland _____	6:00
	Atlanta _____ at Cincinnati _____	7:30
	Baltimore _____ at New York Giants _____	8:00
	Buffalo _____ at Detroit _____	8:00
	Chicago _____ at Miami _____	7:00
	Dallas _____ at Jacksonville _____	8:00
	Minnesota _____ at Pittsburgh _____	7:30
	New England _____ at Washington _____	8:00
	Seattle _____ at Denver _____	7:00
Friday, August 30	Carolina _____ at Cleveland _____	8:00
	Indianapolis _____ at New Orleans _____	6:00
	Philadelphia _____ at New York Jets _____	7:30
	St. Louis _____ at Kansas City _____	7:30
	Tampa Bay _____ at Houston _____	7:00
	Tennessee _____ at Green Bay _____	7:00

FIRST WEEKEND

Thursday, September 5	San Francisco _____ at New York Giants _____	(ESPN) 8:30
Sunday, September 8	New York Jets _____ at Buffalo _____	1:00
(FOX-TV National Weekend)	Baltimore _____ at Carolina _____	1:00
	Minnesota _____ at Chicago (Champaign, Ill.) _____	12:00
	San Diego _____ at Cincinnati _____	1:00
	Kansas City _____ at Cleveland _____	1:00
	Atlanta _____ at Green Bay _____	12:00
	Indianapolis _____ at Jacksonville _____	1:00
	Detroit _____ at Miami _____	1:00
	Philadelphia _____ at Tennessee _____	12:00
	Arizona _____ at Washington _____	1:00
	St. Louis _____ at Denver _____	2:15
	Seattle _____ at Oakland _____	1:15
	New Orleans _____ at Tampa Bay _____	4:15
	Dallas _____ at Houston _____	(ESPN) 7:30
Monday, September 9	Pittsburgh _____ at New England _____	(ABC) 9:00

SECOND WEEKEND

Sunday, September 15	Chicago _____ at Atlanta _____	1:00
(CBS-TV National Weekend)	Tampa Bay _____ at Baltimore _____	1:00
	Detroit _____ at Carolina _____	1:00
	Cincinnati _____ at Cleveland _____	1:00
	Tennessee _____ at Dallas _____	12:00
	Miami _____ at Indianapolis _____	12:00
	Jacksonville _____ at Kansas City _____	12:00
	Green Bay _____ at New Orleans _____	12:00
	New England _____ at New York Jets _____	1:00
	New York Giants _____ at St. Louis _____	3:05
	Arizona _____ at Seattle _____	1:05
	Buffalo _____ at Minnesota _____	3:15
	Houston _____ at San Diego _____	1:15
	Denver _____ at San Francisco _____	1:15
	Oakland _____ at Pittsburgh _____	(ESPN) 8:30
Monday, September 16	Philadelphia _____ at Washington _____	(ABC) 9:00

THIRD WEEKEND
Open Dates:
Baltimore, Jacksonville, Oakland, Pittsburgh

Sunday, September 22	New Orleans _____ at Chicago (Champaign, Ill.) _____	12:00
(FOX-TV National Weekend)	Indianapolis _____ at Houston _____	12:00
	New York Jets _____ at Miami _____	1:00
	Carolina _____ at Minnesota _____	12:00
	Kansas City _____ at New England _____	1:00
	Dallas _____ at Philadelphia _____	1:00
	Cleveland _____ at Tennessee _____	12:00
	San Diego _____ at Arizona _____	1:05
	Buffalo _____ at Denver _____	2:05
	Green Bay _____ at Detroit _____	4:15
	Seattle _____ at New York Giants _____	4:15
	Washington _____ at San Francisco _____	1:15
	Cincinnati _____ at Atlanta _____	(ESPN) 8:30
Monday, September 23	St. Louis _____ at Tampa Bay _____	(ABC) 9:00

FOURTH WEEKEND

Open Dates:
Atlanta, Indianapolis, San Francisco, Washington

Sunday, September 29 (CBS-TV National Weekend)	
Chicago _____ at Buffalo _____	1:00
New Orleans _____ at Detroit _____	1:00
Carolina _____ at Green Bay _____	12:00
New York Jets _____ at Jacksonville _____	1:00
Miami _____ at Kansas City _____	12:00
Houston _____ at Philadelphia _____	1:00
Cleveland _____ at Pittsburgh _____	1:00
Dallas _____ at St. Louis _____	12:00
New York Giants _____ at Arizona _____	1:05
Tampa Bay _____ at Cincinnati _____	4:05
Tennessee _____ at Oakland _____	1:15
New England _____ at San Diego _____	1:15
Minnesota _____ at Seattle _____	(ESPN) 5:30
Monday, September 30 Denver _____ at Baltimore _____	(ABC) 9:00

FIFTH WEEKEND

Open Dates:
Detroit, Houston, Minnesota, Seattle

Sunday, October 6 (FOX-TV National Weekend)	
Tampa Bay _____ at Atlanta _____	1:00
Oakland _____ at Buffalo _____	1:00
Arizona _____ at Carolina _____	1:00
New York Giants _____ at Dallas _____	12:00
Cincinnati _____ at Indianapolis _____	12:00
New England _____ at Miami _____	1:00
Pittsburgh _____ at New Orleans _____	12:00
Washington _____ at Tennessee _____	12:00
San Diego _____ at Denver _____	2:05
Kansas City _____ at New York Jets _____	4:05
Philadelphia _____ at Jacksonville _____	4:15
St. Louis _____ at San Francisco _____	1:15
Baltimore _____ at Cleveland _____	(ESPN) 8:30
Monday, October 7 Green Bay _____ at Chicago (Champaign, Ill.) _____	(ABC) 8:00

SIXTH WEEKEND

Open Dates:
Arizona, Chicago, New York Jets, Philadelphia

Sunday, October 13 (CBS-TV National Weekend)	
Pittsburgh _____ at Cincinnati _____	1:00
Carolina _____ at Dallas _____	12:00
Buffalo _____ at Houston _____	12:00
Baltimore _____ at Indianapolis _____	12:00
Detroit _____ at Minnesota _____	12:00
Green Bay _____ at New England _____	1:00
Atlanta _____ at New York Giants _____	1:00
Jacksonville _____ at Tennessee _____	12:00
New Orleans _____ at Washington _____	1:00
Oakland _____ at St. Louis _____	3:15
Kansas City _____ at San Diego _____	1:15
Cleveland _____ at Tampa Bay _____	4:15
Miami _____ at Denver _____	(ESPN) 6:30
Monday, October 14 San Francisco _____ at Seattle _____	(ABC) 6:00

SEVENTH WEEKEND

Open Dates:
Cincinnati, New England, New York Giants, Tennessee

Sunday, October 20 (FOX-TV National Weekend)	
Carolina _____ at Atlanta _____	1:00
Jacksonville _____ at Baltimore _____	1:00
Chicago _____ at Detroit _____	1:00
Denver _____ at Kansas City _____	12:00
Buffalo _____ at Miami _____	1:00
San Francisco _____ at New Orleans _____	12:00
Minnesota _____ at New York Jets _____	1:00
Tampa Bay _____ at Philadelphia _____	1:00
Seattle _____ at St. Louis _____	12:00
Houston _____ at Cleveland _____	4:05
San Diego _____ at Oakland _____	1:05
Dallas _____ at Arizona _____	1:15
Washington _____ at Green Bay _____	3:15
Monday, October 21 Indianapolis _____ at Pittsburgh _____	(ABC) 9:00

EIGHTH WEEKEND
Open Dates:
Green Bay, Miami, St. Louis, San Diego

Sunday, October 27
(CBS-TV National Weekend)

Pittsburgh _____ at Baltimore _____	1:00
Detroit _____ at Buffalo _____	1:00
Tampa Bay _____ at Carolina _____	1:00
Tennessee _____ at Cincinnati _____	1:00
Seattle _____ at Dallas _____	12:00
Oakland _____ at Kansas City _____	12:00
Chicago _____ at Minnesota _____	12:00
Atlanta _____ at New Orleans _____	12:00
Cleveland _____ at New York Jets _____	1:00
Arizona _____ at San Francisco _____	1:05
Houston _____ at Jacksonville _____	4:15
Denver _____ at New England _____	4:15
Indianapolis _____ at Washington _____	(ESPN) 8:30

Monday, October 28 New York Giants _____ at Philadelphia _____ (ABC) 9:00

NINTH WEEKEND
Open Dates:
Carolina, Denver, Kansas City, New Orleans

Sunday, November 3
(FOX-TV National Weekend)

Baltimore _____ at Atlanta _____	1:00
New England _____ at Buffalo _____	1:00
Philadelphia _____ at Chicago (Champaign, Ill.) _____	12:00
Pittsburgh _____ at Cleveland _____	1:00
Dallas _____ at Detroit _____	1:00
Cincinnati _____ at Houston _____	12:00
Tennessee _____ at Indianapolis _____	1:00
Minnesota _____ at Tampa Bay _____	1:00
New York Jets _____ at San Diego _____	1:05
St. Louis _____ at Arizona _____	2:15
San Francisco _____ at Oakland _____	1:15
Washington _____ at Seattle _____	1:15
Jacksonville _____ at New York Giants _____	(ESPN) 8:30

Monday, November 4 Miami _____ at Green Bay _____ (ABC) 8:00

TENTH WEEKEND
Open Dates:
Buffalo, Cleveland, Dallas, Tampa Bay

Sunday, November 10
(CBS-TV National Weekend)

Cincinnati _____ at Baltimore _____	1:00
New Orleans _____ at Carolina _____	1:00
Detroit _____ at Green Bay _____	12:00
New York Giants _____ at Minnesota _____	12:00
Indianapolis _____ at Philadelphia _____	1:00
Atlanta _____ at Pittsburgh _____	1:00
San Diego _____ at St. Louis _____	12:00
Houston _____ at Tennessee _____	12:00
Seattle _____ at Arizona _____	2:05
Washington _____ at Jacksonville _____	4:05
New England _____ at Chicago (Champaign, Ill.) _____	3:15
Kansas City _____ at San Francisco _____	1:15
Miami _____ at New York Jets _____	(ESPN) 8:30

Monday, November 11 Oakland _____ at Denver _____ (ABC) 7:00

ELEVENTH WEEKEND

Sunday, November 17
(CBS-TV National Weekend)

New Orleans _____ at Atlanta _____	1:00
Cleveland _____ at Cincinnati _____	1:00
Dallas _____ at Indianapolis _____	1:00
Buffalo _____ at Kansas City _____	12:00
Baltimore _____ at Miami _____	1:00
Green Bay _____ at Minnesota _____	12:00
Washington _____ at New York Giants _____	1:00
Arizona _____ at Philadelphia _____	1:00
Pittsburgh _____ at Tennessee _____	12:00
San Francisco _____ at San Diego _____	1:05
Carolina _____ at Tampa Bay _____	4:05
New York Jets _____ at Detroit _____	4:15
Jacksonville _____ at Houston _____	3:15
Denver _____ at Seattle _____	1:15
New England _____ at Oakland _____	(ESPN) 5:30

Monday, November 18 Chicago _____ at St. Louis _____ (ABC) 8:00

TWELFTH WEEKEND

Sunday, November 24
(FOX-TV National Weekend)

Tennessee _____ at Baltimore _____	1:00
Atlanta _____ at Carolina _____	1:00
Detroit _____ at Chicago (Champaign, Ill.) _____	12:00
Jacksonville _____ at Dallas _____	12:00
San Diego _____ at Miami _____	1:00
Minnesota _____ at New England _____	1:00
Cleveland _____ at New Orleans _____	12:00
Buffalo _____ at New York Jets _____	1:00
Cincinnati _____ at Pittsburgh _____	1:00
Green Bay _____ at Tampa Bay _____	1:00
Oakland _____ at Arizona _____	2:05
Kansas City _____ at Seattle _____	1:05
New York Giants _____ at Houston _____	3:15
St. Louis _____ at Washington _____	4:15
Indianapolis _____ at Denver _____	(ESPN) 6:30

Monday, November 25 Philadelphia _____ at San Francisco _____ (ABC) 6:00

THIRTEENTH WEEKEND

Thursday, November 28

New England _____ at Detroit _____	(CBS) 12:30
Washington _____ at Dallas _____	(FOX) 3:05

Sunday, December 1
(FOX-TV National Weekend)

Miami _____ at Buffalo _____	1:00
Baltimore _____ at Cincinnati _____	1:00
Carolina _____ at Cleveland _____	1:00
Chicago _____ at Green Bay _____	12:00
Pittsburgh _____ at Jacksonville _____	1:00
Arizona _____ at Kansas City _____	12:00
Atlanta _____ at Minnesota _____	12:00
Tennessee _____ at New York Giants _____	1:00
Houston _____ at Indianapolis _____	4:05
Denver _____ at San Diego _____	1:05
St. Louis _____ at Philadelphia _____	4:15
Seattle _____ at San Francisco _____	1:15
Tampa Bay _____ at New Orleans _____	(ESPN) 7:30

Monday, December 2 New York Jets _____ at Oakland _____ (ABC) 6:00

FOURTEENTH WEEKEND

Sunday, December 8
(CBS-TV National Weekend)

Cincinnati _____ at Carolina _____	1:00
San Francisco _____ at Dallas _____	12:00
Cleveland _____ at Jacksonville _____	1:00
St. Louis _____ at Kansas City _____	12:00
Buffalo _____ at New England _____	1:00
Houston _____ at Pittsburgh _____	1:00
Atlanta _____ at Tampa Bay _____	1:00
Indianapolis _____ at Tennessee _____	12:00
New York Giants _____ at Washington _____	1:00
Detroit _____ at Arizona _____	2:05
New Orleans _____ at Baltimore _____	4:05
Philadelphia _____ at Seattle _____	1:05
Denver _____ at New York Jets _____	4:15
Oakland _____ at San Diego _____	1:15
Minnesota _____ at Green Bay _____	(ESPN) 7:30

Monday, December 9 Chicago _____ at Miami _____ (ABC) 9:00

FIFTEENTH WEEKEND

Sunday, December 15
(FOX-TV National Weekend)

Seattle _____ at Atlanta _____	1:00
San Diego _____ at Buffalo _____	1:00
New York Jets _____ at Chicago (Champaign, Ill.) _____	12:00
Jacksonville _____ at Cincinnati _____	1:00
Indianapolis _____ at Cleveland _____	1:00
Tampa Bay _____ at Detroit _____	1:00
Baltimore _____ at Houston _____	12:00
Oakland _____ at Miami _____	1:00
Minnesota _____ at New Orleans _____	12:00
Washington _____ at Philadelphia _____	1:00
Carolina _____ at Pittsburgh _____	1:00
Kansas City _____ at Denver _____	2:05
Dallas _____ at New York Giants _____	4:15
Green Bay _____ at San Francisco _____	1:15
Arizona _____ at St. Louis _____	(ESPN) 7:30

Monday, December 16 New England _____ at Tennessee _____ (ABC) 8:00

SIXTEENTH WEEKEND

Saturday, December 21
Miami _____ at Minnesota _____ (CBS) 12:30
San Francisco _____ at Arizona _____ (FOX) 3:00
Philadelphia _____ at Dallas _____ (ESPN) 7:30

Sunday, December 22
(CBS-TV National Weekend)
Detroit _____ at Atlanta _____ 1:00
Chicago _____ at Carolina _____ 1:00
New Orleans _____ at Cincinnati _____ 1:00
Buffalo _____ at Green Bay _____ 12:00
New York Giants _____ at Indianapolis _____ 1:00
Tennessee _____ at Jacksonville _____ 1:00
San Diego _____ at Kansas City _____ 12:00
Houston _____ at Washington _____ 1:00
St. Louis _____ at Seattle _____ 1:05
Cleveland _____ at Baltimore _____ 4:15
Denver _____ at Oakland _____ 1:15
New York Jets _____ at New England _____ (ESPN) 8:30

Monday, December 23
Pittsburgh _____ at Tampa Bay _____ (ABC) 9:00

SEVENTEENTH WEEKEND

Saturday, December 28
Philadelphia _____ at New York Giants _____ (FOX) 1:30
Kansas City _____ at Oakland _____ (CBS) 2:00

Sunday, December 29
(FOX-TV National Weekend)
Cincinnati _____ at Buffalo _____ 1:00
Atlanta _____ at Cleveland _____ 1:00
Minnesota _____ at Detroit _____ 1:00
Tennessee _____ at Houston _____ 12:00
Miami _____ at New England _____ 1:00
Carolina _____ at New Orleans _____ 12:00
Baltimore _____ at Pittsburgh _____ 1:00
Dallas _____ at Washington _____ 1:00
Jacksonville _____ at Indianapolis _____ 4:05
Arizona _____ at Denver _____ 2:15
Green Bay _____ at New York Jets _____ 4:15
Seattle _____ at San Diego _____ 1:15
Tampa Bay _____ at Chicago (Champaign, Ill.) _____ (ESPN) 7:30

Monday, December 30
San Francisco _____ at St. Louis _____ (ABC) 8:00

Wild Card Playoff Games
Site Priorities

Two Wild Card teams (division non-champions with best two records) from each conference and the division champions with the third and fourth-best record in each conference will enter the first round of the playoffs. The division champion with the third-best record will play host to the Wild Card team with the second-best record. The division champion with the fourth-best record will play host to the Wild Card team with the best record. There are no restrictions on intra-division games.

Saturday, January 4, 2003 American Football Conference

_____ at _____ (ABC)

National Football Conference

_____ at _____ (ABC)

Sunday, January 5, 2003 American Football Conference

_____ at _____ (CBS)

National Football Conference

_____ at _____ (FOX)

Divisional Playoff Games
Site Priorities

In each conference, the two division champions with the highest won-lost-tied percentage during the regular season will play host to the Wild Card winners. The division champion with the best record in each conference is assured of playing the lowest seeded Wild Card survivor. There are no restrictions on intra-division games.

Saturday, January 11, 2003 American Football Conference

_____ at _____ (CBS)

National Football Conference

_____ at _____ (FOX)

Sunday, January 12, 2003 American Football Conference

_____ at _____ (CBS)

National Football Conference

_____ at _____ (FOX)

**Championship Games
Site Priorities for
Championship Games**
The home teams will be the surviving playoff winners with the best won-lost-tied percentage during the regular season. A Wild Card team cannot play host unless two Wild Card teams are in the game, in which case the Wild Card team that was seeded highest in the first round of the playoffs will be the home team.

Sunday, January 19, 2003 American Football Conference

_____ at _____ (CBS)

National Football Conference

_____ at _____ (FOX)

Super Bowl XXXVII

Sunday, January 26, 2003 Super Bowl XXXVII at Qualcomm Stadium, San Diego, California

_____ vs. _____ (ABC)

AFC-NFC Pro Bowl

Sunday, February 2, 2003 AFC-NFC Pro Bowl at Aloha Stadium, Honolulu, Hawaii

AFC_____ vs. NFC _____ (ABC)

POSTSEASON GAMES

Saturday, January 4	AFC and NFC Wild Card Playoffs (ABC)
Sunday, January 5	AFC and NFC Wild Card Playoffs (CBS and FOX)
Saturday, January 11	AFC and NFC Divisional Playoffs (CBS and FOX)
Sunday, January 12	AFC and NFC Divisional Playoffs (CBS and FOX)
Sunday, January 19	AFC and NFC Championship Games (CBS and FOX)
Sunday, January 26	Super Bowl XXXVII, Qualcomm Stadium in San Diego, California (ABC)
Sunday, February 2	AFC-NFC Pro Bowl, Aloha Stadium in Honolulu, Hawaii (ABC)

2002 NATIONALLY TELEVISED GAMES
Regular Season

Thursday, September 5	San Francisco at New York Giants (night, ESPN)
Sunday, September 8	St. Louis at Denver (day, FOX)
	Dallas at Houston (night, ESPN)
Monday, September 9	Pittsburgh at New England (night, ABC)
Sunday, September 15	Denver at San Francisco (day, CBS)
	Oakland at Pittsburgh (night, ESPN)
Monday, September 16	Philadelphia at Washington (night, ABC)
Sunday, September 22	Washington at San Francisco (day, FOX)
	Cincinnati at Atlanta (night, ESPN)
Monday, September 23	St. Louis at Tampa Bay (night, ABC)
Sunday, September 29	Tennessee at Oakland (day, CBS)
	Minnesota at Seattle (night, ESPN)
Monday, September 30	Denver at Baltimore (night, ABC)
Sunday, October 6	St. Louis at San Francisco (day, FOX)
	Baltimore at Cleveland (night, ESPN)
Monday, October 7	Green Bay at Chicago (night, ABC)
Sunday, October 13	Oakland at St. Louis (day, CBS)
	Miami at Denver (night, ESPN)
Monday, October 14	San Francisco at Seattle (night, ABC)
Sunday, October 20	Washington at Green Bay (day, FOX)
Monday, October 21	Indianapolis at Pittsburgh (night, ABC)
Sunday, October 27	Denver at New England (day, CBS)
	Indianapolis at Washington (night, ESPN)
Monday, October 28	New York Giants at Philadelphia (night, ABC)
Sunday, November 3	San Francisco at Oakland (day, FOX)
	Jacksonville at New York Giants (night, ESPN)
Monday, November 4	Miami at Green Bay (night, ABC)
Sunday, November 10	New England at Chicago (day, CBS)
	Miami at New York Jets (night, ESPN)
Monday, November 11	Oakland at Denver (night, ABC)
Sunday, November 17	Denver at Seattle (day, CBS)
	New England at Oakland (night, ESPN)
Monday, November 18	Chicago at St. Louis (night, ABC)
Sunday, November 24	St. Louis at Washington (day, FOX)
	Indianapolis at Denver (night, ESPN)
Monday, November 25	Philadelphia at San Francisco (night, ABC)
Thursday, November 28	New England at Detroit (day, CBS)
	Washington at Dallas (day, FOX)
Sunday, December 1	St. Louis at Philadelphia (day, FOX)
	Tampa Bay at New Orleans (night, ESPN)
Monday, December 2	New York Jets at Oakland (night, ABC)
Sunday, December 8	Denver at New York Jets (day, CBS)
	Minnesota at Green Bay (night, ESPN)
Monday, December 9	Chicago at Miami (night, ABC)
Sunday, December 15	Green Bay at San Francisco (day, FOX)
	Arizona at St. Louis (night, ESPN)
Monday, December 16	New England at Tennessee (night, ABC)
Saturday, December 21	Miami at Minnesota (day, CBS)
	San Francisco at Arizona (day, FOX)
	Philadelphia at Dallas (night, ESPN)
Sunday, December 22	Denver at Oakland (day, CBS)
	New York Jets at New England (night, ESPN)
Monday, December 23	Pittsburgh at Tampa Bay (night, ABC)
Saturday, December 28	Philadelphia at New York Giants (day, FOX)
	Kansas City at Oakland (day, CBS)
Sunday, December 29	Green Bay at New York Jets (day, FOX)
	Tampa Bay at Chicago (night, ESPN)
Monday, December 30	San Francisco at St. Louis (night, ABC)

NATIONAL PRIMETIME TELEVISION GAMES AT A GLANCE
(All times local; Thursday/Saturday/Sunday on ESPN, Monday on ABC)

Thursday, September 5	San Francisco at N.Y. Giants (ESPN)	8:30
Sunday, September 8	Dallas at Houston (ESPN)	7:30
Monday, September 9	Pittsburgh at New England (ABC)	9:00
Sunday, September 15	Oakland at Pittsburgh (ESPN)	8:30
Monday, September 16	Philadelphia at Washington (ABC)	9:00
Sunday, September 22	Cincinnati at Atlanta (ESPN)	8:30
Monday, September 23	St. Louis at Tampa Bay (ABC)	9:00
Sunday, September 29	Minnesota at Seattle (ESPN)	5:30
Monday, September 30	Denver at Baltimore (ABC)	9:00
Sunday, October 6	Baltimore at Cleveland (ESPN)	8:30
Monday, October 7	Green Bay at Chicago (ABC)	8:00
Sunday, October 13	Miami at Denver (ESPN)	6:30
Monday, October 14	San Francisco at Seattle (ABC)	6:00
Monday, October 21	Indianapolis at Pittsburgh (ABC)	9:00
Sunday, October 27	Indianapolis at Washington (ESPN)	8:30
Monday, October 28	New York Giants at Philadelphia (ABC)	9:00
Sunday, November 3	Jacksonville at New York Giants (ESPN)	8:30
Monday, November 4	Miami at Green Bay (ABC)	8:00
Sunday, November 10	Miami at New York Jets (ESPN)	8:30
Monday, November 11	Oakland at Denver (ABC)	7:00
Sunday, November 17	New England at Oakland (ESPN)	5:30
Monday, November 18	Chicago at St. Louis (ABC)	8:00
Sunday, November 24	Indianapolis at Denver (ESPN)	6:30
Monday, November 25	Philadelphia at San Francisco (ABC)	6:00
Sunday, December 1	Tampa Bay at New Orleans (ESPN)	7:30
Monday, December 2	New York Jets at Oakland (ABC)	6:00
Sunday, December 8	Minnesota at Green Bay (ESPN)	7:30
Monday, December 9	Chicago at Miami (ABC)	9:00
Sunday, December 15	Arizona at St. Louis (ESPN)	7:30
Monday, December 16	New England at Tennessee (ABC)	8:00
Saturday, December 21	Philadelphia at Dallas (ESPN)	7:30
Sunday, December 22	New York Jets at New England (ESPN)	8:30
Monday, December 23	Pittsburgh at Tampa Bay (ABC)	9:00
Sunday, December 29	Tampa Bay at Chicago (ESPN)	7:30
Monday, December 30	San Francisco at St. Louis (ABC)	8:00

2002

July 8 — Claiming period of 24 hours begins in waiver system.

Mid-July — Preseason training camps open. Clubs not permitted to open official preseason camp earlier than July 5. Veteran players cannot be required to report earlier than 15 days prior to club's first pre-season game or July 15, whichever is later.

July 22* — Signing period ends at 4 P.M., New York time, for Unrestricted Free Agents to whom a June 1 tender was made by Old Club, and for Transition Players. After this date and through 4 P.M., New York time, on November 12, Old Club has exclusive negotiating rights to these players.

*or the first scheduled day of the first NFL training camp, whichever is later.

August 2-5 — Hall of Fame Weekend.

August 3 — American Bowl, Osaka, Japan: San Francisco vs. Washington.

August 5 — Hall of Fame Game, Canton, Ohio: Houston vs. New York Giants.

August 6 — If a Drafted Rookie has not signed with his club by this date, he may not be traded to any other club in 2002.

August 6 — Deadline for players under contract to report to earn a season of free agency credit.

August 8-12 — First Preseason Weekend.

August 10-14 — Deadline for club to provide written notice to certain unsigned players and the NFLPA of its intent to place them on the Exempt List if they fail to report no later than one day prior to the club's second pre-season game. Any player who fails to report prior to the deadline will be ineligible to play or receive compensation for at least three games (preseason or regular season) from the time that he reports.

August 13 — Clubs must be in compliance with NFLEL incentive chart. All bonus exemptions must be identified no later than 4 P.M., New York time.

August 27 — Roster cut-down to maximum of 65 players on Active List by 4 P.M., New York time.

August 28 — All tryouts on this date and for the remainder of the season must be reported to the League office.

September 1 — Roster cut-down to maximum of 53 players on Active/Inactive List by 4 P.M., New York time. Clubs may dress minimum of 42 and maximum of 45 players and Third Quarterback for each regular season and post-season game.

September 1 — Simultaneously with the cut-down to 53 (56 for Houston), clubs that have players in the categories of Active/Physically Unable to Perform or Active/Non-Football Injury or Illness must take one of the following options: place player on Reserve/Physically Unable to Perform or Reserve/Non-Football Injury or Illness, whichever is applicable; ask waivers; terminate; trade; or continue to count him on Active List.

September 2 — After 4 P.M., New York time, clubs may establish a Practice Squad of five players by signing free agents who do not have an accrued season of free agency credit or who were on the 45-player Active List for less than nine regular season games during their only Accrued Season(s). A player cannot participate on the Practice Squad for more than two seasons.

September 3 — All clubs are required to file a personnel (injury) report with their conference Director of Information by 1 P.M., New York time, on this Tuesday and thereafter on each Wednesday before a regular-season game. Such report is to be updated by 1 P.M., New York time, each Thursday. An update must also be reported if there is any change in a player's condition after Thursday.

September 4 — Beginning at 4 P.M., New York time, Team Salary includes all players receiving compensation under their 2002 contracts. Top 51 rule is no longer in effect.

September 5-9 — Regular Season opens.

September 5-10 — Beginning on these dates vested veterans terminated from the Active List or Inactive List (and from Reserve/Injured if the player is placed on Reserve/Injured after the beginning of the regular season) are entitled to receive, after the end of the regular-season schedule, Termination Pay pursuant to the terms of the 1993 CBA.

September 23 — Houston must reduce its Active/Inactive List to a maximum of 53 players by 4 P.M., New York time.

September 24 — Priority on multiple waiver claims is now based on the current season's standing.

October 15 — Beginning the day after the conclusion of the sixth regular season weekend and continuing through the day after the conclusion of the ninth regular season weekend, clubs are permitted to begin practicing players on Reserve/Physically Unable to Perform and Reserve/Non-Football Injury or Illness for a period not to exceed 21 days. Players may be activated during the 21-day practice period or until 4 P.M., New York time, on the day after the conclusion of the 21-day period.

October 15 — All trading ends at 4 P.M., New York time.

October 16 — Players with at least four previous pension-credited seasons are subject to the waiver system for the remainder of the regular season and postseason.

November 4 — Deadline at 4 P.M., New York time, for an increase in a player's 2002 Salary to be counted as Salary for the current year. Any notice of an increase in a player's 2002 Salary received by the NFLMC after this deadline will be treated as a Signing Bonus.

November 12 — Signing period ends at 4 P.M., New York time, for Franchise Players who are eligible to receive Offer Sheets.

November 12 — Deadline for clubs to sign by 4 P.M., New York time, their unsigned Franchise and Transition Players, including Franchise Players who were eligible to receive Offer

	Sheets until this date. If still unsigned after this date, such players are prohibited from playing in NFL in 2002.
November 12	Deadline for clubs to sign by 4 P.M., New York time, their Unrestricted Free Agents to whom June 1 tender was made. If still unsigned after this date, such players are prohibited from playing in NFL in 2002.
November 12	Deadline for clubs to sign by 4 P.M., New York time, their Restricted Free Agents to whom June 1 tender was made. If such players remain unsigned, they are prohibited from playing in NFL in 2002.
November 12	Deadline for clubs to sign Drafted players by 4 P.M., New York time. If such players remain unsigned, they are prohibited from playing in NFL in 2002.
November 30	Deadline for reinstatement of players in Reserve List categories of Retired, Did Not Report, and Exclusive Rights, and of players who were placed on Reserve/Left Squad in a previous season.
December 27	Deadline for waiver requests in 2002, except for "special waiver requests" which have a 10-day claiming period, with termination or assignment delayed until after the Super Bowl.
December 31	Clubs may begin signing free agent players for the 2003 season.

2003

January 4-5	Wild Card Playoff Games.
January 11-12	Divisional Playoff Games.
January 18	Senior Bowl, Mobile, Alabama.
January 19	AFC and NFC Championship Games.
January 26	Super Bowl XXXVII, Qualcomm Stadium, San Diego, California.
†February 3	AFC-NFC Pro Bowl, Honolulu, Hawaii.
†February 10	First day clubs can designate Franchise or Transition players.
†February 20-24	Combine Timing and Testing, RCA Dome, Indianapolis, Indiana.
†February 24	Waiver system begins for 2003. Waivers will expire on the first business day of the new League Year. Players with at least four previous pension-credited seasons that a club desires to terminate are not subject to the waiver system until after the trading deadline.
†February 24	Deadline at 4 P.M., New York time, for clubs to designate Franchise and Transition Players.
†March 3	Expiration date of all player contracts due to expire in 2003.
†March 3	Deadline for exercising options for 2003 on all players who have option clauses in their 2002 contracts.
†March 3	Deadline for submission of Qualifying Offers by clubs to their Restricted Free Agents whose contracts have expired and to whom they desire to retain a Right of First Refusal/Compensation.
†March 3	Deadline for clubs to submit offer of minimum salary to retain exclusive negotiating rights to their players with fewer than three seasons of free agency credit whose contracts have expired.
†March 4	Free Agency period begins.
†March 4	Trading period begins for 2003 after expiration of all 2002 contracts.
†March 4	A claiming period of three business days is in effect for waiver requests made prior to May 1.
March 23-26	NFL Annual Meeting, Arizona Biltmore, Phoenix, Arizona.
April 17	Deadline for signing of Offer Sheets by Restricted Free Agents.
April 24	Deadline for Old Club to exercise Right of First Refusal to Restricted Free Agents.
April 26-27	Annual Player Selection Meeting, New York, N.Y.
May 1	Claiming period of 10 calendar days begins in waiver system.
May 16	Except for a three-day mini-camp held within 15 days of the draft, this is the first day that players eligible for the 2003 Draft are permitted to participate in mini-camps, practices, or meetings. If final examinations at a player's school conclude after this date, the player is prohibited from participating in any activities until after the player's final day of examinations. If the player has left or leaves school, he is prohibited from participating in any club activities until after the final day of examinations at his school.
June 1	Deadline for Old Club to send tender to its unsigned Restricted Free Agents or to extend Qualifying Offer, whichever is greater, in order to retain rights.
June 1	Deadline for Old Club to send tender to its unsigned Unrestricted Free Agents to retain rights if player is not signed by another club by July 22.
June 2	Any unamortized signing bonus amounts will be included in the succeeding year's Team Salary for any players removed from the team's roster other than by trade.
June 15	Deadline for club to withdraw Qualifying Offer to Restricted Free Agents and still retain exclusive negotiating rights by substituting tender of one-year contract at 110 percent of previous year's Paragraph 5 salary (with all other terms carried forward unchanged).

2004

†February 1	Super Bowl XXXVIII, Reliant Stadium, Houston, Texas.

2005

†February 6	Super Bowl XXXIX, ALLTEL Stadium, Jacksonville, Florida.

2006

†February 5	Super Bowl XL, Ford Field, Detroit, Michigan.
†Tentative	

The NFL is online to provide fans and media quick and easy access to all the latest professional football information.

NFL.COM—(http://www.NFL.com or AOL Keyword: NFL.com)

NFL.com, the league's year-round home page on the Internet, enters its sixth season in cyberspace. The site provides NFL information during the regular season, postseason, and offseason, including:

NEWS/STATS: Up-to-the-minute news from around the league, plus game previews, injury reports, and player and team stats.

TEAM AREAS: Customized areas for all 32 clubs, featuring updated rosters, depth carts, and all the latest news from the teams.

GAMEDAY COVERAGE: Live game coverage with play-by-play, scores, and statistics, including graphical drive charts and comprehensive scoreboard that does not require reloading to get the latest information.

VIDEO HIGHLIGHTS: The site showcases NFL Films video highlights of the previous week's games as well as upcoming matchups. Video also supports feature stories and team highlight clips from every game last season.

SUPERBOWL.COM—(http://SuperBowl.com)

Look for SuperBowl.com in late December for complete coverage of the playoffs and Super Bowl XXXVII. The multimedia site follows all postseason action and features audio and video clips of past Super Bowls.

During the week leading up to Super Bowl XXXVII, the site will go 'live' from San Diego, providing coverage of events, press conferences, and chats with Super Bowl players and coaches.

On Super Bowl Sunday, SuperBowl.com will showcase a live Internet cybercast, complete with online commentators calling the action. The site also features digital photos from the game, live public address audio and press-box announcements, and live audio from foreign broadcasts.

NFLEUROPE.COM—(http://NFLEurope.com)

The official site of NFL Europe League provides in-depth information on the six teams and their players, streaming video of one game each weekend, live audio broadcasts of all games, and weekly video highlights of game action. In addition, the site includes weekly player diaries from NFL allocated players, as well as a complete league stats package.

PLAYFOOTBALL.COM—(http://www.playfootball.com)

Play Football.com is the NFL's official web site for kids. It offers boys and girls an interactive sports destination where kids and their families can get actively involved with the NFL, including information on national youth football programs such as Punt, Pass & Kick, and NFL Flag. Youths also can find profiles on NFL players and people behind the scenes of the NFL, vote on weekly MVPs and Plays of the Week, play challenging games, and learn about football strategy and skill.

NFLHS.COM—(http://nflhs.com)

The League's web site dedicated to high school and youth football. NFLHS.com covers high school football on a nation-wide basis and also looks into the high school careers of current and former NFL players and coaches. NFLHS.com goes behind the scenes at major NFL events, such as the Super Bowl and the Draft, and provides coverage from a high school perspective. The site is packed with tips and drills, health and safety information, academic tips and news on the NFL's and its teams' efforts in the community. Whatever you are looking for regarding high school football, we've got it!

PROFOOTBALLHOF.com—(http://www.profootballhof.com)

Profootballhof.com is the official site of the Pro Football Hall of Fame in Canton, Ohio. In addition to a complete visitor's guide to the Hall, the site features bios, stories and Q & A's with Hall of Famers, a detailed archive of football history and information on appearances by members of the Hall.

OFFICIAL NFL TEAM SITES

In addition to a dedicated area on NFL.com, all 32 teams have their own Web sites, which have separate URLs, and are linked from NFL.com.

Arizona Cardinals (www.azcardinals.com)
Atlanta Falcons (www.atlantafalcons.com)
Baltimore Ravens (www.baltimoreravens.com)
Buffalo Bills (www.buffalobills.com)
Carolina Panthers (www.panthers.com)
Cincinnati Bengals (www.bengals.com)
Chicago Bears (www.chicagobears.com)
Cleveland Browns (www.clevelandbrowns.com)
Dallas Cowboys (www.dallascowboys.com)
Denver Broncos (www.denverbroncos.com)
Detroit Lions (www.detroitlions.com)
Green Bay Packers (www.packers.com)
Houston Texans (www.houstontexans.com)
Indianapolis Colts (www.colts.com)
Jacksonville Jaguars (www.jaguars.com)
Kansas City Chiefs (www.kcchiefs.com)
Miami Dolphins (www.miamidolphins.com)
Minnesota Vikings (www.vikings.com)
New England Patriots (www.patriots.com)
New Orleans Saints (www.neworleanssaints.com)
New York Giants (www.giants.com)
New York Jets (www.newyorkjets.com)
Oakland Raiders (www.raiders.com)
Philadelphia Eagles (www.philadelphiaeagles.com)
Pittsburgh Steelers (www.steelers.com)
San Diego Chargers (www.chargers.com)
St. Louis Rams (www.stlouisrams.com)
San Francisco 49ers (www.sf49ers.com)
Seattle Seahawks (www.seahawks.com)
Tampa Bay Buccaneers (www.buccaneers.com)
Tennessee Titans (www.titansonline.com)
Washington Redskins (www.redskins.com)

The NFL rates its passers for statistical purposes against a fixed performance standard based on statistical achievements of all qualified pro passers since 1960. The current system replaced one that rated passers in relation to their position in a total group based on various criteria. The current system, which was adopted in 1973, removes inequities that existed in the former method and, at the same time, provides a means of comparing passing performances from one season to the next.

It is important to remember that the system is used to rate passers, not quarterbacks. Statistics do not reflect leadership, play-calling, and other intangible factors that go into making a successful professional quarterback. Four categories are used as a basis for compiling a rating:

—Percentage of completions per attempt
—Average yards gained per attempt
—Percentage of touchdown passes per attempt
—Percentage of interceptions per attempt

The average standard is 1.000. The bottom is .000. To earn a 2.000 rating, a passer must perform at exceptional levels, i.e., 70 percent in completions, 10 percent in touchdowns, 1.5 percent in interceptions, and 11 yards average gain per pass attempt. The maximum a passer can receive in any category is 2.375.

For example, to gain a 2.375 in completion percentage, a passer would have to complete 77.5 percent of his passes. The NFL record is 70.55 by Ken Anderson (Cincinnati, 1982). To earn a 2.375 in percentage of touchdowns, a passer would have to achieve a percentage of 11.9. The record is 13.9 by Sid Luckman (Chicago, 1943). To gain 2.375 in percentage of interceptions, a passer would have to go the entire season without an interception. The 2.375 figure in average yards is 12.50, compared with the NFL record of 11.17 by Tommy O'Connell (Cleveland, 1957).

In order to make the rating more understandable, the point rating is then converted into a scale of 100, with 158.3 being the highest rating a passer can achieve. In cases where statistical performance has been superior, it is possible for a passer to surpass a 100 rating. For example, take Steve Young's record-setting season in 1994 when he completed 324 of 461 passes for 3,969 yards, 35 touchdowns, and 10 interceptions. The four calculations would be:

—Percentage of Completions—324 of 461 is 70.28 percent. Subtract 30 from the completion percentage (40.28) and multiply the result by 0.05. The result is a point rating of 2.014.
Note: If the result is less than zero (Comp. Pct. less than 30.0), award zero points. If the results are greater than 2.375 (Comp. Pct. greater than 77.5), award 2.375.

—Average Yards Gained Per Attempt—3,969 yards divided by 461 attempts is 8.61. Subtract three yards from yards-per-attempt (5.61) and multiply the result by 0.25. The result is 1.403.
Note: If the result is less than zero (yards per attempt less than 3.0), award zero points. If the result is greater than 2.375 (yards per attempt greater than 12.5), award 2.375 points.

—Percentage of Touchdown Passes—35 touchdowns in 461 attempts is 7.59 percent. Multiply the touchdown percentage by 0.2. The result is 1.518.
Note: If the result is greater than 2.375 (touchdown percentage greater than 11.875), award 2.375.

—Percentage of Interceptions—10 interceptions in 461 attempts is 2.17 percent. Multiply the interception percentage by 0.25 (0.542) and subtract the number from 2.375. The result is 1.833.
Note: If the result is less than zero (interception percentage greater than 9.5), award zero points.

The sum of the four steps is (2.014 + 1.403 + 1.518 + 1.833) 6.768. The sum is then divided by six (1.128) and multiplied by 100. In this case, the result is 112.8. This same formula can be used to determine a passer rating for any player who attempts at least one pass.

The following is a list of qualifying passers who had a single-season passer rating of 100 or higher:

Player, Team	Season	Rating	Att.	Comp.	Pct.	Yds.	Avg.	TD	TD Pct.	Int.	Int. Pct.
Steve Young, San Francisco	1994	112.8	461	324	70.2	3,969	8.61	35	7.6	10	2.2
Joe Montana, San Francisco	1989	112.4	386	271	70.2	3,521	9.12	26	6.7	8	2.1
Milt Plum, Cleveland	1960	110.4	250	151	60.4	2,297	9.19	21	8.4	5	2.0
Sammy Baugh, Washington	1945	109.9	182	128	70.3	1,669	9.17	11	6.0	4	2.2
Kurt Warner, St. Louis	1999	109.2	499	325	65.1	4,353	8.72	41	8.2	13	2.6
Dan Marino, Miami	1984	108.9	564	362	64.2	5,084	9.01	48	8.5	17	3.0
Sid Luckman, Chicago Bears	1943	107.5	202	110	54.5	2,194	10.86	28	13.9	12	5.9
Steve Young, San Francisco	1992	107.0	402	268	66.7	3,465	8.62	25	6.2	7	1.7
Randall Cunningham, Minnesota	1998	106.0	425	259	60.9	3,704	8.72	34	8.0	10	2.4
Bart Starr, Green Bay	1966	105.0	251	156	62.2	2,257	8.99	14	5.6	3	1.2
Roger Staubach, Dallas	1971	104.8	211	126	59.7	1,882	8.92	15	7.1	4	1.9
Y.A. Tittle, N.Y. Giants	1963	104.8	367	221	60.2	3,145	8.57	36	9.8	14	3.8
Steve Young, San Francisco	1997	104.7	356	241	67.7	3,029	8.51	19	5.3	6	1.7
Bart Starr, Green Bay	1968	104.3	171	109	63.7	1,617	9.46	15	8.8	8	4.7
Ken Stabler, Oakland	1976	103.4	291	194	66.7	2,737	9.41	27	9.3	17	5.8
Brian Griese, Denver	2000	102.9	336	216	64.3	2,688	8.00	19	5.7	4	1.2
Joe Montana, San Francisco	1984	102.9	432	279	64.6	3,630	8.40	28	6.5	10	2.3
Charlie Conerly, N.Y. Giants	1959	102.7	194	113	58.2	1,706	8.79	14	7.2	4	2.1
Bert Jones, Baltimore	1976	102.5	343	207	60.3	3,104	9.05	24	7.0	9	2.6
Joe Montana, San Francisco	1987	102.1	398	266	66.8	3,054	7.67	31	7.8	13	3.3
Trent Green, St. Louis	2000	101.8	240	145	60.4	2,063	8.60	16	6.7	5	2.1
Steve Young, San Francisco	1991	101.8	279	180	64.5	2,517	9.02	17	6.1	8	2.9
Len Dawson, Kansas City	1966	101.7	284	159	56.0	2,527	8.90	26	9.2	10	3.5
Vinny Testaverde, N.Y. Jets	1998	101.6	421	259	61.5	3,256	7.73	29	6.9	7	1.7
Steve Young, San Francisco	1993	101.5	462	314	68.0	4,023	8.71	29	6.3	16	3.5
Kurt Warner, St. Louis	2001	101.4	546	375	68.7	4,830	8.85	36	6.6	22	4.0
Jim Kelly, Buffalo	1990	101.2	346	219	63.3	2,829	8.18	24	6.9	9	2.6
Steve Young, San Francisco	1998	101.1	517	322	62.3	4,170	8.07	36	7.0	12	2.3
Chris Chandler, Atlanta	1998	100.9	327	190	58.1	3,154	9.65	25	7.6	12	3.7
Jim Harbaugh, Indianapolis	1995	100.7	314	200	63.7	2,575	8.20	17	5.4	5	1.6

SCHEDULING FORMULA

The NFL expands to 32 teams this season with the addition of the Houston Texans. In addition, the NFL has realigned for the first time since 1970—into eight divisions of four teams each—and a new scheduling formula will guarantee for the first time that all teams play each other on a regular, rotating basis. Although the number of teams will increase to 32, the number of playoff teams will remain the same at 12.

Under the new NFL scheduling formula, every team within a division will play 16 games as follows:

- Home and away against its three division opponents (6 games).
- The four teams from another division within its conference on a rotating three-year cycle (4 games).
- The four teams from a division in the other conference on a rotating four-year cycle (4 games).
- Two intraconference games based on the prior year's standings (2 games). These games will match a first-place team against the first-place teams in the two same-conference divisions the team is not scheduled to play that season. The second-place, third-place, and fourth-place teams in a conference will be matched in the same way each year.

"The new scheduling formula is one of the most positive aspects of realignment," says NFL Commissioner Paul Tagliabue. "The new formula guarantees that NFL fans will see every team play each other on a regular, rotating basis. The formula will eliminate the many aberrations of the past in which teams either did not play for long periods of time or did not play in another team's stadium for many years."

The new schedule format will take each team through a cycle of games—home and away—against every other team in the league. In the next eight seasons, every team will play every other team at least twice—once home and once away. After the 2009 season, a decision will be made on whether to continue with the same rotation or modify it.

In determining how to begin the divisional rotation in 2002, the displacement of teams from their old divisions in the new alignment was taken into account. Preference was given to scheduling games with former division rivals and other regional opponents for clubs realigned from otherwise intact divisions.

The new scheduling format includes the following elements:

- There will be an increased common-opponent emphasis with every team in a division playing against 14 common opponents.
- All teams will play each other on a regular basis, home and away, for a more consistent presentation of attractive games, eliminating the many schedule aberrations of the past.
- Teams are guaranteed to play all non-division opponents in their conference at least once every three years, and at home at least once every six years.
- Every AFC team will play every NFC team once every four years, and at home once every eight years.
- A team's record from the previous year will have less of a bearing on its schedule, with only two (rather than four) opponents being based on the previous year's standing. Thus, the so-called "easy" fifth-place schedules are eliminated.
- The division in which a team resides will be less of a factor in a team's won-loss record with 10 of 16 games each year being against non-division teams.

FUTURE SCHEDULING ROTATION

		2002	2003	2004	2005	2006	2007	2008	2009
AFC EAST	Intraconference	AFCW	AFCS	AFCN	AFCW	AFCS	AFCN	AFCW	AFCS
	Interconference	NFCN	NFCE	NFCW	NFCS	NFCN	NFCE	NFCW	NFCS
AFC NORTH	Intraconference	AFCS	AFCW	AFCE	AFCS	AFCW	AFCE	AFCS	AFCW
	Interconference	NFCS	NFCW	NFCE	NFCN	NFCS	NFCW	NFCE	NFCN
AFC SOUTH	Intraconference	AFCN	AFCE	AFCW	AFCN	AFCE	AFCW	AFCN	AFCE
	Interconference	NFCE	NFCS	NFCN	NFCW	NFCE	NFCS	NFCN	NFCW
AFC WEST	Intraconference	AFCE	AFCN	AFCS	AFCE	AFCN	AFCS	AFCE	AFCN
	Interconference	NFCW	NFCN	NFCS	NFCE	NFCW	NFCN	NFCS	NFCE
NFC EAST	Intraconference	NFCW	NFCS	NFCN	NFCW	NFCS	NFCN	NFCW	NFCS
	Interconference	AFCS	AFCE	AFCN	AFCW	AFCS	AFCE	AFCN	AFCW
NFC NORTH	Intraconference	NFCS	NFCW	NFCE	NFCS	NFCW	NFCE	NFCS	NFCW
	Interconference	AFCE	AFCW	AFCS	AFCN	AFCE	AFCW	AFCS	AFCN
NFC SOUTH	Intraconference	NFCN	NFCE	NFCW	NFCN	NFCE	NFCW	NFCN	NFCE
	Interconference	AFCN	AFCS	AFCW	AFCE	AFCN	AFCS	AFCW	AFCE
NFC WEST	Intraconference	NFCE	NFCN	NFCS	NFCE	NFCN	NFCS	NFCE	NFCN
	Interconference	AFCW	AFCN	AFCE	AFCS	AFCW	AFCN	AFCE	AFCS

AFC EAST NON-DIVISIONAL OPPONENTS 2002-2009

BUFFALO BILLS

	2002		2003		2004		2005	
	Home	Away	Home	Away	Home	Away	Home	Away
Intraconference by Division	OAK	DEN	HOU	JAX	CLE	BAL	DEN	OAK
	SD	KC	IND	TEN	PIT	CIN	KC	SD
Interconference by Division	CHI	GB	PHL	DAL	ARZ	SF	ATL	NO
	DET	MIN	WAS	NYG	STL	SEA	CAR	TB
Intraconference by Position	AFCN	AFCS	AFCN	AFCW	AFCS	AFCW	AFCS	AFCN

	2006		2007		2008		2009	
	Home	Away	Home	Away	Home	Away	Home	Away
Intraconference by Division	JAX	HOU	BAL	CLE	OAK	DEN	HOU	JAX
	TEN	IND	CIN	PIT	SD	KC	IND	TEN
Interconference by Division	GB	CHI	DAL	PHL	SF	ARZ	NO	ATL
	MIN	DET	NYG	WAS	SEA	STL	TB	CAR
Intraconference by Position	AFCW	AFCN	AFCW	AFCS	AFCN	AFCS	AFCN	AFCW

MIAMI DOLPHINS

	2002		2003		2004		2005	
	Home	Away	Home	Away	Home	Away	Home	Away
Intraconference by Division	OAK	DEN	HOU	JAX	CLE	BAL	DEN	OAK
	SD	KC	IND	TEN	PIT	CIN	KC	SD
Interconference by Division	CHI	GB	PHL	DAL	ARZ	SF	ATL	NO
	DET	MIN	WAS	NYG	STL	SEA	CAR	TB
Intraconference by Position	AFCN	AFCS	AFCN	AFCW	AFCS	AFCW	AFCS	AFCN

	2006		2007		2008		2009	
	Home	Away	Home	Away	Home	Away	Home	Away
Intraconference by Division	JAX	HOU	BAL	CLE	OAK	DEN	HOU	JAX
	TEN	IND	CIN	PIT	SD	KC	IND	TEN
Interconference by Division	GB	CHI	DAL	PHL	SF	ARZ	NO	ATL
	MIN	DET	NYG	WAS	SEA	STL	TB	CAR
Intraconference by Position	AFCW	AFCN	AFCW	AFCS	AFCN	AFCS	AFCN	AFCW

NEW ENGLAND PATRIOTS

	2002		2003		2004		2005	
	Home	Away	Home	Away	Home	Away	Home	Away
Intraconference by Division	DEN	OAK	JAX	HOU	BAL	CLE	OAK	DEN
	KC	SD	TEN	IND	CIN	PIT	SD	KC
Interconference by Division	GB	CHI	DAL	PHL	SF	ARZ	NO	ATL
	MIN	DET	NYG	WAS	SEA	STL	TB	CAR
Intraconference by Position	AFCN	AFCS	AFCN	AFCW	AFCS	AFCW	AFCS	AFCN

	2006		2007		2008		2009	
	Home	Away	Home	Away	Home	Away	Home	Away
Intraconference by Division	HOU	JAX	CLE	BAL	DEN	OAK	JAX	HOU
	IND	TEN	PIT	CIN	KC	SD	TEN	IND
Interconference by Division	CHI	GB	PHL	DAL	ARZ	SF	ATL	NO
	DET	MIN	WAS	NYG	STL	SEA	CAR	TB
Intraconference by Position	AFCW	AFCN	AFCW	AFCS	AFCN	AFCS	AFCN	AFCW

NEW YORK JETS

	2002		2003		2004		2005	
	Home	Away	Home	Away	Home	Away	Home	Away
Intraconference by Division	DEN	OAK	JAX	HOU	BAL	CLE	OAK	DEN
	KC	SD	TEN	IND	CIN	PIT	SD	KC
Interconference by Division	GB	CHI	DAL	PHL	SF	ARZ	NO	ATL
	MIN	DET	NYG	WAS	SEA	STL	TB	CAR
Intraconference by Position	AFCN	AFCS	AFCN	AFCW	AFCS	AFCW	AFCS	AFCN

	2006		2007		2008		2009	
	Home	Away	Home	Away	Home	Away	Home	Away
Intraconference by Division	HOU	JAX	CLE	BAL	DEN	OAK	JAX	HOU
	IND	TEN	PIT	CIN	KC	SD	TEN	IND
Interconference by Division	CHI	GB	PHL	DAL	ARZ	SF	ATL	NO
	DET	MIN	WAS	NYG	STL	SEA	CAR	TB
Intraconference by Position	AFCW	AFCN	AFCW	AFCS	AFCN	AFCS	AFCN	AFCW

AFC NORTH NON-DIVISIONAL OPPONENTS 2002-2009

BALTIMORE RAVENS

	2002 Home	2002 Away	2003 Home	2003 Away	2004 Home	2004 Away	2005 Home	2005 Away
Intraconference by Division	JAX	HOU	DEN	OAK	BUF	NE	HOU	JAX
	TEN	IND	KC	SD	MIA	NYJ	IND	TEN
Interconference by Division	NO	ATL	SF	ARZ	DAL	PHL	GB	CHI
	TB	CAR	SEA	STL	NYG	WAS	MIN	DET
Intraconference by Position	AFCW	AFCE	AFCS	AFCE	AFCW	AFCS	AFCE	AFCW

	2006 Home	2006 Away	2007 Home	2007 Away	2008 Home	2008 Away	2009 Home	2009 Away
Intraconference by Division	OAK	DEN	NE	BUF	JAX	HOU	DEN	OAK
	SD	KC	NYJ	MIA	TEN	IND	KC	SD
Interconference by Division	ATL	NO	ARZ	SF	PHL	DAL	CHI	GB
	CAR	TB	STL	SEA	WAS	NYG	DET	MIN
Intraconference by Position	AFCE	AFCS	AFCS	AFCW	AFCW	AFCE	AFCS	AFCE

CINCINNATI BENGALS

	2002 Home	2002 Away	2003 Home	2003 Away	2004 Home	2004 Away	2005 Home	2005 Away
Intraconference by Division	JAX	HOU	DEN	OAK	BUF	NE	HOU	JAX
	TEN	IND	KC	SD	MIA	NYJ	IND	TEN
Interconference by Division	NO	ATL	SF	ARZ	DAL	PHL	GB	CHI
	TB	CAR	SEA	STL	NYG	WAS	MIN	DET
Intraconference by Position	AFCW	AFCE	AFCS	AFCE	AFCW	AFCS	AFCE	AFCW

	2006 Home	2006 Away	2007 Home	2007 Away	2008 Home	2008 Away	2009 Home	2009 Away
Intraconference by Division	OAK	DEN	NE	BUF	JAX	HOU	DEN	OAK
	SD	KC	NYJ	MIA	TEN	IND	KC	SD
Interconference by Division	ATL	NO	ARZ	SF	PHL	DAL	CHI	GB
	CAR	TB	STL	SEA	WAS	NYG	DET	MIN
Intraconference by Position	AFCE	AFCS	AFCS	AFCW	AFCW	AFCE	AFCS	AFCE

CLEVELAND BROWNS

	2002 Home	2002 Away	2003 Home	2003 Away	2004 Home	2004 Away	2005 Home	2005 Away
Intraconference by Division	HOU	JAX	OAK	DEN	NE	BUF	JAX	HOU
	IND	TEN	SD	KC	NYJ	MIA	TEN	IND
Interconference by Division	ATL	NO	ARZ	SF	PHL	DAL	CHI	GB
	CAR	TB	STL	SEA	WAS	NYG	DET	MIN
Intraconference by Position	AFCW	AFCE	AFCS	AFCE	AFCW	AFCS	AFCE	AFCW

	2006 Home	2006 Away	2007 Home	2007 Away	2008 Home	2008 Away	2009 Home	2009 Away
Intraconference by Division	DEN	OAK	BUF	NE	HOU	JAX	OAK	DEN
	KC	SD	MIA	NYJ	IND	TEN	SD	KC
Interconference by Division	NO	ATL	SF	ARZ	DAL	PHL	GB	CHI
	TB	CAR	SEA	STL	NYG	WAS	MIN	DET
Intraconference by Position	AFCE	AFCS	AFCS	AFCW	AFCW	AFCE	AFCS	AFCE

PITTSBURGH STEELERS

	2002 Home	2002 Away	2003 Home	2003 Away	2004 Home	2004 Away	2005 Home	2005 Away
Intraconference by Division	HOU	JAX	OAK	DEN	NE	BUF	JAX	HOU
	IND	TEN	SD	KC	NYJ	MIA	TEN	IND
Interconference by Division	ATL	NO	ARZ	SF	PHL	DAL	CHI	GB
	CAR	TB	STL	SEA	WAS	NYG	DET	MIN
Intraconference by Position	AFCW	AFCE	AFCS	AFCE	AFCW	AFCS	AFCE	AFCW

	2006 Home	2006 Away	2007 Home	2007 Away	2008 Home	2008 Away	2009 Home	2009 Away
Intraconference by Division	DEN	OAK	BUF	NE	HOU	JAX	OAK	DEN
	KC	SD	MIA	NYJ	IND	TEN	SD	KC
Interconference by Division	NO	ATL	SF	ARZ	DAL	PHL	GB	CHI
	TB	CAR	SEA	STL	NYG	WAS	MIN	DET
Intraconference by Position	AFCE	AFCS	AFCS	AFCW	AFCW	AFCE	AFCS	AFCE

AFC SOUTH NON-DIVISIONAL OPPONENTS 2002-2009

HOUSTON TEXANS

	2002		2003		2004		2005	
	Home	Away	Home	Away	Home	Away	Home	Away
Intraconference by Division	BAL	CLE	NE	BUF	OAK	DEN	CLE	BAL
	CIN	PIT	NYJ	MIA	SD	KC	PIT	CIN
Interconference by Division	DAL	PHL	ATL	NO	GB	CHI	ARZ	SF
	NYG	WAS	CAR	TB	MIN	DET	STL	SEA
Intraconference by Position	AFCE	AFCW	AFCW	AFCN	AFCN	AFCE	AFCW	AFCE

	2006		2007		2008		2009	
	Home	Away	Home	Away	Home	Away	Home	Away
Intraconference by Division	BUF	NE	DEN	OAK	BAL	CLE	NE	BUF
	MIA	NYJ	KC	SD	CIN	PIT	NYJ	MIA
Interconference by Division	PHL	DAL	NO	ATL	CHI	GB	SF	ARZ
	WAS	NYG	TB	CAR	DET	MIN	SEA	STL
Intraconference by Position	AFCN	AFCW	AFCE	AFCN	AFCE	AFCW	AFCW	AFCN

INDIANAPOLIS COLTS

	2002		2003		2004		2005	
	Home	Away	Home	Away	Home	Away	Home	Away
Intraconference by Division	BAL	CLE	NE	BUF	OAK	DEN	CLE	BAL
	CIN	PIT	NYJ	MIA	SD	KC	PIT	CIN
Interconference by Division	DAL	PHL	ATL	NO	GB	CHI	ARZ	SF
	NYG	WAS	CAR	TB	MIN	DET	STL	SEA
Intraconference by Position	AFCE	AFCW	AFCW	AFCN	AFCN	AFCE	AFCW	AFCE

	2006		2007		2008		2009	
	Home	Away	Home	Away	Home	Away	Home	Away
Intraconference by Division	BUF	NE	DEN	OAK	BAL	CLE	NE	BUF
	MIA	NYJ	KC	SD	CIN	PIT	NYJ	MIA
Interconference by Division	PHL	DAL	NO	ATL	CHI	GB	SF	ARZ
	WAS	NYG	TB	CAR	DET	MIN	SEA	STL
Intraconference by Position	AFCN	AFCW	AFCE	AFCN	AFCE	AFCW	AFCW	AFCN

JACKSONVILLE JAGUARS

	2002		2003		2004		2005	
	Home	Away	Home	Away	Home	Away	Home	Away
Intraconference by Division	CLE	BAL	BUF	NE	DEN	OAK	BAL	CLE
	PIT	CIN	MIA	NYJ	KC	SD	CIN	PIT
Interconference by Division	PHL	DAL	NO	ATL	CHI	GB	SF	ARZ
	WAS	NYG	TB	CAR	DET	MIN	SEA	STL
Intraconference by Position	AFCE	AFCW	AFCW	AFCN	AFCN	AFCE	AFCW	AFCE

	2006		2007		2008		2009	
	Home	Away	Home	Away	Home	Away	Home	Away
Intraconference by Division	NE	BUF	OAK	DEN	CLE	BAL	BUF	NE
	NYJ	MIA	SD	KC	PIT	CIN	MIA	NYJ
Interconference by Division	DAL	PHL	ATL	NO	GB	CHI	ARZ	SF
	NYG	WAS	CAR	TB	MIN	DET	STL	SEA
Intraconference by Position	AFCN	AFCW	AFCE	AFCN	AFCE	AFCW	AFCW	AFCN

TENNESSEE TITANS

	2002		2003		2004		2005	
	Home	Away	Home	Away	Home	Away	Home	Away
Intraconference by Division	CLE	BAL	BUF	NE	DEN	OAK	BAL	CLE
	PIT	CIN	MIA	NYJ	KC	SD	CIN	PIT
Interconference by Division	PHL	DAL	NO	ATL	CHI	GB	SF	ARZ
	WAS	NYG	TB	CAR	DET	MIN	SEA	STL
Intraconference by Position	AFCE	AFCW	AFCW	AFCN	AFCN	AFCE	AFCW	AFCE

	2006		2007		2008		2009	
	Home	Away	Home	Away	Home	Away	Home	Away
Intraconference by Division	NE	BUF	OAK	DEN	CLE	BAL	BUF	NE
	NYJ	MIA	SD	KC	PIT	CIN	MIA	NYJ
Interconference by Division	DAL	PHL	ATL	NO	GB	CHI	ARZ	SF
	NYG	WAS	CAR	TB	MIN	DET	STL	SEA
Intraconference by Position	AFCN	AFCW	AFCE	AFCN	AFCE	AFCW	AFCW	AFCN

AFC WEST NON-DIVISIONAL OPPONENTS 2002-2009

DENVER BRONCOS

	2002 Home	Away	2003 Home	Away	2004 Home	Away	2005 Home	Away
Intraconference by Division	BUF	NE	CLE	BAL	HOU	JAX	NE	BUF
	MIA	NYJ	PIT	CIN	IND	TEN	NYJ	MIA
Interconference by Division	ARZ	SF	CHI	GB	ATL	NO	PHL	DAL
	STL	SEA	DET	MIN	CAR	TB	WAS	NYG
Intraconference by Position	AFCS	AFCN	AFCE	AFCS	AFCE	AFCN	AFCN	AFCS

	2006 Home	Away	2007 Home	Away	2008 Home	Away	2009 Home	Away
Intraconference by Division	BAL	CLE	JAX	HOU	BUF	NE	CLE	BAL
	CIN	PIT	TEN	IND	MIA	NYJ	PIT	CIN
Interconference by Division	SF	ARZ	GB	CHI	NO	ATL	DAL	PHL
	SEA	STL	MIN	DET	TB	CAR	NYG	WAS
Intraconference by Position	AFCS	AFCE	AFCN	AFCE	AFCS	AFCN	AFCE	AFCS

KANSAS CITY CHIEFS

	2002 Home	Away	2003 Home	Away	2004 Home	Away	2005 Home	Away
Intraconference by Division	BUF	NE	CLE	BAL	HOU	JAX	NE	BUF
	MIA	NYJ	PIT	CIN	IND	TEN	NYJ	MIA
Interconference by Division	ARZ	SF	CHI	GB	ATL	NO	PHL	DAL
	STL	SEA	DET	MIN	CAR	TB	WAS	NYG
Intraconference by Position	AFCS	AFCN	AFCE	AFCS	AFCE	AFCN	AFCN	AFCS

	2006 Home	Away	2007 Home	Away	2008 Home	Away	2009 Home	Away
Intraconference by Division	BAL	CLE	JAX	HOU	BUF	NE	CLE	BAL
	CIN	PIT	TEN	IND	MIA	NYJ	PIT	CIN
Interconference by Division	SF	ARZ	GB	CHI	NO	ATL	DAL	PHL
	SEA	STL	MIN	DET	TB	CAR	NYG	WAS
Intraconference by Position	AFCS	AFCE	AFCN	AFCE	AFCS	AFCN	AFCE	AFCS

OAKLAND RAIDERS

	2002 Home	Away	2003 Home	Away	2004 Home	Away	2005 Home	Away
Intraconference by Division	NE	BUF	BAL	CLE	JAX	HOU	BUF	NE
	NYJ	MIA	CIN	PIT	TEN	IND	MIA	NYJ
Interconference by Division	SF	ARZ	GB	CHI	NO	ATL	DAL	PHL
	SEA	STL	MIN	DET	TB	CAR	NYG	WAS
Intraconference by Position	AFCS	AFCN	AFCE	AFCS	AFCE	AFCN	AFCN	AFCS

	2006 Home	Away	2007 Home	Away	2008 Home	Away	2009 Home	Away
Intraconference by Division	CLE	BAL	HOU	JAX	NE	BUF	BAL	CLE
	PIT	CIN	IND	TEN	NYJ	MIA	CIN	PIT
Interconference by Division	ARZ	SF	CHI	GB	ATL	NO	PHL	DAL
	STL	SEA	DET	MIN	CAR	TB	WAS	NYG
Intraconference by Position	AFCS	AFCE	AFCN	AFCE	AFCS	AFCN	AFCE	AFCS

SAN DIEGO CHARGERS

	2002 Home	Away	2003 Home	Away	2004 Home	Away	2005 Home	Away
Intraconference by Division	NE	BUF	BAL	CLE	JAX	HOU	BUF	NE
	NYJ	MIA	CIN	PIT	TEN	IND	MIA	NYJ
Interconference by Division	SF	ARZ	GB	CHI	NO	ATL	DAL	PHL
	SEA	STL	MIN	DET	TB	CAR	NYG	WAS
Intraconference by Position	AFCS	AFCN	AFCE	AFCS	AFCE	AFCN	AFCN	AFCS

	2006 Home	Away	2007 Home	Away	2008 Home	Away	2009 Home	Away
Intraconference by Division	CLE	BAL	HOU	JAX	NE	BUF	BAL	CLE
	PIT	CIN	IND	TEN	NYJ	MIA	CIN	PIT
Interconference by Division	ARZ	SF	CHI	GB	ATL	NO	PHL	DAL
	STL	SEA	DET	MIN	CAR	TB	WAS	NYG
Intraconference by Position	AFCS	AFCE	AFCN	AFCE	AFCS	AFCN	AFCE	AFCS

NFC EAST NON-DIVISIONAL OPPONENTS 2002-2009

DALLAS COWBOYS

	2002 Home	Away	2003 Home	Away	2004 Home	Away	2005 Home	Away
Intraconference by Division	SF	ARZ	ATL	NO	CHI	GB	ARZ	SF
	SEA	STL	CAR	TB	DET	MIN	STL	SEA
Interconference by Division	JAX	HOU	BUF	NE	CLE	BAL	DEN	OAK
	TEN	IND	MIA	NYJ	PIT	CIN	KC	SD
Intraconference by Position	NFCS	NFCN	NFCW	NFCN	NFCS	NFCW	NFCN	NFCS

	2006 Home	Away	2007 Home	Away	2008 Home	Away	2009 Home	Away
Intraconference by Division	NO	ATL	GB	CHI	SF	ARZ	ATL	NO
	TB	CAR	MIN	DET	SEA	STL	CAR	TB
Interconference by Division	HOU	JAX	NE	BUF	BAL	CLE	OAK	DEN
	IND	TEN	NYJ	MIA	CIN	PIT	SD	KC
Intraconference by Position	NFCN	NFCW	NFCW	NFCS	NFCS	NFCN	NFCW	NFCN

NEW YORK GIANTS

	2002 Home	Away	2003 Home	Away	2004 Home	Away	2005 Home	Away
Intraconference by Division	SF	ARZ	ATL	NO	CHI	GB	ARZ	SF
	SEA	STL	CAR	TB	DET	MIN	STL	SEA
Interconference by Division	JAX	HOU	BUF	NE	CLE	BAL	DEN	OAK
	TEN	IND	MIA	NYJ	PIT	CIN	KC	SD
Intraconference by Position	NFCS	NFCN	NFCW	NFCN	NFCS	NFCW	NFCN	NFCS

	2006 Home	Away	2007 Home	Away	2008 Home	Away	2009 Home	Away
Intraconference by Division	NO	ATL	GB	CHI	SF	ARZ	ATL	NO
	TB	CAR	MIN	DET	SEA	STL	CAR	TB
Interconference by Division	HOU	JAX	NE	BUF	BAL	CLE	OAK	DEN
	IND	TEN	NYJ	MIA	CIN	PIT	SD	KC
Intraconference by Position	NFCN	NFCW	NFCW	NFCS	NFCS	NFCN	NFCW	NFCN

PHILADELPHIA EAGLES

	2002 Home	Away	2003 Home	Away	2004 Home	Away	2005 Home	Away
Intraconference by Division	ARZ	SF	NO	ATL	GB	CHI	SF	ARZ
	STL	SEA	TB	CAR	MIN	DET	SEA	STL
Interconference by Division	HOU	JAX	NE	BUF	BAL	CLE	OAK	DEN
	IND	TEN	NYJ	MIA	CIN	PIT	SD	KC
Intraconference by Position	NFCS	NFCN	NFCW	NFCN	NFCS	NFCW	NFCN	NFCS

	2006 Home	Away	2007 Home	Away	2008 Home	Away	2009 Home	Away
Intraconference by Division	ATL	NO	CHI	GB	ARZ	SF	NO	ATL
	CAR	TB	DET	MIN	STL	SEA	TB	CAR
Interconference by Division	JAX	HOU	BUF	NE	CLE	BAL	DEN	OAK
	TEN	IND	MIA	NYJ	PIT	CIN	KC	SD
Intraconference by Position	NFCN	NFCW	NFCW	NFCS	NFCS	NFCN	NFCW	NFCN

WASHINGTON REDSKINS

	2002 Home	Away	2003 Home	Away	2004 Home	Away	2005 Home	Away
Intraconference by Division	ARZ	SF	NO	ATL	GB	CHI	SF	ARZ
	STL	SEA	TB	CAR	MIN	DET	SEA	STL
Interconference by Division	HOU	JAX	NE	BUF	BAL	CLE	OAK	DEN
	IND	TEN	NYJ	MIA	CIN	PIT	SD	KC
Intraconference by Position	NFCS	NFCN	NFCW	NFCN	NFCS	NFCW	NFCN	NFCS

	2006 Home	Away	2007 Home	Away	2008 Home	Away	2009 Home	Away
Intraconference by Division	ATL	NO	CHI	GB	ARZ	SF	NO	ATL
	CAR	TB	DET	MIN	STL	SEA	TB	CAR
Interconference by Division	JAX	HOU	BUF	NE	CLE	BAL	DEN	OAK
	TEN	IND	MIA	NYJ	PIT	CIN	KC	SD
Intraconference by Position	NFCN	NFCW	NFCW	NFCS	NFCS	NFCN	NFCW	NFCN

NFC NORTH NON-DIVISIONAL OPPONENTS 2002-2009

CHICAGO BEARS

	2002 Home	2002 Away	2003 Home	2003 Away	2004 Home	2004 Away	2005 Home	2005 Away
Intraconference by Division	NO	ATL	ARZ	SF	PHL	DAL	ATL	NO
	TB	CAR	STL	SEA	WAS	NYG	CAR	TB
Interconference by Division	NE	BUF	OAK	DEN	HOU	JAX	BAL	CLE
	NYJ	MIA	SD	KC	IND	TEN	CIN	PIT
Intraconference by Position	NFCE	NFCW	NFCE	NFCS	NFCW	NFCS	NFCW	NFCE

	2006 Home	2006 Away	2007 Home	2007 Away	2008 Home	2008 Away	2009 Home	2009 Away
Intraconference by Division	SF	ARZ	DAL	PHL	NO	ATL	ARZ	SF
	SEA	STL	NYG	WAS	TB	CAR	STL	SEA
Interconference by Division	BUF	NE	DEN	OAK	JAX	HOU	CLE	BAL
	MIA	NYJ	KC	SD	TEN	IND	PIT	CIN
Intraconference by Position	NFCS	NFCE	NFCS	NFCW	NFCE	NFCW	NFCE	NFCS

DETROIT LIONS

	2002 Home	2002 Away	2003 Home	2003 Away	2004 Home	2004 Away	2005 Home	2005 Away
Intraconference by Division	NO	ATL	ARZ	SF	PHL	DAL	ATL	NO
	TB	CAR	STL	SEA	WAS	NYG	CAR	TB
Interconference by Division	NE	BUF	OAK	DEN	HOU	JAX	BAL	CLE
	NYJ	MIA	SD	KC	IND	TEN	CIN	PIT
Intraconference by Position	NFCE	NFCW	NFCE	NFCS	NFCW	NFCS	NFCW	NFCE

	2006 Home	2006 Away	2007 Home	2007 Away	2008 Home	2008 Away	2009 Home	2009 Away
Intraconference by Division	SF	ARZ	DAL	PHL	NO	ATL	ARZ	SF
	SEA	STL	NYG	WAS	TB	CAR	STL	SEA
Interconference by Division	BUF	NE	DEN	OAK	JAX	HOU	CLE	BAL
	MIA	NYJ	KC	SD	TEN	IND	PIT	CIN
Intraconference by Position	NFCS	NFCE	NFCS	NFCW	NFCE	NFCW	NFCE	NFCS

GREEN BAY PACKERS

	2002 Home	2002 Away	2003 Home	2003 Away	2004 Home	2004 Away	2005 Home	2005 Away
Intraconference by Division	ATL	NO	SF	ARZ	DAL	PHL	NO	ATL
	CAR	TB	SEA	STL	NYG	WAS	TB	CAR
Interconference by Division	BUF	NE	DEN	OAK	JAX	HOU	CLE	BAL
	MIA	NYJ	KC	SD	TEN	IND	PIT	CIN
Intraconference by Position	NFCE	NFCW	NFCE	NFCS	NFCW	NFCS	NFCW	NFCE

	2006 Home	2006 Away	2007 Home	2007 Away	2008 Home	2008 Away	2009 Home	2009 Away
Intraconference by Division	ARZ	SF	PHL	DAL	ATL	NO	SF	ARZ
	STL	SEA	WAS	NYG	CAR	TB	SEA	STL
Interconference by Division	NE	BUF	OAK	DEN	HOU	JAX	BAL	CLE
	NYJ	MIA	SD	KC	IND	TEN	CIN	PIT
Intraconference by Position	NFCS	NFCE	NFCS	NFCW	NFCE	NFCW	NFCE	NFCS

MINNESOTA VIKINGS

	2002 Home	2002 Away	2003 Home	2003 Away	2004 Home	2004 Away	2005 Home	2005 Away
Intraconference by Division	ATL	NO	SF	ARZ	DAL	PHL	NO	ATL
	CAR	TB	SEA	STL	NYG	WAS	TB	CAR
Interconference by Division	BUF	NE	DEN	OAK	JAX	HOU	CLE	BAL
	MIA	NYJ	KC	SD	TEN	IND	PIT	CIN
Intraconference by Position	NFCE	NFCW	NFCE	NFCS	NFCW	NFCS	NFCW	NFCE

	2006 Home	2006 Away	2007 Home	2007 Away	2008 Home	2008 Away	2009 Home	2009 Away
Intraconference by Division	ARZ	SF	PHL	DAL	ATL	NO	SF	ARZ
	STL	SEA	WAS	NYG	CAR	TB	SEA	STL
Interconference by Division	NE	BUF	OAK	DEN	HOU	JAX	BAL	CLE
	NYJ	MIA	SD	KC	IND	TEN	CIN	PIT
Intraconference by Position	NFCS	NFCE	NFCS	NFCW	NFCE	NFCW	NFCE	NFCS

NFC SOUTH NON-DIVISIONAL OPPONENTS 2002-2009

ATLANTA FALCONS

	2002 Home	2002 Away	2003 Home	2003 Away	2004 Home	2004 Away	2005 Home	2005 Away
Intraconference by Division	CHI	GB	PHL	DAL	ARZ	SF	GB	CHI
	DET	MIN	WAS	NYG	STL	SEA	MIN	DET
Interconference by Division	BAL	CLE	JAX	HOU	OAK	DEN	NE	BUF
	CIN	PIT	TEN	IND	SD	KC	NYJ	MIA
Intraconference by Position	NFCW	NFCE	NFCN	NFCW	NFCN	NFCE	NFCE	NFCW

	2006 Home	2006 Away	2007 Home	2007 Away	2008 Home	2008 Away	2009 Home	2009 Away
Intraconference by Division	DAL	PHL	SF	ARZ	CHI	GB	PHL	DAL
	NYG	WAS	SEA	STL	DET	MIN	WAS	NYG
Interconference by Division	CLE	BAL	HOU	JAX	DEN	OAK	BUF	NE
	PIT	CIN	IND	TEN	KC	SD	MIA	NYJ
Intraconference by Position	NFCW	NFCN	NFCE	NFCN	NFCW	NFCE	NFCN	NFCW

CAROLINA PANTHERS

	2002 Home	2002 Away	2003 Home	2003 Away	2004 Home	2004 Away	2005 Home	2005 Away
Intraconference by Division	CHI	GB	PHL	DAL	ARZ	SF	GB	CHI
	DET	MIN	WAS	NYG	STL	SEA	MIN	DET
Interconference by Division	BAL	CLE	JAX	HOU	OAK	DEN	NE	BUF
	CIN	PIT	TEN	IND	SD	KC	NYJ	MIA
Intraconference by Position	NFCW	NFCE	NFCN	NFCW	NFCN	NFCE	NFCE	NFCW

	2006 Home	2006 Away	2007 Home	2007 Away	2008 Home	2008 Away	2009 Home	2009 Away
Intraconference by Division	DAL	PHL	SF	ARZ	CHI	GB	PHL	DAL
	NYG	WAS	SEA	STL	DET	MIN	WAS	NYG
Interconference by Division	CLE	BAL	HOU	JAX	DEN	OAK	BUF	NE
	PIT	CIN	IND	TEN	KC	SD	MIA	NYJ
Intraconference by Position	NFCW	NFCN	NFCE	NFCN	NFCW	NFCE	NFCN	NFCW

NEW ORLEANS SAINTS

	2002 Home	2002 Away	2003 Home	2003 Away	2004 Home	2004 Away	2005 Home	2005 Away
Intraconference by Division	GB	CHI	DAL	PHL	SF	ARZ	CHI	GB
	MIN	DET	NYG	WAS	SEA	STL	DET	MIN
Interconference by Division	CLE	BAL	HOU	JAX	DEN	OAK	BUF	NE
	PIT	CIN	IND	TEN	KC	SD	MIA	NYJ
Intraconference by Position	NFCW	NFCE	NFCN	NFCW	NFCN	NFCE	NFCE	NFCW

	2006 Home	2006 Away	2007 Home	2007 Away	2008 Home	2008 Away	2009 Home	2009 Away
Intraconference by Division	PHL	DAL	ARZ	SF	GB	CHI	DAL	PHL
	WAS	NYG	STL	SEA	MIN	DET	NYG	WAS
Interconference by Division	BAL	CLE	JAX	HOU	OAK	DEN	NE	BUF
	CIN	PIT	TEN	IND	SD	KC	NYJ	MIA
Intraconference by Position	NFCW	NFCN	NFCE	NFCN	NFCW	NFCE	NFCN	NFCW

TAMPA BAY BUCCANEERS

	2002 Home	2002 Away	2003 Home	2003 Away	2004 Home	2004 Away	2005 Home	2005 Away
Intraconference by Division	GB	CHI	DAL	PHL	SF	ARZ	CHI	GB
	MIN	DET	NYG	WAS	SEA	STL	DET	MIN
Interconference by Division	CLE	BAL	HOU	JAX	DEN	OAK	BUF	NE
	PIT	CIN	IND	TEN	KC	SD	MIA	NYJ
Intraconference by Position	NFCW	NFCE	NFCN	NFCW	NFCN	NFCE	NFCE	NFCW

	2006 Home	2006 Away	2007 Home	2007 Away	2008 Home	2008 Away	2009 Home	2009 Away
Intraconference by Division	PHL	DAL	ARZ	SF	GB	CHI	DAL	PHL
	WAS	NYG	STL	SEA	MIN	DET	NYG	WAS
Interconference by Division	BAL	CLE	JAX	HOU	OAK	DEN	NE	BUF
	CIN	PIT	TEN	IND	SD	KC	NYJ	MIA
Intraconference by Position	NFCW	NFCN	NFCE	NFCN	NFCW	NFCE	NFCN	NFCW

NFC WEST NON-DIVISIONAL OPPONENTS 2002-2009

ARIZONA CARDINALS

	2002		2003		2004		2005	
	Home	Away	Home	Away	Home	Away	Home	Away
Intraconference by Division	DAL	PHL	GB	CHI	NO	ATL	PHL	DAL
	NYG	WAS	MIN	DET	TB	CAR	WAS	NYG
Interconference by Division	OAK	DEN	BAL	CLE	NE	BUF	JAX	HOU
	SD	KC	CIN	PIT	NYJ	MIA	TEN	IND
Intraconference by Position	NFCN	NFCS	NFCS	NFCE	NFCE	NFCN	NFCS	NFCN

	2006		2007		2008		2009	
	Home	Away	Home	Away	Home	Away	Home	Away
Intraconference by Division	CHI	GB	ATL	NO	DAL	PHL	GB	CHI
	DET	MIN	CAR	TB	NYG	WAS	MIN	DET
Interconference by Division	DEN	OAK	CLE	BAL	BUF	NE	HOU	JAX
	KC	SD	PIT	CIN	MIA	NYJ	IND	TEN
Intraconference by Position	NFCE	NFCS	NFCN	NFCE	NFCN	NFCS	NFCS	NFCE

ST. LOUIS RAMS

	2002		2003		2004		2005	
	Home	Away	Home	Away	Home	Away	Home	Away
Intraconference by Division	DAL	PHL	GB	CHI	NO	ATL	PHL	DAL
	NYG	WAS	MIN	DET	TB	CAR	WAS	NYG
Interconference by Division	OAK	DEN	BAL	CLE	NE	BUF	JAX	HOU
	SD	KC	CIN	PIT	NYJ	MIA	TEN	IND
Intraconference by Position	NFCN	NFCS	NFCS	NFCE	NFCE	NFCN	NFCS	NFCN

	2006		2007		2008		2009	
	Home	Away	Home	Away	Home	Away	Home	Away
Intraconference by Division	CHI	GB	ATL	NO	DAL	PHL	GB	CHI
	DET	MIN	CAR	TB	NYG	WAS	MIN	DET
Interconference by Division	DEN	OAK	CLE	BAL	BUF	NE	HOU	JAX
	KC	SD	PIT	CIN	MIA	NYJ	IND	TEN
Intraconference by Position	NFCE	NFCS	NFCN	NFCE	NFCN	NFCS	NFCS	NFCE

SAN FRANCISCO 49ERS

	2002		2003		2004		2005	
	Home	Away	Home	Away	Home	Away	Home	Away
Intraconference by Division	PHL	DAL	CHI	GB	ATL	NO	DAL	PHL
	WAS	NYG	DET	MIN	CAR	TB	NYG	WAS
Interconference by Division	DEN	OAK	CLE	BAL	BUF	NE	HOU	JAX
	KC	SD	PIT	CIN	MIA	NYJ	IND	TEN
Intraconference by Position	NFCN	NFCS	NFCS	NFCE	NFCE	NFCN	NFCS	NFCN

	2006		2007		2008		2009	
	Home	Away	Home	Away	Home	Away	Home	Away
Intraconference by Division	GB	CHI	NO	ATL	PHL	DAL	CHI	GB
	MIN	DET	TB	CAR	WAS	NYG	DET	MIN
Interconference by Division	OAK	DEN	BAL	CLE	NE	BUF	JAX	HOU
	SD	KC	CIN	PIT	NYJ	MIA	TEN	IND
Intraconference by Position	NFCE	NFCS	NFCN	NFCE	NFCN	NFCS	NFCS	NFCE

SEATTLE SEAHAWKS

	2002		2003		2004		2005	
	Home	Away	Home	Away	Home	Away	Home	Away
Intraconference by Division	PHL	DAL	CHI	GB	ATL	NO	DAL	PHL
	WAS	NYG	DET	MIN	CAR	TB	NYG	WAS
Interconference by Division	DEN	OAK	CLE	BAL	BUF	NE	HOU	JAX
	KC	SD	PIT	CIN	MIA	NYJ	IND	TEN
Intraconference by Position	NFCN	NFCS	NFCS	NFCE	NFCE	NFCN	NFCS	NFCN

	2006		2007		2008		2009	
	Home	Away	Home	Away	Home	Away	Home	Away
Intraconference by Division	GB	CHI	NO	ATL	PHL	DAL	CHI	GB
	MIN	DET	TB	CAR	WAS	NYG	DET	MIN
Interconference by Division	OAK	DEN	BAL	CLE	NE	BUF	JAX	HOU
	SD	KC	CIN	PIT	NYJ	MIA	TEN	IND
Intraconference by Position	NFCE	NFCS	NFCN	NFCE	NFCN	NFCS	NFCS	NFCE

TOP ACTIVE PASSERS
1,000 or more attempts

		Yrs.	Att.	Comp.	Pct. Comp.	Yards	TD	Pct. TD	Had Int.	Pct. Int.	Ratings Pts.
1.	Kurt Warner, St.L.	4	1,403	939	66.9	12,651	98	7.0	53	3.8	103.0
2.	Jeff Garcia, S.F.	3	1,440	896	62.2	10,360	74	5.1	33	2.3	91.5
3.	Brett Favre, G.B.	11	5,442	3,311	60.8	38,627	287	5.3	172	3.2	86.8
4.	Peyton Manning, Ind.	4	2,226	1,357	61.0	16,418	111	5.0	81	3.6	85.1
5.	Mark Brunell, Jax.	8	3,145	1,897	60.3	22,521	125	4.0	79	2.5	85.0
6.	Brian Griese, Den.	4	1,242	753	60.6	8,549	56	4.5	38	3.1	83.6
7.	Brad Johnson, T.B.	8	2,380	1,466	61.6	16,379	92	3.9	68	2.9	83.1
8.	Rich Gannon, Oak.	13	3,295	1,949	59.2	22,256	145	4.4	88	2.7	83.1
9.	Neil O'Donnell, Tenn.	11	3,197	1,844	57.7	21,434	118	3.7	67	2.1	81.7
10.	Randall Cunningham, *	16	4,289	2,429	56.6	29,979	207	4.8	134	3.1	81.5
11.	Steve McNair, Tenn.	7	2,288	1,333	58.3	16,035	86	3.8	61	2.7	81.3
12.	Trent Green, K.C.	4	1,273	719	56.5	9,287	56	4.4	40	3.1	81.1
13.	Steve Beuerlein, Den.	13	3,148	1,793	57.0	22,732	139	4.4	102	3.2	80.9
14.	Chris Chandler, Chi.	14	3,590	2,083	58.0	25,948	161	4.5	127	3.5	80.8
15.	Jeff Blake, Balt.	9	2,533	1,428	56.4	17,199	106	4.2	72	2.8	79.5
16.	Mark Rypien, *	11	2,613	1,466	56.1	18,473	115	4.4	88	3.4	78.9
17.	Donovan McNabb, Phil.	3	1,278	721	56.4	7,546	54	4.2	32	2.5	77.4
18.	Charlie Batch, *	4	1,326	743	56.0	9,016	49	3.7	40	3.0	76.9
19.	Gus Frerotte, Cin.	8	1,990	1,087	54.6	13,970	69	3.5	59	3.0	76.1
20.	Drew Bledsoe, Buff.	9	4,518	2,544	56.3	29,657	166	3.7	138	3.1	75.9
21.	Doug Flutie, S.D.	8	1,925	1,058	55.0	13,249	76	3.9	64	3.3	75.9
22.	Scott Mitchell, *	11	2,346	1,301	55.5	15,692	95	4.0	81	3.5	75.3
23.	Vinny Testaverde, NYJ	15	5,644	3,157	55.9	39,059	241	4.3	230	4.1	74.8
24.	Tim Couch, Cle.	3	1,068	632	59.2	6,970	39	3.7	43	4.0	74.0
25.	Rodney Peete, Car.	13	1,954	1,116	57.1	13,686	61	3.1	78	4.0	72.6
26.	Tony Banks, *	6	2,227	1,202	54.0	14,433	71	3.2	68	3.1	72.0
27.	Kordell Stewart, Pitt.	7	1,941	1,081	55.7	12,173	64	3.3	66	3.4	71.4
28.	Kerry Collins, NYG	7	2,959	1,616	54.6	19,200	100	3.4	104	3.5	71.3
29.	Trent Dilfer, Sea.	8	2,386	1,324	55.5	15,485	89	3.7	95	4.0	71.2
30.	Jon Kitna, Cin.	5	1,711	971	56.8	10,768	61	3.6	67	3.9	71.2

TOP ACTIVE SCORERS
(number in paranteses represents 2-point conversions scored)

		Yrs.	TD	FG	PAT	TP
1.	Gary Anderson, *	20	0	476	705	2,133
2.	Morten Andersen, K.C.	20	0	464	644	2,036
3.	Steve Christie, S.D.	12	0	281	364	1,207
4.	John Carney, N.O.	14	0	290	331	1,201
5.	Jerry Rice, Oak.	17	196	0	(4)	1,184
6.	Matt Stover, Balt.	11	0	267	333	1,134
7.	Jason Elam, Den.	9	0	235	368	1,073
8.	Jason Hanson, Det.	10	0	239	327	1,044
9.	John Kasay, Car.	11	0	231	271	964
10.	Emmitt Smith, Dall.	12	159	0	(1)	956
11.	Mike Hollis, Buff.	7	0	175	239	764
12.	Todd Peterson, Pitt.	8	0	170	233	743
13.	Jeff Wilkins, St.L.	8	0	147	284	725
14.	Adam Vinatieri, N.E.	6	0	160	206 (1)	688
15.	Cary Blanchard, *	7	0	165	188	683
16.	Doug Brien, Minn.	8	0	150	225	675
17.	Marshall Faulk, St.L.	8	110	0	(4)	668
18.	Tim Brown, Oak.	14	100	0	(1)	602
19.	Ryan Longwell, G.B.	5	0	131	203	596
20.	Olindo Mare, Mia.	5	0	136	165	573
21.	Ricky Watters, *	10	91	0	(1)	548
22.	John Hall, NYJ	5	0	125	170	545
23.	Mike Vanderjagt, Ind.	4	0	114	153	495
24.	Terry Allen, *	10	79	0	(2)	478
25.	Joe Nedney, Tenn.	6	0	101	155	458
26.	Curtis Martin, NYJ	7	72	0	(2)	436
27.	Terrell Davis, Den.	7	65	0	(3)	396
	Terance Mathis, *	12	64	0	(6)	396
29.	Marvin Harrison, Ind.	6	62	0	(4)	380
30.	Herman Moore, *	11	62	0	0	376

TOP ACTIVE RUSHERS

		Yrs.	Att.	Yards	TD
1.	Emmitt Smith, Dall.	12	3,798	16,187	148
2.	Jerome Bettis, Pitt.	9	2,686	10,876	53
3.	Ricky Watters, *	10	2,622	10,643	78
4.	Marshall Faulk, St.L.	8	2,155	9,442	79
5.	Curtis Martin, NYJ	7	2,343	9,267	64
6.	Terry Allen, *	10	2,152	8,614	73
7.	Eddie George, Tenn.	6	2,078	7,813	47
8.	Terrell Davis, Den.	7	1,655	7,607	60
9.	Corey Dillon, Cin.	5	1,413	6,209	36
10.	Garrison Hearst, S.F.	9	1,418	6,145	18
11.	Charlie Garner, Oak.	8	1,205	5,471	29
12.	Jamal Anderson, *	8	1,329	5,336	34
13.	Stephen Davis, Wash.	6	1,176	4,970	38
14.	Randall Cunningham, *	16	775	4,928	35
15.	James Stewart, Det.	7	1,247	4,820	44
16.	Warrick Dunn, Atl.	5	1,070	4,200	17
17.	Antowain Smith, N.E.	5	1,047	4,089	38
18.	Lamar Smith, Car.	8	1,102	4,055	31
19.	Mike Alstott, T.B.	6	1,025	3,982	40
20.	Dorsey Levens, *	8	1,006	3,937	28
21.	Edgerrin James, Ind.	3	907	3,924	29
22.	Priest Holmes, K.C.	5	786	3,657	18
23.	Tyrone Wheatley, Oak.	7	918	3,538	30
24.	Fred Taylor, Jax.	4	745	3,470	32
25.	Duce Staley, Phil.	5	835	3,315	12
26.	Ricky Williams, Mia.	3	814	3,129	16
27.	Ahman Green, G.B.	4	628	2,891	20
28.	Terry Kirby, Oak.	9	745	2,824	27
29.	Tiki Barber, NYG	5	629	2,806	15
30.	Steve McNair, Tenn.	7	439	2,594	27

*Free agent; subject to developments.

TOP ACTIVE PASS RECEIVERS

		Yrs.	No.	Yards	TD
1.	Jerry Rice, Oak.	17	1,364	20,386	185
2.	Tim Brown, Oak.	14	937	13,237	95
3.	Larry Centers, Buff.	12	765	6,303	27
4.	Shannon Sharpe, Den.	12	692	8,604	51
5.	Herman Moore, *	11	670	9,174	62
6.	Terance Mathis, *	12	666	8,591	61
7.	Rob Moore, Den.	11	628	9,368	49
8.	Jimmy Smith, Jax.	8	584	8,260	44
9.	Keenan McCardell, *	10	579	7,526	38
10.	Marshall Faulk, St.L.	8	548	5,447	31
11.	Jeff Graham, Atl.	11	542	8,172	30
12.	Eric Metcalf, *	13	541	5,572	31
13.	Isaac Bruce, St.L.	8	540	8,405	56
14.	Ricky Proehl, St.L.	12	537	7,055	42
15.	Marvin Harrison, Ind.	6	522	7,078	62
16.	Keyshawn Johnson, T.B.	6	482	6,248	40
17.	Ed McCaffrey, Den.	11	477	6,324	53
18.	Emmitt Smith, Dall.	12	470	2,923	11
	Rod Smith, Den.	7	470	6,756	44
20.	Johnnie Morton, K.C.	8	469	6,499	35
21.	Ricky Watters, *	10	467	4,248	13
22.	Frank Sanders, Ariz.	7	459	6,179	22
23.	Wayne Chrebet, NYJ	7	456	5,835	30
24.	Curtis Conway, S.D.	9	453	6,335	42
25.	Frank Wycheck, Tenn.	9	448	4,615	24
26.	Sean Dawkins, Minn.	9	445	6,291	25
27.	Shawn Jefferson, Atl.	11	437	6,583	28
28.	Jake Reed, N.O.	11	429	6,639	33
29.	Antonio Freeman, *	7	417	6,510	57
30.	O.J. McDuffie, *	9	415	5,074	29

TOP ACTIVE INTERCEPTORS

		Yrs.	No.	Yards	TD
1.	Rod Woodson, Oak.	15	61	1,240	10
2.	Darrell Green, Wash.	19	54	621	6
3.	Aeneas Williams, St.L.	11	50	722	8
4.	Ray Buchanan, Atl.	9	43	789	4
5.	Terrell Buckley, *	10	41	638	5
6.	LeRoy Butler, G.B.	12	38	533	1
7.	Eric Davis, *	12	37	428	4
	Troy Vincent, Phil.	10	37	596	3
9.	Todd Lyght, Det.	11	35	431	4
10.	Ray Crockett, K.C.	13	34	460	3
11.	Ashley Ambrose, Atl.	10	33	390	2
12.	Donnie Abraham, NYJ	6	31	341	2
	Darryl Williams, *	10	31	691	4
14.	Ryan McNeil, S.D.	9	30	296	2
	Kurt Schulz, *	10	30	244	1
16.	Keith Lyle, Atl.	8	29	336	0
17.	William Thomas, Oak.	11	27	347	2
18.	Doug Evans, Sea.	9	26	321	2
	Otis Smith, N.E.	11	26	624	7
	Jimmy Spencer, Den.	10	26	209	2
21.	Ty Law, N.E.	7	25	438	5
	Dewayne Washington, Pitt.	8	25	511	5
23.	Aaron Glenn, Hou.	8	24	294	3
	Victor Green, *	9	24	529	2
	Rodney Harrison, S.D.	8	24	343	2
	Marcus Robertson, Sea.	11	24	458	0
	Willie Williams, Sea.	9	24	300	4
28.	Dale Carter, N.O.	9	23	231	1
	Sammy Knight, N.O.	5	23	428	4
	Sam Madison, Mia.	5	23	379	1

TOP ACTIVE PUNT RETURNERS
40 or more punt returns

		Yrs.	No.	Yards	Avg.	TD
1.	Jeff Ogden, Mia.	4	55	728	13.2	1
2.	Charlie Rogers, Buff.	3	73	925	12.7	1
3.	Darrien Gordon, *	8	279	3,421	12.3	6
4.	Desmond Howard, Det.	10	235	2,847	12.1	8
5.	Jacquez Green, Wash.	4	55	658	12.0	1
6.	Jermaine Lewis, Hou.	6	231	2,730	11.8	6
7.	Deltha O'Neal, Den.	2	65	759	11.7	1
8.	Arnold Jackson, Ariz.	1	40	461	11.5	0
9.	Troy Brown, N.E.	9	172	1,973	11.5	3
10.	Az-Zahir Hakim, Det.	4	112	1,280	11.4	2
11.	Karl Williams, T.B.	6	155	1,759	11.3	4
12.	Darrell Green, Wash.	19	51	576	11.3	0
13.	Brian Mitchell, Phil.	12	388	4,278	11.0	8
14.	Reggie Barlow, Oak.	6	146	1,581	10.8	2
15.	Tamarick Vanover, S.D.	5	181	1,930	10.7	4
16.	Hank Poteat, Pitt.	2	72	759	10.5	1
17.	Jeff Burris, Cin.	8	100	1,045	10.5	0
18.	Tim Brown, Oak.	14	310	3,217	10.4	3
19.	Joey Galloway, Dall.	7	81	831	10.3	4
20.	Wane McGarity, N.O.	3	58	590	10.2	2
21.	Eric Metcalf, *	13	348	3,454	9.9	10
22.	Tim Dwight, S.D.	4	108	1,063	9.8	3
23.	Glyn Milburn, *	9	304	2,984	9.8	1
24.	Craig Yeast, *	3	57	556	9.8	2
25.	Eddie Kennison, K.C.	6	138	1,343	9.7	3
26.	Amani Toomer, NYG	6	109	1,060	9.7	3
27.	Tiki Barber, NYG	5	121	1,176	9.7	1
28.	Leon Johnson, Chi.	5	119	1,145	9.6	1
29.	Terrell Buckley, *	10	78	746	9.6	1
30.	Derrick Mason, Tenn.	5	141	1,338	9.5	2

TOP ACTIVE KICKOFF RETURNERS
40 or more kickoff returns

		Yrs.	No.	Yards	Avg.	TD
1.	Darrick Vaughn, Atl.	2	100	2,573	25.7	4
2.	Steve Smith, Car.	1	56	1,431	25.6	2
3.	MarTay Jenkins, Ariz.	3	131	3,306	25.2	1
4.	Tim Brown, Oak.	14	49	1,235	25.2	1
5.	Terry Fair, Det.	4	101	2,516	24.9	2
6.	Byron Hanspard, T.B.	2	40	987	24.7	2
7.	Kevin Williams, Hou.	4	41	1,011	24.7	1
8.	Ronney Jenkins, S.D.	2	125	3,072	24.6	3
9.	Michael Bates, Car.	9	347	8,424	24.3	5
10.	Allen Rossum, Atl.	4	171	4,146	24.2	2
11.	Deuce McAllister, N.O.	1	45	1,091	24.2	0
12.	Duce Staley, Phil.	5	48	1,158	24.1	0
13.	Tamarick Vanover, S.D.	5	212	5,099	24.1	4
14.	Glyn Milburn, *	9	407	9,788	24.0	2
15.	Brock Marion, Mia.	9	123	2,951	24.0	0
16.	Charlie Rogers, Buff.	3	134	3,214	24.0	1
17.	Deltha O'Neal, Den.	2	46	1,102	24.0	1
18.	Autry Denson, Chi.	3	43	1,029	23.9	0
19.	Kevin Mathis, N.O.	5	51	1,216	23.8	0
20.	Reggie Swinton, Dall.	1	56	1,327	23.7	0
21.	Chris Cole, Den.	2	59	1,391	23.6	0
22.	Reidel Anthony, Wash.	5	95	2,232	23.5	0
23.	Reggie Barlow, Oak.	6	70	1,634	23.3	1
24.	Troy Walters, Ind.	2	48	1,117	23.3	0
25.	Corey Harris, *	10	238	5,528	23.2	1
26.	Aaron Glenn, Hou.	8	111	2,578	23.2	1
27.	Tim Dwight, S.D.	4	112	2,597	23.2	1
28.	Brian Mitchell, Phil.	12	509	11,735	23.1	4
29.	O.J. McDuffie, *	9	92	2,103	22.9	0
30.	Ahman Green, G.B.	4	63	1,438	22.8	0

TOP ACTIVE PUNTERS
50 or more punts

	Yrs.	No.	Avg.	LG
1. Shane Lechler, Oak.	2	138	46.1	69
2. Darren Bennett, S.D.	6	602	44.5	66
3. Tom Rouen, Den.	9	612	44.0	76
4. Hunter Smith, Ind.	3	191	44.0	65
5. Todd Sauerbrun, Car.	7	503	43.6	73
6. Chris Hanson, Jax.	2	86	43.4	59
7. Sean Landeta, Phil.	17	1,216	43.4	74
8. Tom Tupa, T.B.	13	597	43.3	73
9. Josh Miller, Pitt.	6	433	43.3	75
10. Mitch Berger, St.L.	7	411	43.2	75
11. Chris Gardocki, Cle.	11	825	43.1	72
12. Matt Turk, NYJ	7	561	43.1	77
13. Rodney Williams, NYG	1	91	42.9	90
14. Craig Hentrich, Tenn.	8	609	42.9	78
15. John Jett, Det.	9	640	42.6	62
16. Bryan Barker, Wash.	12	884	42.5	83
17. Lee Johnson, *	17	1,212	42.5	76
18. Mark Royals, Mia.	12	986	42.3	69
19. Toby Gowin, N.O.	5	394	42.3	72
20. Scott Player, Ariz.	4	307	42.3	67
21. Brad Maynard, Chi.	5	467	42.1	64
22. Jeff Feagles, Sea.	14	1,139	41.7	77
23. Kyle Richardson, Minn.	5	383	41.4	67
24. Micah Knorr, Dall.	2	136	41.3	60
25. John Baker, Hou.	2	86	41.2	59
26. Daniel Pope, *	3	199	40.9	64
27. Brian Moorman, Buff.	1	80	40.8	66
28. Jason Baker, S.F.	1	69	40.8	64
29. Josh Bidwell, G.B.	2	160	40.6	68
30. Chris Mohr, Atl.	12	922	40.4	80

TOP ACTIVE QUARTERBACK SACKERS

	Yrs.	No.
1. Bruce Smith, Wash.	17	186.0
2. John Randle, Sea.	12	125.0
3. Trace Armstrong, Oak.	13	99.0
4. Robert Porcher, Det.	10	85.5
5. Michael Strahan, NYG	9	84.5
6. Michael Sinclair, *	10	73.5
7. Michael McCrary, Balt.	9	69.0
8. Rob Burnett, *	12	67.0
9. Kevin Carter, Tenn.	7	64.5
Warren Sapp, T.B.	7	64.5
11. Chad Brown, Sea.	9	64.0
12. Simeon Rice, T.B.	6	62.5
13. Jason Gildon, Pitt.	8	62.0
14. Keith Hamilton, NYG	10	61.5
15. Hugh Douglas, Phil.	7	61.0
Bryant Young, S.F.	8	61.0
17. Tracy Scroggins, *	10	60.5
18. Marco Coleman, *	10	56.5
19. Anthony Pleasant, N.E.	12	54.0
20. Chris Slade, *	9	53.5
21. Peter Boulware, Balt.	5	52.0
Mo Lewis, NYJ	11	52.0
23. Bryan Cox, N.O.	11	51.5
Willie McGinest, N.E.	8	51.5
25. Joe Johnson, G.B.	7	50.5
Dana Stubblefield, S.F.	9	50.5
27. La'Roi Glover, Dall.	6	50.0
28. Santana Dotson, Wash.	10	49.0
29. Tony Brackens, Jax.	6	48.0
Dan Wilkinson, Wash.	8	48.0

COACHES RECORDS

ACTIVE COACHES' CAREER RECORDS (Order Based on Career Victories)
Start of 2002 Season

Coach	Team(s)	Yrs.	Regular Season Won	Lost	Tied	Pct.	Postseason Won	Lost	Pct.	Career Won	Lost	Tied	Pct.
Dan Reeves	Denver Broncos, New York Giants, Atlanta Falcons	21	178	149	1	.544	10	8	.556	188	157	1	.545
Marty Schottenheimer	Cleveland Browns, Kansas City Chiefs, Washington Redskins, San Diego Chargers	16	153	93	1	.621	5	11	.313	158	104	1	.603
Mike Holmgren	Green Bay Packers, Seattle Seahawks	10	99	61	0	.619	9	6	.600	108	67	0	.617
Bill Cowher	Pittsburgh Steelers	10	99	61	0	.619	6	7	.462	105	68	0	.607
Dick Vermeil	Philadelphia Eagles, St. Louis Rams, Kansas City Chiefs	11	82	83	0	.497	6	4	.600	88	87	0	.503
Mike Shanahan	Los Angeles Raiders, Denver Broncos	9	80	52	0	.606	7	2	.778	87	54	0	.617
Jeff Fisher	Tennessee Titans	7	65	53	0	.551	3	2	.600	68	55	0	.553
Tom Coughlin	Jacksonville Jaguars	7	62	50	0	.554	4	4	.500	66	54	0	.550
Dave Wannstedt	Chicago Bears, Miami Dolphins	8	62	66	0	.484	2	3	.400	64	69	0	.481
Tony Dungy	Tampa Bay Buccaneers, Indianapolis Colts	6	54	42	0	.563	2	4	.333	56	46	0	.549
Bill Belichick	Cleveland Browns, New England Patriots	7	52	60	0	.464	4	1	.800	56	61	0	.479
Steve Mariucci	San Francisco 49ers	5	47	33	0	.588	2	3	.400	49	36	0	.576
Jim Fassel	New York Giants	5	44	35	1	.556	2	2	.500	46	37	1	.554
Jon Gruden	Oakland Raiders, Tampa Bay Buccaneers	4	38	26	0	.594	2	2	.500	40	28	0	.588
Brian Billick	Baltimore Ravens	3	30	18	0	.625	5	1	.833	35	19	0	.648
Dom Capers	Carolina Panthers, Houston Texans	4	30	34	0	.469	1	1	.500	31	35	0	.470
Andy Reid	Philadelphia Eagles	3	27	21	0	.563	3	2	.600	30	23	0	.566
Mike Martz	St. Louis Rams	2	24	8	0	.750	2	2	.500	26	10	0	.722
Dick Jauron	Chicago Bears	3	24	24	0	.500	0	1	.000	24	25	0	.490
Mike Sherman	Green Bay Packers	2	21	11	0	.656	1	1	.500	22	12	0	.647
Jim Haslett	New Orleans Saints	2	17	15	0	.531	1	1	.500	18	16	0	.529
Herman Edwards	New York Jets	1	10	6	0	.625	0	1	.000	10	7	0	.588
Dick LeBeau	Cincinnati Bengals	2	10	19	0	.345	0	0	.000	10	19	0	.345
Dave Campo	Dallas Cowboys	2	10	22	0	.313	0	0	.000	10	22	0	.313
Dave McGinnis	Arizona Cardinals	2	8	17	0	.320	0	0	.000	8	17	0	.320
Butch Davis	Cleveland Browns	1	7	9	0	.438	0	0	.000	7	9	0	.438
Gregg Williams	Buffalo Bills	1	3	13	0	.188	0	0	.000	3	13	0	.188
Marty Mornhinweg	Detroit Lions	1	2	14	0	.125	0	0	.000	2	14	0	.125
Bill Callahan	Oakland Raiders	0	0	0	0	.000	0	0	.000	0	0	0	.000
John Fox	Carolina Panthers	0	0	0	0	.000	0	0	.000	0	0	0	.000
Steve Spurrier	Washington Redskins	0	0	0	0	.000	0	0	.000	0	0	0	.000
Mike Tice	Minnesota Vikings	1	0	1	0	.000	0	0	.000	0	1	0	.000

COACHES WITH 100 CAREER VICTORIES (Order Based on Career Victories)
Start of 2002 Season

Coach	Team(s)		Regular Season				Postseason			Career			
		Yrs.	Won	Lost	Tied	Pct.	Won	Lost	Pct.	Won	Lost	Tied	Pct.
Don Shula	Baltimore Colts, Miami Dolphins	33	328	156	6	.676	19	17	.528	347	173	6	.665
George Halas	Chicago Bears	40	318	148	31	.671	6	3	.667	324	151	31	.671
Tom Landry	Dallas Cowboys	29	250	162	6	.605	20	16	.556	270	178	6	.601
Earl (Curly) Lambeau	Green Bay Packers, Chicago Cardinals, Washington Redskins	33	226	132	22	.624	3	2	.600	229	134	22	.623
Chuck Noll	Pittsburgh Steelers	23	193	148	1	.566	16	8	.667	209	156	1	.572
Chuck Knox	Los Angeles Rams, Buffalo Bills, Seattle Seahawks	22	186	147	1	.558	7	11	.389	193	158	1	.550
Dan Reeves	Denver Broncos, New York Giants, Atlanta Falcons	21	178	149	1	.544	10	8	.556	188	157	1	.545
Paul Brown	Cleveland Browns, Cincinnati Bengals	21	166	100	6	.621	4	8	.333	170	108	6	.609
Bud Grant	Minnesota Vikings	18	158	96	5	.620	10	12	.455	168	108	5	.607
Marty Schottenheimer	Cleveland Browns, Kansas City Chiefs, Washington Redskins, San Diego Chargers	16	153	93	1	.621	5	11	.313	158	104	1	.603
Marv Levy	Kansas City Chiefs, Buffalo Bills	17	143	112	0	.561	11	8	.579	154	120	0	.562
Steve Owen	New York Giants	23	151	100	17	.595	2	8	.200	153	108	17	.581
Bill Parcells	New York Giants, New England Patriots, New York Jets	15	138	100	1	.579	11	6	.647	149	106	1	.584
Joe Gibbs	Washington Redskins	12	124	60	0	.674	16	5	.762	140	65	0	.683
Hank Stram	Kansas City Chiefs, New Orleans Saints	17	131	97	10	.571	5	3	.625	136	100	10	.573
Weeb Ewbank	Baltimore Colts, New York Jets	20	130	129	7	.502	4	1	.800	134	130	7	.507
Mike Ditka	Chicago Bears, New Orleans Saints	14	121	95	0	.560	6	6	.500	127	101	0	.557
Jim Mora	New Orleans Saints, Indianapolis Colts	15	125	106	0	.541	0	6	.000	125	112	0	.527
George Seifert	San Francisco 49ers, Carolina Panthers	11	114	62	0	.648	10	5	.667	124	67	0	.649
Sid Gillman	Los Angeles Rams, Los Angeles-San Diego Chargers, Houston Oilers	18	122	99	7	.550	1	5	.167	123	104	7	.541
George Allen	Los Angeles Rams, Washington Redskins	12	116	47	5	.705	2	5	.222	118	54	5	.681
Don Coryell	St. Louis Cardinals, San Diego Chargers	14	111	83	1	.572	3	6	.333	114	89	1	.561
John Madden	Oakland Raiders	10	103	32	7	.750	9	7	.563	112	39	7	.731
Mike Holmgren	Green Bay Packers, Seattle Seahawks	10	99	61	0	.619	9	6	.600	108	67	0	.617
Ray (Buddy) Parker	Chicago Cardinals, Detroit Lions, Pittsburgh Steelers	15	104	75	9	.577	3	1	.750	107	76	9	.581
Vince Lombardi	Green Bay Packers, Washington Redskins	10	96	34	6	.728	9	1	.900	105	35	6	.740
Bill Cowher	Pittsburgh Steelers	10	99	61	0	.619	6	7	.462	105	68	0	.607
Tom Flores	Oakland-Los Angeles Raiders, Seattle Seahawks	12	97	87	0	.527	8	3	.727	105	90	0	.538
Bill Walsh	San Francisco 49ers	10	92	59	1	.609	10	4	.714	102	63	1	.617
Dennis Green	Minnesota Vikings	10	97	63	0	.606	4	8	.333	101	71	0	.587

Active coaches in bold.

The Chicago Bears need six victories to become the first team with 650 total wins.

The Cleveland Browns need three victories to reach 400 total wins.

The Dallas Cowboys need six victories to reach 400 total wins.

The Oakland Raiders need seven victories to reach 400 total wins.

The Seattle Seahawks need nine victories to reach 200 total wins.

Dan Reeves, Atlanta, needs six victories to pass Chuck Knox (193) to move into sixth place all-time in career victories. In 21 seasons, Reeves has 188 career victories.

Bill Cowher, Pittsburgh, needs one victory to reach 100 career regular-season victories. In 10 seasons, Cowher has 99 regular-season victories.

Mike Holmgren, Seattle, needs one victory to reach 100 career regular-season victories. In 10 seasons, Holmgren has 99 regular-season victories.

Brett Favre, Green Bay, needs 1,925 passing yards to pass Vinny Testaverde (39,059), Johnny Unitas (40,239), and Joe Montana (40,551) to move into sixth place all-time (see Testaverde note). In 11 seasons, Favre has passed for 38,627 yards.

Favre has thrown 287 touchdowns passes in 11 seasons and needs 14 to pass Johnny Unitas (290), Warren Moon (291), and John Elway (300) for third all-time.

Favre has led the league in touchdown passes three times in his 11-year career and can tie Johnny Unitas, Len Dawson, and Steve Young (four) for the most seasons leading the league in touchdown passes.

Favre needs 99 completions to pass Joe Montana (3,409) to move into fifth place all-time. Favre has completed 3,311 passes in 11 seasons.

Vinny Testaverde, New York Jets, needs 1,493 passing yards to pass Johnny Unitas (40,239) and Joe Montana (40,551) to move into sixth place all-time (see Favre note). Testaverde has passed for 39,059 yards in 15 seasons.

Testaverde has thrown 241 touchdown passes in 15 seasons and needs 21 to pass John Hadl (244), Boomer Esiason (247), Dan Fouts (254), Sonny Jurgensen (255),and Dave Krieg (261) to move into eighth place all-time.

Testaverde needs 253 completions to pass Dan Fouts (3,297), Brett Favre (3,311), and Joe Montana (3,409) to move into fifth place all-time (see Favre note). In 15 seasons, Testaverde has completed 3,157 passes.

Peyton Manning, Indianapolis, needs 4,000 passing yards to become the first player in NFL history with four consecutive 4,000-yard passing seasons.

Kurt Warner, St. Louis, has led the league in completion percentage each of the past three seasons and can tie Steve Young (four) for the second-longest streak in the category behind Len Dawson (six).

Steve McNair, Tennessee, needs 1,965 passing yards and 406 rushing yards to become the fifth quarterback in NFL history (Randall Cunningham, John Elway, Fran Tarkenton, and Steve Young) to throw for 18,000 yards and rush for 3,000 yards. In seven seasons, McNair has passed for 16,035 yards and rushed for 2,594 yards.

Emmitt Smith, Dallas, needs 540 rushing yards to pass Walter Payton (16,726) to become the NFL's all-time leading rusher. In 12 seasons, Smith has rushed for 16,187 yards.

Smith has 74 career 100-yard rushing games in 12 seasons and needs four to pass Barry Sanders (76) and Walter Payton (77) for the most all-time.

Smith needs two rushing touchdowns to become the first player in NFL history with 150 rushing touchdowns. In 12 seasons, Smith has rushed for 148 touchdowns.

Smith needs 890 combined yards to join Walter Payton (21,803), Jerry Rice (21,017), and Brian Mitchell (20,263) as the only players in NFL history with 20,000 combined yards. Smith

has gained 19,110 combined yards in his 12-year career.

Smith needs 890 total yards from scrimmage to join Walter Payton (21,264) and Jerry Rice (21,011) as the only players in NFL history with 20,000 total scrimmage yards. In 12 seasons, Smith has 19,110 total yards from scrimmage.

Jerome Bettis, Pittsburgh, has rushed for 10,876 yards in nine seasons. Bettis needs 1,245 rushing yards to pass O.J. Simpson (11,236), John Riggins (11,352), Thurman Thomas (12,074), and Franco Harris (12,120) to move into eighth place all-time.

Bettis needs 1,000 rushing yards to move into sole possession of fourth place all-time in 1,000-yard seasons. In nine seasons, Bettis has rushed for 1,000 yards eight times, tied with Tony Dorsett, Franco Harris, and Thurman Thomas.

Curtis Martin, New York Jets, needs 1,000 rushing yards to become the second player in NFL history (Barry Sanders) to rush for 1,000 yards in each of his first eight seasons.

Martin needs 250 carries to become the third player in NFL history (Emmitt Smith and Thurman Thomas) to record eight consecutive seasons with 250 rushing attempts.

Martin needs 733 rushing yards to become the fifteenth player in NFL history to rush for 10,000 yards (see Faulk note). In seven seasons, Martin has gained 9,267 rushing yards.

Marshall Faulk, St. Louis, needs 17 touchdowns to pass Lenny Moore (113), John Riggins (116), Walter Payton (125), and Jim Brown (126) to move into fifth place all-time. In eight seasons, Faulk has scored 110 touchdowns.

Faulk needs 2,000 combined yards to become the first player in NFL history to gain 2,000 combined yards in five consecutive seasons. Faulk is the only player in NFL history to gain 2,000 combined yards four seasons in a row.

Faulk needs 1,644 total yards from scrimmage to pass Ricky Watters (14,891), Eric Dickerson (15,396), Tony Dorsett (16,293), and Thurman Thomas (16,532) to move into sixth place all-time (see Watters note). In eight seasons, Faulk has 14,889 total scrimmage yards.

Faulk needs 2,000 total scrimmage yards to become the first player in NFL history to gain 2,000 yards from scrimmage in five consecutive seasons. Faulk is the only player in NFL history to gain 2,000 total scrimmage yards four seasons in a row.

Faulk has rushed for 9,442 yards in eight seasons and needs 558 yards to become the fifteenth player in NFL history to gain 10,000 rushing yards (see Martin note).

Corey Dillon, Cincinnati, needs 1,000 rushing yards to become the fourth player in NFL history (Barry Sanders, Eric Dickerson, and Curtis Martin) to rush for 1,000 yards in each of his first six seasons.

Ricky Watters, needs nine touchdowns to become the fifteenth player in NFL history to score 100 touchdowns. In 10 seasons, Watters has scored 91 touchdowns.

Watters needs 1,642 yards from scrimmage to pass Eric Dickerson (15,396), Tony Dorsett (16,293), and Thurman Thomas (16,532) to move into sixth place all-time (see Faulk note). In 10 seasons, Watters has 14,891 total scrimmage yards.

Jerry Rice, Oakland, needs four touchdowns to become the first player in NFL history with 200 career touchdowns. In 17 seasons, Rice has scored 196 touchdowns, the most in NFL history.

Rice needs 787 combined yards to pass Walter Payton (21,803) to move into first all-time (see Mitchell note). Rice has 21,017 combined yards in 17 seasons.

Rice needs 254 total yards from scrimmage to pass Walter Payton and become the all-time NFL leader in the category. In 17 seasons, Rice has 21,011 total scrimmage yards.

In 17 seasons, Rice has 1,364 receptions, the most in NFL history, and needs 36 to become the first player with 1,400 career receptions.

Rice needs a reception in his first nine games to become the first player in NFL history with a reception in 250 consecutive games. Rice has a reception in 241 games in a row, the longest streak all-time.

Rice needs 614 receiving yards to become the first player in NFL history with 21,000 receiving yards. Rice has an NFL-best 20,386 yards in 17 seasons.

Rice has led the league in receiving yards six times in his 17-year career and can tie Don Hutson (seven) for the most seasons leading the league in receiving yards.

Rice needs one 200-yard receiving game to tie Lance Alworth (five) for most career 200-yard receiving games. In 17 seasons, Rice has four 200-yard receiving games.

Tim Brown, Oakland, needs 15 receptions to pass Art Monk (940) and Andre Reed (951) to move into third place all-time. Brown has 937 receptions in 14 seasons and needs 63 to become the third receiver in NFL history (Jerry Rice and Cris Carter) with 1,000 career receptions.

Brown needs 1,000 receiving yards to become the second player in NFL history (Jerry Rice) with double-digit 1,000-yard seasons. Brown has nine 1,000-yard receiving seasons in his 14-year career.

Brown needs 768 receiving yards to pass Henry Ellard (13,777), Cris Carter (13,833), and James Lofton (14,004) to move into second place all-time. In 14 seasons, Brown has 13,237 receiving yards.

Brown has 95 touchdown receptions in 14 seasons and needs six to pass Steve Largent (100) to move into third place all-time.

Randy Moss, Minnesota, needs 1,000 receiving yards to become the first player in NFL history with 1,000 receiving yards in each of his first five seasons. Moss is the only player in NFL history with 1,000 receiving yards in each of his first four seasons.

Marvin Harrison, Indianapolis, needs 100 receptions to become the first player in NFL history with four consecutive 100-catch seasons.

Harrison has 522 career receptions in six seasons and needs 74 catches for the most receptions in a player's first seven seasons.

Jimmy Smith, Jacksonville, needs 1,000 receiving yards to tie Lance Alworth (7) for fifth place all-time in 1,000-yard receiving seasons. In nine seasons, Smith has six 1,000-yard seasons.

Frank Wycheck, Tennessee, needs 60 receptions to become the second tight end in NFL history (Shannon Sharpe) with 60 receptions in six consecutive seasons.

Wycheck needs 52 receptions to become the fourth tight end in NFL history (Shannon Sharpe, Ozzie Newsome, and Kellen Winslow) with 500 career receptions. In nine seasons, Wycheck has 448 receptions.

Derrick Mason, Tennessee, needs 2,000 combined yards to become the third player in NFL history (Marshall Faulk and Walter Payton) to gain 2,000 combined yards in three consecutive seasons.

Brian Mitchell, Philadelphia, has 20,263 combined yards in 12 seasons. Mitchell needs 737 yards to join Walter Payton (21,803) and Jerry Rice (21,017) as the only players in NFL history to gain 21,000 combined yards. With 1,541 combined yards, Mitchell can become the all-time leader in the category (see Rice note).

Mitchell needs one kick return touchdown (kickoff or punt) for sole possession of the all-time lead. Mitchell has 12 in his career, tied with Eric Metcalf for the most in league history (see Metcalf note).

Mitchell has eight career punt return touchdowns in 12 seasons and needs two to tie Eric Metcalf (10) for most all-time (see Howard note).

Eric Metcalf, needs one kick return touchdown (kickoff or punt) for sole possession of the all-time lead. Metcalf has 12 in his career, tied with Brian Mitchell for the most in league history (see Mitchell note).

Desmond Howard, Detroit, has eight career punt return touchdowns in 10 seasons and needs two to tie Eric Metcalf (10) for most all-time (see Mitchell note).

Howard needs one kick return touchdown (kickoff or punt) to tie Ollie Matson, Mel Gray and Deion Sanders (nine) for third place all-time. In 10 seasons, Howard has eight kick return touchdowns and needs two to join Eric Metcalf and Brian Mitchell as the only players with double-digit kick return touchdowns.

Michael Bates, Carolina, needs one kickoff return touchdown to tie Ollie Matson, Gale Sayers, Travis Williams and Mel Gray (six) for first place all-time. In nine seasons, Bates has returned five kickoffs for touchdowns.

Morten Andersen, Kansas City, needs 98 points to pass Gary Anderson for first all-time in points scored. In 20 seasons, Andersen has scored 2,036 points.

Andersen has kicked 464 field goals in 20 seasons and needs 13 to pass Gary Anderson (476) for most all-time.

Rod Woodson, Oakland, needs 43 interception return yards to pass Emlen Tunnel (1,282) for the most in NFL history. In 15 seasons, Woodson has 1,240 interception return yards.

Woodson has 61 interceptions in 15 seasons and needs eight to pass Dave Brown (62), Dick LeBeau (62), Ronnie Lott (63), Ken Riley (65), and Dick "Night Train" Lane (68) for third place all-time.

Aeneas Williams, St. Louis, needs two interception returns for a touchdown to pass Ken Houston (9) and tie Rod Woodson (10) for the all-time NFL lead. In 11 seasons, Williams has 8 interception returns for touchdowns.

Jevon Kearse, Tennessee, needs 10 sacks to become the third defensive player in NFL history (Reggie White and Derrick Thomas) to record double-digit sacks in each of his first four seasons.

Bruce Smith, Washington, needs 12.5 sacks to pass Reggie White (198.0) to become the NFL's all-time leader in sacks. In 17 seasons, Smith has 186.0 sacks.

Darrell Green, Washington, can move into a tie for first place all-time (Jackie Slater) for most seasons with one club (20).

Green needs one interception to increase his NFL-record of consecutive seasons with an interception to 20.

67th Annual NFL Draft, April 20-21, 2002
*Denotes Compensatory Selection

ARIZONA CARDINALS
1. Wendell Bryant—12, DT, Wisconsin
2. Levar Fisher—49, LB, North Carolina State
3. Josh McCown—81, QB, Sam Houston State
   *Dennis Johnson—98, DE, Kentucky
4. Nate Dwyer—113, DT, Kansas
5. Jason McAddley—149, WR, Alabama
6. Josh Scobey—185, RB, Kansas State
7. Mike Banks—223, TE, Iowa State

ATLANTA FALCONS
1. T.J. Duckett—18, RB, Michigan State,
   from Washington through Oakland
3. Will Overstreet—80, LB,Tennessee
4. Martin Bibla—116, G, Miami, from Houston
5. Kevin McCadam—148, DB, Virginia Tech
   Kurt Kittner—158, QB, Illinois, from Oakland
6. Kahlil Hill—184, WR, Iowa
7. Michael Coleman—217, WR, Widener, from Dallas
   *Kevin Shaffer—244, T, Tulsa

BALTIMORE RAVENS
1. Ed Reed—24, DB, Miami
2. Anthony Weaver—52, DT, Notre Dame, from Washington
4. Dave Zastudil—112, P, Ohio, from Atlanta through Denver
   Ron Johnson—123, WR, Minnesota
5. Terry Jones—155, TE, Alabama, from Denver
6. Lamont Brightful—195, KR, Eastern Washington
   *Javin Hunter—206, WR, Notre Dame
   *Chester Taylor—207, RB, Toledo
   *Chad Williams—209, DB, Southern Mississippi
7. Wes Pate—236, QB, Stephen F. Austin

BUFFALO BILLS
1. Mike Williams—4, T, Texas
2. Josh Reed—36, WR, Louisiana State
   Ryan Denney—61, DE, Brigham Young, from San Francisco
3. *Coy Wire—97, DB, Stanford
5. Justin Bannan—139, DT, Colorado
6. Kevin Thomas—176, DB, Nevada-Las Vegas
7. Mike Pucillo—215, G, Auburn
   *Rodney Wright—249, WR, Fresno State
   *Jarrett Ferguson—251, RB, Virginia Tech
   *Dominique Stevenson—260, LB, Tennessee

CAROLINA PANTHERS
1. Julius Peppers—2, DE, North Carolina
2. DeShaun Foster—34, RB, UCLA
3. Will Witherspoon—73, LB, Georgia, from Cincinnati
4. Dante Wesley—100, DB, Arkansas-Pine Bluff
5. Randy Fasani—137, QB, Stanford
   Kyle Johnson—145, RB, Syracuse, from Cincinnati
6. Keith Heinrich—174, TE, Sam Houston State
7. Pete Campion—213, G, North Dakota State
   *Brad Franklin—258, DB, Louisiana-Lafayette

CHICAGO BEARS
1. Marc Colombo—29, T, Boston College
3. Roosevelt Williams—72, DB, Tuskegee, from Dallas
   Terrence Metcalf—93, G, Mississippi
4. Alex Brown—104, DE, Florida, from Dallas
5. Bobby Gray—140, DB, Louisiana Tech, from Dallas
   Bryan Knight—165, LB, Pittsburgh
6. Adrian Peterson—199, RB, Georgia Southern, from Miami
   Jamin Elliott—203, WR, Delaware
   *Bryan Fletcher—210, TE, UCLA

CINCINNATI BENGALS
1. Levi Jones—10, T, Arizona State
2. Lamont Thompson—41, DB, Washington State
3. Matt Schobel—67, TE, Texas Christian, from Carolina
4. Travis Dorsch—109, K, Purdue
6. Marquand Manuel—181, DB, Florida
7. Joey Evans—219, DE, North Carolina

CLEVELAND BROWNS
1. William Green—16, RB, Boston College
2. André Davis—47, WR, Virginia Tech
3. Melvin Fowler—76, C, Maryland, from Jacksonville
4. Kevin Bentley—101, LB, Northwestern, from Detroit
   Ben Taylor—111, LB, Virginia Tech
   Darnell Sanders—122, TE, Ohio State, from Oakland
5. Andra Davis—141, LB, Florida, from Minnesota
7. Joaquin Gonzalez—227, T, Miami

DALLAS COWBOYS
1. Roy Williams—8, DB, Oklahoma, from Kansas City
2. Andre Gurode—37, G, Colorado
   Antonio Bryant—63, WR, Pittsburgh, from Chicago
3. Derek Ross—75, DB, Ohio State, from Kansas City
4. Jamar Martin—129, RB, Ohio State, from Chicago
5. Pete Hunter—168, DB, Virginia Union, from New England
6. Tyson Walter—179, T, Ohio State
   *Deveren Johnson—208, WR, Sacred Heart
   *Bob Slowikowski—211, TE, Virginia Tech

DENVER BRONCOS
1. Ashley Lelie—19, WR, Hawaii
2. Clinton Portis—51, RB, Miami
3. Dorsett Davis—96, DT, Mississippi State,
   from New England through Washington and Baltimore
4. Sam Brandon—131, DB, Nevada-Las Vegas,
   from New England
5. Herb Haygood—144, WR, Michigan State,
   from Jacksonville through New England
6. Jeb Putzier—191, TE, Boise State
7. Chris Young—228, DB, Georgia Tech, from Atlanta
   Monsanto Pope—231, DT, Virginia

DETROIT LIONS
1. Joey Harrington—3, QB, Oregon
2. Kalimba Edwards—35, DE, South Carolina
3. André Goodman—68, DB, South Carolina
4. *John Taylor—134, DE, Montana State
5. John Owens—138, TE, Notre Dame
6. Chris Cash—175, DB, Southern California
7. Luke Staley—214, RB, Brigham Young
   *Matt Murphy—252, TE, Maryland
   *Victor Rogers—259, T, Colorado

GREEN BAY PACKERS
1. Javon Walker—20, WR, Florida State, from Seattle
3. Marques Anderson—92, DB, UCLA
4. *Najeh Davenport—135, RB, Miami
5. Aaron Kampman—156, DE, Iowa, from Seattle
   Craig Nall—164, QB, Northwestern State (La.)
6. Mike Houghton—200, G, San Diego State

HOUSTON TEXANS
1. David Carr—1, QB, Fresno State
2. Jabar Gaffney—33, WR, Florida
   Chester Pitts—50, T, San Diego State
3. Fred Weary—66, C, Tennessee
   Charles Hill—83, DT, Maryland
4. Jonathan Wells—99, RB, Ohio State
5. Jarrod Baxter—136, RB, New Mexico
   Ramon Walker—153, DB, Pittsburgh
6. Demarcus Faggins—173, DB, Kansas State
   Howard Green—190, DT, Louisiana State
7. Greg White—229, DE, Minnesota
   Ahmad Miller—261, DT, Nevada-Las Vegas

INDIANAPOLIS COLTS
1. Dwight Freeney—11, DE, Syracuse
2. Larry Tripplett—42, DT, Washington
3. Joseph Jefferson—74, DB, Western Kentucky
4. David Thornton—106, LB, North Carolina
6. David Pugh—182, DT, Virginia Tech
   James Lewis—183, DB, Miami,
       from Kansas City through St. Louis
   Brian Allen—204, RB, Stanford, from St. Louis
7. Josh Mallard—220, DE, Georgia

JACKSONVILLE JAGUARS
1. John Henderson—9, DT, Tennessee
2. Mike Pearson—40, T, Florida
3. Akin Ayodele—89, LB, Purdue,
       from Oakland through Washington
4. David Garrard—108, QB, East Carolina
   Chris Luzar—118, TE, Virginia, from Washington
6. Clenton Ballard—180, DT, Southwest Texas State
7. Kendall Newson—222, WR, Middle Tennessee State
   *Steve Smith—246, DB, Oregon
   *Hayden Epstein—247, K, Michigan

KANSAS CITY CHIEFS
1. Ryan Sims—6, DT, North Carolina, from Dallas
2. Eddie Freeman—43, DT, Alabama-Birmingham
4. Omar Easy—107, RB, Penn State
5. Scott Fujita—143, LB, California
7. Maurice Rodriguez—221, LB, Fresno State

MIAMI DOLPHINS
3. Seth McKinney—90, C, Texas A&M
4. Randy McMichael—114, TE, Georgia, from New Orleans
5. Omare Lowe—161, DB, Washington
   *Sam Simmons—170, WR, Northwestern
7. Leonard Henry—241, RB, East Carolina, from Chicago

MINNESOTA VIKINGS
1. Bryant McKinnie—7, T, Miami
2. Raonall Smith—38, LB, Washington State
3. Willie Offord—70, DB, South Carolina
4. Brian Williams—105, DB, North Carolina State
   *Ed Ta'amu—132, G, Utah
6. Nick Rogers—177, LB, Georgia Tech
7. Chad Beasley—218, DT, Virginia Tech

NEW ENGLAND PATRIOTS
1. Daniel Graham—21, TE, Colorado,
       from Tampa Bay through Oakland and Washington
2. Deion Branch—65, WR, Louisville
4. Rohan Davey—117, QB, Louisiana State, from Denver
   Jarvis Green—126, DE, Louisiana State, from Green Bay
7. Antwoine Womack—237, RB, Virginia,
       from Miami through Dallas
   David Givens—253, WR, Notre Dame

NEW ORLEANS SAINTS
1. Donte' Stallworth—13, WR, Tennessee
   Charles Grant—25, DE, Georgia, from Miami
2. LeCharles Bentley—44, C, Ohio State
3. James Allen—82, LB, Oregon State
4. Keyuo Craver—125, DB, Nebraska, from Miami
5. Mel Mitchell—150, DB, Western Kentucky
6. J.T. O'Sullivan—186, QB, Cal-Davis
   John Gilmore—196, TE, Penn State, from New York Jets
7. Derrius Monroe—224, DE, Virginia Tech

NEW YORK GIANTS
1. Jeremy Shockey—14, TE, Miami, from Tennessee
2. Tim Carter—46, WR, Auburn
3. Jeff Hatch—78, T, Pennsylvania
5. Nick Greisen—152, LB, Wisconsin
6. Wesly Mallard—188, LB, Oregon
7. Daryl Jones—226, WR, Miami
   *Quincy Monk—245, LB, North Carolina

NEW YORK JETS
1. Bryan Thomas—22, DE, Alabama-Birmingham
2. Jon McGraw—57, DB, Kansas State
3. Chris Baker—88, TE, Michigan State
4. Alan Harper—121, DE, Fresno State
5. Jonathan Goodwin—154, G, Michigan, from Washington

OAKLAND RAIDERS
1. Phillip Buchanon—17, DB, Miami, from Atlanta
   Napoleon Harris—23, LB, Northwestern
2. Langston Walker—53, T, California, from Tampa Bay
   Doug Jolley—55, TE, Brigham Young
5. Kenyon Coleman—147, DE, UCLA, from Cleveland
6. Keyon Nash—189, DB, Albany State, Ga., from Cleveland
   Larry Ned—197, RB, San Diego State
7. Ronald Curry—235, QB, North Carolina

PHILADELPHIA EAGLES
1. Lito Sheppard—26, DB, Florida
2. Michael Lewis—58, DB, Colorado
   Sheldon Brown—59, DB, South Carolina, from Miami
3. Brian Westbrook—91, RB, Villanova
4. Scott Peters—124, C, Arizona State
5. Freddie Milons—162, WR, Alabama
6. Tyreo Harrison—198, LB, Notre Dame
7. Raheem Brock—238, DE, Temple

PITTSBURGH STEELERS
1. Kendall Simmons—30, G, Auburn
2. Antwaan Randle El—62, WR, Indiana
3. Chris Hope—94, DB, Florida State
4. Larry Foote—128, LB, Michigan
5. Verron Haynes—166, RB, Georgia
6. Lee Mays—202, WR, Texas-El Paso
7. LaVar Glover—212, DB, Cincinnati, from Houston
   Brett Keisel—242, DE, Brigham Young

ST. LOUIS RAMS
1. Robert Thomas—31, LB, UCLA
2. Travis Fisher—64, DB, Central Florida
3. Lamar Gordon—84, RB, North Dakota State,
       from Washington through Kansas City
   Eric Crouch—95, WR, Nebraska
4. Travis Scott—130, G, Arizona State
5. Courtland Bullard—167, LB, Ohio State
6. Steve Bellisari—205, DB, Ohio State, from New England
7. Chris Massey—243, C, Marshall

SAN DIEGO CHARGERS

1. Quentin Jammer—5, DB, Texas
2. Toniu Fonoti—39, G, Nebraska
   Reche Caldwell—48, WR, Florida, from Atlanta
3. Ben Leber—71, LB, Kansas State
4. Justin Peelle—103, TE, Oregon
5. Terry Charles—142, WR, Portland State
6. Matt Anderle—178, T, Minnesota
7. Seth Burford—216, QB, Cal Poly-San Luis Obispo

SAN FRANCISCO 49ERS

1. Mike Rumph—27, DB, Miami
3. Saleem Rasheed—69, LB, Alabama, from Buffalo
4. Jeff Chandler—102, K, Florida, from Buffalo
   Kevin Curtis—127, DB, Texas Tech
5. Brandon Doman—163, QB, Brigham Young
   *Josh Shaw—172, DT, Michigan State
6. Mark Anelli—201, TE, Wisconsin
7. Eric Heitmann—239, G, Stanford
   *Kyle Kosier—248, T, Arizona State
   *Teddy Gaines—256, DB, Tennessee

SEATTLE SEAHAWKS

1. Jerramy Stevens—28, TE, Washington, from Green Bay
2. Maurice Morris—54, RB, Oregon
   Anton Palepoi—60, DE, Nevada-Las Vegas, from Green Bay
3. Kris Richard—85, DB, Southern California
4. Terreal Bierria—120, DB, Georgia
5. Rocky Bernard—146, DT, Texas A&M, from Indianapolis
   *Ryan Hannam—169, TE, Northern Iowa
   *Matt Hill—171, T, Boise State
6. Craig Jarrett—194, P, Michigan State
7. Jeff Kelly—232, QB, Southern Mississippi

TAMPA BAY BUCCANEERS

3. Marquise Walker—86, WR, Michigan
4. Travis Stephens—119, RB, Tennessee
5. Jermaine Phillips—157, DB, Georgia
6. John Stamper—193, DE, South Carolina
7. Tim Wansley—233, DB, Georgia
   *Tracey Wistrom—250, TE, Nebraska
   *Aaron Lockett—254, WR, Kansas State
   *Zack Quaccia—255, C, Stanford

TENNESSEE TITANS

1. Albert Haynesworth—15, DT, Tennessee,
   from New York Giants
2. Tank Williams—45, DB, Stanford
3. Rocky Calmus—77, LB, Oklahoma
4. Mike Echols—110, DB, Wisconsin, from New York Giants
   Tony Beckham—115, DB, Wisconsin-Stout
   *Rocky Boiman—133, LB, Notre Dame
5. Jake Schifino—151, WR, Akron
6. Justin Hartwig—187, G, Kansas
7. Darrell Hill—225, WR, Northern Illinois
   Carlos Hall—240, DE, Arkansas, from Green Bay

WASHINGTON REDSKINS

1. Patrick Ramsey—32, QB, Tulane, from New England
2. Ladell Betts—56, RB, Iowa, from Baltimore
3. Rashad Bauman—79, DB, Oregon,
   from Cleveland through Jacksonville
   Cliff Russell—87, WR, Utah, from Baltimore
5. Andre Lott—159, DB, Tennessee, from Baltimore
   Robert Royal—160, TE, Louisiana State,
   from New York Jets
6. Reggie Coleman—192, T, Tennessee
7. Jeff Grau—230, TE, UCLA
   Greg Scott—234, DE, Hampton,
   from New York Jets through New England
   *Rock Cartwright—257, RB, Kansas State

NUMBER OF PLAYERS DRAFTED—2002

BY POSITION:
Defensive Backs......................................52
Wide Receivers 33
Linebackers 27
Running Backs.....................................26
Tight Ends..24
Defensive Ends 23
Defensive Tackles...............................19
Tackles...16
Quarterbacks 15
Guards...13
Centers 7
Kickers...3
Punters 2
Kick Returner 1

BY COLLEGE:
Miami 11
Tennessee...10
Florida...8
Georgia..8
Ohio State...8
Virginia Tech 8
Kansas State 6
North Carolina 6
Notre Dame 6
Oregon...6
Stanford 6
UCLA..6
Brigham Young 5
Colorado..5
Louisiana State 5
Michigan State 5
South Carolina 5
Alabama 4
Arizona State...4
Fresno State..4
Michigan 4
Nebraska..4
Nevada-Las Vegas 4
Wisconsin 4
Auburn...3
Iowa...3
Maryland..3
Minnesota..3
Northwestern 3
Pittsburgh..3
San Diego State 3
Virginia...3
Washington..3
Alabama-Birmingham............................2
Boise State..2
Boston College 2
California..2
East Carolina...2
Florida State..2
Georgia Tech 2
Kansas 2
North Carolina State 2
North Dakota State 2
Oklahoma...2
Penn State 2
Purdue 2
Sam Houston State 2
Southern California................................2
Southern Mississippi 2
Syracuse..2
Texas 2

Texas A&M...2
Utah 2
Washington State 2
Western Kentucky 2
Akron..1
Albany State (Ga.) 1
Arkansas..1
Arkansas-Pine Bluff 1
Cal-Davis...1
Cal Poly-San Luis Obispo 1
Central Florida 1
Cincinnati...1
Delaware..1
Eastern Washington 1
Georgia Southern 1
Hampton...1
Hawaii..1
Illinois...1
Indiana...1
Iowa State 1
Kentucky..1
Louisiana-Lafayette 1
Louisiana Tech 1
Louisville..1
Marshall 1
Middle Tennessee State 1
Mississippi...1
Mississippi State 1
Montana State 1
New Mexico 1
Northern Illinois.....................................1
Northern Iowa 1
Northwestern State (La.) 1
Ohio 1
Oregon State 1
Pennsylvania...1
Portland State..1
Sacred Heart..1
Southwest Texas State 1
Stephen F. Austin...................................1
Temple..1
Texas Christian 1
Texas-El Paso 1
Texas Tech 1
Toledo 1
Tulane 1
Tulsa...1
Tuskegee..1
Villanova...1
Virginia Union 1
Widener 1
Wisconsin-Stout.....................................1

BY CONFERENCE:
Southeastern..47
Big Ten..36
Pac 10...32
Big East 27
Big 12..25
ACC 18
Mountain West.......................................15
Conference USA....................................10
WAC 10
Independent..9
MAC...5
Southland..5
Big Sky..3
Gateway..3
Atlantic 10 2
North Central Intercollegiate Athletic 2
Southern Intercollegiate Athletic..............2
Sun Belt..2
Central Intercollegiate Athletic Assoc. 1
Ivy League 1
Middle Atlantic States Collegiate Athletic....1
Mid-Eastern Athletic 1
Northeast..1
Southern...1
Southwestern Athletic 1
Wisconsin Intercollegiate Athletic 1

UNDERCLASSMEN IN THE DRAFT

Year	Entered	Drafted	In Top 10
1989	25	12	3
1990	38	18	5
1991	33	22	2
1992	48	25	5
1993	46	24	5
1994	42	26	6
1995	42	22	2
1996	47	21	4
1997	44	27	7
1998	41	20	3
1999	35	27	5
2000	31	20	4
2001	36	31	5
2002	43	26	2

WAIVERS

The waiver system is a procedure by which player contracts or NFL rights to players are made available by a club to other clubs in the League. During the procedure, the 31 other clubs either file claims to obtain the players or waive the opportunity to do so—thus the term "waiver." Claiming clubs are assigned players on a priority based on the inverse of won-and-lost standing. The claiming period is three business days from the beginning of the League Year through April 30, 10 calendar days from May 1 through the last business day before July 4, and 24 hours after July 4 through the conclusion of the regular season. If a player passes through waivers unclaimed, he becomes a free agent. All waivers are no recall and no withdrawal. Under the Collective Bargaining Agreement, from the beginning of the waiver system each year through the trading deadline (October 15, 2002), any veteran who has acquired four years of pension credit is not subject to the waiver system if the club desires to release him. After the trading deadline, such players are subject to the waiver system.

ACTIVE/INACTIVE LIST

The Active/Inactive List is the principal status for players participating for a club. It consists of all players under contract who are eligible for preseason, regular-season, and postseason games. Teams are permitted to open training camp with no more than 80 players under contract and thereafter must meet two mandatory roster reductions prior to the season opener. Teams will be permitted an Active List of 45 players and an Inactive List of eight players for each regular-season and postseason game. Provided that a club has two quarterbacks on its 45-player Active List, a third quarterback from its Inactive List is permitted to dress for the game, but if he enters the game during the first three quarters, the other two quarterbacks are thereafter prohibited from playing. Teams also are permitted to establish Practice Squads of up to five players who are eligible to participate in practice, but these players remain free agents and are eligible to sign with any other team in the league.

August 27.....................Roster reduction to 65 players
September 1 ....Roster reduction to 53 players
September 2.................Teams establish a Practice Squad of
up to five players

In addition to the squad limits described above, the overall roster limit of 80 players remains in effect throughout the regular season and postseason. The overall limit is applicable to players on a team's Active, Inactive, and certain Exempt Lists, players on the Practice Squad, and players on the Reserve List as Injured, Physically Unable to Perform, Non-Football Illness/Injury, and Suspended by Club.

RESERVE LIST

The Reserve List is a status for players who, for reasons of injury, retirement, military service, or other circumstances, are not immediately available for participation with a club. Players on Reserve/Injured are not eligible to practice or return to the Active/Inactive List in the same season that they are placed on Reserve. Players in the category of Reserve/Retired, Reserve/Did Not Report, Reserve/Exclusive Rights, and players who were placed in the category of Reserve/Left Squad in a previous season may not be reinstated during the period from 30 days before the end of the regular season through the postseason.

TRADES

Unrestricted trading between the AFC and NFC is allowed in 2002 through October 15, after which trading will end until 2003.

ANNUAL ACTIVE PLAYER LIMITS
NFL

Year(s)	Limit
1991-2002	45**
1985-90	45
1983-84	49
1982	45†-49
1978-81	45
1975-77	43
1974	47
1964-73	40
1963	37
1961-62	36
1960	38
1959	36
1957-58	35
1951-56	33
1949-50	32
1948	35
1947	35*-34
1945-46	33
1943-44	28
1940-42	33
1938-39	30
1936-37	25
1935	24
1930-34	20
1926-29	18
1925	16

** 45 plus a third quarterback
† 45 for first two games
* 35 for first three games

AFL

Year(s)	Limit
1966-69	40
1965	38
1964	34
1962-63	33
1960-61	35

NFL FREE AGENCY MOVEMENT

The following chart details veteran free agents who signed with new teams:

	Unrestricted	Restricted	Transition	Franchise	TOTALS
1993	100	8	4	1	113
1994	101	0	4	0	105
1995	154	6	2	1	163
1996	100	4	2	0	106
1997	86	2	2	0	90
1998	112	4	1	2	119
1999	115	2	1	0	118
2000	107	4	0	1	112
2001	93	4	0	2	99

The following procedures will be used to break standings ties for postseason playoffs and to determine regular-season schedules.

Note: Tie games count as one-half win and one-half loss for both clubs.

TO BREAK A TIE WITHIN A DIVISION

If, at the end of the regular season, two or more clubs in the same division finish with the best won-lost-tied percentage, the following steps will be taken until a champion is determined:

TWO CLUBS
1. Head-to-head (best won-lost-tied percentage in games between the clubs.)
2. Best won-lost-tied percentage in games played within the division.
3. Best won-lost-tied percentage in common games.
4. Best won-lost-tied percentage in games played within the conference.
5. Strength of victory.
6. Strength of schedule.
7. Best combined ranking among conference teams in points scored and points allowed.
8. Best combined ranking among all teams in points scored and points allowed.
9. Best net points in common games.
10. Best net points in all games.
11. Best net touchdowns in all games.
12. Coin toss.

THREE OR MORE CLUBS
(Note: If two clubs remain tied after a third club is eliminated during any step, tie-breaker reverts to Step 1 of the two-club format.)
1. Head-to-head (best won-lost-tied percentage in games among the clubs.)
2. Best won-lost-tied percentage in games played within the division.
3. Best won-lost-tied percentage in common games.
4. Best won-lost-tied percentage in games played within the conference.
5. Strength of victory.
6. Strength of schedule.
7. Best combined ranking among conference teams in points scored and points allowed.
8. Best combined ranking among all teams in points scored and points allowed.
9. Best net points in common games.
10. Best net points in all games.
11. Best net touchdowns in all games.
12. Coin toss.

TO BREAK A TIE FOR THE WILD-CARD TEAM

If it is necessary to break ties to determine the two Wild Card clubs from each conference, the following steps will be taken:

A. If all the tied clubs are from the same division, apply division tie-breaker.

B. If the tied clubs are from different divisions, apply the following steps:

TWO CLUBS
1. Head-to-head, if applicable.
2. Best won-lost-tied percentage in the games played within the conference.
3. Best won-lost-tied percentage in common games, minimum of four.
4. Strength of victory.
5. Strength of schedule.
6. Best combined ranking among conference teams in points scored and points allowed.
7. Best combined ranking among all teams in points scored and points allowed.
8. Best net points in conference games.
9. Best net points in all games.
10. Best net touchdowns in all games.
11. Coin toss.

THREE OR MORE CLUBS
1. Apply division tie-breaker to eliminate all but highest ranked club in each division prior to proceeding to Step 2. The original seeding within a division upon application of the division tie-breaker remains the same for all subsequent applications of the procedure that are necessary to identify the Wild Card participants.
2. Head-to-head sweep (apply only if one club has defeated each of the others or one club has lost to each of the others.)
3. Best won-lost-tied percentage in games played within the conference.
4. Best won-lost-tied percentage in common games, minimum of four.
5. Strength of victory.
6. Strength of schedule.
7. Best combined ranking among conference teams in points scored and points allowed.
8. Best combined ranking among all teams in points scored and points allowed.
9. Best net points in conference games.
10. Best net points in all games.
11. Best net touchdowns in all games.
12. Coin toss.

When the first Wild Card team has been identified, the procedure is repeated to name the second Wild Card (i.e., eliminate all but the highest ranked club in each division prior to proceeding to Step 2.) In situations where three teams from the same division are involved in the procedure, the original seeding of the teams remains the same for subsequent applications of the tie-breaker if the top-ranked team in that division qualifies for a Wild Card berth.

OTHER TIE-BREAKING PROCEDURES
1. Only one club advances to the playoffs in any tie-breaking step. Remaining tied clubs revert to the first step of the applicable division or Wild Card tie-breakers. As an example, if two clubs remain tied in any tie-breaker step after all other clubs have been eliminated, the procedure reverts to Step 1 of the two-club format to determine the winner. When one club wins the tie-breaker, all other clubs revert to Step 1 of the applicable two-club or three-club format.
2. In comparing records against common opponents among tied teams, the best won-lost-tied percentage is the deciding factor since teams may have played an unequal number of games.
3. To determine home-field priority among division-titlists, apply Wild Card tie-breakers.
4. To determine home-field priority for Wild Card qualifiers, apply division tie-breakers (if teams are from the same division) or Wild Card tie-breakers (if teams are from different divisions).

TIE-BREAKING PROCEDURE FOR SELECTION MEETING

If two or more clubs are tied in the selection order, the strength-of-schedule tie-breaker is applied, subject to the following exceptions for playoff clubs:
1. The Super Bowl winner is last and the Super Bowl loser next-to-last.
2. Any non-Super Bowl playoff club involved in a tie shall be assigned priority within its segment below that of non-playoff clubs and in the order that the playoff club exited from the playoffs. Thus, within a tied segment a playoff club that loses in the Wild Card game will have priority over a playoff club that loses in the Divisional playoff game, which in turn will have priority over a club that loses in the Conference Championship game. If two tied clubs exited the playoffs in the same round, the tie is broken by strength of schedule.

If any ties cannot be broken by strength of schedule, the divisional or conference tie-breakers, whichever are applicable, are applied. Any ties that still exist are broken by a coin flip.

For the 2002-03 seasons, the NFL will continue to employ a system of Referee Replay Review to aid officiating.

Prior to the two-minute warning of each half, a Coaches' Challenge System will be in effect. After the two-minute warning, and throughout any overtime period, a Referee Review will be initiated by a Replay Assistant from a Replay Booth.

The following procedures will be used:

REVIEWS BY REFEREE: All Replay Reviews will be conducted by the Referee on a field-level monitor after consultation with the other covering official(s), prior to review. A decision will be reversed only when the Referee has *indisputable visual evidence* available to him that warrants the change.

COACHES' CHALLENGE: In each game, a team will be permitted a maximum of two challenges that will initiate Referee Replay reviews. Each challenge will require the use of a team time out. If a challenge is upheld, the time out will be restored to the challenging team. A challenge will never be restored. No challenges will be recognized from a team that has exhausted its time outs.

REPLAY ASSISTANT'S REQUEST FOR REVIEW: After the two-minute warning of each half, and throughout any overtime period, any review will be initiated by a Replay Assistant. There is no limit to the number of reviews that may be initiated by the Replay Assistant. His ability to initiate a review will be unrelated to the number of time outs that either team has remaining, and no time out will be charged for any review initiated by the Replay Assistant.

TIME LIMIT: Each review will be a maximum of 90 seconds in length, timed from when the Referee begins his review of the replay at the field-level monitor.

REVIEWABLE PLAYS: The Replay System will cover the following play situations only:

A) **PLAYS GOVERNED BY SIDELINE, GOAL LINE, END ZONE, AND END LINE:**
   1. Scoring plays, including a runner breaking the plane of the goal line.
   2. Pass complete/incomplete/intercepted at sideline, goal line, end zone, and end line.
   3. Runner/receiver in or out of bounds.
   4. Recovery of loose ball in or out of bounds.

B) **PASSING PLAYS:**
   1. Pass ruled complete/incomplete/intercepted in the field of play.

   2. Touching of a forward pass by an ineligible receiver.
   3. Touching of a forward pass by a defensive player.
   4. Quarterback (Passer) forward pass or fumble.
   5. Illegal forward pass beyond line of scrimmage.
   6. Illegal forward pass after change of possession.
   7. Forward or backward pass thrown from behind line of scrimmage.

C) **OTHER DETECTABLE INFRACTIONS:**
   1. Runner ruled not down by defensive contact.
   2. Forward progress with respect to first down.
   3. Touching of a kick.
   4. Number of players on the field.

INSTANT REPLAY HISTORY

From 1986-1991, a limited system of Instant Replay was used on a year-by-year basis. Replay also was experimented with during the 1996 and 1998 preseasons. For the 1999 season, the NFL introduced a system of Referee Replay Review to aid officiating. That system was extended on a one-year basis for the 2000 season and was approved in March 2001 for the next three years through 2003.

Following are the results of the different systems:

REGULAR SEASON, 1986-1991

Year	Games	Plays Closely Reviewed	Reversals
1986	224	374	38
1987	210	490	57
1988	224	537	53
1989	224	492	65
1990	224	504	73
1991	224	570	90
TOTAL	1,330	2,967	376

PRESEASON, 1996, 1998

Year	Games	Challenges	Reversals
1996	10	13	3
1998	10	10	3
TOTAL	20	23	6

REGULAR SEASON, 1999-2001

Year	Games	Total Replay Reviews	Challenges	Reversals
1999	248	195	133	57
2000	248	247	179	84
2001	248	258	191	89
TOTAL	744	700	503	230

The AFC

**American Football Conference
North Division
Team Colors:** Black, Purple, and Metallic
Gold
11001 Owings Mills Boulevard
Owings Mills, Maryland 21117
Telephone: (410) 654-6200

2002 SCHEDULE
PRESEASON
Aug. 9 **Detroit** 8:00
Aug. 15 **New York Jets** 8:00
Aug. 23 at Philadelphia....................8:00
Aug. 29 at New York Giants 8:00

REGULAR SEASON
Sept. 8 at Carolina..........................1:00
Sept. 15 **Tampa Bay**........................1:00
Sept. 22 Open Date
Sept. 30 **Denver** (Mon.) 9:00
Oct. 6 at Cleveland 8:30
Oct. 13 at Indianapolis 12:00
Oct. 20 **Jacksonville**.......................1:00
Oct. 27 **Pittsburgh**.........................1:00
Nov. 3 at Atlanta.............................1:00
Nov. 10 **Cincinnati** 1:00
Nov. 17 at Miami...............................1:00
Nov. 24 **Tennessee** 1:00
Dec. 1 at Cincinnati 1:00
Dec. 8 **New Orleans**....................4:05
Dec. 15 at Houston 12:00
Dec. 22 **Cleveland** 4:15
Dec. 29 at Pittsburgh......................1:00

Stadium: Ravens Stadium
(opened in 1997)
•**Capacity:** 69,084
1101 Russell Street
Baltimore, Maryland 21230
Playing Surface: Natural Grass
Training Camp: Western Maryland College
2 College Hill
Westminster, Maryland
21157

RAVENS STADIUM

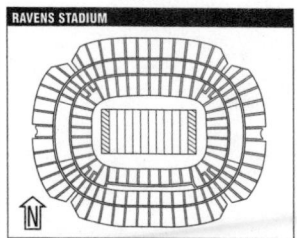

CLUB OFFICIALS
Owner: Arthur B. Modell
President: David Modell
Vice President/Public Relations:
Kevin Byrne
Vice President/Business Development
and Marketing: Dennis Mannion
Senior Vice President of Football
Operations: Ozzie Newsome
Vice President/Administration:
Pat Moriarty
Vice President/CFO: Luis Perez
Senior Director of Broadcast and
Corporate Partnerships: Mark Burdett
Senior Director of Ticket Sales and
Operations: Roy Sommerhof
Director of Operations/Information:
Bob Eller
Director of Publications/Assistant
Director of Public Relations:
Francine Lubera
Director of Player Development:
Earnest Byner
Director of Pro Personnel: James Harris
Director of College Scouting: Phil Savage
Senior Director of Broadcasting and
Video Production: Larry Rosen
Assistant Director of Pro Personnel:
George Kokinis
Scouts: Eric DeCosta, Joe Hortiz,
Ron Marciniak, T.J. McCreight,
Terry McDonough, Vince Newsome,
Art Perkins
Head Trainer: Bill Tessendorf
Equipment Manager: Ed Carroll
Video Director: Jon Dubé

COACHING HISTORY
(51-50-1)
1996-98	Ted Marchibroda	16-31-1
1999-2001	Brian Billick	35-19-0

ATTENDANCE
Home 547,172   Away 515,439
Total 1,062,611
Single-game home record,
69,506 (12/16/01)
Single-season home record, 549,531
(1998)

2002 DRAFT CHOICES
Round	Name	Pos.	College
1	Ed Reed	DB	Miami
2	Anthony Weaver	DT	Notre Dame
4	Dave Zastudil	P	Ohio
	Ron Johnson	WR	Minnesota
5	Terry Jones	TE	Alabama
6	Lamont Brightful	KR	E.Washington
	Javin Hunter	WR	Notre Dame
	Chester Taylor	RB	Toledo
	Chad Williams	DB	S. Mississippi
7	Wes Pate	QB	Stephen F. Austin

BALTIMORE RAVENS

2001 TEAM RECORD
PRESEASON (1-2)

Date	Result	Opponent
8/13	Cancelled	at Philadelphia
8/18	L 3-16	at New York Jets
8/23	L 17-20	Carolina
8/31	W 38-9	New York Giants

REGULAR SEASON (10-6)

Date	Result	Opponent	Att.
9/09	W 17-6	Chicago	69,365
9/23	L 10-21	at Cincinnati	51,121
9/30	W 20-13	at Denver	75,082
10/07	W 26-7	Tennessee	69,494
10/14	L 23-31	at Green Bay	59,866
10/21	L 14-24	at Cleveland	72,818
10/28	W 18-17	Jacksonville	69,439
11/04	W 13-10	at Pittsburgh	62,906
11/12	W 16-10	at Tennessee	68,798
11/18	L 17-27	Cleveland	69,353
11/25	W 24-21	at Jacksonville	53,530
12/02	W 39-27	Indianapolis	69,382
12/16	L 21-26	Pittsburgh	69,506
12/23	W 16-0	Cincinnati	68,987
12/29	L 10-22	at Tampa Bay	65,619
1/07	W 19-3	Minnesota	69,465

POSTSEASON (1-1)

Date	Result	Opponent	Att.
1/13	W 20-3	at Miami	72,251
1/20	L 10-27	at Pittsburgh	63,976

SCORE BY PERIODS

Ravens	29	92	63	119	0	— 303
Opponents	38	77	89	61	0	— 265

2001 TEAM STATISTICS

	Ravens	Opp.
Total First Downs	299	262
Rushing	92	81
Passing	180	161
Penalty	27	20
3rd Down: Made/Att	82/230	70/227
rd Down Pct.	35.7	30.8
4th Down: Made/Att	3/13	6/15
4th Down Pct.	23.1	40.0
Possession Avg.	29:39	30:21
Total Net Yards	5124	4446
Avg. Per Game	320.3	277.9
Total Plays	1080	1010
Avg. Per Play	4.7	4.4
Net Yards Rushing	1810	1411
Avg. Per Game	113.1	88.2
Total Rushes	483	410
Net Yards Passing	3314	3035
Avg. Per Game	207.1	189.7
Sacked/Yards Lost	40/281	45/290
Gross Yards	3595	3325
Att./Completions	557/320	555/321
Completion Pct.	57.5	57.8
Had Intercepted	20	16
Punts/Average	87/38.0	98/41.6
Net Punting Avg.	87/33.6	98/33.6
Penalties/Yards	89/728	105/902
Fumbles/Ball Lost	31/16	22/12
Touchdowns	31	30
Rushing	11	10
Passing	18	16
Returns	2	4

2001 INDIVIDUAL STATISTICS

PASSING

	Att.	Comp.	Yds.	Pct.	TD	Int.	Tkld.	Rate
Grbac	467	265	3033	56.7	15	18	28/215	71.1
Cunningham	89	54	573	60.7	3	2	12/66	81.3
Richardson	1	1	-11	100.0	0	0	0/0	79.2
Ravens	557	320	3595	57.5	18	20	40/281	72.7
Opponents	555	321	3325	57.8	16	16	45/290	72.8

SCORING

	TD R	TD P	TD Rt	PAT	FG	Saf	PTS
Stover	0	0	0	25/25	30/35	0	115
Ismail	0	7	0	0/0	0/0	0	44
Brookins	5	0	0	0/0	0/0	0	30
Allen	3	0	0	0/0	0/0	0	18
T. Taylor	0	3	0	0/0	0/0	0	18
Ayanbadejo	1	1	0	0/0	0/0	0	12
Sharpe	0	2	0	0/0	0/0	0	12
Stokley	0	2	0	0/0	0/0	0	12
Cunningham	1	0	0	0/0	0/0	0	6
Gash	0	1	0	0/0	0/0	0	6
Grbac	1	0	0	0/0	0/0	0	6
Heap	0	1	0	0/0	0/0	0	6
Johnson	0	1	0	0/0	0/0	0	6
Sharper	0	0	1	0/0	0/0	0	6
Woodson	0	0	1	0/0	0/0	0	6
Ravens	11	18	2	25/25	30/35	0	303
Opponents	10	16	4	28/28	19/33	0	265

2-Pt. Conversions: Ismail.
Ravens 1-6, Opponents 0-2.

RUSHING

	Att.	Yds.	Avg.	LG	TD
Allen	168	658	3.9	26	3
Brookins	151	551	3.6	25	5
M. Williams	65	291	4.5	55	0
Ayanbadejo	46	173	3.8	17	1
T. Taylor	5	46	9.2	16	0
Cunningham	14	40	2.9	15	1
Je. Lewis	9	33	3.7	14	0
Grbac	21	18	0.9	6	1
Stokley	1	1	1.0	1	0
Richardson	1	0	0.0	0	0
Gash	2	-1	-.5	0	0
Ravens	483	1810	3.7	55	11
Opponents	410	1411	3.4	38	10

RECEIVING

	No.	Yds.	Avg.	LG	TD
Ismail	74	1059	14.3	77t	7
Sharpe	73	811	11.1	37	2
T. Taylor	42	560	13.3	63	3
Stokley	24	344	14.3	46	2
Ayanbadejo	24	121	5.0	18	1
M. Williams	23	210	9.1	46	0
Allen	17	68	4.0	11	0
Heap	16	206	12.9	24t	1
Gash	9	80	8.9	16	1
Brookins	6	45	7.5	15	0
Johnson	5	57	11.4	25	1
Je. Lewis	4	32	8.0	12	0
Jones	2	13	6.5	13	0
A. Mitchell	1	-11	-11.0	-11	0
Ravens	320	3595	11.2	77t	18
Opponents	321	3325	10.4	90t	16

INTERCEPTIONS

	No.	Yds.	Avg.	LG	TD
Starks	4	9	2.3	9	0
R. Lewis	3	115	38.3	64	0
Woodson	3	57	19.0	47t	1
Harris	2	1	0.5	1	0
Trapp	1	15	15.0	15	0
McCrary	1	1	1.0	1	0
McAlister	1	0	0.0	0	0
Porter	1	-3	-3.0	-3	0
Ravens	16	195	12.2	64	1
Opponents	20	331	16.6	66t	3

PUNTING

	No.	Yds.	Avg.	In 20	LG
Richardson	85	3309	38.9	29	65
Ravens	87	3309	38.0	29	65
Opponents	98	4076	41.6	24	69

PUNT RETURNS

	No.	FC	Yds.	Avg.	LG	TD
Je. Lewis	42	9	519	12.4	62	0
McAlister	5	1	44	8.8	24	0
Lake	1	0	0	0.0	0	0
Ravens	48	10	563	11.7	62	0
Opponents	33	22	183	5.5	30	0

KICKOFF RETURNS

	No.	Yds.	Avg.	LG	TD
Je. Lewis	42	1039	24.7	76	0
Harris	11	235	21.4	34	0
Johnson	2	39	19.5	23	0
Bobo	1	11	11.0	11	0
Brookins	1	23	23.0	23	0
Ravens	57	1347	23.6	76	0
Opponents	64	1393	21.8	51	0

FIELD GOALS

	1-19	20-29	30-39	40-49	50+
Stover	0/0	16/16	9/10	5/9	0/0
Ravens	0/0	16/16	9/10	5/9	0/0
Opponents	0/0	7/7	6/11	6/15	0/0

SACKS

	No.
Boulware	15.0
McCrary	7.5
Sharper	6.0
R. Lewis	3.5
A. Thomas	3.5
Adams	2.0
Siragusa	2.0
Douglas	1.0
Gregg	1.0
S. Taylor	1.0
Trapp	1.0
Webster	0.5
Ravens	45.0
Opponents	40.0

RECORD HOLDERS
INDIVIDUAL RECORDS—CAREER

Category	Name	Performance
Rushing (Yds.)	Byron (Bam) Morris, 1996-97	1,511
Passing (Yds.)	Vinny Testaverde, 1996-97	7,148
Passing (TDs)	Vinny Testaverde, 1996-97	51
Receiving (No.)	Qadry Ismail, 1999-2001	191
Receiving (Yds.)	Qadry Ismail, 1999-2001	2,819
Interceptions	Rod Woodson, 1998-2001	20
	Duane Starks, 1998-2001	20
Punting (Avg.)	Greg Montgomery, 1996-97	43.2
Punt Return (Avg.)	Jermaine Lewis, 1996-2001	11.8
Kickoff Return (Avg.)	Corey Harris, 1998-2001	23.9
Field Goals	Matt Stover, 1996-2001	159
Touchdowns (Tot.)	Jermaine Lewis, 1996-2001	22
Points	Matt Stover, 1996-2001	654

INDIVIDUAL RECORDS—SINGLE SEASON

Category	Name	Performance
Rushing (Yds.)	Jamal Lewis, 2000	1,364
Passing (Yds.)	Vinny Testaverde, 1996	4,177
Passing (TDs)	Vinny Testaverde, 1996	33
Receiving (No.)	Michael Jackson, 1996	76
Receiving (Yds.)	Michael Jackson, 1996	1,201
Interceptions	Rod Woodson, 1999	7
Punting (Avg.)	Kyle Richardson, 1998	43.9
Punt Return (Avg.)	Jermaine Lewis, 2000	16.1
Kickoff Return (Avg.)	Corey Harris, 1998	27.6
Field Goals	Matt Stover, 2000	35
Touchdowns (Tot.)	Michael Jackson, 1996	14
Points	Matt Stover, 2000	135

INDIVIDUAL RECORDS—SINGLE GAME

Category	Name	Performance
Rushing (Yds.)	Priest Holmes, 11-22-98	227
Passing (Yds.)	Vinny Testaverde, 10-27-96	429
Passing (TDs)	Tony Banks, 9-10-00	5
Receiving (No.)	Priest Holmes, 10-11-98	13
Receiving (Yds.)	Qadry Ismail, 12-12-99	268
Interceptions	Many times	2
	Last time by Ray Lewis, 12-23-01	
Field Goals	Matt Stover, 9-21-97, 12-26-99, 10-28-00	5
Touchdowns (Tot.)	Michael Jackson, 12-22-96	3
	Jermaine Lewis, 12-7-97	3
	Qadry Ismail, 12-12-99	3
Points	Michael Jackson, 12-22-96	18
	Matt Stover, 9-21-97	18
	Jermaine Lewis, 12-7-97	18
	Qadry Ismail, 12-12-99	18

2002 VETERAN ROSTER

No.	Name	Pos.	Ht.	Wt.	Birthdate	NFL Exp.	College	Hometown	How Acq.	'01 Games/ Starts
66	Anderson, Bennie	G	6-5	305	2/17/77	2	Tennessee State	St. Louis, Mo.	FA-'01	16/13
28	Baxter, Gary	DB	6-2	204	11/24/78	2	Baylor	Tyler, Texas	D2-'01	6/0
11	Blake, Jeff	QB	6-0	210	12/04/70	11	East Carolina	Sanford, Fla.	FA-'02	1/0*
58	Boulware, Peter	LB	6-4	255	12/18/74	6	Florida State	Columbia, S.C.	D1-'97	16/14
94	Douglas, Marques	DE	6-2	270	3/05/77	4	Howard	Greensboro, N.C.	FA-'01	2/0
62	Flynn, Mike	C-G	6-3	300	6/15/74	5	Maine	Springfield, Mass.	FA-'97	16/16
97	Gregg, Kelly	DT	6-0	285	11/01/76	4	Oklahoma	Edmond, Okla.	FA-'00	8/1
56	Hartwell, Edgerton	LB	6-1	250	5/27/78	2	Western Illinois	Las Vegas, Nev.	D4-'01	16/0
86	Heap, Todd	TE	6-5	252	3/16/80	2	Arizona State	Mesa, Ariz.	D1-'01	12/7
88	Jones, John	TE	6-4	255	4/04/75	3	Indiana (Pa.)	Philadelphia, Pa.	FA-'00	15/2
31	Lewis, Jamal	RB	5-11	231	8/29/79	3	Tennessee	Atlanta, Ga.	D1a-'00	0*
52	Lewis, Ray	LB	6-1	245	5/15/75	7	Miami	Lakeland, Fla.	D1b-'96	16/16
59	Maese, Joe	LS	6-0	241	12/2/78	2	New Mexico	Cortez, Ariz.	D6-'01	15/0
21	McAlister, Chris	CB	6-1	206	6/14/77	4	Arizona	Pasadena, Calif.	D1-'99	16/16
99	McCrary, Michael	DE	6-4	260	7/07/70	10	Wake Forest	Falls Church, Va.	UFA(Sea)-'97	10/10
42	Mitchell, Anthony	S	6-1	211	12/13/74	3	Tuskeegee	Atlanta, Ga.	FA-'99	16/0
64 †	Mulitalo, Edwin	G	6-3	340	9/01/74	4	Arizona	Daly City, Calif.	D4b-'99	14/14
75	Ogden, Jonathan	T	6-8	340	7/31/74	7	UCLA	Washington, D.C.	D1a-'96	16/16
24	Porter, Alvin	CB-S	5-11	175	5/10/77	2	Oklahoma State	Dallas, Texas	FA-'01	16/0
61	Rabach, Casey	C	6-4	301	9/24/77	2	Wisconsin	Sturgeon Bay, Wis.	D3-'01	0*
7	Redman, Chris	QB	6-3	223	7/07/77	3	Louisville	Louisville, Ky.	D3-'00	0*
39	Ricard, Alan	FB	5-11	237	1/17/77	2	Northeast Louisiana	Amite, La.	FA-'00	5/0
80	Stokley, Brandon	WR	5-11	197	6/23/76	4	Southwestern Louisiana	Comeaux, La.	D4a-'99	16/5
3	Stover, Matt	K	5-11	178	1/27/68	13	Louisiana Tech	Dallas, Texas	PB(NYG)-'91	16/0
54	Taylor, Shannon	LB	6-3	247	2/16/75	3	Virginia	Roanoke, Va.	FA-'01	11/0
89	Taylor, Travis	WR	6-1	200	3/30/78	3	Florida	Jacksonville, Fla.	D1b-'00	16/13
96	Thomas, Adalius	DE	6-2	270	8/17/77	3	Southern Mississippi	Equality, Ala.	D6a-'00	16/2
65	Thomas, Jason	G	6-3	300	7/10/77	2	Hampton	Savannah, Ga.	FA-'01	0*
38	Trapp, James	CB	6-0	190	12/28/69	11	Clemson	Lawton, Okla.	UFA(Oak)-'99	10/4

* Blake played 1 game with New Orleans in '01; J. Lewis missed '01 season because of injury; Rabach inactive for 14 games; Redman inactive for 14 games; J. Thomas inactive for 6 games.

† Restricted free agent; subject to developments.

Players lost through Expansion Draft (2): KR Jermaine Lewis (15 games in '01), LB Darren Sharper (16).

Players lost through free agency (4): DT Lional Dalton (Den; 16 games in '01), WR Patrick Johnson (Jax; 4), CB Duane Starks (Ariz; 15), RB Moe Williams (Minn; 15).

Also played with Ravens in '01—DT Sam Adams (14 games), RB Terry Allen (11), FB Obafemi Ayanbadejo (16), G Orlando Bobo (12), RB Jason Brookins (12), DE Rob Burnett (13), QB Randall Cunningham (6), DT Lional Dalton (16), FB Sam Gash (16), QB Elvis Grbac (14), S Corey Harris (16), LS Dale Hellestrae (1), LB Brad Jackson (16), K Danny Kight (10), S Carnell Lake (15), P Kyle Richardson (16), TE Shannon Sharpe (16), DT Tony Siragusa (15), G Kipp Vickers (14), CB-S Reggie Waddell (1), DT Larry Webster (15), T Erik Williams (5), T Sammy Williams (15), S Rod Woodson (16).

2002 FIRST-YEAR ROSTER

Name	Pos.	Ht.	Wt.	Birthdate	College	Hometown	How Acq.
Arah, Obiajulu	LB	6-3	251	7/4/80	Howard	Columbia, Md.	FA
Arnold, Andre	LB	6-4	235	6/5/79	Grambling State	Columbus, Ga.	FA
Bolling, Nathan	DT	6-4	287	1/10/79	Wake Forest	Swanton, Ohio	FA
Bright, Joshua	TE	6-5	235	11/17/79	Delta State	Batesville, Miss.	FA
Brightful, Lamont	DB-KR	5-10	170	1/29/79	Eastern Washington	Oak Harbor, Wash.	D6a
Burrough, Jonathan (1)	TE	6-4	256	8/30/78	New Mexico	Oklahoma City, Okla.	FA-'01
Byrdsong, Shawn	DB	5-10	188	10/2/79	Mississippi State	Longview, Texas	FA
Cox, Alan	P	6-1	196	9/7/76	Washington State	Gunnison, Utah	FA
Davis, Gary	LB	6-0	230	5/17/79	New Mexico	Greenwood, Miss.	FA
Demps, Will	S	5-11	210	11/7/79	San Diego State	Palmdale, Calif.	FA
Farrar, Ken	G	6-5	294	3/25/79	Richmond	Peabody, Mass.	FA
Fladger, Dawani	T	6-4	310	5/23/78	South Carolina State	Mullins, S.C.	FA
Green, Louis	LB	6-3	228	9/23/79	Alcorn State	Lorman, Miss.	FA
Gregory, Sean	RB	5-11	214	2/22/79	Georgia Tech	Homewood, Ill.	FA
Hambrick, Kenyon (1)	WR	6-0	190	5/2/78	Alabama A&M	Huntsville, Ala.	FA-'01
Homer, Derek (1)	RB	5-8	197	11/29/77	Kentucky	Radcliff, Ky.	FA-'01
Humphries, D.J.	WR	6-4	205	12/19/79	Presbyterian	Union, S.C.	FA
Hunter, Dameon	RB	5-11	221	2/18/79	Utah	San Bernadino, Calif.	FA
Hunter, Javin	WR	5-11	190	5/9/80	Notre Dame	Detroit, Mich.	D6b
Hymes, Randy	WR	6-3	211	8/7/79	Grambling State	Houston, Texas	FA
Jenkins, J.R.	K	6-1	195	1/31/79	Marshall	Loganville, Ga.	FA
Johnson, J.R.	LB	6-0	240	6/20/79	Syracuse	Syracuse, N.Y.	FA
Johnson, Ron	WR	6-2	225	5/23/80	Minnesota	Detroit, Mich.	D4b
Jones, Jr., Terry	TE	6-3	265	12/3/79	Alabama	Tuscaloosa, Ala.	D5
Jordan, Omari	DT	6-4	313	4/15/78	Buffalo	Winter Haven, Fla.	FA
Kane, Morgan (1)	RB	6-0	221	3/30/76	Wake Forest	Ottawa, Ontario, Canada	FA
Kemoeatu, Maake	DT	6-5	312	1/10/79	Utah	Kahuku, Hawaii	FA
Kraemer, Mike	LS	6-4	230	9/25/79	Wisconsin-La Crosse	Pulaski, Wis.	FA
Lemon, Cleo	QB	6-2	226	8/16/79	Arkansas State	Greenwood, Miss.	FA
Malone, Robert	DE	6-4	260	10/18/79	Alabama State	Prichard, Ala.	FA
Matavao, Newel	T	6-5	355	9/23/77	Northern State	Hinesville, Ga.	FA
McKibben, Josh	DT	6-2	285	12/14/78	Central Florida	Wauchula, Fla.	FA
Mitchell, Lonny (1)	WR	6-1	200	1/14/77	San Diego State	San Diego, Calif.	FA
Nivens, Damon (1)	T	6-5	301	6/19/75	Southern	Queens, N.Y.	FA
Olford, Jason	CB	5-10	183	7/22/78	Louisiana Tech	Lufkin, Texas	FA
Pate, Wes	QB	6-2	228	3/24/79	Stephen F. Austin	Longview, Texas	D7
Redmon, Tellis	RB	5-11	210	12/19/78	Minnesota	Colleyville, Texas	FA
Reed, Ed	S	5-11	205	9/11/78	Miami	St. Rose, La.	D1
Robinson, Josh	S	5-10	190	1/31/81	Idaho State	San Bernadino, Calif.	FA
Scott, Bart	LB	6-2	235	8/18/80	Southern Illinois	Detroit, Mich.	FA
Scott, Yohance	CB	6-0	189	1/29/79	Utah	Chandler, Ariz.	FA
Simon, Salem	DT	6-3	283	2/21/79	Northwestern	Cleveland, Ohio	FA
Smith, Brian	LS	6-1	280	8/9/80	Hawaii	Thousand Oaks, Calif.	FA
Smith, Lawrence	T	6-3	295	8/16/79	Tennessee State	Atlanta, Ga.	FA
Taylor, Chester	RB	5-11	213	9/22/79	Toledo	River Rouge, Mich.	6c
Taylor, Rod	LB	6-0	257	1/28/79	Alabama-Birmingham	Montgomery, Ala.	FA
Waddell, Reggie	DB	6-0	185	11/14/77	Western Illinois	Houston, Texas	FA-'01
Walker, Jim	G	6-3	292	5/1/76	Utah State	Rigby, Idaho	FA
Weaver, Anthony	DE	6-3	300	7/28/80	Notre Dame	Abilene, Texas	D2
Williams, Chad	S	5-9	207	1/22/79	Southern Miss	Birmingham, Ala.	D6d
Zastudil, Dave	P	6-3	225	10/26/78	Ohio	Bay Village, Ohio	D4a

The term NFL Rookie is defined as a player who is in his first season of professional football and has not been on the roster of another professional football team for any regular-season or postseason games. A Rookie is designated by an "R" on NFL rosters. Players who have been active in another professional football league or players who have NFL experience, including either preseason training camp or being on an Active List or Inactive List, or on Reserve/Injured or Reserve/Physically Unable to Perform for fewer than six regular-season games, are termed NFL First-Year Players. An NFL First-Year Player is designated by a "1" on NFL rosters. Thereafter, a player is credited with an additional year of experience for each season in which he accumulates six games on the Active List or Inactive List, or on Reserve/Injured or Reserve/Physically Unable to Perform.

COACHING STAFF

Head Coach,
Brian Billick

Pro Career: Brian Billick was named the second head coach in Baltimore Ravens history on January 19, 1999, after five years as offensive coordinator for the Minnesota Vikings. In his three years as head coach of the Ravens, Billick has compiled a 35-19 record (.648) including the team's 34-7 Super Bowl XXXV victory over the New York Giants. In 2001, Billick tied Tom Flores for most consecutive playoff wins (5) by a coach at the start of his career. He fell one shy of Joe Gibbs' 6 victories when the Steelers defeated the Ravens 27-10 in a divisional playoff game last season. Baltimore's string of 50 straight games without allowing a 100-yard rusher was broken by Cincinnati's Corey Dillon in 2001. After a number of injuries to key starters on both offense and defense, the 2001 Ravens fell short of defending their title, but under Billick's direction, a good core of young talent will lead the team in 2002. The 48-year old head coach has an impressive resume on both sides of the ball: Baltimore's 2000 defense set the 16-game record for fewest points allowed (165). In 1998, as offensive coordinator of the Minnesota Vikings, he coached an offense that scored an NFL record for most points in a season (556). The Ravens' 2000 defense also became the first team since 1978 to allow fewer than 1,000 rushing yards (970) in a regular season. The team finished the 2000 season ranked first in six categories, including four shutouts and 49 takeaways, and second in three others. In 1999, Baltimore finished 4-0 in December and was in contention for the postseason until week 16. Career record: 35-19.

Background: Prior to his appointment with the Ravens, Billick was Minnesota's offensive coordinator from 1994-98, and tight ends coach in his first two seasons. Billick spent time as a Stanford assistant (1989-1991) after a three-year stint as offensive coordinator at Utah State (1986-88). He coached receivers, tight ends, and quarterbacks at San Diego State (1981-85), also holding a dual responsibility as recruiting coordinator. Billick previously coached at Redlands (1977) and Brigham Young (1978). Billick's NFL career started with the 49ers, where he was assistant director of public relations from 1979-80.

Personal: Born February 28, 1954 in Fairborne, Ohio, Billick earned All-Western Athletic Conference honors and was a honorable mention All-America in 1976 as a tight end at Brigham Young. Played linebacker at Air Force as a freshman before transferring to Brigham Young. In 1977, Billick was drafted by the 49ers in the eleventh round, was released, and had a brief stint with the Dallas Cowboys, but did not play. He and his wife Kim have two daughters—Aubree and Keegan.

ASSISTANT COACHES

Mark Asanovich, asst. strength and conditioning; born May 20, 1959, Duluth, Minn., lives in Pikesville, Md. Attended St. Cloud State. No college or pro playing experience. College coach: Ohio State 1984-85, The Citadel 1986. Pro coach: Minnesota Vikings 1995, Tampa Bay Buccaneers 1996-2001, joined Ravens in 2002.

Matt Cavanaugh, offensive coordinator; born October 27, 1956, Youngstown, Ohio, lives in Owings Mills, Md. Quarterback Pittsburgh 1974-77. Pro quarterback New England Patriots 1978-1982, San Francisco 49ers 1983-85, Philadelphia Eagles 1986-89, New York Giants 1990-91. College coach: Pittsburgh 1993. Pro coach: Arizona Cardinals 1994-95, San Francisco 49ers 1996, Chicago Bears 1997-98, joined Ravens in 1999.

Jim Colletto, offensive line; born October 2, 1944, San Francisco, lives in Finksburg, Md. Fullback-linebacker UCLA 1964-67. No pro playing experience. College coach: UCLA 1967-68, Brown 1969, Xavier 1970-71, Pacific 1972-74, Cal State-Fullerton 1975-79 (head coach), UCLA 1980-1981, Purdue 1982-84, Arizona State 1985-87, Ohio State 1988-1990, Purdue 1991-96 (head coach), Notre Dame 1997-98. Pro coach: Joined Ravens in 1999.

Jeff Friday, strength and conditioning; born October 11, 1966, Milwaukee, Wis., lives in Ellicott City, Md. Attended Wisconsin-Milwaukee. No college or pro playing experience. College coach: Illinois State 1991-92, Northwestern 1992-95. Pro coach: Minnesota Vikings 1996-98, joined Ravens in 1999.

Wade Harman, tight ends-asst. offensive line; born October 1, 1963, Corydon, Iowa, lives in Reisterstown, Md. Linebacker Drake 1985, Utah State 1986. No pro playing experience. College coach: Utah State 1987-1991, Pacific 1992-95, Morningside 1996. Pro coach: Minnesota Vikings 1997-98, joined Ravens in 1999.

Donnie Henderson, secondary; born May 17, 1957, Baltimore, lives in Owings Mills, Md. Defensive back Utah State 1978-79. No pro playing experience. College coach: Utah State 1983-88, Idaho 1989-1990, California 1992-97, Houston 1998. Pro coach: Joined Ravens in 1999.

Mike Nolan, defensive coordinator; born March 7, 1959, Baltimore, lives in Baltimore. Safety Oregon 1978-1980. No pro playing experience. College coach: Oregon 1981, Stanford 1982-83, Rice 1984-85, Louisiana State 1986. Pro coach: Denver Broncos 1987-1992, New York Giants 1993-96, Washington Redskins 1997-99, New York Jets 2000, joined Ravens in 2001.

Paul Ricci, asst. strength and condition-

ing; born November 15, 1969, Elmer, N.J., lives in Owings Mills, Md. Offensive lineman Penn State 1988-89. Pro coach: Seattle Seahawks 1993, Philadelphia Eagles 1995-96, Arizona Cardinals 1996-97, joined Ravens in 2002.

Rex Ryan, defensive line; born December 13, 1962, Ardmore, Okla., lives in Ellicott City, Md. Defensive end Southwest Oklahoma State 1983-86. No pro playing experience. College coach: Eastern Kentucky 1987-88, New Mexico Highlands 1989, Morehead State 1990-93, Cincinnati 1996-97, Oklahoma 1998. Pro coach: Arizona Cardinals 1994-95, joined Ravens in 1999.

David Shaw, quarterbacks-receivers; born July 31, 1972, San Diego, lives in Owings Mills, Md. Wide receiver Stanford 1990-94. No pro playing experience. College coach: Western Washington University 1995-96. Pro coach: Philadelphia Eagles 1997, Oakland Raiders 1998-2001, joined Ravens in 2002.

Matt Simon, running backs; born December 6, 1953, Akron, Ohio, lives in Columbia, Md. Linebacker Eastern New Mexico 1972-75. No pro playing experience. College coach: Washington 1982-1991, New Mexico 1992-94, North Texas 1994-97 (head coach). Pro coach: Denver Broncos 1998, joined Ravens in 1999.

Mike Smith, linebackers; born June 13, 1959, Chicago, lives in Eldersburg, Md. Linebacker East Tennessee 1977-1980. No pro playing experience. College coach: San Diego State 1982-85, Morehead State 1986, Tennessee Tech 1987-1998. Pro coach: Joined Ravens in 1999.

Bennie Thompson, asst. special teams; born February 10, 1963, New Orleans, lives in Owings Mills, Md. Safety Grambling State 1981-84. Pro safety New Orleans 1989-1991, Kansas City Chiefs 1992-93, Cleveland Browns 1994-95, Baltimore Ravens 1996-99. Pro coach: Joined Ravens in 2000.

Phil Zacharias, defensive assistant-defensive line; born February 12, 1959, Sewickley, Pa., lives in Ellicott City, Md. Running back-linebacker Salem College (W. Va.) 1978-1981. No pro playing experience. College coach: Georgetown College 1981, St. Paul College 1982-84, North Carolina 1985, Morehead State 1986-88, Eastern Michigan 1989-1990, Rutgers 1991-93, Stanford 1995-2001. Pro coach: Joined Ravens in 2002.

Gary Zauner, special teams; born November 2, 1950, Milwaukee, lives in Owings Mills, Md. Punter Wisconsin-La Crosse 1968-1972. No pro playing experience. College coach: Brigham Young 1979-1980, San Diego State 1981-86, New Mexico 1987-88, Long Beach State 1990-91. Pro coach: Minnesota Vikings 1994-2001, joined Ravens in 2002.

**American Football Conference
East Division**
Team Colors: Dark Navy, Red, Royal, and Nickel
One Bills Drive
Orchard Park, New York 14127-2296
Telephone: (716) 648-1800

2002 SCHEDULE
PRESEASON
Aug. 9 **Cincinnati** 7:30
Aug. 16 **Minnesota** 7:30
Aug. 24 at Indianapolis 7:00
Aug. 29 at Detroit 8:00

REGULAR SEASON
Sept. 8 **New York Jets** 1:00
Sept. 15 at Minnesota 3:15
Sept. 22 at Denver.............................2:05
Sept. 29 **Chicago** 1:00
Oct. 6 **Oakland** 1:00
Oct. 13 at Houston 12:00
Oct. 20 at Miami...............................1:00
Oct. 27 **Detroit** 1:00
Nov. 3 **New England** 1:00
Nov. 10 Open Date
Nov. 17 at Kansas City 12:00
Nov. 24 at New York Jets 1:00
Dec. 1 **Miami** 1:00
Dec. 8 at New England 1:00
Dec. 15 **San Diego**..........................1:00
Dec. 22 at Green Bay 12:00
Dec. 29 **Cincinnati** 1:00

Stadium: Ralph Wilson Stadium
(opened in1973)
• **Capacity:** 73,967
One Bills Drive
Orchard Park, New York
14127-2296
Playing Surface: AstroTurf
Training Camp: St. John Fisher College
Rochester, New York
14618

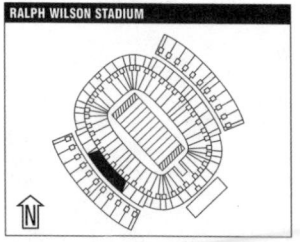

CLUB OFFICIALS
Owner: Ralph C. Wilson, Jr.
President/General Manager: Tom Donahoe
Corporate V.P.: Linda Bogdan
Treasurer: Jeffrey C. Littmann
Vice President/Player Personnel: Dwight Adams
Vice President/Communications: Scott Berchtold
Vice President/Business Development and Marketing: Russ Brandon
Vice President/Operations: Bill Munson
Vice President/Business Administration: Jim Overdorf
Director of Football Operations: Tom Modrak
Director of Pro Personnel: John Guy
Consultant: Christy Wilson Hofmann
Executive Director/Marketing: Marc Honan
Executive Director/Sales: Pete Guelli
Executive Director/Business Development: Karen Marsch
Director of Merchandising: Julie Regan
Director of Ticket Sales: Jerry Foran
Director of Archives: Denny Lynch
Director of Community Programs: Gretchen Geitter
Director of Player Programs: Paul Lancaster
Director of Information Technology: Dan Evans
Director of Guest Services & Event Management: Jan Eberle
Director of Stadium Operations: Joseph Frandina
Director of Security: Bill Bambach
Ticket Director: June Foran
Media Relations Coordinator: Mark Dalton
Business Manager: Don Purdy
Equipment Manager: Dave Hojnowski
Asst. Equipment Manager: Randy Ribbeck
Strength/Conditioning Coordinator: Rusty Jones
Conditioning Assistant: Rich Gray
Trainers: Bud Carpenter, Corey Bennett, Greg McMillen
Video Director: Henry Kunttu
Asst. Video Director: Greg Estes, Matt Smith
Scouts: Brad Forsyth, Tom Gibbons, Joe Haering, David Hinson, Doug Majeski, Bob Ryan, George (Chink) Sengel, David G. Smith, David W. Smith

COACHING HISTORY
(313-336-8)
1960-61	Buster Ramsey	11-16-1
1962-65	Lou Saban	38-18-3
1966-68	Joe Collier*	13-17-1
1968	Harvey Johnson	1-10-1
1969-1970	John Rauch	7-20-1
1971	Harvey Johnson	1-13-0
1972-76	Lou Saban**	32-29-1
1976-77	Jim Ringo	3-20-0
1978-1982	Chuck Knox	38-38-0
1983-85	Kay Stephenson***	10-26-0
1985-86	Hank Bullough****	4-17-0
1986-1997	Marv Levy	123-78-0
1998-2000	Wade Phillips	29-21-0
2001	Gregg Williams	3-13-0

*Released after two games in 1968
**Resigned after five games in 1976
***Released after four games in 1985
****Released after nine games in 1986

ATTENDANCE
Home 494,137 Away 501,582
Total 995,719
Single-game home record, 80,368 (10/4/92)
Single-season home record, 635,889 (1991)

2002 DRAFT CHOICES
Round	Name	Pos.	College
1	Mike Williams	T	Texas
2	Josh Reed	WR	Louisiana State
	Ryan Denney	DE	Brigham Young
3	Coy Wire	DB	Stanford
5	Justin Bannan	DT	Colorado
6	Kevin Thomas	DB	Nevada-Las Vegas
7	Mike Pucillo	G	Auburn
	Rodney Wright	WR	Fresno State
	Jarrett Ferguson	RB	Virgina Tech
	Dominique Stevenson	LB	Tennessee

BUFFALO BILLS

2001 TEAM RECORD
PRESEASON (2-2)

Date	Result	Opponent
8/12	L 10-24	St. Louis
8/18	W 6-3	Philadelphia
8/25	W 20-10	at Cincinnati
8/30	L 0-20	at Pittsburgh

REGULAR SEASON (3-13)

Date	Result	Opponent	Att.
9/09	L 6-24	New Orleans	71,447
9/23	L 26-42	at Indianapolis	56,135
9/30	L 3-20	Pittsburgh	72,874
10/07	L 36-42	New York Jets	72,654
10/18	W 13-10	at Jacksonville	58,893
10/28	L 24-27	at San Diego	63,698
11/04	L 14-30	Indianapolis	63,786
11/11	L 11-21	at New England	60,292
11/18	L 20-23	Seattle	60,836
11/25	L 27-34	Miami	73,063
12/02	L 0-35	at San Francisco	67,252
12/09	W 25-24	Carolina	44,549
12/16	L 9-12	New England(OT)	45,527
12/23	L 30-33	at Atlanta	43,320
12/30	W 14-9	at New York Jets	78,200
1/06	L 7-34	at Miami	73,428

(OT) Overtime

SCORE BY PERIODS

Bills	33	89	56	87	0	—	265
Opponents	91	115	83	128	3	—	420

2001 TEAM STATISTICS

	Bills	Opp.
Total First Downs	287	302
Rushing	75	122
Passing	180	154
Penalty	32	26
3rd Down: Made/Att	75/217	86/205
3rd Down Pct.	34.6	42.0
4th Down: Made/Att	12/24	4/9
4th Down Pct.	50.0	44.4
Possession Avg.	29:00	31:00
Total Net Yards	5137	5292
Avg. Per Game	321.1	330.8
Total Plays	1009	969
Avg. Per Play	5.1	5.5
Net Yards Rushing	1686	2133
Avg. Per Game	105.4	133.3
Total Rushes	406	482
Net Yards Passing	3451	3159
Avg. Per Game	215.7	197.4
Sacked/Yards Lost	46/271	34/219
Gross Yards	3722	3378
Att./Completions	557/327	453/284
Completion Pct.	58.7	62.7
Had Intercepted	20	11
Punts/Average	80/40.8	66/43.0
Net Punting Avg.	80/33.8	66/36.2
Penalties/Yards	123/954	93/835
Fumbles/Ball Lost	26/13	26/8
Touchdowns	31	48
Rushing	9	20
Passing	18	23
Returns	4	5

2001 INDIVIDUAL STATISTICS

PASSING

	Att.	Comp.	Yds.	Pct.	TD	Int.	Tkld.	Rate
Van Pelt	307	178	2056	58.0	12	11	14/73	76.4
Johnson	216	134	1465	62.0	5	7	31/196	76.3
T. Brown	33	15	201	45.5	1	2	1/2	50.2
Moorman	1	0	0	0.0	0	0	0/0	39.6
Bills	557	327	3722	58.7	18	20	46/271	74.7
Opponents	453	284	3378	62.7	23	11	34/219	92.2

SCORING

	TD R	TD P	TD Rt	PAT	FG	Saf	PTS
Arians	0	0	0	16/17	12/21	0	52
P. Price	0	7	0	0/0	0/0	0	42
Moulds	0	5	0	0/0	0/0	0	32
Graham	0	0	0	7/7	6/8	0	25
Centers	2	2	0	0/0	0/0	0	24
Henry	4	0	0	0/0	0/0	0	24
Riemersma	0	3	0	0/0	0/0	0	18
Bryson	2	0	0	0/0	0/0	0	12
Clements	0	0	2	0/0	0/0	0	12
Spoon	0	0	2	0/0	0/0	0	12
S. Jackson	0	1	0	0/0	0/0	0	6
Johnson	1	0	0	0/0	0/0	0	6
Bills	9	18	4	23/24	18/29	0	265
Opponents	20	23	5	48/48	28/37	0	420

2-Pt. Conversions: Moulds.
Bills 1-7, Opponents 0-0.

RUSHING

	Att.	Yds.	Avg.	LG	TD
Henry	213	729	3.4	25	4
Bryson	80	341	4.3	68t	2
Johnson	36	241	6.7	23	1
Centers	34	160	4.7	50	2
P. Price	6	97	16.2	31	0
Morris	20	72	3.6	10	0
Van Pelt	12	33	2.8	15	0
T. Brown	1	10	10.0	10	0
Moulds	3	3	1.0	6	0
Moorman	1	0	0.0	0	0
Bills	406	1686	4.2	68t	9
Opponents	482	2133	4.4	47	20

RECEIVING

	No.	Yds.	Avg.	LG	TD
Centers	80	620	7.8	26	2
Moulds	67	904	13.5	80t	5
P. Price	55	895	16.3	70t	7
Riemersma	53	590	11.1	36	3
Henry	22	179	8.1	40	0
Germany	12	203	16.9	39	0
McDaniel	11	129	11.7	22	0
Bryson	9	59	6.6	23	0
Black	8	90	11.3	25	0
Morris	7	36	5.1	11	0
Crosby	2	16	8.0	9	0
S. Jackson	1	1	1.0	1t	1
Bills	327	3722	11.4	80t	18
Opponents	284	3378	11.9	63t	23

INTERCEPTIONS

	No.	Yds.	Avg.	LG	TD
Clements	3	48	16.0	48t	1
Spoon	2	51	25.5	44t	2
Winfield	2	0	0.0	0	0
Watson	1	23	23.0	23	0
Hansen	1	17	17.0	17	0
Irvin	1	0	0.0	0	0
Tillman	1	0	0.0	0	0
Bills	11	139	12.6	48t	3
Opponents	20	390	19.5	100t	2

PUNTING

	No.	Yds.	Avg.	In 20	LG
Moorman	80	3262	40.8	16	66
Bills	80	3262	40.8	16	66
Opponents	66	2836	43.0	27	77

PUNT RETURNS

	No.	FC	Yds.	Avg.	LG	TD
P. Price	19	8	110	5.8	24	0
Clements	4	1	81	20.3	66t	1
Black	1	0	34	34.0	34	0
Bills	24	9	225	9.4	66t	1
Opponents	40	9	418	10.5	48	0

KICKOFF RETURNS

	No.	Yds.	Avg.	LG	TD
Clements	30	628	20.9	37	0
Black	25	498	19.9	29	0
Bryson	16	299	18.7	32	0
Driver	7	130	18.6	23	0
Watson	5	96	19.2	30	0
Bills	83	1651	19.9	37	0
Opponents	52	987	19.0	72	0

FIELD GOALS

	1-19	20-29	30-39	40-49	50+
Arians	0/0	6/6	2/4	4/11	0/0
Graham	0/0	4/4	0/0	2/4	0/0
Bills	0/0	10/10	2/4	6/15	0/0
Opponents	0/0	7/8	12/15	6/11	3/3

SACKS

	No.
Schobel	6.5
Newman	3.5
Fisher	3.0
Hansen	3.0
Office	3.0
Foreman	2.5
Flowers	2.0
S. Price	2.0
Robertson	2.0
Williams	1.5
Wright	1.5
Clements	1.0
Larsen	1.0
Prioleau	1.0
Jones	0.5
Bills	34.0
Opponents	46.0

RECORD HOLDERS
INDIVIDUAL RECORDS—CAREER

Category	Name	Performance
Rushing (Yds.)	Thurman Thomas, 1988-1999	11,938
Passing (Yds.)	Jim Kelly, 1986-1996	35,467
Passing (TDs)	Jim Kelly, 1986-1996	237
Receiving (No.)	Andre Reed, 1985-1999	941
Receiving (Yds.)	Andre Reed, 1985-1999	13,095
Interceptions	George (Butch) Byrd, 1964-1970	40
Punting (Avg.)	Paul Maguire, 1964-1970	42.1
Punt Return (Avg.)	Clifford Hicks, 1990-92	12.2
Kickoff Return (Avg.)	O.J. Simpson, 1969-1977	30.0
Field Goals	Steve Christie, 1992-2000	234
Touchdowns (Tot.)	Andre Reed, 1985-1999	87
	Thurman Thomas, 1988-1999	87
Points	Steve Christie, 1992-2000	1,011

INDIVIDUAL RECORDS—SINGLE SEASON

Category	Name	Performance
Rushing (Yds.)	O.J. Simpson, 1973	2,003
Passing (Yds.)	Jim Kelly, 1991	3,844
Passing (TDs)	Jim Kelly, 1991	33
Receiving (No.)	Eric Moulds, 2000	94
Receiving (Yds.)	Eric Moulds, 1998	1,368
Interceptions	Billy Atkins, 1961	10
	Tom Janik, 1967	10
Punting (Avg.)	Paul Maguire, 1969	44.5
Punt Return (Avg.)	Keith Moody, 1977	13.1
Kickoff Return (Avg.)	Ed Rutkowski, 1963	30.2
Field Goals	Steve Christie, 1998	33
Touchdowns (Tot.)	O.J. Simpson, 1975	23
Points	Steve Christie, 1998	140

INDIVIDUAL RECORDS—SINGLE GAME

Category	Name	Performance
Rushing (Yds.)	O.J. Simpson, 11-25-76	273
Passing (Yds.)	Joe Ferguson, 10-9-83	419
Passing (TDs)	Jim Kelly, 9-8-91	6
Receiving (No.)	Andre Reed, 11-20-94	15
Receiving (Yds.)	Jerry Butler, 9-23-79	255
Interceptions	Many times	3
	Last time by Mark Kelso, 12-12-92	
Field Goals	Steve Christie, 10-20-96	6
Touchdowns (Tot.)	Cookie Gilchrist, 12-8-63	5
Points	Cookie Gilchrist, 12-8-63	30

2002 VETERAN ROSTER

No.	Name	Pos.	Ht.	Wt.	Birthdate	NFL Exp.	College	Hometown	How Acq.	'01 Games/ Starts
11 t-	Bledsoe, Drew	QB	6-5	240	2/14/72	10	Washington State	Walla Walla, Wash.	T(NE)-'02	2/2*
29	Bostic, Jason	CB	5-9	190	6/30/76	2	Georgia Tech	Ft. Lauderdale, Fla.	FA-'02	0*
79	Brown, Ruben	G	6-3	304	2/13/72	8	Pittsburgh	Lynchburg, Va.	D1-'95	16/16
5	Brown, Travis	QB	6-3	212	7/17/77	3	Northern Arizona	Phoenix, Ariz.	FA-'01	1/0
38	Bryson, Shawn	RB	6-1	228	8/26/76	3	Tennessee	Franklin, N.C.	D3-'99	15/3
65	Carman, Jon	T	6-7	329	1/14/76	2	Georgia Tech	Herndon, Va.	FA-'01	9/2
37	Centers, Larry	FB	6-0	225	6/1/68	13	Stephen F. Austin	Tatum, Texas	FA-'01	16/13
22	Clements, Nate	CB	5-11	204	12/12/79	2	Ohio State	Shaker Heights, Ohio	D1-'01	16/11
63	Conaty, Bill	C	6-2	300	3/8/73	6	Virginia Tech	Pennsauken, N.J.	FA-'97	16/16
41	Crosby, Phillip	FB	6-0	242	11/5/76	2	Tennessee	Bessemer City, N.C.	FA-'01	16/2
25	Driver, Tony	S	6-1	207	8/4/77	2	Notre Dame	Louisville, Ky.	D6a-'01	5/0
98	Edwards, Ron	DT	6-3	305	7/12/79	2	Texas A&M	Houston, Texas	D3a-'01	7/3
72	Farris, Kris	T	6-8	318	3/26/77	2	UCLA	Mission Viejo, Calif.	FA-'01	3/1
70	Fina, John	T	6-5	300	3/11/69	11	Arizona	Tucson, Ariz.	D1-'92	13/12
95	Fisher, Bryce	DT	6-3	268	5/12/77	2	Air Force	Renton, Wash.	D7b-'99	13/2
59	Fletcher, London	LB	5-9	245	5/19/75	5	John Carroll	Cleveland, Ohio	UFA(StL)-'02	16/16*
96	Flowers, Erik	DE	6-4	273	3/1/78	3	Arizona State	San Antonio, Texas	D1-'00	15/5
84	Germany, Reggie	WR	6-1	180	3/19/78	2	Ohio State	St. Louis, Mo.	D7a-'01	16/1
20	Henry, Travis	RB	5-9	220	10/29/78	2	Tennessee	Frostproof, Fla.	D2b-'01	13/12
1	Hollis, Mike	K	5-7	178	5/22/72	8	Idaho	Spokane, Wash.	UFA(Buff)-'02	16/0*
71	Hulsey, Corey	G	6-4	329	7/26/77	2	Clemson	Lula, Ga.	FA-'00	16/12
88	Jackson, Sheldon	TE	6-3	242	7/24/76	4	Nebraska	Diamond Bar, Calif.	D7a-'99	16/1
24	Jenkins, Billy	S	5-10	211	7/8/74	6	Howard	Los Angeles, Calif.	UFA(GB)-'02	12/0*
75	Jennings, Jonas	T	6-3	320	11/21/77	2	Georgia	College Park, Ga.	D3b-'01	12/12
99	Jones, Fred	LB	6-2	246	10/18/77	3	Colorado	San Diego, Calif.	FA-'00	16/0
54	Kazadi, Muadianvita	LB	6-1	236	12/20/73	2	Tulsa	Newton, Kan.	FA-'02	0*
97	Larsen, Leif	DT	6-4	300	4/3/75	3	Texas-El Paso	Tofte, Norway	D6-'00	9/5
86	McDaniel, Jeremy	WR	6-1	195	5/2/76	3	Arizona	New Bern, N.C.	FA-'99	7/0
83	Moore, David	TE	6-2	250	11/11/69	11	Pittsburgh	Morristown, N.J.	FA-'02	16/16*
8	Moorman, Brian	P	6-0	180	2/5/76	2	Pittsburg State	Segdewick, Kan.	FA-'01	16/0
33	Morris, Sammy	RB	6-0	225	3/23/77	3	Texas Tech	San Antonio, Texas	D5-'00	16/1
80	Moulds, Eric	WR	6-2	204	7/17/73	7	Mississippi State	Lucedale, Miss.	D1-'96	16/16
53	Newman, Keith	LB	6-2	248	1/19/77	4	North Carolina	Tampa, Fla.	D4a-'99	16/16
87	O'Leary, Dan	TE-LS	6-3	248	9/1/77	2	Notre Dame	Westlake, Ohio	D6b-'01	8/0
77	Office, Kendrick	DE	6-5	270	8/2/78	2	West Alabama	Butler, Ala.	FA-'01	8/1
60	Ostroski, Jerry	G	6-3	323	7/12/70	9	Tulsa	Broken Arrow, Okla.	FA-'93	7/7
51	Polk, DaShon	LB	6-2	240	3/13/77	3	Arizona	Pacoima, Calif.	D7b-'00	16/1
73	Price, Marcus	T	6-4	314	3/3/72	5	Louisiana State	Port Arthur, Texas	UFA(NO)-'02	12/0*
81	Price, Peerless	WR	5-11	190	10/27/76	4	Tennessee	Dayton, Ohio	D2-'99	16/16
23	Prioleau, Pierson	S	5-11	190	8/6/77	4	Virginia Tech	Alvin, S.C.	FA-'01	6/2
85	Riemersma, Jay	TE	6-5	252	5/17/73	7	Michigan	Zeeland, Mich.	D7b-'96	16/15
92	Robertson, Tyrone	DT	6-4	295	8/15/79	2	Hinds (Miss.) C.C.	Danville, Va.	D7b-'01	12/0
55	Robinson, Eddie	LB	6-1	243	4/13/70	11	Alabama State	New Orleans, La.	FA-'02	16/16*
31 t-	Rogers, Charlie	RB-KR	5-9	177	6/19/76	4	Georgia Tech	Cliffwood, N.J.	T(Hou)-'02	13/0*
94	Schobel, Aaron	DE	6-4	265	9/1/77	2	Texas Christian	Columbus, Texas	D2a-'01	16/11
58	Spoon, Brandon	LB	6-2	244	7/5/78	2	North Carolina	Burlington, N.C.	D4-'01	14/14
74	Sullivan, Marques	T	6-5	323	2/2/78	2	Illinois	Oak Park, Ill.	D5-'01	10/2
67	Teague, Trey	T	6-5	292	12/27/74	5	Tennessee	Jackson, Tenn.	UFA(Den)-'02	16/16*
28	Tillman, Travares	S	6-1	194	10/8/77	3	Georgia Tech	Lyons, Ga.	D2-'00	12/6
10	Van Pelt, Alex	QB	6-1	218	5/1/70	7	Pittsburgh	Pittsburgh, Pa.	FA-'00	12/8
21	Watson, Chris	CB	6-1	188	6/30/77	4	Eastern Illinois	Chicago, Ill.	T(Den)-'00	14/0
93	Williams, Pat	DT	6-3	315	10/24/72	6	Texas A&M	Monroe, La.	FA-'97	13/13
26	Winfield, Antoine	CB	5-9	180	6/24/77	4	Ohio State	Akron, Ohio	D1-'99	16/16

* Bledsoe played 2 games with New England in '01; Bostic last active with Philadelphia in '00; Fletcher played 16 games with St. Louis; Hollis played 16 games with Jacksonville; Jenkins played 6 games with Denver and 6 with Green Bay; Kazadi last active with St.Louis in '97; Moore played 16 games with Tampa Bay; M. Price played 12 games with New Orleans; Robinson played 16 games with Tennessee; Rogers played 13 games with Seattle; Teague played 16 games with Denver.

t- Bills traded for Bledsoe (New England) and Rogers (Houston).

Traded—LB Jay Foreman (16 games in '01) to Houston.

Players lost through Expansion Draft (1): WR Avion Black (14 games in '01).

Players lost through free agency (2): LB Sam Cowart (NYJ; 1 game in '01), LB John Holecek (Atl; 11).

Also played with Bills in '01—K Jake Arians (10 games), CB Lance Brown (14), K Shayne Graham (6), DE Phil Hansen (12), C-G Craig Heimburger (11), S Raion Hill (15), CB Ken Irvin (14), QB Rob Johnson (8), DT Shawn Price (11), LS Mo Unutoa (8), LB Kenyatta Wright (11).

2002 FIRST-YEAR ROSTER

Name	Pos.	Ht.	Wt.	Birthdate	College	Hometown	How Acq.
Alexander, Curtis (1)	RB	5-9	204	6/11/74	Alabama	Memphis, Tenn.	FA-'01
Allen, Reggie (1)	WR	6-0	187	9/11/76	Central Michigan	Flint, Mich.	FA
Bannan, Justin	DT	6-3	300	4/18/79	Colorado	Fair Oaks, Calif.	D5
Brooks, Ahmad	CB	5-8	180	3/13/80	Texas	Abilene, Texas	FA
Brutley, Daryon	CB	5-11	187	5/31/79	Northern Iowa	Eufaula, Ala.	FA
Bryant, Jamarei	CB	5-11	190	4/10/80	Kansas	Phoenix, Ariz.	FA
Burns, Joe	RB	5-9	215	9/15/79	Georgia Tech	Thomasville, Ga.	FA
Coleman, Clarence	WR	5-10	190	6/4/80	Ferris State	Miami, Fla.	FA
Cotton, James (1)	DE	6-2	245	11/7/76	Ohio State	Cleveland, Ohio	FA
Dangerfield, Edward	WR	6-5	212	9/12/79	Louisiana State	Morgan City, La.	FA
Denney, Ryan	DE	6-7	276	6/15/77	Brigham Young	Thorton, Colo.	D2b
Dinkins, David (1)	QB	6-1	215	8/15/78	Morehead State	Pittsburgh, Pa.	FA-'01
Duckett, John	LB	6-1	228	3/31/78	Virginia	Lexington Park, Md.	FA
Early, Michael (1)	C	6-1	305	6/2/77	Norfolk State	Brunswick, Ga.	FA
Ferguson, Jarrett	FB	5-8	222	1/23/79	Virginia Tech	Goodview, Va.	D7c
Hunt, Robert (1)	G	6-4	310	7/22/75	Virginia	Newport News, Va.	FA
Irons, Grant	DE	6-5	270	7/7/79	Notre Dame	The Woodlands, Texas	FA
Mattingly, Chip	LS	6-2	245	7/12/79	Louisville	Louisville, Ky.	FA
Maxie, Demetrious (1)	DT	6-2	280	10/18/73	Texas-El Paso	Downey, Calif.	FA
McDonnell, Brady (1)	TE	6-3	264	7/24/77	Colorado	Quinn, S.D.	FA
Osborne, Scot (1)	TE	6-4	260	10/30/77	William & Mary	Asheville, N.C.	FA-'01
Peterson, Devonte (1)	DT	6-2	275	4/1/78	Catawba	Clinton, N.C.	FA
Priestley, David	QB	6-3	217	7/11/79	Pittsburgh	Los Alamitos, Calif.	FA
Proctor, Milton	S	6-0	211	2/15/79	Kansas State	St. Louis, Mo.	FA
Pucillo, Mike	G	6-4	316	7/14/79	Auburn	Brandon, Fla.	D7a
Reed, Josh	WR	5-10	203	5/1/80	Louisiana State	Rayne, La.	D2a
Robinson, Jimmy (1)	LB	6-2	250	5/4/76	Western Illinois	Milan, Tenn.	FA-'01
Rone, Andre' (1)	WR	5-10	180	4/14/76	Mississippi	Daytona Beach, Fla.	FA
Samuel, Marc	K	5-10	168	12/20/77	Georgetown	Anchorage, Ky.	FA
Schau, Tom (1)	C	6-4	298	12/30/75	Illinois	Hammond, Ind.	FA
Stevenson, Dominique	LB	6-0	231	12/28/77	Tennessee	Gaffney, S.C.	D7d
Thomas, Kevin	CB	5-11	180	7/28/78	Nevada-Las Vegas	Sacramento, Calif.	D6
Williams, Mike	T	6-6	370	1/11/80	Texas	The Colony, Texas	D1
Wire, Coy	S	6-0	209	11/7/78	Stanford	Camp Hill, Pa.	D3
Wright, Rodney	WR	5-9	180	11/18/79	Fresno State	Bakersfield, Calif.	D7b

The term NFL Rookie is defined as a player who is in his first season of professional football and has not been on the roster of another professional football team for any regular-season or postseason games. A Rookie is designated by an "R" on NFL rosters. Players who have been active in another professional football league or players who have NFL experience, including either preseason training camp or being on an Active List or Inactive List, or on Reserve/Injured or Reserve/Physically Unable to Perform for fewer than six regular-season games, are termed NFL First-Year Players. An NFL First-Year Player is designated by a "1" on NFL rosters. Thereafter, a player is credited with an additional year of experience for each season in which he accumulates six games on the Active List or Inactive List, or on Reserve/Injured or Reserve/Physically Unable to Perform.

COACHING STAFF

Head Coach,
Gregg Williams

Pro Career: Became the twelfth head coach in franchise history on February 1, 2001. Spent the previous 11 seasons with the Tennessee organization, including the last four as the Titans' defensive coordinator. Under his leadership in 2000, the Titans' defensive unit led the league in total defense for the first time since joining the NFL, and the 191 points allowed were the third fewest in the NFL since the league adopted a 16-game schedule in 1978. The Tennessee defense also led the league in third-down efficiency (30.8%), fourth-down efficiency (8.3%), and fewest first downs allowed (215). In 2000, the team also established the franchise's single-season records for sacks (55), fewest passing yards allowed (2,424), and fewest offensive touchdowns allowed (17). Williams spent three seasons (1994-96) overseeing the Oilers' linebackers after spending the 1993 campaign as the team's special teams coach. In 1993, Williams's special teams unit had the top-rated punting game and rated sixth in kickoff return defense. From 1990-92, Williams served as the club's first quality control coordinator. Career record: 3-13.

Background: Williams played football (quarterback) and baseball at Northeast Missouri State from 1976-79 where he received his B.S. degree. He later earned his master's degree in education from Central Missouri State. Began his coaching career in the high school ranks as an assistant coach at his hometown of Excelsior Springs (Mo.) High School from 1980-83. He served as head coach at Belton (Mo.) High School from 1984-87. Spent the 1988-89 seasons working with the linebackers as a graduate assistant at the University of Houston for former Oilers head coach Jack Pardee.

Personal: Born July 15, 1958 in Excelsior Springs, Mo. Gregg and his wife Leigh Ann have two sons, Blake (16) and Chase (9), and a daughter, Amy (11).

ASSISTANT COACHES

Miles Aldridge, linebackers; born January 25, 1949, Columbia, S.C., lives in Orchard Park, N.Y. Gardner-Webb 1969-1971. No pro playing experience. College coach: East Tennessee 1973-77, Wichita State 1978, Tulsa 1979, Mississippi 1980-82, Duke 1983-84, Clemson 1985-89, North Carolina State 1990, South Carolina 1991-93, Clemson 1994-95, Arkansas 1996-97, Southwest Louisiana 1998, Middle Tennessee State 1999-2000. Pro coach: Joined Bills in 2001.

Steve Fairchild, running backs; born June 21, 1958 Decatur, Ill., lives in Orchard Park, N.Y. Quarterback Colorado State 1980-81. No pro playing experi-

ence. College coach: Mesa (Colo.) J.C. 1982-83, Ferris State 1984-85, San Diego State 1986, New Mexico 1987-89, San Diego State 1991-92, Colorado State 1997-2000. Pro coach: Joined Bills in 2001.

Kevin Gilbride, offensive coordinator; born August 27, 1951, New Haven, Conn., lives in Orchard Park, N.Y. Quarterback-tight end Southern Connecticut State 1971-73. No pro playing experience. College coach: Idaho State 1974-75, Tufts 1976-77, American International 1978-79, Southern Connecticut State 1980-84, East Carolina 1987-88. Pro coach: Ottawa Rough Riders (CFL) 1985-86, Houston Oilers 1989-1994, Jacksonville Jaguars 1995-96, San Diego Chargers 1997-98, Pittsburgh Steelers 1999-2000, joined Bills in 2002.

Fred Graves, wide receivers; born March 2, 1950, Los Angeles, lives in Orchard Park, N.Y. Halfback-split end Utah 1968-1970. Pro wide receiver Chicago Bears 1971. College coach: Northeast Missouri State 1975-76, Western Illinois 1977-78, New Mexico State 1979-1981, Utah 1982-2000. Pro coach: Joined Bills in 2001.

Jerry Gray, defensive coordinator; born December 16, 1962, Lubbock, Texas, lives in Orchard Park, N.Y. Safety Texas 1981-84. Pro defensive back Los Angeles Rams 1985-1991, Houston Oilers 1992, Tampa Bay Buccaneers 1993. College coach: Southern Methodist 1995-96. Pro coach: Tennessee Titans 1997-2000, joined Bills in 2001.

Steve Jackson, asst. defensive backs-third down specialist; born April 8, 1969, Houston, lives in Orchard Park, N.Y. Defensive back Purdue 1988-1991. Pro defensive back Houston/Tennessee Oilers 1991-98. Pro coach: Joined Bills in 2001.

Rusty Jones, strength and conditioning; born August 14, 1953, Berwick, Maine, lives in Hamburg, N.Y. Attended Springfield College. No college or pro playing experience. College coach: Springfield College 1978-79. Pro coach: Pittsburgh Maulers (USFL) 1983-84, joined Bills in 1985.

Tommy Kaiser, offensive assistant-special teams assistant; born April 9, 1952, lives in Orchard Park, N.Y. Defensive back Houston 1971-73. No pro playing experience. College coach: Houston 1987-1992, Texas Tech 1993, Oklahoma State 1994-2000. Pro coach: Joined Bills in 2001.

Steve Kragthorpe, quarterbacks; born April 28, 1965, Missoula, Mont. lives in Orchard Park, N.Y. Quarterback Eastern New Mexico 1983-84, West Texas A&M 1985-86. No pro playing experience. College coach: Northern Arizona 1990-93, North Texas 1994-95, Boston College 1996, Texas A&M 1997-2000. Pro coach: Joined Bills in 2001.

Chuck Lester, administrative assistant to the head coach-defensive assistant; born May 18, 1955, Chicago, lives in Orchard Park, N.Y. Linebacker Oklahoma 1974. No pro playing experience. College coach: Iowa State 1980-81, Oklahoma 1982-84. Pro coach: Kansas City Chiefs 1984-86 (scout), joined Bills in 1987.

John Levra, defensive line; born October 2, 1937, Arma, Kan., lives in Hamburg, N.Y. Guard-linebacker Pittsburg State 1963-65. No pro playing experience. College coach: New Mexico Highlands 1966-1970, Stephen F. Austin 1971-74, Kansas 1975-78, North Texas State 1979. Pro coach: British Columbia (CFL) 1980, New Orleans Saints 1981-85, Chicago Bears 1986-1992, Denver Broncos 1993-94, Minnesota Vikings 1995-97, joined Bills in 1998.

Dan Neal, tight ends; born August 30, 1949, Corbin, Ky., lives in Orchard Park, N.Y. Offensive line Kentucky 1970-72. Pro offensive lineman Baltimore Colts 1973-74, Chicago Bears 1975-1983. Pro coach: Philadelphia Eagles 1986-1991, Arizona Cardinals 1994-95, New Orleans Saints 1997-99, Tennessee Titans 2000, joined Bills in 2001.

Danny Smith, special teams coordinator; born September 7, 1953, Pittsburgh, lives in Orchard Park, N.Y. Defensive back Edinboro State 1972-75. No pro playing experience. College coach: Edinboro State 1976, Clemson 1979, William & Mary 1980-83, The Citadel 1984-86, Georgia Tech 1987-1994. Pro coach: Philadelphia Eagles 1995-98, Detroit Lions 1999-2000, joined Bills in 2001.

Pat Thomas, defensive backs; born September 1, 1954, Plano, Texas, lives in Orchard Park, N.Y. Defensive back Texas A&M 1972-75. Pro defensive back Los Angeles Rams 1976-1982. College coach: Houston 1985-89. Pro coach: Houston Gamblers (USFL) 1983-84, Houston Oilers 1990-92, Dallas Texans (Arena League) 1993, Indianapolis Colts 1994-97, joined Bills in 2001.

Ronnie Vinklarek, offensive line; born January 21, Orchard Park, N.Y. Attended Southwest Texas State. No college or pro playing experience. College coach: Houston 1988-1993, Valdosta State 1997, Oklahoma State 1998-99. Pro coach: Birmingham Barracudas (CFL) 1995, Tennessee Titans 2000, joined Bills in 2001.

American Football Conference
North Division
Team Colors: Black, Orange, and White
One Paul Brown Stadium
Cincinnati, Ohio 45202-3492
Telephone: (513) 621-3550
Ticket Office (513) 621-TDTD (8383)

2002 SCHEDULE
PRESEASON

Aug. 9 at Buffalo 7:30
Aug. 17 at Indianapolis 7:00
Aug. 24 **New Orleans**.....................7:30
Aug. 29 **Atlanta**..............................7:30

REGULAR SEASON

Sept. 8 **San Diego**...........................1:00
Sept. 15 at Cleveland 1:00
Sept. 22 at Atlanta..............................8:30
Sept. 29 **Tampa Bay**........................4:05
Oct. 6   at Indianapolis 12:00
Oct. 13 **Pittsburgh**...........................1:00
Oct. 20 Open Date
Oct. 27 **Tennessee** 1:00
Nov. 3   at Houston 12:00
Nov. 10 at Baltimore.......................1:00
Nov. 17 **Cleveland** 1:00
Nov. 24 at Pittsburgh.....................1:00
Dec. 1   **Baltimore**...........................1:00
Dec. 8   at Carolina..........................1:00
Dec. 15 **Jacksonville**.......................1:00
Dec. 22 **New Orleans**.....................1:00
Dec. 29 at Buffalo 1:00

Stadium: Paul Brown Stadium
　　　　(opened in 2000)
　　　　• **Capacity:** 65,393
　　　　One Paul Brown Stadium
　　　　Cincinnati, Ohio 45202-3492
Playing Surface: Grass
Training Camp: Georgetown College
　　　　Georgetown, Kentucky
　　　　40324

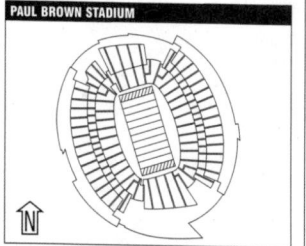

PAUL BROWN STADIUM

CLUB OFFICIALS

President: Mike Brown
Senior Vice President: Pete Brown
Executive Vice President: Katie Blackburn
Vice President: Paul Brown
Vice President: John Sawyer
Business Development: Troy Blackburn
Business Manager: Bill Connelly
Chief Financial Officer: Bill Scanlon
Controller: Johanna Kappner
Managing Director of Paul Brown
　　Stadium: Eric Brown
Director of Technology: Jo Ann Ralstin
Bengals.com Editor: Geoff Hobson
Director of Sales and Public Affairs:
　　Jeff Berding
Director of Corporate Sales and
　　Marketing: Vince Cicero
Ticket Manager: Tim Kelly
Director of Ticket Sales: Kevin Lane
Director of Player Relations: Eric Ball
Director of Football Operations:
　　Jim Lippincott
Director of Player Personnel: Duke Tobin
Public Relations Director: Jack Brennan
Athletic Trainer: Paul Sparling
Equipment Manager: Rob Recker
Video Director: Travis Brammer

COACHING HISTORY
(225-286-1)

1968-1975	Paul Brown	55-59-1
1976-78	Bill Johnson*	18-15-0
1978-79	Homer Rice	8-19-0
1980-83	Forrest Gregg	34-27-0
1984-1991	Sam Wyche	64-68-0
192-96	Dave Shula**	19-52-0
1996-2000	Bruce Coslet***	21-39-0
2000-01	Dick LeBeau	10-19-0

　* Resigned after five games in 1978
　** Released after seven games in 1996
*** Resigned after three games in 2000

ATTENDANCE

Home 446,603　　　　Away 548,483
Total 995,086
Single-game home record,
64,217 (10/14/01)
Single-season home record, 473,288
(1990)

2002 DRAFT CHOICES

Round	Name	Pos.	College
1	Levi Jones	T	Arizona State
2	Lamont Thompson	DB	Washington State
3	Matt Schobel	TE	Texas Christian
4	Travis Dorsch	K	Purdue
6	Marquand Manuel	DB	Florida
7	Joey Evans	DE	North Carolina

CINCINNATI BENGALS

2001 TEAM RECORD
PRESEASON (1-3)

Date	Result	Opponent
8/4	L 13-16	at Chicago
8/10	W 27-24	at Detroit
8/25	L 10-20	Buffalo
8/30	L 17-23	Indianapolis

REGULAR SEASON (6-10)

Date	Result	Opponent	Att.
9/09	W 23-17	New England	51,521
9/23	W 21-10	Baltimore	51,121
9/30	L 14-28	at San Diego	56,048
10/07	L 7-16	at Pittsburgh	62,335
10/14	W 24-14	Cleveland	64,217
10/21	L 0-24	Chicago	63,408
10/28	W 31-27	at Detroit	69,343
11/11	L 13-30	at Jacksonville	57,161
11/18	L 7-20	Tennessee	63,865
11/25	L 0-18	at Cleveland	72,918
12/02	L 13-16	Tampa Bay(OT)	52,135
12/09	L 10-14	Jacksonville	44,920
12/16	L 14-15	at New York Jets	77,745
12/23	L 0-16	at Baltimore	68,987
12/30	W 26-23	Pittsburgh (OT)	63,751
1/06	W 23-21	at Tennessee	68,798

(OT) Overtime

SCORE BY PERIODS

Bengals	27	75	56	65	3 —	226
Opponents	67	83	79	77	3 —	309

2001 TEAM STATISTICS

	Bengals	Opp.
Total First Downs	294	281
Rushing	96	86
Passing	176	173
Penalty	22	22
3rd Down: Made/Att	93/243	86/225
3rd Down Pct.	38.3	38.2
4th Down: Made/Att	6/23	5/13
4th Down Pct.	26.1	38.5
Possession Avg.	29:16	30:44
Total Net Yards	4800	4832
Avg. Per Game	300.0	302.0
Total Plays	1071	1013
Avg. Per Play	4.5	4.8
Net Yards Rushing	1712	1675
Avg. Per Game	107.0	104.7
Total Rushes	441	453
Net Yards Passing	3088	3157
Avg. Per Game	193.0	197.3
Sacked/Yards Lost	28/203	48/320
Gross Yards	3291	3477
Att./Completions	602/322	512/311
Completion Pct.	53.5	60.7
Had Intercepted	26	13
Punts/Average	86/39.6	86/41.2
Net Punting Avg.	86/33.6	86/34.8
Penalties/Yards	103/870	101/837
Fumbles/Ball Lost	28/11	33/15
Touchdowns	25	35
Rushing	11	10
Passing	12	23
Returns	2	2

2001 INDIVIDUAL STATISTICS

PASSING	Att.	Comp.	Yds.	Pct.	TD	Int.	Tkld.	Rate
Kitna	581	313	3216	53.9	12	22	25/185	61.1
Mitchell	12	4	38	33.3	0	3	2/15	3.5
A. Smith	8	5	37	62.5	0	0	1/3	73.4
Dillon	1	0	0	0.0	0	1	0/0	0.0
Bengals	602	322	3291	53.5	12	26	28/203	58.1
Opponents	512	311	3477	60.7	23	13	48/320	85.4

SCORING	TD R	TD P	TD Rt	PAT	FG	Saf	PTS
Dillon	10	3	0	0/0	0/0	0	78
Rackers	0	0	0	23/24	17/28	0	74
Dugans	0	2	0	0/0	0/0	0	14
Scott	0	2	0	0/0	0/0	0	12
Farmer	0	1	0	0/0	0/0	0	6
C. Johnson	0	1	0	0/0	0/0	0	6
Kitna	1	0	0	0/0	0/0	0	6
McGee	0	1	0	0/0	0/0	0	6
Neal	0	1	0	0/0	0/0	0	6
Simmons	0	0	1	0/0	0/0	0	6
Spikes	0	0	1	0/0	0/0	0	6
Warrick	0	1	0	0/0	0/0	0	6
Bengals	11	12	2	23/24	17/28	0	226
Opponents	10	23	2	29/31	22/30	1	309

2-Pt. Conversions: Dugans.
Bengals 1-1, Opponents 1-4.

RUSHING	Att.	Yds.	Avg.	LG	TD
Dillon	340	1315	3.9	96t	10
Bennett	50	232	4.6	36	0
Kitna	27	73	2.7	20	1
Keaton	5	48	9.6	21	0
A. Smith	6	20	3.3	6	0
Warrick	8	14	1.8	13	0
Neal	5	10	2.0	4	0
Bengals	441	1712	3.9	96t	11
Opponents	453	1675	3.7	48	10

RECEIVING	No.	Yds.	Avg.	LG	TD
Warrick	70	667	9.5	33	1
Scott	57	819	14.4	49	2
Dillon	34	228	6.7	17	3
C. Johnson	28	329	11.8	28	1
Dugans	28	251	9.0	31	2
Houshmandzadeh	21	228	10.9	23	0
Bennett	20	150	7.5	15	0
Neal	19	101	5.3	12	1
Farmer	15	228	15.2	27	1
McGee	14	148	10.6	25t	1
Battaglia	13	118	9.1	17	0
McMullen	2	15	7.5	11	0
Keaton	1	9	9.0	9	0
Bengals	322	3291	10.2	49	12
Opponents	311	3477	11.2	47	23

INTERCEPTIONS	No.	Yds.	Avg.	LG	TD
Kaesviharn	3	41	13.7	29	0
Hawkins	3	26	8.7	22	0
J. Smith	2	28	14.0	21	0
Spikes	1	66	66.0	66t	1
D. Williams	1	16	16.0	16	0
C. Carter	1	10	10.0	10	0
Simmons	1	5	5.0	5	0
Roman	1	0	0.0	0	0
Bengals	13	192	14.8	66t	1
Opponents	26	392	15.1	64	0

PUNTING	No.	Yds.	Avg.	In 20	LG
Harris	84	3372	40.1	21	57
Rackers	1	32	32.0	0	32
Bengals	86	3404	39.6	21	57
Opponents	86	3541	41.2	29	76

PUNT RETURNS	No.	FC	Yds.	Avg.	LG	TD
Warrick	18	10	116	6.4	31	0
Houshmandzadeh	12	5	163	13.6	86	0
Farmer	1	1	11	11.0	11	0
Bengals	31	16	290	9.4	86	0
Opponents	47	17	374	8.0	24	0

KICKOFF RETURNS	No.	Yds.	Avg.	LG	TD
Keaton	42	891	21.2	64	0
Houshmandzadeh	10	185	18.5	23	0
Bennett	4	60	15.0	19	0
Ru. Johnson	4	79	19.8	25	0
Gutierrez	2	15	7.5	8	0
Bengals	62	1230	19.8	64	0
Opponents	46	1157	25.2	101t	1

FIELD GOALS	1-19	20-29	30-39	40-49	50+
Rackers	0/0	4/6	8/11	4/9	1/2
Bengals	0/0	4/6	8/11	4/9	1/2
Opponents	0/0	8/8	6/9	7/11	1/2

SACKS	No.
Wilson	9.0
J. Smith	8.5
Simmons	6.5
Spikes	6.0
T. Williams	5.0
D. Williams	3.5
Gibson	3.0
Roman	2.0
Booker	1.5
Ross	1.0
Steele	1.0
Bengals	48.0
Opponents	28.0

RECORD HOLDERS
INDIVIDUAL RECORDS—CAREER

Category	Name	Performance
Rushing (Yds.)	James Brooks, 1984-1991	6,447
Passing (Yds.)	Ken Anderson, 1971-1986	32,838
Passing (TDs)	Ken Anderson, 1971-1986	197
Receiving (No.)	Carl Pickens, 1992-99	530
Receiving (Yds.)	Isaac Curtis, 1973-1984	7,101
Interceptions	Ken Riley, 1969-1983	65
Punting (Avg.)	Dave Lewis, 1970-73	43.8
Punt Return (Avg.)	Mitchell Price, 1990-93	10.4
Kickoff Return (Avg.)	Lemar Parrish, 1970-77	24.7
Field Goals	Jim Breech, 1980-1992	225
Touchdowns (Tot.)	Pete Johnson, 1977-1983	70
Points	Jim Breech, 1980-1992	1,151

INDIVIDUAL RECORDS—SINGLE SEASON

Category	Name	Performance
Rushing (Yds.)	Corey Dillon, 2000	1,435
Passing (Yds.)	Boomer Esiason, 1986	3,959
Passing (TDs)	Ken Anderson, 1981	29
Receiving (No.)	Carl Pickens, 1996	100
Receiving (Yds.)	Eddie Brown, 1988	1,273
Interceptions	Ken Riley, 1976	9
Punting (Avg.)	Dave Lewis, 1970	46.2
Punt Return (Avg.)	Lemar Parrish, 1974	18.8
Kickoff Return (Avg.)	Tremain Mack, 1999	27.1
Field Goals	Doug Pelfrey, 1995	29
Touchdowns (Tot.)	Carl Pickens, 1995	17
Points	Doug Pelfrey, 1995	121

INDIVIDUAL RECORDS—SINGLE GAME

Category	Name	Performance
Rushing (Yds.)	Corey Dillon, 10-22-00	*278
Passing (Yds.)	Boomer Esiason, 10-7-90	490
Passing (TDs)	Boomer Esiason, 12-21-86	5
	Boomer Esiason, 10-29-89	5
Receiving (No.)	Carl Pickens, 10-11-98	13
Receiving (Yds.)	Eddie Brown, 11-6-88	216
Interceptions	Many times	3
	Last time by David Fulcher, 12-17-89	
Field Goals	Doug Pelfrey, 11-6-94	6
Touchdowns (Tot.)	Larry Kinnebrew, 10-28-84	4
	Corey Dillon, 12-4-97	4
Points	Larry Kinnebrew, 10-28-84	24
	Corey Dillon, 12-4-97	24

*NFL Record

2002 VETERAN ROSTER

No.	Name	Pos.	Ht.	Wt.	Birthdate	NFL Exp.	College	Hometown	How Acq.	'01 Games/ Starts
71	Anderson, Willie	T	6-5	340	7/11/75	7	Auburn	Whistler, Ala.	D1-'96	16/16
33	Armour, JoJuan	S	5-11	220	7/10/76	4	Miami (Ohio)	Toledo, Ohio	FA-'00	16/11
23	Bean, Robert	CB	5-11	178	1/6/78	3	Mississippi State	Atlanta, Ga.	D5-'00	15/4
36	Bennett, Brandon	HB	5-11	220	2/3/73	4	South Carolina	Taylors, S.C.	FA-'99	16/1
96	Booker, Vaughn	DE	6-5	300	2/24/68	9	Cincinnati	Cincinnati, Ohio	UFA(GB)-'00	14/13
74	Braham, Rich	C	6-4	305	11/6/70	9	West Virginia	Morgantown, W.Va.	W(Ariz)-'94	16/16
88	Brewer, Sean	TE	6-4	255	10/5/77	2	San Jose State	Riverside, Calif.	D3-'01	0*
21	Burris, Jeff	CB	6-0	190	6/7/72	9	Notre Dame	Rock Hill, S.C.	FA-'02	15/15*
91	Chevrier, Randy	LS-DT	6-2	291	6/6/76	2	McGill (Canada)	St. Leonard, Quebec, Canada	FA-'01	13/0*
4	Covington, Scott	QB	6-3	217	1/17/76	3	Miami	Laguna Niguel, Calif.	FA-'01	0*
98	Curtis, Canute	LB	6-2	257	8/4/74	6	West Virginia	Amityville, N.Y.	FA-'98	16/4
28	Dillon, Corey	HB	6-1	225	10/24/74	6	Washington	Seattle, Wash.	D2-'97	16/16
81	Dugans, Ron	WR	6-2	205	4/27/77	3	Florida State	Tallahassee, Fla.	D3-'00	16/3
83	Farmer, Danny	WR	6-3	215	5/21/77	3	UCLA	Los Angeles, Calif.	W(Pitt)-'00	12/1
95	Foley, Steve	LB	6-3	260	9/9/75	5	Northeast Louisiana	Little Rock, Ark.	D3a-'98	12/12
12	Frerotte, Gus	QB	6-3	225	7/31/71	9	Tulsa	Ford City, Pa.	UFA(Den)-'02	4/1*
99	Gibson, Oliver	DT	6-2	315	3/15/72	8	Notre Dame	Chicago, Ill.	UFA(Pitt)-'99	16/16
63	Goff, Mike	G	6-5	311	1/6/76	5	Iowa	Peru, Ill.	D3b-'98	16/16
62	Gutierrez, Brock	C	6-3	304	9/25/73	6	Central Michigan	Charlotte, Mich.	FA-'98	15/0
26	Hall, Cory	S	6-0	213	12/5/76	4	Fresno State	Bakersfield, Calif.	D3-'99	16/15
8	Harris, Nick	P	6-2	218	7/23/78	2	California	Phoenix, Ariz.	W(Den)-'01	16/0
27	Hawkins, Artrell	CB	5-10	190	11/24/76	5	Cincinnati	Johnstown, Pa.	D2-'98	14/13
22	Heath, Rodney	CB	5-10	177	10/29/74	4	Minnesota	Cincinnati, Ohio	FA-'99	5/5
84	Houshmandzadeh, T.J.	WR	6-1	197	9/26/77	2	Oregon State	Barstow, Calif.	D7-'01	12/1
65	Jackson, John	T	6-6	300	1/4/65	15	Eastern Kentucky	Cincinnati, Ohio	FA-'00	11/0
25	Jennings, Ligarius	CB	5-8	202	11/3/77	2	Tennessee State	Birmingham, Ala.	FA-'01	9/0
85	Johnson, Chad	WR	6-2	192	1/9/78	2	Oregon State	Miami, Fla.	D2-'01	12/3
50	Johnson, Riall	LB	6-3	243	4/20/78	2	Stanford	Lynnwood, Wash.	FA-'01	7/0
32	Johnson, Rudi	HB	5-10	233	10/1/79	2	Auburn	Ettrick, Va.	D4-'01	2/0
34	Kaesviharn, Kevin	CB	6-1	190	8/29/76	2	Augustana (S.D.)	Lakeville, Minn.	FA-'01	10/3
29	Keaton, Curtis	HB-KR	5-10	222	10/18/76	3	James Madison	Columbus, Ohio	D4-'00	13/0
3	Kitna, Jon	QB	6-2	220	9/21/72	6	Central Washington	Tacoma, Wash.	UFA(Sea)-'01	16/15
58	Langford, Jevon	DE	6-3	270	2/16/74	7	Oklahoma State	Washington, D.C.	FA-'01	3/0
77	Leyva, Victor	G	6-4	315	12/18/77	2	Arizona State	Porterville, Calif.	D5-'01	0*
43	McMullen, Kirk	TE	6-4	246	7/19/77	2	Pittsburgh	Imperial, Pa.	FA-'01	7/2
93	Monds, Mario	DT	6-3	325	11/10/76	2	Cincinnati	Fort Pierce, Fla.	W(Wash)-'01	2/0
41	Neal, Lorenzo	FB	5-11	245	12/27/70	10	Fresno State	Fresno, Calif.	FA-'01	16/10
72	O'Dwyer, Matt	G	6-5	310	9/1/72	8	Northwestern	Lincolnshire, Ill.	UFA(NYJ)-'99	12/12
92	Ogbogu, Eric	DE	6-4	270	7/18/75	5	Maryland	Irvington, N.Y.	UFA(NYJ)-'02	15/0*
5	Rackers, Neil	K	6-0	205	8/16/76	3	Illinois	Florissant, Mo.	D6-'00	16/0
79	Rehberg, Scott	G	6-8	325	11/17/73	6	Central Michigan	Kalamazoo, Mich.	FA-'00	14/4
20	Roman, Mark	S	5-11	189	3/26/77	3	Louisiana State	New Iberia, La.	D2-'00	13/8
57	Ross, Adrian	LB	6-2	251	2/19/75	5	Colorado State	Elk Grove, Calif.	FA-'98	16/1
48	St. Louis, Brad	TE-LS	6-3	247	8/19/76	3	Southwest Missouri State	Belton, Mo.	D7-'00	11/0
86	Scott, Darnay	WR	6-1	204	7/7/72	9	San Diego State	St. Louis, Mo.	D2-'94	16/15
56	Simmons, Brian	LB	6-3	248	6/21/75	5	North Carolina	New Bern, N.C.	D1b-'98	16/16
11	Smith, Akili	QB	6-3	220	8/21/75	4	Oregon	San Diego, Calif.	D1-'99	2/1
90	Smith, Justin	DE	6-4	270	9/30/79	2	Missouri	Holt's Summit, Mo.	D1-'01	15/11
59	Spearman, Armegis	LB	6-1	245	4/5/78	3	Mississippi	Bruce, Miss.	FA-'00	0*
51	Spikes, Takeo	LB	6-2	245	12/17/76	5	Auburn	Sandersville, Ga.	D1a-'98	15/15
70	Steele, Glen	DT	6-4	300	10/4/74	5	Michigan	Ligonier, Ind.	D4-'98	16/1
75	Stephens, Jamain	T	6-6	340	1/9/74	7	North Carolina A&T	Lumberton, N.C.	W(Pitt)-'99	9/2
80	Warrick, Peter	WR-PR	5-11	195	6/19/77	3	Florida State	Bradenton, Fla.	D1-'00	16/14
73	Webb, Richmond	T	6-6	325	1/11/67	13	Texas A&M	Dallas, Texas	UFA(Mia)-'01	16/16
97	Whittington, Bernard	DT	6-5	291	8/20/71	9	Indiana	St. Louis, Mo.	UFA(Ind)-'01	16/5
30	Williams, Nick	FB	6-2	267	3/30/77	4	Miami	Farmington Hills, Mich.	D5-'99	4/2
94	Williams, Tony	DT	6-1	294	7/9/75	6	Memphis	Germantown, Tenn.	UFA(Minn)-'01	13/13
55	Wilson, Reinard	DE	6-2	270	12/17/73	6	Florida State	Lake City, Fla.	D1'-97	16/5

* Brewer and Spearman missed '01 season because of injury; Burris played 15 games with Indianapolis; Chevrier played 8 games with Dallas and 5 games with Cincinnati; Covington was inactive for 2 games; Frerotte played 4 games with Denver; Leyva was inactive for 15 games; Ogbogu played 15 games with New York Jets.

Players lost through free agency (1): S Chris Carter (Hou; 16 games in '01).

Also played with Bengals in '01—TE Marco Battaglia (8 games), CB Tom Carter (6), TE Tony McGee (11), QB Scott Mitchell (1), S Daryl Williams (15).

2002 FIRST-YEAR ROSTER

Name	Pos.	Ht.	Wt.	Birthdate	College	Hometown	How Acq.
Archie, Chris	WR	6-4	204	7/9/79	Eastern Michigan	Detroit, Mich.	FA
Bland, Justin	T	6-5	340	2/11/80	Missouri	Chillicothe, Mo.	FA
Dorsch, Travis	K-P	6-6	227	9/4/79	Purdue	Bozeman, Mont.	D4
Edmonds, Chris (1)	LB	6-3	250	1/1/78	West Virginia	Pittsburgh, Pa.	FA-'01
Evans, Joey	DE	6-4	279	8/22/79	North Carolina	Fayetteville, N.C.	D7
Grabowski, John	T	6-5	313	3/23/79	Eastern Michigan	South Holland, Ill.	FA
Grant, Robert	S	6-0	200	8/26/80	Hawaii	Oakland, Calif.	FA
Hoffman, Gavin	QB	6-5	232	12/13/78	Pennsylvania	Wayzata, Minn.	FA
Ivy, Khori (1)	WR	6-3	195	3/16/78	West Virginia	Boca Raton, Fla.	FA
Jackson, Harold	FB	6-1	255	1/31/78	Temple	Wilkes-Barre, Pa.	FA
Johnson, Derrick	DT	6-0	327	7/24/78	Kentucky	Harrodsburg, Ky.	FA
Jones, Levi	T	6-5	306	8/24/79	Arizona State	Eloy, Ariz.	D1
Kelly, Stephon	S	6-2	212	10/20/79	Winston-Salem State	Dorchester, S.C.	FA
Levels, Dwayne	LB	6-2	259	5/9/79	Oklahoma State	Richardson, Texas	FA
Leverette, Kwazeon	WR	6-1	190	12/3/75	Syracuse	Yonkers, N.Y.	FA
Levy, Darcey	WR	6-2	202	7/5/79	Pittsburgh	Aurora, Colo.	FA
Manuel, Marquand	S	6-0	209	7/11/79	Florida	Miami, Fla.	D6
Murray, Jason	FB	6-1	252	11/30/78	Notre Dame	Belle Vernon, Pa.	FA
Myles, Reggie	CB	5-11	185	10/10/79	Alabama	Pascagoula, Miss.	FA
Petty, Jermaine	LB	6-3	261	2/1/78	Arkansas	Inman, S.C.	FA
Prather, Pig	S	6-0	200	8/8/79	Mississippi State	Falkner, Miss.	FA
Redziniak, Ray (1)	C	6-2	297	12/17/78	Illinois	Clark, N.J.	FA
Rodriguez, Tito	LB	6-0	245	8/16/79	Central Florida	Lehigh Acres, Fla.	FA
Sams, Tierre	CB	5-9	169	9/30/77	Fresno State	Fresno, Calif.	FA
Sansbury, Trent	TE	6-2	244	4/5/79	Furman	Lilburn, Ga.	FA
Schobel, Matt	TE	6-5	263	11/4/78	Texas Christian	Columbus, Texas	D3
Slater, Michael	WR	6-1	184	11/7/78	Murray State	Vicksburg, Miss.	FA
Szalay, Thatcher	G	6-4	303	1/18/79	Montana	Whitefish, Mont.	FA
Thompson, Lamont	S	6-1	220	7/30/78	Washington State	Richmond, Calif.	D2

The term NFL Rookie is defined as a player who is in his first season of professional football and has not been on the roster of another professional football team for any regular-season or postseason games. A Rookie is designated by an "R" on NFL rosters. Players who have been active in another professional football league or players who have NFL experience, including either preseason training camp or being on an Active List or Inactive List, or on Reserve/Injured or Reserve/Physically Unable to Perform for fewer than six regular-season games, are termed NFL First-Year Players. An NFL First-Year Player is designated by a "1" on NFL rosters. Thereafter, a player is credited with an additional year of experience for each season in which he accumulates six games on the Active List or Inactive List, or on Reserve/Injured or Reserve/Physically Unable to Perform.p

COACHING STAFF
Head Coach,
Dick LeBeau
Pro Career: LeBeau is entering his third season, and second full season, as head coach of the Bengals. He was named the franchise's eighth head coach on September 25, 2000, following the resignation of Bruce Coslet. He had begun the 2000 season in the role of Bengals assistant head coach/defensive coordinator. A former All-Pro cornerback, LeBeau is in his forty-fourth NFL season, including fourteen as a player and thirteenth as a coach. Upon his promotion to replace Coslet, he became, at age 63, the NFL's oldest rookie head coach since the 1970 merger. The Bengals finished 4-9 under LeBeau last season after starting 0-3 under Coslet. The club showed improvement under LeBeau with a 4-6 record over the last 10 games and a 2-2 mark in the last four. In 2001, the Bengals improved to 6-10. LeBeau began his coaching career as an assistant with the Philadelphia Eagles from 1973-75. He was on the Green Bay Packers staff from 1976-79, and he began the first of two stints with the Bengals in 1980. He was defensive backfield coach through 1983 and was defensive coordinator for eight seasons (1984-1991). LeBeau went to the Pittsburgh Steelers as defensive backs coach in 1992 and was promoted and named Steelers' defensive coordinator for the 1995-96 seasons, when his zone blitz defensive scheme helped power Pittsburgh to Super Bowl XXX. LeBeau left the Steelers in 1997, returning to Cincinnati as assistant head coach/defensive coordinator under Coslet. Career record: 10-19.
Background: LeBeau is a native of London, Ohio, and attended London H.S. He played defensive back at Ohio State from 1955-58, and was a member of OSU's 1957 national championship team. **Personal:** Born September 9, 1937. LeBeau and his wife Nancy live in Cincinnati and have a son, Brandon Grant.

ASSISTANT COACHES
Paul Alexander, offensive line; born February 12, 1960, Rochester, N.Y., lives in Cincinnati. Tackle Cortland State 1979-1981. No pro playing experience. College coach: Penn State 1982-84, Michigan 1985-86, Central Michigan 1987-1991. Pro coach: New York Jets 1992-93, joined Bengals in 1994.
Jim Anderson, running backs; born March 27, 1948, Harrisburg, Pa., lives in Cincinnati. Linebacker-defensive end California Western 1967-1970. No pro playing experience. College coach: California Western 1970-71, Scottsdale (Ariz.) C.C. 1973, Nevada-Las Vegas 1974-75, Southern Methodist 1976-1980, Stanford 1981-83. Pro coach: Joined Bengals in 1984.

Ken Anderson, quarterbacks; born February 15, 1949, Batavia, Ill., lives in Fort Mitchell, Ky. Quarterback Augustana (Ill.) 1967-1970. Pro quarterback Cincinnati Bengals 1971-1986. Pro coach: Joined Bengals in 1992.
Bob Bratkowski, offensive coordinator; born December 22, 1995, San Angelo, Texas, lives in Cincinnati. Wide receiver Washington State. No pro playing experience. College coach: Missouri 1978-1980, Weber State 1981-85, Wyoming 1986, Washington State 1987-88, Miami 1989-1991. Pro coach: Seattle Seahawks 1992-98, Pittsburgh Steelers 1999-2000, joined Bengals in 2001.
Louie Cioffi, defensive assistant; born September 21, 1973, Greenlawn, N.Y., lives in Cincinnati. Attended SUNY-Stony Brook. No college or pro playing experience. College coach: C.W. Post 1995-96. Pro coach: New York Jets 1993-94, joined Bengals in 1997.
Kevin Coyle, cornerbacks; born January 14, 1956, Staten Island, N.Y., lives in Cincinnati. Defensive back Massachusetts 1975-77. No pro playing experience. College coach: Cincinnati 1978-79, Arkansas 1980, U.S. Merchant Marine Academy 1981, Holy Cross 1982-1990, Syracuse 1991-93, Maryland 1994-96, Fresno State 1997-2000. Pro coach: Joined Bengals in 2001.
Mark Duffner, defensive coordinator; born July 19, 1953, Annandale, Va., lives in Cincinnati. Defensive lineman William & Mary 1973-74. No pro playing experience. College coach: Ohio State 1975-76, Cincinnati 1977-1980, Holy Cross 1981-1991 (head coach 1986-1991), Maryland 1992-96 (head coach). Pro coach: Joined Bengals in 1997.
John Garrett, offensive assistant; born March 2, 1965, Danville, Pa., lives in Cincinnati. Wide reciever Columbia 1983-84, Princeton 1987. Pro wide receiver Cincinnati Bengals 1989, San Antonio Riders (World League) 1991. Pro coach: Cincinnati Bengals 1995-98, Arizona Cardinals 1999-2000, joined Bengals in 2001.
Rodney Holman, assistant strength & conditioning; born April 20, 1960, Ypsilanti, Mich., lives in Cincinnati. Tight end Tulane 1978-81. Pro tight end Cincinnati Bengals 1982-92, Detroit Lions 1993-95. Pro coach: New Orleans Saints 1998-99, joined Bengals in 2001.
Tim Krumrie, defensive line; born May 20, 1960, Menomonie, Wis., lives in Cincinnati. Defensive tackle Wisconsin 1979-1982. Pro defensive tackle Cincinnati Bengals 1983-1994. Pro coach: Joined Bengals in 1995.
Steve Mooshagian, wide receivers; born March 27, 1959, Downey, Calif., lives in Cincinnati. Wide receiver Cerritos College 1978-79, Fresno State 1980-81. No pro playing experience. College coach: Fresno State 1985-1994, Fresno City College

1995 (head coach), Nevada 1996, Pittsburgh 1997-98. Pro coach: Joined Bengals in 1999.
Darren Perry, safeties; born December 29, 1968, Norfolk, Va., lives in Cincinnati. Defensive back Penn State 1987-1991. Pro defensive back Pittsburgh Steelers 1992-98, New Orleans Saints 2000. Pro coach: Joined Bengals in 2002.
Al Roberts, special teams; born January 6, 1944, Fresno, Calif., lives in Cincinnati. Running back Washington 1964-65, Puget Sound 1967-68. No pro playing experience. College coach: Washington 1977-1982, 1996, Purdue 1986-87. Pro coach: Los Angeles Express (USFL) 1983-84, Houston Oilers 1984-85, Philadelphia Eagles 1988-1990, New York Jets 1991-93, Arizona Cardinals 1994-95, joined Bengals in 1997.
Bob Surace, offensive assistant; born April 25, 1968, Harrisburg, Pa., lives in Cincinnati. Center Princeton 1987-89. No pro playing experience. College coach: Springfield College 1990-91, Maine Maritime Academy 1992-93, Rensselaer Polytechnic Institute 1995, Western Connecticut State 1996-2001 (head coach 2000-01). Pro coach: Shreveport Pirates (CFL) 1994, joined Bengals in 2002.
Kim Wood, strength; born July 12, 1945, Barrington, Ill., lives in Cincinnati. Running back Wisconsin 1965-68. No pro playing experience. Pro coach: Joined Bengals in 1975.

**American Football Conference
North Division
Team Colors:** Brown, Orange, and White
**76 Lou Groza Blvd.
Berea, Ohio 44017
Telephone:** (440) 891-5000

2002 SCHEDULE
PRESEASON
Aug. 10 at Minnesota 7:00
Aug. 17 **Detroit** 8:00
Aug. 26 at Green Bay 7:00
Aug. 30 **Carolina**...........................8:00

REGULAR SEASON
Sept. 8 **Kansas City** 1:00
Sept. 15 **Cincinnati** 1:00
Sept. 22 at Tennessee 12:00
Sept. 29 at Pittsburgh.......................1:00
Oct. 6 **Baltimore**.........................8:30
Oct. 13 at Tampa Bay 4:15
Oct. 20 **Houston** 4:05
Oct. 27 at New York Jets 1:00
Nov. 3 **Pittsburgh**........................1:00
Nov. 10 Open Date
Nov. 17 at Cincinnati 1:00
Nov. 24 at New Orleans.................12:00
Dec. 1 **Carolina**...........................1:00
Dec. 8 at Jacksonville....................1:00
Dec. 15 **Indianapolis**......................1:00
Dec. 22 at Baltimore.......................4:15
Dec. 29 **Atlanta**..............................1:00

Stadium: Cleveland Browns Stadium
(opened in 1999)
•**Capacity:** 73,300
1085 West 3rd Street
Cleveland, Ohio 44114
Playing Surface: Grass
Headquarters/Training Camp:
76 Lou Groza Boulevard
Berea, Ohio 44017

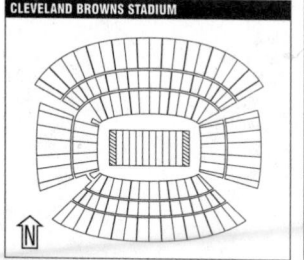
CLEVELAND BROWNS STADIUM

CLUB OFFICIALS
Owner and Chairman: Alfred Lerner
President and Chief Executive Officer:
Carmen Policy
Executive Vice President, Business
Operations and Chief Administrative
Officer: Kofi Bonner
Executive Vice President, Finance:
Doug Jacobs
Executive Vice President, Stadium and
Security: Lew Merletti
Vice President, Operations: Bill Hampton
Assistant Director of Football Operations
& General Counsel: Lal Heneghan
Vice President, Marketing and
Development: Bruce Popko
Assistant Coach-Football Development:
Pete Garcia
Director, College Personnel: Phil Neri
Executive Director of Publicity/Media
Relations: Todd Stewart
Director of New Media: Dan Arthur
Director of Community Relations:
Renee Zidan
Director of Ticket Operations:
John Schulze
Director, Stadium Operations:
Diane Downing
Director, Cleveland Browns Foundation:
Judge George White
Manager of Publicity/Media Relations:
Ken Mather
Manager of New Media: Amy Gretsinger
Facilities Manager: Greg Hipp
Head Athletic Trainer: Mike Colello
Equipment Manager: Bobby Monica
Video Director: Pat Dolan
Head Groundskeeper: Chris Powell

COACHING HISTORY
(397-321-10)
1950-1962 Paul Brown 115-49-5
1963-1970 Blanton Collier 79-38-2
1971-74   Nick Skorich 30-26-2
1975-77   Forrest Gregg* 18-23-0
1977   Dick Modzelewski 0-1-0
1978-1984 Sam Rutigliano** 47-52-0
1984-88   Marty Schottenheimer ..46-31-0
1989-1990 Bud Carson*** 12-14-1
1990   Jim Shofner.....................1-6-0
1991-95   Bill Belichick................37-45-0
1999-2000 Chris Palmer 5-27-0
2001   Butch Davis.....................7-9-0
*Resigned after 13 games in 1977
**Released after eight games in 1984
***Released after nine games in 1990

ATTENDANCE
Home 570,034   Away 507,123
Total 1,077,157
Single-game home record,
85,073 (9/21/70)
Single-season home record, 620,496
(1980)

2002 DRAFT CHOICES
Round	Name	Pos.	College
1	William Green	RB	Boston College
2	André Davis	WR	Virginia Tech
3	Melvin Fowler	C	Maryland
4	Kevin Bentley	LB	Northwestern
	Ben Taylor	LB	Virginia Tech
	Darnell Sanders	TE	Ohio State
5	Andra Davis	LB	Florida
7	Joaquin Gonzalez	T	Miami

CLEVELAND BROWNS

2001 TEAM RECORD
PRESEASON (2-2)

Date	Result	Opponent
8/11	W 10-3	Green Bay
8/18	W 7-6	Tampa Bay
8/24	L 25-27	at Washington
8/31	L 20-23	at Carolina

REGULAR SEASON (7-9)

Date	Result	Opponent	Att.
9/09	L 6-9	Seattle	72,318
9/23	W 24-14	Detroit	73,168
9/30	W 23-14	at Jacksonville	57,875
10/07	W 20-16	San Diego	73,018
10/14	L 14-24	at Cincinnati	64,217
10/21	W 24-14	Baltimore	72,818
11/04	L 21-27	at Chicago(OT)	66,944
11/11	L 12-15	Pittsburgh(OT)	73,218
11/18	W 27-17	at Baltimore	69,353
11/25	W 18-0	Cincinnati	72,918
12/02	L 15-31	Tennessee	72,818
12/09	L 16-27	at New England	60,292
12/16	L 10-15	Jacksonville	72,818
12/23	L 7-30	at Green Bay	59,824
12/30	W 41-38	at Tennessee	68,798
1/06	L 7-28	at Pittsburgh	59,189

(OT) Overtime

SCORE BY PERIODS

Browns	77	83	51	74	0	— 285
Opponents	62	73	89	86	9	— 319

2001 TEAM STATISTICS

	Browns	Opp.
Total First Downs	238	295
Rushing	78	112
assing	139	161
enalty	21	22
3rd Down: Made/Att	68/210	88/235
3rd Down Pct.	32.4	37.4
4th Down: Made/Att	6/12	8/23
4th Down Pct.	50.0	34.8
Possession Avg.	28:16	31:44
Total Net Yards	4152	5297
Avg. Per Game	259.5	331.1
Total Plays	934	1089
Avg. Per Play	4.4	4.9
Net Yards Rushing	1351	2208
Avg. Per Game	84.4	138.0
Total Rushes	417	494
Net Yards Passing	2801	3089
Avg. Per Game	175.1	193.1
Sacked/Yards Lost	51/353	43/288
Gross Yards	3154	3377
Att./Completions	466/279	552/309
Completion Pct.	59.9	56.0
Had Intercepted	21	33
Punts/Average	99/42.9	74/43.2
Net Punting Avg.	99/34.6	74/37.7
Penalties/Yards	94/825	103/779
Fumbles/Ball Lost	24/12	35/9
Touchdowns	31	35
Rushing	8	11
Passing	18	18
Returns	5	6

2001 INDIVIDUAL STATISTICS

PASSING	Att.	Comp.	Yds.	Pct.	TD	Int.	Tkld.	Rate
Couch	454	272	3040	59.9	17	21	51/353	73.1
Holcomb	12	7	114	58.3	1	0	0/0	118.1
Browns	466	279	3154	59.9	18	21	51/353	74.3
Opponents	552	309	3377	56.0	18	33	43/288	60.2

SCORING	TD R	TD P	TD Rt	PAT	FG	Saf	PTS
P. Dawson	0	0	0	29/30	22/25	0	95
K. Johnson	0	9	0	0/0	0/0	0	54
White	5	1	0	0/0	0/0	0	38
J. Jackson	2	0	0	0/0	0/0	0	12
Morgan	0	2	0	0/0	0/0	0	12
Santiago	0	2	0	0/0	0/0	0	12
Sellers	0	2	0	0/0	0/0	0	12
Brown	0	0	1	0/0	0/0	0	6
Bush	0	0	1	0/0	0/0	0	6
J. Dawson	0	1	0	0/0	0/0	0	6
Fuller	0	0	1	0/0	0/0	0	6
Gay	1	0	0	0/0	0/0	0	6
Henry	0	0	1	0/0	0/0	0	6
McCutcheon	0	0	1	0/0	0/0	0	6
O'Hara	0	1	0	0/0	0/0	0	6
Roye	0	0	0	0/0	0/0	1	2
Browns	8	18	5	29/30	22/25	1	285
Opponents	11	18	6	30/32	25/34	0	319

2-Pt. Conversions: White.
Browns 1-1, Opponents 2-2.

RUSHING	Att.	Yds.	Avg.	LG	TD
J. Jackson	195	554	2.8	22	2
White	126	443	3.5	51	5
Gay	51	172	3.4	40	1
Couch	38	128	3.4	15	0
Morgan	2	27	13.5	23	0
Northcutt	3	26	8.7	12	0
Frost	1	1	1.0	1	0
Holcomb	1	0	0.0	0	0
Browns	417	1351	3.2	51	8
Opponents	494	2208	4.5	54	11

RECEIVING	No.	Yds.	Avg.	LG	TD
K. Johnson	84	1097	13.1	55t	9
White	44	418	9.5	45	1
Morgan	30	432	14.4	78	2
J. Dawson	22	281	12.8	44	1
Northcutt	18	211	11.7	26	0
Santiago	17	153	9.0	27	2
Shea	14	86	6.1	12	0
King	11	149	13.5	48	0
Dudley	9	115	12.8	27	0
Sellers	7	73	10.4	28	2
German	7	65	9.3	18	0
J. Jackson	7	56	8.0	16	0
Gay	4	11	2.8	7	0
J. Moreland	3	15	5.0	6	0
O'Hara	1	2	2.0	2t	1
Couch	1	-10	-10.0	-10	0
Browns	279	3154	11.3	78	18
Opponents	309	3377	10.9	71t	18

INTERCEPTIONS	No.	Yds.	Avg.	LG	TD
Henry	10	177	17.7	97t	1
Little	5	33	6.6	15	0
McCutcheon	4	62	15.5	32t	1
Fuller	3	82	27.3	49t	1
R. Jackson	3	52	17.3	52	0
Bush	2	62	31.0	43t	1
Boyer	2	12	6.0	8	0
Ellsworth	1	19	19.0	19	0
J. Miller	1	0	0.0	0	0
Roye	1	0	0.0	0	0
Rudd	1	0	0.0	0	0
Browns	33	499	15.1	97t	4
Opponents	21	242	11.5	69t	3

PUNTING	No.	Yds.	Avg.	In 20	LG
Gardocki	99	4249	42.9	25	69
Browns	99	4249	42.9	25	69
Opponents	74	3198	43.2	28	68

PUNT RETURNS	No.	FC	Yds.	Avg.	LG	TD
Northcutt	15	9	86	5.7	32	0
K. Johnson	14	6	117	8.4	24	0
Chapman	1	0	1	1.0	1	0
R. Jackson	1	0	43	43.0	43	0
Frost	0	1	0	—	—	0
Browns	31	16	247	8.0	43	0
Opponents	52	12	647	12.4	86	1

KICKOFF RETURNS	No.	Yds.	Avg.	LG	TD
Gay	23	513	22.3	42	0
King	14	279	19.9	27	0
White	9	189	21.0	31	0
Morgan	7	175	25.0	51	0
Sellers	4	75	18.8	21	0
Santiago	2	1	0.5	5	0
J. Moreland	1	14	14.0	14	0
Northcutt	1	26	26.0	26	0
Spires	1	13	13.0	13	0
Browns	62	1285	20.7	51	0
Opponents	65	1215	18.7	49	0

FIELD GOALS	1-19	20-29	30-39	40-49	50+
P. Dawson	0/0	10/10	8/9	4/6	0/0
Browns	0/0	10/10	8/9	4/6	0/0
Opponents	0/0	8/9	10/11	5/12	2/2

SACKS	No.
J. Miller	13.0
Rogers	6.0
Warren	5.0
Brown	4.5
Spires	4.0
McKenzie	3.0
McCutcheon	2.0
Mark Smith	2.0
Ellsworth	1.0
Little	1.0
Rainer	1.0
Rudd	0.5
Browns	43.0
Opponents	51.0

RECORD HOLDERS
INDIVIDUAL RECORDS—CAREER

Category	Name	Performance
Rushing (Yds.)	Jim Brown, 1957-1965	12,312
Passing (Yds.)	Brian Sipe, 1974-1983	23,713
Passing (TDs)	Brian Sipe, 1974-1983	154
Receiving (No.)	Ozzie Newsome, 1978-1990	662
Receiving (Yds.)	Ozzie Newsome, 1978-1990	7,980
Interceptions	Thom Darden, 1972-74, 1976-1981	45
Punting (Avg.)	Chris Gardocki, 1999-2001	44.1
Punt Return (Avg.)	Greg Pruitt, 1973-1981	11.8
Kickoff Return (Avg.)	Greg Pruitt, 1973-1981	26.3
Field Goals	Lou Groza, 1950-59, 1961-67	234
Touchdowns (Tot.)	Jim Brown, 1957-1965	126
Points	Lou Groza, 1950-59, 1961-67	1,349

INDIVIDUAL RECORDS—SINGLE SEASON

Category	Name	Performance
Rushing (Yds.)	Jim Brown, 1963	1,863
Passing (Yds.)	Brian Sipe, 1980	4,132
Passing (TDs)	Brian Sipe, 1980	30
Receiving (No.)	Ozzie Newsome, 1983	89
	Ozzie Newsome, 1984	89
Receiving (Yds.)	Webster Slaughter, 1989	1,236
Interceptions	Thom Darden, 1978	10
	Anthony Henry, 2001	10
Punting (Avg.)	Gary Collins, 1965	46.7
Punt Return (Avg.)	Leroy Kelly, 1965	15.6
Kickoff Return (Avg.)	Billy Lefear, 1975	31.7
Field Goals	Matt Stover, 1995	29
Touchdowns (Tot.)	Jim Brown, 1965	21
Points	Jim Brown, 1965	126

INDIVIDUAL RECORDS—SINGLE GAME

Category	Name	Performance
Rushing (Yds.)	Jim Brown, 11-24-57	237
	Jim Brown, 11-19-61	237
Passing (Yds.)	Bernie Kosar, 1-3-87	489
Passing (TDs)	Frank Ryan, 12-12-64	5
	Bill Nelsen, 11-2-69	5
	Brian Sipe, 10-7-79	5
Receiving (No.)	Ozzie Newsome, 10-14-84	14
Receiving (Yds.)	Ozzie Newsome, 10-14-84	191
Interceptions	Many times	3
	Last time by Anthony Henry, 11-18-01	
Field Goals	Don Cockroft, 10-19-75	5
	Matt Stover, 10-29-95	5
Touchdowns (Tot.)	Dub Jones, 11-25-51	*6
Points	Dub Jones, 11-25-51	36

*NFL Record

CLEVELAND BROWNS

2002 VETERAN ROSTER

No.	Name	Pos.	Ht.	Wt.	Birthdate	NFL Exp.	College	Hometown	How Acq.	'01 Games/ Starts
36	Akins, Chris	S	5-11	195	11/29/76	4	Arkansas-Pine Bluff	Little Rock, Ark.	W(GB)-'01	4/0
63	Bedell, Brad	G-T	6-4	299	2/12/77	3	Colorado	Arcadia, Calif.	D6b-'00	15/4
12	Booty, Josh	QB	6-2	217	4/29/78	2	Louisiana State	New Orleans, La.	W(Sea)-'01	0*
52	Boyer, Brant	LB	6-1	230	6/27/71	9	Arizona	Ogden, Utah	UFA(Jax)-'01	16/1
92	Brown, Courtney	DE	6-4	266	2/14/78	3	Penn State	Alvin, S.C.	D1-'00	5/5
23	Bush, Devin	S	6-0	210	7/3/73	8	Florida State	Miami, Fla.	W(StL)-'01	16/7
83	Campbell, Mark	TE	6-6	253	12/6/75	4	Michigan	Clawson, Mich.	FA-'99	0*
26	Carter, Dyshod	CB-S	5-10	197	6/18/78	2	Kansas State	Denver, Colo.	FA-'01	5/0
	Cavil, Kwame	WR	6-2	203	5/3/79	2	Texas	Waco, Texas	FA-'02	0*
69	Chanoine, Roger	T	6-4	295	9/11/76	3	Temple	Linden, N.J.	FA-'99	16/16
27	Chapman, Lamar	CB	6-0	186	11/6/76	3	Kansas State	Liberal, Kan.	D5b-'99	1/0
79	Claybrooks, DeVone	DE-DT	6-3	292	8/15/77	2	East Carolina	Bassett, Va.	FA-'01	0*
2	Couch, Tim	QB	6-4	227	7/31/77	4	Kentucky	Hyden, Ky.	D1-'99	16/16
88	Dawson, JaJuan	WR	6-1	197	11/5/77	3	Tulane	Houston, Texas	D3b-'00	14/0
4	Dawson, Phil	K	5-11	190	1/23/75	4	Texas	Dallas, Texas	FA-'99	16/0
55	Denman, Anthony	LB	6-1	234	10/30/79	2	Notre Dame	Rusk, Texas	FA-'01	11/0
82	Dudley, Rickey	TE	6-6	255	7/15/72	7	Ohio State	Hearne, Texas	UFA(Oak)-'01	4/4
49	Eitzmann, Chris	TE	6-5	255	4/1/77	2	Harvard	Belleville, Kan.	FA-'02	0*
25	Fuller, Corey	CB	5-10	205	5/1/71	8	Florida State	Tallahassee, Fla.	UFA(Minn)-'99	16/16
17	Gardocki, Chris	P	6-1	200	2/7/70	12	Clemson	Stone Mountain, Ga.	UFA(Ind)-'99	16/0
75	Gregory, Damian	DE	6-3	305	1/21/77	3	Illinois State	Lansing, Mich.	W(Mia)-'02	2/0*
24	Griffith, Robert	S	5-11	197	11/30/70	9	San Diego State	San Diego, Calif.	UFA(Minn)-'02	10/9*
73	Ham, Derrick	DE	6-4	270	3/23/75	2	Miami	Merritt Island, Fla.	D4-'01	1/0
37	Henry, Anthony	S	6-0	198	11/3/76	2	South Florida	Fort Myers, Fla.	D4-'01	16/2
10	Holcomb, Kelly	QB	6-2	212	7/9/73	6	Middle Tennessee State	Fayetteville, Tenn.	FA-'01	1/0
50	Holmes, Earl	LB	6-2	245	4/28/73	7	Florida A&M	Tallahassee, Fla.	UFA(Pitt)-'02	16/16*
71	Hyder, Gaylon	G-T	6-5	290	10/18/74	2	Texas Christian	Longview, Texas	FA-'01	0*
29	Jackson, James	RB	5-10	209	8/4/76	2	Miami	Belle Glade, Fla.	D3-'01	11/10
22	Jameson, Michael	CB-S	5-11	186	7/14/79	2	Texas A&M	Killeen, Texas	D6-'01	0*
28	t-Johnson, J. J.	RB	6-1	230	4/20/74	4	Mississippi State	Mobile, Ala.	T(Mia)-'02	10/0*
85	Johnson, Kevin	WR	6-1	195	7/15/76	4	Syracuse	Hamilton Township, N.J.	D2a-'99	16/16
67	Johnson, Tre'	G-T	6-2	326	8/30/71	9	Temple	Peekskill, N.Y.	UFA(Wash)-'01	3/3
51	Jones, Lenoy	LB	6-1	236	8/25/74	7	Texas Christian	Waco, Texas	ED(Tenn)-'01	7/1
84	King, Andre	WR	5-11	195	11/26/73	2	Miami	Fort Lauderdale, Fla.	D7b-'01	7/0
97	Kuehl, Ryan	DT	6-5	290	1/18/72	6	Virginia	Bethesda, Md.	FA-'99	16/0
96	Lang, Kenard	DE	6-4	281	1/31/75	6	Miami	Orlando, Fla.	UFA(Wash)-'02	16/16*
20	Little, Earl	S	6-0	198	3/10/73	5	Miami	Miami, Fla.	W(NO)-'99	16/16
33	McCutcheon, Daylon	CB	5-10	180	12/9/76	4	Southern California	La Puente, Calif.	D3a-'99	16/15
70	McKinley, Alvin	DE-DT	6-3	292	6/9/78	3	Mississippi State	Jackson, Miss.	FA-'01	7/0
62	Mercier, Richard	G-T	6-3	304	5/13/75	3	Miami	Montreal, Quebec, Canada	FA-'01	0*
98	Miller, Arnold	DE	6-3	239	1/3/75	4	Louisiana State	New Orleans, La.	FA-'99	0*
95	Miller, Jamir	LB	6-5	266	11/19/73	3	UCLA	Oakland, Calif.	UFA(Ariz)-'99	16/16
48	Monroe, Rod	TE	6-5	254	7/30/75	3	Cincinnati	Hearne, Texas	FA-'01	7/3
38	Moreland, Earthwind	CB-S	5-11	185	6/13/77	2	Georgia Southern	Atlanta, Ga.	FA-'01	2/0
81	Morgan, Quincy	WR	6-1	209	9/23/77	2	Kansas State	Garland, Texas	D2-'01	16/10
86	Northcutt, Dennis	WR	5-11	175	12/22/77	3	Arizona	Los Angeles, Calif.	D2-'00	11/7
60	O'Hara, Shaun	C	6-3	287	6/23/77	3	Rutgers	Hillsborough, N.J.	FA-'00	16/4
78	Rogers, Tyrone	DT	6-5	236	3/9/74	3	Alabama State	Montgomery, Ala.	FA-'99	16/10
99	Orpheus	DT	6-4	313	1/21/74	7	Florida State	Carrol City, Fla.	UFA(Pitt)-'01	12/10
		LB	6-2	237	2/3/76	6	Alabama	Batesville, Miss.	UFA(Minn)-'01	16/16
		WR	6-1	190	5/8/72	8	Ohio State	Denver, Colo.	FA-'02	4/0*
94										
30	W. CB-S	6-0	202	6/22/78	3	Maryland	Staten Island, N.Y.	D4a-'00	0*	
64	Wohlabaugh	6-3	244	12/5/76	3	Michigan	Ottawa, Ill.	D4b-'00	12/5	
90	Word, Ma...	4	294	8/28/74	6	Auburn	Vicksburg, Miss.	UFA(Ariz)-'01	16/11	
66	Zukauskas, P...	?13	1/13/75	4	California	San Diego, Calif.	D3b-'99	14/2		
			7/26/76	4	Troy State	Washington, D.C.	D6a-'99	0*		
			...'73	5	Eastern Michigan	Flint, Mich.	UFA(GB)-'02	16/3		
				2	Penn State	Damascus, Md.	FA-'02	0*		
					Texas Christian	Midland, Texas	UFA(StL)-'02	16/15*		
					...owa	Des Moines, Iowa	UFA(GB)-'01	15/15		
					...rida	Radford, Fla.	D1-'01	15/15		
					...th Dakota	Los Angeles, Calif.	W(Ind)-'00	16/7		
					...cuse	Hamburg, N.Y.	UFA(NE)-'99	16/16		
					...onville State	Miami, Fla.	FA-'01	0*		
					...College	Boston, Mass.	D7a-'01	1/0		

* Booty inactive for 16 games; Campbell missed '01 season because of injury; Cavil last active with Buffalo in '00; Claybrooks inactive for 6 games; Eitzmann last active with New England in '00; Gregory played 2 games with Miami in '01; Griffith played 10 games with Minnesota; Holmes played 16 games with Pittsburgh; Hyder inactive for 1 game; Jameson missed '01 season because of injury; J.J. Johnson played 10 games with Miami; Lang played 16 games with Washington; Mercier inactive for 13 games; A. Miller missed '01 season because of injury; C. Sanders played 4 games with Tennessee; L. Sanders missed '01 season because of injury; Spriggs missed '01 season because of injury; Thompson last active with Cleveland in '00; Tucker played 16 games with St. Louis; Word missed '01 season because of injury.

t- Browns traded for Johnson (Miami).

Traded—LB Wali Rainer (14 games in '01) to Jacksonville.

Players lost through Expansion Draft (1): G Jeremy McKinney (15 games in '01).

Players lost through free agency (1): DE Greg Spires (TB; 16 games in '01).

Also played with Browns in '01—DE Stalin Colinet (5 games), S Percy Ellsworth (11), S Scott Frost (12), RB Benjamin Gay (16), WR Jammi German (6), CB-S Raymond Jackson (15), DE Keith McKenzie (7), LB Barry Minter (1), TE Jake Moreland (4), G-T Toby Myles (3), TE O.J. Santiago (14), LB Tarek Saleh (13), HB Mike Sellers (9), WR Tony Simmons (1).

2002 FIRST-YEAR ROSTER

Name	Pos.	Ht.	Wt.	Birthdate	College	Hometown	How Acq.
Bentley, Kevin	LB	6-0	243	12/29/79	Northwestern	North Hills, Calif.	D4a
Breedlove, Dimtrius	WR	6-4	210	6/9/78	Evangel	Apopka, Fla.	FA
Caldwell, Cecil (1)	DE-DT	6-1	268	2/23/77	South Carolina	Columbia, S.C.	FA
Claybrooks, Felipe (1)	DE-DT	6-4	260	1/22/78	Georgia Tech	Decatur, Ga.	FA-'01
Davis, Andra	LB	6-1	244	12/23/78	Florida	Live Oak, Fla.	D5
Davis, Andre'	WR	6-1	194	6/12/79	Virginia Tech	Niskayuna, N.Y.	D2
Dean, Konrad	G-T	6-4	297	6/6/79	Akron	Jackson, N.J.	FA
Fair, Carl (1)	RB	6-1	219	6/8/79	Alabama-Birmingham	Starkville, Miss.	FA-'01
Fowler, Melvin	G-T	6-3	300	3/31/79	Maryland	Wheatley Heights, N.Y.	D3
Gibson, Derrick	LB	6-2	240	2/6/75	No College	Haines City, Fla.	FA-'01
Gonzalez, Joaquin	G-T	6-3	293	9/7/79	Miami	Miami, Fla.	D7
Green, William	RB	6-0	221	12/17/79	Boston College	Atlantic City, N.J.	D1
Jackson, Frisman	WR	6-3	205	6/12/79	Western Illinois	Chicago, Ill.	FA
Josiah, Michael	DE-DT	6-4	235	8/13/79	Louisville	Wilsonville, Ala.	FA
Miller, Ben	HB	6-4	270	8/18/79	Air Force	Columbia Station, Ohio	FA
Mitchell, Qasim	G-T	6-6	350	12/3/79	North Carolina A&T	Jacksonville, N.C.	FA
Morrow, Alvin (1)	TE	6-4	260	4/28/78	No College	St. Louis, Mo.	FA-'01
Pearson, Kalvin	CB-S	5-10	190	10/22/78	Grambling	Town Creek, Ala.	FA
Sanders, Darnell	TE	6-4	267	3/16/79	Ohio State	Warrensville Heights, Ohio	D4c
Smith, Mike (1)	LB	6-3	240	10/29/77	Miami	Miami, Fla.	FA
Spears, Calvin	CB-S	6-0	195	8/8/80	Grambling State	Baton Rouge, La.	FA
Sykes, Terrance (1)	G-T	6-6	270	2/24/79	Louisiana Tech	Grenada, Miss.	FA
Taylor, Ben	LB	6-2	236	8/31/78	Virginia Tech	Bellaire, Ohio	D4b
Taylor, Robert	LB	6-4	250	5/17/78	Grambling State	Birmingham, Ala.	FA

The term NFL Rookie is defined as a player who is in his first season of professional football and has not been on the roster of another professional football team for any regular-season or postseason games. A Rookie is designated by an "R" on NFL rosters. Players who have been active in another professional football league or players who have NFL experience, including either preseason training camp or being on an Active List or Inactive List, or on Reserve/Injured or Reserve/Physically Unable to Perform for fewer than six regular-season games, are termed NFL First-Year Players. An NFL First-Year Player is designated by a "1" on NFL rosters. Thereafter, a player is credited with an additional year of experience for each season in which he accumulates six games on the Active List or Inactive List, or on Reserve/Injured or Reserve/Physically Unable to Perform.

COACHING STAFF
Head Coach,
Butch Davis
Pro Career: Named head coach of the Browns on January 30, 2001, and led the Browns to a 7-9 record in his first season as an NFL head coach. Davis came to Cleveland from the University of Miami where Davis rebuilt the Hurricanes program. Davis returned the program back to the college football elite status as Miami defeated Florida in the 2001 Nokia Sugar Bowl, and finished second in both the Associated Press and ESPN/*USA Today* rankings. The tenth full-time head coach in franchise history, Davis has been successful at every previous stop in his coaching career. He has won two Super Bowl championships with the Dallas Cowboys (1992 and 1993) and, at the collegiate level, he won a national championship with the University of Miami (1987). He boasts more than 20 years of coaching experience, including six seasons (1995-2000) as the head coach of Miami, where he compiled a 51-20 record, including a 4-0 mark in bowl games. Davis joined the University of Miami after six years (1989-1994) with the Dallas Cowboys, the last two seasons as the Cowboys' defensive coordinator. Davis was the defensive coordinator on Dallas's 1993 squad that defeated the Buffalo Bills, 30-13, in Super Bowl XXVIII. Davis's 1993 defensive squad helped the Cowboys capture their second consecutive Super Bowl and allowed just one offensive touchdown or less in 12 of 16 games. Prior to being named to the defensive coordinator's post, Davis coached the Dallas defensive line for four seasons. Career record: 7-9.
Background: Davis spent five seasons (1984-88) as the defensive line coach for the University of Miami, including the Hurricanes' 1987 national championship team. Davis started as an assistant on Jimmy Johnson's Oklahoma State teams (1979-1983). Davis was responsible for coaching the receivers and tight ends and serving as the recruiting coordinator. Prior to his tenure at Oklahoma State, Davis was the head coach at Rogers High School in Tulsa, Okla., for one season (1978) after spending time as an assistant at two high schools in Oklahoma and one in Arkansas where he taught biology, anatomy, and physiology. Davis played defensive end for Arkansas (1971-74).
Personal: Born Paul Hilton Davis in Tahlequah, Okla., on November 17, 1951. Earned his bachelor's degree in biology and life science from Arkansas. Davis and his wife Tammy have one son, Andrew, 9.

ASSISTANT COACHES
Bruce Arians, offensive coordinator; born October 3, 1952, Paterson, N.J., lives in Cleveland. Quarterback Virginia Tech 1970-74. No pro playing experience.

College coach: Virginia Tech 1975-77, Mississippi State 1978-1980, Alabama 1981-82, Temple (head coach) 1983-88, Mississippi State 1993-95, Alabama 1997. Pro coach: Kansas City Chiefs 1989-1992, New Orleans Saints 1996, Indianapolis 1998-2000, joined Browns in 2001.
Phil Banko, defensive assistant; born August 9, 1964, Belle Chasse, La., lives in Cleveland. Attended Southern. No college or pro playing experience. College coach: Miami 1998-2000. Pro coach: Joined Browns in 2001.
Todd Bowles, defensive assistant; born November 18, 1963, Elizabeth, N.J., lives in Cleveland. Defensive back Temple 1982-85. Pro defensive back Washington 1986-1990, 1991-93, San Francisco 1990. College coach: Morehouse College 1997, Grambling State 1998-99. Pro coach: New York Jets 2000, joined Browns in 2001.
Keith Butler, linebackers; born May 16, 1956, Anniston, Ala., lives in Cleveland. Linebacker Memphis 1974-77. Pro linebacker Seattle 1978-1987. College coach: Memphis 1990-97, Arkansas State 1998. Pro coach: Joined Browns in 1999.
Foge Fazio, defensive coordinator; born February 28, 1939, Dawmont, W. Va., lives in Cleveland. Linebacker-center Pittsburgh 1957-1960. No pro playing experience. College coach: Boston University 1966-67, Harvard 1968, Pittsburgh 1969-1972, 1977-1985 (head coach 1982-85), Cincinnati 1973-76, Notre Dame 1986-87. Pro coach: Atlanta Falcons 1988-89, New York Jets 1990-94, Minnesota Vikings 1995-98, Washington Redskins 2000, joined Browns in 2001.
Pete Garcia, football development; born September 18, 1961, Havana, Cuba, lives in Cleveland. Attended Miami. No college or pro playing experience. College coach: Miami 1990-2000. Pro coach: Joined Browns in 2001.
Steve Hagen, tight ends; born September 15, 1961, lives in Cleveland. Tight end Cal Lutheran 1979-1982. Pro tight end Boston Breakers (USFL) 1983. College coach: Northern Arizona 1987-88, Notre Dame 1989-1990, Kent State 1991, Nevada 1992-93, Nevada-Las Vegas 1994-95, Wartburg (Iowa) 1996, San Jose State 1997-98, California 1999-2000. Pro coach: Joined Browns in 2001.
Ray Hamilton, defensive line; born January 1, 1951, Omaha, Neb., lives in Cleveland. Nose tackle Oklahoma 1969-1972. Pro defensive lineman New England 1973-1981. College coach: Tennessee 1992. Pro coach: New England Patriots 1985-89, Tampa Bay Buccaneers 1991, Los Angeles Raiders 1993-94, New York Jets 1995-96, New England Patriots 1997-99, New York Jets 2000, joined Browns in 2001.

Todd McNair, running backs; born October 7, 1965, Camden, N.J. lives in Cleveland. Running back Temple 1985-88. Pro running back Kansas City 1989-1993, 1996, Houston 1994-95. Pro coach: Joined the Browns in 2001.
Buddy Morris, head strength and conditioning; born September 29, 1957, South Park, Pa., lives in Cleveland. Attended Pittsburgh. No college or pro playing experience. College coach: Pittsburgh 1980-89, 1997-2001. Pro coach: Joined Browns in 2002
Chuck Pagano, defensive backs; born October 2, 1960, Boulder, Colo., lives in Cleveland. Safety Wyoming 1980-83. No pro playing experience. College coach: Southern California 1984-85, Miami 1986, Boise State 1987-88, East Carolina 1989, Nevada-Las Vegas 1990-91, East Carolina 1992-94, Miami 1995-2000. Pro coach: Joined Browns in 2001.
Rob Phillips, asst. strength and conditioning; born December 3, 1971, Ft. Wayne, Ind., lives in Cleveland. Attended Tennessee. No college or pro playing experience. College coach: Western Carolina 1997-98, Miami 1999-2000. Pro coach: Joined Browns in 2001.
Terry Robiskie, wide receivers; born November 12, 1954, New Orleans, lives in Cleveland. Running back Louisiana State 1973-76. Pro running back Oakland Raiders 1977-79, Miami Dolphins 1980-81. Pro coach: Los Angeles Raiders 1982-1993, Washington Redskins 1994-2000 (head coach 2000), joined Browns in 2001.
Jerry Rosburg, special teams; born November 24, 1955, Fairmont, Minn., lives in Cleveland. No college or pro playing experience. College coach: Northern Michigan 1981-86, Western Michigan 1987-91, Cincinnati 1992-95, Minnesota 1996, Boston College 1997-98, Notre Dame 1999-2000. Pro coach: Joined Browns in 2001.
Carl Smith, quarterbacks; born April 26, 1948, Wasco, Calif., lives in Cleveland. Quarterback Bakersfield College 1966-67, defensive back Cal Poly-San Luis Obispo 1969-1970. No pro playing experience. College coach: Colorado 1972-73, Southwestern Louisiana 1974-78, Lamar 1979-1981, North Carolina State 1982. Pro coach: Philadelphia/Baltimore Stars (USFL) 1983-85, New Orleans Saints 1986-1996, New England Patriots 1997-2000, joined Browns in 2001.
Larry Zierlein, offensive line; born July 12, 1945, Lenora, Kan., lives in Cleveland. No college or pro playing experience. College coach: Fort Hays (Kan.) State College 1970-71, Houston 1978-1986, Tulane 1988-1990, 1995-96, Louisiana State 1993-94, Cincinnati 1997-2000. Pro coach: Washington Commandos (Arena League) 1987, New York/New Jersey Knights (WLAF) 1991-92, joined Browns in 2001.

American Football Conference
West Division
Team Colors: Orange, Broncos Navy
Blue, and White
13655 Broncos Parkway
Englewood, Colorado 80112
Telephone: (303) 649-9000

2002 SCHEDULE
PRESEASON
Aug. 10 at Chicago (Champaign, Ill.) ...7:00
Aug. 19 **San Francisco** 6:00
Aug. 24 at Arizona...............................7:00
Aug. 29 **Seattle**...................................7:00

REGULAR SEASON
Sept. 8 **St. Louis** 2:15
Sept. 15 at San Francisco.................1:15
Sept. 22 **Buffalo** 2:05
Sept. 30 at Baltimore (Mon.) 9:00
Oct. 6 **San Diego**...........................2:05
Oct. 13 **Miami** 6:30
Oct. 20 at Kansas City 12:00
Oct. 27 at New England 4:15
Nov. 3 Open Date
Nov. 11 **Oakland** (Mon.)...................7:00
Nov. 17 at Seattle 1:15
Nov. 24 **Indianapolis**.......................6:30
Dec. 1 at San Diego 1:05
Dec. 8 at New York Jets 4:15
Dec. 15 **Kansas City** 2:05
Dec. 22 at Oakland 1:15
Dec. 29 **Arizona** 2:15

Stadium: INVESCO Field at Mile High
(opened in 2001)
•**Capacity:** 76,125
1700 Eliot Street
Denver, Colorado 80204
Playing Surface: Grass (PAT)
Training Camp: University of Northern
Colorado
Greeley, Colorado 80639

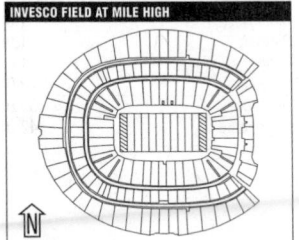

CLUB OFFICIALS
President-Chief Executive Officer:
Pat Bowlen
Executive Vice President of Football
Operations/ Head Coach:
Mike Shanahan
Executive Vice President of Business
Operations: Joe Ellis
FOOTBALL STAFF
General Manager: Ted Sundquist
Director of Football Administration:
Neal Dahlen
Director of Pro Scouting: Rick Smith
Director of College Scouting:
Jim Goodman
Trainer: Steve Antonopulos
Equipment Manager: Doug West
Video Director: Kent Erickson
BUSINESS STAFF
Chief Financial Officer: Allen Fears
General Counsel: Rich Slivka
Vice President of Public Relations:
Jim Saccomano
Vice President of Ticket Operations/
Business Development: Rick Nichols
Vice President of Operations: Bill Harpole
Vice President of Marketing: Greg Carney
Senior Director of Community
Development: Cindy Galloway·
STADIUM MANAGEMENT COMPANY
Vice President and General Manager:
Mac Freeman

COACHING HISTORY
(336-310-10)

1960-61	Frank Filchock	7-20-1
1962-61	Jack Faulkner*	9-22-1
1964-66	Mac Speedie**	6-19-1
1966	Ray Malavasi	4-8-0
1967-1971	Lou Saban***	20-42-3
1971	Jerry Smith	2-3-0
1972-76	John Ralston	34-33-3
1977-1980	Robert (Red) Miller	42-25-0
1981-1992	Dan Reeves	117-79-1
1993-94	Wade Phillips	16-17-0
1995-2001	Mike Shanahan	79-42-0

*Released after four games in 1964
**Resigned after two games in 1966
***Resigned after nine games in 1971

ATTENDANCE
Home 590,756   Away 502,821
Total 1,093,577
Single-game home record,
76,098 (12/23/00)
Single-season home record, 594,813
(2000)

2002 DRAFT CHOICES

Round	Name	Pos.	College
1	Ashley Lelie	WR	Hawaii
2	Clinton Portis	RB	Miami
3	Dorsett Davis	DT	Mississippi State
4	Sam Brandon	DB	Nevada-Las Vegas
5	Herb Haygood	WR	Michigan State
6	Jeb Putzier	TE	Boise State
7	Chris Young	DB	Georgia Tech
	Monsanto Pope	DT	Virginia

DENVER BRONCOS

2001 TEAM RECORD
PRESEASON (3-1)

Date	Result	Opponent
8/11	W 20-6	at Dallas
8/20	L 7-22	at Green Bay
8/25	W 31-24	New Orleans
8/31	W 35-7	San Francisco

REGULAR SEASON (8-8)

Date	Result	Opponent	Att.
9/10	W 31-20	New York Giants	75,735
9/23	W 38-17	at Arizona	50,913
9/30	L 13-20	Baltimore	75,082
10/07	W 20-6	Kansas City	75,037
10/14	L 21-34	at Seattle	61,837
10/21	L 10-27	at San Diego	67,521
10/28	W 31-20	New England	74,750
11/05	L 28-38	at Oakland	62,637
11/11	W 26-16	San Diego	74,951
11/18	L 10-17	Washington	74,622
11/22	W 26-24	at Dallas	64,104
12/02	L 10-21	at Miami	73,938
12/09	W 20-7	Seattle	74,524
12/16	L 23-26	at Kansas City(OT)	77,778
12/30	W 23-17	Oakland	75,582
1/06	L 10-29	at Indianapolis	56,192

(OT) Overtime

SCORE BY PERIODS

Broncos	50	128	89	73	0	— 340
Opponents	65	94	58	119	3	— 339

2001 TEAM STATISTICS

	Broncos	Opp.
Total First Downs	304	292
Rushing	106	86
Passing	174	176
Penalty	24	30
3rd Down: Made/Att	83/219	63/191
3rd Down Pct.	37.9	33.0
4th Down: Made/Att	4/10	4/10
4th Down Pct.	40.0	40.0
Possession Avg.	31:23	28:37
Total Net Yards	4817	4774
Avg. Per Game	301.1	298.4
Total Plays	1034	960
Avg. Per Play	4.7	5.0
Net Yards Rushing	1877	1492
Avg. Per Game	117.3	93.3
Total Rushes	481	406
Net Yards Passing	2940	3282
Avg. Per Game	183.8	205.1
Sacked/Yards Lost	42/268	39/279
Gross Yards	3208	3561
Att./Completions	511/312	515/308
Completion Pct.	61.1	59.8
Had Intercepted	19	22
Punts/Average	82/44.7	77/47.0
Net Punting Avg.	82/36.5	77/38.1
Penalties/Yards	95/917	100/853
Fumbles/Ball Lost	24/8	26/15
Touchdowns	35	38
Rushing	7	9
Passing	26	23
Returns	2	6

2001 INDIVIDUAL STATISTICS

PASSING

	Att.	Comp.	Yds.	Pct.	TD	Int.	Tkld.	Rate
Griese	451	275	2827	61.0	23	19	38/241	78.5
Frerotte	48	30	308	62.5	3	0	3/21	101.7
Jackson	12	7	73	58.3	0	0	1/6	76.0
Broncos	511	312	3208	61.1	26	19	42/268	80.6
Opponents	515	308	3561	59.8	23	22	39/279	77.8

SCORING

	TD R	TD P	TD Rt	PAT	FG	Saf	PTS
Elam	0	0	0	31/31	31/36	0	124
R. Smith	0	11	0	0/0	0/0	0	68
De. Clark	0	6	0	0/0	0/0	0	36
Anderson	4	0	0	0/0	0/0	0	26
Carswell	0	4	0	0/0	0/0	0	26
Hape	0	3	0	0/0	0/0	0	18
Frerotte	1	0	0	0/0	0/0	0	6
Gary	1	0	0	0/0	0/0	0	6
Griese	1	0	0	0/0	0/0	0	6
Kennison	0	1	0	0/0	0/0	0	6
McCaffrey	0	1	0	0/0	0/0	0	6
O'Neal	0	0	1	0/0	0/0	0	6
Walker	0	0	1	0/0	0/0	0	6
Broncos	7	26	2	31/31	31/36	0	340
Opponents	9	23	6	36/37	25/29	0	339

2-Pt. Conversions: Anderson, Carswell, R. Smith. Broncos 3-4, Opponents 0-1.

RUSHING

	Att.	Yds.	Avg.	LG	TD
T. Davis	167	701	4.2	57	0
Anderson	175	678	3.9	62t	4
Gary	57	228	4.0	29	1
Griese	50	173	3.5	24	1
R. Smith	3	27	9.0	17	0
Kasper	3	19	6.3	27	0
Coleman	4	17	4.3	8	0
Frerotte	10	9	0.9	4t	1
Kennison	3	9	3.0	10	0
Jackson	5	7	1.4	4	0
Montgomery	1	5	5.0	5	0
Carter	1	4	4.0	4	0
Hape	2	0	0.0	0	0
Broncos	481	1877	3.9	62t	7
Opponents	406	1492	3.7	60t	9

RECEIVING

	No.	Yds.	Avg.	LG	TD
R. Smith	113	1343	11.9	65t	11
De. Clark	51	566	11.1	39	6
Carswell	34	299	8.8	25	4
Kennison	15	169	11.3	36	1
Hape	15	96	6.4	25	3
T. Davis	12	69	5.8	16	0
Montgomery	11	99	9.0	23	0
Carter	11	83	7.5	17	0
Cole	9	128	14.2	21	0
Kasper	8	84	10.5	21	0
Anderson	8	46	5.8	16	0
McCaffrey	6	94	15.7	28	1
Coleman	6	45	7.5	9	0
Poole	5	38	7.6	10	0
Gary	4	29	7.3	11	0
Dominguez	3	26	8.7	12	0
Griese	1	-6	-6.0	-6	0
Broncos	312	3208	10.3	65t	26
Opponents	308	3561	11.6	72t	23

INTERCEPTIONS

	No.	Yds.	Avg.	LG	TD
O'Neal	9	115	12.8	42	0
Walker	3	60	20.0	39t	1
Spencer	3	25	8.3	18	0
McGlockton	2	17	8.5	17	0
Brown	2	0	0.0	0	0
Mobley	1	17	17.0	17	0
Kennedy	1	6	6.0	6	0
Coghill	1	0	0.0	0	0
Broncos	22	240	10.9	42	1
Opponents	19	256	13.5	56t	2

PUNTING

	No.	Yds.	Avg.	In 20	LG
Rouen	81	3668	45.3	25	64
Broncos	82	3668	44.7	25	64
Opponents	77	3618	47.0	26	90

PUNT RETURNS

	No.	FC	Yds.	Avg.	LG	TD
O'Neal	31	9	405	13.1	86t	1
Broncos	31	9	405	13.1	86t	1
Opponents	48	10	517	10.8	65t	1

KICKOFF RETURNS

	No.	Yds.	Avg.	LG	TD
Cole	48	1127	23.5	52	0
Kasper	14	372	26.6	37	0
Carter	2	44	22.0	24	0
De. Clark	1	11	11.0	11	0
Gary	1	18	18.0	18	0
D. Smith	1	4	4.0	4	0
Broncos	67	1576	23.5	52	0
Opponents	69	1526	22.1	88t	1

FIELD GOALS

	1-19	20-29	30-39	40-49	50+
Elam	0/0	11/11	8/8	10/13	2/4
Broncos	0/0	11/11	8/8	10/13	2/4
Opponents	0/0	12/13	3/3	8/10	2/3

SACKS

	No.
Pryce	7.0
Romanowski	7.0
Washington	4.0
Brown	3.0
Gold	3.0
Hayward	3.0
Wilson	3.0
Berry	2.0
Kennedy	2.0
McGlockton	1.0
Mobley	1.0
Pittman	1.0
Reagor	1.0
Woodall	1.0
Broncos	39.0
Opponents	42.0

RECORD HOLDERS
INDIVIDUAL RECORDS—CAREER

Category	Name	Performance
Rushing (Yds.)	Terrell Davis, 1995-2001	7,607
Passing (Yds.)	John Elway, 1983-1998	51,475
Passing (TDs)	John Elway, 1983-1998	300
Receiving (No.)	Shannon Sharpe, 1990-99	552
Receiving (Yds.)	Shannon Sharpe, 1990-99	6,983
Interceptions	Steve Foley, 1976-1986	44
Punting (Avg.)	Jim Fraser, 1962-64	45.2
Punt Return (Avg.)	Darrien Gordon, 1997-98	12.5
Kickoff Return (Avg.)	Abner Haynes, 1965-66	26.3
Field Goals	Jason Elam, 1993-2001	235
Touchdowns (Tot.)	Terrell Davis, 1995-2001	65
Points	Jason Elam, 1993-2001	1,073

INDIVIDUAL RECORDS—SINGLE SEASON

Category	Name	Performance
Rushing (Yds.)	Terrell Davis, 1998	2,008
Passing (Yds.)	John Elway, 1993	4,030
Passing (TDs)	John Elway, 1997	27
Receiving (No.)	Rod Smith, 2001	113
Receiving (Yds.)	Rod Smith, 2000	1,602
Interceptions	Goose Gonsoulin, 1960	11
Punting (Avg.)	Tom Rouen, 1998	46.9
Punt Return (Avg.)	Floyd Little, 1967	16.9
Kickoff Return (Avg.)	Bill Thompson, 1969	28.5
Field Goals	Jason Elam, 1995, 2001	31
Touchdowns (Tot.)	Terrell Davis, 1998	23
Points	Terrell Davis, 1998	138

INDIVIDUAL RECORDS—SINGLE GAME

Category	Name	Performance
Rushing (Yds.)	Mike Anderson, 12-3-00	251
Passing (Yds.)	Gus Frerotte, 11-19-00	462
Passing (TDs)	Frank Tripucka, 10-28-62	5
	John Elway, 11-18-84	5
	Gus Frerotte, 11-19-00	5
Receiving (No.)	Rod Smith, 9-23-01	14
Receiving (Yds.)	Lionel Taylor, 11-27-60	199
Interceptions	Goose Gonsoulin, 9-18-60	*4
	Willie Brown, 11-15-64	*4
	Deltha O'Neal, 10-7-01	*4
Field Goals	Gene Mingo, 10-6-63	5
	Rich Karlis, 11-20-83	5
	Jason Elam, 9-3-95	5
Touchdowns (Tot.)	Mike Anderson, 12-3-00	4
Points	Mike Anderson, 12-3-00	24

*NFL Record

2002 VETERAN ROSTER

No.	Name	Pos.	Ht.	Wt.	Birthdate	NFL Exp.	College	Hometown	How Acq.	'01 Games/ Starts
38	Anderson, Mike	RB	6-0	230	9/21/73	3	Utah	Winnsboro, S.C.	D6-'00	16/7
92	Berry, Bertrand	DE	6-3	250	8/15/75	5	Notre Dame	Humble, Texas	FA-'01	14/0
11	Beuerlein, Steve	QB	6-3	220	3/7/65	16	Notre Dame	Anaheim, Calif.	FA-'01	0*
77	Brooks, Barrett	T	6-4	320	5/5/72	7	Kansas State	Florissant, Mo.	FA-'02	0*
73	Brown, Cyron	DT	6-5	275	6/28/75	3	Western Illinois	Chicago, Ill.	FA-'98	0*
55	Burns, Keith	LB	6-2	235	5/16/72	9	Oklahoma State	Greeleyville, S.C.	FA-'00	16/0
65	Carlisle, Cooper	T	6-5	295	8/11/77	3	Florida	McComb, Miss.	D4b-'00	16/0
89	Carswell, Dwayne	TE	6-3	260	1/18/72	9	Liberty	Jacksonville, Fla.	FA-'94	16/16
37	Carter, Tony	FB	6-0	235	8/23/72	9	Minnesota	Columbus, Ohio	UFA(NE)-'01	16/6
47	Clark, Darius	S	5-10	204	4/13/77	3	Duke	Tampa, Fla.	FA-'00	7/0
88	#Clark, Desmond	TE	6-3	255	4/20/77	4	Wake Forest	Lakeland, Fla.	D6a-'99	16/4
48	Coghill, George	S	6-0	210	3/30/70	6	Wake Forest	Fredericksburg, Va.	FA-'97	16/0
84	Cole, Chris	WR	6-0	195	11/12/77	3	Texas A&M	Orange, Texas	D3-'00	16/1
21	Coleman, KaRon	RB	5-7	198	5/22/78	3	Stephen F. Austin	Missouri City, Texas	FA-'01	4/0
94	Dalton, Lional	DT	6-1	309	2/21/75	5	Eastern Michigan	Detroit, Mich.	UFA(Balt)-'02	16/3*
30	Davis, Terrell	RB	5-11	210	10/28/72	8	Georgia	San Diego, Calif.	D6b-'95	8/8
81	Dominguez, Matt	TE	6-2	219	6/27/78	2	Sam Houston State	Georgetown, Texas	CFA-'01	12/0
34	Droughns, Reuben	RB	5-11	207	8/21/78	3	Oregon	Anaheim, Calif.	FA-'02	9/3*
1	† Elam, Jason	K	5-11	200	3/8/70	10	Hawaii	Ft. Walton Beach, Fla.	D3b-'93	16/0
64	Friedman, Lennie	G	6-3	285	10/13/76	4	Duke	West Milford, N.J.	D2b-'99	15/14
22	Gary, Olandis	RB	5-11	218	5/18/75	4	Georgia	Washington, D.C.	D4-'99	9/1
52	Gold, Ian	LB	6-0	223	8/23/78	3	Michigan	Ann Arbor, Mich.	D2a-'00	16/0
14	Griese, Brian	QB	6-3	215	3/18/75	5	Michigan	Miami, Fla.	D3-'98	15/15
50	Hamilton, Ben	C	6-4	283	8/18/77	2	Minnesota	Minneapolis, Minn.	D4a-'01	0*
86	Hape, Patrick	FB-TE	6-4	262	6/6/74	6	Alabama	Killen, Ala.	UFA(TB)-'01	15/8
98	Hayward, Reggie	DE	6-5	255	3/14/79	2	Iowa State	Dolton, Ill.	D3-'01	6/2
79	Herndon, Steve	G	6-4	305	5/25/77	2	Georgia	LaGrange, Ga.	FA-'00	5/3
20	Hughley, Delvin	CB	5-10	202	4/18/78	2	Jacksonville State	Anniston, Ala.	FA-'01	0*
67	Humphrey, Jay	G	6-6	314	6/20/76	2	Texas	Richardson, Texas	FA-'02	0*
8	Husak, Todd	QB	6-3	216	7/6/78	3	Stanford	Long Beach, Calif.	FA-'01	0*
17	Jackson, Jarious	QB	6-0	228	5/3/77	3	Notre Dame	Tupelo, Miss.	D7a-'00	1/0
60	Johnson, Garrett	DT	6-3	298	12/31/75	2	Illinois	Belleville, Ill.	FA-'02	0*
90	Johnson, Jerry	DT	6-0	290	7/11/77	3	Florida State	Ft. Pierce, Fla.	D4a-'00	9/0
82	Kasper, Kevin	WR	6-0	193	12/23/77	2	Iowa	Burr Ridge, Ill.	D6-'01	10/5
28	Kennedy, Kenoy	S	6-1	215	11/15/77	3	Arkansas	Terrell, Texas	D2b-'00	16/16
58	Killens, Terry	LB	6-1	235	3/24/74	7	Penn State	Cincinnati, Ohio	UFA(SF)-'02	16/2*
78	Lepsis, Matt	T	6-4	290	1/13/74	6	Colorado	Conroe, Texas	FA-'97	16/16
87	McCaffrey, Ed	WR	6-5	215	8/17/68	14	Stanford	Allentown, Pa.	UFA(SF)-'95	1/1
85	McGeoghan, Phil	WR	6-2	224	7/8/79	2	Maine	Feeding Hills, Mass.	FA-'01	2/0
91	McGlockton, Chester	DT	6-4	334	9/16/69	11	Clemson	Whiteville, N.C.	FA-'01	16/16
23	Middlebrooks, Willie	CB	6-1	200	2/12/79	2	Minnesota	Homestead, Fla.	D1-'01	8/0
51	Mobley, John	LB	6-1	236	10/10/73	7	Kutztown	Chester, Pa.	D1-'96	16/16
83	Montgomery, Scottie	WR	6-1	195	5/26/78	3	Duke	Cherryville, N.C.	FA-'00	8/0
69	Moore, Michael	G	6-2	318	11/1/76	3	Troy State	Fayette, Ala.	FA-'01	0*
15	Moore, Rob	WR	6-3	204	9/15/68	13	Syracuse	Hempstead, N.Y.	FA-'02	0*
66	Nalen, Tom	C	6-3	286	5/13/71	9	Boston College	Foxboro, Mass.	D7c-'94	16/16
62	Neil, Dan	G	6-2	285	10/21/73	6	Texas	Cypress Creek, Texas	D3-'97	15/15
24	O'Neal, Deltha	CB	5-10	196	1/30/77	3	California	Milpitas, Calif.	D1-'00	16/16
95	Pittman, Kavika	DE	6-6	273	10/9/74	7	McNeese State	Leesville, La.	UFA(Dall)-'00	14/14
20	Poole, Tyrone	CB	5-8	188	2/3/72	7	Fort Valley State	La Grange, Ga.	FA-'01	0*
93	Pryce, Trevor	DT	6-5	295	8/3/75	6	Clemson	Winter Park, Fla.	D1-'97	16/16
99	Reagor, Montae	DT	6-3	285	6/29/77	3	Texas Tech	Waxahachie, Texas	D2a-'99	8/0
43	Reese, Izell	S	6-2	190	5/7/74	5	Alabama-Birmingham	Dothan, Ala.	UFA(Dall)-'02	16/4*
16	Rouen, Tom	P	6-3	225	6/9/68	10	Colorado	Hinsdale, Ill.	FA-'93	16/0
74	Salaam, Ephraim	T	6-7	300	6/19/76	5	San Diego State	Sacramento, Calif.	UFA(Atl)-'02	14/13*
84	Sharpe, Shannon	TE	6-2	230	6/26/68	13	Savannah State	Glennville, Ga.	FA-'02	16/15*
80	Smith, Rod	WR	6-0	200	5/15/70	8	Missouri Southern	Texarkana, Ark.	FA-'94	15/14
33	Spencer, Jimmy	CB	5-9	188	3/29/69	11	Florida	Belle Glade, Fla.	FA-'00	16/1
68	Toviessi, Paul	DE	6-6	260	2/26/78	2	Marshall	Alexandria, Va.	D2-'01	0*
27	Walker, Denard	CB	6-1	190	8/9/73	6	Louisiana State	Garland, Texas	UFA(Tenn)-'01	16/15
97	Washington, Keith	DE	6-4	275	12/18/72	8	Nevada-Las Vegas	Dallas, Texas	FA-'01	16/16
56	Wilson, Al	LB	6-0	240	6/21/77	4	Tennessee	Jackson, Tenn.	D1-'99	16/16
72	Winey, Brandon	T	6-6	310	1/27/78	2	Louisiana State	Lake Charles, La.	FA-'01	0*

* Beuerlein inactive for 3 games and missed 13 games in '01 because of injury; Brooks last active with Detroit in '00; C. Brown last

active with Denver in '99; Droughns played 9 games with Detroit in '01; Hamilton inactive for 16 games; Hughley inactive for 2 games; Humphrey last active with Minnesota in '99; Husak inactive for 2 games; G. Johnson last active with New England in '00; Killens played 16 games with San Francisco; M. Moore inactive for 2 games; R. Moore missed '01 season because of injury with Arizona; Poole last active with Indianapolis in '00; Reese played 16 games with Dallas; Sallam played 14 games with Atlanta; Sharpe played 16 games with Baltimore; Toviessi missed '01 season because of injury; Winey inactive for 3 games.

†   Restricted free agent; subject to developments.

Players lost through free agency (2): QB Gus Frerotte (Cin; 4), T Trey Teague (Buff; 16).

Also played with Broncos in '01—S Eric Brown (16 games), C David Diaz-Infante (16), WR Keith Poole (6), LB Lee Woodall (14).

2002 FIRST-YEAR ROSTER

Name	Pos.	Ht.	Wt.	Birthdate	College	Hometown	How Acq.
Adams, Charlie	WR	6-2	190	10/23/79	Hofstra	Camp Hill, Pa.	FA
Bartholomew, Will	FB	5-11	246	10/1/78	Tennessee	Nashville, Tenn.	FA
Brandon, Sam	S	6-2	200	7/5/79	Nevada-Las Vegas	Riverside, Calif.	D4
Brown, Greg (1)	S	6-2	210	7/30/79	Texas	Baton Rouge, La.	FA-'01
Davis, Dorsett	DT	6-5	304	1/24/79	Mississippi State	Cleveland, Miss.	D3
Faulk, Trev	LB	6-2	241	8/6/81	Louisiana State	Lafayette, La.	FA
Gaines, Paris	RB	5-11	228	4/3/78	Fresno State	Vista, Calif.	FA
Hall, Ricky (1)	WR	6-2	200	1/17/76	Virginia	Richmond, Va.	FA-'01
Haygood, Herb	WR	5-11	193	12/29/77	Michigan State	Sarasota, Fla.	D5
Herndon, Kelly (1)	DB	5-10	180	11/3/76	Toledo	Chamberlain, Ohio	FA-'01
Jackson, Kenny (1)	LB	6-2	253	9/30/76	Nevada	Santa Monica, Calif.	FA
Lelie, Ashley	WR	6-3	200	2/16/80	Hawaii	Honolulu, Hawaii	D1
Lies, Michael (1)	T	6-3	295	9/8/75	Kansas	Wichita, Kan.	FA
Peck, Jared	T	6-4	282	5/6/79	North Dakota State	Bloomington, Minn.	FA
Pope, Monsanto	DT	6-3	300	1/27/78	Virginia	Hopewell, Va.	D7b
Portis, Clinton	RB	5-11	205	9/1/81	Miami	Gainesville, Fla.	D2
Putzier, Jeb	TE	6-4	256	1/20/79	Boise State	Eagle, Idaho	D6
Scukanec, Jason	C	6-2	295	12/17/78	Brigham Young	Vancouver, Wash.	FA
Spragan, Donnie	LB	6-3	239	7/12/76	Stanford	Union City, Calif.	FA-'01
Sykes, Jashon	LB	6-2	236	9/25/79	Colorado	Los Angeles, Calif.	FA
Walls, Lenny	CB	6-4	192	9/26/79	Boston College	San Francisco, Calif.	FA
Young, Chris	S	6-0	210	1/23/80	Georgia Tech	Senoia, Ga.	D7a
Young, Sam (1)	CB	5-11	180	8/1/78	Illinois State	Chicago, Ill.	FA

The term NFL Rookie is defined as a player who is in his first season of professional football and has not been on the roster of another professional football team for any regular-season or postseason games. A Rookie is designated by an "R" on NFL rosters. Players who have been active in another professional football league or players who have NFL experience, including either preseason training camp or being on an Active List or Inactive List, or on Reserve/Injured or Reserve/Physically Unable to Perform for fewer than six regular-season games, are termed NFL First-Year Players. An NFL First-Year Player is designated by a "1" on NFL rosters. Thereafter, a player is credited with an additional year of experience for each season in which he accumulates six games on the Active List or Inactive List, or on Reserve/Injured or Reserve/Physically Unable to Perform..

COACHING STAFF
Head Coach,
Mike Shanahan
Pro Career: Became the eleventh head coach in Broncos history on January 31, 1995. Mike Shanahan led the Broncos to back-to-back Super Bowl championships in 1997 and 1998, becoming just the fifth head coach to accomplish that feat. During his NFL career, Shanahan has been a part of teams that have played in six Super Bowls. Shanahan was an assistant with Denver (1984-87, 1989-1991) and San Francisco (1992-94). Returned to Denver as quarterbacks coach on October 16, 1989, after posting 8-12 record as the Los Angeles Raiders' head coach. Career record: 87-54.
Background: Shanahan coached at Oklahoma (1975-76), Northern Arizona (1977), Eastern Illinois (1978), Minnesota (1979), and Florida (1980-83).
Personal: Born in Oak Park, Illinois, on August 24, 1952. He was a wishbone quarterback-defensive back at Eastern Illinois. Mike and his wife, Peggy, have two children—Kyle and Krystal.

ASSISTANT COACHES
Jacob Burney, defensive line; born January 24, 1959, Chattanooga, Tenn., lives in Englewood, Colo. Defensive tackle Tennessee-Chattanooga 1977-1980. No pro playing experience. College coach: New Mexico 1983-86, Tulsa 1987, Mississippi State 1988, Wisconsin 1989, UCLA 1990-92, Tennessee 1993. Pro coach: Cleveland Browns/Baltimore Ravens 1994-98, Carolina Panthers 1999-2001, joined Broncos in 2002.
Frank Bush, special teams; born January 10, 1963, Athens, Ga., lives in Englewood, Colo. Linebacker North Carolina State 1981-84. Pro linebacker Houston Oilers 1985-86. Pro coach: Houston Oilers 1992-94, joined Broncos in 1995.
Larry Coyer, linebackers; born April 19, 1943, Huntington, W. Va., lives in Englewood, Colo. Linebacker Marshall 1962-64. No pro playing experience. College coach: Marshall 1965-67, Iowa 1974-77, Oklahoma State 1978, Iowa State 1979-1983, 1995-96, UCLA 1987-89, Houston 1990, Ohio State 1991-92, East Carolina 1993, Pittsburgh 1997-99. Pro coach: Michigan Panthers (USFL) 1984-85, Memphis Showboats (USFL) 1986, New York Jets 1994, joined Broncos in 2000.
Rick Dennison, offensive line; born June 22, 1958, in Kalispell, Mont., lives in Englewood, Colo. Tight end Colorado State 1976-79. Pro linebacker Denver Broncos 1982-1990. Pro coach: Joined Broncos in 1995.
Karl Dorrell, wide receivers; born December 18, 1968, Alameda, Calif., lives in Englewood, Colo. Wide receiver UCLA 1982-86. No pro playing experience.

College coach: UCLA 1988, Central Florida 1989, Northern Arizona 1990-91, Colorado 1992-93, 1995-98, Arizona State 1994. Pro coach: Joined Broncos in 2000.
George Dyer, asst. to the head coach; born May 4, 1940, Alhambra, Calif., lives in Aurora, Colo. Center-linebacker U.C. Santa Barbara 1961-63. No pro playing experience. College coach: Humboldt State 1964-66, Coalinga (Calif.) J.C. 1967 (head coach), Portland State 1968-1971, Idaho 1972, San Jose State 1973, Michigan State 1977-79, Arizona State 1980-81. Pro coach: Winnipeg Blue Bombers (CFL) 1974-76, Buffalo Bills 1982, Seattle Seahawks 1983-1991, Los Angeles Rams 1992-94, joined Broncos in 1995.
Alex Gibbs, asst. head coach-offensive line; born February 11, 1941, Morganton, N.C., lives in Greenwood Village, Colo. Running back-defensive back Davidson College 1959-1963. No pro playing experience. College coach: Duke 1969-1970, Kentucky 1971-72, West Virginia 1973-74, Ohio State 1975-78, Auburn 1979-1981, Georgia 1982-83. Pro coach: Denver Broncos 1984-87, Los Angeles Raiders 1988-89, San Diego Chargers 1990-91, Indianapolis Colts 1992, Kansas City Chiefs 1993-94, rejoined Broncos in 1995.
David Gibbs, secondary; born January 10, 1968, Mount Airy, N.C., lives in Castle Pines, Colo. Defensive back Colorado 1986-1990. No pro playing experience. College coach: Oklahoma 1991-92, Colorado 1993-94, Kansas 1995-96, Minnesota 1997-2000. Pro coach: Joined Broncos in 2001.
Gary Kubiak, offensive coordinator-quarterbacks; born August 15, 1961, Houston, Texas, lives in Englewood, Colo. Quarterback Texas A&M 1979-1982. Pro quarterback Denver Broncos 1983-1991. College coach: Texas A&M 1992-93. Pro coach: San Francisco 49ers 1994, joined Broncos in 1995.
Anthony Lynn, special teams assistant; born December 21, 1968, McKinney, Texas, lives in Aurora, Colo. Fullback Texas Tech 1987-1990. Pro fullback Denver Broncos 1993, 1997-99, San Francisco 49ers 1995-96. Pro coach: Joined Broncos in 2000.
Pat McPherson, offensive assistant; born April 15, 1969, Santa Clara, Calif., live in Englewood, Colo. Linebacker Santa Clara 1991-92. No pro playing experience. Pro coach: Joined Broncos in 1998.
Keith Millard; asst. defensive line-pass rush specialist; born March 18, 1962, Pleasanton, Calif., lives in Englewood, Colo. Defensive lineman Washington State 1980-84. Pro defensive lineman Minnesota Vikings 1985-1991, Seattle Seahawks 1992, Green Bay Packers 1992, Philadelphia Eagles 1993. College coach: Fort Lewis 1996, Menlo College

1997-2000. Pro coach: San Francisco Demons (XFL) 2001, joined Broncos in 2002.
Ron Milus, nickel backs; born November 25, 1963, Tacoma, Wash., lives in Englewood, Colo. Defensive back Washington 1982-85. No pro playing experience. College coach: Washington 1991-98, Texas A&M 1999. Pro coach: Joined Broncos in 2000.
Brian Pariani, tight ends; born July 2, 1965, San Francisco, lives in Castle Pines, Colo. No college or pro playing experience. College coach: UCLA 1989. Pro coach: San Francisco 49ers 1991-94, joined Broncos in 1995.
Ray Rhodes, defensive coordinator; born October 20, 1950, Mexia, Texas, lives in Aurora, Colo. Running back Texas Christian 1969-1970, wide receiver, defensive back, and kick returner Tulsa 1972-73. Pro wide receiver-defensive back New York Giants 1974-79, San Francisco 49ers 1980. Pro coach: San Francisco 49ers 1981-1991, 1994, Green Bay Packers 1992-93, 1999, Philadelphia Eagles 1995-98, Washington Redskins 2000, joined Broncos in 2001.
Greg Saporta, asst. strength and conditioning; born February 2, 1957, New York, N.Y., lives in Englewood, Colo. Wide receiver Buffalo State 1977-79. No pro playing experience. College coach: Florida 1981-88, 1993-94, North Carolina 1989-1992. Pro coach: Joined Broncos in 1995.
Cedric Smith, asst. strength and conditioning; born May 27, 1968, Enterprise, Ala., lives in Englewood, Colo. Running back Florida 1986-89. Pro fullback Minnesota Vikings 1990, New Orleans Saints 1991, Washington Redskins 1994-95, Arizona Cardinals 1996-98. Pro coach: Joined Broncos in 2001.
Bobby Turner, running backs; born May 6, 1949, East Chicago, Ind., lives in Englewood, Colo. Defensive back Indiana State 1968-1971. No pro playing experience. College coach: Indiana State 1975-1982, Fresno State 1983-88, Ohio State 1989-1990, Purdue 1991-94. Pro coach: Joined Broncos in 1995.
Rich Tuten, strength and conditioning; born December 30, 1953, Columbia, S.C., lives in Englewood, Colo. Nose guard Clemson 1976-78. No pro playing experience. College coach: Florida 1979-1988, 1993-94, North Carolina 1989-1992. Pro coach: Joined Broncos in 1995.
Steve Watson, defensive assistant; born May 28, 1957, Baltimore, lives in Aurora, Colo. Wide receiver Temple 1975-78. Pro wide receiver Denver 1979-1987. Pro coach: Joined Broncos in 2001.

**American Football Conference
South Division
Team Colors:** Deep Steel Blue, Battle
Red, and White
One Reliant Park
Houston, Texas 77054
Telephone: (832) 667-2000

2002 SCHEDULE
PRESEASON
Aug. 5 vs. N. Y. Giants(Canton, Ohio)...8:00
Aug. 10 at New Orleans.......................7:00
Aug. 17 at Kansas City.......................7:30
Aug. 24 **Miami**................................7:00
Aug. 30 **Tampa Bay**...........................7:00
REGULAR SEASON
Sept. 8 **Dallas**................................7:30
Sept. 15 at San Diego 1:15
Sept. 22 **Indianapolis**.....................12:00
Sept. 29 at Philadelphia....................1:00
Oct. 6 Open Date
Oct. 13 **Buffalo**............................12:00
Oct. 20 at Cleveland......................4:05
Oct. 27 at Jacksonville....................4:15
Nov. 3 **Cincinnati**.......................12:00
Nov. 10 at Tennessee....................12:00
Nov. 17 **Jacksonville**......................3:15
Nov. 24 **New York Giants**................3:15
Dec. 1 at Indianapolis....................4:05
Dec. 8 at Pittsburgh.......................1:00
Dec. 15 **Baltimore**........................12:00
Dec. 22 at Washington....................1:00
Dec. 29 **Tennessee**........................12:00

Stadium: Reliant Stadium
(opened in 2002)
• **Capacity:** 69,500
Houston, Texas 77054
Playing Surface: Grass
Training Camp: Reliant Park Practice
Facility

RELIANT STADIUM

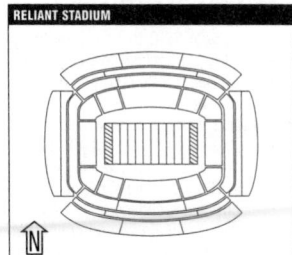

CLUB OFFICIALS
Chairman and CEO: Robert C. McNair
Vice Chairman: Philip Burguieres
Vice Chairman: Chuck Watson
Senior Vice President and General
Manager/Football Operations:
Charley Casserly
Senior Vice President/Chief Development
Officer: Steve Patterson
Senior Vice President/Chief Sales &
Marketing Officer: Jamey Rootes
Senior Vice President/Treasurer and Chief
Financial Officer: Scott Schwinger
Senior Vice President/General Counsel
and Chief Administrative Officer:
Suzanne Thomas
Vice President/Communications:
Tony Wyllie
Vice President/Corporate Sales:
David Peart
Controller: Marilan Logan
Director of Negotiations: Dan Ferens
Director of Pro Scouting: Chuck Banker
Associate Directors of Pro Scouting:
Bobby Grier, Miller McCalmon
Pro Scouting Assistant: Rob Lohman
Coordinator of College Scouting:
Mike Maccagnan
National Scout: George Saimes
College Scouts: Larry Bryan,
Ralph Hawkins, Joel Patten,
Pete Russell, Dave Sears,
Tom Throckmorton
College Scouting Assistant:
Eugene Armstrong
Director of Operations: Barry Asimos
Director of Marketing: Kim Babiak
Director of Client Services: Linda Dodds
Director of Corporate Sales:
Patrick Streko
Director of Security: Ryan Reichert
Director of Ticket Operations:
John Schriever
Director of Community Relations:
Regina Woolfolk
Director of Internet Services &
Publications: Carter Toole
Director of Media Relations:
Brent Williamson
Director of Player Programs: Todd Scott
Director of Information Technology:
Nick Ignatiev
Executive Director, Houston Texans
Foundation: Joanie Haley
Human Resources Administrator:
Glenda Morrison
Head Athletic Trainer: Kevin Bastin
Coordinator of Rehabilitation: Tom Colt
Assistant Athletic Trainer: John Ishop
Director of Equipment Services:
Jay Brunetti
Assistant Equipment Managers:
Matt Grupp, Greg Read
Video Director: Ken Sparacino
Assistant Video Director: Joe Malota
Video Assistant: Robert Wells
Manager of Player Information:
Tom Halligan

2002 DRAFT CHOICES

Round	Name	Pos.	College
1	David Carr	QB	Fresno State
2	Jabar Gaffney	WR	Florida
	Chester Pitts	T	San Diego State
3	Fred Weary	C	Tennessee
	Charles Hill	DT	Maryland
4	Jonathan Wells	RB	Ohio State
5	Jarrod Baxter	RB	New Mexico
	Ramon Walker	DB	Pittsburgh
6	Demarcus Faggins	DB	Kansas City
	Howard Green	DT	Louisiana State
7	Greg White	DE	Minnesota
	Ahmad Miller	DT	Nevada-Las Vegas

PLAYER ACCESS PLAN
The expansion Houston Texans acquired
players four ways, which is similar to the
expansion process of the Cleveland
Browns in 1999.
1. Free agents—The Texans were
allowed to sign previously-terminated free
agents. From December 27 until the end
of the 2001 regular season, Houston was
able to sign a maximum of 10 free agents
(not under contract to other teams) to
2002 contracts.
2. Expansion Draft—Each of the existing 31 NFL clubs was required to submit
a list of five veteran players for selection
by the Texans. Each club could expose
only one player who was placed on
injured reserve after the start of the 2001
regular season, only one player who had
10 or more years of free agency experience, and no more than two players with
"spiked contracts" in 2002. A "spiked
contract" is defined as a contract in
which: A. The 2002 salary cap value is at
least $1.2 million and represents an
increase of at least 75 percent over the
2001 salary cap value; and B. The 2002
cash value is at least $1.2 million and rep-
resents an increase of at least 75 percent
over the 2001 cash value. Neither punters
nor kickers may be part of the list. The
Texans were required to select between
30 and 42 players in the veteran draft or a
fewer number of players with total salaries
of 38 percent of the cap. An existing club
could recall one player from its list after
one of its players is selected. After a second player was selected from a club, that
club could pull back both of its remaining
players.
3. NFL Draft—The Texans were designated 28 choices in the NFL Draft encom-
passing the 2002 and 2003 seasons, 14
in 2002 and 14 in 2003. If the Texans
make the playoffs in 2002, the team will
not have extra picks in 2003.
In the 2002 draft, the Texans were allocated the first pick in each of the seven
rounds. They also received seven additional picks to be allocated in the following
manner: one selection in each of Rounds
2, 3, 4, 5, 6 and 7 after all teams with a
2001 regular-season winning percentage
of less than .500 and the final selection in
Round 7 (after all compensatory selec-

tions).

In the 2003 draft, Houston will receive one regular pick per round based on its 2002 record, the same as all other clubs. The Texans will also receive seven additional picks in the 2003 draft—unless they make the playoffs in 2002, in which case they will receive no extra picks. These picks will vary depending upon Houston's 2002 won-loss percentage, as reflected in the following year's draft order. These additional picks would be allocated in the following manner: If Houston's normal selection is between 1-8, the Texans receive one extra pick in Rounds 3, 4 and 5 and two extra picks in Rounds 6 and 7. If Houston's normal selection is between 9-14, the Texans receive one extra pick in Rounds 4 and 5, two extra picks in Round 6, and three extra picks in Round 7. If Houston's normal selection is between 15-20, the Texans receive one extra pick in Round 5, two extra picks in Round 6, and four extra picks in Round 7.

The first extra Houston pick in any round will fall 16 slots below the club's original choice in that round, but no lower than the end of the round, after any compensatory picks. The second, third or fourth extra pick in a round will be at the end of the round after any compensatory selections.

In 2001 and 2002, Houston was prohibited from trading any draft picks to acquire rights to sign or obtain the contractual release of any non-player personnel (e.g., coach, general manager).

4. Restricted and Unrestricted Free Agents—The Texans were eligible to sign both restricted and unrestricted free agents during the 2002 veteran free agency signing period, which began March 1. They will had the same access to veteran free agents as the other 31 clubs.

During the period from February 18 until July 15, however, the Texans' roster must include at least 30 players acquired from the veteran access draft or a fewer number of players acquired in the veteran draft with total salaries of at least 38 percent of the 2002 salary cap. Any of these players who are released after June 1 are entitled to a supplemental expansion bonus equal to the player's minimum Collective Bargaining Agreement salary even if he subsequently signs with another team.

OTHER PERSONNEL RULES FOR THE TEXANS:

Roster Size, Cutdowns—The Texans have an off-season roster limit of 90 (rest of NFL 80), the first cutdown must be to 70 (others 65), the final cutdown to 56 (others 53), an active/inactive roster limit of 56 through the third week of regular season (others 53).

Waiver Priorities: Through the third weekend of the 2002 regular season, Houston will have waiver priority, and thereafter waiver rights will be based on its 2002 record, the same as all other teams.

NFL Europe League Exemptions: In addition to the 2002 extra roster spots listed above, Houston will receive a number of exemptions equal to the average number of roster exemptions earned by other NFL clubs under the provisions of the NFL Europe League Allocation Policy.

The 2002 Houston Texans access plan is basically the same as that followed by the Cleveland Browns in 1999, with the following exceptions:

• There were no limitations on "spiked contracts" in the Cleveland Browns' 1999 Player Access Plan.

• Players with prior injuries who are exposed in the Veteran Draft must be physically able to play by June 1, 2002 (as opposed to July 1 under the Cleveland plan).

• The existing clubs have reserved the right to adjust the number and/or position of Houston's extra picks in the 2003 NFL Draft if Houston were to lose more than the 14 games Cleveland lost in its first season.

CHRONOLOGY
1997
June 18: The NHL bypasses Chuck Watson and Bob McNair's efforts to bring an expansion hockey club to Houston. The pair moves on to their next project—returning the NFL to Houston.

July 3: Houston Oilers owner Bud Adams gets the green light to move his team to Nashville, Tennessee. U.S. District Judge Lynn Hughes signs the final consent judgment in the lawsuit against the team after all parties involved agree to a settlement.

October 15: NFL Commissioner Paul Tagliabue praises the early plans of Bob McNair and Houston for an expansion franchise at the NFL owners' meetings.

October 17: In reaction to Tagliabue's comments, officials from the Houston Livestock Show and Rodeo (HLS&R) say they will push for the building of a domed stadium that the Rodeo will share with an NFL team, as opposed to renovating the Astrodome. It marks the Rodeo's first public statement in support of McNair's efforts.

1998
March 23: The NFL expansion committee awards an expansion team to Cleveland. McNair, Harris County Judge Robert Eckels and Mayor Lee Brown meet with Tagliabue for the first time as a group at the owners' meeting held in Houston.

May 7: Los Angeles-based entertainment broker Michael Ovitz announces he will spearhead a $750-million proposal to build a stadium in Carson, California, in an effort to bring the NFL back to the Los Angeles area.

June 30: Tagliabue and NFL Stadium Committee head Jerry Richardson visit Houston to see plans for the city's retractable-roof stadium, meeting for several hours with McNair, Houston Sports Authority Jack Rains, Brown, Eckels and HLS&R president Jim Bloodworth.

September 25: The HLS&R votes unanimously to approve paying a $1.5 million annual lease to use the proposed retractable-roof NFL stadium.

October 27: Tagliabue announces that NFL owners will have a decision on the league's newest expansion team by April.

1999
February 16: The NFL Expansion Committee meets, but does not pick a winning bidder from the three finalists. Tagliabue says the decision will come within a month.

March 16: The NFL Expansion Committee votes 29-2 to give Los Angeles until September 15 to work out a feasible stadium and ownership plan. If L.A. cannot get a plan together, the committee will then recommend Houston for the thirty-second franchise.

May 25: Ovitz unveils a new plan for a 60-acre spread of parks, parking garages, and a new stadium where the Los Angeles Memorial Coliseum currently sits. The plan impresses the NFL, but the league remains concerned about a lack of financial planning for the proposed project.

June 3: In a two-hour meeting with Tagliabue, McNair is encouraged to step up his efforts for an expansion team.

July 28: Los Angeles presents an exclusive negotiating agreement to the NFL but the league does not sign it, stating that it does not address the financial situation behind the New Coliseum at Exposition Park.

September 9: NFL executives tell the Houston group to be prepared to come to the owners' meetings in Atlanta on October 6.

September 28: Marvin Davis, one of the bidders for the Los Angeles franchise, bows out of the expansion race.

October 6: The National Football League owners vote 29-0 to award the thirty-second NFL franchise to Houston and Bob McNair for a record amount of $700 million.

November: McNair and Houston NFL executives start the first of 40 separate focus group sessions, which eventually total 500 individual participants. The sessions are conducted in Houston, Galveston, Austin, Beaumont, San Antonio, and Corpus Christi. Fans are asked for their opinions on the image of Houston and its surrounding areas, the image of the NFL and the expectations for the Houston franchise.

November 24: Houston NFL debuts "transition" logo, which serves as the organization's mark until a team name is selected, and the corresponding official logo, team colors, and uniform are developed. The "transition" logo is created by NFL Properties, the New York-based licensing and marketing arm of the NFL.

2000

January 19: Houston NFL hires Charley Casserly as Executive Vice President/General Manager. Casserly comes to Houston after 23 years with the Washington Redskins, the last 10 as general manager. The Redskins captured Super Bowls XVII, XXII, and XXVI during his tenure in Washington.

February: The National Football League begins researching and developing computerized designs for potential logos. Additional focus groups are conducted in Houston and San Antonio.

March 2: Houston NFL announces that its team name search has been narrowed to five choices: Apollos, Bobcats, Stallions, Texans, and Wildcatters. The five names were determined after several months of research conducted jointly by Houston NFL 2002 and National Football League Properties. That research included multiple focus group studies performed in both English and Spanish in Houston, San Antonio, Austin, Galveston, and Beaumont.

March 9: Houston NFL 2002 celebrates the official groundbreaking of the new stadium that will house the team when it begins play in 2002. The 69,500-seat state-of-the-art facility will be the world's first retractable-roof football stadium. Houston NFL 2002 will be a co-tenant of the new stadium with the Houston Livestock Show and Rodeo. Participants in the groundbreaking ceremony include Owner Bob McNair, NFL Commissioner Paul Tagliabue, Houston Livestock Show and Rodeo President Mike Wells, Professional Rodeo Cowboys Association Commissioner Steve Hatchell, Houston Mayor Lee Brown, Harris County Judge Robert Eckels, Harris County Commissioner (Precinct 1) El Franco Lee, Harris County Sports & Convention Corporation Chairman Mike Surface, and Harris County-Houston Sports Authority Chairman Billy Burge.

April: The list of five team names is shaved to three—Apollos, Stallions, and Texans. Color logo designs are presented to focus groups for feedback.

July: McNair reviews logo designs and colors for all three potential names.

August 10: McNair and other club officials view the final proofs of the selected team logo at Giants Stadium in East Rutherford, New Jersey. NFL Properties conducts television and photo testing of the logo as well.

September 6: The NFL's thirty-second franchise is officially christened the Houston Texans before thousands at a downtown rally on Texas Avenue. NFL Commissioner Tagliabue introduces McNair, who then unveils his team's name, colors, and logo to the crowd. The ceremony, televised live on ESPN2, includes simultaneous unveilings in Austin and San Antonio. McNair then heads to Enron Field, where he throws out the first "pitch" (actually a Texans football!) to Houston Astros Owner Drayton McLane before the Astros play the Florida Marlins.

October 26: Reliant Energy acquires the naming rights for Houston's new state-of-the-art football stadium and the sports, entertainment and convention complex currently known as the Astrodomain Complex. Reliant Energy's 32-year agreement to acquire the naming rights for five different buildings and the complex is the most comprehensive naming rights agreement in history. Reliant Park will be a partnership of mutual support between the Harris County Sports and Convention Corporation, the Houston Texans, RodeoHouston, and Reliant Energy. The facilities at Reliant Park will include Reliant Stadium, Reliant Astrodome, Reliant Arena, Reliant Hall, and Reliant Center.

November 1: At its owners' meetings in Atlanta, the NFL announces that Reliant Stadium will host Super Bowl XXXVIII on February 1, 2004. Houston becomes the seventh city to host multiple Super Bowls. Rice Stadium hosted Super Bowl VIII in January, 1974. Jacksonville is awarded Super Bowl XXXIX and Detroit earns Super Bowl XL.

2001

January 21: The Texans introduce Dom Capers as the club's first head coach. Capers comes to Houston from Jacksonville, where he served the previous two seasons as the Jaguars' defensive coordinator. From 1995-98, Capers was the head coach of the expansion Carolina Panthers, leading the team to the NFC West title and a berth in the 1996 NFC Championship Game.

February 2: Chris Palmer is hired as the Texans' first offensive coordinator. Palmer spent the previous two seasons as head coach of the expansion Cleveland Browns.

May 22: The NFL announces its realignment plan for the 2002 season at league meetings in Chicago. The league will realign into eight four-team divisions. The Texans are placed in the AFC South with Indianapolis, Jacksonville, and Tennessee.

September 25: The Texans unveil their team uniforms before a crowd of 12,000 fans in downtown Houston. Local dignitaries and numerous Texan celebrities join Bob McNair on stage for the ceremony. The Houston Texans Cheerleaders also make their debut.

December 29: The Texans sign their first 10 players to contracts—running back Michael Basnight, safety Leomont Evans, tackle Robert Hicks, defensive tackle Jason Nikolao, quarterback Mike Quinn, fullback Matt Snider, cornerback Jason Suttle, linebacker Casey Tisdale, safety Kevin Williams, and tackle Jerry Wisne.

2002

January 14: The Texans hire former Indianapolis Colts defensive coordinator Vic Fangio as their first defensive coordinator.

February 18: The Texans selected (in order) tackle Tony Boselli, tackle Ryan Young, cornerback Aaron Glenn, defensive tackle Gary Walker, linebacker Jamie Sharper, wide receiver-kick returner Jermaine Lewis, cornerback Marcus Coleman, defensive tackle Seth Payne, guard Matt Campbell, safety Matt Stevens, guard Jeremy McKinney, tackle Ryan Schau, running back-kick returner Charlie Rogers, tight end-long snapper Sean McDermott, defensive end Jabari Issa, wide receiver Avion Black, quarterback Danny Wuerffel, linebacker Brian Allen, and tight end Johnny Huggins in the expansion draft.

March 4: The Texans execute the first trade in club history, shipping quarterback Danny Wuerffel to Washington in exchange for defensive tackle Jerry DeLoach.

March 6: The Texans sign their first unrestricted free agent, inking former Colts offensive lineman Steve McKinney.

March 25: The Texans begin their first off-season workout program.

April 20: In their first NFL draft, the Texans selected quarterback David Carr with the first overall selection.

April 25: The Texans held their first minicamp.

2002 VETERAN ROSTER

No.	Name	Pos.	Ht.	Wt.	Birthdate	NFL Exp.	College	Hometown	How Acq.	'01 Games/ Starts
28	Akbar, Hakim	S	6-0	212	8/11/80	2	Washington	Riverside, Calif.	W(NE)-'02	6/0*
50	Aldridge, Allen	LB	6-1	254	5/30/72	9	Houston	Missouri City, Texas	UFA(Det)-'02	16/16*
20	Allen, James	RB	5-10	215	3/28/75	5	Oklahoma	Wynnewood, Okla.	UFA(Chi)-'02	16/7*
4	Baker, John	P	6-2	223	4/22/77	3	North Texas	Brenham, Texas	W(StL)-'02	16/0*
88	Black, Avion	WR	5-11	185	4/24/77	3	Tennessee State	Nashville, Tenn.	ED(Buff)-'02	14/0*
90	Boose, Dorian	DE	6-5	292	1/29/74	5	Washington State	Tacoma, Wash.	FA-'02	8/2*
71	Boselli, Tony	T	6-7	322	4/17/72	8	Southern California	Boulder, Colo.	ED(Jax)-'02	3/3*
85	Bradford, Corey	WR	6-1	197	12/8/75	5	Jackson State	Clinton, La.	UFA(GB)-'02	16/6*
3	Brown, Kris	K	5-11	206	12/23/76	4	Nebraska	Southlake, Texas	RFA(Pitt)-'02	16/0*
36	Carter, Chris	S	6-2	212	9/27/74	6	Texas	Tyler, Texas	UFA(Cin)-'02	16/4*
42	Coleman, Marcus	CB	6-2	210	5/24/74	7	Texas Tech	Dallas, Texas	ED(NYJ)-'02	16/16*
95	t-DeLoach, Jerry	DT	6-2	315	7/17/77	2	California	Valley, Calif.	T(Wash)-'02	15/4*
35	Evans, Leomont	S	6-2	213	7/12/74	5	Clemson	Abbeville, S.C.	FA-'02	0*
56	t-Foreman, Jay	LB	6-1	240	2/18/76	4	Nebraska	Eden Prairie, Minn.	T(Buff)-'02	16/16*
31	Glenn, Aaron	CB	5-9	185	7/16/72	9	Texas A&M	Humble, Texas	ED(NYJ)-'02	13/12*
70	Graham, DeMingo	G	6-3	310	9/10/73	5	Hofstra	Newark, N.J.	UFA(SD)-'02	16/16*
10	Graham, Kent	QB	6-6	248	11/1/68	11	Ohio State	Wheaton, Ill.	UFA(Wash)-'02	3/0*
53	Granville, Billy	LB	6-3	246	3/11/74	5	Duke	Trenton, N.J.	FA-'02	14/0*
33	Groce, Clif	FB	5-11	240	7/30/72	5	Texas A&M	College Station, Texas	FA-'02	0*
75	Herndon, Jimmy	T	6-8	318	8/30/73	7	Houston	Baytown, Texas	UFA(Chi)-'02	16/0*
87	Insley, Trevor	WR	6-0	190	12/25/77	3	Nevada	San Clemente, Calif.	W(Ind)-'02	11/0*
72	Issa, Jabari	DE	6-5	296	4/18/78	3	Washington	San Mateo, Calif.	ED(Ariz)-'02	13/5*
59	Jones, Greg	LB	6-4	248	5/22/74	6	Colorado	Denver, Colo.	UFA(Chi)-'02	16/0*
77	Lane, Max	T	6-6	310	2/22/71	8	Navy	Norborne, Mo.	FA-'02	0*
84	Lewis, Jermaine	WR	5-7	180	10/16/74	7	Maryland	Lanham, Md.	ED(Balt)-'02	15/2*
21	Malbrough, Anthony	CB	5-9	180	12/9/76	2	Texas Tech	Beaumont, Texas	FA-'02	9/1*
48	McDermott, Sean	TE	6-4	250	12/5/76	2	Kansas	Ft. Worth, Texas	ED(TB)-'02	16/0*
66	McKinney, Jeremy	G	6-6	301	1/6/76	3	Iowa	Brighton, Colo.	ED(Cle)-'02	16/9*
76	McKinney, Steve	C-G	6-4	295	10/15/75	5	Texas A&M	Houston, Texas	UFA(Ind)-'02	14/14*
82	Miller, Billy	TE	6-3	230	11/17/74	4	Southern California	Westlake Village, Calif.	FA-'02	6/0*
22	Moreau, Frank	RB	6-2	230	9/9/76	3	Louisville	Elizabethtown, Ky.	FA-'02	5/0*
89	Moreland, Jake	TE	6-3	255	1/18/77	3	Western Michigan	Milwaukee, Wis.	FA-'02	4/0*
79	Overhauser, Chad	G	6-4	214	6/17/75	4	UCLA	Sacramento, Calif.	FA-'02	0*
57	Palmer, Mitch	LS	6-4	259	9/2/73	4	Colorado State	San Diego, Calif.	FA-'02	0*
91	Payne, Seth	DT	6-4	303	2/12/75	5	Cornell	Victor, N.Y.	ED(Jax)-'02	16/16*
98	Posey, Jeff	LB	6-4	249	8/14/75	5	Southern Mississippi	Bassfield, Miss.	UFA(Jax)-'02	11/5*
34	Prentice, Travis	RB	5-11	221	12/8/76	3	Miami (Ohio)	Louisville, Kent.	W(Minn)-'02	14/0*
11	Quinn, Mike	QB	6-4	216	4/15/74	5	Stephen F. Austin	Houston, Texas	FA-'02	0*
83	Rutledge, Rod	TE	6-5	265	8/12/75	5	Alabama	Birmingham, Ala.	UFA(NE)-'02	15/14*
99	Samuel, Khari	LB	6-3	240	10/14/76	4	Massachusetts	Framingham, Mass.	FA-'02	9/0*
65	Schau, Ryan	T	6-6	300	12/30/74	4	Illinois	Bloomington, Ill.	ED(Phil)-'02	2/1*
92	Sears, Corey	DE	6-3	319	4/15/73	4	Mississippi State	Converse, Texas	FA-'02	0*
55	Sharper, Jamie	LB	6-3	240	11/23/74	6	Virginia	Richmond, Va.	ED(Balt)-'02	16/16*
29	t-Shepherd, Jacoby	CB	6-1	195	8/31/79	3	Oklahoma State	Lufkin, Texas	T(StL)-'02	7/0*
30	Simmons, Jason	CB	5-9	198	3/30/76	5	Arizona State	Lawndale, Calif.	UFA(Pitt)-'02	12/0*
81	Simmons, Tony	WR	6-1	212	12/8/74	5	Wisconsin	Chicago, Ill.	UFA(Ind)-'02	7/0*
80	Sinceno, Kaseem	TE	6-4	255	3/26/76	5	Syracuse	Liberty, N.Y.	UFA(Chi)-'02	0*
44	Snider, Matt	FB	6-3	242	1/26/76	4	Richmond	Wynnewood, Pa.	FA-'02	4/0*
7	Stanley, Chad	P	6-3	205	1/29/76	4	Stephen F. Austin	Ore City, Texas	FA-'02	4/0*
26	Stevens, Matt	S	6-0	205	6/15/73	7	Appalachian State	Chapel Hill, N.C.	ED(NE)-'02	15/4*
24	Suttle, Jason	CB	5-10	181	12/2/74	3	Wisconsin	Burnsville, Minn.	FA-'02	0*
96	Walker, Gary	DT	6-2	305	2/28/73	8	Auburn	Carnerville, Ga.	ED(Jax)-'02	16/16*
23	Williams, Kevin	S	6-0	192	8/4/75	4	Oklahoma State	Pine Bluff, Ark.	FA-'02	0*
78	Wisne, Jerry	T	6-7	324	7/28/76	3	Notre Dame	Tulsa, Okla.	FA-'02	0*
52	Wong, Kailee	LB	6-2	250	5/23/76	5	Stanford	Eugene, Ore.	UFA(Minn)-'02	16/16*
74	Young, Ryan	T	6-5	320	6/28/76	4	Kansas State	St. Louis, Mo.	ED(NYJ)-'02	16/16*

* Akbar played 6 games with New England in '01; Aldridge played 16 games with Detroit; J. Allen played 16 games with Chicago; Baker played 16 games with St. Louis; Black played 14 games with Buffalo; Boose played 8 games with Washington; Boselli played 3 games with Jacksonville; Bradford played 16 games with Green Bay; Brown played 16 games with Pittsburgh; Carter played 16 games with Cincinnati; Coleman played 16 games with New York Jets; DeLoach played 15 games with Washington; Evans last active with Washington in '99; Foreman played 16 games with Buffalo; Glenn played 13 games with New York Jets; D. Graham played 16 games with San Diego; K. Graham played 3 games with Washington; Granville played 14 games with Cincinnati; Groce last active with Cincinnati in '00; Hamiter played 1 game with Philadelphia; Herndon played 16 games with Chicago; Insley played 11 games with Indianapolis; Issa played 13 games with Arizona; G. Jones played 16 games with Chicago; Lane last active with New England in '00;

Lewis played 15 games with Baltimore; Malbrough played 9 games with Cleveland; McDermott played 16 games with Tampa Bay; J. McKinney played 16 games with Cleveland; S. McKinney played 14 games with Indianapolis; Miller played 6 games with Denver; Moreau played 5 games with Jacksonville; Moreland played 4 games with Cleveland; Overhauser on practice squad for Atlanta; Palmer last active with Minnesota in '00; Payne played 16 games with Jacksonville; Posey played 4 games with Carolina and 7 games with Jacksonville; Prentice played 14 games with Minnesota; Quinn last active with Miami in '00; Rutledge played 15 games with New England; Samuel played 9 games with Detroit; Schau played 2 games with Philadelphia; Sears last active with St. Louis in '00; Sharper played 16 games with Baltimore; Shepherd played 7 games with St. Louis; J. Simmons played 12 games with Pittsburgh; T. Simmons played 7 games with Indianapolis; Sinceno missed '01 season because of injury with Chicago; Snider played 4 games with Minnesota; Stanley played 4 games with Arizona; Stevens played 15 games with New England; Suttle last active with Denver in '00; Walker played 16 games with Jacksonville; Williams last active with Miami in '00; Wisne inactive 1 game with Minnesota; Wong played 16 games with Minnesota; R. Young played 16 games with N.Y. Jets.

t- Texans traded for DeLoach (Washington), Foreman (Buffalo), and Shepherd (St. Louis).

Traded—KR Charlie Rogers (13 games with Seattle in '01) to Buffalo; QB Danny Wuerffel (1 game with Chicago) to Washington.

2002 FIRST-YEAR ROSTER

Name	Pos.	Ht.	Wt.	Birthdate	College	Hometown	How Acq.
Austin, Larry	CB	5-8	189	5/17/79	Virginia Tech	Norfolk, Va.	FA
Baxter, Jarrod	FB	6-1	245	3/9/79	New Mexico	Albuquerque, N.M.	D5a
Carr, David	QB	6-3	223	7/21/79	Fresno State	Bakersfield, Calif.	D1
Chew, Eric (1)	WR	6-1	183	10/20/75	McNeese State	Alexandria, La.	FA
Davis, Larry (1)	WR	5-9	185	11/5/77	New Mexico	Houston, Texas	FA
Evans, Troy (1)	LB	6-3	243	12/3/77	Cincinnati	Cincinnati, Ohio	FA
Faggins, Demarcus	CB	5-10	178	6/13/79	Kansas State	Irving, Texas	D6a
Finn, Devon (1)	DE	6-5	280	5/6/78	Illinois State	Wheaton, Ill.	FA
Flowers, Delvon	RB	6-0	210	3/19/79	Arizona State	Los Angeles, Calif.	FA
Gaffney, Jabar	WR	6-1	193	12/1/80	Florida	Jacksonville, Fla.	D2a
Gideon, Sherrod (1)	WR	5-11	171	2/21/77	Southern Mississippi	Greenwood, Miss.	FA
Green, Howard	DT	6-2	331	1/12/79	Louisiana State	Donaldsonville, La.	D6b
Harney, Kenny	LB	6-2	239	7/29/80	South Carolina	Allendale, S.C.	FA
Harris, Atnaf	WR	6-1	182	2/27/79	Cal State-Northridge	Fresno, Calif.	FA
Hawkins, Jelani	T	6-4	309	11/26/80	San Jose State	Los Angeles, Calif.	FA
Hill, Charles	DT	6-2	293	11/1/80	Maryland	Palmer Park, Md.	D3b
Jenkins, Michael (1)	RB	5-7	217	9/27/76	Arkansas	Cupertino, Calif.	FA
Jones, Dwaune (1)	WR	6-1	194	7/11/77	Richmond	Washington, D.C.	FA
Jones, Toya (1)	S	6-1	199	10/28/76	Texas A&M	Refugio, Texas	FA
Jones, Tyrone	LB	6-4	240	1/10/80	Texas	Texas City, Texas	FA
Kent, Rashod	TE	6-6	275	6/7/80	Rutgers	Fairmont, W. Va.	FA
Knapp, Joey	TE	6-3	243	2/7/80	Texas-El Paso	Ft. Worth, Texas	FA
Lamar, Jason (1)	LB	6-0	228	11/10/78	Toledo	Detroit, Mich.	FA
Langley, Aron (1)	P	6-0	196	5/31/78	Wyoming	Longmont, Colo.	FA
Lorenti, Chris (1)	C	6-5	290	1/11/78	Central Florida	Port Orange, Fla.	FA
Mackey, Robert	LB	6-3	260	5/31/78	Winston-Salem State	Fort Mill, S.C.	FA
McClain, Jimmy	LB	6-0	231	7/23/80	Troy State	Enterprise, Ala.	FA
Miller, Ahmad	DT	6-3	306	4/10/78	Nevada-Las Vegas	Bradenton, Fla.	D7b
Miller, John	T	6-6	330	9/27/78	Duke	Bassett, Va.	FA
Minardi, John	WR	6-1	196	10/19/79	Colorado	Laguna Niguel, Calif.	FA
Newell, Mike (1)	C	6-4	300	7/22/76	Colorado State	Littleton, Colo.	FA
Phillips, Josh	S	5-11	186	8/6/79	Yale	Orlando, Fla.	FA
Pitts, Chester	G	6-4	320	6/26/79	San Diego State	Los Angeles, Calif.	D2b
Sankey, Ben (1)	QB	6-2	215	12/5/76	Wake Forest	Chicago, Ill.	FA
Stansbury, Ed	FB	6-0	257	5/3/79	UCLA	El Paso, Texas	FA
Thompson, Aaron	LB	6-0	232	5/4/78	Maryland	Baltimore, Md.	FA
Tisdale, Casey (1)	LB	6-6	256	6/18/76	New Mexico	San Diego, Calif.	FA
Tuthill, James (1)	K	6-2	250	3/25/76	Cal Poly-San Luis Obispo	Upland, Calif.	FA
Walker, Ramon	S	6-0	197	11/8/79	Pittsburgh	Akron, Ohio	D5b
Washington, Terrell	LB	6-2	249	9/11/79	Illinois	St. Louis, Mo.	FA
Weary, Fred	G	6-4	308	9/30/77	Tennessee	Montgomery, Ala.	D3a
Wells, Jonathan	RB	6-1	243	7/21/79	Ohio State	River Ridge, La.	D4
White, Greg	LB	6-3	268	7/25/79	Minnesota	Newark, N.J.	D7a

The term NFL Rookie is defined as a player who is in his first season of professional football and has not been on the roster of another professional football team for any regular-season or postseason games. A Rookie is designated by an "R" on NFL rosters. Players who have been active in another professional football league or players who have NFL experience, including either preseason training camp or being on an Active List or Inactive List, or on Reserve/Injured or Reserve/Physically Unable to Perform for fewer than six regular-season games, are termed NFL First-Year Players. An NFL First-Year Player is designated by a "1" on NFL rosters. Thereafter, a player is credited with an additional year of experience for each season in which he accumulates six games on the Active List or Inactive List, or on Reserve/Injured or Reserve/Physically Unable to Perform.

COACHING STAFF
Head Coach,
Dom Capers

Pro Career: The Texans introduced Capers as their first head coach on January 21, 2001. Capers previously spent four seasons (1995-98) as head coach of the Carolina Panthers, guiding that expansion franchise from its infancy to a playoff berth in its second season. Capers compiled a 31-35 record in four seasons as the Panthers' head coach. In 1995, the Panthers' 7-9 record set an NFL mark for most victories by an expansion team. Carolina also posted the first four-game winning streak in expansion history, the first winning home record by an expansion club, and the first win over a defending Super Bowl champion (San Francisco) in expansion annals. In 1996, the Panthers won their final seven regular-season games, resulting in a 12-4 record and the NFC West title. Carolina then defeated defending Super Bowl champion Dallas in the divisional playoffs before losing to Green Bay in the NFC Championship Game. Capers was named Coach of the Year by the *Associated Press,* among numerous other honors. The Panthers posted an 11-21 record the next two seasons, resulting in Capers' dismissal. The Jaguars signed him six weeks later, and the Capers-led defense improved from twenty-fifth in the NFL in total defense in 1998 to fourth in 1999. Capers began his professional career in 1984 with Jim Mora. After winning two USFL titles with the Philadelphia/Baltimore Stars, Capers followed Mora to the Saints, where he served as the defensive backs coach (1986-1991) and helped the franchise to its first three postseason berths. Capers then accepted the defensive coordinator's post with the Pittsburgh Steelers, helping the team win two AFC Central titles. In his three seasons with the Steelers, no team in the NFL yielded fewer touchdowns. Career record: 31-35.

Background: Capers was a star athlete at Meadowbrook (Ohio) High School. Played safety and linebacker at Mount Union College (1968-1971). Capers coached collegiately at Kent State (1972-74), Hawaii (1975-76), San Jose State (1977), California (1978-79), Tennessee (1980-81), and Ohio State (1982-83).

Personal: Born August 7, 1950 in Cambridge, Ohio. He and his wife Karen live in Houston.

ASSISTANT COACHES

Kippy Brown, wide receivers; born March 6, 1955, Sweetwater, Tenn., lives in Houston. Quarterback Memphis State 1974-77. No pro playing experience. College coach: Memphis State 1978-1980, Louisville 1983, Tennessee 1983-89, 1993-94. Pro coach: New York Jets 1990-92, Tampa Bay Buccaneers 1995, Miami Dolphins 1996-99, Green Bay Packers 2000, Memphis Maniax (XFL, head coach) 2001, joined Texans 2002.

Vic Fangio, defensive coordinator; born August 22, 1958, Dunmore, Pa., lives in Houston. East Stroudsburg State University. No pro playing experience. College coach: North Carolina 1983. Pro coach: Philadelphia/Baltimore Stars (USFL) 1984-85, New Orleans Saints 1986-1994, Carolina Panthers 1995-98, Indianapolis Colts 1999-2001, joined Texans in 2002.

Jedd Fisch, defensive quality control; born May 5, 1976, Livingston, N.J., lives in Houston. Attended Florida. No college or pro playing experience. College coach: Florida 1999-2000. Pro coach: Joined Texans in 2001.

Todd Grantham, defensive line; born September 13, 1966, Pulaski, Va., lives in Houston. Guard-tackle Virginia Tech 1984-88. No pro playing experience. College coach: Virginia Tech 1990-95, Michigan State 1996-98. Pro coach: Indianapolis Colts 1999-2001, joined Texans in 2002.

Chick Harris, running backs; born September 21, 1945, Durham, N.C., lives in Houston. Running back Northern Arizona 1966-69. No pro playing experience. College coach: Colorado State 1970-71, Long Beach State 1972-73, Washington 1975-1980. Pro coach: Detroit Wheels (WFL) 1974, Buffalo Bills 1981-82, Seattle Seahawks 1983-1991, Los Angeles Rams 1992-94, Carolina Panthers 1995-2001, joined Texans in 2002.

Reggie Herring, linebackers; born July 3, 1959, Myrtle Beach, S.C., lives in Houston. Linebacker Florida State 1977-1980. No pro playing experience. College coach: Oklahoma State 1981-85, Auburn 1986-1991, Texas Christian 1992-93, Clemson 1993-2001. Pro coach: Joined Texans in 2002.

Jon Hoke, defensive backs; born January 24, 1957, Kettering, Ohio, lives in Houston. Defensive back Ball State 1976-1979. Pro defensive back Chicago Bears 1980. College coach: Bowling Green 1983-86, San Diego State 1987-88, Kent State 1989-1993, Missouri 1994-98, Florida 1999-2001. Pro coach: Joined Texans in 2002.

Joe Marciano, special teams coordinator; born February 10, 1954, Dunmore, Pa., lives in Houston. Quarterback Temple 1972-75. No pro playing experience. College coach: East Stroudsburg 1977, Rhode Island 1978-79, Villanova 1980, Penn State 1981, Temple 1982. Pro coach: Philadelphia/Baltimore Stars (USFL) 1983-85, New Orleans Saints 1986-1995, Tampa Bay Buccaneers 1996-2001, joined Texans in 2002.

Tony Marciano, offensive line; born June 14, 1956, Scranton, Pa., lives in Houston. Offensive line Indiana (Pa.) 1975-77. No pro playing experience. College coach:

Texas Christian 1978-1980, Southern Methodist 1981-87, Brown 1987-88, Richmond 1989-1990, Kent State 1991-92. Pro coach: Toronto Argonauts (CFL) 1994, Calgary Stampeders (CFL) 1995-97, Indianapolis Colts 1998-2001, joined Texans in 2002.

Steve Marshall, asst. offensive line; born June 20, 1956, Hartford, Conn., lives in Houston. Guard-tight end Louisville 1976-78. No pro playing experience. College coach: Plymouth State 1979, Louisville 1980-81, Marshall 1982-83, Louisville 1984, Murray State 1985-86, Virginia Tech 1987-1992, Tennessee 1993-95, UCLA 1996, Texas A&M 1997, North Carolina 1998-99, Colorado 2000-2001. Pro coach: Joined Texans in 2002.

Chris Palmer, offensive coordinator; born September 23, 1949, Brewster, N.Y., lives in Houston. Quarterback Southern Connecticut State 1968-1971. No pro playing experience. College coach: Connecticut 1972-74, Lehigh 1975, Colgate 1976-1982, New Haven 1986-87 (head coach), Boston 1988-89 (head coach). Pro coach: Montreal Concordes (CFL) 1983, New Jersey Generals (USFL) 1984-85, Houston Oilers 1990-92, New England Patriots 1993-96, Jacksonville Jaguars 1997-98, Cleveland Browns 1999-2000 (head coach), joined Texans in 2001.

Dan Riley, strength and conditioning; born October 19, 1949, Syracuse, N.Y., lives in Houston. Attended Keene State. No college or pro playing experience. College coach: Army 1974-77, Penn State 1977-1981. Pro coach: Washington Redskins 1982-2000, joined Texans 2001.

Greg Roman, tight ends; born August 19, 1972, Atlantic City, N.J., lives in Houston. Defensive line-linebacker John Carroll 1990-94. No pro playing experience. Pro coach: Carolina 1995-2001, joined Texans in 2002.

Brian Stewart, asst. defensive backs; born December 4, 1964, San Diego, lives in Houston. Cornerback Northern Arizona 1983, 1986-87. No pro playing experience. College coach: Cal Poly-San Luis Obispo 1993-94, Northern Arizona 1995-96, Missouri 1996, 1998-2000, San Jose State 1997-98, Syracuse 2001. Pro coach: Joined Texans in 2002.

Eric Sutulovich, asst. special teams; born February 28, 1974, Kansas City, Kan., lives in Houston. Tight end Louisiana Tech 1993-95. No pro playing experience. College coach: Louisiana Tech 1997-99, Pittsburgh 2000, Fort Scott 2001. Pro coach: Joined Texans in 2002.

Ray Wright, asst. strength and conditioning; born December 30, 1971, Cleveland, lives in Houston. Running back-wide receiver Duke 1990-95. No pro playing experience. College coach: Cornell 1999, Maryland 2001. Pro coach: Joined Texans in 2002.

American Football Conference
South Division
Team Colors: Royal Blue and White
P.O. Box 535000
Indianapolis, Indiana 46253
Telephone: (317) 297-2658

2002 SCHEDULE
PRESEASON
Aug. 10	at Seattle	7:00
Aug. 17	**Cincinnati**	7:00
Aug. 24	**Buffalo**	7:00
Aug. 30	at New Orleans	6:00

REGULAR SEASON
Sept. 8	at Jacksonville	1:00
Sept. 15	**Miami**	12:00
Sept. 22	at Houston	12:00
Sept. 29	Open Date	
Oct. 6	**Cincinnati**	12:00
Oct. 13	**Baltimore**	12:00
Oct. 21	at Pittsburgh (Mon.)	9:00
Oct. 27	at Washington	8:30
Nov. 3	**Tennessee**	1:00
Nov. 10	at Philadelphia	1:00
Nov. 17	**Dallas**	1:00
Nov. 24	at Denver	6:30
Dec. 1	**Houston**	4:05
Dec. 8	at Tennessee	12:00
Dec. 15	at Cleveland	1:00
Dec. 22	**New York Giants**	1:00
Dec. 29	**Jacksonville**	4:05

Stadium: RCA Dome (opened in 1983)
 • **Capacity:** 56,127
  100 South Capitol Avenue
  Indianapolis, Indiana 46225
Playing Surface: AstroTurf
Training Camp: Rose-Hulman Institute
  5500 Wabash Avenue
  Terre Haute, Indiana
  47803

RCA DOME

CLUB OFFICIALS
Owner and CEO: James Irsay
President: Bill Polian
Head Coach: Tony Dungy
Senior Executive Vice President:
  Pete Ward
General Counsel: Dan Luther
Executive Vice President: Bob Terpening
Senior Vice President-Sales and
  Marketing: Ray Compton
Director of Football Operations:
  Dom Anile
Vice President-Finance: Kurt Humphrey
Vice President-Ticket Operations:
  Larry Hall
Vice President-Public Relations:
  Craig Kelley
Vice President-Business Development:
  Tom Zupancic
Director of Pro Player Personnel:
  Clyde Powers
Director of College Scouting: Mike Butler
Assistant Director of Football Operations:
  Chris Polian
Director of Player Development:
  Steve Champlin
Executive Director of Sponsorship Sales:
  Jay Souers
Director of Ticket Sales/Marketing:
  Greg Hylton
Director of Community
  Development/Player Relations:
  Bill Brooks
Director of Community
  Relations/Marketing: Nicole Duncan
Equipment Manager: Jon Scott
Video Director: Marty Heckscher
Head Trainer: Hunter Smith
Assistant Equipment Manager:
  Mike Mays
Assistant Trainers: Dave Hammer,
  Dave Walston
Assistant Video Director: John Starliper
Purchasing Administrator: Dave Filar

COACHING HISTORY
Baltimore 1953-1983
(352-372-7)
1953	Keith Molesworth	3-9-0
1954-1962	Weeb Ewbank	61-52-1
1963-69	Don Shula	73-26-4
1970-72	Don McCafferty*	26-11-1
1972	John Sandusky	4-5-0
1973-74	Howard Schnellenberger**	4-13-0
1974	Joe Thomas	2-9-0
1975-79	Ted Marchibroda	41-36-0
1980-81	Mike McCormack	9-23-0
1982-84	Frank Kush***	11-28-1
1984	Hal Hunter	0-1-0
1985-86	Rod Dowhower****	5-24-0
1986-1991	Ron Meyer#	36-36-0
1991	Rick Venturi	1-10-0
1992-95	Ted Marchibroda	32-35-0
1996-97	Lindy Infante	12-21-0
1998-2001	Jim Mora	32-34-0

*Released after five games in 1972
**Released after three games in 1974
***Resigned after 15 games in 1984
****Released after 13 games in 1986
#Released after five games in 1991

ATTENDANCE
Home 423,396	Away 548,626

Total 972,022
Single-game home record,
61,139 (10/20/97)
Single-season home record, 481,305
(1984)

2002 DRAFT CHOICES
Round	Name	Pos.	College
1	Dwight Freeney	DE	Syracuse
2	Larry Tripplett	DT	Washington
3	Joseph Jefferson	DB	W. Kentucky
4	David Thornton	LB	North Carolina
6	David Pugh	DT	Virginia Tech
	James Lewis	DB	Miami
	Brian Allen	RB	Stanford
7	Josh Mallard	DE	Georgia

INDIANAPOLIS COLTS

2001 TEAM RECORD
PRESEASON (2-2)

Date	Result	Opponent
8/11	W 28-21	Seattle
8/18	L 26-27	Detroit
8/24	L 21-28	at Minnesota
8/30	W 23-17	at Cincinnati

REGULAR SEASON (6-10)

Date	Result	Opponent	Att.
9/09	W 45-24	at New York Jets	78,606
9/23	W 42-26	Buffalo	56,135
9/30	L 13-44	at New England	60,292
10/14	L 18-23	Oakland	56,972
10/21	L 17-38	New England	56,022
10/25	W 35-28	at Kansas City	74,212
11/04	W 30-14	at Buffalo	63,786
11/11	L 24-27	Miami	57,127
11/18	L 20-34	at New Orleans	70,020
11/25	L 21-40	San Francisco	56,393
12/02	L 27-39	at Baltimore	69,382
12/10	L 6-41	at Miami	73,858
12/16	W 41-27	Atlanta	55,603
12/23	L 28-29	New York Jets	56,302
12/30	L 17-42	at St. Louis	66,084
1/06	W 29-10	Denver	56,192

SCORE BY PERIODS

Colts	70	160	109	74	0 —	413
Opponents	61	200	66	159	0 —	486

2001 TEAM STATISTICS

	Colts	Opp.
Total First Downs	343	323
Rushing	110	108
Passing	206	195
Penalty	27	20
3rd Down: Made/Att	85/205	90/207
3rd Down Pct.	41.5	43.5
4th Down: Made/Att	5/8	7/15
4th Down Pct.	62.5	46.7
Possession Avg.	30:32	29:28
Total Net Yards	5955	5715
Avg. Per Game	372.2	357.2
Total Plays	1025	1004
Avg. Per Play	5.8	5.7
Net Yards Rushing	1966	2115
Avg. Per Game	122.9	132.2
Total Rushes	438	455
Net Yards Passing	3989	3600
Avg. Per Game	249.3	225.0
Sacked/Yards Lost	30/238	40/257
Gross Yards	4227	3857
Att./Completions	557/349	509/311
Completion Pct.	62.7	61.1
Had Intercepted	23	15
Punts/Average	68/44.5	67/42.7
Net Punting Avg.	68/33.8	67/36.6
Penalties/Yards	76/730	96/759
Fumbles/Ball Lost	20/15	16/10
Touchdowns	47	57
Rushing	16	20
Passing	27	30
Returns	4	7

2001 INDIVIDUAL STATISTICS

PASSING

	Att.	Comp.	Yds.	Pct.	TD	Int.	Tkld.	Rate
Manning	547	343	4131	62.7	26	23	29/232	84.1
Rypien	9	5	57	55.6	0	0	1/6	74.8
Dilger	1	1	39	100.0	1	0	0/0	158.3
Colts	557	349	4227	62.7	27	23	30/238	84.9
Opponents	509	311	3857	61.1	30	15	40/257	91.9

SCORING

	TD R	TD P	TD Rt	PAT	FG	Saf	PTS
Vanderjagt	0	0	0	41/42	28/34	0	125
Harrison	0	15	0	0/0	0/0	0	90
Rhodes	9	0	1	0/0	0/0	0	60
Pollard	0	8	0	0/0	0/0	0	48
Manning	4	0	0	0/0	0/0	0	24
James	3	0	0	0/0	0/0	0	20
Pathon	0	2	0	0/0	0/0	0	12
Dilger	0	1	0	0/0	0/0	0	8
Burris	0	0	1	0/0	0/0	0	6
Insley	0	1	0	0/0	0/0	0	6
Nwokorie	0	0	1	0/0	0/0	0	6
Wilkins	0	0	1	0/0	0/0	0	6
McDougal	0	0	0	0/0	0/0	0	2
Colts	16	27	4	41/42	28/34	0	413
Opponents	20	30	7	52/53	30/36	0	486

2-Pt. Conversions: Dilger, James, McDougal. Colts 3-5, Opponents 1-4.

RUSHING

	Att.	Yds.	Avg.	LG	TD
Rhodes	233	1104	4.7	77t	9
James	151	662	4.4	29t	3
Manning	35	157	4.5	33t	4
McDougal	17	48	2.8	12	0
Harrison	1	3	3.0	3	0
Pathon	1	-8	-8.0	-8	0
Colts	438	1966	4.5	77t	16
Opponents	455	2115	4.6	56t	20

RECEIVING

	No.	Yds.	Avg.	LG	TD
Harrison	109	1524	14.0	68	15
Pollard	47	739	15.7	86t	8
Wilkins	34	332	9.8	28	0
Rhodes	34	224	6.6	19	0
Dilger	32	343	10.7	44	1
Wayne	27	345	12.8	43	0
Pathon	24	330	13.8	60t	2
James	24	193	8.0	27	0
Insley	14	165	11.8	26	1
Simmons	2	17	8.5	12	0
McDougal	1	10	10.0	10	0
McKinney	1	5	5.0	5	0
Colts	349	4227	12.1	86t	27
Opponents	311	3857	12.4	91t	30

INTERCEPTIONS

	No.	Yds.	Avg.	LG	TD
Burris	3	69	23.0	30t	1
Macklin	3	15	5.0	11	0
Cota	2	21	10.5	12	0
Peterson	2	18	9.0	13	0
Harper	2	17	8.5	14	0
Phillips	1	18	18.0	18	0
Bashir	1	0	0.0	0	0
Walls	1	0	0.0	0	0
Colts	15	158	10.5	30t	1
Opponents	23	545	23.7	78t	6

PUNTING

	No.	Yds.	Avg.	In 20	LG
H. Smith	68	3023	44.5	12	65
Colts	68	3023	44.5	12	65
Opponents	67	2861	42.7	26	59

PUNT RETURNS

	No.	FC	Yds.	Avg.	LG	TD
Wilkins	21	4	219	10.4	78t	1
Insley	7	8	71	10.1	33	0
Harper	1	0	0	0.0	0	0
Colts	29	12	290	10.0	78t	1
Opponents	35	13	486	13.9	67	1

KICKOFF RETURNS

	No.	Yds.	Avg.	LG	TD
Wilkins	44	1007	22.9	50	0
McDougal	16	362	22.6	40	0
Rhodes	14	356	25.4	88t	1
Finn	3	29	9.7	13	0
Nwokorie	2	15	7.5	9	0
Simmons	2	27	13.5	15	0
Cota	1	0	0.0	0	0
Insley	1	23	23.0	23	0
Pathon	1	13	13.0	13	0
Colts	84	1832	21.8	88t	1
Opponents	87	2006	23.1	64	0

FIELD GOALS

	1-19	20-29	30-39	40-49	50+
Vanderjagt	0/0	7/8	6/6	12/16	3/4
Colts	0/0	7/8	6/6	12/16	3/4
Opponents	0/0	8/8	9/10	13/15	0/3

SACKS

	No.
Bratzke	8.5
Washington	8.0
Nwokorie	5.0
Scioli	4.0
Johnson	3.5
J. Williams	3.0
Peterson	1.5
Thomas	1.5
Morris	1.0
Peter	1.0
Phillips	1.0
Sword	1.0
Bird	0.5
Macklin	0.5
Colts	40.0
Opponents	30.0

RECORD HOLDERS
INDIVIDUAL RECORDS—CAREER

Category	Name	Performance
Rushing (Yds.)	Lydell Mitchell, 1972-77	5,487
Passing (Yds.)	Johnny Unitas, 1956-1972	39,768
Passing (TDs)	Johnny Unitas, 1956-1972	287
Receiving (No.)	Raymond Berry, 1955-1967	631
Receiving (Yds.)	Raymond Berry, 1955-1967	9,275
Interceptions	Bob Boyd, 1960-68	57
Punting (Avg.)	Chris Gardocki, 1994-98	44.8
Punt Return (Avg.)	Ron Gardin, 1970-71	13.5
Kickoff Return (Avg.)	Jim Duncan, 1969-1971	32.5
Field Goals	Dean Biasucci 1984, 1986-1994	176
Touchdowns (Tot.)	Lenny Moore, 1956-1967	113
Points	Dean Biasucci, 1984, 1986-1994	783

INDIVIDUAL RECORDS—SINGLE SEASON

Category	Name	Performance
Rushing (Yds.)	Edgerrin James, 2000	1,709
Passing (Yds.)	Peyton Manning, 2000	4,413
Passing (TDs)	Peyton Manning, 2000	33
Receiving (No.)	Marvin Harrison, 1999	115
Receiving (Yds.)	Marvin Harrison, 1999	1,663
Interceptions	Tom Keane, 1953	11
Punting (Avg.)	Rohn Stark, 1985	45.9
Punt Return (Avg.)	Clarence Verdin, 1989	12.9
Kickoff Return (Avg.)	Jim Duncan, 1970	35.4
Field Goals	Cary Blanchard, 1996	36
Touchdowns (Tot.)	Lenny Moore, 1964	20
Points	Mike Vanderjagt, 1999	145

INDIVIDUAL RECORDS—SINGLE GAME

Category	Name	Performance
Rushing (Yds.)	Edgerrin James, 10-15-00	219
Passing (Yds.)	Peyton Manning, 9-25-00	440
Passing (TDs)	Gary Cuozzo, 11-14-65	5
	Gary Hogeboom, 10-4-87	5
Receiving (No.)	Marvin Harrison, 12-26-99	14
Receiving (Yds.)	Raymond Berry, 11-10-57	224
Interceptions	Many times	3
	Last time by Mike Prior, 12-20-92	
Field Goals	Many times	5
	Last time by Mike Vanderjagt, 1-6-02	
Touchdowns (Tot.)	Many times	4
	Last time by Eric Dickerson, 10-31-88	
Points	Many times	24
	Last time by Eric Dickerson, 10-31-88	

INDIANAPOLIS COLTS

2002 VETERAN ROSTER

No.	Name	Pos.	Ht.	Wt.	Birthdate	NFL Exp.	College	Hometown	How Acq.	'01 Games/ Starts
28	Bashir, Idrees	S	6-2	206	12/7/78	2	Memphis	Decatur, Ga.	D2a-'01	15/15
41	Bird, Cory	CB-S	5-10	216	8/10/78	2	Virginia Tech	Atlantic City, N.J.	D3b-'01	14/0
92	Bratzke, Chad	DE	6-5	272	9/15/71	9	Eastern Kentucky	Brandon, Fla.	UFA(NYG)-'99	15/15
26	Brooks, Rodregis	CB-S	5-9	184	8/30/78	3	Alabama-Birmingham	Alexander City, Ala.	D7b-'00	5/0
97	Cannida, James	DT	6-2	305	1/3/75	5	Nevada	Savannah, Ga.	UFA(TB)-'02	12/2*
31	Crosby, Clifton	CB-S	5-10	172	9/17/74	3	Maryland	Erie, Pa.	FA-'00	14/0
49	Davenport, Joe Dean	TE	6-6	273	10/29/76	2	Arkansas	Springdale, Ark.	FA-'01	3/0
64	DeMulling, Rick	G	6-4	304	7/21/77	2	Idaho	Cheney, Wash.	D7-'01	7/0
71	Diem, Ryan	G	6-6	332	7/1/79	2	Northern Illinois	Carol Stream, Ill.	D4-'01	15/8
34	Doering, Jason	CB-S	6-0	205	4/22/78	2	Wisconsin	Rhinelander, Wis.	D6b-'01	16/1
51	Favors, Greg	LB	6-1	242	9/30/74	5	Mississippi State	Atlanta, Ga.	UFA(Tenn.)-'02	16/12*
36	Finn, Jim	RB	6-0	235	12/9/76	3	Pennsylvania	Teaneck, N.J.	FA-'00	15/0
35	Gay, Ben	RB	6-1	227	2/28/80	2	Garden City (Kan.) C.C.	Houston, Texas	W(Cle)-'02	16/0*
78	Glenn, Tarik	T	6-5	332	5/25/76	6	California	Oakland, Calif.	D1-'97	16/16
84	Haddad, Drew	WR	5-11	185	8/15/78	2	Buffalo	Westlake, Ohio	FA-'01	0*
47	Hampton, Jermaine	CB-S	6-0	205	6/12/79	2	Northern Illinois	Riverdale, Ill.	FA-'01	10/0
25	Harper, Nick	CB-S	5-10	184	9/10/74	2	Fort Valley State	Baldwin, Ga.	FA-'01	13/2
21	Harris, Walt	CB	5-11	195	8/10/74	7	Mississippi State	La Grange, Ga.	UFA(Chi)-'02	15/13*
88	Harrison, Marvin	WR	6-0	178	8/25/72	7	Syracuse	Philadelphia, Pa.	D1-'96	16/16
7 t-	Huard, Brock	QB	6-4	232	4/15/76	4	Washington	Seattle, Wash.	T(Sea)-'02	1/0*
83	Ismail, Qadry	WR	6-0	200	11/8/70	10	Syracuse	Wilkes-Barre, Pa.	FA-'02	16/15*
74	Jackson, Waverly	G	6-2	315	12/19/72	5	Virginia Tech	South Hill, Va.	FA-'98	16/0
32	James, Edgerrin	RB	6-0	214	8/1/78	4	Miami	Immokalee, Fla.	D1-'99	6/6
62	Johnson, Ellis	DT	6-2	288	10/30/73	8	Florida	Wildwood, Fla.	D1-'95	16/16
27	Macklin, David	CB-S	5-9	193	7/14/78	3	Penn State	Newport News, Va.	D3-'00	16/16
18	Manning, Peyton	QB	6-5	230	3/24/76	5	Tennessee	New Orleans, La.	D1-'98	16/16
73	Meadows, Adam	T	6-5	295	1/25/74	6	Georgia	Powder Springs, Ga.	D2-'97	15/15
94	Morris, Rob	LB	6-2	238	1/18/75	3	Brigham Young	Nampa, Idaho	D1-'00	14/14
91	Nwokorie, Chukie	DE	6-3	280	7/10/75	4	Purdue	Lafayette, Ind.	FA-'00	16/5
67	Olsen, Hans	DT	6-4	304	7/31/77	2	Brigham Young	Weiser, Idaho	FA-'01	2/0*
44	Ours, Wes	RB	6-0	284	12/30/77	2	West Virginia	Rawlings, Md.	W(Tenn)-'01	0*
52	Peterson, Mike	LB	6-1	232	6/17/76	4	Florida	Gainesville, Fla.	D2-'99	9/9
81	Pollard, Marcus	TE	6-3	248	2/8/72	8	Bradley	Valley, Ala.	FA-'95	16/16
76	Pyne, Jim	G-C	6-2	297	11/23/71	9	Virginia Tech	Milford, Mass.	UFA(Phil)-'02	5/1*
33	Rhodes, Dominic	RB	5-9	208	1/17/79	2	Midwestern State	Abilene, Texas	FA-'01	15/10
63	Saturday, Jeff	C	6-2	293	6/8/75	4	North Carolina	Tucker, Ga.	FA-'99	16/16
11	Sauter, Cory	QB	6-4	215	11/21/74	3	Minnesota	Hutchinson, Minn.	FA-'02	0*
99	Scioli, Brad	DE	6-3	274	9/6/76	4	Penn State	Bridgeport, Pa.	D5-'99	13/12
17	Smith, Hunter	P	6-2	212	8/9/77	4	Notre Dame	Sherman, Texas	D7a-'99	16/0
48	Snow, Justin	TE	6-3	234	12/21/76	3	Baylor	Abilene, Texas	FA-'00	16/0
30	Stith, Shyrone	RB	5-8	208	4/2/78	3	Virginia Tech	Portsmouth, Va.	FA-'02	0*
98	Sword, Sam	LB	6-1	245	12/4/74	4	Michigan	Saginaw, Mich.	FA-'00	16/2
54	Thompson, Donnel	LB	6-0	234	2/17/78	3	Wisconsin	Madison, Wis.	FA-'01	4/0
13	Vanderjagt, Mike	K	6-5	210	3/24/70	5	West Virginia	Oakville, Ontario, Canada	FA-'98	16/0
42	Walls, Raymond	CB-S	5-10	175	7/24/79	2	Southern Mississippi	Kentwood, La.	D5-'01	4/0
85	Walters, Troy	WR	5-7	174	12/15/76	3	Stanford	Batesburg, S.C.	W(Minn)-'02	6/0*
53	Washington, Marcus	LB	6-3	255	10/17/77	3	Auburn	Auburn, Ala.	D2-'00	16/16
87	Wayne, Reggie	WR	6-0	197	11/17/78	2	Miami	Marrero, La.	D1b-'01	13/9
47	Wiggins, Jermaine	TE	6-2	255	1/18/75	3	Georgia	East Boston, Mass.	W(NE)-'02	16/6*
96	Williams, Josh	DT	6-3	284	8/9/76	3	Michigan	Houston, Texas	D4-'00	16/16

* Cannida played 12 games with Tampa Bay in '01; Favors played 16 games with Tennessee; Gay played 16 games with Cleveland; Haddad missed '01 season because of injury; Harris played 15 games with Chicago; Huard played 1 game with Seattle; Ismail played 16 games with Baltimore; Ours played 2 games with Tennessee; Pyne played 5 games with Philadelphia; Sauter last active with Detroit in '00; Stith was inactive for 9 games; Walters played 6 games with Minnesota; Wiggins played 16 games with New England.

t- Colts traded for Huard (Seattle).

Traded—WR Terrence Wilkins (11 games in '01) to St. Louis.

Players lost through free agency (5): G Steve McKinney (Hou; 14 games in '01); G Larry Moore (Wash; 16), WR Jerome Pathon (NO; 4), LB Ryan Phillips (NE; 13), WR Tony Simmons (Hou; 6).

Also played with Colts in '01—DE Lionel Barnes (6 games), K Doug Brien (1), LB Sean Harris (6), WR Trevor Insley (11), RB Kevin McDougal (9), LB Mike Morton (16), QB Mark Rypien (4), CB Thomas Smith (11), DE Mark Thomas (12), DT Mike Wells (16).

2002 FIRST-YEAR ROSTER

Name	Pos.	Ht.	Wt.	Birthdate	College	Hometown	How Acq.
Albea, Troy (1)	WR	5-11	215	4/30/78	Appalachian State	Lincolnton, Ga.	FA-'01
Allen, Brian	RB	5-9	205	4/20/80	Stanford	Ontario, Calif.	D6c
Allen, Dougie	WR	5-9	170	9/17/79	Kentucky	Lexington, Ky.	FA
Bernard, Walter (1)	CB-S	6-2	200	5/3/78	New Mexico	San Diego, Calif.	FA
Collett, David	K	6-0	190	2/7/80	Tennessee Tech	Soddy-Daisy, Tenn.	FA
Dees, Dempsy (1)	CB-S	5-10	177	10/22/77	Boise State	Yuma, Ariz.	FA
Delamielleure, Todd	LB	5-11	240	1/31/79	Hofstra	Buffalo, N.Y.	FA
Fobbs, Jamaal (1)	WR	5-9	177	9/8/78	Oklahoma State	Monroe, La.	FA
Freeney, Dwight	DE	6-1	268	1/4/78	Syracuse	Hartford, Conn.	D1
Grant, Troy (1)	CB-S	5-9	185	12/5/79	Tennessee Tech	San Antonio, Texas	FA
Herzing, Adam	WR	6-2	197	9/23/80	Cal Poly-San Luis Obispo	San Jose, Calif.	FA
Hicks, Brandon	DT	6-0	282	11/17/77	Bowling Green	Fairborn, Ohio	FA
James, Walter	RB	6-0	213	1/28/80	Illinois State	Naples, Fla.	FA
Jefferson, Joseph	CB-S	6-1	207	2/15/80	Western Kentucky	Russellville, Ky.	D3
Kellett, Gregg	RB	6-3	255	4/12/80	Marshall	Hopatcong, N.J.	FA
Kitchings, Desmond (1)	WR	5-9	178	7/19/78	Furman	Columbia, S.C.	FA-'01
Lacy, Chris	WR	6-0	188	10/12/79	Idaho	Los Angeles, Calif.	FA
Leigeb, Brian (1)	CB-S	6-2	207	10/2/78	Central Michigan	Midland, Mich.	FA
Lewis, James	CB-S	5-10	199	12/19/78	Miami	Piscataway, N.J.	D6b
Mallard, Josh	DE	6-2	254	3/21/79	Georgia	Savannah, Ga.	D7
McGill, Curt	C	6-3	293	8/24/78	Georgia	Dekalb, Ga.	FA
Murphy, Rob (1)	G	6-5	310	1/18/77	Ohio State	Buffalo, N.Y.	FA
Ordway, Jonathan (1)	CB-S	5-10	177	10/19/78	Boston College	Tampa, Fla.	FA
Pugh, David	DT	6-2	270	7/24/79	Virginia Tech	Madison Heights, Va.	D6a
Rhine, Alan (1)	P	5-11	178	3/11/78	Florida	Jacksonville, Fla.	FA
Rodriguez, Christian	LB	6-2	233	5/4/78	Texas A&M	Manhattan, N.Y.	FA
Routzahn, Evan	G	6-5	323	3/1/79	Virginia	Frederick, Md.	FA
Shoals, Donald	WR	5-11	176	12/25/78	Tulsa	Kansas City, Mo.	FA
Smith, Derek	TE	6-4	263	10/1/80	Kentucky	Fort Thomas, Ky.	FA
Souza, Mike	C	6-5	303	4/22/79	Northwestern	Kaneohe, Hawaii	FA
Staine-Pyne, Frank	CB-S	6-0	195	6/18/75	Air Force	Piscataway, N.J.	FA
Stone, John	WR	5-10	178	7/7/79	Wake Forest	Vineland, N.J.	FA
Thornton, David	LB	6-2	230	11/1/78	North Carolina	Goldsboro, N.C.	D4
Tripplett, Larry	DT	6-2	314	1/18/79	Washington	Los Angeles, Calif.	D2
Vollers, Kurt	T	6-7	317	4/4/79	Notre Dame	San Gabriel, Calif.	FA
Wallace, Michael (1)	RB	5-11	243	5/11/79	Army	Seoul, South Korea	FA
Warren, David (1)	DE	6-2	254	10/14/78	Florida State	Tyler, Texas	FA
Williams, Anthony	LB	5-9	216	9/8/78	South Florida	Pahokee, Fla.	FA
Wynn, Browning	TE	6-3	235	12/3/78	Virginia Tech	Kingsport, Tenn.	FA
Zolman, Greg	QB	6-2	216	10/19/78	Vanderbilt	Miamisburg, Ohio	FA

The term NFL Rookie is defined as a player who is in his first season of professional football and has not been on the roster of another professional football team for any regular-season or postseason games. A Rookie is designated by an "R" on NFL rosters. Players who have been active in another professional football league or players who have NFL experience, including either preseason training camp or being on an Active List or Inactive List, or on Reserve/Injured or Reserve/Physically Unable to Perform for fewer than six regular-season games, are termed NFL First-Year Players. An NFL First-Year Player is designated by a "1" on NFL rosters. Thereafter, a player is credited with an additional year of experience for each season in which he accumulates six games on the Active List or Inactive List, or on Reserve/Injured or Reserve/Physically Unable to Perform.

COACHING STAFF
Head Coach,
Tony Dungy

Pro Career: Tony Dungy enters his first season as head coach of the Indianapolis Colts. Dungy was named head coach of the club on January 22, 2002. This season marks his seventh as an NFL head coach. Prior to 2002, Dungy served as head coach (1996-2001) of the Tampa Bay Buccaneers. While at Tampa Bay, he was the most successful head coach in franchise history, compiling a 56-46 record and leading the club to the playoffs four times. During Dungy's tenure, the Buccaneers quickly developed a reputation as one of the NFL's stingiest defenses. This past season, Tampa Bay ranked sixth in total defense and eighth in points allowed with 280. Dungy's defenses with the Buccaneers ranked no lower than eleventh in his six seasons, and the Buccaneers' unit improved from twenty-seventh in the league the season before his arrival to eleventh in 1996. In 2000, the club set a team record with 55 sacks. At 25, Dungy was the NFL's youngest assistant coach when hired by the Pittsburgh Steelers in 1981. In 1982, he was promoted from defensive assistant to defensive backs coach, before becoming the league's youngest defensive coordinator in 1984 at age 28. He served as defensive backs coach at Kansas City (1989-1991) and as defensive coordinator at Minnesota (1992-95). Dungy's defense in Minnesota ranked first in 1993. Dungy, widely considered one of the most respected and popular NFL coaches, also has a reputation for developing Pro-Bowl caliber players, a reputation that began at Pittsburgh and has grown throughout his career. In 2001, the Buccaneers sent six players to the Pro Bowl. In 2000, nine Buccaneers players were selected to the game. Dungy signed with Pittsburgh as a free agent in 1977 and played safety for two seasons. He had 9 interceptions in 30 games for Pittsburgh and played in the club's Super Bowl XIII victory over Dallas. He was traded to San Francisco in 1979 and played 15 games for 49ers. Career record: 56-46.

Background: Starred as a quarterback at University of Minnesota from 1973-76. Finished career as school's all-time leader in attempts, completions, passing yards, and touchdown passes. Two-time team most valuable player, played in Hula Bowl, East-West Shrine Game and Japan Bowl. Attended Parkside High School in Jackson, Michigan.

Personal: Born October 6, 1955, in Jackson, Michigan. Tony and his wife Lauren have five children—daughters Tiara and Jade, and sons James, Eric and, Jordan.

ASSISTANT COACHES

Jim Caldwell, quarterbacks; born January 16, 1955, Beloit, Wis., lives in Indianapolis. Defensive back Iowa 1973-76. No pro playing experience. College coach: Iowa 1977, Southern Illinois 1978-1980, Northwestern 1981, Colorado 1982-84, Louisville 1985, Penn State 1986-1992, Wake Forest 1993-2000. Pro coach: Tampa Bay Buccaneers 2001, joined Colts in 2002.

Clyde Christensen, wide receivers; born January 28, 1958, Covina, Calif., lives in Indianapolis. Quarterback Fresno (Calif.) J.C. 1975, North Carolina 1976-78. No pro playing experience. College coach: East Tennessee State 1980-82, Temple 1983-85, East Carolina 1986-88, Holy Cross 1989-90, South Carolina 1991, Maryland 1992-93, Clemson 1994-95. Pro coach: Tampa Bay Buccaneers 1996-2001, joined Colts in 2002.

Chris Foerster, tight ends; born October 12, 1961, Milwaukee, Wis., lives in Indianapolis. Center Colorado State 1979-1982. No pro playing experience. College coach: Colorado State 1983-87, Stanford 1988-1991, Minnesota 1992. Pro coach: Minnesota Vikings 1993-95, Tampa Bay Buccaneers 1996-2001, joined Colts in 2002.

Richard Howell, asst. strength and conditioning; born February 19, 1972, Bladenboro, N.C., lives in Indianapolis. Quarterback Davidson 1990-93. No pro playing experience. College coach: Davidson 1994-97, North Carolina 1998-99. Pro coach: Barcelona Dragons (NFL Europe) 1999, joined Colts in 2000.

Gene Huey, running backs; born July 20, 1947, Uniontown, Pa., lives in Indianapolis. Defensive back-wide receiver Wyoming 1966-69. No pro playing experience. College coach: Wyoming 1970-74, New Mexico 1975-77, Nebraska 1978-1986, Arizona State 1987, Ohio State 1988-1991. Pro coach: Joined Colts in 1992.

Ron Meeks, defensive coordinator; born August 27, 1954, Jacksonville, Fla., lives in Indianapolis. Defensive back Arkansas State 1975-76. Pro defensive back Hamilton Tiger-Cats (CFL) 1977-79, Ottawa Rough Riders (CFL) 1979, Toronto Argonauts (CFL) 1980-81. College coach: Arkansas State 1984-85, Miami 1986-87, New Mexico State 1988, Fresno State 1989-1990. Pro coach: Dallas Cowboys 1991, Cincinnati Bengals 1992-96, Atlanta Falcons 1997-99, Washington Redskins 2000, St. Louis Rams 2001, joined Colts in 2002.

Tom Moore, offensive coordinator; born November 7, 1938, Owatanna, Minn., lives in Indianapolis. Quarterback Iowa 1957-60. No pro playing experience. College coach: Iowa 1961-62, Dayton 1965-68, Wake Forest 1969, Georgia Tech 1970-71, Minnesota 1972, 1975-76. Pro coach: New York Stars (WFL) 1974, Pittsburgh Steelers 1977-1989, Minnesota Vikings 1990-93, Detroit Lions 1994-96, New Orleans Saints 1997, joined Colts in 1998.

Howard Mudd, offensive line; born February 10, 1942, Midland, Mich., lives in Indianapolis. Guard Hillsdale (Mich.) College 1960-63. Pro offensive lineman San Francisco 49ers 1964-69, Chicago Bears 1969-1970. College coach: California 1972-73. Pro coach: San Diego Chargers 1974-76, San Francisco 49ers 1977, Seattle Seahawks 1978-1982, 1993-97, Cleveland Browns 1983-88, Kansas City Chiefs 1989-1992, joined Colts in 1998.

Mike Murphy, linebackers; born September 25, 1944, New York, N.Y., lives in Indianapolis. Guard-linebacker Huron (S.D.) 1963-66. No pro playing experience. College coach: Vermont 1970-73, Idaho State 1974-76, Western Illinois 1977-78. Pro coach: Saskatchewan Rough Riders (CFL) 1979-1983, Chicago Blitz (USFL) 1984, Detroit Lions 1985-89, Arizona Cardinals 1990-93, Seattle Seahawks 1995-97, joined Colts in 1998.

Russ Purnell, special teams; born June 12, 1948, Chicago, lives in Indianapolis. Center Orange Coast (Calif.) J.C. 1966-67, Whittier College 1968-69. No pro playing experience. College coach: Whittier College 1970-71, Southern California 1982-84. Pro coach: Seattle Seahawks 1986-1994, Tennessee Oilers 1995, Baltimore Ravens 1999-2001, joined Colts in 2002.

John Teerlinck, defensive line; born April 9, 1951, Rochester, N.Y., lives in Indianapolis. Defensive lineman Western Illinois 1970-73. Pro defensive tackle San Diego Chargers 1974-76. College coach: Iowa Lakes J.C. 1977, Eastern Illinois 1978-79, Illinois 1980-82. Pro coach: Chicago Blitz (USFL) 1983, Arizona Wranglers/Outlaws (USFL) 1984-85, Cleveland Browns 1989-1990, Los Angeles Rams 1991, Minnesota Vikings 1992-94, Detroit Lions 1995-96, Denver Broncos 1997-2001, joined Colts in 2002.

Ricky Thomas, offensive assistant; born March 29, 1965, London, England, lives in Indianapolis. Safety Alabama 1983-86. Pro safety Seattle Seahawks 1987. College coach: Kentucky 1996, Gardner-Webb 1996. Pro coach: Tampa Bay Buccaneers 1997-2001, joined Colts in 2002.

Jon Torine, strength and conditioning; born November 16, 1973, Livingston, N.J., lives in Indianapolis. Linebacker Springfield (Mass.) College 1991. No pro playing experience. Pro coach: Buffalo Bills 1995-97, joined Colts in 1998.

Alan Williams, defensive assistant; born November 4, 1969, Norfolk, Va., lives in Indianapolis. Running back William & Mary 1988-1991. No pro playing experience. College coach: William & Mary 1996-2000. Pro coach: Tampa Bay Buccaneers 2001, joined Colts in 2002.

American Football Conference
South Division
Team Colors: Teal, Black, and Gold
ALLTEL Stadium
One ALLTEL Stadium Place
Jacksonville, Florida 32202
Telephone: (904) 633-6000

2002 SCHEDULE
PRESEASON
Aug. 9	at Atlanta	7:30
Aug. 16	**Tampa Bay**	7:00
Aug. 23	at Chicago (Champaign, Ill.)	7:00
Aug. 29	**Dallas**	8:00

REGULAR SEASON
Sept. 8	**Indianapolis**	1:00
Sept. 15	at Kansas City	12:00
Sept. 22	Open Date	
Sept. 29	**New York Jets**	1:00
Oct. 6	**Philadelphia**	4:15
Oct. 13	at Tennessee	12:00
Oct. 20	at Baltimore	1:00
Oct. 27	**Houston**	4:15
Nov. 3	at New York Giants	8:30
Nov. 10	**Washington**	4:05
Nov. 17	at Houston	3:15
Nov. 24	at Dallas	12:00
Dec. 1	**Pittsburgh**	1:00
Dec. 8	**Cleveland**	1:00
Dec. 15	at Cincinnati	1:00
Dec. 22	**Tennessee**	1:00
Dec. 29	at Indianapolis	4:05

Stadium: ALLTEL Stadium
(opened in 1995)
•**Capacity:** 73,000
One ALLTEL Stadium Place
Jacksonville, Florida 32202
Playing Surface: Grass
Training Camp: ALLTEL Stadium
One ALLTEL Stadium Place
Jacksonville, Florida 32202

ALLTEL STADIUM

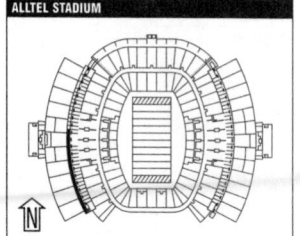

CLUB OFFICIALS
Chairman and Chief Executive Officer:
Wayne Weaver
Senior Vice President/Football
Operations: Paul Vance
Senior Vice President/Marketing:
Dan Connell
Vice President/Chief Financial Officer:
Bill Prescott
Executive Director of Communications
and Broadcasting: Dan Edwards
Executive Director of Sales:
Scott Allerding
Director of Player Personnel:
Rick Reiprish
Director of Pro Scouting: Fran Foley
Director of College Scouting: Gene Smith
Director of Finance: Kim Dodson
Director of Football Operations:
Skip Richardson
Director of Information Technology:
Bruce Swindell
Director of Corporate Sponsorship:
Macky Weaver
Director of Ticket Operations: Tim Bishko
Director of Special Events and
Promotions: Bo Reed
Director of Creative Services:
Jennifer Saalfield
Associate General Counsel:
Joe Pierce
Head Athletic Trainer: Michael Ryan
Video Director: Mike Perkins
Equipment Manager: Drew Hampton
Assistant Director of Pro Scouting:
Matt Littlefield
College Scouts: Louis Clark,
Andy Dengler, David Dougherty,
Chris Driggers, Tim Mingey,
John Wojciechowski

Chair & Chief Executive Officer, Jaguars
Foundation: Delores Barr Weaver
Executive Director: Peter Racine

COACHING HISTORY
(66-54-0)
1995-2001   Tom Coughlin 66-54-0

ATTENDANCE
Home 504,756   Away 493,904
Total 998,660
Single-game home record,
74,143 (12/28/98)
Single-season home record, 561,472
(1998)

2002 DRAFT CHOICES
Round	Name	Pos.	College
1	John Henderson	DT	Tennessee
2	Mike Pearson	T	Florida
3	Akin Ayodele	LB	Purdue
4	David Garrard	QB	East Carolina
	Chris Luzar	TE	Virginia
6	Clenton Ballard	DT	Southwest Texas St.
7	Kendall Newson	WR	Middle Tennessee St.
	Steve Smith	DB	Oregon
	Hayden Epstein	K	Michigan

JACKSONVILLE JAGUARS

2001 TEAM RECORD

PRESEASON (2-2)

Date	Result	Opponent
8/10	W 18-16	Carolina
8/16	L 5-27	at New York Giants
8/23	W 28-23	Kansas City
8/30	L 17-27	at Dallas

REGULAR SEASON (6-10)

Date	Result	Opponent	Att.
9/09	W 21-3	Pittsburgh	63,785
9/23	W 13-6	Tennessee	65,994
9/30	L 14-23	Cleveland	57,875
10/07	L 15-24	at Seattle	54,524
10/18	L 10-13	Buffalo	58,893
10/28	L 17-18	at Baltimore	69,439
11/04	L 24-28	at Tennessee	68,798
11/11	W 30-13	Cincinnati	57,161
11/18	L 7-20	at Pittsburgh	62,644
11/25	L 21-24	Baltimore	53,530
12/03	L 21-28	Green Bay	66,908
12/09	W 14-10	at Cincinnati	44,920
12/16	W 15-10	at Cleveland	72,818
12/23	W 33-23	at Minnesota	64,150
12/30	L 26-30	Kansas City	59,396
1/06	L 13-33	at Chicago	66,944

SCORE BY PERIODS

Jaguars	49	83	90	72	0	—	294
Opponents	43	89	75	79	0	—	286

2001 TEAM STATISTICS

	Jaguars	Opp.
Total First Downs	289	300
Rushing	85	89
Passing	181	193
Penalty	23	18
3rd Down: Made/Att	70/198	87/227
3rd Down Pct.	35.4	38.3
4th Down: Made/Att	3/12	5/18
4th Down Pct.	25.0	27.8
Possession Avg.	28:01	31:59
Total Net Yards	4840	5070
Avg. Per Game	302.5	316.9
Total Plays	969	1056
Avg. Per Play	5.0	4.8
Net Yards Rushing	1600	1611
Avg. Per Game	100.0	100.7
Total Rushes	372	469
Net Yards Passing	3240	3459
Avg. Per Game	202.5	216.2
Sacked/Yards Lost	63/430	43/298
Gross Yards	3670	3757
Att./Completions	534/321	544/354
Completion Pct.	60.1	65.1
Had Intercepted	14	12
Punts/Average	82/43.6	83/40.5
Net Punting Avg.	82/37.1	83/35.0
Penalties/Yards	97/710	96/834
Fumbles/Ball Lost	29/13	28/12
Touchdowns	34	30
Rushing	11	15
Passing	20	13
Returns	3	2

2001 INDIVIDUAL STATISTICS

PASSING	Att.	Comp.	Yds.	Pct.	TD	Int.	Tkld.	Rate
Brunell	473	289	3309	61.1	19	13	57/387	84.1
Quinn	61	32	361	52.5	1	1	6/43	69.1
Jaguars	534	321	3670	60.1	20	14	63/430	82.4
Opponents	544	354	3757	65.1	13	12	43/298	83.9

SCORING	TD R	TD P	TD Rt	PAT	FG	Saf	PTS
Hollis	0	0	0	29/31	18/28	0	83
Mack	9	1	0	0/0	0/0	0	60
Ji. Smith	0	8	0	0/0	0/0	0	48
McCardell	0	6	0	0/0	0/0	0	38
Joseph	0	2	1	0/0	0/0	0	18
Brady	0	2	0	0/0	0/0	0	12
Battles	0	0	1	0/0	0/0	0	6
Beasley	0	0	1	0/0	0/0	0	6
Brunell	1	0	0	0/0	0/0	0	6
Jones	0	1	0	0/0	0/0	0	6
Moreau	1	0	0	0/0	0/0	0	6
Brackens	0	0	0	0/0	0/0	1	2
Holmes	0	0	0	1/1	0/0	0	1
Jaguars	11	20	3	30/32	18/28	2	294
Opponents	15	13	2	28/28	26/35	0	286

2-Pt. Conversions: McCardell.
Jaguars 1-2, Opponents 0-2.

RUSHING	Att.	Yds.	Avg.	LG	TD
Mack	213	877	4.1	54	9
Joseph	68	294	4.3	27	0
Brunell	39	224	5.7	38	1
Taylor	30	116	3.9	24	0
Quinn	8	42	5.3	27	0
Moreau	8	27	3.4	14	1
Gibson	2	19	9.5	18	0
Whitted	1	4	4.0	4	0
Hanson	2	0	0.0	0	0
Ji. Smith	1	-3	-3.0	-3	0
Jaguars	372	1600	4.3	54	11
Opponents	469	1611	3.4	40	15

RECEIVING	No.	Yds.	Avg.	LG	TD
Ji. Smith	112	1373	12.3	35t	8
McCardell	93	1110	11.9	45	6
Brady	36	386	10.7	20t	2
Mack	23	165	7.2	25	1
Dawkins	20	234	11.7	28	0
Joseph	18	183	10.2	29t	2
Jones	8	140	17.5	40	1
Washington	5	36	7.2	12	0
Whitted	2	17	8.5	10	0
Gibson	2	13	6.5	9	0
Taylor	2	13	6.5	11	0
Jaguars	321	3670	11.4	45	20
Opponents	354	3757	10.6	63	13

INTERCEPTIONS	No.	Yds.	Avg.	LG	TD
Nickerson	3	4	1.3	2	0
Beasley	3	0	0.0	0	0
Battles	2	26	13.0	26	0
Craft	2	4	2.0	4	0
Darius	1	39	39.0	39	0
McCree	1	10	10.0	10	0
Jaguars	12	83	6.9	39	0
Opponents	14	299	21.4	97t	2

PUNTING	No.	Yds.	Avg.	In 20	LG
Hanson	82	3577	43.6	24	59
Jaguars	82	3577	43.6	24	59
Opponents	83	3359	40.5	31	68

PUNT RETURNS	No.	FC	Yds.	Avg.	LG	TD
Gibson	38	22	333	8.8	24	0
Jaguars	38	22	333	8.8	24	0
Opponents	38	15	295	7.8	43	0

KICKOFF RETURNS	No.	Yds.	Avg.	LG	TD
Gibson	26	511	19.7	35	0
Joseph	17	428	25.2	95t	1
Ross	8	150	18.8	26	0
Mack	2	49	24.5	31	0
Meier	2	14	7.0	8	0
Boyd	1	0	0.0	0	0
Prince	1	4	4.0	4	0
Spicer	1	8	8.0	8	0
Jaguars	58	1164	20.1	95t	1
Opponents	64	1266	19.8	49	0

FIELD GOALS	1-19	20-29	30-39	40-49	50+
Hollis	0/0	4/5	8/11	6/11	0/1
Jaguars	0/0	4/5	8/11	6/11	0/1
Opponents	0/0	11/12	4/5	10/15	1/3

SACKS	No.
Brackens	11.0
Walker	7.5
Hardy	5.5
Payne	5.0
Wynn	5.0
K. Thomas	3.0
Spicer	2.0
Battles	1.0
McCree	1.0
Slaughter	1.0
Westmoreland	1.0
Jaguars	43.0
Opponents	63.0

RECORD HOLDERS

INDIVIDUAL RECORDS—CAREER

Category	Name	Performance
Rushing (Yds.)	Fred Taylor, 1998-2001	3,470
Passing (Yds.)	Mark Brunell, 1995-2001	22,116
Passing (TDs)	Mark Brunell, 1995-2001	125
Receiving (No.)	Jimmy Smith, 1995-2001	584
Receiving (Yds.)	Jimmy Smith, 1995-2001	8,260
Interceptions	Aaron Beasley, 1996-2001	15
Punting (Avg.)	Bryan Barker, 1995-2000	43.5
Punt Return (Avg.)	Chris Hudson, 1995-98	10.9
Kickoff Return (Avg.)	Reggie Barlow, 1997-2000	23.3
Field Goals	Mike Hollis, 1995-2001	175
Touchdowns (Tot.)	Jimmy Smith, 1995-2001	46
Points	Mike Hollis, 1995-2001	764

INDIVIDUAL RECORDS—SINGLE SEASON

Category	Name	Performance
Rushing (Yds.)	Fred Taylor, 2000	1,399
Passing (Yds.)	Mark Brunell, 1996	4,367
Passing (TDs)	Mark Brunell, 1998	20
Receiving (No.)	Jimmy Smith, 1999	116
Receiving (Yds.)	Jimmy Smith, 1999	1,636
Interceptions	Aaron Beasley, 1999	6
Punting (Avg.)	Bryan Barker, 1998	45.0
Punt Return (Avg.)	Reggie Barlow, 1998	12.9
Kickoff Return (Avg.)	Reggie Barlow, 1998	24.9
Field Goals	Mike Hollis, 1997, 1999	31
Touchdowns (Tot.)	Fred Taylor, 1998	17
Points	Mike Hollis, 1997	134

INDIVIDUAL RECORDS—SINGLE GAME

Category	Name	Performance
Rushing (Yds.)	Fred Taylor, 11-19-00	234
Passing (Yds.)	Mark Brunell, 9-22-96	432
Passing (TDs)	Mark Brunell, 11-29-98	4
Receiving (No.)	Keenan McCardell, 10-20-96	16
Receiving (Yds.)	Jimmy Smith, 9-10-00	291
Interceptions	Deon Figures, 8-31-97	2
	Aaron Beasley, 9-12-99	2
	Rayna Stewart, 9-10-00	2
Field Goals	Mike Hollis, 12-1-96, 11-30-97, 9-10-00	5
Touchdowns (Tot.)	James Stewart, 10-12-97	5
Points	James Stewart, 10-12-97	30

2002 VETERAN ROSTER

No.	Name	Pos.	Ht.	Wt.	Birthdate	NFL Exp.	College	Hometown	How Acq.	'01 Games/ Starts
26	Battles, Ainsley	S	5-10	195	11/6/78	3	Vanderbilt	Lilburn, Ga.	W(Pitt)-'01	13/11
42	Boyd, James	S	5-11	201	10/17/77	2	Penn State	Chesapeake, Va.	D3b-'01	16/0
90	Brackens, Tony	DE	6-4	264	12/26/74	7	Texas	Fairfield, Texas	D2a-'96	12/12
80	Brady, Kyle	TE	6-6	273	1/14/72	8	Penn State	New Cumberland, Pa.	UFA(NYJ)-'99	16/16
8	Brunell, Mark	QB	6-1	217	9/17/70	10	Washington	Santa Maria, Calif.	T(GB)-'95	15/15
25	Bryant, Fernando	CB	5-10	171	3/26/77	4	Alabama	Murfreesboro, Tenn.	D1-'99	10/9
72	Chambers, Derrick	G-T	6-4	317	1/28/78	2	Florida	Shelby, N.C.	FA-'01	0*
55	Clark, Danny	LB	6-2	240	5/9/77	3	Illinois	Country Club Hills, Ill.	D7d-'00	13/3
60	Clayton, Carey	C	6-3	278	8/31/77	2	Texas-El Paso	Dyersburg, Tenn.	FA-'02	0*
93	Colinet, Stalin	DE	6-6	288	7/17/74	6	Boston College	New York, N.Y.	FA-'02	16/11
36	Cox, Renard	DB	6-0	191	3/3/78	2	Maryland	Richmond, Va.	FA-'01	5/0
29	Craft, Jason	CB	5-10	180	2/13/76	4	Colorado State	Denver, Colo.	D5-'99	16/8
20	Darius, Donovin	S	6-1	214	8/12/75	5	Syracuse	Camden, N.J.	D1b-'98	11/11
78	Fordham, Todd	T-G	6-5	307	10/9/73	6	Florida State	Tifton, Ga.	FA-'97	12/12
85	Gibson, Damon	WR-KR	5-9	177	2/25/75	3	Iowa	Houston, Texas	FA-'01	16/0
2	Hanson, Chris	P	6-1	211	10/25/76	3	Marshall	Riverdale, Ga.	FA-'01	16/0
3	Holmes, Jaret	K	6-0	223	3/3/76	2	Auburn	Clinton, Miss.	W-'00	4/0
84	Johnson, Patrick	WR	5-10	180	8/10/76	5	Oregon	Redlands, Calif.	UFA(Balt)-'02	0*
35	Joseph, Elvis	RB	6-1	215	8/30/78	2	Southern	New Orleans, La.	FA-'01	14/3
64	Koch, Aaron	G-T	6-3	302	2/21/78	3	Oregon State	Keizer, Ore.	W-'00	16/1
34	Mack, Stacey	RB-FB	6-1	236	6/26/75	4	Temple	Orlando, Fla.	FA-'99	16/11
32	McCree, Marlon	S	5-11	198	3/17/77	2	Kentucky	Daytona Beach, Fla.	D7b-'01	13/11
63	Meester, Brad	G	6-3	304	3/23/77	3	Northern Iowa	Parkersburg, Iowa	D2-'00	16/16
92	Meier, Rob	DE	6-5	280	8/29/77	3	Washington State	W. Vancouver, B.C., Canada	D7b-'00	16/0
68	Miller, Jeff	T	6-4	362	11/23/72	3	Mississippi	Vero Beach, Fla.	FA-'02	0*
83	Mitchell, Pete	TE	6-2	248	10/9/71	8	Boston College	Birmingham, Mich.	FA-'02	5/1
96	Morabito, Tim	DT	6-3	296	10/12/73	5	Boston College	Garnerville, N.Y.	FA-'02	0*
65	Naeole, Chris	G	6-3	313	12/25/74	6	Colorado	Kaaava, Hawaii	UFA(NO)-'02	16/16*
89	Prince, Ryan	TE	6-4	255	5/16/78	2	Weber State	Farmington, Utah	FA-'02	8/2
58	Rainer, Wali	LB	6-2	247	4/19/77	4	Virginia	Charlotte, N.C.	T(Cle)-'02	14/14*
10	Robinson, Roderick	QB	6-3	235	5/17/76	2	Arkansas-Pine Bluff	Memphis, Tenn.	W(Ind)-'01	0*
18	Shannon, Larry	WR	6-4	210	2/2/75	2	East Carolina	Starke, Fla.	FA-'02	0*
16	Shaw, Bobby	WR	6-0	183	4/23/75	5	California	San Francisco, Calif.	UFA(Pitt)-'02	16/0*
53	Slaughter, T.J.	LB	6-0	231	2/20/77	3	Southern Mississippi	Birmingham, Ala.	D3-'00	9/8
33	Smith, Detron	FB	5-10	230	2/25/74	7	Texas A&M	Dallas, Texas	UFA(Den)-'02	15/0*
82	Smith, Jimmy	WR	6-1	203	2/9/69	10	Jackson State	Jackson, Miss.	FA-'95	16/16
94	Smith, Larry	DT-DE	6-5	290	12/4/74	4	Florida State	Folkston, Ga.	D2-'99	7/0
81	Soward, R. Jay	WR	5-11	182	1/16/78	2	Southern California	Rialto, Calif.	D1-'00	0*
95	Spicer, Paul	DE	6-4	279	8/18/75	3	Saginaw Valley State	Indianapolis, Ind.	FA-'00	16/4
99	Stroud, Marcus	DT	6-6	322	6/25/78	2	Georgia	Barney, Ga.	D1-'01	16/0
28	Taylor, Fred	RB	6-1	228	1/27/76	5	Florida	Belle Glade, Fla.	D1a-'98	2/2
59	Thomas, Edward	LB	6-1	226	9/27/74	3	Georgia Southern	Thomasville, Ga.	FA-'00	16/4
41	Thomas, Kiwaukee	CB	5-11	187	6/19/77	3	Georgia Southern	Perry, Ga.	D5-'00	16/5
57	Tuipala, Joseph	LB	6-1	243	9/13/76	2	San Diego State	Ridgecrest, Calif.	FA-'01	12/0
70	Venzke, Patrick	T	6-6	306	4/6/75	2	Idaho	Essen, Germany	FA-'01	0*
66	Wade, John	C-G	6-5	302	1/25/75	5	Marshall	Harrisonburg, Va.	D5-'98	15/0
31	Washington, Patrick	FB	6-2	242	3/4/78	2	Virginia	Washington, D.C.	FA-'01	16/6
50	Wesley, Joe	LB	6-1	234	11/10/76	3	Louisiana State	Brookhaven, Miss.	FA-'01	6/0
52	Westmoreland, Eric	LB	6-0	227	3/11/77	2	Tennessee	Jasper, Tenn.	D3a-'01	11/2
22	White, Reggie	RB	6-0	228	7/11/79	2	Oklahoma State	Liberty, Texas	FA-'01	5/0
77	Wiegert, Zach	G-T	6-5	315	8/16/72	8	Nebraska	Fremont, Neb.	FA-'99	16/16
74	Williams, Maurice	T	6-5	300	1/26/79	2	Michigan	Detroit, Mich.	D2-'01	16/16
88	Zelenka, Joe	TE-LS	6-3	263	3/9/76	4	Wake Forest	Cleveland, Ohio	FA-'01	16/0
79	Ziemann, Chris	T	6-8	305	9/20/76	2	Michigan	Aurora, Ill.	FA-'02	0*

* Chambers inactive for 11 games; Clayton last active with San Diego in '00; Johnson played 4 games with Baltimore in '01; Miller last active with Green Bay in '95; Morabito missed '01 season because of injury; Naeole played 16 games with New Orleans; Rainer played 14 games with Cleveland; Robinson inactive for 11 games with Jacksonville; Shannon last active with Miami in '99; Shaw played 16 games with Pittsburgh; D. Smith played 15 games with Denver; Soward inactive for 2 games; Venzke inactive for 12 games; Ziemann last active with N.Y. Giants in '00.

t- Jaguars traded for Rainer (Cle).

Players lost in Expansion Draft (3): T Tony Boselli (3 games in '01), DT Seth Payne (16), DT Gary Walker (16).

Players lost through free agency (7): WR Sean Dawkins (Minn; 16 games in '01), LB Kevin Hardy (Dall; 16), K Mike Hollis (Buff; 16), LB Jeff Posey (Hou; 11), QB Jonathan Quinn (KC; 6), C-G Jeff Smith (Tenn; 16), DE Renaldo Wynn (Wash; 16).

Also played with Jaguars in '01—CB Aaron Beasley (12 games), S Delvin Brown (5), TE Damon Jones (7), WR Keenan McCardell (16), RB Frank Moreau (3), LB Hardy Nickerson (15), T Gannon Shepherd (1), K Jim Tarle (9), WR Alvis Whitted (11), T Steve Zahursky (1).

2002 FIRST-YEAR ROSTER

Name	Pos.	Ht.	Wt.	Birthdate	College	Hometown	How Acq.
Ayodele, Akin	LB	6-2	252	9/17/79	Purdue	Grand Prairie, Texas	D3
Ballard, Clenton	DT	6-3	315	4/17/79	Southwest Texas State	San Antonio, Texas	D6
Branch, Bruce	CB	5-11	184	9/14/78	Penn State	Richmond, Va.	FA
Bristol, Mark (1)	T	6-6	308	8/8/77	Mansfield (Pa.)	Philadelphia, Pa.	FA
Broomfield, Donald (1)	DT	6-3	309	6/10/76	Clemson	Olustee, Fla.	FA
Bullock, Chrys	G	6-4	319	3/21/80	Tulane	Metairie, La.	FA
Burroughs, Noah (1)	S	6-1	204	6/11/76	Buffalo	Hempstead, N.Y.	FA
Bush, Jovon	DT	6-4	308	4/27/79	Clemson	Hardeeville, S.C.	FA
Chatman, Jermaine	CB	5-11	181	2/15/80	Arizona	Compton, Calif.	FA
Douglas, Henry(1)	WR	6-0	173	3/3/77	North Carolina A&T	Southern Pines, N.C.	FA
Ellis, Victor	LB	6-1	235	11/24/79	Alabama	Chattanooga, Tenn.	FA
Epstein, Hayden	K	6-2	214	11/16/80	Michigan	Cardiff, Calif.	D7c
Fontana, Stevan (1)	TE	6-5	266	6/3/78	Northern Arizona	San Anselmo, Calif.	FA-'02
Garner, Randy (1)	DE	6-4	275	11/28/77	Arkansas	Douglasville, Texas	FA-'01
Garrard, David	QB	6-1	237	2/14/78	East Carolina	Durham, N.C.	D4a
Gray, Quinn	QB	6-3	246	5/21/79	Florida A&M	Fort Lauderdale, Fla.	FA
Hamilton, Aaron (1)	DE	6-5	280	12/9/73	Westmar (Iowa)	Austin, Texas	FA
Henderson, John	DT	6-7	316	1/9/79	Tennessee	Nashville, Tenn.	D1
Jones, Garrick	T	6-5	305	12/2/78	Arkansas State	Little Rock, Ark.	FA
Luzar, Chris	TE	6-7	260	2/12/79	Virginia	Williamsburg, Va.	D4b
Mills, Javor	DE	6-4	265	5/11/79	Auburn	Wilmington, Del.	FA
Muldrow, Marquise	G	6-2	323	7/11/78	Arizona State	Glendale, Ariz.	FA
Newson, Kendall	WR	6-1	195	3/5/80	Middle Tennessee State	Decatur, Ga.	D7a
Ofahengaue, Tevita (1)	TE	6-2	259	7/9/74	Brigham Young	Laie, Hawaii	FA-'01
Parchman, Corey	WR	6-1	181	2/23/79	Ball State	Indianapolis, Ind.	FA
Pearson, Mike	T	6-7	303	8/2/80	Florida	Seffner, Fla.	D2
Redmond, Jimmy (1)	WR	6-0	192	8/18/77	McNeese State	Blue Springs, Mo.	FA
Ross, Micah (1)	WR	6-3	219	1/13/76	Jacksonville	Jacksonville, Fla.	FA-'01
Schorejs, Derek (1)	K	6-0	220	5/14/73	Bowling Green	Westerville, Ohio	FA
Smith Steve	CB	6-1	190	6/28/79	Oregon	Palos Verdes, Calif.	D7b
Spears, Ellis	WR	6-2	182	9/17/80	Grambling State	Zachary, La.	FA
Stephens, Conner	LB	6-4	250	8/26/80	Mississippi State	Ackerman, Miss.	FA
Sweeney, Matt (1)	DT	6-2	295	5/24/77	Miami	Lafayette, N.J.	W(TB)
Tate, Adam	RB	6-1	234	5/22/78	Utah	Alhambra, Calif.	FA
Watkins, James(1)	S	6-4	220	9/22/77	Tennessee State	Hillsboro, Ala.	FA
Wheeler, Damen (1)	CB	5-9	180	9/3/77	Colorado	Sacramento, Calif.	FA-'01
White, Fred (1)	S	5-10	207	3/18/77	Tennessee	Griffin, Ga.	FA

The term NFL Rookie is defined as a player who is in his first season of professional football and has not been on the roster of another professional football team for any regular-season or postseason games. A Rookie is designated by an "R" on NFL rosters. Players who have been active in another professional football league or players who have NFL experience, including either preseason training camp or being on an Active List or Inactive List, or on Reserve/Injured or Reserve/Physically Unable to Perform for fewer than six regular-season games, are termed NFL First-Year Players. An NFL First-Year Player is designated by a "1" on NFL rosters. Thereafter, a player is credited with an additional year of experience for each season in which he accumulates six games on the Active List or Inactive List, or on Reserve/Injured or Reserve/Physically Unable to Perform.

COACHING STAFF
Head Coach,
Tom Coughlin
Pro Career: Under Tom Coughlin, who has the second-longest tenure with his team among NFL head coaches, the Jaguars have the most victories of any NFL expansion team in its first seven seasons. They are also the only expansion team in NFL history to advance to the playoffs four times in their first five seasons. After a 4-12 inaugural season, Coughlin's team went 9-7 in year two on the way to the AFC Championship Game, and 11-5 and into the playoffs in both 1997 and 1998. In 1999, Coughlin posted an NFL-best 14-2 mark in the regular season and a second AFC Championship Game appearance. Coughlin became the first head coach of the Jaguars on February 21, 1994, following a successful three seasons as head coach at Boston College. A veteran of 30 years in coaching, including 17 at the collegiate level and seven as an NFL assistant, Coughlin previously coached wide receivers for the Philadelphia Eagles (1984-85), Green Bay Packers (1986-87), and New York Giants (1988-1990). He was a member of the Giants' Super Bowl XXV champion coaching staff prior to being named head coach at Boston College in 1991. In three seasons at Boston College, he turned a struggling program into a top-20 team, posting a 21-13-1 record. Coughlin's previous 14 seasons as a college coach were at Rochester Institute of Technology 1970-73 (head coach), Syracuse 1974-1980, and Boston College 1981-83. Career record: 66-54.
Background: Played wingback for Syracuse from 1965-67 under coach Ben Schwartzwalder, along with teammates Larry Csonka and Floyd Little. Received Syracuse 1967 Orange Key Award as outstanding scholar athlete, and graduated with bachelor's degree in education (1968). Received master's degree in education from Syracuse (1969).
Personal: Born August 31, 1947, Waterloo, N.Y. Was star for Waterloo Central High School. Tom and his wife, Judy, reside in Jacksonville, and have two daughters, Keli and Katie, two sons, Tim and Brian, and a daughter-in-law, Andrea.

ASSISTANT COACHES
John Bonamego, special teams coordinator; born August 14, 1963, Waynesboro, Pa., lives in Jacksonville. Wide receiver-quarterback Central Michigan 1985-86. No pro playing experience. College coach: Maine 1988-1991, Lehigh 1992, Army 1993-98. Pro coach: Joined Jaguars in 1999.
Perry Fewell, secondary; born November 7, 1962, Gastonia, N.C., lives in Jacksonville. Defensive back Lenoir-Rhyne 1981-84. No pro playing experience. College coach: Army 1987, 1992-

94, Kent State 1988-1991, Vanderbilt 1995-97. Pro coach: Joined Jaguars in 1998.
Greg Finnegan, asst. strength and conditioning; born February 21, 1969, Toledo, Ohio, lives in Jacksonville. Center Cornell 1988-1992. No pro playing experience. College coach: Kansas State 1993, Boston College 1994-97. Pro coach: Joined Jaguars in 1998.
John Hufnagel, quarterbacks; born September 13, 1951, Pittsburgh, lives in Jacksonville. Quarterback Penn State 1969-1972. Pro quarterback Denver Broncos 1973-75, Calgary Stampeders (CFL) 1976-79, Saskatchewan Roughriders (CFL) 1980-83, 1987, Winnipeg Blue Bombers (CFL) 1984-86. Pro coach: Saskatchewan Roughriders (CFL) 1988, Calgary Stampeders (CFL) 1990-96, New Jersey Red Dogs (Arena League) 1997-98, Cleveland Browns 1999-2000, Indianapolis Colts 2001, joined Jaguars in 2002.
Jerald Ingram, running backs; born December 24, 1960, Beaver, Pa., lives in Jacksonville. Fullback Michigan 1979-1984. No pro playing experience. College coach: Ball State 1985-1990, Boston College 1991-93. Pro coach: Joined Jaguars in 1995.
Ty Knott, offensive quality control; born December 9, 1965, Los Angeles, lives in Jacksonville. Defensive back Oregon Tech 1988-89. No pro playing experience. College coach: Whittier College 1994-95, Indiana (Penn.) 1997-99, Mt. San Antonio (Calif.) J.C. 2000, Greenville 2001. Pro coach: Joined Jaguars in 2002.
Mike Maser, offensive line; born March 2, 1947, Clayton, N.Y., lives in Jacksonville. Guard Buffalo 1967-1970. No pro playing experience. College coach: Marshall 1973, Bluefield State College 1974-78, Maine 1979-1980, Boston College 1981-1993. Pro coach: Joined Jaguars in 1995.
John McNulty, wide receivers; born May 29, 1968, Scranton, Pa., lives in Jacksonville. Safety Penn State 1987-1990. No pro playing experience. College coach: Michigan 1991-94, Connecticut 1995-97. Pro coach: Joined Jaguars in 1998.
Jerry Palmieri, strength and conditioning; born October 30, 1958, Englewood, N.J., lives in Jacksonville. No college or pro playing experience. College coach: Oklahoma State 1984-87, Kansas State 1988-1992, Boston College 1993-94. Pro coach: Joined Jaguars in 1995.
John Pease, asst. head coach-defensive coordinator; born October 14, 1943, Pittsburgh, lives in Jacksonville. Wingback Utah 1963-64. No pro playing experience. College coach: Fullerton (Calif.) J.C. 1970-73, Long Beach State 1974-76, Utah 1977, Washington 1978-1983. Pro coach: Philadelphia/Baltimore Stars (USFL) 1983-85, New Orleans Saints 1986-1994, joined Jaguars in

1995.
Mike Priefer, asst. special teams; born August 21, 1966, Cleveland, lives in Jacksonville. Attended Navy. No college or pro playing experience. College coach: Navy 1994-96, Youngstown State 1997-98, Virginia Military Institute 1999, Northern Illinois 2000-2001. Pro coach: Joined Jaguars in 2002.
Lucious Selmon, defensive line; born March 15, 1951, Muskogee, Okla., lives in Jacksonville. Defensive tackle Oklahoma 1970-73. Pro defensive tackle Memphis Southmen (WFL) 1974-75. College coach: Oklahoma 1976-1994. Pro coach: Joined Jaguars in 1995.
Tony Sparano, tight ends; born October 7, 1961, West Haven, Conn., lives in Jacksonville. Center New Haven 1978-1981. No pro playing experience. College coach: New Haven 1984-87, Boston University 1988-1993, New Haven 1994-98 (head coach). Pro coach: Cleveland Browns 1999-2000, Washington Redskins 2001, joined Jaguars in 2002.
Mike Sullivan, defensive quality control; born January 28, 1967, Santa Maria, Calif., lives in Jacksonville. Defensive back Army 1987-88. No pro playing experience. College coach: Mt. San Jacinto (Calif.) J.C. 1993, Humboldt State 1994, Army 1995-96, 1999-2000, Youngstown State 1997-98, Ohio University 2001. Pro coach: Joined Jaguars in 2002.
Steve Szabo, linebackers; born September 11, 1943, Chicago, lives in Jacksonville. Halfback/defensive back Navy 1961-64. No pro playing experience. College coach: Johns Hopkins 1969, Toledo 1970, Iowa 1971-73, Syracuse 1974-76, Iowa State 1977-78, Ohio State 1979-1981, Western Michigan 1982-84, Edinboro 1985-87 (head coach), Northern Iowa 1988, Colorado State 1989-1990, Boston College 1991-93. Pro coach: Joined Jaguars in 1995.

American Football Conference
West Division
Team Colors: Red, Gold, and White
One Arrowhead Drive
Kansas City, Missouri 64129
Telephone: (816) 920-9300

2002 SCHEDULE
PRESEASON
Aug. 10 at San Francisco.................6:00
Aug. 17 Houston 7:30
Aug. 24 at Seattle............................7:00
Aug. 30 **St. Louis** 7:30

REGULAR SEASON
Sept. 8 at Cleveland 1:00
Sept. 15 **Jacksonville**.....................12:00
Sept. 22 at New England 1:00
Sept. 29 **Miami** 12:00
Oct. 6 at New York Jets 4:05
Oct. 13 at San Diego 1:15
Oct. 20 **Denver**...........................12:00
Oct. 27 **Oakland** 12:00
Nov. 3 Open Date
Nov. 10 at San Francisco.................1:15
Nov. 17 **Buffalo**...........................12:00
Nov. 24 at Seattle...........................1:05
Dec. 1 **Arizona** 12:00
Dec. 8 **St. Louis** 12:00
Dec. 15 at Denver...........................2:05
Dec. 22 **San Diego**.......................12:00
Dec. 28 at Oakland (Sat.) 2:00

Stadium: Arrowhead Stadium
(opened in 1972)
•**Capacity:** 79,451
One Arrowhead Drive
Kansas City, Missouri 64129
Playing Surface: Grass
Training Camp: University of
Wisconsin-River Falls
River Falls, Wisconsin
54022

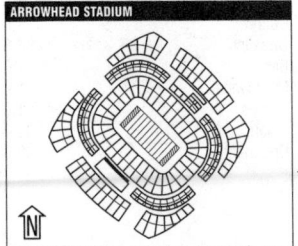

ARROWHEAD STADIUM

CLUB OFFICIALS
Founder: Lamar Hunt
Chairman of the Board: Jack Steadman
President: Carl Peterson
Executive Vice President/Assistant
General Manager: Dennis Thum
Vice President of Football
Operations/Player Personnel: Lynn Stiles
Senior Vice President: Dennis Watley
Secretary: Jim Seigfried
Director of Finance/Treasurer: Dale Young
Vice President of Sales and Marketing:
Wallace Bennett
Director of Pro Personnel: Bill Kuharich
Director of College Scouting: Chuck Cook
Director of Public Relations: Bob Moore
Associate Director of Public Relations:
Pete Moris
Director of Operations: Steve Schneider
Director of Development: Ken Blume
Director of Corporate Sales: Anita Bailey
Director of Sales: Gary Spani
Director of Player Development:
Lamonte Winston
Director of Community Relations:
Brenda Sniezek
Director of Ticket Operations:
Doug Hopkins
Director of Special Events: Julie Dorn
Equipment Manager: Mike Davidson
Asst. Equipment Managers: Allen Wright,
Chris Shropshire
Head Athletic Trainer: Dave Kendall
Assistant Trainers: Bud Epps,
Keith Abrams
Director of Video Operations: Mike Portz
Video Assistants: Todd Weger,
Andrew Hearne

COACHING HISTORY
Dallas Texans 1960-62
(336-299-12)
1960-1974 Hank Stram 129-79-10
1975-77 Paul Wiggin* 11-24-0
1977 Tom Bettis 1-6-0
1978-1982 Marv Levy 31-42-0
1983-86 John Mackovic 30-35-0
1987-88 Frank Gansz...................8-22-1
1989-1998 Marty Schottenheimer...104-65-1
1999-2000 Gunther Cunningham 16-16-0
2001 Dick Vermeil....................6-10-0
*Released after seven games in 1977

ATTENDANCE
Home 617,473   Away 511,757
Total 1,129,230
Single-game home record,
82,893* (10/2/00)
Single-season home record, 629,569
(1999)
*Arrowhead Stadium attendance: 78,502;
Kauffman Stadium attendance: 4,391

2002 DRAFT CHOICES
Round	Name	Pos.	College
1	Ryan Sims	DT	North Carolina
2	Eddie Freeman	DT	Ala.-Birmingham
4	Omar Easy	RB	Penn State
5	Scott Fujita	LB	California
7	Maurice Rodriguez	LB	Fresno State

2001 TEAM RECORD

PRESEASON (2-2)

Date	Result	Opponent
8/12	W 20-0	Washington
8/18	W 10-9	Chicago
8/23	L 23-28	at Jacksonville
8/31	L 17-21	at St. Louis

REGULAR SEASON (6-10)

Date	Result	Opponent	Att.
9/09	L 24-27	Oakland	78,844
9/23	L 3-13	New York Giants	77,666
9/30	W 45-13	at Washington	76,573
10/07	L 6-20	at Denver	75,037
10/14	L 17-20	Pittsburgh	78,413
10/21	L 16-24	at Arizona	35,916
10/25	L 28-35	Indianapolis	74,212
11/04	W 25-20	at San Diego	58,789
11/11	L 7-27	at New York Jets	78,234
11/25	W 19-7	Seattle	77,357
11/29	L 10-23	Philadelphia	77,087
12/09	L 26-28	at Oakland	60,784
12/16	W 26-23	Denver (OT)	77,778
12/23	W 20-17	San Diego	76,131
12/30	W 30-26	at Jacksonville	59,396
1/06	L 18-21	at Seattle	58,460

(OT) Overtime

SCORE BY PERIODS

Chiefs	56	92	64	105	3	— 320
Opponents	43	115	103	83	0	— 344

2001 TEAM STATISTICS

	Chiefs	Opp.
Total First Downs	324	296
Rushing	119	111
Passing	178	167
Penalty	27	18
3rd Down: Made/Att	70/195	86/218
3rd Down Pct.	35.9	39.4
4th Down: Made/Att	5/16	5/8
4th Down Pct.	31.3	62.5
Possession Avg.	29:07	30:53
Total Net Yards	5673	5304
Avg. Per Game	354.6	331.5
Total Plays	1015	1003
Avg. Per Play	5.6	5.3
Net Yards Rushing	2008	2140
Avg. Per Game	125.5	133.8
Total Rushes	448	481
Net Yards Passing	3665	3164
Avg. Per Game	229.1	197.8
Sacked/Yards Lost	39/198	31/239
Gross Yards	3863	3403
Att./Completions	528/300	491/296
Completion Pct.	56.8	60.3
Had Intercepted	24	13
Punts/Average	75/40.5	79/41.0
Net Punting Avg.	75/35.3	79/35.6
Penalties/Yards	68/602	87/761
Fumbles/Ball Lost	19/9	23/13
Touchdowns	34	37
Rushing	16	15
Passing	17	19
Returns	1	3

2001 INDIVIDUAL STATISTICS

PASSING	Att.	Comp.	Yds.	Pct.	TD	Int.	Tkld.	Rate
Green	523	296	3783	56.6	17	24	39/198	71.1
Collins	4	3	40	75.0	0	0	0/0	106.3
Gonzalez	1	1	40	100.0	0	0	0/0	118.8
Chiefs	528	300	3863	56.8	17	24	39/198	71.7
Opponents	491	296	3403	60.3	19	13	31/239	83.1

SCORING	TD R	TD P	TD Rt	PAT	FG	Saf	PTS
Peterson	0	0	0	27/28	27/35	0	108
Holmes	8	2	0	0/0	0/0	0	60
Richardson	7	0	0	0/0	0/0	0	42
Gonzalez	0	6	0	0/0	0/0	0	38
Alexander	0	3	0	0/0	0/0	0	18
Parker	0	2	0	0/0	0/0	0	12
Kennison	0	0	0	0/0	0/0	0	2
Ricks	0	1	0	0/0	0/0	1	8
Cloud	1	0	0	0/0	0/0	0	6
Dunn	0	1	0	0/0	0/0	0	6
Minnis	0	1	0	0/0	0/0	0	6
Thomas	0	1	0	0/0	0/0	0	6
Warfield	0	0	1	0/0	0/0	0	6
Green	0	0	0	0/0	0/0	0	2
Chiefs	16	17	1	27/28	27/35	1	320
Opponents	15	19	3	35/35	27/34	1	344

2-Pt. Conversions: Gonzalez, Green, Kennison. Chiefs 3-6, Opponents 2-2.

RUSHING	Att.	Yds.	Avg.	LG	TD
Holmes	327	1555	4.8	41	8
Richardson	66	191	2.9	19	7
Green	35	158	4.5	16	0
Cloud	7	54	7.7	16	1
Alexander	2	16	8.0	15	0
Kennison	2	13	6.5	14	0
Hall	2	10	5.0	6	0
Gonzalez	1	9	9.0	9	0
Collins	2	6	3.0	7	0
Parker	3	6	2.0	7	0
Stryzinski	1	-10	-10.0	-10	0
Chiefs	448	2008	4.5	41	16
Opponents	481	2140	4.4	77t	15

RECEIVING	No.	Yds.	Avg.	LG	TD
Gonzalez	73	917	12.6	36	6
Holmes	62	614	9.9	67t	2
Minnis	33	511	15.5	56	1
Richardson	30	265	8.8	47	0
Alexander	27	470	17.4	46	3
Thomas	19	247	13.0	28	1
Ricks	18	252	14.0	40	1
Kennison	16	322	20.1	65	0
Parker	15	199	13.3	44	2
Dunn	4	54	13.5	28	1
J. Williams	2	11	5.5	9	0
Green	1	1	1.0	1	0
Chiefs	300	3863	12.9	67t	17
Opponents	296	3403	11.5	49	19

INTERCEPTIONS	No.	Yds.	Avg.	LG	TD
Warfield	4	61	15.3	51t	1
Woods	3	48	16.0	25	0
Wesley	2	44	22.0	30	0
Patton	2	5	2.5	5	0
Crockett	1	8	8.0	8	0
Cadrez	1	0	0.0	0	0
Chiefs	13	166	12.8	51t	1
Opponents	24	296	12.3	61t	1

PUNTING	No.	Yds.	Avg.	In 20	LG
Stryzinski	73	2976	40.8	27	76
Peterson	2	61	30.5	0	34
Chiefs	75	3037	40.5	27	76
Opponents	79	3238	41.0	19	65

PUNT RETURNS	No.	FC	Yds.	Avg.	LG	TD
Hall	32	6	235	7.3	26	0
Parker	11	2	91	8.3	14	0
Warfield	1	0	0	0.0	0	0
Chiefs	44	8	326	7.4	26	0
Opponents	31	18	288	9.3	88t	1

KICKOFF RETURNS	No.	Yds.	Avg.	LG	TD
Hall	43	969	22.5	71	0
Cloud	8	174	21.8	33	0
Beisel	3	35	11.7	14	0
Belser	3	58	19.3	24	0
Dunn	2	34	17.0	18	0
Atkins	1	0	0.0	0	0
Parker	1	22	22.0	22	0
Chiefs	61	1292	21.2	71	0
Opponents	65	1474	22.7	88t	1

FIELD GOALS	1-19	20-29	30-39	40-49	50+
Peterson	0/0	9/11	9/10	8/12	1/2
Chiefs	0/0	9/11	9/10	8/12	1/2
Opponents	0/0	6/6	10/10	8/15	3/3

SACKS	No.
Clemons	7.0
Hicks	3.5
Owens	3.0
Patton	3.0
Ransom	3.0
Edwards	2.0
Wesley	2.0
Browning	1.5
Cadrez	1.5
Downing	1.5
Bartee	1.0
Maslowski	1.0
Woods	1.0
Chiefs	31.0
Opponents	39.0

RECORD HOLDERS
INDIVIDUAL RECORDS—CAREER

Category	Name	Performance
Rushing (Yds.)	Christian Okoye, 1987-1992	4,897
Passing (Yds.)	Len Dawson, 1962-1975	28,507
Passing (TDs)	Len Dawson, 1962-1975	237
Receiving (No.)	Henry Marshall, 1976-1987	416
Receiving (Yds.)	Otis Taylor, 1965-1975	7,306
Interceptions	Emmitt Thomas, 1966-1978	58
Punting (Avg.)	Jerrel Wilson, 1963-1977	43.6
Punt Return (Avg.)	Noland Smith, 1967-69	11.1
Kickoff Return (Avg.)	Noland Smith, 1967-69	26.8
Field Goals	Nick Lowery, 1980-1993	329
Touchdowns (Tot.)	Otis Taylor, 1965-1975	60
Points	Nick Lowery, 1980-1993	1,466

INDIVIDUAL RECORDS—SINGLE SEASON

Category	Name	Performance
Rushing (Yds.)	Priest Holmes, 2001	1,555
Passing (Yds.)	Bill Kenney, 1983	4,348
Passing (TDs)	Len Dawson, 1964	30
Receiving (No.)	Tony Gonzalez, 2000	93
Receiving (Yds.)	Derrick Alexander, 2000	1,391
Interceptions	Emmitt Thomas, 1974	12
Punting (Avg.)	Jerrel Wilson, 1965	46.0
Punt Return (Avg.)	Abner Haynes, 1960	15.4
Kickoff Return (Avg.)	Dave Grayson, 1962	29.7
Field Goals	Nick Lowery, 1990	34
Touchdowns (Tot.)	Abner Haynes, 1962	19
Points	Nick Lowery, 1990	139

INDIVIDUAL RECORDS—SINGLE GAME

Category	Name	Performance
Rushing (Yds.)	Barry Word, 10-14-90	200
Passing (Yds.)	Elvis Grbac, 11-5-00	504
Passing (TDs)	Len Dawson, 11-1-64	6
Receiving (No.)	Ed Podolak, 10-7-73	12
Receiving (Yds.)	Stephone Paige, 12-22-85	309
Interceptions	Bobby Ply, 10-16-62	*4
	Bobby Hunt, 12-4-64	*4
	Deron Cherry, 9-29-85	*4
Field Goals	Many times	5
	Last time by Nick Lowery, 9-21-93	
Touchdowns (Tot.)	Abner Haynes, 11-26-61	5
Points	Abner Haynes, 11-26-61	30

*NFL Record

2002 VETERAN ROSTER

No.	Name	Pos.	Ht.	Wt.	Birthdate	NFL Exp.	College	Hometown	How Acq.	'01 Games/ Starts
72	Alford, Darnell	T	6-4	328	6/11/77	3	Boston College	Fredericksburg, Va.	D6-'00	2/0
26	Allen, Taje	CB	5-11	185	11/6/73	6	Texas	Lubbock, Texas	UFA(StL)-'01	16/0
69	Allotey, Victor	G	6-3	338	4/8/75	4	Indiana	Brooklyn, N.Y.	FA-'01	0*
64	Andersen, Jason	T	6-6	310	9/3/75	4	Brigham Young	Hayward, Calif.	FA-'02	0*
8	Andersen, Morten	K	6-2	205	8/19/60	21	Michigan State	Copenhagen, Denmark	UFA(NYG)-'02	16/0*
50	Atkins, Larry	S	6-3	225	7/21/75	4	UCLA	Venice, Calif.	D3b-'99	12/0
24	Bartee, William	CB	6-1	196	6/25/77	3	Oklahoma	Daytona Beach, Fla.	D2-'00	16/5
96	Beisel, Monty	LB	6-3	267	8/20/78	2	Kansas State	Douglass, Kan.	FA-'01	16/0
29	Belser, Jason	S	5-10	191	5/28/70	11	Oklahoma	Kansas City, Mo.	FA-'01	16/0
23	Blaylock, Derrick	RB	5-9	200	8/23/79	2	Stephen F. Austin	Atlanta, Ga.	D5b-'01	0*
93	Browning, John	DE	6-4	289	9/30/73	7	West Virginia	Miami, Fla.	D3-'96	6/6
56	Bush, Lew	LB	6-2	249	12/2/69	10	Washington State	Atlanta, Ga.	UFA(Minn)-'00	12/11
51	Cadrez, Glenn	LB	6-2	241	1/2/70	11	Houston	El Centro, Calif.	FA-'01	16/5
99	Clemons, Duane	DE	6-5	278	5/23/74	7	California	Riverside, Calif.	FA-'00	16/5
34	Cloud, Michael	RB	5-10	205	7/1/75	4	Boston College	Portsmouth, R.I.	D2-'99	15/0
15	Collins, Todd	QB	6-4	219	11/5/71	8	Michigan	Walpole, Mass.	W(Buff)-'98	1/0
39	Crockett, Ray	CB	5-10	184	1/5/67	14	Baylor	Dallas, Texas	FA-'01	14/12
79	Downing, Eric	DT	6-3	314	9/16/78	2	Syracuse	Ahoskie, N.C.	D3a-'01	15/9
89	Dunn, Jason	TE	6-4	260	11/15/73	6	Eastern Kentucky	Harrodsburg, Ky.	FA-'00	15/5
83	Gammon, Kendall	TE	6-4	255	10/23/68	11	Pittsburg State	Wichita, Kan.	UFA(NO)-'00	16/0
7	Germaine, Joe	QB	6-2	220	8/11/75	4	Ohio State	Denver, Colo.	D1-'97	0*
88	Gonzalez, Tony	TE	6-4	248	2/27/76	6	California	Huntington Beach, Calif.	D1-'97	16/16
10	Green, Trent	QB	6-3	210	7/9/70	9	Indiana	Cedar Rapids, Iowa	T(StL)-'01	16/16
20	Hall, Dante	WR-KR	5-8	193	9/1/78	3	Texas A&M	Lufkin, Texas	D5a-'00	13/0
40	Harris, Corey	CB	5-10	191	11/28/76	2	North Alabama	Jacksonville, Fla.	FA-'01	4/0
98	Hicks, Eric	DE	6-6	280	6/17/76	5	Maryland	Erie, Pa.	FA-'98	16/16
94	Hobgood-Chittick, Nate	DT	6-3	290	11/30/74	5	North Carolina	Allentown, Pa	FA-'01	10/1
31	Holmes, Priest	RB	5-9	205	10/7/73	6	Texas	Fort Smith, Ark.	UFA(Balt)-'01	16/16
14	Jackson, Curtis	WR	5-10	194	9/22/73	2	Texas	Fort Worth, Texas	FA-'02	2/0*
11	Jones, Reggie	WR	6-0	195	5/8/71	5	Louisiana State	Kansas City, Mo.	FA-'01	0*
73	Jones, Willie	T	6-6	355	12/17/75	4	Grambling State	Pahokee, Fla.	FA-'00	12/0
52	Jordan, Richard	LB	6-1	257	12/1/74	4	Missouri Southern	Hillsboro, Texas	FA-'01	0*
87	Kennison, Eddie	WR	6-1	190	1/20/73	7	Louisiana State	Lake Charles, La.	FA-'01	5/1
57	Maslowski, Mike	LB	6-1	243	7/11/74	4	Wisconsin-La Crosse	Thorp, Wis.	FA-'99	8/0
75	McCleary, Norris	DT	6-6	305	5/10/77	2	East Carolina	Shelby, N.C.	FA-'00	10/0
22	McClellion, Central	CB	6-0	190	9/15/75	2	Ohio State	Boynton Beach, Calif.	FA-'02	6/0*
81	Minnis, Marvin	WR	6-1	172	2/6/77	2	Florida State	Miami, Fla.	D1-'01	13/11
84	Morris, Sylvester	WR	6-3	216	10/6/77	3	Jackson State	New Orleans, La.	D1-'00	0*
80	Morton, Johnnie	WR	6-0	190	10/7/71	9	Southern California	Torrance, Calif.	FA-'02	16/16*
97	Owens, Ritchie	DE	6-6	288	5/22/72	8	Lehigh	Philadelphia, Pa.	UFA(Mia)-'01	16/1
85	Parker, Larry	WR	6-1	206	7/14/76	4	Southern California	Bakersfield, Calif.	D4-'99	12/4
53	Patton, Marvcus	LB	6-2	239	5/1/67	13	UCLA	Lawndale, Calif.	UFA(Wash)-'99	16/15
12	Quinn, Jonathan	QB	6-6	239	2/27/75	5	Middle Tennessee State	Turlock, Calif.	UFA(Jax)-'01	6/1*
95	Ransom, Derrick	DE	6-3	310	9/13/76	5	Cincinnati	Indianapolis, Ind.	D6-'98	16/16
49	Richardson, Tony	FB	6-1	232	12/17/71	8	Auburn	Daleville, Ala.	FA-'95	14/7
77 t-	Roaf, Willie	T	6-5	312	4/18/70	10	Louisiana Tech	Pine Bluff, Ark.	T(NO)-'02	7/7*
91	Sands, Terdell	DT	6-7	340	10/31/79	2	Tennessee–Chattanooga	Chattanooga, Tenn.	D7b-'01	0*
41	Shields, Paul	FB	6-1	238	1/31/76	3	Arizona	Camp Springs, Md.	FA-'02	0*
68	Shields, Will	G	6-3	315	9/15/71	10	Nebraska	Lawton, Okla.	D3-'93	16/16
70	Spears, Marcus	T	6-4	316	9/28/71	9	Northwestern State (La.)	Scotlandville, La.	FA-'97	16/16
35	Stephens, Reggie	CB	5-9	190	2/21/75	3	Rutgers	Shreveport, La.	FA-'02	0*
55	Stills, Gary	LB	6-2	235	7/11/74	4	West Virginia	Trenton, N.J.	D3a-'99	10/0
4	Stryzinski, Dan	P	6-2	203	5/15/65	13	Indiana	Vincennes, Ind.	UFA(Atl)-'01	16/0
76	Tait, John	T	6-6	320	1/26/75	3	Brigham Young	Phoenix, Ariz.	D1-'99	16/16
65	Threats, Jabbar	DE	6-5	268	4/26/75	3	Michigan State	Springfield, Ohio	FA-'01	0*
44	Warfield, Eric	CB	6-0	198	3/3/76	4	Nebraska	Texarkana, Ark.	D7a-'98	16/16
54	Waters, Brian	C	6-3	315	2/18/77	3	North Texas	Waxahachie, Texas	FA-'00	16/8
25	Wesley, Greg	S	6-2	208	3/19/78	3	Arkansas-Pine Bluff	England, Ark.	D3-'00	16/16
30	West, Lyle	S	6-0	215	12/20/76	3	San Jose State	Columbus, Ga.	FA-'02	0*
62	Wiegman, Casey	C	6-2	285	7/20/75	6	Iowa	Parkersburg, Iowa	UFA(Chi)-'01	15/15
60	Willis, Donald	G	6-3	330	7/15/73	5	North Carolina A&T	Goleta, Calif.	FA-'00	14/4
21	Woods, Jerome	S	6-2	207	3/17/73	7	Memphis	Memphis, Tenn.	D1-'96	16/16
67	Wyman, Devin	DT	6-7	330	8/29/73	4	Kentucky State	Lynwood, Calif.	FA-'02	0*

* Allotey inactive for 1 game; J. Andersen last active with Miami in '00; M. Andersen played 16 games with N.Y. Giants in '01; Blaylock inactive for 16 games; Germaine inactive for 16 games; Jackson played 2 games with New England; R. Jones inactive for 2 games; Jordan last active with Detroit in '99; McClellion played 6 games with Washington; Morris missed '01 season because of injury; Morton played 16 games with Detroit; Quinn played 6 games with Jacksonville; Roaf played 7 games with New Orleans; Sands missed '01 season on the Non-Football Injury List; P. Shields last active with Indianapolis in '00; Stephens last active with New York Giants in '00; Threats last active in Jacksonville in '98; West last active with New York Giants in '00; D. Wyman last active with New England in '97.

t- Chiefs traded for Roaf (NO).

Players lost through free agency (4): LB Donnie Edwards (SD; 16 games in '01), K Todd Peterson (Pitt; 16), WR Mikhael Ricks (Det; 16), T Victor Riley (NO; 7).

Also played with Chiefs in '01—WR Derrick Alexander (16 games), DT Tyrone Williams (7).

2002 FIRST-YEAR ROSTER

Name	Pos.	Ht.	Wt.	Birthdate	College	Hometown	How Acq.
Allen, Ian (1)	G	6-4	320	7/22/78	Purdue	Newark, N.J.	FA
Baber, Billy (1)	TE	6-3	258	1/17/79	Virginia	Charlottesville, Va.	D5a
Baggett, Jason	T	6-5	310	12/25/79	Louisiana State	Baytown, Texas	FA
Bingham, T.J.	DE	6-3	259	5/28/77	Ouachita Baptist	Houston, Texas	FA
Blakley, Dwayne	TE	6-4	256	8/10/79	Missouri	St. Joseph, Mo.	FA
Boerigter, Marc (1)	WR	6-3	215	5/4/78	Hastings	Sioux Center, Iowa	FA
Capel, John (1)	WR	5-11	163	11/27/78	Florida	Brooksville, Fla.	FA-'01
Crittendon, Aaron	T	6-4	343	3/27/79	Missouri	St. Joseph, Mo.	FA
Easy, Omar	FB	6-1	244	10/29/77	Penn State	Everett, Mass.	D4
Finley, Clint	S	6-0	205	3/27/77	Nebraska	Cuero, Texas	FA
Freeman, Eddie	DT	6-5	310	1/4/78	Alabama-Birmingham	Mobile, Ala.	D2
Fujita, Scott	LB	6-5	248	4/28/79	California	Ventura, Calif.	D5
Harts, Shaunard (1)	S	5-11	207	8/4/78	Boise State	Pittsburg, Calif.	D7a
Hawkins, Ahmad (1)	CB	5-10	185	12/10/78	Virginia	Hampton, Va.	FA-'01
Hayes, Chad	TE	6-6	258	1/26/79	Maine	Old Town, Maine	FA
Hobbs, Gary	T	6-4	340	5/13/80	Arkansas	Ft. Smith, Ark.	FA
Julien, Jarmar	RB	5-11	235	12/11/79	San Jose State	San Jose, Calif.	FA
Klemic, Dave (1)	WR	5-11	186	6/16/78	Northeastern	Philadelphia, Pa.	FA-'01
Landry, Michael	DE	6-3	266	12/22/78	Southern	Donaldson, La.	FA
Ludwig, Brandon	G-C	6-3	285	4/23/79	California	Modesto, Calif.	FA
Lynch, Shawn	C	6-4	271	7/2/79	Duke	West Palm Beach, Fla.	FA
Moses, J.J. (1)	WR	5-9	178	9/12/79	Iowa State	Waterloo, Iowa	FA-'01
Newson, Tony	LB	6-0	227	9/11/79	Utah State	Las Vegas, Nev.	FA
Rebstock, Pete	WR	5-8	188	8/10/78	Colorado State	Englewood, Colo.	FA
Robertson, Harold	LB	6-2	223	2/13/79	Texas A&M	Dallas, Texas	FA
Robertson, Wes (1)	LB	6-2	229	11/19/78	Rutgers	Camden, N.J.	FA
Rodriguez, Maurice	LB	6-1	237	8/30/78	Fresno State	Visalia, Calif.	D7
Rogers, Kirk	WR	5-11	186	8/22/78	Hardin-Simmons	Olney, Texas	FA
Roth, Josh (1)	FB	6-0	238	3/15/78	Buffalo	Conewango Valley, N.Y.	FA
Sims, Ryan	DT	6-4	311	5/4/80	North Carolina	Spartanburg, S.C.	D1
Tynes, Lawrence (1)	K	6-0	187	5/3/78	Troy State	Greenock, Scotland	FA
Wulfeck, Adam	P	6-0	228	7/26/80	Cincinnati	Ft. Mitchell, Ky.	FA

The term NFL Rookie is defined as a player who is in his first season of professional football and has not been on the roster of another professional football team for any regular-season or postseason games. A Rookie is designated by an "R" on NFL rosters. Players who have been active in another professional football league or players who have NFL experience, including either preseason training camp or being on an Active List or Inactive List, or on Reserve/Injured or Reserve/Physically Unable to Perform for fewer than six regular-season games, are termed NFL First-Year Players. An NFL First-Year Player is designated by a "1" on NFL rosters. Thereafter, a player is credited with an additional year of experience for each season in which he accumulates six games on the Active List or Inactive List, or on Reserve/Injured or Reserve/Physically Unable to Perform.

COACHING STAFF
Head Coach,
Dick Vermeil
Pro Career: Dick Vermeil was named the ninth head coach in Chiefs franchise history on January 12, 2001. Vermeil joins Bill Parcells, Dan Reeves, and Don Shula as the only coaches in NFL history to guide two different teams to the Super Bowl. In 1999, he led St. Louis to a win in Super Bowl XXXIV and guided Philadelphia to Super Bowl XV after the 1980 season. In his third season in St. Louis, he led the Rams to a 13-3 record and their lone Super Bowl victory. Honored as the NFL's coach of the year after both Super Bowl seasons. Entered league as the first special teams coach in NFL history with the L.A. Rams (1969). Career record: 88-87. **Background:** Vermeil played quarterback, and graduated, from San Jose State from 1956-57 after transferring from Napa (Calif.) Junior College. He owns the distinction of being named "Coach of the Year" on four levels: high school, junior college, NCAA Division I, and the NFL. Was head coach at UCLA from 1974-75. He is the only coach to have guided a team to a victory in both the Rose Bowl and the Super Bowl. **Personal:** Born October 30, 1936 in Calistoga, Calif. Vermeil and his wife Carol reside in Kansas City, Mo. They have three children and 11 grandchildren.

ASSISTANT COACHES
Irv Eatman, assistant offensive line; born January 1, 1961, Birmingham, Ala., lives in Lee's Summit, Mo. Defensive end-offensive tackle UCLA 1979-1982. Pro offensive tackle Philadelphia/Baltimore Stars (USFL) 1983-85, Kansas City Chiefs 1986-1990, New York Jets 1991-92, L.A. Rams 1993, Atlanta Falcons 1994, Houston Oilers 1995-96. Pro coach: Green Bay Packers 1999, Pittsburgh Steelers 2000, joined Chiefs in 2001.
Frank Gansz, Jr., special teams; born August 8, 1962, Greenville, S.C., lives in Overland Park, Kan. Defensive back The Citadel 1981-84. No pro playing experience. College coach: Kansas 1987, Pittsburgh 1988-89, Army 1990-91, Houston 1993-97. Pro coach: New York-New Jersey Knights (WLAF) 1992, Oakland Raiders 1998-99, joined Chiefs in 2001.
Peter Giunta, defensive backs; born August 11, 1956, Salem, Mass., lives in Leawood, Kan. Running back-defensive back Northeastern 1975-76. No pro playing experience. College coach: Penn State 1981-83, Brown 1984-87, Lehigh 1988-1990. Pro coach: Philadelphia Eagles 1991-94, N.Y. Jets 1995-96, St. Louis Rams 1997-2000, joined Chiefs in 2001.
Carl Hairston, defensive line; born December 15, 1952, Martinsville, Va., lives in Independence, Mo. Defensive end Maryland-Eastern Shore 1972-75. Pro defensive end Philadelphia Eagles 1976-

1983, Cleveland Browns 1984-89, Phoenix Cardinals 1990. Pro coach: Kansas City Chiefs 1995-96, St. Louis Rams 1997-2000, rejoined Chiefs in 2001.
Jeff Hurd, strength and conditioning; born April 24, 1958, Pomona, Calif., lives in Overland Park, Kan. Attended Fort Hays State. No college or pro playing experience. College coach: Fort Hays State 1984, Delta State 1985, Clemson 1986, Western Michigan 1987-1993, Tulsa 1994. Pro coach: Jacksonville Jaguars 1995-97, joined Chiefs in 1998.
Charlie Joiner, receivers; born October 14, 1947, Many, La., lives in Overland Park, Kan. Wide receiver Grambling State 1965-68. Pro defensive back-wide receiver Houston Oilers 1969-1972, Cincinnati Bengals 1972-75, San Diego Chargers 1976-1986. Inducted into Pro Football Hall of Fame 1996. Pro coach: San Diego Chargers 1987-1991, Buffalo Bills 1992-2000, joined Chiefs in 2001.
Bob Karmelowicz, defensive line; born July 22, 1949, New Britain, Conn., lives in Leawood, Kan. Nose tackle Bridgeport 1968-1971. No pro playing experience. College coach: Arizona State 1975-79, Massachusetts 1980, Texas-El Paso 1981, Illinois 1982-86, Washington State 1987-88, Miami 1989-1991. Pro coach: Cincinnati Bengals 1992-93, Washington Redskins 1994-96, joined Chiefs in 1997.
Billy Long, asst. strength and conditioning coach; born June 23, 1959, Phenix City, Ala., lives in Lee's Summit, Mo. College coach: Alabama State 1981-86, Arkansas-Pine Bluff 1987-1991, Southern 1992-2000. Pro coach: Joined Chiefs in 2001.
Greg Robinson, defensive coordinator; born October 9, 1951, Los Angeles, Calif., lives in Leawood, Kan. Linebacker-tight end Pacific 1973-74. No pro playing experience. College coach: Pacific 1975-76, Cal State-Fullerton 1977-79, North Carolina State 1980-81, UCLA 1982-89. Pro coach: New York Jets 1990-94, Denver Broncos 1995-2000, joined Chiefs in 2001.
Keith Rowen, tight ends; born September 2, 1952, New York, N.Y., lives in Overland Park, Kan. Offensive tackle Stanford 1972-74. No pro playing experience. College coach: Stanford 1974-75, Long Beach State 1977-78, Arizona 1979-1982. Pro coach: Boston/New Orleans Breakers (USFL) 1983-84, Cleveland Browns 1984, Indianapolis Colts 1985-88, New England Patriots 1989, Atlanta Falcons 1990-93, Minnesota Vikings 1994-96, Oakland Raiders 1997-98, joined Chiefs in 1999.
Al Saunders, asst. head coach-offensive coordinator; born February 1, 1947, London, England, lives in Overland Park, Kan. Wide receiver-defensive back San Jose State 1966-68. No pro playing experience. College coach: Southern California 1970-71, Missouri 1972, Utah State 1973-75, California 1976-1981, Tennessee 1982. Pro coach: San Diego Chargers 1983-88 (head coach 1986-88), Kansas City Chiefs 1989-

1998, St. Louis Rams 1999-2000, rejoined Chiefs in 2001.
James Saxon, running backs; born March 23, 1966, Beaufort, S.C., lives in Independence, Mo. Running back American River J.C. (S.C.) 1985, San Jose State 1986-87. Pro running back Kansas City Chiefs 1988-1991, Miami Dolphins 1992-94, Philadelphia Eagles 1995. College coach: Rutgers 1997-98, Menlo College 1999. Pro coach: Buffalo Bills 2000, joined Chiefs in 2001.
Terry Shea, quarterbacks; born June 12, 1946, San Mateo, Calif., lives in Leawood, Kan. Quarterback Oregon 1965-67. No pro playing experience. College coach: Oregon 1968-69; Mt. Hood J.C. (Ore.) 1970-75, Utah State 1976-1981, San Jose State 1984-86, 1990-91 (head coach 1990-91), California 1987-89, Stanford 1992-94, Rutgers 1996-2000 (head coach 1996-2000). Pro coach: British Columbia Lions 1995 (CFL), joined Chiefs in 2001.
Mike Solari, offensive line; born January 16, 1955, Daly City, Calif., lives in Leawood, Kan. Offensive lineman San Diego State 1975-76. No pro playing experience. College coach: Mira Vista (Calif.) J.C. 1977-78, U.S. International 1979, Boise State 1980, Cincinnati 1981-82, Kansas 1983-85, Pittsburgh 1986, Alabama 1990-91. Pro coach: Dallas Cowboys 1987-88, Phoenix Cardinals 1989, San Francisco 49ers 1992-96, joined Chiefs in 1997.
Jason Verduzco, offensive assistant-quality control; born April 3, 1970, Walnut Creek, Calif., lives in Leawood, Kan. Quarterback Illinois 1989-1993. Pro quarterback: British Columbia Lions (CFL) 1993. College coach: Hamilton College (N.Y.) 1994-96, Illinois 1997-99. Pro coach: Washington Redskins 2000, joined Chiefs in 2001.
Joe Vitt, linebackers; born August 23, 1954, Syracuse, N.Y., lives in Kansas City, Mo. Linebacker Towson State 1973-75. No pro playing experience. Pro coach: Baltimore Colts 1979-1981, Seattle Seahawks 1982-1991, L.A. Rams 1992-94, Philadelphia Eagles 1995-98, Green Bay Packers 1999, joined Chiefs in 2000.
Darvin Wallis, defensive assistant-quality control; born February 14, 1949, Ft. Branch, Ind., lives in Overland Park, Kan. Defensive end Arizona 1970-71. No pro playing experience. College coach: Adams State 1976-77, Tulane 1978-79, Mississippi 1980-81. Pro coach: Cleveland Browns 1982-88, joined Chiefs in 1989.
Mike White, director of football administration; born January 4, 1936, Berkeley, Calif., lives in Kansas City, Mo. Wide receiver California 1955-57. No pro playing experience. College coach: California 1958-1963, 1972-77 (head coach 1972-77), Stanford 1964-1971, Illinois 1980-87 (head coach). Pro coach: San Francisco 49ers 1978-79, Los Angeles-Oakland Raiders 1990-96 (head coach 1995-96), St. Louis Rams 1997-99, joined Chiefs in 2001.

**American Football Conference
East Division
Team Colors:** Aqua, Coral, Blue, and
White
**7500 S.W. 30th Street
Davie, Florida 33314
Telephone:** (954) 452-7000

2002 SCHEDULE
PRESEASON
Aug. 12 at Tampa Bay 8:00
Aug. 15 **New Orleans**........................7:00
Aug. 24 at Houston 7:00
Aug. 29 **Chicago** 7:00

REGULAR SEASON
Sept. 8 **Detroit** 1:00
Sept. 15 at Indianapolis 12:00
Sept. 22 **New York Jets** 1:00
Sept. 29 at Kansas City 12:00
Oct. 6 **New England** 1:00
Oct. 13 at Denver.............................6:30
Oct. 20 **Buffalo**................................1:00
Oct. 27 Open Date
Nov. 4 at Green Bay (Mon.)...........8:00
Nov. 10 at New York Jets 8:30
Nov. 17 **Baltimore**...........................1:00
Nov. 24 **San Diego**..........................1:00
Dec. 1 at Buffalo 1:00
Dec. 9 **Chicago** (Mon.)..................9:00
Dec. 15 **Oakland** 1:00
Dec. 21 at Minnesota (Sat.)...........12:30
Dec. 29 at New England 1:00

Stadium: Pro Player Stadium
(opened in 1987)
• **Capacity:** 75,192
2269 Dan Marino Blvd.
Miami, Florida 33056
Playing Surface: Grass (PAT)
Training Camp: Nova University
7500 S.W. 30th Street
Davie, Florida 33314

PRO PLAYER STADIUM

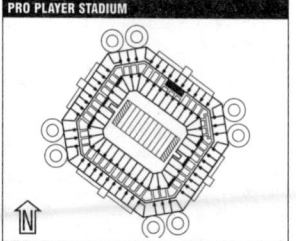

CLUB OFFICIALS
Owner/Chairman of the Board:
H. Wayne Huizenga
President: Eddie J. Jones
Head Coach: Dave Wannstedt
Executive Vice President & Chief
Operating Officer: Bryan Wiedmeier
Senior Vice President-Finance &
Administration: Jill R. Strafaci
Senior Vice President-Football
Operations/Player Personnel:
Rick Spielman
Senior Vice President-Operations:
Bill Galante
Senior Vice President-Media Relations:
Harvey Greene
Senior Vice President-Sales & Marketing:
Jim Ross
Director of Pro Personnel: George Paton
Director of College Scouting:
Ron Labadie
Staff Counsel: Matt Thomas
Senior Director of Community & Alumni
Relations: Fudge Browne
Senior Director of Ticket Operations:
Andy Major
Senior Director of Business Development:
Jim Frevola
Director of Player Programs: Jamie Allen
Director of Media Relations: Neal Gulkis
Director of Publications & Internet:
Scott Stone
Director of Operations: Rhett Ticconi
Director of Information Technology:
Tery Howard
Cheerleader Director: Dorie Grogan
Director of Special Events: Jeff Griffith
Director of Records & Archives:
Kristin Hingston
Head Athletic Trainer: Kevin O'Neill
Equipment Manager: Tony Egues
Video Director: Dave Hack
Team Security Investigator:
Stuart Weinstein

COACHING HISTORY
(350-229-4)
1966-69   George Wilson.............15-39-2
1970-1995 Don Shula 274-147-2
1996-99   Jimmy Johnson...........38-31-0
2000-01   Dave Wannstedt 23-12-0

ATTENDANCE
Home 588,127   Away 520,786
Total 1,108,913
Single-game home record,
75,283 (10/27/96)
Single-season home record, 592,161
(1999)

2002 DRAFT CHOICES
Round	Name	Pos.	College
3	Seth McKinney	C	Texas A&M
4	Randy McMichael	TE	Georgia
5	Omare Lowe	DB	Washington
	Sam Simmons	WR	Northwestern
7	Leonard Henry	RB	East Carolina

2001 TEAM RECORD

PRESEASON (1-4)

Date	Result	Opponent
8/6	L 10-17	vs. St. Louis, at Canton, Ohio
8/13	W 17-14	at Tampa Bay
8/18	L 20-23	San Diego (OT)
8/25	L 12-17	at Green Bay
8/31	L 7-20	Minnesota

REGULAR SEASON (11-5)

Date	Result	Opponent	Att.
9/09	W 31-23	at Tennessee	68,798
9/23	W 18-15	Oakland	73,404
9/30	L 10-42	at St. Louis	66,046
10/07	W 30-10	New England	73,024
10/14	L 17-21	at New York Jets	78,823
10/28	W 24-20	at Seattle	59,108
11/04	W 23-6	Carolina	72,597
11/11	W 27-24	at Indianapolis	57,127
11/18	L 0-24	New York Jets	74,259
11/25	W 34-27	at Buffalo	73,063
12/02	W 21-10	Denver	73,938
12/10	W 41-6	Indianapolis	73,858
12/16	L 0-21	at San Francisco	68,223
12/22	L 13-20	at New England	60,292
12/30	W 21-14	Atlanta	73,619
1/06	W 34-7	Buffalo	73,428

(OT) Overtime

POSTSEASON (0-1)

1/13	L	3-20	Baltimore	72,251

SCORE BY PERIODS

Dolphins	65	110	27	142	0	—	344
Opponents	58	91	86	55	0	—	290

2001 TEAM STATISTICS

	Dolphins	Opp.
Total First Downs	263	283
Rushing	95	97
Passing	154	148
Penalty	14	38
3rd Down: Made/Att	89/215	70/201
3rd Down Pct.	41.4	34.8
4th Down: Made/Att	9/14	6/15
4th Down Pct.	64.3	40.0
Possession Avg.	30:04	29:56
Total Net Yards	4821	4608
Avg. Per Game	301.3	288.0
Total Plays	953	957
Avg. Per Play	5.1	4.8
Net Yards Rushing	1664	1779
Avg. Per Game	104.0	111.2
Total Rushes	473	453
Net Yards Passing	3157	2829
Avg. Per Game	197.3	176.8
Sacked/Yards Lost	27/178	37/230
Gross Yards	3335	3059
Att./Completions	453/275	467/262
Completion Pct.	60.7	56.1
Had Intercepted	19	17
Punts/Average	81/41.0	86/44.1
Net Punting Avg.	81/37.6	86/36.0
Penalties/Yards	107/914	82/623
Fumbles/Ball Lost	26/19	27/11
Touchdowns	41	35
Rushing	14	9
Passing	20	22
Returns	7	4

2001 INDIVIDUAL STATISTICS

PASSING	Att.	Comp.	Yds.	Pct.	TD	Int.	Tkld.	Rate
Fiedler	450	273	3290	60.7	20	19	27/178	80.3
Lucas	3	2	45	66.7	0	0	0/0	109.7
Dolphins	453	275	3335	60.7	20	19	27/178	80.6
Opponents	467	262	3059	56.1	22	17	37/230	76.7

SCORING	TD R	TD P	TD Rt	PAT	FG	Saf	PTS
Mare	0	0	0	39/40	19/21	0	96
L. Smith	6	2	0	0/0	0/0	0	48
Chambers	0	7	0	0/0	0/0	0	42
Fiedler	4	0	0	0/0	0/0	0	24
Minor	2	1	1	0/0	0/0	0	24
McKnight	0	3	0	0/0	0/0	0	20
Gadsden	0	3	0	0/0	0/0	0	18
Konrad	1	1	0	0/0	0/0	0	12
Marion	0	0	2	0/0	0/0	0	12
Weaver	0	2	0	0/0	0/0	0	12
Lucas	1	0	0	0/0	0/0	0	6
Mixon	0	0	1	0/0	0/0	0	6
Ogden	0	1	0	0/0	0/0	0	6
Surtain	0	0	1	0/0	0/0	0	6
J. Taylor	0	0	1	0/0	0/0	0	6
Thomas	0	0	1	0/0	0/0	0	6
Dolphins	14	20	7	39/40	19/21	0	344
Opponents	9	22	4	32/34	16/22	0	290

2-Pt. Conversions: McKnight.
Dolphins 1-1, Opponents 0-1.

RUSHING	Att.	Yds.	Avg.	LG	TD
L. Smith	313	968	3.1	25	6
Fiedler	73	321	4.4	26	4
Minor	59	281	4.8	56t	2
McKnight	6	39	6.5	18	0
J. Johnson	5	22	4.4	9	0
Konrad	5	22	4.4	18t	1
Ward	2	21	10.5	16	0
Lucas	8	6	0.8	3	1
Mare	1	-5	-5.0	-5	0
Chambers	1	-11	-11.0	-11	0
Dolphins	473	1664	3.5	56t	14
Opponents	453	1779	3.9	44	9

RECEIVING	No.	Yds.	Avg.	LG	TD
McKnight	55	684	12.4	40	3
Gadsden	55	674	12.3	61	3
Chambers	48	883	18.4	74t	7
L. Smith	30	234	7.8	65t	2
Minor	29	263	9.1	29	1
Ward	21	209	10.0	20	0
Weaver	18	215	11.9	27	2
Ogden	6	73	12.2	18	1
Konrad	5	52	10.4	17	1
Goodwin	4	27	6.8	9	0
J. Johnson	4	21	5.3	7	0
Dolphins	275	3335	12.1	74t	20
Opponents	262	3059	11.7	80t	22

INTERCEPTIONS	No.	Yds.	Avg.	LG	TD
Marion	5	227	45.4	100t	2
Surtain	3	74	24.7	41	1
Thomas	2	51	25.5	34t	1
Madison	2	0	0.0	0	0
Mixon	1	56	56.0	56t	1
J. Taylor	1	4	4.0	4	0
Freeman	1	0	0.0	0	0
Galyon	1	0	0.0	0	0
Walker	1	0	0.0	0	0
Dolphins	17	412	24.2	100t	5
Opponents	19	254	13.4	63t	3

PUNTING	No.	Yds.	Avg.	In 20	LG
Turk	81	3321	41.0	28	77
Dolphins	81	3321	41.0	28	77
Opponents	86	3789	44.1	12	73

PUNT RETURNS	No.	FC	Yds.	Avg.	LG	TD
Ogden	32	11	377	11.8	48	0
Ward	9	2	88	9.8	18	0
Cousin	1	0	0	0.0	0	0
Madison	1	0	6	6.0	6	0
Dolphins	43	13	471	11.0	48	0
Opponents	30	14	136	4.5	23	0

KICKOFF RETURNS	No.	Yds.	Avg.	LG	TD
Chambers	36	811	22.5	47	0
Marion	17	371	21.8	55	0
Dyer	2	24	12.0	14	0
J. Johnson	1	16	16.0	16	0
E. Perry	1	0	0.0	0	0
Dolphins	57	1222	21.4	55	0
Opponents	59	1189	20.2	50	0

FIELD GOALS	1-19	20-29	30-39	40-49	50+
Mare	1/1	8/8	8/8	2/4	0/0
Dolphins	1/1	8/8	8/8	2/4	0/0
Opponents	0/0	5/6	4/5	6/9	1/2

SACKS	No.
J. Taylor	8.5
Bromell	6.5
Gardener	4.0
T. Bowens	3.0
Thomas	3.0
Cousin	2.0
Mixon	2.0
Greenwood	1.5
D. Bowens	1.0
Freeman	1.0
Galyon	1.0
Rodgers	1.0
Surtain	1.0
Grant	0.5
Haley	0.5
Ogunleye	0.5
Dolphins	37.0
Opponents	27.0

RECORD HOLDERS
INDIVIDUAL RECORDS—CAREER

Category	Name	Performance
Rushing (Yds.)	Larry Csonka, 1968-1974, 1979	6,737
Passing (Yds.)	Dan Marino, 1983-1999	*61,361
Passing (TDs)	Dan Marino, 1983-1999	*420
Receiving (No.)	Mark Clayton, 1983-1992	550
Receiving (Yds.)	Mark Duper, 1982-1992	8,869
Interceptions	Jake Scott, 1970-75	35
Punting (Avg.)	John Kidd, 1994-97	44.2
Punt Return (Avg.)	Jeff Ogden, 2000-01	13.7
Kickoff Return (Avg.)	Mercury Morris, 1969-1975	26.5
Field Goals	Pete Stoyanovich, 1989-1995	176
Touchdowns (Tot.)	Mark Clayton, 1983-1992	82
Points	Garo Yepremian, 1970-78	830

INDIVIDUAL RECORDS—SINGLE SEASON

Category	Name	Performance
Rushing (Yds.)	Delvin Williams, 1978	1,258
Passing (Yds.)	Dan Marino, 1984	*5,084
Passing (TDs)	Dan Marino, 1984	*48
Receiving (No.)	O.J. McDuffie, 1998	90
Receiving (Yds.)	Mark Clayton, 1984	1,389
Interceptions	Dick Westmoreland, 1967	10
Punting (Avg.)	John Kidd, 1996	46.3
Punt Return (Avg.)	Jeff Ogden, 2000	17.0
Kickoff Return (Avg.)	Duriel Harris, 1976	32.9
Field Goals	Olindo Mare, 1999	*39
Touchdowns (Tot.)	Mark Clayton, 1984	18
Points	Olindo Mare, 1999	144

INDIVIDUAL RECORDS—SINGLE GAME

Category	Name	Performance
Rushing (Yds.)	Mercury Morris, 9-30-73	197
Passing (Yds.)	Dan Marino, 10-23-88	521
Passing (TDs)	Bob Griese, 11-24-77	6
	Dan Marino, 9-21-86	6
Receiving (No.)	Jim Jensen, 11-6-88	12
Receiving (Yds.)	Mark Duper, 11-10-85	217
Interceptions	Dick Anderson, 12-3-73	*4
Field Goals	Olindo Mare, 10-17-99	6
Touchdowns (Tot.)	Paul Warfield, 12-15-73	4
	Mark Ingram, 11-27-94	4
Points	Paul Warfield, 12-15-73	24
	Mark Ingram, 11-27-94	24

*NFL Record

2002 VETERAN ROSTER

No.	Name	Pos.	Ht.	Wt.	Birthdate	NFL Exp.	College	Hometown	How Acq.	'01 Games/ Starts
65	Andrew, Troy	C	6-4	297	12/12/77	2	Duke	Klein, Texas	FA-'01	8/0
83	Baker, Robert	WR	5-11	198	5/14/76	2	Auburn	Gainesville, Fla.	FA-'01	0*
35	Barnes, Marlon	RB	5-10	211	3/13/76	2	Colorado	Millington, Tenn.	FA-'02	0*
96	Bowens, David	DE	6-3	260	7/3/77	4	Western Illinois	Orchard Lake, Mich.	FA-'01	9/0
95	Bowens, Tim	DT	6-4	320	2/7/73	9	Mississippi	Okolona, Miss.	D1-'94	15/15
62	Bundren, Jim	G	6-3	303	10/6/74	4	Clemson	Wilmington, Del.	FA-'02	0*
64	Cesario, Anthony	G	6-5	305	7/19/76	3	Colorado State	Pueblo, Colo.	FA-'01	0*
84	Chambers, Chris	WR	5-11	210	8/12/78	2	Wisconsin	Bedford, Ohio	D2-'01	16/7
64	Chester, Larry	DT	6-2	310	10/17/75	5	Temple	Hammond, La.	UFA(Car)-'02	11/5*
63	Dixon, Mark	G	6-4	300	11/26/70	5	Virginia	Jamestown, N.C.	FA-'98	10/10
45	Donaldson, Cedric	CB	5-9	180	2/12/78	2	Louisiana State	Jackson, Miss.	FA-'02	0*
46	Draper, Shawn	TE	6-3	280	7/5/79	2	Alabama	Huntsville, Ala.	D5-'01	0*
33	Dyer, Deon	FB	5-11	255	10/2/77	3	North Carolina	Tidewater, Va.	D4-'00	16/0
47	Edwards, Robert	RB	5-11	220	10/2/74	4	Georgia	Tennille, Ga.	FA-'02	0*
9	Fiedler, Jay	QB	6-2	225	12/29/71	7	Dartmouth	Oceanside, N.Y.	UFA(Jax)-'00	16/16
21	Fletcher, Jamar	CB	5-9	184	8/28/79	2	Wisconsin	Hazelwood, Mo.	D1-'01	14/2
27	Freeman, Arturo	S	6-0	196	10/27/76	3	South Carolina	Orangeburg, S.C.	D5-'00	16/4
86	Gadsden, Oronde	WR	6-2	215	8/20/71	5	Winston-Salem State	Charleston, S.C.	FA-'98	14/14
58	Galyon, Scot	LB	6-2	238	3/23/74	7	Tennessee	Seymour, Tenn.	UFA(NYG)-'00	16/2
42	Gamble, Trent	S	5-9	195	7/24/77	3	Wyoming	Parker, Colo.	FA-'00	1/0
92	Gardener, Daryl	DE	6-6	310	2/25/73	7	Baylor	Lawton, Okla.	D1-'96	8/8
97	Grant, Ernest	DT	6-5	315	5/17/76	3	Arkansas-Pine Bluff	Atlanta, Ga.	D6-'00	11/3
79	Green, Cornell	T	6-6	320	8/25/76	3	Central Florida	St. Petersburg, Fla.	FA-'02	0*
40	Green, Ray	CB	6-3	187	3/22/77	3	South Carolina	Charleston, S.C.	FA-'01	4/0
52	Greenwood, Morlon	LB	6-0	242	7/17/78	2	Syracuse	Freeport, N.Y.	D3b-'01	14/12
94	Haley, Jermaine	DT	6-4	305	2/23/73	3	Butte College	Hanford, Calif.	D7a-'99	12/5
51	Hendricks, Tommy	LB	6-2	233	10/23/78	3	Michigan	Houston, Texas	FA-'00	16/1
16	Johnson, Albert	WR	5-9	190	11/11/77	2	Southern Methodist	Missouri City, Texas	FA-'01	0*
44	Konrad, Rob	FB	6-3	255	11/12/76	4	Syracuse	Danvers, Mass.	D2b-'99	12/9
6	Lucas, Ray	QB	6-3	225	8/6/72	5	Rutgers	Harrison, N.J.	UFA(NYJ)-'01	10/0
29	Madison, Sam	CB	5-11	185	4/23/74	6	Louisville	Monticello, Fla.	D2-'97	13/13
10	Mare, Olindo	K	5-10	195	6/6/73	6	Syracuse	Cooper City, Fla.	FA-'97	16/0
31	Marion, Brock	S	5-11	205	6/11/70	10	Nevada	Bakersfield, Calif.	UFA(Dall)-'98	15/15
85	Mayes, Alonzo	TE	6-4	260	6/4/75	5	Oklahoma State	Oklahoma City, Okla.	T(Chi)-'00	0*
11	McDonald, Darnell	WR	6-3	199	5/26/78	2	Kansas State	Fairfax, Va.	FA-'02	0*
43	McGarrahan, Scott	S	6-1	200	2/12/74	5	New Mexico	Arlington, Texas	FA-'01	16/0
80	McKnight, James	WR	6-1	198	6/17/72	9	Liberty	Apopka, Fla.	UFA(Dall)-'01	16/15
8	McNown, Cade	QB	6-1	210	1/12/77	4	UCLA	West Linn, Ore.	T(Chi)-'01	0*
28	Minor, Travis	RB	5-10	201	6/30/79	2	Florida State	Baton Rouge, La.	D3a-'01	16/0
57	Moore, Corey	LB	5-11	225	3/20/77	2	Virginia Tech	Brownsville, Tenn.	FA-'01	1/0
66	Nails, Jamie	G	6-6	360	6/3/75	5	Florida A&M	Baxley, Ga.	FA-'02	0*
88	Ogden, Jeff	WR	6-0	187	2/22/75	6	Eastern Washington	Snohomish, Wash.	T(Dall)-'00	16/0
90	Ogunleye, Adewale	DE	6-4	270	8/9/77	3	Indiana	Staten Island, N.Y.	FA-'00	7/0
89	Perry, Ed	TE	6-4	270	9/1/74	6	James Madison	Richmond, Va.	D6d-'97	16/0
75	Perry, Todd	G	6-5	305	11/28/70	10	Kentucky	Elizabethtown, Ky.	UFA(Chi)-'01	16/16
59	Rodgers, Derrick	LB	6-1	235	10/14/71	6	Arizona State	New Orleans, La.	D3b-'97	14/14
3	Royals, Mark	P	6-5	215	6/22/65	14	Appalachian State	Mathews, Va.	FA-'02	16/0*
61	Ruddy, Tim	C	6-3	300	4/27/72	9	Notre Dame	Dunmore, Pa.	D2b-'94	15/15
56	Russell, Twan	LB	6-1	220	4/25/74	6	Miami	Ft. Lauderdale, Fla.	FA-'00	16/2
14	Sanford, Sulecio	WR	5-10	190	3/23/76	2	Middle Tennessee State	Milledgeville, Ga.	FA-'02	0*
72	Searcy, Leon	G	6-4	320	12/21/69	11	Miami	Orlando, Fla.	FA-'02	0*
20	Shields, Scott	S	6-4	229	3/29/76	3	Weber State	San Diego, Calif.	FA-'02	0*
74	Smith, Brent	T	6-5	315	11/21/73	6	Mississippi State	Pontotoc, Miss.	D3d-'97	0*
76	Spriggs, Marcus	T	6-3	315	5/30/74	6	Houston	Jackson, Miss.	UFA(Buff)-'01	1/1
23	Surtain, Patrick	CB	5-11	192	6/19/76	5	Southern Mississippi	New Orleans, La.	D2a-'98	16/16
98	Taylor, Henry	DT	6-2	295	11/29/75	4	South Carolina	Barnwell, S.C.	FA-'01	3/0
99	Taylor, Jason	DE	6-6	260	9/1/74	6	Akron	Woodland Hills, Pa.	D3a-'97	16/16
54	Thomas, Zach	LB	5-11	235	9/1/73	7	Texas Tech	Pampa, Texas	D5c-'96	15/15
71	Wade, Todd	T	6-8	325	10/30/76	3	Mississippi	Jackson, Miss.	D2-'00	15/15
73	Wallace, Al	DE	6-5	260	3/25/74	4	Maryland	Delray Beach, Fla.	FA-'02	0*
87	Ward, Dedric	WR	5-9	190	9/29/74	6	Northern Iowa	Cedar Rapids, Iowa	UFA(NYJ)-'01	13/1
82	Weaver, Jed	TE	6-4	262	8/11/76	4	Oregon	Redmond, Ore.	W(Phil)-'00	16/7
34 t-	Williams, Ricky	RB	5-10	230	5/21/77	4	Texas	San Diego, Calif.	T(NO)-'02	16/16*
22	Wooden, Shawn	S	5-11	205	10/23/73	7	Notre Dame	Abington, Pa.	FA-'01	13/0

* Baker last active with Miami in '01 postseason; Barnes last active with Chicago in '00; Bundren last active with Cleveland in '00; Cesario inactive for 1 game; Chester played 11 games with Carolina; Donaldson last active with Chicago in '00; Draper inactive for 16 games; R. Edwards last active with New England in '98; C. Green inactive for 9 games with N.Y. Jets; Johnson missed '01 season because of injury; Mayes missed '01 season because of injury; McDonald last active with Tampa Bay in '99; Nails last active with Buffalo in '00; Royals played 16 games with Tampa Bay; Sanford missed '00 season because of injury with Chicago; Searcy missed '01 season because of injury with Baltimore; Shields last active with Pittsburgh in '00; Smith missed '01 season because of injury; Wallace last active wth Philadelphia in '98; Williams played 16 games with New Orleans.

t- Dolphins traded for Williams (NO).

Players lost through free agency (7): DE Lorenzo Bromell (Minn; 16 games with '01), CB Terry Cousin (Car; 16), T Spencer Folau (NO; 16), DE Kenny Mixon (Minn; 16), RB Lamar Smith (Car; 16), P Matt Turk (NYJ; 16), S Brian Walker (Det; 13).

Also played with Dolphins in '01—TE Hunter Goodwin (16), G Heath Irwin (16), RB J.J. Johnson (10), CB Ben Kelly (2), T Harry Swayne (13).

2002 FIRST-YEAR ROSTER

Name	Pos.	Ht.	Wt.	Birthdate	College	Hometown	How Acq.
Brown, Delvin (1)	CB	6-0	205	9/17/79	Miami	Miami, Fla.	FA
Daniels, Ronney (1)	WR	6-1	210	9/17/76	Auburn	Lake Wales, Fla.	FA
Getherall, Joey (1)	WR	5-7	170	11/7/78	Notre Dame	Hacienda Heights, Calif.	FA
Henry, Leonard	RB	6-1	206	1/5/78	East Carolina	Clinton, N.C.	D7
Hooks, Margin (1)	WR	5-11	190	2/10/78	Brigham Young	Waco, Texas	FA
Jerman, Greg	T	6-5	296	1/24/79	Baylor	El Paso, Texas	FA
Kalapinski, Matt (1)	FB	6-1	227	9/8/79	Maryland	Marshfield, Mass.	FA
Kelly, Rod (1)	DE	6-5	260	7/5/79	Northeastern State (Okla.)	Houston, Texas	FA
Kustok, Zak	QB	6-1	213	2/24/79	Northwestern	Orland Park, Ill.	FA
Lethridge, Zebbie (1)	CB	6-0	202	1/31/75	Texas Tech	Lubbock, Texas	FA
Levcik, Tim	QB	6-6	234	4/27/80	Robert Morris	Ford Cliff, Pa.	FA
Lowe, Omare	CB	6-1	196	4/20/78	Washington	Maple Valley, Wash.	D5a
McKinney, Seth	CB	6-3	300	6/12/79	Texas A&M	Austin, Texas	D3
McMichael, Randy	TE	6-3	247	6/28/79	Georgia	Fort Valley, Ga.	D4
Mitchell, Corey	T	6-4	310	5/15/79	Massachusetts	Utica, N.Y.	FA
Pisetsky, Vitaly (1)	K	5-10	219	6/28/79	Wisconsin	New York, N.Y.	FA
Pitts, Otis (1)	DT	6-0	307	4/27/76	Louisiana Tech	Boosier City, La.	FA
Rollins, Kevin (1)	LB	6-1	240	2/1/78	Toledo	Twinsburg, Ohio	FA
Romero, Dario (1)	DT	6-3	305	4/13/78	Eastern Washington	Spokane, Wash.	FA
Roussel, Casey	P	6-1	219	10/28/79	Tulane	Paulina, La.	FA
Seaverns, Justin	LB	6-1	227	7/2/80	Appalachian State	Cartersville, Ga.	FA
Simmons, Sam	WR	5-9	200	11/25/79	Northwestern	Kansas City, Kan.	D5b
Symonette, Joshua (1)	LB	5-10	180	5/8/78	Tennessee Tech	Stone Mountain, Ga.	FA
Terry, Shawn	WR	6-1	176	1/26/79	West Virginia	Homestead, Fla.	FA
Wadley, Shannon	LB	6-1	228	12/21/76	South Carolina	Swainsboro, Ga.	FA
Westbrooks, Jerry (1)	RB	6-2	230	8/27/77	Ohio State	Boca Raton, Fla.	FA

The term NFL Rookie is defined as a player who is in his first season of professional football and has not been on the roster of another professional football team for any regular-season or postseason games. A Rookie is designated by an "R" on NFL rosters. Players who have been active in another professional football league or players who have NFL experience, including either preseason training camp or being on an Active List or Inactive List, or on Reserve/Injured or Reserve/Physically Unable to Perform for fewer than six regular-season games, are termed NFL First-Year Players. An NFL First-Year Player is designated by a "1" on NFL rosters. Thereafter, a player is credited with an additional year of experience for each season in which he accumulates six games on the Active List or Inactive List, or on Reserve/Injured or Reserve/Physically Unable to Perform.

COACHING STAFF

Head Coach,
Dave Wannstedt

Pro Career: Was named the fourth head coach in Miami history on January 16, 2000. Last year, Wannstedt led the Dolphins to their second consecutive 11-5 record while reaching the postseason for a NFL-high fifth straight year. The team's 22-10 regular-season mark under Wannstedt is the best by the Dolphins in consecutive seasons since 1984-85. In 2000, Wannstedt guided the Dolphins to a regular-season record of 11-5 and the team's first AFC East title since 1994. Led the Chicago Bears to a 41-57 record in six seasons (1993-98) as head coach. Served as the Dolphins' assistant head coach in 1999. Began his NFL coaching career as linebackers coach with the Dolphins in 1989. Spent seven weeks in that post during the offseason before joining Jimmy Johnson in Dallas as the Cowboys' defensive coordinator prior to the 1989 season. In 1992 the Cowboys led the league in total defense as they went on to capture the first of two straight Super Bowl titles. Named Bears head coach in 1993, in 1994 Wannstedt was named NFC coach of the year as Chicago went 9-7 and won its first playoff game since 1990. Career record: 64-69.

Background: Wannstedt coached collegiately at Pittsburgh (1975-78), Oklahoma State (1979-1982), Southern California (1983-85), and Miami (1986-88). Wannstedt lettered three seasons (1971-73) as an offensive lineman at Pittsburgh. Wannstedt was selected by Green Bay in the fifteenth round of the 1974 NFL Draft. He spent the 1974 season on the Packers' injured reserve list with a neck injury.

Personal: Wannstedt was born in Pittsburgh, on May 21, 1952. He and his wife, Jan, have two daughters, Keri and Jami.

ASSISTANT COACHES

Keith Armstrong, special teams; born December 15, 1963, Trenton, N.J., lives in Miami. Running back-defensive back Temple 1983-86. No pro playing experience. College coach: Temple 1986, Miami 1987-88, Oklahoma State 1990-92, Notre Dame 1993. Pro coach: Atlanta Falcons 1994-96, Chicago Bears 1997-2000, joined Dolphins in 2001.

Jim Bates, defensive coordinator; born May 31, 1946, Pontiac, Mich., lives in Miami. Linebacker Tennessee 1964-67. No pro playing experience. College coach: Tennessee 1968, Southern Mississippi 1972, Villanova 1973-74, Kansas State 1975-76, West Virginia 1977, Texas Tech 1978-1983, Tennessee 1989, Florida 1990. Pro coach: San Antonio Gunslingers (USFL) 1984-85 (head coach 1985), Arizona Outlaws (USFL) 1986, Detroit Drive (AFL) 1988, Cleveland Browns 1991-93, 1995, Atlanta Falcons

1994, Dallas Cowboys 1996-99, joined Dolphins in 2000.

Doug Blevins, kicking; born August 3, 1963, Abingdon, Va., lives in Vero Beach, Fla. No college or pro playing experience. College coach: Tennessee 1982-83, Emory & Henry College 1984-85, East Tennessee State 1986-87. Pro coach: World League kicking coordinator 1995-97, joined Dolphins in 1997.

Clarence Brooks, defensive line; born May 20, 1951, New York, N.Y., lives in Miami. Guard Massachusetts 1970-73. No pro playing experience. College coach: Massachusetts 1976-1980, Syracuse 1981-89, Arizona 1990-92. Pro coach: Chicago Bears 1993-98, Cleveland Browns 1999, joined Dolphins in 2000.

Joel Collier, running backs; born December 25, 1963, Buffalo, lives in Plantation, Fla. Linebacker Northern Colorado 1984-87. No pro playing experience. College coach: Syracuse 1988-89. Pro coach: Tampa Bay Buccaneers 1990, New England Patriots 1991-93, joined Dolphins in 1994.

Robert Ford, wide receivers; born June 21, 1951, Belton, Texas, lives in Pembroke Pines, Fla. Wide receiver Houston 1970-72. No pro playing experience. College coach: Western Illinois 1974-76, New Mexico 1977-79, Oregon State 1980-1981, Mississippi State 1982-83, Kansas 1986, Texas Tech 1987-88, Texas A&M 1989-1990. Pro coach: Houston Gamblers (USFL) 1985, Dallas Cowboys 1991-97, joined Dolphins in 1998.

John Gamble, strength and conditioning; born June 26, 1957, Richmond, Va., lives in Weston, Fla. No pro playing experience. College coach: Hampton Institute 1975-78. No pro playing experience. College coach: Virginia 1982-1993. Pro coach: Joined Dolphins in 1994.

Judd Garrett, offensive quality control; born June 25, 1967, Abington, Pa., lives in Miami. Running back Princeton 1987-89. Pro running back London Monarchs (WLAF) 1991-92, Dallas Cowboys 1993, Las Vegas Posse (CFL) 1994, San Antonio Texans (CFL) 1995. College coach: Princeton 1990. Pro coach: New Orleans Saints 1997-99, joined Dolphins in 2000.

Pat Jones, tight ends; born November 4, 1947, Memphis, Tenn., lives in Ft. Lauderdale, Fla. Nose guard Arkansas Tech 1965, linebacker-nose guard Arkansas 1966-67. No pro playing experience. College coach: Arkansas 1974-75, Southern Methodist 1976-77, Pittsburgh 1978, Oklahoma State 1979-1994 (head coach 1984-1994). Pro coach: Joined Dolphins in 1996.

Bill Lewis, defensive nickel package; born August 5, 1941, Bristol, Pa., lives in Ft. Lauderdale, Fla. Quarterback East Stroudsburg State 1959-1962. No pro playing experience. College coach: East Stroudsburg State 1963-65, Pittsburgh

1966-68, Wake Forest 1969-1970, Georgia Tech 1971-72, 1992-94 (head coach), Arkansas 1973-76, Wyoming 1977-79, Georgia 1980-88, East Carolina 1989-1991 (head coach). Pro coach: Joined Dolphins in 1996.

Robert Nunn, asst. defensive line-defensive quality control; born June 10, 1965, Apache, Okla., lives in Miami. Linebacker Oklahoma State 1983-84 and 1986-87. No pro playing experience. College coach: Northeastern Oklahoma 1988, Tennessee 1989-1990, Georgia Military College 1991-99 (head coach 1992-99). Pro coach: Joined Dolphins in 2000.

Mel Phillips, secondary; born January 6, 1942, Shelby, N.C., lives in Miami Lakes, Fla. Defensive back-running back North Carolina A&T 1964-65. Pro defensive back San Francisco 49ers 1966-1977. Pro coach: Detroit Lions 1980-84, joined Dolphins in 1985.

Brad Roll, asst. strength and conditioning; born July 4, 1958, Houston, lives in Ft. Lauderdale, Fla. Center Blinn (Tex.) J.C. 1976-77, Stephen F. Austin 1978-79. No pro playing experience. College coach: Stephen F. Austin 1980, Southwestern Louisiana 1981-86, Kansas 1987-88, Miami 1989-1992. Pro coach: Tampa Bay Buccaneers 1993-95, joined Dolphins in 1996.

Bob Sanders, linebackers; born December 5, 1953, Jacksonville, N.C., lives in Miami. Linebacker Davidson College 1973-75. No pro playing experience. College coach: Georgia Tech 1978, East Carolina 1980-82, Richmond 1983-84, Duke 1985-89, Florida 1990-2000. Pro coach: Joined Dolphins in 2001.

Mike Shula, quarterbacks; born June 3, 1965, Baltimore, lives in Miami. Quarterback Alabama 1983-86. No pro playing experience. Pro coach: Tampa Bay Buccaneers 1988-1990, 1996-99, Miami Dolphins 1991-92, Chicago Bears 1993-95, rejoined Dolphins in 2000.

Norv Turner, asst. head coach-offensive coordinator; born May 17, 1952, LeJeune, N.C., lives in Miami. Quarterback Oregon 1971-74. No pro playing experience. College coach: Oregon 1975, Southern California 1976-1984. Pro coach: Los Angeles Rams 1985-1990, Dallas 1991-93, Washington 1994-2000 (head coach), San Diego Chargers 2001, joined Dolphins in 2002.

Tony Wise, offensive line; born December 28, 1951, Albany, N.Y., lives in Miami. Offensive lineman Ithaca College 1971-72. No pro playing experience. College coach: Albany State 1973, Bridgeport 1974, Central Connecticut State 1975, Washington State 1976, Pittsburgh 1977-78, Oklahoma State 1979-1983, Syracuse 1984, Miami 1985-88. Pro coach: Dallas Cowboys 1989-1992, Chicago Bears 1993-98, Carolina Panthers 1999-2000, joined Dolphins in 2001.

NEW ENGLAND PATRIOTS

**American Football Conference
East Division
Team Colors:** Blue, Red, Silver, and White
**CMGI Field
One Patriot Place
Foxboro, Massachusetts 02035
Telephone:** (508) 543-8200

2002 SCHEDULE
PRESEASON
Aug. 10 at New York Giants 8:00
Aug. 17 **Philadelphia** 8:00
Aug. 23 **Carolina**............................8:00
Aug. 29 at Washington 8:00

REGULAR SEASON
Sept. 9 **Pittsburgh** (Mon.) 9:00
Sept. 15 at New York Jets 1:00
Sept. 22 **Kansas City** 1:00
Sept. 29 at San Diego 1:15
Oct. 6 at Miami............................1:00
Oct. 13 **Green Bay**..........................1:00
Oct. 20 Open Date
Oct. 27 **Denver**..............................4:15
Nov. 3 at Buffalo 1:00
Nov. 10 at Chicago (Champaign, Ill.) .3:15
Nov. 17 at Oakland........................5:30
Nov. 24 **Minnesota** 1:00
Nov. 28 at Detroit (Thurs.).............12:30
Dec. 8 **Buffalo**.............................1:00
Dec. 16 at Tennessee (Mon.)...........8:00
Dec. 22 **New York Jets** 8:30
Dec. 29 **Miami**...............................1:00

Stadium: CMGI Field (opened in 2002)
 •**Capacity:** 68,000
  One Patriot Place
  Foxboro, Massachusetts 02035
Playing Surface: Grass
Training Camp: Bryant College
           Smithfield, Rhode Island
           02917

CMGI FIELD

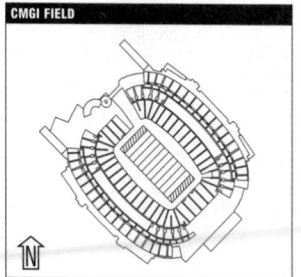

CLUB OFFICIALS
Owner & Chairman: Robert K. Kraft
Vice Chairman: Jonathan A. Kraft
Senior Vice President & Chief Operating
 Officer: Andrew Wasynczuk
Vice President of Corporate Marketing
 and Broadcast Sales: Daniel A. Kraft
Vice President-Finance:
 James Hausmann
Vice President of Corporate and
 Community Affairs:
 Meg Vaillancourt
Vice President of Marketing & Special
 Events: Lou Imbriano
Director of Legal & Business Affairs:
 Jack Mula
Director of Player Personnel: Scott Pioli
Assistant Director of Pro Scouting:
 Andre Tippett
Director of Operations: Chris Caminiti
Director of Media Relations:
 Stacey James
Director of Finance: Jim Nolan
Director of Ticketing: MaryRuth Hughey
General Manager of CMGI Field:
 Dan Murphy
Director of Stadium Operations:
 Charles London
Head Trainer: Jim Whalen
Equipment Manager: Don Brocher
Video Director: Jimmy Dee

COACHING HISTORY
**Boston 1960-1970
(301-338-9)**

1960-61	Lou Saban*	7-12-0
1961-68	Mike Holovak	53-47-9
1969-1970	Clive Rush**	5-16-0
1970-72	John Mazur***	9-21-0
1972	Phil Bengtson	1-4-0
1973-78	Chuck Fairbanks****	46-41-0
1978	Hank Bullough-Ron Erhardt#	0-1-0
1979-1981	Ron Erhardt	21-27-0
1981-84	Ron Meyer##	18-16-0
1984-89	Raymond Berry	51-41-0
1990	Rod Rust	1-15-0
1991-92	Dick MacPherson	8-24-0
1993-96	Bill Parcells	34-34-0
1997-99	Pete Carroll	28-23-0
2000-01	Bill Belichick	19-16-0

  *Released after five games in 1961
 **Released after seven games in 1970
***Resigned after nine games in 1972
****Suspended for final regular-season game in 1978
 #Co-coaches
 ##Released after eight games in 1984

ATTENDANCE
Home 477,375   Away 487,916
Total 965,291
Single-game home record,
61,457 (12/5/71)
Single-season home record, 482,572
(1986)

2002 DRAFT CHOICES
Round	Name	Pos.	College
1	Daniel Graham	TE	Colorado
2	Deion Branch	WR	Louisville
4	Rohan Davey	QB	Louisiana State
	Jarvis Green	DE	Louisiana State
7	Antwoine Womack	RB	Virginia
	David Givens	WR	Notre Dame

2001 TEAM RECORD
PRESEASON (3-1)

Date	Result	Opponent
8/10	W 14-0	New York Giants
8/18	W 23-8	at Carolina
8/25	L 3-20	at Tampa Bay
8/30	W 33-13	Washington

REGULAR SEASON (11-5)

Date	Result	Opponent	Att.
9/09	L 17-23	at Cincinnati	51,521
9/23	L 3-10	New York Jets	60,292
9/30	W 44-13	Indianapolis	60,292
10/07	L 10-30	at Miami	73,024
10/14	W 29-26	San Diego(OT)	60,292
10/21	W 38-17	at Indianapolis	56,022
10/28	L 20-31	at Denver	74,750
11/04	W 24-10	at Atlanta	45,572
11/11	W 21-11	Buffalo	60,292
11/18	L 17-24	St. Louis	60,292
11/25	W 34-17	New Orleans	60,292
12/02	W 17-16	at New York Jets	78,712
12/09	W 27-16	Cleveland	60,292
12/16	W 12-9	at Buffalo(OT)	45,527
12/22	W 20-13	Miami	60,292
1/06	W 38-6	at Carolina	71,907

(OT) Overtime

POSTSEASON (3-0)

Date	Result	Opponent	Att.
1/19	W 16-13	Oakland (OT)	60,292
1/27	W 24-17	at Pittsburgh	64,704
2/3	W 20-17	vs. St. Louis, at New Orleans	72,922

SCORE BY PERIODS

Patriots	74	133	58	100	6	— 371
Opponents	54	51	94	73	0	— 272

2001 TEAM STATISTICS

	Patriots	Opp.
Total First Downs	292	303
Rushing	101	99
Passing	163	171
Penalty	28	33
3rd Down: Made/Att	91/221	80/215
3rd Down Pct.	41.2	37.2
4th Down: Made/Att	7/17	5/15
4th Down Pct.	41.2	33.3
Possession Avg.	30:48	29:12
Total Net Yards	4882	5352
Avg. Per Game	305.1	334.5
Total Plays	1001	1016
Avg. Per Play	4.9	5.3
Net Yards Rushing	1793	1855
Avg. Per Game	112.1	115.9
Total Rushes	473	429
Net Yards Passing	3089	3497
Avg. Per Game	193.1	218.6
acked/Yards Lost	46/237	41/234
Gross Yards	3326	3731
Att./Completions	482/306	546/299
Completion Pct.	63.5	54.8
Had Intercepted	15	22
Punts/Average	74/41.1	73/39.5
Net Punting Avg.	74/38.1	73/31.6
Penalties/Yards	92/802	93/839
Fumbles/Ball Lost	29/13	23/13
Touchdowns	43	26
Rushing	15	7
Passing	21	15
Returns	7	4

2001 INDIVIDUAL STATISTICS

PASSING

	Att.	Comp.	Yds.	Pct.	TD	Int.	Tkld.	Rate
Brady	413	264	2843	63.9	18	12	41/216	86.5
Bledsoe	66	40	400	60.6	2	2	5/21	75.3
Patten	2	1	60	50.0	1	1	0/0	95.8
Faulk	1	1	23	100.0	0	0	0/0	118.8
Patriots	482	306	3326	63.5	21	15	46/237	85.3
Opponents	546	299	3731	54.8	15	22	41/234	68.6

SCORING

	TD R	TD P	TD Rt	PAT	FG	Saf	PTS
Vinatieri	0	0	0	41/42	24/30	0	113
A. Smith	12	1	0	0/0	0/0	0	78
Brown	0	5	2	0/0	0/0	0	42
Patten	1	4	0	0/0	0/0	0	30
Wiggins	0	4	0	0/0	0/0	0	24
M. Edwards	1	2	0	0/0	0/0	0	18
Faulk	1	2	0	0/0	0/0	0	18
Law	0	0	2	0/0	0/0	0	12
O. Smith	0	0	2	0/0	0/0	0	12
Buckley	0	0	1	0/0	0/0	0	6
Glenn	0	1	0	0/0	0/0	0	6
C. Johnson	0	1	0	0/0	0/0	0	6
Pass	0	1	0	0/0	0/0	0	6
Patriots	15	21	7	41/42	24/30	0	371
Opponents	7	15	4	22/22	30/41	0	272

2-Pt. Conversions: None.
Patriots 0-1, Opponents 2-4.

RUSHING

	Att.	Yds.	Avg.	LG	TD
A. Smith	287	1157	4.0	44	12
Faulk	41	169	4.1	24	1
M. Edwards	51	141	2.8	14	1
Redmond	35	119	3.4	16	0
Brown	11	91	8.3	31	0
Patten	5	67	13.4	29t	1
Brady	36	43	1.2	12	0
Bledsoe	5	18	3.6	8	0
Pass	1	7	7.0	7	0
L. Johnson	1	-19	-19.0	-19	0
Patriots	473	1793	3.8	44	15
Opponents	429	1855	4.3	58	7

RECEIVING

	No.	Yds.	Avg.	LG	TD
Brown	101	1199	11.9	60t	5
Patten	51	749	14.7	91t	4
Faulk	30	189	6.3	28	2
M. Edwards	25	166	6.6	17	2
A. Smith	19	192	10.1	41t	1
Glenn	14	204	14.6	23	1
Wiggins	14	133	9.5	31	4
C. Johnson	14	111	7.9	24t	1
Redmond	13	132	10.2	17	0
Pass	6	66	11.0	23t	1
Rutledge	5	35	7.0	9	0
Small	4	29	7.3	11	0
Emanuel	4	25	6.3	16	0
Coleman	2	50	25.0	46	0
Jackson	2	16	8.0	12	0
Brady	1	23	23.0	23	0
Cox	1	7	7.0	7	0
Patriots	306	3326	10.9	91t	21
Opponents	299	3731	12.5	68	15

PUNTING

	No.	Yds.	Avg.	In 20	LG
Walter	49	1964	40.1	24	58
L. Johnson	24	1045	43.5	3	76
Vinatieri	1	33	33.0	1	33
Patriots	74	3042	41.1	28	76
Opponents	73	2885	39.5	18	61

INTERCEPTIONS

	No.	Yds.	Avg.	LG	TD
O. Smith	5	181	36.2	78t	2
Law	3	91	30.3	46t	2
Buckley	3	76	25.3	52t	1
Vrabel	2	27	13.5	15	0
Milloy	2	21	10.5	21	0
Bruschi	2	7	3.5	4	0
Pleasant	2	0	0.0	0	0
Phifer	1	14	14.0	14	0
Stevens	1	9	9.0	9	0
T. Jones	1	-4	-4.0	-4	0
Patriots	22	422	19.2	78t	5
Opponents	15	273	18.2	49t	2

PUNT RETURNS

	No.	FC	Yds.	Avg.	LG	TD
Brown	29	15	413	14.2	85t	2
Faulk	4	0	27	6.8	10	0
Patriots	33	15	440	13.3	85t	2
Opponents	26	17	124	4.8	26	0

KICKOFF RETURNS

	No.	Yds.	Avg.	LG	TD
Faulk	33	662	20.1	42	0
Pass	10	222	22.2	33	0
Kelly	7	123	17.6	28	0
Jackson	2	30	15.0	19	0
Patten	2	44	22.0	24	0
Redmond	2	57	28.5	30	0
Brown	1	13	13.0	13	0
Bruschi	1	10	10.0	10	0
Edwards	1	23	23.0	23	0
Patriots	59	1184	20.1	42	0
Opponents	75	1658	22.1	64	0

FIELD GOALS

	1-19	20-29	30-39	40-49	50+
Vinatieri	1/1	8/8	7/8	7/12	1/1
Patriots	1/1	8/8	7/8	7/12	1/1
Opponents	2/2	11/12	8/9	7/14	2/4

SACKS

	No.
Hamilton	7.0
McGinest	6.0
Pleasant	6.0
Milloy	3.0
Seymour	3.0
Vrabel	3.0
Bruschi	2.0
Phifer	2.0
O. Smith	2.0
Buckley	1.0
T. Jones	1.0
Law	1.0
Mitchell	1.0
Parker	1.0
Patriots	41.0
Opponents	46.0

RECORD HOLDERS

INDIVIDUAL RECORDS—CAREER

Category	Name	Performance
Rushing (Yds.)	Sam Cunningham, 1973-79, 1981-82	5,453
Passing (Yds.)	Drew Bledsoe, 1993-2001	29,657
Passing (TDs)	Steve Grogan, 1975-1990	182
Receiving (No.)	Stanley Morgan, 1977-1989	534
Receiving (Yds.)	Stanley Morgan, 1977-1989	10,352
Interceptions	Raymond Clayborn, 1977-1989	36
Punting (Avg.)	Tom Tupa, 1996-97	44.7
Punt Return (Avg.)	Mack Herron, 1973-75	12.0
Kickoff Return (Avg.)	Allen Carter, 1975-76	27.2
Field Goals	Gino Cappelletti, 1960-1970	176
Touchdowns (Tot.)	Stanley Morgan, 1977-1989	68
Points	Gino Cappelletti, 1960-1970	1,130

INDIVIDUAL RECORDS—SINGLE SEASON

Category	Name	Performance
Rushing (Yds.)	Curtis Martin, 1995	1,487
Passing (Yds.)	Drew Bledsoe, 1994	4,555
Passing (TDs)	Vito (Babe) Parilli, 1964	31
Receiving (No.)	Troy Brown, 2001	101
Receiving (Yds.)	Stanley Morgan, 1986	1,491
Interceptions	Ron Hall, 1964	11
Punting (Avg.)	Tom Tupa, 1997	45.8
Punt Return (Avg.)	Mack Herron, 1974	14.8
Kickoff Return (Avg.)	Raymond Clayborn, 1977	31.0
Field Goals	Tony Franklin, 1986	32
Touchdowns (Tot.)	Curtis Martin, 1996	17
Points	Gino Cappelletti, 1964	155

INDIVIDUAL RECORDS—SINGLE GAME

Category	Name	Performance
Rushing (Yds.)	Tony Collins, 9-18-83	212
Passing (Yds.)	Drew Bledsoe, 11-13-94	426
Passing (TDs)	Vito (Babe) Parilli, 11-15-64	5
	Vito (Babe) Parilli, 10-15-67	5
	Steve Grogan, 9-9-79	5
Receiving (No.)	Terry Glenn, 10-3-99	13
Receiving (Yds.)	Terry Glenn, 10-3-99	214
Interceptions	Many times	3
	Last time by Roland James, 10-23-83	
Field Goals	Gino Cappelletti, 10-4-64	6
Touchdowns (Tot.)	Many times	3
	Last time by Curtis Martin, 11-3-96	
Points	Gino Cappelletti, 12-18-65	28

2002 VETERAN ROSTER

No.	Name	Pos.	Ht.	Wt.	Birthdate	NFL Exp.	College	Hometown	How Acq.	'01 Games/ Starts
75	Anderson, Maurice	DT	6-3	280	1/19/75	2	Virginia	Nottoway, Va.	FA-'01	0*
63	Andruzzi, Joe	G	6-3	315	8/23/75	6	Southern Connecticut St.	Staten Island, N.Y.	FA-'00	16/16
99	Ayi, Kole	LB	6-1	231	9/27/78	2	Massachusetts	Nashua, N.H.	W(NYG)-'01	1/0
12	Brady, Tom	QB	6-4	220	8/3/77	3	Michigan	San Mateo, Calif.	D6b-'00	15/14
80	Brown, Troy	WR	5-10	193	7/2/71	10	Marshall	Blackville, S.C.	D8-'93	16/13
54	Bruschi, Tedy	LB	6-1	245	6/9/73	7	Arizona	Roseville, Calif.	D3-'96	15/9
58	Chatham, Matt	LB	6-4	250	6/28/77	3	South Dakota	Sioux City, Iowa	W(StL)-'00	11/0
30	Cherry, Je'Rod	S	6-1	205	5/30/73	7	California	Berkeley, Calif.	FA-'01	16/0
85	Cleeland, Cameron	TE	6-4	272	8/15/75	5	Washington	Sedro Woolley, Wash.	UFA(NO)-'02	9/7*
84	Coleman, Fred	WR	6-0	190	1/31/75	2	Washington	Tyler, Texas	FA-'01	8/0
77	Compton, Mike	G-C	6-6	310	9/18/70	10	West Virginia	Richlands, Va.	UFA(Det)-'01	16/16
43	Dragos, Scott	FB	6-2	245	10/28/75	3	Boston College	Old Rochester, Mass.	UFA(Chi)-'02	6/0*
44	Edwards, Marc	FB	6-0	245	11/17/74	6	Notre Dame	Cincinnati, Ohio	UFA(Cle)-'01	16/13
33	Faulk, Kevin	RB	5-8	202	6/5/76	4	Louisiana State	Carencro, La.	D2-'99	15/1
88	Fauria, Christian	TE	6-4	245	9/22/71	8	Colorado	Encino, Calif.	UFA(Sea)-'02	16/11*
91	Hamilton, Bobby	DE	6-5	280	7/1/71	8	Southern Mississippi	Columbia, Miss.	UFA(NYJ)-'00	16/15
23	Harris, Antwan	S	5-9	192	5/29/77	3	Virginia	Raleigh, N.C.	D6a-'00	11/1
22	Hayes, Chris	S	6-0	206	5/7/72	6	Washington State	San Bernadino, Calif.	FA-'02	16/1*
81	Hayes, Donald	WR	6-4	208	7/13/75	5	Wisconsin	Madison, Wis.	UFA(Car)-'02	16/15*
49	Holloway, Jabari	TE	6-2	258	12/18/78	2	Notre Dame	Riverdale, Ga.	D4b-'01	0*
19	Huard, Damon	QB	6-3	220	7/9/73	6	Washington	Puyallup, Wash.	UFA(Mia)-'01	0*
53	Izzo, Larry	LB	5-10	228	9/26/74	7	Rice	Houston, Texas	UFA(Mia)-'01	16/0
52	Johnson, Ted	LB	6-4	253	12/4/72	8	Colorado	Alameda, Calif.	D2-'95	12/5
74	Jones, Kenyatta	T	6-3	305	1/18/79	2	South Florida	Gainesville, Fla.	D4a-'01	5/0
34	Jones, Tebucky	FS	6-2	218	10/6/74	5	Syracuse	New Britain, Conn.	D1b-'98	16/12
59	Katzenmoyer, Andy	LB	6-3	260	12/2/77	4	Ohio State	Westerville, Ohio	D1b-'99	0*
31	Kelly, Ben	CB	5-9	185	9/15/78	3	Colorado	Cleveland, Ohio	W(Mia)-'01	2/0
37	Kelly, Rob	S	6-0	199	6/24/74	5	Ohio State	Mt. Vernon, Ohio	FA-'02	0*
70	Klemm, Adrian	T	6-3	312	5/21/77	3	Hawaii	Los Angeles, Calif.	D2-'00	0*
29	Knight, Tom	CB	6-0	195	12/29/74	6	Iowa	Marlton, N.J.	UFA(Ariz)-'02	8/8*
24	Law, Ty	CB	5-11	199	2/10/74	8	Michigan	Aliquippa, Pa.	D1-'95	16/16
72	Light, Matt	T	6-4	305	6/23/78	2	Purdue	Greenville, Ohio	D2-'01	14/12
48	Love, Arther	TE	6-4	250	9/18/77	2	South Carolina State	Soperton, Ga.	D6a-'01	0*
96	Lyle, Rick	DE-DT	6-5	290	2/26/71	9	Missouri	Hickman Hills, Mo.	UFA(NYJ)-'02	16/3*
90	Martin, Steve	DT	6-4	319	5/31/74	7	Missouri	St. Paul, Minn.	UFA(NYJ)-'02	16/15*
55	McGinest, Willie	DE	6-5	270	12/11/71	9	Southern California	Long Beach, Calif.	D1-'94	11/5
36	Milloy, Lawyer	S	6-0	207	11/14/73	7	Washington	Tacoma, Wash.	D2-'96	16/16
46	Moore, Marty	LB	6-1	245	3/19/71	9	Kentucky	Bell County, Ky.	FA-'02	3/0
25	Myers, Leonard	CB	5-10	195	12/18/78	2	Miami	Fort Lauderdale , Fla.	D6b-'01	7/0
92	Nugent, David	DE	6-4	295	10/27/77	3	Purdue	Collierville, Tenn.	D6c-'00	9/1
35	Pass, Patrick	FB	5-10	217	12/31/77	3	Georgia	Tucker, Ga.	D7b-'00	16/0
86	Patten, David	WR	5-10	190	8/19/74	6	Western Carolina	Hopkins, S.C.	UFA(Cle)-'01	16/14
66	Paxton, Lonie	LS	6-2	260	3/13/78	3	Sacramento State	Corona, Calif.	FA-'00	16/0
51	Phillips, Ryan	LB	6-4	250	2/7/74	6	Idaho	Renton, Wash.	UFA(Ind)-'02	13/6*
98	Pleasant, Anthony	DE	6-5	280	1/27/68	13	Tennessee State	Century, Fla.	UFA(SF)-'01	16/16
38	Porter, Daryl	S	5-9	188	1/16/74	5	Boston College	Ft. Lauderdale, Fla.	UFA(Tenn)-'02	14/3*
21	Redmond, J.R.	RB	5-11	215	9/28/77	3	Arizona State	Carson, Calif.	D3-'00	12/0
64	Robinson-Randall, Greg	T	6-5	322	6/23/78	3	Michigan State	La Marque, Texas	D4-'00	16/16
67	Ruegamer, Grey	C-G	6-4	300	6/1/76	4	Arizona State	Las Vegas, Nevada	FA-'00	14/1
94	Sayler, Jace	DL	6-5	295	2/27/79	2	Michigan State	McHenry, Ill.	FA-'01	2/1
93	Seymour, Richard	DT	6-6	305	10/6/79	2	Georgia	Gadsden, S.C.	D1-'01	13/10
32	Smith, Antowain	RB	6-2	230	3/14/72	6	Houston	Montgomery, Ala.	UFA(Buff)-'01	16/15
45	Smith, Otis	CB	5-11	196	10/22/65	13	Missouri	Mataire, La.	FA-'00	15/15
71	Sullivan, Chris	DL	6-4	285	3/14/73	7	Boston College	North Attleboro, Mass.	FA-'01	0*
62	Tylski, Rich	G	6-4	306	2/27/71	8	Utah State	San Diego, Calif.	FA-'02	12/10*
4	Vinatieri, Adam	K	6-0	200	12/28/72	7	South Dakota State	Rapid City, S.D.	FA-'96	16/0
50	Vrabel, Mike	LB	6-4	250	8/14/75	6	Ohio State	Akron, Ohio	UFA(Pitt)-'01	16/12
13	Walter, Ken	P	6-1	195	8/15/72	6	Kent State	Euclid, Ohio	FA-'01	11/0
28	Williams, Brock	CB	5-10	195	8/11/79	2	Notre Dame	Hammond, La.	D3-'01	0*
76	Williams, Grant	T	6-7	320	5/10/74	7	Louisiana Tech	Clinton, Miss.	UFA(Sea)-'00	14/4
14	Williams, Walter	RB	6-0	210	9/8/77	2	Grambling State	Baton Rouge, La.	FA-'01	0*
65	Woody, Damien	C	6-3	320	11/3/77	4	Boston College	Beaverdam, Va.	D1a-'99	16/15

* Anderson last active with N.Y. Jets in '00; Cleeland played 9 games with New Orleans in '01; Dragos played 6 games with Chicago; Fauria played 16 games with Seattle; C. Hayes played 16 games with N.Y. Jets; D. Hayes played 16 games with Carolina; Holloway

missed '01 season because of injury; Huard was inactive for 9 games; Katzenmoyer missed '01 season because of injury; R. Kelly played last active with New Orleans in '00; Klemm was inactive for 5 games; Knight played 8 games with Arizona; Love was inactive for 6 games; Lyle played 16 games with N.Y. Jets; Martin played 16 games with N.Y. Jets; Phillips played 13 games with Indianapolis; Porter played 14 games with Tennessee; Sullivan was inactive for 3 games; Tylski played 12 games with Pittsburgh; B. Williams missed '01 season because of injury; W. Williams missed '01 season because of injury.

Traded—QB Drew Bledsoe (2 games in '01) to Buffalo.

Players lost through Expansion Draft (1): S Matt Stevens (15 games in '01).

Players lost through free agency (4): LB Bryan Cox (NO; 11 games in '01), DT Brandon Mitchell (Sea; 16), DT Riddick Parker (NYJ; 13), TE Rod Rutledge (Hou; 15).

Also played with Patriots in '01—S Hakim Akbar (6 games), CB Terrell Buckley (15), WR Bert Emanuel (2), LB Rob Homberg (2), WR Curtis Jackson (2), P Lee Johnson (5), LB Roman Phifer (16), CB Terrance Shaw (13), WR Torrance Small (3), LB T.J. Turner (2), TE Jermaine Wiggins (16).

2002 FIRST-YEAR ROSTER

Name	Pos.	Ht.	Wt.	Birthdate	College	Hometown	How Acq.
Ashworth, Tom (1)	G-T	6-6	295	10/10/77	Colorado	Englewood, Colo.	FA-'01
Benjamin, Ryan (1)	LS	6-1	260	11/17/77	South Florida	New Port Richey, Fla.	FA
Branch, Deion	WR	5-9	191	7/18/79	Louisville	Albany, Ga.	D2
Clare, Mike (1)	G	6-3	320	1/9/79	Harvard	Rutherford, N.J.	FA
Davey, Rohan	QB	6-2	245	4/14/75	Louisiana State	Miami, Fla.	D4a
Downey, Patrick (1)	C	6-2	300	6/21/74	New Hampshire	Beverly, Mass.	FA
Farris, Jimmy (1)	WR	6-0	200	4/13/78	Montana	Lewiston, Idaho	FA-'01
Gali, Setema (1)	DE	6-4	245	7/2/76	Brigham Young	Orem, Utah	FA-'01
Givens, David	WR	6-0	217	8/16/80	Notre Dame	Humble, Texas	D7b
Graham, Daniel	TE	6-3	248	11/16/78	Colorado	Denver, Colo.	D1
Green, Jarvis	DE	6-3	272	1/12/79	Louisiana State	Donaldsonville, La.	D4b
Inzer, Drew (1)	G-T	6-4	305	12/5/79	Brown	North Smithfield, R.I.	FA-'01
Lockhart, Radell (1)	DE	6-2	250	5/11/79	Catawba	Charlotte, N.C.	FA
McCready, Scott (1)	WR	6-0	200	2/1/77	South Florida	Tampa, Fla.	FA-'01
Neal, Stephen (1)	G-T	6-4	290	10/9/76	Cal State-Bakersfield	San Diego, Calif.	FA-'01
Taylor, T.C.	WR	6-3	219	9/22/78	Jackson State	Magnolia, Miss.	FA
Tuitele, Maugaula (1)	LB	6-1	255	5/26/78	Colorado State	Torrance, Calif.	FA-'01
Umholtz, Tony (1)	P	6-0	195	12/13/76	South Florida	Osceola, Fla.	FA
Womack, Antwoine	RB	5-11	214	3/20/78	Virginia	Hampton, Va.	D7a

The term NFL Rookie is defined as a player who is in his first season of professional football and has not been on the roster of another professional football team for any regular-season or postseason games. A Rookie is designated by an "R" on NFL rosters. Players who have been active in another professional football league or players who have NFL experience, including either preseason training camp or being on an Active List or Inactive List, or on Reserve/Injured or Reserve/Physically Unable to Perform for fewer than six regular-season games, are termed NFL First-Year Players. An NFL First-Year Player is designated by a "1" on NFL rosters. Thereafter, a player is credited with an additional year of experience for each season in which he accumulates six games on the Active List or Inactive List, or on Reserve/Injured or Reserve/Physically Unable to Perform.

COACHING STAFF
Head Coach,
Bill Belichick
Pro Career: Bill Belichick returned to New England when Patriots owner Robert Kraft named the fourteenth head coach in Patriots history on January 27, 2000. Belichick, who was a defensive assistant for the Patriots when the team last won a conference title in 1996, inherited a team whose win total had eroded with each passing year since then. He immediately began rebuilding the foundation by instilling a new team philosophy that was fortified with the acquistion of dozens of new players. It took just two seasons to reverse their course and return to NFL prominence, as the Patriots closed out the 2001 season by winning a franchise-record nine consecutive games, including playoff victories over Oakland, at Pittsburgh, and in Super Bowl XXXVI against the Rams to claim the first Super Bowl title in franchise history. Long renowed as one of the league's premier defensive coaches after years a defensive assistant, Belichick is now recognized as one of the NFL's premier game strategists and, with last year's performance, has been lauded for completing one of the best coaching efforts in NFL history. Including last season's Super Bowl title, Belichick's coaching contributions have led to three Super Bowls, four conference championships, and six division titles since 1986. The 27-year NFL coaching veteran, Belichick launched his career in 1975 as a special assistant with the Baltimore Colts. He was an assistant special teams coach with Detroit (1976-77) and Denver (1978). In 1979, he joined the New York Giants as the special teams coach. In 1981-82, he took on the dual responsibilities of coaching both special teams and linebackers. By 1985, he was named defensive coordinator. Throughout the next six seasons, he was credited with creating one of the greatest defensive units of all-time. Their success as a unit contributed to the Giants winning two Super Bowl titles in four seasons, in 1986 and again in 1990. Following Super Bowl XXV, Belichick was named head coach of the Cleveland Browns in 1991. At the age of 37, he became the youngest head coach in the league. By 1994, Belichick had assembled one of the league's most dominant defenses. That year, the Browns finished 11-5 after the team allowed a league-low 204 total points. The Browns qualified for the playoffs and eliminated the Patriots in the first round. In 1996, Belichick joined New England and was a key contributor to the team's rebound from a 6-10 season in 1995 to an 11-5 division championship season. It was the team's first division title in 10 years. The Patriots hosted two playoff games in which the defense allowed just nine total points. The unit's dominance propelled

the Patriots to victories over Pittsburgh (28-3) and Jacksonville (20-6) en route to Super Bowl XXXI against Green Bay. He spent three seasons with the New York Jets from 1997 to 1999. In his first season in New York, the Jets defense played a key factor in the Jets rise from 1-15 in 1996 to 9-7. In 1998, the defense was a critical factor in the team's ability to claim its first AFC East title with a franchise-best 12-4 regular-season record. The Jets advanced to the AFC Championship Game, but lost to the eventual Super Bowl champion Denver Broncos. In 1999, the Jets won seven of their final nine games, allowing only 18.4 points per game during that span. Career record: 56-61.
Background: Belichick was a center/tight end at Wesleyan 1971-74.
Personal: Born April 16, 1952, Nashville. Bill and his wife, Debby, have three children—Amanda, Stephen, and Brian.

ASSISTANT COACHES
Romeo Crennel, defensive coordinator-defensive line; born June 18, 1947, Lynchburg, Va., lives in Foxboro. Offensive-defensive tackle, linebacker Western Kentucky 1966-69. No pro playing experience. College coach: Western Kentucky 1970-74, Texas Tech 1975-77, Mississippi 1978-79, Georgia Tech 1980. Pro coach: New York Giants 1981-1992, New England Patriots 1993-96, New York Jets 1997-99, Cleveland Browns 2000, rejoined Patriots in 2001.
Brian Daboll, wide receivers; born Welland, Ontario, lives in Attleboro, Mass. Safety Rochester 1994-96. No pro playing experience. College coach: William & Mary 1997, Michigan State 1998-99. Pro coach: Joined Patriots in 2000.
Jeff Davidson, asst. offensive line-tight ends; born October 3, 1967, Akron, Ohio, lives in Franklin, Mass. Offensive lineman Ohio State 1986-89. Pro offensive lineman Denver Broncos 1990-92, New Orleans Saints 1994. Pro coach: New Orleans Saints 1995-96, joined the Patriots in 1997.
Ivan Fears, running backs; born November 15, 1954, Portsmouth, Va., lives in Foxboro, Mass. Running back William & Mary 1973-75. No pro playing experience. College coach: William & Mary 1977-1980, Syracuse 1981-1990. Pro coach: New England Patriots 1991-92, Chicago Bears 1993-98, rejoined Patriots in 1999.
Pepper Johnson, inside linebackers; born July 29, 1964, Detroit, in Foxboro, Mass. Linebacker Ohio State 1982-85. Pro linebacker New York Giants 1986-1992, Cleveland Browns 1993-95, Detroit 1996, New York Jets 1997-98. Pro coach: Joined the Patriots in 2000.
Eric Mangini, defensive backs; born January 10, 1971, Hartford, Conn., lives in Medfield, Mass. Nose tackle Wesleyan (Conn.) 1989-1990, 1992-93. No pro

playing experience. Pro coach: Cleveland Browns 1995, Baltimore Ravens 1996, New York Jets 1997-99, joined Patriots in 2000.
Markus Paul, asst. strength and conditioning; born April 1, 1966, Orlando, Fla., lives in Plainville, Mass. Safety Syracuse 1984-88. Pro safety Chicago Bears 1989-1993, Tampa Bay Buccaneers 1993. Pro coach: New Orleans 1998-99, joined Patriots in 2000.
Rob Ryan, outside linebackers; born December 13, 1962, Ardmore, Okla., lives in Franklin, Mass. Linebacker Oklahoma State 1984, Southwestern Oklahoma State 1985-86. No pro playing experience. College coach: Western Kentucky 1987, Ohio State 1988, Tennessee State 1989-1993, Hutchinson (Kan.) C.C. 1996, Oklahoma State 1997-99. Pro coach: Arizona Cardinals 1994-95, joined Patriots in 2000.
Dante Scarnecchia, asst. head coach-offensive line; born February 15, 1948, Los Angeles, lives in Wrentham, Mass. Center-guard California Western (now U.S. International) 1968-1970. No pro playing experience. College coach: California Western 1970-72, Iowa State 1973-74, Southern Methodist 1975-76, 1980-81, Pacific 1977-78, Northern Arizona 1979. Pro coach: New England Patriots 1982-88, Indianapolis Colts 1989-1990, rejoined the Patriots in 1991.
Brad Seely, special teams; born September 6, 1956, Vinton, Iowa, lives in Wrentham, Mass. Tackle-guard South Dakota State 1974-77. No pro playing experience. College coach: Colorado State 1980, Southern Methodist 1981, North Carolina State 1982, Pacific 1983, Oklahoma State 1984-88. Pro coach: Indianapolis Colts 1989-1993, New York Jets 1994, Carolina Panthers 1995-98, joined Patriots in 1999.
Charlie Weis, offensive coordinator-quarterbacks; born March 30, 1956, Trenton, N.J., lives in Cumberland, R.I. Attended Notre Dame. No college or pro playing experience. College coach: South Carolina 1985-88. Pro coach: New York Giants 1988-1992, New England Patriots 1993-96, New York Jets 1997-99, rejoined Patriots in 2000.
Mike Woicik, strength and conditioning; born September 26, 1956, Baltimore, lives in Foxboro, Mass. Attended Boston College. No college or pro playing experience. College coach: Springfield College 1978-79, Syracuse 1980-89. Pro coach: Dallas Cowboys 1990-96, New Orleans Saints 1997-99, joined Patriots in 2000.

**American Football Conference
East Division**
Team Colors: Green and White
1000 Fulton Avenue
Hempstead, New York 11550
Telephone: (516) 560-8100

2002 SCHEDULE
PRESEASON
Aug. 8	at Pittsburgh	8:00
Aug. 15	at Baltimore	8:00
Aug. 24	**New York Giants**	8:00
Aug. 30	**Philadelphia**	7:30

REGULAR SEASON
Sept. 8	at Buffalo	1:00
Sept. 15	**New England**	1:00
Sept. 22	at Miami	1:00
Sept. 29	at Jacksonville	1:00
Oct. 6	**Kansas City**	4:05
Oct. 13	Open Date	
Oct. 20	**Minnesota**	1:00
Oct. 27	**Cleveland**	1:00
Nov. 3	at San Diego	1:05
Nov. 10	**Miami**	8:30
Nov. 17	at Detroit	4:15
Nov. 24	**Buffalo**	1:00
Dec. 2	at Oakland (Mon.)	6:00
Dec. 8	**Denver**	4:15
Dec. 15	at Chicago (Champaign, Ill.)	12:00
Dec. 22	at New England	8:30
Dec. 29	**Green Bay**	4:15

Stadium: Giants Stadium
(opened in 1976)
• **Capacity:** 79,466
East Rutherford, New Jersey
07073
Playing Surface: Natural Grass
Training Camp: 1000 Fulton Avenue
Hempstead, New York
11550

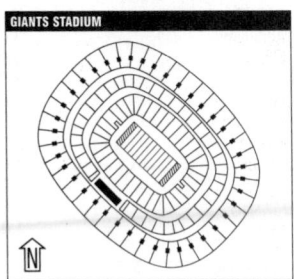
GIANTS STADIUM

CLUB OFFICIALS
Owner and CEO:
Robert Wood Johnson IV
President: Jay Cross
General Manager: Terry Bradway
Assistant General Manager/Director
of Pro Personnel: Mike Tannenbaum
Vice President-Public Relations:
Ron Colangelo
Vice President-Finance and CFO:
Michael Gerstle
Vice President-Operations: Michael Kensil
Vice President-Business Operations:
Robert Parente
Vice President-Stadium Development:
Thad Sheely
Vice President-Marketing and Sales:
Lee Stacey
Senior Pro Scout/AFC: JoJo Wooden
Pro Scout/NFC: Brian Gaine
Salary Cap Analyst/Pro Personnel
Assistant: Dawn Aponte
Pro Personnel Assistant: Chris Shea
Director of College Scouting: Jessie Kaye
National Scout: Joey Clinkscales
Senior Personnel Scout: Dick Haley
Scouting Coordinator: John Griffin
Personnel Scouts: Jeff Bauer,
Joe Bommarito, Ron Brockington,
Jim Cochran, Michael Davis, Sid Hall,
Brendan Prophett, Bob Schmitz,
Gary Smith
Head Athletic Trainer: Dave Price
Assistant Head Athletic Trainer:
John Mellody
Assistant Head Athletic Trainer:
Bill Peters
Video Director: John Seiter
Assistant Video Director: Jim Space
Director of Player Programs:
Kevin Winston
Director of Security: Steve Yarnell
Equipment Manager: Clay Hampton
Assistant Equipment Manager:
Gus Granneman
Senior Director of Marketing: Marc Riccio
Director of Community Relations:
Eve Barth
Community Relations Manager:
Kimberlee Fields
Directors of Marketing and New
Business Development: Tracy Belmear,
Bob Brennafleck
Director of Ticket Operations:
John Buschhorn
Assistant Director of Tickets:
Carolanne Cappola
Director of Internet and Publications:
Ken Ilchuk
Director of Media Relations:
Douglas Miller
Coordinator of Media Relations:
Jared Winley
Media Relations Assistant: Kristin Ianiero
Controller: Mike Minarczyk
Director of Information Technology:
Tom Murphy

COACHING HISTORY
New York Titans 1960-62
(285-349-8)
1960-61	Sammy Baugh	14-14-0
1962	Clyde (Bulldog) Turner	5-9-0
1963-1973	Weeb Ewbank	73-78-6
1974-75	Charley Winner*	9-14-0
1975	Ken Shipp	1-4-0
1976	Lou Holtz**	3-10-0
1976	Mike Holovak	0-1-0
1977-1982	Walt Michaels	41-49-1
1983-89	Joe Walton	54-59-1
1990-93	Bruce Coslet	26-39-0
1994	Pete Carroll	6-10-0
1995-96	Rich Kotite	4-28-0
1997-99	Bill Parcells	30-20-0
2000	Al Groh	9-7-0
2001	Herman Edwards	10-7-0

*Released after nine games in 1975
**Resigned after 13 games in 1976

ATTENDANCE
Home 627,603   Away 515,126
Total 1,142,729
Single-game home record,
78,823 (10/14/01)
Single-season home record, 627,603
(2001)

2002 DRAFT CHOICES
Round	Name	Pos.	College
1	Bryan Thomas	DE	Alabama-Birmingham
2	Jon McGraw	DB	Kansas State
3	Chris Baker	TE	Michigan State
4	Alan Harper	DE	Fresno State
5	Jonathan Goodwin	G	Michigan

2001 TEAM RECORD

PRESEASON (2-2)

Date	Result	Opponent
8/11	L 10-20	Atlanta
8/18	W 16-3	Baltimore
8/25	W 17-14	at New York Giants
8/30	L 12-13	at Philadelphia

REGULAR SEASON (10-6)

Date	Result	Opponent	Att.
9/09	L 24-45	Indianapolis	78,606
9/23	W 10-3	at New England	60,292
10/01	L 17-19	San Francisco	78,722
10/07	W 42-36	at Buffalo	72,654
10/14	W 21-17	Miami	78,823
10/21	L 14-34	St. Louis	78,766
10/28	W 13-12	at Carolina	72,642
11/04	W 16-9	at New Orleans	70,020
11/11	W 27-7	Kansas City	78,234
11/18	W 24-0	at Miami	74,259
12/02	L 16-17	New England	78,712
12/09	L 7-18	at Pittsburgh	62,884
12/16	W 15-14	Cincinnati	77,745
12/23	W 29-28	at Indianapolis	56,302
12/30	L 9-1	Buffalo	78,200
1/06	W 24-22	at Oakland	62,011

POSTSEASON (0-1)

1/12	L 24-38	at Oakland	61,503

SCORE BY PERIODS

Jets	78	85	80	65	0	—	308
Opponents	38	123	77	57	0	—	295

2001 TEAM STATISTICS

	Jets	Opp.
Total First Downs	274	284
Rushing	105	116
Passing	151	155
Penalty	18	13
3rd Down: Made/Att	76/200	101/227
3rd Down Pct.	38.0	44.5
4th Down: Made/Att	6/12	9/18
4th Down Pct.	50.0	50.0
Possession Avg.	29:13	30:47
Total Net Yards	4795	5153
Avg. Per Game	299.7	322.1
Total Plays	928	1030
Avg. Per Play	5.2	5.0
Net Yards Rushing	2054	2154
Avg. Per Game	128.4	134.6
Total Rushes	445	481
Net Yards Passing	2741	2999
Avg. Per Game	171.3	187.4
Sacked/Yards Lost	19/130	33/171
Gross Yards	2871	3170
Att./Completions	464/272	516/313
Completion Pct.	58.6	60.7
Had Intercepted	14	20
Punts/Average	76/39.0	75/40.7
Net Punting Avg.	76/31.6	75/35.4
Penalties/Yards	62/507	85/700
Fumbles/Ball Lost	22/7	29/19
Touchdowns	34	33
Rushing	11	15
Passing	17	14
Returns	6	4

2001 INDIVIDUAL STATISTICS

PASSING	Att.	Comp.	Yds.	Pct.	TD	Int.	Tkld.	Rate
Testaverde	441	260	2752	59.0	15	14	18/122	75.3
Pennington	20	10	92	50.0	1	0	1/8	79.6
Jordan	1	0	0	0.0	0	0	0/0	39.6
C. Martin	1	1	18	100.0	1	0	0/0	158.3
Tupa	1	1	9	100.0	0	0	0/0	104.2
Jets	464	272	2871	58.6	17	14	19/130	76.4
Opponents	516	313	3170	60.7	14	20	33/171	71.1

SCORING	TD R	TD P	TD Rt	PAT	FG	Saf	PTS
Hall	0	0	0	32/32	24/31	0	104
C. Martin	10	0	0	0/0	0/0	0	60
Coles	0	7	0	0/0	0/0	0	42
Becht	0	5	0	0/0	0/0	0	30
Anderson	0	2	0	0/0	0/0	0	12
Jordan	1	1	0	0/0	0/0	0	12
Abraham	0	0	1	0/0	0/0	0	6
Chrebet	0	1	0	0/0	0/0	0	6
Dearth	0	1	0	0/0	0/0	0	6
A. Glenn	0	0	1	0/0	0/0	0	6
J. Glenn	0	1	0	0/0	0/0	0	6
V. Green	0	0	1	0/0	0/0	0	6
C. Hayes	0	0	1	0/0	0/0	0	6
Lewis	0	0	1	0/0	0/0	0	6
Jets	11	17	6	32/32	24/31	0	308
Opponents	15	14	4	27/30	22/27	1	295

2-Pt. Conversions: None.
Jets 0-2, Opponents 1-3.

RUSHING	Att.	Yds.	Avg.	LG	TD
C. Martin	333	1513	4.5	47	10
Jordan	39	292	7.5	46t	1
Coles	10	108	10.8	20	0
Anderson	26	102	3.9	12	0
Testaverde	31	25	0.8	12	0
Pennington	1	11	11.0	11	0
Sowell	4	9	2.3	4	0
Moss	1	-6	-6.0	-6	0
Jets	445	2054	4.6	47	11
Opponents	481	2154	4.5	56t	15

RECEIVING	No.	Yds.	Avg.	LG	TD
Coles	59	868	14.7	40t	7
Chrebet	56	750	13.4	36	1
C. Martin	53	320	6.0	27	0
Anderson	40	252	6.3	22	2
Becht	36	321	8.9	24	5
Swayne	13	203	15.6	27	0
Jordan	7	44	6.3	25t	1
Dearth	3	10	3.3	9	1
Hatchette	2	44	22.0	29	0
Moss	2	40	20.0	33	0
Sowell	1	19	19.0	19	0
Jets	272	2871	10.6	40t	17
Opponents	313	3170	10.1	70t	14

INTERCEPTIONS	No.	Yds.	Avg.	LG	TD
A. Glenn	5	82	16.4	60t	1
V. Green	3	76	25.3	63t	1
Jones	3	27	9.0	18	0
Farrior	2	84	42.0	47	0
Robinson	2	58	29.0	30	0
Coleman	2	41	20.5	36	0
Lewis	1	17	17.0	17	0
Henderson	1	5	5.0	5	0
Burton	1	0	0.0	0	0
Jets	20	390	19.5	63t	2
Opponents	14	222	15.9	49	1

PUNTING	No.	Yds.	Avg.	In 20	LG
Tupa	67	2575	38.4	21	59
Parks	5	238	47.6	1	56
Pope	4	153	38.3	2	47
Jets	76	2966	39.0	24	59
Opponents	75	3056	40.7	28	65

PUNT RETURNS	No.	FC	Yds.	Avg.	LG	TD
Morton	13	7	113	8.7	33	0
Yeast	13	6	122	9.4	35	0
Moss	6	0	82	13.7	23	0
A. Glenn	2	1	6	3.0	4	0
Jets	34	14	323	9.5	35	0
Opponents	34	11	446	13.1	78t	1

KICKOFF RETURNS	No.	Yds.	Avg.	LG	TD
Yeast	29	663	22.9	50	0
Morton	12	247	20.6	33	0
Coles	9	211	23.4	34	0
Jordan	3	62	20.7	23	0
Dearth	1	7	7.0	7	0
Henderson	1	0	0.0	0	0
Sowell	1	6	6.0	6	0
Jets	56	1196	21.4	50	0
Opponents	63	1355	21.5	65	0

FIELD GOALS	1-19	20-29	30-39	40-49	50+
Hall	1/1	8/8	5/7	7/9	3/6
Jets	1/1	8/8	5/7	7/9	3/6
Opponents	1/1	9/10	5/5	6/10	1/1

SACKS	No.
Abraham	13.0
Ellis	5.0
Lyle	3.5
Lewis	3.0
S. Martin	2.5
Burton	2.0
Farrior	1.0
Jones	1.0
Mickens	1.0
Reed	1.0
Jets	33.0
Opponents	19.0

RECORD HOLDERS
INDIVIDUAL RECORDS—CAREER

Category	Name	Performance
Rushing (Yds.)	Freeman McNeil, 1981-1992	8,074
Passing (Yds.)	Joe Namath, 1965-1976	27,057
Passing (TDs)	Joe Namath, 1965-1976	170
Receiving (No.)	Don Maynard, 1960-1972	627
Receiving (Yds.)	Don Maynard, 1960-1972	11,732
Interceptions	Bill Baird, 1963-69	34
Punting (Avg.)	Curley Johnson, 1961-68	42.8
Punt Return (Avg.)	Dick Christy, 1961-63	16.2
Kickoff Return (Avg.)	Bobby Humphery, 1984-89	22.8
Field Goals	Pat Leahy, 1974-1991	304
Touchdowns (Tot.)	Don Maynard, 1960-1972	88
Points	Pat Leahy, 1974-1991	1,470

INDIVIDUAL RECORDS—SINGLE SEASON

Category	Name	Performance
Rushing (Yds.)	Curtis Martin, 2001	1,513
Passing (Yds.)	Joe Namath, 1967	4,007
Passing (TDs)	Vinny Testaverde, 1998	29
Receiving (No.)	Al Toon, 1988	93
Receiving (Yds.)	Don Maynard, 1967	1,434
Interceptions	Dainard Paulson, 1964	12
Punting (Avg.)	Curley Johnson, 1965	45.3
Punt Return (Avg.)	Dick Christy, 1961	21.3
Kickoff Return (Avg.)	Bobby Humphery, 1984	30.7
Field Goals	Jim Turner, 1968	34
Touchdowns (Tot.)	Art Powell, 1960	14
	Don Maynard, 1965	14
	Emerson Boozer, 1972	14
Points	Jim Turner, 1968	145

INDIVIDUAL RECORDS—SINGLE GAME

Category	Name	Performance
Rushing (Yds.)	Curtis Martin, 12-3-00	203
Passing (Yds.)	Joe Namath, 9-24-72	496
Passing (TDs)	Joe Namath, 9-24-72	6
Receiving (No.)	Clark Gaines, 9-21-80	17
Receiving (Yds.)	Don Maynard, 11-17-68	228
Interceptions	Many times	3
	Last time by Marcus Coleman, 10-23-00	
Field Goals	Jim Turner, 11-3-68	6
	Bobby Howfield, 12-3-72	6
Touchdowns (Tot.)	Wesley Walker, 9-21-86	4
Points	Wesley Walker, 9-21-86	24

2002 VETERAN ROSTER

No.	Name	Pos.	Ht.	Wt.	Birthdate	NFL Exp.	College	Hometown	How Acq.	'01 Games/ Starts
29	Abraham, Donnie	CB	5-10	192	10/8/73	7	East Tennessee State	Orangeburg, S.C.	UFA(TB)-'02	15/5*
94	Abraham, John	DE	6-4	256	5/6/78	3	South Carolina	Lamar, S.C.	D1b-'00	16/15
20	Anderson, Richie	FB	6-2	230	9/13/71	10	Penn State	Sandy Spring, Md.	D6-'93	16/16
21	Beasley, Aaron	CB	6-0	205	7/7/73	7	West Virginia	Pottstown, Pa.	UFA(Jax)-'02	12/12*
88	Becht, Anthony	TE	6-5	272	8/8/77	3	West Virginia	Drexel Hill, Pa.	D1d-'00	16/16
80	Chrebet, Wayne	WR	5-10	188	8/14/73	8	Hofstra	Garfield, N.J.	FA-'95	15/15
87	Coles, Laveranues	WR-KR	5-11	196	12/29/77	3	Florida State	Jacksonville, Fla.	D3-'00	16/16
56	Cowart, Sam	LB	6-2	245	2/26/75	5	Florida State	Jacksonville, Fla.	UFA(Buff)-'02	1/1*
51	Darling, James	LB	6-0	250	12/29/74	6	Washington State	Kettle Falls, Tenn.	UFA(Phil)-'01	16/0
85	Dearth, James	TE-LS	6-4	270	1/22/76	2	Tarleton State	Scurrey, Texas	FA-'01	16/0
76	Elliott, Jumbo (John)	T	6-7	305	4/1/65	14	Michigan	Lake Ronkonkoma, N.Y.	UFA(NYG)-'96	0*
92	Ellis, Shaun	DT-DE	6-5	294	6/24/77	3	Tennessee	Anderson, S.C.	D1a-'00	16/16
69	Fabini, Jason	T	6-7	304	8/25/74	5	Cincinnati	Ft. Wayne, Ind.	D4-'98	16/16
72	Ferguson, Jason	DT	6-3	305	11/28/74	6	Georgia	Nettleton, Miss.	D7b-'97	0*
25	Ferguson, Nick	S	5-11	201	11/27/74	3	Georgia Tech	Miami, Fla.	FA-'00	16/1
42	Garnes, Sam	S	6-3	225	7/12/74	6	Cincinnati	Bronx, N.Y.	FA-'02	16/16*
58	Glenn, Jason	LB	6-0	231	8/20/79	2	Texas A&M	Aldine, Texas	W(Det)-'01	15/0
9	Hall, John	K	6-3	228	3/17/74	6	Wisconsin	Port Charlotte, Fla.	FA-'97	15/0
23	Henderson, Jamie	CB	6-2	202	1/1/79	2	Georgia	Carrollton, Ga.	D4-'01	16/0
55	Jones, Marvin	LB	6-2	244	6/28/72	10	Florida State	Miami, Fla.	D1-'93	16/16
34	Jordan, LaMont	RB-KR	5-10	230	11/11/78	2	Maryland	Forestville, Md.	D2-'01	16/0
57	Lewis, Mo	LB	6-3	258	10/21/69	12	Georgia	Peachtree, Ga.	D3-'91	16/16
63	Machado, J.P.	C-G	6-4	300	1/6/76	4	Illinois	Monmouth, Ill.	D6b-'99	16/3
28	Martin, Curtis	RB	5-11	210	5/1/73	8	Pittsburgh	Pittsburgh, Pa.	RFA(NE)-'98	16/16
68	Mawae, Kevin	C	6-4	289	1/23/71	9	Louisiana State	Leesville, La.	UFA(SEA)-'98	16/16
67	McKenzie, Kareem	T	6-6	327	5/24/79	2	Penn State	Willingboro, N.J.	D3-'01	8/0
24	Mickens, Ray	CB	5-8	180	1/4/73	7	Texas A&M	El Paso, Texas	D3-'96	16/4
26	Morton, Chad	RB-KR	5-8	186	4/4/77	3	Southern California	Torrance, Calif.	T(NO)-'01	8/0
50	Moses, Kelvin	LB	6-0	239	9/3/76	2	Wake Forest	Heartsville, S.C.	FA-'01	16/0
83	Moss, Santana	WR-KR	5-10	185	6/1/79	2	Miiami	Miami, Fla.	D1-'01	5/0
97	Parker, Riddick	DE-DT	6-3	295	7/14/76	6	North Carolina	Emporia, Va.	UFA(NE)-'02	13/0*
10	Pennington, Chad	QB	6-3	225	6/26/76	3	Marshall	Knoxville, Tenn.	D1c-'00	2/0
93	Reed, James	DT	6-0	286	2/3/77	2	Iowa State	Saginaw, Mich.	D7a-'01	16/2
22	Robinson, Damien	S	6-2	223	12/23/73	6	Iowa	Dallas, Texas	UFA(TB)-'01	14/14
27	Scott, Tony	CB	5-10	193	10/3/76	3	North Carolina State	Lawndale, N.C.	D6-'00	7/0
33	Sowell, Jerald	FB	6-0	237	1/21/74	6	Tulane	Baker, La.	W(GB)-'97	16/0
82	Swayne, Kevin	WR	6-1	191	1/17/75	2	Wayne State	Riverside, Calif.	FA-'01	15/1
79	Szott, Dave	G	6-4	289	12/12/67	13	Penn State	Clifton, N.J.	UFA(Wash)-'02	16/16*
16	Testaverde, Vinny	QB	6-5	235	11/13/63	16	Miami	Floral Park, N.Y.	FA-'98	16/16
77	Thomas, Randy	G	6-4	301	1/19/76	4	Mississippi State	East Point, Ga.	D2-'99	13/13
1	Turk, Matt	P	6-5	250	6/16/68	8	Wisconsin-Whitewater	Greenfield, Wis.	UFA(Mia)-'02	16/0*
75	Webster, Larry	DT	6-5	315	11/8/69	10	Maryland	Elkton, Md.	FA-'02	15/0*
95	White, Steve	DE	6-2	271	10/25/73	7	Tennessee	Memphis, Tenn.	UFA(TB)-'02	16/1*
86	Wilcox, Daniel	TE	6-1	245	3/23/77	2	Appalachian State	Atlanta, Ga.	FA-'01	1/0
11	Woodbury, Tory	QB	6-2	208	7/12/78	2	Winston-Salem State	Winston-Salem, N.C.	FA-'01	10/0

* D. Abraham played 15 games with Tampa Bay in '01; Beasley played 12 games with Jacksonville; Cowart played 1 game with Buffalo; Elliott last active with N.Y. Jets in '00; J. Ferguson missed '01 season because of injury; Garnes played 16 games with N.Y. Giants; Parker played 13 games with New England; Szott played 16 games with Washington; Turk played 16 games with Miami; Webster played 15 games with Baltimore; White played 16 games with Tampa Bay.

Traded—G David Loverne (16 games in '01) to Washington.

Players lost through Expansion Draft (3): CB Marcus Coleman (16 games in '01), CB Aaron Glenn (14), T Ryan Young (16).

Players lost through free agency (4): LB James Farrior (Pitt; 16 games in '01), DE Rick Lyle (NE; 16), DT STeve Martin (NE; 16), DE Eric Ogbogu (Cin; 15).

Also played for Jets in '01—NT Tom Barndt (5 games), DT Shane Burton (15), S Victor Green (16), WR Matthew Hatchette (11), S Chris Hayes (16), WR Windrell Hayes (1), G Kerry Jenkins (16), P Tommy Parks (1), P Daniel Pope (1), LB Joe Todd (1), P Tom Tupa (15), WR Craig Yeast (11).

2002 FIRST-YEAR ROSTER

Name	Pos.	Ht.	Wt.	Birthdate	College	Hometown	How Acq.
Alston, Corey (1)	WR	6-1	213	8/26/79	Western Michigan	Camden, N.J.	FA-'01
Amitrano, John	P	5-10	195	8/4/76	Southern Illinois	Valley Stream, N.Y.	FA
Bailey, Kory	WR	6-1	195	3/31/79	North Carolina	Durham, N.C.	FA
Baker, Chris	TE	6-3	258	11/18/79	Michigan State	Saline, Mich.	D3
Boyd, Danny (1)	K	5-11	216	6/1/78	Louisiana State	Bradenton, Fla.	FA-'01
Bradley, Scott	LB	6-1	220	1/29/80	Boston College	Hanover, Mass.	FA
Brooks, Jay	CB	5-9	160	1/30/78	Texas A&M	Killeen, Texas	FA
Burrow, Jamie	LB	6-1	250	11/4/78	Nebraska	Ames, Iowa	FA
Cash, Ataveus	WR	6-1	205	5/2/79	Hampton	Washington, D.C.	FA
Clelland, Lance	C	6-6	320	6/30/79	Northwestern	Reisterstown, Md.	FA
Cooper, Joe	LB	6-0	240	1/22/79	Ohio State	Columbus, Ohio	FA
Davison, Andrew	CB	5-11	185	12/9/79	Kansas	Detroit, Mich.	FA
Farmer, Matt (1)	WR	6-0	190	6/2/77	Air Force	Pella, Iowa	FA-'00
Flowers, Little John	RB	6-0	215	1/31/80	Michigan State	Kalamazoo, Mich.	FA
Floyd, Marcus	CB	5-9	180	10/12/78	Indiana	Bartow, Fla.	FA
Franz, Todd (1)	CB	6-0	194	4/12/76	Tulsa	Weatherford, Okla.	FA-'01
Goodspeed, Dan (1)	T-G	6-6	300	5/20/77	Kent State	Union Town, Ohio	FA-'01
Goodwin, Jonathan	G	6-3	318	12/2/78	Michigan	Columbia, S.C.	D5
Hannen, Corey	T	6-5	305	11/12/78	Iowa State	Hiawatha, Iowa	FA
Harper, Alan	DT	6-1	285	9/6/79	Fresno State	Fontana, Calif.	D4
Jackson, Marlion (1)	RB	6-2	240	10/11/77	Saginaw Valley State	Detroit, Mich.	FA-'00
Janssen, Jeremiah	LB	6-3	235	7/19/79	St. Norbert	De Pere, Wis.	FA
Kleinhesselink, Riley (1)	DE	6-5	275	9/27/77	Northwestern College	Orange City, Iowa	FA-'01
Knutson, Matt	T	6-7	315	6/14/79	North Dakota	Minot, N.D.	FA
Kuhns, Chad	FB	6-1	240	10/17/78	Wisconsin	Bellevue, Ohio	FA
Kulaga, Jay	T	6-5	300	5/25/78	Illinois	Seminole, Fla.	FA
Mason, Tavon	WR	5-11	180	4/16/80	Virginia	Baltimore, Md.	FA
McCann, Kyle	QB	6-5	215	9/10/78	Iowa	Kreston, Iowa	FA
McGraw, Jon	S	6-3	206	4/2/79	Kansas State	Manhattan, Kan.	D2
Mercer, Giradie (1)	DT	6-2	285	3/19/76	Marshall	Washington, D.C.	FA-'01
Moore, Brandon	DT	6-3	295	6/3/80	Illinois	Gary, Ind.	FA
Newman, David (1)	TE	6-6	245	8/6/78	Louisiana Tech	St. Joseph, La.	FA-'01
Ornstein, Gus (1)	QB	6-3	225	11/23/74	Rowan	Tenalfy, N.J.	FA-'01
O'Sullivan, Dennis (1)	C	6-3	300	1/28/76	Tulane	Stony Point, N.Y.	FA-'01
Pittman, Jonathan (1)	WR	5-11	184	3/3/78	Brigham Young	Bullflower, Calif.	T(TB)
Price, Idris	LB	5-11	235	9/30/76	New Haven	Norwalk, Conn.	FA
Reese, John	RB	6-1	220	4/15/80	Columbia	St. Louis, Mo.	FA
Rooths, James (1)	CB	5-11	210	9/3/76	Shepherd	Baltimore, Md.	FA-'01
Scott, Brian	WR	6-3	214	4/21/79	South Carolina	Darlington, S.C.	FA
Shanahan, Doug	S	6-0	198	1/11/79	Hofstra	Farmingville, N.Y.	FA
Smith, Chris	T	6-8	285	10/9/79	California-Davis	Lodi, Calif.	FA
Thomas, Bryan	DE	6-4	266	6/7/79	Alabama-Birmingham	Birmingham, Ala.	D1
Viger, David (1)	G	6-4	281	5/13/75	Navy	Vista, Calif.	FA-'01

The term NFL Rookie is defined as a player who is in his first season of professional football and has not been on the roster of another professional football team for any regular-season or postseason games. A Rookie is designated by an "R" on NFL rosters. Players who have been active in another professional football league or players who have NFL experience, including either preseason training camp or being on an Active List or Inactive List, or on Reserve/Injured or Reserve/Physically Unable to Perform for fewer than six regular-season games, are termed NFL First-Year Players. An NFL First-Year Player is designated by a "1" on NFL rosters. Thereafter, a player is credited with an additional year of experience for each season in which he accumulates six games on the Active List or Inactive List, or on Reserve/Injured or Reserve/Physically Unable to Perform.

COACHING STAFF

Head Coach,
Herman Edwards

Pro Career: On January 28, 2001, Edwards was named the Jets' thirteenth full-time head coach. Edwards took over control of the Jets after having served as the assistant head coach-defensive backs coach for Tampa Bay the past five seasons. In 2001, he led the Jets to a 10-6 regular-season mark and, after clinching one of the AFC Wild Card positions, became the first head coach in team history to make the playoffs in his first season. The 1999 Buccaneers faced eventual Super Bowl XXXIV-champion St. Louis Rams in the NFC Championship Game and held the prolific Rams offense to 11 points. Before joining Tampa Bay, Edwards worked for the Kansas City Chiefs for six seasons in several different roles. In 1995 he worked as a scout in the pro personnel department. During the 1992-94 seasons he worked as the team's defensive backs coach. In 1990-91, Edwards was a talent scout for the Chiefs while assisting the defensive backs coach. Edwards began his pro coaching career as a participant in the NFL's Minority Coaching Fellowship program with the Kansas City Chiefs in the summer of 1989. Career record: 10-7.

Background: Played cornerback collegiately for California (1972), (1974), Monterrey Peninsula (Calif.) J.C. 1973, and San Diego State (1975-76). Professionally, Edwards played for the Philadelphia Eagles (1977-1985), Los Angeles Rams (1986), and Atlanta Falcons (1986). He was the defensive backs coach at San Jose State (1987-89).

Personal: Born April 27, 1954, Monmouth, N.J. Edwards and his wife Lia have one son, Marcus.

ASSISTANT COACHES

Bill Bradley, secondary; born January 24, 1947, Palestine, Texas, lives on Long Island, N.Y. Quarterback-defensive back-punter-kicker-returner-holder Texas 1966-68. Pro safety-punter-returner-holder Philadelphia Eagles 1969-1977, St. Louis Cardinals 1978. College coach: Texas 1987. Pro coach: San Antonio Gunslingers (USFL) 1983-84, Memphis Showboats (USFL) 1985, Cagary Stampeders (CFL) 1988-1990, San Antonio Riders (WLAF) 1991-92, Sacramento Gold Miners (CFL) 1993-94, San Antonio Texans (CFL) 1995, Toronto Argonauts (CFL) 1996-97, Buffalo Bills 1998-2000, joined Jets in 2001.

Rubin Carter, defensive line; born December 12, 1952, Ft. Lauderdale, Fla., lives on Long Island, N.Y. Defensive tackle Miami 1970-74. Pro defensive tackle Denver Broncos 1975-1986. College coach: Howard 1989-1993, San Jose State 1995-96, Maryland 1997-98. Pro coach: Denver Broncos 1987-88, Washington Redskins 1999-2000, joined Jets in 2001.

Ted Cottrell, defensive coordinator; born June 13, 1947, Chester, Pa., lives on Long Island, N.Y. Linebacker Delaware Valley College 1966-68. Pro linebacker Atlanta Falcons 1969-1970, Winnipeg Blue Bombers (CFL) 1971. College coach: Rutgers 1973-1980, 1983. Pro coach: Kansas City Chiefs 1981-82, New Jersey Generals (USFL) 1983-84, Buffalo Bills 1986-89, 1995-2000, Arizona Cardinals 1990-94, joined Jets in 2001.

Paul Hackett, offensive coordinator; born July 5, 1947, Burlington, Vt., lives on Long Island, N.Y. Quarterback Cal-Davis 1965-68. No pro playing experience. College coach: Cal-Davis 1970-71, California 1972-75, Southern California 1976-1980, Pittsburgh 1989-1992 (head coach 1990-92), Southern California 1998-2000 (head coach). Pro coach: Cleveland Browns 1981-82, San Francisco 49ers 1983-85, Dallas Cowboys 1986-88, Kansas City Chiefs 1993-97, joined Jets in 2001.

Bishop Harris, running backs; born November 23, 1941, Phenix City, Ala., lives in Douglaston, N.Y. Running back-defensive back North Carolina College 1960-63. No pro playing experience. College coach: Duke 1972-75, North Carolina State 1977-79, Louisiana State 1980-83, Notre Dame 1984-85, Minnesota 1986-1990, North Carolina Central 1991-92 (head coach). Pro coach: Denver Broncos 1993-94, Oakland Raiders 1995-97, Buffalo Bills 1998-99, joined Jets in 2001.

Mike Henning, quality control-offensive assistant; born January 30, 1973, Houston, lives in Garden City, N.Y. Quarterback Cal Poly-San Luis Obispo 1991-94. No pro playing experience. College coach: C.W. Post 1998-99. Pro coach: Joined Jets in 2001.

John Lott, strength and conditioning; born May 9, 1964, Denton, Texas, lives on Long Island, N.Y. Offensive lineman North Texas 1983-86. Pro offensive lineman Pittsburgh Steelers 1987. College coach: North Texas 1989, Houston 1990-96. Pro coach: Joined Jets in 1997.

Doug Marrone, offensive line; born July 25, 1964, Bronx, N.Y., lives on Long Island, N.Y. Offensive lineman Syracuse 1982-86. Pro offensive lineman Miami Dolphins 1987, New Orleans Saints 1989, London Monarchs (NFLE) 1992. College coach: Cortland State 1992, U.S. Coast Guard 1993, Northeastern 1994, Georgia Tech 1995-99, Georgia 2000, Tennessee 2001. Pro coach: Joined Jets in 2002.

David Merritt, defensive assistant; born September 8, 1971, Raleigh, N.C., lives on Long Island, N.Y. Linebacker North Carolina State 1989-1992. Pro linebacker Miami Dolphins 1993, Arizona Cardinals 1993-96, Rhein Fire (NFLE) 1997. College coach: Chattanooga 1997, Virginia Military Institute 1998-2000. Pro coach: Joined Jets in 2001.

Phil Pettey, tight ends; born April 17, 1961, Kenosha, Wis., lives on Long Island, N.Y. Guard Missouri 1984-86. Pro guard Washington Redskins 1987. College coach: Louisiana State 1990, Pittsburgh 1991, Southern California 1999. Pro coach: New Orleans Saints 2000, joined Jets in 2001.

Eric Price, quality control-offensive assistant; born September 12, 1966, Pullman, Wash., lives on Long Island, N.Y. Wide receiver Dixie (Utah) J.C. 1986-87, Weber State 1988-89. No pro playing experience. College coach: Weber State 1990, Washington State 1991, Hawaii 1991, Miami 1992-93, Cal Poly-San Luis Obispo 1994-95, Northern Arizona 1996-97, Washington State 1998-2000. Pro coach: Joined Jets in 2001.

Jimmy Raye, senior offensive assistant; born March 26, 1946, Fayetteville, N.C., lives on Long Island, N.Y. Quarterback Michigan State 1965-67. Pro defensive back Philadelphia Eagles 1969. College coach: Michigan State 1971-75, Wyoming 1976. Pro coach: San Francisco 49ers 1977, Detroit Lions 1978-79, Atlanta Falcons 1980-82, 1987-89, Los Angeles Rams 1983-84, 1991, Tampa Bay Buccaneers 1985-86, New England Patriots 1990, Kansas City Chiefs 1992-2000, Washington Redskins 2001, joined Jets in 2002.

Mose Rison, wide receiver; born July 22, 1956, Flint, Mich., lives on Long Island, N.Y. Running back Central Michigan 1974-77. No pro playing experience. College coach: Central Michigan 1981-87, U.S. Naval Academy 1988-89, Rutgers 1990-94, Stanford 1995-2000. Pro coach: Joined Jets in 2001.

Bob Sutton, linebackers; born January 23, 1951, Ypsilanti, Mich., lives on Long Island, N.Y. Attended Eastern Michigan. No college or pro playing experience. College coach: Michigan 1972-73, Syracuse 1974, Western Michigan 1975-76, Illinois 1977-79, North Carolina State 1982, Army 1983-1999 (head coach 1991-99). Pro coach: Joined Jets in 2000.

Mike Westhoff, special teams; born January 10, 1948, Pittsburgh, lives in Garden City, N.Y. Center-linebacker Wichita State 1967-69. No pro playing experience. College coach: Indiana 1974-75, Dayton 1976, Indiana State 1977, Northwestern 1978-1980, Texas Christian 1981. Pro coach: Baltimore/Indianapolis Colts 1982-84, Arizona Outlaws (USFL) 1985, Miami Dolphins 1986-2000, joined Jets in 2001.

**American Football Conference
West Division**
Team Colors: Silver and Black
**1220 Harbor Bay Parkway
Alameda, California 94502
Telephone:** (510) 864-5000

2002 SCHEDULE
PRESEASON
Aug. 9   at Dallas.................................8:00
Aug. 15   at Tennessee.........................7:00
Aug. 24   **San Francisco** 6:00
Aug. 29   **Arizona** 6:00

REGULAR SEASON
Sept. 8   **Seattle**...............................1:15
Sept. 15   at Pittsburgh.......................8:30
Sept. 22   Open Date
Sept. 29   **Tennessee** 1:15
Oct. 6   at Buffalo 1:00
Oct. 13   at St. Louis.........................3:15
Oct. 20   **San Diego**...........................1:05
Oct. 27   at Kansas City 12:00
Nov. 3   **San Francisco** 1:15
Nov. 11   at Denver (Mon.) 7:00
Nov. 17   **New England** 5:30
Nov. 24   at Arizona...........................2:05
Dec. 2   **New York Jets** (Mon.) 6:00
Dec. 8   at San Diego 1:15
Dec. 15   at Miami.............................1:00
Dec. 22   **Denver**...............................1:15
Dec. 28   **Kansas City** (Sat.).............2:00

Stadium: Network Associates Coliseum
            (opened in 1966)
            •**Capacity:** 63,132
Playing Surface: Grass
Training Camp: Napa Valley Marriott
                Napa, California 94558

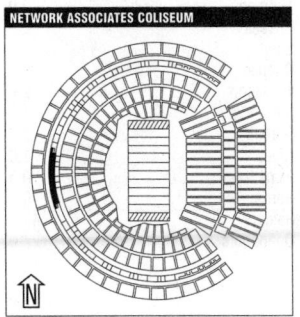
NETWORK ASSOCIATES COLISEUM

CLUB OFFICIALS
Owner: Al Davis
Chief Executive: Amy Trask
Executive Assistant: Al LoCasale
General Counsel: Jeff Birren
Senior Assistant: Bruce Allen
Personnel Executive: Mike Lombardi
Personnel Executive: Chet Franklin
Legal Affairs: Jeff Birren,
    Roxanne Kosarzycki
Finance: Marc Badain, Tom Blanda,
    Derek Person
Special Projects: Jim Otto
Senior Administrator: Morris Bradshaw
Senior Executive: John Herrera
Public Relations Director: Mike Taylor
Player Development and Community
    Relations: Terry Burton
Public Relations: Craig Long
Ticket Operations: Peter Eiges
Head Trainer: H. Rod Martin
Assistant Trainer: Scott Touchet
Assistant Trainer: Mark Mayer
Equipment Manager: Bob Romanski
Video Director: Dave Nash

COACHING HISTORY
**Oakland 1960-1981
Los Angeles 1982-1994
(393-264-11)**

1960-61	Eddie Erdelatz*	6-10-0
1961-62	Marty Feldman**	2-15-0
1962	Red Conkright	1-8-0
1963-65	Al Davis	23-16-3
1966-68	John Rauch	35-10-1
1969-1978	John Madden	112-39-7
1979-1987	Tom Flores	91-56-0
1988-89	Mike Shanahan***	8-12-0
1989-1994	Art Shell	56-41-0
1995-96	Mike White	15-17-0
1997	Joe Bugel	4-12-0
1998-2001	Jon Gruden	40-28-0

*Released after two games in 1961
**Released after five games in 1962
***Released after four games in 1989

ATTENDANCE
Home 458,539   Away 560,213
Total 1,018,752
Single-game home record,
62,637 (11/5/01)
Single-season home record, 458,539
(2001)

2002 DRAFT CHOICES
Round	Name	Pos.	College
1	Phillip Buchanon	DB	Miami
	Napoleon Harris	LB	Northwestern
2	Langston Walker	T	California
	Doug Jolley	TE	Brigham Young
5	Kenyon Coleman	DE	UCLA
6	Keyon Nash	DB	Albany State
	Larry Ned	RB	San Diego St.
7	Ronald Curry	QB	North Carolina

2001 TEAM RECORD

PRESEASON (3-2)

Date	Result	Opponent
8/4	W 21-14	Dallas
8/11	W 10-7	at Arizona
8/19	L 17-20	at San Francisco
8/27	L 6-21	vs. Dallas, at Mexico City
8/31	W 24-13	Green Bay

REGULAR SEASON (10-6)

Date	Result	Opponent	Att.
9/09	W 27-24	at Kansas City	78,844
9/23	L 15-18	at Miami	73,404
9/30	W 38-14	Seattle	54,629
10/07	W 28-21	Dallas	61,535
10/14	W 23-18	at Indianapolis	56,972
10/28	W 20-10	at Philadelphia	65,342
11/05	W 38-28	Denver	62,637
11/11	L 27-34	at Seattle	67,231
11/18	W 34-24	San Diego	61,960
11/25	W 28-10	at New York Giants	78,756
12/02	L 31-34	Arizona(OT)	46,601
12/09	W 28-26	Kansas City	60,784
12/15	W 13-6	at San Diego	67,349
12/22	L 10-13	Tennessee	61,934
12/30	L 17-23	at Denver	75,582
1/06	L 22-24	New York Jets	62,011

(OT) Overtime

POSTSEASON (1-1)

1/12	W 38-24	New York Jets	61,503
1/19	L 13-16	at New England (OT)	60,292

SCORE BY PERIODS

Raiders	87	116	97	99	0	—	399
Opponents	53	83	83	105	3	—	327

2001 TEAM STATISTICS

	Raiders	Opp.
Total First Downs	316	296
Rushing	102	104
Passing	195	166
Penalty	19	26
3rd Down: Made/Att	81/209	67/210
3rd Down Pct.	38.8	31.9
4th Down: Made/Att	8/13	9/20
4th Down Pct.	61.5	45.0
Possession Avg.	30:56	29:04
Total Net Yards	5361	5071
Avg. Per Game	335.1	316.9
Total Plays	1030	1002
Avg. Per Play	5.2	5.1
Net Yards Rushing	1654	1988
Avg. Per Game	103.4	124.3
Total Rushes	450	433
Net Yards Passing	3707	3083
Avg. Per Game	231.7	192.7
Sacked/Yards Lost	27/155	41/204
Gross Yards	3862	3287
Att./Completions	553/364	528/290
Completion Pct.	65.8	54.9
Had Intercepted	9	17
Punts/Average	74/45.6	83/40.9
Net Punting Avg.	74/35.6	83/34.6
Penalties/Yards	107/897	81/621
Fumbles/Ball Lost	27/16	18/7
Touchdowns	46	36
Rushing	14	17
Passing	27	16
Returns	5	3

2001 INDIVIDUAL STATISTICS

PASSING	Att.	Comp.	Yds.	Pct.	TD	Int.	Tkld.	Rate
Gannon	549	361	3828	65.8	27	9	27/155	95.5
Tuiasosopo	4	3	34	75.0	0	0	0/0	100.0
Raiders	553	364	3862	65.8	27	9	27/155	95.5
Opponents	528	290	3287	54.9	16	17	41/204	70.5

	TD	TD	TD				
SCORING	R	P	Rt	PAT	FG	Saf	PTS
Janikowski	0	0	0	42/42	23/28	0	111
Brown	0	9	1	0/0	0/0	0	60
Rice	0	9	0	0/0	0/0	0	54
Crockett	6	0	0	0/0	0/0	0	36
Wheatley	5	1	0	0/0	0/0	0	36
Garner	1	2	0	0/0	0/0	0	18
R. Williams	0	3	0	0/0	0/0	0	18
Gannon	2	0	0	0/0	0/0	0	14
Dorsett	0	0	2	0/0	0/0	0	12
Ritchie	0	2	0	0/0	0/0	0	12
Daluiso	0	0	0	1/2	3/4	0	10
Allen	0	0	1	0/0	0/0	0	6
J. Brigham	0	1	0	0/0	0/0	0	6
Kirby	0	0	1	0/0	0/0	0	6
Raiders	14	27	5	43/44	26/32	0	399
Opponents	17	16	3	28/29	25/33	0	327

2-Pt. Conversions: Gannon.
Raiders 1-2, Opponents 4-7.

RUSHING	Att.	Yds.	Avg.	LG	TD
Garner	211	839	4.0	38	1
Wheatley	88	276	3.1	22	5
Gannon	63	231	3.7	17	2
Crockett	57	145	2.5	10	6
Jordan	13	59	4.5	37	0
Kirby	10	49	4.9	20	0
Brown	4	39	9.8	19	0
Porter	2	13	6.5	7	0
Lechler	1	2	2.0	2	0
Tuiasosopo	1	1	1.0	1	0
Raiders	450	1654	3.7	38	14
Opponents	433	1988	4.6	88t	17

RECEIVING	No.	Yds.	Avg.	LG	TD
Brown	91	1165	12.8	46t	9
Rice	83	1139	13.7	40t	9
Garner	72	578	8.0	27	2
R. Williams	33	298	9.0	49	3
Porter	19	220	11.6	21	0
Ritchie	19	154	8.1	17	2
J. Brigham	12	85	7.1	17	1
Wheatley	12	61	5.1	11	1
Jordan	9	63	7.0	19	0
Kirby	9	62	6.9	9	0
Jett	2	19	9.5	10	0
Crockett	2	10	5.0	8	0
Dunn	1	8	8.0	8	0
Raiders	364	3862	10.6	49	27
Opponents	290	3287	11.3	67t	16

INTERCEPTIONS	No.	Yds.	Avg.	LG	TD
James	5	72	14.4	33	0
Thomas	3	46	15.3	33	0
Dorsett	2	65	32.5	39t	2
Woodson	1	64	64.0	34	0
Pope	1	22	22.0	22	0
Allen	1	19	19.0	19	0
Gibson	1	9	9.0	9	0
Smith	1	9	9.0	9	0
Cooper	1	0	0.0	0	0
Russell	1	0	0.0	0	0
Raiders	17	306	18.0	41	2
Opponents	9	147	16.3	51t	1

PUNTING	No.	Yds.	Avg.	In 20	LG
Lechler	73	3375	46.2	23	65
Raiders	74	3375	45.6	23	65
Opponents	83	3394	40.9	24	76

PUNT RETURNS	No.	FC	Yds.	Avg.	LG	TD
Dunn	19	11	169	8.9	23	0
Brown	6	21	111	18.5	88t	1
Woodson	4	0	47	11.8	16	0
Porter	0	0	12	—	12	0
Raiders	29	32	339	11.7	88t	1
Opponents	34	5	502	14.8	55	0

KICKOFF RETURNS	No.	Yds.	Avg.	LG	TD
Kirby	46	1066	23.2	90t	1
Dunn	20	458	22.9	40	0
Raiders	66	1524	23.1	90t	1
Opponents	75	1657	22.1	93t	1

FIELD GOALS	1-19	20-29	30-39	40-49	50+
Janikowski	0/0	7/7	9/10	6/9	1/2
Daluiso	0/0	1/2	1/1	1/1	0/0
Raiders	0/0	8/9	10/11	7/10	1/2
Opponents	0/0	11/12	9/11	4/7	1/3

SACKS	No.
Upshaw	7.0
Coleman	6.0
Bryant	5.0
Jackson	4.0
Biekert	3.0
Thomas	3.0
Russell	2.5
Smith	2.5
Cooper	2.0
Woodson	2.0
Alexander	1.0
Dorsett	1.0
Taves	1.0
Armstrong	0.5
Harris	0.5
Raiders	41.0
Opponents	27.0

RECORD HOLDERS
INDIVIDUAL RECORDS—CAREER

Category	Name	Performance
Rushing (Yds.)	Marcus Allen, 1982-1992	8,545
Passing (Yds.)	Ken Stabler, 1970-79	19,078
Passing (TDs)	Ken Stabler, 1970-79	150
Receiving (No.)	Tim Brown, 1988-2001	937
Receiving (Yds.)	Tim Brown, 1988-2001	13,237
Interceptions	Willie Brown, 1967-1978	39
	Lester Hayes, 1977-1986	39
Punting (Avg.)	Shane Lechler, 2000-01	46.1
Punt Return (Avg.)	Claude Gibson, 1963-65	12.6
Kickoff Return (Avg.)	Jack Larscheid, 1960-61	28.4
Field Goals	Chris Bahr, 1980-88	162
Touchdowns (Tot.)	Tim Brown, 1988-2001	100
Points	George Blanda, 1967-1975	863

INDIVIDUAL RECORDS—SINGLE SEASON

Category	Name	Performance
Rushing (Yds.)	Marcus Allen, 1985	1,759
Passing (Yds.)	Jeff George, 1997	3,917
Passing (TDs)	Daryle Lamonica, 1969	34
Receiving (No.)	Tim Brown 1997	104
Receiving (Yds.)	Tim Brown, 1997	1,408
Interceptions	Lester Hayes, 1980	13
Punting (Avg.)	Shane Lechler, 2001	46.2
Punt Return (Avg.)	Claude Gibson, 1964	14.4
Kickoff Return (Avg.)	Harold Hart, 1975	30.5
Field Goals	Jeff Jaeger, 1993	35
Touchdowns (Tot.)	Marcus Allen, 1984	18
Points	Jeff Jaeger, 1993	132

INDIVIDUAL RECORDS—SINGLE GAME

Category	Name	Performance
Rushing (Yds.)	Napoleon Kaufman, 10-19-97	227
Passing (Yds.)	Jeff Hostetler, 10-31-93	424
Passing (TDs)	Tom Flores, 12-22-63	6
	Daryle Lamonica, 10-19-69	6
Receiving (No.)	Tim Brown, 12-21-97	14
Receiving (Yds.)	Art Powell, 12-22-63	247
Interceptions	Many times	3
	Last time by Terry McDaniel, 10-9-94	
Field Goals	Jeff Jaeger, 12-11-94	5
	Sebastian Janikowski, 10-29-00	5
Touchdowns (Tot.)	Art Powell, 12-22-63	4
	Marcus Allen, 9-24-84	4
	Harvey Williams, 11-16-97	4
Points	Art Powell, 12-22-63	24
	Marcus Allen, 9-24-84	24
	Harvey Williams, 11-16-97	24

2002 VETERAN ROSTER

No.	Name	Pos.	Ht.	Wt.	Birthdate	NFL Exp.	College	Hometown	How Acq.	'01 Games/ Starts
69	Ackerman, Tom	G-C	6-3	300	9/6/72	7	Eastern Washington	Bellingham, Wash.	FA-'02	16/0*
93	Armstrong, Trace	DE	6-4	275	10/5/65	14	Florida	Birmingham, Ala.	FA-'02	3/0
77	Ashmore, Darryl	G-T	6-6	310	11/1/69	10	Northwestern	Peoria, Ill.	FA-'98	14/1
70	Badger, Brad	T	6-4	320	1/11/75	6	Stanford	Corvalllis, Ore.	FA-'02	13/12*
85	Barlow, Reggie	WR	6-0	190	1/22/73	6	Alabama State	Montgomery, Ala.	FA-'01	0*
50	Barton, Eric	LB	6-2	245	9/29/77	4	Maryland	Alexandria, Va.	D5-'99	16/1
54	Biekert, Greg	LB	6-2	255	3/14/69	10	Colorado	Longmont, Colo	D7-'93	16/16
27	Branch, Calvin	S	5-11	195	5/8/74	5	Colorado State	Spring, Texas	FA-'02	0*
87	Brigham, Jeremy	TE	6-6	255	3/22/75	5	Washington	Scottsdale, Ariz.	D5-'98	14/3
55	Brooks, Bobby	LB	6-2	240	3/3/76	3	Fresno State	Vallejo, Calif	FA-'99	16/0
52	Brown, Cornell	LB	6-1	240	3/15/75	5	Virginia Tech	Lynchburg, Va.	FA-'02	0*
81	Brown, Tim	WR	6-0	195	7/22/66	15	Notre Dame	Dallas, Texas	D1-'88	16/16
94	Bryant, Tony	DE	6-6	275	9/3/76	4	Florida State	Marathon, Fla.	D2-'99	16/16
57	Coleman, Rod	DT	6-2	285	8/16/76	4	East Carolina	Philadelphia, Pa.	D5-'99	14/6
79	Collins, Mo	T	6-4	325	9/22/76	5	Florida	Charlotte, N.C.	D1-'98	5/4
75	Cooper, Chris	DT	6-5	275	12/27/77	2	Nebraska-Omaha	Lincoln, Neb.	D6-'01	12/1
32	Crockett, Zack	RB	6-2	240	12/2/72	8	Florida State	Pompano Beach, Fla.	UFA(Jax)-'99	16/1
	Davis, Billy	WR	6-1	205	7/6/72	7	Pittsburgh	El Paso, Texas	FA-'02	0*
51	Dixon, Gerald	LB	6-2	255	6/20/69	10	South Carolina	Rock Hill, S.C.	UFA(SD)-'02	16/15*
33	Dorsett, Anthony	S	5-11	205	9/14/73	7	Pittsburgh	Aliquippa, Pa.	UFA(Tenn)-'00	16/16
89	Fulcher, Mondriel	TE	6-3	250	10/15/76	3	Miami	Coffeyville, Kan.	D7-'00	13/1
12	Gannon, Rich	QB	6-3	210	12/20/65	15	Delaware	Philadelphia, Pa.	UFA(KC)-'99	16/16
25	Garner, Charlie	RB	5-10	190	2/13/72	9	Tennessee	Fairfax, Va.	UFA(SF)-'01	16/16
36	Gibson, Derrick	S	6-2	215	3/22/79	2	Florida State	Miami, Fla.	D1-'01	16/0
95	Grant, DeLawrence	DE	6-3	280	11/18/79	2	Oregon State	Compton, Calif	D3-'01	2/0
37	Harris, Johnnie	S	6-2	210	8/21/72	4	Mississippi State	Chicago, Ill.	FA-'99	16/5
67	Harris, Jon	DE	6-7	310	6/9/74	3	Virginia	Inwood, N.Y.	FA-'02	0*
	Hatchette, Matthew	WR	6-2	201	5/1/74	5	Langston	Cleveland, Ohio	FA-'01	11/0*
23	Hill, Madre	RB	6-1	205	1/2/76	2	Arkansas	Malvern, Ark.	FA-'02	0*
4	Howard, Eddie	P-K	6-2	230	10/6/72	3	Idaho	Covina, Calif.	FA-'02	0*
14	Hoying, Bobby	QB	6-3	220	9/20/72	7	Ohio State	St. Henry, Ohio	T(Phil)-'99	0*
92	Ioane, Junior	DT	6-4	320	7/21/77	3	Arizona State	Mt. Pleasant, Utah	D4-'00	3/0
20	James, Tory	CB	6-2	190	5/18/73	7	Louisiana State	Marrero, La.	UFA(Den)-'00	16/2
11	Janikowski, Sebastian	K	6-2	255	3/3/78	4	Florida State	Daytona Beach, Fla.	D1-'00	15/0
39	Jennings, Brandon	CB	6-0	190	7/15/78	3	Texas A&M	Channelview, Texas	FA-'00	8/0
82	Jett, James	WR	5-10	170	12/28/70	10	West Virginia	Kearneysville, W. Va.	FA-'93	11/0
41	Johnson, Eric	CB	6-0	190	4/30/76	3	Nebraska	Phoenix, Ariz	FA-'00	7/0
28	Jordan, Randy	RB	5-11	220	6/6/70	9	North Carolina	Manson, N.C.	FA-'98	16/0
72	Kennedy, Lincoln	T	6-6	335	2/12/71	10	Washington	San Diego, Calif.	T(Atl)-'96	15/15
42	Kirby, Terry	RB	6-1	225	1/20/70	10	Virginia	Tabb. Va.	FA-'00	11/0
83	Knight, Marcus	WR	6-1	180	6/19/78	2	Michigan	Sylacauga, Ala.	FA-'00	5/1
9	Lechler, Shane	P	6-2	225	8/7/76	3	Texas A&M	East Bernard, Texas	D5-'00	16/0
38	Love, Clarence	CB	5-10	180	6/16/76	2	Toledo	Jackson, Mich.	FA-'02	0*
73	Middleton, Frank	G	6-4	330	10/25/74	6	Arizona	Beaumont, Texas	UFA(TB)-'01	13/12
3	Mirer, Rick	QB	6-3	210	3/19/70	10	Notre Dame	Goshen, Ind.	FA-'02	0*
98	Mohring, Mike	DT	6-5	305	3/22/74	6	Pittsburgh	Glen Cove, N.Y.	FA-'02	9/0*
97	Parrella, John	DT	6-3	300	11/22/69	10	Nebraska	Topeka, Kan.	FA-'02	16/16*
84	Porter, Jerry	WR	6-2	220	7/14/78	3	West Virginia	Washington, D.C.	D2-'00	15/1
80	Rice, Jerry	WR	6-2	195	10/13/62	18	Mississippi Valley State	Crawford, Miss.	FA-'01	16/15
40	Ritchie, Jon	FB	6-1	250	9/4/74	5	Stanford	Mechanicsburgh, Pa.	D3-'98	15/10
63	Robbins, Barret	C	6-3	320	8/26/73	8	Texas Christian	Houston, Texas	D2-'95	2/2
53	Romanowski, Bill	LB	6-4	245	4/2/66	15	Boston College	Vernon, Conn.	FA-'02	16/16*
22	Shaw, Terrance	CB	6-0	200	1/11/73	8	Stephen F. Austin	Marshall, Texas	FA-'02	13/2*
65	Sims, Barry	T	6-5	300	12/1/74	4	Utah	Park City, Utah	FA-'99	15/15
78	Slaughter, Chad	T	6-8	340	6/4/78	2	Alcorn State	Dallas, Texas	FA-'02	0*
56	Smith, Travian	LB	6-4	240	8/26/75	5	Oklahoma	Tatum, Texas	D5-'98	16/2
64	Staat, Jeremy	T-G	6-4	305	10/10/76	4	Arizona State	Bakersfield, Calif.	FA-'02	0*
74	Stinchcomb, Matt	T	6-6	310	6/3/77	4	Georgia	Liiburn, Ga.	D1-'99	15/1
99	Taves, Josh	DE	6-7	285	5/13/72	3	Northeastern	Yarmouth, Mass.	FA-'00	8/3
59	Thomas, William	LB	6-2	225	8/13/68	12	Texas A&M	Amarillo, Texas	FA-'00	16/15
62	Treu, Adam	C	6-5	300	6/24/74	6	Nebraska	Lincoln, Neb.	D3-'97	16/14
8	Tuiasosopo, Marques	QB	6-1	220	3/22/79	2	Washington	Woodinville, Wash.	D2-'01	1/0
91	Upshaw, Regan	DE	6-4	260	8/12/75	7	California	Pittsburg, Calif.	UFA(Jax)-'00	16/15
6	Van Dyke, Alex	WR	6-0	210	7/24/74	5	Nevada	Sacramento, Calif.	FA-'02	0*
47	Wheatley, Tyrone	RB	6-0	235	1/19/72	8	Michigan	Inkster, Mich.	FA-'99	11/2

86	Williams, Roland	TE	6-5	255	4/27/75	6	Syracuse	Rochester, N.Y.	T(StL)-'01	16/15
76	Wisniewski, Steve	G	6-4	305	4/7/67	14	Penn State	Houston, Texas	D2-'89	16/16
24	Woodson, Charles	CB	6-1	200	10/7/76	5	Michigan	Fremont, Ohio	D1-'98	16/15
26	Woodson, Rod	S	6-2	205	3/10/65	15	Purdue	Fort Wayne, Ind.	FA-'02	16/16*

* Ackerman last active with New Orleans in '00; Badger played 13 games with Minnesota in '01; Barlow last active with Jacksonville in '00; Branch last active with Raiders in '00; C. Brown last active with Baltimore '00; Davis last active with Baltimore in '00; Dixon played 16 games with San Diego; Harris last active with Green Bay in '99; Hatchette played 11 games with N.Y. Jets; Hill last active with Cleveland in '99; Howard last active with San Francisco in '99; Hoying inactive for 5 games; Love last active with Baltimore in '99; Mirer inactive 10 games with San Francisco; Mohring played 9 games with San Diego; Parrella played 16 games with San Diego; Romanowski played 16 games with Denver; Shaw played 13 games with New England; Slaughter last active with N.Y. Jets in '00; Staat last active with Pittsburgh in '00; Van Dyke last active with Philadelphia in '00; R. Woodson played 16 games with Baltimore.

Retired—Eric Allen, 14-year cornerback, 16 games in '01.

Players lost through free agency (3): C Aaron Graham (Tenn; 14), DT Grady Jackson (NO; 16), QB Rodney Peete (Car; 1).

Also played with the Raiders in '01—K Brad Daluiso (1 game), WR David Dunn (10), CB James Hasty (1), DE Darren Mickell (2), T Toby Myles (1), S Marquez Pope (16), DT Darrell Russell (11), RB Jermaine Williams (1).

2002 FIRST-YEAR ROSTER

Name	Pos.	Ht.	Wt.	Birthdate	College	Hometown	How Acq.
Angel, Chris	CB-S	6-0	205	7/5/79	Western Oregon	Albany, Ore.	FA
Barnett, Melvin	RB	6-0	245	11/16/79	Baylor	Cuero, Texas	FA
Buchanon, Phillip	CB	5-9	185	9/19/80	Miami	Fort Meyers, Fla.	D1a
Christenson, Brandon (1)	TE	6-5	260	5/10/77	Northwestern Oklahoma State	Clinton, Okla.	FA
Coleman, Kenyon	DE	6-4	285	4/10/79	Southern California	Alta Loma, Calif.	D5
Combs, Derek (1)	CB	6-0	195	2/28/79	Ohio State	Urbancrest, Ohio	FA
Curry, Ronald	QB	6-1	220	5/28/79	North Carolina	Hampton, Va.	D7
Ekiyor, Emil (1)	DE	6-4	250	12/25/74	Central Florida	Daytona Beach, Fla.	FA
Emanuel, Jim (1)	LB	6-1	235	3/26/76	Hofstra	Denver, Colo.	FA
Fields, Marcus	RB	6-2	225	2/18/79	California	Stockton, Calif.	FA
Ford, Willie	DB	6-2	200	5/12/78	Syracuse	Falmouth, Mass.	FA
Harris, Napoleon	LB	6-2	255	2/25/79	Northwestern	Dixmoor, Ill.	D1b
Jolley, Doug	TE	6-4	250	1/2/79	Brigham Young	St. George, Utah	D2b
McKenzie, Kevin (1)	WR	5-11	195	9/20/75	Washington State	Long Beach, Calif.	FA
Nash, Keyon	CB-S	6-3	215	3/11/79	Albany State (Ga.)	Colquitt, Ga.	D6a
Ned, Larry	RB	5-11	215	8/23/78	San Diego State	Moreno Valley, Calif.	D6b
Perryman, Raymond (1)	S	5-11	195	11/27/78	Northern Arizona	Phoenix, Ariz.	FA
Pickens, Derrick	DT-DE	6-1	295	7/19/80	Iowa	Houston, Texas	FA
Slaughter, Chad (1)	G-T	6-7	345	6/4/78	Alcorn State	Dallas, Texas	FA
Thurmon, Elijah (1)	WR	6-4	205	8/2/78	Howard	Severn, Md.	FA
Walker, Langston	T	6-8	345	9/3/79	California	Oakland, Calif.	D2a
White, Ted (1)	QB	6-2	225	5/29/76	Howard	Baton Rouge, La.	FA
Whiting, Teag	G-T	6-3	320	4/16/79	Brigham Young	Salt Lake City, Utah	FA
Williams, Marcus (1)	TE	6-5	230	12/12/77	Washington State	Oakland, Calif.	FA
Williams, Royd	WR	6-2	210	3/13/79	Alabama-Birmingham	Birmingham, Ala.	FA
Wong, Joe (1)	G-T	6-6	315	2/24/76	Brigham Young	Honolulu, Hawaii	FA

The term NFL Rookie is defined as a player who is in his first season of professional football and has not been on the roster of another professional football team for any regular-season or postseason games. A Rookie is designated by an "R" on NFL rosters. Players who have been active in another professional football league or players who have NFL experience, including either preseason training camp or being on an Active List or Inactive List, or on Reserve/Injured or Reserve/Physically Unable to Perform for fewer than six regular-season games, are termed NFL First-Year Players. An NFL First-Year Player is designated by a "1" on NFL rosters. Thereafter, a player is credited with an additional year of experience for each season in which he accumulates six games on the Active List or Inactive List, or on Reserve/Injured or Reserve/Physically Unable to Perform.

COACHING STAFF

Head Coach,
Bill Callahan

Pro career: Bill Callahan became the 13th Head Coach in Oakland Raiders history on March 12, 2002. Callahan, 45, spent the past four seasons as offensive coordinator for the Raiders. In addition to serving as offensive coordinator, Callahan also coached the Raiders' offensive line for the past three seasons and doubled as tight ends coach in 1998. In 2001, with Callahan as offensive coordinator, the Raiders captured their second consecutive American Football Conference Western Division title, finishing second in the AFC (fourth in NFL) in passing at 231.7 yards per game and fourth in the conference in total offense (seventh in NFL) with 335.1 yards per game average. Last year under Callahan's tutelage, the Raiders allowed only 27 sacks, the least ever in franchise history in a 16-game regular season as Oakland advanced to the divisional round of the AFC playoffs. The Raiders offense also produced a 3,000-yard passer for the third straight season (Rich Gannon, 3,828) and two 1,000-yard receivers (Tim Brown, 1,165 and Jerry Rice, 1,139). Under Callahan, the Raiders led the NFL in rushing in 2000, averaging 154.4 yards per game as Oakland advanced to the AFC Championship Game. The Raiders also led the NFL in first downs rushing with 128, ranked second in rushing touchdowns, and ranked third in both scoring and total offense. In 1999 under Callahan, the Raiders were third in the NFL in rushing yards and fifth in total offense. Prior to joining the Raiders, Callahan coached offensive line for the Philadelphia Eagles from 1995-97, where he worked with former Raiders head coach Jon Gruden. In 1995 and 1996, Callahan's offensive line unit helped the Eagles rank second in NFC in rushing.

Background: Callahan was a three-year starter at quarterback at Illinois Benedictine (1975-77), where he was a NAIA honorable mention All-American in his final two seasons. Coached collegiately at Illinois (1980-86) and Northern Arizona (1987-88), before being named offensive coordinator at Southern Illinois (1989), where his offensive unit set 18 school records. From 1990-94, Callahan was offensive line coach at Wisconsin when Badger linemen earned nine first team All-Big Ten honors.

Personal: Born July 31, 1956, in Chicago. Callahan and his wife Valerie have four children—Brian, Daniel, Cathryn and Jaclyn.

ASSISTANT COACHES

Fred Biletnikoff, wide receivers; born February 23, 1943, Erie, Pa., lives in San Ramon, Calif. Wide receiver Florida State 1962-64. Pro wide receiver Oakland Raiders 1965-1978, Montreal Alouettes (CFL) 1980. Inducted into Pro Football Hall of Fame in 1988. College coach: Palomar (Calif.) J.C. 1983, Diablo Valley (Calif.) J.C. 1984, 1986. Pro coach: Oakland Invaders (USFL) 1985, Calgary Stampeders (CFL) 1987-88, joined Raiders in 1989.

Chuck Bresnahan, defensive coordinator; born September 8, 1960, Springfield, Mass., lives in Alameda, Calif. Linebacker Navy 1979-1982. No pro playing experience. College coach: Navy 1983, 1986, Georgia Tech 1987-1991, Maine 1992-93. Pro coach: Cleveland Browns 1994-95, Indianapolis Colts 1996-97, joined Raiders in 1998.

Willie Brown, squad development; born December 2, 1940, Yazoo City, Miss., lives in Tracy, Calif. Defensive back Grambling 1959-1962. Pro defensive back Denver Broncos 1963-66, Oakland Raiders 1967-78. Inducted into Pro Football Hall of Fame in 1984. College coach: Long Beach State 1990-91 (head coach 1991). Pro coach: Oakland/Los Angeles Raiders 1979-1988, rejoined Raiders in 1995.

Bob Casullo, special teams; born March 24, 1951, Little Falls, N.Y., lives in Alameda, Calif. Running back Brockport State College 1970-73. No pro playing experience. College coach: Syracuse 1985-1994, Georgia Tech 1995-98, Michigan State 1999. Pro coach: Joined Raiders in 2000.

Garrett Giemont, strength and conditioning; born August 31, 1957, Fullerton, Calif., lives in San Francisco. Attended Fullerton College. No college or pro playing experience. Pro coach: Los Angeles Rams 1990-91, joined Raiders in 1995.

Chris Griswold, quality control-defense; born February 23, 1973, Hornell, N.Y., lives in Alameda. Defensive lineman Hobart College 1992-96. No pro playing experience. College coach: Allegheny 1998, Princeton 1999-2001. Pro coach: Joined Raiders in 2002.

Jim Harbaugh, offensive assistant; born December 23, 1963, Toledo, Ohio, lives in Alameda, Calif. Quarterback Michigan 1983-87. Pro quarterback Chicago Bears 1987-1993, Indianapolis Colts 1994-97, Baltimore Ravens 1998, San Diego Chargers 1999-2000, Carolina Panthers 2001. Pro coach: Joined Raiders in 2002.

Aaron Kromer, asst. offensive line; born April 30, 1967, Sandusky, Ohio, lives in Alameda, Calif. Offensive tackle Miami (Ohio) 1986-89. No pro playing experience. College coach: Miami (Ohio) 1990-98, Northwestern 1999-2000. Pro coach: Joined Raiders in 2001.

Ron Lynn, defensive backs; born December 6, 1944, Youngstown, Ohio, lives in Pleasanton, Calif. Quarterback Mount Union College 1963-66. No pro playing experience. Pro coach: Oakland Invaders (USFL) 1983-85, San Diego Chargers 1986-1991, Cincinnati Bengals 1992-93, Washington Redskins 1994-96, New England Patriots 1997-99, joined Raiders in 2000.

Don Martin, quality control-defense; born September 17, 1949, Carrollton, Mo., lives in Oakland. Running back Yale 1968-1970. Pro defensive back New England Patriots 1973, Kansas City Chiefs 1975, Tampa Bay Buccaneers 1976. College coach: Yale 1981-1996. Pro coach: Joined Raiders in 1998.

John Morton, quality control-offense; born September 24, 1969, Pontiac, Mich., lives in Castro Valley, Calif. Wide receiver Western Michigan 1991-92, Grand Rapids (Mich.) C.C. 1989-1990. Pro wide receiver Los Angeles Raiders 1993-94, Toronto Argonauts (CFL) 1995-96, Frankfurt Galaxy (WLAF) 1997. Pro coach: Joined Raiders in 1998.

Jay Norvell, tight ends; born March 28, 1963, Madison, Wis., lives in Alameda. Defensive back Iowa 1982-85. Pro defensive back Chicago Bears 1987. College coach: Iowa 1986, Northern Iowa 1988, Wisconsin 1989-93, Iowa State 1995-97. Pro coach: Indianapolis Colts 1998-2001, joined Raiders in 2002.

Fred Pagac, linebackers; born April 26, 1952, Richeyville, Pa., lives in Alameda, Calif. Tight end Ohio State 1971-73. Pro tight end Chicago Bears 1974-75, Tampa Bay Buccaneers 1976-77. College coach: Ohio State 1982-2000. Pro coach: Joined Raiders in 2001.

Skip Peete, running backs, born January 30, 1963, Mesa, Ariz., lives in Alameda, Calif. Wide receiver Arizona 1981-82, Kansas 1984-85. Pro wide receiver New York Jets 1987. College coach: Pittsburgh 1988-92, Michigan State 1993-94, Rutgers 1995, UCLA 1996-97. Pro coach: Joined Raiders in 1998.

Marc Trestman, senior assistant; born January 15, 1956, Minneapolis, lives in Alameda, Calif. Quarterback Minnesota 1974-75, Moorhead (Minn.) State 1977. No pro playing experience. College coach: Miami 1981-84. Pro coach: Minnesota Vikings 1985-86, 1990-91, Tampa Bay Buccaneers 1987, Cleveland Browns 1988-89, San Francisco 49ers 1995-96, Detroit Lions 1997, Arizona Cardinals 1998-2000, joined Raiders in 2001.

Chris Turner, quality control-offense; born February 28, 1969, Fairfield, Calif., lives in Martinez, Calif. No pro playing experience. College coach: San Jose State 1993, Notre Dame 1994, Bucknell 1995-2001. Pro coach: Joined Raiders in 2002.

Mike Waufle, defensive line; born June 27, 1954, Hornell, N.Y., lives in Oakland. Defensive lineman Bakersfield J.C. 1975-76, Utah State 1977-78. No pro playing experience. College coach: Alfred 1979, Utah State 1980-84, Fresno State 1985-88, UCLA 1989, Oregon State 1990-91, California 1992-97. Pro coach: Joined Raiders in 1998.

American Football Conference
North Division
Team Colors: Black and Gold
3400 South Water Street
Pittsburgh, Pennsylvania 15203
Telephone: (412) 432-7800

2002 SCHEDULE
PRESEASON

Aug. 8	**New York Jets**	8:00
Aug. 18	at Washington	8:00
Aug. 24	at Detroit	12:30
Aug. 29	**Minnesota**	7:30

REGULAR SEASON

Sept. 9	at New England (Mon.)	9:00
Sept. 15	**Oakland**	8:30
Sept. 22	Open Date	
Sept. 29	**Cleveland**	1:00
Oct. 6	at New Orleans	12:00
Oct. 13	at Cincinnati	1:00
Oct. 21	**Indianapolis** (Mon.)	9:00
Oct. 27	at Baltimore	1:00
Nov. 3	at Cleveland	1:00
Nov. 10	**Atlanta**	1:00
Nov. 17	at Tennessee	12:00
Nov. 24	**Cincinnati**	1:00
Dec. 1	at Jacksonville	1:00
Dec. 8	**Houston**	1:00
Dec. 15	**Carolina**	1:00
Dec. 23	at Tampa Bay (Mon.)	9:00
Dec. 29	**Baltimore**	1:00

Stadium: Heinz Field (opened in 2001)
  • Capacity: 64,450
  100 Art Rooney Ave.
  Pittsburgh, Pennsylvania 15212
Playing Surface: Grass
Training Camp: St. Vincent College
  Latrobe, Pennsylvania
  15650

HEINZ FIELD

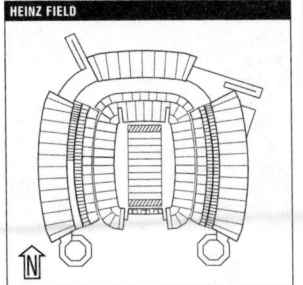

CLUB OFFICIALS
President: Daniel M. Rooney
Vice President/General Counsel:
  Arthur J. Rooney II
Vice President: John R. McGinley
Vice President: Arthur J. Rooney, Jr.
Administration Advisor: Charles H. Noll
Communications Coordinator: Ron Wahl
Public Relations/Media Manager:
  David Lockett
Director of Business: Mark Hart
Business Coordinator/Contract
  Negotiator: Omar Khan
Business Accounting Coordinator:
  Jim Ellenberger
Director of Football Operations:
  Kevin Colbert
College Personnel Coordinator: Bill Baker
Pro Personnel Coordinator: Doug Whaley
College Scouts: Kelvin Fisher,
  Mark Gorscak, Phil Kreidler, Bob Lane,
  Bruce McNorton, Dan Rooney
Office/Ticket Coordinator:
  Geraldine R. Glenn
Director of Marketing: Tony Quatrini
Player Development Coordinator:
  Arthony Griggs
Trainers: John Norwig, Ryan Grove
Equipment Manager: Rodgers Freyvogel

COACHING HISTORY
Pittsburgh Pirates 1933-1940
(475-490-20)

1933	Forrest (Jap) Douds	3-6-2
1934	Luby DiMelio	2-10-0
1935-36	Joe Bach	10-14-0
1937-39	Johnny (Blood) McNally*	6-19-0
1939-1940	Walt Kiesling	3-13-3
1941	Bert Bell**	0-2-0
	Aldo (Buff) Donelli***	0-5-0
1941-44	Walt Kiesling****	13-20-2
1945	Jim Leonard	2-8-0
1946-47	Jock Sutherland	13-10-1
1948-1951	Johnny Michelosen	20-26-2
1952-53	Joe Bach	11-13-0
1954-56	Walt Kiesling	14-22-0
1957-1964	Raymond (Buddy) Parker	51-48-6
1965	Mike Nixon	2-12-0
1966-68	Bill Austin	11-28-3
1969-1991	Chuck Noll	209-156-1
1992-2001	Bill Cowher	105-68-0

  *Released after three games in 1939
  **Resigned after two games in 1941
  ***Released after five games in 1941
  ****Co-coach with Earle (Greasy) Neale in
  Philadelphia-Pittsburgh merger in 1943 and
  with Phil Handler in Chicago Cardinals-
  Pittsburgh merger in 1944

ATTENDANCE
Home 509,726   Away 544,907
Total 1,054,633
Single-game home record,
63,763 (10/29/01)
Single-season home record, 509,726
(2001)

2002 DRAFT CHOICES

Round	Name	Pos.	College
1	Kendall Simmons	G	Auburn
2	Antwaan Randle El	WR	Indiana
3	Chris Hope	DB	Florida State
4	Larry Foote	LB	Michigan
5	Verron Haynes	RB	Georgia
6	Lee Mays	WR	Texas-El Paso
7	LaVar Glover	DB	Cincinnati
	Brett Keisel	DE	Brigham Young

PITTSBURGH STEELERS

2001 TEAM RECORD

PRESEASON (3-1)

Date	Result	Opponent
8/3	W 17-16	at Atlanta
8/16	L 10-24	at Minnesota
8/25	W 20-7	Detroit
8/30	W 20-0	Buffalo

REGULAR SEASON (13-3)

Date	Result	Opponent	Att.
9/09	L 3-21	at Jacksonville	63,785
9/30	W 20-3	at Buffalo	72,874
10/07	W 16-7	Cincinnati	62,335
10/14	W 20-17	at Kansas City	78,413
10/21	W 17-10	at Tampa Bay	65,588
10/29	W 34-7	Tennessee	63,763
11/04	L 10-13	Baltimore	62,906
11/11	W 15-12	at Cleveland(OT)	73,218
11/18	W 20-7	Jacksonville	62,644
11/25	W 34-24	at Tennessee	68,801
12/02	W 21-16	Minnesota	62,661
12/09	W 18-7	New York Jets	62,884
12/16	W 26-21	at Baltimore	69,506
12/23	W 47-14	Detroit	62,809
12/30	L 23-26	at Cincinnati(OT)	63,751
1/06	W 28-7	Cleveland	59,189

(OT) Overtime

POSTSEASON (1-1)

Date	Result	Opponent	Att.
1/20	W 27-10	Baltimore	63,976
1/27	L 17-24	New England	64,704

SCORE BY PERIODS

Steelers	60	108	102	79	3 —	352
Opponents	33	81	13	82	3 —	212

2001 TEAM STATISTICS

	Steelers	Opp.
Total First Downs	314	254
Rushing	148	70
Passing	150	160
Penalty	16	24
3rd Down: Made/Att	106/232	68/199
3rd Down Pct.	45.7	34.2
4th Down: Made/Att	6/12	4/17
4th Down Pct.	50.0	23.5
Possession Avg.	34:10	25:50
Total Net Yards	5887	4137
Avg. Per Game	367.9	258.6
Total Plays	1065	919
Avg. Per Play	5.5	4.5
Net Yards Rushing	2774	1195
Avg. Per Game	173.4	74.7
Total Rushes	580	339
Net Yards Passing	3113	2942
Avg. Per Game	194.6	183.9
Sacked/Yards Lost	31/182	55/367
Gross Yards	3295	3309
Att./Completions	454/274	525/295
Completion Pct.	60.4	56.2
Had Intercepted	12	16
Punts/Average	63/41.4	87/42.3
Net Punting Avg.	63/34.6	87/36.3
Penalties/Yards	86/737	71/585
Fumbles/Ball Lost	28/9	27/12
Touchdowns	38	26
Rushing	17	5
Passing	16	19
Returns	5	2

2001 INDIVIDUAL STATISTICS

PASSING

	Att.	Comp.	Yds.	Pct.	TD	Int.	Tkld.	Rate
Stewart	442	266	3109	60.2	14	11	29/175	81.7
Maddox	9	7	154	77.8	1	1	1/4	116.2
Bettis	2	1	32	50.0	1	0	0/0	135.4
Ward	1	0	0	0.0	0	0	1/3	39.6
Steelers	454	274	3295	60.4	16	12	31/182	83.4
Opponents	525	295	3309	56.2	19	16	55/367	74.5

SCORING

	TD R	TD P	TD Rt	PAT	FG	Saf	PTS
K. Brown	0	0	0	34/37	30/44	0	124
Burress	0	6	0	0/0	0/0	0	36
Stewart	5	0	0	0/0	0/0	0	30
Bettis	4	0	0	0/0	0/0	0	24
Fuamatu-Ma'afala	3	1	0	0/0	0/0	0	24
Ward	0	4	0	0/0	0/0	0	24
Edwards	1	0	1	0/0	0/0	0	12
Scott	0	0	2	0/0	0/0	0	12
Shaw	0	2	0	0/0	0/0	0	12
Zereoue	1	1	0	0/0	0/0	0	12
Bowers	1	0	0	0/0	0/0	0	6
Cushing	0	1	0	0/0	0/0	0	6
Gildon	0	0	1	0/0	0/0	0	6
Kreider	1	0	0	0/0	0/0	0	6
Maddox	1	0	0	0/0	0/0	0	6
Tuman	0	1	0	0/0	0/0	0	6
Washington	0	0	1	0/0	0/0	0	6
Steelers	17	16	5	34/37	30/44	0	352
Opponents	5	19	2	23/24	9/20	2	212

2-Pt. Conversions: None.
Steelers 0-1, Opponents 1-2.

RUSHING

	Att.	Yds.	Avg.	LG	TD
Bettis	225	1072	4.8	48	4
Stewart	96	537	5.6	48t	5
Fuamatu-Ma'afala	120	453	3.8	46	3
Zereoue	85	441	5.2	32	1
Bowers	18	84	4.7	21t	1
Ward	10	83	8.3	36	0
Kreider	7	29	4.1	12	1
Edwards	5	28	5.6	12t	1
Witman	5	24	4.8	14	0
Maddox	6	9	1.5	8	1
Martin	1	8	8.0	8	0
K. Brown	1	6	6.0	6	0
Miller	1	0	0.0	0	0
Steelers	580	2774	4.8	48t	17
Opponents	339	1195	3.5	36	5

RECEIVING

	No.	Yds.	Avg.	LG	TD
Ward	94	1003	10.7	34	4
Burress	66	1008	15.3	43	6
Shaw	24	409	17.0	90t	2
Edwards	19	283	14.9	57	0
Fuamatu-Ma'afala	16	127	7.9	54	1
Zereoue	13	154	11.8	62	1
Bruener	12	98	8.2	21	0
Bettis	8	48	6.0	16	0
Tuman	7	96	13.7	32t	1
Witman	6	32	5.3	12	0
Cushing	5	24	4.8	9	1
Kreider	2	5	2.5	5	0
Blackwell	1	8	8.0	8	0
Bowers	1	0	0.0	0	0
Steelers	274	3295	12.0	90t	16
Opponents	295	3309	11.2	80t	19

INTERCEPTIONS

	No.	Yds.	Avg.	LG	TD
Scott	5	204	40.8	62	2
Alexander	4	39	9.8	22	0
Townsend	2	7	3.5	7	0
Logan	2	2	1.0	2	0
Washington	1	15	15.0	15	0
Clancy	1	3	3.0	3	0
Gildon	1	0	0.0	0	0
Steelers	16	270	16.9	62	2
Opponents	12	101	8.4	39	0

PUNTING

	No.	Yds.	Avg.	In 20	LG
Miller	59	2505	42.5	23	64
K. Brown	3	106	35.3	0	46
Steelers	63	2611	41.4	23	64
Opponents	87	3677	42.3	28	57

PUNT RETURNS

	No.	FC	Yds.	Avg.	LG	TD
Poteat	36	14	292	8.1	39	0
Edwards	10	0	83	8.3	28	0
Shaw	4	1	45	11.3	23	0
Steelers	50	15	420	8.4	39	0
Opponents	28	14	334	11.9	62	0

KICKOFF RETURNS

	No.	Yds.	Avg.	LG	TD
Edwards	20	462	23.1	81	0
Poteat	16	250	15.6	30	0
Jackson	6	125	20.8	25	0
Blackwell	2	36	18.0	20	0
Logan	1	9	9.0	9	0
Shaw	1	2	2.0	2	0
Steelers	46	884	19.2	81	0
Opponents	73	1561	21.4	95t	1

FIELD GOALS

	1-19	20-29	30-39	40-49	50+
K. Brown	0/0	7/7	15/20	6/15	2/2
Steelers	0/0	7/7	15/20	6/15	2/2
Opponents	0/0	3/5	4/6	2/7	0/2

SACKS

	No.
Gildon	12.0
K. Bell	9.0
Porter	9.0
A. Smith	8.0
von Oelhoffen	4.0
Alexander	2.0
Bailey	2.0
Holmes	2.0
Logan	2.0
Townsend	2.0
Flowers	1.0
Hampton	1.0
Washington	1.0
Steelers	55.0
Opponents	31.0

RECORD HOLDERS
INDIVIDUAL RECORDS—CAREER

Category	Name	Performance
Rushing (Yds.)	Franco Harris, 1972-1983	11,950
Passing (Yds.)	Terry Bradshaw, 1970-1983	27,989
Passing (TDs)	Terry Bradshaw, 1970-1983	212
Receiving (No.)	John Stallworth, 1974-1987	537
Receiving (Yds.)	John Stallworth, 1974-1987	8,723
Interceptions	Mel Blount, 1970-1983	57
Punting (Avg.)	Bobby Joe Green, 1960-61	45.7
Punt Return (Avg.)	Bobby Gage, 1949-1950	14.9
Kickoff Return (Avg.)	Lynn Chandnois, 1950-56	29.6
Field Goals	Gary Anderson, 1982-1994	309
Touchdowns (Tot.)	Franco Harris, 1972-1983	100
Points	Gary Anderson, 1982-1994	1,343

INDIVIDUAL RECORDS—SINGLE SEASON

Category	Name	Performance
Rushing (Yds.)	Barry Foster, 1992	1,690
Passing (Yds.)	Terry Bradshaw, 1979	3,724
Passing (TDs)	Terry Bradshaw, 1978	28
Receiving (No.)	Hines Ward, 2001	94
Receiving (Yds.)	Yancey Thigpen, 1997	1,398
Interceptions	Mel Blount, 1975	11
Punting (Avg.)	Bobby Joe Green, 1961	47.0
Punt Return (Avg.)	Bobby Gage, 1949	16.0
Kickoff Return (Avg.)	Lynn Chandnois, 1952	35.2
Field Goals	Norm Johnson, 1995	34
Touchdowns (Tot.)	Louis Lipps, 1985	15
Points	Norm Johnson, 1995	141

INDIVIDUAL RECORDS—SINGLE GAME

Category	Name	Performance
Rushing (Yds.)	John Fuqua, 12-20-70	218
Passing (Yds.)	Bobby Layne, 12-3-58	409
Passing (TDs)	Terry Bradshaw, 11-15-81	5
	Mark Malone, 9-8-85	5
Receiving (No.)	Courtney Hawkins, 11-1-98	14
Receiving (Yds.)	Buddy Dial, 10-22-61	235
Interceptions	Jack Butler, 12-13-53	*4
Field Goals	Gary Anderson, 10-23-88	6
Touchdowns (Tot.)	Ray Mathews, 10-17-54	4
	Roy Jefferson, 11-3-68	4
Points	Ray Mathews, 10-17-54	24
	Roy Jefferson, 11-3-68	24

*NFL Record

2002 VETERAN ROSTER

No.	Name	Pos.	Ht.	Wt.	Birthdate	NFL Exp.	College	Hometown	How Acq.	'01 Games/ Starts
27	Alexander, Brent	S	5-11	200	7/10/71	9	Tennessee State	Gallatin, Tenn.	UFA(Car)-'00	16/16
46	Allred, John	TE	6-4	246	9/9/74	5	Southern California	Encinitas, Calif.	FA-'02	0*
94	Bailey, Rodney	DE	6-3	297	10/7/79	2	Ohio State	Cleveland, Ohio	D6a-'01	16/1
97	Bell, Kendrell	LB	6-1	248	7/2/78	2	Georgia	Augusta, Ga.	D2-'01	16/16
36	Bettis, Jerome	RB	5-11	256	2/16/72	10	Notre Dame	Detroit, Mich.	T(StL)-'96	11/11
33	Bowers, R.J.	FB	6-0	245	2/10/74	2	Grove City (Pa.)	West Middlesex, Pa.	FA-'01	3/0
87	Bruener, Mark	TE	6-4	262	9/16/72	8	Washington	Aberdeen, Wash.	D1-'95	9/9
80	Burress, Plaxico	WR	6-5	228	8/12/77	3	Michigan State	Virginia Beach, Va.	D1-'00	16/16
96	Clancy, Kendrick	NT	6-1	289	9/17/78	3	Mississippi	Tuscaloosa, Ala.	D3a-'00	16/4
73	Combs, Chris	DE	6-5	290	12/15/76	3	Duke	Roanoke, Va.	D6a-'00	2/0
48	Cushing, Matt	TE	6-3	260	7/2/75	4	Illinois	South Bend, Ind.	FA-'99	13/3
81	Edwards, Troy	WR	5-9	196	4/7/77	4	Louisiana Tech	Shreveport, La.	D1-'99	16/0
66	Faneca, Alan	G	6-5	310	12/7/76	5	Louisiana State	New Orleans, La.	D1-'98	15/15
50	Farrior, James	LB	6-2	245	1/6/75	6	Virginia	Ettrick, Va.	UFA(NYJ)-'02	16/16*
57	Fiala, John	LB	6-2	239	11/25/73	5	Washington	Kirkland, Wash.	FA-'98	15/0
41	Flowers, Lee	S	6-0	215	1/14/73	8	Georgia Tech	Columbia, S.C.	D5a-'95	15/15
45	Fuamatu-Ma'afala, Chris	RB	6-0	255	3/4/77	5	Utah	Honolulu, Hawaii	D6a-'98	16/5
72	Gandy, Wayne	T	6-5	308	2/10/71	9	Auburn	Haines City, Fla.	UFA(StL)-'99	15/15
85	Geason, Cory	TE	6-4	270	8/12/75	3	Tulane	St. James, La.	FA-'99	7/0
92	Gildon, Jason	LB	6-4	252	7/31/72	9	Oklahoma State	Altus, Okla.	D3-'94	16/16
53	Haggans, Clark	LB	6-3	247	1/10/77	3	Colorado State	Torrance, Calif.	D5a-'00	16/1
98	Hampton, Casey	DT	6-1	318	9/3/77	2	Texas	Galveston, Texas	D1-'01	16/11
64	Hartings, Jeff	C	6-3	294	9/7/72	7	Penn State	St. Henry, Ohio	UFA(Det)-'01	16/16
83	Jackson, Lenzie	WR	6-0	195	6/17/77	4	Arizona State	Milpitas, Calif.	FA-'01	12/0
35	Kreider, Dan	FB	5-11	247	3/11/77	3	New Hampshire	Mount Joy, Pa.	FA-'00	13/1
90	Kurpeikis, Justin	LB	6-3	248	7/17/77	2	Penn State	Pittsburgh, Pa.	FA-'01	3/0
31	Logan, Mike	DB	6-1	209	9/15/74	6	West Virginia	McKeesport, Pa.	UFA(Jax)-'01	16/1
8	Maddox, Tommy	QB	6-4	220	9/2/71	6	UCLA	Hurst, Texas	FA-'01	3/0
17	Martin, Tee	QB	6-1	225	7/25/78	3	Tennessee	Mobile, Ala.	D5b-'00	1/0
4	Miller, Josh	P	6-3	220	7/14/70	7	Arizona	East Brunswick, N.J.	FA-'96	16/0
78	Nkwenti, Mathias	T	6-3	300	5/11/78	2	Temple	Rockville, Md.	D4-'01	1/0
56	Okobi, Chukky	C-G	6-1	305	10/18/78	2	Purdue	Hamden, Conn.	D5-'01	1/0
2	Peterson, Todd	K	5-10	177	2/4/70	8	Georgia	Duluth, Ga.	UFA(Pitt)-'02	16/0*
55	Porter, Joey	LB	6-3	249	3/22/77	4	Colorado State	Bakersfield, Calif.	D3a-'99	15/15
22	Poteat, Hank	CB	5-10	195	8/30/77	3	Pittsburgh	Harrisburg, Pa.	D3b-'00	13/0
79	Ross, Oliver	G	6-5	314	9/27/74	3	Iowa State	Culver City, Calif.	FA-'00	16/7
54	Schneck, Mike	LS	6-1	246	8/4/77	4	Wisconsin	Whitefish Bay, Wis.	FA-'99	16/0
30	Scott, Chad	DB	6-1	201	9/6/74	6	Maryland	Capitol Heights, Md.	D1-'97	15/15
91	Smith, Aaron	DE	6-5	293	4/9/76	4	Northern Colorado	Colorado Springs, Colo.	D4-'99	16/16
77	Smith, Marvel	T	6-5	310	8/6/78	3	Arizona State	Oakland, Calif.	D2-'00	16/16
10	Stewart, Kordell	QB	6-1	217	10/16/72	8	Colorado	Marrero, La.	D2-'95	16/16
26	Townsend, Deshea	CB	5-10	191	9/8/75	5	Alabama	Batesville, Miss.	D4a-'98	16/1
84	Tuman, Jerame	TE	6-4	252	3/24/76	4	Michigan	Liberal, Kan.	D5a-'99	16/7
68	Vincent, Keydrick	G	6-4	330	4/13/78	2	Mississippi	Bartow, Fla.	FA-'01	5/1
67	von Oelhoffen, Kimo	DT-DE	6-3	297	1/30/71	8	Boise State	Kaunakakai, Hawaii	UFA(Cin)-'00	15/15
86	Ward, Hines	WR	6-0	200	3/8/76	5	Georgia	Forest Park, Ga.	D3b-'98	16/16
20	Washington, Dewayne	CB	6-0	193	12/27/72	9	North Carolina State	Durham, N.C.	UFA(Minn)-'98	16/16
21	Zereoue, Amos	RB	5-8	207	10/8/76	4	West Virginia	Hempstead, N.Y.	D3c-'99	14/0

* Allred last active with Chicago in '00; Farrior played 16 games with N. Y. Jets in '01; Peterson played 16 games with Kansas City.

\# Unrestricted free agent; subject to developments.

Players lost through free agency (4): K Kris Brown (Hou; 16 games in '01), LB Earl Holmes (Cle; 16), WR Bobby Shaw (Jax; 16), CB Jason Simmons (Hou; 12).

Also played with Steelers in '01—WR Tim Baker (3 games), S Myron Bell (16), WR Will Blackwell (1), C Roger Duffy (8), FB Jon Witman (15).

2002 FIRST-YEAR ROSTER

Name	Pos.	Ht.	Wt.	Birthdate	College	Hometown	How Acq.
Anderson, Matt	C	6-3	302	8/22/78	Texas	Cuero, Texas	FA
Bouton, Will	LB	6-1	230	7/15/79	Furman	Greenville, S.C.	FA
Brockmeier, Leon	T	6-6	315	11/4/78	Northwestern	Tallahassee, Fla.	FA
Brown, Demetrius (1)	WR	6-3	210	4/10/76	Wisconsin	Pahokee, Fla.	FA-'01
Burr, Josh	T	6-9	320	9/18/76	South Dakota	Lancaster, Wis.	FA
Clinton, Eugene (1)	DB	6-1	187	9/5/76	Mississippi State	Jackson, Miss.	FA
Cole, Travis	QB	6-2	210	6/14/79	Minnesota	Lake Oswego, Ore.	FA
Collins, McAllister (1)	C	6-2	307	4/23/79	Northern Illinois	Washington, D.C.	FA
Connor, Rameel (1)	DE	6-3	289	6/26/77	Illinois	Chicago, Ill.	FA-'01
Dales, Burke	P	6-2	215	2/16/77	Concordia	Montreal, Quebec, Canada	FA
Davis, Dallas	WR	5-8	178	10/17/78	Colorado State	Fort Collins, Colo.	FA
Eason, Nijrel (1)	C	6-1	205	5/20/79	Arizona State	Long Beach, Calif.	FA
Flick, D.J.	WR	5-10	175	4/27/80	Slippery Rock	Montgomery, Pa.	FA
Foote, Larry	LB	6-0	234	6/12/80	Michigan	Detroit, Mich.	D4
Glover, LaVar	DB	5-9	175	12/17/78	Cincinnati	Dayton, Ohio	D7a
Griffin, Pernell	LB	6-1	247	10/8/79	East Carolina	Williamston, N.C.	FA
Harrison, James	LB	6-0	243	5/4/78	Kent State	Akron, Ohio	FA
Haynes, Verron	FB	5-9	223	2/17/79	Georgia	Bronx, N.Y.	D5
Holleyman, Bary	DE	6-3	284	3/20/79	Oklahoma	Oklahoma City, Okla.	FA
Hope, Chris	S	5-11	204	9/29/80	Florida State	Rock Hill, S.C.	D3
Johnson, Jay	LB	6-1	237	4/1/78	SUNY-Brockport	Sanborn, N.Y.	FA
Jones, Bob	DL-LS	6-3	270	9/3/78	Penn State	Wadsworth, Ohio	FA
Jones, Jermese	T	6-5	333	2/1/78	Virginia	Durham, N.C.	FA
Keisel, Brett	DE	6-5	269	9/19/78	Brigham Young	Greybull, Wyo.	D7b
Mays, Lee	WR	6-1	192	9/18/78	Texas-El Paso	Houston, Texas	D6
McCray, Antwon	RB	5-11	203	9/5/79	Toledo	Carnegie, Pa.	FA
O'Donnell, Joe (1)	K	5-10	215	2/11/75	Maryland	Rural Ridge, Pa.	FA
Randle El, Antwaan	WR	5-9	184	8/17/79	Indiana	Markham, Ill.	D2
Schultz, Scott (1)	DL	6-2	297	4/19/77	North Dakota	Saskatchewan, Canada	FA
Simmons, Kendall	G	6-2	313	3/11/79	Auburn	Ripley, Miss.	D1
Totten, Erik	S	5-9	188	1/21/80	Western Washington	Maple Valley, Wash.	FA
Tuipulotu, Albert	FB	5-11	240	2/27/79	Portland State	San Mateo, Calif.	FA
Walker, Bryan (1)	TE	6-5	270	3/2/77	Southeast Missouri	St. Louis, Mo.	FA
Williams, Payton (1)	DB	5-9	181	11/19/78	Fresno State	Riverside, Calif.	FA-'01
Woodyard, Ashante	CB	6-0	210	12/29/78	Purdue	La Grange, Ga.	FA

The term NFL Rookie is defined as a player who is in his first season of professional football and has not been on the roster of another professional football team for any regular-season or postseason games. A Rookie is designated by an "R" on NFL rosters. Players who have been active in another professional football league or players who have NFL experience, including either preseason training camp or being on an Active List or Inactive List, or on Reserve/Injured or Reserve/Physically Unable to Perform for fewer than six regular-season games, are termed NFL First-Year Players. An NFL First-Year Player is designated by a "1" on NFL rosters. Thereafter, a player is credited with an additional year of experience for each season in which he accumulates six games on the Active List or Inactive List, or on Reserve/Injured or Reserve/Physically Unable to Perform.

COACHING STAFF
Head Coach,
Bill Cowher

Pro Career: Became the fifteenth head coach in Steelers history when he replaced Chuck Noll on January 21, 1992. In 1995, at age 38, he was the youngest coach to lead his team to a Super Bowl. Cowher is only the second coach in NFL history to lead his team to the playoffs in each of his first six seasons as head coach, joining Pro Football Hall of Fame member Paul Brown. During Cowher's 17-year coaching career, teams he has been associated with have made the postseason 13 times. Began his NFL career as a free-agent linebacker with the Philadelphia Eagles in 1979, and then signed with the Cleveland Browns the following year. Cowher played three seasons (1980-82) in Cleveland before being traded back to the Eagles, where he played two more years (1983-84). Cowher began his coaching career in 1985 at age 28 under Marty Schottenheimer with the Browns. He was the Browns' special teams coach in 1985-86 and secondary coach in 1987-88 before following Schottenheimer to the Kansas City Chiefs in 1989 as defensive coordinator. Career record: 105-68.

Background: Excelled in football, basketball, and track for Carlynton High in Crafton, Pa. Was a three-year starter at linebacker for North Carolina State, serving as captain and earning team MVP honors as a senior. Graduated in 1979 with education degree.

Personal: Born in Pittsburgh, on May 8, 1957. His wife Kaye, also a North Carolina State graduate, played professional basketball for the New York Stars of the Women's Professional Basketball League with twin sister Faye. Bill and Kaye live in Pittsburgh and have three daughters—Meagan Lyn, Lauren Marie, and Lindsay Morgan.

ASSISTANT COACHES

Mike Archer, linebackers; born July 26, 1953, State College, Pa., lives in Pittsburgh. Safety/punter Miami 1972-75. No pro playing experience. College coach: Miami 1978-1983, Louisiana State 1984-1990 (head coach 1987-1990), Virginia 1991-92, Kentucky 1993-95. Pro coach: Joined Steelers in 1996.

Tom Clements, quarterbacks; born June 18, 1953, McKees Rocks, Pa., lives in Pittsburgh. Quarterback Notre Dame 1972-74. Pro quarterback Ottawa Rough Riders (CFL) 1975-78, Hamilton Tiger-Cats (CFL) 1979, 1981-82, Kansas City Chiefs 1980, Winnipeg Blue Bombers (CFL) 1983-87. College coach: Notre Dame 1992-95. Pro coach: New Orleans Saints 1997-99, Kansas City Chiefs 2000, joined Steelers in 2001.

Russ Grimm, offensive line; born May 2, 1959, Scottdale, Pa., lives in Pittsburgh. Center Pittsburgh 1977-1980. Pro guard Washington Redskins 1981-1991. Pro coach: Washington Redskins 1992-2000, joined Steelers in 2001.

Dick Hoak, running backs; born December 8, 1939, Jeannette, Pa., lives in Greensburg, Pa. Halfback-quarterback Penn State 1958-1960. Pro running back Pittsburgh Steelers 1961-1970. Pro coach: Joined Steelers in 1972.

Kenny Jackson, wide receivers; born February 15, 1962, Neptune, N.J., lives in Pittsburgh. Wide receiver Penn State 1980-83. Pro wide receiver Philadelphia Eagles 1984-88, 1991-92, Houston Oilers 1989. College coach: Penn State 1993-2000. Pro coach: Joined Steelers in 2001.

Tim Lewis, defensive coordinator; born December 18, 1961, Quakertown, Pa., lives in Pittsburgh. Defensive back Pittsburgh 1979-1982. Pro cornerback Green Bay Packers 1983-86. College coach: Texas A&M 1987-88, Southern Methodist 1989-1992, Pittsburgh 1993-94. Pro coach: Joined Steelers in 1995.

John Mitchell, defensive line; born October 14, 1951, Mobile, Ala., lives in Pittsburgh. Defensive end Eastern Arizona J.C. 1969-1970, Alabama 1971-72. No pro playing experience. College coach: Alabama 1973-76, Arkansas 1977-1982, Temple 1986, Louisiana State 1987-1990. Pro coach: Birmingham Stallions (USFL) 1983-85, Cleveland Browns 1991-93, joined Steelers in 1994.

Mike Mularkey, offensive coordinator; born November 19, 1961, Ft. Lauderdale, Fla., lives in Pittsburgh. Tight end Florida 1979-1982. Pro tight end Minnesota Vikings 1983-88, Pittsburgh Steelers 1989-1991. College coach: Concordia 1993. Pro coach: Tampa Bay Buccaneers 1994-95, joined Steelers in 1996.

Willy Robinson, defensive backs; born February 10, 1956, Fort Carson, Colo., lives in Pittsburgh. Defensive back Fresno State 1976-77. No pro playing experience. College coach: San Jose State 1979, Fresno State 1980-1992, Miami 1993-94, Oregon State 1999. Pro coach: Seattle Seahawks 1995-98, joined Steelers in 2000.

Kevin Spencer, special teams; born November 2, 1953, Queens, N.Y., lives in Pittsburgh. Outside linebacker Springfield College 1971. No pro playing experience. College coach: SUNY-Cortland 1975-76, Cornell 1979-1980, Ithaca 1981-86, Wesleyan 1978-1991. Pro coach: Cleveland Browns 1991-94, Oakland Raiders 1995-97, Indianapolis Colts 1998-2001, joined Steelers in 2002.

Ken Whisenhunt, tight ends; born February 29, 1962, Atlanta, lives in Pittsburgh. Tight end-quarterback Georgia Tech 1980-84. Pro tight end Atlanta Falcons 1985-88, Washington Redskins 1989-1990, New York Jets 1991-93. College coach: Vanderbilt 1995-96. Pro coach: Baltimore Ravens 1997-98, Cleveland Browns 1999, New York Jets 2000, joined Steelers in 2001.

American Football Conference
West Division
Team Colors: Navy Blue, White, and Gold
P.O. Box 609609
San Diego, California 92160-9609
Telephone: (858) 874-4500

2002 SCHEDULE
PRESEASON

Aug. 10	**Arizona**	7:00
Aug. 16	**Seattle**	8:00
Aug. 22	at St. Louis	8:00
Aug. 28	at San Francisco	6:00

REGULAR SEASON

Sept. 8	at Cincinnati	1:00
Sept. 15	**Houston**	1:15
Sept. 22	at Arizona	1:05
Sept. 29	**New England**	1:15
Oct. 6	at Denver	2:05
Oct. 13	**Kansas City**	1:15
Oct. 20	at Oakland	1:05
Oct. 27	Open Date	
Nov. 3	**New York Jets**	1:05
Nov. 10	at St. Louis	12:00
Nov. 17	**San Francisco**	1:05
Nov. 24	at Miami	1:00
Dec. 1	**Denver**	1:05
Dec. 8	**Oakland**	1:15
Dec. 15	at Buffalo	1:00
Dec. 22	at Kansas City	12:00
Dec. 29	**Seattle**	1:15

Stadium: Qualcomm Stadium
(opened in 1967)
•**Capacity:** 70,000
9449 Friars Road
San Diego, California 92108
Playing Surface: Grass
Training Camp: University of California-
San Diego, Third College
La Jolla, California 92037

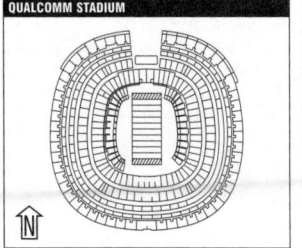

QUALCOMM STADIUM

CLUB OFFICIALS
Chairman of the Board: Alex G. Spanos
President/CEO: Dean A. Spanos
Executive Vice President:
  Michael A. Spanos
Executive Vice President & General
  Manager: John Butler
Executive Vice President-Finance:
  Jeremiah T. Murphy
Vice President of Football Operations:
  Ed McGuire
Vice President-Chief Financial &
  Administrative Officer:
  Jeanne M. Bonk
Vice President & Chief Marketing Officer:
  Ken Derrett
Assistant General Manager & Director
  of Pro Personnel: A.J. Smith
Director of Player Personnel: Buddy Nix
Director of College Scouting:
  Jimmy Raye
Head Athletic Trainer: James Collins
Director of Video Operations:
  Brian Duddy
Equipment Manager: Bob Wick
Director of Business & Stadium
  Operations: John Hinek
Director of Public Relations: Bill Johnston
Director of Public Affairs &
  Corporate/Community Relations:
  Kimberley Layton
Director of Security & Player Programs:
  Dick Lewis
Director of Ticket Sales and Services:
  Jerry McBurney
Director of Marketing & Events:
  Sean O'Connor
Director of Marketing Partnerships:
  Dennis O'Leary
Controller: Marsha Wells

COACHING HISTORY
Los Angeles 1960
(303-332-11)

1960-69	Sid Gillman*	83-51-6
1969-1970	Charlie Waller	9-7-3
1971	Sid Gillman**	4-6-0
1971-73	Harland Svare***	7-17-2
1973	Ron Waller	1-5-0
1974-78	Tommy Prothro****	21-39-0
1978-1986	Don Coryell#	72-60-0
1986-88	Al Saunders	17-22-0
1989-1991	Dan Henning	16-32-0
1992-96	Bobby Ross	50-36-0
1997-98	Kevin Gilbride	6-16-0
1998	June Jones	3-7-0
1999-2001	Mike Riley	14-34-0

*Retired after nine games in 1969
**Resigned after 10 games in 1971
***Resigned after eight games in 1973
****Resigned after four games in 1978
#Resigned after eight games in 1986
##Released after six games in 1998

ATTENDANCE
Home 542,660   Away 514,978
Total 1,057,638
Single-game home record,
69,288 (11/7/99)
Single-season home record, 546,533
(1999)

2002 DRAFT CHOICES

Round	Name	Pos.	College
1	Quentin Jammer	DB	Texas
2	Toniu Fonoti	G	Nebraska
	Reche Caldwell	WR	Florida
3	Ben Leber	LB	Kansas State
4	Justin Peelle	TE	Oregon
5	Terry Charles	WR	Portland St.
6	Matt Anderle	T	Minnesota
7	Seth Burford	QB	Cal Poly-SLO

2001 TEAM RECORD
PRESEASON (3-1)

Date	Result	Opponent
8/11	W 25-24	San Francisco
8/18	W 23-20	at Miami
8/25	W 13-10	St. Louis (OT)
8/31	L 3-16	at Arizona

REGULAR SEASON (5-11)

Date	Result	Opponent	Att.
9/09	W 30-3	Washington	60,629
9/23	W 32-21	at Dallas	63,430
9/30	W 28-14	Cincinnati	56,048
10/07	L 16-20	at Cleveland	73,018
10/14	L 26-29	at New England(OT)	60,292
10/21	W 27-10	Denver	67,521
10/28	W 27-24	Buffalo	63,698
11/04	L 20-25	Kansas City	58,789
11/11	L 16-26	at Denver	74,951
11/18	L 24-34	at Oakland	61,960
11/25	L 17-20	Arizona	49,398
12/02	L 10-13	at Seattle(OT)	55,466
12/09	L 14-24	at Philadelphia	65,438
12/15	L 6-13	Oakland	67,349
12/23	L 17-20	at Kansas City	76,131
12/30	L 22-25	Seattle	51,412

(OT) Overtime

SCORE BY PERIODS

Chargers	81	51	81	119	0	— 332
Opponents	60	109	46	100	6	— 321

2001 TEAM STATISTICS

	Chargers	Opp.
Total First Downs	290	290
Rushing	92	99
Passing	177	166
Penalty	21	25
3rd Down: Made/Att	79/221	84/224
3rd Down Pct.	35.7	37.5
4th Down: Made/Att	3/4	7/12
4th Down Pct.	75.0	58.3
Possession Avg.	30:15	29:45
Total Net Yards	5200	4904
Avg. Per Game	325.0	306.5
Total Plays	1010	1025
Avg. Per Play	5.1	4.8
Net Yards Rushing	1695	1504
Avg. Per Game	105.9	94.0
Total Rushes	435	449
Net Yards Passing	3505	3400
Avg. Per Game	219.1	212.5
Sacked/Yards Lost	27/180	41/218
Gross Yards	3685	3618
Att./Completions	548/309	535/317
Completion Pct.	56.4	59.3
Had Intercepted	18	19
Punts/Average	78/42.4	90/42.1
Net Punting Avg.	78/36.9	90/36.8
Penalties/Yards	97/777	79/632
Fumbles/Ball Lost	26/11	33/12
Touchdowns	35	35
Rushing	13	10
Passing	16	24
Returns	6	1

2001 INDIVIDUAL STATISTICS

PASSING	Att.	Comp.	Yds.	Pct.	TD	Int.	Tkld.	Rate
Flutie	521	294	3464	56.4	15	18	25/168	72.0
Brees	27	15	221	55.6	1	0	2/12	94.8
Chargers	548	309	3685	56.4	16	18	27/180	73.1
Opponents	535	317	3618	59.3	24	19	41/218	79.8

SCORING	TD R	TD P	TD Rt	PAT	FG	Saf	PTS
Richey	0	0	0	26/26	21/32	0	89
Tomlinson	10	0	0	0/0	0/0	0	60
Conway	1	6	0	0/0	0/0	0	42
Christie	0	0	0	6/6	9/11	0	33
J. Graham	0	5	0	0/0	0/0	0	30
F. Jones	0	4	0	0/0	0/0	0	24
Dwight	1	0	1	0/0	0/0	0	12
Jenkins	0	0	2	0/0	0/0	0	12
Flutie	1	0	0	0/0	0/0	0	6
Harris	0	0	1	0/0	0/0	0	6
Heiden	0	1	0	0/0	0/0	0	6
Johnson	0	0	1	0/0	0/0	0	6
Perry	0	0	1	0/0	0/0	0	6
Chargers	13	16	6	32/32	30/43	0	332
Opponents	10	24	1	31/33	26/35	0	321

2-Pt. Conversions: None.
Chargers 0-3, Opponents 1-2.

RUSHING	Att.	Yds.	Avg.	LG	TD
Tomlinson	339	1236	3.6	54	10
Flutie	53	192	3.6	16	1
Conway	7	116	16.6	67t	1
Fletcher	29	107	3.7	16	0
Dwight	2	24	12.0	16t	1
Brees	2	18	9.0	13	0
McCrary	2	3	1.5	2	0
Jenkins	1	-1	-1.0	-1	0
Chargers	435	1695	3.9	67t	13
Opponents	449	1504	3.3	26	10

RECEIVING	No.	Yds.	Avg.	LG	TD
Conway	71	1125	15.8	72t	6
Tomlinson	59	367	6.2	27	0
J. Graham	52	811	15.6	61t	5
F. Jones	35	388	11.1	34	4
Dwight	25	406	16.2	78	0
Fletcher	23	184	8.0	27	0
Gaylor	14	217	15.5	31	0
McCrary	13	71	5.5	12	0
Heiden	8	55	6.9	16	1
R. Jones	5	29	5.8	11	0
Batteaux	3	25	8.3	17	0
Harris	1	7	7.0	7	0
Chargers	309	3685	11.9	78	16
Opponents	317	3618	11.4	80t	24

INTERCEPTIONS	No.	Yds.	Avg.	LG	TD
McNeil	8	55	6.9	33	0
R. Harrison	2	51	25.5	22	0
Perry	2	37	18.5	37t	1
Cody	2	3	1.5	3	0
Beckett	1	8	8.0	8	0
Dixon	1	6	6.0	6	0
Seau	1	2	2.0	2	0
Fontenot	1	0	0.0	0	0
Molden	1	0	0.0	0	0
Chargers	19	162	8.5	37t	1
Opponents	18	135	7.5	41	0

PUNTING	No.	Yds.	Avg.	In 20	LG
Bennett	78	3308	42.4	25	62
Chargers	78	3308	42.4	25	62
Opponents	90	3789	42.1	25	63

PUNT RETURNS	No.	FC	Yds.	Avg.	LG	TD
Dwight	24	12	271	11.3	84t	1
Milburn	17	4	139	8.2	19	0
R. Jones	3	0	5	1.7	5	0
Chargers	44	16	415	9.4	84t	1
Opponents	32	15	346	10.8	40	0

KICKOFF RETURNS	No.	Yds.	Avg.	LG	TD
Jenkins	58	1541	26.6	93t	2
R. Jones	4	126	31.5	74	0
Carson	1	10	10.0	10	0
Fletcher	1	11	11.0	11	0
Harris	1	19	19.0	19	0
Whitman	1	9	9.0	9	0
Chargers	66	1716	26.0	93t	2
Opponents	64	1671	26.1	70	0

FIELD GOALS	1-19	20-29	30-39	40-49	50+
Richey	0/0	13/15	4/7	3/7	1/3
Christie	0/0	4/4	3/5	2/2	0/0
Chargers	0/0	17/19	7/12	5/9	1/3
Opponents	1/1	11/11	6/6	7/16	1/1

SACKS	No.
Wiley	13.0
Johnson	9.5
R. Harrison	3.5
Carson	3.0
Dixon	2.0
Parrella	2.0
Dingle	1.0
Fontenot	1.0
L. Harrison	1.0
Moreno	1.0
Rogers	1.0
Ruff	1.0
Seau	1.0
Tanuvasa	1.0
Chargers	41.0
Opponents	27.0

RECORD HOLDERS
INDIVIDUAL RECORDS—CAREER

Category	Name	Performance
Rushing (Yds.)	Paul Lowe, 1960-67	4,963
Passing (Yds.)	Dan Fouts, 1973-1987	43,040
Passing (TDs)	Dan Fouts, 1973-1987	254
Receiving (No.)	Charlie Joiner, 1976-1986	586
Receiving (Yds.)	Lance Alworth, 1962-1970	9,585
Interceptions	Gill Byrd, 1983-1992	42
Punting (Avg.)	Darren Bennett, 1995-2001	44.5
Punt Return (Avg.)	Darrien Gordon, 1993-96	13.6
Kickoff Return (Avg.)	Leslie (Speedy) Duncan, 1964-1970	25.3
Field Goals	John Carney, 1990-2000	261
Touchdowns (Tot.)	Lance Alworth, 1962-1970	83
Points	John Carney, 1990-2000	1,076

INDIVIDUAL RECORDS—SINGLE SEASON

Category	Name	Performance
Rushing (Yds.)	Natrone Means, 1994	1,350
Passing (Yds.)	Dan Fouts, 1981	4,802
Passing (TDs)	Dan Fouts, 1981	33
Receiving (No.)	Tony Martin, 1995	90
Receiving (Yds.)	Lance Alworth, 1965	1,602
Interceptions	Charlie McNeil, 1961	9
Punting (Avg.)	Darren Bennett, 2000	46.2
Punt Return (Avg.)	Leslie (Speedy) Duncan, 1965	15.5
Kickoff Return (Avg.)	Keith Lincoln, 1962	28.4
Field Goals	John Carney, 1994	34
Touchdowns (Tot.)	Chuck Muncie, 1981	19
Points	John Carney, 1994	135

INDIVIDUAL RECORDS—SINGLE GAME

Category	Name	Performance
Rushing (Yds.)	Gary Anderson, 12-18-88	217
Passing (Yds.)	Dan Fouts, 10-19-80, 12-11-82	444
Passing (TDs)	Dan Fouts, 11-22-81	6
Receiving (No.)	Kellen Winslow, 10-7-84	15
Receiving (Yds.)	Wes Chandler, 12-20-82	260
Interceptions	Many times	3
	Last time by Dwayne Harper, 11-27-95	
Field Goals	John Carney, 9-5-93, 9-18-93	6
	Greg Davis, 10-5-97	6
Touchdowns (Tot.)	Kellen Winslow, 11-22-81	5
Points	Kellen Winslow, 11-22-81	30

2002 VETERAN ROSTER

No.	Name	Pos.	Ht.	Wt.	Birthdate	NFL Exp.	College	Hometown	How Acq.	'01 Games/ Starts
81	Alexander, Stephen	TE	6-4	250	11/7/75	5	Oklahoma	Chickasha, Okla.	UFA(Wash)-'02	7/5*
86	Batteaux, Patrick	WR	6-0	195	4/18/78	2	Texas Christian	Missouri City, Texas	FA-'01	5/0
42	Beckett, Rogers	S	6-3	205	1/31/77	3	Marshall	Apopka, Fla.	D2-'00	16/16
2	Bennett, Darren	P	6-5	235	1/9/65	8	No College	Perth, Australia	FA-'95	16/0
50	Binn, David	LS	6-3	250	2/6/72	9	California	San Mateo, Calif.	FA-'94	16/0
9	Brees, Drew	QB	6-0	213	1/15/79	2	Purdue	Austin, Texas	D2-'01	1/0
96	Carson, Leonardo	DT	6-2	305	2/11/77	3	Auburn	Mobile, Ala.	D4b-'00	16/13
30	Carswell, Robert	S	5-11	215	10/26/78	2	Clemson	Lithonia, Ga.	D7b-'01	16/0
8	Christie, Steve	K	6-0	195	11/13/67	13	William & Mary	Oakville, Ontario, Canada	FA-'01	5/0
27	Cody, Tay	CB	5-9	180	10/6/77	2	Florida State	Blakely, Ga.	D3-'01	14/11
80	Conway, Curtis	WR	6-1	196	1/13/71	10	Southern California	Los Angeles, Calif.	UFA(Chi)-'00	16/16
15	Dickenson, Dave	QB	5-11	185	1/11/73	2	Montana	Great Falls, Mont.	FA-'01	0*
90	Dingle, Adrian	DE	6-3	272	6/25/77	4	Clemson	Holly Hill, S.C.	D5a-'99	14/0
85	Dwight, Tim	WR-KR	5-8	180	7/13/75	5	Iowa	Iowa City, Iowa	T(Atl)-'01	10/2
54	Edwards, Donnie	LB	6-2	227	4/6/73	7	UCLA	San Diego, Calif.	UFA(KC)-'02	16/16*
69	Ellis, Ed	G-T	6-7	325	10/13/75	6	Buffalo	Hamden, Conn.	UFA(Wash)-'01	16/2
92	Fisk, Jason	DT	6-3	295	9/4/72	8	Stanford	Davis, Calif.	UFA(Tenn)-'02	16/16*
41	Fletcher, Terrell	RB	5-8	196	9/14/73	8	Wisconsin	St. Louis, Mo.	D2b-'95	13/0
7	Flutie, Doug	QB	5-10	180	10/23/62	9	Boston College	Natick, Mass.	FA-'01	16/16
95	Fontenot, Al	DE	6-4	287	9/17/70	10	Baylor	Houston, Texas	UFA(Ind)-'99	16/2
82	Gaylor, Trevor	WR	6-3	195	11/3/77	3	Miami (Ohio)	St. Louis, Mo.	D4a-'00	7/3
73	Gorin, Brandon	T	6-6	304	7/17/78	2	Purdue	Muncie, Ind.	D7a-'01	0*
64	Hallen, Bob	G	6-4	295	3/9/75	5	Kent State	Mentor, Ohio	UFA(Atl)-'02	15/12*
22	Harrison, Lloyd	CB	5-10	190	6/21/77	3	North Carolina State	Floral Park, N.Y.	W(Wash)-'01	12/1
37	Harrison, Rodney	S	6-1	220	12/15/72	9	Western Illinois	Chicago Heights, Ill.	D5b-'94	14/14
83	Heiden, Steve	TE	6-5	270	9/21/76	4	South Dakota State	Rushford, Minn.	D3-'99	16/10
53	Humphrey, Deon	LB	6-3	240	5/7/76	3	Florida State	Lake Worth, Fla.	FA-'00	11/0
28	Jenkins, Ronney	RB	5-11	188	5/25/77	3	Northern Arizona	Oxnard, Calif.	FA-'00	16/0
99	Johnson, Raylee	DE	6-3	272	6/1/70	10	Arkansas	Fordyce, Ark.	D4a-'93	16/16
61	Keathley, Michael	G	6-4	296	3/9/78	2	Texas Christian	Glen Rose, Texas	FA-'01	16/0
44	McCrary, Fred	FB	6-0	245	9/19/72	6	Mississippi State	Naples, Fla.	FA-'99	16/12
77	McIntosh, Damion	T	6-4	325	3/21/77	3	Kansas State	Hollywood, Fla.	D3-'00	15/14
47	McNeil, Ryan	CB	6-2	210	10/4/70	10	Miami	Westwood, Fla.	FA-'01	16/16
25	Molden, Alex	CB	5-10	190	8/4/73	7	Oregon	Colorado Springs, Colo.	UFA(NO)-'01	6/3
57	Moreno, Zeke	LB	6-2	246	10/10/78	2	Southern California	Chula Vista, Calif.	D5b-'01	16/0
70	Parker, Vaughn	T	6-3	300	6/5/71	9	UCLA	Buffalo, N.Y.	D2b-'94	16/16
31	Perry, Jason	S	6-0	200	8/1/76	4	North Carolina State	Passaic, N.J.	D4-'99	14/3
52	Polk, Carlos	LB	6-2	250	2/22/77	2	Nebraska	Rockford, Ill.	D4-'01	6/0
66	Raymer, Cory	C	6-3	300	3/3/73	8	Wisconsin	Fond du Lac, Wis.	UFA(Wash)-'02	16/16*
5	Richey, Wade	K	6-3	205	5/19/76	5	Louisiana State	Lafayette, La.	RFA(SF)-'01	16/0
59	Rogers, Sam	LB	6-3	245	5/30/70	9	Colorado	Pontiac, Mich.	UFA(Buff)-'01	15/0
56	Ruff, Orlando	LB	6-3	247	9/26/76	4	Furman	Winnsboro, S.C.	FA-'99	16/15
33	Sanchez, Davis	CB	5-10	180	8/7/74	2	Oregon	Vancouver, B.C., Canada	FA-'01	12/2
55	Seau, Junior	LB	6-3	250	1/19/69	13	Southern California	Oceanside, Calif.	D1-'90	16/16
68	Silvers, Elliott	T	6-7	348	2/19/78	2	Washington	Agoura, Calif.	D5a-'01	1/0
21	Tomlinson, LaDainian	RB	5-10	221	6/23/79	2	Texas Christian	Waco, Texas	D1-'01	16/16
87	Vanover, Tamarick	WR-KR	6-0	220	2/25/74	6	Florida State	Tallahassee, Fla.	FA-'02	0*
84	Whitman, Josh	TE	6-4	245	8/5/78	2	Illinois	Lafayette, Ind.	FA-'01	4/1
75	Wiley, Marcellus	DE	6-4	275	11/30/74	6	Columbia	Los Angeles, Calif.	UFA(Buff)-'01	14/14
76	Williams, Jamal	DT	6-3	305	4/28/76	4	Oklahoma State	Washington, D.C.	D2(Supp)-'98	3/3

* Alexander played 7 games with Washington in '01; Dickenson inactive for 16 games; Edwards played 16 games with Kansas City; Fisk played 16 games with Tennessee; Gorin inactive for 16 games; Hallen played 15 games with Atlanta; Raymer played 16 games with Washington; Vanover last active with Kansas City in '99.

Players lost through free agency (6): LB Gerald Dixon (Oak; 16 games in '01), G DeMingo Graham (Hou; 16), LB John Holecek (Atl; 11), C Kendyl Jacox (NO; 16), DT Mike Mohring (Oak; 9), DT John Parrella (Oak; 16).

Also played with the Chargers in '01—C Carey Clayton (1 game), WR Jeff Graham (14), FB Derrick Harris (16), TE Freddie Jones (14), WR Reggie Jones (9), RB Glyn Milburn (6), G Raleigh Roundtree (16), DT Maa Tanuvasa (2), CB Scott Turner (4).

2002 FIRST-YEAR ROSTER

Name	Pos.	Ht.	Wt.	Birthdate	College	Hometown	How Acq.
Anderle, Matt	T	6-6	327	7/14/79	Minnesota	St. Paul, Minn.	D6
Ball, Jason	C	6-2	301	3/21/79	New Hampshire	Londonderry, N.H.	FA
Burford, Seth	QB	6-3	241	3/11/79	Cal Poly	Oakdale, Calif.	D7
Caldwell, Reche	WR	5-11	194	3/28/79	Florida	Tampa, Fla.	D2b
Charles, Terry	WR	6-3	207	7/8/79	Portland State	Long Beach, Calif.	D5
Chatman, Jesse	RB	5-8	232	9/22/79	Eastern Washington	Seattle, Wash.	FA
Demaree, Chris	DE	6-4	260	3/12/80	Kentucky	Louisville, Ky.	FA
Dennard, Ryan	WR	6-3	220	2/27/79	Arizona State	Albuquerque, N.M.	FA
Fletcher, Anthony	DT	6-2	297	4/16/80	UCLA	San Dimas, Calif.	FA
Fonoti, Toniu	G	6-4	349	11/26/81	Nebraska	Hauula, Hawaii	D2a
Foreman, Tyree	FB	5-11	230	11/6/79	Virginia	Sandy Spring, Md.	FA
Fox, Vernon	S	5-9	201	10/9/79	Fresno State	Las Vegas, Nev.	FA
Gilliam, Dondre (1)	WR	6-0	185	2/9/77	Millersville	Aberdeen, Md.	FA-'01
Goodspeed, Joey (1)	FB	6-1	247	2/22/78	Notre Dame	Oswego, Ill.	FA
Green, Donny (1)	LB	6-2	238	9/18/77	Virginia	Hampton, Va.	FA
Guenther, Eric (1)	LB	6-2	240	5/4/77	Illinois	Westlake, Calif.	FA-'01
Hebert, Jason	S	5-11	190	8/17/79	Rice	Spring, Texas	FA
Hendricks, Bart (1)	QB	6-0	210	8/30/78	Boise State	Reno, Nev.	FA-'01
Jammer, Quentin	CB	5-11	204	6/19/79	Texas	Angleton, Texas	D1
Kirk-Hughes, Antwan	G	6-3	315	12/16/79	Texas	Waxahachie, Texas	FA
Leber, Ben	LB	6-3	244	12/7/78	Kansas State	Vermillion, S.D.	D3
Machado, Jeff	G	6-3	305	12/6/79	Oklahoma State	Cedar Rapids, Iowa	FA
Norman, Josh	TE	6-2	236	7/27/80	Oklahoma	Midland, Texas	FA
Okanlawon, Tony	CB	5-10	185	3/4/79	Maryland	Forestville, Md.	FA
Osika, Craig	C	6-3	293	12/4/79	Indiana	Hobart, Ind.	FA
Peelle, Justin	TE	6-4	255	3/15/79	Oregon	Dublin, Calif.	D4
Pitts, DeRonnie (1)	WR	5-11	190	4/5/78	Stanford	Saginaw, Mich.	FA-'01
Poli-Dixon, Brian	WR	6-5	210	4/21/79	UCLA	Tucson, Ariz.	FA
Rekuc, Brad (1)	LB	6-2	240	12/6/77	Weber State	Phoenix, Ariz.	FA-'01
Sanders, Vaughn (1)	RB	5-11	212	3/19/77	Hofstra	Cedarhurst, N.Y.	FA
Scott, Dequincy (1)	DT	6-1	283	3/5/78	Southern Mississippi	Laplace, La.	FA-'01
Sikyala, Mukala (1)	RB	5-9	212	9/20/78	Maryland	Silver Springs, Md.	FA
Simmons, Antuan	CB	5-9	189	3/31/79	Southern California	Sacramento, Calif.	FA
Sims, Doug (1)	DT	6-3	340	10/20/78	Hawaii	Berkeley, Calif.	FA
Thomas, Lew	RB	6-0	213	4/30/80	Vanderbilt	Atlanta, Ga.	FA
Turner, Nate (1)	WR	6-2	210	5/26/78	Nevada-Las Vegas	Compton, Calif.	FA-'01
Tuupo, Tupo	DE	6-3	276	12/17/78	Washington State	Menlo Park, Calif.	FA
Williams, Levron	RB	6-3	224	12/12/79	Indiana	Evansville, Ind.	FA
Witherspoon, Terry (1)	FB	5-11	250	8/22/77	Clemson	Monroe, N.C.	W(Dall)-'02

The term NFL Rookie is defined as a player who is in his first season of professional football and has not been on the roster of another professional football team for any regular-season or postseason games. A Rookie is designated by an "R" on NFL rosters. Players who have been active in another professional football league or players who have NFL experience, including either preseason training camp or being on an Active List or Inactive List, or on Reserve/Injured or Reserve/Physically Unable to Perform for fewer than six regular-season games, are termed NFL First-Year Players. An NFL First-Year Player is designated by a "1" on NFL rosters. Thereafter, a player is credited with an additional year of experience for each season in which he accumulates six games on the Active List or Inactive List, or on Reserve/Injured or Reserve/Physically Unable to Perform.

COACHING STAFF
Head Coach,
Marty Schottenheimer
Pro Career: Marty Schottenheimer was named the thirteenth head coach in Chargers history on January 29, 2002. In fifteen full seasons as a head coach in the NFL, Schottenheimer has led his teams to twelve winning seasons. He is tenth on the NFL's all-time list with 158 wins, and his 11 playoff appearances is fifth in NFL history. Schottenheimer spent the 2001 as the Washington Redskins head coach and director of football operations. In his 10 years as head coach of the Kansas City Chiefs (1989-1998), he had a record of 104-65-1 and advanced to the playoffs seven times. The Cleveland Browns went to the playoffs all four full seasons (1985-88) he was coach. In 1986, Schottenheimer was the consensus AFC coach of the year. He coached with the Portland Storm (WFL) in 1974, New York Giants (1975-77), and Detroit Lions (1978-79), and Cleveland Browns (1980-84). In 1984, he took over as the Browns' head coach midway through the season. Played linebacker for Buffalo (1965-68) and Boston Patriots (1969-1970). Career record: 158-104-1.
Background: Schottenheimer was an All-America linebacker at Pittsburgh (1962-64). After leaving the Chiefs in 1998, he joined ESPN as a pro football analyst.
Personal: Born September 23, 1943 in Canonsburg, Pa. Marty and his wife Patricia have one daughter, Kristen, and one son, Brian, who is the Chargers' quarterbacks coach.

ASSISTANT COACHES
Bill Arnsparger, associate head coach-defense; born December 16, 1926, in Paris, Ky., lives in San Diego. Tackle Miami (Ohio) 1946-49. No college or pro playing experience. College coach: Miami (Ohio) 1950, Ohio State 1951-53, Kentucky 1954-1961, Tulane 1962-63, Louisiana State 1984-86 (head coach). Pro coach: Baltimore Colts 1964-69, Miami Dolphins 1970-73, 1976-1983, New York Giants 1974-76 (head coach), San Diego Chargers 1992, Washington Redskins 1999-2001, re-joined Chargers in 2002.
Tim Brewster, tight ends; born October 13, 1960, Phillipsburg, N.J., lives in San Diego. Tight end Illinois 1980-83. No pro playing experience. College coach: Purdue 1986, North Carolina 1989-1997, Texas 1998-2001. Pro coach: Joined Chargers in 2002.
Cam Cameron, offensive coordinator; born February 6, 1961, Chapel Hill, N.C., lives in San Diego. Quarterback Indiana 1980-83. No pro playing experience. College coach: Michigan 1984-1993, Indiana 1997-2001 (head coach). Pro coach: Washington Redskins 1994-96, joined Chargers in 2002.
Pete Carmichael, Jr., offensive assistant-

quality control; born October 6, 1971, Farmingham, Mass., lives in San Diego. Attended Boston College. No college or pro playing experience. College coach: New Hampshire 1994, Louisiana Tech 1995-99. Pro coach: Cleveland Browns 2000, Washington Redskins 2001, joined Chargers in 2002.
Steve Crosby, special teams; born July 3, 1950, Great Bend, Kan., lives in San Diego. Running back Fort Hayes State 1970-73. Pro running back New York Giants 1974-76. College coach: Vanderbilt 1998-2001. Pro coach: Miami Dolphins 1979-1982, Atlanta Falcons 1983-84, 1986-89, Cleveland Browns 1985, 1991-95, New England Patriots 1990, joined Chargers in 2002.
Jerry Holmes, defensive backs; born December 22, 1957, Hampton, Va., lives in San Diego. Defensive back Chowon (N.J.) J.C. 1976-77, West Virginia 1978-79. Pro defensive back New York Jets 1980-83, 1986-87, Pittsburgh Maulers (USFL) 1984, New Jersey Generals (USFL) 1985, Detroit Lions 1988-89, Green Bay Packers 1990-91. College coach: Hampton 1992-94, West Virginia 1995-98. Pro coach: Cleveland Browns 1999-2000, Washington Redskins 2001, joined Chargers in 2002.
Hudson Houck, offensive line; born January 7, 1943, Los Angeles, lives in San Diego. Center Southern California 1962-64. No pro playing experience. College coach: Southern California 1970-72, 1976-1982, Stanford 1973-75. Pro coach: Los Angeles Rams 1983-1991, Seattle Seahawks 1992, Dallas Cowboys 1993-2001, joined Chargers in 2002.
Dale Lindsey, defensive coordinator; born January 18, 1943, Bedford Ind., lives in San Diego. Linebacker Western Kentucky 1961-64. Pro linebacker Cleveland Browns 1965-1973. College coach: Southern Methodist 1988-89. Pro coach: Green Bay Packers 1986-87, New England Patriots 1990, Tampa Bay Buccaneers 1991, San Diego Chargers 1992-96, Washington Redskins 1997-98, Chicago Bears 1999-2001, re-joined Chargers in 2002.
James Lofton, wide receivers; born July 5, 1956, Fort Ord, Calif., lives in San Diego. Wide receiver Stanford 1975-77. Pro wide receiver Green Bay Packers 1978-1986, Los Angeles Raiders 1987-88, Buffalo Bills 1989-1992, Los Angeles Rams 1993, Philadelphia Eagles 1993. Pro coach: Joined Chargers in 2002.
Greg Manusky, linebackers; born August 12, 1966, Wilkes-Barre, Pa., lives in San Diego. Linebacker Colgate 1983-87. Pro linebacker Washington Redskins 1988-1990, Minnesota Vikings 1991-93, Kansas City Chiefs 1994-99. Pro coach: Washington Redskins 2001, joined Chargers in 2002.
Wayne Nunnely, defensive line; born March 29, 1952, Los Angeles, lives in

San Diego. Fullback Nevada-Las Vegas 1972-75. No pro playing experience. College coach: Nevada-Las Vegas 1976, 1982-89 (head coach 1986-89), Cal Poly-Pomona 1977-78, Cal State-Fullerton 1979, Pacific 1980-81, Southern California 1991-92, UCLA 1993-94. Pro coach: New Orleans Saints 1995-96, joined Chargers in 1997.
John Pagano, defensive assistant-quality control; born March 30, 1967, Boulder, Colo., lives in San Diego. Linebacker Mesa State College 1985-88. No pro playing experience. College coach: Mesa State College 1989, Nevada-Las Vegas 1990-91, Louisiana Tech 1994, Mississippi 1995. Pro coach: New Orleans Saints 1996-97, Indianapolis Colts 1998-2001, joined Chargers in 2002.
Joe Pascale, special projects; born April 4, 1946, New York, N.Y., lives in San Diego. Linebacker Connecticut 1963-66. No pro playing experience. College coach: Connecticut 1967-68, Rhode Island 1969-1973, Idaho State 1974-76 (head coach 1976), Princeton 1977-79. Pro coach: Montreal Alouettes (CFL) 1980-81, Ottawa Rough Riders (CFL) 1982-83, New Jersey Generals (USFL) 1984-85, St. Louis/Phoenix Cardinals 1986-1993, Cincinnati Bengals 1994-96, joined Chargers in 1997.
Dave Redding, strength and conditioning; born June 14, 1952, North Platte, Neb., lives in San Diego. Defensive end Nebraska 1972-75. No pro playing experience. College coach: Nebraska 1976, Washington State 1977, Missouri 1978-1981. Pro coach: Cleveland Browns 1982-88, Kansas City Chiefs 1989-1997, Washington Redskins 2001, joined Chargers in 2002.
Matt Schiotz, asst. strength and conditioning; born June 8, 1971, Menomonie, Wis., lives in San Diego. Attended Wisconsin-La Crosse. No college or pro playing experience. College coach: Kansas 1995-96, Southern California 1998-2000. Pro coach: Kansas City Chiefs 1997, Washington Redskins 2001, joined Chargers in 2002.
Brian Schottenheimer, quarterbacks; born October 16, 1973, Denver, lives in San Diego. Quarterback Kansas 1992, Florida 1993-96. No pro playing experience. College coach: Syracuse 1999, Southern California 2000. Pro coach: St. Louis Rams 1997, Kansas City Chiefs 1998, Washington Redskins 2001, joined Chargers in 2002.
Clarence Shelmon, running backs; born September 17, 1952, Bossier City, La., lives in San Diego. Running back Houston 1971-75. No pro playing experience. College coach: Army 1978-1980, Indiana 1981-83, Arizona 1984-86, Southern California 1987-1990. Pro coach: Los Angeles Rams 1991, Seattle Seahawks 1992-97, Dallas Cowboys 1998-2001, joined Chargers in 2002.

American Football Conference
South Division
Team Colors: Navy, Titans Blue, Red, Silver
460 Great Circle Road
Nashville, Tennessee 37228
Telephone: (615) 565-4000

2002 SCHEDULE
PRESEASON

Aug. 10	**St. Louis**	7:00
Aug. 15	**Oakland**	7:00
Aug. 23	at Minnesota	7:00
Aug. 30	at Green Bay	7:00

REGULAR SEASON

Sept. 8	**Philadelphia**	12:00
Sept. 15	at Dallas	12:00
Sept. 22	**Cleveland**	12:00
Sept. 29	at Oakland	1:15
Oct. 6	**Washington**	12:00
Oct. 13	**Jacksonville**	12:00
Oct. 20	Open Date	
Oct. 27	at Cincinnati	1:00
Nov. 3	at Indianapolis	1:00
Nov. 10	**Houston**	12:00
Nov. 17	**Pittsburgh**	12:00
Nov. 24	at Baltimore	1:00
Dec. 1	at New York Giants	1:00
Dec. 8	**Indianapolis**	12:00
Dec. 16	**New England** (Mon.)	8:00
Dec. 22	at Jacksonville	1:00
Dec. 29	at Houston	12:00

Stadium: Coliseum
(opened in 1999)
•**Capacity:** 68,804
One Titans Way
Nashville, Tennessee 37213
Playing Surface: Natural Grass
Training Camp: Baptist Sports Park
460 Great Circle Road
Nashville, Tennessee
37228

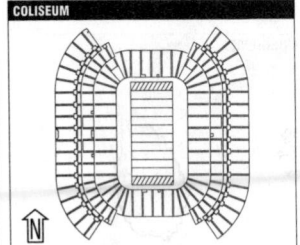

COLISEUM

CLUB OFFICIALS
Owner/Chairman of the Board/CEO:
K.S. (Bud) Adams, Jr.
Executive Assistant to Owner/
Chairman of the Board/CEO:
Thomas S. Smith
President/Chief Operating Officer:
Jeff Diamond
Executive V.P./General Manager and
Director Of Football Operations:
Floyd Reese
Executive V.P. of Administration:
Don MacLachlan
Executive V.P./General Counsel:
Steve Underwood
Asst. General Counsel: Elza Bullock
Vice President/Finance:
Robert McBurnett
Vice President/Community Affairs:
Bob Hyde
Director of Player Personnel:
Rich Snead
Director of College Scouting:
Mike Ackerley
Director of Sales and Operations:
Stuart Spears
Asst. Director of Sales and Operations:
Brent Akers
Director of Broadcasting: Mike Keith
Director of Marketing: Ralph Ockenfels
Controller: Jenneen Kaufman
Director of Information Systems:
Russ Hudson
Director of Internet
Operations/Publications: Gary Glenn
Director of Media Relations:
Robbie Bohren
Asst. Director of Media Relations:
William Bryant
Director of Security: Steve Berk
Director of Ticket Operations:
Marty Collins
Director of Player Development/Pro
Personnel: Al Smith
Director of Cheerleading and
Entertainment: Meeka Gabriel
V.P. and G.M. of Adelphia
Coliseum/Facilities: Bill Dickerson
Suite and Club Services Manager:
Bill Wainwright
Head Athletic Trainer: Brad Brown
Assistant Athletic Trainers:
Don Moseley, Geoff Kaplan
Equipment Manager: Paul Noska
Video Director: Anthony Pastrana

COACHING HISTORY
Houston 1960-1996
(305-328-6)

1960-61	Lou Rymkus*	12-7-1
1961	Wally Lemm	10-0-0
1962-63	Frank (Pop) Ivy	17-12-0
1964	Sammy Baugh	4-10-0
1965	Hugh Taylor	4-10-0
1966-1970	Wally Lemm	28-40-4
1971	Ed Hughes	4-9-1
1972-73	Bill Peterson**	1-18-0
1973-74	Sid Gillman	8-15-0
1975-1980	O.A. (Bum) Phillips	59-38-0
1981-83	Ed Biles***	8-23-0
1983	Chuck Studley	2-8-0
1984-85	Hugh Campbell****	8-22-0
1985-89	Jerry Glanville	35-35-0
1990-94	Jack Pardee#	44-35-0
1994-2001	Jeff Fisher	68-55-0

* Released after five games in 1961
** Released after five games in 1973
*** Resigned after six games in 1983
**** Released after 14 games in 1985
\# Released after 10 games in 1994

ATTENDANCE
Home 537,496   Away 533,490
Total 1,070,986
Single-game home record,
68,804 (12/16/01)
Single-season home record, 537,496
(2001)

2002 DRAFT CHOICES

Round	Name	Pos.	College
1	Albert Haynesworth	DT	Tennessee
2	Tank Williams	DB	Stanford
3	Rocky Calmus	LB	Oklahoma
4	Mike Echols	DB	Wisconsin
	Tony Beckham	DB	Wisconsin-Stout
	Rocky Boiman	LB	Notre Dame
5	Jake Schifino	WR	Akron
6	Justin Hartwig	G	Kansas
7	Darrell Hill	WR	Northern Illinois
	Carlos Hall	DE	Arkansas

2001 TEAM RECORD
PRESEASON (3-1)

Date	Result	Opponent
8/11	W 27-24	Chicago
8/17	W 23-10	at St. Louis
8/23	L 14-20	Philadelphia
8/30	W 28-25	at Detroit

REGULAR SEASON (7-9)

Date	Result	Opponent	Att.
9/09	L 23-31	Miami	68,798
9/23	L 6-13	at Jacksonville	65,994
10/07	L 7-26	at Baltimore	69,494
10/14	W 31-28	Tampa Bay(OT)	68,798
10/21	W 27-24	at Detroit	76,940
10/29	L 7-34	at Pittsburgh	63,763
11/04	W 28-24	Jacksonville	68,798
11/12	L 10-16	Baltimore	68,798
11/18	W 20-7	at Cincinnati	63,865
11/25	L 24-34	Pittsburgh	68,801
12/02	W 31-15	at Cleveland	72,818
12/09	L 24-42	at Minnesota	64,271
12/16	W 26-20	Green Bay	68,804
12/22	W 13-10	at Oakland	61,934
12/30	L 38-41	Cleveland	68,798
1/06	L 21-23	Cincinnati	68,798

(OT) Overtime

SCORE BY PERIODS

Titans	84	73	90	86	3 —	336
Opponents	61	127	74	126	0 —	388

2001 TEAM STATISTICS

	Titans	Opp.
Total First Downs	288	300
Rushing	87	79
Passing	179	192
Penalty	22	29
3rd Down: Made/Att	98/233	74/212
3rd Down Pct.	42.1	34.9
4th Down: Made/Att	2/15	7/14
4th Down Pct.	13.3	50.0
Possession Avg.	31:29	28:31
Total Net Yards	5352	5515
Avg. Per Game	334.5	344.7
Total Plays	1026	996
Avg. Per Play	5.2	5.5
Net Yards Rushing	1794	1431
Avg. Per Game	112.1	89.4
Total Rushes	468	405
Net Yards Passing	3558	4084
Avg. Per Game	222.4	255.3
Sacked/Yards Lost	43/309	32/175
Gross Yards	3867	4259
Att./Completions	515/307	559/328
Completion Pct.	59.6	58.7
Had Intercepted	17	13
Punts/Average	85/42.0	82/41.3
Net Punting Avg.	85/37.0	82/35.7
Penalties/Yards	119/1025	88/832
Fumbles/Ball Lost	18/11	21/11
Touchdowns	39	46
Rushing	12	17
Passing	23	27
Returns	4	2

2001 INDIVIDUAL STATISTICS

PASSING

	Att.	Comp.	Yds.	Pct.	TD	Int.	Tkld.	Rate
McNair	431	264	3350	61.3	21	12	37/251	90.2
O'Donnell	76	42	496	55.3	2	2	6/58	73.1
Volek	3	0	0	0.0	0	0	0/0	39.6
Green	2	0	0	0.0	0	2	0/0	0.0
Hentrich	2	0	0	0.0	0	1	0/0	0.0
Wycheck	1	1	21	100.0	0	0	0/0	118.8
Titans	515	307	3867	59.6	23	17	43/309	84.2
Opponents	559	328	4259	58.7	27	13	32/175	89.1

SCORING

	TD R	TD P	TD Rt	PAT	FG	Saf	PTS
Nedney	0	0	0	34/35	20/28	0	94
Mason	0	9	1	0/0	0/0	0	62
K. Dyson	0	7	0	0/0	0/0	0	44
George	5	0	0	0/0	0/0	0	30
McNair	5	0	0	0/0	0/0	0	30
Wycheck	0	4	0	0/0	0/0	0	24
Green	1	1	0	0/0	0/0	0	12
Mitchell	0	0	2	0/0	0/0	0	12
Bennett	0	1	0	0/0	0/0	0	8
Hicks	1	0	0	0/0	0/0	0	6
Kinney	0	1	0	0/0	0/0	0	6
Myers	0	0	1	0/0	0/0	0	6
Fisk	0	0	0	0/0	0/0	1	2
Titans	12	23	4	34/35	20/28	1	336
Opponents	17	27	2	44/44	22/29	0	388

2-Pt. Conversions: Bennett, K. Dyson, Mason. Titans 3-4, Opponents 1-2.

RUSHING

	Att.	Yds.	Avg.	LG	TD
George	315	939	3.0	27	5
McNair	75	414	5.5	24	5
Hicks	56	341	6.1	51	1
Green	15	71	4.7	21	1
O'Donnell	6	28	4.7	15	0
Wycheck	1	1	1.0	1	0
Titans	468	1794	3.8	51	12
Opponents	405	1431	3.5	48t	17

RECEIVING

	No.	Yds.	Avg.	LG	TD
Mason	73	1128	15.5	71t	9
Wycheck	60	672	11.2	30	4
K. Dyson	54	825	15.3	68t	7
George	37	279	7.5	25	0
Kinney	25	263	10.5	24	1
Bennett	24	329	13.7	50	1
Green	12	64	5.3	10	1
Sanders	5	74	14.8	22	0
Hicks	5	22	4.4	9	0
McCareins	3	88	29.3	36	0
Meier	3	31	10.3	18	0
Natkin	2	42	21.0	27	0
Berlin	2	28	14.0	19	0
Coleman	1	19	19.0	19	0
Ours	1	3	3.0	3	0
Titans	307	3867	12.6	71t	23
Opponents	328	4259	13.0	78	27

INTERCEPTIONS

	No.	Yds.	Avg.	LG	TD
A. Dyson	3	36	12.0	36	0
Rolle	3	3	1.0	3	0
Bulluck	2	21	10.5	21	0
Robinson	2	13	6.5	13	0
Godfrey	1	5	5.0	5	0
Booker	1	0	0.0	0	0
Favors	1	0	0.0	0	0
Titans	13	78	6.0	36	0
Opponents	17	163	9.6	45t	2

PUNTING

	No.	Yds.	Avg.	In 20	LG
Hentrich	85	3567	42.0	28	70
Titans	85	3567	42.0	28	70
Opponents	82	3388	41.3	25	58

PUNT RETURNS

	No.	FC	Yds.	Avg.	LG	TD
Mason	20	19	128	6.4	20	0
J. Walker	14	4	125	8.9	36	0
McCareins	2	0	29	14.5	18	0
Titans	36	23	282	7.8	36	0
Opponents	36	20	264	7.3	31	0

KICKOFF RETURNS

	No.	Yds.	Avg.	LG	TD
Mason	34	748	22.0	101t	1
Berlin	13	253	19.5	32	0
Coleman	11	251	22.8	34	0
McCareins	4	70	17.5	21	0
J. Walker	3	33	11.0	19	0
Green	2	20	10.0	12	0
Bennett	1	11	11.0	11	0
Kinney	1	14	14.0	14	0
Long	1	10	10.0	10	0
Rolle	1	3	3.0	3	0
Titans	71	1413	19.9	101t	1
Opponents	57	1418	24.9	81	0

FIELD GOALS

	1-19	20-29	30-39	40-49	50+
Nedney	0/0	6/6	5/5	8/15	1/2
Titans	0/0	6/6	5/5	8/15	1/2
Opponents	0/0	4/4	15/17	2/7	1/1

SACKS

	No.
Kearse	10.0
Evans	5.5
Fisk	2.5
Carter	2.0
Rolle	2.0
Smith	2.0
Favors	1.5
Morris	1.5
Bulluck	1.0
Chamberlin	1.0
Ford	1.0
Godfrey	1.0
Robinson	1.0
Titans	32.0
Opponents	43.0

RECORD HOLDERS
INDIVIDUAL RECORDS—CAREER

Category	Name	Performance
Rushing (Yds.)	Earl Campbell, 1978-1984	8,574
Passing (Yds.)	Warren Moon, 1984-1993	33,685
Passing (TDs)	Warren Moon, 1984-1993	196
Receiving (No.)	Ernest Givins, 1986-1994	542
Receiving (Yds.)	Ernest Givins, 1986-1994	7,935
Interceptions	Jim Norton, 1960-68	45
Punting (Avg.)	Greg Montgomery, 1988-1993	43.6
Punt Return (Avg.)	Billy Johnson, 1974-1980	13.2
Kickoff Return (Avg.)	Bobby Jancik, 1962-67	26.5
Field Goals	Al Del Greco, 1991-2000	246
Touchdowns (Tot.)	Earl Campbell, 1978-1984	73
Points	Al Del Greco, 1991-2000	1,060

INDIVIDUAL RECORDS—SINGLE SEASON

Category	Name	Performance
Rushing (Yds.)	Earl Campbell, 1980	1,934
Passing (Yds.)	Warren Moon, 1991	4,690
Passing (TDs)	George Blanda, 1961	36
Receiving (No.)	Charley Hennigan, 1964	101
Receiving (Yds.)	Charley Hennigan, 1961	1,746
Interceptions	Fred Glick, 1963	12
	Mike Reinfeldt, 1979	12
Punting (Avg.)	Craig Hentrich, 1998	47.2
Punt Return (Avg.)	Billy Johnson, 1977	15.4
Kickoff Return (Avg.)	Ken Hall, 1960	31.3
Field Goals	Al Del Greco, 1998	36
Touchdowns (Tot.)	Earl Campbell, 1979	19
Points	Al Del Greco, 1998	136

INDIVIDUAL RECORDS—SINGLE GAME

Category	Name	Performance
Rushing (Yds.)	Billy Cannon, 12-10-61	216
	Eddie George, 8-31-97	216
Passing (Yds.)	Warren Moon, 12-16-90	527
Passing (TDs)	George Blanda, 11-19-61	*7
Receiving (No.)	Charley Hennigan, 10-13-61	13
	Haywood Jeffires, 10-13-91	13
Receiving (Yds.)	Charley Hennigan, 10-13-61	272
Interceptions	Many times	3
	Last time by Samari Rolle, 12-26-99	
Field Goals	Roy Gerela, 9-28-69	5
	Al Del Greco, 12-3-00	5
Touchdowns (Tot.)	Billy Cannon, 12-10-61	5
Points	Billy Cannon, 12-10-61	30

*NFL Record

TENNESSEE TITANS

2002 VETERAN ROSTER

No.	Name	Pos.	Ht.	Wt.	Birthdate	NFL Exp.	College	Hometown	How Acq.	'01 Games/ Starts
38	Alexander, Dan	RB-FB	6-0	252	3/17/78	2	Nebraska	Wentzville, Mo.	D6a-'01	7/0
83	Bennett, Drew	WR	6-5	203	8/26/78	2	UCLA	Orinde, Calif.	FA-'01	14/1
82	Berlin, Eddie	WR	5-11	194	1/14/78	2	Northern Iowa	Urbandale, Iowa	D5-'01	11/0
53	Bulluck, Keith	LB	6-3	232	4/4/77	3	Syracuse	New City, N.Y.	D1-'00	15/3
93	Carter, Kevin	DE	6-5	280	9/21/73	8	Florida	Tallahassee, Fla.	T(StL)-'01	16/16
57	Chamberlin, Frank	LB	6-1	246	1/2/78	3	Boston College	Mahwah, N.J.	D5b-'00	16/0
80	Coleman, Chris	WR	6-0	205	5/8/77	3	North Carolina State	Murphy, N.C.	FA-'00	16/0
33	Comella, Greg	FB	6-1	248	7/29/75	5	Stanford	Wellesley, Mass.	UFA(NYG)-'02	16/13*
	Daft, Kevin	QB	6-1	207	11/19/75	2	California-Davis	Tustin, Calif.	FA-'02	0*
66	DiNapoli, Gennaro	G	6-3	295	5/25/75	5	Virginia Tech	Manhasset, N.Y.	T(Oak)-'00	5/2
22	Dyson, Andre	CB	5-10	187	5/25/79	2	Utah	Clearfield, Utah	D2-'01	14/12
87	Dyson, Kevin	WR	6-1	199	6/23/75	5	Utah	Clearfield, Utah	D1-'98	16/16
92	Ford, Henry	DT	6-3	295	10/30/71	9	Arkansas	Ft. Worth, Texas	D1-'94	16/0
27	George, Eddie	RB	6-3	240	9/24/73	7	Ohio State	Philadelphia, Pa.	D1-'96	16/16
26	George, Tony	S	5-11	206	8/10/75	3	Florida	Cincinnati, Ohio	FA-'02	0*
56	Godfrey, Randall	LB	6-2	245	4/6/73	7	Georgia	Valdosta, Ga.	UFA(Dall)-'00	14/14
	Graham, Aaron	C	6-4	300	5/22/73	6	Nebraska	Denton, Texas	UFA(Oak)-'02	14/0*
20	Green, Mike	RB	6-0	249	9/2/76	3	Houston	Houston, Texas	FA-'01	16/1
70	Haayer, Adam	T	6-6	301	2/22/77	2	Minnesota	Wyoming, Minn.	D6b-'01	0*
61	Hall, Barry	T	6-6	311	11/23/77	2	Middle Tennessee State	Fairmount, Ga.	FA-'01	0*
15	Hentrich, Craig	P-K	6-3	198	5/18/71	9	Notre Dame	Alton, Ill.	UFA(GB)-'98	16/0
42	#Hicks, Skip	RB	6-0	230	10/13/74	5	UCLA	Burkburnett, Texas	W(Chi)-'01	9/0
	Holcombe, Robert	RB	5-11	215	12/11/75	5	Illinois	Mesa, Ariz.	UFA(StL)-'02	16/0*
72	Hopkins, Brad	T	6-3	305	9/5/70	10	Illinois	Moline, Ill.	D1-'93	14/14
90	Kearse, Jevon	DE	6-4	265	9/3/76	4	Florida	Ft. Myers, Fla.	D1-'99	16/16
88	Kinney, Erron	TE	6-5	280	7/28/77	3	Florida	Ashland, Va.	D3a-'00	13/12
85	Mason, Derrick	WR	5-10	188	1/17/74	6	Michigan State	Detroit, Mich.	D4a-'97	15/15
76	Mathews, Jason	T	6-5	300	2/9/71	9	Texas A&M	Orange, Texas	FA-'98	16/2
74	Matthews, Bruce	G-C	6-5	305	8/8/61	20	Southern California	Arcadia, Calif.	D1-'83	16/16
86	McCareins, Justin	WR	6-2	205	12/11/78	2	Northern Illinois	Naperville, Ill.	D4-'01	4/1
9	McNair, Steve	QB	6-2	225	2/14/73	8	Alcorn State	Mt. Olive, Miss.	D1-'95	15/15
84	Meier, Shad	TE	6-4	253	6/7/78	2	Kansas State	Pittsburg, Kan.	D3-'01	11/1
71	Miller, Fred	T	6-7	315	2/6/73	7	Baylor	Houston, Texas	UFA(StL)-'00	16/16
30	Mitchell, Donald	CB	5-9	182	12/14/76	4	Southern Methodist	Beaumont, Texas	D4b-'99	12/3
28	Morris, Aric	S	5-10	212	7/22/77	3	Michigan State	Oak Park, Mich.	D5a-'00	16/10
32	Myers, Bobby	S	6-1	191	11/10/76	3	Wisconsin	Hamden, Conn.	D4a-'00	1/1
6	Nedney, Joe	K	6-5	220	3/22/73	7	San Jose State	San Jose, Calif.	UFA(Car)-'01	16/0
14	O'Donnell, Neil	QB	6-3	228	7/3/66	13	Maryland	Madison, N.J.	UFA(Cin)-'99	5/1
75	Olson, Benji	G	6-3	315	6/5/75	5	Washington	Port Orchard, Wash.	D5-'98	16/16
69	Piller, Zach	G	6-5	315	5/2/76	4	Florida	Tallahassee, Fla.	D3-'99	14/9
21	Rolle, Samari	CB	6-0	175	8/10/76	5	Florida State	Miami, Fla.	D2-'98	14/14
95	Salave'a, Joe	DT	6-3	295	3/23/75	5	Arizona	San Diego, Calif.	D4-'98	11/0
31	Schulters, Lance	S	6-2	207	5/27/75	5	Hofstra	Brooklyn, N.Y.	UFA(SF)-'02	16/16*
37	Sidney, Dainon	CB	6-0	188	5/30/75	5	Alabama-Birmingham	Atlanta, Ga.	D3-'98	1/1
59	Sirmon, Peter	LB	6-2	246	2/18/77	3	Oregon	Walla Walla, Wash.	D4b-'00	16/0
51	Smith, Jeff	C	6-3	320	5/25/73	7	Tennessee	Decatur, Tenn.	UFA(Jax)-'02	16/16*
98	Smith, Robaire	DE-DT	6-4	280	11/15/77	3	Michigan State	Flint, Mich.	D6-'00	10/0
94	Thomas, Juqua	DE	6-2	252	5/15/78	2	Oklahoma State	Houston, Texas	FA-'01	7/0
78	Thornton, John	DT	6-2	300	10/2/76	4	West Virginia	Philadelphia, Pa.	D2-'99	3/0
58	Thweatt, Byron	LB	6-2	233	3/21/77	2	Virginia	Chesterfield, Va.	FA-'01	5/0
12	Volek, Billy	QB	6-2	214	4/28/76	3	Fresno State	Fresno, Calif.	FA-'00	1/0
29	Walker, Joe	S	5-10	204	3/19/77	2	Nebraska	Arlington, Texas	FA-'01	16/3
89	Wycheck, Frank	TE	6-3	250	10/14/71	10	Maryland	Philadelphia, Pa.	W(Wash)-'95	16/16

* Comella played 16 games with N.Y. Giants in '01; Daft last active with San Francisco in '00; T. George last active with New England in '00; Graham plaeyd 14 games with Oakland; Haayer missed '01 season because of injury; Hall was inactive for 16 games; Holcombe played 16 games with St. Louis; Schulters played 16 games with San Francisco; J. Smith played 16 games with Jacksonville.

Players lost through free agency (3): LB Greg Favors (Ind; 16 games in '01), DT Jason Fisk (SD; 16), S Daryl Porter (NE; 14).

Also played with the Titans in '01—S Blaine Bishop (5 games), CB Michael Booker (16), DT Josh Evans (16), CB DeRon Jenkins (15), TE Mike Leach (4), C Kevin Long (15), FB Wes Ours (3), S Perry Phenix (12), LB Eddie Robinson (16), WR Chris Sanders (4).

2002 FIRST-YEAR ROSTER

Name	Pos.	Ht.	Wt.	Birthdate	College	Hometown	How Acq.
Aldridge, Kevin	DE	6-1	271	3/3/80	Southern Methodist	Jacksonville, Texas	FA
Bandy, Nate	TE	6-7	238	9/5/78	Tennessee-Chattanooga	Atlantic City, N.J.	FA
Beckham, Tony	CB	6-1	195	10/1/78	Wisconsin-Stout	Ocala, Fla.	D4b
Benn, Kyle	C	6-2	300	4/4/79	Washington	Edmonds, Wash.	FA
Boiman, Rocky	LB	6-4	242	1/24/80	Notre Dame	Cincinnati, Ohio	D4c
Bradford, Antuian	LB	6-0	231	11/21/79	Vanderbilt	Batesville, Miss.	FA
Bush, Marlon	DT	6-1	281	12/3/79	Alabama-Birmingham	Athens, Ala.	FA
Calmus, Rocky	LB	6-3	243	8/1/79	Oklahoma	Jenks, Okla.	D3
Carson, Elliott (1)	TE	6-5	266	6/20/78	Vanderbilt	Lebanon, Tenn.	FA
Cooper, Rafael (1)	RB	5-11	205	1/8/75	Louisville	Detroit, Mich.	FA
Davis, Wade (1)	CB	5-11	185	7/20/77	Weber State	Aurora, Colo.	FA
Dewalt, Dedrick	WR	5-8	188	6/3/79	Boston College	Chicago, Ill.	FA
Echols, Mike	CB	5-10	190	10/13/78	Wisconsin	Youngstown, Ohio	D4a
Hall, Carlos	DE	6-4	259	1/16/79	Arkansas	Moro, Ark.	D7b
Hartwig, Justin	G	6-4	300	11/21/78	Kansas	West Des Moines, Iowa	D6
Haynesworth, Albert	DT	6-6	320	6/17/81	Tennessee	Hartsville, S.C.	D1
Hill, Darrell	WR	6-3	197	6/19/79	Northern Illinois	Chicago, Ill.	D7a
Iglesias, Orlando	WR	6-3	215	12/3/77	Houston	Miami, Fla.	FA
Jackson, Nate	S	5-10	170	12/25/79	Hawaii	Oahu, Hawaii	FA
Judge, Joe	S	5-11	203	3/10/78	McNeese State	Kaplan, La.	FA
Kassell, Brad	LB	6-3	240	1/7/80	North Texas State	Llano, Texas	FA
Kocurek, Kris (1)	DT	6-4	293	11/15/78	Texas Tech	Caldwell, Texas	FA
Martin, Matt	T	6-6	272	10/12/79	Kansas State	Huntington Beach, Calif.	FA
Miller, Dicenzo	RB	5-10	215	7/9/80	Mississippi State	Weir, Miss.	FA
Morrow, Nate	LB	6-3	248	12/10/78	Vanderbilt	New Concord, Ohio	FA
Natkin, Brian (1)	TE	6-4	250	1/3/78	Texas-El Paso	San Antonio, Texas	FA
Newman, Billy	S	5-10	204	12/10/78	Washington State	Laguna Niguel, Calif.	FA
Patu, Saul (1)	DT	6-3	272	6/8/78	Oregon	Seattle, Wash.	FA
Raynock, Chase (1)	T	6-6	305	9/29/77	Montana	Billings, Mont.	FA
Sanders, Chris (1)	QB	6-1	214	12/22/77	Tennessee-Chattanooga	Flower Mound, Texas	FA
Schifino, Jake	WR	6-1	200	11/15/79	Akron	Pittsburgh, Pa.	D5
Simon, John	RB	5-11	202	12/11/78	Louisiana Tech	Baton Rouge, La.	FA
Smith, Marcus	CB	5-9	183	8/17/80	Memphis	Memphis, Tenn.	FA
Snelling, Robby (1)	TE	6-2	244	8/14/78	Boise State	Burney, Calif.	FA
Thomas, Tarlos (1)	T	6-5	323	8/23/77	Florida State	Monticello, Fla.	FA
Watson, Ryan	DT	6-2	300	11/25/78	Appalachian State	Tampa, Fla.	FA
Williams, Tank	S	6-3	223	6/30/80	Stanford	Bay St. Louis, Miss.	D2
Witczak, Jason (1)	K	6-1	188	5/24/78	Southeast Missouri State	North Fond Du Lac, Wis.	FA

The term NFL Rookie is defined as a player who is in his first season of professional football and has not been on the roster of another professional football team for any regular-season or postseason games. A Rookie is designated by an "R" on NFL rosters. Players who have been active in another professional football league or players who have NFL experience, including either preseason training camp or being on an Active List or Inactive List, or on Reserve/Injured or Reserve/Physically Unable to Perform for fewer than six regular-season games, are termed NFL First-Year Players. An NFL First-Year Player is designated by a "1" on NFL rosters. Thereafter, a player is credited with an additional year of experience for each season in which he accumulates six games on the Active List or Inactive List, or on Reserve/Injured or Reserve/Physically Unable to Perform.

TENNESSEE TITANS

COACHING STAFF
Head Coach,
Jeff Fisher
Pro Career: Became the franchise's fifteenth head coach on January 5, 1995 after closing his first campaign as head coach/defensive coordinator. He replaced Jack Pardee on November 14, 1994, serving the remaining six games as head coach. Fisher is the franchise's winningest coach with 68 victories and is the fourth youngest NFL coach (43) to reach the 60-regular season win plateau since 1960 (Don Shula, John Madden, and Bill Cowher). Over the past three seasons, Fisher has led the Titans to an AFC Championship in 1999, an AFC Central Division title in 2000 and the league's second best record. In 2000, Fisher became only the fifth coach in NFL history to lead his team to consecutive 13-win seasons, joining Mike Holmgren, George Seifert, Marv Levy, and Mike Ditka. Fisher originally joined the Oilers in 1994 as the defensive coordinator after serving as defensive backs coach for the San Francisco 49ers (1992-93). Prior to heading up the 49ers' secondary, Fisher served as the defensive coordinator for the Los Angeles Rams (1991). He began his coaching career with the Philadelphia Eagles in 1986, where he handled defensive backs until becoming the NFL's youngest defensive coordinator in 1988. Drafted by Chicago in the seventh round in 1981, he spent five seasons as a cornerback and kick returner for the Bears (1981-85). Assisted defensive coordinator Buddy Ryan in Bears' 1985 Super Bowl championship season after being placed on injured reserve with ankle injury. Career record: 68-55.
Background: Played at Southern California (1977-1980) for John Robinson in a star-studded defensive backfield that included Ronnie Lott, Dennis Smith, and Joey Browner. Member of the USC team that won the national championship in 1978. Also served as the Trojans' backup placekicker and was a Pac-10 All-Academic selection in 1980.
Personal: Born February 25, 1958, in Culver City, Calif. Jeff and his wife, Juli, have three children, sons Brandon and Trenton, and daughter Tara. The family resides in Franklin, Tenn.

ASSISTANT COACHES
Chuck Cecil, defensive assistant-quality control; born November 8, 1964, Red Bluff, Calif., lives in Nashville. Defensive back Arizona 1983-87. Pro safety Green Bay Packers 1988-1992, Phoenix Cardinals 1993, Houston Oilers 1995. Pro coach: Joined Titans in 2001.
Gunther Cunningham, asst. head coach-linebackers; born June 19, 1946, Munich, Germany, lives in Nashville. Linebacker-placekicker Oregon 1966-68. No pro playing experience. College coach:

Oregon 1969-1971, Arkansas 1972, Stanford 1973, California 1977-1980. Pro coach: Hamilton Tiger-Cats (CFL) 1981, Baltimore-Indianapolis Colts 1982-84, San Diego Chargers 1985-1990, Los Angeles Raiders 1991-94, Kansas City Chiefs 1995-2000 (head coach 1999-2000), joined Titans in 2001.
Mike Heimerdinger, offensive coordinator; born October 13, 1952, DeKalb, Ill., lives in Brentwood, Tenn. Wide receiver Eastern Illinois 1970-74. No pro playing experience. College coach: Florida 1980, Air Force 1981, North Texas State 1982, Florida 1983-87, Cal State-Fullerton 1988, Rice 1989-1993, Duke 1994. Pro coach: Denver Broncos 1995-99, joined Titans in 2000.
George Henshaw, asst. head coach; born January 22, 1948, Richmond, Va., lives in Nashville. Defensive tackle West Virginia 1967-69. No pro playing experience. College coach: West Virginia 1970-75, Florida State 1976-1982, Alabama 1983-86, Tulsa 1987 (head coach). Pro coach: Denver Broncos 1988-1992, New York Giants 1993-96, joined Titans/Oilers in 1997.
Ned James, offensive assistant-quality control; born Jan. 18, 1964, Syracuse, N.Y., lives in Franklin, Tenn. Quarterback New Mexico 1985-86. Pro quarterback Dallas Texans (Arena League) 1990. College coach: Arizona State 1987, Long Beach State 1988, Texas Christian 1989-1990, Winona State 1992-94, Indiana 2000, New Mexico 2001. Pro coach: London Monarchs (WLAF) 1992, Seattle Seahawks 1995-97, New Orleans Saints 1998-99, New Jersey Gladiators (Arena League) 2001, joined Titans in 2002.
Craig Johnson, quarterbacks; born March 3, 1960, Rome, N.Y., lives in Nashville. Quarterback Wyoming 1978-1982. No pro playing experience. College coach: Wyoming 1983, Arkansas 1984, Army 1985, Rutgers 1986-88, Virginia Military Institute 1989-1991, Northwestern 1992-96, Maryland 1997-99. Pro coach: Joined Titans in 2000.
Alan Lowry, special teams; born November 21, 1950, Miami, Okla., lives in Franklin, Tenn. Defensive back-quarterback Texas 1970-72. No pro playing experience. College coach: Virginia Tech 1974, Wyoming 1975, Texas 1977-1981. Pro coach: Dallas Cowboys 1982-1990, Tampa Bay Buccaneers 1991, San Francisco 49ers 1992-95, joined Titans/Oilers in 1996.
Mike Munchak, offensive line; born March 5, 1960, Scranton, Pa., lives in Brentwood, Tenn. Guard-tackle Penn State 1979-1981. Pro guard Houston Oilers 1982-1993. Pro coach: Joined Titans/Oilers in 1994.
Jim Schwartz, defensive coordinator; born June 2, 1966, Baltimore, lives in Nashville. Linebacker Georgetown 1984-88. No pro playing experience. College

coach: Maryland 1989, Minnesota 1990, North Carolina Central 1991, Colgate 1992. Pro coach: Cleveland Browns/Baltimore Ravens 1995-98, joined Titans in 1999.
Sherman Smith, running backs; born November 1, 1954, Youngstown, Ohio, lives in Franklin, Tenn. Quarterback Miami (Ohio) 1972-75. Pro running back Seattle Seahawks 1976-1982, San Diego Chargers 1983-84. College coach: Miami (Ohio) 1990-91, Illinois 1992-94. Pro coach: Joined Titans/Oilers in 1995.
Steve Walters, wide receivers; born June 16, 1948, Jonesboro, Ark., lives in Nashville. Quarterback-defensive back Arkansas 1967-1970. No pro playing experience. College coach: Tampa 1973, Northeastern Louisana 1974-75, Morehead State 1976, Tulsa 1977-78, Memphis State 1979, Southern Methodist 1980-81, Alabama 1985. Pro coach: New England Patriots 1982-84, 1997-98, New Orleans 1986-1996, joined Titans in 1999.
Jim Washburn, defensive line; born December 2, 1949, Shelby, N.C., lives in Nashville. Offensive lineman Gardner-Webb 1969-1973. No pro playing experience. College coach: Southern Methodist 1976, Lees McRae J.C. 1977-78, Livingston 1979, New Mexico 1980-82, South Carolina 1983-88, Purdue 1989, Arkansas 1994-97, Houston 1998. Pro coach: London Monarchs (WLAF) 1991, Charlotte Rage (AFL) 1993, joined Titans in 1999.
Steve Watterson, strength and rehabilitation; born November 27, 1956, Newport, R.I., lives in Brentwood, Tenn. Attended Rhode Island. No college or pro playing experience. Pro coach: Philadelphia Eagles 1984-85, joined Titans/Oilers in 1986.
Everett Withers, defensive backs; born June 15, 1963, Charlotte, lives in Nashville. Defensive back Appalachian State 1981-85. No pro playing experience. College coach: Austin Peay 1988-1990, Tulane 1991, Southern Mississippi 1992-93, Louisville 1995-97, Texas 1998-2000. Pro coach: New Orleans Saints 1994, joined Titans in 2001.

The NFC

National Football Conference
West Division
Team Colors: Cardinal Red, Black, and White
P.O. Box 888
Phoenix, Arizona 85001-0888
Telephone: (602) 379-0101

2002 SCHEDULE
PRESEASON
Aug. 10	at San Diego	7:00
Aug. 17	**Green Bay**	7:00
Aug. 24	**Denver**	7:00
Aug. 29	at Oakland	6:00

REGULAR SEASON
Sept. 8	at Washington	1:00
Sept. 15	at Seattle	1:05
Sept. 22	**San Diego**	1:05
Sept. 29	**New York Giants**	1:05
Oct. 6	at Carolina	1:00
Oct. 13	Open Date	
Oct. 20	**Dallas**	1:15
Oct. 27	at San Francisco	1:05
Nov. 3	**St. Louis**	2:15
Nov. 10	**Seattle**	2:05
Nov. 17	at Philadelphia	1:00
Nov. 24	**Oakland**	2:05
Dec. 1	at Kansas City	12:00
Dec. 8	**Detroit**	2:05
Dec. 15	at St. Louis	7:30
Dec. 21	**San Francisco (Sat.)**	3:00
Dec. 29	at Denver	2:15

Stadium: Sun Devil Stadium
 • **Capacity:** 73,014
 Fifth Street
 Tempe, Arizona 85287
Playing Surface: Grass
Training Camp: Northern Arizona University
 Flagstaff, Arizona 86011

SUN DEVIL STADIUM

CLUB OFFICIALS
President: William V. Bidwill
Vice Chairman: Thomas J. Guilfoil
Vice President: Larry Wilson
Vice President: William V. Bidwill, Jr.
Vice President/General Counsel:
 Michael Bidwill
Vice President/Sales and Marketing:
 Ron Minegar
Vice President: Nicole Bidwill
Treasurer and Chief Financial Officer:
 Charley Schlegel
General Manager: Bob Ferguson
Assistant to the President: Rod Graves
Public Relations Director: Paul Jensen
Media Coordinator: Greg Gladysiewski
Internet Coordinator: Luke Sacks
Director of Players Programs:
 Anthony Edwards
Director of Community Relations:
 Luis Zendejas
Director of Security: Rick Knight
Director of Operations: Steve Walsh
Director of Cardinals Charities:
 Pat Tankersley
Information Services Director: Mark Feller
Director of Broadcasting: Craig Amazeen
Director of Ticketing: Steve Bomar
Director of Ticket Sales: Jamie Brandt
Director of Group Sales: Scott Bull
Director of Corporate and Broadcast
 Sales: Joe Castor
Director of Corporate Sales: Joe Hickey
Director of Marketing and Promotions:
 Lisa Manning
Director of Cheerleading:
 Molly Handy-Young
Trainer: John Omohundro
Assistant Trainers:
 Jim Shearer, Jeff Herndon
Equipment Manager: Mark Ahlemeier
Assistant Equipment Manager:
 Steve Christensen

COACHING HISTORY
Chicago 1920-1959, St. Louis 1960-1987
(435-607-39)
1920-22	John (Paddy) Driscoll	17-8-4
1923-24	Arnold Horween	13-8-1
1925-26	Norman Barry	16-8-2
1927	Guy Chamberlin	3-7-1
1928	Fred Gillies	1-5-0
1929	Dewey Scanlon	6-6-1
1930	Ernie Nevers	5-6-2
1931	LeRoy Andrews*	0-1-0
1931	Ernie Nevers	5-3-0
1932	Jack Chevigny	2-6-2
1933-34	Paul Schissler	6-15-1
1935-38	Milan Creighton	16-26-4
1939	Ernie Nevers	1-10-0
1940-42	Jimmy Conzelman	8-22-3
1943-45	Phil Handler**	1-29-0
1946-48	Jimmy Conzelman	27-10-0
1949	Phil Handler-Buddy Parker***	2-4-0
1949	Raymond (Buddy) Parker	4-1-1
1950-51	Earl (Curly) Lambeau****	7-15-0
1951	Phil Handler-Cecil Isbell#	1-1-0
1952	Joe Kuharich	4-8-0
1953-54	Joe Stydahar	3-20-1
1955-57	Ray Richards	14-21-1
1958-1961	Frank (Pop) Ivy##	17-29-2
1961	Chuck Drulis-Ray Prochaska-Ray Willsey###	2-0-0
1962-65	Wally Lemm	27-26-3
1966-1970	Charley Winner	35-30-5
1971-72	Bob Hollway	8-18-2
1973-77	Don Coryell	42-29-1
1978-79	Bud Wilkinson####	9-20-0
1979	Larry Wilson	2-1-0
1980-85	Jim Hanifan	39-50-1
1986-89	Gene Stallings@	23-34-1
1989	Hank Kuhlmann	0-5-0
1990-93	Joe Bugel	20-44-0
1994-95	Buddy Ryan	12-20-0
1996-2000	Vince Tobin@@	29-44-00
2000-01	Dave McGinnis	8-17-0

 * Resigned after one game in 1931
 ** Co-coach with Walt Kiesling in Chicago
  Cardinals-Pittsburgh merger in 1944
 *** Co-coaches for first six games in 1949
 **** Resigned after 10 games in 1951
 # Co-coaches
 ## Resigned after 12 games in 1961
 ### Co-coaches
 #### Released after 13 games in 1979
 @ Released after 11 games in 1989
 @@ Released after seven games in 2000

ATTENDANCE
Home 307,317	Away 525,884

Total 833,201
Single-game home record,
73,025 (9/19/93)
Single-season home record, 497,330
(1994)

2002 DRAFT CHOICES
Round	Name	Pos.	College
1	Wendell Bryant	DT	Wisconsin
2	Levar Fisher	LB	North Carolina St.
3	Josh McCown	QB	Sam Houston St.
	Dennis Johnson	DE	Kentucky
4	Nate Dwyer	DT	Kansas
5	Jason McAddley	WR	Alabama
6	Josh Scobey	RB	Kansas State
7	Mike Banks	TE	Iowa State

2001 TEAM RECORD
PRESEASON (3-1)

Date	Result	Opponent
8/11	L	7-10 Oakland
8/18	W	16-13 at Seattle (OT)
8/25	W	24-20 at Chicago
8/31	W	16-3 San Diego

REGULAR SEASON (7-9)

Date	Result	Opponent	Att.
9/23	L	17-38 Denver	50,913
9/30	L	14-34 Atlanta	28,878
10/07	W	21-20 at Philadelphia	66,360
10/14	L	13-20 at Chicago	66,944
10/21	W	24-16 Kansas City	35,916
10/28	L	3-17 at Dallas	63,114
11/04	L	7-21 Philadelphia	33,430
11/11	L	10-17 New York Giants	36,917
11/18	W	45-38 Detroit	32,322
11/25	W	20-17 at San Diego	49,398
12/02	W	34-31 at Oakland (OT)	46,601
12/09	L	10-20 Washington	40,056
12/15	L	13-17 at New York Giants	77,913
12/23	W	17-10 Dallas	48,883
12/30	W	30-7 at Carolina	72,025
1/06	L	17-20 at Washington	61,721

(OT) Overtime

SCORE BY PERIODS

Cardinals	51	110	30	101	3 —	295
Opponents	57	114	72	100	0 —	343

2001 TEAM STATISTICS

	Cardinals	Opp.
Total First Downs	277	319
Rushing	77	124
Passing	177	179
Penalty	23	16
3rd Down: Made/Att	57/196	84/220
3rd Down Pct.	29.1	38.2
4th Down: Made/Att	10/20	12/24
4th Down Pct.	50.0	50.0
Possession Avg.	27:45	32:15
Total Net Yards	4898	5685
Avg. Per Game	306.1	355.3
Total Plays	955	1071
Avg. Per Play	5.1	5.3
Net Yards Rushing	1449	2087
Avg. Per Game	90.6	130.4
Total Rushes	400	496
Net Yards Passing	3449	3598
Avg. Per Game	215.6	224.9
Sacked/Yards Lost	29/204	19/128
Gross Yards	3653	3726
Att./Completions	526/304	556/337
Completion Pct.	57.8	60.6
Had Intercepted	14	17
Punts/Average	87/41.0	75/43.3
Net Punting Avg.	87/33.7	75/34.1
Penalties/Yards	72/620	110/980
Fumbles/Ball Lost	26/13	27/7
Touchdowns	33	39
Rushing	10	10
Passing	18	26
Returns	5	3

2001 INDIVIDUAL STATISTICS

PASSING

	Att.	Comp.	Yds.	Pct.	TD	Int.	Tkld.	Rate
Plummer	525	304	3653	57.9	18	14	29/204	79.6
Sanders	1	0	0	0.0	0	0	0/0	39.6
Cardinals	526	304	3653	57.8	18	14	29/204	79.5
Opponents	556	337	3726	60.6	26	17	19/128	83.4

SCORING

	TD R	TD P	TD Rt	PAT	FG	Saf	PTS
Gramatica	0	0	0	25/25	16/20	0	73
Boston	0	8	0	0/0	0/0	0	48
Jones	5	0	0	0/0	0/0	0	30
Pittman	5	0	0	0/0	0/0	0	30
Oglesby	0	0	0	7/7	5/6	0	22
Jenkins	0	3	0	0/0	0/0	0	18
Hardy	0	2	0	0/0	0/0	0	12
McKinnon	0	0	2	0/0	0/0	0	12
Mitchell	0	2	0	0/0	0/0	0	12
Sanders	0	2	0	0/0	0/0	0	12
Makovicka	0	1	0	0/0	0/0	0	6
Vanden Bosch	0	0	1	0/0	0/0	0	6
Wakefield	0	0	1	0/0	0/0	0	6
Wilson	0	0	1	0/0	0/0	0	6
Plummer	0	0	0	0/0	0/0	0	2
Cardinals	10	18	5	32/32	21/26	0	295
Opponents	10	26	3	36/36	23/32	0	343

2-Pt. Conversions: Plummer.
Cardinals 1-1, Opponents 2-3.

RUSHING

	Att.	Yds.	Avg.	LG	TD
Pittman	241	846	3.5	42	5
Jones	112	380	3.4	21	5
Plummer	35	163	4.7	21	0
Boston	5	35	7.0	17	0
Makovicka	1	19	19.0	19	0
Jenkins	3	4	1.3	16	0
Gruttadauria	1	1	1.0	1	0
McKinley	1	1	1.0	1	0
Player	1	0	0.0	0	0
Cardinals	400	1449	3.6	42	10
Opponents	496	2087	4.2	41	10

RECEIVING

	No.	Yds.	Avg.	LG	TD
Boston	98	1598	16.3	61t	8
Pittman	42	264	6.3	27	0
Sanders	41	618	15.1	68t	2
Jenkins	32	518	16.2	53	3
Mitchell	25	196	7.8	24t	2
Jones	21	151	7.2	18	0
Makovicka	16	95	5.9	25	1
Hardy	11	79	7.2	13	2
Jackson	9	44	4.9	16	0
Bush	8	80	10.0	16	0
McKinley	1	10	10.0	10	0
Cardinals	304	3653	12.0	68t	18
Opponents	337	3726	11.1	79t	26

INTERCEPTIONS

	No.	Yds.	Avg.	LG	TD
Lassiter	9	80	8.9	25	0
Wilson	2	97	48.5	61t	1
Barrett	2	30	15.0	23	0
Knight	1	43	43.0	43	0
McKinnon	1	24	24.0	24t	1
Wakefield	1	20	20.0	20t	1
Chavous	1	0	0.0	0	0
Cardinals	17	294	17.3	61t	3
Opponents	14	157	11.2	43	1

PUNTING

	No.	Yds.	Avg.	In 20	LG
Player	67	2779	41.5	17	58
Stanley	19	751	39.5	4	54
Gramatica	1	41	41.0	0	41
Cardinals	87	3571	41.0	21	58
Opponents	75	3251	43.3	22	64

PUNT RETURNS

	No.	FC	Yds.	Avg.	LG	TD
Jackson	40	0	461	11.5	55	0
Lassiter	3	1	11	3.7	10	0
Cardinals	43	1	472	11.0	55	0
Opponents	48	17	481	10.0	45	0

KICKOFF RETURNS

	No.	Yds.	Avg.	LG	TD
Jenkins	49	1120	22.9	70	0
Pittman	6	161	26.8	44	0
Shipp	6	118	19.7	26	0
Jackson	2	46	23.0	24	0
Burke	1	15	15.0	15	0
Bush	1	9	9.0	9	0
Makovicka	1	7	7.0	7	0
McKinley	1	11	11.0	11	0
Cardinals	67	1487	22.2	70	0
Opponents	53	967	18.2	94t	1

FIELD GOALS

	1-19	20-29	30-39	40-49	50+
Gramatica	1/1	7/7	3/4	4/7	1/1
Oglesby	1/1	2/2	1/2	1/1	0/0
Cardinals	2/2	9/9	4/6	5/8	1/1
Opponents	0/0	7/9	8/9	7/12	1/2

SACKS

	No.
Fredrickson	4.0
Wakefield	2.5
Burke	2.0
R. Davis	2.0
McKinnon	2.0
Lassiter	1.0
Sanyika	1.0
Tosi	1.0
Walz	1.0
Bell	0.5
Hill	0.5
Thompson	0.5
Vanden Bosch	0.5
Wilson	0.5
Cardinals	19.0
Opponents	29.0

RECORD HOLDERS
INDIVIDUAL RECORDS—CAREER

Category	Name	Performance
Rushing (Yds.)	Ottis Anderson, 1979-1986	7,999
Passing (Yds.)	Jim Hart, 1966-1983	34,639
Passing (TDs)	Jim Hart, 1966-1983	209
Receiving (No.)	Larry Centers, 1990-98	535
Receiving (Yds.)	Roy Green, 1979-1990	8,497
Interceptions	Larry Wilson, 1960-1972	52
Punting (Avg.)	Jerry Norton, 1959-1961	44.9
Punt Return (Avg.)	Charley Trippi, 1947-1955	13.7
Kickoff Return (Avg.)	Ollie Matson, 1952, 1954-58	28.5
Field Goals	Jim Bakken, 1962-1978	282
Touchdowns (Tot.)	Roy Green, 1979-1990	70
Points	Jim Bakken, 1962-1978	1,380

INDIVIDUAL RECORDS—SINGLE SEASON

Category	Name	Performance
Rushing (Yds.)	Ottis Anderson, 1979	1,605
Passing (Yds.)	Neil Lomax, 1984	4,614
Passing (TDs)	Charley Johnson, 1963	28
	Neil Lomax, 1984	28
Receiving (No.)	Larry Centers, 1995	101
Receiving (Yds.)	David Boston, 2001	1,596
Interceptions	Bob Nussbaumer, 1949	12
Punting (Avg.)	Jerry Norton, 1960	45.6
Punt Return (Avg.)	John (Red) Cochran, 1949	20.9
Kickoff Return (Avg.)	Ollie Matson, 1958	35.5
Field Goals	Greg Davis, 1995	30
Touchdowns (Tot.)	John David Crow, 1962	17
Points	Jim Bakken, 1967	117
	Neil O'Donoghue, 1984	117

INDIVIDUAL RECORDS—SINGLE GAME

Category	Name	Performance
Rushing (Yds.)	LeShon Johnson, 9-22-96	214
Passing (Yds.)	Boomer Esiason, 11-10-96 (OT)	522
Passing (TDs)	Jim Hardy, 10-2-50	6
	Charley Johnson, 9-26-65, 11-2-69	6
Receiving (No.)	Sonny Randle, 11-4-62	16
Receiving (Yds.)	Sonny Randle, 11-4-62	256
Interceptions	Bob Nussbaumer, 11-13-49	*4
	Jerry Norton, 11-20-60	*4
	Kwamie Lassiter, 12-27-98	*4
Field Goals	Jim Bakken, 9-24-67	*7
Touchdowns (Tot.)	Ernie Nevers, 11-28-29	*6
Points	Ernie Nevers, 11-28-29	*40

*NFL Record

ARIZONA CARDINALS

2002 VETERAN ROSTER

No.	Name	Pos.	Ht.	Wt.	Birthdate	NFL Exp.	College	Hometown	How Acq.	'01 Games/ Starts
36	Barrett, David	CB	5-10	198	12/22/77	3	Arkansas	Osceola, Ark.	D4-'00	16/9
94	Bell, Marcus	DT	6-2	330	6/1/79	2	Memphis	Memphis, Tenn.	D4b-'01	13/0
61	Borum, Jarvis	T	6-7	324	9/16/78	2	North Carolina State	Columbia, S.C.	FA-'01	1/0
89	Boston, David	WR	6-2	236	8/19/78	4	Ohio State	Humble, Texas	D1a-'99	16/16
71	Bowers, Andy	DE	6-5	286	2/22/76	2	Utah	Salt Lake City, Utah	FA-'01	1/1
95	Burke, Thomas	DE	6-3	261	10/12/76	4	Wisconsin	Poplar, Wis.	D3-'99	12/9
87	Bush, Steve	TE-LS	6-3	274	7/4/74	6	Arizona State	Paradise Valley, Ariz.	FA-'01	9/7
65	Clement, Anthony	T	6-8	328	4/10/76	5	Southwestern Louisiana	Lafayette, La.	D2b-'98	16/16
62	Cook, Michael	T	6-6	347	6/23/78	2	Boston College	Walpole, Mass.	FA-'01	0*
75	Davis, Leonard	G	6-6	372	9/5/78	2	Texas	Wortham, Texas	D1-'01	16/16
98	Davis, Russell	DT	6-4	316	3/28/75	4	North Carolina	Fayetteville, N.C.	W(Chi)-'00	16/16
67	Dishman, Chris	G	6-3	340	2/27/74	6	Nebraska	Cozad, Neb.	D4-'97	16/5
79	Fatafehi, Mario	DT	6-2	300	1/27/79	2	Kansas State	Honolulu, Hawaii	D5-'01	7/1
59	Fredrickson, Rob	LB	6-4	239	5/13/71	9	Michigan State	St. Joseph, Mich.	UFA(Oak)-'99	15/15
86	Gilmore, Bryan	WR	6-0	193	7/21/78	2	Midwestern State	Lufkin, Texas	FA-'00	3/0
7	Gramatica, Bill	K	5-10	187	7/1/78	2	South Florida	LaBelle, Fla.	D4a-'01	13/0
14	Greisen, Chris	QB	6-3	227	7/2/76	4	Northwest Missouri State	Sturgeon Bay, Wis.	D7-'99	0*
60	Gruttadauria, Mike	C	6-3	280	12/6/72	7	Central Florida	Tarpon Springs, Fla.	UFA(StL)-'00	15/15
45	Hill, Renaldo	CB	5-11	183	11/12/78	2	Michigan State	Detroit, Mich.	D7a-'01	14/1
84	Jackson, Arnold	WR	5-8	173	4/9/77	2	Louisville	Jacksonville, Fla.	FA-'01	16/1
82	Jenkins, MarTay	WR	6-0	206	2/28/75	4	Nebraska-Omaha	Waterloo, Iowa	W(Dall)-'99	13/3
85	Jones, Freddie	TE	6-4	271	9/16/74	6	North Carolina	Landover, Md.	FA-'02	14/9*
26	Jones, Thomas	RB	5-10	220	8/19/78	3	Virginia	Big Stone Gap, Va.	D1-'00	16/2
66	Kendall, Pete	G	6-5	288	7/9/73	7	Boston College	Weymouth, Mass.	UFA(Sea)-'01	11/11
42	#Lassiter, Kwamie	S	6-0	207	12/3/69	8	Kansas	Newport News, Va.	FA-'95	16/16
41	Lucas, Justin	CB-S	5-10	198	7/15/76	4	Abilene Christian	Victoria, Texas	FA-'99	13/4
34	† Makovicka, Joel	FB	5-11	251	10/6/75	4	Nebraska	Brainard, Neb.	D4-'99	16/14
39	† McKinley, Dennis	FB	6-2	247	11/3/76	4	Mississippi State	Weir, Miss.	D6b-'99	14/0
57	McKinnon, Ronald	LB	6-0	248	9/20/73	7	North Alabama	Elba, Ala.	FA-'96	16/16
83	Mitchell, Tywan	TE	6-5	256	12/10/75	3	Minnesota State-Mankato	Crete, Ill.	FA-'99	16/4
10	Player, Scott	P	6-1	221	12/17/69	5	Florida State	St. Augustine, Fla.	FA-'98	12/0
16	Plummer, Jake	QB	6-2	212	12/19/74	6	Arizona State	Boise, Idaho	D2-'97	16/16
23	† Rhinehart, Coby	CB	5-11	196	2/7/77	3	Southern Methodist	Dallas, Texas	D6a-'99	13/0
51	Rutledge, Johnny	LB	6-3	239	1/4/77	4	Florida	Belle Glade, Fla.	D2-'99	14/0
81	Sanders, Frank	WR	6-2	215	2/17/73	8	Auburn	Fort Lauderdale, Fla.	D2-'95	15/13
54	Sanyika, Sekou	LB	6-3	240	3/17/78	3	California	Hercules, Calif.	D7-'00	16/1
70	Shelton, L.J.	T	6-6	335	3/21/76	4	Eastern Michigan	Rochester Hills, Mich.	D1b-'99	16/16
31	Shipp, Marcel	RB	5-11	219	8/8/78	2	Massachusetts	Paterson, N.J.	FA-'01	11/0
50	Starkey, Jason	C	6-4	297	7/15/77	3	Marshall	Barboursville, W. Va.	FA-'00	14/1
22	Starks, Duane	CB	5-10	172	5/23/74	5	Miami	Miami, Fla.	UFA(Balt)-'02	15/15*
44	Stone, Michael	CB	5-11	197	2/13/78	2	Memphis	Southfield, Mich.	D2b-'01	7/0
92	Tanner, Barron	DT	6-3	346	9/14/73	5	Oklahoma	Athens, Texas	FA-'00	16/16
55	Thompson, Ray	LB	6-3	217	11/21/77	3	Tennessee	New Orleans, La.	D2-'00	14/14
78	Tosi, Mao	DT	6-6	312	12/12/76	3	Idaho	Anchorage, Alaska	D5a-'00	11/1
93	Vanden Bosch, Kyle	DE	6-4	263	11/17/78	2	Nebraska	Larchwood, Iowa	D2a-'01	3/3
97	Wakefield, Fred	DE	6-7	288	9/17/78	2	Illinois	Tuscola, Ill.	FA-'01	16/12
22	Wilson, Adrian	DB	6-3	217	10/12/79	2	North Carolina State	High Point, N.C.	D3-'01	16/0
56	Woods, LeVar	LB	6-3	245	3/15/78	2	Iowa	Larchwood, Iowa	FA-'01	15/0

* Cook was inactive for 1 game; Greisen inactive for 16 games; F. Jones played 14 games with San Diego in '01; Starks played 15 games with Baltimore.

† Restricted free agent; subject to developments.

Unrestricted free agent; subject to developments.

Players lost through Expansion Draft (1): DE Jabari Issa (13 games in '01).

Players lost through free agency (3): CB Corey Chavous (Minn; 14 games in '01); CB Tom Knight (NE; 8), RB Michael Pittman (TB; 15).

Also played with Cardinals in '01—TE Terry Hardy (8 games), TE-LS Trey Junkin (16), K Cedric Oglesby (3), G Yusuf Scott (5), P Chad Stanley (4), S Pat Tillman (12), LB Zack Walz (14).

2002 FIRST-YEAR ROSTER

Name	Pos.	Ht.	Wt.	Birthdate	College	Hometown	How Acq.
Anderson, Damien	RB	5-10	212	7/17/79	Northwestern	Wilmington, Ill.	FA
Anderson, Kurt	G	6-3	302	8/6/78	Michigan	Evanston, Ill.	FA
Banks, Mike	TE	6-4	260	11/5/79	Iowa State	Boone, Iowa	D7
Bryant, Wendell	DT	6-4	308	9/12/80	Wisconsin	St. Louis, Mo.	D1
Burton, Charles	LB	6-1	237	5/6/79	Syracuse	Sugarland, Texas	FA
Dawson, Dan	S	6-1	219	6/13/78	Rice	Bauxite, Ark.	FA
Duncan, Tim	K	6-1	209	6/12/79	Oklahoma	Clinton, Okla.	FA
Dwyer, Nate	DT	6-3	313	9/30/78	Kansas	Stillwater, Minn.	D4
Fisher, Levar	LB	6-1	228	11/29/79	North Carolina State	Beaufort, N.C.	D2
Gallimore, Justin	CB	5-9	202	8/17/78	Colorado State	Denver, Colo.	FA
Grace, Steve	C	6-3	293	2/13/79	Arizona	Honolulu, Hawaii	FA
Guy, Daniel (1)	WR	6-2	211	12/11/77	Jackson State	Memphis, Tenn.	FA
Harris, Quentin	S	6-0	215	1/26/77	Syracuse	Wilkes Barre, Pa.	FA
Haws, Robert	T	6-8	320	3/7/77	Northern Arizona	Eagar, Ariz.	FA
Hodel, Nathan (1)	TE-LS	6-2	245	11/12/77	Illinois	Fairfield, Ill.	FA
Johnson, Dennis	DE	6-5	258	12/4/79	Kentucky	Harrodsburg, Ky.	D3b
Joyce, Eric	CB	5-9	192	1/21/78	Tennessee State	Nashville, Tenn.	FA
McAddley, Jason	WR	6-1	201	7/28/79	Alabama	Oak Ridge, Tenn.	D5
McCown, Josh	QB	6-4	229	7/4/79	Sam Houston State	Jacksonville, Texas	D3a
McCray, William	FB	5-11	232	1/31/79	Florida State	Jacksonville, Fla.	FA
Moody, Thomas	G	6-3	323	7/21/78	Florida	Seville, Fla.	FA
Moore, Alton	DE	6-6	255	11/11/79	Alabama	Bay Minette, Ala.	FA
O'Connor, Sean	G	6-3	295	9/14/78	Syracuse	Morristown, N.J.	FA
Padget, Jason (1)	C	6-3	295	3/23/79	Louisville	Avondale, Ariz.	FA
Parker, Ezekiel	WR	5-10	194	12/19/78	Louisville	Athens, Ga.	FA
Parsons, Preston	QB	6-3	222	2/19/79	Northern Arizona	Beaverton. Ore.	FA
Poole, Nathan (1)	WR	6-2	212	2/1/77	Marshall	Danville, Va.	FA
Procell, Jarrett (1)	DE	6-2	275	11/4/77	Louisiana Tech	Bossier City, La.	FA
Scobey, Josh	RB	5-11	216	12/11/79	Kansas State	Oklahoma City, Okla.	D6
Soliday, Jake	WR	6-1	193	11/16/78	Northern Iowa	Mansfield, Ohio	FA
White, Anthony (1)	RB	6-0	195	5/1/77	Kentucky	Twinsburg, Ohio	FA
Wragge, Tony	G	6-3	311	8/14/79	New Mexico State	Creighton, Neb.	FA
Young, Michael (1)	LB	6-2	247	6/1/78	Illinois	St. Louis, Mo.	FA

The term NFL Rookie is defined as a player who is in his first season of professional football and has not been on the roster of another professional football team for any regular-season or postseason games. A Rookie is designated by an "R" on NFL rosters. Players who have been active in another professional football league or players who have NFL experience, including either preseason training camp or being on an Active List or Inactive List, or on Reserve/Injured or Reserve/Physically Unable to Perform for fewer than six regular-season games, are termed NFL First-Year Players. An NFL First-Year Player is designated by a "1" on NFL rosters. Thereafter, a player is credited with an additional year of experience for each season in which he accumulates six games on the Active List or Inactive List, or on Reserve/Injured or Reserve/Physically Unable to Perform.

COACHING STAFF
Head Coach,
Dave McGinnis
Pro Career: Named Arizona Cardinals' thirty-eighth head coach on December 18, 2000 after serving as team's interim head coach for final nine games of 2000 season and as defensive coordinator since 1996. Prior to joining Arizona in 1996, the Snyder, Texas, native spent 10 seasons (1986-1995) as linebackers coach of the Chicago Bears. In his decade with the Bears, Chicago played in nine playoff games and the defense ranked among the top six teams in fewest yards allowed seven times. McGinnis was part of a defensive staff that led the NFL in fewest points allowed in 1986 and 1988 and ranked first or second in total defense from 1986-88. In addition, McGinnis coached Pro Bowl players at all three linebacker positions—outside linebackers Otis Wilson and Wilber Marshall, and middle linebacker Mike Singletary, a 1998 Pro Football Hall of Fame inductee who made the Pro Bowl every season under McGinnis' tutelage. Career record: 8-17.
Background: Prior to joining the Bears, McGinnis spent 13 years coaching at the major college level. His first assignment was as a freshman coach at his alma mater, Texas Christian University, in 1973-74. In 1975 he moved to Missouri to coach the linebackers and secondary. After spending the 1978-1981 seasons at Indiana State as secondary coach, McGinnis returned to TCU in 1982 for one season as defensive backfield coach before joining Kansas State as defensive ends and linebackers coach from 1983-85. McGinnis was a three-time letterman (1970-72) and two-year starter (1971-72) at defensive back at Texas Christian where he earned academic all-Southwest Conference honors twice (1971-72) and earned a bachelor's degree in business administration. His 5 interceptions as a junior tied for the conference lead.
Personal: Born August 7, 1951, in Independence, Kansas. McGinnis attended Snyder High School in west Texas. He resides in Phoenix with his wife, Kim.

ASSISTANT COACHES
Geep Chryst, quarterbacks; born June 25, 1962, Madison, Wis., lives in Phoenix. Linebacker Princeton 1981-84. Pro linebacker Orlando Thunder (World League) 1992. College coach: Wisconsin-Platteville 1987. Pro Coach: Orlando Thunder (World League) 1991, Chicago Bears 1991-95, Arizona Cardinals 1996-98, San Diego Chargers 1999-2000, rejoined Cardinals in 2001.
Mike Devlin, asst. offensive line-offensive quality control; born November 16, 1979, Blacksburg, Va., lives in Phoenix. Center Iowa. Pro center Buffalo Bills 1993-95, Arizona Cardinals 1996-99. Pro coach: Joined Cardinals in 2000.

Jeff FitzGerald, linebackers; born April 18, 1960, Burbank, Calif., lives in Phoenix. Attended Oregon State. No college or pro playing experience. College coach: Cincinnati 1985-86, Alabama 1987-89, San Diego State 1994-97. Pro coach: Tampa Bay Buccaneers 1990-93, Washington Redskins 1998-99, joined Cardinals in 2000.
Joe Greene, defensive line; born September 24, 1946, Temple, Tex., lives in Phoenix. Defensive tackle North Texas State 1966-68. Pro defensive tackle Pittsburgh Steelers 1969-1981. Inducted into Pro Football Hall of Fame in 1987. Pro coach: Pittsburgh Steelers 1987-1991, Miami Dolphins 1992-95, joined Cardinals in 1996.
Pete Hoener, tight ends; born June 14, 1951, Peoria, Ill., lives in Phoenix. Defensive end Bradley 1969-1970. No pro playing experience. College coach: Missouri 1975-76, Illinois State 1977, Indiana State 1978-1984, Illinois 1987-88, Purdue 1989-1991, Texas Christian 1991-97, Iowa State 1998-99, Texas A&M 2000. Pro Coach: St. Louis Cardinals 1985-86; rejoined Cardinals in 2001.
Hank Kuhlmann, special teams; born October 6, 1937, Webster Groves, Mo., lives in Phoenix. Running back Missouri 1956-59. No pro playing experience. College coach: Missouri 1962-1971, Notre Dame 1975-77. Pro coach: Green Bay Packers 1972-74, Chicago Bears 1978-1982, Birmingham Stallions (USFL) 1983-85, St. Louis/Phoenix Cardinals 1986-89, Tampa Bay Buccaneers 1991, Indianapolis Colts 1994-97, rejoined Cardinals in 1998.
Stan Kwan, special teams assistant and defensive quality control; born November 2, 1967, lives in Phoenix. No college or pro playing experience. Pro coach: San Diego Chargers 1991-96, Detroit Lions 1997-2000, joined Cardinals in 2001.
Larry Marmie, defensive coordinator; born October 17, 1942, Barnesville, Ohio, lives in Phoenix. Quarterback Eastern Kentucky 1962-65. No pro playing experience. College coach: Eastern Kentucky 1967-68, 1972-76, Morehead State 1968-1971, Tulsa 1977-78, North Carolina 1979-1982, Tennessee 1983-84, 1992-94, Arizona State 1988-1991 (head coach), UCLA 1995. Pro coach: Joined Cardinals in 1996.
Rich Olson, offensive coordinator; born July 7, 1948, Wilmington, Calif., lives in Phoenix. Quarterback-free safety Washington State 1968-69. No pro playing experience. College coach: Washington State 1970, Fresno State 1976, Southern California 1977, Southern Methodist 1978-1980, Arkansas 1981-83, Fresno State 1984-1991, Miami 1992-94. Pro coach: Seattle Seahawks 1995-98, Washington Redskins 1999-2000, joined Cardinals in 2001.

Kevin Ramsey, defensive backs; born September 5, 1961, St. Louis, lives in Phoenix. Defensive back Indiana State 1979-1983. No pro playing experience. College coach: Kansas State 1986-1990, Northwestern 1990-92, West Virginia 1993-94, Tennessee 1995-98, Georgia 1999-2000. Pro coach: Joined Cardinals in 2001.
Bob Rogucki, strength and conditioning; born September 27, 1953, Clarksburg, W. Va., lives in Phoenix. No college or pro playing experience. College coach: Penn State 1981, Weber State 1982, Army 1983-89. Pro coach: Joined Cardinals in 1990.
Johnny Roland, running backs; born May 21, 1943, Corpus Christi, Texas, lives in Phoenix. Running back Missouri 1961-65. Pro running back St. Louis Cardinals 1966-1972, New York Giants 1973. College coach: Notre Dame 1975. Pro coach: Green Bay Packers 1974, Philadelphia Eagles 1976-78, Chicago Bears 1983-1992, New York Jets 1993-94, St. Louis Rams 1995-96, joined Cardinals in 1997.
Jerry Sullivan, wide receivers; born July 13, 1944, Miami, lives in Phoenix. Quarterback Florida State 1963-64. No pro playing experience. College coach: Kansas State 1971-72, Texas Tech 1973-75, South Carolina 1976-1982, Indiana 1983, Louisiana State 1984-1990, Ohio State 1991. Pro coach: San Diego Chargers 1992-96, Detroit Lions 1997-2000, joined Cardinals in 2001.
George Warhop, offensive line; born September 19, 1961, Riverside, Calif., lives in Phoenix. Guard Mt. San Jacinto (Calif.) J.C. 1979-80. Pro center Cincinnati Bengals 1981-82. College coach: Cincinnati 1983, Kansas 1984-86, Vanderbilt 1987-89, New Mexico 1990, Southern Methodist 1993, Boston College 1994-95. Pro coach: London Monarchs (World League) 1991-92, St. Louis Rams 1996-97, joined Cardinals in 1998.

National Football Conference
South Division
Team Colors: Black, Red, Silver, and White
4400 Falcon Parkway
Flowery Beach, Georgia 30542
Telephone: (770) 965-3115

2002 SCHEDULE
PRESEASON
Aug. 9   **Jacksonville**....................7:30
Aug. 17 **New York Giants**..............4:00
Aug. 24 at Dallas...........................7:00
Aug. 29 at Cincinnati 7:30

REGULAR SEASON
Sept. 8   at Green Bay 12:00
Sept. 15 **Chicago**.........................1:00
Sept. 22 **Cincinnati**......................8:30
Sept. 29 OPEN DATE
Oct. 6   **Tampa Bay**.....................1:00
Oct. 13   at New York Giants...........1:00
Oct. 20   **Carolina**.........................1:00
Oct. 27   at New Orleans................12:00
Nov. 3   **Baltimore**.......................1:00
Nov. 10   at Pittsburgh 1:00
Nov. 17   **New Orleans**..................1:00
Nov. 24   at Carolina 1:00
Dec. 1   at Minnesota 12:00
Dec. 8   at Tampa Bay 1:00
Dec. 15   **Seattle**...........................1:00
Dec. 22   **Detroit**............................1:00
Dec. 29   at Cleveland 1:00

Stadium: Georgia Dome
(opened in 1992)
•**Capacity:** 71,228
One Georgia Dome Drive
Atlanta, Georgia 30313
Playing Surface: Artificial turf
Training Camp: Furman University
3300 Poinsett Highway
Greenville, South Carolina
29613

GEORGIA DOME

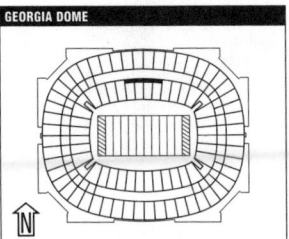

CLUB OFFICIALS
Owner; Chairman, President & CEO:
Arthur M. Blank
Executive Vice President-Head Coach:
Dan Reeves
Executive Vice President–Marketing:
Dick Sullivan
Vice President-Community Affairs:
Susan Bass
Vice President of Football Operations:
Ron Hill
Vice President of Finance: Greg Beadles
Controller: Wallace Norman
Vice President of Marketing and Sales:
Rob Jackson
Vice President of Special Events
Marketing: Tommy Nobis
Director of Corporate Sales and
Sponsorships: Mark Fuhrman
Logistics Coordinator: Spencer Treadwell
Director of Communications:
Aaron Salkin
Director of Media Relations: Frank Kleha
Director of Ticket Operations:
Jack Ragsdale
Dirctor of Ticket Sales: Dave Cohen
Assistant Director of Ticket Operations:
Brent Coleman
Executive Director of the Atlanta Falcons
Youth Foundation: Carol Breeding
Director of Community Relations:
Chris Demos
Player Programs Coordinator:
Billy (White Shoes) Johnson
Director of Information Systems:
Brian Xanders
Director of Player Personnel/Pro:
Les Sneed
Director of Player Personnel/College:
Reed Johnson
Area Scouts: Ken Blair, Billy Campfield,
Dick Corrick, Boyd Dowler, Bill
Groman, Bob Harrison
National Scout: Mike Hagan
Pro Scout: Roy Farmer
Regional Scout: Jeff Smith
Head Athletic Trainer: Ron Medlin
Assistant Athletic Trainers: Harold King,
Thomas Reed
Video Director: Mike Crews
Assistant Video Director: Jonah Bassett
Equipment Manager: Brian Boigner
Senior Equipment Director/Gameday
Coordinator: Horace Daniel

COACHING HISTORY
(216-333-5)
1966-68	Norb Hecker*	4-26-1
1968-1974	Norm Van Brocklin**	..37-49-3
1974-76	Marion Campbell***	6-19-0
1976	Pat Peppler	3-6-0
1977-1982	Leeman Bennett	47-44-0
1983-86	Dan Henning	22-41-1
1987-89	Marion Campbell****	.11-32-0
1989	Jim Hanifan	0-4-0
1990-93	Jerry Glanville	28-38-0
1994-96	June Jones	19-30-0
1997-2001	Dan Reeves	39-44-0

*Released after three games in 1968
**Released after eight games in 1974
***Released after five games in 1976
****Retired after 12 games in 1989

ATTENDANCE
Home 422,732   Away 480,685
Total 903,417
Single-game home record,
70,452 (11/11/01)
Single-season home record, 553,979
(1992)

2002 DRAFT CHOICES
Round	Name	Pos.	College
1	T.J. Duckett	RB	Michigan State
3	Will Overstreet	LB	Tennessee
4	Martin Bibla	G	Miami
5	Kevin McCadam	DB	Virginia Tech
	Kurt Kittner	QB	Illinois
6	Kahlil Hill	WR	Iowa
7	Michael Coleman	WR	Widener
	Kevin Shaffer	T	Tulsa

ATLANTA FALCONS

2001 TEAM RECORD
PRESEASON (3-1)

Date	Result	Opponent
8/3	L 16-17	Pittsburgh
8/11	W 20-10	at New York Jets
8/17	W 27-6	at Washington
8/31	W 36-7	Tampa Bay

REGULAR SEASON (7-9)

Date	Result	Opponent	Att.
9/09	L 13-16	at San Francisco(OT)	65,989
9/23	W 24-16	Carolina	49,312
9/30	W 34-14	at Arizona	28,878
10/07	L 3-31	Chicago	47,640
10/14	L 31-37	San Francisco(OT)	48,100
10/21	W 20-13	at New Orleans	70,020
11/04	L 10-24	New England	45,572
11/11	W 20-13	Dallas	70,452
11/18	W 23-20	at Green Bay	59,849
11/25	W 10-7	at Carolina	72,234
12/02	L 6-35	St. Louis	60,787
12/09	L 10-28	New Orleans	68,826
12/16	L 27-41	at Indianapolis	55,603
12/23	W 33-30	Buffalo	43,320
12/30	L 14-21	at Miami	73,619
1/06	L 13-31	at St. Louis	66,033

(OT) Overtime

SCORE BY PERIODS

Falcons	98	61	40	92	0 —	291
Opponents	68	120	64	116	9 —	377

2001 TEAM STATISTICS

	Falcons	Opp.
Total First Downs	280	298
Rushing	85	95
Passing	165	184
Penalty	30	19
3rd Down: Made/Att	89/217	93/201
3rd Down Pct.	41.0	46.3
4th Down: Made/Att	5/17	2/8
4th Down Pct.	29.4	25.0
Possession Avg.	31:18	28:42
Total Net Yards	5070	5845
Avg. Per Game	316.9	365.3
Total Plays	988	957
Avg. Per Play	5.1	6.1
Net Yards Rushing	1762	1943
Avg. Per Game	110.1	121.4
Total Rushes	439	405
Net Yards Passing	3308	3902
Avg. Per Game	206.8	243.9
Sacked/Yards Lost	64/387	37/230
Gross Yards	3695	4132
Att./Completions	485/278	515/331
Completion Pct.	57.3	64.3
Had Intercepted	17	18
Punts/Average	69/38.8	71/43.3
Net Punting Avg.	69/36.1	71/34.2
Penalties/Yards	90/754	97/852
Fumbles/Ball Lost	27/11	23/12
Touchdowns	29	46
Rushing	9	13
Passing	19	29
Returns	1	4

2001 INDIVIDUAL STATISTICS

PASSING	Att.	Comp.	Yds.	Pct.	TD	Int.	Tkld.	Rate
Chandler	365	223	2847	61.1	16	14	41/261	84.1
Vick	113	50	785	44.2	2	3	21/113	62.7
D. Johnson	5	3	23	60.0	1	0	2/13	110.8
Mohr	2	2	40	100.0	0	0	0/0	118.8
Falcons	485	278	3695	57.3	19	17	64/387	80.0
Opponents	515	331	4132	64.3	29	18	37/230	93.3

SCORING	TD R	TD P	TD Rt	PAT	FG	Saf	PTS
Feely	0	0	0	28/28	29/37	0	115
M. Smith	5	1	0	0/0	0/0	0	36
Christian	2	2	0	0/0	0/0	0	24
Crumpler	0	3	0	0/0	0/0	0	18
Finneran	0	3	0	0/0	0/0	0	18
Martin	0	3	0	0/0	0/0	0	18
Jefferson	0	2	0	0/0	0/0	0	14
Anderson	1	1	0	0/0	0/0	0	12
Mathis	0	2	0	0/0	0/0	0	12
Kozlowski	0	1	0	0/0	0/0	0	6
Rackley	0	1	0	0/0	0/0	0	6
Vaughn	0	0	1	0/0	0/0	0	6
Vick	1	0	0	0/0	0/0	0	6
Falcons	9	19	1	28/28	29/37	0	291
Opponents	13	29	4	44/44	19/24	0	377

2-Pt. Conversions: Jefferson.
Falcons 1-1, Opponents 0-1.

RUSHING	Att.	Yds.	Avg.	LG	TD
M. Smith	237	760	3.2	58	5
Vick	31	289	9.3	35	1
Christian	44	284	6.5	53	2
Anderson	55	190	3.5	14	1
Thomas	37	126	3.4	21	0
Chandler	25	84	3.4	22	0
D. Johnson	5	12	2.4	8	0
McCord	2	11	5.5	8	0
Jervey	3	6	2.0	2	0
Falcons	439	1762	4.0	58	9
Opponents	405	1943	4.8	68t	13

RECEIVING	No.	Yds.	Avg.	LG	TD
Mathis	51	564	11.1	34	2
Christian	45	392	8.7	42	2
Martin	37	548	14.8	63t	3
Jefferson	37	539	14.6	48	2
Crumpler	25	330	13.2	57t	3
Finneran	23	491	21.3	52	3
M. Smith	19	230	12.1	79t	1
R. Kelly	16	142	8.9	25	0
Kozlowski	15	270	18.0	46	1
Anderson	3	111	37.0	94t	1
McCord	3	53	17.7	26	0
Thomas	2	26	13.0	15	0
Rackley	1	1	1.0	1t	1
Feely	1	-2	-2.0	-2	0
Falcons	278	3695	13.3	94t	19
Opponents	331	4132	12.5	65t	29

INTERCEPTIONS	No.	Yds.	Avg.	LG	TD
Buchanan	5	85	17.0	33	0
Ambrose	5	43	8.6	27	0
Brooking	2	17	8.5	9	0
Crockett	1	7	7.0	7	0
Gordon	1	7	7.0	7	0
Wiley	1	1	1.0	1	0
Carty	1	0	0.0	0	0
Vaughn	1	0	0.0	0	0
Dronett	1	-6	-6.0	-6	0
Falcons	18	154	8.6	33	0
Opponents	17	330	19.4	56t	3

PUNTING	No.	Yds.	Avg.	In 20	LG
Mohr	69	2680	38.8	25	55
Falcons	69	2680	38.8	25	55
Opponents	71	3074	43.3	24	64

PUNT RETURNS	No.	FC	Yds.	Avg.	LG	TD
Gordon	31	6	437	14.1	74	0
Hudson	2	1	26	13.0	22	0
Kozlowski	1	0	0	0.0	0	0
Falcons	34	7	463	13.6	74	0
Opponents	17	26	130	7.6	30	0

KICKOFF RETURNS	No.	Yds.	Avg.	LG	TD
Vaughn	61	1491	24.4	96t	1
Crumpler	3	32	10.7	14	0
Kozlowski	3	35	11.7	14	0
McCord	2	39	19.5	23	0
Garza	1	1	1.0	1	0
Falcons	70	1598	22.8	96t	1
Opponents	64	1286	20.1	37	0

FIELD GOALS	1-19	20-29	30-39	40-49	50+
Feely	1/1	8/8	14/15	4/9	2/4
Falcons	1/1	8/8	14/15	4/9	2/4
Opponents	0/0	9/9	7/7	3/8	0/0

SACKS	No.
Kerney	12.0
B. Smith	8.0
Dronett	5.5
Brooking	3.5
Jasper	3.5
T. Hall	2.5
Bradford	1.0
Wiley	1.0
Falcons	37.0
Opponents	64.0

RECORD HOLDERS
INDIVIDUAL RECORDS—CAREER

Category	Name	Performance
Rushing (Yds.)	Gerald Riggs, 1982-88	6,631
Passing (Yds.)	Steve Bartkowski, 1975-1985	23,468
Passing (TDs)	Steve Bartkowski, 1975-1985	154
Receiving (No.)	Terance Mathis, 1994-2001	573
Receiving (Yds.)	Terance Mathis, 1994-2001	7,349
Interceptions	Rolland Lawrence, 1973-1980	39
Punting (Avg.)	Rick Donnelly, 1985-89	42.6
Punt Return (Avg.)	Darrien Gordon, 2001	14.1
Kickoff Return (Avg.)	Darrick Vaughn, 2000-01	25.7
Field Goals	Morten Andersen, 1995-2000	139
Touchdowns (Tot.)	Terance Mathis, 1994-2001	57
Points	Morten Andersen, 1995-2000	620

INDIVIDUAL RECORDS—SINGLE SEASON

Category	Name	Performance
Rushing (Yds.)	Jamal Anderson, 1998	1,846
Passing (Yds.)	Jeff George, 1995	4,143
Passing (TDs)	Steve Bartkowski, 1980	31
Receiving (No.)	Terance Mathis, 1994	111
Receiving (Yds.)	Alfred Jenkins, 1981	1,358
Interceptions	Scott Case, 1988	10
Punting (Avg.)	Billy Lothridge, 1968	44.3
Punt Return (Avg.)	Darrien Gordon, 2001	14.1
Kickoff Return (Avg.)	Darrick Vaughn, 2000	27.7
Field Goals	Morten Andersen, 1995	31
Touchdowns (Tot.)	Jamal Anderson, 1998	16
Points	Morten Andersen, 1995	122

INDIVIDUAL RECORDS—SINGLE GAME

Category	Name	Performance
Rushing (Yds.)	Gerald Riggs, 9-2-84	202
Passing (Yds.)	Steve Bartkowski, 11-15-81	416
Passing (TDs)	Wade Wilson, 12-13-92	5
Receiving (No.)	William Andrews, 11-15-81	15
Receiving (Yds.)	Terance Mathis, 12-13-98	198
Interceptions	Many times	2
	Last time by Ashley Ambrose, 11-18-01	
Field Goals	Norm Johnson, 11-13-94	6
Touchdowns (Tot.)	Many times	3
	Last time by Jamal Anderson, 11-1-98	
Points	Norm Johnson, 11-13-94	20

ATLANTA FALCONS

2002 VETERAN ROSTER

No.	Name	Pos.	Ht.	Wt.	Birthdate	NFL Exp.	College	Hometown	How Acq.	'01 Games/ Starts
33	Ambrose, Ashley	CB	5-10	187	9/17/70	11	Mississippi Valley State	New Orleans, La.	UFA(NO)-'00	16/16
24	Bolden, Juran	CB	6-2	207	6/27/74	6	Mississippi Delta	Tampa, Fla.	FA-'02	0*
56	Brooking, Keith	LB	6-2	245	10/30/75	5	Georgia Tech	Senoia, Ga.	D1-'98	16/16
34	Buchanan, Ray	CB	5-9	186	9/29/71	10	Louisville	Chicago, Ill.	UFA(Ind)-'97	16/16
29	Carpenter, Keion	S	5-11	205	10/31/77	4	Virginia Tech	Baltimore, Md.	FA-'02	15/10*
35	Carty, Johndale	S	6-0	196	8/27/77	4	Utah State	Miami, Fla.	D4-'99	16/2
44	Christian, Bob	FB	5-11	232	11/14/68	10	Northwestern	Florissant, Mo.	UFA(Car)-'97	16/8
71	Claridge, Travis	T-G	6-5	300	3/23/78	3	Southern California	Vancouver, Wash.	D2-'00	14/11
83	Crumpler, Alge	TE	6-2	262	12/23/77	2	North Carolina	Wilmington, N.C.	D2-'01	16/12
54 †	Draft, Chris	LB	5-11	232	2/26/76	4	Stanford	Anaheim, Calif.	W(SF)-'00	13/10
75	Dronett, Shane	DE	6-6	300	1/12/71	11	Texas	Baton Rouge, La.	FA-'97	15/15
28	Dunn, Warrick	RB	5-9	180	1/5/75	6	Florida State	Orange, Texas	UFA(TB)-'02	16/16*
4	Feely, Jay	K	5-10	206	5/23/76	2	Michigan	Odessa, Fla.	FA-'01	16/0
86	Finneran, Brian	WR	6-5	210	1/31/76	3	Villanova	Mission Viejo, Calif.	FA-'00	16/1
79	Flemons, Ronald	DE	6-5	265	10/20/79	2	Texas A&M	San Antonio, Texas	D7c-'01	1/0
65	Forney, Kynan	G	6-2	305	9/8/78	2	Hawaii	Nacogdoches, Texas	D7b-'01	12/8
63	Garza, Roberto	C	6-2	296	3/2/79	2	Texas A&M-Kingsville	Rio Hondo, Texas	D4a-'01	16/4
81	Graham, Jeff	WR	6-2	206	2/14/69	12	Ohio State	Dayton, Ohio	FA-'02	14/11*
42	Hall, Corey	CB-S	6-4	203	1/17/79	2	Appalachian State	Athens, Ga.	D7a-'01	3/0
98	Hall, Travis	DT	6-5	295	8/3/72	8	Brigham Young	Kenai, Alaska	D6-'95	16/16
59	Holecek, John	LB	6-2	242	5/7/72	8	Illinois	Steger, Ill.	UFA(Buff)-'02	11/0*
95	Jasper, Ed	DT	6-2	293	1/18/73	6	Texas A&M	Tyler, Texas	FA-'99	16/1
84	Jefferson, Shawn	WR	5-11	185	2/22/69	12	Central Florida	Jacksonville, Fla.	UFA(NE)-'00	16/6
36	Jervey, Travis	RB	6-0	222	5/5/72	8	Citadel	Columbia, S.C.	FA-'01	16/0
11	Johnson, Doug	QB	6-2	225	10/27/77	3	Florida	Gainesville, Fla.	FA-'00	3/0
51 †	Kelly, Jeff	LB	5-11	242	12/13/75	4	Kansas State	La Grange, Texas	D6-'99	0*
89	Kelly, Reggie	TE	6-3	255	2/22/77	4	Mississippi State	Aberdeen, Miss.	D2-'99	14/13
97	Kerney, Patrick	DE	6-5	273	12/30/76	4	Virginia	Newtown, N.J.	D1-'99	16/16
85	Kozlowski, Brian	TE	6-3	250	10/4/70	9	Connecticut	Rochester, N.Y.	FA-'97	16/0
38	Layne, George	FB	5-11	250	10/9/78	2	Texas Christian	Alvin, Texas	FA-'01	2/0
41	Lyle, Keith	S	6-2	210	4/17/72	9	Virginia	Vienna, Va.	UFA(Wash)-'02	16/0*
22	McBurrows, Gerald	S	5-11	208	10/7/73	8	Kansas	Detroit, Mich.	UFA(StL)-'99	14/8
62 †	McClure, Todd	C	6-1	286	2/16/77	4	Louisiana State	Baton Rouge, La.	D7-'99	15/15
88	McCord, Quentin	WR	5-10	188	6/26/78	2	Kentucky	La Grange, Ga.	D7d-'01	7/0
80	McGriff, Travis	WR	5-10	185	6/24/76	4	Florida	St. Louis, Mo.	FA-'02	5/0*
96	Miller, Brandon	DT	6-0	299	11/27/75	3	Georgia	Greensboro, Ga.	FA-'02	0*
13	Mohr, Chris	P	6-5	215	5/11/66	13	Alabama	Atlanta, Ga.	FA-'01	16/0
90	Moore, Ron	DT	6-2	312	8/10/77	2	Northwestern Oklahoma St.	Sanford, Fla.	FA-'01	1/0
49	Neil, Dallas	TE	6-1	235	9/30/76	2	Montana	Great Falls, Mont.	FA-'02	0*
61	Page, Craig	C	6-3	303	1/17/76	3	Georgia Tech	Jupiter, Fla.	FA-'02	0*
82	Philyaw, Mareno	WR	6-2	208	12/19/77	3	Troy State	Atlanta, Ga.	D6-'00	0*
48	Rackley, Derek	TE	6-4	250	7/18/77	3	Minnesota	Apple Valley, Minn.	FA-'00	16/0
23	Rossum, Allen	CB	5-8	178	10/22/75	5	Notre Dame	Dallas, Texas	UFA(GB)-'02	6/0*
53	Simoneau, Mark	LB	6-0	234	1/16/77	3	Kansas State	Smith Center, Kan.	D3-'00	16/5
91	Smith, Brady	DE	6-5	274	6/5/73	7	Colorado State	Barrington, Ill.	UFA(NO)-'00	15/15
43	Smith, Maurice	RB	6-0	235	2/14/77	3	North Carolina A&T	Palmyra, N.C.	FA-'00	16/12
52	Stewart, Matt	LB	6-3	232	8/31/79	2	Vanderbilt	Columbus, Ohio	D4b-'01	16/12
55	Thierry, John	DE	6-4	262	9/4/71	9	Alcorn State	Houston, Texas	UFA(GB)-'02	12/12*
66	Thompson, Michael	T	6-4	295	2/11/77	3	Tennessee State	Savannah, Ga.	D4-'00	2/1
50	Ulmer, Artie	LB	6-3	247	7/30/73	5	Valdosta State	Rincon, Ga.	FA-'01	15/0
37	Vaughn, Darrick	CB	5-11	193	10/2/78	3	Southwest Texas	Aldine, Texas	D7-'00	16/0
7	Vick, Michael	QB	6-0	215	6/28/80	2	Virginia Tech	Newport News, Va.	D1-'01	8/2
24	Weary, Fred	CB	5-10	181	4/12/74	5	Florida	Jacksonville, Fla.	UFA(NO)-'02	14/14*
74	Weiner, Todd	T	6-4	300	9/16/75	5	Kansas State	Coral Springs, Fla.	UFA(Sea)-'02	16/3*
70	Whitfield, Bob	T	6-5	310	10/18/71	11	Stanford	Carson, Calif.	D1a-'92	16/16
87	Whitted, Alvis	WR	6-0	186	9/4/74	4	North Carolina State	Durham, N.C.	FA-'02	11/0*

* Bolden last active with Kansas City in '99; Carpenter played 15 games with Buffalo in '01; Dunn played 16 games with Tampa Bay; Graham played 14 games with San Diego; Holecek played 11 games with Buffalo; J. Kelly missed '01 season because of injury; Lyle played 16 games with Washington; McGriff played 5 games with Denver; Miller last active with Indianapolis in '00; Neil last active with Atlanta in '00; Page last active with Dallas in '00; Philyaw spent '01 season on Reserve/Non-Football injury list; Rossum played 6 games with Green Bay; Thierry played 12 games with Green Bay; Weary played 14 games with New Orleans; Weiner played 16 games with Seattle; Whitted played 11 games with Jacksonville.

† Restricted free agent; subject to developments.

Players lost through free agency (4): LB Henri Crockett (Minn; 16 games in '01), C Bob Hallen (SD; 15), T Ephraim Salaam (Den; 14), DE Chuck Wiley (Minn; 16).

Also played with Falcons in '01—RB Jamal Anderson (3 games), S Ronnie Bradford (14), S Marty Carter (5), QB Chris Chandler (14), CB Darrien Gordon (16), CB Conrad Hamilton (6), LB Antony Jordan (4), WR Tony Martin (11), WR Terance Mathis (16), DT Shawn Swayda (10), RB Rodney Thomas (12), CB Elijah Williams (5).

2002 FIRST-YEAR ROSTER

Name	Pos.	Ht.	Wt.	Birthdate	College	Hometown	How Acq.
Allen, Matt (1)	P	6-4	246	10/23/77	Troy State	Montgomery, Ala.	FA
Bibla, Martin	G	6-3	306	10/4/79	Miami	Mountaintop, Pa.	D4
Bonner, Dusty	QB	6-2	230	10/27/78	Valdosta State	Valdosta, Ga.	FA
Coleman, Michael	WR	5-11	190	7/9/80	Widener	Wilmington, Del.	D7a
Dalton, Antico (1)	LB	6-1	238	12/31/75	Hampton	Eden, N.C.	FA
Davis, Curt	DE	6-3	277	12/12/78	Arkansas	Monroe, La.	FA
Duckett, T.J.	RB	6-0	254	2/17/81	Michigan State	Kalamazoo, Mich.	D1
English, R.J.	WR	6-2	213	5/16/79	Pittsburgh	Waterford, Pa.	FA
Grant, Karim	LB	6-4	243	12/25/76	Acadia (Canada)	Scarborough, Ontario, Canada	FA
Harris, Corey	S	5-9	197	3/31/78	Arkansas	Friendswood, Texas	FA
Hill, Kahlil	WR	6-2	200	3/18/79	Iowa	Iowa City, Iowa	D6
Holmes, Brian	K	5-11	195	10/9/77	Samford	Stone Mountain, Ga.	FA
Kadela, Dave (1)	T	6-6	294	5/6/78	Virginia Tech	Dearborn, Mich.	FA-'01
Kanoa, Manly	G	6-4	315	10/22/79	Hawaii	Honolulu, Hawaii	FA
Kittner, Kurt	QB	6-2	221	1/23/80	Illinois	Schaumburg, Ill.	D5b
Lessman, Curt	C	6-3	294	3/28/79	Northwest Missouri State	Sioux City, Iowa	FA
McCadam, Kevin	S	6-1	219	3/6/79	Virginia Tech	Lakeside, Calif.	D5a
McFadden, Marques (1)	G-T	6-5	320	9/12/78	Arizona	St. Louis, Mo.	FA
Mills, Shawn (1)	WR	6-1	184	2/10/77	Southern Mississippi	Enid, Okla.	FA-'01
Overstreet, Will	LB	6-2	259	10/7/79	Tennessee	Jackson, Miss.	D3
Perry, Fred (1)	DE	6-1	235	1/5/75	Southern Arkansas	Fort Smith, Ark.	FA
Sadler, Adrian (1)	CB	5-9	184	3/10/78	Rice	Texarkana, Texas	FA
Shaffer, Kevin	T	6-5	290	3/2/80	Tulsa	Leola, Pa.	D7b
Shepherd, Gannon (1)	T	6-8	317	1/4/77	Duke	Flint, Mich.	FA
Sims, Eric	CB	5-11	180	8/10/79	Eastern Kentucky	Ellsville, Miss.	FA
Togiai, Jerry	NT	6-2	310	8/2/75	Kansas State	Laie, Hawaii	FA
Williams, Terrance	HB	5-10	185	9/18/78	Central Florida	Clearwater, Fla.	FA
Wingrove, Ryan	DE	6-3	250	7/3/79	Bowling Green	Parkersburg, W. Va.	FA

The term NFL Rookie is defined as a player who is in his first season of professional football and has not been on the roster of another professional football team for any regular-season or postseason games. A Rookie is designated by an "R" on NFL rosters. Players who have been active in another professional football league or players who have NFL experience, including either preseason training camp or being on an Active List or Inactive List, or on Reserve/Injured or Reserve/Physically Unable to Perform for fewer than six regular-season games, are termed NFL First-Year Players. An NFL First-Year Player is designated by a "1" on NFL rosters. Thereafter, a player is credited with an additional year of experience for each season in which he accumulates six games on the Active List or Inactive List, or on Reserve/Injured or Reserve/Physically Unable to Perform.

COACHING STAFF
Head Coach,
Dan Reeves

Pro Career: Head coach Dan Reeves, the NFL's winningest active coach with 189 career victories, heads into his sixth season as head coach of Atlanta. Reeves led the Falcons to their first-ever Super Bowl appearance in 1998 in only its second season with Atlanta since taking over on January 20,1997. Reeves led the Falcons to the NFC West title with a 14-2 record and a franchise record 442 points. Reeves was named NFL coach of the year in 1998 for the fifth time in his coaching career. Reeves had been the head coach of the New York Giants from 1993-96. Prior to that, he compiled a 117-79-1 record as head coach of the Denver Broncos from 1981-92, earning NFL coach of the year honors in 1982, 1988 and 1991. He led the Broncos to three Super Bowl berths, four AFC Championship games, and five AFC West Division titles. In his first year in New York, he earned NFL coach of the year honors, taking the Giants from 6-10 to an 11-5 mark, including a wild-card playoff victory. Overall, Reeves has participated in 48 playoff games and nine Super Bowls as an NFL player, assistant coach, and head coach. He was the only NFL coach in the 1980s to take his team to back-to-back Super Bowls. Career record: 188-157-1.

Background: Reeves was a member of the Dallas Cowboys' coaching staff (1970-1980), spending a total of 16 years under Tom Landry as a player and coach. In 1977, he was named offensive coordinator of Landry's staff. Reeves began his pro career as a free agent running back for Dallas in 1965. Prior to that he was a quarterback at South Carolina from 1962-64, and was inducted into the school's hall of fame in 1978.

Personal: Born January 19, 1944, Americus, Ga. Dan and his wife, Pam, live in Atlanta, and have three children—Dana, Laura, and Lee.

ASSISTANT COACHES

Dennis Allen, defensive quality control; born September 22, 1972, Hurst, Texas, lives in Atlanta. Safety Texas A&M 1992-95. No pro playing experience. College coach: Texas A&M 1996-99, Tulsa 2000-01. Pro coach: Joined Falcons in 2002.

Marvin Bass, asst. to head coach-pro personnel; born August 28, 1919, Norfolk, Va., lives in Suwanee, Ga. Tackle William & Mary 1940-42. No pro playing experience. College coach: William & Mary 1944-48, 1950-51 (head coach), North Carolina 1949, 1953-55, South Carolina 1956-59, 1961-65, Georgia Tech 1960, Richmond 1963. Pro coach: Washington Redskins 1952, Montreal Beavers (Continental League) 1966-67, Montreal Alouettes (CFL) 1968, Buffalo Bills 1969-71, Birmingham Americans

(WFL) 1974-75, Denver Broncos 1982-92. Joined Falcons in 1997.

Jack Burns, quarterbacks; born January 3, 1949, Tampa, lives in Suwanee, Ga. Safety Florida 1967-1970. No pro playing experience. College coach: Florida 1971-73, 1975, Louisville 1974, 1985-88, Texas 1976, Vanderbilt 1977-78, Auburn 1979-1980. Pro coach: Tampa Bay Bandits (USFL) 1983, Washington Redskins 1989-1991, Minnesota Vikings 1992-93, joined Falcons in 1997.

Rocky Colburn, asst. strength and conditioning; born May 24, 1963, Dallas, Ore., lives in Lawrenceville, Ga. Safety Alabama 1981-83. No pro playing experience. College coach: Alabama 1984, 1987-1992, Samford 1986. Pro coach: Joined Falcons 1999.

James Daniel, tight ends; born January 17, 1953, Wetumpka, Ala., lives in Suwanee, Ga. Offensive guard Alabama State 1970-73. No pro playing experience. College coach: Auburn 1981-1992. Pro coach: New York Giants 1993-96, joined Falcons in 1997.

Billy Davis, linebackers; born November 5, 1965, Youngstown, Ohio, lives in TBA. Quarterback Cincinnati 1984-88. No pro playing experience. College coach: Michigan State 1990-91. Pro coach: Pittsburgh Steelers 1992-94, Carolina Panthers 1995-98, Cleveland Browns 1999, Green Bay Packers 2000, joined Falcons in 2001.

Joe DeCamillis, special teams; born June 29, 1965, Arvada, Colo., lives in Alpharetta, Ga. No college or pro playing experience. College coach: Wyoming 1988. Pro coach: Denver Broncos 1989, Miami Dolphins 1990, New York Giants 1993-96, joined Falcons in 1997.

Bill Johnson, defensive line; born June 23, 1955, Monroe, Louisiana, lives in TBA. Defensive lineman Northwestern (La.) State 1976-79. No pro playing experience. College coach: Northwestern (La.) State 1980-81, McNeese State 1985-86, Miami 1987, Louisiana Tech 1988-89, Arkansas 1990-91, 2000, Texas A&M 1992-99. Pro coach: Joined Falcons in 2001.

Mike Johnson, wide receivers; born May 2, 1967, Los Angeles, lives in Atlanta. Quarterback Arizona State 1985-86, Akron 1988-89. Pro quarterback Arizona Cardinals 1990, San Antonio Riders (World League) 1991-92, British Columbia Lions (CFL) 1992-93, Shreveport Pirates (CFL) 1994-95. College coach: Oregon State 1997-99. Pro coach: San Diego Chargers 2000-01, joined Falcons in 2002.

Pete Mangurian, offensive line; born June 17, 1955, Los Angeles, lives in TBA. Defensive lineman Louisiana State 1975-78. No pro playing experience. College coach: Southern Methodist 1979-1980, New Mexico State 1981, Stanford 1982-83, Louisiana State 1984-87, Cornell

1998-2000 (head coach). Pro coach: Denver Broncos 1988-1992, New York Giants 1993-96, Atlanta Falcons 1997, rejoined Falcons in 2001.

Al Miller, strength and conditioning; born August 29, 1947, El Dorado, Ark., lives in Alpharetta, Ga. Wide receiver Northeast Louisiana 1965-69. No pro playing experience. College coach: Northwestern State (La.) 1974-78, Mississippi State 1980, Northeast Louisiana 1981, Alabama 1982-84. Pro coach: Denver Broncos 1987-92, New York Giants 1993-96, joined Falcons in 1997.

Wade Phillips, defensive coordinator; born June 21, 1947, Orange, Texas, lives in Atlanta. Linebacker Houston 1966-68. No pro playing experience. College coach: Houston 1969, Oklahoma State 1973-74, Kansas 1975. Pro coach: Houston Oilers 1976-1980, New Orleans 1981-85 (head coach last four games of 1985), Philadelphia Eagles 1986-88, Denver Broncos 1989-94 (head coach 1993-94), Buffalo Bills 1995-2000 (head coach 1998-2000), joined Falcons in 2002.

Warren (Rennie) Simmons, asst. offensive line; born February 25, 1942, Poughkeepsie, N.Y., lives in Gainesville, Ga. Center San Diego State 1961-65. No pro playing experience. College coach: Cal State-Fullerton 1974-78, Cerritos (Calif.) J.C. 1978-80, Vanderbilt 1995. Pro coach: Washington Redskins 1981-93, Los Angeles Rams 1994, Houston Oilers 1996, joined Falcons in 1997.

Emmitt Thomas, secondary; born June 3, 1943, Angleton, Texas, lives in Atlanta. Quarterback-receiver, Bishop (Texas) College 1963-65. Pro defensive back Kansas City Chiefs 1966-1978. College coach: Central Missouri State 1979-1980. Pro coach: St. Louis Cardinals 1981-85, Washington Redskins 1986-1994, Philadelphia Eagles 1995-98, Green Bay Packers 1999, Minnesota Vikings 2000-01, joined Falcons in 2002.

Ed West, offensive quality control; born August 2, 1961, Leighton, Ala., lives in Woodstock, Ga. Tight end Auburn 1980-83. Pro tight end Green Bay Packers 1984-1994, Philadelphia Eagles 1995-96, Atlanta Falcons 1997. Pro coach: Joined Falcons in 1998.

Ollie Wilson, running backs; born March 3, 1951, Worcester, Mass., lives in Atlanta. Wide receiver Springfield 1971-73. No pro playing experience. College coach: Springfield 1975, Northeastern 1976-1982, California 1983-1990. Pro coach: Atlanta Falcons 1991-96, San Diego Chargers 1997-2001, re-joined Falcons in 2002.

**National Football Conference
South Division
Team Colors:** Black, Panther Blue, and
Silver
**800 South Mint Street
Charlotte, North Carolina 28202-1502
Telephone:** (704) 358-7000

2002 SCHEDULE
PRESEASON
Aug. 10 **Washington** 8:00
Aug. 17 **Dallas** 8:00
Aug. 23 at New England 8:00
Aug. 30 at Cleveland 8:00

REGULAR SEASON
Sept. 8 **Baltimore**...........................1:00
Sept. 15 **Detroit** 1:00
Sept. 22 at Minnesota 12:00
Sept. 29 at Green Bay 12:00
Oct. 6 **Arizona** 1:00
Oct. 13 at Dallas...........................12:00
Oct. 20 at Atlanta...........................1:00
Oct. 27 **Tampa Bay**........................1:00
Nov. 3 OPEN DATE
Nov. 10 **New Orleans**.....................1:00
Nov. 17 at Tampa Bay 4:05
Nov. 24 **Atlanta**..............................1:00
Dec. 1 at Cleveland 1:00
Dec. 8 **Cincinnati** 1:00
Dec. 15 at Pittsburgh.......................1:00
Dec. 22 **Chicago** 1:00
Dec. 29 at New Orleans.................12:00

Stadium: Ericsson Stadium
(opened in 1996)
• **Capacity:** 73,250
Charlotte, North Carolina
28202-1502
Playing Surface: Grass
Training Camp: Wofford College
Spartanburg,
South Carolina 29303

ERICSSON STADIUM

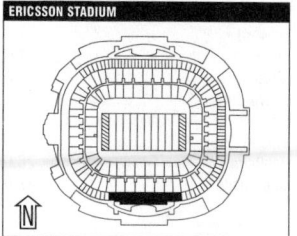

CLUB OFFICIALS
Founder/Owner: Jerry Richardson
President: Mark Richardson
President Carolinas Stadium Corp.:
Jon Richardson
General Manager: Marty Hurney
Director of Marketing and Sponsorships:
Charles Waddell
Counsel: Richard Thigpen
Chief Financial Officer: Dave Olsen
Controller: Lisa Garber
Director of Player Personnel:
Jack Bushofsky
Director of Pro Scouting: Mark Koncz
Pro Scouts: Hal Hunter,
Kenny Roberson
Director of College Scouting: Tony Softli
College Scouts: Brian Adams,
Hal Athon, Ryan Cowden,
Jay Mondock, Jeff Morrow,
Mike Sabao, Joe Schoen
Director of Communications:
Charlie Dayton
Communications Assistant:
Bruce Speight
Public Relations Assistant:
Deedee Thomason
Media Relations Assistant: Ted Crews
Director of Ticket Sales: Phil Youtsey
Director of Player Relations: Donnie Shell
Director of Community Relations/Family
Programs: B.J. Harrison Waymer
Director of Special Events: Leslie Matz
Director of Information Systems:
Roger Goss
Salary Cap Analyst/Negotiatior:
Rob Rogers
Video Director: Mark Hobbs
Assistant Video Director: Jeff Mueller
Head Trainer: Ryan Vermillion
Assistant Trainers:
Mark Shermansky, Mike Hooper
Equipment Manager: Jackie Miles
Assistant Equipment Manager: Don Toner
Director of Security: Gene Brown
Stadium Operations Manager: Scott Paul
Facilities Manger: Matthew Getz
Head Groundskeeper: Tom Vaughn
Human Resources/Office Manager:
Jackie Jeffries

COACHING HISTORY
(47-67-0)
1995-98 Dom Capers 31-35-0
1999-2001 George Seifert 16-32-0

ATTENDANCE
Home 560,599   Away 503,966
Total 1,064,565
Single-game home record,
76,136 (12/10/95)
Single-season home record, 570,035
(2000)

2002 DRAFT CHOICES
Round	Name	Pos.	College
1	Julius Peppers	DE	North Carolina
2	DeShaun Foster	RB	UCLA
3	Will Witherspoon	LB	Georgia
4	Dante Wesley	DB	Arkansas-Pine Bluff
5	Randy Fasani	QB	Stanford
	Kyle Johnson	RB	Syracuse
6	Keith Heinrich	TE	Sam Houston St.
7	Pete Campion	G	North Dakota State
	Brad Franklin	DB	Louisiana-Lafayette

CAROLINA PANTHERS

2001 TEAM RECORD
PRESEASON (2-2)

Date	Result	Opponent
8/10	L 16-18	at Jacksonville
8/18	L 8-23	New England
8/23	W 20-17	at Baltimore
8/31	W 23-20	Cleveland

REGULAR SEASON (1-15)

Date	Result	Opponent	Att.
9/09	W 24-13	at Minnesota	64,108
9/23	L 16-24	at Atlanta	49,312
9/30	L 7-28	Green Bay	73,120
10/07	L 14-24	at San Francisco	66,944
10/14	L 25-27	New Orleans	72,049
10/21	L 14-17	at Washington(OT)	74,480
10/28	L 12-13	New York Jets	72,642
11/04	L 6-23	at Miami	72,597
11/11	L 14-48	at St. Louis	66,069
11/18	L 22-25	San Francisco(OT)	72,665
11/25	L 7-10	Atlanta	72,234
12/02	L 23-27	at New Orleans	70,020
12/09	L 24-25	at Buffalo	44,549
12/23	L 32-38	St. Louis	72,438
12/30	L 7-30	Arizona	72,025
1/06	L 6-38	New England	71,907

(OT) Overtime

SCORE BY PERIODS

Panthers	50	83	52	68	0 —	253
Opponents	78	114	112	100	6 —	410

2001 TEAM STATISTICS

	Panthers	Opp.
Total First Downs	236	304
Rushing	68	106
Passing	144	187
Penalty	24	11
3rd Down: Made/Att	67/219	97/233
3rd Down Pct.	30.6	41.6
4th Down: Made/Att	5/21	7/10
4th Down Pct.	23.8	70.0
Possession Avg.	27:30	32:30
Total Net Yards	4254	5943
Avg. Per Game	265.9	371.4
Total Plays	965	1057
Avg. Per Play	4.4	5.6
Net Yards Rushing	1372	2301
Avg. Per Game	85.8	143.8
Total Rushes	354	521
Net Yards Passing	2882	3642
Avg. Per Game	180.1	227.6
Sacked/Yards Lost	32/216	26/167
Gross Yards	3098	3809
Att./Completions	579/314	510/306
Completion Pct.	54.2	60.0
Had Intercepted	22	24
Punts/Average	94/47.0	85/40.7
Net Punting Avg.	94/38.9	85/34.6
Penalties/Yards	87/747	96/793
Fumbles/Ball Lost	33/13	27/12
Touchdowns	27	48
Rushing	9	13
Passing	12	25
Returns	6	10

2001 INDIVIDUAL STATISTICS

PASSING	Att.	Comp.	Yds.	Pct.	TD	Int.	Tkld.	Rate
Weinke	540	293	2931	54.3	11	19	26/177	62.0
Lytle	30	17	133	56.7	1	3	3/24	39.3
Craig	8	4	34	50.0	0	0	2/15	61.5
Huntley	1	0	0	0.0	0	0	1/0	39.6
Panthers	579	314	3098	54.2	12	22	32/216	60.6
Opponents	510	306	3809	60.0	25	24	26/167	79.9

	TD	TD	TD				
SCORING	R	P	Rt	PAT	FG	Saf	PTS
Kasay	0	0	0	22/23	23/28	0	91
Weinke	6	0	0	0/0	0/0	0	36
Walls	0	5	0	0/0	0/0	0	30
Huntley	2	1	0	0/0	0/0	0	18
Smith	0	0	3	0/0	0/0	0	18
Hayes	0	2	0	0/0	0/0	0	12
Mangum	0	2	0	0/0	0/0	0	12
Anderson	0	0	1	0/0	0/0	0	6
Biakabutuka	1	0	0	0/0	0/0	0	6
Byrd	0	1	0	0/0	0/0	0	6
Crawford	0	0	1	0/0	0/0	0	6
Evans	0	0	1	0/0	0/0	0	6
Muhammad	0	1	0	0/0	0/0	0	6
Panthers	9	12	6	22/23	23/28	0	253
Opponents	13	25	10	43/44	25/30	0	410

2-Pt. Conversions: None.
Panthers 0-4, Opponents 2-4.

RUSHING	Att.	Yds.	Avg.	LG	TD
Huntley	165	665	4.0	25	2
Biakabutuka	53	230	4.3	27	1
Goings	66	197	3.0	16	0
Weinke	37	128	3.5	23	6
Hoover	17	71	4.2	10	0
Smith	4	43	10.8	39	0
Craig	3	20	6.7	13	0
Hetherington	5	12	2.4	8	0
Lytle	2	8	4.0	4	0
Sauerbrun	1	0	0.0	0	0
Byrd	1	-2	-2.0	-2	0
Panthers	354	1372	3.9	39	9
Opponents	521	2301	4.4	71t	13

RECEIVING	No.	Yds.	Avg.	LG	TD
Hayes	52	597	11.5	48	2
Muhammad	50	585	11.7	43	1
Walls	43	452	10.5	25	5
Byrd	37	492	13.3	42	1
Hoover	26	185	7.1	19	0
Hetherington	23	124	5.4	15	0
Huntley	21	101	4.8	23	1
Mangum	15	89	5.9	11	2
Jeffers	14	127	9.1	21	0
Biakabutuka	12	121	10.1	47	0
Smith	10	154	15.4	33	0
Goings	8	39	4.9	11	0
Broughton	2	22	11.0	13	0
Crawford	1	10	10.0	10	0
Panthers	314	3098	9.9	48	12
Opponents	306	3809	12.4	94t	25

INTERCEPTIONS	No.	Yds.	Avg.	LG	TD
Evans	8	126	15.8	49	1
Grant	5	96	19.2	43	0
Hitchcock	3	65	21.7	35	0
Minter	2	32	16.0	30	0
Buckner	1	29	29.0	29	0
Howard	1	16	16.0	16	0
Morgan	1	10	10.0	10	0
Anderson	1	0	0.0	0	0
Towns	1	0	0.0	0	0
J. Williams	1	0	0.0	0	0
Panthers	24	374	15.6	49	1
Opponents	22	432	19.6	76t	6

PUNTING	No.	Yds.	Avg.	In 20	LG
Sauerbrun	93	4419	47.5	35	73
Panthers	94	4419	47.0	35	73
Opponents	85	3457	40.7	24	59

PUNT RETURNS	No.	FC	Yds.	Avg.	LG	TD
Smith	34	10	364	10.7	70t	1
Byrd	5	2	56	11.2	22	0
Panthers	39	12	420	10.8	70t	1
Opponents	42	19	425	10.1	68t	1

KICKOFF RETURNS	No.	Yds.	Avg.	LG	TD
Smith	56	1431	25.6	99t	2
Byrd	10	225	22.5	26	0
Hetherington	4	31	7.8	12	0
Broughton	3	46	15.3	26	0
Crawford	1	8	8.0	8	0
Hoover	1	8	8.0	8	0
Huntley	1	20	20.0	20	0
Panthers	76	1769	23.3	99t	2
Opponents	60	1340	22.3	46	0

FIELD GOALS	1-19	20-29	30-39	40-49	50+
Kasay	0/0	10/10	4/4	7/9	2/5
Panthers	0/0	10/10	4/4	7/9	2/5
Opponents	2/2	9/9	7/9	7/10	0/0

SACKS	No.
Rucker	9.0
Buckner	4.5
Slade	2.5
Gilbert	2.0
Jenkins	2.0
Grant	1.0
Howard	1.0
Lucas	1.0
Morgan	1.0
J. Williams	1.0
Chester	0.5
Wilson	0.5
Panthers	26.0
Opponents	32.0

RECORD HOLDERS
INDIVIDUAL RECORDS—CAREER

Category	Name	Performance
Rushing (Yds.)	Tshimanga Biakabutuka, 1996-2001	2,530
Passing (Yds.)	Steve Beuerlein, 1996-2000	12,690
Passing (Tds)	Steve Beuerlein, 1996-2000	86
Receiving (No.)	Muhsin Muhammad, 1996-2001	368
Receiving (Yds.)	Muhsin Muhammad, 1996-2001	4,686
Interceptions	Eric Davis, 1996-2000	25
Punting (Avg.)	Ken Walter, 1997-2000	40.4
Punt Return (Avg.)	Winslow Oliver, 1996-98	10.7
Kickoff Return (Avg.)	Michael Bates, 1996-2000	25.7
Field Goals	John Kasay, 1995-2001	149
Touchdowns (Tot.)	Wesley Walls, 1996-2001	40
Points	John Kasay, 1995-2001	617

INDIVIDUAL RECORDS—SINGLE SEASON

Category	Name	Performance
Rushing (Yds.)	Anthony Johnson, 1996	1,120
Passing (Yds.)	Steve Beuerlein, 1999	4,436
Passing (Tds)	Steve Beuerlein, 1999	36
Receiving (No.)	Muhsin Muhammad, 2000	102
Receiving (Yds.)	Muhsin Muhammad, 1999	1,253
Interceptions	Doug Evans, 2001	8
Punting (Avg.)	Todd Sauerbrun, 2001	47.5
Punt Return (Avg.)	Winslow Oliver, 1996	11.5
Kickoff Return (Avg.)	Michael Bates, 1996	30.2
Field Goals	John Kasay, 1996	37
Touchdowns (Tot.)	Wesley Walls, 1999	12
	Patrick Jeffers, 1999	12
Points	John Kasay, 1996	145

INDIVIDUAL RECORDS—SINGLE GAME

Category	Name	Performance
Rushing (Yds.)	Richard Huntley, 1-6-02	168
Passing (Yds.)	Steve Beuerlein, 12-12-99	373
Passing (Tds)	Steve Beuerlein, 1-2-00	5
Receiving (No.)	Muhsin Muhammad, 12-18-99, 11-27-00	11
Receiving (Yds.)	Muhsin Muhammad, 9-13-98	192
Interceptions	Many times	2
	Last time by Deon Grant, 1-6-02	
Field Goals	John Kasay, 9-1-96, 9-8-96	5
Touchdowns (Tot.)	Fred Lane, 11-2-97	3
	Tshimanga Biakabutuka, 10-3-99	3
	Muhsin Muhammad, 12-18-99	3
Points	Fred Lane, 11-2-97	18
	Tshimanga Biakabutuka, 10-3-99	18
	Muhsin Muhammad, 12-18-99	18

CAROLINA PANTHERS

2002 VETERAN ROSTER

No.	Name	Pos.	Ht.	Wt.	Birthdate	NFL Exp.	College	Hometown	How Acq.	'01 Games/ Starts
43	Allen, Brian	LB	6-0	232	4/1/78	2	Florida State	Lake City, Fla.	W(Hou)-'02	3/0*
46	Anderson, Rashard	CB	6-2	204	6/14/77	3	Jackson State	Forest, Miss.	D1-'00	15/9
24	Bates, Michael	RB	5-10	189	12/19/69	10	Arizona	Tucson, Ariz.	FA-'02	16/0*
22	Brown, Dee	RB	5-10	209	5/12/78	2	Syracuse	Lake Brantley, Fla.	D6-'01	0*
99	Buckner, Brentson	DT	6-2	305	9/30/71	9	Clemson	Columbus, Ga.	UFA(SF)-'01	16/10
98	Burton, Shane	DE	6-6	305	1/18/74	7	Tennessee	Catawba, N.C.	FA-'02	15/13*
82	Byrd, Isaac	WR	6-1	188	11/16/74	6	Kansas	St. Louis, Mo.	W(Tenn)-'00	15/5
40	Cooper, Jarrod	S	6-0	210	3/31/78	2	Kansas State	Pearland, Texas	D5-'01	16/0
21	Cousin, Terry	CB	5-9	181	3/11/75	6	South Carolina	Miami, Fla.	UFA(Mia)-'02	14/2*
84	Crawford, Casey	TE	6-6	255	8/1/77	3	Virginia	Falls Church, Va.	FA-'00	3/1
65	Donnalley, Kevin	G	6-5	310	6/10/68	12	North Carolina	Raleigh, N.C.	UFA(Mia)-'01	6/6
58	Fields, Mark	LB	6-2	244	11/9/72	8	Washington State	Los Angeles, Calif.	FA-'02	14/12*
74	Fletcher, Derrick	G	6-6	350	9/9/75	3	Baylor	Aldine, Texas	FA-'02	0*
94	Gilbert, Sean	DT	6-5	318	4/10/70	10	Pittsburgh	Aliquippa, Pa.	FFA(Wash)-'98	9/9
37	Goings, Nick	RB	6-0	225	1/26/78	2	Pittsburgh	Dublin, Ohio	FA-'01	13/2
27	Grant, Deon	S	6-2	207	3/14/79	3	Tennessee	Augusta, Ga.	D2-'00	16/16
88	Hankton, Karl	WR	6-2	202	7/24/70	4	Trinity College (Ill.)	New Orleans, La.	FA-'00	11/0
28	Harper, Deveron	CB	5-11	187	11/15/77	3	Notre Dame	Orangeburg, S.C.	FA-'00	8/1
45	Hoover, Brad	FB	6-2	225	11/11/76	3	Western Carolina	Thomasville, N.C.	FA-'00	16/7
23	Howard, Reggie	CB	6-0	190	5/17/77	3	Memphis State	Memphis, Tenn.	W(NO)-'00	11/0
50	Jackson, Brad	LB	6-0	230	1/11/75	4	Cincinnati	Akron, Ohio	FA-'02	16/5*
78	James, Jeno	G	6-3	292	1/12/77	3	Auburn	Montgomery, Ala.	D6-'00	14/6
83	Jeffers, Patrick	WR	6-3	218	2/2/73	7	Virginia	Fort Worth, Texas	RFA(Dall)-'99	9/0
25	Jenkins, DeRon	CB	5-11	192	11/14/73	7	Tennessee	St. Louis, Mo.	FA-'02	15/6*
77	Jenkins, Kris	DT	6-4	315	8/3/79	2	Maryland	Ypsilanti, Mich.	D2-'01	16/11
76	Jordan, Leander	G	6-3	320	9/15/77	3	Indiana (Pa.)	Pittsburgh, Pa.	D3-'00	13/5
4	Kasay, John	K	5-10	198	10/27/69	12	Georgia	Athens, Ga.	UFA(Sea)-'95	16/0
56	Kyle, Jason	LB	6-3	242	5/12/72	8	Arizona State	Tempe, Ariz.	UFA(SF)-'01	16/0
86	Mangum, Kris	TE	6-4	249	8/15/73	5	Mississippi	Magee, Miss.	D7-'97	16/10
91	Milem, John	DE	6-7	290	6/9/75	3	Lenoir-Rhyne	Concord, N.C.	W(SF)-'01	2/0
52	Minor, Kory	LB	6-1	247	12/14/76	3	Notre Dame	La Puente, Calif.	FA-'99	11/2
30	Minter, Mike	S	5-10	188	1/15/74	6	Nebraska	Lawton, Okla.	D2-'97	14/14
60	Mitchell, Jeff	C	6-4	300	1/29/74	6	Florida	Dallas, Texas	UFA(Balt)-'01	15/15
33	Montgomery, Joe	RB	5-10	230	6/8/76	4	Ohio State	Oak Lawn, Ill.	FA-'02	0*
55	Morgan, Dan	LB	6-2	233	12/19/78	2	Miami	Coral Springs, Fla.	D1-'01	11/11
87	Muhammad, Muhsin	WR	6-2	217	5/5/73	7	Michigan State	Lansing, Mich.	D2-'96	11/11
53	Navies, Hannibal	LB	6-2	240	7/19/77	4	Colorado	Oakland, Calif.	D4-'99	5/5
63	Nesbit, Jamar	G	6-4	330	12/17/76	4	South Carolina	Summerville, S.C.	FA-'99	16/16
9	Peete, Rodney	QB	6-0	230	3/16/66	14	Southern California	Shawnee Mission, Kan.	UFA(Oak)-'02	1/0*
39	Richardson, Damien	S	6-1	210	4/3/76	5	Arizona State	Fresno, Calif.	D6-'98	16/2
93	Rucker, Micheal	DE	6-5	258	2/28/75	4	Nebraska	St. Joseph, Mo.	D2b-'99	16/16
10	Sauerbrun, Todd	P	5-10	211	1/4/73	8	West Virginia	Garden City, N.Y.	FA-'01	16/0
26	Smith, Lamar	RB	5-11	224	11/29/70	9	Houston	Fort Wayne, Ind.	UFA(Mia)-'02	16/16*
89	Smith, Steve	WR	5-9	179	5/12/79	2	Utah	Lynwood, Calif.	D3-'01	15/1
75	Steussie, Todd	T	6-6	308	12/1/70	9	California	Aguora, Calif.	FA-'01	16/16
70	Terry, Chris	T	6-5	295	8/8/75	4	Georgia	Jacksonville, Fla.	D2a-'99	15/15
57	Towns, Lester	LB	6-1	252	8/28/77	3	Washington	Pasadena, Calif.	D7-'00	16/15
15	Turner, Jim	WR	6-4	212	11/13/75	5	Syracuse	Jacksonville, Fla.	FA-'01	0*
73	Tuten, Melvin	T	6-7	320	11/11/71	6	Syracuse	Washington, D.C.	W(Den)-'00	15/1
85	Walls, Wesley	TE	6-5	250	2/26/66	14	Mississippi	Pontotoc, Miss.	UFA(NO)-'96	14/14
62	Washington, T.J.	G-T	6-4	340	7/1/74	2	Virginia Tech	Onley, Va.	FA-'01	0*
16	Weinke, Chris	QB	6-4	232	7/31/72	2	Florida State	St. Paul, Minn.	D4-'01	15/15
96	Williams, Jay	DE	6-3	280	10/13/71	7	Wake Forest	Washington, D.C.	UFA(StL)-'00	16/13
66	Williams, Louis	C	6-4	291	4/11/79	2	Louisiana State	Ft. Walton Beach, Fla.	D7a-'01	0*

* Allen played 3 games with St. Louis in '01; Bates played 16 games with Washington; Brown missed '01 season because of injury; Burton played 15 games with N.Y. Jets; Cousin played 14 games with Miami; Fields played 14 games with St. Louis; Fletcher last active with Washington in '00; Jackson played 16 games with Baltimore; D. Jenkins played 15 games with Tennessee; Montgomery last active with N.Y. Giants in '00; Peete played 1 game with Oakland; L. Smith played 16 games with Miami; Turner did not play in 1 game; Washington inactive for 6 games; L. Williams inactive for 5 games.

Retired—Jim Harbaugh, 15-year quarterback (0 games in '01).

Players lost through free agency (4): TE Luther Broughton (Chi; 15 games in '01), DT Larry Chester (Mia; 11), WR Donald Hayes (NE; 16), FB Chris Hetherington (StL; 16).

Also played with Carolina in '01—RB Tshimanga Biakabutuka (5 games), QB Dameyune Craig (2), CB Doug Evans (16), LB Darren Hambrick (9), LB Michael Hawkes (2), Nate Hemsley (9), CB Jimmy Hitchcock (16), LB Rob Holmberg (1), RB Richard Huntley (14), DE Cedric Killings (4), DT Al Lucas (7), QB Matt Lytle (3), DE Jason Peter (6), S Perry Phenix (2), LB Jeff Posey (4), DE Chris Slade (15), LB Dean Wells (13), DE Gillis Wilson (5).

2002 FIRST-YEAR ROSTER

Name	Pos.	Ht.	Wt.	Birthdate	College	Hometown	How Acq.
Amato, Ken	LB	6-2	242	5/18/77	Montana State	Miami, Fla.	FA
Baker, Tim (1)	WR	6-4	208	10/23/77	Texas Tech	Borger, Texas	FA
Benoit, Jermaine (1)	DE	6-3	270	7/11/75	Central Florida	Tampa, Fla.	FA
Black, Nathan	WR	6-0	190	6/20/78	Northwestern St. (La.)	Baton Rouge, La.	FA
Brackins, Eric	LB	6-1	235	11/4/78	Michigan	Pigeon Forge, Tenn.	FA
Bright, Anthony (1)	WR	6-1	170	3/28/77	Valencia (Fla.) C.C.	Gainesville, Fla.	FA-'01
Campion, Pete	T	6-4	307	12/3/79	North Dakota State	Fergus Falls, Minn.	D7
Cecere, Mike (1)	DE	6-2	279	5/10/78	Delaware	Fairfield, N.J.	FA
Coleman, Ben	DT	6-5	300	8/20/79	Florida A&M	St. Paul, Minn.	FA
Cooper, Deke (1)	S	6-3	215	10/18/77	Notre Dame	Evansville, Ind.	FA
Fasani, Randy	QB	6-3	234	9/18/78	Stanford	Loomis, Calif.	D5
Ford, Lonnie	DE	6-2	255	2/21/79	Southern California	San Diego, Calif.	FA
Foster, DeShaun	RB	6-0	222	1/10/80	UCLA	Tustin, Calif.	D2
Franklin, Brad	CB	6-1	190	12/22/79	Louisiana-Lafayette	Baton Rouge, La.	D7
Fritz, Luke (1)	G	6-4	296	8/10/78	Eastern Washington	Oliver, B.C., Canada	FA
Gary, Guilian	WR	6-0	183	6/5/80	Maryland	Horseheads, N.Y.	FA
Greenwood, Billy Dee	S	6-0	186	12/21/78	North Carolina	Norwalk, Conn.	FA
Harris, Terrell	WR	5-11	191	4/3/80	Tulane	Marrero, La.	FA
Heinrich, Keith	TE	6-5	255	3/19/79	Sam Houston State	Tomball, Texas	D6
Inkrott, Mark	TE	6-4	246	12/13/78	Findlay (Ohio)	Ottawa, Ohio	FA
Johnson, Kyle	FB	6-0	242	12/15/78	Syracuse	Woodbridge, N.J.	D5
Kiernan, Scott (1)	G	6-3	310	8/16/74	Syracuse	Cos Cob, Conn.	FA
Marriott, Jeff (1)	DT	6-4	294	3/3/77	Missouri	Chillicothe, Mo.	FA
Money, Shannon	G	6-3	295	9/26/79	Arkansas	Conway, Ark.	FA
Monroe, Aries	LB	6-2	233	1/23/80	Alabama	Tallahassee, Fla.	FA
O'Neal, Mike (1)	P	6-0	185	10/19/75	Idaho	San Diego, Calif.	FA
Peppers, Julius	DE	6-6	283	1/18/80	North Carolina	Bailey, N.C.	D1
Pounds, Tavarreus	LB	6-0	236	10/10/78	Auburn	Villa Rica, Ga.	FA
Purtill, Tyler (1)	K	6-3	225	2/1/78	Georgetown	Glastonbury, Conn.	FA
Rasmussen, Kemp	DE	6-3	255	5/25/79	Indiana	Hadley, Mich.	FA
Ray, Bryan(1)	DE	6-3	272	3/8/78	Wake Forest	Olney, Md.	FA
Sandlin, Kenny	C	6-2	313	12/1/78	Arkansas	Van Buren, Ark.	FA
Tate, Darian	DT	6-3	288	11/16/79	Walsh (Ohio)	Chicago, Ill.	FA
Tolhurst, Ryan	WR	5-11	193	7/10/79	Richmond	Wexford, Pa.	FA
Watkins, Mike (1)	QB	6-4	220	12/10/78	Louisville	Louisville, Ky.	FA
Wesley, Dante	CB	6-0	211	4/5/79	Arkansas-Pine Bluff	Pine Bluff, Ark.	D4
Witherspoon, Will	LB	6-1	231	8/19/80	Georgia	Panama City, Fla.	D3

The term NFL Rookie is defined as a player who is in his first season of professional football and has not been on the roster of another professional football team for any regular-season or postseason games. A Rookie is designated by an "R" on NFL rosters. Players who have been active in another professional football league or players who have NFL experience, including either preseason training camp or being on an Active List or Inactive List, or on Reserve/Injured or Reserve/Physically Unable to Perform for fewer than six regular-season games, are termed NFL First-Year Players. An NFL First-Year Player is designated by a "1" on NFL rosters. Thereafter, a player is credited with an additional year of experience for each season in which he accumulates six games on the Active List or Inactive List, or on Reserve/Injured or Reserve/Physically Unable to Perform.

COACHING STAFF
Head Coach,
John Fox

Pro Career: Became the third coach in Carolina Panthers history on January 25, 2002. Prior to joining Carolina he served as the defensive coordinator for the New York Giants from 1997-2001. His 2001 defense ranked first in the NFL in third-down efficiency, fifth in sacks per pass attempt, and included Michael Strahan, who set an NFL record with 22.5 sacks. In 2000, Fox helped the Giants win the NFC and reach Super Bowl XXXV with a defense that finished fifth in the NFL in both scoring defense and in yards allowed per game, and second in rushing defense. Against Minnesota in the NFC Championship Game, the Giants 41-0 victory was the first shutout in a conference championship game since 1986. From 1997-2000, the Giants had 125 takeaways, the second-highest total in the NFC, and ranked fifth in the NFL with 184 sacks. Before joining the Giants he was a consultant for the St. Louis Rams in 1996 and the defensive coordinator for the Oakland Raiders from 1994-1995. From 1992-1993, he worked as the defensive backs coach for the San Diego Chargers. Fox began his NFL coaching career with the Pittsburgh Steelers as their defensive backs coach from 1989-91.

Background: Defensive back at San Diego State (1976-77). Coached at San Diego State (1978), U.S. International (1979), Boise State (1980), Long Beach State (1981), Utah (1982), Kansas (1983), Iowa State (1984), and Pittsburgh (1986-88). Fox entered the pro ranks in 1985 as the secondary coach for the Los Angeles Express (USFL). Received bachelor's degree in physical education and earned a teaching credential from San Diego State (1977).

Personal: Born February 8, 1955, in Virginia Beach, Va. He and his wife, Robin, have three sons—Mathew, Mark, and Cody, and a daughter, Halle—and live in Charlotte, N.C.

ASSISTANT COACHES

Paul Boudreau, offensive line; born December 30, 1949, Arlington Mass., lives in Charlotte. Offensive lineman Boston College 1971-73. No pro playing experience. College coach: Boston College 1974-75, Maine 1976-78, Dartmouth 1979-1981, Navy 1982. Pro coach: Edmonton Eskimos (CFL) 1983-86, New Orleans Saints 1987-1993, Detroit Lions 1994-96, New England Patriots 1997-98, Miami Dolphins 1999-2000, joined Panthers in 2001.

Don Breaux, tight ends; born August 3, 1940, Jennings, La., lives in Charlotte. Quarterback McNeese State 1959-1961. Pro quarterback Denver Broncos 1963, San Diego Chargers 1964-65. College coach: Florida State 1966-67, Arkansas 1968-1971, 1977-1980, Florida 1973-74, Texas 1975-76. Pro coach: Houston Oilers 1972, Washington Redskins 1981-1993, New York Jets 1994, joined Panthers in 1995.

Jack Del Rio, Jr., defensive coordinator; born April 4, 1963, Castro Valley, Calif., lives in Charlotte. Linebacker Southern California 1981-84. Pro linebacker New Orleans Saints 1985-86, Kansas City Chiefs 1987-88, Dallas Cowboys 1989-1991, Minnesota Vikings 1992-95. Pro coach: New Orleans Saints 1997-98, Baltimore Ravens 1999-2001, joined Panthers in 2002.

Dan Henning, offensive coordinator-quarterbacks; born June 21, 1942, Bronx, N.Y., lives in Charlotte. Quarterback William & Mary 1962-64. Pro quarterback San Diego Chargers 1964, 1966-67. College coach: Florida State 1968-1970, 1974, Virginia Tech 1971, 1973, Boston College 1994-96 (head coach). Pro coach: Houston Oilers 1972, New York Jets 1976-78, 1998-2000, Miami Dolphins 1979-1980, Washington Redskins 1981-1982, 1987-88, Atlanta Falcons 1983-86 (head coach), San Diego Chargers 1989-1991 (head coach), Detroit Lions 1992-93, Buffalo Bills 1997, joined Panthers in 2002.

Mike McCoy, offensive assistant; born April 1, 1972, San Francisco, Calif., lives in Charlotte. Quarterback Long Beach State 1990-91, Utah 1992-94. Pro quarterback Amsterdam Admirals (NFLE) 1997, Calgary Stampeders (CFL) 1999. Pro coach: Joined Panthers in 1999.

Sam Mills, linebackers; born June 3, 1959, Neptune, N.J., lives in Charlotte. Linebacker Montclair State 1977-1980. Pro linebacker Philadelphia/Baltimore Stars (USFL) 1983-85, New Orleans Saints 1986-1994, Carolina Panthers 1995-97. Pro coach: Joined Panthers in 1999.

Scott O'Brien, asst. head coach-special teams; born June 25, 1957, Superior, Wis., lives in Charlotte. Defensive end Wisconsin-Superior 1975-78. Pro defensive end Green Bay Packers 1979, Toronto Argonauts (CFL) 1979. College coach: Wisconsin-Superior 1980-82, Nevada-Las Vegas 1983-85, Rice 1986, Pittsburgh 1987-1990. Pro coach: Cleveland Browns/Baltimore Ravens 1991-98, joined Panthers in 1999.

Rod Perry, secondary; born September 11, 1953, Fresno, Calif., lives in Charlotte. Defensive back Colorado 1972-74. Pro cornerback Los Angeles Rams 1975-1982, Cleveland Browns 1983-84. College coach: Columbia 1985, Fresno City College 1986, Fresno State 1987-88. Pro coach: Seattle Seahawks 1989-1991, Los Angeles Rams 1992-94, Houston Oilers 1995-96, San Diego Chargers 1997-2001, joined Panthers in 2002.

Alvin Reynolds, defensive assistant; born June 24, 1959, Pineville, La., lives in Charlotte. Safety Indiana State 1978-1981. No pro playing experience. College coach: Indiana State 1982-1992. Pro coach: Denver Broncos 1993-95, Baltimore Ravens 1996-98, joined Panthers in 1999.

Darrin Simmons, special teams assistant-asst. strength and conditioning; born April 9, 1973, Elkhart, Kan., lives in Charlotte. Punter Kansas 1993-95. No pro playing experience. College coach: Kansas 1996, Minnesota 1997. Pro coach: Baltimore Ravens 1998, joined Panthers in 1999.

Jerry Simmons, strength and conditioning; born June 15, 1954, Elkhart, Kan., lives in Charlotte. Linebacker Fort Hays State 1976-77. No pro playing experience. College coach: Fort Hays State 1978, Clemson 1980, Rice 1981-82, Southern California 1983-87. Pro coach: New England Patriots 1988-1990, Cleveland Browns/Baltimore Ravens 1991-98, joined Panthers in 1999.

Jim Skipper, running backs; born January 23, 1949, Breaux Bridge, La., lives in Charlotte. Defensive back Whittier College 1971-72. No pro playing experience. College coach: Cal Poly-Pomona 1974-76, San Jose State 1977-78, Pacific 1979, Oregon 1980-82. Pro coach: Philadelphia/Baltimore Stars (USFL) 1983-85, New Orleans Saints 1986-1995, Arizona Cardinals 1996, New York Giants 1997-2000, San Francisco Demons (XFL) 2001 (head coach), joined Panthers in 2002.

Sal Sunseri, defensive assistant; born August 1, 1959, Pittsburgh, lives in Charlotte. Linebacker Pittsburgh 1979-1981. College coach: Pittsburgh 1985-1992, Iowa Wesleyan 1993, Louisville 1995-97, Alabama A&M 1998-99, Louisiana State 2000, Michigan State 2001. Pro coach: Joined Panthers in 2002.

Mike Trgovac, defensive line; born February 27, 1959, Youngstown, Ohio, lives in Charlotte. Defensive lineman Michigan 1977-1980. No pro playing experience. College coach: Michigan 1984-85, Ball State 1986-88, Navy 1989, Colorado State 1990-91, Notre Dame 1992-94. Pro coach: Philadelphia Eagles 1995-98, Green Bay Packers 1999, Washington Redskins 2000-01, joined Panthers in 2002.

Richard Williamson, wide receivers; born April 13, 1941, Ft. Deposit, Ala., lives in Charlotte. Receiver Alabama 1961-62. No pro playing experience. College coach: Alabama 1963-67, 1970-71, Arkansas 1968-69, 1972-74, Memphis State 1975-1980 (head coach). Pro coach: Kansas City Chiefs 1983-86, Tampa Bay Buccaneers 1987-1991 (interim head coach 1990, head coach 1991), Cincinnati Bengals 1992-94, joined Panthers in 1995.

**National Football Conference
North Division**
Team Colors: Navy Blue, Orange, and
White
Halas Hall at Conway Park
1000 Football Drive
Lake Forest, Illinois 60045
Telephone: (847) 295-6600

2002 SCHEDULE
PRESEASON
Aug. 10	**Denver**	7:00
Aug. 16	at St. Louis	7:00
Aug. 23	**Jacksonville**	7:00
Aug. 29	at Miami	7:00

REGULAR SEASON
Sept. 8	**Minnesota**	12:00
Sept. 15	at Atlanta	1:00
Sept. 22	**New Orleans**	12:00
Sept. 29	at Buffalo	1:00
Oct. 7	**Green Bay (Mon.)**	8:00
Oct. 13	OPEN DATE	
Oct. 20	at Detroit	1:00
Oct. 27	at Minnesota	12:00
Nov. 3	**Philadelphia**	12:00
Nov. 10	**New England**	3:15
Nov. 18	at St. Louis (Mon.)	8:00
Nov. 24	**Detroit**	12:00
Dec. 1	at Green Bay	12:00
Dec. 9	at Miami (Mon.)	9:00
Dec. 15	**New York Jets**	12:00
Dec. 22	at Carolina	1:00
Dec. 29	**Tampa Bay**	7:30

Stadium: Memorial Stadium
(opened in 1923)
• **Capacity:** 70,904
Champaign, Illinois 61820
Playing Surface: Grass
Training Camp: Olivet-Nazarene
University
Bourbonnais, Illinois
60901

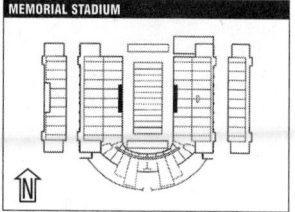

MEMORIAL STADIUM

CLUB OFFICIALS
Chairman Emeritus:
Edward W. McCaskey
Chairman of the Board:
Michael B. McCaskey
Secretary: Virginia H. McCaskey
President and CEO: Ted Phillips
General Manager: Jerry Angelo
Vice President: Tim McCaskey
Director of Pro Personnel: Bobby DePaul
Assistant Director of Pro Personnel:
Morocco Brown
Director of College Scouting:
Greg Gabriel
Director of Player Contracts and Legal
Affairs: Cliff Stein
Chief Marketing Officer: Dave Greeley
Chief Financial Officer: Karen Zust
Director of Administration: Bill McGrane
Director of Special Projects:
Pat McCaskey
Director of Business Development:
Brian McCaskey
Director of Ticket Operations:
George McCaskey
Director of Community Relations:
John Bostrom
Director of Public Relations: Scott Hagel
Assistant Director of Public Relations:
Jim Christman
Public Relations Assistant: Roger Hacker
Director of Player Development:
Dwayne Joseph
Video Director: Dean Pope
Assistant Video Directors:
Dave Hendrickson, Craig Podolski
Head Athletic Trainer: Tim Bream
Assistant Trainers: Chris Hanks,
Bobby Slater, Reggie Barnes
Physical Development
Coordinator: Russ Riederer
Asstistant Physical Development
Coordinator/Assistant Linebackers
Coach: Steve Little
Head Equipment Manager: Tony Medlin
Assistant Equipment Managers:
Carl Piekarski, Jamal Nelson
Scouts: Chris Ballard, Marty Barrett,
Phil Emery, Pat Roberts, Jeff Shiver
BLESTO Scout: Ted Monago

COACHING HISTORY
Decatur Staleys 1920,
Chicago Staleys 1921
(644-457-42)
1920-29	George Halas	84-31-19
1930-32	Ralph Jones	24-10-7
1933-1942	George Halas*	88-24-4
1942-45	Hunk Anderson- Luke Johnsos**	24-12-2
1946-1955	George Halas	76-43-2
1956-57	John (Paddy) Driscoll	14-10-1
1958-1967	George Halas	76-53-6
1968-1971	Jim Dooley	20-36-0
1972-74	Abe Gibron	11-30-1
1975-77	Jack Pardee	20-23-0
1978-1981	Neill Armstrong	30-35-0
1982-1992	Mike Ditka	112-68-0
1993-98	Dave Wannstedt	41-57-0
1999-2001	Dick Jauron	24-25-0

*Retired after five games to enter U.S. Navy
**Co-coaches

ATTENDANCE
Home 527,151	Away 523,463

Total 1,050,614
Single-game home record,
66,900 (9/5/93)
Single-season home record, 527,769
(1999)

2002 DRAFT CHOICES
Round	Name	Pos.	College
1	Marc Colombo	T	Boston College
3	Roosevelt Williams	DB	Tuskegee
	Terrence Metcalf	G	Mississippi
4	Alex Brown	DE	Florida
5	Bobby Gray	DB	Louisiana Tech
5	Bryan Knight	LB	Pittsburgh
6	Adrian Peterson	RB	Georgia Southern
	Jamin Elliott	WR	Delaware
	Bryan Fletcher	TE	UCLA

2001 TEAM RECORD

PRESEASON (1-3)

Date	Result	Opponent
8/4	W 16-13	Cincinnati
8/11	L 24-27	at Tennessee
8/18	L 9-10	at Kansas City
8/25	L 20-24	Arizona

REGULAR SEASON (13-3)

Date	Result	Opponent	Att.
9/09	L 6-17	at Baltimore	69,365
9/23	W 17-10	Minnesota	66,944
10/07	W 31-3	at Atlanta	47,640
10/14	W 20-13	Arizona	66,944
10/21	W 24-0	at Cincinnati	63,408
10/28	W 37-31	San Francisco(OT)	66,944
11/04	W 27-21	Cleveland(OT)	66,944
11/11	L 12-20	Green Bay	66,944
11/18	W 27-24	at Tampa Bay	65,612
11/25	W 13-6	at Minnesota	64,221
12/02	W 13-10	Detroit	66,944
12/09	L 7-17	at Green Bay	59,869
12/16	W 27-3	Tampa Bay	66,944
12/23	W 20-15	at Washington	78,884
12/30	W 24-0	at Detroit	76,067
1/06	W 33-13	Jacksonville	66,944

(OT) Overtime

POSTSEASON (0-1)

1/19	L 19-33	Philadelphia	66,944

SCORE BY PERIODS

Bears	38	96	71	121	12 —	338
Opponents	48	31	71	53	0 —	203

2001 TEAM STATISTICS

	Bears	Opp.
Total First Downs	277	277
Rushing	100	71
Passing	153	191
Penalty	24	15
3rd Down: Made/Att	74/225	80/223
3rd Down Pct.	32.9	35.9
4th Down: Made/Att	10/21	4/17
4th Down Pct.	47.6	23.5
Possession Avg.	30:35	29:25
Total Net Yards	4694	4978
Avg. Per Game	293.4	311.1
Total Plays	1020	1023
Avg. Per Play	4.6	4.9
Net Yards Rushing	1742	1313
Avg. Per Game	108.9	82.1
Total Rushes	475	373
Net Yards Passing	2952	3665
Avg. Per Game	184.5	229.1
Sacked/Yards Lost	17/120	48/294
Gross Yards	3072	3959
Att./Completions	528/315	602/355
Completion Pct.	59.7	59.0
Had Intercepted	16	20
Punts/Average	88/42.5	90/40.7
Net Punting Avg.	88/37.0	90/32.2
Penalties/Yards	63/622	97/808
Fumbles/Ball Lost	21/8	34/17
Touchdowns	37	21
Rushing	12	6
Passing	20	12
Returns	5	3

2001 INDIVIDUAL STATISTICS

PASSING

PASSING	Att.	Comp.	Yds.	Pct.	TD	Int.	Tkld.	Rate
Miller	395	228	2299	57.7	13	10	11/72	74.9
Matthews	129	84	694	65.1	5	6	6/48	72.3
Booker	2	1	34	50.0	1	0	0/0	135.4
Johnson	1	1	18	100.0	0	0	0/0	118.8
Maynard	1	1	27	100.0	1	0	0/0	158.3
Bears	528	315	3072	59.7	20	16	17/120	76.0
Opponents	602	355	3959	59.0	12	20	48/294	71.4

SCORING

SCORING	TD R	TD P	TD Rt	PAT	FG	Saf	PTS
Edinger	0	0	0	34/34	26/31	0	112
Booker	0	8	0	0/0	0/0	0	48
Thomas	7	0	0	0/0	0/0	0	44
Johnson	4	0	0	0/0	0/0	0	24
Terrell	0	4	0	0/0	0/0	0	24
Allen	1	1	0	0/0	0/0	0	12
Baxter	0	2	0	0/0	0/0	0	12
Brown	0	0	2	0/0	0/0	0	12
M. Robinson	0	2	0	0/0	0/0	0	12
Urlacher	0	1	1	0/0	0/0	0	12
Bates	0	1	0	0/0	0/0	0	6
Harris	0	0	1	0/0	0/0	0	6
McQuarters	0	0	1	0/0	0/0	0	6
Shelton	0	1	0	0/0	0/0	0	6
Bears	12	20	5	34/34	26/31	1	338
Opponents	6	12	3	19/20	18/28	1	203

2-Pt. Conversions: Thomas.
Bears 1-1, Opponents 1-1.

RUSHING

RUSHING	Att.	Yds.	Avg.	LG	TD
Thomas	278	1183	4.3	46	7
Allen	135	469	3.5	19	1
Johnson	20	99	5.0	34	4
Booker	4	8	2.0	13	0
Matthews	4	5	1.3	3	0
Denson	1	4	4.0	4	0
Milburn	3	3	1.0	4	0
Maynard	1	-10	-10.0	-10	0
Miller	29	-19	-.7	3	0
Bears	475	1742	3.7	46	12
Opponents	373	1313	3.5	29	6

RECEIVING

RECEIVING	No.	Yds.	Avg.	LG	TD
Booker	100	1071	10.7	66t	8
White	45	428	9.5	32	0
Terrell	34	415	12.2	62	4
Allen	30	203	6.8	34t	1
M. Robinson	23	269	11.7	34t	2
Thomas	22	178	8.1	23	0
Baxter	22	148	6.7	19	2
Shelton	12	76	6.3	16	1
Davis	11	68	6.2	14	0
Bates	9	160	17.8	40	1
Milburn	3	9	3.0	7	0
Merritt	2	20	10.0	13	0
Urlacher	1	27	27.0	27t	1
Johnson	1	0	0.0	0	0
Bears	315	3072	9.8	66t	20
Opponents	355	3959	11.2	60t	12

INTERCEPTIONS

INTERCEPTIONS	No.	Yds.	Avg.	LG	TD
Brown	5	81	16.2	33t	2
Urlacher	3	60	20.0	41	0
McQuarters	3	47	15.7	43	0
Parrish	3	36	12.0	26	0
Colvin	2	22	11.0	14	0
Traylor	1	67	67.0	67	0
Harris	1	45	45.0	39t	1
Azumah	1	14	14.0	14	0
Holdman	1	0	0.0	0	0
Bears	20	372	18.6	67	3
Opponents	16	187	11.7	97t	1

PUNTING

PUNTING	No.	Yds.	Avg.	In 20	LG
Maynard	87	3709	42.6	36	60
Edinger	1	34	34.0	1	34
Bears	88	3743	42.5	37	60
Opponents	90	3662	40.7	21	56

PUNT RETURNS

PUNT RETURNS	No.	FC	Yds.	Avg.	LG	TD
Johnson	28	10	255	9.1	35	0
McQuarters	12	1	96	8.0	16	0
Milburn	4	3	33	8.3	20	0
Denson	1	0	5	5.0	5	0
Azumah	0	0	16	—	16	0
Bears	45	14	405	9.0	35	0
Opponents	45	14	327	7.3	32	0

KICKOFF RETURNS

KICKOFF RETURNS	No.	Yds.	Avg.	LG	TD
Denson	23	534	23.2	37	0
Johnson	14	286	20.4	33	0
Milburn	6	152	25.3	37	0
Azumah	4	65	16.3	23	0
Dogins	1	6	6.0	6	0
Newkirk	1	8	8.0	8	0
Powell	1	1	1.0	1	0
Terrell	1	8	8.0	8	0
Bears	51	1060	20.8	37	0
Opponents	66	1353	20.5	39	0

FIELD GOALS

FIELD GOALS	1-19	20-29	30-39	40-49	50+
Edinger	0/0	6/7	7/8	13/16	0/0
Bears	0/0	6/7	7/8	13/16	0/0
Opponents	0/0	7/7	5/7	6/14	0/0

SACKS

SACKS	No.
Colvin	10.5
Daniels	9.0
Urlacher	6.0
B. Robinson	4.5
Brown	3.0
Green	3.0
Azumah	2.0
Boone	2.0
Traylor	2.0
Holdman	1.5
Washington	1.5
McQuarters	1.0
Newkirk	1.0
Parrish	1.0
Bears	48.0
Opponents	17.0

RECORD HOLDERS
INDIVIDUAL RECORDS—CAREER

Category	Name	Performance
Rushing (Yds.)	Walter Payton, 1975-1987	*16,726
Passing (Yds.)	Sid Luckman, 1939-1950	14,686
Passing (TDs)	Sid Luckman, 1939-1950	137
Receiving (No.)	Walter Payton, 1975-1987	492
Receiving (Yds.)	Johnny Morris, 1958-1967	5,059
Interceptions	Gary Fencik, 1976-1987	38
Punting (Avg.)	George Gulyanics, 1947-1952	44.5
Punt Return (Avg.)	Ray (Scooter) McLean, 1940-47	14.8
Kickoff Return (Avg.)	Gale Sayers, 1965-1971	*30.6
Field Goals	Kevin Butler, 1985-1995	243
Touchdowns (Tot.)	Walter Payton, 1975-1987	125
Points	Kevin Butler, 1985-1995	1,116

INDIVIDUAL RECORDS—SINGLE SEASON

Category	Name	Performance
Rushing (Yds.)	Walter Payton, 1977	1,852
Passing (Yds.)	Erik Kramer, 1995	3,838
Passing (TDs)	Erik Kramer, 1995	29
Receiving (No.)	Marty Booker, 2001	100
Receiving (Yds.)	Marcus Robinson, 1999	1,400
Interceptions	Mark Carrier, 1990	10
Punting (Avg.)	Bobby Joe Green, 1963	46.5
Punt Return (Avg.)	Harry Clark, 1943	15.8
Kickoff Return (Avg.)	Gale Sayers, 1967	37.7
Field Goals	Kevin Butler, 1985	31
Touchdowns (Tot.)	Gale Sayers, 1965	22
Points	Kevin Butler, 1985	144

INDIVIDUAL RECORDS—SINGLE GAME

Category	Name	Performance
Rushing (Yds.)	Walter Payton, 11-20-77	275
Passing (Yds.)	Johnny Lujack, 12-11-49	468
Passing (TDs)	Sid Luckman, 11-14-43	*7
Receiving (No.)	Jim Keane, 10-23-49	14
Receiving (Yds.)	Harlon Hill, 10-31-54	214
Interceptions	Many times	3
	Last time by Mark Carrier, 12-9-90	
Field Goals	Roger LeClerc, 12-3-61	5
	Mac Percival, 10-20-68	5
Touchdowns (Tot.)	Gale Sayers, 12-12-65	*6
Points	Gale Sayers, 12-12-65	36

*NFL Record

2002 VETERAN ROSTER

No.	Name	Pos.	Ht.	Wt.	Birthdate	NFL Exp.	College	Hometown	How Acq.	'01 Games/ Starts
27	Abdullah, Rabih	RB	6-0	227	4/27/75	5	Lehigh	Roselle, N.J.	UFA(TB)-'02	16/0*
24	Austin, Reggie	CB	5-9	178	1/21/77	2	Wake Forest	Atlanta, Ga.	D4-'00	9/0
23	Azumah, Jerry	CB	5-10	195	9/1/77	4	New Hampshire	Worcester, Mass.	D5c-'99	16/5
84	Baxter, Fred	TE	6-3	265	6/14/71	10	Auburn	Brundidge, Ala.	W(NYJ)-'01	14/14
86	Booker, Marty	WR	5-11	215	7/31/76	4	Northeast Louisiana	Jonesboro-Hodge, La.	D3c-'99	16/16
70	Boone, Alfonso	DT	6-4	325	1/11/76	2	Mt. San Antonio (Calif.) J.C.	Saginaw, Mich.	W(Det)-'00	11/0
85	Broughton, Luther	TE	6-0	248	11/30/74	6	Furman	Huger, S.C.	UFA(Car)-'02	15/0*
30	Brown, Mike	S	5-10	202	2/13/78	3	Nebraska	Scottsdale, Ariz.	D2-'00	16/16
10	Burris, Henry	QB	6-0	185	6/4/75	2	Temple	Spiro, Okla.	FA-'02	0*
55	Caldwell, Mike	LB	6-2	237	8/31/71	10	Middle Tennessee State	Oak Ridge, Tenn.	UFA(Phil)-'02	16/16*
12	Chandler, Chris	QB	6-4	228	10/12/65	15	Washington	Everett, Wash.	FA-'02	14/14*
59	Colvin, Rosevelt	LB	6-3	254	9/5/77	4	Purdue	Indianapolis, Ind.	D4b-'99	16/13
76	Cook, Damion	T	6-6	343	4/16/79	2	Bethune-Cookman	Sunrise, Fla.	W(Balt)-'01	0*
93	Daniels, Phillip	DE	6-5	290	3/4/73	7	Georgia	Donalsonville, Ga.	UFA(Sea)-'00	16/16
82	Davis, John	TE	6-4	264	5/14/73	6	Emporia State	Jasper, Texas	W(Min)-'01	16/7
73	Dogins, Kevin	C	6-1	305	12/7/72	6	Texas A&M-Kingsville	Eagle Lake, Texas	W(TB)-'01	16/0
2	Edinger, Paul	K	5-10	162	1/17/78	3	Michigan State	Lakeland, Fla.	D6b-'00	16/0
69	Gandy, Mike	G	6-4	304	1/3/79	2	Notre Dame	Garland, Texas	D3-'01	0*
43	Green, Mike	S	6-0	176	12/6/76	3	Northwestern State (La.)	Ruston, La.	D7b-'00	16/2
8	Hilbert, Jon	K	6-2	220	7/15/75	2	Louisville	Boonville, Ind.	UFA(Dall)-'02	8/0*
53	Holdman, Warrick	LB	6-1	246	11/22/75	4	Texas A&M	Alief, Texas	D4a-'99	16/15
52	Howard, Bobbie	LB	5-10	230	6/14/77	2	Notre Dame	Rand, W. Va.	W(TB)-'00	16/0
32	Johnson, Leon	RB	6-0	216	7/13/74	5	North Carolina	Morgantown, N.C.	UFA(NYJ)-'01	12/0
57	Kreutz, Olin	C	6-2	285	6/9/77	4	Washington	Honolulu, Hawaii	D3-'98	16/16
44	Leach, Mike	FB	6-2	240	10/18/76	3	William & Mary	Jefferson Township, N.J.	FA-'02	4/0*
89	Lyman, Dustin	TE	6-4	250	8/5/76	3	Wake Forest	Boulder, Colo.	D3b-'00	4/0
65	Mannelly, Patrick	T-LS	6-5	270	4/18/75	5	Duke	Atlanta, Ga.	D6b-'98	15/0
4	Maynard, Brad	P	6-1	190	2/9/74	6	Ball State	Sheridan, Ind.	UFA(NYG)-'01	16/0
26	McMillon, Todd	CB	5-10	183	9/26/74	3	Northern Arizona	Bellflower, Calif.	FA-'00	8/0
21	McQuarters, R.W.	CB	5-9	198	12/21/76	5	Oklahoma State	Tulsa, Okla.	T(SF)-'00	16/16
22	Merrill, Than	S	6-2	212	12/17/77	2	Yale	Fresno, Calif.	W(TB)-'01	15/0
81	Merritt, Ahmad	WR	5-10	193	2/5/77	2	Wisconsin	Chicago, Ill.	FA-'00	2/0
15	Miller, Jim	QB	6-2	215	2/9/71	9	Michigan State	Waterford, Mich.	W(Det)-'98	14/13
36	Pritchett, Stanley	FB	6-2	242	12/22/72	7	South Carolina	Atlanta, Ga.	W(Phil)-'01	7/0
91	Riley, Karon	DE	6-2	264	8/23/78	2	Minnesota	Detroit, Mich.	D4-'01	5/0
74	Robertson, Bernard	T	6-3	308	6/9/79	2	Tulane	New Orleans, La.	D5-'01	0*
98	Robinson, Bryan	DE	6-4	300	6/22/74	6	Fresno State	Toledo, Ohio	W(StL)-'98	16/16
88	Robinson, Marcus	WR	6-3	215	2/27/75	6	South Carolina	Ft. Valley, Ga.	D4b-'97	6/4
31	Shelton, Daimon	FB	6-0	258	9/15/72	6	Sacramento State	Duarte, Calif.	UFA(Jax)-'01	16/9
99	Tafoya, Joe	DE	6-4	270	9/6/77	2	Arizona	Pittsburg, Calif.	W(TB)-'01	5/0
83	Terrell, David	WR	6-3	215	3/13/79	2	Michigan	Richmond, Va.	D1-'01	16/6
35	Thomas, Anthony	RB	6-2	227	11/11/77	2	Michigan	Winnfield, La.	D2-'01	14/10
94	Traylor, Keith	DT	6-2	304	9/3/69	11	Central State (Okla.)	Little Rock, Ark.	UFA(Den)-'01	16/15
64	Tucker, Rex	G	6-5	315	12/20/76	4	Texas A&M	Midland, Texas	D3a-'99	16/16
54	Urlacher, Brian	LB	6-3	244	5/25/78	3	New Mexico	Lovington, N.M.	D1-'00	16/16
58	Villarrial, Chris	G	6-4	308	6/9/73	7	Indiana (Pa.)	Hershey, Pa.	D5-'96	16/16
92	Washington, Ted	DT	6-5	330	4/13/68	12	Louisville	Tampa, Fla.	UFA(Buff)-'01	16/15
33	Whigham, Larry	S	6-2	210	6/23/72	9	Northeast Louisiana	Hattiesburg, Miss.	UFA(NE)-'01	14/0
80	White, Dez	WR	6-0	219	8/23/79	3	Georgia Tech	Orange Park, Fla.	D3a-'00	14/6
71	Williams, James	T	6-7	331	3/29/68	12	Cheyney State (Pa.)	Allerdice, Pa.	FA-'91	16/16
72	Wiltz, Jason	DT-DE	6-4	300	11/23/76	4	Nebraska	New Orleans, La.	W(NYJ)-'02	0*
37	Young, Floyd	CB	5-10	179	11/23/75	7	Texas A&M-Kingsville	New Orleans, La.	FA-'02	0*

* Abdullah played 16 games with Tampa Bay in '01; Broughton played 15 games with Carolina; Burris inactive for 10 games with Green Bay; Caldwell played 16 games with Philadelphia; Chandler played 14 games with Atlanta; Cook inactive for 14 games; Gandy inactive for 16 games; Hilbert played 8 games with Dallas; Leach played 4 games with Tennessee; Robertson inactive for 16 games; Wiltz last active with New York Jets in '00; Young last active with Tampa Bay in '00.

Players lost through free agency (8): RB James Allen (Hou; 16 games in '01), FB Scott Dragos (NE; 6), CB Walt Harris (Ind; 15), T Jimmy Herndon (Hou; 16), LB Greg Jones (Hou; 16), S Tony Parrish (SF; 16), DE Carl Powell (Wash; 16); TE Kaseem Sinceno (Hou; 0).

Also played with Bears in '01—T Blake Brockermeyer (16), QB Shane Matthews (4), KR-PR Glyn Milburn (4), DT Robert Newkirk (11), LB Khari Samuel (1), DT Henry Taylor (1), QB Danny Wuerffel (1).

2002 FIRST-YEAR ROSTER

Name	Pos.	Ht.	Wt.	Birthdate	College	Hometown	How Acq.
Barnes, Leo (1)	S	6-0	210	6/2/79	Southern Mississippi	Hattiesburg, Miss.	FA
Bennett, Stan (1)	G	6-4	285	7/16/79	Villanova	Rancho Santa Margarita, Calif.	FA
Brown, Alex	DE	6-3	260	6/4/79	Florida	White Springs, Fla.	D4
Brown, Chris (1)	T	6-5	329	1/21/78	Georgia Tech	Augusta, Ga.	FA
Butkus, Luke	C	6-4	290	6/26/79	Illinois	Steger, Ill.	FA
Christian, Kenny (1)	WR	6-1	198	7/11/78	Eastern Michigan	Arcadia, Fla.	FA
Coleman, Travis	DB	5-11	180	1/4/80	Hampton	Goldsboro, N.C.	FA
Collins, Mike	G	6-6	318	8/27/78	Wake Forest	Hickory, N.C.	FA
Colombo, Marc	T	6-7	313	10/8/78	Boston College	Bridgewater, Mass.	D1
Davis, Adam (1)	G	6-4	309	1/11/77	Oklahoma State	Hobart, Okla.	FA
Dawson, Curry	DT	6-6	280	8/4/79	Angelo State	Water Valley, Texas	FA
Elliott, Jamin	WR	6-0	181	10/5/79	Delaware	Portsmouth, Va.	D6b
Evans, Jerris	WR	5-11	185	10/9/78	Missouri Southern	St. Joseph, Mo.	FA
Fitts, Steve	P	6-0	192	2/7/80	Illinois	Gaston, S.C.	FA
Fletcher, Bryan	TE	6-5	235	3/23/79	UCLA	St. Louis, Mo.	D6c
Gray, Bobby	S	6-0	209	4/30/78	Louisiana Tech	Aldine, Texas	D5a
Grzeskowiak, Jeff	T	6-5	309	11/9/78	Akron	North Olmstead, Ohio	FA
Hicks, Maurice	RB	5-10	200	7/22/78	North Carolina A&T	Emporia, Va.	FA
Jones, Rodney	DT	6-2	295	9/18/77	Alabama-Birmingham	Birmingham, Ala.	FA
Johnson, Eric (1)	DB	6-0	215	8/14/77	Western Kentucky	Shallotte, N.C.	FA-'01
Johnson, Kiah	LB	6-3	235	9/20/78	Texas A&M-Kingsville	Houston, Texas	FA
Johnson, Tim (1)	LB	6-0	236	2/7/78	Youngstown State	Fairfield, Ala.	FA-'01
Kirby, Charles (1)	FB	6-1	240	11/27/74	Virginia	Fayetteville, N.C.	FA
Knight, Bryan	LB	6-2	240	1/22/79	Pittsburgh	Buffalo, N.Y.	D5b
Lemons, Devon (1)	LB	6-2	232	3/20/79	Texas Tech	Pampa, Texas	FA-'01
Lewis, Brad	QB	6-3	215	2/7/79	West Virginia	Shadyside, Ohio	FA
Lukins, Tony	CB	5-11	186	2/18/79	New Mexico State	El Paso, Texas	FA
Mastrole, Ken (1)	QB	6-3	249	2/25/77	Rhode Island	Ft. Lauderdale, Fla.	FA
Matthews, Roshaun (1)	DE	6-3	260	4/22/77	Southern	Baton Rouge, La.	FA-'01
McCoo, Eric	RB	5-10	209	9/6/80	Penn State	Red Bank, N.J.	FA
Metcalf, Terrence	T-G	6-3	318	1/28/78	Mississippi	Clarksdale, Miss.	D3
North, Ramondo (1)	WR	5-11	176	3/30/77	North Carolina A&T	Charlotte, N.C.	FA-'01
Peterson, Adrian	RB	5-10	214	7/1/79	Georgia Southern	Alachua, Fla.	D6a
Sanford, Robert (1)	RB	5-10	228	4/17/79	Western Michigan	Miami, Fla.	FA
Shepherd, Edell	WR	6-1	170	5/18/80	San Jose State	Los Angeles, Calif.	FA
Singleton, Adrian	S	6-2	210	12/9/78	Alabama-Birmingham	Mobile, Ala.	FA
Spencer, Willie (1)	WR	6-3	226	4/4/77	Tiffin	Massillon, Ohio	FA-'01
Tugbenyoh, Mawuko (1)	LB	5-11	245	4/9/78	California	Concord, Calif.	FA
Volk, Dave	T	6-5	300	8/1/78	Nebraska	Battle Creek, Neb.	FA
Warner, Josh (1)	T	6-5	305	5/15/79	SUNY-Brockport	Cato, N.Y.	FA
Williams, Roosevelt	CB	5-11	204	9/10/78	Tuskegee	Jacksonville, Fla.	D2

The term NFL Rookie is defined as a player who is in his first season of professional football and has not been on the roster of another professional football team for any regular-season or postseason games. A Rookie is designated by an "R" on NFL rosters. Players who have been active in another professional football league or players who have NFL experience, including either preseason training camp or being on an Active List or Inactive List, or on Reserve/Injured or Reserve/Physically Unable to Perform for fewer than six regular-season games, are termed NFL First-Year Players. An NFL First-Year Player is designated by a "1" on NFL rosters. Thereafter, a player is credited with an additional year of experience for each season in which he accumulates six games on the Active List or Inactive List, or on Reserve/Injured or Reserve/Physically Unable to Perform.

CHICAGO BEARS

COACHING STAFF

Head Coach,
Dick Jauron
Pro Career: Named eleventh head coach in franchise history on January 24, 1999. Earned NFL coach of the year honors in 2001 after leading the Bears to the greatest single-season turnaround in team history with a 13-3 record. Jauron directed the team to its first division title since 1990 and coached the team in its first playoff game since 1994. In 2000, Jauron became the first Bears coach in history to beat the Packers at Lambeau Field in each of his first two trips with a 27-24 win on October 1, 2000. Jauron guided the Bears to four wins in their final eight games to finish at 5-11 in 2000. Chicago posted six victories during Jauron's rookie season of 1999. As Jacksonville's inaugural defensive coordinator, he was instrumental in the early success of the Jaguars, which included three playoff berths in the franchise's first four seasons and a run to the 1996 AFC Championship Game. Jauron coached defensive backs for nine years in Green Bay (1986-1994) before moving to Jacksonville. Spent several years away from NFL before joining the Buffalo Bills' coaching staff in 1985. Moved to Green Bay the following season and served as the defensive backs coach under three different head coaches (Forrest Gregg, 1986-87; Lindy Infante, 1988-91; Mike Holmgren, 1992-94). Jauron accepted the defensive coordinator post with the expansion Jaguars in 1995 and helped lead the team to three consecutive playoff berths after their opening season. Career record: 24-25.
Background: Played running back at Yale from 1970-72 where he held the school's career rushing mark with 2,947 for 27 seasons. Drafted by the Detroit Lions in the fourth round of the 1973 draft. Jauron played eight years as a defensive back in the NFL with the Detroit Lions (1973-77) and Cincinnati Bengals (1978-1980), earning a trip to the 1975 Pro Bowl.
Personal: Born October 7, 1950, Peoria, Ill. Dick and his wife Gail live in Lake Forest, Ill. And have two daughters—Kacy and Amy.

ASSISTANT COACHES

Vance Bedford, defensive backs; born August 20, 1958, Houston, lives in Gurnee, Ill. Defensive back Texas 1977-79, 1981. Pro defensive back St. Louis Cardinals 1982, Oklahoma Outlaws (USFL) 1984. College coach: Navarro (Texas) J.C. 1986, Colorado State 1987-1992, Oklahoma State 1993-94, Michigan 1995-98. Pro coach: Joined Bears in 1999.
Greg Blache, defensive coordinator; born March 9, 1949, New Orleans, lives in Lake Bluff, Ill. Attended Notre Dame. No college or pro playing experience. College coach: Notre Dame 1973-75, 1981-83, Tulane

1976-1980, Southern 1986, Kansas 1987. Pro coach: Jacksonville Bulls (USFL) 1984-85, Green Bay Packers 1988-1993, Indianapolis Colts 1994-98, joined Bears in 1999.
Chuck Bullough, asst. defensive line-asst. special teams; born March 3, 1968, East Lansing, Mich., lives in Hainsville, Ill. Linebacker Michigan State 1988-1991. Pro linebacker Miami dolphins 1993-94. College coach: Michigan State 1997-98. Pro coach: Joined Bears in 1999.
Pete Carmichael, offensive assistant; born March 4, 1941, North Plainfield, N.J., lives in Grayslake, Ill. Quarterback Dayton 1961, Montclair State College 1962-63. No pro playing experience. College coach: Virginia Military Institute 1965-66, New Hampshire 1967, Boston College 1968-1972, 1981-1993, Trenton State College 1973 (head coach), Columbia 1974-77, Merchant Marine Academy 1977-1980 (head coach). Pro coach: Jacksonville Jaguars 1995-99, Cleveland Browns 2000, joined Bears in 2001.
Charlie Coiner, offensive quality control; born Waynesboro, Va., lives in Evanston, Ill. Attended Catawba College, Appalachian State. No college or pro playing experience. College coach: Appalachian State 1983-86, Minnesota 1987, Louisville 1995-97, Tennessee-Chattanooga 1998, Louisiana State 1999, Texas Southern 2000. Pro coach: Joined Bears in 2001.
Pat Flaherty, tight ends; born April 27, 1956, Hanover, Pa., lives in Waukegan, Ill. Center East Stroudsburg 1976-79. No pro playing experience. College coach: East Stroudsburg 1980-81, Penn State 1982-83, Rutgers 1984-1991, East Carolina 1992, Wake Forest 1993-98, Iowa 1999. Pro coach: Washington Redskins 2000, joined Bears in 2001.
Todd Haley, wide receivers; born February 28, 1967, Atlanta, lives in Gurnee, Ill. Attended Florida and Miami. No college or pro playing experience. Pro coach: New York Jets 1996-2000, joined Bears in 2001.
Gary Moeller, linebackers; born January 26, 1941, Lima, Ohio, lives in Ponte Verda, Fla. Center Ohio State 1960-62. No pro playing experience. College coach: Miami (Ohio) 1967, Michigan 1969-1976, 1980-1994 (head coach 1990-94), Illinois 1977-79 (head coach). Pro coach: Cincinnati Bengals 1995-96, Detroit Lions 1997-2000 (interim head coach in 2000), Jacksonville Jaguars 2001, joined Bears in 2002.
Earle Mosley, running backs; born December 20, 1946, Darby, Pa., lives in Buffalo Grove, Ill. Defensive back West Chester State 1970-72. No pro playing experience. College coach: West Chester State 1979, Rutgers 1980-83, Northwestern 1984-87, Temple 1988-1991, Notre Dame 1992-96, Stanford

1997-98. Pro coach: Joined Bears in 1999.
Rex Norris, defensive line; born December 10, 1939, Tipton, Ind., lives in Libertyville, Ill. Linebacker San Angelo (Texas) J.C. 1959-1960, East Texas State 1961-62. No pro playing experience. College coach: Navarro (Texas) J.C. 1970-71, Texas A&M 1972, Oklahoma 1973-1983, Arizona State 1984, Florida 1988-89, Tennessee 1990-91, Texas 1992-93. Pro coach: Detroit Lions 1985-87, Denver Broncos 1994, Tennessee Oilers 1995-98, joined Bears in 1999.
John Shoop, offensive coordinator; born August 1, 1969, Pittsburgh, lives in Libertyville, Ill. Quarterback University of the South 1987-1990. No pro playing experience. College coach: Dartmouth 1991, Vanderbilt 1992-94. Pro coach: Carolina Panthers 1995-98, joined Bears in 1999.
Mike Sweatman, special teams; born October 23, 1947, Kansas City, Mo., lives in Lake Bluff, Ill. Linebacker Kansas 1964-67. No pro playing experience. College coach: Kansas 1973-74, 1979-1982, Tulsa 1977-78, Tennessee 1983. Pro coach: Minnesota Vikings 1984, New York Giants 1985-1992, New England Patriots 1993-96, New York Jets 1997-2000, joined Bears in 2001.
Bob Wylie, offensive line; born February 16, 1951, West Warwick, R.I., lives in Lake Bluff, Ill. Linebacker Colorado 1969-1971. No pro playing experience. College coach: Brown 1980-82, Holy Cross 1983-84, Ohio 1985-87, Colorado State 1988-89, Cincinnati 1996. Pro coach: New York Jets 1990-91, Tampa Bay Buccaneers 1992-95, Cincinnati Bengals 1997-98, joined Bears in 1999.

National Football Conference
East Division
Team Colors: Royal Blue, Metallic Silver
Blue, and White
Cowboys Center
One Cowboys Parkway
Irving, Texas 75063
Telephone: (972) 556-9900

2002 SCHEDULE
PRESEASON
Aug. 9   **Oakland** 8:00
Aug. 17 at Carolina.........................8:00
Aug. 24 **Atlanta**...............................7:00
Aug. 29 at Jacksonville....................8:00

REGULAR SEASON
Sept. 8   at Houston 7:30
Sept. 15 **Tennessee** 12:00
Sept. 22 at Philadelphia....................1:00
Sept. 29 at St. Louis.......................12:00
Oct. 6   **New York Giants** 12:00
Oct. 13   **Carolina**...........................12:00
Oct. 20   at Arizona...........................1:15
Oct. 27   **Seattle** 12:00
Nov. 3   at Detroit 1:00
Nov. 10 OPEN DATE
Nov. 17 at Indianapolis 1:00
Nov. 24 **Jacksonville**.....................12:00
Nov. 28 **Washington (Thurs.)**..........3:05
Dec. 8   **San Francisco** 12:00
Dec. 15 at New York Giants 4:15
Dec. 21 **Philadelphia (Sat.)** 7:30
Dec. 29 at Washington 1:00

Stadium: Texas Stadium (opened in 1971)
  • **Capacity:** 65,639
  2401 E. Airport Freeway
  Irving, Texas 75062
Playing Surface: Sportfield Turf
Training Camp: Alamodome
  San Antonio, Texas 78203

TEXAS STADIUM

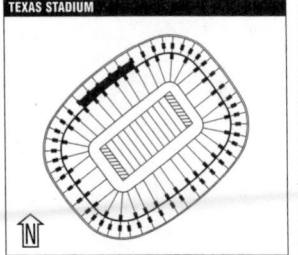

CLUB OFFICIALS
Owner/President/General Manager:
  Jerry Jones
Chief Operating Officer/Executive Vice
  President-Player Personnel:
  Stephen Jones
Vice President/Director of Charities and
  Special Events: Charlotte Anderson
Vice President/Director of
  Marketing/Legal/Internet:
  Jerry Jones, Jr.
CFO: George Mitchell
Public Relations Director: Rich Dalrymple
Assistant Director of Public Relations:
  Brett Daniels
Director of College and Pro Scouting:
  Larry Lacewell
Assistant Director of College Scouting:
  Tom Ciskowski
Assistant Director of Pro Scouting:
  Bryan Broaddus
Director of Operations: Bruce Mays
Ticket Manager: Carol Padgett
Trainer: Jim Maurer
Equipment Manager: Mike McCord
Video Director: Robert Blackwell
Cheerleader Director: Kelli Finglass

COACHING HISTORY
(394-279-6)
1960-1988	Tom Landry	270-178-6
1989-1993	Jimmy Johnson	51-37-0
1994-97	Barry Switzer	45-26-0
1998-99	Chan Gailey	18-16-0
2000-01	Dave Campo	10-22-0

ATTENDANCE
Home 465,396   Away 542,606
Total 1,008,002
Single-game home record,
65,180 (11/12/95)
Single-season home record, 518,167
(1995)

2002 DRAFT CHOICES
Round	Name	Pos.	College
1	Roy Williams	DB	Oklahoma
2	Andre Gurode	G	Colorado
	Antonio Bryant	WR	Pittsburgh
3	Derek Ross	DB	Ohio State
4	Jamar Martin	RB	Ohio State
5	Pete Hunter	DB	Virginia Union
6	Tyson Walter	T	Ohio State
	Deveren Johnson	WR	Sacred Heart
	Bob Slowikowski	TE	Virginia Tech

2001 TEAM RECORD
PRESEASON (2-3)

Date	Result	Opponent
8/4	L 14-21	at Oakland
8/11	L 6-20	Denver
8/18	L 10-16	at New Orleans
8/27	W 21-6	vs. Oakland, at Mexico City
8/30	W 27-17	Jacksonville

REGULAR SEASON (5-11)

Date	Result	Opponent	Att.
9/09	L 6-10	Tampa Bay	61,521
9/23	L 21-32	San Diego	63,430
9/30	L 18-40	at Philadelphia	66,621
10/07	L 21-28	at Oakland	61,535
10/15	W 9-7	Washington	63,941
10/28	W 17-3	Arizona	63,114
11/04	L 24-27	at N.Y. Giants(OT)	78,673
11/11	L 13-20	at Atlanta	70,452
11/18	L 3-36	Philadelphia	63,204
11/22	L 24-26	Denver	64,104
12/02	W 20-14	at Washington	85,112
12/09	W 20-13	New York Giants	61,821
12/16	L 3-29	at Seattle	63,366
12/23	L 10-17	at Arizona	48,883
12/30	W 27-21	San Francisco	64,366
1/06	L 10-15	at Detroit	77,512

(OT) Overtime

SCORE BY PERIODS

Cowboys	38	81	45	82	0 —	246
Opponents	60	131	54	90	3 —	338

2001 TEAM STATISTICS

	Cowboys	Opp.
Total First Downs	247	272
Rushing	114	90
Passing	110	160
Penalty	23	22
3rd Down: Made/Att	71/215	76/214
3rd Down Pct.	33.0	35.5
4th Down: Made/Att	4/16	8/15
4th Down Pct.	25.0	53.3
Possession Avg.	30:13	29:47
Total Net Yards	4402	4599
Avg. Per Game	275.1	287.4
Total Plays	952	985
Avg. Per Play	4.6	4.7
Net Yards Rushing	2184	1710
Avg. Per Game	136.5	106.9
Total Rushes	505	472
Net Yards Passing	2218	2889
Avg. Per Game	138.6	180.6
Sacked/Yards Lost	34/190	24/130
Gross Yards	2408	3019
Att./Completions	413/210	489/287
Completion Pct.	50.8	58.7
Had Intercepted	20	9
Punts/Average	81/38.7	79/41.7
Net Punting Avg.	81/31.1	79/34.5
Penalties/Yards	91/744	69/634
Fumbles/Ball Lost	25/14	29/16
Touchdowns	26	37
Rushing	8	12
Passing	14	20
Returns	4	5

2001 INDIVIDUAL STATISTICS

PASSING	Att.	Comp.	Yds.	Pct.	TD	Int.	Tkld.	Rate
Carter	176	90	1072	51.1	5	7	12/56	63.0
Wright	98	48	529	49.0	5	5	5/30	61.1
Leaf	88	45	494	51.1	1	3	12/82	57.7
Stoerner	49	26	314	53.1	3	5	5/22	53.8
Galloway	1	1	-1	100.0	0	0	0/0	79.2
Knorr	1	0	0	0.0	0	0	0/0	39.6
Cowboys	413	210	2408	50.8	14	20	34/190	59.9
Opponents	489	287	3019	58.7	20	9	24/130	82.7

SCORING	TD R	TD P	TD Rt	PAT	FG	Saf	PTS
Seder	1	0	0	12/12	11/17	0	51
Hilbert	0	0	0	12/12	11/16	0	45
Galloway	0	3	0	0/0	0/0	0	18
Smith	3	0	0	0/0	0/0	0	18
Chiaverini	0	2	0	0/0	0/0	0	12
Coakley	0	0	2	0/0	0/0	0	12
T. Hambrick	2	0	0	0/0	0/0	0	12
Harris	0	2	0	0/0	0/0	0	12
Ismail	0	2	0	0/0	0/0	0	12
Swinton	0	1	1	0/0	0/0	0	12
Carter	1	0	0	0/0	0/0	0	6
Edwards	0	0	1	0/0	0/0	0	6
Lucky	0	1	0	0/0	0/0	0	6
McGarity	0	1	0	0/0	0/0	0	6
Stoerner	1	0	0	0/0	0/0	0	6
Thomas	0	1	0	0/0	0/0	0	6
Wiley	1	0	0	0/0	0/0	0	6
Cowboys	8	14	4	24/24	22/33	0	246
Opponents	12	20	5	33/34	27/36	1	338

2-Pt. Conversions: None.
Cowboys 0-2, Opponents 0-3.

RUSHING	Att.	Yds.	Avg.	LG	TD
Smith	261	1021	3.9	44	3
T. Hambrick	113	579	5.1	80	2
Wiley	34	247	7.3	58	0
Carter	45	150	3.3	17	1
Wright	17	57	3.4	12	0
Thomas	6	40	6.7	24	0
Galloway	3	32	10.7	16	0
Ismail	8	31	3.9	11	0
Stoerner	9	27	3.0	13	1
Seder	1	8	8.0	8t	1
Chiaverini	1	3	3.0	3	0
Knorr	1	0	0.0	0	0
Taylor	1	0	0.0	0	0
Swinton	1	-4	-4.0	-4	0
Leaf	4	-7	-1.8	0	0
Cowboys	505	2184	4.3	80	8
Opponents	472	1710	3.6	48	12

RECEIVING	No.	Yds.	Avg.	LG	TD
Ismail	53	834	15.7	80t	2
Galloway	52	699	13.4	47t	3
Smith	17	116	6.8	22	0
Wiley	16	99	6.2	17	1
Harris	15	141	9.4	28	2
Lucky	13	96	7.4	16	1
Chiaverini	10	107	10.7	21	2
Huggins	8	36	4.5	10	0
Swinton	7	117	16.7	45t	1
McGarity	6	45	7.5	11t	1
Thomas	5	19	3.8	6	1
T. Hambrick	4	62	15.5	27	0
Rambo	3	28	9.3	14	0
Witherspoon	1	9	9.0	9	0
Cowboys	210	2408	11.5	80t	14
Opponents	287	3019	10.5	78	20

INTERCEPTIONS	No.	Yds.	Avg.	LG	TD
Woodson	3	11	3.7	6	0
Coakley	2	39	19.5	29t	2
Hawthorne	2	28	14.0	22	0
Edwards	1	71	71.0	71t	1
Reese	1	42	42.0	42	0
Cowboys	9	191	21.2	71t	3
Opponents	20	344	17.2	50t	4

PUNTING	No.	Yds.	Avg.	In 20	LG
Knorr	78	3135	40.2	25	57
Cowboys	81	3135	38.7	25	57
Opponents	79	3298	41.7	29	62

PUNT RETURNS	No.	FC	Yds.	Avg.	LG	TD
Swinton	31	8	414	13.4	65t	1
McGarity	6	2	38	6.3	17	0
Rambo	2	0	15	7.5	13	0
Galloway	1	0	6	6.0	6	0
Ismail	1	3	20	20.0	20	0
Cowboys	41	13	493	12.0	65t	1
Opponents	38	18	493	13.0	74	0

KICKOFF RETURNS	No.	Yds.	Avg.	LG	TD
Swinton	56	1327	23.7	77	0
Wiley	4	90	22.5	40	0
Rambo	2	30	15.0	19	0
Evans	1	7	7.0	7	0
Larrimore	1	22	22.0	22	0
Cowboys	64	1476	23.1	77	0
Opponents	54	1164	21.6	61	0

FIELD GOALS	1-19	20-29	30-39	40-49	50+
Seder	0/0	5/5	3/5	3/6	0/1
Hilbert	0/0	3/3	6/6	2/7	0/0
Cowboys	0/0	8/8	9/11	5/13	0/1
Opponents	2/2	10/10	6/8	8/11	1/5

SACKS	No.
Ellis	6.0
Myers	3.5
Noble	3.5
Frisch	3.0
Reese	3.0
Zellner	3.0
Dixon	1.0
Evans	1.0
Cowboys	24.0
Opponents	34.0

RECORD HOLDERS
INDIVIDUAL RECORDS—CAREER

Category	Name	Performance
Rushing (Yds.)	Emmitt Smith, 1990-2001	16,187
Passing (Yds.)	Troy Aikman, 1989-2000	32,942
Passing (TDs)	Troy Aikman, 1989-2000	165
Receiving (No.)	Michael Irvin, 1988-1999	750
Receiving (Yds.)	Michael Irvin, 1988-1999	11,904
Interceptions	Mel Renfro, 1964-1977	52
Punting (Avg.)	Mike Saxon, 1985-1992	41.5
Punt Return (Avg.)	Deion Sanders, 1995-99	13.3
Kickoff Return (Avg.)	Mel Renfro, 1964-1977	26.4
Field Goals	Rafael Septien, 1978-1986	162
Touchdowns (Tot.)	Emmitt Smith, 1990-2001	159
Points	Emmitt Smith, 1990-2001	956

INDIVIDUAL RECORDS—SINGLE SEASON

Category	Name	Performance
Rushing (Yds.)	Emmitt Smith, 1995	1,773
Passing (Yds.)	Danny White, 1983	3,980
Passing (TDs)	Danny White, 1983	29
Receiving (No.)	Michael Irvin, 1995	111
Receiving (Yds.)	Michael Irvin, 1995	1,603
Interceptions	Everson Walls, 1981	11
Punting (Avg.)	Sam Baker, 1962	45.4
Punt Return (Avg.)	Bob Hayes, 1968	20.8
Kickoff Return (Avg.)	Mel Renfro, 1965	30.0
Field Goals	Richie Cunningham, 1997	34
Touchdowns (Tot.)	Emmitt Smith, 1995	25
Points	Emmitt Smith, 1995	150

INDIVIDUAL RECORDS—SINGLE GAME

Category	Name	Performance
Rushing (Yds.)	Emmitt Smith, 10-31-93	237
Passing (Yds.)	Don Meredith, 11-10-63	460
Passing (TDs)	Many times	5
	Last time by Troy Aikman, 9-12-99	
Receiving (No.)	Lance Rentzel, 11-19-67	13
Receiving (Yds.)	Bob Hayes, 11-13-66	246
Interceptions	Herb Adderley, 9-26-71	3
	Lee Roy Jordan, 11-4-73	3
	Dennis Thurman, 12-13-81	3
Field Goals	Chris Boniol, 11-18-96	*7
Touchdowns (Tot.)	Many times	4
	Last time by Emmitt Smith, 9-4-95	
Points	Many times	24
	Last time by Emmitt Smith, 9-4-95	

*NFL Record

2002 VETERAN ROSTER

No.	Name	Pos.	Ht.	Wt.	Birthdate	NFL Exp.	College	Hometown	How Acq.	'01 Games/ Starts
76	Adams, Flozell	T	6-7	335	5/18/75	5	Michigan State	Bellwood, Ill.	D2-'98	16/16
43	Adams, Keith	LB	5-11	223	11/22/79	2	Clemson	College Park, Ga.	FA-'01	4/0
73	Allen, Larry	G	6-3	326	11/27/71	9	Sonoma State	Compton, Calif.	D2-'94	16/16
33	Bell, Jason	CB	6-0	182	4/1/78	2	UCLA	Long Beach, Calif.	FA-'01	16/0
99	Blade, Willie	DT	6-3	315	2/7/79	2	Mississippi State	Warner Robins, Ga.	D3-'01	0*
50	Brooks, Jamal	LB	6-2	240	11/9/76	2	Hampton	Grenada Hills, Calif.	FA-'01	16/1
17	Carter, Quincy	QB	6-2	231	10/13/77	2	Georgia	Decatur, Ga.	D2a-'01	8/8
85	Chiaverini, Darrin	WR	6-2	210	10/12/77	4	Colorado	Orange County, Calif.	T(Cle)-'01	16/0
52	Coakley, Dexter	LB	5-10	230	10/20/72	6	Appalachian State	Mt. Pleasant, S.C.	D3a-'97	15/15
70	Collins, Javiar	T	6-6	314	4/13/78	2	Northwestern	St. Paul, Minn.	FA-'01	0*
25	Criss, Shad	CB	5-10	190	1/11/76	2	Missouri	Denison, Texas	FA-'02	0*
41	Dennis, Pat	CB	6-0	213	6/30/78	3	Louisiana-Monroe	Shreveport, La.	W(KC)-'01	11/0
24	Dixon, Tony	S	6-1	213	6/18/79	2	Alabama	Reform, Ala.	D2b-'01	8/0
79	Dorsey, Char-ron	T	6-6	347	11/5/78	2	Florida State	Jacksonville, Fla.	D7c-'01	8/2
27	Edwards, Mario	CB	6-0	191	12/1/75	3	Florida State	Pascagoula, Miss.	D6-'00	16/15
96	Ekuban, Ebenezer	DE	6-3	282	5/29/76	4	North Carolina	Riverdale, Md.	D1-'99	1/1
98	Ellis, Greg	DE	6-6	275	8/14/75	5	North Carolina	Wendell, N.C.	D1-'98	16/16
92	Evans, Demetric	DE	6-3	286	9/3/79	2	Georgia	Haynesville, La.	FA-'01	16/0
66	Fricke, Ben	G-C	6-0	280	11/13/75	4	Houston	Austin, Texas	FA-'99	5/0
90	Frisch, Byron	DE	6-5	267	12/17/76	3	Brigham Young	Bonita, Calif.	FA-'01	13/0
84	Galloway, Joey	WR	5-11	197	11/20/71	8	Ohio State	Bellaire, Ohio	T(Sea)-'00	16/16
61	Garmon, Kelvin	G	6-2	329	10/26/76	3	Baylor	Haltom, Texas	D7-'99	16/16
63	Gibson, Aaron	T	6-6	380	9/27/77	4	Wisconsin	Indianapolis, Ind.	W(Det)-'01	7/6*
97	Glover, La'Roi	DT	6-2	285	7/4/74	7	San Diego State	San, Diego, Calif.	UFA(NO)-'02	16/16*
23	Goodrich, Dwayne	CB	5-11	200	5/29/78	3	Tennessee	Oak Lawn, Ill.	D2-'00	0*
56	Grant, Orantes	LB	6-0	230	3/18/78	3	Georgia	Atlanta, Ga.	D7-'00	10/1
42	Hambrick, Troy	RB	6-1	255	11/6/76	3	Savannah State	Pasco, Fla.	FA-'00	16/11
51	Hardy, Kevin	LB	6-4	249	7/24/73	7	Illinois	Evansville, Ind.	UFA(Jax)-'02	9/9*
38	Hawthorne, Duane	CB	5-10	175	8/26/76	4	Northern Illinois	St. Louis, Mo.	FA-'99	16/11
49	Huggins, J.J.	TE	6-3	245	3/29/76	2	Alabama State	Zachary, La.	W(Hou)-'02	10/2
81	Ismail, Raghib	WR	5-11	183	11/18/69	10	Notre Dame	Wilkes Barre, Pa.	UFA(Car)-'99	14/13
71	Jackson, Alcender	G	6-3	311	5/18/77	3	Louisiana State	Moss Point, Miss.	FA-'00	0*
57	Johnson, Paris	LB	6-3	220	1/18/76	2	Miami (Ohio)	Chicago, Ill.	FA-'02	0*
4	Knorr, Micah	P	6-2	199	1/9/75	3	Utah State	Orange, Calif.	FA-'00	16/0
68	Lehr, Matt	G-C	6-2	292	4/25/79	2	Virginia Tech	Woodbridge, Va.	D5-'01	8/0
15	Lucas, Anthony	WR	6-3	204	11/20/76	2	Arkansas	Tallulah, La.	W(GB)-'01	0*
86	Lucky, Mike	TE	6-6	273	11/23/75	4	Arizona	Antioch, Calif.	D7a-'99	16/5
58	Mackey, Louis	LB	6-1	225	12/29/77	2	Akron	Albany, Calif.	FA-'01	1/0
82	McGee, Tony	TE	6-4	248	4/21/71	10	Michigan	Terre Haute, Ind.	FA-'02	11/9*
72	Missouri, Dwayne	DE	6-5	260	12/23/78	2	Northwestern	San Antonio, Texas	FA-'01	3/0
94	Myers, Michael	DE-DT	6-2	292	1/20/76	5	Alabama	Vicksburg, Miss.	D4-'98	16/16
59	Nguyen, Dat	LB	5-11	243	9/25/75	4	Texas A&M	Rockport, Texas	D3-'99	16/16
60	Nix, John	DT	6-1	326	11/24/76	2	Southern Mississippi	Lucedale, Miss.	D7b-'01	16/0
75	Noble, Brandon	DT	6-2	304	4/10/74	4	Penn State	Virginia Beach, Va.	FA-'99	16/16
77	Page, Solomon	T	6-5	321	2/27/76	4	West Virginia	Pittsburgh, Pa.	D2-'99	14/14
87	Rambo, Ken-Yon	WR	6-1	195	10/4/78	2	Ohio State	Cerritos, Calif.	FA-'01	13/0
88	Robinson, Jeff	TE	6-4	275	2/20/70	10	Idaho	Spokane, Wash.	UFA(StL)-'02	16/6*
21	Scott, Lynn	S	6-0	210	6/23/77	2	Northwestern Oklahoma	Turpin, Okla.	FA-'01	14/0
6	Seder, Tim	K	5-9	197	9/17/74	3	Ashland University	Ashland, Ohio	FA-'00	8/0
22	Smith, Emmitt	RB	5-9	216	5/15/69	13	Florida	Escambia, Fla.	D1-'90	14/14
55	Steele, Markus	LB	6-3	240	7/24/79	2	Southern California	New Bedford, Ohio	D4-'01	15/10
5	Stoerner, Clint	QB	6-2	210	12/29/77	3	Arkansas	Baytown, Texas	FA-'00	4/2
80	Swinton, Reggie	WR	6-0	175	7/24/75	2	Murray State	Little Rock, Ark.	FA-'01	15/1
44	Thomas, Robert	FB	6-1	273	12/1/74	5	Henderson State	Jacksonville, Ark.	FA-'98	5/5
30	Westbrook, Bryant	CB	6-0	198	12/19/74	6	Texas	Oceanside, Calif.	UFA(Det)-'02	10/3*
83	Whalen, James	TE	6-4	228	12/11/77	3	Kentucky	Portland, Ore.	FA-'00	0*
32	Wiley, Michael	RB	5-11	203	1/5/78	3	Ohio State	Spring Valley, Calif.	D5-'00	16/0
89	Williams, Randal	WR	6-3	214	5/21/78	2	New Hampshire	Bronx, N.Y.	W(Jax)-'01	7/0
28	Woodson, Darren	S	6-1	219	4/25/69	11	Arizona State	Phoenix, Ariz.	D2b-'92	16/16
2	Wright, Anthony	QB	6-1	207	2/14/76	4	South Carolina	Vanceboro, N.C.	FA-'00	4/3
18	Yamini, Bashir	WR	6-3	201	9/10/77	2	Iowa	Dolton, Ill.	FA-'01	0*
93	Zellner, Peppi	DE	6-5	262	3/14/75	4	Fort Valley State (Ga.)	Forsythe, Ga.	D4b-'99	16/15

* Blade missed '01 season because of injury; Collins was inactive for 16 games; Criss last active with Jacksonville in '00; Gibson played 6 games with Detroit and 1 with Dallas in '01; Glover played 16 games with New Orleans; Goodrich missed '01 season because of injury; Hardy played 9 games with Jacksonville; Jackson was inactive for 16 games; Johnson last active with Arizona in '99; Lucas missed '01 season because of injury; McGee played 11 games with Cincinnati; Robinson played 16 games with St. Louis; Westbrook played 10 games with Detroit; Whalen missed '01 season because of injury; Yamini missed '01 season because of injury.

Players lost through free agency (1): S Izell Reese (Den; 16 games in '01).

Also played with Cowboys in '01—DT Randy Chevrier (8 games), LB Darren Hambrick (5), TE Jackie Harris (13), K Jon Hilbert (8), TE J.J. Huggins (10), CB Kareem Larrimore (4), QB Ryan Leaf (4), WR Wane McGarity (3), TE Mike Solwold (8), C Mark Stepnoski (16), S George Teague (16), DE Dimitrius Underwood (4), FB Terry Witherspoon (3).

2002 FIRST-YEAR ROSTER

Name	Pos.	Ht.	Wt.	Birthdate	College	Hometown	How Acq.
Abram, Dashawn	CB	6-2	201	5/28/79	Wyoming	Columbus, Ohio	FA
Bryant, Antonio	WR	6-1	188	3/9/81	Pittsburgh	Miami, Fla.	D2b
Bryant, Darius	DT	6-1	287	1/21/79	North Carolina State	Suffolk, Va.	FA
Campbell, Khary	LB	6-1	230	4/4/79	Bowling Green	Toledo, Ohio	FA
Clemons, Sam	QB	6-1	207	10/10/78	Western Illinois	El Dorado Hills, Calif.	FA
Collins, Dan (1)	G	6-4	300	7/27/76	Boston College	Raynham, Mass.	FA
Copeland, Jeremaine (1)	WR	6-1	200	2/19/77	Tennessee	Harriman, Tenn.	FA
Cundiff, Billy	K	6-1	201	3/30/80	Drake	Harlan, Iowa	FA
Dantzler, Woodrow	RB	5-10	209	10/4/79	Clemson	Orangeburg, S.C.	FA
Davis, Keith	S	5-10	193	12/30/78	Sam Houston	Italy, Texas	FA
DeRonde, Kevin	DE	6-5	259	8/15/78	Iowa State	Pella, Iowa	FA
Filipovic, Filip	P	6-2	216	11/5/77	South Dakota	Howland, Ohio	FA
Flowers, Richmond (1)	WR	5-11	193	5/4/78	Tennessee-Chattanooga	Birmingham, Ala.	FA-'01
Gamble, Jason (1)	G	6-3	289	9/12/75	Clemson	Darby, Kan.	FA
Gurode, Andre	G-C	6-4	316	3/6/78	Colorado	Houston, Texas	D2a
Haywood, Ennis	RB	5-10	224	12/5/79	Iowa State	Dallas, Texas	FA
Hunter, Pete	CB	6-2	202	5/25/80	Virginia Union	Atlantic City, N.J.	D5
Hutchinson, Chad	QB	6-5	230	2/21/77	Stanford	Del Mar, Calif.	FA
Johnson, DeVeren	WR	6-4	211	9/21/78	Sacred Heart	San Diego, Calif.	D6b
Martin, Jamar	FB	5-11	244	4/12/80	Ohio State	Canton, Ohio	D4
Ortega, Travis (1)	S	6-2	220	5/11/77	Rice	Rockdale, Texas	FA
Ranek, Josh	RB	5-7	207	5/11/78	South Dakota State	Tyndall, S.D.	FA
Ross, Derek	CB	5-10	197	1/5/80	Ohio State	Rock Hill, S.C.	D3
Slaten, Joey	T	6-6	321	4/17/79	Southern Methodist	Seguin, Texas	FA
Slowikowski, Bob	TE	6-5	261	10/30/79	Virginia Tech	Pittsburgh, Pa.	D6c
Stewart, Daleroy (1)	DT	6-4	318	11/2/78	Southern Mississippi	Vero Beach, Fla.	D6-'01
Szaferski, Maciek	P	6-3	240	3/4/75	St. Francis	Warsaw, Poland	FA
Taylor, Tony (1)	RB	5-9	191	3/9/78	Northwestern Louisiana	Pineville, La.	FA-'01
Walter, Tyson	T	6-4	300	3/17/78	Ohio State	Bainbridge, Ohio	D6a
Weatherington, Colston (1)	DE	6-5	289	10/29/77	Central Missouri State	Graceville, Fla.	D7a-'01
Williams, Roy	S	6-0	219	8/14/80	Oklahoma	Union City, Calif.	D1
Zimmerman, Scott (1)	LB	6-0	235	4/29/77	Northern Colorado	Westminster, Colo.	FA-'01

The term NFL Rookie is defined as a player who is in his first season of professional football and has not been on the roster of another professional football team for any regular-season or postseason games. A Rookie is designated by an "R" on NFL rosters. Players who have been active in another professional football league or players who have NFL experience, including either preseason training camp or being on an Active List or Inactive List, or on Reserve/Injured or Reserve/Physically Unable to Perform for fewer than six regular-season games, are termed NFL First-Year Players. An NFL First-Year Player is designated by a "1" on NFL rosters. Thereafter, a player is credited with an additional year of experience for each season in which he accumulates six games on the Active List or Inactive List, or on Reserve/Injured or Reserve/Physically Unable to Perform.

COACHING STAFF
Head Coach,
Dave Campo

Pro Career: Dave Campo became the fifth head coach in Cowboys history on January 26, 2000, after eleven seasons as an assistant with the club. In his two seasons at the helm, the club posted a 10-22 record. Campo has participated in three Super Bowls, four NFC Championship Games, and won six division titles. He joined four NFL head coaches who have been a part of three or more Super Bowl titles in their coaching careers. That group includes Mike Shanahan, Bill Belichick, and Mike Holmgren. From 1995-99, Campo directed the Dallas defense. Prior to that, Campo served as the Cowboys' secondary coach (1991-94) and was a defensive assistant (1989-1990). Career record: 10-22.

Background: Campo was a defensive back at Central Connecticut State from 1967-1970 and twice earned All-East honors at shortstop. He began his coaching career at Central Connecticut State, coaching linebackers (1971-72). He then moved to Albany State (1973), Bridgeport (1974), Pittsburgh (1975), Washington State (1976), Boise State (1977-79), Oregon State (1980), Weber State (1981-82), Iowa State (1983), Syracuse (1984-86), and Miami (1987-88).

Personal: Born in New London, Conn., on July 18, 1947. Was a standout at Robert E. Fitch High School in Groton, Conn. Dave and his wife, Kay, have six children—Angie, Eric, Becky, Tommy, Shelbie, and Michael.

ASSISTANT COACHES

Joe Avezzano, special teams; born November 17, 1943, Yonkers, N.Y., lives in Irving, Texas. Guard Florida State 1961-65. Pro center Boston Patriots 1966. College coach: Florida State 1968, Iowa State 1969-1972, Pittsburgh 1973-76, Tennessee 1977-79, Oregon State 1980-84 (head coach), Texas 1985-88. Pro coach: Joined Cowboys in 1990.

Bill Bates, defensive nickel package-asst. special teams; born June 6, 1961, Knoxville, Tenn., lives in Plano, Texas. Defensive back Tennessee 1979-1982. Pro defensive back Dallas Cowboys 1983-1997. Pro coach: Joined Cowboys in 1998.

Wes Chandler, wide receivers; born August 22, 1956, New Smyrna Beach, Fla., lives in Grapevine, Tex. Wide receiver Florida 1974-77. Pro wide receiver New Orleans Saints 1978-1981, San Diego Chargers 1981-87, San Francisco 49ers 1988. College coach: Central Florida 1994-95. Pro coach: Orlando Thunder (NFL Europe) 1992, Rhein Fire (NFLE) 1995-97, Frankfurt Galaxy (NFLE) 1998, Berlin Thunder (NFLE) 1999 (head coach), joined Cowboys in 2000.

Bruce Coslet, offensive coordinator; born August 5, 1946, Oakdale, Calif., lives in Irving, Tex. Tight end Pacific 1965-67. Pro tight end Cincinnati Bengals 1969-1976. Pro coach: San Francisco 49ers 1980, Cincinnati Bengals 1981-89, 1994-2000 (head coach 1996-2000), New York Jets 1990-93 (head coach), joined Cowboys in 2002.

Gary Gibbs, linebackers; born August 13, 1952, Spring Branch, Tex., lives in Irving, Texas. Linebacker Oklahoma 1972-74. No pro playing experience. College coach: Oklahoma 1975-1994 (head coach 1989-1994), Georgia 2000, Louisiana State 2001. Pro coach: Joined Cowboys in 2002.

Galen Hall, running backs; born August 14, 1940, Altoona, Pa., lives in Irving, Tex. Quarterback Penn State 1958-1961. Pro quarterback Washington Redskins 1962, N.Y. Jets 1963. College coach: West Virginia 1964-65, Oklahoma 1966-1983, Florida (head coach) 1984-89. Pro coach: Orlando Thunder (World League) 1991-92 (head coach 1992), Charlotte Rage (Arena League) 1994 (head coach), Rhein Fire (NFLE) 1995-2000 (head coach), Orlando Rage (XFL) 2001 (head coach), joined Cowboys in 2002.

Steve Hoffman, kickers-quality control; born September 8, 1958, Camden, N.J., lives in Irving, Texas. Quarterback-running back-wide receiver Dickinson College 1979-1982. Pro punter Washington Federals (USFL) 1983. College coach: Miami 1985-87. Pro coach: Joined Cowboys in 1989.

Jim Jeffcoat, defensive ends; born April 1, 1961, Cliffwood, N.J., lives in Dallas. Defensive end Arizona State 1979-1982. Pro defensive end Dallas Cowboys 1983-1994, Buffalo Bills 1995-97. Pro coach: Joined Cowboys in 1998.

Joe Juraszek, strength and conditioning; born June 8, 1958, Chicago, lives in Coppell, Texas. Linebacker-defensive end New Mexico 1976-1980. No pro playing experience. College coach: Oklahoma 1981-86, 1993-96, Texas Tech 1987-1992. Pro coach: Joined Cowboys in 1997.

Andre Patterson, defensive tackles; born June 12, 1960, Camden, Ark., lives in Grapevine, Tex. Offensive lineman Contra Costa (Calif.) J.C. 1978-1980, Montana 1981. No pro playing experience. College coach: Montana 1982, Weber State 1988, Western Washington 1989, Cornell 1990, Washington State 1992-93, Cal Poly-San Luis Obispo 1994-96 (head coach). Pro coach: New England Patriots 1997, Minnesota Vikings 1998-99, joined Cowboys in 2000.

Clancy Pendergast, secondary; born November 29, 1967, Phoenix, lives in Plano, Texas. No college or pro playing experience. College coach: Mississippi State 1991, Southern California 1992, Oklahoma 1993-94. Pro coach: Houston

Oilers 1995, joined Cowboys in 1996.

Greg Seamon, tight ends-offensive quality control; born July 24, 1955, Bright, Ind., lives in Irving, Tex. Quarterback Franklin College 1973. No pro playing experience. College coach: Purdue 1981-82, Army 1983-84, Pacific 1985-86, Navy 1987-88, Akron 1991-94, Cincinnati 1995-98, Miami (Ohio) 1999-2000. Pro coach: Joined Cowboys in 2002.

Frank Verducci, offensive line; born March 17, 1957, Glen Ridge, N.J., lives in Irving, Tex. Tight end-fullback U.S. Merchant Marine Academy-Kings Point 1975. No pro playing experience. College coach: Colorado State 1980, Maryland 1981-83, Northern Illinois 1984, Iowa 1985-86, 1989-1998, Northwestern 1987-88. Pro coach: Cincinnati Bengals 1999-2001, joined Cowboys in 2002.

Wade Wilson, quarterbacks; born February 1, 1959, Commerce, Texas, lives in Coppell, Tex. Quarterback East Texas State 1977-1980. Pro quarterback Minnesota Vikings 1981-1991, Atlanta Falcons 1992, New Orleans Saints 1993-94, Dallas Cowboys 1995-97, Oakland Raiders 1998-99. Pro coach: Joined Cowboys in 2000.

Mike Zimmer, defensive coordinator; born June 5, 1956, Peoria, Ill., lives in Colleyville, Texas. Quarterback-linebacker Illinois State 1974-76. No pro playing experience. College coach: Missouri 1979-1980, Weber State 1981-88, Washington State 1989-1993. Pro coach: Joined Cowboys in 1994.

National Football Conference
North Division
Team Colors: Honolulu Blue and Silver
Detroit Lions Practice &
Training Facility
222 Republic Drive
Allen Park, Michigan 48101
Telephone: (313) 216-4000

2002 SCHEDULE
PRESEASON
Aug. 9   at Baltimore.........................8:00
Aug. 17   at Cleveland 8:00
Aug. 24   **Pittsburgh**.......................12:30
Aug. 29   **Buffalo**..............................8:00

REGULAR SEASON
Sept. 8   at Miami............................1:00
Sept. 15   at Carolina.........................1:00
Sept. 22   **Green Bay**........................4:15
Sept. 29   **New Orleans**....................1:00
Oct. 6   OPEN DATE
Oct. 13   at Minnesota 12:00
Oct. 20   **Chicago** 1:00
Oct. 27   at Buffalo 1:00
Nov. 3   **Dallas**................................1:00
Nov. 10   at Green Bay 12:00
Nov. 17   **New York Jets** 4:15
Nov. 24   at Chicago (Champaign, Ill.) 12:00
Nov. 28   **New England (Thurs.)**......12:30
Dec. 8   at Arizona...........................2:05
Dec. 15   **Tampa Bay**........................1:00
Dec. 22   at Atlanta............................1:00
Dec. 29   **Minnesota** 1:00

Stadium: Ford Field (opened in 2002)
        • **Capacity:** 65,000
        2001 St. Antoine
        Detroit, Michigan 48226
Playing Surface: FieldTurf
Training Camp: 222 Republic Drive
        Allen Park, Michigan
        48101

FORD FIELD

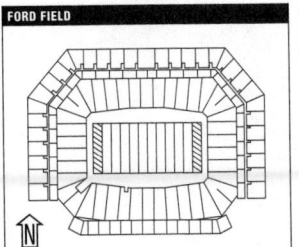

CLUB OFFICIALS
Chairman and Owner: William Clay Ford
Vice Chairman: William Clay Ford, Jr.
President and CEO: Matt Millen
Senior Vice President: Bill Keenist
Senior Vice President: Kevin Warren
Assistant to President/Finance & Special
  Projects: Kent Newhart
Vice President of Stadium Development
  and Salary Cap: Tom Lewand
Executive Director of Player Personnel:
  Bill Tobin
Vice President of Finance and Chief
  Financial Officer: Tom Lesnau
Vice President of Ticket
  Sales/Operations: Jennifer Manzo
Secretary: David Hempstead
Senior Director of Community Affairs:
  Tim Pendell
Director of Media Relations:
  Matt Barnhart
Senior Director of Football
  Administration/Staff Counsel:
  Martin Mayhew
Director of Pro Personnel: Sheldon White
Director of College Scouting:
  Russ Bolinger
Scouts: Dennis Gentry,
  Hessley Hempstead, Chad Henry,
  Scott McEwen, Lance Newmark,
  Charlie Sanders, Dave Uryus
Director of Broadcasting and New Media:
  Bryan Bender
Director of Ticket Operations:
  Mark Graham
Head Athletic Trainer: Al Bellamy
Equipment Manager: Mark Glenn
Video Director: Steve Hermans

COACHING HISTORY
Portsmouth Spartans 1930-33
(466-496-32)
1930	Hal (Tubby) Griffen	5-6-3
1931-36	George (Potsy) Clark	49-20-6
1937-38	Earl (Dutch) Clark	14-8-0
1939	Elmer (Gus) Henderson	6-5-0
1940	George (Potsy) Clark	5-5-1
1941-42	Bill Edwards*	4-9-1
1942	John Karcis	0-8-0
1943-47	Charles (Gus) Dorais	20-31-2
1948-1950	Alvin (Bo) McMillin	12-24-0
1951-56	Raymond (Buddy) Parker	50-24-2
1957-1964	George Wilson	55-45-6
1965-66	Harry Gilmer	10-16-2
1967-1972	Joe Schmidt	43-35-7
1973	Don McCafferty	6-7-1
1974-76	Rick Forzano**	15-17-0
1976-77	Tommy Hudspeth	11-13-0
1978-1984	Monte Clark	43-63-1
1985-88	Darryl Rogers***	18-40-0
1988-1996	Wayne Fontes	67-71-0
1997-2000	Bobby Ross****	27-32-0
2000	Gary Moeller	4-3-0
2001	Marty Mornhinweg	2-14-0

*Released after three games in 1942
**Resigned after four games in 1976
***Released after 11 games in 1988
****Resigned after nine games in 2000

ATTENDANCE
Home 601,821   Away 487,459
Total 1,089,280
Single-game home record,
80,444 (12/20/81)
Single-season home record, 644,904
(1980)

2002 DRAFT CHOICES
Round	Name	Pos.	College
1	Joey Harrington	QB	Oregon
2	Kalimba Edwards	DE	South Carolina
3	André Goodman	DB	South Carolina
4	John Taylor	DE	Montana State
5	John Owens	TE	Notre Dame
6	Chris Cash	DB	Southern California
7	Luke Staley	RB	Brigham Young
	Matt Murphy	TE	Maryland
	Victor Rogers	T	Colorado

DETROIT LIONS

2001 TEAM RECORD
PRESEASON (1-3)

Date	Result	Opponent
8/10	L 24-27	Cincinnati
8/18	W 27-26	at Indianapolis
8/25	L 7-20	at Pittsburgh
8/30	L 25-28	Tennessee

REGULAR SEASON (2-14)

Date	Result	Opponent	Att.
9/09	L 6-28	at Green Bay	59,523
9/23	L 14-24	at Cleveland	73,168
10/08	L 0-35	St. Louis	77,765
10/14	L 26-31	at Minnesota	64,048
10/21	L 24-27	Tennessee	76,940
10/28	L 27-31	Cincinnati	69,343
11/04	L 13-21	at San Francisco	67,605
11/11	L 17-20	Tampa Bay	74,268
11/18	L 38-45	at Arizona	32,322
11/22	L 27-29	Green Bay	77,730
12/02	L 10-13	at Chicago	66,944
12/09	L 12-15	at Tampa Bay	65,514
12/16	W 27-24	Minnesota	72,190
12/23	L 14-47	at Pittsburgh	62,809
12/30	L 0-24	Chicago	76,067
1/06	W 15-10	Dallas	77,512

SCORE BY PERIODS

Lions	47	79	67	77	0	— 270
Opponents	101	125	90	108	0	— 424

2001 TEAM STATISTICS

	Lions	Opp.
Total First Downs	289	321
Rushing	74	99
Passing	184	189
Penalty	31	33
3rd Down: Made/Att	76/222	87/210
3rd Down Pct.	34.2	41.4
4th Down: Made/Att	12/25	6/13
4th Down Pct.	48.0	46.2
Possession Avg.	28:34	31:26
Total Net Yards	4994	5521
Avg. Per Game	312.1	345.1
Total Plays	1026	1015
Avg. Per Play	4.9	5.4
Net Yards Rushing	1398	1993
Avg. Per Game	87.4	124.6
Total Rushes	351	470
Net Yards Passing	3596	3528
Avg. Per Game	224.8	220.5
Sacked/Yards Lost	66/373	31/224
Gross Yards	3969	3752
Att./Completions	609/343	514/312
Completion Pct.	56.3	60.7
Had Intercepted	24	16
Punts/Average	75/43.0	72/42.6
Net Punting Avg.	75/35.2	72/36.5
Penalties/Yards	116/1081	95/896
Fumbles/Ball Lost	24/14	19/6
Touchdowns	30	52
Rushing	8	15
Passing	18	30
Returns	4	7

2001 INDIVIDUAL STATISTICS

PASSING

PASSING	Att.	Comp.	Yds.	Pct.	TD	Int.	Tkld.	Rate
Batch	341	198	2392	58.1	12	12	33/176	76.8
Detmer	151	92	906	60.9	3	10	12/75	56.9
McMahon	115	53	671	46.1	3	1	21/122	69.9
Warren	2	0	0	0.0	0	1	0/0	0.0
Lions	609	343	3969	56.3	18	24	66/373	69.6
Opponents	514	312	3752	60.7	30	16	31/224	89.6

SCORING

SCORING	TD R	TD P	TD Rt	PAT	FG	Saf	PTS
Hanson	0	0	0	23/23	21/30	0	86
Sloan	0	7	0	0/0	0/0	0	42
Warren	3	1	0	0/0	0/0	0	26
Morton	0	4	0	0/0	0/0	0	24
Schlesinger	3	0	0	0/0	0/0	0	18
Crowell	0	2	0	0/0	0/0	0	12
Stewart	1	1	0	0/0	0/0	0	12
McMahon	1	0	0	0/0	0/0	0	8
Anderson	0	1	0	0/0	0/0	0	6
Bailey	0	0	1	0/0	0/0	0	6
Droughns	0	1	0	0/0	0/0	0	6
Fair	0	0	1	0/0	0/0	0	6
Hall	0	0	1	0/0	0/0	0	6
Howard	0	1	0	0/0	0/0	0	6
Lyght	0	0	1	0/0	0/0	0	6
Lions	8	18	4	23/23	21/30	0	270
Opponents	15	30	7	49/50	19/27	1	424

2-Pt. Conversions: McMahon, Warren.
Lions 2-7, Opponents 2-2.

RUSHING

RUSHING	Att.	Yds.	Avg.	LG	TD
Stewart	143	685	4.8	38	1
Warren	61	191	3.1	34	3
Schlesinger	47	154	3.3	26	3
McMahon	27	145	5.4	22	1
Droughns	30	72	2.4	15	0
Batch	12	45	3.8	12	0
Cason	11	31	2.8	19	0
Detmer	9	26	2.9	9	0
Howard	5	25	5.0	7	0
Crowell	1	6	6.0	6	0
Morton	1	6	6.0	6	0
Olivo	1	6	6.0	6	0
Foster	2	6	3.0	3	0
Jett	1	0	0.0	0	0
Lions	351	1398	4.0	38	8
Opponents	470	1993	4.2	96t	15

RECEIVING

RECEIVING	No.	Yds.	Avg.	LG	TD
Morton	77	1154	15.0	76	4
Schlesinger	60	466	7.8	38	0
Warren	40	336	8.4	36	1
Sloan	37	409	11.1	27	7
Stewart	23	242	10.5	56	1
Crowell	22	289	13.1	46t	2
Foster	22	283	12.9	36	0
Emanuel	17	221	13.0	29	0
Anderson	12	211	17.6	69	1
Howard	10	133	13.3	36t	1
Trejo	5	61	12.2	20	0
Mitchell	5	29	5.8	12	0
Moore	4	76	19.0	25	0
Cason	4	32	8.0	9	0
Droughns	4	21	5.3	8t	0
Waerig	1	6	6.0	6	0
Lions	343	3969	11.6	76	18
Opponents	312	3752	12.0	68t	30

INTERCEPTIONS

INTERCEPTIONS	No.	Yds.	Avg.	LG	TD
Lyght	4	72	18.0	59t	1
Bailey	2	74	37.0	74t	1
Fair	2	29	14.5	26t	1
Schulz	2	22	11.0	19	0
Claiborne	2	11	5.5	6	0
Rice	2	9	4.5	8	0
Carter	1	0	0.0	0	0
Westbrook	1	0	0.0	0	0
Lions	16	217	13.6	74t	3
Opponents	24	376	15.7	93t	3

PUNTING

PUNTING	No.	Yds.	Avg.	In 20	LG
Jett	58	2512	43.3	16	62
Araguz	17	713	41.9	6	55
Lions	75	3225	43.0	22	62
Opponents	72	3065	42.6	24	61

PUNT RETURNS

PUNT RETURNS	No.	FC	Yds.	Avg.	LG	TD
Howard	22	19	201	9.1	34	0
Fair	4	2	37	9.3	21	0
Foster	3	0	17	5.7	9	0
Lions	29	21	255	8.8	34	0
Opponents	39	16	387	9.9	84t	1

KICKOFF RETURNS

KICKOFF RETURNS	No.	Yds.	Avg.	LG	TD
Howard	57	1446	25.4	91	0
Fair	10	187	18.7	32	0
Foster	9	182	20.2	36	0
Morton	1	4	4.0	4	0
Olivo	1	40	40.0	40	0
Raiola	1	11	11.0	11	0
Schlesinger	1	10	10.0	10	0
Warren	0	-4	—	-4	0
Lions	80	1876	23.5	91	0
Opponents	53	1143	21.6	53	0

FIELD GOALS

FIELD GOALS	1-19	20-29	30-39	40-49	50+
Hanson	1/1	2/2	8/8	6/12	4/7
Lions	1/1	2/2	8/8	6/12	4/7
Opponents	0/1	2/2	11/13	5/10	1/1

SACKS

SACKS	No.
Porcher	11.0
Claiborne	4.0
Hall	4.0
S. Rogers	3.0
Scroggins	2.0
Aldridge	1.0
Boyd	1.0
Campbell	1.0
Green	1.0
Rice	1.0
Spellman	1.0
Lions	31.0
Opponents	66.0

RECORD HOLDERS
INDIVIDUAL RECORDS—CAREER

Category	Name	Performance
Rushing (Yds.)	Barry Sanders, 1989-1998	15,269
Passing (Yds.)	Bobby Layne, 1950-58	15,710
Passing (TDs)	Bobby Layne, 1950-58	118
Receiving (No.)	Herman Moore, 1991-2001	670
Receiving (Yds.)	Herman Moore, 1991-2001	9,174
Interceptions	Dick LeBeau, 1959-1972	62
Punting (Avg.)	Yale Lary, 1952-53, 1956-1964	44.3
Punt Return (Avg.)	Jack Christiansen, 1951-58	12.8
Kickoff Return (Avg.)	Pat Studstill, 1961-67	25.7
Field Goals	Eddie Murray, 1980-1991	243
Touchdowns (Tot.)	Barry Sanders, 1989-1998	109
Points	Eddie Murray, 1980-1991	1,113

INDIVIDUAL RECORDS—SINGLE SEASON

Category	Name	Performance
Rushing (Yds.)	Barry Sanders, 1997	2,053
Passing (Yds.)	Scott Mitchell, 1995	4,338
Passing (TDs)	Scott Mitchell, 1995	32
Receiving (No.)	Herman Moore, 1995	*123
Receiving (Yds.)	Herman Moore, 1995	1,686
Interceptions	Don Doll, 1950	12
	Jack Christiansen, 1953	12
Punting (Avg.)	Yale Lary, 1963	48.9
Punt Return (Avg.)	Jack Christiansen, 1952	21.5
Kickoff Return (Avg.)	Tom Watkins, 1965	34.4
Field Goals	Jason Hanson, 1993	34
Touchdowns (Tot.)	Barry Sanders, 1991	17
Points	Jason Hanson, 1995	132

INDIVIDUAL RECORDS—SINGLE GAME

Category	Name	Performance
Rushing (Yds.)	Barry Sanders, 11-13-94	237
Passing (Yds.)	Charlie Batch, 11-18-01	436
Passing (TDs)	Gary Danielson, 12-9-78	5
Receiving (No.)	Herman Moore, 12-4-95	14
Receiving (Yds.)	Cloyce Box, 12-3-50	302
Interceptions	Don Doll, 10-23-49	*4
Field Goals	Garo Yepremian, 11-13-66	6
	Jason Hanson, 10-17-99	6
Touchdowns (Tot.)	Dutch Clark, 10-22-34	4
	Cloyce Box, 12-3-50	4
	Barry Sanders, 11-24-91	4
Points	Dutch Clark, 10-22-34	24
	Cloyce Box, 12-3-50	24
	Barry Sanders, 11-24-91	24

*NFL Record

2002 VETERAN ROSTER

No.	Name	Pos.	Ht.	Wt.	Birthdate	NFL Exp.	College	Hometown	How Acq.	'01 Games/ Starts
88	Anderson, Scotty	WR	6-2	184	11/24/79	2	Grambling State	Jonesboro, La.	D5a-'01	9/4
76	Backus, Jeff	T	6-5	308	9/21/77	2	Michigan	Norcross, Ga.	D1-'01	16/16
89	Banta, Bradford	TE	6-6	255	12/14/70	9	Southern California	Baton Rouge, La.	UFA(NYJ)-'01	16/0
79	Beverly, Eric	C	6-3	294	3/28/74	5	Miami (Ohio)	Bedford Heights, Ohio	FA-'97	16/16
65	Blaise, Kerlin	G	6-5	323	12/25/74	5	Miami	Orlando, Fla.	FA-'98	7/0
39	Campbell, Lamar	S	5-11	183	8/29/76	5	Wisconsin	Chester, Pa.	FA-'98	12/12
31	Cason, Aveion	RB	5-10	210	7/12/79	2	Illinois State	St. Petersburg, Fla.	FA-'01	6/0
50	Claiborne, Chris	LB	6-3	255	7/26/78	4	Southern California	Riverside, Calif.	D1a-'99	16/16
82	Crowell, Germane	WR	6-3	216	9/13/76	5	Virginia	Winston Salem, N.C.	D2a-'98	5/4
14	Detmer, Ty	QB	6-0	194	10/30/67	11	Brigham Young	San Antonio, Texas	T(Cle)-'01	4/3
95 †	DeVries, Jared	DE	6-4	280	6/11/76	4	Iowa	Aplington, Iowa	D3-'99	11/0
12	Dreisbach, Scott	QB	6-3	210	12/16/75	4	Michigan	Mishawaka, Ind.	FA-'01	0*
94	Elliss, Luther	DT	6-5	305	3/22/73	8	Utah	Mancos, Colo.	D1-'95	14/13
83 #	Emanuel, Bert	WR	5-10	185	10/26/70	9	Rice	Houston, Texas	FA-'01	6/4
23	Fair, Terry	CB	5-9	184	7/20/76	5	Tennessee	Phoenix, Ariz.	D1-'98	12/12
87	Foster, Larry	WR	5-10	196	11/7/76	3	Louisiana State	Harvey, La.	FA-'00	13/5
59	Gooch, Jeff	LB	5-11	225	10/31/74	7	Austin Peay	Nashville, Tenn.	FA-'02	13/0*
54	Green, Barrett	LB	6-0	232	10/29/77	3	West Virginia	West Palm Beach, Fla.	D2-'00	14/10
81	Hakim, Az-Zahir	WR	5-10	178	6/3/77	5	San Diego State	Los Angeles, Calif.	UFA(StL)-'02	16/2*
96	Hall, James	DE	6-2	271	2/4/77	3	Michigan	New Orleans, La.	FA-'00	16/0
4	Hanson, Jason	K	5-11	182	6/17/70	11	Washington State	Spokane, Wash.	D2b-'92	16/0
25	Harris, Corey	S	5-11	200	10/25/69	11	Vanderbilt	Indianapolis, Ind.	FA-'02	0*
64	Hopson, Tyrone	G	6-2	305	5/28/76	3	Eastern Kentucky	Owensboro, Ky.	FA-'01	0*
80	Howard, Desmond	WR	5-10	185	5/15/70	11	Michigan	Cleveland, Ohio	FA-'99	14/1
40	Iwuoma, Chidi	CB	5-8	180	2/19/78	2	California	Pasadena, Calif.	FA-'01	14/1
19	Jett, John	P	6-0	197	11/11/68	10	East Carolina	Reedville, Va.	UFA(Dall)-'97	13/0
75	Joyce, Matt	T	6-7	305	3/30/72	8	Richmond	Scottsdale, Ariz.	FA-'01	16/12
67	Kirschke, Travis	DT	6-3	287	9/6/74	6	UCLA	Yorba Linda, Calif.	FA-'97	16/2
58	Kriewaldt, Clint	LB	6-1	236	3/16/76	4	Wisconsin-Stevens Point	Shiocton, Wis.	D6-'99	14/1
24	Lyght, Todd	CB	6-0	190	2/9/69	12	Notre Dame	Flint, Mich.	UFA(StL)-'01	16/16
73	McDougle, Stockar	G	6-6	350	1/11/77	3	Oklahoma	Deerfield Beach, Fla.	D1-'00	9/3
8	McMahon, Mike	QB	6-2	213	2/8/79	2	Rutgers	Wexford, Pa.	D5b-'01	8/3
26	Olivo, Brock	FB	6-0	232	6/24/76	5	Missouri	Washington, Mo.	FA-'98	16/0
91	Porcher, Robert	DE	6-3	282	7/30/69	11	South Carolina State	Wando, S.C.	D1-'92	16/16
93	Pritchett, Kelvin	DT	6-3	319	10/24/69	12	Mississippi	Atlanta, Ga.	UFA(Jax)-'99	16/1
51	Raiola, Dominic	C	6-1	303	12/30/78	2	Nebraska	Honolulu, Hawaii	D2a-'01	16/0
86	Ricks, Mikhael	TE	6-5	237	11/14/74	5	Stephen F. Austin	Anahuac, Texas	UFA(KC)-'02	16/0*
92	Rogers, Shaun	DT	6-4	331	3/12/79	2	Texas	La Porte, Texas	D2b-'01	16/16
59 #	Samuel, Khari	LB	6-3	240	10/14/76	4	Massachusetts	Framingham, Mass.	FA-'01	9/0
30	Schlesinger, Cory	FB	6-0	246	6/23/72	8	Nebraska	Duncan, Neb.	D6b-'95	16/13
84	Schroeder, Bill	WR	6-3	205	1/9/71	8	Wisconsin-La Crosse	Sheboygan, Wis.	UFA(GB)-'02	14/14*
62	Semple, Tony	G	6-5	303	12/20/70	9	Memphis	Lincoln, Ill.	D5-'94	15/12
66	Stai, Brenden	G	6-4	312	3/30/72	8	Nebraska	Yorba Linda, Calif.	FA-'01	16/16
34	Stewart, James	RB	6-1	226	12/27/71	8	Tennessee	Morristown, Tenn.	UFA(Jax)-'00	11/10
36	Trejo, Stephen	FB	6-2	258	11/20/77	2	Arizona State	Casa Grande, Ariz.	FA-'01	14/0
46	Waerig, John	TE	6-2	264	4/8/76	2	Maryland	Philadelphia, Pa.	FA-'01	1/0
28	Walker, Bracy	S	6-0	206	10/28/70	9	North Carolina	Fayetteville, N.C.	FA-'02	15/0*
45	Walker, Brian	S	6-0	206	5/31/72	8	Washington State	Widefield, Colo.	FA-'02	13/13*
25	Warren, Lamont	RB	5-11	202	1/4/73	8	Colorado	Los Angeles, Calif.	FA-'01	16/3
99	Williams, Brian	LB	6-1	257	12/17/72	8	Southern California	Dallas, Texas	W(NO)-'01	2/1
27	Wyrick, Jimmy	CB	5-9	179	12/31/76	3	Minnesota	De Soto, Texas	FA-'00	16/0

* Dreisbach inactive for 2 games; Gooch played 13 games with Tampa Bay in '01; Hakim played 16 games with St. Louis; Harris played 16 games with Baltimore; Hopson inactive for 3 games; Ricks played 16 games with Kansas City; Schroeder played 14 games with Green Bay; Bracy Walker played 15 games with Kansas City; Brian Walker played 13 games with Miami.

† Restricted free agent; subject to developments.

Unrestricted free agent; subject to developments.

Retired—Robert Bailey, 11-year cornerback, 9 games in '01; Stephen Boyd 7-year linebacker, 4 games; Tracy Scroggins, 10-year defensive end, 16 games.

Players lost through free agency (3): LB Allen Aldridge (Hou; 16 games in '01), TE David Sloan (NO; 15), CB Bryant Westbrook (Dall; 10).

Also played with the Lions in '01—P Leo Araguz (3), QB Charlie Batch (10), S Tommy Bennett (8), S Marty Carter (9), RB Reuben Droughns (9), LB Scott Kowalkowski (15), CB Ray McElroy (4), TE Pete Mitchell (5), WR Herman Moore (4), WR Johnnie Morton (16), DE Alonzo Spellman (5).

2002 FIRST-YEAR ROSTER

Name	Pos.	Ht.	Wt.	Birthdate	College	Hometown	How Acq.
Brown, Pierre	WR	6-0	190	7/19/79	Wayne State	West Bloomfield, Mich.	FA
Cash, Chris	CB	5-11	170	7/13/80	Southern California	Stockton, Calif.	D6
Cason, Aveion (1)	RB	5-10	210	7/12/79	Illinois State	St. Petersburg, Fla.	FA
Chapman, Robert	LB	6-3	240	1/19/79	Southern	Houma, La.	FA
Clemons, Crance	CB	5-9	175	12/20/79	Texas-El Paso	Pearland, Texas	FA
Collins, Mike	DT	6-3	310	1/19/78	Ohio State	Columbus, Ohio	FA
Drummond, Eddie	WR	5-9	185	4/12/80	Penn State	Pittsburgh, Pa.	FA
Edmonds, Aaron	P	6-1	193	6/23/77	Brigham Young	Provo, Utah	FA
Edwards, Kalimba	DE	6-5	264	12/26/79	South Carolina	Atlanta, Ga.	D2
Goodman, André	CB	5-10	182	8/8/78	South Carolina	Greenville, S.C.	D3
Glantzis, Chris	DE	6-4	259	12/9/78	Bowling Green	Mentor, Ohio	FA
Grim, Latef (1)	WR	6-0	188	9/26/78	Pittsburgh	Stockton, Calif.	FA
Harrington, Joey	QB	6-4	220	10/21/78	Oregon	Portland, Ore.	D1
Herron, Anthony (1)	DE	6-3	280	9/24/79	Iowa	Bolingbrook, Ill.	FA
Howard, Abdual	S	6-0	210	1/27/79	Florida State	Quincy, Fla.	FA
Howard, Marcel	T	6-6	320	10/25/78	Iowa State	Davenport, Iowa	FA
Jackson, Ken	DT	6-1	308	9/14/77	Mississippi	Oxford, Miss.	FA
Kroeker, Dustin (1)	T	6-5	290	10/4/78	Cal Poly-San Luis Obispo	Shafter, Calif.	FA
Lake, Antwan	DE	6-4	285	7/10/79	West Virginia	Seaforo, Del.	FA
Lovelady, Josh (1)	G	6-3	330	1/28/78	Houston	Midfield, Texas	FA
McCall, James	T	6-4	319	8/28/79	Hampton	Southfield, Mich.	FA
Mitchell, Labrone	WR	6-2	205	9/19/77	Georgia	Marietta, Ga.	FA
Mungro, James	RB	5-9	214	2/13/78	Syracuse	Syracuse, N.Y.	FA
Murphy, Chaz (1)	LB	6-3	237	3/30/77	Kansas	Galveston, Texas	FA
Murphy, Matt	TE	6-5	253	2/23/80	Maryland	New Haven, Mich.	D7b
Owens, John	TE	6-3	266	1/10/80	Notre Dame	Washington, D.C.	D5
Pavich, Dave	K	6-1	175	10/21/78	Kent	Kent, Ohio	FA
Philpot, Ken	LB	6-1	248	9/18/79	Eastern Michigan	Chicago, Ill.	FA
Rogers, Victor	T	6-6	331	10/10/78	Colorado	Federal Way, Wash.	D7c
Rogers, Wayne (1)	LB	6-1	232	2/10/78	Houston	Waco, Texas	FA
Ryan, Kris	FB	6-0	235	11/20/79	Pennsylvania	Pittsburgh, Pa.	FA
Staley, Luke	RB	6-1	227	9/16/80	Brigham Young	Tualatin, Ore.	D7a
Taylor, John	DE	6-3	260	8/29/79	Montana State	Denver, Colo.	D4
Thornhill, Josh	LB	6-2	243	1/19/80	Michigan State	Lansing, Mich.	FA
Waerig, John (1)	TE	6-2	264	4/8/76	Maryland	Philadelphia, Pa.	FA

The term NFL Rookie is defined as a player who is in his first season of professional football and has not been on the roster of another professional football team for any regular-season or postseason games. A Rookie is designated by an "R" on NFL rosters. Players who have been active in another professional football league or players who have NFL experience, including either preseason training camp or being on an Active List or Inactive List, or on Reserve/Injured or Reserve/Physically Unable to Perform for fewer than six regular-season games, are termed NFL First-Year Players. An NFL First-Year Player is designated by a "1" on NFL rosters. Thereafter, a player is credited with an additional year of experience for each season in which he accumulates six games on the Active List or Inactive List, or on Reserve/Injured or Reserve/Physically Unable to Perform.

COACHING STAFF

Head Coach,
Marty Mornhinweg

Pro Career: Named Lions' twenty-first head coach January 25, 2001. Joined the Lions after spending four years as offensive coordinator for San Francisco 49ers (1997-2000). The 49ers' offense was ranked fourth overall in 2000, accumulating 6,040 total yards, and they led the NFL in rushing two consecutive seasons (1998-99), including a team record 2,544 yards in 1998. Mornhinweg began his pro coaching career with the Green Bay Packers (1995-96). He was the Packers' offensive assistant-quality control coach in 1995 and was the team's quarterbacks coach in 1996 when the team went on to win Super Bowl XXXI. Played quarterback briefly for the Denver Dynamite (Arena Football League) in 1986. Career record: 2-14.

Background: Played quarterback for Montana (1981-84) where he was the school's starter four consecutive seasons and established 15 school passing records. Began coaching career at Montana in 1985. Moved on as an assistant to Texas-El Paso (1986-87), Northern Arizona (1988), Southeast Missouri State (1989-1990), Missouri (1991-93), and Northern Arizona (1994).

Personal: Born March 29, 1962 in Edmond, Okla. Marty and wife, Lindsay, have four children—Madison, Molly Lynn, Skyler, and Bobby Cade—and live in Plymouth, Michigan.

ASSISTANT COACHES

Jason Arapoff, strength and conditioning; born July, 8 1965, Weymouth, Mass., lives in Plymouth, Mich. Defensive back Springfield College 1985-88. No pro playing experience. Pro coach: Washington Redskins 1992-2000, joined Lions in 2001.

Malcolm Blacken, asst. strength and conditioning; born October 12, 1965, Richmond, Va., lives in Troy, Mich. Running back Virginia Tech 1984-88. No pro playing experience. College coach: South Carolina 1990-91, George Mason 1992-95, Virginia 1995. Pro coach: Washington Redskins 1996-2000, joined Lions in 2001.

Maurice Carthon, offensive coordinator; born April 24, 1961, Chicago, lives in Detroit. Running back Arkansas State 1979-1982. Pro running back New Jersey Generals (USFL) 1983-85, New York Giants 1985-1991, Indianapolis Colts 1992. Pro coach: New England Patriots 1994-96, New York Jets 1997-2000, joined Lions in 2001.

Don Clemons, defensive assistant-quality control; born February 15, 1954, Newark, N.J., lives in Rochester, Mich. Defensive end Muhlenberg (Pa.) 1973-76. No pro playing experience. College coach: Kutztown State 1977-78, New Mexico

1979, Arizona State 1980-84. Pro coach: Joined Lions in 1985.

Charles Haley, defensive line; born January 6, 1964, Gladys, Va., lives in Auburn Hills, Mich. Defensive end James Madison 1982-85. Pro defensive end San Francisco 49ers 1986-1991, 1998-99, Dallas Cowboys 1992-96. Pro coach: San Francisco 49ers 2000, joined Lions in 2001.

Kevin Higgins, quarterbacks; born December 1, 1955, New York, N.Y., lives in Northville, Mich. Defensive back West Chester (Pa.) 1973-76. No pro playing experience. College coach: Gettysburg College 1981-84, Richmond 1985-87, Lehigh 1988-2000 (head coach 1994-2000). Pro coach: Joined Lions in 2001.

Ray Horton, secondary; born April 12, 1960, Tacoma, Wash., lives in Allen Park, Mich. Defensive back Washington 1979-1982. Pro defensive back Cincinnati Bengals 1983-88, Dallas Cowboys 1989-1992. Pro coach: Washington Redskins 1994-96, Cincinnati Bengals 1997-2001, joined Lions in 2002.

Larry Kirksey, wide receivers; born January 6, 1951, Harlan, Ky., lives in Farmington Hills, Mich. Wide receiver Eastern Kentucky 1969-1972. No pro playing experience. College coach: Miami (Ohio) 1974-76, Kentucky 1977-1981, Kansas 1982, Kentucky State 1983 (head coach), Florida 1984-88, Pittsburgh 1989, Alabama 1990-93, Texas A&M 2000. Pro coach: San Francisco 49ers 1994-99, joined Lions in 2001.

Sean Kugler, tight ends; born August 9, 1966, Lockport, N.Y., lives in Waterford, Mich. Offensive lineman Texas-El Paso 1985-88. Pro offensive lineman Sacramento Surge (WLAF) 1991. College coach: Texas-El Paso 1993-2000. Pro coach: Joined Lions in 2001.

Sherman Lewis, special assistant-offense; born June 29, 1942, Louisville, Ky., lives in Novi, Mich. Running back Michigan State 1960-63. Pro running back Toronto Argonauts (CFL) 1964-65, New York Jets 1966. College coach: Michigan State 1969-1982. Pro coach: San Francisco 49ers 1983-1991, Green Bay Packers 1992-99, Minnesota Vikings 2000-01, joined Lions in 2002.

John Marshall, asst. defensive; born October 2, 1945, Arroyo Grande, Calif., lives in Commerce, Mich. Linebacker Washington State 1964. No pro playing experience. College coach: Oregon 1970-76, Southern California 1977-79. Pro coach: Green Bay Packers 1980-82, Atlanta Falcons 1983-85, Indianapolis Colts 1986-88, San Francisco 49ers 1989-1998, Carolina Panthers 1999-2001, joined Lions in 2002.

Carl Mauck, offensive line; born July 7, 1947, McLeansboro, Ill., lives in Plymouth, Mich. Linebacker-center Southern Illinois 1966-68. Pro center Baltimore Colts 1969, Miami Dolphins

1970, San Diego Chargers 1971-72, Houston Oilers 1975-1981. Pro coach: New Orleans Saints 1982-85, Kansas City Chiefs 1986-88, Tampa Bay Buccaneers 1991, San Diego Chargers 1992-95, Arizona Cardinals 1996-97, Buffalo Bills 1998-2000, joined Lions in 2001.

Mike McHugh, offensive assistant-quality control; born December 12, 1957, Pottston, Pa., lives in Plymouth, Mich. Attended Findlay. No college or playing experience. College coach: Eastern Michigan 1989-1992, Missouri 1993-98, Oregon 1999-2000. Pro coach: Joined Lions in 2001.

Glenn Pires, linebackers; born September 13, 1958, New Bedford, Mass., lives in Novi, Mich. Offensive line Springfield College 1976-79. No pro playing experience. College coach: Syracuse 1983-84, 1989-1994, Dartmouth 1985-88, Michigan State 1995. Pro coach: Arizona Cardinals 1996-2000, joined Lions in 2001.

Chuck Preifer, special teams; born July 26, 1944, Cleveland, lives in Farmington, Mich. Attended John Carroll. No college or pro playing experience. College coach: Miami (Ohio) 1977, North Carolina 1978-1983, Kent State 1986, Georgia Tech 1987-1991. Pro coach: Green Bay Packers 1984-85, San Diego Chargers 1992-96, joined Lions in 1997.

Kurt Schottenheimer, defensive coordinator; born October 1, 1949, in McDonald, Pa., lives in Detroit. Defensive back Miami 1969-1970. No pro playing experience. College coach: William Paterson 1974, Michigan State 1978-1982, Tulane 1983, Louisiana State 1984-85, Notre Dame 1986. Pro coach: Cleveland Browns 1987-88, Kansas City Chiefs 1989-2000, Washington Redskins 2001, joined Lions in 2002.

Richard Selcer, defensive nickel; born August 22, 1937, Cincinnati, lives in Dearborn, Mich. Running back Notre Dame 1955-59. No pro playing experience. College coach: Xavier 1962-64, 1970-71 (head coach 1970-71), Cincinnati 1965-66, Brown 1967-69, Wisconsin 1972-74, Kansas State 1975-77, Southwestern Louisiana 1978-1980. Pro coach: Houston Oilers 1981-83, Cincinnati Bengals 1984-1991, Los Angeles/St. Louis Rams 1992-96, joined Lions in 1997.

National Football Conference
North Division
Team Colors: Dark Green, Gold, and White
1265 Lombardi Avenue
Green Bay, Wisconsin 54304
Telephone: (920) 496-5700

2002 SCHEDULE
PRESEASON
Aug. 10	at Philadelphia	7:30
Aug. 17	at Arizona	7:00
Aug. 26	**Cleveland**	7:00
Aug. 30	**Tennessee**	7:00

REGULAR SEASON
Sept. 8	**Atlanta**	12:00
Sept. 15	at New Orleans	12:00
Sept. 22	at Detroit	4:15
Sept. 29	**Carolina**	12:00
Oct. 7	at Chicago (Champaign,Ill.)(Mon.)	8:00
Oct. 13	at New England	1:00
Oct. 20	**Washington**	3:15
Oct. 27	OPEN DATE	
Nov. 4	**Miami (Mon.)**	8:00
Nov. 10	**Detroit**	12:00
Nov. 17	at Minnesota	12:00
Nov. 24	at Tampa Bay	1:00
Dec. 1	**Chicago**	12:00
Dec. 8	**Minnesota**	7:30
Dec. 15	at San Francisco	1:15
Dec. 22	**Buffalo**	12:00
Dec. 29	at New York Jets	4:15

Stadium: Lambeau Field (opened in 1957)
  •Capacity: 62,500
  1265 Lombardi Avenue
  Green Bay, Wisconsin 54304
Playing Surface: Grass
Training Camp: St. Norbert College
  De Pere, Wisconsin 54115

LAMBEAU FIELD

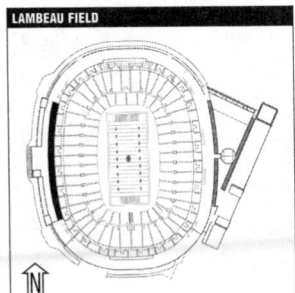

CLUB OFFICIALS
President and CEO: Bob Harlan
Vice President: John Fabry
Secretary: Peter Platten
Treasurer: John Underwood
Exec. V.P./General Manager/Head Coach:
  Mike Sherman
Executive Vice President and Chief
  Operating Officer: John Jones
Vice President of Football Operations:
  Mark Hatley
Vice President of Player Finance/General
  Counsel: Andrew Brandt
Director of College Scouting:
  John Dorsey
Director of Pro Personnel:
  Reggie McKenzie
Personnel Analyst to General Manager:
  John Schneider
Assistant to General Manager/Director of
  Football Administration:
  Bruce Warwick
Consultant: Ron Wolf
Exec. Director of Public Relations:
  Lee Remmel
Associate Director of Public Relations:
  Jeff Blumb
Assistant Director of Public Relations/
  Travel Coordinator: Aaron Popkey
Public Relations Assistants:
  Zak Gilbert, Sarah Koenig
Director of Player Development:
  Edgar Bennett
Director of Family Programs:
  Sherry Schuldes
Manager of Community Relations:
  TBA
Ticket Director: Mark Wagner
Director of Corporate Sponsorships:
  Craig Benzel
Director of Premium Guest Services:
  Jennifer Ark
Director of Special Events:
  Dee Geurts-Bengtson
Director of Administrative Affairs:
  Mark Schiefelbein
Director of Finance:
  Vicki Vannieuwenhoven
Director of Accounting: Duke Copp
Director of Computer Services:
  Wayne Wichlacz
Corporate Security Officer: Jerry Parins
Corporate Counsel: Jason Wied
Assistant Director of Pro Personnel:
  Sean Howard
Pro Personnel Assistant: Marc Lillibridge
Assistant Director of College Scouting:
  Shaun Herock
College Scouts: Lee Gissendaner,
  Brian Gutekunst, Alonzo Highsmith,
  Lenny McGill, Sam Seale, Red Cochran
Scouting Coordinator: Danny Mock
Director of Research and Development:
  Mike Eayrs
Video Director: Bob Eckberg
Head Trainer: Pepper Burruss
Equipment Manager: Gordon (Red) Batty
Stadium Manager: Ted Eisenreich

COACHING HISTORY
(603-475-36)
1921-1949	Earl (Curly) Lambeau	.212-106-21
1950-53	Gene Ronzani*	14-31-1
1953	Hugh Devore-	
	Ray (Scooter) McLean**	0-2-0
1954-57	Lisle Blackbourn	17-31-0
1958	Ray (Scooter) McLean	1-10-1
1959-1967	Vince Lombardi	98-30-4
1968-1970	Phil Bengtson	20-21-1
1971-74	Dan Devine	25-28-4
1975-1983	Bart Starr	53-77-3
1984-87	Forrest Gregg	25-37-1
1988-1991	Lindy Infante	24-40-0
1992-98	Mike Holmgren	84-42-0
1999	Ray Rhodes	8-8-0
2000-01	Mike Sherman	22-12-0

  *Resigned after 10 games in 1953
**Co-coaches

ATTENDANCE
Home 478,433   Away 554,849
Total 1,033,282
Single-game home record,
60,766 (9/1/97)
Single-season home record, 482,988
(1996)

2002 DRAFT CHOICES
Round	Name	Pos.	College
1	Javon Walker	WR	Florida State
3	Marques Anderson	DB	UCLA
4	Najeh Davenport	RB	Miami
5	Aaron Kampman	DE	Iowa
	Craig Nall	QB	Northwestern St., La.
6	Mike Houghton	G	San Diego State

2001 TEAM RECORD
PRESEASON (2-2)

Date	Result	Opponent
8/11	L 3-10	at Cleveland
8/20	W 22-7	Denver
8/25	W 17-12	Miami
8/31	L 13-24	at Oakland

REGULAR SEASON (12-4)

Date	Result	Opponent	Att.
9/09	W 28-6	Detroit	59,523
9/24	W 37-0	Washington	59,771
9/30	W 28-7	at Carolina	73,120
10/07	L 10-14	at Tampa Bay	65,510
10/14	W 31-23	Baltimore	59,866
10/21	L 13-35	at Minnesota	64,165
11/04	W 21-20	Tampa Bay	59,861
11/11	W 20-12	at Chicago	66,944
11/18	L 20-23	Atlanta	59,849
11/22	W 29-27	at Detroit	77,730
12/03	W 28-21	at Jacksonville	66,908
12/09	W 17-7	Chicago	59,869
12/16	L 20-26	at Tennessee	68,804
12/23	W 30-7	Cleveland	59,824
12/30	W 24-13	Minnesota	59,870
1/06	W 34-25	at New York Giants	78,601

POSTSEASON (1-1)

1/13	W 25-15	San Francisco	59,825
1/20	L 17-45	at St. Louis	66,338

SCORE BY PERIODS

Packers	89	90	111	100	0	—	390
Opponents	37	106	34	89	0	—	266

2001 TEAM STATISTICS

	Packers	Opp.
Total First Downs	282	278
Rushing	72	83
Passing	187	176
Penalty	23	19
3rd Down: Made/Att	72/197	93/238
3rd Down Pct.	36.5	39.1
4th Down: Made/Att	3/6	9/22
4th Down Pct.	50.0	40.9
Possession Avg.	29:32	30:28
Total Net Yards	5463	4937
Avg. Per Game	341.4	308.6
Total Plays	942	1041
Avg. Per Play	5.8	4.7
Net Yards Rushing	1693	1769
Avg. Per Game	105.8	110.6
Total Rushes	410	406
Net Yards Passing	3770	3168
Avg. Per Game	235.6	198.0
Sacked/Yards Lost	22/151	52/337
Gross Yards	3921	3505
Att./Completions	510/314	583/341
Completion Pct.	61.6	58.5
Had Intercepted	15	20
Punts/Average	82/42.5	86/42.4
Net Punting Avg.	82/36.5	86/37.4
Penalties/Yards	80/633	104/921
Fumbles/Ball Lost	28/12	36/19
Touchdowns	47	28
Rushing	11	10
Passing	32	14
Returns	4	4

2001 INDIVIDUAL STATISTICS

PASSING	Att.	Comp.	Yds.	Pct.	TD	Int.	Tkld.	Rate
Favre	510	314	3921	61.6	32	15	22/151	94.1
Packers	510	314	3921	61.6	32	15	22/151	94.1
Opponents	583	341	3505	58.5	14	20	52/337	69.6

SCORING	TD R	TD P	TD Rt	PAT	FG	Saf	PTS
Longwell	0	0	0	44/45	20/31	0	104
Green	9	2	0	0/0	0/0	0	66
Franks	0	9	0	0/0	0/0	0	54
Schroeder	0	9	0	0/0	0/0	0	54
Freeman	0	6	0	0/0	0/0	0	38
Bradford	0	2	0	0/0	0/0	0	12
Driver	1	1	0	0/0	0/0	0	12
Favre	1	0	0	0/0	0/0	0	6
Lee	0	1	0	0/0	0/0	0	6
Levens	0	1	0	0/0	0/0	0	6
Martin	0	1	0	0/0	0/0	0	6
McKenzie	0	0	1	0/0	0/0	0	6
Mealey	0	0	1	0/0	0/0	0	6
Rossum	0	0	1	0/0	0/0	0	6
T. Williams	0	0	1	0/0	0/0	0	6
Thierry	0	0	0	0/0	0/0	1	2
Packers	11	32	4	44/45	20/31	1	390
Opponents	10	14	4	20/20	22/28	1	266

2-Pt. Conversions: A. Freeman.
Packers 1-2, Opponents 5-8.

RUSHING	Att.	Yds.	Avg.	LG	TD
Green	304	1387	4.6	83t	9
Levens	44	165	3.8	40	0
Favre	38	56	1.5	14	1
Driver	3	38	12.7	31t	1
Mealey	11	37	3.4	9	0
Henderson	6	11	1.8	4	0
Schroeder	1	6	6.0	6	0
Goodman	1	-1	-1.0	-1	0
Pederson	1	-1	-1.0	-1	0
Freeman	1	-5	-5.0	-5	0
Packers	410	1693	4.1	83t	11
Opponents	406	1769	4.4	61	10

RECEIVING	No.	Yds.	Avg.	LG	TD
Green	62	594	9.6	42	2
Schroeder	53	918	17.3	67t	9
Freeman	52	818	15.7	63	6
Franks	36	322	8.9	31	9
Bradford	31	526	17.0	56	2
Levens	24	159	6.6	19	1
Henderson	21	193	9.2	26	0
Driver	13	167	12.8	37	1
Martin	13	144	11.1	31	1
Lee	3	32	10.7	23	1
T. Davis	3	14	4.7	7	0
Mealey	2	31	15.5	19	0
Collins	1	3	3.0	3	0
Packers	314	3921	12.5	67t	32
Opponents	341	3505	10.3	47t	14

INTERCEPTIONS	No.	Yds.	Avg.	LG	TD
Sharper	6	78	13.0	23	0
T. Williams	4	117	29.3	69t	1
Wayne	3	55	18.3	35	0
McKenzie	2	38	19.0	38t	1
Jue	2	35	17.5	35	0
Harris	2	12	6.0	8	0
Thibodeaux	1	9	9.0	9	0
Packers	20	344	17.2	69t	2
Opponents	15	252	16.8	98t	2

PUNTING	No.	Yds.	Avg.	In 20	LG
Bidwell	82	3485	42.5	21	68
Packers	82	3485	42.5	21	68
Opponents	86	3644	42.4	33	70

PUNT RETURNS	No.	FC	Yds.	Avg.	LG	TD
Freeman	17	7	114	6.7	29	0
Rossum	11	8	109	9.9	55t	1
Lee	3	0	6	2.0	6	0
Ferguson	1	2	4	4.0	4	0
Sharper	1	3	18	18.0	18	0
Packers	33	20	251	7.6	55t	1
Opponents	34	19	288	8.5	37	0

KICKOFF RETURNS	No.	Yds.	Avg.	LG	TD
Rossum	23	431	18.7	27	0
Levens	14	362	25.9	53	0
Henderson	6	62	10.3	14	0
Mealey	4	63	15.8	24	0
Ferguson	2	32	16.0	16	0
Freeman	2	28	14.0	24	0
Akins	1	0	0.0	0	0
Flanigan	1	9	9.0	9	0
Goodman	1	21	21.0	21	0
Packers	54	1008	18.7	53	0
Opponents	76	1520	20.0	43	0

FIELD GOALS	1-19	20-29	30-39	40-49	50+
Longwell	0/0	3/4	9/10	7/14	1/3
Packers	0/0	3/4	9/10	7/14	1/3
Opponents	0/0	4/5	10/11	7/9	1/3

SACKS	No.
Gbaja-Biamila	13.5
Holliday	7.0
Wayne	5.5
Flanigan	4.5
S. Dotson	3.5
Thierry	3.5
Harris	2.5
Diggs	2.0
Lyon	2.0
McBride	2.0
Reynolds	2.0
Sharper	2.0
Butler	1.0
Packers	52.0
Opponents	22.0

RECORD HOLDERS
INDIVIDUAL RECORDS—CAREER

Category	Name	Performance
Rushing (Yds.)	Jim Taylor, 1958-1966	8,207
Passing (Yds.)	Brett Favre, 1992-2001	38,627
Passing (TDs)	Brett Favre, 1992-2001	287
Receiving (No.)	Sterling Sharpe, 1988-1994	595
Receiving (Yds.)	James Lofton, 1978-1986	9,656
Interceptions	Bobby Dillon, 1952-59	52
Punting (Avg.)	Craig Hentrich, 1994-97	42.8
Punt Return (Avg.)	Desmond Howard, 1996, 1999	13.8
Kickoff Return (Avg.)	Travis Williams, 1967-1970	26.7
Field Goals	Chris Jacke, 1989-1996	173
Touchdowns (Tot.)	Don Hutson, 1935-1945	105
Points	Don Hutson, 1935-1945	823

INDIVIDUAL RECORDS—SINGLE SEASON

Category	Name	Performance
Rushing (Yds.)	Jim Taylor, 1962	1,474
Passing (Yds.)	Lynn Dickey, 1983	4,458
Passing (TDs)	Brett Favre, 1996	39
Receiving (No.)	Sterling Sharpe, 1993	112
Receiving (Yds.)	Robert Brooks, 1995	1,497
Interceptions	Irv Comp, 1943	10
Punting (Avg.)	Craig Hentrich, 1997	45.0
Punt Return (Avg.)	Billy Grimes, 1950	19.1
Kickoff Return (Avg.)	Travis Williams, 1967	*41.1
Field Goals	Chester Marcol, 1972	33
	Ryan Longwell, 2000	33
Touchdowns (Tot.)	Jim Taylor, 1962	19
Points	Paul Hornung, 1960	*176

INDIVIDUAL RECORDS—SINGLE GAME

Category	Name	Performance
Rushing (Yds.)	Dorsey Levens, 11-23-97	190
Passing (Yds.)	Lynn Dickey, 10-12-80	418
Passing (TDs)	Many times	5
	Last time by Brett Favre, 9-27-98	
Receiving (No.)	Don Hutson, 11-22-42	14
Receiving (Yds.)	Billy Howton, 10-21-56	257
Interceptions	Bobby Dillon, 11-26-53	*4
	Willie Buchanon, 9-24-78	*4
Field Goals	Chris Jacke, 11-11-90, 10-14-96	5
	Ryan Longwell, 9-24-00	5
Touchdowns (Tot.)	Paul Hornung, 12-12-65	5
Points	Paul Hornung, 10-8-61	33

*NFL Record

GREEN BAY PACKERS

2002 VETERAN ROSTER

No.	Name	Pos.	Ht.	Wt.	Birthdate	NFL Exp.	College	Hometown	How Acq.	'01 Games/ Starts
85	Bailey, Karsten	WR	6-0	205	4/26/77	3	Auburn	Sharpsburg, Ga.	FA-'02	0*
9	Bidwell, Josh	P	6-3	220	3/13/76	3	Oregon	Winston, Ore.	D4b-'99	16/0
28	Bowen, Matt	S	6-1	208	11/12/76	3	Iowa	Glen Elyn, Ill.	FA-'01	6/0*
39	Brookins, Jason	RB	6-2	235	1/5/76	2	Lane College	Mexico, Mo.	FA-'02	12/3*
93	Brown, Gilbert	DT	6-2	339	2/22/71	9	Kansas	Detroit, Mich.	W(Minn)-'93	11/11
36	Butler, LeRoy	S	6-0	204	7/19/68	13	Florida State	Jacksonville, Fla.	D2-'90	9/9
76	Clifton, Chad	T	6-5	327	6/26/76	3	Tennessee	Martin, Tenn.	D2-'00	14/13
60	Davis, Rob	LS	6-3	286	12/10/68	7	Shippensburg	Greenbelt, Md.	FA-'97	16/0
81	Davis, Tyrone	TE	6-4	260	6/30/72	7	Virginia	Halifax, Va.	FA-'97	4/2
59	Diggs, Na'il	LB	6-4	238	7/8/78	3	Ohio State	Los Angeles, Calif.	D4a-'00	16/16
72	Dotson, Earl	T	6-4	317	12/17/70	10	Texas A&I	Beaumont, Texas	FA-'01	12/0
80	Driver, Donald	WR	6-0	185	2/2/75	4	Alcorn State	Houston, Texas	D7b-'99	13/2
24	Edwards, Antuan	CB-S	6-1	210	5/26/77	4	Clemson	Starkville, Miss.	D1-'99	3/0
4	Favre, Brett	QB	6-2	225	10/10/69	12	Southern Mississippi	Kiln, Miss.	T(Atl)-'92	16/16
89	Ferguson, Robert	WR	6-1	209	12/17/79	2	Texas A&M	Houston, Texas	D2-'01	1/0
63	Ferrario, Bill	G	6-2	315	9/22/78	2	Wisconsin	Scranton, Pa.	D4-'01	0*
73	Fields, Aaron	DE	6-4	260	1/9/76	2	Troy State	Notasulga, Ala.	FA-'02	3/0*
58	Flanagan, Mike	C	6-5	297	11/10/73	7	UCLA	Sacramento, Calif.	D3a-'96	16/16
75	#Flanigan, Jim	DT	6-2	290	8/27/71	9	Notre Dame	Brussels, Wis.	FA-'01	16/8
88	Franks, Bubba	TE	6-6	260	1/6/78	3	Miami	Big Spring, Texas	D1-'00	16/14
49	French, Rufus	TE	6-4	253	3/15/78	2	Mississippi	Amory, Miss.	FA-'02	0*
47	Frost, Scott	S	6-3	211	1/4/75	5	Nebraska	Wood River, Neb.	FA-'01	12/0*
94	Gbaja-Biamila, Kabeer	DE	6-4	253	9/24/77	3	San Diego State	Los Angeles, Calif.	FA-'00	16/0
57	Gizzi, Chris	LB	6-0	235	3/8/75	3	Air Force	Cleveland, Ohio	FA-'00	12/1
83	t- Glenn, Terry	WR	5-11	195	7/23/74	7	Ohio State	Columbus, Ohio	T(NE)-'02	4/1*
29	Goodman, Herbert	RB	5-11	205	8/31/77	3	Graceland	Homestead, Fla.	FA-'00	7/0
30	Green, Ahman	RB	6-0	217	2/16/77	5	Nebraska	Omaha, Neb.	T(Sea)-'00	16/16
16	Hayes, Windrell	WR	5-11	198	12/14/76	3	Southern California	Stockton, Calif.	FA-'02	1/0*
33	Henderson, William	FB	6-1	253	2/19/71	8	North Carolina	Chester, Va.	D3b-'95	16/8
90	Holliday, Vonnie	DE	6-5	290	12/11/75	5	North Carolina	Camden, S.C.	D1-'98	16/16
56	Holmberg, Rob	LB	6-3	240	5/6/71	9	Penn State	Mt. Pleasant, Pa.	FA-'01	7/2*
97	Hunt, Cletidus	DT-DE	6-4	300	1/2/76	4	Kentucky State	Memphis, Tenn.	D3b-'99	12/4
91	Johnson, Joe	DE	6-4	270	7/11/72	9	Louisville	St. Louis, Mo.	UFA(NO)-'02	16/16*
55	Jones, Robert	LB	6-2	246	9/27/69	11	East Carolina	Nottoway, Va.	FA-'01	15/9*
78	Jordan, Kevin	T	6-5	312	11/7/78	2	Fresno State	Harbor City, Calif.	FA-'01	0*
21	Jue, Bhawoh	CB-S	6-0	200	5/24/79	2	Penn State	Chantilly, Va.	D3a-'01	15/7
82	Lee, Charles	WR	6-2	205	11/19/77	3	Central Florida	Homestead, Fla.	D7c-'00	7/0
8	Longwell, Ryan	K	6-0	200	8/16/74	6	California	Bend, Ore.	W(SF)-'97	16/0
98	Lyon, Billy	DE-DT	6-5	295	12/10/73	5	Marshall	Erlanger, Ky.	FA-'98	12/0
51	Marshall, Torrance	LB	6-2	255	6/12/77	2	Oklahoma	Miami, Fla.	D3b-'01	14/1
87	Martin, David	TE	6-4	250	3/13/79	2	Tennessee	Norfolk, Va.	D6-'01	14/1
27	McBride, Tod	CB	6-1	200	1/26/76	4	UCLA	Walnut, Calif.	W(Sea)-'99	16/0
34	McKenzie, Mike	CB	6-0	190	4/26/76	4	Memphis	Miami, Fla.	D3a-'99	16/16
40	McLeod, Kevin	FB	6-0	250	10/17/74	2	Auburn	Clarkston, Ga.	FA-'02	0*
32	Mealey, Rondell	RB	6-0	224	2/24/77	3	Louisiana State	Destrehan, La.	D7e-'00	11/0
18	Pederson, Doug	QB	6-3	220	1/31/68	10	Northeast Louisiana	Ferndale, Wash.	FA-'01	16/0
99	Reynolds, Jamal	DE	6-3	266	2/20/79	2	Florida State	Aiken, S.C.	D1-'01	6/0
62	Rivera, Marco	G	6-4	310	4/26/72	7	Penn State	Elmont, N.Y.	D6-'96	16/16
46	Sessions, Anthony	LB	6-0	223	2/16/79	2	Tennessee	Warner Robins, Ga.	FA-'02	0*
42	Sharper, Darren	S	6-2	207	11/3/75	6	William & Mary	Richmond, Va.	D2-'97	16/16
65	Tauscher, Mark	T-G	6-3	320	6/17/77	3	Wisconsin	Auburndale, Wis.	D7a-'00	16/16
22	Thibodeaux, Keith	CB	5-11	189	5/16/74	5	Northwestern State (La.)	Opelousas, La.	FA-'01	7/0*
77	Tomich, Jared	DE	6-3	281	4/24/74	5	Nebraska	Schereville, Ind.	FA-'01	0*
68	Wahle, Mike	G	6-6	310	3/29/77	5	Navy	Lake Arrowhead, Calif.	SD2-'98	16/16
95	Walker, Rod	DT	6-3	320	2/4/76	2	Troy State	Milton, Fla.	T(Tenn)-'01	11/0
96	Warren, Steve	DT	6-1	300	1/22/78	3	Nebraska	Springfield, Mo.	D3-'00	0*
54	Wayne, Nate	LB	6-0	237	1/12/75	5	Mississippi	Macon, Miss.	T(Den)-'00	12/12
37	Williams, Tyrone	CB	5-11	193	5/31/73	7	Nebraska	Bradenton, Fla.	D3b-'96	16/16
52	Winters, Frank	C	6-3	305	1/23/64	16	Western Illinois	Union City, N.J.	PB(KC)-'92	4/0

* Bailey last active with Seattle in '00; Bowen played 1 game with St. Louis; Brookins played 12 games with Baltimore; Ferrario inactive for 16 games; Fields played 3 games with Dallas; French last active with Seattle in '99; Frost played 12 games with Cleveland; Glenn played 4 games with New England; Hayes played 1 game with N.Y. Jets; Holmberg played 2 games with New England and 1 game with Carolina; Johnson played 16 games with New Orleans; Jones played 15 games with Washington; Jordan missed '01 season because of injury; McLeod last active with Tampa Bay in '99; Sessions missed '01 season because of injury with

Washington; Thibodeaux played 5 games with Minnesota; Tomich last active with New Orleans in '00; Warren missed '01 season because of injury.

\#   Unrestricted free agent; subject to developments.

t-   Packers traded for Glenn (NE).

Players lost through free agency (6): WR Corey Bradford (Hou; 16 games in '01), S Billy Jenkins (Buff; 6), CB-KR Allen Rossum (Atl; 6), WR Bill Schroeder (Det; 16), T-G Barry Stokes (Cle; 16), DE John Thierry (Atl; 12).

Also played with Packers in '01—S Chris Akins (11 games), TE Bobby Collins (4), DT Santana Dotson (16), WR Antonio Freeman (16), LB Bernardo Harris (16), RB Dorsey Levens (15), LB Andre O'Neal (2), LB K.D. Williams (12).

2002 FIRST-YEAR ROSTER

Name	Pos.	Ht.	Wt.	Birthdate	College	Hometown	How Acq.
Anderson, Marques	S	5-11	211	5/26/79	UCLA	Long Beach, Calif.	D3
Atkinson, Algie	LB	6-5	251	8/5/80	Kansas	Evanston, Ill.	FA
Barry, Kevin	G	6-4	325	7/20/79	Arizona	Racine, Wis.	FA
Bironas, Rob	K	6-0	198	1/29/78	Georgia Southern	Louisville, Ky.	FA
Brady, Marcus	QB	6-0	191	9/24/79	Cal State-Northridge	San Diego, Calif.	FA
Bryant, Terry (1)	DT	6-3	282	2/5/78	Clemson	Savannah, Ga.	FA
Davenport, Najeh	FB	6-1	246	2/8/79	Miami	Miami, Fla.	D4
Dozier, Joey (1)	RB	6-0	255	2/23/77	New Mexico State	Topeka, Kan.	FA
Eby, Andy	C	6-3	300	4/26/79	Kansas State	Olathe, Kan.	FA
Elder, Scott	P	6-1	210	7/31/80	Oklahoma State	Harahan, La.	FA
Fisher, Tony	RB	6-1	222	10/12/79	Notre Dame	Euclid, Ohio	FA
Gall, Chris (1)	FB	6-0	240	4/4/76	Indiana	Oak Park, Ill.	FA
Gilmore, John	DE	6-4	283	10/8/77	Tennessee State	Missouri City, Texas	FA
Heupel, Josh (1)	QB	6-2	215	3/22/78	Oklahoma	Aberdeen, S.D.	FA
Hollingshed, Adrian	LB	6-2	250	10/13/77	Georgia	Fort Valley, Ga.	FA
Hood, Kerry (1)	WR	6-1	195	12/16/78	South Carolina	Atlanta, Ga.	FA
Houghton, Mike	G-T	6-5	313	12/1/79	San Diego State	San Diego, Calif.	D6
Kampman, Aaron	DT-DE	6-4	286	11/30/79	Iowa	Kelsey, Iowa	D5a
Kehl, Ed (1)	G-LS	6-4	310	8/3/72	Brigham Young	Sandy, Utah	FA
Kocher, Ken	DT	6-3	328	7/30/80	UCLA	San Diego, Calif.	FA
Lenon, Paris (1)	LB	6-2	230	11/26/77	Richmond	Lynchburg, Va.	FA
Lewis, Richard	WR-KR	5-11	176	5/23/80	North Dakota State	St. Paul, Minn.	FA
McMillan, Seneca	CB	5-11	190	7/10/78	Nicholls State	Orlando, Fla.	FA
Menafee, Cornell (1)	LB	6-2	247	11/26/76	Mississippi State	Opelika, Ala.	FA
Nall, Craig	QB	6-3	227	4/21/79	Northwestern State (La.)	Alexandria, La.	D5b
Seymour, Bill	TE	6-3	259	11/9/78	Michigan	Mishawaka, Ind.	FA
Stuber, Tim (1)	G-T	6-5	315	2/2/78	Colorado State	Northglenn, Colo.	FA
Swiney, Erwin	CB	6-0	186	10/8/78	Nebraska	Lincoln, Neb.	FA
Tarver, Hurley (1)	CB	6-0	180	11/30/75	Central Oklahoma	Fort Worth, Texas	FA
Unertl, Jeremy	S	6-1	210	9/15/78	Wisconsin-La Crosse	Lomira, Wis.	FA
Walker, Javon	WR	6-3	210	10/14/78	Florida State	Lafayette, La.	D1
Watton, Chris (1)	G-C	6-3	305	10/6/77	Baylor	Foley, Ala.	FA
White, George (1)	S	6-1	209	11/17/77	Boston College	North Royalton, Ohio	FA
Wilkins, Marcus	LB	6-2	226	1/2/80	Texas	Austin, Texas	FA
Williams, Travis (1)	WR	6-3	196	5/22/78	Navy	Lexington, N.C.	FA

The term NFL Rookie is defined as a player who is in his first season of professional football and has not been on the roster of another professional football team for any regular-season or postseason games. A Rookie is designated by an "R" on NFL rosters. Players who have been active in another professional football league or players who have NFL experience, including either preseason training camp or being on an Active List or Inactive List, or on Reserve/Injured or Reserve/Physically Unable to Perform for fewer than six regular-season games, are termed NFL First-Year Players. An NFL First-Year Player is designated by a "1" on NFL rosters. Thereafter, a player is credited with an additional year of experience for each season in which he accumulates six games on the Active List or Inactive List, or on Reserve/Injured or Reserve/Physically Unable to Perform.

COACHING STAFF

**Executive Vice President/
General Manager/Head Coach,
Mike Sherman**

Pro Career: Named the thirteenth head coach in Packers history January 18, 2000. Added general manager responsibilities in 2001 following the retirement of Ron Wolf. Sherman has gone 21-11 (.656) in the regular season since taking over the Packers' reins in 2000; no other head coach has had a better winning percentage during his first two seasons in Green Bay, including Vince Lombardi (15-9, .625). Has won 16 of his last 20 regular-season games, including a 12-4 record in 2001 as he returned the Packers to the playoffs for the first time since 1998. Ended initial season at 9-7 after posting 4-0 December mark. Joined Pro Football Hall of Fame members Curly Lambeau and Lombardi, along with Mike Holmgren, as the only head coaches in team history to post a winning record in their first seasons. Previously had served as Green Bay's tight ends coach for two seasons (1997-98) before following Holmgren to the Seattle Seahawks in 1999 as offensive coordinator-tight ends coach. Career record: 22-12.

Background: After coaching for three seasons at the high school level, Sherman coached collegiately at Pittsburgh (1981-82), Tulane (1983-84), Holy Cross (1985-88), Texas A&M (1989-1993, 1995-96), and UCLA (1994). Played offensive guard and tackle, as well as linebacker at Central Connecticut State (1974, 1976-77), where he holds a bachelor's degree in English. Was a prep star at Algonquin Regional High School in Northboro, Mass.

Personal: Born December 19, 1954, in Norwood, Mass.. He and his wife, Karen, have four children—Sarah, Emily, Matthew, and Benjamin—and live in Green Bay.

ASSISTANT COACHES

Larry Beightol, offensive line; born November 21, 1942, Pittsburgh, lives in Green Bay. Guard-linebacker Catawba College 1960-63. No pro playing experience. College coach: William & Mary 1968-1971, North Carolina State 1972-75, Auburn 1976, Arkansas 1977-78, 1980-82, Louisiana Tech 1979 (head coach), Missouri 1983-84. Pro coach: Atlanta Falcons 1985-86, Tampa Bay Buccaneers 1987-88, San Diego Chargers 1989, New York Jets 1990-94, Houston Oilers 1995, Miami Dolphins 1996-98, joined Packers in 1999.

Darrell Bevell, offensive assistant; born January 6, 1970, Yuma, Ariz., lives in De Pere, Wis. Quarterback Northern Arizona 1989, Wisconsin 1992-95. No pro playing experience. College coach: Westmar 1996, Iowa State 1997, Connecticut 1998-99. Pro coach: Joined Packers in 2000.

Sylvester Croom, running backs; born September 25, 1954, Tuscaloosa, Ala., lives in Green Bay. Center Alabama 1971-74. Pro center New Orleans Saints 1975. College coach: Alabama 1976-1986. Pro coach: Tampa Bay Buccaneers 1987-1990, Indianapolis Colts 1991, San Diego Chargers 1992-96, Detroit Lions 1997-2000, joined Packers in 2001.

Ed Donatell, defensive coordinator; born February 4, 1957, Akron, Ohio, lives in Green Bay. Defensive back Glenville State 1975-78. No pro playing experience. College coach: Kent State 1979-1980, Washington 1981-82, Pacific 1983-85, Idaho 1986-88, Cal State-Fullerton 1989. Pro coach: New York Jets 1990-94, Denver Broncos 1995-99, joined Packers in 2000.

Stan Drayton, quality control-special teams/offense; born March 11, 1971, Cleveland, lives in De Pere, Wis. Running back Allegheny 1990-92. No pro playing experience. College coach: Allegheny 1993, Eastern Michigan 1994, Pennsylvania 1995, Villanova 1996-2000. Pro coach: Joined Packers in 2001.

Jethro Franklin, defensive line; born October 25, 1965, St. Lazaire, France, lives in De Pere, Wis. Defensive end San Jose (Calif.) C.C. 1984-85, Fresno State 1986-87. Pro defensive end Seattle Seahawks 1989. College coach: Fresno State 1991-98, UCLA 1999. Pro coach: Joined Packers in 2000.

Jeff Jagodzinski, tight ends; born October 12, 1963, Milwaukee, Wis., lives in Green Bay. Running back Wisconsin-Whitewater 1981-84. No pro playing experience. College coach: Wisconsin-Whitewater 1985, Northern Illinois 1986, Louisiana State 1987-88, East Carolina 1989-1996, Boston College 1997-98. Pro coach: Joined Packers in 1999.

Brad Miller, defensive assistant-quality control; born May 30, 1963, Pasadena, Calif., lives in De Pere, Wis. Tight end-safety Oregon State 1981-84. No pro playing experience. College coach: Riverside (Calif.) C.C. 1986-1993, Portland State 1994. Pro coach: Birmingham Barracudas (CFL) 1995, Edmonton Eskimos (CFL) 1996-2000, joined Packers in 2001.

Frank Novak, special teams; born May 18, 1938, Leominster, Mass., lives in De Pere, Wis. Quarterback Northern Michigan 1959-1961. No pro playing experience. College coach: Northern Michigan 1966-1972, East Carolina 1973, Virginia 1974-75, Western Illinois 1976-77, Holy Cross 1978-1983, Missouri 1988. Pro coach: Oklahoma Outlaws (USFL) 1984, Birmingham Stallions (USFL) 1985, Houston Oilers 1989-1994, Detroit Lions 1995-96, San Diego Chargers 1997-98, joined Packers in 2000.

Bo Pelini, linebackers; born December 13, 1967, Youngstown, Ohio, lives in Green Bay. Defensive back Ohio State 1987-1990. No pro playing experience.

College coach: Iowa 1991-92. Pro coach: San Francisco 49ers 1994-96, New England Patriots 1997-99, joined Packers in 2000.

Tom Rossley, offensive coordinator; born August 9, 1946, Painesville, Ohio, lives in De Pere, Wis. Wide receiver Cincinnati 1966-68. No pro playing experience. College coach: Arkansas 1972, Rice 1976, 1978-1981, Cincinnati 1977, Holy Cross 1986-87, Southern Methodist 1988-89, 1991-96 (head coach 1991-96). Pro coach: Montreal Concorde (CFL) 1982-84, San Antonio Gunslingers (USFL) 1985, Denver Dynamite (Arena) 1987, Atlanta Falcons 1990, Chicago Bears 1997-98, Kansas City Chiefs 1999, joined Packers in 2000.

Barry Rubin, strength and conditioning; born June 25, 1957, Monroe, La., lives in Green Bay. Running back-punter Louisiana State 1976-77, tight end-punter Northwestern (La.) State 1978-1980. No pro playing experience. College coach: Northeast Louisiana 1981-83, 1987-1990, 1994, Louisiana State 1984-85. Pro coach: Joined Packers in 1995.

Pat Ruel, asst. offensive line; born December 5, 1950, Washington, D.C., lives in Green Bay. Guard Miami 1971-72. No pro playing experience. College coach: Miami 1973-76, Arkansas 1977-78, Washington State 1979-1981, Texas A&M 1982-84, Northern Illinois 1985-87, Kansas 1988-1996, Michigan State 1998-99. Pro coach: Detroit Lions 2000, joined Packers in 2001.

Ray Sherman, wide receivers; born November 27, 1951, Berkeley, Calif., lives in Green Bay. Wide receiver Laney (Calif.) J.C. 1969-1970, Fresno State 1971-72. No pro playing experience. College coach: San Jose State 1974, California 1975, 1981, Michigan State 1976-77, Wake Forest 1978-1980, Purdue 1982-85, Georgia 1986-87. Pro coach: Houston Oilers 1988-89, Atlanta Falcons 1990, San Francisco 49ers 1991-93, New York Jets 1994, Minnesota Vikings 1995-97, 1999, Pittsburgh Steelers 1998, joined Packers in 2000.

Bob Slowik, assistant head coach-defensive backs; born May 16, 1954, Pittsburgh, lives in Green Bay. Defensive back Delaware 1973-76. No pro playing experience. College coach: Delaware 1977-78, Florida 1979-1982, Drake 1983, Rutgers 1984-89, East Carolina 1990-91. Pro coach: Dallas Cowboys 1992, Chicago Bears 1993-98, Cleveland Browns 1999, joined Packers in 2000.

Lionel Washington, asst. defensive backs; born October 21, 1960, New Orleans, lives in De Pere, Wis. Defensive back Tulane 1979-1982. Pro defensive back St. Louis Cardinals 1983-86, Los Angeles/Oakland Raiders 1987-1994, 1997, Denver Broncos 1995-96. Pro coach: Joined Packers in 1999.

**National Football Conference
North Division**
Team Colors: Purple, Gold, and White
9520 Viking Drive
Eden Prairie, Minnesota 55344
Telephone: (952) 828-6500

2002 SCHEDULE
PRESEASON
Aug. 10	**Cleveland**	7:00
Aug. 16	at Buffalo	7:30
Aug. 23	**Tennessee**	7:00
Aug. 29	at Pittsburgh	7:30

REGULAR SEASON
Sept. 8	at Chicago (Champaign, Ill.)	12:00
Sept. 15	**Buffalo**	3:15
Sept. 22	**Carolina**	12:00
Sept. 29	at Seattle	5:30
Oct. 6	OPEN DATE	
Oct. 13	**Detroit**	12:00
Oct. 20	at New York Jets	1:00
Oct. 27	**Chicago**	12:00
Nov. 3	at Tampa Bay	1:00
Nov. 10	**New York Giants**	12:00
Nov. 17	**Green Bay**	12:00
Nov. 24	at New England	1:00
Dec. 1	**Atlanta**	12:00
Dec. 8	at Green Bay	7:30
Dec. 15	at New Orleans	12:00
Dec. 21	**Miami (Sat.)**	12:30
Dec. 29	at Detroit	1:00

Stadium: Hubert H. Humphrey Metrodome
(opened in 1982)
 • **Capacity:** 64,121
500 11th Avenue South
Minneapolis, Minnesota 55415
Playing Surface: AstroTurf
Training Camp: Minnesota State-Mankato
Mankato, Minnesota
56001

HUBERT H. HUMPHREY METRODOME

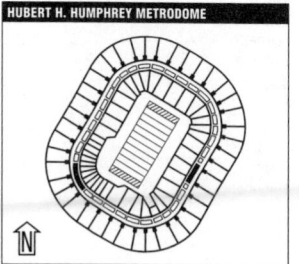

CLUB OFFICIALS
Owners: Red & Charline McCombs
President: Gary Woods
Executive Vice President: Mike Kelly
Vice President of Football Operations:
 Rob Brzezinski
Vice President of Sales and Marketing:
 Steve LaCroix
Vice President of Finance: Steve Poppen
Director of Pro Scouting: Paul Wiggin
Director of College Scouting:
 Scott Studwell
Director of Football Operations:
 Dave Blando
Senior Consultant/Player Personnel:
 Frank Gilliam
Director of Community Relations:
 Brad Madson
Director of Public Relations: Bob Hagan
Director of Operations: Breck Spinner
Director of Ticket Sales: Phil Huebner
Equipment Manager: Dennis Ryan
Head Athletic Trainer: Chuck Barta
Senior Consultant/Medical Services:
 Fred Zamberletti
Digital Video Director: Bob Marcus

COACHING HISTORY
(356-289-9)
1961-66	Norm Van Brocklin	29-51-4
1967-1983	Bud Grant	161-99-5
1984	Les Steckel	3-13-0
1985	Bud Grant	7-9-0
1986-1991	Jerry Burns	55-46-0
1992-2001	Dennis Green*	101-70-0
2001	Mike Tice	0-1-0

*Resigned after 15 games in 2001

ATTENDANCE
Home 504,472   Away 524,297
Total 1,028,769
Single-game home record,
64,471 (11/22/98)
Single-season home record, 510,741
(1998)

2002 DRAFT CHOICES
Round	Name	Pos.	College
1	Bryant McKinnie	T	Miami
2	Raonall Smith	LB	Washington St.
3	Willie Offord	DB	South Carolina
4	Brian Williams	DB	N. Carolina St.
	Ed Ta'amu	G	Utah
6	Nick Rogers	LB	Georgia Tech
7	Chad Beasley	DT	Virginia Tech

2001 TEAM RECORD

PRESEASON (4-0)

Date	Result	Opponent
8/11	W 28-21	vs. New Orleans, at San Antonio
8/16	W 24-10	Pittsburgh
8/24	W 28-21	Indianaplois
8/31	W 20-7	at Miami

REGULAR SEASON (5-11)

Date	Result	Opponent	Att
9/09	L 13-24	Carolina	64,108
9/23	L 10-17	at Chicago	66,944
9/30	W 20-16	Tampa Bay	64,105
10/07	L 15-28	at New Orleans	70,020
10/14	W 31-26	Detroit	64,048
10/21	W 35-13	Green Bay	64,165
10/28	L 14-41	at Tampa Bay	65,558
11/11	L 17-48	at Philadelphia	65,638
11/19	W 28-16	New York Giants	64,283
11/25	L 6-13	Chicago	64,214
12/02	L 16-21	at Pittsburgh	62,661
12/09	W 42-24	Tennessee	64,271
12/16	L 24-27	at Detroit	72,190
12/23	L 3-33	Jacksonville	64,150
12/30	L 13-24	at Green Bay	59,870
1/07	L 3-19	at Baltimore	69,465

SCORE BY PERIODS

Vikings	44	77	83	86	0	— 290
Opponents	77	111	84	118	0	— 390

2001 TEAM STATISTICS

	Vikings	Opp.
Total First Downs	288	312
Rushing	88	127
Passing	179	166
Penalty	21	19
3rd Down: Made/Att	88/210	82/204
3rd Down Pct.	41.9	40.2
4th Down: Made/Att	8/18	6/10
4th Down Pct.	44.4	60.0
Possession Avg.	29:11	30:49
Total Net Yards	5185	5666
Avg. Per Game	324.1	354.1
Total Plays	978	985
Avg. Per Play	5.3	5.8
Net Yards Rushing	1609	2299
Avg. Per Game	100.6	143.7
Total Rushes	376	477
Net Yards Passing	3576	3367
Avg. Per Game	223.5	210.4
Sacked/Yards Lost	47/278	30/204
Gross Yards	3854	3571
Att./Completions	555/335	478/291
Completion Pct.	60.4	60.9
Had Intercepted	23	8
Punts/Average	72/42.1	72/40.3
Net Punting Avg.	72/33.4	72/34.7
Penalties/Yards	109/835	92/874
Fumbles/Ball Lost	35/16	22/10
Touchdowns	35	42
Rushing	10	21
Passing	23	16
Returns	2	5

2001 INDIVIDUAL STATISTICS

PASSING

	Att.	Comp.	Yds.	Pct.	TD	Int.	Tkld.	Rate
Culpepper	366	235	2612	64.2	14	13	33/186	83.3
Wynn	98	48	418	49.0	1	6	10/65	38.6
Bouman	89	51	795	57.3	8	4	4/27	98.3
Berger	1	0	0	0.0	0	0	0/0	39.6
Moss	1	1	29	100.0	0	0	0/0	118.8
Vikings	555	335	3854	60.4	23	23	47/278	77.9
Opponents	478	291	3571	60.9	16	8	30/204	88.1

SCORING

	TD R	TD P	TD Rt	PAT	FG	Saf	PTS
Anderson	0	0	0	29/30	15/18	0	74
Moss	0	10	0	0/0	0/0	0	60
C. Carter	0	6	0	0/0	0/0	0	36
Culpepper	5	0	0	0/0	0/0	0	34
Bennett	2	1	0	0/0	0/0	0	18
Chamberlain	0	3	0	0/0	0/0	0	18
Prentice	2	0	0	0/0	0/0	0	12
Reed	1	0	0	0/0	0/0	0	8
T. Carter	0	0	1	0/0	0/0	0	6
Chapman	0	1	0	0/0	0/0	0	6
Jordan	0	1	0	0/0	0/0	0	6
Kleinsasser	0	1	0	0/0	0/0	0	6
Wong	0	0	1	0/0	0/0	0	6
Vikings	10	23	2	29/30	15/18	0	290
Opponents	21	16	5	39/39	33/38	0	390

2-Pt. Conversions: Culpepper 2, Reed.
Vikings 3-5, Opponents 0-3.

RUSHING

	Att.	Yds.	Avg.	LG	TD
Bennett	172	682	4.0	31t	2
Culpepper	71	416	5.9	34	5
Chapman	63	195	3.1	19	0
Kleinsasser	23	72	3.1	11	1
Morrow	12	67	5.6	15	0
Bouman	9	61	6.8	21	0
Wynn	8	61	7.6	14	0
Moss	3	38	12.7	18	0
Prentice	14	13	0.9	6	2
C. Carter	1	4	4.0	4	0
Vikings	376	1609	4.3	34	10
Opponents	477	2299	4.8	61	21

RECEIVING

	No.	Yds.	Avg.	LG	TD
Moss	82	1233	15.0	73t	10
C. Carter	73	871	11.9	52	6
Chamberlain	57	666	11.7	47t	3
Bennett	29	226	7.8	80t	1
Reed	27	309	11.4	27	1
Kleinsasser	24	184	7.7	18	0
Chapman	16	135	8.4	38t	1
Morrow	13	142	10.9	28	0
Walsh	9	67	7.4	19	0
Jordan	3	11	3.7	4	1
Prentice	1	10	10.0	10	0
Culpepper	1	0	0.0	0	0
Vikings	335	3854	11.5	80t	23
Opponents	291	3571	12.3	69	16

INTERCEPTIONS

	No.	Yds.	Avg.	LG	TD
Griffith	2	25	12.5	14	0
E. Kelly	2	-7	-3.5	2	0
Wong	1	27	27.0	27t	1
Sawyer	1	2	2.0	2	0
McDaniel	1	0	0.0	0	0
Thomas	1	0	0.0	0	0
Vikings	8	47	5.9	27t	1
Opponents	23	219	9.5	59t	2

PUNTING

	No.	Yds.	Avg.	In 20	LG
Berger	47	2046	43.5	10	67
Johnson	25	983	39.3	9	59
Vikings	72	3029	42.1	19	67
Opponents	72	2904	40.3	22	62

PUNT RETURNS

	No.	FC	Yds.	Avg.	LG	TD
Jacquet	29	6	219	7.6	23	0
Walters	11	3	69	6.3	16	0
Morgan	4	0	17	4.3	6	0
Walsh	1	0	2	2.0	2	0
Vikings	45	9	307	6.8	23	0
Opponents	34	7	366	10.8	34	0

KICKOFF RETURNS

	No.	Yds.	Avg.	LG	TD
Jacquet	46	1012	22.0	53	0
Walters	18	425	23.6	40	0
Morrow	6	109	18.2	28	0
Morgan	4	78	19.5	24	0
Prentice	1	2	2.0	2	0
Walsh	1	10	10.0	10	0
Worthen	1	11	11.0	11	0
Vikings	77	1647	21.4	53	0
Opponents	59	1266	21.5	93t	1

FIELD GOALS

	1-19	20-29	30-39	40-49	50+
Anderson	0/0	7/7	2/4	6/7	0/0
Vikings	0/0	7/7	2/4	6/7	0/0
Opponents	1/1	13/13	8/8	8/10	3/6

SACKS

	No.
Hovan	6.0
Johnstone	5.5
Sawyer	5.0
Wong	3.0
Chukwurah	2.5
Garnett	2.0
Robbins	2.0
T. Carter	1.0
Colinet	1.0
Hall	1.0
McDaniel	1.0
Vikings	30.0
Opponents	47.0

RECORD HOLDERS
INDIVIDUAL RECORDS—CAREER

Category	Name	Performance
Rushing (Yds.)	Robert Smith, 1993-2000	6,818
Passing (Yds.)	Fran Tarkenton, 1961-66, 1972-78	33,098
Passing (TDs)	Fran Tarkenton, 1961-66, 1972-78	239
Receiving (No.)	Cris Carter, 1990-2001	1,004
Receiving (Yds.)	Cris Carter, 1990-2001	12,383
Interceptions	Paul Krause, 1968-79	53
Punting (Avg.)	Harry Newsome, 1990-93	43.8
Punt Return (Avg.)	David Palmer, 1994-2000	9.4
Kickoff Return (Avg.)	Charlie West, 1968-73	25.5
Field Goals	Fred Cox, 1963-77	282
Touchdowns (Tot.)	Cris Carter, 1990-2001	110
Points	Fred Cox, 1963-77	1,365

INDIVIDUAL RECORDS—SINGLE SEASON

Category	Name	Performance
Rushing (Yds.)	Robert Smith, 2000	1,521
Passing (Yds.)	Warren Moon, 1994	4,264
Passing (TDs)	Randall Cunningham, 1998	34
Receiving (No.)	Cris Carter, 1994, 1995	122
Receiving (Yds.)	Randy Moss, 2000	1,437
Interceptions	Paul Krause, 1975	10
Punting (Avg.)	Bobby Walden, 1964	46.4
Punt Return (Avg.)	David Palmer, 1995	13.2
Kickoff Return (Avg.)	John Gilliam, 1972	26.3
Field Goals	Gary Anderson, 1998	35
Touchdowns (Tot.)	Chuck Foreman, 1975	22
Points	Gary Anderson, 1998	164

INDIVIDUAL RECORDS—SINGLE GAME

Category	Name	Performance
Rushing (Yds.)	Chuck Foreman, 10-24-76	200
Passing (Yds.)	Tommy Kramer, 11-2-86	490
Passing (TDs)	Joe Kapp, 9-28-69	*7
Receiving (No.)	Rickey Young, 12-16-79	15
Receiving (Yds.)	Sammy White, 11-7-76	210
Interceptions	Many Times	3
	Last time by Jack Del Rio, 12-5-93	
Field Goals	Rich Karlis, 11-5-89	*7
Touchdowns (Tot.)	Chuck Foreman, 12-20-75	4
	Ahmad Rashad, 9-2-79	4
Points	Chuck Foreman, 12-20-75	24
	Ahmad Rashad, 9-2-79	24

*NFL Record

2002 VETERAN ROSTER

No.	Name	Pos.	Ht.	Wt.	Birthdate	NFL Exp.	College	Hometown	How Acq.	'01 Games/ Starts
82	Bates, D'Wayne	WR	6-2	215	12/4/75	4	Northwestern	Aiken, S.C.	W(Chi)-'02	11/1*
23	Bennett, Michael	RB	5-9	211	8/13/78	2	Wisconsin	Milwaukee, Wis.	D1-'01	13/13
78	Birk, Matt	C	6-4	308	7/23/76	5	Harvard	St. Paul, Minn.	D6-'98	16/16
8	Bouman, Todd	QB	6-2	229	8/1/72	5	St. Cloud State	Ruthton, Minn.	FA-'97	5/3
26	Bradford, Ronnie	S	5-10	198	10/1/70	10	Colorado	Commerce City, Colo.	FA-'02	14/14*
4	Brien, Doug	K	6-0	180	11/24/70	9	California	Concord, Calif.	UFA(TB)-'02	2/0*
91	Bromell, Lorenzo	DE	6-6	268	9/23/75	5	Clemson	Georgetown, S.C.	UFA(Mia)-'02	16/1*
22	Carter, Tyrone	S	5-8	190	3/31/76	3	Minnesota	Pompano Beach, Fla.	D4b-'00	15/7
87	Chamberlain, Byron	TE	6-1	242	10/17/71	7	Wayne State	Fort Worth, Texas	UFA(Den)-'01	16/15
34	Chapman, Doug	RB	5-10	213	8/22/77	3	Marshall	Chesterfield, Va.	D3-'00	16/3
21	Chavous, Corey	CB	6-1	206	1/5/76	5	Vanderbilt	Aiken, S.C.	UFA(Ariz)-'02	14/14*
50	Chukwurah, Patrick	DE	6-1	250	3/1/79	2	Wyoming	Irving, Texas	D5-'01	16/3
73	Crawford, Brian	T	6-6	324	9/27/77	2	Western Oregon	Lake Oswego, Ore.	D7-'01	0*
52	Crockett, Henri	LB	6-2	238	10/28/74	6	Florida State	Pompano Beach, Fla.	UFA(Atl)-'02	16/15*
11	Culpepper, Daunte	QB	6-4	260	1/28/77	4	Central Florida	Ocala, Fla.	D1a-'99	11/11
86	Dawkins, Sean	WR	6-4	218	2/3/71	10	California	Sunnyvale, Calif.	UFA(Jax)-'02	16/3*
71	Dixon, David	G	6-5	359	1/5/69	9	Arizona State	Auckland, New Zealand	FA-'94	15/14
92	Garnett, Winfield	DT	6-6	320	7/24/76	2	Ohio State	Harvey, Ill.	FA-'01	12/2
83	Goodwin, Hunter	TE	6-5	270	10/10/72	7	Texas A&M	Bellville, Texas	FA-'02	16/11*
55	Hall, Lemanski	LB	6-0	234	11/24/70	8	Alabama	Valley, Ala.	UFA(Dall)-'00	16/13
93	Holland, Darius	DT	6-5	330	11/10/73	7	Colorado	Las Cruces, N.M.	FA-'02	0*
99	Hovan, Chris	DT	6-2	294	5/12/78	3	Boston College	Rocky River, Ohio	D1-'00	16/16
90	Howard, Willie	DE	6-3	298	12/26/77	2	Stanford	Mountain View, Calif.	D2-'01	8/0
13	James, Cedric	WR	6-1	199	3/19/79	2	Texas Christian	Kennedale, Texas	D4b-'01	0*
51	Johnstone, Lance	DE	6-4	253	6/11/73	7	Temple	Germantown, Pa.	FA-'01	16/5
25	Kelly, Eric	CB	5-10	197	1/15/77	2	Kentucky	Panama, Fla.	D3-'01	16/11
61	Kelly, Lewis	T	6-4	306	4/21/77	3	South Carolina State	Lithonia, Ga.	D7c-'00	4/0
47	Keys, Isaac	LB	6-4	265	6/6/78	2	Morehouse College	Florissant, Mo.	FA-'01	0*
40	Kleinsasser, Jim	TE	6-3	274	1/31/77	4	North Dakota	Carrington, N.D.	D2-'99	11/11
63	Lacina, Corbin	G	6-4	314	11/2/70	9	Augustana	St. Paul, Minn.	FA-'99	16/16
43	Liddiard, Brody	TE	6-4	234	6/12/77	3	Colorado	San Diego, Calif.	FA-'01	16/0
62	Lindsay, Everett	G	6-4	302	9/18/70	9	Mississippi	Raleigh, N.C.	T(Cle)-'01	16/8
76	Liwienski, Chris	T	6-5	321	8/2/75	4	Indiana	Sterling Heights, Mich.	FA-'99	16/16
69	Malano, Mike	G	6-2	304	10/16/76	2	San Diego State	Scottsdale, Ariz.	D7a-'00	0*
85	McWilliams, Johnny	TE	6-4	271	12/14/72	6	Southern California	Ontario, Calif.	FA-'02	0*
79	Mixon, Kenny	DE	6-4	275	5/31/75	5	Louisiana State	Pineville, La.	UFA(Mia)-'02	16/16*
31	Morgan, Don	S	5-11	202	9/18/75	2	Nevada	Stockton, Calif.	FA-'01	16/2
33	Morrow, Harold	FB	5-11	232	2/24/73	7	Auburn	Maplesville, Ala.	W(Dall)-'96	16/2
84	Moss, Randy	WR	6-4	204	2/13/77	5	Marshall	Rand, W. Va.	D1-'98	16/16
56	Nelson, Jim	LB	6-1	234	4/16/75	4	Penn State	Waldorf, Md.	W(GB)-'00	16/2
96	O'Neal, Andre	LB	6-1	235	12/12/75	3	Marshall	Decatur, Ga.	FA-'01	4/1
5	Richardson, Kyle	P	6-2	210	3/2/73	6	Arkansas State	Farmington, Mo.	FA-'02	16/0*
98	Robbins, Fred	DT	6-4	313	3/25/77	3	Wake Forest	Pensacola, Fla.	D2a-'00	16/12
97	Sawyer, Talance	DE	6-2	270	6/14/76	4	Nevada-Las Vegas	Bastrop, La.	D6a-'99	16/16
41	Scott, Carey	CB	5-11	207	8/11/78	2	Kentucky State	Savannah, Ga.	D6-'01	0*
28	Tate, Robert	CB	5-10	193	10/19/73	6	Cincinnati	Harrisburg, Pa.	D6-'97	16/5
68	Waddell, Bennitte	T	6-5	308	5/26/77	2	Tuskegee	Sanford, N.C.	FA-'01	0*
81	Walsh, Chris	WR	6-1	199	12/12/68	10	Stanford	Concord, Calif.	FA-'94	16/0
94	Wiley, Chuck	DE	6-5	277	3/6/75	4	Louisiana State	Baton Rouge, La.	UFA(Atl)-'02	16/11*
30	Williams, Moe	RB	6-1	210	7/26/74	7	Kentucky	Columbus, Ga.	UFA(Balt)-'02	15/2*
54	Wilson, Antonio	LB	6-2	247	12/29/77	3	Texas A&M-Commerce	Dallas, Texas	D4a-'00	10/0
60	Withrow, Cory	C	6-2	281	4/5/75	3	Washington State	Spokane, Wash.	FA-'99	16/1
95	Worthen, Shawn	DT	6-0	316	9/12/78	2	Texas Christian	San Antonio, Texas	D4a-'01	4/0
20	Wright, Kenny	CB	6-1	205	9/14/77	4	Northwestern State	Ruston, La.	D4a-'99	15/8
3	Wynn, Spergon	QB	6-3	226	8/10/78	3	Southwest Texas State	Bellaire, Texas	T(Cle)-'01	3/2

* Bates played 11 games with Chicago in '01; Bradford played 14 games with Atlanta; Brien played 2 games with Tampa Bay; Bromell played 16 games with Miami; Chavous played 14 games with Arizona; Crawford was inactive with 16 games; Crockett played 16 games for Atlanta; Dawkins played 16 games with Jacksonville; Goodwin played 16 games with Miami; Holland was last active with Cleveland in '00; James missed '01 season because of injury; Keys missed '01 season because of injury; Malano missed '00 season because of injury; McWilliams was last active with Minnesota in '00; Mixon played 16 games with Miami; Richardson played 16 games with Baltimore; Scott missed '01 season because of injury; Waddell missed '01 season because of injury; Wiley played 16 games with Atlanta; Williams played 15 games with Baltimore.

Retired—Cris Carter, 15-year wide receiver, 16 games in '01.

Players lost through free agency (4): CB Dale Carter (NO; 9 games in '01), S Robert Griffith (Cle; 10), WR Jake Reed (NO; 16), LB Kailee Wong (Hou; 16).

Also played with Vikings in '01—K Gary Anderson (16 games), T Brad Badger (13), P Mitch Berger (12), DE Stalin Colinet (11), G Calvin Collins (7), DE Jeff Hazuga (3), WR-PR Nate Jacquet (10), P Lee Johnson (4), S Henry Jones (5), TE Andrew Jordan (16), LB Ed McDaniel (14), LB Pete Monty (6), RB Travis Prentice (14), CB Wasswa Serwanga (7), FB Matt Snider (4), CB-S Keith Thibodeaux (5), S Orlando Thomas (13), KR-RB Troy Walters (6), LB Fearon Wright (7).

2002 FIRST-YEAR ROSTER

Name	Pos.	Ht.	Wt.	Birthdate	College	Hometown	How Acq.
Allen, David (1)	RB	5-9	195	2/9/78	Kansas State	Euless, Texas	FA
Allen, Jeremy	RB	5-11	241	9/5/79	Iowa	Indianapolis, Ind.	FA
Ashe, Tyler	K	5-11	178	2/14/78	Wake Forest	Shelby, N.C.	FA
Beasley, Chad	DT	6-5	303	11/13/78	Virginia Tech	Gate City, Va.	D7
Bell, Atrews	WR	5-11	218	1/10/78	Florida State	Jacksonville, Fla.	FA
Brewer, Jack	S	6-0	194	1/8/79	Minnesota	Grapevine, Texas	FA
Campbell, Kelly	WR	5-10	171	7/23/80	Georgia Tech	Atlanta, Ga.	FA
Cercone, Matt (1)	TE	6-5	252	11/30/75	Arizona State	Bakersfield, Calif.	FA
Clark, Kenny (1)	WR	6-1	227	5/14/78	Central Florida	Ocala, Fla.	FA
Daniels, Carlos	RB	6-2	262	3/11/79	Western Illinois	Farrell, Pa.	FA
Davis, Nick	WR	6-0	180	10/6/79	Wisconsin	Manchester, Mich.	FA
France, Todd	K	6-3	185	2/13/80	Toledo	Maumee, Ohio	FA
Hebert, Kyries	S	6-3	205	10/9/80	Louisiana-Lafayette	Eunice, La.	FA
Hill, Shaun	QB	6-3	223	1/9/80	Maryland	Parsons, Kan.	FA
Kostrewa, Jeff (1)	TE	6-5	261	11/21/78	Wisconsin-La Crosse	Kenosha, Wis.	FA
Krager, Dane	LB	6-2	227	5/18/79	Angelo State	Austin, Texas	FA
Lewis, Devin	WR	6-2	205	7/22/79	Southern	New Orleans, La.	FA
Louisdor, Mesene (1)	CB	5-10	182	12/3/75	Central Michigan	Miami, Fla.	FA
McKinnie, Bryant	T	6-8	343	9/23/79	Miami	Woodbury, N.J.	D1
Miller, Romaro (1)	QB	6-1	195	9/12/78	Mississippi	Shannon, Miss.	FA
Morton, Brian (1)	P	6-6	231	9/23/78	Duke	Auburndale, Fla.	FA
Murphy, Nick	P	5-11	188	10/22/79	Arizona State	Scottsdale, Ariz.	FA
Offord, Willie	S	6-1	215	12/22/78	South Carolina	Palatka, Fla.	D3
Rogers, Nick	LB	6-2	251	5/31/79	Georgia Tech	East Point, Ga.	D6
Russell, Brian (1)	S	6-2	204	2/5/78	San Diego State	West Covina, Calif.	FA
Smith, Raonall	LB	6-2	244	10/22/79	Washington State	Gig Harbor, Wash.	D2
Ta'amu, Ed	G	6-1	335	11/8/79	Utah	Honolulu, Hawaii	D4b
Williams, Brian	S	5-11	207	7/2/79	North Carolina State	Guilford, N.C.	D4a
Wofford, James (1)	RB	6-0	186	6/6/78	Nevada-Las Vegas	Bakersfield, Calif.	FA
Yates, Max	LB	6-3	228	10/30/79	Marshall	Newport News, Va.	FA

The term NFL Rookie is defined as a player who is in his first season of professional football and has not been on the roster of another professional football team for any regular-season or postseason games. A Rookie is designated by an "R" on NFL rosters. Players who have been active in another professional football league or players who have NFL experience, including either preseason training camp or being on an Active List or Inactive List, or on Reserve/Injured or Reserve/Physically Unable to Perform for fewer than six regular-season games, are termed NFL First-Year Players. An NFL First-Year Player is designated by a "1" on NFL rosters. Thereafter, a player is credited with an additional year of experience for each season in which he accumulates six games on the Active List or Inactive List, or on Reserve/Injured or Reserve/Physically Unable to Perform.

COACHING STAFF
Head Coach,
Mike Tice

Pro Career: Named the Vikings sixth head coach on January 10, 2002. Tice has been associated with the team since 1992, playing tight end from 1992-93 and 1995, coaching the tight ends in 1996 and the offensive line from 1997-2001. Tice added the title of assistant head coach for the 2001 season and was made the interim head coach for the Vikings last regular season game of the 2001 season against Baltimore. Tice is the first Vikings alumni player to hold the title of the franchise's head coach. In five seasons coaching the offensive line, Tice guided five different players—Matt Birk, Jeff Christy, Randall McDaniel, Todd Steussie, Korey Stringer—to 10 Pro Bowl appearances. In 1998, the offensive line paved the way for numerous NFL and Vikings records including a League record for points scored in a season (556) and set Vikings records for total yards (6,264) and fewest sacks allowed in a 16-game season (25). Career record: 0-1.

Background: Played quarterback at the University of Maryland from 1977-1980. Tice completed 71of 140 passes for 928 yards with 5 touchdowns as a senior and 896 yards and 5 touchdowns as a junior. Over his 14-year NFL career, Tice caught 107 passes for 894 yards and 11 touchdowns and blocked for running backs that rushed for over 1,000 yards in a season five times. Tice played three seasons with the Vikings (1992-93, 1995), ten years with the Seattle Seahawks (1981-88, 1990-91), and one season with the Washington Redskins (1989) and made 109 starts in 177 games played.

Personal: Born February 2, 1959 in Bayshore, N.Y. Attended Central Islip High School on Long Island. He and wife Diane have two children, Adrienne and Nathan, and live in Edina, Minn.

ASSISTANT COACHES

Charlie Baggett, wide receivers; born January 21, 1953, Fayetteville, N.C., lives in Eden Prairie, Minn. Quarterback Michigan State 1972-75. No pro playing experience. College coach: Bowling Green 1977-1980, Minnesota 1981-82, Michigan State 1983-1992, 1995-98. Pro coach: Houston Oilers 1993-94, Green Bay Packers 1999, joined Vikings in 2000.

Brian Baker, linebackers; born June 20, 1962, Baltimore, lives in Eden Prairie, Minn. Linebacker Maryland 1980-83. No pro playing experience. College coach: Maryland 1984-85, Army 1986, Georgia Tech 1987-1995. Pro coach: San Diego Chargers 1996, Detroit Lions 1997-2000, joined Vikings in 2001.

Pete Bercich, defensive assistant-quality control; born December 23, 1971, Joliet, Ill., lives in Lakeville, Minn. Linebacker Notre Dame 1990-93. Pro linebacker Minnesota Vikings 1994-2000. Pro coach: Joined Vikings in 2002.

Dean Dalton, running backs; born July 27, 1963, Platteville, Wis., lives in Eden Prairie, Minn. Defensive back Air Force Academy 1981-82, Western Illinois 1983-84. No pro playing experience. College coach: Western Illinois 1984-85, Wisconsin 1986-87, Texas Southern 1988-89, Purdue 1990. Pro coach: Joined Vikings in 1999.

Jay Hayes, special teams; born March 3, 1960, South Fayette, Pa., lives in Eden Prairie, Minn. Defensive end Idaho 1978-1981. Pro defensive end-linebacker Michigan Panthers (USFL) 1984, Memphis Showboats (USFL) 1985. College coach: Notre Dame 1988-1991, California 1992-94, Wisconsin 1995-98. Pro coach: Pittsburgh Steelers 1999-2001, joined Vikings in 2002.

Chuck Knox, Jr., defensive backfield; born February 19, 1965, Englewood, N.J., lives in Eden Prairie, Minn. Running back Arizona 1984-88. No pro playing experience. Pro coach: Los Angeles Rams 1993-94, Philadelphia Eagles 1995-98, Green Bay Packers 1999, joined Vikings in 2000.

Daryl Lawrence, asst. strength & conditioning; born October 20, 1965, Chicago Heights, Ill., lives in Shakopee, Minn. Attended Illinois State. No college or pro playing experience. College coach: Illinois State 1995-96, Army 1998-99. Pro coach: Minnesota Vikings 1997, rejoined Vikings in 2000.

Scott Linehan, offensive coordinator; born September 17, 1963, Sunnyside, Wash., lives in Chanhassen, Minn. Quarterback Idaho 1982-86. No pro playing experience. College coach: Idaho 1988-1990, Nevada-Las Vegas 1991, Idaho 1992-93, Washington 1994-98, Louisville 1999-2001. Pro coach: Joined Vikings in 2002.

Steve Loney, offensive line; born April 26, 1952, Marshalltown, Iowa, lives in Savage, Minn. Offensive line Iowa State 1970-73. No pro playing experience. College coach: Missouri Western College 1975-76, Moorhead State 1979-1983, The Citadel 1984-86, Colorado State 1989-1992, Connecticut 1994, Iowa State 1995-97, 2000, Minnesota 1998-99. Pro coach: Phoenix Cardinals 1993, joined Vikings in 2002.

George O'Leary, asst. head coach-defensive line; born August 17, 1946, Manhattan, N.Y., lives in Edina, Minn. No college or pro playing experience. College coach: Syracuse 1980-86, Georgia Tech 1987-1991, 1994-2001 (head coach 1994-2001). Pro coach: San Diego Chargers 1992-93, joined Vikings in 2002.

Jim Panagos, offensive assistant-quality control; born March 23, 1971, Brooklyn, N.Y., lives in Eden Prairie, Minn. Defensive line Maryland 1989-1992. No pro playing experience. College coach: Maryland 1993. Pro coach: Joined Vikings in 2002.

Willie Shaw, defensive coordinator-secondary; born January 11, 1944, Glenmora, La., lives in Eden Prairie, Minn. Cornerback New Mexico 1966-68. No pro playing experience. College coach: San Diego (Calif.) C.C. 1970-73, Stanford 1974-76, 1989-1991, Long Beach State 1977-78, Oregon 1979, Arizona State 1980-84. Pro coach: Detroit Lions 1985-88, Minnesota Vikings 1992-93, San Diego Chargers 1994, St. Louis Rams 1995-96, New Orleans Saints 1997, Oakland Raiders 1998-99, Kansas City Chiefs 2000, rejoined Vikings in 2001.

John Tice, tight ends-asst. offensive line; born June 22, 1960, Bayshore, N.Y., lives in Eden Prairie, Minn. Tight end Maryland 1978-1982. Pro tight end New Orleans Saints 1983-1992. Pro coach: Joined Vikings in 1999.

Steve Wetzel, strength and conditioning; born May 11, 1963, Washington D.C., lives in Eden Prairie, Minn. Attended Slippery Rock. No college or pro playing experience. College coach: Maryland 1985-89, George Mason 1990. Pro coach: Washington Redskins 1990-91, joined Vikings in 1992.

Alex Wood, quarterbacks; born March 14, 1955, Massillon, Ohio, lives in Eden Prairie, Minn. Running back Iowa 1974-77. No pro playing experience. College coach: Iowa 1978, Kent 1979-1980, Southern Illinois 1981, Southern 1982-84, Wyoming 1985-86, Washington State 1987-88, Miami 1989-1992, Wake Forest 1993-94, James Madison (head coach) 1995-98. Pro coach: Joined Vikings in 1999.

National Football Conference
South Division
Team Colors: Old Gold, Black, and White
5800 Airline Drive
Metairie, Louisiana 70003
Telephone: (504) 733-0255

2002 SCHEDULE
PRESEASON

Aug. 10	**Houston**	7:00
Aug. 15	at Miami	7:00
Aug. 24	at Cincinnati	7:30
Aug. 30	**Indianapolis**	6:00

REGULAR SEASON

Sept. 8	at Tampa Bay	4:15
Sept. 15	**Green Bay**	12:00
Sept. 22	at Chicago (Champaign, Ill.)	12:00
Sept. 29	at Detroit	1:00
Oct. 6	**Pittsburgh**	12:00
Oct. 13	at Washington	1:00
Oct. 20	**San Francisco**	12:00
Oct. 27	**Atlanta**	12:00
Nov. 3	OPEN DATE	
Nov. 10	at Carolina	1:00
Nov. 17	at Atlanta	1:00
Nov. 24	**Cleveland**	12:00
Dec. 1	**Tampa Bay**	7:30
Dec. 8	at Baltimore	4:05
Dec. 15	**Minnesota**	12:00
Dec. 22	at Cincinnati	1:00
Dec. 29	**Carolina**	12:00

Stadium: Louisiana Superdome
(opened in 1975)
• **Capacity:** 68,390
1500 Poydras Street
New Orleans, Louisiana 70112
Playing Surface: AstroTurf
Training Camp: Nicholls State University
Thibodaux, LA 70310

LOUISIANA SUPERDOME

CLUB OFFICIALS
Owner: Tom Benson
General Manager of Football Operations:
Mickey Loomis
Director of Administration:
Arnold D. Fielkow
Assistant General Manager of Football
Operations: Charles Bailey
Director of Player Personnel:
Rick Mueller
College Scouting Coordinator:
Rick Thompson
Regional Scouting Supervisor:
Pat Mondock
Pro Scouts: Mike Baugh, Grant Neill,
Bill Quinter
Area Scouts: Mike Faulkiner,
Cornell Gowdy, Tim Heffelfinger,
Mark Sadowski, James Jefferson,
Barrett Wiley
Combine Scout: Andy Weidl
Football Operations Assistant: Ryan Pace
Equipment Manager: Dan Simmons
Head Athletic Trainer: Scottie B. Patton
Video Director: Dave Desposito
Director of Player Development:
Ricky Porter
Offensive Administrative Assistant:
John (Chip) Beake
Defensive Administrative Assistant:
T.D. Cox
Director of Media & Public Relations:
Greg Bensel
New Media Manager: Ricky Zeller
Media & Public Relations Managers:
Paul Corliss, Justin Macione,
Chris Pika
Director of Community Relations:
Vernon Cheek
Director of Photography:
Michael C. Hebert
Chief Financial Officer: Dennis Lauscha
Director of Sales & Marketing:
Wayne Hodes
Director of Regional Sales & Marketing:
Mike Feder
Manager of Ticket Sales & Services:
Mike Stanfield
Director of Team Logistics & Box Office
Manager: James Nagaoka
Director of Information Technology:
Bruce Reid, Jr.
Stadium Operations Manager:
Robert Sergent
Facility Manager: Terry Ashburn

COACHING HISTORY
(210-321-5)

1967-70	Tom Fears*	13-34-2
1970-72	J.D. Roberts	7-25-3
1973-75	John North**	11-23-0
1975	Ernie Hefferle	1-7-0
1976-77	Hank Stram	7-21-0
1978-80	Dick Nolan***	15-29-0
1980	Dick Stanfel	1-3-0
1981-85	O.A. (Bum) Phillips****	27-42-0
1985	Wade Phillips	1-3-0
1986-96	Jim Mora#	93-78-0
1996	Rick Venturi	1-7-0
1997-99	Mike Ditka	15-33-0
2000-01	Jim Haslett	18-16-0

*Released after seven games in 1970
**Released after six games in 1975
***Released after 12 games in 1980
****Resigned after 12 games in 1985
#Resigned after eight games in 1996

ATTENDANCE
Home 528,343   Away 543,365
Total 1,071,708
Single-game home record,
70,940 (9/2/79)
Single-season home record, 548,728
(1992)

2002 DRAFT CHOICES

Round	Name	Pos.	College
1	Donté Stallworth	WR	Tennessee
	Charles Grant	DE	Georgia
2	LeCharles Bentley	C	Ohio State
3	James Allen	LB	Oregon State
4	Keyuo Craver	DB	Nebraska
5	Mel Mitchell	DB	Western Kentucky
6	J.T. O'Sullivan	QB	Cal-Davis
	John Gilmore	TE	Penn State
7	Derrius Monroe	DE	Virginia Tech

NEW ORLEANS SAINTS

2001 TEAM RECORD
PRESEASON (1-3)

Date	Result	Opponent
8/11	L 21-28	vs.Minnesota, at San Antonio
8/18	W 16-10	Dallas
8/25	L 24-31	at Denver
9/1	L 14-28	Seattle

REGULAR SEASON (7-9)

Date	Result	Opponent	Att.
9/09	W 24-6	at Buffalo	71,447
9/30	L 13-21	at New York Giants	78,451
10/07	W 28-15	Minnesota	70,020
10/14	W 27-25	at Carolina	72,049
10/21	L 13-20	Atlanta	70,020
10/28	W 34-31	at St. Louis	66,189
11/04	L 9-16	New York Jets	70,020
11/11	L 27-28	at San Francisco	68,083
11/18	W 34-20	Indianapolis	70,020
11/25	L 17-34	at New England	60,292
12/02	W 27-23	Carolina	70,020
12/09	W 28-10	at Atlanta	68,826
12/17	L 21-34	St. Louis	70,332
12/23	L 21-48	at Tampa Bay	65,526
12/30	L 10-40	Washington	70,020
1/06	L 0-38	San Francisco	70,020

SCORE BY PERIODS

Saints	53	77	108	95	0 —	333
Opponents	120	120	47	122	0 —	409

2001 TEAM STATISTICS

	Saints	Opp.
Total First Downs	294	284
Rushing	87	88
Passing	184	169
Penalty	23	27
3rd Down: Made/Att	89/227	80/201
3rd Down Pct.	39.2	39.8
4th Down: Made/Att	6/18	3/12
4th Down Pct.	33.3	25.0
Possession Avg.	29:24	30:36
Total Net Yards	5226	5070
Avg. Per Game	326.6	316.9
Total Plays	1031	948
Avg. Per Play	5.1	5.3
Net Yards Rushing	1712	1715
Avg. Per Game	107.0	107.2
Total Rushes	419	443
Net Yards Passing	3514	3355
Avg. Per Game	219.6	209.7
Sacked/Yards Lost	50/330	53/323
Gross Yards	3844	3678
Att./Completions	562/313	452/278
Completion Pct.	55.7	61.5
Had Intercepted	22	15
Punts/Average	76/41.8	67/43.5
Net Punting Avg.	76/35.8	67/38.3
Penalties/Yards	119/1025	100/877
Fumbles/Ball Lost	35/13	28/15
Touchdowns	36	47
Rushing	8	15
Passing	27	30
Returns	1	2

2001 INDIVIDUAL STATISTICS

PASSING	Att.	Comp.	Yds.	Pct.	TD	Int.	Tkld.	Rate
Brooks	558	312	3832	55.9	26	22	50/330	76.4
McAllister	2	1	12	50.0	1	0	0/0	108.3
Blake	1	0	0	0.0	0	0	0/0	39.6
Horn	1	0	0	0.0	0	0	0/0	39.6
Saints	562	313	3844	55.7	27	22	50/330	76.7
Opponents	452	278	3678	61.5	30	15	53/323	95.5

SCORING	TD R	TD P	TD Rt	PAT	FG	Saf	PTS
Carney	0	0	0	32/32	27/31	0	113
Horn	0	9	0	0/0	0/0	0	54
R. Williams	6	1	0	0/0	0/0	0	42
W. Jackson	0	5	0	0/0	0/0	0	32
Cleeland	0	4	0	0/0	0/0	0	24
Bo. Williams	0	3	0	0/0	0/0	0	18
Connell	0	2	0	0/0	0/0	0	12
McAllister	1	1	0	0/0	0/0	0	12
T. Smith	0	2	0	0/0	0/0	0	12
Brooks	1	0	0	0/0	0/0	0	6
Oldham	0	0	1	0/0	0/0	0	6
Saints	8	27	1	32/32	27/31	1	333
Opponents	15	30	2	42/42	27/31	0	409

2-Pt. Conversions: W. Jackson.
Saints 1-4, Opponents 2-5.

RUSHING	Att.	Yds.	Avg.	LG	TD
R. Williams	313	1245	4.0	46	6
Brooks	80	358	4.5	26	1
McAllister	16	91	5.7	54t	1
T. Smith	5	8	1.6	6	0
Connell	1	6	6.0	6	0
Horn	1	4	4.0	4	0
McAfee	1	2	2.0	2	0
Blake	1	-1	-1.0	-1	0
Carney	1	-1	-1.0	-1	0
Saints	419	1712	4.1	54t	8
Opponents	443	1715	3.9	55	15

RECEIVING	No.	Yds.	Avg.	LG	TD
Horn	83	1265	15.2	56	9
W. Jackson	81	1046	12.9	63	5
R. Williams	60	511	8.5	42	1
R. Wilson	21	277	13.2	44	0
Bo. Williams	20	202	10.1	26	3
McAllister	15	166	11.1	22t	1
Cleeland	13	138	10.6	19t	4
Connell	12	191	15.9	46t	2
T. Smith	4	30	7.5	12	2
L. Hall	2	15	7.5	9	0
Stachelski	1	5	5.0	5	0
McGarity	1	-2	-2.0	-2	0
Saints	313	3844	12.3	63	27
Opponents	278	3678	13.2	86t	30

INTERCEPTIONS	No.	Yds.	Avg.	LG	TD
S. Knight	6	114	19.0	40	0
Bellamy	3	21	7.0	21	0
Mathis	2	34	17.0	23	0
Howard	1	37	37.0	37	0
Clemons	1	3	3.0	3	0
Oldham	1	0	0.0	0	0
Thomas	1	0	0.0	0	0
Saints	15	209	13.9	40	0
Opponents	22	189	8.6	36t	1

PUNTING	No.	Yds.	Avg.	In 20	LG
Gowin	76	3180	41.8	24	62
Saints	76	3180	41.8	24	62
Opponents	67	2917	43.5	19	70

PUNT RETURNS	No.	FC	Yds.	Avg.	LG	TD
McGarity	19	9	183	9.6	42	0
Lewis	14	0	81	5.8	32	0
McAllister	4	4	24	6.0	10	0
Saints	37	13	288	7.8	42	0
Opponents	36	18	316	8.8	70t	1

KICKOFF RETURNS	No.	Yds.	Avg.	LG	TD
McAllister	45	1091	24.2	63	0
Lewis	32	762	23.8	68	0
McAfee	6	144	24.0	34	0
Ackerman	2	11	5.5	11	0
Whitehead	2	19	9.5	12	0
Saints	87	2027	23.3	68	0
Opponents	66	1472	22.3	86	0

FIELD GOALS	1-19	20-29	30-39	40-49	50+
Carney	0/0	7/7	11/11	8/12	1/1
Saints	0/0	7/7	11/11	8/12	1/1
Opponents	0/0	9/9	8/9	5/8	5/5

SACKS	No.
Clemons	13.5
Johnson	9.0
Glover	8.0
Howard	6.0
Hand	3.5
Oldham	2.5
Bellamy	2.0
K. Mitchell	2.0
Whitehead	2.0
D. Smith	1.5
Chase	1.0
S. Knight	1.0
Mathis	1.0
Saints	53.0
Opponents	50.0

RECORD HOLDERS
INDIVIDUAL RECORDS—CAREER

Category	Name	Performance
Rushing (Yds.)	George Rogers, 1981-84	4,267
Passing (Yds.)	Archie Manning, 1971-1982	21,734
Passing (TDs)	Archie Manning, 1971-1982	115
Receiving (No.)	Eric Martin, 1985-1993	532
Receiving (Yds.)	Eric Martin, 1985-1993	7,854
Interceptions	Dave Waymer, 1980-89	37
Punting (Avg.)	Mark Royals, 1997-98	45.7
Punt Return (Avg.)	Mel Gray, 1986-88	13.4
Kickoff Return (Avg.)	Walter Roberts, 1967	26.3
Field Goals	Morten Andersen, 1982-1994	302
Touchdowns (Tot.)	Dalton Hilliard, 1986-1993	53
Points	Morten Andersen, 1982-1994	1,318

INDIVIDUAL RECORDS—SINGLE SEASON

Category	Name	Performance
Rushing (Yds.)	George Rogers, 1981	1,674
Passing (Yds.)	Jim Everett, 1995	3,970
Passing (TDs)	Jim Everett, 1995	26
	Aaron Brooks, 2001	26
Receiving (No.)	Joe Horn, 2000	94
Receiving (Yds.)	Joe Horn, 2000	1,340
Interceptions	Dave Whitsell, 1967	10
Punting (Avg.)	Mark Royals, 1997	45.9
Punt Return (Avg.)	Mel Gray, 1987	14.7
Kickoff Return (Avg.)	Don Shy, 1969	27.9
	Mel Gray, 1986	27.9
Field Goals	Morten Andersen, 1985	31
Touchdowns (Tot.)	Dalton Hilliard, 1989	18
Points	Morten Andersen, 1987	121

INDIVIDUAL RECORDS—SINGLE GAME

Category	Name	Performance
Rushing (Yds.)	George Rogers, 9-4-83	206
Passing (Yds.)	Aaron Brooks, 12-3-00	441
Passing (TDs)	Billy Kilmer, 11-2-69	6
Receiving (No.)	Tony Galbreath, 9-10-78	14
Receiving (Yds.)	Wes Chandler, 9-2-79	205
Interceptions	Tommy Myers, 9-3-78	3
	Dave Waymer, 10-6-85	3
	Reggie Sutton, 10-18-87	3
	Gene Atkins, 12-22-91	3
	Sammy Knight, 9-9-01	3
Field Goals	Many times	5
	Last time by John Carney, 10-28-01	
Touchdowns (Tot.)	Many times	3
	Last time by Ricky Williams, 10-22-00	
Points	Many times	18
	Last time by Ricky Williams, 10-22-00	

2002 VETERAN ROSTER

No.	Name	Pos.	Ht.	Wt.	Birthdate	NFL Exp.	College	Hometown	How Acq.	'01 Games/ Starts
20	Bellamy, Jay	S	5-11	200	7/8/72	9	Rutgers	Aberdeen, N.J.	UFA(Sea)-'01	16/16
2	Brooks, Aaron	QB	6-4	205	3/24/76	4	Virginia	Newport News, Va.	T(GB)-'00	16/16
3	Carney, John	K	5-11	180	4/20/64	13	Notre Dame	West Palm Beach, Fla.	FA-'01	15/0
21	Carter, Dale	CB	6-1	194	11/28/69	10	Tennessee	Covington, Ga.	UFA(Minn)-'02	9/8*
92	Chase, Martin	DT	6-2	310	12/19/74	5	Oklahoma	Lawton, Okla.	W(Balt)-'00	16/3
56	Clemons, Charlie	LB	6-2	250	7/4/72	6	Georgia	Griffin, Ga.	RFA(StL)-'00	16/15
51	Cox, Bryan	LB	6-4	250	2/1/68	12	Western Illinois	East St. Louis, Ill.	UFA(NE)-'02	11/7*
12	Delhomme, Jake	QB	6-2	205	1/10/75	4	Louisiana-Lafayette	Lafayette, La.	FA-'99	0*
71	Folau, Spencer	T	6-5	315	4/5/73	6	Idaho	Redwood City, Calif.	UFA(Mia)-'02	16/15*
62	Fontenot, Jerry	C	6-3	300	11/21/66	14	Texas A&M	Lafayette, La.	UFA(Chi)-'97	16/16
37	Gleason, Steve	S	5-11	215	3/19/77	2	Washington State	Gonzaga, Calif.	FA-'01	7/0
4	Gowin, Toby	P	5-10	167	3/30/75	6	North Texas	Jacksonville, Texas	RFA(Dall)-'00	16/0
81	Hall, Lamont	TE	6-4	260	11/16/74	4	Clemson	Clover, S.C.	T(GB)-'00	16/6
99	Hand, Norman	DT	6-3	310	9/4/72	8	Mississippi	Walterboro, S.C.	UFA(SD)-'00	13/13
36	Hawthorne, Michael	CB	6-3	196	1/26/77	3	Purdue	Sarasota, Fla.	D6b-'00	11/2
52	Hodge, Sedrick	LB	6-4	244	9/13/78	2	North Carolina	Atlanta, Ga.	D3a-'01	16/0
57	Holden, Curtis	LB	6-2	232	3/17/79	2	Washington State	San Francisco, Calif.	FA-'01	12/0
87	Horn, Joe	WR	6-1	206	1/16/72	7	Itawamba (Miss.) J.C.	New Haven, Conn.	UFA(KC)-'00	16/16
47	Houser, Kevin	LS	6-2	250	8/23/77	3	Ohio State	Westlake, Ohio	D7-'00	16/0
93	Howard, Darren	DE	6-3	281	11/19/76	3	Kansas State	St. Petersburg, Fla.	D2-'00	16/0
27	Irvin, Ken	CB	5-11	186	7/11/72	8	Memphis	Lindale, Ga.	FA-'02	14/14*
91	Jackson, Grady	DT	6-2	330	1/21/73	6	Knoxville	Greensboro, Ala.	UFA(Oak)-'02	16/16*
64	Jacox, Kendyl	C-G	6-2	330	6/10/75	5	Kansas State	Dallas, Texas	UFA(NO)-'02	16/16*
29	Knight, Sammy	S	6-0	205	9/10/75	6	Southern California	Riverside, Calif.	FA-'97	16/16
7	Lewis, Jeff	QB	6-2	215	4/17/73	5	Northern Arizona	Scottsdale, Ariz.	FA-'02	0*
84	Lewis, Michael	WR	5-8	165	11/14/71	2	No College	New Orleans, La.	FA-'01	8/0
23	Mathis, Kevin	CB	5-9	185	4/29/74	6	Texas A&M-Commerce	Gainesville, Texas	T(Dall)-'00	14/13
25	McAfee, Fred	RB	5-10	193	6/20/68	11	Mississippi College	Philadelphia, Miss.	UFA(TB)-'00	16/0
26	McAllister, Deuce	RB	6-1	221	12/27/78	2	Mississippi	Lena, Miss.	D1-'01	16/4
67	Miller, Bubba	C-G	6-1	305	1/24/73	7	Tennessee	Franklin, Tenn.	UFA(Phil)-'02	0*
85	Mitchell, Johnny	TE	6-3	241	1/20/71	5	Nebraska	Chicago, Ill.	FA-'01	0*
30	Moronkola, Dee	CB-S	5-9	190	7/1/77	2	Washington State	Richmond, Calif.	FA-'02	0*
31	Newsome, Richard	S	5-11	202	12/6/77	2	Michigan State	Fostoria, Ohio	FA-'01	11/0
33	Norris, Moran	FB	6-1	250	6/16/78	2	Kansas	Houston, Texas	D4-'01	5/0
89	Ojo, Onome	WR	6-4	205	6/3/77	2	California-Davis	San Francisco, Calif.	D5-'01	0*
80	Pathon, Jerome	WR	6-0	182	12/16/75	5	Washington	N. Vancouver, B.C., Canada	UFA(Ind)-'02	4/3*
86	Reed, Jake	WR	6-3	213	9/28/67	12	Grambling State	Covington, Ga.	UFA(Minn)-'02	16/0*
76	Reyes, Tutan	T	6-3	299	10/28/77	3	Mississippi	Queens, N.Y.	D5a-'00	1/0
66	Riley, Victor	T	6-5	328	11/4/74	5	Auburn	Swansea, S.C.	UFA(KC)-'02	7/5*
74	Sanderson, Scott	T	6-6	295	7/25/74	6	Washington State	Concord, Calif.	FA-'01	0*
88	Sloan, David	TE	6-6	260	6/8/72	8	New Mexico	Tollhouse, Calif.	UFA(Det)-'02	15/15*
54	Smith, Darrin	LB	6-1	230	4/15/70	10	Miami	Miami, Fla.	FA-'00	16/16
90	Smith, Kenny	DT	6-4	295	9/8/77	2	Alabama	Meridian, Miss.	D3b-'01	6/0
44	Smith, Terrelle	FB	6-0	246	3/12/78	2	Arizona State	Mareno Valley, Calif.	D4-'01	14/9
22	Thomas, Fred	CB	5-9	184	9/11/73	7	Tennessee-Martin	Bruce, Miss.	UFA(Sea)-'00	16/16
68	Turley, Kyle	T	6-5	300	9/24/75	5	San Diego State	Moreno Valley, Calif.	D1-'98	16/16
98	Whitehead, Willie	DE	6-3	285	1/26/73	4	Auburn	Tuskegee, Ala.	FA-'99	14/0
82	Williams, Boo	TE	6-4	235	6/22/79	2	Arkansas	Tallahassee, Fla.	FA-'01	11/4
63	Williams, Wally	G-C	6-2	321	2/20/71	10	Florida A&M	Tallahassee, Fla.	UFA(Balt)-'99	15/15
49	Wilson, Jerry	CB	5-10	190	7/17/73	7	Southern	Lake Charles, La.	FA-'01	1/0

* Carter played 9 games for Minnesota in '01; Cox played 11 games with New England; Delhomme was inactive for 16 games; Folau played 16 games with Miami; Irvin played 14 games with Buffalo; G. Jackson played 16 games with Oakland; Jacox played 16 games with San Diego; J. Lewis last active with Carolina in '00; Miller missed '01 season because of injury with Philadelphia; J. Mitchell was inactive for 2 games; Moronkola last active with Jacksonville in '99; Ojo inactive for 16 games; Pathon played 4 games with Indianapolis; Reed played 16 games with Minnesota; Riley played 7 games with Kansas City; Sanderson inactive for 6 games; Sloan played 15 games with Detroit.

Traded—T Willie Roaf (7 games in '01) to Kansas City; RB Ricky Williams (16) to Miami.

Players lost to free agency (6): TE Cameron Cleeland (NE; 9 games in '01), DT La'Roi Glover (Dall; 16), DE Joe Johnson (GB; 16), G Chris Naeole (Jax; 16), T Marcus Price (Buff; 12), CB Fred Weary (Atl; 14).

Also played with Saints in '01—C-G Tom Ackerman (16 games), QB Jeff Blake (1), LB Phil Clarke (13), WR Albert Connell (11), CB Steve Israel (9), WR Willie Jackson (16), WR Wane McGarity (12), LB Keith Mitchell (15), S Chris Oldham (16), T Daryl Terrell (16), WR Robert Wilson (15).

2002 FIRST-YEAR ROSTER

Name	Pos.	Ht.	Wt.	Birthdate	College	Hometown	How Acq.
Adams, Jonathan	RB	6-0	219	1/26/79	Arkansas State	Osceola, Ark.	FA
Alexander, Hilton (1)	WR	6-2	185	6/15/78	Morris Brown	Atlanta, Ga.	FA
Alexander, P.J.	T	6-4	297	12/23/78	Syracuse	Tallahassee, Fla.	FA
Allen, James	LB	6-2	240	11/11/79	Oregon State	Portland, Ore.	D3
Bentley, LeCharles	G-C	6-2	299	11/7/79	Ohio State	Cleveland, Ohio	D2
Bradley, Roylin (1)	LB	6-2	232	7/15/78	Texas A&M	LaMarque, Texas	FA
Carroll, Travis	LB	6-4	240	10/26/78	Florida	Jacksonville, Fla.	FA
Carter, Tim (1)	CB	6-0	183	7/15/78	Tulane	Tallahassee, Fla.	FA-'01
Chaney, Jeff (1)	RB	5-10	205	11/16/76	Florida State	Lake Wales, Fla.	FA
Chase, Jeff (1)	G-T	6-4	295	3/23/76	Texas A&M-Kingsville	Rowland Heights, Calif.	FA
Cook, Shane (1)	T	6-6	303	12/14/76	Colorado	Lakewood, Colo.	FA
Craver, Keyuo	CB	5-10	195	8/22/80	Nebraska	Harleton, Texas	D4
Cutolo, Frank	WR	5-10	181	1/8/78	Eastern Illinois	Boca Raton, Fla.	FA
Elstrom, Todd	WR	6-2	200	12/26/79	Washington	Puyallup, Wash.	FA
Fenderson, James (1)	RB	5-9	200	10/24/76	Hawaii	Oahu, Hawaii	FA-'01
Gilmore, John	TE	6-3	265	9/21/79	Penn State	West Lawn, Pa.	D6b
Grant, Charles	DE	6-3	282	9/3/78	Georgia	Colquitt, Ga.	D1b
Hadenfeldt, Dan (1)	P	5-11	195	8/7/76	Nebraska	West Des Moines, Iowa	FA
House, Kevin	CB	5-11	175	1/9/79	South Carolina	Tampa, Fla.	FA
Jackson, Jonathan (1)	LB	6-2	248	9/2/77	Oregon State	Las Vegas, Nev.	FA-'01
Johnson, Dirk (1)	P	6-0	205	6/1/75	Northern Colorado	Montrose, Calif.	FA
Jones, J.J. (1)	LB	6-1	230	6/7/78	Arkansas	Manolia, Ark.	FA
Knight, Roger (1)	LB	6-0	245	10/11/78	Wisconsin	Brooklyn, N.Y.	FA-'01
Lacey, Chonn	S	6-2	218	5/15/79	Temple	Pottstown, Pa.	FA
LeClair, Andrew	LB	6-5	244	10/26/78	North Dakota State	Mayville, N.D.	FA
Lewis, Derrick	WR	6-2	185	10/30/75	San Diego State	New Orleans, La.	FA
Miles, Jermaine (1)	DE	6-4	270	8/16/74	Georgia Tech	Brooklyn, N.Y.	FA
Mitchell, Mel	S	6-1	220	2/2/79	Western Kentucky	Rockledge, Fla.	D5
Monroe, Derrius	DE	6-4	269	7/21/78	Virginia Tech	Tallahassee, Fla.	D7
Montgomery, Jerry	DT	6-3	300	9/19/79	Iowa	Mesquite, Nev.	FA
Noah, Abdul-Salam (1)	DT	6-4	280	9/19/78	San Jose State	Los Angeles, Calif.	FA
O'Sullivan, J.T.	QB	6-2	220	8/25/79	California-Davis	Carmichael, Calif.	D6a
Reed, Jeff	K	5-11	215	4/9/79	North Carolina	Charlotte, N.C.	FA
Robinson, Jimmy (1)	WR	6-1	201	10/22/76	Kentucky	Stone Mountain, Ga.	FA
Romero, John (1)	C-G	6-4	316	10/3/76	California	San Leandro, Calif.	FA
Seals, Richard (1)	DT	6-3	305	3/18/76	Utah	Houston, Texas	FA
Sherrod, Rick	S	6-2	195	1/19/79	West Virginia	Charleston, W. Va.	FA
Smith, Demetrius	FB	6-2	255	8/6/79	Southwest Missouri State	Oaklawn, Ill.	FA
Stallworth, Donte'	WR	6-0	197	11/10/80	Tennessee	Sacramento, Calif.	D1a
Valletta, Chris (1)	G	6-2	285	3/1/78	Texas A&M	Plano, Texas	FA
White, Mitch (1)	T	6-4	311	3/25/78	Oregon State	San Diego, Calif.	D6-'01
Wiggins, Bruce (1)	C	6-3	286	10/13/77	Arizona	Houston, Texas	FA
Wiliams, Richard (1)	WR	5-11	180	4/16/77	Arizona State	Miami, Fla.	FA
Williams, Ricky	RB	5-7	195	8/1/78	Texas Tech	Duncanville, Texas	FA

The term NFL Rookie is defined as a player who is in his first season of professional football and has not been on the roster of another professional football team for any regular-season or postseason games. A Rookie is designated by an "R" on NFL rosters. Players who have been active in another professional football league or players who have NFL experience, including either preseason training camp or being on an Active List or Inactive List, or on Reserve/Injured or Reserve/Physically Unable to Perform for fewer than six regular-season games, are termed NFL First-Year Players. An NFL First-Year Player is designated by a "1" on NFL rosters. Thereafter, a player is credited with an additional year of experience for each season in which he accumulates six games on the Active List or Inactive List, or on Reserve/Injured or Reserve/Physically Unable to Perform.

NEW ORLEANS SAINTS

COACHING STAFF
Head Coach,
Jim Haslett
Pro Career: Named the thirteenth head coach in Saints history on February 3, 2000. He enters his third season as head coach with the second-best winning percentage (.531) in club history. In 2000, led the Saints to a 10-6 record and their first-ever playoff victory. Previously coached the Pittsburgh Steelers (1997-99), the Saints (1995-96), Los Angeles Raiders (1993-94), and the Sacramento Surge (1991-92). Haslett was a second-round draft choice of the Buffalo Bills in 1979, when he captured *Associated Press* defensive rookie of the year honors. He concluded his playing career with the New York Jets in 1987. Haslett began his initial coaching at the University of Buffalo (1988-1990). Career record: 18-16.
Background: Haslett was a three-time All-America at defensive end at Indiana University of Pennsylvania (1975-78).
Personal: Born December 9, 1955 in Pittsburgh. He and his wife Beth, have three children—Kelsey, Elizabeth, and Chase.

ASSISTANT COACHES
Hubbard Alexander, wide receivers; born February 14, 1939, Winston-Salem, N.C., lives in Metairie, La. Center Tennessee State 1958-1961. No pro playing experience. College coach: Tennessee State 1962-63, Vanderbilt 1974-78, Miami 1979-1988. Pro coach: Dallas Cowboys 1989-1997, Minnesota Vikings 1998-99, joined Saints in 2000.
Dave Atkins, running backs; born May 18, 1949, Victoria, Texas, lives in Destrehan, La. Running back Texas-El Paso 1970-72. Pro running back San Francisco 49ers 1973, Honolulu Hawaiians (WFL) 1974, San Diego Chargers 1975. College coach: Texas El-Paso 1979-1980, San Diego State 1981-85. Pro coach: Philadelphia Eagles 1986-1992, New England Patriots 1993, Arizona Cardinals 1994-95, New Orleans Saints 1996, Minnesota Vikings 1997-99, rejoined Saints in 2000.
Joe Baker, asst. secondary; born June 29, 1969, Glen Ridge, N.J., lives in New Orleans. Wide receiver Princeton 1987-1990. No pro playing experience. College coach: East Stroudsburg 1991, Samford 1993, Wisconsin 1999. Pro coach: Birmingham Fire (WFL) 1992, Jacksonville Jaguars 1994-98, joined Saints in 2000.
Greg Brown, defensive assistant; born October 10, 1957, Denver, lives in River Ridge, Colo. (Ariz.) C.C. 1976-77, Texas-El Paso 1978-79. No pro playing experience. College coach: Wyoming 1987-88, Purdue 1989-1990, Colorado 1991-93. Pro coach: Tampa Bay Buccaneers 1984-86, Atlanta Falcons 1994, San Diego Chargers 1995-96, Tennessee Oilers 1997-98, San Francisco

49ers 1999, Atlanta Falcons 2000-01, joined Saints in 2002.
Sam Clancy, defensive line; born May 29, 1958, Pittsburgh, lives in Destrehan, La. No college playing experience. Pro defensive lineman Seattle Seahawks 1982-83, Pittsburgh Maulers (USFL) 1984-85, Cleveland Browns 1985-88, Indianapolis Colts 1989-1993. Pro coach: Barcelona Dragons (NFLE) 1995-99, joined Saints in 2000.
Al Everest, special teams; born August 22, 1950, Santa Barbara, Calif., lives in Destrehan, La. Safety Southern Methodist 1970-71. No pro playing experience. College coach: Southern Methodist 1972, North Texas State 1973-74, Cameron (Okla.) 1974-75, U.S. International 1981-87. Pro coach: Arkansas Miners (PSFL) 1991-92, Birmingham Barracudas (CFL) 1995, Arizona Cardinals 1996-99, joined Saints in 2000.
Rock Gullickson, strength and conditioning; born April 11, 1955, Moorhead, Minn., lives in Destrehan, La. Guard Moorhead (Minn.) State 1973-76. College coach: Moorhead State 1978, Mayville (N.D.) State 1979-1980, South Dakota State 1981, Montana State 1982-89, Rutgers 1990-92, Texas 1993-97, Louisville 1998-99. Pro coach: Joined Saints in 2000.
Jack Henry, offensive line; born March 14, 1946, Wilmerding, Pa., lives in Destrehan, La. Linebacker Penn State 1964-65, guard Indiana (Penn.) 1967-68. No pro playing experience. College coach: West Virginia 1970, 1978-79, Edinboro 1973, Louisville 1974, Millersville 1975-76, Southern Illinois 1977, Appalachian State 1980, Wake Forest 1981-85, Indiana (Penn.) 1986-89, Pittsburgh 1993-95. Pro coach: Pittsburgh Steelers 1990-91, San Diego Chargers 1996, Detroit Lions 1997-99, joined Saints in 2000.
Jim Hostler, asst. wide receivers; born November 11, 1966, Pittsburgh, lives in Destrehan, La. Defensive back Indiana (Penn.) 1986-89. No pro playing experience. College coach: Indiana (Penn.) 1990-92, 1994-99, Juniata (Penn.) 1993. Pro coach: Kansas City Chiefs 2000, joined Saints in 2001.
Danny Langsdorf, offensive assistant; born June 28, 1972, Fargo, N.D., lives in New Orleans. Quarterback Boise State 1991-93, Linfield College 1994-95. No pro playing experience. College coach: Cal Lutheran 1996, Oregon State 1997-98. Pro coach: Edmonton Eskimos (CFL) 1999-2001, joined Saints in 2002.
Evan Marcus, asst. strength and conditioning; born January 2, 1968, Cranford, N.J., lives in River Ridge, La. Tackle Ithaca College 1986-1990. No pro playing experience. College coach: Arizona State 1990-91, Rutgers 1993, Maryland 1994, Texas 1995-97, Louisville 1998-99. Pro coach: Joined Saints in 2000.

Mike McCarthy, offensive coordinator; born November 10, 1963, Pittsburgh, lives in Destrehan, La. Tight end Baker 1985-86. No pro playing experience. College coach: Fort Hays State 1987-88, Pittsburgh 1989-1992. Pro coach: Kansas City Chiefs 1993-98, Green Bay Packers 1999, joined Saints in 2000.
Winston Moss, linebackers; born December 24, 1965, Miami, lives in Kenner, La. Linebacker Miami 1983-86. Pro linebacker Tampa Bay Buccaneers 1987-1990, Los Angeles Raiders 1991-94, Seattle Seahawks 1995-97. Pro coach: Seattle Seahawks 1998, joined Saints in 2000.
Bob Palcic, tight ends; born July 2, 1948, Gownada, N.Y., lives in Destrehan, La. Linebacker Dayton 1968-1970. No pro playing experience. College coach: Dayton 1974-75, Ball State 1976-77, Wisconsin 1978-1981, Arizona 1984-85, Ohio State 1986-1991, Southern California 1992, UCLA 1993. Pro coach: Atlanta Falcons 1994-96, Detroit Lions 1997-98, Cleveland Browns 1999, joined Saints in 2000.
Mike Riley, asst. head coach-secondary; born July 6, 1953, Wallace, Idaho, lives in New Orleans. Defensive back Alabama 1971-74. No pro playing experience. College coach: California 1975, Whitworth College 1976, Linfield College 1977-1982, Northern Colorado 1986, Southern California 1993-96, Oregon State 1997-98 (head coach). Pro coach: Winnipeg Blue Bombers (CFL) 1983-85, 1987-1990 (head coach 1987-1990), San Antonio Riders (World League) 1991-92, San Diego Chargers 1999-2001 (head coach), joined Saints in 2002.
Mike Sheppard, quarterbacks; born October 29, 1951, Tulsa, Okla., lives in Destrehan, La. Wide receiver Cal Lutheran 1969-1972. No pro playing experience. College coach: Cal Lutheran 1974-76, Brigham Young 1977-78, U.S. International 1979, Idaho State 1980-81, Long Beach State 1982, 1984-86, Kansas 1983, New Mexico 1987-1991, California 1992. Pro coach: Cleveland Browns 1993-95, Baltimore Ravens 1996, San Diego Chargers 1997-98, Seattle Seahawks 1999-2000, Buffalo Bills 2001, joined Saints in 2002.
Rick Venturi, defensive coordinator; born February 23, 1946, Taylorville, Ill., lives in Destrehan, La. Quarterback-defensive back Northwestern 1965-67. No pro playing experience. College coach: Northwestern 1968-1972, 1978-1980 (head coach), Purdue 1973-76, Illinois 1977. Pro coach: Hamilton Tiger-Cats (CFL) 1981, Indianapolis Colts 1982-1993 (interim head coach for final 11 games of 1991), Cleveland Browns 1994-95, joined Saints in 1996 (interim head coach for final eight games of 1996).

**National Football Conference
East Division
Team Colors:** Blue, Red, and White
**Giants Stadium
East Rutherford, New Jersey 07073
Telephone:** (201) 935-8111

2002 SCHEDULE
PRESEASON
Aug. 5   vs. Houston 8:00
Aug. 10 **New England** 8:00
Aug. 17 at Atlanta............................4:00
Aug. 24 at New York Jets 8:00
Aug. 29 **Baltimore** 8:00

REGULAR SEASON
Sept. 5   **San Francisco (Thurs.)**......8:30
Sept. 15 at St. Louis.........................3:05
Sept. 22 **Seattle**..............................4:15
Sept. 29 at Arizona...........................1:05
Oct. 6   at Dallas.........................12:00
Oct. 13   **Atlanta**.............................1:00
Oct. 20   OPEN DATE
Oct. 28   at Philadelphia (Mon.).........9:00
Nov. 3   **Jacksonville**.....................8:30
Nov. 10   at Minnesota 12:00
Nov. 17   **Washington** 1:00
Nov. 24   at Houston 3:15
Dec. 1   **Tennessee** 1:00
Dec. 8   at Washington 1:00
Dec. 15   **Dallas** 4:15
Dec. 22   at Indianapolis....................1:00
Dec. 28   **Philadelphia (Sat.)** 1:30

Stadium: Giants Stadium (opened in 1976)
 •**Capacity:** 80,242
   East Rutherford, New Jersey
   07073
Playing Surface: Natural Grass
Training Camp: University at Albany
                1400 Washington Avenue
                Albany, N.Y. 12222

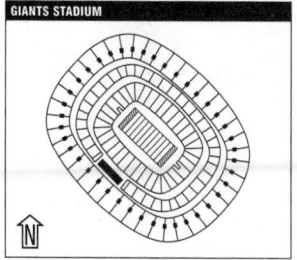

GIANTS STADIUM

CLUB OFFICIALS
President/Co-CEO: Wellington T. Mara
Chairman/Co-CEO: Preston Robert Tisch
Executive Vice President/General
   Counsel: John K. Mara, Esq.
Treasurer: Jonathan Tisch
Vice President-General Manager:
   Ernie Accorsi
Vice President-Chief Financial Officer:
   Christine Procops
Vice President-Marketing: Rusty Hawley
Vice-President-Communications:
   Pat Hanlon
Assistant General Manager:
   Kevin Abrams
Director of College Player Personnel:
   Jerry Reese
Director of Pro Player Personnel:
   David Gettleman
Assistant Director of Pro Player
   Personnel: Ken Sternfeld
Director of College Scouting: Jerry Shay
Director of Research and Development:
   Raymond J. Walsh, Jr.
Director of Player Development:
   Greg Gabriel
Pro Personnel Assistant: Geoff Mazza
Director of Promotions: Frank Mara
Ticket Manager: John Gorman
Director of Administration: Jim Phelan
Controller: Steven Hamrahi
Director of Community Relations:
   Allison Stangeby
Director of Creative Services:
   Doug Murphy
Director of Public Relations:
   Peter John-Baptiste
Assistant Director of Communications:
   Avis Roper
Head Athletic Trainer: Ronnie Barnes
Assistant Athletic Trainers: John
   Johnson, Steve Kennelly,
   Byron Hansen
Equipment Manager: Ed Wagner, Jr.

COACHING HISTORY
(573-479-33)
Year	Coach	Record
1925	Bob Folwell	8-4-0
1926	Joe Alexander	8-4-1
1927-28	Earl Potteiger	15-8-3
1929-1930	LeRoy Andrews*	24-5-1
1930	Benny Friedman-Steve Owen	2-0-0
1931-1953	Steve Owen	153-108-17
1954-1960	Jim Lee Howell	55-29-4
1961-68	Allie Sherman	57-54-4
1969-1973	Alex Webster	29-40-1
1974-76	Bill Arnsparger**	7-28-0
1976-78	John McVay	14-23-0
1979-1982	Ray Perkins	24-35-0
1983-1990	Bill Parcells	85-52-1
1991-92	Ray Handley	14-18-0
1993-96	Dan Reeves	32-34-0
1997-2001	Jim Fassel	46-37-1

*Released after 15 games in 1930
**Released after games in 1976

ATTENDANCE
Home 627,985   Away 521,034
Total 1,149,019
Single-game home record,
78,821 (10/22/01)
Single-season home record, 627,985
(2001)

2002 DRAFT CHOICES
Round	Name	Pos.	College
1	Jeremy Shockey	TE	Miami
2	Tim Carter	WR	Auburn
3	Jeff Hatch	T	Pennsylvania
5	Nick Greisen	LB	Wisconsin
6	Wesly Mallard	LB	Oregon
7	Daryl Jones	WR	Miami
	Quincy Monk	LB	North Carolina

2001 TEAM RECORD
PRESEASON (1-3)
Date	Result	Opponent
8/10	L 0-14	at New England
8/16	W 27-5	Jacksonville
8/25	L 14-17	New York Jets
8/31	L 9-38	at Baltimore

REGULAR SEASON (7-9)
Date	Result	Opponent	Att.
9/10	L 20-31	at Denver	75,735
9/23	W 13-3	at Kansas City	77,666
9/30	W 21-13	New Orleans	78,451
10/07	W 23-9	Washington	78,651
10/14	L 14-15	at St. Louis	65,992
10/22	L 9-10	Philadelphia	78,821
10/28	L 21-35	at Washington	80,316
11/04	W 27-24	Dallas (OT)	78,673
11/11	W 17-10	at Arizona	36,917
11/19	L 16-28	at Minnesota	64,283
11/25	L 10-28	Oakland	78,756
12/09	L 13-20	at Dallas	61,821
12/15	W 17-13	Arizona	77,913
12/23	W 27-24	Seattle	78,119
12/30	L 21-24	at Philadelphia	65,885
1/06	L 25-34	Green Bay	78,601
(OT) Overtime			

SCORE BY PERIODS
Giants	63	94	34	100	3 —	294
Opponents	88	80	60	93	0 —	321

2001 TEAM STATISTICS
	Giants	Opp.
Total First Downs	295	268
Rushing	93	83
Passing	189	161
Penalty	13	24
3rd Down: Made/Att	78/220	66/218
3rd Down Pct.	35.5	30.3
4th Down: Made/Att	6/13	11/19
4th Down Pct.	46.2	57.9
Possession Avg.	29:43	30:17
Total Net Yards	5335	4975
Avg. Per Game	333.4	310.9
Total Plays	1028	995
Avg. Per Play	5.2	5.0
Net Yards Rushing	1777	1545
Avg. Per Game	111.1	96.6
Total Rushes	424	428
Net Yards Passing	3558	3430
Avg. Per Game	222.4	214.4
Sacked/Yards Lost	36/206	46/320
Gross Yards	3764	3750
Att./Completions	568/327	521/298
Completion Pct.	57.6	57.2
Had Intercepted	16	15
Punts/Average	96/42.2	90/41.8
Net Punting Avg.	96/34.9	90/35.6
Penalties/Yards	97/905	100/695
Fumbles/Ball Lost	41/13	29/13
Touchdowns	32	36
Rushing	11	7
Passing	19	25
Returns	2	4

2001 INDIVIDUAL STATISTICS
PASSING
	Att.	Comp.	Yds.	Pct.	TD	Int.	Tkld.	Rate
Collins	568	327	3764	57.6	19	16	36/206	77.1
Giants	568	327	3764	57.6	19	16	36/206	77.1
Opponents	521	298	3750	57.2	25	15	46/320	83.7

SCORING
	TD R	TD P	TD Rt	PAT	FG	Saf	PTS
Andersen	0	0	0	29/30	23/28	0	98
Dayne	7	0	0	0/0	0/0	0	44
Hilliard	0	6	0	0/0	0/0	0	36
Toomer	0	5	0	0/0	0/0	0	30
Barber	4	0	0	0/0	0/0	0	26
Jurevicius	0	3	0	0/0	0/0	0	18
Rivers	0	2	0	0/0	0/0	0	12
Campbell	0	1	0	0/0	0/0	0	6
Comella	0	1	0	0/0	0/0	0	6
Dixon	0	1	0	0/0	0/0	0	6
Sehorn	0	0	1	0/0	0/0	0	6
Strahan	0	0	1	0/0	0/0	0	6
Pochman	0	0	0	0/0	0/2	0	0
Giants	11	19	2	29/30	23/30	0	294
Opponents	7	25	4	34/34	23/31	0	321

2-Pt. Conversions: Barber, Dayne.
Giants 2-2, Opponents 1-2.

RUSHING
	Att.	Yds.	Avg.	LG	TD
Barber	166	865	5.2	36	4
Dayne	180	690	3.8	61	7
Washington	28	89	3.2	22	0
Collins	39	73	1.9	11	0
Hilliard	1	21	21.0	21	0
R. Williams	2	16	8.0	11	0
Comella	4	15	3.8	9	0
Toomer	3	8	2.7	9	0
Dixon	1	0	0.0	0	0
Giants	424	1777	4.2	61	11
Opponents	428	1545	3.6	44	7

RECEIVING
	No.	Yds.	Avg.	LG	TD
Toomer	72	1054	14.6	60t	5
Barber	72	577	8.0	44	0
Hilliard	52	659	12.7	38	6
Jurevicius	51	706	13.8	46t	3
Comella	39	253	6.5	26	1
Campbell	13	148	11.4	25	1
Dixon	8	227	28.4	62	1
Dayne	8	67	8.4	21	0
Washington	4	25	6.3	16	0
Davis	3	34	11.3	20	0
Rivers	3	11	3.7	8	2
Cross	1	5	5.0	5	0
Collins	1	-2	-2.0	-2	0
Giants	327	3764	11.5	76	19
Opponents	298	3750	12.6	76t	25

INTERCEPTIONS
	No.	Yds.	Avg.	LG	TD
Allen	4	27	6.8	17	0
Sehorn	3	34	11.3	34t	1
S. Williams	3	25	8.3	20	0
Short	1	21	21.0	21	0
Jones	1	14	14.0	14	0
Garnes	1	5	5.0	5	0
Thomas	1	3	3.0	3	0
Peterson	1	0	0.0	0	0
Giants	15	129	8.6	34t	1
Opponents	16	181	11.3	71t	2

PUNTING
	No.	Yds.	Avg.	In 20	LG
R. Williams	91	3905	42.9	25	90
Pochman	5	146	29.2	3	39
Giants	96	4051	42.2	28	90
Opponents	90	3761	41.8	31	64

PUNT RETURNS
	No.	FC	Yds.	Avg.	LG	TD
Barber	38	12	338	8.9	23	0
Toomer	8	1	41	5.1	15	0
Dixon	1	0	-3	-3.0	-3	0
Giants	47	13	376	8.0	23	0
Opponents	45	9	543	12.1	89t	1

KICKOFF RETURNS
	No.	Yds.	Avg.	LG	TD
Dixon	34	645	19.0	43	0
Carter	8	155	19.4	31	0
Stoutmire	8	127	15.9	24	0
Washington	6	99	16.5	22	0
Campbell	2	8	4.0	8	0
McDaniel	1	17	17.0	17	0
Rivers	1	11	11.0	11	0
Giants	60	1062	17.7	43	0
Opponents	66	1593	24.1	68	0

FIELD GOALS
	1-19	20-29	30-39	40-49	50+
Andersen	0/0	8/8	7/8	6/7	2/5
Pochman	0/0	0/0	0/0	0/0	0/2
Giants	0/0	8/8	7/8	6/7	2/7
Opponents	0/0	7/7	9/10	6/12	1/2

SACKS
	No.
Strahan	22.5
Barrow	6.0
Hamilton	6.0
K. Holmes	3.5
Griffin	2.5
Armstead	1.5
Ferrara	1.0
Sehorn	1.0
Short	1.0
S. Williams	1.0
Giants	46.0
Opponents	36.0

RECORD HOLDERS
INDIVIDUAL RECORDS—CAREER

Category	Name	Performance
Rushing (Yds.)	Rodney Hampton, 1990-97	6,897
Passing (Yds.)	Phil Simms, 1979-1993	33,462
Passing (TDs)	Phil Simms, 1979-1993	199
Receiving (No.)	Joe Morrison, 1959-1972	395
Receiving (Yds.)	Frank Gifford, 1952-1964	5,434
Interceptions	Emlen Tunnell, 1948-1958	74
Punting (Avg.)	Don Chandler, 1956-1964	43.8
Punt Return (Avg.)	Ward Cuff, 1941-45	12.1
Kickoff Return (Avg.)	Rocky Thompson, 1971-73	27.2
Field Goals	Pete Gogolak, 1966-1974	126
Touchdowns (Tot.)	Frank Gifford, 1952-1964	78
Points	Pete Gogolak, 1966-1974	646

INDIVIDUAL RECORDS—SINGLE SEASON

Category	Name	Performance
Rushing (Yds.)	Joe Morris, 1986	1,516
Passing (Yds.)	Phil Simms, 1984	4,044
Passing (TDs)	Y.A. Tittle, 1963	36
Receiving (No.)	Amani Toomer, 1999	79
Receiving (Yds.)	Homer Jones, 1967	1,209
Interceptions	Otto Schnellbacher, 1951	11
	Jim Patton, 1958	11
Punting (Avg.)	Don Chandler, 1959	46.6
Punt Return (Avg.)	Merle Hapes, 1942	15.5
Kickoff Return (Avg.)	John Salscheider, 1949	31.6
Field Goals	Ali Haji-Sheikh, 1983	35
Touchdowns (Tot.)	Joe Morris, 1985	21
Points	Ali Haji-Sheikh, 1983	127

INDIVIDUAL RECORDS—SINGLE GAME

Category	Name	Performance
Rushing (Yds.)	Gene Roberts, 11-12-50	218
Passing (Yds.)	Phil Simms, 10-13-85	513
Passing (TDs)	Y.A. Tittle, 10-28-62	*7
Receiving (No.)	Tiki Barber, 1-2-00	13
Receiving (Yds.)	Del Shofner, 10-28-62	269
Interceptions	Many times	3
	Last time by Terry Kinard, 9-20-87	
Field Goals	Joe Danelo, 10-18-81	6
Touchdowns (Tot.)	Ron Johnson, 10-2-72	4
	Earnest Gray, 9-7-80	4
	Rodney Hampton, 9-24-95	4
Points	Ron Johnson, 10-2-72	24
	Earnest Gray, 9-7-80	24
	Rodney Hampton, 9-24-95	24

*NFL Record

2002 VETERAN ROSTER

No.	Name	Pos.	Ht.	Wt.	Birthdate	NFL Exp.	College	Hometown	How Acq.	'01 Games/ Starts
25	Allen, Will	CB	5-10	192	8/5/78	2	Syracuse	Syracuse, N.Y.	D1-'01	13/12
21	Barber, Tiki	RB	5-10	200	4/7/75	6	Virginia	Roanoke, Va.	D2-'97	14/9
58	Barrow, Mike	LB	6-2	240	4/19/70	10	Miami	Homestead, Fla.	FA-'00	16/16
20	Bennett, Sean	RB	6-1	230	11/9/75	2	Northwestern	Evansville, Ind.	FA-'02	0*
67	Bober, Chris	T	6-5	305	12/24/76	3	Nebraska-Omaha	Omaha, Neb.	FA-'00	16/0
22	Brown, Ralph	CB	5-10	185	9/16/78	3	Nebraska	Hacienda Heights, Calif.	D5-'00	8/0
89	Campbell, Dan	TE	6-5	260	4/13/76	4	Texas A&M	Glen Rose, Texas	D3-'99	16/13
5	Collins, Kerry	QB	6-5	245	12/30/72	8	Penn State	Lebanon, Pa.	UFA(NO)-'99	16/16
82	Davis, Thabiti	WR	6-2	205	3/24/75	3	Wake Forest	Charlotte, N.C.	FA-'00	16/0
27	Dayne, Ron	RB	5-10	253	3/14/78	3	Wisconsin	Berlin, N.J.	D1-'00	16/7
86	Dixon, Ron	WR	6-0	190	5/28/76	3	Lambuth	Wildwood, Fla.	D3-'00	15/0
95	Ferrara, Frank	DE	6-3	270	12/7/75	2	Rhode Island	Staten Island, N.Y.	FA-'01	9/0
97	Griffin, Cornelius	DT	6-3	300	12/3/76	3	Alabama	Brundidge, Ala.	D2-'00	16/16
75	Hamilton, Keith	DT	6-6	295	5/25/71	11	Pittsburgh	Lynchburg, Va.	D4-'92	13/13
88	Hilliard, Ike	WR	5-11	195	4/5/76	6	Florida	Patterson, La.	D1-'97	14/9
90	Holmes, Kenny	DE	6-4	270	10/24/73	6	Miami	Vero Beach, Fla.	UFA(Tenn)-'01	16/16
94	Johnson, Dwight	DE	6-4	285	1/30/77	4	Baylor	Waco, Texas	FA-'02	0*
55	Jones, Dhani	LB	6-1	240	2/22/78	3	Michigan	Potomac, Md.	D6-'00	16/0
99	Kolodziej, Ross	DT	6-2	287	5/11/78	2	Wisconsin	Stevens Point, Wis.	D7-'01	9/1
70	Legree, Lance	DT	6-1	285	12/22/77	2	Notre Dame	St. Stephens, S.C.	FA-'01	14/2
59	Lewis, Kevin	LB	6-1	230	10/6/78	3	Duke	Orlando, Fla.	FA-'01	9/0
3	Palmer, Jesse	QB	6-2	219	10/5/78	2	Florida	Toronto, Ontario, Canada	D4b-'01	0*
28	Patmon, DeWayne	S	6-0	190	4/25/79	2	Michigan	San Diego, Calif.	FA-'01	7/0
24	Peterson, William	CB	6-0	197	6/15/79	2	Western Illinois	Uniontown, Pa.	FA-'01	16/5
77	Petitgout, Luke	T	6-6	310	6/16/76	4	Notre Dame	Georgetown, Del.	D1-'99	16/16
9	Pochman, Owen	K	6-0	180	8/2/77	2	Brigham Young	Mercer Island, Wash.	W(NE)-'01	10/0
83	Rivers, Marcellus	TE	6-4	231	10/26/78	2	Oklahoma State	Oklahoma City, Okla.	FA-'01	16/0
78	Rosenthal, Mike	G	6-7	315	6/10/77	4	Notre Dame	Granger, Ind.	D5-'99	7/0
96	Scott, Cedric	DE	6-5	274	10/19/77	2	Southern Mississippi	Gulfport, Miss.	D4a-'01	9/0
31	Sehorn, Jason	CB	6-2	215	4/15/71	10	Southern California	Mt. Shasta, Calif.	D2-'94	13/13
69	Seubert, Rich	T	6-5	295	3/30/79	2	Western Illinois	Rozellville, Wis.	FA-'01	2/0
53	Short, Brandon	LB	6-3	255	7/11/77	3	Penn State	McKeesport, Pa.	D4-'00	16/16
23	Stoutmire, Omar	S	5-11	198	7/9/74	6	Fresno State	Long Beach, Calif.	FA-'00	16/0
92	Strahan, Michael	DE	6-5	275	11/21/71	10	Texas Southern	Westbury, Texas	D2-'93	16/16
81	Toomer, Amani	WR	6-3	208	9/8/74	7	Michigan	Berkeley, Calif.	D2-'96	16/14
29	Washington, Damon	RB	5-11	193	2/20/77	3	Colorado State	San Diego, Calif.	FA-'00	10/0
57	White, Clayton	LB	5-11	225	12/2/77	2	North Carolina State	Dunn, N.C.	FA-'01	16/0
66	Whittle, Jason	G	6-4	305	3/7/75	4	Southwest Missouri State	Springfield, Mo.	FA-'98	16/2
2	Williams, Rodney	P	6-0	178	4/25/77	2	Georgia Tech	Decatur, Ga.	FA-'01	15/0
36	Williams, Shaun	S	6-2	215	10/10/76	5	UCLA	Encino, Calif.	D1-'98	16/16
38	Wright, Adam	FB	6-1	230	12/18/77	2	Nebraska-Omaha	Omaha, Neb.	FA-'01	0*
52	Zeigler, Dusty	C	6-5	305	9/27/73	7	Notre Dame	Rincon, Ga.	UFA(Buff)-'00	16/16

* Bennett missed '01 season because of injury; Johnson last active with Philadelphia in '00; Palmer was inactive for 16 games; Wright missed '01 season because of injury.

Retired—Howard Cross, 13-year tight end, 16 games in '01.

Players lost to free agency (3): K Morten Anderson (KC; 16 games in '01), FB Greg Comella (Tenn; 16), WR Joe Jurevicius (TB; 14).

Also played with Giants in '01—LB Jessie Armstead (16 games), S Sam Garnes (16), LB Jack Golden (16).

2002 FIRST-YEAR ROSTER

Name	Pos.	Ht.	Wt.	Birthdate	College	Hometown	How Acq.
Badger, Tony	CB	5-10	170	7/26/80	West Alabama	Enterprise, Ala.	FA
Bryant, Matt	K	5-9	191	5/21/75	Baylor	Orange, Texas	FA
Bryant, Taman (1)	TE	6-4	230	3/17/77	Rowan College	Vineland, N.J.	FA-'01
Carter, Jonathan (1)	WR	5-11	173	3/20/79	Troy State	Lineville, Ala.	FA-'01
Carter, Tim	WR	5-11	190	9/21/79	Auburn	Lakewood, Fla.	D2
Clark, Ryan	S	5-11	192	10/12/79	Louisiana State	Marrero, La.	FA
Coggins, Nate	S	6-0	202	9/25/78	West Georgia	Atlanta, Ga.	FA
Colbert, Nick	LB	6-2	226	10/17/77	Troy State	Enterprise, Ala.	FA
Coleman, Calvin	CB	5-10	181	12/16/78	Montana	Niceville, Fla.	FA
Crable, Rachman	DT	6-3	282	8/26/79	Ball State	Indianapolis, Ind.	FA
Crummey, Pat	G	6-3	288	8/1/80	Youngstown State	Van Wert, Ohio	FA
Deterding, Ryan	T	6-5	265	12/23/78	Chadron State	Cambridge, Neb.	FA
Dinkins, Darnell	QB	6-3	234	1/20/77	Pittsburgh	Pittsburgh, Pa.	FA
Dorris, Derek	WR	6-2	206	12/1/78	Texas Tech	Azle, Texas	FA
Fisher, Ryan	DT	6-2	297	8/6/77	Oklahoma	Arlington, Texas	FA
Golden, Tad	S	6-1	200	1/6/80	Tennessee	Lithonia, Ga.	FA
Greisen, Nick	LB	6-1	242	8/10/79	Wisconsin	Sturgeon Bay, Wis.	D5
Guthrie, Sean	DE	6-4	269	7/14/79	Boston College	Miami, Fla.	FA
Harris, Brad	DT	6-3	267	12/31/79	Pittsburg State	Pontotoc, Miss.	FA
Hatch, Jeff	T	6-6	302	9/28/79	Pennsylvania	Millersville, Md.	D3
Hopkins, Tam	G-T	6-4	315	3/22/78	Ohio State	Winter Park, Fla.	FA
Hotchkiss, Josh	LB	6-1	244	8/26/78	Western State (Colo.)	Gunnison, Colo.	FA
Jones, Daryl	WR	5-9	175	2/2/79	Miami	Dallas, Texas	D7a
Joyce, Delvin	RB	5-7	181	9/21/78	James Madison	Martinsville, Va.	FA
Kernek, Aaron	FB	6-2	224	4/11/79	Austin College	Bowie, Texas	FA-'01
Key, KaRon	FB	5-9	235	7/16/79	Tennessee State	Nashville, Tenn.	W(Tenn)
Layow, Matt	DE	6-4	244	3/22/77	Kentucky	Miami, Fla.	FA
LeBlanc, Clarence (1)	S	6-3	200	3/26/77	Louisiana State	River Ridge, La.	FA-'01
Lindstrom, Gabe	DE	6-4	221	5/25/76	Toledo	Bisbee, Ariz.	FA
Littleton, Jody	P	6-1	235	10/23/75	Baylor	Brighton, Colo.	FA
Mallard, Wesly	LB	6-1	221	11/21/78	Oregon	Columbus, Ga.	D6
Maurer, Martin (1)	TE	6-4	252	10/23/78	Oregon State	Jacksonville, Ore.	FA
Mitchell, David	CB	6-1	195	10/18/79	Ohio State	Westerville, Ohio	FA
Mitrione, Matt	DT	6-2	295	7/15/78	Purdue	Springfield, Ill.	FA
Monk, Quincy	LB	6-3	250	1/30/79	North Carolina	Jacksonville, N.C.	D7b
Pierce, Dwayne	G	6-2	319	5/14/78	Louisiana State	New Orleans, La.	FA
Rice, Brad	LB	6-1	231	1/14/79	Idaho	Lewiston, Idaho	FA
Riley, Sean	WR	5-9	153	8/17/74	Western Michigan	Houston, Texas	FA
Sandoval, Vincent	T	6-4	313	4/10/79	Oregon State	Palmdale, Calif.	FA
Shockey, Jeremy	TE	6-5	252	8/18/80	Miami	Ada, Okla.	D1
Smith, Omar	G	6-2	296	9/8/77	Kentucky	Miramar, Fla.	FA
Stackhouse, Charles	FB	6-2	252	4/11/80	Mississippi	West Memphis, Ark.	FA
Stambaugh, Phil (1)	QB	6-2	218	8/10/78	Lehigh	Roseto, Pa.	FA
Stamer, Josh	LB	6-1	235	10/11/77	South Dakota	Sutherland, Iowa	FA
Stensrud, Andy	T	6-8	272	9/26/78	Iowa State	Lake Mills, Iowa	FA
Thompson, David	WR	6-3	194	8/7/78	Holy Cross	Terrytown, N.Y.	FA
Tucker, Marshaun	WR	5-10	184	10/6/79	Oregon	Chula Vista, Calif.	FA
Van Dyke, Jason	P	5-10	193	2/2/74	Adams State	Loveland, Colo.	FA
Wagner, Terence	C	6-2	290	5/26/79	Sacramento State	Carmichael, Calif.	FA
Warren, Antonio	RB	5-9	201	11/25/75	Cal Poly-San Luis Obispo	San Francisco, Calif.	FA
Welsh, John	QB	6-1	223	1/20/78	Idaho	Oak Forest, Ill.	FA

The term NFL Rookie is defined as a player who is in his first season of professional football and has not been on the roster of another professional football team for any regular-season or postseason games. A Rookie is designated by an "R" on NFL rosters. Players who have been active in another professional football league or players who have NFL experience, including either preseason training camp or being on an Active List or Inactive List, or on Reserve/Injured or Reserve/Physically Unable to Perform for fewer than six regular-season games, are termed NFL First-Year Players. An NFL First-Year Player is designated by a "1" on NFL rosters. Thereafter, a player is credited with an additional year of experience for each season in which he accumulates six games on the Active List or Inactive List, or on Reserve/Injured or Reserve/Physically Unable to Perform.

COACHING STAFF
Head Coach,
Jim Fassel
Pro Career: Was named the fifteenth head coach in Giants history on January 15, 1997. Enters his sixth season as head coach of the Giants. In 2000, the Giants won their last five regular-season games en route to the best record in the NFC and the franchise's first Super Bowl appearance in 10 seasons. In 1998, the Giants finished 8-8 by winning five of their last six games. In 1997, Fassel led his squad to a 10-5-1 record and a berth in the playoffs while capturing the NFC East title. He was named coach of the year by 11 media outlets as the Giants became the fifteenth team in NFL history to finish in first place in their division the season after finishing last. Fassel entered the NFL with the Giants in 1991 as quarterbacks coach, then as offensive coordinator in 1992. Fassel spent two campaigns as assistant head coach/offensive coordinator for the Denver Broncos (1993 and 1994), the 1995 season as quarterbacks coach for the Oakland Raiders, and was the offensive coordinator and quarterbacks coach for the Arizona Cardinals in 1996. Fassel has been credited with an ability to develop quarterbacks, including John Elway, Kent Graham, and Boomer Esiason. Career record: 46-37-1.
Background: Fassel began coaching in 1973 at his alma mater, Fullerton College, then was a player-coach for the Hawaii Hawaiians of the World Football League in 1974. He coached at Utah (1976), Weber State (1977-78), and Stanford (1979-1983). At Stanford, Fassel was credited with recruiting and coaching John Elway. Fassel entered the pro arena in 1984 as offensive coordinator for the New Orleans Breakers of the USFL, then returned to Utah as head coach (1985-89).
Personal: A native of Anaheim, California, Fassel led Fullerton College to the junior college national championship in 1967. He also played collegiately at Southern California with Seattle Seahawks head coach Mike Holmgren and at Long Beach State. He was drafted by the Chicago Bears in the seventh round of the 1972 NFL draft and played briefly with Chicago, the Houston Oilers, and San Diego Chargers. Born August 31, 1949 in Anaheim, Calif. Fassel and his wife, Kitty, have four children—John, Brian, Jana, and Mike.

ASSISTANT COACHES
Dave Brazil, senior defensive analyst; born March 25, 1936, Detroit, lives in East Rutherford, N.J. No college or pro playing experience. College coach: Holy Cross 1968, Tulsa 1969-1970, Eastern Michigan 1971-73, Boston College 1980, Kent State 1981-82. Pro coach: Detroit Wheels (WFL) 1974, Chicago Wind (WFL) 1975, Kansas City Chiefs 1984-88,

Pittsburgh Steelers 1989-1991, joined Giants in 1992.
John Dunn, strength and conditioning; born July 22, 1956, Wayne, N.J., lives in Wayne, N.J. Guard Penn State 1974-77. No pro playing experience. College coach: Penn State 1978. Pro coach: Washington Redskins 1984-86, Los Angeles Raiders 1987-89, San Diego Chargers 1990-96, joined Giants in 1997.
Johnnie Lynn, defensive coordinator; born December 19, 1956, Los Angeles, lives in Wayne, N.J. Defensive back UCLA 1975-78. Pro defensive back New York Jets 1979-1986. College coach: Arizona 1988-1993. Pro coach: Tampa Bay Buccaneers 1994-95, San Francisco 49ers 1996, joined Giants in 1997.
Denny Marcin, defensive line; born April 24, 1942, Cleveland, lives in Wayne, N.J. Defensive and offensive line Miami (Ohio) 1961-64. No pro playing experience. College coach: Miami (Ohio) 1974-77, North Carolina 1978-1987, Illinois 1988-1996. Pro coach: Joined Giants in 1997.
Jim McNally, offensive line; born December 13, 1943, Buffalo, lives in Cedar Grove, N.J. Guard Buffalo 1961-65. No pro playing experience. College coach: Buffalo 1966-1970, Marshall 1971-74, Boston College 1975-77, Wake Forest 1978-79. Pro coach: Cincinnati Bengals 1980-1994, Carolina Panthers 1995-98, joined Giants in 1999.
Tom Olivadotti, linebackers; born September 22, 1945, Long Beach, N.J., lives in Glennrock, N.J. Defensive back-wide receiver Upsala 1963-66. No pro playing experience. College coach: Princeton 1975-77, Boston College 1978-79, Miami 1980-83. Pro coach: Cleveland Browns 1985-86, Miami Dolphins 1987-1995, Minnesota Vikings 1996-99, joined Giants in 2000.
Sean Payton, offensive coordinator-quarterbacks; born December 29, 1963, San Mateo, Calif., lives in Wayne, N.J. Quarterback Eastern Illinois 1982-86. Pro quarterback Ottawa Rough Riders (CFL) 1987, Chicago Bears 1987. College coach: San Diego State 1988-89, 1992-93, Indiana State 1990-91, Miami (Ohio) 1994-95, Illinois 1996. Pro coach: Philadelphia Eagles 1997-98, joined Giants in 1999.
Mike Pope, tight ends; born March 15, 1942, Monroe, N.C., lives in Somerset, N.J. Quarterback Lenoir-Rhyne 1962-64. No pro playing experience. College coach: Florida State 1970-74, Texas Tech 1975-77, Mississippi 1978-1982. Pro coach: New York Giants 1983-1991, Cincinnati Bengals 1992-93, New England Patriots 1994-96, Washington Redskins 1997-99, joined Giants in 2000.
Bruce Read, special teams; born January 26, 1962, in Santa Rosa, Calif., lives in East Rutherford, N.J. Attended Oregon Institute of Technology, Portland State. No college or pro playing experience. College

coach: Oregon Institute of Technology 1980, Portland State 1981-84, Montana 1985-1996, Oregon State 1997-98. Pro coach: San Diego Chargers 1999-2001, joined Giants in 2002.
Jay Robertson, offensive assistant; born February 20, 1940, Chicago, lives in Mahwah, N.J. Center Northwestern 1960-62. No pro playing experience. College coach: Northwestern 1967-1975, Northern Illinois 1976, Wisconsin 1980-1981, Notre Dame 1982-1983, West Point 1984-1991. Pro coach: Indianapolis Colts 1992-1993, 1997, joined Giants in 2001.
Jimmy Robinson, wide receivers; born January 3, 1953, Atlanta, lives in Wayne, N.J. Wide receiver Georgia Tech 1972-74. Pro wide receiver Atlanta Falcons 1975, New York Giants 1976-79, San Francisco 49ers 1980, Denver Broncos 1981. College coach: Georgia Tech 1986-89. Pro coach: Memphis Showboats (USFL) 1984-85, Atlanta Falcons 1990-93, Indianapolis Colts 1994-97, joined Giants in 1998.
Rod Rust, defensive quality control; born August 2, 1928, Weber City, Iowa., lives in Ocean City, N.J. Center-linebacker Iowa State 1947-49. No pro playing experience. College coach: New Mexico 1960-62, Stanford 1963-66, North Texas State 1967-1972 (head coach). Pro coach: Montreal Alouettes (CFL) 1973-75, Philadelphia Eagles 1976-77, Kansas City Chiefs 1978-1982, 1988, New England Patriots 1983-87, 1990 (head coach 1990), Pittsburgh Steelers 1989, New York Giants 1992, Winnepeg Blue Bombers (CFL) 1994, Atlanta Falcons 1995-96, Montreal Alouettes (CFL) 1997-2001, joined Giants in 2002.
Craig Stoddard, asst. strength and conditioning; born February 8, 1972, North Tarrytown, N.Y., lives in Hackensack, N.J. Linebacker Springfield College 1990-93. No pro playing experience. College coach: Penn State 1995-96. Pro coach: San Diego Chargers 1994, joined Giants in 1997.
Eric Studesville, running backs; born May 29, 1967, Madison, Wis., lives in Clifton, N.J. Defensive back Wisconsin-Whitewater 1985-88. No pro playing experience. College coach: Wingate 1994, Kent State 1995-96. Pro coach: Chicago Bears 1997-2000, joined Giants in 2001.
DeWayne Walker, defensive backs; born December 3, 1960, Los Angeles, lives in East Rutherford, N.J. Cornerback Pasadena (Calif.) C.C. 1978-79, Minnesota 1980-81. Pro cornerback Edmonton Eskimos (CFL) 1982, Oakland Invaders (USFL) 1985. College coach: Mt. San Antonio (Calif.) C.C. 1988-1992, Utah State 1993, Brigham Young 1994, Oklahoma State 1995, California 1996-97, Southern California 2001. Pro coach: New England Patriots 1998-2000, joined Giants in 2002.

**National Football Conference
East Division**
Team Colors: Midnight Green, Silver, Black, and White
**NovaCare Complex
One NovaCare Way
Philadelphia, Pennsylvania 19145**
Telephone: (215) 463-2500

2002 SCHEDULE
PRESEASON
Aug. 10 **Green Bay**..........................7:30
Aug. 17 at New England 8:00
Aug. 23 **Baltimore**...........................8:00
Aug. 30 at New York Jets 7:30

REGULAR SEASON
Sept. 8 at Tennessee 12:00
Sept. 16 at Washington (Mon.).............9:00
Sept. 22 **Dallas**....................................1:00
Sept. 29 **Houston**................................1:00
Oct. 6   at Jacksonville 4:15
Oct. 13 OPEN DATE
Oct. 20 **Tampa Bay** 1:00
Oct. 28 **New York Giants (Mon.)** 9:00
Nov. 3   at Chicago (Champaign, Ill.) ...12:00
Nov. 10 **Indianapolis** 1:00
Nov. 17 **Arizona** 1:00
Nov. 25 at San Francisco (Mon.) 6:00
Dec. 1   **St. Louis** 4:15
Dec. 8   at Seattle................................1:05
Dec. 15 **Washington** 1:00
Dec. 21 at Dallas (Sat.) 7:30
Dec. 28 at New York Giants (Sat.) 1:30

Stadium: Veterans Stadium
(opened in 1971)
• **Capacity:** 65,352
3501 South Broad Street
Philadelphia, Pennsylvania 19148
Playing Surface: NexTurf
Training Camp: Lehigh University
Bethlehem, Pennsylvania
18015

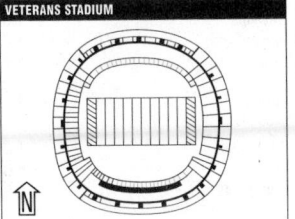

VETERANS STADIUM

CLUB OFFICIALS
Chairman/Chief Executive Officer:
Jeffrey Lurie
President: Joe Banner
Head Coach/Executive Vice President of
Football Operations: Andy Reid
Director of Player Personnel:
Tom Heckert
Senior Vice President/Business
Operations: Len Komoroski
Senior Vice President/Chief Financial
Officer: Don Smolenski
Vice President, Corporate Sales:
Dave Rowan
Vice President, Sales: Jason Gonella
Executive Director of Eagles Youth
Partnership: Sarah Martinez-Helfman
Director of Pro Personnel: Scott Cohen
Director of College Scouting: Marc Ross
Coordinator of Football Media Relations:
Derek Boyko
Media Relations Assistants: Rich Burg,
Bob Lange
Manager of Community Relations:
Julie Dubin
Director of Human Resourses:
Eric Newman
Director, Broadcasting/Exec. Producer
Eagles Television Network:
Rob Alberino
Ticket Manager: Leo Carlin
Director of Merchandise:
Steve Strawbridge
Travel Coordinator: Tracey Bucher
Director of Security:
Anthony (Butch) Buchanico
Head Athletic Trainer: Rick Burkholder
Asst. Athletic Trainers: Eric Sugarman,
Chris Peduzzi
Video Director: Mike Dougherty
Head Equipment Manager: John Hatfield

COACHING HISTORY
(430-502-25)
1933-35   Lud Wray 9-21-1
1936-1940 Bert Bell 10-44-2
1941-1950 Earle (Greasy) Neale* ...66-44-5
1951   Alvin (Bo) McMillin** 2-0-0
1951   Wayne Millner...............2-8-0
1952-55   Jim Trimble..................25-20-3
1956-57   Hugh Devore 7-16-1
1958-1960 Lawrence (Buck) Shaw..20-16-1
1961-63   Nick Skorich 15-24-3
1964-68   Joe Kuharich 28-41-1
1969-1971 Jerry Williams*** 7-22-2
1971-72   Ed Khayat.....................8-15-2
1973-75   Mike McCormack 16-25-1
1976-1982 Dick Vermeil 57-51-0
1983-85   Marion Campbell**** ...17-29-1
1985   Fred Bruney.....................1-0-0
1986-1990 Buddy Ryan 43-38-1
1991-94   Rich Kotite...................37-29-0
1995-98   Ray Rhodes..................30-36-1
1999-2001 Andy Reid...................30-22-0
*Co-coach with Walt Kiesling in Philadelphia-
Pittsburgh merger in 1943
**Retired after two games in 1951
***Released after three games in 1971
****Released after 15 games in 1985

ATTENDANCE
Home 524,691   Away 514,465
Total 1,039,156
Single-game home record,
72,111 (11/1/81)
Single-season home record, 557,325
(1980)

2002 DRAFT CHOICES
Round	Name	Pos.	College
1	Lito Sheppard	DB	Florida
2	Michael Lewis	DB	Colorado
	Sheldon Brown	DB	South Carolina
3	Brian Westbrook	RB	Villanova
4	Scott Peters	C	Arizona State
5	Freddie Milons	WR	Alabama
6	Tyreo Harrison	LB	Notre Dame
7	Raheem Brock	DE	Temple

2001 TEAM RECORD
PRESEASON (2-1)

Date	Result	Opponent
8/13	Cancelled	Baltimore
8/18	L 3-6	at Buffalo
8/23	W 20-14	at Tennessee
8/30	W 13-12	New York Jets

REGULAR SEASON (11-5)

Date	Result	Opponent	Att.
9/09	L 17-20	St. Louis(OT)	66,243
9/23	W 27-3	at Seattle	62,826
9/30	W 40-18	Dallas	66,621
10/07	L 20-21	Arizona	66,360
10/22	W 10-9	at New York Giants	78,821
10/28	L 10-20	Oakland	65,342
11/04	W 21-7	at Arizona	33,430
11/11	W 48-17	Minnesota	65,638
11/18	W 36-3	at Dallas	63,204
11/25	L 3-13	Washington	65,666
11/29	W 23-10	at Kansas City	77,087
12/09	W 24-14	San Diego	65,438
12/16	W 20-6	at Washington	84,936
12/22	L 3-13	at San Francisco	68,124
12/30	W 24-21	New York Giants	65,885
1/06	W 17-13	at Tampa Bay	65,541

(OT) Overtime

POSTSEASON (2-1)

Date	Result	Opponent	Att.
1/12	W 31-9	Tampa Bay	65,847
1/19	W 33-19	at Chicago	66,944
1/27	L 24-29	at St. Louis	66,502

SCORE BY PERIODS

Eagles	58	144	40	101	0 —	343
Opponents	50	72	30	53	3 —	208

2001 TEAM STATISTICS

	Eagles	Opp.
Total First Downs	256	262
Rushing	90	88
Passing	146	150
Penalty	20	24
3rd Down: Made/Att	68/220	71/232
3rd Down Pct.	30.9	30.6
4th Down: Made/Att	9/13	7/13
4th Down Pct.	69.2	53.8
Possession Avg.	28:39	31:21
Total Net Yards	4923	4701
Avg. Per Game	307.7	293.8
Total Plays	974	1017
Avg. Per Play	5.1	4.6
Net Yards Rushing	1778	1837
Avg. Per Game	111.1	114.8
Total Rushes	412	455
Net Yards Passing	3145	2864
Avg. Per Game	196.6	179.0
Sacked/Yards Lost	40/282	45/283
Gross Yards	3427	3147
Att./Completions	522/300	517/288
Completion Pct.	57.5	55.7
Had Intercepted	14	14
Punts/Average	97/43.5	104/40.6
Net Punting Avg.	97/36.4	104/34.6
Penalties/Yards	100/768	85/741
Fumbles/Ball Lost	20/10	39/19
Touchdowns	38	20
Rushing	6	6
Passing	27	13
Returns	5	1

2001 INDIVIDUAL STATISTICS

PASSING

PASSING	Att.	Comp.	Yds.	Pct.	TD	Int.	Tkld.	Rate
McNabb	493	285	3233	57.8	25	12	39/273	84.3
Detmer	14	5	51	35.7	0	1	1/9	17.3
Feeley	14	10	143	71.4	2	1	0/0	114.0
F. Mitchell	1	0	0	0.0	0	0	0/0	39.6
Eagles	522	300	3427	57.5	27	14	40/282	83.4
Opponents	517	288	3147	55.7	13	14	45/283	71.0

SCORING

SCORING	TD R	TD P	TD Rt	PAT	FG	Saf	PTS
Akers	0	0	0	37/38	26/31	0	115
Thrash	0	8	0	0/0	0/0	0	48
Lewis	0	6	0	0/0	0/0	0	36
Pinkston	0	4	0	0/0	0/0	0	24
Staley	2	2	0	0/0	0/0	0	24
Buckhalter	2	0	0	0/0	0/0	0	12
D. Douglas	0	2	0	0/0	0/0	0	12
Martin	0	2	0	0/0	0/0	0	12
McNabb	2	0	0	0/0	0/0	0	12
Bartrum	0	1	0	0/0	0/0	0	6
Dawkins	0	0	1	0/0	0/0	0	6
Hampton	0	0	1	0/0	0/0	0	6
B. Mitchell	0	0	1	0/0	0/0	0	6
F. Mitchell	0	1	0	0/0	0/0	0	6
Moore	0	0	1	0/0	0/0	0	6
Stewart	0	1	0	0/0	0/0	0	6
Trotter	0	0	1	0/0	0/0	0	6
Eagles	6	27	5	37/38	26/31	0	343
Opponents	6	13	1	17/17	23/32	0	208

2-Pt. Conversions: None.
Eagles 0-0, Opponents 1-3.

RUSHING

RUSHING	Att.	Yds.	Avg.	LG	TD
Staley	166	604	3.6	44t	2
Buckhalter	129	586	4.5	48	2
McNabb	82	482	5.9	33	2
Thrash	6	57	9.5	24	0
Martin	9	27	3.0	8	0
B. Mitchell	7	9	1.3	11	0
Detmer	8	6	0.8	14	0
Smart	2	6	3.0	6	0
Pinkston	1	5	5.0	5	0
F. Mitchell	2	-4	-2.0	12	0
Eagles	412	1778	4.3	48	6
Opponents	455	1837	4.0	80	6

RECEIVING

RECEIVING	No.	Yds.	Avg.	LG	TD
Thrash	63	833	13.2	64t	8
Staley	63	626	9.9	46t	2
Pinkston	42	586	14.0	62t	4
Lewis	41	422	10.3	33	6
Martin	24	124	5.2	17	2
F. Mitchell	21	283	13.5	29	1
Buckhalter	13	130	10.0	26	0
Brown	7	95	13.6	18	0
B. Mitchell	6	122	20.3	56	0
D. Douglas	5	77	15.4	27	2
Stewart	5	52	10.4	15	1
Thomason	5	33	6.6	11	0
Scott	2	26	13.0	18	0
Reader	2	14	7.0	11	0
Bartrum	1	4	4.0	4t	1
Eagles	300	3427	11.4	64t	27
Opponents	288	3147	10.9	76	13

INTERCEPTIONS

INTERCEPTIONS	No.	Yds.	Avg.	LG	TD
Vincent	3	0	0.0	0	0
Trotter	2	64	32.0	50t	1
Harris	2	22	11.0	14	0
Dawkins	2	15	7.5	15	0
Moore	2	2	1.0	2	0
Hampton	1	33	33.0	33t	1
Cook	1	11	11.0	11	0
Taylor	1	5	5.0	5	0
Eagles	14	152	10.9	50t	2
Opponents	14	99	7.1	25	0

PUNTING

PUNTING	No.	Yds.	Avg.	In 20	LG
Landeta	97	4221	43.5	26	64
Eagles	97	4221	43.5	26	64
Opponents	104	4225	40.6	26	61

PUNT RETURNS

PUNT RETURNS	No.	FC	Yds.	Avg.	LG	TD
B. Mitchell	39	22	467	12.0	54	0
Brown	5	0	30	6.0	11	0
Cook	0	0	11	—	11	0
Eagles	44	22	508	11.5	54	0
Opponents	56	16	488	8.7	30	0

KICKOFF RETURNS

KICKOFF RETURNS	No.	Yds.	Avg.	LG	TD
B. Mitchell	41	1025	25.0	94t	1
Thrash	5	101	20.2	34	0
D. Douglas	2	32	16.0	18	0
Buckhalter	1	28	28.0	28	0
Lewis	0	-10	—	-10	0
Reese	0	-11	—	-11	0
Eagles	49	1165	23.8	94t	1
Opponents	67	1430	21.3	59	0

FIELD GOALS

FIELD GOALS	1-19	20-29	30-39	40-49	50+
Akers	1/1	9/9	7/8	7/10	2/3
Eagles	1/1	9/9	7/8	7/10	2/3
Opponents	0/0	10/10	5/10	8/12	0/0

SACKS

SACKS	No.
H. Douglas	9.5
Simon	7.5
Burgess	6.0
Trotter	3.5
Caldwell	3.0
Kalu	3.0
Whiting	2.5
Grasmanis	2.0
Dawkins	1.5
Vincent	1.5
Cook	1.0
Emmons	1.0
Moore	1.0
Taylor	1.0
Da. Walker	1.0
Eagles	45.0
Opponents	40.0

RECORD HOLDERS
INDIVIDUAL RECORDS—CAREER

Category	Name	Performance
Rushing (Yds.)	Wilbert Montgomery, 1977-1984	6,538
Passing (Yds.)	Ron Jaworski, 1977-1986	26,963
Passing (TDs)	Ron Jaworski, 1977-1986	175
Receiving (No.)	Harold Carmichael, 1971-1983	589
Receiving (Yds.)	Harold Carmichael, 1971-1983	8,978
Interceptions	Bill Bradley, 1969-1976	34
	Eric Allen, 1988-1994	34
Punting (Avg.)	Joe Muha, 1946-1950	42.9
Punt Return (Avg.)	Steve Van Buren, 1944-1951	13.9
Kickoff Return (Avg.)	Steve Van Buren, 1944-1951	26.7
Field Goals	Paul McFadden, 1984-87	91
Touchdowns (Tot.)	Harold Carmichael, 1971-1983	79
Points	Bobby Walston, 1951-1962	881

INDIVIDUAL RECORDS—SINGLE SEASON

Category	Name	Performance
Rushing (Yds.)	Wilbert Montgomery, 1979	1,512
Passing (Yds.)	Randall Cunningham, 1988	3,808
Passing (TDs)	Sonny Jurgensen, 1961	32
Receiving (No.)	Irving Fryar, 1996	88
Receiving (Yds.)	Mike Quick, 1983	1,409
Interceptions	Bill Bradley, 1971	11
Punting (Avg.)	Joe Muha, 1948	47.2
Punt Return (Avg.)	Steve Van Buren, 1944	15.3
Kickoff Return (Avg.)	Al Nelson, 1972	29.1
Field Goals	Paul McFadden, 1984	30
Touchdowns (Tot.)	Steve Van Buren, 1945	18
Points	David Akers, 2000	121

INDIVIDUAL RECORDS—SINGLE GAME

Category	Name	Performance
Rushing (Yds.)	Steve Van Buren, 11-27-49	205
Passing (Yds.)	Randall Cunningham, 9-17-89	447
Passing (TDs)	Adrian Burk, 10-17-54	*7
Receiving (No.)	Don Looney, 12-1-40	14
Receiving (Yds.)	Tommy McDonald, 12-10-60	237
Interceptions	Russ Craft, 9-24-50	*4
Field Goals	Tom Dempsey, 11-12-72	6
Touchdowns (Tot.)	Many times	4
	Last time by Irving Fryar, 10-20-96	
Points	Bobby Walston, 10-17-54	25

*NFL Record

2002 VETERAN ROSTER

No.	Name	Pos.	Ht.	Wt.	Birthdate	NFL Exp.	College	Hometown	How Acq.	'01 Games/ Starts
2	Akers, David	K	5-10	200	12/9/74	4	Louisville	Lexington, Ky.	FA-'99	16/0
56	Barber, Shawn	LB	6-2	237	1/14/75	5	Richmond	Hermitage, Va.	UFA(Wash)-'02	3/3*
88	Bartrum, Mike	TE-LS	6-4	245	6/23/70	9	Marshall	Pomeroy, Ohio	FA-'00	16/0
24	Bishop, Blaine	S	5-9	203	7/24/70	10	Ball State	Indianapolis, Ind.	FA-'02	5/4*
85	Brown, Na	WR	6-0	196	2/22/77	4	North Carolina	Reidsville, N.C.	D4c-'99	16/2
74	Brzezinski, Doug	G	6-4	305	3/11/76	4	Boston College	Detroit, Mich.	D3-'99	16/1
28	Buckhalter, Correll	RB	6-0	222	10/6/78	2	Nebraska	Collins, Miss.	D4-'01	15/6
59	Burgess, Derrick	LB-DE	6-2	266	8/12/78	2	Mississippi	Greenbelt, Md.	D3-'01	16/4
55	Caver, Quinton	LB	6-4	230	8/22/78	2	Arkansas	Anniston, Ala.	D2-'01	11/0
42	Cook, Rashard	S	5-11	197	4/18/77	4	Southern California	San Diego, Calif.	W(Chi)-'99	16/3
29	Crutchfield, Darrel	CB	6-0	177	2/26/79	2	Clemson	Jacksonville, Fla.	FA-'01	4/0
20	Dawkins, Brian	S	5-11	200	10/13/73	7	Clemson	Jacksonville, Fla.	D2b-'96	15/15
10	Detmer, Koy	QB	6-1	195	7/5/73	6	Colorado	San Antonio, Texas	D7a-'97	16/0
82	Douglas, Dameane	WR	6-0	195	3/15/76	4	California	Hanford, Calif.	W(Oak)-'99	16/0
53	Douglas, Hugh	LB-DE	6-2	280	8/23/71	8	Central State (Ohio)	Mansfield, Ohio	T(NYJ)-'98	15/15
51	Emmons, Carlos	LB	6-5	250	9/3/73	7	Arkansas State	Greenwood, Miss.	UFA(Pitt)-'00	16/15
14	Feeley, A.J.	QB	6-3	217	5/16/77	2	Oregon	Ontario, Ore.	D5b-'01	1/0
63	Fraley, Hank	C-G	6-2	300	9/21/77	3	Robert Morris	Gaithersburg, Md.	W(Pitt)-'00	16/15
52	Gardner, Barry	LB	6-0	248	12/13/76	4	Northwestern	Harvey, Ill.	D2-'99	16/0
96	Grasmanis, Paul	DT	6-3	298	8/2/74	7	Notre Dame	Jenison, Mich.	UFA(Den)-'00	14/2
41	Hampton, William	CB	5-10	190	3/7/75	2	Murray State	Little Rock, Ark.	FA-'00	13/0
31	Harris, Al	CB	6-1	185	12/7/74	5	Texas A&M-Kingsville	Pompano Beach, Fla.	W(TB)-'98	16/2
27	Jones, Julian	S	6-0	190	6/8/78	2	Missouri	Oklahoma City, Okla.	FA-'01	0*
94	Kalu, N.D.	DE	6-3	265	8/3/75	6	Rice	San Antonio, Texas	UFA(Wash)-'01	14/1
7	Landeta, Sean	P	6-0	215	1/6/62	18	Towson State	Towson, Md.	UFA(GB)-'99	16/0
89	Lewis, Chad	TE	6-6	252	10/5/71	5	Brigham Young	Orem, Utah	W(StL)-'99	15/15
38	Martin, Cecil	FB	6-0	235	7/8/75	4	Wisconsin	Evanston, Ill.	D6a-'99	16/15
71	Mayberry, Jermane	G-T	6-4	325	8/29/73	7	Texas A&M-Kingsville	Floresville, Texas	D1-'96	16/15
5	McNabb, Donovan	QB	6-2	226	11/25/76	4	Syracuse	Chicago, Ill.	D1-'99	16/16
30	Mitchell, Brian	RB-KR	5-10	221	8/18/68	13	Southwestern Louisiana	Plaquemine, La.	FA-'00	16/0
84	Mitchell, Freddie	WR	5-11	184	11/28/78	2	UCLA	Lakeland, Fla.	D1-'01	15/1
43	#Moore, Damon	S	5-11	215	9/15/76	4	Ohio State	Fostoria, Ohio	D4b-'99	16/16
19	Morey, Sean	WR	5-11	194	2/26/76	2	Brown	Marshfield, Mass.	FA-'01	0*
87	Pinkston, Todd	WR	6-2	170	4/23/77	3	Southern Mississippi	Forest, Miss.	D2a-'00	15/15
34	Reader, Jamie	FB	6-0	238	5/4/74	2	Akron	Monessen, Pa.	W(NYJ)-'01	16/0
58	Reese, Ike	LB	6-2	222	10/16/73	5	Michigan State	Cincinnati, Ohio	D5-'98	16/0
69	Runyan, Jon	T	6-7	330	11/27/73	7	Michigan	Flint, Mich.	UFA(Tenn)-'00	16/16
86	Scott, Gari	WR	6-0	191	6/2/78	3	Michigan State	Riviera Beach, Fla.	D4-'00	3/0
90	Simon, Corey	DT	6-2	293	3/2/77	3	Florida State	Pompano Beach, Fla.	D1-'00	16/16
25	Smart, Rod	RB	5-11	191	1/9/77	2	Western Kentucky	Lakeland, Fla.	FA-'01	6/0
22	Staley, Duce	RB	5-11	220	2/27/75	6	South Carolina	Columbia, S.C.	D3-'97	13/10
81	Stewart, Tony	TE	6-5	255	8/9/79	2	Penn State	Allentown, Pa.	D5a-'01	3/1
21	Taylor, Bobby	CB	6-3	216	12/28/73	8	Notre Dame	Longview, Texas	D2a-'95	16/14
78	Thomas, Hollis	DT	6-0	306	1/10/74	7	Northern Illinois	St. Louis, Mo.	FA-'96	14/14
72	Thomas, Tra	T	6-7	349	11/20/74	5	Florida State	Deland, Fla.	D1-'98	15/15
83	Thomason, Jeff	TE	6-5	255	12/30/69	10	Oregon	Newport Beach, Calif.	T(GB)-'00	14/0
80	Thrash, James	WR	6-0	200	4/28/75	6	Missouri Southern	Denver, Colo.	UFA(Wash)-'01	15/15
23	Vincent, Troy	CB	6-1	200	6/8/71	11	Wisconsin	Trenton, N.J.	TFA(Mia)-'96	15/15
97	Walker, Darwin	DT	6-3	294	6/15/77	3	Tennessee	Walterboro, S.C.	W(Ariz)-'00	10/0
76	Welbourn, John	G-T	6-5	318	3/30/76	4	California	Palos Verdes, Calif.	D4a-'99	15/15
98	Whiting, Brandon	DE-DT	6-3	285	7/30/76	5	California	Long Beach, Calif.	D4a-'98	13/12
66	Williams, Bobbie	G	6-3	320	9/25/76	3	Arkansas	Jefferson, Texas	D2b-'00	1/1

* Barber played 3 games with Washington in '01; Bishop played 5 games with Tennessee; Jones missed '01 season because of injury; Morey played 3 playoff games with Philadelphia in '01.

\# Unrestricted free agent; subject to developments.

Players lost through Expansion Draft (1): T Ryan Schau (2 games in '01).

Players lost through free agency (4): LB Mike Caldwell (Chi; 16 games in '01), C-G Bubba Miller (NO; 0), C Jim Pyne (Ind; 5), LB Jeremiah Trotter (Wash; 16).

Also played with Eagles in '01—DE Uhuru Hamiter (1 game), S Tim Hauck (16).

PHILADELPHIA EAGLES

2002 FIRST-YEAR ROSTER

Name	Pos.	Ht.	Wt.	Birthdate	College	Hometown	How Acq.
Brock, Raheem	DE	6-4	257	6/10/78	Temple	Philadelphia, Pa.	D7
Brown, Sheldon	CB	5-10	196	3/19/79	South Carolina	Richburg, S.C.	D2b
Cheek, Steve (1)	P	6-4	200	4/18/77	Humboldt State	Westfield, N.J.	FA
Dickerson, Kori	TE	6-4	240	12/6/78	Southern California	Los Angeles, Calif.	FA
Edwards, Steve	T	6-5	350	2/20/79	Central Florida	Chicago, Ill.	FA
Elisara, Pita (1)	G-T	6-4	280	11/16/76	Indiana	American Samoa	FA
Ena, Justin	LB	6-3	247	11/20/77	Brigham Young	Shelton, Wash.	FA
Foye, David (1)	WR	6-1	208	6/24/78	Marshall	Charleston, W. Va.	FA
Harrison, Tyreo	LB	6-2	238	5/15/80	Notre Dame	Sulphur Springs, Texas	D6
Hart, Clinton (1)	S	6-0	205	7/20/77	Central Florida C.C.	Bushnell, Fla.	FA
Hasselbeck, Tim (1)	QB	6-1	211	4/6/78	Boston College	Westwood, Mass.	FA
Hicks, Artis	T	6-4	303	11/28/78	Memphis State	Jackson, Tenn.	FA
Johnson, Carlos	WR	5-9	167	11/14/79	Valdosta State	Moultrie, Ga.	FA
Ledford, Dwayne (1)	C-G	6-4	295	11/2/76	East Carolina	Marion, N.C.	FA
Lewis, Michael	S	6-1	211	4/29/80	Colorado	Richmond, Texas	D2a
McCoy, Ivory	DE	6-3	240	1/12/79	Michigan State	Chicago, Ill.	FA
McDonald, Brian (1)	WR-KR	5-9	175	2/21/77	Louisville	Louisville, Ky.	FA
McIntyre, Corey	FB	6-0	245	1/25/79	West Virginia	Indiantown, Fla.	FA
McKie, Jason	FB	5-11	239	5/22/80	Temple	Gulf Breeze, Fla.	FA
Meng, Eric (1)	K	6-1	192	11/29/74	Georgia Southern	Jupiter, Fla.	FA
Milons, Freddie	WR	5-11	190	6/27/80	Alabama	Starkville, Miss.	D5
Moore, Josh (1)	T	6-4	317	5/25/78	Furman	Clinton, S.C.	FA
Nielsen, Ryan	DT	6-5	280	3/20/79	Southern California	Simi Valley, Calif.	FA
Parry, Josh (1)	LB	6-2	250	4/5/78	San Jose State	Sonora, Calif.	FA
Peters, Scott	C-G	6-3	300	11/23/78	Arizona State	Pleasanton, Calif.	D4
Roberson, Marcus	DT	6-4	285	11/29/80	Washington	Compton, Calif.	FA
Rogers, Kendrick (1)	T	6-5	311	10/10/76	Alabama A&M	Mobile, Ala.	FA-'01
Romero, Frank	G	6-4	300	11/24/79	Oklahoma	Moore, Okla.	FA
Scott, Sean (1)	WR	6-2	190	9/25/78	Millersville	Philadelphia, Pa.	FA-'01
Sheppard, Lito	CB	5-10	194	4/8/81	Florida	Jacksonville, Fla.	D1
Slechta, Jeremy	DT	6-6	285	5/12/80	Nebraska	La Vista, Neb.	FA
Story, Lawrence	WR	6-4	205	12/24/78	Jackson State	Birmingham, Ala.	FA
Strohmeyer, Dax (1)	LB	6-4	235	1/31/77	Rutgers	Upper Saddle River, N.J.	FA-'01
Westbrook, Brian	RB-KR	5-8	200	9/2/79	Villanova	Ft. Washington, Md.	D3

The term NFL Rookie is defined as a player who is in his first season of professional football and has not been on the roster of another professional football team for any regular-season or postseason games. A Rookie is designated by an "R" on NFL rosters. Players who have been active in another professional football league or players who have NFL experience, including either preseason training camp or being on an Active List or Inactive List, or on Reserve/Injured or Reserve/Physically Unable to Perform for fewer than six regular-season games, are termed NFL First-Year Players. An NFL First-Year Player is designated by a "1" on NFL rosters. Thereafter, a player is credited with an additional year of experience for each season in which he accumulates six games on the Active List or Inactive List, or on Reserve/Injured or Reserve/Physically Unable to Perform.

COACHING STAFF

Head Coach/Executive Vice President of Football Operations, Andy Reid

Pro Career: Andy Reid was named the twentieth head coach in franchise history on January 11, 1999. On May 7, 2001, Reid was given the title of head coach/executive vice president of football operations. Reid has been simply masterful in turning the Eagles into one of the NFL's elite teams. Last year, he captured the team's first NFC East division title since 1988. His Eagles also reached the NFC Championship Game for the first time since 1980 and he tied the club's all-time record for postseason victories with 3, joining Greasy Neale and Dick Vermeil. After a 5-11 mark in his first season, he led the 2000 Eagles to the greatest turnaround in franchise history, finishing second in the NFC East at 11-5 and earning a trip to the NFC Divisional Playoffs. For his efforts, Reid was named the NFL's coach of the year by the Maxwell Football Club, The Sporting News, and Football Digest. Reid came to the Eagles after spending the previous seven seasons as an assistant coach with the Green Bay Packers under Mike Holmgren. With Green Bay, Reid helped the Packers reach the playoffs six consecutive times from 1993-98. During that span, Green Bay defeated New England in Super Bowl XXXI and reached the NFL's title game again the following year after earning the NFC crown with a victory against San Francisco. In his 10-year NFL coaching career, Reid's teams have made the playoff eight times. He has coached in the Super Bowl twice and in the NFC Championship Game four times. Career record: 30-23.

Background: Coached at Brigham Young (1982), San Francisco State (1983-85), Northern Arizona (1986), Texas-El Paso (1987-88), and Missori (1989-1991). San Francisco State led the nation in passing offense and total offense for three consecutive years while Reid served as the school's offensive coordinator, offensive line coach, and strength coach. Reid first met Holmgren, who was a member of BYU's coaching staff, when Reid was an offensive tackle and guard on three Cougars Holiday Bowl teams. Reid graduating with a bachelor's degree in physical education. He also received a master's degree in professional leadership in physical education and athletics.

Personal: Born in Los Angeles on March 19, 1958, Reid and his wife Tammy have five children—Garrett, Britt, Crosby, Drew Ann, and Spencer.

ASSISTANT COACHES

Tommy Brasher, defensive line; born Dec. 30, 1940, El Dorado, Ark., lives in Newtown Square, Pa. Linebacker Arkansas 1962-63. No pro playing experience. College coach: Arkansas 1970,

Virginia Tech 1971, Northeast Louisiana 1974, 1976, Southern Methodist 1977-1981. Pro coach: Shreveport Steamer (WFL) 1975, New England Patriots 1982-84, Philadelphia Eagles 1985, Atlanta Falcons 1986-89, Tampa Bay Buccaneers 1990, Seattle Seahawks 1992-98, rejoined Eagles in 1999.

Juan Castillo, offensive line; born October 8, 1959, Port Isabel, Texas, lives in Mount Laurel, N.J. Linebacker Texas A&I (now Texas A&M-Kingsville) 1978-1980. Pro linebacker San Antonio Gunslingers (USFL) 1984-85. College coach: Texas A&M-Kingsville 1982-85, 1990-94. Pro coach: Joined Eagles in 1995.

Brad Childress, offensive coordinator; born June 27, 1956, Aurora, Ill., lives in Cinnaminson, N.J. Eastern Illinois 1975-78. No pro playing experience. College coach: Illinois 1978-1984, Northern Arizona 1986-89, Utah 1990, Wisconsin 1991-98. Pro coach: Indianapolis Colts 1985, joined Eagles in 1999.

David Culley, wide receivers; born September 17, 1955, Sparta, Tenn., lives in Sewell, N.J. Quarterback Vanderbilt 1973-77. No pro playing experience. College coach: Austin Peay 1978, Vanderbilt 1979-1981, Middle Tennessee State 1982, Tennessee-Chattanooga 1983, Western Kentucky 1984, Southwestern Louisiana 1985-88, Texas-El Paso 1989-1990, Texas A&M 1991-93. Pro coach: Tampa Bay Buccaneers 1994-95, Pittsburgh Steelers 1996-1998, joined Eagles in 1999.

Leslie Frazier, defensive backs; born April 3, 1959, Columbus, Miss., lives in Cherry Hill, N.J. Defensive back Alcorn State 1979-1980. Pro defensive back Chicago Bears 1981-86. College coach: Trinity (Ill.) College 1988-1996 (head coach), Illinois 1997-98. Pro coach: Joined Eagles in 1999.

John Harbaugh, special teams; born September 23, 1962, Perrysburg, Ohio, lives in Newtown Square, Pa. Defensive back Miami (Ohio) 1980-83. No pro playing experience. College coach: Western Michigan 1984-86, Pittsburgh 1987, Morehead State 1988, Cincinnati 1989-1996, Indiana 1997. Pro coach: Joined Eagles in 1998.

Jim Johnson, defensive coordinator; born May 26, 1941, Maywood, Ill., lives in Newtown Square, Pa. Quarterback Missouri 1959-1962. Pro tight end Buffalo Bills 1963-64. College coach: Missouri Southern 1967-68 (head coach), Drake 1969-1972, Indiana 1973-76, Notre Dame 1977-1980. Pro coach: Oklahoma Outlaws (USFL) 1984, Jacksonville Bulls (USFL) 1985, Phoenix Cardinals 1986-1993, Indianapolis Colts 1994-97, Seattle Seahawks 1998, joined Eagles in 1999.

Mike Kelly, offensive assistant-quality control; born February 2, 1958, Waterbury, Conn., lives in Bridgeport, Pa. Quarterback Bluffton (Ohio) College

1976-79. No pro playing experience. College coach: Edinboro 1982, Marietta College 1983-85, Ohio Wesleyan 1986, Capital University 1987-89, San Francisco State 1990-91, Valdosta State 1997-99. Pro coach: Winnipeg Blue Bombers (CFL) 1992-96, Orlando Rage (XFL) 2001, joined Eagles in 2002.

Sean McDermott, defense assistant-quality control; born March 21, 1974, Omaha, Neb., lives in Conshohocken, Pa. Safety William & Mary 1994-97. No pro playing experience. College coach: William & Mary 1998. Pro coach: Joined Eagles in 1998.

Tom Melvin, tight ends; born October 1, 1961, Redwood City, Calif., lives in Cinnaminson, N.J. Offensive lineman San Francisco State 1982-83. No pro playing experience. College coach: San Francisco State 1984-85, Northern Arizona 1986-87, California-Santa Barbara 1988-1990, Occidental College 1991-98. Pro coach: Joined Eagles in 1999.

Ron Rivera, linebackers; born January 7, 1962, Fort Ord, Calif., lives in Cherry Hill, N.J. Linebacker California 1980-83. Pro linebacker Chicago Bears 1984-1992. Pro coach: Chicago Bears 1997-98, joined Eagles in 1999.

Pat Shurmur, quarterbacks; born April 14, 1965, Dearborn Heights, Mich., lives in Cinnaminson, N.J. Center Michigan State 1983-87. No pro playing experience. College coach: Michigan State 1988-1997, Stanford 1998. Pro coach: Joined Eagles in 1999.

Steve Spagnuolo, defensive backs; born December 21, 1959, Witinsville, Mass., lives in Haddon Heights, N.J. Wide receiver Springfield College 1979-1981. No pro playing experience. College coach: Massachusetts 1982-83, Lafayette 1984-86, Connecticut 1987-1991, Maine 1993, Rutgers 1994-95, Bowling Green 1996-97. Pro coach: Barcelona Dragons (World League) 1992, Frankfurt Galaxy (NFL Europe) 1998, joined Eagles in 1999.

Dave Toub, special teams quality control; born June 1, 1962, Ossining, N.Y., lives in Philadelphia. Offensive lineman Springfield College 1980-81, Texas-El Paso 1983-84. No pro playing experience. College coach: Texas-El Paso 1987-89, Missouri 1989-2000. Pro coach: Joined Eagles in 2001.

Ted Williams, running backs; born November 17, 1943, Lyons, Texas, lives in Sicklerville, N.J. No college or pro playing experience. College coach: UCLA 1980-89, Washington State 1991-93, Arizona 1994. Pro coach: Joined Eagles in 1995.

Mike Wolf, strength and conditioning; born May 15, 1965, Allentown, Pa., lives in Medford, N.J. Center Penn State 1983-87. No pro playing experience. College coach: Vanderbilt 1988-89, Lehigh 1990, Penn State 1991. Pro coach: Minnesota Vikings 1992-94, joined Eagles in 1995.

**National Football Conference
West Division**
Team Colors: New Century Gold,
Millennium Blue, and White
**One Rams Way
St. Louis, Missouri 63045**
Telephone: (314) 982-7267

2002 SCHEDULE
PRESEASON
Aug. 10 at Tennessee 7:00
Aug. 16 **Chicago** 7:00
Aug. 22 **San Diego**.........................8:00
Aug. 30 at Kansas City 7:30

REGULAR SEASON
Sept. 8   at Denver...........................2:15
Sept. 15 **New York Giants**................3:05
Sept. 23 at Tampa Bay (Mon.)..........9:00
Sept. 29 **Dallas** 12:00
Oct. 6   at San Francisco.................1:15
Oct. 13 **Oakland** 3:15
Oct. 20 **Seattle**.............................12:00
Oct. 27 OPEN DATE
Nov. 3   at Arizona............................2:15
Nov. 10 **San Diego** 12:00
Nov. 18 **Chicago (Mon.)**..................8:00
Nov. 24 at Washington 4:15
Dec. 1   at Philadelphia....................4:15
Dec. 8   at Kansas City 12:00
Dec. 15 **Arizona** 7:30
Dec. 22 at Seattle............................1:05
Dec. 30 **San Francisco (Mon.)**........8:00

Stadium: Edward Jones Dome
(opened in 1995)
•**Capacity:** 66,000
701 Convention Plaza
St. Louis, Missouri 63101
Playing Surface: Astro Turf
Training Camp: Western Illinois University
Thompson Hall
Macomb, Illinois 61455

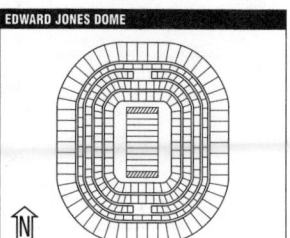

EDWARD JONES DOME

CLUB OFFICIALS
Owner/Chairman: Georgia Frontiere
Owner/Vice Chairman: Stan Kroenke
President: John Shaw
President-Football Operations:
Jay Zygmunt
Senior Vice President-Administration and
General Counsel: Bob Wallace
Treasurer: Jeff Brewer
Vice President-Finance:
Adrian Barr-Bracy
General Manager: Charley Armey
Vice President-Sales and Marketing:
Phil Thomas
Director-Scouting:
Lawrence McCutcheon
Vice President-Ticket Operations:
Michael T. Naughton
Vice President of Operations:
John Oswald
Director of Football Administration:
Samir Suleiman
Director of Public Relations: Rick Smith
Assistant Director of Public Relations:
Duane Lewis
Head Trainer: Jim Anderson
Assistant Trainers: Dake Walden,
Ron DuBuque
Equipment Manager: Todd Hewitt
Scouts: Dick Daniels, Mel Foels,
Ryan Grigson, Tom Marino,
John Mancini, David Razzano

COACHING HISTORY
Cleveland 1937-1945,
Los Angeles 1946-1994
(472-424-20)
1937-38	Hugo Bezdek*	1-13-0
1938	Art Lewis	4-4-0
1939-1942	Earl (Dutch) Clark	..16-26-2
1944	Aldo (Buff) Donelli	4-6-0
1945-46	Adam Walsh	16-5-1
1947	Bob Snyder	6-6-0
1948-49	Clark Shaughnessy	..14-8-3
1950-52	Joe Stydahar**	19-9-0
1952-54	Hamp Pool	23-11-2
1955-59	Sid Gillman	28-32-1
1960-62	Bob Waterfield***	...9-24-1
1962-65	Harland Svare	14-31-3
1966-1970	George Allen	49-19-4
1971-72	Tommy Prothro	14-12-2
1973-77	Chuck Knox	57-20-1
1978-1982	Ray Malavasi	43-36-0
1983-1991	John Robinson	79-74-0
1992-94	Chuck Knox	15-33-0
1995-96	Rich Brooks	13-19-0
1997-99	Dick Vermeil	25-26-0
2000-01	Mike Martz	26-10-0

*Released after three games in 1938
**Resigned after one game in 1952
***Resigned after eight games in 1962

ATTENDANCE
Home 519,733   Away 547,716
Total 1,067,449
Single-game home record,
66,273 (12/10/00)
Single-season home record, 520,926
(1999)

2002 DRAFT CHOICES
Round	Name	Pos.	College
1	Robert Thomas	LB	UCLA
2	Travis Fisher	DB	Central Florida
3	Lamar Gordon	RB	North Dakota St.
	Eric Crouch	WR	Nebraska
4	Travis Scott	G	Arizona State
5	Courtland Bullard	LB	Ohio State
6	Steve Bellisari	DB	Ohio State
7	Chris Massey	C	Marshall

2001 TEAM RECORD

PRESEASON (3-2)

Date	Result	Opponent
8/6	W 17-10	vs. Miami, at Canton, Ohio
8/12	W 24-10	at Buffalo
8/17	L 10-23	Tennessee
8/25	L 10-13	at San Diego (OT)
8/31	W 21-17	Kansas City

REGULAR SEASON (14-2)

Date	Result	Opponent	Att.
9/09	W 20-17	at Philadelphia(OT)	66,243
9/23	W 30-26	at San Francisco	67,536
9/30	W 42-10	Miami	66,046
10/08	W 35-0	at Detroit	77,765
10/14	W 15-14	New York Giants	65,992
10/21	W 34-14	at New York Jets	78,766
10/28	L 31-34	New Orleans	66,189
11/11	W 48-14	Carolina	66,069
11/18	W 24-17	at New England	60,292
11/26	L 17-24	Tampa Bay	66,198
12/02	W 35-6	at Atlanta	60,787
12/09	W 27-14	San Francisco	66,218
12/17	W 34-21	at New Orleans	70,332
12/23	W 38-32	at Carolina	72,438
12/30	W 42-17	Indianapolis	66,084
1/06	W 31-13	Atlanta	66,033

(OT) Overtime

POSTSEASON (2-1)

1/20	W 45-17	Green Bay	66,338
1/27	W 29-24	Philadelphia	66,502
2/3	L 17-20	vs. New England, at New Orleans	72,922

SCORE BY PERIODS

Rams	140	165	103	92	3	—	503
Opponents	51	85	66	71	0	—	273

2001 TEAM STATISTICS

	Rams	Opp.
Total First Downs	357	256
Rushing	104	77
Passing	236	153
Penalty	17	26
3rd Down: Made/Att	96/192	69/209
3rd Down Pct.	50.0	33.0
4th Down: Made/Att	8/11	11/23
4th Down Pct.	72.7	47.8
Possession Avg.	31:45	28:15
Total Net Yards	6690	4471
Avg. Per Game	418.1	279.4
Total Plays	1007	952
Avg. Per Play	6.6	4.7
Net Yards Rushing	2027	1374
Avg. Per Game	126.7	85.9
Total Rushes	416	366
Net Yards Passing	4663	3097
Avg. Per Game	291.4	193.6
Sacked/Yards Lost	40/240	45/251
Gross Yards	4903	3348
Att./Completions	551/379	541/314
Completion Pct.	68.8	58.0
Had Intercepted	22	21
Punts/Average	43/42.1	79/42.0
Net Punting Avg.	43/34.9	79/34.9
Penalties/Yards	107/847	100/830
Fumbles/Ball Lost	38/22	21/13
Touchdowns	62	31
Rushing	20	11
Passing	37	16
Returns	5	4

2001 INDIVIDUAL STATISTICS

PASSING	Att.	Comp.	Yds.	Pct.	TD	Int.	Tkld.	Rate
Warner	546	375	4830	68.7	36	22	38/233	101.4
Martin	3	3	22	100.0	0	0	2/7	97.2
Faulk	1	0	0	0.0	0	0	0/0	39.6
Hakim	1	1	51	100.0	1	0	0/0	158.3
Rams	551	379	4903	68.8	37	22	40/240	102.2
Opponents	541	314	3348	58.0	16	21	45/251	69.9

SCORING	TD R	TD P	TD Rt	PAT	FG	Saf	PTS
Faulk	12	9	0	0/0	0/0	0	128
Wilkins	0	0	0	58/58	23/29	0	127
Holt	0	7	0	0/0	0/0	0	42
Bruce	0	6	0	0/0	0/0	0	36
Canidate	6	0	0	0/0	0/0	0	36
Proehl	0	5	0	0/0	0/0	0	32
Conwell	1	4	0	0/0	0/0	0	30
Hakim	0	3	0	0/0	0/0	0	18
Bly	0	0	2	0/0	0/0	0	12
Williams	0	0	2	0/0	0/0	0	12
Hodgins	0	1	0	0/0	0/0	0	6
Holcombe	1	0	0	0/0	0/0	0	6
Manumaleuna	0	1	0	0/0	0/0	0	6
McCleon	0	0	1	0/0	0/0	0	6
Robinson	0	1	0	0/0	0/0	0	6
Rams	20	37	5	58/58	23/29	0	503
Opponents	11	16	4	27/27	20/26	0	273

2-Pt. Conversions: Faulk, Proehl.
Rams 2-4, Opponents 0-4.

RUSHING	Att.	Yds.	Avg.	LG	TD
Faulk	260	1382	5.3	71t	12
Canidate	78	441	5.7	45	6
Warner	28	60	2.1	23	0
Hakim	11	50	4.5	12	0
Holcombe	13	42	3.2	11	1
Conwell	7	28	4.0	13	1
Bruce	4	23	5.8	10	0
Hodgins	2	5	2.5	5	0
Proehl	1	5	5.0	5	0
Baker	1	0	0.0	0	0
Holt	2	0	0.0	2	0
Watson	1	0	0.0	0	0
Martin	8	-9	-1.1	-1	0
Rams	416	2027	4.9	71t	20
Opponents	366	1374	3.8	30	11

RECEIVING	No.	Yds.	Avg.	LG	TD
Faulk	83	765	9.2	65t	9
Holt	81	1363	16.8	51	7
Bruce	64	1106	17.3	51t	6
Proehl	40	563	14.1	37	5
Hakim	39	374	9.6	33	3
Conwell	38	431	11.3	47	4
Canidate	17	154	9.1	29	0
Robinson	11	108	9.8	26	1
Hodgins	4	24	6.0	11t	1
Holcombe	1	14	14.0	14	0
Manumaleuna	1	1	1.0	1t	1
Rams	379	4903	12.9	65t	37
Opponents	314	3348	10.7	49t	16

INTERCEPTIONS	No.	Yds.	Avg.	LG	TD
Bly	6	150	25.0	93t	2
Williams	4	69	17.3	42t	2
McCleon	4	66	16.5	43	0
Fletcher	2	18	9.0	18	0
Wistrom	2	-4	-2.0	0	0
Fields	1	30	30.0	30	0
Young	1	25	25.0	25	0
Herring	1	15	15.0	15	0
Rams	21	369	17.6	93t	4
Opponents	22	307	14.0	52t	1

PUNTING	No.	Yds.	Avg.	In 20	LG
Baker	43	1809	42.1	9	58
Rams	43	1809	42.1	9	58
Opponents	79	3317	42.0	17	64

PUNT RETURNS	No.	FC	Yds.	Avg.	LG	TD
Hakim	36	12	330	9.2	32	0
Bly	7	6	71	11.0	32	0
Butler	0	0	-1	—	-1	0
Rams	43	18	400	9.3	32	0
Opponents	17	6	167	9.8	19	0

KICKOFF RETURNS	No.	Yds.	Avg.	LG	TD
Canidate	36	748	20.8	40	0
Murphy	8	174	21.8	29	0
Bly	6	128	21.3	32	0
Cason	4	73	18.3	26	0
Archuleta	1	0	0.0	0	0
Rams	55	1123	20.4	40	0
Opponents	86	2194	25.5	99t	2

FIELD GOALS	1-19	20-29	30-39	40-49	50+
Wilkins	0/0	11/11	5/5	6/12	1/1
Rams	0/0	11/11	5/5	6/12	1/1
Opponents	0/0	6/7	6/6	6/8	2/5

SACKS	No.
Little	14.5
Wistrom	9.0
Young	6.5
Fletcher	4.5
Jackson	3.0
Ahanotu	2.0
Archuleta	2.0
Moran	2.0
Coady	1.0
Pickett	0.5
Rams	45.0
Opponents	40.0

RECORD HOLDERS
INDIVIDUAL RECORDS—CAREER

Category	Name	Performance
Rushing (Yds.)	Eric Dickerson, 1983-87	7,245
Passing (Yds.)	Jim Everett, 1986-1993	23,758
Passing (TDs)	Roman Gabriel, 1962-1972	154
Receiving (No.)	Henry Ellard, 1983-1993	593
Receiving (Yds.)	Henry Ellard, 1983-1993	9,761
Interceptions	Ed Meador, 1959-1970	46
Punting (Avg.)	Danny Villanueva, 1960-64	44.2
Punt Return (Avg.)	Henry Ellard, 1983-1992	11.3
Kickoff Return (Avg.)	Tom Wilson, 1956-1961	27.1
Field Goals	Mike Lansford, 1982-1990	158
Touchdowns (Tot.)	Marshall Faulk, 1999-2001	59
Points	Mike Lansford, 1982-1990	789

INDIVIDUAL RECORDS—SINGLE SEASON

Category	Name	Performance
Rushing (Yds.)	Eric Dickerson, 1984	*2,105
Passing (Yds.)	Kurt Warner, 2001	4,830
Passing (TDs)	Kurt Warner, 1999	41
Receiving (No.)	Isaac Bruce, 1995	119
Receiving (Yds.)	Isaac Bruce, 1995	1,781
Interceptions	Dick (Night Train) Lane, 1952	*14
Punting (Avg.)	Danny Villanueva, 1962	45.5
Punt Return (Avg.)	Woodley Lewis, 1952	18.5
Kickoff Return (Avg.)	Verda (Vitamin T) Smith, 1950	33.7
Field Goals	David Ray, 1973	30
Touchdowns (Tot.)	Marshall Faulk, 2000	*26
Points	Marshall Faulk, 2000	160

INDIVIDUAL RECORDS—SINGLE GAME

Category	Name	Performance
Rushing (Yds.)	Willie Ellison, 12-5-71	247
Passing (Yds.)	Norm Van Brocklin, 9-28-51	*554
Passing (TDs)	Many times	5
	Last time by Kurt Warner, 10-10-99	
Receiving (No.)	Tom Fears, 12-3-50	18
Receiving (Yds.)	Willie Anderson, 11-26-89	*336
Interceptions	Many times	3
	Last time by Keith Lyle, 12-15-96	
Field Goals	Bob Waterfield, 12-9-51	5
	Jeff Wilkins, 10-1-00	5
Touchdowns (Tot.)	Many times	4
	last time by Marshall Faulk, 12-30-01	
Points	Many times	24
	last time by Marshall Faulk, 12-30-01	

*NFL Record

2002 VETERAN ROSTER

No.	Name	Pos.	Ht.	Wt.	Birthdate	NFL Exp.	College	Hometown	How Acq.	'01 Games/ Starts
31	Archuleta, Adam	S	6-0	215	11/27/77	2	Arizona State	Chandler, Ariz.	D1b-'01	13/12
17	Berger, Mitch	P	6-4	220	6/24/72	8	Colorado	Vancouver, B.C., Canada	FA-'02	12/0*
32	Bly, Dre'	CB	5-9	190	5/22/77	4	North Carolina	Chesapeake, Va.	D2-'99	16/4
93	Brown, Jonathan	DE	6-3	270	11/28/75	2	Tennessee	Tulsa, Okla.	FA-'01	3/1
80	Bruce, Isaac	WR	6-0	188	11/10/72	9	Memphis	Fort Lauderdale, Fla.	D2a-'94	16/16
10	Bulger, Marc	QB	6-3	215	4/5/77	2	West Virginia	Pittsburgh, Pa.	FA-'01	0*
95	Burrough, John	DE	6-4	276	5/17/72	7	Wyoming	Pinedale, Wyo.	FA-'02	0*
23	Butler, Jerametrius	CB	5-10	181	11/28/78	2	Kansas State	Dallas, Texas	D5-'01	16/0
24	Canidate, Trung	RB	5-11	205	3/3/77	3	Arizona	Phoenix, Ariz.	D1-'00	16/2
38	Coady, Rich	S	6-1	215	1/26/76	4	Texas A&M	Dallas, Texas	D3-'99	12/2
56	Cohen, Dustin	LB	6-3	241	12/22/76	2	Miami (Ohio)	Cincinnati, Ohio	FA-'01	4/0
84	Conwell, Ernie	TE	6-2	265	8/17/72	7	Washington	Kent, Wash.	D2b-'96	16/13
58	Davis, Don	LB	6-1	234	12/17/72	7	Kansas	Olathe, Kan.	UFA(TB)-'01	12/8
59	Duncan, Jamie	LB	6-1	238	7/20/75	5	Vanderbilt	Wilmington, Del.	UFA(TB)-'02	15/15*
28	Faulk, Marshall	RB	5-10	211	2/26/73	9	San Diego State	New Orleans, La.	T(Ind)-'99	14/14
65	Garcia, Frank	C	6-2	302	1/28/72	8	Washington	Phoenix, Ariz.	UFA(Car)-'01	13/2
30	Gary, Willie	S	5-10	195	11/1/78	2	Kentucky	Valdosta, Ga.	FA-'01	7/0
20	Herring, Kim	S	6-0	200	9/10/75	6	Penn State	Solon, Ohio	UFA(Balt)-'01	16/15
44	Hetherington, Chris	RB	6-3	244	11/27/72	6	Yale	North Branford, Conn.	UFA(Car)-'02	16/1*
42	Hodgins, James	RB	6-1	270	4/30/77	4	San Jose State	San Jose, Calif.	FA-'99	16/10
81	Holt, Torry	WR	6-0	190	6/5/76	4	North Carolina State	Greensboro, N.C.	D1-'99	16/14
63	Irwin, Heath	G	6-4	301	6/27/73	7	Colorado	Boulder, Colo.	FA-'02	16/7*
97	Jackson, Tyoka	DT	6-2	280	11/22/71	8	Penn State	Forrestville, Md.	UFA(TB)-'01	16/0
92	Lewis, Damione	DT	6-2	301	3/1/78	2	Miami	Sulphur Springs, Texas	D1a-'01	9/3
91	Little, Leonard	DE	6-3	257	10/19/74	5	Tennessee	Asheville, N.C.	D3-'98	13/3
15	Looker, Dane	WR	6-0	194	5/5/76	2	Washington	Puyallup, Wash.	FA-'02	0*
86	Manumaleuna, Brandon	TE	6-2	288	1/4/80	2	Arizona	Lomita, Calif.	D4b-'01	16/0
12	Martin, Jamie	QB	6-2	205	2/8/70	8	Weber State	Arroyo Grande, Calif.	FA-'01	5/0
21	McCleon, Dexter	CB	5-10	195	10/9/73	6	Clemson	Meridian, Miss.	D2-'97	16/16
67	McCollum, Andy	C	6-4	300	6/2/70	9	Toledo	Richfield, Ohio	UFA(NO)-'99	16/16
83	Murphy, Yo	WR	5-10	187	5/11/73	3	Idaho	Idaho Falls, Idaho	FA-'01	16/0
71	Noa, Kaulana	T	6-3	307	12/29/76	3	Hawaii	Honokaa, Hawaii	D4-'00	0*
61	Nütten, Tom	G	6-5	304	8/14/71	6	Western Michigan	Magog, Quebec, Canada	FA-'98	15/14
76	Pace, Orlando	T	6-7	325	11/4/75	6	Ohio State	Sandusky, Ohio	D1-'97	16/16
79	Pickett, Ryan	DT	6-2	310	10/8/79	2	Ohio State	Zephyrhills, Fla.	D1c-'01	11/0
52	Polley, Tommy	LB	6-3	240	1/11/78	2	Florida State	Baltimore, Md.	D2-'01	16/11
87	Proehl, Ricky	WR	6-0	190	3/7/68	13	Wake Forest	Hillsborough, N.J.	UFA(Chi)-'98	16/3
70	St. Clair, John	T	6-4	315	7/15/77	3	Virginia	Roanoke, Va.	D3-'00	0*
41	Sorensen, Nick	S	6-2	205	7/31/78	2	Virginia Tech	Vienna, Va.	FA-'01	7/0
73	Spikes, Cameron	G	6-2	323	11/6/76	4	Texas A&M	Bryan, Texas	D5-'99	5/0
62	Timmerman, Adam	G	6-4	300	8/14/71	8	South Dakota State	Cherokee, Iowa	UFA(GB)-'99	16/16
13	Warner, Kurt	QB	6-2	220	6/22/71	5	Northern Iowa	Burlington, Iowa	FA-'98	16/16
14	Wilkins, Jeff	K	6-2	205	4/19/72	9	Youngstown State	Austintown, Ohio	RFA(SF)-'97	16/0
82 t-	Wilkins, Terrence	WR	5-10	180	7/29/75	4	Virginia	Falls Church, Va.	T(Ind)-'02	11/4*
35	Williams, Aeneas	CB	5-11	200	1/29/68	12	Southern	New Orleans, La.	T(Ariz)-'01	16/16
98	Wistrom, Grant	DE	6-4	272	7/3/76	5	Nebraska	Webb City, Mo.	D1-98	15/15
66	Young, Brian	DE	6-2	290	7/8/77	3	Texas-El Paso	El Paso, Texas	D5-'00	16/16
90	Zgonina, Jeff	DT	6-2	305	5/24/70	10	Purdue	Mundelein, Ill.	UFA(Ind)-'99	13/13

*   Berger played 12 games with Minnesota in '01; Bulger inactive for 16 games in '01; Burrough last active with Minnesota in '00; Duncan played in 15 games with Tampa Bay; Hetherington played 16 games with Carolina; Irwin played 16 games with Miami; Looker last active with New England in '00; Noa inactive for 16 games; St. Clair inactive for 16 games; T. Wilkins played 11 games with Indianapolis.

t-Rams traded for T. Wilkins (Ind).

Traded—CB Jacoby Shepherd (7 games in '01) to Houston.

Players lost through Expansion Draft (1): LB Brian Allen (3 games in '01).

Players lost through free agency (7): LB London Fletcher (Buff; 16 games in '01), WR Az-Zahir Hakim (Det; 16), RB Robert Holcombe (Tenn; 16), T Rod Jones (Wash; 6), DE Sean Moran (SF; 16), TE Jeff Robinson (Dall; 16), T Ryan Tucker (Cle; 16).

Also played with Rams in '01—DE Chidi Ahanotu (16 games), LB Kole Ayi (6), P John Baker (16), S Matt Bowen (1), LB O.J. Brigance (8), WR Aveion Cason (1), LB Mark Fields (14), RB Justin Watson (11).

2002 FIRST-YEAR ROSTER

Name	Pos.	Ht.	Wt.	Birthdate	College	Hometown	How Acq.
Almanzar, Luis (1)	DE	6-3	295	12/15/76	Southwest Missouri State	Jersey City, N.J.	FA
Baker, Eugene (1)	WR	6-2	183	3/18/76	Kent State	Pittsburgh, Pa.	FA
Bellisari, Steve	S	6-3	220	4/21/80	Ohio State	Boca Raton, Fla.	D6
Bradley, Carl (1)	DT	6-1	290	2/22/79	Virginia Tech	Lynchburg, Va.	FA
Broyles, James	G	6-1	312	5/18/78	Southwest Missouri State	Rensselaer, Ind.	FA
Bullard, Courtland	LB	6-3	234	8/2/78	Ohio State	Miami, Fla.	D5
Cole, Giles (1)	TE	6-6	255	2/4/76	Texas A&M-Kingsville	Orange, Texas	FA
Crouch, Eric	WR	6-0	205	11/16/78	Nebraska	Omaha, Neb.	D3b
Cunningham, Alonzo	G	6-4	316	5/21/79	Iowa	Iowa City, Iowa	FA
Douglas, Maurice	RB	6-1	245	6/6/79	Southwest Missouri State	Eureka, Mo.	FA
Fisher, Travis	CB	5-10	189	9/12/79	Central Florida	Tallahassee, Fla.	D2
Gatrell, Rob (1)	G	6-4	300	3/14/77	Fresno State	Brentwood, Calif.	FA
Gavadza, Jason (1)	TE	6-3	249	1/31/76	Kent State	Toronto, Ontario, Canada	FA
Glaze, Marques	RB	5-10	193	6/2/80	Bloomsburg State	Robesonia, Pa.	FA
Gordon, Lamar	RB	6-1	214	1/7/80	North Dakota State	Milwaukee, Wis.	D3a
Hall, Darran (1)	WR	5-10	175	9/8/75	Colorado State	San Diego, Calif.	FA
Hall, Joe	RB	6-0	293	11/3/79	Kansas State	Lynwood, Calif.	FA
Hawkes, Michael (1)	LB	6-0	228	4/11/77	Virginia Tech	Blackstone, Va.	FA
Helming, Ryan (1)	QB	6-2	220	12/14/77	Northern Iowa	Springfield, Mo.	FA
Hollenbeck, Joey	G	6-4	290	2/26/80	Washington State	Enumclaw, Wash.	FA
Howard, Todd	CB	5-10	190	2/20/80	Michigan	Bolingbrook, Ill.	FA
King, Andy	G	6-4	310	11/9/78	Illinois State	Lincoln, Ill.	FA
Malan, Michael	RB	5-11	235	4/8/80	Brown	St. Louis, Mo.	FA
Massey, Chris	C	6-0	245	8/21/79	Marshall	Chesapeake, W. Va.	D7
Oliver, Chris	WR	6-2	210	5/25/80	Iowa	Flossmoor, Ill.	FA
Pack, Derick	LB	6-1	230	2/10/79	James Madison	Princeton, W. Va.	FA
Robinson, Robbie	S	5-11	200	12/7/78	Colorado	Oceanside, Calif.	FA
Rogers, Ronald	CB	5-10	180	7/12/78	Western Michigan	Miami, Fla.	FA
St. Paul, Francis (1)	WR	5-10	185	4/25/79	Northern Arizona	Los Angeles, Calif.	FA-'01
Scott, Travis	G	6-6	300	8/9/79	Arizona State	Mesa, Ariz.	D4
Sigmund, John (1)	TE	6-4	265	7/2/78	Wisconsin	Sewell, N.J.	FA
Sternke, Kevin (1)	P	6-2	189	11/23/78	Wisconsin	Green Bay, Wis.	FA
Taylor, Chris (1)	WR	5-10	183	4/25/79	Texas A&M	Madisonville, Texas	FA
Thomas, Robert	LB	6-0	229	7/17/80	UCLA	Imperial, Calif.	D1
Whitley, James (1)	CB	5-11	190	5/13/79	Michigan	Norfolk, Va.	FA
Williams, Brian (1)	LB	6-0	246	7/8/78	Northwest Missouri State	Kansas City, Mo.	FA

The term NFL Rookie is defined as a player who is in his first season of professional football and has not been on the roster of another professional football team for any regular-season or postseason games. A Rookie is designated by an "R" on NFL rosters. Players who have been active in another professional football league or players who have NFL experience, including either preseason training camp or being on an Active List or Inactive List, or on Reserve/Injured or Reserve/Physically Unable to Perform for fewer than six regular-season games, are termed NFL First-Year Players. An NFL First-Year Player is designated by a "1" on NFL rosters. Thereafter, a player is credited with an additional year of experience for each season in which he accumulates six games on the Active List or Inactive List, or on Reserve/Injured or Reserve/Physically Unable to Perform.

COACHING STAFF
Head Coach,
Mike Martz
Pro Career: Named 21st head coach of the Rams on February 2, 2000. Has led Rams to playoffs in each of first two seasons as head coach, including berth in Super Bowl XXXVI. Offensive mastermind behind one of most explosive offenses in NFL history during past three seasons, as Rams are only franchise in league history to score at least 500 points in three different seasons (526 in 1999, 540 in 2000, 503 in 2001). Rams have led league in scoring and total offense in each of past three seasons while producing the past three NFL Most Valuable Players (QB Kurt Warner in 1999 and 2001, RB Marshall Faulk in 2000). Rejoined Rams in 1999 after two seasons as quarterbacks coach of Washington Redskins (1997-98). In second tour with Rams, as he began NFL career with team in 1992 as offensive assistant. Coached tight ends, receivers, and quarterbacks through 1996 season. Career record: 26-10.

Background: Played tight end at Fresno State 1972 after transferring from the University of California-Santa Barbara, which dropped football a season earlier. Began coaching career in 1973 at Bullard High School in Fresno, California, before moving to the collegiate ranks as an assistant at San Diego Mesa C.C. (1974, 1976-77), San Jose State (1975), and Santa Ana College (1978) before returning to his alma mater in 1979. Served as assistant at University of Pacific (1980-81) and Minnesota (1982) before moving to Arizona State, where he coached quarterbacks and receivers from 1983-87, and was offensive coordinator from 1987-1991.

Personal: Born May 13, 1951 in Sioux Falls, S.D. Graduated summa cum laude at Fresno State in 1973. Lives with wife Julie in Chesterfield, Mo., and has three sons and one daughter.

ASSISTANT COACHES
Bobby April, special teams; born April 15, 1953, New Orleans, lives in St. Louis. Linebacker-defensive end Nicholls State 1972-75. No pro playing experience. College coach: Southern Mississippi 1978, Tulane 1979, Arizona 1980-86, Southern California 1987-1990. Pro coach: Atlanta Falcons 1991-93, Pittsburgh Steelers 1994-95, New Orleans Saints 1996-99, joined Rams in 2001.

Chris Clausen, strength and conditioning coordinator; born February 21, 1958, Evergreen Park, Ill., lives in St. Louis. Cornerback Indiana 1976-79. No pro playing experience. College coach: San Diego State 1987-88. Pro coach: San Diego Chargers 1989-1991, joined Rams in 1992.

Henry Ellard, wide receivers; born July 21, 1961, Fresno, Calif., lives in St. Louis.

Wide receiver Fresno State 1979-1982. Pro wide receiver-punt returner Los Angeles Rams 1983-1993, Washington Redskins 1994-97, New England Patriots 1998, Washington Redskins 1998. College coach: Fresno State 2000. Pro coach: Joined Rams in 2001.

Mike Haluchak, linebackers; born November 28, 1949, Concord, Calif., lives in St. Louis. Linebacker Southern California 1967-1970. No pro playing experience. College coach: Southern California 1976-77, Cal State-Fullerton 1978, Pacific 1979-1980, California 1981, North Carolina State 1982. Pro coach: Oakland Invaders (USFL) 1983-85, San Diego Chargers 1986-1991, Cincinnati Bengals 1992-93, Washington Redskins 1994-96, New York Giants 1997-99, joined Rams in 2000.

Jim Hanifan, offensive line; born September 21, 1933, Compton, Calif., lives in St. Charles, Mo. Tight end California 1952-54. Pro tight end Toronto Argonauts (USFL) 1955. College coach: Yuba City (Calif.) J.C. 1959-1961, Glendale (Calif.) J.C. 1964-65, Utah 1966-69, California 1970-71, San Diego State 1972. Pro coach: St. Louis Cardinals 1973-78, 1980-85 (head coach), San Diego Chargers 1979, Atlanta Falcons 1987-89, Washington Redskins 1990-96, joined Rams in 1997.

Bobby Jackson, associate head coach-offensive coordinator-running backs; born February 16, 1940, Forsyth, Ga., lives in Chesterfield, Mo. Linebacker-running back Samford 1959-1962. No pro playing experience. College coach: Florida State 1965-69, Kansas State 1970-74, Louisville 1975-76, Tennessee 1977-1982. Pro coach: Atlanta Falcons 1983-86, San Diego Chargers 1987-1991, Phoenix Cardinals 1992-93, Washington Redskins 1994-99, joined Rams in 2000.

Bill Kollar, defensive line; born November 27, 1952, Warren, Ohio, lives in St. Louis. Defensive end Montana State 1971-74. Pro defensive end Cincinnati Bengals 1974-76, Tampa Bay Buccaneers 1977-1981. College coach: Illinois 1985-87, Purdue 1988-89. Pro coach: Tampa Bay Buccaneers 1984, Atlanta Falcons 1990-2000, joined Rams in 2001.

Dana LeDuc, strength and conditioning; born March 22, 1953, Tacoma, Wash., lives in St. Charles, Mo. Attended Texas. No college or pro playing experience. College coach: Texas 1977-1992, Miami 1993-94. Pro coach: Seattle Seahawks 1995-98, joined Rams in 1999.

Carlos Mainord, defensive backs; born August 26, 1944, Greenville, Texas, lives in St. Louis. Linebacker Navarro J.C. (Texas) 1962-63, McMurry College 1964-65. No pro playing experience. College coach: McMurry College 1966-68, Texas Tech 1969, 1983-85, 1987-1992, Ranger (Texas) J.C. 1970-77 (head coach, 1972-77), Rice 1978-1982, Miami 1986. Pro

coach; Chicago Bears 1993-98, New Orleans 1999, Carolina Panthers 2000-01, joined Rams in 2001.

John Matsko, asst. head coach-offensive line; born February 2, 1951, Cleveland, lives in Lake St. Louis, Mo. Fullback Kent State 1970-73. No pro playing experience. College coach Kent State 1973, Miami (Ohio) 1974-75, 1977, North Carolina 1978-1984, Navy 1985, Arizona 1986, Southern California 1987-1991. Pro coach: Phoenix Cardinals 1992-93, New Orleans Saints 1994-96, New York Giants 1997-98, joined Rams in 1999.

Wilbert Montgomery, tight ends; born September 16, 1954, Greenville, Miss., lives in Chesterfield, Mo. Running back Abilene Christian 1973-76. Pro running back Philadelphia Eagles 1977-1984, Detroit Lions 1985-86. Pro coach: Joined Rams in 1997.

John Ramsdell, quarterbacks; born August 16, 1954, Lafayette, Ind., lives in Chesterfield, Mo. Running back Springfield (Mass.) College 1972-75. No pro playing experience. College coach: San Francisco State 1976-77, Long Beach State 1978, Pacific 1979-1982, Oregon 1983-1994. Pro coach: Joined Rams in 1995.

Matt Sheldon, defensive assistant-quality control; born February 26, 1969, Berwyn, Ill., lives in Chesterfield, Mo. Cornerback Minnesota 1987-1991. No pro playing experience. College coach: Wisconsin 1997-99. Pro coach: Joined Rams in 2001.

Lovie Smith, defensive coordinator; born May 8, 1958, Gladewater, Texas, lives in St. Louis. Linebacker Tulsa 1976-79. No pro playing experience. College coach: Tulsa 1983-86, Wisconsin 1987, Arizona State 1988-1991, Kentucky 1992, Tennessee 1993-94, Ohio State 1995. Pro coach: Tampa Bay Buccaneers 1996-2000, joined Rams in 2001.

Ken Zampese, passing game; born July 19, 1967, Santa Maria, Calif., lives in O'Fallon, Mo. Wide receiver San Diego 1985-88. No pro playing experience. College coach: San Diego 1989, Southern California 1990-91, Northern Arizona 1992-95, Miami (Ohio) 1996-97. Pro coach: Philadelphia Eagles 1988, Green Bay Packers 1999, joined Rams in 2000.

National Football Conference
West Division
Team Colors: Metalllic Gold,
Cardinal Red, and Beige
4949 Centennial Boulevard
Santa Clara, California 95054
Telephone: (408) 562-4949

2002 SCHEDULE
PRESEASON
Aug. 3	vs. Washington (Tokyo, Japan)	10:00
Aug. 10	**Kansas City**	6:00
Aug. 19	at Denver	6:00
Aug. 24	at Oakland	6:00
Aug. 28	**San Diego**	6:00

REGULAR SEASON
Sept. 5	at New York Giants (Thurs.)	8:30
Sept. 15	**Denver**	1:15
Sept. 22	**Washington**	1:15
Sept. 29	OPEN DATE	
Oct. 6	**St. Louis**	1:15
Oct. 14	at Seattle (Mon.)	6:00
Oct. 20	at New Orleans	12:00
Oct. 27	**Arizona**	1:05
Nov. 3	at Oakland	1:15
Nov. 10	**Kansas City**	1:15
Nov. 17	at San Diego	1:05
Nov. 25	**Philadelphia (Mon.)**	6:00
Dec. 1	**Seattle**	1:15
Dec. 8	at Dallas	12:00
Dec. 15	**Green Bay**	1:15
Dec. 21	at Arizona (Sat.)	3:00
Dec. 30	at St. Louis (Mon.)	8:00

Stadium: 3Com Park (opened in 1958)
• **Capacity:** 69,734
San Francisco, California
94124
Playing Surface: Grass
Training Camp: University of the Pacific
Stockton, California
95211

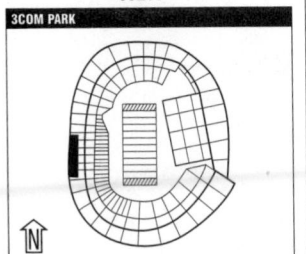

CLUB OFFICIALS
Owner: Denise DeBartolo York
Owner's Representative: Dr. John York
President/CEO: Peter Harris
General Manager: Terry Donahue
COO: Les Schmidt
Vice President/Director of Football
Administration: John McVay
Consultant: Bill Walsh
Pro Personnel Director: Bill McPherson
Vice President/Business Development:
David Goldman
Senior Director of Communications:
Rodney Knox
Director of Public Relations:
Kirk Reynolds
Ticket Manager: Lynn Carrozzi
Director of Stadium Operations:
Murlan (Mo) Fowell
Video Director: Robert Yanagi
Trainer: Lindsy McLean
Equipment Manager: Kevin Lartigue

COACHING HISTORY
(439-334-13)
1950-54	Lawrence (Buck) Shaw	33-25-2
1955	Norman (Red) Strader	4-8-0
1956-58	Frankie Albert	19-17-1
1959-1963	Howard (Red) Hickey*	27-27-1
1963-67	Jack Christiansen	26-38-3
1968-1975	Dick Nolan	56-56-5
1976	Monte Clark	8-6-0
1977	Ken Meyer	5-9-0
1978	Pete McCulley**	1-8-0
1978	Fred O'Connor	1-6-0
1979-1988	Bill Walsh	102-63-1
1989-1996	George Seifert	108-35-0
1997-2001	Steve Mariucci	49-36-0

*Resigned after three games in 1963
**Released after nine games in 1978

ATTENDANCE
Home 539,756   Away 509,068
Total 1,048,824
Single-game home record,
69,014 (11/13/94)
Single-season home record, 544,228
(1999)

2002 DRAFT CHOICES
Round	Name	Pos.	College
1	Mike Rumph	DB	Miami
3	Saleem Rasheed	LB	Alabama
4	Jeff Chandler	K	Florida
	Kevin Curtis	DB	Texas Tech
5	Brandon Doman	QB	Brigham Young
	Josh Shaw	DT	Michigan State
6	Mark Anelli	TE	Wisconsin
7	Eric Heitmann	G	Stanford
	Kyle Kosier	T	Arizona State
	Teddy Gaines	DB	Tennessee

SAN FRANCISCO 49ERS

2001 TEAM RECORD
PRESEASON (1-3)

Date	Result	Opponent
8/11	L 24-25	at San Diego
8/19	W 20-17	Oakland
8/25	L 18-28	Seattle
8/31	L 7-35	at Denver

REGULAR SEASON (12-4)

Date	Result	Opponent	Att.
9/09	W 16-13	Atlanta(OT)	65,989
9/23	L 26-30	St. Louis	67,536
10/01	W 19-17	at New York Jets	78,722
10/07	W 24-14	Carolina	66,944
10/14	W 37-31	at Atlanta(OT)	48,100
10/28	L 31-37	at Chicago(OT)	66,944
11/04	W 21-13	Detroit	67,605
11/11	W 28-27	New Orleans	68,083
11/18	W 25-22	at Carolina(OT)	72,665
11/25	W 40-21	at Indianapolis	56,393
12/02	W 35-0	Buffalo	67,252
12/09	L 14-27	at St. Louis	66,218
12/16	W 21-0	Miami	68,223
12/22	W 13-3	Philadelphia	68,124
12/30	L 21-27	at Dallas	64,366
1/06	W 38-0	at New Orleans	70,020

(OT) Overtime

POSTSEASON (0-1)
1/3	L 15-25	at Green Bay	59,825

SCORE BY PERIODS

49ers	52	139	82	124	12	—	409
Opponents	75	72	70	59	6	—	282

2001 TEAM STATISTICS

	49ers	Opp.
Total First Downs	328	289
Rushing	121	89
Passing	184	179
Penalty	23	21
3rd Down: Made/Att	95/213	78/210
3rd Down Pct.	44.6	37.1
4th Down: Made/Att	9/17	11/19
4th Down Pct.	52.9	57.9
Possession Avg.	31:49	28:11
Total Net Yards	5689	4954
Avg. Per Game	355.6	309.6
Total Plays	1041	988
Avg. Per Play	5.5	5.0
Net Yards Rushing	2244	1571
Avg. Per Game	140.3	98.2
Total Rushes	509	389
Net Yards Passing	3445	3383
Avg. Per Game	215.3	211.4
Sacked/Yards Lost	26/114	32/220
Gross Yards	3559	3603
Att./Completions	506/318	567/332
Completion Pct.	62.8	58.6
Had Intercepted	12	24
Punts/Average	69/40.8	72/41.4
Net Punting Avg.	69/35.4	72/36.0
Penalties/Yards	82/669	95/812
Fumbles/Ball Lost	19/7	24/10
Touchdowns	51	30
Rushing	16	9
Passing	32	18
Returns	3	3

2001 INDIVIDUAL STATISTICS

PASSING	Att.	Comp.	Yds.	Pct.	TD	Int.	Tkld.	Rate
Garcia	504	316	3538	62.7	32	12	26/114	94.8
Rattay	2	2	21	100.0	0	0	0/0	110.4
49ers	506	318	3559	62.8	32	12	26/114	95.0
Opponents	567	332	3603	58.6	18	24	32/220	70.3

SCORING	TD R	TD P	TD Rt	PAT	FG	Saf	PTS
Cortez	0	0	0	47/47	18/25	0	101
Owens	0	16	0	0/0	0/0	0	96
Stokes	0	7	0	0/0	0/0	0	42
Barlow	4	1	0	0/0	0/0	0	30
Garcia	5	0	0	0/0	0/0	0	30
Hearst	4	1	0	0/0	0/0	0	30
Johnson	0	3	0	0/0	0/0	0	20
T. Jackson	1	2	0	0/0	0/0	0	18
Bronson	0	0	2	0/0	0/0	0	12
Beasley	1	0	0	0/0	0/0	0	6
Peterson	0	0	1	0/0	0/0	0	6
P. Smith	1	0	0	0/0	0/0	0	6
Streets	0	1	0	0/0	0/0	0	6
Swift	0	1	0	0/0	0/0	0	6
49ers	16	32	3	47/47	18/25	0	409
Opponents	9	18	3	23/23	23/27	1	282

2-Pt. Conversions: Johnson.
49ers 1-3, Opponents 4-6.

RUSHING	Att.	Yds.	Avg.	LG	TD
Hearst	252	1206	4.8	43t	4
Barlow	125	512	4.1	25	4
Garcia	72	254	3.5	25	5
T. Jackson	22	138	6.3	15	1
Beasley	23	73	3.2	16	1
P. Smith	4	27	6.8	13t	1
Owens	4	21	5.3	12	0
Sutherland	1	16	16.0	16	0
Baker	1	0	0.0	0	0
Rattay	5	-3	-.6	1	0
49ers	509	2244	4.4	43t	16
Opponents	389	1571	4.0	39	9

RECEIVING	No.	Yds.	Avg.	LG	TD
Owens	93	1412	15.2	60t	16
Stokes	54	585	10.8	47	7
Hearst	41	347	8.5	60t	1
Johnson	40	362	9.1	24	3
Streets	28	345	12.3	52	1
Barlow	22	247	11.2	61t	1
Beasley	16	99	6.2	15	0
T. Jackson	12	91	7.6	14	2
Swift	11	66	6.0	13	1
Sutherland	1	5	5.0	5	0
49ers	318	3559	11.2	61t	32
Opponents	332	3603	10.9	63	18

INTERCEPTIONS	No.	Yds.	Avg.	LG	TD
Bronson	7	165	23.6	97t	2
Plummer	7	45	6.4	24	0
Webster	3	61	20.3	31	0
Schulters	3	0	0.0	0	0
Winborn	2	40	20.0	29	0
Holman	1	19	19.0	19	0
D. Smith	1	0	0.0	0	0
49ers	24	330	13.8	97t	2
Opponents	12	232	19.3	74t	3

PUNTING	No.	Yds.	Avg.	In 20	LG
Baker	69	2813	40.8	21	64
49ers	69	2813	40.8	21	64
Opponents	72	2981	41.4	25	68

PUNT RETURNS	No.	FC	Yds.	Avg.	LG	TD
Sutherland	21	19	147	7.0	19	0
C. Wilson	2	0	4	2.0	3	0
49ers	23	19	151	6.6	19	0
Opponents	34	14	290	8.5	34	0

KICKOFF RETURNS	No.	Yds.	Avg.	LG	TD
Sutherland	50	1140	22.8	65	0
C. Wilson	6	127	21.2	34	0
P. Smith	3	37	12.3	16	0
Lewis	2	32	16.0	19	0
49ers	61	1336	21.9	65	0
Opponents	68	1408	20.7	46	0

FIELD GOALS	1-19	20-29	30-39	40-49	50+
Cortez	1/2	6/7	6/7	4/8	1/1
49ers	1/2	6/7	6/7	4/8	1/1
Opponents	0/0	11/11	6/6	6/8	0/2

SACKS	No.
Carter	6.5
Engelberger	4.0
Stubblefield	4.0
Young	3.5
Peterson	3.0
D. Smith	3.0
Okeafor	2.5
R. Heard	1.0
McGrew	1.0
Schulters	1.0
Setzer	1.0
Ulbrich	0.5
Webster	0.5
Winborn	0.5
49ers	32.0
Opponents	26.0

RECORD HOLDERS

INDIVIDUAL RECORDS—CAREER

Category	Name	Performance
Rushing (Yds.)	Joe Perry, 1950-1960, 1963	7,344
Passing (Yds.)	Joe Montana, 1979-1992	35,124
Passing (TDs)	Joe Montana, 1979-1992	244
Receiving (No.)	Jerry Rice, 1985-2000	*1,281
Receiving (Yds.)	Jerry Rice, 1985-2000	*19,247
Interceptions	Ronnie Lott, 1981-1990	51
Punting (Avg.)	Tommy Davis, 1959-1969	44.7
Punt Return (Avg.)	Dana McLemore, 1982-87	10.8
Kickoff Return (Avg.)	Abe Woodson, 1958-1964	29.4
Field Goals	Ray Wersching, 1977-1987	190
Touchdowns (Tot.)	Jerry Rice, 1985-2000	*187
Points	Jerry Rice, 1985-2000	1,130

INDIVIDUAL RECORDS—SINGLE SEASON

Category	Name	Performance
Rushing (Yds.)	Garrison Hearst, 1998	1,570
Passing (Yds.)	Jeff Garcia, 2000	4,278
Passing (TDs)	Steve Young, 1998	36
Receiving (No.)	Jerry Rice, 1995	122
Receiving (Yds.)	Jerry Rice, 1995	*1,848
Interceptions	Dave Baker, 1960	10
	Ronnie Lott, 1986	10
Punting (Avg.)	Tommy Davis, 1965	45.8
Punt Return (Avg.)	Dana McLemore, 1982	22.3
Kickoff Return (Avg.)	Joe Arenas, 1953	34.4
Field Goals	Jeff Wilkins, 1996	30
Touchdowns (Tot.)	Jerry Rice, 1987	23
Points	Jerry Rice, 1987	138

INDIVIDUAL RECORDS—SINGLE GAME

Category	Name	Performance
Rushing (Yds.)	Charlie Garner, 9-24-00	201
Passing (Yds.)	Joe Montana, 10-14-90	476
Passing (TDs)	Joe Montana, 10-14-90	6
Receiving (No.)	Terrell Owens, 12-17-00	*20
Receiving (Yds.)	Jerry Rice, 12-18-95	289
Interceptions	Dave Baker, 12-4-60	*4
Field Goals	Ray Wersching, 10-16-83	6
	Jeff Wilkins, 9-29-96	6
Touchdowns (Tot.)	Jerry Rice, 10-14-90	5
Points	Jerry Rice, 10-14-90	30

*NFL Record

2002 VETERAN ROSTER

No.	Name	Pos.	Ht.	Wt.	Birthdate	NFL Exp.	College	Hometown	How Acq.	'01 Games/ Starts
7	Baker, Jason	P	6-1	195	5/17/78	2	Iowa	Fort Wayne, Ind.	FA-'01	16/0
32	Barlow, Kevan	RB	6-1	238	1/7/79	2	Pittsburgh	Pittsburgh, Pa.	D3-'01	15/0
4	Bayes, Andrew	P	6-3	200	2/11/78	2	East Carolina	Hyattsville, Md.	FA-'02	0*
40	Beasley, Fred	FB	6-0	246	9/18/74	5	Auburn	Montgomery, Ala.	D6-'98	15/12
31	Bronson, Zack	S	6-1	201	1/28/74	6	McNeese State	Jasper, Texas	FA-'97	16/16
65	Brown, Ray	G	6-5	318	12/12/62	17	Arkansas State	Marion, Ark.	UFA(Wash)-'96	16/16
90	Bryant, Junior	DE-DT	6-4	278	1/16/71	8	Notre Dame	Omaha, Neb.	FA-'93	0*
19	Carmazzi, Giovanni	QB	6-3	224	4/14/77	3	Hofstra	Sacramento, Calif.	D3a-'00	0*
96	Carter, Andre	DE	6-4	265	5/12/79	2	California	San Jose, Calif.	D1-'01	15/15
6	Cortez, Jose	K	5-11	205	5/27/75	2	Oregon State	Van Nuys, Calif.	FA-'01	16/0
76	Costa, Dave	T	6-5	307	9/8/78	2	Wisconsin	Ellwood City, Pa.	FA-'01	14/0
75	Davis, Jerome	DE	6-5	290	2/4/74	4	Minnesota	Detroit, Mich.	FA-'02	0*
63	Deese, Derrick	T	6-3	289	5/17/70	11	Southern California	Culver City, Calif.	FA-'92	16/16
59	Elam, Shane	LB	6-1	240	11/6/77	2	Mississippi	Covington, Tenn.	FA-'02	4/0
95	Engelberger, John	DE	6-4	260	10/18/76	3	Virginia Tech	Blacksburg, Va.	D2a-'00	15/14
74	Fiore, Dave	G	6-4	290	8/10/74	7	Hofstra	Waldwick, N.J.	FA-'98	16/16
5	Garcia, Jeff	QB	6-1	195	2/24/70	4	San Jose State	Gilroy, Calif.	FA-'99	16/16
78	Gragg, Scott	T	6-8	325	2/28/72	8	Montana	Silverton, Ore.	UFA(NYG)-'00	16/16
38	Heard, Ronnie	S	6-3	215	10/5/76	3	Mississippi	Baycity, Texas	FA-'00	16/0
20	Hearst, Garrison	RB	5-11	215	1/4/71	10	Georgia	Lincolnton, Ga.	UFA(Cin)-'97	16/16
26	Holman, Rashad	CB	5-11	191	1/17/78	2	Louisville	Louisville, Ky.	D6b-'01	16/1
22 †	Jackson, Terry	FB	6-0	232	1/10/76	4	Florida	Gainesville, Fla.	D5-'99	16/1
86	Jennings, Brian	TE-LS	6-5	245	10/14/76	3	Arizona State	Mesa, Ariz.	D7b-'00	16/0
82	Johnson, Eric	TE	6-3	256	9/15/79	2	Yale	Needham, Mass.	D7b-'01	16/14
28	Keith, John	S	6-0	207	2/4/77	3	Furman	Newnan, Ga.	D4-'00	1/0
43	Lewis, Jonas	RB	5-9	210	12/27/76	3	San Diego State	San Diego, Calif.	FA-'00	1/0
57	Lincoln, Alex	LB	6-0	251	11/17/77	2	Auburn	Mobile, Ala.	D7a-'01	0*
61	McCurley, Jeff	C	6-5	290	6/25/79	2	Pittsburgh	Bessemer, Pa.	FA-'01	0*
92	McGrew, Reggie	DT	6-1	312	12/16/76	4	Florida	Mayo, Fla.	D1-'99	12/0
71	Moran, Sean	DE	6-4	275	6/5/73	7	Colorado State	Denver, Colo.	UFA(StL)-'02	16/1*
62	Newberry, Jeremy	C	6-5	304	3/23/76	5	California	Antioch, Calif.	D2-'98	15/15
91 †	Okeafor, Chike	DE	6-4	254	3/27/76	4	Purdue	West Lafayette, Ind.	D3-'99	14/3
81	Owens, Terrell	WR	6-3	226	12/7/73	7	Tennessee-Chattanooga	Alexander City, Ala.	D3-'96	16/16
21	Parker, Anthony	CB	6-1	200	12/4/75	4	Weber State	Denver, Colo.	D4-'99	5/0
30	Parrish, Tony	S	5-11	210	11/23/75	5	Washington	Hunington Beach, Calif.	FA-'02	16/16*
98	Peterson, Julian	LB	6-3	235	7/28/78	3	Michigan State	Hillcrest Heights, Md.	D1a-'00	14/14
29	Plummer, Ahmed	CB	5-11	191	3/26/76	3	Ohio State	Wyoming, Ohio	D1b-'00	15/15
13	Rattay, Tim	QB	6-0	215	3/15/77	3	Louisiana Tech	Elyria, Ohio	D7a-'00	3/0
93	Schlecht, John	DT	6-0	290	5/23/78	2	Minnesota	St. Paul, Minn.	FA-'01	8/0
90	Setzer, Bobby	DE	6-4	280	6/16/76	2	Boise State	Kelso, Wash.	FA-'01	14/0
50	Smith, Derek	LB	6-2	245	1/18/75	6	Arizona State	American Fork, Utah	UFA(Wash)-'01	14/14
27	Smith, Paul	RB	5-11	234	1/31/78	3	Texas-El Paso	El Paso, Texas	D5a-'00	15/0
64	Stephenson, Milford	G-T	6-2	300	2/8/77	2	Kansas State	Houston, Texas	FA-'01	0*
54	Stewart, Quincy	LB	6-1	220	3/27/78	2	Louisiana Tech	Tyler, Texas	FA-'01	16/0
83	Stokes, J.J.	WR	6-4	217	10/6/72	8	UCLA	San Diego, Calif.	D1-'95	16/16
60	Stone, Ron	G	6-5	320	7/20/71	9	Boston College	West Roxbury, Mass.	FA-'02	15/15*
89	Streets, Tai	WR	6-2	206	4/20/77	4	Michigan	Matteson, Ill.	D6-'99	16/3
94	Stubblefield, Dana	DT	6-2	290	11/14/70	10	Kansas	Cleves, Ohio	FA-'01	16/16
25	Sutherland, Vinny	KR-HB	5-8	188	4/22/78	2	Purdue	West Palm Beach, Fla.	FA-'01	15/0
88	Swift, Justin	TE	6-3	265	8/14/75	3	Kansas State	Overland Park, Kan.	FA-'99	16/2
52	Turner, T.J.	LB	6-3	255	10/1/78	2	Michigan State	Dayton, Ohio	FA-'02	2/0*
53	Ulbrich, Jeff	LB	6-0	249	2/17/77	3	Hawaii	San Jose, Calif.	D3b-'00	14/14
36	Webster, Jason	CB	5-9	180	9/8/77	3	Texas A&M	Houston, Texas	D2b-'00	16/16
23	Williams, Jimmy	CB	5-10	189	3/10/79	2	Vanderbilt	Baton Rouge, La.	FA-'01	10/0
77	Willig, Matt	T	6-8	315	1/21/69	11	Southern California	Santa Fe Springs, Calif.	UFA(StL)-'00	15/0
84	Wilson, Cedrick	WR	5-10	179	12/17/78	2	Tennessee	Memphis, Tenn.	D6a-'01	6/0
55	Winborn, Jamie	LB	5-11	242	5/14/79	2	Vanderbilt	Wetumpka, Ala.	D2-'01	14/4
97	Young, Bryant	DT	6-3	291	1/27/72	9	Notre Dame	Chicago Heights, Ill.	D1-'94	16/16

* Bayes last active with Tampa Bay in '00; Bryant missed '01 season because of injury; Carmazzi missed '01 season because of injury; Davis missed '01 season because of injury with Detroit; Lincoln missed '01 season because of injury; McCurley missed '01 season because of injury; Moran played 16 games with St. Louis; Parrish played 16 games with Chicago; Stephenson was inactive for 6 games; Stone played 15 games with N.Y. Giants; Turner played 2 games with New England.

† Restricted free agent; subject to developments.

Players lost through free agency (2): LB Terry Killens (Den; 16 games in '01), S Lance Schulters (16).

Also played for the 49ers in '01—CB Tyrone Drakeford (1 game), G Ben Lynch (11), CB George McCullough (15), DE John Milem (2), CB Jason Suttle (1).

2002 FIRST-YEAR ROSTER

Name	Pos.	Ht.	Wt.	Birthdate	College	Hometown	How Acq.
Anelli, Mark	TE	6-3	265	6/5/79	Wisconsin	Addison, Ill.	D6
Anthony, Cornelius (1)	LB	6-0	235	7/3/78	Texas A&M	Missouri City, Texas	FA-'01
Blades, Al (1)	S	6-2	205	3/19/77	Miami	Plantation, Fla.	FA-'01
Chandler, Jeff	K	6-2	218	6/18/79	Florida	Jacksonville, Fla.	D4a
Cloman, Scott (1)	WR	6-3	200	11/6/75	Southern	Compton, Calif.	FA-'01
Cockerham, Billy (1)	QB	6-1	215	3/18/77	Minnesota	Concord, Calif.	FA
Curtis, Kevin	S	6-2	212	7/28/80	Texas Tech	Lubbock, Texas	D4b
Doman, Brandon	QB	6-1	210	12/29/76	Brigham Young	Salt Lake City, Utah	D5a
Fernandez, Ryan	CB	5-11	180	8/2/80	Stanford	Oakland, Calif.	FA
Feugill, John (1)	T	6-6	287	12/20/75	Maryland	Methuen, Mass.	FA-'01
Fletcher, Ryan	DT	6-2	288	6/18/79	Hofstra	Glen Cove, N.Y.	FA
Gaines, Teddy	CB	5-11	165	9/12/79	Tennessee	Kingsport, Tenn.	D7c
Garcia, Aaron (1)	QB	6-1	200	10/28/70	Sacramento State	Sacramento, Calif.	FA
Harris, Kenny	CB	5-11	190	5/6/79	Northern Iowa	Buffalo, N.Y.	FA
Hart, Mike	TE	6-6	260	11/25/78	Duke	Sayville, N.Y.	FA
Haugabrook, Brian	WR	6-2	204	10/18/78	Florida	Wildwood, Fla.	FA
Hay, Shawn (1)	DE	6-4	250	8/8/78	South Florida	Miami, Fla.	FA
Heitmann, Eric	G	6-3	305	2/24/80	Stanford	Katy, Texas	D7a
Holloway, Menson (1)	DE	6-2	284	7/12/78	Texas-El Paso	El Paso, Texas	D6c-'01
Isom, Jasen (1)	FB	6-0	225	1/7/77	Western Illinois	Wheatley Heights, Md.	FA
Jackson, Nate	WR	6-3	217	6/4/79	Menlo College	San Jose, Calif.	FA
Jennings, Mike	WR	5-11	170	9/7/79	Florida State	Jacksonville, Fla.	FA
Jones, Ontei (1)	DB	5-10	195	5/10/79	Oklahoma	Miami, Fla.	FA
Jordan, James (1)	WR	6-2	225	6/11/78	Louisiana Tech	Kenner, La.	FA
Kosier, Kyle	T	6-5	293	1/27/78	Arizona State	Peoria, Ariz.	D7b
Lee, Austin	T	6-6	275	12/13/78	Stanford	Post Falls, Idaho	FA
McCullough, Saladin (1)	RB	5-9	195	7/17/75	Oregon	Pasadena, Calif.	FA
Moore, Brandon	LB	6-1	242	1/16/79	Oklahoma	Baldwin, N.Y.	FA
O'Neal, Donnie	WR	6-2	188	11/14/79	Arizona State	Olathe, Kan.	FA
Pinkney, Cleveland (1)	DT	6-1	300	9/14/77	South Carolina	Sumter, S.C.	FA
Rasheed, Saleem	LB	6-2	229	6/15/81	Alabama	Birmingham, Ala.	D3
Rheem, Jamie (1)	K	6-2	215	9/12/77	Kansas State	Wichita, Kan.	FA
Robertson, Jamal (1)	RB	5-10	210	1/10/77	Ohio Northern	Dayton, Ohio	FA
Rumph, Mike	CB	6-2	205	11/8/79	Miami	Boynton Beach, Fla.	D1
Sanders, Darryl	DE	6-2	272	1/8/79	Virginia	Leonardtown, Md.	FA
Shaw, Josh	DT	6-2	279	9/7/79	Michigan State	Fort Lauderdale, Fla.	D5b
Simonton, Ken	RB	5-8	195	6/7/79	Oregon State	Pittsburg, Calif.	FA
Smith, Brian (1)	S	6-1	202	7/15/79	Massachusetts	Wilmington, Del.	FA
Stanley, Matt	FB	6-3	245	4/27/79	UCLA	Columbus, Ohio	FA
Steele, Ben (1)	TE	6-5	241	5/27/78	Mesa State	Palisade, Colo.	FA-'01
Strong, Frank	S	6-1	222	1/14/80	Southern California	Stockton, Calif.	FA
Ward, Chad (1)	G	6-4	321	1/12/77	Washington	Kennewick, Wash.	FA-'01

The term NFL Rookie is defined as a player who is in his first season of professional football and has not been on the roster of another professional football team for any regular-season or postseason games. A Rookie is designated by an "R" on NFL rosters. Players who have been active in another professional football league or players who have NFL experience, including either preseason training camp or being on an Active List or Inactive List, or on Reserve/Injured or Reserve/Physically Unable to Perform for fewer than six regular-season games, are termed NFL First-Year Players. An NFL First-Year Player is designated by a "1" on NFL rosters. Thereafter, a player is credited with an additional year of experience for each season in which he accumulates six games on the Active List or Inactive List, or on Reserve/Injured or Reserve/Physically Unable to Perform.

SAN FRANCISCO 49ERS

COACHING STAFF

Head Coach,
Steve Mariucci

Pro Career: Became the thirteenth head coach in 49ers history on January 16, 1997. One of thirteen head coaches since the NFL-AFL merger in 1970 to lead his team to a division title in his first season. He established an NFL mark for consecutive wins by a rookie head coach with an 11-game winning streak. He served as quarterbacks coach for the Green Bay Packers (1992-95). His first pro position was in 1985 when he was receivers coach for the USFL's Orlando Renegades. Later that fall, he had a brief stint with the Los Angeles Rams as quality control coach. Career record: 49-36.

Background: Three-time All-America quarterback at Northern Michigan. Began his coaching career at his alma mater (1978-79), and moved to Cal State-Fullerton (1980-82), and Louisville (1983-84). Joined the Southern California staff in 1986, then moved to California in 1987. In 1990-91, he served as the Bears' offensive coordinator. Became the head coach at California in 1996 and guided the squad to a 5-0 start and a berth in the Aloha Bowl.

Personal: Born November 4, 1955, in Iron Mountain, Mich. He and his wife, Gayle, have four children—Tyler, Adam, Stephen, and Brielle—and live in Saratoga, Calif.

ASSISTANT COACHES

Jerry Attaway, physical development; born January 3, 1946, Susanville, Calif., lives in San Jose, Calif. Defensive back Yuba (Calif.) J.C. 1964-65, UC Davis 1967. No pro playing experience. College coach: UC Davis 1970-71, Idaho 1972-74, Utah State 1975-77, Southern California 1978-1982. Pro coach: Joined 49ers in 1983.

Tom Batta, tight ends; born October 6, 1942, in Youngstown, Ohio, lives in Livermore, Calif. Offensive-defensive lineman Kent State 1961-63. No pro playing experience. College coach: Akron 1973, Colorado 1974-78, Kansas 1979-1982, North Carolina State 1983. Pro coach: Minnesota Vikings 1984-1993, Indianapolis Colts 1994-97, Pittsburgh Steelers 1998, joined 49ers in 1999.

Christopher Beake, defensive assistant; born September 10, 1972, Highlands Ranch, Colo., lives in Mountain View, Calif. Quarterback Air Force 1991-92. No pro playing experience. College coach: Air Force 1994-95. Pro coach: Joined 49ers in 1999.

Dwaine Board, defensive line; born November 29, 1956, Rocky Mount, Va., lives in Redwood City, Calif. Defensive lineman North Carolina A&T 1974-77. Pro defensive lineman San Francisco 49ers 1979-1987, New Orleans Saints 1988. Pro coach: Joined 49ers in 1991.

Bruce DeHaven, special teams; born September 6, 1948, Trousdale, Kan., lives in Livermore, Calif. Attended Southwestern (Kan.) College. No college or pro playing experience. College coach: Kansas 1979-1981, New Mexico State 1982. Pro coach: New Jersey Generals (USFL) 1983, Pittsburgh Maulers (USFL) 1984, Orlando Renegades (USFL) 1985, Buffalo Bills 1987-1999, joined 49ers in 2000.

Terrell Jones, strength development; born April 25, 1961, Chicago, lives in San Jose, Calif. Attended San Jose State. No college or pro playing experience. College coach: San Jose (Calif.) C.C. 1998-2000. Pro coach: Joined 49ers in 2000.

Greg Knapp, offensive coordinator; born March 5, 1963, Long Beach, Calif., lives in Los Gatos, Calif. Quarterback Cal State-Sacramento 1982-85. No pro playing experience. College coach: Cal State-Sacramento 1986-1994. Pro coach: Joined 49ers in 1995.

Brett Maxie, secondary; born January 13, 1962, Dallas, lives in Santa Clara, Calif. Safety Texas Southern 1980-84. Pro safety New Orleans Saints 1985-1993, Atlanta Falcons 1994, Carolina Panthers 1995-96, San Francisco 49ers 1997. Pro coach: Carolina Panthers 1998, joined 49ers in 1999.

Jim Mora, defensive coordinator; born November 19, 1961, Los Angeles, lives in Los Gatos, Calif. Defensive back Washington 1980-83. No pro playing experience. College coach: Washington 1984. Pro coach: San Diego Chargers 1985-1991, New Orleans Saints 1992-96, joined 49ers in 1997.

Pat Morris, offensive line; born April 7, 1954, Cleveland, lives in Mountain View, Calif. Offensive lineman Southern California 1972-75. No pro playing experience. College coach: Southern California 1976-77, 1983-86, Northern Arizona 1978, Minnesota 1979-1982, Michigan State 1987-1994, Stanford 1995-96. Pro coach: Joined 49ers in 1997.

Dan Quinn, defensive quality control; born Orange, N.J., lives in Santa Clara, Calif. Defensive lineman Salisbury State 1990-93. No pro playing experience. College coach: William & Mary 1994, Virginia Military Institute 1995, Hofstra 1997-2000. Pro coach: Joined 49ers in 2001.

Tom Rathman, running backs; born October 7, 1962, Grand Island, Neb., lives in Redwood City, Calif. Running back Nebraska 1983-85. Pro running back San Francisco 49ers 1986-1993, Los Angeles Raiders 1994. College coach: Menlo College 1996. Pro coach: Joined 49ers in 1997.

Richard Smith, linebackers; born October 17, 1955, Los Angeles, lives in Pleasanton, Calif. Offensive lineman Rio Hondo (Calif.) J.C. 1975-76, Fresno State 1977-78. No pro playing experience. College coach: Rio Hondo J.C. 1979-1980, Cal State-Fullerton 1981-83, California 1984-86, Arizona 1987. Pro coach: Houston Oilers 1988-1992, Denver Broncos 1993-96, joined 49ers in 1997.

George Stewart, wide receivers; born December 29, 1958, Little Rock, Ark., lives in Santa Clara, Calif. Guard Arkansas 1977-1980. No pro playing experience. College coach: Minnesota 1984-85, Notre Dame 1986-88. Pro coach: Pittsburgh Steelers 1989-1991, Tampa Bay Buccaneers 1992-95, joined 49ers in 1996.

Andy Sugarman, offensive assistant; born May 23, 1972, San Francisco, lives in Mountain View, Calif. Attended California. No college or pro playing experience. College coach: California 1990-97. Pro coach: Joined 49ers in 1998.

Ted Tollner, quarterbacks; born May 29, 1940, San Francisco, lives in Santa Clara, Calif. Quarterback Cal Poly-San Luis Obispo 1959-1961. No pro playing experience. College coach: College of San Mateo 1971-72 (head coach), San Diego State 1973-1980, 1994-2001 (head coach 1994-2001), Brigham Young 1981, Southern California 1982-86 (head coach 1983-86). Pro coach: Buffalo Bills 1987-88, San Diego Chargers 1989-1991, joined 49ers in 2002.

National Football Conference
West Division
Team Colors: Seahawks Blue, Seahawks
Navy, Seahawks Bright Green
11220 N.E. 53RD Street
Kirkland, Washington, 98033
Telephone: (504) 733-0255

2002 SCHEDULE
PRESEASON

Aug. 10	**Indianapolis**	7:00
Aug. 16	at San Diego	8:00
Aug. 24	**Kansas City**	7:00
Aug. 29	at Denver	7:00

REGULAR SEASON

Sept. 8	at Oakland	1:15
Sept. 15	**Arizona**	1:05
Sept. 22	at New York Giants	4:15
Sept. 29	**Minnesota**	5:30
Oct. 6	OPEN DATE	
Oct. 14	**San Francisco (Mon.)**	6:00
Oct. 20	at St. Louis	12:00
Oct. 27	at Dallas	12:00
Nov. 3	**Washington**	1:15
Nov. 10	at Arizona	2:05
Nov. 17	**Denver**	1:15
Nov. 24	**Kansas City**	1:05
Dec. 1	at San Francisco	1:15
Dec. 8	**Philadelphia**	1:05
Dec. 15	at Atlanta	1:00
Dec. 22	**St. Louis**	1:05
Dec. 29	at San Diego	1:15

Stadium: Seahawks Stadium
(opened in 2002)
•**Capacity:** 67,000
Playing Surface: FieldTurf
Training Camp: Eastern Washington Univ.
Cheney, Washington 99004

SEAHAWKS STADIUM

CLUB OFFICIALS
Chairman: Paul Allen
President: Bob Whitsitt
Executive VP of Football Operations/
General Manager & Head Coach:
Mike Holmgren
Sr. Vice President: Mike Reinfeldt
VP/Community Outreach, I.S., Facilities:
Mike Flood
General Counsel: Lance Lopes
Sr. VP/Marketing: Duane McLean
VP/Marketing: Mike Sheehan
VP/Football Operations: Ted Thompson
VP/Corporate Sales: Scott Patrick
VP/Communications: Gary Wright
Director of Pro Personnel: Will Lewis
Director of College Scouting:
Scot McCloughan
Director of Public Relations: Dave Pearson
Asst. Director of Public Relations:
Lane Gammel
Director of Community Outreach:
Sandy Gregory
Director of Player Programs: Nesby Glasgow
Director of Broadcasting: Mike Wacker
Director of Sponsor Sales: Kevin Williams
Director of Ticket Sales/Operations:
Chuck Arnold
Director of Football Administration:
Gary Reynolds
Football Operations Coordinator/Team Travel:
Bill Nayes
Video Director Football: Thom Fermstad
Head Athletic Trainer: Paul Federici
Equipment Manager: Erik Kennedy

COACHING HISTORY
(191-221-0)

1976-1982	Jack Patera*	35-59-0
1982	Mike McCormack	4-3-0
1983-1991	Chuck Knox	83-67-0
1992-94	Tom Flores	14-34-0
1995-98	Dennis Erickson	31-33-0
1999-2001	Mike Holmgren	24-25-0

*Released after two games in 1982

ATTENDANCE
Home 446,322   Away 562,122
Total 1,008,444
Single-game home record,
68,681 (12/16/00)
Single-season home record, 522,656
(1999)

2002 DRAFT CHOICES

Round	Name	Pos.	College
1	Jerramy Stevens	TE	Washington
2	Maurice Morris	RB	Oregon
	Anton Palepoi	DE	Nevada-Las Vegas
3	Kris Richard	DB	Southern California
4	Terreal Bierria	DB	Georgia
5	Rocky Bernard	DT	Texas A&M
	Ryan Hannam	TE	Northern Iowa
	Matt Hill	T	Boise State
6	Craig Jarrett	P	Michigan State
7	Jeff Kelly	QB	So. Mississippi

SEATTLE SEAHAWKS

2001 TEAM RECORD
PRESEASON (2-2)

Date	Result	Opponent
8/11	L 21-28	at Indianapolis
8/18	L 13-16	Arizona (OT)
8/25	W 28-18	at San Francisco
9/1	W 28-14	New Orleans

REGULAR SEASON (9-7)

Date	Result	Opponent	Att.
9/09	W 9-6	at Cleveland	72,318
9/23	L 3-27	Philadelphia	62,826
9/30	L 14-38	at Oakland	54,629
10/07	W 24-15	Jacksonville	54,524
10/14	W 34-21	Denver	61,837
10/28	L 20-24	Miami	59,108
11/04	L 14-27	at Washington	82,352
11/11	W 34-27	Oakland	67,231
11/18	W 23-20	at Buffalo	60,836
11/25	L 7-19	at Kansas City	77,357
12/02	W 13-10	San Diego (OT)	55,466
12/09	L 7-20	at Denver	74,524
12/16	W 29-3	Dallas	63,366
12/23	L 24-27	at New York Giants	78,119
12/30	W 25-22	at San Diego	51,412
1/06	W 21-18	Kansas City	58,460

(OT) Overtime

SCORE BY PERIODS

Seahawks	64	107	75	52	3	— 301
Opponents	53	123	74	74	0	— 324

2001 TEAM STATISTICS

	Seahawks	Opp.
Total First Downs	274	300
Rushing	107	91
Passing	141	186
Penalty	26	23
3rd Down: Made/Att	77/213	92/223
3rd Down Pct.	36.2	41.3
4th Down: Made/Att	8/17	6/11
4th Down Pct.	47.1	54.5
Possession Avg.	29:51	30:09
Total Net Yards	4772	5206
Avg. Per Game	298.3	325.4
Total Plays	980	1028
Avg. Per Play	4.9	5.1
Net Yards Rushing	1936	1721
Avg. Per Game	121.0	107.6
Total Rushes	469	427
Net Yards Passing	2836	3485
Avg. Per Game	177.3	217.8
Sacked/Yards Lost	49/328	38/248
Gross Yards	3164	3733
Att./Completions	462/258	563/339
Completion Pct.	55.8	60.2
Had Intercepted	12	14
Punts/Average	86/43.4	76/42.3
Net Punting Avg.	86/36.4	76/36.1
Penalties/Yards	66/579	101/805
Fumbles/Ball Lost	24/9	28/13
Touchdowns	34	34
Rushing	15	9
Passing	15	20
Returns	4	5

2001 INDIVIDUAL STATISTICS

PASSING	Att.	Comp.	Yds.	Pct.	TD	Int.	Tkld.	Rate
Hasselbeck	321	176	2023	54.8	7	8	38/251	70.9
Dilfer	122	73	1014	59.8	7	4	10/72	92.0
Huard	17	9	127	52.9	1	0	1/5	96.9
Feagles	2	0	0	0.0	0	0	0	39.6
Seahawks	462	258	3164	55.8	15	12	49/328	77.2
Opponents	563	339	3733	60.2	20	14	38/248	81.4

SCORING	TD R	TD P	TD Rt	PAT	FG	Saf	PTS
Alexander	14	2	0	0/0	0/0	0	96
Lindell	0	0	0	33/33	20/32	0	93
D. Jackson	0	8	0	0/0	0/0	0	48
Mili	0	2	0	0/0	0/0	0	12
Fauria	0	1	0	0/0	0/0	0	8
Bannister	0	0	1	0/0	0/0	0	6
Charlton	0	0	1	0/0	0/0	0	6
Randle	0	0	1	0/0	0/0	0	6
Robinson	0	1	0	0/0	0/0	0	6
Tongue	0	0	1	0/0	0/0	0	6
Watters	1	0	0	0/0	0/0	0	6
J. Williams	0	1	0	0/0	0/0	0	6
Seahawks	15	15	4	33/33	20/32	1	301
Opponents	9	20	5	31/31	29/36	0	324

2-Pt. Conversions: Fauria.
Seahawks 1-1, Opponents 1-3.

RUSHING	Att.	Yds.	Avg.	LG	TD
Alexander	309	1318	4.3	88t	14
Watters	72	318	4.4	40	1
Hasselbeck	40	141	3.5	17	0
Strong	17	55	3.2	12	0
Graham	12	43	3.6	19	0
Dilfer	11	17	1.5	11	0
Robinson	4	13	3.3	6	0
Evans	2	11	5.5	7	0
Huard	1	11	11.0	11	0
D. Jackson	1	9	9.0	9	0
Seahawks	469	1936	4.1	88t	15
Opponents	427	1721	4.0	57	9

RECEIVING	No.	Yds.	Avg.	LG	TD
D. Jackson	70	1081	15.4	64	8
Alexander	44	343	7.8	28t	2
Robinson	39	536	13.7	42	1
Engram	29	400	13.8	31	0
Fauria	21	188	9.0	30	1
Strong	17	141	8.3	35	0
J. Williams	12	212	17.7	49	1
Watters	11	107	9.7	34	0
Mili	8	98	12.3	41	2
Bannister	4	50	12.5	17	0
Rogers	1	7	7.0	7	0
Graham	1	6	6.0	6	0
Dilfer	1	-5	-5.0	-5	0
Seahawks	258	3164	12.3	64	15
Opponents	339	3733	11.0	65	20

INTERCEPTIONS	No.	Yds.	Avg.	LG	TD
W. Williams	4	24	6.0	24	0
Tongue	3	67	22.3	55t	1
Charlton	2	43	21.5	38t	1
Robertson	2	30	15.0	25	0
Kacyvenski	1	22	22.0	22	0
Lucas	1	0	0.0	0	0
Springs	1	0	0.0	0	0
Seahawks	14	186	13.3	55t	2
Opponents	12	36	3.0	10	0

PUNTING	No.	Yds.	Avg.	In 20	LG
Feagles	85	3730	43.9	26	68
Seahawks	86	3730	43.4	26	68
Opponents	76	3212	42.3	25	64

PUNT RETURNS	No.	FC	Yds.	Avg.	LG	TD
Rogers	25	10	244	9.8	34	0
Engram	6	3	96	16.0	28	0
Joseph	2	1	12	6.0	12	0
Seahawks	33	14	352	10.7	34	0
Opponents	43	11	462	10.7	86t	1

KICKOFF RETURNS	No.	Yds.	Avg.	LG	TD
Rogers	50	1120	22.4	64	0
J. Williams	9	175	19.4	31	0
Joseph	4	83	20.8	24	0
Evans	3	40	13.3	20	0
Graham	3	56	18.7	20	0
Engram	1	6	6.0	6	0
Fauria	1	0	0.0	0	0
Strong	1	16	16.0	16	0
Seahawks	72	1496	20.8	64	0
Opponents	64	1273	19.9	90t	1

FIELD GOALS	1-19	20-29	30-39	40-49	50+
Lindell	0/0	7/8	4/5	6/14	3/5
Seahawks	0/0	7/8	4/5	6/14	3/5
Opponents	0/0	12/12	7/8	9/12	1/4

SACKS	No.
Randle	11.0
C. Brown	8.5
Cochran	4.5
Sinclair	3.5
Terry	2.5
Simmons	2.0
Bell	1.0
Charlton	1.0
Eaton	1.0
Joseph	1.0
Kirkland	1.0
Tongue	1.0
Seahawks	38.0
Opponents	49.0

RECORD HOLDERS
INDIVIDUAL RECORDS—CAREER

Category	Name	Performance
Rushing (Yds.)	Chris Warren, 1990-97	6,706
Passing (Yds.)	Dave Krieg, 1980-1991	26,132
Passing (TDs)	Dave Krieg, 1980-1991	195
Receiving (No.)	Steve Largent, 1976-1989	819
Receiving (Yds.)	Steve Largent, 1976-1989	13,089
Interceptions	Dave Brown, 1976-1986	50
Punting (Avg.)	Rick Tuten, 1991-97	43.8
Punt Return (Avg.)	Charlie Rogers, 1999-2001	12.7
Kickoff Return (Avg.)	Steve Broussard, 1995-98	23.2
Field Goals	Norm Johnson, 1982-1990	159
Touchdowns (Tot.)	Steve Largent, 1976-1989	101
Points	Norm Johnson, 1982-1990	810

INDIVIDUAL RECORDS—SINGLE SEASON

Category	Name	Performance
Rushing (Yds.)	Chris Warren, 1994	1,545
Passing (Yds.)	Warren Moon, 1997	3,678
Passing (TDs)	Dave Krieg, 1984	32
Receiving (No.)	Brian Blades, 1994	81
Receiving (Yds.)	Steve Largent, 1985	1,287
Interceptions	John Harris, 1981	10
	Kenny Easley, 1984	10
Punting (Avg.)	Rick Tuten, 1995	45.0
Punt Return (Avg.)	Charlie Rogers, 1999	14.5
Kickoff Return (Avg.)	Charlie Rogers, 2000	24.9
Field Goals	Todd Peterson, 1999	34
Touchdowns (Tot.)	Chris Warren, 1995	16
	Shaun Alexander, 2001	16
Points	Todd Peterson, 1999	134

INDIVIDUAL RECORDS—SINGLE GAME

Category	Name	Performance
Rushing (Yds.)	Shaun Alexander, 11-11-01	266
Passing (Yds.)	Dave Krieg, 11-20-83	418
Passing (TDs)	Dave Krieg, 12-2-84, 9-15-85, 11-28-88	5
	Warren Moon, 10-26-97	5
Receiving (No.)	Steve Largent, 10-18-87	15
Receiving (Yds.)	Steve Largent, 10-18-87	261
Interceptions	Kenny Easley, 9-3-84	3
	Eugene Robinson, 12-6-92	3
	Darryl Williams, 9-21-97	3
Field Goals	Norm Johnson, 9-20-87, 12-18-88	5
Touchdowns (Tot.)	Daryl Turner, 9-15-85	4
	Curt Warner, 12-11-88	4
Points	Daryl Turner, 9-15-85	24
	Curt Warner, 12-11-88	24

2002 VETERAN ROSTER

No.	Name	Pos.	Ht.	Wt.	Birthdate	NFL Exp.	College	Hometown	How Acq.	'01 Games/ Starts
37	Alexander, Shaun	RB	5-11	229	8/30/77	3	Alabama	Florence, Ky.	D1a-'00	16/12
85	Bannister, Alex	WR	6-5	207	4/23/79	2	Eastern Kentucky	Cincinnati, Ohio	D5-'01	16/0
55	Bell, Marcus	LB	6-1	245	7/19/77	3	Arizona	St. Johns, Ariz.	D4a-'00	14/0
83	Bownes, Fabien	WR	5-11	191	2/29/72	8	Western Illinois	Aurora, Ill.	W(Chi)-'00	16/0
94	Brown, Chad	LB	6-2	245	7/12/70	10	Colorado	Altadena, Calif.	UFA(Pitt)-'97	16/16
23	Charlton, Ike	CB	5-11	204	10/6/77	3	Virginia Tech	Orlando, Fla.	D2-'00	15/1
78	Cochran, Antonio	DT	6-4	292	6/21/76	4	Georgia	Montezuma, Ga.	D4-'99	16/2
52	Darche, Jean-Philippe	LS	6-0	246	2/28/75	3	McGill	Montreal, Quebec, Canada	FA-'00	16/0
4	Dilfer, Trent	QB	6-4	225	3/13/72	9	Fresno State	Santa Cruz, Calif.	UFA(Balt)-'01	6/4
90	Eaton, Chad	DT	6-5	303	4/6/72	7	Washington State	Puyallup, Wash.	UFA(NE)-'01	16/16
84	Engram, Bobby	WR	5-10	188	1/7/73	7	Penn State	Camden, S.C.	UFA(Chi)-'01	16/4
33	Evans, Doug	CB	6-1	188	5/13/70	10	Louisiana Tech	Haynesville, La.	UFA(Car)-'02	16/16*
44	Evans, Heath	FB	6-0	252	12/30/78	2	Auburn	West Palm Beach, Fla.	D3-'01	16/0
10	Feagles, Jeff	P	6-1	211	3/7/66	15	Miami	Anaheim, Calif.	UFA(Ariz)-'98	16/0
29	Fuller, Curtis	S	5-10	191	7/25/78	2	Texas Christian	North Richland Hill, Texas	D4b-'01	10/1
35	Graham, Jay	RB	6-0	225	7/14/75	6	Tennessee	Concord, N.C.	FA-'01	11/0
6	Graham, Shayne	K	6-0	192	12/9/77	2	Virginia Tech	Dublin, Va.	FA-'02	6/0*
62	Gray, Chris	G-C	6-4	308	6/19/70	10	Auburn	Birmingham, Ala.	UFA(Chi)-'98	16/16
8	Hasselbeck, Matt	QB	6-4	223	9/25/75	4	Boston College	Westwood, Mass.	T(GB)-'01	13/12
95	Hilliard, John	DE	6-2	296	4/16/76	3	Mississippi State	Houston, Texas	D6c-'00	16/8
57	Huff, Orlando	LB	6-2	250	8/14/78	2	Fresno State	Upland, Calif.	D4a-'01	12/0
76	Hutchinson, Steve	G	6-5	313	11/1/77	2	Michigan	Fort Lauderdale, Fla.	D1b-'01	16/16
82	Jackson, Darrell	WR	6-0	201	12/6/78	3	Florida	Dayton, Ohio	D3-'00	16/16
71	Jones, Walter	T	6-5	308	1/19/74	6	Florida State	Aliceville, Ala.	D1b-'97	16/16
58	Kacyvenski, Isaiah	LB	6-1	252	10/3/77	3	Harvard	Endicott, N.Y.	D4b-'00	16/0
26	Kelly, Maurice	S	6-2	212	10/9/72	3	East Tennessee State	Orangebury, S.C.	FA-'00	8/3
92	King, Lamar	DE	6-3	311	8/10/75	4	Saginaw Valley State	Baltimore, Md.	D1-'99	8/8
99	Kirkland, Levon	LB	6-1	275	2/17/69	11	Clemson	Lamar, S.C.	UFA(Pitt)-'01	16/16
5	Leaf, Ryan	QB	6-5	248	5/15/76	5	Washington State	Great Falls, Mont.	FA-'02	4/3*
9	Lindell, Rian	K	6-3	237	1/20/77	3	Washington State	Vancouver, Wash.	FA-'00	16/0
21	Lucas, Ken	CB	6-0	205	1/23/79	2	Mississippi	Cleveland, Miss.	D2-'01	16/8
36	McDonald, Ramos	CB	6-0	196	4/30/76	4	New Mexico	Dallas, Texas	FA-'02	3/0*
75	McIntosh, Chris	T	6-6	308	2/20/77	3	Wisconsin	Pewaukee, Wis.	D1b-'00	10/3
89	Mili, Itula	TE	6-4	260	4/20/73	6	Brigham Young	Laie, Hawaii	D6-'97	16/5
53	Miller, Keith	LB	6-1	245	7/9/76	2	California	San Diego, Calif.	FA-'02	0*
22	Miranda, Paul	CB	5-10	185	5/2/76	4	Central Florida	Thomasville, Ga.	FA-'00	8/2
97	Mitchell, Brandon	DT	6-3	290	6/19/75	6	Texas A&M	Abbeville, La.	UFA(NE)-'02	16/11*
49	Neufeld, Ryan	TE	6-4	254	11/22/75	3	UCLA	Morgan Hill, Calif.	FA-'02	0*
68	Norman, Dennis	T	6-5	312	1/26/80	2	Princeton	Marlton, N.J.	D7b-'01	0*
93	Randle, John	DT	6-1	287	12/12/67	13	Texas A&I	Hearne, Texas	UFA(Minn)-'01	15/14
31	Robertson, Marcus	S	5-11	206	10/2/69	12	Iowa State	Pasadena, Calif.	UFA(Tenn)-'01	12/12
81	Robinson, Koren	WR	6-1	205	3/19/80	2	North Carolina State	Belmont, N.C.	D1a-'01	16/13
51	Simmons, Anthony	LB	6-0	242	6/20/76	5	Clemson	Spartanburg, S.C.	D1-'98	16/16
24	Springs, Shawn	CB	6-0	204	3/11/75	6	Ohio State	Silver Springs, Md.	D1a-'97	8/7
87	Stewart, Russell	TE	6-4	249	9/25/77	2	Stanford	Bellevue, Wash.	FA-'01	0*
38	Strong, Mack	FB	6-0	245	9/11/71	8	Georgia	Columbus, Ga.	FA-'93	16/13
59	Terry, Tim	LB	6-2	240	7/26/74	4	Temple	Hempstead, N.Y.	FA-'00	16/0
61	Tobeck, Robbie	C-G	6-4	297	3/6/70	9	Washington State	Tarpon Springs, Fla.	UFA(Atl)-'00	16/16
25	Tongue, Reggie	S	6-0	204	4/11/73	7	Oregon State	Fairbanks, Alaska	UFA(KC)-'00	16/16
69	Wedderburn, Floyd	G	6-5	333	5/5/76	4	Penn State	Upper Darby, Pa.	D5a-'99	16/0
88	Williams, James	WR	5-10	186	3/6/78	3	Marshall	Vicksburg, Miss.	D6a-'00	6/2
27	Williams, Willie	CB	5-9	182	12/26/70	10	Western Carolina	Columbia, S.C.	UFA(Pitt)-'97	14/14
77	Womack, Floyd	T	6-4	333	11/15/78	2	Mississippi State	Cleveland, Miss.	D4c-'01	5/0
98	Woodard, Cedric	DT	6-2	320	9/5/77	3	Texas	Sweeny, Texas	W(Balt)-'00	16/0

* D. Evans played 16 games with Carolina in '01; S. Graham played 6 games with Buffalo; Leaf played 4 games with Dallas; McDonald played 3 games with N.Y. Giants; Miller last active with St. Louis in '00; Mitchell played 16 games with New England; Neufeld last active with Jacksonville in '00; Norman was inactive for 16 games; Stewart was inactive for 16 games.

Traded—QB Brock Huard (1 game in '01) to Indianapolis.

Players lost through Expansion Draft (1): RB Charlie Rogers (13 games).

Players lost through free agency (2): TE Christian Fauria (NE, 16 games in '01), T Todd Weiner (Atl, 16).

Also played with Seahawks in '01: DE Matt LaBounty (2), DE Michael Sinclair (16), RB Ricky Watters (5).

2002 FIRST-YEAR ROSTER

Name	Pos.	Ht.	Wt.	Birthdate	College	Hometown	How Acq.
Arnaud, Robert (1)	RB	5-11	205	10/3/76	Georgia	Marrow, Ga.	FA
Bernard, Rocky	DE	6-3	293	4/19/79	Texas A&M	Baytown, Texas	D5a
Bierria, Terreal	S	6-3	211	10/10/80	Georgia	Slidell, La.	D4
Blackmon, Harold (1)	CB	5-11	216	5/20/78	Northwestern	Chicago, Ill.	D7a-'01
Brown, Joe (1)	DT	6-6	302	3/5/77	Ohio State	Tucson, Ariz.	FA-'01
Clemens, Kevin (1)	FB	6-0	271	6/20/76	Grand Valley State	Kankakee, Ill.	FA
Cook, Kerwin (1)	WR	6-1	185	12/21/79	Tulane	Ferriday, La.	FA-'01
Davis, Shockmain (1)	WR	6-0	208	8/20/77	Angelo State	Port Arthur, Texas	FA
Elling, Aaron (1)	P	6-1	207	5/31/78	Wyoming	Laramie, Wyo.	FA
Forte, Shawn (1)	S	6-1	206	1/20/77	Maryland	Poughkeepsie, N.Y.	FA
Gray, Brian (1)	S	6-1	216	1/10/76	Brigham Young	Hawthorne, Calif.	FA
Grimes, Reggie (1)	DE	6-4	302	11/7/76	Alabama	Nashville, Tenn.	FA-'01
Hannam, Ryan	TE	6-2	248	2/24/80	Northern Iowa	St. Ansgar, Iowa	D5b
Hargrove, Reggie	DE	6-2	280	8/28/74	Louisville	Durham, N.C.	FA
Heyward-Johnson, Keith	CB	5-11	185	2/2/79	Oregon State	Woodland Hills, Calif.	FA
Hill, Matt	T	6-6	304	11/10/78	Boise State	Grangeville, Idaho	D5c
Hodge, Damon (1)	WR	6-1	208	2/16/77	Alabama State	Thomaston, Ala.	FA
Jarrett, Craig	P	6-2	215	7/17/79	Michigan State	Martinsville, Ind.	D6
Kelly, Jeff	QB	6-1	212	9/7/79	Southern Mississippi	Deerpark, Ala.	D7
Lewis, D.D.	LB	6-1	241	1/8/79	Texas	Houston, Texas	FA
McElrath, Nakoa	WR	6-2	195	4/18/79	Washington State	La Jolla, Calif.	W(Jax)
Miller, Keith (1)	LB	6-1	245	7/9/76	California	San Diego, Calif.	FA
Morris, Maurice	RB	5-11	202	12/1/79	Oregon	Chester, S.C.	D2a
Nelson, Corey (1)	WR	6-1	193	10/9/77	Boise State	Rohnert Park, Calif.	FA
Neufeld, Ryan (1)	TE	6-4	254	11/22/75	UCLA	Morgan Hill, Calif.	FA
Niklos, John	FB	6-2	233	6/19/79	Western Illinois	Worthington, Ohio	FA
Palepoi, Anton	DE	6-3	283	11/19/78	Nevada-Las Vegas	Salt Lake City, Utah	D2b
Peko, Tupe (1)	C-G	6-4	300	9/19/78	Michigan State	Whittier, Calif.	FA-'01
Pendergrass, Jon	WR	6-0	205	10/7/78	Southern Illinois	Springfield, Ill.	FA
Perry, Merceda	LB	6-5	246	7/2/79	North Carolina	Asheboro, N.C.	W(Jax)
Phillips, Rodnick (1)	RB	5-11	222	11/17/77	Southern Methodist	Galveston, Texas	FA-'01
Rawlings, Josh (1)	G	6-4	315	4/11/77	Minnesota	Fort Gratiot, Mich.	FA
Richard, Kris	CB	5-11	190	10/28/78	Southern California	Carson, Calif.	D3
Smith, Ron	DT	6-3	308	8/18/78	Lane College	St. Louis, Mo.	FA
Stevens, Jerramy	TE	6-7	265	11/13/79	Washington	Olympia, Wash.	D1
Tharpe, Nigel (1)	DT	6-4	291	3/24/78	Iowa State	Detroit, Mich.	FA-'01
Van Dyke, Ryan	QB	6-5	226	2/13/80	Michigan State	Marshall, Mich.	FA
Watkins, T.J.	T	6-3	305	10/3/78	Clemson	North Augusta, S.C.	FA
Wright, Damion	G	6-3	323	2/13/79	Weber State	Aurora, Colo.	FA

The term NFL Rookie is defined as a player who is in his first season of professional football and has not been on the roster of another professional football team for any regular-season or postseason games. A Rookie is designated by an "R" on NFL rosters. Players who have been active in another professional football league or players who have NFL experience, including either preseason training camp or being on an Active List or Inactive List, or on Reserve/Injured or Reserve/Physically Unable to Perform for fewer than six regular-season games, are termed NFL First-Year Players. An NFL First-Year Player is designated by a "1" on NFL rosters. Thereafter, a player is credited with an additional year of experience for each season in which he accumulates six games on the Active List or Inactive List, or on Reserve/Injured or Reserve/Physically Unable to Perform.

COACHING STAFF

Executive Vice President of Football Operations/General Manager & Head Coach,

Mike Holmgren

Pro Career: Named to his current position as the Seahawks' executive vice president of football operations/general manager and head coach on January 8, 1999. In addition to his coaching duties, Holmgren oversees all facets of the team's football operations, including scouting, personnel, salary cap, player negotiations, as well as regular coaching responsibilities. In his first season, Holmgren guided the Seahawks to their first postseason appearance since 1988. The Seahawks also won their first postseason game since 1984. Holmgren joined Seattle after serving as the head coach of the Green Bay Packers (1992-98). By winning at least one game in five consecutive postseasons (1993-97) Holmgren joined John Madden (1973-77) as the only coaches in league history to accomplish that feat. In 16 NFL seasons (1999-2001 head coach, 1992-98 head coach Green Bay, 1986-1991 assistant coach San Francisco) Holmgren's teams have posted a 170-84-1 (.669) record, posted double-digit win totals 10 times, made the postseason 12 times, won three Super Bowls (XXIII, XXIV, and XXXI), and reached another (XXXII). Career record: 108-67.

Background: Quarterback at Southern California (1966-69) and was drafted by the St. Louis Cardinals in the eighth round of the 1970 NFL Draft. He served as an assistant coach at San Francisco State (1981) and Brigham Young (1982-85). Earned his bachelor degree in business finance at Southern California.

Personal: Born June 15, 1948, in San Francisco. He and his wife, Kathy, live in Mercer Island, Wash., and have four daughters—Calla, Jenny, Emily, and Gretchen.

ASSISTANT COACHES

Larry Brooks, defensive line; born June 10, 1950, Prince George, Va., lives in Kirkland, Wash. Defensive lineman Virginia State 1968-1971. Pro defensive tackle Los Angeles Rams 1972-1982. College coach: Virginia State 1992-93. Pro coach: Los Angeles Rams 1983-1990, Green Bay Packers 1994-98, joined Seahawks in 1999.

Jerry Colquitt, offensive quality control; born June 28, 1972, Oak Ridge, Tenn., lives in Kirkland, Wash. Quarterback Tennessee 1991-94. Quarterback Frankfurt Galaxy (NFL Europe) 1997. College coach: Tennessee 1996-98. Pro coach: Joined Seahawks in 1999.

Nolan Cromwell, wide receivers; born January 30, 1955, Smith Center, Kan., lives in Bellevue, Wash. Quarterback-safety Kansas 1973-76. Pro defensive back Los Angeles Rams 1977-1987. Pro

coach: Los Angeles Rams 1991, Green Bay Packers 1992-98, joined Seahawks in 1999.

Ken Flajole, defensive backs; born October 4, 1954, Seattle, lives in Kirkland, Wash. Linebacker Wenatchee (Wash.) Valley C.C. 1973-74, Pacific Lutheran 1975-76. No pro playing experience. College coach: Pacific Lutheran 1977-78, Washington 1979, Montana 1980-85, Texas-El Paso 1986-88, Missouri 1989-1993, Richmond 1994, Hawaii 1995, Nevada 1996-97. Pro coach: Green Bay Packers 1998, joined Seahawks in 1999.

Gil Haskell, offensive coordinator; born September 24, 1943, San Francisco, lives in Kirkland. Defensive back San Francisco State 1961, 1963-65. No pro playing experience. College coach: Southern California 1978-1982. Pro coach: Los Angeles Rams 1983-1991, Green Bay Packers 1992-97, Carolina Panthers 1998-99, joined Seahawks in 2000.

Johnny Holland, linebackers; born March 11, 1965, Belleville, Texas, lives in Kirkland. Linebacker Texas A&M 1983-86. Pro linebacker Green Bay Packers 1987-1993. Pro coach: Green Bay Packers 1995-99, joined Seahawks in 2000.

Kent Johnston, strength and conditioning; born February 21, 1956, Mexia, Texas, lives in Bellevue, Wash. Defensive back Stephen F. Austin 1974-77. No pro playing experience. College coach: Northwestern State (La.) 1979, Northeast Louisiana 1980-81, Alabama 1983-86. Pro coach: Tampa Bay Buccaneers 1987-1991, Green Bay Packers 1992-98, joined Seahawks in 1999.

Jim Lind, tight ends; born Novemeber 11, 1947, Isle, Minn., lives in Bellevue, Wash. Linebacker Bethel College 1965-66, defensive back Bemidji State 1971-72. No pro playing experience. College coach: St. Cloud State 1977-78, St. John's (Minn.) 1979-1980, Brigham Young 1981-82, Minnesota-Morris 1983-86 (head coach), Wisconsin-Eau Claire 1987-1991 (head coach). Pro coach: Green Bay Packers 1992-98, joined Seahawks in 1999.

Clayton Lopez, defensive quality control; born May 26, 1971, Los Angeles, lives in Kirkland, Wash. Safety Nevada 1991-94. No pro playing experience. College coach: Nevada 1995-98. Pro coach: Joined Seahawks in 1999.

Tom Lovat, asst. head coach-offensive line; born December 28, 1938, Bingham, Utah, lives in Bellevue, Wash. Guard-linebacker Utah 1958-1960. No pro playing experience. College coach: Utah 1967, 1972-76 (head coach 1974-76), Idaho State 1968-1970, Stanford 1977-79, Wyoming 1989. Pro coach: Saskatchewan Roughriders (CFL) 1971, Green Bay Packers 1980, 1992-98, St. Louis/Phoenix Cardinals 1981-84, 1990-91, Indianapolis Colts 1985-88, joined Seahawks in 1999.

Mark Michaels, asst. special teams; born

Aug. 15, 1963, Kingston, Pa., lives in Bothell, Wash. Defensive lineman Connecticut 1983-86. No pro playing experience. College coach: New Haven 1987-1990, Brown 1993-97, Massachusetts 1998. Pro coach: Helsinki Roosters (Finnish Maple League) 1991, Utah Pioneers (Professional Spring Football League) 1992, Cleveland Browns 1999-2000, joined Seahawks in 2001.

Stump Mitchell, running backs; born March 15, 1959, St. Mary's, Ga., lives in Kirkland, Wash. Tailback The Citadel 1977-1980. Running back St. Louis/Phoenix Cardinals 1981-89. College coach: Morgan State 1995-98 (head coach 1996-98). Pro coach: San Antonio Rough Riders (WLAF) 1991, joined Seahawks in 1999.

Pete Rodriguez, special teams coordinator; born July 25, 1940, Chicago, lives in Kirkland, Wash. Guard-linebacker Denver 1959-1960, Western State (Colo.) 1961-63. No pro playing experience. College coach: Western State (Colo.) 1964, Arizona 1968-69, Western Illinois 1970-73, 1979-1982 (head coach), Florida State 1974-75, Iowa State 1976-78, Northern Iowa 1986. Pro coach: Michigan Panthers (USFL) 1983-84, Denver Gold (USFL) 1985, Jacksonville Bulls (USFL) 1986, Ottawa Rough Riders (CFL) 1987, Los Angeles Raiders 1988-89, Phoenix Cardinals 1990-93, Washington Redskins 1994-97, joined Seahawks in 1998.

Zerick Rollins, defensive assistant; born June 20, 1975, Houston, lives in Bothell, Wash. Defensive end Texas A&M 1995-97. No pro playing experience. Graduate assistant Texas A&M 1997-2000.

Steve Sidwell, defensive coordinator; born August 30, 1944, Winfield, Kan., lives in Kirkland. Linebacker Colorado 1962-65. No pro playing experience. College coach: Colorado 1966-1973, Nevada-Las Vegas 1974-75, Southern Methodist 1976-1981. Pro coach: New England Patriots 1982-84, 1997-99, Indianapolis Colts 1985, New Orleans Saints 1986-1994, Houston Oilers 1995-96, joined Seahawks in 2000.

Rod Springer, asst. strength & conditioning; born September 19, 1960, Oklahoma City, Okla., lives in Kirkland. Attended Tarrleton State. No college or pro playing experience. College coach: Alabama 1985-86. Pro coach: Joined Seahawks in 1999.

Jim Zorn, quarterbacks; born May 10, 1953, Whittier, Calif., lives in Mercer Island, Wash. Quarterback Cal Poly-Pomona 1973-75. Pro quarterback Seattle Seahawks 1975-1984, Green Bay Packers 1985, Winnipeg Blue Bombers (CFL) 1986, Tampa Bay Buccaneers 1987. College coach: Boise State 1989-1991, Utah State 1992-94, Minnesota 1995-96. Pro coach: Seattle Seahawks 1997, Detroit Lions 1998-2000, rejoined Seahawks in 2001.

National Football Conference
South Division
Team Colors: Buccaneer Red,Pewter,
Black, and Orange
One Buccaneer Place
Tampa, Florida 33607
Telephone: (813) 870-2700

2002 SCHEDULE
PRESEASON
Aug. 12 **Miami** 8:00
Aug. 16 at Jacksonville....................7:00
Aug. 24 **Washington** 8:00
Aug. 30 at Houston 7:00

REGULAR SEASON
Sept. 8 **New Orleans**.....................4:15
Sept. 15 at Baltimore.......................1:00
Sept. 23 **St. Louis (Mon.)**.................9:00
Sept. 29 at Cincinnati 4:05
Oct. 6 at Atlanta...........................1:00
Oct. 13 **Cleveland** 4:15
Oct. 20 at Philadelphia...................1:00
Oct. 27 at Carolina..........................1:00
Nov. 3 **Minnesota** 1:00
Nov. 10 OPEN DATE
Nov. 17 **Carolina**............................4:05
Nov. 24 **Green Bay**..........................1:00
Dec. 1 at New Orleans..................7:30
Dec. 8 **Atlanta** 1:00
Dec. 15 at Detroit 1:00
Dec. 23 **Pittsburgh (Mon.)** 9:00
Dec. 29 at Chicago (Champaign, Ill.) ..7:30

Stadium: Raymond James Stadium
(opened in 1998)
•**Capacity:** 65,657
Tampa, Florida 33607
Playing Surface: Grass
Training Camp: Disney's Wide World of
Sports
Lake Buena Vista, Florida

RAYMOND JAMES STADIUM

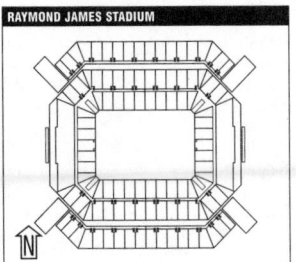

CLUB OFFICIALS
Owner/President: Malcolm Glazer
Executive Vice President: Bryan Glazer
Executive Vice President: Joel Glazer
Executive Vice President: Edward Glazer
General Manager: Rich McKay
Assistant General Manager:
John Idzik
Director of Player Personnel:
Tim Ruskell
Director of College Scouting:
Ruston Webster
Executive Director of the Glazer Family
Foundation: Veronica (Roni) Costello
Director of Communications:
Reggie Roberts
Director of Marketing: George Woods
Director of Community Relations:
Stephanie Waller
Director of Legal Affairs:
Nathan Whitaker
Director of Player Development:
Cedric Saunders
Director of Special Events: Maury Wilks
Director of Security: Andre Trescastro
College Scouts: Joe DiMarzo, Jr.,
Frank Dorazio, Dennis Hickey,
Mike Yowarsky
Pro Scout: Lloyd Lee
Director of Pro Personnel:
Mark Dominik
National Combine Scout: Seth Turner
Assistant to Head Coach-Football
Operations: Mark Arteaga
Director of Ticketing and Customer
Relations: Mike Newquist
Director of Human Resources/Sales:
Gene Magrini
Internet Manager: Scott Smith
Communications Manager: Jeff Kamis
Trainer: Todd Toriscelli
Director of Rehabilitation: Scott Trulock
Equipment Manager: Tim Sain
Assistant Equipment Manager:
Mark Meschede
Video Director: Dave Levy
Assistant Video Director: Pat Brazil

COACHING HISTORY
(151-262-1)
1976-1984 John McKay.................45-91-1
1985-86 Leeman Bennett............4-28-0
1987-1990 Ray Perkins*...............19-41-0
1990-91 Richard Williamson 4-15-0
1992-95 Sam Wyche 23-41-0
1996-2001 Tony Dungy.................56-46-0
*Released after 13 games in 1990

ATTENDANCE
Home 513,684   Away 506,195
Total 1,019,879
Single-game home record,
73,523 (12/7/97)
Single-season home record, 545,980
(1979)

2002 DRAFT CHOICES
Round	Name	Pos.	College
3	Marquise Walker	WR	Michigan
4	Travis Stephens	RB	Tennessee
5	Jermaine Phillips	DB	Georgia
6	John Stamper	DE	South Carolina
7	Tim Wansley	DB	Georgia
	Tracey Wistrom	TE	Nebraska
	Aaron Lockett	WR	Kansas State
	Zack Quaccia	C	Stanford

TAMPA BAY BUCCANEERS

2001 TEAM RECORD

PRESEASON (1-3)

Date	Result	Opponent
8/13	L 14-17	Miami
8/18	L 6-7	at Cleveland
8/25	W 20-3	New England
8/31	L 7-36	at Atlanta

REGULAR SEASON (9-7)

Date	Result	Opponent	Att.
9/09	W 10-6	at Dallas	61,521
9/30	L 16-20	at Minnesota	64,105
10/07	W 14-10	Green Bay	65,510
10/14	L 28-31	at Tennessee(OT)	68,798
10/21	L 10-17	Pittsburgh	65,588
10/28	W 41-14	Minnesota	65,558
11/04	L 20-21	at Green Bay	59,861
11/11	W 20-17	at Detroit	74,268
11/18	L 24-27	Chicago	65,612
11/26	W 24-17	at St. Louis	66,198
12/02	W 16-13	at Cincinnati(OT)	52,135
12/09	W 15-12	Detroit	65,514
12/16	L 3-27	at Chicago	66,944
12/23	W 48-21	New Orleans	65,526
12/29	W 22-10	Baltimore	65,619
1/06	L 13-17	Philadelphia	65,541

(OT) Overtime

POSTSEASON (0-1)

1/12	L 9-31	at Philadelphia	65,847

SCORE BY PERIODS

Buccaneers	39	130	50	102	3 —	324
Opponents	33	63	86	95	3 —	280

2001 TEAM STATISTICS

	Buccaneers	Opp.
Total First Downs	298	262
Rushing	84	86
Passing	189	156
Penalty	25	20
3rd Down: Made/Att	80/228	78/216
3rd Down Pct.	35.1	36.1
4th Down: Made/Att	11/17	4/13
4th Down Pct.	64.7	30.8
Possession Avg.	31:40	28:20
Total Net Yards	4694	4653
Avg. Per Game	293.4	290.8
Total Plays	1046	950
Avg. Per Play	4.5	4.9
Net Yards Rushing	1371	1702
Avg. Per Game	85.7	106.4
Total Rushes	407	415
Net Yards Passing	3323	2951
Avg. Per Game	207.7	184.4
Sacked/Yards Lost	47/298	42/272
Gross Yards	3621	3223
Att./Completions	592/362	493/273
Completion Pct.	61.1	55.4
Had Intercepted	12	28
Punts/Average	83/40.7	78/41.5
Net Punting Avg.	83/34.2	78/34.3
Penalties/Yards	77/672	91/742
Fumbles/Ball Lost	20/10	22/11
Touchdowns	34	29
Rushing	17	8
Passing	13	20
Returns	4	1

2001 INDIVIDUAL STATISTICS

PASSING

PASSING	Att.	Comp.	Yds.	Pct.	TD	Int.	Tkld.	Rate
B. Johnson	559	340	3406	60.8	13	11	44/269	77.7
King	31	21	210	67.7	0	1	3/29	73.3
Gramatica	1	0	0	0.0	0	0	0/0	39.6
Royals	1	1	5	100.0	0	0	0/0	87.5
Buccaneers	592	362	3621	61.1	13	12	47/298	77.4
Opponents	493	273	3223	55.4	20	28	42/272	65.3

SCORING

SCORING	TD R	TD P	TD Rt	PAT	FG	Saf	PTS
Gramatica	0	0	0	28/28	23/29	0	97
Alstott	10	1	0	0/0	0/0	0	70
Dunn	3	3	0	0/0	0/0	0	36
Moore	0	4	0	0/0	0/0	0	24
B. Johnson	3	0	0	0/0	0/0	0	18
Brien	0	0	0	2/2	5/6	0	17
Stecker	1	1	0	0/0	0/0	0	12
Williams	0	1	1	0/0	0/0	0	12
Barber	0	0	1	0/0	0/0	0	6
Green	0	1	0	0/0	0/0	0	6
K. Johnson	0	1	0	0/0	0/0	0	6
Murphy	0	1	0	0/0	0/0	0	6
Quarles	0	0	1	0/0	0/0	0	6
Yoder	0	0	1	0/0	0/0	0	6
King	0	0	0	0/0	0/0	1	2
Buccaneers	17	13	4	30/30	28/35	0	324
Opponents	8	20	1	25/25	25/29	0	280

2-Pt. Conversions: Alstott 2, King.
Buccaneers 3-4, Opponents 3-4.

RUSHING

RUSHING	Att.	Yds.	Avg.	LG	TD
Alstott	165	680	4.1	39t	10
Dunn	158	447	2.8	21t	3
B. Johnson	39	120	3.1	21	3
Stecker	24	72	3.0	17	1
Abdullah	11	40	3.6	12	0
Anthony	3	22	7.3	16	0
Cook	2	2	1.0	2	0
King	5	-12	-2.4	0	0
Buccaneers	407	1371	3.4	39t	17
Opponents	415	1702	4.1	63t	8

RECEIVING

RECEIVING	No.	Yds.	Avg.	LG	TD
K. Johnson	106	1266	11.9	47	1
Dunn	68	557	8.2	31	3
Green	36	402	11.2	35	1
Moore	35	285	8.1	29	4
Alstott	35	231	6.6	19t	1
Williams	24	314	13.1	42	1
Cook	17	89	5.2	16	0
Anthony	13	162	12.5	35	0
Stecker	10	101	10.1	35t	1
Murphy	8	71	8.9	20	1
Wynn	4	69	17.3	36	0
Yoder	4	48	12.0	24	0
Abdullah	2	26	13.0	14	0
Buccaneers	362	3621	10.0	47	13
Opponents	273	3223	11.8	67t	20

INTERCEPTIONS

INTERCEPTIONS	No.	Yds.	Avg.	LG	TD
Barber	10	86	8.6	36t	1
Abraham	6	98	16.3	46	0
Jackson	4	42	10.5	29	0
Brooks	3	65	21.7	53	0
Lynch	3	21	7.0	15	0
Quarles	1	98	98.0	98t	1
Duncan	1	9	9.0	9	0
Buccaneers	28	419	15.0	98t	2
Opponents	12	74	6.2	25	0

PUNTING

PUNTING	No.	Yds.	Avg.	In 20	LG
Royals	83	3382	40.7	26	61
Buccaneers	83	3382	40.7	26	61
Opponents	78	3234	41.5	19	58

PUNT RETURNS

PUNT RETURNS	No.	FC	Yds.	Avg.	LG	TD
Williams	35	13	366	10.5	84t	1
Anthony	3	1	12	4.0	7	0
Jackson	0	0	18	—	18	0
Buccaneers	38	14	396	10.4	84t	1
Opponents	44	12	380	8.6	55t	1

KICKOFF RETURNS

KICKOFF RETURNS	No.	Yds.	Avg.	LG	TD
Murphy	20	445	22.3	39	0
Smith	16	355	22.2	45	0
Stecker	9	259	28.8	86	0
Abdullah	5	92	18.4	29	0
Williams	2	35	17.5	22	0
Washington	1	22	22.0	22	0
White	1	0	0.0	0	0
Buccaneers	54	1208	22.4	86	0
Opponents	63	1321	21.0	77	0

FIELD GOALS

FIELD GOALS	1-19	20-29	30-39	40-49	50+
Gramatica	0/0	9/10	9/9	5/7	0/3
Brien	0/0	2/2	1/1	2/3	0/0
Buccaneers	0/0	11/12	10/10	7/10	0/3
Opponents	0/0	7/7	6/7	11/13	1/2

SACKS

SACKS	No.
S. Rice	11.0
Sapp	6.0
White	5.0
McFarland	3.5
Jones	3.0
Jackson	2.5
Darby	2.0
Duncan	2.0
Quarles	2.0
Kelly	1.5
Barber	1.0
Lynch	1.0
Singleton	1.0
Gooch	0.5
Buccaneers	42.0
Opponents	47.0

RECORD HOLDERS
INDIVIDUAL RECORDS—CAREER

Category	Name	Performance
Rushing (Yds.)	James Wilder, 1981-89	5,957
Passing (Yds.)	Vinny Testaverde, 1987-1992	14,820
Passing (TDs)	Vinny Testaverde, 1987-1992	77
Receiving (No.)	James Wilder, 1981-89	430
Receiving (Yds.)	Mark Carrier, 1987-1992	5,018
Interceptions	Donnie Abraham, 1996-2001	31
Punting (Avg.)	Tommy Barnhardt, 1996-98	42.6
Punt Return (Avg.)	Jacquez Green, 1998-2001	12.0
Kickoff Return (Avg.)	Reidel Anthony, 1997-2001	23.5
Field Goals	Michael Husted, 1993-98	117
Touchdowns (Tot.)	Mike Alstott, 1996-2001	50
Points	Michael Husted, 1993-98	502

INDIVIDUAL RECORDS—SINGLE SEASON

Category	Name	Performance
Rushing (Yds.)	James Wilder, 1984	1,544
Passing (Yds.)	Doug Williams, 1981	3,563
Passing (TDs)	Trent Dilfer, 1997, 1998	21
Receiving (No.)	Keyshawn Johnson, 2001	106
Receiving (Yds.)	Mark Carrier, 1989	1,422
Interceptions	Ronde Barber, 2001	10
Punting (Avg.)	Mark Royals, 1999	43.1
Punt Return (Avg.)	Karl Williams, 1996	21.1
Kickoff Return (Avg.)	Karl Williams, 1996	27.4
Field Goals	Martin Gramatica, 2000	28
Touchdowns (Tot.)	James Wilder, 1984	13
Points	Martin Gramatica, 2000	126

INDIVIDUAL RECORDS—SINGLE GAME

Category	Name	Performance
Rushing (Yds.)	James Wilder, 11-6-83	219
Passing (Yds.)	Doug Williams, 11-16-80	486
Passing (TDs)	Steve DeBerg, 9-13-87	5
Receiving (No.)	James Wilder, 9-15-85	13
Receiving (Yds.)	Mark Carrier, 12-6-87	212
Interceptions	Ronde Barber, 12-23-01	3
Field Goals	Many times	4
	Last time by Martin Gramatica, 12-23-01	
Touchdowns (Tot.)	Jimmie Giles, 10-20-85	4
Points	Jimmie Giles, 10-20-85	24

2002 VETERAN ROSTER

No.	Name	Pos.	Ht.	Wt.	Birthdate	NFL Exp.	College	Hometown	How Acq.	'01 Games/ Starts
40	Alstott, Mike	FB	6-1	248	12/21/73	7	Purdue	Joliet, Ill.	D2-'96	16/16
20	Barber, Ronde	CB	5-10	184	4/7/75	6	Virginia	Roanoke, Va.	D3b-'97	16/16
81	Battaglia, Marco	TE	6-3	249	1/25/73	7	Rutgers	Queens, N.Y.	UFA(Wash)-'02	11/1*
55	Brooks, Derrick	LB	6-0	235	4/18/73	8	Florida State	Pensacola, Fla.	D1b-'95	16/16
23 #	Chamblin, Corey	CB	5-10	189	5/29/77	2	Tennessee Tech	Birmingham, Ala.	FA-'02	0*
62	Christy, Jeff	C	6-2	285	2/3/69	10	Pittsburgh	Freeport, Pa.	UFA(Minn)-'00	15/15
60	Coleman, Cosey	G	6-4	322	10/27/78	3	Tennessee	Clarkston, Ga.	D2-'00	16/16
43	Cook, Jameel	FB	5-10	237	2/8/79	2	Illinois	Miami, Fla.	D6a-'01	16/3
76	Curry, DeMarcus	T	6-5	332	4/30/75	3	Auburn	Columbus, Ga.	FA-'99	3/0
91	Darby, Chartric	DT	6-0	270	10/22/75	2	South Carolina State	North, S.C.	FA-'00	13/0
22	Gibson, David	S	6-1	210	11/5/77	3	Southern California	Santa Ana, Calif.	D6-'00	13/0
58	Golden, Jack	LB	6-1	240	1/28/77	3	Oklahoma State	Harvey, Ill.	W(NYG)-'02	16/0*
7	Gramatica, Martín	K	5-8	170	11/27/75	4	Kansas State	LaBelle, Fla.	D3-'99	14/0
84	Green, E.G.	WR	5-11	188	6/28/75	4	Florida State	Ft. Walton Beach, Fla.	FA-'02	0*
68	Grice, Shane	G	6-1	307	12/20/76	2	Mississippi	Shannon, Miss.	FA-'01	1/0
1	Hamilton, Joe	QB	5-10	190	3/13/77	3	Georgia Tech	Alvin, S.C.	D7-'00	0*
29	Hanspard, Byron	RB	5-10	200	1/23/76	4	Texas Tech	Desoto, Texas	FA-'02	0*
65	Hochstein, Russ	G	6-4	300	10/7/77	2	Nebraska	Hartington, Neb.	D5-'01	0*
38	Howell, John	S	5-11	204	4/28/78	2	Colorado State	Mullen, Neb.	D4-'01	14/1
34 †	Jackson, Dexter	S	6-1	203	7/28/77	4	Florida State	Quincy, Fla.	D4-'99	15/15
70	Jenkins, Kerry	G	6-5	305	9/6/73	5	Troy State	Tuscaloosa, Ala.	FA-'02	16/16*
14	Johnson, Brad	QB	6-5	226	9/13/68	11	Florida State	Black Mountain, N.C.	UFA(Wash)-'01	16/16
19	Johnson, Keyshawn	WR	6-4	212	7/22/72	7	Southern California	Los Angeles, Calif.	T(NYJ)-'00	15/15
11	Johnson, Rob	QB	6-4	212	3/18/73	8	Southern California	El Toro, Calif.	FA-'02	8/8*
57	Jones, Chris	LB	5-10	229	9/30/76	2	Clemson	Monroe, Ga.	FA-'02	0*
78	Jones, Marcus	DE	6-6	278	8/15/73	7	North Carolina	Jacksonville, N.C.	D1b-'96	15/15
85	Jurevicius, Joe	WR	6-5	230	12/23/74	5	Penn State	Mentor Lake, Ohio	UFA(NYG)-'02	14/9*
25	Kelly, Brian	CB	5-11	193	1/14/76	5	Southern California	Aurora, Colo.	D2b-'98	16/11
10	King, Shaun	QB	6-0	225	5/29/77	4	Tulane	St. Petersburg, Fla.	D2-'99	3/0
47	Lynch, John	S	6-2	220	9/25/71	10	Stanford	Solana Beach, Calif.	D3-'93	16/16
66	Mack, Kendell	G	6-4	322	7/18/75	2	Auburn	Pineville, S.C.	FA-'00	0*
92	McFarland, Anthony	DT	6-0	300	12/18/77	4	Louisiana State	Winnsboro, La.	D1-'99	14/14
87	Murphy, Frank	WR	6-0	206	2/11/77	2	Kansas State	Callahan, Fla.	FA-'00	11/0
69 #	Pierson, Pete	T	6-5	315	2/4/71	8	Washington	Portland, Ore.	D5-'94	16/0
32	Pittman, Michael	RB	6-0	218	8/14/75	5	Fresno State	San Diego, Calif.	UFA(Ariz)-'02	15/14*
83	Poole, Keith	WR	6-0	193	6/18/74	6	Arizona State	Clovis, Calif.	FA-'02	6/0*
53	Quarles, Shelton	LB	6-1	225	9/11/71	6	Vanderbilt	Whites Creek, Tenn.	FA-'97	16/16
97	Rice, Simeon	DE	6-5	268	2/24/74	7	Illinois	Chicago, Ill.	UFA(Ariz)-'01	16/16
99	Sapp, Warren	DT	6-2	303	12/19/72	8	Miami	Apopka, Fla.	D1a-'95	16/16
51	Singleton, Alshermond	LB	6-2	228	8/7/75	6	Temple	Irvington, N.J.	D4-'97	16/0
26	Smith, Dwight	CB	5-10	201	8/13/78	2	Akron	Detroit, Mich.	D3-'01	15/0
94	Spires, Greg	DE	6-1	265	8/12/74	5	Florida State	Cape Coral, Fla.	UFA(Cle)-'02	16/4*
27	Stecker, Aaron	RB	5-10	205	11/13/75	3	Western Illinois	Green Bay, Wis.	FA-'00	13/0
67	Walker, Kenyatta	T	6-5	302	2/1/79	2	Florida	Meridian, Miss.	D1-'01	16/16
93	Warner, Ron	DE	6-2	265	9/26/75	2	Kansas	Independence, Kan.	FA-'01	0*
75	Washington, Todd	C-G	6-3	324	7/19/76	5	Virginia Tech	Melfa, Va.	D4-'98	15/1
52	Webster, Nate	LB	5-11	225	11/29/77	3	Miami	Miami, Fla.	D3-'00	16/1
86 #	Williams, Karl	WR	5-10	177	4/10/71	7	Texas A&M-Kingsville	Garland, Texas	FA-'96	15/3
71	Wunsch, Jerry	T	6-6	339	1/21/74	6	Wisconsin	Wausau, Wis.	D2-'97	16/16
96	Wyms, Ellis	DE	6-3	279	4/12/79	2	Mississippi State	Indianola, Miss.	D6b-'01	4/0
88	Wynn, Milton	WR	6-2	207	9/21/78	2	Washington State	Lancaster, Calif.	W(StL)-'01	1/0
80	Yoder, Todd	TE	6-4	250	3/18/78	3	Vanderbilt	New Palestine, Ind.	FA-'00	16/1

* Battaglia played 8 games with Cincinnati and 3 games with Washington in '01; Chamblin last active with Jacksonville in '99; Golden played 16 games with N.Y. Giants; Green last active with Indianapolis in '00; Hamilton was inactive for 16 games; Hanspard last active with Atlanta in '99; Hochstein was inactive for 16 games; Jenkins played 16 games with N.Y. Jets; R. Johnson played 8 games with Buffalo; C. Jones missed '00 season because of injury with Denver; Jurevicius played 14 games with N.Y. Giants; Mack missed '01 season because of injury; Pittman played 15 games with Arizona; Poole played 6 games with Denver; Spires played 16 games with Cleveland; Warner last active with New Orleans in '98.

† Restricted free agent; subject to developments.

Unrestricted free agent; subject to developments.

Players lost through Expansion Draft (1): TE Sean McDermott (16 games).

Players lost through free agency (8)—RB Rabih Abdullah (Chi; 16 games in '01), WR Reidel Anthony (Wash; 13), K Doug Brien (Minn; 2), DT James Cannida (Ind; 11), LB Jamie Duncan (StL; 15), RB Warrick Dunn (Atl; 13), WR Jacquez Green (Wash; 12), DE Steve White (NYJ; 16).

Retired—Randall McDaniel, 14-year guard, 16 games in '01.

Also played with Buccaneers in '01—CB Donnie Abraham (15 games), LB Marq Cerqua (3), LB Jeff Gooch (13), TE Dave Moore (16), P Mark Royals (16), S Eric Vance (10).

2002 FIRST-YEAR ROSTER

Name	Pos.	Ht.	Wt.	Birthdate	College	Hometown	How Acq.
Abrams, Mike	P	6-2	236	1/15/79	Virginia	Aiken, S.C.	FA
Alexander, Bennie	CB	5-9	182	9/8/78	Florida	Raiford, Fla.	FA
Cerimele, Mike (1)	FB	5-9	237	11/28/77	Penn State	Allentown, Pa.	FA
Daniel, Darryl (1)	WR	5-11	190	1/24/76	Syracuse	Lancaster, Pa.	FA
Duncan, Howard	G	6-4	324	11/15/80	Oklahoma	Kansas City, Kan.	FA
Fitzgerald, Markese	CB	5-10	184	4/25/79	Miami	St. Petersburg, Fla.	FA
Gilmore, Zain	RB	6-0	215	10/30/79	Missouri	Tampa, Fla.	FA
Gruber, Brian (1)	T	6-7	316	10/10/77	Vanderbilt	Houston, Texas	FA
Gurley, Buck (1)	DT	6-2	295	4/7/78	Florida	Tallahassee, Fla.	FA
Hardaway, Eddie (1)	WR	6-1	195	10/7/77	C.W. Post	Amityville, N.Y.	FA
Hogan, Andy	LS	6-0	213	6/30/78	Georgia	Athens, Ga.	FA
Ivy, Corey (1)	CB	5-8	183	3/29/77	Oklahoma	Moore, Okla.	FA
Kelly, Jermale (1)	WR	6-2	200	6/14/77	South Carolina	Greenville, S.C.	FA
Leaverton, David (1)	P	6-4	210	4/1/78	Tennessee	Midland, Texas	T(NYJ)
Lockett, Aaron	WR	5-7	155	9/6/78	Kansas State	Tulsa, Okla.	D7c
Mackenzie, Mike (1)	DT	6-2	269	3/16/78	Colorado State	Miami, Fla.	FA
McCaslin, Eugene (1)	LB	6-1	228	7/12/77	Florida	Tampa, Fla.	FA
Midget, Anthony (1)	CB	5-11	193	2/2/78	Virginia Tech	Clewiston, Fla.	FA
Morgan, Tim (1)	P	6-5	212	4/27/77	San Jose State	Vallejo, Calif.	FA
Nece, Ryan	LB	6-3	224	2/24/79	UCLA	San Bernardino, Calif.	FA
Phillips, Jermaine	S	6-1	214	3/27/79	Georgia	Roswell, Ga.	D5
Quaccia, Zack	G	6-4	309	4/20/79	Stanford	Oakdale, Calif.	D7d
Roberg, Mike (1)	TE	6-4	263	9/18/77	Idaho	Spokane, Wash.	FA
Rogers, Sterling	LB	6-1	223	12/26/79	Southwest Texas State	Houston, Texas	FA
Smith, Corey	DE	6-2	250	11/2/79	North Carolina State	Richmond, Va.	FA
Smith, Justin	LB	6-0	218	6/5/79	Indiana	Indianapolis, Ind.	FA
Stamper, John	DE	6-4	265	8/30/78	South Carolina	Andrews, S.C.	D6
Stephens, Travis	RB	5-8	194	6/26/78	Tennessee	Clarksville, Tenn.	D4
Sumter, Glenn	S	6-1	192	2/22/80	Memphis	Detroit, Mich.	FA
Vaughn, Damian (1)	TE	6-4	252	6/14/75	Miami (Ohio)	Orrville, Ohio	FA
Walker, Marquise	WR	6-2	219	12/11/78	Michigan	Syracuse, N.Y.	D3
Wansley, Tim	CB	5-8	180	11/11/78	Georgia	Buford, Ga.	D7a
White, Jamal	LB	6-3	223	9/12/80	Kentucky	Cincinnati, Ohio	FA
Wistrom, Tracey	TE	6-4	245	8/28/78	Nebraska	Webb City, Mo.	D7b

The term NFL Rookie is defined as a player who is in his first season of professional football and has not been on the roster of another professional football team for any regular-season or postseason games. A Rookie is designated by an "R" on NFL rosters. Players who have been active in another professional football league or players who have NFL experience, including either preseason training camp or being on an Active List or Inactive List, or on Reserve/Injured or Reserve/Physically Unable to Perform for fewer than six regular-season games, are termed NFL First-Year Players. An NFL First-Year Player is designated by a "1" on NFL rosters. Thereafter, a player is credited with an additional year of experience for each season in which he accumulates six games on the Active List or Inactive List, or on Reserve/Injured or Reserve/Physically Unable to Perform.

COACHING STAFF

Head Coach,
Jon Gruden

Pro Career: Gruden was named the seventh head coach in Buccaneers history on February 18, 2002, when he signed a five-year contract. Gruden, the NFL's youngest head coach at 39, guided the Oakland Raiders to AFC West division titles in each of his final two seasons as head coach. He steered the Raiders to a 40-28 mark in his four seasons (1998-2001) with the club, including postseason appearances in 2000 and 2001. Under Gruden, the Raiders advanced to the AFC title game in 2000 and lost last season in a divisional playoff game to eventual Super Bowl champion New England. Gruden's offenses have finished among the league's Top 10 in each of the last three seasons. Prior to his four seasons with Oakland, Gruden spent 1995-97 as offensive coordinator for the Philadelphia Eagles and three years (1992-94) as wide receivers coach for Green Bay Packers. Worked as offensive assistant for San Francisco 49ers in 1990. Career record: 40-28.

Background: Was a three-year letterman at quarterback at the University of Dayton, graduating in 1985 with a degree in communications. The Flyers had a 24-7 record in Gruden's three varsity seasons there. Attended South Bend Clay High School in Indiana. Was wide receivers coach for University of Pittsburgh in 1991, wide receivers coach at University of Pacific in 1989, and passing game coordinator at Southeast Missouri State in 1988. Began coaching career as a graduate assistant at the University of Tennessee (1986-87).

Personal: Born August 17, 1963 in Sandusky, Ohio. Jon and his wife Cindy, have three sons, Jon II (8), Michael (5) and Jayson (2).

ASSISTANT COACHES

Joe Barry, linebackers; born July 5, 1970, Boulder, Colo., lives in Tampa. Linebacker Southern California 1991-93. No pro playing experience. College coach: Southern California 1994-95, Northern Arizona 1996-98, Nevada-Las Vegas 1999. Pro coach: San Francisco 49ers 2000, joined Buccaneers in 2001.

Jeremy Bates, offensive quality control; born August 27, 1976, Sevierville, Tenn., lives in Tampa. Quarterback Tennessee 1995, Rice 1996-99. No pro playing experience. Pro coach: Joined Buccaneers in 2002.

Richard Bisaccia, special teams; born June 3, 1960, Yonkers, N.Y., lives in Tampa. Defensive back Yankton College 1979-1982, Philadelphia Stars (USFL) 1983. College coach: Wayne State College 1983-87, South Carolina 1988-1993, Clemson 1994-98, Mississippi 1999-2001. Pro coach: Joined

Buccaneers in 2002.

Michael Christianson, assistant offensive line-offensive quality control; born April 7, 1965, Kuna, Idaho, lives in Tampa. Linebacker Portland State 1987-88, Tight end-offensive tackle Western Oregon 1989-1991. No pro playing experience. College coach: Western Oregon 1991-94, Lewis & Clark 1995, Portland State 1996-98, Montana State 2000. Pro coach: Joined Buccaneers in 2002.

Monte Kiffin, defensive coordinator; born February 29, 1940, Lexington, Neb., lives in Tampa. Offensive/defensive tackle Nebraska 1959-63. Pro defensive end Winnipeg Blue Bombers (CFL) 1965. College coach: Nebraska 1966-76, Arkansas 1977-79, North Carolina State 1980-82 (head coach). Pro coach: Green Bay Packers 1983, Buffalo Bills 1984-85, Minnesota Vikings 1986-89, 1991-94, New York Jets 1990, New Orleans Saints 1995, joined Buccaneers in 1996.

Richard Mann, wide receivers; born April 20, 1947, Aliquippa, Pa., lives in Tampa. Wide receiver Arizona State 1966-68. No pro playing experience. College coach: Arizona State 1974-79, Louisville 1980-81. Pro coach: Baltimore/Indianapolis Colts 1982-84, Cleveland Browns 1985-1993, New York Jets 1994-96, Baltimore Ravens 1997-98, Kansas City Chiefs 1999-2000, Washington Redskins 2001, joined Buccaneers in 2002.

Rod Marinelli, asst. head coach-defensive line; born July 13, 1949, Rosemead, Calif., lives in Tampa. Offensive/defensive tackle Utah 1968, offensive tackle California Lutheran 1970-72 (military service 1969-70). No pro playing experience. College coach: Utah State 1976-82, California 1983-91, Arizona State 1992-94, Southern California 1995. Pro coach: Joined Buccaneers in 1996.

Mike Morris, asst. strength and conditioning; born May 7, 1964, Ayer, Mass., lives in Tampa. Wide receiver Syracuse 1981-85. No pro playing experience. Pro coach: New England Patriots 1997-99, joined Buccaneers in 2002.

Raheem Morris, defensive quality control; born September 3, 1976, Irvington, N.J., lives in Tampa. Safety Hofstra 1994-97. No pro playing experience. College coach: Hofstra 1998, 2000-2001, Cornell 1999. Pro coach: New York Jets 2001, joined Buccaneers in 2002.

Bill Muir, offensive coordinator-offensive line; born October 26, 1942, Pittsburgh, Pa., lives in Tampa. Tackle Susquehanna 1962-64. No pro playing experience. College coach: Susquehanna 1965, Delaware Valley 1966-67, Rhode Island 1970-71, Idaho State 1972-73, Southern Methodist 1976-77. Pro coach: Orlando (Continental Football League) 1968-69, Houston Shreveport Steamer (WFL) 1975, New England Patriots 1982-88, Indianapolis Colts 1989-1991, Philadelphia Eagles 1992-94, New York

Jets 1995-2001, joined Buccaneers in 2002.

Johnny Parker, strength and conditioning; born February 1, 1947, Greenville, S.C., lives in Tampa. Attended Mississippi. No college or pro playing experience. College coach: South Carolina 1974-76, Indiana 1977-79, Louisiana State 1980, Mississippi 1981-83. Pro coach: New York Giants 1984-1992, New England Patriots 1993-99, joined Buccaneers in 2002.

Stan Parrish, quarterbacks; born September 20, 1946, Cleveland, Ohio, lives in Tampa. Defensive back Heidelberg College 1964-67. No pro playing experience. College coach: Heidelberg College 1968, Purdue 1975-76, 1983, Wabash College 1977-1982, Marshall 1984-85, Kansas State 1986-88, Rutgers 1990-95, Michigan 1996-2001. Pro coach: Joined Buccaneers in 2002.

Mike Tomlin, defensive backs; born March 15, 1972, Hampton, Va., lives in Tampa. Wide receiver William & Mary 1991-94. No pro playing experience. College coach: Virginia Military Institute 1995, Memphis 1996, Tennessee-Martin 1997, Arkansas State 1997-98, Cincinnati 1999-2000. Pro coach: Joined Buccaneers in 2001.

Art Valero, tight ends; born May 12, 1958, Whittier, Calif., lives in Tampa. Offensive lineman Boise State 1979-1980. No pro playing experience. College coach: Boise State 1981-82, Iowa State 1983, Long Beach State 1984-86, New Mexico 1987-89, Idaho 1990-94, Louisville 1998-2001. Pro coach: Kansas City Chiefs 1994, Buffalo Bills 1996, joined Buccaneers in 2002.

Kirby Wilson, running backs; born August 24, 1961, Los Angeles, Calif., lives in Tampa. Running back-wide receiver Pasadena (Calif.) C.C. 1979-1980, Illinois 1981-82. Pro cornerback Winnipeg Blue Bombers (CFL) 1983, Toronto Argonauts (CFL) 1984. College coach: Pasadena (Calif.) C.C. 1985, Southwest (Calif.) C.C. 1989-1990, Southern Illinois 1991-92, Wyoming 1993-94, Iowa State 1995-96, Southern California 2001. Pro coach: New England Patriots 1997-99, Washington Redskins 2000, joined Buccaneers in 2002.

WASHINGTON REDSKINS

National Football Conference
East Division
Team Colors: Burgundy and Gold
Redskin Park
21300 Redskin Park Drive
Ashburn, Virginia 20147
Telephone: (703) 726-7088

2002 SCHEDULE
PRESEASON
Aug. 3	vs. San Francisco	10:00
Aug. 10	at Carolina	8:00
Aug. 18	**Pittsburgh**	8:00
Aug. 24	at Tampa Bay	8:00
Aug. 29	**New England**	8:00

REGULAR SEASON
Sept. 8	at Cincinnati	1:00
Sept. 8	**Arizona**	1:00
Sept. 16	**Philadelphia (Mon.)**	9:00
Sept. 22	at San Francisco	1:15
Sept. 29	OPEN DATE	
Oct. 6	at Tennessee	12:00
Oct. 13	**New Orleans**	1:00
Oct. 20	at Green Bay	3:15
Oct. 27	**Indianapolis**	8:30
Nov. 3	at Seattle	1:15
Nov. 10	at Jacksonville	4:05
Nov. 17	at New York Giants	1:00
Nov. 24	**St. Louis**	4:15
Nov. 28	at Dallas (Thurs.)	3:05
Dec. 8	**New York Giants**	1:00
Dec. 15	at Philadelphia	1:00
Dec. 22	**Houston**	1:00
Dec. 29	**Dallas**	1:00

Stadium: FedEx Field (opened in 1997)
 • **Capacity:** 86,484
  1600 FedEx Way
  Landover, Maryland 20785
Playing Surface: Natural Grass
Training Camp: Dickinson College
   Carlisle, Pennsylvania
   17013

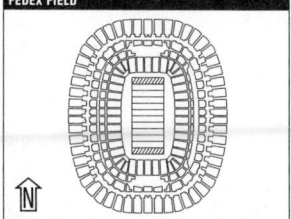

FEDEX FIELD

CLUB OFFICIALS
Owner: Daniel M. Snyder
Chief Operating Officer: David Pauken
Chief Marketing Officer: Steve Baldacci
Assistant General Manager:
 Bobby Mitchell
Senior Vice President: Karl Swanson
Senior Vice President, Stadium
 Operations: Michael Dillow
Vice President, Football Operations:
 Joe Mendes
Vice President, Football Operations:
 Pepper Rodgers
Contract Negotiator/Salary Cap:
 Mark Levin
Salary Cap Assistant: Dustin Nelson
Director of Player Personnel:
 Vinny Cerrato
Director of Pro Personnel:
 Scott Campbell
Pro Scouts: Louis Riddick,
 Dennis Murphy
Pro Personnel Assistant: Tim Gribble
Director of College Scouting: Ron Nay
College Scouts: Trent Baalke,
 Jim Nagy, Reggie Cobb,
 Shemy Schembechler
Director of Player Development:
 John Jefferson
Director of Public Relations:
 Michelle Tessier
Director of Publications: Casey Husband
Director of Community Affairs:
 Alex Hahn
Director of Football Administration:
 Jamie Speronis
Special Assistant of Football
 Administration: Bubba Tyer
Video Director: Rob Porteus
Assistant Video Director: Mike Bracken
Director of Ticket Operations: Jeff Ritter
Head Trainer: Dean Kleinschmidt
Assistant Trainer: Eric Steward,
 Larry Hess
Equipment Manager: Brad Berlin
Assistant Equipment Manager:
 Anders Beutel

COACHING HISTORY
Boston 1932-36
(509-447-27)
1932	Lud Wray	4-4-2
1933-34	William (Lone Star) Dietz	11-11-2
1935	Eddie Casey	2-8-1
1936-1942	Ray Flaherty	56-23-3
1943	Arthur (Dutch) Bergman	7-4-1
1944-45	Dudley DeGroot	14-6-1
1946-48	Glen (Turk) Edwards	16-18-1
1949	John Whelchel*	3-3-1
1949-1951	Herman Ball**	4-16-0
1951	Dick Todd	5-4-0
1952-53	Earl (Curly) Lambeau	10-13-1
1954-58	Joe Kuharich	26-32-2
1959-1960	Mike Nixon	4-18-2
1961-65	Bill McPeak	21-46-3
1966-68	Otto Graham	17-22-3
1969	Vince Lombardi	7-5-2
1970	Bill Austin	6-8-0
1971-77	George Allen	69-35-1
1978-1980	Jack Pardee	24-24-0
1981-1992	Joe Gibbs	140-65-0
1993	Richie Petitbon	4-12-0
1994-2000	Norv Turner***	50-60-1
2000	Terry Robiskie	1-2-0
2001	Marty Schottenheimer	8-8-0

*Released after seven games in 1949
**Released after three games in 1951
***Released after 13 games in 2000

ATTENDANCE
Home 661,970   Away 511,933
Total 1,173,903
Single-game home record,
84,936 (12/16/01)
Single-season home record, 661,970
(2001)

2002 DRAFT CHOICES
Round	Name	Pos.	College
1	Patrick Ramsey	QB	Tulane
2	Ladell Betts	RB	Iowa
3	Rashad Bauman	DB	Oregon
	Cliff Russell	WR	Utah
5	Andre Lott	DB	Tennessee
	Robert Royal	TE	Louisiana State
6	Reggie Coleman	T	Tennessee
7	Jeff Grau	TE	UCLA
	Greg Scott	DE	Hampton
	Rock Cartwright	RB	Kansas State

<footer>**2002 NFL Record & Fact Book**   **229**</footer>

2001 TEAM RECORD
PRESEASON (1-3)

Date	Result	Opponent
8/12	L 0-20	at Kansas City
8/17	L 6-27	Atlanta
8/24	W 27-25	Cleveland
8/30	L 13-33	at New England

REGULAR SEASON (8-8)

Date	Result	Opponent	Att.
9/09	L 3-30	at San Diego	60,629
9/24	L 0-37	at Green Bay	59,771
9/30	L 13-45	Kansas City	76,573
10/07	L 9-23	at New York Giants	78,651
10/15	L 7-9	at Dallas	63,941
10/21	W 17-14	Carolina (OT)	74,480
10/28	W 35-21	New York Giants	80,316
11/04	W 27-14	Seattle	82,352
11/18	W 17-10	at Denver	74,622
11/25	W 13-3	at Philadelphia	65,666
12/02	L 14-20	Dallas	85,112
12/09	W 20-10	at Arizona	40,056
12/16	L 6-20	Philadelphia	84,936
12/23	L 15-20	Chicago	78,884
12/30	W 40-10	at New Orleans	70,020
1/06	W 20-17	Arizona	61,721

(OT) Overtime

SCORE BY PERIODS

Redskins	65	80	54	79	3 —	281
Opponents	63	91	39	76	0 —	269

2001 TEAM STATISTICS

	Redskins	Opp.
Total First Downs	241	271
Rushing	104	103
Passing	122	149
Penalty	15	19
3rd Down: Made/Att	79/223	76/210
3rd Down Pct.	35.4	36.2
4th Down: Made/Att	4/13	5/17
4th Down Pct.	30.8	29.4
Possession Avg.	30:15	29:45
Total Net Yards	4435	4846
Avg. Per Game	277.2	302.9
Total Plays	960	982
Avg. Per Play	4.6	4.9
Net Yards Rushing	1948	1869
Avg. Per Game	121.8	116.8
Total Rushes	490	484
Net Yards Passing	2487	2977
Avg. Per Game	155.4	186.1
Sacked/Yards Lost	38/229	25/139
Gross Yards	2716	3116
Att./Completions	432/235	473/262
Completion Pct.	54.4	55.4
Had Intercepted	13	23
Punts/Average	91/41.5	77/42.3
Net Punting Avg.	91/34.7	77/34.7
Penalties/Yards	104/828	83/672
Fumbles/Ball Lost	33/15	31/11
Touchdowns	25	33
Rushing	10	10
Passing	13	19
Returns	2	4

2001 INDIVIDUAL STATISTICS

PASSING	Att.	Comp.	Yds.	Pct.	TD	Int.	Tkld.	Rate
Banks	370	198	2386	53.5	10	10	29/173	71.3
George	42	23	168	54.8	0	3	6/38	34.6
Graham	19	13	131	68.4	2	0	2/16	122.9
Lockett	1	1	31	100.0	1	0	0/0	158.3
Metcalf	0	0	0	—	0	0	1/2	—
Redskins	432	235	2716	54.4	13	13	38/229	71.1
Opponents	473	262	3116	55.4	19	23	25/139	68.8

SCORING	TD R	TD P	TD Rt	PAT	FG	Saf	PTS
Conway	0	0	0	22/22	26/33	0	100
Davis	5	0	0	0/0	0/0	0	32
Gardner	0	4	0	0/0	0/0	0	24
Westbrook	0	4	0	0/0	0/0	0	24
Carter	3	0	0	0/0	0/0	0	18
Banks	2	0	0	0/0	0/0	0	12
Flemister	0	2	0	0/0	0/0	0	12
Rasby	0	2	0	0/0	0/0	0	12
Arrington	0	0	1	0/0	0/0	0	6
Metcalf	0	0	1	0/0	0/0	0	6
Thompson	0	1	0	0/0	0/0	0	6
Bennett	0	0	0	0/0	0/0	0	2
Redskins	10	13	2	22/22	26/33	1	256
Opponents	10	19	4	33/33	24/29	0	303

2-Pt. Conversions: Bennett, Davis.
Redskins 2-3, Opponents 0-0.

RUSHING	Att.	Yds.	Avg.	LG	TD
Davis	356	1432	4.0	32	5
Carter	63	308	4.9	30	3
Banks	47	152	3.2	17	2
Bennett	10	39	3.9	8	0
Gardner	1	16	16.0	16	0
Westbrook	2	8	4.0	8	0
George	4	0	0.0	2	0
Graham	7	-7	-1.0	0	0
Redskins	490	1948	4.0	32	10
Opponents	484	1869	3.9	46	10

RECEIVING	No.	Yds.	Avg.	LG	TD
Westbrook	57	664	11.6	76t	4
Gardner	46	741	16.1	85t	4
Davis	28	205	7.3	29	0
Lockett	22	293	13.3	34	0
Flemister	18	196	10.9	33	2
Bennett	15	112	7.5	30	0
Carter	13	83	6.4	15	0
Rasby	10	128	12.8	27	2
Johnson	9	129	14.3	32	0
Alexander	9	85	9.4	21	0
Metcalf	4	19	4.8	9	0
Thompson	3	52	17.3	31t	1
Battaglia	1	9	9.0	9	0
Redskins	235	2716	11.6	85t	13
Opponents	262	3116	11.9	64t	19

INTERCEPTIONS	No.	Yds.	Avg.	LG	TD
Smoot	5	36	7.2	36	0
Arrington	3	120	40.0	67t	1
Bailey	3	17	5.7	12	0
Shade	2	9	4.5	9	0
Terrell	2	0	0.0	0	0
Wilkinson	2	0	0.0	0	0
Lang	1	14	14.0	14	0
Ohalete	1	12	12.0	12	0
Leverette	1	1	1.0	1	0
Da. Green	1	0	0.0	0	0
Lyle	1	0	0.0	0	0
Pierce	1	0	0.0	0	0
Redskins	23	209	9.1	67t	1
Opponents	13	247	19.0	61t	2

PUNTING	No.	Yds.	Avg.	In 20	LG
Barker	90	3747	41.6	27	59
Conway	1	28	28.0	1	28
Redskins	91	3775	41.5	28	59
Opponents	77	3260	42.3	20	72

PUNT RETURNS	No.	FC	Yds.	Avg.	LG	TD
Metcalf	33	5	412	12.5	89t	1
Lockett	5	3	14	2.8	11	0
Bates	2	2	5	2.5	5	0
McClellion	1	0	0	0.0	0	0
Redskins	41	10	431	10.5	89t	1
Opponents	44	16	434	9.9	84t	1

KICKOFF RETURNS	No.	Yds.	Avg.	LG	TD
Bates	49	1150	23.5	41	0
Carter	8	111	13.9	27	0
Johnson	4	51	12.8	18	0
Thompson	3	17	5.7	17	0
Metcalf	1	25	25.0	25	0
Redskins	65	1354	20.8	41	0
Opponents	54	945	17.5	44	0

FIELD GOALS	1-19	20-29	30-39	40-49	50+
Conway	0/0	8/8	8/11	8/12	2/2
Redskins	0/0	8/8	8/11	8/12	2/2
Opponents	0/0	9/9	10/10	3/7	2/3

SACKS	No.
Smith	5.0
M. Coleman	4.5
Lang	4.0
Wilkinson	4.0
Mitchell	2.0
DeLoach	1.0
Lyle	1.0
Mason	1.0
Pierce	1.0
Terrell	1.0
Arrington	0.5
Redskins	25.0
Opponents	38.0

RECORD HOLDERS

INDIVIDUAL RECORDS—CAREER

Category	Name	Performance
Rushing (Yds.)	John Riggins, 1976-79, 1981-85	7,472
Passing (Yds.)	Joe Theismann, 1974-1985	25,206
Passing (TDs)	Sammy Baugh, 1937-1952	187
Receiving (No.)	Art Monk, 1980-1993	888
Receiving (Yds.)	Art Monk, 1980-1993	12,028
Interceptions	Darrell Green, 1983-2001	54
Punting (Avg.)	Sammy Baugh, 1937-1952	*45.1
Punt Return (Avg.)	Johnny Williams, 1952-53	12.8
Kickoff Return (Avg.)	Bobby Mitchell, 1962-68	28.5
Field Goals	Mark Moseley, 1974-1986	263
Touchdowns (Tot.)	Charley Taylor, 1964-1977	90
Points	Mark Moseley, 1974-1986	1,206

INDIVIDUAL RECORDS—SINGLE SEASON

Category	Name	Performance
Rushing (Yds.)	Stephen Davis, 2001	1,432
Passing (Yds.)	Jay Schroeder, 1986	4,109
Passing (TDs)	Sonny Jurgensen, 1967	31
Receiving (No.)	Art Monk, 1984	106
Receiving (Yds.)	Bobby Mitchell, 1963	1,436
Interceptions	Dan Sandifer, 1948	13
Punting (Avg.)	Sammy Baugh, 1940	*51.4
Punt Return (Avg.)	Johnny Williams, 1952	15.3
Kickoff Return (Avg.)	Mike Nelms, 1981	29.7
Field Goals	Mark Moseley, 1983	33
Touchdowns (Tot.)	John Riggins, 1983	24
Points	Mark Moseley, 1983	161

INDIVIDUAL RECORDS—SINGLE GAME

Category	Name	Performance
Rushing (Yds.)	Gerald Riggs, 9-17-89	221
Passing (Yds.)	Sammy Baugh, 10-31-43	446
Passing (TDs)	Sammy Baugh, 10-31-43, 11-23-47	6
	Mark Rypien, 11-10-91	6
Receiving (No.)	Art Monk, 12-15-85, 11-4-90	13
	Kelvin Bryant, 12-7-86	13
Receiving (Yds.)	Anthony Allen, 10-4-87	255
Interceptions	Sammy Baugh, 11-14-43	*4
	Dan Sandifer, 10-31-48	*4
Field Goals	Many times	5
	Last time by Chip Lohmiller, 10-25-92	
Touchdowns (Tot.)	Dick James, 12-17-61	4
	Larry Brown, 12-16-73	4
Points	Dick James, 12-17-61	24
	Larry Brown, 12-16-73	24

*NFL Record

2002 VETERAN ROSTER

No.	Name	Pos.	Ht.	Wt.	Birthdate	NFL Exp.	College	Hometown	How Acq.	'01 Games/ Starts
77	Albright, Ethan	LS	6-5	268	5/1/71	8	North Carolina	Greensboro, N.C.	FA-'01	16/0
84	Anthony, Reidel	WR	5-11	180	10/20/76	6	Florida	South Bay, Fla.	UFA(TB)-'02	13/4*
98	Armstead, Jessie	LB	6-1	240	10/26/70	10	Miami	Dallas, Texas	UFA(NYG)-'02	16/16*
74	Arp, Donovan	DT	6-3	293	1/12/78	2	Louisville	Salt Lake City, Utah	FA-'01	0*
56	Arrington, LaVar	LB	6-3	246	6/20/78	3	Penn State	Pittsburgh, Pa.	D1-'00	14/14
24	Bailey, Champ	CB	6-0	192	6/22/78	4	Georgia	Folkston, Ga.	D1-'99	16/16
4	Barker, Bryan	P	6-1	200	6/28/64	13	Santa Clara	Jacksonville Beach, Fla.	UFA(Jax)-'01	16/0
54	Brandt, David	G-T	6-4	309	9/25/77	2	Michigan	Grant Rapids, Mich.	FA-'01	13/1
5	Conway, Brett	K	6-2	207	3/8/75	6	Penn State	Lilburn, Ga.	UFA(NYJ)-'01	16/0
91	Cowsette, Delbert	DT	6-1	288	9/3/77	2	Maryland	Cleveland, Ohio	FA-'00	16/0
57	Curry, Donte'	LB	6-1	233	7/22/78	2	Morris Brown	College Park, Ga.	FA-'00	8/0
48	Davis, Stephen	RB	6-0	235	3/1/74	7	Auburn	Spartanburg, S.C.	D4-'96	16/16
19	Doering, Chris	WR	6-4	195	5/19/73	5	Florida	Gainesville, Fla.	FA-'02	0*
71	Dotson, Santana	DT	6-5	287	12/19/69	11	Baylor	Houston, Texas	FA-'02	16/13*
89	Flemister, Zeron	TE	6-4	249	9/8/76	3	Iowa	Sioux City, Iowa	FA-'00	16/1
87	Gardner, Rod	WR	6-2	218	10/26/77	2	Clemson	Jacksonville, Fla.	D1-'01	16/16
28	Green, Darrell	CB	5-9	187	2/15/60	20	Texas A&I	Houston, Texas	D1-'83	16/4
80	Green, Jacquez	WR	5-10	175	1/15/76	5	Florida	Fort Valley, Ga.	UFA(TB)-'02	12/10*
25	Greer, Donovan	CB	5-9	178	9/11/74	5	Texas A&M	Houston, Texas	UFA(Buff)-'01	2/0
76	Jansen, Jon	T	6-6	311	1/28/76	4	Michigan	Clawson, Mich.	D2-'99	16/16
47	Johnson, Bryan	FB	6-1	234	1/18/79	2	Boise State	Pocatello, Idaho	FA-'00	16/1
61	Jones, Rod	T-G	6-5	335	1/11/74	7	Kansas	Detroit, Mich.	UFA(StL)-'02	6/1*
93	Leverette, Otis	DE	6-6	275	5/31/78	2	Alabama-Birmingham	Americus, Ga.	FA-'01	4/0
83	Lockett, Kevin	WR	6-0	186	9/8/74	6	Kansas State	Tulsa, Okla.	UFA(KC)-'01	16/0
66 t-	Loverne, David	G	6-3	299	5/22/76	3	San Jose State	Concord, Calif.	T(NYJ)-'02	16/0*
97	Marshall, Lemar	LB	6-2	208	12/17/76	2	Michigan State	Cincinnati, Ohio	FA-'01	0*
53	Mason, Eddie	LB	6-0	233	1/9/72	6	North Carolina	Siler City, N.C.	UFA(Jax)-'99	15/1
6	Matthews, Shane	QB	6-3	196	6/1/70	9	Florida	Pascagoula, Miss.	FA-'02	4/3*
55	Mitchell, Kevin	LB	6-1	250	1/1/71	8	Syracuse	Harrisburg, Pa.	UFA(NO)-'00	13/13
52	Moore, Larry	G-T	6-2	296	6/1/75	5	Brigham Young	La Mesa, Calif.	UFA(Ind)-'02	11/1*
26	Ohalete, Ifeanyi	DB	6-2	217	5/22/79	2	Southern California	Springfield, Ill.	FA-'01	16/0
58	Pierce, Antonio	LB	6-1	232	10/26/78	2	Arizona	Long Beach, Calif.	FA-'01	16/7
71	Powell, Carl	DE-DT	6-2	272	1/4/74	4	Louisville	Detroit, Mich.	UFA(Chi)-'02	16/0*
86	Rasby, Walter	TE	6-3	256	9/7/72	9	Wake Forest	Charlotte, N.C.	UFA(Det)-'01	16/11
18	Rosenfels, Sage	QB	6-4	216	3/6/78	2	Iowa State	Maquoketa, Iowa	D4-'01	0*
60	Samuels, Chris	T	6-5	303	7/28/77	3	Alabama	Mobile, Ala.	D1-'00	16/16
22	Serwanga, Kato	CB	6-0	202	7/23/76	4	California	Kampala, Uganda	FA-'01	11/0
29	Shade, Sam	S	6-0	205	6/14/73	8	Alabama	Birmingham, Ala.	UFA(Cin)-'99	16/15
78	Smith, Bruce	DE	6-4	261	6/18/63	18	Virginia Tech	Norfolk, Va.	UFA(Buff)-'00	14/14
21	Smoot, Fred	CB	5-11	172	4/17/79	2	Mississippi State	Jackson, Miss.	D2-'01	14/13
31	Terrell, David	CB	6-0	187	7/8/75	3	Texas-El Paso	Cedar Hill, Texas	FA-'00	16/16
88 †	Thompson, Derrius	WR	6-2	216	7/5/77	3	Baylor	Cedar Hill, Texas	FA-'99	16/0
54	Trotter, Jeremiah	LB	6-1	262	1/20/77	5	Stephen F. Austin	Hooks, Texas	UFA(Phil)-'02	16/16*
68	Tucker, Ross	T-G	6-4	305	3/2/79	2	Princeton	Wyomissing, Pa.	FA-'01	3/0
70	Vickers, Kipp	G-T	6-2	300	8/27/69	8	Miami	Holiday, Fla.	FA-'02	16/14*
95	Wilkinson, Dan	DT	6-4	325	3/13/73	9	Ohio State	Dayton, Ohio	T(Cin)-'98	16/16
17 t-	Wuerffel, Danny	QB	6-1	212	5/27/74	6	Florida	Pensacola, Fla.	T(Hou)-'02	1/0*
97	Wynn, Renaldo	DL	6-3	280	9/3/74	6	Notre Dame	Chicago, Ill.	UFA(Jax)-'02	16/16*

* Anthony played 13 games with Tampa Bay in '01; Armstead played 16 games with N.Y. Giants; Arp inactive for 10 games; Doering last active with Denver in '99; Dotson played 16 games with Green Bay; Green played 12 games with Tampa Bay; Jones played 6 games with St. Louis; Loverne played 16 games with N.Y. Jets; Marshall inactive for 2 games; Matthews played 4 games with Chicago; Moore played 11 games with Indianapolis; Powell played 16 games with Chicago; Rosenfels inactive for 14 games; Trotter played 16 games with Philadelphia; Wuerffel played 1 game with Chicago; Vickers played 16 games with Baltimore; Wynn played 16 games with Jacksonville.

† Restricted free agent; subject to developments.

t- Redskins traded for Loverne (NYJ) and Wuerffel (Hou).

Traded—DT Jerry DeLoach (15 games in '01) to Houston.

Players lost through Expansion Draft (1): G Matthew Campbell (11 games in '01)

Players lost through free agency (9): TE Stephen Alexander (SD; 7 games in '01), LB Shawn Barber (Phil; 3), TE Marco Battaglia (TB; 3), QB Kent Graham (Hou; 3), LB Robert Jones (Hou; 15), DE-DT Kenard Lang (Cle; 16), S Keith Lyle (Atl; 16), C Cory Raymer (SD; 16), G-T Dave Szott (NYJ; 16).

Also played with Redskins in '01—QB Tony Banks (15), KR Michael Bates (16), FB Donnell Bennett (16), RB Ki-Jana Carter (14), G Ben Coleman (15), DE Marco Coleman (12), QB Jeff George (2), LB Donny Green (1), PR Eric Metcalf (10), WR Michael Westbrook (16), DE-DT Tyrone Williams (4).

2002 FIRST-YEAR ROSTER

Name	Pos.	Ht.	Wt.	Birthdate	College	Hometown	How Acq.
Bauman, Rashad	CB	5-8	181	5/7/79	Oregon	Phoenix, Ariz.	D3
Beck, Wil	DT	6-2	329	11/10/79	Idaho	Veradale, Wash.	FA
Betts, Ladell	RB	5-10	221	8/27/79	Iowa	Blue Springs, Mo.	D2
Boldin, Ron	G-T	6-5	318	4/6/78	Florida State	Pahokee, Fla.	FA
Buttone, Thad (1)	FB	6-0	257	5/21/79	Troy State	Atlanta, Ga.	FA
Cartwright, Rock	FB	5-7	239	12/3/79	Kansas State	Conroe, Texas	D7
Coleman, Reggie	T	6-5	297	11/4/78	Tennessee	Jonesboro, Ark.	D7
Dailey, Jauron (1)	LB	6-3	232	2/20/78	Florida A&M	Miami, Fla.	FA-'01
Engelhardt, Tim (1)	DT	6-2	296	5/12/78	New Mexico State	Edwards Air Force Base, Calif.	FA
Finney, Shamar	LB	6-3	241	1/13/80	Penn State	Shelby, N.C.	FA
Floyd, Otis (1)	LB	6-1	237	6/13/76	Louisville	South Field, Mich.	FA
Frantz, Dan (1)	K-P	6-1	192	7/9/77	Portland State	Vancouver, Wash.	FA
Gillespie, Robert	RB	5-9	190	11/2/79	Florida	Hattiesburg, Miss.	FA
Grant, Kenneth (1)	CB	6-0	205	1/7/79	Kentucky	Austin, Texas	FA
Grant, Tony	LS	6-2	257	12/31/78	Michigan State	Bay City, Mich.	FA
Grau, Jeff	LS	6-3	257	12/16/79	UCLA	Torrance, Calif.	D7
Harper, Scott (1)	T	6-5	294	12/13/77	Marshall	Grand Bay, Ala.	FA-'01
Hires, Leon (1)	T-G	6-4	297	12/6/77	Florida	Bradenton, Fla.	FA
Israel, Ron	CB-S	6-0	212	1/5/78	Notre Dame	Lawnside, N.J.	FA
Jackson, Bernard	DT	6-4	281	5/10/80	Tennessee	Louisville, Ky.	FA
Jackson, Ladairis (1)	DE	6-2	261	6/16/79	Oregon State	Gardena, Calif.	FA
Johnson, Emmett	WR	6-3	202	3/17/80	Virginia Tech	Chesapeake, Va.	FA
Joseph, Ricot	DB	6-0	185	3/13/80	Central Florida	Lake Worth, Fla.	FA
Keith, Dustin (1)	C	6-5	295	8/8/77	Virginia	Yorktown, Va.	FA
Landrigan, Charlie	FB	5-11	232	10/24/78	Southern California	Mission Viejo, Calif.	FA
Lott, Andre	CB-S	5-10	194	5/31/79	Tennessee	Memphis, Tenn.	D7
Marshall, Lemar (1)	LB	6-2	228	12/17/76	Michigan State	Cincinnati, Ohio	FA-'01
Martin, Du'Shon	DB	6-0	207	4/28/79	Appalachian State	Atlanta, Ga.	FA
McCants, Darnerien (1)	WR	6-3	210	8/1/78	Delaware State	Odenton, Md.	D5-'01
Mercer, Ivan (1)	TE	6-6	227	9/19/79	Miami	Antelope Valley, Calif.	FA
Paige, Melvin	G-T	6-5	315	10/23/79	South Carolina	Dillon, S.C.	FA
Powell, Sean (1)	DT	6-1	298	1/23/74	New Mexico State	Long Beach, Calif.	FA
Ramsey, Patrick	QB	6-2	217	2/14/79	Tulane	Ruston, La.	D1
Royal, Robert	TE	6-4	253	5/15/79	Louisiana State	New Orleans, La.	D6
Russell, Cliff	WR	5-11	186	2/8/79	Utah	Ewa Beach, Hawaii	D3
Scott, Greg	DE	6-4	258	10/2/79	Hampton	Courtland, Va.	D7
Simmons, Terrence (1)	G-T	6-8	310	5/3/76	Alabama State	Prichard, Ala.	FA-'01
Skaggs, Justin (1)	WR	6-2	202	4/22/79	Evangel	Wentzville, Mo.	FA-'01
Smith, Akil	T-G	6-4	301	12/28/79	Clemson	Richmond, Va.	FA
Smith, Chandler (1)	DB	6-1	201	3/29/76	Southern Mississippi	Vicksburg, Miss.	FA
Smith, Wayne	T-G	6-2	305	11/17/79	Appalachian State	Pembroke Pines, Fla.	FA
Stephens, Leonard (1)	TE	6-3	249	7/9/78	Howard	Princeton Junction, N.J.	FA
Sulfsted, Alex (1)	T-G	6-3	320	12/21/77	Miami (Ohio)	Cincinnati, Ohio	FA-'01
Thomas, Anthony	DT-DE	6-2	319	3/1/79	Arizona	Pasadena, Calif.	FA
Washington, Mark (1)	CB	5-8	187	4/16/73	Rutgers	Temple Hills, Md.	FA
Watkins, Jimmy	RB	6-0	203	11/25/78	Applachian State	Elberten, Ga.	FA
Watson, Kenny (1)	HB	5-11	214	3/13/78	Penn State	Harrisburg, Pa.	FA-'01

The term NFL Rookie is defined as a player who is in his first season of professional football and has not been on the roster of another professional football team for any regular-season or postseason games. A Rookie is designated by an "R" on NFL rosters. Players who have been active in another professional football league or players who have NFL experience, including either preseason training camp or being on an Active List or Inactive List, or on Reserve/Injured or Reserve/Physically Unable to Perform for fewer than six regular-season games, are termed NFL First-Year Players. An NFL First-Year Player is designated by a "1" on NFL rosters. Thereafter, a player is credited with an additional year of experience for each season in which he accumulates six games on the Active List or Inactive List, or on Reserve/Injured or Reserve/Physically Unable to Perform.

COACHING STAFF
Head Coach,
Steve Spurrier
Pro Career: Steve Spurrier joined the Washington Redskins as the organization's twenty-third head coach in January 2002. The former Heisman Trophy winner amassed a stunning 122-27-1 record in his 12 years as head coach of the University of Florida Gators, including the 1996 national championship. Spurrier's teams won seven Southeastern Conference titles, and he had 10 or more wins in nine of his seasons with the Gators. His list of achievements include the best win total in history for a major college coach over his first 12 seasons, and reaching 100 career victories faster than any major college coach in the 20th century. He began his coaching career in 1978 as quarterbacks coach at his alma mater, Florida, before moving to Georgia Tech as offensive coordinator and quarterbacks coach for the 1979 season. He joined the Duke Blue Devils in the same capacity from 1980-82, and then moved on to the USFL as the head coach of the Tampa Bay Bandits. With the Bandits from 1983-85, Spurrier compiled a 35-19 record with two straight playoff appearances. His 1984 team was the first in pro football history to produce a 4,000-yard passer and two 1,000-yard rushers in the same season. He returned to Duke as head coach in 1987 and turned around a moribund program to produce winning seasons after his initial 5-6 year. During his three-year tenure, he compiled a 20-13-1 record and in 1989 led the team to its first Atlantic Coast Conference (ACC) title in 24 years. In each of his three seasons, the Blue Devils averaged more than 300 yards per game passing, the only team in ACC history to accomplish that feat.
Background: He began coaching following the completion of a 10-year career as an NFL quarterback on the heels of his 1966 Heisman Trophy. He was the Florida Gators starting quarterback for three years and was voted first team All-American in both 1865 and 1966. He was named to the National Collegiate Football Hall of Fame in 1986. As the first-round pick of the 49ers in the 1967 NFL Draft, he played quarterback for San Francisco from 1967-1975 and for the Tampa Bay Buccaneers in 1976.
Personal: Spurrier was born April 20, 1945 in Miami Beach, Florida. Steve and his wife Jerri have four children and seven grandchildren.

ASSISTANT COACHES
Noah Brindise, asst. quarterbacks; born March 3, 1975, St. Thomas, Virgin Islands, lives in Potomac Falls, Va. Quarterback Florida 1995-97. No pro playing experience. College coach: Ursinius College (Pa.) 1998, Florida 1999-

2001. Pro coach: Joined Redskins in 2002.
DeChon Burns, asst. defensive line-quality control; born June 6, 1970, Riverdale, Calif., lives in Sterling, Va. Cornerback Southern California 1989-90. No pro playing experience. College coach: Southern California 1992-1993, Florida 2001. Pro coach: Joined Redskins in 2002.
George Catavolos, defensive backs; born May 8, 1945, Chicago, lives in Zionsville, Ind. Defensive back Purdue 1964-67. No pro playing experience. College coach: Purdue 1967-68, 1971-76, Middle Tennessee State 1969, Louisville 1970, Kentucky 1977-1981, Tennessee 1982-83. Pro coach: Indianapolis Colts 1984-1994, 1998-2001, Carolina Panthers 1995-97, joined Redskins in 2002.
Jim Collins, asst. special teams; born September 30, 1952, Greensboro, N.C., lives in Leesburg, Va. Attended Elon College. No college or pro playing experience. College Coach: Lees-McRae (Kan.) J.C. 1980, Appalachian State 1981-82, Duke 1983, 1985-89, Jacksonville State 1984, Florida 1990-2001. Pro coach: Joined Redskins in 2002.
George Edwards, linebackers; born January 16, 1967, Siler City, N.C., lives in Coppell, Texas. Linebacker Duke 1985-89. No pro playing experience. College coach: Florida 1990-91, Appalachian State 1992-95, Duke 1996, Georgia 1997. Pro coach: Dallas Cowboys 1998-2001, joined Redskins in 2002.
John Hastings, asst. strength and conditioning; born July 5, 1964, Newport News, Va., lives in Ashburn, Va. Attended Ohio University. No college or pro playing experience. Pro coach: San Diego Chargers 1990-2001, joined Redskins in 2002.
Kim Helton, offensive line; born July 28, 1948, Pensacola, Fla., lives in Hamilton, Va. Center Florida 1967-1970. No pro playing experience. College coach: Florida 1972-78, Miami 1979-1982, Houston (head coach) 1993-99. Pro coach: Tampa Bay Buccaneers 1983-86, Houston Oilers 1987-89, Los Angeles Raiders 1990-92, joined Redskins in 2002.
Lawson Holland, tight ends; born September 29, 1952, Mooresville, N.C., lives in Leesburg, Va. Quarterback Clemson 1970-74. No pro playing experience. College Coach: Clemson 1975, 1979-1985, Duke 1977, North Carolina 1986-87, Wake Forest 1988-91, Oklahoma State 1992-94, Florida 1995-2001. Pro coach: Joined Redskins in 2002.
Ricky Hunley, defensive line; born November 11, 1961, Petersburg, Va., lives in Ashburn, Va. Linebacker Arizona 1980-83. Pro linebacker Denver Broncos 1984-1987, Los Angeles Raiders 1989-1990. College coach: Southern California 1992-93, Missouri 1994-2000, Florida 2001. Pro coach: Joined Redskins in

2002.
John Hunt, asst. offensive line; born November 6, 1962, Orlando, Fla., lives in Ashburn, Va. Guard Florida 1980-83. Pro guard Dallas Cowboys 1984, Tampa Bay Buccaneers 1985. College coach: Florida 1989-1991, 1999-2001. Pro coach: Joined Redskins in 2002.
Hue Jackson, running backs; born October 22, 1965, Los Angeles, lives in Ashburn, Va. Quarterback Pacific 1985-1986. No pro playing experience. College coach: Pacific 1987-89, Cal State-Fullerton 1990, Arizona State 1992-95, California 1996, Southern California 1997-2000. Pro coach: London Monarchs (WFL) 1991, joined Redskins in 2001.
Marvin Lewis, asst. head coach-defensive coordinator; born September 23, 1958, McDonald, Pa., lives in Finksburg, Md. Linebacker Idaho State 1977-1980. No pro playing experience. College coach: Idaho State 1981-84, Long Beach State 1985-86, New Mexico 1987-89, Pittsburgh 1990-91. Pro coach: Pittsburgh Steelers 1992-95, Baltimore Ravens 1999-2001, joined Redskins in 2002.
Chip Morton, strength and conditioning; born November 27, 1962, Hamden, Conn., lives in Ashburn, Va. Attended North Carolina. No college or pro experience. College coach: Ohio State 1985-86, Penn State 1987-1992. Pro coach: San Diego Chargers 1992-94, Carolina Panthers 1995-98, Baltimore Ravens 1999-2001, joined Redskins in 2002.
Kirk Olivadotti, asst. defensive backs; born January 1, 1974, Wilmington, Del., lives in Ashburn, Va. Wide receiver Purdue 1992-1996. No pro playing experience. College coach: Maine Maritime Academy 1997, Indiana State 1998-99. Pro coach: Joined Redskins in 2000.
Steve Spurrier Jr., wide receivers; born September 26, 1971, Palo Alto, Calif., lives in Leesburg, Va.. Wide receiver Duke 1992-93. No pro playing experience. College coach: Florida 1994-1996, Oklahoma 1999-2001. Pro coach: Joined Redskins in 2002.
Mike Stock, special teams; born September 29, 1939, Baberton, Ohio, lives in Leesburg, Va. Fullback Northwestern 1957-60. Pro running back Saskatchewan Roughriders (CFL) 1961. College coach: Northwestern 1961, Buffalo 1966-67, Navy 1968, Notre Dame 1969-1974, 1984-1986, Wisconsin 1975-78, Eastern Michigan 1979-1983 (head coach), Ohio State 1992-94. Pro coach: Cincinnati Bengals 1987-1991, Kansas City Chiefs 1995-2000, joined Redskins in 2001.

2001 Season in Review

2001 TRADES

Quarterback **Matt Hasselbeck** and Green Bay's first-round selection in 2001 (#17) from the Packers to Seattle for the Seahawks' first-round selection in 2001 (#10) and third-round selection in 2001 (#72). (3/5)

Quarterback **Eric Zeier** from Tampa Bay to Atlanta for the Falcons' seventh-round selection in 2001. (3/6)

Linebacker **Jeff Gooch** from Tampa Bay to St. Louis for Denver's fifth-round selection in 2001. (3/19)

Defensive end **Kevin Carter** from St. Louis to Tennessee for the Titans' first-round selection in 2001 (#29). (4/4)

San Diego's first-round selection in 2001 (#1) from the Chargers to Atlanta for wide receiver **Tim Dwight**, the Falcons' first-round selection in 2001 (#5), the Falcons' third-round selection in 2001 (#67), and the Falcons' second-round selection in 2002. (4/20)

Tight end **Roland Williams** from St. Louis to Oakland for the Raiders' fourth-round selection in 2001. (4/21)

San Francisco's second-round selection in 2001 (#41), the 49ers' third-round selection in 2001 (#71), and the 49ers' fourth-round selection in 2001 (#105) from the 49ers to Green Bay for the Packers' second-round selection in 2001 (#47), the Packers' third-round selection in 2001 (#80), New Orleans' third-round selection in 2001 (#82), the Packers' sixth-round selection in 2001 (#179), and St. Louis's seventh-round selection in 2001 (#222). (4/21)

Quarterback **Trent Green** and St. Louis's first-round selection in 2001 (#150) from St. Louis to Kansas City for the Chiefs' first-round selection in 2001 (#12). (4/21)

Dallas's first-round selection in 2001 (#7) and Oakland's sixth-round selection in 2001 (#191) from Seattle to San Francisco for the 49ers' first-round selection in 2001 (#9), New Orleans's third-round selection in 2001 (#82), and St. Louis's seventh-round selection in 2001 (#222). (4/21)

Buffalo's first-round selection in 2001 (#14) from the Bills to Tampa Bay for the Buccaneers' first-round selection in 2001 (#21) and the Buccaneers' second-round selection in 2001 (#51). (4/21)

Pittsburgh's first-round selection in 2001 (#16) from the Steelers to the New York Jets for the Jets' first-round selection in 2001 (#19), the Jets' fourth-round selection in 2001 (#111), and the Jets' sixth-round selection in 2001 (#181). (4/21)

Indianapolis's first-round selection in 2001 (#22) from the Colts to the New York Giants for the Giants' first-round

selection in 2001 (#30), the Giants' third-round selection in 2001 (#91), and the Giants' sixth-round selection in 2001 (#193). (4/21)

Dallas's second-round selection in 2001 (#37) from the Cowboys to Indianapolis for the Colts' second-round selection in 2001 (#52) and the Colts' third-round selection in 2001 (#81). (4/21)

New England's second-round selection in 2001 (#39) from the Patriots to Pittsburgh for the Steelers' second-round selection in 2001 (#50) and the Steelers' fourth-round selection in 2001 (#112). (4/21)

Defensive back **Aeneas Williams** from Arizona to St. Louis for the Rams' second-round selection in 2001 (#54) and Oakland's fourth-round selection in 2001 (#123). (4/21)

Detroit's second-round selection in 2001 (#48) from the Lions to New England for Pittsburgh's second-round selection in 2001 (#50) and San Francisco's sixth-round selection in 2001 (#173). (4/21)

Tampa Bay's second-round selection in 2001 (#51) from Buffalo to Denver for the Broncos' second-round selection in 2001 (#58) and the Bills' fourth-round selection in 2001 (#110). (4/21)

Indianapolis's second-round selection in 2001 (#52) from Dallas to Miami for the Dolphins' second-round selection in 2001 (#56) and the Dolphins' fourth-round selection in 2001 (#122). (4/21)

New Orleans's second-round selection in 2001 (#53) from the Saints to Dallas for the Cowboys' third-round selection in 2001 (#70) and Indianapolis's third-round selection in 2001 (#81). (4/21)

The New York Giants' second-round selection in 2001 (#61) from the Giants to Detroit for the Lions' third-round selection in 2001 (#78) and the Lions' fourth-round selection in 2001 (#114). (4/21)

New England's third-round selection in 2001 (#69) from the Patriots to Minnesota for the Vikings' third-round selection in 2001 (#86) and the Vikings' fourth-round selection in 2001 (#119). (4/21)

Miami's second-round selection in 2002 from the Dolphins to Philadelphia for the Eagles' third-round selection in 2001 (#88) and the Eagles' sixth-round selection in 2001 (#187). (4/21)

San Diego's fourth-round selection in 2001 (#96) from the Chargers to New England for Pittsburgh's fourth-round selection in 2001 (#112) and the Patriots' fifth-round selection in 2001 (#139). (4/22)

Washington's fifth-round selection in 2001 (#145) from the Redskins to St. Louis for Denver's fifth-round selection in 2001 (#154) and the Rams' sixth-round

selection in 2001 (#186). (4/22)

The New York Jets' fifth-round selection in 2001 (#149) from New England to Detroit for the Lions' sixth-round selection in 2001 (#180) and the Lions' seventh-round selection in 2001 (#216). (4/22)

New England's sixth-round selection in 2001 (#170) from the Patriots to Jacksonville for the Jaguars' fifth-round selection in 2002. (4/22)

Atlanta's fourth-round selection in 2002 from the Falcons to Denver for Washington's seventh-round selection in 2001 (#215), Green Bay's seventh-round selection in 2001 (#219), and the Broncos' seventh-round selection in 2001 (#226). (4/22)

Running back **Robert Arnaud** from New Orleans to Washington for a future unannounced selection choice. (7/20)

Linebacker **Henri Crockett** from Denver to Atlanta for the Falcons' seventh-round selection in 2002. (8/2)

Tight end **Bobby Collins** from Buffalo to Green Bay for Defensive End **David Bowens.** (8/7)

Tackle **Everett Lindsay** from Cleveland to Minnesota for the Vikings' seventh-round selection in 2002. (8/15)

Quarterback **Cade McNown** and Chicago's earliest selection in the seventh round of 2002 from the Bears to Miami for the Dolphins' sixth-round selection in 2002 and an unannounced future selection choice. (8/22)

Running back **Chad Morton** from New Orleans to the New York Jets for defensive back **Earthwind Moreland** and the Jets' sixth-round selection in 2002. (8/23)

Wide receiver **Darrin Chiaverini** from Cleveland to Dallas for Miami's seventh-round selection in 2002. (8/28)

Running back **Travis Prentice**, quarterback **Spergon Wynn**, and Minnesota's seventh-round selection in 2002 from Cleveland to Minnesota for the Vikings' fifth-round selection in 2002 and an unannounced future selection choice. (9/2)

Quarterback **Ty Detmer** and Cleveland's sixth-round selection in 2002 from the Browns to Detroit for the Lions' fourth-round selection in 2002 and the Lions' sixth-round selection in 2002. (9/2)

Defensive back **Perry Phenix** from Tennessee to Carolina for the Panthers' seventh-round selection in 2002. (9/2)

Defensive tackle **Rod Walker** from Tennessee to Green Bay for the Packers' seventh-round selection in 2002. (9/2)

Quarterback **Joe Germaine** from St. Louis to Kansas City for the Chiefs' sixth-round selection in 2002. (9/3)

Defensive end **Stalin Colinet** and an unannounced future selection choice from Cleveland to the Vikings for an unannounced future selection choice. (10/16)

2002 TRADES

Quarterback **Danny Wuerffel** from Houston to Washington for defensive tackle **Jerry DeLoach**. (3/4)

Running back **Ricky Williams** and the Saints' fourth-round selection in 2002 from New Orleans to Miami for the Dolphins' first-round selection in 2002, their fourth-round selection in 2002, and an unannounced future selection choice. (3/8)

Running back **J.J. Johnson** from Miami to Cleveland for an unannounced future selection choice. (3/11)

Wide receiver **Terry Glenn** from New England to Green Bay for the Packers' fourth-round selection in 2002. (3/11)

Tackle **Willie Roaf** from New Orleans to Kansas City for an unannounced future selection choice. (3/27)

Defensive back **Jacoby Shepherd** from St. Louis to Houston for an unannounced future selection choice. (3/28)

Tackle **David Loverne** and the New York Jets' fifth-round selection in 2002 from the Jets to Washington for the Redskins' fifth-round selection in 2002. (4/9)

Wide receiver **Terrence Wilkins** from Indianapolis to St. Louis for Kansas City's sixth-round selection in 2002. (4/15)

Linebacker **Jay Foreman** from Buffalo to Houston for running back **Charlie Rogers**. (4/18)

Quarterback **Brock Huard** from Seattle to Indianapolis for the Colts' fifth-round selection in 2002 (#146). (4/19)

Dallas's first-round selection in 2002 (#6) from Dallas to Kansas City for the Chiefs' first-round selection in 2002 (#8), the Chiefs' third-round selection in 2002 (#75), and an unannounced future selection choice. (4/20)

Tennessee's first-round selection in 2002 (#14) from the Titans to the New York Giants for the Giants' first-round selection in 2002 (#15) and the Giants' fourth-round selection in 2002 (#110). (4/20)

Washington's first-round selection in 2002 (#18) from the Redskins to Oakland for Tampa Bay's first-round selection in 2002 (#21) and the Raiders' third-round selection in 2002 (#89). (4/20)

Atlanta's first-round selection in 2002 (#17) from the Falcons to Oakland for Washington's first-round selection in 2002 (#18) and the Raiders' fifth-round selection in 2002 (#158). (4/20)

Seattle's first-round selection in 2002 (#20) and fifth-round selection in 2002 (#156) from the Seahawks to Green Bay for the Packers' first-round selection in 2002 (#28) and the Packers' second-round selection in 2002 (#60). (4/20)

Tampa Bay's first-round selection in 2002 (#21) from Washington to New England for the Patriots' first-round selection in 2002 (#32), the Patriots' third-round selection in 2002 (#96), and the Patriots' seventh-round selection in 2002 (#234). (4/20)

Washington's second-round selection in 2002 (#52) and New England's third-round selection in 2002 (#96) from the Redskins to Baltimore for the Ravens' second-round selection in 2002 (#56), the Ravens' third-round selection in 2002 (#87), and the Ravens' fifth-round selection in 2002 (#159). (4/20)

San Francisco's second-round selection in 2002 (#61) from the 49ers to Buffalo for the Bills' third-round selection in 2002 (#69) and the Bills' fourth-round selection in 2002 (#102). (4/20)

Chicago's second-round selection in 2002 (#63) and Chicago's fourth-round selection in 2002 (#129) from the Bears to Dallas for the Cowboys' third-round selection in 2002 (#72), the Cowboys' fourth-round selection in 2002 (#104), and the Cowboys' fifth-round selection in 2002 (#140). (4/20)

Carolina's third-round selection in 2002 (#67) from the Panthers to Cincinnati for the Bengals' third-round selection in 2002 (#73) and the Bengals' fifth-round selection in 2002 (#145). (4/20)

Linebacker **Wali Rainer** and Cleveland's third-round selection in 2002 (#79) from the Browns to Jacksonville for the Jaguars' third-round selection in 2002 (#76). (4/20)

Cleveland's third-round selection in 2002 (#79) from Jacksonville to Washington for Oakland's third-round selection in 2002 (#89) and the Redskins' fourth-round selection in 2002 (#118). (4/20)

New England's third-round selection in 2002 (#112) from Baltimore to Denver for Atlanta's fourth-round selection in 2002 (#112) and the Broncos' fifth-round selection in 2002 (#155). (4/20)

Houston's fourth-round selection in 2002 (#116) from the Texans to Atlanta for the Falcons' third-round selection in 2003. (4/21)

Denver's fourth-round selection in 2002 (#117) from the Broncos to New England for the Patriots' fourth-round selection in 2002 (#131) and Jacksonville's fifth-round selection in 2002 (#144). (4/21)

Oakland's fourth-round selection in 2002 (#122) from the Raiders to Cleveland for the Browns' fifth-round selection in 2002 (#147) and the Browns' sixth-round selection in 2002 (#189). (4/21)

New England's fifth-round selection in 2002 (#168) from the Patriots to Dallas for Miami's seventh-round selection in 2002 (#237) and the Cowboys' fifth-round selection in 2003. (4/21)

Quarterback **Drew Bledsoe** from New England to Buffalo for the Bills' first-round selection in 2003. (4/22)

Punter **David Leaverton** from the New York Jets to Tampa Bay for wide receiver **Jonathan Pittman**. (4/23)

PRESEASON STANDINGS
AMERICAN FOOTBALL CONFERENCE

Eastern Division

	W	L	T	Pct.	Pts.	OP
New England	3	1	0	.750	73	41
Buffalo	2	2	0	.500	36	57
Indianapolis	2	2	0	.500	98	93
N.Y. Jets	2	2	0	.500	55	50
Miami	1	4	0	.200	66	91

Central Division

	W	L	T	Pct.	Pts.	OP
Pittsburgh	3	1	0	.750	67	47
Tennessee	3	1	0	.750	92	79
Cleveland	2	2	0	.500	62	59
Jacksonville	2	2	0	.500	68	93
Baltimore	1	2	0	.333	58	45
Cincinnati	1	3	0	.250	67	83

Western Division

	W	L	T	Pct.	Pts.	OP
Denver	3	1	0	.750	93	59
San Diego	3	1	0	.750	64	70
Oakland	3	2	0	.600	78	75
Kansas City	2	2	0	.500	70	58
Seattle	2	2	0	.500	90	76

AFC PRESEASON RECORDS—TEAM BY TEAM

Eastern Division

BUFFALO (2-2)

10	St. Louis	24
6	Philadelphia	3
20	at Cincinnati	10
0	at Pittsburgh	20
36		57

INDIANAPOLIS (2-2)

28	Seattle	21
26	Detroit	27
21	at Minnesota	28
23	at Cincinnati	17
98		93

MIAMI (1-4)

10	St. Louis (a)	17
17	at Tampa Bay	14
20	San Diego (OT)	23
12	at Green Bay	17
7	Minnesota	20
66		91

NEW ENGLAND (3-1)

14	N.Y. Giants	0
23	at Carolina	8
3	at Tampa Bay	20
33	Washington	13
73		41

N.Y. JETS (2-2)

10	Atlanta	20
16	Baltimore	3
17	at N.Y. Giants	14
12	at Philadelphia	13
55		50

Central Division

BALTIMORE (1-2)

	at Philadelphia (b)	
3	at N.Y. Jets	16
17	Carolina	20
38	N.Y. Giants	9
58		45

CINCINNATI (1-3)

13	at Chicago (OT)	16
27	at Detroit	24
10	Buffalo	20
17	Indianapolis	23
67		83

CLEVELAND (2-2)

10	Green Bay	3
7	Tampa Bay	6
25	at Washington	27
20	at Carolina	23
62		59

JACKSONVILLE (2-2)

18	Carolina	16
5	at N.Y. Giants	27
28	Kansas City	23
17	at Dallas	27
68		93

PITTSBURGH (3-1)

17	at Atlanta	16
10	at Minnesota	24
20	Detroit	7
20	Buffalo	0
67		47

TENNESSEE (3-1)

27	Chicago	24
23	at St. Louis	10
14	Philadelphia	20
28	at Detroit	25
92		79

Western Division

DENVER (3-1)

20	at Dallas	6
7	at Green Bay	22
31	New Orleans	24
35	San Francisco	7
93		59

KANSAS CITY (2-2)

20	Washington	0
10	Chicago	9
23	at Jacksonville	28
17	at St. Louis	21
70		58

OAKLAND (3-2)

21	Dallas	14
10	at Arizona	7
17	at San Francisco	20
6	vs. Dallas (c)	21
24	Green Bay	13
78		75

SAN DIEGO (3-1)

25	San Francisco	24
23	at Miami (OT)	20
13	St. Louis (OT)	10
3	at Arizona	16
64		70

SEATTLE (2-2)

21	at Indianapolis	28
13	Arizona (OT)	16
28	at San Francisco	18
28	New Orleans	14
90		76

(a) Pro Football Hall of Fame Game at Canton, Ohio
(b) Game canceled
(c) American Bowl at Mexico City, Mexico

NFC PRESEASON RECORDS—TEAM BY TEAM

Eastern Division
ARIZONA (3-1)

7	Oakland	10
16	at Seattle (OT)	13
24	at Chicago	20
16	San Diego	3
63		46

DALLAS (2-3)

14	at Oakland	21
6	Denver	20
10	at New Orleans	16
21	Oakland (c)	6
27	Jacksonville	17
78		80

N.Y. GIANTS (1-3)

0	at New England	14
27	Jacksonville	5
14	N.Y. Jets	17
9	at Baltimore	38
50		74

PHILADELPHIA (2-1)

	Baltimore (b)	
3	at Buffalo	6
20	at Tennessee	14
13	N.Y. Jets	12
36		32

WASHINGTON (1-3)

0	at Kansas City	20
6	Atlanta	27
27	Cleveland	25
13	at New England	33
46		105

Central Division
CHICAGO (1-3)

16	Cincinnati (OT)	13
24	at Tennessee	27
9	at Kansas City	10
20	Arizona	24
69		74

DETROIT (1-3)

24	Cincinnati	27
27	at Indianapolis	26
7	at Pittsburgh	20
25	Tennessee	28
83		101

GREEN BAY (2-2)

3	at Cleveland	10
22	Denver	7
17	Miami	12
13	at Oakland	24
55		53

MINNESOTA (4-0)

28	at New Orleans	21
24	Pittsburgh	10
28	Indianapolis	21
20	at Miami	7
100		59

TAMPA BAY (1-3)

14	Miami	17
6	at Cleveland	7
20	New England	3
7	at Atlanta	36
47		63

Western Division
ATLANTA (3-1)

16	Pittsburgh	17
20	at N.Y. Jets	10
27	at Washington	6
36	Tampa Bay	7
99		40

CAROLINA (2-2)

16	at Jacksonville	18
8	New England	23
20	at Baltimore	17
23	Cleveland	20
67		78

NEW ORLEANS (1-3)

21	Minnesota	28
16	Dallas	10
24	at Denver	31
14	at Seattle	28
75		97

ST. LOUIS (3-2)

17	Miami (a)	10
24	at Buffalo	10
10	Tennessee	23
10	at San Diego (OT)	13
21	Kansas City	17
82		73

SAN FRANCISCO (1-3)

24	at San Diego	25
20	Oakland	17
18	Seattle	28
7	at Denver	35
69		105

(a) Pro Football Hall of Fame Game at Canton, Ohio
(b) Game canceled
(c) American Bowl at Mexico City, Mexico

PRESEASON STANDINGS
NATIONAL FOOTBALL CONFERENCE
Eastern Division

	W	L	T	Pct.	Pts.	OP
Arizona	3	1	0	.750	63	46
Philadelphia	2	1	0	.667	36	32
Dallas	2	3	0	.400	78	80
N.Y. Giants	1	3	0	.250	50	74
Washington	1	3	0	.250	46	105

Central Division

	W	L	T	Pct.	Pts.	OP
Minnesota	4	0	0	1.000	100	59
Green Bay	2	2	0	.500	55	53
Chicago	1	3	0	.250	69	74
Detroit	1	3	0	.250	83	101
Tampa Bay	1	3	0	.250	47	63

Western Division

	W	L	T	Pct.	Pts.	OP
Atlanta	3	1	0	.750	99	40
St. Louis	3	2	0	.600	82	73
Carolina	2	2	0	.500	67	78
New Orleans	1	3	0	.250	75	97
San Francisco	1	3	0	.250	69	105

AMERICAN FOOTBALL CONFERENCE

BALTIMORE (10-6)

17	CHICAGO	6
10	at Cincinnati	21
20	at Denver	13
26	TENNESSEE	7
23	at Green Bay	31
14	at Cleveland	24
18	JACKSONVILLE	17
13	at Pittsburgh	10
16	at Tennessee	10
17	CLEVELAND	27
24	at Jacksonville	21
39	INDIANAPOLIS	27
21	PITTSBURGH	26
16	CINCINNATI	0
10	at Tampa Bay	22
19	MINNESOTA	3
303		**265**

BUFFALO (3-13)

6	NEW ORLEANS	24
26	at Indianapolis	42
3	PITTSBURGH	20
36	NEW YORK JETS	42
13	at Jacksonville	10
24	at San Diego	27
14	INDIANAPOLIS	30
11	at New England	21
20	SEATTLE	23
27	MIAMI	34
0	at San Francisco	35
25	CAROLINA	24
9	NEW ENGLAND (OT)	12
30	at Atlanta	33
14	at New York Jets	9
7	at Miami	34
265		**420**

CINCINNATI (6-10)

23	NEW ENGLAND	17
21	BALTIMORE	10
14	at San Diego	28
7	at Pittsburgh	16
24	CLEVELAND	14
0	CHICAGO	24
31	at Detroit	27
13	at Jacksonville	30
7	TENNESSEE	20
0	at Cleveland	18
13	TAMPA BAY (OT)	16
10	JACKSONVILLE	14
14	at New York Jets	15
0	at Baltimore	16
26	PITTSBURGH (OT)	23
23	at Tennessee	21
226		**309**

CLEVELAND (7-9)

6	SEATTLE	9
24	DETROIT	14
23	at Jacksonville	14
20	SAN DIEGO	16
14	at Cincinnati	24
24	BALTIMORE	14
21	at Chicago (OT)	27
12	PITTSBURGH (OT)	15
27	at Baltimore	17
18	CINCINNATI	0
15	TENNESSEE	31
16	at New England	27
10	JACKSONVILLE	15
7	at Green Bay	30
41	at Tennessee	38
7	at Pittsburgh	28
285		**319**

DENVER (8-8)

31	NEW YORK GIANTS	20
38	at Arizona	17
13	BALTIMORE	20
20	KANSAS CITY	6
21	at Seattle	34
10	at San Diego	27
31	NEW ENGLAND	20
28	at Oakland	38
26	SAN DIEGO	16
10	WASHINGTON	17
26	at Dallas	24
10	at Miami	21
20	SEATTLE	7
23	at Kansas City (OT)	26
23	OAKLAND	17
10	at Indianapolis	29
340		**339**

INDIANAPOLIS (6-10)

45	at New York Jets	24
42	BUFFALO	26
13	at New England	44
18	OAKLAND	23
17	NEW ENGLAND	38
35	at Kansas City	28
30	at Buffalo	14
24	MIAMI	27
20	at New Orleans	34
21	SAN FRANCISCO	40
27	at Baltimore	39
6	at Miami	41
41	ATLANTA	27
28	NEW YORK JETS	29
17	at St. Louis	42
29	DENVER	10
413		**486**

JACKSONVILLE (6-10)

21	PITTSBURGH	3
13	TENNESSEE	6
14	CLEVELAND	23
15	at Seattle	24
10	BUFFALO	13
17	at Baltimore	18
24	at Tennessee	28
30	CINCINNATI	13
7	at Pittsburgh	20
21	BALTIMORE	24
21	GREEN BAY	28
14	at Cincinnati	10
15	at Cleveland	10
33	at Minnesota	3
26	KANSAS CITY	30
13	at Chicago	33
294		**286**

KANSAS CITY (6-10)

24	OAKLAND	27
3	NEW YORK GIANTS	13
45	at Washington	13
6	at Denver	20
17	PITTSBURGH	20
16	at Arizona	24
28	INDIANAPOLIS	35
25	at San Diego	20
7	at New York Jets	27
19	SEATTLE	7
10	PHILADELPHIA	23
26	at Oakland	28
26	DENVER (OT)	23
20	SAN DIEGO	17
30	at Jacksonville	26
18	at Seattle	21
320		**344**

MIAMI (11-5)

31	at Tennessee	23
18	OAKLAND	15
10	at St. Louis	42
30	NEW ENGLAND	10
17	at New York Jets	21
24	at Seattle	20
23	CAROLINA	6
27	at Indianapolis	24
0	NEW YORK JETS	24
34	at Buffalo	27
21	DENVER	10
41	INDIANAPOLIS	6
0	at San Francisco	21
13	at New England	20
21	ATLANTA	14
34	BUFFALO	7
344		**290**

NEW ENGLAND (11-5)

17	at Cincinnati	23
3	NEW YORK JETS	10
44	INDIANAPOLIS	13
10	at Miami	30
29	SAN DIEGO (OT)	26
38	at Indianapolis	17
20	at Denver	31
24	at Atlanta	10
21	BUFFALO	11
17	ST. LOUIS	24
34	NEW ORLEANS	17
17	at New York Jets	16
27	CLEVELAND	16
12	at Buffalo (OT)	9
20	MIAMI	13
38	at Carolina	6
371		**272**

N.Y. JETS (10-6)

24	INDIANAPOLIS	45
10	at New England	3
17	SAN FRANCISCO	19
42	at Buffalo	36
21	MIAMI	17
14	ST. LOUIS	34
13	at Carolina	12
27	KANSAS CITY	7
24	at Miami	0
16	at New Orleans	9
16	NEW ENGLAND	17
7	at Pittsburgh	18
15	CINCINNATI	14
29	at Indianapolis	28
9	BUFFALO	14
24	at Oakland	22
308		**295**

OAKLAND (10-6)

27	at Kansas City	24
15	at Miami	18
38	SEATTLE	14
28	DALLAS	21
23	at Indianapolis	18
20	at Philadelphia	10
38	DENVER	28
27	at Seattle	34
34	SAN DIEGO	24
28	at New York Giants	10
31	ARIZONA (OT)	34
28	KANSAS CITY	26
13	at San Diego	6
10	TENNESSEE	13
17	at Denver	23
22	NEW YORK JETS	24
399		**327**

PITTSBURGH (13-3)

3	at Jacksonville	21
20	at Buffalo	3
16	CINCINNATI	7
20	at Kansas City	17
17	at Tampa Bay	10
34	TENNESSEE	7
10	BALTIMORE	13
15	at Cleveland (OT)	12
20	JACKSONVILLE	7
34	at Tennessee	24
21	MINNESOTA	16
18	NEW YORK JETS	7
26	at Baltimore	21
47	DETROIT	14
23	at Cincinnati (OT)	26
28	CLEVELAND	7
352		**212**

SAN DIEGO (5-11)

30	WASHINGTON	3
32	at Dallas	21
28	CINCINNATI	14
16	at Cleveland	20
26	at New England (OT)	29
27	DENVER	10
27	BUFFALO	24
20	KANSAS CITY	25
16	at Denver	26
24	at Oakland	34
17	ARIZONA	20
10	at Seattle (OT)	13
14	at Philadelphia	24
6	OAKLAND	13
17	at Kansas City	20
22	SEATTLE	25
332		**321**

SEATTLE (9-7)

9	at Cleveland	6
3	PHILADELPHIA	27
14	at Oakland	38
24	JACKSONVILLE	15
34	DENVER	21
20	MIAMI	24
14	at Washington	27
34	OAKLAND	27
23	at Buffalo	20
7	at Kansas City	19
13	SAN DIEGO (OT)	10
7	at Denver	20
29	DALLAS	3
24	at New York Giants	27
25	at San Diego	22
21	KANSAS CITY	18
301		**324**

TENNESSEE (7-9)

23	MIAMI	31
6	at Jacksonville	13
7	at Baltimore	26
31	TAMPA BAY (OT)	28
27	at Detroit	24
7	at Pittsburgh	34
28	JACKSONVILLE	24
10	BALTIMORE	16
20	at Cincinnati	7
24	PITTSBURGH	34
31	at Cleveland	15
24	at Minnesota	42
26	GREEN BAY	20
13	at Oakland	10
38	CLEVELAND	41
21	CINCINNATI	23
336		**388**

NATIONAL FOOTBALL CONFERENCE

ARIZONA (7-9)
17	DENVER	38
14	ATLANTA	34
21	at Philadelphia	20
13	at Chicago	20
24	KANSAS CITY	16
3	at Dallas	17
7	PHILADELPHIA	21
10	NEW YORK GIANTS	17
45	DETROIT	38
20	at San Diego	17
34	at Oakland (OT)	31
10	WASHINGTON	20
13	at New York Giants	17
17	DALLAS	10
30	at Carolina	7
17	at Washington	20
295		**343**

ATLANTA (7-9)
13	at San Francisco (OT)	16
24	CAROLINA	16
34	at Arizona	14
3	CHICAGO	31
31	SAN FRANCISCO (OT)	37
20	at New Orleans	13
10	NEW ENGLAND	24
20	DALLAS	13
23	at Green Bay	20
10	at Carolina	7
6	ST. LOUIS	35
10	NEW ORLEANS	28
27	at Indianapolis	41
33	BUFFALO	30
14	at Miami	21
13	at St. Louis	31
291		**377**

CAROLINA (1-15)
24	at Minnesota	13
16	at Atlanta	24
7	GREEN BAY	28
14	at San Francisco	24
25	NEW ORLEANS	27
14	at Washington (OT)	17
12	NEW YORK JETS	13
6	at Miami	23
14	at St. Louis	48
22	SAN FRANCISCO (OT)	25
7	ATLANTA	10
23	at New Orleans	27
24	at Buffalo	25
32	ST. LOUIS	38
7	ARIZONA	30
6	NEW ENGLAND	38
253		**410**

CHICAGO (13-3)
6	at Baltimore	17
17	MINNESOTA	10
31	at Atlanta	3
20	ARIZONA	13
24	at Cincinnati	0
37	SAN FRANCISCO (OT)	31
27	CLEVELAND (OT)	21
12	GREEN BAY	20
27	at Tampa Bay	24
13	at Minnesota	6
13	DETROIT	10
7	at Green Bay	17
27	TAMPA BAY	3
20	at Washington	15
24	at Detroit	0
33	JACKSONVILLE	13
338		**203**

DALLAS (5-11)
6	TAMPA BAY	10
21	SAN DIEGO	32
18	at Philadelphia	40
21	at Oakland	28
9	WASHINGTON	7
17	ARIZONA	13
24	at New York Giants (OT)	27
13	at Atlanta	20
3	PHILADELPHIA	36
24	DENVER	26
20	at Washington	14
20	NEW YORK GIANTS	13
3	at Seattle	29
10	at Arizona	17
27	SAN FRANCISCO	21
10	at Detroit	15
246		**338**

DETROIT (2-14)
6	at Green Bay	28
14	at Cleveland	24
0	ST. LOUIS	35
26	at Minnesota	31
24	TENNESSEE	27
27	CINCINNATI	31
13	at San Francisco	21
17	TAMPA BAY	20
38	at Arizona	45
27	GREEN BAY	29
10	at Chicago	13
12	at Tampa Bay	15
27	MINNESOTA	24
14	at Pittsburgh	47
0	CHICAGO	24
15	DALLAS	10
270		**424**

GREEN BAY (12-4)
28	DETROIT	6
37	WASHINGTON	0
28	at Carolina	7
10	at Tampa Bay	14
31	BALTIMORE	23
13	at Minnesota	35
21	TAMPA BAY	20
20	at Chicago	12
20	ATLANTA	23
29	at Detroit	27
28	at Jacksonville	21
17	CHICAGO	7
20	at Tennessee	26
30	CLEVELAND	7
24	MINNESOTA	13
34	at New York Giants	25
390		**266**

MINNESOTA (5-11)
13	CAROLINA	24
10	at Chicago	17
20	TAMPA BAY	16
15	at New Orleans	28
31	DETROIT	26
35	GREEN BAY	13
14	at Tampa Bay	41
17	at Philadelphia	48
28	NEW YORK GIANTS	16
6	CHICAGO	13
16	at Pittsburgh	21
42	TENNESSEE	24
24	at Detroit	27
3	JACKSONVILLE	33
13	at Green Bay	24
3	at Baltimore	19
290		**390**

NEW ORLEANS (7-9)
24	at Buffalo	6
13	at New York Giants	21
28	MINNESOTA	15
27	at Carolina	25
13	ATLANTA	20
34	at St. Louis	31
9	NEW YORK JETS	16
27	at San Francisco	28
34	INDIANAPOLIS	20
17	at New England	34
27	CAROLINA	23
28	at Atlanta	10
21	ST. LOUIS	34
21	at Tampa Bay	48
10	WASHINGTON	40
0	SAN FRANCISCO	38
333		**409**

N.Y. GIANTS (7-9)
20	at Denver	31
13	at Kansas City	3
21	NEW ORLEANS	13
23	WASHINGTON	9
14	at St. Louis	15
9	PHILADELPHIA	10
21	at Washington	35
27	DALLAS (OT)	24
17	at Arizona	10
16	at Minnesota	28
10	OAKLAND	28
13	at Dallas	20
17	ARIZONA	13
27	SEATTLE	24
21	at Philadelphia	24
25	GREEN BAY	34
294		**321**

PHILADELPHIA (11-5)
17	ST. LOUIS (OT)	20
27	at Seattle	3
40	DALLAS	18
20	ARIZONA	21
10	at New York Giants	9
10	OAKLAND	20
21	at Arizona	7
48	MINNESOTA	17
36	at Dallas	3
3	WASHINGTON	13
23	at Kansas City	10
24	SAN DIEGO	14
20	at Washington	6
3	at San Francisco	13
24	NEW YORK GIANTS	21
17	at Tampa Bay	13
343		**208**

ST. LOUIS (14-2)
20	at Philadelphia (OT)	17
30	at San Francisco	26
42	MIAMI	10
35	at Detroit	0
15	NEW YORK GIANTS	14
34	at New York Jets	14
31	NEW ORLEANS	34
48	CAROLINA	14
24	at New England	17
17	TAMPA BAY	24
35	at Atlanta	6
27	SAN FRANCISCO	14
34	at New Orleans	21
38	at Carolina	32
42	INDIANAPOLIS	17
31	ATLANTA	13
503		**273**

SAN FRANCISCO (12-4)
16	ATLANTA (OT)	13
26	ST. LOUIS	30
19	at New York Jets	17
24	CAROLINA	14
37	at Atlanta	31
31	at Chicago (OT)	37
21	DETROIT	13
28	NEW ORLEANS	27
25	at Carolina (OT)	22
40	at Indianapolis	21
35	BUFFALO	0
14	at St. Louis	27
21	MIAMI	0
13	PHILADELPHIA	3
21	at Dallas	27
38	at New Orleans	0
409		**282**

TAMPA BAY (9-7)
10	at Dallas	6
16	at Minnesota	20
14	GREEN BAY	10
28	at Tennessee (OT)	31
10	PITTSBURGH	17
41	MINNESOTA	14
20	at Green Bay	21
20	at Detroit	17
24	CHICAGO	27
24	at St. Louis	17
16	at Cincinnati (OT)	13
15	DETROIT	12
3	at Chicago	27
48	NEW ORLEANS	21
22	BALTIMORE	10
13	PHILADELPHIA	17
324		**280**

WASHINGTON (8-8)
3	at San Diego	30
0	at Green Bay	37
13	KANSAS CITY	45
9	at New York Giants	23
7	at Dallas	9
17	CAROLINA (OT)	14
35	NEW YORK GIANTS	21
27	SEATTLE	14
17	at Denver	10
13	at Philadelphia	3
14	DALLAS	20
20	at Arizona	10
6	PHILADELPHIA	20
15	CHICAGO	20
40	at New Orleans	10
20	ARIZONA	17
256		**303**

FINAL STANDINGS

AMERICAN FOOTBALL CONFERENCE

Eastern Division	W	L	T	Pct.	Pts.	OP
New England	11	5	0	.688	371	272
* Miami	11	5	0	.688	344	290
* New York Jets	10	6	0	.625	308	295
Indianapolis	6	10	0	.375	413	486
Buffalo	3	13	0	.188	265	420
Central Division						
# Pittsburgh	13	3	0	.813	352	212
* Baltimore	10	6	0	.625	303	265
Cleveland	7	9	0	.438	285	319
Tennessee	7	9	0	.438	336	388
Jacksonville	6	10	0	.375	294	286
Cincinnati	6	10	0	.375	226	309
Western Division						
Oakland	10	6	0	.625	399	327
Seattle	9	7	0	.563	301	324
Denver	8	8	0	.500	340	339
Kansas City	6	10	0	.375	320	344
San Diego	5	11	0	.313	332	321

NATIONAL FOOTBALL CONFERENCE

Eastern Division	W	L	T	Pct.	Pts.	OP
Philadelphia	11	5	0	.688	343	208
Washington	8	8	0	.500	256	303
New York Giants	7	9	0	.438	294	321
Arizona	7	9	0	.438	295	343
Dallas	5	11	0	.313	246	338
Central Division						
Chicago	13	3	0	.813	338	203
* Green Bay	12	4	0	.750	390	266
* Tampa Bay	9	7	0	.563	324	280
Minnesota	5	11	0	.313	290	390
Detroit	2	14	0	.125	270	424
Western Division						
# St. Louis	14	2	0	.875	503	273
* San Francisco	12	4	0	.750	409	282
New Orleans	7	9	0	.438	333	409
Atlanta	7	9	0	.438	291	377
Carolina	1	15	0	.063	253	410

*Wild-Card qualifier for playoffs
#Top playoff seed in conference

New England finished ahead of Miami based on better division record (6-2 to Dolphins' 5-3). Baltimore was second Wild Card ahead of N.Y. Jets based on better record against common opponents (3-2 to Jets' 2-2). Cleveland finished ahead of Tennessee based on better division record (5-5 to Titans' 3-7). Jacksonville finished ahead of Cincinnati based on head-to-head record (2-0). N.Y. Giants finished ahead of Arizona based on head-to-head record (2-0). Green Bay was first Wild Card ahead of San Francisco based on better conference record (9-3 to 49ers' 8-4). New Orleans finished ahead of Atlanta based on better division record (4-4 to Falcons' 3-5).

WILD-CARD PLAYOFFS

AFC
OAKLAND 38, New York Jets 24
Baltimore 20, MIAMI 3
NFC
PHILADELPHIA 31, Tampa Bay 9
GREEN BAY 25, San Francisco 15

DIVISIONAL PLAYOFFS

AFC
NEW ENGLAND 16, Oakland 13 (OT)
PITTSBURGH 27, Baltimore 10
NFC
Philadelphia 33, CHICAGO 19
ST. LOUIS 45, Green Bay 17

CHAMPIONSHIP GAMES

AFC
New England 24, PITTSBURGH 17
NFC
ST. LOUIS 29, Philadelphia 24

SUPER BOWL XXXVI

New England (AFC) 20, St. Louis (NFC) 17
at Louisiana Superdome, New Orleans, Louisiana

AFC-NFC PRO BOWL

AFC 38, NFC 30
at Aloha Stadium, Honolulu, Hawaii

Home teams in playoff games are indicated in CAPS.

FIRST WEEK SUMMARIES

American Football Conference

Eastern Division

	W	L	T	Pct.	Pts.	OP
Indianapolis	1	0	0	1.000	45	24
Miami	1	0	0	1.000	31	23
Buffalo	0	1	0	.000	6	24
New England	0	1	0	.000	17	23
N.Y. Jets	0	1	0	.000	24	45

Central Division

	W	L	T	Pct.	Pts.	OP
Baltimore	1	0	0	1.000	17	6
Cincinnati	1	0	0	1.000	23	17
Jacksonville	1	0	0	1.000	21	3
Cleveland	0	1	0	.000	6	9
Pittsburgh	0	1	0	.000	3	21
Tennessee	0	1	0	.000	23	31

Western Division

	W	L	T	Pct.	Pts.	OP
Denver	1	0	0	1.000	31	20
Oakland	1	0	0	1.000	27	24
San Diego	1	0	0	1.000	30	3
Seattle	1	0	0	1.000	9	6
Kansas City	0	1	0	.000	24	27

National Football Conference

Eastern Division

	W	L	T	Pct.	Pts.	OP
Arizona	0	0	0	.000	0	0
Dallas	0	1	0	.000	6	10
N.Y.-Giants	0	1	0	.000	20	31
Philadelphia	0	1	0	.000	17	20
Washington	0	1	0	.000	3	30

Central Division

	W	L	T	Pct.	Pts.	OP
Green Bay	1	0	0	1.000	28	6
Tampa Bay	1	0	0	1.000	10	6
Chicago	0	1	0	.000	6	17
Detroit	0	1	0	.000	6	28
Minnesota	0	1	0	.000	13	24

Western Division

	W	L	T	Pct.	Pts.	OP
Carolina	1	0	0	1.000	24	13
New Orleans	1	0	0	1.000	24	6
St. Louis	1	0	0	1.000	20	17
San Francisco	1	0	0	1.000	16	13
Atlanta	0	1	0	.000	13	16

SUNDAY, SEPTEMBER 9

SAN FRANCISCO 16, ATLANTA 13 (OT)—at 3Com Park, attendance 65,989. Jose Cortez made his 49ers' debut a memorable one when he kicked the tying field goal with eight seconds left in regulation, then converted the winning kick 4:04 into overtime. J.J. Stokes (47 yards), Terrell Owens (40), and Tai Streets (52) each turned short passes into long gains during the 49ers' final three scoring drives. Cortez sent the game into overtime with a 20-yard field goal, and his 24-yard field goal four plays after Streets' heroics lifted the 49ers to victory. Garcia was 26 of 40 for 335 yards and 1 touchdown, with 1 interception for the 49ers, which gained 260 of its 429 total yards in the fourth quarter and overtime. Chris Chandler was 11 of 18 for 121 yards.

Atlanta	7	3	3	0	0	— 13
San Francisco	0	3	0	10	3	— 16

Atl	—	J. Anderson 1 run (Feely kick)
SF	—	FG Cortez 39
Atl	—	FG Feely 28
Atl	—	FG Feely 24
SF	—	Stokes 16 pass from Garcia (Cortez kick)
SF	—	FG Cortez 20
SF	—	FG Cortez 24

CAROLINA 24, MINNESOTA 13—at Metrodome, attendance 64,108. Chris Weinke passed for 1 touchdown and ran for another in the Panthers' victory. Early in the fourth quarter, Deon Grant's interception gave Carolina the ball at the Vikings' 34 and led to Weinke's 1-yard sneak for an 11-point lead with 9:52 to go. Minnesota's last chance ended when Culpepper fumbled the ball out of the end zone for a touchback with 3:32 left. Weinke, a 29-year-old rookie who became the oldest drafted rookie to start

in his NFL debut since 1967, was 13 of 22 for 223 yards and 1 touchdown, with 1 interception. Rookie Steve Smith returned the opening kickoff 93 yards for a touchdown. Culpepper was 22 of 38 for 236 yards, with 3 interceptions.

Carolina	7	3	7	7	— 24
Minnesota	0	0	13	0	— 13

Car	—	Smith 93 kickoff return (Kasay kick)
Car	—	FG Kasay 23
Minn	—	Culpepper 7 run (Anderson kick)
Minn	—	Carter 12 pass from Culpepper (kick blocked)
Car	—	Muhammad 16 pass from Weinke (Kasay kick)
Car	—	Weinke 1 run (Kasay kick)

BALTIMORE 17, CHICAGO 6—at PSINet Stadium, attendance 69,365. The Super Bowl XXXV-champion Ravens opened the season with a strong defensive performance. Baltimore permitted a pair of field goals to the Bears, yet trailed 6-3 late in the third quarter. But Elvis Grbac completed 5 of 6 passes on an 87-yard drive, capped by a 6-yard touchdown pass to Sam Gash. The 10-6 advantage was enough for Baltimore's defense, which intercepted 2 passes late, including 1 by Ray Lewis that led to Terry Allen's clinching 1-yard touchdown run with 2:36 left. Grbac was 24 of 30 for 262 yards and 1 touchdown. Shane Matthews was 24 of 39 for 138 yards, with 2 interceptions.

Chicago	3	0	3	0	— 6
Baltimore	0	3	7	7	— 17

Chi	—	FG Edinger 20
Balt	—	FG Stover 37
Chi	—	FG Edinger 46
Balt	—	Gash 6 pass from Grbac (Stover kick)
Balt	—	Allen 1 run (Stover kick)

GREEN BAY 28, DETROIT 6—at Lambeau Field, attendance 59,523. Ahman Green rushed for 2 first-quarter touchdowns, and the Packers built a big first-quarter lead before coasting to the victory. Green ran 31 yards for a touchdown just 2:33 into the game, and 83 yards for a touchdown run to put the Packers ahead 21-0 with 4:29 still to play in the first quarter. Green went on to run for 157 yards on 17 carries. Brett Favre was 22 of 28 for 260 yards. Bill Schroeder had 4 receptions for 104 yards. Charlie Batch was 20 of 39 for 276 yards, with 2 interceptions. Johnnie Morton caught 5 passes for 111 yards.

Detroit	3	3	0	0	— 6
Green Bay	21	0	7	0	— 28

GB	—	A. Green 31 run (Longwell kick)
GB	—	Schroeder 23 pass from Favre (Longwell kick)
GB	—	A. Green 83 run (Longwell kick)
Det	—	FG Hanson 49
Det	—	FG Hanson 39
GB	—	Franks 1 pass from Favre (Longwell kick)

INDIANAPOLIS 45, N.Y. JETS 24—at Giants Stadium, attendance 78,606. Edgerrin James rushed for 135 yards and 2 touchdowns to key the Colts' victory. Peyton Manning tossed a 21-yard touchdown pass to Jerome Pathon with 1:29 left before the half, and Terrence Wilkins returned a punt 78 yards for a score just 20 seconds before halftime for a 31-14 lead. With 5:35 to play, Vinny Testaverde and guard David Loverne, who was lined up at fullback in the short-yardage situation, collided and the ball popped loose. Defensive end Chukie Nwokorie grabbed the ball and rumbled 95 yards for the game-clinching touchdown. Manning was 22 of 32 for 231 yards and 2 touchdowns, with 2 interceptions. Testaverde

was 17 of 25 for 175 yards and 2 touchdowns.

Indianapolis	3	28	7	7	— 45
N.Y. Jets	7	7	3	7	— 24

NYJ	—	Coles 38 pass from Testaverde (Hall kick)
Ind	—	FG Vanderjagt 37
Ind	—	James 29 run (Vanderjagt kick)
Ind	—	James 1 run (Vanderjagt kick)
NYJ	—	Martin 6 run (Hall kick)
Ind	—	Pathon 21 pass from Manning (Vanderjagt kick)
Ind	—	Wilkins 78 punt return (Vanderjagt kick)
NYJ	—	FG Hall 22
Ind	—	Pollard 4 pass from Manning (Vanderjagt kick)
NYJ	—	Anderson 5 pass from Testaverde (Hall kick)
Ind	—	Nwokorie 95 fumble return (Vanderjagt kick)

CINCINNATI 23, NEW ENGLAND 17—at Paul Brown Stadium, attendance 51,521. Corey Dillon rushed for 104 yards and a touchdown to lead the Bengals to the victory. Cincinnati scored on all of its third-quarter possessions, capped by Jon Kitna's 25-yard touchdown pass to Tony McGee for a 23-10 lead. New England 's comeback attempt was stalled when Drew Bledsoe was stopped inches short of a first down on a quarterback sneak on fourth-and-2 with 2:41 to play. Kitna was 18 of 27 for 204 yards. Scott had 104 yards on 5 catches. Bledsoe was 22 of 38 for 241 yards and 2 touchdowns.

New England	0	10	0	7	— 17
Cincinnati	0	10	13	0	— 23

NE	—	T. Brown 14 pass from Bledsoe (Vinatieri kick)
Cin	—	FG Rackers 36
NE	—	FG Vinatieri 39
Cin	—	Dillon 5 run (Rackers kick)
Cin	—	FG Rackers 47
Cin	—	FG Rackers 33
Cin	—	McGee 25 pass from Kitna (Rackers kick)
NE	—	Wiggins 8 pass from Bledsoe (Vinatieri kick)

NEW ORLEANS 24, BUFFALO 6—at Ralph Wilson Stadium, attendance 71,447. Aaron Brooks passed for 3 second-half touchdowns to rally the Saints. The Saints trailed 6-0 at halftime, and had just 65 yards, but Aaron Brooks' 46-yard touchdown pass to Albert Connell started the spree early in the third quarter, followed by 2 Sammy Knight interceptions, which led directly to 10 points and a 17-6 lead. Brooks was 18 of 29 for 209 yards and 3 touchdowns. Rob Johnson was 16 of 27 for 160 yards, with 3 interceptions. Knight tied a club record with all 3 interceptions.

New Orleans	0	0	17	7	— 24
Buffalo	3	3	0	0	— 6

Buff	—	FG Arians 37
Buff	—	FG Arians 22
NO	—	Connell 46 pass from Brooks (Carney kick)
NO	—	FG Carney 31
NO	—	Cleeland 12 pass from Brooks (Carney kick)
NO	—	R. Williams 19 pass from Brooks (Carney kick)

OAKLAND 27, KANSAS CITY 24—at Arrowhead Stadium, attendance 78,844. Sebastian Janikowski's 31-yard field goal with 15 seconds left capped a wild finish. Rich Gannon's 15-yard touchdown pass to Jon Ritchie with 3:19 left snapped a 17-17 tie. But Kansas City countered with a 10-play, 80-yard march to a touchdown, capped by Green's 30-yard strike to rookie Marvin Minnis with 1:21 to play. David Dunn returned the ensuing kickoff 40 yards to the Chiefs' 49, and Gannon and Brown teamed on a 33-yard pass play to set up the winning kick. Gannon was 31 of 46 for 341 yards and 2 touchdowns, with 1 interception. Brown had 8 catches for 133 yards and 1 touchdown, while Jerry Rice caught 8 passes for 87 yards in his Oakland debut. Green was 16 of 37 for 222 yards and 1 touchdown, with 1 interception.

Oakland	6	0	8	13	—	27
Kansas City	7	7	3	7	—	24

KC — Warfield 51 interception return (Peterson kick)
Oak — FG Janikowski 43
Oak — FG Janikowski 43
KC — Richardson 3 run (Peterson kick)
KC — FG Peterson 31
Oak — T. Brown 33 pass from Gannon (Gannon run)
Oak — FG Janikowski 36
Oak — Ritchie 15 pass from Gannon (Janikowski kick)
KC — Minnis 30 pass from Green (Peterson kick)
Oak — FG Janikowski 31

JACKSONVILLE 21, PITTSBURGH 3—at ALLTEL Stadium, attendance 63,785. Mark Brunell passed for 3 touchdowns, all in the second quarter, to lead the Jaguars. Following 2 touchdown passes to Jimmy Smith, Hardy Nickerson forced Hines Ward to fumble. Marlon McCree recovered to set up Brunell's third touchdown pass. The rest of the game was played in a rainstorm. Pittsburgh drove into Jacksonville territory on three of its six second-half possessions, but turned the ball over on an interception, fumble, and once on downs. Brunell was 15 of 26 for 198 yards. Smith had 8 receptions for 126 yards. Kordell Stewart was 21 of 37 for 181 yards, with 2 interceptions.

Pittsburgh	0	3	0	0	—	3
Jacksonville	0	21	0	0	—	21

Pitt — FG Brown 41
Jax — J. Smith 34 pass from Brunell (Hollis kick)
Jax — J. Smith 15 pass from Brunell (Hollis kick)
Jax — Jones 1 pass from Brunell (Hollis kick)

ST. LOUIS 20, PHILADELPHIA 17 (OT)—at Veterans Stadium, attendance 66,243. Jeff Wilkins kicked a 26-yard field goal 7:56 into overtime for the Rams. The Eagles trailed 17-3 when Troy Vincent's interception at Philadelphia's 2-yard line with 2:13 left in the third quarter started an 18-play, 98-yard touchdown drive got them back into the game, capped by Donovan McNabb's 1-yard toss to Cecil Martin with 10:01 to play. McNabb passed or carried on all nine plays of the Eagles' next possession, a 69-yard drive, to the tying touchdown with 3:59 to play. Philadelphia was forced to punt after taking the ball first in overtime. Kurt Warner completed passes of 20 and 27 yards to Isaac Bruce to move into field-goal range to set up Wilkins' winning kick. Warner was 28 of 42 for 308 yards and 1 touchdown, with 2 interceptions. McNabb was 32 of 48 for 312 yards and 2 touchdowns, with 1 interception.

St. Louis	7	7	3	0	3	— 20
Philadelphia	3	0	0	14	0	— 17

StL — Faulk 7 run (Wilkins kick)
Phil — FG Akers 50
StL — Conwell 2 pass from Warner (Wilkins kick)
StL — FG Wilkins 20

Phil — Martin 1 pass from McNabb (Akers kick)
Phil — Martin 7 pass from McNabb (Akers kick)
StL — FG Wilkins 26

SEATTLE 9, CLEVELAND 6—at Cleveland Browns Stadium, attendance 72,318. Rian Lindell kicked a 52-yard field goal with three seconds remaining to lift the Seahawks. The defenses dominated a game in which the two teams combined for only 490 total yards. The Browns reached Seattle's 7 with 3:06 left while trailing 6-3, but had to settle for Phil Dawson's game-tying field goal at the 2:14 mark. Charlie Rogers broke free for a 49-yard kickoff return to set up Lindell's winning kick. Matt Hasselbeck was 20 of 34 for 178 yards in his first NFL start, with 2 interceptions. Tim Couch was 17 of 33 for 176 yards, with 1 interception.

Seattle	0	3	3	3	—	9
Cleveland	0	3	0	3	—	6

Cle — FG Dawson 48
Sea — FG Lindell 49
Sea — FG Lindell 23
Cle — FG Dawson 22
Sea — FG Lindell 52

TAMPA BAY 10, DALLAS 6—at Texas Stadium, attendance 61,521. Brad Johnson ran 1 yard for the game's only touchdown early in the fourth quarter to help the Buccaneers win for the first time ever in Dallas. The Cowboys had a chance to score late, starting at the Buccaneers' 39 with 2:00 left, but Quincy Carter's fourth-down pass from the 38 was intercepted by John Lynch, and the Buccaneers ran out the last 1:15 to secure the victory. Carter, a rookie in his first NFL start, was 9 of 19 for 34 yards, with 2 interceptions. Brad Johnson was 26 of 35 for 195 yards, with 1 interception. Tampa Bay's defense allowed 127 yards.

Tampa Bay	3	0	0	7	—	10
Dallas	3	0	3	0	—	6

TB — FG Gramatica 39
Dall — FG Seder 22
Dall — FG Seder 46
TB — B. Johnson 1 run (Gramatica kick)

SAN DIEGO 30, WASHINGTON 3—at Qualcomm Stadium, attendance 60,629. Rookie LaDainian Tomlinson rushed for 2 touchdowns in his first NFL game to lead the Chargers to an easy victory. Tim Dwight returned a punt 84 yards for a touchdown just 3:29 into the game as the Chargers matched their win total from 2000. Tomlinson, who carried 36 times for 113 yards, had a 3-yard touchdown run to put the Chargers ahead 17-0 in the second quarter and capped the scoring with a 1-yard touchdown run in the fourth period. The Redskins managed only 8 first downs, fumbled 7 times, losing 2, and suffered 2 interceptions. Doug Flutie was 10 of 18 for 129 yards, with 2 interceptions. Jeff George was 8 of 18 for 66 yards before giving way to Tony Banks.

Washington	0	0	3	0	—	3
San Diego	10	10	0	10	—	30

SD — Dwight 84 punt return (Richey kick)
SD — FG Richey 21
SD — Tomlinson 3 run (Richey kick)
SD — FG Richey 48
Wash — FG Conway 40
SD — FG Richey 32
SD — Tomlinson 1 run (Richey kick)

SUNDAY NIGHT, SEPTEMBER 9

MIAMI 31, TENNESSEE 23—at Adelphia Coliseum, attendance 68,798. Jay Fiedler passed for 2 touchdowns to lead the Dolphins to their tenth consecutive victory on Kickoff Weekend. Miami's string of 10

opening-game victories is second in NFL history to the 17 in a row that Dallas won from 1965-1981. The Titans cut the deficit to 24-14 on Steve McNair's 29-yard touchdown pass to Derrick Mason, but McNair injured his shoulder on the play and did not return to the game. His backup, Neil O'Donnell, passed for 110 yards and a touchdown but also suffered 2 interceptions, 1 of which was returned 34 yards for a touchdown by Zach Thomas in the fourth quarter. Fiedler was 12 of 20 for 225 and 2 touchdowns. McNair was 7 of 19 for 118 yards and 1 touchdown, with 1 interception, and O'Donnell was 9 of 21 for 110 yards and 1 touchdown, with 2 interceptions.

Miami	10	7	7	7	—	31
Tennessee	0	7	7	9	—	23

Mia — FG Mare 37
Mia — L. Smith 4 run (Mare kick)
Tenn — Myers 14 fumble return (Nedney kick)
Mia — Gadsden 23 pass from Fiedler (Mare kick)
Mia — L. Smith 65 pass from Fiedler (Mare kick)
Tenn — Mason 29 pass from McNair (Nedney kick)
Mia — Z. Thomas 34 interception return (Mare kick)
Tenn — Kinney 18 pass from O'Donnell (kick failed)
Tenn — FG Nedney 51

MONDAY NIGHT, SEPTEMBER 10

DENVER 31, N.Y. GIANTS 20—at INVESCO Field at Mile High, attendance 75,244. Brian Griese passed for 3 touchdowns, and Denver began play in its new stadium by upending the defending NFC champions. Denver snapped a 14-14 tie on Griese's 25-yard touchdown pass to Rod Smith midway through the third quarter. Jason Elam kicked a 37-yard field goal and Mike Anderson ran 6 yards for a touchdown as the Broncos built their advantage to as much as 17 points in the fourth quarter. Ed McCaffrey broke his leg after catching a pass on the go-ahead touchdown drive in the third quarter and was lost for the rest of the season. Griese was 21 of 29 for 330 yards and Terrell Davis rushed for 101 yards to help the Broncos amass 473 total yards. Smith caught 9 passes for 115 yards and 3 touchdowns. Collins was 19 of 34 for 258 yards and 2 touchdowns.

N.Y. Giants	0	7	7	6	—	20
Denver	7	7	3	14	—	31

Den — Hape 1 pass from Griese (Elam kick)
NYG — Toomer 43 pass from Collins (Andersen kick)
Den — McCaffrey 16 pass from Griese (Elam kick)
NYG — Toomer 11 pass from Collins (Andersen kick)
Den — R. Smith 25 pass from Griese (Elam kick)
Den — FG Elam 37
Den — Anderson 6 run (Elam kick)
NYG — Rivers 1 pass from Collins (kick blocked)

In the wake of the September 11 terrorist attacks, Commissioner Paul Tagliabue postponed the Week 2 games scheduled for September 16-17. The Commissioner later re-scheduled the Week 2 games for the weekend of January 6-7 to conclude the regular season.

SECOND WEEK SUMMARIES
American Football Conference

Eastern Division	W	L	T	Pct.	Pts.	OP
Indianapolis	2	0	0	1.000	87	50

Miami	2	0	0	1.000	49	38
N.Y. Jets	1	1	0	.500	34	48
Buffalo	0	2	0	.000	32	66
New England	0	2	0	.000	20	33

Central Division

Cincinnati	2	0	0	1.000	44	27
Jacksonville	2	0	0	1.000	34	9
Baltimore	1	1	0	.500	27	27
Cleveland	1	1	0	.500	30	23
Pittsburgh	0	1	0	.000	3	21
Tennessee	0	2	0	.000	29	44

Western Division

Denver	2	0	0	1.000	69	37
San Diego	2	0	0	1.000	62	24
Oakland	1	1	0	.500	42	42
Seattle	1	1	0	.500	12	33
Kansas City	0	2	0	.000	27	40

National Football Conference

Eastern Division

	W	L	T	Pct.	Pts.	OP
N.Y. Giants	1	1	0	.500	33	34
Philadelphia	1	1	0	.500	44	23
Arizona	0	1	0	.000	17	38
Dallas	0	2	0	.000	27	42
Washington	0	2	0	.000	3	67

Central Division

Green Bay	2	0	0	1.000	65	6
Tampa Bay	1	0	0	1.000	10	6
Chicago	1	1	0	.500	23	27
Detroit	0	2	0	.000	20	52
Minnesota	0	2	0	.000	23	41

Western Division

St. Louis	2	0	0	1.000	50	43
New Orleans	1	0	0	1.000	24	6
Atlanta	1	1	0	.500	37	32
Carolina	1	1	0	.500	40	37
San Francisco	1	1	0	.500	42	43

SUNDAY, SEPTEMBER 23

CINCINNATI 21, BALTIMORE 10—at Paul Brown Stadium, attendance 49,632. Jon Kitna passed for 1 touchdown and ran for another as the Bengals stunned the Ravens, handing them their first loss in 13 regular-season and postseason games. Kitna accounted for both of his touchdowns in a span of 3:28 of the third quarter. After Patrick Johnson fumbled the second-half kickoff, the Bengals began their possession at the Ravens' 18-yard line and scored on Kitna's 1-yard toss to Corey Dillon to put Cincinnati ahead. On the next play, Todd Heap lost a fumble at the Ravens' 33. Six plays later, Kitna ran 2 yards for a touchdown on a quarterback draw for a 14-3 advantage. Takeo Spikes' 66-yard interception return for a touchdown with 6:04 left. The Ravens controlled the ball for 28 of the final 31 plays, but failed to produce a point. Kitna was 19 of the 30 for 154 yards and 1 touchdown. Grbac established club records with 33 attempts and 63 completions en route to passing for 326 yards, but he was intercepted 3 times.

Baltimore	3	0	0	7	—	10
Cincinnati	0	0	14	7	—	21

Balt	—	FG Stover 38
Cin	—	Dillon 1 pass from Kitna (Rackers kick)
Cin	—	Kitna 2 run (Rackers kick)
Balt	—	P. Johnson 2 pass from Grbac (Stover kick)
Cin	—	Spikes 66 interception return (Rackers kick)

INDIANAPOLIS 42, BUFFALO 26—at RCA Dome, attendance 56,135. Peyton Manning passed for 421 yards and accounted for 5 touchdowns. The Colts scored touchdowns on six consecutive possessions to turn the game into a rout, capped by Manning's 1-yard run for a touchdown with 5:57 left in the third quarter. Manning was 23 of 29 for 421 yards and 4 touchdowns, with 2 interceptions. Pathon had 9 receptions for 168 yards and Harrison had 7 receptions for 146 yards. James added 111 yards on the ground, and Indianapolis finished with 555 total yards. The Bills were whistled for a club-record-tying 19 penalties for 133 yards. Rob Johnson was 24 of 37 for 257 yards and 1 touchdown, with 1 interception.

Buffalo	7	10	3	6	—	26
Indianapolis	14	21	7	0	—	42

Buff	—	Clements 48 interception return (Arians kick)
Ind	—	James 1 run (Vanderjagt kick)
Ind	—	Pathon 60 pass from Manning (Vanderjagt kick)
Buff	—	Henry 4 run (Arians kick)
Ind	—	Harrison 39 pass from Manning (Vanderjagt kick)
Ind	—	Harrison 39 pass from Manning (Vanderjagt kick)
Buff	—	FG Arians 48
Ind	—	Harrison 7 pass from Manning (Vanderjagt kick)
Buff	—	FG Arians 49
Ind	—	Manning 1 run (Vanderjagt kick)
Buff	—	P. Price 40 pass from Johnson (pass failed)

ATLANTA 24, CAROLINA 16—at Georgia Dome, attendance 47,807. Chris Chandler passed for 2 touchdowns and backup Michael Vick ran for another for the Falcons. It was 10-10 before Atlanta took the lead for good on its first play of the second half. Todd Sauerbrun's 52-yard punt pinned the Falcons back at their 6-yard line, but Chandler found Jamal Anderson wide open for a pass completion at the 35. He sprinted the remaining 65 yards for a touchdown and a 17-10 lead. Vick led Atlanta on a scoring drive in the second quarter, then in the fourth quarter came into the game on third-and-goal from Carolina's 2-yard line. He rolled left and bulled his way into the end zone for a 24-13 lead with 12:36 to go. Chandler was 11 of 14 for 244 yards and 2 touchdowns, with 1 interception. Chris Weinke was 27 of 41 for 276 yards and ran for a touchdown. Muhsin Muhammad had 10 catches for 132 yards.

Carolina	3	7	3	3	—	16
Atlanta	7	3	7	7	—	24

Atl	—	Martin 12 pass from Chandler (Feely kick)
Car	—	FG Kasay 30
Car	—	Weinke 5 run (Kasay kick)
Atl	—	FG Feely 25
Atl	—	Anderson 94 pass from Chandler (Feely kick)
Car	—	FG Kasay 26
Atl	—	Vick 2 run (Feely kick)
Car	—	FG Kasay 31

CLEVELAND 24, DETROIT 14—at Cleveland Browns Stadium, attendance 73,168. Tim Couch passed for 3 touchdowns and the Browns' defense intercepted former teammate Ty Detmer 7 times in Cleveland's victory. Detmer earned the Lions' starting nod over Charlie Batch, but was picked off seven of the last nine times the Lions had the ball. Tim Couch helped the Browns build a 24-7 lead, including a 34-yard touchdown pass to Quincy Morgan. Anthony Henry had 3 of Cleveland's 7 interceptions. James Jackson had 124 yards on 31 carries. Detmer was 22 of 42 for 212 yards. Morton caught 6 passes for 100 yards. Detroit stymied itself with 15 penalties for 115 yards.

Detroit	0	0	7	7	—	14
Cleveland	7	7	10	0	—	24

Cle	—	K. Johnson 4 pass from Couch (Dawson kick)

Cle	—	O'Hara 2 pass from Couch (Dawson kick)
Cle	—	FG Dawson 33
Det	—	Fair 26 interception return (Hanson kick)
Cle	—	Morgan 34 pass from Couch (Dawson kick)
Det	—	Morton 14 pass from Detmer (Hanson kick)

CHICAGO 17, MINNESOTA 10—at Soldier Field, attendance 66,944. Jim Miller came off the bench to pass for 2 touchdowns and rally the Bears to the victory. The loss gave the Vikings an 0-2 record for the first time in 17 years. Miller, who entered the game in the second quarter after starter Shane Matthews bruised his ribs, directed 45- and 54-yard scoring drives, capped by a 15-yard touchdown pass to Marty Booker that tied the score. Chicago got the ball back at the Vikings' 45 after a fake punt failed on Minnesota's next possession, and Miller needed only five plays to produce the decisive touchdown on a 24-yard pass to Marcus Robinson at the 3:39 mark. Matthews was 5 of 9 for 33 yards, while Miller was 18 of 29 for 204 yards and 2 touchdowns. Culpepper was 24 of 36 for 233 yards and 1 touchdown.

Minnesota	3	0	7	0	—	10
Chicago	0	0	3	14	—	17

Minn	—	FG Anderson 20
Minn	—	Jordan 3 pass from Culpepper (Anderson kick)
Chi	—	FG Edinger 45
Chi	—	Booker 15 pass from Miller (Edinger kick)
Chi	—	M. Robinson 24 pass from Miller (Edinger kick)

N.Y. GIANTS 13, KANSAS CITY 3—at Arrowhead Stadium, attendance 77,666. Ron Dayne's 7-yard touchdown run in the second quarter helped lift the Giants. Shaun Williams' end-zone interception began a 9-play, 80-yard drive capped by Dayne's touchdown run on the first play of the second quarter. The 10-0 advantage was enough for New York's defense, which limited the Chiefs to 11 first downs and 266 yards. Todd Peterson missed a 49-yard field-goal attempt midway through the fourth quarter, and the Giants ran out the last 7:21 of the clock, including a fourth-down conversion, to preserve the victory. Kerry Collins was 20 of 34 for 208 yards, with 3 interceptions. Trent Green was 17 of 34 for 184 yards, with 1 interception.

N.Y. Giants	3	10	0	0	—	13
Kansas City	0	0	3	0	—	3

NYG	—	FG Andersen 42
NYG	—	Dayne 7 run (Andersen kick)
NYG	—	FG Andersen 34
KC	—	FG Peterson 33

N.Y. JETS 10, NEW ENGLAND 3—at Foxboro Stadium, attendance 60,292. Curtis Martin's 8-yard touchdown run broke a 3-3 tie in the third quarter and lifted the Jets. John Hall's 26-yard field goal tied the game as time expired in the first half. Steve Martin's fumble recovery at the Patriots' 7 sparked the Jets to a 12-play, 93-yard drive capped by Curtis Martin's touchdown with 2:29 left in the quarter. James Farrior's end-zone interception thwarted one drive, and New England's last chance ended with Tom Brady's fourth-down incompletion from the 29 as time ran out. Brady was in the game because Bledsoe was injured during an 8-yard scramble. The backup quarterback completed 5 of his first 6 passes, but a spike and three consecutive incompletions ended the Patriots' hopes. Vinny Testaverde was 16 of 28 for 137 yards. Martin rushed for 106 yards. Bledsoe was 18 of 28 for 159 yards, with 2 interceptions, while Brady was 5 of 10 for 46 yards.

N.Y. Jets	0	3	7	0	—	10
New England	3	0	0	0	—	3

NE — FG Vinatieri 24
NYJ — FG Hall 26
NYJ — C. Martin 8 run (Hall kick)

MIAMI 18, OAKLAND 15—at Pro Player Stadium, attendance 73,404. Jay Fiedler's 2-yard touchdown run with five seconds remaining atoned for a crucial error earlier in the fourth quarter and lifted the Dolphins to a dramatic victory. On the Dolphins' first possession of the fourth quarter, Anthony Dorsett intercepted Fiedler's pass and returned it 26 yards for a touchdown with 12:41 left. A 2-point conversion attempt failed, leaving Oakland with a 15-10 advantage. It was still that way when Miami began its final possession at its 20-yard line with 1:41 left and no time outs. Fiedler completed three passes to the Raiders' 25. With 27 seconds left, the Dolphins had a first-and-goal at the 9. Fielder scrambled 7 yards to the 2, then spiked the ball to stop the clock with 12 seconds to go. He rolled right on the next play and dove into the end zone for the decisive score. Fiedler was 16 of 34 for 217 yards, with 2 interceptions. Rich Gannon was 14 of 25 for 125 yards.

Oakland	3	3	3	6	—	15
Miami	0	7	3	8	—	18

Oak — FG Janikowski 42
Oak — FG Janikowski 25
Mia — Fiedler 2 run (Mare kick)
Oak — FG Janikowski 45
Mia — FG Mare 27
Oak — Dorsett 26 interception return (run failed)
Mia — Fiedler 2 run (McKnight run)

PHILADELPHIA 27, SEATTLE 3—at Husky Stadium, attendance 62,826. Donovan McNabb passed for 2 touchdowns and ran for another in the Eagles' victory. McNabb teamed with James Thrash on a pair of touchdown passes in the second quarter, and the Seahawks never threatened. After halftime they had 23 total yards, punted all seven times they had the ball, and failed to cross midfield. McNabb was 24 of 37 for 283 yards and 2 touchdowns. Thrash had career bests of 10 receptions and 165 yards. Matt Hasselbeck was 9 of 24 for 62 yards.

Philadelphia	3	14	0	10	—	27
Seattle	0	3	0	0	—	3

Phil — FG Akers 48
Phil — Thrash 64 pass from McNabb (Akers kick)
Sea — FG Lindell 41
Phil — Thrash 23 pass from McNabb (Akers kick)
Phil — FG Akers 21
Phil — McNabb 3 run (Akers kick)

ST. LOUIS 30, SAN FRANCISCO 26—at 3Com Park, attendance 67,536. Kurt Warner passed for 321 yards and 3 touchdowns to lead the Rams past the 49ers. Warner's 39-yard touchdown pass to Isaac Bruce in the opening minute of the fourth quarter gave the Rams a 30-16 lead. San Francisco answered with Jeff Garcia's 10-yard touchdown pass to Terry Jackson, then pulled within four points by converting Bruce's fumble into a 33-yard field goal with 6:47 left. The 49ers would not get the ball again, however. Marshall Faulk converted three consecutive third downs with an 8-yard catch, a 12-yard run, and a 9-yard run. Warner was 24 of 35 for 321 yards and 3 touchdowns, with 1 interception. Faulk had 105 rushing yards. Bruce had 8 catches for 144 yards. Garcia was 19 of 34 for just 121 yards and 1 touchdown, with 1 interception.

St. Louis	9	3	10	8	—	30

San Francisco	0	16	0	10	—	26

StL — FG Wilkins 44
StL — Robinson 1 pass from Warner (pass failed)
StL — FG Wilkins 40
SF — Garcia 10 run (Cortez kick)
SF — Barlow 1 run (run failed)
SF — FG Cortez 52
StL — Hakim 25 pass from Warner (Wilkins kick)
StL — FG Wilkins 25
StL — Bruce 39 pass from Warner (Proehl pass from Warner)
SF — Jackson 10 pass from Garcia (Cortez kick)
SF — FG Cortez 33

SAN DIEGO 32, DALLAS 21—at Texas Stadium, attendance 63,430. Doug Flutie passed for 353 yards and 2 touchdowns as the Chargers, who won only one game all of 2000, improved to 2-0. Flutie passed for touchdowns on his team's first two possessions as San Diego built a 14-0 lead. Anthony Wright passed for 2 touchdowns in the second quarter to pull Dallas within six points, but they could get no closer. Tim Dwight scooted 16 yards around left end to cap an 83-yard touchdown drive midway through the third quarter. Flutie was 23 of 38 for 353 yards and 2 touchdowns. Wright was 12 of 25 for 193 yards and 3 touchdowns, with 3 interceptions.

San Diego	14	6	6	6	—	32
Dallas	0	14	0	7	—	21

SD — F. Jones 11 pass from Flutie (Richey kick)
SD — Conway 7 pass from Flutie (Richey kick)
SD — FG Richey 22
Dall — Ismail 80 pass from Wright (Seder kick)
SD — FG Richey 24
Dall — McGarity 11 pass from Wright (Seder kick)
SD — Dwight 16 run (pass failed)
SD — FG Richey 23
Dall — Lucky 7 pass from Wright (Seder kick)
SD — FG Richey 43

JACKSONVILLE 13, TENNESSEE 6—at ALLTEL Stadium, attendance 65,994. Stacey Mack ran 22 yards for the game's only touchdown in the second quarter to key the Jaguars' victory. Mack, the backup running back who entered the game after starter Fred Taylor was injured, had runs of 12 and 4 yards before bursting off right tackle for the go-ahead touchdown with 4:56 left in the half. The Titans reached the Jaguars' 9 in the final moments, but Neil O'Donnell threw incomplete on four consecutive attempts. Brunell was 17 of 27 for 235 yards. O'Donnell, playing in place of injured Steve McNair, was 21 of 36 for 215 yards.

Tennessee	3	3	0	0	—	6
Jacksonville	3	7	3	0	—	13

Tenn — FG Nedney 22
Jax — FG Hollis 35
Tenn — FG Nedney 43
Jax — Mack 22 run (Hollis kick)
Jax — FG Hollis 39

SUNDAY NIGHT, SEPTEMBER 23
DENVER 38, ARIZONA 17—at Sun Devil Stadium, attendance 50,913. Brian Griese passed for 3 touchdowns and Rod Smith had a club-record 14 receptions in the Broncos' victory. With the game-time temperature in Sun Devil Stadium a withering 103 degrees, the Broncos rallied from a 10-0 deficit to take a 17-10 lead at halftime capped by Griese's 10-yard touchdown pass to Smith with 32 seconds left

in the half. Griese and Smith teamed for a 34-yard touchdown pass on the play after a Thomas Jones fumble to give the Broncos a 24-10 lead. Griese equaled a club record by completing 17 consecutive passes. He was 22 of 31 for 242 yards and 3 touchdowns. Smith had 162 receiving yards. Jake Plummer was 16 of 28 for 242 yards and 1 touchdown, with 1 interception. David Boston had 8 catches for 145 yards.

Denver	0	17	14	7	—	38
Arizona	3	7	0	7	—	17

Ariz — FG Gramatica 28
Ariz — Jones 1 run (Gramatica kick)
Den — FG Elam 49
Den — FG Elam 41
Den — FG Elam 35
Den — Smith 10 pass from Griese (Carswell pass from Griese)
Den — Smith 34 pass from Griese (Elam kick)
Den — Hape 1 pass from Griese (Elam kick)
Den — Gary 9 run (Elam kick)
Ariz — Hardy 6 pass from Plummer (Gramatica kick)

MONDAY NIGHT, SEPTEMBER 24
GREEN BAY 37, WASHINGTON 0—at Lambeau Field, attendance 59,771. Brett Favre passed for 3 touchdowns as the Packers handed the Redskins their second consecutive defeat. The Redskins suffered their first shutout since 1993, while the Packers recorded their first shutout since the same year. Ahman Green rushed for 116 yards to become the first player in the club history to open the season with back-to-back 100-yard rushing games. Green Bay had a huge edge in first downs (23-8). Favre was 20 of 31 for 236 yards and 3 touchdowns, with 1 interception. Jeff George was 15 of 24 for 102 yards, with 1 interception.

Washington	0	0	0	0	—	0
Green Bay	7	3	10	17	—	37

GB — Freeman 12 pass from Favre (Longwell kick)
GB — FG Longwell 28
GB — FG Longwell 32
GB — Schroeder 41 pass from Favre (Longwell kick)
GB — Franks 4 pass from Favre (Longwell kick)
GB — FG Longwell 30
GB — Mealey 27 fumble return (Longwell kick)

THIRD WEEK SUMMARIES
American Football Conference

Eastern Division	W	L	T	Pct.	Pts.	OP
Indianapolis	2	1	0	.667	100	94
Miami	2	1	0	.667	59	80
New England	1	2	0	.333	64	46
N.Y. Jets	1	2	0	.333	51	67
Buffalo	0	3	0	.000	35	86
Central Division						
Baltimore	2	1	0	.667	47	40
Cincinnati	2	1	0	.667	58	55
Cleveland	2	1	0	.667	53	37
Jacksonville	2	1	0	.667	48	32
Pittsburgh	1	1	0	.500	23	24
Tennessee	0	2	0	.000	29	44
Western Division						
San Diego	3	0	0	1.000	90	38
Denver	2	1	0	.667	82	57
Oakland	2	1	0	.667	80	56
Kansas City	1	2	0	.333	72	53
Seattle	1	2	0	.333	26	71

National Football Conference

Eastern Division	W	L	T	Pct.	Pts.	OP
N.Y. Giants	2	1	0	.667	54	47
Philadelphia	2	1	0	.667	84	41

Arizona	0	2 0	.000	31	72
Dallas	0	3 0	.000	45	82
Washington	0	3 0	.000	16	112

Central Division

Green Bay	3	0 0	1.000	93	13
Chicago	1	1 0	.500	23	27
Tampa Bay	1	1 0	.500	26	26
Minnesota	1	2 0	.333	43	57
Detroit	0	2 0	.000	20	52

Western Division

St. Louis	3	0 0	1.000	92	53
Atlanta	2	1 0	.667	71	46
San Francisco	2	1 0	.667	61	60
New Orleans	1	1 0	.500	37	27
Carolina	1	2 0	.333	47	65

SUNDAY, SEPTEMBER 30

ATLANTA 34, ARIZONA 14—at Sun Devil Stadium, attendance 28,878. Chris Chandler passed for 3 touchdowns to lead Atlanta. Atlanta built a 27-point advantage in the fourth period when Maurice Smith scored 2 touchdowns, the second coming on a 79-yard pass from Chandler. Smith was in the game because Jamal Anderson suffered a season-ending knee injury on the game's opening drive. Smith had 108 yards on 2 receptions. Chandler was 20 of 28 for 286 yards and 3 touchdowns. Mathis became the Falcons' all-time leader with 57 touchdown catches. Jake Plummer was 23 of 35 for 276 yards and 1 touchdown, with 3 interceptions.

Atlanta	10	3	7	14 —	34
Arizona	0	0	7	7 —	14

Atl	—	Mathis 17 pass from Chandler (Feely kick)
Atl	—	FG Feely 34
Atl	—	FG Feely 55
Ariz	—	Pittman 24 run (Gramatica kick)
Atl	—	Mathis 10 pass from Chandler (Feely kick)
Atl	—	M. Smith 1 run (Feely kick)
Atl	—	M. Smith 79 pass from Chandler (Feely kick)
Ariz	—	Hardy 12 pass from Plummer (Gramatica kick)

BALTIMORE 20, DENVER 13—at INVESCO Field at Mile High, attendance 75,082. Elvis Grbac passed for 2 touchdowns in the second half to rally the Ravens past the Broncos. Chester McGlockton intercepted Grbac's pass on the first play of the game and returned it 17 yards to Baltimore's 3, setting up Brian Griese's touchdown pass to Dwayne Carswell 20 seconds into the game. Denver led 13-6 and had the ball midway through the third quarter when Duane Starks' interception sparked two consecutive scoring drives. Denver drove to Baltimore's 19-yard line on its next possession, but Griese's pass fell incomplete from there on fourth-and-1, and Corey Harris intercepted a pass on the final possession with 1:32 left to secure Baltimore's victory. Grbac was 17 of 30 for 221 yards and 2 touchdowns, with 1 interception. Griese was 17 of 33 for 191 yards and 1 touchdown, with 3 interceptions.

Baltimore	3	3	7	7 —	20
Denver	10	0	3	0 —	13

Den	—	Carswell 3 pass from Griese (Elam kick)
Balt	—	FG Stover 29
Den	—	FG Elam 43
Balt	—	FG Stover 26
Den	—	FG Elam 49
Balt	—	Ismail 20 pass from Grbac (Stover kick)
Balt	—	T. Taylor 3 pass from Grbac (Stover kick)

SAN DIEGO 28, CINCINNATI 14—at Qualcomm Stadium, attendance 56,048. The Chargers improved to 3-0 when LaDainian Tomlinson broke open a close game by scoring touchdowns on three consecutive second-half possessions. The Chargers had just 245 total yards and the Bengals only 237. On the final touchdown drive, Tomlinson ran for 49 of 59 yards on a six-play drive that culminated in his 3-yard scoring run 45 seconds into the fourth quarter. Doug Flutie was 12 of 19 for 133 yards and 1 touchdown. Tomlinson finished with 107 yards on 21 carries, with all but 19 yards coming after halftime. Jon Kitna was 18 of 32 for 135 yards and 2 touchdowns, with 3 interceptions.

Cincinnati	0	7	0	7 —	14
San Diego	0	7	14	7 —	28

SD	—	Conway 19 pass from Flutie (Richey kick)
Cin	—	Johnson 8 pass from Kitna (Rackers kick)
SD	—	Tomlinson 4 run (Richey kick)
SD	—	Tomlinson 2 run (Richey kick)
SD	—	Tomlinson 3 run (Richey kick)
Cin	—	Warrick 7 pass from Kitna (Rackers kick)

CLEVELAND 23, JACKSONVILLE 14—at ALLTEL Stadium, attendance 57,875. Tim Couch passed for 249 yards and Phil Dawson made 3 field goals, including the go-ahead kick from 30 yards with 5:13 remaining, to help the Browns to victory. Couch completed all 4 of his passes for 56 yards on the decisive 66-yard drive, which began at Cleveland's 21-yard line with 11:32 left and took 11 plays, consuming 6:19. Daylon McCutcheon returned an interception 32 yards for a touchdown with 35 seconds left to seal the victory. Couch was 24 of 34 for 249 yards, with 1 interception. Quinn was 15 of 30 for 136 yards in relief of Mark Brunell, who took a hard hit after throwing an interception in the first half.

Cleveland	3	10	0	10 —	23
Jacksonville	0	0	14	0 —	14

Cle	—	FG Dawson 35
Cle	—	White 4 run (Dawson kick)
Cle	—	FG Dawson 28
Jax	—	McCardell 8 pass from Quinn (Hollis kick)
Jax	—	Beasley 40 fumble return (Hollis kick)
Cle	—	FG Dawson 30
Cle	—	McCutcheon 32 interception return (Dawson kick)

GREEN BAY 28, CAROLINA 7—at Ericsson Stadium, attendance 67,417. Brett Favre passed for 308 yards and 3 touchdowns as the Packers improved to 3-0. All of Favre's touchdown passes came in the second half after Green Bay trailed by one point. Two fumbles by Steve Smith led to Favre's first 2 touchdowns and a 21-7 lead. Favre was 25 of 39 for 308 yards and 3 touchdowns, with 2 interceptions. Chris Weinke was 18 of 30 for 160 yards and 1 touchdown.

Green Bay	0	6	15	7 —	28
Carolina	0	7	0	0 —	7

Car	—	Walls 3 pass from Weinke (Kasay kick)
GB	—	FG Longwell 42
GB	—	FG Longwell 48
GB	—	Schroeder 12 pass from Favre (Freeman pass from Favre)
GB	—	Franks 6 pass from Favre (Longwell kick)
GB	—	Bradford 5 pass from Favre (Longwell kick)

NEW ENGLAND 44, INDIANAPOLIS 13—at Foxboro Stadium, attendance 56,280. Antowain Smith ran for 2 touchdowns and the Patriots' defense returned 2 interceptions for touchdowns.

Smith opened the scoring with a 4-yard touchdown run in the first quarter and closed it with a 2-yard touchdown run in the fourth quarter. In between, Otis Smith and Ty Law helped turn the game into a rout by returning interceptions of Peyton Manning for touchdowns. Otis Smith's 78-yard return came 1:42 before halftime and gave New England a 17-0 lead. Tom Brady was 13 of 23 for 168 yards in his first career start in place of injured Drew Bledsoe. Manning was 20 of 34 for 196 yards and 1 touchdown, with 3 interceptions.

Indianapolis	0	0	7	6 —	13
New England	7	13	3	21 —	44

NE	—	A. Smith 4 run (Vinatieri kick)
NE	—	FG Vinatieri 47
NE	—	O. Smith 78 interception return (Vinatieri kick)
NE	—	FG Vinatieri 48
NE	—	FG Vinatieri 35
Ind	—	Manning 10 run (Vanderjagt kick)
NE	—	Faulk 8 run (Vinatieri kick)
NE	—	Law 23 interception return (Vinatieri kick)
Ind	—	Pollard 17 pass from Manning (pass failed)
NE	—	A. Smith 2 run (Vinatieri kick)

KANSAS CITY 45, WASHINGTON 13—at FedEx Field, attendance 76,573. Priest Holmes rushed for 147 yards and scored 3 touchdowns as the Chiefs rolled past the Redskins. Kansas City scored touchdowns on its final four possessions of the first half to take a 28-10 lead at intermission. Then the Chiefs added a pair of touchdowns and a field goal on their first three possessions of the second half to turn the game into a rout. Holmes caught a 24-yard touchdown pass, then ran 7 and 24 yards for touchdowns, all within a span of 3:53. The Redskins managed only 218 total yards, though they reached the end zone for the first time this season when Tony Banks tossed a 26-yard touchdown pass to Rod Gardner 3:39 before halftime. Trent Green was 21 of 26 for 307 yards and 3 touchdowns. Holmes, who also had 78 yards on 5 receptions, accounted for 225 of the Chiefs' 546 total yards. Banks, who took over at quarterback when deposed starter Jeff George was released earlier in the week, was 11 of 27 for 116 yards and 1 touchdown, with 1 interception.

Kansas City	0	28	7	10 —	45
Washington	3	7	3	0 —	13

Wash	—	FG Conway 30
KC	—	Richardson 4 run (Peterson kick)
KC	—	Holmes 24 pass from Green (Peterson kick)
Wash	—	Gardner 26 pass from Banks (Conway kick)
KC	—	Holmes 7 run (Peterson kick)
KC	—	Holmes 24 run (Peterson kick)
Wash	—	FG Conway 28
KC	—	Gonzalez 3 pass from Green (Peterson kick)
KC	—	FG Peterson 33
KC	—	Thomas 3 pass from Green (Peterson kick)

ST. LOUIS 42, MIAMI 10—at Dome at America's Center, attendance 66,046. Kurt Warner passed for 4 touchdowns and Marshall Faulk scored 3 times in the Rams' rout. Both teams entered the game 2-0, but St. Louis had little trouble while amassing 441 total yards. The key play of the game came when Warner and Faulk teamed on a 1-yard touchdown pass as time ran out in the second quarter. The Rams were leading 14-10 but eschewed a field-goal attempt after driving from their 32-yard line to a fourth-and-goal at the Dolphins' 1 with three seconds left in the half. Jay Fiedler completed a 24-yard touchdown pass to James McKnight in the first quarter, but also lost 2 fumbles, including a costly one when he was sacked by London Fletcher after Miami reached the Rams' 6-yard line with the score tied in the second quarter. Warner was 24 of 31 for 328 yards and 4 touchdowns. Faulk ran for 88 yards and caught 6 passes for 72 yards. Holt had 111 yards on 4 receptions. Fiedler was 19 of 27 for 204 yards and 1 touchdown, with 2 interceptions

Miami	7	3	0	0	—	10
St. Louis	7	14	7	14	—	42

StL	—	Proehl 3 pass from Warner (Wilkins kick)
Mia	—	McKnight 24 pass from Fiedler (Mare kick)
StL	—	Faulk 10 pass from Warner (Wilkins kick)
Mia	—	FG Mare 26
StL	—	Faulk 1 pass from Warner (Wilkins kick)
StL	—	Faulk 1 run (Wilkins kick)
StL	—	Holt 45 pass from Warner (Wilkins kick)
StL	—	Canidate 9 run (Wilkins kick)

N.Y. GIANTS 21, NEW ORLEANS 13—at Giants Stadium, attendance 78,451. Ron Dayne rushed for 111 yards and a touchdown, and the Giants withstood the Saints' last-ditch effort at a tying touchdown to preserve the victory. Kerry Collins' 46-yard touchdown pass to Joe Jurevicius gave the Giants a 21-10 lead with 6:05 to play. It was 21-13 when Collins lost a fumble at New Orleans' 30-yard line with 3:17 left. With Brooks passing for 51 yards and scrambling for 10, the Saints marched to a first down at New York's 9 with 15 seconds remaining. After an intentional spike and 2 incompletions, it was fourth-and-goal from the 9 with four seconds to play. Brooks dropped back to pass, scrambled from pressure, and found Jackson for an apparent touchdown pass as time ran out. But Jackson was whistled for offensive pass interference on the play—another penalty for illegal touching was declined—and, by rule, the game ended. Collins was 9 of 18 for 135 yards, and 1 touchdown. Brooks was 28 of 54 for 291 yards and 1 touchdown, with 1 interception. Jackson had 8 receptions for 105 yards.

New Orleans	0	3	0	10	—	13
N.Y. Giants	0	14	0	7	—	21

NYG	—	Dayne 6 run (Andersen kick)
NYG	—	Barber 14 run (Andersen kick)
NO	—	FG Carney 32
NO	—	W. Jackson 32 pass from Brooks (Carney kick)
NYG	—	Jurevicius 46 pass from Collins (Andersen kick)
NO	—	FG Carney 30

PITTSBURGH 20, BUFFALO 3—at Ralph Wilson Stadium, attendance 72,874. Dewayne Washington returned a fumble 63 yards for a touchdown to spark the Steelers past the Bills. The game was scoreless until Brent Alexander forced Travis Henry to fumble on second-and-5 from the Steelers' 35-yard line late in the first quarter. Washington picked up the loose ball and raced the distance to give Pittsburgh the lead. The Steelers' defense limited the Bills to 172 yards. Kordell Stewart was 15 of 22 for 107 yards. Pittsburgh gained 170 rushing yards, led by Jerome Bettis' 114 yards on 22 carries. Rob Johnson was 13 of 22 for 104 yards before leaving the game with a bruised hip in the fourth quarter, and Alex Van Pelt was 3 of 5 for 44 yards, with 1 interception.

Pittsburgh	7	3	0	10	—	20
Buffalo	0	3	0	0	—	3

Pitt	—	Washington 63 fumble return (K. Brown kick)
Pitt	—	FG K. Brown 30

Buff	—	FG Arians 23
Pitt	—	FG K. Brown 52
Pitt	—	Fuamatu-Ma'afala 22 run (K. Brown kick)

OAKLAND 38, SEATTLE 14—at Network Associates Coliseum, attendance 54,629. Jerry Rice caught 2 of Rich Gannon's 3 touchdown passes as the Raiders coasted to the victory. Rice, the NFL's all-time leading receiver, had his first touchdown catches for Oakland after playing 15 seasons for San Francisco. On the Raiders' second possession, which began at their 33-yard line midway through the first quarter, he had catches of 17 and 7 yards before grabbing a 33-yard touchdown to complete the drive. His 14-yard touchdown catch 1:57 before halftime put Oakland ahead 24-0. Shaun Alexander, who was in the game because Ricky Watters injured his shoulder in the first quarter, scored a touchdown for Seattle. Gannon was 19 of 28 for 217 yards and 3 touchdowns. Hasselbeck was 14 of 28 for 167 yards, with 1 interception. Dilfer was 2 for 2 for 49 yards, and Huard was 9 of 17 passes for 127 yards and 1 touchdown. Jackson had 125 yards on 5 receptions.

Seattle	0	0	7	7	—	14
Oakland	7	17	14	0	—	38

Oak	—	Rice 33 pass from Gannon (Janikowski kick)
Oak	—	FG Janikowski 20
Oak	—	Allen 26 fumble return (Janikowski kick)
Oak	—	Rice 14 pass from Gannon (Janikowski kick)
Oak	—	Gannon 1 run (Janikowski kick)
Oak	—	Wheatley 3 pass from Gannon (Janikowski kick)
Sea	—	Alexander 4 run (Lindell kick)
Sea	—	Fauria 3 pass from Huard (Lindell kick)

MINNESOTA 20, TAMPA BAY 16—at Metrodome, attendance 64,105. Daunte Culpepper ran 8 yards for the winning touchdown with 1:03 remaining to lift the Vikings to their first victory. The Buccaneers had taken a 16-13 lead on Warrick Dunn's 6-yard touchdown run 2:20 into the fourth quarter. After an exchange of possessions, the Vikings began the winning drive from their 4-yard line with 6:21 to play. Culpepper teamed with Byron Chamberlain on a 37-yard completion to the 3 with 1:08 remaining. A false start penalty moved the ball back to the 8, but Culpepper ran up the middle to put Minnesota ahead. After the ensuing kickoff, Tampa Bay took over at its 25-yard line with 59 seconds left. Brad Johnson's 9-yard strike to Keyshawn Johnson and a neutral-zone infraction on Minnesota gave the Buccaneers a first down at the 18 with 25 seconds left, but Eric Kelly's interception at the 3 on second down clinched the win. Culpepper was 20 of 44 for 322 yards and 1 touchdown, with 2 interceptions. Brad Johnson was 20 of 34 for 224 yards, with 1 interception.

Tampa Bay	3	3	3	7	—	16
Minnesota	7	3	3	7	—	20

TB	—	FG Gramatica 25
Minn	—	C. Carter 13 pass from Culpepper (Anderson kick)
Minn	—	FG Anderson 24
TB	—	FG Gramatica 25
TB	—	FG Gramatica 49
Minn	—	FG Anderson 29
TB	—	Dunn 6 run (Gramatica kick)
Minn	—	Culpepper 8 run (Anderson kick)

SUNDAY NIGHT, SEPTEMBER 30
PHILADELPHIA 40, DALLAS 18—at Veterans Stadium, attendance 66,621. Donovan McNabb passed

for 3 touchdowns, and the Eagles overwhelmed the Cowboys with a 26-point second quarter. Brian Mitchell fumbled twice to set up two Dallas field goals,. but his 28-yard kickoff return led to a 62-yard touchdown drive capped by McNabb's 10-yard touchdown pass to Chad Lewis with 3:49 left in the first quarter, and Philadelphia never trailed again. The Eagles turned the game into a rout by scoring 16 points in a span of 4:41 of the second quarter, following 3 Dallas fumbles, to make it 30-6 with 5:43 left before intermission. McNabb was 14 of 28 for 162 yards and 3 touchdowns. Wright, starting in place of injured Quincy Carter, was just 7 of 23 for 33 yards, with 1 interception. Clint Stoerner was 4 of 7 for 44 yards and 2 touchdowns. Hambrick had an 80-yard run late in the game to finish with 107 yards on 10 carries.

Dallas	6	0	0	12	—	18
Philadelphia	7	26	7	0	—	40

Dall	—	FG Seder 41
Dall	—	FG Seder 43
Phil	—	Lewis 10 pass from McNabb (Akers kick)
Phil	—	Lewis 17 pass from McNabb (Akers kick)
Phil	—	Moore 10 fumble return (Akers kick)
Phil	—	Pinkston 10 pass from McNabb(kick failed)
Phil	—	FG Akers 40
Phil	—	FG Akers 19
Phil	—	Buckhalter 3 run (Akers kick)
Dall	—	R. Thomas 5 pass from Stoerner (pass failed)
Dall	—	Wiley 11 pass from Stoerner (pass failed)

MONDAY NIGHT, OCTOBER 1
SAN FRANCISCO 19, N.Y. JETS 17—at Giants Stadium, attendance 78,722. Jeff Garcia passed for 1 touchdown and Jose Cortez kicked 4 field goals. San Francisco kept the ball on the ground for 43 of its 65 plays from scrimmage, amassing 233 rushing yards and maintaining possession for 36:08 of the game's 60 minutes. Garrison Hearst ran for 95 yards on 20 carries, and rookie Kevan Barlow added 83 yards on only 9 carries. Cortez kicked field goals on four of the next five possessions following Garcia's touchdown pass to help the 49ers build a 19-10 lead. Curtis Martin's second touchdown came with 50 seconds left. Garcia was 16 of 20 for 141 yards and 1 touchdown. Vinny Testaverde was 11 of 24 for 192 yards.

San Francisco	0	13	3	3	—	19
N.Y. Jets	7	0	3	7	—	17

NYJ	—	C. Martin 2 run (Hall kick)
SF	—	Owens 6 pass from Garcia (Cortez kick)
SF	—	FG Cortez 19
SF	—	FG Cortez 49
NYJ	—	FG Hall 24
SF	—	FG Cortez 35
SF	—	FG Cortez 29
NYJ	—	C. Martin 1 run (Hall kick)

FOURTH WEEK SUMMARIES
American Football Conference

Eastern Division	W	L	T	Pct.	Pts.	OP
Miami	3	1	0	.750	89	90
Indianapolis	2	1	0	.667	100	94
N.Y. Jets	2	2	0	.500	93	103
New England	1	3	0	.250	74	76
Buffalo	0	4	0	.000	71	128
Central Division						
Baltimore	3	1	0	.750	73	47
Cleveland	3	1	0	.750	73	53
Pittsburgh	2	1	0	.667	39	31
Cincinnati	2	2	0	.500	65	71

				Pct.	Pts.	OP
Jacksonville	2	2	0	.500	63	56
Tennessee	0	3	0	.000	36	70

Western Division

Denver	3	1	0	.750	102	63
Oakland	3	1	0	.750	108	77
San Diego	3	1	0	.750	106	58
Seattle	2	2	0	.500	50	86
Kansas City	1	3	0	.250	78	73

National Football Conference

Eastern Division

	W	L	T	Pct.	Pts.	OP
N.Y. Giants	3	1	0	.750	77	56
Philadelphia	2	2	0	.500	104	62
Arizona	1	2	0	.333	52	92
Dallas	0	4	0	.000	66	110
Washington	0	4	0	.000	25	135

Central Division

Green Bay	3	1	0	.750	103	27
Chicago	2	1	0	.667	54	30
Tampa Bay	2	1	0	.667	40	36
Minnesota	1	3	0	.250	58	85
Detroit	0	3	0	.000	20	87

Western Division

St. Louis	4	0	0	1.000	127	53
San Francisco	3	1	0	.750	85	74
New Orleans	2	1	0	.667	65	42
Atlanta	2	2	0	.500	74	77
Carolina	1	3	0	.250	61	89

SUNDAY, OCTOBER 7

ARIZONA 21, PHILADELPHIA 20—at Veterans Stadium, attendance 66,360. Jake Plummer's 35-yard touchdown pass to MarTay Jenkins with nine seconds remaining gave the Cardinals a dramatic victory. The Cardinals snapped a nine-game losing streak. Donovan McNabb passed for 2 touchdowns and David Akers kicked 2 field goals, the second of which came from 28 yards and gave the Eagles a 20-14 lead with 1:13 left in the game. Arizona, which was out of time outs, began the ensuing drive at its 26-yard line at the 1:09 mark and soon faced second-and-15 from the 21. But Plummer completed a 16-yard pass to Jenkins for a first down, intentionally spiked the ball to stop the clock, and then found Jenkins again for 28 yards and a first down at Philadelphia's 35 with 28 seconds to go. Another spike and 2 incompletions made it fourth-and-10 with 17 seconds left before Plummer and Jenkins teamed one more time on the winning pass. Plummer was 18 of 32 for 238 yards and 2 touchdowns, with 1 interception. Jenkins had 6 receptions for 119 yards. McNabb was 19 of 29 for 280 yards and 2 touchdowns, with 1 interception. Correll Buckhalter had 134 yards on 21 rushes.

Arizona	14	0	0	7	—	21
Philadelphia	7	10	0	3	—	20

Ariz	—	Vanden Bosch 9 fumble recovery (Gramatica kick)
Ariz	—	Makovicka 2 pass from Plummer (Gramatica kick)
Phil	—	Pinkston 13 pass from McNabb (Akers kick)
Phil	—	FG Akers 42
Phil	—	Pinkston 2 pass from McNabb (Akers kick)
Phil	—	FG Akers 28
Ariz	—	Jenkins 35 pass from Plummer (Gramatica kick)

CHICAGO 31, ATLANTA 3—at Georgia Dome, attendance 46,483. Wide receiver Marty Booker passed for 1 touchdown and caught another, and the Bears utilized big plays on both sides of the ball to rout the Falcons. The game was scoreless early in the second quarter when Booker took a lateral pass from Jim Miller, and then fired a 34-yard touchdown strike to Marcus Robinson to give Chicago a lead it would not relinquish. Booker also was on the receiving end of a 63-yard touchdown pass from Miller on the first play of the fourth quarter as the Bears opened a 17-0 lead. Phillip Daniels forced Michael Vick to fumble and Brian Urlacher picked up the ball and raced 90 yards for a touchdown and a 24-0 lead. The sack was 1 of 7 recorded by the Bears' defense, and the turnover was 1 of 5 it forced. Miller was 17 of 26 for 196 yards and 1 touchdown, with 2 interceptions. Robinson caught 9 passes for 114 yards. Chris Chandler was 7 of 12 for 75, with 3 interceptions and suffered a concussion before giving way to Vick, who was 12 of 18 for 186 yards.

Chicago	0	10	0	21	—	31
Atlanta	0	0	0	3	—	3

Chi	—	Robinson 34 pass from Booker (Edinger kick)
Chi	—	FG Edinger 42
Chi	—	Booker 63 pass from Miller (Edinger kick)
Chi	—	Urlacher 90 fumble return (Edinger kick)
Atl	—	FG Feely 44
Chi	—	A. Thomas 32 run (Edinger kick)

PITTSBURGH 16, CINCINNATI 7—at Heinz Field, attendance 62,335. Jerome Bettis rushed for 153 yards to lead the Steelers to a victory in the first game ever at Heinz Field. Bettis carried 23 times and helped Pittsburgh amass 274 of its 412 total yards on the ground, while the Steelers' defense permitted just 214 total yards. Pittsburgh led just 13-7 with 4:45 left, but dashed Cincinnati's comeback hopes by driving to Kris Brown's clinching 48-yard field goal at the 1:52 mark, keyed by Kordell Stewart's 24-yard pass to Hines Ward for a first down at the Bengals' 33. Stewart was 15 of 24 for 151 yards. Bettis surpassed the 10,000-yard rushing mark for his career and finished the game at 10,099. Kitna was 19 of 34 for 164 yards and 1 touchdown, with 1 interception.

Cincinnati	0	0	0	7	—	7
Pittsburgh	0	10	0	6	—	16

Pitt	—	FG Brown 26
Pitt	—	Stewart 8 run (Brown kick)
Pitt	—	FG Brown 42
Cin	—	Neal 1 pass from Kitna (Rackers kick)
Pitt	—	FG Brown 48

OAKLAND 28, DALLAS 21—at Network Associates Coliseum, attendance 61,535. Tyrone Wheatley rushed for 2 touchdowns for the Raiders. The game, previously scheduled for October 21, was moved up two weeks to avoid a conflict with the Oakland A's during the baseball playoffs. Oakland marched to touchdowns the first three times it had the ball and never trailed. Wheatley scored from 1 yard out to cap an 18-play, 72-yard drive that consumed 9:49 following the second-half kickoff to take a 28-7 lead. Kicker Tim Seder's 8-yard touchdown run on a fake field goal and Darrin Chiaverini's touchdown catch brought the Cowboys close, but the Raiders covered an onside kick with 1:21 left to secure the victory. Rich Gannon was 21 of 28 for 209 yards and 1 touchdown. Tim Brown had 7 receptions for 114 yards. Anthony Wright was 14 of 22 for 126 yards and 2 touchdowns in relief of Quincy Carter, who had returned to the lineup after missing two games with a thumb injury. Carter was 1 of 5 for 4 yards before injuring his hamstring in the first quarter.

Dallas	0	7	7	7	—	21
Oakland	7	14	7	0	—	28

Oak	—	Rice 5 pass from Gannon (Janikowski kick)
Oak	—	Crockett 3 run (Janikowski kick)
Dall	—	Galloway 40 pass from Wright (Seder kick)
Oak	—	Wheatley 4 run (Janikowski kick)
Oak	—	Wheatley 1 run (Janikowski kick)
Dall	—	Seder 8 run (Seder kick)
Dall	—	Chiaverini 3 pass from Wright (Seder kick)

TAMPA BAY 14, GREEN BAY 10—at Raymond James Stadium, attendance 65,510. Mike Alstott ran 39 yards for the go-ahead touchdown with 6:45 left in the game, and the Buccaneers' defense kept the Packers out of the end zone in the closing seconds to preserve the victory. Alstott's touchdown run capped a 95-yard drive. Dexter Jackson's interception stopped Green Bay's next possesion, but the Packers got the ball back and reached Tampa Bay's 13-yard line with 44 seconds left. Anthony McFarland's 5-yard sack of Favre pushed Green Bay back to the 18-yard line. After an incompletion, Favre's fourth-down pass was batted down in the end zone by John Lynch as time expired. Brad Johnson was 23 of 29 for 184 yards. Favre was 20 of 35 for 258 yards and 1 touchdown, with 3 interceptions, 1 of which was returned 98 yards by Shelton Quarles. Bill Schroeder had 4 catches for 119 yards.

Green Bay	0	7	3	0	—	10
Tampa Bay	0	7	0	7	—	14

TB	—	Quarles 98 interception return (Gramatica kick)
GB	—	Schroeder 67 pass from Favre (Longwell kick)
GB	—	FG Longwell 35
TB	—	Alstott 39 run (Gramatica kick)

SEATTLE 24, JACKSONVILLE 15—at Husky Stadium, attendance 54,524. Shaun Alexander rushed for 176 yards and 2 touchdowns to lead the Seahawks to the victory. Alexander, starting in place of injured Ricky Watters, carried 31 times and had touchdown runs of 14 and 3 as Seattle built a 21-12 halftime lead. The Jaguars pulled within 21-15, but Elvis Joseph lost a fumble on fourth-and-1 from Seattle's 35, leading to Rian Lindell's 25-yard field goal with 7:39 left. Dilfer, making his first start in place of injured Matt Hasselbeck, was 15 of 23 for 219 yards and 1 touchdown, with 1 interception. Brunell was 21 of 39 for 233 yards and 1 touchdown.

Jacksonville	3	9	3	0	—	15
Seattle	14	7	0	3	—	24

Jax	—	FG Hollis 32
Sea	—	Mili 1 pass from Dilfer (Lindell kick)
Sea	—	Alexander 14 run (Lindell kick)
Jax	—	FG Hollis 48
Jax	—	Joseph 18 pass from Brunell (run failed)
Sea	—	Alexander 3 run (Lindell kick)
Jax	—	FG Hollis 48
Sea	—	FG Lindell 25

DENVER 20, KANSAS CITY 6—at INVESCO Field at Mile High, attendance 73,506. Mike Anderson rushed for 155 yards and cornerback Deltha O'Neal tied an NFL record with 4 interceptions in the Broncos' victory. Anderson, who rushed for 1,487 yards as a rookie in 2000 but began 2001 as a backup to Terrell Davis, started his third game in place of the injured veteran and raced 62 yards for a touchdown with 5:49 left in the first quarter. Anderson's touchdown burst came three plays after O'Neal intercepted Trent Green's pass in the end zone. O'Neal intercepted Green three times in the second half. He returned the second theft 42 yards to the Chiefs' 4-yard line. Brian Griese tossed a touchdown pass to Rod Smith on the next play for a 20-6 lead with 8:11 left, and he returned his final one 27 yards to the Chiefs' 46 with 1:46 to go. Griese was 11 of 20 for 121 yards and 1 touchdown, with 1 interception. Smith had 8 receptions for 110 yards. Green was 25 of 40 for 283 yards, with 4 interceptions. Tony Gonzalez had 8 receptions for 129 yards.

Kansas City	0	6	0	0	—	6
Denver	7	3	3	7	—	20

Den	—	Anderson 62 run (Elam kick)
KC	—	FG Peterson 23
Den	—	FG Elam 48
KC	—	FG Peterson 35
Den	—	FG Elam 24
Den	—	R. Smith 4 pass from Griese (Elam kick)

NEW ORLEANS 28, MINNESOTA 15—at Louisiana Superdome, attendance 70,020. Ricky Williams rushed for 136 yards to lift the Saints. Williams carried 30 times and had a 1-yard touchdown run midway through the second quarter to cap a 74-yard drive and give New Orleans the lead for good. John Carney kicked 5 field goals without a miss, and Chris Oldham returned a fumble 38 yards for a touchdown in the third quarter. Ths Saints' defense limited the Vikings to 34 rushing yards and registered 6 sacks. Aaron Brooks was 15 of 30 for 210 yards, with 1 interception. Daunte Culpepper was 23 of 34 for 332 yards and 2 touchdowns, with 1 interception.

Minnesota	7	0	8	0	—	15
New Orleans	6	9	10	3	—	28

NO	—	FG Carney 50
NO	—	FG Carney 23
Minn	—	Moss 29 pass from Culpepper (Anderson kick)
NO	—	R. Williams 1 run (run failed)
NO	—	FG Carney 45
NO	—	FG Carney 29
NO	—	Oldham 38 fumble return (Carney kick)
Minn	—	Chamberlain 19 pass from Culpepper (Culpepper run)
NO	—	FG Carney 33

MIAMI 30, NEW ENGLAND 10—at Pro Player Stadium, attendance 72,713. Lamar Smith rushed for 144 yards and a touchdown in the Dolphins' rout. Miami kept the ball on the ground much of the game, gaining 209 of its 296 total yards via that route. Smith had 29 carries as the Dolphins ran on 44 of their 65 plays from scrimmage and controlled the ball for 36:21. Late in the third quarter, Jason Taylor picked up a fumbled snap at the Patriots' 1-yard line and scored the touchdown that broke open the game at 27-10. Fiedler was 11 of 21 for 87 yards and 1 touchdown, with 1 interception. Tom Brady was 12 of 24 for 86 yards in his second NFL start.

New England	7	3	0	0	—	10
Miami	7	10	10	3	—	30

NE	—	A. Smith 9 run (Vinatieri kick)
Mia	—	L. Smith 7 run (Mare kick)
Mia	—	FG Mare 19
NE	—	FG Vinatieri 37
Mia	—	Weaver 14 pass from Fiedler (Mare kick)
Mia	—	FG Mare 34
Mia	—	Taylor 1 fumble return (Mare kick)
Mia	—	FG Mare 27

N.Y. JETS 42, BUFFALO 36—at Ralph Wilson Stadium, attendance 72,654. Curtis Martin rushed for 135 yards and 2 touchdowns as the Jets dropped the Bills to 0-4. The Jets' defense forced the Bills to turn over the ball 5 times, and the Jets converted the miscues into 28 points. Buffalo pulled within 28-22 thanks to 2 touchdown passes by Alex Van Pelt, but the Jets regained command with 2 touchdowns in a 64-second span late in the third quarter. First, Vinny Testaverde's 36-yard completion to Wayne Chrebet set up his 2-yard touchdown toss to Anthony Becht, and two plays later, Mo Lewis picked up Larry Centers' fumble at the Bills' 15-yard line and returned it

for a touchdown and a 42-22 lead. Matthew Hatchette covered an onside kickoff with seven seconds left to preserve the victory. Testaverde was 15 of 25 for 173 yards and 2 touchdowns. Van Pelt, who entered the game after starter Rob Johnson pinched a nerve in his neck, was 23 of 41 for 268 yards and 3 touchdowns, with 1 interception. Centers caught 12 passes for 75 yards, while Eric Moulds had 5 receptions for 107 yards and Peerless Price had 4 for 103. Travis Henry added 113 yards rushing.

N.Y. Jets	21	7	14	0	—	42
Buffalo	6	9	7	14	—	36

NYJ	—	C. Martin 16 run (Hall kick)
NYJ	—	Anderson 4 pass from Testaverde (Hall kick)
Buff	—	Moulds 46 pass from Johnson (pass failed)
NYJ	—	Abraham 7 fumble return (Hall kick)
Buff	—	FG Arians 28
NYJ	—	C. Martin 4 run (Hall kick)
Buff	—	Riemersma 3 pass from Van Pelt (pass failed)
Buff	—	Price 70 pass from Van Pelt (Arians kick)
NYJ	—	Becht 2 pass from Testaverde (Hall kick)
NYJ	—	Lewis 15 fumble return (Hall kick)
Buff	—	Centers 2 run (Arians kick)
Buff	—	Centers 6 pass from Van Pelt (Arians kick)

CLEVELAND 20, SAN DIEGO 16—at Cleveland Browns Stadium, attendance 73,018. Tim Couch's 19-yard touchdown pass to Kevin Johnson with 1:15 remaining lifted the Browns to their third consecutive victory and ended San Diego's three-game winning streak. The Chargers led 16-10 with 8:32 left, but Cleveland countered with Phil Dawson's 27-yard field goal with 4:58 to go and quickly forced a punt to begin the winning drive from midfield at the 3:52 mark. The touchdown pass came on third-and-6 from San Diego's 19. The Chargers had one last possession. Doug Flutie kept his team's hopes alive by scrambling 11 yards for a first down on fourth-and-10, then completing 2 passes to reach the Browns' 45 with 14 seconds left. But time ran out after 2 desperation passes fell incomplete in the end zone. Couch was 14 of 27 for 203 yards and 1 touchdown. Flutie was 17 of 37 for 149 yards. LaDainian Tomlinson ran for 102 yards to give him three 100-yard outings in his first four NFL games.

San Diego	3	0	7	6	—	16
Cleveland	0	10	0	10	—	20

SD	—	FG Richey 23
Cle	—	FG P. Dawson 31
Cle	—	J. Jackson 12 run (P. Dawson kick)
SD	—	Tomlinson 2 run (Richey kick)
SD	—	FG Richey 21
SD	—	FG Richey 38
Cle	—	FG P. Dawson 27
Cle	—	K. Johnson 19 pass from Couch (P. Dawson kick)

BALTIMORE 26, TENNESSEE 7—at PSINet Stadium, attendance 69,494. Terry Allen rushed for 108 yards and a touchdown, and the Ravens' defense handed Tennessee its third consecutive defeat. The Ravens built a 17-0 lead by halftime, which was more than enough for Baltimore's defense, which forced the Titans to punt on each of their first six possessions before Joe Nedney was short on a 46-yard field-goal attempt as time ran out in the first half. It was more of the same in the second half, when Tennessee punted each of the first four times it had the ball after the intermission, and had just 185 total

yards for the game. Elvis Grbac was 15 of 31 for 259 yards and 1 touchdown. Allen owned 108 of the Ravens' 207 rushing yards. Steve McNair was 17 of 32 for 154 yards, with 1 interception. Tennessee offensive lineman Bruce Matthews played in the 283rd game, the most by a non-kicker in NFL history.

Tennessee	0	0	7	0	—	7
Baltimore	7	10	3	6	—	26

Balt	—	Allen 9 run (Stover kick)
Balt	—	Ismail 77 pass from Grbac (Stover kick)
Balt	—	FG Stover 26
Balt	—	FG Stover 25
Tenn	—	Mitchell 26 blocked punt return (Nedney kick)
Balt	—	Brookins 1 run (pass failed)

N.Y. GIANTS 23, WASHINGTON 9—at Giants Stadium, attendance 78,651. Kerry Collins' 1-yard touchdown pass to Dan Campbell broke a tie early in the fourth quarter, and the Giants went on to hand the Redskins their fourth consecutive defeat. Damon Washington's 22-yard scamper on the opening play of the fourth quarter led to Collins' touchdown pass to Campbell. Jason Sehorn thwarted two Washington drives after that with interceptions, including one he returned 34 yards for the clinching touchdown with 2:57 left. The Giants' defense limited the Redskins to 9 first downs, 181 total yards, registed 4 sacks, and forced 5 turnovers. Collins was 15 of 29 for 177 yards and 1 touchdown, with 2 interceptions. Washington, a reserve running back, had only 1 carry in his first two seasons for the Giants before running 25 times for 90 yards. He had 22 carries for 80 yards in the second half, which Ron Dayne sat out with a sprained neck. Tiki Barber, normally the starting running back, was inactive with a hamstring injury. Tony Banks was 13 of 31 for 151 yards, with 2 interceptions.

Washington	3	3	3	0	—	9
N.Y. Giants	3	6	0	14	—	23

NYG	—	FG Andersen 50
Wash	—	FG Conway 35
NYG	—	FG Andersen 26
Wash	—	FG Conway 55
NYG	—	FG Andersen 22
Wash	—	FG Conway 41
NYG	—	Campbell 1 pass from Collins (Andersen kick)
NYG	—	Sehorn 34 interception return (Andersen kick)

SUNDAY NIGHT, OCTOBER 7
SAN FRANCISCO 24, CAROLINA 14—at 3Com Park, attendance 66,944. Jeff Garcia and Terrell Owens combined on a pair of third-quarter touchdown passes to rally the 49ers. After Doug Evans returned an interception 39 yards for a touchdown to give the Panthers a 14-10 lead 1:06 into the second half, Garcia and Owens teamed up 3 times on the ensuing 8-play, 67-yard drive, including a 29-yard touchdown that put San Francisco in front with 9:11 left in the third quarter. The next time the 49ers had the ball, Owens had a 26-yard reception to spark an 80-yard drive capped by his 20-yard touchdown grab for a 10-point lead 2:36 before the end of the quarter. Garcia was 17 of 31 for 212 yards and 2 touchdowns, with 1 interception. Owens had 8 receptions for 118 yards. Chris Weinke was 29 of 47 for 275 yards and 1 touchdown, with 3 interceptions. .

Carolina	0	7	7	0	—	14
San Francisco	0	10	14	0	—	24

SF	—	Garcia 1 run (Cortez kick)
Car	—	Walls 10 pass from Weinke (Kasay kick)
SF	—	FG Cortez 40

250

Car — Evans 39 interception return (Kasay kick)
SF — Owens 29 pass from Garcia (Cortez kick)
SF — Owens 20 pass from Garcia (Cortez kick)

MONDAY NIGHT, OCTOBER 8

ST. LOUIS 35, DETROIT 0—at Pontiac Silverdome, attendance 77,765. Kurt Warner passed for 3 touchdowns as the Rams overwhelmed the Lions. Dre' Bly's 93-yard interception return for a touchdown gave St. Louis a 21-0 lead 3:04 before halftime. Detroit drove inside St. Louis territory on three of its four second-half possessions, but came away empty each time, turning over the ball on an interception, a fumble, and on downs. Warner was 29 of 37 for 291 yards and 3 touchdowns. Detmer played the first half and was 15 of 18 for 149 yards, with 1 interception. Charlie Batch was 11 of 16 for 113 yards, with 1 interception.

St. Louis	7	14	0	14	— 35
Detroit	0	0	0	0	— 0

StL — Hakim 15 pass from Warner (Wilkins kick)
StL — Holt 36 pass from Warner (Wilkins kick)
StL — Bly 93 interception return (Wilkins kick)
StL — Conwell 1 pass from Warner (Wilkins kick)
StL — Faulk 7 run (Wilkins kick)

FIFTH WEEK SUMMARIES
American Football Conference

Eastern Division	W	L	T	Pct.	Pts.	OP
Miami	3	2	0	.600	106	111
N.Y. Jets	3	2	0	.600	114	120
Indianapolis	2	2	0	.500	118	117
New England	2	3	0	.400	103	102
Buffalo	0	4	0	.000	71	128
Central Division						
Pittsburgh	3	1	0	.750	59	48
Baltimore	3	2	0	.600	96	78
Cincinnati	3	2	0	.600	89	85
Cleveland	3	2	0	.600	87	77
Jacksonville	2	2	0	.500	63	56
Tennessee	1	3	0	.250	67	98
Western Division						
Oakland	4	1	0	.800	131	95
Denver	3	2	0	.600	123	97
San Diego	3	2	0	.600	132	87
Seattle	3	2	0	.600	84	107
Kansas City	1	4	0	.200	95	93

National Football Conference

Eastern Division	W	L	T	Pct.	Pts.	OP
N.Y. Giants	3	2	0	.600	91	71
Philadelphia	2	2	0	.500	104	62
Arizona	1	3	0	.250	65	112
Dallas	1	4	0	.200	75	117
Washington	0	5	0	.000	32	144
Central Division						
Green Bay	4	1	0	.800	134	50
Chicago	3	1	0	.750	74	43
Tampa Bay	2	2	0	.500	68	67
Minnesota	2	3	0	.400	89	111
Detroit	0	4	0	.000	46	118
Western Division						
St. Louis	5	0	0	1.000	142	67
San Francisco	4	1	0	.800	122	105
New Orleans	3	1	0	.750	92	67
Atlanta	2	3	0	.400	105	114
Carolina	1	4	0	.200	86	116

SUNDAY, OCTOBER 14

CHICAGO 20, ARIZONA 13—at Soldier Field, attendance 66,944. R.W. McQuarters returned a fumble 69 yards for the decisive touchdown in the Bears'

---

third consecutive victory. Chicago led 13-6 when the Cardinals drove to a first down at the Bears' 30-yard line midway through the third quarter. Mike Brown stopped Michael Pittman for a 1-yard loss, and the ball popped loose. McQuarters picked it up and never broke stride en route to the end zone for a 14-point lead with 7:33 left in the quarter. Jim Miller was 15 of 21 for 116 yards, with 2 interceptions. Plummer was 20 of 37 for 216 yards and 1 touchdown.

Arizona	0	6	0	7	— 13
Chicago	3	10	7	0	— 20

Chi — FG Edinger 46
Ariz — FG Gramatica 40
Chi — Allen 1 run (Edinger kick)
Ariz — FG Gramatica 47
Chi — FG Edinger 43
Chi — McQuarters 69 fumble return (Edinger kick)
Ariz — Sanders 7 pass from Plummer (Gramatica kick)

GREEN BAY 31, BALTIMORE 23—at Lambeau Field, attendance 59,866. Brett Favre passed for 337 yards and 3 touchdowns to lead the Packers. Green Bay shredded the Ravens' vaunted defense for 391 yards, including 230 yards in a first half in which Favre passed for 198 yards and 2 touchdowns to help give his team a 17-7 lead. Baltimore pulled within seven points with 5:46 left in the third quarter, but Favre responded by completing 4 of 6 passes for 57 yards on an 80-yard drive capped by Ahman Green's 1-yard touchdown run in the final minute of the period. Favre's 2-yard touchdown pass to Bubba Franks with 6:59 left built the lead to 21 points, which was enough to withstand 2 late touchdowns engineered by reserve Randall Cunningham. Favre was 27 of 34 for 337 yards and 3 touchdowns. Freeman had 9 catches for 138 yards. Baltimore's Elvis Grbac was 11 of 21 for 138 yards, with 1 touchdown, with 2 interceptions. Cunningham was 5 of 10 for 70 yards.

Baltimore	7	0	3	13	— 23
Green Bay	0	17	7	7	— 31

Balt — Taylor 18 pass from Grbac (Stover kick)
GB — Franks 2 pass from Favre (Longwell kick)
GB — FG Longwell 33
GB — Freeman 8 pass from Favre (Longwell kick)
Balt — FG Stover 28
GB — Green 1 run (Longwell kick)
GB — Franks 2 pass from Favre (Longwell kick)
Balt — Brookins 1 run (Stover kick)
Balt — Cunningham 11 run (pass failed)

CINCINNATI 24, CLEVELAND 14—at Paul Brown Stadium, attendance 64,217. Corey Dillon rushed for 140 yards and a touchdown as the Bengals snapped the Browns' three-game winning streak. Cincinnati had sizeable advantages in total yards (400-211) and time of possession (36:23-23:37). Dillon's 5-yard touchdown run 43 seconds into the fourth quarter gave the Bengals a 21-7 lead, and they had the ball for 7:25 the next time they had the ball, driving 76 yards in 16 plays to Neil Rackers' 21-yard field goal with 1:55 left. Kitna was 20 of 38 for 201 yards and 1 touchdown. Kevin Johnson caught 8 passes for 153 yards.

Cleveland	7	0	0	7	— 14
Cincinnati	3	0	10	11	— 24

Cin — FG Rackers 27
Cle — Johnson 30 pass from Couch (P. Dawson kick)
Cin — Scott 5 pass from Kitna (Rackers kick)
Cin — FG Rackers 42

Cin — Dillon 5 run (Dugans pass from Kitna)
Cin — FG Rackers 21
Cle — Sellers 3 pass from Couch (P. Dawson kick)

SEATTLE 34, DENVER 21—at Husky Stadium, attendance 61,837. Shaun Alexander rushed for 142 yards and scored 2 touchdowns in the Seahawks' victory. Alexander broke off a 60-yard touchdown run only 3:06 into the game. Reggie Tongue added to Seattle's lead with a 55-yard interception return for a touchdown, and Alexander's 1-yard touchdown run 3:14 before halftime put the Seahawks ahead 24-7. Alex Bannister's blocked punt and 9-yard return for a touchdown in the third quarter helped run the game out of reach. Trent Dilfer was 12 of 18 for 110 yards. The Seahawks ran the ball on 26 of their 31 plays after the intermission. Griese was 24 of 36 for 209 yards and 2 touchdowns, with 3 interceptions.

Denver	0	14	0	7	— 21
Seattle	10	14	7	3	— 34

Sea — Alexander 60 run (Lindell kick)
Sea — FG Lindell 44
Sea — Tongue 55 interception return (Lindell kick)
Den — Kennison 8 pass from Griese (Elam kick)
Den — R. Smith 1 pass from Griese (Elam kick)
Sea — Alexander 1 run (Lindell kick)
Sea — Bannister 9 blocked punt return (Lindell kick)
Sea — FG Lindell 23
Den — O'Neal 86 punt return (Elam kick)

MINNESOTA 31, DETROIT 26—at Metrodome, attendance 64,048. Daunte Culpepper rushed for 2 touchdowns and passed for another to carry the Vikings. Culpepper had 2 touchdown runs in the first half, then teamed with Cris Carter on a 47-yard touchdown pass for a seemingly insurmountable 31-6 lead 4:35 into the second half. But Detroit dominated the rest of the way, driving 74, 59, and 93 yards to touchdowns the next three times it had the ball to pull within 31-26 with 6:18 still to play. The Lions began their last possession at their 20-yard line with no time outs and 1:34 left. Charlie Batch completed 4 of 6 passes to march his team to Minnesota's 46 at the 15-second mark, but time ran out after Batch's 20-yard completion to Germane Crowell. Culpepper was 20 of 27 for 244 yards and 1 touchdown, with 1 interception, and had a team-high 83 rushing yards. Carter caught 8 passes for 111 yards. Batch was 31 of 41 for 345 yards and 3 touchdowns. Crowell caught 9 passes for 125 yards and James Stewart ran for 108 yards.

Detroit	3	3	7	13	— 26
Minnesota	7	17	7	0	— 31

Minn — Culpepper 7 run (Anderson kick)
Det — FG Hanson 19
Minn — Prentice 1 run (Anderson kick)
Minn — FG Anderson 41
Det — FG Hanson 51
Minn — Culpepper 33 run (Anderson kick)
Minn — C. Carter 47 pass from Culpepper (Anderson kick)
Det — Stewart 15 pass from Batch (Hanson kick)
Det — Crowell 16 pass from Batch (pass failed)
Det — Morton 20 pass from Batch (Hanson kick)

N.Y. JETS 21, MIAMI 17—at Giants Stadium, attendance 78,823. Vinny Testaverde passed for 2 touchdowns and Curtis Martin ran for another as the Jets overcame a 17-point halftime deficit to defeat the Dolphins for the seventh consecutive time. Miami outgained the Jets 250 total yards to 27 in the first half, and maintaining possession for 22:01. But the roles were reversed in the second half, when the Jets amassed 241 yards to the Dolphins' 98 and held the ball for 18:11. Martin's 27-yard touchdown run came one play after a Lamar Smith fumble and cut the deficit to 17-14 only 3:56 into the second half. Testaverde and Laveranues Coles teamed on another touchdown pass, this time from 25 yards 2:52 into the fourth quarter, to give the Jets the lead. Late in the game, Miami drove from its 43-yard line to a first-and-goal at New York's 6 with 1:17 left. But Fiedler's pass was intercepted in the end zone by Marvin Jones. Victor Green picked off Fiedler again at New York's 21 with 28 seconds left to end the Dolphins' last chance. Testaverde was 15 of 22 for 168 yards and 2 touchdowns, and Martin rushed for 120 yards. Fiedler was 23 of 34 for 213 yards and 1 touchdown, with 2 interceptions.

Miami	7	10	0	0	—	17
N.Y. Jets	0	0	14	7	—	21

Mia	—	Smith 14 pass from Fiedler (Mare kick)
Mia	—	Minor 29 run (Mare kick)
Mia	—	FG Mare 26
NYJ	—	Coles 22 pass from Testaverde (Hall kick)
NYJ	—	C. Martin 27 run (Hall kick)
NYJ	—	Coles 25 pass from Testaverde (Hall kick)

NEW ORLEANS 27, CAROLINA 25—at Ericsson Stadium, attendance 46,744. Ricky Williams ran 1 yard for the winning touchdown as time expired to give the Saints a dramatic victory. Williams' run spoiled a comeback by the Panthers, who turned over the ball on three first-half possessions en route to falling behind 17-0. Carolina chipped away at the deficit, though, and took its only lead of the game at 25-20 when Steve Smith returned a punt 70 yards for a touchdown with 1:48 left in the game. But New Orleans began the ensuing possession at its 18-yard line and drove 82 yards in 13 plays to the winning score. The key plays were Aaron Brooks' 14-yard pass to Willie Jackson on fourth-and-10 from the Saints' 45 with 53 seconds left, and his 22-yard pass to Joe Horn to the 5. After 2 defensive penalties, New Orleans had a first-and-goal at the 1 with six seconds to play. Brooks' pass fell incomplete in the end zone with one second left before Williams took a pitch on second down and scooted around left end for the decisive touchdown. Brooks was 14 of 40 for 180 yards and 2 touchdowns, with 1 interception. Williams had 31 carries for 147 yards. Chris Weinke was 21 of 39 for 196 yards and 2 touchdowns, with 1 interception.

New Orleans	10	7	3	7	—	27
Carolina	0	6	6	13	—	25

NO	—	Cleeland 11 pass from Brooks (Carney kick)
NO	—	FG Carney 30
NO	—	Cleeland 16 pass from Brooks (Carney kick)
Car	—	FG Kasay 46
Car	—	FG Kasay 52
Car	—	Hayes 9 pass from Weinke (pass failed)
NO	—	FG Carney 39
Car	—	Walls 23 pass from Weinke (pass failed)
Car	—	Smith 70 punt return (Kasay kick)
NO	—	R. Williams 1 run (Carney kick)

ST. LOUIS 15, N.Y. GIANTS 14—at Dome at America's Center, attendance 65,992. Backup Trung Canidate ran 1 yard for a touchdown with 4:16 left to give the Rams a hard-fought victory over the Giants. The Giants limited St. Louis' high-powered offense to 3 field goals in the first three quarters and took a 14-9 lead on Kerry Collins' 25-yard touchdown pass to Ike Hilliard 1:27 into the fourth period. The Rams began the winning march from their 23-yard line with 8:34 to play. With Marshall Faulk on the sideline with a sprained knee suffered late in the third quarter, Kurt Warner passed on each of the first 11 plays of the decisive drive, completing 6 to move his team to the Giants' 24. Warner's next pass fell incomplete in the end zone, but Sam Garnes was whistled for interfering with Canidate, and the penalty gave St. Louis a first-and-goal at the 1. Canidate ran for the go-ahead touchdown on the next play. Joe Jurevicius fumbled at the Rams' 31 in the closing minutes, and Grant Wistrom recovered to secure the Rams' victory. Warner was 28 of 46 for 316 yards, with 1 interception. Collins was 18 of 32 for 250 yards and 1 touchdown, with 1 interception. Jurevicius had 6 receptions for 101 yards.

N.Y. Giants	7	0	0	7	—	14
St. Louis	6	3	0	6	—	15

NYG	—	Dayne 4 run (Andersen kick)
StL	—	FG Wilkins 28
StL	—	FG Wilkins 33
StL	—	FG Wilkins 25
NYG	—	Hilliard 25 pass from Collins (Andersen kick)
StL	—	Canidate 1 run (pass failed)

PITTSBURGH 20, KANSAS CITY 17—at Arrowhead Stadium, attendance 78,413. Jerome Bettis rushed for 112 yards, and the Steelers built an 18-point lead through three quarters before holding on for their third consecutive victory. Chad Scott's 61-yard interception return for a touchdown four plays into the second half, and runs of 10 and 30 yards by Bettis on a 68-yard drive capped by Kordell Stewart's 5-yard touchdown pass to Hines Ward gave the Steelers a 20-2 lead. Then the Chiefs' offense came to life, marching 60 and 73 yards to touchdowns the next two times it had the ball. Priest Holmes capped the drives with touchdown runs of 29 yards and 1 yard, the latter pulling Kansas City within three points with 2:39 to play. But the Chiefs did not get the ball back. Amos Zereoue's 10-yard run on third-and-3 from Pittsburgh's 27-yard line at the two-minute warning enabled the Steelers to run out the clock. Stewart was 15 of 25 for 141 yards and 1 touchdown. Bettis gained 83 of his 112 yards after halftime and helped Pittsburgh. Green was 16 of 33 for 127 yards, with 1 interception. Holmes rushed for 150 yards on 26 carries.

Pittsburgh	0	6	14	0	—	20
Kansas City	0	2	0	15	—	17

Pitt	—	FG Brown 42
Pitt	—	FG Brown 55
KC	—	Safety, Ricks blocked punt out of end zone
Pit	—	Scott 61 interception return (Brown kick)
Pit	—	Ward 5 pass from Stewart (Brown kick)
KC	—	Holmes 26 run (Peterson kick)
KC	—	Holmes 1 run (Gonzalez pass from Green)

NEW ENGLAND 29, SAN DIEGO 26 (OT)—at Foxboro Stadium, attendance 59,093. The Patriots erased a 10-point deficit late in regulation, then won on Adam Vinatieri's 44-yard field goal 4:05 into overtime. New England beat San Diego for the tenth consecutive time dating to 1973. The Chargers led 26-16 fourth-quarter lead, but New England countered with a 15-play, 69-yard drive capped by Vinatieri's 23-yard field goal with 3:35 to play. The Patriots' defense forced a punt, and Troy Brown's 40-yard return gave New England good field position at its 40-yard line with 2:10 left. Tom Brady completed passes of 3, 12, and 16 yards to Brown to give the Patriots a first down at San Diego's 29 with 56 seconds to go. Brady teamed with David Patten on a 26-yard strike to the 3, then tossed the tying touchdown pass to Jermaine Wiggins with 36 seconds left. The Chargers took possession first in the extra session but punted, and the Patriots began the decisive drive from their 23. They used a 37-yard pass-interference penalty and on third-and-5 from the 35, Brady completed a first-down pass to Kevin Faulk to the 26, and Vinatieri made the winning kick three plays later. Brady was 33 of 54 for 364 yards and 2 touchdowns. Brown had 11 receptions for 117 yards, and Terry Glenn caught 7 passes for 110 yards. Flutie was 20 of 32 for 270 yards and 1 touchdown. Curtis Conway caught 4 passes for 117 yards.

San Diego	3	3	7	13	0	—	26
New England	3	6	7	10	3	—	29

NE	—	FG Vinatieri 26
SD	—	FG Richey 21
NE	—	Glenn 21 pass from Brady (kick failed)
SD	—	FG Richey 27
SD	—	Tomlinson 1 run (Richey kick)
NE	—	A. Smith 1 run (Vinatieri kick)
SD	—	Heiden 3 pass from Flutie (run failed)
SD	—	Harris 6 fumble return (Richey kick)
NE	—	FG Vinatieri 23
NE	—	Wiggins 3 pass from Brady (Vinatieri kick)
NE	—	FG Vinatieri 44

SAN FRANCISCO 37, ATLANTA 31 (OT)—at Georgia Dome, attendance 46,727. Jeff Garcia and Terrell Owens teamed on 3 touchdown passes, including the winning, 52-yard strike 8:44 into overtime, as the 49ers came from behind to beat the Falcons. The 49ers, who also beat the Falcons in overtime in week 1, had 517 yards in all. San Francisco, which trailed by as many as 14 points during the first half, rallied to take a 24-23 advantage on Kevan Barlow's 2-yard touchdown run with 4:44 left in regulation. Atlanta needed only six plays, however, to regain the lead, capped by Chris Chandler's 47-yard touchdown strike to Brian Finneran. Chandler's 2-point conversion pass to Shawn Jefferson made it 31-24 with 2:22 left. Garcia completed 5 passes and scrambled twice for 14 yards to help move the ball to the Falcons' 17 with 22 seconds left. An intentional spike stopped the clock before Garcia found Owens for the tying touchdown pass with 17 seconds to go., and Garcia found Owens down the right sideline in overtime for the winning touchdown. Garcia was 27 of 41 for 332 yards and 3 touchdowns, and ran for 70 yards. Owens caught 9 passes for 183 yards, all after halftime. Chandler was 19 of 36 for 268 yards and 2 touchdowns, with 1 interception.

San Francisco	0	7	10	14	6	—	37
Atlanta	14	6	0	11	0	—	31

Atl	—	Christian 5 pass from Chandler (Feely kick)
Atl	—	M. Smith 3 run (Feely kick)
SF	—	Garcia 7 run (Cortez kick)
Atl	—	FG Feely 39
Atl	—	FG Feely 24
SF	—	FG Cortez 27
SF	—	Owens 33 pass from Garcia (Cortez kick)

Atl — FG Feely 36
SF — Barlow 2 run (Cortez kick)
Atl — Finneran 47 pass from Chandler
(Jefferson pass from Chandler)
SF — Owens 17 pass from Garcia
(Cortez kick)
SF — Owens 52 pass from Garcia

TENNESSEE 31, TAMPA BAY 28 (OT)—at Adelphia Coliseum, attendance 68,798. Joe Nedney's 49-yard field goal 2:38 into overtime ended the Titans' three-game losing streak and spoiled a dramatic comeback. Eddie George's 4-yard touchdown run gave Tennessee a 28-14 lead midway through the fourth quarter, but Tampa Bay rallied. Nedney missed a potential, game-clinching 47-yard field goal with 2:08 left and a 28-21 lead, and Tampa Bay took over possession at its 38-yard line. Brad Johnson passed on every down of the ensuing 11-play march, before teaming with Dave Moore on the tying, 5-yard touchdown pass with 54 seconds to go. The Buccaneers won the overtime coin toss, but a penalty on the kickoff forced them to start from their 9-yard line. After three consecutive incompletions and a punt, the Titans began the winning drive at the Buccaneers' 46. Steve McNair completed a 14-yard pass to Drew Bennett on first down, and Nedney came on for the winning kick. McNair was 15 of 23 for 230 yards and 1 touchdown, with 1 interception. Brad Johnson passed on each of his team's final 26 plays and finished 24 of 50 for 287 yards and 3 touchdowns, with 1 interception. Keyshawn Johnson had 8 receptions for 140 yards.

| Tampa Bay | 0 | 7 | 14 | 0 | — | 28 |
| Tennessee | 7 | 10 | 0 | 11 | 3 | — | 31 |

Tenn — K. Dyson 1 pass from McNair
(Nedney kick)
TB — Dunn 5 run (Gramatica kick)
Tenn — McNair 1 run (Nedney kick)
Tenn — FG Nedney 44
TB — Dunn 26 pass from B. Johnson
(Gramatica kick)
Tenn — FG Nedney 45
Tenn — George 4 run (K. Dyson pass from McNair)
TB — Green 6 pass from B. Johnson (Gramatica kick)
TB — Moore 5 pass from B. Johnson (Gramatica kick)
Tenn — FG Nedney 49

SUNDAY NIGHT, OCTOBER 14
OAKLAND 23, INDIANAPOLIS 18—at RCA Dome, attendance 56,972. Rich Gannon passed for 243 yards and Anthony Dorsett returned an interception 39 yards for a touchdown to highlight the Raiders' victory. Dorsett's interception return 5:24 before halftime gave Oakland a 13-3 lead. They closest the Colts came was two points when Mike Vanderjagt kicked a 34-yard field goal with 13:57 to play in the game, but they were forced to punt on their next possession. The Raiders then executed a 14-play, 61-yard drive that culminated in Sebastian Janikowski's 37-yard field goal and took the clock down to just 2:22 left. Tory James' interception at Oakland's 44 with 55 seconds left sealed the victory. Gannon was 18 of 32 for 243 yards. Tim Brown caught 7 passes for 145 yards. Manning was 26 of 41 for 241 yards and 2 touchdowns, with 1 interception. Edgerrin James rushed for 116 yards on 26 carries.

| Oakland | 3 | 10 | 7 | 3 | — | 23 |
| Indianapolis | 0 | 9 | 6 | 3 | — | 18 |

Oak — FG Janikowski 39
Oak — FG Janikowski 42
Ind — FG Vanderjagt 47
Oak — Dorsett 39 interception return (Janikowski kick)

Ind — Harrison 3 pass from Manning
(kick failed)
Oak — Wheatley 1 run (Janikowski kick)
Ind — Harrison 6 pass from Manning
(run failed)
Ind — FG Vanderjagt 34
Oak — FG Janikowski 37

MONDAY NIGHT, OCTOBER 15
DALLAS 9, WASHINGTON 7—at Texas Stadium, attendance 63,941. Tim Seder's 26-yard field goal as time expired lifted the Cowboys to their first victory and sent the Redskins to their fifth consecutive defeat. The Cowboys' victory was their eighth in a row over their division rivals dating to 1997. Tony Banks' 31-yard touchdown pass to Michael Westbrook put the Redskins ahead 7-3 2:44 into the fourth period. The Cowboys countered with Seder's 39-yard field goal with 6:32 left to make it 7-6, and Stephen Davis, carrying for the sixth time on the eight-play drive, lost a fumble at Dallas' 33 with 2:39 to play. Troy Hambrick's 2-yard run to the 24 converted a key third down with 1:10 remaining. Emmitt Smith then had back-to-back runs of 3 and 13 yards to set up Seder's winning kick. Anthony Wright was 15 of 28 for 177 yards, with 1 interception, while Smith had 107 yards on 25 carries. Banks was 10 of 18 for 132 yards.

| Washington | 0 | 0 | 0 | 7 | — | 7 |
| Dallas | 0 | 3 | 0 | 6 | — | 9 |

Dall — FG Seder 28
Wash — Westbrook 31 pass from Banks
(Conway kick)
Dall — FG Seder 39
Dall — FG Seder 26

SIXTH WEEK SUMMARIES
American Football Conference

Eastern Division	W	L	T	Pct.	Pts.	OP
Miami	3	2	0	.600	106	111
New England	3	3	0	.500	141	119
N.Y. Jets	3	3	0	.500	128	154
Indianapolis	2	3	0	.400	135	155
Buffalo	1	4	0	.200	84	138
Central Division						
Pittsburgh	4	1	0	.800	76	58
Cleveland	4	2	0	.667	111	91
Baltimore	3	3	0	.500	110	102
Cincinnati	3	3	0	.500	89	109
Jacksonville	2	3	0	.400	73	69
Tennessee	2	3	0	.400	94	122
Western Division						
Oakland	4	1	0	.800	131	95
San Diego	4	2	0	.667	159	97
Seattle	3	2	0	.600	84	107
Denver	3	3	0	.500	133	124
Kansas City	1	5	0	.167	111	117

National Football Conference

Eastern Division	W	L	T	Pct.	Pts.	OP
Philadelphia	3	2	0	.600	114	71
N.Y. Giants	3	3	0	.500	100	81
Arizona	2	3	0	.400	89	128
Dallas	1	4	0	.200	75	117
Washington	1	5	0	.167	49	158
Central Division						
Chicago	4	1	0	.800	98	43
Green Bay	4	2	0	.667	147	85
Minnesota	3	3	0	.500	124	124
Tampa Bay	2	3	0	.400	78	84
Detroit	0	5	0	.000	70	145
Western Division						
St. Louis	6	0	0	1.000	176	81
San Francisco	4	1	0	.800	122	105
New Orleans	3	2	0	.600	105	87
Atlanta	3	3	0	.500	125	127
Carolina	1	5	0	.167	100	133

THURSDAY NIGHT, OCTOBER 18

BUFFALO 13, JACKSONVILLE 10—at ALLTEL Stadium, attendance 58,893. Jake Arians kicked a 46-yard field goal with 1:03 left to lift the Bills to their first victory. Rob Johnson's 27-yard touchdown pass to Eric Moulds in the third quarter gave Buffalo a 10-7 lead, and it stayed that way until the Jaguars' Mike Hollis kicked a 41-yard field goal to tie the game with 3:54 left in the game. The Bills began the ensuing possession at their 23-yard line, and Johnson scrambled 12 yards for a first down. Johnson completed short passes to Larry Centers for 2 more first downs on the 10-play, 48-yard drive before Arians came on for the go-ahead kick on fourth-and-1 from Jacksonville's 29. Tillman's interception sealed Buffalo's victory with 44 seconds left. Johnson was 23 of 30 for 238 yards and 1 touchdown. Mark Brunell was 16 of 26 for 150 yards and 1 touchdown, with 2 interceptions.

| Buffalo | 0 | 3 | 7 | 3 | — | 13 |
| Jacksonville | 0 | 0 | 7 | 3 | — | 10 |

Buff — FG Arians 30
Jax — Brady 20 pass from Brunell (Hollis kick)
Buff — Moulds 27 pass from Johnson
(Arians kick)
Jax — FG Hollis 41
Buff — FG Arians 46

SUNDAY, OCTOBER 21
ATLANTA 20, NEW ORLEANS 13—at Louisiana Superdome, attendance 70,020. Chris Chandler's 39-yard touchdown pass to Shawn Jefferson broke a 10-10 tie late in the fourth quarter and helped lift the Falcons. The Falcons' decisive drive began at Atlanta's 49-yard line at the outset of the final quarter. Chandler converted a third-and-5 from the Saints' 46 by completing a pass to Brian Finneran, then teamed with Jefferson for a touchdown on the next play. Jay Feely added a 38-yard field goal with 2:34 remaining. New Orleans recovered an onside kick after John Carney's field goal with 30 seconds left, and drove to the Falcons' 33 before Aaron Brooks' final pass fell incomplete in the end zone as time expired. Chandler was 14 of 20 for 187 yards and 2 touchdowns, with 1 interception. Brooks was 23 of 39 for 249 yards and 1 touchdown, with 1 interception.

| Atlanta | 10 | 0 | 0 | 10 | — | 20 |
| New Orleans | 0 | 10 | 0 | 3 | — | 13 |

Atl — Crumpler 57 pass from Chandler
(Feely kick)
Atl — FG Feely 31
NO — FG Carney 23
NO — Cleeland 19 pass from Brooks
(Carney kick)
Atl — Jefferson 39 pass from Chandler
(Feely kick)
Atl — FG Feely 38
NO — FG Carney 31

CLEVELAND 24, BALTIMORE 14—at Cleveland Browns Stadium, attendance 72,818. The Browns' defense recorded 7 sacks and Tim Couch passed for 2 touchdowns in a span of 1:56 of the third quarter as the Browns stunned the Ravens. The Browns managed only 10 first downs and 219 total yards but did not turn over the ball and made the most of their few scoring opportunities. Ben Gay returned the game's opening kickoff 42 yards to set up James Jackson's 11-yard touchdown run, Anthony Henry's second-quarter interception led to Phil Dawson's 33-yard field goal. Cleveland had a 10-6 lead before marching 80 yards the first time it had the ball in second half, with Couch's 28-yard touchdown pass to Kevin Johnson capping the drive 7:16 into the third quarter. Four plays later, Greg Spires recovered Elvis Grbac's fumble at Baltimore's 36-yard line. Couch teamed with Quincy Morgan for a touchdown pass on the next play to make it 24-6. Couch was 11 of 18 for 149 yards and 2 touchdowns. Grbac was 16 of 20 for 142 yards, with 2 interceptions, before being injured. Cunningham was 11 of 25 for 120 yards and 1 touchdown. Matt Stover's 21-yard field goal 5:11 before halftime gave him an NFL-record 32 consecutive games with at least 1 field goal.

| Baltimore | 0 | 6 | 0 | 8 | — | 14 |
| Cleveland | 7 | 3 | 14 | 0 | — | 24 |

Cle	—	J. Jackson 11 run (P. Dawson kick)
Balt	—	FG Stover 21
Cle	—	FG P. Dawson 33
Balt	—	FG Stover 38
Cle	—	Johnson 28 pass from Couch (P. Dawson kick)
Cle	—	Morgan 36 pass from Couch (P. Dawson kick)
Balt	—	Ismail 22 pass from Cunningham (Ismail pass from Cunningham)

WASHINGTON 17, CAROLINA 14 (OT)—at FedEx Field, attendance 74,480. The Redskins ended their five-game losing streak when Brett Conway kicked a 23-yard field goal 1:52 into overtime. To win, Washington had to rally from a 14-0 deficit in the fourth quarter. First, LaVar Arrington returned an interception 67 yards for a touchdown with 10:10 left to pull the Redskins within seven points. Then, Washington's defense forced a punt, and Tony Banks teamed with Rod Gardner on an 85-yard touchdown pass on the next play to tie the game with 7:25 to go. Conway's 32-yard field-goal attempt was wide right in regulation, but Washington won the overtime coin toss and Banks completed back-to-back passes of 32 yards to Bryan Johnson and 47 yards to Gardner to push the ball to the Panthers' 5 and allow Conway to redeem himself. Banks was 17 of 30 for 346 yards and 1 touchdown, with 1 interception. Gardner had 208 yards on 6 receptions. Chris Weinke was 24 of 35 for 226 yards and 1 touchdown, with 4 interceptions—all in Redskins' territory. Tshimanga Biakabutuka had 20 carries for 121 yards and 1 touchdown but broke his foot and was lost for the rest of the season.

| Carolina | 7 | 0 | 0 | 7 | 0 | — | 14 |
| Washington | 0 | 0 | 0 | 14 | 3 | — | 17 |

Car	—	Walls 2 pass from Weinke (Kasay kick)
Car	—	Biakabutuka 10 run (Kasay kick)
Wash	—	Arrington 67 interception return (Conway kick)
Wash	—	Gardner 85 pass from Banks (Conway kick)
Wash	—	FG Conway 23

CHICAGO 24, CINCINNATI 0—at Paul Brown Stadium, attendance 63,408. Anthony Thomas rushed for a club rookie-record 188 yards to lead the Bears to their first shutout since 1993. Thomas carried 22 times and had a 23-yard touchdown run to close the scoring 5:55 into the fourth quarter. The Bears' defense forced Cincinnati to punt on seven of its first eight drives . On their next possession, the Bengals drove from their 30-yard line to Chicago's 2, but 4 consecutive incompletions ended the threat. Jim Miller was 23 of 30 for 232 yards and 2 touchdowns. Jon Kitna was 19 of 46 for 244 yards, with 1 interception.

| Chicago | 3 | 7 | 7 | 7 | — | 24 |
| Cincinnati | 0 | 0 | 0 | 0 | — | 0 |

Chi	—	FG Edinger 48
Chi	—	Baxter 1 pass from Miller (Edinger kick)
Chi	—	Booker 13 pass from Miller (Edinger kick)
Chi	—	Thomas 23 run (Edinger kick)

SAN DIEGO 27, DENVER 10—at Qualcomm Stadium, attendance 67,521. Ronney Jenkins returned the opening kickoff 88 yards for a touchdown to spark the Chargers to the victory. The Chargers put the game away by converting 2 turnovers, a fumble recovery by Jason Perry and interception by Al Fontenot, into 2 Doug Flutie-to-Jeff Graham touchdowns, the latter with 8:36 to play. Flutie was 21 of 32 for 280 yards and 2 touchdowns, with 1 interception. Graham had 7 catches for 107 yards. Griese was 26 of 41 for 212 yards and 1 touchdown, with 2 interceptions.

| Denver | 0 | 7 | 3 | 0 | — | 10 |
| San Diego | 8 | 6 | 7 | 7 | — | 27 |

SD	—	Jenkins 88 kickoff return (Richey kick)
SD	—	FG Richey 21
SD	—	FG Richey 51
Den	—	Clark 6 pass from Griese (Elam kick)
Den	—	FG Elam 45
SD	—	Graham 17 pass from Flutie (Richey kick)
SD	—	Graham 20 pass from Flutie (Richey kick)

MINNESOTA 35, GREEN BAY 13—at Metrodome, attendance 64,165. Daunte Culpepper ran for 1 touchdown and passed for another to pace the Vikings. Culpepper teamed with Cris Carter on a 43-yard touchdown strike to open the scoring 6:42 into the second quarter. Two plays later, Kailee Wong intercepted Brett Favre's pass and returned the ball 27 yards for a touchdown and a 14-0 lead. Culpepper was 18 of 27 for 184 yards and 1 touchdown. Favre was 21 of 35 for 169 yards and 2 touchdowns, with 1 interception.

| Green Bay | 0 | 0 | 7 | 6 | — | 13 |
| Minnesota | 0 | 20 | 0 | 15 | — | 35 |

Minn	—	Carter 43 pass from Culpepper (Anderson kick)
Minn	—	Wong 27 interception return (Anderson kick)
Minn	—	FG Anderson 42
Minn	—	FG Anderson 36
GB	—	Franks 2 pass from Favre (Longwell kick)
Minn	—	Culpepper 14 run (Reed pass from Culpepper)
Minn	—	Kleinsasser 2 run (Anderson kick)
GB	—	Lee 3 pass from Favre (pass failed)

ARIZONA 24, KANSAS CITY 16—at Sun Devil Stadium, attendance 35,916. The Cardinals scored touchdowns on three consecutive second-half possessions, then thwarted Kansas City's comeback bid with an end zone interception in the game's final seconds. Arizona led 24-9 with 9:43 to play, but the Chiefs cut the deficit to 24-16 and got the ball at their 1-yard line with 1:06 remaining following a 54-yard punt by Scott Player. In rapid succession, Green completed passes of 25 yards to Tony Gonzalez, 43 yards to Alexander, and 20 yards to Marvin Minnis to push the ball to the Cardinals' 11 with 21 seconds left. After an intentional spike, Green teamed with Holmes on a 9-yard pass to the 2, then spiked the ball again to stop the clock with five seconds remaining. But on fourth down, Green's pass in the end zone for Minnis was batted away by Adrian Wilson and into the hands of Corey Chavous. Plummer was 16 of 25 for 228 yards and 1 touchdown. Boston caught 7 passes for 131 yards. Green was 21 of 44 for 352 yards and 1 touchdown, with 2 interceptions.

| Kansas City | 3 | 6 | 0 | 7 | — | 16 |
| Arizona | 0 | 3 | 7 | 14 | — | 24 |

KC	—	FG Peterson 49
Ariz	—	FG Gramatica 30
KC	—	FG Peterson 29
KC	—	FG Peterson 33
Ariz	—	Pittman 24 run (Gramatica kick)
Ariz	—	Boston 23 pass from Plummer (Gramatica kick)
Ariz	—	T. Jones 13 run (Gramatica kick)
KC	—	Alexander 34 pass from Green (Peterson kick)

NEW ENGLAND 38, INDIANAPOLIS 17—at RCA Dome, attendance 56,022. The Patriots routed the Colts for the second time in four weeks when wide receiver David Patten became the first NFL player since Walter Payton in 1979 to account for touchdowns running, passing, and receiving in the same game. New England, which beat Indianapolis 44-13 in Foxboro in week 3, jumped to a 7-0 lead 4:25 into the game when Patten raced 29 yards around right end on the Patriots' first play. The score was set up when Brandon Mitchell blocked a field goal that cornerback Leonard Myers scooped up and returned 35 yards. Midway through the second quarter, the Patriots took over possession at their 9-yard line. Patten hauled in a pass from Tom Brady and turned it into a 91-yard touchdown for a 14-3 advantage. After New England forced a punt, Patten was responsible for another 1-play drive, taking a lateral pass from Brady and tossing a 60-yard touchdown pass to Troy Brown. The Colts had 2 field-goal tries blocked and lost 2 fumbles. Patten, who added a 6-yard touchdown catch to close the scoring in the fourth quarter, had 4 receptions for 117 yards and finished with 206 yards rushing, passing, and receiving. Brady was 16 of 20 for 202 yards and 3 touchdowns. Peyton Manning was 22 of 34 for 335 yards and 1 touchdown. Marvin Harrison caught 8 passes for 157 yards and Edgerrin James rushed for 143 yards.

| New England | 7 | 21 | 3 | 7 | — | 38 |
| Indianapolis | 3 | 3 | 11 | 0 | — | 17 |

NE	—	Patten 29 run (Vinatieri kick)
Ind	—	FG Vanderjagt 42
NE	—	Patten 91 pass from Brady (Vinatieri kick)
NE	—	T. Brown 60 pass from Patten (Vinatieri kick)
NE	—	Wiggins 2 pass from Brady (Vinatieri kick)
Ind	—	FG Vanderjagt 42
Ind	—	Harrison 2 pass from Manning (Dilger pass from Manning)
Ind	—	FG Vinatieri 43
Ind	—	FG Vanderjagt 24
NE	—	Patten 6 pass from Brady (Vinatieri kick)

PITTSBURGH 17, TAMPA BAY 10—at Raymond James Stadium, attendance 65,588. Jerome Bettis rushed and passed for touchdowns to key the Steelers' fourth consecutive victory. Pittsburgh trailed 3-0 before Bettis began to sweep right on third-and-2 from the Buccaneers' 32-yard line. He pulled up and tossed a touchdown pass to Jerame Tuman to give the Steelers the lead. In the second half, Bettis rushed for 118 yards, including a 46-yard touchdown run 2:17 into the third quarter to open an 11-point advantage. Kordell Stewart was 10 of 16 for 100 yards, with 2 interceptions. The Steelers' defense recorded 10 sacks. Brad Johnson was 24 of 40 for 283 yards and 1 touchdown, with 1 interception. Keyshawn Johnson caught 10 passes for 159 yards.

| Pittsburgh | 0 | 7 | 10 | 0 | — | 17 |
| Tampa Bay | 0 | 3 | 0 | 7 | — | 10 |

| TB | — | FG Gramatica 31 |

Pitt — Tuman 32 pass from Bettis (Brown kick)
Pitt — Bettis 46 run (Brown kick)
Pitt — FG Brown 35
TB — Murphy 5 pass from B. Johnson (Gramatica kick)

ST. LOUIS 34, N.Y. JETS 14—at Giants Stadium, attendance 78,766. Trung Canidate led the Rams by rushing for 195 yards and 2 touchdowns in his first NFL start. The game was tied at 7-7 in the second quarter when Canidate, playing in place of injured Marshall Faulk, took a pitch from Az-Zahir Hakim, who had run 12 yards around right end to the Jets' 44-yard line. Canidate raced untouched the rest of the way for a touchdown to put St. Louis ahead for good. St. Louis put the game away by holding the ball for 12:49 in a third quarter in which it recorded 11 first downs and totaled 166 yards on 24 plays to no first downs and 8 yards on 3 plays for the Jets, including a touchdown by Canidate when he took a direct snap. A surprise onside kick led to another field goal for a 34-7 lead. Kurt Warner was 18 of 27 for 215 yards and 1 touchdown. Vinny Testaverde was 9 of 13 for 74 yards and 1 touchdown, with 1 interception, and backup Chad Pennington was 9 of 14 for 68 yards and 1 touchdown.

St. Louis	0	21	10	3	—	34
N.Y. Jets	0	7	0	7	—	14

StL — Hakim 15 pass from Warner (Wilkins kick)
NYJ — Becht 5 pass from Testaverde (Hall kick)
StL — Canidate 44 run (Wilkins kick)
StL — A. Williams 42 interception return (Wilkins kick)
StL — FG Wilkins 47
StL — Canidate 12 run (Wilkins kick)
StL — FG Wilkins 24
NYJ — Becht 7 pass from Pennington (Hall kick)

TENNESSEE 27, DETROIT 24—at Pontiac Silverdome, attendance 76,940. The Titans outlasted the Lions when Joe Nedney kicked his fourth field goal of the game from 46 yards with five seconds to play. The Titans took a 24-17 lead on Steve McNair's 6-yard touchdown pass to Frank Wycheck. Wycheck set up the score by taking a lateral pitch from McNair and completing a 21-yard toss to Desmond Mason. Charlie Batch fired a touchdown pass to Desmond Howard to tie the game with 1:18 to go. McNair answered with an 18-yard pass to Mason to midfield, then ran 22 yards two plays later to position Nedney for his winning kick. McNair was 15 of 35 for 216 yards and 1 touchdown, with 2 interceptions. Wycheck had 7 catches for 100 yards. Batch was 25 of 42 for 338 yards and 3 touchdowns, with 1 interception. Johnnie Morton had 9 catches for 113 yards.

Tennessee	3	6	8	10	—	27
Detroit	0	14	0	10	—	24

Tenn — FG Nedney 38
Tenn — FG Nedney 46
Det — Morton 18 pass from Batch (Hanson kick)
Det — Crowell 46 pass from Batch (Hanson kick)
Tenn — FG Nedney 30
Tenn — Mitchell 69 blocked field goal return (Bennett pass from McNair)
Det — FG Hanson 23
Tenn — Wycheck 6 pass from McNair (Nedney kick)
Det — Howard 36 pass from Batch (Hanson kick)
Tenn — FG Nedney 46

MONDAY NIGHT, OCTOBER 22
PHILADELPHIA 10, N.Y. GIANTS 9—at Giants Stadium, attendance 78,821. Donovan McNabb's 18-yard touchdown pass to James Thrash with 1:52 remaining lifted the Eagles past the Giants, ending Philadelphia's nine-game losing streak to its division rivals. The Giants outgained the Eagles 238-215 in all, but managed only 3 first downs and 59 total yards in the final two periods. In the first half the Giants had lengthy marches of 15, 11, and 13 plays, but each drive stalled iand the Giants had to settle for 3 short field goals by Morten Andersen and a 9-0 lead. The Giants led 9-3 in the fourth quarter, but a 27-yard punt by Rodney Williams gave Philadelphia the ball at the Giants' 40-yard line with 5:52 left. McNabb scrambled for 7 yards to start the winning drive, and he ended it six plays later with the go-ahead touchdown pass to Thrash. Jeremiah Trotter sacked Kerry Collins, forcing a fumble that Brandon Whiting recovered at the Giants' 36 with 1:05 to play. McNabb was 15 of 26 for 154 yards and 1 touchdown, with 1 interception. Collins was 21 of 33 for 162 yards, but had only 41 yards in the second half.

Philadelphia	0	0	3	7	—	10
N.Y. Giants	3	6	0	0	—	9

NYG — FG Andersen 24
NYG — FG Andersen 21
NYG — FG Andersen 24
Phil — FG Akers 25
Phil — Thrash 18 pass from McNabb (Akers kick)

SEVENTH WEEK SUMMARIES
American Football Conference

Eastern Division	W	L	T	Pct.	Pts.	OP
Miami	4	2	0	.667	130	131
N.Y. Jets	4	3	0	.571	141	166
Indianapolis	3	3	0	.500	170	183
New England	3	4	0	.429	161	150
Buffalo	1	5	0	.167	108	165
Central Division						
Pittsburgh	5	1	0	.833	110	65
Cleveland	4	2	0	.667	111	91
Baltimore	4	3	0	.571	128	119
Cincinnati	4	3	0	.571	120	136
Jacksonville	2	4	0	.333	90	87
Tennessee	2	4	0	.333	101	156
Western Division						
Oakland	5	1	0	.833	151	105
San Diego	5	2	0	.714	186	121
Denver	4	3	0	.571	164	144
Seattle	3	3	0	.500	104	131
Kansas City	1	6	0	.143	139	152

National Football Conference

Eastern Division	W	L	T	Pct.	Pts.	OP
Philadelphia	3	3	0	.500	124	91
N.Y. Giants	3	4	0	.429	121	116
Arizona	2	4	0	.333	92	145
Dallas	2	4	0	.333	92	120
Washington	2	5	0	.286	84	179
Central Division						
Chicago	5	1	0	.833	135	74
Green Bay	4	2	0	.667	147	85
Tampa Bay	3	3	0	.500	119	98
Minnesota	3	4	0	.429	138	165
Detroit	0	6	0	.000	97	176
Western Division						
St. Louis	6	1	0	.857	207	115
New Orleans	4	2	0	.667	139	118
San Francisco	4	2	0	.667	153	142
Atlanta	3	3	0	.500	125	127
Carolina	1	6	0	.143	112	146

THURSDAY NIGHT, OCTOBER 25
INDIANAPOLIS 35, KANSAS CITY 28—at Arrowhead Stadium, attendance 74,212. Dominic Rhodes made the big plays as the Colts held off the Chiefs in a wild second half. Indianapolis led just 7-3 at halftime before a barrage of scoring over the final two periods. Rhodes returned a kickoff 88 yards for a touchdown to give the Colts a 17-6 lead with 4:50 remaining in the third quarter. The Chiefs trimmed the deficit to 28-21 on Green's 11-yard touchdown pass to Larry Parker with 4:45 left in the game, then drove from their 47-yard line to a first down at the Colts' 11 the next time they had the ball. But Green's third-down pass from there was intercepted in the end zone by Idrees Bashir with 2:01 to go. Three plays later, Rhodes burst 77 yards off right tackle for the clinching touchdown at the 1:02 mark. Larry Parker caught a 5-yard reception with four seconds left. Rhodes was in the game because starter Edgerrin James suffered a season-ending knee injury on the previous series. James ran for 102 yards on 24 carries. Manning was 19 of 30 for 201 yards and 2 touchdowns. Trent Green was 22 of 43 for 324 yards and 3 touchdowns, with 3 interceptions.

Indianapolis	0	7	10	18	—	35
Kansas City	0	3	11	14	—	28

Ind — Pollard 6 pass from Manning (Vanderjagt kick)
KC — FG T. Peterson 48
Ind — FG Vanderjagt 50
KC — FG T. Peterson 22
Ind — Rhodes 88 kickoff return (Vanderjagt kick)
KC — Gonzalez 35 pass from Green (Green run)
Ind — FG Vanderjagt 42
Ind — Harrison 47 pass from Manning (James pass from Manning)
KC — Parker 11 pass from Green (T. Peterson kick)
Ind — Rhodes 77 run (Vanderjagt kick)
KC — Parker 5 pass from Green (T. Peterson kick)

SUNDAY, OCTOBER 28
DALLAS 17, ARIZONA 3—at Texas Stadium, attendance 63,114. Third-string quarterback Clint Stoerner ran 6 yards for the tie-breaking touchdown in the Cowboys' victory. A 47-yard pass-interference penalty against the Cardinals' Corey Chavous gave the Cowboys a first down at Arizona's 5 in the third quarter. The ball was at the 6 three plays later when Stoerner ran up the middle on a quarterback draw for the go-ahead touchdown. Jake Plummer's ill-advised pass was intercepted by Dexter Coakley, whose 10-yard touchdown return gave Dallas a 17-3 lead. Arizona drove inside Cowboys' territory on each of their three possessions after that, but came away empty each time after Plummer's fourth-down passes fell incomplete. Stoerner, who made his first NFL start because of injuries to Quincy Carter and Anthony Wright, was 9 of 18 for 93 yards, with 1 interception. Plummer was 25 of 42 for 233 yards, with 2 interceptions. David Boston caught 9 passes for 108 yards.

Arizona	3	0	0	0	—	3
Dallas	0	3	14	0	—	17

Ariz — FG Gramatica 27
Dall — FG Seder 31
Dall — Stoerner 6 run (Seder kick)
Dall — Coakley 10 interception return (Seder kick)

SAN DIEGO 27, BUFFALO 24—at Qualcomm Stadium, attendance 63,698. Doug Flutie beat his former teammates when he scrambled 13 yards for the winning touchdown with 1:10 left. Flutie played for the Bills from 1998-2000 but was released during the offseason when the Bills decided to keep Rob Johnson. Flutie exacted revenge after Johnson had rallied Buffalo from a 10-point deficit. The Bills' quarterback completed a 61-yard touchdown pass to

Peerless Price, then guided a 12-play, 68-yard drive capped by Travis Henry's 3-yard touchdown run for a 24-20 lead with 1:30 to go. But San Diego's Ronney Jenkins brought back the ensuing kickoff 72 yards to the Bills' 26-yard line, and a penalty against Buffalo on the return pushed the ball to the 13. Flutie scrambled up the middle for the go-ahead touchdown on the next play. Still, the Chargers' victory wasn't secured until the final seconds. Johnson scrambled twice for 18 yards and completed a 25-yard pass to Jay Riemersma as the Bills drove to San Diego's 26-yard line with 15 seconds left. But Jake Arians' 44-yard game-tying field-goal attempt was blocked by Ed Ellis. Flutie was 21 of 33 for 254 yards and 1 touchdown. Curtis Conway caught 9 passes for 120 yards. Johnson was 24 of 37 for 310 yards and 1 touchdown, with 1 interception. Price had 8 receptions for 151 yards.

Buffalo	0	10	0	14 — 24
San Diego	3	0	14 — 27	
SD	—	FG Richey 37		
SD	—	F. Jones 1 pass from Flutie (Richey kick)		
SD	—	FG Richey 25		
Buff	—	R. Johnson 1 run (Arians kick)		
Buff	—	FG Arians 41		
SD	—	Perry 37 interception return (Richey kick)		
Buff	—	P. Price 61 pass from Johnson (Arians kick)		
Buff	—	Henry 3 run (Arians kick)		
SD	—	Flutie 13 run (Richey kick)		

CINCINNATI 31, DETROIT 27—at Pontiac Silverdome, attendance 69,343. Corey Dillon rushed for 184 yards and scored 3 touchdowns to carry the Bengals and stake the Lions to their worse start in 46 years. Dillon raced 96 yards for a touchdown on the game's first play, then had an 8-yard touchdown catch in the second quarter as Cincinnati built a 21-6 lead. Detroit rallied to take a 27-24 lead, but Dillon answered with a 1-yard run to put Cincinnati back in front with 8:06 to play. The Lions had the ball four times after that, but never moved it out of their own territory. Jon Kitna was 17 of 27 for 204 yards and 2 touchdowns, with 2 interceptions. Dillon finished with 204 yards from scrimmage. Batch was 20 of 35 for 239 yards and 2 touchdowns, with 2 interceptions.

Cincinnati	7	14	3	7 — 31
Detroit	3	10	14	0 — 27
Cin	—	Dillon 96 run (Rackers kick)		
Det	—	FG Hanson 51		
Cin	—	Dillon 8 pass from Kitna (Rackers kick)		
Det	—	FG Hanson 24		
Cin	—	D. Scott 30 pass from Kitna (Rackers kick)		
Det	—	Warren 1 run (Hanson kick)		
Det	—	Sloan 1 pass from Batch (pass failed)		
Cin	—	FG Rackers 39		
Det	—	Sloan 1 pass from Batch (Warren pass from Batch)		
Cin	—	Dillon 1 run (Rackers kick)		

BALTIMORE 18, JACKSONVILLE 17—at PSINet Stadium, attendance 69,439. Randall Cunningham tossed a 2-yard touchdown pass to Qadry Ismail with 4:07 to go, lifting the Ravens to a come-from-behind victory. Mark Brunell passed for 2 touchdowns in a span of 1:27 late to give Jacksonville a 17-6 lead seven seconds into the final period. But the 38-year-old Cunningham, making his first start for Baltimore in place of injured Elvis Grbac, engineered 2 touchdown drives to take a 18-17 lead. The Jaguars drove from their 20 to the Ravens' 44 on the ensuing possession, but Brunell's fourth-down pass

from there fell incomplete at the 1:46 mark. A 17-yard punt gave Jacksonville one last chance from its 42 with 19 seconds left, but the clock ran out after 3 incomplete passes. Cunningham was 23 of 31 for 222 yards and 1 touchdown, with 1 interception. Brunell was 25 of 37 for 306 yards and 2 touchdowns. Jimmy Smith (7 catches for 119 yards) and Keenan McCardell (10 receptions for 118 yards) each surpassed the 100-yard receiving mark.

Jacksonville	0	3	7	7 — 17
Baltimore	0	3	3	12 — 18
Balt	—	FG Stover 49		
Jax	—	FG Hollis 40		
Balt	—	FG Stover 28		
Jax	—	Smith 35 pass from Brunell (Hollis kick)		
Jax	—	Mack 11 pass from Brunell (Hollis kick)		
Balt	—	Brookins 2 run (pass failed)		
Balt	—	Ismail 2 pass from Cunningham (pass failed)		

MIAMI 24, SEATTLE 20—at Husky Stadium, attendance 59,108. Jay Fiedler's 39-yard touchdown pass to James McKnight with 6:16 left lifted the Dolphins. Rian Lindell's 42-yard field goal gave Seattle a three-point lead with 8:37 left. The Dolphins needed only five plays to counter with the decisive touchdown. Fiedler began the drive with a 6-yard pass to McKnight, then had a 21-yard toss to Chris Chambers two plays later for a first down at the Seahawks' 39-yard line. After Smith was stopped for no gain, Fiedler and McKnight teamed again for the go-ahead score. Late in the game, Seattle elected to try a field goal from Miami's 10-yard line instead of going for it on fourth-and-4. But Lindell's 28-yard attempt sailed wide left, and the Dolphins ran out the last 1:56 to secure the victory. Fiedler was 15 of 21 for 213 yards and 1 touchdown, with 2 interceptions. Hasselbeck was 16 of 28 for 230 yards and 2 touchdowns. Darrell Jackson caught 5 passes for 121 yards.

Miami	0	10	7	7 — 24
Seattle	0	14	3	3 — 20
Mia	—	FG Mare 46		
Mia	—	Minor fumble recovery in end zone (Mare kick)		
Sea	—	Mili 15 pass from Hasselbeck (Lindell kick)		
Sea	—	Jackson 17 pass from Hasselbeck (Lindell kick)		
Sea	—	FG Lindell 36		
Mia	—	L. Smith 1 run (Mare kick)		
Sea	—	FG Lindell 42		
Mia	—	McKnight 39 pass from Fiedler (Mare kick)		

TAMPA BAY 41, MINNESOTA 14—at Raymond James Stadium, attendance 65,558. Mike Alstott ran for 3 touchdowns and Brad Johnson passed for 2 in the Buccaneers' rout. Tampa Bay punted the first time it had the ball, then scored on each of its next seven possessions. Tampa Bay had big advantages in first downs (26-11), total yards (446-192), and time of possession (38:04-21:56). Brad Johnson was 18 of 25 for 214 yards and 2 touchdowns. Alstott had 129 rushing yards. Daunte Culpepper was 13 of 24 for 150 yards and 1 touchdown, with 1 interception.

Minnesota	0	0	8	6 — 14
Tampa Bay	7	21	13	0 — 41
TB	—	Alstott 3 run (Gramatica kick)		
TB	—	Alstott 6 run (Gramatica kick)		
TB	—	Stecker 35 pass from B. Johnson (Gramatica kick)		
TB	—	Moore 5 pass from B. Johnson (Gramatica kick)		
TB	—	FG Gramatica 44		
TB	—	FG Gramatica 48		
Minn	—	Prentice 1 run (Culpepper run)		
TB	—	Alstott 10 run (Gramatica kick)		
Minn	—	Moss 25 pass from Culpepper (pass failed)		

DENVER 31, NEW ENGLAND 20—at INVESCO Field at Mile High, attendance 72,349. Brian Griese passed for 2 touchdowns in the third quarter as the Broncos rallied from a 10-point deficit to win. Tom Brady completed 2 touchdown passes in the first half, then Adam Vinatieri capped New England's first possession of the second half with a 44-yard field goal. But Denver began its comeback on the next play from scrimmage, when Griese teamed with Rod Smith on a 65-yard touchdown pass to pull the Broncos within 20-17. The next time Denver had the ball, Griese marched his team 80 yards in 9 plays, capping the drive with a 6-yard touchdown pass to Dwayne Carswell to give the Broncos their first lead 3:35 before the end of the quarter. Denver's defense secured the victory by intercepting Brady on each of the Patriots' ensuing four possessions. Deltha O'Neal and Denard Walker each had 2 interceptions, including 1 Walker returned for a 39-yard touchdown with 2:24 left. Griese was 19 of 30 for 283 yards and 2 touchdowns, with 2 interceptions, while Smith had 6 catches for 159 yards. Brady was 25 of 38 for 203 yards and 2 touchdowns, with 4 interceptions. He had not been intercepted in 162 career passes before Denver's flurry of second-half interceptions. It was the longest such streak to begin a career in NFL history.

New England	10	7	3	0 — 20
Denver	7	3	14	7 — 31
NE	—	FG Vinatieri 24		
NE	—	Patten 30 pass from Brady (Vinatieri kick)		
Den	—	Anderson 8 run (Elam kick)		
Den	—	FG Elam 50		
NE	—	Brown 4 pass from Brady (Vinatieri kick)		
NE	—	FG Vinatieri 44		
Den	—	R. Smith 65 pass from Griese (Elam kick)		
Den	—	Carswell 6 pass from Griese (Elam kick)		
Den	—	Walker 39 interception return (Elam kick)		

NEW ORLEANS 34, ST. LOUIS 31—at Dome at America's Center, attendance 66,189. John Carney's 27-yard field goal with one second left gave the Saints a dramatic victory over the Rams, who entered the game unbeaten but were done in by their mistakes. The Rams appeared on their way to their seventh consecutive victory after taking a 24-6 halftime advantage. But New Orleans erupted for 25 unanswered points in the third quarter to take the lead. Deuce McAllister's 46-yard kickoff return to begin the second half and Sammy Knight's interception on the next possession helped cut the deficit to 24-16 only 3:21 into the third period. St. Louis turned over the ball again on the ensuing kickoff when Dre' Bly lost a fumble at the 18. Five plays later, Brooks' 6-yard touchdown pass to Horn pulled New Orleans within two points. Brooks' 49-yard touchdown pass to Willie Jackson the next time the Saints had the ball put New Orleans ahead for the first time at 28-24, and Darren Howard's interception and 37-yard return led to another 44-yard field goal by Carney with 3:54 still to play in the quarter. Warner bounced back to throw a tying, 4-yard touchdown pass to Torry Holt with 7:20 left in the game. Chris Oldham picked up Trung Canidate's fumble and returned it 43 yards to the Rams' 36-yard line. Five plays later, Carney's 30-yard field-goal try was blocked by Bly with 1:48 left, but Bly was penalized for being offsides, resulting in a first down for the Saints. Brooks kept the ball on three consecutive plays to run out most of the clock before Carney's winning kick. Fittingly, the Rams lost another fumble on the ensuing kickoff. They finished with 474 total yards, but turned the ball over 8 times. Brooks was 20 of 31 for 254 yards and 3 touchdowns. Horn had 8 catches for 121 yards. Warner was 29 of 47 for 385 yards and 1 touchdown, with 4 interceptions. Canidate, starting in place of injured Marshall Faulk, caught 10 passes for 107 yards. Isaac Bruce had 7 catches for 179 yards.

New Orleans	3	3	25	3	—	34
St. Louis	14	10	0	7	—	31

StL	—	Bruce 51 pass from Hakim (Wilkins kick)
StL	—	Conwell 2 run (Wilkins kick)
NO	—	FG Carney 33
StL	—	Canidate 1 run (Wilkins kick)
NO	—	FG Carney 44
StL	—	FG Wilkins 54
NO	—	Horn 46 pass from Brooks (Carney kick)
NO	—	FG Carney 44
NO	—	Horn 6 pass from Brooks (run failed)
NO	—	W. Jackson 49 pass from Brooks (pass failed)
NO	—	FG Carney 23
StL	—	Holt 8 pass from Warner (Wilkins kick)
NO	—	FG Carney 27

WASHINGTON 35, N.Y. GIANTS 21—at FedEx Field, attendance 80,316. Tony Banks passed for 2 touchdowns as the Redskins stunned the Giants. Washington led 17-14 in the third quarter when Kevin Lockett took a lateral pass and tossed a 31-yard touchdown pass to Derrius Thompson for a 24-14 lead. It was 27-21 before Tony Banks secured the victory with a 76-yard touchdown pass to Michael Westbrook with 6:41 left in the game. Banks was 11 of 19 for 190 yards and 2 touchdowns, while Stephen Davis added 107 yards on 29 rushes. Eric Metcalf's 89-yard punt return for a touchdown gave Washington a 14-0 lead. It was Metcalf's first punt return since he played for Carolina in 1999—he did not play in 2000 and signed with the Redskins only four days before the game with the Giants—and gave him an NFL record 12 punt and kickoff returns in his career. Collins was 32 of 52 for 346 yards and 3 touchdowns, with 1 interception. Amani Toomer caught 9 passes for 109 yards.

N.Y. Giants	0	14	0	7	—	21
Washington	14	3	10	8	—	35

Wash	—	Gardner 12 pass from Banks (Conway kick)
Wash	—	Metcalf 89 punt return (Conway kick)
NYG	—	Toomer 6 pass from Collins (Andersen kick)
NYG	—	Hilliard 27 pass from Collins (Andersen kick)
Wash	—	FG Conway 43
Wash	—	Thompson 31 pass from Lockett (Conway kick)
Wash	—	FG Conway 20
NYG	—	Comella 1 pass from Collins (Andersen kick)
Wash	—	Westbrook 76 pass from Banks (Bennett pass from Banks)

N.Y. JETS 13, CAROLINA 12—at Ericsson Stadium, attendance 59,253. John Hall's 34-yard field goal with 4:53 remaining lifted the Jets. The Jets outgained Carolina 358-162 but stymied themselves with 4 turnovers. The Jets lone touchdown occurred when Jamie Henderson blocked a punt that teammate Chris Hayes returned 7 yards for a score. The Panthers led 12-7 in the third quarter on the strength of 2 field goals by John Kasay and Rashard Anderson's 94-yard fumble return for a touchdown. But Kasay's extra-point try after the touchdown hit the right upright and bounced away, which would prove critical. Hall pulled the Jets within two points by making a 43-yard field goal midway through the third quarter, and they capitalized on a turnover in the final quarter to take the lead. After Tom Tupa's 41-yard punt backed up the Panthers at their 1-yard line, Chris Weinke's deep pass for Muhsin Muhammad was intercepted by Aaron Glenn. Glenn returned the ball 22 yards to set up Hall's go-ahead field goal. Vinny Testaverde was 21 of 34 for 181 yards, with 3 interceptions, and Curtis Martin rushed for 159 yards. Weinke was 12 of 34 for 76 yards, with 1 interception.

N.Y. Jets	7	0	3	3	—	13
Carolina	6	3	3	0	—	12

Car	—	Anderson 94 fumble return (kick failed)
NYJ	—	Hayes 7 blocked punt return (Hall kick)
Car	—	FG Kasay 45
Car	—	FG Kasay 45
NYJ	—	FG Hall 43
NYJ	—	FG Hall 34

OAKLAND 20, PHILADELPHIA 10—at Veterans Stadium, attendance 65,342. The Raiders utilized a powerful rushing game and a stifling defense to extend their winning streak over NFC opponents to 10 games. The Raiders ran the ball on 47 of its 74 plays from scrimmage and maintained possession for 40:09. Philadelphia punted on each of its first five possessions and managed only 195 total yards. But Oakland recovered an onside-kick attempt after Duce Staley's touchdown, and 6 consecutive runs by Zack Crockett ran out the clock. Rich Gannon was 17 of 26 for 158 yards. Donovan McNabb was 12 of 27 for 133 yards.

Oakland	7	3	7	3	—	20
Philadelphia	0	3	0	7	—	10

Oak	—	Garner 2 run (Janikowski kick)
Oak	—	FG Janikowski 42
Phil	—	FG Akers 34
Oak	—	Crockett 1 run (Janikowski kick)
Oak	—	FG Janikowski 32
Phil	—	Staley 3 run (Akers kick)

CHICAGO 37, SAN FRANCISCO 31 (OT)—at Soldier Field, attendance 66,944. Mike Brown returned an interception 33 yards for a touchdown just 16 seconds into overtime to give the Bears a dramatic comeback victory. San Francisco led 28-9 after Zack Bronson returned an interception 97 yards for a touchdown midway through the third quarter and Jose Cortez's 40-yard field goal gave the 49ers a 31-16 lead with 7:47 to play. Shane Matthews' 13-yard touchdown pass to David Terrell pulled the Bears within eight points with 4:08 left. After San Francisco failed to make a first down, Chicago took over possession at its 33-yard line with 2:46 left. Ten plays later, Matthews completed a 4-yard pass to John Davis on fourth-and-three from the 49ers' 8 for a first down, and two plays later teamed with Terrell on a touchdown pass to make it 31-29 with 26 seconds left. Anthony Thomas then ran for a 2-point conversion. San Francisco won the overtime coin toss and elected to receive, but Jeff Garcia's pass on the first play from the 20-yard line bounced off Terrell Owens' hands and into the arms of Brown, who raced to the end zone for the winning touchdown, ending the shortest overtime in NFL history. Matthews was 25 of 31 for 166 yards and 3 touchdowns, with 1 interception, after replacing injured starter Jim Miller. Thomas finished with 127 yards. Garcia was 21 of 29 for 269 yards and 2 touchdowns, with 2 interceptions. Garrison Hearst had 4 receptions for 105 yards.

San Francisco	14	0	14	3	0	—	31
Chicago	0	9	7	15	6	—	37

SF	—	Peterson 26 fumble return (Cortez kick)
SF	—	Swift 1 pass from Garcia (Cortez kick)
Chi	—	Safety, ball snapped out of end zone
Chi	—	Shelton 3 pass from Matthews (Edinger kick)
SF	—	Hearst 60 pass from Garcia (Cortez kick)
SF	—	Bronson 97 interception return (Cortez kick)
Chi	—	Thomas 19 run (Edinger kick)
SF	—	FG Cortez 40
Chi	—	Terrell 13 pass from Matthews (Edinger kick)
Chi	—	Terrell 4 pass from Matthews (Thomas run)
Chi	—	M. Brown 33 interception return

MONDAY NIGHT, OCTOBER 29
PITTSBURGH 34, TENNESSEE 7—at Heinz Field, attendance 63,763. Kordell Stewart passed for 232 yards and a touchdown and ran for another touchdown to lead the Steelers to their fifth consecutive victory. The Steelers outgained Tennessee 405-214 in total yards and ended a seven-game losing streak to Tennessee. Stewart's 3-yard touchdown pass to Hines Ward followed Brent Alexander's second-quarter interception and gave the Steelers the lead for good. Pittsburgh scored on its first three second-half possessions to take a 34-7 lead. Stewart was 13 of 22 for 232 yards and 1 touchdown. Burress caught 6 passes for 151 yards. McNair was 14 of 23 for 175 yards and 1 touchdown, with 2 interceptions.

Tennessee	0	7	0	0	—	7
Pittsburgh	7	10	10	7	—	34

Pitt	—	Bettis 1 run (Brown kick)
Tenn	—	Wycheck 4 pass from McNair (Nedney kick)
Pitt	—	Ward 3 pass from Stewart (Brown kick)
Pitt	—	FG Brown 42
Pitt	—	Bettis 7 run (Brown kick)
Pitt	—	FG Brown 27
Pitt	—	Stewart 2 run (Brown kick)

EIGHTH WEEK SUMMARIES
American Football Conference

Eastern Division	W	L	T	Pct.	Pts.	OP
Miami	5	2	0	.714	153	137
N.Y. Jets	5	3	0	.625	157	175
Indianapolis	4	3	0	.571	200	197
New England	4	4	0	.500	185	160
Buffalo	1	6	0	.143	122	195
Central Division						
Pittsburgh	5	2	0	.714	120	78
Baltimore	5	3	0	.625	141	129
Cincinnati	4	3	0	.571	120	136
Cleveland	4	3	0	.571	132	118
Tennessee	3	4	0	.429	129	180
Jacksonville	2	5	0	.286	114	115
Western Division						
Oakland	6	1	0	.857	189	133
San Diego	5	3	0	.625	206	146
Denver	4	4	0	.500	192	182
Seattle	3	4	0	.429	118	158
Kansas City	2	6	0	.250	164	172

National Football Conference

Eastern Division	W	L	T	Pct.	Pts.	OP
Philadelphia	4	3	0	.571	145	98

N.Y. Giants	4	4	0	.500	148	140
Washington	3	5	0	.375	111	193
Arizona	2	5	0	.286	99	166
Dallas	2	5	0	.286	116	147
Central Division						
Chicago	6	1	0	.857	162	95
Green Bay	5	2	0	.714	168	105
Minnesota	3	4	0	.429	138	165
Tampa Bay	3	4	0	.429	139	119
Detroit	0	7	0	.000	110	197
Western Division						
St. Louis	6	1	0	.857	207	115
San Francisco	5	2	0	.714	174	155
New Orleans	4	3	0	.571	148	134
Atlanta	3	4	0	.429	135	151
Carolina	1	7	0	.125	118	169

SUNDAY, NOVEMBER 4

BALTIMORE 13, PITTSBURGH 10—at Heinz Field, attendance 62,906. Matt Stover made 2 fourth-quarter field goals and Kris Brown missed 4 of 5 field-goal tries to end Pittsburgh's five-game winning streak. The Steelers led 10-7 until Stover kicked a 25-yard field goal to tie the score three seconds into the fourth quarter. Brown missed a 48-yard field-goal attempt with 4:22 left, and the Ravens took over at their 38-yard line. Randall Cunningham completed a 26-yard pass to Shannon Sharpe to move the ball into Pittsburgh territory, and Stover kicked a 40-yard field goal six plays later to give Baltimore the lead with 1:49 to go. Kordell Stewart completed 5 passes on the ensuing drive to help the Steelers march from their 38 to the Ravens' 17, but Brown was wide right on the 35-yard field-goal attempt with 14 seconds left for his fourth consecutive miss. Cunningham was 14 of 22 for 158 yards and 1 touchdown, with 1 interception, in his second start in place of injured Elvis Grbac, but Baltimore managed only 10 first downs and 183 total yards. Stewart was 22 of 37 for 236 yards and 1 touchdown.

Baltimore	0	7	0	6	—	13
Pittsburgh	3	7	0	0	—	10

Pitt	—	FG K. Brown 38
Balt	—	Sharpe 13 pass from Cunningham (Stover kick)
Pitt	—	Burress 21 pass from Stewart (K. Brown kick)
Balt	—	FG Stover 25
Balt	—	FG Stover 39

MIAMI 23, CAROLINA 6—at Pro Player Stadium, attendance 72,597. Jay Fiedler passed for 287 yards and a touchdown as the Dolphins handed the Panthers their seventh consecutive defeat. Patrick Surtain returned an interception 29 yards for a touchdown and Olindo Mare kicked 2 field goals as Miami built a 13-6 halftime lead and coasted to the victory. Carolina's offense managed only 68 total yards during the final two quarters. Jay Fiedler was 20 of 33 for 287 yards and 1 touchdown, with 1 interception. Chris Weinke was 9 of 21 for 158 yards, 1 interception, before leaving with a strained shoulder. Dameyune Craig was 4 of 8 for 34 yards before spraining his foot, and Matt Lytle was 2 of 4 for 7 yards.

Carolina	3	3	0	0	—	6
Miami	3	10	0	10	—	23

Mia	—	FG Mare 36
Car	—	FG Kasay 27
Mia	—	Surtain 29 interception return (Mare kick)
Car	—	FG Kasay 20
Mia	—	FG Mare 45
Mia	—	Konrad 5 pass from Fiedler (Mare kick)
Mia	—	FG Mare 29

CHICAGO 27, CLEVELAND 21 (OT)—at Soldier Field, attendance 66,944. Mike Brown returned an interception 16 yards for a touchdown 2:50 into overtime to give the Bears a stunning victory in a game they trailed by 14 points with less than 30 seconds remaining in regulation. It was the second consecutive week that Brown capped a comeback with an interception in overtime. Chicago trailed 21-7 before Shane Matthews tossed a 9-yard touchdown pass to Marty Booker with just 28 seconds left. The Bears then successfully executed an onside kick that Bobby Howard recovered at the Browns' 47-yard line with 24 seconds to go. Matthews completed back-to-back passes of 4 and 9 yards to James Allen, but Chicago had to use its last time out with the ball at the 34 and just eight seconds left. Matthews heaved a desperation pass into the end zone that was batted by Percy Ellsworth and caught by a diving Allen, who was trailing the play, for the tying touchdown as time expired. The Bears got the ball first in overtime but punted. On the Browns' third play, Tim Couch's pass from Cleveland's 23-yard line was tipped in the air by Bryan Robinson and into the arms of Brown, whose touchdown gave the Bears their sixth consecutive victory. Matthews was 30 of 50 for a career-best 357 yards and 2 touchdowns, with 3 interceptions. Couch was 14 of 23 for 211 yards and 2 touchdowns, with 1 interception.

Cleveland	7	0	14	0	—	21
Chicago	0	7	0	14	6	—	27

Cle	—	C. Brown 25 fumble return (P. Dawson kick)
Chi	—	Thomas 2 run (Edinger kick)
Cle	—	Sellers 3 pass from Couch (P. Dawson kick)
Cle	—	K. Johnson 55 pass from Couch (P. Dawson kick)
Chi	—	Booker 9 pass from Matthews (Edinger kick)
Chi	—	Allen 34 pass from Matthews (Edinger kick)
Chi	—	M. Brown 16 interception return

N.Y. GIANTS 27, DALLAS 24 (OT)—at Giants Stadium, attendance 78,673. The Giants rallied from 17 points down at halftime to beat the Cowboys on Morten Andersen's 42-yard field goal 7:48 into overtime. Dallas led 24-7 at intermission largely on the strength of interception returns for touchdowns by Dexter Coakley (29 yards) and Mario Edwards (71 yards). But the Giants erased the deficit with the help of 4 interceptions and a blocked punt in the second half. First, Will Peterson intercepted Clint Stoerner's pass in the end zone when the Cowboys were well into field-goal range on their first possession of the third quarter. Kerry Collins teamed with Joe Jurevicius on a 34-yard touchdown pass to make it 24-14. Jason Sehorn and Dhani Jones picked off Stoerner's passes on each of Dallas' next two possessions, with the latter leading to Andersen's 40-yard field goal 4:19 into the fourth quarter. Thabiti Davis blocked a punt the next time the Cowboys had the ball, the Giants needed only 2 plays to march 14 yards, tying the score on Collins' 9-yard touchdown pass to Ike Hilliard with 8:19 left in the game. In overtime, the Giants began the winning drive from their 15 after forcing a punt. A 33-yard pass from Collins to Hilliard was the key plan to set up Andersen for his winning kick. Collins was 24 of 34 for 280 yards and 3 touchdowns, with 2 interceptions. Stoerner was 13 of 23 for 177 yards and 1 touchdown, with 4 interceptions and was replaced by Ryan Leaf, who was 4 of 8 for 85 yards. Raghib Ismail caught 6 passes for 107 yards.

Dallas	10	14	0	0	0	—	24
N.Y. Giants	0	7	7	10	3	—	27

Dall	—	FG Seder 22
Dall	—	Galloway 16 pass from Stoerner (Seder kick)
Dall	—	Coakley 29 interception return (Seder kick)
NYG	—	Jurevicius 4 pass from Collins (Andersen kick)
Dall	—	Edwards 71 interception return (Seder kick)
NYG	—	Jurevicius 34 pass from Collins (Andersen kick)
NYG	—	FG Andersen 40
NYG	—	Hilliard 9 pass from Collins (Andersen kick)
NYG	—	FG Andersen 42

SAN FRANCISCO 21, DETROIT 13—at 3Com Park, attendance 67,605. Jeff Garcia passed for 3 touchdowns, including 2 in the second half to Terrell Owens, as the 49ers rallied to keep the Lions winless. The 49ers took the lead for good on Garcia's 30-yard touchdown pass to Owens 4:39 into the third quarter. The pair teamed again on a 7-yard touchdown pass three plays into the fourth quarter. The Lions turned over the ball on downs with 1:14 remaining. San Francisco had sizeable advantages in first downs (27-12), total yards (427-131), and maintained possession for 38:33. Garcia was 26 of 35 for 296 yards and 3 touchdowns, with 2 interceptions. Owens had 9 receptions for 125 yards. Charlie Batch was 8 of 20 for 74 yards, and rookie Mike McMahon was 2 of 4 for 16 yards in his NFL debut.

Detroit	7	3	3	0	—	13
San Francisco	0	7	7	7	—	21

Det	—	Bailey 74 interception return (Hanson kick)
Det	—	FG Hanson 39
SF	—	Johnson 4 pass from Garcia (Cortez kick)
SF	—	Owens 30 pass from Garcia (Cortez kick)
Det	—	FG Hanson 45
SF	—	Owens 7 pass from Garcia (Cortez kick)

INDIANAPOLIS 30, BUFFALO 14—at Ralph Wilson Stadium, attendance 63,786. Peyton Manning passed for 1 touchdown and ran for another and the Colts' defense recorded 6 sacks in their victory. It was 7-7 when Manning called a naked bootleg on third-and-1 from the Bills' 33-yard line and ran around left end for the touchdown that gave the Colts the lead 9:18 before the half. After that, the Colts relied mostly on the running of Dominic Rhodes to protect their lead. The rookie carried on 19 of Indianapolis' 30 plays after halftime and finished with 100 yards in his first start in place of injured Edgerrin James. Manning was 17 of 27 for 199 yards and 1 touchdown. Rob Johnson was 17 of 33 for 172 yards and 1 touchdown.

Indianapolis	0	17	7	6	—	30
Buffalo	0	7	0	7	—	14

Ind	—	Pollard 15 pass from Manning (Vanderjagt kick)
Buff	—	Clements 66 punt return (Arians kick)
Ind	—	Manning 33 run (Vanderjagt kick)
Ind	—	FG Vanderjagt 34
Ind	—	Rhodes 1 run (Vanderjagt kick)
Ind	—	FG Vanderjagt 41
Buff	—	Riemersma 27 pass from Johnson (Arians kick)
Ind	—	FG Vanderjagt 47

TENNESSEE 28, JACKSONVILLE 24—at Adelphia Coliseum, attendance 68,798. Steve McNair passed for 2 touchdowns and ran for 2 more, including the game winner from 1 yard with 44 seconds remaining, for the Titans. Tennessee trailed 17-7 at half-time, but scored touchdowns on three of its four second-half possessions. The Jaguars rallied to take a 24-21 lead on Frank Moreau's 4-yard touchdown run with 3:05 to play, but with McNair passing on every play, the Titans marched from their 41-yard line to a first down at Jacksonville's 11 with 1:15 left. McNair scrambled for 6 yards and Eddie George ran for 4 yards to make it first-and-goal at the 1 before McNair kept the ball for the winning touchdown. McNair was 27 of 34 for 241 yards and 2 touchdowns. Jevon Kearse had 3 sacks. Mark Brunell was 21 of 32 for 261 yards and 1 touchdown, with 1 interception. Jimmy Smith caught 7 passes for 120 yards.

| Jacksonville | 0 | 17 | 0 | 7 | — | 24 |
| Tennessee | 7 | 0 | 7 | 14 | — | 28 |

Tenn	—	Dyson 20 pass from McNair (Nedney kick)
Jax	—	Mack 1 run (Hollis kick)
Jax	—	Brady 3 pass from Brunell (Hollis kick)
Jax	—	FG Hollis 38
Tenn	—	McNair 5 run (Nedney kick)
Tenn	—	Mason 5 pass from McNair (Nedney kick)
Jax	—	Moreau 4 run (Hollis kick)
Tenn	—	McNair 1 run (Nedney kick)

KANSAS CITY 25, SAN DIEGO 20—at Qualcomm Stadium, attendance 58,789. Tony Richardson ran 1 yard for a touchdown with 1:26 left for the Chiefs. San Diego trailed 19-0 at halftime, but rallied behind rookie Drew Brees, who made his NFL debut after Doug Flutie left the game with a concussion in the second quarter. Wade Richey kicked 2 field goals and LaDainian Tomlinson ran 8 yards for a touchdown before Brees gave the Chargers their first score of the game with a 20-yard touchdown pass to Freddie Jones with 6:10 left. The Chiefs began the next possession at their 29-yard line and Green completed an 11-yard pass to Larry Parker on third-and-6 from the Chargers' 42. Holmes carried on 5 consecutive plays to push the ball to the 1 before Richardson put Kansas City in front. Brees had one more chance and drove San Diego from its 32 to the Chiefs' 41 with 13 seconds left. He scrambled for 13 yards on the next play but was called for an illegal forward pass at the end of the run, and by rule the game ended. Green was 13 of 25 for 146 yards, with 1 interception. Holmes ran for 181 yards as the Chiefs ended a four-game losing streak. Brees was 15 of 27 for 221 yards and 1 touchdown, while Flutie was 6 of 16 for 61 yards, with 1 interception.

| Kansas City | 9 | 10 | 0 | 6 | — | 25 |
| San Diego | 0 | 0 | 10 | 10 | — | 20 |

KC	—	FG Peterson 37
KC	—	Richardson 1 run (kick blocked)
KC	—	Holmes 3 run (Peterson kick)
KC	—	FG Peterson 28
SD	—	FG Richey 48
SD	—	Tomlinson 8 run (Richey kick)
SD	—	FG Richey 35
SD	—	F. Jones 20 pass from Brees (Richey kick)
KC	—	Richardson 1 run (pass failed)

NEW ENGLAND 24, ATLANTA 10—at Georgia Dome, attendance 44,229. Tom Brady passed for 3 touchdowns to lead the Patriots. New England trailed 7-0 before turning the game in its favor with a 17-point second quarter. First, Brady capped a 16-play, 75-yard drive that consumed 8:35 with a 4-yard touchdown pass to Kevin Faulk to tie the score. The Patriots converted three third downs and a fourth down en route to the touchdown. An Otis Smith interception led to Adam Vinatieri's 48-yard field goal and a 10-7 lead, and Brady tossed a 15-yard

touchdown pass to Marc Edwards at the end of a 10-play, 89-yard drive with 15 seconds remaining in the half. Brady's 44-yard touchdown pass to Troy Brown in the final minute of the third quarter helped keep the game out of Atlanta's reach. Brady was 21 of 31 for 250 yards and 3 touchdowns, and Antowain Smith rushed for 117 yards. The Patriots' defense ensured the win with 9 sacks. Chandler was 8 of 20 for 95 yards and 1 touchdown, with 1 interception, before leaving with bruised ribs. Vick was 2 of 9 for 56 yards.

| New England | 0 | 17 | 7 | 0 | — | 24 |
| Atlanta | 7 | 0 | 0 | 3 | — | 10 |

Atl	—	Jefferson 15 pass from Chandler (Feely kick)
NE	—	Faulk 4 pass from Brady (Vinatieri kick)
NE	—	FG Vinatieri 48
NE	—	Edwards 15 pass from Brady (Vinatieri kick)
NE	—	Brown 44 pass from Brady (Vinatieri kick)
Atl	—	FG Feely 20

PHILADELPHIA 21, ARIZONA 7—at Sun Devil Stadium, attendance 33,430. Brian Mitchell returned the opening kickoff 94 yards for a touchdown to spark the Eagles. Mitchell's big return was his twelfth kickoff or punt return for a touchdown in his career, tying Eric Metcalf for the NFL record. Metcalf had his twelfth just one week earlier for the Redskins against the Giants. Arizona cut the deficit to 14-7 on an 80-yard drive highlighted by Jake Plummer's 52-yard pass to David Boston and capped by his 2-yard touchdown toss to Tywan Mitchell, but Donovan McNabb's 54-yard touchdown pass to James Thrash three plays later made it 21-7. The Cardinals punted on their next five possessions and committed 2 late turnovers, including Michael Pittman's fumble into the end zone after Arizona had driven to Philadelphia's 1. McNabb was 19 of 33 for 238 yards and 2 touchdowns, with 1 interception. Plummer was 24 of 41 for 293 yards and 1 touchdown, with 1 interception. Boston had 8 catches for 138 yards.

| Philadelphia | 7 | 14 | 0 | 0 | — | 21 |
| Arizona | 0 | 7 | 0 | 0 | — | 7 |

Phil	—	B. Mitchell 94 kickoff return (Akers kick)
Phil	—	Thrash 8 pass from McNabb (Akers kick)
Ariz	—	T. Mitchell 2 pass from Plummer (Gramatica kick)
Phil	—	Thrash 54 pass from McNabb (Akers kick)

WASHINGTON 27, SEATTLE 14—at Fed Ex Field, attendance 82,352. The resurgent Redskins won their third consecutive game behind 142 rushing yards from Stephen Davis. Washington dominated much of the game, amassing 230 yards on the ground and maintaining possession for 39:18. Davis carried 32 times and scored the Redskins' first rushing touchdown of the season when he capped a 69-yard drive with a 1-yard run to give the Redskins a 20-7 lead. Tony Banks completed a 13-yard strike to Michael Westbrook to extend the lead to 27-7 midway through the third quarter. Banks was 15 of 23 for 152 yards and 2 touchdowns, with 1 interception. Matt Hasselbeck was 6 of 12 for 127 yards, with 2 interceptions in the first half before being replaced. Trent Dilfer was 8 of 18 for 121 yards and 1 touchdown.

| Seattle | 7 | 0 | 7 | 0 | — | 14 |
| Washington | 10 | 10 | 7 | 0 | — | 27 |

| Wash | — | Rasby 7 pass from Banks (Conway kick) |
| Sea | — | Alexander 41 run (Lindell kick) |

Wash	—	FG Conway 43
Wash	—	FG Conway 23
Wash	—	Davis 1 run (Conway kick)
Wash	—	Westbrook 13 pass from Banks (Conway kick)
Sea	—	Jackson 46 pass from Dilfer (Lindell kick)

GREEN BAY 21, TAMPA BAY 20—at Lambeau Field, attendance 59,861. Allen Rossum returned a punt 55 yards for a touchdown with 3:03 left to lift the Packers. The Packers' defense limited the Buccaneers to only 194 total yards and recorded 7 sacks. Green Bay, which beat Tampa Bay at home for the twelfth consecutive year, trailed 17-7 until Ahman Green raced 63 yards for a touchdown to cut the deficit to three points with 4:40 left in the third quarter. Martin Gramatica's 49-yard field goal gave the Buccaneers led 20-14 midway through the fourth quarter. The teams exchanged punts on the next two possessions, but Mark Royals' 45-yard kick from Tampa Bay's 10-yard line was brought back the distance by Rossum. Brad Johnson's desperation pass into the end zone was batted away by Sharper as time ran out. Brett Favre was 16 of 27 for 180 yards and 1 touchdown, with 2 interceptions. Green had a career-high 169 rushing yards. Brad Johnson was 18 of 30 for 177 yards and 2 touchdowns.

| Tampa Bay | 0 | 10 | 7 | 3 | — | 20 |
| Green Bay | 7 | 0 | 7 | 7 | — | 21 |

GB	—	Freeman 21 pass from Favre (Longwell kick)
TB	—	FG Gramatica 33
TB	—	Moore 11 pass from B. Johnson (Gramatica kick)
TB	—	Alstott 19 pass from B. Johnson (Gramatica kick)
GB	—	Green 63 run (Longwell kick)
TB	—	FG Gramatica 49
GB	—	Rossum 55 punt return (Longwell kick)

SUNDAY NIGHT, NOVEMBER 4
N.Y. JETS 16, NEW ORLEANS 9—at Louisiana Superdome, attendance 70,020. Vinny Testaverde passed for a touchdown and John Hall kicked 3 field goals in the Jets' victory. Ricky Williams' 1-yard touchdown run midway through the third quarter was set up by Kevin Mathis' fumble recovery and cut the deficit to 13-7. Testaverde was called for intentional grounding in the end zone, an automatic safety that made it 13-9. John Hall's third field goal of the game, from 23 yards with 2:37 left in the game, upped the Jets' lead to 16-9, and the Jets withstood a late scoring threat by the Saints, who marched to New York's 6 with 1:14 left. On second-and-3 from there, Aaron Brooks gained 1 yard, and Damien Robinson and Kyle Turley were whistled for offsetting facemask penalties. But Turley also was assessed 15 yards for unnecessary roughness, moving the ball back to the 20. Brooks threw 2 incomplete passes, then was sacked by John Abraham. It was Abraham's fourth sack of the game and the Jets' sixth sack. Testaverde was 13 of 22 for 145 yards and 1 touchdown, with 1 interception. Brooks was 12 of 28 for 164 yards, with 2 interceptions.

| N.Y. Jets | 6 | 7 | 0 | 3 | — | 16 |
| New Orleans | 0 | 0 | 9 | 0 | — | 9 |

NYJ	—	FG Hall 39
NYJ	—	FG Hall 47
NYJ	—	Coles 7 pass from Testaverde (Hall kick)
NO	—	R. Williams 1 run (Carney kick)
NO	—	Safety, Testaverde penalized for intentional grounding in end zone
NYJ	—	FG Hall 23

MONDAY NIGHT, NOVEMBER 5

OAKLAND 38, DENVER 28—at Network Associates Coliseum, attendance 62,637. Rich Gannon passed for 3 touchdowns and Zack Crockett ran for 2 as the Raiders extended their winning streak to five games and ended a seven-game losing streak against the Broncos. Gannon teamed with Tim Brown on 2 of his scoring tosses. Brian Griese's 11-yard touchdown pass to Desmond Clark with 10:41 left, and Griese's 2-point conversion pass to Rod Smith trimmed the Raiders' lead to 28-20. But Oakland secured its first victory over the Broncos since 1997 by scoring 10 points in 22 seconds. After Sebastian Janikowski kicked a 31-yard field goal with 7:28 left in the game, William Thomas intercepted Griese's pass on the first play of the ensuing possession and returned the ball 33 yards to set up Crockett's second touchdown. Gannon was 25 of 34 for 242 yards and 3 touchdowns. Griese was 22 of 32 for 221 yards and 2 touchdowns, with 2 interceptions. Smith had 10 receptions for 91 yards.

Denver	3	6	16	—	28
Oakland	7	14	7	10	—	38

Oak	—	T. Brown 11 pass from Gannon (Janikowski kick)
Den	—	FG Elam 39
Den	—	FG Elam 21
Oak	—	Crockett 1 run (Janikowski kick)
Oak	—	Ritchie 4 pass from Gannon (Janikowski kick)
Den	—	R. Smith 2 pass from Griese (pass failed)
Oak	—	T. Brown 19 pass from Gannon (Janikowski kick)
Den	—	Clark 11 pass from Griese (R. Smith pass from Griese)
Oak	—	FG Janikowski 31
Oak	—	Crockett 3 run (Janikowski kick)
Den	—	R. Smith 26 pass from Frerotte (Anderson run)

NINTH WEEK SUMMARIES
American Football Conference

Eastern Division	W	L	T	Pct.	Pts.	OP
Miami	6	2	0	.750	180	161
N.Y. Jets	6	3	0	.667	184	158
New England	5	4	0	.556	206	171
Indianapolis	4	4	0	.500	224	224
Buffalo	1	7	0	.125	133	216
Central Division						
Pittsburgh	6	2	0	.750	135	90
Baltimore	6	3	0	.667	157	139
Cincinnati	4	4	0	.500	133	166
Cleveland	4	4	0	.500	144	133
Jacksonville	3	5	0	.375	144	128
Tennessee	3	5	0	.375	139	196
Western Division						
Oakland	6	2	0	.750	216	167
Denver	5	4	0	.556	218	198
San Diego	5	4	0	.556	222	172
Seattle	4	4	0	.500	152	185
Kansas City	2	7	0	.222	171	199

National Football Conference

Eastern Division	W	L	T	Pct.	Pts.	OP
Philadelphia	5	3	0	.625	193	115
N.Y. Giants	5	4	0	.556	165	150
Washington	3	5	0	.375	111	193
Arizona	2	6	0	.250	109	183
Dallas	2	6	0	.250	129	167
Central Division						
Chicago	6	2	0	.750	174	115
Green Bay	6	2	0	.750	188	117
Tampa Bay	4	4	0	.500	159	136
Minnesota	3	5	0	.375	155	213
Detroit	0	8	0	.000	127	217
Western Division						
St. Louis	7	1	0	.875	255	129
San Francisco	6	2	0	.750	202	182

Atlanta	4	4	0	.500	155	164
New Orleans	4	4	0	.500	175	162
Carolina	1	8	0	.111	132	217

SUNDAY, NOVEMBER 11

NEW ENGLAND 21, BUFFALO 11—at Foxboro Stadium, attendance 57,294. Antowain Smith ran for 100 yards and 2 touchdowns against his former teammates to lead the Patriots. Buffalo rallied from a 14-3 deficit behind backup Alex Van Pelt, who entered the game in the fourth quarter after Rob Johnson separated his shoulder. Van Pelt teamed with Peerless Price on a 17-yard touchdown pass with 2:43 left, then narrowed the Bills' deficit to three points with a 2-point conversion pass to Eric Moulds. But New England recovered the ensuing onside kick, and Smith sealed the victory by running 42 yards for a touchdown with 1:52 left. Tom Brady was 15 of 21 for 107 yards and 1 touchdown, with 1 interception. Johnson was 14 of 27 for 167 yards, with 1 interception, and Van Pelt was 2 of 7 for 37 yards and 1 touchdown, with 1 interception.

Buffalo	0	3	0	8	—	11
New England	7	7	0	7	—	21

NE	—	Faulk 6 pass from Brady (Vinatieri kick)
Buff	—	FG Arians 24
NE	—	A. Smith 1 run (Vinatieri kick)
Buff	—	Price 17 pass from Van Pelt (Moulds pass from Van Pelt)
NE	—	A. Smith 42 run (Vinatieri kick)

ST. LOUIS 48, CAROLINA 14—at Dome at America's Center, attendance 66,069. Marshall Faulk returned to the Rams' lineup and shredded the Panthers' defense, rushing for 183 yards and 2 touchdowns on only 15 carries in the first half. Faulk, who had been sidelined since suffering a bruised bone in his knee in week 5, broke free for a 71-yard touchdown run in the game's third play, and St. Louis had a 7-0 lead. Faulk's 58-yard run midway through the first quarter set up Robert Holcombe's 1-yard touchdown run. Faulk added a 6-yard touchdown run 2:41 into the second quarter and called it a day at halftime with the Rams leading 31-7. His backup, Trung Canidate, had a 23-yard touchdown run in the third quarter and went on to rush for 145 yards. St. Louis amassed 337 yards on the ground in all, and outgained Carolina 493-146. Warner was 14 of 20 for 144 yards and 1 touchdown, with 3 interceptions. Matt Lytle was 15 of 26 for 126 yards and 1 touchdown, with 2 interceptions, in his first career start.

Carolina	0	7	7	0	—	14
St. Louis	21	10	14	3	—	48

StL	—	Faulk 71 run (Wilkins kick)
StL	—	Holcombe 1 run (Wilkins kick)
StL	—	Bruce 26 pass from Warner (Wilkins kick)
StL	—	Faulk 6 run (Wilkins kick)
StL	—	FG Wilkins 25
Car	—	Smith 99 kickoff return (Kasay kick)
StL	—	A. Williams 16 interception return (Wilkins kick)
StL	—	Canidate 23 run (Wilkins kick)
Car	—	Mangum 4 pass from Lytle (Kasay kick)
StL	—	FG Wilkins 35

JACKSONVILLE 30, CINCINNATI 13—at ALLTEL Stadium, attendance 57,161. The Jaguars ended a five-game losing streak when Mark Brunell passed for 2 touchdowns and Stacey Mack ran for 2 touchdowns. Trailing 13-7, Jacksonville turned up the game by scoring touchdowns on three consecutive possessions in the third quarter, capped by Brunell's 20-yard touchdown strike to Keenan McCardell in

the final minute of the third quarter. Brunell was 20 of 32 for 189 yards and 2 touchdowns. Jon Kitna was 28 of 48 for 303 yards, with 1 interception.

Cincinnati	0	13	0	0	—	13
Jacksonville	7	0	21	2	—	30

Jax	—	Mack 1 run (Hollis kick)
Cin	—	FG Rackers 26
Cin	—	Dillon 7 run (Rackers kick)
Cin	—	FG Rackers 52
Jax	—	Ji. Smith 5 pass from Brunell (Hollis kick)
Jax	—	Mack 2 run (Hollis kick)
Jax	—	McCardell 20 pass from Brunell (Hollis kick)
Jax	—	Safety, Brackens sacked Kitna in end zone

ATLANTA 20, DALLAS 13—at Georgia Dome, attendance 69,010. Third-string quarterback Doug Johnson tossed a 1-yard touchdown pass to Brian Kozlowski with 5:20 left to carry the Falcons. Dallas led 13-10 when Darrien Gordon returned a punt 74 yards to the Cowboys' 15-yard line midway through the final quarter. Four runs by Maurice Smith moved the ball to the 1 before Johnson and Kozlowski teamed on the go-ahead scoring pass. Jay Feely's 19-yard field goal with 1:11 to go followed a 41-yard punt return by Gordon. The Cowboys crossed midfield on their final possession, but Ryan Leaf's pass from the Falcons' 46 was intercepted by Keith Brooking with eight seconds left. Johnson replaced rookie Michael Vick, who was ineffective while starting his first NFL game for injured Chris Chandler. Vick was 4 of 12 for 32 yards and 1 touchdown, while Johnson was 3 of 4 for 23 yards and 1 touchdown. Maurice Smith had 148 yards on 27 carries. Leaf, the fourth quarterback to start for Dallas in the first eight games of the season, was 14 of 22 for 114 yards and 1 touchdown, with 1 interception. Troy Hambrick, subbing for injured Emmitt Smith, rushed for 127 yards on 20 carries.

Dallas	3	10	0	0	—	13
Atlanta	7	0	3	10	—	20

Dall	—	FG Seder 28
Atl	—	Crumpler 9 pass from Vick (Feely kick)
Dall	—	FG Seder 47
Dall	—	Harris 3 pass from Leaf (Seder kick)
Atl	—	FG Feely 31
Atl	—	Kozlowski 1 pass from Johnson (Feely kick)
Atl	—	FG Feely 19

GREEN BAY 20, CHICAGO 12—at Soldier Field, attendance 66,944. Brett Favre passed for 2 touchdowns, and the Packers pulled even with the Bears and snapped Chicago's six-game winning string. Green Bay led 20-12 before Chicago mounted its final drive beginning from its 20-yard line with 4:19 left in the game. The Bears held the ball for 14 plays and converted 2 third downs and a fourth down on a drive that reached the Packers' 15. But Jim Miller's passes fell incomplete on third and fourth downs. Favre was 19 of 32 for 268 yards and 2 touchdowns, with 1 interception. Schroeder caught 4 passes for 100 yards. Miller was 28 of 47 for 201 yards.

Green Bay	0	10	7	3	—	20
Chicago	6	3	3	0	—	12

Chi	—	FG Edinger 37
Chi	—	FG Edinger 47
GB	—	FG Longwell 40
GB	—	Schroeder 41 pass from Favre (Longwell kick)
Chi	—	FG Edinger 38
GB	—	Freeman 9 pass from Favre (Longwell kick)

Chi — FG Edinger 41
GB — FG Longwell 31

N.Y. JETS 27, KANSAS CITY 7—at Giants Stadium, attendance 78,234. Curtis Martin rushed for 113 yards and 3 touchdowns to power the Jets. Victor Green's interception and 13-yard return led to Martin's 25-yard touchdown run just 24 seconds before halftime. It was 17-0 before Martin's 5-yard touchdown run midway through the third quarter. Vinny Testaverde was 17 of 27 for 170 yards, with 1 interception, while the Jets' defense forced 4 turnovers. Trent Green was 16 of 31 for 143 yards and 1 touchdown, with 3 interceptions.

Kansas City	0	0	0	7	—	7
N.Y. Jets	0	14	13	0	—	27

NYJ — C. Martin 1 run (Hall kick)
NYJ — C. Martin 25 run (Hall kick)
NYJ — FG Hall 51
NYJ — C. Martin 5 run (Hall kick)
NYJ — FG Hall 31
KC — Gonzalez 6 pass from Green (Peterson kick)

MIAMI 27, INDIANAPOLIS 24—at RCA Dome, attendance 57,127. Jay Fiedler's 29-yard touchdown pass to Chris Chambers with 7:16 left lifted the Dolphins. Peyton Manning and Marvin Harrison teamed on 3 touchdown passes for the Colts, including a 40-yard strike midway through the third quarter to break a 17-17 tie. But late in the period, Zach Thomas intercepted Manning's pass to set up a field goal. On the ensuing possession, Manning suffered an injured jaw, and backup quarterback Mark Rypien and Dominic Rhodes failed to execute a handoff on the next play. The resulting fumble was recovered by Jason Taylor. It took Miami only seven plays to cover 59 yards and take the lead for good on Fiedler's touchdown pass to Chambers. Manning returned to the game for the Colts' final two possessions, but Indianapolis could not drive further than Miami's 40. Fiedler was 17 of 29 for 259 yards and 2 touchdowns. Chambers had 3 receptions for 113 yards, including the first career touchdown catches. Manning was 20 of 33 for 253 yards and 3 touchdowns, with 2 interceptions. Harrison had 9 receptions for 174 yards.

Miami	7	10	0	10	—	27
Indianapolis	3	7	14	0	—	24

Ind — FG Vanderjagt 25
Mia — Minor 56 run (Mare kick)
Ind — Harrison 8 pass from Manning (Vanderjagt kick)
Mia — Chambers 74 pass from Fiedler (Mare kick)
Mia — FG Mare 31
Ind — Harrison 11 pass from Manning (Vanderjagt kick)
Ind — Harrison 40 pass from Manning (Vanderjagt kick)
Mia — FG Mare 31
Mia — Chambers 29 pass from Fiedler (Mare kick)

PHILADELPHIA 48, MINNESOTA 17—at Veterans Stadium, attendance 65,638. Donovan McNabb passed for 3 touchdowns and ran for another for the Eagles. A 91-yard march capped by McNabb's 12-yard touchdown run on the first play of the second quarter gave the Eagles a 14-0 lead en route to a 31-10 halftime lead. Duce Staley raced 44 yards for a touchdown on the Eagles' second play of the second half. McNabb was 19 of 29 for 223 yards and 3 touchdowns. Staley ran for 146 yards. Daunte Culpepper was 21 of 35 for 285 yards and 2 touchdowns, with 1 interception.

Minnesota	0	10	0	7	—	17
Philadelphia	7	24	7	10	—	48

Phil — Thrash 14 pass from McNabb (Akers kick)
Phil — McNabb 12 run (Akers kick)
Minn — FG Anderson 43
Phil — FG Akers 36
Phil — Thrash 17 pass from McNabb (Akers kick)
Phil — Buckhalter 1 run (Akers kick)
Minn — C. Carter 5 pass from Culpepper (Anderson kick)
Phil — Staley 44 run (Akers kick)
Phil — FG Akers 21
Phil — Bartrum 4 pass from McNabb (Akers kick)
Minn — Moss 29 pass from Culpepper (Anderson kick)

SAN FRANCISCO 28, NEW ORLEANS 27—at 3Com Park, attendance 68,083. Jeff Garcia passed for 252 yards and 4 touchdowns to lead the 49ers to a key victory. The Saints took a 24-21 lead before Ricky Williams lost a fumble at his 30-yard line. Four plays later, Garcia's 10-yard touchdown pass to Eric Johnson put the 49ers ahead for good with 11:06 to play. Carney's fourth field goal, a 36-yard kick on the ensuing possession, made it a one-point game, but New Orleans could not move past its 25 on its final drive, and San Francisco ran out the last 3:39. Garcia was 21 of 34 for 252 yards and 4 touchdowns. Garrison Hearst finished with 145 rushing yards. Terrell Owens caught 8 passes for 100 yards. Brooks was 22 of 37 for 347 yards and 2 touchdowns. Williams rushed for 121 yards for the Saints. Willie Jackson had 11 receptions for 167 yards.

New Orleans	3	11	10	3	—	27
San Francisco	7	14	0	7	—	28

NO — FG Carney 43
SF — Owens 25 pass from Garcia (Cortez kick)
SF — Owens 5 pass from Garcia (Cortez kick)
NO — Horn 22 pass from Brooks (Jackson pass from Brooks)
SF — Barlow 61 pass from Garcia (Cortez kick)
NO — FG Carney 42
NO — FG Carney 35
NO — Horn 6 pass from Brooks (Carney kick)
SF — E. Johnson 10 pass from Garcia (Cortez kick)
NO — FG Carney 36

N.Y. GIANTS 17, ARIZONA 10—at Sun Devil Stadium, attendance 36,917. Tiki Barber (118 yards) and Ron Dayne combined to rush for 167 yards for the Giants. The Giants played ball control, running on 41 of their 67 plays. The Cardinals pulled within four points on Bill Gramatica's 32-yard field goal midway through the third quarter, but could get no closer. After Gramatica's field goal, Arizona crossed midfield just once. Kerry Collins was 15 of 24 for 155 yards and 1 touchdown, with 1 interception. Plummer was 13 of 26 for 172 yards and 1 touchdown, with 1 interception. David Boston had 9 receptions for 137 yards.

N.Y. Giants	7	7	0	3	—	17
Arizona	0	7	3	0	—	10

NYG — Dayne 3 run (Andersen kick)
NYG — Hilliard 27 pass from Collins (Andersen kick)
Ariz — Boston 38 pass from Plummer (Gramatica kick)
Ariz — FG Gramatica 32
NYG — FG Andersen 25

PITTSBURGH 15, CLEVELAND 12 (OT)—at Cleveland Browns Stadium, attendance 73,218. Kris

Brown kicked 5 field goals, including the game winner in overtime, for the Steelers. Brown, who missed 4 field-goal tries in a loss to Baltimore one week earlier, helped Pittsburgh overcome an early 9-0 deficit to tie the game at 12-12. He could have won it late in regulation, but his 45-yard field-goal attempt was wide left with 1:37 left. The Steelers won the overtime coin toss and Jerome Bettis rumbled 27 yards on the first play of the extra session to move the ball into Browns territory, then carried on 6 of the next 7 plays to reach the 14-yard line to set up Brown's winning kick. The Steelers' defense limited Cleveland to only 187 total yards, and registered 7 sacks. Bettis finished with 163 yards on 29 carries, while Kordell Stewart was 18 of 32 for 188 yards. Tim Couch was 18 of 33 for 166 yards and 1 touchdown.

Pittsburgh	3	3	3	3	3	—	15
Cleveland	9	0	3	0	0	—	12

Cle — Safety, Bettis tackled by Roye in end zone
Cle — Santiago 12 pass from Couch (P. Dawson kick)
Pitt — FG K. Brown 31
Pitt — FG K. Brown 27
Pitt — FG K. Brown 37
Cle — FG P. Dawson 40
Pitt — FG K. Brown 37
Pitt — FG K. Brown 32

DENVER 26, SAN DIEGO 16—at INVESCO Field at Mile High, attendance 74,951. Brian Griese passed for 2 touchdowns in a 39-second span late in the first half to spark the Broncos to the victory. Following Griese's first touchdown, John Mobley intercepted Doug Flutie's pass and returned it 17 yards to the Chargers' 3-yard line. Griese teamed with Dwayne Carswell for a touchdown pass on the next snap, and Denver's lead was 20-0 just 32 seconds before halftime. The Broncos led by as much as 26-3 before withstanding San Diego's fourth-quarter rally, as Flutie was intercepted on the Chargers' final three possessions. Griese was 21 of 31 for 224 yards and 2 touchdowns. Flutie was 12 of 31 for 165 yards and 1 touchdown, with 4 interceptions. Conway had 3 catches for 111 yards.

San Diego	0	0	3	13	—	16
Denver	3	17	6	0	—	26

Den — FG Elam 25
Den — FG Elam 29
Den — De. Clark 18 pass from Griese (Elam kick)
Den — Carswell 3 pass from Griese (Elam kick)
Den — FG Elam 26
SD — FG Richey 29
Den — FG Elam 33
SD — Conway 72 pass from Flutie (Richey kick)
SD — R. Johnson 45 fumble return (run failed)

TAMPA BAY 20, DETROIT 17—at Pontiac Silverdome, attendance 74,268. Martin Gramatica's 37-yard field goal lifted the Buccaneers to the victory. The Lions fell to 0-8, but the last five losses were by a total of 23 points. Detroit had erased a 10-point, fourth-quarter deficit to tie the game on Charlie Batch's 8-yard touchdown pass to Reuben Droughns with 1:49 left. But Brad Johnson completed an 18-yard pass to Keyshawn Johnson on third-and-3 from the 27, and two plays later teamed with Warrick Dunn on a 23-yard pass play to the Lions' 26 to set up Gramatica's winning kick. Brad Johnson was 20 of 37 for 188 yards and 1 touchdown. Batch was 21 of 39 for 239 yards and 1 touchdown, with 2 interceptions.

Tampa Bay	0	10	7	3	—	20

Detroit		0	0	7	10	—	17

TB — FG Gramatica 37
TB — Dunn 12 pass from
B. Johnson (Gramatica kick)
Det — Schlesinger 1 run
(Hanson kick)
TB — K. Williams 84 punt return (Gramatica kick)
Det — FG Hanson 38
Det — Droughns 8 pass from Batch
(Hanson kick)
TB — FG Gramatica 35

SUNDAY NIGHT, NOVEMBER 11

SEATTLE 34, OAKLAND 27—at Husky Stadium, attendance 67,231. Shaun Alexander rushed for a club-record 266 yards and 3 touchdowns as the Seahawks ended the Raiders' five-game winning streak. Oakland led 20-13 in the third quarter before Alexander took over. He capped a 61-yard drive with a 6-yard touchdown run to tie the game. The next time possession, he broke free for an 88-yard touchdown run, longest in club history, to put Seattle ahead for good. Later, his 10-yard run opened a 34-20 lead. Alexander, who carried 35 times, had the fourth-highest single-game rushing total in NFL history. Matt Hasselbeck was 15 of 23 for 181 yards and 1 touchdown. Gannon was 24 of 38 for 257 yards and 2 touchdowns.

Oakland	3	7	10	7	—	27
Seattle	6	7	14	7	—	34

Sea — FG Lindell 33
Oak — FG Janikowski 52
Sea — FG Lindell 20
Oak — T. Brown 4 pass from Gannon
(Janikowski kick)
Sea — Jackson 9 pass from Hasselbeck
(Lindell kick)
Oak — Kirby 90 kickoff return (Janikowski kick)
Oak — FG Janikowski 37
Sea — Alexander 6 run (Lindell kick)
Sea — Alexander 88 run (Lindell kick)
Sea — Alexander 10 run (Lindell kick)
Oak — R. Williams 5 pass from Gannon
(Janikowski kick)

MONDAY NIGHT, NOVEMBER 12

BALTIMORE 16, TENNESSEE 10—at Adelphia Coliseum, attendance 68,798. The Ravens won their third consecutive game with a dramatic goal-line stand on the game's final play. Matt Stover kicked 2 field goals in the fourth quarter to break a 10-10 tie, including a 30-yarder with 3:06 left, before the Titans began their last drive at their 22-yard line. McNair completed 7 of 9 passes for 59 yards as Tennessee marched to a first-and-goal at Baltimore's 6 with 24 seconds left and no timeouts. After back-to-back incomplete passes, McNair hit Dyson on a 5-yard pass to the 1. Both teams scrambled to the line of scrimmage, and McNair sneaked into the end zone. But officials ruled that Peter Boulware had made contact with a Titans' player before the snap, negating the play. With three seconds left on the clock, McNair tried another sneak from inside the 1, but was stopped by a pile of defenders, and the game ended. McNair was 27 of 48 for 256 yards and 1 touchdown. Grbac was 15 of 27 for 192 yards and 1 touchdown, with 1 interception. Ismail had 129 yards on 8 receptions. Derrick Mason caught 12 passes for 99 yards.

Baltimore	0	0	10	6	—	16
Tennessee	0	0	10	0	—	10

Tenn — FG Nedney 27
Balt — FG Stover 31
Tenn — Dyson 22 pass from McNair (Nedney kick)

Balt — Ismail 57 pass from Grbac (Stover kick)
Balt — FG Stover 33
Balt — FG Stover 30

TENTH WEEK SUMMARIES
American Football Conference

Eastern Division	W	L	T	Pct.	Pts.	OP
N.Y. Jets	7	3	0	.700	208	182
Miami	6	3	0	.667	180	185
New England	5	5	0	.500	223	195
Indianapolis	4	5	0	.444	244	258
Buffalo	1	8	0	.111	153	239

Central Division	W	L	T	Pct.	Pts.	OP
Pittsburgh	7	2	0	.778	155	97
Baltimore	6	4	0	.600	174	166
Cleveland	5	4	0	.556	171	150
Cincinnati	4	5	0	.444	140	186
Tennessee	4	5	0	.444	159	203
Jacksonville	3	6	0	.333	151	148

Western Division	W	L	T	Pct.	Pts.	OP
Oakland	7	2	0	.778	250	191
Seattle	5	4	0	.556	175	205
Denver	5	5	0	.500	228	215
San Diego	5	5	0	.500	246	206
Kansas City	2	7	0	.222	171	199

National Football Conference

Eastern Division	W	L	T	Pct.	Pts.	OP
Philadelphia	6	3	0	.667	229	118
N.Y. Giants	5	5	0	.500	181	178
Washington	4	5	0	.444	128	203
Arizona	3	6	0	.333	154	221
Dallas	2	7	0	.222	132	203

Central Division	W	L	T	Pct.	Pts.	OP
Chicago	7	2	0	.778	201	139
Green Bay	6	3	0	.667	208	140
Minnesota	4	5	0	.444	183	229
Tampa Bay	4	5	0	.444	183	163
Detroit	0	9	0	.000	165	262

Western Division	W	L	T	Pct.	Pts.	OP
St. Louis	8	1	0	.889	279	146
San Francisco	7	2	0	.778	227	204
Atlanta	5	4	0	.556	178	184
New Orleans	5	4	0	.556	209	182
Carolina	1	9	0	.100	154	242

SUNDAY, NOVEMBER 18

ATLANTA 23, GREEN BAY 20—at Lambeau Field, attendance 59,849. Chris Chandler passed for 352 yards and 2 touchdowns for the Falcons. Green Bay narrowed a 13-point deficit to 16-13 before Chandler completed 5 of 6 passes on a 78-yard drive in the fourth quarter that was capped by a 12-yard touchdown toss to Brian Finneran with 8:49 left. The Packers countered on Brett Favre's 39-yard touchdown pass to Antonio Freeman at the 6:31 mark, then had two more chances to tie or win. But the first ended with a punt and the second was stopped when Ashley Ambrose intercepted Favre's long pass at the Falcons' 2-yard line with 1:08 left. Chandler was 29 of 50 for 352 yards and 2 touchdowns, with 2 interceptions. Favre was 16 of 29 for 262 yards and 2 touchdowns, with 3 interceptions. Corey Bradford had 117 yards on 3 catches.

Atlanta	6	10	0	7	—	23
Green Bay	3	7	3	7	—	20

Atl — FG Feely 26
Atl — FG Feely 39
GB — FG Longwell 39
Atl — Christian 21 pass from Chandler
(Feely kick)
Atl — FG Feely 32
GB — Schroeder 4 pass from Favre
(Longwell kick)
GB — FG Longwell 45
Atl — Finneran 12 pass from Chandler
(Feely kick)

GB — Freeman 39 pass from Favre
(Longwell kick)

CHICAGO 27, TAMPA BAY 24—at Raymond James Stadium, attendance 65,612. Marty Booker caught 3 touchdown passes, and the Bears held on to win when Martin Gramatica missed a 48-yard field-goal attempt on the final play. The victory propelled the Bears back into first place in the NFC Central. Booker, who had 7 receptions for 165 yards, grabbed scoring tosses of 28, 44, and 66 yards—the latter 2 coming only 1:40 apart in the third quarter—as Chicago took a 27-16 lead. But the Buccaneers rallied to within a field goal when Brad Johnson ran 1 yard for a touchdown with 2:29 left, then teamed with Mike Alstott on a 2-point conversion pass. An unsportsmanlike conduct pentalty by R.W. McQuarters put the Buccaneers in field-goal range, but Gramatica had his kick bounce off the right upright as time ran out. Miller was 14 of 25 for 228 yards and 3 touchdowns, with 1 interception. Johnson was 40 of 56 for 399 yards, with 2 interceptions, most of them to Dunn (12 receptions for 138 yards) and Keyshawn Johnson (12 catches for 89 yards).

Chicago	0	7	13	7	—	27
Tampa Bay	3	6	0	15	—	24

TB — FG Gramatica 25
TB — FG Gramatica 38
Chi — Booker 28 pass from Miller
(Edinger kick)
TB — FG Gramatica 26
Chi — Booker 44 pass from Miller
(Edinger kick)
Chi — Booker 66 pass from Miller
(Edinger kick)
Chi — FG Edinger 26
TB — Alstott 1 run (Gramatica kick)
Chi — FG Edinger 40
TB — B. Johnson 1 run (Alstott pass
from B. Johnson)

CLEVELAND 27, BALTIMORE 17—at PSINet Stadium, attendance 69,353. The Browns' defense helped Cleveland complete a surprising season sweep of the Ravens. Cleveland jumped to a big first-half lead, then held on to win. The key plays were interceptions by Anthony Henry and Devin Bush on back-to-back drives. The Browns secured the victory with a 12-play, 68-yard touchdown drive that consumed 5:51 of the fourth quarter, capped by Jamel White's 1-yard run with 4:02 left. Tim Couch was 19 of 30 for 144 yards, with 3 interceptions. Grbac was 23 of 44 for 261 yards and 2 touchdowns, with 4 interceptions.

Cleveland	3	17	0	7	—	27
Baltimore	3	7	10	0	—	17

Cle — FG P. Dawson 29
Cle — Gay 7 run (P. Dawson kick)
Cle — Bush 43 interception return
(P. Dawson kick)
Balt — Stokley 21 pass from Grbac
(Stover kick)
Cle — FG P. Dawson 42
Balt — Heap 24 pass from Grbac (Stover kick)
Balt — FG Stover 42
Cle — White 1 run (P. Dawson kick)

ARIZONA 45, DETROIT 38—at Sun Devil Stadium, attendance 32,322. Jake Plummer passed for 4 touchdowns to rally the Cardinals from a 10-point, fourth-quarter deficit and hand the Lions another frustrating defeat. Detroit built a 31-21 lead, but the Cardinals scored on consecutive possessions to go ahead for good with 10:04 left. From there, Kwamie Lassiter intercepted 2 passes and tipped a pass that was Fred Wakefield intercepted and returned for a touchdown. Plummer was 21 of 33 for 334 yards and 4 touchdowns, with 1 interception. Frank Sanders had 7 catches for 127 yards. Batch was 36 of 62 for a club-record 436 yards and 3 touchdowns, with 3 interceptions. Lamont Warren had 11 catches for 64 yards, and Johnnie Morton had 7 for 153 yards.

Detroit	0	14	17	7	—	38
Arizona	7	7	7	24	—	45

Ariz	—	T. Jones 3 run (Gramatica kick)
Det	—	Schlesinger 1 run (Hanson kick)
Det	—	Sloan 2 pass from Batch (Hanson kick)
Ariz	—	Boston 13 pass from Plummer (Gramatica kick)
Det	—	Warren 3 run (Hanson kick)
Ariz	—	Sanders 68 pass from Plummer (Gramatica kick)
Det	—	Sloan 1 pass from Batch (Hanson kick)
Det	—	FG Hanson 49
Ariz	—	Boston 18 pass from Plummer (Gramatica kick)
Ariz	—	Jenkins 3 pass from Plummer (Gramatica kick)
Ariz	—	Wakefield 20 interception return (Gramatica kick)
Ariz	—	FG Gramatica 50
Det	—	Warren 6 pass from Batch (Hanson kick)

NEW ORLEANS 34, INDIANAPOLIS 20—at Louisiana Superdome, attendance 70,020. Aaron Brooks passed for 2 touchdowns and ran for another as the Saints overcame a 14-point fourth-quarter deficit to win. Peyton Manning, playing his first professional game in the stadium where his father Archie played in the 1970s, completed an 86-yard touchdown pass to Marcus Pollard on the first play of the game, and took a 14-0 lead later in the quarter. But the Saints took the lead for good when Brooks and Eddie Williams teamed on a 12-yard touchdown pass following the second-half kickoff. It was 27-20 when Ricky Williams ran 14 yards for the final tally with 4:40 left. Brooks was 19 of 22 for 249 yards and 2 touchdowns. Williams rushed 28 times for 120 yards, while Joe Horn had 8 catches for 148 yards. Manning was 18 of 28 for 262 yards and 1 touchdown, with 1 interception. Pollard had 3 catches for 126 yards.

Indianapolis	14	3	0	3	—	20
New Orleans	0	17	7	10	—	34

Ind	—	Pollard 86 pass from Manning (Vanderjagt kick)
Ind	—	Rhodes 1 run (Vanderjagt kick)
NO	—	E. Williams 8 pass from Brooks (Carney kick)
NO	—	FG Carney 46
NO	—	Brooks 7 run (Carney kick)
Ind	—	FG Vanderjagt 52
NO	—	E. Williams 12 pass from Brooks (Carney kick)
NO	—	FG Carney 48
Ind	—	FG Vanderjagt 41
NO	—	R. Williams 14 run (Carney kick)

PITTSBURGH 20, JACKSONVILLE 7—at Heinz Field, attendance 62,644. Kordell Stewart ran for 1 touchdown and passed for another as the Steelers won for the sixth time in seven games and the Jaguars lost for the sixth time in seven games. Pittsburgh led 6-0 before Stewart teamed with Hines Ward on a 28-yard touchdown pass with 19 seconds left in the third quarter. But Jacksonville immediately pulled close again when Elvis Joseph returned the ensuing kickoff 95 yards for a touchdown. Late in the game, the Jaguars were driving to a potential go-ahead touchdown when Joey Porter sacked Jonathan Quinn, forcing a fumble that Casey

Hampton recovered at the Steelers' 21-yard line with 4:01 left. Jerome Bettis (40 yards) and Amos Zereoue (28 yards) broke off long runs on the next two plays, and Stewart soon ran 7 yards for the clinching touchdown with 1:56 to play. Stewart was 21of 33 for 266 yards and 1 touchdown. Ward caught 9 passes for 112 yards. Quinn started in place of injured Mark Brunell for Jacksonville and was 17 of 31 for 225 yards.

Jacksonville	0	0	7	0	—	7
Pittsburgh	3	3	7	7	—	20

Pitt	—	FG K. Brown 48
Pitt	—	FG K. Brown 28
Pitt	—	Ward 28 pass from Stewart (K. Brown kick)
Jax	—	Joseph 95 kickoff return (Hollis kick)
Pitt	—	Stewart 7 run (K. Brown kick)

N.Y. JETS 24, MIAMI 0—at Pro Player Stadium, attendance 74,259. The Jets continued their mastery over Miami beating their division rivals for the eighth consecutive time to move into first place in the AFC East. The Jets managed only 162 total yards, but forced 5 turnovers while handing Miami its first home shutout in 31 years. The Jets intercepted 3 passes, 2 of which were returned for touchdowns by Aaron Glenn and Victor Green. The Dolphins drove inside the Jets' 40-yard line five times, but were stymied by 3 interceptions, a fumble, and a missed field goal. Testaverde was 10 of 21 for 76 yards and 1 touchdown. Jay Fiedler was 24 of 36 for 188 yards, with 3 interceptions.

N.Y. Jets	7	7	3	7	—	24
Miami	0	0	0	0	—	0

NYJ	—	Glenn 60 interception return (Hall kick)
NYJ	—	Coles 17 pass from Testaverde (Hall kick)
NYJ	—	Green 63 interception return (Hall kick)
NYJ	—	FG Hall 43

PHILADELPHIA 36, DALLAS 3—at Texas Stadium, attendance 63,204. Jeremiah Trotter and William Hampton returned interceptions for touchdowns as the Eagles. Philadelphia led 13-0 in the closing seconds of the second quarter when Trotter stepped in front of Ryan Leaf's ill-advised sideline pass and returned the interception 50 yards for a touchdown as time ran out in the half. The Eagles' forced 4 turnovers and had 3 sacks. Donovan McNabb was 16 of 32 for 129 yards and 1 touchdown, with 1 interception. Duce Staley rushed for 102 yards. Leaf was 11 of 26 for 102 yards, with 2 interceptions.

Philadelphia	0	20	6	10	—	36
Dallas	0	0	0	3	—	3

Phil	—	Lewis 2 pass from McNabb (Akers kick)
Phil	—	FG Akers 24
Phil	—	FG Akers 46
Phil	—	Trotter 50 interception return (Akers kick)
Phil	—	FG Akers 26
Phil	—	FG Akers 28
Dall	—	FG Hilbert 30
Phil	—	FG Akers 30
Phil	—	Hampton 33 interception return (Akers kick)

OAKLAND 34, SAN DIEGO 24—at Network Associates Coliseum, attendance 61,960. Jerry Rice caught 3 touchdown passes, including the decisive 20-yard score at 2:46 left, to help carry the Raiders. Rice also had touchdown catches of 12 yards in the first quarter and 30 yards on the first play of the fourth quarter, but the score was tied at 24-24 late in the game largely because of two big

plays: Curtis Conway's 67-yard touchdown run on a reverse and Ronney Jenkins' 93-yard kickoff return for a touchdown. Follwoing Rice's third touchdown, Doug Flutie fumbled and Sebastian Janikowski added a field goal with 55 seconds left. Gannon was 25 of 38 for 311 yards and 4 touchdowns, with 1 interception, while Rice caught 8 passes for 131 yards. Flutie was 12 of 27 for 98 yards, with 1 interception.

San Diego	7	0	10	7	—	24
Oakland	14	0	3	17	—	34

Oak	—	T. Brown 10 pass from Gannon (Janikowski kick)
SD	—	Conway 67 run (Richey kick)
Oak	—	Rice 12 pass from Gannon (Janikowski kick)
SD	—	FG Richey 26
Oak	—	FG Janikowski 24
SD	—	Jenkins 93 kickoff return (Richey kick)
Oak	—	Rice 30 pass from Gannon (Janikowski kick)
SD	—	Tomlinson 1 run (Richey kick)
Oak	—	Rice 20 pass from Gannon (Janikowski kick)
Oak	—	FG Janikowski 25

SAN FRANCISCO 25, CAROLINA 22 (OT)—at Ericsson Stadium, attendance 58,054. Jose Cortez' 26-yard field goal 4:41 into overtime lifted the 49ers and handed the Panthers their ninth consecutive defeat. Carolina led 22-14 when San Francisco gained possession at its 34-yard line with 1:46 left. Jeff Garcia completed a pair of passes to move the ball quickly into Carolina territory, then kept the drive alive by teaming with Tai Streets for an 8-yard gain on fourth-and-4 from the 46. Four plays later, Garcia found Eric Johnson for a 21-yard gain to the 7, then hit Terrell Owens for a touchdown to pull the 49ers within 22-20 with one second left. Garcia and Johnson teamed again on a tying 2-point conversion pass to send the game to overtime. The 49ers won the toss and Garrison Hearst ran 31 yards from the 40 to position Cortez. Garcia was 34 of 54 for 302 yards and 3 touchdowns, with 2 interceptions. Chris Weinke was 22 of 41 for 177 yards and 2 touchdowns.

San Francisco	0	7	7	8	3	—	25
Carolina	7	3	3	9	0	—	22

Car	—	Huntley 13 pass from Weinke (Kasay kick)
SF	—	Stokes 14 pass from Garcia (Cortez kick)
Car	—	FG Kasay 25
Car	—	FG Kasay 41
SF	—	Stokes 9 pass from Garcia (Cortez kick)
Car	—	Walls 24 pass from Weinke (pass failed)
Car	—	FG Kasay 28
SF	—	Owens 7 pass from Garcia (E. Johnson pass from Garcia)
SF	—	FG Cortez 26

SEATTLE 23, BUFFALO 20—at Ralph Wilson Stadium, attendance 60,836. Shaun Alexander ran 1 yard for the go-ahead touchdown in the third quarter, and the Seahawks went on to hand the Bills their fourth consecutive defeat. The game was tied at 10-10 at halftime, but Seattle opened the second half by marching 70 yards in 8 plays to Alexander's touchdown and Rian Lindell kept them at arm's length by kicking 2 field goals. Seattle recovered an onside kickoff in the final minute to seal the victory. Hasselbeck was 16 of 23 for 134 yards and 1 touchdown. Alex Van Pelt, making his first start in place of injured Rob Johnson, was 28 of 42 for 316 yards and 2 touchdowns. Peerless Price had 10 catches for 138 yards.

Seattle	3	7	7	6 —	23
Buffalo	0	10	3	7 —	20

Sea — FG Lindell 40
Sea — K. Robinson 7 pass from Hasselbeck (Lindell kick)
Buff — P. Price 16 pass from Van Pelt (Arians kick)
Buff — FG Arians 25
Sea — Alexander 1 run (Lindell kick)
Buff — FG Arians 26
Sea — FG Lindell 38
Sea — FG Lindell 51
Buff — Riemersma 6 pass from Van Pelt (Arians kick)

TENNESSEE 20, CINCINNATI 7—at Paul Brown Stadium, attendance 63,865. Derrick Mason returned the opening kickoff 101 yards for a touchdown to spark the Titans. After Mason's big return, Tennessee forced a punt, then drove 57 yards to Joe Nedney's 41-yard field goal for a 10-0 lead. Cincinnati managed only 37 yards on its first six second-half possessions. Steve McNair was 16 of 25 for 172 yards and a touchdown, with 1 interception, and had a game-high 68 rushing yards. Kitna was 23 of 42 for 234 yards and 1 touchdown, with 2 interceptions.

Tennessee	10	0	7	3 —	20
Cincinnati	7	0	0	0 —	7

Tenn — Mason 101 kickoff return (Nedney kick)
Tenn — FG Nedney 41
Cin — Dugans 10 pass from Kitna (Rackers kick)
Tenn — K. Dyson 28 pass from McNair (Nedney kick)
Tenn — FG Nedney 37

WASHINGTON 17, DENVER 10—at INVESCO Field at Mile High, attendance 74,622. The surging Redskins won their fourth in a row when backup Kent Graham came off the bench to pass for 2 touchdowns in the fourth quarter. Washington trailed 10-0 when Tony Banks suffered a concussion with 1:50 left in the second quarter. With snow falling, Graham completed 2 fourth-quarter touchdown passes, the second with 2:48 left, to win it. The Redskins' defense allowed just 10 first downs and 186 total yards. Graham was 12 of 18 for 123 yards and 2 touchdowns in his relief stint for Banks, who was 4 of 13 for 27 yards. Westbrook caught 9 passes for 104 yards. Griese was 11 of 31 for 114 yards and 1 touchdown.

Washington	0	3	0	14 —	17
Denver	0	10	0	0 —	10

Den — FG Elam 33
Den — R. Smith 1 pass from Griese (Elam kick)
Wash — FG Conway 48
Wash — Westbrook 5 pass from Graham (Conway kick)
Wash — Flemister 3 pass from Graham (Conway kick)

SUNDAY NIGHT, NOVEMBER 18
ST. LOUIS 24, NEW ENGLAND 17—at Foxboro Stadium, attendance 59,884. Kurt Warner passed for 401 yards and 3 touchdowns to lead the Rams. The game turned late in the second quarter, when the Patriots led 10-7 and were about to extend their advantage, when Antowain Smith lost a fumble at St. Louis' 3-yard line just 2:12 before halftime. Warner teamed with Marshall Faulk on a 9-yard touchdown pass to put the Rams ahead for good. St. Louis made it 24-10 after Jeff Wilkins kicked a 35-yard field goal in the third quarter and Warner tossed an 11-yard touchdown pass to James Hodgins with

10:32 left. Tom Brady's 10-yard touchdown pass to David Patten cut the deficit to 24-17 with 7:46 left, but they never got the ball back again. Faulk converted three straight third downs with a pass reception and two runs, and the Rams held the ball for the final 14 plays. Warner was 30 of 42 for 401 yards and 3 touchdowns, with 2 interceptions. Isaac Bruce caught 7 passes for 130 yards. Brady was 19 of 27 for 185 yards and 1 touchdown, with 2 interceptions.

St. Louis	7	7	3	7 —	24
New England	7	3	0	7 —	17

StL — Holt 16 pass from Warner (Wilkins kick)
NE — Buckley 52 interception return (Vinatieri kick)
NE — FG Vinatieri 33
StL — M. Faulk 9 pass from Warner (Wilkins kick)
StL — FG Wilkins 35
StL — Hodgins 11 pass from Warner (Wilkins kick)
NE — Patten 10 pass from Brady (Vinatieri kick)

MONDAY NIGHT, NOVEMBER 19
MINNESOTA 28, N.Y. GIANTS 16—at Metrodome, attendance 64,283. Daunte Culpepper tossed 4 touchdown passes, 3 of them to Randy Moss, to carry the Vikings. The Giants rallied to take leads of 10-7 and 16-14 before the Vikings held the ball for an 8:54 stretch of the third and fourth quarters, taking the lead for good when Culpepper and Cris Carter teamed on a 1-yard touchdown pass 5:57 into the final quarter. Culpepper found Moss on a crossing patternfor the clinching 57-yard touchdown with 6:32 left. Culpepper was 26 of 38 for 277 yards and 4 touchdowns, with 2 interceptions. Moss had 10 catches for 171 yards, and Carter had 10 for 46 yards. Kerry Collins was 21 of 37 for 321 yards, with 2 interceptions. Ike Hilliard had 6 catches for 106 yards.

N.Y. Giants	10	3	3	0 —	16
Minnesota	7	7	14	0 —	28

Minn — Moss 28 pass from Culpepper (Anderson kick)
NYG — FG Andersen 43
NYG — Barber 1 run (Andersen kick)
Minn — Moss 25 pass from Culpepper (Anderson kick)
NYG — FG Andersen 36
NYG — FG Andersen 51
Minn — Carter 1 pass from Culpepper (Anderson kick)
Minn — Moss 57 pass from Culpepper (Anderson kick)

ELEVENTH WEEK SUMMARIES
American Football Conference

Eastern Division	W	L	T	Pct.	Pts.	OP
Miami	7	3	0	.700	214	212
N.Y. Jets	7	3	0	.700	208	182
New England	6	5	0	.545	257	212
Indianapolis	4	6	0	.400	265	298
Buffalo	1	9	0	.100	180	273
Central Division						
Pittsburgh	8	2	0	.800	189	121
Baltimore	7	4	0	.636	198	187
Cleveland	6	4	0	.600	189	150
Cincinnati	4	6	0	.400	140	204
Tennessee	4	6	0	.400	183	237
Jacksonville	3	7	0	.300	172	172
Western Division						
Oakland	8	2	0	.800	278	201
Denver	6	5	0	.545	254	239
Seattle	5	5	0	.500	182	224
San Diego	5	6	0	.455	263	226
Kansas City	3	7	0	.300	190	206

National Football Conference

Eastern Division	W	L	T	Pct.	Pts.	OP
Philadelphia	6	4	0	.600	232	131
Washington	5	5	0	.500	141	206
N.Y. Giants	5	6	0	.455	191	206
Arizona	4	6	0	.400	174	238
Dallas	2	8	0	.200	156	229
Central Division						
Chicago	8	2	0	.800	214	145
Green Bay	7	3	0	.700	237	167
Tampa Bay	5	5	0	.500	207	180
Minnesota	4	6	0	.400	189	242
Detroit	0	10	0	.000	192	291
Western Division						
St. Louis	8	2	0	.800	296	170
San Francisco	8	2	0	.800	267	225
Atlanta	6	4	0	.600	188	191
New Orleans	5	5	0	.500	226	216
Carolina	1	10	0	.091	161	252

THURSDAY, NOVEMBER 22
DENVER 26, DALLAS 24—at Texas Stadium, attendance 64,104. The Broncos built a 23-point lead, then withstood a furious fourth-quarter rally. Jason Elam's fourth field goal of the game, from 28 yards, gave the Broncos a seemingly secure 26-3 advantage with 11:13 left in the game. But Troy Hambrick's 1-yard touchdown run with 8:12 to go, followed 43 seconds later by Reggie Swinton's 65-yard punt return for a touchdown clipped the lead to 26-17. Dallas eschewed a 2-point conversion attempt. When Hambrick capped a 56-yard drive with another 1-yard scoring run with 1:10 left, the deficit was two. But Denver survived the scare by recovering the ensuing onside kickoff. Griese was 17 of 29 for 171 yards and 1 touchdown, with 1 interception. Mike Anderson rushed for 118 yards. Leaf was 16 of 32 for 193 yards.

Denver	3	14	6	3 —	26
Dallas	3	0	0	21 —	24

Den — FG Elam 24
Dall — FG Hilbert 43
Den — Anderson 1 run (Elam kick)
Den — Carswell 4 pass from Griese (Elam kick)
Den — FG Elam 50
Den — FG Elam 46
Den — FG Elam 28
Dall — Hambrick 1 run (Hilbert kick)
Dall — Swinton 65 punt return (Hilbert kick)
Dall — Hambrick 1 run (Hilbert kick)

GREEN BAY 29, DETROIT 27—at Pontiac Silverdome, attendance 77,730. Ahman Green scored 2 touchdowns, and the Packers kept the Lions winless by stopping a two-point conversion attempt in the final seconds. Green Bay led 29-13 when Mike McMahon replaced injured Charlie Batch to play the Lions with 6:56 to play. Detroit converted three fourth downs before Lamont Warren carried 1 yard for a touchdown on the eighteenth play of a 71-yard march. McMahon ran for a 2-point conversion to pull the Lions within 29-21, and Detroit got the ball back when Todd Lyght recovered the onside kick with 1:10 left. On fourth-and-8, McMahon completed a 29-yard touchdown pass to Scotty Anderson to make it 29-27 with 10 seconds to go. But the potential game-tying conversion attempt failed when McMahon's pass for Cory Schlesinger fell incomplete. Favre was 18 of 26 for 252 yards and 2 touchdowns, and Ahman Green rushed for 102 yards. McMahon was 9 of 20 for 89 yards and 1 touchdown, while Batch was 8 of 19 for 118 yards, with 1 interception. James Stewart had 102 rushing yards.

Green Bay	7	10	7	5 —	29
Detroit	3	10	0	14 —	27

GB	—	Green 26 run (Longwell kick)				
Det	—	FG Hanson 33				
Det	—	FG Hanson 54				
GB	—	FG Longwell 46				
Det	—	Hall 8 fumble return (Hanson kick)				
GB	—	Martin 1 pass from Favre (Longwell kick)				
GB	—	Green 35 pass from Favre (Longwell kick)				
GB	—	Safety, Warren recovered Batch fumble in end zone				
GB	—	FG Longwell 39				
Det	—	Warren 1 run (McMahon run)				
Det	—	Anderson 29 pass from McMahon (pass failed)				

SUNDAY, NOVEMBER 25

ARIZONA 20, SAN DIEGO 17—at Qualcomm Stadium, attendance 49,398. Bill Gramatica's 42-yard field goal with one second remaining lifted the Cardinals. The Chargers managed only 3 first-half points on four trips inside Cardinals' territory—Wade Richey made a 26-yard field goal but missed from 25 and 27 yards. San Diego rallied twice to tie the score in the final quarter, the last time at 17-17 on Doug Flutie's 28-yard touchdown pass to Jeff Graham with 1:54 to play. But Jake Plummer completed a 20-yard pass to Tywan Mitchell to move the ball into Chargers' territory and three plays later scrambled 13 yards for a first down to position Gramatica for the winning kick. Plummer was 19 of 31 for 241 yards and 1 touchdown, with 2 interceptions. Boston had 6 receptions for 121 yards. Flutie was 33 of 44 for 308 yards and 2 touchdowns. LaDainian Tomlinson caught 13 passes for 72 yards.

Arizona	0	7	3	10	—	20
San Diego	3	0	0	14	—	17

SD	—	FG Richey 26
Ariz	—	Boston 37 pass from Plummer (Gramatica kick)
Ariz	—	FG Gramatica 18
SD	—	Conway 6 pass from Flutie (Richey kick)
Ariz	—	Pittman 1 run (Gramatica kick)
SD	—	Graham 28 pass from Flutie (Richey kick)
Ariz	—	FG Gramatica 42

ATLANTA 10, CAROLINA 7—at Ericsson Stadium, attendance 50,219. The Falcons handed the Panthers their tenth loss in a row. The Falcons had a 99-yard second-quarter driver, capped by Bob Christian's 4-yard touchdown run for a 10-0 lead just 2:09 before halftime. The Panthers had a chance to tie, but Chris Weinke was stopped short on a fourth-and-1 sneak from the Falcons' 45-yard line following the two-minute warning. Chris Chandler was 14 of 27 for 132 yards. Christian had 78 yards on only 4 carries. Weinke was 17 of 31 for 171 yards, with 2 interceptions.

Atlanta	3	7	0	0	—	10
Carolina	0	0	0	7	—	7

Atl	—	FG Feely 39
Atl	—	Christian 4 run (Feely kick)
Car	—	Weinke 12 run (Kasay kick)

BALTIMORE 24, JACKSONVILLE 21—at ALLTEL Stadium, attendance 53,530. Elvis Grbac's 3-yard touchdown pass to Shannon Sharpe with nine seconds left gave the Ravens the victory. The Jaguars had rallied from a 17-point, third-quarter deficit to take a 21-17 lead on Stacey Mack's 3-yard touchdown run with 1:32 to play. Grbac completed 2 of 8 passes on the ensuing drive, capped by Sharpe's grab in the back of the end zone. Grbac was 21 of 30 for 259 yards and 1 touchdown, with 1 interception. Brunell was 23 of 38 for 259 yards and 1

touchdown.

Baltimore	3	7	7	7	—	24
Jacksonville	0	0	7	14	—	21

Balt	—	FG Stover 41
Balt	—	Brookins 2 run (Stover kick)
Balt	—	Brookins 1 run (Stover kick)
Jax	—	Mack 4 run (Hollis kick)
Jax	—	Ji. Smith 12 pass from Brunell (Hollis kick)
Jax	—	Mack 3 run (Hollis kick)
Balt	—	Sharpe 3 pass from Grbac (Stover kick)

CLEVELAND 18, CINCINNATI 0—at Cleveland Browns Stadium, attendance 72,918. The Browns forced 7 turnovers en route to their first shutout since 1994. Tim Couch and Kevin Johnson teamed on a 6-yard pass for the game's lone touchdown 26 seconds before halftime. The Bengals had the ball inside Cleveland territory on seven occasions, only to come up empty each time. Couch was 16 of 27 for 189 yards and 1 touchdown, with 2 interceptions. Johnson had 6 catches for 113 yards. Scott Mitchell was in the game in place of Jon Kitna, who was 8 of 19 for 85 yards, with 2 interceptions. Mitchell was 4 of 12 for 38 yards, with 3 interceptions. Akili Smith (1 of 2 for 2 yards). In addition to the 5 interceptions, Cincinnati also lost 2 fumbles.

Cincinnati	0	0	0	0	—	0
Cleveland	3	9	0	6	—	18

Cle	—	FG P. Dawson 23
Cle	—	FG P. Dawson 27
Cle	—	Johnson 6 pass from Couch (kick failed)
Cle	—	FG P. Dawson 23
Cle	—	FG P. Dawson 33

MIAMI 34, BUFFALO 27—at Ralph Wilson Stadium, attendance 73,063. Jay Fiedler passed for 3 touchdowns in the fourth quarter, including a game-winning, 32-yard strike to Chris Chambers with 48 seconds left, as the Dolphins handed the Bills their fifth consecutive defeat. Buffalo led 21-10 before Fiedler's heroics. Olindo Mare tied the game with a 39-yard field goal with 1:11 left, and when Buffalo's Nate Clements lost a fumble on the ensuing kickoff, setting up Chambers' winning catch. Fiedler was 18 of 31 for 262 yards and 3 touchdowns. Oronde Gadsden had 8 catches for 118 yards, while Chambers caught 5 passes for 101 yards. Alex Van Pelt was 21 of 34 for 309 yards and 3 touchdowns, with 1 interception. Eric Moulds caught 6 passes for 196 yards.

Miami	7	3	0	24	—	34
Buffalo	7	7	7	6	—	27

Mia	—	L. Smith 1 run (Mare kick)
Buff	—	Moulds 80 pass from Van Pelt (Arians kick)
Mia	—	FG Mare 25
Buff	—	Jackson 1 pass from Van Pelt (Arians kick)
Buff	—	Moulds 54 pass from Van Pelt (Arians kick)
Mia	—	Weaver 8 pass from Fiedler (Mare kick)
Buff	—	Henry 8 run (kick failed)
Mia	—	Chambers 22 pass from Fiedler (Mare kick)
Mia	—	FG Mare 39
Mia	—	Chambers 32 pass from Fiedler (Mare kick)

NEW ENGLAND 34, NEW ORLEANS 17—at Foxboro Stadium, attendance 57,117. Tom Brady passed for 4 touchdowns to lead the Patriots past the Saints. Brady tossed a 41-yard touchdown pass to Antowain Smith on the sixth play of the game, then teamed with Troy Brown (8 yards) and Charles

Johnson (24 yards) for touchdown passes as New England built a 20-0 halftime lead. Brady was 19 of 26 for 258 yards and 4 touchdowns. Smith finished with 111 yards on 24 carries. Brooks was 16 of 39 for 307 yards and 1 touchdown, with 2 interceptions.

New Orleans	0	0	10	7	—	17
New England	7	13	0	14	—	34

NE	—	A. Smith 41 pass from Brady (Vinatieri kick)
NE	—	T. Brown 8 pass from Brady (pass failed)
NE	—	C. Johnson 24 pass from Brady (Vinatieri kick)
NO	—	FG Carney 31
NO	—	R. Williams 3 run (Carney kick)
NE	—	Edwards 2 pass from Brady (Vinatieri kick)
NO	—	Jackson 7 pass from Brooks (Carney kick)
NE	—	A. Smith 3 run (Vinatieri kick)

OAKLAND 28, N.Y. GIANTS 10—at Giants Stadium, attendance 78,756. Rich Gannon passed for 3 touchdowns to lead the Raiders. Charlie Garner broke free for a 38-yard run on the first snap and seven plays later Zack Crockett ran 1 yard for a touchdown. Tim Brown grabbed a 46-yard scoring pass from Gannon 1:51 before the halftime to give the Raiders a 21-3 lead. Gannon was 13 of 20 for 221 yards and 3 touchdowns. Brown caught 6 passes for 117 yards. Kerry Collins was 19 of 38 for 184 yards. Tiki Barber rushed for 124 yards.

Oakland	7	14	0	7	—	28
N.Y. Giants	3	0	7	0	—	10

Oak	—	Crockett 1 run (Janikowski kick)
NYG	—	FG Andersen 47
Oak	—	Garner 21 run from Gannon (Janikowski kick)
Oak	—	T. Brown 46 pass from Gannon (Janikowski kick)
NYG	—	Barber 12 run (Andersen kick)
Oak	—	T. Brown 19 pass from Gannon (Janikowski kick)

PITTSBURGH 34, TENNESSEE 24—at Adelphia Coliseum, attendance 68,801. Kordell Stewart passed for 2 touchdowns and ran for another for the Steelers. An 81-yard kickoff return Troy Edwards returned the ensuing kickoff 81 yards to the Titans' 17 to set up Stewart's 25-yard touchdown pass to Amos Zereoue to put the Steelers ahead for good with 6:40 left in the third quarter. Chad Scott's 45-yard interception return with 3:23 to play clinched the victory. Stewart was 19 of 31 for 254 yards and 2 touchdowns. Plaxico Burress had 8 catches for 114 yards. Steve McNair was 23 of 37 for 334 yards and 2 touchdowns, with 2 interceptions. Derrick Mason had 7 catches for 114 yards, and Kevin Dyson had 4 for 112 yards.

Pittsburgh	3	7	14	10	—	34
Tennessee	7	7	3	7	—	24

Pitt	—	FG Brown 39
Tenn	—	Dyson 68 pass from McNair (Nedney kick)
Tenn	—	Wycheck 4 pass from McNair (Nedney kick)
Pitt	—	Burress 4 pass from Stewart (Brown kick)
Pitt	—	Stewart 48 run (Brown kick)
Tenn	—	FG Nedney 49
Pitt	—	Zereoue 25 pass from Stewart (Brown kick)
Pitt	—	FG Brown 37
Tenn	—	McNair 1 run (Nedney kick)
Pitt	—	Scott 45 interception return (Brown kick)

SAN FRANCISCO 40, INDIANAPOLIS 21—at RCA Dome, attendance 56,393. Jeff Garcia passed for 2 touchdowns and Garrison Hearst ran for 2 to lead the 49ers to their fourth consecutive victory. San Francisco trailed 21-20 until its defense came up with a critical play late in the third quarter. Zack Bronson intercepted Peyton Manning's pass and returned it 48 yards for the touchdown that put the 49ers ahead for good . Manning was intercepted again on the next possession by Rashad Holman. Garcia teamed with Terrell Owens on a 35-yard touchdown pass to open the fourth quarter, and Hearst secured the victory with a 43-yard touchdown run with 5:52 left. The Colts committed 5 turnovers, which San Francisco converted into 23 points. Garcia was 14 of 22 for 179 yards and 2 touchdowns, with 1 interception. Owens had 6 receptions for 103 yards. Hearst had 106 yards on only 12 attempts for the 49ers. Manning was 31 of 51 for 370 yards and 2 touchdowns, with 4 interceptions. Marvin Harrison caught 8 passes for 128 yards, and Dominic Rhodes rushed for 104 yards.

San Francisco	3	17	7	13	—	40
Indianapolis	7	7	0	7	—	21

Ind	—	Rhodes 1 run (Vanderjagt kick)
SF	—	FG Cortez 30
SF	—	Stokes 5 pass from Garcia (Cortez kick)
Ind	—	Harrison 15 pass from Manning (Vanderjagt kick)
SF	—	Hearst 28 run (Cortez kick)
SF	—	FG Cortez 46
Ind	—	Rhodes 1 run (Vanderjagt kick)
SF	—	Bronson 48 interception return (Cortez kick)
SF	—	Owens 35 pass from Garcia (pass failed)
SF	—	Hearst 43 run (Cortez kick)

KANSAS CITY 19, SEATTLE 7—at Arrowhead Stadium, attendance 77,357. Trent Green passed for 256 yards and Priest Holmes rushed for 120 yards to carry the Chiefs past the Seahawks. The well-balanced attack helped Kansas City dominate Seattle in terms total yards (433-204). In the fourth quarter, Green and Holmes teamed on a 55-yard completion that led to Mike Cloud's game-clinching, 15-yard touchdown run with 5:45 to play. Green was 16 of 26 for 256 yards. Hasselbeck was 16 of 26 for 162 yards and 1 touchdown.

Seattle	0	7	0	0	—	7
Kansas City	3	7	0	9	—	19

KC	—	FG Peterson 23
KC	—	Richardson 1 run (Peterson kick)
Sea	—	Alexander 28 pass from Hasselbeck (Lindell kick)
KC	—	FG Peterson 26
KC	—	Cloud 15 run (run failed)

WASHINGTON 13, PHILADELPHIA 3—at Veterans Stadium, attendance 65,666. The Redskins made NFL history as they won their fifth in a row, following five consecutive losses to begin the season. Ki-Jana Carter ran 5 yards for the only touchdown in the second quarter and Washington's defense limited Philadelphia to only 7 first downs and 186 yards. Trailing 10-3, the Eagles were twice stopped on fourth down inside Redskins' territory. The Redskins kept the ball on the ground for 45 of their 65 plays and had possession for 37:49. Tony Banks was 12 of 18 for 96 yards. Donovan McNabb was 15 of 27 for 92 yards.

Washington	0	10	0	3	—	13
Philadelphia	0	0	3	0	—	3

Wash	—	Carter 5 run (Conway kick)
Wash	—	FG Conway 43
Phil	—	FG Akers 49
Wash	—	FG Conway 32

SUNDAY NIGHT, NOVEMBER 25
CHICAGO 13, MINNESOTA 6—at Metrodome, attendance 64,214. James Allen rushed for 107 yards, and the Bears' defense kept the Vikings out of the end zone as Chicago completed a season sweep. Minnesota failed to score a touchdown for the first time in 98 regular-season games. Allen, playing because Anthony Thomas was injured, had 80 yards in the first half, when the Bears built a 10-0 lead. Allen had back-to-back runs of 9 and 13 yards on the ensuing possession to help Chicago take the clock all the way down to 16 seconds. Jim Miller was 10 of 21 for 97 yards. Culpepper was 26 of 46 for 209 yards, with 1 interception.

Chicago	0	10	0	3	—	13
Minnesota	0	0	3	3	—	6

Chi	—	Johnson 1 run (Edinger kick)
Chi	—	FG Edinger 30
Minn	—	FG Anderson 44
Chi	—	FG Edinger 43
Minn	—	FG Anderson 21

MONDAY NIGHT, NOVEMBER 26
TAMPA BAY 24, ST. LOUIS 17—at Dome at America's Center, attendance 66,198. Warrick Dunn's 21-yard touchdown run 3:47 into the fourth quarter lifted the Buccaneers to an upset of the mistake-prone Rams. With the score 17-17, Tampa Bay countered with a 9-play, 90-yard drive capped by Dunn's decisive run. St. Louis had four possessions thereafter, but the first two ended with punts and the last two were stymied by interceptions, including John Lynch's game-clinching theft with 2:26 left. Johnson was 21 of 34 for 185 yards, with 1 interception. Warner was 19 of 39 for 291 yards and 1 touchdown, with 2 interceptions. Torry Holt had 8 receptions for 139 yards.

Tampa Bay	0	10	7	7	—	24
St. Louis	3	6	8	0	—	17

StL	—	FG Wilkins 44
TB	—	Alstott 7 run (Gramatica kick)
StL	—	FG Wilkins 42
TB	—	FG Gramatica 36
StL	—	FG Wilkins 24
TB	—	M. Alstott 8 run (Gramatica kick)
StL	—	Manumaleuna 1 pass from Warner (Faulk run)
TB	—	Dunn 21 run (Gramatica kick)

TWELFTH WEEK SUMMARIES
American Football Conference

Eastern Division	W	L	T	Pct.	Pts.	OP
Miami	8	3	0	.727	235	222
N.Y. Jets	7	4	0	.636	224	199
New England	7	5	0	.583	274	228
Indianapolis	4	7	0	.364	292	337
Buffalo	1	10	0	.091	180	308
Central Division						
Pittsburgh	9	2	0	.818	210	137
Baltimore	8	4	0	.667	237	214
Cleveland	6	5	0	.545	204	181
Tennessee	5	6	0	.455	214	252
Cincinnati	4	7	0	.364	153	220
Jacksonville	3	8	0	.273	193	200
Western Division						
Oakland	8	3	0	.727	309	235
Seattle	6	5	0	.545	195	234
Denver	6	6	0	.500	264	260
San Diego	5	7	0	.417	273	239
Kansas City	3	8	0	.273	200	229

National Football Conference

Eastern Division	W	L	T	Pct.	Pts.	OP
Philadelphia	7	4	0	.636	255	141
Arizona	5	6	0	.455	208	269
N.Y. Giants	5	6	0	.455	191	206
Washington	5	6	0	.455	155	226
Dallas	3	8	0	.273	176	243
Central Division						
Chicago	9	2	0	.818	227	155
Green Bay	8	3	0	.727	265	188
Tampa Bay	6	5	0	.545	223	193
Minnesota	4	7	0	.364	205	263
Detroit	0	11	0	.600	202	304
Western Division						
St. Louis	9	2	0	.818	331	176
San Francisco	9	2	0	.818	302	225
Atlanta	6	5	0	.545	194	226
New Orleans	6	5	0	.545	253	239
Carolina	1	11	0	.083	184	279

THURSDAY NIGHT, NOVEMBER 29
PHILADELPHIA 23, KANSAS CITY 10—at Arrowhead Stadium, attendance 77,087. Donovan McNabb passed for 2 touchdowns to pace the Eagles. Philadelphia, recovered a surprise onside kickoff to open the game, drove to a field goal, and never looked back. McNabb's second touchdown pass, a 1-yard strike to Tony Stewart midway through the third quarter, helped the Eagles to a 20-3 lead. The Chiefs still had four possessions after that, but they ended with a punt, a fumble, an interception, and a fourth-down incompletion. McNabb was 18 of 26 for 269 yards and 2 touchdowns, with 1 interception. Green was 21 of 35 for 213 yards and 1 touchdown, with 1 interception. Priest Holmes had 8 receptions for 100 yards.

Philadelphia	3	10	7	3	—	23
Kansas City	0	3	7	0	—	10

Phil	—	FG Akers 24
Phil	—	Staley 46 pass from McNabb (Akers kick)
Phil	—	FG Akers 33
KC	—	FG Peterson 29
Phil	—	Stewart 1 pass from McNabb (Akers kick)
KC	—	Alexander 3 pass from Green (Peterson kick)
Phil	—	FG Akers 38

SUNDAY, DECEMBER 2
ARIZONA 34, OAKLAND 31 (OT)—at Network Associates Coliseum, attendance 46,601. The Cardinals won their third consecutive game, stunning the Raiders when Bill Gramatica kicked a 36-yard field goal 7:29 into overtime. Arizona led 23-21 before a wild finish to the fourth quarter led to the extra session. First, Sebastian Janikowski kicked a 24-yard field goal to give his team the lead with 1:47 left. The advantage lasted only 29 seconds, however, because Jake Plummer completed a short pass to David Boston four plays later, and the receiver turned it into a 50-yard touchdown. Plummer's 2-point conversion run gave the Cardinals a 31-24 lead. The Raiders began the next possession at their 22-yard line with 1:10 left, and on fourth-and-goal from the 2, Gannon and Rice teamed on the tying touchdown pass with 12 seconds to go. David Dunn muffed a punt in overtime, and LeVar Woods recovered at the Raiders' 25 to set up Gramatica's winning kick. Plummer was 22 of 38 for 249 yards and 1 touchdown. Boston had 6 receptions for 106 yards. Gannon was 29 of 45 for 302 yards and 3 touchdowns, with 2 interceptions.

Arizona	7	13	0	11	3	—	34
Oakland	7	0	7	17	0	—	31

Oak	—	T. Brown 5 pass from Gannon (Janikowski kick)
Ariz	—	T. Jones 5 run (Gramatica kick)
Ariz	—	Pittman 1 run (Gramatica kick)
Ariz	—	FG Gramatica 23
Ariz	—	FG Gramatica 26
Oak	—	Crockett 1 run (Janikowski kick)
Ariz	—	FG Gramatica 33

Oak	—	T. Brown 22 pass from Gannon (Janikowski kick)
Oak	—	FG Janikowski 24
Ariz	—	Boston 50 pass from Plummer (Plummer run)
Oak	—	Rice 2 pass from Gannon (Janikowski kick)
Ariz	—	FG Gramatica 36

NEW ORLEANS 27, CAROLINA 23—at Louisiana Superdome, attendance 70,020. Aaron Brooks tossed a 17-yard touchdown pass to Joe Horn with 1:35 left to end the Saints' four-game losing streak. Carolina had erased a 10-point, fourth-quarter deficit and taken a 23-20 lead on John Kasay's third field goal of the game, a 51-yard kick with 2:40 left. But beginning from its 26-yard line, New Orleans needed only four plays to march to the winning score. Carolina still had one more possession, but Chris Weinke went to the sidelines after being sacked for a 6-yard loss by Charlie Clemons, and backup Matt Lytle's pass on the final play was intercepted by Fred Thomas. New Orleans finished a big advantage in total yards (432-150). Brooks was 26 of 40 for 330 yards and 3 touchdowns, with 1 interception, while Horn had 13 catches for 150 yards. Ricky Williams added 102 yards. Weinke was 11 of 19 for 161 yards and ran for 2 touchdowns.

Carolina	7	0	3	13	—	23
New Orleans	0	10	3	14	—	27

Car	—	Weinke 6 run (Kasay kick)
NO	—	FG Carney 42
NO	—	T. Smith 4 pass from Brooks (Carney kick)
NO	—	FG Carney 24
Car	—	FG Kasay 47
NO	—	Connell 14 pass from Brooks (Carney kick)
Car	—	FG Kasay 23
Car	—	Weinke 1 run (Kasay kick)
Car	—	FG Kasay 51
NO	—	Horn 17 pass from Brooks (Carney kick)

DALLAS 20, WASHINGTON 14—at FedEx Field, attendance 85,112. The Cowboys dealt a severe blow to the playoff hopes of the resurgent Redskins by beating their division rivals for the second time this season and the ninth consecutive time dating to 1997. Emmitt Smith rushed for 102 yards and 2 touchdowns. Dallas broke a 7-7 tie by scoring on its next three possessions. Dallas recovered an onside kick to secure the victory. The Cowboys had a season-best 215 of their 337 total yards on the ground. Smith eclipsed the 100-yard mark for the first time since being in a victory over Washington in week 5. Carter was 7 of 14 for 130 yards and 1 touchdown, with 1 interception. Banks was 17 of 32 for 216 yards and 1 touchdown, with 1 interception.

Dallas	7	0	13	—	20
Washington	0	0	7	7	—	14

Dall	—	E. Smith 5 run (Hilbert kick)
Wash	—	Banks 1 run (Conway kick)
Dall	—	FG Hilbert 38
Dall	—	Ismail 64 pass from Carter (Hilbert kick)
Dall	—	FG Hilbert 39
Wash	—	Gardner 15 pass from Banks (Conway kick)

CHICAGO 13, DETROIT 10—at Soldier Field, attendance 66,944. Leon Johnson ran 1 yard for the go-ahead touchdown with 5:34 left, and the Bears held on to win when Jason Hanson missed a tying field-goal attempt from 40 yards with 21 seconds remaining. Chicago trailed 10-6 in the final quarter before embarking on a time-consuming touchdown drive from its 45-yard line with 12:18 to go, high-

lighted by the Lions' jumping offside on fourth-and-6, Chicago decided to go for it on fourth-and-1, and Johnson carried 6 yards to convert the first down. Eight plays later, Johnson ran for the touchdown. Jim Miller was 17 of 34 for 124 yards, with 1 interception. McMahon was 4 of 9 for 42 yards and 1 touchdown in the game because Charlie Batch suffered a season-ending separated shoulder. Batch was 18 of 28 for 214 yards.

Detroit	7	0	3	0	—	10
Chicago	0	3	0	10	—	13

Det	—	Stewart 3 run (Hanson kick)
Chi	—	FG Edinger 46
Det	—	FG Hanson 36
Chi	—	FG Edinger 26
Chi	—	L. Johnson 1 run (Edinger kick)

MIAMI 21, DENVER 10—at Pro Player Stadium, attendance 73,938. The Dolphins blitzed the Broncos for 3 touchdowns in a span of 4:46 of the fourth quarter. Jay Fiedler capped a 58-yard drive with an 11-yard touchdown pass to Chris Chambers 1:15 into the fourth quarter to pull Miami within 10-7. Jason Taylor pressured Brian Griese into an interception that Kenny Mixon returned 56 yards for the go-ahead touchdown with 9:51 left. Miami recovered a fumble on the ensuing kickoff and Lamar Smith ran 1 yard for a touchdown. Fiedler was 18 of 28 for 176 yards and 1 touchdown. Griese was 18 of 33 for 135 yards and 1 touchdown, with 1 interception.

Denver	0	3	7	0	—	10
Miami	0	0	0	21	—	21

Den	—	FG Elam 45
Den	—	Clark 4 pass from Griese (Elam kick)
Mia	—	Chambers 11 pass from Fiedler (Mare kick)
Mia	—	Mixon 56 interception return (Mare kick)
Mia	—	L. Smith 1 run (Mare kick)

BALTIMORE 39, INDIANAPOLIS 27—at PSINet Stadium, attendance 69,382. Elvis Grbac passed for 268 yards and 2 touchdowns in the Ravens' victory. Peyton Manning passed for 2 third-quarter touchdowns for the Colts, including a 57-yard bomb to Marvin Harrison that gave Indianapolis a 27-26 lead 1:06 before the end of the quarter. But Corey Harris returned the ensuing kickoff 34 yards to Indianapolis' 48-yard line, and it took Baltimore only six plays from there to take the lead for good, on a 5-yard touchdown pass to Qadry Ismail with 13:29 to play. Rod Woodson returned an interception 47 yards for the clinching touchdown at the 1:34 mark. It was Woodson's tenth career interception return for a touchdown, breaking the NFL record he shared with Ken Houston. Grbac was 23 of 39 for 268 yards and 2 touchdowns, with 1 interception. Williams had 111 rushing yards. Manning was 27 of 48 for 310 yards and 2 touchdowns, with 1 interception.

Indianapolis	3	7	17	0	—	27
Baltimore	3	13	10	13	—	39

Balt	—	FG Stover 26
Ind	—	FG Vanderjagt 33
Balt	—	Ayanbadejo 5 pass from Grbac (Stover kick)
Ind	—	Burris 30 interception return (Vanderjagt kick)
Balt	—	FG Stover 30
Balt	—	FG Stover 29
Balt	—	FG Stover 27
Ind	—	FG Vanderjagt 25
Ind	—	Pollard 40 pass from Manning (Vanderjagt kick)
Balt	—	Ayanbadejo 9 pass from Grbac (Stover kick)
Ind	—	Harrison 57 pass from Manning (Vanderjagt kick)

Balt	—	Ismail 5 pass from Grbac (pass failed)
Balt	—	Woodson 47 interception return (Stover kick)

PITTSBURGH 21, MINNESOTA 16—at Heinz Field, attendance 62,661. The Steelers built an 18-point lead, then held off a furious fourth-quarter rally by the Vikings to win their fourth consecutive game. Troy Edwards scored on a touchdown run midway through the third quarter, then forced a fumble on the ensuing kickoff that was recovered by teammate Myron Bell and led to Amos Zereoue's 4-yard touchdown run for a 21-3 lead. Todd Bouman relieved injured Daunte Culpepper early in the fourth quarter and led Minnesota to 13 points to cut the deficit to 21-16 at the 3:22 mark. The Vikings reached the Steelers' 5 in the final moments, but 2 penalties and a pass that lost 4 yards moved the ball to the 20, and a fourth-down pass fell incomplete with 1:43 left. Chris Fuamatu-Ma'afala sealed the victory by racing 46 yards for a first down on the game's final possession. Stewart was 13 of 19 for 157 yards, with 1 interception. Bouman was 11 of 15 for 200 yards and 2 touchdowns, with 1 interception. Culpepper was 12 of 17 for 140 yards, with 1 interception. Randy Moss had 8 catches for 144 yards.

Minnesota	3	0	0	13	—	16
Pittsburgh	0	7	14	0	—	21

Minn	—	FG Anderson 25
Pitt	—	Bettis 1 run (K. Brown kick)
Pitt	—	Edwards 12 run (K. Brown kick)
Pitt	—	Zereoue 4 run (K. Brown kick)
Minn	—	Bennett 80 pass from Bouman (Anderson kick)
Minn	—	Moss 12 pass from Bouman (pass failed)

NEW ENGLAND 17, N.Y. JETS 16—at Giants Stadium, attendance 78,712. Adam Vinatieri's 28-yard field goal with 6:29 left capped a second-half rally that lifted the Patriots to the victory. New England trailed 13-0 until Mike Vrabel's interception and 12-yard return gave the Patriots possession at their 43-yard line 2:35 into the second half, after which the Patriots scored on three consecutive possessions. The Patriots had been outgained 219-67 in the first half, but outgained the Jets 197-63 in the second. Brady, who completed 20 of 28 passes for 213 yards, was 15 of 17 for 150 yards after halftime. Vinny Testaverde was 19 of 33 for 184 yards and 1 touchdown, with 2 interceptions. Curtis Martin eclipsed the 1,000-yard rushing barrier for the season. He joined Barry Sanders (10) and Eric Dickerson (7) as the only players to run for more than 1,000 yards in each of their first seven seasons.

New England	0	0	14	3	—	17
N.Y. Jets	10	3	3	0	—	16

NYJ	—	Coles 34 pass from Testaverde (Hall kick)
NYJ	—	FG Hall 19
NYJ	—	FG Hall 40
NE	—	A. Smith 4 run (Vinatieri kick)
NYJ	—	FG Hall 50
NE	—	Edwards 4 run (Vinatieri kick)
NE	—	FG Vinatieri 28

ST. LOUIS 35, ATLANTA 6—at Georgia Dome, attendance 59,318. Kurt Warner passed for 4 touchdowns, including 3 to Marshall Faulk, as the Rams routed the Falcons. St. Louis led 7-3 when Warner teamed with Faulk for the first time, capping a 10-play, 80-yard touchdown drive with a 19-yard touchdown pass 3:32 before the end of the first quarter. It was 14-6 at halftime, then the Rams put the game away with touchdowns on their first two possessions of the third quarter. Warner opened the second half with consecutive completions of 21 yards to

Torry Holt and 16 yards to Isaac Bruce before going back to Holt for a 45-yard touchdown bomb just 1:38 into the second half. After a punt pinned St. Louis back on its 3-yard line, the Rams drove 97 yards in 10 plays, with Warner's 9-yard touchdown pass to Faulk opening a 28-6 advantage. Faulk's 65-yard scoring catch in the fourth quarter made him the thirteenth player in league history to record 100 career touchdowns. He had 6 catches for 128 yards. Warner was 17 of 23 for 342 yards and 4 touchdowns. Chris Chandler was 14 of 18 for 123 yards, with 1 interception, in the first half for the Falcons, who had their three-game winning streak halted. Michael Vick was 7 of 18 for 94 yards and ran for 52 yards.

| St. Louis | 14 | 0 | 14 | 7 | — | 35 |
| Atlanta | 3 | 3 | 0 | 0 | — | 6 |

StL	—	Bly 56 interception return (Wilkins kick)
Atl	—	FG Feely 41
StL	—	Faulk 19 pass from Warner (Wilkins kick)
Atl	—	FG Feely 24
StL	—	Holt 45 pass from Warner (Wilkins kick)
StL	—	Faulk 9 pass from Warner (Wilkins kick)
StL	—	Faulk 65 pass from Warner (Wilkins kick)

SEATTLE 13, SAN DIEGO 10 (OT)—at Husky Stadium, attendance 55,466. Kicker Rian Lindell atoned for 2 misses late in regulation by making a 24-yard field goal 6:23 into overtime. The game was tied at 10-10 when Lindell missed 2 field-goal attempts, before setting up his overtime heroics. During the last 11:50 of regulation and overtime, the Seahawks controlled the ball for 34 snaps (including penalties and field goals) and 16:23, while the Chargers had possession for only 3 plays and 1:50. Hasselbeck was 19 of 35 for 202 yards. Doug Flutie was 19 of 33 for 195 yards, with 2 interceptions.

| San Diego | 0 | 3 | 7 | 0 | 0 | — | 10 |
| Seattle | 7 | 0 | 3 | 0 | 3 | — | 13 |

Sea	—	Alexander 1 run (Lindell kick)
SD	—	FG Christie 26
SD	—	Tomlinson 1 run (Christie kick)
Sea	—	FG Lindell 43
Sea	—	FG Lindell 24

TAMPA BAY 16, CINCINNATI 13 (OT)—at Paul Brown Stadium, attendance 52,135. Martin Gramatica's 21-yard field goal 5:06 into overtime lifted the Buccaneers to back-to-back victories for the first time in 2001. The winning kick came after John Lynch forced Corey Dillon to fumble on Cincinnati's first play of the extra session and pounced on the ball at the Bengals' 3-yard line. Tampa Bay did not attempt another play from scrimmage, but immediately turned to Gramatica. The ending spoiled a fourth-quarter comeback in which Cincinnati erased a 13-3 deficit with 10 points in the final 4:29 of regulation., capped by Corey Dillon taking a short pass from Kitna and fighting his way into the end zone for the tying touchdown with six seconds left. Mark Royals pinned the Bengals at the 4 with a punt, setting up Lynch's big play. Brad Johnson was 26 of 33 for 231 yards. The Buccaneers' defense allowed only 201 total yards. Kitna was 19 of 38 for 144 yards and 1 touchdown, with 1 interception.

| Tampa Bay | 0 | 7 | 3 | 3 | 3 | — | 16 |
| Cincinnati | 3 | 0 | 0 | 10 | 0 | — | 13 |

Cin	—	FG Rackers 23
TB	—	Yoder 11 blocked punt return (Gramatica kick)
TB	—	FG Gramatica 38
TB	—	FG Gramatica 48

Cin	—	FG Rackers 41
Cin	—	Dillon 6 pass from Kitna (Rackers kick)
TB	—	FG Gramatica 21

TENNESSEE 31, CLEVELAND 15—at Cleveland Browns Stadium, attendance 72,818. Steve McNair passed for 3 touchdowns to help the Titans. Tennessee was in command from the start after recovering a fumble on the opening kickoff and quickly marching 19 yards to Eddie George's 1-yard touchdown run 2:59 into the first quarter. Later in the period, McNair tossed a 43-yard touchdown pass to Derrick Mason for a 14-0 lead. McNair was 11 of 17 for 244 yards and 3 touchdowns despite sitting out much of the second quarter after injuring his left arm. Kevin Dyson had 6 catches for 110 yards, while Mason had 3 for 122 yards. Tim Couch was 17 of 26 for 110 yards and 1 touchdown, with 1 interception, and Kelly Holcomb was 7 of 12 for 114 yards and 1 score.

| Tennessee | 14 | 3 | 14 | 0 | — | 31 |
| Cleveland | 0 | 7 | 0 | 8 | — | 15 |

Tenn	—	George 1 run (Nedney kick)
Tenn	—	Mason 43 pass from McNair (Nedney kick)
Tenn	—	FG Nedney 29
Cle	—	Johnson 10 pass from Couch (P. Dawson kick)
Tenn	—	Bennett 5 pass from McNair (Nedney kick)
Tenn	—	Mason 71 pass from McNair (Nedney kick)
Cle	—	Johnson 20 pass from Holcomb (White run)

SUNDAY NIGHT, DECEMBER 2
SAN FRANCISCO 35, BUFFALO 0—at 3Com Park, attendance 67,252. The 49ers utilized a balanced offense and an opportunistic defense to overwhelm the Bills. On offense, Garrison Hearst rushed for 124 yards and a touchdown and Jeff Garcia passed for 189 yards and 2 touchdowns as San Francisco amassed 409 total yards and controlled the ball for 39:48. On defense, Ahmed Plummer intercepted a pair of passes, and the 49ers forced 5 turnovers while limiting Buffalo to only 191 total yards. Plummer's interceptions led to 14 points, and Paul Smith's fourth-quarter fumble recovery on special teams led to his 13-yard run for his first NFL touchdown. Garcia was 19 of 27 for 189 yards and 2 touchdowns. Alex Van Pelt was 21 of 38 for 168 yards, with 4 interceptions.

| Buffalo | 0 | 0 | 0 | 0 | — | 0 |
| San Francisco | 0 | 14 | 7 | 14 | — | 35 |

SF	—	Hearst 1 run (Cortez kick)
SF	—	Streets 23 pass from Garcia (Cortez kick)
SF	—	Owens 17 pass from Garcia (Cortez kick)
SF	—	Beasley 3 run (Cortez kick)
SF	—	P. Smith 13 run (Cortez kick)

MONDAY NIGHT, DECEMBER 3
GREEN BAY 28, JACKSONVILLE 21—at ALLTEL Stadium, attendance 66,908. Brett Favre scrambled 6 yards for the winning touchdown with 1:30 remaining as the Packers came from behind. Jacksonville led 21-7 before Favre ignited his team's comeback with a 43-yard touchdown pass to Bill Schroeder with 2:38 left in the third quarter. Then, after Torrance Marshall recovered Elvis Joseph's fumble on the ensuing kickoff at the Jaguars' 32-yard line, it took Favre only three plays to tie the game. Jacksonville had a couple of excellent chances to break the deadlock, but Brunell was intercepted in the end zone by Tyrone Williams early

in the fourth quarter, and Mike Hollis' 42-yard field-goal attempt bounced off the left upright with 5:12 left. After an exchange of punts, Green Bay took over possession at its 44 with 2:03 to go and moments later Favre ran around left end for the decisive score. Favre was 24 of 42 for 362 yards and 3 touchdowns. Schroeder had 106 yards on 6 receptions, while Freeman added 104 yards on 3 catches. Brunell was 26 of 45 for 311 yards and 1 touchdown, with 2 interceptions. Jimmy Smith caught 8 passes for 116 yards.

| Green Bay | 0 | 7 | 14 | 7 | — | 28 |
| Jacksonville | 3 | 10 | 8 | 0 | — | 21 |

Jax	—	FG Hollis 34
Jax	—	Joseph 29 pass from Brunell (Hollis kick)
Jax	—	FG Hollis 30
GB	—	Green 13 pass from Favre (Longwell kick)
Jax	—	Battles 60 fumble return (McCardell pass from Brunell)
GB	—	Schroeder 43 pass from Favre (Longwell kick)
GB	—	Franks 1 pass from Favre (Longwell kick)
GB	—	Favre 6 run (Longwell kick)

THIRTEENTH WEEK SUMMARIES
American Football Conference

Eastern Division	W	L	T	Pct.	Pts.	OP
Miami	9	3	0	.750	276	228
New England	8	5	0	.615	301	244
N.Y. Jets	7	5	0	.583	231	217
Indianapolis	4	8	0	.333	298	378
Buffalo	2	10	0	.167	205	332
Central Division						
Pittsburgh	10	2	0	.833	228	144
Baltimore	8	4	0	.667	237	214
Cleveland	6	6	0	.500	220	208
Tennessee	5	7	0	.417	238	294
Cincinnati	4	8	0	.333	163	234
Jacksonville	4	8	0	.333	207	210
Western Division						
Oakland	9	3	0	.750	337	261
Denver	7	6	0	.538	284	267
Seattle	6	6	0	.500	202	254
San Diego	5	8	0	.385	287	263
Kansas City	3	9	0	.250	226	257

National Football Conference

Eastern Division	W	L	T	Pct.	Pts.	OP
Philadelphia	8	4	0	.667	279	155
Washington	6	6	0	.500	175	236
Arizona	5	7	0	.417	218	289
N.Y. Giants	5	7	0	.417	204	226
Dallas	4	8	0	.333	196	256
Central Division						
Chicago	9	3	0	.750	234	172
Green Bay	9	3	0	.750	282	195
Tampa Bay	7	5	0	.583	238	205
Minnesota	5	7	0	.417	247	287
Detroit	0	12	0	.000	214	319
Western Division						
St. Louis	10	2	0	.833	358	190
San Francisco	9	3	0	.750	316	252
New Orleans	7	5	0	.583	281	249
Atlanta	6	6	0	.500	204	254
Carolina	1	12	0	.077	208	304

SUNDAY, DECEMBER 9
BUFFALO 25, CAROLINA 24—at Ralph Wilson Stadium, attendance 44,549. Travis Henry's 1-yard touchdown run midway through the fourth quarter capped an 18-point comeback. Chris Weinke ran and passed for touchdowns to help stake his team to a 24-6 lead late in the first half. But Buffalo began chipping away at its deficit when Alex Van Pelt teamed with Peerless Price on a 7-yard touchdown pass one second before halftime. In the third quar-

ter, Brandon Spoon intercepted Weinke's pass and returned it 44 yards for a touchdown to make it 24-19. Price's 24-yard punt return early in the fourth quarter then set up the winning 51-yard drive that Henry capped with his touchdown run with 7:51 to go. Van Pelt was 20 of 29 for 277 yards and 1 touchdown, with 1 interception, while Henry finished with 101 yards on 27 carries. Weinke was 15 of 30 for 153 yards and 1 touchdown, with 1 interception. Muhsin Muhammad had 8 receptions for 104 yards.

Carolina	3	21	0	0	—	24
Buffalo	3	10	6	6	—	25
Car	—	FG Kasay 37				
Buff	—	FG Graham 20				
Car	—	Weinke 1 run (Kasay kick)				
Car	—	Huntley 2 run (Kasay kick)				
Buff	—	FG Graham 27				
Car	—	Mangum 2 pass from Weinke (Kasay kick)				
Buff	—	P. Price 7 pass from Van Pelt (Graham kick)				
Buff	—	Spoon 44 interception return (pass failed)				
Buff	—	Henry 1 run (pass failed)				

GREEN BAY 17, CHICAGO 7—at Lambeau Field, attendance 59,869. Ahman Green rushed for 125 yards and a touchdown for the Packers. The game was tied at 7-7 in the third quarter when Green Bay began a drive when the Packers drove 91 yards, capped by Green's 12-yard jaunt. Darren Sharper intercepted a pass on the Bears' next possession, which led to Ryan Longwell's 27-yard field goal and a 10-point lead. Chicago's offense penetrated no further than Green Bay's 44 after that. The Packers' defense allowed only 189 total yards. Favre was 15 of 27 for 207 yards and 1 touchdown, with 1 interception. He became the first quarterback in NFL history to surpass 3,000 yards in 10 consecutive seasons. Jim Miller was 18 of 33 for 139 yards, with 1 interception.

Chicago	0	0	7	0	—	7
Green Bay	7	0	7	3	—	17
GB	—	Freeman 3 pass from Favre (Longwell kick)				
Chi	—	Thomas 19 run (Edinger kick)				
GB	—	A. Green 12 run (Longwell kick)				
GB	—	FG Longwell 27				

NEW ENGLAND 27, CLEVELAND 16—at Foxboro Stadium, attendance 54,797. Antowain Smith ran for 2 touchdowns and Troy Brown returned a punt 85 yards for a touchdown to highlight the Patriots' third consecutive victory. Brown's big punt return came 3:28 before the end of the half and gave the Patriots the lead for good. He also had a 20-yard return to set up Smith's 5-yard touchdown run that sealed the outcome with 2:43 left. Tom Brady was 19 of 28 for 218 yards, with 2 interceptions. Brown had 125 yards on 4 punt returns and added 89 yards on 7 receptions. Tim Couch was 20 of 39 for 244 yards, with 3 interceptions.

Cleveland	10	0	3	3	—	16
New England	3	17	0	7	—	27
NE	—	FG Vinatieri 54				
Cle	—	FG P. Dawson 27				
Cle	—	Fuller 49 interception return (P. Dawson kick)				
NE	—	A. Smith 1 run (Vinatieri kick)				
NE	—	T. Brown 85 punt return (Vinatieri kick)				
NE	—	FG Vinatieri 38				
Cle	—	FG P. Dawson 39				
Cle	—	FG P. Dawson 47				
NE	—	A. Smith 5 run (Vinatieri kick)				

TAMPA BAY 15, DETROIT 12—at Raymond James Stadium, attendance 65,514. Keyshawn Johnson's first touchdown catch of the season, a 13-yard toss from Brad Johnson with 45 seconds remaining, lifted the Buccaneers to their third consecutive victory and kept the Lions winless. Keyshawn Johnson, who led the NFL by week's end with 93 receptions but went without a touchdown on his first 92, leaped over Jimmy Wyrick to cap a dramatic 15-play, 80-yard drive that staved off defeat. Trailing 12-7, Brad Johnson, who completed 8 of 12 passes on the winning march with 4 completions going to Keyshawn Johnson, lofted the winning pass while being sandwiched by two Lions defenders. The drive included 2 fourth-dwon conversions. Ronde Barber recovered Desmond Howard's fumble on the ensuing kickoff to secure the victory. Detroit lost by three points or less for the fifth time. Jason Hanson kicked 4 field goals to provide all of the Lions' points. Rookie Mike McMahon, making his first NFL start in place of injured Charlie Batch, was 11 of 25 for 165 yards. Brad Johnson was 31 of 54 passes for 305 yards and 1 touchdown, with 2 interceptions. Keyshawn Johnson caught 10 passes for 101 yards.

Detroit	0	3	6	3	—	12
Tampa Bay	0	7	0	8	—	15
TB	—	Alstott 24 run (Gramatica kick)				
Det	—	FG Hanson 39				
Det	—	FG Hanson 30				
Det	—	FG Hanson 50				
Det	—	FG Hanson 42				
TB	—	K. Johnson 13 pass from B. Johnson (Alstott pass from B. Johnson)				

JACKSONVILLE 14, CINCINNATI 10—at Paul Brown Stadium, attendance 44,920. Mark Brunell passed for 2 touchdowns, including an 11-yard strike to Keenan McCardell 33 seconds into the fourth quarter, to lead the Jaguars. The Jaguars trailed 10-7 late in the third quarter when they began the winning touchdown drive from the Bengals' 38-yard line. Brunell was sacked on the first two plays of the march, but on third-and-19 from the 47, he teamed with McCardell on a 29-yard completion. The decisive touchdown pass came three plays into the fourth quarter. Brunell was 23 of 32 for 242 yards and 2 touchdowns, with 1 interception. Smith caught 9 passes for 119 yards. Jon Kitna was 16 of 30 for 147 yards, with 1 interception. The Bengals' defense recorded 8 sacks.

Jacksonville	7	0	0	7	—	14
Cincinnati	0	7	3	0	—	10
Jax	—	Ji. Smith 17 pass from Brunell (Hollis kick)				
Cin	—	Dillon 9 run (Rackers kick)				
Cin	—	FG Rackers 47				
Jax	—	McCardell 11 pass from Brunell (Hollis kick)				

OAKLAND 28, KANSAS CITY 26—at Network Associates Coliseum, attendance 60,784. Regan Upshaw sacked Trent Green on a potential game-tying, 2-point conversion attempt with 1:38 left to preserve the Raiders' victory. Oakland led 28-20 and stopped the Chiefs on a fourth-and-goal from the 4-yard line 2:58 left in the game. But three plays later, Rich Gannon fumbled, and the ball was recovered by Greg Wesley, giving Kansas City another chance from Oakland's 27 with 1:49 to go. The Chiefs scored, but Upshaw thwarted the conversion attempt and Jerry Porter recovered the ensuing onside kick attempt for the Raiders. The 39-year-old Jerry Rice caught an 8-yard touchdown pass in the second quarter and surpassed 20,000 receiving yards for his career. Thirty-five-year-old Tim Brown entered the season as one of only four players in NFL history to return more than 300 punts in his career. But he had not brought back a kick since

1998 before taking Dan Stryzinski's punt and racing 88 yards to give Oakland a 28-17 lead 3:26 into the second half. Gannon was 18 of 24 for 195 yard and 1 touchdown, with 1 interception. Green was 15 of 32 for 253 yards and 2 touchdowns, with 1 interception. Priest Holmes rushed for 168 yards caught 5 passes for 109 yards.

Kansas City	10	7	3	6	—	26
Oakland	7	14	7	0	—	28
KC	—	Holmes 10 run (Peterson kick)				
KC	—	FG Peterson 43				
Oak	—	Wheatley 6 run (Janikowski kick)				
KC	—	Holmes 67 pass from Green (Peterson kick)				
Oak	—	Gannon 5 run (Janikowski kick)				
Oak	—	Rice 8 pass from Gannon (Janikowski kick)				
Oak	—	Brown 88 punt return (Janikowski kick)				
KC	—	FG Peterson 36				
KC	—	Gonzalez 24 pass from Green (pass failed)				

NEW ORLEANS 28, ATLANTA 10—at Georgia Dome, attendance 68,826. Deuce McAllister ran for 1 touchdown and passed for another to spark the Saints. McAllister, a backup to Ricky Williams, touched the ball only twice against the Falcons. On the first, he took a pitch from Aaron Brooks and threw a 12-yard touchdown pass to Willie Jackson to tie the game at 7-7 late in the first quarter. On the second, he ran 54 yards on his only carry of the day for the clinching touchdown with 8:16 remaining in the game. The Saints' defense recorded 9 sacks. Brooks was 20 of 30 for 279 yards and 1 touchdown. Chris Chandler was 18 of 32 for 233 yards, with 1 interception.

New Orleans	14	0	0	14	—	28
Atlanta	7	3	0	0	—	10
Atl	—	M. Smith 1 run (Feely kick)				
NO	—	W. Jackson 12 pass from McAllister (Carney kick)				
NO	—	R. Williams 1 run (Carney kick)				
Atl	—	FG Feely 22				
NO	—	Horn 50 pass from Brooks (Carney kick)				
NO	—	McAllister 54 run (Carney kick)				

DALLAS 20, N.Y. GIANTS 13—at Texas Stadium, attendance 61,821. Quincy Carter's 3-yard touchdown pass to Jackie Harris 2:06 into the fourth quarter lifted the Cowboys to a victory over the reeling Giants. Carter teamed with Raghib Ismail on a 41-yard pass play midway through the third quarter, and Emmitt Smith ran 1 yard for the tying touchdown on the next play. Late in the same quarter, punter Rodney Williams was tackled after a fumbled snap on fourth down, and the Cowboys took just five plays to cover 26 yards for the final touchdown. Carter was 17 of 26 for 194 yards and 1 touchdown, with 1 interception. Kerry Collins was 13 of 26 for 122 yards and 1 touchdown, with 1 interception.

N.Y. Giants	6	7	0	0	—	13
Dallas	3	3	7	7	—	20
NYG	—	FG Andersen 35				
Dall	—	FG Hilbert 48				
NYG	—	FG Andersen 41				
NYG	—	Rivers 2 pass from Collins (Andersen kick)				
Dall	—	FG Hilbert 41				
Dall	—	Smith 1 run (Hilbert kick)				
Dall	—	Harris 3 pass from Carter (Hilbert kick)				

PITTSBURGH 18, N.Y. JETS 7—at Heinz Field, attendance 62,884. The Steelers won their fifth consecutive game in methodical fashion over the Jets.

Chris Fuamatu-Ma'afala, carrying the rushing load in place of injured Jerome Bettis, ran for a touchdown and Kris Brown kicked 4 field goals as Pittsburgh. Pittsburgh maintained possession for 36:53, and the defense allowed just 220 total yards. The Jets had only one scoring threat in the second half, which came up empty when Vinny Testaverde's fourth-down pass from the Steelers' 12-yard line fell incomplete with 50 seconds left. Kordell Stewart was 20 of 36 for 214 yards. Testaverde was 15 of 26 for 141 yards.

N.Y. Jets	0	7	0	0	—	7
Pittsburgh	3	9	0	6	—	18

Pitt	—	FG Brown 26
Pit	—	Fuamatu-Ma'afala 1 run (kick failed)
NYJ	—	Chrebet 18 pass from Martin (Hall kick)
Pitt	—	FG Brown 33
Pitt	—	FG Brown 38
Pitt	—	FG Brown 20

PHILADELPHIA 24, SAN DIEGO 14—at Veterans Stadium, attendance 65,438. Brian Dawkins' 49-yard fumble return for a touchdown highlighted the Eagles' victory. The score was tied at 7-7 nine minutes into the game when LaDainian Tomlinson fumbled a pitchout. Dawkins scooped up the ball near midfield and raced for the touchdown that put Philadelphia ahead for good with 5:47 left in the opening quarter. Philadelphia's defense took over in the second half. After allowing 282 total yards in the first two quarters, the Eagles limited San Diego to only 19 total yards on its first six second-half drives before a march resulted in a missed field goal. McNabb was 22 of 44 for 221 yards and 2 touchdowns, with 1 interception. Flutie was 20 of 44 for 307 yards and 2 touchdowns, with 2 interceptions. Graham had 5 catches for 110 yards.

San Diego	7	7	0	0	—	14
Philadelphia	14	7	0	3	—	24

Phil	—	Lewis 1 pass from McNabb (Akers kick)
SD	—	Graham 61 pass from Flutie (Christie kick)
Phil	—	Dawkins 49 fumble return (Akers kick)
Phil	—	Staley 8 pass from McNabb (Akers kick)
SD	—	Graham 10 pass from Flutie (Christie kick)
Phil	—	FG Akers 37

ST. LOUIS 27, SAN FRANCISCO 14—at Dome at America's Center, attendance 66,218. Kurt Warner passed for 2 touchdowns and Marshall Faulk scored 2 to pace the Rams. St. Louis had little trouble dispatching the 49ers for the sixth consecutive time by holding the 49ers to season lows for points (14) and total yards (220). Aeneas Williams intercepted Jeff Garcia's pass on the third play of the game, and Faulk capped the 12-play, 41-yard march with a 6-yard run. Warner was 26 of 42 for 294 yards and 2 touchdowns, with 1 interception. Proehl had 6 catches for 109 yards. Garcia was 13 of 36 for 146 yards, with 2 interceptions.

San Francisco	0	7	0	7	—	14
St. Louis	14	7	3	3	—	27

StL	—	Faulk 6 run (Wilkins kick)
StL	—	Proehl 15 pass from Warner (Wilkins kick)
SF	—	Hearst 1 run (Cortez kick)
StL	—	Faulk 3 pass from Warner (Wilkins kick)
StL	—	FG Wilkins 22
StL	—	FG Wilkins 39
SF	—	Garcia 1 run (Cortez kick)

MINNESOTA 42, TENNESSEE 24—at Metrodome, attendance 64,271. Todd Bouman passed for 348 yards and 4 touchdowns in his first NFL start to keep the Vikings' flickering playoff hopes alive and deal the Titans' chances a severe blow. Bouman, who prior to the previous week hadn't attempted a pass in more than three seasons, started in place of injured Daunte Culpepper and rallied from an early 10-0 deficit. He tossed touchdown passes of 6 yards to Byron Chamberlain and 20 yards to Jake Reed to give Minnesota a 14-10 lead at intermission, and he helped break open the game by teaming with Doug Chapman on a 38-yard touchdown pass for a 28-10 advantage late in the third quarter. The Vikings had 496 of the game's 949 yards. Bouman was 21 of 31 for 348 yards and 4 touchdowns, with 1 interception. Michael Bennett rushed for a career-best 113 yards and 2 touchdowns. Moss caught 7 passes for 158 yards and 2 touchdowns. McNair was 25 of 36 for 302 yards and 2 touchdowns.

Tennessee	10	0	0	14	—	24
Minnesota	0	14	14	14	—	42

Tenn	—	George 13 run (Nedney kick)
Tenn	—	FG Nedney 37
Minn	—	Chamberlain 6 pass from Bouman (Anderson kick)
Minn	—	Reed 20 pass from Bouman (Anderson kick)
Minn	—	Bennett 31 run (Anderson kick)
Minn	—	Chapman 38 pass from Bouman (Anderson kick)
Tenn	—	Mason 15 pass from McNair (Nedney kick)
Minn	—	Bennett 10 run (Anderson kick)
Tenn	—	Wycheck 9 pass from McNair (Nedney kick)
Minn	—	Moss 73 pass from Bouman (Anderson kick)

WASHINGTON 20, ARIZONA 10—at Sun Devil Stadium, attendance 40,056. Stephen Davis rushed for 110 yards and a touchdown in the Redskins' victory. Tony Banks added a touchdown pass and Brett Conway had 2 field goals for Washington, who won for the sixth time in seven games. The Redskins led 13-3 until Davis, who carried 26 times and became the first player in club history to surpass 1,000 rushing yards in three consecutive seasons, capped a 58-yard drive with a 1-yard touchdown run to put the game out of reach with 8:20 left. The scoring run came one play after Banks' 40-yard completion to Rod Gardner. Banks was 19 of 26 for 210 yards and 1 touchdown. Jake Plummer was 20 of 34 for 253 yards and 1 touchdown, with 1 interception. David Boston had 6 catches for 132 yards.

Washington	0	10	0	10	—	20
Arizona	0	3	0	7	—	10

Wash	—	Flemister 2 pass from Banks (Conway kick)
Ariz	—	FG Gramatica 24
Wash	—	FG Conway 22
Wash	—	FG Conway 42
Wash	—	S. Davis 1 run (Conway kick)
Ariz	—	Jenkins 10 pass from Plummer (Gramatica kick)

SUNDAY NIGHT, DECEMBER 9

DENVER 20, SEATTLE 7—at INVESCO Field at Mile High, attendance 74,524. The Broncos vaulted past the Seahawks and into second place in the AFC West by winning a key divisional matchup. Brian Griese and Gus Frerotte each tossed touchdown passes for Denver, while Terrell Davis added 109 yards on the ground. Griese was 11 of 17 for 81 yards and 1 touchdown, with 1 interception, and Frerotte was 10 of 20 for 77 yards and 1 touchdown. Davis, who had a 57-yard run to set up a field goal in the third quarter, carried 19 times and ran for

more than 100 yards for the seventh consecutive time against the Seahawks. Hasselbeck was 17 of 37 for 243 yards and 1 touchdown, with 2 interceptions.

Seattle	0	7	0	0	—	7
Denver	7	3	10	0	—	20

Den	—	De. Clark 11 pass from Griese (Elam kick)
Den	—	FG Elam 42
Sea	—	D. Jackson 24 pass from Hasselbeck (Lindell kick)
Den	—	Hape 1 pass from Frerotte (Elam kick)
Den	—	FG Elam 20

MONDAY NIGHT, DECEMBER 10

MIAMI 41, INDIANAPOLIS 6—at Pro Player Stadium, attendance 73,858. Jay Fiedler passed for 3 touchdowns and ran for another as the AFC East-leading Dolphins ended any slim hopes the Colts still had for making the playoffs. Miami dominated from the start, taking the opening kickoff and marching 84 yards in 13 plays on a drive that consumed 7:46 and was capped by backup quarterback Ray Lucas' 2-yard touchdown run. Fiedler was 18 of 26 for 191 yards and 3 touchdowns. Lamar Smith added 107 yards on 28 carries. Peyton Manning was 19 of 32 for 173 yards, with 3 interceptions, and the Dolphins converted all 3 interceptions into touchdowns. Brock Marion had 2 interceptions and recovered a fumble.

Indianapolis	0	3	3	0	—	6
Miami	7	13	0	21	—	41

Mia	—	Lucas 2 run (Mare kick)
Mia	—	Chambers 2 pass from Fiedler (Mare kick)
Mia	—	Fiedler 9 run (kick blocked)
Ind	—	FG Vanderjagt 35
Ind	—	FG Vanderjagt 40
Mia	—	Chambers 32 pass from Fiedler (Mare kick)
Mia	—	Gadsden 9 pass from Fiedler (Mare kick)
Mia	—	Konrad 18 run (Fiedler kick)

FOURTEENTH WEEK SUMMARIES

American Football Conference

Eastern Division	W	L	T	Pct.	Pts.	OP
Miami	9	4	0	.692	276	249
New England	9	5	0	.643	313	253
N.Y. Jets	8	5	0	.615	246	231
Indianapolis	5	8	0	.385	339	405
Buffalo	2	11	0	.154	214	344
Central Division						
Pittsburgh*	11	2	0	.846	254	165
Baltimore	8	5	0	.615	258	240
Cleveland	6	7	0	.462	230	223
Tennessee	6	7	0	.462	264	314
Jacksonville	5	8	0	.385	222	220
Cincinnati	4	9	0	.308	177	249
Western Division						
Oakland*	10	3	0	.769	350	267
Seattle	7	6	0	.538	231	257
Denver	7	7	0	.500	307	293
San Diego	5	9	0	.357	293	276
Kansas City	4	9	0	.308	252	280

National Football Conference

Eastern Division	W	L	T	Pct.	Pts.	OP
Philadelphia	9	4	0	.692	299	161
N.Y. Giants	6	7	0	.462	221	239
Washington	6	7	0	.462	181	256
Arizona	5	8	0	.385	231	306
Dallas	4	9	0	.308	199	285
Central Division						
Chicago#	10	3	0	.769	261	175
Green Bay	9	4	0	.692	302	221
Tampa Bay	7	6	0	.538	241	232
Minnesota	5	8	0	.385	271	314

Detroit	1	12	0	.077	241	343
Western Division						
St. Louis#	11	2	0	.846	392	211
San Francisco#	10	3	0	.769	337	252
New Orleans	7	6	0	.538	302	283
Atlanta	6	7	0	.462	231	295
Carolina	1	12	0	.077	208	304

*Clinched division title
#Clinched playoff berth

SATURDAY, DECEMBER 15

N.Y. GIANTS 17, ARIZONA 13—at Giants Stadium, attendance 77,913. Kerry Collins' 4-yard touchdown pass to Amani Toomer with 25 seconds left lifted the Giants. Collins also had a 26-yard touchdown pass to Ron Dixon in the first quarter to help stake the Giants to a 10-6 lead, which they held midway through the final quarter. Bill Gramatica had a pair of field goals, but the rookie kicker hurt his leg while celebrating a 42-yard kick midway through the first quarter and was not available for long field goals or kickoffs in the second half. But a short punt in the fourth quarter positioned Arizona for a 43-yard touchdown drive, and the Cardinals took a 13-10 lead on Jake Plummer's fourth-and-16, 24-yard toss to Tywan Mitchell with 4:04 left. Kerry Collins completed 6 of 9 passes for 56 yards on the winning march, including third-down completions to Ike Hilliard and Tiki Barber for first downs. Collins was 14 of 32 for 147 yards and 2 touchdowns. Plummer was 27 of 45 for 207 yards and 1 touchdown.

Arizona	3	3	0	7	—	13
N.Y. Giants	7	0	0	10	—	17

Ariz	—	FG Gramatica 42
NYG	—	Dixon 26 pass from Collins (Andersen kick)
Ariz	—	FG Gramatica 23
NYG	—	FG Andersen 39
Ariz	—	Mitchell 24 pass from Plummer (Gramatica kick)
NYG	—	Toomer 4 pass from Collins (Andersen kick)

OAKLAND 13, SAN DIEGO 6—at Qualcomm Stadium, attendance 67,349. The Raiders clinched their second consecutive AFC West title by turning away the Chargers twice late in the game. Trailing 10-6, San Diego marched from its 43-yard line to the Raiders' 2 with 6:04 left in the game. But William Thomas stepped in front of Doug Flutie's pass to stymie the threat. Thomas returned the ball 11 yards before lateraling to teammate Charles Woodson, who tacked on another 30 yards. The takeaway led to Sebastian Janikowski's second field goal of the game with 1:07 left, for a seven-point lead. The Chargers still had one last chance, but Jeff Graham dropped Flutie's fourth-down pass from the 23, sealing San Diego's seventh consecutive defeat. Gannon was 20 of 28 for 221 yards and 1 touchdown, with 1 interception. Flutie was 19 of 37 for 215 yards, with 3 interceptions.

Oakland	3	0	7	3	—	13
San Diego	0	3	0	3	—	6

Oak	—	FG Janikowski 20
SD	—	FG Christie 29
Oak	—	Rice 40 pass from Gannon (Janikowski kick)
SD	—	FG Christie 31
Oak	—	FG Janikowski 31

SUNDAY, DECEMBER 16

INDIANAPOLIS 41, ATLANTA 27—at RCA Dome, attendance 55,603. Peyton Manning passed for 325 yards and 3 touchdowns and Dominic Rhodes rushed for 177 yards and 2 scores to lead the Colts. Leading 28-20, Rhodes countered with his second 11-yard touchdown run of the game only five plays later, and Mike Vanderjagt added 2 ield goals on the

Colts' next two possessions. Manning was 23 of 35 for 325 yards and 3 touchdowns, with 1 interception, while the rookie Rhodes carried 29 times for 177 yards. Marcus Pollard had 5 receptions for 101 yards. Chandler was 23 of 39 for 249 yards and 2 touchdowns.

Atlanta	0	14	3	10	—	27
Indianapolis	7	21	0	13	—	41

Ind	—	Rhodes 11 run (Vanderjagt kick)
Ind	—	Pollard 1 pass from Manning (Vanderjagt kick)
Atl	—	Christian 3 run (Feely kick)
Ind	—	Dilger 12 pass from Manning (Vanderjagt kick)
Atl	—	Finneran 18 pass from Chandler (Feely kick)
Ind	—	Insley 19 pass from Manning (Vanderjagt kick)
Atl	—	FG Feely 35
Atl	—	FG Feely 32
Ind	—	Rhodes 11 run (Vanderjagt kick)
Atl	—	Martin 11 pass from Chandler (Feely kick)
Ind	—	FG Vanderjagt 39
Ind	—	FG Vanderjagt 42

N.Y. JETS 15, CINCINNATI 14—at Giants Stadium, attendance 77,745. Vinny Testaverde passed for 2 fourth-quarter touchdowns as the Jets rallied. Corey Dillon scored 2 touchdowns—including a 1-yard run to cap a 20-play, 80-yard drive that consumed 12:00 the first time Cincinnati had the ball—to help stake the Bengals to a 14-3 second-half lead. But Testaverde countered Dillon's second touchdown, a 3-yard run 1:57 before the end of the third quarter, by directing a 68-yard touchdown drive. The Jets quickly forced a punt and Lamont Jordan gained 16 yards after taking a direct snap from center to highlight a 69-yard drive that ended with Testaverde's 2-yard touchdown pass to Anthony Becht in 6:57 to play. The one-point advantage stood up when Damien Robinson and James Farrior each had an interception. Testaverde was 17 of 28 for 196 yards and 2 touchdowns. Akili Smith was 4 of 6 for 35 yards and engineered the 12-minute first quarter drive while making his first start of the season, but injured his hamstring and was replaced by Jon Kitna, who was 10 of 17 for 93 yards, with 3 interceptions.

Cincinnati	7	0	7	0	—	14
N.Y. Jets	0	3	0	12	—	15

Cin	—	Dillon 1 run (Rackers kick)
NYJ	—	FG Hall 24
Cin	—	Dillon 3 run (Rackers kick)
NYJ	—	Dearth 1 pass from Testaverde (pass failed)
NYJ	—	Becht 2 pass from Testaverde (pass failed)

SEATTLE 29, DALLAS 3—at Husky Stadium, attendance 63,366. Ricky Watters rushed for 104 yards and a touchdown in his return to the starting lineup, but also suffered a season-ending ankle injury. Watters was named the starter for the rest of the season over 1,000-yard rusher Shaun Alexander earlier in the week, and responded by capping the opening drive with a 1-yard touchdown run 4:43 into the game. But two plays into the fourth quarter, with Seattle leading 12-3, Watters was injured on his twenty-eighth carry of the game. Alexander came on and helped secure the Seahawks' victory by running 7 yards for a touchdown and a 22-3 lead with 6:37 to play. Matt Hasselbeck was 13 of 25 for 152 yards. Carter was 14 of 33 for 135 yards, with 1 interception.

Dallas	0	3	0	0	—	3
Seattle	10	0	2	17	—	29

Sea	—	Watters 1 run (Lindell kick)
Sea	—	FG Lindell 22
Dall	—	FG Hilbert 37
Sea	—	Safety, Brooks kicked fumble out of end zone
Sea	—	FG Lindell 37
Sea	—	Alexander 7 run (Lindell kick)
Sea	—	Charlton 38 interception return (Lindell kick)

KANSAS CITY 26, DENVER 23 (OT)—at Arrowhead Stadium, attendance 77,778. Todd Peterson kicked 4 field goals, including the game winner from 32 yards 5:56 into overtime, to lift the Chiefs. Jason Elam had forced overtime by kicking his third field goal, from 49 yards, with 1:13 to play in regulation. In overtime, Kansas City quickly drove to Denver's 13, and Peterson made a 31-yard field goal, apparently to win the game. But a holding penalty forced Peterson to try again from 41 yards, and the kick bounced off the right upright. After the Broncos went three-and-out, Trent Green and Marvin Minnis teamed on a 56-yard pass play to Denver's 14 to begin the Chiefs' next possession. Peterson immediately came on for the winning kick. Green was 17 of 21 for 292 yards and 1 touchdown, with 1 interception. Priest Holmes ran for 121 yards and a touchdown. Gus Frerotte, playing in place of injured starter Brian Griese, was 16 of 22 for 181 yards and 1 touchdown. But Frerotte separated his shoulder while diving into the end zone on a 4-yard touchdown run in the third quarter and gave way to Jarious Jackson, who was 7 of 12 for 73 yards.

Denver	0	10	7	6	0	— 23
Kansas City	10	3	7	3	3	— 26

KC	—	FG Peterson 51
KC	—	Holmes 12 run (Peterson kick)
Den	—	R. Smith 11 pass from Frerotte (Elam kick)
KC	—	FG Peterson 43
Den	—	FG Elam 34
KC	—	Alexander 24 pass from Green (Peterson kick)
Den	—	Frerotte 4 run (Elam kick)
KC	—	FG Peterson 41
Den	—	FG Elam 49
KC	—	FG Peterson 32

TENNESSEE 26, GREEN BAY 20—at Adelphia Coliseum, attendance 68,804. Steve McNair passed for 2 touchdowns for the Titans. Tennessee, struggling to keep its AFC playoff hopes alive, spotted Green Bay a 10-2 lead before McNair completed 6 of 7 passes for 57 yards on a 60-yard drive that he capped with a 4-yard touchdown pass to Mike Green 3:30 into the second quarter. Late in the half, Jevon Kearse sacked Brett Favre, forcing a fumble that Daryl Porter recovered at Green Bay's 35-yard line. McNair teamed with Derrick Mason for a touchdown pass on the next play to put the Titans ahead for good with 2:36 left in the half. Favre brought his team close by tossing a 16-yard touchdown pass to Bill Schroeder with 6:42 left, but the Packers final drive stalled after reaching Tennessee's 46. Hicks finished with 142 yards while spelling hobbled starter Eddie George. McNair was 25 of 35 for 283 yards and 2 touchdowns and Mason caught 8 passes for 107 yards. Favre was 21 of 39 for 201 yards and 2 touchdowns, with 1 interception.

Green Bay	10	3	0	7	—	20
Tennessee	2	13	3	8	—	26

Tenn	—	Safety, A. Green tackled by Fisk in end zone
GB	—	FG Longwell 33
GB	—	Driver 7 pass from Favre (Longwell kick)

Tenn — M. Green 4 pass from McNair (pass failed)
Tenn — Mason 35 pass from McNair (Nedney kick)
GB — FG Longwell 54
Tenn — FG Nedney 24
Tenn — Hicks 22 run (Mason pass from McNair)
GB — Schroeder 16 pass from Favre (Longwell kick)

JACKSONVILLE 15, CLEVELAND 10—at Cleveland Browns Stadium, attendance 72,818. Mike Hollis kicked 2 field goals in the fourth quarter, and the Jaguars survived a bizarre finish. After Cleveland pulled within 9-7 on Anthony Henry's 97-yard interception return for a touchdown 2:28 before the end of the third quarter, but Hollis' 37-yard field goal with 2:57 to go gave Jacksonville a 15-10 lead. Cleveland had one more possession and marched from its 34-yard line to Jacksonville's 12 with 1:08 left. On fourth-and-2, Tim Couch apparently completed a 3-yard pass to Quincy Morgan for a first down, but after Couch spiked the ball to stop the clock, the first-down call on the field was overturned by instant replay, giving the Jaguars possession with 48 seconds left. Officials cleared the field and declared the game over when the hometown fans became unruly, only to call the teams back from the locker room nearly half an hour later. Before only several thousand fans remaining in the stands, and with several offensive players lined up on defense for Cleveland, Mark Brunell took a knee twice to end the game. Brunell was 20 of 35 for 202 yards and 1 touchdown, with 2 interceptions, while Stacey Mack added 115 yards on 28 carries. Couch was 21 of 30 for 184 yards, with 1 interception.

Jacksonville	9	0	0	6	—	15
Cleveland	0	0	7	3	—	10

Jax — Ji. Smith 4 pass from Brunell (kick failed)
Jax — FG Hollis 43
Clev — Henry 97 interception return (P. Dawson kick)
Jax — FG Hollis 46
Clev — FG P. Dawson 29
Jax — FG Hollis 37

SAN FRANCISCO 21, MIAMI 0—at 3Com Park, attendance 68,223. Kevan Barlow had 2 short touchdown runs and the 49ers posted their second consecutive home shutout. Barlow capped a back-breaking, 17-play, 98-yard drive with a 1-yard touchdown run in the third quarter. The 49ers' defense forced 4 turnovers and had 6 sacks and allowed 174 yards. Hearst had 103 yards on 26 carries. The 49ers maintained possession for 39:12. Jeff Garcia was 14 of 20 for 133 yards and 1 touchdown. Jay Fiedler was 16 of 28 for 149 yards, with 3 interceptions.

Miami	0	0	0	0	—	0
San Francisco	14	0	7	0	—	21

SF — Barlow 2 run (Cortez kick)
SF — Johnson 12 pass from Garcia (Cortez kick)
SF — Barlow 1 run (Cortez kick)

DETROIT 27, MINNESOTA 24—at Pontiac Silverdome, attendance 72,190. Mike McMahon passed for 241 yards and ran for 74 to lead the Lions to their first victory. After a series of agonizingly close defeats, Detroit built a 20-7 halftime lead, fell behind, but regained it on Cory Schlesinger's 1-yard run for the go-ahead touchdown with 10:36 to play. Todd Bouman's incomplete pass on fourth-and-10 from the Lions' 42 ended the Vikings' last hope with three seconds left. Mike McMahon, making his second start in place of injured Charlie Batch, was 15 of 28

for 241 yards. Bouman was 18 of 38 for 243 yards and 2 touchdowns, with 2 interceptions. Moss had 7 catches for 144 yards.

Minnesota	7	0	17	0	—	24
Detroit	14	6	0	7	—	27

Det — Lyght 59 interception return (Hanson kick)
Minn — T. Carter 46 fumble return (Anderson kick)
Det — McMahon 1 run (Hanson kick)
Det — FG Hanson 44
Det — FG Hanson 36
Minn — FG Anderson 27
Minn — Moss 66 pass from Bouman (Anderson kick)
Minn — Moss 13 pass from Bouman (Anderson kick)
Det — Schlesinger 1 run (Hanson kick)

NEW ENGLAND 12, BUFFALO 9 (OT)—at Ralph Wilson Stadium, attendance 45,527. The Patriots won a battle of field goals when Adam Vinatieri kicked his fourth of the game, from 23 yards 5:45 into overtime. New England won its fourth in a row and pulled within a half-game of first-place Miami in the AFC East. Shayne Graham's third field goal of the game came from 41 yards and put Buffalo ahead for the first time with 5:57 to play. But New England drove 56 yards to Vinatieri's tying, 25-yard field goal with 2:45 left. The Bills had the ball first in overtime but punted, and the Patriots began the winning drive from their 20-yard line. Antowain Smith burst 38 yards off left tackle to Buffalo's 3 to set up the decisive kick. Tom Brady was 19 of 35 for 237 yards, with 1 interception. Alex Van Pelt was 22 of 44 for 219 yards, with 1 interception.

New England	3	3	0	3	3	—	12
Buffalo	0	0	3	6	0	—	9

NE — FG Vinatieri 40
NE — FG Vinatieri 32
Buff — FG Graham 41
Buff — FG Graham 25
Buff — FG Graham 41
NE — FG Vinatieri 25
NE — FG Vinatieri 23

PHILADELPHIA 20, WASHINGTON 6—at FedEx Field, attendance 84,936. Donovan McNabb passed for 2 touchdowns to carry the Eagles. The Redskins led 6-0 until McNabb capped an 11-play, 66-yard drive with a 4-yard touchdown pass to Freddie Mitchell midway through the second quarter. McNabb's 62-yard touchdown pass to Todd Pinkston midway through the third quarter opened a 17-6 advantage. Meanwhile, Philadelphia's defense was turning away Washington time and again in Eagles' territory, including 2 missed field goals and reaching the Eagles' 20, 21, and 2, but two were thwarted by interceptions and another ended with an incomplete pass on fourth down. McNabb was 16 of 34 for 235 yards and 2 touchdowns, with 3 interceptions. Tony Banks was 17 of 36 for 213 yards, with 2 interceptions, and Stephen Davis rushed for 111 yards.

Philadelphia	0	10	7	3	—	20
Washington	3	3	0	0	—	6

Wash — FG Conway 47
Wash — FG Conway 25
Phil — F. Mitchell 4 pass from McNabb (Akers kick)
Phil — FG Akers 40
Phil — Pinkston 62 pass from McNabb (Akers kick)
Phil — FG Akers 49

CHICAGO 27, TAMPA BAY 3—at Soldier Field, attendance 66,944. The Bears clinched their first playoff berth since 1994. Chicago never trailed, scoring first on Paul Edinger's 30-yard field goal

after driving 68 yards on its second possession. After Tampa Bay tied the game on Martin Gramatica's 25-yard field goal midway through the second quarter, the Bears countered with a 64-yard touchdown march to take the lead for good. Most of the yardage came on a 62-yard strike from Jim Miller to David Terrell to the Buccaneers' 2-yard line, and Miller capped the drive with a 2-yard touchdown pass to Marty Booker 4:36 before intermission. Anthony Thomas rushed for 146 of his game-high 173 yards in the final two quarters. The Buccaneers managed only 4 first downs on six second-half possessions. Miller was 14 of 29 for 190 yards and 2 touchdowns, with 1 interception. Brad Johnson was 18 of 40 for 191 yards, with 2 interceptions. Keyshawn Johnson caught 7 passes for 119 yards.

Tampa Bay	0	3	0	0	—	3
Chicago	3	10	7	7	—	27

Chi — FG Edinger 30
TB — FG Gramatica 25
Chi — Booker 2 pass from Miller (Edinger kick)
Chi — FG Edinger 46
Chi — Baxter 18 pass from Miller (Edinger kick)
Chi — Thomas 5 run (Edinger kick)

SUNDAY NIGHT, DECEMBER 16
PITTSBURGH 26, BALTIMORE 21—at PSINet Stadium, attendance 69,506. Kordell Stewart passed for 333 yards and 2 touchdowns as the Steelers beat the Ravens to clinch the AFC Central title. Pittsburgh outgained the Ravens 476-207 in total yards and controlled the ball for 41:05 of the game's 60 minutes. Stewart had a 25-yard touchdown pass to Plaxico Burress to put Pittsburgh ahead for good 1:52 before halftime, then teamed with Bobby Shaw on a 90-yard touchdown strike for a 19-7 advantage with 8:53 to go in the game. After the Ravens pulled within five points on Elvis Grbac's 14-yard touchdown pass to Qadry Ismail 2:17 later, the Steelers countered with Dan Kreider's 4-yard touchdown run with 3:05 to play. Grbac's 5-yard touchdown pass with 1:14 left, but Pittsburgh covered the ensuing onside kick. Stewart was 20 of 31 for 333 yards and 2 touchdowns, and also ran for 55 yards. Burress caught 8 passes for 164 yards, while Shaw had 100 yards on only 2 receptions. Grbac was 20 of 38 for 159 yards and 2 touchdowns, with 1 interception. Ravens kicker Matt Stover, who missed his only field-goal try from 48 yards in the second quarter, had his NFL-record string of 38 consecutive games with a field goal broken.

Pittsburgh	3	10	0	13	—	26
Baltimore	0	7	0	14	—	21

Pitt — FG Brown 22
Balt — Grbac 2 run (Stover kick)
Pitt — FG Brown 33
Pitt — Burress 25 pass from Stewart (Brown kick)
Pitt — Shaw 90 pass from Stewart (run failed)
Balt — Ismail 14 pass from Grbac (Stover kick)
Pitt — Kreider 4 run (Brown kick)
Balt — Stokley 5 pass from Grbac (Stover kick)

MONDAY NIGHT, DECEMBER 17
ST. LOUIS 34, NEW ORLEANS 21—at Louisiana Superdome, attendance 70,332. Kurt Warner passed for 4 touchdowns as St. Louis avenged an earlier loss to the Saints. After building a 28-14 lead in the third quarter, they held off their division rivals with the help of 2 fourth-quarter field goals from Jeff Wilkins. Three of Warner's touchdown passes went to Isaac Bruce. His other scoring toss was a 4-yard pass to Marshall Faulk to break a 14-14 tie just 28

seconds before intermission. New Orleans hampered its cause by committing 16 penalties. Warner was 23 of 32 for 338 yards and 4 touchdowns. Faulk had 105 yards from scrimmage. Aaron Brooks was 23 of 40 for 269 yards and 3 touchdowns, with 2 interceptions. Willie Jackson had 8 catches for 156 yards.

St. Louis	7	14	7	6	—	34
New Orleans	7	7	7	0	—	21

NO	—	Smith 4 pass from Brooks (Carney kick)
StL	—	Bruce 6 pass from Warner (Wilkins kick)
StL	—	Bruce 11 pass from Warner (Wilkins kick)
NO	—	Horn 6 pass from Brooks (Carney kick)
StL	—	Faulk 4 pass from Warner (Wilkins kick)
StL	—	Bruce 40 pass from Warner (Wilkins kick)
NO	—	Jackson 28 pass from Brooks (Carney kick)
StL	—	FG Wilkins 43
StL	—	FG Wilkins 27

FIFTEENTH WEEK SUMMARIES
American Football Conference

Eastern Division	W	L	T	Pct.	Pts.	OP
New England	10	5	0	.667	333	266
Miami	9	5	0	.643	289	269
N.Y. Jets	9	5	0	.643	275	259
Indianapolis	5	9	0	.357	367	434
Buffalo	2	12	0	.143	244	377

Central Division	W	L	T	Pct.	Pts.	OP
Pittsburgh*	12	2	0	.857	301	179
Baltimore	9	5	0	.643	274	240
Tennessee	7	7	0	.500	277	324
Cleveland	6	8	0	.429	237	253
Jacksonville	6	8	0	.429	255	223
Cincinnati	4	10	0	.286	177	265

Western Division	W	L	T	Pct.	Pts.	OP
Oakland*	10	4	0	.714	360	280
Denver	7	7	0	.500	307	293
Seattle	7	7	0	.500	255	284
Kansas City	5	9	0	.357	272	297
San Diego	5	10	0	.333	310	296

National Football Conference

Eastern Division	W	L	T	Pct.	Pts.	OP
Philadelphia	9	5	0	.643	302	174
N.Y. Giants	7	7	0	.500	248	263
Arizona	6	8	0	.429	248	316
Washington	6	8	0	.429	196	276
Dallas	4	10	0	.286	209	302

Central Division	W	L	T	Pct.	Pts.	OP
Chicago#	11	3	0	.786	281	190
Green Bay#	10	4	0	.714	332	228
Tampa Bay	8	6	0	.571	289	253
Minnesota	5	9	0	.357	274	347
Detroit	1	13	0	.071	255	390

Western Division	W	L	T	Pct.	Pts.	OP
St. Louis#	12	2	0	.857	430	243
San Francisco#	11	3	0	.786	350	255
Atlanta	7	7	0	.500	264	325
New Orleans	7	7	0	.500	323	331
Carolina	1	13	0	.071	240	342

*Clinched division title
#Clinched playoff berth

SATURDAY, DECEMBER 22
NEW ENGLAND 20, MIAMI 13—at Foxboro Stadium, attendance 60,292. The streaking Patriots built a 20-0 lead, then held on to jump past the Dolphins and into first place in the AFC East. New England, which won its fifth in a row and seventh in the past eight, scored all its points in a 14-minute span of the second quarter. The Patriots' offense stalled in the second half, punting on each of its four full pos-

sessions, and the Dolphins made it close when Jay Fiedler tossed a 10-yard touchdown pass to Jeff Ogden with 1:28 left. But Fred Coleman recovered the ensuing onside kick, and Tom Brady took a knee three times to end the game. Brady was 11 of 19 for 108 yards and 1 touchdown. Smith had 156 rushing yards. Fiedler was 21 of 37 for 320 yards and 1 touchdown. Chris Chambers had 7 catches for 124 yards.

Miami	0	3	0	10	—	13
New England	0	20	0	0	—	20

NE	—	A. Smith 2 run (Vinatieri kick)
NE	—	Pass 23 pass from Brady (Vinatieri kick)
NE	—	FG Vinatieri 32
NE	—	FG Vinatieri 23
Mia	—	FG Mare 36
Mia	—	FG Mare 36
Mia	—	Ogden 10 pass from Fiedler (Mare kick)

SAN FRANCISCO 13, PHILADELPHIA 3—at 3Com Park, attendance 68,124. Jeff Garcia and Terrell Owens teamed for the game's only touchdown, and the 49ers' defense executed a prolonged goal-line stand. After Jose Cortez kicked a 32-yard field goal to give San Francisco a 6-3 lead in the final minute of the third quarter, the Eagles responded with their best drive of the day, marching from their 40 to a first-and-goal at the 49ers' 9 early in the fourth quarter. Donovan McNabb completed an 8-yard pass to James Thrash before Duce Staley was dropped for a 1-yard loss on second down. On third down, McNabb and Thrash teamed on a 1-yard completion, and on fourth down McNabb was pushed out of bounds at the 1. But Lance Schulters was called for holding on the play, giving the Eagles a first-and-goal inside the 1. Staley was stopped for no gain two times before McNabb's third-down pass was intercepted by Derek Smith in the end zone for a touchback. After that, the 49ers needed only 7 plays to go 80 yards against Philadelphia's defense, capping the drive with Garcia's 32-yard scoring pass to Owens with 6:52 left. Garcia was 14 of 24 for 136 yards and 1 touchdown. McNabb was 23 of 34 for 232 yards, with 1 interception.

Philadelphia	0	3	0	0	—	3
San Francisco	0	3	3	7	—	13

Phil	—	FG Akers 20
SF	—	FG Cortez 21
SF	—	FG Cortez 32
SF	—	Owens 32 pass from Garcia (Cortez kick)

SATURDAY NIGHT, DECEMBER 22
TENNESSEE 13, OAKLAND 10—at Network Associates Coliseum, attendance 61,934. The Titans edged the Raiders when Joe Nedney made a 21-yard field goal with 1:47 left and Sebastian Janikowski missed a 42-yard try with six seconds remaining. With the score 10-10, Janikowski missed a 33-yard attempt and the Titans drove 74 yards in 13 plays to Nedney's go-ahead field goal. Oakland still had time for one more possession, but the left-footed kicker, who didn't practice all week because of a groin strain, pulled his attempt wide right. It was the third miss of the game for Janikowski, who had entered the game having made 21 of 23 field-goal attempts. Steve McNair was 15 of 27 for 178 yards and 1 touchdown, with 2 interceptions. Gannon was 29 of 50 for 249 yards and 1 touchdown, with 1 interception.

Tennessee	0	0	10	3	—	13
Oakland	0	0	0	10	—	10

Tenn	—	FG Nedney 22
Tenn	—	K. Dyson 30 pass from McNair (Nedney kick)

Oak	—	Williams 4 pass from Gannon (Janikowski kick)
Oak	—	FG Janikowski 35
Tenn	—	FG Nedney 21

SUNDAY, DECEMBER 23
ATLANTA 33, BUFFALO 30—at Georgia Dome, attendance 43,320. Jay Feely kicked a 52-yard field goal as time expired to give the Falcons a wild victory over the Bills. Chris Chandler passed for a club-record 431 yards and 2 touchdowns, the last a 49-yard strike to Alge Crumpler to give the Falcons their biggest lead at 30-20 with 11:56 left. The Bills cut the deficit to 30-23 and Alex Van Pelt completed 7 of 11 passes on the ensuing 82-yard drive, including a 3-yard touchdown pass to Eric Moulds to tie the game with only 48 seconds to play. But that was plenty of time for Atlanta after Darrick Vaughn returned the ensuing kickoff to the Falcons' 43. From midfield with nine seconds left, Chandler completed a 16-yard pass to Brian Finneran, and Atlanta called its last time out with two seconds remaining to set up Feely's game winner. Chandler was 28 of 40 for 431 yards and 2 touchdowns, with 2 interceptions. Van Pelt was 17 of 31 for 208 yards, with 170 coming in the fourth quarter, and 1 touchdown. Shawn Bryson rushed for 130 yards and 2 touchdowns .

Buffalo	7	7	6	10	—	30
Atlanta	10	3	10	10	—	33

Atl	—	M. Smith 1 run (Feely kick)
Buff	—	Bryson 15 run (Graham kick)
Atl	—	FG Feely 32
Buff	—	Spoon 7 interception return (Graham kick)
Atl	—	FG Feely 32
Atl	—	FG Feely 43
Buff	—	Bryson 68 run (pass failed)
Atl	—	Martin 63 pass from Chandler (Feely kick)
Atl	—	Crumpler 49 pass from Chandler (Feely kick)
Buff	—	FG Graham 28
Buff	—	Moulds 3 pass from Van Pelt (Graham kick)
Atl	—	FG Feely 52

CHICAGO 20, WASHINGTON 15—at FedEx Field, attendance 78,884. Linebacker Brian Urlacher caught a 27-yard touchdown pass from Brad Maynard out of field-goal formation for the decisive points in the Bears' victory. Chicago, trailing 15-13, lined up for an apparent 45-yard, game-tying field-goal attempt by Paul Edinger with 10:01 remaining in the fourth quarter. But Maynard, the Bears' punter and their holder on field-goal attempts, took the snap, rolled to his right, and lofted a pass to Urlacher down the right sideline. Urlacher, a former two-way player in college, hauled in his first NFL reception and scored the go-ahead touchdown with 9:55 to play. The Redskins reached the Bears' 3, but Urlacher stopped Stephen Davis for no gain on second down. Banks threw incomplete on third and fourth down. Maynard took an intentional safety with 20 seconds left to close the scoring. Jim Miller was 13 of 26 for 98 yards. Banks was 23 of 43 for 236 yards.

Chicago	3	7	0	10	—	20
Washington	7	3	3	2	—	15

Chi	—	FG Edinger 39
Wash	—	Davis 3 run (Conway kick)
Chi	—	L. Johnson 32 run (Edinger kick)
Wash	—	FG Conway 34
Wash	—	FG Conway 26
Chi	—	Urlacher 27 pass from Maynard (Edinger kick)
Chi	—	FG Edinger 37
Wash	—	Safety, Maynard ran out of the end zone

BALTIMORE 16, CINCINNATI 0—at PSINet Stadium, attendance 68,987. Terry Allen rushed for 91 yards and the game's lone touchdown. Allen's touchdown run capped an 80-yard drive 1:25 into the second quarter and gave Baltimore a 10-0 lead. The Ravens posted their first shutout of the season after blanking a league-high four opponents in 2000. The Bengals punted 8 times and turned over the ball 4 times. Their three best drives reached Baltimore's 17-, 20-, and 7-yard lines, but each ended in interceptions, including 2 by Ray Lewis. Elvis Grbac was 16 of 30 for 181 yards and Jon Kitna was 16 of 30 for 153 yards, with 3 interceptions. Corey Dillon rushed for 127 yards on 24 carries. He became the first runner to eclipse the 100-yard barrier against the Ravens since the 1998 season, a span of 51 games.

Cincinnati	0	0	0	0	—	0
Baltimore	3	10	0	3	—	16

Balt — FG Stover 43
Balt — Allen 4 run (Stover kick)
Balt — FG Stover 29
Balt — FG Stover 33

GREEN BAY 30, CLEVELAND 7—at Lambeau Field, attendance 59,824. The Packers clinched at least a wild-card playoff berth. Brett Favre passed for 3 touchdowns and Tyrone Williams returned an interception 69 yards for a critical touchdown, but it was the running of Ahman Green and Dorsey Levens in 24 degree temperatures that made the difference. Green ran for 150 yards on 21 carries and Levens added 72 yards on 9 attempts. Favre, who improved to 28-0 at home when the game-time temperature is 34 degrees or below, was 18 of 28 for 139 yards and 3 touchdowns. Tim Couch was 22 of 33 for 203 yards and 1 touchdown, with 3 interceptions. Jamel White rushed for 131 yards.

Cleveland	0	7	0	0	—	7
Green Bay	13	10	0	7	—	30

GB — Franks 1 pass from Favre (kick blocked)
GB — Franks 4 pass from Favre (Longwell kick)
Cle — White 3 pass from Couch (P. Dawson kick)
GB — FG Longwell 39
GB — Ty. Williams 69 interception return (Longwell kick)
GB — Levens 16 pass from Favre (Longwell kick)

ARIZONA 17, DALLAS 10—at Sun Devil Stadium, attendance 48,883. Michael Pittman ran 1 yard for the go-ahead touchdown in the second quarter and the Cardinals held off the Cowboys. Dallas dominated the game statistically, recording 21 first downs to only 11 for Arizona, running 70 plays to 52, gaining 343 total yards to 209, and maintaining possession for 37:14 to 22:46. But the Cowboys were done in by 9 penalties, poor special-teams play, and 3 turnovers. The Cowboys drove into Cardinals' territory three times on four second-half possessions, but a bad snap thwarted one field-goal attempt and Jon Hilbert missed another try from 41 yards. Carter was 16 of 28 for 176 yards and 1 touchdown, with 2 interceptions, while Emmitt Smith added 128 rushing yards. Jake Plummer was 17 of 31 for 144 yards.

Dallas	3	7	0	0	—	10
Arizona	0	17	0	0	—	17

Dall — FG Hilbert 27
Ariz — R. McKinnon 24 interception return (Oglesby kick)
Dall — Swinton 45 pass from Carter (Hilbert kick)
Ariz — Pittman 1 run (Oglesby kick)

Ariz — FG Oglesby 34

PITTSBURGH 47, DETROIT 14—at Heinz Field, attendance 62,809. Kordell Stewart passed for 3 touchdowns and ran for another as the Steelers extended their winning streak to seven games and clinched a first-round bye. Stewart tossed a 5-yard touchdown pass to Hines Ward as the Steelers increased their lead to 27-14 at halftime. Pittsburgh broke open the game with a field goal and a touchdown on its first two possessions of the second half, the latter coming on Stewart's 19-yard pass to Plaxico Burress. Stewart was 17 of 26 for 226 yards and 3 touchdowns, while Chris Fuamatu-Ma'afala added 126 rushing yards on 26 carries. Mike McMahon was 12 of 28 for 118 yards and 2 touchdowns, with 1 interception.

Detroit	7	7	0	0	—	14
Pittsburgh	14	13	10	10	—	47

Pitt — Gildon 27 fumble return (Brown kick)
Det — Sloan 10 pass from McMahon (Hanson kick)
Pitt — Cushing 4 pass from Stewart (Brown kick)
Pitt — Stewart 2 run (kick failed)
Pitt — Ward 5 pass from Stewart (Brown kick)
Det — Sloan 1 pass from McMahon (Hanson kick)
Pitt — FG Brown 37
Pitt — Burress 19 pass from Stewart (Brown kick)
Pitt — FG Brown 31
Pitt — Maddox 5 run (Brown kick)

JACKSONVILLE 33, MINNESOTA 3—at Metrodome, attendance 64,150. Stacey Mack rushed for 111 yards and 2 touchdowns in the Jaguars' rout. Mack had a 3-yard touchdown run as Jacksonville built a 16-0 second-quarter lead. The Jaguars amassed 23 first downs and 423 total yards, did not turn over the ball, and scored on seven of their eight full possessions. Mark Brunell was 17 of 24 for 217 yards and 1 touchdown. Jimmy Smith caught 8 passes for 122 yards. Todd Bouman lasted only one series before an injured thumb forced him to the sidelines. Third-string quarterback Spergon Wynn was 24 of 39 for 218 yards, with 1 interception.

Jacksonville	10	6	7	10	—	33
Minnesota	0	3	0	0	—	3

Jax — FG Hollis 39
Jax — Mack 3 run (Hollis kick)
Jax — FG Hollis 23
Jax — FG Hollis 21
Minn — FG Anderson 32
Jax — McCardell 10 pass from Brunell (Hollis kick)
Jax — FG Hollis 21
Jax — Mack 2 run (Hollis kick)

TAMPA BAY 48, NEW ORLEANS 21—at Raymond James Stadium, attendance 65,526. Brad Johnson passed for 3 touchdowns, and Tampa Bay built a 30-0 halftime lead en route to an easy victory over the Saints. The Buccaneers got an immediate spark when Aaron Stecker returned the opening kickoff 86 yards to the Saints' 14-yard line. Two plays later, Johnson's 14-yard touchdown pass to Karl Williams gave the Buccaneers the lead only 1:06 into the game. Ronde Barber's interception on the ensuing possession and his 10-yard return to New Orleans' 12 led to Mike Alstott's 1-yard touchdown run, and the rout was on. Johnson was 16 of 31 for 207 yards and 3 touchdowns. Alstott rushed for 101 yards on 24 carries. Aaron Brooks was 21 of 38 for 248 yards and 3 touchdowns, all in the second half,

with 4 interceptions. Barber had 3 of the interceptions.

New Orleans	0	0	14	7	—	21
Tampa Bay	17	13	3	15	—	48

TB — K. Williams 14 pass from B. Johnson (Gramatica kick)
TB — Alstott 1 run (Gramatica kick)
TB — FG Gramatica 20
TB — FG Gramatica 24
TB — Dunn 17 pass from B. Johnson (Gramatica kick)
TB — FG Gramatica 32
NO — Horn 11 pass from Brooks (Carney kick)
TB — FG Gramatica 27
NO — E. Williams 16 pass from Brooks (Carney kick)
TB — Moore 4 pass from B. Johnson (Gramatica kick)
NO — Horn 10 pass from Brooks (Carney kick)
TB — Barber 36 interception return (King kick)

ST. LOUIS 38, CAROLINA 32—at Ericsson Stadium, attendance 47,873. Marshall Faulk rushed for 202 yards and 2 touchdowns as the Rams won their fourth in a row and the Panthers fell to 1-13. Faulk's 4-yard touchdown run 2:06 before halftime gave the Rams the lead for good at 14-10. Moments later, Dre' Bly picked up a loose ball at the Panthers' 44-yard line after an errant field-goal snap. Bly ran 15 yards before lateraling to teammate Dexter McCleon, who covered the remaining 29 yards for a 21-10 advantage 41 seconds before halftime. The Panthers made it close with 10 points on their final two possessions, but McCleon recovered an onside kick with 27 seconds left to preserve the victory. Warner was 18 of 23 for 217 yards and 2 touchdowns, with 2 interceptions. Marshall Faulk, who ran for 183 yards in only two quarters of a rout of Carolina in week 9, had 252 yards from scrimmage. Chris Weinke was 24 of 51 for 312 yards and 1 touchdown.

St. Louis	7	14	10	7	—	38
Carolina	7	6	10	9	—	32

Car — Byrd 27 pass from Weinke (Kasay kick)
StL — Proehl 6 pass from Warner (Wilkins kick)
Car — FG Kasay 22
StL — Faulk 4 run (Wilkins kick)
StL — McCleon 29 lateral from Bly (Wilkins kick)
Car — FG Kasay 29
Car — FG Kasay 30
StL — FG Wilkins 34
StL — Faulk 70 run (Wilkins kick)
Car — Huntley 4 run (Kasay kick)
StL — Conwell 4 pass from Warner (Wilkins kick)
Car — Crawford recovered fumble in end zone (pass failed)
Car — FG Kasay 46

KANSAS CITY 20, SAN DIEGO 17—at Arrowhead Stadium, attendance 76,131. Tony Richardson's 1-yard touchdown run with 48 seconds left lifted the Chiefs to the victory. Kansas City won back-to-back games for the first time all season, while the Chargers' losing streak reached eight games. Trailing 17-13, Trent Green's pass was intercepted by Leonardo Carson, but the play was wiped out when Rodney Harrison was called for roughing the passer, giving the Chiefs first-and-goal at the 4. Priest Holmes ran 1 yard and Green passed incomplete, but Harrison was cited again, this time for holding, and Kansas City had another first-and-goal at the 1 with 1:00 remaining. Richardson was stopped once for no gain, then scored the winning touchdown. Green was 19 of 28 for 203 yards and 1 touchdown, with 2 interceptions. Doug Flutie was 15 of 27 for 175 yards and 2 touchdowns and LaDainian Tomlinson rushed for 145 yards.

San Diego	7	0	7	3	—	17
Kansas City	7	0	3	10	—	20

KC — Dunn 3 pass from Green (Peterson kick)
SD — F. Jones 3 pass from Flutie (Christie kick)
KC — FG Peterson 33
SD — Conway 4 pass from Flutie (Christie kick)
KC — FG Peterson 41
SD — FG Christie 27
KC — T. Richardson 1 run (Peterson kick)

N.Y. GIANTS 27, SEATTLE 24—at Giants Stadium, attendance 78,119. Kerry Collins kept the Giants' playoff hopes alive when he tossed a 7-yard touchdown pass to Ike Hilliard with 20 seconds remaining. The winning play capped a dramatic 96-yard drive that began with the Giants trailing 24-20 and just 2:52 left in the game. Dave Thomas intercepted Matt Hasselbeck's pass on the next play from scrimmage to secure the victory. Collins was 30 of 47 for 338 yards and 1 touchdown. Toomer caught 8 passes for 124 yards, and Hilliard had 7 receptions for 105 yards. Hasselbeck was 15 of 26 for 185 yards and 1 touchdown, with 1 interception.

Seattle	7	10	7	0	—	24
N.Y. Giants	7	10	0	10	—	27

Sea — Alexander 29 run (Lindell kick)
NYG — Dayne 31 run (Andersen kick)
Sea — FG Lindell 20
NYG — Strahan 13 fumble return (Andersen kick)
Sea — Randle recovered fumble in end zone (Lindell kick)
NYG — FG Andersen 32
Sea — Alexander 16 pass from Hasselbeck (Lindell kick)
NYG — FG Andersen 33
NYG — Hilliard 7 pass from Collins (Andersen kick)

SUNDAY NIGHT, DECEMBER 23
N.Y. JETS 29, INDIANAPOLIS 28—at RCA Dome, attendance 56,302. The Jets pulled out another one-point victory when Vinny Testaverde completed a 6-yard touchdown pass to Anthony Becht with 58 seconds left. The Jets trailed 28-22 when they began a drive at their 24-yard line with 2:39 remaining before finding Becht for the decisive touchdown. Indianapolis moved from its 20 to its 40 on the next possession, but Peyton Manning's pass for Marvin Harrison on fourth-and-3 was completed for no gain with 15 seconds left. Testaverde was 28 of 47 for 285 yards and 2 touchdowns, with 2 interceptions. Martin ran for 122 yards and Chrebet caught 8 passes for 118 yards as the Jets amassed 451 total yards. Manning was 25 of 35 for 228 yards and 1 touchdown for the Colts, who had 393 total yards. Dominic Rhodes rushed for 126 yards, and Harrison had 12 receptions for 127 yards.

N.Y. Jets	3	10	6	10	—	29
Indianapolis	0	10	7	11	—	28

NYJ — FG Hall 47
NYJ — Jordan 25 pass from Testaverde (Hall kick)
Ind — Rhodes 46 run (Vanderjagt kick)
NYJ — FG Hall 22
Ind — FG Vanderjagt 50
NYJ — FG Hall 48

Ind — Pollard 28 pass from Manning (Vanderjagt kick)
NYJ — FG Hall 46
NYJ — FG Hall 24
Ind — Harrison 39 pass from Dilger (McDougal run)
Ind — FG Vanderjagt 43
NYJ — Becht 6 pass from Testaverde (Hall kick)

SIXTEENTH WEEK SUMMARIES
American Football Conference

Eastern Division	W	L	T	Pct.	Pts.	OP
Miami	10	5	0	.667	310	283
New England#	10	5	0	.667	333	266
N.Y. Jets	9	6	0	.600	284	273
Indianapolis	5	10	0	.333	384	476
Buffalo	3	12	0	.200	258	386
Central Division						
Pittsburgh*	12	3	0	.800	324	205
Baltimore	9	6	0	.600	284	262
Cleveland	7	8	0	.467	278	291
Tennessee	7	8	0	.467	315	365
Jacksonville	6	9	0	.400	281	253
Cincinnati	5	10	0	.333	203	288
Western Division						
Oakland*	10	5	0	.667	377	303
Denver	8	7	0	.533	330	310
Seattle	8	7	0	.533	280	306
Kansas City	6	9	0	.400	302	323
San Diego	5	11	0	.313	332	321

National Football Conference

Eastern Division	W	L	T	Pct.	Pts.	OP
Philadelphia*	10	5	0	.667	326	195
Arizona	7	8	0	.467	278	323
N.Y. Giants	7	8	0	.467	269	287
Washington	7	8	0	.467	236	286
Dallas	5	10	0	.333	236	325
Central Division						
Chicago#	12	3	0	.800	305	190
Green Bay#	11	4	0	.733	356	241
Tampa Bay#	9	6	0	.600	311	263
Minnesota	5	10	0	.333	287	371
Detroit	1	14	0	.067	255	414
Western Division						
St. Louis*	13	2	0	.867	472	260
San Francisco#	11	4	0	.733	371	282
Atlanta	7	8	0	.467	278	346
New Orleans	7	8	0	.467	333	371
Carolina	1	14	0	.067	247	372

*Clinched division title
#Clinched playoff berth

SATURDAY NIGHT, DECEMBER 29
TAMPA BAY 22, BALTIMORE 10—at Raymond James Stadium, attendance 65,619. Defense and special teams that made the big plays in the Buccaneers' victory. After Doug Brien's 38-yard field goal pulled Tampa Bay within 7-6 midway through the second quarter, the Buccaneers forced a punt, which was blocked by Todd Yoder and recovered by Rabih Abdullah. Moments later, Brien's 24-yard field goal gave Tampa Bay the lead for good. On the ensuing possession, Derrick Brooks intercepted Elvis Grbac's pass and returned it 53 yards to the Ravens' 1-yard line, setting up Johnson's sneak for a 16-7 lead. Brad Johnson was 13 of 29 for 90 yards. Grbac was 21 of 37 for 205 yards and 1 touchdown, with 2 interceptions. Tampa Bay clinched the sixth and final NFC playoff berth when Atlanta lost at Miami the next day.

Baltimore	0	7	0	3	—	10
Tampa Bay	3	13	0	6	—	22

TB — FG Brien 42
Balt — Taylor 14 pass from Grbac (Stover kick)
TB — FG Brien 38
TB — FG Brien 24

TB — B. Johnson 1 run (Brien kick)
Balt — FG Stover 24
TB — Alstott 32 run (pass failed)

SUNDAY, DECEMBER 30
ARIZONA 30, CAROLINA 7—at Ericsson Stadium, attendance 43,272. Jake Plummer and David Boston teamed on a pair of touchdown passes in less than three minutes of the second quarter to key the Cardinals' rout. Arizona led 10-0 when Boston hauled in Plummer's 61-yard pass for a touchdown 12:36 before halftime. Two plays later, David Barrett's interception and 24-yard return set up the Cardinals at the Panthers' 23-yard line. Thomas Jones carried three times to move the ball to the 5, and Plummer's strike to Boston made it 24-0 at the 9:46 mark. Plummer was 12 of 23 for 173 yards and 2 touchdowns. Boston finished with 7 catches for 127 yards. Chris Weinke was 36 of 63 for 223 yards and 1 touchdown, with 1 interception, for Carolina, which lost its fourteenth consecutive game. The 63 pass attempts were the most ever by a rookie in an NFL game.

Arizona	7	20	3	0	—	30
Carolina	0	7	0	0	—	7

Ariz — McKinnon 25 fumble return (Oglesby kick)
Ariz — FG Oglesby 41
Ariz — Boston 61 pass from Plummer (Oglesby kick)
Ariz — Boston 5 pass from Plummer (Oglesby kick)
Car — Hayes 7 pass from Weinke (Kasay kick)
Ariz — FG Oglesby 18
Ariz — FG Oglesby 26

MIAMI 21, ATLANTA 14—at Pro Player Stadium, attendance 73,559. The Dolphins executed a goal-line stand late in the fourth quarter to secure a playoff berth for the fifth consecutive season. Miami took a 21-7 lead into the fourth quarter, but Michael Vick, who replaced the injured Chris Chandler in the second quarter, completed a 48-yard pass to Shawn Jefferson, setting up a 1-yard touchdown pass to Derek Rackley with 9:16 left. After forcing a punt, the Falcons began their final drive at their 23-yard line. Vick's 34-yard pass to Terance Mathis moved the ball into Dolphins' territory, and his 10-yard run around left end gave Atlanta a first-and-goal at the 4 with 2:29 to play. Two runs netted 3 yards before Bob Christian was stopped a foot short of the goal line, setting up fourth-and-goal with 53 seconds left. Christian got the ball again but was stuffed by Ernest Grant and a host of others, and the Dolphins were in the playoffs. Fiedler was 16 of 29 for 191 yards and 2 touchdowns, with 1 interception. Vick was 11 of 20 for 214 yards and 1 touchdown, with 2 interceptions, and rushed for 63 yards.

Atlanta	7	0	0	7	—	14
Miami	7	14	0	0	—	21

Atl — M. Smith 2 run (Feely kick)
Mia — Marion 26 interception return (Mare kick)
Mia — Minor 17 pass from Fiedler (Mare kick)
Mia — Gadsden 2 pass from Fiedler (Mare kick)
Atl — Rackley 1 pass from Vick (Feely kick)

BUFFALO 14, N.Y. JETS 9—at Giants Stadium, attendance 78,200. The Bills kept the Jets from securing a playoff berth with the upset. Larry Centers ran 5 yards for a touchdown and Alex Van Pelt teamed with Peerless Price on a 22-yard touchdown pass as Buffalo built a 14-6 lead. The Jets had one more chance when a bad punt snap gave them possession at midfield with 47 seconds to go, and they reached Buffalo's 24 at the 13-second mark. Testaverde's short pass was caught over the middle by Curtis Martin, who was tackled at the 17. The Jets scrambled to get off another play as time ran out, but Testaverde's pass for Kevin Swayne was incomplete. Alex Van Pelt was 16 of 27 for 185 yards and 1 touchdown. Shawn Bryson rushed for 107 yards. Testaverde was 20 of 38 for 235 yards, with 2 interceptions, and Martin added 115 yards on 19 carries.

Buffalo	0	7	7	0	—	14
N.Y. Jets	3	3	0	3	—	9

NYJ	—	FG Hall 33
NYJ	—	FG Hall 28
Buff	—	Centers 5 run (Graham kick)
Buff	—	P. Price 22 pass from Van Pelt (Graham kick)
NYJ	—	FG Hall 32

CHICAGO 24, DETROIT 0—at Pontiac Silverdome, attendance 76,067. Jim Miller passed for 2 touchdowns in the first quarter to trigger the Bears' easy victory. Miller completed 6 of 8 passes for 140 yards and 2 touchdowns on the first two possessions. Chicago's defense recorded its second shutout of the season. Miller was 17 of 30 for 252 yards and 2 touchdowns. Marty Booker caught 9 passes for 115 yards, while Bates added 4 for 107 yards. Ty Detmer, starting in place of injured Mike McMahon, was 31 of 51 for 303 yards, with 2 interceptions.

Chicago	14	3	0	7	—	24
Detroit	0	0	0	0	—	0

Chi	—	Bates 28 pass from Miller (Edinger kick)
Chi	—	Terrell 20 pass from Miller (Edinger kick)
Chi	—	FG Edinger 38
Chi	—	Harris 39 interception return (Edinger kick)

CLEVELAND 41, TENNESSEE 38—at Adelphia Coliseum, attendance 68,798. The Browns scored 17 points in the last 9:21 of the fourth quarter to overcome the Titans. Cleveland countered Eddie George's second touchdown by driving 54 yards in 9 plays and capping the march on Jamel White's 2-yard touchdown run to trim its deficit to 38-31. After the Browns forced a punt, Tim Couch and Quincy Morgan teamed on a 78-yard completion that led to Couch's game-tying, 4-yard touchdown pass to Kevin Johnson with 5:37 to play. Cleveland's defense held again, and White carried 6 times on the ensuing 8-play drive, and a key roughing-the-passer penalty positioned Phil Dawson for the winning 44-yard field goal with 55 seconds left. Couch was 20 of 27 for 336 yards, along with 3 touchdowns, with 1 interception. Steve McNair was 16 of 25 for 274 yards and 2 touchdowns. George rushed for 130 yards.

Cleveland	14	10	0	17	—	41
Tennessee	14	10	7	7	—	38

Cle	—	J. Dawson 33 pass from Couch (P. Dawson kick)
Tenn	—	Green 17 run (Nedney kick)
Cle	—	Santiago 20 pass from Couch (P. Dawson kick)
Tenn	—	Dyson 40 pass from McNair (Nedney kick)
Cle	—	FG P. Dawson 30
Tenn	—	Mason 59 pass from McNair (Nedney kick)
Cle	—	White 1 run (P. Dawson kick)
Tenn	—	FG Nedney 31
Tenn	—	George 7 run (Nedney kick)
Tenn	—	George 20 run (Nedney kick)
Cle	—	White 2 run (P. Dawson kick)

Cle	—	Johnson 4 pass from Couch (P. Dawson kick)
Cle	—	FG P. Dawson 44

ST. LOUIS 42, INDIANAPOLIS 17—at Dome at America's Center, attendance 66,084. Marshall Faulk scored 4 touchdowns as the Rams won to clinch the NFC West. Faulk rushed for 118 yards and got lots of help from St. Louis' other explosive position players. Kurt Warner broke open a close game by passing for 3 touchdowns in the final 8:44 of the first half and Torry Holt caught 7 passes for 203 yards, including a pair of touchdowns. Faulk had 3 1-yard touchdown runs and caught a 5-yard scoring pass from Warner that made the score 28-14 with 1:45 to go in the second quarter. Warner was 23 of 30 for 359 yards and 3 touchdowns, with 1 interception, and St. Louis amassed 483 total yards. Peyton Manning was 15 of 28 for 195 yards, with 1 interception.

Indianapolis	7	7	3	0	—	17
St. Louis	7	28	0	7	—	42

StL	—	Faulk 1 run (Wilkins kick)
Ind	—	Rhodes 1 run (Vanderjagt kick)
StL	—	Faulk 1 run (Wilkins kick)
Ind	—	Manning 1 run (Vanderjagt kick)
StL	—	Holt 21 pass from Warner (Wilkins kick)
StL	—	Faulk 5 pass from Warner (Wilkins kick)
StL	—	Holt 46 pass from Warner (Wilkins kick)
Ind	—	FG Vanderjagt 48
StL	—	Faulk 1 run (Wilkins kick)

KANSAS CITY 30, JACKSONVILLE 26—at ALLTEL Stadium, attendance 59,396. Trent Green passed for 2 touchdowns to Tony Gonzalez, and the Chiefs won their third consecutive game by holding off the Jaguars. The Jaguars drove to the Chiefs' 8, but the march stalled because of a penalty and a fourth-down completion that came up 2 yards short. After Kansas City took an intentional safety with 46 seconds left, the Jaguars had one final chance. They reached the Chiefs' 13 with 12 seconds to go, but Brunell's final two attempts fell incomplete as time ran out. Green was 26 of 35 for 294 yards and 2 touchdowns, with 2 interceptions. Eddie Kennison had 6 catches for 121 yards. Brunell was 22 of 37 for 283 yards and 1 touchdown, with 1 interception, while McCardell had 7 catches for 132 yards.

Kansas City	7	10	10	3	—	30
Jacksonville	7	10	0	9	—	26

KC	—	Holmes 6 run (Peterson kick)
Jax	—	Mack 3 run (Hollis kick)
Jax	—	Brunell 3 run (Hollis kick)
KC	—	Gonzalez 1 pass from Green (Peterson kick)
Jax	—	FG Hollis 28
KC	—	FG Peterson 47
KC	—	FG Peterson 40
KC	—	Gonzalez 12 pass from Green (Peterson kick)
Jax	—	McCardell 20 pass from Brunell (Hollis kick)
KC	—	FG Peterson 29
Jax	—	Safety, Stryzinski ran out of end zone

GREEN BAY 24, MINNESOTA 13—at Lambeau Field, attendance 59,870. Ahman Green ran 4 yards for the go-ahead touchdown with 6:28 left, and the Packers kept their division-title hopes alive. Green Bay trailed 13-10 before driving 79 yards in seven plays to Green's touchdown. Mike McKenzie intercepted Wynn's pass on the ensuing possession and returned the ball 38 yards for the clinching touch-

down with 5:25 to play. Favre was 18 of 29 for 169 yards in a game that began with the temperature at 19 degrees, and improved his record to 30-0 in games played at home with the temperature 34 degrees or below. Wynn, starting because of injuries to Daunte Culpepper and Todd Bouman, was 11 of 30 for 114 yards and 1 touchdown, with 3 interceptions. Michael Bennett gained 104 yards on 25 carries.

Minnesota	0	3	3	7	—	13
Green Bay	0	7	0	17	—	24

Minn	—	FG Anderson 44
GB	—	Driver 31 run (Longwell kick)
Minn	—	FG Anderson 42
GB	—	FG Longwell 24
Minn	—	Chamberlain 47 pass from Wynn (Anderson kick)
GB	—	Green 4 run (Longwell kick)
GB	—	McKenzie 38 interception return (Longwell kick)

PHILADELPHIA 24, N.Y. GIANTS 21—at Veterans Stadium, attendance 65,885. David Akers kicked a 35-yard field goal with seven seconds left and the Eagles survived a scare on the game's final play to win the NFC East and officially eliminate the defending-conference-champion Giants from the playoffs. Ron Dayne's 16-yard touchdown run helped the Giants take a 21-14 lead with 2:43 to play. The Eagles needed only 54 seconds to tie the score, capped by Donovan McNabb's 7-yard touchdown pass to Chad Lewis with 1:49 left. The Giants quickly went three-plays-and-out, giving Philadelphia another possession beginning from its 29-yard line with 58 seconds left. McNabb's 25-yard completion to Thrash moved the ball into Giants territory, and his 11-yard keeper positioned Akers for the go-ahead kick. The Eagles' advantage seemed safe when the Giants had only seven seconds remaining as they took the snap from their 20-yard line following the ensuing kickoff. But Kerry Collins completed a short pass to Tiki Barber, who flipped the ball to Ron Dixon, who looped behind him at the 34. Dixon streaked untouched down the left sideline for 60 yards until he was pushed out of bounds by Damon Moore at Philadelphia's 6-yard line with time having expired. McNabb was 21 of 39 for 270 yards and 3 touchdowns, with 1 interception. Thrash caught 7 passes for 143 yards and a touchdown. Collins was 22 of 39 for 301 yards and 1 touchdown.

N.Y. Giants	0	0	10	11	—	21
Philadelphia	7	0	17	—	24

Phil	—	Lewis 5 pass from McNabb (Akers kick)
NYG	—	Toomer 60 pass from Collins (Andersen kick)
NYG	—	FG Andersen 25
Phil	—	Thrash 57 pass from McNabb (Akers kick)
NYG	—	FG Andersen 32
NYG	—	Dayne 16 run (Barber run)
Phil	—	Lewis 7 pass from McNabb (Akers kick)
Phil	—	FG Akers 35

DENVER 23, OAKLAND 17—at INVESCO Field at Mile High, attendance 75,582. The Broncos held off the Raiders when Kenoy Kennedy intercepted Rich Gannon's pass in the end zone as time ran out. Oakland led 17-13 until Brian Griese and Rod Smith teamed on a 12-yard touchdown pass that gave the Broncos the lead for good at 20-17 with 9:59 left. Jason Elam increased the Broncos' lead to six points with 1:32 to play before the Raiders mounted a last-ditch effort beginning from their 25-yard line. Gannon completed seven consecutive passes to move the ball to Denver's 17 with 16 seconds left. Facing fourth-and-1 from there with seven seconds left,

Kennedy made his game-saving play. Gannon was 35 of 49 for 313 yards and 2 touchdowns, with 2 interceptions. Griese was 19 of 26 for 142 yards and 1 touchdown.

| Oakland | 3 | 7 | 7 | 0 | — | 17 |
| Denver | 3 | 10 | 0 | 10 | — | 23 |

Oak	—	FG Janikowski 28
Den	—	FG Elam 27
Den	—	FG Elam 25
Oak	—	Garner 6 pass from Gannon (Janikowski kick)
Den	—	Griese 5 run (Elam kick)
Oak	—	Brigham 1 pass from Gannon (Janikowski kick)
Den	—	R. Smith 12 pass from Griese (Elam kick)
Den	—	FG Elam 42

CINCINNATI 26, PITTSBURGH 23 (OT)—at Paul Brown Stadium, attendance 63,751. The Bengals stunned the Steelers by overcoming a 13-point deficit in the final 2:46 of regulation and winning on Neil Rackers' 31-yard field goal 10:52 into overtime. Despite losing, the Steelers clinched the top seed in the AFC playoffs when Oakland lost later in the day. Jon Kitna tossed a 6-yard touchdown pass to Ron Dugans with 2:46 left in the fourth quarter to trim Cincinnati's deficit to 23-17, and on fourth-and-goal, Kitna's pass for Corey Dillon fell incomplete, but Cincinnati got a reprieve when Chad Scott was penalized for defensive holding. A penalty against the Bengals on the next play moved the ball back to the 18, but Kitna teamed with Danny Farmer on the tying touchdown pass with 37 seconds to play. The game remained tied when Rackers pushed the extra-point attempt off the right upright. He got off the hook in overtime when the Bengals drove 86 yards from their 1 the first time they had the ball. in overtime, highlighted by Brandon Bennett 's 36-yard run on the second play of the march. Kitna was 35 of 68 for 411 yards and 2 touchdowns, with 1 interception, to help Cincinnati amass 544 total yards against the league's top-ranked defense. Darnay Scott had 113 yards on 7 receptions, while Peter Warrick added 109 yards on 10 catches. Stewart was 19 of 35 for 251 yards and 3 touchdowns, with 4 interceptions, 3 of them coming on consecutive possessions in the fourth quarter. Plaxico Burress caught 6 passes for 102 yards.

| Pittsburgh | 14 | 3 | 6 | 0 | 0 | — | 23 |
| Cincinnati | 0 | 0 | 13 | 3 | 3 | — | 26 |

Pitt	—	Burress 42 pass from Stewart (Brown kick)
Pitt	—	Burress 28 pass from Stewart (Brown kick)
Cin	—	Simmons 56 fumble return (Rackers kick)
Pitt	—	FG Brown 38
Cin	—	FG Rackers 34
Pitt	—	Fuamatu-Ma'afala 37 pass from Stewart (Brown kick)
Cin	—	Dugans 6 pass from Kitna (Rackers kick)
Cin	—	Farmer 18 pass from Kitna (kick failed)
Cin	—	FG Rackers 31

DALLAS 27, SAN FRANCISCO 21—at Texas Stadium, attendance 64,366. Quincy Carter passed for 2 touchdowns and ran for another for the Cowboys. San Francisco led 14-10 at halftime, but Dallas began the third period by driving 75 yards in 10 plays and taking the lead for good on Carter's 1-yard sneak. The next time the Cowboys had the ball, Carter teamed with Joey Galloway on a 47-yard touchdown bomb for a 24-14 advantage. The 49ers narrowed the gap when Jeff Garcia and J.J. Stokes teamed on a 3-yard touchdown pass in the final

minute, but Dallas recovered the ensuing onside kick. Carter was 15 of 25 for a career-best 241 yards, while Emmitt Smith added 26 carries for 126 yards on the ground. Galloway caught 6 passes for 146 yards. Garcia was 21 of 36 for 229 yards and 2 touchdowns.

| San Francisco | 0 | 14 | 0 | 7 | — | 21 |
| Dallas | 0 | 10 | 14 | 3 | — | 27 |

Dall	—	FG Hilbert 22
SF	—	Garcia 6 run (Cortez kick)
Dall	—	Chiaverini 2 pass from Carter (Hilbert kick)
SF	—	Stokes 7 pass from Garcia (Cortez kick)
Dall	—	Carter 1 run (Hilbert kick)
Dall	—	Galloway 47 pass from Carter (Hilbert kick)
Dall	—	FG Hilbert 20
SF	—	Stokes 3 pass from Garcia (Cortez kick)

SEATTLE 25, SAN DIEGO 22—at Qualcomm Stadium, attendance 51,412. Rian Lindell kicked a 54-yard field goal as time expired to keep the Seahawks in the chase for a wild-card playoff berth. The Chargers ended their season with nine consecutive losses after a 5-2 start, and head coach Mike Riley was fired the next day. Steve Christie's fifth field goal of the game, from 36 yards, tied the score at 22-22 with just 16 seconds left to play, apparently forcing overtime. But Seattle averted the extra session when Charlie Rogers returned the ensuing kickoff 64 yards to San Diego's 36 with six seconds to play, and Lindell came on for his winning kick. Trent Dilfer was 14 of 23 for 267 yards and 3 touchdowns. Darrell Jackson caught 5 passes for 114 yards and James Williams had 4 for 101 yards. Doug Flutie was 34 of 53 for 377 yards and 1 touchdown, with 2 interceptions.

| Seattle | 0 | 14 | 8 | 3 | — | 25 |
| San Diego | 10 | 3 | 3 | 6 | — | 22 |

SD	—	Conway 4 pass from Flutie (Christie kick)
SD	—	FG Christie 32
SD	—	FG Christie 25
Sea	—	D. Jackson 43 pass from Dilfer (Lindell kick)
Sea	—	D. Jackson 48 pass from Dilfer (Lindell kick)
SD	—	FG Christie 40
Sea	—	Williams 37 pass from Dilfer (Fauria pass from Dilfer)
SD	—	FG Christie 41
SD	—	FG Christie 36
Sea	—	FG Lindell 54

SUNDAY NIGHT, DECEMBER 30

WASHINGTON 40, NEW ORLEANS 10—at Louisiana Superdome, attendance 70,020. The Redskins spotted New Orleans an early 10-0 lead, then roared back to beat the reeling Saints their third consecutive defeat. Stephen Davis rushed for 111 yards and a touchdown, backup Ki-Jana Carter added 2 scoring runs. The Redskins had only 263 total yards but took advantage of several New Orleans miscues, converting 3 interceptions and a fumble recovery into 13 points and scoring 14 more points after the Saints turned over the ball on downs. New Orleans had been eliminated from playoff consideration when Tampa Bay won a day earlier. Tony Banks was 9 of 15 for 94 yards, with 1 interception. Aaron Brooks was 14 of 28 for 127 yards and 1 touchdown, with 3 interceptions.

| Washington | 0 | 13 | 17 | 10 | — | 40 |
| New Orleans | 10 | 0 | 0 | 0 | — | 10 |

| NO | — | McAllister 22 pass from Brooks (Carney kick) |
| NO | — | FG Carney 29 |

Wash	—	Davis 6 run (Conway kick)
Wash	—	FG Conway 53
Wash	—	FG Conway 22
Wash	—	FG Conway 37
Wash	—	Banks 2 run (Conway kick)
Wash	—	Carter 2 run (Conway kick)
Wash	—	FG Conway 37
Wash	—	Carter 1 run (Conway kick)

SEVENTEENTH WEEK SUMMARIES

American Football Conference

Eastern Division	W	L	T	Pct.	Pts.	OP
New England*	11	5	0	.688	371	272
Miami#	11	5	0	.688	344	290
N.Y. Jets#	10	6	0	.625	308	295
Indianapolis	6	10	0	.375	413	486
Buffalo	3	13	0	.188	265	420
Central Division						
Pittsburgh*	13	3	0	.813	352	212
Baltimore#	10	6	0	.625	303	265
Cleveland	7	9	0	.438	285	319
Tennessee	7	9	0	.438	336	388
Jacksonville	6	10	0	.375	294	286
Cincinnati	6	10	0	.375	226	309
Western Division						
Oakland*	10	6	0	.625	399	327
Seattle	9	7	0	.563	301	324
Denver	8	8	0	.500	340	339
Kansas City	6	10	0	.375	320	344
San Diego	5	11	0	.313	332	321

National Football Conference

Eastern Division	W	L	T	Pct.	Pts.	OP
Philadelphia*	11	5	0	.688	343	208
Washington	8	8	0	.500	256	303
N.Y. Giants	7	9	0	.438	294	321
Arizona	7	9	0	.438	295	343
Dallas	5	11	0	.313	246	338
Central Division						
Chicago*	13	3	0	.813	338	203
Green Bay#	12	4	0	.750	390	266
Tampa Bay#	9	7	0	.563	324	280
Minnesota	5	11	0	.313	290	390
Detroit	2	14	0	.125	270	424
Western Division						
St. Louis*	14	2	0	.875	503	273
San Francisco#	12	4	0	.750	409	282
New Orleans	7	9	0	.438	333	409
Atlanta	7	9	0	.438	291	377
Carolina	1	15	0	.063	253	410

*Clinched division title
#Clinched playoff berth

SUNDAY, JANUARY 6

CHICAGO 33, JACKSONVILLE 13—at Soldier Field, attendance 66,944. Anthony Thomas rushed for 160 yards and 2 touchdowns as the Bears clinched their first division title in 11 years. Thomas had a 2-yard touchdown run to help Chicago forge a 13-0 halftime lead. Keith Traylor then helped put the game away by intercepting Mark Brunell's pass on the Jaguars' first possession of the second half and rumbling 67 yards to set up Jim Miller's 9-yard touchdown pass to David Terrell. Miller was 19 of 28 for 159 yards and 1 touchdown. Brunell was 19 of 36 for 189 yards and 2 touchdowns, with 3 interceptions.

| Jacksonville | 0 | 0 | 6 | 7 | — | 13 |
| Chicago | 3 | 10 | 10 | 10 | — | 33 |

Chi	—	FG Edinger 47
Chi	—	A. Thomas 2 run (Edinger kick)
Chi	—	FG Edinger 23
Chi	—	Terrell 9 pass from Miller (Edinger kick)
Jax	—	McCardell 15 pass from Brunell (kick failed)
Chi	—	FG Edinger 25
Chi	—	FG Edinger 22
Chi	—	A. Thomas 2 run (Edinger kick)

Jax — J. Smith 3 pass from Brunell
(Holmes kick)

CINCINNATI 23, TENNESSEE 21—at Adelphia Coliseum, attendance 68,798. Neil Rackers kicked a 34-yard field goal with 20 seconds remaining to lift the Bengals to the victory. Cincinnati rallied from a 14-0 first-half deficit to take a 20-14 lead , but Neil O'Donnell, who relieved starter Steve McNair in the second half, put the Titans back on top with a 35-yard touchdown pass to Derrick Mason in the final minute of the third quarter. However, Jon Kitna teamed with Darnay Scott on a 39-yard completion to set up Rackers' winning kick. Kitna was 28 of 47 for 340 yards, with 1 interception. Scott had 9 catches for 152 yards. McNair was 11 of 18 for 173 yards and 1 touchdown and O'Donnell was 7 of 14 for 134 yards and 1 touchdown. Mason caught 9 passes for 186 yards.

Cincinnati	0	14	6	3 —	23
Tennessee	7	7	7	0 —	21

Tenn	—	Mason 41 pass from McNair (Nedney kick)
Tenn	—	McNair 6 run (Nedney kick)
Cin	—	Dillon 2 run (Rackers kick)
Cin	—	Dillon 34 run (Rackers kick)
Cin	—	FG Rackers 30
Cin	—	FG Rackers 33
Tenn	—	Mason 35 pass from O'Donnell (Nedney kick)
Cin	—	FG Rackers 34

DETROIT 15, DALLAS 10—at Pontiac Silverdome, attendance 77,512. Ty Detmer passed for 2 touchdowns, including the winning, 16-yard strike to Johnnie Morton with 5:37 left, as Detroit won for only the second time this season. A bobbled snap on the extra-point attempt had the Lions facing a 10-9 deficit when they began possession on their 34-yard line with 9:08 left in the game. Cory Schlesinger (20 yards) and Aveion Cason (19 yards) reeled off long runs as Detroit quickly moved into Cowboys' territory, and Detmer capped the 6-play, 66-yard drive with the go-ahead touchdown pass to Morton. Detmer was 24 of 40 for 242 yards and 2 touchdowns. Emmitt Smith became the first player to rush for 1,000 yards in 11 consecutive seasons. The game was the last to be played at the Pontiac Silverdome, which had housed the Lions since 1974.

Dallas	0	7	0	3 —	10
Detroit	0	6	3	6 —	15

Dall	—	Smith 2 run (Hilbert kick)
Det	—	Sloan 20 pass from Detmer (pass failed)
Det	—	FG Hanson 47
Dall	—	FG Hilbert 33
Det	—	Morton 16 from Detmer (pass failed)

GREEN BAY 34, N.Y. GIANTS 25—at Giants Stadium, attendance 78,601. Brett Favre passed for 2 touchdowns and Ahman Green ran for 2 touchdowns to pace the Packers. It was 17-10 at halftime before Green Bay broke open the game with 17 points in the third quarter. On consecutive possessions, Green ran 1 yard for a touchdown, Ryan Longwell kicked a 43-yard field goal, and Favre teamed with Corey Bradford on a 54-yard touchdown pass to make it 34-10. Favre was 15 of 30 for 315 yards and 2 touchdowns. Green ran for 101 yards on 23 carries, while Schroeder had 5 catches for 102 yards and Bradford 3 for 111. Collins was 36 of 59 for 386 yards and 2 touchdowns, with 2 interceptions. Michael Strahan sacked Favre with 2:42 left in the game to break Mark Gastineau's 17-year-old NFL record for sacks in a season. Strahan finished with 22 1/2 sacks. Gastineau had 22 sacks

in 1984.

Green Bay	14	3	17	0 —	34
N.Y. Giants	7	3	0	15 —	25

GB	—	Schroeder 26 pass from Favre (Longwell kick)
GB	—	Green 25 run (Longwell kick)
NYG	—	Hilliard 8 pass from Collins (Andersen kick)
NYG	—	FG Andersen 27
GB	—	FG Longwell 44
GB	—	Green 1 run (Longwell kick)
GB	—	FG Longwell 43
GB	—	Bradford 54 pass from Favre (Longwell kick)
NYG	—	Barber 10 run (Andersen kick)
NYG	—	Dayne 1 run (Dayne run)

INDIANAPOLIS 29, DENVER 10—at RCA Dome, attendance 56,192. Peyton Manning and Marvin Harrison teamed on a pair of touchdown passes as the Colts concluded a disappointing season. Indianapolis led just 9-7 before Manning capped a 12-play, 89-yard drive with a 20-yard touchdown pass to Harrison 4:20 before halftime. Ryan Phillips intercepted Brian Griese on the next play from scrimmage, leading to Mike Vanderjagt's fourth field goal of the first half and to give the Colts a 19-7 lead at the intermission. Manning was 16 of 30 for 191 yards and 2 touchdowns, with 1 interception. Harrison had 9 catches for 128 yards. Rookie Dominic Rhodes rushed for 141 yards to finish with 1,104 yards despite starting just 10 games. Indianapolis finished the season just 6-10, and head coach Jim Mora was fired two days later. Griese was 16 of 32 for 151 yards and 1 touchdown, with 4 interceptions.

Denver	0	7	3	0 —	10
Indianapolis	9	10	3	7 —	29

Ind	—	FG Vanderjagt 22
Ind	—	FG Vanderjagt 40
Ind	—	FG Vanderjagt 45
Den	—	Clark 1 pass from Griese (Elam kick)
Ind	—	Harrison 20 pass from Manning (Vanderjagt kick)
Ind	—	FG Vanderjagt 22
Ind	—	FG Vanderjagt 25
Den	—	FG Elam 25
Ind	—	Harrison 43 pass from Manning (Vanderjagt kick)

MIAMI 34, BUFFALO 7—at Pro Player Stadium, attendance 73,428. Lamar Smith ran for 158 yards and a touchdown to help the Dolphins. It was 13-7 before the Dolphins put the game out of reach with touchdowns on consecutive possessions to open the fourth quarter. Jay Fiedler tossed a 16-yard touchdown pass to James McKnight three plays into the final quarter, then capped a 43-yard drive following Scott Galyon's interception with an 18-yard touchdown run with 8:03 to play. The Dolphins entered the game aware that New England's victory earlier in the day ended their chance at a division title, but they still needed to win to assure themselves of playing a wild-card game at home. Fiedler was 9 of 16 for 110 yards and 1 touchdown. Travis Brown, who relieved injured Alex Van Pelt, was 15 of 33 for 201 yards and 1 touchdown, with 2 interceptions.

Buffalo	0	0	7	0 —	7
Miami	3	10	0	21 —	34

Mia	—	FG Mare 22
Mia	—	L. Smith 6 run (Mare kick)
Mia	—	FG Mare 20
Buff	—	Centers 12 pass from T. Brown (Graham kick)
Mia	—	McKnight 16 pass from Fiedler (Mare kick)

Mia	—	Fiedler 18 run (Mare kick)
Mia	—	Marion 100 interception return (Mare kick)

NEW ENGLAND 38, CAROLINA 6—at Ericsson Stadium, attendance 21,070. The Patriots clinched the AFC East title by winning their sixth consecutive game as the Panthers became the first team in NFL history to lose fifteen consecutive games within one season. New England scored touchdowns via rushing, passing, on defense, and on special teams in the rout. Troy Brown helped break open the game by returning a punt 68 yards for a touchdown midway through the third quarter, and Antowain Smith added a 32-yard touchdown run for a 24-6 lead. Tom Brady's 5-yard touchdown pass to Jermaine Wiggins and Otis Smith's 76-yard interception return for a touchdown punctuated New England's victory. Brady was 17 of 29 for 198 yards and 1 touchdown, with 2 interceptions. Weinke was 15 of 36 for 144 yards, with 3 interceptions. Richard Huntley rushed for a club-record 168 yards for the Panthers.

New England	10	0	14	14 —	38
Carolina	0	3	3	0 —	6

NE	—	FG Vinatieri 19
NE	—	Law 46 interception return (Vinatieri kick)
Car	—	FG Kasay 29
NE	—	T. Brown 68 punt return (Vinatieri kick)
Car	—	FG Kasay 40
NE	—	A. Smith 32 run (Vinatieri kick)
NE	—	Wiggins 5 pass from Brady (Vinatieri kick)
NE	—	O. Smith 76 interception return (Vinatieri kick)

N.Y. JETS 24, OAKLAND 22—at Network Associates Coliseum, attendance 62,011. John Hall kicked a 53-yard field goal with 59 seconds left to give the Jets a dramatic victory that lifted them into the playoffs. Brad Daluiso, signed earlier in the week to replace injured Sebastian Janikowski, kicked 3 field goals but also missed a 28-yard try and an extra-point attempt. Daluiso had given the Raiders a 22-21 lead by kicking a 37-yard field goal with 6:05 left, before Hall drilled his winning kick. Testaverde was 18 of 29 for 230 yards and 1 touchdown, with 2 interceptions, and Coles caught 5 passes for 111 yards for the Jets, who earned a return trip to Oakland the following week for a wild-card playoff game. Rich Gannon was 23 of 38 for 224 yards and 1 touchdown for the Raiders, whose third consecutive loss cost them a bye in the opening round of the postseason.

N.Y. Jets	7	7	7	3 —	24
Oakland	3	13	3	3 —	22

NYJ	—	Coles 40 pass from Testaverde (Hall kick)
Oak	—	FG Daluiso 23
Oak	—	Wheatley 3 run (kick failed)
NYJ	—	J. Glenn 4 blocked punt return (Hall kick)
Oak	—	R. Williams 18 pass from Gannon (Daluiso kick)
Oak	—	FG Daluiso 44
NYJ	—	L. Jordan 46 run (Hall kick)
Oak	—	FG Daluiso 37
NYJ	—	FG Hall 53

PITTSBURGH 28, CLEVELAND 7—at Heinz Field, attendance 59,189. Troy Edwards returned a fumble for a touchdown to spark the Steelers to the victory. Edwards, a backup wide receiver playing on special teams, picked up the loose ball on the second half's opening kickoff and returned it for a touchdown to put Pittsburgh ahead for good just 16 seconds into the third quarter. Backup quarterback Tommy Maddox added a 40-yard touchdown pass to Bobby Shaw and reserve running back R.J. Bowers added a 21-yard, fourth-quarter touchdown run to help break open the game. The Steelers, already having clinched the AFC Central division title and the top seed in the conference playoffs, went with reserves much of the game. Kordell Stewart was 8 of 16 for 72 yards, with 2 interceptions, and Maddox was 6 of 8 for 97 yards and 1 touchdown, with 1 intercepiton. Chris Fuamatu-Ma'afala rushed for 98 yards. Tim Couch was 13 of 26 for 150 yards, with 2 inteceptions.

Cleveland	7	0	0	0	—	7
Pittsburgh	0	7	14	7	—	28

Cle	—	White 3 run (P. Dawson kick)
Pitt	—	Fuamatu-Ma'afala 17 run (K. Brown kick)
Pitt	—	Edwards 32 fumble return (K. Brown kick)
Pitt	—	Shaw 40 pass from Maddox (K. Brown kick)
Pitt	—	Bowers 21 run (K. Brown kick)

ST. LOUIS 31, ATLANTA 13—at Dome at America's Center, attendance 66,033. The Rams secured the top seed in the NFC playoffs with another overwhelming offensive performance. Kurt Warner passed for 280 yards and 3 touchdowns and Marshall Faulk rushed for 168 yards and a touchdown for St. Louis, which amassed 458 total yards. Warner was 25 of 30 for 280 yards and 3 touchdowns, with 3 interceptions, and ended the season with 4,830 passing yards, the second-highest total in NFL history. Faulk had 226 yards from scrimmage to finish the year at 2,147. He became the first player to surpass 2,000 yards four consecutive seasons. Michael Vick was 12 of 30 for 176 yards and rushed for 58 yards in his second career start. But he also suffered an interception, lost 2 fumbles, and was sacked 7 times.

Atlanta	0	6	7	0	—	13
St. Louis	10	7	14	0	—	31

StL	—	FG Wilkins 24
StL	—	Proehl 12 pass from Warner (Wilkins kick)
Atl	—	FG Feely 49
StL	—	Conwell 15 pass from Warner (Wilkins kick)
Atl	—	FG Feely 33
StL	—	Faulk 3 run (Wilkins kick)
Atl	—	Vaughn 96 kickoff return (Feely kick)
StL	—	Proehl 8 pass from Warner (Wilkins kick)

SAN FRANCISCO 38, NEW ORLEANS 0—at Louisiana Superdome, attendance 70,020. Jeff Garcia passed for 263 yards and 4 touchdowns for the 49ers. The game was scoreless until Garcia and Terrell Owens teamed on a 56-yard touchdown pass midway through the first quarter. The next time San Francisco got the ball, the two combined on a 60-yard touchdown strike, and the rout was on. The 49ers' defense forced 6 turnovers, permitted only 11 first downs and 126 total yards, and recorded their third shutout in six weeks. The Saints ended the season with four losses in which then allowed 160 points. Garcia was 14 of 21 for 263 yards and 4 touchdowns. Aaron Brooks was 21 of 33 for 119 yards, with 4 interceptions.

San Francisco	14	7	3	14	—	38
New Orleans	0	0	0	0	—	0

SF	—	Owens 56 pass from Garcia (Cortez kick)
SF	—	Owens 60 pass from Garcia (Cortez kick)
SF	—	T. Jackson 6 pass from Garcia (Cortez kick)
SF	—	FG Cortez 39
SF	—	Stokes 6 pass from Garcia (Cortez kick)
SF	—	T. Jackson 9 run (Cortez kick)

SEATTLE 21, KANSAS CITY 18—at Husky Stadium, attendance 58,460. Trent Dilfer passed for 2 touchdowns to lead the Seahawks past the Chiefs, but the victory wasn't enough to carry Seattle to the playoffs. Its wild-card hopes were dashed when the New York Jets edged Oakland Sunday and Baltimore beat Minnesota Monday night. Dilfer staked the Seahawks to a 14-0 lead with touchdown passes of 12 and 18 yards to Darrell Jackson, and Shaun Alexander raced 44 yards for a touchdown with 39 seconds left in the third quarter to give Seattle a 21-10 advantage. Dilfer was 22 of 38 for 248 yards and 2 touchdowns, with 2 interceptions, while winning for the fifteenth consecutive time as a starter. Alexander rushed for 127 yards. Green was 15 of 33 for 184 yards and 1 touchdown, with 1 interception. Priest Holmes ran for 117 yards for the Chiefs.

Kansas City	0	0	10	8	—	18
Seattle	0	14	7	0	—	21

Sea	—	Jackson 12 pass from Dilfer (Lindell kick)
Sea	—	Jackson 18 pass from Dilfer (Lindell kick)
KC	—	Ricks 1 pass from Green (Peterson kick)
KC	—	FG Peterson 27
Sea	—	S. Alexander 44 run (Lindell kick)
KC	—	Richardson 1 run (Kennison pass from Green)

WASHINGTON 20, ARIZONA 17—at FedEx Field, attendance 61,721. Stephen Davis rushed for 148 yards, including the winning, 2-yard touchdown with 3:11 left, as the Redskins came from behind to finish the season at .500. Arizona led 17-6 before the Redskins mounted a comeback. Banks was 13 of 25 for 154 yards and 1 touchdown, with 1 interception. Davis finished the game with a career-high 38 carries. Plummer was 11 of 25 for 154 yards, with 1 interception.

Arizona	7	10	0	0	—	17
Washington	0	6	6	8	—	20

Ariz	—	Wilson 61 interception return (Oglesby kick)
Wash	—	FG Conway 36
Ariz	—	Jones 4 run (Oglesby kick)
Wash	—	FG Conway 33
Ariz	—	FG Oglesby 26
Wash	—	Rasby 5 pass from Banks (pass failed)
Wash	—	Davis 2 run (Davis run)

SUNDAY NIGHT, JANUARY 6
PHILADELPHIA 17, TAMPA BAY 13—at Raymond James Stadium, attendance 65,541. Rookie third-string quarterback A.J. Feeley threw 2 touchdown passes to Dameane Douglas in a 26-second span late in the fourth quarter to rally the Eagles. The Buccaneers led 13-3 until Feeley completed 5 of 6 passes on a 61-yard drive capped by his 2-yard touchdown pass to Douglas with 2:12 remaining in the game. Karl Williams then fumbled the ensuing kickoff, and Philadelphia's Tim Hauck recovered at the Buccaneers' 24-yard line. After an incomplete pass, Feeley and Douglas teamed on the go-ahead touchdown pass with 1:46 left. With the Eagles and Buccaneers locked into playoff position and slated to play each other in Philadelphia the following weekend, the two teams rested many of their starters. Feeley was 10 of 14 for 143 yards and 2 touch-

downs, with 1 interception, in his first NFL action. King was 19 of 28 for 148 yards, with 1 interception, in relief of starter Brad Johnson, who led the Buccaneers to a 3-0 only series.

Philadelphia	0	3	0	14	—	17
Tampa Bay	3	10	0	0	—	13

TB	—	FG Brien 42
TB	—	Stecker 4 run (Brien kick)
Phil	—	FG Akers 47
TB	—	FG Brien 23
Phil	—	D. Douglas 2 pass from Feeley (Akers kick)
Phil	—	D. Douglas 24 pass from Feeley (Akers kick)

MONDAY NIGHT, JANUARY 7
BALTIMORE 19, MINNESOTA 3—at PSINet Stadium, attendance 69,465. The Ravens earned the right to defend their Super Bowl XXXV championship by securing the last AFC wild-card playoff berth with the victory. Jamie Sharper returned a fumble 8 yards for a touchdown for Baltimore, whose win eliminated Seattle from postseason consideration. The Seahawks had remained in the chase by beating Kansas City on Sunday. But after spotting Minnesota, playing its first game under new coach Mike Tice after Dennis Green was fired earlier in the week, a first-quarter field goal, the Ravens shut down the Vikings. Terry Allen gained 133 yards on 23 carries. The game's lone touchdown came when Peter Boulware sacked Spergon Wynn late in the fourth quarter and forced Wynn to fumble. Jamie Sharper picked up the loose ball and ran 8 yards for the score with 1:37 to play. Elvis Grbac was 10 of 27 for 160 yards. Wynn was 13 of 29 passes for 86 yards, with 2 interceptions.

Minnesota	3	0	0	0	—	3
Baltimore	0	9	3	7	—	19

Minn	—	FG Anderson 26
Balt	—	FG Stover 21
Balt	—	FG Stover 20
Balt	—	FG Stover 38
Balt	—	FG Stover 20
Balt	—	Sharper 8 fumble return (Stover kick)

For postseason summaries, please refer to the following—the playoff summaries are located on pages 508-518, the Super Bowl summary on 496, and the Pro Bowl summary on 519.

2001 PRO FOOTBALL AWARDS

ASSOCIATED PRESS
Most Valuable Player	Kurt Warner
Offensive Player of the Year	Marshall Faulk
Defensive Player of the Year	Michael Strahan
Offensive Rookie of the Year	Anthony Thomas
Defensive Rookie of the Year	Kendrell Bell
Coach of the Year	Dick Jauron
Comeback Player of the Year	Garrison Hearst

THE SPORTING NEWS
Player of the Year	Marshall Faulk
Rookie of the Year	Kendrell Bell
Coach of the Year	Dick Jauron

THE FOOTBALL NEWS
Offensive Player of the Year	Curtis Martin (AFC)
	Marshall Faulk (NFC)
Defensive Player of the Year	Ray Lewis (AFC)
	Brian Urlacher (NFC)
Coach of the Year	Bill Cowher (AFC)
	Dick Jauron (NFC)
Offensive Rookie of the Year	Chris Chambers
Defensive Rookie of the Year	Kendrell Bell

PRO FOOTBALL WEEKLY/PFWA
Executive of the Year	Charlie Armey
Most Valuable Player	Marshall Faulk
Defensive Most Valuable Player	Michael Strahan
Offensive Rookie of the Year	Anthony Thomas
Defensive Rookie of the Year	Kendrell Bell
Coach of the Year	Dick Jauron
Assistant Coach of the Year	Mike Mularkey
Golden Toe	Todd Sauerbrun
Comeback Player of the Year	Garrison Hearst
Most Improved Player of the Year	Kordell Stewart

FOOTBALL DIGEST
Offensive Player of the Year	Kurt Warner
Defensive Player of the Year	Brian Urlacher
Offensive Rookie of the Year	Chris Chambers
Defensive Rookie of the Year	Kendrell Bell
Coach of the Year	Dick Jauron
Comeback Player of the Year	Garrison Hearst
Rookie Coach of the Year	Butch Davis

SPORTS ILLUSTRATED
Player of the Year	Marshall Faulk
Coach of the Year	Dick Jauron
Rookie of the Year	Kendrell Bell

COLLEGE & PRO FOOTBALL NEWSWEEKLY
Offensive Player of the Year	Marshall Faulk
Defensive Player of the Year	Michael Strahan
Coach of the Year	Bill Belichick

MAXWELL CLUB PLAYER OF THE YEAR
(Bert Bell Trophy)	Marshall Faulk

MAXWELL CLUB COACH OF THE YEAR
(Earle "Greasy" Neale Trophy)	Dick Jauron

MILLER LITE AWARD
Player of the Year	Marshall Faulk

WALTER PAYTON/NFL MAN OF THE YEAR
Man of the Year	Jerome Bettis

SUPER BOWL MOST VALUABLE PLAYER
Pete Rozelle Trophy	Tom Brady

AFC-NFC PRO BOWL PLAYER OF THE GAME
Dan McGuire Award	Rich Gannon

2001 ALL-PRO TEAMS

2001 PFW/PFWA ALL-PRO TEAM
Selected by *Pro Football Weekly* and the Professional Football Writers of America

Offense:
Kurt Warner, St. Louis	Quarterback
Marshall Faulk, St. Louis	Running Back
Curtis Martin, New York Jets	Running Back
David Boston, Arizona	Wide Receiver
Terrell Owens, San Francisco	Wide Receiver
Tony Gonzalez, Kansas City	Tight End
Jonathan Ogden, Balitmore	Tackle
Orlando Pace, St. Louis	Tackle
Larry Allen, Dallas	Guard
Alan Faneca, Pittsburgh	Guard
Kevin Mawae, New York Jets	Center

Defense:
John Abraham, New York Jets	End
Michael Strahan, New York Giants	End
Warren Sapp, Tampa Bay	Tackle
Sam Adams, Baltimore	Tackle
Jason Gildon, Pittsburgh	Linebacker
Jamir Miller, Cleveland	Linebacker
Brian Urlacher, Chicago	Linebacker
Ronde Barber, Tampa Bay	Cornerback
Aeneas Williams, St. Louis	Cornerback
John Lynch, Tampa Bay	Safety
Brian Dawkins, Philadelphia	Safety

Special Teams:
David Akers, Philadelphia	Kicker
Todd Sauerbrun, Carolina	Punter
Steve Smith, Carolina	Kick Returner
Troy Brown, New England	Punt Returner
Larry Whigham, Chicago	Special Teams Player

2001 ASSOCIATED PRESS ALL-PRO TEAM
Selected by the *Associated Press*

Offense:
Kurt Warner, St. Louis	Quarterback
Marshall Faulk, St. Louis	Running Back
Priest Holmes, Kansas City	Running Back
David Boston, Arizona	Wide Receiver
Terrell Owens, San Francisco	Wide Receiver
Tony Gonzalez, Kansas City	Tight End
Orlando Pace, St. Louis	Tackle
Walter Jones, Seattle	Tackle
Larry Allen, Dallas	Guard
Alan Faneca, Pittsburgh	Guard
Kevin Mawae, New York Jets	Center

Defense:
Michael Strahan, New York Giants	End
John Abraham, New York Jets	End
Warren Sapp, Tampa Bay	Tackle
Ted Washington, Chicago	Tackle
Jamir Miller, Cleveland	Linebacker
Jason Gildon, Pittsburgh	Linebacker
Ray Lewis, Baltimore	Linebacker
Brian Urlacher, Chicago	Linebacker
Ronde Barber, Tampa Bay	Cornerback
Aeneas Williams, St. Louis	Cornerback
Brian Dawkins, Philadelphia	Safety
Mike Brown, Chicago	Safety

Specialists:

David Akers, Philadelphia	Kicker
Steve Smith, Carolina	Kick Returner
Todd Sauerbrun, Carolina	Punter

2001 ALL-NFL TEAM

Selected by the *Associated Press*, *Pro Football Weekly*, and the Professional Football Writers of America

Offense:

Kurt Warner, St. Louis (AP, PFW)	Quarterback
Marshall Faulk, St. Louis (AP, PFW)	Running Back
Priest Holmes, Kansas City (AP)	Running Back
Curtis Martin, New York Jets (PFW)	Running Back
David Boston, Arizona (AP, PFW)	Wide Receiver
Terrell Owens, San Francisco (AP, PFW)	Wide Receiver
Tony Gonzalez, Kansas City (AP, PFW)	Tight End
Orlando Pace, St. Louis (AP, PFW)	Tackle
Walter Jones, Seattle (AP)	Tackle
Jonathan Ogden, Balitmore (PFW)	Tackle
Larry Allen, Dallas (AP, PFW)	Guard
Alan Faneca, Pittsburgh (AP, PFW)	Guard
Kevin Mawae, New York Jets (AP, PFW)	Center

Defense:

John Abraham, New York Jets (AP, PFW)	End
Michael Strahan, New York Giants (AP, PFW)	End
Warren Sapp, Tampa Bay (AP, PFW)	Tackle
Ted Washington, Chicago (AP)	Tackle
Sam Adams, Baltimore (PFW)	Tackle
Jason Gildon, Pittsburgh (AP, PFW)	Linebacker
Jamir Miller, Cleveland (AP, PFW)	Linebacker
Brian Urlacher, Chicago (AP, PFW)	Linebacker
Ray Lewis, Baltimore (AP)	Linebacker
Ronde Barber, Tampa Bay (AP, PFW)	Cornerback
Aeneas Williams, St. Louis (AP, PFW)	Cornerback
Brian Dawkins, Philadelphia (AP, PFW)	Safety
Mike Brown, Chicago (AP)	Safety
John Lynch, Tampa Bay (PFW)	Safety

Special Teams:

David Akers, Philadelphia (AP, PFW)	Kicker
Todd Sauerbrun, Carolina (AP, PFW)	Punter
Steve Smith, Carolina (AP, PFW)	Kick Returner
Troy Brown, New England (PFW)	Punt Returner
Larry Whigham, Chicago (PFW)	Special Teams Player

2001 FOOTBALL NEWS ALL-AFC TEAM

Selected by *Football News*

Offense:

Rich Gannon, Oakland	Quarterback
Priest Holmes, Kansas City	Running Back
Curtis Martin, New York Jets	Running Back
Hines Ward, Pittsburgh	Wide Receiver
Marvin Harrison, Indianapolis	Wide Receiver
Tony Gonzalez, Kansas City	Tight End
Walter Jones, Seattle	Tackle
Jonathan Ogden, Baltimore	Tackle
Alan Faneca, Pittsburgh	Guard
Will Shields, Kansas City	Guard
Kevin Mawae, New York Jets	Center

Defense:

Marcellus Wiley, San Diego	End
John Abraham, New York Jets	End
Trevor Pryce, Denver	Tackle
Sam Adams, Baltimore	Tackle
Jason Gildon, Pittsburgh	Linebacker
Joey Porter, Pittsburgh	Linebacker
Ray Lewis, Baltimore	Linebacker
Charles Woodson, Oakland	Cornerback
Ty Law, New England	Cornerback
Rodney Harrison, San Diego	Safety
Lawyer Milloy, New England	Safety

Specialists:

Troy Brown, New England	Punt Returner
Matt Turk, Miami	Punter
Ronney Jenkins, San Diego	Kick Returner
Jason Elam, Denver	Kicker

2001 FOOTBALL NEWS ALL-NFC TEAM

Offense:

Kurt Warner, St. Louis	Quarterback
Marshall Faulk, St. Louis	Running Back
Ahman Green, Green Bay	Running Back
David Boston, Arizona	Wide Receiver
Terrell Owens, San Francisco	Wide Receiver
Byron Chamberlain, Minnesota	Tight End
Orlando Pace, St. Louis	Tackle
James Williams, Chicago	Tackle
Larry Allen, Dallas	Guard
Ray Brown, San Francisco	Guard
Matt Birk, Minnesota	Center

Defense:

Michael Strahan, New York Giants	End
Hugh Douglas, Philadelphia	End
Ted Washington, Chicago	Tackle
Bryant Young, San Francisco	Tackle
Derrick Brooks, Tampa Bay	Linebacker
LaVar Arrington, Washington	Linebacker
Brian Urlacher, Chicago	Linebacker
Aeneas Williams, St. Louis	Cornerback
Troy Vincent, Philadelphia	Cornerback
Mike Brown, Chicago	Safety
Brian Dawkins, Philadelphia	Safety

Specialists:

Darrien Gordon, Atlanta	Punt Returner
Todd Sauerbrun, Carolina	Punter
Steve Smith, Carolina	Kick Returner
David Akers, Philadelphia	Kicker

2001 PFW/PFWA ALL-ROOKIE TEAM

Selected by *Pro Football Weekly* and the Professional Football Writers of America

Offense:

Chris Weinke, Carolina	Quarterback
Anthony Thomas, Chicago	Running Back
LaDainian Tomlinson, San Diego	Running Back
Chris Chambers, Miami	Wide Receiver
Rod Gardner, Washington	Wide Receiver
Eric Johnson, San Francisco	Tight End
Jeff Backus, Detroit	Tackle
Kenyatta Walker, Tampa Bay	Tackle
Leonard Davis, Arizona	Guard
Steve Hutchinson, Detroit	Guard
Dominic Raiola, Detroit	Center

Defense:

Justin Smith, Cincinnati	Lineman
Shaun Rogers, Detroit	Lineman
Richard Seymour, New England	Lineman
Gerard Warren, Cleveland	Lineman
Kendrell Bell, Pittsburgh	Linebacker
Dan Morgan, Carolina	Linebacker
Tommy Polley, St. Louis	Linebacker
Anthony Henry, Cleveland	Cornerback
Fred Smoot, Washington	Cornerback
Adam Archuleta, St. Louis	Safety
Idrees Bashir, Indianapolis	Safety

Special Teams:

Jay Feely, Atlanta	Kicker
Jason Baker, San Francisco	Punter
Steve Smith, Carolina	Kick Returner
Steve Smith, Carolina	Punt Returner
Jamie Winborn, San Francisco	Special Teams Player

2001 PLAYERS OF THE WEEK/MONTH

2001 AFC PLAYERS OF THE WEEK

	Offense	Defense	Special Teams
Week 1	QB Brian Griese, Denver	LB Zach Thomas, Miami	KR Tim Dwight, San Diego
Week 2	QB Peyton Manning, Indianapolis	LB Takeo Spikes, Cincinnati	K Wade Richey, San Diego
Week 3	RB Priest Holmes, Kansas City	S Corey Harris, Baltimore	K Phil Dawson, Cleveland
Week 4	RB Shaun Alexander, Seattle	CB Deltha O'Neal, Denver	P Matt Turk, Miami
Week 5	QB Tom Brady, New England	LB Marvin Jones, New York Jets	K Joe Nedney, Tennessee
Week 6	WR David Patten, New England	LB Joey Porter, Pittsburgh	K Joe Nedney, Tennessee
Week 7	RB Corey Dillon, Cincinnati	CB Denard Walker, Denver	P Tom Tupa, New York Jets
Week 8	QB Steve McNair, Tennessee	DE John Abraham, New York Jets	K Matt Stover, Baltimore
Week 9	RB Shaun Alexander, Seattle	LB Jason Gildon, Pittsburgh	P Tom Rouen, Denver
Week 10	QB Rich Gannon, Oakland	CB Anthony Henry, Cleveland	KR Derrick Mason, Tennessee
Week 11	QB Tom Brady, New England	LB William Thomas, Oakland	KR Troy Edwards, Pittsburgh
Week 12	QB Steve McNair, Tennessee	DE Adalius Thomas, Baltimore	P Matt Turk, Miami
Week 13	RB Priest Holmes, Kansas City	S Brock Marion, Miami	PR Tim Brown, Oakland
Week 14	QB Kordell Stewart, Pittsburgh	LB William Thomas, Oakland	K Adam Vinatieri, New England
Week 15	QB Vinny Testaverde, New York Jets	LB Ray Lewis, Baltimore	P Ken Walter, New England
Week 16	QB Jon Kitna, Cincinnati	LB Zach Thomas, Miami	KR Charlie Rogers, Seattle
Week 17	RB Lamar Smith, Miami	LB Peter Boulware, Baltimore	K John Hall, New York Jets

2001 AFC PLAYERS OF THE MONTH

	Offense	Defense	Special Teams
September	QB Brian Griese, Denver	CB Ryan McNeil, San Diego	K Sebastian Janikowski, Oakland
October	RB Jerome Bettis, Pittsburgh	CB Deltha O'Neal, Denver	KR Ronney Jenkins, San Diego
November	QB Rich Gannon, Oakland	DE John Abraham, New York Jets	K Jason Elam, Denver
December	QB Kordell Stewart, Pittsburgh	S Brock Marion, Miami	PR Troy Brown, New England

2001 NFC PLAYERS OF THE WEEK

	Offense	Defense	Special Teams
Week 1	RB Ahman Green, Green Bay	S Sammy Knight, New Orleans	K Jose Cortez, San Francisco
Week 2	RB Jamal Anderson, Atlanta	LB London Fletcher, St. Louis	P Sean Landeta, Philadelphia
Week 3	QB Kurt Warner, St. Louis	DE Michael Strahan, New York Giants	LB K.D. Williams, Green Bay
Week 4	RB Ricky Williams, New Orleans	LB Brian Urlacher, Chicago	K John Carney, New Orleans
Week 5	QB Brett Favre, Green Bay	DE Michael Strahan, New York Giants	K Tim Seder, Dallas
Week 6	WR Rod Gardner, Washington	LB Keith Brooking, Atlanta	P Todd Sauerbrun, Carolina
Week 7	QB Shane Matthews, Chicago	S Sammy Knight, New Orleans	K John Carney, New Orleans
Week 8	RB Ahman Green, Green Bay	S Mike Brown, Chicago	KR Brian Mitchell, Philadelphia
Week 9	QB Jeff Garcia, San Francisco	CB Ronde Barber, Tampa Bay	PR Darrien Gordon, Atlanta
Week 10	WR Randy Moss, Minnesota	LB London Fletcher, St. Louis	K David Akers, Philadelphia
Week 11	RB Garrison Hearst, San Francisco	DT Warren Sapp, Tampa Bay	K Bill Gramatica, Arizona
Week 12	QB Kurt Warner, St. Louis	S Mike Brown, Chicago	K Bill Gramatica, Arizona
			K Martin Gramatica, Tampa Bay
Week 13	QB Todd Bouman, Minnesota	CB Aeneas Williams, St. Louis	P Sean Landeta, Philadelphia
Week 14	RB Anthony Thomas, Chicago	DE Grant Wistrom, St. Louis	PR Darrien Gordon, Atlanta
Week 15	QB Chris Chandler, Atlanta	CB Ronde Barber, Tampa Bay	LB Brian Urlacher, Chicago
Week 16	QB Quincy Carter, Dallas	LB Derrick Brooks, Tampa Bay	TE Todd Yoder, Tampa Bay
Week 17	RB Marshall Faulk, St. Louis	DE Andre Carter, San Francisco	KR Dorsey Levens, Green Bay

2001 NFC PLAYERS OF THE MONTH

	Offense	Defense	Special Teams
September	RB Marshall Faulk, St. Louis	DE Kabeer Gbaja-Biamila, Green Bay	P Rodney Williams, New York Giants
October	RB Ricky Williams, New Orleans	DE Michael Strahan, New York Giants	K John Carney, New Orleans
November	QB Jeff Garcia, San Francisco	S Kwamie Lassiter, Arizona	P Brad Maynard, Chicago
December	RB Marshall Faulk, St. Louis	DE Simeon Rice, Tampa Bay	P Todd Sauerbrun, Carolina

2001 PLAYOFF PLAYERS OF THE WEEK

Round	Offense	Defense	Special Teams
Wild Card	WR Jerry Rice, Oakland	S Damon Moore, Philadelphia	P Josh Bidwell, Green Bay
Divisional	QB Donovan McNabb, Philadelphia	CB Aeneas Williams, St. Louis	K Adam Vinatieri, New England
Championship	RB Marshall Faulk, St. Louis	DE Grant Wistrom, St. Louis	PR Troy Brown, New England

2001 NFL ROOKIES OF THE MONTH

	Offense (College)	Defense (College)
September	RB LaDainian Tomlinson, San Diego (Texas Christian)	CB Fred Smoot, Washington (Mississippi State)
October	RB Anthony Thomas, Chicago (Michigan)	LB Kendrell Bell, Pittsburgh (Georgia)
November	WR Chris Chambers, Miami (Wisconsin)	LB Kendrell Bell, Pittsburgh (Georgia)
December	RB Dominic Rhodes, Indianapolis (Midwestern State)	DE Andre Carter, San Francisco (California)

TEN BEST RUSHING PERFORMANCES, 2001

	Att.	Yards	TD
1. Shaun Alexander	35	266	3
Seattle vs. Oakland, Nov. 11			
2. Marshall Faulk	30	202	2
St. Louis vs. Carolina, Dec. 23			
3. Trung Canidate	23	195	2
St. Louis vs. New York Jets, Oct. 21			
4. Anthony Thomas	22	188	1
Chicago vs. Cincinnati, Oct. 21			
5. Corey Dillon	27	184	2
Cincinnati vs. Detroit, Oct. 28			
6. Marshall Faulk	15	183	2
St. Louis vs. Carolina, Nov. 11			
7. Priest Holmes	30	181	1
Kansas City vs. San Diego, Nov. 4			
8. Dominic Rhodes	29	177	2
Indianapolis vs. Atlanta, Dec. 16			
9. Shaun Alexander	31	176	2
Seattle vs. Jacksonville, Oct. 7			
10. Anthony Thomas	31	173	1
Chicago vs. Tampa Bay, Dec. 16			

100-YARD RUSHING PERFORMANCES, 2001

First Week
Ahman Green, Green Bay — 157 yards vs. Detroit
Edgerrin James, Indianapolis — 135 yards vs. New York Jets
LaDainian Tomlinson, San Diego — 113 yards vs. Washington
Corey Dillon, Cincinnati — 104 yards vs. New England
Terrell Davis, Denver — 101 yards vs. New York Giants

Second Week
James Jackson, Cleveland — 124 yards vs. Detroit
Ahman Green, Green Bay — 116 yards vs. Washington
Edgerrin James, Indianapolis — 111 yards vs. Buffalo
Curtis Martin, New York Jets — 106 yards vs. New England
Marshall Faulk, St. Louis — 105 yards vs. San Francisco

Third Week
Priest Holmes, Kansas City — 147 yards vs. Washington
Jerome Bettis, Pittsburgh — 114 yards vs. Buffalo
Ron Dayne, New York Giants — 111 yards vs. New Orleans
Troy Hambrick, Dallas — 107 yards vs. Philadelphia
LaDainian Tomlinson, San Diego — 107 yards vs. Cincinnati

Fourth Week
Shaun Alexander, Seattle — 176 yards vs. Jacksonville
Mike Anderson, Denver — 155 yards vs. Kansas City
Jerome Bettis, Pittsburgh — 153 yards vs. Cincinnati
Lamar Smith, Miami — 144 yards vs. New England
Ricky Williams, New Orleans — 136 yards vs. Minnesota
Curtis Martin, New York Jets — 135 yards vs. Buffalo
Correll Buckhalter, Philadelphia — 134 yards vs. Arizona
Travis Henry, Buffalo — 113 yards vs. New York Jets
Terry Allen, Baltimore — 108 yards vs. Tennessee
LaDainian Tomlinson, San Diego — 102 yards vs. Cleveland

Fifth Week
Priest Holmes, Kansas City — 150 yards vs. Pittsburgh
Ricky Williams, New Orleans — 147 yards vs. Carolina
Shaun Alexander, Seattle — 142 yards vs. Denver
Corey Dillon, Cincinnati — 140 yards vs. Cleveland
Curtis Martin, New York Jets — 120 yards vs. Miami
Edgerrin James, Indianapolis — 116 yards vs. Oakland
Jerome Bettis, Pittsburgh — 112 yards vs. Kansas City
James Stewart, Detroit — 108 yards vs. Minnesota
Emmitt Smith, Dallas — 107 yards vs. Washington

Sixth Week
Trung Canidate, St. Louis — 195 yards vs. New York Jets
Anthony Thomas, Chicago — 188 yards vs. Cincinnati
Jerome Bettis, Pittsburgh — 143 yards vs. Tampa Bay
Edgerrin James, Indianapolis — 143 yards vs. New England
Tshimanga Biakabutuka, Carolina — 121 yards vs. Washington

Seventh Week
Corey Dillon, Cincinnati — 184 yards vs. Detroit
Curtis Martin, New York Jets — 159 yards vs. Carolina
Mike Alstott, Tampa Bay — 129 yards vs. Minnesota
Anthony Thomas, Chicago — 127 yards vs. San Francisco
Stephen Davis, Washington — 107 yards vs. New York Giants
Edgerrin James, Indianapolis — 102 yards vs. Kansas City

Eighth Week
Priest Holmes, Kansas City — 181 yards vs. San Diego
Ahman Green, Green Bay — 169 yards vs. Tampa Bay
Stephen Davis, Washington — 142 yards vs. Seattle
Antowain Smith, New England — 117 yards vs. Atlanta
Dominic Rhodes, Indianapolis — 100 yards vs. Buffalo

Ninth Week
Shaun Alexander, Seattle — 266 yards vs. Oakland
Marshall Faulk, St. Louis — 183 yards vs. Carolina
Jerome Bettis, Pittsburgh — 163 yards vs. Cleveland
Maurice Smith, Atlanta — 148 yards vs. Dallas
Duce Staley, Philadelphia — 146 yards vs. Minnesota
Trung Canidate, St. Louis — 145 yards vs. Carolina
Garrison Hearst, San Francisco — 145 yards vs. New Orleans
Troy Hambrick, Dallas — 127 yards vs. Atlanta
Ricky Williams, New Orleans — 121 yards vs. San Francisco
Tiki Barber, New York Giants — 118 yards vs. Arizona
Curtis Martin, New York Jets — 113 yards vs. Kansas City
Antowain Smith, New England — 100 yards vs. Buffalo

Tenth Week
Ricky Williams, New Orleans — 120 yards vs. Indianapolis
Duce Staley, Philadelphia — 102 yards vs. Dallas

Eleventh Week
Tiki Barber, New York Giants — 124 yards vs. Oakland
Priest Holmes, Kansas City — 120 yards vs. Seattle
Mike Anderson, Denver — 118 yards vs. Dallas
Antowain Smith, New England — 111 yards vs. New Orleans
James Allen, Chicago — 107 yards vs. Minnesota
Garrison Hearst, San Francisco — 106 yards vs. Indianapolis
Dominic Rhodes, Indianapolis — 104 yards vs. San Francisco
Ahman Green, Green Bay — 102 yards vs. Detroit
James Stewart, Detroit — 102 yards vs. Green Bay

Twelfth Week
Garrison Hearst, San Francisco — 124 yards vs. Buffalo
Moe Williams, Baltimore — 111 yards vs. Indianapolis
Emmitt Smith, Dallas — 102 yards vs. Washington
Ricky Williams, New Orleans — 102 yards vs. Carolina

Thirteenth Week
Priest Holmes, Kansas City — 168 yards vs. Oakland
Ahman Green, Green Bay — 125 yards vs. Chicago
Michael Bennett, Minnesota — 113 yards vs. Tennessee
Tiki Barber, New York Giants — 110 yards vs. Dallas
Stephen Davis, Washington — 110 yards vs. Arizona
Terrell Davis, Denver — 109 yards vs. Seattle
Lamar Smith, Miami — 107 yards vs. Indianapolis
Travis Henry, Buffalo — 101 yards vs. Carolina

Fourteenth Week
Dominic Rhodes, Indianapolis — 177 yards vs. Atlanta
Anthony Thomas, Chicago — 173 yards vs. Tampa Bay
Skip Hicks, Tennessee — 142 yards vs. Green Bay
Priest Holmes, Kansas City — 121 yards vs. Denver
Stacey Mack, Jacksonville — 115 yards vs. Cleveland
Stephen Davis, Washington — 111 yards vs. Philadelphia
Ricky Watters, Seattle — 104 yards vs. Dallas
Garrison Hearst, San Francisco — 103 yards vs. Miami

Fifteenth Week
Marshall Faulk, St. Louis — 202 yards vs. Carolina
Antowain Smith, New England — 156 yards vs. Miami
Ahman Green, Green Bay — 150 yards vs. Cleveland
LaDainian Tomlinson, San Diego — 145 yards vs. Kansas City
Jamel White, Cleveland — 131 yards vs. Green Bay
Shawn Bryson, Buffalo — 130 yards vs. Atlanta

Emmitt Smith, Dallas	128 yards vs. Arizona
Corey Dillon, Cincinnati	127 yards vs. Baltimore
Chris Fuamatu-Ma'afala, Pittsburgh	126 yards vs. Detroit
Dominic Rhodes, Indianapolis	126 yards vs. New York Jets
Curtis Martin, New York Jets	122 yards vs. Indianapolis
Stacey Mack, Jacksonville	111 yards vs. Minnesota
Mike Alstott, Tampa Bay	101 yards vs. New Orleans

Sixteenth Week

Eddie George, Tennessee	130 yards vs. Cleveland
Emmitt Smith, Dallas	126 yards vs. San Francisco
Stacey Mack, Jacksonville	125 yards vs. Kansas City
Curtis Martin, New York Jets	123 yards vs. Buffalo
Marshall Faulk, St. Louis	118 yards vs. Indianapolis
Stephen Davis, Washington	111 yards vs. New Orleans
Shawn Bryson, Buffalo	107 yards vs. New York Jets
Michael Bennett, Minnesota	104 yards vs. Green Bay

Seventeenth Week

Marshall Faulk, St. Louis	168 yards vs. Atlanta
Richard Huntley, Carolina	168 yards vs. New England
Anthony Thomas, Chicago	160 yards vs. Jacksonville
Lamar Smith, Miami	158 yards vs. Buffalo
Stephen Davis, Washington	148 yards vs. Arizona
Dominic Rhodes, Indianapolis	141 yards vs. Denver
Terry Allen, Baltimore	133 yards vs. Minnesota
Shaun Alexander, Seattle	127 yards vs. Kansas City
Priest Holmes, Kansas City	117 yards vs. Seattle
Ahman Green, Green Bay	101 yards vs. New York Giants

Times 100 or More (124)

Green, Holmes, Martin, 7; S. Davis, 6; Bettis, Faulk, James, Rhodes, R. Williams, 5; Alexander, Dillon, Hearst, A. Smith, E. Smith, Thomas, Tomlinson, 4; Barber, Mack, L. Smith, 3; T. Allen, Alstott, Anderson, Bennett, Bryson, Canidate, T. Davis, Hambrick, Henry, M. Smith, Staley, Stewart, 2.

TEN BEST PASSING PERFORMANCES, 2001

	Att.	Comp.	Yards	TD
1. Charlie Batch Detroit vs. Arizona, Nov. 18	62	36	436	3
2. Chris Chandler Atlanta vs. Buffalo, Dec. 23	40	28	431	2
3. Peyton Manning Indianapolis vs. Buffalo, Sept. 23	29	23	421	4
4. Jon Kitna Cincinnati vs. Pittsburgh, Dec. 30	68	35	411	2
5. Kurt Warner St. Louis vs. New England, Nov. 18	42	30	401	3
6. Brad Johnson Tampa Bay vs. Chicago, Nov. 18	56	40	399	0
7. Kerry Collins New York Giants vs. Green Bay, Jan. 6	59	36	386	1
8. Kurt Warner St. Louis vs. New Orleans, Oct. 28	47	29	385	1
9. Doug Flutie San Diego vs. Seattle, Dec. 30	53	34	377	1
10. Peyton Manning Indianapolis vs. San Francisco, Nov. 25	51	31	370	1

300-YARD PASSING PERFORMANCES, 2001

First Week

Rich Gannon, Oakland	341 yards vs. Kansas City
Jeff Garcia, San Francisco	335 yards vs. Atlanta
Brian Griese, Denver	330 yards vs. New York Giants
Donovan McNabb, Philadelphia	312 yards vs. St. Louis
Kurt Warner, St. Louis	308 yards vs. Philadelphia

Second Week

Peyton Manning, Indianapolis	421 yards vs. Buffalo
Doug Flutie, San Diego	348 yards vs. Dallas
Elvis Grbac, Baltimore	326 yards vs. Cincinnati
Kurt Warner, St. Louis	321 yards vs. San Francisco

Third Week

Kurt Warner, St. Louis	328 yards vs. Miami
Daunte Culpepper, Minnesota	322 yards vs. Tampa Bay
Brett Favre, Green Bay	308 yards vs. Carolina
Trent Green, Kansas City	307 yards vs. Washington

Fourth Week

Daunte Culpepper, Minnesota	332 yards vs. New Orleans

Fifth Week

Tom Brady, New England	364 yards vs. San Diego
Charlie Batch, Detroit	345 yards vs. Minnesota
Brett Favre, Green Bay	337 yards vs. Baltimore
Jeff Garcia, San Francisco	332 yards vs. Atlanta
Kurt Warner, St. Louis	316 yards vs. New York Giants

Sixth Week

Trent Green, Kansas City	352 yards vs. Arizona
Tony Banks, Washington	346 yards vs. Carolina
Charlie Batch, Detroit	338 yards vs. Tennessee
Peyton Manning, Indianapolis	335 yards vs. New England

Seventh Week

Kurt Warner, St. Louis	385 yards vs. New Orleans
Kerry Collins, New York Giants	346 yards vs. Washington
Trent Green, Kansas City	324 yards vs. Indianapolis
Rob Johnson, Buffalo	310 yards vs. San Diego
Mark Brunell, Jacksonville	306 yards vs. Baltimore

Eighth Week

Shane Matthews, Chicago	357 yards vs. Cleveland

Ninth Week

Aaron Brooks, New Orleans	347 yards vs. San Francisco
Jon Kitna, Cincinnati	303 yards vs. Jacksonville

Tenth Week

Charlie Batch, Detroit	436 yards vs. Arizona
Kurt Warner, St. Louis	401 yards vs. New England
Brad Johnson, Tampa Bay	399 yards vs. Chicago
Chris Chandler, Atlanta	352 yards vs. Green Bay

Jake Plummer, Arizona 334 yards vs. Detroit
Kerry Collins, New York Giants 321 yards vs. Minnesota
Alex Van Pelt, Buffalo 316 yards vs. Seattle
Rich Gannon, Oakland 311 yards vs. San Diego
Jeff Garcia, San Francisco 305 yards vs. Carolina
Eleventh Week
Peyton Manning, Indianapolis 370 yards vs. San Francisco
Steve McNair, Tennessee 334 yards vs. Pittsburgh
Alex Van Pelt, Buffalo 309 yards vs. Miami
Doug Flutie, San Diego 308 yards vs. Arizona
Aaron Brooks, New Orleans 307 yards vs. New England
Twelfth Week
Brett Favre, Green Bay 362 yards vs. Jacksonville
Kurt Warner, St. Louis 342 yards vs. Atlanta
Aaron Brooks, New Orleans 330 yards vs. Carolina
Mark Brunell, Jacksonville 311 yards vs. Green Bay
Peyton Manning, Indianapolis 310 yards vs. Baltimore
Rich Gannon, Oakland 302 yards vs. Arizona
Thirteenth Week
Todd Bouman, Minnesota 348 yards vs. Tennessee
Doug Flutie, San Diego 307 yards vs. Philadelphia
Brad Johnson, Tampa Bay 305 yards vs. Detroit
Steve McNair, Tennessee 302 yards vs. Minnesota
Fourteenth Week
Kurt Warner, St. Louis 338 yards vs. New Orleans
Kordell Stewart, Pittsburgh 333 yards vs. Baltimore
Peyton Manning, Indianapolis 325 yards vs. Atlanta
Fifteenth Week
Chris Chandler, Atlanta 431 yards vs. Buffalo
Kerry Collins, New York Giants 338 yards vs. Seattle
Jay Fiedler, Miami 320 yards vs. New England
Chris Weinke, Carolina 312 yards vs. St. Louis
Sixteenth Week
Jon Kitna, Cincinnati 411 yards vs. Pittsburgh
Doug Flutie, San Diego 377 yards vs. Seattle
Kurt Warner, St. Louis 359 yards vs. Indianapolis
Tim Couch, Cleveland 336 yards vs. Tennessee
Rich Gannon, Oakland 313 yards vs. Denver
Kerry Collins, New York Giants 303 yards vs. Philadelphia
Ty Detmer, Detroit 303 yards vs. Chicago
Seventeenth Week
Kerry Collins, New York Giants 386 yards vs. Green Bay
Jon Kitna, Cincinnati 340 yards vs. Tennessee
Brett Favre, Green Bay 315 yards vs. New York Giants

Times 300 or More (72)
Warner, 9; Collins, Manning, 5; Favre, Flutie, Gannon, 4;
Batch, Brooks, Garcia, Green, Kitna, 3; Brunell, Chandler,
Culpepper, B. Johnson, McNair, Van Pelt, 2.

TEN BEST RECEIVING PERFORMANCES, 2001

	No.	Yards	TD
1. Rod Gardner	6	208	1
Washington vs. Carolina, Oct. 21			
2. Torry Holt	7	203	2
St. Louis vs. Indianapolis, Dec. 30			
3. Eric Moulds	6	196	2
Buffalo vs. Miami, Nov. 25			
4. Derrick Mason	9	186	2
Tennessee vs. Cincinnati, Jan. 6			
5. Terrell Owens	9	183	3
San Francisco vs. Atlanta, Oct. 14			
6. Isaac Bruce	7	179	1
St. Louis vs. New Orleans, Oct. 28			
7. Marvin Harrison	9	174	3
Indianapolis vs. Miami, Nov. 11			
8. Randy Moss	10	171	3
Minnesota vs. New York Giants, Nov. 19			
9. Jerome Pathon	9	168	1
Indianapolis vs. Buffalo, Sept. 23			
10. Willie Jackson	11	167	0
New Orleans vs. San Francisco, Nov. 11			

100-YARD RECEIVING PERFORMANCES, 2001

First Week
Tim Brown, Oakland 133 yards vs. Kansas City
Jimmy Smith, Jacksonville 126 yards vs. Pittsburgh
Rod Smith, Denver 115 yards vs. New York Giants
Johnnie Morton, Detroit 111 yards vs. Green Bay
Troy Brown, New England 106 yards vs. Cincinnati
Darnay Scott, Cincinnati 104 yards vs. New England
Bill Schroeder, Green Bay 104 yards vs. Detroit
Second Week
Jerome Pathon, Indianapolis 168 yards vs. Buffalo
James Thrash, Philadelphia 165 yards vs. Seattle
Rod Smith, Denver 162 yards vs. Arizona
Marvin Harrison, Indianapolis 146 yards vs. Buffalo
David Boston, Arizona 145 yards vs. Denver
Isaac Bruce, St. Louis 144 yards vs. San Francisco
Muhsin Muhammad, Carolina 132 yards vs. Atlanta
Johnnie Morton, Detroit 100 yards vs. Cleveland
Third Week
Darrell Jackson, Seattle 125 yards vs. Oakland
Torry Holt, St. Louis 111 yards vs. Miami
Maurice Smith, Atlanta 108 yards vs. Arizona
Willie Jackson, New Orleans 105 yards vs. New York Giants
Fourth Week
Tony Gonzalez, Kansas City 129 yards vs. Denver
MarTay Jenkins, Arizona 119 yards vs. Philadelphia
Bill Schroeder, Green Bay 119 yards vs. Tampa Bay
Terrell Owens, San Francisco 118 yards vs. Carolina
Tim Brown, Oakland 114 yards vs. Dallas
Marcus Robinson, Chicago 114 yards vs. Atlanta
Rod Smith, Denver 110 yards vs. Kansas City
Eric Moulds, Buffalo 107 yards vs. New York Jets
Peerless Price, Buffalo 103 yards vs. New York Jets
Fifth Week
Terrell Owens, San Francisco 183 yards vs. Atlanta
Kevin Johnson, Cleveland 153 yards vs. Cincinnati
Tim Brown, Oakland 145 yards vs. Indianapolis
Keyshawn Johnson, Tampa Bay 140 yards vs. Tennessee
Antonio Freeman, Green Bay 138 yards vs. Baltimore
Germane Crowell, Detroit 125 yards vs. Minnesota
Troy Brown, New England 117 yards vs. San Diego
Curtis Conway, San Diego 117 yards vs. New England
Cris Carter, Minnesota 111 yards vs. Detroit
Terry Glenn, New England 110 yards vs. San Diego
Sixth Week
Rod Gardner, Washington 208 yards vs. Carolina

Keyshawn Johnson, Tampa Bay	159 yards vs. Pittsburgh
Marvin Harrison, Indianapolis	157 yards vs. New England
David Boston, Arizona	131 yards vs. Kansas City
Troy Brown, New England	120 yards vs. Indianapolis
David Patten, New England	117 yards vs. Indianapolis
Johnnie Morton, Detroit	113 yards vs. Tennessee
Jeff Graham, San Diego	107 yards vs. Denver
Frank Wycheck, Tennessee	100 yards vs. Detroit

Seventh Week

Isaac Bruce, St. Louis	179 yards vs. New Orleans
Rod Smith, Denver	159 yards vs. New England
Plaxico Burress, Pittsburgh	151 yards vs. Tennessee
Peerless Price, Buffalo	151 yards vs. San Diego
Joe Horn, New Orleans	121 yards vs. St. Louis
Darrell Jackson, Seattle	121 yards vs. Miami
Curtis Conway, San Diego	120 yards vs. Buffalo
Jimmy Smith, Jacksonville	119 yards vs. Baltimore
Keenan McCardell, Jacksonville	118 yards vs. Baltimore
Amani Toomer, New York Giants	109 yards vs. Washington
David Boston, Arizona	108 yards vs. Dallas
Trung Canidate, St. Louis	107 yards vs. New Orleans
Garrison Hearst, San Francisco	105 yards vs. Chicago

Eighth Week

David Boston, Arizona	138 yards vs. Philadelphia
Terrell Owens, San Francisco	125 yards vs. Detroit
Jimmy Smith, Jacksonville	120 yards vs. Tennessee
Raghib Ismail, Dallas	107 yards vs. New York Giants
Oronde Gadsden, Miami	102 yards vs. Carolina

Ninth Week

Marvin Harrison, Indianapolis	174 yards vs. Miami
Willie Jackson, New Orleans	167 yards vs. San Francisco
David Boston, Arizona	137 yards vs. New York Giants
Qadry Ismail, Baltimore	129 yards vs. Tennessee
Chris Chambers, Miami	113 yards vs. Indianapolis
Curtis Conway, San Diego	111 yards vs. Denver
Darrell Jackson, Seattle	102 yards vs. Oakland
Terrell Owens, San Francisco	100 yards vs. New Orleans
Bill Schroeder, Green Bay	100 yards vs. Chicago

Tenth Week

Randy Moss, Minnesota	171 yards vs. New York Giants
Marty Booker, Chicago	165 yards vs. Tampa Bay
Johnnie Morton, Detroit	153 yards vs. Arizona
Joe Horn, New Orleans	148 yards vs. Indianapolis
Warrick Dunn, Tampa Bay	138 yards vs. Chicago
Peerless Price, Buffalo	138 yards vs. Seattle
Jerry Rice, Oakland	131 yards vs. San Diego
Isaac Bruce, St. Louis	130 yards vs. New England
Frank Sanders, Arizona	127 yards vs. Detroit
Marcus Pollard, Indianapolis	126 yards vs. New Orleans
Corey Bradford, Green Bay	117 yards vs. Atlanta
Hines Ward, Pittsburgh	112 yards vs. Jacksonville
Ike Hilliard, New York Giants	106 yards vs. Minnesota
Michael Westbrook, Washington	104 yards vs. Denver

Eleventh Week

Eric Moulds, Buffalo	196 yards vs. Miami
Torry Holt, St. Louis	139 yards vs. Tampa Bay
Marvin Harrison, Indianapolis	128 yards vs. San Francisco
David Boston, Arizona	121 yards vs. San Diego
Tim Brown, Oakland	117 yards vs. New York Giants
Oronde Gadsden, Miami	116 yards vs. Buffalo
Plaxico Burress, Pittsburgh	114 yards vs. Tennessee
Derrick Mason, Tennessee	114 yards vs. Pittsburgh
Kevin Johnson, Cleveland	113 yards vs. Cincinnati
Kevin Dyson, Tennessee	112 yards vs. Pittsburgh
Terrell Owens, San Francisco	103 yards vs. Indianapolis
Chris Chambers, Miami	101 yards vs. Buffalo

Twelfth Week

Joe Horn, New Orleans	150 yards vs. Carolina
Randy Moss, Minnesota	144 yards vs. Pittsburgh

Marshall Faulk, St. Louis	128 yards vs. Atlanta
Derrick Mason, Tennessee	122 yards vs. Cleveland
Jimmy Smith, Jacksonville	116 yards vs. Green Bay
Kevin Dyson, Tennessee	110 yards vs. Cleveland
David Boston, Arizona	106 yards vs. Oakland
Bill Schroeder, Green Bay	106 yards vs. Jacksonville
Antonio Freeman, Green Bay	104 yards vs. Jacksonville
Priest Holmes, Kansas City	100 yards vs. Philadelphia

Thirteenth Week

Randy Moss, Minnesota	158 yards vs. Tennessee
Joe Horn, New Orleans	138 yards vs. Atlanta
David Boston, Arizona	132 yards vs. Washington
Hines Ward, Pittsburgh	124 yards vs. New York Jets
Jimmy Smith, Jacksonville	119 yards vs. Cincinnati
Raghib Ismail, Dallas	118 yards vs. New York Giants
Jeff Graham, San Diego	110 yards vs. Philadelphia
Priest Holmes, Kansas City	109 yards vs. Oakland
Ricky Proehl, St. Louis	109 yards vs. San Francisco
Darrell Jackson, Seattle	104 yards vs. Denver
Muhsin Muhammad, Carolina	104 yards vs. Buffalo
Keyshawn Johnson, Tampa Bay	101 yards vs. Detroit

Fourteenth Week

Plaxico Burress, Pittsburgh	164 yards vs. Baltimore
Willie Jackson, New Orleans	156 yards vs. St. Louis
Randy Moss, Minnesota	144 yards vs. Detroit
Keyshawn Johnson, Tampa Bay	119 yards vs. Chicago
Derrick Mason, Tennessee	107 yards vs. Green Bay
Marcus Pollard, Indianapolis	101 yards vs. Atlanta
Bobby Shaw, Pittsburgh	100 yards vs. Baltimore
Rod Smith, Denver	100 yards vs. Kansas City

Fifteenth Week

Marvin Harrison, Indianapolis	127 yards vs. New York Jets
Chris Chambers, Miami	124 yards vs. New England
Amani Toomer, New York Giants	124 yards vs. Seattle
Jimmy Smith, Jacksonville	122 yards vs. Minnesota
Wayne Chrebet, New York Jets	118 yards vs. Indianapolis
Ike Hilliard, New York Giants	105 yards vs. Seattle
Duce Staley, Philadelphia	103 yards vs. San Francisco

Sixteenth Week

Torry Holt, St. Louis	203 yards vs. Indianapolis
Curtis Conway, San Diego	156 yards vs. Seattle
Joey Galloway, Dallas	146 yards vs. San Francisco
James Thrash, Philadelphia	143 yards vs. New York Giants
Keenan McCardell, Jacksonville	132 yards vs. Kansas City
David Boston, Arizona	127 yards vs. Carolina
Eddie Kennison, Kansas City	121 yards vs. Jacksonville
Marty Booker, Chicago	115 yards vs. Detroit
Darrell Jackson, Seattle	114 yards vs. San Diego
Darnay Scott, Cincinnati	113 yards vs. Pittsburgh
Peter Warrick, Cincinnati	109 yards vs. Pittsburgh
Jerry Rice, Oakland	108 yards vs. Denver
D'Wayne Bates, Chicago	107 yards vs. Detroit
Plaxico Burress, Pittsburgh	102 yards vs. Cincinnati
James Williams, Seattle	101 yards vs. San Diego

Seventeenth Week

Derrick Mason, Tennessee	186 yards vs. Cincinnati
Darnay Scott, Cincinnati	152 yards vs. Tennessee
Marvin Harrison, Indianapolis	128 yards vs. Denver
Terrell Owens, San Francisco	116 yards vs. New Orleans
Corey Bradford, Green Bay	111 yards vs. New York Giants
Laveranues Coles, New York Jets	111 yards vs. Oakland
Bill Schroeder, Green Bay	102 yards vs. New York Giants

Times 100 or More (159)
Boston, 9; Harrison, Owens, J. Smith, 6; D. Jackson, Schroeder, R. Smith, 5; Ti. Brown, Burress, Conway, Horn, Key. Johnson, Mason, Morton, Moss, 4; Tr. Brown, Bruce, Chambers, Holt, W. Jackson, Price, Scott, 3; Booker, Bradford, Dyson, Freeman, Gadsden, Graham, Hilliard, Holmes, R. Ismail, Kev. Johnson, McCardell, Moulds, Muhammad, Pollard, Rice, Thrash, Tooomer, Ward, 2.

TOP QUARTERBACK SACK PERFORMANCES, 2001
(2.5 or More Sacks Per Game Needed to Qualify)

First Week
Kabeer Gbaja-Biamila, Green Bay	3.0 vs. Detroit
Joe Johnson, New Orleans	3.0 vs. Buffalo

Second Week
None

Third Week
Charlie Clemons, New Orleans	3.0 vs. New York Giants
Michael Strahan, New York Giants	3.0 vs. New Orleans

Fourth Week
Kabeer Gbaja-Biamila, Green Bay	3.0 vs. Tampa Bay
Leonard Little, St. Louis	3.0 vs. Detroit
Rosevelt Colvin, Chicago	2.5 vs. Atlanta

Fifth Week
Michael Strahan, New York Giants	4.0 vs. St. Louis
Chris Hovan, Minnesota	2.5 vs. Detroit

Sixth Week
Joey Porter, Pittsburgh	4.0 vs. Tampa Bay
Kimo von Oelhoffen, Pittsburgh	3.0 vs. Tampa Bay
Rick Lyle, New York Jets	2.5 vs. St. Louis

Seventh Week
Marcus Washington, Indianapolis	2.5 vs. Kansas City

Eighth Week
John Abraham, New York Jets	4.0 vs. New Orleans
Courtney Brown, Cleveland	3.0 vs. Chicago
Jevon Kearse, Tennessee	3.0 vs. Jacksonville

Ninth Week
Jamie Sharper, Baltimore	3.5 vs. Tennessee
Jason Gildon, Pittsburgh	3.0 vs. Cleveland
Hugh Douglas, Philadelphia	2.5 vs. Minnesota
Patrick Kerney, Atlanta	2.5 vs. Dallas

Tenth Week
Raylee Johnson, San Diego	3.0 vs. Oakland

Eleventh Week
None

Twelfth Week
None

Thirteenth Week
James Hall, Detroit	3.5 vs. Tampa Bay
Reggie Hayward, Denver	3.0 vs. Seattle
Justin Smith, Cincinnati	3.0 vs. Jacksonville

Fourteenth Week
Jamir Miller, Cleveland	3.0 vs. Jacksonville
Chike Okeafor, San Francisco	2.5 vs. Miami
Grant Wistrom, St. Louis	2.5 vs. New Orleans

Fifteenth Week
Reinard Wilson, Cincinnati	3.0 vs. Baltimore

Sixteenth Week
Michael Strahan, New York Giants	3.5 vs. Philadelphia

Seventeenth Week
Peter Boulware, Baltimore	4.0 vs. Minnesota
Chad Bratzke, Indianapolis	3.0 vs. Denver

AMERICAN FOOTBALL CONFERENCE OFFENSE

	Balt.	Buff.	Cin.	Cle.	Den.	Ind.	Jax.	KC	Mia.	NE	NYJ	Oak.	Pitt.	SD	Sea.	Tenn.
First Downs	299	287	294	238	304	343	289	324	263	292	274	316	314	290	274	288
Rushing	92	75	96	78	106	110	85	119	95	101	105	102	148	92	107	87
Passing	180	180	176	139	174	206	181	178	154	163	151	195	150	177	141	179
Penalty	27	32	22	21	24	27	23	27	14	28	18	19	16	21	26	22
Rushes	483	406	441	417	481	438	372	448	473	473	445	450	580	435	469	468
Net Yds. Gained	1810	1686	1712	1351	1877	1966	1600	2008	1664	1793	2054	1654	2774	1695	1936	1794
Avg. Gain	3.7	4.2	3.9	3.2	3.9	4.5	4.3	4.5	3.5	3.8	4.6	3.7	4.8	3.9	4.1	3.8
Avg. Yds. per Game	113.1	105.4	107.0	84.4	117.3	122.9	100.0	125.5	104.0	112.1	128.4	103.4	173.4	105.9	121.0	112.1
Passes Attempted	557	557	602	466	511	557	534	528	453	482	464	553	454	548	462	515
Completed	320	327	322	279	312	349	321	300	275	306	272	364	274	309	258	307
% Completed	57.5	58.7	53.5	59.9	61.1	62.7	60.1	56.8	60.7	63.5	58.6	65.8	60.4	56.4	55.8	59.6
Total Yds. Gained	3595	3722	3291	3154	3208	4227	3670	3863	3335	3326	2871	3862	3295	3685	3164	3867
Times Sacked	40	46	28	51	42	30	63	39	27	46	19	27	31	27	49	43
Yds. Lost	281	271	203	353	268	238	430	198	178	237	130	155	182	180	328	309
Net Yds. Gained	3314	3451	3088	2801	2940	3989	3240	3665	3157	3089	2741	3707	3113	3505	2836	3558
Avg. Yds. per Game	207.1	215.7	193.0	175.1	183.8	249.3	202.5	229.1	197.3	193.1	171.3	231.7	194.6	219.1	177.3	222.4
Net Yds. per Pass Play	5.55	5.72	4.90	5.42	5.32	6.80	5.43	6.46	6.58	5.85	5.67	6.39	6.42	6.10	5.55	6.38
Yds. Gained per Comp.	11.23	11.38	10.22	11.30	10.28	12.11	11.43	12.88	12.13	10.87	10.56	10.61	12.03	11.93	12.26	12.60
Combined Net Yds. Gained	5124	5137	4800	4152	4817	5955	4840	5673	4821	4882	4795	5361	5887	5200	4772	5352
% Total Yds. Rushing	35.3	32.8	35.7	32.5	39.0	33.0	33.1	35.4	34.5	36.7	42.8	30.9	47.1	32.6	40.6	33.5
% Total Yds. Passing	64.7	67.2	64.3	67.5	61.0	67.0	66.9	64.6	65.5	63.3	57.2	69.1	52.9	67.4	59.4	66.5
Avg. Yds. per Game	320.3	321.1	300.0	259.5	301.1	372.2	302.5	354.6	301.3	305.1	299.7	335.1	367.9	325.0	298.3	334.5
Ball Control Plays	1080	1009	1071	934	1034	1025	969	1015	953	1001	928	1030	1065	1010	980	1026
Avg. Yds. per Play	4.7	5.1	4.5	4.4	4.7	5.8	5.0	5.6	5.1	4.9	5.2	5.2	5.5	5.1	4.9	5.2
Avg. Time of Poss.	29:39	29:00	29:16	28:16	31:23	30:32	28:01	29:07	30:04	30:48	29:13	30:56	34:10	30:15	29:51	31:29
Third Down Efficiency	35.7	34.6	38.3	32.4	37.9	41.5	35.4	35.9	41.4	41.2	38.0	38.8	45.7	35.7	36.2	42.1
Had Intercepted	20	20	26	21	19	23	14	24	19	15	14	9	12	18	12	17
Yds. Opp Returned	331	390	392	242	256	545	299	296	254	273	222	147	101	135	36	163
Ret. by Opp. for TD	3	2	0	3	2	6	2	1	3	2	1	1	0	0	0	2
Punts	87	80	86	99	82	68	82	75	81	74	76	74	63	78	86	85
Yds. Punted	3309	3262	3404	4249	3668	3023	3577	3037	3321	3042	2966	3375	2611	3308	3730	3567
Avg. Yds. per Punt	38.0	40.8	39.6	42.9	44.7	44.5	43.6	40.5	41.0	41.1	39.0	45.6	41.4	42.4	43.4	42.0
Punt Returns	48	24	31	31	31	29	38	44	43	33	34	29	50	44	33	36
Yds. Returned	563	225	290	247	405	290	333	326	471	440	323	339	420	415	352	282
Avg. Yds. per Return	11.7	9.4	9.4	8.0	13.1	10.0	8.8	7.4	11.0	13.3	9.5	11.7	8.4	9.4	10.7	7.8
Returned for TD	0	1	0	0	1	1	0	0	0	2	0	1	0	1	0	0
Kickoff Returns	57	83	62	62	67	84	58	61	57	59	56	66	46	66	72	71
Yds. Returned	1347	1651	1230	1285	1576	1832	1164	1292	1222	1184	1196	1524	884	1716	1496	1413
Avg. Yds. per Return	23.6	19.9	19.8	20.7	23.5	21.8	20.1	21.2	21.4	20.1	21.4	23.1	19.2	26.0	20.8	19.9
Returned for TD	0	0	0	0	0	1	1	0	0	0	0	1	0	2	0	1
Fumbles	31	26	28	24	24	20	29	19	26	29	22	27	28	26	24	18
Lost	16	13	11	12	8	15	13	9	19	13	7	16	9	11	9	11
Out of Bounds	0	1	2	1	5	0	1	0	2	2	1	1	5	1	3	0
Own Rec. for TD	0	0	0	0	0	0	0	0	1	0	0	0	0	0	0	0
Opp. Rec. by	12	8	15	8	15	10	12	13	11	13	19	7	12	12	13	11
Opp. Rec. for TD	1	0	1	1	0	1	2	0	1	0	2	1	3	2	1	1
Penalties	89	123	103	94	95	76	97	68	107	92	62	107	86	97	66	119
Yds. Penalized	728	954	870	825	917	730	710	602	914	802	507	897	737	777	579	1025
Total Points Scored	303	265	226	285	340	413	294	320	344	371	308	399	352	332	301	336
Total TDs	31	31	26	31	35	47	34	34	41	43	34	46	38	35	34	39
TDs Rushing	11	9	11	8	7	16	11	16	14	15	11	14	17	13	15	12
TDs Passing	18	18	12	18	26	27	20	17	20	21	17	27	16	16	15	23
TDs on Ret. and Rec.	2	4	2	5	2	4	3	1	7	7	6	5	5	6	4	4
Extra Point Kicks	25	23	23	29	31	41	30	27	39	41	32	43	34	32	33	34
Extra Point Kicks Att.	25	24	24	30	31	42	32	28	40	42	32	44	37	32	33	35
2Pt Conversions	1	1	1	1	3	3	1	3	1	0	1	0	0	0	1	3
2Pt Conversions Att.	6	7	1	1	4	5	2	6	1	1	2	2	1	3	1	4
Safeties	0	0	0	1	0	0	2	1	0	0	0	0	0	0	1	1
Field Goals Made	30	18	17	22	31	28	18	27	19	24	24	26	30	30	20	20
Field Goals Attempted	35	29	28	25	36	34	28	35	21	30	31	32	44	43	32	28
% Successful	85.7	62.1	60.7	88.0	86.1	82.4	64.3	77.1	90.5	80.0	77.4	81.3	68.2	69.8	62.5	71.4

AMERICAN FOOTBALL CONFERENCE DEFENSE

	Balt.	Buff.	Cin.	Cle.	Den.	Ind.	Jax.	KC	Mia.	NE	NYJ	Oak.	Pitt.	SD	Sea.	Tenn.
First Downs	262	302	281	295	292	323	300	296	283	303	284	296	254	290	300	300
Rushing	81	122	86	112	86	108	89	111	97	99	116	104	70	99	91	79
Passing	161	154	173	161	176	195	193	167	148	171	155	166	160	166	186	192
Penalty	20	26	22	22	30	20	18	18	38	33	13	26	24	25	23	29
Rushes	410	482	453	494	406	455	469	481	453	429	481	433	339	449	427	405
Net Yds. Gained	1411	2133	1675	2208	1492	2115	1611	2140	1779	1855	2154	1988	1195	1504	1721	1431
Avg. Gain	3.4	4.4	3.7	4.5	3.7	4.6	3.4	4.4	3.9	4.3	4.5	4.6	3.5	3.3	4.0	3.5
Avg. Yds. per Game	88.2	133.3	104.7	138.0	93.3	132.2	100.7	133.8	111.2	115.9	134.6	124.3	74.7	94.0	107.6	89.4
Passes Attempted	555	453	512	552	515	509	544	491	467	546	516	528	525	535	563	559
Completed	321	284	311	309	308	311	354	296	262	299	313	290	295	317	339	328
% Completed	57.8	62.7	60.7	56.0	59.8	61.1	65.1	60.3	56.1	54.8	60.7	54.9	56.2	59.3	60.2	58.7
Total Yds. Gained	3325	3378	3477	3377	3561	3857	3757	3403	3059	3731	3170	3287	3309	3618	3733	4259
Times Sacked	45	34	48	43	39	40	43	31	37	41	33	41	55	41	38	32
Yds. Lost	290	219	320	288	279	257	298	239	230	234	171	204	367	218	248	175
Net Yds. Gained	3035	3159	3157	3089	3282	3600	3459	3164	2829	3497	2999	3083	2942	3400	3485	4084
Avg. Yds. per Game	189.7	197.4	197.3	193.1	205.1	225.0	216.2	197.8	176.8	218.6	187.4	192.7	183.9	212.5	217.8	255.3
Net Yds. per Pass Play	5.06	6.49	5.64	5.19	5.92	6.56	5.89	6.06	5.61	5.96	5.46	5.42	5.07	5.90	5.80	6.91
Yds. Gained per Comp.	10.36	11.89	11.18	10.93	11.56	12.40	10.61	11.50	11.68	12.48	10.13	11.33	11.22	11.41	11.01	12.98
Combined Net Yds. Gained	4446	5292	4832	5297	4774	5715	5070	5304	4608	5352	5153	5071	4137	4904	5206	5515
% Total Yds. Rushing	31.7	40.3	34.7	41.7	31.3	37.0	31.8	40.3	38.6	34.7	41.8	39.2	28.9	30.7	33.1	25.9
% Total Yds. Passing	68.3	59.7	65.3	58.3	68.7	63.0	68.2	59.7	61.4	65.3	58.2	60.8	71.1	69.3	66.9	74.1
Avg. Yds. per Game	277.9	330.8	302.0	331.1	298.4	357.2	316.9	331.5	288.0	334.5	322.1	316.9	258.6	306.5	325.4	344.7
Ball Control Plays	1010	969	1013	1089	960	1004	1056	1003	957	1016	1030	1002	919	1025	1028	996
Avg. Yds. per Play	4.4	5.5	4.8	4.9	5.0	5.7	4.8	5.3	4.8	5.3	5.0	5.1	4.5	4.8	5.1	5.5
Avg. Time of Poss.	30:21	31:00	30:44	31:44	28:37	29:28	31:59	30:53	29:56	29:12	30:47	29:04	25:50	29:45	30:09	28:31
Third Down Efficiency	30.8	42.0	38.2	37.4	33.0	43.5	38.3	39.4	34.8	37.2	44.5	31.9	34.2	37.5	41.3	34.9
Intercepted By	16	11	13	33	22	15	12	13	17	22	20	17	16	19	14	13
Yds. Returned By	195	139	192	499	240	158	83	166	412	422	390	306	270	162	186	78
Returned for TD	1	3	1	4	1	1	0	1	5	5	2	2	2	1	2	0
Punts	98	66	86	74	77	67	83	79	86	73	75	83	87	90	76	82
Yds. Punted	4076	2836	3541	3198	3618	2861	3359	3238	3789	2885	3056	3394	3677	3789	3212	3388
Avg. Yds. per Punt	41.6	43.0	41.2	43.2	47.0	42.7	40.5	41.0	44.1	39.5	40.7	40.9	42.3	42.1	42.3	41.3
Punt Returns	33	40	47	52	48	35	38	31	30	26	34	34	28	32	43	36
Yds. Returned	183	418	374	647	517	486	295	288	136	124	446	502	334	346	462	264
Avg. Yds. per Return	5.5	10.5	8.0	12.4	10.8	13.9	7.8	9.3	4.5	4.8	13.1	14.8	11.9	10.8	10.7	7.3
Returned for TD	0	0	0	1	1	1	0	1	0	0	1	0	0	0	1	0
Kickoff Returns	64	52	46	65	69	87	64	65	59	75	63	75	73	64	64	57
Yds. Returned	1393	987	1157	1215	1526	2006	1266	1474	1189	1658	1355	1657	1561	1671	1273	1418
Avg. Yds. per Return	21.8	19.0	25.2	18.7	22.1	23.1	19.8	22.7	20.2	22.1	21.5	22.1	21.4	26.1	19.9	24.9
Returned for TD	0	0	1	0	1	0	0	1	0	0	0	1	1	0	1	0
Fumbles	22	26	33	35	26	16	28	23	27	23	29	18	27	33	28	21
Lost	12	8	15	9	15	10	12	13	11	13	19	7	12	12	13	11
Out of Bounds	2	4	2	5	1	0	2	0	0	1	1	3	1	2	2	0
Own Rec. for TD	0	0	0	0	0	0	0	0	0	0	0	0	0	0	0	0
Opp. Rec. by	16	13	11	12	8	15	13	9	19	13	7	16	8	11	9	11
Opp. Rec. for TD	0	3	0	2	1	0	0	0	1	2	2	0	1	1	2	0
Penalties	105	93	101	103	100	96	96	87	82	93	85	81	71	79	101	88
Yds. Penalized	902	835	837	779	853	759	834	761	623	839	700	621	585	632	805	832
Total Points Scored	265	420	309	319	339	486	286	344	290	272	295	327	212	321	324	388
Total TDs	30	48	35	35	38	57	30	37	35	26	33	36	26	35	34	46
TDs Rushing	10	20	10	11	9	20	15	15	9	7	15	17	5	10	9	17
TDs Passing	16	23	23	18	23	30	13	19	22	15	14	16	19	24	20	27
TDs on Ret. and Rec.	4	5	2	6	6	7	2	3	4	4	4	3	2	1	5	2
Extra Point Kicks	28	48	29	30	36	52	28	35	32	22	27	28	23	31	31	44
Extra Point Kicks Att.	28	48	31	32	37	53	28	35	34	22	30	29	24	33	31	44
2Pt Conversions	0	0	1	2	0	1	0	2	0	2	1	4	1	1	1	1
2Pt Conversions Att.	2	0	4	2	1	4	2	2	1	4	3	7	2	2	3	2
Safeties	0	0	1	0	0	0	0	1	0	0	1	0	2	0	0	0
Field Goals Made	19	28	22	25	25	30	26	27	16	30	22	25	9	26	29	22
Field Goals Attempted	33	37	30	34	29	36	35	34	22	41	27	33	20	35	36	29
% Successful	57.6	75.7	73.3	73.5	86.2	83.3	74.3	79.4	72.7	73.2	81.5	75.8	45.0	74.3	80.6	75.9

NATIONAL FOOTBALL CONFERENCE OFFENSE

	Ariz.	Atl.	Car.	Chi.	Dall.	Det.	GB	Minn.	NO	NYG	Phil.	StL	SF	TB	Wash.
First Downs	277	280	236	277	247	289	282	288	294	295	256	357	328	298	241
Rushing	77	85	68	100	114	74	72	88	87	93	90	104	121	84	104
Passing	177	165	144	153	110	184	187	179	184	189	146	236	184	189	122
Penalty	23	30	24	24	23	31	23	21	23	13	20	17	23	25	15
Rushes	400	439	354	475	505	351	410	376	419	424	412	416	509	407	490
Net Yds. Gained	1449	1762	1372	1742	2184	1398	1693	1609	1712	1777	1778	2027	2244	1371	1948
Avg. Gain	3.6	4.0	3.9	3.7	4.3	4.0	4.1	4.3	4.1	4.2	4.3	4.9	4.4	3.4	4.0
Avg. Yds. per Game	90.6	110.1	85.8	108.9	136.5	87.4	105.8	100.6	107.0	111.1	111.1	126.7	140.3	85.7	121.8
Passes Attempted	526	485	579	528	413	609	510	555	562	568	522	551	506	592	432
Completed	304	278	314	315	210	343	314	335	313	327	300	379	318	362	235
% Completed	57.8	57.3	54.2	59.7	50.8	56.3	61.6	60.4	55.7	57.6	57.5	68.8	62.8	61.1	54.4
Total Yds. Gained	3653	3695	3098	3072	2408	3969	3921	3854	3844	3764	3427	4903	3559	3621	2716
Times Sacked	29	64	32	17	34	66	22	47	50	36	40	40	26	47	38
Yds. Lost	204	387	216	120	190	373	151	278	330	206	282	240	114	298	229
Net Yds. Gained	3449	3308	2882	2952	2218	3596	3770	3576	3514	3558	3145	4663	3445	3323	2487
Avg. Yds. per Game	215.6	206.8	180.1	184.5	138.6	224.8	235.6	223.5	219.6	222.4	196.6	291.4	215.3	207.7	155.4
Net Yds. per Pass Play	6.21	6.03	4.72	5.42	4.96	5.33	7.09	5.94	5.74	5.89	5.60	7.89	6.48	5.20	5.29
Yds. Gained per Comp.	12.02	13.29	9.87	9.75	11.47	11.57	12.49	11.50	12.28	11.51	11.42	12.94	11.19	10.00	11.56
Combined Net															
Yds. Gained	4898	5070	4254	4694	4402	4994	5463	5185	5226	5335	4923	6690	5689	4694	4435
% Total Yds. Rushing	29.6	34.8	32.3	37.1	49.6	28.0	31.0	31.0	32.8	33.3	36.1	30.3	39.4	29.2	43.9
% Total Yds. Passing	70.4	65.2	67.7	62.9	50.4	72.0	69.0	69.0	67.2	66.7	63.9	69.7	60.6	70.8	56.1
Avg. Yds. per Game	306.1	316.9	265.9	293.4	275.1	312.1	341.4	324.1	326.6	333.4	307.7	418.1	355.6	293.4	277.2
Ball Control Plays	955	988	965	1020	952	1026	942	978	1031	1028	974	1007	1041	1046	960
Avg. Yds. per Play	5.1	5.1	4.4	4.6	4.6	4.9	5.8	5.3	5.1	5.2	5.1	6.6	5.5	4.5	4.6
Avg. Time of Poss.	27:45	31:18	27:30	30:35	30:13	28:34	29:32	29:11	29:24	29:43	28:39	31:45	31:49	31:40	30:15
Third Down Efficiency	29.1	41.0	30.6	32.9	33.0	34.2	36.5	41.9	39.2	35.5	30.9	50.0	44.6	35.1	35.4
Had Intercepted	14	17	22	16	20	24	15	23	22	16	14	22	12	12	13
Yds. Opp Returned	157	330	432	187	344	376	252	219	189	181	99	307	232	74	247
Ret. by Opp. for TD	1	3	6	1	4	3	2	2	1	2	0	1	3	0	2
Punts	87	69	94	88	81	75	82	72	76	96	97	43	69	83	91
Yds. Punted	3571	2680	4419	3743	3135	3225	3485	3029	3180	4051	4221	1809	2813	3382	3775
Avg. Yds. per Punt	41.0	38.8	47.0	42.5	38.7	43.0	42.5	42.1	41.8	42.2	43.5	42.1	40.8	40.7	41.5
Punt Returns	43	34	39	45	41	29	33	45	37	47	44	43	23	38	41
Yds. Returned	472	463	420	405	493	255	251	307	288	376	508	400	151	396	431
Avg. Yds. per Return	11.0	13.6	10.8	9.0	12.0	8.8	7.6	6.8	7.8	8.0	11.5	9.3	6.6	10.4	10.5
Returned for TD	0	0	1	0	1	0	1	0	0	0	0	0	0	1	1
Kickoff Returns	67	70	76	51	64	80	54	77	87	60	49	55	61	54	65
Yds. Returned	1487	1598	1769	1060	1476	1876	1008	1647	2027	1062	1165	1123	1336	1208	1354
Avg. Yds. per Return	22.2	22.8	23.3	20.8	23.1	23.5	18.7	21.4	23.3	17.7	23.8	20.4	21.9	22.4	20.8
Returned for TD	0	1	2	0	0	0	0	0	0	0	1	0	0	0	0
Fumbles	26	27	33	21	25	24	28	35	35	41	20	38	19	20	33
Lost	13	11	13	8	14	14	12	16	13	13	10	22	7	10	15
Out of Bounds	1	1	3	2	3	1	3	1	3	4	0	2	2	4	0
Own Rec. for TD	0	0	1	0	0	0	0	0	0	0	0	0	0	0	0
Opp. Rec. by	6	12	11	17	16	6	19	9	15	13	19	13	10	11	11
Opp. Rec. for TD	2	0	1	2	0	1	1	1	1	1	1	2	1	0	1
Penalties	72	90	87	63	91	116	80	109	119	97	100	107	82	77	104
Yds. Penalized	620	754	747	622	744	1081	633	835	1025	905	768	847	669	672	828
Total Points Scored	295	291	253	338	246	270	390	290	333	294	343	503	409	324	256
Total TDs	33	29	27	37	26	30	47	35	36	32	38	62	51	34	25
TDs Rushing	10	9	9	12	8	8	11	10	8	11	6	20	16	17	10
TDs Passing	18	19	12	20	14	18	32	23	27	19	27	37	32	13	13
TDs on Ret. and Rec.	5	1	6	5	4	4	4	2	1	2	5	5	3	4	2
Extra Point Kicks	32	28	22	34	24	23	44	29	32	29	37	58	47	30	22
Extra Point Kicks Att.	32	28	23	34	24	23	45	30	32	30	38	58	47	30	22
2Pt Conversions	1	1	0	1	0	2	1	3	1	2	0	2	1	3	2
2Pt Conversions Att.	1	1	4	1	2	7	2	5	4	2	0	4	3	4	3
Safeties	0	0	0	1	0	0	1	0	1	0	0	0	0	0	1
Field Goals Made	21	29	23	26	22	21	20	15	27	23	26	23	18	28	26
Field Goals Attempted	26	37	28	31	33	30	31	18	31	30	31	29	25	35	33
% Successful	80.8	78.4	82.1	83.9	66.7	70.0	64.5	83.3	87.1	76.7	83.9	79.3	72.0	80.0	78.8

NATIONAL FOOTBALL CONFERENCE DEFENSE

	Ariz.	Atl.	Car.	Chi.	Dall.	Det.	GB	Minn.	NO	NYG	Phil.	StL	SF	TB	Wash.
First Downs	319	298	304	277	272	321	278	312	284	268	262	256	289	262	271
Rushing	124	95	106	71	90	99	83	127	88	83	88	77	89	86	103
Passing	179	184	187	191	160	189	176	166	169	161	150	153	179	156	149
Penalty	16	19	11	15	22	33	19	19	27	24	24	26	21	20	19
Rushes	496	405	521	373	472	470	406	477	443	428	455	366	389	415	484
Net Yds. Gained	2087	1943	2301	1313	1710	1993	1769	2299	1715	1545	1837	1374	1571	1702	1869
Avg. Gain	4.2	4.8	4.4	3.5	3.6	4.2	4.4	4.8	3.9	3.6	4.0	3.8	4.0	4.1	3.9
Avg. Yds. per Game	130.4	121.4	143.8	82.1	106.9	124.6	110.6	143.7	107.2	96.6	114.8	85.9	98.2	106.4	116.8
Passes Attempted	556	515	510	602	489	514	583	478	452	521	517	541	567	493	473
Completed	337	331	306	355	287	312	341	291	278	298	288	314	332	273	262
% Completed	60.6	64.3	60.0	59.0	58.7	60.7	58.5	60.9	61.5	57.2	55.7	58.0	58.6	55.4	55.4
Total Yds. Gained	3726	4132	3809	3959	3019	3752	3505	3571	3678	3750	3147	3348	3603	3223	3116
Times Sacked	19	37	26	48	24	31	52	30	53	46	45	45	32	42	25
Yds. Lost	128	230	167	294	130	224	337	204	323	320	283	251	220	272	139
Net Yds. Gained	3598	3902	3642	3665	2889	3528	3168	3367	3355	3430	2864	3097	3383	2951	2977
Avg. Yds. per Game	224.9	243.9	227.6	229.1	180.6	220.5	198.0	210.4	209.7	214.4	179.0	193.6	211.4	184.4	186.1
Net Yds. per Pass Play	6.26	7.07	6.79	5.64	5.63	6.47	4.99	6.63	6.64	6.05	5.10	5.28	5.65	5.52	5.98
Yds. Gained per Comp.	11.06	12.48	12.45	11.15	10.52	12.03	10.28	12.27	13.23	12.58	10.93	10.66	10.85	11.81	11.89
Combined Net Yds. Gained	5685	5845	5943	4978	4599	5521	4937	5666	5070	4975	4701	4471	4954	4653	4846
% Total Yds. Rushing	36.7	33.2	38.7	26.4	37.2	36.1	35.8	40.6	33.8	31.1	39.1	30.7	31.7	36.6	38.6
% Total Yds. Passing	63.3	66.8	61.3	73.6	62.8	63.9	64.2	59.4	66.2	68.9	60.9	69.3	68.3	63.4	61.4
Avg. Yds. per Game	355.3	365.3	371.4	311.1	287.4	345.1	308.6	354.1	316.9	310.9	293.8	279.4	309.6	290.8	302.9
Ball Control Plays	1071	957	1057	1023	985	1015	1041	985	948	995	1017	952	988	950	982
Avg. Yds. per Play	5.3	6.1	5.6	4.9	4.7	5.4	4.7	5.8	5.3	5.0	4.6	4.7	5.0	4.9	4.9
Avg. Time of Poss.	32:15	28:42	32:30	29:25	29:47	31:26	30:28	30:49	30:36	30:17	31:21	28:15	28:11	28:20	29:45
Third Down Efficiency	38.2	46.3	41.6	35.9	35.5	41.4	39.1	40.2	39.8	30.3	30.6	33.0	37.1	36.1	36.2
Intercepted By	17	18	24	20	9	16	20	8	15	15	14	21	24	28	23
Yds. Returned By	294	154	374	372	191	217	344	47	209	129	152	369	330	419	209
Returned for TD	3	0	1	3	3	3	2	1	0	1	2	4	2	2	1
Punts	75	71	85	90	79	72	86	72	67	90	104	79	72	78	77
Yds. Punted	3251	3074	3457	3662	3298	3065	3644	2904	2917	3761	4225	3317	2981	3234	3260
Avg. Yds. per Punt	43.3	43.3	40.7	40.7	41.7	42.6	42.4	40.3	43.5	41.8	40.6	42.0	41.4	41.5	42.3
Punt Returns	48	17	42	45	38	39	34	34	36	45	56	17	34	44	44
Yds. Returned	481	130	425	327	493	387	288	366	316	543	488	167	290	380	434
Avg. Yds. per Return	10.0	7.6	10.1	7.3	13.0	9.9	8.5	10.8	8.8	12.1	8.7	9.8	8.5	8.6	9.9
Returned for TD	0	0	1	0	0	1	0	0	1	1	0	0	0	1	1
Kickoff Returns	53	64	60	66	54	53	76	59	66	66	67	86	68	63	54
Yds. Returned	967	1286	1340	1353	1164	1143	1520	1266	1472	1593	1430	2194	1408	1321	945
Avg. Yds. per Return	18.2	20.1	22.3	20.5	21.6	21.6	20.0	21.5	22.3	24.1	21.3	25.5	20.7	21.0	17.5
Returned for TD	1	0	0	0	0	0	0	1	0	0	0	2	0	0	0
Fumbles	27	23	27	34	29	19	36	22	28	29	39	21	24	22	31
Lost	7	12	12	17	16	6	19	10	15	13	19	13	10	11	11
Out of Bounds	3	1	3	2	1	2	2	2	2	2	1	1	1	0	6
Own Rec. for TD	0	0	0	0	0	0	0	0	0	0	1	0	0	0	0
Opp. Rec. by	13	11	12	8	13	14	12	15	13	13	13	22	7	10	15
Opp. Rec. for TD	1	1	2	2	1	2	2	2	0	1	1	0	0	0	1
Penalties	110	97	96	97	69	95	104	92	100	100	85	100	95	91	83
Yds. Penalized	980	852	793	808	634	896	921	874	877	695	741	830	812	742	672
Total Points Scored	343	377	410	203	338	424	266	390	409	321	208	273	282	280	303
Total TDs	39	46	48	21	37	52	28	42	47	36	20	31	30	29	33
TDs Rushing	10	13	13	6	12	15	10	21	15	7	6	11	9	8	10
TDs Passing	26	29	25	12	20	30	14	16	30	25	13	16	18	20	19
TDs on Ret. and Rec.	3	4	10	3	5	7	4	5	2	4	1	4	3	1	4
Extra Point Kicks	36	44	43	19	33	49	20	39	42	34	17	27	23	25	33
Extra Point Kicks Att.	36	44	44	20	34	50	20	39	42	34	17	27	23	25	33
2Pt Conversions	2	0	2	1	0	2	5	0	2	1	1	0	4	3	0
2Pt Conversions Att.	3	1	4	1	3	2	8	3	5	2	3	4	6	4	0
Safeties	0	0	0	1	1	1	1	0	0	0	0	0	1	0	0
Field Goals Made	23	19	25	18	27	19	22	33	27	23	23	20	23	25	24
Field Goals Attempted	32	24	30	28	36	27	28	38	31	31	32	26	27	29	29
% Successful	71.9	79.2	83.3	64.3	75.0	70.4	78.6	86.8	87.1	74.2	71.9	76.9	85.2	86.2	82.8

AFC, NFC, AND NFL SUMMARY

	AFC Offense Total	AFC Offense Average	AFC Defense Total	AFC Defense Average	NFC Offense Total	NFC Offense Average	NFC Defense Total	NFC Defense Average	NFL Total	NFL Average
First Downs	4689	293.1	4661	291.3	4245	283.0	4273	284.9	8934	288.2
Rushing	1598	99.9	1550	96.9	1361	90.7	1409	93.9	2959	95.5
Passing	2724	170.3	2724	170.3	2549	169.9	2549	169.9	5273	170.1
Penalty	367	22.9	387	24.2	335	22.3	315	21.0	702	22.6
Rushes	7279	454.9	7066	441.6	6387	425.8	6600	440.0	13666	440.8
Net Yds. Gained	29374	1835.9	28412	1775.8	26066	1737.7	27028	1801.9	55440	1788.4
Avg. Gain	—	4.0	—	4.0	—	4.1	—	4.1	—	4.1
Avg. Yds. per Game	—	114.7	—	111.0	—	108.6	—	112.6	—	111.8
Passes Attempted	8243	515.2	8370	523.1	7938	529.2	7811	520.7	16181	522.0
Completed	4895	305.9	4937	308.6	4647	309.8	4605	307.0	9542	307.8
% Completed	—	59.4	—	59.0	—	58.5	—	59.0	—	59.0
Total Yds. Gained	56135	3508.4	56301	3518.8	53504	3566.9	53338	3555.9	109639	3536.7
Times Sacked	608	38.0	641	40.1	588	39.2	555	37.0	1196	38.6
Yds. Lost	3941	246.3	4037	252.3	3618	241.2	3522	234.8	7559	243.8
Net Yds. Gained	52194	3262.1	52264	3266.5	49886	3325.7	49816	3321.1	102080	3292.9
Avg. Yds. per Game	—	203.9	—	204.2	—	207.9	—	207.6	—	205.8
Net Yds. per Pass Play	—	5.90	—	5.80	—	5.85	—	5.95	—	5.87
Yds. Gained per Comp.	—	11.47	—	11.40	—	11.51	—	11.58	—	11.49
Combined Net Yds. Gained	81568	5098.0	80676	5042.3	75952	5063.5	76844	5122.9	157520	5081.3
% Total Yds. Rushing	—	36.0	—	35.2	—	34.3	—	35.2	—	35.2
% Total Yds. Passing	—	64.0	—	64.8	—	65.7	—	64.8	—	64.8
Avg. Yds. per Game	—	318.6	—	315.1	—	316.5	—	320.2	—	317.6
Ball Control Plays	16130	1008.1	16077	1004.8	14913	994.2	14966	997.7	31043	1001.4
Avg. Yds. per Play	—	5.1	—	5.0	—	5.1	—	5.1	—	5.1
Third Down Efficiency	—	38.2	—	37.5	—	36.6	—	37.4	—	37.4
Interceptions	283	17.7	273	17.1	262	17.5	272	18.1	545	17.6
Yds. Returned	4082	255.1	3898	243.6	3626	241.7	3810	254.0	7708	248.6
Returned for TD	28	1.8	31	1.9	31	2.1	28	1.9	59	1.9
Punts	1276	79.8	1282	80.1	1203	80.2	1197	79.8	2479	80.0
Yds. Punted	53449	3340.6	53917	3369.8	50518	3367.9	50050	3336.7	103967	3353.8
Avg. Yds. per Punt	—	41.9	—	42.1	—	42.0	—	41.8	—	41.9
Punt Returns	578	36.1	587	36.7	582	38.8	573	38.2	1160	37.4
Yds. Returned	5721	357.6	5822	363.9	5616	374.4	5515	367.7	11337	365.7
Avg. Yds. per Return	—	9.9	—	9.9	—	9.6	—	9.6	—	9.8
Returned for TD	7	0.4	6	0.4	5	0.3	6	0.4	12	0.4
Kickoff Returns	1027	64.2	1042	65.1	970	64.7	955	63.7	1997	64.4
Yds. Returned	22012	1375.8	22806	1425.4	21196	1413.1	20402	1360.1	43208	1393.8
Avg. Yds. per Return	—	21.4	—	21.9	—	21.9	—	21.4	—	21.6
Returned for TD	6	0.4	6	0.4	4	0.3	4	0.3	10	0.3
Fumbles	401	25.1	415	25.9	425	28.3	411	27.4	826	26.6
Lost	192	12.0	192	12.0	191	12.7	191	12.7	383	12.4
Out of Bounds	25	1.6	26	1.6	30	2.0	29	1.9	55	1.8
Own Rec. for TD	1	0.1	1	0.1	1	0.1	1	0.1	2	0.1
Opp. Rec.	191	11.9	191	11.9	188	12.5	188	12.5	379	12.2
Opp. Rec. for TD	17	1.1	15	0.9	14	0.9	16	1.1	31	1.0
Penalties	1481	92.6	1461	91.3	1394	92.9	1414	94.3	2875	92.7
Yds. Penalized	12574	785.9	12197	762.3	11750	783.3	12127	808.5	24324	784.6
Total Points Scored	5189	324.3	5197	324.8	4835	322.3	4827	321.8	10024	323.4
Total TDs	578	36.1	581	36.3	542	36.1	539	35.9	1120	36.1
TDs Rushing	200	12.5	199	12.4	165	11.0	166	11.1	365	11.8
TDs Passing	311	19.4	322	20.1	324	21.6	313	20.9	635	20.5
TDs on Ret. and Rec.	67	4.2	60	3.8	53	3.5	60	4.0	120	3.9
Extra Point Kicks	517	32.3	524	32.8	491	32.7	484	32.3	1008	32.5
Extra Point Kicks Att.	531	33.2	539	33.7	496	33.1	488	32.5	1027	33.1
2Pt Conversions	20	1.3	17	1.1	20	1.3	23	1.5	40	1.3
2Pt Conversions Att.	47	2.9	41	2.6	43	2.9	49	3.3	90	2.9
Safeties	6	0.4	5	0.3	4	0.3	5	0.3	10	0.3
Field Goals Made	384	24.0	381	23.8	348	23.2	351	23.4	732	23.6
Field Goals Attempted	511	31.9	511	31.9	448	29.9	448	29.9	959	30.9
% Successful	—	75.1	—	74.6	—	77.7	—	78.3	—	76.3

CLUB LEADERS

	Offense	Defense
First Downs	StL 357	Pitt. 254
Rushing	Pitt. 148	Pitt. 70
Passing	StL 236	Mia. 148
Penalty	Buff. 32	Car. 11
Rushes	Pitt. 580	Pitt. 339
Net Yds. Gained	Pitt. 2774	Pitt. 1195
Avg. Gain	StL 4.9	SD 3.3
Passes Attempted	Det. 609	NO 452
Completed	StL 379	Mia. & Wash. 262
% Completed	StL 68.8	NE 54.8
Total Yds. Gained	StL 4903	Dall. 3019
Times Sacked	Chi. 17	Pitt. 55
Yds. Lost	SF 114	Pitt. 367
Net Yds. Gained	StL 4663	Mia. 2829
Net Yds. per Pass Play	StL 7.9	GB 5.0
Yds. Gained per Comp.	Atl. 13.3	NYJ 10.1
Combined Net Yds. Gained	StL 6690	Pitt. 4137
% Total Yds. Rushing	Dall. 49.6	Tenn. 25.9
% Total Yds. Passing	Det. 72.0	NYJ 58.2
Ball Control Plays	Balt. 1080	Pitt. 919
Avg. Yds. per Play	StL 6.6	Balt. 4.4
Avg. Time of Poss.	Pitt. 34:10	—
Third Down Efficiency	StL 50.0	NYG 30.3
Interceptions	—	Cle. 33
Yds. Returned	—	Cle. 499
Returned for TD	—	Mia. & NE 5
Punts	Cle. 99	—
Yds. Punted	Car. 4419	—
Avg. Yds. per Punt	Car. 47.0	—
Punt Returns	Pitt. 50	Atl. & StL 17
Yds. Returned	Balt. 563	NE 124
Avg. Yds. per Return	Atl. 13.6	Mia. 4.5
Returned for TD	NE 2	—
Kickoff Returns	NO 87	Cin. 46
Yds. Returned	NO 2027	Wash. 945
Avg. Yds. per Return	SD 26.0	Wash. 17.5
Returned for TD	Car. & SD 2	—
Total Points Scored	StL 503	Chi. 203
Total TDs	StL 62	Phil. 20
TDs Rushing	StL 20	Pitt. 5
TDs Passing	StL 37	Chi. 12
TDs on Ret. and Rec.	Mia. & NE 7	Phil. & SD & TB 1
Extra Point Kicks	StL 58	Phil. 17
2-Point Conversions	Den. & Ind. & KC & Minn. & TB & Tenn. 3	—
Safeties	Jax. 2	—
Field Goals Made	Den. 31	Pitt. 9
Field Goals Attempted	Pitt. 44	Pitt. 20
% Successful	Mia. 90.5	Pitt. 45.0

NFL CLUB RANKINGS BY YARDS

	Offense			Defense		
	Total	Rush	Pass	Total	Rush	Pass
Arizona	18	27	13	28	24	26
Atlanta	15	16	17	30	21	30
Baltimore	14	11	16	2	4	8
Buffalo	13	22	12	21	26	13
Carolina	30	29	26	31	31	28
Chicago	26T	17	24	15	2	29
Cincinnati	23	18T	23	9	11	12
Cleveland	31	31	28	22	29	10
Dallas	29	3	31	4	13	3
Denver	22	10	25	8	6	16
Detroit	16	28	6	26	23	25
Green Bay	6	21	3	12	16	15
Indianapolis	2	7	2	29	25	27
Jacksonville	20	26	18	16T	10	22
Kansas City	5	6	5	23	27	14
Miami	21	23	19	5	17	*1
Minnesota	12	25	7	27	30	18
New England	19	13	22	24	19	24
New Orleans	10	18T	10	16T	14	17
N.Y. Giants	9	15	8T	14	8	21
N.Y. Jets	24	4	29	19	28	7
Oakland	7	24	4	18	22	9
Philadelphia	17	14	20	7	18	2
Pittsburgh	3	*1	21	*1	*1	4
St. Louis	*1	5	*1	3	3	11
San Diego	11	20	11	11	7	20
San Francisco	4	2	14	13	9	19
Seattle	25	9	27	20	15	23
Tampa Bay	26T	30	15	6	12	5
Tennessee	8	12	8T	25	5	31
Washington	28	8	30	10	20	6

T = Tied for position
* = League Leader

AFC TAKEAWAYS/GIVEAWAYS

	Takeaways			Giveaways			Net
	Int	Fum	Total	Int	Fum	Total	Diff.
N.Y. Jets	20	19	39	14	7	21	+18
Denver	22	15	37	19	8	27	+10
Cleveland	33	9	42	21	12	33	+9
New England	22	13	35	15	13	28	+7
Pittsburgh	16	12	28	12	9	21	+7
Seattle	14	13	27	12	9	21	+6
San Diego	19	12	31	18	11	29	+2
Oakland	17	7	24	9	16	25	-1
Jacksonville	12	12	24	14	13	27	-3
Tennessee	13	11	24	17	11	28	-4
Kansas City	13	13	26	24	9	33	-7
Baltimore	16	12	28	20	16	36	-8
Cincinnati	13	15	28	26	11	37	-9
Miami	17	11	28	19	19	38	-10
Indianapolis	15	10	25	23	15	38	-13
Buffalo	11	8	19	20	13	33	-14
AFC Totals	273	192	465	283	192	475	-10

NFC TAKEAWAYS/GIVEAWAYS

	Takeaways			Giveaways			Net
	Int	Fum	Total	Int	Fum	Total	Diff.
Tampa Bay	28	11	39	12	10	22	+17
San Francisco	24	10	34	12	7	19	+15
Chicago	20	17	37	16	8	24	+13
Green Bay	20	19	39	15	12	27	+12
Philadelphia	14	19	33	14	10	24	+9
Washington	23	11	34	13	15	28	+6
Atlanta	18	12	30	17	11	28	+2
Carolina	24	12	36	22	13	35	+1
N.Y. Giants	15	13	28	16	13	29	-1
Arizona	17	7	24	14	13	27	-3
New Orleans	15	15	30	22	13	35	-5
Dallas	9	16	25	20	14	34	-9
St. Louis	21	13	34	22	22	44	-10
Detroit	16	6	22	24	14	38	-16
Minnesota	8	10	18	23	16	39	-21
NFC Totals	272	191	463	262	191	453	+10

SCORING

POINTS
NFC: 128 Marshall Faulk, St. Louis
AFC: 125 Mike Vanderjagt, Indianapolis

TOUCHDOWNS
NFC: 21 Marshall Faulk, St. Louis
AFC: 16 Shaun Alexander, Seattle

EXTRA POINT KICKS
NFC: 58 Jeff Wilkins, St. Louis
AFC: 42 Sebastian Janikowski, Oakland

TWO-POINT EXTRA POINT PLAYS
NFC: 2 Mike Alstott, Tampa Bay
     2 Daunte Culpepper, Minnesota
AFC: 1 many players

FIELD GOALS
AFC: 31 Jason Elam, Denver
NFC: 29 Jay Feely, Atlanta

FIELD GOAL ATTEMPTS
AFC: 44 Kris Brown, Pittsburgh
NFC: 37 Jay Feely, Atlanta

LONGEST FIELD GOAL
AFC: 55 Kris Brown, Pittsburgh at Kansas City, October 14
NFC: 55 Jay Feely, Atlanta at Arizona, September 30
     55 Brett Conway, Washington at N.Y. Giants, October 7

MOST POINTS, GAME
NFC: 24 Marshall Faulk, St. Louis vs. Indianapolis, December 30 (4 TD)
AFC: 18 Marvin Harrison, Indianapolis vs. Buffalo, September 23 (3 TD)
     18 LaDainian Tomlinson, San Diego vs. Cincinnati, September 30 (3 TD)
     18 Priest Holmes, Kansas City at Washington, September 30 (3 TD)
     18 David Patten, New England at Indianapolis, October 21 (3 TD)
     18 Corey Dillon, Cincinnati at Detroit, October 28 (3 TD)
     18 Curtis Martin, N.Y. Jets vs. Kansas City, November 11 (3 TD)
     18 Marvin Harrison, Indianapolis vs. Miami, November 11 (3 TD)
     18 Shaun Alexander, Seattle vs. Oakland, November 11 (3 TD)
     18 Jerry Rice, Oakland vs. San Diego, November 18 (3 TD)

TEAM LEADERS, POINTS
AFC: BALTIMORE, 115, Matt Stover; BUFFALO, 52, Jake Arians; CINCINNATI, 78, Corey Dillon; CLEVELAND, 95, Phil Dawson; DENVER, 124, Jason Elam; INDIANAPOLIS, 125, Mike Vanderjagt; JACKSONVILLE, 83, Mike Hollis; KANSAS CITY, 108, Todd Peterson; MIAMI, 96, Olindo Mare; NEW ENGLAND, 113, Adam Vinatieri; N.Y. JETS, 104, John Hall; OAKLAND, 111, Sebastian Janikowski; PITTSBURGH, 124, Kris Brown; SAN DIEGO, 89, Wade Richey; SEATTLE, 96, Shaun Alexander; TENNESSEE, 94, Joe Nedney

NFC: ARIZONA, 73, Bill Gramatica; ATLANTA, 115, Jay Feely; CAROLINA, 91, John Kasay; CHICAGO, 112, Paul Edinger; DALLAS, 51, Tim Seder; DETROIT, 86, Jason Hanson; GREEN BAY, 104, Ryan Longwell; MINNESOTA, 74, Gary Anderson; NEW ORLEANS, 113, John Carney; N.Y. GIANTS, 98, Morten Andersen; PHILADELPHIA, 115, David Akers; ST. LOUIS, 128, Marshall Faulk; SAN FRANCISCO, 101, Jose Cortez; TAMPA BAY, 97, Martin Gramatica; WASHINGTON, 100, Brett Conway

TEAM CHAMPION
NFC: 503 St. Louis
AFC: 413 Indianapolis

NFL TOP TEN SCORERS—KICKERS

	XP	XPA	FG	FGA	PTS
Wilkins, Jeff, StL	58	58	23	29	127
Vanderjagt, Mike, Ind.	41	42	28	34	125
Brown, Kris, Pitt.	34	37	30	44	124
Elam, Jason, Den.	31	31	31	36	124
Akers, David, Phil.	37	38	26	31	115
Feely, Jay, Atl.	28	28	29	37	115
Stover, Matt, Balt.	25	25	30	35	115
Carney, John, NO	32	32	27	31	113
Vinatieri, Adam, NE	41	42	24	30	113
Edinger, Paul, Chi.	34	34	26	31	112

NFL TOP TEN SCORERS—NONKICKERS

	TD	TDR	TDP	TDM	X2G	PTS
Faulk, Marshall, StL	21	12	9	0	1	128
Alexander, Shaun, Sea.	16	14	2	0	0	96
Owens, Terrell, SF	16	0	16	0	0	96
Harrison, Marvin, Ind.	15	0	15	0	0	90
Dillon, Corey, Cin.	13	10	3	0	0	78
Smith, Antowain, NE	13	12	1	0	0	78
Alstott, Mike, TB	11	10	1	0	2	70
Smith, Rod, Den.	11	0	11	0	1	68
Green, Ahman, GB	11	9	2	0	0	66
Mason, Derrick, Tenn.	10	0	9	1	1	62

AFC—INDIVIDUAL SCORERS

KICKERS

	XP	XPA	FG	FGA	PTS
Vanderjagt, Mike, Ind.	41	42	28	34	125
Brown, Kris, Pitt.	34	37	30	44	124
Elam, Jason, Den.	31	31	31	36	124
Stover, Matt, Balt.	25	25	30	35	115
Vinatieri, Adam, NE	41	42	24	30	113
Janikowski, Sebastian, Oak.	42	42	23	28	111
Peterson, Todd, KC	27	28	27	35	108
Hall, John, NYJ	32	32	24	31	104
Mare, Olindo, Mia.	39	40	19	21	96
Dawson, Phil, Cle.	29	30	22	25	95
Nedney, Joe, Tenn.	34	35	20	28	94
Lindell, Rian, Sea.	33	33	20	32	93
Richey, Wade, SD	26	26	21	32	89
Hollis, Mike, Jax.	29	31	18	28	83
Rackers, Neil, Cin.	23	24	17	28	74
Arians, Jake, Buff.	16	17	12	21	52
Christie, Steve, SD	6	6	9	11	33
Graham, Shayne, Buff.	7	7	6	8	25
Daluiso, Brad, Oak.	1	2	3	4	10
Holmes, Jaret, Jax.	1	1	0	0	1

NONKICKERS

	TD	TDR	TDP	TDM	X2G	PTS
Alexander, Shaun, Sea.	16	14	2	0	0	96
Harrison, Marvin, Ind.	15	0	15	0	0	90
Dillon, Corey, Cin.	13	10	3	0	0	78
Smith, Antowain, NE	13	12	1	0	0	78
Smith, Rod, Den.	11	0	11	0	1	68
Mason, Derrick, Tenn.	10	0	9	1	1	62
Brown, Tim, Oak.	10	0	9	1	0	60

Player						
Holmes, Priest, KC	10	8	2	0	0	60
Mack, Stacey, Jax.	10	9	1	0	0	60
Martin, Curtis, NYJ	10	10	0	0	0	60
Rhodes, Dominic, Ind.	10	9	0	1	0	60
Tomlinson, LaDainian, SD	10	10	0	0	0	60
Johnson, Kevin, Cle.	9	0	9	0	0	54
Rice, Jerry, Oak.	9	0	9	0	0	54
Jackson, Darrell, Sea.	8	0	8	0	0	48
Pollard, Marcus, Ind.	8	0	8	0	0	48
Smith, Jimmy, Jax.	8	0	8	0	0	48
Smith, Lamar, Mia.	8	6	2	0	0	48
Dyson, Kevin, Tenn.	7	0	7	0	1	44
Ismail, Qadry, Balt.	7	0	7	0	1	44
Brown, Troy, NE	7	0	5	2	0	42
Chambers, Chris, Mia.	7	0	7	0	0	42
Coles, Laveranues, NYJ	7	0	7	0	0	42
Conway, Curtis, SD	7	1	6	0	0	42
Price, Peerless, Buff.	7	0	7	0	0	42
Richardson, Tony, KC	7	7	0	0	0	42
Gonzalez, Tony, KC	6	0	6	0	1	38
McCardell, Keenan, Jax.	6	0	6	0	1	38
White, Jamel, Cle.	6	5	1	0	1	38
Burress, Plaxico, Pitt.	6	0	6	0	0	36
Clark, Desmond, Den.	6	0	6	0	0	36
Crockett, Zack, Oak.	6	6	0	0	0	36
Wheatley, Tyrone, Oak.	6	5	1	0	0	36
Moulds, Eric, Buff.	5	0	5	0	1	32
Becht, Anthony, NYJ	5	0	5	0	0	30
Brookins, Jason, Balt.	5	5	0	0	0	30
George, Eddie, Tenn.	5	5	0	0	0	30
Graham, Jeff, SD	5	0	5	0	0	30
McNair, Steve, Tenn.	5	5	0	0	0	30
Patten, David, NE	5	1	4	0	0	30
Stewart, Kordell, Pitt.	5	5	0	0	0	30
Anderson, Mike, Den.	4	4	0	0	1	26
Carswell, Dwayne, Den.	4	0	4	0	1	26
Bettis, Jerome, Pitt.	4	4	0	0	0	24
Centers, Larry, Buff.	4	2	2	0	0	24
Fiedler, Jay, Mia.	4	4	0	0	0	24
Fuamatu-Ma'afala, Chris, Pitt.	4	3	1	0	0	24
Henry, Travis, Buff.	4	4	0	0	0	24
Jones, Freddie, SD	4	0	4	0	0	24
Manning, Peyton, Ind.	4	4	0	0	0	24
Minor, Travis, Mia.	4	2	1	1	0	24
Ward, Hines, Pitt.	4	0	4	0	0	24
Wiggins, Jermaine, NE	4	0	4	0	0	24
Wycheck, Frank, Tenn.	4	0	4	0	0	24
James, Edgerrin, Ind.	3	3	0	0	1	20
McKnight, James, Mia.	3	0	3	0	1	20
Alexander, Derrick, KC	3	0	3	0	0	18
Allen, Terry, Balt.	3	3	0	0	0	18
Edwards, Marc, NE	3	1	2	0	0	18
Faulk, Kevin, NE	3	1	2	0	0	18
Gadsden, Oronde, Mia.	3	0	3	0	0	18
Garner, Charlie, Oak.	3	1	2	0	0	18
Hape, Patrick, Den.	3	0	3	0	0	18
Joseph, Elvis, Jax.	3	0	2	1	0	18
Riemersma, Jay, Buff.	3	0	3	0	0	18
Taylor, Travis, Balt.	3	0	3	0	0	18
Williams, Roland, Oak.	3	0	3	0	0	18
Dugans, Ron, Cin.	2	0	2	0	1	14
Gannon, Rich, Oak.	2	2	0	0	0	14
Anderson, Richie, NYJ	2	0	2	0	0	12
Ayanbadejo, Obafemi, Balt.	2	1	1	0	0	12
Brady, Kyle, Jax.	2	0	2	0	0	12
Bryson, Shawn, Buff.	2	2	0	0	0	12
Clements, Nate, Buff.	2	0	0	2	0	12
Dorsett, Anthony, Oak.	2	0	0	2	0	12
Dwight, Tim, SD	2	1	0	1	0	12
Edwards, Troy, Pitt.	2	1	0	1	0	12
Green, Mike, Tenn.	2	1	1	0	0	12
Jackson, James, Cle.	2	2	0	0	0	12
Jenkins, Ronney, SD	2	0	0	2	0	12
Jordan, LaMont, NYJ	2	1	1	0	0	12
Konrad, Rob, Mia.	2	1	1	0	0	12
Law, Ty, NE	2	0	0	2	0	12
Marion, Brock, Mia.	2	0	0	2	0	12
Mili, Itula, Sea.	2	0	2	0	0	12
Mitchell, Donald, Tenn.	2	0	0	2	0	12
Morgan, Quincy, Cle.	2	0	2	0	0	12
Parker, Larry, KC	2	0	2	0	0	12
Pathon, Jerome, Ind.	2	0	2	0	0	12
Ritchie, Jon, Oak.	2	0	2	0	0	12
Santiago, O.J., Cle.	2	0	2	0	0	12
Scott, Chad, Pitt.	2	0	0	2	0	12
Scott, Darnay, Cin.	2	0	2	0	0	12
Sellers, Mike, Cle.	2	0	2	0	0	12
Sharpe, Shannon, Balt.	2	0	2	0	0	12
Shaw, Bobby, Pitt.	2	0	2	0	0	12
Smith, Otis, NE	2	0	0	2	0	12
Spoon, Brandon, Buff.	2	0	2	0	0	12
Stokley, Brandon, Balt.	2	0	2	0	0	12
Weaver, Jed, Mia.	2	0	2	0	0	12
Zereoue, Amos, Pitt.	2	1	1	0	0	12
Bennett, Drew, Tenn.	1	0	1	0	1	8
Dilger, Ken, Ind.	1	0	1	0	1	8
Fauria, Christian, Sea.	1	0	1	0	1	8
Kennison, Eddie, KC	1	0	1	0	1	8
Ricks, Mikhael, KC	1	0	1	0	0	*8
Abraham, John, NYJ	1	0	0	1	0	6
Allen, Eric, Oak.	1	0	0	1	0	6
Bannister, Alex, Sea.	1	0	0	1	0	6
Battles, Ainsley, Jax.	1	0	0	1	0	6
Beasley, Aaron, Jax.	1	0	0	1	0	6
Bowers, R.J., Pitt.	1	1	0	0	0	6
Brigham, Jeremy, Oak.	1	0	1	0	0	6
Brown, Courtney, Cle.	1	0	0	1	0	6
Brunell, Mark, Jax.	1	1	0	0	0	6
Buckley, Terrell, NE	1	0	0	1	0	6
Burris, Jeff, Ind.	1	0	0	1	0	6
Bush, Devin, Cle.	1	0	0	1	0	6
Charlton, Ike, Sea.	1	0	0	1	0	6
Chrebet, Wayne, NYJ	1	0	1	0	0	6
Cloud, Mike, KC	1	1	0	0	0	6
Cunningham, Randall, Balt.	1	1	0	0	0	6
Cushing, Matt, Pitt.	1	0	1	0	0	6
Dawson, JaJuan, Cle.	1	0	1	0	0	6
Dearth, James, NYJ	1	0	1	0	0	6
Dunn, Jason, KC	1	0	1	0	0	6
Farmer, Danny, Cin.	1	0	1	0	0	6
Flutie, Doug, SD	1	1	0	0	0	6
Frerotte, Gus, Den.	1	1	0	0	0	6
Fuller, Corey, Cle.	1	0	0	1	0	6
Gary, Olandis, Den.	1	1	0	0	0	6
Gash, Sam, Balt.	1	0	1	0	0	6
Gay, Benjamin, Cle.	1	1	0	0	0	6
Gildon, Jason, Pitt.	1	0	0	1	0	6
Glenn, Aaron, NYJ	1	0	0	1	0	6
Glenn, Jason, NYJ	1	0	0	1	0	6
Glenn, Terry, NE	1	0	1	0	0	6
Grbac, Elvis, Balt.	1	1	0	0	0	6
Green, Victor, NYJ	1	0	0	1	0	6
Griese, Brian, Den.	1	1	0	0	0	6
Harris, Derrick, SD	1	0	0	1	0	6
Hayes, Chris, NYJ	1	0	0	1	0	6
Heap, Todd, Balt.	1	0	1	0	0	6
Heiden, Steve, SD	1	0	1	0	0	6
Henry, Anthony, Cle.	1	0	0	1	0	6
Hicks, Skip, Tenn.	1	1	0	0	0	6
Insley, Trevor, Ind.	1	0	1	0	0	6

Name					
Jackson, Sheldon, Buff.	1	0	1	0	0	6
Johnson, Chad, Cin.	1	0	1	0	0	6
Johnson, Charles, NE	1	0	1	0	0	6
Johnson, Patrick, Balt.	1	0	1	0	0	6
Johnson, Raylee, SD	1	0	0	1	0	6
Johnson, Rob, Buff.	1	1	0	0	0	6
Jones, Damon, Jax.	1	0	1	0	0	6
Kinney, Erron, Tenn.	1	0	1	0	0	6
Kirby, Terry, Oak.	1	0	0	1	0	6
Kitna, Jon, Cin.	1	1	0	0	0	6
Kreider, Dan, Pitt.	1	1	0	0	0	6
Lewis, Mo, NYJ	1	0	0	1	0	6
Lucas, Ray, Mia.	1	1	0	0	0	6
Maddox, Tommy, Pitt.	1	1	0	0	0	6
McCaffrey, Ed, Den.	1	0	1	0	0	6
McCutcheon, Daylon, Cle.	1	0	0	1	0	6
McGee, Tony, Cin.	1	0	1	0	0	6
Minnis, Snoop, KC	1	0	1	0	0	6
Mixon, Kenny, Mia.	1	0	0	1	0	6
Moreau, Frank, Jax.	1	1	0	0	0	6
Myers, Bobby, Tenn.	1	0	0	1	0	6
Neal, Lorenzo, Cin.	1	0	1	0	0	6
Nwokorie, Chukie, Ind.	1	0	0	1	0	6
Ogden, Jeff, Mia.	1	0	1	0	0	6
O'Hara, Shaun, Cle.	1	0	1	0	0	6
O'Neal, Deltha, Den.	1	0	0	1	0	6
Pass, Patrick, NE	1	0	1	0	0	6
Perry, Jason, SD	1	0	0	1	0	6
Randle, John, Sea.	1	0	0	1	0	6
Robinson, Koren, Sea.	1	0	1	0	0	6
Sharper, Jamie, Balt.	1	0	0	1	0	6
Simmons, Brian, Cin.	1	0	0	1	0	6
Spikes, Takeo, Cin.	1	0	0	1	0	6
Surtain, Patrick, Mia.	1	0	0	1	0	6
Taylor, Jason, Mia.	1	0	0	1	0	6
Thomas, Chris, KC	1	0	1	0	0	6
Thomas, Zach, Mia.	1	0	0	1	0	6
Tongue, Reggie, Sea.	1	0	0	1	0	6
Tuman, Jerame, Pitt.	1	0	1	0	0	6
Walker, Denard, Den.	1	0	0	1	0	6
Warfield, Eric, KC	1	0	0	1	0	6
Warrick, Peter, Cin.	1	0	1	0	0	6
Washington, Dewayne, Pitt.	1	0	0	1	0	6
Watters, Ricky, Sea.	1	1	0	0	0	6
Wilkins, Terrence, Ind.	1	0	0	1	0	6
Williams, James, Sea.	1	0	1	0	0	6
Woodson, Rod, Balt.	1	0	0	1	0	6
Brackens, Tony, Jax.	0	0	0	0	0	*2
Fisk, Jason, Tenn.	0	0	0	0	0	*2
Green, Trent, KC	0	0	0	0	1	2
McDougal, Kevin, Ind.	0	0	0	0	1	2
Roye, Orpheus, Cle.	0	0	0	0	0	*2

* Safety
Team safety credited to Jacksonville and Seattle.

NFC—INDIVIDUAL SCORERS
KICKERS

	XP	XPA	FG	FGA	PTS
Wilkins, Jeff, StL	58	58	23	29	127
Akers, David, Phil.	37	38	26	31	115
Feely, Jay, Atl.	28	28	29	37	115
Carney, John, NO	32	32	27	31	113
Edinger, Paul, Chi.	34	34	26	31	112
Longwell, Ryan, GB	44	45	20	31	104
Cortez, Jose, SF	47	47	18	25	101
Conway, Brett, Wash.	22	22	26	33	100
Andersen, Morten, NYG	29	30	23	28	98
Gramatica, Martin, TB	28	28	23	29	97
Kasay, John, Car.	22	23	23	28	91

Hanson, Jason, Det.	23	23	21	30	86
Anderson, Gary, Minn.	29	30	15	18	74
Gramatica, Bill, Ariz	25	25	16	20	73
Seder, Tim, Dall.	12	12	11	17	#51
Hilbert, Jon, Dall.	12	12	11	16	45
Oglesby, Cedric, Ariz	7	7	5	6	22
Brien, Doug, TB	2	2	5	6	17
Pochman, Owen, NYG	0	0	0	2	0

Also scored touchdown.

NONKICKERS

	TD	TDR	TDP	TDM	X2G	PTS
Faulk, Marshall, StL	21	12	9	0	1	128
Owens, Terrell, SF	16	0	16	0	0	96
Alstott, Mike, TB	11	10	1	0	2	70
Green, Ahman, GB	11	9	2	0	0	66
Moss, Randy, Minn.	10	0	10	0	0	60
Franks, Bubba, GB	9	0	9	0	0	54
Horn, Joe, NO	9	0	9	0	0	54
Schroeder, Bill, GB	9	0	9	0	0	54
Booker, Marty, Chi.	8	0	8	0	0	48
Boston, David, Ariz	8	0	8	0	0	48
Thrash, James, Phil.	8	0	8	0	0	48
Dayne, Ron, NYG	7	7	0	0	1	44
Thomas, Anthony, Chi.	7	7	0	0	1	44
Holt, Torry, StL	7	0	7	0	0	42
Sloan, David, Det.	7	0	7	0	0	42
Stokes, J.J., SF	7	0	7	0	0	42
Williams, Ricky, NO	7	6	1	0	0	42
Freeman, Antonio, GB	6	0	6	0	1	38
Bruce, Isaac, StL	6	0	6	0	0	36
Canidate, Trung, StL	6	6	0	0	0	36
Carter, Cris, Minn.	6	0	6	0	0	36
Dunn, Warrick, TB	6	3	3	0	0	36
Hilliard, Ike, NYG	6	0	6	0	0	36
Lewis, Chad, Phil.	6	0	6	0	0	36
Smith, Maurice, Atl.	6	5	1	0	0	36
Weinke, Chris, Car.	6	6	0	0	0	36
Culpepper, Daunte, Minn.	5	5	0	0	2	34
Davis, Stephen, Wash.	5	5	0	0	1	32
Jackson, Willie, NO	5	0	5	0	1	32
Proehl, Ricky, StL	5	0	5	0	1	32
Barlow, Kevan, SF	5	4	1	0	0	30
Conwell, Ernie, StL	5	1	4	0	0	30
Garcia, Jeff, SF	5	5	0	0	0	30
Hearst, Garrison, SF	5	4	1	0	0	30
Jones, Thomas, Ariz	5	5	0	0	0	30
Pittman, Michael, Ariz	5	5	0	0	0	30
Toomer, Amani, NYG	5	0	5	0	0	30
Walls, Wesley, Car.	5	0	5	0	0	30
Barber, Tiki, NYG	4	4	0	0	1	26
Warren, Lamont, Det.	4	3	1	0	1	26
Christian, Bob, Atl.	4	2	2	0	0	24
Cleeland, Cameron, NO	4	0	4	0	0	24
Gardner, Rod, Wash.	4	0	4	0	0	24
Johnson, Leon, Chi.	4	4	0	0	0	24
Moore, Dave, TB	4	0	4	0	0	24
Morton, Johnnie, Det.	4	0	4	0	0	24
Pinkston, Todd, Phil.	4	0	4	0	0	24
Staley, Duce, Phil.	4	2	2	0	0	24
Terrell, David, Chi.	4	0	4	0	0	24
Westbrook, Michael, Wash.	4	0	4	0	0	24
Johnson, Eric, SF	3	0	3	0	1	20
Bennett, Michael, Minn.	3	2	1	0	0	18
Carter, Ki-Jana, Wash.	3	3	0	0	0	18
Chamberlain, Byron, Minn.	3	0	3	0	0	18
Crumpler, Alge, Atl.	3	0	3	0	0	18
Finneran, Brian, Atl.	3	0	3	0	0	18
Galloway, Joey, Dall.	3	0	3	0	0	18

Player						Pts
Hakim, Az-Zahir, StL	3	0	3	0	0	18
Huntley, Richard, Car.	3	2	1	0	0	18
Jackson, Terry, SF	3	1	2	0	0	18
Jenkins, MarTay, Ariz	3	0	3	0	0	18
Johnson, Brad, TB	3	3	0	0	0	18
Jurevicius, Joe, NYG	3	0	3	0	0	18
Martin, Tony, Atl.	3	0	3	0	0	18
Schlesinger, Cory, Det.	3	3	0	0	0	18
Smith, Emmitt, Dall.	3	3	0	0	0	18
Smith, Steve, Car.	3	0	0	3	0	18
Williams, Boo, NO	3	0	3	0	0	18
Jefferson, Shawn, Atl.	2	0	2	0	1	14
Allen, James, Chi.	2	1	1	0	0	12
Anderson, Jamal, Atl.	2	1	1	0	0	12
Banks, Tony, Wash.	2	2	0	0	0	12
Baxter, Fred, Chi.	2	0	2	0	0	12
Bly, Dre', StL	2	0	0	2	0	12
Bradford, Corey, GB	2	0	2	0	0	12
Bronson, Zack, SF	2	0	0	2	0	12
Brown, Mike, Chi.	2	0	0	2	0	12
Buckhalter, Correll, Phil.	2	2	0	0	0	12
Chiaverini, Darrin, Dall.	2	0	2	0	0	12
Coakley, Dexter, Dall.	2	0	0	2	0	12
Connell, Albert, NO	2	0	2	0	0	12
Crowell, Germane, Det.	2	0	2	0	0	12
Douglas, Dameane, Phil.	2	0	2	0	0	12
Driver, Donald, GB	2	1	1	0	0	12
Flemister, Zeron, Wash.	2	0	2	0	0	12
Hambrick, Troy, Dall.	2	2	0	0	0	12
Hardy, Terry, Ariz	2	0	2	0	0	12
Harris, Jackie, Dall.	2	0	2	0	0	12
Hayes, Donald, Car.	2	0	2	0	0	12
Ismail, Raghib, Dall.	2	0	2	0	0	12
Mangum, Kris, Car.	2	0	2	0	0	12
Martin, Cecil, Phil.	2	0	2	0	0	12
Mathis, Terance, Atl.	2	0	2	0	0	12
McAllister, Deuce, NO	2	1	1	0	0	12
McKinnon, Ronald, Ariz	2	0	0	2	0	12
McNabb, Donovan, Phil.	2	2	0	0	0	12
Mitchell, Tywan, Ariz	2	0	2	0	0	12
Prentice, Travis, Minn.	2	2	0	0	0	12
Rasby, Walter, Wash.	2	0	2	0	0	12
Rivers, Marcellus, NYG	2	0	2	0	0	12
Robinson, Marcus, Chi.	2	0	2	0	0	12
Sanders, Frank, Ariz	2	0	2	0	0	12
Smith, Terrelle, NO	2	0	2	0	0	12
Stecker, Aaron, TB	2	1	1	0	0	12
Stewart, James, Det.	2	1	1	0	0	12
Swinton, Reggie, Dall.	2	0	1	1	0	12
Urlacher, Brian, Chi.	2	0	1	1	0	12
Williams, Aeneas, StL	2	0	0	2	0	12
Williams, Karl, TB	2	0	1	1	0	12
McMahon, Mike, Det.	1	1	0	0	1	8
Reed, Jake, Minn.	1	0	1	0	1	8
Anderson, Rashard, Car.	1	0	0	1	0	6
Anderson, Scotty, Det.	1	0	1	0	0	6
Arrington, LaVar, Wash.	1	0	0	1	0	6
Bailey, Robert, Det.	1	0	0	1	0	6
Barber, Ronde, TB	1	0	0	1	0	6
Bartrum, Mike, Phil.	1	0	1	0	0	6
Bates, D'Wayne, Chi.	1	0	1	0	0	6
Beasley, Fred, SF	1	1	0	0	0	6
Biakabutuka, Tim, Car.	1	1	0	0	0	6
Brooks, Aaron, NO	1	1	0	0	0	6
Byrd, Isaac, Car.	1	0	1	0	0	6
Campbell, Dan, NYG	1	0	1	0	0	6
Carter, Quincy, Dall.	1	1	0	0	0	6
Carter, Tyrone, Minn.	1	0	0	1	0	6
Chapman, Doug, Minn.	1	0	1	0	0	6
Comella, Greg, NYG	1	0	1	0	0	6
Crawford, Casey, Car.	1	0	0	1	0	6
Dawkins, Brian, Phil.	1	0	0	1	0	6
Dixon, Ron, NYG	1	0	1	0	0	6
Droughns, Reuben, Det.	1	0	1	0	0	6
Edwards, Mario, Dall.	1	0	0	1	0	6
Evans, Doug, Car.	1	0	0	1	0	6
Fair, Terry, Det.	1	0	0	1	0	6
Favre, Brett, GB	1	1	0	0	0	6
Green, Jacquez, TB	1	0	1	0	0	6
Hall, James, Det.	1	0	0	1	0	6
Hampton, William, Phil.	1	0	0	1	0	6
Harris, Walt, Chi.	1	0	0	1	0	6
Hodgins, James, StL	1	0	1	0	0	6
Holcombe, Robert, StL	1	1	0	0	0	6
Howard, Desmond, Det.	1	0	1	0	0	6
Johnson, Keyshawn, TB	1	0	1	0	0	6
Jordan, Andrew, Minn.	1	0	1	0	0	6
Kleinsasser, Jimmy, Minn.	1	1	0	0	0	6
Kozlowski, Brian, Atl.	1	0	1	0	0	6
Lee, Charles, GB	1	0	1	0	0	6
Levens, Dorsey, GB	1	0	1	0	0	6
Lucky, Mike, Dall.	1	0	1	0	0	6
Lyght, Todd, Det.	1	0	0	1	0	6
Makovicka, Joel, Ariz	1	0	1	0	0	6
Manumaleuna, Brandon, StL	1	0	1	0	0	6
Martin, David, GB	1	0	1	0	0	6
McCleon, Dexter, StL	1	0	0	1	0	6
McGarity, Wane, Dall.†	1	0	1	0	0	6
McKenzie, Mike, GB	1	0	0	1	0	6
McQuarters, R.W., Chi.	1	0	0	1	0	6
Mealey, Rondell, GB	1	0	0	1	0	6
Metcalf, Eric, Wash.	1	0	0	1	0	6
Mitchell, Brian, Phil.	1	0	0	1	0	6
Mitchell, Freddie, Phil.	1	0	1	0	0	6
Moore, Damon, Phil.	1	0	0	1	0	6
Muhammad, Muhsin, Car.	1	0	1	0	0	6
Murphy, Frank, TB	1	0	0	1	0	6
Oldham, Chris, NO	1	0	0	1	0	6
Peterson, Julian, SF	1	0	0	1	0	6
Quarles, Shelton, TB	1	0	0	1	0	6
Rackley, Derek, Atl.	1	0	1	0	0	6
Robinson, Jeff, StL	1	0	1	0	0	6
Rossum, Allen, GB	1	0	0	1	0	6
Sehorn, Jason, NYG	1	0	0	1	0	6
Shelton, Daimon, Chi.	1	0	1	0	0	6
Smith, Paul, SF	1	1	0	0	0	6
Stewart, Tony, Phil.	1	0	1	0	0	6
Stoerner, Clint, Dall.	1	1	0	0	0	6
Strahan, Michael, NYG	1	0	0	1	0	6
Streets, Tai, SF	1	0	1	0	0	6
Swift, Justin, SF	1	0	1	0	0	6
Thomas, Robert, Dall.	1	0	1	0	0	6
Thompson, Derrius, Wash.	1	0	1	0	0	6
Trotter, Jeremiah, Phil.	1	0	0	1	0	6
Vanden Bosch, Kyle, Ariz	1	0	0	1	0	6
Vaughn, Darrick, Atl.	1	0	0	1	0	6
Vick, Michael, Atl.	1	1	0	0	0	6
Wakefield, Fred, Ariz	1	0	0	1	0	6
Wiley, Michael, Dall.	1	0	1	0	0	6
Williams, Tyrone, GB	1	0	0	1	0	6
Wilson, Adrian, Ariz	1	0	0	1	0	6
Wong, Kailee, Minn.	1	0	0	1	0	6
Yoder, Todd, TB	1	0	0	1	0	6
Bennett, Donnell, Wash.	0	0	0	0	1	2
King, Shaun, TB	0	0	0	0	1	2
Plummer, Jake, Ariz	0	0	0	0	1	2
Thierry, John, GB	0	0	0	0	0	*2

* Safety

Team safety credited to Chicago, New Orleans, and Washington.

AMERICAN FOOTBALL CONFERENCE—SCORING

	TD	TDR	TDP	TDM	XKG	XKAtt	X2G	X2Att	FG	FGA	SAF	POINTS
Indianapolis	47	16	27	4	41	42	3	5	28	34	0	413
Oakland	46	14	27	5	43	44	1	2	26	32	0	399
New England	43	15	21	7	41	42	0	1	24	30	0	371
Pittsburgh	38	17	16	5	34	37	0	1	30	44	0	352
Miami	41	14	20	7	39	40	1	1	19	21	0	344
Denver	35	7	26	2	31	31	3	4	31	36	0	340
Tennessee	39	12	23	4	34	35	3	4	20	28	1	336
San Diego	35	13	16	6	32	32	0	3	30	43	0	332
Kansas City	34	16	17	1	27	28	3	6	27	35	1	320
N.Y. Jets	34	11	17	6	32	32	0	2	24	31	0	308
Baltimore	31	11	18	2	25	25	1	6	30	35	0	303
Seattle	34	15	15	4	33	33	1	1	20	32	1	301
Jacksonville	34	11	20	3	30	32	1	2	18	28	2	294
Cleveland	31	8	18	5	29	30	1	1	22	25	1	285
Buffalo	31	9	18	4	23	24	1	7	18	29	0	265
Cincinnati	25	11	12	2	23	24	1	1	17	28	0	226
AFC Total	578	200	311	67	517	531	20	47	384	511	6	5189
AFC Average	36.1	12.5	19.4	4.2	32.3	33.2	1.3	2.9	24.0	31.9	0.4	324.3

NATIONAL FOOTBALL CONFERENCE—SCORING

	TD	TDR	TDP	TDM	XKG	XKAtt	X2G	X2Att	FG	FGA	SAF	POINTS
St. Louis	62	20	37	5	58	58	2	4	23	29	0	503
San Francisco	51	16	32	3	47	47	1	3	18	25	0	409
Green Bay	47	11	32	4	44	45	1	2	20	31	1	390
Philadelphia	38	6	27	5	37	38	0	0	26	31	0	343
Chicago	37	12	20	5	34	34	1	1	26	31	1	338
New Orleans	36	8	27	1	32	32	1	4	27	31	1	333
Tampa Bay	34	17	13	4	30	30	3	4	28	35	0	324
Arizona	33	10	18	5	32	32	1	1	21	26	0	295
N.Y. Giants	32	11	19	2	29	30	2	2	23	30	0	294
Atlanta	29	9	19	1	28	28	1	1	29	37	0	291
Minnesota	35	10	23	2	29	30	3	5	15	18	0	290
Detroit	30	8	18	4	23	23	2	7	21	30	0	270
Washington	25	10	13	2	22	22	2	3	26	33	1	256
Carolina	27	9	12	6	22	23	0	4	23	28	0	253
Dallas	26	8	14	4	24	24	0	2	22	33	0	246
NFC Total	542	165	324	53	491	496	20	43	348	448	4	4835
NFC Average	36.1	11.0	21.6	3.5	32.7	33.1	1.3	2.9	23.2	29.9	0.3	322.3
NFL Total	1120	365	635	120	1008	1027	40	90	732	959	10	10024
NFL Average	36.1	11.8	20.5	3.9	32.5	33.1	1.3	2.9	23.6	30.9	0.3	323.4

FIELD GOALS

FIELD GOAL PERCENTAGE
AFC: .905   Olindo Mare, Miami
NFC: .871   John Carney, New Orleans

FIELD GOALS
AFC: 31   Jason Elam, Denver
NFC: 29   Jay Feely, Atlanta

FIELD GOAL ATTEMPTS
AFC: 44   Kris Brown, Pittsburgh
NFC: 37   Jay Feely, Atlanta

FIELD GOALS, GAME
AFC: 5   Kris Brown, Pittsburgh at Cleveland, November 11 (6 attempts) - (OT)
       5   John Hall, N.Y. Jets at Indianapolis, December 23 (6 attempts)
       5   Steve Christie, San Diego vs. Seattle, December 30 (5 attempts)
       5   Mike Vanderjagt, Indianapolis vs. Denver, January 6 (5 attempts)
NFC: 5   John Carney, New Orleans vs. Minnesota, October 7 (5 attempts)
       5   John Carney, New Orleans at St. Louis, October 28 (5 attempts)
       5   David Akers, Philadelphia at Dallas, November 18 (5 attempts)

LONGEST FIELD GOAL
AFC: 55   Kris Brown, Pittsburgh at Kansas City, October 14
NFC: 55   Jay Feely, Atlanta at Arizona, September 30
       55   Brett Conway, Washington at N.Y. Giants, October 7

AVERAGE YARDS MADE
NFC: 39.9   Jason Hanson, Detroit
AFC: 37.4   Mike Vanderjagt, Indianapolis

AMERICAN FOOTBALL CONFERENCE—FIELD GOALS

	FG	FGA	Pct	Long
Miami	19	21	.905	46
Cleveland	22	25	.880	48
Denver	31	36	.861	50
Baltimore	30	35	.857	49
Indianapolis	28	34	.824	52
Oakland	26	32	.813	52
New England	24	30	.800	54
N.Y. Jets	24	31	.774	53
Kansas City	27	35	.771	51
Tennessee	20	28	.714	51
San Diego	30	43	.698	51
Pittsburgh	30	44	.682	55
Jacksonville	18	28	.643	48
Seattle	20	32	.625	54
Buffalo	18	29	.621	49
Cincinnati	17	28	.607	52
AFC Total	384	511	—	55
AFC Average	24.0	31.9	.751	—

NATIONAL FOOTBALL CONFERENCE—FIELD GOALS

	FG	FGA	Pct	Long
New Orleans	27	31	.871	50
Chicago	26	31	.839	48
Philadelphia	26	31	.839	50
Minnesota	15	18	.833	44
Carolina	23	28	.821	52
Arizona	21	26	.808	50
Tampa Bay	28	35	.800	49
St. Louis	23	29	.793	54
Washington	26	33	.788	55
Atlanta	29	37	.784	55
N.Y. Giants	23	30	.767	51
San Francisco	18	25	.720	52
Detroit	21	30	.700	54
Dallas	22	33	.667	46
Green Bay	20	31	.645	54
NFC Total	348	448	—	55
NFC Average	23.2	29.9	.777	—
League Total	732	959	—	55
League Average	23.6	30.9	.763	—

AFC—INDIVIDUAL FIELD GOALS

	1-19 Yards	20-29 Yards	30-39 Yards	40-49 Yards	50 or Longer	Totals	Avg Yds Att	Avg Yds Made	Avg Yds Miss	Long
Mare, Olindo, Mia.	1-1 1.000	8-8 1.000	8-8 1.000	2-4 .500	0-0 —	19-21 .905	32.5	31.2	45.5	46
Dawson, Phil, Cle.	0-0 —	10-10 1.000	8-9 .889	4-6 .667	0-0 —	22-25 .880	33.0	31.6	43.7	48
Elam, Jason, Den.	0-0 —	11-11 1.000	8-8 1.000	10-13 .769	2-4 .500	31-36 .861	37.9	35.8	50.8	50
Stover, Matt, Balt.	0-0 —	16-16 1.000	9-10 .900	5-9 .556	0-0 —	30-35 .857	32.9	31.2	42.8	49
Vanderjagt, Mike, Ind.	0-0 —	7-8 .875	6-6 1.000	12-16 .750	3-4 .750	28-34 .824	38.5	37.4	44.0	52
Janikowski, Sebastian, Oak.	0-0 —	7-7 1.000	9-10 .900	6-9 .667	1-2 .500	23-28 .821	35.6	34.0	43.0	52
Vinatieri, Adam, NE	1-1 1.000	8-8 1.000	7-8 .875	7-12 .583	1-1 1.000	24-30 .800	36.5	34.5	44.2	54
Hall, John, NYJ	1-1 1.000	8-8 1.000	5-7 .714	7-9 .778	3-6 .500	24-31 .774	37.2	35.4	43.3	53
Peterson, Todd, KC	0-0 —	9-11 .818	9-10 .900	8-12 .667	1-2 .500	27-35 .771	36.1	34.9	40.0	51
Nedney, Joe, Tenn.	0-0 —	6-6 1.000	5-5 1.000	8-15 .533	1-2 .500	20-28 .714	39.6	36.6	47.1	51
Brown, Kris, Pitt.	0-0 —	7-7 1.000	15-20 .750	6-15 .400	2-2 1.000	30-44 .682	37.4	35.7	40.9	55
Richey, Wade, SD	0-0 —	13-15 .867	4-7 .571	3-7 .429	1-3 .333	21-32 .656	33.9	30.5	40.5	51
Hollis, Mike, Jax.	0-0 —	4-5 .800	8-11 .727	6-11 .545	0-1 .000	18-28 .643	37.3	35.7	40.2	48
Lindell, Rian, Sea.	0-0 —	7-8 .875	4-5 .800	6-14 .429	3-5 .600	20-32 .625	38.8	35.9	43.8	54
Rackers, Neil, Cin.	0-0 —	4-6 .667	8-11 .727	4-9 .444	1-2 .500	17-28 .607	36.9	35.1	39.6	52
Arians, Jake, Buff.	0-0 —	6-6 1.000	2-4 .500	4-11 .364	0-0 —	12-21 .571	37.9	33.3	44.1	49
(Nonqualifiers)										
Christie, Steve, SD	0-0 —	4-4 1.000	3-5 .600	2-2 1.000	0-0 —	9-11 .818	32.5	31.9	35.5	41
Graham, Shayne, Buff.	0-0 —	4-4 1.000	0-0 —	2-4 .500	0-0 —	6-8 .750	34.3	30.3	46.0	41
Daluiso, Brad, Oak.	0-0 —	1-2 .500	1-1 1.000	1-1 1.000	0-0 —	3-4 .750	33.0	34.7	28.0	44
AFC Totals	3-3 1.000	140-150 .933	119-145 .821	103-179 .575	19-34 .559	384-511 .751	36.3	34.3	42.5	55
League Totals	9-10 .900	253-267 .948	230-271 .849	202-338 .598	38-73 .521	732-959 .763	36.5	34.5	43.2	55

Leader based on overall percentage, minimum 16 field goals

NFC—INDIVIDUAL FIELD GOALS

	1-19 Yards	20-29 Yards	30-39 Yards	40-49 Yards	50 or Longer	Totals	Avg Yds Att	Avg Yds Made	Avg Yds Miss	Long
Carney, John, NO	0-0 —	7-7 1.000	11-11 1.000	8-12 .667	1-1 1.000	27-31 .871	36.3	34.9	45.3	50
Akers, David, Phil.	1-1 1.000	9-9 1.000	7-8 .875	7-10 .700	2-3 .667	26-31 .839	35.8	34.3	44.0	50
Edinger, Paul, Chi.	0-0 —	6-7 .857	7-8 .875	13-16 .813	0-0 —	26-31 .839	37.6	37.3	39.2	48
Anderson, Gary, Minn.	0-0 —	7-7 1.000	2-4 .500	6-7 .857	0-0 —	15-18 .833	34.1	33.1	39.3	44
Andersen, Morten, NYG	0-0 —	8-8 1.000	7-8 .875	6-7 .857	2-5 .400	23-28 .821	37.1	34.4	49.8	51
Kasay, John, Car.	0-0 —	10-10 1.000	4-4 1.000	7-9 .778	2-5 .400	23-28 .821	37.1	34.5	49.4	52
Gramatica, Bill, Ariz	1-1 1.000	7-7 1.000	3-4 .750	4-7 .571	1-1 1.000	16-20 .800	34.6	32.5	42.8	50
Gramatica, Martin, TB	0-0 —	9-10 .900	9-9 1.000	5-7 .714	0-3 .000	23-29 .793	36.1	33.7	45.3	49
Wilkins, Jeff, StL	0-0 —	11-11 1.000	5-5 1.000	6-12 .500	1-1 1.000	23-29 .793	35.1	33.0	43.2	54
Conway, Brett, Wash.	0-0 —	8-8 1.000	8-11 .727	8-12 .667	2-2 1.000	26-33 .788	36.5	35.2	41.6	55
Feely, Jay, Atl.	1-1 1.000	8-8 1.000	14-15 .933	4-9 .444	2-4 .500	29-37 .784	36.4	33.9	45.6	55
Cortez, Jose, SF	1-2 .500	6-7 .857	6-7 .857	4-8 .500	1-1 1.000	18-25 .720	34.2	33.4	36.1	52
Hanson, Jason, Det.	1-1 1.000	2-2 1.000	8-8 1.000	6-12 .500	4-7 .571	21-30 .700	42.3	39.9	47.9	54
Hilbert, Jon, Dall.	0-0 —	3-3 1.000	6-6 1.000	2-7 .286	0-0 —	11-16 .688	36.8	33.5	44.2	43
Seder, Tim, Dall.	0-0 —	5-5 1.000	3-5 .600	3-6 .500	0-1 .000	11-17 .647	36.1	33.2	41.5	46
Longwell, Ryan, GB	0-0 —	3-4 .750	9-10 .900	7-14 .500	1-3 .333	20-31 .645	39.6	37.5	43.5	54
(Nonqualifiers)										
Brien, Doug, TB	0-0 —	2-2 1.000	1-1 1.000	2-3 .667	0-0 —	5-6 .833	34.8	33.8	40.0	42
Oglesby, Cedric, Ariz	1-1 1.000	2-2 1.000	1-2 .500	1-1 1.000	0-0 —	5-6 .833	30.0	29.0	35.0	41
Pochman, Owen, NYG	0-0 —	0-0 —	0-0 —	0-0 —	0-2 .000	0-2 .000	59.0	—	59.0	0
NFC Totals	6-7 .857	113-117 .966	111-126 .881	99-159 .623	19-39 .487	348-448 .777	36.8	34.7	43.9	55
League Totals	9-10 .900	253-267 .948	230-271 .849	202-338 .598	38-73 .521	732-959 .763	36.5	34.5	43.2	55

Leader based on overall percentage, minimum 16 field goals

RUSHING

YARDS

AFC:	1555	Priest Holmes, Kansas City
NFC:	1432	Stephen Davis, Washington

YARDS, GAME

AFC:	266	Shaun Alexander, Seattle vs. Oakland, November 11 (35 attempts, 3 TD)
NFC:	202	Marshall Faulk, St. Louis at Carolina, December 23 (30 attempts, 2 TD)

LONGEST

AFC:	96	Corey Dillon, Cincinnati at Detroit, October 28 - TD
NFC:	83	Ahman Green, Green Bay vs. Detroit, September 9 - TD

ATTEMPTS

NFC:	356	Stephen Davis, Washington
AFC:	340	Corey Dillon, Cincinnati

ATTEMPTS, GAME

NFC:	38	Stephen Davis, Washington vs. Arizona, January 6 (148 yards, 1 TD)
AFC:	36	LaDainian Tomlinson, San Diego vs. Washington, September 9 (113 yards, 2 TD)

YARDS PER ATTEMPT

NFC:	5.3	Marshall Faulk, St. Louis
AFC:	4.8	Jerome Bettis, Pittsburgh

TOUCHDOWNS

AFC:	14	Shaun Alexander, Seattle
NFC:	12	Marshall Faulk, St. Louis

TEAM LEADERS, YARDS

AFC: BALTIMORE, 658, Terry Allen; BUFFALO, 729, Travis Henry; CINCINNATI, 1315, Corey Dillon; CLEVELAND, 554, James Jackson; DENVER, 701, Terrell Davis; INDIANAPOLIS, 1104, Dominic Rhodes; JACKSONVILLE, 877, Stacey Mack; KANSAS CITY, 1555, Priest Holmes; MIAMI, 968, Lamar Smith; NEW ENGLAND, 1157, Antowain Smith; N.Y. JETS, 1513, Curtis Martin; OAKLAND, 839, Charlie Garner; PITTSBURGH, 1072, Jerome Bettis; SAN DIEGO, 1236, LaDainian Tomlinson; SEATTLE, 1318, Shaun Alexander; TENNESSEE, 939, Eddie George

NFC: ARIZONA, 846, Michael Pittman; ATLANTA, 760, Maurice Smith; CAROLINA, 665, Richard Huntley; CHICAGO, 1183, Anthony Thomas; DALLAS, 1021, Emmitt Smith; DETROIT, 685, James Stewart; GREEN BAY, 1387, Ahman Green; MINNESOTA, 682, Michael Bennett; NEW ORLEANS, 1245, Ricky Williams; N.Y. GIANTS, 865, Tiki Barber; PHILADELPHIA, 604, Duce Staley; ST. LOUIS, 1382, Marshall Faulk; SAN FRANCISCO, 1206, Garrison Hearst; TAMPA BAY, 680, Mike Alstott; WASHINGTON, 1432, Stephen Davis

TEAM CHAMPION

AFC:	2774	Pittsburgh
NFC:	2244	San Francisco

NFL TOP TEN RUSHERS

	Att	Yards	Avg	Long	TD
Holmes, Priest, KC	327	1555	4.8	41	8
Martin, Curtis, NYJ	333	1513	4.5	47	10
Davis, Stephen, Wash	356	1432	4.0	32	5
Green, Ahman, GB	304	1387	4.6	83t	9
Faulk, Marshall, StL	260	1382	5.3	71t	12
Alexander, Shaun, Sea	309	1318	4.3	88t	14
Dillon, Corey, Cin	340	1315	3.9	96t	10
Williams, Ricky, NO	313	1245	4.0	46	6
Tomlinson, LaDainian, SD	339	1236	3.6	54	10
Hearst, Garrison, SF	252	1206	4.8	43t	4

AFC—INDIVIDUAL RUSHERS

	Att	Yards	Avg	Long	TD
Holmes, Priest, KC	327	1555	4.8	41	8
Martin, Curtis, NYJ	333	1513	4.5	47	10
Alexander, Shaun, Sea.	309	1318	4.3	88t	14
Dillon, Corey, Cin.	340	1315	3.9	96t	10
Tomlinson, LaDainian, SD	339	1236	3.6	54	10
Smith, Antowain, NE	287	1157	4.0	44	12
Rhodes, Dominic, Ind.	233	1104	4.7	77t	9
Bettis, Jerome, Pitt.	225	1072	4.8	48	4
Smith, Lamar, Mia.	313	968	3.1	25	6
George, Eddie, Tenn.	315	939	3.0	27	5
Mack, Stacey, Jax.	213	877	4.1	54	9
Garner, Charlie, Oak.	211	839	4.0	38	1
Henry, Travis, Buff.	213	729	3.4	25	4
Davis, Terrell, Den.	167	701	4.2	57	0
Anderson, Mike, Den.	175	678	3.9	62t	4
James, Edgerrin, Ind.	151	662	4.4	29t	3
Allen, Terry, Balt.	168	658	3.9	26	3
Jackson, James, Cle.	195	554	2.8	22	2
Brookins, Jason, Balt.	151	551	3.6	25	5
Stewart, Kordell, Pitt.	96	537	5.6	48t	5
Fuamatu-Ma'afala, Chris, Pitt.	120	453	3.8	46	3
White, Jamel, Cle.	126	443	3.5	51	5
Zereoue, Amos, Pitt.	85	441	5.2	32	1
McNair, Steve, Tenn.	75	414	5.5	24	5
Bryson, Shawn, Buff.	80	341	4.3	68t	2
Hicks, Skip, Tenn.	56	341	6.1	51	1
Fiedler, Jay, Mia.	73	321	4.4	26	4
Watters, Ricky, Sea.	72	318	4.4	40	1
Joseph, Elvis, Jax.	68	294	4.3	27	0
Jordan, LaMont, NYJ	39	292	7.5	46t	1
Williams, Moe, Buff.	65	291	4.5	55	0
Minor, Travis, Mia.	59	281	4.8	56t	2
Wheatley, Tyrone, Oak.	88	276	3.1	22	5
Johnson, Rob, Buff.	36	241	6.7	23	1
Bennett, Brandon, Cin.	50	232	4.6	36	0
Gannon, Rich, Oak.	63	231	3.7	17	2
Gary, Olandis, Den.	57	228	4.0	29	1
Brunell, Mark, Jax.	39	224	5.7	38	1
Flutie, Doug, SD	53	192	3.6	16	1
Richardson, Tony, KC	66	191	2.9	19	7
Ayanbadejo, Obafemi, Balt.	46	173	3.8	17	1
Griese, Brian, Den.	50	173	3.5	24	1
Gay, Benjamin, Cle.	51	172	3.4	40	1
Faulk, Kevin, NE	41	169	4.1	24	1
Centers, Larry, Buff.	34	160	4.7	50	2
Green, Trent, KC	35	158	4.5	16	0
Manning, Peyton, Ind.	35	157	4.5	33t	4
Crockett, Zack, Oak.	57	145	2.5	10	6
Edwards, Marc, NE	51	141	2.8	14	1
Hasselbeck, Matt, Sea.	40	141	3.5	17	0
Couch, Tim, Cle.	38	128	3.4	15	0
Redmond, J.R., NE	35	119	3.4	16	0
Conway, Curtis, SD	7	116	16.6	67t	1
Taylor, Fred, Jax.	30	116	3.9	24	0
Coles, Laveranues, NYJ	10	108	10.8	20	0

Player	Att	Yards	Avg	Long	TD
Fletcher, Terrell, SD	29	107	3.7	16	0
Anderson, Richie, NYJ	26	102	3.9	12	0
Price, Peerless, Buff.	6	97	16.2	31	0
Brown, Troy, NE	11	91	8.3	31	0
Bowers, R.J., Pitt.	18	84	4.7	21t	1
Ward, Hines, Pitt.	10	83	8.3	36	0
Kitna, Jon, Cin.	27	73	2.7	20	1
Morris, Sammy, Buff.	20	72	3.6	10	0
Green, Mike, Tenn.	15	71	4.7	21	1
Patten, David, NE	5	67	13.4	29t	1
Jordan, Randy, Oak.	13	59	4.5	37	0
Strong, Mack, Sea.	17	55	3.2	12	0
Cloud, Mike, KC	7	54	7.7	16	1
Kirby, Terry, Oak.	10	49	4.9	20	0
Keaton, Curtis, Cin.	5	48	9.6	21	0
McDougal, Kevin, Ind.	17	48	2.8	12	0
Taylor, Travis, Balt.	5	46	9.2	16	0
Brady, Tom, NE	36	43	1.2	12	0
Graham, Jay, Sea.	12	43	3.6	19	0
Quinn, Jonathan, Jax.	8	42	5.3	27	0
Cunningham, Randall, Balt.	14	40	2.9	15	1
Brown, Tim, Oak.	4	39	9.8	19	0
McKnight, James, Mia.	6	39	6.5	18	0
Lewis, Jermaine, Balt.	9	33	3.7	14	0
Van Pelt, Alex, Buff.	12	33	2.8	15	0
Kreider, Dan, Pitt.	7	29	4.1	12	1
Edwards, Troy, Pitt.	5	28	5.6	12t	1
O'Donnell, Neil, Tenn.	6	28	4.7	15	0
Moreau, Frank, Jax.	8	27	3.4	14	1
Morgan, Quincy, Cle.	2	27	13.5	23	0
Smith, Rod, Den.	3	27	9.0	17	0
Northcutt, Dennis, Cle.	3	26	8.7	12	0
Testaverde, Vinny, NYJ	31	25	0.8	12	0
Dwight, Tim, SD	2	24	12.0	16t	1
Witman, Jon, Pitt.	5	24	4.8	14	0
Johnson, J.J., Mia.	5	22	4.4	9	0
Kennison, Eddie, Den.-KC	5	22	4.4	14	0
Konrad, Rob, Mia.	5	22	4.4	18t	1
Ward, Dedric, Mia.	2	21	10.5	16	0
Smith, Akili, Cin.	6	20	3.3	6	0
Gibson, Damon, Jax.	2	19	9.5	18	0
Kasper, Kevin, Den.	3	19	6.3	27	0
Bledsoe, Drew, NE	5	18	3.6	8	0
Brees, Drew, SD	2	18	9.0	13	0
Grbac, Elvis, Balt.	21	18	0.9	6	1
Coleman, KaRon, Den.	4	17	4.3	8	0
Dilfer, Trent, Sea.	11	17	1.5	11	0
Alexander, Derrick, KC	2	16	8.0	15	0
Warrick, Peter, Cin.	8	14	1.8	13	0
Porter, Jerry, Oak.	2	13	6.5	7	0
Robinson, Koren, Sea.	4	13	3.3	6	0
Evans, Heath, Sea.	2	11	5.5	7	0
Huard, Brock, Sea.	1	11	11.0	11	0
Pennington, Chad, NYJ	1	11	11.0	11	0
Brown, Travis, Buff.	1	10	10.0	10	0
Hall, Dante, KC	2	10	5.0	6	0
Neal, Lorenzo, Cin.	5	10	2.0	4	0
Frerotte, Gus, Den.	10	9	0.9	4t	1
Gonzalez, Tony, KC	1	9	9.0	9	0
Jackson, Darrell, Sea.	1	9	9.0	9	0
Maddox, Tommy, Pitt.	6	9	1.5	8	1
Sowell, Jerald, NYJ	4	9	2.3	4	0
Martin, Tee, Pitt.	1	8	8.0	8	0
Jackson, Jarious, Den.	5	7	1.4	4	0
Pass, Patrick, NE	1	7	7.0	7	0
Brown, Kris, Pitt.	1	6	6.0	6	0
Collins, Todd S., KC	2	6	3.0	7	0
Lucas, Ray, Mia.	8	6	0.8	3	1
Parker, Larry, KC	3	6	2.0	7	0
Montgomery, Scottie, Den.	1	5	5.0	5	0
Carter, Tony, Den.	1	4	4.0	4	0
Whitted, Alvis, Jax.	1	4	4.0	4	0
Harrison, Marvin, Ind.	1	3	3.0	3	0
McCrary, Fred, SD	2	3	1.5	2	0
Moulds, Eric, Buff.	3	3	1.0	6	0
Lechler, Shane, Oak.	1	2	2.0	2	0
Frost, Scott, Cle.	1	1	1.0	1	0
Stokley, Brandon, Balt.	1	1	1.0	1	0
Tuiasosopo, Marques, Oak.	1	1	1.0	1	0
Wycheck, Frank, Tenn.	1	1	1.0	1	0
Hanson, Chris, Jax.	2	0	0.0	0	0
Hape, Patrick, Den.	2	0	0.0	0	0
Holcomb, Kelly, Cle.	1	0	0.0	0	0
Miller, Josh, Pitt.	1	0	0.0	0	0
Moorman, Brian, Buff.	1	0	0.0	0	0
Richardson, Kyle, Balt.	1	0	0.0	0	0
Gash, Sam, Balt.	2	-1	-0.5	0	0
Jenkins, Ronney, SD	1	-1	-1.0	-1	0
Smith, Jimmy, Jax.	1	-3	-3.0	-3	0
Mare, Olindo, Mia.	1	-5	-5.0	-5	0
Moss, Santana, NYJ	1	-6	-6.0	-6	0
Pathon, Jerome, Ind.	1	-8	-8.0	-8	0
Stryzinski, Dan, KC	1	-10	-10.0	-10	0
Chambers, Chris, Mia.	1	-11	-11.0	-11	0
Johnson, Lee, NE	1	-19	-19.0	-19	0

t = Touchdown
Leader based on most yards gained

NFC—INDIVIDUAL RUSHERS

Player	Att	Yards	Avg	Long	TD
Davis, Stephen, Wash.	356	1432	4.0	32	5
Green, Ahman, GB	304	1387	4.6	83t	9
Faulk, Marshall, StL	260	1382	5.3	71t	12
Williams, Ricky, NO	313	1245	4.0	46	6
Hearst, Garrison, SF	252	1206	4.8	43t	4
Thomas, Anthony, Chi.	278	1183	4.3	46	7
Smith, Emmitt, Dall.	261	1021	3.9	44	3
Barber, Tiki, NYG	166	865	5.2	36	4
Pittman, Michael, Ariz	241	846	3.5	42	5
Smith, Maurice, Atl.	237	760	3.2	58	5
Dayne, Ron, NYG	180	690	3.8	61	7
Stewart, James, Det.	143	685	4.8	38	1
Bennett, Michael, Minn.	172	682	4.0	31t	2
Alstott, Mike, TB	165	680	4.1	39t	10
Huntley, Richard, Car.	165	665	4.0	25	2
Staley, Duce, Phil.	166	604	3.6	44t	2
Buckhalter, Correll, Phil.	129	586	4.5	48	2
Hambrick, Troy, Dall.	113	579	5.1	80	2
Barlow, Kevan, SF	125	512	4.1	25	4
McNabb, Donovan, Phil.	82	482	5.9	33	2
Allen, James, Chi.	135	469	3.5	19	1
Dunn, Warrick, TB	158	447	2.8	21t	3
Canidate, Trung, StL	78	441	5.7	45	6
Culpepper, Daunte, Minn.	71	416	5.9	34	5
Jones, Thomas, Ariz	112	380	3.4	21	5
Brooks, Aaron, NO	80	358	4.5	26	1
Carter, Ki-Jana, Wash.	63	308	4.9	30	3
Vick, Michael, Atl.	31	289	9.3	35	1
Christian, Bob, Atl.	44	284	6.5	53	2
Garcia, Jeff, SF	72	254	3.5	25	5
Wiley, Michael, Dall.	34	247	7.3	58	0
Biakabutuka, Tim, Car.	53	230	4.3	27	1
Goings, Nick, Car.	66	197	3.0	16	0
Chapman, Doug, Minn.	63	195	3.1	19	0
Warren, Lamont, Det.	61	191	3.1	34	3
Anderson, Jamal, Atl.	55	190	3.5	14	1
Levens, Dorsey, GB	44	165	3.8	40	0
Plummer, Jake, Ariz	35	163	4.7	21	0
Schlesinger, Cory, Det.	47	154	3.3	26	3

Banks, Tony, Wash.	47	152	3.2	17	2	Jervey, Travis, Atl.	3	6	2.0	2	0
Carter, Quincy, Dall.	45	150	3.3	17	1	Morton, Johnnie, Det.	1	6	6.0	6	0
McMahon, Mike, Det.	27	145	5.4	22	1	Olivo, Brock, Det.	1	6	6.0	6	0
Jackson, Terry, SF	22	138	6.3	15	1	Schroeder, Bill, GB	1	6	6.0	6	0
Weinke, Chris, Car.	37	128	3.5	23	6	Smart, Rod, Phil.	2	6	3.0	6	0
Thomas, Rodney, Atl.	37	126	3.4	21	0	Hodgins, James, StL	2	5	2.5	5	0
Johnson, Brad, TB	39	120	3.1	21	3	Matthews, Shane, Chi.	4	5	1.3	3	0
Johnson, Leon, Chi.	20	99	5.0	34	4	Pinkston, Todd, Phil.	1	5	5.0	5	0
McAllister, Deuce, NO	16	91	5.7	54t	1	Proehl, Ricky, StL	1	5	5.0	5	0
Washington, Damon, NYG	28	89	3.2	22	0	Carter, Cris, Minn.	1	4	4.0	4	0
Chandler, Chris, Atl.	25	84	3.4	22	0	Denson, Autry, Chi.	1	4	4.0	4	0
Beasley, Fred, SF	23	73	3.2	16	1	Horn, Joe, NO	1	4	4.0	4	0
Collins, Kerry, NYG	39	73	1.9	11	0	Jenkins, MarTay, Ariz	3	4	1.3	16	0
Droughns, Reuben, Det.	30	72	2.4	15	0	Chiaverini, Darrin, Dall.	1	3	3.0	3	0
Kleinsasser, Jimmy, Minn.	23	72	3.1	11	1	Milburn, Glyn, Chi.	3	3	1.0	4	0
Stecker, Aaron, TB	24	72	3.0	17	1	Cook, Jameel, TB	2	2	1.0	2	0
Hoover, Brad, Car.	17	71	4.2	10	0	McAfee, Fred, NO	1	2	2.0	2	0
Morrow, Harold, Minn.	12	67	5.6	15	0	Gruttadauria, Mike, Ariz	1	1	1.0	1	0
Bouman, Todd, Minn.	9	61	6.8	21	0	McKinley, Dennis, Ariz	1	1	1.0	1	0
Wynn, Spergon, Minn.	8	61	7.6	14	0	Baker, Jason, SF	1	0	0.0	0	0
Warner, Kurt, StL	28	60	2.1	23	0	Baker, John, StL	1	0	0.0	0	0
Thrash, James, Phil.	6	57	9.5	24	0	Dixon, Ron, NYG	1	0	0.0	0	0
Wright, Anthony, Dall.	17	57	3.4	12	0	George, Jeff, Wash.	4	0	0.0	2	0
Favre, Brett, GB	38	56	1.5	14	1	Holt, Torry, StL	2	0	0.0	2	0
Hakim, Az-Zahir, StL	11	50	4.5	12	0	Jett, John, Det.	1	0	0.0	0	0
Batch, Charlie, Det.	12	45	3.8	12	0	Knorr, Micah, Dall.	1	0	0.0	0	0
Smith, Steve, Car.	4	43	10.8	39	0	Player, Scott, Ariz	1	0	0.0	0	0
Holcombe, Robert, StL	13	42	3.2	11	1	Sauerbrun, Todd, Car.	1	0	0.0	0	0
Abdullah, Rabih, TB	11	40	3.6	12	0	Taylor, Tony, Dall.	1	0	0.0	0	0
Thomas, Robert, Dall.	6	40	6.7	24	0	Watson, Justin, StL	1	0	0.0	0	0
Bennett, Donnell, Wash.	10	39	3.9	8	0	Blake, Jeff, NO	1	-1	-1.0	-1	0
Driver, Donald, GB	3	38	12.7	31t	1	Carney, John, NO	1	-1	-1.0	-1	0
Moss, Randy, Minn.	3	38	12.7	18	0	Goodman, Herbert, GB	1	-1	-1.0	-1	0
Mealey, Rondell, GB	11	37	3.4	9	0	Pederson, Doug, GB	1	-1	-1.0	-1	0
Boston, David, Ariz	5	35	7.0	17	0	Byrd, Isaac, Car.	1	-2	-2.0	-2	0
Galloway, Joey, Dall.	3	32	10.7	16	0	Rattay, Tim, SF	5	-3	-0.6	1	0
Cason, Aveion, Det.	11	31	2.8	19	0	Mitchell, Freddie, Phil.	2	-4	-2.0	12	0
Ismail, Raghib, Dall.	8	31	3.9	11	0	Swinton, Reggie, Dall.	1	-4	-4.0	-4	0
Conwell, Ernie, StL	7	28	4.0	13	1	Freeman, Antonio, GB	1	-5	-5.0	-5	0
Martin, Cecil, Phil.	9	27	3.0	8	0	Graham, Kent, Wash.	7	-7	-1.0	0	0
Smith, Paul, SF	4	27	6.8	13t	1	Leaf, Ryan, Dall.	4	-7	-1.8	0	0
Stoerner, Clint, Dall.	9	27	3.0	13	1	Martin, Jamie, StL	8	-9	-1.1	-1	0
Detmer, Ty, Det.	9	26	2.9	9	0	Maynard, Brad, Chi.	1	-10	-10.0	-10	0
Howard, Desmond, Det.	5	25	5.0	7	0	King, Shaun, TB	5	-12	-2.4	0	0
Bruce, Isaac, StL	4	23	5.8	10	0	Miller, Jim, Chi.	29	-19	-0.7	3	0
Anthony, Reidel, TB	3	22	7.3	16	0						
Hilliard, Ike, NYG	1	21	21.0	21	0	t = Touchdown					
Owens, Terrell, SF	4	21	5.3	12	0	Leader based on most yards gained					
Craig, Dameyune, Car.	3	20	6.7	13	0						
Makovicka, Joel, Ariz	1	19	19.0	19	0						
Gardner, Rod, Wash.	1	16	16.0	16	0						
Sutherland, Vinny, SF	1	16	16.0	16	0						
Williams, Rodney, NYG	2	16	8.0	11	0						
Comella, Greg, NYG	4	15	3.8	9	0						
Prentice, Travis, Minn.	14	13	0.9	6	2						
Hetherington, Chris, Car.	5	12	2.4	8	0						
Johnson, Doug, Atl.	5	12	2.4	8	0						
Henderson, William, GB	6	11	1.8	4	0						
McCord, Quentin, Atl.	2	11	5.5	8	0						
Mitchell, Brian, Phil.	7	9	1.3	11	0						
Booker, Marty, Chi.	4	8	2.0	13	0						
Lytle, Matt, Car.	2	8	4.0	4	0						
Seder, Tim, Dall.	1	8	8.0	8t	1						
Smith, Terrelle, NO	5	8	1.6	6	0						
Toomer, Amani, NYG	3	8	2.7	9	0						
Westbrook, Michael, Wash.	2	8	4.0	8	0						
Connell, Albert, NO	1	6	6.0	6	0						
Crowell, Germane, Det.	1	6	6.0	6	0						
Detmer, Koy, Phil.	8	6	0.8	14	0						
Foster, Larry, Det.	2	6	3.0	3	0						

AMERICAN FOOTBALL CONFERENCE—RUSHING

	Att	Yards	Avg	Long	TD
Pittsburgh	580	2774	4.8	48t	17
N.Y. Jets	445	2054	4.6	47	11
Kansas City	448	2008	4.5	41	16
Indianapolis	438	1966	4.5	77t	16
Seattle	469	1936	4.1	88t	15
Denver	481	1877	3.9	62t	7
Baltimore	483	1810	3.7	55	11
Tennessee	468	1794	3.8	51	12
New England	473	1793	3.8	44	15
Cincinnati	441	1712	3.9	96t	11
San Diego	435	1695	3.9	67t	13
Buffalo	406	1686	4.2	68t	9
Miami	473	1664	3.5	56t	14
Oakland	450	1654	3.7	38	14
Jacksonville	372	1600	4.3	54	11
Cleveland	417	1351	3.2	51	8
AFC Total	7279	29374	4.0	96t	200
AFC Average	454.9	1835.9	4.0	—	12.5

NATIONAL FOOTBALL CONFERENCE—RUSHING

	Att	Yards	Avg	Long	TD
San Francisco	509	2244	4.4	43t	16
Dallas	505	2184	4.3	80	8
St. Louis	416	2027	4.9	71t	20
Washington	490	1948	4.0	32	10
Philadelphia	412	1778	4.3	48	6
N.Y. Giants	424	1777	4.2	61	11
Atlanta	439	1762	4.0	58	9
Chicago	475	1742	3.7	46	12
New Orleans	419	1712	4.1	54t	8
Green Bay	410	1693	4.1	83t	11
Minnesota	376	1609	4.3	34	10
Arizona	400	1449	3.6	42	10
Detroit	351	1398	4.0	38	8
Carolina	354	1372	3.9	39	9
Tampa Bay	407	1371	3.4	39t	17
NFC Total	6387	26066	4.1	83t	165
NFC Average	425.8	1737.7	4.1	—	11.0
League Total	13666	55440	—	96t	365
League Average	440.8	1788.4	4.1	—	11.8

PASSING

HIGHEST RATING
NFC: 101.4 Kurt Warner, St. Louis
AFC: 95.5 Rich Gannon, Oakland

COMPLETION PERCENTAGE
NFC: 68.7 Kurt Warner, St. Louis
AFC: 65.8 Rich Gannon, Oakland

ATTEMPTS
AFC: 581 Jon Kitna, Cincinnati
NFC: 568 Kerry Collins, N.Y. Giants

COMPLETIONS
NFC: 375 Kurt Warner, St. Louis
AFC: 361 Rich Gannon, Oakland

YARDS
NFC: 4830 Kurt Warner, St. Louis
AFC: 4131 Peyton Manning, Indianapolis

YARDS, GAME
NFC: 436 Charlie Batch, Detroit at Arizona, November 18 (36-62, 3 TD)
AFC: 421 Peyton Manning, Indianapolis vs. Buffalo, September 23 (23-29, 4 TD)

LONGEST
NFC: 94 Chris Chandler (to Jamal Anderson) Atlanta vs. Carolina, September 23 - TD
AFC: 91 Tom Brady (to David Patten) New England at Indianapolis, October 21 - TD

YARDS PER ATTEMPT
NFC: 8.85 Kurt Warner, St. Louis
AFC: 7.77 Steve McNair, Tennessee

TOUCHDOWN PASSES
NFC: 36 Kurt Warner, St. Louis
AFC: 27 Rich Gannon, Oakland

TOUCHDOWN PASSES, GAME
AFC: 4 Peyton Manning, Indianapolis vs. Buffalo, September 23 (23-29, 421 yards)
4 Rich Gannon, Oakland vs. San Diego, November 18 (25-38, 311 yards)
4 Tom Brady, New England vs. New Orleans, November 25 (19-26, 258 yards)
NFC: 4 Kurt Warner, St. Louis vs. Miami, September 30 (24-31, 328 yards)
4 Jeff Garcia, San Francisco vs. New Orleans, November 11 (21-34, 252 yards)
4 Jake Plummer, Arizona vs. Detroit, November 18 (21-33, 334 yards)
4 Daunte Culpepper, Minnesota vs. N.Y. Giants, November 19 (26-38, 277 yards)
4 Kurt Warner, St. Louis at Atlanta, December 2 (17-23, 342 yards)
4 Todd Bouman, Minnesota vs. Tennessee, December 9 (21-31, 348 yards)
4 Kurt Warner, St. Louis at New Orleans, December 17 (23-32, 338 yards)
4 Jeff Garcia, San Francisco at New Orleans, January 6 (14-21, 263 yards)

LOWEST INTERCEPTION PERCENTAGE
NFC: 2.0 Brad Johnson, Tampa Bay
AFC: 1.6 Rich Gannon, Oakland

TEAM CHAMPION (MOST NET YARDS)
NFC: 4663 St. Louis
AFC: 3989 Indianapolis

NFL TOP TEN PASSERS

	Att	Comp	Pct Comp	Yds	Avg Gain	TD	Pct TD	Long	Int	Pct Int	Sack	Yds Lost	Rating Points
Warner, Kurt, StL	546	375	68.7	4830	8.85	36	6.6	65t	22	4.0	38	233	101.4
Gannon, Rich, Oak.	549	361	65.8	3828	6.97	27	4.9	49	9	1.6	27	155	95.5
Garcia, Jeff, SF	504	316	62.7	3538	7.02	32	6.3	61t	12	2.4	26	114	94.8
Favre, Brett, GB	510	314	61.6	3921	7.69	32	6.3	67t	15	2.9	22	151	94.1
McNair, Steve, Tenn.	431	264	61.3	3350	7.77	21	4.9	71t	12	2.8	37	251	90.2
Brady, Tom, NE	413	264	63.9	2843	6.88	18	4.4	91t	12	2.9	41	216	86.5
McNabb, Donovan, Phil.	493	285	57.8	3233	6.56	25	5.1	64t	12	2.4	39	273	84.3
Manning, Peyton, Ind.	547	343	62.7	4131	7.55	26	4.8	86t	23	4.2	29	232	84.1
Chandler, Chris, Atl.	365	223	61.1	2847	7.80	16	4.4	94t	14	3.8	41	261	84.1
Brunell, Mark, Jax.	473	289	61.1	3309	7.00	19	4.0	44	13	2.7	57	387	84.1

AFC—INDIVIDUAL PASSERS

	Att	Comp	Pct Comp	Yds	Avg Gain	TD	Pct TD	Long	Int	Pct Int	Sack	Yds Lost	Rating Points
Gannon, Rich, Oak.	549	361	65.8	3828	6.97	27	4.9	49	9	1.6	27	155	95.5
McNair, Steve, Tenn.	431	264	61.3	3350	7.77	21	4.9	71t	12	2.8	37	251	90.2
Brady, Tom, NE	413	264	63.9	2843	6.88	18	4.4	91t	12	2.9	41	216	86.5
Manning, Peyton, Ind.	547	343	62.7	4131	7.55	26	4.8	86t	23	4.2	29	232	84.1
Brunell, Mark, Jax.	473	289	61.1	3309	7.00	19	4.0	44	13	2.7	57	387	84.1
Stewart, Kordell, Pitt.	442	266	60.2	3109	7.03	14	3.2	90t	11	2.5	29	175	81.7
Fiedler, Jay, Mia.	450	273	60.7	3290	7.31	20	4.4	74t	19	4.2	27	178	80.3
Griese, Brian, Den.	451	275	61.0	2827	6.27	23	5.1	65t	19	4.2	38	241	78.5
Van Pelt, Alex, Buff.	307	178	58.0	2056	6.70	12	3.9	80t	11	3.6	14	73	76.4
Testaverde, Vinny, NYJ	441	260	59.0	2752	6.24	15	3.4	40t	14	3.2	18	122	75.3
Couch, Tim, Cle.	454	272	59.9	3040	6.70	17	3.7	78	21	4.6	51	353	73.1
Flutie, Doug, SD	521	294	56.4	3464	6.65	15	2.9	78	18	3.5	25	168	72.0
Green, Trent, KC	523	296	56.6	3783	7.23	17	3.3	67t	24	4.6	39	198	71.1
Grbac, Elvis, Balt.	467	265	56.7	3033	6.49	15	3.2	77t	18	3.9	28	215	71.1
Hasselbeck, Matt, Sea.	321	176	54.8	2023	6.30	7	2.2	64	8	2.5	38	251	70.9

	Att	Comp	Pct Comp	Yds	Avg Gain	TD	Pct TD	Long	Int	Pct Int	Sack	Yds Lost	Rating Points
Kitna, Jon, Cin.	581	313	53.9	3216	5.54	12	2.1	49	22	3.8	25	185	61.1
(Nonqualifiers)													
Holcomb, Kelly, Cle.	12	7	58.3	114	9.50	1	8.3	25	0	0.0	0	0	118.1
Frerotte, Gus, Den.	48	30	62.5	308	6.42	3	6.3	26t	0	0.0	3	21	101.7
Huard, Brock, Sea.	17	9	52.9	127	7.47	1	5.9	44	0	0.0	1	5	96.9
Brees, Drew, SD	27	15	55.6	221	8.19	1	3.7	40	0	0.0	2	12	94.8
Dilfer, Trent, Sea.	122	73	59.8	1014	8.31	7	5.7	54	4	3.3	10	72	92.0
Cunningham, Randall, Balt.	89	54	60.7	573	6.44	3	3.4	30	2	2.2	12	66	81.3
Pennington, Chad, NYJ	20	10	50.0	92	4.60	1	5.0	24	0	0.0	1	8	79.6
Johnson, Rob, Buff.	216	134	62.0	1465	6.78	5	2.3	61t	7	3.2	31	196	76.3
Jackson, Jarious, Den.	12	7	58.3	73	6.08	0	0.0	19	0	0.0	1	6	76.0
Bledsoe, Drew, NE	66	40	60.6	400	6.06	2	3.0	58	2	3.0	5	21	75.3
O'Donnell, Neil, Tenn.	76	42	55.3	496	6.53	2	2.6	35t	2	2.6	6	58	73.1
Quinn, Jonathan, Jax.	61	32	52.5	361	5.92	1	1.6	45	1	1.6	6	43	69.1
Brown, Travis, Buff.	33	15	45.5	201	6.09	1	3.0	34	2	6.1	1	2	50.2
Mitchell, Scott, Cin.	12	4	33.3	38	3.17	0	0.0	16	3	25.0	2	15	3.5
(Fewer than 10 attempts)													
Bettis, Jerome, Pitt.	2	1	50.0	32	16.00	1	50.0	32t	0	0.0	0	0	135.4
Collins, Todd S., KC	4	3	75.0	40	10.00	0	0.0	26	0	0.0	0	0	106.3
Dilger, Ken, Ind.	1	1	100.0	39	39.00	1	100.0	39t	0	0.0	0	0	158.3
Dillon, Corey, Cin.	1	0	0.0	0	0.00	0	0.0	0	1	100.0	0	0	0.0
Faulk, Kevin, NE	1	1	100.0	23	23.00	0	0.0	23	0	0.0	0	0	118.8
Feagles, Jeff, Sea.	2	0	0.0	0	0.00	0	0.0	0	0	0.0	0	0	39.6
Gonzalez, Tony, KC	1	1	100.0	40	40.00	0	0.0	40	0	0.0	0	0	118.8
Green, Mike, Tenn.	2	0	0.0	0	0.00	0	0.0	0	2	100.0	0	0	0.0
Hentrich, Craig, Tenn.	2	0	0.0	0	0.00	0	0.0	0	1	50.0	0	0	0.0
Jordan, LaMont, NYJ	1	0	0.0	0	0.00	0	0.0	0	0	0.0	0	0	39.6
Lucas, Ray, Mia.	3	2	66.7	45	15.00	0	0.0	28	0	0.0	0	0	109.7
Maddox, Tommy, Pitt.	9	7	77.8	154	17.11	1	11.1	57	1	11.1	1	4	116.2
Martin, Curtis, NYJ	1	1	100.0	18	18.00	1	100.0	18t	0	0.0	0	0	158.3
Moorman, Brian, Buff.	1	0	0.0	0	0.00	0	0.0	0	0	0.0	0	0	39.6
Patten, David, NE	2	1	50.0	60	30.00	1	50.0	60t	1	50.0	0	0	95.8
Richardson, Kyle, Balt.	1	1	100.0	-11	-11.00	0	0.0	-11	0	0.0	0	0	79.2
Rypien, Mark, Ind.	9	5	55.6	57	6.33	0	0.0	21	0	0.0	1	6	74.8
Smith, Akili, Cin.	8	5	62.5	37	4.63	0	0.0	14	0	0.0	1	3	73.4
Tuiasosopo, Marques, Oak.	4	3	75.0	34	8.50	0	0.0	15	0	0.0	0	0	100.0
Tupa, Tom, NYJ	1	1	100.0	9	9.00	0	0.0	9	0	0.0	0	0	104.2
Volek, Billy, Tenn.	3	0	0.0	0	0.00	0	0.0	0	0	0.0	0	0	39.6
Ward, Hines, Pitt.	1	0	0.0	0	0.00	0	0.0	0	0	0.0	1	3	39.6
Wycheck, Frank, Tenn.	1	1	100.0	21	21.00	0	0.0	21	0	0.0	0	0	118.8

t = Touchdown
Leader based on rating points, minimum 224 attempts

NFC—INDIVIDUAL PASSERS

	Att	Comp	Pct Comp	Yds	Avg Gain	TD	Pct TD	Long	Int	Pct Int	Sack	Yds Lost	Rating Points
Warner, Kurt, StL	546	375	68.7	4830	8.85	36	6.6	65t	22	4.0	38	233	101.4
Garcia, Jeff, SF	504	316	62.7	3538	7.02	32	6.3	61t	12	2.4	26	114	94.8
Favre, Brett, GB	510	314	61.6	3921	7.69	32	6.3	67t	15	2.9	22	151	94.1
McNabb, Donovan, Phil.	493	285	57.8	3233	6.56	25	5.1	64t	12	2.4	39	273	84.3
Chandler, Chris, Atl.	365	223	61.1	2847	7.80	16	4.4	94t	14	3.8	41	261	84.1
Culpepper, Daunte, Minn.	366	235	64.2	2612	7.14	14	3.8	57t	13	3.6	33	186	83.3
Plummer, Jake, Ariz	525	304	57.9	3653	6.96	18	3.4	68t	14	2.7	29	204	79.6
Johnson, Brad, TB	559	340	60.8	3406	6.09	13	2.3	47	11	2.0	44	269	77.7
Collins, Kerry, NYG	568	327	57.6	3764	6.63	19	3.3	76	16	2.8	36	206	77.1
Batch, Charlie, Det.	341	198	58.1	2392	7.01	12	3.5	76	12	3.5	33	176	76.8
Brooks, Aaron, NO	558	312	55.9	3832	6.87	26	4.7	63	22	3.9	50	330	76.4
Miller, Jim, Chi.	395	228	57.7	2299	5.82	13	3.3	66t	10	2.5	11	72	74.9
Banks, Tony, Wash.	370	198	53.5	2386	6.45	10	2.7	85t	10	2.7	29	173	71.3
Weinke, Chris, Car.	540	293	54.3	2931	5.43	11	2.0	48	19	3.5	26	177	62.0
(Nonqualifiers)													
Graham, Kent, Wash.	19	13	68.4	131	6.89	2	10.5	16	0	0.0	2	16	122.9
Feeley, A.J., Phil.	14	10	71.4	143	10.21	2	14.3	27	1	7.1	0	0	114.0
Bouman, Todd, Minn.	89	51	57.3	795	8.93	8	9.0	80t	4	4.5	4	27	98.3
King, Shaun, TB	31	21	67.7	210	6.77	0	0.0	42	1	3.2	3	29	73.3
Matthews, Shane, Chi.	129	84	65.1	694	5.38	5	3.9	34t	6	4.7	6	48	72.3
McMahon, Mike, Det.	115	53	46.1	671	5.83	3	2.6	69	1	0.9	21	122	69.9
Carter, Quincy, Dall.	176	90	51.1	1072	6.09	5	2.8	64t	7	4.0	12	56	63.0
Vick, Michael, Atl.	113	50	44.2	785	6.95	2	1.8	52	3	2.7	21	113	62.7

Wright, Anthony, Dall.	98	48	49.0	529	5.40	5	5.1	80t	5	5.1	5	30	61.1
Leaf, Ryan, Dall.	88	45	51.1	494	5.61	1	1.1	38	3	3.4	12	82	57.7
Detmer, Ty, Det.	151	92	60.9	906	6.00	3	2.0	27	10	6.6	12	75	56.9
Stoerner, Clint, Dall.	49	26	53.1	314	6.41	3	6.1	28	5	10.2	5	22	53.8
Lytle, Matt, Car.	30	17	56.7	133	4.43	1	3.3	28	3	10.0	3	24	39.3
Wynn, Spergon, Minn.	98	48	49.0	418	4.27	1	1.0	47t	6	6.1	10	65	38.6
George, Jeff, Wash.	42	23	54.8	168	4.00	0	0.0	17	3	7.1	6	38	34.6
Detmer, Koy, Phil.	14	5	35.7	51	3.64	0	0.0	16	1	7.1	1	9	17.3
(Fewer than 10 attempts)													
Berger, Mitch, Minn.	1	0	0.0	0	0.00	0	0.0	0	0	0.0	0	0	39.6
Blake, Jeff, NO	1	0	0.0	0	0.00	0	0.0	0	0	0.0	0	0	39.6
Booker, Marty, Chi.	2	1	50.0	34	17.00	1	50.0	34t	0	0.0	0	0	135.4
Craig, Dameyune, Car.	8	4	50.0	34	4.25	0	0.0	18	0	0.0	2	15	61.5
Faulk, Marshall, StL	1	0	0.0	0	0.00	0	0.0	0	0	0.0	0	0	39.6
Galloway, Joey, Dall.	1	1	100.0	-1	-1.00	0	0.0	-1	0	0.0	0	0	79.2
Gramatica, Martin, TB	1	0	0.0	0	0.00	0	0.0	0	0	0.0	0	0	39.6
Hakim, Az-Zahir, StL	1	1	100.0	51	51.00	1	100.0	51t	0	0.0	0	0	158.3
Horn, Joe, NO	1	0	0.0	0	0.00	0	0.0	0	0	0.0	0	0	39.6
Huntley, Richard, Car.	1	0	0.0	0	0.00	0	0.0	0	0	0.0	1	0	39.6
Johnson, Doug, Atl.	5	3	60.0	23	4.60	1	20.0	14	0	0.0	2	13	110.8
Johnson, Leon, Chi.	1	1	100.0	18	18.00	0	0.0	18	0	0.0	0	0	118.8
Knorr, Micah, Dall.	1	0	0.0	0	0.00	0	0.0	0	0	0.0	0	0	39.6
Lockett, Kevin, Wash.	1	1	100.0	31	31.00	1	100.0	31t	0	0.0	0	0	158.3
Martin, Jamie, StL	3	3	100.0	22	7.33	0	0.0	10	0	0.0	2	7	97.2
Maynard, Brad, Chi.	1	1	100.0	27	27.00	1	100.0	27t	0	0.0	0	0	158.3
McAllister, Deuce, NO	2	1	50.0	12	6.00	1	50.0	12t	0	0.0	0	0	108.3
Metcalf, Eric, Wash.	0	0	—	0	—	0	—	—	0	—	1	2	—
Mitchell, Freddie, Phil.	1	0	0.0	0	0.00	0	0.0	0	0	0.0	0	0	39.6
Mohr, Chris, Atl.	2	2	100.0	40	20.00	0	0.0	42	0	0.0	0	0	118.8
Moss, Randy, Minn.	1	1	100.0	29	29.00	0	0.0	29	0	0.0	0	0	118.8
Rattay, Tim, SF	2	2	100.0	21	10.50	0	0.0	20	0	0.0	0	0	110.4
Royals, Mark, TB	1	1	100.0	5	5.00	0	0.0	5	0	0.0	0	0	87.5
Sanders, Frank, Ariz	1	0	0.0	0	0.00	0	0.0	0	0	0.0	0	0	39.6
Warren, Lamont, Det.	2	0	0.0	0	0.00	0	0.0	0	1	50.0	0	0	0.0

t = Touchdown
Leader based on rating points, minimum 224 attempts

AMERICAN FOOTBALL CONFERENCE—PASSING

	Att	Comp	Pct Comp	Gross Yards	Sacked	Yds Lost	Net Yards	Yds/ Att	Yards/ Comp	TD	Pct TD	Long	Int	Pct Int
Indianapolis	557	349	62.7	4227	30	238	3989	7.59	12.11	27	4.85	86t	23	4.1
Tennessee	515	307	59.6	3867	43	309	3558	7.51	12.60	23	4.47	71t	17	3.3
Kansas City	528	300	56.8	3863	39	198	3665	7.32	12.88	17	3.22	67t	24	4.5
Oakland	553	364	65.8	3862	27	155	3707	6.98	10.61	27	4.88	49	9	1.6
Buffalo	557	327	58.7	3722	46	271	3451	6.68	11.38	18	3.23	80t	20	3.6
San Diego	548	309	56.4	3685	27	180	3505	6.72	11.93	16	2.92	78	18	3.3
Jacksonville	534	321	60.1	3670	63	430	3240	6.87	11.43	20	3.75	45	14	2.6
Baltimore	557	320	57.5	3595	40	281	3314	6.45	11.23	18	3.23	77t	20	3.6
Miami	453	275	60.7	3335	27	178	3157	7.36	12.13	20	4.42	74t	19	4.2
New England	482	306	63.5	3326	46	237	3089	6.90	10.87	21	4.36	91t	15	3.1
Pittsburgh	454	274	60.4	3295	31	182	3113	7.26	12.03	16	3.52	90t	12	2.6
Cincinnati	602	322	53.5	3291	28	203	3088	5.47	10.22	12	1.99	49	26	4.3
Denver	511	312	61.1	3208	42	268	2940	6.28	10.28	26	5.09	65t	19	3.7
Seattle	462	258	55.8	3164	49	328	2836	6.85	12.26	15	3.25	64	12	2.6
Cleveland	466	279	59.9	3154	51	353	2801	6.77	11.30	18	3.86	78	21	4.5
N.Y. Jets	464	272	58.6	2871	19	130	2741	6.19	10.56	17	3.66	40t	14	3.0
AFC Total	8243	4895	—	56135	608	3941	52194	—	—	311	—	91t	283	—
AFC Average	515.2	305.9	59.4	3508.4	38.0	246.3	3262.1	6.81	11.47	19.4	3.8	—	17.7	3.4

NATIONAL FOOTBALL CONFERENCE—PASSING

	Att	Comp	Pct Comp	Gross Yards	Sacked	Yds Lost	Net Yards	Yds/ Att	Yards/ Comp	TD	Pct TD	Long	Int	Pct Int
St. Louis	551	379	68.8	4903	40	240	4663	8.90	12.94	37	6.72	65t	22	4.0
Detroit	609	343	56.3	3969	66	373	3596	6.52	11.57	18	2.96	76	24	3.9
Green Bay	510	314	61.6	3921	22	151	3770	7.69	12.49	32	6.27	67t	15	2.9
Minnesota	555	335	60.4	3854	47	278	3576	6.94	11.50	23	4.14	80t	23	4.1
New Orleans	562	313	55.7	3844	50	330	3514	6.84	12.28	27	4.80	63	22	3.9
N.Y. Giants	568	327	57.6	3764	36	206	3558	6.63	11.51	19	3.35	76	16	2.8
Atlanta	485	278	57.3	3695	64	387	3308	7.62	13.29	19	3.92	94t	17	3.5
Arizona	526	304	57.8	3653	29	204	3449	6.94	12.02	18	3.42	68t	14	2.7
Tampa Bay	592	362	61.1	3621	47	298	3323	6.12	10.00	13	2.20	47	12	2.0
San Francisco	506	318	62.8	3559	26	114	3445	7.03	11.19	32	6.32	61t	12	2.4
Philadelphia	522	300	57.5	3427	40	282	3145	6.57	11.42	27	5.17	64t	14	2.7
Carolina	579	314	54.2	3098	32	216	2882	5.35	9.87	12	2.07	48	22	3.8
Chicago	528	315	59.7	3072	17	120	2952	5.82	9.75	20	3.79	66t	16	3.0
Washington	432	235	54.4	2716	38	229	2487	6.29	11.56	13	3.01	85t	13	3.0
Dallas	413	210	50.8	2408	34	190	2218	5.83	11.47	14	3.39	80t	20	4.8
NFC Total	7938	4647	—	53504	588	3618	49886	—	—	324	—	94t	262	—
NFC Average	529.2	309.8	58.5	3566.9	39.2	241.2	3325.7	6.74	11.51	21.6	4.1	—	17.5	3.3
League Total	16181	9542	—	109639	1196	7559	102,080	—	—	635	—	94t	545	—
League Average	522.0	307.8	59.0	3536.7	38.6	243.8	3292.9	6.78	11.49	20.5	3.9	—	17.6	3.4

PASS RECEIVING

RECEPTIONS
AFC: 113 Rod Smith, Denver
NFC: 106 Keyshawn Johnson, Tampa Bay

RECEPTIONS, GAME
AFC: 14 Rod Smith, Denver at Arizona, September 23 (162 yards, 2 TD)
NFC: 13 Joe Horn, New Orleans vs. Carolina, December 2 (150 yards, 1 TD)

YARDS
NFC: 1598 David Boston, Arizona
AFC: 1524 Marvin Harrison, Indianapolis

YARDS, GAME
NFC: 208 Rod Gardner, Washington vs. Carolina, October 21 (6 receptions, 1 TD) - (OT)
AFC: 196 Eric Moulds, Buffalo vs. Miami, November 25 (6 receptions, 2 TD)

LONGEST
NFC: 94 Jamal Anderson (from Chris Chandler) Atlanta vs. Carolina, September 23 - TD
AFC: 91 David Patten (from Tom Brady) New England at Indianapolis, October 21 - TD

YARDS PER RECEPTION
AFC: 18.4 Chris Chambers, Miami
NFC: 17.3 Bill Schroeder, Green Bay

TOUCHDOWNS
NFC: 16 Terrell Owens, San Francisco
AFC: 15 Marvin Harrison, Indianapolis

TEAM LEADERS, RECEPTIONS
AFC: BALTIMORE, 74, Qadry Ismail; BUFFALO, 80, Larry Centers ; CINCINNATI, 70, Peter Warrick; CLEVELAND, 84, Kevin Johnson; DENVER, 113, Rod Smith; INDIANAPOLIS, 109, Marvin Harrison; JACKSONVILLE, 112, Jimmy Smith; KANSAS CITY, 73, Tony Gonzalez; MIAMI, 55, Oronde Gadsden, James McKnight; NEW ENGLAND, 101, Troy Brown; N.Y. JETS, 59, Laveranues Coles; OAKLAND, 91, Tim Brown; PITTSBURGH, 94, Hines Ward; SAN DIEGO, 71, Curtis Conway; SEATTLE, 70, Darrell Jackson; TENNESSEE, 73, Derrick Mason

NFC: ARIZONA, 98, David Boston; ATLANTA, 51, Terance Mathis; CAROLINA, 52, Donald Hayes; CHICAGO, 100, Marty Booker; DALLAS, 53, Raghib Ismail; DETROIT, 77, Johnnie Morton; GREEN BAY, 62, Ahman Green; MINNESOTA, 82, Randy Moss; NEW ORLEANS, 83, Joe Horn; N.Y. GIANTS, 72, Tiki Barber, Amani Toomer; PHILADELPHIA, 63, Duce Staley, James Thrash; ST. LOUIS, 83, Marshall Faulk; SAN FRANCISCO, 93, Terrell Owens; TAMPA BAY, 106, Keyshawn Johnson; WASHINGTON, 57, Michael Westbrook

NFL TOP TEN PASS RECEIVERS

	No	Yards	Avg	Long	TD
Smith, Rod, Den.	113	1343	11.9	65t	11
Smith, Jimmy, Jax.	112	1373	12.3	35t	8
Harrison, Marvin, Ind.	109	1524	14.0	68	15
Johnson, Keyshawn, TB	106	1266	11.9	47	1
Brown, Troy, NE	101	1199	11.9	60t	5
Booker, Marty, Chi.	100	1071	10.7	66t	8
Boston, David, Ariz	98	1598	16.3	61t	8
Ward, Hines, Pitt.	94	1003	10.7	34	4
McCardell, Keenan, Jax.	93	1110	11.9	45	6
Owens, Terrell, SF	93	1412	15.2	60t	16

NFL TOP TEN RECEIVERS BY YARDS

	Yards	No	Avg	Long	TD
Boston, David, Ariz	1598	98	16.3	61t	8
Harrison, Marvin, Ind.	1524	109	14.0	68	15
Owens, Terrell, SF	1412	93	15.2	60t	16
Smith, Jimmy, Jax.	1373	112	12.3	35t	8
Holt, Torry, StL	1363	81	16.8	51	7
Smith, Rod, Den.	1343	113	11.9	65t	11
Johnson, Keyshawn, TB	1266	106	11.9	47	1
Horn, Joe, NO	1265	83	15.2	56	9
Moss, Randy, Minn.	1233	82	15.0	73t	10
Brown, Troy, NE	1199	101	11.9	60t	5

AFC—INDIVIDUAL RECEIVERS

	No	Yards	Avg	Long	TD
Smith, Rod, Den.	113	1343	11.9	65t	11
Smith, Jimmy, Jax.	112	1373	12.3	35t	8
Harrison, Marvin, Ind.	109	1524	14.0	68	15
Brown, Troy, NE	101	1199	11.9	60t	5
Ward, Hines, Pitt.	94	1003	10.7	34	4
McCardell, Keenan, Jax.	93	1110	11.9	45	6
Brown, Tim, Oak.	91	1165	12.8	46t	9
Johnson, Kevin, Cle.	84	1097	13.1	55t	9
Rice, Jerry, Oak.	83	1139	13.7	40t	9
Centers, Larry, Buff.	80	620	7.8	26	2
Ismail, Qadry, Balt.	74	1059	14.3	77t	7
Mason, Derrick, Tenn.	73	1128	15.5	71t	9
Gonzalez, Tony, KC	73	917	12.6	36	6
Sharpe, Shannon, Balt.	73	811	11.1	37	2
Garner, Charlie, Oak.	72	578	8.0	27	2
Conway, Curtis, SD	71	1125	15.8	72t	6
Jackson, Darrell, Sea.	70	1081	15.4	64	8
Warrick, Peter, Cin.	70	667	9.5	33	1
Moulds, Eric, Buff.	67	904	13.5	80t	5
Burress, Plaxico, Pitt.	66	1008	15.3	43	6
Holmes, Priest, KC	62	614	9.9	67t	2
Wycheck, Frank, Tenn.	60	672	11.2	30	4
Coles, Laveranues, NYJ	59	868	14.7	40t	7
Tomlinson, LaDainian, SD	59	367	6.2	27	0
Scott, Darnay, Cin.	57	819	14.4	49	2
Chrebet, Wayne, NYJ	56	750	13.4	36	1
Price, Peerless, Buff.	55	895	16.3	70t	7
McKnight, James, Mia.	55	684	12.4	40	3
Gadsden, Oronde, Mia.	55	674	12.3	61	3
Dyson, Kevin, Tenn.	54	825	15.3	68t	7
Riemersma, Jay, Buff.	53	590	11.1	36	3
Martin, Curtis, NYJ	53	320	6.0	27	0
Graham, Jeff, SD	52	811	15.6	61t	5
Patten, David, NE	51	749	14.7	91t	4
Clark, Desmond, Den.	51	566	11.1	39	6
Chambers, Chris, Mia.	48	883	18.4	74t	7
Pollard, Marcus, Ind.	47	739	15.7	86t	8
White, Jamel, Cle.	44	418	9.5	45	1
Alexander, Shaun, Sea.	44	343	7.8	28t	2
Taylor, Travis, Balt.	42	560	13.3	63	3
Anderson, Richie, NYJ	40	252	6.3	22	2
Robinson, Koren, Sea.	39	536	13.7	42	1

Player	No	Yds	Avg	Long	TD
George, Eddie, Tenn.	37	279	7.5	25	0
Brady, Kyle, Jax.	36	386	10.7	20t	2
Becht, Anthony, NYJ	36	321	8.9	24	5
Jones, Freddie, SD	35	388	11.1	34	4
Wilkins, Terrence, Ind.	34	332	9.8	28	0
Carswell, Dwayne, Den.	34	299	8.8	25	4
Dillon, Corey, Cin.	34	228	6.7	17	3
Rhodes, Dominic, Ind.	34	224	6.6	19	0
Minnis, Snoop, KC	33	511	15.5	56	1
Williams, Roland, Oak.	33	298	9.0	49	3
Dilger, Ken, Ind.	32	343	10.7	44	1
Kennison, Eddie, Den.-KC	31	491	15.8	65	1
Morgan, Quincy, Cle.	30	432	14.4	78	2
Richardson, Tony, KC	30	265	8.8	47	0
Smith, Lamar, Mia.	30	234	7.8	65t	2
Faulk, Kevin, NE	30	189	6.3	28	2
Engram, Bobby, Sea.	29	400	13.8	31	0
Minor, Travis, Mia.	29	263	9.1	29	1
Johnson, Chad, Cin.	28	329	11.8	28	1
Dugans, Ron, Cin.	28	251	9.0	31	2
Alexander, Derrick, KC	27	470	17.4	46	3
Wayne, Reggie, Ind.	27	345	12.8	43	0
Dwight, Tim, SD	25	406	16.2	78	0
Kinney, Erron, Tenn.	25	263	10.5	24	1
Edwards, Marc, NE	25	166	6.6	17	2
Shaw, Bobby, Pitt.	24	409	17.0	90t	2
Stokley, Brandon, Balt.	24	344	14.3	46	2
Pathon, Jerome, Ind.	24	330	13.8	60t	2
Bennett, Drew, Tenn.	24	329	13.7	50	1
James, Edgerrin, Ind.	24	193	8.0	27	0
Ayanbadejo, Obafemi, Balt.	24	121	5.0	18	1
Williams, Moe, Balt.	23	210	9.1	46	0
Fletcher, Terrell, SD	23	184	8.0	27	0
Mack, Stacey, Jax.	23	165	7.2	25	1
Dawson, JaJuan, Cle.	22	281	12.8	44	1
Henry, Travis, Buff.	22	179	8.1	40	0
Houshmandzadeh, T.J., Cin.	21	228	10.9	23	0
Ward, Dedric, Mia.	21	209	10.0	20	0
Fauria, Christian, Sea.	21	188	9.0	30	1
Dawkins, Sean, Jax.	20	234	11.7	28	0
Bennett, Brandon, Cin.	20	150	7.5	15	0
Edwards, Troy, Pitt.	19	283	14.9	57	0
Thomas, Chris, KC	19	247	13.0	28	1
Porter, Jerry, Oak.	19	220	11.6	21	0
Smith, Antowain, NE	19	192	10.1	41t	1
Ritchie, Jon, Oak.	19	154	8.1	17	2
Neal, Lorenzo, Cin.	19	101	5.3	12	1
Ricks, Mikhael, KC	18	252	14.0	40	1
Weaver, Jed, Mia.	18	215	11.9	27	2
Northcutt, Dennis, Cle.	18	211	11.7	26	0
Joseph, Elvis, Jax.	18	183	10.2	29t	1
Santiago, O.J., Cle.	17	153	9.0	27	2
Strong, Mack, Sea.	17	141	8.3	35	0
Allen, Terry, Balt.	17	68	4.0	11	0
Heap, Todd, Balt.	16	206	12.9	24t	1
Fuamatu-Ma'afala, Chris, Pitt.	16	127	7.9	54	1
Farmer, Danny, Cin.	15	228	15.2	27	1
Parker, Larry, KC	15	199	13.3	44	2
Hape, Patrick, Den.	15	96	6.4	25	3
Gaylor, Trevor, SD	14	217	15.5	31	0
Glenn, Terry, NE	14	204	14.6	23	1
Insley, Trevor, Ind.	14	165	11.8	26	1
McGee, Tony, Cin.	14	148	10.6	25t	1
Wiggins, Jermaine, NE	14	133	9.5	31	4
Johnson, Charles, NE	14	111	7.9	24t	1
Shea, Aaron, Cle.	14	86	6.1	12	0
Swayne, Kevin, NYJ	13	203	15.6	27	0
Zereoue, Amos, Pitt.	13	154	11.8	62	1
Redmond, J.R., NE	13	132	10.2	17	0
McCrary, Fred, SD	13	71	5.5	12	0
Williams, James, Sea.	12	212	17.7	49	1
Germany, Reggie, Buff.	12	203	16.9	39	0
Bruener, Mark, Pitt.	12	98	8.2	21	0
Brigham, Jeremy, Oak.	12	85	7.1	17	1
Davis, Terrell, Den.	12	69	5.8	16	0
Green, Mike, Tenn.	12	64	5.3	10	1
Wheatley, Tyrone, Oak.	12	61	5.1	11	1
King, Andre, Cle.	11	149	13.5	48	0
McDaniel, Jeremy, Buff.	11	129	11.7	22	0
Watters, Ricky, Sea.	11	107	9.7	34	0
Montgomery, Scottie, Den.	11	99	9.0	23	0
Carter, Tony, Den.	11	83	7.5	17	0
Cole, Chris, Den.	9	128	14.2	21	0
Dudley, Rickey, Cle.	9	115	12.8	27	0
Gash, Sam, Balt.	9	80	8.9	16	1
Jordan, Randy, Oak.	9	63	7.0	19	0
Kirby, Terry, Oak.	9	62	6.9	9	0
Bryson, Shawn, Buff.	9	59	6.6	23	0
Jones, Damon, Jax.	8	140	17.5	40	1
Mili, Itula, Sea.	8	98	12.3	41	2
Black, Avion, Buff.	8	90	11.3	25	0
Kasper, Kevin, Den.	8	84	10.5	21	0
Heiden, Steve, SD	8	55	6.9	16	1
Bettis, Jerome, Pitt.	8	48	6.0	16	0
Anderson, Mike, Den.	8	46	5.8	16	0
Tuman, Jerame, Pitt.	7	96	13.7	32t	1
Sellers, Mike, Cle.	7	73	10.4	28	2
German, Jammi, Cle.	7	65	9.3	18	0
Jackson, James, Cle.	7	56	8.0	16	0
Jordan, LaMont, NYJ	7	44	6.3	25t	1
Morris, Sammy, Buff.	7	36	5.1	11	0
McCaffrey, Ed, Den.	6	94	15.7	28	1
Ogden, Jeff, Mia.	6	73	12.2	18	1
Pass, Patrick, NE	6	66	11.0	23t	1
Brookins, Jason, Balt.	6	45	7.5	15	0
Coleman, KaRon, Den.	6	45	7.5	9	0
Witman, Jon, Pitt.	6	32	5.3	12	0
Sanders, Chris D., Tenn.	5	74	14.8	22	0
Johnson, Patrick, Balt.	5	57	11.4	25	1
Konrad, Rob, Mia.	5	52	10.4	17	1
Poole, Keith, Den.	5	38	7.6	10	0
Washington, Patrick, Jax.	5	36	7.2	12	0
Rutledge, Rod, NE	5	35	7.0	9	0
Jones, Reggie, SD	5	29	5.8	11	0
Cushing, Matt, Pitt.	5	24	4.8	9	1
Hicks, Skip, Tenn.	5	22	4.4	9	0
Dunn, Jason, KC	4	54	13.5	28	1
Bannister, Alex, Sea.	4	50	12.5	17	0
Lewis, Jermaine, Balt.	4	32	8.0	12	0
Gary, Olandis, Den.	4	29	7.3	11	0
Small, Torrance, NE	4	29	7.3	11	0
Goodwin, Hunter, Mia.	4	27	6.8	9	0
Johnson, J.J., Mia.	4	21	5.3	7	0
Gay, Benjamin, Cle.	4	11	2.8	7	0
McCareins, Justin, Tenn.	3	88	29.3	36	0
Meier, Shad, Tenn.	3	31	10.3	18	0
Dominguez, Matt, Den.	3	26	8.7	12	0
Batteaux, Pat, SD	3	25	8.3	17	0
Moreland, Jake, Cle.	3	15	5.0	6	0
Dearth, James, NYJ	3	10	3.3	9	1
Coleman, Fred, NE	2	50	25.0	46	0
Hatchette, Matt, NYJ	2	44	22.0	29	0
Natkin, Brian, Tenn.	2	42	21.0	27	0
Moss, Santana, NYJ	2	40	20.0	33	0
Berlin, Eddie, Tenn.	2	28	14.0	19	0
Jett, James, Oak.	2	19	9.5	10	0
Simmons, Tony, Ind.	2	17	8.5	12	0
Whitted, Alvis, Jax.	2	17	8.5	10	0
Crosby, Phillip, Buff.	2	16	8.0	9	0
Jackson, Curtis, NE	2	16	8.0	12	0

Player	No	Yards	Avg	Long	TD
McMullen, Kirk, Cin.	2	15	7.5	11	0
Gibson, Damon, Jax.	2	13	6.5	9	0
Jones, John, Balt.	2	13	6.5	13	0
Taylor, Fred, Jax.	2	13	6.5	11	0
Williams, Jermaine, KC	2	11	5.5	9	0
Crockett, Zack, Oak.	2	10	5.0	8	0
Kreider, Dan, Pitt.	2	5	2.5	5	0
Brady, Tom, NE	1	23	23.0	23	0
Coleman, Chris, Tenn.	1	19	19.0	19	0
Sowell, Jerald, NYJ	1	19	19.0	19	0
McDougal, Kevin, Ind.	1	10	10.0	10	0
Keaton, Curtis, Cin.	1	9	9.0	9	0
Blackwell, Will, Pitt.	1	8	8.0	8	0
Dunn, David, Oak.	1	8	8.0	8	0
Cox, Bryan, NE	1	7	7.0	7	0
Harris, Derrick, SD	1	7	7.0	7	0
Rogers, Charlie, Sea.	1	7	7.0	7	0
Graham, Jay, Sea.	1	6	6.0	6	0
McKinney, Steve, Ind.	1	5	5.0	5	0
Ours, Wes, Tenn.	1	3	3.0	3	0
O'Hara, Shaun, Cle.	1	2	2.0	2t	1
Green, Trent, KC	1	1	1.0	1	0
Jackson, Sheldon, Buff.	1	1	1.0	1t	1
Bowers, R.J., Pitt.	1	0	0.0	0	0
Dilfer, Trent, Sea.	1	-5	-5.0	-5	0
Griese, Brian, Den.	1	-6	-6.0	-6	0
Couch, Tim, Cle.	1	-10	-10.0	-10	0
Mitchell, Anthony, Balt.	1	-11	-11.0	-11	0

t = Touchdown
Leader based on receptions

NFC—INDIVIDUAL RECEIVERS

Player	No	Yards	Avg	Long	TD
Johnson, Keyshawn, TB	106	1266	11.9	47	1
Booker, Marty, Chi.	100	1071	10.7	66t	8
Boston, David, Ariz	98	1598	16.3	61t	8
Owens, Terrell, SF	93	1412	15.2	60t	16
Horn, Joe, NO	83	1265	15.2	56	9
Faulk, Marshall, StL	83	765	9.2	65t	9
Moss, Randy, Minn.	82	1233	15.0	73t	10
Holt, Torry, StL	81	1363	16.8	51	7
Jackson, Willie, NO	81	1046	12.9	63	5
Morton, Johnnie, Det.	77	1154	15.0	76	4
Carter, Cris, Minn.	73	871	11.9	52	6
Toomer, Amani, NYG	72	1054	14.6	60t	5
Barber, Tiki, NYG	72	577	8.0	44	0
Dunn, Warrick, TB	68	557	8.2	31	3
Bruce, Isaac, StL	64	1106	17.3	51t	6
Thrash, James, Phil.	63	833	13.2	64t	8
Staley, Duce, Phil.	63	626	9.9	46t	2
Green, Ahman, GB	62	594	9.6	42	2
Williams, Ricky, NO	60	511	8.5	42	1
Schlesinger, Cory, Det.	60	466	7.8	38	0
Chamberlain, Byron, Minn.	57	666	11.7	47t	3
Westbrook, Michael, Wash.	57	664	11.6	76t	4
Stokes, J.J., SF	54	585	10.8	47	7
Schroeder, Bill, GB	53	918	17.3	67t	9
Ismail, Raghib, Dall.	53	834	15.7	80t	2
Freeman, Antonio, GB	52	818	15.7	63	6
Galloway, Joey, Dall.	52	699	13.4	47t	3
Hilliard, Ike, NYG	52	659	12.7	38	6
Hayes, Donald, Car.	52	597	11.5	48	2
Jurevicius, Joe, NYG	51	706	13.8	46t	3
Mathis, Terance, Atl.	51	564	11.1	34	2
Muhammad, Muhsin, Car.	50	585	11.7	43	1
Gardner, Rod, Wash.	46	741	16.1	85t	4
White, Dez, Chi.	45	428	9.5	32	0
Christian, Bob, Atl.	45	392	8.7	42	2
Walls, Wesley, Car.	43	452	10.5	25	5
Pinkston, Todd, Phil.	42	586	14.0	62t	4
Pittman, Michael, Ariz	42	264	6.3	27	0
Sanders, Frank, Ariz	41	618	15.1	68t	2
Lewis, Chad, Phil.	41	422	10.3	33	6
Hearst, Garrison, SF	41	347	8.5	60t	1
Proehl, Ricky, StL	40	563	14.1	37	5
Johnson, Eric, SF	40	362	9.1	24	3
Warren, Lamont, Det.	40	336	8.4	36	1
Hakim, Az-Zahir, StL	39	374	9.6	33	3
Comella, Greg, NYG	39	253	6.5	26	1
Conwell, Ernie, StL	38	431	11.3	47	4
Martin, Tony, Atl.	37	548	14.8	63t	3
Jefferson, Shawn, Atl.	37	539	14.6	48	2
Byrd, Isaac, Car.	37	492	13.3	42	1
Sloan, David, Det.	37	409	11.1	27	7
Green, Jacquez, TB	36	402	11.2	35	1
Franks, Bubba, GB	36	322	8.9	31	9
Moore, Dave, TB	35	285	8.1	29	4
Alstott, Mike, TB	35	231	6.6	19t	1
Terrell, David, Chi.	34	415	12.2	62	4
Jenkins, MarTay, Ariz	32	518	16.2	53	3
Bradford, Corey, GB	31	526	17.0	56	2
Allen, James, Chi.	30	203	6.8	34t	1
Bennett, Michael, Minn.	29	226	7.8	80t	1
Streets, Tai, SF	28	345	12.3	52	1
Davis, Stephen, Wash.	28	205	7.3	29	0
Reed, Jake, Minn.	27	309	11.4	27	1
Hoover, Brad, Car.	26	185	7.1	19	0
Crumpler, Alge, Atl.	25	330	13.2	57t	3
Mitchell, Tywan, Ariz	25	196	7.8	24t	2
Williams, Karl, TB	24	314	13.1	42	1
Kleinsasser, Jimmy, Minn.	24	184	7.7	18	0
Levens, Dorsey, GB	24	159	6.6	19	1
Martin, Cecil, Phil.	24	124	5.2	17	2
Finneran, Brian, Atl.	23	491	21.3	52	3
Robinson, Marcus, Chi.	23	269	11.7	34t	2
Stewart, James, Det.	23	242	10.5	56	1
Hetherington, Chris, Car.	23	124	5.4	15	0
Lockett, Kevin, Wash.	22	293	13.3	34	0
Crowell, Germane, Det.	22	289	13.1	46t	2
Foster, Larry, Det.	22	283	12.9	36	0
Barlow, Kevan, SF	22	247	11.2	61t	1
Thomas, Anthony, Chi.	22	178	8.1	23	0
Baxter, Fred, Chi.	22	148	6.7	19	2
Mitchell, Freddie, Phil.	21	283	13.5	29	1
Wilson, Robert, NO	21	277	13.2	44	0
Emanuel, Bert, NE-Det.	21	246	11.7	29	0
Henderson, William, GB	21	193	9.2	26	0
Jones, Thomas, Ariz	21	151	7.2	18	0
Huntley, Richard, Car.	21	101	4.8	23	1
Williams, Boo, NO	20	202	10.1	26	3
Smith, Maurice, Atl.	19	230	12.1	79t	1
Flemister, Zeron, Wash.	18	196	10.9	33	2
Canidate, Trung, StL	17	154	9.1	29	0
Smith, Emmitt, Dall.	17	116	6.8	22	0
Cook, Jameel, TB	17	89	5.2	16	0
Kelly, Reggie, Atl.	16	142	8.9	25	0
Chapman, Doug, Minn.	16	135	8.4	38t	1
Beasley, Fred, SF	16	99	6.2	15	0
Wiley, Michael, Dall.	16	99	6.2	17	1
Makovicka, Joel, Ariz	16	95	5.9	25	1
Kozlowski, Brian, Atl.	15	270	18.0	46	1
McAllister, Deuce, NO	15	166	11.1	22t	1
Harris, Jackie, Dall.	15	141	9.4	28	2
Bennett, Donnell, Wash.	15	112	7.5	30	0
Mangum, Kris, Car.	15	89	5.9	11	2
Battaglia, Marco, Cin.-Was.	14	127	9.1	17	0
Jeffers, Patrick, Car.	14	127	9.1	21	0
Driver, Donald, GB	13	167	12.8	37	1
Anthony, Reidel, TB	13	162	12.5	35	0

Player	No.	Yds	Avg	Long	TD
Campbell, Dan, NYG	13	148	11.4	25	1
Martin, David, GB	13	144	11.1	31	1
Morrow, Harold, Minn.	13	142	10.9	28	0
Cleeland, Cameron, NO	13	138	10.6	19t	4
Buckhalter, Correll, Phil.	13	130	10.0	26	0
Lucky, Mike, Dall.	13	96	7.4	16	1
Carter, Ki-Jana, Wash.	13	83	6.4	15	0
Anderson, Scotty, Det.	12	211	17.6	69	1
Connell, Albert, NO	12	191	15.9	46t	2
Biakabutuka, Tim, Car.	12	121	10.1	47	0
Jackson, Terry, SF	12	91	7.6	14	2
Shelton, Daimon, Chi.	12	76	6.3	16	1
Robinson, Jeff, StL	11	108	9.8	26	1
Hardy, Terry, Ariz	11	79	7.2	13	2
Davis, John, Chi.	11	68	6.2	14	0
Swift, Justin, SF	11	66	6.0	13	1
Smith, Steve, Car.	10	154	15.4	33	0
Howard, Desmond, Det.	10	133	13.3	36t	1
Rasby, Walter, Wash.	10	128	12.8	27	2
Chiaverini, Darrin, Dall.	10	107	10.7	21	2
Stecker, Aaron, TB	10	101	10.1	35t	1
Bates, D'Wayne, Chi.	9	160	17.8	40	1
Johnson, Bryan, Wash.	9	129	14.3	32	0
Alexander, Stephen, Wash.	9	85	9.4	21	0
Walsh, Chris, Minn.	9	67	7.4	19	0
Jackson, Arnold, Ariz	9	44	4.9	16	0
Dixon, Ron, NYG	8	227	28.4	62	1
Bush, Steve, Ariz	8	80	10.0	16	0
Murphy, Frank, TB	8	71	8.9	20	1
Dayne, Ron, NYG	8	67	8.4	21	0
Goings, Nick, Car.	8	39	4.9	11	0
Huggins, J.J., Dall.	8	36	4.5	10	0
Swinton, Reggie, Dall.	7	117	16.7	45t	1
Brown, Na, Phil.	7	95	13.6	18	0
McGarity, Wane, Dall.-NO	7	43	6.1	11t	1
Mitchell, Brian, Phil.	6	122	20.3	56	0
Douglas, Dameane, Phil.	5	77	15.4	27	2
Trejo, Stephen, Det.	5	61	12.2	20	0
Stewart, Tony, Phil.	5	52	10.4	15	1
Thomason, Jeff, Phil.	5	33	6.6	11	0
Mitchell, Pete, Det.	5	29	5.8	12	0
Thomas, Robert, Dall.	5	19	3.8	6	1
Moore, Herman, Det.	4	76	19.0	25	0
Wynn, Milton, TB	4	69	17.3	36	0
Hambrick, Troy, Dall.	4	62	15.5	27	0
Yoder, Todd, TB	4	48	12.0	24	0
Cason, Aveion, Det.	4	32	8.0	9	0
Smith, Terrelle, NO	4	30	7.5	12	2
Washington, Damon, NYG	4	25	6.3	16	0
Hodgins, James, StL	4	24	6.0	11t	1
Droughns, Reuben, Det.	4	21	5.3	8t	1
Metcalf, Eric, Wash.	4	19	4.8	9	0
Anderson, Jamal, Atl.	3	111	37.0	94t	1
McCord, Quentin, Atl.	3	53	17.7	26	0
Thompson, Derrius, Wash.	3	52	17.3	31t	1
Davis, Thabiti, NYG	3	34	11.3	20	0
Lee, Charles, GB	3	32	10.7	23	1
Rambo, Ken-Yon, Dall.	3	28	9.3	14	0
Davis, Tyrone, GB	3	14	4.7	7	0
Jordan, Andrew, Minn.	3	11	3.7	4	1
Rivers, Marcellus, NYG	3	11	3.7	8	2
Milburn, Glyn, Chi.	3	9	3.0	7	0
Mealey, Rondell, GB	2	31	15.5	19	0
Abdullah, Rabih, TB	2	26	13.0	14	0
Scott, Gari, Phil.	2	26	13.0	18	0
Thomas, Rodney, Atl.	2	26	13.0	15	0
Broughton, Luther, Car.	2	22	11.0	13	0
Merritt, Ahmad, Chi.	2	20	10.0	13	0
Hall, Lamont, NO	2	15	7.5	9	0
Reader, Jamie, Phil.	2	14	7.0	11	0
Urlacher, Brian, Chi.	1	27	27.0	27t	1
Holcombe, Robert, StL	1	14	14.0	14	0
Crawford, Casey, Car.	1	10	10.0	10	0
McKinley, Dennis, Ariz	1	10	10.0	10	0
Prentice, Travis, Minn.	1	10	10.0	10	0
Witherspoon, Terry, Dall.	1	9	9.0	9	0
Waerig, John, Det.	1	6	6.0	6	0
Cross, Howard, NYG	1	5	5.0	5	0
Stachelski, Dave, NO	1	5	5.0	5	0
Sutherland, Vinny, SF	1	5	5.0	5	0
Bartrum, Mike, Phil.	1	4	4.0	4t	1
Collins, Bobby, GB	1	3	3.0	3	0
Manumaleuna, Brandon, StL	1	1	1.0	1t	1
Rackley, Derek, Atl.	1	1	1.0	1t	1
Culpepper, Daunte, Minn.	1	0	0.0	0	0
Johnson, Leon, Chi.	1	0	0.0	0	0
Collins, Kerry, NYG	1	-2	-2.0	-2	0
Feely, Jay, Atl.	1	-2	-2.0	-2	0

t = Touchdown
Leader based on receptions

INTERCEPTIONS

INTERCEPTIONS
AFC: 10 Anthony Henry, Cleveland
NFC: 10 Ronde Barber, Tampa Bay

INTERCEPTIONS, GAME
AFC: 4 Deltha O'Neal, Denver vs. Kansas City, October 7 (69 yards, 0 TD)
NFC: 3 Sammy Knight, New Orleans at Buffalo, September 9 (40 yards, 0 TD)
3 Ronde Barber, Tampa Bay vs. New Orleans, December 23 (56 yards, 1 TD)

YARDS
AFC: 227 Brock Marion, Miami
NFC: 165 Zack Bronson, San Francisco

LONGEST
AFC: 100 Brock Marion, Miami vs. Buffalo, January 6 - TD
NFC: 98 Shelton Quarles, Tampa Bay vs. Green Bay, October 7 - TD

TOUCHDOWNS
AFC: 2 Anthony Dorsett, Oakland
2 Ty Law, New England
2 Brock Marion, Miami
2 Chad Scott, Pittsburgh
2 Otis Smith, New England
2 Brandon Spoon, Buffalo
NFC: 2 Dre' Bly, St. Louis
2 Zack Bronson, San Francisco
2 Mike Brown, Chicago
2 Dexter Coakley, Dallas
2 Aeneas Williams, St. Louis

TEAM LEADERS, INTERCEPTIONS
AFC: BALTIMORE, 4, Duane Starks; BUFFALO, 3, Nate Clements; CINCINNATI, 3, Artrell Hawkins, Kevin Kaesviharn; CLEVELAND, 10, Anthony Henry; DENVER, 9, Deltha O'Neal; INDIANAPOLIS, 3, Jeff Burris, David Macklin; JACKSONVILLE, 3, Aaron Beasley, Hardy Nickerson; KANSAS CITY, 4, Eric Warfield; MIAMI, 5, Brock Marion; NEW ENGLAND, 5, Otis Smith; N.Y. JETS, 5, Aaron Glenn; OAKLAND, 5, Tory James; PITTSBURGH, 5, Chad Scott; SAN DIEGO, 8, Ryan McNeil; SEATTLE, 4, Willie Williams; TENNESSEE, 3, Andre Dyson, Samari Rolle

NFC: ARIZONA, 9, Kwamie Lassiter; ATLANTA, 5, Ashley Ambrose, Ray Buchanan; CAROLINA, 8, Doug Evans; CHICAGO, 5, Mike Brown; DALLAS, 3, Darren Woodson; DETROIT, 4, Todd Lyght; GREEN BAY, 6, Darren Sharper; MINNESOTA, 2, Robert Griffith, Eric Kelly; NEW ORLEANS, 6, Sammy Knight; N.Y. GIANTS, 4, Will Allen; PHILADELPHIA, 3, Troy Vincent; ST. LOUIS, 6, Dre' Bly; SAN FRANCISCO, 7, Zack Bronson, Ahmed Plummer; TAMPA BAY, 10, Ronde Barber; WASHINGTON, 3, Fred Smoot

TEAM CHAMPION
AFC: 33 Cleveland
NFC: 28 Tampa Bay

NFL TOP TEN INTERCEPTORS

	No	Yards	Avg	Long	TD
Barber, Ronde, TB	10	86	8.6	36t	1
Henry, Anthony, Cle.	10	177	17.7	97t	1
Lassiter, Kwamie, Ariz	9	80	8.9	25	0
O'Neal, Deltha, Den.	9	115	12.8	42	0
Evans, Doug, Car.	8	126	15.8	49	1
McNeil, Ryan, SD	8	55	6.9	33	0
Bronson, Zack, SF	7	165	23.6	97t	2
Plummer, Ahmed, SF	7	45	6.4	24	0
Abraham, Donnie, TB	6	98	16.3	46	0
Bly, Dre', StL	6	150	25.0	93t	2
Knight, Sammy, NO	6	114	19.0	40	0
Sharper, Darren, GB	6	78	13.0	23	0

AFC—INDIVIDUAL INTERCEPTORS

	No	Yards	Avg	Long	TD
Henry, Anthony, Cle.	10	177	17.7	97t	1
O'Neal, Deltha, Den.	9	115	12.8	42	0
McNeil, Ryan, SD	8	55	6.9	33	0
Marion, Brock, Mia.	5	227	45.4	100t	2
Scott, Chad, Pitt.	5	204	40.8	62	2
Smith, Otis, NE	5	181	36.2	78t	2
Glenn, Aaron, NYJ	5	82	16.4	60t	1
James, Tory, Oak.	5	72	14.4	33	0
Little, Earl, Cle.	5	33	6.6	15	0
McCutcheon, Daylon, Cle.	4	62	15.5	32t	1
Warfield, Eric, KC	4	61	15.3	51t	1
Alexander, Brent, Pitt.	4	39	9.8	22	0
Williams, Willie, Sea.	4	24	6.0	24	0
Starks, Duane, Balt.	4	9	2.3	9	0
Lewis, Ray, Balt.	3	115	38.3	64	0
Law, Ty, NE	3	91	30.3	46t	2
Fuller, Corey, Cle.	3	82	27.3	49t	1
Buckley, Terrell, NE	3	76	25.3	52t	1
Green, Victor, NYJ	3	76	25.3	63t	1
Surtain, Patrick, Mia.	3	74	24.7	41	1
Burris, Jeff, Ind.	3	69	23.0	30t	1
Tongue, Reggie, Sea.	3	67	22.3	55t	1
Walker, Denard, Den.	3	60	20.0	39t	1
Woodson, Rod, Balt.	3	57	19.0	47t	1
Jackson, Raymond, Cin.	3	52	17.3	52	0
Clements, Nate, Buff.	3	48	16.0	48t	1
Woods, Jerome, KC	3	48	16.0	25	0
Thomas, William, Oak.	3	46	15.3	33	0
Kaesviharn, Kevin, Cin.	3	41	13.7	29	0
Dyson, Andre, Tenn.	3	36	12.0	36	0
Jones, Marvin, NYJ	3	27	9.0	18	0
Hawkins, Artrell, Cin.	3	26	8.7	22	0
Spencer, Jimmy, Den.	3	25	8.3	18	0
Macklin, David, Ind.	3	15	5.0	11	0
Nickerson, Hardy, Jax.	3	4	1.3	2	0
Rolle, Samari, Tenn.	3	3	1.0	3	0
Beasley, Aaron, Jax.	3	0	0.0	0	0
Farrior, James, NYJ	2	84	42.0	47	0
Dorsett, Anthony, Oak.	2	65	32.5	39t	2
Bush, Devin, Cle.	2	62	31.0	43t	1
Robinson, Damien, NYJ	2	58	29.0	30	0
Harrison, Rodney, SD	2	51	25.5	22	0
Spoon, Brandon, Buff.	2	51	25.5	44t	2
Thomas, Zach, Mia.	2	51	25.5	34t	1
Wesley, Greg, KC	2	44	22.0	30	0
Charlton, Ike, Sea.	2	43	21.5	38t	1
Coleman, Marcus, NYJ	2	41	20.5	36	0
Perry, Jason, SD	2	37	18.5	37t	1
Robertson, Marcus, Sea.	2	30	15.0	25	0
Smith, Justin, Cin.	2	28	14.0	21	0
Vrabel, Mike, NE	2	27	13.5	15	0
Battles, Ainsley, Jax.	2	26	13.0	26	0
Bulluck, Keith, Tenn.	2	21	10.5	21	0

Player	No	Yards	Avg	Long	TD
Cota, Chad, Ind.	2	21	10.5	12	0
Milloy, Lawyer, NE	2	21	10.5	21	0
Peterson, Mike, Ind.	2	18	9.0	13	0
Harper, Nicholas, Ind.	2	17	8.5	14	0
McGlockton, Chester, Den.	2	17	8.5	17	0
Robinson, Eddie, Tenn.	2	13	6.5	13	0
Boyer, Brant, Cle.	2	12	6.0	8	0
Bruschi, Tedy, NE	2	7	3.5	4	0
Townsend, Deshea, Pitt.	2	7	3.5	7	0
Patton, Marvcus, KC	2	5	2.5	5	0
Craft, Jason, Jax.	2	4	2.0	4	0
Cody, Tay, SD	2	3	1.5	3	0
Logan, Mike, Pitt.	2	2	1.0	2	0
Harris, Corey, Balt.	2	1	0.5	1	0
Brown, Eric, Den.	2	0	0.0	0	0
Madison, Sam, Mia.	2	0	0.0	0	0
Pleasant, Anthony, NE	2	0	0.0	0	0
Winfield, Antoine, Buff.	2	0	0.0	0	0
Spikes, Takeo, Cin.	1	66	66.0	66t	1
Woodson, Charles, Oak.	1	64	64.0	34	0
Mixon, Kenny, Mia.	1	56	56.0	56t	1
Darius, Donovin, Jax.	1	39	39.0	39	0
Watson, Chris, Buff.	1	23	23.0	23	0
Kacyvenski, Isaiah, Sea.	1	22	22.0	22	0
Pope, Marquez, Oak.	1	22	22.0	22	0
Allen, Eric, Oak.	1	19	19.0	19	0
Ellsworth, Percy, Cle.	1	19	19.0	19	0
Phillips, Ryan, Ind.	1	18	18.0	18	0
Hansen, Phil, Buff.	1	17	17.0	17	0
Lewis, Mo, NYJ	1	17	17.0	17	0
Mobley, John, Den.	1	17	17.0	17	0
Williams, Darryl, Cin.	1	16	16.0	16	0
Trapp, James, Balt.	1	15	15.0	15	0
Washington, Dewayne, Pitt.	1	15	15.0	15	0
Phifer, Roman, NE	1	14	14.0	14	0
Carter, Chris, Cin.	1	10	10.0	10	0
McCree, Marlon, Jax.	1	10	10.0	10	0
Gibson, Derrick, Oak.	1	9	9.0	9	0
Smith, Travian, Oak.	1	9	9.0	9	0
Stevens, Matt, NE	1	9	9.0	9	0
Beckett, Rogers, SD	1	8	8.0	8	0
Crockett, Ray, KC	1	8	8.0	8	0
Dixon, Gerald, SD	1	6	6.0	6	0
Kennedy, Kenoy, Den.	1	6	6.0	6	0
Godfrey, Randall, Tenn.	1	5	5.0	5	0
Henderson, Jamie, NYJ	1	5	5.0	5	0
Simmons, Brian, Cin.	1	5	5.0	5	0
Taylor, Jason, Mia.	1	4	4.0	4	0
Clancy, Kendrick, Pitt.	1	3	3.0	3	0
Seau, Junior, SD	1	2	2.0	2	0
McCrary, Michael, Balt.	1	1	1.0	1	0
Bashir, Idrees, Ind.	1	0	0.0	0	0
Booker, Michael, Tenn.	1	0	0.0	0	0
Burton, Shane, NYJ	1	0	0.0	0	0
Cadrez, Glenn, KC	1	0	0.0	0	0
Coghill, George, Den.	1	0	0.0	0	0
Cooper, Chris, Oak.	1	0	0.0	0	0
Favors, Greg, Tenn.	1	0	0.0	0	0
Fontenot, Albert, SD	1	0	0.0	0	0
Freeman, Arturo, Mia.	1	0	0.0	0	0
Galyon, Scott, Mia.	1	0	0.0	0	0
Gildon, Jason, Pitt.	1	0	0.0	0	0
Irvin, Ken, Buff.	1	0	0.0	0	0
Lucas, Ken, Sea.	1	0	0.0	0	0
McAlister, Chris, Balt.	1	0	0.0	0	0
Miller, Jamir, Cle.	1	0	0.0	0	0
Molden, Alex, SD	1	0	0.0	0	0
Roman, Mark, Cin.	1	0	0.0	0	0
Roye, Orpheus, Cle.	1	0	0.0	0	0
Rudd, Dwayne, Cle.	1	0	0.0	0	0
Russell, Darrell, Oak.	1	0	0.0	0	0
Springs, Shawn, Sea.	1	0	0.0	0	0
Tillman, Travares, Buff.	1	0	0.0	0	0
Walker, Brian, Mia.	1	0	0.0	0	0
Walls, Raymond, Ind.	1	0	0.0	0	0
Porter, Alvin, Balt.	1	-3	-3.0	-3	0
Jones, Tebucky, NE	1	-4	-4.0	-4	0

t = Touchdown
Leader based on interceptions

NFC—INDIVIDUAL INTERCEPTORS

Player	No	Yards	Avg	Long	TD
Barber, Ronde, TB	10	86	8.6	36t	1
Lassiter, Kwamie, Ariz	9	80	8.9	25	0
Evans, Doug, Car.	8	126	15.8	49	1
Bronson, Zack, SF	7	165	23.6	97t	2
Plummer, Ahmed, SF	7	45	6.4	24	0
Bly, Dre', StL	6	150	25.0	93t	2
Knight, Sammy, NO	6	114	19.0	40	0
Abraham, Donnie, TB	6	98	16.3	46	0
Sharper, Darren, GB	6	78	13.0	23	0
Grant, Deon, Car.	5	96	19.2	43	0
Buchanan, Ray, Atl.	5	85	17.0	33	0
Brown, Mike, Chi.	5	81	16.2	33t	2
Ambrose, Ashley, Atl.	5	43	8.6	27	0
Smoot, Fred, Wash.	5	36	7.2	36	0
Williams, Tyrone, GB	4	117	29.3	69t	1
Lyght, Todd, Det.	4	72	18.0	59t	1
Williams, Aeneas, StL	4	69	17.3	42t	2
McCleon, Dexter, StL	4	66	16.5	43	0
Jackson, Dexter, TB	4	42	10.5	29	0
Allen, Will, NYG	4	27	6.8	17	0
Arrington, LaVar, Wash.	3	120	40.0	67t	1
Brooks, Derrick, TB	3	65	21.7	53	0
Hitchcock, Jimmy, Car.	3	65	21.7	35	0
Webster, Jason, SF	3	61	20.3	31	0
Urlacher, Brian, Chi.	3	60	20.0	41	0
Wayne, Nate, GB	3	55	18.3	35	0
McQuarters, R.W., Chi.	3	47	15.7	43	0
Parrish, Tony, Chi.	3	36	12.0	26	0
Sehorn, Jason, NYG	3	34	11.3	34t	1
Williams, Shaun, NYG	3	25	8.3	20	0
Bellamy, Jay, NO	3	21	7.0	21	0
Lynch, John, TB	3	21	7.0	15	0
Bailey, Champ, Wash.	3	17	5.7	12	0
Woodson, Darren, Dall.	3	11	3.7	6	0
Schulters, Lance, SF	3	0	0.0	0	0
Vincent, Troy, Phil.	3	0	0.0	0	0
Wilson, Adrian, Ariz	2	97	48.5	61t	1
Bailey, Robert, Det.	2	74	37.0	74t	1
Trotter, Jeremiah, Phil.	2	64	32.0	50t	1
Winborn, Jamie, SF	2	40	20.0	29	0
Coakley, Dexter, Dall.	2	39	19.5	29t	2
McKenzie, Mike, GB	2	38	19.0	38t	1
Jue, Bhawoh, GB	2	35	17.5	35	0
Mathis, Kevin, NO	2	34	17.0	23	0
Minter, Mike, Car.	2	32	16.0	30	0
Barrett, David, Ariz	2	30	15.0	23	0
Fair, Terry, Det.	2	29	14.5	26t	1
Hawthorne, Duane, Dall.	2	28	14.0	22	0
Griffith, Robert, Minn.	2	25	12.5	14	0
Colvin, Rosevelt, Chi.	2	22	11.0	14	0
Harris, Al, Phil.	2	22	11.0	14	0
Schulz, Kurt, Det.	2	22	11.0	19	0
Fletcher, London, StL	2	18	9.0	18	0
Brooking, Keith, Atl.	2	17	8.5	9	0
Dawkins, Brian, Phil.	2	15	7.5	15	0
Harris, Bernardo, GB	2	12	6.0	8	0
Claiborne, Chris, Det.	2	11	5.5	6	0

Rice, Ron, Det.	2	9	4.5	8	0
Shade, Sam, Wash.	2	9	4.5	9	0
Moore, Damon, Phil.	2	2	1.0	2	0
Terrell, David, Wash.	2	0	0.0	0	0
Wilkinson, Dan, Wash.	2	0	0.0	0	0
Wistrom, Grant, StL	2	-4	-2.0	0	0
Kelly, Eric, Minn.	2	-7	-3.5	2	0
Quarles, Shelton, TB	1	98	98.0	98t	1
Edwards, Mario, Dall.	1	71	71.0	71t	1
Traylor, Keith, Chi.	1	67	67.0	67	0
Harris, Walt, Chi.	1	45	45.0	39t	1
Knight, Tom, Ariz	1	43	43.0	43	0
Reese, Izell, Dall.	1	42	42.0	42	0
Howard, Darren, NO	1	37	37.0	37	0
Hampton, William, Phil.	1	33	33.0	33t	1
Fields, Mark, StL	1	30	30.0	30	0
Buckner, Brentson, Car.	1	29	29.0	29	0
Wong, Kailee, Minn.	1	27	27.0	27t	1
Young, Brian, StL	1	25	25.0	25	0
McKinnon, Ronald, Ariz	1	24	24.0	24t	1
Short, Brandon, NYG	1	21	21.0	21	0
Wakefield, Fred, Ariz	1	20	20.0	20t	1
Holman, Rashad, SF	1	19	19.0	19	0
Howard, Reggie, Car.	1	16	16.0	16	0
Herring, Kim, StL	1	15	15.0	15	0
Azumah, Jerry, Chi.	1	14	14.0	14	0
Jones, Dhani, NYG	1	14	14.0	14	0
Lang, Kenard, Wash.	1	14	14.0	14	0
Ohalete, Ifeanyi, Wash.	1	12	12.0	12	0
Cook, Rashard, Phil.	1	11	11.0	11	0
Morgan, Dan, Car.	1	10	10.0	10	0
Duncan, Jamie, TB	1	9	9.0	9	0
Thibodeaux, Keith, GB	1	9	9.0	9	0
Crockett, Henri, Atl.	1	7	7.0	7	0
Gordon, Darrien, Atl.	1	7	7.0	7	0
Garnes, Sam, NYG	1	5	5.0	5	0
Taylor, Bobby, Phil.	1	5	5.0	5	0
Clemons, Charlie, NO	1	3	3.0	3	0
Thomas, Dave, NYG	1	3	3.0	3	0
Sawyer, Talance, Minn.	1	2	2.0	2	0
Leverette, Otis, Wash.	1	1	1.0	1	0
Wiley, Chuck, Atl.	1	1	1.0	1	0
Anderson, Rashard, Car.	1	0	0.0	0	0
Carter, Marty, Det.	1	0	0.0	0	0
Carty, Johndale, Atl.	1	0	0.0	0	0
Chavous, Corey, Ariz	1	0	0.0	0	0
Green, Darrell, Wash.	1	0	0.0	0	0
Holdman, Warrick, Chi.	1	0	0.0	0	0
Lyle, Keith, Wash.	1	0	0.0	0	0
McDaniel, Ed, Minn.	1	0	0.0	0	0
Oldham, Chris, NO	1	0	0.0	0	0
Peterson, Will, NYG	1	0	0.0	0	0
Pierce, Antonio, Wash.	1	0	0.0	0	0
Smith, Derek M., SF	1	0	0.0	0	0
Thomas, Fred, NO	1	0	0.0	0	0
Thomas, Orlando, Minn.	1	0	0.0	0	0
Towns, Lester, Car.	1	0	0.0	0	0
Vaughn, Darrick, Atl.	1	0	0.0	0	0
Westbrook, Bryant, Det.	1	0	0.0	0	0
Williams, Jay, Car.	1	0	0.0	0	0
Dronett, Shane, Atl.	1	-6	-6.0	-6	0

t = Touchdown
Leader based on interceptions

AMERICAN FOOTBALL CONFERENCE—INTERCEPTIONS

	No	Yards	Avg	Long	TD
Cleveland	33	499	15.1	97t	4
Denver	22	240	10.9	42	1
New England	22	422	19.2	78t	5
N.Y. Jets	20	390	19.5	63t	2
San Diego	19	162	8.5	37t	1
Miami	17	412	24.2	100t	5
Oakland	17	306	18.0	41	2
Baltimore	16	195	12.2	64	1
Pittsburgh	16	270	16.9	62	2
Indianapolis	15	158	10.5	30t	1
Seattle	14	186	13.3	55t	2
Cincinnati	13	192	14.8	66t	1
Kansas City	13	166	12.8	51t	1
Tennessee	13	78	6.0	36	0
Jacksonville	12	83	6.9	39	0
Buffalo	11	139	12.6	48t	3
AFC Total	273	3898	14.3	100t	31
AFC Average	17.1	243.6	14.3	—	1.9

NATIONAL FOOTBALL CONFERENCE—INTERCEPTIONS

	No	Yards	Avg	Long	TD
Tampa Bay	28	419	15.0	98t	2
Carolina	24	374	15.6	49	1
San Francisco	24	330	13.8	97t	2
Washington	23	209	9.1	67t	1
St. Louis	21	369	17.6	93t	4
Chicago	20	372	18.6	67	3
Green Bay	20	344	17.2	69t	2
Atlanta	18	154	8.6	33	0
Arizona	17	294	17.3	61t	3
Detroit	16	217	13.6	74t	3
New Orleans	15	209	13.9	40	0
N.Y. Giants	15	129	8.6	34t	1
Philadelphia	14	152	10.9	50t	2
Dallas	9	191	21.2	71t	3
Minnesota	8	47	5.9	27t	1
NFC Total	272	3810	14.0	98t	28
NFC Average	18.1	254.0	14.0	—	1.9
League Total	545	7708	—	100t	59
League Average	17.6	248.6	14.1	—	1.9

PUNTING

AVERAGE YARDS PER PUNT
NFC: 47.5   Todd Sauerbrun, Carolina
AFC: 46.2   Shane Lechler, Oakland

NET AVERAGE YARDS PER PUNT
NFC: 38.9   Todd Sauerbrun, Carolina
AFC: 38.1   Ken Walter, New England

LONGEST
NFC: 90   Rodney Williams, N.Y. Giants at Denver, September 10
AFC: 77   Matt Turk, Miami at Buffalo, November 25

PUNTS
AFC: 99   Chris Gardocki, Cleveland
NFC: 97   Sean Landeta, Philadelphia

PUNTS, GAME
AFC: 10   Jeff Feagles, Seattle vs. Philadelphia, September 23 (466 yards)
      10   Craig Hentrich, Tennessee at Baltimore, October 7 (402 yards)
NFC: 10   Todd Sauerbrun, Carolina vs. N.Y. Jets, October 28 (445 yards)
      10   Sean Landeta, Philadelphia at Arizona, November 4 (476 yards)
      10   Sean Landeta, Philadelphia vs. San Diego, December 9 (414 yards)

TEAM CHAMPION
NFC: 47.0   Carolina
AFC: 45.6   Oakland

AMERICAN FOOTBALL CONFERENCE—PUNTING

	Total Punts	Yards	Long	Avg	TB	Blk	Opp Ret	Return Yards	In 20	Net Avg
Oakland	74	3375	65	45.6	12	1	34	502	23	35.6
Denver	82	3668	64	44.7	8	1	48	517	25	36.5
Indianapolis	68	3023	65	44.5	12	0	35	486	12	33.8
Jacksonville	82	3577	59	43.6	12	0	38	295	24	37.1
Seattle	86	3730	68	43.4	7	1	43	462	26	36.4
Cleveland	99	4249	69	42.9	9	0	52	647	25	34.6
San Diego	78	3308	62	42.4	4	0	32	346	25	36.9
Tennessee	85	3567	70	42.0	8	0	36	264	28	37.0
Pittsburgh	63	2611	64	41.4	5	1	28	334	23	34.6
New England	74	3042	76	41.1	5	0	26	124	28	38.1
Miami	81	3321	77	41.0	7	0	30	136	28	37.6
Buffalo	80	3262	66	40.8	7	0	40	418	16	33.8
Kansas City	75	3037	76	40.5	5	0	31	288	27	35.3
Cincinnati	86	3404	57	39.6	7	1	47	374	21	33.6
N.Y. Jets	76	2966	59	39.0	6	0	34	446	24	31.6
Baltimore	87	3309	65	38.0	10	2	33	183	29	33.6
AFC Total	1276	53449	77	—	124	7	587	5822	384	—
AFC Average	79.8	3340.6	—	41.9	7.8	0.4	36.7	363.9	24.0	35.4

NATIONAL FOOTBALL CONFERENCE—PUNTING

	Total Punts	Yards	Long	Avg	TB	Blk	Opp Ret	Return Yards	In 20	Net Avg
Carolina	94	4419	73	47.0	17	1	42	425	35	38.9
Philadelphia	97	4221	64	43.5	10	0	56	488	26	36.4
Detroit	75	3225	62	43.0	10	0	39	387	22	35.2
Chicago	88	3743	60	42.5	8	0	45	327	37	37.0
Green Bay	82	3485	68	42.5	10	0	34	288	21	36.5
N.Y. Giants	96	4051	90	42.2	8	0	45	543	28	34.9
St. Louis	43	1809	58	42.1	7	0	17	167	9	34.9
Minnesota	72	3029	67	42.1	13	0	34	366	19	33.4
New Orleans	76	3180	62	41.8	7	0	36	316	24	35.8
Washington	91	3775	59	41.5	9	0	44	434	28	34.7
Arizona	87	3571	58	41.0	8	0	48	481	21	33.7
San Francisco	69	2813	64	40.8	4	0	34	290	21	35.4
Tampa Bay	83	3382	61	40.7	8	0	44	380	26	34.2
Atlanta	69	2680	55	38.8	3	0	17	130	25	36.1
Dallas	81	3135	57	38.7	6	3	38	493	25	31.1
NFC Total	1203	50518	90	—	128	4	573	5515	367	—
NFC Average	80.2	3367.9	—	42.0	8.5	0.3	38.2	367.7	24.5	35.3
NFL Total	2479	103967	90	—	252	11	1160	11337	751	—
NFL Average	80.0	3353.8	—	41.9	8.1	0.4	37.4	365.7	24.2	35.3

NFL TOP TEN PUNTERS

	No	Yards	Long	Avg	Total Punts	TB	Blk	Opp Ret	Return Yards	In 20	Net Avg
Sauerbrun, Todd, Car.	93	4419	73	47.5	94	17	1	42	425	35	38.9
Lechler, Shane, Oak.	73	3375	65	46.2	74	12	1	34	502	23	35.6
Rouen, Tom, Den.	81	3668	64	45.3	82	8	1	48	517	25	36.5
Smith, Hunter, Ind.	68	3023	65	44.5	68	12	0	35	486	12	33.8
Feagles, Jeff, Sea.	85	3730	68	43.9	86	7	1	43	462	26	36.4
Hanson, Chris, Jax.	82	3577	59	43.6	82	12	0	38	295	24	37.1
Berger, Mitch, Minn.	47	2046	67	43.5	47	10	0	25	302	10	32.9
Landeta, Sean, Phil.	97	4221	64	43.5	97	10	0	56	488	26	36.4
Jett, John, Det.	58	2512	62	43.3	58	6	0	30	332	16	35.5
Gardocki, Chris, Cle.	99	4249	69	42.9	99	9	0	52	647	25	34.6

AFC—INDIVIDUAL PUNTERS

	No	Yards	Long	Avg	Total Punts	TB	Blk	Opp Ret	Return Yards	In 20	Net Avg
Lechler, Shane, Oak.	73	3375	65	46.2	74	12	1	34	502	23	35.6
Rouen, Tom, Den.	81	3668	64	45.3	82	8	1	48	517	25	36.5
Smith, Hunter, Ind.	68	3023	65	44.5	68	12	0	35	486	12	33.8
Feagles, Jeff, Sea.	85	3730	68	43.9	86	7	1	43	462	26	36.4
Hanson, Chris, Jax.	82	3577	59	43.6	82	12	0	38	295	24	37.1
Gardocki, Chris, Cle.	99	4249	69	42.9	99	9	0	52	647	25	34.6
Miller, Josh, Pitt.	59	2505	64	42.5	60	5	1	26	310	23	34.9
Bennett, Darren, SD	78	3308	62	42.4	78	4	0	32	346	25	36.9
Hentrich, Craig, Tenn.	85	3567	70	42.0	85	8	0	36	264	28	37.0
Turk, Matt, Mia.	81	3321	77	41.0	81	7	0	30	136	28	37.6
Moorman, Brian, Buff.	80	3262	66	40.8	80	7	0	40	418	16	33.8
Stryzinski, Dan, KC	73	2976	76	40.8	73	5	0	30	277	27	35.6
Harris, Nick, Cin.	84	3372	57	40.1	85	6	1	47	374	21	33.9
Walter, Ken, NE	49	1964	58	40.1	49	2	0	17	59	24	38.1
Richardson, Kyle, Balt.	85	3309	65	38.9	87	10	2	33	183	29	33.6
Tupa, Tom, NYJ	67	2575	59	38.4	67	5	0	29	333	21	32.0
(Nonqualifiers)											
Parks, Tommy, NYJ	5	238	56	47.6	5	1	0	4	105	1	22.6
Pope, Daniel, NYJ	4	153	47	38.3	4	0	0	1	8	2	36.3
Brown, Kris, Pitt.	3	106	46	35.3	3	0	0	2	24	0	27.3
Peterson, Todd, KC	2	61	34	30.5	2	0	0	1	11	0	25.0
Vinatieri, Adam, NE	1	33	33	33.0	1	0	0	0	0	1	33.0
Rackers, Neil, Cin.	1	32	32	32.0	1	1	0	0	0	0	12.0

NFC—INDIVIDUAL PUNTERS

	No	Yards	Long	Avg	Total Punts	TB	Blk	Opp Ret	Return Yards	In 20	Net Avg
Sauerbrun, Todd, Car.	93	4419	73	47.5	94	17	1	42	425	35	38.9
Berger, Mitch, Minn.	47	2046	67	43.5	47	10	0	25	302	10	32.9
Landeta, Sean, Phil.	97	4221	64	43.5	97	10	0	56	488	26	36.4
Jett, John, Det.	58	2512	62	43.3	58	6	0	30	332	16	35.5
Williams, Rodney, NYG	91	3905	90	42.9	91	8	0	43	521	25	35.4
Maynard, Brad, Chi.	87	3709	60	42.6	87	8	0	45	327	36	37.0
Bidwell, Josh, GB	82	3485	68	42.5	82	10	0	34	288	21	36.5
Baker, John, StL	43	1809	58	42.1	43	7	0	17	167	9	34.9
Gowin, Toby, NO	76	3180	62	41.8	76	7	0	36	316	24	35.8
Barker, Bryan, Wash.	90	3747	59	41.6	90	9	0	44	434	27	34.8
Player, Scott, Ariz	67	2779	58	41.5	67	7	0	35	377	17	33.8
Johnson, Lee, NE-Minn.	49	2028	76	41.4	49	6	0	18	129	12	36.3
Baker, Jason, SF	69	2813	64	40.8	69	4	0	34	290	21	35.4
Royals, Mark, TB	83	3382	61	40.7	83	8	0	44	380	26	34.2
Knorr, Micah, Dall.	78	3135	57	40.2	81	6	3	38	493	25	31.1
Mohr, Chris, Atl.	69	2680	55	38.8	69	3	0	17	130	25	36.1
(Nonqualifiers)											
Stanley, Chad, Ariz	19	751	54	39.5	19	1	0	12	82	4	34.2
Araguz, Leo, Det.	17	713	55	41.9	17	4	0	9	55	6	34.0
Pochman, Owen, NYG	5	146	39	29.2	5	0	0	2	22	3	24.8
Gramatica, Bill, Ariz	1	41	41	41.0	1	0	0	1	22	0	19.0
Edinger, Paul, Chi.	1	34	34	34.0	1	0	0	0	0	1	34.0
Conway, Brett, Wash.	1	28	28	28.0	1	0	0	0	0	1	28.0

Leader based on average, minimum 40 punts

PUNT RETURNS

YARDS PER RETURN
AFC: 14.2 Troy Brown, New England
NFC: 14.1 Darrien Gordon, Atlanta

YARDS
AFC: 519 Jermaine Lewis, Baltimore
NFC: 467 Brian Mitchell, Philadelphia

YARDS, GAME
NFC: 139 Darrien Gordon, Atlanta vs. Dallas, November 11 (3 returns, 0 TD)
AFC: 126 T.J. Houshmandzadeh, Cincinnati at Cleveland, November 25 (5 returns, 0 TD)

LONGEST
NFC: 89 Eric Metcalf, Washington vs. N.Y. Giants, October 28 - TD
AFC: 88 Tim Brown, Oakland vs. Kansas City, December 9 - TD

RETURNS
AFC: 42 Jermaine Lewis, Baltimore
NFC: 40 Arnold Jackson, Arizona

RETURNS, GAME
NFC: 7 Brian Mitchell, Philadelphia at Seattle, September 23 (86 yards, 0 TD)
       7 Eric Metcalf, Washington at Denver, November 18 (54 yards, 0 TD)
       7 Nate Jacquet, Minnesota vs. Chicago, November 25 (39 yards, 0 TD)
AFC: 6 Hank Poteat, Pittsburgh at Buffalo, September 30 (91 yards, 0 TD)
       6 Craig Yeast, N.Y. Jets at Carolina, October 28 (59 yards, 0 TD)
       6 Jermaine Lewis, Baltimore vs. Cincinnati, December 23 (59 yards, 0 TD)

FAIR CATCHES
AFC: 22 Damon Gibson, Jacksonville
NFC: 22 Brian Mitchell, Philadelphia

TOUCHDOWNS
AFC: 2 Troy Brown, New England
NFC: 1 Eric Metcalf, Washington
       1 Allen Rossum, Green Bay
       1 Steve Smith, Carolina
       1 Reggie Swinton, Dallas
       1 Karl Williams, Tampa Bay

TEAM CHAMPION
NFC: 13.6 Atlanta
AFC: 13.3 New England

NFL TOP TEN PUNT RETURNERS

	No	FC	Yards	Avg	Long	TD
Brown, Troy, NE	29	15	413	14.2	85t	2
Gordon, Darrien, Atl.	31	6	437	14.1	74	0
Swinton, Reggie, Dall.	31	8	414	13.4	65t	1
O'Neal, Deltha, Den.	31	9	405	13.1	86t	1
Metcalf, Eric, Wash.	33	5	412	12.5	89t	1
Lewis, Jermaine, Balt.	42	9	519	12.4	62	0
Mitchell, Brian, Phil.	39	22	467	12.0	54	0
Ogden, Jeff, Mia.	32	11	377	11.8	48	0
Jackson, Arnold, Ariz	40	0	461	11.5	55	0
Dwight, Tim, SD	24	12	271	11.3	84t	1

AFC—INDIVIDUAL PUNT RETURNERS

	No	FC	Yards	Avg	Long	TD
Brown, Troy, NE	29	15	413	14.2	85t	2
O'Neal, Deltha, Den.	31	9	405	13.1	86t	1
Lewis, Jermaine, Balt.	42	9	519	12.4	62	0
Ogden, Jeff, Mia.	32	11	377	11.8	48	0
Dwight, Tim, SD	24	12	271	11.3	84t	1
Wilkins, Terrence, Ind.	21	4	219	10.4	78t	1
Rogers, Charlie, Sea.	25	10	244	9.8	34	0
Gibson, Damon, Jax.	38	22	333	8.8	24	0
Milburn, Glyn, Chi.-SD	21	7	172	8.2	20	0
Poteat, Hank, Pitt.	36	14	292	8.1	39	0
Hall, Dante, KC	32	6	235	7.3	26	0
Mason, Derrick, Tenn.	20	19	128	6.4	20	0
(Nonqualifiers)						
Dunn, David, Oak.	19	11	169	8.9	23	0
Price, Peerless, Buff.	19	8	110	5.8	24	0
Warrick, Peter, Cin.	18	10	116	6.4	31	0
Northcutt, Dennis, Cle.	15	9	86	5.7	32	0
Walker, Joe, Tenn.	14	4	125	8.9	36	0
Johnson, Kevin, Cle.	14	6	117	8.4	24	0
Yeast, Craig, NYJ	13	6	122	9.4	35	0
Morton, Chad, NYJ	13	7	113	8.7	33	0
Houshmandzadeh, T.J., Cin.	12	5	163	13.6	86	0
Parker, Larry, KC	11	2	91	8.3	14	0
Edwards, Troy, Pitt.	10	0	83	8.3	28	0
Ward, Dedric, Mia.	9	2	88	9.8	18	0
Insley, Trevor, Ind.	7	8	71	10.1	33	0
Brown, Tim, Oak.	6	21	111	18.5	88t	1
Engram, Bobby, Sea.	6	3	96	16.0	28	0
Moss, Santana, NYJ	6	0	82	13.7	23	0
McAlister, Chris, Balt.	5	1	44	8.8	24	0
Clements, Nate, Buff.	4	1	81	20.3	66t	1
Woodson, Charles, Oak.	4	0	47	11.8	16	0
Shaw, Bobby, Pitt.	4	1	45	11.3	23	0
Faulk, Kevin, NE	4	0	27	6.8	10	0
Jones, Reggie, SD	3	0	5	1.7	5	0
McCareins, Justin, Tenn.	2	0	29	14.5	18	0
Joseph, Kerry, Sea.	2	1	12	6.0	12	0
Glenn, Aaron, NYJ	2	1	6	3.0	4	0
Jackson, Raymond, Cle.	1	0	43	43.0	43	0
Black, Avion, Buff.	1	0	34	34.0	34	0
Farmer, Danny, Cin.	1	1	11	11.0	11	0
Madison, Sam, Mia.	1	0	6	6.0	6	0
Chapman, Lamar, Cle.	1	0	1	1.0	1	0
Cousin, Terry, Mia.	1	0	0	0.0	0	0
Harper, Nicholas, Ind.	1	0	0	0.0	0	0
Lake, Carnell, Balt.	1	0	0	0.0	0	0
Warfield, Eric, KC	1	0	0	0.0	0	0
Porter, Jerry, Oak.	0	0	12	—	12	0
Frost, Scott, Cle.	0	1	0	—	—	0

t = Touchdown
Leader based on average return, minimum 20 returns

NFC—INDIVIDUAL PUNT RETURNERS

	No	FC	Yards	Avg	Long	TD
Gordon, Darrien, Atl.	31	6	437	14.1	74	0
Swinton, Reggie, Dall.	31	8	414	13.4	65t	1
Metcalf, Eric, Wash.	33	5	412	12.5	89t	1
Mitchell, Brian, Phil.	39	22	467	12.0	54	0
Jackson, Arnold, Ariz	40	0	461	11.5	55	0
Smith, Steve, Car.	34	10	364	10.7	70t	1
Williams, Karl, TB	35	13	366	10.5	84t	1
Hakim, Az-Zahir, StL	36	12	330	9.2	32	0
Howard, Desmond, Det.	22	19	201	9.1	34	0
Johnson, Leon, Chi.	28	10	255	9.1	35	0
Barber, Tiki, NYG	38	12	338	8.9	23	0
McGarity, Wane, Dall.-N.O.	25	11	221	8.8	42	0
Jacquet, Nate, Minn.	29	6	219	7.6	23	0
Sutherland, Vinny, SF	21	19	147	7.0	19	0
(Nonqualifiers)						
Freeman, Antonio, GB	17	7	114	6.7	29	0
Lewis, Michael, NO	14	0	81	5.8	32	0
McQuarters, R.W., Chi.	12	1	96	8.0	16	0
Rossum, Allen, GB	11	8	109	9.9	55t	1
Walters, Troy, Minn.	11	3	69	6.3	16	0
Toomer, Amani, NYG	8	1	41	5.1	15	0
Bly, Dre', StL	7	6	71	10.1	32	0
Byrd, Isaac, Car.	5	2	56	11.2	22	0
Brown, Na, Phil.	5	0	30	6.0	11	0
Lockett, Kevin, Wash.	5	3	14	2.8	11	0
Fair, Terry, Det.	4	2	37	9.3	21	0
McAllister, Deuce, NO	4	4	24	6.0	10	0
Morgan, Don, Minn.	4	0	17	4.3	6	0
Foster, Larry, Det.	3	0	17	5.7	9	0
Anthony, Reidel, TB	3	1	12	4.0	7	0
Lassiter, Kwamie, Ariz	3	1	11	3.7	10	0
Lee, Charles, GB	3	0	6	2.0	6	0
Hudson, Chris, Atl.	2	1	26	13.0	22	0
Rambo, Ken-Yon, Dall.	2	0	15	7.5	13	0
Bates, Michael, Wash.	2	2	5	2.5	5	0
Wilson, Cedrick, SF	2	0	4	2.0	3	0
Ismail, Raghib, Dall.	1	3	20	20.0	20	0
Sharper, Darren, GB	1	3	18	18.0	18	0
Galloway, Joey, Dall.	1	0	6	6.0	6	0
Denson, Autry, Chi.	1	0	5	5.0	5	0
Ferguson, Robert, GB	1	2	4	4.0	4	0
Walsh, Chris, Minn.	1	0	2	2.0	2	0
Kozlowski, Brian, Atl.	1	0	0	0.0	0	0
McClellion, Central, Wash.	1	0	0	0.0	0	0
Dixon, Ron, NYG	1	0	-3	-3.0	-3	0
Jackson, Dexter, TB	0	0	18	—	18	0
Azumah, Jerry, Chi.	0	0	16	—	16	0
Cook, Rashard, Phil.	0	0	11	—	11	0
Butler, Jerametrius, StL	0	0	-1	—	-1	0

t = Touchdown
Leader based on average return, minimum 20 returns

AMERICAN FOOTBALL CONFERENCE—PUNT RETURNS

	No	FC	Yards	Avg	Long	TD
New England	33	15	440	13.3	85t	2
Denver	31	9	405	13.1	86t	1
Baltimore	48	10	563	11.7	62	0
Oakland	29	32	339	11.7	88t	1
Miami	43	13	471	11.0	48	0
Seattle	33	14	352	10.7	34	0
Indianapolis	29	12	290	10.0	78t	1
N.Y. Jets	34	14	323	9.5	35	0
San Diego	44	16	415	9.4	84t	1
Buffalo	24	9	225	9.4	66t	1
Cincinnati	31	16	290	9.4	86	0
Jacksonville	38	22	333	8.8	24	0
Pittsburgh	50	15	420	8.4	39	0
Cleveland	31	16	247	8.0	43	0
Tennessee	36	23	282	7.8	36	0
Kansas City	44	8	326	7.4	26	0
AFC Total	578	244	5721	9.9	88t	7
AFC Average	36.1	15.3	357.6	9.9	—	0.4

NATIONAL FOOTBALL CONFERENCE—PUNT RETURNS

	No	FC	Yards	Avg	Long	TD
Atlanta	34	7	463	13.6	74	0
Dallas	41	13	493	12.0	65t	1
Philadelphia	44	22	508	11.5	54	0
Arizona	43	1	472	11.0	55	0
Carolina	39	12	420	10.8	70t	1
Washington	41	10	431	10.5	89t	1
Tampa Bay	38	14	396	10.4	84t	1
St. Louis	43	18	400	9.3	32	0
Chicago	45	14	405	9.0	35	0
Detroit	29	21	255	8.8	34	0
N.Y. Giants	47	13	376	8.0	23	0
New Orleans	37	13	288	7.8	42	0
Green Bay	33	20	251	7.6	55t	1
Minnesota	45	9	307	6.8	23	0
San Francisco	23	19	151	6.6	19	0
NFC Total	582	206	5616	9.6	89t	5
NFC Average	38.8	13.7	374.4	9.6	—	0.3
League Total	1160	450	11337	—	89t	12
League Average	37.4	14.5	365.7	—	9.8	0.4

KICKOFF RETURNS

YARDS PER RETURN
AFC:	26.6	Ronney Jenkins, San Diego
NFC:	25.6	Steve Smith, Carolina

YARDS
AFC:	1541	Ronney Jenkins, San Diego
NFC:	1491	Darrick Vaughn, Atlanta

YARDS, GAME
NFC:	252	Steve Smith, Carolina at St. Louis, November 11 (7 returns, 1 TD)
AFC:	250	Ronney Jenkins, San Diego at Oakland, November 18 (6 returns, 1 TD)

LONGEST
AFC:	101	Derrick Mason, Tennessee at Cincinnati, November 18 - TD
NFC:	99	Steve Smith, Carolina at St. Louis, November 11 - TD

RETURNS
NFC:	61	Darrick Vaughn, Atlanta
AFC:	58	Ronney Jenkins, San Diego

RETURNS, GAME
NFC:	9	Nate Jacquet, Minnesota at Philadelphia, November 11 (237 yards, 0 TD)
AFC:	8	Terrence Wilkins, Indianapolis at Baltimore, December 2 (173 yards, 0 TD)

TOUCHDOWNS
AFC:	2	Ronney Jenkins, San Diego
NFC:	2	Steve Smith, Carolina

TEAM CHAMPION
AFC:	26.0	San Diego
NFC:	23.8	Philadelphia

NFL TOP TEN KICKOFF RETURNERS
	No	Yards	Avg	Long	TD
Jenkins, Ronney, SD	58	1541	26.6	93t	2
Smith, Steve, Car.	56	1431	25.6	99t	2
Howard, Desmond, Det.	57	1446	25.4	91	0
Mitchell, Brian, Phil.	41	1025	25.0	94t	1
Lewis, Jermaine, Balt.	42	1039	24.7	76	0
Vaughn, Darrick, Atl.	61	1491	24.4	96t	1
McAllister, Deuce, NO	45	1091	24.2	63	0
Lewis, Michael, NO	32	762	23.8	68	0
Swinton, Reggie, Dall.	56	1327	23.7	77	0
Cole, Chris, Den.	48	1127	23.5	52	0

AFC—INDIVIDUAL KICKOFF RETURNERS
	No	Yards	Avg	Long	TD
Jenkins, Ronney, SD	58	1541	26.6	93t	2
Lewis, Jermaine, Balt.	42	1039	24.7	76	0
Cole, Chris, Den.	48	1127	23.5	52	0
Kirby, Terry, Oak.	46	1066	23.2	90t	1
Edwards, Troy, Pitt.	20	462	23.1	81	0
Dunn, David, Oak.	20	458	22.9	40	0
Wilkins, Terrence, Ind.	44	1007	22.9	50	0
Yeast, Craig, NYJ	29	663	22.9	50	0
Hall, Dante, KC	43	969	22.5	71	0
Chambers, Chris, Mia.	36	811	22.5	47	0
Rogers, Charlie, Sea.	50	1120	22.4	64	0
Gay, Benjamin, Cle.	23	513	22.3	42	0
Mason, Derrick, Tenn.	34	748	22.0	101t	1
Keaton, Curtis, Cin.	42	891	21.2	64	0
Clements, Nate, Buff.	30	628	20.9	37	0

Faulk, Kevin, NE	33	662	20.1	42	0
Black, Avion, Buff.	25	498	19.9	29	0
Gibson, Damon, Jax.	26	511	19.7	35	0
(Nonqualifiers):					
Joseph, Elvis, Jax.	17	428	25.2	95t	1
Marion, Brock, Mia.	17	371	21.8	55	0
McDougal, Kevin, Ind.	16	362	22.6	40	0
Bryson, Shawn, Buff.	16	299	18.7	32	0
Poteat, Hank, Pitt.	16	250	15.6	30	0
Kasper, Kevin, Den.	14	372	26.6	37	0
Rhodes, Dominic, Ind.	14	356	25.4	88t	1
King, Andre, Cle.	14	279	19.9	27	0
Berlin, Eddie, Tenn.	13	253	19.5	32	0
Morton, Chad, NYJ	12	247	20.6	33	0
Coleman, Chris, Tenn.	11	251	22.8	34	0
Harris, Corey, Balt.	11	235	21.4	34	0
Pass, Patrick, NE	10	222	22.2	33	0
Houshmandzadeh, T.J., Cin.	10	185	18.5	23	0
Coles, Laveranues, NYJ	9	211	23.4	34	0
White, Jamel, Cle.	9	189	21.0	31	0
Williams, James, Sea.	9	175	19.4	31	0
Cloud, Mike, KC	8	174	21.8	33	0
Ross, Micah, Jax.	8	150	18.8	26	0
Morgan, Quincy, Cle.	7	175	25.0	51	0
Driver, Tony, Buff.	7	130	18.6	23	0
Kelly, Ben, NE	7	123	17.6	28	0
Jackson, Lenzie, Pitt.	6	125	20.8	25	0
Watson, Chris, Buff.	5	96	19.2	30	0
Jones, Reggie, SD	4	126	31.5	74	0
Joseph, Kerry, Sea.	4	83	20.8	24	0
Johnson, Rudi, Cin.	4	79	19.8	25	0
Sellers, Mike, Cle.	4	75	18.8	21	0
McCareins, Justin, Tenn.	4	70	17.5	21	0
Bennett, Brandon, Cin.	4	60	15.0	19	0
Jordan, LaMont, NYJ	3	62	20.7	23	0
Belser, Jason, KC	3	58	19.3	24	0
Graham, Jay, Sea.	3	56	18.7	20	0
Evans, Heath, Sea.	3	40	13.3	20	0
Beisel, Monty, KC	3	35	11.7	14	0
Walker, Joe, Tenn.	3	33	11.0	19	0
Finn, Jim, Ind.	3	29	9.7	13	0
Redmond, J.R., NE	2	57	28.5	30	0
Mack, Stacey, Jax.	2	49	24.5	31	0
Carter, Tony, Den.	2	44	22.0	24	0
Patten, David, NE	2	44	22.0	24	0
Johnson, Patrick, Balt.	2	39	19.5	23	0
Blackwell, Will, Pitt.	2	36	18.0	20	0
Dunn, Jason, KC	2	34	17.0	18	0
Jackson, Curtis, NE	2	30	15.0	19	0
Simmons, Tony, Ind.	2	27	13.5	15	0
Dyer, Deon, Mia.	2	24	12.0	14	0
Green, Mike, Tenn.	2	20	10.0	12	0
Gutierrez, Brock, Cin.	2	15	7.5	8	0
Nwokorie, Chukie, Ind.	2	15	7.5	9	0
Meier, Rob, Jax.	2	14	7.0	8	0
Santiago, O.J., Cle.	2f	1	0.5	5	0
Northcutt, Dennis, Cle.	1	26	26.0	26	0
Brookins, Jason, Balt.	1	23	23.0	23	0
Edwards, Marc, NE	1	23	23.0	23	0
Insley, Trevor, Ind.	1	23	23.0	23	0
Parker, Larry, KC	1	22	22.0	22	0
Harris, Derrick, SD	1	19	19.0	19	0
Gary, Olandis, Den.	1	18	18.0	18	0
Johnson, J.J., Mia.	1	16	16.0	16	0
Strong, Mack, Sea.	1	16	16.0	16	0
Kinney, Erron, Tenn.	1	14	14.0	14	0
Moreland, Jake, Cle.	1	14	14.0	14	0
Brown, Troy, NE	1	13	13.0	13	0
Pathon, Jerome, Ind.	1	13	13.0	13	0
Spires, Greg, Cle.	1	13	13.0	13	0

Bennett, Drew, Tenn.	1	11	11.0	11	0	Wiley, Michael, Dall.	4	90	22.5	40	0
Bobo, Orlando, Balt.	1	11	11.0	11	0	Morgan, Don, Minn.	4	78	19.5	24	0
Clark, Desmond, Den.	1	11	11.0	11	0	Cason, Aveion, StL	4	73	18.3	26	0
Fletcher, Terrell, SD	1	11	11.0	11	0	Azumah, Jerry, Chi.	4	65	16.3	23	0
Bruschi, Tedy, NE	1	10	10.0	10	0	Mealey, Rondell, GB	4	63	15.8	24	0
Carson, Leonardo, SD	1	10	10.0	10	0	Johnson, Bryan, Wash.	4	51	12.8	18	0
Long, Kevin, Tenn.	1	10	10.0	10	0	Hetherington, Chris, Car.	4	31	7.8	12	0
Logan, Mike, Pitt.	1	9	9.0	9	0	Broughton, Luther, Car.	3	46	15.3	26	0
Whitman, Josh, SD	1	9	9.0	9	0	Smith, Paul, SF	3	37	12.3	16	0
Spicer, Paul, Jax.	1	8	8.0	8	0	Kozlowski, Brian, Atl.	3	35	11.7	14	0
Dearth, James, NYJ	1	7	7.0	7	0	Crumpler, Alge, Atl.	3	32	10.7	14	0
Engram, Bobby, Sea.	1	6	6.0	6	0	Thompson, Derrius, Wash.	3	17	5.7	17	0
Sowell, Jerald, NYJ	1	6	6.0	6	0	Jackson, Arnold, Ariz	2	46	23.0	24	0
Prince, Ryan, Jax.	1	4	4.0	4	0	McCord, Quentin, Atl.	2	39	19.5	23	0
Smith, Detron, Den.	1	4	4.0	4	0	Williams, Karl, TB	2	35	17.5	22	0
Rolle, Samari, Tenn.	1	3	3.0	3	0	Douglas, Dameane, Phil.	2	32	16.0	18	0
Shaw, Bobby, Pitt.	1	2	2.0	2	0	Ferguson, Robert, GB	2	32	16.0	16	0
Atkins, Larry, KC	1	0	0.0	0	0	Lewis, Jonas, SF	2	32	16.0	19	0
Boyd, James, Jax.	1	0	0.0	0	0	Rambo, Ken-Yon, Dall.	2	30	15.0	19	0
Cota, Chad, Ind.	1	0	0.0	0	0	Freeman, Antonio, GB	2	28	14.0	24	0
Fauria, Christian, Sea.	1	0	0.0	0	0	Whitehead, Willie, NO	2	19	9.5	12	0
Henderson, Jamie, NYJ	1	0	0.0	0	0	Ackerman, Tom, NO	2	11	5.5	11	0
Perry, Ed, Mia.	1f	0	0.0	0	0	Campbell, Dan, NYG	2	8	4.0	8	0
						Olivo, Brock, Det.	1	40	40.0	40	0

t = Touchdown
f = Fair Catch
Leader based on average return, minimum 20 returns

NFC—INDIVIDUAL KICKOFF RETURNERS

	No	Yards	Avg	Long	TD
Smith, Steve, Car.	56	1431	25.6	99t	2
Howard, Desmond, Det.	57	1446	25.4	91	0
Mitchell, Brian, Phil.	41	1025	25.0	94t	1
Vaughn, Darrick, Atl.	61	1491	24.4	96t	1
McAllister, Deuce, NO	45	1091	24.2	63	0
Lewis, Michael, NO	32	762	23.8	68	0
Swinton, Reggie, Dall.	56	1327	23.7	77	0
Bates, Michael, Wash.	49	1150	23.5	41	0
Denson, Autry, Chi.	23	534	23.2	37	0
Jenkins, MarTay, Ariz	49	1120	22.9	70	0
Sutherland, Vinny, SF	50	1140	22.8	65	0
Murphy, Frank, TB	20	445	22.3	39	0
Jacquet, Nate, Minn.	46	1012	22.0	53	0
Canidate, Trung, StL	36	748	20.8	40	0
Dixon, Ron, NYG	34	645	19.0	43	0
Rossum, Allen, GB	23	431	18.7	27	0

(Nonqualifiers)

Walters, Troy, Minn.	18	425	23.6	40	0
Smith, Dwight, TB	16	355	22.2	45	0
Levens, Dorsey, GB	14	362	25.9	53	0
Johnson, Leon, Chi.	14	286	20.4	33	0
Byrd, Isaac, Car.	10	225	22.5	26	0
Fair, Terry, Det.	10	187	18.7	32	0
Stecker, Aaron, TB	9	259	28.8	86	0
Foster, Larry, Det.	9	182	20.2	36	0
Murphy, Yo, StL	8	174	21.8	29	0
Carter, Jonathan, NYG	8	155	19.4	31	0
Stoutmire, Omar, NYG	8	127	15.9	24	0
Carter, Ki-Jana, Wash.	8	111	13.9	27	0
Pittman, Michael, Ariz	6	161	26.8	44	0
Milburn, Glyn, Chi.	6	152	25.3	37	0
McAfee, Fred, NO	6	144	24.0	34	0
Bly, Dre', StL	6	128	21.3	32	0
Wilson, Cedrick, SF	6	127	21.2	34	0
Shipp, Marcel, Ariz	6	118	19.7	26	0
Morrow, Harold, Minn.	6	109	18.2	28	0
Washington, Damon, NYG	6	99	16.5	22	0
Henderson, William, GB	6	62	10.3	14	0
Thrash, James, Phil.	5	101	20.2	34	0
Abdullah, Rabih, TB	5	92	18.4	29	0

Continuation of right column list:

Buckhalter, Correll, Phil.	1	28	28.0	28	0
Metcalf, Eric, Wash.	1	25	25.0	25	0
Larrimore, Kareem, Dall.	1	22	22.0	22	0
Washington, Todd, TB	1	22	22.0	22	0
Goodman, Herbert, GB	1	21	21.0	21	0
Huntley, Richard, Car.	1	20	20.0	20	0
McDaniel, Emmanuel, NYG	1	17	17.0	17	0
Burke, Tom, Ariz	1	15	15.0	15	0
McKinley, Dennis, Ariz	1	11	11.0	11	0
Raiola, Dominic, Det.	1	11	11.0	11	0
Rivers, Marcellus, NYG	1	11	11.0	11	0
Worthen, Shawn, Minn.	1	11	11.0	11	0
Schlesinger, Cory, Det.	1	10	10.0	10	0
Walsh, Chris, Minn.	1	10	10.0	10	0
Bush, Steve, Ariz	1	9	9.0	9	0
Flanigan, Jim, GB	1	9	9.0	9	0
Crawford, Casey, Car.	1	8	8.0	8	0
Hoover, Brad, Car.	1	8	8.0	8	0
Newkirk, Robert, Chi.	1	8	8.0	8	0
Terrell, David, Chi.	1	8	8.0	8	0
Evans, Demetric, Dall.	1	7	7.0	7	0
Makovicka, Joel, Ariz	1	7	7.0	7	0
Dogins, Kevin, Chi.	1	6	6.0	6	0
Morton, Johnnie, Det.	1	4	4.0	4	0
Prentice, Travis, Minn.	1	2	2.0	2	0
Garza, Roberto, Atl.	1	1	1.0	1	0
Powell, Carl, Chi.	1f	1	1.0	1	0
Akins, Chris, GB	1	0	0.0	0	0
Archuleta, Adam, StL	1	0	0.0	0	0
White, Steve, TB	1f	0	0.0	0	0
Snider, Matt, Minn.	0f	0	—	—	0
Warren, Lamont, Det.	0	-4	—	-4	0
Lewis, Chad, Phil.	0	-10	—	-10	0
Reese, Ike, Phil.	0	-11	—	-11	0

t = Touchdown
f = Fair Catch
Leader based on average return, minimum 20 returns

AMERICAN FOOTBALL CONFERENCE—KICKOFF RETURNS

	No	Yards	Avg	Long	TD
San Diego	66	1716	26.0	93t	2
Baltimore	57	1347	23.6	76	0
Denver	67	1576	23.5	52	0
Oakland	66	1524	23.1	90t	1
Indianapolis	84	1832	21.8	88t	1
Miami	57	1222	21.4	55	0
N.Y. Jets	56	1196	21.4	50	0
Kansas City	61	1292	21.2	71	0
Seattle	72	1496	20.8	64	0
Cleveland	62	1285	20.7	51	0
Jacksonville	58	1164	20.1	95t	1
New England	59	1184	20.1	42	0
Tennessee	71	1413	19.9	101t	1
Buffalo	83	1651	19.9	37	0
Cincinnati	62	1230	19.8	64	0
Pittsburgh	46	884	19.2	81	0
AFC Total	1027	22012	21.4	101t	6
AFC Average		64.2	1375.8	21.4	—	0.4

NATIONAL FOOTBALL CONFERENCE—KICKOFF RETURNS

	No	Yards	Avg	Long	TD
Philadelphia	49	1165	23.8	94t	1
Detroit	80	1876	23.5	91	0
New Orleans	87	2027	23.3	68	0
Carolina	76	1769	23.3	99t	2
Dallas	64	1476	23.1	77	0
Atlanta	70	1598	22.8	96t	1
Tampa Bay	54	1208	22.4	86	0
Arizona	67	1487	22.2	70	0
San Francisco	61	1336	21.9	65	0
Minnesota	77	1647	21.4	53	0
Washington	65	1354	20.8	41	0
Chicago	51	1060	20.8	37	0
St. Louis	55	1123	20.4	40	0
Green Bay	54	1008	18.7	53	0
N.Y. Giants	60	1062	17.7	43	0
NFC Total	970	21196	21.9	99t	4
NFC Average	64.7	1413.1	21.9	—	0.3
League Total	1997	43208	—	101t	10
League Average	64.4	1393.8	21.6	—	0.3

FUMBLES

MOST FUMBLES

NFC:	23	Kerry Collins, N.Y. Giants
AFC:	13	Rich Gannon, Oakland
	13	Jon Kitna, Cincinnati

MOST FUMBLES, GAME

AFC:	3	Jon Kitna, Cincinnati at Jacksonville, November 11
	3	Trent Green, Kansas City at N.Y. Jets, November 11
	3	Jonathan Quinn, Jacksonville at Pittsburgh, November 18
NFC:	3	many times

OWN FUMBLES RECOVERED

AFC:	7	Jon Kitna, Cincinnati
NFC:	7	Kerry Collins, N.Y. Giants
	7	Daunte Culpepper, Minnesota
	7	Stephen Davis, Washington

OWN FUMBLES RECOVERED, GAME

AFC:	3	Jon Kitna, Cincinnati at Jacksonville, November 11 (0 yards, 0 TD)
NFC:	2	many times

OPPONENTS' FUMBLES RECOVERED

NFC:	5	Sammy Knight, New Orleans
AFC:	4	Corey Harris, Balt.imore
	4	Jason Taylor, Miami

OPPONENTS' FUMBLES RECOVERED, GAME

AFC:	2	Donnie Edwards, Kansas City vs. Oakland, September 9 (0 yards, 0 TD)
	2	Samari Rolle, Tennessee at Jacksonville, September 23 (26 yards, 0 TD)
	2	Jason Taylor, Miami vs. New England, October 7 (1 yard, 1 TD)
	2	Kimo von Oelhoffen, Pittsburgh vs. Jacksonville, November 18 (0 yards, 0 TD)
NFC:	2	Dwight Smith, Tampa Bay at St. Louis, November 26 (0 yards, 0 TD)
	2	Vonnie Holliday, Green Bay at Tennessee, December 16 (0 yards, 0 TD)

YARDS

NFC:	101	Brian Urlacher, Chicago
AFC:	95	Chukie Nwokorie, Indianapolis

LONGEST

AFC:	95	Chukie Nwokorie, Indianapolis at N.Y. Jets, September 9 - TD
NFC:	94	Rashard Anderson, Carolina vs. N.Y. Jets, October 28 - TD

AFC—TOUCHDOWNS ON FUMBLE RECOVERIES

Abraham, John, NYJ	1
Allen, Eric, Oak.	1
Battles, Ainsley, Jax.	1
Beasley, Aaron, Jax.	1
Brown, Courtney, Cle.	1
Edwards, Troy, Pitt.	1
Gildon, Jason, Pitt.	1
Harris, Derrick, SD	1
Johnson, Raylee, SD	1
Lewis, Mo, NYJ	1
Minor, Travis, Mia.	1
Myers, Bobby, Tenn.	1
Nwokorie, Chukie, Ind.	1
Randle, John, Sea.	1
Sharper, Jamie, Balt.	1
Simmons, Brian, Cin.	1
Taylor, Jason, Mia.	1
Washington, Dewayne, Pitt.	1

NFC—TOUCHDOWNS ON FUMBLE RECOVERIES

Anderson, Rashard, Car.	1
Carter, Tyrone, Minn.	1
Crawford, Casey, Car.	1
Dawkins, Brian, Phil.	1
Hall, James, Det.	1
McCleon, Dexter, StL	1
McKinnon, Ronald, Ariz	1
McQuarters, R.W., Chi.	1
Mealey, Rondell, GB	1
Moore, Damon, Phil.	1
Oldham, Chris, NO	1
Peterson, Julian, SF	1
Strahan, Michael, NYG	1
Urlacher, Brian, Chi.	1
Vanden Bosch, Kyle, Ariz	1

AFC FUMBLES—INDIVIDUAL

	Fum	Own Rec	Opp Rec	Yards	Tot Rec
Abraham, John, NYJ	0	0	3	7	3
Alexander, Shaun, Sea.	4	3	0	8	3
Allen, Eric, Oak.	0	0	1	26	1
Allen, Terry, Balt.	1	0	0	0	0
Anderson, Mike, Den.	1	0	0	0	0
Anderson, Richie, NYJ	1	0	0	0	0
Anderson, Bennie, Balt.	0	1	0	0	1
Andruzzi, Joe, NE	0	1	0	0	1
Ayanbadejo, Obafemi, Balt.	1	2	0	0	2
Bannister, Alex, Sea.	0	0	1	0	1
Barndt, Tom, NYJ	0	0	1	0	1
Battaglia, Marco, Cin.	1	0	0	0	0
Battles, Ainsley, Jax.	0	0	2	60	2
Bean, Robert, Cin.	0	0	1	10	1
Beasley, Aaron, Jax.	0	0	1	40	1
Beckett, Rogers, SD	0	0	1	1	1
Bell, Myron, Pitt.	0	0	1	0	1
Bennett, Brandon, Cin.	1	0	0	0	0
Berry, Bert, Den.	0	0	2	1	2
Bettis, Jerome, Pitt.	3	2	0	0	2
Biekert, Greg, Oak.	0	0	1	0	1
Black, Avion, Buff.	0	0	1	0	1
Bledsoe, Drew, NE	1	1	0	0	1
Bobo, Orlando, Balt.	1	0	0	0	0
Boulware, Peter, Balt.	0	0	1	0	1
Boyd, James, Jax.	0	1	0	47	1
Brackens, Tony, Jax.	0	0	1	1	1
Brady, Tom, NE	12	4	0	-18	4
Braham, Rich, Cin.	1	0	0	-22	0

Bratzke, Chad, Ind.	0	0	1	0	1	Fisk, Jason, Tenn.	0	0	1	0	1
Brees, Drew, SD	2	1	0	0	1	Fletcher, Terrell, SD	1	0	0	0	0
Brookins, Jason, Balt.	3	2	0	0	2	Flutie, Doug, SD	7	5	0	-8	5
Brown, Chad, Sea.	0	0	1	3	1	Flynn, Mike, Balt.	1	1	0	-3	1
Brown, Courtney, Cle.	0	0	2	25	2	Folau, Spencer, Mia.	0	1	0	0	1
Brown, Eric, Den.	0	0	1	0	1	Foreman, Jay, Buff.	0	0	2	0	2
Brown, Kris, Pitt.	1	1	0	0	1	Freeman, Arturo, Mia.	0	0	2	-5	2
Brown, Tim, Oak.	1	0	0	0	0	Frerotte, Gus, Den.	2	1	0	0	1
Brown, Travis, Buff.	1	0	0	0	0	Fuller, Corey, Cle.	0	0	1	0	1
Brown, Troy, NE	2	1	0	0	1	Gadsden, Oronde, Mia.	1	1	0	0	1
Bruener, Mark, Pitt.	0	1	0	0	1	Galyon, Scott, Mia.	0	0	1	0	1
Brunell, Mark, Jax.	8	2	0	-8	2	Gannon, Rich, Oak.	13	3	0	-8	3
Bruschi, Tedy, NE	1	0	1	0	1	Garner, Charlie, Oak.	2	0	0	0	0
Bulluck, Keith, Tenn.	0	0	2	0	2	Gay, Benjamin, Cle.	4	1	0	0	1
Burnett, Rob, Balt.	0	0	1	0	1	George, Eddie, Tenn.	8	3	0	0	3
Burns, Keith, Den.	0	0	2	0	2	Germany, Reggie, Buff.	0	1	0	0	1
Burress, Plaxico, Pitt.	1	0	0	0	0	Gibson, Damon, Jax.	3	1	0	0	1
Bush, Devin, Cle.	0	0	1	0	1	Gibson, Oliver, Cin.	0	0	1	0	1
Cadrez, Glenn, KC	0	0	1	20	1	Gildon, Jason, Pitt.	0	0	2	27	2
Carson, Leonardo, SD	0	0	2	0	2	Glenn, Aaron, NYJ	1	1	1	2	2
Carswell, Dwayne, Den.	0	1	0	0	1	Gold, Ian, Den.	0	0	2	0	2
Carswell, Robert, SD	0	1	0	0	1	Graham, DeMingo, SD	0	1	0	0	1
Carter, Tony, Den.	1	1	0	0	1	Graham, Jeff, SD	1	0	0	0	0
Carter, Chris, Cin.	0	0	2	12	2	Gray, Chris, Sea.	0	2	0	0	2
Centers, Larry, Buff.	2	0	0	0	0	Grbac, Elvis, Balt.	9	2	0	-2	2
Chambers, Chris, Mia.	2	0	0	0	0	Green, Mike, Tenn.	1	1	0	0	1
Clark, Desmond, Den.	3	0	0	0	0	Green, Trent, KC	11	5	0	-5	5
Clements, Nate, Buff.	1	0	0	0	0	Green, Victor, NYJ	0	0	1	0	1
Clemons, Duane, KC	0	0	1	0	1	Griese, Brian, Den.	7	2	0	-1	2
Cochran, Antonio, Sea.	0	0	1	0	1	Hall, Cory, Cin.	0	0	1	73	1
Cole, Chris, Den.	2	0	0	0	0	Hall, Dante, KC	2	1	0	0	1
Coleman, Fred, NE	0	0	1	0	1	Hamilton, Bobby, NE	0	0	1	0	1
Coleman, Marcus, NYJ	0	0	1	0	1	Hampton, Casey, Pitt.	0	0	1	0	1
Coleman, Roderick, Oak.	0	0	1	0	1	Hanson, Chris, Jax.	1	1	0	-25	1
Coles, Laveranues, NYJ	1	1	0	0	1	Hardy, Kevin, Jax.	0	0	1	0	1
Compton, Mike, NE	1	0	0	-15	0	Harper, Nicholas, Ind.	1	0	1	0	1
Conaty, Bill, Buff.	0	1	0	0	1	Harris, Corey, KC	0	0	1	-4	1
Conway, Curtis, SD	1	0	0	0	0	Harris, Corey, Balt.	0	0	4	8	4
Cota, Chad, Ind.	0	0	1	9	1	Harris, Derrick, SD	0	0	1	6	1
Couch, Tim, Cle.	9	6	0	-10	6	Harrison, Rodney, SD	0	0	1	0	1
Cousin, Terry, Mia.	0	0	1	0	1	Hartwell, Edgerton, Balt.	0	1	0	0	1
Cox, Bryan, NE	0	0	1	9	1	Hasselbeck, Matt, Sea.	6	0	0	-16	0
Crockett, Zack, Oak.	1	0	0	0	0	Hawkins, Artrell, Cin.	0	0	1	0	1
Crosby, Clifton, Ind.	0	0	1	0	1	Heap, Todd, Balt.	1	0	0	0	0
Crosby, Phillip, Buff.	0	1	0	0	1	Heath, Rodney, Cin.	0	0	1	0	1
Cunningham, Randall, Balt.	4	3	0	-9	3	Hellestrae, Dale, Balt.	1	0	0	-11	0
Curtis, Canute, Cin.	0	0	1	3	1	Henry, Travis, Buff.	5	2	0	0	2
Davis, Eric, Den.	0	0	1	0	1	Hicks, Eric, KC	0	0	1	0	1
Davis, Terrell, Den.	2	1	0	0	1	Hill, Raion, Buff.	0	0	1	0	1
Dawkins, Sean, Jax.	1	0	0	0	0	Holmes, Earl, Pitt.	0	0	1	0	1
Dilfer, Trent, Sea.	3	0	0	-3	0	Holmes, Priest, KC	4	0	0	0	0
Dilger, Ken, Ind.	2	0	0	0	0	Houshmandzadeh, T.J., Cin.	3	0	0	0	0
Dillon, Corey, Cin.	5	1	0	0	1	Hulsey, Corey, Buff.	0	1	0	0	1
Dorsett, Anthony, Oak.	0	1	0	0	1	Hutchinson, Steve, Sea.	0	1	0	0	1
Dugans, Ron, Cin.	0	1	0	0	1	Ismail, Qadry, Balt.	1	0	0	0	0
Dunn, David, Oak.	3	0	0	0	0	Izzo, Larry, NE	0	0	1	0	1
Dwight, Tim, SD	1	1	0	0	1	Jackson, Brad, Balt.	0	0	1	0	1
Dyer, Deon, Mia.	0	1	0	0	1	Jackson, Grady, Oak.	0	0	1	0	1
Eaton, Chad, Sea.	0	0	1	0	1	Jackson, James, Cle.	1	0	0	0	0
Edwards, Donnie, KC	0	0	3	0	3	Jackson, Jarious, Den.	2	2	0	-1	2
Edwards, Marc, NE	3	1	0	0	1	Jacox, Kendyl, SD	1	2	0	-18	2
Edwards, Troy, Pitt.	1	0	1	32	1	James, Edgerrin, Ind.	3	1	0	0	1
Fabini, Jason, NYJ	0	1	0	0	1	Jenkins, Ronney, SD	1	0	1	0	1
Farmer, Danny, Cin.	1	0	0	0	0	Johnson, Kevin, Cle.	2	2	0	0	2
Faulk, Kevin, NE	2	1	0	0	1	Johnson, Lee, NE	1	0	0	0	0
Fauria, Christian, Sea.	2	0	0	0	0	Johnson, Patrick, Balt.	1	0	0	0	0
Feagles, Jeff, Sea.	2	2	0	0	2	Johnson, Raylee, SD	0	0	2	46	2
Ferguson, Nick, NYJ	0	0	1	0	1	Johnson, Rob, Buff.	6	1	0	-4	1
Fiala, John, Pitt.	0	0	1	0	1	Johnson, Ted, NE	0	0	1	0	1
Fiedler, Jay, Mia.	6	0	0	0	0	Jones, Damon, Jax.	1	1	0	0	1

Player						Player					
Jones, Marvin, NYJ	1	0	1	0	1	Poteat, Hank, Pitt.	4	2	0	0	2
Jones, Reggie, SD	2	1	0	0	1	Price, Peerless, Buff.	2	1	0	0	1
Jones, Willie, KC	0	1	0	0	1	Quinn, Jonathan, Jax.	4	0	0	0	0
Joseph, Elvis, Jax.	2	1	0	0	1	Rainer, Wali, Cle.	0	0	1	0	1
Joseph, Kerry, Sea.	1	0	0	0	0	Randle, John, Sea.	0	0	1	0	1
Kennedy, Lincoln, Oak.	0	2	0	2	2	Ransom, Derrick, KC	0	0	1	0	1
Kennison, Eddie, Den.-KC	1	1	0	0	1	Reed, James, NYJ	0	0	1	0	1
King, Andre, Cle.	1	0	0	0	0	Rhodes, Dominic, Ind.	6	0	0	-3	0
King, Lamar, Sea.	0	0	1	0	1	Rice, Jerry, Oak.	1	1	0	0	1
Kirby, Terry, Oak.	1	0	0	0	0	Richardson, Tony, KC	0	0	1	0	1
Kitna, Jon, Cin.	13	7	0	-13	7	Richardson, Kyle, Balt.	1	2	0	0	2
Lake, Carnell, Balt.	1	0	1	0	1	Robinson, Damien, NYJ	1	0	1	4	1
Lechler, Shane, Oak.	1	1	0	0	1	Robinson, Eddie, Tenn.	0	0	2	-1	2
Lewis, Jermaine, Balt.	2	0	0	0	0	Robinson, Koren, Sea.	2	1	0	-3	1
Lewis, Mo, NYJ	0	0	2	15	2	Rogers, Charlie, Sea.	2	0	0	0	0
Lewis, Ray, Balt.	0	0	1	0	1	Rolle, Samari, Tenn.	0	0	2	34	2
Logan, Mike, Pitt.	0	1	1	14	2	Roman, Mark, Cin.	0	0	1	-1	1
Long, Kevin, Tenn.	0	1	0	0	1	Ross, Adrian, Cin.	0	1	0	0	1
Lucas, Ken, Sea.	0	0	1	0	1	Ross, Micah, Jax.	1	0	0	0	0
Lyle, Rick, NYJ	0	0	1	0	1	Ross, Oliver, Pitt.	0	2	0	0	2
Mack, Stacey, Jax.	3	2	0	0	2	Roundtree, Raleigh, SD	0	1	0	2	1
Maddox, Tommy, Pitt.	1	0	0	0	0	Ruff, Orlando, SD	0	0	1	0	1
Manning, Peyton, Ind.	7	2	1	-2	3	Scott, Darnay, Cin.	0	1	0	0	1
Marion, Brock, Mia.	1	0	1	1	1	Seymour, Richard, NE	0	0	1	0	1
Martin, Curtis, NYJ	2	3	0	0	3	Sharpe, Shannon, Balt.	1	0	0	0	0
Martin, Steve, NYJ	0	0	2	0	2	Sharper, Jamie, Balt.	0	0	1	8	1
Mason, Derrick, Tenn.	2	1	0	0	1	Shaw, Bobby, Pitt.	1	0	0	0	0
Mawae, Kevin, NYJ	1	0	0	-5	0	Shea, Aaron, Cle.	0	1	0	0	1
McCardell, Keenan, Jax.	1	0	0	0	0	Simmons, Brian, Cin.	0	0	0	56	0
McCree, Marlon, Jax.	0	1	1	2	2	Sims, Barry, Oak.	0	1	0	0	1
McGarrahan, Scott, Mia.	0	1	0	0	1	Sinclair, Michael, Sea.	0	0	1	12	1
McKnight, James, Mia.	3	0	0	0	0	Smith, Antowain, NE	4	1	0	0	1
McNair, Steve, Tenn.	5	1	0	-15	1	Smith, Detron, Den.	0	0	1	0	1
Meester, Brad, Jax.	0	1	0	21	1	Smith, Jimmy, Jax.	1	1	0	0	1
Mickens, Ray, NYJ	0	0	1	0	1	Smith, Akili, Cin.	0	1	0	0	1
Middleton, Frank, Oak.	0	1	0	0	1	Smith, Lamar, Mia.	6	0	0	0	0
Milburn, Glyn, Chi.-S.D.	2	1	0	0	1	Smith, Larry, Jax.	0	0	1	0	1
Miller, Josh, Pitt.	1	0	0	-9	0	Smith, Mark, Cle.	0	0	1	0	1
Milloy, Lawyer, NE	0	0	1	0	1	Smith, Otis, NE	0	1	1	0	2
Minor, Travis, Mia.	0	1	0	0	1	Smith, Rod, Den.	1	0	0	0	0
Miranda, Paul, Sea.	0	0	1	0	1	Smith, Travian, Oak.	1	0	1	0	1
Mobley, John, Den.	0	0	3	8	3	Spears, Marcus, KC	0	2	0	1	2
Moore, Larry, Ind.	0	2	0	0	2	Spencer, Jimmy, Den.	0	0	1	0	1
Moreau, Frank, Jax.	1	0	0	0	0	Spicer, Paul, Jax.	0	0	1	3	1
Morgan, Quincy, Cle.	3	0	0	0	0	Spires, Greg, Cle.	0	0	1	0	1
Morris, Sammy, Buff.	1	1	0	0	1	Springs, Shawn, Sea.	0	0	1	0	1
Moulds, Eric, Buff.	1	1	0	0	1	Steele, Glen, Cin.	0	0	1	0	1
Myers, Bobby, Tenn.	0	0	1	14	1	Stevens, Matt, NE	0	1	0	0	1
Neil, Dan, Den.	0	1	0	0	1	Stewart, Kordell, Pitt.	11	5	0	-11	5
Nickerson, Hardy, Jax.	0	0	1	0	1	Stills, Gary, KC	0	0	1	0	1
Northcutt, Dennis, Cle.	3	1	0	0	1	Stokley, Brandon, Balt.	1	1	0	0	1
Nwokorie, Chukie, Ind.	0	0	3	95	3	Surtain, Patrick, Mia.	1	0	2	0	2
O'Donnell, Neil, Tenn.	1	0	0	0	0	Taylor, Fred, Jax.	1	0	0	0	0
O'Dwyer, Matt, Cin.	0	1	0	0	1	Taylor, Jason, Mia.	0	0	4	7	4
Ogbogu, Eric, NYJ	0	0	1	0	1	Taylor, Shannon, Balt.	0	0	1	0	1
Ogden, Jeff, Mia.	3	0	0	0	0	Teague, Trey, Den.	0	1	0	0	1
O'Neal, Deltha, Den.	2	0	0	0	0	Testaverde, Vinny, NYJ	12	5	0	-28	5
Ostroski, Jerry, Buff.	0	1	0	0	1	Thomas, Kiwaukee, Jax.	0	0	1	0	1
Parker, Riddick, NE	0	0	1	0	1	Thomas, Randy, NYJ	0	1	0	0	1
Parrella, John, SD	0	0	1	0	1	Thomas, William, Oak.	0	0	2	11	2
Pass, Patrick, NE	0	0	1	0	1	Tillman, Travares, Buff.	0	0	1	17	1
Patten, David, NE	1	0	0	0	0	Tomlinson, LaDainian, SD	8	0	0	0	0
Perry, Ed, Mia.	1	0	0	0	0	Tongue, Reggie, Sea.	0	0	2	23	2
Perry, Jason, SD	0	0	1	7	1	Unutoa, Morris, Buff.	1	0	0	-13	0
Peterson, Mike, Ind.	0	0	1	0	1	Van Pelt, Alex, Buff.	5	1	0	0	1
Phifer, Roman, NE	0	0	2	0	2	von Oelhoffen, Kimo, Pitt.	0	0	2	0	2
Pittman, Kavika, Den.	0	0	1	9	1	Walker, Bracy, KC	0	0	1	0	1
Pleasant, Anthony, NE	1	0	0	0	0	Walker, Denard, Den.	1	1	0	0	1
Porter, Daryl, Tenn.	0	0	2	0	2	Walker, Gary, Jax.	0	0	1	3	1
Porter, Joey, Pitt.	0	0	1	0	1	Walker, Joe, Tenn.	1	0	1	0	1

Player	Fum	Own Rec	Opp Rec	Yards	Tot Rec
Ward, Dedric, Mia.	1	0	0	0	0
Ward, Hines, Pitt.	1	0	0	0	0
Warfield, Eric, KC	1	0	0	0	0
Warrick, Peter, Cin.	3	1	0	0	1
Washington, Dewayne, Pitt.	0	0	1	63	1
Washington, Keith, Den.	0	0	1	0	1
Watson, Chris, Buff.	1	0	1	0	1
Watters, Ricky, Sea.	1	1	0	0	1
Weaver, Jed, Mia.	1	0	0	0	0
Webb, Richmond, Cin.	0	1	0	0	1
Weiner, Todd, Sea.	0	1	0	-3	1
Wesley, Greg, KC	0	0	2	0	2
Westmoreland, Eric, Jax.	0	0	1	0	1
Wheatley, Tyrone, Oak.	3	0	0	0	0
White, Jamel, Cle.	1	0	0	0	0
Wiggins, Jermaine, NE	0	1	0	0	1
Wilkins, Terrence, Ind.	1	0	0	0	0
Williams, Darryl, Cin.	0	0	1	0	1
Williams, Jamal, SD	0	0	1	0	1
Williams, James, Sea.	1	1	0	7	1
Williams, Josh, Ind.	0	0	1	0	1
Williams, Moe, Balt.	1	0	0	0	0
Williams, Maurice, Jax.	0	3	0	0	3
Williams, Tony, Cin.	0	0	2	0	2
Williams, Willie, Sea.	0	0	1	0	1
Wilson, Reinard, Cin.	0	0	2	0	2
Winfield, Antoine, Buff.	0	0	1	5	1
Woodbury, Tory, NYJ	0	0	1	0	1
Woodson, Rod, Balt.	0	0	1	0	1
Woody, Damien, NE	0	1	0	0	1
Wright, Kenyatta, Buff.	0	0	1	0	1
Yeast, Craig, NYJ	2	1	0	0	1
Young, Ryan, NYJ	0	1	0	0	1
Zelenka, Joe, Jax.	1	0	0	-26	0
Zereoue, Amos, Pitt.	3	1	0	0	1

Yards includes aborted plays, own recoveries, and opponents' recoveries.

NFC FUMBLES—INDIVIDUAL

Player	Fum	Own Rec	Opp Rec	Yards	Tot Rec
Abdullah, Rabih, TB	0	0	1	0	1
Abraham, Donnie, TB	0	0	1	0	1
Ackerman, Tom, NO	1	0	0	0	0
Adams, Flozell, Dall.	0	1	0	0	1
Ahanotu, Chidi, StL	0	0	1	0	1
Akins, Chris, GB	1	0	0	0	0
Allen, James, Chi.	1	0	0	0	0
Allen, Will, NYG	0	0	1	0	1
Alstott, Mike, TB	2	0	0	0	0
Ambrose, Ashley, Atl.	0	1	1	0	2
Anderson, Jamal, StL	1	0	0	0	0
Anderson, Rashard, Car.	0	1	2	97	3
Anthony, Reidel, TB	1	1	0	0	1
Archuleta, Adam, StL	2	0	1	24	1
Arrington, LaVar, Wash.	0	0	2	0	2
Azumah, Jerry, Chi.	0	0	1	0	1
Badger, Brad, Minn.	0	1	0	0	1
Bailey, Champ, Wash.	0	0	1	0	1
Baker, John, StL	1	0	0	-9	0
Banks, Tony, Wash.	10	1	0	-22	1
Banta, Brad, Det.	1	0	0	-6	0
Barber, Tiki, NYG	8	6	0	2	6
Barber, Ronde, TB	0	0	2	0	2
Barlow, Kevan, SF	1	0	0	0	0
Barrow, Micheal, NYG	0	0	2	13	2
Batch, Charlie, Det.	6	2	0	0	2
Bates, Michael, Wash.	4	2	0	0	2
Baxter, Fred, Chi.	0	1	0	0	1
Beasley, Fred, SF	1	0	0	0	0
Bennett, Donnell, Wash.	1	1	0	0	1
Bennett, Michael, Minn.	0	1	0	0	1
Beverly, Eric, Det.	2	0	0	-21	0
Biakabutuka, Tim, Car.	3	1	0	2	1
Bly, Dre', StL	1	0	1	15	1
Booker, Marty, Chi.	2	0	0	0	0
Boone, Alfonso, Chi.	0	0	1	6	1
Boston, David, Ariz	1	0	0	0	0
Bouman, Todd, Minn.	1	0	0	0	0
Bradford, Corey, GB	1	0	0	0	0
Brockermeyer, Blake, Chi.	0	2	0	0	2
Bronson, Zack, SF	1	0	1	0	1
Brooking, Keith, Atl.	0	0	2	-6	2
Brooks, Aaron, NO	13	6	0	-50	6
Brown, Mike, Chi.	0	0	1	5	1
Bruce, Isaac, StL	4	0	0	0	0
Buchanan, Ray, Atl.	0	0	1	0	1
Buckhalter, Correll, Phil.	2	1	1	0	2
Buckner, Brentson, Car.	1	1	0	0	1
Burgess, Derrick, Phil.	0	0	1	0	1
Burke, Tom, Ariz	0	0	1	0	1
Campbell, Lamar, Det.	0	0	1	0	1
Canidate, Trung, StL	3	2	0	0	2
Carter, Andre, SF	0	0	1	1	1
Carter, Cris, Minn.	2	0	0	0	0
Carter, Ki-Jana, Wash.	1	2	0	0	2
Carter, Quincy, Dall.	5	2	0	-4	2
Carter, Tyrone, Minn.	0	0	1	46	1
Cason, Aveion, StL-Det.	2	0	0	0	0
Chamberlain, Byron, Minn.	1	1	0	0	1
Chandler, Chris, Atl.	8	4	0	-8	4
Chapman, Doug, Minn.	1	2	0	0	2
Chester, Larry, Car.	0	0	1	0	1
Chevrier, Randy, Dall.	1	0	0	-26	0
Claiborne, Chris, Det.	0	0	1	0	1
Cleeland, Cameron, NO	1	0	0	0	0
Clemons, Charlie, NO	0	0	1	0	1
Coakley, Dexter, Dall.	0	0	1	0	1
Colinet, Stalin, Cle.-Minn.	0	0	1	0	1
Collins, Kerry, NYG	23	7	0	-48	7
Colvin, Rosevelt, Chi.	0	0	1	0	1
Comella, Greg, NYG	2	3	0	0	3
Connell, Albert, NO	0	1	0	0	1
Conwell, Ernie, StL	2	1	0	0	1
Cook, Rashard, Phil.	0	0	1	0	1
Craig, Dameyune, Car.	1	1	0	-15	1
Crawford, Casey, Car.	0	1	0	0	1
Crowell, Germane, Det.	1	1	0	0	1
Crumpler, Alge, Atl.	1	2	0	0	2
Culpepper, Daunte, Minn.	16	7	0	-17	7
Daniels, Phillip, Chi.	0	0	2	0	2
Darby, Chartric, TB	0	0	1	0	1
Davis, Don, StL	0	1	0	0	1
Davis, Stephen, Wash.	6	7	0	0	7
Dawkins, Brian, Phil.	0	0	2	49	2
Dayne, Ron, NYG	2	2	0	-17	2
Deese, Derrick, SF	0	1	0	0	1
Denson, Autry, Chi.	1	0	0	0	0
Detmer, Ty, Det.	3	1	0	0	1
Dixon, David, Minn.	0	1	0	0	1
Dixon, Ron, NYG	2	0	0	0	0
Dronett, Shane, Atl.	1	0	1	0	1
Dunn, Warrick, TB	2	0	0	0	0
Edwards, Antuan, GB	0	0	1	-2	1
Edwards, Mario, Dall.	0	0	1	2	1
Ellis, Greg, Dall.	0	0	2	0	2
Faulk, Marshall, StL	3	2	0	0	2
Favre, Brett, GB	16	6	0	-38	6
Flanagan, Mike, GB	2	0	0	-18	0

Player						Player					
Foster, Larry, Det.	1	1	0	0	1	Kyle, Jason, Car.	1	0	1	-26	1
Fraley, Hank, Phil.	1	0	0	-17	0	Lang, Kenard, Wash.	0	0	2	-3	2
Freeman, Antonio, GB	1	1	0	0	1	Leaf, Ryan, Dall.	4	0	0	-1	0
Frost, Scott, Cle.-GB	0	0	1	0	1	Legree, Lance, NYG	0	0	1	0	1
Galloway, Joey, Dall.	1	1	0	0	1	Lewis, Chad, Phil.	2	1	0	0	1
Garcia, Jeff, SF	9	5	0	-1	5	Lewis, Damione, StL	0	0	1	0	1
Gardner, Rod, Wash.	1	0	0	0	0	Lewis, Michael, NO	6	2	0	0	2
Garmon, Kelvin, Dall.	0	1	0	0	1	Little, Leonard, StL	0	0	1	0	1
Gbaja-Biamila, Kabeer, GB	0	0	1	0	1	Lockett, Kevin, Wash.	1	0	0	0	0
George, Jeff, Wash.	2	1	0	0	1	Lyght, Todd, Det.	0	0	1	0	1
Gleason, Steve, NO	0	0	1	0	1	Lynch, John, TB	0	0	1	0	1
Glover, La'Roi, NO	1	1	1	12	2	Makovicka, Joel, Ariz	1	1	0	0	1
Goings, Nick, Car.	1	0	0	0	0	Marshall, Torrance, GB	0	0	1	0	1
Gordon, Darrien, Atl.	4	3	0	0	3	Matthews, Shane, Chi.	4	2	0	-6	2
Gragg, Scott, SF	0	1	0	0	1	McAfee, Fred, NO	0	1	2	0	3
Graham, Kent, Wash.	2	1	0	-3	1	McAllister, Deuce, NO	1	1	0	0	1
Grant, Orantes, Dall.	0	0	1	0	1	McBurrows, Gerald, Atl.	0	0	1	15	1
Green, Ahman, GB	5	2	0	0	2	McClellion, Central, Wash.	1	0	0	0	0
Green, Michael, Chi.	0	0	1	0	1	McCleon, Dexter, StL	0	0	1	29	1
Griffin, Cornelius, NYG	0	0	1	0	1	McClure, Todd, Atl.	0	1	0	0	1
Gruttadauria, Mike, Ariz	1	1	0	0	1	McDaniel, Emmanuel, NYG	0	0	1	0	1
Hakim, Az-Zahir, StL	8	1	0	-12	1	McGarity, Wane, Dall.-NO	2	0	0	0	0
Hall, James, Det.	0	0	2	8	2	McKinnon, Ronald, Ariz	0	0	2	25	2
Hall, Lamont, NO	1	0	0	0	0	McMahon, Mike, Det.	5	0	0	0	0
Hall, Lemanski, Minn.	0	0	2	0	2	McNabb, Donovan, Phil.	8	3	0	-7	3
Hall, Travis, Atl.	0	0	1	0	1	McQuarters, R.W., Chi.	0	0	1	69	1
Hambrick, Darren, Car.	0	0	1	0	1	Mealey, Rondell, GB	0	0	1	27	1
Hambrick, Troy, Dall.	1	1	1	0	2	Metcalf, Eric, Wash.	4	1	0	0	1
Hampton, William, Phil.	0	0	1	0	1	Miller, Jim, Chi.	7	3	0	-17	3
Hardy, Terry, Ariz	1	0	0	0	0	Minter, Mike, Car.	0	0	2	0	2
Harris, Bernardo, GB	0	0	3	0	3	Mitchell, Brian, Phil.	3	1	0	0	1
Harris, Walt, Chi.	0	0	2	0	2	Mitchell, Jeff, Car.	0	2	0	0	2
Hauck, Tim, Phil.	0	0	1	0	1	Moore, Damon, Phil.	0	0	2	10	2
Hawkes, Michael, Car.	0	0	1	0	1	Morgan, Dan, Car.	0	0	1	0	1
Hayes, Donald, Car.	1	1	0	0	1	Morgan, Don, Minn.	1	0	0	0	0
Hearst, Garrison, SF	1	1	0	0	1	Morrow, Harold, Minn.	1	2	1	0	3
Henderson, William, GB	0	2	0	0	2	Morton, Johnnie, Det.	1	0	0	0	0
Holcombe, Robert, StL	1	0	0	0	0	Muhammad, Muhsin, Car.	2	2	0	0	2
Holliday, Vonnie, GB	0	0	3	11	3	Murphy, Frank, TB	2	0	0	0	0
Holmes, Kenny, NYG	0	0	4	12	4	Myers, Michael, Dall.	0	0	1	0	1
Holt, Torry, StL	2	1	0	2	1	Naeole, Chris, NO	0	1	0	0	1
Hoover, Brad, Car.	1	0	0	0	0	Nelson, Jim, Minn.	0	1	0	-1	1
Horn, Joe, NO	1	0	0	0	0	Nesbit, Jamar, Car.	0	1	0	0	1
Hovan, Chris, Minn.	0	0	1	0	1	Newsome, Richard, NO	0	0	1	0	1
Howard, Bobbie, Chi.	0	0	1	0	1	Noble, Brandon, Dall.	0	0	2	6	2
Howard, Desmond, Det.	1	0	0	0	0	Ohalete, Ifeanyi, Wash.	0	1	0	0	1
Howell, John, TB	0	1	0	0	1	Oldham, Chris, NO	0	0	2	81	2
Hunt, Cletidus, GB	0	0	1	0	1	Olivo, Brock, Det.	0	0	1	0	1
Huntley, Richard, Car.	3	1	0	0	1	O'Neal, Andre, GB	0	0	1	0	1
Jackson, Terry, SF	1	0	0	0	0	Pace, Orlando, StL	0	1	0	0	1
Jackson, Tyoka, StL	0	0	1	0	1	Parker, Glenn, NYG	0	1	0	0	1
Jacquet, Nate, Minn.	4	2	0	0	2	Parrish, Tony, Chi.	0	0	2	35	2
Jenkins, Kris, Car.	0	0	1	0	1	Peterson, Julian, SF	0	0	2	26	2
Jenkins, MarTay, Ariz	5	2	0	0	2	Petitgout, Luke, NYG	0	1	0	0	1
Jennings, Brian, SF	1	0	0	-18	0	Pierce, Antonio, Wash.	0	0	1	0	1
Johnson, Doug, Atl.	2	0	0	0	0	Pittman, Michael, Ariz	5	0	0	0	0
Johnson, Eric, SF	1	0	0	0	0	Plummer, Ahmed, SF	0	0	1	0	1
Johnson, Brad, TB	4	2	0	-1	2	Plummer, Jake, Ariz	8	5	0	-3	5
Johnson, Joe, NO	0	0	2	0	2	Prentice, Travis, Minn.	1	1	0	0	1
Johnson, Keyshawn, TB	2	0	0	0	0	Rattay, Tim, SF	1	1	0	0	1
Johnson, Leon, Chi.	2	2	0	0	2	Reader, Jamie, Phil.	0	0	1	0	1
Jones, Marcus, TB	0	0	1	0	1	Rivera, Marco, GB	0	1	0	0	1
Jones, Thomas, Ariz	2	2	0	0	2	Robinson, Bryan, Chi.	0	0	1	1	1
Joyce, Matt, Det.	0	2	0	0	2	Rucker, Mike, Car.	0	0	1	0	1
Junkin, Trey, Ariz	1	0	0	-19	0	Runyan, Jon, Phil.	0	1	0	0	1
Kerney, Patrick, Atl.	0	0	1	0	1	Samuels, Chris, Wash.	0	1	0	0	1
Kleinsasser, Jimmy, Minn.	2	0	0	0	0	Sanders, Frank, Ariz	1	0	0	0	0
Knight, Sammy, NO	0	0	5	0	5	Sanyika, Sekou, Ariz	0	1	0	0	1
Knorr, Micah, Dall.	0	0	1	0	1	Sapp, Warren, TB	0	0	2	0	2
Kreutz, Olin, Chi.	1	0	0	-9	0	Sawyer, Talance, Minn.	0	0	2	0	2

Player					
Schlesinger, Cory, Det.	1	1	0	0	1
Schroeder, Bill, GB	1	0	0	0	0
Schulters, Lance, SF	0	1	1	20	2
Scott, Lynn, Dall.	0	0	2	0	2
Seder, Tim, Dall.	0	1	0	-6	1
Sehorn, Jason, NYG	0	0	0	35	1
Shade, Sam, Wash.	0	0	1	0	1
Sharper, Darren, GB	1	0	1	17	1
Shelton, Daimon, Chi.	2	0	0	0	0
Short, Brandon, NYG	0	0	1	0	1
Simoneau, Mark, Atl.	0	0	1	0	1
Singleton, Alshermond, TB	0	1	0	0	1
Smith, Bruce, Wash.	0	0	1	0	1
Smith, Derek M., SF	0	0	2	3	2
Smith, Dwight, TB	2	0	2	0	2
Smith, Emmitt, Dall.	1	1	0	0	1
Smith, Maurice, Atl.	1	2	0	0	2
Smith, Paul, SF	1	0	1	0	1
Smith, Steve, Car.	8	4	0	2	4
Smith, Terrelle, NO	1	1	0	0	1
Smoot, Fred, Wash.	0	0	1	0	1
Staley, Duce, Phil.	3	1	0	-5	1
Stecker, Aaron, TB	0	1	0	0	1
Stepnoski, Mark, Dall.	1	0	0	0	0
Stewart, Matt, Atl.	0	0	1	0	1
Stoerner, Clint, Dall.	1	0	0	-1	0
Stone, Ron, NYG	0	1	0	1	1
Strahan, Michael, NYG	0	0	1	13	1
Sutherland, Vinny, SF	1	0	0	0	0
Swinton, Reggie, Dall.	4	1	0	0	1
Tauscher, Mark, GB	0	1	0	0	1
Taylor, Bobby, Phil.	0	0	3	0	3
Terrell, David, Wash.	0	0	1	0	1
Thierry, John, GB	0	0	2	0	2
Thomas, Anthony, Chi.	0	1	0	0	1
Thomas, Hollis, Phil.	0	0	1	0	1
Thomas, Robert, Dall.	0	0	1	0	1
Thomason, Jeff, Phil.	0	1	0	0	1
Thompson, Derrius, Wash.	0	0	1	0	1
Thrash, James, Phil.	1	1	0	0	1
Timmerman, Adam, StL	0	1	0	0	1
Toomer, Amani, NYG	2	1	0	0	1
Trotter, Jeremiah, Phil.	0	0	1	0	1
Tucker, Ryan, StL	0	1	0	0	1
Turley, Kyle, NO	0	2	0	0	2
Urlacher, Brian, Chi.	0	0	2	101	2
Vanden Bosch, Kyle, Ariz	0	0	1	9	1
Vaughn, Darrick, Atl.	3	1	1	0	2
Vick, Michael, Atl.	6	0	0	0	0
Vincent, Troy, Phil.	0	0	1	0	1
Walls, Wesley, Car.	0	1	0	0	1
Walsh, Chris, Minn.	0	0	1	0	1
Walters, Troy, Minn.	2	0	0	0	0
Walz, Zack, Ariz	0	0	1	0	1
Warner, Kurt, StL	10	2	0	-14	2
Warren, Lamont, Det.	1	0	0	0	1
Washington, Damon, NYG	2	1	0	0	1
Washington, Ted, Chi.	0	0	1	0	1
Washington, Todd, TB	1	0	0	-9	0
Wayne, Nate, GB	0	0	2	0	2
Weinke, Chris, Car.	11	1	0	-2	1
White, Steve, TB	1	0	0	0	0
Whitfield, Bob, Atl.	0	1	1	5	2
Whiting, Brandon, Phil.	0	0	3	0	3
Wiley, Michael, Dall.	1	0	1	0	1
Williams, Aeneas, StL	0	1	3	0	4
Williams, Brian, NO	0	1	0	0	1
Williams, Ricky, NO	8	2	0	4	2
Williams, Karl, TB	3	0	0	0	0
Williams, K.D., GB	0	0	1	0	1
Williams, Tyrone, GB	0	0	1	0	1
Winborn, Jamie, SF	0	0	1	17	1
Wistrom, Grant, StL	0	0	1	17	1
Woods, LeVar, Ariz	0	0	1	0	1
Woodson, Darren, Dall.	0	0	1	0	1
Wright, Anthony, Dall.	4	0	0	0	0
Wynn, Spergon, Minn.	3	0	0	-2	0
Zeigler, Dusty, NYG	0	1	0	0	1
Zellner, Peppi, Dall.	0	0	1	0	1
Zgonina, Jeff, StL	0	0	2	0	2

Yards includes aborted plays, own recoveries, and opponents' recoveries.

SACKS

MOST SACKS
NFC:	22.5	Michael Strahan, N.Y. Giants
AFC:	15.0	Peter Boulware, Balt.imore

MOST SACKS, GAME
AFC:	4.0	Joey Porter, Pittsburgh at Tampa Bay, October 21
	4.0	John Abraham, N.Y. Jets at New Orleans, November 4
	4.0	Peter Boulware, Balt.imore vs. Minnesota, January 7
NFC:	4.0	Michael Strahan, N.Y. Giants at St. Louis, October 14

TEAM LEADERS, SACKS
AFC: BALTIMORE, 15.0, Peter Boulware; BUFFALO, 6.5, Aaron Schobel; CINCINNATI, 9.0, Reinard Wilson; CLEVELAND, 13.0, Jamir Miller; DENVER, 7.0, Trevor Pryce, Bill Romanowski; INDIANAPOLIS, 8.5, Chad Bratzke; JACKSONVILLE, 11.0, Tony Brackens; KANSAS CITY, 7.0, Duane Clemons; MIAMI, 8.5, Jason Taylor; NEW ENGLAND, 7.0, Bobby Hamilton; N.Y. JETS, 13.0, John Abraham; OAKLAND, 7.0, Regan Upshaw; PITTSBURGH, 12.0, Jason Gildon; SAN DIEGO, 13.0, Marcellus Wiley; SEATTLE, 11.0, John Randle; TENNESSEE, 10.0, Jevon Kearse

NFC: ARIZONA, 4.0, Rob Fredrickson; ATLANTA, 12.0, Patrick Kerney; CAROLINA, 9.0, Mike Rucker; CHICAGO, 10.5, Rosevelt Colvin; DALLAS, 6.0, Greg Ellis; DETROIT, 11.0, Robert Porcher; GREEN BAY, 13.5, Kabeer Gbaja-Biamila; MINNESOTA, 6.0, Chris Hovan; NEW ORLEANS, 13.5, Charlie Clemons; N.Y. GIANTS, 22.5, Michael Strahan; PHILADELPHIA, 9.5, Hugh Douglas; ST. LOUIS, 14.5, Leonard Little; SAN FRANCISCO, 6.5, Andre Carter; TAMPA BAY, 11.0, Simeon Rice; WASHINGTON, 5.0, Bruce Smith

TEAM CHAMPION
AFC:	55	Pittsburgh
NFC:	53	New Orleans

NFL TOP TEN LEADERS—SACKS

Strahan, Michael, NYG	22.5
Boulware, Peter, Balt.	15.0
Little, Leonard, StL	14.5
Clemons, Charlie, NO	13.5
Gbaja-Biamila, Kabeer, GB	13.5
Abraham, John, NYJ	13.0
Miller, Jamir, Cle.	13.0
Wiley, Marcellus, SD	13.0
Gildon, Jason, Pitt.	12.0
Kerney, Patrick, Atl.	12.0

AMERICAN FOOTBALL CONFERENCE—SACKS

	Sacks	Yards
Pittsburgh	55	367
Cincinnati	48	320
Baltimore	45	290
Cleveland	43	288
Jacksonville	43	298
New England	41	234
Oakland	41	204
San Diego	41	218
Indianapolis	40	257
Denver	39	279
Seattle	38	248
Miami	37	230
Buffalo	34	219
N.Y. Jets	33	171
Tennessee	32	175
Kansas City	31	239
AFC Total	641	4037
AFC Average	40.1	252.3

NATIONAL FOOTBALL CONFERENCE—SACKS

	Sacks	Yards
New Orleans	53	323
Green Bay	52	337
Chicago	48	294
N.Y. Giants	46	320
Philadelphia	45	283
St. Louis	45	251
Tampa Bay	42	272
Atlanta	37	230
San Francisco	32	220
Detroit	31	224
Minnesota	30	204
Carolina	26	167
Washington	25	139
Dallas	24	130
Arizona	19	128
NFC Total	555	3522
NFC Average	37.0	234.8
League Total	1196	7559
League Average	38.6	243.8

AFC—INDIVIDUAL SACKS

Boulware, Peter, Balt.	15.0
Abraham, John, NYJ	13.0
Miller, Jamir, Cle.	13.0
Wiley, Marcellus, SD	13.0
Gildon, Jason, Pitt.	12.0
Brackens, Tony, Jax.	11.0
Randle, John, Sea.	11.0
Kearse, Jevon, Tenn.	10.0
Johnson, Raylee, SD	9.5
Bell, Kendrell, Pitt.	9.0
Porter, Joey, Pitt.	9.0
Wilson, Reinard, Cin.	9.0
Bratzke, Chad, Ind.	8.5
Brown, Chad, Sea.	8.5
Smith, Justin, Cin.	8.5
Taylor, Jason, Mia.	8.5
Smith, Aaron, Pitt.	8.0
Washington, Marcus, Ind.	8.0
McCrary, Michael, Balt.	7.5
Walker, Gary, Jax.	7.5
Clemons, Duane, KC	7.0
Hamilton, Bobby, NE	7.0
Pryce, Trevor, Den.	7.0
Romanowski, Bill, Den.	7.0
Upshaw, Regan, Oak.	7.0
Bromell, Lorenzo, Mia.	6.5
Schobel, Aaron, Buff.	6.5
Simmons, Brian, Cin.	6.5
Coleman, Roderick, Oak.	6.0
McGinest, Willie, NE	6.0
Pleasant, Anthony, NE	6.0
Rogers, Tyrone, Cle.	6.0
Sharper, Jamie, Balt.	6.0
Spikes, Takeo, Cin.	6.0
Evans, Josh, Tenn.	5.5
Hardy, Kevin, Jax.	5.5
Bryant, Tony, Oak.	5.0
Ellis, Shaun, NYJ	5.0
Nwokorie, Chukie, Ind.	5.0
Payne, Seth, Jax.	5.0
Warren, Gerard, Cle.	5.0
Williams, Tony, Cin.	5.0
Wynn, Renaldo, Jax.	5.0
Brown, Courtney, Cle.	4.5
Cochran, Antonio, Sea.	4.5
Gardener, Daryl, Mia.	4.0
Jackson, Grady, Oak.	4.0
Scioli, Brad, Ind.	4.0
Spires, Greg, Cle.	4.0
von Oelhoffen, Kimo, Pitt.	4.0
Washington, Keith, Den.	4.0
Harrison, Rodney, SD	3.5
Hicks, Eric, KC	3.5
Johnson, Ellis, Ind.	3.5
Lewis, Ray, Balt.	3.5
Lyle, Rick, NYJ	3.5
Newman, Keith, Buff.	3.5
Sinclair, Michael, Sea.	3.5
Thomas, Adalius, Balt.	3.5
Williams, Darryl, Cin.	3.5
Biekert, Greg, Oak.	3.0
Bowens, Tim, Mia.	3.0
Brown, Eric, Den.	3.0
Carson, Leonardo, SD	3.0
Fisher, Bryce, Buff.	3.0
Gibson, Oliver, Cin.	3.0
Gold, Ian, Den.	3.0
Hansen, Phil, Buff.	3.0
Hayward, Reggie, Den.	3.0

Lewis, Mo, NYJ	3.0
McKenzie, Keith, Cle.	3.0
Milloy, Lawyer, NE	3.0
Office, Kendrick, Buff.	3.0
Owens, Rich, KC	3.0
Patton, Marvcus, KC	3.0
Ransom, Derrick, KC	3.0
Seymour, Richard, NE	3.0
Thomas, Kiwaukee, Jax.	3.0
Thomas, William, Oak.	3.0
Thomas, Zach, Mia.	3.0
Vrabel, Mike, NE	3.0
Williams, Josh, Ind.	3.0
Wilson, Al, Den.	3.0
Fisk, Jason, Tenn.	2.5
Foreman, Jay, Buff.	2.5
Martin, Steve, NYJ	2.5
Russell, Darrell, Oak.	2.5
Smith, Travian, Oak.	2.5
Terry, Tim, Sea.	2.5
Adams, Sam, Balt.	2.0
Alexander, Brent, Pitt.	2.0
Bailey, Rodney, Pitt.	2.0
Berry, Bert, Den.	2.0
Bruschi, Tedy, NE	2.0
Burton, Shane, NYJ	2.0
Carter, Kevin, Tenn.	2.0
Cooper, Chris, Oak.	2.0
Cousin, Terry, Mia.	2.0
Dixon, Gerald, SD	2.0
Edwards, Donnie, KC	2.0
Flowers, Erik, Buff.	2.0
Holmes, Earl, Pitt.	2.0
Kennedy, Kenoy, Den.	2.0
Logan, Mike, Pitt.	2.0
McCutcheon, Daylon, Cle.	2.0
Mixon, Kenny, Mia.	2.0
Parrella, John, SD	2.0
Phifer, Roman, NE	2.0
Price, Shawn, Buff.	2.0
Robertson, Tyrone, Buff.	2.0
Rolle, Samari, Tenn.	2.0
Roman, Mark, Cin.	2.0
Simmons, Anthony, Sea.	2.0
Siragusa, Tony, Balt.	2.0
Smith, Mark, Cle.	2.0
Smith, Otis, NE	2.0
Smith, Robaire, Tenn.	2.0
Spicer, Paul, Jax.	2.0
Townsend, Deshea, Pitt.	2.0
Wesley, Greg, KC	2.0
Woodson, Charles, Oak.	2.0
Booker, Vaughn, Cin.	1.5
Browning, John, KC	1.5
Cadrez, Glenn, KC	1.5
Downing, Eric, KC	1.5
Favors, Greg, Tenn.	1.5
Greenwood, Morlon, Mia.	1.5
Morris, Aric, Tenn.	1.5
Peterson, Mike, Ind.	1.5
Thomas, Mark, Ind.	1.5
Williams, Pat, Buff.	1.5
Wright, Kenyatta, Buff.	1.5
Alexander, Elijah, Oak.	1.0
Bartee, William, KC	1.0
Battles, Ainsley, Jax.	1.0
Bell, Marcus, Sea.	1.0
Bowens, David, Mia.	1.0
Buckley, Terrell, NE	1.0
Bulluck, Keith, Tenn.	1.0

		NFC—INDIVIDUAL SACKS	
Chamberlin, Frank, Tenn.	1.0		
Charlton, Ike, Sea.	1.0	Strahan, Michael, NYG	22.5
Clements, Nate, Buff.	1.0	Little, Leonard, StL	14.5
Dingle, Adrian, SD	1.0	Clemons, Charlie, NO	13.5
Dorsett, Anthony, Oak.	1.0	Gbaja-Biamila, Kabeer, GB	13.5
Douglas, Marques, Balt.	1.0	Kerney, Patrick, Atl.	12.0
Eaton, Chad, Sea.	1.0	Porcher, Robert, Det.	11.0
Ellsworth, Percy, Cle.	1.0	Rice, Simeon, TB	11.0
Farrior, James, NYJ	1.0	Colvin, Rosevelt, Chi.	10.5
Flowers, Lethon, Pitt.	1.0	Douglas, Hugh, Phil.	9.5
Fontenot, Albert, SD	1.0	Daniels, Phillip, Chi.	9.0
Ford, Henry, Tenn.	1.0	Johnson, Joe, NO	9.0
Freeman, Arturo, Mia.	1.0	Rucker, Mike, Car.	9.0
Galyon, Scott, Mia.	1.0	Wistrom, Grant, StL	9.0
Godfrey, Randall, Tenn.	1.0	Glover, La'Roi, NO	8.0
Gregg, Kelly, Balt.	1.0	Smith, Brady, Atl.	8.0
Hampton, Casey, Pitt.	1.0	Simon, Corey, Phil.	7.5
Harrison, Lloyd, SD	1.0	Holliday, Vonnie, GB	7.0
Jones, Marvin, NYJ	1.0	Carter, Andre, SF	6.5
Jones, Tebucky, NE	1.0	Young, Brian, StL	6.5
Joseph, Kerry, Sea.	1.0	Barrow, Micheal, NYG	6.0
Kirkland, Levon, Sea.	1.0	Burgess, Derrick, Phil.	6.0
Larsen, Leif, Buff.	1.0	Ellis, Greg, Dall.	6.0
Law, Ty, NE	1.0	Hamilton, Keith, NYG	6.0
Little, Earl, Cle.	1.0	Hovan, Chris, Minn.	6.0
Maslowski, Mike, KC	1.0	Howard, Darren, NO	6.0
McCree, Marlon, Jax.	1.0	Sapp, Warren, TB	6.0
McGlockton, Chester, Den.	1.0	Urlacher, Brian, Chi.	6.0
Mickens, Ray, NYJ	1.0	Dronett, Shane, Atl.	5.5
Mitchell, Brandon, NE	1.0	Johnstone, Lance, Minn.	5.5
Mobley, John, Den.	1.0	Wayne, Nate, GB	5.5
Moreno, Zeke, SD	1.0	Sawyer, Talance, Minn.	5.0
Morris, Rob, Ind.	1.0	Smith, Bruce, Wash.	5.0
Parker, Riddick, NE	1.0	White, Steve, TB	5.0
Peter, Christian, Ind.	1.0	Buckner, Brentson, Car.	4.5
Phillips, Ryan, Ind.	1.0	Coleman, Marco, Wash.	4.5
Pittman, Kavika, Den.	1.0	Flanigan, Jim, GB	4.5
Prioleau, Pierson, Buff.	1.0	Fletcher, London, StL	4.5
Rainer, Wali, Cle.	1.0	Robinson, Bryan, Chi.	4.5
Reagor, Montae, Den.	1.0	Claiborne, Chris, Det.	4.0
Reed, James, NYJ	1.0	Engelberger, John, SF	4.0
Robinson, Eddie, Tenn.	1.0	Fredrickson, Rob, Ariz	4.0
Rodgers, Derrick, Mia.	1.0	Hall, James, Det.	4.0
Rogers, Sam, SD	1.0	Lang, Kenard, Wash.	4.0
Ross, Adrian, Cin.	1.0	Stubblefield, Dana, SF	4.0
Ruff, Orlando, SD	1.0	Wilkinson, Dan, Wash.	4.0
Seau, Junior, SD	1.0	Brooking, Keith, Atl.	3.5
Slaughter, T.J., Jax.	1.0	Dotson, Santana, GB	3.5
Steele, Glen, Cin.	1.0	Hand, Norman, NO	3.5
Surtain, Patrick, Mia.	1.0	Holmes, Kenny, NYG	3.5
Sword, Sam, Ind.	1.0	Jasper, Edward, Atl.	3.5
Tanuvasa, Maa, SD	1.0	McFarland, Anthony, TB	3.5
Taves, Josh, Oak.	1.0	Myers, Michael, Dall.	3.5
Taylor, Shannon, Balt.	1.0	Noble, Brandon, Dall.	3.5
Tongue, Reggie, Sea.	1.0	Thierry, John, GB	3.5
Trapp, James, Balt.	1.0	Trotter, Jeremiah, Phil.	3.5
Washington, Dewayne, Pitt.	1.0	Young, Bryant, SF	3.5
Westmoreland, Eric, Jax.	1.0	Brown, Mike, Chi.	3.0
Woodall, Lee, Den.	1.0	Caldwell, Mike, Phil.	3.0
Woods, Jerome, KC	1.0	Frisch, Byron, Dall.	3.0
Armstrong, Trace, Oak.	0.5	Green, Michael, Chi.	3.0
Bird, Cory, Ind.	0.5	Jackson, Tyoka, StL	3.0
Grant, Ernest, Mia.	0.5	Jones, Marcus, TB	3.0
Haley, Jermaine, Mia.	0.5	Kalu, N. D., Phil.	3.0
Harris, Johnnie, Oak.	0.5	Peterson, Julian, SF	3.0
Jones, Fred, Buff.	0.5	Reese, Izell, Dall.	3.0
Macklin, David, Ind.	0.5	Rogers, Shaun, Det.	3.0
Ogunleye, Adewale, Mia.	0.5	Smith, Derek M., SF	3.0
Rudd, Dwayne, Cle.	0.5	Wong, Kailee, Minn.	3.0
Webster, Larry, Balt.	0.5	Zellner, Peppi, Dall.	3.0

Chukwurah, Patrick, Minn.	2.5	Mason, Eddie, Wash.	1.0
Griffin, Cornelius, NYG	2.5	Mathis, Kevin, NO	1.0
Hall, Travis, Atl.	2.5	McDaniel, Ed, Minn.	1.0
Harris, Bernardo, GB	2.5	McGrew, Reggie, SF	1.0
Jackson, Dexter, TB	2.5	McQuarters, R.W., Chi.	1.0
Okeafor, Chike, SF	2.5	Moore, Damon, Phil.	1.0
Oldham, Chris, NO	2.5	Morgan, Dan, Car.	1.0
Slade, Chris, Car.	2.5	Newkirk, Robert, Chi.	1.0
Wakefield, Fred, Ariz	2.5	Parrish, Tony, Chi.	1.0
Whiting, Brandon, Phil.	2.5	Pierce, Antonio, Wash.	1.0
Ahanotu, Chidi, StL	2.0	Rice, Ron, Det.	1.0
Archuleta, Adam, StL	2.0	Sanyika, Sekou, Ariz	1.0
Azumah, Jerry, Chi.	2.0	Schulters, Lance, SF	1.0
Bellamy, Jay, NO	2.0	Sehorn, Jason, NYG	1.0
Boone, Alfonso, Chi.	2.0	Setzer, Bobby, SF	1.0
Burke, Tom, Ariz	2.0	Short, Brandon, NYG	1.0
Darby, Chartric, TB	2.0	Singleton, Alshermond, TB	1.0
Davis, Russell, Ariz	2.0	Spellman, Alonzo, Det.	1.0
Diggs, Na'il, GB	2.0	Taylor, Bobby, Phil.	1.0
Duncan, Jamie, TB	2.0	Terrell, David, Wash.	1.0
Garnett, Winfield, Minn.	2.0	Tosi, Mao, Ariz	1.0
Gilbert, Sean, Car.	2.0	Walker, Darwin, Phil.	1.0
Grasmanis, Paul, Phil.	2.0	Walz, Zack, Ariz	1.0
Jenkins, Kris, Car.	2.0	Wiley, Chuck, Atl.	1.0
Lyon, Billy, GB	2.0	Williams, Jay, Car.	1.0
McBride, Tod, GB	2.0	Williams, Shaun, NYG	1.0
McKinnon, Ronald, Ariz	2.0	Arrington, LaVar, Wash.	0.5
Mitchell, Keith, NO	2.0	Bell, Marcus, Ariz	0.5
Mitchell, Kevin, Wash.	2.0	Chester, Larry, Car.	0.5
Moran, Sean, StL	2.0	Gooch, Jeff, TB	0.5
Quarles, Shelton, TB	2.0	Hill, Renaldo, Ariz	0.5
Reynolds, Jamal, GB	2.0	Pickett, Ryan, StL	0.5
Robbins, Fred, Minn.	2.0	Thompson, Raynoch, Ariz	0.5
Scroggins, Tracy, Det.	2.0	Ulbrich, Jeff, SF	0.5
Sharper, Darren, GB	2.0	Vanden Bosch, Kyle, Ariz	0.5
Traylor, Keith, Chi.	2.0	Webster, Jason, SF	0.5
Whitehead, Willie, NO	2.0	Wilson, Adrian, Ariz	0.5
Armstead, Jessie, NYG	1.5	Wilson, Gillis, Car.	0.5
Dawkins, Brian, Phil.	1.5	Winborn, Jamie, SF	0.5
Holdman, Warrick, Chi.	1.5		
Kelly, Brian, TB	1.5		
Smith, Darrin, NO	1.5		
Vincent, Troy, Phil.	1.5		
Washington, Ted, Chi.	1.5		
Aldridge, Allen, Det.	1.0		
Barber, Ronde, TB	1.0		
Boyd, Stephen, Det.	1.0		
Bradford, Ronnie, Atl.	1.0		
Butler, LeRoy, GB	1.0		
Campbell, Lamar, Det.	1.0		
Carter, Tyrone, Minn.	1.0		
Chase, Martin, NO	1.0		
Coady, Rich, StL	1.0		
Colinet, Stalin, Minn.	1.0		
Cook, Rashard, Phil.	1.0		
DeLoach, Jerry, Wash.	1.0		
Dixon, Tony, Dall.	1.0		
Emmons, Carlos, Phil.	1.0		
Evans, Demetric, Dall.	1.0		
Ferrara, Frank, NYG	1.0		
Grant, Deon, Car.	1.0		
Green, Barrett, Det.	1.0		
Hall, Lemanski, Minn.	1.0		
Heard, Ronnie, SF	1.0		
Howard, Reggie, Car.	1.0		
Knight, Sammy, NO	1.0		
Lassiter, Kwamie, Ariz	1.0		
Lucas, Al, Car.	1.0		
Lyle, Keith, Wash.	1.0		
Lynch, John, TB	1.0		

2001 NFL PAID ATTENDANCE BREAKDOWN

	Games	Attendance	Average
NFL Preseason Total	63	3,656,928	58,046
NFL Regular-Season Total	248	16,166,258	65,187
NFL Postseason Total	12	766,905	63,909
NFL All Games	323	20,590,091	63,746

1.1-MILLION CLUB

During the 2001 season, five teams drew more than 1.1 million paid attendance home and away during the regular season. The Washington Redskins led the league for the third consecutive season by drawing 1,173,903 fans in 2001, and set an NFL home attendance record for the second year in a row with 661,970 fans.

Team	Total Paid Home Attendance	Total Paid Visiting Attendance	Total Paid Attendance
Washington	661,970	511,933	1,173,903
New York Giants	627,985	521,034	1,149,019
New York Jets	627,603	515,126	1,142,729
Kansas City	617,473	511,757	1,129,230
Miami	588,127	520,786	1,108,913

For complete year-by-year attendance records, see pages 581-582.

Inside the Numbers

GREATEST COMEBACKS IN NFL HISTORY
(Most Points Overcome To Win Game)

REGULAR SEASON GAMES

FROM 28 POINTS BEHIND TO WIN:
December 7, 1980, at San Francisco

New Orleans	14	21	0	0	0	— 35
San Francisco	0	7	14	14	3	— 38

- NO — Harris 33 pass from Manning (Ricardo kick)
- NO — Childs 21 pass from Manning (Ricardo kick)
- NO — Holmes 1 run (Ricardo kick)
- SF — Solomon 57 punt return (Wersching kick)
- NO — Holmes 1 run (Ricardo kick)
- NO — Harris 41 pass from Manning (Ricardo kick)
- SF — Montana 1 run (Wersching kick)
- SF — Clark 71 pass from Montana (Wersching kick)
- SF — Solomon 14 pass from Montana (Wersching kick)
- SF — Elliott 7 run (Wersching kick)
- SF — FG Wersching 36

FROM 26 POINTS BEHIND TO WIN:
September 21, 1997, at Buffalo

Indianapolis	14	12	0	9	— 35
Buffalo	0	10	6	21	— 37

- Ind — Bailey 10 pass from Harbaugh (Blanchard kick)
- Ind — Faulk 10 run (Blanchard kick)
- Ind — FG Blanchard 39
- Ind — FG Blanchard 36
- Ind — FG Blanchard 49
- Ind — FG Blanchard 22
- Buff — Johnson 16 pass from Collins (Christie kick)
- Buff — FG Christie 27
- Buff — A. Smith 15 run (2-pt attempt failed)
- Ind — FG Blanchard 25
- Buff — Early 4 pass from Collins (Christie kick)
- Buff — A. Smith 1 run (Christie kick)
- Buff — A. Smith 54 run (Christie kick)
- Ind — Harrison 2 pass from Justin (2-pt attempt failed)

FROM 25 POINTS BEHIND TO WIN:
November 8, 1987, at St. Louis

Tampa Bay	7	7	14	0	— 28
St. Louis	0	3	0	28	— 31

- TB — Carrier 5 pass from DeBerg (Igwebuike kick)
- TB — Carter 3 pass from DeBerg (Igwebuike kick)
- StL — FG Gallery 31
- TB — Smith 34 pass from DeBerg (Igwebuike kick)
- TB — Smith 3 run (Igwebuike kick)

- StL — Awalt 4 pass from Lomax (Gallery kick)
- StL — Noga 23 fumble recovery (Gallery kick)
- StL — J. Smith 11 pass from Lomax (Gallery kick)
- StL — J. Smith 17 pass from Lomax (Gallery kick)

FROM 24 POINTS BEHIND TO WIN:
October 27, 1946, at Washington

Philadelphia	0	0	14	14	— 28
Washington	10	14	0	0	— 24

- Wash — Rosato 2 run (Poillon kick)
- Wash — FG Poillon 28
- Wash — Rosato 4 run (Poillon kick)
- Wash — Lapka recovered fumble in end zone (Poillon kick)
- Phil — Steele 1 run (Lio kick)
- Phil — Pritchard 45 pass from Thompson (Lio kick)
- Phil — Steinke 7 pass from Thompson (Lio kick)
- Phil — Ferrante 30 pass from Thompson (Lio kick)

FROM 24 POINTS BEHIND TO WIN:
October 20, 1957, at Detroit

Baltimore	7	14	6	0	— 27
Detroit	0	3	7	21	— 31

- Balt — Mutscheller 15 pass from Unitas (Rechichar kick)
- Det — FG Martin 47
- Balt — Moore 72 pass from Unitas (Rechichar kick)
- Balt — Mutscheller 52 pass from Unitas (Rechichar kick)
- Balt — Moore 4 pass from Unitas (kick failed)
- Det — Junker 14 pass from Rote (Layne kick)
- Det — Cassady 26 pass from Layne (Layne kick)
- Det — Johnson 1 run (Layne kick)
- Det — Cassady 29 pass from Layne (Layne kick)

FROM 24 POINTS BEHIND TO WIN:
October 25, 1959, at Minneapolis

Philadelphia	0	0	21	7	— 28
Chicago Cardinals	7	10	7	0	— 24

- Cardinals — Crow 10 pass from Roach (Conrad kick)
- Cardinals — J. Hill 77 blocked field goal return (Conrad kick)
- Cardinals — FG Conrad 15
- Cardinals — Lane 37 interception return (Conrad kick)
- Phil — Barnes 1 run (Walston kick)
- Phil — McDonald 29 pass from Van Brocklin (Walston kick)
- Phil — Barnes 2 run (Walston kick)
- Phil — McDonald 22 pass from Van Brocklin (Walston kick)

FROM 24 POINTS BEHIND TO WIN:
October 23, 1960, at Denver

Boston	10	7	7	0	— 24
Denver	0	0	14	17	— 31

- Bos — FG Cappelletti 12

- Bos — Colclough 10 pass from Songin (Cappelletti kick)
- Bos — Wells 6 pass from Songin (Cappelletti kick)
- Bos — Miller 47 pass from Songin (Cappelletti kick)
- Den — Carmichael 21 pass from Tripucka (Mingo kick)
- Den — Jessup 19 pass from Tripucka (Mingo kick)
- Den — Carmichael 35 lateral from Taylor, pass from Tripucka (Mingo kick)
- Den — Taylor 8 pass from Tripucka (Mingo kick)
- Den — FG Mingo 9

FROM 24 POINTS BEHIND TO WIN:
December 15, 1974, at Miami

New England	21	3	0	3	— 27
Miami	0	17	7	10	— 34

- NE — Hannah recovered fumble in end zone (J. Smith kick)
- NE — Sanders 23 interception return (J. Smith kick)
- NE — Herron 4 pass from Plunkett (J. Smith kick)
- NE — FG J. Smith 46
- Mia — Nottingham 1 run (Yepremian kick)
- Mia — Baker 37 pass from Morrall (Yepremian kick)
- Mia — FG Yepremian 28
- Mia — Baker 46 pass from Morrall (Yepremian kick)
- NE — FG J. Smith 34
- Mia — Nottingham 2 run (Yepremian kick)
- Mia — FG Yepremian 40

FROM 24 POINTS BEHIND TO WIN:
December 4, 1977, at Minnesota

San Francisco	0	10	14	3	— 27
Minnesota	0	0	7	21	— 28

- SF — Delvin Williams 2 run (Wersching kick)
- SF — FG Wersching 31
- SF — Dave Williams 80 kickoff return (Wersching kick)
- SF — Delvin Williams 5 run (Wersching kick)
- Minn — McClanahan 15 pass from Lee (Cox kick)
- Minn — Rashad 8 pass from Kramer (Cox kick)
- Minn — Tucker 9 pass from Kramer (Cox kick)
- SF — FG Wersching 31
- Minn — S. White 69 pass from Kramer (Cox kick)

FROM 24 POINTS BEHIND TO WIN:
September 23, 1979, at Denver

Seattle	10	10	14	0	— 34
Denver	0	10	21	6	— 37

- Sea — FG Herrera 28
- Sea — Doornink 5 run (Herrera kick)
- Den — FG Turner 27

Sea — Doornink 5 run (Herrera kick)
Den — Armstrong 2 run (Turner kick)
Sea — FG Herrera 22
Sea — McCullum 13 pass from Zorn (Herrera kick)
Sea — Smith 1 run (Herrera kick)
Den — Studdard 2 pass from Morton (Turner kick)
Den — Moses 11 pass from Morton (Turner kick)
Den — Upchurch 35 pass from Morton (Turner kick)
Den — Lytle 1 run (kick failed)

FROM 24 POINTS BEHIND TO WIN:
September 23, 1979, at Cincinnati

Houston	0	10	17	0	3 —	30
Cincinnati	14	10	0	3	0 —	27

Cin — Johnson 1 run (Bahr kick)
Cin — Alexander 2 run (Bahr kick)
Cin — Johnson 1 run (Bahr kick)
Cin — FG Bahr 52
Hou — Burrough 35 pass from Pastorini (Fritsch kick)
Hou — FG Fritsch 33
Hou — Campbell 8 run (Fritsch kick)
Hou — Caster 22 pass from Pastorini (Fritsch kick)
Hou — FG Fritsch 47
Cin — FG Bahr 55
Hou — FG Fritsch 29

FROM 24 POINTS BEHIND TO WIN:
November 22, 1982, at Los Angeles

San Diego	10	14	0	0 —	24
L.A. Raiders	0	7	14	7 —	28

SD — FG Benirschke 19
SD — Scales 29 pass from Fouts (Benirschke kick)
SD — Muncie 2 run (Benirschke kick)
SD — Muncie 1 run (Benirschke kick)
Raiders — Christensen 1 pass from Plunkett (Bahr kick)
Raiders — Allen 3 run (Bahr kick)
Raiders — Allen 6 run (Bahr kick)
Raiders — Hawkins 1 run (Bahr kick)

FROM 24 POINTS BEHIND TO WIN:
September 26, 1988, at Denver

L.A. Raiders	0	0	14	13	3 —	30
Denver	7	17	0	3	0 —	27

Den — Dorsett 1 run (Karlis kick)
Den — Dorsett 1 run (Karlis kick)
Den — Sewell 7 pass from Elway (Karlis kick)
Den — FG Karlis 39
Raiders — Smith 40 pass from Schroeder (Bahr kick)
Raiders — Smith 42 pass from Schroeder (Bahr kick)
Raiders — FG Bahr 28
Raiders — Allen 4 run (Bahr kick)
Den — FG Karlis 25
Raiders — FG Bahr 44
Raiders — FG Bahr 35

FROM 24 POINTS BEHIND TO WIN:
December 6, 1992, at Tampa

L.A. Rams	0	3	21	7 —	31
Tampa Bay	6	21	0	0 —	27

TB — FG Murray 34
TB — FG Murray 47
TB — Armstrong 81 pass from Testaverde (Murray kick)
TB — Jones 26 fumble recovery (Murray kick)
Rams — FG Zendejas 18
TB — Carrier 10 pass from Testaverde (Murray kick)
Rams — Anderson 40 pass from Everett (Zendejas kick)
Rams — Chadwick 27 pass from Everett (Zendejas kick)
Rams — Lang 1 run (Zendejas kick)
Rams — Carter 8 pass from Everett (Zendejas kick)

POSTSEASON GAMES

FROM 32 POINTS BEHIND TO WIN:
AFC First-Round Playoff Game
January 3, 1993, at Buffalo

Houston	7	21	7	3	0 —	38
Buffalo	3	0	28	7	3 —	41

Hou — Jeffires 3 pass from Moon (Del Greco kick)
Buff — FG Christie 36
Hou — Slaughter 7 pass from Moon (Del Greco kick)
Hou — Duncan 26 pass from Moon (Del Greco kick)
Hou — Jeffires 27 pass from Moon (Del Greco kick)
Hou — McDowell 58 interception return (Del Greco kick)
Buff — Davis 1 run (Christie kick)
Buff — Beebe 38 pass from Reich (Christie kick)
Buff — Reed 26 pass from Reich (Christie kick)
Buff — Reed 18 pass from Reich (Christie kick)
Buff — Reed 17 pass from Reich (Christie kick)
Hou — FG Del Greco 26
Buff — FG Christie 32

FROM 20 POINTS BEHIND TO WIN:
Western Conference Playoff Game
December 22, 1957, at San Francisco

Detroit	0	7	14	10 —	31
San Francisco	14	10	3	0 —	27

SF — Owens 34 pass from Tittle (Soltau kick)
SF — McElhenny 47 pass from Tittle (Soltau kick)
Det — Junker 4 pass from Rote (Martin kick)
SF — Wilson 12 pass from Tittle (Soltau kick)
SF — FG Soltau 25
SF — FG Soltau 10
Det — Tracy 2 run (Martin kick)
Det — Tracy 58 run (Martin kick)
Det — Gedman 3 run (Martin kick)
Det — FG Martin 14

FROM 18 POINTS BEHIND TO WIN:
NFC Divisional Playoff Game
December 23, 1972, at San Francisco

Dallas	3	10	0	17 —	30
San Francisco	7	14	7	0 —	28

SF — Washington 97 kickoff return (Gossett kick)
Dall — FG Fritsch 37
SF — Schreiber 1 run (Gossett kick)
SF — Schreiber 1 run (Gossett kick)
Dall — FG Fritsch 45
Dall — Alworth 28 pass from Morton (Fritsch kick)
SF — Schreiber 1 run (Gossett kick)
Dall — FG Fritsch 27
Dall — Parks 20 pass from Staubach (Fritsch kick)
Dall — Sellers 10 pass from Staubach (Fritsch kick)

FROM 18 POINTS BEHIND TO WIN:
AFC Divisional Playoff Game
January 4, 1986, at Miami

Cleveland	7	7	7	0 —	21
Miami	3	0	14	7 —	24

Mia — FG Reveiz 51
Cle — Newsome 16 pass from Kosar (Bahr kick)
Cle — Byner 21 run (Bahr kick)
Cle — Byner 66 run (Bahr kick)
Mia — Moore 6 pass from Marino (Reveiz kick)
Mia — Davenport 31 run (Reveiz kick)
Mia — Davenport 1 run (Reveiz kick)

RECORDS FOR NFL TEAMS FOR MOST POINTS IN A GAME (REGULAR SEASON ONLY)

Note: When the record has been achieved more than once, only the most recent game is shown; summaries are listed in alphabetical order by conference. Bold face indicates team holding record.

BALTIMORE RAVENS
November 26, 2000, at Baltimore

Cleveland	7	0	0	0	— 7
Baltimore	7	24	6	7	— 44

TD: Balt—Jamal Lewis 2, Sam Gash, Patrick Johnson, Priest Holmes; Cle—Travis Prentice. TD Passes: Balt—Trent Dilfer 2. FG: Balt—Matt Stover 3.

BUFFALO BILLS
September 18, 1966, at Buffalo

Miami	3	7	0	14	— 24
Buffalo	21	27	3	7	— 58

TD: Buff—Bobby Burnett 2, Butch Byrd 2, Jack Spikes 2, Bobby Crockett, Jack Kemp; Mia—Dave Kocourek, Bo Roberson, John Roderick. TD Passes: Buff—Jack Kemp, Daryle Lamonica; Mia—George Wilson 3. FG: Buff—Booth Lusteg; Mia—Gene Mingo.

CINCINNATI BENGALS
December 17, 1989, at Cincinnati

Houston	0	0	0	7	— 7
Cincinnati	21	10	21	9	— 61

TD: Cin—Eddie Brown 2, Eric Ball, James Brooks, Ira Hillary, Rodney Holman, Tim McGee, Craig Taylor; Hou—Lorenzo White. TD Passes: Cin—Boomer Esiason 4, Erik Wilhelm. FG: Cin—Jim Breech 2.

CLEVELAND BROWNS
November 7, 1954, at Cleveland

Washington	0	3	0	0	— 3
Cleveland	13	14	21	14	— 62

TD: Cle—Darrell Brewster 2, Mo Bassett, Ken Gorgal, Otto Graham, Dub Jones, Dante Lavelli, Curley Morrison. TD Passes: Cle—George Ratterman 3, Otto Graham. FG: Cle—Lou Groza 2; Wash—Vic Janowicz.

DENVER BRONCOS
October 6, 1963, at Denver

San Diego	13	7	0	14	— 34
Denver	3	14	9	24	— 50

TD: Den—Lionel Taylor 2, Goose Gonsoulin, Gene Prebola, Donnie Stone; SD—Keith Lincoln 2, Lance Alworth, Paul Lowe, Jacque MacKinnon. TD Passes: Den—John McCormick 3; SD—Tobin Rote 3, John Hadl 2. FG: Den—Gene Mingo 5.

INDIANAPOLIS COLTS
December 12, 1976, at Baltimore

Buffalo	3	3	7	7	— 20
Baltimore Colts	7	13	28	10	— 58

TD: Balt—Roger Carr, Raymond Chester, Glenn Doughty, Roosevelt Leaks, Derrel Luce, Lydell Mitchell, Howard Stevens; Buff—Bob Chandler, O.J. Simpson. TD Passes: Balt—Bert Jones 3; Buff—Gary Marangi. FG: Balt—Toni Linhart 3; Buff—George Jakowenko 2.

JACKSONVILLE JAGUARS
December 3, 2000, at Jacksonville

Cleveland	0	0	0	0	— 0
Jacksonville	3	17	21	7	— 48

TD: Jax—Fred Taylor 3, Keenan McCardell, Mark Brunell, Shyrone Stith. TD Passes: Jax—Mark Brunell. FG: Jax—Mike Hollis 2.

KANSAS CITY CHIEFS
September 7, 1963, at Denver

Kansas City	14	14	21	10	— 59
Denver	0	7	0	0	— 7

TD: KC—Chris Burford 2, Frank Jackson 2, Dave Grayson, Abner Haynes, Sherrill Headrick, Curtis McClinton; Den—Lionel Taylor. TD Passes: KC—Len Dawson 4, Curtis McClinton; Den—Mickey Slaughter. FG: KC—Tommy Brooker.

MIAMI DOLPHINS
November 24, 1977, at St. Louis

Miami	14	14	20	7	— 55
St. Louis Cardinals	7	0	0	7	— 14

TD: Mia—Nat Moore 3, Gary Davis, Duriel Harris, Leroy Harris, Benny Malone, Andre Tillman; StL—Ike Harris, Terry Metcalf. TD Passes: Mia—Bob Griese 6; StL—Jim Hart.

NEW ENGLAND PATRIOTS
September 9, 1979, at New England

New York Jets	3	0	0	0	— 3
New England	14	21	7	14	— 56

TD: NE—Harold Jackson 3, Stanley Morgan 2, Allan Clark, Andy Johnson, Don Westbrook. TD Passes: NE—Steve Grogan 5, Tom Owen. FG: NYJ—Pat Leahy.

NEW YORK JETS
November 17, 1985, at New York

Tampa Bay	14	7	7	0	— 28
New York Jets	17	24	14	7	— 62

TD: NYJ—Mickey Shuler 3, Johnny Hector 2, Tony Paige, Al Toon, Wesley Walker; TB—James Wilder 2, Kevin House, Calvin Magee. TD Passes: NYJ—Ken O'Brien 5; TB—Steve DeBerg 2. FG: NYJ—Pat Leahy 2.

OAKLAND RAIDERS
December 24, 2000, at Oakland

Carolina	3	6	0	0	— 9
Oakland	7	17	14	14	— 52

TD: Oak—Jeremy Brigham 2, Rickey Dudley 2, Tim Brown, Eric Allen, Darrien Gordon. TD Passes: Oak—Rich Gannon 5. FG: Oak—Sebastian Janikowski 2; Car—Joe Nedney 3.

PITTSBURGH STEELERS
November 30, 1952, at Pittsburgh

New York Giants	0	0	7	0	— 7
Pittsburgh	14	14	7	28	— 63

TD: Pitt—Lynn Chandnois 2, Dick Hensley 2, Jack Butler, George Hays, Ray Mathews, Ed Modzelewski, Elbie Nickel; NYG—Bill Stribling. TD Passes: Pitt—Jim Finks 4, Gary Kerkorian; NYG—Tom Landry.

SAN DIEGO CHARGERS
December 22, 1963, at San Diego

Denver	7	10	3	0	— 20
San Diego	10	16	10	22	— 58

TD: SD—Paul Lowe 2, Chuck Allen, Bobby Jackson, Dave Kocourek, Keith Lincoln, Jacque MacKinnon; Den—Billy Joe, Donnie Stone. TD Passes: SD—John Hadl, Tobin Rote; Den—Don Breaux. FG: SD—George Blair 3; Den—Gene Mingo 2.

TENNESSEE TITANS
December 9, 1990, at Houston

Cleveland	0	7	7	0	— 14
Houston Oilers	14	31	7	6	— 58

TD: Hou—Lorenzo White 4, Ernest Givins, Leonard Harris, Tony Jones, Terry Kinard; Cle—Eric Metcalf 2. TD Passes: Hou—Warren Moon 2, Cody Carlson; Cle—Bernie Kosar. FG: Hou—Teddy Garcia.

ARIZONA CARDINALS
November 13, 1949, at New York

Chicago Cardinals	7	31	14	13	— 65
New York Bulldogs	7	0	6	7	— 20

TD: Chi—Red Cochran 2, Pat Harder 2, Bill Dewell, Mel Kutner, Bob Ravensburg, Vic Schwall, Charlie Trippi; NY—Joe Golding, Frank Muehlheuser, Johnny Rauch. TD Passes: Chi—Paul Christman 3, Jim Hardy 3; NY—Bobby Layne. FG: Chi—Pat Harder.

ATLANTA FALCONS
September 16, 1973, at New Orleans

Atlanta	0	24	21	17	— 62
New Orleans	0	0	7	0	— 7

TD: Atl—Ken Burrow 2, Eddie Ray 2, Wes Chesson, Tom Hayes, Art Malone, Joe Profit; NO—Bill Butler. TD Passes: Atl—Dick Shiner 3, Bob Lee; NO—Archie Manning. FG: Atl—Nick Mike-Mayer 2.

CAROLINA PANTHERS
January 2, 2000, at Carolina

New Orleans	0	0	0	13 —	13
Carolina	10	7	14	14 —	45

TD: Car—Patrick Jeffers 2, Wesley Walls 2, Michael Bates, Muhsin Muhammad; NO—Jake Delhomme, Eddie Kennison. TD Passes: Car—Steve Beuerlein 5; NO—Jake Delhomme. FG: Car—Richie Cunningham.

CHICAGO BEARS
December 7, 1980, at Chicago

Green Bay	0	7	0	0 —	7
Chicago	0	28	13	20 —	61

TD: Chi—Walter Payton 3, Brian Baschnagel, Robin Earl, Roland Harper, Willie McClendon, Len Walterscheid, Rickey Watts; GB—James Lofton. TD Passes: Chi—Vince Evans 3; GB—Lynn Dickey.

DALLAS COWBOYS
October 12, 1980, at Dallas

San Francisco	0	7	0	7 —	14
Dallas	14	24	14	7 —	59

TD: Dall—Drew Pearson 3, Ron Springs 2, Tony Dorsett, Billy Joe DuPree, Robert Newhouse; SF—Dwight Clark 2. TD Passes: Dall—Danny White 4; SF—Steve DeBerg 2. FG: Dall—Rafael Septien.

DETROIT LIONS
November 27, 1997, at Detroit

Chicago	14	6	0	0 —	20
Detroit	3	14	17	21 —	55

TD: Det—Herman Moore, Johnnie Morton, Ron Rivers, Barry Sanders 3, Tracy Scroggins; Chi—Raymont Harris, Ricky Proehl. TD Passes: Det—Scott Mitchell 2; Chi—Erik Kramer. FG: Det—Jason Hanson 2; Chi—Jeff Jaeger 2.

GREEN BAY PACKERS
October 7, 1945, at Milwaukee

Detroit	0	7	7	7 —	21
Green Bay	0	41	9	7 —	57

TD: GB—Don Hutson 4, Charley Brock, Irv Comp, Ted Fritsch, Clyde Goodnight; Det—Chuck Fenenbock, John Greene, Bob Westfall. TD Passes: GB—Tex McKay 4, Lou Brock, Irv Comp; Det—Dave Ryan.

MINNESOTA VIKINGS
October 18, 1970, at Minnesota

Dallas	3	3	0	7 —	13
Minnesota	14	20	17	3 —	54

TD: Minn—Clint Jones 2, Ed Sharockman 2, John Beasley, Dave Osborn; Dall—Calvin Hill. TD Pass: Minn—Gary Cuozzo. FG: Minn—Fred Cox 4; Dall—Mike Clark 2.

NEW ORLEANS SAINTS
November 21, 1976, at Seattle

New Orleans	3	17	28	3 —	51
Seattle	6	0	7	14 —	27

TD: NO—Bobby Douglass 2, Tony Galbreath, Chuck Muncie, Tom Myers, Elex Price; Sea—Sherman Smith 2, Steve Largent, Jim Zorn. TD Pass: Sea—Bill Munson. FG: NO—Rich Szaro 3.

NEW YORK GIANTS
November 26, 1972, at New York

Philadelphia	3	7	0	0 —	10
New York Giants	14	24	10	14 —	62

TD: NYG—Don Herrmann 2, Ron Johnson 2, Bob Tucker 2, Randy Johnson; Phil—Harold Jackson. TD Passes: NYG—Norm Snead 3, Randy Johnson 2; Phil—John Reaves. FG: NYG—Pete Gogolak 2; Phil—Tom Dempsey.

PHILADELPHIA EAGLES
November 6, 1934, at Philadelphia

Cincinnati Reds	0	0	0	0 —	0
Philadelphia	26	6	12	20 —	64

TD: Phil—Joe Carter 3, Swede Hanson 3, Marvin Ellstrom, Roger Kirkman, Ed Matesic, Ed Storm. TD Passes: Phil—Ed Matesic 2, Albert Weiner 2, Marvin Elstrom.

ST. LOUIS RAMS
October 22, 1950, at Los Angeles

Baltimore	13	0	7	7 —	27
Los Angeles Rams	21	14	14	21 —	70

TD: LA—Bob Boyd 2, Vitamin T. Smith 2, Tom Fears, Elroy (Crazylegs) Hirsch, Dick Hoerner, Ralph Pasquariello, Dan Towler, Bob Waterfield; Balt—Chet Mutryn 2, Adrian Burk, Billy Stone. TD Passes: LA—Norm Van Brocklin 2, Bob Waterfield 2, Glenn Davis; Balt—Adrian Burk 3.

SAN FRANCISCO 49ERS
October 18, 1992, at San Francisco

Atlanta	7	3	0	7 —	17
San Francisco	21	21	14	0 —	56

TD: SF—Jerry Rice 3, Ricky Watters 3, Brent Jones, Tom Rathman; Atl—Michael Haynes, Jason Phillips. TD Passes: SF—Steve Young 3; Atl—Chris Miller, Wade Wilson. FG: Atl—Norm Johnson.

SEATTLE SEAHAWKS
October 30, 1977, at Seattle

Buffalo	3	0	7	7 —	17
Seattle	14	28	7	7 —	56

TD: Sea—Steve Largent 2, Duke Fergerson, Al Hunter, David Sims, Sherman Smith, Don Testerman, Jim Zorn; Buff—Joe Ferguson, John Kimbrough. TD Passes: Sea—Jim Zorn 4; Buff—Joe Ferguson. FG: Buff—Carson Long.

TAMPA BAY BUCCANEERS
December 23, 2001, at Tampa Bay

New Orleans	0	0	7	14 —	21
Tampa Bay	17	13	3	15 —	48

TD: TB—Mike Alstott, Ronde Barber, Warrick Dunn, Dave Moore, Karl Williams; NO—Joe Horn 2, Eddie Williams. TD Passes: TB—Brad Johnson 3; NO—Aaron Brooks 3. FG: TB—Martin Gramatica 4.

WASHINGTON REDSKINS
November 27, 1966, at Washington

New York Giants	0	14	14	13 —	41
Washington	13	21	14	24 —	72

TD: Wash—A.D. Whitfield 3, Brig Owens 2, Charley Taylor 2, Rickie Harris, Joe Don Looney, Bobby Mitchell; NYG—Allen Jacobs, Homer Jones, Dan Lewis, Joe Morrison, Aaron Thomas, Gary Wood. TD Passes: Wash—Sonny Jurgensen 3; NYG—Gary Wood 2, Tom Kennedy. FG: Wash—Charlie Gogolak.

TEAMS THAT FINISHED IN FIRST PLACE IN THEIR DIVISION THE SEASON AFTER FINISHING IN LAST PLACE

Season	Team	Record	Previous Season
1967	Houston	9-4-1	*3-11-0
1968	Minnesota	8-6-0	3- 8-3
1970	Cincinnati	8-6-0	4- 9-1
1970	San Francisco	10-3-1	4- 8-2
1972	Green Bay	10-4-0	4- 8-2
1975	Baltimore	10-4-0	2-12-0
1979	Tampa Bay	10-6-0	5-11-0
1981	Cincinnati	12-4-0	6-10-0
1987	Indianapolis	9-6-0	3-13-0
1988	Cincinnati	12-4-0	4-11-0
1990	Cincinnati	9-7-0	8- 8-0
1991	Denver	12-4-0	5-11-0
1992	San Diego	11-5-0	4-12-0
1993	Detroit	10-6-0	5-11-0
1997	N.Y. Giants	10-5-1	6-10-0
1999	Indianapolis	13-3-0	3-13-0
1999	St. Louis	13-3-0	4-12-0
2000	New Orleans	10-6-0	3-13-0
2001	Chicago	13-3-0	5-11-0
2001	New England	11-5-0	5-11-0

*tied for last place

RECORDS OF NFL TEAMS SINCE 1970 AFL-NFL MERGER

AFC	W	L	T	Pct.	Division Titles	Playoff Berths	Postseason Record	Super Bowl Record
Miami	315	171	2	.648	12	21	20-19	2-3
Oakland	293	189	6	.607	11	17	20-14	3-0
Pittsburgh	291	196	1	.597	15	19	22-15	4-1
Denver	281	201	6	.582	9	14	16-12	2-4
Jacksonville**	62	50	0	.554	2	4	4-4	0-0
Kansas City	241	240	7	.501	4	9	3-9	0-0
Baltimore***	46	49	1	.484	0	2	5-1	1-0
Buffalo	234	252	2	.482	7	13	12-13	0-4
Tennessee	230	256	2	.473	3	12	10-12	0-1
Cleveland+	206	231	3	.472	6	10	4-10	0-0
New England	228	260	0	.467	5	10	9-9	1-2
Cincinnati	217	271	0	.445	5	7	5-7	0-2
San Diego	210	273	5	.435	5	7	6-7	0-1
N.Y. Jets	210	276	2	.432	1	7	4-7	0-0
Indianapolis	209	277	2	.430	6	10	6-9	1-0

NFC	W	L	T	Pct.	Division Titles	Playoff Berths	Postseason Record	Super Bowl Record
San Francisco	295	190	3	.608	16	20	24-15	5-0
Dallas	295	193	0	.605	15	22	31-17	5-3
Minnesota	287	199	2	.590	14	21	15-21	0-3
Washington	283	203	2	.582	6	14	19-11	3-2
St. Louis	266	218	4	.549	10	17	15-16	1-2
Chicago	243	244	1	.499	7	11	7-10	1-0
Green Bay	236	244	8	.492	4	9	11-8	1-1
Philadelphia	234	247	7	.487	3	12	8-12	0-1
N.Y. Giants	233	252	3	.481	5	9	12-7	2-1
Seattle*	188	216	0	.465	2	5	3-5	0-0
Detroit	217	267	4	.449	3	9	1-9	0-0
Arizona	199	283	6	.414	2	4	1-4	0-0
Atlanta	200	284	4	.413	2	6	4-6	0-1
Carolina**	46	66	0	.411	1	1	1-1	0-0
New Orleans	197	287	0	.407	2	5	1-5	0-0
Tampa Bay*	148	255	1	.368	3	7	3-7	0-0

*Entered NFL in 1976.
**Entered NFL in 1995.
***Entered NFL in 1996.
+Did not play 1996-98.
Oakland totals include L.A. Raiders, 1982-1994.
Tennessee totals include Houston, 1970-1996.
Indianapolis totals include Baltimore, 1970-1983.
St. Louis totals include L.A. Rams, 1970-1994.
Arizona totals include St. Louis, 1970-1987, and Phoenix, 1988-1993.
Tie games before 1972 are not calculated in won-lost percentage.

HOME RECORDS OF NFL TEAMS SINCE 1970 AFL-NFL MERGER

AFC	W	L	T	Pct.
Miami	180	62	1	.743
Pittsburgh	176	68	0	.721
Denver	173	68	4	.716
Oakland	161	81	2	.665
Jacksonville**	37	19	0	.661
Kansas City	145	95	3	.603
Baltimore***	27	20	1	.573
Buffalo	137	107	1	.561
Cincinnati	135	109	0	.553
New England	134	110	0	.549
Tennessee	133	110	1	.547
Cleveland+	115	102	2	.530
San Diego	121	120	2	.502
Indianapolis	112	130	2	.463
N.Y. Jets	110	132	1	.455

NFC	W	L	T	Pct.
Dallas	169	75	0	.693
Minnesota	167	77	1	.684
Washington	160	81	2	.663
San Francisco	156	86	2	.644
Green Bay	145	94	5	.605
St. Louis	143	99	2	.591
Chicago	143	100	1	.588
Detroit	139	104	1	.572
Philadelphia	133	109	3	.549
Seattle*	111	92	0	.547
N.Y. Giants	132	112	1	.541
Atlanta	122	122	1	.500
Carolina**	27	29	0	.482
Arizona	115	125	3	.479
Tampa Bay*	94	107	1	.468
New Orleans	108	135	1	.444

*Entered NFL in 1976.
**Entered NFL in 1995.
***Entered NFL in 1996.
+Did not play 1996-98.
Oakland totals include L.A. Raiders, 1982-1994.
Tennessee totals include Houston, 1970-1996.
Indianapolis totals include Baltimore, 1970-1983.
St. Louis totals include L.A. Rams, 1970-1994.
Arizona totals include St. Louis, 1970-1987, and Phoenix, 1988-1993.
Tie games before 1972 are not calculated in won-lost percentage.

ROAD RECORDS OF NFL TEAMS SINCE 1970 AFL-NFL MERGER

AFC	W	L	T	Pct.
Miami	135	109	1	.553
Oakland	132	108	4	.549
Pittsburgh	115	128	1	.473
Denver	108	133	2	.449
Jacksonville**	25	31	0	.446
Cleveland+	91	129	1	.414
N.Y. Jets	100	144	1	.410
Buffalo	97	145	1	.401
Kansas City	96	145	4	.400
Tennessee	97	146	1	.399
Indianapolis	97	147	0	.398
Baltimore***	19	29	0	.396
New England	94	150	0	.385
San Diego	89	153	3	.369
Cincinnati	82	162	0	.336

NFC	W	L	T	Pct.
San Francisco	139	104	1	.572
Dallas	126	118	0	.516
St. Louis	123	119	2	.508
Washington	123	122	0	.502
Minnesota	120	122	1	.496
Philadelphia	101	138	4	.424
N.Y. Giants	101	140	2	.420
Chicago	100	144	0	.410
Seattle*	77	124	0	.383
Green Bay	91	150	3	.379
New Orleans	89	152	3	.370
Arizona	84	158	3	.348
Carolina**	19	37	0	.339
Atlanta	78	162	3	.325
Detroit	78	163	3	.325
Tampa Bay*	54	148	0	.267

*Entered NFL in 1976.
**Entered NFL in 1995.
***Entered NFL in 1996.
+Did not play 1996-98.
Oakland totals include L.A. Raiders, 1982-1994.
Tennessee totals include Houston, 1970-1996.
Indianapolis totals include Baltimore, 1970-1983.
St. Louis totals include L.A. Rams, 1970-1994.
Arizona totals include St. Louis, 1970-1987, and Phoenix,1988-1993.
Tie games before 1972 are not calculated in won-lost percentage.

RECORDS OF TEAMS ON OPENING DAY, 1933-2001

AFC	W	L	T	Pct.	Longest W Strk.	Longest L Strk.	Current Streak
Jacksonville	6	1	0	.857	6	1	W- 6
Denver	26	15	1	.634	4	4	W- 1
Miami	21	14	1	.600	10	5	W-10
San Diego	24	18	0	.571	6	6	W- 1
Kansas City	23	19	0	.548	7	4	L- 3
Oakland	23	19	0	.548	5	5	W- 2
Cleveland	26	23	0	.531	5	5	L- 4
Indianapolis	26	23	1	.531	8	8	W- 3
Pittsburgh	32	31	4	.507	4	3	L- 2
Baltimore	3	3	0	.500	1	3	W- 2
Tennessee	21	21	0	.500	4	3	L- 2
Cincinnati	16	18	0	.471	4	4	W- 1
New England	19	23	0	.452	6	3	L- 2
Buffalo	17	25	0	.405	6	5	L- 1
N.Y. Jets	17	25	0	.405	3	5	L- 1
NFC							
Dallas	30	11	1	.732	17	3	L- 2
N.Y. Giants	39	26	4	.600	4	3	L- 1
Minnesota	23	17	1	.575	5	3	L- 1
Chicago	39	29	1	.574	9	6	L- 2
St. Louis	36	28	0	.563	5	6	W- 3
Green Bay	36	30	3	.545	5	6	W- 1
Detroit	35	32	2	.522	7	4	L- 1
San Francisco	26	25	1	.510	5	3	W- 1
Atlanta	18	18	0	.500	5	3	L- 1
Washington	32	33	4	.492	6	5	L- 1
Tampa Bay	11	15	0	.423	3	5	W- 2
Arizona	27	40	1	.403	6	7	L- 2
Philadelphia	27	40	1	.403	5	9	L- 1
Carolina	2	5	0	.286	1	4	W- 1
New Orleans	10	25	0	.286	2	6	W- 1
Seattle	7	19	0	.269	3	8	W- 1

Kansas City totals include Dallas Texans, 1960-62.
Oakland totals include L.A. Raiders, 1982-1994.
San Diego totals include L.A. Chargers, 1960.
Indianapolis totals include Baltimore, 1953-1983.
Tennessee totals include Houston, 1960-1996.
New England totals include Boston, 1960-1970.
St. Louis totals include Cleveland, 1937-1942 and 1944-45, and L.A. Rams, 1946-1994.
Detroit totals include Portsmouth, 1933.
Arizona totals include Chi. Cardinals, 1933-1959, St. Louis, 1960-1987, and Phoenix, 1988-1993.
NOTE: All tied games occurred prior to 1972, when calculation of ties in percentages as half-win, half-loss was begun.

INSIDE THE NUMBERS

RECORDS OF NFL TEAMS, 1992-2001

AFC	W	L	T	Pct.	Division Titles	Playoff Berths	Postseason Record	Super Bowl Record
Pittsburgh	99	61	0	.619	6	7	6-7	0-1
Miami	97	63	0	.606	3	8	5-8	0-0
Denver	96	64	0	.600	2	5	7-3	2-0
Kansas City	94	66	0	.588	3	5	2-5	0-0
Jacksonville	62	50	0	.554	2	4	4-4	0-0
Buffalo	88	72	0	.550	2	6	6-6	0-2
Tennessee	88	72	0	.550	2	4	3-4	0-1
Oakland	83	77	0	.519	2	3	3-3	0-0
Baltimore	46	49	1	.484	0	2	5-1	1-0
New England	77	83	0	.481	3	5	6-4	1-1
Indianapolis	74	86	0	.463	1	4	2-4	0-0
N.Y. Jets	70	90	0	.438	1	2	1-2	0-0
San Diego	70	90	0	.438	2	3	3-3	0-1
Cleveland	42	70	0	.375	0	1	1-1	0-0
Cincinnati	50	110	0	.313	0	0	0-0	0-0

Oakland totals include L.A. Raiders, 1992-94
Tennessee totals include Houston, 1992-96

NFC	W	L	T	Pct.	Division Titles	Playoff Berths	Postseason Record	Super Bowl Record
San Francisco	107	53	0	.669	5	8	8-7	1-0
Green Bay	104	56	0	.650	3	7	10-6	1-1
Minnesota	97	63	0	.606	4	8	4-8	0-0
Dallas	93	67	0	.581	6	7	11-4	3-0
Philadelphia	82	77	1	.516	1	5	5-5	0-0
N.Y. Giants	81	78	1	.509	2	3	3-3	0-1
Tampa Bay	77	83	0	.481	1	4	2-4	0-0
St. Louis	74	86	0	.463	2	3	5-2	1-1
Detroit	72	88	0	.450	1	5	0-5	0-0
Washington	71	88	1	.447	1	2	2-2	0-0
Chicago	69	91	0	.431	1	2	1-2	0-0
New Orleans	69	91	0	.431	1	2	1-2	0-0
Seattle	69	91	0	.431	1	1	0-1	0-0
Atlanta	68	92	0	.425	1	2	2-2	0-1
Carolina	46	66	0	.411	1	1	1-1	0-0
Arizona	59	101	0	.369	0	1	1-1	0-0

Arizona totals include Phoenix, 1992-93
St. Louis totals include L.A. Rams, 1992-94
Seattle was in the AFC from 1992-2001

HOME RECORDS, 1992-2001

AFC	W-L-T	Pct.
Denver	61-19-0	.763
Kansas City	59-21-0	.738
Pittsburgh	58-22-0	.725
Miami	55-25-0	.688
Jacksonville	37-19-0	.661
Buffalo	51-29-0	.638
Tennessee	46-34-0	.575
Baltimore	27-20-1	.573
Oakland	45-35-0	.563
New England	44-36-0	.550
Indianapolis	43-37-0	.538
San Diego	40-40-0	.500
N.Y. Jets	36-44-0	.450
Cincinnati	33-47-0	.413
Cleveland	23-33-0	.411

NFC	W-L-T	Pct.
Green Bay	67-13-0	.838
San Francisco	62-18-0	.775
Minnesota	57-23-0	.713
Dallas	56-24-0	.700
Philadelphia	49-31-0	.613
Tampa Bay	49-31-0	.613
Detroit	47-33-0	.588
N.Y. Giants	45-35-0	.563
Atlanta	44-36-0	.550
Washington	41-38-1	.519
Chicago	41-39-0	.513
St. Louis	41-39-0	.513
Seattle	41-39-0	.513
Carolina	27-29-0	.482
Arizona	38-42-0	.475
New Orleans	35-45-0	.438

Arizona totals include Phoenix, 1992-93
Oakland totals include L.A. Raiders, 1992-94
St. Louis totals include L.A. Rams, 1992-94
Tennessee totals include Houston, 1992-96
Seattle was in the AFC from 1992-2001

ROAD RECORDS, 1992-2001

AFC	W-L-T	Pct.
Miami	42-38-0	.525
Tennessee	42-38-0	.525
Pittsburgh	41-39-0	.513
Oakland	38-42-0	.475
Buffalo	37-43-0	.463
Jacksonville	25-31-0	.446
Denver	35-45-0	.438
Kansas City	35-45-0	.438
N.Y. Jets	34-46-0	.425
New England	33-47-0	.413
Baltimore	19-29-0	.396
Indianapolis	31-49-0	.388
San Diego	30-50-0	.375
Cleveland	19-37-0	.339
Cincinnati	17-63-0	.213

NFC	W-L-T	Pct.
San Francisco	45-35-0	.563
Minnesota	40-40-0	.500
Dallas	37-43-0	.463
Green Bay	37-43-0	.463
N.Y. Giants	36-43-1	.456
New Orleans	34-46-0	.425
Philadelphia	33-46-1	.419
St. Louis	33-47-0	.413
Washington	30-50-0	.375
Chicago	28-52-0	.350
Seattle	28-52-0	.350
Tampa Bay	28-52-0	.350
Carolina	19-37-0	.339
Detroit	25-55-0	.313
Atlanta	24-56-0	.300
Arizona	21-59-0	.263

Arizona totals include Phoenix, 1992-93
Oakland totals include L.A. Raiders, 1992-94
St. Louis totals include L.A. Rams, 1992-94
Tennessee totals include Houston, 1992-96
Seattle was in the AFC from 1992-2001

RECORDS BY MONTHS, 1992-2001

	Sept.	Oct.	Nov.	Dec.	Total	
AFC	W-L-T	W-L-T	W-L-T	W-L-T	W-L-T	Pct.
Pittsburgh	20-16-0	29- 9-0	27-16-0	23-20-0	99-61-0	.619
Miami	26- 7-0	27-14-0	24-19-0	20-23-0	97-63-0	.606
Denver	24-15-0	23-15-0	31-10-0	18-24-0	96-64-0	.600
Kansas City	27-12-0	20-17-0	24-19-0	23-18-0	94-66-0	.588
Jacksonville	15-12-0	12-16-0	17-10-0	18-12-0	62-50-0	.554
Buffalo	20-14-0	23-17-0	26-18-0	19-23-0	88-72-0	.550
Tennessee	16-20-0	23-15-0	22-21-0	27-16-0	88-72-0	.550
Oakland	18-21-0	27-10-0	19-22-0	19-24-0	83-77-0	.519
Baltimore	13-10-0	7-16-0	12-13-1	14-10-0	46-49-1	.484
New England	15-20-0	16-26-0	21-20-0	25-17-0	77-83-0	.481
Indianapolis	15-19-0	21-20-0	13-29-0	25-18-0	74-86-0	.463
N.Y. Jets	14-23-0	17-23-0	24-16-0	15-28-0	70-90-0	.438
San Diego	21-17-0	16-22-0	15-27-0	18-24-0	70-90-0	.438
Cleveland	14-12-0	12-15-0	9-20-0	7-23-0	42-70-0	.375
Cincinnati	9-28-0	8-31-0	14-28-0	19-23-0	50-110-0	.313

Oakland totals include L.A. Raiders, 1992-94
Tennessee totals include Houston, 1992-96
September totals include August; December totals include January

	Sept.	Oct.	Nov.	Dec.	Total	
NFC	W-L-T	W-L-T	W-L-T	W-L-T	W-L-T	Pct.
San Francisco	25-12-0	25-14-0	30-11-0	27-16-0	107-53-0	.669
Green Bay	26-13-0	18-16-0	27-16-0	33-11-0	104-56-0	.650
Minnesota	26-12-0	24-14-0	24-17-0	23-20-0	97-63-0	.606
Dallas	20-15-0	27-12-0	24-20-0	22-20-0	93-67-0	.581
Philadelphia	17-19-0	24-16-0	20-23-1	21-19-0	82-77-1	.516
N.Y. Giants	20-17-0	20-20-0	16-25-1	25-16-0	81-78-1	.509
Tampa Bay	18-20-0	13-24-0	22-20-0	24-19-0	77-83-0	.481
St. Louis	23-15-0	15-23-0	13-28-0	23-20-0	74-86-0	.463
Detroit	19-20-0	16-20-0	19-25-0	18-23-0	72-88-0	.450
Washington	16-21-0	19-21-0	15-25-1	21-21-0	71-88-1	.447
Chicago	11-27-0	22-16-0	18-24-0	18-24-0	69-91-0	.431
New Orleans	14-23-0	20-19-0	18-23-0	17-26-0	69-91-0	.431
Seattle	18-21-0	13-24-0	20-21-0	18-25-0	69-91-0	.431
Atlanta	12-26-0	15-24-0	24-17-0	17-25-0	68-92-0	.425
Carolina	8-16-0	10-19-0	14-16-0	14-15-0	46-66-0	.411
Arizona	9-26-0	13-27-0	20-23-0	17-25-0	59-101-0	.369

Arizona totals include Phoenix, 1992-93
St. Louis totals include L.A. Rams, 1992-94
Seattle was in the AFC from 1992-2001
September totals include August; December totals include January

TAKEAWAYS/GIVEAWAYS, 1992-2001

AFC	Takeaways			Giveaways			Net.Diff.
	Int.	Fum.	Total	Int.	Fum.	Total	
Kansas City	177	165	342	142	113	255	87
Pittsburgh	191	150	341	154	121	275	66
N.Y. Jets	189	149	338	190	122	312	26
Denver	177	132	309	157	129	286	23
Jacksonville	96	98	194	96	76	172	22
Miami	190	127	317	169	134	303	14
New England	178	128	306	184	128	312	- 6
Tennessee	165	144	309	167	148	315	- 6
Baltimore	109	72	181	110	79	189	- 8
Oakland	155	122	277	162	137	299	-22
Cleveland	114	83	197	131	91	222	-25
Buffalo	165	123	288	183	132	315	-27
Cincinnati	144	120	264	160	133	293	-29
San Diego	188	110	298	215	122	337	-39
Indianapolis	133	114	247	177	128	305	-58

Oakland totals include L.A. Raiders, 1992-94
Tennessee totals include Houston, 1992-96

NFC	Takeaways			Giveaways			Net.Diff.
	Int.	Fum.	Total	Int.	Fum.	Total	
San Francisco	201	110	311	136	112	248	63
N.Y. Giants	184	121	305	147	108	255	50
Philadelphia	187	142	329	158	148	306	23
Washington	187	121	308	180	107	287	21
Dallas	161	115	276	133	123	256	20
Green Bay	194	124	318	174	125	299	19
Minnesota	176	136	312	178	122	300	12
Tampa Bay	168	130	298	172	119	291	7
Seattle	189	130	319	178	141	319	0
Detroit	171	115	286	174	113	287	- 1
Carolina	129	104	233	134	110	244	-11
Chicago	149	138	287	173	135	308	-21
New Orleans	165	147	312	205	140	345	-33
Atlanta	152	126	278	189	125	314	-36
St. Louis	201	104	305	196	158	354	-49
Arizona	157	130	287	218	151	369	-82

Arizona totals include Phoenix, 1992-93
St. Louis totals include L.A. Rams, 1992-94
Seattle was in the AFC from 1992-2001

BEST TAKEAWAY/GIVEAWAY DIFFERENTIAL, SEASON
+43 Washington, 1983
+26 Kansas City, 1990
+25 N.Y. Giants, 1997

HIGH AND LOW SINGLE-GAME YARDAGE TOTALS, 1992-2001
Most Total Yards, Game
615 Arizona vs. Washington, Nov. 10, 1996 (OT)
614 St. Louis vs. San Diego, Oct. 1, 2000
598 San Francisco vs. Buffalo, Sept. 13, 1992
590 San Francisco vs. Atlanta, Oct. 18, 1992
579 Buffalo vs. Seattle, Dec. 23, 2000
Fewest Total Yards, Game
40 Cleveland vs. Pittsburgh, Sept. 12, 1999
53 Cleveland vs. Jacksonville, Dec. 3, 2000
62 Seattle vs. Dallas, Oct. 11, 1992
82 Denver vs. Philadelphia, Sept. 20, 1992
87 Seattle vs. Philadelphia, Dec. 13, 1992 (OT)
Most Yards Rushing, Game
407 Cincinnati vs. Denver, Oct. 22, 2000
337 St. Louis vs. Carolina, Nov. 11, 2001
328 San Francisco vs. Detroit, Dec. 14, 1998
319 Seattle vs. Oakland, Nov. 11, 2001
315 Buffalo vs. Atlanta, Nov. 22, 1992
Fewest Yards Rushing, Game
4 Buffalo vs. Tennessee, Nov. 23, 1997
  Cincinnati vs. Baltimore, Sept. 24, 2000

8 Oakland vs. Kansas City, Dec. 3, 1995
  Dallas vs. New Orleans, Dec. 6, 1998
9 Cleveland vs. Pittsburgh, Sept. 12, 1999
Most Yards Passing, Game
507 Arizona vs. Washington, Nov. 10, 1996 (OT)
475 San Francisco vs. L.A. Rams, Nov. 28, 1993
474 Kansas City vs. Oakland, Nov. 5, 2000
473 N.Y. Jets vs. Baltimore, Dec. 24, 2000
456 Miami vs. New England, Sept. 4, 1994
Fewest Yards Passing, Game
-19 San Diego vs. Kansas City, Sept. 20, 1998
-9 Cleveland vs. Jacksonville, Dec. 3, 2000
9 Dallas vs. Tennessee, Dec. 25, 2000
12 Carolina vs. Buffalo, Sept. 10, 1995
   Philadelphia vs. Seattle, Sept. 6, 1998

NFL INDIVIDUAL LEADERS, 1992-2001

Points		Passing Yards	
Gary Anderson	1,123	Brett Favre	38,627
Jason Elam	1,073	Drew Bledsoe	29,657
Morten Andersen	1,071	Vinny Testaverde	26,793
Matt Stover	1,053	Dan Marino	25,975
Two tied	1,044	Troy Aikman	25,860

Touchdowns		TD Passes	
Emmitt Smith	135	Brett Favre	287
Marshall Faulk	110	Steve Young	181
Cris Carter	102	Vinny Testaverde	178
Jerry Rice	99	Drew Bledsoe	166
Ricky Watters	91	Dan Marino	154

Field Goals		Receptions	
Matt Stover	251	Cris Carter	905
John Carney	250	Tim Brown	839
Morten Andersen	247	Jerry Rice	838
Gary Anderson	247	Larry Centers	746
Steve Christie	243	Shannon Sharpe	663

Rushes		Reception Yards	
Emmitt Smith	3,192	Tim Brown	11,685
Jerome Bettis	2,686	Jerry Rice	11,314
Ricky Watters	2,622	Cris Carter	11,008
Curtis Martin	2,343	Herman Moore	9,039
Barry Sanders	2,185	Michael Irvin	8,936

Rushing Yards		Receiving TDs	
Emmitt Smith	13,687	Cris Carter	102
Barry Sanders	10,947	Jerry Rice	92
Jerome Bettis	10,876	Tim Brown	82
Ricky Watters	10,643	Carl Pickens	63
Marshall Faulk	9,442	Two tied	62

Rushing TDs		Interceptions	
Emmitt Smith	125	Rod Woodson	45
Marshall Faulk	79	Aeneas Williams	44
Ricky Watters	78	Ray Buchanan	43
Terry Allen	71	Terrell Buckley	41
Curtis Martin	64	Troy Vincent	37

Pass Attempts		Sacks	
Brett Favre	5,437	John Randle	114.5
Drew Bledsoe	4,518	Bruce Smith	108.0
Vinny Testaverde	3,842	Kevin Greene	97.5
Troy Aikman	3,660	Chris Doleman	89.0
Dan Marino	3,628	Reggie White	88.0

Completions	
Brett Favre	3,311
Drew Bledsoe	2,544
Troy Aikman	2,280
Vinny Testaverde	2,237
Dan Marino	2,169

NFL GAMES IN WHICH A TEAM HAS SCORED 60 OR MORE POINTS

(Home team in capitals)

Regular Season

WASHINGTON 72, New York Giants 41	November 27, 1966
LOS ANGELES RAMS 70, Baltimore 27	October 22, 1950
Chicago Cardinals 65, NEW YORK BULLDOGS 20	November 13, 1949
LOS ANGELES RAMS 65, Detroit 24	October 29, 1950
PHILADELPHIA 64, Cincinnati 0	November 6, 1934
CHICAGO CARDINALS 63, New York Giants 35	October 17, 1948
AKRON 62, Oorang 0	October 29, 1922
PITTSBURGH 62, New York Giants 7	November 30, 1952
CLEVELAND 62, New York Giants 14	December 6, 1953
CLEVELAND 62, Washington 3	November 7, 1954
NEW YORK GIANTS 62, Philadelphia 10	November 26, 1972
Atlanta 62, NEW ORLEANS 7	September 16, 1973
NEW YORK JETS 62, Tampa Bay 28	November 17, 1985
CHICAGO 61, San Francisco 20	December 12, 1965
Cincinnati 61, HOUSTON 17	December 17, 1972
CHICAGO 61, Green Bay 7	December 7, 1980
CINCINNATI 61, Houston 7	December 17, 1989
ROCK ISLAND 60, Evansville 0	October 15, 1922
CHICAGO CARDINALS 60, Rochester 0	October 7, 1923

Postseason

Chicago Bears 73, WASHINGTON 0	December 8, 1940
JACKSONVILLE 62, Miami 7	January 15, 2000

YOUNGEST AND OLDEST PLAYERS IN NFL IN 2001

10 Youngest Players	Birthdate	Games	Starts	Position
Hakim Akbar, New England	08/11/1980	6	0	DB
Kendrell Bell, Pittsburgh	07/17/1980	16	16	LB
Michael Vick, Atlanta	06/28/1980	8	2	QB
Koren Robinson, Seattle	03/19/1980	16	13	WR
Todd Heap, Baltimore	03/16/1980	12	6	TE
Benjamin Gay, Cleveland	02/28/1980	16	0	RB
Brandon Manumaleuna, St. Louis	01/04/1980	16	0	TE
Robert Ferguson, Green Bay	12/17/1979	1	0	WR
Nate Clements, Buffalo	12/12/1979	16	11	CB
Scotty Anderson, Detroit	11/24/1979	9	4	WR

10 Oldest Players	Birthdate	Games	Starts	Position
Gary Anderson, Minnesota	07/16/1959	16	0	K
Darrell Green, Washington	02/15/1960	16	4	DB
Morten Andersen, Atlanta	08/19/1960	16	0	K
Trey Junkin, Arizona	01/23/1961	16	0	TE
Bruce Matthews, Tennessee	08/08/1961	16	16	C-G
Lee Johnson, N.E.-Minn.	11/27/1961	9	0	P
Sean Landeta, Philadelphia	01/06/1962	16	0	P
Dale Hellestrae, Baltimore	07/11/1962	1	0	T
Mark Rypien, Indianapolis	10/02/1962	4	0	QB
Jerry Rice, Oakland	10/13/1962	16	15	WR

YOUNGEST AND OLDEST REGULAR STARTERS BY POSITION IN 2001

Minimum: 8 Games Started

	Youngest		Oldest	
QB	10/13/1977	Quincy Carter, Dall.	10/23/1962	Doug Flutie, S.D.
RB	06/23/1979	LaDainian Tomlinson, S.D.	02/21/1968	Terry Allen, Balt.
WR	03/19/1980	Koren Robinson, Sea.	10/13/1962	Jerry Rice, Oak.
TE	09/15/1979	Eric Johnson, S.F.	02/26/1966	Wesley Walls, Car.
T	11/03/1977	Damien Woody, N.E.	03/30/1963	Lomas Brown, N.Y.G.
G	07/01/1979	Ryan Diem, Ind.	12/12/1962	Ray Brown, S.F.
C	02/01/1979	Kenyatta Walker, T.B.	08/08/1961	Bruce Matthews, Tenn.
DE	09/30/1979	Justin Smith, Cin.	06/18/1963	Bruce Smith, Wash.
DT	10/06/1979	Richard Seymour, N.E.	05/14/1967	Tony Siragusa, Balt.
LB	07/17/1980	Kendrell Bell, Pitt.	09/01/1965	Hardy Nickerson, Jax.
CB	12/12/1979	Nate Clements, Buff.	10/22/1965	Otis Smith, N.E.
S	03/14/1979	Deon Grant, Car.	03/10/1965	Rod Woodson, Balt.

OLDEST INDIVIDUAL SINGLE-SEASON OR SINGLE-GAME RECORDS IN NFL RECORD & FACT BOOK

Most Points, Game—40, Ernie Nevers, Chi. Cardinals vs. Chi. Bears, Nov. 28, 1929 (6-td, 4-pat)

Most Touchdowns Rushing, Game—6, Ernie Nevers, Chi. Cardinals vs. Chi. Bears, Nov. 28, 1929

Highest Punting Average, Season (Qualifiers)—51.40, Sammy Baugh, Washington, 1940 (35-1,799)

Highest Punting Average, Rookie, Season (Qualifiers)—45.92, Frank Sinkwich, Detroit, 1943 (12-551)

Highest Punting Average, Game (minimum: 4 punts)—61.75, Bob Cifers, Detroit vs. Chi. Bears, Nov. 24, 1946 (4-247)

Highest Average Gain, Pass Receptions, Season (minimum: 24 receptions)—32.58, Don Currivan, Boston, 1947 (24-782)

Highest Average Gain, Passing, Game (minimum: 20 passes)—18.58, Sammy Baugh, Washington vs. Boston, Oct. 31, 1948 (24-446)

Most Touchdowns, Fumble Recoveries, Game—2, Fred (Dippy) Evans, Chi. Bears vs. Washington, Nov. 28, 1948

Most Yards Gained, Intercepted Passes, Rookie, Season—301, Don Doll, Detroit, 1949

Most Passes Had Intercepted, Game—8, Jim Hardy, Chi. Cardinals vs. Philadelphia, Sept. 24, 1950

Highest Average Gain, Rushing, Game (minimum: 10 attempts)—17.09, Marion Motley, Cleveland vs. Pittsburgh, Oct. 29, 1950 (11-188)

Highest Kickoff Return Average, Game (minimum: 3 returns)—73.50, Wally Triplett, Detroit vs. Los Angeles, Oct. 29, 1950 (4-294)

Highest Punt Return Average, Season (Qualifiers)—23.00, Herb Rich, Baltimore, 1950 (12-276)

Highest Punt Return Average, Rookie, Season (Qualifiers)—23.00, Herb Rich, Baltimore, 1950 (12-276)

Most Yards Passing, Game—554, Norm Van Brocklin, Los Angeles vs. N.Y. Yanks, Sept. 28, 1951

Most Touchdowns, Punt Returns, Rookie, Season—4, Jack Christiansen, Detroit, 1951

Most Interceptions By, Season—14, Dick (Night Train) Lane, Los Angeles, 1952

Most Interceptions By, Rookie, Season—14, Dick (Night Train) Lane, Los Angeles, 1952

Highest Average Gain, Passing, Season (Qualifiers)—11.17, Tommy O'Connell, Cleveland, 1957 (110-1,229)

Most Points, Season—176, Paul Hornung, Green Bay, 1960 (15-td, 41-pat,15-fg)

Most Yards Gained, Pass Receptions, Rookie, Season—1,473, Bill Groman, Houston, 1960

EMMITT SMITH'S CAREER RUSHING VS. EACH OPPONENT

Opponent	Games	Rushes	Yards	Yards Per Rush	Yards Per Game	TD
Arizona	24	512	2,204	4.3	91.8	25
Atlanta	7	143	695	4.9	99.3	9
Baltimore	1	11	48	4.4	48.0	0
Buffalo	1	15	25	1.7	25.0	1
Carolina	3	47	247	5.3	82.3	2
Chicago	4	67	322	4.8	80.5	1
Cincinnati	4	73	238	3.3	59.5	1
Cleveland	2	58	224	3.9	112.0	1
Denver	4	81	278	3.4	69.5	3
Detroit	4	82	353	4.3	88.3	5
Green Bay	6	139	567	4.1	94.5	6
Indianapolis	3	73	298	4.1	99.3	4
Jacksonville	2	48	177	3.7	88.5	1
Kansas City	3	56	193	3.4	64.3	2
Miami	3	69	228	3.3	76.0	0
Minnesota	5	82	538	6.6	107.6	8
New England	2	46	160	3.5	80.0	0
New Orleans	5	104	387	3.7	77.4	3
N.Y. Giants	22	441	1,858	4.2	84.5	18
N.Y. Jets	3	54	256	4.7	85.3	0
Oakland	4	95	346	3.6	86.5	7
Philadelphia	24	514	2,384	4.6	99.3	13
Pittsburgh	3	89	349	3.9	116.3	2
St. Louis	2	40	134	3.4	67.0	1
San Diego	3	41	155	3.8	51.7	2
San Francisco	8	147	579	3.9	72.4	5
Seattle	3	51	191	3.7	63.7	2
Tampa Bay	4	72	289	4.0	72.3	2
Tennessee	4	61	181	3.0	45.3	1
Washington	22	487	2,283	4.7	103.8	23
Totals	185	3,798	16,187	4.3	87.5	148

Arizona totals include eight games vs. Phoenix
Oakland totals include one game vs. L.A. Raiders
St. Louis totals include two games vs. L.A. Rams
Tennessee totals include two games vs. Houston

JEROME BETTIS' CAREER RUSHING VS. EACH OPPONENT

Opponent	Games	Rushes	Yards	Yards Per Rush	Yards Per Game	TD
Arizona	3	73	309	4.2	103.0	4
Atlanta	8	160	686	4.3	85.8	2
Baltimore	10	199	762	3.8	76.2	2
Buffalo	4	56	274	4.9	68.5	3
Carolina	4	81	305	3.8	76.3	3
Chicago	4	90	358	4.0	89.5	2
Cincinnati	12	287	1,278	4.5	106.5	8
Cleveland	6	146	645	4.4	107.5	3
Dallas	1	15	63	4.2	63.0	0
Denver	2	57	216	3.8	108.0	1
Detroit	2	49	180	3.7	90.0	0
Green Bay	4	68	193	2.8	48.3	0
Indianapolis	2	41	195	4.8	97.5	1
Jacksonville	12	241	854	3.5	71.2	3
Kansas City	6	150	632	4.2	105.3	1
Miami	3	46	188	4.1	62.7	0
Minnesota	1	19	81	4.3	81.0	1
New England	2	40	128	3.2	64.0	0
New Orleans	5	103	513	5.0	102.6	1
N.Y. Giants	3	56	160	2.9	53.3	0
N.Y. Jets	2	33	119	3.6	59.5	1
Oakland	2	34	141	4.1	70.5	0
Philadelphia	3	60	241	4.0	80.3	1
Pittsburgh	1	16	76	4.8	76.0	1
St. Louis	1	19	129	6.8	129.0	2
San Diego	3	52	160	3.1	53.3	0
San Francisco	8	116	454	3.9	56.8	5
Seattle	2	39	177	4.5	88.5	0

RICKY WATTERS' CAREER RUSHING VS. EACH OPPONENT

Opponent	Games	Rushes	Yards	Yards Per Rush	Yards Per Game	TD
Tampa Bay	3	47	229	4.9	76.3	1
Tennessee	12	202	737	3.6	61.4	5
Washington	5	91	393	4.3	78.6	2
Totals	136	2,686	10,876	4.0	80.0	53

Arizona totals include one game vs. Phoenix
Oakland totals include one game vs. L.A. Raiders
Tennessee totals include three games vs. Houston

Opponent	Games	Rushes	Yards	Yards Per Rush	Yards Per Game	TD
Arizona	9	195	723	3.7	80.3	6
Atlanta	8	141	663	4.7	82.9	8
Baltimore	1	11	37	3.4	37.0	0
Buffalo	4	74	276	3.7	69.0	1
Carolina	2	31	96	3.1	48.0	1
Chicago	2	35	112	3.2	56.0	0
Cincinnati	3	64	309	4.8	103.0	5
Cleveland	2	29	180	6.2	90.0	0
Dallas	10	205	837	4.1	83.7	5
Denver	9	132	487	3.7	54.1	6
Detroit	4	59	231	3.9	57.8	2
Green Bay	3	64	244	3.8	81.3	1
Indianapolis	3	47	235	5.0	78.3	1
Jacksonville	2	39	124	3.2	62.0	1
Kansas City	7	139	580	4.2	82.9	4
Miami	2	36	232	6.4	116.0	1
Minnesota	3	29	82	2.8	27.3	1
New England	1	19	104	5.5	104.0	1
New Orleans	8	169	780	4.6	97.5	1
N.Y. Giants	7	149	640	4.3	91.4	5
N.Y. Jets	4	61	244	4.0	61.0	2
Oakland	9	164	649	4.0	72.1	3
Philadelphia	5	56	244	4.4	48.8	1
Pittsburgh	4	80	239	3.0	59.8	0
St. Louis	8	150	583	3.9	72.9	7
San Diego	8	153	481	3.1	60.1	3
San Francisco	1	14	42	3.0	42.0	0
Seattle	1	21	69	3.3	69.0	2
Tampa Bay	5	74	305	4.1	61.0	3
Tennessee	1	14	63	4.5	63.0	0
Washington	8	168	752	4.5	94.0	7
Totals	144	2,622	10,643	4.1	73.9	78

Arizona totals include two games vs. Phoenix
Oakland totals include one game vs. L.A. Raiders
St. Louis totals include six games vs. L.A. Rams

MARSHALL FAULK'S CAREER RUSHING VS. EACH OPPONENT

Opponent	Games	Rushes	Yards	Yards Per Rush	Yards Per Game	TD
Arizona	1	12	46	3.8	46.0	0
Atlanta	7	131	886	6.8	126.6	4
Baltimore	3	55	290	5.3	96.7	2
Buffalo	10	194	690	3.6	69.0	5
Carolina	7	136	795	5.8	113.6	5
Chicago	1	10	54	5.4	54.0	0
Cincinnati	6	103	350	3.4	58.3	3
Cleveland	2	38	194	5.1	97.0	2
Denver	1	14	78	5.6	78.0	1
Detroit	3	37	124	3.4	41.3	1
Green Bay	1	17	116	6.8	116.0	0
Indianapolis	1	25	118	4.7	118.0	3
Jacksonville	1	22	54	2.5	54.0	1
Kansas City	2	37	138	3.7	69.0	1
Miami	10	181	676	3.7	67.6	4
Minnesota	2	48	237	4.9	118.5	6
New England	10	154	537	3.5	53.7	1
New Orleans	7	153	716	4.7	102.3	6
N.Y. Giants	2	24	93	3.9	46.5	0
N.Y. Jets	10	186	710	3.8	71.0	5

Oakland	1	14	41	2.9	41.0	2
Philadelphia	3	42	252	6.0	84.0	4
Pittsburgh	2	35	116	3.3	58.0	0
St. Louis	1	19	177	9.3	177.0	3
San Diego	5	69	201	2.9	40.2	1
San Francisco	8	152	706	4.6	88.3	7
Seattle	5	98	364	3.7	72.8	4
Tampa Bay	4	66	278	4.2	69.5	4
Tennessee	2	39	233	6.0	116.5	3
Washington	3	44	172	3.9	57.3	1
Totals	121	2,155	9,442	4.4	78.0	79

Tennessee totals include one game vs. Houston

CURTIS MARTIN'S CAREER RUSHING VS. EACH OPPONENT

Opponent	Games	Rushes	Yards	Yards Per Rush	Yards Per Game	TD
Arizona	2	65	223	3.4	111.5	1
Atlanta	2	39	145	3.7	72.5	2
Baltimore	3	61	157	2.6	52.3	0
Buffalo	14	326	1,200	3.7	85.7	8
Carolina	3	72	354	4.9	118.0	4
Chicago	2	31	108	3.5	54.0	1
Cincinnati	1	24	78	3.3	78.0	0
Cleveland	1	19	102	5.4	102.0	1
Dallas	2	46	204	4.4	102.0	0
Denver	5	73	253	3.5	50.6	3
Detroit	1	16	52	3.3	52.0	1
Green Bay	2	48	175	3.6	87.5	1
Indianapolis	14	332	1,540	4.6	110.0	7
Jacksonville	2	42	154	3.7	77.0	1
Kansas City	3	63	186	3.0	62.0	3
Miami	13	266	969	3.6	74.5	9
Minnesota	1	21	104	5.0	104.0	0
New England	8	196	833	4.3	104.1	5
New Orleans	2	52	178	3.4	89.0	2
N.Y. Giants	2	14	13	0.9	6.5	0
N.Y. Jets	6	163	737	4.5	122.8	7
Oakland	3	59	184	3.1	61.3	0
Pittsburgh	3	53	237	4.5	79.0	0
St. Louis	1	14	63	4.5	63.0	0
San Diego	2	41	138	3.4	69.0	0
San Francisco	3	66	197	3.0	65.7	2
Seattle	2	51	195	3.8	97.5	2
Tampa Bay	2	26	116	4.5	58.0	0
Tennessee	1	27	123	4.6	123.0	1
Washington	2	37	249	6.7	124.5	3
Totals	108	2,343	9,267	4.0	85.8	64

JERRY RICE'S CAREER RECEIVING VS. EACH OPPONENT

Opponent	Games	Rec.	Yards	Yards/ Rec.	Yards/ Game	TD
Arizona	8	42	656	15.6	82.0	8
Atlanta	29	175	2,731	15.6	94.2	25
Baltimore	1	6	58	9.7	58.0	1
Buffalo	4	14	158	11.3	39.5	1
Carolina	10	58	783	13.5	78.3	4
Chicago	6	31	500	16.1	83.3	7
Cincinnati	5	32	508	15.9	101.6	4
Cleveland	3	19	275	14.5	91.7	4
Dallas	9	54	795	14.7	88.3	7
Denver	7	37	522	14.1	74.6	2
Detroit	9	42	559	13.3	62.1	2
Green Bay	8	47	716	15.2	89.5	7
Indianapolis	5	26	458	17.6	91.6	5
Jacksonville	1	2	17	8.5	17.0	0
Kansas City	6	30	353	11.8	58.8	3
Miami	4	19	311	16.4	77.8	5
Minnesota	10	55	919	16.7	91.9	10
New England	5	24	409	17.0	81.8	6
New Orleans	30	147	2,025	13.8	67.5	14

N.Y. Giants	9	40	615	15.4	68.3	5
N.Y. Jets	5	24	409	17.0	81.8	3
Oakland	5	23	408	17.7	81.6	3
Philadelphia	7	33	524	15.9	74.9	5
Pittsburgh	5	29	280	9.7	56.0	4
St. Louis	30	158	2,409	15.2	80.3	20
San Diego	6	44	730	16.6	121.7	10
Seattle	5	25	448	17.9	89.6	6
Tampa Bay	8	47	710	15.1	88.8	10
Tennessee	6	40	414	10.4	69.0	2
Washington	8	41	686	16.7	85.8	2
Totals	254	1,364	20,386	14.9	80.3	185

Arizona totals include one game vs. St. Louis, four games vs. Phoenix
Oakland totals include four games vs. L.A. Raiders
St. Louis totals include 20 games vs. L.A. Rams
Tennessee totals include four games vs. Houston

TIM BROWN'S CAREER RECEIVING VS. EACH OPPONENT

Opponent	Games	Rec.	Yards	Yards/ Rec.	Yards/ Game	TD
Arizona	2	7	76	10.9	38.0	2
Atlanta	5	24	393	16.4	78.6	3
Baltimore	2	9	99	11.0	49.5	2
Buffalo	7	24	536	22.3	76.6	5
Carolina	2	13	181	13.9	90.5	1
Chicago	4	17	192	11.3	48.0	2
Cincinnati	7	24	434	18.1	62.0	6
Cleveland	3	5	83	16.6	27.7	0
Dallas	4	25	338	13.5	84.5	1
Denver	26	128	1,669	13.0	64.2	13
Detroit	2	6	48	8.0	24.0	1
Green Bay	3	13	161	12.4	53.7	0
Indianapolis	4	20	329	16.5	82.3	0
Jacksonville	2	19	224	11.8	112.0	1
Kansas City	25	122	1,754	14.4	70.2	6
Miami	9	46	583	12.7	64.8	5
Minnesota	4	16	175	10.9	43.8	1
New England	1	2	46	23.0	46.0	0
New Orleans	5	20	268	13.4	53.6	3
N.Y. Giants	4	17	371	21.8	92.8	4
N.Y. Jets	7	48	708	14.8	101.1	5
Philadelphia	3	12	158	13.2	52.7	1
Pittsburgh	4	16	181	11.3	45.3	0
St. Louis	4	11	203	18.5	50.8	1
San Diego	27	115	1,474	12.8	54.6	8
San Francisco	4	17	284	16.7	71.0	3
Seattle	26	103	1,591	15.4	61.2	13
Tampa Bay	3	13	180	13.8	60.0	1
Tennessee	6	26	322	12.4	53.7	5
Washington	3	19	176	9.3	58.7	2
Totals	208	937	13,237	14.1	63.6	95

St. Louis totals include three games vs. L.A. Rams
Tennessee totals include three games vs. Houston

SHANNON SHARPE'S CAREER RECEIVING VS. EACH OPPONENT

Opponent	Games	Rec.	Yards	Yards/Rec.	Yards/Game	TD
Arizona	3	11	138	12.5	46.0	1
Atlanta	2	10	163	16.3	81.5	1
Baltimore	1	9	161	17.9	161.0	0
Buffalo	5	25	414	16.6	82.8	1
Carolina	1	8	174	21.8	174.0	0
Chicago	4	11	146	13.3	36.5	1
Cincinnati	9	39	407	10.4	45.2	4
Cleveland	9	40	499	12.5	55.4	1
Dallas	4	19	281	14.8	70.3	3
Denver	1	5	50	10.0	50.0	0
Detroit	1	1	33	33.0	33.0	0
Green Bay	4	16	130	8.1	32.5	0
Indianapolis	3	7	91	13.0	30.3	1
Jacksonville	6	23	293	12.7	48.8	3
Kansas City	18	86	1,028	12.0	57.1	10
Miami	3	16	139	8.7	46.3	0
Minnesota	5	14	248	17.7	49.6	0
New England	6	14	155	11.1	25.8	2
New Orleans	1	5	39	7.8	39.0	1
N.Y. Giants	2	8	59	7.4	29.5	0
N.Y. Jets	5	22	275	12.5	55.0	1
Oakland	18	55	706	12.8	39.2	4
Philadelphia	3	15	91	6.1	30.3	1
Pittsburgh	8	17	226	13.3	28.3	1
St. Louis	2	9	89	9.9	44.5	0
San Diego	18	72	1,037	14.4	57.6	9
San Francisco	2	12	134	11.2	67.0	0
Seattle	17	51	661	13.0	38.9	6
Tampa Bay	4	20	172	8.6	43.0	0
Tennessee	7	32	373	11.7	53.3	0
Washington	4	20	192	9.6	48.0	0
Totals	176	692	8,604	12.4	48.9	51

Arizona totals includes one game vs. Phoenix
Oakland totals includes 10 games vs. L.A. Raiders
St. Louis totals includes one game vs. L.A. Rams
Tennessee totals includes three games vs. Houston

GARY ANDERSON'S CAREER KICKING VS. EACH OPPONENT

Opponent	Games	FG	FGA	FG%	Long FG	XP	XPA	Pts.
Arizona	8	14	19	73.7	44	22	22	64
Atlanta	7	8	10	80.0	39	26	26	50
Baltimore	2	7	7	100.0	46	2	2	23
Buffalo	10	17	20	85.0	49	21	21	72
Carolina	5	7	9	77.8	48	14	15	35
Chicago	12	19	23	82.6	50	25	25	82
Cincinnati	26	39	48	81.3	52	60	60	177
Cleveland	26	35	52	67.3	49	47	47	152
Dallas	13	22	28	78.6	49	27	27	93
Denver	11	19	23	82.6	42	24	24	81
Detroit	13	19	26	73.1	44	35	35	92
Green Bay	12	18	23	78.3	48	27	28	81
Indianapolis	8	11	13	84.6	53	22	22	55
Jacksonville	2	4	4	100.0	53	5	5	17
Kansas City	10	23	29	79.3	49	24	24	93
Miami	10	16	21	76.2	49	24	24	72
Minnesota	5	3	7	42.9	44	10	10	19
New England	8	10	10	100.0	49	20	20	50
New Orleans	9	20	22	90.9	51	19	19	79
N.Y. Giants	9	10	12	83.3	46	22	22	52
N.Y. Jets	8	13	19	68.4	45	24	24	63
Oakland	5	5	12	41.7	37	8	8	23
Philadelphia	5	6	8	75.0	52	11	11	29
Pittsburgh	1	1	2	50.0	25	1	1	4
St. Louis	8	9	11	81.8	46	22	22	49
San Diego	14	25	27	92.6	55	41	42	116
San Francisco	5	8	11	72.7	50	12	12	36
Seattle	10	13	15	86.7	43	10	10	49
Tampa Bay	12	16	20	80.0	44	24	24	72
Tennessee	27	47	52	90.4	54	56	58	197
Washington	8	12	13	92.3	49	20	21	56
Totals	309	476	596	79.9	55	705	711	2,133

Arizona totals include one game vs. St. Louis, one game vs. Phoenix
Indianapolis totals include one game vs. Baltimore
Oakland totals include three games vs. L.A. Raiders
Tennessee totals include 25 games vs. Houston
St. Louis totals include three games vs. L.A. Rams

MORTEN ANDERSEN'S CAREER KICKING VS. EACH OPPONENT

Opponent	Games	FG	FGA	FG%	Long FG	XP	XPA	Pts.
Arizona	14	23	24	95.8	52	36	37	105
Atlanta	25	40	51	78.4	49	56	58	176
Baltimore	1	2	3	66.7	41	1	1	7
Buffalo	4	7	11	63.6	50	7	7	28
Carolina	12	22	28	78.6	51	23	23	89
Chicago	6	5	8	62.5	60	14	14	29
Cincinnati	5	5	8	62.5	49	17	17	32
Cleveland	4	7	8	87.5	53	7	7	28
Dallas	13	22	30	73.3	54	22	22	88
Denver	6	4	8	50.0	55	18	20	30
Detroit	10	11	17	64.7	50	19	19	52
Green Bay	7	11	12	91.7	52	17	17	50
Indianapolis	3	3	5	60.0	46	11	11	20
Jacksonville	2	1	2	50.0	44	3	3	6
Kansas City	6	11	12	91.7	50	10	10	43
Miami	5	5	7	71.4	35	15	15	30
Minnesota	11	18	23	78.3	51	18	18	72
New England	6	10	12	83.3	54	16	16	46
New Orleans	13	22	28	78.6	55	31	31	97
N.Y. Giants	9	17	20	85.0	45	15	15	66
N.Y. Jets	6	10	11	90.9	53	12	12	42
Oakland	7	8	10	80.0	51	14	14	38
Philadelphia	13	24	29	82.8	56	21	21	93
Pittsburgh	6	7	10	70.0	50	10	10	31
St. Louis	36	53	62	85.5	51	87	89	246
San Diego	4	3	7	42.9	35	9	9	18
San Francisco	37	60	72	83.3	59	59	61	239
Seattle	6	9	10	90.0	47	12	12	39
Tampa Bay	16	24	32	75.0	50	35	35	107
Tennessee	6	9	13	69.2	47	13	13	40
Washington	9	11	17	64.7	50	16	16	49
Totals	308	464	590	78.6	60	644	653	2,036

Arizona totals include five games vs. St. Louis, four games vs. Phoenix
Oakland totals include four games vs. L.A. Raiders
St. Louis totals include 23 games vs. L.A. Rams
Tennessee totals include five games vs. Houston

BRETT FAVRE'S CAREER PASSING VS. EACH OPPONENT

Opponent	Games	Att.	Cmp.	Pct.	Yards	Avg. Gain	TD	Int.	Sacked
Arizona	2	65	38	58.5	588	9.05	3	1	3/21
Atlanta	3	116	78	67.2	859	7.41	5	5	6/45
Baltimore	2	75	49	65.3	597	7.96	5	2	3/14
Buffalo	3	93	59	63.4	639	6.87	7	1	5/44
Carolina	5	207	127	61.4	1,521	7.35	14	10	10/73
Chicago	20	632	399	63.1	4,719	7.47	39	20	34/213
Cincinnati	3	117	76	65.0	902	7.71	6	2	9/68
Cleveland	3	89	61	68.5	572	6.43	6	0	4/22
Dallas	6	240	138	57.5	1,383	5.76	11	4	12/91
Denver	3	93	47	50.5	635	6.83	5	8	2/12
Detroit	20	702	437	62.3	5,308	7.56	34	26	39/246
Indianapolis	2	61	41	67.2	664	10.89	5	3	5/43
Jacksonville	2	72	44	61.1	564	7.83	5	1	3/19
Kansas City	2	83	47	56.6	527	6.35	3	4	8/50
Miami	3	122	76	62.3	809	6.63	4	2	7/28
Minnesota	19	606	364	60.1	3,957	6.53	28	19	42/278
New England	2	81	48	59.3	533	6.58	4	2	5/42
New Orleans	2	62	39	62.9	458	7.39	5	0	8/39
N.Y. Giants	4	132	77	58.3	1,002	7.59	6	3	7/44
N.Y. Jets	2	62	34	54.8	335	5.40	3	1	2/14
Oakland	2	75	42	56.0	523	6.97	5	3	5/24
Philadelphia	7	240	133	55.4	1,716	7.15	10	12	16/93
Pittsburgh	3	90	59	65.6	745	8.28	4	1	7/44
St. Louis	7	219	130	59.4	1,471	6.72	10	10	15/124
San Diego	3	78	47	60.3	550	7.05	6	3	5/56
San Francisco	4	151	87	57.6	1,176	7.79	7	5	7/49
Seattle	2	69	34	49.3	389	5.64	5	4	5/28
Tampa Bay	20	684	427	62.4	4,642	6.79	33	15	39/210
Tennessee	3	90	53	58.9	607	6.74	6	2	7/18
Washington	2	36	20	55.6	236	6.56	3	3	2/21
Totals	161	5,442	3,311	60.8	38,627	7.10	287	172	322/2,073

Oakland totals include one game vs. L.A. Raiders
St. Louis totals include four games vs. L.A. Rams
Tennessee totals include one game vs. Houston

VINNY TESTAVERDE'S CAREER PASSING VS. EACH OPPONENT

Opponent	Games	Att.	Cmp.	Pct.	Yards	Avg. Gain	TD	Int.	Sacked
Arizona	7	238	127	53.4	1,487	6.25	9	7	23/179
Atlanta	5	121	62	51.2	939	7.76	4	7	11/73
Baltimore	1	69	36	52.2	481	6.97	2	3	1/8
Buffalo	9	259	147	56.8	1,751	6.76	10	6	9/65
Carolina	3	92	57	62.0	676	7.35	3	5	6/29
Chicago	11	316	155	49.1	1,951	6.17	12	17	27/212
Cincinnati	9	283	161	56.9	1,911	6.75	17	13	6/46
Cleveland	1	50	27	54.0	370	7.40	2	4	2/21
Dallas	3	78	49	62.8	583	7.47	3	3	10/89
Denver	3	101	54	53.5	705	6.98	5	3	4/29
Detroit	12	268	152	56.7	1,835	6.85	10	14	16/154
Green Bay	11	348	206	59.2	2,719	7.81	12	15	29/205
Indianapolis	13	425	228	53.6	3,192	7.51	23	17	23/206
Jacksonville	6	214	131	61.2	1,666	7.79	9	8	13/67
Kansas City	4	109	62	56.9	672	6.17	4	2	2/15
Miami	9	291	170	58.4	1,751	6.02	12	8	12/78
Minnesota	10	247	119	48.2	1,483	6.00	8	13	20/153
New England	11	318	194	61.0	2,347	7.38	20	10	22/117
New Orleans	7	187	95	50.8	1,359	7.27	7	8	16/110
N.Y. Giants	3	100	58	58.0	583	5.83	3	5	9/56
N.Y. Jets	4	137	77	56.2	946	6.91	3	4	5/54
Oakland	4	109	61	56.0	792	7.27	2	5	9/72
Philadelphia	3	95	45	47.4	516	5.43	3	8	6/44
Pittsburgh	11	310	170	54.8	2,024	6.53	12	15	17/97
St. Louis	7	151	95	62.9	1,152	7.63	10	7	12/83
San Diego	3	112	65	58.0	718	6.41	3	3	10/60
San Francisco	4	100	46	46.0	646	6.46	3	2	7/65
Seattle	2	84	58	69.0	646	7.69	4	2	0/0
Tampa Bay	2	69	39	56.5	437	6.33	3	3	1/3
Tennessee	9	304	182	59.9	2,268	7.46	19	11	15/138
Washington	2	59	29	49.2	453	7.68	4	2	4/24
Totals	189	5,644	3,157	55.9	39,059	6.92	241	230	347/2,552

Arizona totals include one game vs. St. Louis, four games vs. Phoenix
Oakland totals include one game vs. L.A. Raiders
St. Louis totals include four games vs. L.A. Rams
Tennessee totals include seven games vs. Houston

HIGHEST NFL POSTSEASON PASSER RATINGS (MINIMUM: 150 ATTEMPTS)

Player	Games	Att.	Cmp.	Pct.	Yards	Avg. Gain	TD	Int.	Rating
Bart Starr	10	213	130	61.0	1,753	8.23	15	3	104.8
Joe Montana	23	734	460	62.7	5,772	7.86	45	21	95.6
Ken Anderson	6	166	110	66.3	1,321	7.96	9	6	93.5
Kurt Warner	7	268	169	63.1	2,221	8.29	15	10	92.3
Joe Theismann	10	211	128	60.7	1,782	8.45	11	7	91.4
Troy Aikman	16	502	320	63.7	3,849	7.67	23	17	88.3
Brett Favre	16	522	318	60.9	3,940	7.55	29	19	87.7
Steve Young	22	471	292	62.0	3,326	7.06	20	13	85.8
Warren Moon	10	403	259	64.3	2,870	7.12	17	14	84.9
Ken Stabler	13	351	203	57.8	2,641	7.52	19	13	84.2

HIGHEST NFL POSTSEASON PASSER RATINGS, ACTIVE PLAYERS (MINIMUM: 150 ATTEMPTS)

Player	Games	Att.	Cmp.	Pct.	Yards	Avg. Gain	TD	Int.	Rating
Kurt Warner	7	268	169	63.1	2,221	8.29	15	10	92.3
Brett Favre	16	522	318	60.9	3,940	7.55	29	19	87.7
Vinny Testaverde	5	189	114	60.3	1,320	6.98	6	5	81.0
Donovan McNabb	5	169	104	61.5	969	5.73	8	5	80.7
Neil O'Donnell	8	274	159	58.1	1,709	6.24	9	8	75.2
Randall Cunningham	12	365	192	52.6	2,426	6.65	12	9	74.3
Mark Rypien	8	234	126	53.9	1,776	7.59	8	10	72.2
Jim Harbaugh	5	163	83	51.0	906	5.56	6	5	67.2
Kerry Collins	5	156	86	55.1	933	5.98	8	9	66.0
Mark Brunell	9	255	127	49.8	1,550	6.08	10	10	65.6

STARTING RECORDS OF ACTIVE NFL QUARTERBACKS

Minimum: 10 starts

	W - L - T	Pct.
Kurt Warner	35- 8-0	.814
Tom Brady	11- 3-0	.786
Jay Fiedler	22-10-0	.688
Jim Miller	13- 6-0	.684
Shaun King	14- 7-0	.667
Brett Favre	103-54-0	.656
Donovan McNabb	24-14-0	.632
Brad Johnson	41-25-0	.621
Kordell Stewart	43-27-0	.614
Randall Cunningham	82-52-1	.611
Steve McNair	48-31-0	.608
Mark Rypien	47-31-0	.603
Doug Flutie	35-25-0	.583
Mark Brunell	57-42-0	.576
Rich Gannon	61-45-0	.575
Elvis Grbac	40-30-0	.571
Trent Dilfer	49-39-0	.557
Daunte Culpepper	15-12-0	.556
Neil O'Donnell	54-45-0	.545
Shane Matthews	8- 7-0	.533
Rodney Peete	37-35-0	.514
Drew Bledsoe	63-60-0	.512
Kerry Collins	45-43-0	.511
Brian Griese	19-19-0	.500
Jon Kitna	24-24-0	.500
Peyton Manning	32-32-0	.500
Aaron Brooks	10-11-0	.476
Jeff Garcia	20-22-0	.476
Steve Beuerlein	45-52-0	.464
Chris Chandler	62-75-0	.453
Scott Mitchell	32-39-0	.451
Kent Graham	17-21-0	.447
Vinny Testaverde	79-98-1	.447
Tony Banks	33-42-0	.440
Ty Detmer	11-14-0	.440
Dave Brown	26-34-0	.433
Gus Frerotte	25-33-1	.432
Matt Hasselbeck	5- 7-0	.417
Jeff Blake	32-45-0	.416
Charlie Batch	19-27-0	.413
Todd Collins	7-10-0	.412
Trent Green	14-21-0	.400
Jake Plummer	25-41-0	.379
Rob Johnson	10-17-0	.370
Rick Mirer	22-38-0	.367
Tom Tupa	4- 9-0	.308
Paul Justin	3- 7-0	.300
Tim Couch	11-26-0	.297
Alex Van Pelt	3- 8-0	.273
Bobby Hoying	3- 9-1	.269
Cade McNown	3-12-0	.200
Ryan Leaf	4-17-0	.190
Akili Smith	3-13-0	.188
Doug Pederson	3-14-0	.176
Chris Weinke	1-14-0	.067

ALL-TIME RANKINGS OF PLAYERS IN FOUR CATEGORIES THAT DETERMINE NFL PASSER RATING

Minimum: 1,500 Attempts

COMPLETION PERCENTAGE	Pct.	Att.	Comp.
Steve Young	64.28	4,149	2,667
Joe Montana	63.24	5,391	3,409
Brad Johnson	61.60	2,380	1,466
Troy Aikman	61.46	4,715	2,898
Peyton Manning	60.96	2,226	1,357
Brett Favre	60.84	5,442	3,311
Mark Brunell	60.32	3,145	1,897
Jim Kelly	60.14	4,779	2,874
Ken Stabler	59.85	3,793	2,270
Danny White	59.69	2,950	1,761

AVERAGE YARDS PER PASS	Avg.	Att.	Yards
Otto Graham	8.63	1,565	13,499
Sid Luckman	8.42	1,744	14,686
Norm Van Brocklin	8.16	2,895	23,611
Steve Young	7.98	4,149	33,124
Ed Brown	7.85	1,987	15,600
Bart Starr	7.85	3,149	24,718
Johnny Unitas	7.76	5,186	40,239
Earl Morrall	7.74	2,689	20,809
Dan Fouts	7.68	5,604	43,040
Len Dawson	7.67	3,741	28,711

TOUCHDOWN PERCENTAGE	Pct.	Att.	TD
Sid Luckman	7.86	1,744	137
Frank Ryan	6.99	2,133	149
Len Dawson	6.39	3,741	239
Daryle Lamonica	6.31	2,601	164
Sammy Baugh	6.24	2,995	187
Charley Conerly	6.11	2,833	173
Bob Waterfield	6.00	1,617	97
Earl Morrall	5.99	2,689	161
Sonny Jurgensen	5.98	4,262	255
Norm Van Brocklin	5.98	2,895	173

INTERCEPTION PERCENTAGE	Pct.	Att.	Int.
Neil O'Donnell	2.10	3,197	67
Steve Bono	2.47	1,701	42
Mark Brunell	2.51	3,145	79
Joe Montana	2.58	5,391	139
Steve Young	2.58	4,149	107
Bernie Kosar	2.59	3,365	87
Steve McNair	2.67	2,288	61
Rich Gannon	2.67	3,295	88
Ken O'Brien	2.72	3,602	98
Jeff Blake	2.84	2,533	72

NFL INDIVIDUAL LEADERS OVER RECENT SEASONS

Last 2 Seasons		Last 3 Seasons		Last 4 Seasons	
Points					
288	Marshall Faulk	391	Mike Vanderjagt	495	Mike Vanderjagt
250	Matt Stover	366	Matt Stover	476	Ryan Longwell
246	Mike Vanderjagt	362	Marshall Faulk	470	Jason Elam
236	David Akers	357	Olindo Mare	456	Olindo Mare
235	Ryan Longwell	348	Ryan Longwell	453	Two tied
Touchdowns					
47	Marshall Faulk	59	Marshall Faulk	69	Marshall Faulk
29	Marvin Harrison	41	Marvin Harrison	54	Randy Moss
29	Terrell Owens	38	Edgerrin James	48	Marvin Harrison
25	Randy Moss	37	Randy Moss	48	Terrell Owens
24	Two tied	34	Eddie George	40	Three tied
Field Goals					
65	Matt Stover	93	Matt Stover	114	Matt Stover
55	David Akers	87	Mike Vanderjagt	114	Mike Vanderjagt
55	Kris Brown	86	Olindo Mare	108	Olindo Mare
54	Joe Nedney	80	Kris Brown	108	Adam Vinatieri
53	Two tied	78	Three tied	107	Ryan Longwell
Rushes					
718	Eddie George	1,038	Eddie George	1,386	Eddie George
688	Stephen Davis	1,016	Curtis Martin	1,385	Curtis Martin
655	Corey Dillon	978	Stephen Davis	1,203	Emmitt Smith
649	Curtis Martin	918	Corey Dillon	1,195	Jerome Bettis
622	Lamar Smith	907	Edgerrin James	1,180	Corey Dillon
Rushing Yards					
2,750	Stephen Davis	4,181	Curtis Martin	5,468	Curtis Martin
2,750	Corey Dillon	4,155	Stephen Davis	5,441	Marshall Faulk
2,741	Marshall Faulk	4,122	Marshall Faulk	5,080	Corey Dillon
2,717	Curtis Martin	3,950	Corey Dillon	5,046	Eddie George
2,562	Ahman Green	3,924	Edgerrin James	4,953	Emmitt Smith
Rushing Touchdowns					
30	Marshall Faulk	37	Marshall Faulk	43	Marshall Faulk
20	Lamar Smith	33	Stephen Davis	36	Emmitt Smith
19	Four tied	29	Edgerrin James	33	Stephen Davis
		28	Eddie George	33	Eddie George
		24	Two tied	32	Two tied
Passes					
1,118	Peyton Manning	1,685	Brett Favre	2,236	Brett Favre
1,097	Kerry Collins	1,651	Peyton Manning	2,226	Peyton Manning
1,090	Brett Favre	1,537	Rich Gannon	1,928	Jake Plummer
1,065	Jeff Garcia	1,513	Elvis Grbac	1,891	Rich Gannon
1,062	Donovan McNabb	1,494	Jon Kitna	1,781	Kerry Collins
Completions					
700	Peyton Manning	1,031	Peyton Manning	1,357	Peyton Manning
671	Jeff Garcia	993	Brett Favre	1,340	Brett Favre
652	Brett Favre	949	Rich Gannon	1,155	Rich Gannon
645	Rich Gannon	935	Kurt Warner	1,099	Jake Plummer
638	Kerry Collins	896	Jeff Garcia	1,067	Mark Brunell
Passing Yards					
8,544	Peyton Manning	12,679	Peyton Manning	16,418	Peyton Manning
8,259	Kurt Warner	12,612	Kurt Warner	16,036	Brett Favre
7,816	Jeff Garcia	11,824	Brett Favre	13,403	Rich Gannon
7,733	Brett Favre	11,098	Rich Gannon	12,651	Kurt Warner
7,374	Kerry Collins	10,591	Elvis Grbac	12,610	Mark Brunell

Last 2 Seasons		Last 3 Seasons		Last 4 Seasons	
Touchdown Passes					
63	Jeff Garcia	98	Kurt Warner	111	Peyton Manning
59	Peyton Manning	85	Peyton Manning	105	Brett Favre
57	Kurt Warner	79	Rich Gannon	98	Kurt Warner
55	Rich Gannon	74	Brett Favre	89	Rich Gannon
52	Brett Favre	74	Jeff Garcia	74	Jeff Garcia
Receptions					
213	Rod Smith	326	Marvin Harrison	397	Jimmy Smith
211	Marvin Harrison	319	Jimmy Smith	385	Marvin Harrison
203	Jimmy Smith	292	Rod Smith	378	Rod Smith
190	Terrell Owens	266	Keyshawn Johnson	349	Keyshawn Johnson
187	Keenan McCardell	265	Keenan McCardell	338	Tim Brown
Reception Yards					
2,998	Torry Holt	4,600	Marvin Harrison	5,404	Jimmy Smith
2,945	Rod Smith	4,222	Jimmy Smith	5,396	Randy Moss
2,937	Marvin Harrison	4,083	Randy Moss	5,376	Marvin Harrison
2,863	Terrell Owens	3,965	Rod Smith	5,187	Rod Smith
2,754	David Boston	3,786	Torry Holt	4,714	Terrell Owens
Receiving Touchdowns					
29	Marvin Harrison	41	Marvin Harrison	53	Randy Moss
29	Terrell Owens	36	Randy Moss	48	Marvin Harrison
25	Randy Moss	33	Terrell Owens	47	Terrell Owens
20	Tim Brown	28	Cris Carter	40	Cris Carter
19	Rod Smith	27	Isaac Bruce	35	Two tied
Interceptions					
15	Darren Sharper	20	Donnie Abraham	22	Ray Buchanan
13	Donnie Abraham	18	Darren Sharper	22	Sam Madison
12	Ronde Barber	16	Dexter McCleon	21	Donnie Abraham
12	Dexter McCleon	15	Four tied	20	Four tied
11	Two tied				
Sacks					
32.0	Michael Strahan	37.5	Michael Strahan	52.5	Michael Strahan
25.5	Jason Gildon	36.0	Jevon Kearse	45.5	Robert Porcher
25.0	La'Roi Glover	35.0	Simeon Rice	45.0	Jason Gildon
24.5	Hugh Douglas	35.0	Warren Sapp	45.0	Simeon Rice
23.5	Marcellus Wiley	34.0	Two tied	43.5	La'Roi Glover

NFL TEAM LEADERS OVER RECENT SEASONS

Highest Won-Lost Percentage					
.750	St. Louis	.771	St. Louis	.641	Miami
.688	Five tied	.688	Tennessee	.641	Minnesota
		.646	Miami	.641	St. Louis
		.625	Three tied	.641	Tennessee
				.625	Green Bay
Most Points					
1,043	St. Louis	1,569	St. Louis	1,854	St. Louis
878	Oakland	1,268	Oakland	1,642	Minnesota
842	Indianapolis	1,265	Indianapolis	1,640	Denver
825	Denver	1,139	Denver	1,575	Indianapolis
797	San Francisco	1,100	Green Bay	1,571	San Francisco
Most Total Yards					
13,765	St. Louis	20,177	St. Louis	24,649	St. Louis
12,096	Indianapolis	17,822	Indianapolis	23,909	San Francisco
11,729	San Francisco	17,109	San Francisco	23,203	Minnesota
11,371	Denver	16,939	Minnesota	22,938	Indianapolis
11,287	Kansas City	16,830	Oakland	22,746	Denver

Last 2 Seasons	Last 3 Seasons	Last 4 Seasons

Most Rushing Yards

5,022	Pittsburgh	7,013	Pittsburgh	9,047	Pittsburgh
4,188	Denver	6,208	Oakland	8,684	San Francisco
4,137	Dallas	6,188	Dallas	8,520	Denver
4,124	Oakland	6,140	San Francisco	8,202	Dallas
4,045	San Francisco	6,077	Cincinnati	7,935	Oakland

Most Passing Yards

9,895	St. Louis	14,248	St. Louis	17,335	St. Louis
8,271	Indianapolis	12,337	Indianapolis	15,967	Indianapolis
7,814	Kansas City	11,397	Minnesota	15,725	Minnesota
7,684	San Francisco	11,348	Green Bay	15,458	Green Bay
7,448	Green Bay	11,053	Kansas City	15,225	San Francisco

*Fewest Turnovers

38	San Francisco	67	Pittsburgh	94	Jacksonville
42	Pittsburgh	70	San Francisco	99	Pittsburgh
45	Oakland	74	Jacksonville	99	Tennessee
46	Tampa Bay	74	Oakland	100	Denver
52	Denver	80	Two tied	100	San Francisco

*Fewest Points Allowed

430	Baltimore	707	Baltimore	1,042	Baltimore
453	Philadelphia	784	Tampa Bay	1,079	Tampa Bay
467	Pittsburgh	787	Pittsburgh	1,090	Pittsburgh
516	Miami	810	Philadelphia	1,117	Miami
549	Tampa Bay	830	Jacksonville	1,154	Philadelphia

*Fewest Total Yards Allowed

8,413	Baltimore	12,635	Baltimore	17,932	Baltimore
8,850	Pittsburgh	13,648	Miami	18,078	Tampa Bay
9,244	Miami	13,733	Tampa Bay	18,083	Miami
9,320	Washington	13,734	Pittsburgh	18,454	Buffalo
9,328	Tennessee	13,763	Buffalo	18,697	Pittsburgh

*Fewest Rushing Yards Allowed

2,381	Baltimore	3,612	Baltimore	5,317	Baltimore
2,701	N.Y. Giants	4,247	San Diego	5,387	San Diego
2,821	Tennessee	4,260	St. Louis	5,981	Tennessee
2,888	Pittsburgh	4,261	N.Y. Giants	6,114	Denver
2,926	San Diego	4,371	Tennessee	6,265	N.Y. Giants

*Fewest Passing Yards Allowed

5,582	Dallas	8,657	Miami	11,581	Miami
5,598	Washington	8,701	Buffalo	11,738	Tampa Bay
5,729	Miami	8,888	Pittsburgh	11,899	Buffalo
5,854	Philadelphia	8,976	Tampa Bay	12,035	Philadelphia
5,931	N.Y. Jets	8,980	Dallas	12,209	Pittsburgh

Most Opponents' Turnovers

81	Denver	111	Tampa Bay	139	N.Y. Jets
80	Tampa Bay	110	Philadelphia	137	Denver
77	Baltimore	109	N.Y. Jets	137	Tampa Bay
74	Carolina	108	Baltimore	136	Carolina
74	N.Y. Jets	108	Green Bay	134	Seattle

Cleveland excluded from last four seasons' lists.

LONGEST WINNING STREAKS SINCE 1970

16	Miami, 1971-73	(1 in 1971, 14 in 1972, 1 in 1973)
16	Miami, 1983-84	(5 in 1983, 11 in 1984)
15	San Francisco, 1989-90	(5 in 1989, 10 in 1990)
14	Oakland, 1976-77	(10 in 1976, 4 in 1977)
14	Denver, 1997-98	(1 in 1997, 13 in 1998)
13	Minnesota, 1974-75	(3 in 1974, 10 in 1975)
13	Chicago, 1984-85	(1 in 1984, 12 in 1985)
13	N.Y. Giants, 1989-90	(3 in 1989, 10 in 1990)
12	Washington, 1990-91	(1 in 1990, 11 in 1991)
11	Pittsburgh, 1975	
11	Baltimore, 1975-76	(9 in 1975, 2 in 1976)
11	Chicago, 1986-87	(7 in 1986, 4 in 1987)
11	Houston, 1993	
11	San Francisco, 1997	
11	Jacksonville, 1999	
11	Indianapolis, 1999	
10	Miami, 1973	
10	Pittsburgh, 1976-77	(9 in 1976, 1 in 1977)
10	Denver, 1984	
10	San Francisco, 1994	
10	Minnesota, 1999-00	(3 in 1999, 7 in 2000)

NFL PLAYOFF APPEARANCES BY SEASONS

Team	Number of Seasons in Playoffs
Dallas	26
N.Y. Giants	25
St. Louis	25
Cleveland	23
Minnesota	23
Chicago	22
Miami	21
San Francisco	21
Green Bay	20
Oakland	20
Pittsburgh	20
Washington	20
Buffalo	17
Tennessee	17
Philadelphia	16
Indianapolis	15
Denver	14
Detroit	14
Kansas City	13
San Diego	12
New England	11
N.Y. Jets	9
Cincinnati	7
Tampa Bay	7
Arizona	6
Atlanta	6
New Orleans	5
Seattle	5
Jacksonville	4
Baltimore	2
Carolina	1

TEAMS IN SUPER BOWL CONTENTION (1978-2001)

	With 3 Weeks to Play	With 2 Weeks to Play	With 1 Week to Play
2001	23	16	13
2000	19	17	16
1999	23	20	16
1998	22	19	14
1997	22	18	14
1996	23	21	13
1995	*27	21	*18
1994	25	*22	15
1993	20	18	16
1992	20	16	14
1991	20	18	13
1990	23	20	15
1989	21	18	17
1988	21	18	15
1987	19	19	15
1986	19	17	14
1985	21	18	13
1984	18	14	13
1983	24	19	15
1982	20	17	16
1981	21	20	16
1980	20	14	12
1979	19	15	13
1978	20	17	12

RECORD OF TEAMS ON THE ROAD (1970-2001)

Year	W	L	T	Pct
1970	72	101	9	.420
1971	74	100	8	.429
1972	87	90	5	.492
1973	66	109	7	.382
1974	82	99	1	.453
1975	81	101	0	.445
1976	83	112	1	.426
1977	83	113	0	.423
1978	93	130	1	.417
1979	92	132	0	.411
1980	101	122	1	.453
1981	84	139	1	.377
1982	57	68	1	.456
1983	104	119	1	.467
1984	94	129	1	.422
1985	80	144	0	.357
1986	104	118	2	.469
1987	95	114	1	.455
1988	92	131	1	.413
1989	95	128	1	.426
1990	93	131	0	.415
1991	92	132	0	.411
1992	88	136	0	.393
1993	101	123	0	.451
1994	96	128	0	.429
1995	96	144	0	.400
1996	91	149	0	.379
1997	93	145	2	.392
1998	89	151	0	.371
1999	100	148	0	.403
2000	110	138	0	.444
2001	112	136	0	.452

GAMES DECIDED BY 7 POINTS OR LESS AND 3 POINTS OR LESS (1970-2001)

	Games Decided by 7 Points or Less	Games Decided by 3 Points or Less
1970	59 of 182 (32.4%)	34 of 182 (18.7%)
1971	76 of 182 (41.8%)	35 of 182 (19.2%)
1972	71 of 182 (39.0%)	38 of 182 (20.9%)
1973	60 of 182 (32.9%)	28 of 182 (15.4%)
1974	91 of 182 (50.0%)	37 of 182 (20.3%)
1975	62 of 182 (34.1%)	35 of 182 (19.2%)
1976	73 of 196 (37.2%)	38 of 196 (19.4%)
1977	85 of 196 (43.4%)	36 of 196 (18.4%)
1978	108 of 224 (48.2%)	49 of 224 (21.9%)
1979	104 of 224 (46.4%)	51 of 224 (22.8%)
1980	108 of 224 (48.2%)	58 of 224 (25.9%)
1981	91 of 224 (40.6%)	60 of 224 (26.8%)
1982	61 of 126 (48.4%)	33 of 126 (26.2%)
1983	106 of 224 (47.3%)	54 of 224 (24.1%)
1984	95 of 224 (42.4%)	58 of 224 (25.9%)
1985	87 of 224 (38.8%)	38 of 224 (17.0%)

1986	106 of 224 (47.3%)	48 of 224 (21.4%)
1987	99 of 210 (47.1%)	40 of 210 (19.0%)
1988	113 of 224 (50.4%)	62 of 224 (27.7%)
1989	107 of 224 (47.8%)	55 of 224 (24.6%)
1990	97 of 224 (43.3%)	54 of 224 (24.1%)
1991	112 of 224 (50.0%)	57 of 224 (25.4%)
1992	88 of 224 (39.3%)	48 of 224 (21.4%)
1993	*105 of 224 (46.9%)	53 of 224 (23.7%)
1994	115 of 224 (51.3%)	60 of 224 (26.8%)
1995	115 of 240 (47.9%)	61 of 240 (25.4%)
1996	109 of 240 (45.4%)	47 of 240 (19.6%)
1997	111 of 240 (46.3%)	67 of 240 (27.9%)
1998	113 of 240 (47.1%)	50 of 240 (20.8%)
1999	115 of 248 (46.4%)	**64 of 248 (25.8%)
2000	109 of 248 (44.0%)	61 of 248 (24.6%)
2001	121 of 248 (48.8%)	62 of 248 (25.0%)

*Week record: Dec. 11-13, 1993 (Week 15), 12 of 14 games (86%) decided by 7 points or less.
**Week record: Oct. 10-11, 1999 (Week 5), 10 of 14 games (71%) decided by 3 points or less.

2001 RECORDS OF TEAMS IN CLOSE GAMES

AFC	Overall Record	Decided by 8 Pts. or Less	Decided By 3 Pts. or Less
Baltimore	10-6	5-2	3-0
Buffalo	3-13	3-6	2-4
Cincinnati	6-10	4-3	2-2
Cleveland	7-9	2-4	1-2
Denver	8-8	2-3	1-1
Indianapolis	6-10	1-3	0-2
Jacksonville	6-10	3-6	0-3
Kansas City	6-10	4-6	2-4
Miami	11-5	6-2	2-0
New England	11-5	4-3	3-0
N.Y. Jets	10-6	8-3	4-2
Oakland	10-6	5-6	2-4
Pittsburgh	13-3	5-2	2-2
San Diego	5-11	1-8	1-5
Seattle	9-7	6-2	5-1
Tennessee	7-9	5-5	3-2

NFC	Overall Record	Decided by 8 Pts. or Less	Decided By 3 Pts. or Less
Arizona	7-9	6-4	3-1
Atlanta	7-9	6-3	3-1
Carolina	1-15	0-9	0-6
Chicago	13-3	8-1	2-0
Dallas	5-11	4-7	1-2
Detroit	2-14	2-9	1-5
Green Bay	12-4	5-3	2-1
Minnesota	5-11	2-4	0-1
New Orleans	7-9	3-4	2-1
N.Y. Giants	7-9	5-4	2-3
Philadelphia	11-5	3-2	2-2
St. Louis	14-2	5-2	2-1
San Francisco	12-4	6-3	4-0
Tampa Bay	9-7	6-6	3-3
Washington	8-8	3-3	2-1

SUPER BOWL CHAMPIONS THAT DID NOT MAKE PLAYOFFS THE FOLLOWING YEAR

Denver—Super Bowl XXXIII champions did not make playoffs in the 1999 season.

N.Y. Giants—Super Bowl XXV champions did not make playoffs in the 1991 season.

Washington—Super Bowl XXII champions did not make playoffs in the 1988 season.

N.Y. Giants—Super Bowl XXI champions did not make playoffs in the 1987 season.

San Francisco—Super Bowl XVI champions did not make playoffs in the 1982 season.

Oakland—Super Bowl XV champions did not make playoffs in the 1981 season.

Pittsburgh—Super Bowl XIV champions did not make playoffs in the 1980 season.

Kansas City—Super Bowl IV champions did not make playoffs in the 1970 season.

Green Bay—Super Bowl II champions did not make playoffs in the 1968 season.

NON-DIVISION WINNERS THAT PLAYED IN SUPER BOWL

2000	Baltimore Ravens	Super Bowl XXXV
	(Defeated N.Y. Giants, 34-7)	
1999	Tennessee Titans	Super Bowl XXXIV
	(Lost to St. Louis, 23-16)	
1997	Denver Broncos	Super Bowl XXXII
	(Defeated Green Bay, 31-24)	
1992	Buffalo Bills	Super Bowl XXVII
	(Lost to Dallas, 52-17)	
1985	New England Patriots	Super Bowl XX
	(Lost to Chicago, 46-10)	
1980	Oakland Raiders	Super Bowl XV
	(Defeated Philadelphia, 27-10)	
1975	Dallas Cowboys	Super Bowl X
	(Lost to Pittsburgh, 21-17)	
1969	Kansas City Chiefs	Super Bowl IV
	(Defeated Minnesota, 23-7)	

TEAMS AT OR UNDER .500 IN POSTSEASON PLAY

1999	Dallas Cowboys	8-8
1999	Detroit Lions	8-8
1991	New York Jets	8-8
1990	New Orleans Saints	8-8
1985	Cleveland Browns	8-8
1982	Cleveland Browns	4-5
1982	Detroit Lions	4-5
1969	Houston Oilers	6-6-2

COLDEST NFL GAMES ON RECORD

-13 degrees (-48 degree wind chill)—December 31, 1967, Lambeau Field, Green Bay, Wisconsin, NFL Championship (Green Bay 21, Dallas 17)

-9 degrees (-59 degree wind chill)—January 10, 1982, Riverfront Stadium, Cincinnati, Ohio, AFC Championship (Cincinnati 27, San Diego 7)

0 degrees (-32 degree wind chill)—January 15, 1994, Rich Stadium, Orchard Park, New York, AFC Divisional Playoff (Buffalo 29, Los Angeles Raiders 23)

1 degree (wind chill not recorded)—January 4, 1981, Cleveland Stadium, Cleveland, Ohio, AFC Divisional Playoff (Oakland 14, Cleveland 12)

TEAM LEADERS

Offense	Most Scored		Fewest Scored	
1st Quarter	140	St. Louis	27	Cincinnati
2nd Quarter	165	St. Louis	51	San Diego
3rd Quarter	111	Green Bay	27	Miami
4th Quarter	142	Miami	52	Seattle

Defense	Most Allowed		Fewest Allowed	
1st Quarter	120	New Orleans	33	Pittsburgh
				Tampa Bay
2nd Quarter	200	Indianapolis	31	Chicago
3rd Quarter	112	Carolina	13	Pittsburgh
4th Quarter	159	Indianapolis	53	Chicago
				Philadelphia

2001 NFL SCORE BY QUARTERS

AFC Offense	1	2	3	4	OT	PTS
Indianapolis	70	160	109	74	0	413
Oakland	87	116	97	99	0	399
New England	74	133	58	100	6	371
Pittsburgh	60	108	102	79	3	352
Miami	65	110	27	142	0	344
Denver	50	128	89	73	0	340
Tennessee	84	73	90	86	3	336
San Diego	81	51	81	119	0	332
Kansas City	56	92	64	105	3	320
N.Y. Jets	78	85	80	65	0	308
Baltimore	29	92	63	119	0	303
Seattle	64	107	75	52	3	301
Jacksonville	49	83	90	72	0	294
Cleveland	77	83	51	74	0	285
Buffalo	33	89	56	87	0	265
Cincinnati	27	75	56	65	3	226

NFC Offense	1	2	3	4	OT	PTS
St. Louis	140	165	103	92	3	503
San Francisco	52	139	82	124	12	409
Green Bay	89	90	111	100	0	390
Philadelphia	58	144	40	101	0	343
Chicago	38	96	71	121	12	338
New Orleans	53	77	108	95	0	333
Tampa Bay	39	130	50	102	3	324
Arizona	51	110	30	101	3	295
N.Y. Giants	63	94	34	100	3	294
Atlanta	98	61	40	92	0	291
Minnesota	44	77	83	86	0	290
Detroit	47	79	67	77	0	270
Washington	40	71	59	83	3	256
Carolina	50	83	52	68	0	253
Dallas	38	81	45	82	0	246

AFC Defense	1	2	3	4	OT	PTS
Pittsburgh	33	81	13	82	3	212
Baltimore	38	77	89	61	0	265
New England	54	51	94	73	0	272
Jacksonville	43	89	75	79	0	286
Miami	58	91	86	55	0	290
N.Y. Jets	38	123	77	57	0	295
Cincinnati	67	83	79	77	3	309
Cleveland	62	73	89	86	9	319
San Diego	60	109	46	100	6	321
Seattle	53	123	74	74	0	324
Oakland	53	83	83	105	3	327
Denver	65	94	58	119	3	339
Kansas City	43	115	103	83	0	344
Tennessee	61	127	74	126	0	388
Buffalo	91	115	83	128	3	420
Indianapolis	61	200	66	159	0	486

NFC Defense	1	2	3	4	OT	PTS
Chicago	48	31	71	53	0	203
Philadelphia	50	72	30	53	3	208
Green Bay	37	106	34	89	0	266
St. Louis	51	85	66	71	0	273
Tampa Bay	33	63	86	95	3	280
San Francisco	75	72	70	59	6	282
Washington	61	104	34	104	0	303
N.Y. Giants	88	80	60	93	0	321
Dallas	60	131	54	90	3	338
Arizona	57	114	72	100	0	343
Atlanta	68	120	64	116	9	377
Minnesota	77	111	84	118	0	390
New Orleans	120	120	47	122	0	409
Carolina	78	114	112	100	6	410
Detroit	101	125	90	108	0	424
NFL Totals	**1,884**	**3,082**	**2,163**	**2,835**	**60**	**10,024**

LARGEST TRADES IN NFL HISTORY
(Based on number of players or draft choices involved)

18—October 13, 1989—RB Herschel Walker from the Dallas Cowboys to Minnesota. Dallas also traded its third-round choice in 1990, its tenth-round choice in 1990, and its third-round choice in 1991 to Minnesota. Minnesota traded LB Jesse Solomon, LB David Howard, CB Issiac Holt, and DE Alex Stewart along with its first-round choice in 1990, its second-round choice in 1990, its sixth-round choice in 1990, its first-round choice in 1991, its second-round choice in 1991, its first-round choice in 1992, its second-round choice in 1992, and its third-round choice in 1992 to Dallas. Minnesota traded RB Darrin Nelson to Dallas, which traded Nelson to San Diego for the Chargers' fifth-round choice in 1990, which Dallas then sent to Minnesota.

15—March 26, 1953—T Mike McCormack, DT Don Colo, LB Tom Catlin, DB John Petitbon, and G Herschell Forester from Baltimore to Cleveland for DB Don Shula, DB Bert Rechichar, DB Carl Taseff, LB Ed Sharkey, E Gern Nagler, QB Harry Agganis, T Dick Batten, T Stu Sheets, G Art Spinney, and G Elmer Willhoite.

15—January 28, 1971—LB Marlin McKeever, first- and third-round choices in 1971, and third-, fourth-, fifth-, sixth-, and seventh-round choices in 1972 from Washington to the Los Angeles Rams for LB Maxie Baughan, LB Jack Pardee, LB Myron Pottios, RB Jeff Jordan, G John Wilbur, DT Diron Talbert, and a fifth-round choice in 1971.

12—June 13, 1952—Selection rights to Les Richter from the Dallas Texans to the Los Angeles Rams for RB Dick Hoerner, DB Tom Keane, DB George Sims, C Joe Reid, HB Billy Baggett, T Jack Halliday, FB Dick McKissack, LB Vic Vasicek, E Richard Wilkins, C Aubrey Phillips, and RB Dave Anderson.

10—March 23, 1959—HB Ollie Matson from the Chicago Cardinals to the Los Angeles Rams for T Frank Fuller, DE Glenn Holtzman, T Ken Panfil, DT Art Hauser, E John Tracey, FB Larry Hickman, HB Don Brown, the Rams second-round choice in 1960, and a player to be delivered during the 1959 training camp.

10—October 31, 1987—RB Eric Dickerson from the Los Angeles Rams to Indianapolis. The rights to LB Cornelius Bennett from Indianapolis to Buffalo. Indianapolis running back Owen Gill and the Colts' first- and second-round choices in 1988 and second-round choice in 1989, plus Bills running back Greg Bell and Buffalo's first-round choice in 1988 and first- and second-round choices in 1989 to the Rams.

2001 TOP 100 TELEVISION MARKETS
(NFL TEAM MARKETS IN BOLD)

RANK	DMA	TV HHLDS	% of U.S TV HHLDS	Cable TV HHLDS	% of Cable Penetration
1	**New York**	6,935,610	6.787	5,526,970	80
2	Los Angeles	5,354,150	5.240	3,913,920	73
3	**Chicago**	3,244,850	3.175	2,309,540	71
4	**Philadelphia**	2,703,480	2.646	2,274,490	84
5	**San Francisco-Oak-San Jose**	2,431,720	2.380	1,897,140	78
6	**Boston (Manchester)**	2,242,240	2.194	1,877,130	84
7	**Dallas-Ft. Worth**	2,069,010	2.025	1,394,900	67
8	**Washington, DC (Hagrstwn)**	2,047,340	2.004	1,616,210	79
9	**Detroit**	1,873,620	1.834	1,433,470	77
10	**Atlanta**	1,857,220	1.817	1,537,220	83
11	**Houston**	1,747,350	1.710	1,244,300	71
12	**Seattle-Tacoma**	1,605,900	1.572	1,307,930	81
13	**Minneapolis-St. Paul**	1,510,130	1.478	961,190	64
14	**Tampa-St. Pete (Sarasota)**	1,507,790	1.476	1,240,340	82
15	**Cleveland**	1,488,270	1.456	1,190,400	80
16	**Miami-Ft. Lauderdale**	1,468,630	1.437	1,197,650	82
17	**Phoenix**	1,441,660	1.411	1,048,990	73
18	**Denver**	1,312,300	1.284	967,700	74
19	Sacramnto-Stktn-Modesto	1,187,000	1.162	894,740	75
20	**Pittsburgh**	1,128,810	1.105	978,270	87
21	Orlando-Daytona Bch-Melbrn	1,126,000	1.102	980,520	87
22	**St. Louis**	1,121,410	1.097	797,140	71
23	Portland, OR	1,017,760	0.996	739,150	73
24	**Baltimore**	1,010,160	0.989	773,340	77
25	**San Diego**	996,220	0.975	873,670	88
26	**Indianapolis**	974,390	0.954	758,650	78
27	Hartford & New Haven	923,740	0.904	830,020	90
28	**Charlotte**	903,950	0.885	739,780	82
29	Raleigh-Durham (Fayetvlle)	873,440	0.855	687,870	79
30	**Kansas City**	835,580	0.818	645,990	77
31	**Nashville**	830,800	0.813	659,960	79
32	**Cincinnati**	828,650	0.811	608,350	73
33	Milwaukee	827,570	0.810	597,080	72
34	Columbus, OH	772,160	0.756	597,940	77
35	Greenvll-Spart-Ashevll-And	734,600	0.719	586,160	80
36	Salt Lake City	732,380	0.717	475,080	65
37	San Antonio	693,810	0.679	535,620	77
38	Grand Rapids-Kalmzoo-B.Crk	683,120	0.668	514,090	75
39	Birmingham (Ann,Tusc)	673,940	0.660	560,080	83
40	Memphis	641,630	0.628	489,050	76
41	Norfolk-Portsmth-Newpt Nws	638,190	0.625	540,870	85
42	**New Orleans**	636,340	0.623	529,110	83
43	West Palm Beach-Ft. Pierce	632,600	0.619	574,910	91
44	**Buffalo**	618,660	0.605	529,480	86
45	Oklahoma City	604,240	0.591	466,910	77
46	Harrisburg-Lncstr-Leb-York	604,210	0.591	517,400	86
47	Greensboro-H.Point-W.Salem	600,000	0.587	487,360	81
48	Louisville	587,450	0.575	458,640	78
49	Providence-New Bedford	572,880	0.561	417,250	83
50	Albuquerque-Santa Fe	570,460	0.558	474,830	73

2001 TOP 100 TELEVISION MARKETS
(NFL TEAM MARKETS IN BOLD)

RANK	DMA	TV HHLDS	% of U.S TV HHLDS	Cable TV HHLDS	% of Cable Penetration
51	Las Vegas	559,330	0.547	438,000	78
52	Wilkes Barre-Scranton	550,340	0.539	492,970	90
53	**Jacksonville, Brunswick**	**548,750**	**0.537**	**456,710**	**83**
54	Fresno-Visalia	519,200	0.508	321,200	62
55	Dayton	515,160	0.504	421,970	82
56	Albany-Schenectady-Troy	508,470	0.498	422,760	83
57	Little Rock-Pine Bluff	491,830	0.481	401,080	82
58	Austin	491,820	0.481	368,380	75
59	Tulsa	490,160	0.480	366,250	75
60	Richmond-Petersburg	489,320	0.479	380,830	78
61	Charleston-Huntington	481,200	0.471	428,670	89
62	Mobile-Pensacola (Ft Walt)	468,680	0.459	408,780	87
63	Knoxville	461,950	0.452	384,770	83
64	Flint-Saginaw-Bay City	448,990	0.439	353,150	79
65	Wichita-Hutchinson Plus	444,710	0.435	363,250	82
66	Lexington	424,010	0.415	367,900	87
67	Toledo	413,910	0.405	326,710	79
68	Roanoke-Lynchburg	407,480	0.399	347,980	85
69	**Green Bay-Appleton**	**398,510**	**0.390**	**281,220**	**71**
70	Des Moines-Ames	393,980	0.386	293,800	75
71	Tucson (Sierra Vista)	391,930	0.384	283,800	72
72	Honolulu	382,720	0.375	348,530	91
73	Paducah-C.Gird-Harbg-Mt VN	376,780	0.369	296,460	79
74	Rochester, NY	376,740	0.369	300,400	80
75	Omaha	375,070	0.367	301,800	81
76	Shreveport	371,020	0.363	306,260	83
77	Spokane	370,060	0.362	273,850	74
78	Springfield, MO	369,070	0.361	262,950	71
79	Portland-Auburn	362,660	0.355	308,620	85
80	Syracuse	361,650	0.354	298,730	83
81	Ft. Myers-Naples	352,240	0.345	312,220	89
82	Huntsville-Decatur (Flor)	351,860	0.344	295,620	84
83	Champaign&Sprngfld-Decatur	345,420	0.338	296,970	86
84	Madison	329,190	0.322	243,180	74
85	Columbia, SC	324,060	0.317	247,630	76
86	Chattanooga	323,170	0.316	275,330	85
87	South Bend-Elkhart	318,770	0.312	230,210	72
88	Jackson, MS	307,850	0.301	248,080	81
89	Cedar Rapids-Wtrlo-IWC&Dub	307,310	0.301	236,740	77
90	Davenport-R.Island-Moline	303,370	0.297	240,640	79
91	Burlington-Plattsburgh	300,650	0.294	243,670	81
92	Colorado Springs-Pueblo	298,600	0.292	243,050	81
93	Tri-Cities, TN-VA	295,260	0.289	257,930	87
94	Waco-Temple-Bryan	286,720	0.281	239,190	83
95	Johnstown-Altoona	283,140	0.277	261,550	92
96	Baton Rouge	280,130	0.274	238,400	85
97	Evansville	276,070	0.270	224,280	81
98	El Paso	275,850	0.270	192,350	70
99	Youngstown	272,500	0.267	221,960	82
100	Savannah	260,340	0.255	224,010	86
TOTAL NFL MARKETS		**46,572,000**	**45.578**		
TOTAL TOP 100 MARKETS		**87,761,420**	**85.890**		

RETIRED UNIFORM NUMBERS IN NFL
AFC

Baltimore:	None	
Buffalo:	Jim Kelly	12
Cincinnati:	Bob Johnson	54
Cleveland:	Otto Graham	14
	Jim Brown	32
	Ernie Davis	45
	Don Fleming	46
	Lou Groza	76
Denver:	John Elway	7
	Frank Tripucka	18
	Floyd Little	44
Houston:	None	
Indianapolis:	Johnny Unitas	19
	Buddy Young	22
	Lenny Moore	24
	Art Donovan	70
	Jim Parker	77
	Raymond Berry	82
	Gino Marchetti	89
Jacksonville:	None	
Kansas City:	Jan Stenerud	3
	Len Dawson	16
	Abner Haynes	28
	Stone Johnson	33
	Mack Lee Hill	36
	Willie Lanier	63
	Bobby Bell	78
	Buck Buchanan	86
Miami:	Bob Griese	12
	Dan Marino	13
New England:	Gino Cappelletti	20
	Mike Haynes	40
	Steve Nelson	57
	John Hannah	73
	Jim Hunt	79
	Bob Dee	89
New York Jets:	Joe Namath	12
	Don Maynard	13
Oakland:	None	
Pittsburgh:	Ernie Stautner	70
San Diego:	Dan Fouts	14
Tennessee:	Earl Campbell	34
	Jim Norton	43
	Mike Munchak	63
	Elvin Bethea	65

NFC

Arizona:	Larry Wilson	8
	Stan Mauldin	77
	J.V. Cain	88
	Marshall Goldberg	99
Atlanta:	Steve Bartowski	10
	William Andrews	31
	Jeff Van Note	57
	Tommy Nobis	60
Carolina:	None	
Chicago:	Bronko Nagurski	3
	George McAfee	5
	George Halas	7
	Willie Galimore	28
	Walter Payton	34
	Gale Sayers	40
	Brian Piccolo	41
	Sid Luckman	42
	Dick Butkus	51
	Bill Hewitt	56
	Bill George	61
	Bulldog Turner	66
	Red Grange	77

Dallas:	None	
Detroit:	Dutch Clark	7
	Bobby Layne	22
	Doak Walker	37
	Joe Schmidt	56
	Chuck Hughes	85
	Charlie Sanders	88
Green Bay:	Tony Canadeo	3
	Don Hutson	14
	Bart Starr	15
	Ray Nitschke	66
Minnesota:	Fran Tarkenton	10
	Mick Tingelhoff	53
	Jim Marshall	70
	Korey Stringer	77
	Alan Page	88
New Orleans:	Jim Taylor	31
	Doug Atkins	81
New York Giants:	Ray Flaherty	1
	Tuffy Leemans	4
	Mel Hein	7
	Phil Simms	11
	Y.A. Tittle	14
	Frank Gifford	16
	Al Blozis	32
	Joe Morrison	40
	Charlie Conerly	42
	Ken Strong	50
	Lawrence Taylor	56
Philadelphia:	Steve Van Buren	15
	Tom Brookshier	40
	Pete Retzlaff	44
	Chuck Bednarik	60
	Al Wistert	70
	Jerome Brown	99
St. Louis:	Bob Waterfield	7
	Eric Dickerson	29
	Merlin Olsen	74
	Jackie Slater	78
	Jack Youngblood	85
San Francisco:	John Brodie	12
	Joe Montana	16
	Joe Perry	34
	Jimmy Johnson	37
	Hugh McElhenny	39
	Charlie Krueger	70
	Leo Nomellini	73
	Bob St. Clair	79
	Dwight Clark	87
Seattle:	"Fans/the twelfth man"	12
	Steve Largent	80
Tampa Bay:	Lee Roy Selmon	63
Washington:	Sammy Baugh	33

ALL-TIME REGULAR-SEASON RECORDS OF CURRENT NFL TEAMS

AFC
BALTIMORE RAVENS

Season	All Games			Home Games			Road Games		
	W	L	T	W	L	T	W	L	T
1996	4	12		4	4		0	8	
1997	6	9	1	3	4	1	3	5	
1998	6	10		4	4		2	6	
1999	8	8		4	4		4	4	
2000	12	4		6	2		6	2	
2001	10	6		6	2		4	4	
	46	49	1	27	20	1	19	29	

BUFFALO BILLS

Season	All Games			Home Games			Road Games		
	W	L	T	W	L	T	W	L	T
1960	5	8	1	3	4		2	4	1
1961	6	8		2	5		4	3	
1962	7	6	1	3	3	1	4	3	
1963	7	6	1	4	2	1	3	4	
1964	12	2		6	1		6	1	
1965	10	3	1	5	2		5	1	1
1966	9	4	1	4	2	1	5	2	
1967	4	10		2	5		2	5	
1968	1	12	1	1	6		0	6	1
1969	4	10		4	3		0	7	
1970	3	10	1	1	6		2	4	1
1971	1	13		1	6		0	7	
1972	4	9	1	2	4	1	2	5	
1973	9	5		5	2		4	3	
1974	9	5		5	2		4	3	
1975	8	6		3	4		5	2	
1976	2	12		1	6		1	6	
1977	3	11		1	6		2	5	
1978	5	11		4	4		1	7	
1979	7	9		3	5		4	4	
1980	11	5		6	2		5	3	
1981	10	6		7	1		3	5	
1982	4	5		4	1		0	4	
1983	8	8		3	5		5	3	
1984	2	14		2	6		0	8	
1985	2	14		2	6		0	8	
1986	4	12		3	5		1	7	
1987	7	8		4	4		3	4	
1988	12	4		8	0		4	4	
1989	9	7		6	2		3	5	
1990	13	3		8	0		5	3	
1991	13	3		7	1		6	2	
1992	11	5		6	2		5	3	
1993	12	4		6	2		6	2	
1994	7	9		4	4		3	5	
1995	10	6		6	2		4	4	
1996	10	6		7	1		3	5	
1997	6	10		4	4		2	6	
1998	10	6		6	2		4	4	
1999	11	5		6	2		5	3	
2000	8	8		5	3		3	5	
2001	3	13		1	7		2	6	
	299	321	8	171	140	4	128	181	4

CINCINNATI BENGALS

Season	All Games			Home Games			Road Games		
	W	L	T	W	L	T	W	L	T
1968	3	11		2	5		1	6	
1969	4	9	1	4	3		0	6	1
1970	8	6		5	2		3	4	
1971	4	10		3	4		1	6	
1972	8	6		4	3		4	3	
1973	10	4		7	0		3	4	
1974	7	7		4	3		3	4	
1975	11	3		6	1		5	2	
1976	10	4		6	1		4	3	
1977	8	6		5	2		3	4	
1978	4	12		3	5		1	7	
1979	4	12		4	4		0	8	
1980	6	10		3	5		3	5	
1981	12	4		6	2		6	2	
1982	7	2		4	0		3	2	
1983	7	9		4	4		3	5	
1984	8	8		5	3		3	5	
1985	7	9		5	3		2	6	
1986	10	6		6	2		4	4	
1987	4	11		1	7		3	4	
1988	12	4		8	0		4	4	
1989	8	8		5	3		3	5	
1990	9	7		5	3		4	4	
1991	3	13		3	5		0	8	
1992	5	11		3	5		2	6	
1993	3	13		3	5		0	8	
1994	3	13		2	6		1	7	
1995	7	9		3	5		4	4	
1996	8	8		6	2		2	6	
1997	7	9		6	2		1	7	
1998	3	13		1	7		2	6	
1999	4	12		2	6		2	6	
2000	4	12		3	5		1	7	
2001	6	10		4	4		2	6	
	224	291	1	141	117		83	174	1

CLEVELAND BROWNS*

Season	All Games			Home Games			Road Games		
	W	L	T	W	L	T	W	L	T
1950	10	2		5	1		5	1	
1951	11	1		6	0		5	1	
1952	8	4		4	2		4	2	
1953	11	1		6	0		5	1	
1954	9	3		5	1		4	2	
1955	9	2	1	5	1		4	1	1
1956	5	7		1	5		4	2	
1957	9	2	1	6	0		3	2	1
1958	9	3		4	2		5	1	
1959	7	5		3	3		4	2	
1960	8	3	1	4	2		4	1	1
1961	8	5	1	4	3		4	2	1
1962	7	6	1	4	2	1	3	4	
1963	10	4		5	2		5	2	
1964	10	3	1	5	1	1	5	2	
1965	11	3		5	2		6	1	
1966	9	5		5	2		4	3	
1967	9	5		6	1		3	4	
1968	10	4		5	2		5	2	
1969	10	3	1	5	1	1	5	2	
1970	7	7		4	3		3	4	
1971	9	5		4	3		5	2	
1972	10	4		4	3		6	1	
1973	7	5	2	5	1	1	2	4	1
1974	4	10		3	4		1	6	
1975	3	11		3	4		0	7	
1976	9	5		6	1		3	4	
1977	6	8		2	5		4	3	
1978	8	8		5	3		3	5	
1979	9	7		5	3		4	4	
1980	11	5		6	2		5	3	
1981	5	11		3	5		2	6	
1982	4	5		2	2		2	3	
1983	9	7		6	2		3	5	
1984	5	11		2	6		3	5	
1985	8	8		5	3		3	5	
1986	12	4		6	2		6	2	

Season	W	L	T	W	L	T	W	L	T
1987	10	5		5	2		5	3	
1988	10	6		6	2		4	4	
1989	9	6	1	5	2	1	4	4	
1990	3	13		2	6		1	7	
1991	6	10		3	5		3	5	
1992	7	9		4	4		3	5	
1993	7	9		4	4		3	5	
1994	11	5		6	2		5	3	
1995	5	11		3	5		2	6	
1999	2	14		0	8		2	6	
2000	3	13		2	6		1	7	
2001	7	9		4	4		3	5	
	386	302	10	208	135	5	178	167	5

*Did not play from 1996-98.

DENVER BRONCOS

	All Games			Home Games			Road Games		
Season	W	L	T	W	L	T	W	L	T
1960	4	9	1	2	4	1	2	5	
1961	3	11		2	5		1	6	
1962	7	7		3	4		4	3	
1963	2	11	1	2	5		0	6	1
1964	2	11	1	2	4	1	0	7	
1965	4	10		2	5		2	5	
1966	4	10		3	4		1	6	
1967	3	11		1	6		2	5	
1968	5	9		3	4		2	5	
1969	5	8	1	4	2	1	1	6	
1970	5	8	1	3	3	1	2	5	
1971	4	9	1	2	4	1	2	5	
1972	5	9		3	4		2	5	
1973	7	5	2	3	3	1	4	2	1
1974	7	6	1	3	3	1	4	3	
1975	6	8		5	2		1	6	
1976	9	5		6	1		3	4	
1977	12	2		6	1		6	1	
1978	10	6		6	2		4	4	
1979	10	6		6	2		4	4	
1980	8	8		4	4		4	4	
1981	10	6		8	0		2	6	
1982	2	7		1	4		1	3	
1983	9	7		6	2		3	5	
1984	13	3		7	1		6	2	
1985	11	5		6	2		5	3	
1986	11	5		7	1		4	4	
1987	10	4	1	7	1		3	3	1
1988	8	8		6	2		2	6	
1989	11	5		6	2		5	3	
1990	5	11		4	4		1	7	
1991	12	4		7	1		5	3	
1992	8	8		7	1		1	7	
1993	9	7		5	3		4	4	
1994	7	9		4	4		3	5	
1995	8	8		6	2		2	6	
1996	13	3		8	0		5	3	
1997	12	4		8	0		4	4	
1998	14	2		8	0		6	2	
1999	6	10		3	5		3	5	
2000	11	5		6	2		5	3	
2001	8	8		6	2		2	6	
	320	298	10	197	111	7	123	187	3

INDIANAPOLIS COLTS*

	All Games			Home Games			Road Games		
Season	W	L	T	W	L	T	W	L	T
1953	3	9		2	4		1	5	
1954	3	9		2	4		1	5	
1955	5	6	1	4	1	1	1	5	
1956	5	7		4	2		1	5	
1957	7	5		4	2		3	3	

Season	W	L	T	W	L	T	W	L	T
1958	9	3		6	0		3	3	
1959	9	3		4	2		5	1	
1960	6	6		4	2		2	4	
1961	8	6		5	2		3	4	
1962	7	7		3	4		4	3	
1963	8	6		4	3		4	3	
1964	12	2		7	1		5	1	
1965	10	3	1	5	2		5	1	1
1966	9	5		5	2		4	3	
1967	11	1	2	6	0	1	5	1	1
1968	13	1		6	1		7	0	
1969	8	5	1	4	2	1	4	3	
1970	11	2	1	5	1	1	6	1	
1971	10	4		5	2		5	2	
1972	5	9		2	5		3	4	
1973	4	10		3	4		1	6	
1974	2	12		0	7		2	5	
1975	10	4		5	2		5	2	
1976	11	3		6	1		5	2	
1977	10	4		6	1		4	3	
1978	5	11		2	6		3	5	
1979	5	11		3	5		2	6	
1980	7	9		2	6		5	3	
1981	2	14		1	7		1	7	
1982	0	8	1	0	3	1	0	5	
1983	7	9		3	5		4	4	
1984	4	12		2	6		2	6	
1985	5	11		4	4		1	7	
1986	3	13		1	7		2	6	
1987	9	6		4	4		5	2	
1988	9	7		6	2		3	5	
1989	8	8		6	2		2	6	
1990	7	9		3	5		4	4	
1991	1	15		0	8		1	7	
1992	9	7		4	4		5	3	
1993	4	12		2	6		2	6	
1994	8	8		5	3		3	5	
1995	9	7		5	3		4	4	
1996	9	7		6	2		3	5	
1997	3	13		2	6		1	7	
1998	3	13		3	5		0	8	
1999	13	3		7	1		6	2	
2000	10	6		6	2		4	4	
2001	6	10		3	5		3	5	
	342	361	7	187	164	5	155	197	2

*includes Baltimore Colts (1953-1983).

JACKSONVILLE JAGUARS

	All Games			Home Games			Road Games		
Season	W	L	T	W	L	T	W	L	T
1995	4	12		2	6		2	6	
1996	9	7		7	1		2	6	
1997	11	5		7	1		4	4	
1998	11	5		7	1		4	4	
1999	14	2		7	1		7	1	
2000	7	9		4	4		3	5	
2001	6	10		3	5		3	5	
	62	50		37	19		25	31	

KANSAS CITY CHIEFS*

	All Games			Home Games			Road Games		
Season	W	L	T	W	L	T	W	L	T
1960	8	6		5	2		3	4	
1961	6	8		4	3		2	5	
1962	11	3		6	1		5	2	
1963	5	7	2	4	3		1	4	2
1964	7	7		4	3		3	4	
1965	7	5	2	5	2		2	3	2
1966	11	2	1	4	2	1	7	0	
1967	9	5		4	3		5	2	

Season	All Games W	L	T	Home Games W	L	T	Road Games W	L	T
1968	12	2		6	1		6	1	
1969	11	3		6	1		5	2	
1970	7	5	2	4	1	2	3	4	
1971	10	3	1	7	0		3	3	1
1972	8	6		3	4		5	2	
1973	7	5	2	5	1	1	2	4	1
1974	5	9		1	6		4	3	
1975	5	9		3	4		2	5	
1976	5	9		1	6		4	3	
1977	2	12		1	6		1	6	
1978	4	12		3	5		1	7	
1979	7	9		3	5		4	4	
1980	8	8		3	5		5	3	
1981	9	7		5	3		4	4	
1982	3	6		2	2		1	4	
1983	6	10		5	3		1	7	
1984	8	8		5	3		3	5	
1985	6	10		5	3		1	7	
1986	10	6		6	2		4	4	
1987	4	11		3	4		1	7	
1988	4	11	1	4	4		0	7	1
1989	8	7	1	5	3		3	4	1
1990	11	5		6	2		5	3	
1991	10	6		6	2		4	4	
1992	10	6		7	1		3	5	
1993	11	5		7	1		4	4	
1994	9	7		5	3		4	4	
1995	13	3		8	0		5	3	
1996	9	7		5	3		4	4	
1997	13	3		8	0		5	3	
1998	7	9		5	3		2	6	
1999	9	7		6	2		3	5	
2000	7	9		5	3		2	6	
2001	6	10		3	5		3	5	
	328	288	12	193	116	4	135	172	8

*includes Dallas Texans (1960-62).

MIAMI DOLPHINS

Season	All Games W	L	T	Home Games W	L	T	Road Games W	L	T
1966	3	11		2	5		1	6	
1967	4	10		4	3		0	7	
1968	5	8	1	1	5	1	4	3	
1969	3	10	1	2	4	1	1	6	
1970	10	4		6	1		4	3	
1971	10	3	1	6	1		4	2	1
1972	14	0		7	0		7	0	
1973	12	2		7	0		5	2	
1974	11	3		7	0		4	3	
1975	10	4		5	2		5	2	
1976	6	8		3	4		3	4	
1977	10	4		6	1		4	3	
1978	11	5		7	1		4	4	
1979	10	6		6	2		4	4	
1980	8	8		5	3		3	5	
1981	11	4	1	6	1	1	5	3	
1982	7	2		4	0		3	2	
1983	12	4		7	1		5	3	
1984	14	2		7	1		7	1	
1985	12	4		8	0		4	4	
1986	8	8		4	4		4	4	
1987	8	7		4	3		4	4	
1988	6	10		4	4		2	6	
1989	8	8		4	4		4	4	
1990	12	4		7	1		5	3	
1991	8	8		5	3		3	5	
1992	11	5		6	2		5	3	
1993	9	7		4	4		5	3	
1994	10	6		6	2		4	4	
1995	9	7		5	3		4	4	

Season	All Games W	L	T	Home Games W	L	T	Road Games W	L	T
1996	8	8		4	4		4	4	
1997	9	7		6	2		3	5	
1998	10	6		7	1		3	5	
1999	9	7		5	3		4	4	
2000	11	5		5	3		6	2	
2001	11	5		7	1		4	4	
	330	210	4	189	79	3	141	131	1

NEW ENGLAND PATRIOTS*

Season	All Games W	L	T	Home Games W	L	T	Road Games W	L	T
1960	5	9		3	4		2	5	
1961	9	4	1	4	2	1	5	2	
1962	9	4	1	6	1		3	3	1
1963	7	6	1	5	1	1	2	5	
1964	10	3	1	4	2	1	6	1	
1965	4	8	2	1	4	2	3	4	
1966	8	4	2	4	2	1	4	2	1
1967	3	10	1	2	4		1	6	1
1968	4	10		2	5		2	5	
1969	4	10		2	5		2	5	
1970	2	12		1	6		1	6	
1971	6	8		5	2		1	6	
1972	3	11		2	5		1	6	
1973	5	9		3	4		2	5	
1974	7	7		3	4		4	3	
1975	3	11		2	5		1	6	
1976	11	3		6	1		5	2	
1977	9	5		6	1		3	4	
1978	11	5		5	3		6	2	
1979	9	7		6	2		3	5	
1980	10	6		6	2		4	4	
1981	2	14		2	6		0	8	
1982	5	4		3	1		2	3	
1983	8	8		5	3		3	5	
1984	9	7		5	3		4	4	
1985	11	5		7	1		4	4	
1986	11	5		4	4		7	1	
1987	8	7		5	3		3	4	
1988	9	7		7	1		2	6	
1989	5	11		3	5		2	6	
1990	1	15		0	8		1	7	
1991	6	10		4	4		2	6	
1992	2	14		1	7		1	7	
1993	5	11		3	5		2	6	
1994	10	6		5	3		5	3	
1995	6	10		3	5		3	5	
1996	11	5		6	2		5	3	
1997	10	6		6	2		4	4	
1998	9	7		6	2		3	5	
1999	8	8		5	3		3	5	
2000	5	11		3	5		2	6	
2001	11	5		6	2		5	3	
	291	328	9	167	140	6	124	188	3

*includes Boston Patriots (1960-1970).

NEW YORK JETS*

Season	All Games W	L	T	Home Games W	L	T	Road Games W	L	T
1960	7	7		3	4		4	3	
1961	7	7		5	2		2	5	
1962	5	9		2	5		3	4	
1963	5	8	1	4	2	1	1	6	
1964	5	8	1	5	1	1	0	7	
1965	5	8	1	3	3	1	2	5	
1966	6	6	2	4	3		2	3	2
1967	8	5	1	4	2	1	4	3	
1968	11	3		6	1		5	2	
1969	10	4		5	2		5	2	
1970	4	10		2	5		2	5	

Season	All Games W	L	T	Home Games W	L	T	Road Games W	L	T
1971	6	8		4	3		2	5	
1972	7	7		4	3		3	4	
1973	4	10		2	4		2	6	
1974	7	7		3	4		4	3	
1975	3	11		1	6		2	5	
1976	3	11		2	5		1	6	
1977	3	11		1	6		2	5	
1978	8	8		4	4		4	4	
1979	8	8		6	2		2	6	
1980	4	12		2	6		2	6	
1981	10	5	1	6	2		4	3	1
1982	6	3		3	1		3	2	
1983	7	9		2	6		5	3	
1984	7	9		3	5		4	4	
1985	11	5		7	1		4	4	
1986	10	6		5	3		5	3	
1987	6	9		4	4		2	5	
1988	8	7	1	5	2	1	3	5	
1989	4	12		1	7		3	5	
1990	6	10		3	5		3	5	
1991	8	8		4	4		4	4	
1992	4	12		3	5		1	7	
1993	8	8		3	5		5	3	
1994	6	10		4	4		2	6	
1995	3	13		2	6		1	7	
1996	1	15		0	8		1	7	
1997	9	7		5	3		4	4	
1998	12	4		7	1		5	3	
1999	8	8		4	4		4	4	
2000	9	7		5	3		4	4	
2001	10	6		3	5		7	1	
	279	341	8	151	157	5	128	184	3

*includes New York Titans (1960-62).

OAKLAND RAIDERS*

Season	All Games W	L	T	Home Games W	L	T	Road Games W	L	T
1960	6	8		3	4		3	4	
1961	2	12		1	6		1	6	
1962	1	13		1	6		0	7	
1963	10	4		6	1		4	3	
1964	5	7	2	5	2		0	5	2
1965	8	5	1	5	2		3	3	1
1966	8	5	1	3	3	1	5	2	
1967	13	1		7	0		6	1	
1968	12	2		6	1		6	1	
1969	12	1	1	7	0		5	1	1
1970	8	4	2	6	1		2	3	2
1971	8	4	2	5	1	1	3	3	1
1972	10	3	1	5	1	1	5	2	
1973	9	4	1	5	2		4	2	1
1974	12	2		6	1		6	1	
1975	11	3		6	1		5	2	
1976	13	1		7	0		6	1	
1977	11	3		6	1		5	2	
1978	9	7		4	4		5	3	
1979	9	7		6	2		3	5	
1980	11	5		6	2		5	3	
1981	7	9		4	4		3	5	
1982	8	1		4	0		4	1	
1983	12	4		6	2		6	2	
1984	11	5		6	2		5	3	
1985	12	4		7	1		5	3	
1986	8	8		3	5		5	3	
1987	5	10		3	5		2	5	
1988	7	9		3	5		4	4	
1989	8	8		7	1		1	7	
1990	12	4		6	2		6	2	
1991	9	7		5	3		4	4	
1992	7	9		5	3		2	6	
1993	10	6		5	3		5	3	
1994	9	7		4	4		5	3	
1995	8	8		4	4		4	4	
1996	7	9		4	4		3	5	
1997	4	12		2	6		2	6	
1998	8	8		4	4		4	4	
1999	8	8		5	3		3	5	
2000	12	4		7	1		5	3	
2001	10	6		5	3		5	3	
	370	247	11	205	106	3	165	141	8

*includes Los Angeles Raiders (1982-1994).

PITTSBURGH STEELERS

Season	All Games W	L	T	Home Games W	L	T	Road Games W	L	T
1933	3	6	2	2	3		1	3	2
1934	2	10		1	5		1	5	
1935	4	8		2	5		2	3	
1936	6	6		4	1		2	5	
1937	4	7		2	4		2	3	
1938	2	9		0	5		2	4	
1939	1	9	1	1	4		0	5	1
1940	2	7	2	1	2	2	1	5	
1941	1	9	1	1	4		0	5	1
1942	7	4		3	2		4	2	
1945	2	8		1	4		1	4	
1946	5	5	1	4	1		1	4	1
1947	8	4		5	1		3	3	
1948	4	8		4	2		0	6	
1949	6	5	1	3	2	1	3	3	
1950	6	6		2	4		4	2	
1951	4	7	1	1	4	1	3	3	
1952	5	7		2	4		3	3	
1953	6	6		3	3		3	3	
1954	5	7		4	2		1	5	
1955	4	8		3	2		1	6	
1956	5	7		3	3		2	4	
1957	6	6		4	2		2	4	
1958	7	4	1	5	1		2	3	1
1959	6	5	1	3	2	1	3	3	
1960	5	6	1	4	2		1	4	1
1961	6	8		4	3		2	5	
1962	9	5		4	3		5	2	
1963	7	4	3	5	0	2	2	4	1
1964	5	9		2	5		3	4	
1965	2	12		1	6		1	6	
1966	5	8	1	3	3	1	2	5	
1967	4	9	1	1	6		3	3	1
1968	2	11	1	1	6		1	5	1
1969	1	13		1	6		0	7	
1970	5	9		4	3		1	6	
1971	6	8		5	2		1	6	
1972	11	3		7	0		4	3	
1973	10	4		7	1		3	3	
1974	10	3	1	5	2		5	1	1
1975	12	2		6	1		6	1	
1976	10	4		6	1		4	3	
1977	9	5		6	1		3	4	
1978	14	2		7	1		7	1	
1979	12	4		8	0		4	4	
1980	9	7		6	2		3	5	
1981	8	8		5	3		3	5	
1982	6	3		4	0		2	3	
1983	10	6		4	4		6	2	
1984	9	7		6	2		3	5	
1985	7	9		5	3		2	6	
1986	6	10		4	4		2	6	
1987	8	7		4	3		4	4	
1988	5	11		4	4		1	7	
1989	9	7		4	4		5	3	

Season	W	L	T	W	L	T	W	L	T
1990	9	7		6	2		3	5	
1991	7	9		5	3		2	6	
1992	11	5		7	1		4	4	
1993	9	7		6	2		3	5	
1994	12	4		7	1		5	3	
1995	11	5		6	2		5	3	
1996	10	6		7	1		3	5	
1997	11	5		7	1		4	4	
1998	7	9		5	3		2	6	
1999	6	10		2	6		4	4	
2000	9	7		4	4		5	3	
2001	13	3		7	1		6	2	
	448	449	19	266	180	8	182	269	11

*includes Pittsburgh Pirates (1933-1940).

SAN DIEGO CHARGERS*

	All Games			Home Games			Road Games		
Season	W	L	T	W	L	T	W	L	T
1960	10	4		5	2		5	2	
1961	12	2		6	1		6	1	
1962	4	10		3	4		1	6	
1963	11	3		6	1		5	2	
1964	8	5	1	4	3		4	2	1
1965	9	2	3	4	1	2	5	1	1
1966	7	6	1	5	2		2	4	1
1967	8	5	1	5	2	1	3	3	
1968	9	5		4	3		5	2	
1969	8	6		5	2		3	4	
1970	5	6	3	2	3	2	3	3	1
1971	6	8		6	1		0	7	
1972	4	9	1	2	5		2	4	1
1973	2	11	1	2	5		0	6	1
1974	5	9		3	4		2	5	
1975	2	12		1	6		1	6	
1976	6	8		3	4		3	4	
1977	7	7		3	4		4	3	
1978	9	7		5	3		4	4	
1979	12	4		7	1		5	3	
1980	11	5		6	2		5	3	
1981	10	6		5	3		5	3	
1982	6	3		3	1		3	2	
1983	6	10		4	4		2	6	
1984	7	9		4	4		3	5	
1985	8	8		6	2		2	6	
1986	4	12		2	6		2	6	
1987	8	7		4	3		4	4	
1988	6	10		3	5		3	5	
1989	6	10		4	4		2	6	
1990	6	10		3	5		3	5	
1991	4	12		3	5		1	7	
1992	11	5		6	2		5	3	
1993	8	8		4	4		4	4	
1994	11	5		5	3		6	2	
1995	9	7		5	3		4	4	
1996	8	8		5	3		3	5	
1997	4	12		2	6		2	6	
1998	5	11		4	4		1	7	
1999	8	8		4	4		4	4	
2000	1	15		1	7		0	8	
2001	5	11		4	4		1	7	
	296	321	11	168	141	5	128	180	6

*includes Los Angeles Chargers (1960).

TENNESSEE TITANS*

	All Games			Home Games			Road Games		
Season	W	L	T	W	L	T	W	L	T
1960	10	4		6	1		4	3	
1961	10	3	1	6	1		4	2	1
1962	11	3		6	1		5	2	
1963	6	8		4	3		2	5	
1964	4	10		3	4		1	6	
1965	4	10		3	4		1	6	
1966	3	11		3	4		0	7	
1967	9	4	1	5	2		4	2	1
1968	7	7		3	4		4	3	
1969	6	6	2	4	2	1	2	4	1
1970	3	10	1	1	6		2	4	1
1971	4	9	1	3	3	1	1	6	
1972	1	13		1	6		0	7	
1973	1	13		0	7		1	6	
1974	7	7		3	4		4	3	
1975	10	4		5	2		5	2	
1976	5	9		3	4		2	5	
1977	8	6		5	2		3	4	
1978	10	6		5	3		5	3	
1979	11	5		6	2		5	3	
1980	11	5		6	2		5	3	
1981	7	9		5	3		2	6	
1982	1	8		1	4		0	4	
1983	2	14		2	6		0	8	
1984	3	13		2	6		1	7	
1985	5	11		4	4		1	7	
1986	5	11		4	4		1	7	
1987	9	6		5	2		4	4	
1988	10	6		7	1		3	5	
1989	9	7		6	2		3	5	
1990	9	7		6	2		3	5	
1991	11	5		7	1		4	4	
1992	10	6		5	3		5	3	
1993	12	4		7	1		5	3	
1994	2	14		2	6		0	8	
1995	7	9		3	5		4	4	
1996	8	8		2	6		6	2	
1997	8	8		6	2		2	6	
1998	8	8		3	5		5	3	
1999	13	3		8	0		5	3	
2000	13	3		7	1		6	2	
2001	7	9		3	5		4	4	
	300	322	6	176	136	2	124	186	4

*includes Houston Oilers (1960-1996) and Tennessee Oilers (1997-98).

NFC
ARIZONA CARDINALS*

	All Games			Home Games			Road Games		
Season	W	L	T	W	L	T	W	L	T
1920	6	2	2	5	1	1	1	1	1
1921	3	3	2	3	3	1	0	0	1
1922	8	3		8	3		0	0	
1923	8	4		8	3		0	1	
1924	5	4	1	5	3	1	0	1	
1925	11	2	1	11	2		0	0	1
1926	5	6	1	3	3		2	3	1
1927	3	7	1	2	3	1	1	4	
1928	1	5		1	1		0	4	
1929	6	6	1	3	2		3	4	1
1930	5	6	2	3	2		2	4	2
1931	5	4		3	0		2	4	
1932	2	6	2	1	2	1	1	4	1
1933	1	9	1	0	4	1	1	5	
1934	5	6		2	2		3	4	
1935	6	4	2	2	2		4	2	2
1936	3	8	1	3	1	1	0	7	
1937	5	5	1	1	3		4	2	1
1938	2	9		1	4		1	5	
1939	1	10		0	4		1	6	
1940	2	7	2	2	1	1	0	6	1
1941	3	7	1	0	3	1	3	4	
1942	3	8		2	2		1	6	
1943	0	10		0	3		0	7	

Season	W	L	T	W	L	T	W	L	T
1945	1	9		0	3		1	6	
1946	6	5		2	2		4	3	
1947	9	3		5	0		4	3	
1948	11	1		5	1		6	0	
1949	6	5	1	2	3	1	4	2	
1950	5	7		3	3		2	4	
1951	3	9		1	5		2	4	
1952	4	8		2	4		2	4	
1953	1	10	1	0	5	1	1	5	
1954	2	10		2	4		0	6	
1955	4	7	1	3	2	1	1	5	
1956	7	5		4	2		3	3	
1957	3	9		0	6		3	3	
1958	2	9	1	1	4	1	1	5	
1959	2	10		2	4		0	6	
1960	6	5	1	3	2	1	3	3	
1961	7	7		3	4		4	3	
1962	4	9	1	2	4	1	2	5	
1963	9	5		3	4		6	1	
1964	9	3	2	4	1	1	5	2	1
1965	5	9		2	5		3	4	
1966	8	5	1	5	1	1	3	4	
1967	6	7	1	3	3	1	3	4	
1968	9	4	1	4	2	1	5	2	
1969	4	9	1	3	4		1	5	1
1970	8	5	1	6	1		2	4	1
1971	4	9	1	1	5	1	3	4	
1972	4	9	1	2	5		2	4	1
1973	4	9	1	2	4	1	2	5	
1974	10	4		5	2		5	2	
1975	11	3		6	1		5	2	
1976	10	4		6	1		4	3	
1977	7	7		4	3		3	4	
1978	6	10		3	5		3	5	
1979	5	11		3	5		2	6	
1980	5	11		2	6		3	5	
1981	7	9		5	3		2	6	
1982	5	4		1	3		4	1	
1983	8	7	1	4	3	1	4	4	
1984	9	7		5	3		4	4	
1985	5	11		4	4		1	7	
1986	4	11	1	3	5		1	6	1
1987	7	8		4	3		3	5	
1988	7	9		4	4		3	5	
1989	5	11		2	6		3	5	
1990	5	11		3	5		2	6	
1991	4	12		2	6		2	6	
1992	4	12		3	5		1	7	
1993	7	9		4	4		3	5	
1994	8	8		5	3		3	5	
1995	4	12		3	5		1	7	
1996	7	9		5	3		2	6	
1997	4	12		3	5		1	7	
1998	9	7		5	3		4	4	
1999	6	10		4	4		2	6	
2000	3	13		3	5		0	8	
2001	7	9		3	5		4	4	
	431	594	39	248	260	22	183	334	17

*includes Chicago Cardinals (1920-1959), St. Louis Cardinals (1960-1987), and Phoenix Cardinals (1988-1993).

ATLANTA FALCONS

Season	All Games			Home Games			Road Games		
	W	L	T	W	L	T	W	L	T
1966	3	11		1	6		2	5	
1967	1	12	1	1	5	1	0	7	
1968	2	12		1	6		1	6	
1969	6	8		4	3		2	5	
1970	4	8	2	3	4		1	4	2
1971	7	6	1	4	3		3	3	1
1972	7	7		4	3		3	4	
1973	9	5		4	3		5	2	
1974	3	11		2	5		1	6	
1975	4	10		3	4		1	6	
1976	4	10		3	4		1	6	
1977	7	7		4	3		3	4	
1978	9	7		7	1		2	6	
1979	6	10		3	5		3	5	
1980	12	4		6	2		6	2	
1981	7	9		4	4		3	5	
1982	5	4		2	3		3	1	
1983	7	9		4	4		3	5	
1984	4	12		2	6		2	6	
1985	4	12		3	5		1	7	
1986	7	8	1	2	5	1	5	3	
1987	3	12		2	6		1	6	
1988	5	11		2	6		3	5	
1989	3	13		3	5		0	8	
1990	5	11		5	3		0	8	
1991	10	6		6	2		4	4	
1992	6	10		5	3		1	7	
1993	6	10		4	4		2	6	
1994	7	9		5	3		2	6	
1995	9	7		7	1		2	6	
1996	3	13		2	6		1	7	
1997	7	9		3	5		4	4	
1998	14	2		8	0		6	2	
1999	5	11		4	4		1	7	
2000	4	12		3	5		1	7	
2001	7	9		3	5		4	4	
	212	327	5	129	142	2	83	185	3

CAROLINA PANTHERS

Season	All Games			Home Games			Road Games		
	W	L	T	W	L	T	W	L	T
1995	7	9		5	3		2	6	
1996	12	4		8	0		4	4	
1997	7	9		2	6		5	3	
1998	4	12		2	6		2	6	
1999	8	8		5	3		3	5	
2000	7	9		5	3		2	6	
2001	1	15		0	8		1	7	
	46	66		27	29		19	37	

CHICAGO BEARS*

Season	All Games			Home Games			Road Games		
	W	L	T	W	L	T	W	L	T
1920	10	1	2	6	0	1	4	1	1
1921	9	1	1	9	1	1	0	0	
1922	9	3		7	1		2	2	
1923	9	2	1	7	1	1	2	1	
1924	6	1	4	5	0	3	1	1	1
1925	9	5	3	7	1	1	2	4	2
1926	12	1	3	10	0	2	2	1	1
1927	9	3	2	7	1	1	2	2	1
1928	7	5	1	6	3		1	2	1
1929	4	9	2	1	5	2	3	4	
1930	9	4	1	5	2	1	4	2	
1931	8	5		6	3		2	2	
1932	7	1	6	6	1	1	1	0	5
1933	10	2	1	6	0		4	2	1
1934	13	0		5	0		8	0	
1935	6	4	2	1	2	2	5	2	
1936	9	3		3	1		6	2	
1937	9	1	1	4	1		5	0	1
1938	6	5		2	3		4	2	
1939	8	3		4	1		4	2	
1940	8	3		5	0		3	3	
1941	10	1		5	1		5	0	
1942	11	0		6	0		5	0	

Season	W	L	T	W	L	T	W	L	T
1943	8	1	1	5	0		3	1	1
1944	6	3	1	4	0	1	2	3	
1945	3	7		2	3		1	4	
1946	8	2	1	4	1	1	4	1	
1947	8	4		4	2		4	2	
1948	10	2		5	1		5	1	
1949	9	3		5	1		4	2	
1950	9	3		6	0		3	3	
1951	7	5		3	3		4	2	
1952	5	7		3	3		2	4	
1953	3	8	1	1	4	1	2	4	
1954	8	4		4	2		4	2	
1955	8	4		5	1		3	3	
1956	9	2	1	6	0		3	2	1
1957	5	7		2	4		3	3	
1958	8	4		5	1		3	3	
1959	8	4		4	2		4	2	
1960	5	6	1	4	2		1	4	1
1961	8	6		5	2		3	4	
1962	9	5		4	3		5	2	
1963	11	1	2	6	0	1	5	1	1
1964	5	9		2	5		3	4	
1965	9	5		5	2		4	3	
1966	5	7	2	4	1	2	1	6	
1967	7	6	1	3	3	1	4	3	
1968	7	7		2	5		5	2	
1969	1	13		1	6		0	7	
1970	6	8		3	4		3	4	
1971	6	8		4	3		2	5	
1972	4	9	1	1	5	1	3	4	
1973	3	11		1	6		2	5	
1974	4	10		4	3		0	7	
1975	4	10		3	4		1	6	
1976	7	7		4	3		3	4	
1977	9	5		5	2		4	3	
1978	7	9		4	4		3	5	
1979	10	6		6	2		4	4	
1980	7	9		5	3		2	6	
1981	6	10		4	4		2	6	
1982	3	6		2	2		1	4	
1983	8	8		5	3		3	5	
1984	10	6		6	2		4	4	
1985	15	1		8	0		7	1	
1986	14	2		7	1		7	1	
1987	11	4		6	2		5	2	
1988	12	4		7	1		5	3	
1989	6	10		4	4		2	6	
1990	11	5		7	1		4	4	
1991	11	5		6	2		5	3	
1992	5	11		4	4		1	7	
1993	7	9		3	5		4	4	
1994	9	7		5	3		4	4	
1995	9	7		5	3		4	4	
1996	7	9		6	2		1	7	
1997	4	12		2	6		2	6	
1998	4	12		3	5		1	7	
1999	6	10		3	5		3	5	
2000	5	11		3	5		2	6	
2001	13	3		7	1		6	2	
	630	442	42	370	185	24	260	257	18

*includes Decatur Staleys (1920) and Chicago Staleys (1921).

DALLAS COWBOYS

	All Games			Home Games			Road Games		
Season	W	L	T	W	L	T	W	L	T
1960	0	11	1	0	6		0	5	1
1961	4	9	1	2	4	1	2	5	
1962	5	8	1	2	4	1	3	4	
1963	4	10		3	4		1	6	
1964	5	8	1	2	4	1	3	4	

Season	W	L	T	W	L	T	W	L	T
1965	7	7		5	2		2	5	
1966	10	3	1	6	1		4	2	1
1967	9	5		5	2		4	3	
1968	12	2		5	2		7	0	
1969	11	2	1	6	0	1	5	2	
1970	10	4		6	1		4	3	
1971	11	3		6	1		5	2	
1972	10	4		5	2		5	2	
1973	10	4		6	1		4	3	
1974	8	6		5	2		3	4	
1975	10	4		5	2		5	2	
1976	11	3		6	1		5	2	
1977	12	2		6	1		6	1	
1978	12	4		7	1		5	3	
1979	11	5		6	2		5	3	
1980	12	4		8	0		4	4	
1981	12	4		8	0		4	4	
1982	6	3		3	2		3	1	
1983	12	4		6	2		6	2	
1984	9	7		5	3		4	4	
1985	10	6		7	1		3	5	
1986	7	9		3	5		4	4	
1987	7	8		3	4		4	4	
1988	3	13		1	7		2	6	
1989	1	15		0	8		1	7	
1990	7	9		5	3		2	6	
1991	11	5		6	2		5	3	
1992	13	3		7	1		6	2	
1993	12	4		6	2		6	2	
1994	12	4		6	2		6	2	
1995	12	4		6	2		6	2	
1996	10	6		6	2		4	4	
1997	6	10		5	3		1	7	
1998	10	6		6	2		4	4	
1999	8	8		7	1		1	7	
2000	5	11		3	5		2	6	
2001	5	11		4	4		1	7	
	362	258	6	205	104	4	157	154	2

DETROIT LIONS*

	All Games			Home Games			Road Games		
Season	W	L	T	W	L	T	W	L	T
1930	5	6	3	5	1	2	0	5	1
1931	11	3		8	0		3	3	
1932	6	2	4	3	0	2	3	2	2
1933	6	5		4	1		2	4	
1934	10	3		6	2		4	1	
1935	7	3	2	5	0	1	2	3	1
1936	8	4		5	1		3	3	
1937	7	4		4	2		3	2	
1938	7	4		4	3		3	1	
1939	6	5		4	2		2	3	
1940	5	5	1	3	3		2	2	1
1941	4	6	1	3	2		1	4	1
1942	0	11		0	7		0	4	
1943	3	6	1	2	2	1	1	4	
1944	6	3	1	4	2		2	1	1
1945	7	3		4	1		3	2	
1946	1	10		1	5		0	5	
1947	3	9		2	4		1	5	
1948	2	10		2	4		0	6	
1949	4	8		2	4		2	4	
1950	6	6		4	2		2	4	
1951	7	4	1	3	3	1	4	1	
1952	9	3		6	1		3	2	
1953	10	2		5	1		5	1	
1954	9	2	1	5	0	1	4	2	
1955	3	9		3	4		0	5	
1956	9	3		5	1		4	2	
1957	8	4		5	1		3	3	

Year	W	L	T	W	L	T	W	L	T
1958	4	7	1	2	4		2	3	1
1959	3	8	1	2	4		1	4	1
1960	7	5		5	1		2	4	
1961	8	5	1	2	5		6	0	1
1962	11	3		7	0		4	3	
1963	5	8	1	3	3	1	2	5	
1964	7	5	2	3	3	1	4	2	1
1965	6	7	1	2	4	1	4	3	
1966	4	9	1	3	4		1	5	1
1967	5	7	2	3	4		2	3	2
1968	4	8	2	1	4	2	3	4	
1969	9	4	1	5	2		4	2	1
1970	10	4		6	1		4	3	
1971	7	6	1	3	4		4	2	1
1972	8	5	1	5	2		3	3	1
1973	6	7	1	4	3		2	4	1
1974	7	7		5	2		2	5	
1975	7	7		4	3		3	4	
1976	6	8		5	2		1	6	
1977	6	8		5	2		1	6	
1978	7	9		5	3		2	6	
1979	2	14		2	6		0	8	
1980	9	7		6	2		3	5	
1981	8	8		7	1		1	7	
1982	4	5		2	3		2	2	
1983	9	7		6	2		3	5	
1984	4	11	1	2	5	1	2	6	
1985	7	9		6	2		1	7	
1986	5	11		1	7		4	4	
1987	4	11		1	6		3	5	
1988	4	12		2	6		2	6	
1989	7	9		4	4		3	5	
1990	6	10		3	5		3	5	
1991	12	4		8	0		4	4	
1992	5	11		3	5		2	6	
1993	10	6		5	3		5	3	
1994	9	7		6	2		3	5	
1995	10	6		7	1		3	5	
1996	5	11		4	4		1	7	
1997	9	7		6	2		3	5	
1998	5	11		4	4		1	7	
1999	8	8		6	2		2	6	
2000	9	7		4	4		5	3	
2001	2	14		2	6		0	8	
	459	486	32	284	201	14	175	285	18

*includes Portsmouth Spartans (1930-33).

GREEN BAY PACKERS

Season	All Games			Home Games			Road Games		
	W	L	T	W	L	T	W	L	T
1921	3	2	1	2	1		1	1	1
1922	4	3	3	4	1	1	0	2	2
1923	7	2	1	4	2	1	3	0	
1924	7	4		5	0		2	4	
1925	8	5		6	0		2	5	
1926	7	3	3	4	1	2	3	2	1
1927	7	2	1	6	1		1	1	1
1928	6	4	3	2	2	2	4	2	1
1929	12	0	1	5	0		7	0	1
1930	10	3	1	6	0		4	3	1
1931	12	2		8	0		4	2	
1932	10	3	1	5	0	1	5	3	
1933	5	7	1	3	2	1	2	5	
1934	7	6		4	2		3	4	
1935	8	4		5	2		3	2	
1936	10	1	1	5	1		5	0	1
1937	7	4		3	2		4	2	
1938	8	3		4	2		4	1	
1939	9	2		4	1		5	1	
1940	6	4	1	4	2		2	2	1
1941	10	1		4	1		6	0	
1942	8	2	1	4	1		4	1	1
1943	7	2	1	2	1	1	5	1	
1944	8	2		5	0		3	2	
1945	6	4		4	1		2	3	
1946	6	5		2	3		4	2	
1947	6	5	1	4	2		2	3	1
1948	3	9		2	4		1	5	
1949	2	10		1	5		1	5	
1950	3	9		3	3		0	6	
1951	3	9		2	4		1	5	
1952	6	6		3	3		3	3	
1953	2	9	1	1	5		1	4	1
1954	4	8		2	4		2	4	
1955	6	6		5	1		1	5	
1956	4	8		2	4		2	4	
1957	3	9		1	5		2	4	
1958	1	10	1	1	4	1	0	6	
1959	7	5		4	2		3	3	
1960	8	4		4	2		4	2	
1961	11	3		6	1		5	2	
1962	13	1		7	0		6	1	
1963	11	2	1	6	1		5	1	1
1964	8	5	1	4	3		4	2	1
1965	10	3	1	6	1		4	2	1
1966	12	2		6	1		6	1	
1967	9	4	1	4	2	1	5	2	
1968	6	7	1	2	5		4	2	1
1969	8	6		5	2		3	4	
1970	6	8		4	3		2	5	
1971	4	8	2	3	3	1	1	5	1
1972	10	4		4	3		6	1	
1973	5	7	2	3	2	2	2	5	
1974	6	8		4	3		2	5	
1975	4	10		3	4		1	6	
1976	5	9		4	3		1	6	
1977	4	10		2	5		2	5	
1978	8	7	1	5	2	1	3	5	
1979	5	11		4	4		1	7	
1980	5	10	1	4	4		1	6	1
1981	8	8		4	4		4	4	
1982	5	3	1	3	1		2	2	1
1983	8	8		5	3		3	5	
1984	8	8		5	3		3	5	
1985	8	8		5	3		3	5	
1986	4	12		1	7		3	5	
1987	5	9	1	2	5	1	3	4	
1988	4	12		2	6		2	6	
1989	10	6		6	2		4	4	
1990	6	10		3	5		3	5	
1991	4	12		2	6		2	6	
1992	9	7		6	2		3	5	
1993	9	7		6	2		3	5	
1994	9	7		7	1		2	6	
1995	11	5		7	1		4	4	
1996	13	3		8	0		5	3	
1997	13	3		8	0		5	3	
1998	11	5		7	1		4	4	
1999	8	8		5	3		3	5	
2000	9	7		6	2		3	5	
2001	12	4		7	1		5	3	
	580	464	36	336	187	16	244	277	20

MINNESOTA VIKINGS

Season	All Games			Home Games			Road Games		
	W	L	T	W	L	T	W	L	T
1961	3	11		3	4		0	7	
1962	2	11	1	1	5	1	1	6	
1963	5	8	1	3	4		2	4	1
1964	8	5	1	4	3		4	2	1

Year	W	L	T	W	L	T	W	L	T
1965	7	7		2	5		5	2	
1966	4	9	1	2	5		2	4	1
1967	3	8	3	1	4	2	2	4	1
1968	8	6		4	3		4	3	
1969	12	2		7	0		5	2	
1970	12	2		7	0		5	2	
1971	11	3		5	2		6	1	
1972	7	7		3	4		4	3	
1973	12	2		7	0		5	2	
1974	10	4		4	3		6	1	
1975	12	2		7	0		5	2	
1976	11	2	1	6	0	1	5	2	
1977	9	5		5	2		4	3	
1978	8	7	1	5	3		3	4	1
1979	7	9		5	3		2	6	
1980	9	7		5	3		4	4	
1981	7	9		5	3		2	6	
1982	5	4		4	1		1	3	
1983	8	8		3	5		5	3	
1984	3	13		2	6		1	7	
1985	7	9		4	4		3	5	
1986	9	7		5	3		4	4	
1987	8	7		5	3		3	4	
1988	11	5		7	1		4	4	
1989	10	6		8	0		2	6	
1990	6	10		4	4		2	6	
1991	8	8		4	4		4	4	
1992	11	5		5	3		6	2	
1993	9	7		4	4		5	3	
1994	10	6		6	2		4	4	
1995	8	8		6	2		2	6	
1996	9	7		5	3		4	4	
1997	9	7		5	3		4	4	
1998	15	1		8	0		7	1	
1999	10	6		6	2		4	4	
2000	11	5		7	1		4	4	
2001	5	11		5	3		0	8	
	339	266	9	194	110	4	145	156	5

NEW ORLEANS SAINTS

	All Games			Home Games			Road Games		
Season	W	L	T	W	L	T	W	L	T
1967	3	11		2	5		1	6	
1968	4	9	1	3	4		1	5	1
1969	5	9		3	4		2	5	
1970	2	11	1	2	5		0	6	1
1971	4	8	2	2	4	1	2	4	1
1972	2	11	1	2	5		0	6	1
1973	5	9		5	2		0	7	
1974	5	9		4	3		1	6	
1975	2	12		2	5		0	7	
1976	4	10		2	5		2	5	
1977	3	11		2	5		1	6	
1978	7	9		3	5		4	4	
1979	8	8		3	5		5	3	
1980	1	15		0	8		1	7	
1981	4	12		2	6		2	6	
1982	4	5		2	3		2	2	
1983	8	8		5	3		3	5	
1984	7	9		3	5		4	4	
1985	5	11		3	5		2	6	
1986	7	9		4	4		3	5	
1987	12	3		6	1		6	2	
1988	10	6		5	3		5	3	
1989	9	7		5	3		4	4	
1990	8	8		5	3		3	5	
1991	11	5		6	2		5	3	
1992	12	4		6	2		6	2	
1993	8	8		4	4		4	4	
1994	7	9		3	5		4	4	

Year	W	L	T	W	L	T	W	L	T
1995	7	9		4	4		3	5	
1996	3	13		2	6		1	7	
1997	6	10		3	5		3	5	
1998	6	10		4	4		2	6	
1999	3	13		3	5		0	8	
2000	10	6		3	5		7	1	
2001	7	9		3	5		4	4	
	209	316	5	116	148	1	93	168	4

NEW YORK GIANTS

	All Games			Home Games			Road Games		
Season	W	L	T	W	L	T	W	L	T
1925	8	4		7	2		1	2	
1926	8	4	1	5	2	1	3	2	
1927	11	1	1	7	1		4	0	1
1928	4	7	2	1	2	2	3	5	
1929	13	1	1	7	1		6	0	1
1930	13	4		6	2		7	2	
1931	7	6	1	4	2	1	3	4	
1932	4	6	2	3	2	1	1	4	1
1933	11	3		7	0		4	3	
1934	8	5		5	1		3	4	
1935	9	3		4	2		5	1	
1936	5	6	1	3	3	1	2	3	
1937	6	3	2	4	2	1	2	1	1
1938	8	2	1	6	1		2	1	1
1939	9	1	1	6	0		3	1	1
1940	6	4	1	4	3		2	1	1
1941	8	3		5	2		3	1	
1942	5	5	1	3	2	1	2	3	
1943	6	3	1	4	2		2	1	1
1944	8	1	1	5	1		3	0	1
1945	3	6	1	2	4		1	2	1
1946	7	3	1	5	1	1	2	2	
1947	2	8	2	2	3	1	0	5	1
1948	4	8		2	4		2	4	
1949	6	6		2	4		4	2	
1950	10	2		5	1		5	1	
1951	9	2	1	5	1		4	1	1
1952	7	5		2	4		5	1	
1953	3	9		2	4		1	5	
1954	7	5		4	2		3	3	
1955	6	5	1	4	1	1	2	4	
1956	8	3	1	4	1	1	4	2	
1957	7	5		3	3		4	2	
1958	9	3		5	1		4	2	
1959	10	2		5	1		5	1	
1960	6	4	2	1	3	2	5	1	
1961	10	3	1	4	2	1	6	1	
1962	12	2		6	1		6	1	
1963	11	3		5	2		6	1	
1964	2	10	2	2	5		0	5	2
1965	7	7		3	4		4	3	
1966	1	12	1	1	6		0	6	1
1967	7	7		5	2		2	5	
1968	7	7		3	4		4	3	
1969	6	8		5	2		1	6	
1970	9	5		5	2		4	3	
1971	4	10		1	6		3	4	
1972	8	6		4	3		4	3	
1973	2	11	1	2	4	1	0	7	
1974	2	12		0	7		2	5	
1975	5	9		2	5		3	4	
1976	3	11		3	4		0	7	
1977	5	9		3	4		2	5	
1978	6	10		5	3		1	7	
1979	6	10		4	4		2	6	
1980	4	12		2	6		2	6	
1981	9	7		4	4		5	3	
1982	4	5		2	3		2	2	

Season	W	L	T	W	L	T	W	L	T
1983	3	12	1	1	7		2	5	1
1984	9	7		6	2		3	5	
1985	10	6		6	2		4	4	
1986	14	2		8	0		6	2	
1987	6	9		5	3		1	6	
1988	10	6		5	3		5	3	
1989	12	4		7	1		5	3	
1990	13	3		7	1		6	2	
1991	8	8		5	3		3	5	
1992	6	10		4	4		2	6	
1993	11	5		6	2		5	3	
1994	9	7		4	4		5	3	
1995	5	11		3	5		2	6	
1996	6	10		3	5		3	5	
1997	10	5	1	6	2		4	3	1
1998	8	8		5	3		3	5	
1999	7	9		4	4		3	5	
2000	12	4		5	3		7	1	
2001	7	9		5	3		2	6	
	557	459	33	315	211	16	242	248	17

PHILADELPHIA EAGLES

	All Games			Home Games			Road Games		
Season	W	L	T	W	L	T	W	L	T
1933	3	5	1	2	3	1	1	2	
1934	4	7		2	4		2	3	
1935	2	9		0	5		2	4	
1936	1	11		1	6		0	5	
1937	2	8	1	0	5	1	2	3	
1938	5	6		2	3		3	3	
1939	1	9	1	1	3	1	0	6	
1940	1	10		1	4		0	6	
1941	2	8	1	1	4	1	1	4	
1942	2	9		0	5		2	4	
1944	7	1	2	3	1	2	4	0	
1945	7	3		6	0		1	3	
1946	6	5		3	2		3	3	
1947	8	4		6	1		2	3	
1948	9	2	1	6	0		3	2	1
1949	11	1		6	0		5	1	
1950	6	6		2	4		4	2	
1951	4	8		1	5		3	3	
1952	7	5		4	2		3	3	
1953	7	4	1	5	0	1	2	4	
1954	7	4	1	5	1		2	3	1
1955	4	7	1	4	2		0	5	1
1956	3	8	1	2	3	1	1	5	
1957	4	8		3	3		1	5	
1958	2	9	1	2	4		0	5	1
1959	7	5		5	1		2	4	
1960	10	2		5	1		5	1	
1961	10	4		5	2		5	2	
1962	3	10	1	2	5		1	5	1
1963	2	10	2	1	5	1	1	5	1
1964	6	8		3	4		3	4	
1965	5	9		2	5		3	4	
1966	9	5		5	2		4	3	
1967	6	7	1	5	2		1	5	1
1968	2	12		1	6		1	6	
1969	4	9	1	2	5		2	4	1
1970	3	10	1	3	3	1	0	7	
1971	6	7	1	3	4		3	3	1
1972	2	11	1	0	6	1	2	5	
1973	5	8	1	4	3		1	5	1
1974	7	7		5	2		2	5	
1975	4	10		2	5		2	5	
1976	4	10		2	5		2	5	
1977	5	9		4	3		1	6	
1978	9	7		5	3		4	4	
1979	11	5		5	3		6	2	

Season	W	L	T	W	L	T	W	L	T
1980	12	4		7	1		5	3	
1981	10	6		6	2		4	4	
1982	3	6		1	4		2	2	
1983	5	11		1	7		4	4	
1984	6	9	1	5	3		1	6	1
1985	7	9		4	4		3	5	
1986	5	10	1	2	5	1	3	5	
1987	7	8		4	4		3	4	
1988	10	6		5	3		5	3	
1989	11	5		6	2		5	3	
1990	10	6		6	2		4	4	
1991	10	6		4	4		6	2	
1992	11	5		8	0		3	5	
1993	8	8		3	5		5	3	
1994	7	9		5	3		2	6	
1995	10	6		6	2		4	4	
1996	10	6		5	3		5	3	
1997	6	9	1	6	2		0	7	1
1998	3	13		3	5		0	8	
1999	5	11		4	4		1	7	
2000	11	5		5	3		6	2	
2001	11	5		4	4		7	1	
	413	485	24	237	217	12	176	268	12

ST. LOUIS RAMS*

	All Games			Home Games			Road Games		
Season	W	L	T	W	L	T	W	L	T
1937	1	10		0	5		1	5	
1938	4	7		2	2		2	5	
1939	5	5	1	3	2	1	2	3	
1940	4	6	1	3	1	1	1	5	
1941	2	9		1	4		1	5	
1942	5	6		3	2		2	4	
1944	4	6		1	2		3	4	
1945	9	1		4	0		5	1	
1946	6	4	1	3	2		3	2	1
1947	6	6		3	3		3	3	
1948	6	5	1	3	2	1	3	3	
1949	8	2	2	5	1		3	1	2
1950	9	3		5	1		4	2	
1951	8	4		5	2		3	2	
1952	9	3		5	1		4	2	
1953	8	3	1	5	1		3	2	1
1954	6	5	1	3	2	1	3	3	
1955	8	3	1	5	1		3	2	1
1956	4	8		4	2		0	6	
1957	6	6		5	1		1	5	
1958	8	4		4	2		4	2	
1959	2	10		0	6		2	4	
1960	4	7	1	2	3	1	2	4	
1961	4	10		4	3		0	7	
1962	1	12	1	0	7		1	5	1
1963	5	9		3	4		2	5	
1964	5	7	2	3	2	2	2	5	
1965	4	10		3	4		1	6	
1966	8	6		5	2		3	4	
1967	11	1	2	5	1	1	6	0	1
1968	10	3	1	5	2		5	1	1
1969	11	3		5	2		6	1	
1970	9	4	1	3	3	1	6	1	
1971	8	5	1	4	2	1	4	3	
1972	6	7	1	4	3		2	4	1
1973	12	2		7	0		5	2	
1974	10	4		6	1		4	3	
1975	12	2		6	1		6	1	
1976	10	3	1	5	2		5	1	1
1977	10	4		7	0		3	4	
1978	12	4		6	2		6	2	
1979	9	7		4	4		5	3	
1980	11	5		6	2		5	3	

Season	All Games W	L	T	Home Games W	L	T	Road Games W	L	T
1981	6	10		4	4		2	6	
1982	2	7		1	4		1	3	
1983	9	7		5	3		4	4	
1984	10	6		5	3		5	3	
1985	11	5		6	2		5	3	
1986	10	6		6	2		4	4	
1987	6	9		3	4		3	5	
1988	10	6		4	4		6	2	
1989	11	5		6	2		5	3	
1990	5	11		2	6		3	5	
1991	3	13		2	6		1	7	
1992	6	10		4	4		2	6	
1993	5	11		3	5		2	6	
1994	4	12		3	5		1	7	
1995	7	9		4	4		3	5	
1996	6	10		4	4		2	6	
1997	5	11		2	6		3	5	
1998	4	12		2	6		2	6	
1999	13	3		8	0		5	3	
2000	10	6		5	3		5	3	
2001	14	2		6	2		8	0	
	457	402	20	250	174	10	207	228	10

*includes Cleveland Rams (1937-1942, 1944-45) and Los Angeles Rams (1946-1994).

SAN FRANCISCO 49ERS

Season	All Games W	L	T	Home Games W	L	T	Road Games W	L	T
1950	3	9		3	3		0	6	
1951	7	4	1	5	1		2	3	1
1952	7	5		3	3		4	2	
1953	9	3		5	1		4	2	
1954	7	4	1	4	2		3	2	1
1955	4	8		2	4		2	4	
1956	5	6	1	3	3		2	3	1
1957	8	4		5	1		3	3	
1958	6	6		4	2		2	4	
1959	7	5		4	2		3	3	
1960	7	5		3	3		4	2	
1961	7	6	1	5	1	1	2	5	
1962	6	8		1	6		5	2	
1963	2	12		2	5		0	7	
1964	4	10		3	4		1	6	
1965	7	6	1	4	2	1	3	4	
1966	6	6	2	4	2	1	2	4	1
1967	7	7		3	4		4	3	
1968	7	6	1	3	3	1	4	3	
1969	4	8	2	3	3	1	1	5	1
1970	10	3	1	5	1	1	5	2	
1971	9	5		4	3		5	2	
1972	8	5	1	4	2	1	4	3	
1973	5	9		3	4		2	5	
1974	6	8		3	4		3	4	
1975	5	9		2	5		3	4	
1976	8	6		4	3		4	3	
1977	5	9		3	4		2	5	
1978	2	14		2	6		0	8	
1979	2	14		2	6		0	8	
1980	6	10		4	4		2	6	
1981	13	3		7	1		6	2	
1982	3	6		0	5		3	1	
1983	10	6		4	4		6	2	
1984	15	1		7	1		8	0	
1985	10	6		5	3		5	3	
1986	10	5	1	6	2		4	3	1
1987	13	2		6	1		7	1	
1988	10	6		4	4		6	2	
1989	14	2		6	2		8	0	
1990	14	2		6	2		8	0	
1991	10	6		7	1		3	5	
1992	14	2		7	1		7	1	
1993	10	6		6	2		4	4	
1994	13	3		7	1		6	2	
1995	11	5		6	2		5	3	
1996	12	4		6	2		6	2	
1997	13	3		8	0		5	3	
1998	12	4		8	0		4	4	
1999	4	12		3	5		1	7	
2000	6	10		4	4		2	6	
2001	12	4		7	1		5	3	
	415	318	13	225	141	7	190	177	6

SEATTLE SEAHAWKS

Season	All Games W	L	T	Home Games W	L	T	Road Games W	L	T
1976	2	12		1	6		1	6	
1977	5	9		3	4		2	5	
1978	9	7		5	3		4	4	
1979	9	7		5	3		4	4	
1980	4	12		0	8		4	4	
1981	6	10		5	3		1	7	
1982	4	5		3	2		1	3	
1983	9	7		5	3		4	4	
1984	12	4		7	1		5	3	
1985	8	8		5	3		3	5	
1986	10	6		7	1		3	5	
1987	9	6		6	2		3	4	
1988	9	7		5	3		4	4	
1989	7	9		3	5		4	4	
1990	9	7		5	3		4	4	
1991	7	9		5	3		2	6	
1992	2	14		1	7		1	7	
1993	6	10		4	4		2	6	
1994	6	10		3	5		3	5	
1995	8	8		5	3		3	5	
1996	7	9		4	4		3	5	
1997	8	8		4	4		4	4	
1998	8	8		6	2		2	6	
1999	9	7		5	3		4	4	
2000	6	10		3	5		3	5	
2001	9	7		6	2		3	5	
	188	216		111	92		77	124	

TAMPA BAY BUCCANEERS

Season	All Games W	L	T	Home Games W	L	T	Road Games W	L	T
1976	0	14		0	7		0	7	
1977	2	12		1	6		1	6	
1978	5	11		3	5		2	6	
1979	10	6		5	3		5	3	
1980	5	10	1	2	5	1	3	5	
1981	9	7		6	2		3	5	
1982	5	4		4	1		1	3	
1983	2	14		1	7		1	7	
1984	6	10		6	2		0	8	
1985	2	14		2	6		0	8	
1986	2	14		1	7		1	7	
1987	4	11		2	5		2	6	
1988	5	11		3	5		2	6	
1989	5	11		2	6		3	5	
1990	6	10		4	4		2	6	
1991	3	13		3	5		0	8	
1992	5	11		3	5		2	6	
1993	5	11		3	5		2	6	
1994	6	10		4	4		2	6	
1995	7	9		5	3		2	6	
1996	6	10		5	3		1	7	
1997	10	6		5	3		5	3	
1998	8	8		6	2		2	6	
1999	11	5		7	1		4	4	

	W	L	T		W	L	T		W	L	T
2000	10	6			6	2			4	4	
2001	9	7			5	3			4	4	
	148	255	1		94	107	1		54	148	

WASHINGTON REDSKINS*

	All Games			Home Games			Road Games		
Season	W	L	T	W	L	T	W	L	T
1932	4	4	2	2	3	1	2	1	1
1933	5	5	2	4	2		1	3	2
1934	6	6		4	3		2	3	
1935	2	8	1	2	5		0	3	1
1936	7	5		4	3		3	2	
1937	8	3		4	2		4	1	
1938	6	3	2	3	1	1	3	2	1
1939	8	2	1	5	0	1	3	2	
1940	9	2		6	0		3	2	
1941	6	5		4	2		2	3	
1942	10	1		5	1		5	0	
1943	6	3	1	4	2		2	1	1
1944	6	3	1	4	2		2	1	1
1945	8	2		6	0		2	2	
1946	5	5	1	3	2	1	2	3	
1947	4	8		4	2		0	6	
1948	7	5		4	2		3	3	
1949	4	7	1	3	3		1	4	1
1950	3	9		1	5		2	4	
1951	5	7		2	4		3	3	
1952	4	8		1	5		3	3	
1953	6	5	1	3	3		3	2	1
1954	3	9		3	3		0	6	
1955	8	4		3	3		5	1	
1956	6	6		4	2		2	4	
1957	5	6	1	2	3	1	3	3	
1958	4	7	1	3	2	1	1	5	
1959	3	9		2	4		1	5	
1960	1	9	2	1	4	1	0	5	1
1961	1	12	1	1	6		0	6	1
1962	5	7	2	3	4		2	3	2
1963	3	11		1	6		2	5	
1964	6	8		4	3		2	5	
1965	6	8		3	4		3	4	
1966	7	7		4	3		3	4	
1967	5	6	3	2	4	1	3	2	2
1968	5	9		3	4		2	5	
1969	7	5	2	4	2	1	3	3	1
1970	6	8		4	3		2	5	
1971	9	4	1	4	2	1	5	2	
1972	11	3		6	1		5	2	
1973	10	4		7	0		3	4	
1974	10	4		6	1		4	3	
1975	8	6		5	2		3	4	
1976	10	4		5	2		5	2	
1977	9	5		5	2		4	3	
1978	8	8		5	3		3	5	
1979	10	6		6	2		4	4	
1980	6	10		4	4		2	6	
1981	8	8		5	3		3	5	
1982	8	1		3	1		5	0	
1983	14	2		7	1		7	1	
1984	11	5		7	1		4	4	
1985	10	6		5	3		5	3	
1986	12	4		7	1		5	3	
1987	11	4		6	1		5	3	
1988	7	9		4	4		3	5	
1989	10	6		4	4		6	2	
1990	10	6		7	1		3	5	
1991	14	2		7	1		7	1	
1992	9	7		6	2		3	5	
1993	4	12		3	5		1	7	
1994	3	13		0	8		3	5	
1995	6	10		4	4		2	6	
1996	9	7		5	3		4	4	
1997	8	7	1	5	2	1	3	5	
1998	6	10		4	4		2	6	
1999	10	6		6	2		4	4	
2000	8	8		4	4		4	4	
2001	8	8		4	4		4	4	
	487	432	27	281	190	11	206	242	16

*includes Boston Braves (1932) and Boston Redskins (1933-36).

History

The Professional Football Hall of Fame is located in Canton, Ohio, site of the organizational meeting on September 17, 1920, from which the National Football League evolved. The NFL recognized Canton as the Hall of Fame site on April 27, 1961. Canton area individuals, foundations, and companies donated almost $400,000 in cash and services to provide funds for the construction of the original two-building complex, which was dedicated on September 7, 1963. Since that time, the Hall added three buildings with major expansion projects in 1971, 1978, and 1995. The Hall's largest-ever expansion, a $9.2 million project, was completed in early fall 1995. With the new fifth building, the Hall's size is now 82,307-square feet, more than four times its original size.

The expanded Hall represents the sport of pro football in many ways—through (1) GameDay Stadium, a dynamic two-part turntable theater featuring NFL action in Cinemascope for the first time, (2) a standard theater showing NFL films hourly, (3) six large exhibition areas where the history of pro football is detailed in memento, picture, and story form, (4) an extensive archive and information center, and (5) a new and enlarged museum store.

Throughout the years, the Pro Football Hall of Fame has become an extremely popular tourist attraction. At the end of 2001, a total of 7,054,806 fans had visited the Hall of Fame.

New members of the Pro Football Hall of Fame are elected annually by a 38-member National Board of Selectors, made up of media representatives from every league city, six at-large representatives, and a representative of the Pro Football Writers of America. Between four and seven new members are elected each year. An affirmative vote of approximately 80 percent is needed for election.

Any fan may nominate any eligible player or contributor simply by writing to the Pro Football Hall of Fame. Players must be retired five years to be eligible, while a coach needs only to be retired with no time limit specified. Contributors (administrators, owners, *et al.*) may be elected while they are still active.

The charter class of 17 enshrinees was elected in 1963 and the honor roll now stands at 216 with the election of a five-man class in 2002. That class consists of George Allen, Dave Casper, Dan Hampton, Jim Kelly, and John Stallworth.

ROSTER OF MEMBERS

HERB ADDERLEY
Cornerback. 6-0, 205. Born in Philadelphia, Pennsylvania, June 8, 1939. Michigan State. Inducted in 1980. 1961-69 Green Bay Packers, 1970-72 Dallas Cowboys. **Highlights:** 48 interceptions, 7 touchdowns. Played in four Super Bowls, five Pro Bowls.

GEORGE ALLEN
Coach. Born in Detroit, Michigan, April 29, 1918. Died December 31, 1990. Alma College, Marquette, Michigan. Inducted in 2002. 1966-1970 Los Angeles Rams, 1971-77 Washington Redskins. **Highlights:** 118-54-5 overall record. Never suffered a losing season, and ranked tenth in coaching victories at time of retirement.

LANCE ALWORTH
Wide receiver. 6-0, 184. Born in Houston, Texas, August 3, 1940. Arkansas. Inducted in 1978. 1962-1970 San Diego Chargers, 1971-72 Dallas Cowboys. **Highlights:** 542 receptions for 10,266 yards, 85 touchdowns. All-AFL seven times, seven All-Star games.

DOUG ATKINS
Defensive end. 6-8, 275. Born in Humboldt, Tennessee, May 8, 1930. Tennessee. Inducted in 1982. 1953-54 Cleveland Browns, 1955-1966 Chicago Bears, 1967-69 New Orleans Saints. **Highlights:** Eight Pro Bowls, All-NFL four times. Played for 17 years, 205 games.

MORRIS (RED) BADGRO
End. 6-0, 190. Born in Orillia, Washington, December 1, 1902. Died July 13, 1998. Southern California. Inducted in 1981. 1927 New York Yankees, 1930-35 New York Giants, 1936 Brookly Dodgers. **Highlights:** All-NFL four times. Scored first touchdown in NFL Championship Game series.

LEM BARNEY
Cornerback. 6-0, 190. Born in Gulfport, Mississippi, September 8, 1945. Jackson State. Inducted in 1992. 1967-1977 Detroit Lions. **Highlights:** 56 interceptions for 1,077 yards, 11 touchdowns (7 defensive, 4 special teams). Seven Pro Bowls, All-NFL/NFC four times.

CLIFF BATTLES
Halfback. 6-1, 195. Born in Akron, Ohio, May 1, 1910. Died April 28, 1981. West Virginia Wesleyan. Inducted in 1968. 1932 Boston Braves, 1933-36 Boston Redskins, 1937 Washington Redskins. **Highlights:** NFL rushing champion 1932, 1937. First to gain more than 200 yards in a game, 1933.

SAMMY BAUGH
Quarterback. 6-2, 180. Born in Temple, Texas, March 17, 1914. Texas Christian. Inducted in 1963. 1937-1952 Washington Redskins. **Highlights:** Charter enshrinee. Six-time NFL passing leader. NFL passing, punting, interception champ, 1943.

CHUCK BEDNARIK
Center-linebacker. 6-3, 230. Born in Bethlehem, Pennsylvania, May 1, 1925. Pennsylvania. Inducted in 1967. 1949-1962 Philadelphia Eagles. **Highlights:** Eight Pro Bowls. Missed three games in 14 years. Named NFL all-time center, 1969.

MORRIS (RED) BADGRO
End. 6-0, 190. Born in Orillia, Washington, December 1, 1902. Died July 13, 1998. Southern California. Inducted in 1981. 1927 New York Yankees, 1930-35 New York Giants, 1936 Brookly Dodgers. **Highlights:** All-NFL four times. Scored first touchdown in NFL Championship Game series.

BERT BELL
Team owner. Commissioner. Born in Philadelphia, Pennsylvania, February 25, 1895. Died October 11, 1959. Pennsylvania. Inducted in 1963. 1933-1940 Philadelphia Eagles, 1941-42 Pittsburgh Steelers, 1943 Phil-Pitt, 1944 Card-Pitt, 1945-46 Pittsburgh Steelers. Commissioner, 1946-1959. **Highlights:** Charter enshrinee. Built NFL image as commissioner, 1946-1959. Set up long-term television policies.

BOBBY BELL
Linebacker. 6-4, 225. Born in Shelby, North Carolina, June 17, 1940. Minnesota. Inducted in 1983. 1963-1974 Kansas City Chiefs. **Highlights:** 26 interceptions. All-AFL/AFC eight times. Nine career touchdowns, 1 on onside kick return.

RAYMOND BERRY
End. 6-2, 187. Born in Corpus Christi, Texas, February 27, 1933. Southern Methodist. Inducted in 1973. 1955-1967 Baltimore Colts. **Highlights:** 631 receptions for 9,275 yards, 68 touchdowns. Set NFL title game mark with 12 catches for 178 yards, 1958.

CHARLES W. BIDWILL SR.
Team owner. Born in Chicago, Illinois, September 16, 1895. Died April 19, 1947. Loyola of Chicago. Inducted in 1967. 1933-1943 Chicago Cardinals, 1944 Card-Pitt, 1945-47 Chicago Cardinals. **Highlights:** Guiding light for NFL during depression years. Built famous "Dream Backfield."

FRED BILETNIKOFF
Wide receiver. 6-1, 190. Born in Erie, Pennsylvania, February 23, 1943. Florida State. Inducted in 1988. 1965-1978 Oakland Raiders. **Highlights:** 589 receptions for 8,974 yards, 76 touchdowns. 40 catches 10 straight years. MVP, Super Bowl XI.

GEORGE BLANDA
Quarterback-kicker. 6-2, 215. Born in Youngwood, Pennsylvania, September 17, 1927. Kentucky. Inducted in 1981. 1949-1958 Chicago Bears, 1950 Baltimore Colts, 1960-66 Houston Oilers, 1967-1975 Oakland Raiders. **Highlights:** 2,002 career points. 26-season, 340-game career longest in NFL history.

MEL BLOUNT
Cornerback. 6-3, 205. Born in Vidalia, Georgia, April 10, 1948. Southern University. Inducted in 1989. 1970-1983 Pittsburgh Steelers. **Highlights:** 57 interceptions for 736 yards. NFL defensive MVP, 1975. Played in five Pro Bowls.

TERRY BRADSHAW
Quarterback. 6-3, 210. Born in Shreveport, Louisiana, September 2, 1948. Louisiana Tech. Inducted in 1989. 1970-1983 Pittsburgh Steelers. **Highlights:** 27,989 yards passing, 212 touchdowns. MVP in Super Bowls XIII, XIV.

JIM BROWN
Fullback. 6-2, 228. Born in St. Simons, Georgia, February 17, 1936. Syracuse. Inducted in 1971. 1957-1965 Cleveland Browns. **Highlights:** 12,312 yards rushing, 756 points. Led NFL rushers eight years. Nine consecutive Pro Bowls.

PAUL BROWN
Coach. Born in Norwalk, Ohio, September 7, 1908. Died August 5, 1991. Miami (Ohio). Inducted in 1967. 1946-49 Cleveland Browns (AAFC), 1950-1962 Cleveland Browns. **Highlights:** Built Cleveland dynasty with 167-53-8 record, four AAFC titles, three NFL crowns. Returned to coaching with Cincinnati Bengals after induction, 1968-1975.

ROOSEVELT BROWN
Tackle. 6-3, 255. Born in Charlottes-ville, Virginia, October 20, 1932. Morgan State. Inducted in 1975. 1953-1965 New York Giants. **Highlights:** All-NFL eight consecutive years, nine Pro Bowls. NFL's lineman of year, 1956.

WILLIE BROWN
Cornerback. 6-1, 210. Born in Yazoo City, Mississippi, December 2, 1940. Grambling. Inducted in 1984. 1963-66 Denver Broncos, 1967-1978 Oakland Raiders. **Highlights:** 54 interceptions for 472 yards. Scored on 75-yard interception in Super Bowl XI.

BUCK BUCHANAN
Defensive tackle. 6-7, 274. Born in Gainesville, Alabama, September 10, 1940. Died July 16, 1992. Grambling. Inducted in 1990. 1963-1975 Kansas City Chiefs. **Highlights:** Led Chiefs defensive efforts in Super Bowl I, IV. Did not miss a game in 13 years.

NICK BUONICONTI
Linebacker. 5-11, 220. Born in Springfield, Massachusetts, December 15, 1940. Notre Dame. Inducted in 2001. 1962-68 Boston Patriots, 1969-1974, 1976 Miami Dolphins. **Highlights:** All-AFL/AFC eight times. Named to AFL's All-Time Team.

DICK BUTKUS
Linebacker. 6-3, 245. Born in Chicago, Illinois, December 9, 1942. Illinois. Inducted in 1979. 1965-1973 Chicago Bears. **Highlights:** All-NFL six years, eight consecutive Pro Bowls. 25 fumble recoveries.

EARL CAMPBELL
Running back. 5-11, 233. Born in Tyler, Texas, March 29, 1955. Texas. Inducted in 1991. 1978-1984 Houston Oilers, 1984-85 New Orleans Saints. **Highlights:** 9,407 yards rushing, 74 touchdowns. 1,934 yards rushing in 1980, including four games with at least 200 yards.

TONY CANADEO
Halfback. 5-11, 195. Born in Chicago, Illinois, May 5, 1919. Gonzaga. Inducted in 1974. 1941-44, 1946-1952 Green Bay Packers. **Highlights:** Two-way player. Third player to rush for 1,000 yards in single season, 1949.

JOE CARR
NFL president. Born in Columbus, Ohio, October 22, 1880. Died May 20, 1939. Did not attend college. Inducted in 1963. President, 1921-1939 National Football League. **Highlights:** Charter enshrinee. NFL co-organizer, 1920. Introduced standard player's contract.

DAVE CASPER
Tight end. 6-4, 240. Born in Bemidji, Minnesota, February 2, 1952. Notre Dame. Inducted in 2002. 1974-1980 Oakland Raiders, 1980-83 Houston Oilers, 1983 Minnesota Vikings, 1984 Los Angeles Raiders. **Highlights:** 378 receptions for 5,216 yards, 52 touchdowns. Five consecutive Pro Bowls.

GUY CHAMBERLIN
End. Coach. 6-2, 196. Born in Blue Springs, Nebraska, January 16, 1894. Died April 4, 1967. Nebraska. Inducted in 1965. 1919 Canton Bulldogs, 1920 Decatur Staleys, 1921 Chicago Staleys, player-coach 1922-23 Canton Bulldogs, 1924 Cleveland Bulldogs, 1925-26 Frankford Yellow Jackets, 1927-28 Chicago Cardinals. **Highlights:** Player-coach of four NFL championship teams. Six-year coaching record of 58-16-7.

JACK CHRISTIANSEN
Safety. 6-1, 185. Born in Sublette, Kansas, December 20, 1928. Died June 29, 1986. Colorado State. Inducted in 1970. 1951-58 Detroit Lions. **Highlights:** 46 interceptions. NFL interception leader, 1953, 1957. Eight punt returns for touchdowns.

EARL (DUTCH) CLARK
Quarterback. 6-0, 185. Born in Fowler, Colorado, October 11, 1906. Died August 5, 1978. Colorado College. Inducted in 1963. 1931-32 Portsmouth Spartans, 1934-38 Detroit Lions. **Highlights:** Charter enshrinee. NFL scoring champion three years. Led Lions to 1935 NFL title.

GEORGE CONNOR
Tackle-linebacker. 6-3, 240. Born in Chicago, Illinois, January 21, 1925. Holy Cross, Notre Dame. Inducted in 1975. 1948-1955 Chicago Bears. **Highlights:** All-NFL at three positions—T, DT, LB. All-NFL five years. Played in first four Pro Bowls.

JIMMY CONZELMAN
Quarterback. Coach. Team owner. 6-0, 180. Born in St. Louis, Missouri, March 6, 1898. Died July 31, 1970. Washington of St. Louis. Inducted in 1964. 1920 Decatur Staleys, 1921-22 Rock Island Independents, 1923-24 Milwaukee Badgers; owner-coach 1925-26 Detroit Panthers; player-coach 1927-29, coach 1930 Providence Steam Roller; coach 1940-42, 1946-48 Chicago Cardinals. **Highlights:** Player-coach of four NFL teams in 1920's. Coached Cardinals to 1947 NFL crown.

LOU CREEKMUR
Tackle-guard. 6-4, 255. Born in Hopelawn, New Jersey, January 22, 1927. William & Mary. Inducted in 1996. 1950-59 Detroit Lions. **Highlights:** All-NFL six times, twice at guard and four times at tackle. Selected to eight Pro Bowls and played on three NFL championship teams.

LARRY CSONKA
Running back. 6-3, 235. Born in Stow, Ohio, December 25, 1946. Syracuse. Inducted in 1987. 1968-1974, 1979 Miami Dolphins, 1976-78 New York Giants. **Highlights:** 8,081 yards rushing, 68 touchdowns. MVP Super Bowl VIII. Only 21 fumbles in 1,891 carries and 106 receptions.

AL DAVIS
Team, League Administrator. Born in Brockton, Massachusetts, July 4, 1929. Wittenberg, Syracuse. Inducted in 1992. 1963-1981, 1995-present Oakland Raiders, 1982-1994 Los Angeles Raiders, 1966 American Football League. **Highlights:** Only person to serve in pros as personnel assistant, scout, assistant coach, head coach, general manager, commissioner, team owner/CEO.

WILLIE DAVIS
Defensive end. 6-3, 245. Born in Lisbon, Louisiana, July 24, 1934. Grambling. Inducted in 1981. 1958-59 Cleveland Browns, 1960-69 Green Bay Packers. **Highlights:** All-NFL five seasons, five Pro Bowls. Did not miss game in 12-year career.

LEN DAWSON
Quarterback. 6-0, 190. Born in Alliance, Ohio, June 20, 1935. Purdue. Inducted in 1987. 1957-59 Pittsburgh Steelers, 1960-61 Cleveland Browns, 1962 Dallas Texans, 1963-1975 Kansas City Chiefs. **Highlights:** 28,711 yards passing, 239 touchdowns. Four AFL passing crowns. MVP, Super Bowl IV.

ERIC DICKERSON
Running back. 6-3, 220. Born in Sealy, Texas, September 2, 1960. Southern Methodist. Inducted in 1999. 1983-87 Los Angeles Rams, 1987-1991 Indianapolis Colts, 1992 Los Angeles Raiders, 1993 Atlanta Falcons. **Highlights:** Rushed for 13,259 career yards, including an NFL record 2,105 yards in 1984. All-Pro five times, six Pro Bowls.

DAN DIERDORF
Tackle. 6-3, 290. Born in Canton, Ohio, June 29, 1949. Michigan. Inducted in 1996. 1971-1983 St. Louis Cardinals. **Highlights:** All-Pro five times, played in six Pro Bowls, named NFL's best blocker three times.

MIKE DITKA
Tight end. 6-3, 225. Born in Carnegie, Pennsylvania, October 18, 1939. Pittsburgh. Inducted in 1988. 1961-66 Chicago Bears, 1967-68 Philadelphia Eagles, 1969-1972 Dallas Cowboys. **Highlights:** 427 receptions for 5,812 yards, 43 touchdowns. First tight end selected to Hall of Fame. Five consecutive Pro Bowls.

ART DONOVAN
Defensive tackle. 6-3, 265. Born in Bronx, New York, June 5, 1925. Boston College. Inducted in 1968. 1950 Baltimore Colts, 1951 New York Yanks, 1952 Dallas Texans, 1953-1961 Baltimore Colts. **Highlights:** Five Pro Bowls. Vital part of Baltimore's climb to powerhouse status in 1950s.

TONY DORSETT
Running back. 5-11, 184. Born in Rochester, Pennsylvania, April 7, 1954. Pittsburgh. Inducted in 1994. 1977-1987 Dallas Cowboys, 1988 Denver Broncos. **Highlights:** 12,739 yards rushing, 398 receptions, 91 touchdowns. Ran record 99 yards for touchdown vs. Minnesota, January, 1983.

JOHN (PADDY) DRISCOLL
Quarterback. 5-11, 160. Born in Evanston, Illinois, January 11, 1896. Died June 29, 1968. Northwestern. Inducted in 1965. 1919 Hammond Pros, 1920 Decatur Staleys, 1920-25 Chicago Cardinals, 1926-29 Chicago Bears. **Highlights:** All-NFL seven times. Dropkicked record 4 field goals in one game, 1925.

BILL DUDLEY
Halfback. 5-10, 182. Born in Bluefield, Virginia, December 24, 1921. Virginia. Inducted in 1966. 1942, 1945-46 Pittsburgh Steelers, 1947-49 Detroit Lions, 1950-51, 1953 Washington Redskins. **Highlights:** Won NFL rushing, interception, punt return titles, 1946. All-NFL 1942, 1946, and 1947.

ALBERT GLEN (TURK) EDWARDS
Tackle. 6-2, 260. Born in Mold, Washington, September 28, 1907. Died January 12, 1973. Washington State. Inducted in 1969. 1932 Boston Braves, 1933-36 Boston Redskins, 1937-1940 Washington Redskins. **Highlights:** All-NFL 1932-34, 1936, 1937. Steamrolling blocker, smothering tackler.

WEEB EWBANK
Coach. Born in Richmond, Indiana, May 6, 1907. Died November 17, 1998. Miami (Ohio). Inducted in 1978. 1954-1962 Baltimore Colts, 1963-1973 New York Jets. **Highlights:** Only coach to win championships in both NFL, AFL. Led both Colts (1958) and Jets (1968) to championships.

TOM FEARS
End. 6-2, 215. Born in Guadalajara, Mexico, December 3, 1923. Died January 4, 2000. Santa Clara, UCLA. Inducted in 1970. 1948-1956 Los Angeles Rams. **Highlights:** 400 receptions for 5,397 yards, 38 touchdowns. Led NFL receivers first three seasons. Had then-record 18 receptions in single game.

JIM FINKS
Administrator. Born in St. Louis, Missouri, August 31, 1927. Died May 8, 1994. Tulsa. Inducted 1995. 1964-1973 Minnesota Vikings, 1974-1982 Chicago Bears, 1986-1993 New Orleans Saints. **Highlights:** Developed Vikings, Bears, Saints—all teams with losing records—into winners.

RAY FLAHERTY
Coach. Born in Spokane, Washington, September 1, 1903. Died July 19, 1994. Gonzaga. Inducted in 1976. 1936 Boston Redskins, 1937-1942 Washington Redskins, 1946-48 New York Yankees (AAFC), 1949 Chicago Hornets (AAFC). **Highlights:** 82-41-5 coaching record. Introduced screen pass in 1937 title game and platoon system.

LEN FORD
Defensive end. 6-4, 260. Born in Washington, D.C., February 18, 1926. Died March 14, 1972. Morgan State, Michigan. Inducted in 1976. 1948-49 Los Angeles Dons (AAFC), 1950-57 Cleveland Browns, 1958 Green Bay Packers. **Highlights:** All-NFL five times, four Pro Bowls. Recovered 20 opponents' fumbles.

DAN FORTMANN
Guard. 6-0, 210. Born in Pearl River, New York, April 11, 1916. Died May 23, 1995. Colgate. Inducted in 1965. 1936-1943 Chicago Bears. **Highlights:** At 20, became youngest starter in NFL. All-NFL six consecutive years.

DAN FOUTS
Quarterback. 6-3, 210. Born in San Francisco, California, June 10, 1951. Oregon. Inducted in 1993. 1973-1987 San Diego Chargers. **Highlights:** 43,040 passing yards, 254 touchdowns. Six Pro Bowls, NFL MVP, 1982.

FRANK GATSKI
Center. 6-3, 240. Born in Farmington, West Virginia, March 18, 1922. Marshall, Auburn. Inducted in 1985. 1946-49 Cleveland Browns (AAFC), 1950-56 Cleveland Browns, 1957 Detroit Lions. **Highlights:** Never missed game in high school, college, or pro football. Played 11 championship games, winning eight.

BILL GEORGE
Linebacker. 6-2, 230. Born in Waynesburg, Pennsylvania, October 27, 1930. Died September 30, 1982. Wake Forest. Inducted in 1974. 1952-1965 Chicago Bears, 1966 Los Angeles Rams. **Highlights:** All-NFL eight years, eight consecutive Pro Bowls. 14 years of service, longest of any Bears player.

JOE GIBBS
Coach. Born in Mocksville, North Carolina, November 25, 1940. Cerritos (Calif.) J.C., San Diego State. Inducted in 1996. 1981-1992 Washington Redskins. **Highlights:** 124-60-0 record in regular season, 16-5 in postseason, including four Super Bowl appearances—winning three. Won 10 or more games eight times.

FRANK GIFFORD
Halfback. 6-1, 195. Born in Santa Monica, California, August 16, 1930. Southern California. Inducted in 1977. 1952-1960, 1962-64 New York Giants. **Highlights:** Starred on both offense and defense. Seven Pro Bowls, 1956 NFL player of the year.

SID GILLMAN
Coach. Born in Minneapolis, Minnesota, October 26, 1911. Ohio State. Inducted in 1983. 1955-59 Los Angeles Rams, 1960 Los Angeles Chargers, 1961-69, 1971 San Diego Chargers, 1973-74 Houston Oilers. **Highlights:** 123-104-7 coaching record. First to win division titles in both NFL, AFL.

OTTO GRAHAM
Quarterback. 6-1, 195. Born in Waukegan, Illinois, December 6, 1921. Northwestern. Inducted in 1965. 1946-49 Cleveland Browns (AAFC), 1950-55 Cleveland Browns. **Highlights:** 23,584 passing yards, 174 touchdowns. Guided Browns to 10 division or league crowns in 10 years.

HAROLD (RED) GRANGE
Halfback. 6-0, 185. Born in Forksville, Pennsylvania, June 13, 1903. Died January 28, 1991. Illinois. Inducted in 1963. 1925 Chicago Bears, 1926 New York Yankees (AFL), 1927 New York Yankees, 1929-1934 Chicago Bears. **Highlights:** Nicknamed "Galloping Ghost." Name produced first huge pro football crowds.

BUD GRANT
Coach. Born in Superior, Wisconsin, May 20, 1927. Minnesota. Inducted in 1994. 1967-1983, 1985 Minnesota Vikings. **Highlights:** 168-108-5 coaching record. Led Vikings to 11 division championships, four Super Bowls.

JOE GREENE
Defensive tackle. 6-4, 260. Born in Temple, Texas, September 24, 1946. North Texas State. Inducted in 1987. 1969-1981 Pittsburgh Steelers. **Highlights:** NFL defensive player of the year, 1972, 1974. Four-time Super Bowl champion, 10 Pro Bowls.

FORREST GREGG
Tackle. 6-4, 250. Born in Birthright, Texas, October 18, 1933. Southern Methodist. Inducted in 1977. 1956, 1958-1970 Green Bay Packers, 1971 Dallas Cowboys. **Highlights:** Played 188 consecutive games. Nine Pro Bowls. Played on six NFL championship teams, three Super Bowl winners.

BOB GRIESE
Quarterback. 6-1, 190. Born in Evansville, Indiana, February 3, 1945. Purdue. Inducted in 1990. 1967-1980 Miami Dolphins. **Highlights:** 25,092 passing yards, 192 touchdowns. Led Miami to three AFC titles, Super Bowl VII, VIII wins.

LOU GROZA
Tackle-kicker. 6-3, 250. Born in Martins Ferry, Ohio, January 25, 1924. Died November 29, 2000. Ohio State. Inducted in 1974. 1946-49 Cleveland Browns (AAFC), 1950-59, 1961-67 Cleveland Browns. **Highlights:** 1,608 points in 21 years. Nine Pro Bowls, All-NFL six years. NFL player of the year, 1954.

JOE GUYON
Halfback. 6-1, 180. Born on White Earth Indian Reservation, Minnesota, November 26, 1892. Died November 27, 1971. Carlisle, Georgia Tech. Inducted in 1966. 1919-1920 Canton Bulldogs, 1921 Cleveland Indians, 1922-23 Oorang Indians, 1924 Rock Island Independents, 1924-25 Kansas City Cowboys, 1927 New York Giants. **Highlights:** Touchdown pass gave Giants victory over Bears to win 1927 championship.

GEORGE HALAS
End. Coach. Team owner. Born in Chicago, Illinois, February 2, 1895. Died October 31, 1983. Illinois. Inducted in 1963. Player-coach 1920 Decatur Staleys, 1921 Chicago Staleys, 1922-29 Chicago Bears; coach 1933-1942, 1946-1955, 1958-1967 Chicago Bears. **Highlights:** Charter enshrinee. 324 coaching wins. Only person associated with NFL throughout first 50 years. Coached Bears 40 seasons, won six NFL titles.

JACK HAM
Linebacker. 6-1, 225. Born in Johnstown, Pennsylvania, December 23, 1948. Penn State. Inducted in 1988. 1971-1982 Pittsburgh Steelers. **Highlights:** Won four Super Bowls, 21 opponents' fumbles recovered, 32 interceptions. Eight consecutive Pro Bowls.

DAN HAMPTON
Defensive tackle-defensive end. 6-5, 264. Born in Oklahoma City, Oklahoma, September 19, 1957. Arkansas. Inducted in 2002. 1979-1990 Chicago Bears. **Highlights:** A versatile player, he earned all-pro honors at both defensive tackle and defensive end. Named to four Pro Bowls.

JOHN HANNAH
Guard. 6-3, 265. Born in Canton, Georgia, April 4, 1951. Alabama. Inducted in 1991. 1973-1985 New England Patriots. **Highlights:** Renowned as premier guard of era. All-Pro 10 years, nine Pro Bowls.

FRANCO HARRIS
Running back. 6-2, 225. Born in Fort Dix, New Jersey, March 7, 1950. Penn State. Inducted in 1990. 1972-1983 Pittsburgh Steelers, 1984 Seattle Seahawks. **Highlights:** 12,120 rushing yards, 100 total touchdowns. 1,556 rushing yards in 19 postseason games. MVP in Super Bowl IX.

MIKE HAYNES
Cornerback. 6-2, 195. Born in Denison, Texas, July 1, 1953. Arizona State. Inducted in 1997. 1976-1982 New England Patriots, 1983-89 Los Angeles Raiders. **Highlights:** Defensive rookie of the year. Selected to nine Pro Bowls and intercepted 46 passes, plus one pick in Super Bowl XVIII.

ED HEALEY
Tackle. 6-3, 220. Born in Indian Orchard, Massachusetts, December 28, 1894. Died December 9, 1978. Dartmouth. Inducted in 1964. 1920-22 Rock Island Independents, 1922-27 Chicago Bears. **Highlights:** Two-way star. Perennial all-pro with Bears.

MEL HEIN
Center. 6-2, 225. Born in Redding, California, August 22, 1909. Died January 31, 1992. Washington State. Inducted in 1963. 1931-1945 New York Giants. **Highlights:** Charter enshrinee. 60-minute regular for 15 years. All-NFL eight consecutive years.

TED HENDRICKS
Linebacker. 6-7, 235. Born in Guatemala City, Guatemala, November 1, 1947. Miami. Inducted in 1990. 1969-1973 Baltimore Colts, 1974 Green Bay Packers, 1975-1981 Oakland Raiders, 1982-83 Los Angeles Raiders. **Highlights:** 25 blocked field goals, extra points, and punts, 26 interceptions. Played in 215 consecutive games.

WILBUR (PETE) HENRY
Tackle. 6-0, 250. Born in Mansfield, Ohio, October 31, 1897. Died February 7, 1952. Washington & Jefferson. Inducted in 1963. 1920-23, 1925-26 Canton Bulldogs, 1927 New York Giants, 1927-28 Pottsville Maroons. **Highlights:** Largest player of his time at 250 pounds. Bulwark of Canton's championship lines.

ARNIE HERBER
Quarterback. 6-0, 200. Born in Green Bay, Wisconsin, April 2, 1910. Died October 14, 1969. Wisconsin, Regis College. Inducted in 1966. 1930-1940 Green Bay Packers, 1944-45 New York Giants. **Highlights:** NFL passing leader 1932, 1934, 1936. Came out of retirement to lead 1944 Giants to NFL Eastern crown.

BILL HEWITT
End. 5-11, 191. Born in Bay City, Michigan, October 8, 1909. Died January 14, 1947. Michigan. Inducted in 1971. 1932-36 Chicago Bears, 1937-39 Philadelphia Eagles, 1943 Phil-Pitt. **Highlights:** First to be named all-NFL with two teams—1933, 1934, 1936 Bears; 1937 Eagles.

CLARKE HINKLE
Fullback. 5-11, 201. Born in Toronto, Ohio, April 10, 1909. Died November 9, 1988. Bucknell. Inducted in 1964. 1932-1941 Green Bay Packers. **Highlights:** 3,860 yards rushing, 379 points. Fullback on offense, linebacker on defense.

ELROY (CRAZYLEGS) HIRSCH
Halfback-end. 6-2, 190. Born in Wausau, Wisconsin, June 17, 1923. Wisconsin, Michigan. Inducted in 1968. 1946-48 Chicago Rockets (AAFC), 1949-1957 Los Angeles Rams. **Highlights:** 387 receptions for 7,029 yards, 60 touchdowns. Key part of Rams' revolutionary "three end" offense, 1949.

PAUL HORNUNG
Halfback. 6-2, 220. Born in Louisville, Kentucky, December 23, 1935. Notre Dame. Inducted in 1986. 1957-1962, 1964-66 Green Bay Packers. **Highlights:** 760 points. Led NFL scorers three years, including record 176 points, 1960. Record 19 points scored in 1961 NFL title game.

KEN HOUSTON
Safety. 6-3, 198. Born in Lufkin, Texas, November 12, 1944. Prairie View A&M. Inducted in 1986. 1967-1972 Houston Oilers, 1973-1980 Washington Redskins. **Highlights:** 49 interceptions, 898 yards, 9 touchdowns. NFL's premier strong safety of 1970s. 12 Pro Bowls.

ROBERT (CAL) HUBBARD
Tackle. 6-5, 250. Born in Keytesville, Missouri, October 31, 1900. Died October 17, 1977. Centenary, Geneva. Inducted in 1963. 1927-28 New York Giants, 1929-1933, 1935 Green Bay Packers, 1936 New York Giants, 1936 Pittsburgh Pirates. **Highlights:** Charter enshrinee. Most feared lineman of his time. All-NFL six years, 1927-29, 1931-33.

SAM HUFF
Linebacker. 6-1, 230. Born in Morgantown, West Virginia, October 4, 1934. West Virginia. Inducted in 1982. 1956-1963 New York Giants, 1964-67, 1969 Washington Redskins. **Highlights:** 30 interceptions. Played in six NFL title games, five Pro Bowls. Redskins player-coach, 1969.

LAMAR HUNT
Team owner. Born in El Dorado, Arkansas, August 2, 1932. Southern Methodist. Inducted in 1972. 1960-62 Dallas Texans, 1963-present Kansas City Chiefs. **Highlights:** Driving force behind organization of AFL. Spearheaded merger negotiations with NFL, 1966.

DON HUTSON
End. 6-1, 180. Born in Pine Bluff, Arkansas, January 31, 1913. Died June 26, 1997. Alabama. Inducted in 1963. 1935-1945 Green Bay Packers. **Highlights:** 488 receptions for 7,991 yards, 99 touchdowns. NFL receiving champion eight years. NFL MVP, 1941, 1942.

JIMMY JOHNSON
Cornerback. 6-2, 187. Born in Dallas, Texas, March 31, 1938. UCLA. Inducted in 1994. 1961-1976 San Francisco 49ers. **Highlights:** 47 interceptions for 615 yards. Five Pro Bowls. Opposing passers avoided throwing in his area.

JOHN HENRY JOHNSON
Fullback. 6-2, 225. Born in Waterproof, Louisiana, November 24, 1929. St. Mary's, Arizona State. Inducted in 1987. 1954-56 San Francisco 49ers, 1957-59 Detroit Lions, 1960-65 Pittsburgh Steelers, 1966 Houston Oilers. **Highlights:** 6,803 yards rushing, 55 total touchdowns. Member of San Francisco's "Million-Dollar" backfield.

CHARLIE JOINER
Wide receiver. 5-11, 180. Born in Many, Louisiana, October 14, 1947. Grambling. Inducted in 1996. 1969-1972 Houston Oilers, 1972-75 Cincinnati Bengals, 1976-1986 San Diego Chargers. **Highlights:** 750 receptions for 12,146 yards and 65 touchdowns. Played 18 seasons, 239 games, most ever for wide receiver.

DAVID (DEACON) JONES
Defensive end. 6-5, 260. Born in Eatonville, Florida, December 9, 1938. South Carolina State, Mississippi Vocational. Inducted in 1980. 1961-1971 Los Angeles Rams, 1972-73 San Diego Chargers, 1974 Washington Redskins. **Highlights:** Specialized in quarterback "sacks," a term he invented. Unanimous all-league five consecutive years.

STAN JONES
Guard-defensive tackle. 6-1, 250. Born in Altoona, Pennsylvania, November 24, 1931. Maryland. Inducted in 1991. 1954-1965 Chicago Bears, 1966 Washington Redskins. **Highlights:** Seven consecutive Pro Bowls. First to rely on weightlifting for football preparation.

HENRY JORDAN
Defensive tackle, 6-3, 240. Born in Emporia, Virginia, January 26, 1935. Died February 21, 1977. Virginia. Inducted in 1995. 1957-58 Cleveland Browns, 1959-1969 Green Bay Packers. **Highlights:** Fixture at DT during Packers' dynasty. Played in four Pro Bowls, seven NFL title games, Super Bowls I, II.

SONNY JURGENSEN
Quarterback. 6-0, 203. Born in Wilmington, North Carolina, August 23, 1934. Duke. Inducted in 1983. 1957-1963 Philadelphia Eagles, 1964-1974 Washington Redskins. **Highlights:** 32,224 yards passing, 255 touchdowns, 82.63 passer rating. Surpassed 3,000 yards passing in five seasons.

JIM KELLY
Quarterback. 6-3, 217. Born in Pittsburgh, Pennsylvania, February 14, 1960. Miami. Inducted in 2002. 1986-1996 Buffalo Bills. **Highlights:** Passed for more than 3,000 yards eight times. Mastered the no-huddle offense that propelled Bills to four consecutive Super Bowls.

LEROY KELLY
Running back. 6-0, 205. Born in Philadelphia, Pennsylvania, May 20, 1942. Morgan State. Inducted in 1994. 1964-1973 Cleveland Browns. **Highlights:** 7,274 yards rushing, 90 total touchdowns, 1,000-yard rusher first three years as starter. Punt return champion, 1965.

WALT KIESLING
Guard. Coach. 6-2, 245. Born in St. Paul, Minnesota, March 27, 1903. Died March 2, 1962. St. Thomas (Minnesota). Inducted in 1966. 1926-27 Duluth Eskimos, 1928 Pottsville Maroons, 1929-1933 Chicago Cardinals, 1934 Chicago Bears, 1935-36 Green Bay Packers, 1937-38 Pittsburgh Pirates; coach, 1939 Pittsburgh Pirates, 1940-42 Pittsburgh Steelers; co-coach, 1943 Phil-Pitt, 1944 Card-Pitt; coach, 1954-56 Pittsburgh Steelers. **Highlights:** 34-year career as pro player, assistant coach, head coach. Led Steelers to first winning season, 1942.

FRANK (BRUISER) KINARD
Tackle. 6-1, 210. Born in Pelahatchie, Mississippi, October 23, 1914. Died September 7, 1985. Mississippi. Inducted in 1971. 1938-1943 Brooklyn Dodgers, 1944 Brooklyn Tigers, 1946-47 New York Yankees (AAFC). **Highlights:** First man to earn both All-NFL, All-AAFC honors. Out because of injury only once.

PAUL KRAUSE
Safety. 6-3, 200. Born in Flint, Michigan, February 19, 1942. Iowa. Inducted in 1998. 1964-67 Washington Redskins, 1968-1979 Minnesota Vikings. **Highlights:** NFL all-time leader with 81 interceptions. Played in eight Pro Bowls. Starting safety in four Super Bowls.

EARL (CURLY) LAMBEAU
Coach. Born in Green Bay, Wisconsin, April 9, 1898. Died June 1, 1965. Notre Dame. Inducted in 1963. 1919-1949 Green Bay Packers, 1950-51 Chicago Cardinals, 1952-53 Washington Redskins. **Highlights:** 229-134-22 coaching record with six NFL championships. Founded pre-NFL Packers, 1919.

JACK LAMBERT
Linebacker. 6-4, 220. Born in Mantua, Ohio, July 8, 1952. Kent State. Inducted in 1990. 1974-1984 Pittsburgh Steelers. **Highlights:** Leader of 'Steel Curtain.' NFL defensive player of year in 1976, nine Pro Bowls.

TOM LANDRY
Coach. Born in Mission, Texas, September 11, 1924. Died February 12, 2000. Texas. Inducted in 1990. 1960-1988 Dallas Cowboys. **Highlights:** 270-178-6 coaching record. 20 consecutive winning seasons. Innovator on offense and defense.

DICK (NIGHT TRAIN) LANE
Cornerback. 6-2, 210. Born in Austin, Texas, April 16, 1928. Died January 29, 2002. Scottsbluff Junior College. Inducted in 1974. 1952-53 Los Angeles Rams, 1954-59 Chicago Cardinals, 1960-65 Detroit Lions. **Highlights:** 68 interceptions for 1,207 yards, 5 touchdowns. Record 14 interceptions as rookie. Seven Pro Bowls.

JIM LANGER
Center. 6-2, 255. Born in Little Falls, Minnesota, May 16, 1948. South Dakota State. Inducted in 1987. 1970-79 Miami Dolphins, 1980-81 Minnesota Vikings. **Highlights:** Played every offensive down in Dolphins' perfect 1972 season. Six Pro Bowls.

WILLIE LANIER
Linebacker. 6-1, 245. Born in Clover, Virginia, August 21, 1945. Morgan State. Inducted in 1986. 1967-1977 Kansas City Chiefs. **Highlights:** 27 interceptions. Defensive star in Super Bowl IV upset. Nicknamed 'Contact' for ferocious tackling.

STEVE LARGENT
Wide receiver. 5-11, 191. Born in Tulsa, Oklahoma, September 28, 1954, Tulsa. Inducted in 1995. 1976-1989 Seattle Seahawks. **Highlights:** 819 receptions for 13,089 yards, 100 touchdowns. Receptions in 177 consecutive games.

YALE LARY
Defensive back-punter. 5-11, 189. Born in Fort Worth, Texas, November 24, 1930. Texas A&M. Inducted in 1979. 1952-53, 1956-1964 Detroit Lions. **Highlights:** 50 interceptions. Three NFL punting crowns, three touchdowns on punt returns. Nine Pro Bowls.

DANTE LAVELLI
End. 6-0, 199. Born in Hudson, Ohio, February 23, 1923. Ohio State. Inducted in 1975. 1946-49 Cleveland Browns (AAFC), 1950-56 Cleveland Browns. **Highlights:** 386 receptions for 6,488 yards, 62 touchdowns. 24 catches in six NFL title games.

BOBBY LAYNE
Quarterback. 6-2, 190. Born in Santa Ana, Texas, December 19, 1926. Died December 1, 1986. Texas. Inducted in 1967. 1948 Chicago Bears, 1949 New York Bulldogs, 1950-58 Detroit Lions, 1958-1962 Pittsburgh Steelers. **Highlights:** 26,768 yards passing, 196 touchdowns, 2,451 yards rushing. Late touchdown pass won 1953 NFL title game.

ALPHONSE (TUFFY) LEEMANS
Fullback. 6-0, 200. Born in Superior, Wisconsin, November 12, 1912. Died January 19, 1979. Oregon, George Washington. Inducted in 1978. 1936-1943 New York Giants. **Highlights:** 3,132 yards rushing, 2,318 yards passing, 422 yards receiving. Led NFL rushers as rookie, 1936.

MARV LEVY
Coach. Born in Chicago, Illinois, August 3, 1925. Coe College, Harvard. Inducted in 2001. 1978-1982 Kansas City Chiefs, 1986-1997 Buffalo Bills. **Highlights:** Led Bills to unprecedented four consecutive Super Bowls. Had 154-120 record. Coaching victories ranked 10th when retired.

BOB LILLY
Defensive tackle. 6-5, 260. Born in Olney, Texas, July 26, 1939. Texas Christian. Inducted in 1980. 1961-1974 Dallas Cowboys. **Highlights:** Eleven Pro Bowls. Played 196 consecutive games. Foundation of great Dallas defensive units.

LARRY LITTLE
Guard. 6-1, 265. Born in Groveland, Georgia, November 2, 1945. Bethune-Cookman. Inducted in 1993. 1967-68 San Diego Chargers, 1969-1980 Miami Dolphins. **Highlights:** Five Pro Bowls, started in three Super Bowls. Epitome of powerful Dolphins rushing game of 1970s.

VINCE LOMBARDI
Coach. Born in Brooklyn, New York, June 11, 1913. Died September 3, 1970. Fordham. Inducted in 1971. 1959-1967 Green Bay Packers, 1969 Washington Redskins. **Highlights:** 105-35-6 coaching record in 10 years, including five NFL titles and victories in Super Bowls I and II.

HOWIE LONG
Defensive end. 6-5, 268. Born in Somerville, Massachusetts, January 6, 1960. Villanova. Inducted in 2000. 1981-1993 Oakland/Los Angeles Raiders. **Highlights:** All-Pro 1983, 1984, 1985. Named All-AFC four times, 1983-1986. Eight Pro Bowls.

RONNIE LOTT
Cornerback-safety. 6-0, 203. Born in Albuquerque, New Mexico, May 8, 1959. Southern California. Inducted in 2000. 1981-1990 San Francisco 49ers, 1991-92 Los Angeles Raiders, 1993-94 New York Jets. **Highlights:** Ten Pro Bowls, 63 career interceptions, and was named to the NFL's 75th Anniversary Team.

SID LUCKMAN
Quarterback. 6-0, 195. Born in Brooklyn, New York, November 21, 1916. Died July 5, 1998. Columbia. Inducted in 1965. 1939-1950 Chicago Bears. **Highlights:** 137 touchdown passes. All-NFL five times. League MVP in 1943.

WILLIAM ROY (LINK) LYMAN
Tackle. 6-2, 252. Born in Table Rock, Nebraska, November 30, 1898. Died December 28, 1972. Nebraska. Inducted in 1964. 1922-23, 1925 Canton Bulldogs, 1924 Cleveland Bulldogs, 1925 Frankford Yellow Jackets, 1926-28, 1930-31, 1933-34 Chicago Bears. **Highlights:** Played for four NFL champions. In 16 seasons of college and pro football, played on one losing team.

TOM MACK
Guard. 6-3, 250. Born in Cleveland, Ohio, November 1, 1943. Michigan. Inducted in 1999. 1966-1978 Los Angeles Rams. **Highlights:** Never missed a game in entire 184-game career. Elected to 11 Pro Bowls.

JOHN MACKEY
Tight end. 6-2, 224. Born in New York, New York, September 24, 1941. Syracuse. Inducted in 1992. 1963-1971 Baltimore Colts, 1972 San Diego Chargers. **Highlights:** 331 receptions for 5,236 yards, 38 touchdowns. Second tight end to enter Hall of Fame.

TIM MARA
Team owner. Born in New York, New York, July 29, 1887. Died February 17, 1959. Did not attend college. Inducted in 1963. 1925-1959 New York Giants. **Highlights:** Charter enshrinee. Founder of New York Giants. Built team into powerhouse winning four NFL titles, 10 division titles.

WELLINGTON MARA
Team owner. Born in New York, New York, August 14, 1916. Fordham. Inducted in 1997. 1937-present New York Giants. **Highlights:** Lifetime contributor to NFL and New York Giants. Worked as Giants' ballboy, secretary, vice-president, president and co-CEO. NFC president 1984-present.

GINO MARCHETTI
Defensive end. 6-4, 245. Born in Smithers, West Virginia, January 2, 1927. San Francisco. Inducted in 1972. 1952 Dallas Texans, 1953-1964, 1966 Baltimore Colts. **Highlights:** Named top defensive end of NFL's first 50 years. 10 consecutive Pro Bowls. All-NFL seven times.

GEORGE PRESTON MARSHALL
Team owner. Born in Grafton, West Virginia, October 11, 1896. Died August 9, 1969. Randolph-Macon. Inducted in 1963. 1932 Boston Braves, 1933-36 Boston Redskins, 1937-1969 Washington Redskins. **Highlights:** Charter enshrinee. Sponsored progressive rules changes. Organized first team band, pioneered halftime shows.

OLLIE MATSON
Halfback. 6-2, 220. Born in Trinity, Texas, May 1, 1930. San Francisco. Inducted in 1972. 1952, 1954-58 Chicago Cardinals, 1959-1962 Los Angeles Rams, 1963 Detroit Lions, 1964-66 Philadelphia Eagles. **Highlights:** Nine touchdowns on kickoff, punt returns. Traded for nine players in 1959.

DON MAYNARD
Wide receiver. 6-1, 185. Born in Crosbyton, Texas, January 25, 1935. Texas Western. Inducted in 1987. 1958 New York Giants, 1960-62 New York Titans, 1963-1972 New York Jets, 1973 St. Louis Cardinals. **Highlights:** 633 receptions for 11,834 yards, 88 touchdowns. At least 50 catches and 1,000 yards in five different seasons.

GEORGE McAFEE
Halfback. 6-0, 177. Born in Corbin, Kentucky, March 13, 1918. Duke. Inducted in 1966. 1940-41, 1945-1950 Chicago Bears. **Highlights:** Two-way star. 25 interceptions, 234 points. Career punt-return average of 12.78 yards per return.

MIKE McCORMACK
Tackle. 6-4, 250. Born in Chicago, Illinois, June 21, 1930. Kansas. Inducted in 1984. 1951 New York Yanks, 1954-1962 Cleveland Browns. **Highlights:** Excelled as offensive right tackle for eight years. Six Pro Bowls.

TOMMY McDONALD
Wide receiver. 5-9, 175. Born in Roy, New Mexico, July 26, 1934. Oklahoma. Inducted in 1998. 1957-1963 Philadelphia Eagles, 1964 Dallas Cowboys, 1965-66 Los Angeles Rams, 1967 Atlanta Falcons, 1968 Cleveland Browns. **Highlights:** Recorded 495 receptions for 8,410 yards, 84 touchdowns.

HUGH McELHENNY
Halfback. 6-1, 198. Born in Los Angeles, California, December 31, 1928. Washington. Inducted in 1970. 1952-1960 San Francisco 49ers, 1961-62 Minnesota Vikings, 1963 New York Giants, 1964 Detroit Lions. **Highlights:** 5,281 rushing yards, 360 points. Totaled 11,369 yards rushing, receiving, and returning kicks.

JOHNNY (BLOOD) McNALLY
Halfback. 6-0, 185. Born in New Richmond, Wisconsin, November 27, 1903. Died November 28, 1985. Notre Dame, St. John's (Minnesota). Inducted in 1963. 1925-26 Milwaukee Badgers, 1926-27 Duluth Eskimos, 1928 Pottsville Maroons, 1929-1933, 1935-36 Green Bay Packers, 1934 Pittsburgh Pirates; player-coach, 1937-38 Pittsburgh Pirates. **Highlights:** 49 touchdowns, 296 points in 14 seasons with five teams.

MIKE MICHALSKE
Guard. 6-0, 209. Born in Cleveland, Ohio, April 24, 1903. Died October 26, 1983. Penn State. Inducted in 1964. 1926 New York Yankees (AFL), 1927-28 New York Yankees, 1929-1935, 1937 Green Bay Packers. **Highlights:** Anchored Packers' championship lines, 1929-1931. First guard enshrined in Canton.

WAYNE MILLNER
End. 6-0, 191. Born in Roxbury, Massachusetts, January 31, 1913. Died November 19, 1976. Notre Dame. Inducted in 1968. 1936 Boston Redskins, 1937-1941, 1945 Washington Redskins. **Highlights:** Redskins' all-time leader with 124 catches when retired. 55- and 78-yard touchdown receptions in 1937 NFL Championship Game.

BOBBY MITCHELL
Running back-wide receiver. 6-0, 195. Born in Hot Springs, Arkansas, June 6, 1935. Illinois. Inducted in 1983. 1958-1961 Cleveland Browns, 1962-68 Washington Redskins. **Highlights:** 91 touchdowns, including 8 on kickoff and punt returns. 14,078 combined yards.

RON MIX
Tackle. 6-4, 255. Born in Los Angeles, California, March 10, 1938. Southern California. Inducted in 1979. 1960 Los Angeles Chargers, 1961-69 San Diego Chargers, 1971 Oakland Raiders. **Highlights:** All-AFL nine times. Only two holding penalties in 10 years with the Chargers.

JOE MONTANA
Quarterback. 6-2, 200. Born in New Eagle, Pennsylvania, June, 11, 1956. Notre Dame. Inducted in 2000. 1979-1992 San Francisco 49ers, 1993-94 Kansas City Chiefs. **Highlights:** MVP in Super Bowl's XVI, XIX, and XXIV. Eight Pro Bowls and All-NFL three times.

LENNY MOORE
Flanker-running back. 6-1, 198. Born in Reading, Pennsylvania, November 25, 1933. Penn State. Inducted in 1975. 1956-1967 Baltimore Colts. **Highlights:** From 1963-65, scored touchdowns in record 18 consecutive games. 113 career touchdowns, 12,451 combined net yards.

MARION MOTLEY
Fullback. 6-1, 238. Born in Leesburg, Georgia, June 5, 1920. Died June 27, 1999. South Carolina State, Nevada. Inducted in 1968. 1946-49 Cleveland Browns (AAFC), 1950-53 Cleveland Browns, 1955 Pittsburgh Steelers. **Highlights:** AAFC's all-time rushing champion. Led league in rushing in first NFL season.

MIKE MUNCHAK
Guard. 6-3, 281. Born in Scranton, Pennsylvania, March 5, 1960. Penn State. Inducted in 2001. 1982-1993 Houston Oilers. **Highlights:** Devastating blocker, All-AFC seven times, elected to nine Pro Bowls.

ANTHONY MUÑOZ
Tackle. 6-6, 278. Born in Ontario, California, August 19, 1958. Southern California. Inducted in 1998. 1980-1992 Cincinnati Bengals. **Highlights:** All-Pro choice 11 consecutive years, 1981-1991. Selected to 11 straight Pro Bowls.

GEORGE MUSSO
Guard-tackle. 6-2, 270. Born in Collinsville, Illinois. April 8, 1910. Died September 5, 2000. Millikin. Inducted in 1982. 1933-1944 Chicago Bears. **Highlights:** First player to achieve All-NFL status at two positions—tackle in 1935 and guard in 1937.

BRONKO NAGURSKI
Fullback. 6-2, 225. Born in Rainy River, Ontario, Canada, November 3, 1908. Died January 7, 1990. Minnesota. Inducted in 1963. 1930-37, 1943 Chicago Bears. **Highlights:** Charter enshrinee. 2,778 rushing yards in nine seasons. All-NFL three times.

JOE NAMATH
Quarterback. 6-2, 200. Born in Beaver Falls, Pennsylvania, May 31, 1943. Alabama. Inducted in 1985. 1965-1976 New York Jets, 1977 Los Angeles Rams. **Highlights:** First quarterback to pass for more than 4,000 yards in season, 1967. Guaranteed, delivered victory over Colts in Super Bowl III.

EARLE (GREASY) NEALE
Coach. Born in Parkersburg, West Virginia, November 5, 1891. Died November 2, 1973. West Virginia Wesleyan. Inducted in 1969. 1941-42, 1944-1950 Philadelphia Eagles; co-coach, 1943 Phil-Pitt. **Highlights:** Turned Eagles into winners with three consecutive division crowns, NFL championships in 1948 and 1949.

ERNIE NEVERS
Fullback. 6-1, 205. Born in Willow River, Minnesota, June 11, 1903. Died May 3, 1976. Stanford. Inducted in 1963. 1926-27 Duluth Eskimos, 1929-1931 Chicago Cardinals. **Highlights:** Charter enshrinee. Holds NFL's longest-standing record, 40 points in one game in 1929.

OZZIE NEWSOME
Tight end. 6-2, 232. Born in Muscle Shoals, Alabama, March 16, 1956. Alabama. Inducted in 1999. 1978-1990 Cleveland Browns. **Highlights:** Leading tight end receiver in NFL history with 662 receptions for 7,980 yards.

RAY NITSCHKE
Linebacker. 6-3, 235. Born in Elmwood Park, Illinois, December 29, 1936. Died March 8, 1998. Illinois. Inducted in 1978. 1958-1972 Green Bay Packers. **Highlights:** MVP of 1962 title game. Named NFL's all-time linebacker in 1969.

CHUCK NOLL
Coach. Born in Cleveland, Ohio, January 5, 1932. Dayton. Inducted in 1993. 1969-1991 Pittsburgh Steelers. **Highlights:** Coached for 23 years. Only coach to win four Super Bowl titles (IX, X, XIII, XIV).

LEO NOMELLINI
Defensive tackle. 6-3, 264. Born in Lucca, Italy, June 19, 1924. Died October 17, 2000. Minnesota. Inducted in 1969. 1950-1963 San Francisco 49ers. **Highlights:** Played every 49ers game for 14 seasons. 10 Pro Bowls.

MERLIN OLSEN
Defensive tackle. 6-5, 270. Born in Logan, Utah, September 15, 1940. Utah State. Inducted in 1982. 1962-1976 Los Angeles Rams. **Highlights:** Member of the Fearsome "Foursome." Named" to 14 consecutive Pro Bowls, Rams' all-time team.

JIM OTTO
Center. 6-2, 255. Born in Wausau, Wisconsin, January 5, 1938. Miami. Inducted in 1980. 1960-1974 Oakland Raiders. **Highlights:** Named AFL's all-time center. Played in 210 games, 12 AFL All-Star Games or Pro Bowls, six AFL/AFC title games.

STEVE OWEN
Tackle. Coach. 6-2, 235. Born in Cleo Springs, Oklahoma, April 21, 1898. Died May 17, 1964. Phillips. Inducted in 1966. 1924-25 Kansas City Cowboys, 1925 Cleveland Bulldogs, 1926-1931, 1933 New York Giants; coach, 1930-1953 New York Giants. **Highlights:** Both player and coach. Coached Giants to record of 155-108-17, eight divisional titles, two NFL championships.

ALAN PAGE
Defensive tackle. 6-4, 225. Born in Canton, Ohio, August 7, 1945. Notre Dame. Inducted in 1988. 1967-1978 Minnesota Vikings, 1978-1981 Chicago Bears. **Highlights:** Dominating defensive tackle played in 218 consecutive games, four Super Bowls. Won league MVP honors in 1971.

CLARENCE (ACE) PARKER
Quarterback. 5-11, 168. Born in Portsmouth, Virginia, May 17, 1912. Duke. Inducted in 1972. 1937-1941 Brooklyn Dodgers, 1945 Boston Yanks, 1946 New York Yankees (AAFC). **Highlights:** Two-way threat. Two-time All-NFL performer, league MVP in 1940.

JIM PARKER
Guard-tackle. 6-3, 273. Born in Macon, Georgia, April 3, 1934. Ohio State. Inducted in 1973. 1957-1967 Baltimore Colts. **Highlights:** First full-time offensive lineman elected to Hall of Fame. All-NFL eight consecutive years, eight Pro Bowls.

WALTER PAYTON
Running back. 5-10, 202. Born in Columbia, Mississippi, July 25, 1954. Died November 1, 1999. Jackson State. Inducted in 1993. 1975-1987 Chicago Bears. **Highlights:** NFL's all-time leading rusher with 16,726 yards and combined net yardage with 21,803.

JOE PERRY
Fullback. 6-0, 200. Born in Stevens, Arkansas, January 22, 1927. Compton Junior College. Inducted in 1969. 1948-49 San Francisco 49ers (AAFC), 1950-1960, 1963 San Francisco 49ers, 1961-62 Baltimore Colts. **Highlights:** First player in NFL history to gain 1,000 yards two consecutive seasons. 12,505 combined yards.

PETE PIHOS
End. 6-1, 210. Born in Orlando, Florida, October 22, 1923. Indiana. Inducted in 1970. 1947-1955 Philadelphia Eagles. **Highlights:** Three-time NFL receiving champion. Caught winning touchdown in 1949 NFL Championship Game.

HUGH (SHORTY) RAY
Supervisor of officials 1938-1952. Born in Highland Park, Illinois, September 21, 1884. Died September 16, 1956. Illinois. Inducted in 1966. **Highlights:** Supervisor of Officials, 1938-1952. Streamlined rules to improve game tempo, player safety.

DAN REEVES
Team owner. Born in New York, New York, June 30, 1912. Died April 15, 1971. Georgetown. Inducted in 1967. 1941-45 Cleveland Rams, 1946-1971 Los Angeles Rams. **Highlights:** Moved Rams to Los Angeles in 1946 and opened up West Coast to pro football. First postwar owner to sign African-American player.

MEL RENFRO
Cornerback-safety. 6-0, 192. Born in Houston, Texas, December 30, 1941. Oregon. Inducted in 1996. 1964-1977 Dallas Cowboys. **Highlights:** 52 interceptions for 626 yards and 3 touchdowns. Also added 842 yards on punt returns, 2,246 yards on kickoff returns. Elected to Pro Bowl first 10 seasons.

JOHN RIGGINS
Running back. 6-2, 240. Born in Seneca, Kansas, August 4, 1949. Kansas. Inducted in 1992. 1971-75 New York Jets, 1976-79, 1981-85 Washington Redskins. **Highlights:** 11,352 rushing yards, 116 total touchdowns. MVP of Super Bowl XVII with 166 rushing yards including game-winning 43-yard touchdown.

JIM RINGO
Center. 6-2, 230. Born in Orange, New Jersey, November 21, 1931. Syracuse. Inducted in 1981. 1953-1963 Green Bay Packers, 1964-67 Philadelphia Eagles. **Highlights:** Ten-time Pro Bowl selection, six-time All-NFL selection. Started in then-record 182 consecutive games.

ANDY ROBUSTELLI
Defensive end. 6-0, 230. Born in Stamford, Connecticut, December 6, 1925. Arnold College. Inducted in 1971. 1951-55 Los Angeles Rams, 1956-1964 New York Giants. **Highlights:** Anchored defense in eight championship games. Named NFL's top player in 1962.

PRO FOOTBALL HALL OF FAME

ART ROONEY
Team owner. Born in Coulterville, Pennsylvania, January 27, 1901. Died August 25, 1988. Georgetown, Duquesne. Inducted in 1964. 1933-39 Pittsburgh Pirates, 1940-42, 1945-1988 Pittsburgh Steelers, 1943 Phil-Pitt, 1944 Card-Pitt. **Highlights:** Founded Pittsburgh Pirates in 1933 and renamed them Steelers in 1940. Team won four Super Bowls in 1970s.

DAN ROONEY
Team owner. Born in Pittsburgh, Pennsylvania, July, 20, 1932. Duquesne. Inducted in 2000. 1955-present Pittsburgh Steelers. **Highlights:** Has been on the board of directors for the NFL Trust Fund, NFL Films, and Scheduling Committee. Played a key role in the labor agreement reached in 1993 between the NFL owners and players.

PETE ROZELLE
Commissioner. Born in South Gate, California, March 1, 1926. Died December 6, 1996. Compton Junior College, San Francisco. Inducted in 1985. Commissioner, 1960-1989. **Highlights:** Negotiated first league-wide television contract in 1962. Generally recognized as premiere commissioner in all of sports. Credited with making NFL the nation's most popular sport.

BOB ST. CLAIR
Tackle. 6-9, 265. Born in San Francisco, California, February 18, 1931. San Francisco, Tulsa. Inducted in 1990. 1953-1963 San Francisco 49ers. **Highlights:** Exceptional offensive lineman. Also played goal-line defense and had 10 blocked field goals, 1956.

GALE SAYERS
Running back. 6-0, 200. Born in Wichita, Kansas, May 30, 1943. Kansas. Inducted in 1977. 1965-1971 Chicago Bears. **Highlights:** Broke into league by scoring rookie-record 22 touchdowns. Led league in rushing in 1966, 1969. MVP of three Pro Bowls.

JOE SCHMIDT
Linebacker. 6-0, 222. Born in Pittsburgh, Pennsylvania, January 18, 1932. Pittsburgh. Inducted in 1973. 1953-1965 Detroit Lions. **Highlights:** 24 interceptions. Lions' team captain for nine years. Mastered middle linebacker position that evolved in 1950s.

TEX SCHRAMM
Team president-general manager. Born in San Gabriel, California, June 2, 1920. Texas. Inducted in 1991. 1947-1956 Los Angeles Rams. 1960-1989 Dallas Cowboys. **Highlights:** Played prominent role in AFL-NFL merger. Chairman of Competition Committee from 1966-1988.

LEE ROY SELMON
Defensive end. 6-3, 250. Born in Eufaula, Oklahoma, October 20, 1954. Oklahoma. Inducted in 1995. 1976-1984 Tampa Bay Buccaneers. **Highlights:** 78½ sacks, 380 quarterback pressures, forced 28 fumbles. Six consecutive Pro Bowl selections.

BILLY SHAW
Guard. 6-2, 258. Born in Natchez, Mississippi, December 15, 1938. Georgia Tech. Inducted in 1999. 1961-69 Buffalo Bills. **Highlights:** First player who played entire career in AFL to be elected to Hall of Fame. Named to AFL's all-time team.

ART SHELL
Tackle. 6-5, 285. Born in Charleston, South Carolina, November 26, 1946. Maryland State-Eastern Shore. Inducted in 1989. 1968-1981 Oakland Raiders, 1982 Los Angeles Raiders. **Highlights:** Cornerstone of Raiders' offensive line in 1970s. 207 regular-season games, 24 post-season games, eight Pro Bowls.

DON SHULA
Coach. Born in Grand River, Ohio, January 4, 1930. John Carroll. Inducted in 1997. 1963-69 Baltimore Colts, 1970-1995 Miami Dolphins. **Highlights:** Won more games (347) than any coach in NFL history. Won two Super Bowl titles, including Super Bowl VII when Dolphins recorded NFL's only perfect season (17-0).

O.J. SIMPSON
Running back. 6-1, 212. Born in San Francisco, California, July 9, 1947. City College (San Francisco), Southern California. Inducted in 1985. 1969-1977 Buffalo Bills, 1978-79 San Francisco 49ers. **Highlights:** In 1973, became first player to rush for 2,000 yards in season. Finished career with four rushing titles, 11,236 yards.

MIKE SINGLETARY
Linebacker. 6-0, 230. Born in Houston, Texas, October 9, 1958. Baylor. Inducted in 1998. 1981-1992 Chicago Bears. **Highlights:** All-Pro choice eight times and All-NFC nine consecutive seasons. Selected to 10 Pro Bowls.

JACKIE SLATER
Tackle. 6-4, 277. Born in Jackson, Mississippi, May 27, 1954. Jackson State. Inducted in 2001. 1976-1995 Los Angeles/St. Louis Rams. **Highlights:** Played 20 seasons, 259 games. Blocked for seven different 1,000-yard rushers. Seven Pro Bowls.

JACKIE SMITH
Tight end. 6-4, 232. Born in Columbia, Mississippi, February 23, 1940. Northwestern State (Louisiana). Inducted in 1994. 1963-1977 St. Louis Cardinals, 1978 Dallas Cowboys. **Highlights:** 480 receptions for 7,918 yards, 40 touchdowns. Third tight end to be elected to Hall of Fame.

JOHN STALLWORTH
Wide receiver. 6-2, 191. Born in Tuscaloosa, Alabama, July 15, 1952. Alabama A&M. Inducted in 2002. 1974-1987 Pittsburgh Steelers. **Highlights:** 537 receptions for 8,723 yards, 63 touchdowns. Scored go-ahead touchdown in Super Bowl XIV on 73-yard reception.

BART STARR
Quarterback. 6-1, 200. Born in Montgomery, Alabama, January 9, 1934. Alabama. Inducted in 1977. 1956-1971 Green Bay Packers. **Highlights:** Quarterbacked Packers to six division titles, five NFL titles, and first two Super Bowls in which he was MVP.

ROGER STAUBACH
Quarterback. 6-3, 202. Born in Cincinnati, Ohio, February 5, 1942. New Mexico Military Institute, Navy. Inducted in 1985. 1969-1979 Dallas Cowboys. **Highlights:** Led Cowboys to four NFC titles and victories in Super Bowls VI, XII. When retired, 83.4 career passer rating was best of all time.

ERNIE STAUTNER
Defensive tackle. 6-2, 235. Born in Prinzing-by-Cham, Bavaria, April 20, 1925. Boston College. Inducted in 1969. 1950-1963 Pittsburgh Steelers. **Highlights:** Played in nine Pro Bowls and won the best lineman award in 1957. Recorded 3 safeties.

JAN STENERUD
Kicker. 6-2, 190. Born in Fetsund, Norway, November 26, 1942. Montana State. Inducted in 1991. 1967-1979 Kansas City Chiefs, 1980-83 Green Bay Packers, 1984-85 Minnesota Vikings. **Highlights:** 1,699 points on 580 extra points, 373 field goals. First pure placekicker to enter Hall of Fame.

DWIGHT STEPHENSON
Center. 6-2, 255. Born in Murfreesboro, North Carolina, November 20, 1957. Alabama. Inducted in 1998. 1980-87 Miami Dolphins. **Highlights:** Recognized as premier center of his time. All-Pro, All-AFC five straight years. Selected to five Pro Bowls.

KEN STRONG
Halfback. 5-11, 210. Born in West Haven, Connecticut, April 21, 1906. Died October 5, 1979. New York University. Inducted in 1967. 1929-1932 Staten Island Stapletons, 1933-35, 1939, 1944-47 New York Giants, 1936-37 New York Yanks (AFL). **Highlights:** Scored 17 points to lead Giants to victory in 1934 'Sneakers' game, led NFL with 64 points, 1933.

JOE STYDAHAR
Tackle. 6-4, 230. Born in Kaylor, Pennsylvania, March 17, 1912. Died March 23, 1977. West Virginia. Inducted in 1967. 1936-1942, 1945-46 Chicago Bears. **Highlights:** One of stalwarts of Bears' 'Monsters of the Midway.' Played on five divisional, three NFL championship teams.

LYNN SWANN
Wide receiver. 5-11, 180. Born in Alcoa, Tennessee, March 7, 1952. Southern California. Inducted in 2001. 1974-1982 Pittsburgh Steelers. **Highlights:** All-AFC three times. Selected to three Pro Bowls. MVP, Super Bowl X.

FRAN TARKENTON
Quarterback. 6-0, 185. Born in Richmond, Virginia, February 3, 1940. Georgia. Inducted in 1986. 1961-66, 1972-78 Minnesota Vikings, 1967-1971 New York Giants. **Highlights:** At retirement, held NFL records for attempts (6,467), completions (3,686), yards (47,003), and touchdowns (342). Four touchdowns passes in first NFL game.

CHARLEY TAYLOR
Running back-wide receiver. 6-3, 210. Born in Grand Prairie, Texas, September 28, 1941. Arizona State. Inducted in 1984. 1964-1975, 1977 Washington Redskins. **Highlights:** Won rookie of year honors as running back. Switched to wide receiver and won receiving titles in 1966, 1967.

JIM TAYLOR
Fullback. 6-0, 216. Born in Baton Rouge, Louisiana, September 20, 1935. Louisiana State. Inducted in 1976. 1958-1966 Green Bay Packers, 1967 New Orleans Saints. **Highlights:** 8,597 rushing yards, 558 points. In 1962, led league in rushing and scoring with 19 touchdowns.

LAWRENCE TAYLOR
Linebacker. 6-3, 237. Born in Williamsburg, Virginia, February 4, 1959. North Carolina. Inducted in 1999. 1981-1993 New York Giants. **Highlights:** Redefined the position of outside linebacker. All-Pro nine times, 10 Pro Bowls. NFL MVP in 1986.

JIM THORPE
Halfback. 6-1, 190. Born in Prague, Oklahoma, May 28, 1888. Died March 28, 1953. Carlisle. Inducted in 1963. 1915-17, 1919-1920, 1926 Canton Bulldogs, 1921 Cleveland Indians, 1922-23 Oorang Indians, 1924 Rock Island Independents, 1925 New York Giants, 1928 Chicago Cardinals. **Highlights:** Charter enshrinee. First president of American Professional Football Association, 1920. Played for 12 seasons.

Y.A. TITTLE
Quarterback. 6-0, 200. Born in Marshall, Texas, October 24, 1926. Louisiana State. Inducted in 1971. 1948-49 Baltimore Colts (AAFC), 1950 Baltimore Colts, 1951-1960 San Francisco 49ers, 1961-64 New York Giants. **Highlights:** 33,070 yards, 242 touchdowns. 33 touchdown passes in 1962 and 36 in 1963. Two-time league MVP.

GEORGE TRAFTON
Center. 6-2, 235. Born in Chicago, Illinois, December 6, 1896. Died September 5, 1971. Notre Dame. Inducted in 1964. 1920 Decatur Staleys, 1921 Chicago Staleys, 1922-1932 Chicago Bears. **Highlights:** First center to snap with one hand. Named top NFL center of 1920s.

CHARLEY TRIPPI
Halfback-quarterback. 6-0, 185. Born in Pittston, Pennsylvania, December 14, 1922. Georgia. Inducted in 1968. 1947-1955 Chicago Cardinals. **Highlights:** One of football's most versatile performers. Played halfback five years, quarterback for two, defense for two.

EMLEN TUNNELL
Safety. 6-1, 200. Born in Bryn Mawr, Pennsylvania, March 29, 1925. Died July 22, 1975. Toledo, Iowa. Inducted in 1967. 1948-1958 New York Giants, 1959-1961 Green Bay Packers. **Highlights:** 79 interceptions. Gained more yards on kickoff, punt, and interception returns (924) in 1952 than that season's NFL rushing leader.

CLYDE (BULLDOG) TURNER
Center. 6-2, 235. Born in Plains, Texas, March 10, 1919. Died October 30, 1998. Hardin-Simmons. Inducted in 1966. 1940-1952 Chicago Bears. **Highlights:** Anchored defense for four NFL championship teams, including 4 interceptions in five title games.

JOHNNY UNITAS
Quarterback. 6-1, 195. Born in Pittsburgh, Pennsylvania, May 7, 1933. Louisville. Inducted in 1979. 1956-1972 Baltimore Colts, 1973 San Diego Chargers. **Highlights:** 40,239 passing yards, 290 touchdowns. Led Colts to two NFL championships. Passed for at least one touchdown in 47 consecutive games.

GENE UPSHAW
Guard. 6-5, 255. Born in Robstown, Texas, August 15, 1945. Texas A & I. Inducted in 1987. 1967-1981 Oakland Raiders. **Highlights:** Premier guard of his era played in 10 AFL/AFC Championship Games, three Super Bowls, seven Pro Bowls.

NORM VAN BROCKLIN
Quarterback. 6-1, 190. Born in Eagle Butte, South Dakota, March 15, 1926. Died May 2, 1983. Oregon. Inducted in 1971. 1949-1957 Los Angeles Rams, 1958-1960 Philadelphia Eagles. **Highlights:** NFL-record 554 yards passing in 1951 season opener. Guided Eagles to NFL crown as league MVP in 1960.

STEVE VAN BUREN
Halfback. 6-1, 200. Born in La Ceiba, Honduras, December 28, 1920. Louisiana State. Inducted in 1965. 1944-1951 Philadelphia Eagles. **Highlights:** Four-time rushing champion. Won 1944 punt-return title and was 1945 kickoff-return champion.

DOAK WALKER
Halfback. 5-11, 173. Born in Dallas, Texas, January 1, 1927. Died September 27, 1998. Southern Methodist. Inducted in 1986. 1950-55 Detroit Lions. **Highlights:** 534 points. Won two NFL scoring titles. Had winning 67-yard scoring run in 1952 title game.

BILL WALSH
Coach. Born in Los Angeles, California, November 30, 1931. San Jose State. Inducted in 1993. 1979-1988 San Francisco 49ers. **Highlights:** 102-63-1 coaching record. Guided 49ers to three Super Bowl titles (XVI, XIX, XXIII) in 10 years.

PAUL WARFIELD
Wide receiver. 6-0, 188. Born in Warren, Ohio, November 28, 1942. Ohio State. Inducted in 1983. 1964-69, 1976-77 Cleveland Browns, 1970-74 Miami Dolphins. **Highlights:** 8,565 yards receiving, 85 touchdowns. Eight-time Pro Bowl player. Key to both Cleveland and Miami offenses.

BOB WATERFIELD
Quarterback. 6-2, 200. Born in Elmira, New York, July 26, 1920. Died March 25, 1983. UCLA. Inducted in 1965. 1945 Cleveland Rams, 1946-1952 Los Angeles Rams. **Highlights:** NFL MVP as rookie in 1945 and led Rams to NFL title. Grabbed 20 interceptions in limited defensive duties.

MIKE WEBSTER
Center. 6-2, 260. Born in Tomahawk, Wisconsin, March 18, 1952. Wisconsin. Inducted in 1997. 1974-1988 Pittsburgh Steelers, 1989-1990 Kansas City Chiefs. **Highlights:** Played in 245 games, nine Pro Bowls, and won four Super Bowls during 17-year career.

ARNIE WEINMEISTER
Defensive tackle. 6-4, 235. Born in Rhein, Saskatchewan, Canada, March 23, 1923. Died June 29, 2000. Washington. Inducted in 1984. 1948-49 New York Yankees (AAFC), 1950-53 New York Giants. **Highlights:** Dominant defensive tackle of his time. Four-time All-NFL selection, four Pro Bowls.

RANDY WHITE
Defensive tackle. 6-4, 265. Born in Pittsburgh, Pennsylvania, January 15, 1953. Maryland. Inducted in 1994. 1975-1988 Dallas Cowboys. **Highlights:** Missed only one game in 14 seasons. Co-MVP of Super Bowl XII. Nine-time Pro Bowl selection.

DAVE WILCOX
Linebacker. 6-3, 241. Born in Ontario, Oregon, September, 29, 1942. Boise State, Oregon. Inducted in 2000. 1964-1974 San Francisco 49ers. **Highlights:** Seven Pro Bowls, All-NFL five times. Missed only one game because of injury.

BILL WILLIS
Guard. 6-2, 215. Born in Columbus, Ohio, October 5, 1921. Ohio State. Inducted in 1977. 1946-49 Cleveland Browns (AAFC), 1950-53 Cleveland Browns. **Highlights:** Two-way player who excelled on defense. Four-time All-NFL player, played in three Pro Bowls.

LARRY WILSON
Safety. 6-0, 190. Born in Rigby, Idaho, March 24, 1938. Utah. Inducted in 1978. 1960-1972 St. Louis Cardinals. **Highlights:** 52 interceptions. Had interception in seven consecutive games in 1966. Made "safety blitz" famous.

KELLEN WINSLOW
Tight end. 6-5, 250. Born in St. Louis, Missouri, November 5, 1957. Inducted in 1995. 1979-1987 San Diego Chargers **Highlights:** 541 receptions for 6,741 yards, 45 touchdowns. 13 catches, blocked field goal in 1981 playoff win over Miami.

ALEX WOJCIECHOWICZ
Center. 6-0, 235. Born in South River, New Jersey, August 12, 1915. Died July 13, 1992. Fordham. Inducted in 1968. 1938-1946 Detroit Lions, 1946-1950 Philadelphia Eagles. **Highlights:** One of league's first iron men. Played both ways for eight years with Lions.

WILLIE WOOD
Safety. 5-10, 190. Born in Washington, D.C., December 23, 1936. Southern California. Inducted in 1989. 1960-1971 Green Bay Packers. **Highlights:** 48 interceptions. Competed in six NFL Championship Games and Super Bowls I and II.

RON YARY
Tackle. 6-5, 255. Born in Chicago, Illinois, July 16, 1946. Cerritos (Calif.) J.C., Southern California. Inducted in 2001. 1968-1981 Minnesota Vikings, 1982 Los Angeles Rams. **Highlights:** All-Pro six consecutive seasons, All-NFC eight consecutive years. Named to seven Pro Bowls. Started in four Super Bowls and five NFL/NFC Championship Games.

JACK YOUNGBLOOD
Defensive end. 6-4, 247. Born in Jacksonville, Florida, January 26, 1950. Florida. Inducted in 2001. 1971-1984 Los Angeles Rams. **Highlights:** Played in club-record 201 consecutive games. Played in five NFC Championship Games, one Super Bowl. Named All-Pro five times, All-NFC seven times. Elected to seven consecutive Pro Bowls.

ENSHRINEES BY YEAR OF INDUCTION
*Deceased
(Date of enshrinement in parentheses)

1963 CHARTER CLASS
(September 7, 1963)
Sammy Baugh
Bert Bell*
Joe Carr*
Earl (Dutch) Clark*
Harold (Red) Grange*
George Halas*
Mel Hein*
Wilbur (Pete) Henry*
Robert (Cal) Hubbard*
Don Hutson*
Earl (Curly) Lambeau*
Tim Mara*
George Preston Marshall*
John (Blood) McNally*
Bronko Nagurski*
Ernie Nevers*
Jim Thorpe*

CLASS OF 1964
(September 6, 1964)
Jimmy Conzelman*
Ed Healey*
Clarke Hinkle*
William Roy (Link) Lyman*
Mike Michalske*
Art Rooney*
George Trafton*

CLASS OF 1965
(September 12, 1965)
Guy Chamberlin*
John (Paddy) Driscoll*
Dan Fortmann*
Otto Graham
Sid Luckman*
Steve Van Buren*
Bob Waterfield*

CLASS OF 1966
(September 17, 1966)
Bill Dudley
Joe Guyon*
Arnie Herber*
Walt Kiesling*
George McAfee*
Steve Owen*
Hugh (Shorty) Ray*
Clyde (Bulldog) Turner*

CLASS OF 1967
(August 5, 1967)
Chuck Bednarik
Charles W. Bidwill Sr.*
Paul Brown*
Bobby Layne*
Dan Reeves*
Ken Strong*
Joe Stydahar*
Emlen Tunnell*

CLASS OF 1968
(August 3, 1968)
Cliff Battles*
Art Donovan
Elroy (Crazylegs) Hirsch
Wayne Millner*
Marion Motley*
Charley Trippi
Alex Wojciechowicz*

CLASS OF 1969
(September 13, 1969)
Albert Glen (Turk) Edwards*
Earle (Greasy) Neale*
Leo Nomellini*
Joe Perry
Ernie Stautner

CLASS OF 1970
(August 8, 1970)
Jack Christiansen*
Tom Fears*
Hugh McElhenny
Pete Pihos

CLASS OF 1971
(July 31, 1971)
Jim Brown
Bill Hewitt*
Frank (Bruiser) Kinard*
Vince Lombardi*
Andy Robustelli
Y. A. Tittle
Norm Van Brocklin*

CLASS OF 1972
(July 29, 1972)
Lamar Hunt
Gino Marchetti
Ollie Matson
Clarence (Ace) Parker

CLASS OF 1973
(July 28, 1973)
Raymond Berry
Jim Parker
Joe Schmidt

CLASS OF 1974
(July 27, 1974)
Tony Canadeo
Bill George*
Lou Groza*
Dick (Night Train) Lane*

CLASS OF 1975
(August 2, 1975)
Roosevelt Brown
George Connor
Dante Lavelli
Lenny Moore

CLASS OF 1976
(July 24, 1976)
Ray Flaherty*
Len Ford*
Jim Taylor

CLASS OF 1977
(July 30, 1977)
Frank Gifford
Forrest Gregg
Gale Sayers
Bart Starr
Bill Willis

CLASS OF 1978
(July 29, 1978)
Lance Alworth
Weeb Ewbank*
Alphonse (Tuffy) Leemans*
Ray Nitschke*
Larry Wilson

CLASS OF 1979
(July 28, 1979)
Dick Butkus
Yale Lary
Ron Mix
Johnny Unitas

CLASS OF 1980
(August 2, 1980)
Herb Adderley
David (Deacon) Jones
Bob Lilly
Jim Otto

CLASS OF 1981
(August 1, 1981)
Morris (Red) Badgro*
George Blanda
Willie Davis
Jim Ringo

CLASS OF 1982
(August 7, 1982)
Doug Atkins
Sam Huff
George Musso*
Merlin Olsen

CLASS OF 1983
(July 30, 1983)
Bobby Bell
Sid Gillman
Sonny Jurgensen
Bobby Mitchell
Paul Warfield

CLASS OF 1984
(July 28, 1984)
Willie Brown
Mike McCormack
Charley Taylor
Arnie Weinmeister*

CLASS OF 1985
(August 3, 1985)
Frank Gatski
Joe Namath
Pete Rozelle*
O. J. Simpson
Roger Staubach

CLASS OF 1986
(August 2, 1986)
Paul Hornung
Ken Houston
Willie Lanier
Fran Tarkenton
Doak Walker*

CLASS OF 1987
(August 8, 1987)
Larry Csonka
Len Dawson
Joe Greene
John Henry Johnson
Jim Langer
Don Maynard
Gene Upshaw

CLASS OF 1988
(July 30, 1988)
Fred Biletnikoff
Mike Ditka
Jack Ham
Alan Page

CLASS OF 1989
(August 5, 1989)
Mel Blount
Terry Bradshaw
Art Shell
Willie Wood

CLASS OF 1990
(August 4, 1990)
Buck Buchanan*
Bob Griese
Franco Harris
Ted Hendricks
Jack Lambert
Tom Landry*
Bob St. Clair

CLASS OF 1991
(July 27, 1991)
Earl Campbell
John Hannah
Stan Jones
Tex Schramm
Jan Stenerud

CLASS OF 1992
(August 1, 1992)
Lem Barney
Al Davis
John Mackey
John Riggins

CLASS OF 1993
(July 31, 1993)
Dan Fouts
Larry Little
Chuck Noll
Walter Payton*
Bill Walsh

CLASS OF 1994
(July 30, 1994)
Tony Dorsett
Bud Grant
Jimmy Johnson
Leroy Kelly
Jackie Smith
Randy White

CLASS OF 1995
(July 29, 1995)
Jim Finks*
Henry Jordan*
Steve Largent
Lee Roy Selmon
Kellen Winslow

CLASS OF 1996
(July 27, 1996)
Lou Creekmur
Dan Dierdorf
Joe Gibbs
Charlie Joiner
Mel Renfro

CLASS OF 1997
(July 26, 1997)
Mike Haynes
Wellington Mara
Don Shula
Mike Webster

CLASS OF 1998
(August 1, 1998)
Paul Krause
Tommy McDonald
Anthony Muñoz
Mike Singletary
Dwight Stephenson

CLASS OF 1999
(August 7, 1999)
Eric Dickerson
Tom Mack
Ozzie Newsome
Billy Shaw
Lawrence Taylor

CLASS OF 2000
(July 29, 2000)
Howie Long
Ronnie Lott
Joe Montana
Dan Rooney
Dave Wilcox

CLASS OF 2001
(August 4, 2001)
Nick Buoniconti
Marv Levy
Mike Munchak
Jackie Slater
Lynn Swann
Ron Yary
Jack Youngblood

CLASS OF 2002
(August 3, 2002)
George Allen*
Dave Casper
Dan Hampton
Jim Kelly
John Stallworth

1869
Rutgers and Princeton played a college soccer football game, the first ever, November 6. The game used modified London Football Association rules. During the next seven years, rugby gained favor with the major eastern schools over soccer, and modern football began to develop from rugby.

1876
At the Massasoit convention, the first rules for American football were written. Walter Camp, who would become known as the father of American football, first became involved with the game.

1892
In an era in which football was a major attraction of local athletic clubs, an intense competition between two Pittsburgh-area clubs, the Allegheny Athletic Association (AAA) and the Pittsburgh Athletic Club (PAC), led to the making of the first professional football player. Former Yale All-America guard William (Pudge) Heffelfinger was paid $500 by the AAA to play in a game against the PAC, becoming the first person to be paid to play football, November 12. The AAA won the game 4-0 when Heffelfinger picked up a PAC fumble and ran 35 yards for a touchdown.

1893
The Pittsburgh Athletic Club signed one of its players, probably halfback Grant Dibert, to the first known pro football contract, which covered all of the PAC's games for the year.

1895
John Brallier became the first football player to openly turn pro, accepting $10 and expenses to play for the Latrobe YMCA against the Jeannette Athletic Club.

1896
The Allegheny Athletic Association team fielded the first completely professional team for its abbreviated two-game season.

1897
The Latrobe Athletic Associa-tion football team went entire-ly professional, becoming the first team to play a full season with only professionals.

1898
A touchdown was changed from four points to five.

1899
Chris O'Brien formed a neighborhood team, which played under the name the Morgan Athletic Club, on the south side of Chicago. The team later became known as the Normals, then the Racine (for a street in Chicago) Cardinals, the Chicago Cardinals, the St. Louis Cardinals, the Phoenix Cardinals, and, in 1994, the Arizona Cardinals. The team remains the oldest continuing operation in pro football.

1900
William C. Temple took over the team payments for the Duquesne Country and Athletic Club, becoming the first known individual club owner.

1902
Baseball's Philadelphia Athletics, managed by Connie Mack, and the Philadelphia Phillies formed professional football teams, joining the Pittsburgh Stars in the first attempt at a pro football league, named the National Football League. The Athletics won the first night football game ever played, 39-0 over Kanaweola AC at Elmira, New York, November 21.

All three teams claimed the pro championship for the year, but the league president, Dave Berry, named the Stars the champions. Pitcher Rube Waddell was with the Athletics, and pitcher Christy Mathewson a fullback for Pittsburgh.

The first World Series of pro football, actually a five-team tournament, was played among a team made up of players from both the Athletics and the Phillies, but simply named New York; the New York Knickerbockers; the Syracuse AC; the Warlow AC; and the Orange (New Jersey) AC at New York's original Madison Square Garden. New York and Syracuse played the first indoor football game before 3,000, December 28.

Syracuse, with Glen (Pop) Warner at guard, won 6-0 and went on to win the tournament.

1903
The Franklin (Pa.) Athletic Club won the second and last World Series of pro football over the Oreos AC of Asbury Park, New Jersey; the Watertown Red and Blacks; and the Orange AC.

Pro football was popularized in Ohio when the Massillon Tigers, a strong amateur team, hired four Pittsburgh pros to play in the season-ending game against Akron. At the same time, pro football declined in the Pittsburgh area, and the emphasis on the pro game moved west from Pennsylvania to Ohio.

1904
A field goal was changed from five points to four.

Ohio had at least seven pro teams, with Massillon winning the Ohio Independent Championship, that is, the pro title. Talk surfaced about forming a state-wide league to end spiraling salaries brought about by constant bidding for players and to write universal rules for the game. The feeble attempt to start the league failed.

Halfback Charles Follis signed a contract with the Shelby (Ohio) AC, making him the first known black pro football player.

1905
The Canton AC, later to become known as the Bulldogs, became a professional team. Massillon again won the Ohio League championship.

1906
The forward pass was legalized. The first authenticated pass completion in a pro game came on October 27, when George (Peggy) Parratt of Massillon threw a completion to Dan (Bullet) Riley in a victory over a combined Benwood-Moundsville team.

Arch-rivals Canton and Massillon, the two best pro teams in America, played twice, with Canton winning the first game but Massillon winning the second and the Ohio League championship. A bet-ting scandal and the financial disaster wrought upon the two clubs by paying huge salaries caused a temporary decline in interest in pro football in the two cities and, somewhat, throughout Ohio.

1909
A field goal dropped from four points to three.

1912
A touchdown was increased from five points to six.

Jack Cusack revived a strong pro team in Canton.

1913
Jim Thorpe, a former football and track star at the Carlisle Indian School (Pa.) and a double gold medal winner at the 1912 Olympics in Stockholm, played for the Pine Village Pros in Indiana.

1915
Massillon again fielded a major team, reviving the old rivalry with Canton. Cusack signed Thorpe to play for Canton for $250 a game.

1916
With Thorpe and former Carlisle teammate Pete Calac starring, Canton went 9-0-1, won the Ohio League championship, and was acclaimed the pro football champion.

1917
Despite an upset by Massillon, Canton again won the Ohio League championship.

1919
Canton again won the Ohio League championship, despite the team having been turned over from Cusack to Ralph Hay. Thorpe and Calac were joined in the backfield by Joe Guyon.

Earl (Curly) Lambeau and George Calhoun organized the Green Bay Packers. Lambeau's employer at the Indian Packing Company provided $500 for equipment and allowed the team to use the company field for practices. The Packers went 10-1.

1920
Pro football was in a state of confusion due to three major problems: dramatically rising salaries; players continually

jumping from one team to another following the highest offer; and the use of college players still enrolled in school. A league in which all the members would follow the same rules seemed the answer. An organizational meeting, at which the Akron Pros, Canton Bulldogs, Cleveland Indians, and Dayton Triangles were represented, was held at the Jordan and Hupmobile auto showroom in Canton, Ohio, August 20. This meeting resulted in the formation of the American Professional Football Conference.

A second organizational meeting was held in Canton, September 17. The teams were from four states—Akron, Canton, Cleveland, and Dayton from Ohio; the Hammond Pros and Muncie Flyers from Indiana; the Rochester Jeffersons from New York; and the Rock Island Independents, Decatur Staleys, and Racine Cardinals from Illinois. The name of the league was changed to the American Professional Football Association. Hoping to capitalize on his fame, the members elected Thorpe president; Stanley Cofall of Cleveland was elected vice president. A membership fee of $100 per team was charged to give an appearance of respectability, but no team ever paid it. Scheduling was left up to the teams, and there were wide variations, both in the overall number of games played and in the number played against APFA member teams.

Four other teams—the Buffalo All-Americans, Chicago Tigers, Columbus Panhandles, and Detroit Heralds—joined the league sometime during the year. On September 26, the first game featuring an APFA team was played at Rock Island's Douglas Park. A crowd of 800 watched the Independents defeat the St. Paul Ideals 48-0. A week later, October 3, the first game matching two APFA teams was held. At Triangle Park, Dayton defeated Columbus 14-0, with Lou Partlow of Dayton scoring the first touchdown in a game between Association teams. The same day, Rock Island defeated Muncie 45-0.

By the beginning of December, most of the teams in the APFA had abandoned their hopes for a championship, and some of them, including the Chicago Tigers and Detroit Heralds, had finished their seasons, disbanded, and had their franchises canceled by the Association. Four teams—Akron, Buffalo, Canton, and Decatur—still had championship as-pirations, but a series of late-season games among them left Akron as the only undefeated team in the Association. At one of these games, Akron sold tackle Bob Nash to Buffalo for $300 and five percent of the gate receipts—the first APFA player deal.

1921
At the league meeting in Akron, April 30, the championship of the 1920 season was awarded to the Akron Pros. The APFA was reorganized, with Joe Carr of the Columbus Panhandles named president and Carl Storck of Dayton secretary-treasurer. Carr moved the Association's headquarters to Columbus, drafted a league constitution and by-laws, gave teams territorial rights, restricted player movements, developed membership criteria for the franchises, and issued standings for the first time, so that the APFA would have a clear champion.

The Association's membership increased to 22 teams, including the Green Bay Packers, who were awarded to John Clair of the Acme Packing Company.

Thorpe moved from Canton to the Cleveland Indians, but he was hurt early in the season and played very little.

A.E. Staley turned the Decatur Staleys over to player-coach George Halas, who moved the team to Cubs Park in Chicago. Staley paid Halas $5,000 to keep the name Staleys for one more year. Halas made halfback Ed (Dutch) Sternaman his partner.

Player-coach Fritz Pollard of the Akron Pros became the first black head coach.

The Staleys claimed the APFA championship with a 9-1-1 record, as did Buffalo at 9-1-2. Carr ruled in favor of the Staleys, giving Halas his first championship.

1922
After admitting the use of players who had college eligibility remaining during the 1921 season, Clair and the Green Bay management withdrew from the APFA, January 28. Curly Lambeau promised to obey league rules and then used $50 of his own money to buy back the franchise. Bad weather and low attendance plagued the Packers, and Lambeau went broke, but local merchants arranged a $2,500 loan for the club. A public nonprofit corporation was set up to operate the team, with Lambeau as head coach and manager.

The American Professional Football Association changed its name to the National Football League, June 24. The Chicago Staleys became the Chicago Bears.

The NFL fielded 18 teams, including the new Oorang Indians of Marion, Ohio, an all-Indian team featuring Thorpe, Joe Guyon, and Pete Calac, and sponsored by the Oorang dog kennels.

Canton, led by player-coach Guy Chamberlin and tackles Link Lyman and Wilbur (Pete) Henry, emerged as the league's first true powerhouse, going 10-0-2.

1923
For the first time, all of the franchises considered to be part of the NFL fielded teams. Thorpe played his second and final season for the Oorang Indians. Against the Bears, Thorpe fumbled, and Halas picked up the ball and returned it 98 yards for a touchdown, a record that would last until 1972.

Canton had its second consecutive undefeated season, going 11-0-1 for the NFL title.

1924
The league had 18 franchises, including new ones in Kansas City, Kenosha, and Frankford, a section of Philadelphia. League champion Canton, successful on the field but not at the box office, was purchased by the owner of the Cleveland franchise, who kept the Canton franchise inactive,

while using the best players for his Cleveland team, which he renamed the Bulldogs. Cleveland won the title with a 7-1-1 record.

1925
Five new franchises were admitted to the NFL—the New York Giants, who were awarded to Tim Mara and Billy Gibson for $500; the Detroit Panthers, featuring Jimmy Conzelman as owner, coach, and tailback; the Providence Steam Roller; a new Canton Bulldogs team; and the Pottsville Maroons, who had been perhaps the most successful independent pro team. The NFL established its first player limit, at 16 players.

Late in the season, the NFL made its greatest coup in gaining national recognition. Shortly after the University of Illinois season ended in November, All-America halfback Harold (Red) Grange signed a contract to play with the Chicago Bears. On Thanksgiving Day, a crowd of 36,000—the largest in pro football history—watched Grange and the Bears play the Chicago Cardinals to a scoreless tie at Wrigley Field. At the beginning of December, the Bears left on a barnstorming tour that saw them play eight games in 12 days, in St. Louis, Philadelphia, New York City, Washington, Boston, Pittsburgh, Detroit, and Chicago. A crowd of 73,000 watched the game against the Giants at the Polo Grounds, helping assure the future of the troubled NFL franchise in New York. The Bears then played nine more games in the South and West, including a game in Los Angeles, in which 75,000 fans watched them defeat the Los Angeles Tigers in the Los Angeles Memorial Coliseum.

Pottsville and the Chicago Cardinals were the top contenders for the league title, with Pottsville winning a late-season meeting 21-7. Pottsville scheduled a game against a team of former Notre Dame players for Shibe Park in Philadelphia. Frankford lodged a protest not only because the game was in Frankford's protected territory, but because it was being played the same day as a Yellow Jackets home game. Carr gave three different notices forbidding Pottsville to play the game, but Pottsville played anyway, December 12. That day, Carr fined the club, suspended it from all rights and privileges (including the right to play for the NFL championship), and re-turned its franchise to the league. The Cardinals, who ended the season with the best record in the league, were named the 1925 champions.

1926
Grange's manager, C.C. Pyle, told the Bears that Grange wouldn't play for them unless he was paid a five-figure salary and given one-third ownership of the team. The Bears refused. Pyle leased Yankee Stadium in New York City, then petitioned for an NFL franchise. After he was refused, he started the first American Football League. It lasted one season and included Grange's New York Yankees and eight other teams. The AFL champion Philadelphia Quakers played a December game against the New York Giants, seventh in the NFL, and the Giants won 31-0. At the end of the season, the AFL folded.

Halas pushed through a rule that prohibited any team from signing a player whose college class had not graduated.

The NFL grew to 22 teams, including the Duluth Eskimos, who signed All-America fullback Ernie Nevers of Stanford, giving the league a gate attraction to rival Grange. The 15-member Eskimos, dubbed the Iron Men of the North, played 29 exhibition and league games, 28 on the road, and Nevers played in all but 29 minutes of them.

Frankford edged the Bears for the championship, despite Halas having obtained John (Paddy) Driscoll from the Cardinals. On December 4, the Yellow Jackets scored in the final two minutes to defeat the Bears 7-6 and move ahead of them in the standings.

1927
At a special meeting in Cleveland, April 23, Carr decided to secure the NFL's future by eliminating the financially weaker teams and consolidating the quality players onto a limited number of more successful teams. The new-look NFL dropped to 12 teams, and the center of gravity of the league left the Midwest, where the NFL had started, and began to emerge in the large cities of the East. One of the new teams was Grange's New York Yankees, but Grange suffered a knee injury and the Yankees finished in the middle of the pack. The NFL championship was won by the cross-town rival New York Giants, who posted 10 shutouts in 13 games.

1928
Grange and Nevers both retired from pro football, and Duluth disbanded, as the NFL was reduced to only 10 teams. The Providence Steam Roller of Jimmy Conzelman and Pearce Johnson won the championship, playing in the Cycledrome, a 10,000-seat oval that had been built for bicycle races.

1929
Chris O'Brien sold the Chicago Cardinals to David Jones, July 27.

The NFL added a fourth official, the field judge, July 28.

Grange and Nevers returned to the NFL. Nevers scored six rushing touchdowns and four extra points as the Cardinals beat Grange's Bears 40-6, November 28. The 40 points set a record that remains the NFL's oldest.

Providence became the first NFL team to host a game at night under floodlights, against the Cardinals, November 3.

The Packers added back Johnny Blood (McNally), tackle Cal Hubbard, and guard Mike Michalske, and won their first NFL championship, edging the Giants, who featured quarterback Benny Friedman.

1930
Dayton, the last of the NFL's original franchises, was purchased by William B. Dwyer and John C. Depler, moved to Brooklyn, and renamed the Dodgers. The Portsmouth, Ohio, Spartans entered the league.

The Packers edged the Giants for the title, but the most improved team was the Bears. Halas retired as a player and replaced himself as coach of the Bears with Ralph Jones, who refined the T-formation by introducing wide ends and a halfback in motion. Jones also introduced rookie All-America fullback-tackle Bronko Nagurski.

The Giants defeated a team of former Notre Dame players coached by Knute Rockne 22-0 before 55,000 at the Polo Grounds, December 14. The proceeds went to the New York Unemployment Fund to help those suffering because of the Great Depression, and the easy victory helped give the NFL credibility with the press and the public.

1931
The NFL decreased to 10 teams, and halfway through the season the Frankford franchise folded. Carr fined the Bears, Packers, and Portsmouth $1,000 each for using players whose college classes had not graduated.

The Packers won an unprecedented third consecutive title, beating out the Spartans, who were led by rookie backs Earl (Dutch) Clark and Glenn Presnell.

1932
George Preston Marshall, Vincent Bendix, Jay O'Brien, and M. Dorland Doyle were awarded a franchise for Boston, July 9. Despite the presence of two rookies—halfback Cliff Battles and tackle Glen (Turk) Edwards—the new team, named the Braves, lost money and Marshall was left as the sole owner at the end of the year.

NFL membership dropped to eight teams, the lowest in history. Official statistics were kept for the first time. The Bears and the Spartans finished the season in the first-ever tie for first place. After the season finale, the league office arranged for an additional regular-season game to determine the league champion. The game was moved indoors to Chicago Stadium because of bitter cold and heavy snow. The arena allowed only an 80-yard field that came right to the walls. The goal posts were moved from the end lines to the goal lines and, for safety, inbounds lines or hashmarks where the ball would be put in play were drawn 10 yards from the walls that butted against the sidelines. The Bears won 9-0, December 18, scoring the winning touchdown on a two-yard pass from Nagurski to Grange. The Spartans claimed Nagurski's pass was thrown from less than five yards behind the line of scrimmage, violating the existing passing rule, but the play stood.

1933
The NFL, which long had followed the rules of college football, made a number of significant changes from the college game for the first time and began to develop rules serving its needs and the style of play it preferred. The innovations from the 1932 championship game—inbounds line or hashmarks and goal posts on the goal lines—were adopted. Also the forward pass was legalized from anywhere behind the line of scrimmage, February 25.

Marshall and Halas pushed through a proposal that divided the NFL into two divisions, with the winners to meet in an annual championship game, July 8.

Three new franchises joined the league—the Pittsburgh Pirates of Art Rooney, the Philadelphia Eagles of Bert Bell and Lud Wray, and the Cincinnati Reds. The Staten Island Stapletons suspended operations for a year, but never returned to the league.

Halas bought out Sternaman, became sole owner of the Bears, and reinstated himself as head coach. Marshall changed the name of the Boston Braves to the Redskins. David Jones sold the Chicago Cardinals to Charles W. Bidwill.

In the first NFL Championship Game scheduled before the season, the Western Division champion Bears defeated the Eastern Division champion Giants 23-21 at Wrigley Field, December 17.

1934
G.A. (Dick) Richards pur-

chased the Portsmouth Spartans, moved them to Detroit, and renamed them the Lions.

Professional football gained new prestige when the Bears were matched against the best college football players in the first Chicago College All-Star Game, August 31. The game ended in a scoreless tie before 79,432 at Soldier Field.

The Cincinnati Reds lost their first eight games, then were suspended from the league for defaulting on payments. The St. Louis Gunners, an independent team, joined the NFL by buying the Cincinnati franchise and went 1-2 the last three weeks.

Rookie Beattie Feathers of the Bears became the NFL's first 1,000-yard rusher, gaining 1,004 on 101 carries. The Thanksgiving Day game between the Bears and the Lions became the first NFL game broadcast nationally, with Graham McNamee the announcer for NBC radio.

In the championship game, on an extremely cold and icy day at the Polo Grounds, the Giants trailed the Bears 13-3 in the third quarter before changing to basketball shoes for better footing. The Giants won 30-13 in what has come to be known as the Sneakers Game, December 9.

The player waiver rule was adopted, December 10.

1935
The NFL adopted Bert Bell's proposal to hold an annual draft of college players, to begin in 1936, with teams selecting in an inverse order of finish, May 19. The inbounds line or hashmarks were moved nearer the center of the field, 15 yards from the sidelines.

All-America end Don Hutson of Alabama joined Green Bay. The Lions defeated the Giants 26-7 in the NFL Championship Game, December 15.

1936
There were no franchise transactions for the first year since the formation of the NFL. It also was the first year in which all member teams played the same number of games.

The Eagles made University of Chicago halfback and Heisman Trophy winner Jay

Berwanger the first player ever selected in the NFL draft, February 8. The Eagles traded his rights to the Bears, but Berwanger never played pro football. The first player selected to actually sign was the number-two pick, Riley Smith of Alabama, who was selected by Boston.

A rival league was formed, and it became the second to call itself the American Football League. The Boston Shamrocks were its champions.

Because of poor attendance, Marshall, the owner of the host team, moved the Championship Game from Boston to the Polo Grounds in New York. Green Bay defeated the Redskins 21-6, December 13.

1937
Homer Marshman was granted a Cleveland franchise, named the Rams, February 12. Marshall moved the Redskins to Washington, D.C., February 13. The Redskins signed TCU All-America tailback Sammy Baugh, who led them to a 28-21 victory over the Bears in the NFL Championship Game, December 12.

The Los Angeles Bulldogs had an 8-0 record to win the AFL title, but then the 2-year-old league folded.

1938
At the suggestion of Halas, Hugh (Shorty) Ray became a technical advisor on rules and officiating to the NFL. A new rule called for a 15-yard penalty for roughing the passer.

Rookie Byron (Whizzer) White of the Pittsburgh Pirates led the NFL in rushing. The Giants defeated the Packers 23-17 for the NFL title, December 11.

Marshall, *Los Angeles Times* sports editor Bill Henry, and promoter Tom Gallery established the Pro Bowl game between the NFL champion and a team of pro all-stars.

1939
The New York Giants defeated the Pro All-Stars 13-10 in the first Pro Bowl, at Wrigley Field, Los Angeles, January 15.

Carr, NFL president since 1921, died in Columbus, May

20. Carl Storck was named acting president, May 25.

An NFL game was televised for the first time when NBC broadcast the Brooklyn Dodgers-Philadelphia Eagles game from Ebbets Field to the approximately 1,000 sets then in New York.

Green Bay defeated New York 27-0 in the NFL Championship Game, December 10 at Milwaukee. NFL attendance exceeded 1 million in a season for the first time, reaching 1,071,200.

1940
A six-team rival league, the third to call itself the American Football League, was formed, and the Columbus Bullies won its championship.

Halas' Bears, with additional coaching by Clark Shaughnessy of Stanford, defeated the Redskins 73-0 in the NFL Championship Game, December 8. The game, which was the most decisive victory in NFL history, popularized the Bears' T-formation with a man-in-motion. It was the first championship carried on network radio, broadcast by Red Barber to 120 stations of the Mutual Broadcasting System, which paid $2,500 for the rights.

Art Rooney sold the Pittsburgh franchise to Alexis Thompson, December 9, then bought part interest in the Philadelphia Eagles.

1941
Elmer Layden was named the first Commissioner of the NFL, March 1; Storck, the acting president, resigned, April 5. NFL headquarters were moved to Chicago.

Bell and Rooney traded the Eagles to Thompson for the Pirates, then re-named their new team the Steelers. Homer Marshman sold the Rams to Daniel F. Reeves and Fred Levy, Jr.

The league by-laws were revised to provide for playoffs in case there were ties in division races, and sudden-death overtimes in case a playoff game was tied after four quarters. An official *NFL Record Manual* was published for the first time.

Columbus again won the championship of the AFL, but

the two-year-old league then folded.

The Bears and the Packers finished in a tie for the Western Division championship, setting up the first divisional playoff game in league history. The Bears won 33-14, then defeated the Giants 37-9 for the NFL championship, December 21.

1942
Players departing for service in World War II depleted the rosters of NFL teams. Halas left the Bears in midseason to join the Navy, and Luke Johnsos and Heartley (Hunk) Anderson served as co-coaches as the Bears went 11-0 in the regular season. The Redskins defeated the Bears 14-6 in the NFL Championship Game, December 13.

1943
The Cleveland Rams, with co-owners Reeves and Levy in the service, were granted permission to suspend operations for one season, April 6. Levy transferred his stock in the team to Reeves, April 16.

The NFL adopted free substitution, April 7. The league also made the wearing of helmets mandatory and approved a 10-game schedule for all teams.

Philadelphia and Pittsburgh were granted permission to merge for one season, June 19. The team, known as Phil-Pitt (and called the Steagles by fans), divided home games between the two cities, and Earle (Greasy) Neale of Philadelphia and Walt Kiesling of Pittsburgh served as co-coaches. The merger automatically dissolved the last day of the season, December 5.

Ted Collins was granted a franchise for Boston, to become active in 1944.

Sammy Baugh led the league in passing, punting, and interceptions. He led the Redskins to a tie with the Giants for the Eastern Division title, and then to a 28-0 victory in a divisional playoff game. The Bears beat the Redskins 41-21 in the NFL Championship Game, December 26.

1944
Collins, who had wanted a

franchise in Yankee Stadium in New York, named his new team in Boston the Yanks. Cleveland resumed operations. The Brooklyn Dodgers changed their name to the Tigers.

Coaching from the bench was legalized, April 20.

The Cardinals and the Steelers were granted permission to merge for one year under the name Card-Pitt, April 21. Phil Handler of the Cardinals and Walt Kiesling of the Steelers served as co-coaches. The merger automatically dissolved the last day of the season, December 3.

In the NFL Championship Game, Green Bay defeated the New York Giants 14-7, December 17.

1945
The inbounds lines or hashmarks were moved from 15 yards away from the sidelines to nearer the center of the field—20 yards from the sidelines.

Brooklyn and Boston merged into a team that played home games in both cities and was known simply as The Yanks. The team was coached by former Boston head coach Herb Kopf. In December, the Brooklyn franchise withdrew from the NFL to join the new All-America Football Conference; all the players on its active and reserve lists were assigned to The Yanks, who once again became the Boston Yanks.

Halas rejoined the Bears late in the season after service with the U.S. Navy. Although Halas took over much of the coaching duties, Anderson and Johnsos remained the coaches of record throughout the season.

Steve Van Buren of Philadelphia led the NFL in rushing, kickoff returns, and scoring.

After the Japanese surrendered ending World War II, a count showed that the NFL service roster, limited to men who had played in league games, totaled 638, 21 of whom had died in action.

Rookie quarterback Bob Waterfield led Cleveland to a 15-14 victory over Washington in the NFL Championship Game, December 16.

1946
The contract of Commissioner Layden was not renewed, and Bert Bell, the co-owner of the Steelers, replaced him, January 11. Bell moved the league headquarters from Chicago to the Philadelphia suburb of Bala-Cynwyd.

Free substitution was withdrawn and substitutions were limited to no more than three men at a time. Forward passes were made automatically incomplete upon striking the goal posts, January 11.

The NFL took on a truly national appearance for the first time when Reeves was granted permission by the league to move his NFL champion Rams to Los Angeles.

Halfback Kenny Washington (March 21) and end Woody Strode (May 7) signed with the Los Angeles Rams to become the first African-Americans to play in the NFL in the modern era. Guard Bill Willis (August 6) and running back Marion Motley (August 9) joined the AAFC with the Cleveland Browns.

The rival All-America Football Conference began play with eight teams. The Cleveland Browns, coached by Paul Brown, won the AAFC's first championship, defeating the New York Yankees 14-9.

Bill Dudley of the Steelers led the NFL in rushing, interceptions, and punt returns, and won the league's most valuable player award.

Backs Frank Filchock and Merle Hapes of the Giants were questioned about an attempt by a New York man to fix the championship game with the Bears. Bell suspended Hapes but allowed Filchock to play; he played well, but Chicago won 24-14, December 15.

1947
The NFL added a fifth official, the back judge.

A bonus choice was made for the first time in the NFL draft. One team each year would select the special choice before the first round began. The Chicago Bears won a lottery and the rights to the first choice and drafted back Bob Fenimore of Oklahoma A&M.

The Cleveland Browns again won the AAFC title,

defeating the New York Yankees 14-3.

Charles Bidwill, Sr., owner of the Cardinals, died April 19, but his wife and sons retained ownership of the team. On December 28, the Cardinals won the NFL Championship Game 28-21 over the Philadelphia Eagles, who had beaten Pittsburgh 21-0 in a playoff.

1948
Plastic helmets were prohibited. A flexible artificial tee was permitted at the kickoff. Officials other than the referee were equipped with whistles, not horns, January 14.

Fred Mandel sold the Detroit Lions to a syndicate headed by D. Lyle Fife, January 15.

Halfback Fred Gehrke of the Los Angeles Rams painted horns on the Rams' helmets, the first modern helmet emblems in pro football.

The Cleveland Browns won their third straight championship in the AAFC, going 14-0 and then defeating the Buffalo Bills 49-7.

In a blizzard, the Eagles defeated the Cardinals 7-0 in the NFL Championship Game, December 19.

1949
Alexis Thompson sold the champion Eagles to a syndicate headed by James P. Clark, January 15. The Boston Yanks became the New York Bulldogs, sharing the Polo Grounds with the Giants.

Free substitution was adopted for one year, January 20.

The NFL had two 1,000-yard rushers in the same season for the first time—Steve Van Buren of Philadelphia and Tony Canadeo of Green Bay.

The AAFC played its season with a one-division, seven-team format. On December 9, Bell announced a mer-ger agreement in which three AAFC franchises—Cleveland, San Francisco, and Baltimore—would join the NFL in 1950. The Browns won their fourth consecutive AAFC title, defeating the 49ers 21-7, December 11.

In a heavy rain, the Eagles defeated the Rams 14-0 in the NFL Championship Game, December 18.

1950
Unlimited free substitution was restored, opening the way for the era of two platoons and specialization in pro football, January 20.

Curly Lambeau, founder of the franchise and Green Bay's head coach since 1921, resigned under fire, February 1.

The name National Football League was restored after about three months as the National-American Football League. The American and National conferences were created to replace the Eastern and Western divisions, March 3.

The New York Bulldogs became the Yanks and divided the players of the former AAFC Yankees with the Giants. A special allocation draft was held in which the 13 teams drafted the remaining AAFC players, with special consideration for Baltimore, which received 15 choices compared to 10 for other teams.

The Los Angeles Rams became the first NFL team to have all of its games—both home and away—televised. The Washington Redskins followed the Rams in arranging to televise their games; other teams made deals to put selected games on television.

In the first game of the season, former AAFC champion Cleveland defeated NFL champion Philadelphia 35-10. For the first time, deadlocks occurred in both conferences and playoffs were necessary. The Browns defeated the Giants in the American and the Rams defeated the Bears in the National. Cleveland defeated Los Angeles 30-28 in the NFL Championship Game, December 24.

1951
The Pro Bowl game, dormant since 1942, was revived under a new format matching the all-stars of each conference at the Los Angeles Memorial Coliseum. The American Conference defeated the National Conference 28-27, January 14.

Abraham Watner returned the Baltimore franchise and its player contracts back to the NFL for $50,000. Baltimore's former players were made available for drafting at the same time as college players, January 18.

A rule was passed that no tackle, guard, or center would be eligible to catch a forward pass, January 18.

The Rams reversed their television policy and televised only road games.

The NFL Championship Game was televised coast-to-coast for the first time, December 23. The DuMont Network paid $75,000 for the rights to the game, in which the Rams defeated the Browns 24-17.

1952
Ted Collins sold the New York Yanks' franchise back to the NFL, January 19. A new franchise was awarded to a group in Dallas after it purchased the assets of the Yanks, January 24. The new Texans went 1-11, with the owners turning the franchise back to the league in midseason. For the last five games of the season, the commissioner's office operated the Texans as a road team, using Hershey, Pennsylvania, as a home base. At the end of the season the franchise was canceled, the last time an NFL team failed.

The Pittsburgh Steelers abandoned the Single-Wing for the T-formation, the last pro team to do so.

The Detroit Lions won their first NFL championship in 17 years, defeating the Browns 17-7 in the title game, December 28.

1953
A Baltimore group headed by Carroll Rosenbloom was granted a franchise and was awarded the holdings of the defunct Dallas organization, January 23. The team, named the Colts, put together the largest trade in league history, acquiring 10 players from Cleveland in exchange for five.

The names of the American and National conferences were changed to the Eastern and Western conferences, January 24.

Jim Thorpe died, March 28.

Mickey McBride, founder of the Cleveland Browns, sold the franchise to a syndicate headed by Dave R. Jones, June 10.

The NFL policy of blacking out home games was upheld by Judge Allan K. Grim of the U.S. District Court in Philadelphia, November 12.

The Lions again defeated the Browns in the NFL Championship Game, winning 17-16, December 27.

1954
The Canadian Football League began a series of raids on NFL teams, signing quarterback Eddie LeBaron and defensive end Gene Brito of Washington and defensive tackle Arnie Weinmeister of the Giants, among others.

Fullback Joe Perry of the 49ers became the first player in league history to gain 1,000 yards rushing in consecutive seasons.

Cleveland defeated Detroit 56-10 in the NFL Championship Game, December 26.

1955
The sudden-death overtime rule was used for the first time in a preseason game between the Rams and Giants at Portland, Oregon, August 28. The Rams won 23-17 three minutes into overtime.

A rule change declared the ball dead immediately if the ball carrier touched the ground with any part of his body except his hands or feet while in the grasp of an opponent.

The Baltimore Colts made an 80-cent phone call to Johnny Unitas and signed him as a free agent. Another quarterback, Otto Graham, played his last game as the Browns defeated the Rams 38-14 in the NFL Championship Game, December 26. Graham had quarterbacked the Browns to 10 championship-game appearances in 10 years.

NBC replaced DuMont as the network for the title game, paying a rights fee of $100,000.

1956
The NFL Players Association was founded.

Grabbing an opponent's facemask (other than the ball carrier) was made illegal. Using radio receivers to communicate with players on the field was prohibited. A natural leather ball with white end stripes replaced the white ball

with black stripes for night games.

The Giants moved from the Polo Grounds to Yankee Stadium.

Halas retired as coach of the Bears, and was replaced by Paddy Driscoll.

CBS became the first network to broadcast some NFL regular-season games to selected television markets across the nation.

The Giants routed the Bears 47-7 in the NFL Championship Game, December 30.

1957
Pete Rozelle was named general manager of the Rams. Anthony J. Morabito, founder and co-owner of the 49ers, died of a heart attack during a game against the Bears at Kezar Stadium, October 28. An NFL-record crowd of 102,368 saw the 49ers-Rams game at the Los Angeles Memorial Coliseum, November 10.

The Lions came from 20 points down to post a 31-27 playoff victory over the 49ers, December 22. Detroit defeated Cleveland 59-14 in the NFL Championship Game, December 29.

1958
The bonus selection in the draft was eliminated, January 29. The last selection was quarterback King Hill of Rice by the Chicago Cardinals.

Halas reinstated himself as coach of the Bears.

Jim Brown of Cleveland gained an NFL-record 1,527 yards rushing. In a divisional playoff game, the Giants held Brown to eight yards and defeated Cleveland 10-0.

Baltimore, coached by Weeb Ewbank, defeated the Giants 23-17 in the first sudden-death overtime in an NFL Championship Game, December 28. The game ended when Colts fullback Alan Ameche scored on a one-yard touchdown run after 8:15 of overtime.

1959
Vince Lombardi was named head coach of the Green Bay Packers, January 28. Tim Mara, the co-founder of the Giants, died, February 17.

Lamar Hunt of Dallas

announced his intentions to form a second pro football league. The first meeting was held in Chicago, August 14, and consisted of Hunt representing Dallas; Bob Howsam, Denver; K.S. (Bud) Adams, Houston; Barron Hilton, Los Angeles; Max Winter and Bill Boyer, Minneapolis; and Harry Wismer, New York City. They made plans to begin play in 1960.

The new league was named the American Football League, August 22. Buffalo, owned by Ralph Wilson, became the seventh franchise, October 28. Boston, owned by William H. Sullivan, became the eighth team, November 22. The first AFL draft, lasting 33 rounds, was held, November 22. Joe Foss was named AFL Commissioner, November 30. An additional draft of 20 rounds was held by the AFL, December 2.

NFL Commissioner Bert Bell died of a heart attack suffered at Franklin Field, Philadelphia, during the last two minutes of a game between the Eagles and the Steelers, October 11. Treasurer Austin Gunsel was named president in the office of the commissioner, October 14.

The Colts again defeated the Giants in the NFL Championship Game, 31-16, December 27.

1960
Pete Rozelle was elected NFL Commissioner as a compromise choice on the twenty-third ballot, January 26. Rozelle moved the league offices to New York City.

Hunt was elected AFL president for 1960, January 26. Minneapolis withdrew from the AFL, January 27, and the same ownership was given an NFL franchise for Minnesota (to start in 1961), January 28. Dallas received an NFL franchise for 1960, January 28. Oakland received an AFL franchise, January 30.

The AFL adopted the two-point option on points after touchdown, January 28. A no-tampering verbal pact, relative to players' contracts, was agreed to between the NFL and AFL, February 9.

The NFL owners voted to allow the transfer of the Chicago Cardinals to St. Louis, March 13.

The AFL signed a five-year television contract with ABC, June 9.

The Boston Patriots defeated the Buffalo Bills 28-7 before 16,000 at Buffalo in the first AFL preseason game, July 30. The Denver Broncos defeated the Patriots 13-10 before 21,597 at Boston in the first AFL regular-season game, September 9.

Philadelphia defeated Green Bay 17-13 in the NFL Championship Game, December 26.

1961

The Houston Oilers defeated the Los Angeles Chargers 24-16 before 32,183 in the first AFL Championship Game, January 1.

Detroit defeated Cleveland 17-16 in the first Playoff Bowl, or Bert Bell Benefit Bowl, between second-place teams in each conference in Miami, January 7.

End Willard Dewveall of the Bears played out his option and joined the Oilers, becoming the first player to move deliberately from one league to the other, January 14.

Ed McGah, Wayne Valley, and Robert Osborne bought out their partners in the ownership of the Raiders, January 17. The Chargers were transferred to San Diego, February 10. Dave R. Jones sold the Browns to a group headed by Arthur B. Modell, March 22. The Howsam brothers sold the Broncos to a group headed by Calvin Kunz and Gerry Phipps, May 26.

NBC was awarded a two-year contract for radio and television rights to the NFL Championship Game for $615,000 annually, $300,000 of which was to go directly into the NFL Player Benefit Plan, April 5.

Canton, Ohio, where the league that became the NFL was formed in 1920, was chosen as the site of the Pro Football Hall of Fame, April 27. Dick McCann, a former Redskins executive, was named executive director.

A bill legalizing single-network television contracts by professional sports leagues was introduced in Congress by Representative Emanuel Celler. It passed the House and Senate and was signed into law by President John F. Kennedy, September 30.

Houston defeated San Diego 10-3 for the AFL championship, December 24. Green Bay won its first NFL championship since 1944, defeating the New York Giants 37-0, December 31.

1962

The Western Division defeated the Eastern Division 47-27 in the first AFL All-Star Game, played before 20,973 in San Diego, January 7.

Both leagues prohibited grabbing any player's facemask. The AFL voted to make the scoreboard clock the official timer of the game.

The NFL entered into a single-network agreement with CBS for telecasting all regular-season games for $4.65 million annually, January 10.

Judge Roszel Thompson of the U.S. District Court in Baltimore ruled against the AFL in its antitrust suit against the NFL, May 21. The AFL had charged the NFL with monopoly and conspiracy in areas of expansion, television, and player signings. The case lasted two and a half years, the trial two months.

McGah and Valley acquired controlling interest in the Raiders, May 24. The AFL assumed financial responsibility for the New York Titans, November 8. With Commissioner Rozelle as referee, Daniel F. Reeves regained ownership of the Rams, outbidding his partners in sealed-envelope bidding for the team, November 27.

The Dallas Texans defeated the Oilers 20-17 for the AFL championship at Houston after 17 minutes, 54 seconds of overtime on a 25-yard field goal by Tommy Brooker, December 23. The game lasted a record 77 minutes, 54 seconds.

Judge Edward Weinfeld of the U.S. District Court in New York City upheld the legality of the NFL's television blackout within a 75-mile radius of home games and denied an injunction that would have forced the championship game between the Giants and the Packers to be televised in the New York City area, December 28. The Packers beat the Giants 16-7 for the NFL title, December 30.

1963

The Dallas Texans transferred to Kansas City, becoming the Chiefs, February 8. The New York Titans were sold to a five-man syndicate headed by David (Sonny) Werblin, March 28. Weeb Ewbank became the Titans' new head coach and the team's name was changed to the Jets, April 15. They began play in Shea Stadium.

NFL Properties, Inc., was founded to serve as the licensing arm of the NFL.

Rozelle indefinitely suspended Green Bay halfback Paul Hornung and Detroit defensive tackle Alex Karras for placing bets on their own teams and on other NFL games; he also fined five other Detroit players $2,000 each for betting on one game in which they did not participate, and the Detroit Lions Football Company $2,000 on each of two counts for failure to report information promptly and for lack of sideline supervision.

Paul Brown, head coach of the Browns since their inception, was fired and replaced by Blanton Collier. Don Shula replaced Weeb Ewbank as head coach of the Colts.

The AFL allowed the Jets and Raiders to select players from other franchises in hopes of giving the league more competitive balance, May 11.

NBC was awarded exclusive network broadcasting rights for the 1963 AFL Championship Game for $926,000, May 23.

The Pro Football Hall of Fame was dedicated at Canton, Ohio, September 7.

The U.S. Fourth Circuit Court of Appeals reaffirmed the lower court's finding for the NFL in the $10-million suit brought by the AFL, ending three and a half years of litigation, November 21.

Jim Brown of Cleveland rushed for an NFL single-season record 1,863 yards.

Boston defeated Buffalo 26-8 in the first divisional playoff game in AFL history, December 28.

The Bears defeated the Giants 14-10 in the NFL Championship Game, a record sixth and last title for Halas in his thirty-sixth season as the Bears' coach, December 29.

1964

The Chargers defeated the Patriots 51-10 in the AFL Championship Game, January 5.

William Clay Ford, the Lions' president since 1961, purchased the team, January 10. A group representing the late James P. Clark sold the Eagles to a group headed by Jerry Wolman, January 21. Carroll Rosenbloom, the majority owner of the Colts since 1953, acquired complete ownership of the team, January 23.

The AFL signed a five-year, $36-million television contract with NBC to begin with the 1965 season, January 29. Commissioner Rozelle negotiated an agreement on behalf of the NFL clubs to purchase Ed Sabol's Blair Motion Pictures, which was renamed NFL Films, March 5.

Hornung and Karras were reinstated by Rozelle, March 16.

CBS submitted the winning bid of $14.1 million per year for the NFL regular-season television rights for 1964 and 1965, January 24. CBS acquired the rights to the champion-ship games for 1964 and 1965 for $1.8 million per game, April 17.

Pete Gogolak of Cornell signed a contract with Buffalo, becoming the first soccer-style kicker in pro football.

Buffalo defeated San Diego 20-7 in the AFL Championship Game, December 26. Cleveland defeated Baltimore 27-0 in the NFL Championship Game, December 27.

1965

The NFL teams pledged not to sign college seniors until completion of all their games, including bowl games, and empowered the Commissioner to discipline the clubs up to as much as the loss of an entire draft list for a violation of the pledge, February 15.

The NFL added a sixth official, the line judge, February 19. The color of the officials' penalty flags was changed from white to bright gold, April

5.

Atlanta was awarded an NFL franchise for 1966, with Rankin Smith, Sr., as owner, June 30. Miami was awarded an AFL franchise for 1966, with Joe Robbie and Danny Thomas as owners, August 16.

Field Judge Burl Toler became the first black official in NFL history, September 19.

According to a Harris survey, sports fans chose professional football (41 percent) as their favorite sport, overtaking baseball (38 percent) for the first time, October.

Green Bay defeated Baltimore 13-10 in sudden-death overtime in a Western Conference playoff game. Don Chandler kicked a 25-yard field goal for the Packers after 13 minutes, 39 seconds of overtime, December 26. The Packers then defeated the Browns 23-12 in the NFL Championship Game, January 2.

In the AFL Championship Game, the Bills again defeated the Chargers, 23-0, December 26.

CBS acquired the rights to the NFL regular-season games in 1966 and 1967, with an option for 1968, for $18.8 million per year, December 29.

1966
The AFL-NFL war reached its peak, as the leagues spent a combined $7 million to sign their 1966 draft choices. The NFL signed 75 percent of its 232 draftees, the AFL 46 percent of its 181. Of the 111 common draft choices, 79 signed with the NFL, 28 with the AFL, and 4 went unsigned.

Buddy Young became the first African-American to work in the league office when Commissioner Rozelle named him director of player relations, February 1.

The rights to the 1966 and 1967 NFL Championship Games were sold to CBS for $2 million per game, February 14.

Foss resigned as AFL Commissioner, April 7. Al Davis, the head coach and general manager of the Raiders, was named to replace him, April 8.

Goal posts offset from the goal line, painted bright yellow, and with uprights 20 feet above the cross-bar were made standard in the NFL, May 16.

A series of secret meetings regarding a possible AFL-NFL merger were held in the spring between Hunt of Kansas City and Tex Schramm of Dallas. Rozelle announced the merger, June 8. Under the agreement, the two leagues would combine to form an expanded league with 24 teams, to be increased to 26 in 1968 and to 28 by 1970 or soon thereafter. All existing franchises would be retained, and no franchises would be transferred outside their metropolitan areas. While maintaining separate schedules through 1969, the leagues agreed to play an annual AFL-NFL World Championship Game beginning in January, 1967, and to hold a combined draft, also beginning in 1967. Preseason games would be held between teams of each league starting in 1967. Official regular-season play would start in 1970 when the two leagues would officially merge to form one league with two conferences. Rozelle was named Commissioner of the expanded league setup.

Davis rejoined the Raiders, and Milt Woodard was named president of the AFL, July 25.

The St. Louis Cardinals moved into newly constructed Busch Memorial Stadium.

Barron Hilton sold the Chargers to a group headed by Eugene Klein and Sam Schulman, August 25.

Congress approved the AFL-NFL merger, passing legislation exempting the agreement itself from antitrust action, October 21.

New Orleans was awarded an NFL franchise to begin play in 1967, November 1. John Mecom, Jr., of Houston was designated majority stockholder and president of the franchise, December 15.

The NFL was realigned for the 1967-69 seasons into the Capitol and Century Divisions in the Eastern Conference and the Central and Coastal Divisions in the Western Conference, December 2. New Orleans and the New York Giants agreed to switch divisions in 1968 and return to the 1967 alignment in 1969.

The rights to the Super Bowl for four years were sold to CBS and NBC for $9.5 million, December 13.

1967
Green Bay earned the right to represent the NFL in the first AFL-NFL World Championship Game by defeating Dallas 34-27, January 1. The same day, Kansas City defeated Buffalo 31-7 to represent the AFL. The Packers defeated the Chiefs 35-10 before 61,946 fans at the Los Angeles Memorial Coliseum in the first game between AFL and NFL teams, January 15. The winning players' share for the Packers was $15,000 each, and the losing players' share for the Chiefs was $7,500 each. The game was televised by both CBS and NBC.

The "sling-shot" goal post and a six-foot-wide border around the field were made standard in the NFL, February 22.

Baltimore made Bubba Smith, a Michigan State defensive lineman, the first choice in the first combined AFL-NFL draft, March 14.

The AFL awarded a franchise to begin play in 1968 to Cincinnati, May 24. A group with Paul Brown as part owner, general manager, and head coach, was awarded the Cincinnati franchise, September 27.

Arthur B. Modell, the president of the Cleveland Browns, was elected president of the NFL, May 28.

Defensive back Emlen Tunnell of the New York Giants became the first black player to enter the Pro Football Hall of Fame, August 5.

An AFL team defeated an NFL team for the first time, when Denver beat Detroit 13-7 in a preseason game, August 5.

Green Bay defeated Dallas 21-17 for the NFL championship on a last-minute 1-yard quarterback sneak by Bart Starr in 13-below-zero temperature at Green Bay, December 31. The same day, Oakland defeated Houston 40-7 for the AFL championship.

1968
Green Bay defeated Oakland 33-14 in Super Bowl II at Miami, January 14. The game had the first $3-million gate in pro football history.

Vince Lombardi resigned as head coach of the Packers, but remained as general manager, January 28.

Art McNally, a nine-year NFL game official, was named Supervisor of Officials, April 8. Werblin sold his shares in the Jets to his partners Don Lillis, Leon Hess, Townsend Martin, and Phil Iselin, May 21. Lillis assumed the presidency of the club, but then died July 23. Iselin was appointed president, August 6.

Halas retired for the fourth and last time as head coach of the Bears, May 27.

The Oilers left Rice Stadium for the Astrodome and became the first NFL team to play its home games in a domed stadium.

The movie *Heidi* became a footnote in sports history when NBC didn't show the last :50 of the Jets-Raiders game in order to permit the children's special to begin on time. The Raiders scored two touchdowns in the last 42 seconds to win 43-32, November 17.

Ewbank became the first coach to win titles in both the NFL and AFL when his Jets defeated the Raiders 27-23 for the AFL championship, December 29. The same day, Baltimore defeated Cleveland 34-0.

1969
The AFL established a playoff format for the 1969 season, with the winner in one division playing the runner-up in the other, January 11.

An AFL team won the Super Bowl for the first time, as the Jets defeated the Colts 16-7 at Miami, January 12 in Super Bowl III. The title Super Bowl was recognized by the NFL for the first time.

Vince Lombardi became part owner, executive vice-president, and head coach of the Washington Redskins, February 7.

Wolman sold the Eagles to Leonard Tose, May 1.

Baltimore, Cleveland, and Pittsburgh agreed to join the AFL teams to form the 13-team American Football Conference of the NFL in 1970, May 17. The NFL also agreed on a playoff format that would include one "wild-card" team per conference—the second-place team with the best record.

Monday Night Football was signed for 1970. ABC acquired the rights to televise 13 NFL regular-season Monday night games in 1970, 1971, and 1972.

George Preston Marshall, president emeritus of the Redskins, died at 72, August 9.

The NFL marked its fiftieth year by the wearing of a special patch by each of the 16 teams.

1970

Kansas City defeated Minnesota 23-7 in Super Bowl IV at New Orleans, January 11. The gross receipts of approximately $3.8 million were the largest ever for a one-day sports event.

Four-year television contracts, under which CBS would televise all NFC games and NBC all AFC games (except Monday night games) and the two would divide televising the Super Bowl and AFC-NFC Pro Bowl games, were announced, January 26.

Art Modell resigned as president of the NFL, March 12. Milt Woodard resigned as president of the AFL, March 13. Lamar Hunt was elected president of the AFC and George Halas was elected president of the NFC, March 19.

The merged 26-team league adopted rules changes putting names on the backs of players' jerseys, making a point after touchdown worth only one point, and making the scoreboard clock the official timing device of the game, March 18.

The Players Negotiating Committee and the NFL Players Association announced a four-year agreement guaranteeing approximately $4,535,000 annually to player pension and insurance benefits, August 3. The owners also agreed to contribute $250,000 annually to improve or implement items such as disability payments, widows' benefits, maternity benefits, and dental benefits. The agreement also provided for increased preseason game

and per diem payments, averaging approximately $2.6 million annually.

The Pittsburgh Steelers moved into Three Rivers Stadium. The Cincinnati Bengals moved to Riverfront Stadium.

Lombardi died of cancer at 57, September 3.

The Super Bowl trophy was renamed the Vince Lombardi trophy, September 10.

Tom Dempsey of New Orleans kicked a game-winning NFL-record 63-yard field goal against Detroit, November 8.

1971

Baltimore defeated Dallas 16-13 on Jim O'Brien's 32-yard field goal with five seconds to go in Super Bowl V at Miami, January 17. The NBC telecast was viewed in an estimated 23,980,000 homes, the largest audience ever for a one-day sports event.

The NFC defeated the AFC 27-6 in the first AFC-NFC Pro Bowl at Los Angeles, January 24.

The Boston Patriots changed their name to the New England Patriots, March 25. Their new stadium, Schaefer Stadium, was dedicated in a 20-14 preseason victory over the Giants.

The Philadelphia Eagles left Franklin Field and played their games at the new Veterans Stadium.

The San Francisco 49ers left Kezar Stadium and moved their games to Candlestick Park.

Daniel F. Reeves, the president and general manager of the Rams, died at 58, April 15.

The Dallas Cowboys moved from the Cotton Bowl into their new home, Texas Stadium, October 24.

Miami defeated Kansas City 27-24 in sudden-death overtime in an AFC Divisional Playoff Game, December 25. Garo Yepremian kicked a 37-yard field goal for the Dolphins after 22 minutes, 40 seconds of overtime, as the game lasted 82 minutes, 40 seconds overall, making it the longest game in history.

1972

Dallas defeated Miami 24-3 in Super Bowl VI at New Orleans, January 16. The CBS telecast

was viewed in an estimated 27,450,000 homes, the top-rated one-day telecast ever.

The inbounds lines or hashmarks were moved nearer the center of the field, 23 yards, 1 foot, 9 inches from the sidelines, March 23. The method of determining won-lost percentage in standings changed. Tie games, previously not counted in the standings, were made equal to a half-game won and a half-game lost, May 24.

Robert Irsay purchased the Los Angeles Rams and transferred ownership of the club to Carroll Rosen-bloom in exchange for the Baltimore Colts, July 13.

William V. Bidwill purchased the stock of his brother Charles (Stormy) Bidwill to become the sole owner of the St. Louis Cardinals, September 2.

The National District Attorneys Association endorsed the position of professional leagues in opposing proposed legalization of gambling on professional team sports, September 28.

Franco Harris' "Immaculate Reception" gave the Steelers their first postseason win ever, 13-7 over the Raiders, December 23.

1973

Rozelle announced that all Super Bowl VII tickets were sold and that the game would be telecast in Los Angeles, site of the game, on an experimental basis, January 3.

Miami defeated Washington 14-7 in Super Bowl VII at Los Angeles, completing a 17-0 season, the first perfect-record regular-season and postseason mark in NFL history, January 14. The NBC telecast was viewed by approximately 75 million people.

The AFC defeated the NFC 33-28 in the Pro Bowl in Dallas, the first time since 1942 that the game was played outside Los Angeles, January 21.

A jersey numbering system was adopted, April 5: 1-19 for quarterbacks and specialists, 20-49 for running backs and defensive backs, 50-59 for centers and linebackers, 60-79 for defensive linemen and interior offensive linemen other than centers, and 80-89

for wide receivers and tight ends. Players who had been in the NFL in 1972 could continue to use old numbers.

NFL Charities, a nonprofit organi-zation, was created to derive an income from monies generated from NFL Properties' licensing of NFL trademarks and team names, June 26. NFL Charities was set up to support education and charitable activities and to supply economic support to persons formerly associated with professional football who were no longer able to support themselves.

Congress adopted experimental legislation (for three years) requiring any NFL game that had been declared a sell-out 72 hours prior to kickoff to be made available for local televising, September 14. The legislation provided for an annual review to be made by the Federal Communications Commission.

The Buffalo Bills moved their home games from War Memorial Stadium to Rich Stadium in nearby Orchard Park. The Giants tied the Eagles 23-23 in the final game in Yankee Stadium, September 23. The Giants played the rest of their home games at the Yale Bowl in New Haven, Connecticut.

A rival league, the World Football League, was formed and was reported in operation, October 2. It had plans to start play in 1974.

O.J. Simpson of Buffalo became the first player to rush for more than 2,000 yards in a season, gaining 2,003.

1974

Miami defeated Minnesota 24-7 in Super Bowl VIII at Houston, the second consecutive Super Bowl championship for the Dolphins, January 13. The CBS telecast was viewed by approximately 75 million people.

Rozelle was given a 10-year contract effective January 1, 1973, February 27.

Tampa Bay was awarded a franchise to begin operation in 1976, April 24.

Sweeping rules changes were adopted to add action and tempo to games: one sudden-death overtime period was added for preseason and regular-season games; the goal posts were moved from the goal line to the end lines; kickoffs were moved from the 40- to the 35-yard line; after missed field goals from beyond the 20, the ball was to be returned to the line of scrimmage; restrictions were placed on members of the punting team to open up return possibilities; roll-blocking and cutting of wide receivers was eliminated; the extent of downfield contact a defender could have with an eligible receiver was restricted; the penalties for offensive holding, illegal use of the hands, and tripping were reduced from 15 to 10 yards; wide receivers blocking back toward the ball within three yards of the line of scrimmage were prevented from blocking below the waist, April 25.

Seattle was awarded an NFL franchise to begin play in 1976, June 4. Lloyd W. Nordstrom, president of the Seattle Seahawks, and Hugh Culverhouse, president of the Tampa Bay Buccaneers, signed franchise agreements, December 5.

The Birmingham Americans defeated the Florida Blazers 22-21 in the WFL World Bowl, winning the league championship, December 5.

1975
Pittsburgh defeated Minnesota 16-6 in Super Bowl IX at New Orleans, the Steelers' first championship since entering the NFL in 1933. The NBC telecast was viewed by approximately 78 million people.

The Memphis Southmen of the WFL signed Larry Csonka, Jim Kiick, and Paul Warfield of Miami, March 31.

The divisional winners with the highest won-loss percentage were made the home team for the divisional playoffs, and the surviving winners with the highest percentage made home teams for the championship games, June 26.

Referees were equipped with wireless microphones for all preseason, regular-season, and playoff games.

The Lions moved to the new Pontiac Silverdome. The Giants played their home games in Shea Stadium. The Saints moved into the Louisiana Superdome.

The World Football League folded, October 22.

1976
Pittsburgh defeated Dallas 21-17 in Super Bowl X in Miami. The Steelers joined Green Bay and Miami as the only teams to win two Super Bowls; the Cowboys became the first wild-card team to play in the Super Bowl. The CBS telecast was viewed by an estimated 80 million people, the largest television audience in history.

Lloyd Nordstrom, the president of the Seahawks, died at 66, January 20. His brother Elmer succeeded him as majority representative of the team.

The owners awarded Super Bowl XII, to be played on January 15, 1978, to New Orleans. They also adopted the use of two 30-second clocks for all games, visible to both players and fans to note the official time between the ready-for-play signal and snap of the ball, March 16.

A veteran player allocation was held to stock the Seattle and Tampa Bay franchises with 39 players each, March 30-31. In the college draft, Seattle and Tampa Bay each received eight extra choices, April 8-9.

The Giants moved into new Giants Stadium in East Rutherford, New Jersey.

The Steelers defeated the College All-Stars in a storm-shortened Chicago College All-Star Game, the last of the series, July 23. St. Louis defeated San Diego 20-10 in a preseason game before 38,000 in Korakuen Stadium, Tokyo, in the first NFL game outside of North America, August 16.

1977
Oakland defeated Minnesota 32-14 in Super Bowl XI at Pasadena, January 9. The paid attendance was a pro record 103,438. The NBC telecast was viewed by 81.9 million people, the largest ever to view a sports event. The victory was the fifth consecutive for the AFC in the Super Bowl.

The NFL Players Association and the NFL Management Council ratified a collective bargaining agreement extending until 1982, covering five football seasons while continuing the pension plan—including years 1974, 1975, and 1976—with contributions totaling more than $55 million. The total cost of the agreement was estimated at $107 million. The agreement called for a college draft at least through 1986; contained a no-strike, no-suit clause; established a 43-man active player limit; reduced pension vesting to four years; provided for increases in minimum salaries and preseason and postseason pay; improved insurance, medical, and dental benefits; modified previous practices in player movement and control; and reaffirmed the NFL Commissioner's disciplinary authority. Additionally, the agreement called for the NFL member clubs to make payments totaling $16 million in the next 10 years to settle various legal disputes, February 25.

The San Francisco 49ers were sold to Edward J. DeBartolo, Jr., March 28.

A 16-game regular season, 4-game preseason was adopted to begin in 1978, March 29. A second wild-card team was adopted for the playoffs beginning in 1978, with the wild-card teams to play each other and the winners advancing to a round of eight postseason series.

The Seahawks were permanently aligned in the AFC Western Division and the Buccaneers in the NFC Central Division, March 31.

The owners awarded Super Bowl XIII, to be played on January 21, 1979, to Miami, to be played in the Orange Bowl; Super Bowl XIV, to be played January 20, 1980, was awarded to Pasadena, to be played in the Rose Bowl, June 14.

Rules changes were adopted to open up the passing game and to cut down on injuries. Defenders were permitted to make contact with eligible receivers only once; the head slap was outlawed; offensive linemen were prohibited from thrusting their hands to an opponent's neck, face, or head; and wide receivers were prohibited from clipping, even in the legal clipping zone.

Rozelle negotiated contracts with the three television networks to televise all NFL regular-season and postseason games, plus selected preseason games, for four years beginning with the 1978 season. ABC was awarded yearly rights to 16 Monday night games, four prime-time games, the AFC-NFC Pro Bowl, and the Hall of Fame games. CBS received the rights to all NFC regular-season and postseason games (except those in the ABC package) and to Super Bowls XIV and XVI. NBC received the rights to all AFC regular-season and postseason games (except those in the ABC package) and to Super Bowls XIII and XV. Industry sources considered it the largest single television package ever negotiated, October 12.

Chicago's Walter Payton set a single-game rushing record with 275 yards (40 carries) against Minnesota, November 20.

1978
Dallas defeated Denver 27-10 in Super Bowl XII, held indoors for the first time, at the Louisiana Superdome in New Orleans, January 15. The CBS telecast was viewed by more than 102 million people, meaning the game was watched by more viewers than any other show of any kind in the history of television. Dallas' victory was the first for the NFC in six years.

According to a Louis Harris Sports Survey, 70 percent of the nation's sports fans said they followed football, compared to 54 percent who followed baseball. Football increased its lead as the country's favorite, 26 percent to 16 percent for baseball, January 19.

A seventh official, the side judge, was added to the officiating crew, March 14.

The NFL continued a trend toward opening up the game. Rules changes permitted a defender to maintain contact with a receiver within five yards of the line of scrimmage, but restricted contact beyond that point. The pass-blocking rule was interpreted to permit the extending of arms and open hands, March 17.

A study on the use of instant replay as an officiating aid was made during seven nationally televised preseason games.

The NFL played for the first time in Mexico City, with the Saints defeating the Eagles 14-7 in a preseason game, August 5.

Bolstered by the expansion of the regular-season schedule from 14 to 16 weeks, NFL paid attendance exceeded 12 million (12,771,800) for the first time. The per-game average of 57,017 was the third-highest in league history and the most since 1973.

1979

Pittsburgh defeated Dallas 35-31 in Super Bowl XIII at Miami to become the first team ever to win three Super Bowls, January 21. The NBC telecast was viewed in 35,090,000 homes, by an estimated 96.6 million fans.

The owners awarded three future Super Bowl sites: Super Bowl XV to the Louisiana Superdome in New Orleans, to be played on January 25, 1981; Super Bowl XVI to the Pontiac Silverdome in Pontiac, Michigan, to be played on January 24, 1982; and Super Bowl XVII to Pasadena's Rose Bowl, to be played on January 30, 1983, March 13.

NFL rules changes emphasized additional player safety. The changes prohibited players on the receiving team from blocking below the waist during kickoffs, punts, and field-goal attempts; prohibited the wearing of torn or altered equipment and exposed pads that could be hazardous; extended the zone in which there could be no crackback blocks; and instructed officials to quickly whistle a play dead when a quarterback was clearly in the grasp of a tackler, March 16.

Rosenbloom, the president of the Rams, drowned at 72, April 2. His widow, Georgia, assumed control of the club.

1980

Pittsburgh defeated the Los Angeles Rams 31-19 in Super Bowl XIV at Pasadena to

become the first team to win four Super Bowls, January 20. The game was viewed in a record 35,330,000 homes.

The AFC-NFC Pro Bowl, won 37-27 by the NFC, was played before 48,060 fans at Aloha Stadium in Honolulu, Hawaii. It was the first time in the 30-year history of the Pro Bowl that the game was played in a non-NFL city.

Rules changes placed greater restrictions on contact in the area of the head, neck, and face. Under the heading of "personal foul," players were prohibited from directly striking, swinging, or clubbing on the head, neck, or face. Starting in 1980, a penalty could be called for such contact whether or not the initial contact was made below the neck area.

CBS, with a record bid of $12 million, won the national radio rights to 26 NFL regular-season games, including Monday Night Football, and all 10 postseason games for the 1980-83 seasons.

The Los Angeles Rams moved their home games to Anaheim Stadium in nearby Orange County, California.

The Oakland Raiders joined the Los Angeles Coliseum Commission's antitrust suit against the NFL. The suit contended the league violated antitrust laws in declining to approve a proposed move by the Raiders from Oakland to Los Angeles.

NFL regular-season attendance of nearly 13.4 million set a record for the third year in a row. The average paid attendance for the 224-game 1980 regular season was 59,787, the highest in the league's 61-year history. NFL games in 1980 were played before 92.4 percent of total stadium capacity.

Television ratings in 1980 were the second-best in NFL history, trailing only the combined ratings of the 1976 season. All three networks posted gains, and NBC's 15.0 rating was its best ever. CBS and ABC had their best ratings since 1977, with 15.3 and 20.8 ratings, respectively. CBS Radio reported a record audience of 7 million for Monday night and special games.

1981

Oakland defeated Philadelphia 27-10 in Super Bowl XV at the Louisiana Superdome in New Orleans, to become the first wild-card team to win a Super Bowl, January 25.

Edgar F. Kaiser, Jr., purchased the Denver Broncos from Gerald and Allan Phipps, February 26.

The owners adopted a disaster plan for re-stocking a team should the club be involved in a fatal accident, March 20.

The owners awarded Super Bowl XVIII to Tampa, to be played in Tampa Stadium on January 22, 1984, June 3.

A CBS-New York Times poll showed that 48 percent of sports fans preferred football to 31 percent for baseball.

The NFL teams hosted 167 representatives from 44 predominantly black colleges during training camps for a total of 289 days. The program was adopted for renewal during each training camp period.

NFL regular-season attendance—13.6 million for an average of 60,745—set a record for the fourth year in a row. It also was the first time the per-game average exceeded 60,000. NFL games in 1981 were played before 93.8 percent of total stadium capacity.

ABC and CBS set all-time rating highs. ABC finished with a 21.7 rating and CBS with a 17.5 rating. NBC was down slightly to 13.9.

1982

San Francisco defeated Cincinnati 26-21 in Super Bowl XVI at the Pontiac Silverdome, in the first Super Bowl held in the North, January 24. The CBS telecast achieved the highest rating of any televised sports event ever, 49.1 with a 73.0 share. The game was viewed by a record 110.2 million fans. CBS Radio reported a record 14 million listeners for the game.

The NFL signed a five-year contract with the three television networks (ABC, CBS, and NBC) to televise all NFL regular-season and postseason games starting with the 1982 season.

The owners awarded the 1983, 1984, and 1985 AFC-

NFC Pro Bowls to Honolulu's Aloha Stadium.

A jury ruled against the NFL in the antitrust trial brought by the Los Angeles Coliseum Commission and the Oakland Raiders, May 7. The verdict cleared the way for the Raiders to move to Los Angeles, where they defeated Green Bay 24-3 in their first preseason game, August 29.

The 1982 season was reduced from a 16-game schedule to nine as the result of a 57-day players' strike. The strike was called by the NFLPA at midnight on Monday, September 20, following the Green Bay at New York Giants game. Play resumed November 21-22 following ratification of the Collective Bargaining Agreement by NFL owners, November 17 in New York.

Under the Collective Bargaining Agreement, which was to run through the 1986 season, the NFL draft was extended through 1992 and the veteran free-agent system was left basically unchanged. A minimum salary schedule for years of experience was established; training camp and postseason pay were increased; players' medical, insurance, and retirement benefits were increased; and a severance-pay system was introduced to aid in career transition, a first in professional sports.

Despite the players' strike, the average paid attendance in 1982 was 58,472, the fifth-highest in league history.

The owners awarded the sites of two Super Bowls, December 14: Super Bowl XIX, to be played on January 20, 1985, to Stanford University Stadium in Stanford, California, with San Francisco as host team; and Super Bowl XX, to be played on January 26, 1986, to the Louisiana Superdome in New Orleans.

1983

Because of the shortened season, the NFL adopted a format of 16 teams competing in a Super Bowl Tournament for the 1982 playoffs. The NFC's number-one seed, Washington, defeated the AFC's number-two seed, Miami, 27-17 in Super Bowl XVII at the Rose

Bowl in Pasadena, January 30.

Super Bowl XVII was the second-highest rated live television program of all time, giving the NFL a sweep of the top 10 live television programs in television history. The game was viewed in more than 40 million homes, the largest ever for a live telecast.

George Halas, the owner of the Bears and the last surviving member of the NFL's second organizational meeting, died at 88, October 31.

1984
The Los Angeles Raiders defeated Washington 38-9 in Super Bowl XVIII at Tampa Stadium, January 22. The game achieved a 46.4 rating and 71.0 share.

An 11-man group headed by H.R. (Bum) Bright purchased the Dallas Cowboys from Clint Murchison, Jr., March 20. Club president Tex Schramm was designated as managing general partner.

Wellington Mara was named president of the NFC, March 20.

Patrick Bowlen purchased a majority interest in the Denver Broncos from Edgar Kaiser, Jr., March 21.

The Colts relocated to Indianapolis, March 28. Their new home became the Hoosier Dome.

The owners awarded two Super Bowl sites at their May 23-25 meetings: Super Bowl XXI, to be played on January 25, 1987, to the Rose Bowl in Pasadena; and Super Bowl XXII, to be played on January 31, 1988, to San Diego Jack Murphy Stadium.

The New York Jets moved their home games to Giants Stadium in East Rutherford, New Jersey.

Alex G. Spanos purchased a majority interest in the San Diego Chargers from Eugene V. Klein, August 28.

Houston defeated Pittsburgh 23-20 to mark the one-hundredth overtime game in regular-season play since overtime was adopted in 1974, December 2.

On the field, many all-time records were set: Dan Marino of Miami passed for 5,084 yards and 48 touchdowns; Eric Dickerson of the Los Angeles Rams rushed for 2,105 yards; Art Monk of Washington caught 106 passes; and Walter Payton of Chicago broke Jim Brown's career rushing mark, finishing the season with 13,309 yards.

According to a CBS Sports/New York Times survey, 53 percent of the nation's sports fans said they most enjoyed watching football, compared to 18 percent for baseball, December 2-4.

NFL paid attendance exceeded 13 million for the fifth consecutive complete regular season when 13,398,112, an average of 59,813, attended games. The figure was the second-highest in league history. Teams averaged 42.4 points per game, the second-highest total since the 1970 merger.

1985
San Francisco defeated Miami 38-16 in Super Bowl XIX at Stanford Stadium in Stanford, California, January 20. The game was viewed on television by more people than any other live event in history. President Ronald Reagan, who took his second oath of office before tossing the coin for the game, was one of 115,936,000 viewers. The game drew a 46.4 rating and a 63.0 share. In addition, 6 million people watched the Super Bowl in the United Kingdom and a similar number in Italy. Super Bowl XIX had a direct economic impact of $113.5 million on the San Francisco Bay area.

NBC Radio and the NFL entered into a two-year agreement granting NBC the radio rights to a 37-game package in each of the 1985-86 seasons, March 6. The package included 27 regular-season games and 10 postseason games.

The owners awarded two Super Bowl sites at their annual meeting, March 10-15: Super Bowl XXIII, to be played on January 22, 1989, to the proposed Dolphins Stadium in Miami; and Super Bowl XXIV, to be played on January 28, 1990, to the Louisiana Superdome in New Orleans.

Norman Braman, in partnership with Edward Leibowitz, bought the Philadelphia Eagles from Leonard Tose, April 29.

Bruce Smith, a Virginia Tech defensive lineman selected by Buffalo, was the first player chosen in the fiftieth NFL draft, April 30.

A group headed by Tom Benson, Jr., was approved to purchase the New Orleans Saints from John W. Mecom, Jr., June 3.

The NFL owners adopted a resolution calling for a series of overseas preseason games, beginning in 1986, with one game to be played in England/Europe and/or one game in Japan each year. The game would be a fifth preseason game for the clubs involved and all arrangements and selection of the clubs would be under the control of the Commissioner, May 23.

The league-wide conversion to videotape from movie film for coach-ing study was approved.

Commissioner Rozelle was authorized to extend the commitment to Honolulu's Aloha Stadium for the AFC-NFC Pro Bowl for 1988, 1989, and 1990, October 15.

The NFL set a single-weekend paid attendance record when 902,657 tickets were sold for the weekend of October 27-28.

A Louis Harris poll in December revealed that pro football remained the sport most followed by Americans. Fifty-nine percent of those surveyed followed pro football, compared with 54 percent who followed baseball.

The Chicago-Miami Monday game had the highest rating, 29.6, and share, 46.0, of any prime-time game in NFL history, December 2. The game was viewed in more than 25 million homes.

The NFL showed a ratings increase on all three networks for the season, gaining 4 percent on NBC, 10 on CBS, and 16 on ABC.

1986
Chicago defeated New England 46-10 in Super Bowl XX at the Louisiana Superdome, January 26. The Patriots had earned the right to play the Bears by becoming the first wild-card team to win three consecutive games on the road. The NBC telecast replaced the final episode of M*A*S*H as the most-viewed television program in history, with an audience of 127 million viewers, according to A.C. Nielsen figures. In addition to drawing a 48.3 rating and a 70 percent share in the United States, Super Bowl XX was televised to 59 foreign countries and beamed via satellite to the QE II. An estimated 300 million Chinese viewed a tape delay of the game in March. NBC Radio figures indicated an audience of 10 million for the game.

The owners adopted limited use of instant replay as an officiating aid, prohibited players from wearing or otherwise displaying equipment, apparel, or other items that carry commercial names, names of organizations, or personal messages of any type, March 11.

After an 11-week trial, a jury in U.S. District Court in New York awarded the United States Football League one dollar in its $1.7 billion antitrust suit against the NFL. The jury rejected all of the USFL's television-related claims, which were the self-proclaimed heart of the USFL's case. The jury deliberated five days, July 29.

Chicago defeated Dallas 17-6 at Wembley Stadium in London in the first American Bowl. The game drew a sellout crowd of 82,699 and the NBC national telecast in this country produced a 12.4 rating and 36 percent share, making it the highest daytime preseason television audience ever with 10.65-million viewers, August 3.

ABC's NFL Monday Night Football, in its seventeenth season, became the longest-running prime-time series in the history of the network.

1987
The New York Giants defeated Denver 39-20 in Super Bowl XXI and captured their first NFL title since 1956. The game, played in Pasadena's Rose Bowl, drew a sellout crowd of 101,063. According to A.C. Nielsen figures, the CBS broadcast of the game was viewed in the U.S. on television by 122.64-million peo-

ple, making the telecast the second most-watched television show of all-time behind Super Bowl XX. The game was watched live or on tape in 55 foreign countries and NBC Radio's broadcast of the game was heard by a record 10.1 million people.

New three-year TV contracts with ABC, CBS, and NBC were announced for 1987-89 at the NFL annual meeting in Maui, Hawaii, March 15. Commissioner Rozelle and Broadcast Committee Chairman Art Modell also announced a three-year contract with ESPN to televise 13 prime-time games each season. The ESPN contract was the first with a cable network. However, NFL games on ESPN also were scheduled for regular television in the city of the visiting team and in the home city if the game was sold out 72 hours in advance.

A special payment program was adopted to benefit nearly 1,000 former NFL players who participated in the League before the current Bert Bell NFL Pension Plan was created and made retroactive to the 1959 season. Players covered by the new program spent at least five years in the League and played all or part of their career prior to 1959. Each vested player would receive $60 per month for each year of service in the League for life.

NFL and CBS Radio jointly announced agreement granting CBS the radio rights to a 40-game package in each of the next three NFL seasons, 1987-89, April 7.

NFL owners awarded Super Bowl XXV, to be played on January 27, 1991, to Tampa Stadium, May 20.

Over 400 former NFL players from the pre-1959 era received first payments from NFL owners, July 1.

The NFL's debut on ESPN produced the two highest-rated and most-watched sports programs in basic cable history. The Chicago at Miami game on August 16 drew an 8.9 rating in 3.81 million homes. Those records fell two weeks later when the Los Angeles Raiders at Dallas game achieved a 10.2 cable rating in 4.36 million homes.

The 1987 season was reduced from a 16-game season to 15 as the result of a 24-day players' strike. The strike was called by the NFLPA on Tuesday, September 22, following the New England at New York Jets game. Games scheduled for the third weekend were canceled but the games of weeks four, five, and six were played with replacement teams. Striking players returned for the seventh week of the season, October 25.

In a three-team deal involving 10 players and/or draft choices, the Los Angeles Rams traded running back Eric Dickerson to the Indianapolis Colts for six draft choices and two players. Buffalo obtained the rights to linebacker Cornelius Bennett from Indianapolis, sending Greg Bell and three draft choices to the Rams. The Colts added Owen Gill and three draft choices of their own to complete the deal with the Rams, October 31.

The Chicago at Minnesota game became the highest-rated and most-watched sports program in basic cable history when it drew a 14.4 cable rating in 6.5 million homes, December 6.

1988
Washington defeated Denver 42-10 in Super Bowl XXII to earn its second victory this decade in the NFL Championship Game. The game, played for the first time in San Diego Jack Murphy Stadium, drew a sellout crowd of 73,302. According to A.C. Nielsen figures, the ABC broadcast of the game was viewed in the U.S. on television by 115,000,000 people. The game was seen live or on tape in 60 foreign countries, including the People's Republic of China, and CBS's radio broadcast of the game was heard by 13.7 million people.

In a unanimous 3-0 decision, the 2nd Circuit Court of Appeals in New York upheld the verdict of the jury that in July, 1986, had awarded the United States Football League one dollar in its $1.7 billion antitrust suit against the NFL. In a 91-page opinion, Judge Ralph K. Winter said the USFL sought through court decree

the success it failed to gain among football fans, March 10.

By a 23-5 margin, owners voted to continue the instant replay system for the third consecutive season with the Instant Replay Official to be assigned to a regular seven-man, on-the-field crew. At the NFL annual meeting in Phoenix, Arizona, a 45-second clock was also approved to replace the 30-second clock. For a normal sequence of plays, the interval between plays was changed to 45 seconds from the time the ball is signaled dead until it is snapped on the succeeding play.

NFL owners approved the transfer of the Cardinals' franchise from St. Louis to Phoenix; approved two supplemental drafts each year—one prior to training camp and one prior to the regular season; and voted to initiate an annual series of games in Japan/Asia as early as the 1989 preseason, March 14-18.

The NFL Annual Selection Meeting returned to a separate two-day format and for the first time originated on a Sunday. ESPN drew a 3.6 rating during their seven-hour coverage of the draft, which was viewed in 1.6 million homes, April 24-25.

Art Rooney, founder and owner of the Steelers, died at 87, August 25.

Johnny Grier became the first African-American referee in NFL history, September 4.

Commissioner Rozelle announced that two teams would play a preseason game as part of the American Bowl series on August 6, 1989, in the Korakuen Tokyo Dome in Japan, December 16.

1989
San Francisco defeated Cincinnati 20-16 in Super Bowl XXIII. The game, played for the first time at Joe Robbie Stadium in Miami, was attended by a sellout crowd of 75,129. NBC's telecast of the game was watched by an estimated 110,780,000 viewers, according to A.C. Nielsen, making it the sixth most-watched program in television history. The game was seen live or on tape

in 60 foreign countries, including an estimated 300 million in China. The CBS Radio broadcast of the game was heard by 11.2 million people.

Commissioner Rozelle announced his retirement, pending the naming of a successor, March 22 at the NFL annual meeting in Palm Desert, California.

Following the announcement, AFC president Lamar Hunt and NFC president Wellington Mara announced the formation of a six-man search committee composed of Art Modell, Robert Parins, Dan Rooney, and Ralph Wilson. Hunt and Mara served as co-chairmen.

By a 24-4 margin, owners voted to continue the instant replay system for the fourth straight season. A strengthened policy regarding anabolic steroids and masking agents was announced by Commissioner Rozelle. NFL clubs called for strong disciplinary measures in cases of feigned injuries and adopted a joint proposal by the Long-Range Planning and Finance committees regarding player personnel rules, March 19-23.

Two hundred twenty-nine unconditional free agents signed with new teams under management's Plan B system, April 1.

Jerry Jones purchased a majority interest in the Dallas Cowboys from H.R. (Bum) Bright, April 18.

Tex Schramm was named president of the new World League of American Football to work with a six-man committee of Dan Rooney, chairman; Norman Braman, Lamar Hunt, Victor Kiam, Mike Lynn, and Bill Walsh, April 18.

NFL and CBS Radio jointly announced agreement extending CBS's radio rights to an annual 40-game package through the 1994 season, April 18.

NFL owners awarded Super Bowl XXVI, to be played on January 26, 1992, to Minneapolis, May 24.

As of opening day, September 10, of the 229 Plan B free agents, 111 were active and 23 others were on teams' reserve lists. Ninety-two others were waived and three retired.

Art Shell was named head coach of the Los Angeles Raiders making him the NFL's first black head coach since Fritz Pollard coached the Akron Pros in 1921, October 3.

The site of the New England Patriots at San Francisco 49ers game scheduled for Candlestick Park on October 22 was switched to Stanford Stadium in the aftermath of the Bay Area Earthquake of October 17. The change was announced on October 19.

Paul Tagliabue became the seventh chief executive of the NFL on October 26 when he was chosen to succeed Commissioner Pete Rozelle on the sixth ballot of a three-day meeting in Cleveland, Ohio.

In all, 12 ballots were required to select Tagliabue. Two were conducted at a meeting in Chicago on July 6, and four at a meeting in Dallas on October 10-11. On the twelfth ballot, with Seattle absent, Tagliabue received more than the 19 affirmative votes required for election from among the 27 clubs present.

The transfer from Commissioner Rozelle to Commissioner Tagliabue took place at 12:01 A.M. on Sunday, November 5.

NFL Charities donated $1 million through United Way to benefit Bay Area earthquake victims, November 6.

NFL paid attendance of 17,399,538 was the highest total in league history. This included a total of 13,625,662 for an average of 60,829—both NFL records—for the 224-game regular season.

1990

San Francisco defeated Denver 55-10 in Super Bowl XXIV at the Louisiana Superdome, January 28. San Francisco joined Pittsburgh as the NFL's only teams to win four Super Bowls.

The NFL announced revisions in its 1990 draft eligibility rules. College juniors became eligible but must renounce their collegiate football eligibility before applying for the NFL Draft, February 16.

Commissioner Tagliabue announced NFL teams will play their 16-game schedule over 17 weeks in 1990 and 1991 and 16 games over 18 weeks in 1992 and 1993, February 27.

The NFL revised its playoff format to include two additional wild-card teams (one per conference), which raised the total to six wild-card teams.

Commissioner Tagliabue and Broadcast Committee Chairman Art Modell announced a four-year contract with Turner Broadcasting to televise nine Sunday-night games.

New four-year TV agreements were ratified for 1990-93 for ABC, CBS, NBC, ESPN, and TNT at the NFL annual meeting in Orlando, Florida, March 12. The contracts totaled $3.6 billion, the largest in TV history.

The NFL announced plans to expand its American Bowl series of preseason games. In addition to games in London and Tokyo, American Bowl games were scheduled for Berlin, Germany, and Montreal, Canada, in 1990.

For the fifth straight year, NFL owners voted to continue a limited system of Instant Replay. Beginning in 1990, the replay official will have a two-minute time limit to make a decision. The vote was 21-7, March 12.

Commissioner Tagliabue announced the formation of a Committee on Expansion and Realignment, March 13. He also named a Player Advisory Council, comprised of 12 former NFL players, March 14.

One-hundred eighty-four Plan B unconditional free agents signed with new teams, April 2.

Commissioner Tagliabue appointed Dr. John Lombardo as the League's Drug Advisor for Anabolic Steroids, April 25 and named Dr. Lawrence Brown as the League's Advisor for Drugs of Abuse, May 17.

NFL owners awarded Super Bowl XXVIII, to be played in 1994, to the proposed Georgia Dome, May 23.

Commissioner Tagliabue named NFL referee Jerry Seeman as NFL Director of Officiating, replacing Art McNally, who announced his retirement after 31 years on the field and at the league office, July 12.

NFL International Week was celebrated with four preseason games in seven days in Tokyo, London, Berlin, and Montreal. More than 200,000 fans on three continents attended the four games, August 4-11.

Commissioner Tagliabue announced the NFL Teacher of the Month program in which the League furnishes grants and scholarships in recognition of teachers who provided a positive influence upon NFL players in elementary and secondary schools, September 20.

For the first time since 1957, every NFL club won at least one of its first four games, October 1.

The Super Bowl Most Valuable Player trophy was renamed the Pete Rozelle trophy, October 8.

NFL total paid attendance of 17,665,671 was the highest total in League history. The regular-season total paid attendance of 13,959,896 and average of 62,321 for 224 games were the highest ever, surpassing the previous records set in the 1989 season.

1991

The New York Giants defeated Buffalo 20-19 in Super Bowl XXV to capture their second title in five years. The game was played before a sellout crowd of 73,813 at Tampa Stadium and became the first Super Bowl decided by one point, January 26. The ABC broadcast of the game was seen by more than 112-million people in the United States and was seen live or taped in 60 other countries.

NFL playoff games earned the top television rating spot of the week for each week of the month-long playoffs, January 29.

New York businessman Robert Tisch purchased a 50 percent interest in the New York Giants from Mrs. Helen Mara Nugent and her children, Tim Mara and Maura Mara Concannon, February 2.

NFL owners awarded Super Bowl XXVII, to be played on January 31, 1993, to Pasadena, March 19.

NFL clubs voted to continue a limited system of Instant Replay for the sixth consecutive year. The vote was 21-7, March 19.

The NFL launched the World League of American Football, the first sports league to operate on a weekly basis on two separate continents, March 23.

NFL Charities presented a $250,000 donation to the United Service Organization. The donation was the second largest single grant ever by NFL Charities, April 5.

Commissioner Tagliabue named Harold Henderson as Executive Vice President for Labor Relations and Chairman of the NFL Management Council Executive Committee, April 8.

NFL clubs approved a recommendation by the Expansion and Realignment Committee to add two teams for the 1994 season, resulting in six divisions of five teams each, May 22.

NFL clubs awarded Super Bowl XXIX, to be played on January 29, 1995, to Miami, May 23.

"NFL International Week" featured six 1990 playoff teams playing nationally televised games in London, Berlin, and Tokyo on July 28 and August 3-4. The games drew more than 150,000 fans.

Paul Brown, founder of the Cleveland Browns and Cincinnati Bengals, died at age 82, August 5.

NFL clubs approved a resolution establishing an international division. A three-year financial plan for the World League was approved by NFL clubs at a meeting in Dallas, October 23.

1992

The NFL agreed to provide a minimum of $2.5 million in financial support to the NFL Alumni Association and assistance to NFL Alumni-related programs. The agreement included contributions from NFL Charities to the Pre-59ers and Dire Need Programs for former players, January 25.

The Washington Redskins defeated the Buffalo Bills 37-24 in Super Bowl XXVI to capture their third world championship in 10 years, January 26. The game was played before a sellout crowd of

63,130 at the Hubert H. Humphrey Metrodome in Minneapolis and attracted the second largest television audience in Super Bowl history. The CBS broadcast was seen by more than 123 million people nationally, second only to the 127 million who viewed Super Bowl XX.

The use in officiating of a limited system of Instant Replay was not approved. The vote was 17-11 in favor of approval (21 votes were required). Instant Replay had been used for six consecutive years (1986-1991), March 18.

St. Louis businessman James Orthwein purchased controlling interest in the New England Patriots from Victor Kiam, May 11.

In a Harris Poll taken during the NFL offseason, professional football again was declared the nation's most popular sport. Professional football finished atop similar surveys conducted by Harris in 1985 and 1989, May 23.

NFL clubs accepted the report of the Expansion Committee at a league meeting in Pasadena. The report names five cities as finalists for the two expansion teams—Baltimore, Charlotte, Jacksonville, Memphis, and St. Louis, May 19.

At a league meeting in Dallas, NFL clubs approved a proposal by the World League Board of Directors to restructure the World League and place future emphasis on its international success, September 17.

NFL teams played their 16-game regular-season schedule over 18 weeks for the only time in league history.

1993
The NFL and lawyers for the players announced a settlement of various lawsuits and an agreement on the terms of a seven-year deal that included a new player system to be in place through the 1999 season, January 6.

Commissioner Tagliabue announced the establishment of the "NFL World Partnership Program" to develop amateur football internationally through a series of clinics conducted by former NFL players and coaches, January 14.

As part of Super Bowl XXVII, the NFL announced the creation of the first NFL Youth Education Town, a facility located in south central Los Angeles for inner city youth. January 25.

The Dallas Cowboys defeated the Buffalo Bills 52-17 in Super Bowl XXVII to capture their first NFL title since 1978. The game was played before a crowd of 98,374 at the Rose Bowl in Pasadena, California. The NBC broadcast of the game was the most watched program in television history and was seen by 133,400,000 people in the United States. The rating for the game was 45.1, the tenth highest for any televised sports event. The game also was seen live or taped in 101 other countries, January 31.

NFL clubs awarded Super Bowl XXX to the city of Phoenix, to be played on January 28, 1996, at Sun Devil Stadium, March 23.

The NFL and the NFL Players Association officially signed a 7-year Collective Bargaining Agreement in Washington, D.C., which guarantees more than $1 billion in pension, health, and post-career benefits for current and retired players—the most extensive benefits plan in pro sports. It was the NFL's first CBA since the 1982 agreement that expired in 1987, June 29.

NFL Enterprises, a newly formed division of the NFL responsible for NFL Films, home video, and special domestic and international television programming was announced, August 19.

NFL announced plans to allow fans, for the first time ever, to join players and coaches in selecting the annual AFC and NFC Pro Bowl teams, October 12.

NFL clubs unanimously awarded the league's twenty-ninth franchise to the Carolina Panthers and owner Jerry Richardson at a meeting in Chicago. NFL clubs also awarded Super Bowl XXXI to New Orleans and Super Bowl XXXII to San Diego, October 26.

At the same meeting in Chicago, NFL clubs approved

a plan to form a European league with joint venture partners, October 27.

Don Shula became the winningest coach in NFL history when Miami beat Philadelphia to give Shula his 325th victory, one more than George Halas, November 14.

NFL clubs awarded the league's thirtieth franchise to the Jacksonville Jaguars and owner Wayne Weaver at a meeting in Chicago, November 30.

The NFL announced new 4-year television agreements with ABC, ESPN, TNT, and NFL newcomer FOX, which took over the NFC package from CBS, December 18.

The NFL completed its new TV agreements by announcing that NBC would retain the rights to the AFC package, December 20.

1994
The Dallas Cowboys defeated the Buffalo Bills 30-13 in Super Bowl XXVIII to become the fifth team to win back-to-back Super Bowl titles. The game was viewed by the largest U.S. audience in television history—134.8 million people. The game's 45.5 rating was the highest for a Super Bowl since 1987 and the tenth highest-rated Super Bowl ever, January 30.

NFL clubs unanimously approved the transfer of New England Patriots from James Orthwein to Robert Kraft at a meeting in Orlando, February 22.

In a move to increase offensive production, NFL clubs at the league's annual meeting in Orlando adopted a package of changes, including modifications in line play, chucking rules, and the roughing-the-passer rule, plus the adoption of the two-point conversion and moving the spot of the kickoff back to the 30-yard line, March 22.

NFL clubs approved the transfer of the majority interest in the Miami Dolphins from the Robbie family to H. Wayne Huizenga, March 23.

The NFL and FOX announced the formation of a joint venture to create a six-team World League to begin play in Europe in April, 1995, March 23.

The Carolina Panthers earned the right to select first in the 1995 NFL draft by winning a coin toss with the Jacksonville Jaguars. The Jaguars received the second selection in the 1995 draft, April 24.

NFL clubs approved the transfer of the Philadelphia Eagles from Norman Braman to Jeffrey Lurie, May 6.

The NFL launched "NFL Sunday Ticket," a new season subscription service for satellite television dish owners, June 1.

An all-time NFL record crowd of 112,376 attended the American Bowl game between Dallas and Houston in Mexico City. It concluded the biggest American Bowl series in NFL history with four games attracting a record 256,666 fans, August 15.

The NFL reached agreement on a new seven-year contract with its game officials, September 22.

The NFL Management Council and the NFL Players Association announced an agreement on the formulation and implementation of the most comprehensive drug and alcohol policy in sports, October 28.

At an NFL meeting in Chicago, Commissioner Tagliabue slotted the two new expansion teams into the AFC Central (Jacksonville Jaguars) and NFC West (Carolina Panthers) for the 1995 season only. He also appointed a special committee on realignment to make recommendations on the 1996 season and beyond, November 2.

1995
The San Francisco 49ers became the first team to win five Super Bowls when they defeated the San Diego Chargers 49-26 in Super Bowl XXIX at Joe Robbie Stadium in Miami, January 29.

Carolina and Jacksonville stocked their expansion rosters with a total of 66 players from other NFL teams in a veteran player allocation draft in New York, February 16.

CBS Radio and the NFL agreed to a new four-year contract for an annual 53-game package of games, continuing a relationship that spanned 15 of the past 17 years, February 22.

NFL clubs approved the transfer of the Tampa Bay Buccaneers from the estate of the late Hugh Culverhouse to South Florida businessman Malcolm Glazer, March 13.

A series of safety-related rules changes were adopted at a league meeting in Phoenix, primarily related to the use of the helmet against defenseless players, March 14.

After a two-year hiatus, the World League of American Football returned to action with six teams in Europe, April 8.

The NFL became the first major sports league to establish a site on the Internet system of on-line computer communication, April 10.

The transfer of the Rams from Los Angeles to St. Louis was approved by a vote of the NFL clubs at a meeting in Dallas, April 12.

ABC's *NFL Monday Night Football* finished the 1994-95 television season as the fifth highest-rated show out of 146 with a 17.8 average rating, the highest finish in the 25-year history of the series, April 18.

In an ABC News Poll taken during the NFL offseason, America's sports fans chose football as their favorite spectator sport by more than a 2-to-1 margin over basketball and baseball (35%-16%-12%), April 26.

The Frankfurt Galaxy defeated the Amsterdam Admirals 26-22 to win the 1995 World Bowl before a crowd of 23,847 in Amsterdam's Olympic Stadium, June 23.

Former NFL quarterback and Rhein Fire general manager Oliver Luck was named President of the World League, July 13.

The transfer of the Raiders from Los Angeles to Oakland was approved by a vote of the NFL clubs at a meeting in Chicago, July 22.

Jacksonville Municipal Stadium opened in Jacksonville, Florida before a sold-out crowd of more than 70,000 as the St. Louis Rams defeated the Jacksonville Jaguars 27-10 in their first preseason game, August 18.

NFL Charities and 50 NFL players donated $1 million to the United Negro College Fund in honor of the fiftieth anniversary of the UNCF and the inte-

gration of the modern NFL, September 15.

The Pro Football Hall Of Fame in Canton, Ohio, completed an $8.9 million expansion including a $4 million contribution by the NFL clubs, October 14.

The Trans World Dome opened in St. Louis with a sold-out crowd of 65,598 as the Rams defeated the Carolina Panthers 28-17, November 12.

NFL paid attendance totaled 963,521 for 15 games in Week 12, the highest weekend total in the league's 76-year history, November 19-20.

On the field, many significant records and milestones were achieved: Miami's Dan Marino surpassed Pro Football Hall of Famer Fran Tarkenton in four major passing categories—attempts, completions, yards, and touchdowns—to become the NFL's all-time career leader. San Francisco's Jerry Rice became the all-time reception and receiving-yardage leader with career totals of 942 catches and 15,123 yards. Dallas' Emmitt Smith scored 25 touchdowns, breaking the season record of 24 set by Washington's John Riggins in 1983.

1996

The Dallas Cowboys won their third Super Bowl title in four years when they defeated the Pittsburgh Steelers 27-17 in Super Bowl XXX at Sun Devil Stadium in Tempe, Arizona. The game was viewed by the largest audience in U.S. television history—138.5 million people, January 28.

An agreement between the NFL and the city of Cleveland regarding the Cleveland Browns' relocation was approved by a vote of the NFL clubs, February 9. According to the agreement, the city of Cleveland retained the Browns' heritage and records, including the name, logo, colors, history, playing records, trophies, and memorabilia, and committed to building a new 72,000-seat stadium for a reactivated Browns' franchise to begin play there no later than 1999. Art Modell received approval to move his franchise to Balti-

more and rename it.

NFL total paid attendance for all 1995 games reached a record level for the seventh consecutive year, exceeding 19 million for the first time (19,202,757), March 7.

The transfer of the Oilers from Houston to Nashville for the 1998 season was approved by a vote of the NFL clubs at a meeting in Atlanta, April 30.

The Scottish Claymores defeated the Frankfurt Galaxy 32-27 to win the 1996 World Bowl in front of 38,982 at Murrayfield Stadium in Edinburgh, Scotland, June 23.

The NFL returned to Baltimore when the new Baltimore Ravens defeated the Philadelphia Eagles 17-9 in a preseason game before a crowd of 63,804 at Memorial Stadium, August 3.

Ericsson Stadium opened in Charlotte, North Carolina with a crowd of 65,350 as the Carolina Panthers defeated the Chicago Bears 30-12 in a preseason game, August 3.

NFL owners awarded Super Bowl XXXIII, to be played on January 31, 1999, to South Florida; Super Bowl XXXIV, to be played on January, 30, 2000, to Atlanta; and Super Bowl XXXV, to be played on January 28, 2001, to Tampa, October 31.

Points scored totaled 762 and NFL paid attendance totaled 964,079 for 15 games in Week 11, the highest weekend totals in either category in the league's 77-year history, November 10-11.

Former NFL Commissioner Pete Rozelle died at his home in Rancho Santa Fe, California. Rozelle, regarded as the premiere commissioner in sports history, led the NFL for 29 years, from 1960-1989, December 6.

1997

Indianapolis Colts owner Robert Irsay died from complications related to a stroke he suffered in 1995. Irsay acquired the club in 1972 when he traded his Los Angeles Rams to Carrol Rosenbloom for the Colts. He later moved the Colts from Baltimore to Indianapolis in 1984, January 14.

The Green Bay Packers won

their first NFL title in 29 years by defeating the New England Patriots 35-21 in Super Bowl XXXI at the Louisiana Superdome in New Orleans. The game was viewed by the fourth-largest audience in U.S. television history—128 million people, January 26.

The rules governing cross-ownership were modified, permitting NFL club owners to also own teams in other sports in their home market or markets without NFL teams. The vote was 24-5 (one abstention) in favor of approval, March 11.

Washington Redskins owner Jack Kent Cooke died at his home in Washington, D.C. Cooke became majority owner in 1974 and the Redskins won three Super Bowls under his leadership, April 6.

The Barcelona Dragons defeated the Rhein Fire 38-24 to win the 1997 World Bowl in front of 31,100 fans at Estadi Olimpic de Montjuic in Barcelona, Spain, June 22.

NFL clubs approved the transfer of the Seattle Seahawks from Ken Behring to Paul Allen, August 19.

Jack Kent Cooke Stadium opened in Raljon, Maryland with a crowd of 78,270 as the Washington Redskins defeated the Arizona Cardinals 19-13 in overtime, September 14.

The 10,000th regular-season game in NFL history was played when the Seattle Seahawks defeated the Tennessee Oilers 16-13 at the Kingdome in Seattle, October 5.

Atlanta Falcons owner Rankin Smith died of heart failure three days prior to his seventy-third birthday. Smith was the founder of the Falcons and was instrumental in bringing Super Bowls XXVIII and XXXIV to Atlanta, October 26.

NFL paid attendance totaled 999,778 for 15 games in Week 12, the highest weekend total in league history, November 16-17.

1998

The NFL reached agreement on record eight-year television contracts with four networks. ABC (*Monday Night Football*) and FOX (NFC) retained their previous rights, CBS took over the AFC package from NBC, and ESPN won the right to broadcast the entire Sunday night cable package, January 13.

The World League was renamed the NFL Europe League, January 22.

The Denver Broncos won their first Super Bowl by defeating the defending champion Green Bay Packers 31-24 in Super Bowl XXXII at Qualcomm Stadium in San Diego. The game tied Super Bowl XXVII for the third-largest audience in U.S. television history with 133.4 million viewers, January 25.

The NFL clubs approved an extension of the Collective Bargaining Agreement through 2003. The extended CBA also created a $100 million fund for youth football, March 22.

The NFL clubs unanimously approved an expansion team for Cleveland to fulfill the commitment to return the Browns to the field in 1999, March 23.

A total of $25.1 million, the largest NFL postseason pool ever, was divided among 737 players who participated in the 1997 playoffs, March 24.

The Rhein Fire defeated the Frankfurt Galaxy 34-10 to win the 1998 World Bowl in front of 47,846 fans in Frankfurt's Waldstadion—the biggest crowd to witness a World Bowl since 1991, June 14.

NFL clubs approved the transfer of the Minnesota Vikings from a 10-man ownership group to Red McCombs, July 28.

The NFL Stadium at Camden Yards opened in Baltimore, Maryland before a crowd of 65,938 as the Baltimore Ravens defeated the Chicago Bears 19-14 in a preseason game, August 8.

NFL paid attendance totaled 997,835 for 15 games in Week 1, the highest opening weekend total in league history and the second-highest total ever. In 1997, paid attendance totaled 999,778 for 15 games in Week 12, September 6-7.

Raymond James Stadium opened in Tampa, Florida before a crowd of 62,410 as the Tampa Bay Buccaneers defeated the Chicago Bears 27-15, September 20.

A Harris Poll says 55 percent of adults follow professional football, up 4 percent from 1997 and 6 percent from

1992, October 15.

NFL owners awarded Super Bowl XXXVI, to be played on January 27, 2002, to New Orleans, October 28.

Tennessee Oilers owner Bud Adams announced the team will change its name to the Tennessee Titans following the 1998 season. The NFL announced that the name Oilers will be retired—a first in league history, November 14.

1999

The Denver Broncos won their second consecutive Super Bowl title by defeating the NFC champion Atlanta Falcons 34-19 in Super Bowl XXXIII at Pro Player Stadium in Miami. The game was viewed by 127.5 million viewers, the sixth most-watched program in U.S. television history, January 31.

Jim Pyne, a center allocated by the Detroit Lions, was the first selection of the Cleveland Browns in the 1999 NFL Expansion Draft. The Browns eventually selected 37 players, February 9.

CBS Radio/Westwood One agreed to a 3-year extension of their exclusive national radio rights to NFL games, March 11.

NFL paid attendance of 19,741,493 for all games played during the 1998 season was the highest in league history, topping the 19,202,757 fans who paid to attend games in 1995. The 1998 regular-season total paid attendance of 15,364,873 for an average of 64,020 were also records, March 15.

By a vote of 28-3, the owners adopted an instant replay system as an officiating aid for the 1999 season, March 17.

New York Jets owner Leon Hess died from complications of a blood disease. Hess had been involved in the ownership of the Jets since 1963 and was sole owner of the club since 1984, May 9.

A group led by Washington area businessman Daniel Snyder is approved by NFL clubs as the new owner of the Washington Redskins at a league meeting in Atlanta, May 25.

NFL owners awarded Super Bowl XXXVII, to be played on January 26, 2003, to San

Diego, May 26.

The Frankfurt Galaxy became the first team in NFL Europe League history to win a second World Bowl by defeating the Barcelona Dragons 38-24 at Rheinstadion, in Düsseldorf, Germany, June 27.

The Cleveland Browns returned to the field for the first time since 1995 and defeated the Dallas Cowboys 20-17 in overtime in the annual Hall of Fame Game at Canton, Ohio, August 9.

Cleveland Browns Stadium opened in Cleveland, Ohio before a crowd of 71,398 as the Minnesota Vikings defeated the Browns in a preseason game, 24-17, August 21.

Adelphia Coliseum opened in Nashville, Tennessee before a crowd of 65,729 with the Tennessee Titans defeating the Atlanta Falcons 17-3 in a preseason game, August 26.

Houston, Texas and owner Robert McNair were awarded the NFL's thirty-second franchise in a vote of the NFL clubs at a league meeting in Atlanta. The team will begin play in 2002. The NFL clubs also voted to realign into eight divisions of four teams each for the 2002 season, October 6.

Walter Payton, the NFL's all-time leading rusher, died of liver cancer at the age of 45. Payton played for the Chicago Bears from 1975-1987 and rushed for an NFL-record 16,726 yards, November 1.

Former NFL Commissioner Pete Rozelle, who guided a still-developing league to its position today as America's most popular sport, was named by *The Sporting News* as the most powerful person in sports in the 20th Century, December 15.

2000

New York businessman Robert Wood Johnson IV was approved by NFL clubs as the new owner of the New York Jets at a league meeting, January 18.

The St. Louis Rams won their first Super Bowl by defeating the AFC champion Tennessee Titans 23-16 in Super Bowl XXXIV at the Georgia Dome in Atlanta. The game was viewed by 130.7 million

viewers, the fifth most-watched program in U.S. television history, January 30.

For the first time in league history, paid attendance topped 16 million for the regular season and more than 65,000 per game, an increase of 1,300 per game over 1998. Paid attendance for all NFL games increased in 1999 for the third year in a row and was the highest ever in the 80-year history of the league. It marked the first time in league history that the 20-million paid attendance mark was reached for all games in a season, March 27.

The Rhein Fire won their second World Bowl in three years, defeating the Scottish Claymores 13-10 to win World Bowl 2000 in front of 35,680 at Frankfurt's Waldstadion, June 25.

More than 100 of the 136 living members of the Pro Football Hall of Fame gathered to celebrate Pro Football's Greatest Reunion in Canton, Ohio, July 28-31.

Paul Brown Stadium opened in Cincinnati, Ohio with a crowd of 56,180 as the Cincinnati Bengals defeated the Chicago Bears 24-20 in a preseason game, August 19.

Cincinnati's Corey Dillon set a single-game rushing record with 278 yards (22 carries) against Denver, breaking the previous record of 275 yards by Chicago's Walter Payton in 1977, October 22.

Minnesota's Gary Anderson converted a 21-yard field goal against Buffalo to pass George Blanda as the NFL's all-time scoring leader with 2,004 points, October 22.

NFL owners awarded Super Bowl XXXVIII, to be played on February 1, 2004, to Houston; Super Bowl XXXIX, to be played on February 6, 2005, to Jacksonville; and Super Bowl XL, to be played on February 5, 2006, to Detroit, November 1.

The NFL named Mike Pereira as Director of Officiating and Larry Upson as Director of Officiating Operations to replace retiring Senior Director of Officiating Jerry Seeman, December 1.

San Francisco's Terrell Owens set a single-game receiving record with 20 receptions (283 yards) against Chicago, surpassing the previous mark of 18 by Tom Fears of the Los Angeles Rams in 1950, December 17.

2001

NFL clubs approved additional league-wide revenue sharing at a special league meeting in Dallas. The teams agreed to pool the visiting team share of gate receipts for all preseason and regular-season games and divide the pool equally starting in 2002, January 17.

The Baltimore Ravens won their first Super Bowl by defeating the NFC champion New York Giants 34-7 in Super Bowl XXXV at Raymond James Stadium in Tampa. The game was witnessed by 131.2 million viewers, the fifth most-watched program in U.S. television history, January 28.

The *Sports Business Daily* named NFL Commissioner Paul Tagliabue the 2000 Sports Industrialist of the Year, February 28.

The NFL set an all-time paid attendance record in 2000 for the third consecutive year, reaching the 20-million paid attendance mark for only the second time in league history. Regular-season paid attendance of 16,387,289 for an average of 66,078 per game also was an all-time record for the third consecutive season. The Washington Redskins set an all-time NFL regular-season home paid attendance record with a total of 656,599 for eight games, breaking the record of 634,204 held by the 1980 Detroit Lions, March 26.

A jury ruled for the NFL in a lawsuit brought against the league by the Oakland Raiders. The state court jury in Los Angeles rejected the Raiders' claims that the NFL destroyed their 1995 Hollywood Park stadium deal and that they own the Los Angeles market, May 21.

NFL owners unanimously approved a realignment plan for the league starting in 2002. With the addition of the Houston Texans, the league's 32 teams will be divided into eight four-team divisions. Seven clubs change divisions, and the Seattle Seahawks change conferences, moving from the AFC to the NFC. A

new scheduling format ensures that every team meets every other team in the league at least once every four years, May 22.

The Berlin Thunder won their first World Bowl, defeating the Barcelona Dragons 24-17 to win World Bowl IX in front of 32,116 at Amsterdam ArenA, June 30.

Heinz Field opened in Pittsburgh, Pennsylvania before a crowd of 57,829 with the Pittsburgh Steelers defeating the Detroit Lions 20-7 in a preseason game; and INVESCO Field at Mile High opened in Denver, Colorado before a crowd of 74,063 with the Denver Broncos defeating the New Orleans Saints 31-24 in a preseason game, August 25.

President George W. Bush became the first United States President to be involved in an NFL regular-season pregame coin toss as he helped kick off the 2001 season from the White House. Via satellite, President Bush tossed the coin for the 10 regular-season games that started at 1:00 PM ET, September 9.

In the wake of the September 11 terrorist attacks, Commissioner Paul Tagliabue postponed the games scheduled for September 16-17, September 13.

The league's 16-game regular season was retained when the postponed Week 2 games were rescheduled for the weekend of January 6-7, September 18.

The NFL and its game officials agreed to a new six-year Collective Bargaining Agreement, ending a two-week lockout of the regular officials, who returned to work on September 23, September 19.

The NFL announced that the Super Bowl would be rescheduled from January 27 to February 3 in order to retain the full playoff format for the 2002 season. It will be the first Super Bowl played in February, October 3.

President Bush designated Super Bowl XXXVI as a "National Special Security Event," allowing all security for the game to be coordinated by the Secret Service, November 26.

George Young, the NFL's senior vice president of foot-

ball operations and former general manager of the New York Giants, died at the age of 71. During Young's 19-year tenure with the Giants, the team earned eight playoff berths and won Super Bowl XXI and XXV. Young was named NFL Executive of the Year an unprecedented five times, December 8.

2002

The NFL and the NFL Players Association agreed to a fourth extension of the 1993 Collective Bargaining Agreement through 2007, January 7.

In an AFC Wild Card matchup, the Oakland Raiders defeated the New York Jets 38-24 in the NFL's first-ever primetime playoff game, January 12.

In a special meeting in New Orleans, NFL owners voted unanimously to approve the purchase of the Atlanta Falcons to Home Depot co-founder Arthur Blank, February 2.

The New England Patriots won their first Super Bowl by defeating the NFC champion St. Louis Rams 20-17 in Super Bowl XXXVI at the Louisiana Superdome in New Orleans. The game marked the first time in Super Bowl history that the winning points came on the final play, a 48-yard field goal by Patriots kicker Adam Vinatieri. Super Bowl XXXVI was viewed by 131.7 million viewers, the fifth-most watched program in U.S. television history, February 3.

Tennessee Titans head coach Jeff Fisher was named co-chairman of the NFL Competition Committee, February 6.

Tony Boselli, a five-time Pro Bowl tackle allocated by the Jacksonville Jaguars, was the first selection of the Houston Texans in the 2002 NFL Expansion Draft. The Texans selected 19 players, February 18.

The NFL and Westwood One/CBS Radio Sports announced the renewal of a multiyear agreement for Westwood One/CBS Radio Sports to continue as the exclusive network radio home of the NFL, April 9.

NFL Europe kicked off its tenth season with a record

254 players allocated by NFL clubs, April 13-14.

NFL COMMISSIONERS AND PRESIDENTS*

1920....	Jim Thorpe, President
1921-39...	Joe Carr, President
1939-41.	Carl Storck, President
1941-46..........	Elmer Layden, Commissioner
1946-59.................	Bert Bell, Commissioner
1960-89............	Pete Rozelle, Commissioner
1989-present..	Paul Tagliabue, Commissioner

NFL treasurer Austin Gunsel served as president in the office of the commissioner following the death of Bert Bell (Oct. 11, 1959) until the election of Pete Rozelle (Jan. 26, 1960).

2001

AMERICAN CONFERENCE

Eastern Division

	W	L	T	Pct.	Pts.	OP
New England	11	5	0	.688	371	272
Miami*	11	5	0	.688	344	290
N.Y. Jets*	10	6	0	.625	308	295
Indianapolis	6	10	0	.375	413	486
Buffalo	3	13	0	.188	265	420

Central Division

	W	L	T	Pct.	Pts.	OP
Pittsburgh#	13	3	0	.813	352	212
Baltimore*	10	6	0	.625	303	265
Cleveland	7	9	0	.438	285	319
Tennessee	7	9	0	.438	336	388
Jacksonville	6	10	0	.375	294	286
Cincinnati	6	10	0	.375	226	309

Western Division

	W	L	T	Pct.	Pts.	OP
Oakland	10	6	0	.625	399	327
Seattle	9	7	0	.563	301	324
Denver	8	8	0	.500	340	339
Kansas City	6	10	0	.375	320	344
San Diego	5	11	0	.313	332	321

NATIONAL CONFERENCE

Eastern Division

	W	L	T	Pct.	Pts.	OP
Philadelphia	11	5	0	.688	343	208
Washington	8	8	0	.500	256	303
N.Y. Giants	7	9	0	.438	294	321
Arizona	7	9	0	.438	295	343
Dallas	5	11	0	.313	246	338

Central Division

	W	L	T	Pct.	Pts.	OP
Chicago	13	3	0	.813	338	203
Green Bay*	12	4	0	.750	390	266
Tampa Bay*	9	7	0	.563	324	280
Minnesota	5	11	0	.313	290	390
Detroit	2	14	0	.125	270	424

Western Division

	W	L	T	Pct.	Pts.	OP
St. Louis#	14	2	0	.875	503	273
San Francisco*	12	4	0	.750	409	282
New Orleans	7	9	0	.438	333	409
Atlanta	7	9	0	.438	291	377
Carolina	1	15	0	.063	253	410

*Wild-Card qualifier for playoffs; #Top playoff seed in conference
New England finished ahead of Miami based on better division record (6-2 to Dolphins' 5-3). Baltimore was second Wild Card ahead of N.Y. Jets based on better record against common opponents (3-2 to Jets' 2-2). Cleveland finished ahead of Tennessee based on better division record (5-5 to Titans' 3-7). Jacksonville finished ahead of Cincinnati based on head-to-head record (2-0). N.Y. Giants finished ahead of Arizona based on head-to-head record (2-0). Green Bay was first Wild Card ahead of San Francisco based on better conference record (9-3 to 49ers' 8-4). New Orleans finished ahead of Atlanta based on better division record (4-4 to Falcons' 3-5).
Wild-Card playoffs: OAKLAND 38, New York Jets 24; Baltimore 20, MIAMI 3
Divisional playoffs: NEW ENGLAND 16, Oakland 13 (OT); PITTSBURGH 27, Baltimore 10
AFC Championship: New England 24, PITTSBURGH 17
Wild-Card playoffs: PHILADELPHIA 31, Tampa Bay 9; GREEN BAY 25, San Francisco 15
Divisional playoffs: Philadelphia 33, CHICAGO 19; ST. LOUIS 45, Green Bay 17
NFC Championship: ST. LOUIS 29, Philadelphia 24
Super Bowl XXXVI: New England (AFC) 20, St. Louis (NFC) 17 at Louisiana Superdome, New Orleans, Louisiana

In Past Standings section, home teams in playoff games are indicated by capital letters.

2000

AMERICAN CONFERENCE

Eastern Division

	W	L	T	Pct.	Pts.	OP
Miami	11	5	0	.688	323	226
Indianapolis*	10	6	0	.625	429	326
N.Y. Jets	9	7	0	.563	321	321
Buffalo	8	8	0	.500	315	350
New England	5	11	0	.313	276	338

Central Division

	W	L	T	Pct.	Pts.	OP
Tennessee#	13	3	0	.813	346	191
Baltimore*	12	4	0	.750	333	165
Pittsburgh	9	7	0	.563	321	255
Jacksonville	7	9	0	.438	367	327
Cincinnati	4	12	0	.250	185	359
Cleveland	3	13	0	.188	161	419

Western Division

	W	L	T	Pct.	Pts.	OP
Oakland	12	4	0	.750	479	299
Denver*	11	5	0	.688	485	369
Kansas City	7	9	0	.438	355	354
Seattle	6	10	0	.375	320	405
San Diego	1	15	0	.063	269	440

NATIONAL CONFERENCE

Eastern Division

	W	L	T	Pct.	Pts.	OP
N.Y. Giants#	12	4	0	.750	328	246
Philadelphia*	11	5	0	.688	351	245
Washington	8	8	0	.500	281	269
Dallas	5	11	0	.313	294	361
Arizona	3	13	0	.188	210	443

Central Division

	W	L	T	Pct.	Pts.	OP
Minnesota	11	5	0	.688	397	371
Tampa Bay*	10	6	0	.625	388	269
Green Bay	9	7	0	.563	353	323
Detroit	9	7	0	.563	307	307
Chicago	5	11	0	.313	216	355

Western Division

	W	L	T	Pct.	Pts.	OP
New Orleans	10	6	0	.625	354	305
St. Louis*	10	6	0	.625	540	471
Carolina	7	9	0	.438	310	310
San Francisco	6	10	0	.375	388	422
Atlanta	4	12	0	.250	252	413

*Wild-Card qualifier for playoffs; #Top playoff seed in conference
Green Bay finished ahead of Detroit based on better division record (5-3 to Lions' 3-5). New Orleans finished ahead of St. Louis based on better division record (7-1 to Rams' 5-3). Tampa Bay was second Wild Card based on head-to-head victory over St. Louis (1-0).
Wild-Card playoffs: MIAMI 23, Indianapolis 17 (OT); BALTIMORE 21, Denver 3
Divisional playoffs: OAKLAND 27, Miami 0; Baltimore 24, TENNESSEE 10
AFC Championship: Baltimore 16, OAKLAND 3
Wild-Card playoffs: NEW ORLEANS 31, St. Louis 28; PHILADELPHIA 21, Tampa Bay 3
Divisional playoffs: MINNESOTA 34, New Orleans 16; N.Y. GIANTS 20, Philadelphia 10
NFC Championship: N.Y. GIANTS 41, Minnesota 0
Super Bowl XXXV: Baltimore (AFC) 34, N.Y. Giants (NFC) 7 at Raymond James Stadium, Tampa, Florida

1999

AMERICAN CONFERENCE

Eastern Division

	W	L	T	Pct.	Pts.	OP
Indianapolis	13	3	0	.813	423	333
Buffalo*	11	5	0	.688	320	229
Miami*	9	7	0	.563	326	336
N.Y. Jets	8	8	0	.500	308	309
New England	8	8	0	.500	299	284

Central Division

	W	L	T	Pct.	Pts.	OP
Jacksonville#	14	2	0	.875	396	217
Tennessee*	13	3	0	.813	392	324
Baltimore	8	8	0	.500	324	277
Pittsburgh	6	10	0	.375	317	320
Cincinnati	4	12	0	.250	283	460
Cleveland	2	14	0	.125	217	437

Western Division

	W	L	T	Pct.	Pts.	OP
Seattle	9	7	0	.563	338	298
Kansas City	9	7	0	.563	390	322
San Diego	8	8	0	.500	269	316
Oakland	8	8	0	.500	390	329
Denver	6	10	0	.375	314	318

NATIONAL CONFERENCE

Eastern Division

	W	L	T	Pct.	Pts.	OP
Washington	10	6	0	.625	443	377
Dallas*	8	8	0	.500	352	276
N.Y. Giants	7	9	0	.438	299	358
Arizona	6	10	0	.375	245	382
Philadelphia	5	11	0	.313	272	357

Central Division

	W	L	T	Pct.	Pts.	OP
Tampa Bay	11	5	0	.688	270	235
Minnesota*	10	6	0	.625	399	335
Detroit*	8	8	0	.500	322	323
Green Bay	8	8	0	.500	357	341
Chicago	6	10	0	.375	272	341

Western Division

	W	L	T	Pct.	Pts.	OP
St. Louis#	13	3	0	.813	526	242
Carolina	8	8	0	.500	421	381
Atlanta	5	11	0	.313	285	380
San Francisco	4	12	0	.250	295	453
New Orleans	3	13	0	.188	260	434

*Wild-Card qualifier for playoffs; #Top playoff seed in conference
Miami was third Wild Card ahead of Kansas City based on better record against common opponents (6-1 to Chiefs' 5-3). N.Y. Jets finished ahead of New England based on better division record (4-4 to Patriots' 2-6). Seattle finished ahead of Kansas City based on head-to-head sweep (2-0). San Diego finished ahead of Oakland based on better division record (5-3 to Raiders' 3-5). Dallas was second Wild Card based on better record against common opponents (3-2 to Lions' 3-3) and better conference record than Carolina (7-5 to Panthers' 6-6). Detroit was third Wild Card based on better conference record than Green Bay (7-5 to Packers' 6-6) and better conference record than Carolina (7-5 to Panthers' 6-6).

Wild-Card playoffs: TENNESSEE 22, Buffalo 16;
Miami 20, SEATTLE 17
Divisional playoffs: JACKSONVILLE 62, Miami 7;
Tennessee 19, INDIANAPOLIS 16
AFC Championship: Tennessee 33, JACKSONVILLE 14
Wild-Card playoffs: WASHINGTON 27, Detroit 13;
MINNESOTA 27, Dallas 10
Divisional playoffs: TAMPA BAY 14, Washington 13;
ST. LOUIS 49, Minnesota 37
NFC Championship: ST. LOUIS 11, Tampa Bay 6
Super Bowl XXXIV: St. Louis (NFC) 23, Tennessee (AFC) 16
at Georgia Dome, Atlanta, Georgia

1998

AMERICAN CONFERENCE

Eastern Division

	W	L	T	Pct.	Pts.	OP
N.Y. Jets	12	4	0	.750	416	266
Miami*	10	6	0	.625	321	265
Buffalo*	10	6	0	.625	400	333
New England*	9	7	0	.563	337	329
Indianapolis	3	13	0	.188	310	444

Central Division

	W	L	T	Pct.	Pts.	OP
Jacksonville	11	5	0	.688	392	338
Tennessee	8	8	0	.500	330	320
Pittsburgh	7	9	0	.438	263	303
Baltimore	6	10	0	.375	269	335
Cincinnati	3	13	0	.188	268	452

Western Division

	W	L	T	Pct.	Pts.	OP
Denver#	14	2	0	.875	501	309
Oakland	8	8	0	.500	288	356
Seattle	8	8	0	.500	372	310
Kansas City	7	9	0	.438	327	363
San Diego	5	11	0	.313	241	342

NATIONAL CONFERENCE

Eastern Division

	W	L	T	Pct.	Pts.	OP
Dallas	10	6	0	.625	381	275
Arizona*	9	7	0	.563	325	378
N.Y. Giants	8	8	0	.500	287	309
Washington	6	10	0	.375	319	421
Philadelphia	3	13	0	.188	161	344

Central Division

	W	L	T	Pct.	Pts.	OP
Minnesota#	15	1	0	.938	556	296
Green Bay*	11	5	0	.688	408	319
Tampa Bay	8	8	0	.500	314	295
Detroit	5	11	0	.313	306	378
Chicago	4	12	0	.250	276	368

Western Division

	W	L	T	Pct.	Pts.	OP
Atlanta	14	2	0	.875	442	289
San Francisco*	12	4	0	.750	479	328
New Orleans	6	10	0	.375	305	359
Carolina	4	12	0	.250	336	413
St. Louis	4	12	0	.250	285	378

*Wild-Card qualifier for playoffs; #Top playoff seed in conference
Miami finished ahead of Buffalo based on better net division points (6 to Bills' 0). Oakland finished ahead of Seattle based on head-to-head sweep (2-0). Carolina finished ahead of St. Louis based on head-to-head sweep (2-0).

Wild-Card playoffs: MIAMI 24, Buffalo 17;
JACKSONVILLE 25, New England 10
Divisional playoffs: DENVER 38, Miami 3;
N.Y. JETS 34, Jacksonville 24
AFC Championship: DENVER 23, N.Y. Jets 10
Wild-Card playoffs: Arizona 20, DALLAS 7;
SAN FRANCISCO 30, Green Bay 27
Divisional playoffs: ATLANTA 20, San Francisco 18;
MINNESOTA 41, Arizona 21
NFC Championship: Atlanta 30, MINNESOTA 27 (OT)
Super Bowl XXXIII: Denver (AFC) 34, Atlanta (NFC) 19,
at Pro Player Stadium, Miami, Florida

1997

AMERICAN CONFERENCE

Eastern Division

	W	L	T	Pct.	Pts.	OP
New England	10	6	0	.625	369	289
Miami*	9	7	0	.563	339	327
N.Y. Jets	9	7	0	.563	348	287
Buffalo	6	10	0	.375	255	367
Indianapolis	3	13	0	.188	313	401

Central Division

	W	L	T	Pct.	Pts.	OP
Pittsburgh	11	5	0	.688	372	307
Jacksonville*	11	5	0	.688	394	318
Tennessee	8	8	0	.500	333	310
Cincinnati	7	9	0	.438	355	405
Baltimore	6	9	1	.406	326	345

Western Division

	W	L	T	Pct.	Pts.	OP
Kansas City#	13	3	0	.813	375	232
Denver*	12	4	0	.750	472	287
Seattle	8	8	0	.500	365	362
Oakland	4	12	0	.250	324	419
San Diego	4	12	0	.250	266	425

NATIONAL CONFERENCE

Eastern Division

	W	L	T	Pct.	Pts.	OP
N.Y. Giants	10	5	1	.656	307	265
Washington	8	7	1	.531	327	289
Philadelphia	6	9	1	.406	317	372
Dallas	6	10	0	.375	304	314
Arizona	4	12	0	.250	283	379

Central Division

	W	L	T	Pct.	Pts.	OP
Green Bay	13	3	0	.813	422	282
Tampa Bay*	10	6	0	.625	299	263
Detroit*	9	7	0	.563	379	306
Minnesota*	9	7	0	.563	354	359
Chicago	4	12	0	.250	263	421

Western Division

	W	L	T	Pct.	Pts.	OP
San Francisco#	13	3	0	.813	375	265
Carolina	7	9	0	.438	265	314
Atlanta	7	9	0	.438	320	361
New Orleans	6	10	0	.375	237	327
St. Louis	5	11	0	.313	299	359

*Wild-Card qualifier for playoffs; #Top playoff seed in conference
Miami finished ahead of N.Y. Jets based on head-to-head sweep
(2-0). Pittsburgh finished ahead of Jacksonville based on better
net division points (78 to Jaguars' 23). Oakland finished ahead of
San Diego based on better division record (2-6 to Chargers' 1-7).
San Francisco was top playoff seed based on better conference
record than Green Bay (11-1 to Packers' 10-2). Detroit finished
ahead of Minnesota based on head-to-head sweep (2-0). Caroli-
na finished ahead of Atlanta based on head-to-head sweep (2-0).
Wild-Card playoffs: DENVER 42, Jacksonville 17;
    NEW ENGLAND 17, Miami 3
Divisional playoffs: PITTSBURGH 7, New England 6;
    Denver 14, KANSAS CITY 10
AFC Championship: Denver 24, PITTSBURGH 21
Wild-Card playoffs: Minnesota 23, N.Y. GIANTS 22;
    TAMPA BAY 20, Detroit 10
Divisional playoffs: SAN FRANCISCO 38, Minnesota 22;
    GREEN BAY 21, Tampa Bay 7
NFC Championship: Green Bay 23, SAN FRANCISCO 10
Super Bowl XXXII: Denver (AFC) 31, Green Bay (NFC) 24,
    at Qualcomm Stadium, San Diego, California

1996

AMERICAN CONFERENCE

Eastern Division

	W	L	T	Pct.	Pts.	OP
New England	11	5	0	.688	418	313
Buffalo	10	6	0	.625	319	266
Indianapolis*	9	7	0	.563	317	334
Miami	8	8	0	.500	339	325
N.Y. Jets	1	15	0	.063	279	454

Central Division

	W	L	T	Pct.	Pts.	OP
Pittsburgh	10	6	0	.625	344	257
Jacksonville*	9	7	0	.563	325	335
Cincinnati	8	8	0	.500	372	369
Houston	8	8	0	.500	345	319
Baltimore	4	12	0	.250	371	441

Western Division

	W	L	T	Pct.	Pts.	OP
Denver#	13	3	0	.813	391	275
Kansas City	9	7	0	.563	297	300
San Diego	8	8	0	.500	310	376
Oakland	7	9	0	.438	340	293
Seattle	7	9	0	.438	317	376

NATIONAL CONFERENCE

Eastern Division

	W	L	T	Pct.	Pts.	OP
Dallas	10	6	0	.625	286	250
Philadelphia*	10	6	0	.625	363	341
Washington	9	7	0	.563	364	312
Arizona	7	9	0	.438	300	397
N.Y. Giants	6	10	0	.375	242	297

Central Division

	W	L	T	Pct.	Pts.	OP
Green Bay#	13	3	0	.813	456	210
Minnesota*	9	7	0	.563	298	315
Chicago	7	9	0	.438	283	305
Tampa Bay	6	10	0	.375	221	293
Detroit	5	11	0	.313	302	368

Western Division

	W	L	T	Pct.	Pts.	OP
Carolina	12	4	0	.750	367	218
San Francisco*	12	4	0	.750	398	257
St. Louis	6	10	0	.375	303	409
Atlanta	3	13	0	.188	309	461
New Orleans	3	13	0	.188	229	339

*Wild-Card qualifier for playoffs; #Top playoff seed in conference
Jacksonville was second Wild Card ahead of Indianapolis and
    Kansas City based on better conference record (7-5 to Colts' 6-6
    and Chiefs' 5-7). Indianapolis was third Wild Card based on
    head-to-head victory over Kansas City (1-0). Cincinnati finished
    ahead of Houston based on better net division points (19 to Oil-
    ers' 11). Oakland finished ahead of Seattle based on better divi-
    sion record (3-5 to Seahawks' 2-6). Dallas finished ahead of
    Philadelphia based on better record against common opponents
    (8-5 to Eagles' 7-6). Minnesota was third Wild Card based on
    better conference record than Washington (8-4 to Redskins'
    6-6). Carolina finished ahead of San Francisco based on head-to-
    head sweep (2-0). Atlanta finished ahead of New Orleans based
    on head-to-head sweep (2-0).
Wild-Card playoffs: Jacksonville 30, BUFFALO 27;
    PITTSBURGH 42, Indianapolis 14
Divisional playoffs: Jacksonville 30, DENVER 27;
    NEW ENGLAND 28, Pittsburgh 3
AFC Championship: NEW ENGLAND 20, Jacksonville 6
Wild-Card playoffs: DALLAS 40, Minnesota 15;
    SAN FRANCISCO 14, Philadelphia 0
Divisional playoffs: GREEN BAY 35, San Francisco 14;
    CAROLINA 26, Dallas 17
NFC Championship: GREEN BAY 30, Carolina 13
Super Bowl XXXI: Green Bay (NFC) 35, New England (AFC) 21,
    at Louisiana Superdome, New Orleans, Louisiana

1995

AMERICAN CONFERENCE

Eastern Division

	W	L	T	Pct.	Pts.	OP
Buffalo	10	6	0	.625	350	335
Indianapolis*	9	7	0	.563	331	316
Miami*	9	7	0	.563	398	332
New England	6	10	0	.375	294	377
N.Y. Jets	3	13	0	.188	233	384

Central Division

	W	L	T	Pct.	Pts.	OP
Pittsburgh	11	5	0	.688	407	327
Cincinnati	7	9	0	.438	349	374
Houston	7	9	0	.438	348	324
Cleveland	5	11	0	.313	289	356
Jacksonville	4	12	0	.250	275	404

Western Division

	W	L	T	Pct.	Pts.	OP
Kansas City#	13	3	0	.813	358	241
San Diego*	9	7	0	.563	321	323
Seattle	8	8	0	.500	363	366
Denver	8	8	0	.500	388	345
Oakland	8	8	0	.500	348	332

NATIONAL CONFERENCE

Eastern Division

	W	L	T	Pct.	Pts.	OP
Dallas#	12	4	0	.750	435	291
Philadelphia*	10	6	0	.625	318	338
Washington	6	10	0	.375	326	359
N.Y. Giants	5	11	0	.313	290	340
Arizona	4	12	0	.250	275	422

Central Division

	W	L	T	Pct.	Pts.	OP
Green Bay	11	5	0	.688	404	314
Detroit*	10	6	0	.625	436	336
Chicago	9	7	0	.563	392	360
Minnesota	8	8	0	.500	412	385
Tampa Bay	7	9	0	.438	238	335

Western Division

	W	L	T	Pct.	Pts.	OP
San Francisco	11	5	0	.688	457	258
Atlanta*	9	7	0	.563	362	349
St. Louis	7	9	0	.438	309	418
Carolina	7	9	0	.438	289	325
New Orleans	7	9	0	.438	319	348

*Wild-Card qualifier for playoffs; #Top playoff seed in conference
Indianapolis finished ahead of Miami based on head-to-head sweep (2-0). San Diego was first Wild Card based on head-to-head victory over Indianapolis (1-0). Cincinnati finished ahead of Houston based on better division record (4-4 to Oilers' 3-5). Seattle finished ahead of Denver and Oakland based on best head-to-head record (3-1 to Broncos' 2-2 and Raiders' 1-3). Denver finished ahead of Oakland based on head-to-head sweep (2-0). Philadelphia was first Wild Card ahead of Detroit based on better conference record (9-3 to Lions' 7-5). San Francisco was second playoff seed ahead of Green Bay based on better conference record (8-4 to Packers' 7-5). Atlanta was third Wild Card ahead of Chicago based on better record against common opponents (4-2 to Bears' 3-3). St. Louis finished ahead of Carolina and New Orleans based on best head-to-head record (3-1 to Panthers' 1-3 and Saints' 2-2). Carolina finished ahead of New Orleans based on better conference record (4-8 to 3-9).
Wild-Card playoffs: BUFFALO 37, Miami 22;
    Indianapolis 35, SAN DIEGO 20
Divisional playoffs: PITTSBURGH 40, Buffalo 21;
    Indianapolis 10, KANSAS CITY 7
AFC Championship: PITTSBURGH 20, Indianapolis 16
Wild-Card playoffs: PHILADELPHIA 58, Detroit 37;
    GREEN BAY 37, Atlanta 20
Divisional playoffs: Green Bay 27, SAN FRANCISCO 17;
    DALLAS 30, Philadelphia 11
NFC Championship: DALLAS 38, Green Bay 27
Super Bowl XXX: Dallas (NFC) 27, Pittsburgh (AFC)17,
    at Sun Devil Stadium, Tempe, Arizona

1994

AMERICAN CONFERENCE

Eastern Division

	W	L	T	Pct.	Pts.	OP
Miami	10	6	0	.625	389	327
New England*	10	6	0	.625	351	312
Indianapolis	8	8	0	.500	307	320
Buffalo	7	9	0	.438	340	356
N.Y. Jets	6	10	0	.375	264	320

Central Division

	W	L	T	Pct.	Pts.	OP
Pittsburgh#	12	4	0	.750	316	234
Cleveland*	11	5	0	.688	340	204
Cincinnati	3	13	0	.188	276	406
Houston	2	14	0	.125	226	352

Western Division

	W	L	T	Pct.	Pts.	OP
San Diego	11	5	0	.688	381	306
Kansas City*	9	7	0	.563	319	298
L.A. Raiders	9	7	0	.563	303	327
Denver	7	9	0	.438	347	396
Seattle	6	10	0	.375	287	323

NATIONAL CONFERENCE

Eastern Division

	W	L	T	Pct.	Pts.	OP
Dallas	12	4	0	.750	414	248
N.Y. Giants	9	7	0	.563	279	305
Arizona	8	8	0	.500	235	267
Philadelphia	7	9	0	.438	308	308
Washington	3	13	0	.188	320	412

Central Division

	W	L	T	Pct.	Pts.	OP
Minnesota	10	6	0	.625	356	314
Green Bay*	9	7	0	.563	382	287
Detroit*	9	7	0	.563	357	342
Chicago*	9	7	0	.563	271	307
Tampa Bay	6	10	0	.375	251	351

Western Division

	W	L	T	Pct.	Pts.	OP
San Francisco#	13	3	0	.813	505	296
New Orleans	7	9	0	.438	348	407
Atlanta	7	9	0	.438	317	385
L.A. Rams	4	12	0	.250	286	365

*Wild-Card qualifier for playoffs; #Top playoff seed in conference
Miami finished ahead of New England based on head-to-head sweep (2-0). Kansas City finished ahead of L.A. Raiders based on head-to-head sweep (2-0). Green Bay was first Wild Card based on best head-to-head record (3-1) vs. Detroit (2-2) and Chicago (1-3) and better conference record (8-4) than N.Y. Giants (6-6). Detroit was second Wild Card based on better division record (4-4) than Chicago (3-5) and head-to-head victory over N.Y. Giants (1-0). Chicago was third Wild Card based on better record against common opponents (4-4) than N.Y. Giants (3-5). New Orleans finished ahead of Atlanta based on head-to-head sweep (2-0).
Wild-Card playoffs: MIAMI 27, Kansas City 17;
    CLEVELAND 20, New England 13
Divisional playoffs: PITTSBURGH 29, Cleveland 9;
    SAN DIEGO 22, Miami 21
AFC Championship: San Diego 17, PITTSBURGH 13
Wild-Card playoffs: GREEN BAY 16, Detroit 12;
    Chicago 35, MINNESOTA 18
Divisional playoffs: SAN FRANCISCO 44, Chicago 15;
    DALLAS 35, Green Bay 9
NFC Championship: SAN FRANCISCO 38, Dallas 28
Super Bowl XXIX: San Francisco (NFC) 49, San Diego (AFC) 26,
    at Joe Robbie Stadium, Miami, Florida

1993

AMERICAN CONFERENCE

Eastern Division

	W	L	T	Pct.	Pts.	OP
Buffalo#	12	4	0	.750	329	242
Miami	9	7	0	.563	349	351
N.Y. Jets	8	8	0	.500	270	247
New England	5	11	0	.313	238	286
Indianapolis	4	12	0	.250	189	378

Central Division

	W	L	T	Pct.	Pts.	OP
Houston	12	4	0	.750	368	238
Pittsburgh*	9	7	0	.563	308	281
Cleveland	7	9	0	.438	304	307
Cincinnati	3	13	0	.188	187	319

Western Division

	W	L	T	Pct.	Pts.	OP
Kansas City	11	5	0	.688	328	291
L.A. Raiders*	10	6	0	.625	306	326
Denver*	9	7	0	.563	373	284
San Diego	8	8	0	.500	322	290
Seattle	6	10	0	.375	280	314

NATIONAL CONFERENCE

Eastern Division

	W	L	T	Pct.	Pts.	OP
Dallas#	12	4	0	.750	376	229
N.Y. Giants*	11	5	0	.688	288	205
Philadelphia	8	8	0	.500	293	315
Phoenix	7	9	0	.438	326	269
Washington	4	12	0	.250	230	345

Central Division

	W	L	T	Pct.	Pts.	OP
Detroit	10	6	0	.625	298	292
Minnesota*	9	7	0	.563	277	290
Green Bay*	9	7	0	.563	340	282
Chicago	7	9	0	.438	234	230
Tampa Bay	5	11	0	.313	237	376

Western Division

	W	L	T	Pct.	Pts.	OP
San Francisco	10	6	0	.625	473	295
New Orleans	8	8	0	.500	317	343
Atlanta	6	10	0	.375	316	385
L.A. Rams	5	11	0	.313	221	367

Wild-Card qualifier for playoffs; #Top playoff seed in conference
Buffalo was top playoff seed based on head-to-head victory over Houston (1-0). Denver was second Wild Card, and Pittsburgh was third Wild Card ahead of Miami, based on better conference record (8-4 to Steelers' 7-5 to Dolphins' 6-6). San Francisco was second playoff seed based on head-to-head victory over Detroit (1-0). Minnesota finished ahead of Green Bay based on head-to-head sweep (2-0).

Wild-Card playoffs: KANSAS CITY 27, Pittsburgh 24 (OT);
  L.A. RAIDERS 42, Denver 24
Divisional playoffs: BUFFALO 29, L.A. Raiders 23;
  Kansas City 28, HOUSTON 20
AFC Championship: BUFFALO 30, Kansas City 13
Wild-Card playoffs: Green Bay 28, DETROIT 24;
  N.Y. GIANTS 17, Minnesota 10
Divisional playoffs: SAN FRANCISCO 44, N.Y. Giants 3;
  DALLAS 27, Green Bay 17
NFC Championship: DALLAS 38, San Francisco 21
Super Bowl XXVIII: Dallas (NFC) 30, Buffalo (AFC) 13,
  at Georgia Dome, Atlanta, Georgia

1992

AMERICAN CONFERENCE

Eastern Division

	W	L	T	Pct.	Pts.	OP
Miami	11	5	0	.688	340	281
Buffalo*	11	5	0	.688	381	283
Indianapolis	9	7	0	.563	216	302
N.Y. Jets	4	12	0	.250	220	315
New England	2	14	0	.125	205	363

Central Division

	W	L	T	Pct.	Pts.	OP
Pittsburgh#	11	5	0	.688	299	225
Houston*	10	6	0	.625	352	258
Cleveland	7	9	0	.438	272	275
Cincinnati	5	11	0	.313	274	364

Western Division

	W	L	T	Pct.	Pts.	OP
San Diego	11	5	0	.688	335	241
Kansas City*	10	6	0	.625	348	282
Denver	8	8	0	.500	262	329
L.A. Raiders	7	9	0	.438	249	281
Seattle	2	14	0	.125	140	312

NATIONAL CONFERENCE

Eastern Division

	W	L	T	Pct.	Pts.	OP
Dallas	13	3	0	.813	409	243
Philadelphia*	11	5	0	.688	354	245
Washington*	9	7	0	.563	300	255
N.Y. Giants	6	10	0	.375	306	367
Phoenix	4	12	0	.250	243	332

Central Division

	W	L	T	Pct.	Pts.	OP
Minnesota	11	5	0	.688	374	249
Green Bay	9	7	0	.563	276	296
Tampa Bay	5	11	0	.313	267	365
Chicago	5	11	0	.313	295	361
Detroit	5	11	0	.313	273	332

Western Division

	W	L	T	Pct.	Pts.	OP
San Francisco#	14	2	0	.875	431	236
New Orleans*	12	4	0	.750	330	202
Atlanta	6	10	0	.375	327	414
L.A. Rams	6	10	0	.375	313	383

Wild-Card qualifier for playoffs; #Top playoff seed in conference
Pittsburgh was top playoff seed, and Miami was second playoff seed ahead of San Diego, based on conference record (10-2 to Dolphins' 9-3 to Chargers' 9-5). Miami finished ahead of Buffalo based on better conference record (9-3 to Bills' 7-5). Houston was second Wild Card based on head-to-head victory over Kansas City (1-0). Washington was third Wild Card based on better conference record than Green Bay (7-5 to Packers' 6-6). Tampa Bay finished ahead of Chicago and Detroit based on better conference record (5-9 to Bears' 4-8 and Lions' 3-9). Atlanta finished ahead of L.A. Rams based on better record against common opponents (5-7 to Rams' 4-8).

Wild-Card playoffs: SAN DIEGO 17, Kansas City 0;
  BUFFALO 41, Houston 38 (OT)
Divisional playoffs: Buffalo 24, PITTSBURGH 3;
  MIAMI 31, San Diego 0
AFC Championship: Buffalo 29, MIAMI 10
Wild-Card playoffs: Washington 24, MINNESOTA 7;
  Philadelphia 36, NEW ORLEANS 20
Divisional playoffs: SAN FRANCISCO 20, Washington 13;
  DALLAS 34, Philadelphia 10
NFC Championship: Dallas 30, SAN FRANCISCO 20
Super Bowl XXVII: Dallas (NFC) 52, Buffalo (AFC) 17,
  at Rose Bowl, Pasadena, California

1991

AMERICAN CONFERENCE

Eastern Division

	W	L	T	Pct.	Pts.	OP
Buffalo#	13	3	0	.813	458	318
N.Y. Jets*	8	8	0	.500	314	293
Miami	8	8	0	.500	343	349
New England	6	10	0	.375	211	305
Indianapolis	1	15	0	.063	143	381

Central Division

	W	L	T	Pct.	Pts.	OP
Houston	11	5	0	.688	386	251
Pittsburgh	7	9	0	.438	292	344
Cleveland	6	10	0	.375	293	298
Cincinnati	3	13	0	.188	263	435

Western Division

	W	L	T	Pct.	Pts.	OP
Denver	12	4	0	.750	304	235
Kansas City*	10	6	0	.625	322	252
L.A. Raiders*	9	7	0	.563	298	297
Seattle	7	9	0	.438	276	261
San Diego	4	12	0	.250	274	342

NATIONAL CONFERENCE

Eastern Division

	W	L	T	Pct.	Pts.	OP
Washington#	14	2	0	.875	485	224
Dallas*	11	5	0	.688	342	310
Philadelphia	10	6	0	.625	285	244
N.Y. Giants	8	8	0	.500	281	297
Phoenix	4	12	0	.250	196	344

Central Division

	W	L	T	Pct.	Pts.	OP
Detroit	12	4	0	.750	339	295
Chicago*	11	5	0	.688	299	269
Minnesota	8	8	0	.500	301	306
Green Bay	4	12	0	.250	273	313
Tampa Bay	3	13	0	.188	199	365

Western Division

	W	L	T	Pct.	Pts.	OP
New Orleans	11	5	0	.688	341	211
Atlanta*	10	6	0	.625	361	338
San Francisco	10	6	0	.625	393	239
L.A. Rams	3	13	0	.188	234	390

*Wild-Card qualifier for playoffs; #Top playoff seed in conference
N.Y. Jets finished ahead of Miami based on head-to-head sweep
(2-0). Chicago was first Wild Card based on better conference
record than Dallas (9-3 to Cowboys' 8-4). Atlanta finished ahead
of San Francisco based on head-to-head sweep (2-0), and was
third Wild Card ahead of Philadelphia based on better conference
record (7-5 to Eagles' 6-6).
Wild-Card playoffs: KANSAS CITY 10, L.A. Raiders 6;
HOUSTON 17, N.Y. Jets 10
Divisional playoffs: DENVER 26, Houston 24;
BUFFALO 37, Kansas City 14
AFC Championship: BUFFALO 10, Denver 7
Wild-Card playoffs: Atlanta 27, NEW ORLEANS 20;
Dallas 17, CHICAGO 13
Divisional playoffs: WASHINGTON 24, Atlanta 7;
DETROIT 38, Dallas 6
NFC Championship: WASHINGTON 41, Detroit 10
Super Bowl XXVI: Washington (NFC) 37, Buffalo (AFC) 24,
at Hubert H. Humphrey Metrodome, Minneapolis, Minnesota

1990

AMERICAN CONFERENCE

Eastern Division

	W	L	T	Pct.	Pts.	OP
Buffalo#	13	3	0	.813	428	263
Miami*	12	4	0	.750	336	242
Indianapolis	7	9	0	.438	281	353
N.Y. Jets	6	10	0	.375	295	345
New England	1	15	0	.063	181	446

Central Division

	W	L	T	Pct.	Pts.	OP
Cincinnati	9	7	0	.563	360	352
Houston*	9	7	0	.563	405	307
Pittsburgh	9	7	0	.563	292	240
Cleveland	3	13	0	.188	228	462

Western Division

	W	L	T	Pct.	Pts.	OP
L.A. Raiders	12	4	0	.750	337	268
Kansas City*	11	5	0	.688	369	257
Seattle	9	7	0	.563	306	286
San Diego	6	10	0	.375	315	281
Denver	5	11	0	.313	331	374

NATIONAL CONFERENCE

Eastern Division

	W	L	T	Pct.	Pts.	OP
N.Y. Giants	13	3	0	.813	335	211
Philadelphia*	10	6	0	.625	396	299
Washington*	10	6	0	.625	381	301
Dallas	7	9	0	.438	244	308
Phoenix	5	11	0	.313	268	396

Central Division

	W	L	T	Pct.	Pts.	OP
Chicago	11	5	0	.688	348	280
Tampa Bay	6	10	0	.375	264	367
Detroit	6	10	0	.375	373	413
Green Bay	6	10	0	.375	271	347
Minnesota	6	10	0	.375	351	326

Western Division

	W	L	T	Pct.	Pts.	OP
San Francisco#	14	2	0	.875	353	239
New Orleans*	8	8	0	.500	274	275
L.A. Rams	5	11	0	.313	345	412
Atlanta	5	11	0	.313	348	365

*Wild-Card qualifier for playoffs; #Top playoff seed in conference
Cincinnati finished ahead of Houston and Pittsburgh based on best
head-to-head record (3-1 to Oilers' 2-2 to Steelers' 1-3). Houston was Wild Card based on better conference record (8-4) than
Seattle (7-5) and Pittsburgh (6-6). Philadelphia finished ahead of
Washington based on better division record (5-3 to Redskins'
4-4). Tampa Bay was second in NFC Central based on best head-
to-head record (3-1 against Detroit (2-4), Green Bay (3-3), and
Minnesota (2-4). Detroit finished third based on best net division
points (minus 8) against Green Bay (minus 40). Green Bay fin-
ished ahead of Minnesota based on better conference record
(5-7 to Vikings' 4-8). The L.A. Rams finished ahead of Atlanta
based on net points in division (plus 1 to Falcons' minus 31).
Wild-Card playoffs: MIAMI 17, Kansas City 16;
CINCINNATI 41, Houston 14
Divisional playoffs: BUFFALO 44, Miami 34;
L.A. RAIDERS 20, Cincinnati 10
AFC Championship: BUFFALO 51, L.A. Raiders 3
Wild-Card playoffs: Washington 20, PHILADELPHIA 6;
CHICAGO 16, New Orleans 6
Divisional playoffs: SAN FRANCISCO 28, Washington 10;
N.Y. GIANTS 31, Chicago 3
NFC Championship: N.Y. Giants 15, SAN FRANCISCO 13
Super Bowl XXV: N.Y. Giants (NFC) 20, Buffalo (AFC) 19,
at Tampa Stadium, Tampa, Florida

1989

AMERICAN CONFERENCE

Eastern Division

	W	L	T	Pct.	Pts.	OP
Buffalo	9	7	0	.563	409	317
Indianapolis	8	8	0	.500	298	301
Miami	8	8	0	.500	331	379
New England	5	11	0	.313	297	391
N.Y. Jets	4	12	0	.250	253	411

Central Division

	W	L	T	Pct.	Pts.	OP
Cleveland	9	6	1	.594	334	254
Houston*	9	7	0	.563	365	412
Pittsburgh*	9	7	0	.563	265	326
Cincinnati	8	8	0	.500	404	285

Western Division

	W	L	T	Pct.	Pts.	OP
Denver#	11	5	0	.688	362	226
Kansas City	8	7	1	.531	318	286
L.A. Raiders	8	8	0	.500	315	297
Seattle	7	9	0	.438	241	327
San Diego	6	10	0	.375	266	290

NATIONAL CONFERENCE

Eastern Division

	W	L	T	Pct.	Pts.	OP
N.Y. Giants	12	4	0	.750	348	252
Philadelphia*	11	5	0	.688	342	274
Washington	10	6	0	.625	386	308
Phoenix	5	11	0	.313	258	377
Dallas	1	15	0	.063	204	393

Central Division

	W	L	T	Pct.	Pts.	OP
Minnesota	10	6	0	.625	351	275
Green Bay	10	6	0	.625	362	356
Detroit	7	9	0	.438	312	364
Chicago	6	10	0	.375	358	377
Tampa Bay	5	11	0	.313	320	419

Western Division

	W	L	T	Pct.	Pts.	OP
San Francisco#	14	2	0	.875	442	253
L.A. Rams*	11	5	0	.688	426	344
New Orleans	9	7	0	.563	386	301
Atlanta	3	13	0	.188	279	437

*Wild-Card qualifier for playoffs; #Top playoff seed in conference
Indianapolis finished ahead of Miami based on better conference record (7-5 vs. Dolphins' 6-8). Houston finished ahead of Pittsburgh based on head-to-head sweep (2-0). The L.A. Rams did not play San Francisco in the divisional playoffs because, from 1970-1989, two teams from the same division could not meet prior to the conference championship game. Philadelphia was first Wild Card ahead of L.A. Rams based on better record against common opponents (6-3 to Rams' 5-4). Minnesota finished ahead of Green Bay based on better division record (6-2 vs. Packers' 5-3).

Wild-Card playoff: Pittsburgh 26, HOUSTON 23 (OT)
Divisional playoffs: CLEVELAND 34, Buffalo 30;
  DENVER 24, Pittsburgh 23
AFC Championship: DENVER 37, Cleveland 21
Wild-Card playoff: L.A. Rams 21, PHILADELPHIA 7
Divisional playoffs: L.A. Rams 19, N.Y. GIANTS 13 (OT);
  SAN FRANCISCO 41, Minnesota 13
NFC Championship: SAN FRANCISCO 30, L.A. Rams 3
Super Bowl XXIV: San Francisco (NFC) 55, Denver (AFC) 10,
  at Louisiana Superdome, New Orleans, Louisiana

1988

AMERICAN CONFERENCE

Eastern Division

	W	L	T	Pct.	Pts.	OP
Buffalo	12	4	0	.750	329	237
Indianapolis	9	7	0	.563	354	315
New England	9	7	0	.563	250	284
N.Y. Jets	8	7	1	.531	372	354
Miami	6	10	0	.375	319	380

Central Division

	W	L	T	Pct.	Pts.	OP
Cincinnati#	12	4	0	.750	448	329
Cleveland*	10	6	0	.625	304	288
Houston*	10	6	0	.625	424	365
Pittsburgh	5	11	0	.313	336	421

Western Division

	W	L	T	Pct.	Pts.	OP
Seattle	9	7	0	.563	339	329
Denver	8	8	0	.500	327	352
L.A. Raiders	7	9	0	.438	325	369
San Diego	6	10	0	.375	231	332
Kansas City	4	11	1	.281	254	320

NATIONAL CONFERENCE

Eastern Division

	W	L	T	Pct.	Pts.	OP
Philadelphia	10	6	0	.625	379	319
N.Y. Giants	10	6	0	.625	359	304
Washington	7	9	0	.438	345	387
Phoenix	7	9	0	.438	344	398
Dallas	3	13	0	.188	265	381

Central Division

	W	L	T	Pct.	Pts.	OP
Chicago#	12	4	0	.750	312	215
Minnesota*	11	5	0	.688	406	233
Tampa Bay	5	11	0	.313	261	350
Detroit	4	12	0	.250	220	313
Green Bay	4	12	0	.250	240	315

Western Division

	W	L	T	Pct.	Pts.	OP
San Francisco	10	6	0	.625	369	294
L.A. Rams*	10	6	0	.625	407	293
New Orleans	10	6	0	.625	312	283
Atlanta	5	11	0	.313	244	315

*Wild-Card qualifier for playoffs; #Top playoff seed in conference
Cincinnati was top playoff seed ahead of Buffalo based on head-to-head victory (1-0). Indianapolis finished ahead of New England based on better record against common opponents (7-5 to Patriots' 6-6). Cleveland finished ahead of Houston based on better division record (4-2 to Oilers' 3-3). Houston did not play Cincinnati, and Minnesota did not play Chicago in the divisional playoffs because, from 1970-1989, two teams from the same division could not meet prior to the conference championship game. Philadelphia finished first in NFC East based on head-to-head sweep of N.Y. Giants (2-0). Washington finished third in NFC East based on better division record (4-4) than Phoenix (3-5). Detroit finished fourth in NFC Central based on head-to-head sweep of Green Bay (2-0). San Francisco finished first in NFC West based on better head-to-head record (3-1) against L.A. Rams (2-2) and New Orleans (1-3). L.A. Rams finished second in NFC West based on better division record (4-2) than New Orleans (3-3) and earned Wild-Card position based on better conference record (8-4) than N.Y. Giants (9-5) and New Orleans (6-6).

Wild-Card playoff: Houston 24, CLEVELAND 23
Divisional playoffs: CINCINNATI 21, Seattle 13;
  BUFFALO 17, Houston 10
AFC Championship: CINCINNATI 21, Buffalo 10
Wild-Card playoff: MINNESOTA 28, L.A. Rams 17
Divisional playoffs: CHICAGO 20, Philadelphia 12;
  SAN FRANCISCO 34, Minnesota 9
NFC Championship: San Francisco 28, CHICAGO 3
Super Bowl XXIII: San Francisco (NFC) 20, Cincinnati (AFC) 16,
  at Joe Robbie Stadium, Miami, Florida

1987

AMERICAN CONFERENCE

Eastern Division

	W	L	T	Pct.	Pts.	OP
Indianapolis	9	6	0	.600	300	238
New England	8	7	0	.533	320	293
Miami	8	7	0	.533	362	335
Buffalo	7	8	0	.467	270	305
N.Y. Jets	6	9	0	.400	334	360

Central Division

	W	L	T	Pct.	Pts.	OP
Cleveland	10	5	0	.667	390	239
Houston*	9	6	0	.600	345	349
Pittsburgh	8	7	0	.533	285	299
Cincinnati	4	11	0	.267	285	370

Western Division

	W	L	T	Pct.	Pts.	OP
Denver#	10	4	1	.700	379	288
Seattle*	9	6	0	.600	371	314
San Diego	8	7	0	.533	253	317
L.A. Raiders	5	10	0	.333	301	289
Kansas City	4	11	0	.267	273	388

NATIONAL CONFERENCE

Eastern Division

	W	L	T	Pct.	Pts.	OP
Washington	11	4	0	.733	379	285
Dallas	7	8	0	.467	340	348
St. Louis	7	8	0	.467	362	368
Philadelphia	7	8	0	.467	337	380
N.Y. Giants	6	9	0	.400	280	312

Central Division

	W	L	T	Pct.	Pts.	OP
Chicago	11	4	0	.733	356	282
Minnesota*	8	7	0	.533	336	335
Green Bay	5	9	1	.367	255	300
Tampa Bay	4	11	0	.267	286	360
Detroit	4	11	0	.267	269	384

Western Division

	W	L	T	Pct.	Pts.	OP
San Francisco#	13	2	0	.867	459	253
New Orleans*	12	3	0	.800	422	283
L.A. Rams	6	9	0	.400	317	361
Atlanta	3	12	0	.200	205	436

Wild-Card qualifier for playoffs; #Top playoff seed in conference
New England finished ahead of Miami based on head-to-head sweep (2-0). Houston was first Wild Card ahead of Seattle based on better conference record (7-4 to Seahawks' 5-6). Chicago was second playoff seed of Washington based on better conference record (9-2 to Redskins' 9-3). Dallas finished ahead of St. Louis and Philadelphia based on better division record (4-4 to Cardinals' 3-5 and Eagles' 3-5). St. Louis finished ahead of Philadelphia based on better conference record (7-7 to Eagles' 4-7). Tampa Bay finished ahead of Detroit based on better division record (3-4 to Lions' 2-5).
Wild-Card playoff: HOUSTON 23, Seattle 20 (OT)
Divisional playoffs: CLEVELAND 38, Indianapolis 21; DENVER 34, Houston 10
AFC Championship: DENVER 38, Cleveland 33
Wild-Card playoff: Minnesota 44, NEW ORLEANS 10
Divisional playoffs: Minnesota 36, SAN FRANCISCO 24; Washington 21, CHICAGO 17
NFC Championship: WASHINGTON 17, Minnesota 10
Super Bowl XXII: Washington (NFC) 42, Denver (AFC) 10, at San Diego Jack Murphy Stadium, San Diego, California
Note: 1987 regular season was reduced from 16 to 15 games for each team due to players' strike.

1986

AMERICAN CONFERENCE

Eastern Division

	W	L	T	Pct.	Pts.	OP
New England	11	5	0	.688	412	307
N.Y. Jets*	10	6	0	.625	364	386
Miami	8	8	0	.500	430	405
Buffalo	4	12	0	.250	287	348
Indianapolis	3	13	0	.188	229	400

Central Division

	W	L	T	Pct.	Pts.	OP
Cleveland#	12	4	0	.750	391	310
Cincinnati	10	6	0	.625	409	394
Pittsburgh	6	10	0	.375	307	336
Houston	5	11	0	.313	274	329

Western Division

	W	L	T	Pct.	Pts.	OP
Denver	11	5	0	.688	378	327
Kansas City*	10	6	0	.625	358	326
Seattle	10	6	0	.625	366	293
L.A. Raiders	8	8	0	.500	323	346
San Diego	4	12	0	.250	335	396

NATIONAL CONFERENCE

Eastern Division

	W	L	T	Pct.	Pts.	OP
N.Y. Giants#	14	2	0	.875	371	236
Washington*	12	4	0	.750	368	296
Dallas	7	9	0	.438	346	337
Philadelphia	5	10	1	.344	256	312
St. Louis	4	11	1	.281	218	351

Central Division

	W	L	T	Pct.	Pts.	OP
Chicago	14	2	0	.875	352	187
Minnesota	9	7	0	.563	398	273
Detroit	5	11	0	.313	277	326
Green Bay	4	12	0	.250	254	418
Tampa Bay	2	14	0	.125	239	473

Western Division

	W	L	T	Pct.	Pts.	OP
San Francisco	10	5	1	.656	374	247
L.A. Rams*	10	6	0	.625	309	267
Atlanta	7	8	1	.469	280	280
New Orleans	7	9	0	.438	288	287

Wild-Card qualifier for playoffs; #Top playoff seed in conference
Denver was second playoff seed ahead of New England based on head-to-head victory (1-0). N.Y. Jets were first Wild Card based on better conference record (8-4) than Kansas City (9-5), Seattle (7-5), and Cincinnati (7-5). Kansas City was second Wild Card based on better conference record (9-5) than Seattle (7-5) and Cincinnati (7-5). N.Y. Giants were top playoff seed based on better conference record than Chicago (11-1 to Bears' 10-2). Washington did not play the N.Y. Giants in the divisional playoffs because, from 1970-1989, two teams from the same division could not meet prior to the conference championship game.
Wild-Card playoff: N.Y. JETS 35, Kansas City 15
Divisional playoffs: CLEVELAND 23, N.Y. Jets 20 (OT); DENVER 22, New England 17
AFC Championship: Denver 23, CLEVELAND 20 (OT)
Wild-Card playoff: WASHINGTON 19, L.A. Rams 7
Divisional playoffs: Washington 27, CHICAGO 13 N.Y. GIANTS 49, San Francisco 3
NFC Championship: N.Y. GIANTS 17, Washington 0
Super Bowl XXI: N.Y. Giants (NFC) 39, Denver (AFC) 20, at Rose Bowl, Pasadena, California

1985

AMERICAN CONFERENCE

Eastern Division

	W	L	T	Pct.	Pts.	OP
Miami	12	4	0	.750	428	320
N.Y. Jets*	11	5	0	.688	393	264
New England*	11	5	0	.688	362	290
Indianapolis	5	11	0	.313	320	386
Buffalo	2	14	0	.125	200	381

Central Division

	W	L	T	Pct.	Pts.	OP
Cleveland	8	8	0	.500	287	294
Cincinnati	7	9	0	.438	441	437
Pittsburgh	7	9	0	.438	379	355
Houston	5	11	0	.313	284	412

Western Division

	W	L	T	Pct.	Pts.	OP
L.A. Raiders#	12	4	0	.750	354	308
Denver	11	5	0	.688	380	329
Seattle	8	8	0	.500	349	303
San Diego	8	8	0	.500	467	435
Kansas City	6	10	0	.375	317	360

NATIONAL CONFERENCE

Eastern Division

	W	L	T	Pct.	Pts.	OP
Dallas	10	6	0	.625	357	333
N.Y. Giants*	10	6	0	.625	399	283
Washington	10	6	0	.625	297	312
Philadelphia	7	9	0	.438	286	310
St. Louis	5	11	0	.313	278	414

Central Division

	W	L	T	Pct.	Pts.	OP
Chicago#	15	1	0	.938	456	198
Green Bay	8	8	0	.500	337	355
Minnesota	7	9	0	.438	346	359
Detroit	7	9	0	.438	307	366
Tampa Bay	2	14	0	.125	294	448

Western Division

	W	L	T	Pct.	Pts.	OP
L.A. Rams	11	5	0	.688	340	277
San Francisco*	10	6	0	.625	411	263
New Orleans	5	11	0	.313	294	401
Atlanta	4	12	0	.250	282	452

*Wild-Card qualifier for playoffs; #Top playoff seed in conference

L.A. Raiders were top playoff seed ahead of Miami based on better record against common opponents (5-1 to 4-2). N.Y. Jets were first Wild Card based on better conference record (9-3) than New England (8-4) and Denver (8-4). New England was second Wild Card ahead of Denver based on better record against common opponents (4-2 to Broncos' 3-3). Cincinnati finished ahead of Pittsburgh based on head-to-head sweep (2-0). Seattle finished ahead of San Diego based on head-to-head sweep (2-0). Dallas finished ahead of N.Y. Giants and Washington based on better head-to-head record (4-0 to Giants' 1-3 and Redskins' 1-3). N.Y. Giants were first Wild Card based on better conference record (8-4) than San Francisco (7-5) and Washington (6-6). San Francisco was second Wild Card based on head-to-head victory over Washington (1-0). Minnesota finished ahead of Detroit based on better division record (3-5 to Lions' 2-6).

Wild-Card playoff: New England 26, N.Y. JETS 14

Divisional playoffs: MIAMI 24, Cleveland 21; New England 27, L.A. RAIDERS 20

AFC Championship: New England 31, MIAMI 14

Wild-Card playoff: N.Y. GIANTS 17, San Francisco 3

Divisional playoffs: L.A. RAMS 20, Dallas 0; CHICAGO 21, N.Y. Giants 0

NFC Championship: CHICAGO 24, L.A. Rams 0

Super Bowl XX: Chicago (NFC) 46, New England (AFC) 10, at Louisiana Superdome, New Orleans, Louisiana

1984

AMERICAN CONFERENCE

Eastern Division

	W	L	T	Pct.	Pts.	OP
Miami#	14	2	0	.875	513	298
New England	9	7	0	.563	362	352
N.Y. Jets	7	9	0	.438	332	364
Indianapolis	4	12	0	.250	239	414
Buffalo	2	14	0	.125	250	454

Central Division

	W	L	T	Pct.	Pts.	OP
Pittsburgh	9	7	0	.563	387	310
Cincinnati	8	8	0	.500	339	339
Cleveland	5	11	0	.313	250	297
Houston	3	13	0	.188	240	437

Western Division

	W	L	T	Pct.	Pts.	OP
Denver	13	3	0	.813	353	241
Seattle*	12	4	0	.750	418	282
L.A. Raiders*	11	5	0	.688	368	278
Kansas City	8	8	0	.500	314	324
San Diego	7	9	0	.438	394	413

NATIONAL CONFERENCE

Eastern Division

	W	L	T	Pct.	Pts.	OP
Washington	11	5	0	.688	426	310
N.Y. Giants*	9	7	0	.563	299	301
St. Louis	9	7	0	.563	423	345
Dallas	9	7	0	.563	308	308
Philadelphia	6	9	1	.406	278	320

Central Division

	W	L	T	Pct.	Pts.	OP
Chicago	10	6	0	.625	325	248
Green Bay	8	8	0	.500	390	309
Tampa Bay	6	10	0	.375	335	380
Detroit	4	11	1	.281	283	408
Minnesota	3	13	0	.188	276	484

Western Division

	W	L	T	Pct.	Pts.	OP
San Francisco#	15	1	0	.938	475	227
L.A. Rams*	10	6	0	.625	346	316
New Orleans	7	9	0	.438	298	361
Atlanta	4	12	0	.250	281	382

*Wild-Card qualifier for playoffs; #Top playoff seed in conference

N.Y. Giants finished ahead of St. Louis and Dallas based on best head-to-head record (3-1 to Cardinals' 2-2 and Cowboys' 1-3). St. Louis finished ahead of Dallas based on better division record (5-3 to Cowboys' 3-5).

Wild-Card playoff: SEATTLE 13, L.A. Raiders 7

Divisional playoffs: MIAMI 31, Seattle 10; Pittsburgh 24, DENVER 17

AFC Championship: MIAMI 45, Pittsburgh 28

Wild-Card playoff: N.Y. Giants 16, L.A. RAMS 13

Divisional playoffs: SAN FRANCISCO 21, N.Y. Giants 10; Chicago 23, WASHINGTON 19

NFC Championship: SAN FRANCISCO 23, Chicago 0

Super Bowl XIX: San Francisco (NFC) 38, Miami (AFC) 16, at Stanford Stadium, Stanford, California

1983

AMERICAN CONFERENCE
Eastern Division

	W	L	T	Pct.	Pts.	OP
Miami	12	4	0	.750	389	250
New England	8	8	0	.500	274	289
Buffalo	8	8	0	.500	283	351
Baltimore	7	9	0	.438	264	354
N.Y. Jets	7	9	0	.438	313	331

Central Division

	W	L	T	Pct.	Pts.	OP
Pittsburgh	10	6	0	.625	355	303
Cleveland	9	7	0	.563	356	342
Cincinnati	7	9	0	.438	346	302
Houston	2	14	0	.125	288	460

Western Division

	W	L	T	Pct.	Pts.	OP
L.A. Raiders#	12	4	0	.750	442	338
Seattle*	9	7	0	.563	403	397
Denver*	9	7	0	.563	302	327
San Diego	6	10	0	.375	358	462
Kansas City	6	10	0	.375	386	367

NATIONAL CONFERENCE
Eastern Division

	W	L	T	Pct.	Pts.	OP
Washington#	14	2	0	.875	541	332
Dallas*	12	4	0	.750	479	360
St. Louis	8	7	1	.531	374	428
Philadelphia	5	11	0	.313	233	322
N.Y. Giants	3	12	1	.219	267	347

Central Division

	W	L	T	Pct.	Pts.	OP
Detroit	9	7	0	.563	347	286
Green Bay	8	8	0	.500	429	439
Chicago	8	8	0	.500	311	301
Minnesota	8	8	0	.500	316	348
Tampa Bay	2	14	0	.125	241	380

Western Division

	W	L	T	Pct.	Pts.	OP
San Francisco	10	6	0	.625	432	293
L.A. Rams*	9	7	0	.563	361	344
New Orleans	8	8	0	.500	319	337
Atlanta	7	9	0	.438	370	389

*Wild-Card qualifier for playoffs; #Top playoff seed in conference
L.A. Raiders were top playoff seed ahead of Miami based on head-to-head victory (1-0). Seattle was second Wild Card ahead of Denver based on better division record (5-3 to Broncos' 3-5) after Cleveland was eliminated from three-way tie based on head-to-head record (Seattle and Denver 2-1 to Browns' 0-2). Seattle did not play the L.A. Raiders in the divisional playoffs because, from 1970-1989, two teams from the same division could not meet prior to the conference championship game. New England finished ahead of Buffalo based on head-to-head sweep (2-0). Baltimore finished ahead of N.Y. Jets based on better conference record (5-9 to Jets' 4-8). San Diego finished ahead of Kansas City based on head-to-head sweep (2-0). Green Bay finished ahead of Chicago based on better record against common opponents (5-5 to Bears' 4-6) after Minnesota was eliminated from three-way tie based on conference record (Chicago 7-7 and Green Bay 6-6 to Vikings' 4-8).
Wild-Card playoff: SEATTLE 31, Denver 7
Divisional playoffs: Seattle 27, MIAMI 20;
    L.A. RAIDERS 38, Pittsburgh 10
AFC Championship: L.A. RAIDERS 30, Seattle 14
Wild-Card playoff: L.A. Rams 24, DALLAS 17
Divisional playoffs: SAN FRANCISCO 24, Detroit 23;
    WASHINGTON 51, L.A. Rams 7
NFC Championship: WASHINGTON 24, San Francisco 21
Super Bowl XVIII: L.A. Raiders (AFC) 38, Washington (NFC) 9,
    at Tampa Stadium, Tampa, Florida

1982

AMERICAN CONFERENCE

	W	L	T	Pct.	Pts.	OP
L.A. Raiders#	8	1	0	.889	260	200
Miami	7	2	0	.778	198	131
Cincinnati	7	2	0	.778	232	177
Pittsburgh	6	3	0	.667	204	146
San Diego	6	3	0	.667	288	221
N.Y. Jets	6	3	0	.667	245	166
New England	5	4	0	.556	143	157
Cleveland	4	5	0	.444	140	182
Buffalo	4	5	0	.444	150	154
Seattle	4	5	0	.444	127	147
Kansas City	3	6	0	.333	176	184
Denver	2	7	0	.222	148	226
Houston	1	8	0	.111	136	245
Baltimore	0	8	1	.056	113	236

NATIONAL CONFERENCE

	W	L	T	Pct.	Pts.	OP
Washington#	8	1	0	.889	190	128
Dallas	6	3	0	.667	226	145
Green Bay	5	3	1	.611	226	169
Minnesota	5	4	0	.556	187	198
Atlanta	5	4	0	.556	183	199
St. Louis	5	4	0	.556	135	170
Tampa Bay	5	4	0	.556	158	178
Detroit	4	5	0	.444	181	176
New Orleans	4	5	0	.444	129	160
N.Y. Giants	4	5	0	.444	164	160
San Francisco	3	6	0	.333	209	206
Chicago	3	6	0	.333	141	174
Philadelphia	3	6	0	.333	191	195
L.A. Rams	2	7	0	.222	200	250

As the result of a 57-day players' strike, the 1982 NFL regular season schedule was reduced from 16 weeks to 9. At the conclusion of the regular season, the NFL conducted a 16-team postseason Super Bowl Tournament. Eight teams from each conference were seeded 1-8 based on their records during the season.
#Top playoff seed in conference
Miami finished ahead of Cincinnati based on better conference record (6-1 to Bengals' 6-2). Pittsburgh finished ahead of San Diego based on better record against common opponents (3-1 to Chargers' 2-1) after N.Y. Jets were eliminated from three-way tie based on conference record (Pittsburgh and San Diego 5-3 to Jets' 2-3). Cleveland finished ahead of Buffalo and Seattle based on better conference record (4-3 to Bills' 3-3 to Seahawks' 3-5). Buffalo finished ahead of Seattle based on better conference record (3-3 to Seahawks' 3-5). Minnesota (4-1), Atlanta (4-3), St. Louis (5-4), Tampa Bay (3-3) seeds were determined by best won-lost record in conference games. Detroit finished ahead of New Orleans and the N.Y. Giants based on best conference record (4-4 to Saints' 3-5 to Giants' 3-5). San Francisco finished ahead of Chicago, and Chicago finished ahead of Philadelphia, based on conference record (49ers' 2-3 to Bears' 2-5 to Eagles' 1-5).
First round playoff: MIAMI 28, New England 13;
    L.A. RAIDERS 27, Cleveland 10;
    N.Y. Jets 44, CINCINNATI 17;
    San Diego 31, PITTSBURGH 28
Second round playoff: N.Y. Jets 17, L.A. RAIDERS 14;
    MIAMI 34, San Diego 13
AFC Championship: MIAMI 14, N.Y. Jets 0
First round playoff: WASHINGTON 31, Detroit 7;
    GREEN BAY 41, St. Louis 16;
    MINNESOTA 30, Atlanta 24;
    DALLAS 30, Tampa Bay 17
Second round playoff: WASHINGTON 21, Minnesota 7;
    DALLAS 37, Green Bay 26
NFC Championship: WASHINGTON 31, Dallas 17
Super Bowl XVII: Washington (NFC) 27, Miami (AFC) 17,
    at Rose Bowl, Pasadena, California

1981

AMERICAN CONFERENCE

Eastern Division

	W	L	T	Pct.	Pts.	OP
Miami	11	4	1	.719	345	275
N.Y. Jets*	10	5	1	.656	355	287
Buffalo*	10	6	0	.625	311	276
Baltimore	2	14	0	.125	259	533
New England	2	14	0	.125	322	370

Central Division

	W	L	T	Pct.	Pts.	OP
Cincinnati#	12	4	0	.750	421	304
Pittsburgh	8	8	0	.500	356	297
Houston	7	9	0	.438	281	355
Cleveland	5	11	0	.313	276	375

Western Division

	W	L	T	Pct.	Pts.	OP
San Diego	10	6	0	.625	478	390
Denver	10	6	0	.625	321	289
Kansas City	9	7	0	.563	343	290
Oakland	7	9	0	.438	273	343
Seattle	6	10	0	.375	322	388

NATIONAL CONFERENCE

Eastern Division

	W	L	T	Pct.	Pts.	OP
Dallas	12	4	0	.750	367	277
Philadelphia*	10	6	0	.625	368	221
N.Y. Giants*	9	7	0	.563	295	257
Washington	8	8	0	.500	347	349
St. Louis	7	9	0	.438	315	408

Central Division

	W	L	T	Pct.	Pts.	OP
Tampa Bay	9	7	0	.563	315	268
Detroit	8	8	0	.500	397	322
Green Bay	8	8	0	.500	324	361
Minnesota	7	9	0	.438	325	369
Chicago	6	10	0	.375	253	324

Western Division

	W	L	T	Pct.	Pts.	OP
San Francisco#	13	3	0	.813	357	250
Atlanta	7	9	0	.438	426	355
Los Angeles	6	10	0	.375	303	351
New Orleans	4	12	0	.250	207	378

*Wild-Card qualifier for playoffs; #Top playoff seed in conference
Baltimore finished ahead of New England based on head-to-head sweep (2-0). San Diego finished ahead of Denver based on better division record (6-2 to Broncos' 5-3). Buffalo was second Wild Card based on head-to-head victory over Denver (1-0). Detroit finished ahead of Green Bay based on better record against common opponents (5-5 to Packers' 4-6).
Wild-Card playoff: Buffalo 31, N.Y. JETS 27
Divisional playoffs: San Diego 41, MIAMI 38 (OT);
CINCINNATI 28, Buffalo 21
AFC Championship: CINCINNATI 27, San Diego 7
Wild-Card playoff: N.Y. Giants 27, PHILADELPHIA 21
Divisional playoffs: DALLAS 38, Tampa Bay 0;
SAN FRANCISCO 38, N.Y. Giants 24
NFC Championship: SAN FRANCISCO 28, Dallas 27
Super Bowl XVI: San Francisco (NFC) 26, Cincinnati (AFC) 21,
at Silverdome, Pontiac, Michigan

1980

AMERICAN CONFERENCE

Eastern Division

	W	L	T	Pct.	Pts.	OP
Buffalo	11	5	0	.688	320	260
New England	10	6	0	.625	441	325
Miami	8	8	0	.500	266	305
Baltimore	7	9	0	.438	355	387
N.Y. Jets	4	12	0	.250	302	395

Central Division

	W	L	T	Pct.	Pts.	OP
Cleveland	11	5	0	.688	357	310
Houston*	11	5	0	.688	295	251
Pittsburgh	9	7	0	.563	352	313
Cincinnati	6	10	0	.375	244	312

Western Division

	W	L	T	Pct.	Pts.	OP
San Diego#	11	5	0	.688	418	327
Oakland*	11	5	0	.688	364	306
Kansas City	8	8	0	.500	319	336
Denver	8	8	0	.500	310	323
Seattle	4	12	0	.250	291	408

NATIONAL CONFERENCE

Eastern Division

	W	L	T	Pct.	Pts.	OP
Philadelphia	12	4	0	.750	384	222
Dallas*	12	4	0	.750	454	311
Washington	6	10	0	.375	261	293
St. Louis	5	11	0	.313	299	350
N.Y. Giants	4	12	0	.250	249	425

Central Division

	W	L	T	Pct.	Pts.	OP
Minnesota	9	7	0	.563	317	308
Detroit	9	7	0	.563	334	272
Chicago	7	9	0	.438	304	264
Tampa Bay	5	10	1	.344	271	341
Green Bay	5	10	1	.344	231	371

Western Division

	W	L	T	Pct.	Pts.	OP
Atlanta#	12	4	0	.750	405	272
Los Angeles*	11	5	0	.688	424	289
San Francisco	6	10	0	.375	320	415
New Orleans	1	15	0	.063	291	487

*Wild-Card qualifier for playoffs; #Top playoff seed in conference
San Diego was top playoff seed based on better conference record than Cleveland and Buffalo (9-3 to Browns' 8-4 and Bills' 8-4). Cleveland was second playoff seed based on better record against common opponents (5-2 to Bills' 5-3). Cleveland finished ahead of Houston based on better conference record (8-4 to Oilers' 7-5). Oakland was first Wild Card based on better conference record than Houston (9-3 to Oilers' 7-5). San Diego finished ahead of Oakland based on better net points in division games (plus 60 net points to Raiders' plus 37). Oakland did not play San Diego in the divisional playoffs because, from 1970-1989, two teams from the same division could not meet prior to the conference championship game. Kansas City finished ahead of Denver based on head-to-head sweep (2-0). Atlanta was top playoff seed based on head-to-head victory over Philadelphia (1-0). Philadelphia finished ahead of Dallas based on better net points in division games (plus 84 net points to Cowboys' plus 50). Minnesota finished ahead of Detroit based on better conference record (8-4 to Lions' 9-5). Tampa Bay finished ahead of Green Bay based on better head-to-head record (1-0-1 to Packers' 0-1-1).
Wild-Card playoff: OAKLAND 27, Houston 7
Divisional playoffs: SAN DIEGO 20, Buffalo 14;
Oakland 14, CLEVELAND 12
AFC Championship: Oakland 34, SAN DIEGO 27
Wild-Card playoff: DALLAS 34, Los Angeles 13
Divisional playoffs: PHILADELPHIA 31, Minnesota 16;
Dallas 30, ATLANTA 27
NFC Championship: PHILADELPHIA 20, Dallas 7
Super Bowl XV: Oakland (AFC) 27, Philadelphia (NFC) 10,
at Louisiana Superdome, New Orleans, Louisiana

1979

AMERICAN CONFERENCE

Eastern Division

	W	L	T	Pct.	Pts.	OP
Miami	10	6	0	.625	341	257
New England	9	7	0	.563	411	326
N.Y. Jets	8	8	0	.500	337	383
Buffalo	7	9	0	.438	268	279
Baltimore	5	11	0	.313	271	351

Central Division

	W	L	T	Pct.	Pts.	OP
Pittsburgh	12	4	0	.750	416	262
Houston*	11	5	0	.688	362	331
Cleveland	9	7	0	.563	359	352
Cincinnati	4	12	0	.250	337	421

Western Division

	W	L	T	Pct.	Pts.	OP
San Diego#	12	4	0	.750	411	246
Denver*	10	6	0	.625	289	262
Seattle	9	7	0	.563	378	372
Oakland	9	7	0	.563	365	337
Kansas City	7	9	0	.438	238	262

NATIONAL CONFERENCE

Eastern Division

	W	L	T	Pct.	Pts.	OP
Dallas#	11	5	0	.688	371	313
Philadelphia*	11	5	0	.688	339	282
Washington	10	6	0	.625	348	295
N.Y. Giants	6	10	0	.375	237	323
St. Louis	5	11	0	.313	307	358

Central Division

	W	L	T	Pct.	Pts.	OP
Tampa Bay	10	6	0	.625	273	237
Chicago*	10	6	0	.625	306	249
Minnesota	7	9	0	.438	259	337
Green Bay	5	11	0	.313	246	316
Detroit	2	14	0	.125	219	365

Western Division

	W	L	T	Pct.	Pts.	OP
Los Angeles	9	7	0	.563	323	309
New Orleans	8	8	0	.500	370	360
Atlanta	6	10	0	.375	300	388
San Francisco	2	14	0	.125	308	416

*Wild-Card qualifier for playoffs; #Top playoff seed in conference
San Diego was top playoff seed based on head-to-head victory over
  Pittsburgh (1-0). Seattle finished ahead of Oakland based on
  head-to-head sweep (2-0). Dallas finished ahead of Philadelphia
  based on better conference record (10-2 to Eagles' 9-3).
  Philadelphia did not play Dallas in the divisional playoffs because,
  from 1970-1989, two teams from the same division could not
  meet prior to the conference championship game. Tampa Bay fin-
  ished ahead of Chicago based on a better division record (6-2 to
  Bears' 5-3). Chicago was second Wild Card ahead of Washington
  based on better net points in all games (57 to Redskins' 53).
Wild-Card playoff: HOUSTON 13, Denver 7
Divisional playoffs: Houston 17, SAN DIEGO 14;
  PITTSBURGH 34, Miami 14
AFC Championship: PITTSBURGH 27, Houston 13
Wild-Card playoff: PHILADELPHIA 27, Chicago 17
Divisional playoffs: TAMPA BAY 24, Philadelphia 17;
  Los Angeles 21, DALLAS 19
NFC Championship: Los Angeles 9, TAMPA BAY 0
Super Bowl XIV: Pittsburgh (AFC) 31, Los Angeles (NFC) 19,
  at Rose Bowl, Pasadena, California

1978

AMERICAN CONFERENCE

Eastern Division

	W	L	T	Pct.	Pts.	OP
New England	11	5	0	.688	358	286
Miami*	11	5	0	.688	372	254
N.Y. Jets	8	8	0	.500	359	364
Buffalo	5	11	0	.313	302	354
Baltimore	5	11	0	.313	239	421

Central Division

	W	L	T	Pct.	Pts.	OP
Pittsburgh#	14	2	0	.875	356	195
Houston*	10	6	0	.625	283	298
Cleveland	8	8	0	.500	334	356
Cincinnati	4	12	0	.250	252	284

Western Division

	W	L	T	Pct.	Pts.	OP
Denver	10	6	0	.625	282	198
Oakland	9	7	0	.563	311	283
Seattle	9	7	0	.563	345	358
San Diego	9	7	0	.563	355	309
Kansas City	4	12	0	.250	243	327

NATIONAL CONFERENCE

Eastern Division

	W	L	T	Pct.	Pts.	OP
Dallas	12	4	0	.750	384	208
Philadelphia*	9	7	0	.563	270	250
Washington	8	8	0	.500	273	283
St. Louis	6	10	0	.375	248	296
N.Y. Giants	6	10	0	.375	264	298

Central Division

	W	L	T	Pct.	Pts.	OP
Minnesota	8	7	1	.531	294	306
Green Bay	8	7	1	.531	249	269
Detroit	7	9	0	.438	290	300
Chicago	7	9	0	.438	253	274
Tampa Bay	5	11	0	.313	241	259

Western Division

	W	L	T	Pct.	Pts.	OP
Los Angeles#	12	4	0	.750	316	245
Atlanta*	9	7	0	.563	240	290
New Orleans	7	9	0	.438	281	298
San Francisco	2	14	0	.125	219	350

*Wild-Card qualifier for playoffs; #Top playoff seed in conference
New England finished ahead of Miami based on better division
  record (6-2 to Dolphins' 5-3). Buffalo finished ahead of Baltimore
  based on head-to-head sweep (2-0). Oakland finished ahead of
  Seattle and San Diego based on better record against common
  opponents (6-2 to Seahawks' 5-3 and Chargers' 4-4). Atlanta
  was first Wild Card based on better conference record than
  Philadelphia (8-4 to Eagles' 6-6). Houston did not play Pittsburgh, and Atlanta did not play Los Angeles in the divisional playoffs because, from 1970-1989, two teams from the same division could not meet prior to the conference championship game.
  St. Louis finished ahead of N.Y. Giants based on better division
  record (3-5 to Giants' 2-6). Minnesota finished ahead of Green
  Bay based on better head-to-head record (1-0-1). Detroit finished
  ahead of Chicago based on better division record (4-4 to Bears'
  3-5).
Wild-Card playoff: Houston 17, MIAMI 9
Divisional playoffs: Houston 31, NEW ENGLAND 14;
  PITTSBURGH 33, Denver 10
AFC Championship: PITTSBURGH 34, Houston 5
Wild-Card playoff: ATLANTA 14, Philadelphia 13
Divisional playoffs: DALLAS 27, Atlanta 20;
  LOS ANGELES 34, Minnesota 10
NFC Championship: Dallas 28, LOS ANGELES 0
Super Bowl XIII: Pittsburgh (AFC) 35, Dallas (NFC) 31,
  at Orange Bowl, Miami, Florida

1977

AMERICAN CONFERENCE

Eastern Division

	W	L	T	Pct.	Pts.	OP
Baltimore	10	4	0	.714	295	221
Miami	10	4	0	.714	313	197
New England	9	5	0	.643	278	217
Buffalo	3	11	0	.214	160	313
N.Y. Jets	3	11	0	.214	191	300

Central Division

	W	L	T	Pct.	Pts.	OP
Pittsburgh	9	5	0	.643	283	243
Cincinnati	8	6	0	.571	238	235
Houston	8	6	0	.571	299	230
Cleveland	6	8	0	.429	269	267

Western Division

	W	L	T	Pct.	Pts.	OP
Denver#	12	2	0	.857	274	148
Oakland*	11	3	0	.786	351	230
San Diego	7	7	0	.500	222	205
Seattle	5	9	0	.357	282	373
Kansas City	2	12	0	.143	225	349

NATIONAL CONFERENCE

Eastern Division

	W	L	T	Pct.	Pts.	OP
Dallas#	12	2	0	.857	345	212
Washington	9	5	0	.643	196	189
St. Louis	7	7	0	.500	272	287
Philadelphia	5	9	0	.357	220	207
N.Y. Giants	5	9	0	.357	181	265

Central Division

	W	L	T	Pct.	Pts.	OP
Minnesota	9	5	0	.643	231	227
Chicago*	9	5	0	.643	255	253
Detroit	6	8	0	.429	183	252
Green Bay	4	10	0	.286	134	219
Tampa Bay	2	12	0	.143	103	223

Western Division

	W	L	T	Pct.	Pts.	OP
Los Angeles	10	4	0	.714	302	146
Atlanta	7	7	0	.500	179	129
San Francisco	5	9	0	.357	220	260
New Orleans	3	11	0	.214	232	336

Wild-Card qualifier for playoffs; #Top playoff seed in conference

Baltimore finished ahead of Miami based on better conference record (9-3 to Dolphins' 8-4). Buffalo finished ahead of N.Y. Jets based on better strength of schedule (.582 to Jets' .536). Cincinnati finished ahead of Houston based on better division record (6-3 to Oilers' 5-4). Oakland did not play Denver in the divisional playoffs because, from 1970-1989, two teams from the same division could not meet prior to the conference championship game. Minnesota finished ahead of Chicago based on fewer losses by common opponents (11 losses to 14 losses by the Bears' opponents). Chicago won Wild Card ahead of Washington based on better net points in conference games (48 to Redskins' 4). Philadelphia finished ahead of N.Y. Giants based on head-to-head sweep (2-0).

Divisional playoffs: DENVER 34, Pittsburgh 21; Oakland 37, BALTIMORE 31 (OT)
AFC Championship: DENVER 20, Oakland 17
Divisional playoffs: DALLAS 37, Chicago 7; Minnesota 14, LOS ANGELES 7
NFC Championship: DALLAS 23, Minnesota 6
Super Bowl XII: Dallas (NFC) 27, Denver (AFC) 10, at Louisiana Superdome, New Orleans, Louisiana

1976

AMERICAN CONFERENCE

Eastern Division

	W	L	T	Pct.	Pts.	OP
Baltimore	11	3	0	.786	417	246
New England*	11	3	0	.786	376	236
Miami	6	8	0	.429	263	264
N.Y. Jets	3	11	0	.214	169	383
Buffalo	2	12	0	.143	245	363

Central Division

	W	L	T	Pct.	Pts.	OP
Pittsburgh	10	4	0	.714	342	138
Cincinnati	10	4	0	.714	335	210
Cleveland	9	5	0	.643	267	287
Houston	5	9	0	.357	222	273

Western Division

	W	L	T	Pct.	Pts.	OP
Oakland#	13	1	0	.929	350	237
Denver	9	5	0	.643	315	206
San Diego	6	8	0	.429	248	285
Kansas City	5	9	0	.357	290	376
Tampa Bay	0	14	0	.000	125	412

NATIONAL CONFERENCE

Eastern Division

	W	L	T	Pct.	Pts.	OP
Dallas	11	3	0	.786	296	194
Washington*	10	4	0	.714	291	217
St. Louis	10	4	0	.714	309	267
Philadelphia	4	10	0	.286	165	286
N.Y. Giants	3	11	0	.214	170	250

Central Division

	W	L	T	Pct.	Pts.	OP
Minnesota#	11	2	1	.821	305	176
Chicago	7	7	0	.500	253	216
Detroit	6	8	0	.429	262	220
Green Bay	5	9	0	.357	218	299

Western Division

	W	L	T	Pct.	Pts.	OP
Los Angeles	10	3	1	.750	351	190
San Francisco	8	6	0	.571	270	190
Atlanta	4	10	0	.286	172	312
New Orleans	4	10	0	.286	253	346
Seattle	2	12	0	.143	229	429

Wild-Card qualifier for playoffs; #Top playoff seed in conference

Baltimore finished ahead of New England based on better division record (7-1 to Patriots' 6-2). Pittsburgh finished ahead of Cincinnati based on head-to-head sweep (2-0). Washington finished ahead of St. Louis based on head-to-head sweep (2-0). Atlanta finished ahead of New Orleans based on better division record (2-4 to Saints' 1-5).

Divisional playoffs: OAKLAND 24, New England 21; Pittsburgh 40, BALTIMORE 14
AFC Championship: OAKLAND 24, Pittsburgh 7
Divisional playoffs: MINNESOTA 35, Washington 20; Los Angeles 14, DALLAS 12
NFC Championship: MINNESOTA 24, Los Angeles 13
Super Bowl XI: Oakland (AFC) 32, Minnesota (NFC) 14, at Rose Bowl, Pasadena, California

1975

AMERICAN CONFERENCE
Eastern Division

	W	L	T	Pct.	Pts.	OP
Baltimore	10	4	0	.714	395	269
Miami	10	4	0	.714	357	222
Buffalo	8	6	0	.571	420	355
N.Y. Jets	3	11	0	.214	258	433
New England	3	11	0	.214	258	358

Central Division

	W	L	T	Pct.	Pts.	OP
Pittsburgh#	12	2	0	.857	373	162
Cincinnati*	11	3	0	.786	340	246
Houston	10	4	0	.714	293	226
Cleveland	3	11	0	.214	218	372

Western Division

	W	L	T	Pct.	Pts.	OP
Oakland	11	3	0	.786	375	255
Denver	6	8	0	.429	254	307
Kansas City	5	9	0	.357	282	341
San Diego	2	12	0	.143	189	345

NATIONAL CONFERENCE
Eastern Division

	W	L	T	Pct.	Pts.	OP
St. Louis	11	3	0	.786	356	276
Dallas*	10	4	0	.714	350	268
Washington	8	6	0	.571	325	276
N.Y. Giants	5	9	0	.357	216	306
Philadelphia	4	10	0	.286	225	302

Central Division

	W	L	T	Pct.	Pts.	OP
Minnesota	12	2	0	.857	377	180
Detroit	7	7	0	.500	245	262
Chicago	4	10	0	.286	191	379
Green Bay	4	10	0	.286	226	285

Western Division

	W	L	T	Pct.	Pts.	OP
Los Angeles#	12	2	0	.857	312	135
San Francisco	5	9	0	.357	255	286
Atlanta	4	10	0	.286	240	289
New Orleans	2	12	0	.143	165	360

Wild-Card qualifier for playoffs; #Top playoff seed in conference
Baltimore finished ahead of Miami based on head-to-head sweep (2-0). Cincinnati did not play Pittsburgh in the divisional playoffs because, from 1970-1989, two teams from the same division could not meet prior to the conference championship game. N.Y. Jets finished ahead of New England based on head-to-head sweep (2-0). Los Angeles was top playoff seed based on better strength of schedule than Minnesota (.383 to Vikings' .332). Chicago finished ahead of Green Bay based on better division record (2-4 to Bears' 1-5).
Divisional playoffs: PITTSBURGH 28, Baltimore 10; OAKLAND 31, Cincinnati 28
AFC Championship: PITTSBURGH 16, Oakland 10
Divisional playoffs: LOS ANGELES 35, St. Louis 23; Dallas 17, MINNESOTA 14
NFC Championship: Dallas 37, LOS ANGELES 7
Super Bowl X: Pittsburgh (AFC) 21, Dallas (NFC) 17, at Orange Bowl, Miami, Florida

From 1933-1974, sites for league/conference championship games alternated by division.

1974

AMERICAN CONFERENCE
Eastern Division

	W	L	T	Pct.	Pts.	OP
Miami	11	3	0	.786	327	216
Buffalo*	9	5	0	.643	264	244
New England	7	7	0	.500	348	289
N.Y. Jets	7	7	0	.500	279	300
Baltimore	2	12	0	.143	190	329

Central Division

	W	L	T	Pct.	Pts.	OP
Pittsburgh	10	3	1	.750	305	189
Houston	7	7	0	.500	236	282
Cincinnati	7	7	0	.500	283	259
Cleveland	4	10	0	.286	251	344

Western Division

	W	L	T	Pct.	Pts.	OP
Oakland	12	2	0	.857	355	228
Denver	7	6	1	.536	302	294
Kansas City	5	9	0	.357	233	293
San Diego	5	9	0	.357	212	285

NATIONAL CONFERENCE
Eastern Division

	W	L	T	Pct.	Pts.	OP
St. Louis	10	4	0	.714	285	218
Washington*	10	4	0	.714	320	196
Dallas	8	6	0	.571	297	235
Philadelphia	7	7	0	.500	242	217
N.Y. Giants	2	12	0	.143	195	299

Central Division

	W	L	T	Pct.	Pts.	OP
Minnesota	10	4	0	.714	310	195
Detroit	7	7	0	.500	256	270
Green Bay	6	8	0	.429	210	206
Chicago	4	10	0	.286	152	279

Western Division

	W	L	T	Pct.	Pts.	OP
Los Angeles	10	4	0	.714	263	181
San Francisco	6	8	0	.429	226	236
New Orleans	5	9	0	.357	166	263
Atlanta	3	11	0	.214	111	271

Wild-Card qualifier for playoffs
New England finished ahead of N.Y. Jets based on better record against common opponents (5-4 to Jets' 4-5). Houston finished ahead of Cincinnati based on head-to-head sweep (2-0). Kansas City finished ahead of San Diego based on better record against common opponents (4-6 to Chargers' 3-7). St. Louis finished ahead of Washington based on head-to-head sweep (2-0).
Divisional playoffs: OAKLAND 28, Miami 26; PITTSBURGH 32, Buffalo 14
AFC Championship: Pittsburgh 24, OAKLAND 13
Divisional playoffs: MINNESOTA 30, St. Louis 14; LOS ANGELES 19, Washington 10
NFC Championship: MINNESOTA 14, Los Angeles 10
Super Bowl IX: Pittsburgh (AFC) 16, Minnesota (NFC) 6, at Tulane Stadium, New Orleans, Louisiana

1973

AMERICAN CONFERENCE

Eastern Division

	W	L	T	Pct.	Pts.	OP
Miami	12	2	0	.857	343	150
Buffalo	9	5	0	.643	259	230
New England	5	9	0	.357	258	300
N.Y. Jets	4	10	0	.286	240	306
Baltimore	4	10	0	.286	226	341

Central Division

	W	L	T	Pct.	Pts.	OP
Cincinnati	10	4	0	.714	286	231
Pittsburgh*	10	4	0	.714	347	210
Cleveland	7	5	2	.571	234	255
Houston	1	13	0	.071	199	447

Western Division

	W	L	T	Pct.	Pts.	OP
Oakland	9	4	1	.679	292	175
Kansas City	7	5	2	.571	231	192
Denver	7	5	2	.571	354	296
San Diego	2	11	1	.179	188	386

NATIONAL CONFERENCE

Eastern Division

	W	L	T	Pct.	Pts.	OP
Dallas	10	4	0	.714	382	203
Washington*	10	4	0	.714	325	198
Philadelphia	5	8	1	.393	310	393
St. Louis	4	9	1	.321	286	365
N.Y. Giants	2	11	1	.179	226	362

Central Division

	W	L	T	Pct.	Pts.	OP
Minnesota	12	2	0	.857	296	168
Detroit	6	7	1	.464	271	247
Green Bay	5	7	2	.429	202	259
Chicago	3	11	0	.214	195	334

Western Division

	W	L	T	Pct.	Pts.	OP
Los Angeles	12	2	0	.857	388	178
Atlanta	9	5	0	.643	318	224
San Francisco	5	9	0	.357	262	319
New Orleans	5	9	0	.357	163	312

*Wild-Card qualifier for playoffs
Cincinnati finished ahead of Pittsburgh based on better conference record (8-3 to Steelers' 7-4). N.Y. Jets finished ahead of Baltimore based on head-to-head sweep (2-0). Kansas City finished ahead of Denver based on better division record (4-2 to Broncos' 3-2-1). Dallas finished ahead of Washington based on better point differential in head-to-head games (13 points). San Francisco finished ahead of New Orleans based on better division record (2-4 to Saints' 1-5).
Divisional playoffs: OAKLAND 33, Pittsburgh 14; MIAMI 34, Cincinnati 16
AFC Championship: MIAMI 27, Oakland 10
Divisional playoffs: MINNESOTA 27, Washington 20; DALLAS 27, Los Angeles 16
NFC Championship: Minnesota 27, DALLAS 10
Super Bowl VIII: Miami (AFC) 24, Minnesota (NFC) 7, at Rice Stadium, Houston, Texas

1972

AMERICAN CONFERENCE

Eastern Division

	W	L	T	Pct.	Pts.	OP
Miami	14	0	0	1.000	385	171
N.Y. Jets	7	7	0	.500	367	324
Baltimore	5	9	0	.357	235	252
Buffalo	4	9	1	.321	257	377
New England	3	11	0	.214	192	446

Central Division

	W	L	T	Pct.	Pts.	OP
Pittsburgh	11	3	0	.786	343	175
Cleveland*	10	4	0	.714	268	249
Cincinnati	8	6	0	.571	299	229
Houston	1	13	0	.071	164	380

Western Division

	W	L	T	Pct.	Pts.	OP
Oakland	10	3	1	.750	365	248
Kansas City	8	6	0	.571	287	254
Denver	5	9	0	.357	325	350
San Diego	4	9	1	.321	264	344

NATIONAL CONFERENCE

Eastern Division

	W	L	T	Pct.	Pts.	OP
Washington	11	3	0	.786	336	218
Dallas*	10	4	0	.714	319	240
N.Y. Giants	8	6	0	.571	331	247
St. Louis	4	9	1	.321	193	303
Philadelphia	2	11	1	.179	145	352

Central Division

	W	L	T	Pct.	Pts.	OP
Green Bay	10	4	0	.714	304	226
Detroit	8	5	1	.607	339	290
Minnesota	7	7	0	.500	301	252
Chicago	4	9	1	.321	225	275

Western Division

	W	L	T	Pct.	Pts.	OP
San Francisco	8	5	1	.607	353	249
Atlanta	7	7	0	.500	269	274
Los Angeles	6	7	1	.464	291	286
New Orleans	2	11	1	.179	215	361

*Wild-Card qualifier for playoffs
Dallas did not play Washington in the divisional playoffs because, from 1970-1989, two teams from the same division could not meet prior to the conference championship game.
Divisional playoffs: PITTSBURGH 13, Oakland 7; MIAMI 20, Cleveland 14
AFC Championship: Miami 21, PITTSBURGH 17
Divisional playoffs: Dallas 30, SAN FRANCISCO 28; WASHINGTON 16, Green Bay 3
NFC Championship: WASHINGTON 26, Dallas 3
Super Bowl VII: Miami (AFC) 14, Washington (NFC) 7, at Memorial Coliseum, Los Angeles, California

1971

AMERICAN CONFERENCE
Eastern Division

	W	L	T	Pct.	Pts.	OP
Miami	10	3	1	.769	315	174
Baltimore*	10	4	0	.714	313	140
New England	6	8	0	.429	238	325
N.Y. Jets	6	8	0	.429	212	299
Buffalo	1	13	0	.071	184	394

Central Division

	W	L	T	Pct.	Pts.	OP
Cleveland	9	5	0	.643	285	273
Pittsburgh	6	8	0	.429	246	292
Houston	4	9	1	.308	251	330
Cincinnati	4	10	0	.286	284	265

Western Division

	W	L	T	Pct.	Pts.	OP
Kansas City	10	3	1	.769	302	208
Oakland	8	4	2	.667	344	278
San Diego	6	8	0	.429	311	341
Denver	4	9	1	.308	203	275

NATIONAL CONFERENCE
Eastern Division

	W	L	T	Pct.	Pts.	OP
Dallas	11	3	0	.786	406	222
Washington*	9	4	1	.692	276	190
Philadelphia	6	7	1	.462	221	302
St. Louis	4	9	1	.308	231	279
N.Y. Giants	4	10	0	.286	228	362

Central Division

	W	L	T	Pct.	Pts.	OP
Minnesota	11	3	0	.786	245	139
Detroit	7	6	1	.538	341	286
Chicago	6	8	0	.429	185	276
Green Bay	4	8	2	.333	274	298

Western Division

	W	L	T	Pct.	Pts.	OP
San Francisco	9	5	0	.643	300	216
Los Angeles	8	5	1	.615	313	260
Atlanta	7	6	1	.538	274	277
New Orleans	4	8	2	.333	266	347

*Wild-Card qualifier for playoffs
New England finished ahead of N.Y. Jets based on better strength of schedule (.537 to Jets' .510).
Divisional playoffs: Miami 27, KANSAS CITY 24 (OT); Baltimore 20, CLEVELAND 3
AFC Championship: MIAMI 21, Baltimore 0
Divisional playoffs: Dallas 20, MINNESOTA 12; SAN FRANCISCO 24, Washington 20
NFC Championship: DALLAS 14, San Francisco 3
Super Bowl VI: Dallas (NFC) 24, Miami (AFC) 3, at Tulane Stadium, New Orleans, Louisiana

From 1920-1971, tie games were not included in winning percentage.

1970

AMERICAN CONFERENCE
Eastern Division

	W	L	T	Pct.	Pts.	OP
Baltimore	11	2	1	.846	321	234
Miami*	10	4	0	.714	297	228
N.Y. Jets	4	10	0	.286	255	286
Buffalo	3	10	1	.231	204	337
Boston Patriots	2	12	0	.143	149	361

Central Division

	W	L	T	Pct.	Pts.	OP
Cincinnati	8	6	0	.571	312	255
Cleveland	7	7	0	.500	286	265
Pittsburgh	5	9	0	.357	210	272
Houston	3	10	1	.231	217	352

Western Division

	W	L	T	Pct.	Pts.	OP
Oakland	8	4	2	.667	300	293
Kansas City	7	5	2	.583	272	244
San Diego	5	6	3	.455	282	278
Denver	5	8	1	.385	253	264

NATIONAL CONFERENCE
Eastern Division

	W	L	T	Pct.	Pts.	OP
Dallas	10	4	0	.714	299	221
N.Y. Giants	9	5	0	.643	301	270
St. Louis	8	5	1	.615	325	228
Washington	6	8	0	.429	297	314
Philadelphia	3	10	1	.231	241	332

Central Division

	W	L	T	Pct.	Pts.	OP
Minnesota	12	2	0	.857	335	143
Detroit*	10	4	0	.714	347	202
Green Bay	6	8	0	.429	196	293
Chicago	6	8	0	.429	256	261

Western Division

	W	L	T	Pct.	Pts.	OP
San Francisco	10	3	1	.769	352	267
Los Angeles	9	4	1	.692	325	202
Atlanta	4	8	2	.333	206	261
New Orleans	2	11	1	.154	172	347

*Wild-Card qualifier for playoffs
Miami did not play Baltimore, and Detroit did not play Minnesota, in the divisional playoffs because, from 1970-1989, two teams from the same division could not meet prior to the conference championship game. Green Bay finished ahead of Chicago based on better division record (2-4 to Bears' 1-5).
Divisional playoffs: BALTIMORE 17, Cincinnati 0; OAKLAND 21, Miami 14
AFC Championship: BALTIMORE 27, Oakland 17
Divisional playoffs: DALLAS 5, Detroit 0; San Francisco 17, MINNESOTA 14
NFC Championship: Dallas 17, SAN FRANCISCO 10
Super Bowl V: Baltimore (AFC) 16, Dallas (NFC) 13, at Orange Bowl, Miami, Florida

1969 NFL

EASTERN CONFERENCE
Capitol Division

	W	L	T	Pct.	Pts.	OP
Dallas	11	2	1	.846	369	223
Washington	7	5	2	.583	307	319
New Orleans	5	9	0	.357	311	393
Philadelphia	4	9	1	.308	279	377

Century Division

	W	L	T	Pct.	Pts.	OP
Cleveland	10	3	1	.769	351	300
N.Y. Giants	6	8	0	.429	264	298
St. Louis	4	9	1	.308	314	389
Pittsburgh	1	13	0	.071	218	404

WESTERN CONFERENCE
Coastal Division

	W	L	T	Pct.	Pts.	OP
Los Angeles	11	3	0	.786	320	243
Baltimore	8	5	1	.615	279	268
Atlanta	6	8	0	.429	276	268
San Francisco	4	8	2	.333	277	319

Central Division

	W	L	T	Pct.	Pts.	OP
Minnesota	12	2	0	.857	379	133
Detroit	9	4	1	.692	259	188
Green Bay	8	6	0	.571	269	221
Chicago	1	13	0	.071	210	339

Conference championships: Cleveland 38, DALLAS 14;
 MINNESOTA 23, Los Angeles 20
NFL championship: MINNESOTA 27, Cleveland 7
Super Bowl IV: Kansas City (AFL) 23, Minnesota (NFL) 7,
 at Tulane Stadium, New Orleans, Louisiana

1969 AFL

EASTERN DIVISION

	W	L	T	Pct.	Pts.	OP
N.Y. Jets	10	4	0	.714	353	269
Houston	6	6	2	.500	278	279
Boston Patriots	4	10	0	.286	266	316
Buffalo	4	10	0	.286	230	359
Miami	3	10	1	.231	233	332

WESTERN DIVISION

	W	L	T	Pct.	Pts.	OP
Oakland	12	1	1	.923	377	242
Kansas City	11	3	0	.786	359	177
San Diego	8	6	0	.571	288	276
Denver	5	8	1	.385	297	344
Cincinnati	4	9	1	.308	280	367

Divisional playoffs: Kansas City 13, N.Y. JETS 6;
 OAKLAND 56, Houston 7
AFL championship: Kansas City 17, OAKLAND 7

1968 NFL

EASTERN CONFERENCE
Capitol Division

	W	L	T	Pct.	Pts.	OP
Dallas	12	2	0	.857	431	186
N.Y. Giants	7	7	0	.500	294	325
Washington	5	9	0	.357	249	358
Philadelphia	2	12	0	.143	202	351

Century Division

	W	L	T	Pct.	Pts.	OP
Cleveland	10	4	0	.714	394	273
St. Louis	9	4	1	.692	325	289
New Orleans	4	9	1	.308	246	327
Pittsburgh	2	11	1	.154	244	397

WESTERN CONFERENCE
Coastal Division

	W	L	T	Pct.	Pts.	OP
Baltimore	13	1	0	.929	402	144
Los Angeles	10	3	1	.769	312	200
San Francisco	7	6	1	.538	303	310
Atlanta	2	12	0	.143	170	389

Central Division

	W	L	T	Pct.	Pts.	OP
Minnesota	8	6	0	.571	282	242
Chicago	7	7	0	.500	250	333
Green Bay	6	7	1	.462	281	227
Detroit	4	8	2	.333	207	241

Conference championships: CLEVELAND 31, Dallas 20;
 BALTIMORE 24, Minnesota 14
NFL championship: Baltimore 34, CLEVELAND 0
Super Bowl III: N.Y. Jets (AFL) 16, Baltimore (NFL) 7,
 at Orange Bowl, Miami, Florida

1968 AFL

EASTERN DIVISION

	W	L	T	Pct.	Pts.	OP
N.Y. Jets	11	3	0	.786	419	280
Houston	7	7	0	.500	303	248
Miami	5	8	1	.385	276	355
Boston Patriots	4	10	0	.286	229	406
Buffalo	1	12	1	.077	199	367

WESTERN DIVISION

	W	L	T	Pct.	Pts.	OP
Oakland	12	2	0	.857	453	233
Kansas City	12	2	0	.857	371	170
San Diego	9	5	0	.643	382	310
Denver	5	9	0	.357	255	404
Cincinnati	3	11	0	.214	215	329

Western Division playoff: OAKLAND 41, Kansas City 6
AFL championship: N.Y. JETS 27, Oakland 23

1967 NFL

EASTERN CONFERENCE
Capitol Division

	W	L	T	Pct.	Pts.	OP
Dallas	9	5	0	.643	342	268
Philadelphia	6	7	1	.462	351	409
Washington	5	6	3	.455	347	353
New Orleans	3	11	0	.214	233	379

Century Division

	W	L	T	Pct.	Pts.	OP
Cleveland	9	5	0	.643	334	297
N.Y. Giants	7	7	0	.500	369	379
St. Louis	6	7	1	.462	333	356
Pittsburgh	4	9	1	.308	281	320

WESTERN CONFERENCE
Coastal Division

	W	L	T	Pct.	Pts.	OP
Los Angeles	11	1	2	.917	398	196
Baltimore	11	1	2	.917	394	198
San Francisco	7	7	0	.500	273	337
Atlanta	1	12	1	.077	175	422

Central Division

	W	L	T	Pct.	Pts.	OP
Green Bay	9	4	1	.692	332	209
Chicago	7	6	1	.538	239	218
Detroit	5	7	2	.417	260	259
Minnesota	3	8	3	.273	233	294

*Los Angeles finished ahead of Baltimore based on better point dif-
 ferential in head-to-head games (net 24 points).*
Conference championships: DALLAS 52, Cleveland 14;
 GREEN BAY 28, Los Angeles 7
NFL championship: GREEN BAY 21, Dallas 17
Super Bowl II: Green Bay (NFL) 33, Oakland (AFL) 14,
 at Orange Bowl, Miami, Florida

1967 AFL

EASTERN DIVISION

	W	L	T	Pct.	Pts.	OP
Houston	9	4	1	.692	258	199
N.Y. Jets	8	5	1	.615	371	329
Buffalo	4	10	0	.286	237	285
Miami	4	10	0	.286	219	407
Boston Patriots	3	10	1	.231	280	389

WESTERN DIVISION

	W	L	T	Pct.	Pts.	OP
Oakland	13	1	0	.929	468	233
Kansas City	9	5	0	.643	408	254
San Diego	8	5	1	.615	360	352
Denver	3	11	0	.214	256	409

AFL championship: OAKLAND 40, Houston 7

1966 NFL

EASTERN CONFERENCE

	W	L	T	Pct.	Pts.	OP
Dallas	10	3	1	.769	445	239
Cleveland	9	5	0	.643	403	259
Philadelphia	9	5	0	.643	326	340
St. Louis	8	5	1	.615	264	265
Washington	7	7	0	.500	351	355
Pittsburgh	5	8	1	.385	316	347
Atlanta	3	11	0	.214	204	437
N.Y. Giants	1	12	1	.077	263	501

WESTERN CONFERENCE

	W	L	T	Pct.	Pts.	OP
Green Bay	12	2	0	.857	335	163
Baltimore	9	5	0	.643	314	226
Los Angeles	8	6	0	.571	289	212
San Francisco	6	6	2	.500	320	325
Chicago	5	7	2	.417	234	272
Detroit	4	9	1	.308	206	317
Minnesota	4	9	1	.308	292	304

NFL championship: Green Bay 34, DALLAS 27
Super Bowl I: Green Bay (NFL) 35, Kansas City (AFL) 10,
 at Memorial Coliseum, Los Angeles, California

1966 AFL

EASTERN DIVISION

	W	L	T	Pct.	Pts.	OP
Buffalo	9	4	1	.692	358	255
Boston Patriots	8	4	2	.677	315	283
N.Y. Jets	6	6	2	.500	322	312
Houston	3	11	0	.214	335	396
Miami	3	11	0	.214	213	362

WESTERN DIVISION

	W	L	T	Pct.	Pts.	OP
Kansas City	11	2	1	.846	448	276
Oakland	8	5	1	.615	315	288
San Diego	7	6	1	.538	335	284
Denver	4	10	0	.286	196	381

AFL championship: Kansas City 31, BUFFALO 7

1965 NFL

EASTERN CONFERENCE	W	L	T	Pct.	Pts.	OP	WESTERN CONFERENCE	W	L	T	Pct.	Pts.	OP
Cleveland	11	3	0	.786	363	325	Green Bay	10	3	1	.769	316	224
Dallas	7	7	0	.500	325	280	Baltimore	10	3	1	.769	389	284
N.Y. Giants	7	7	0	.500	270	338	Chicago	9	5	0	.643	409	275
Washington	6	8	0	.429	257	301	San Francisco	7	6	1	.538	421	402
Philadelphia	5	9	0	.357	363	359	Minnesota	7	7	0	.500	383	403
St. Louis	5	9	0	.357	296	309	Detroit	6	7	1	.462	257	295
Pittsburgh	2	12	0	.143	202	397	Los Angeles	4	10	0	.286	269	328

Western Conference playoff: GREEN BAY 13, Baltimore 10 (OT)
NFL championship: GREEN BAY 23, Cleveland 12

1965 AFL

EASTERN DIVISION	W	L	T	Pct.	Pts.	OP	WESTERN DIVISION	W	L	T	Pct.	Pts.	OP
Buffalo	10	3	1	.769	313	226	San Diego	9	2	3	.818	340	227
N.Y. Jets	5	8	1	.385	285	303	Oakland	8	5	1	.615	298	239
Boston Patriots	4	8	2	.333	244	302	Kansas City	7	5	2	.583	322	285
Houston	4	10	0	.286	298	429	Denver	4	10	0	.286	303	392

AFL championship: Buffalo 23, SAN DIEGO 0

1964 NFL

EASTERN CONFERENCE	W	L	T	Pct.	Pts.	OP	WESTERN CONFERENCE	W	L	T	Pct.	Pts.	OP
Cleveland	10	3	1	.769	415	293	Baltimore	12	2	0	.857	428	225
St. Louis	9	3	2	.750	357	331	Green Bay	8	5	1	.615	342	245
Philadelphia	6	8	0	.429	312	313	Minnesota	8	5	1	.615	355	296
Washington	6	8	0	.429	307	305	Detroit	7	5	2	.583	280	260
Dallas	5	8	1	.385	250	289	Los Angeles	5	7	2	.417	283	339
Pittsburgh	5	9	0	.357	253	315	Chicago	5	9	0	.357	260	379
N.Y. Giants	2	10	2	.167	241	399	San Francisco	4	10	0	.286	236	330

NFL championship: CLEVELAND 27, Baltimore 0

1964 AFL

EASTERN DIVISION	W	L	T	Pct.	Pts.	OP	WESTERN DIVISION	W	L	T	Pct.	Pts.	OP
Buffalo	12	2	0	.857	400	242	San Diego	8	5	1	.615	341	300
Boston Patriots	10	3	1	.769	365	297	Kansas City	7	7	0	.500	366	306
N.Y. Jets	5	8	1	.385	278	315	Oakland	5	7	2	.417	303	350
Houston	4	10	0	.286	310	355	Denver	2	11	1	.154	240	438

AFL championship: BUFFALO 20, San Diego 7

1963 NFL

EASTERN CONFERENCE	W	L	T	Pct.	Pts.	OP	WESTERN CONFERENCE	W	L	T	Pct.	Pts.	OP
N.Y. Giants	11	3	0	.786	448	280	Chicago	11	1	2	.917	301	144
Cleveland	10	4	0	.714	343	262	Green Bay	11	2	1	.846	369	206
St. Louis	9	5	0	.643	341	283	Baltimore	8	6	0	.571	316	285
Pittsburgh	7	4	3	.636	321	295	Detroit	5	8	1	.385	326	265
Dallas	4	10	0	.286	305	378	Minnesota	5	8	1	.385	309	390
Washington	3	11	0	.214	279	398	Los Angeles	5	9	0	.357	210	350
Philadelphia	2	10	2	.167	242	381	San Francisco	2	12	0	.143	198	391

NFL championship: CHICAGO 14, N.Y. Giants 10

1963 AFL

EASTERN DIVISION	W	L	T	Pct.	Pts.	OP	WESTERN DIVISION	W	L	T	Pct.	Pts.	OP
Boston Patriots	7	6	1	.538	327	257	San Diego	11	3	0	.786	399	255
Buffalo	7	6	1	.538	304	291	Oakland	10	4	0	.714	363	282
Houston	6	8	0	.429	302	372	Kansas City	5	7	2	.417	347	263
N.Y. Jets	5	8	1	.385	249	399	Denver	2	11	1	.154	301	473

Eastern Division playoff: Boston 26, BUFFALO 8
AFL championship: SAN DIEGO 51, Boston 10

1962 NFL

EASTERN CONFERENCE	W	L	T	Pct.	Pts.	OP	WESTERN CONFERENCE	W	L	T	Pct.	Pts.	OP
N.Y. Giants	12	2	0	.857	398	283	Green Bay	13	1	0	.929	415	148
Pittsburgh	9	5	0	.643	312	363	Detroit	11	3	0	.786	315	177
Cleveland	7	6	1	.538	291	257	Chicago	9	5	0	.643	321	287
Washington	5	7	2	.417	305	376	San Francisco	6	8	0	.429	282	331
Dallas Cowboys	5	8	1	.385	398	402	Minnesota	2	11	1	.154	254	410
St. Louis	4	9	1	.308	287	361	Los Angeles	1	12	1	.077	220	334
Philadelphia	3	10	1	.231	282	356							

NFL championship: Green Bay 16, N.Y. GIANTS 7

1962 AFL

EASTERN DIVISION	W	L	T	Pct.	Pts.	OP	WESTERN DIVISION	W	L	T	Pct.	Pts.	OP
Houston	11	3	0	.786	387	270	Dallas Texans	11	3	0	.786	389	233
Boston Patriots	9	4	1	.692	346	295	Denver	7	7	0	.500	353	334
Buffalo	7	6	1	.538	309	272	San Diego	4	10	0	.286	314	392
N.Y. Titans	5	9	0	.357	278	423	Oakland	1	13	0	.071	213	370

AFL championship: Dallas Texans 20, HOUSTON 17 (OT)

1961 NFL

EASTERN CONFERENCE	W	L	T	Pct.	Pts.	OP	WESTERN CONFERENCE	W	L	T	Pct.	Pts.	OP
N.Y. Giants	10	3	1	.769	368	220	Green Bay	11	3	0	.786	391	223
Philadelphia	10	4	0	.714	361	297	Detroit	8	5	1	.615	270	258
Cleveland	8	5	1	.615	319	270	Baltimore	8	6	0	.571	302	307
St. Louis	7	7	0	.500	279	267	Chicago	8	6	0	.571	326	302
Pittsburgh	6	8	0	.429	295	287	San Francisco	7	6	1	.538	346	272
Dallas Cowboys	4	9	1	.308	236	380	Los Angeles	4	10	0	.286	263	333
Washington	1	12	1	.077	174	392	Minnesota	3	11	0	.214	285	407

NFL championship: GREEN BAY 37, N.Y. Giants 0

1961 AFL

EASTERN DIVISION	W	L	T	Pct.	Pts.	OP	WESTERN DIVISION	W	L	T	Pct.	Pts.	OP
Houston	10	3	1	.769	513	242	San Diego	12	2	0	.857	396	219
Boston Patriots	9	4	1	.692	413	313	Dallas Texans	6	8	0	.429	334	343
N.Y. Titans	7	7	0	.500	301	390	Denver	3	11	0	.214	251	432
Buffalo	6	8	0	.429	294	342	Oakland	2	12	0	.143	237	458

AFL championship: Houston 10, SAN DIEGO 3

1960 NFL

EASTERN CONFERENCE	W	L	T	Pct.	Pts.	OP	WESTERN CONFERENCE	W	L	T	Pct.	Pts.	OP
Philadelphia	10	2	0	.833	321	246	Green Bay	8	4	0	.667	332	209
Cleveland	8	3	1	.727	362	217	Detroit	7	5	0	.583	239	212
N.Y. Giants	6	4	2	.600	271	261	San Francisco	7	5	0	.583	208	205
St. Louis	6	5	1	.545	288	230	Baltimore	6	6	0	.500	288	234
Pittsburgh	5	6	1	.455	240	275	Chicago	5	6	1	.455	194	299
Washington	1	9	2	.100	178	309	L.A. Rams	4	7	1	.364	265	297
							Dallas Cowboys	0	11	1	.000	177	369

NFL championship: PHILADELPHIA 17, Green Bay 13

1960 AFL

EASTERN CONFERENCE	W	L	T	Pct.	Pts.	OP	WESTERN CONFERENCE	W	L	T	Pct.	Pts.	OP
Houston	10	4	0	.714	379	285	L.A. Chargers	10	4	0	.714	373	336
N.Y. Titans	7	7	0	.500	382	399	Dallas Texans	8	6	0	.571	362	253
Buffalo	5	8	1	.385	296	303	Oakland	6	8	0	.429	319	388
Boston	5	9	0	.357	286	349	Denver	4	9	1	.308	309	393

AFL championship: HOUSTON 24, L.A. Chargers 16

1959

EASTERN CONFERENCE	W	L	T	Pct.	Pts.	OP	WESTERN CONFERENCE	W	L	T	Pct.	Pts.	OP
N.Y. Giants	10	2	0	.833	284	170	Baltimore	9	3	0	.750	374	251
Cleveland	7	5	0	.583	270	214	Chi. Bears	8	4	0	.667	252	196
Philadelphia	7	5	0	.583	268	278	Green Bay	7	5	0	.583	248	246
Pittsburgh	6	5	1	.545	257	216	San Francisco	7	5	0	.583	255	237
Washington	3	9	0	.250	185	350	Detroit	3	8	1	.273	203	275
Chi. Cardinals	2	10	0	.167	234	324	Los Angeles	2	10	0	.167	242	315

NFL championship: BALTIMORE 31, N.Y. Giants 16

1958

EASTERN CONFERENCE	W	L	T	Pct.	Pts.	OP	WESTERN CONFERENCE	W	L	T	Pct.	Pts.	OP
N.Y. Giants	9	3	0	.750	246	183	Baltimore	9	3	0	.750	381	203
Cleveland	9	3	0	.750	302	217	Chi. Bears	8	4	0	.667	298	230
Pittsburgh	7	4	1	.636	261	230	Los Angeles	8	4	0	.667	344	278
Washington	4	7	1	.364	214	268	San Francisco	6	6	0	.500	257	324
Chi. Cardinals	2	9	1	.182	261	356	Detroit	4	7	1	.364	261	276
Philadelphia	2	9	1	.182	235	306	Green Bay	1	10	1	.091	193	382

Eastern Conference playoff: N.Y. GIANTS 10, Cleveland 0
NFL championship: Baltimore 23, N.Y. GIANTS 17 (OT)

1957

EASTERN CONFERENCE	W	L	T	Pct.	Pts.	OP	WESTERN CONFERENCE	W	L	T	Pct.	Pts.	OP
Cleveland	9	2	1	.818	269	172	Detroit	8	4	0	.667	251	231
N.Y. Giants	7	5	0	.583	254	211	San Francisco	8	4	0	.667	260	264
Pittsburgh	6	6	0	.500	161	178	Baltimore	7	5	0	.583	303	235
Washington	5	6	1	.455	251	230	Los Angeles	6	6	0	.500	307	278
Philadelphia	4	8	0	.333	173	230	Chi. Bears	5	7	0	.417	203	211
Chi. Cardinals	3	9	0	.250	200	299	Green Bay	3	9	0	.250	218	311

Western Conference playoff: Detroit 31, SAN FRANCISCO 27
NFL championship: DETROIT 59, Cleveland 14

1956

EASTERN CONFERENCE	W	L	T	Pct.	Pts.	OP	WESTERN CONFERENCE	W	L	T	Pct.	Pts.	OP
N.Y. Giants	8	3	1	.727	264	197	Chi. Bears	9	2	1	.818	363	246
Chi. Cardinals	7	5	0	.583	240	182	Detroit	9	3	0	.750	300	188
Washington	6	6	0	.500	183	225	San Francisco	5	6	1	.455	233	284
Cleveland	5	7	0	.417	167	177	Baltimore	5	7	0	.417	270	322
Pittsburgh	5	7	0	.417	217	250	Green Bay	4	8	0	.333	264	342
Philadelphia	3	8	1	.273	143	215	Los Angeles	4	8	0	.333	291	307

NFL championship: N.Y. GIANTS 47, Chi. Bears 7

1955

EASTERN CONFERENCE	W	L	T	Pct.	Pts.	OP	WESTERN CONFERENCE	W	L	T	Pct.	Pts.	OP
Cleveland	9	2	1	.818	349	218	Los Angeles	8	3	1	.727	260	231
Washington	8	4	0	.667	246	222	Chi. Bears	8	4	0	.667	294	251
N.Y. Giants	6	5	1	.545	267	223	Green Bay	6	6	0	.500	258	276
Chi. Cardinals	4	7	1	.364	224	252	Baltimore	5	6	1	.455	214	239
Philadelphia	4	7	1	.364	248	231	San Francisco	4	8	0	.333	216	298
Pittsburgh	4	8	0	.333	195	285	Detroit	3	9	0	.250	230	275

NFL championship: Cleveland 38, LOS ANGELES 14

1954

EASTERN CONFERENCE	W	L	T	Pct.	Pts.	OP	WESTERN CONFERENCE	W	L	T	Pct.	Pts.	OP
Cleveland	9	3	0	.750	336	162	Detroit	9	2	1	.818	337	189
Philadelphia	7	4	1	.636	284	230	Chi. Bears	8	4	0	.667	301	279
N.Y. Giants	7	5	0	.583	293	184	San Francisco	7	4	1	.636	313	251
Pittsburgh	5	7	0	.417	219	263	Los Angeles	6	5	1	.545	314	285
Washington	3	9	0	.250	207	432	Green Bay	4	8	0	.333	234	251
Chi. Cardinals	2	10	0	.167	183	347	Baltimore	3	9	0	.250	131	279

NFL championship: CLEVELAND 56, Detroit 10

1953

EASTERN CONFERENCE	W	L	T	Pct.	Pts.	OP	WESTERN CONFERENCE	W	L	T	Pct.	Pts.	OP
Cleveland	11	1	0	.917	348	162	Detroit	10	2	0	.833	271	205
Philadelphia	7	4	1	.636	352	215	San Francisco	9	3	0	.750	372	237
Washington	6	5	1	.545	208	215	Los Angeles	8	3	1	.727	366	236
Pittsburgh	6	6	0	.500	211	263	Chi. Bears	3	8	1	.273	218	262
N.Y. Giants	3	9	0	.250	179	277	Baltimore	3	9	0	.250	182	350
Chi. Cardinals	1	10	1	.091	190	337	Green Bay	2	9	1	.182	200	338

NFL championship: DETROIT 17, Cleveland 16

1952

AMERICAN CONFERENCE	W	L	T	Pct.	Pts.	OP	NATIONAL CONFERENCE	W	L	T	Pct.	Pts.	OP
Cleveland	8	4	0	.667	310	213	Detroit	9	3	0	.750	344	192
N.Y. Giants	7	5	0	.583	234	231	Los Angeles	9	3	0	.750	349	234
Philadelphia	7	5	0	.583	252	271	San Francisco	7	5	0	.583	285	221
Pittsburgh	5	7	0	.417	300	273	Green Bay	6	6	0	.500	295	312
Chi. Cardinals	4	8	0	.333	172	221	Chi. Bears	5	7	0	.417	245	326
Washington	4	8	0	.333	240	287	Dallas Texans	1	11	0	.083	182	427

National Conference playoff: DETROIT 31, Los Angeles 21
NFL championship: Detroit 17, CLEVELAND 7

1951

AMERICAN CONFERENCE	W	L	T	Pct.	Pts.	OP	NATIONAL CONFERENCE	W	L	T	Pct.	Pts.	OP
Cleveland	11	1	0	.917	331	152	Los Angeles	8	4	0	.667	392	261
N.Y. Giants	9	2	1	.818	254	161	Detroit	7	4	1	.636	336	259
Washington	5	7	0	.417	183	296	San Francisco	7	4	1	.636	255	205
Pittsburgh	4	7	1	.364	183	235	Chi. Bears	7	5	0	.583	286	282
Philadelphia	4	8	0	.333	234	264	Green Bay	3	9	0	.250	254	375
Chi. Cardinals	3	9	0	.250	210	287	N.Y. Yanks	1	9	2	.100	241	382

NFL championship: LOS ANGELES 24, Cleveland 17

1950

AMERICAN CONFERENCE	W	L	T	Pct.	Pts.	OP	NATIONAL CONFERENCE	W	L	T	Pct.	Pts.	OP
Cleveland	10	2	0	.833	310	144	Los Angeles	9	3	0	.750	466	309
N.Y. Giants	10	2	0	.833	268	150	Chi. Bears	9	3	0	.750	279	207
Philadelphia	6	6	0	.500	254	141	N.Y. Yanks	7	5	0	.583	366	367
Pittsburgh	6	6	0	.500	180	195	Detroit	6	6	0	.500	321	285
Chi. Cardinals	5	7	0	.417	233	287	Green Bay	3	9	0	.250	244	406
Washington	3	9	0	.250	232	326	San Francisco	3	9	0	.250	213	300
							Baltimore	1	11	0	.083	213	462

American Conference playoff: CLEVELAND 8, N.Y. Giants 3
National Conference playoff: LOS ANGELES 24, Chi. Bears 14
NFL championship: CLEVELAND 30, Los Angeles 28

1949

EASTERN DIVISION	W	L	T	Pct.	Pts.	OP	WESTERN DIVISION	W	L	T	Pct.	Pts.	OP
Philadelphia	11	1	0	.917	364	134	Los Angeles	8	2	2	.800	360	239
Pittsburgh	6	5	1	.545	224	214	Chi. Bears	9	3	0	.750	332	218
N.Y. Giants	6	6	0	.500	287	298	Chi. Cardinals	6	5	1	.545	360	301
Washington	4	7	1	.364	268	339	Detroit	4	8	0	.333	237	259
N.Y. Bulldogs	1	10	1	.091	153	368	Green Bay	2	10	0	.167	114	329

NFL championship: Philadelphia 14, LOS ANGELES 0

1948

EASTERN DIVISION	W	L	T	Pct.	Pts.	OP	WESTERN DIVISION	W	L	T	Pct.	Pts.	OP
Philadelphia	9	2	1	.818	376	156	Chi. Cardinals	11	1	0	.917	395	226
Washington	7	5	0	.583	291	287	Chi. Bears	10	2	0	.833	375	151
N.Y. Giants	4	8	0	.333	297	388	Los Angeles	6	5	1	.545	327	269
Pittsburgh	4	8	0	.333	200	243	Green Bay	3	9	0	.250	154	290
Boston	3	9	0	.250	174	372	Detroit	2	10	0	.167	200	407

NFL championship: PHILADELPHIA 7, Chi. Cardinals 0

1947

EASTERN DIVISION	W	L	T	Pct.	Pts.	OP	WESTERN DIVISION	W	L	T	Pct.	Pts.	OP
Philadelphia	8	4	0	.667	308	242	Chi. Cardinals	9	3	0	.750	306	231
Pittsburgh	8	4	0	.667	240	259	Chi. Bears	8	4	0	.667	363	241
Boston	4	7	1	.364	168	256	Green Bay	6	5	1	.545	274	210
Washington	4	8	0	.333	295	367	Los Angeles	6	6	0	.500	259	214
N.Y. Giants	2	8	2	.200	190	309	Detroit	3	9	0	.250	231	305

Eastern Division playoff: Philadelphia 21, PITTSBURGH 0
NFL championship: CHI. CARDINALS 28, Philadelphia 21

1946

EASTERN DIVISION	W	L	T	Pct.	Pts.	OP	WESTERN DIVISION	W	L	T	Pct.	Pts.	OP
N.Y. Giants	7	3	1	.700	236	162	Chi. Bears	8	2	1	.800	289	193
Philadelphia	6	5	0	.545	231	220	Los Angeles	6	4	1	.600	277	257
Washington	5	5	1	.500	171	191	Green Bay	6	5	0	.545	148	158
Pittsburgh	5	5	1	.500	136	117	Chi. Cardinals	6	5	0	.545	260	198
Boston	2	8	1	.200	189	273	Detroit	1	10	0	.091	142	310

NFL championship: Chi. Bears 24, N.Y. GIANTS 14

1945

EASTERN DIVISION	W	L	T	Pct.	Pts.	OP	WESTERN DIVISION	W	L	T	Pct.	Pts.	OP
Washington	8	2	0	.800	209	121	Cleveland	9	1	0	.900	244	136
Philadelphia	7	3	0	.700	272	133	Detroit	7	3	0	.700	195	194
N.Y. Giants	3	6	1	.333	179	198	Green Bay	6	4	0	.600	258	173
Boston	3	6	1	.333	123	211	Chi. Bears	3	7	0	.300	192	235
Pittsburgh	2	8	0	.200	79	220	Chi. Cardinals	1	9	0	.100	98	228

NFL championship: CLEVELAND 15, Washington 14

1944

EASTERN DIVISION	W	L	T	Pct.	Pts.	OP	WESTERN DIVISION	W	L	T	Pct.	Pts.	OP
N.Y. Giants	8	1	1	.889	206	75	Green Bay	8	2	0	.800	238	141
Philadelphia	7	1	2	.875	267	131	Chi. Bears	6	3	1	.667	258	172
Washington	6	3	1	.667	169	180	Detroit	6	3	1	.667	216	151
Boston	2	8	0	.200	82	233	Cleveland	4	6	0	.400	188	224
Brooklyn	0	10	0	.000	69	166	Card-Pitt	0	10	0	.000	108	328

NFL championship: Green Bay 14, N.Y. GIANTS 7

1943

EASTERN DIVISION	W	L	T	Pct.	Pts.	OP	WESTERN DIVISION	W	L	T	Pct.	Pts.	OP
Washington	6	3	1	.667	229	137	Chi. Bears	8	1	1	.889	303	157
N.Y. Giants	6	3	1	.667	197	170	Green Bay	7	2	1	.778	264	172
Phil-Pitt	5	4	1	.556	225	230	Detroit	3	6	1	.333	178	218
Brooklyn	2	8	0	.200	65	234	Chi. Cardinals	0	10	0	.000	95	238

Eastern Division playoff: Washington 28, N.Y. GIANTS 0
NFL championship: CHI. BEARS 41, Washington 21

1942

EASTERN DIVISION	W	L	T	Pct.	Pts.	OP	WESTERN DIVISION	W	L	T	Pct.	Pts.	OP
Washington	10	1	0	.909	227	102	Chi. Bears	11	0	0	1.000	376	84
Pittsburgh	7	4	0	.636	167	119	Green Bay	8	2	1	.800	300	215
N.Y. Giants	5	5	1	.500	155	139	Cleveland	5	6	0	.455	150	207
Brooklyn	3	8	0	.273	100	168	Chi. Cardinals	3	8	0	.273	98	209
Philadelphia	2	9	0	.182	134	239	Detroit	0	11	0	.000	38	263

NFL championship: WASHINGTON 14, Chi. Bears 6

1941

EASTERN DIVISION	W	L	T	Pct.	Pts.	OP	WESTERN DIVISION	W	L	T	Pct.	Pts.	OP
N.Y. Giants	8	3	0	.727	238	114	Chi. Bears	10	1	0	.909	396	147
Brooklyn	7	4	0	.636	158	127	Green Bay	10	1	0	.909	258	120
Washington	6	5	0	.545	176	174	Detroit	4	6	1	.400	121	195
Philadelphia	2	8	1	.200	119	218	Chi. Cardinals	3	7	1	.300	127	197
Pittsburgh	1	9	1	.100	103	276	Cleveland	2	9	0	.182	116	244

Western Division playoff: CHI. BEARS 33, Green Bay 14
NFL championship: CHI. BEARS 37, N.Y. Giants 9

1940

EASTERN DIVISION	W	L	T	Pct.	Pts.	OP	WESTERN DIVISION	W	L	T	Pct.	Pts.	OP
Washington	9	2	0	.818	245	142	Chi. Bears	8	3	0	.727	238	152
Brooklyn	8	3	0	.727	186	120	Green Bay	6	4	1	.600	238	155
N.Y. Giants	6	4	1	.600	131	133	Detroit	5	5	1	.500	138	153
Pittsburgh	2	7	2	.222	60	178	Cleveland	4	6	1	.400	171	191
Philadelphia	1	10	0	.091	111	211	Chi. Cardinals	2	7	2	.222	139	222

NFL championship: Chi. Bears 73, WASHINGTON 0

1939

EASTERN DIVISION	W	L	T	Pct.	Pts.	OP	WESTERN DIVISION	W	L	T	Pct.	Pts.	OP
N.Y. Giants	9	1	1	.900	168	85	Green Bay	9	2	0	.818	233	153
Washington	8	2	1	.800	242	94	Chi. Bears	8	3	0	.727	298	157
Brooklyn	4	6	1	.400	108	219	Detroit	6	5	0	.545	145	150
Philadelphia	1	9	1	.100	105	200	Cleveland	5	5	1	.500	195	164
Pittsburgh	1	9	1	.100	114	216	Chi. Cardinals	1	10	0	.091	84	254

NFL championship: GREEN BAY 27, N.Y. Giants 0

1938

EASTERN DIVISION	W	L	T	Pct.	Pts.	OP	WESTERN DIVISION	W	L	T	Pct.	Pts.	OP
N.Y. Giants	8	2	1	.800	194	79	Green Bay	8	3	0	.727	223	118
Washington	6	3	2	.667	148	154	Detroit	7	4	0	.636	119	108
Brooklyn	4	4	3	.500	131	161	Chi. Bears	6	5	0	.545	194	148
Philadelphia	5	6	0	.455	154	164	Cleveland	4	7	0	.364	131	215
Pittsburgh	2	9	0	.182	79	169	Chi. Cardinals	2	9	0	.182	111	168

NFL championship: N.Y. GIANTS 23, Green Bay 17

1937

EASTERN DIVISION	W	L	T	Pct.	Pts.	OP	WESTERN DIVISION	W	L	T	Pct.	Pts.	OP
Washington	8	3	0	.727	195	120	Chi. Bears	9	1	1	.900	201	100
N.Y. Giants	6	3	2	.667	128	109	Green Bay	7	4	0	.636	220	122
Pittsburgh	4	7	0	.364	122	145	Detroit	7	4	0	.636	180	105
Brooklyn	3	7	1	.300	82	174	Chi. Cardinals	5	5	1	.500	135	165
Philadelphia	2	8	1	.200	86	177	Cleveland	1	10	0	.091	75	207

NFL championship: Washington 28, CHI. BEARS 21

1936

EASTERN DIVISION	W	L	T	Pct.	Pts.	OP	WESTERN DIVISION	W	L	T	Pct.	Pts.	OP
Boston	7	5	0	.583	149	110	Green Bay	10	1	1	.909	248	118
Pittsburgh	6	6	0	.500	98	187	Chi. Bears	9	3	0	.750	222	94
N.Y. Giants	5	6	1	.455	115	163	Detroit	8	4	0	.667	235	102
Brooklyn	3	8	1	.273	92	161	Chi. Cardinals	3	8	1	.273	74	143
Philadelphia	1	11	0	.083	51	206							

NFL championship: Green Bay 21, Boston 6, at Polo Grounds, N.Y.

1935

EASTERN DIVISION	W	L	T	Pct.	Pts.	OP	WESTERN DIVISION	W	L	T	Pct.	Pts.	OP
N.Y. Giants	9	3	0	.750	180	96	Detroit	7	3	2	.700	191	111
Brooklyn	5	6	1	.455	90	141	Green Bay	8	4	0	.667	181	96
Pittsburgh	4	8	0	.333	100	209	Chi. Bears	6	4	2	.600	192	106
Boston	2	8	1	.200	65	123	Chi. Cardinals	6	4	2	.600	99	97
Philadelphia	2	9	0	.182	60	179							

NFL championship: DETROIT 26, N.Y. Giants 7
One game between Boston and Philadelphia was canceled.

1934

EASTERN DIVISION	W	L	T	Pct.	Pts.	OP	WESTERN DIVISION	W	L	T	Pct.	Pts.	OP
N.Y. Giants	8	5	0	.615	147	107	Chi. Bears	13	0	0	1.000	286	86
Boston	6	6	0	.500	107	94	Detroit	10	3	0	.769	238	59
Brooklyn	4	7	0	.364	61	153	Green Bay	7	6	0	.538	156	112
Philadelphia	4	7	0	.364	127	85	Chi. Cardinals	5	6	0	.455	80	84
Pittsburgh	2	10	0	.167	51	206	St. Louis	1	2	0	.333	27	61
							Cincinnati	0	8	0	.000	10	243

NFL championship: N.Y. GIANTS 30, Chi. Bears 13

1933

EASTERN DIVISION	W	L	T	Pct.	Pts.	OP	WESTERN DIVISION	W	L	T	Pct.	Pts.	OP
N.Y. Giants	11	3	0	.786	244	101	Chi. Bears	10	2	1	.833	133	82
Brooklyn	5	4	1	.556	93	54	Portsmouth	6	5	0	.545	128	87
Boston	5	5	2	.500	103	97	Green Bay	5	7	1	.417	170	107
Philadelphia	3	5	1	.375	77	158	Cincinnati	3	6	1	.333	38	110
Pittsburgh	3	6	2	.333	67	208	Chi. Cardinals	1	9	1	.100	52	101

NFL championship: CHI. BEARS 23, N.Y. Giants 21

1932

	W	L	T	Pct.
Chicago Bears	7	1	6	.875
Green Bay Packers	10	3	1	.769
Portsmouth Spartans	6	2	4	.750
Boston Braves	4	4	2	.500
New York Giants	4	6	2	.400
Brooklyn Dodgers	3	9	0	.250
Chicago Cardinals	2	6	2	.250
Staten Island Stapletons	2	7	3	.222

Chicago Bears and Portsmouth finished regularly scheduled games tied for first place. Bears won playoff game, which counted in standings, 9-0.

1931

	W	L	T	Pct.
Green Bay Packers	12	2	0	.857
Portsmouth Spartans	11	3	0	.786
Chicago Bears	8	5	0	.615
Chicago Cardinals	5	4	0	.556
New York Giants	7	6	1	.538
Providence Steam Roller	4	4	3	.500
Staten Island Stapletons	4	6	1	.400
Cleveland Indians	2	8	0	.200
Brooklyn Dodgers	2	12	0	.143
Frankford Yellow Jackets	1	6	1	.143

1930

	W	L	T	Pct.
Green Bay Packers	10	3	1	.769
New York Giants	13	4	0	.765
Chicago Bears	9	4	1	.692
Brooklyn Dodgers	7	4	1	.636
Providence Steam Roller	6	4	1	.600
Staten Island Stapletons	5	5	2	.500
Chicago Cardinals	5	6	2	.455
Portsmouth Spartans	5	6	3	.455
Frankford Yellow Jackets	4	13	1	.222
Minneapolis Red Jackets	1	7	1	.125
Newark Tornadoes	1	10	1	.091

1929

	W	L	T	Pct.
Green Bay Packers	12	0	1	1.000
New York Giants	13	1	1	.929
Frankford Yellow Jackets	10	4	5	.714
Chicago Cardinals	6	6	1	.500
Boston Bulldogs	4	4	0	.500
Staten Island Stapletons	3	4	3	.429
Providence Steam Roller	4	6	2	.400
Orange Tornadoes	3	5	4	.375
Chicago Bears	4	9	2	.308
Buffalo Bisons	1	7	1	.125
Minneapolis Red Jackets	1	9	0	.100
Dayton Triangles	0	6	0	.000

1928

	W	L	T	Pct.
Providence Steam Roller	8	1	2	.889
Frankford Yellow Jackets	11	3	2	.786
Detroit Wolverines	7	2	1	.778
Green Bay Packers	6	4	3	.600
Chicago Bears	7	5	1	.583
New York Giants	4	7	2	.364
New York Yankees	4	8	1	.333
Pottsville Maroons	2	8	0	.200
Chicago Cardinals	1	5	0	.167
Dayton Triangles	0	7	0	.000

1927

	W	L	T	Pct.
New York Giants	11	1	1	.917
Green Bay Packers	7	2	1	.778
Chicago Bears	9	3	2	.750
Cleveland Bulldogs	8	4	1	.667
Providence Steam Roller	8	5	1	.615
New York Yankees	7	8	1	.467
Frankford Yellow Jackets	6	9	3	.400
Pottsville Maroons	5	8	0	.385
Chicago Cardinals	3	7	1	.300
Dayton Triangles	1	6	1	.143
Duluth Eskimos	1	8	0	.111
Buffalo Bisons	0	5	0	.000

1926

	W	L	T	Pct.
Frankford Yellow Jackets	14	1	2	.933
Chicago Bears	12	1	3	.923
Pottsville Maroons	10	2	2	.833
Kansas City Cowboys	8	3	0	.727
Green Bay Packers	7	3	3	.700
Los Angeles Buccaneers	6	3	1	.667
New York Giants	8	4	1	.667
Duluth Eskimos	6	5	3	.545
Buffalo Rangers	4	4	2	.500
Chicago Cardinals	5	6	1	.455
Providence Steam Roller	5	7	1	.417
Detroit Panthers	4	6	2	.400
Hartford Blues	3	7	0	.300
Brooklyn Lions	3	8	0	.273
Milwaukee Badgers	2	7	0	.222
Akron Pros	1	4	3	.200
Dayton Triangles	1	4	1	.200
Racine Tornadoes	1	4	0	.200
Columbus Tigers	1	6	0	.143
Canton Bulldogs	1	9	3	.100
Hammond Pros	0	4	0	.000
Louisville Colonels	0	4	0	.000

1925

	W	L	T	Pct.
Chicago Cardinals	11	2	1	.846
Pottsville Maroons	10	2	0	.833
Detroit Panthers	8	2	2	.800
New York Giants	8	4	0	.667
Akron Indians	4	2	2	.667
Frankford Yellow Jackets	13	7	0	.650
Chicago Bears	9	5	3	.643
Rock Island Independents	5	3	3	.625
Green Bay Packers	8	5	0	.615
Providence Steam Roller	6	5	1	.545
Canton Bulldogs	4	4	0	.500
Cleveland Bulldogs	5	8	1	.385
Kansas City Cowboys	2	5	1	.286
Hammond Pros	1	4	0	.200
Buffalo Bisons	1	6	2	.143
Duluth Kelleys	0	3	0	.000
Rochester Jeffersons	0	6	1	.000
Milwaukee Badgers	0	6	0	.000
Dayton Triangles	0	7	1	.000
Columbus Tigers	0	9	0	.000

1924

	W	L	T	Pct.
Cleveland Bulldogs	7	1	1	.875
Chicago Bears	6	1	4	.857
Frankford Yellow Jackets	11	2	1	.846
Duluth Kelleys	5	1	0	.833
Rock Island Independents	5	2	2	.714
Green Bay Packers	7	4	0	.636
Racine Legion	4	3	3	.571
Chicago Cardinals	5	4	1	.556
Buffalo Bisons	6	5	0	.545
Columbus Tigers	4	4	0	.500
Hammond Pros	2	2	1	.500
Milwaukee Badgers	5	8	0	.385
Akron Indians	2	6	0	.250
Dayton Triangles	2	6	0	.250
Kansas City Blues	2	7	0	.222
Kenosha Maroons	0	4	1	.000
Minneapolis Marines	0	6	0	.000
Rochester Jeffersons	0	7	0	.000

1923

	W	L	T	Pct.
Canton Bulldogs	11	0	1	1.000
Chicago Bears	9	2	1	.818
Green Bay Packers	7	2	1	.778
Milwaukee Badgers	7	2	3	.778
Cleveland Indians	3	1	3	.750
Chicago Cardinals	8	4	0	.667
Duluth Kelleys	4	3	0	.571
Buffalo All-Americans	5	4	3	.556
Columbus Tigers	5	4	1	.556
Racine Legion	4	4	2	.500
Toledo Maroons	3	3	2	.500
Rock Island Independents	2	3	3	.400
Minneapolis Marines	2	5	2	.286
St. Louis All-Stars	1	4	2	.200
Hammond Pros	1	5	1	.167
Dayton Triangles	1	6	1	.143
Akron Indians	1	6	0	.143
Oorang Indians	1	10	0	.091
Louisville Brecks	0	3	0	.000
Rochester Jeffersons	0	4	0	.000

1922

	W	L	T	Pct.
Canton Bulldogs	10	0	2	1.000
Chicago Bears	9	3	0	.750
Chicago Cardinals	8	3	0	.727
Toledo Maroons	5	2	2	.714
Rock Island Independents	4	2	1	.667
Racine Legion	6	4	1	.600
Dayton Triangles	4	3	1	.571
Green Bay Packers	4	3	3	.571
Buffalo All-Americans	5	4	1	.556
Akron Pros	3	5	2	.375
Milwaukee Badgers	2	4	3	.333
Oorang Indians	3	6	0	.333
Minneapolis Marines	1	3	0	.250
Louisville Brecks	1	3	0	.250
Evansville Crimson Giants	0	3	0	.000
Rochester Jeffersons	0	4	1	.000
Hammond Pros	0	5	1	.000
Columbus Panhandles	0	8	0	.000

1921

	W	L	T	Pct.
Chicago Staleys	9	1	1	.900
Buffalo All-Americans	9	1	2	.900
Akron Pros	8	3	1	.727
Canton Bulldogs	5	2	3	.714
Rock Island Independents	4	2	1	.667
Evansville Crimson Giants	3	2	0	.600
Green Bay Packers	3	2	1	.600
Dayton Triangles	4	4	1	.500
Chicago Cardinals	3	3	2	.500
Rochester Jeffersons	2	3	0	.400
Cleveland Indians	3	5	0	.375
Washington Senators	1	2	0	.333
Cincinnati Celts	1	3	0	.250
Hammond Pros	1	3	1	.250
Minneapolis Marines	1	3	0	.250
Detroit Heralds	1	5	1	.167
Columbus Panhandles	1	8	0	.111
Tonawanda Kardex	0	1	0	.000
Muncie Flyers	0	2	0	.000
Louisville Brecks	0	2	0	.000
New York Giants	0	2	0	.000

1920*

	W	L	T	Pct.
Akron Pros	8	0	3	1.000
Decatur Staleys	10	1	2	.909
Buffalo All-Americans	9	1	1	.900
Chicago Cardinals	6	2	2	.750
Rock Island Independents	6	2	2	.750
Dayton Triangles	5	2	2	.714
Rochester Jeffersons	6	3	2	.667
Canton Bulldogs	7	4	2	.636
Detroit Heralds	2	3	3	.400
Cleveland Tigers	2	4	2	.333
Chicago Tigers	2	5	1	.286
Hammond Pros	2	5	0	.286
Columbus Panhandles	2	6	2	.250
Muncie Flyers	0	1	0	.000

*No official standings were maintained for the 1920 season, and the championship was awarded to the Akron Pros in a League meeting on April 30, 1921. Clubs played schedules that included games against nonleague opponents.

RS=REGULAR SEASON
PS=POSTSEASON

*ARIZONA vs. ATLANTA
RS: Cardinals lead series, 13-8
1966—Falcons, 16-10 (A)
1968—Cardinals, 17-12 (StL)
1971—Cardinals, 26-9 (A)
1973—Cardinals, 32-10 (A)
1975—Cardinals, 23-20 (StL)
1978—Cardinals, 42-21 (StL)
1980—Falcons, 33-27 (StL) OT
1981—Falcons, 41-20 (A)
1982—Cardinals, 23-20 (A)
1986—Falcons, 33-13 (A)
1987—Cardinals, 34-21 (A)
1989—Cardinals, 34-20 (P)
1990—Cardinals, 24-13 (A)
1991—Cardinals, 16-10 (P)
1992—Falcons, 20-17 (A)
1993—Cardinals, 27-10 (A)
1994—Falcons, 10-6 (Atl)
1995—Cardinals, 40-37 (Ariz) OT
1997—Cardinals, 29-26 (Ariz)
1999—Falcons, 37-14 (Atl)
2001—Falcons, 34-14 (Ariz)
(RS Pts.—Cardinals 488, Falcons 453)
*Franchise known as Phoenix prior to
1994 and in St. Louis prior to 1988*

*ARIZONA vs. BALTIMORE
RS: Series tied, 1-1
1997—Cardinals, 16-13 (B)
2000—Ravens, 13-7 (B)
(RS Pts.—Ravens 26, Cardinals 23)

*ARIZONA vs. BUFFALO
RS: Bills lead series, 4-3
1971—Cardinals, 28-23 (B)
1975—Bills, 32-14 (StL)
1981—Cardinals, 24-0 (StL)
1984—Cardinals, 37-7 (StL)
1986—Bills, 17-10 (B)
1990—Bills, 45-14 (B)
1999—Bills, 31-21 (A)
(RS Pts.—Bills 155, Cardinals 148)
*Franchise known as Phoenix prior to
1994 and in St. Louis prior to 1988*

ARIZONA vs. CAROLINA
RS: Series tied, 1-1
1995—Panthers, 27-7 (C)
2001—Cardinals, 30-7 (C)
(RS Pts.—Cardinals 37, Panthers 34)

*ARIZONA vs. **CHICAGO
RS: Bears lead series, 53-26-6
(NP denotes Normal Park;
Wr denotes Wrigley Field;
Co denotes Comiskey Park;
So denotes Soldier Field;
all Chicago)
1920—Cardinals, 7-6 (NP)
    Staleys, 10-0 (Wr)
1921—Tie, 0-0 (Wr)
1922—Cardinals, 6-0 (Co)
    Cardinals, 9-0 (Co)
1923—Bears, 3-0 (Wr)
1924—Bears, 6-0 (Wr)
    Bears, 21-0 (Co)
1925—Cardinals, 9-0 (Co)
    Tie, 0-0 (Wr)
1926—Bears, 16-0 (Wr)
    Bears, 10-0 (So)
    Tie, 0-0 (Wr)

1927—Bears, 9-0 (NP)
    Cardinals, 3-0 (Wr)
1928—Bears, 15-0 (NP)
    Bears, 34-0 (Wr)
1929—Tie, 0-0 (Wr)
    Cardinals, 40-6 (Co)
1930—Bears, 32-6 (Co)
    Bears, 6-0 (Wr)
1931—Bears, 26-13 (Wr)
    Bears, 18-7 (Wr)
1932—Tie, 0-0 (Wr)
    Bears, 34-0 (Wr)
1933—Bears, 12-9 (Wr)
    Bears, 22-6 (Wr)
1934—Bears, 20-0 (Wr)
    Bears, 17-6 (Wr)
1935—Tie, 7-7 (Wr)
    Bears, 13-0 (Wr)
1936—Bears, 7-3 (Wr)
    Cardinals, 14-7 (Wr)
1937—Bears, 16-7 (Wr)
    Bears, 42-28 (Wr)
1938—Bears, 16-13 (So)
    Bears, 34-28 (Wr)
1939—Bears, 44-7 (Wr)
    Bears, 48-7 (Co)
1940—Cardinals, 21-7 (Co)
    Bears, 31-23 (Wr)
1941—Bears, 53-7 (Wr)
    Bears, 34-24 (Co)
1942—Bears, 41-14 (Wr)
    Bears, 21-7 (Co)
1943—Bears, 20-0 (Wr)
    Bears, 35-24 (Co)
1945—Cardinals, 16-7 (Wr)
    Bears, 28-20 (Co)
1946—Bears, 34-17 (Co)
    Cardinals, 35-28 (Wr)
1947—Cardinals, 31-7 (Co)
    Cardinals, 30-21 (Wr)
1948—Bears, 28-17 (Co)
    Cardinals, 24-21 (Wr)
1949—Bears, 17-7 (Co)
    Bears, 52-21 (Wr)
1950—Bears, 27-6 (Wr)
    Cardinals, 20-10 (Co)
1951—Cardinals, 28-14 (Co)
    Cardinals, 24-14 (Wr)
1952—Cardinals, 21-10 (Co)
    Bears, 10-7 (Wr)
1953—Cardinals, 24-17 (Wr)
1954—Bears, 29-7 (Co)
1955—Cardinals, 53-14 (Co)
1956—Bears, 10-3 (Wr)
1957—Bears, 14-6 (Co)
1958—Bears, 30-14 (Wr)
1959—Bears, 31-7 (So)
1965—Bears, 34-13 (Wr)
1966—Cardinals, 24-17 (StL)
1967—Bears, 30-3 (Wr)
1969—Cardinals, 20-17 (StL)
1972—Bears, 27-10 (StL)
1975—Cardinals, 34-20 (So)
1977—Cardinals, 16-13 (StL)
1978—Bears, 17-10 (So)
1979—Bears, 42-6 (So)
1982—Cardinals, 10-7 (So)
1984—Cardinals, 38-21 (StL)
1990—Bears, 31-21 (P)
1994—Bears, 19-16 (A) OT

1998—Cardinals, 20-7 (A)
2001—Bears, 20-13 (A)
(RS Pts.—Bears 1,594, Cardinals 1,047)
*Franchise known as Phoenix prior to
1994, in St. Louis prior to 1988, and in
Chicago prior to 1960*
**Franchise in Decatur prior to 1921 and
known as Staleys prior to 1922*

*ARIZONA vs. CINCINNATI
RS: Bengals lead series, 5-2
1973—Bengals, 42-24 (C)
1979—Bengals, 34-28 (C)
1985—Cardinals, 41-27 (StL)
1988—Bengals, 21-14 (C)
1994—Cardinals, 28-7 (A)
1997—Bengals, 24-21 (C)
2000—Bengals, 24-13 (C)
(RS Pts.—Bengals 179, Cardinals 169)
*Franchise known as Phoenix prior to
1994 and in St. Louis prior to 1988*

*ARIZONA vs. CLEVELAND
RS: Browns lead series, 32-11-3
1950—Browns, 34-24 (Cle)
    Browns, 10-7 (Chi)
1951—Browns, 34-17 (Chi)
    Browns, 49-28 (Cle)
1952—Browns, 28-13 (Cle)
    Browns, 10-0 (Chi)
1953—Browns, 27-7 (Chi)
    Browns, 27-16 (Cle)
1954—Browns, 31-7 (Cle)
    Browns, 35-3 (Chi)
1955—Browns, 26-20 (Chi)
    Browns, 35-24 (Cle)
1956—Cardinals, 9-7 (Chi)
    Cardinals, 24-7 (Cle)
1957—Browns, 17-7 (Chi)
    Browns, 31-0 (Cle)
1958—Browns, 35-28 (Cle)
    Browns, 38-24 (Chi)
1959—Browns, 34-7 (Cle)
    Browns, 17-7 (Cle)
1960—Browns, 28-27 (Cle)
    Tie, 17-17 (StL)
1961—Browns, 20-17 (Cle)
    Browns, 21-10 (StL)
1962—Browns, 34-7 (StL)
    Browns, 38-14 (Cle)
1963—Cardinals, 20-14 (Cle)
    Browns, 24-10 (StL)
1964—Tie, 33-33 (Cle)
    Cardinals, 28-19 (StL)
1965—Cardinals, 49-13 (Cle)
    Browns, 27-24 (StL)
1966—Cardinals, 34-28 (Cle)
    Browns, 38-10 (StL)
1967—Browns, 20-16 (Cle)
    Browns, 20-16 (StL)
1968—Cardinals, 27-21 (Cle)
    Cardinals, 27-16 (StL)
1969—Tie, 21-21 (Cle)
    Browns, 27-21 (StL)
1974—Cardinals, 29-7 (StL)
1979—Browns, 38-20 (StL)
1985—Cardinals, 27-24 (Cle) OT
1988—Browns, 29-21 (P)
1994—Browns, 32-0 (Cle)
2000—Cardinals, 29-21 (A)
(RS Pts.—Browns 1,162, Cardinals 826)
Franchise known as Phoenix prior to

*1994, in St. Louis prior to 1988,
and in Chicago prior to 1960*
*ARIZONA vs. DALLAS
RS: Cowboys lead series, 52-26-1
PS: Cardinals lead series, 1-0
1960—Cardinals, 12-10 (StL)
1961—Cardinals, 31-17 (D)
          Cardinals, 31-13 (StL)
1962—Cardinals, 28-24 (D)
          Cardinals, 52-20 (StL)
1963—Cardinals, 34-7 (D)
          Cowboys, 28-24 (StL)
1964—Cardinals, 16-6 (D)
          Cowboys, 31-13 (StL)
1965—Cardinals, 20-13 (StL)
          Cowboys, 27-13 (D)
1966—Tie, 10-10 (StL)
          Cowboys, 31-17 (D)
1967—Cowboys, 46-21 (D)
1968—Cowboys, 27-10 (StL)
1969—Cowboys, 24-3 (D)
1970—Cardinals, 20-7 (StL)
          Cardinals, 38-0 (D)
1971—Cowboys, 16-13 (StL)
          Cowboys, 31-12 (D)
1972—Cowboys, 33-24 (D)
          Cowboys, 27-6 (StL)
1973—Cowboys, 45-10 (D)
          Cowboys, 30-3 (StL)
1974—Cardinals, 31-28 (StL)
          Cowboys, 17-14 (D)
1975—Cowboys, 37-31 (D) OT
          Cardinals, 31-17 (StL)
1976—Cardinals, 21-17 (StL)
          Cowboys, 19-14 (D)
1977—Cowboys, 30-24 (StL)
          Cardinals, 24-17 (D)
1978—Cowboys, 21-12 (D)
          Cowboys, 24-21 (StL) OT
1979—Cowboys, 22-21 (StL)
          Cowboys, 22-13 (D)
1980—Cowboys, 27-24 (StL)
          Cowboys, 31-21 (D)
1981—Cowboys, 30-17 (D)
          Cardinals, 20-17 (StL)
1982—Cowboys, 24-7 (StL)
1983—Cowboys, 34-17 (StL)
          Cowboys, 35-17 (D)
1984—Cardinals, 31-20 (D)
          Cowboys, 24-17 (StL)
1985—Cardinals, 21-10 (StL)
          Cowboys, 35-17 (D)
1986—Cowboys, 31-7 (StL)
          Cowboys, 37-6 (D)
1987—Cardinals, 24-13 (StL)
          Cowboys, 21-16 (D)
1988—Cowboys, 17-14 (P)
          Cardinals, 16-10 (D)
1989—Cardinals, 19-10 (D)
          Cardinals, 24-20 (P)
1990—Cardinals, 20-3 (P)
          Cowboys, 41-10 (D)
1991—Cowboys, 17-9 (P)
          Cowboys, 27-7 (D)
1992—Cowboys, 31-20 (D)
          Cowboys, 16-10 (P)
1993—Cowboys, 17-10 (P)
          Cowboys, 20-15 (D)
1994—Cowboys, 38-3 (D)
          Cowboys, 28-21 (A)

1995—Cowboys, 34-20 (D)
          Cowboys, 37-13 (A)
1996—Cowboys, 17-3 (D)
          Cowboys, 10-6 (A)
1997—Cardinals, 25-22 (A) OT
          Cowboys, 24-6 (D)
1998—Cowboys, 38-10 (D)
          Cowboys, 35-28 (A)
          **Cardinals, 20-7 (D)
1999—Cowboys, 35-7 (D)
          Cardinals, 13-9 (A)
2000—Cardinals, 32-31 (A)
          Cowboys, 48-7 (D)
2001—Cowboys, 17-3 (D)
          Cardinals, 17-10 (A)
(RS Pts.—Cowboys 1,845, Cardinals 1,368)
(PS Pts.—Cardinals 20, Cowboys 7)
**Franchise known as Phoenix prior to
1994 and in St. Louis prior to 1988
**NFC First-Round Playoff*
*ARIZONA vs. DENVER
RS: Broncos lead series, 5-0-1
1973—Tie, 17-17 (StL)
1977—Broncos, 7-0 (D)
1989—Broncos, 37-0 (P)
1991—Broncos, 24-19 (D)
1995—Broncos, 38-6 (D)
2001—Broncos, 38-17 (A)
(RS Pts.—Broncos 161, Cardinals 59)
**Franchise known as Phoenix prior to
1994 and in St. Louis prior to 1988*
*ARIZONA vs. **DETROIT
RS: Lions lead series, 28-20-5
1930—Tie, 0-0 (Port)
          Cardinals, 23-0 (C)
1931—Spartans, 13-3 (Port)
          Cardinals, 20-19 (C)
1932—Tie, 7-7 (Port)
1933—Spartans, 7-6 (Port)
1934—Lions, 6-0 (D)
          Lions, 17-13 (C)
1935—Tie, 10-10 (D)
          Lions, 7-6 (C)
1936—Lions, 39-0 (D)
          Lions, 14-7 (C)
1937—Lions, 16-7 (C)
          Lions, 16-7 (D)
1938—Lions, 10-0 (D)
          Lions, 7-3 (C)
1939—Lions, 21-3 (D)
          Lions, 17-3 (C)
1940—Tie, 0-0 (Buffalo)
          Lions, 43-14 (C)
1941—Tie, 14-14 (C)
          Lions, 21-3 (D)
1942—Cardinals, 13-0 (C)
          Cardinals, 7-0 (D)
1943—Lions, 35-17 (D)
          Lions, 7-0 (Buffalo)
1945—Lions, 10-0 (Milwaukee)
          Lions, 26-0 (D)
1946—Cardinals, 34-14 (C)
          Cardinals, 36-14 (D)
1947—Cardinals, 45-21 (C)
          Cardinals, 17-7 (D)
1948—Cardinals, 56-20 (C)
          Cardinals, 28-14 (D)
1949—Lions, 24-7 (C)
          Cardinals, 42-19 (D)
1959—Lions, 45-21 (D)

1961—Lions, 45-14 (StL)
1967—Cardinals, 38-28 (StL)
1969—Lions, 20-0 (D)
1970—Lions, 16-3 (D)
1973—Lions, 20-16 (StL)
1975—Cardinals, 24-13 (D)
1978—Cardinals, 21-14 (StL)
1980—Lions, 20-7 (D)
          Cardinals, 24-23 (StL)
1989—Cardinals, 16-13 (D)
1993—Lions, 26-20 (D)
          Lions, 21-14 (Phx)
1995—Cardinals, 20-17 (D)
1998—Cardinals, 17-15 (D)
1999—Cardinals, 23-19 (A)
2001—Cardinals, 45-38 (A)
(RS Pts.—Lions 908, Cardinals 784)
**Franchise known as Phoenix prior to
1994, in St. Louis prior to 1988,
and in Chicago prior to 1960
**Franchise in Portsmouth prior to 1934
and known as the Spartans*
*ARIZONA vs. GREEN BAY
RS: Packers lead series, 41-21-4
PS: Packers lead series, 1-0
1921—Tie, 3-3 (C)
1922—Cardinals, 16-3 (C)
1924—Cardinals, 3-0 (C)
1925—Cardinals, 9-6 (C)
1926—Cardinals, 13-7 (GB)
          Packers, 3-0 (C)
1927—Packers, 13-0 (GB)
          Tie, 6-6 (C)
1928—Packers, 20-0 (GB)
1929—Packers, 9-2 (GB)
          Packers, 7-6 (C)
          Packers, 12-0 (C)
1930—Packers, 14-0 (GB)
          Cardinals, 13-6 (C)
1931—Packers, 26-7 (GB)
          Cardinals, 21-13 (C)
1932—Packers, 15-7 (GB)
          Packers, 19-9 (C)
1933—Packers, 14-6 (C)
1934—Packers, 15-0 (GB)
          Cardinals, 9-0 (Mil)
          Cardinals, 6-0 (C)
1935—Packers, 7-6 (GB)
          Cardinals, 3-0 (Mil)
          Cardinals, 9-7 (C)
1936—Packers, 10-7 (GB)
          Packers, 24-0 (Mil)
          Tie, 0-0 (C)
1937—Cardinals, 14-7 (GB)
          Packers, 34-13 (Mil)
1938—Packers, 28-7 (GB)
          Packers, 24-22 (Buffalo)
1939—Packers, 14-10 (Mil)
          Packers, 27-20 (Mil)
1940—Packers, 31-6 (Mil)
          Packers, 28-7 (C)
1941—Packers, 14-13 (Mil)
          Packers, 17-9 (GB)
1942—Packers, 17-13 (C)
          Packers, 55-24 (GB)
1943—Packers, 28-7 (C)
          Packers, 35-14 (Mil)
1945—Packers, 33-14 (GB)
1946—Packers, 19-7 (C)
          Cardinals, 24-6 (GB)

1947—Cardinals, 14-10 (GB)
Cardinals, 21-20 (C)
1948—Cardinals, 17-7 (Mil)
Cardinals, 42-7 (C)
1949—Cardinals, 39-17 (Mil)
Cardinals, 41-21 (C)
1955—Packers, 31-14 (GB)
1956—Packers, 24-21 (C)
1962—Packers, 17-0 (Mil)
1963—Packers, 30-7 (StL)
1967—Packers, 31-23 (StL)
1969—Packers, 45-28 (GB)
1971—Tie, 16-16 (StL)
1973—Packers, 25-21 (GB)
1976—Cardinals, 29-0 (StL)
1982—**Packers, 41-16 (GB)
1984—Packers, 24-23 (GB)
1985—Cardinals, 43-28 (StL)
1988—Packers, 26-17 (P)
1990—Packers, 24-21 (P)
1999—Packers, 49-24 (GB)
2000—Packers, 29-3 (A)
(RS Pts.—Packers 1,156, Cardinals 850)
(PS Pts.—Packers 41, Cardinals 16)
*Franchise known as Phoenix prior to
1994, in St. Louis prior to 1988,
and in Chicago prior to 1960
**NFC First-Round Playoff

*ARIZONA vs. **INDIANAPOLIS
RS: Series tied, 6-6
1961—Colts, 16-0 (B)
1964—Colts, 47-27 (B)
1968—Colts, 27-0 (B)
1972—Cardinals, 10-3 (B)
1976—Cardinals, 24-17 (StL)
1978—Colts, 30-17 (StL)
1980—Cardinals, 17-10 (B)
1981—Cardinals, 35-24 (B)
1984—Cardinals, 34-33 (I)
1990—Cardinals, 20-17 (P)
1992—Colts, 16-13 (I)
1996—Colts, 20-13 (I)
(RS Pts.—Colts 260, Cardinals 210)
*Franchise known as Phoenix prior to
1994 and in St. Louis prior to 1988
**Franchise in Baltimore prior to 1984

ARIZONA vs. JACKSONVILLE
RS: Jaguars lead series, 1-0
2000—Jaguars, 44-10 (J)
(RS Pts.—Jaguars 44, Cardinals 10)

*ARIZONA vs. KANSAS CITY
RS: Chiefs lead series, 5-2-1
1970—Tie, 6-6 (KC)
1974—Chiefs, 17-13 (StL)
1980—Chiefs, 21-13 (StL)
1983—Chiefs, 38-14 (KC)
1986—Cardinals, 23-14 (StL)
1995—Chiefs, 24-3 (A)
1998—Chiefs, 34-24 (KC)
2001—Cardinals, 24-16 (A)
(RS Pts.—Chiefs 170, Cardinals 120)
*Franchise known as Phoenix prior to
1994 and in St. Louis prior to 1988

*ARIZONA vs. MIAMI
RS: Dolphins lead series, 8-0
1972—Dolphins, 31-10 (M)
1977—Dolphins, 55-14 (StL)
1978—Dolphins, 24-10 (M)
1981—Dolphins, 20-7 (StL)
1984—Dolphins, 36-28 (StL)

1990—Dolphins, 23-3 (M)
1996—Dolphins, 38-10 (A)
1999—Dolphins, 19-16 (M)
(RS Pts.—Dolphins 246, Cardinals 98)
*Franchise known as Phoenix prior to
1994 and in St. Louis prior to 1988

*ARIZONA vs. MINNESOTA
RS: Series tied, 8-8
PS: Vikings lead series, 2-0
1963—Cardinals, 56-14 (M)
1967—Cardinals, 34-24 (M)
1969—Vikings, 27-10 (StL)
1972—Cardinals, 19-17 (M)
1974—Vikings, 28-24 (StL)
**Vikings, 30-14 (M)
1977—Cardinals, 27-7 (M)
1979—Cardinals, 37-7 (StL)
1981—Cardinals, 30-17 (StL)
1983—Cardinals, 41-31 (StL)
1991—Vikings, 34-7 (M)
Vikings, 28-0 (P)
1994—Cardinals, 17-7 (A)
1995—Vikings, 30-24 (A) OT
1996—Vikings, 41-17 (M)
1997—Vikings, 20-19 (A)
1998—**Vikings, 41-21 (M)
2000—Vikings, 31-14 (M)
(RS Pts.—Cardinals 376, Vikings 363)
(PS Pts.—Vikings 71, Cardinals 35)
*Franchise known as Phoenix prior to
1994 and in St. Louis prior to 1988
**NFC Divisional Playoff

*ARIZONA vs. **NEW ENGLAND
RS: Cardinals lead series, 6-4
1970—Cardinals, 31-0 (StL)
1975—Cardinals, 24-17 (StL)
1978—Patriots, 16-6 (StL)
1981—Cardinals, 27-20 (NE)
1984—Cardinals, 33-10 (NE)
1990—Cardinals, 34-14 (P)
1991—Cardinals, 24-10 (P)
1993—Patriots, 23-21 (P)
1996—Patriots, 31-0 (NE)
1999—Patriots, 27-3 (A)
(RS Pts.—Cardinals 203, Patriots 168)
*Franchise known as Phoenix prior to
1994 and in St. Louis prior to 1988
**Franchise in Boston prior to 1971

*ARIZONA vs. NEW ORLEANS
RS: Cardinals lead series, 12-11
1967—Cardinals, 31-20 (StL)
1968—Cardinals, 21-20 (NO)
Cardinals, 31-17 (StL)
1969—Saints, 51-42 (StL)
1970—Cardinals, 24-17 (StL)
1974—Saints, 14-0 (NO)
1977—Cardinals, 49-31 (StL)
1980—Cardinals, 40-7 (NO)
1981—Cardinals, 30-3 (StL)
1982—Cardinals, 21-7 (NO)
1983—Saints, 28-17 (NO)
1984—Saints, 34-24 (NO)
1985—Cardinals, 28-16 (StL)
1986—Saints, 16-7 (StL)
1987—Cardinals, 24-19 (StL)
1990—Saints, 28-7 (NO)
1991—Saints, 27-3 (P)
1992—Saints, 30-21 (P)
1993—Saints, 20-17 (P)
1996—Cardinals, 28-14 (NO)

1997—Saints, 27-10 (NO)
1998—Cardinals, 19-17 (A)
2000—Saints, 21-10 (A)
(RS Pts.—Cardinals 504, Saints 484)
*Franchise known as Phoenix prior to
1994 and in St. Louis prior to 1988

*ARIZONA vs. N.Y. GIANTS
RS: Giants lead series, 77-39-2
1926—Giants, 20-0 (NY)
1927—Giants, 28-7 (NY)
1929—Giants, 24-21 (NY)
1930—Giants, 25-12 (NY)
Giants, 13-7 (C)
1935—Cardinals, 14-13 (NY)
1936—Giants, 14-6 (NY)
1938—Giants, 6-0 (NY)
1939—Giants, 17-7 (NY)
1941—Cardinals, 10-7 (NY)
1942—Giants, 21-7 (NY)
1943—Giants, 24-13 (NY)
1946—Giants, 28-24 (NY)
1947—Giants, 35-31 (NY)
1948—Cardinals, 63-35 (NY)
1949—Giants, 41-38 (C)
1950—Cardinals, 17-3 (C)
Giants, 51-21 (NY)
1951—Giants, 28-17 (NY)
Giants, 10-0 (C)
1952—Cardinals, 24-23 (NY)
Giants, 28-6 (C)
1953—Giants, 21-7 (NY)
Giants, 23-20 (C)
1954—Giants, 41-10 (C)
Giants, 31-17 (NY)
1955—Cardinals, 28-17 (C)
Giants, 10-0 (NY)
1956—Cardinals, 35-27 (C)
Giants, 23-10 (NY)
1957—Giants, 27-14 (NY)
Giants, 28-21 (C)
1958—Giants, 37-7 (Buffalo)
Cardinals, 23-6 (NY)
1959—Giants, 9-3 (NY)
Giants, 30-20 (Minn)
1960—Giants, 35-14 (StL)
Cardinals, 20-13 (NY)
1961—Cardinals, 21-10 (NY)
Giants, 24-9 (StL)
1962—Giants, 31-14 (StL)
Giants, 31-28 (NY)
1963—Giants, 38-21 (StL)
Cardinals, 24-17 (NY)
1964—Giants, 34-17 (NY)
Tie, 10-10 (StL)
1965—Giants, 14-10 (NY)
Giants, 28-15 (StL)
1966—Cardinals, 24-19 (StL)
Cardinals, 20-17 (NY)
1967—Giants, 37-20 (StL)
Giants, 37-14 (NY)
1968—Cardinals, 28-21 (NY)
1969—Cardinals, 42-17 (StL)
Giants, 49-6 (NY)
1970—Giants, 35-17 (NY)
Giants, 34-17 (StL)
1971—Giants, 21-20 (StL)
Cardinals, 24-7 (NY)
1972—Giants, 27-21 (NY)
Giants, 13-7 (StL)
1973—Cardinals, 35-27 (StL)

Giants, 24-13 (New Haven)
1974—Cardinals, 23-21 (New Haven)
Cardinals, 26-14 (StL)
1975—Cardinals, 26-14 (StL)
Cardinals, 20-13 (NY)
1976—Cardinals, 27-21 (StL)
Cardinals, 17-14 (NY)
1977—Cardinals, 28-0 (StL)
Giants, 27-7 (NY)
1978—Cardinals, 20-10 (StL)
Giants, 17-0 (NY)
1979—Cardinals, 27-14 (NY)
Cardinals, 29-20 (StL)
1980—Giants, 41-35 (StL)
Cardinals, 23-7 (NY)
1981—Giants, 34-14 (NY)
Giants, 20-10 (StL)
1982—Cardinals, 24-21 (StL)
1983—Tie, 20-20 (StL) OT
Cardinals, 10-6 (NY)
1984—Giants, 16-10 (NY)
Cardinals, 31-21 (StL)
1985—Giants, 27-17 (NY)
Giants, 34-3 (StL)
1986—Giants, 13-6 (StL)
Giants, 27-7 (NY)
1987—Giants, 30-7 (NY)
Cardinals, 27-24 (StL)
1988—Cardinals, 24-17 (P)
Giants, 44-7 (NY)
1989—Giants, 35-7 (NY)
Giants, 20-13 (P)
1990—Giants, 20-19 (NY)
Giants, 24-21 (P)
1991—Giants, 20-9 (NY)
Giants, 21-14 (P)
1992—Giants, 31-21 (NY)
Cardinals, 19-0 (P)
1993—Giants, 19-17 (NY)
Cardinals, 17-6 (P)
1994—Giants, 20-17 (A)
Cardinals, 10-9 (NY)
1995—Giants, 27-21 (NY) OT
Giants, 10-6 (A)
1996—Giants, 16-8 (NY)
Cardinals, 31-23 (A)
1997—Giants, 27-13 (A)
Giants, 19-10 (NY)
1998—Giants, 34-7 (NY)
Giants, 23-19 (A)
1999—Cardinals, 14-3 (A)
Cardinals, 34-24 (NY)
2000—Giants, 21-16 (NY)
Giants, 31-7 (A)
2001—Giants, 17-10 (A)
Giants, 17-13 (NY)
(RS Pts.—Giants 2,598, Cardinals 1,989)
*Franchise known as Phoenix prior to
1994, in St. Louis prior to 1988,
and in Chicago prior to 1960

*ARIZONA vs. N.Y. JETS
RS: Jets lead series, 3-2
1971—Cardinals, 17-10 (StL)
1975—Cardinals, 37-6 (NY)
1978—Jets, 23-10 (NY)
1996—Jets, 31-21 (A)
1999—Jets, 12-7 (NY)
(RS Pts.—Cardinals 92, Jets 82)
*Franchise known as Phoenix prior to
1994 and in St. Louis prior to 1988

*ARIZONA vs. **OAKLAND
RS: Raiders lead series, 3-2
1973—Raiders, 17-10 (StL)
1983—Cardinals, 34-24 (LA)
1989—Raiders, 16-14 (LA)
1998—Raiders, 23-20 (A)
2001—Cardinals, 34-31 (O) OT
(RS Pts.—Cardinals 112, Raiders 111)
*Franchise known as Phoenix prior to
1994 and in St. Louis prior to 1988
**Franchise in Los Angeles from
1982-1994

*ARIZONA vs. PHILADELPHIA
RS: Cardinals lead series, 52-51-5
PS: Series tied, 1-1
1935—Cardinals, 12-3 (C)
1936—Cardinals, 13-0 (C)
1937—Tie, 6-6 (P)
1938—Eagles, 7-0 (Erie, Pa.)
1941—Eagles, 21-14 (P)
1945—Eagles, 21-6 (P)
1947—Cardinals, 45-21 (P)
**Cardinals, 28-21 (C)
1948—Cardinals, 21-14 (C)
**Eagles, 7-0 (P)
1949—Eagles, 28-3 (P)
1950—Eagles, 45-7 (C)
Cardinals, 14-10 (P)
1951—Eagles, 17-14 (C)
1952—Eagles, 10-7 (P)
Cardinals, 28-22 (C)
1953—Eagles, 56-17 (C)
Eagles, 38-0 (P)
1954—Eagles, 35-16 (C)
Eagles, 30-14 (P)
1955—Tie, 24-24 (C)
Eagles, 27-3 (P)
1956—Cardinals, 20-6 (P)
Cardinals, 28-17 (C)
1957—Eagles, 38-21 (C)
Cardinals, 31-27 (P)
1958—Tie, 21-21 (C)
Eagles, 49-21 (P)
1959—Eagles, 28-24 (Minn)
Eagles, 27-17 (P)
1960—Eagles, 31-27 (P)
Eagles, 20-6 (StL)
1961—Eagles, 30-27 (P)
Eagles, 20-7 (StL)
1962—Cardinals, 27-21 (P)
Cardinals, 45-35 (StL)
1963—Cardinals, 28-24 (P)
Cardinals, 38-14 (StL)
1964—Cardinals, 38-13 (P)
Cardinals, 36-34 (StL)
1965—Eagles, 34-27 (P)
Eagles, 28-24 (StL)
1966—Cardinals, 16-13 (StL)
Cardinals, 41-10 (P)
1967—Cardinals, 48-14 (StL)
1968—Cardinals, 45-17 (P)
1969—Eagles, 34-30 (StL)
1970—Cardinals, 35-20 (P)
Cardinals, 23-14 (StL)
1971—Eagles, 37-20 (StL)
Eagles, 19-7 (P)
1972—Tie, 6-6 (P)
Cardinals, 24-23 (StL)
1973—Cardinals, 34-23 (P)
Eagles, 27-24 (StL)

1974—Cardinals, 7-3 (StL)
Cardinals, 13-3 (P)
1975—Cardinals, 31-20 (StL)
Cardinals, 24-23 (P)
1976—Cardinals, 33-14 (StL)
Cardinals, 17-14 (P)
1977—Cardinals, 21-17 (P)
Cardinals, 21-16 (StL)
1978—Cardinals, 16-10 (P)
Eagles, 14-10 (StL)
1979—Eagles, 24-20 (StL)
Eagles, 16-13 (P)
1980—Cardinals, 24-14 (StL)
Eagles, 17-3 (P)
1981—Eagles, 52-10 (StL)
Eagles, 38-0 (P)
1982—Cardinals, 23-20 (P)
1983—Cardinals, 14-11 (P)
Cardinals, 31-7 (StL)
1984—Cardinals, 34-14 (P)
Cardinals, 17-16 (StL)
1985—Eagles, 30-7 (P)
Eagles, 24-14 (StL)
1986—Cardinals, 13-10 (StL)
Tie, 10-10 (P) OT
1987—Eagles, 28-23 (StL)
Cardinals, 31-19 (P)
1988—Eagles, 31-21 (P)
Eagles, 23-17 (Phx)
1989—Eagles, 17-5 (Phx)
Eagles, 31-14 (P)
1990—Cardinals, 23-21 (P)
Eagles, 23-21 (Phx)
1991—Cardinals, 26-10 (P)
Eagles, 34-14 (Phx)
1992—Eagles, 31-14 (Phx)
Eagles, 7-3 (P)
1993—Eagles, 23-17 (P)
Cardinals, 16-3 (Phx)
1994—Eagles, 17-7 (P)
Cardinals, 12-6 (A)
1995—Eagles, 31-19 (A)
Eagles, 21-20 (P)
1996—Cardinals, 36-30 (A)
Eagles, 29-19 (P)
1997—Eagles, 13-10 (P) OT
Cardinals, 31-21 (A)
1998—Cardinals, 17-3 (A)
Cardinals, 20-17 (P) OT
1999—Cardinals, 25-24 (P)
Cardinals, 21-17 (A)
2000—Eagles, 33-14 (A)
Eagles, 34-9 (P)
2001—Cardinals, 21-20 (P)
Eagles, 21-7 (A)
(RS Pts.—Eagles 2,281, Cardinals 2,092)
(PS Pts.—Eagles 28, Cardinals 28)
*Franchise known as Phoenix prior to
1994, in St. Louis prior to 1988,
and in Chicago prior to 1960
**NFL Championship

*ARIZONA vs. **PITTSBURGH
RS: Steelers lead series, 30-22-3
1933—Pirates, 14-13 (C)
1935—Pirates, 17-13 (P)
1936—Cardinals, 14-6 (C)
1937—Cardinals, 13-7 (P)
1939—Cardinals, 10-0 (P)
1940—Tie, 7-7 (P)
1942—Steelers, 19-3 (P)

1945—Steelers, 23-0 (P)
1946—Steelers, 14-7 (P)
1948—Cardinals, 24-7 (P)
1950—Steelers, 28-17 (C)
     Steelers, 28-7 (P)
1951—Steelers, 28-14 (C)
1952—Steelers, 34-28 (C)
     Steelers, 17-14 (P)
1953—Steelers, 31-28 (P)
     Steelers, 21-17 (C)
1954—Cardinals, 17-14 (C)
     Steelers, 20-17 (P)
1955—Steelers, 14-7 (P)
     Cardinals, 27-13 (C)
1956—Steelers, 14-7 (P)
     Cardinals, 38-27 (C)
1957—Steelers, 29-20 (P)
     Steelers, 27-2 (C)
1958—Steelers, 27-20 (C)
     Steelers, 38-21 (P)
1959—Cardinals, 45-24 (C)
     Steelers, 35-20 (P)
1960—Steelers, 27-14 (P)
     Cardinals, 38-7 (StL)
1961—Steelers, 30-27 (P)
     Cardinals, 20-0 (StL)
1962—Steelers, 26-17 (StL)
     Steelers, 19-7 (P)
1963—Steelers, 23-10 (P)
     Cardinals, 24-23 (StL)
1964—Cardinals, 34-30 (StL)
     Cardinals, 21-20 (P)
1965—Cardinals, 20-7 (P)
     Cardinals, 21-17 (StL)
1966—Steelers, 30-9 (P)
     Cardinals, 6-3 (StL)
1967—Cardinals, 28-14 (P)
     Tie, 14-14 (StL)
1968—Tie, 28-28 (StL)
     Cardinals, 20-10 (P)
1969—Cardinals, 27-14 (P)
     Cardinals, 47-10 (StL)
1972—Steelers, 25-19 (StL)
1979—Steelers, 24-21 (StL)
1985—Steelers, 23-10 (P)
1988—Cardinals, 31-14 (Phx)
1994—Cardinals, 20-17 (A) OT
1997—Steelers, 26-20 (A) OT
(RS Pts.—Steelers 1,064, Cardinals 1,023)
*Franchise known as Phoenix prior to 1994, in St. Louis prior to 1988, and in Chicago prior to 1960
**Steelers known as Pirates prior to 1941

*ARIZONA vs. **ST. LOUIS
RS: Rams lead series, 23-21-2
PS: Rams lead series, 1-0
1937—Cardinals, 6-0 (Clev)
     Cardinals, 13-7 (Chi)
1938—Cardinals, 7-6 (Clev)
     Cardinals, 31-17 (Chi)
1939—Rams, 24-0 (Chi)
     Rams, 14-0 (Clev)
1940—Rams, 26-14 (Clev)
     Cardinals, 17-7 (Chi)
1941—Rams, 10-6 (Clev)
     Cardinals, 7-0 (Chi)
1942—Cardinals, 7-0 (Buffalo)
     Rams, 7-3 (Clev)
1945—Rams, 21-0 (Clev)
     Rams, 35-21 (Chi)

1946—Cardinals, 34-10 (Chi)
     Rams, 17-14 (LA)
1947—Rams, 27-7 (LA)
     Cardinals, 17-10 (Chi)
1948—Cardinals, 27-22 (LA)
     Cardinals, 27-24 (Chi)
1949—Tie, 28-28 (Chi)
     Cardinals, 31-27 (LA)
1951—Rams, 45-21 (LA)
1953—Tie, 24-24 (Chi)
1954—Rams, 28-17 (LA)
1958—Rams, 20-14 (Chi)
1960—Cardinals, 43-21 (LA)
1965—Rams, 27-3 (StL)
1968—Rams, 24-13 (StL)
1970—Rams, 34-13 (LA)
1972—Cardinals, 24-14 (StL)
1975—***Rams, 35-23 (LA)
1976—Cardinals, 30-28 (LA)
1979—Rams, 21-0 (LA)
1980—Rams, 21-13 (StL)
1984—Rams, 16-13 (StL)
1985—Rams, 46-14 (LA)
1986—Rams, 16-10 (StL)
1987—Rams, 27-24 (StL)
1988—Cardinals, 41-27 (LA)
1989—Rams, 37-14 (LA)
1991—Cardinals, 24-14 (LA)
1992—Cardinals, 20-14 (LA)
1993—Cardinals, 38-10 (P)
1994—Rams, 14-12 (LA)
1996—Cardinals, 31-28 (A) OT
1998—Cardinals, 20-17 (StL)
(RS Pts.—Rams 912, Cardinals 793)
(PS Pts.—Rams 35, Cardinals 23)
*Franchise known as Phoenix prior to 1994, in St. Louis prior to 1988, and in Chicago prior to 1960
**Franchise in Los Angeles prior to 1995 and in Cleveland prior to 1946
***NFC Divisional Playoff

*ARIZONA vs. SAN DIEGO
RS: Chargers lead series, 6-3
1971—Chargers, 20-17 (SD)
1976—Chargers, 43-24 (SD)
1983—Cardinals, 44-14 (StL)
1987—Chargers, 28-24 (SD)
1989—Chargers, 24-13 (P)
1992—Chargers, 27-21 (P)
1995—Chargers, 28-25 (SD)
1998—Cardinals, 16-13 (A)
2001—Cardinals, 20-17 (SD)
(RS Pts.—Chargers 214, Cardinals 204)
*Franchise known as Phoenix prior to 1994, in St. Louis prior to 1988,

*ARIZONA vs. SAN FRANCISCO
RS: 49ers lead series, 12-9
1951—Cardinals, 27-21 (SF)
1957—Cardinals, 20-10 (SF)
1962—49ers, 24-17 (StL)
1964—Cardinals, 23-13 (SF)
1968—49ers, 35-17 (SF)
1971—49ers, 26-14 (StL)
1974—Cardinals, 34-9 (SF)
1976—Cardinals, 23-20 (StL) OT
1978—Cardinals, 16-10 (SF)
1979—Cardinals, 13-10 (StL)
1980—49ers, 24-21 (SF) OT
1982—49ers, 31-20 (StL)
1983—49ers, 42-27 (StL)

1986—49ers, 43-17 (SF)
1987—49ers, 34-28 (SF)
1988—Cardinals, 24-23 (P)
1991—49ers, 14-10 (SF)
1992—Cardinals, 24-14 (P)
1993—49ers, 28-14 (SF)
1999—49ers, 24-10 (A)
2000—49ers, 27-20 (SF)
(RS Pts.—49ers 482, Cardinals 419)
*Franchise known as Phoenix prior to 1994, in St. Louis prior to 1988, and in Chicago prior to 1960

*ARIZONA vs. SEATTLE
RS: Cardinals lead series, 5-1
1976—Cardinals, 30-24 (S)
1983—Cardinals, 33-28 (StL)
1989—Cardinals, 34-24 (S)
1993—Cardinals, 30-27 (S) OT
1995—Cardinals, 20-14 (A) OT
1998—Seahawks, 33-14 (S)
(RS Pts.—Cardinals 161, Seahawks 150)
*Franchise known as Phoenix prior to 1994 and in St. Louis prior to 1988

*ARIZONA vs. TAMPA BAY
RS: Series tied, 7-7
1977—Buccaneers, 17-7 (TB)
1981—Buccaneers, 20-10 (TB)
1983—Cardinals, 34-27 (TB)
1985—Buccaneers, 16-0 (TB)
1986—Cardinals, 30-19 (TB)
     Cardinals, 21-17 (StL)
1987—Cardinals, 31-28 (StL)
     Cardinals, 31-14 (TB)
1988—Cardinals, 30-24 (TB)
1989—Buccaneers, 14-13 (P)
1992—Buccaneers, 23-7 (TB)
     Buccaneers, 7-3 (P)
1996—Cardinals, 13-9 (A)
1997—Buccaneers, 19-18 (TB)
(RS Pts.—Buccaneers 254, Cardinals 248)
*Franchise known as Phoenix prior to 1994 and in St. Louis prior to 1988

*ARIZONA vs. **TENNESSEE
RS: Cardinals lead series, 4-3
1970—Cardinals, 44-0 (StL)
1974—Cardinals, 31-27 (H)
1979—Cardinals, 24-17 (H)
1985—Oilers, 20-10 (StL)
1988—Oilers, 38-20 (H)
1994—Cardinals, 30-12 (H)
1997—Oilers, 41-14 (A)
(RS Pts.—Cardinals 173, Titans 155)
*Franchise known as Phoenix prior to 1994 and in St. Louis prior to 1988
**Franchise in Houston prior to 1997; known as Oilers prior to 1999

*ARIZONA vs. **WASHINGTON
RS: Redskins lead series, 69-44-2
1932—Cardinals, 9-0 (B)
     Braves, 8-6 (C)
1933—Redskins, 10-0 (C)
     Tie, 0-0 (B)
1934—Redskins, 9-0 (B)
1935—Cardinals, 6-0 (B)
1936—Redskins, 13-10 (B)
1937—Redskins, 21-14 (W)
1939—Redskins, 28-7 (W)
1940—Redskins, 28-21 (W)
1942—Redskins, 28-0 (W)
1943—Redskins, 13-7 (W)

1945—Redskins, 24-21 (W)
1947—Redskins, 45-21 (W)
1949—Cardinals, 38-7 (C)
1950—Cardinals, 38-28 (W)
1951—Redskins, 7-3 (C)
 Redskins, 20-17 (W)
1952—Redskins, 23-7 (C)
 Cardinals, 17-6 (W)
1953—Redskins, 24-13 (C)
 Redskins, 28-17 (W)
1954—Cardinals, 38-16 (C)
 Redskins, 37-20 (W)
1955—Cardinals, 24-10 (W)
 Redskins, 31-0 (C)
1956—Cardinals, 31-3 (W)
 Redskins, 17-14 (C)
1957—Redskins, 37-14 (C)
 Cardinals, 44-14 (W)
1958—Cardinals, 37-10 (C)
 Redskins, 45-31 (W)
1959—Cardinals, 49-21 (C)
 Redskins, 23-14 (W)
1960—Cardinals, 44-7 (StL)
 Cardinals, 26-14 (W)
1961—Cardinals, 24-0 (W)
 Cardinals, 38-24 (StL)
1962—Redskins, 24-14 (W)
 Tie, 17-17 (StL)
1963—Cardinals, 21-7 (W)
 Cardinals, 24-20 (StL)
1964—Cardinals, 23-17 (W)
 Cardinals, 38-24 (StL)
1965—Cardinals, 37-16 (W)
 Redskins, 24-20 (StL)
1966—Cardinals, 23-7 (StL)
 Redskins, 26-20 (W)
1967—Cardinals, 27-21 (W)
1968—Cardinals, 41-14 (StL)
1969—Redskins, 33-17 (W)
1970—Cardinals, 27-17 (StL)
 Redskins, 28-27 (W)
1971—Redskins, 24-17 (StL)
 Redskins, 20-0 (W)
1972—Redskins, 24-10 (W)
 Redskins, 33-3 (StL)
1973—Cardinals, 34-27 (StL)
 Redskins, 31-13 (W)
1974—Cardinals, 17-10 (W)
 Cardinals, 23-20 (StL)
1975—Redskins, 27-17 (W)
 Cardinals, 20-17 (StL) OT
1976—Redskins, 20-10 (W)
 Redskins, 16-10 (StL)
1977—Redskins, 24-14 (W)
 Redskins, 26-20 (StL)
1978—Redskins, 28-10 (StL)
 Cardinals, 27-17 (W)
1979—Redskins, 17-7 (StL)
 Redskins, 30-28 (W)
1980—Redskins, 23-0 (W)
 Redskins, 31-7 (StL)
1981—Cardinals, 40-30 (StL)
 Redskins, 42-21 (W)
1982—Redskins, 12-7 (StL)
 Redskins, 28-0 (W)
1983—Redskins, 38-14 (StL)
 Redskins, 45-7 (W)
1984—Cardinals, 26-24 (StL)
 Redskins, 29-27 (W)
1985—Redskins, 27-10 (W)

 Redskins, 27-16 (StL)
1986—Redskins, 28-21 (W)
 Redskins, 20-17 (StL)
1987—Redskins, 28-21 (W)
 Redskins, 34-17 (StL)
1988—Cardinals, 30-21 (P)
 Redskins, 33-17 (W)
1989—Redskins, 30-28 (W)
 Redskins, 29-10 (P)
1990—Redskins, 31-0 (W)
 Redskins, 38-10 (P)
1991—Redskins, 34-0 (W)
 Redskins, 20-14 (P)
1992—Cardinals, 27-24 (P)
 Redskins, 41-3 (W)
1993—Cardinals, 17-10 (W)
 Cardinals, 36-6 (P)
1994—Cardinals, 19-16 (W) OT
 Cardinals, 17-15 (A)
1995—Redskins, 27-7 (W)
 Cardinals, 24-20 (A)
1996—Cardinals, 37-34 (W) OT
 Cardinals, 27-26 (A)
1997—Redskins, 19-13 (W) OT
 Redskins, 38-28 (A)
1998—Cardinals, 29-27 (A)
 Cardinals, 45-42 (W)
1999—Redskins, 24-10 (A)
 Redskins, 28-3 (W)
2000—Cardinals, 16-15 (A)
 Redskins, 20-3 (W)
2001—Redskins, 20-10 (A)
 Redskins, 20-17 (W)
(RS Pts.—Redskins 2,552, Cardinals 2,131)
*Franchise known as Phoenix prior to
1994, in St. Louis prior to 1988,
and in Chicago prior to 1960
**Franchise in Boston prior to 1937 and
known as Braves prior to 1933

ATLANTA vs. ARIZONA
RS: Cardinals lead series, 13-8;
See Arizona vs. Atlanta
ATLANTA vs. BALTIMORE
RS: Ravens lead series, 1-0
1999—Ravens, 19-13 (A) OT
(RS Pts.—Ravens 19, Falcons 13)
ATLANTA vs. BUFFALO
RS: Series tied, 4-4
1973—Bills, 17-6 (A)
1977—Bills, 3-0 (B)
1980—Falcons, 30-14 (B)
1983—Falcons, 31-14 (A)
1989—Falcons, 30-28 (A)
1992—Bills, 41-14 (B)
1995—Bills, 23-17 (B)
2001—Falcons, 33-30 (A)
(RS Pts.—Bills 170, Falcons 161)
ATLANTA vs. CAROLINA
RS: Falcons lead series, 9-5
1995—Falcons, 23-20 (A) OT
 Panthers, 21-17 (C)
1996—Panthers, 29-6 (C)
 Falcons, 20-17 (A)
1997—Panthers, 9-6 (A)
 Panthers, 21-12 (C)
1998—Falcons, 19-14 (C)
 Falcons, 51-23 (A)
1999—Falcons, 27-20 (A)
 Panthers, 34-28 (C)

2000—Falcons, 15-10 (C)
 Falcons, 13-12 (A)
2001—Falcons, 24-16 (A)
 Falcons, 10-7 (C)
(RS Pts.—Falcons 271, Panthers 253)
ATLANTA vs. CHICAGO
RS: Series tied, 10-10
1966—Bears, 23-6 (C)
1967—Bears, 23-14 (A)
1968—Falcons, 16-13 (C)
1969—Falcons, 48-31 (A)
1970—Bears, 23-14 (A)
1972—Falcons, 37-21 (C)
1973—Falcons, 46-6 (A)
1974—Falcons, 13-10 (A)
1976—Falcons, 10-0 (C)
1977—Falcons, 16-10 (C)
1978—Bears, 13-7 (C)
1980—Falcons, 28-17 (A)
1983—Falcons, 20-17 (C)
1985—Bears, 36-0 (C)
1986—Bears, 13-10 (A)
1990—Bears, 30-24 (A)
1992—Bears, 41-31 (A)
1993—Bears, 6-0 (C)
1998—Falcons, 20-13 (A)
2001—Bears, 31-3 (A)
(RS Pts.—Bears 377, Falcons 363)
ATLANTA vs. CINCINNATI
RS: Bengals lead series, 7-2
1971—Falcons, 9-6 (C)
1975—Bengals, 21-14 (A)
1978—Bengals, 37-7 (C)
1981—Bengals, 30-28 (A)
1984—Bengals, 35-14 (C)
1987—Bengals, 16-10 (A)
1990—Falcons, 38-17 (A)
1993—Bengals, 21-17 (C)
1996—Bengals, 41-31 (C)
(RS Pts.—Bengals 224, Falcons 168)
ATLANTA vs. CLEVELAND
RS: Browns lead series, 8-2
1966—Browns, 49-17 (A)
1968—Browns, 30-7 (C)
1971—Falcons, 31-14 (C)
1976—Browns, 20-17 (A)
1978—Browns, 24-16 (A)
1981—Browns, 28-17 (C)
1984—Browns, 23-7 (A)
1987—Browns, 38-3 (C)
1990—Browns, 13-10 (C)
1993—Falcons, 17-14 (A)
(RS Pts.—Browns 253, Falcons 142)
ATLANTA vs. DALLAS
RS: Cowboys lead series, 12-7
PS: Cowboys lead series, 2-0
1966—Cowboys, 47-14 (A)
1967—Cowboys, 37-7 (D)
1969—Cowboys, 24-17 (A)
1970—Cowboys, 13-0 (D)
1974—Cowboys, 24-0 (A)
1976—Falcons, 17-10 (A)
1978—*Cowboys, 27-20 (D)
1980—*Cowboys, 30-27 (A)
1985—Cowboys, 24-10 (D)
1986—Falcons, 37-35 (A)
1987—Falcons, 21-10 (D)
1988—Cowboys, 26-20 (D)
1989—Falcons 27-21 (A)
1990—Falcons, 26-7 (A)

1991—Cowboys, 31-27 (D)
1992—Cowboys, 41-17 (A)
1993—Falcons, 27-14 (A)
1995—Cowboys, 28-13 (A)
1996—Cowboys, 32-28 (D)
1999—Cowboys, 24-7 (D)
2001—Falcons, 20-13 (A)
(RS Pts.—Cowboys 461, Falcons 335)
(PS Pts.—Cowboys 57, Falcons 47)
*NFC Divisional Playoff

ATLANTA vs. DENVER
RS: Broncos lead series, 7-3
PS: Broncos lead series, 1-0
1970—Broncos, 24-10 (D)
1972—Broncos, 23-20 (A)
1975—Falcons, 35-21 (A)
1979—Broncos, 20-17 (A) OT
1982—Falcons, 34-27 (D)
1985—Broncos, 44-28 (A)
1988—Broncos, 30-14 (A)
1994—Broncos, 32-28 (D)
1997—Broncos, 29-21 (A)
1998—*Broncos, 34-19 (Miami)
2000—Broncos, 42-14 (D)
(RS Pts.—Broncos 289, Falcons 224)
(PS Pts.—Broncos 34, Falcons 19)
*Super Bowl XXXIII

ATLANTA vs. DETROIT
RS: Lions lead series, 21-7
1966—Lions, 28-10 (D)
1967—Lions, 24-3 (D)
1968—Lions, 24-7 (A)
1969—Lions, 27-21 (D)
1971—Lions, 41-38 (D)
1972—Lions, 26-23 (A)
1973—Lions, 31-6 (D)
1975—Lions, 17-14 (A)
1976—Lions, 24-10 (D)
1977—Falcons, 17-6 (A)
1978—Lions, 14-0 (A)
1979—Lions, 24-23 (D)
1980—Falcons, 43-28 (A)
1983—Falcons, 30-14 (D)
1984—Lions, 27-24 (A) OT
1985—Lions, 28-27 (A)
1986—Falcons, 20-6 (D)
1987—Lions, 30-13 (A)
1988—Lions, 31-17 (D)
1989—Lions, 31-24 (A)
1990—Lions, 21-14 (D)
1993—Lions, 30-13 (D)
1994—Lions, 31-28 (D) OT
1995—Falcons, 34-22 (A)
1996—Lions, 28-24 (D)
1997—Lions, 28-17 (D)
1998—Falcons, 24-17 (D)
2000—Lions, 13-10 (D)
(RS Pts.—Lions 657, Falcons 548)

ATLANTA vs. GREEN BAY
RS: Series tied, 10-10
PS: Packers lead series, 1-0
1966—Packers, 56-3 (Mil)
1967—Packers, 23-0 (Mil)
1968—Packers, 38-7 (A)
1969—Packers, 28-10 (GB)
1970—Packers, 27-24 (GB)
1971—Falcons, 28-21 (A)
1972—Falcons, 10-9 (Mil)
1974—Falcons, 10-3 (A)
1975—Packers, 22-13 (GB)

1976—Packers, 24-20 (A)
1979—Falcons, 25-7 (A)
1981—Falcons, 31-17 (GB)
1982—Packers, 38-7 (A)
1983—Falcons, 47-41 (A) OT
1988—Falcons, 20-0 (A)
1989—Packers, 23-21 (Mil)
1991—Falcons, 35-31 (A)
1992—Falcons, 24-10 (A)
1994—Packers, 21-17 (Mil)
1995—*Packers, 37-20 (GB)
2001—Falcons, 23-20 (GB)
(RS Pts.—Packers 459, Falcons 375)
(PS Pts.—Packers 37, Falcons 20)
*NFC First-Round Playoff

ATLANTA vs. *INDIANAPOLIS
RS: Colts lead series, 11-1
1966—Colts, 19-7 (A)
1967—Colts, 38-31 (B)
　　　Colts, 49-7 (A)
1968—Colts, 28-20 (A)
　　　Colts, 44-0 (B)
1969—Colts, 21-14 (A)
　　　Colts, 13-6 (B)
1974—Colts, 17-7 (A)
1986—Colts, 28-23 (A)
1989—Colts, 13-9 (I)
1998—Falcons, 28-21 (A)
2001—Colts, 41-27 (I)
(RS Pts.—Colts 332, Falcons 179)
*Franchise in Baltimore prior to 1984

ATLANTA vs. JACKSONVILLE
RS: Jaguars lead series, 2-0
1996—Jaguars, 19-17 (J)
1999—Jaguars, 30-7 (A)
(RS Pts.—Jaguars 49, Falcons 24)

ATLANTA vs. KANSAS CITY
RS: Chiefs lead series, 4-1
1972—Chiefs, 17-14 (A)
1985—Chiefs, 38-10 (KC)
1991—Chiefs, 14-3 (KC)
1994—Chiefs, 30-10 (A)
2000—Falcons, 29-13 (A)
(RS Pts.—Chiefs 112, Falcons 66)

ATLANTA vs. MIAMI
RS: Dolphins lead series, 7-2
1970—Dolphins, 20-7 (A)
1974—Dolphins, 42-7 (M)
1980—Dolphins, 20-17 (A)
1983—Dolphins, 31-24 (M)
1986—Falcons, 20-14 (M)
1992—Dolphins, 21-17 (M)
1995—Dolphins, 21-20 (M)
1998—Falcons, 38-16 (A)
2001—Dolphins, 21-14 (M)
(RS Pts.—Dolphins 206, Falcons 164)

ATLANTA vs. MINNESOTA
RS: Vikings lead series, 13-6
PS: Series tied, 1-1
1966—Falcons, 20-13 (M)
1967—Falcons, 21-20 (A)
1968—Vikings, 47-7 (M)
1969—Falcons, 10-3 (A)
1970—Vikings, 37-7 (A)
1971—Vikings, 24-7 (M)
1973—Falcons, 20-14 (A)
1974—Vikings, 23-10 (M)
1975—Vikings, 38-0 (M)
1977—Vikings, 14-7 (A)
1980—Vikings, 24-23 (M)

1981—Falcons, 31-30 (A)
1982—*Vikings, 30-24 (M)
1984—Vikings, 27-20 (M)
1985—Falcons, 14-13 (A)
1987—Vikings, 24-13 (M)
1989—Vikings, 43-17 (M)
1991—Vikings, 20-19 (A)
1996—Vikings, 23-17 (A)
1998—**Falcons, 30-27 (M) OT
1999—Vikings, 17-14 (A)
(RS Pts.—Vikings 454, Falcons 277)
(PS Pts.—Vikings 57, Falcons 54)
*NFC First-Round Playoff
**NFC Championship

ATLANTA vs. NEW ENGLAND
RS: Falcons lead series, 6-4
1972—Patriots, 21-20 (NE)
1977—Patriots, 16-10 (A)
1980—Falcons, 37-21 (NE)
1983—Falcons, 24-13 (A)
1986—Patriots, 25-17 (NE)
1989—Falcons, 16-15 (A)
1992—Falcons, 34-0 (A)
1995—Falcons, 30-17 (A)
1998—Falcons, 41-10 (NE)
2001—Patriots, 24-10 (A)
(RS Pts.—Falcons 239, Patriots 162)

ATLANTA vs. NEW ORLEANS
RS: Falcons lead series, 38-27
PS: Falcons lead series, 1-0
1967—Saints, 27-24 (NO)
1969—Falcons, 45-17 (A)
1970—Falcons, 14-3 (NO)
　　　Falcons, 32-14 (A)
1971—Falcons, 28-6 (A)
　　　Falcons, 24-20 (NO)
1972—Falcons, 21-14 (NO)
　　　Falcons, 36-20 (A)
1973—Falcons, 62-7 (NO)
　　　Falcons, 14-10 (A)
1974—Saints, 14-13 (NO)
　　　Saints, 13-3 (A)
1975—Falcons, 14-7 (A)
　　　Saints, 23-7 (NO)
1976—Saints, 30-0 (NO)
　　　Falcons, 23-20 (A)
1977—Saints, 21-20 (NO)
　　　Falcons, 35-7 (A)
1978—Falcons, 20-17 (NO)
　　　Falcons, 20-17 (A)
1979—Falcons, 40-34 (NO) OT
　　　Saints, 37-6 (A)
1980—Falcons, 41-14 (NO)
　　　Falcons, 31-13 (A)
1981—Falcons, 27-0 (A)
　　　Falcons, 41-10 (NO)
1982—Falcons, 35-0 (A)
　　　Saints, 35-6 (NO)
1983—Saints, 19-17 (A)
　　　Saints, 27-10 (NO)
1984—Falcons, 36-28 (NO)
　　　Saints, 17-13 (A)
1985—Falcons, 31-24 (A)
　　　Falcons, 16-10 (NO)
1986—Falcons, 31-10 (NO)
　　　Saints, 14-9 (A)
1987—Saints, 38-0 (A)
1988—Saints, 29-21 (A)
　　　Saints, 10-9 (NO)
1989—Saints, 20-13 (NO)

Saints, 26-17 (A)
1990—Falcons, 28-27 (A)
Saints, 10-7 (NO)
1991—Saints, 27-6 (A)
Falcons, 23-20 (NO) OT
*Falcons, 27-20 (NO)
1992—Saints, 10-7 (A)
Saints, 22-14 (NO)
1993—Saints, 34-31 (A)
Falcons, 26-15 (NO)
1994—Saints, 33-32 (NO)
Saints, 29-20 (A)
1995—Falcons, 27-24 (NO) OT
Falcons, 19-14 (A)
1996—Falcons, 17-15 (A)
Falcons, 31-15 (NO)
1997—Falcons, 23-17 (NO)
Falcons, 20-3 (A)
1998—Falcons, 31-23 (A)
Falcons, 27-17 (NO)
1999—Falcons, 20-17 (NO)
Falcons, 35-12 (A)
2000—Saints, 21-19 (A)
Saints, 23-7 (NO)
2001—Falcons, 20-13 (NO)
Saints, 28-10 (A)
(RS Pts.—Falcons 1,405, Saints 1,191)
(PS Pts.—Falcons 27, Saints 20)
*NFC First-Round Playoff

ATLANTA vs. N.Y. GIANTS
RS: Series tied, 7-7
1966—Falcons, 27-16 (NY)
1968—Falcons, 24-21 (A)
1971—Giants, 21-17 (A)
1974—Falcons, 14-7 (New Haven)
1977—Falcons, 17-3 (A)
1978—Falcons, 23-20 (A)
1979—Giants, 24-3 (NY)
1981—Giants, 27-24 (A) OT
1982—Falcons, 16-14 (NY)
1983—Giants, 16-13 (A) OT
1984—Giants, 19-7 (A)
1988—Giants, 23-16 (A)
1998—Falcons, 34-20 (NY)
2000—Giants, 13-6 (A)
(RS Pts.—Giants 244, Falcons 241)

ATLANTA vs. N.Y. JETS
RS: Series tied, 4-4
1973—Falcons, 28-20 (NY)
1980—Jets, 14-7 (A)
1983—Falcons, 27-21 (NY)
1986—Jets, 28-14 (A)
1989—Jets, 27-7 (NY)
1992—Falcons, 20-17 (A)
1995—Falcons, 13-3 (A)
1998—Jets, 28-3 (NY)
(RS Pts.—Jets 158, Falcons 119)

ATLANTA vs. *OAKLAND
RS: Raiders lead series, 7-3
1971—Falcons, 24-13 (A)
1975—Raiders, 37-34 (A) OT
1979—Raiders, 50-19 (O)
1982—Raiders, 38-14 (A)
1985—Raiders, 34-24 (A)
1988—Falcons, 12-6 (LA)
1991—Falcons, 21-17 (A)
1994—Raiders, 30-17 (LA)
1997—Raiders, 36-31 (A)
2000—Raiders, 41-14 (O)
(RS Pts.—Raiders 302, Falcons 210)

*Franchise in Los Angeles from
1982-1994
ATLANTA vs. PHILADELPHIA
RS: Eagles lead series, 10-9-1
PS: Falcons lead series, 1-0
1966—Eagles, 23-10 (P)
1967—Eagles, 38-7 (A)
1969—Falcons, 27-3 (P)
1970—Tie, 13-13 (P)
1973—Falcons, 44-27 (P)
1976—Eagles, 14-13 (A)
1978—*Falcons, 14-13 (A)
1979—Falcons, 14-10 (P)
1980—Falcons, 20-17 (P)
1981—Eagles, 16-13 (P)
1983—Eagles, 28-24 (A)
1984—Falcons, 26-10 (A)
1985—Eagles, 23-17 (P) OT
1986—Eagles, 16-0 (A)
1988—Falcons, 27-24 (P)
1990—Eagles, 24-23 (A)
1994—Falcons, 28-21 (A)
1996—Eagles, 33-18 (A)
1997—Falcons, 20-17 (A)
1998—Falcons, 17-12 (A)
2000—Eagles, 38-10 (P)
(RS Pts.—Eagles 407, Falcons 371)
(PS Pts.—Falcons 14, Eagles 13)
*NFC First-Round Playoff

ATLANTA vs. PITTSBURGH
RS: Steelers lead series, 11-1
1966—Steelers, 57-33 (A)
1968—Steelers, 41-21 (A)
1970—Falcons, 27-16 (A)
1974—Steelers, 24-17 (P)
1978—Steelers, 31-7 (P)
1981—Steelers, 34-20 (A)
1984—Steelers, 35-10 (P)
1987—Steelers, 28-12 (A)
1990—Steelers, 21-9 (P)
1993—Steelers, 45-17 (A)
1996—Steelers, 20-17 (A)
1999—Steelers, 13-9 (P)
(RS Pts.—Steelers 365, Falcons 199)

ATLANTA vs. *ST. LOUIS
RS: Rams lead series, 45-23-2
1966—Rams, 19-14 (A)
1967—Rams, 31-3 (A)
Rams, 20-3 (LA)
1968—Rams, 27-14 (LA)
Rams, 17-10 (A)
1969—Rams, 17-7 (LA)
Rams, 38-6 (A)
1970—Tie, 10-10 (LA)
Rams, 17-7 (A)
1971—Tie, 20-20 (A)
Rams, 24-16 (A)
1972—Falcons, 31-3 (A)
Rams, 20-7 (LA)
1973—Rams, 31-0 (LA)
Falcons, 15-13 (A)
1974—Rams, 21-0 (A)
Rams, 30-7 (A)
1975—Rams, 22-7 (LA)
Rams, 16-7 (A)
1976—Rams, 30-14 (A)
Rams, 59-0 (LA)
1977—Falcons, 17-6 (A)
Rams, 23-7 (LA)
1978—Rams, 10-0 (LA)

Falcons, 15-7 (A)
1979—Rams, 20-14 (LA)
Rams, 34-13 (A)
1980—Falcons, 13-10 (A)
Rams, 20-17 (LA) OT
1981—Rams, 37-35 (A)
Rams, 21-16 (LA)
1982—Falcons, 34-17 (A)
1983—Rams, 27-21 (LA)
Rams, 36-13 (A)
1984—Falcons, 30-28 (LA)
Rams, 24-10 (A)
1985—Rams, 17-6 (LA)
Falcons, 30-14 (A)
1986—Falcons, 26-14 (A)
Rams, 14-7 (LA)
1987—Falcons, 24-20 (A)
Rams, 33-0 (LA)
1988—Rams, 33-0 (A)
Rams, 22-7 (LA)
1989—Falcons, 31-21 (A)
Rams, 26-14 (LA)
1990—Rams, 44-24 (LA)
Falcons, 20-13 (A)
1991—Falcons, 31-14 (A)
Falcons, 31-14 (LA)
1992—Falcons, 30-28 (A)
Rams, 38-27 (LA)
1993—Falcons, 30-24 (A)
Falcons, 13-0 (LA)
1994—Falcons, 31-13 (A)
Falcons, 8-5 (LA)
1995—Rams, 21-19 (StL)
Falcons, 31-6 (A)
1996—Rams, 59-16 (StL)
Rams, 34-27 (A)
1997—Falcons, 34-31 (A)
Falcons, 27-21 (StL)
1998—Falcons, 37-15 (A)
Falcons, 21-10 (StL)
1999—Rams, 35-7 (StL)
Rams, 41-13 (A)
2000—Rams, 41-20 (A)
Rams, 45-29 (StL)
2001—Rams, 35-6 (A)
Rams, 31-13 (StL)
(RS Pts.—Rams 1,647, Falcons 1,133)
*Franchise in Los Angeles prior to 1995

ATLANTA vs. SAN DIEGO
RS: Falcons lead series, 5-1
1973—Falcons, 41-0 (SD)
1979—Falcons, 28-26 (SD)
1988—Chargers, 10-7 (A)
1991—Falcons, 13-10 (SD)
1994—Falcons, 10-9 (A)
1997—Falcons, 14-3 (SD)
(RS Pts.—Falcons 113, Chargers 58)

ATLANTA vs. SAN FRANCISCO
RS: 49ers lead series, 44-25-1
PS: Falcons lead series, 1-0
1966—49ers, 44-7 (A)
1967—49ers, 38-7 (SF)
49ers, 34-28 (A)
1968—49ers, 28-13 (SF)
49ers, 14-12 (A)
1969—Falcons, 24-12 (A)
Falcons, 21-7 (SF)
1970—Falcons, 21-20 (A)
49ers, 24-20 (SF)
1971—Falcons, 20-17 (A)

49ers, 24-3 (SF)
1972—49ers, 49-14 (A)
49ers, 20-0 (SF)
1973—49ers, 13-9 (A)
Falcons, 17-3 (SF)
1974—49ers, 16-10 (A)
49ers, 27-0 (SF)
1975—Falcons, 17-3 (SF)
Falcons, 31-9 (A)
1976—49ers, 15-0 (SF)
Falcons, 21-16 (A)
1977—Falcons, 7-0 (SF)
49ers, 10-3 (A)
1978—Falcons, 20-17 (SF)
Falcons, 21-10 (A)
1979—49ers, 20-15 (SF)
Falcons, 31-21 (A)
1980—Falcons, 20-17 (SF)
Falcons, 35-10 (A)
1981—Falcons, 34-17 (A)
49ers, 17-14 (SF)
1982—Falcons, 17-7 (SF)
1983—49ers, 24-20 (SF)
Falcons, 28-24 (A)
1984—49ers, 14-5 (SF)
49ers, 35-17 (A)
1985—49ers, 35-16 (SF)
49ers, 38-17 (A)
1986—Tie, 10-10 (A) OT
49ers, 20-0 (SF)
1987—49ers, 25-17 (A)
49ers, 35-7 (SF)
1988—Falcons, 34-17 (SF)
49ers, 13-3 (A)
1989—49ers, 45-3 (SF)
49ers, 23-10 (A)
1990—49ers, 19-13 (SF)
49ers, 45-35 (A)
1991—Falcons, 39-34 (SF)
Falcons, 17-14 (A)
1992—49ers, 56-17 (SF)
49ers, 41-3 (A)
1993—49ers, 37-30 (SF)
Falcons, 27-24 (A)
1994—49ers, 42-3 (A)
49ers, 50-14 (SF)
1995—49ers, 41-10 (SF)
Falcons, 28-27 (A)
1996—49ers, 39-17 (SF)
49ers, 34-10 (A)
1997—49ers, 34-7 (SF)
49ers, 35-28 (A)
1998—49ers, 31-20 (SF)
Falcons, 31-19 (A)
*Falcons, 20-18 (A)
1999—49ers, 26-7 (SF)
Falcons, 34-29 (A)
2000—Falcons, 36-28 (A)
49ers, 16-6 (SF)
2001—49ers, 16-13 (SF) OT
49ers, 37-31 (A) OT
(RS Pts.—49ers 1,711, Falcons 1,175)
(PS Pts.—Falcons 20, 49ers 18)
*NFC Divisional Playoff

ATLANTA vs. SEATTLE
RS: Seahawks lead series, 5-2
1976—Seahawks, 30-13 (S)
1979—Seahawks, 31-28 (A)
1985—Seahawks, 30-26 (S)
1988—Seahawks, 31-20 (A)

1991—Falcons, 26-13 (A)
1997—Falcons, 24-17 (S)
2000—Seahawks, 30-10 (A)
(RS Pts.—Seahawks 182, Falcons 147)

ATLANTA vs. TAMPA BAY
RS: Buccaneers lead series, 9-8
1977—Falcons, 17-0 (TB)
1978—Buccaneers, 14-9 (TB)
1979—Falcons, 17-14 (A)
1981—Buccaneers, 24-23 (TB)
1984—Buccaneers, 23-6 (TB)
1986—Falcons, 23-20 (TB) OT
1987—Buccaneers, 48-10 (TB)
1988—Falcons, 17-10 (A)
1990—Buccaneers, 23-17 (TB)
1991—Falcons, 43-7 (A)
1992—Falcons, 35-7 (TB)
1993—Buccaneers, 31-24 (A)
1994—Falcons, 34-13 (A)
1995—Falcons, 24-21 (TB)
1997—Buccaneers, 31-10 (A)
1999—Buccaneers, 19-10 (TB)
2000—Buccaneers, 27-14 (A)
(RS Pts.—Falcons 333, Buccaneers 332)

ATLANTA vs. *TENNESSEE
RS: Series tied, 5-5
1972—Falcons, 20-10 (A)
1976—Oilers, 20-14 (H)
1978—Falcons, 20-14 (A)
1981—Falcons, 31-27 (H)
1984—Falcons, 42-10 (A)
1987—Oilers, 37-33 (H)
1990—Falcons, 47-27 (A)
1993—Oilers, 33-17 (H)
1996—Oilers, 23-13 (A)
1999—Titans, 30-17 (T)
(RS Pts.—Falcons 254, Titans 231)
*Franchise in Houston prior to 1997;
known as Oilers prior to 1999

ATLANTA vs. WASHINGTON
RS: Redskins lead series, 13-4-1
PS: Redskins lead series, 1-0
1966—Redskins, 33-20 (W)
1967—Tie, 20-20 (A)
1969—Redskins, 27-20 (W)
1972—Redskins, 24-13 (W)
1975—Redskins, 30-27 (A)
1977—Redskins, 10-6 (W)
1978—Falcons, 20-17 (A)
1979—Redskins, 16-7 (A)
1980—Falcons, 10-6 (A)
1983—Redskins, 37-21 (W)
1984—Redskins, 27-14 (W)
1985—Redskins, 44-10 (A)
1987—Falcons, 21-20 (A)
1989—Redskins, 31-30 (A)
1991—Redskins, 56-17 (W)
*Redskins, 24-7 (W)
1992—Redskins, 24-17 (W)
1993—Redskins, 30-17 (W)
1994—Falcons, 27-20 (W)
(RS Pts.—Redskins 472, Falcons 317)
(PS Pts.—Redskins 24, Falcons 7)
*NFC Divisional Playoff

BALTIMORE vs. ARIZONA
RS: Series tied, 1-1;
See Arizona vs. Baltimore

BALTIMORE vs. ATLANTA
RS: Ravens lead series, 1-0;

See Atlanta vs. Baltimore

BALTIMORE vs. BUFFALO
RS: Bills lead series, 1-0
1999—Bills, 13-10 (Balt)
(RS Pts.—Bills 13, Ravens 10)

BALTIMORE vs. CAROLINA
RS: Panthers lead series, 1-0
1996—Panthers, 27-16 (C)
(RS Pts.—Panthers 27, Ravens 16)

BALTIMORE vs. CHICAGO
RS: Series tied, 1-1
1998—Bears, 24-3 (C)
2001—Ravens, 17-6 (B)
(RS Pts.—Bears 30, Ravens 20)

BALTIMORE vs. CINCINNATI
RS: Ravens lead series, 8-4
1996—Bengals, 24-21 (B)
Bengals, 21-14 (C)
1997—Ravens, 23-10 (B)
Bengals, 16-14 (C)
1998—Ravens, 31-24 (B)
Ravens, 20-13 (C)
1999—Ravens, 34-31 (C)
Ravens, 22-0 (B)
2000—Ravens, 37-0 (B)
Ravens, 27-7 (C)
2001—Bengals, 21-10 (C)
Ravens, 16-0 (B)
(RS Pts.—Ravens 269, Bengals 167)

BALTIMORE vs. CLEVELAND
RS: Ravens lead series, 4-2
1999—Ravens, 17-10 (B)
Ravens, 41-9 (C)
2000—Ravens, 12-0 (C)
Ravens, 44-7 (B)
2001—Browns, 24-14 (C)
Browns, 27-17 (B)
(RS Pts.—Ravens 145, Browns 77)

BALTIMORE vs. DALLAS
RS: Ravens lead series, 1-0
2000—Ravens, 27-0 (B)
(RS Pts.—Ravens 27, Cowboys 0)

BALTIMORE vs. DENVER
RS: Series tied, 1-1
PS: Ravens lead series, 1-0
1996—Broncos, 45-34 (D)
2000—*Ravens, 21-3 (B)
2001—Ravens, 20-13 (D)
(RS Pts.—Broncos 58, Ravens 54)
(PS Pts.—Ravens 21, Broncos 3)
*AFC First-Round Playoff

BALTIMORE vs. DETROIT
RS: Ravens lead series, 1-0
1998—Ravens, 19-10 (B)
(RS Pts.—Ravens 19, Lions 10)

BALTIMORE vs. GREEN BAY
RS: Packers lead series, 2-0
1998—Packers, 28-10 (GB)
2001—Packers, 31-23 (GB)
(RS Pts.—Packers 59, Ravens 33)

BALTIMORE vs. INDIANAPOLIS
RS: Ravens lead series, 2-1
1996—Colts, 26-21 (I)
1998—Ravens, 38-31 (B)
2001—Ravens, 39-27 (B)
(RS Pts.—Ravens 98, Colts 84)

BALTIMORE vs. JACKSONVILLE
RS: Jaguars lead series, 8-4
1996—Jaguars, 30-27 (J)
Jaguars, 28-25 (B) OT

1997—Jaguars, 28-27 (B)
Jaguars, 29-27 (J)
1998—Jaguars, 24-10 (J)
Jaguars, 45-19 (B)
1999—Jaguars, 6-3 (J)
Jaguars, 30-23 (B)
2000—Ravens, 39-36 (B)
Ravens, 15-10 (J)
2001—Ravens, 18-17 (B)
Ravens, 24-21 (J)
(RS Pts.—Jaguars 304, Ravens 257)
BALTIMORE vs. KANSAS CITY
RS: Chiefs lead series, 1-0;
1999—Chiefs, 35-8 (B)
(RS Pts.—Chiefs 35, Ravens 8)
BALTIMORE vs. MIAMI
RS: Dolphins lead series, 2-0
PS: Ravens lead series, 1-0
1997—Dolphins, 24-13 (B)
2000—Dolphins, 19-6 (M)
2001—*Ravens, 20-3 (M)
(RS Pts.—Dolphins 43, Ravens 19)
(PS Pts.—Ravens 20, Dolphins 3)
*AFC First-Round Playoff
BALTIMORE vs. MINNESOTA
RS: Series tied, 1-1
1998—Vikings, 38-28 (B)
2001—Ravens, 19-3 (B)
(RS Pts.—Ravens 47, Vikings 41)
BALTIMORE vs. NEW ENGLAND
RS: Patriots lead series, 2-0
1996—Patriots, 46-38 (B)
1999—Patriots, 20-3 (NE)
(RS Pts.—Patriots 66, Ravens 41)
BALTIMORE vs. NEW ORLEANS
RS: Ravens lead series, 2-0
1996—Ravens, 17-10 (B)
1999—Ravens, 31-8 (B)
(RS Pts.—Ravens 48, Saints 18)
BALTIMORE vs. N.Y. GIANTS
RS: Ravens lead series, 1-0
PS: Ravens lead series, 1-0
1997—Ravens, 24-23 (NY)
2000—*Ravens, 34-7 (Tampa)
(RS Pts.—Ravens 24, Giants 23)
(PS Pts.—Ravens 34, Giants 7)
*Super Bowl XXXV
BALTIMORE vs. N.Y. JETS
RS: Ravens lead series, 2-1
1997—Jets, 19-16 (NY) OT
1998—Ravens, 24-10 (NY)
2000—Ravens, 34-20 (B)
(RS Pts.—Ravens 74, Jets 49)
BALTIMORE vs. OAKLAND
RS: Ravens lead series, 2-0
PS: Ravens lead series, 1-0
1996—Ravens, 19-14 (B)
1998—Ravens, 13-10 (B)
2000—*Ravens, 16-3 (O)
(RS Pts.—Ravens 32, Raiders 24)
(PS Pts.—Ravens 16, Raiders 3)
*AFC Championship
BALTIMORE vs. PHILADELPHIA
RS: Series tied, 0-0-1
1997—Tie, 10-10 (B) OT
(RS Pts.—Ravens 10, Eagles 10)
BALTIMORE vs. PITTSBURGH
RS: Steelers lead series, 8-4
PS: Steelers lead series, 1-0
1996—Steelers, 31-17 (P)

Ravens, 31-17 (B)
1997—Steelers, 42-34 (B)
Steelers, 37-0 (P)
1998—Steelers, 20-13 (B)
Steelers, 16-6 (P)
1999—Steelers, 23-20 (B)
Ravens, 31-24 (P)
2000—Ravens, 16-0 (P)
Steelers, 9-6 (B)
2001—Ravens, 13-10 (P)
Steelers, 26-21 (B)
*Steelers, 27-10 (P)
(RS Pts.—Steelers 255, Ravens 208)
(PS Pts.—Steelers 27, Ravens 10)
*AFC Divisional Playoff
BALTIMORE vs. ST. LOUIS
RS: Series tied, 1-1
1996—Ravens, 37-31 (B) OT
1999—Rams, 27-10 (StL)
(RS Pts.—Rams 58, Ravens 47)
BALTIMORE vs. SAN DIEGO
RS: Chargers lead series, 2-1
1997—Chargers, 21-17 (SD)
1998—Chargers, 14-13 (SD)
2000—Ravens, 24-3 (B)
(RS Pts.—Ravens 54, Chargers 38)
BALTIMORE vs. SAN FRANCISCO
RS: 49ers lead series, 1-0
1996—49ers, 38-20 (SF)
(RS Pts.—49ers 38, Ravens 20)
BALTIMORE vs. SEATTLE
RS: Ravens lead series, 1-0
1997—Ravens, 31-24 (B)
(RS Pts.—Ravens 31, Seahawks 24)
BALTIMORE vs. TAMPA BAY
RS: Buccaneers lead series, 1-0
2001—Buccaneers, 22-10 (TB)
(RS Pts.—Buccaneers 22, Ravens 10)
BALTIMORE vs. *TENNESSEE
RS: Series tied, 6-6
PS: Ravens lead series, 1-0
1996—Oilers, 29-13 (H)
Oilers, 24-21 (B)
1997—Ravens, 36-10 (T)
Ravens, 21-19 (B)
1998—Oilers, 12-8 (B)
Oilers, 16-14 (T)
1999—Titans, 14-11 (T)
Ravens, 41-14 (B)
2000—Titans, 14-6 (B)
Ravens, 24-23 (T)
**Ravens, 24-10 (T)
2001—Ravens, 26-7 (B)
Ravens, 16-10 (T)
(RS Pts.—Ravens 237, Titans 192)
(PS Pts.—Ravens 24, Titans 10)
*Franchise in Houston prior to 1997;
known as Oilers prior to 1999
**AFC Divisional Playoff
BALTIMORE vs. WASHINGTON
RS: Series tied, 1-1
1997—Ravens, 20-17 (W)
2000—Redskins, 10-3 (W)
(RS Pts.—Redskins 27, Ravens 23)

BUFFALO vs. ARIZONA
RS: Bills lead series, 4-3;
See Arizona vs. Buffalo
BUFFALO vs. ATLANTA
RS: Series tied, 4-4;

See Atlanta vs. Buffalo
BUFFALO vs. BALTIMORE
RS: Bills lead series, 1-0;
See Baltimore vs. Buffalo
BUFFALO vs. CAROLINA
RS: Bills lead series, 3-0
1995—Bills, 31-9 (B)
1998—Bills, 30-14 (C)
2001—Bills, 25-24 (B)
(RS Pts.—Bills 86, Panthers 47)
BUFFALO vs. CHICAGO
RS: Bears lead series, 5-3
1970—Bears, 31-13 (C)
1974—Bills, 16-6 (B)
1979—Bears, 7-0 (B)
1988—Bears, 24-3 (C)
1991—Bills, 35-20 (B)
1994—Bears, 20-13 (C)
1997—Bears, 20-3 (C)
2000—Bills, 20-3 (B)
(RS Pts.—Bears 131, Bills 103)
BUFFALO vs. CINCINNATI
RS: Series tied, 9-9
PS: Bengals lead series, 2-0
1968—Bengals, 34-23 (C)
1969—Bills, 16-13 (B)
1970—Bengals, 43-14 (B)
1973—Bengals, 16-13 (B)
1975—Bengals, 33-24 (C)
1978—Bills, 5-0 (B)
1979—Bills, 51-24 (B)
1980—Bills, 14-0 (C)
1981—Bengals, 27-24 (C) OT
*Bengals, 28-21 (C)
1983—Bills, 10-6 (C)
1984—Bengals, 52-21 (C)
1985—Bengals, 23-17 (B)
1986—Bengals, 36-33 (C) OT
1988—Bengals, 35-21 (C)
**Bengals, 21-10 (C)
1989—Bills, 24-7 (B)
1991—Bills, 35-16 (B)
1996—Bills, 31-17 (B)
1998—Bills, 33-20 (C)
(RS Pts.—Bills 409, Bengals 402)
(PS Pts.—Bengals 49, Bills 31)
*AFC Divisional Playoff
**AFC Championship
BUFFALO vs. CLEVELAND
RS: Browns lead series, 7-4
PS: Browns lead series, 1-0
1972—Browns, 27-10 (C)
1974—Bills, 15-10 (C)
1977—Browns, 27-16 (B)
1978—Browns, 41-20 (C)
1981—Bills, 22-13 (B)
1984—Browns, 13-10 (B)
1985—Browns, 17-7 (B)
1986—Browns, 21-17 (B)
1987—Browns, 27-21 (C)
1989—*Browns, 34-30 (C)
1990—Bills, 42-0 (C)
1995—Bills, 22-19 (C)
(RS Pts.—Browns 215, Bills 202)
(PS Pts.—Browns 34, Bills 30)
*AFC Divisional Playoff
BUFFALO vs. DALLAS
RS: Series tied, 3-3
PS: Cowboys lead series, 2-0
1971—Cowboys, 49-37 (B)

1976—Cowboys, 17-10 (D)
1981—Cowboys, 27-14 (D)
1984—Bills, 14-3 (B)
1992—*Cowboys, 52-17 (Pasadena)
1993—Bills, 13-10 (D)
      **Cowboys, 30-13 (Atlanta)
1996—Bills, 10-7 (B)
(RS Pts.—Cowboys 113, Bills 98)
(PS Pts.—Cowboys 82, Bills 30)
*Super Bowl XXVII
**Super Bowl XXVIII

BUFFALO vs. DENVER
RS: Bills lead series, 17-12-1
PS: Bills lead series, 1-0
1960—Broncos, 27-21 (B)
      Tie, 38-38 (D)
1961—Broncos, 22-10 (B)
      Bills, 23-10 (D)
1962—Broncos, 23-20 (B)
      Bills, 45-38 (D)
1963—Bills, 30-28 (D)
      Bills, 27-17 (B)
1964—Bills, 30-13 (D)
      Bills, 30-19 (D)
1965—Bills, 30-15 (D)
      Bills, 31-13 (B)
1966—Bills, 38-21 (B)
1967—Bills, 17-16 (D)
      Broncos, 21-20 (B)
1968—Broncos, 34-32 (D)
1969—Bills, 41-28 (B)
1970—Broncos, 25-10 (B)
1975—Bills, 38-14 (B)
1977—Broncos, 26-6 (D)
1979—Broncos, 19-16 (B)
1981—Bills, 9-7 (B)
1984—Broncos, 37-7 (B)
1987—Bills, 21-14 (B)
1989—Broncos, 28-14 (B)
1990—Bills, 29-28 (B)
1991—*Bills, 10-7 (B)
1992—Bills, 27-17 (B)
1994—Bills, 27-20 (B)
1995—Broncos, 22-7 (D)
1997—Broncos, 23-20 (B) OT
(RS Pts.—Bills 714, Broncos 663)
(PS Pts.—Bills 10, Broncos 7)
*AFC Championship

BUFFALO vs. DETROIT
RS: Lions lead series, 3-2-1
1972—Tie, 21-21 (B)
1976—Lions, 27-14 (D)
1979—Bills, 20-17 (D)
1991—Lions, 17-14 (B) OT
1994—Lions, 35-21 (D)
1997—Bills, 22-13 (D)
(RS Pts.—Lions 130, Bills 112)

BUFFALO vs. GREEN BAY
RS: Bills lead series, 6-2
1974—Bills, 27-7 (GB)
1979—Bills, 19-12 (B)
1982—Packers, 33-21 (Mil)
1988—Bills, 28-0 (B)
1991—Bills, 34-24 (Mil)
1994—Bills 29-20 (B)
1997—Packers, 31-21 (GB)
2000—Bills 27-18 (B)
(RS Pts.—Bills 206, Packers 145)

BUFFALO vs. *INDIANAPOLIS
RS: Bills lead series, 34-28-1

1970—Tie, 17-17 (Balt)
      Colts, 20-14 (Buff)
1971—Colts, 43-0 (Buff)
      Colts, 24-0 (Balt)
1972—Colts, 17-0 (Buff)
      Colts, 35-7 (Balt)
1973—Bills, 31-13 (Buff)
      Bills, 24-17 (Balt)
1974—Bills, 27-14 (Balt)
      Bills, 6-0 (Balt)
1975—Bills, 38-31 (Balt)
      Colts, 42-35 (Buff)
1976—Colts, 31-13 (Buff)
      Colts, 58-20 (Balt)
1977—Colts, 17-14 (Balt)
      Colts, 31-13 (Buff)
1978—Bills, 24-17 (Buff)
      Bills, 21-14 (Balt)
1979—Bills, 31-13 (Balt)
      Colts, 14-13 (Buff)
1980—Colts, 17-12 (Buff)
      Colts, 28-24 (Balt)
1981—Bills, 35-3 (Balt)
      Bills, 23-17 (Buff)
1982—Bills, 20-0 (Buff)
1983—Bills, 28-23 (Buff)
      Bills, 30-7 (Balt)
1984—Colts, 31-17 (I)
      Bills, 21-15 (Buff)
1985—Colts, 49-17 (I)
      Bills, 21-9 (Buff)
1986—Bills, 24-13 (Buff)
      Colts, 24-14 (I)
1987—Colts, 47-6 (Buff)
      Bills, 27-3 (I)
1988—Bills, 34-23 (Buff)
      Colts, 17-14 (I)
1989—Colts, 37-14 (I)
      Bills, 30-7 (Buff)
1990—Bills, 26-10 (Buff)
      Bills, 31-7 (I)
1991—Bills, 42-6 (Buff)
      Bills, 35-7 (I)
1992—Bills, 38-0 (Buff)
      Colts, 16-13 (I) OT
1993—Bills, 23-9 (Buff)
      Bills, 30-10 (I)
1994—Colts, 27-17 (Buff)
      Colts, 10-9 (I)
1995—Bills, 20-14 (Buff)
      Bills, 16-10 (I)
1996—Bills, 16-13 (Buff) OT
      Colts, 13-10 (I) OT
1997—Bills, 37-35 (B)
      Bills, 9-6 (I)
1998—Bills, 31-24 (I)
      Bills, 34-11 (B)
1999—Colts, 31-14 (I)
      Bills, 31-6 (B)
2000—Colts, 18-16 (B)
      Colts, 44-20 (I)
2001—Colts, 42-26 (I)
      Colts, 30-14 (B)
(RS Pts.—Bills 1,317, Colts 1,237)
*Franchise in Baltimore prior to 1984

BUFFALO vs. JACKSONVILLE
RS: Bills lead series, 2-1
PS: Jaguars lead series, 1-0
1996—*Jaguars, 30-27 (B)
1997—Jaguars, 20-14 (B)

1998—Bills, 17-16 (B)
2001—Bills, 13-10 (J)
(RS Pts.—Jaguars 46, Bills 44)
(PS Pts.—Jaguars 30, Bills 27)
*AFC First-Round Playoff

BUFFALO vs. *KANSAS CITY
RS: Bills lead series, 18-14-1
PS: Bills lead series, 2-1
1960—Texans, 45-28 (B)
      Texans, 24-7 (D)
1961—Bills, 27-24 (B)
      Bills, 30-20 (D)
1962—Texans, 41-21 (D)
      Bills, 23-14 (B)
1963—Tie, 27-27 (B)
      Bills, 35-26 (KC)
1964—Bills, 34-17 (B)
      Bills, 35-22 (KC)
1965—Bills, 23-7 (KC)
      Bills, 34-25 (B)
1966—Chiefs, 42-20 (B)
      Bills, 29-14 (KC)
      **Chiefs, 31-7 (B)
1967—Chiefs, 23-13 (KC)
1968—Chiefs, 18-7 (B)
1969—Chiefs, 29-7 (B)
      Chiefs, 22-19 (KC)
1971—Chiefs, 22-9 (KC)
1973—Bills, 23-14 (B)
1976—Bills, 50-17 (B)
1978—Bills, 28-13 (B)
      Chiefs, 14-10 (KC)
1982—Bills, 14-9 (B)
1983—Bills, 14-9 (KC)
1986—Chiefs, 20-17 (B)
      Bills, 17-14 (KC)
1991—Chiefs, 33-6 (KC)
      ***Bills, 37-14 (B)
1993—Chiefs, 23-7 (KC)
      ****Bills, 30-13 (B)
1994—Bills, 44-10 (B)
1996—Bills, 20-9 (B)
1997—Chiefs, 22-16 (KC)
2000—Bills, 21-17 (KC)
(RS Pts.—Bills 715, Chiefs 686)
(PS Pts.—Bills 74, Chiefs 58)
*Franchise in Dallas prior to 1963 and
known as Texans
**AFC Championship
***AFC Divisional Playoff
****AFC Championship

BUFFALO vs. MIAMI
RS: Dolphins lead series, 46-25-1
PS: Bills lead series, 3-1
1966—Bills, 58-24 (B)
      Bills, 29-0 (M)
1967—Bills, 35-13 (B)
      Dolphins, 17-14 (M)
1968—Tie, 14-14 (M)
      Dolphins, 21-17 (B)
1969—Dolphins, 24-6 (M)
      Bills, 28-3 (B)
1970—Dolphins, 33-14 (B)
      Dolphins, 45-7 (M)
1971—Dolphins, 29-14 (B)
      Dolphins, 34-0 (M)
1972—Dolphins, 24-23 (M)
      Dolphins, 30-16 (B)
1973—Dolphins, 27-6 (M)
      Dolphins, 17-0 (B)

1974—Dolphins, 24-16 (B)
    Dolphins, 35-28 (M)
1975—Dolphins, 35-30 (B)
    Dolphins, 31-21 (M)
1976—Dolphins, 30-21 (B)
    Dolphins, 45-27 (M)
1977—Dolphins, 13-0 (B)
    Dolphins, 31-14 (M)
1978—Dolphins, 31-24 (M)
    Dolphins, 25-24 (B)
1979—Dolphins, 9-7 (B)
    Dolphins, 17-7 (M)
1980—Bills, 17-7 (B)
    Dolphins, 17-14 (M)
1981—Bills, 31-21 (B)
    Dolphins, 16-6 (M)
1982—Dolphins, 9-7 (B)
    Dolphins, 27-10 (M)
1983—Dolphins, 12-0 (B)
    Bills, 38-35 (M) OT
1984—Dolphins, 21-17 (B)
    Dolphins, 38-7 (M)
1985—Dolphins, 23-14 (B)
    Dolphins, 28-0 (M)
1986—Dolphins, 27-14 (M)
    Dolphins, 34-24 (B)
1987—Bills, 34-31 (M) OT
    Bills, 27-0 (B)
1988—Bills, 9-6 (B)
    Bills, 31-6 (M)
1989—Bills, 27-24 (M)
    Bills, 31-17 (B)
1990—Dolphins, 30-7 (M)
    Bills, 24-14 (B)
    *Bills, 44-34 (B)
1991—Bills, 35-31 (B)
    Bills, 41-27 (M)
1992—Dolphins, 37-10 (B)
    Bills, 26-20 (M)
    **Bills, 29-10 (M)
1993—Dolphins, 22-13 (B)
    Bills, 47-34 (M)
1994—Bills, 21-11 (B)
    Bills, 42-31 (M)
1995—Dolphins, 23-6 (M)
    Bills, 23-20 (B)
    ***Bills, 37-22 (B)
1996—Dolphins, 21-7 (B)
    Dolphins, 16-14 (M)
1997—Bills, 9-6 (B)
    Dolphins, 30-13 (M)
1998—Dolphins, 13-7 (M)
    Bills, 30-24 (B)
    ***Dolphins, 24-17 (M)
1999—Bills, 23-18 (M)
    Bills, 23-3 (B)
2000—Dolphins, 22-13 (M)
    Dolphins, 33-6 (B)
2001—Dolphins, 34-27 (B)
    Dolphins, 34-7 (M)
(RS Pts.—Dolphins 1,634, Bills 1,332)
(PS Pts.—Bills 127, Dolphins 90)
*AFC Divisional Playoff
**AFC Championship
***AFC First-Round Playoff
BUFFALO vs. MINNESOTA
RS: Vikings lead series, 7-2
1971—Vikings, 19-0 (M)
1975—Vikings, 35-13 (B)
1979—Vikings, 10-3 (M)

1982—Bills, 23-22 (B)
1985—Vikings, 27-20 (B)
1988—Bills, 13-10 (B)
1994—Vikings, 21-17 (B)
1997—Vikings, 34-13 (B)
2000—Vikings, 31-27 (M)
(RS Pts.—Vikings 209, Bills 129)
BUFFALO vs. *NEW ENGLAND
RS: Patriots lead series, 43-39-1
PS: Patriots lead series, 1-0
1960—Bills, 13-0 (Bos)
    Bills, 38-14 (Buff)
1961—Patriots, 23-21 (Buff)
    Patriots, 52-21 (Bos)
1962—Tie, 28-28 (Buff)
    Patriots, 21-10 (Bos)
1963—Bills, 28-21 (Buff)
    Patriots, 17-7 (Bos)
    **Patriots, 26-8 (Buff)
1964—Patriots, 36-28 (Buff)
    Bills, 24-14 (Bos)
1965—Bills, 24-7 (Buff)
    Bills, 23-7 (Bos)
1966—Patriots, 20-10 (Buff)
    Patriots, 14-3 (Bos)
1967—Patriots, 23-0 (Buff)
    Bills, 44-16 (Bos)
1968—Patriots, 16-7 (Buff)
    Patriots, 23-6 (Bos)
1969—Bills, 23-16 (Buff)
    Patriots, 35-21 (Bos)
1970—Bills, 45-10 (Bos)
    Patriots, 14-10 (Buff)
1971—Patriots, 38-33 (NE)
    Bills, 27-20 (Buff)
1972—Bills, 38-14 (Buff)
    Bills, 27-24 (NE)
1973—Bills, 31-13 (NE)
    Bills, 37-13 (Buff)
1974—Bills, 30-28 (Buff)
    Bills, 29-28 (NE)
1975—Bills, 45-31 (Buff)
    Bills, 34-14 (NE)
1976—Patriots, 26-22 (Buff)
    Patriots, 20-10 (NE)
1977—Bills, 24-14 (NE)
    Patriots, 20-7 (Buff)
1978—Patriots, 14-10 (Buff)
    Patriots, 26-24 (NE)
1979—Patriots, 26-6 (Buff)
    Bills, 16-13 (NE) OT
1980—Bills, 31-13 (Buff)
    Patriots, 24-2 (NE)
1981—Bills, 20-17 (Buff)
    Bills, 19-10 (NE)
1982—Patriots, 30-19 (NE)
1983—Patriots, 31-0 (Buff)
    Patriots, 21-7 (NE)
1984—Patriots, 21-17 (Buff)
    Patriots, 38-10 (NE)
1985—Patriots, 17-14 (Buff)
    Patriots, 14-3 (NE)
1986—Patriots, 23-3 (Buff)
    Patriots, 22-19 (NE)
1987—Patriots, 14-7 (Buff)
    Patriots, 13-7 (Buff)
1988—Bills, 16-14 (NE)
    Bills, 23-20 (Buff)
1989—Bills, 31-10 (Buff)
    Patriots, 33-24 (NE)

1990—Bills, 27-10 (NE)
    Bills, 14-0 (Buff)
1991—Bills, 22-17 (Buff)
    Patriots, 16-13 (NE)
1992—Bills, 41-7 (NE)
    Bills, 16-7 (Buff)
1993—Bills, 38-14 (Buff)
    Bills, 13-10 (NE) OT
1994—Bills, 38-35 (NE)
    Patriots, 41-17 (Buff)
1995—Patriots, 27-14 (NE)
    Patriots, 35-25 (Buff)
1996—Bills, 17-10 (Buff)
    Patriots, 28-25 (NE)
1997—Patriots, 33-6 (NE)
    Patriots, 31-10 (Buff)
1998—Bills, 13-10 (Buff)
    Patriots, 25-21 (NE)
1999—Bills, 17-7 (Buff)
    Bills, 13-10 (NE) OT
2000—Bills, 16-13 (NE) OT
    Patriots, 13-10 (Buff) OT
2001—Patriots, 21-11 (NE)
    Patriots, 12-9 (Buff) OT
(RS Pts.—Patriots 1,626, Bills 1,602)
(PS Pts.—Patriots 26, Bills 8)
*Franchise in Boston prior to 1971
**Division Playoff
BUFFALO vs. NEW ORLEANS
RS: Bills lead series, 4-3
1973—Bills, 13-0 (NO)
1980—Bills, 35-26 (NO)
1983—Bills, 27-21 (B)
1989—Saints, 22-19 (B)
1992—Bills, 20-16 (NO)
1998—Bills, 45-33 (NO)
2001—Saints, 24-6 (B)
(RS Pts.—Saints 155, Bills 152)
BUFFALO vs. N.Y. GIANTS
RS: Bills lead series, 5-3
PS: Giants lead series, 1-0
1970—Giants, 20-6 (NY)
1975—Giants, 17-14 (B)
1978—Bills, 41-17 (B)
1987—Bills, 6-3 (B) OT
1990—Bills, 17-13 (NY)
    *Giants, 20-19 (Tampa)
1993—Bills, 17-14 (B)
1996—Bills, 23-20 (NY) OT
1999—Giants, 19-17 (B)
(RS Pts.—Bills 141, Giants 123)
(PS Pts.—Giants 20, Bills 19)
*Super Bowl XXV
BUFFALO vs. *N.Y. JETS
RS: Bills lead series, 46-36
PS: Bills lead series, 1-0
1960—Titans, 27-3 (NY)
    Titans, 17-13 (B)
1961—Bills, 41-31 (B)
    Titans, 21-14 (NY)
1962—Titans, 17-6 (B)
    Bills, 20-3 (NY)
1963—Bills, 45-14 (B)
    Bills, 19-10 (NY)
1964—Bills, 34-24 (B)
    Bills, 20-7 (NY)
1965—Bills, 33-21 (B)
    Jets, 14-12 (NY)
1966—Bills, 33-23 (NY)
    Bills, 14-3 (B)

1967—Bills, 20-17 (B)
Jets, 20-10 (NY)
1968—Bills, 37-35 (B)
Jets, 25-21 (NY)
1969—Jets, 33-19 (B)
Jets, 16-6 (NY)
1970—Bills, 34-31 (B)
Bills, 10-6 (NY)
1971—Jets, 28-17 (NY)
Jets, 20-7 (B)
1972—Jets, 41-24 (B)
Jets, 41-3 (NY)
1973—Bills, 9-7 (B)
Bills, 34-14 (NY)
1974—Bills, 16-12 (B)
Jets, 20-10 (NY)
1975—Bills, 42-14 (B)
Bills, 24-23 (NY)
1976—Jets, 17-14 (NY)
Jets, 19-14 (B)
1977—Jets, 24-19 (B)
Bills, 14-10 (NY)
1978—Jets, 21-20 (B)
Jets, 45-14 (NY)
1979—Bills, 46-31 (B)
Bills, 14-12 (NY)
1980—Bills, 20-10 (B)
Bills, 31-24 (NY)
1981—Bills, 31-0 (B)
Jets, 33-14 (NY)
**Bills, 31-27 (NY)
1983—Jets, 34-10 (B)
Bills, 24-17 (NY)
1984—Jets, 28-26 (B)
Jets, 21-17 (NY)
1985—Jets, 42-3 (NY)
Jets, 27-7 (B)
1986—Jets, 28-24 (B)
Jets, 14-13 (NY)
1987—Jets, 31-28 (B)
Bills, 17-14 (NY)
1988—Bills, 37-14 (NY)
Bills, 9-6 (B) OT
1989—Bills, 34-3 (B)
Bills, 37-0 (NY)
1990—Bills, 30-7 (NY)
Bills, 30-27 (B)
1991—Bills, 23-20 (NY)
Bills, 24-13 (B)
1992—Bills, 24-20 (NY)
Jets, 24-17 (B)
1993—Bills, 19-10 (NY)
Bills, 16-14 (B)
1994—Jets, 23-3 (B)
Jets, 22-17 (NY)
1995—Bills, 29-10 (B)
Bills, 28-26 (NY)
1996—Bills, 25-22 (NY)
Bills, 35-10 (B)
1997—Bills, 28-22 (NY)
Bills, 20-10 (B)
1998—Jets, 34-12 (NY)
Jets, 17-10 (B)
1999—Bills, 17-3 (B)
Jets, 17-7 (NY)
2000—Jets, 27-14 (NY)
Bills, 23-20 (B)
2001—Jets, 42-36 (B)
Bills, 14-9 (NY)
(RS Pts.—Bills 1,688, Jets 1,609)

(PS Pts.—Bills 31, Jets 27)
*Jets known as Titans prior to 1963
**AFC First-Round Playoff
BUFFALO vs. *OAKLAND
RS: Raiders lead series, 16-15
PS: Bills lead series, 2-0
1960—Bills, 38-9 (B)
Raiders, 20-7 (O)
1961—Raiders, 31-22 (B)
Bills, 26-21 (O)
1962—Bills, 14-6 (B)
Bills, 10-6 (O)
1963—Raiders, 35-17 (O)
Bills, 12-0 (B)
1964—Bills, 23-20 (B)
Raiders, 16-13 (O)
1965—Bills, 17-12 (B)
Bills, 17-14 (O)
1966—Bills, 31-10 (O)
1967—Raiders, 24-20 (B)
Raiders, 28-21 (O)
1968—Raiders, 48-6 (B)
Raiders, 13-10 (O)
1969—Raiders, 50-21 (O)
1972—Raiders, 28-16 (O)
1974—Bills, 21-20 (B)
1977—Raiders, 34-13 (O)
1980—Bills, 24-7 (B)
1983—Raiders, 27-24 (B)
1987—Raiders, 34-21 (LA)
1988—Bills, 37-21 (B)
1990—Bills, 38-24 (B)
**Bills, 51-3 (B)
1991—Bills, 30-27 (LA) OT
1992—Raiders, 20-3 (LA)
1993—Raiders, 25-24 (B)
***Bills, 29-23 (B)
1998—Bills, 44-21 (B)
1999—Raiders, 20-14 (B)
(RS Pts.—Raiders 671, Bills 634)
(PS Pts.—Bills 80, Raiders 26)
*Franchise in Los Angeles from
1982-1994
**AFC Championship
***AFC Divisional Playoff
BUFFALO vs. PHILADELPHIA
RS: Bills lead series, 5-4
1973—Bills, 27-26 (B)
1981—Eagles, 20-14 (B)
1984—Eagles, 27-17 (B)
1985—Eagles, 21-17 (B)
1987—Eagles, 17-7 (P)
1990—Bills, 30-23 (B)
1993—Bills, 10-7 (P)
1996—Bills, 24-17 (P)
1999—Bills, 26-0 (B)
(RS Pts.—Bills 172, Eagles 158)
BUFFALO vs. PITTSBURGH
RS: Steelers lead series, 9-8
PS: Steelers lead series, 2-1
1970—Steelers, 23-10 (P)
1972—Steelers, 38-21 (B)
1974—*Steelers, 32-14 (P)
1975—Bills, 30-21 (P)
1978—Steelers, 28-17 (B)
1979—Steelers, 28-0 (P)
1980—Bills, 28-13 (B)
1982—Bills, 13-0 (B)
1985—Steelers, 30-24 (P)
1986—Bills, 16-12 (B)

1988—Bills, 36-28 (B)
1991—Bills, 52-34 (B)
1992—Bills, 28-20 (B)
*Bills, 24-3 (P)
1993—Steelers, 23-0 (P)
1994—Steelers, 23-10 (P)
1995—*Steelers, 40-21 (P)
1996—Steelers, 24-6 (P)
1999—Bills, 24-21 (B)
2001—Steelers, 20-3 (B)
(RS Pts.—Steelers 386, Bills 318)
(PS Pts.—Steelers 75, Bills 59)
*AFC Divisional Playoff
BUFFALO vs. *ST. LOUIS
RS: Series tied, 4-4
1970—Rams, 19-0 (B)
1974—Rams, 19-14 (LA)
1980—Bills, 10-7 (B) OT
1983—Rams, 41-17 (LA)
1989—Bills, 23-20 (B)
1992—Bills, 40-7 (B)
1995—Bills, 45-27 (StL)
1998—Rams, 34-33 (B)
(RS Pts.—Bills 182, Rams 174)
*Franchise in Los Angeles prior to 1995
BUFFALO vs. *SAN DIEGO
RS: Chargers lead series, 18-8-2
PS: Bills lead series, 2-1
1960—Chargers, 24-10 (B)
Bills, 32-3 (LA)
1961—Chargers, 19-11 (B)
Chargers, 28-10 (SD)
1962—Bills, 35-10 (B)
Bills, 40-20 (SD)
1963—Chargers, 14-10 (SD)
Chargers, 23-13 (B)
1964—Bills, 30-3 (B)
Bills, 27-24 (SD)
**Bills, 20-7 (B)
1965—Chargers, 34-3 (B)
Tie, 20-20 (SD)
**Bills, 23-0 (SD)
1966—Chargers, 27-7 (SD)
Tie, 17-17 (B)
1967—Chargers, 37-17 (B)
1968—Chargers, 21-6 (B)
1969—Chargers, 45-6 (SD)
1971—Chargers, 20-3 (SD)
1973—Chargers, 34-7 (SD)
1976—Chargers, 34-13 (B)
1979—Chargers, 27-19 (SD)
1980—Bills, 26-24 (SD)
***Chargers, 20-14 (SD)
1981—Bills, 28-27 (SD)
1985—Chargers, 14-9 (B)
Chargers, 40-7 (SD)
1998—Chargers, 16-14 (SD)
2000—Bills, 27-24 (B) OT
2001—Chargers, 27-24 (SD)
(RS Pts.—Chargers 656, Bills 471)
(PS Pts.—Bills 57, Chargers 27)
*Franchise in Los Angeles prior to 1961
**AFL Championship
***AFC Divisional Playoff
BUFFALO vs. SAN FRANCISCO
RS: Series tied, 4-4
1972—Bills, 27-20 (B)
1980—Bills, 18-13 (SF)
1983—49ers, 23-10 (B)
1989—49ers, 21-10 (SF)

1992—Bills, 34-31 (SF)
1995—49ers, 27-17 (SF)
1998—Bills, 26-21 (B)
2001—49ers, 35-0 (SF)
(RS Pts.—49ers 191, Bills 142)
BUFFALO vs. SEATTLE
RS: Seahawks lead series, 6-3
1977—Seahawks, 56-17 (S)
1984—Seahawks, 31-28 (S)
1988—Bills, 13-3 (S)
1989—Seahawks, 17-16 (S)
1995—Bills, 27-21 (B)
1996—Seahawks, 26-18 (S)
1999—Seahawks, 26-16 (S)
2000—Bills, 42-23 (S)
2001—Seahawks, 23-20 (B)
(RS Pts.—Seahawks 226, Bills 197)
BUFFALO vs. TAMPA BAY
RS: Buccaneers lead series, 5-2
1976—Bills, 14-9 (TB)
1978—Buccaneers, 31-10 (TB)
1982—Buccaneers, 24-23 (TB)
1986—Buccaneers, 34-28 (TB)
1988—Buccaneers, 10-5 (TB)
1991—Bills, 17-10 (TB)
2000—Buccaneers, 31-17 (TB)
(RS Pts.—Buccaneers 149, Bills 114)
BUFFALO vs. *TENNESSEE
RS: Titans lead series, 22-14
PS: Bills lead series, 2-1
1960—Bills, 25-24 (B)
    Oilers, 31-23 (H)
1961—Bills, 22-12 (H)
    Oilers, 28-16 (B)
1962—Oilers, 28-23 (B)
    Oilers, 17-14 (H)
1963—Oilers, 31-20 (B)
    Oilers, 28-14 (H)
1964—Bills, 48-17 (H)
    Bills, 24-10 (B)
1965—Bills, 19-17 (B)
    Bills, 29-18 (H)
1966—Bills, 27-20 (B)
    Bills, 42-20 (H)
1967—Oilers, 20-3 (B)
    Oilers, 10-3 (H)
1968—Oilers, 30-7 (B)
    Oilers, 35-6 (H)
1969—Oilers, 17-3 (B)
    Oilers, 28-14 (H)
1971—Oilers, 20-14 (B)
1974—Oilers, 21-9 (B)
1976—Oilers, 13-3 (B)
1978—Oilers, 17-10 (H)
1983—Bills, 30-13 (B)
1985—Bills, 20-0 (B)
1986—Oilers, 16-7 (H)
1987—Bills, 34-30 (B)
1988—**Bills, 17-10 (B)
1989—Bills, 47-41 (H) OT
1990—Oilers, 27-24 (H)
1992—Oilers, 27-3 (H)
    ***Bills, 41-38 (B) OT
1993—Bills, 35-7 (B)
1994—Bills, 15-7 (H)
1995—Oilers, 28-17 (B)
1997—Oilers, 31-14 (T)
1999—***Titans, 22-16 (T)
2000—Bills, 16-13 (B)
(RS Pts.—Titans 754, Bills 678)

(PS Pts.—Bills 74, Titans 70)
*Franchise in Houston prior to 1997;
known as Oilers prior to 1999
**AFC Divisional Playoff
***AFC First-Round Playoff
BUFFALO vs. WASHINGTON
RS: Bills lead series, 5-4
PS: Redskins lead series, 1-0
1972—Bills, 24-17 (W)
1977—Redskins, 10-0 (B)
1981—Bills, 21-14 (B)
1984—Redskins, 41-14 (W)
1987—Redskins, 27-7 (B)
1990—Redskins, 29-14 (W)
1991—*Redskins, 37-24 (Minneapolis)
1993—Bills, 24-10 (B)
1996—Bills, 38-13 (B)
1999—Bills, 34-17 (W)
(RS Pts.—Redskins 178, Bills 176)
(PS Pts.—Redskins 37, Bills 24)
*Super Bowl XXVI

CAROLINA vs. ARIZONA
RS: Series tied, 1-1;
See Arizona vs. Carolina
CAROLINA vs. ATLANTA
RS: Falcons lead series, 9-5;
See Atlanta vs. Carolina
CAROLINA vs. BALTIMORE
RS: Panthers lead series, 1-0;
See Baltimore vs. Carolina
CAROLINA vs. BUFFALO
RS: Bills lead series, 3-0;
See Buffalo vs. Carolina
CAROLINA vs. CHICAGO
RS: Bears lead series, 1-0
1995—Bears, 31-27 (Chi)
(RS Pts.—Bears 31, Panthers 27)
CAROLINA vs. CINCINNATI
RS: Panthers lead series, 1-0
1999—Panthers, 27-3 (Car)
(RS Pts.—Panthers 27, Bengals 3)
CAROLINA vs. CLEVELAND
RS: Panthers lead series, 1-0
1999—Panthers, 31-17 (Cle)
(RS Pts.—Panthers 31, Browns 17)
CAROLINA vs. DALLAS
RS: Cowboys lead series, 2-1
PS: Panthers lead series, 1-0
1996—*Panthers, 26-17 (C)
1997—Panthers, 23-13 (D)
1998—Cowboys, 27-20 (D)
2000—Cowboys, 16-13 (C) OT
(RS Pts.—Cowboys 56, Panthers 56)
(PS Pts.—Panthers 26, Cowboys 17)
*NFC Divisional Playoff
CAROLINA vs. DENVER
RS: Broncos lead series, 1-0
1997—Broncos, 34-0 (D)
(RS Pts.—Broncos 34, Panthers 0)
CAROLINA vs. DETROIT
RS: Lions lead series, 1-0
1999—Lions, 24-9 (C)
(RS Pts.—Lions 24, Panthers 9)
CAROLINA vs. GREEN BAY
RS: Packers lead series, 3-2
PS: Packers lead series, 1-0
1996—*Packers, 30-13 (GB)
1997—Packers, 31-10 (C)
1998—Packers, 37-30 (C)

1999—Panthers, 33-31 (GB)
2000—Panthers, 31-14 (C)
2001—Packers, 28-7 (C)
(RS Pts.—Packers 141, Panthers 111)
(PS Pts.—Packers 30, Panthers 13)
*NFC Championship
CAROLINA vs. INDIANAPOLIS
RS: Panthers lead series, 2-0
1995—Panthers, 13-10 (C)
1998—Panthers, 27-19 (I)
(RS Pts.—Panthers 40, Colts 29)
CAROLINA vs. JACKSONVILLE
RS: Jaguars lead series, 2-0
1996—Jaguars, 24-14 (J)
1999—Jaguars, 22-20 (C)
(RS Pts.—Jaguars 46, Panthers 34)
CAROLINA vs. KANSAS CITY
RS: Chiefs lead series, 2-0
1997—Chiefs, 35-14 (C)
2000—Chiefs, 15-14 (KC)
(RS Pts.—Chiefs 50, Panthers 28)
CAROLINA vs. MIAMI
RS: Dolphins lead series, 2-0
1998—Dolphins, 13-9 (C)
2001—Dolphins, 23-6 (M)
(RS Pts.—Dolphins 36, Panthers 15)
CAROLINA vs. MINNESOTA
RS: Vikings lead series, 3-1
1996—Vikings, 14-12 (M)
1997—Vikings, 21-14 (M)
2000—Vikings, 31-17 (M)
2001—Vikings, 24-13 (M)
(RS Pts.—Vikings 79, Panthers 67)
CAROLINA vs. NEW ENGLAND
RS: Series tied, 1-1
1995—Panthers, 20-17 (NE) OT
2001—Patriots, 38-6 (C)
(RS Pts.—Patriots 55, Panthers 26)
CAROLINA vs. NEW ORLEANS
RS: Saints lead series, 8-6
1995—Panthers, 20-3 (C)
    Saints, 34-26 (NO)
1996—Panthers, 22-20 (NO)
    Panthers, 19-7 (C)
1997—Panthers, 13-0 (NO)
    Saints, 16-13 (C)
1998—Saints, 19-14 (NO)
    Panthers, 31-17 (C)
1999—Saints, 19-10 (NO)
    Panthers, 45-13 (C)
2000—Saints, 24-6 (NO)
    Saints, 20-10 (C)
2001—Saints, 27-25 (C)
    Saints, 27-23 (NO)
(RS Pts.—Panthers 277, Saints 246)
CAROLINA vs. N.Y. GIANTS
RS: Panthers lead series, 1-0
1995—Panthers, 27-17 (C)
(RS Pts.—Panthers 27, Giants 17)
CAROLINA vs. N.Y. JETS
RS: Jets lead series, 2-1
1995—Panthers, 26-15 (C)
1998—Jets, 48-21 (NY)
2001—Jets, 13-12 (C)
(RS Pts.—Jets 76, Panthers 59)
CAROLINA vs. OAKLAND
RS: Series tied, 1-1
1997—Panthers, 38-14 (C)
2000—Raiders, 52-9 (O)
(RS Pts.—Raiders 66, Panthers 47)

CAROLINA vs. PHILADELPHIA
RS: Series tied, 1-1
1996—Eagles, 20-9 (P)
1999—Panthers, 33-7 (C)
(RS Pts.—Panthers 42, Eagles 27)
CAROLINA vs. PITTSBURGH
RS: Series tied, 1-1
1996—Bears, 18-14 (C)
1999—Steelers, 30-20 (P)
(RS Pts.—Steelers 44, Panthers 38)
CAROLINA vs. ST. LOUIS
RS: Series tied, 7-7
1995—Rams, 31-10 (C)
    Rams, 28-17 (StL)
1996—Panthers, 45-13 (C)
    Panthers, 20-10 (StL)
1997—Panthers, 16-10 (StL)
    Rams, 30-18 (C)
1998—Panthers, 24-20 (StL)
    Panthers, 20-13 (C)
1999—Rams, 35-10 (StL)
    Rams, 34-21 (C)
2000—Panthers, 27-24 (StL)
    Panthers, 16-3 (C)
2001—Rams, 48-14 (StL)
    Rams, 38-32 (C)
(RS Pts.—Rams 337, Panthers 290)
CAROLINA vs. SAN DIEGO
RS: Panthers lead series, 2-0
1997—Panthers, 26-7 (SD)
2000—Panthers, 30-22 (C)
(RS Pts.—Panthers 56, Chargers 29)
CAROLINA vs. SAN FRANCISCO
RS: Series tied, 7-7
1995—Panthers, 13-7 (SF)
    49ers, 31-10 (C)
1996—Panthers, 23-7 (C)
    Panthers, 30-24 (SF)
1997—49ers, 34-21 (C)
    49ers, 27-19 (SF)
1998—49ers, 25-23 (SF)
    49ers, 31-28 (C) OT
1999—Panthers, 31-29 (SF)
    Panthers, 41-24 (C)
2000—Panthers, 38-22 (SF)
    Panthers, 34-16 (C)
2001—49ers, 24-14 (SF)
    49ers, 25-22 (C) OT
(RS Pts.—Panthers 347, 49ers 326)
CAROLINA vs. SEATTLE
RS: Panthers lead series, 1-0
2000—Panthers, 26-3 (C)
(RS Pts.—Panthers 26, Seahawks 3)
CAROLINA vs. TAMPA BAY
RS: Buccaneers lead series, 2-1
1995—Buccaneers, 20-13 (C)
1996—Panthers, 24-0 (C)
1998—Buccaneers, 16-13 (TB)
(RS Pts.—Panthers 50, Buccaneers 36)
CAROLINA vs. *TENNESSEE
RS: Panthers lead series, 1-0
1996—Panthers, 31-6 (H)
(RS Pts.—Panthers 31, Titans 6)
*Franchise in Houston prior to 1997;
known as Oilers prior to 1999
CAROLINA vs. WASHINGTON
RS: Redskins lead series, 6-0
1995—Redskins, 20-17 (W)
1997—Redskins, 24-10 (C)
1998—Redskins, 28-25 (C)

1999—Redskins, 38-36 (W)
2000—Redskins, 20-17 (W)
2001—Redskins, 17-14 (W) OT
(RS Pts.—Redskins 147, Panthers 119)

CHICAGO vs. ARIZONA
RS: Bears lead series, 53-26-6;
See Arizona vs. Chicago
CHICAGO vs. ATLANTA
RS: Series tied, 10-10;
See Atlanta vs. Chicago
CHICAGO vs. BALTIMORE
RS: Series tied, 1-1;
See Baltimore vs. Chicago
CHICAGO vs. BUFFALO
RS: Bears lead series, 5-3;
See Buffalo vs. Chicago
CHICAGO vs. CAROLINA
RS: Bears lead series, 1-0;
See Carolina vs. Chicago
CHICAGO vs. CINCINNATI
RS: Bengals lead series, 4-3
1972—Bengals, 13-3 (Chi)
1980—Bengals, 17-14 (Chi) OT
1986—Bears, 44-7 (Cin)
1989—Bears, 17-14 (Chi)
1992—Bengals, 31-28 (Chi) OT
1995—Bengals, 16-10 (Cin)
2001—Bears, 24-0 (Cin)
(RS Pts.—Bears 140, Bengals 98)
CHICAGO vs. CLEVELAND
RS: Browns lead series, 8-4
1951—Browns, 42-21 (Cle)
1954—Browns, 39-10 (Chi)
1960—Browns, 42-0 (Cle)
1961—Bears, 17-14 (Chi)
1967—Browns, 24-0 (Cle)
1969—Browns, 28-24 (Chi)
1972—Bears, 17-0 (Cle)
1980—Browns, 27-21 (Cle)
1986—Bears, 41-31 (Chi)
1989—Browns, 27-7 (Cle)
1992—Browns, 27-14 (Cle)
2001—Bears, 27-21 (Chi) OT
(RS Pts.—Browns 322, Bears 199)
CHICAGO vs. DALLAS
RS: Cowboys lead series, 9-8
PS: Cowboys lead series, 2-0
1960—Bears, 17-7 (C)
1962—Bears, 34-33 (D)
1964—Cowboys, 24-10 (C)
1968—Cowboys, 34-3 (C)
1971—Bears, 23-19 (C)
1973—Cowboys, 20-17 (C)
1976—Cowboys, 31-21 (D)
1977—*Cowboys, 37-7 (D)
1979—Cowboys, 24-20 (D)
1981—Cowboys, 10-9 (D)
1984—Cowboys, 23-14 (C)
1985—Bears, 44-0 (D)
1986—Bears, 24-10 (D)
1988—Bears, 17-7 (C)
1991—**Cowboys, 17-13 (C)
1992—Cowboys, 27-14 (D)
1996—Bears, 22-6 (C)
1997—Cowboys, 27-3 (D)
1998—Bears, 13-12 (D)
(RS Pts.—Cowboys 314, Bears 305)
(PS Pts.—Cowboys 54, Bears 20)
*NFC Divisional Playoff

**NFC First-Round Playoff
CHICAGO vs. DENVER
RS: Broncos lead series, 6-5
1971—Broncos, 6-3 (D)
1973—Bears, 33-14 (D)
1976—Broncos, 28-14 (C)
1978—Broncos, 16-7 (D)
1981—Bears, 35-24 (C)
1983—Bears, 31-14 (C)
1984—Bears, 27-0 (C)
1987—Broncos, 31-29 (D)
1990—Bears, 16-13 (D) OT
1993—Broncos, 13-3 (C)
1996—Broncos, 17-12 (D)
(RS Pts.—Bears 210, Broncos 176)
CHICAGO vs. *DETROIT
RS: Bears lead series, 81-58-5
1930—Spartans, 7-6 (P)
    Bears, 14-6 (C)
1931—Bears, 9-6 (C)
    Spartans, 3-0 (P)
1932—Tie, 13-13 (C)
    Tie, 7-7 (P)
    Bears, 9-0 (C)
1933—Bears, 17-14 (C)
    Bears, 17-7 (P)
1934—Bears, 19-16 (D)
    Bears, 10-7 (C)
1935—Tie, 20-20 (C)
    Lions, 14-2 (D)
1936—Bears, 12-10 (C)
    Lions, 13-7 (D)
1937—Bears, 28-20 (C)
    Bears, 13-0 (D)
1938—Lions, 13-7 (C)
    Lions, 14-7 (D)
1939—Lions, 10-0 (C)
    Bears, 23-13 (D)
1940—Bears, 7-0 (C)
    Lions, 17-14 (D)
1941—Bears, 49-0 (C)
    Bears, 24-7 (D)
1942—Bears, 16-0 (C)
    Bears, 42-0 (D)
1943—Bears, 27-21 (D)
    Bears, 35-14 (C)
1944—Tie, 21-21 (C)
    Lions, 41-21 (D)
1945—Lions, 16-10 (D)
    Lions, 35-28 (C)
1946—Bears, 42-6 (C)
    Bears, 45-24 (D)
1947—Bears, 33-24 (C)
    Bears, 34-14 (D)
1948—Bears, 28-0 (C)
    Bears, 42-14 (D)
1949—Bears, 27-24 (C)
    Bears, 28-7 (D)
1950—Bears, 35-21 (D)
    Bears, 6-3 (C)
1951—Bears, 28-23 (C)
    Lions, 41-28 (D)
1952—Bears, 24-23 (C)
    Lions, 45-21 (D)
1953—Lions, 20-16 (C)
    Lions, 13-7 (D)
1954—Lions, 48-23 (D)
    Bears, 28-24 (C)
1955—Bears, 24-14 (D)
    Bears, 21-20 (C)

1956—Lions, 42-10 (D)
Bears, 38-21 (C)
1957—Bears, 27-7 (D)
Lions, 21-13 (C)
1958—Bears, 20-7 (D)
Bears, 21-16 (C)
1959—Bears, 24-14 (D)
Bears, 25-14 (C)
1960—Bears, 28-7 (C)
Lions, 36-0 (D)
1961—Bears, 31-17 (D)
Lions, 16-15 (C)
1962—Lions, 11-3 (D)
Bears, 3-0 (C)
1963—Bears, 37-21 (D)
Bears, 24-14 (C)
1964—Lions, 10-0 (C)
Bears, 27-24 (D)
1965—Bears, 38-10 (C)
Bears, 17-10 (D)
1966—Lions, 14-3 (D)
Tie, 10-10 (C)
1967—Bears, 14-3 (C)
Bears, 27-13 (D)
1968—Lions, 42-0 (D)
Lions, 28-10 (C)
1969—Lions, 13-7 (D)
Lions, 20-3 (C)
1970—Lions, 28-14 (D)
Lions, 16-10 (C)
1971—Bears, 28-23 (D)
Lions, 28-3 (C)
1972—Lions, 38-24 (C)
Lions, 14-0 (D)
1973—Lions, 30-7 (C)
Lions, 40-7 (D)
1974—Bears, 17-9 (C)
Lions, 34-17 (D)
1975—Lions, 27-7 (D)
Bears, 25-21 (C)
1976—Bears, 10-3 (C)
Lions, 14-10 (D)
1977—Bears, 30-20 (C)
Bears, 31-14 (D)
1978—Bears, 19-0 (D)
Lions, 21-17 (C)
1979—Bears, 35-7 (C)
Lions, 20-0 (D)
1980—Bears, 24-7 (C)
Bears, 23-17 (D) OT
1981—Lions, 48-17 (D)
Lions, 23-7 (C)
1982—Lions, 17-10 (D)
Bears, 20-17 (C)
1983—Lions, 31-17 (D)
Lions, 38-17 (C)
1984—Bears, 16-14 (C)
Bears, 30-13 (D)
1985—Bears, 24-3 (C)
Bears, 37-17 (D)
1986—Bears, 13-7 (C)
Bears, 16-13 (D)
1987—Bears, 30-10 (C)
1988—Bears, 24-7 (D)
Bears, 13-12 (C)
1989—Bears, 47-27 (D)
Lions, 27-17 (C)
1990—Bears, 23-17 (C) OT
Lions, 38-21 (D)
1991—Bears, 20-10 (C)

Lions, 16-6 (D)
1992—Bears, 27-24 (C)
Lions, 16-3 (D)
1993—Bears, 10-6 (D)
Lions, 20-14 (C)
1994—Lions, 21-16 (D)
Bears, 20-10 (C)
1995—Bears, 24-17 (C)
Lions, 27-7 (D)
1996—Lions, 35-16 (D)
Bears, 31-14 (C)
1997—Lions, 32-7 (C)
Lions, 55-20 (D)
1998—Bears, 31-27 (C)
Lions, 26-3 (D)
1999—Lions, 21-17 (D)
Bears, 28-10 (C)
2000—Lions, 21-14 (C)
Bears, 23-20 (D)
2001—Bears, 13-10 (C)
Bears, 24-0 (D)
(RS Pts.—Bears 2,673, Lions 2,509)
*Franchise in Portsmouth prior to 1934
and known as the Spartans
CHICAGO vs. GREEN BAY
RS: Bears lead series, 83-73-6
PS: Bears lead series, 1-0
1921—Staleys, 20-0 (C)
1923—Bears, 3-0 (GB)
1924—Bears, 3-0 (C)
1925—Packers, 14-10 (GB)
Bears, 21-0 (C)
1926—Tie, 6-6 (GB)
Bears, 19-13 (C)
Tie, 3-3 (C)
1927—Bears, 7-6 (GB)
Bears, 14-6 (C)
1928—Tie, 12-12 (GB)
Packers, 16-6 (C)
Packers, 6-0 (C)
1929—Packers, 23-0 (GB)
Packers, 14-0 (C)
Packers, 25-0 (C)
1930—Packers, 7-0 (GB)
Packers, 13-12 (C)
Bears, 21-0 (C)
1931—Packers, 7-0 (GB)
Packers, 6-2 (C)
Bears, 7-6 (C)
1932—Tie, 0-0 (GB)
Packers, 2-0 (C)
Bears, 9-0 (C)
1933—Bears, 14-7 (GB)
Bears, 10-7 (C)
Bears, 7-6 (C)
1934—Bears, 24-10 (GB)
Bears, 27-14 (C)
1935—Packers, 7-0 (GB)
Packers, 17-14 (C)
1936—Bears, 30-3 (GB)
Packers, 21-10 (C)
1937—Bears, 14-2 (GB)
Packers, 24-14 (C)
1938—Bears, 2-0 (GB)
Packers, 24-17 (C)
1939—Packers, 21-16 (GB)
Bears, 30-27 (C)
1940—Bears, 41-10 (GB)
Bears, 14-7 (C)
1941—Bears, 25-17 (GB)

Packers, 16-14 (C)
**Bears, 33-14 (C)
1942—Bears, 44-28 (GB)
Bears, 38-7 (C)
1943—Tie, 21-21 (GB)
Bears, 21-7 (C)
1944—Packers, 42-28 (GB)
Bears, 21-0 (C)
1945—Packers, 31-21 (GB)
Bears, 28-24 (C)
1946—Bears, 30-7 (GB)
Bears, 10-7 (C)
1947—Packers, 29-20 (GB)
Bears, 20-17 (C)
1948—Bears, 45-7 (GB)
Bears, 7-6 (C)
1949—Bears, 17-0 (GB)
Bears, 24-3 (C)
1950—Packers, 31-21 (GB)
Bears, 28-14 (C)
1951—Bears, 31-20 (GB)
Bears, 24-13 (C)
1952—Bears, 24-14 (GB)
Packers, 41-28 (C)
1953—Bears, 17-13 (GB)
Tie, 21-21 (C)
1954—Bears, 10-3 (GB)
Bears, 28-23 (C)
1955—Packers, 24-3 (GB)
Bears, 52-31 (C)
1956—Bears, 37-21 (GB)
Bears, 38-14 (C)
1957—Packers, 21-17 (GB)
Bears, 21-14 (C)
1958—Bears, 34-20 (GB)
Bears, 24-10 (C)
1959—Packers, 9-6 (GB)
Bears, 28-17 (C)
1960—Bears, 17-14 (GB)
Packers, 41-13 (C)
1961—Packers, 24-0 (GB)
Packers, 31-28 (C)
1962—Packers, 49-0 (GB)
Packers, 38-7 (C)
1963—Bears, 10-3 (GB)
Bears, 26-7 (C)
1964—Packers, 23-12 (GB)
Packers, 17-3 (C)
1965—Packers, 23-14 (GB)
Bears, 31-10 (C)
1966—Packers, 17-0 (C)
Packers, 13-6 (GB)
1967—Packers, 13-10 (GB)
Packers, 17-13 (C)
1968—Bears, 13-10 (GB)
Packers, 28-27 (C)
1969—Packers, 17-0 (GB)
Packers, 21-3 (C)
1970—Packers, 20-19 (GB)
Bears, 35-17 (C)
1971—Packers, 17-14 (C)
Packers, 31-10 (GB)
1972—Packers, 20-17 (GB)
Packers, 23-17 (C)
1973—Bears, 31-17 (GB)
Packers, 21-0 (C)
1974—Bears, 10-9 (C)
Packers, 20-3 (Mil)
1975—Bears, 27-14 (C)
Packers, 28-7 (GB)

1976—Bears, 24-13 (C)
Bears, 16-10 (GB)
1977—Bears, 26-0 (GB)
Bears, 21-10 (C)
1978—Packers, 24-14 (GB)
Bears, 14-0 (C)
1979—Bears, 6-3 (C)
Bears, 15-14 (GB)
1980—Packers, 12-6 (GB) OT
Bears, 61-7 (C)
1981—Packers, 16-9 (C)
Packers, 21-17 (GB)
1983—Packers, 31-28 (GB)
Bears, 23-21 (C)
1984—Bears, 9-7 (GB)
Packers, 20-14 (C)
1985—Bears, 23-7 (C)
Bears, 16-10 (GB)
1986—Bears, 25-12 (GB)
Bears, 12-10 (C)
1987—Bears, 26-24 (GB)
Bears, 23-10 (C)
1988—Bears, 24-6 (GB)
Bears, 16-0 (C)
1989—Packers, 14-13 (GB)
Packers, 40-28 (C)
1990—Bears, 31-13 (GB)
Bears, 27-13 (C)
1991—Bears, 10-0 (GB)
Bears, 27-13 (C)
1992—Bears, 30-10 (GB)
Packers, 17-3 (C)
1993—Packers, 17-3 (GB)
Bears, 30-17 (C)
1994—Packers, 33-6 (C)
Packers, 40-3 (GB)
1995—Packers, 27-24 (C)
Packers, 35-28 (GB)
1996—Packers, 37-6 (C)
Packers, 28-17 (GB)
1997—Packers, 38-24 (GB)
Packers, 24-23 (C)
1998—Packers, 26-20 (GB)
Packers, 16-13 (C)
1999—Bears, 14-13 (GB)
Packers, 35-19 (C)
2000—Bears, 27-24 (GB)
Packers, 28-6 (C)
2001—Packers, 20-12 (C)
Packers, 17-7 (GB)
(RS Pts.—Bears 2,727, Packers 2,571)
(PS Pts.—Bears 33, Packers 14)
*Bears known as Staleys prior to 1922
**Division Playoff
CHICAGO vs. *INDIANAPOLIS
RS: Colts lead series, 21-17
1953—Colts, 13-9 (B)
Colts, 16-14 (C)
1954—Bears, 28-9 (C)
Bears, 28-13 (B)
1955—Colts, 23-17 (B)
Bears, 38-10 (C)
1956—Colts, 28-21 (B)
Bears, 58-27 (C)
1957—Colts, 21-10 (B)
Colts, 29-14 (C)
1958—Colts, 51-38 (B)
Colts, 17-0 (C)
1959—Bears, 26-21 (B)
Colts, 21-7 (C)

1960—Colts, 42-7 (B)
Colts, 24-20 (C)
1961—Bears, 24-10 (C)
Bears, 21-20 (B)
1962—Bears, 35-15 (C)
Bears, 57-0 (B)
1963—Bears, 10-3 (C)
Bears, 17-7 (B)
1964—Colts, 52-0 (B)
Colts, 40-24 (C)
1965—Colts, 26-21 (C)
Bears, 13-0 (B)
1966—Bears, 27-17 (C)
Colts, 21-16 (B)
1967—Colts, 24-3 (C)
1968—Colts, 28-7 (B)
1969—Colts, 24-21 (C)
1970—Colts, 21-20 (B)
1975—Colts, 35-7 (C)
1983—Colts, 22-19 (B) OT
1985—Bears, 17-10 (C)
1988—Bears, 17-13 (I)
1991—Bears, 31-17 (I)
2000—Bears, 27-24 (C)
(RS Pts.—Colts 794, Bears 769)
*Franchise in Baltimore prior to 1984
CHICAGO vs. JACKSONVILLE
RS: Bears lead series, 2-1
1995—Bears, 30-27 (J)
1998—Jaguars, 24-23 (C)
2001—Bears, 33-13 (C)
(RS Pts.—Bears 86, Jaguars 64)
CHICAGO vs. KANSAS CITY
RS: Bears lead series, 5-3
1973—Chiefs, 19-7 (KC)
1977—Bears, 28-27 (C)
1981—Bears, 16-13 (KC) OT
1987—Bears, 31-28 (C)
1990—Chiefs, 21-10 (C)
1993—Bears, 19-17 (KC)
1996—Chiefs, 14-10 (KC)
1999—Bears, 20-17 (C)
(RS Pts.—Chiefs 156, Bears 141)
CHICAGO vs. MIAMI
RS: Dolphins lead series, 5-3
1971—Dolphins, 34-3 (M)
1975—Dolphins, 46-13 (C)
1979—Dolphins, 31-16 (M)
1985—Dolphins, 38-24 (M)
1988—Bears, 34-7 (C)
1991—Dolphins, 16-13 (C) OT
1994—Bears, 17-14 (M)
1997—Bears, 36-33 (M) OT
(RS Pts.—Dolphins 219, Bears 156)
CHICAGO vs. MINNESOTA
RS: Vikings lead series, 44-35-2
PS: Bears lead series, 1-0
1961—Vikings, 37-13 (M)
Bears, 52-35 (C)
1962—Bears, 13-0 (M)
Bears, 31-30 (C)
1963—Bears, 28-7 (M)
Tie, 17-17 (C)
1964—Bears, 34-28 (M)
Vikings, 41-14 (C)
1965—Bears, 45-37 (M)
Vikings, 24-17 (C)
1966—Bears, 13-10 (M)
Bears, 41-28 (C)
1967—Bears, 17-7 (M)

Tie, 10-10 (C)
1968—Bears, 27-17 (M)
Bears, 26-24 (C)
1969—Vikings, 31-0 (C)
Vikings, 31-14 (M)
1970—Vikings, 24-0 (C)
Vikings, 16-13 (M)
1971—Bears, 20-17 (M)
Vikings, 27-10 (C)
1972—Bears, 13-10 (C)
Vikings, 23-10 (M)
1973—Vikings, 22-13 (C)
Vikings, 31-13 (M)
1974—Vikings, 11-7 (C)
Vikings, 17-0 (C)
1975—Vikings, 28-3 (M)
Vikings, 13-9 (C)
1976—Vikings, 20-19 (M)
Bears, 14-13 (C)
1977—Vikings, 22-16 (M) OT
Bears, 10-7 (C)
1978—Vikings, 24-20 (C)
Vikings, 17-14 (M)
1979—Bears, 26-7 (C)
Vikings, 30-27 (M)
1980—Vikings, 34-14 (C)
Bears, 13-7 (M)
1981—Vikings, 24-21 (M)
Bears, 10-9 (C)
1982—Vikings, 35-7 (M)
1983—Vikings, 23-14 (C)
Bears, 19-13 (M)
1984—Bears, 16-7 (C)
Bears, 34-3 (M)
1985—Bears, 33-24 (M)
Bears, 27-9 (C)
1986—Bears, 23-0 (C)
Vikings, 23-7 (M)
1987—Bears, 27-7 (C)
Bears, 30-24 (M)
1988—Vikings, 31-7 (C)
Vikings, 28-27 (M)
1989—Bears, 38-7 (C)
Vikings, 27-16 (M)
1990—Bears, 19-16 (C)
Vikings, 41-13 (M)
1991—Bears, 10-6 (C)
Bears, 34-17 (M)
1992—Vikings, 21-20 (M)
Vikings, 38-10 (C)
1993—Vikings, 10-7 (M)
Vikings, 19-12 (C)
1994—Vikings, 42-14 (C)
Vikings, 33-27 (M) OT
*Bears, 35-18 (M)
1995—Bears, 31-14 (C)
Bears, 14-6 (M)
1996—Vikings, 20-14 (C)
Bears, 15-13 (M)
1997—Vikings, 27-24 (C)
Vikings, 29-22 (M)
1998—Vikings, 31-28 (C)
Vikings, 48-22 (M)
1999—Bears, 24-22 (M)
Vikings, 27-24 (C) OT
2000—Vikings, 30-27 (M)
Vikings, 28-16 (C)
2001—Bears, 17-10 (C)
Bears, 13-6 (M)
RS Pts.—Vikings 1,688, Bears 1,503)

(PS Pts.—Bears 35, Vikings 18)
*NFC First-Round Playoff
CHICAGO vs. NEW ENGLAND
RS: Patriots lead series, 5-3
PS: Bears lead series, 1-0
1973—Patriots, 13-10 (C)
1979—Patriots, 27-7 (C)
1982—Bears, 26-13 (C)
1985—Bears, 20-7 (C)
    *Bears, 46-10 (New Orleans)
1988—Patriots, 30-7 (NE)
1994—Patriots, 13-3 (C)
1997—Patriots, 31-3 (NE)
2000—Bears, 24-17 (C)
(RS Pts.—Patriots 151, Bears 100)
(PS Pts.—Bears 46, Patriots 10)
*Super Bowl XX
CHICAGO vs. NEW ORLEANS
RS: Bears lead series, 10-9
PS: Bears lead series, 1-0
1968—Bears, 23-17 (NO)
1970—Bears, 24-3 (NO)
1971—Bears, 35-14 (C)
1973—Saints, 21-16 (NO)
1974—Bears, 24-10 (C)
1975—Bears, 42-17 (NO)
1977—Saints, 42-24 (C)
1980—Bears, 22-3 (C)
1982—Saints, 10-0 (C)
1983—Saints, 34-31 (NO) OT
1984—Bears, 20-7 (C)
1987—Saints, 19-17 (C)
1990—*Bears, 16-6 (C)
1991—Bears, 20-17 (NO)
1992—Saints, 28-6 (NO)
1994—Bears, 17-7 (C)
1996—Saints, 27-24 (NO)
1997—Saints, 20-17 (C)
1999—Bears, 14-10 (C)
2000—Saints, 31-10 (C)
(RS Pts.—Bears 386, Saints 337)
(PS Pts.—Bears 16, Saints 6)
*NFC First-Round Playoff
CHICAGO vs. N.Y. GIANTS
RS: Bears lead series, 25-17-2
PS: Bears lead series, 5-3
1925—Bears, 19-7 (NY)
    Giants, 9-0 (C)
1926—Bears, 7-0 (C)
1927—Giants, 13-7 (NY)
1928—Bears, 13-0 (C)
1929—Giants, 26-14 (C)
    Giants, 34-0 (NY)
    Giants, 14-9 (C)
1930—Giants, 12-0 (C)
    Bears, 12-0 (NY)
1931—Bears, 6-0 (C)
    Bears, 12-6 (NY)
    Giants, 25-6 (C)
1932—Bears, 28-8 (NY)
    Bears, 6-0 (C)
1933—Bears, 14-10 (C)
    Giants, 3-0 (NY)
    *Bears, 23-21 (C)
1934—Bears, 27-7 (C)
    Bears, 10-9 (NY)
    *Giants, 30-13 (NY)
1935—Bears, 20-3 (NY)
    Giants, 3-0 (C)
1936—Bears, 25-7 (NY)

1937—Tie, 3-3 (NY)
1939—Giants, 16-13 (NY)
1940—Bears, 37-21 (NY)
1941—*Bears, 37-9 (C)
1942—Bears, 26-7 (NY)
1943—Bears, 56-7 (NY)
1946—Giants, 14-0 (NY)
    *Bears, 24-14 (NY)
1948—Bears, 35-14 (C)
1949—Giants, 35-28 (NY)
1956—Tie, 17-17 (NY)
    *Giants, 47-7 (NY)
1962—Giants, 26-24 (C)
1963—*Bears, 14-10 (C)
1965—Bears, 35-14 (NY)
1967—Bears, 34-7 (C)
1969—Giants, 28-24 (NY)
1970—Bears, 24-16 (NY)
1974—Bears, 16-13 (C)
1977—Bears, 12-9 (NY) OT
1985—**Bears, 21-0 (C)
1987—Bears, 34-19 (C)
1990—**Giants, 31-3 (NY)
1991—Bears, 20-17 (C)
1992—Giants, 27-14 (C)
1993—Giants, 26-20 (C)
1995—Bears, 27-24 (NY)
2000—Giants, 14-7 (C)
(RS Pts.—Bears 741, Giants 570)
(PS Pts.—Giants 162, Bears 142)
*NFL Championship
**NFC Divisional Playoff
CHICAGO vs. N.Y. JETS
RS: Bears lead series, 4-3
1974—Jets, 23-21 (C)
1979—Bears, 23-13 (C)
1985—Bears, 19-6 (NY)
1991—Bears, 19-13 (C) OT
1994—Bears, 19-7 (NY)
1997—Jets, 23-15 (C)
2000—Jets, 17-10 (NY)
(RS Pts.—Bears 126, Jets 102)
CHICAGO vs. *OAKLAND
RS: Raiders lead series, 6-4
1972—Raiders, 28-21 (O)
1976—Raiders, 28-27 (C)
1978—Raiders, 25-19 (C) OT
1981—Bears, 23-6 (O)
1984—Bears, 17-6 (C)
1987—Bears, 6-3 (LA)
1990—Raiders, 24-10 (LA)
1993—Raiders, 16-14 (C)
1996—Bears, 19-17 (C)
1999—Raiders, 24-17 (O)
(RS Pts.—Raiders 177, Bears 173)
*Franchise in Los Angeles from
1982-1994
CHICAGO vs. PHILADELPHIA
RS: Bears lead series, 24-6-1
PS: Eagles lead series, 2-1
1933—Tie, 3-3 (P)
1935—Bears, 39-0 (P)
1936—Bears, 17-0 (P)
    Bears, 28-7 (P)
1938—Bears, 28-6 (P)
1939—Bears, 27-14 (C)
1941—Bears, 49-14 (P)
1942—Bears, 45-14 (C)
1944—Bears, 28-7 (P)
1946—Bears, 21-14 (C)

1947—Bears, 40-7 (C)
1948—Eagles, 12-7 (P)
1949—Bears, 38-21 (C)
1955—Bears, 17-10 (C)
1961—Eagles, 16-14 (P)
1963—Bears, 16-7 (C)
1968—Bears, 29-16 (P)
1970—Bears, 20-16 (C)
1972—Bears, 21-12 (P)
1975—Bears, 15-13 (C)
1979—*Eagles, 27-17 (P)
1980—Eagles, 17-14 (P)
1983—Bears, 7-6 (P)
    Bears, 17-14 (C)
1986—Bears, 13-10 (C) OT
1987—Bears, 35-3 (P)
1988—**Bears, 20-12 (C)
1989—Bears, 27-13 (C)
1993—Bears, 17-6 (P)
1994—Eagles, 30-22 (C)
1995—Bears, 20-14 (C)
1999—Eagles, 20-16 (C)
2000—Eagles, 13-9 (P)
2001—**Eagles, 33-19 (C)
(RS Pts.—Bears 699, Eagles 355)
(PS Pts.—Eagles 72, Bears 56)
*NFC First-Round Playoff
**NFC Divisional Playoff
CHICAGO vs. *PITTSBURGH
RS: Bears lead series, 16-6-1
1934—Bears, 28-0 (P)
1935—Bears, 23-7 (P)
1936—Bears, 27-9 (P)
    Bears, 26-6 (C)
1937—Bears, 7-0 (P)
1939—Bears, 32-0 (P)
1941—Bears, 34-7 (C)
1945—Bears, 28-7 (C)
1947—Bears, 49-7 (C)
1949—Bears, 30-21 (C)
1958—Steelers, 24-10 (P)
1959—Bears, 27-21 (C)
1963—Tie, 17-17 (P)
1967—Steelers, 41-13 (P)
1969—Bears, 38-7 (C)
1971—Bears, 17-15 (C)
1975—Steelers, 34-3 (P)
1980—Steelers, 38-3 (P)
1986—Bears, 13-10 (C) OT
1989—Bears, 20-0 (P)
1992—Bears, 30-6 (C)
1995—Steelers, 37-34 (C) OT
1998—Steelers, 17-12 (P)
(RS Pts.—Bears 521, Steelers 331)
*Steelers known as Pirates prior to 1941
CHICAGO vs. *ST. LOUIS
RS: Bears lead series, 47-32-3
PS: Series tied, 1-1
1937—Bears, 20-2 (Clev)
    Bears, 15-7 (C)
1938—Rams, 14-7 (C)
    Rams, 23-21 (Clev)
1939—Bears, 30-21 (Clev)
    Bears, 35-21 (C)
1940—Bears, 21-14 (Clev)
    Bears, 47-25 (C)
1941—Bears, 48-21 (Clev)
    Bears, 31-13 (C)
1942—Bears, 21-7 (Clev)
    Bears, 47-0 (C)

1944—Rams, 19-7 (Clev)
    Bears, 28-21 (C)
1945—Rams, 17-0 (Clev)
    Rams, 41-21 (C)
1946—Tie, 28-28 (C)
    Bears, 27-21 (LA)
1947—Bears, 41-21 (LA)
    Rams, 17-14 (C)
1948—Bears, 42-21 (C)
    Bears, 21-6 (LA)
1949—Rams, 31-16 (C)
    Rams, 27-24 (LA)
1950—Bears, 24-20 (LA)
    Bears, 24-14 (C)
    **Rams, 24-14 (LA)
1951—Rams, 42-17 (C)
1952—Rams, 31-7 (LA)
    Rams, 40-24 (C)
1953—Rams, 38-24 (LA)
    Bears, 24-21 (C)
1954—Rams, 42-38 (LA)
    Bears, 24-13 (C)
1955—Bears, 31-20 (LA)
    Bears, 24-3 (C)
1956—Bears, 35-24 (LA)
    Bears, 30-21 (C)
1957—Bears, 34-26 (C)
    Bears, 16-10 (LA)
1958—Bears, 31-10 (C)
    Rams, 41-35 (LA)
1959—Rams, 28-21 (C)
    Bears, 26-21 (LA)
1960—Bears, 34-27 (C)
    Tie, 24-24 (LA)
1961—Bears, 21-17 (LA)
    Bears, 28-24 (C)
1962—Bears, 27-23 (LA)
    Bears, 30-14 (C)
1963—Bears, 52-14 (LA)
    Bears, 6-0 (C)
1964—Bears, 38-17 (C)
    Bears, 34-24 (LA)
1965—Rams, 30-28 (LA)
    Bears, 31-6 (C)
1966—Rams, 31-17 (LA)
    Bears, 17-10 (C)
1967—Bears, 28-17 (C)
1968—Bears, 17-16 (LA)
1969—Rams, 9-7 (C)
1971—Rams, 17-3 (LA)
1972—Tie, 13-13 (C)
1973—Rams, 26-0 (C)
1975—Rams, 38-10 (LA)
1976—Rams, 20-12 (LA)
1977—Bears, 24-23 (C)
1979—Bears, 27-23 (C)
1981—Rams, 24-7 (C)
1982—Bears, 34-26 (LA)
1983—Rams, 21-14 (LA)
1984—Rams, 29-13 (LA)
1985—***Bears, 24-0 (C)
1986—Rams, 20-17 (C)
1988—Rams, 23-3 (LA)
1989—Bears, 20-10 (C)
1990—Bears, 38-9 (C)
1993—Rams, 20-6 (LA)
1994—Bears, 27-13 (C)
1995—Rams, 34-28 (StL)
1996—Bears, 35-9 (C)
1997—Bears, 13-10 (StL)

1998—Rams, 20-12 (C)
1999—Rams, 34-12 (StL)
(RS Pts.—Bears 1,897, Rams 1,679)
(PS Pts.—Bears 38, Rams 24)
*Franchise in Los Angeles prior to 1995
and in Cleveland prior to 1946
**Conference Playoff
***NFC Championship
CHICAGO vs. SAN DIEGO
RS: Series tied, 4-4
1970—Chargers, 20-7 (C)
1974—Chargers, 28-21 (SD)
1978—Chargers, 40-7 (SD)
1981—Bears, 20-17 (C) OT
1984—Chargers, 20-7 (SD)
1993—Bears, 16-13 (SD)
1996—Bears, 27-14 (C)
1999—Bears, 23-20 (SD) OT
(RS Pts.—Chargers 172, Bears 128)
CHICAGO vs. SAN FRANCISCO
RS: Series tied, 26-26-1
PS: 49ers lead series, 3-0
1950—Bears, 32-20 (SF)
    Bears, 17-0 (C)
1951—Bears, 13-7 (C)
1952—49ers, 40-16 (C)
    Bears, 20-17 (SF)
1953—49ers, 35-28 (C)
    Bears, 24-14 (SF)
1954—49ers, 31-24 (C)
    Bears, 31-27 (SF)
1955—49ers, 20-19 (C)
    Bears, 34-23 (SF)
1956—Bears, 31-7 (C)
    Bears, 38-21 (SF)
1957—49ers, 21-17 (C)
    49ers, 21-17 (SF)
1958—Bears, 28-6 (C)
    Bears, 27-14 (SF)
1959—49ers, 20-17 (SF)
    Bears, 14-3 (C)
1960—Bears, 27-10 (C)
    49ers, 25-7 (SF)
1961—Bears, 31-0 (C)
    49ers, 41-31 (SF)
1962—Bears, 30-14 (SF)
    49ers, 34-27 (C)
1963—49ers, 20-14 (SF)
    Bears, 27-7 (C)
1964—49ers, 31-21 (SF)
    Bears, 23-21 (C)
1965—49ers, 52-24 (SF)
    Bears, 61-20 (C)
1966—Tie, 30-30 (C)
    49ers, 41-14 (SF)
1967—Bears, 28-14 (SF)
1968—Bears, 27-19 (C)
1969—49ers, 42-21 (SF)
1970—49ers, 37-16 (C)
1971—49ers, 13-0 (SF)
1972—Bears, 34-21 (C)
1974—Bears, 34-0 (C)
1975—49ers, 31-3 (SF)
1976—Bears, 19-12 (SF)
1978—Bears, 16-13 (SF)
1979—Bears, 28-27 (SF)
1981—49ers, 28-17 (SF)
1983—Bears, 13-3 (C)
1984—*49ers, 23-0 (SF)
1985—Bears, 26-10 (SF)

1987—49ers, 41-0 (SF)
1988—Bears, 10-9 (C)
    *49ers, 28-3 (C)
1989—49ers, 26-0 (SF)
1991—49ers, 52-14 (SF)
1994—**49ers, 44-15 (SF)
2000—49ers, 17-0 (SF)
2001—Bears, 37-31 (C) OT
(RS Pts.—49ers 1,196, Bears 1,100)
(PS Pts.—49ers 95, Bears 18)
*NFC Championship
**NFC Divisional Playoff
CHICAGO vs. SEATTLE
RS: Seahawks lead series, 5-2
1976—Bears, 34-7 (S)
1978—Seahawks, 31-29 (C)
1982—Seahawks, 20-14 (S)
1984—Seahawks, 38-9 (S)
1987—Seahawks, 34-21 (C)
1990—Bears, 17-0 (C)
1999—Seahawks, 14-13 (C)
(RS Pts.—Seahawks 144, Bears 137)
CHICAGO vs. TAMPA BAY
RS: Bears lead series, 33-15
1977—Bears, 10-0 (TB)
1978—Buccaneers, 33-19 (TB)
    Bears, 14-3 (C)
1979—Buccaneers, 17-13 (C)
    Bears, 14-0 (TB)
1980—Bears, 23-0 (C)
    Bears, 14-13 (TB)
1981—Bears, 28-17 (C)
    Buccaneers, 20-10 (TB)
1982—Buccaneers, 26-23 (TB) OT
1983—Bears, 17-10 (C)
    Bears, 27-0 (TB)
1984—Bears, 34-14 (C)
    Bears, 44-9 (TB)
1985—Bears, 38-28 (C)
    Bears, 27-19 (TB)
1986—Bears, 23-3 (TB)
    Bears, 48-14 (C)
1987—Bears, 20-3 (C)
    Bears, 27-26 (TB)
1988—Bears, 28-10 (C)
    Bears, 27-15 (TB)
1989—Buccaneers, 42-35 (TB)
    Buccaneers, 32-31 (C)
1990—Bears, 26-6 (TB)
    Bears, 27-14 (C)
1991—Bears, 21-20 (TB)
    Bears, 27-0 (C)
1992—Bears, 31-14 (C)
    Buccaneers, 20-17 (TB)
1993—Bears, 47-17 (C)
    Buccaneers, 13-10 (TB)
1994—Bears, 21-9 (C)
    Bears, 20-6 (TB)
1995—Bears, 25-6 (TB)
    Bears, 31-10 (C)
1996—Bears, 13-10 (C)
    Buccaneers, 34-19 (TB)
1997—Bears, 13-7 (C)
    Buccaneers, 31-15 (TB)
1998—Buccaneers, 27-15 (TB)
    Buccaneers, 31-17 (C)
1999—Buccaneers, 6-3 (TB)
    Buccaneers, 20-6 (C)
2000—Buccaneers, 41-0 (TB)
    Bears, 13-10 (C)

2001—Bears, 27-24 (TB)
    Bears, 27-3 (C)
(RS Pts.—Bears 1,065, Buccaneers 733)
CHICAGO vs. *TENNESSEE
RS: Series tied, 4-4
1973—Bears, 35-14 (C)
1977—Oilers, 47-0 (H)
1980—Oilers, 10-6 (C)
1986—Bears, 20-7 (H)
1989—Oilers, 33-28 (C)
1992—Oilers, 24-7 (H)
1995—Bears, 35-32 (C)
1998—Bears, 23-20 (T)
(RS Pts.—Titans 187, Bears 154)
*Franchise in Houston prior to 1997;
known as Oilers prior to 1999*
CHICAGO vs. *WASHINGTON
RS: Bears lead series, 19-15-1
PS: Redskins lead series, 4-3
1932—Tie, 7-7 (B)
1933—Bears, 7-0 (C)
    Redskins, 10-0 (B)
1934—Bears, 21-0 (B)
1935—Bears, 30-14 (B)
1936—Bears, 26-0 (B)
1937—**Redskins, 28-21 (C)
1938—Bears, 31-7 (C)
1940—Redskins, 7-3 (W)
    **Bears, 73-0 (W)
1941—Bears, 35-21 (C)
1942—**Redskins, 14-6 (W)
1943—Redskins, 21-7 (W)
    **Bears, 41-21 (C)
1945—Redskins, 28-21 (W)
1946—Bears, 24-20 (C)
1947—Bears, 56-20 (W)
1948—Bears, 48-13 (C)
1949—Bears, 31-21 (W)
1951—Bears, 27-0 (W)
1953—Bears, 27-24 (W)
1957—Redskins, 14-3 (C)
1964—Redskins, 27-20 (W)
1968—Redskins, 38-28 (C)
1971—Bears, 16-15 (C)
1974—Redskins, 42-0 (W)
1976—Bears, 33-7 (C)
1978—Bears, 14-10 (W)
1980—Bears, 35-21 (C)
1981—Redskins, 24-7 (C)
1984—***Bears, 23-19 (W)
1985—Bears, 45-10 (C)
1986—***Redskins, 27-13 (C)
1987—***Redskins, 21-17 (C)
1988—Bears, 34-14 (W)
1989—Redskins, 38-14 (W)
1990—Redskins, 10-9 (W)
1991—Redskins, 20-7 (C)
1996—Redskins, 10-3 (W)
1997—Redskins, 31-8 (C)
1999—Redskins, 48-22 (W)
2001—Bears, 20-15 (W)
(RS Pts.—Bears 719, Redskins 607)
(PS Pts.—Bears 194, Redskins 130)
*Franchise in Boston prior to 1937 and
known as Braves prior to 1933*
***NFL Championship*
****NFC Divisional Playoff*

CINCINNATI vs. ARIZONA
RS: Bengals lead series, 5-2;
See Arizona vs. Cincinnati
CINCINNATI vs. ATLANTA
RS: Bengals lead series, 7-2;
See Atlanta vs. Cincinnati
CINCINNATI vs. BALTIMORE
RS: Ravens lead series, 8-4;
See Baltimore vs. Cincinnati
CINCINNATI vs. BUFFALO
RS: Series tied, 9-9
PS: Bengals lead series, 2-0;
See Buffalo vs. Cincinnati
CINCINNATI vs. CAROLINA
RS: Panthers lead series, 1-0;
See Carolina vs. Cincinnati
CINCINNATI vs. CHICAGO
RS: Bengals lead series, 4-3;
See Chicago vs. Cincinnati
CINCINNATI vs. CLEVELAND
RS: Browns lead series, 29-28
1970—Browns, 30-27 (Cle)
    Bengals, 14-10 (Cin)
1971—Browns, 27-24 (Cin)
    Browns, 31-27 (Cle)
1972—Browns, 27-6 (Cle)
    Browns, 27-24 (Cin)
1973—Browns, 17-10 (Cle)
    Bengals, 34-17 (Cin)
1974—Bengals, 33-7 (Cin)
    Bengals, 34-24 (Cle)
1975—Bengals, 24-17 (Cin)
    Browns, 35-23 (Cle)
1976—Bengals, 45-24 (Cle)
    Bengals, 21-6 (Cin)
1977—Browns, 13-3 (Cin)
    Bengals, 10-7 (Cle)
1978—Browns, 13-10 (Cle) OT
    Bengals, 48-16 (Cin)
1979—Browns, 28-27 (Cle)
    Bengals, 16-12 (Cin)
1980—Browns, 31-7 (Cle)
    Browns, 27-24 (Cin)
1981—Browns, 20-17 (Cin)
    Bengals, 41-21 (Cle)
1982—Bengals, 23-10 (Cin)
1983—Browns, 17-7 (Cle)
    Bengals, 28-21 (Cin)
1984—Bengals, 12-9 (Cin)
    Bengals, 20-17 (Cle) OT
1985—Bengals, 27-10 (Cin)
    Browns, 24-6 (Cle)
1986—Bengals, 30-13 (Cle)
    Browns, 34-3 (Cin)
1987—Browns, 34-0 (Cin)
    Browns, 38-24 (Cle)
1988—Bengals, 24-17 (Cin)
    Browns, 23-16 (Cle)
1989—Bengals, 21-14 (Cin)
    Bengals, 21-0 (Cle)
1990—Bengals, 34-13 (Cle)
    Bengals, 21-14 (Cin)
1991—Browns, 14-13 (Cle)
    Bengals, 23-21 (Cin)
1992—Bengals, 30-10 (Cin)
    Browns, 37-21 (Cle)
1993—Browns, 27-14 (Cle)
    Browns, 28-17 (Cin)
1994—Browns, 28-20 (Cin)
    Browns, 37-13 (Cle)
1995—Browns, 29-26 (Cin) OT
    Browns, 26-10 (Cle)

1999—Bengals, 18-17 (Cle)
    Bengals, 44-28 (Cin)
2000—Browns, 24-7 (Cin)
    Bengals, 12-3 (Cle)
2001—Bengals, 24-14 (Cin)
    Browns, 18-0 (Cle)
(RS Pts.—Bengals 1,158, Browns 1,156)
CINCINNATI vs. DALLAS
RS: Cowboys lead series, 5-3
1973—Cowboys, 38-10 (D)
1979—Cowboys, 38-13 (D)
1985—Bengals, 50-24 (C)
1988—Bengals, 38-24 (D)
1991—Cowboys, 35-23 (D)
1994—Cowboys, 23-20 (C)
1997—Bengals, 31-24 (C)
2000—Cowboys, 23-6 (D)
(RS Pts.—Cowboys 229, Bengals 191)
CINCINNATI vs. DENVER
RS: Broncos lead series, 14-7
1968—Bengals, 24-10 (C)
    Broncos, 10-7 (D)
1969—Broncos, 30-23 (C)
    Broncos, 27-16 (D)
1971—Bengals, 24-10 (D)
1972—Bengals, 21-10 (D)
1973—Broncos, 28-10 (D)
1975—Bengals, 17-16 (D)
1976—Bengals, 17-7 (C)
1977—Broncos, 24-13 (C)
1979—Broncos, 10-0 (D)
1981—Bengals, 38-21 (C)
1983—Broncos, 24-17 (D)
1984—Bengals, 20-17 (D)
1986—Broncos, 34-28 (D)
1991—Broncos, 45-14 (D)
1994—Broncos, 15-13 (D)
1996—Broncos, 14-10 (C)
1997—Broncos, 38-20 (D)
1998—Broncos, 33-26 (C)
2000—Bengals, 31-21 (C)
(RS Pts.—Broncos 447, Bengals 386)
CINCINNATI vs. DETROIT
RS: Bengals lead series, 5-3
1970—Lions, 38-3 (D)
1974—Lions, 23-19 (C)
1983—Bengals, 17-9 (C)
1986—Bengals, 24-17 (D)
1989—Bengals, 42-7 (C)
1992—Lions, 19-13 (C)
1998—Bengals, 34-28 (D) OT
2001—Bengals, 31-27 (D)
(RS Pts.—Bengals 183, Lions 168)
CINCINNATI vs. GREEN BAY
RS: Packers lead series, 5-4
1971—Packers, 20-17 (GB)
1976—Bengals, 28-7 (C)
1977—Bengals, 17-7 (Mil)
1980—Packers, 14-9 (GB)
1983—Bengals, 34-14 (C)
1986—Bengals, 34-28 (Mil)
1992—Packers, 24-23 (GB)
1995—Packers, 24-10 (GB)
1998—Packers, 13-6 (C)
(RS Pts.—Bengals 178, Packers 151)
CINCINNATI vs. *INDIANAPOLIS
RS: Colts lead series, 11-8
PS: Colts lead series, 1-0
1970—**Colts, 17-0 (B)
1972—Colts, 20-19 (C)

1974—Bengals, 24-14 (B)
1976—Colts, 28-27 (B)
1979—Colts, 38-28 (B)
1980—Bengals, 34-33 (C)
1981—Bengals, 41-19 (B)
1982—Bengals, 20-17 (B)
1983—Colts, 34-31 (C)
1987—Bengals, 23-21 (I)
1989—Colts, 23-12 (C)
1990—Colts, 34-20 (C)
1992—Colts, 21-17 (C)
1993—Colts, 9-6 (C)
1994—Colts, 17-13 (C)
1995—Bengals, 24-21 (I) OT
1996—Bengals, 31-24 (C)
1997—Bengals, 28-13 (I)
1998—Colts, 39-26 (I)
1999—Colts, 31-10 (I)
(RS Pts.—Colts 456, Bengals 434)
(PS Pts.—Colts 17, Bengals 0)
*Franchise in Baltimore prior to 1984
**AFC Divisional Playoff
CINCINNATI vs. JACKSONVILLE
RS: Jaguars lead series, 9-5
1995—Bengals, 24-17 (C)
        Bengals, 17-13 (J)
1996—Bengals, 28-21 (C)
        Jaguars, 30-27 (J)
1997—Jaguars, 21-13 (J)
        Bengals, 31-26 (C)
1998—Jaguars, 24-11 (J)
        Jaguars, 34-17 (C)
1999—Jaguars, 41-10 (J)
        Jaguars, 24-7 (J)
2000—Jaguars, 13-0 (J)
        Bengals, 17-14 (C)
2001—Jaguars, 30-13 (J)
        Jaguars, 14-10 (C)
(RS Pts.—Jaguars 322, Bengals 225)
CINCINNATI vs. KANSAS CITY
RS: Chiefs lead series, 11-9
1968—Chiefs, 13-3 (KC)
        Chiefs, 16-9 (C)
1969—Bengals, 24-19 (C)
        Chiefs, 42-22 (KC)
1970—Chiefs, 27-19 (C)
1972—Bengals, 23-16 (KC)
1973—Bengals, 14-6 (C)
1974—Bengals, 33-6 (C)
1976—Bengals, 27-24 (KC)
1977—Bengals, 27-7 (KC)
1978—Chiefs, 24-23 (C)
1979—Chiefs, 10-7 (C)
1980—Bengals, 20-6 (KC)
1983—Chiefs, 20-15 (KC)
1984—Chiefs, 27-22 (C)
1986—Chiefs, 24-14 (KC)
1987—Bengals, 30-27 (C) OT
1988—Chiefs, 31-28 (KC)
1989—Bengals, 21-17 (KC)
1993—Chiefs, 17-15 (KC)
(RS Pts.—Bengals 396, Chiefs 379)
CINCINNATI vs. MIAMI
RS: Dolphins lead series, 12-3
PS: Dolphins lead series, 1-0
1968—Dolphins, 24-22 (C)
        Bengals, 38-21 (M)
1969—Bengals, 27-21 (C)
1971—Dolphins, 23-13 (C)
1973—*Dolphins, 34-16 (M)

1974—Dolphins, 24-3 (M)
1977—Bengals, 23-17 (C)
1978—Dolphins, 21-0 (M)
1980—Dolphins, 17-16 (M)
1983—Dolphins, 38-14 (M)
1987—Dolphins, 20-14 (C)
1989—Dolphins, 20-13 (C)
1991—Dolphins, 37-13 (M)
1994—Dolphins, 23-7 (C)
1995—Dolphins, 26-23 (C)
2000—Dolphins, 31-16 (C)
(RS Pts.—Dolphins 363, Bengals 242)
(PS Pts.—Dolphins 34, Bengals 16)
*AFC Divisional Playoff
CINCINNATI vs. MINNESOTA
RS: Vikings lead series, 5-4
1973—Bengals, 27-0 (C)
1977—Vikings, 42-10 (M)
1980—Bengals, 14-0 (C)
1983—Vikings, 20-14 (M)
1986—Bengals, 24-20 (C)
1989—Vikings, 29-21 (M)
1992—Vikings, 42-7 (C)
1995—Bengals, 27-24 (C)
1998—Vikings, 24-3 (M)
(RS Pts.—Vikings 201, Bengals 147)
CINCINNATI vs. *NEW ENGLAND
RS: Patriots lead series, 10-8
1968—Patriots, 33-14 (B)
1969—Patriots, 25-14 (C)
1970—Bengals, 45-7 (C)
1972—Bengals, 31-7 (NE)
1975—Bengals, 27-10 (C)
1978—Patriots, 10-3 (C)
1979—Patriots, 20-14 (C)
1984—Patriots, 20-14 (NE)
1985—Patriots, 34-23 (NE)
1986—Bengals, 31-7 (NE)
1988—Bengals, 27-21 (NE)
1990—Bengals, 41-7 (C)
1991—Bengals, 29-7 (C)
1992—Bengals, 20-10 (C)
1993—Patriots, 7-2 (NE)
1994—Patriots, 31-28 (C)
2000—Patriots, 16-13 (NE)
2001—Bengals, 23-17 (C)
(RS Pts.—Bengals 393, Patriots 295)
*Franchise in Boston prior to 1971
CINCINNATI vs. NEW ORLEANS
RS: Saints lead series, 5-4
1970—Bengals, 26-6 (C)
1975—Bengals, 21-0 (NO)
1978—Saints, 20-18 (C)
1981—Saints, 17-7 (NO)
1984—Bengals, 24-21 (NO)
1987—Saints, 41-24 (C)
1990—Saints, 21-7 (C)
1993—Saints, 20-13 (NO)
1996—Bengals, 30-15 (C))
(RS Pts.—Bengals 170, Saints 161)
CINCINNATI vs. N.Y. GIANTS
RS: Bengals lead series, 4-2
1972—Bengals, 13-10 (C)
1977—Bengals, 30-13 (C)
1985—Bengals, 35-30 (C)
1991—Bengals, 27-24 (C)
1994—Giants, 27-20 (NY)
1997—Giants, 29-27 (NY)
(RS Pts.—Bengals 152, Giants 133)

CINCINNATI vs. N.Y. JETS
RS: Jets lead series, 11-6
PS: Jets lead series, 1-0
1968—Jets, 27-14 (NY)
1969—Jets, 21-7 (C)
        Jets, 40-7 (NY)
1971—Jets, 35-21 (NY)
1973—Bengals, 20-14 (C)
1976—Bengals, 42-3 (NY)
1981—Bengals, 31-30 (NY)
1982—*Jets, 44-17 (C)
1984—Jets, 43-23 (NY)
1985—Jets, 29-20 (C)
1986—Bengals, 52-21 (C)
1987—Jets, 27-20 (NY)
1988—Bengals, 36-19 (C)
1990—Bengals, 25-20 (C)
1992—Jets, 17-14 (NY)
1993—Jets, 17-12 (NY)
1997—Bengals, 31-14 (C)
2001—Jets, 15-14 (NY)
(RS Pts.—Jets 409, Bengals 372)
(PS Pts.—Jets 44, Bengals 17)
*AFC First-Round Playoff
CINCINNATI vs. *OAKLAND
RS: Raiders lead series, 16-7
PS: Raiders lead series, 2-0
1968—Raiders, 31-10 (O)
        Raiders, 34-0 (C)
1969—Bengals, 31-17 (C)
        Raiders, 37-17 (O)
1970—Bengals, 31-21 (C)
1971—Raiders, 31-27 (O)
1972—Raiders, 20-14 (C)
1974—Raiders, 30-27 (O)
1975—Bengals, 14-10 (C)
        **Raiders, 31-28 (O)
1976—Raiders, 35-20 (O)
1978—Raiders, 34-21 (O)
1980—Raiders, 28-17 (O)
1982—Bengals, 31-17 (C)
1983—Raiders, 20-10 (C)
1985—Raiders, 13-6 (LA)
1988—Bengals, 45-21 (LA)
1989—Raiders, 28-7 (LA)
1990—Raiders, 24-7 (LA)
        **Raiders, 20-10 (LA)
1991—Raiders, 38-14 (C)
1992—Bengals, 24-21 (C) OT
1993—Bengals, 16-10 (C)
1995—Raiders, 20-17 (C)
1998—Raiders, 27-10 (O)
(RS Pts.—Raiders 567, Bengals 416)
(PS Pts.—Raiders 51, Bengals 38)
*Franchise in Los Angeles from
1982-1994
**AFC Divisional Playoff
CINCINNATI vs. PHILADELPHIA
RS: Bengals lead series, 6-3
1971—Bengals, 37-14 (C)
1975—Bengals, 31-0 (P)
1979—Bengals, 37-13 (C)
1982—Bengals, 18-14 (P)
1988—Bengals, 28-24 (P)
1991—Eagles, 17-10 (P)
1994—Bengals, 33-30 (C)
1997—Eagles, 44-42 (P)
2000—Eagles, 16-7 (P)
(RS Pts.—Bengals 243, Eagles 172)

CINCINNATI vs. PITTSBURGH
RS: Steelers lead series, 36-27
1970—Steelers, 21-10 (P)
    Bengals, 34-7 (C)
1971—Steelers, 21-10 (P)
    Steelers, 21-13 (C)
1972—Bengals, 15-10 (C)
    Steelers, 40-17 (P)
1973—Bengals, 19-7 (C)
    Steelers, 20-13 (P)
1974—Bengals, 17-10 (C)
    Steelers, 27-3 (P)
1975—Steelers, 30-24 (C)
    Steelers, 35-14 (C)
1976—Steelers, 23-6 (P)
    Steelers, 7-3 (C)
1977—Steelers, 20-14 (P)
    Bengals, 17-10 (C)
1978—Bengals, 28-3 (C)
    Steelers, 7-6 (P)
1979—Bengals, 34-10 (C)
    Steelers, 37-17 (P)
1980—Bengals, 30-28 (C)
    Bengals, 17-16 (P)
1981—Bengals, 34-7 (C)
    Bengals, 17-10 (P)
1982—Steelers, 26-20 (P) OT
1983—Steelers, 24-14 (C)
    Bengals, 23-10 (P)
1984—Steelers, 38-17 (P)
    Bengals, 22-20 (C)
1985—Bengals, 37-24 (P)
    Bengals, 26-21 (C)
1986—Bengals, 24-22 (C)
    Steelers, 30-9 (P)
1987—Steelers, 23-20 (P)
    Steelers, 30-16 (C)
1988—Bengals, 17-12 (P)
    Bengals, 42-7 (C)
1989—Bengals, 41-10 (C)
    Bengals, 26-16 (P)
1990—Bengals, 27-3 (C)
    Bengals, 16-12 (P)
1991—Steelers, 33-27 (C) OT
    Steelers, 17-10 (P)
1992—Steelers, 20-0 (P)
    Steelers, 21-9 (C)
1993—Steelers, 34-7 (P)
    Steelers, 24-16 (C)
1994—Steelers, 14-10 (P)
    Steelers, 38-15 (C)
1995—Bengals, 27-9 (P)
    Steelers, 49-31 (C)
1996—Steelers, 20-10 (P)
    Bengals, 34-24 (C)
1997—Steelers, 26-10 (C)
    Steelers, 20-3 (P)
1998—Bengals, 25-20 (C)
    Bengals, 25-24 (P)
1999—Steelers, 17-3 (C)
    Bengals, 27-20 (P)
2000—Steelers, 15-0 (P)
    Steelers, 48-28 (C)
2001—Steelers, 16-7 (P)
    Bengals, 26-23 (C) OT
(RS Pts.—Steelers 1,312, Bengals 1,134)

CINCINNATI vs. *ST. LOUIS
RS: Bengals lead series, 5-4
1972—Rams, 15-12 (LA)
1976—Bengals, 20-12 (C)
1978—Bengals, 20-19 (LA)
1981—Bengals, 24-10 (C)
1984—Rams, 24-14 (C)
1990—Bengals, 34-31 (LA) OT
1993—Bengals, 15-3 (C)
1996—Rams, 26-16 (StL)
1999—Rams, 38-10 (C)
(RS Pts.—Rams 178, Bengals 165)
*Franchise in Los Angeles prior to 1995

CINCINNATI vs. SAN DIEGO
RS: Chargers lead series, 16-9
PS: Bengals lead series, 1-0
1968—Chargers, 29-13 (SD)
    Chargers, 31-10 (C)
1969—Bengals, 34-20 (C)
    Bengals, 21-14 (SD)
1970—Bengals, 17-14 (SD)
1971—Bengals, 31-0 (C)
1973—Bengals, 20-13 (SD)
1974—Chargers, 20-17 (C)
1975—Bengals, 47-17 (C)
1977—Chargers, 24-3 (SD)
1978—Chargers, 22-13 (C)
1979—Chargers, 26-24 (C)
1980—Chargers, 31-14 (C)
1981—Bengals, 40-17 (SD)
    *Bengals, 27-7 (C)
1982—Chargers, 50-34 (SD)
1985—Chargers, 44-41 (C)
1987—Chargers, 10-9 (C)
1988—Bengals, 27-10 (C)
1990—Bengals, 21-16 (SD)
1992—Chargers, 27-10 (SD)
1994—Chargers, 27-10 (SD)
1996—Chargers, 27-14 (SD)
1997—Bengals, 38-31 (C)
1999—Chargers, 34-7 (C)
2001—Chargers, 28-14 (SD)
(RS Pts.—Chargers 589, Bengals 522)
(PS Pts.—Bengals 27, Chargers 7)
*AFC Championship

CINCINNATI vs. SAN FRANCISCO
RS: 49ers lead series, 7-2
PS: 49ers lead series, 2-0
1974—Bengals, 21-3 (SF)
1978—49ers, 28-12 (SF)
1981—49ers, 21-3 (C)
    *49ers, 26-21 (Detroit)
1984—49ers, 23-17 (SF)
1987—49ers, 27-26 (C)
1988—**49ers, 20-16 (Miami)
1990—49ers, 20-17 (C) OT
1993—49ers, 21-8 (SF)
1996—49ers, 28-21 (SF)
1999—Bengals, 44-30 (C)
(RS Pts.—49ers 201, Bengals 169)
(PS Pts.—49ers 46, Bengals 37)
*Super Bowl XVI
**Super Bowl XXIII

CINCINNATI vs. SEATTLE
RS: Seahawks lead series, 8-7
PS: Bengals lead series, 1-0
1977—Bengals, 42-20 (C)
1981—Bengals, 27-21 (C)
1982—Bengals, 24-10 (C)
1984—Seahawks, 26-6 (C)
1985—Seahawks, 28-24 (C)
1986—Bengals, 34-7 (C)
1987—Bengals, 17-10 (S)
1988—*Bengals, 21-13 (C)
1989—Seahawks, 24-17 (C)
1990—Seahawks, 31-16 (S)
1991—Seahawks, 13-7 (C)
1992—Bengals, 21-3 (S)
1993—Seahawks, 19-10 (C)
1994—Bengals, 20-17 (S) OT
1995—Seahawks, 24-21 (S)
1999—Seahawks, 37-20 (S)
(RS Pts.—Bengals 306, Seahawks 290)
(PS Pts.—Bengals 21, Seahawks 13)
*AFC Divisional Playoff

CINCINNATI vs. TAMPA BAY
RS: Buccaneers lead series, 4-3
1976—Bengals, 21-0 (C)
1980—Buccaneers, 17-12 (C)
1983—Bengals, 23-17 (TB)
1989—Bengals, 56-23 (C)
1995—Buccaneers, 19-16 (TB)
1998—Buccaneers, 35-0 (C)
2001—Buccaneers, 16-13 (C) OT
(RS Pts.—Bengals 141, Buccaneers 127)

CINCINNATI vs. *TENNESSEE
RS: Titans lead series, 36-29-1
PS: Bengals lead series, 1-0
1968—Oilers, 27-17 (C)
1969—Tie, 31-31 (H)
1970—Oilers, 20-13 (C)
    Bengals, 30-20 (H)
1971—Oilers, 10-6 (H)
    Bengals, 28-13 (C)
1972—Bengals, 30-7 (C)
    Bengals, 61-17 (H)
1973—Bengals, 24-10 (C)
    Bengals, 27-24 (H)
1974—Oilers, 34-21 (C)
    Oilers, 20-3 (H)
1975—Bengals, 21-19 (H)
    Bengals, 23-19 (C)
1976—Bengals, 27-7 (H)
    Bengals, 31-27 (C)
1977—Bengals, 13-10 (C) OT
    Oilers, 21-16 (H)
1978—Bengals, 28-13 (H)
    Oilers, 17-10 (H)
1979—Oilers, 30-27 (C) OT
    Oilers, 42-21 (H)
1980—Oilers, 13-10 (C)
    Oilers, 23-3 (H)
1981—Oilers, 17-10 (H)
    Bengals, 34-21 (C)
1982—Bengals, 27-6 (C)
    Bengals, 35-27 (H)
1983—Bengals, 55-14 (H)
    Bengals, 38-10 (C)
1984—Bengals, 13-3 (C)
    Bengals, 31-13 (H)
1985—Oilers, 44-27 (H)
    Bengals, 45-27 (C)
1986—Bengals, 31-28 (C)
    Oilers, 32-28 (H)
1987—Oilers, 31-29 (H)
    Oilers, 21-17 (H)
1988—Bengals, 44-21 (C)
    Oilers, 41-6 (H)
1989—Oilers, 26-24 (H)
    Bengals, 61-7 (C)
1990—Oilers, 48-17 (H)
    Bengals, 40-20 (C)
    **Bengals, 41-14 (C)
1991—Oilers, 30-7 (C)

Oilers, 35-3 (H)
1992—Oilers, 38-24 (C)
Oilers, 26-10 (H)
1993—Oilers, 28-12 (H)
Oilers, 38-3 (C)
1994—Oilers, 20-13 (H)
Bengals, 34-31 (C)
1995—Oilers, 38-28 (C)
Bengals, 32-25 (H)
1996—Oilers, 30-27 (C) OT
Bengals, 21-13 (H)
1997—Oilers, 30-7 (T)
Bengals, 41-14 (C)
1998—Oilers, 23-14 (C)
Oilers, 44-14 (T)
1999—Titans, 36-35 (T)
Titans, 24-14 (C)
2000—Titans, 23-14 (C)
Titans, 35-3 (T)
2001—Titans, 20-7 (C)
Bengals, 23-21 (T)
(RS Pts.—Titans 1,553, Bengals 1,519)
(PS Pts.—Bengals 41, Titans 14)
*Franchise in Houston prior to 1997;
known as Oilers prior to 1999
**AFC First-Round Playoff
CINCINNATI vs. WASHINGTON
RS: Redskins lead series, 4-2
1970—Redskins, 20-0 (W)
1974—Bengals, 28-17 (C)
1979—Redskins, 28-14 (W)
1985—Redskins, 27-24 (W)
1988—Bengals, 20-17 (C) OT
1991—Redskins, 34-27 (C)
(RS Pts.—Redskins 143, Bengals 113)

CLEVELAND vs. ARIZONA
RS: Browns lead series, 32-11-3;
See Arizona vs. Cleveland
CLEVELAND vs. ATLANTA
RS: Browns lead series, 8-2;
See Atlanta vs. Cleveland
CLEVELAND vs. BALTIMORE
RS: Ravens lead series, 4-2;
See Baltimore vs. Cleveland
CLEVELAND vs. BUFFALO
RS: Browns lead series, 7-4
PS: Browns lead series, 1-0;
See Buffalo vs. Cleveland
CLEVELAND vs. CAROLINA
RS: Panthers lead series, 1-0;
See Carolina vs. Cleveland
CLEVELAND vs. CHICAGO
RS: Browns lead series, 8-4;
See Chicago vs. Cleveland
CLEVELAND vs. CINCINNATI
RS: Browns lead series, 29-28;
See Cincinnati vs. Cleveland
CLEVELAND vs. DALLAS
RS: Browns lead series, 15-9
PS: Browns lead series, 2-1
1960—Browns, 48-7 (D)
1961—Browns, 25-7 (C)
Browns, 38-17 (D)
1962—Browns, 19-10 (C)
Cowboys, 45-21 (D)
1963—Browns, 41-24 (D)
Browns, 27-17 (C)
1964—Browns, 27-6 (C)
Browns, 20-16 (D)

1965—Browns, 23-17 (C)
Browns, 24-17 (D)
1966—Browns, 30-21 (C)
Cowboys, 26-14 (D)
1967—Cowboys, 21-14 (C)
*Cowboys, 52-14 (D)
1968—Cowboys, 28-7 (C)
*Browns, 31-20 (C)
1969—Browns, 42-10 (C)
*Browns, 38-14 (D)
1970—Cowboys, 6-2 (C)
1974—Cowboys, 41-17 (D)
1979—Browns, 26-7 (C)
1982—Cowboys, 31-14 (D)
1985—Cowboys, 20-7 (D)
1988—Browns, 24-21 (C)
1991—Cowboys, 26-14 (C)
1994—Browns, 19-14 (D)
(RS Pts.—Browns 543, Cowboys 455)
(PS Pts.—Cowboys 86, Browns 83)
*Conference Championship
CLEVELAND vs. DENVER
RS: Broncos lead series, 14-5
PS: Broncos lead series, 3-0
1970—Browns, 27-13 (D)
1971—Broncos, 27-0 (C)
1972—Browns, 27-20 (D)
1974—Browns, 23-21 (C)
1975—Broncos, 16-15 (D)
1976—Broncos, 44-13 (D)
1978—Broncos, 19-7 (C)
1980—Broncos, 19-16 (C)
1981—Broncos, 23-20 (D) OT
1983—Broncos, 27-6 (D)
1984—Broncos, 24-14 (C)
1986—*Broncos, 23-20 (C) OT
1987—*Broncos, 38-33 (D)
1988—Broncos, 30-7 (D)
1989—Browns, 16-13 (C)
*Broncos, 37-21 (D)
1990—Browns, 30-29 (D)
1991—Broncos, 17-7 (C)
1992—Broncos, 12-0 (C)
1993—Broncos, 29-14 (C)
1994—Broncos, 26-14 (D)
2000—Broncos, 44-10 (D)
(RS Pts.—Broncos 453, Browns 266)
(PS Pts.—Broncos 98, Browns 74)
*AFC Championship
CLEVELAND vs. DETROIT
RS: Lions lead series, 12-4
PS: Lions lead series, 3-1
1952—Lions, 17-6 (D)
*Lions, 17-7 (C)
1953—*Lions, 17-16 (D)
1954—Lions, 14-10 (C)
*Browns, 56-10 (C)
1957—Lions, 20-7 (D)
*Lions, 59-14 (D)
1958—Lions, 30-10 (C)
1963—Lions, 38-10 (D)
1964—Browns, 37-21 (C)
1967—Lions, 31-14 (D)
1969—Lions, 28-21 (C)
1970—Lions, 41-24 (C)
1975—Lions, 21-10 (D)
1983—Browns, 31-26 (D)
1986—Browns, 24-21 (C)
1989—Lions, 13-10 (D)
1992—Lions, 24-14 (D)

1995—Lions, 38-20 (D)
2001—Browns, 24-14 (C)
(RS Pts.—Lions 397, Browns 272)
(PS Pts.—Lions 103, Browns 93)
*NFL Championship
CLEVELAND vs. GREEN BAY
RS: Packers lead series, 9-6
PS: Packers lead series, 1-0
1953—Browns, 27-0 (Mil)
1955—Browns, 41-10 (C)
1956—Browns, 24-7 (Mil)
1961—Packers, 49-17 (C)
1964—Packers, 28-21 (Mil)
1965—*Packers, 23-12 (GB)
1966—Packers, 21-20 (C)
1967—Packers, 55-7 (Mil)
1969—Browns, 20-7 (C)
1972—Packers, 26-10 (C)
1980—Browns, 26-21 (C)
1983—Packers, 35-21 (Mil)
1986—Packers, 17-14 (C)
1992—Browns, 17-6 (C)
1995—Packers, 31-20 (C)
2001—Packers, 30-7 (GB)
(RS Pts.—Packers 343, Browns 292)
(PS Pts.—Packers 23, Browns 12)
*NFL Championship
CLEVELAND vs. *INDIANAPOLIS
RS: Browns lead series, 13-8
PS: Series tied, 2-2
1956—Colts, 21-7 (C)
1959—Browns, 38-31 (B)
1962—Colts, 36-14 (C)
1964—**Browns, 27-0 (C)
1968—Browns, 30-20 (B)
**Colts, 34-0 (C)
1971—Browns, 14-13 (B)
***Colts, 20-3 (C)
1973—Browns, 24-14 (C)
1975—Colts, 21-7 (B)
1978—Browns, 45-24 (B)
1979—Browns, 13-10 (B)
1980—Browns, 28-27 (B)
1981—Browns, 42-28 (C)
1983—Browns, 41-23 (C)
1986—Browns, 24-9 (I)
1987—Colts, 9-7 (C)
***Browns, 38-21 (C)
1988—Browns, 23-17 (C)
1989—Colts, 23-17 (I) OT
1991—Browns, 31-0 (I)
1992—Colts, 14-3 (I)
1993—Colts, 23-10 (I)
1994—Browns, 21-14 (I)
1999—Colts, 29-28 (C)
(RS Pts.—Browns 467, Colts 406)
(PS Pts.—Colts 75, Browns 68)
*Franchise in Baltimore prior to 1984
**NFL Championship
***AFC Divisional Playoff
CLEVELAND vs. JACKSONVILLE
RS: Jaguars lead series, 7-1
1995—Jaguars, 23-15 (C)
Jaguars, 24-21 (J)
1999—Jaguars, 24-7 (J)
Jaguars, 24-14 (C)
2000—Jaguars, 27-7 (C)
Jaguars, 48-0 (J)
2001—Browns, 23-14 (J)
Jaguars, 15-10 (C)

(RS Pts.—Jaguars 199, Browns 97)

CLEVELAND vs. KANSAS CITY
RS: Browns lead series, 8-7-2
1971—Chiefs, 13-7 (KC)
1972—Chiefs, 31-7 (C)
1973—Tie, 20-20 (KC)
1975—Browns, 40-14 (C)
1976—Chiefs, 39-14 (KC)
1977—Browns, 44-7 (C)
1978—Chiefs, 17-3 (KC)
1979—Browns, 27-24 (KC)
1980—Browns, 20-13 (C)
1984—Chiefs, 10-6 (KC)
1986—Browns, 20-7 (C)
1988—Browns, 6-3 (KC)
1989—Tie, 10-10 (C) OT
1990—Chiefs, 34-0 (KC)
1991—Browns, 20-15 (C)
1994—Chiefs, 20-13 (KC)
1995—Browns, 35-17 (C)
(RS Pts.—Chiefs 294, Browns 292)

CLEVELAND vs. MIAMI
RS: Dolphins lead series, 6-4
PS: Dolphins lead series, 2-0
1970—Browns, 28-0 (M)
1972—*Dolphins, 20-14 (M)
1973—Dolphins, 17-9 (C)
1976—Browns, 17-13 (C)
1979—Browns, 30-24 (C) OT
1985—*Dolphins, 24-21 (M)
1986—Browns, 26-16 (C)
1988—Dolphins, 38-31 (M)
1989—Dolphins, 13-10 (M) OT
1990—Dolphins, 30-13 (C)
1992—Dolphins, 27-23 (C)
1993—Dolphins, 24-14 (C)
(RS Pts.—Dolphins 202, Browns 201)
(PS Pts.—Dolphins 44, Browns 35)
*AFC Divisional Playoff

CLEVELAND vs. MINNESOTA
RS: Vikings lead series, 8-3
PS: Vikings lead series, 1-0
1965—Vikings, 27-17 (C)
1967—Browns, 14-10 (C)
1969—Vikings, 51-3 (M)
        *Vikings, 27-7 (M)
1973—Vikings, 26-3 (M)
1975—Vikings, 42-10 (C)
1980—Vikings, 28-23 (M)
1983—Vikings, 27-21 (C)
1986—Browns, 23-20 (M)
1989—Browns, 23-17 (C) OT
1992—Vikings, 17-13 (C)
1995—Vikings, 27-11 (M)
(RS Pts.—Vikings 292, Browns 161)
(PS Pts.—Vikings 27, Browns 7)
*NFL Championship

CLEVELAND vs. NEW ENGLAND
RS: Browns lead series, 11-6
PS: Browns lead series, 1-0
1971—Browns, 27-7 (C)
1974—Browns, 21-14 (NE)
1977—Browns, 30-27 (C) OT
1980—Patriots, 34-17 (NE)
1982—Browns, 10-7 (C)
1983—Browns, 30-0 (NE)
1984—Patriots, 17-16 (C)
1985—Browns, 24-20 (C)
1987—Browns, 20-10 (NE)
1991—Browns, 20-0 (NE)

1992—Browns, 19-17 (NE)
1993—Patriots, 20-17 (C)
1994—Browns, 13-6 (C)
        *Browns, 20-13 (C)
1995—Patriots, 17-14 (NE)
1999—Patriots, 19-7 (C)
2000—Browns, 19-11 (C)
2001—Patriots, 27-16 (NE)
(RS Pts.—Browns 320, Patriots 253)
(PS Pts.—Browns 20, Patriots 13)
*AFC First-Round Playoff

CLEVELAND vs. NEW ORLEANS
RS: Browns lead series, 10-3
1967—Browns, 42-7 (NO)
1968—Browns, 24-10 (NO)
        Browns, 35-17 (C)
1969—Browns, 27-17 (NO)
1971—Browns, 21-17 (NO)
1975—Browns, 17-16 (C)
1978—Browns, 24-16 (NO)
1981—Browns, 20-17 (C)
1984—Saints, 16-14 (C)
1987—Saints, 28-21 (NO)
1990—Saints, 25-20 (NO)
1993—Browns, 17-13 (C)
1999—Browns, 21-16 (NO)
(RS Pts.—Browns 303, Saints 215)

CLEVELAND vs. N.Y. GIANTS
RS: Browns lead series, 25-18-2
PS: Series tied, 1-1
1950—Giants, 6-0 (C)
        Giants, 17-13 (NY)
        *Browns, 8-3 (C)
1951—Browns, 14-13 (C)
        Browns, 10-0 (NY)
1952—Giants, 17-9 (C)
        Giants, 37-34 (NY)
1953—Browns, 7-0 (NY)
        Browns, 62-14 (C)
1954—Browns, 24-14 (C)
        Browns, 16-7 (NY)
1955—Browns, 24-14 (C)
        Tie, 35-35 (NY)
1956—Giants, 21-9 (C)
        Browns, 24-7 (NY)
1957—Browns, 6-3 (C)
        Browns, 34-28 (NY)
1958—Giants, 21-17 (C)
        Giants, 13-10 (NY)
        *Giants, 10-0 (NY)
1959—Giants, 10-6 (C)
        Giants, 48-7 (NY)
1960—Giants, 17-13 (C)
        Browns, 48-34 (NY)
1961—Giants, 37-21 (C)
        Tie, 7-7 (NY)
1962—Browns, 17-7 (C)
        Giants, 17-13 (NY)
1963—Browns, 35-24 (NY)
        Giants, 33-6 (C)
1964—Browns, 42-20 (C)
        Browns, 52-20 (NY)
1965—Browns, 38-14 (NY)
        Browns, 34-21 (C)
1966—Browns, 28-7 (NY)
        Browns, 49-40 (C)
1967—Giants, 38-34 (NY)
        Browns, 24-14 (C)
1968—Browns, 45-10 (C)
1969—Browns, 28-17 (C)

        Giants, 27-14 (NY)
1973—Browns, 12-10 (C)
1977—Browns, 21-7 (NY)
1985—Browns, 35-33 (NY)
1991—Giants, 13-10 (NY)
1994—Giants, 16-13 (C)
2000—Giants, 24-3 (C)
(RS Pts.—Browns 1,003, Giants 832)
(PS Pts.—Giants 13, Browns 8)
*Conference Playoff

CLEVELAND vs. N.Y. JETS
RS: Browns lead series, 9-6
PS: Browns lead series, 1-0
1970—Browns, 31-21 (C)
1972—Browns, 26-10 (NY)
1976—Browns, 38-17 (C)
1978—Browns, 37-34 (C) OT
1979—Browns, 25-22 (NY) OT
1980—Browns, 17-14 (C)
1981—Jets, 14-13 (C)
1983—Browns, 10-7 (C)
1984—Jets, 24-20 (C)
1985—Jets, 37-10 (NY)
1986—*Browns, 23-20 (C) OT
1988—Jets, 23-3 (C)
1989—Browns, 38-24 (C)
1990—Jets, 24-21 (NY)
1991—Jets, 17-14 (C)
1994—Browns, 27-7 (C)
(RS Pts.—Browns 330, Jets 295)
(PS Pts.—Browns 23, Jets 20)
*AFC Divisional Playoff

CLEVELAND vs. *OAKLAND
RS: Raiders lead series, 9-4
PS: Raiders lead series, 2-0
1970—Raiders, 23-20 (O)
1971—Raiders, 34-20 (C)
1973—Browns, 7-3 (O)
1974—Raiders, 40-24 (C)
1975—Raiders, 38-17 (O)
1977—Raiders, 26-10 (C)
1979—Raiders, 19-14 (O)
1980—**Raiders, 14-12 (C)
1982—***Raiders, 27-10 (LA)
1985—Raiders, 21-20 (C)
1986—Raiders, 27-14 (LA)
1987—Browns, 24-17 (LA)
1992—Browns, 28-16 (LA)
1993—Browns, 19-16 (LA)
2000—Raiders, 36-10 (O)
(RS Pts.—Raiders 316, Browns 227)
(PS Pts.—Raiders 41, Browns 22)
*Franchise in Los Angeles from
1982-1994
**AFC Divisional Playoff
***AFC First-Round Playoff

CLEVELAND vs. PHILADELPHIA
RS: Browns lead series, 31-13-1
1950—Browns, 35-10 (P)
        Browns, 13-7 (C)
1951—Browns, 20-17 (C)
        Browns, 24-9 (P)
1952—Browns, 49-7 (P)
        Eagles, 28-20 (C)
1953—Browns, 37-13 (C)
        Eagles, 42-27 (P)
1954—Eagles, 28-10 (P)
        Browns, 6-0 (C)
1955—Browns, 21-17 (C)
        Eagles, 33-17 (P)

1956—Browns, 16-0 (P)
    Browns, 17-14 (C)
1957—Browns, 24-7 (C)
    Eagles, 17-7 (P)
1958—Browns, 28-14 (C)
    Browns, 21-14 (P)
1959—Browns, 28-7 (C)
    Browns, 28-21 (P)
1960—Browns, 41-24 (P)
    Eagles, 31-29 (C)
1961—Eagles, 27-20 (P)
    Browns, 45-24 (C)
1962—Eagles, 35-7 (P)
    Tie, 14-14 (C)
1963—Browns, 37-7 (C)
    Browns, 23-17 (P)
1964—Browns, 28-20 (P)
    Browns, 38-24 (C)
1965—Browns, 35-17 (P)
    Browns, 38-34 (C)
1966—Browns, 27-7 (C)
    Eagles, 33-21 (P)
1967—Eagles, 28-24 (P)
1968—Browns, 47-13 (C)
1969—Browns, 27-20 (P)
1972—Browns, 27-17 (P)
1976—Browns, 24-3 (C)
1979—Browns, 24-19 (P)
1982—Eagles, 24-21 (C)
1988—Browns, 19-3 (C)
1991—Eagles, 32-30 (C)
1994—Browns, 26-7 (P)
2000—Eagles, 35-24 (C)
(RS Pts.—Browns 1,144, Eagles 820)
CLEVELAND vs. PITTSBURGH
RS: Browns lead series, 54-44
PS: Steelers lead series, 1-0
1950—Browns, 30-17 (P)
    Browns, 45-7 (C)
1951—Browns, 17-0 (C)
    Browns, 28-0 (P)
1952—Browns, 21-20 (P)
    Browns, 29-28 (C)
1953—Browns, 34-16 (C)
    Browns, 20-16 (P)
1954—Steelers, 55-27 (P)
    Browns, 42-7 (C)
1955—Browns, 41-14 (C)
    Browns, 30-7 (P)
1956—Browns, 14-10 (P)
    Steelers, 24-16 (C)
1957—Browns, 23-12 (P)
    Browns, 24-0 (C)
1958—Browns, 45-12 (P)
    Browns, 27-10 (C)
1959—Steelers, 17-7 (P)
    Steelers, 21-20 (C)
1960—Browns, 28-20 (C)
    Steelers, 14-10 (P)
1961—Browns, 30-28 (P)
    Steelers, 17-13 (C)
1962—Browns, 41-14 (P)
    Browns, 35-14 (C)
1963—Browns, 35-23 (C)
    Steelers, 9-7 (P)
1964—Steelers, 23-7 (C)
    Browns, 30-17 (P)
1965—Browns, 24-19 (C)
    Browns, 42-21 (P)
1966—Browns, 41-10 (C)

    Steelers, 16-6 (P)
1967—Browns, 21-10 (C)
    Browns, 34-14 (P)
1968—Browns, 31-24 (C)
    Browns, 45-24 (P)
1969—Browns, 42-31 (C)
    Browns, 24-3 (P)
1970—Browns, 15-7 (C)
    Steelers, 28-9 (P)
1971—Browns, 27-17 (C)
    Steelers, 26-9 (P)
1972—Browns, 26-24 (C)
    Steelers, 30-0 (P)
1973—Steelers, 33-6 (P)
    Browns, 21-16 (C)
1974—Steelers, 20-16 (P)
    Steelers, 26-16 (C)
1975—Steelers, 42-6 (C)
    Steelers, 31-17 (P)
1976—Steelers, 31-14 (P)
    Browns, 18-16 (C)
1977—Steelers, 28-14 (C)
    Steelers, 35-31 (P)
1978—Steelers, 15-9 (P) OT
    Steelers, 34-14 (C)
1979—Steelers, 51-35 (C)
    Steelers, 33-30 (P) OT
1980—Browns, 27-26 (C)
    Steelers, 16-13 (P)
1981—Steelers, 13-7 (P)
    Steelers, 32-10 (C)
1982—Browns, 10-9 (C)
    Steelers, 37-21 (P)
1983—Steelers, 44-17 (P)
    Browns, 30-17 (C)
1984—Browns, 20-10 (C)
    Steelers, 23-20 (P)
1985—Browns, 17-7 (C)
    Steelers, 10-9 (P)
1986—Browns, 27-24 (P)
    Browns, 37-31 (C) OT
1987—Browns, 34-10 (C)
    Browns, 19-13 (P)
1988—Browns, 23-9 (P)
    Browns, 27-7 (C)
1989—Browns, 51-0 (P)
    Steelers, 17-7 (C)
1990—Browns, 13-3 (C)
    Steelers, 35-0 (P)
1991—Browns, 17-14 (C)
    Steelers, 17-10 (P)
1992—Browns, 17-9 (C)
    Steelers, 23-13 (P)
1993—Browns, 28-23 (C)
    Steelers, 16-9 (P)
1994—Steelers, 17-10 (C)
    Steelers, 17-7 (P)
    *Steelers, 29-9 (P)
1995—Steelers, 20-3 (P)
    Steelers, 20-17 (C)
1999—Steelers, 43-0 (C)
    Browns, 16-15 (P)
2000—Browns, 23-20 (C)
    Steelers, 22-0 (P)
2001—Steelers, 15-12 (C) OT
    Steelers, 28-7 (P)
(RS Pts.—Browns 2,047, Steelers 1,899)
(PS Pts.—Steelers 29, Browns 9)
AFC Divisional Playoff

CLEVELAND vs. *ST. LOUIS
RS: Series tied, 8-8
PS: Browns lead series, 2-1
1950—**Browns, 30-28 (C)
1951—Browns, 38-23 (LA)
    **Rams, 24-17 (LA)
1952—Browns, 37-7 (C)
1955—**Browns, 38-14 (LA)
1957—Browns, 45-31 (C)
1958—Browns, 30-27 (LA)
1963—Browns, 20-6 (C)
1965—Rams, 42-7 (LA)
1968—Rams, 24-6 (C)
1973—Rams, 30-17 (LA)
1977—Rams, 9-0 (C)
1978—Browns, 30-19 (C)
1981—Rams, 27-16 (LA)
1984—Rams, 20-17 (LA)
1987—Browns, 30-17 (C)
1990—Rams, 38-23 (C)
1993—Browns, 42-14 (LA)
1999—Rams, 34-3 (StL)
(RS Pts.—Rams 368, Browns 361)
(PS Pts.—Browns 85, Rams 66)
Franchise in Los Angeles prior to 1995
**NFL Championship*
CLEVELAND vs. SAN DIEGO
RS: Chargers lead series, 10-7-1
1970—Chargers, 27-10 (C)
1972—Browns, 21-17 (SD)
1973—Tie, 16-16 (C)
1974—Chargers, 36-35 (SD)
1976—Browns, 21-17 (C)
1977—Chargers, 37-14 (SD)
1981—Chargers, 44-14 (C)
1982—Chargers, 30-13 (C)
1983—Browns, 30-24 (SD) OT
1985—Browns, 21-7 (SD)
1986—Browns, 47-17 (C)
1987—Chargers, 27-24 (SD) OT
1990—Chargers, 24-14 (C)
1991—Browns, 30-24 (SD) OT
1992—Chargers, 14-13 (C)
1995—Chargers, 31-13 (SD)
1999—Chargers, 23-10 (SD)
2001—Browns, 20-16 (C)
(RS Pts.—Chargers 431, Browns 366)
CLEVELAND vs. SAN FRANCISCO
RS: Browns lead series, 9-6
1950—Browns, 34-14 (C)
1951—49ers, 24-10 (SF)
1953—Browns, 23-21 (C)
1955—Browns, 38-3 (SF)
1959—49ers, 21-20 (SF)
1962—Browns, 13-10 (SF)
1968—Browns, 33-21 (SF)
1970—49ers, 34-31 (SF)
1974—Browns, 7-0 (C)
1978—Browns, 24-7 (C)
1981—Browns, 15-12 (SF)
1984—49ers, 41-7 (C)
1987—49ers, 38-24 (SF)
1990—Browns, 20-17 (SF)
1993—Browns, 23-13 (C)
(RS Pts.—Browns 319, 49ers 279)
CLEVELAND vs. SEATTLE
RS: Seahawks lead series, 10-4
1977—Seahawks, 20-19 (S)
1978—Seahawks, 47-24 (S)
1979—Seahawks, 29-24 (C)

1980—Browns, 27-3 (S)
1981—Seahawks, 42-21 (S)
1982—Browns, 21-7 (S)
1983—Seahawks, 24-9 (C)
1984—Seahawks, 33-0 (S)
1985—Seahawks, 31-13 (S)
1988—Seahawks, 16-10 (C)
1989—Browns, 17-7 (S)
1993—Seahawks, 22-5 (S)
1994—Browns, 35-9 (C)
2001—Seahawks, 9-6 (C)
(RS Pts.—Seahawks 299, Browns 231)
CLEVELAND vs. TAMPA BAY
RS: Browns lead series, 5-0
1976—Browns, 24-7 (TB)
1980—Browns, 34-27 (TB)
1983—Browns, 20-0 (C)
1989—Browns, 42-31 (TB)
1995—Browns, 22-6 (C)
(RS Pts.—Browns 142, Buccaneers 71)
CLEVELAND vs. *TENNESSEE
RS: Browns lead series, 31-26
PS: Titans lead series, 1-0
1970—Browns, 28-14 (C)
        Browns, 21-10 (H)
1971—Browns, 31-0 (C)
        Browns, 37-24 (H)
1972—Browns, 23-17 (H)
        Browns, 20-0 (C)
1973—Browns, 42-13 (C)
        Browns, 23-13 (H)
1974—Browns, 20-7 (C)
        Oilers, 28-24 (H)
1975—Oilers, 40-10 (C)
        Oilers, 21-10 (H)
1976—Browns, 21-7 (H)
        Browns, 13-10 (C)
1977—Browns, 24-23 (H)
        Oilers, 19-15 (C)
1978—Oilers, 16-13 (C)
        Oilers, 14-10 (H)
1979—Oilers, 31-10 (H)
        Browns, 14-7 (C)
1980—Oilers, 16-7 (C)
        Browns, 17-14 (H)
1981—Oilers, 9-3 (C)
        Oilers, 17-13 (H)
1982—Browns, 20-14 (H)
1983—Browns, 25-19 (C) OT
        Oilers, 34-27 (H)
1984—Browns, 27-10 (C)
        Browns, 27-20 (H)
1985—Browns, 21-6 (H)
        Browns, 28-21 (C)
1986—Browns, 23-20 (H)
        Browns, 13-10 (C) OT
1987—Oilers, 15-10 (C)
        Browns, 40-7 (H)
1988—Oilers, 24-17 (H)
        Browns, 28-23 (C)
        **Oilers, 24-23 (C)
1989—Browns, 28-17 (C)
        Browns, 24-20 (H)
1990—Oilers, 35-23 (C)
        Oilers, 58-14 (H)
1991—Oilers, 28-24 (H)
        Oilers, 17-14 (C)
1992—Browns, 24-14 (H)
        Oilers, 17-14 (C)
1993—Oilers, 27-20 (C)

Oilers, 19-17 (H)
1994—Browns, 11-8 (H)
        Browns, 34-10 (C)
1995—Browns, 14-7 (H)
        Oilers, 37-10 (C)
1999—Titans, 26-9 (T)
        Titans, 33-21 (C)
2000—Titans, 24-10 (T)
        Titans, 24-0 (C)
2001—Titans, 31-15 (C)
        Titans, 41-38 (T)
(RS Pts.—Browns 1,122, Titans 1,083)
(PS Pts.—Titans 24, Browns 23)
*Franchise in Houston prior to 1997;
known as Oilers prior to 1999
**AFC First-Round Playoff
CLEVELAND vs. WASHINGTON
RS: Browns lead series, 32-9-1
1950—Browns, 20-14 (C)
        Browns, 45-21 (W)
1951—Browns, 45-0 (C)
1952—Browns, 19-15 (C)
        Browns, 48-24 (W)
1953—Browns, 30-14 (W)
        Browns, 27-3 (C)
1954—Browns, 62-3 (C)
        Browns, 34-14 (W)
1955—Redskins, 27-17 (C)
        Browns, 24-14 (W)
1956—Redskins, 20-9 (W)
        Redskins, 20-17 (C)
1957—Browns, 21-17 (C)
        Tie, 30-30 (W)
1958—Browns, 20-10 (W)
        Browns, 21-14 (C)
1959—Browns, 34-7 (C)
        Browns, 31-17 (W)
1960—Browns, 31-10 (W)
        Browns, 27-16 (C)
1961—Browns, 31-7 (C)
        Browns, 17-6 (W)
1962—Redskins, 17-16 (C)
        Redskins, 17-9 (W)
1963—Browns, 37-14 (C)
        Browns, 27-20 (W)
1964—Browns, 27-13 (W)
        Browns, 34-24 (C)
1965—Browns, 17-7 (W)
        Browns, 24-16 (C)
1966—Browns, 38-14 (W)
        Browns, 14-3 (C)
1967—Browns, 42-37 (C)
1968—Browns, 24-21 (W)
1969—Browns, 27-23 (C)
1971—Browns, 20-13 (W)
1975—Redskins, 23-7 (C)
1979—Redskins, 13-9 (C)
1985—Redskins, 14-7 (C)
1988—Browns, 17-13 (W)
1991—Redskins, 42-17 (W)
(RS Pts.—Browns 1,073, Redskins 667)

DALLAS vs. ARIZONA
RS: Cowboys lead series, 52-26-1
PS: Cardinals lead series, 1-0;
See Arizona vs. Dallas
DALLAS vs. ATLANTA
RS: Cowboys lead series, 12-7
PS: Cowboys lead series, 2-0;
See Atlanta vs. Dallas

DALLAS vs. BALTIMORE
RS: Ravens lead series, 1-0;
See Baltimore vs. Dallas
DALLAS vs. BUFFALO
RS: Series tied, 3-3
PS: Cowboys lead series, 2-0;
See Buffalo vs. Dallas
DALLAS vs. CAROLINA
RS: Cowboys lead series, 2-1
PS: Panthers lead series, 1-0;
See Carolina vs. Dallas
DALLAS vs. CHICAGO
RS: Cowboys lead series, 9-8
PS: Cowboys lead series, 2-0;
See Chicago vs. Dallas
DALLAS vs. CINCINNATI
RS: Cowboys lead series, 5-3;
See Cincinnati vs. Dallas
DALLAS vs. CLEVELAND
RS: Browns lead series, 15-9
PS: Browns lead series, 2-1;
See Cleveland vs. Dallas
DALLAS vs. DENVER
RS: Series tied, 4-4
PS: Cowboys lead series, 1-0
1973—Cowboys, 22-10 (Den)
1977—Cowboys, 14-6 (Dall)
        *Cowboys, 27-10 (New Orleans)
1980—Broncos, 41-20 (Den)
1986—Broncos, 29-14 (Den)
1992—Cowboys, 31-27 (Den)
1995—Cowboys, 31-21 (Dall)
1998—Broncos, 42-23 (Den)
2001—Broncos, 26-24 (Dall)
(RS Pts.—Broncos 202, Cowboys 179)
(PS Pts.—Cowboys 27, Broncos 10)
*Super Bowl XII
DALLAS vs. DETROIT
RS: Series tied, 7-7
PS: Series tied, 1-1
1960—Lions, 23-14 (Det)
1963—Cowboys, 17-14 (Dal)
1968—Cowboys, 59-13 (Dal)
1970—*Cowboys, 5-0 (Dal)
1972—Cowboys, 28-24 (Dal)
1975—Cowboys, 36-10 (Det)
1977—Cowboys, 37-0 (Dal)
1981—Lions, 27-24 (Det)
1985—Lions, 26-21 (Det)
1986—Cowboys, 31-7 (Det)
1987—Lions, 27-17 (Det)
1991—Lions, 34-10 (Det)
        *Lions, 38-6 (Det)
1992—Cowboys, 37-3 (Det)
1994—Lions, 20-17 (Dal) OT
2001—Lions, 15-10 (Det)
(RS Pts.—Cowboys 358, Lions 243)
(PS Pts.—Lions 38, Cowboys 11)
*NFC Divisional Playoff
DALLAS vs. GREEN BAY
RS: Cowboys lead series, 10-9
PS: Cowboys lead series, 4-2
1960—Packers, 41-7 (GB)
1964—Packers, 45-21 (D)
1965—Packers, 13-3 (Mil)
1966—*Packers, 34-27 (D)
1967—*Packers, 21-17 (GB)
1968—Packers, 28-17 (D)
1970—Cowboys, 16-3 (D)
1972—Packers, 16-13 (Mil)

1975—Packers, 19-17 (D)
1978—Cowboys, 42-14 (Mil)
1980—Cowboys, 28-7 (Mil)
1982—**Cowboys, 37-26 (D)
1984—Cowboys, 20-6 (D)
1989—Packers, 31-13 (GB)
    Packers, 20-10 (D)
1991—Cowboys, 20-17 (Mil)
1993—Cowboys, 36-14 (D)
    ***Cowboys, 27-17 (D)
1994—Cowboys, 42-31 (D)
    ***Cowboys, 35-9 (D)
1995—Cowboys, 34-24 (D)
    ****Cowboys, 38-27 (D)
1996—Cowboys, 21-6 (D)
1997—Packers, 45-17 (GB)
1999—Cowboys, 27-13 (D)
(RS Pts.—Cowboys 404, Packers 393)
(PS Pts.—Cowboys 181, Packers 134)
*NFL Championship
**NFC Second-Round Playoff
***NFC Divisional Playoff
****NFC Championship

DALLAS vs. *INDIANAPOLIS
RS: Cowboys lead series, 7-4
PS: Colts lead series, 1-0
1960—Colts, 45-7 (D)
1967—Colts, 23-17 (B)
1969—Cowboys, 27-10 (D)
1970—**Colts, 16-13 (Miami)
1972—Cowboys, 21-0 (B)
1976—Cowboys, 30-27 (D)
1978—Cowboys, 38-0 (D)
1981—Cowboys, 37-13 (B)
1984—Cowboys, 22-3 (D)
1993—Cowboys, 27-3 (I)
1996—Colts, 25-24 (D)
1999—Colts, 34-24 (I)
(RS Pts.—Cowboys 274, Colts 183)
(PS Pts.—Colts 16, Cowboys 13)
*Franchise in Baltimore prior to 1984
**Super Bowl V

DALLAS VS. JACKSONVILLE
RS: Series tied, 1-1
1997—Cowboys, 26-22 (D)
2000—Jaguars, 23-17 (D) OT
(RS Pts.—Jaguars 45, Cowboys 43)

DALLAS vs. KANSAS CITY
RS: Cowboys lead series, 4-3
1970—Cowboys, 27-16 (KC)
1975—Chiefs, 34-31 (D)
1983—Cowboys, 41-21 (D)
1989—Chiefs, 36-28 (KC)
1992—Cowboys, 17-10 (D)
1995—Cowboys, 24-12 (D)
1998—Chiefs, 20-17 (KC)
(RS Pts.—Cowboys 185, Chiefs 149)

DALLAS vs. MIAMI
RS: Dolphins lead series, 6-3
PS: Cowboys lead series, 1-0
1971—*Cowboys, 24-3 (New Orleans)
1973—Dolphins, 14-7 (D)
1978—Dolphins, 23-16 (M)
1981—Cowboys, 28-27 (D)
1984—Dolphins, 28-21 (M)
1987—Dolphins, 20-14 (D)
1989—Dolphins, 17-14 (D)
1993—Dolphins, 16-14 (D)
1996—Cowboys, 29-10 (M)
1999—Cowboys, 20-0 (D)

(RS Pts.—Cowboys 163, Dolphins 155)
(PS Pts.—Cowboys 24, Dolphins 3)
*Super Bowl VI

DALLAS vs. MINNESOTA
RS: Series tied, 9-9
PS: Cowboys lead series, 4-2
1961—Cowboys, 21-7 (D)
    Cowboys, 28-0 (M)
1966—Cowboys, 28-17 (D)
1968—Cowboys, 20-7 (M)
1970—Vikings, 54-13 (M)
1971—*Cowboys, 20-12 (M)
1973—**Vikings, 27-10 (D)
1974—Vikings, 23-21 (D)
1975—*Cowboys, 17-14 (M)
1977—Cowboys, 16-10 (M) OT
    **Cowboys, 23-6 (D)
1978—Vikings, 21-10 (D)
1979—Cowboys, 36-20 (M)
1982—Vikings, 31-27 (M)
1983—Cowboys, 37-24 (M)
1987—Vikings, 44-38 (D) OT
1988—Vikings, 43-3 (D)
1993—Cowboys, 37-20 (M)
1995—Cowboys, 23-17 (M) OT
1996—***Cowboys, 40-15 (D)
1998—Vikings, 46-36 (D)
1999—Vikings, 27-17 (M)
    ***Vikings, 27-10 (M)
2000—Vikings, 27-15 (D)
(RS Pts.—Vikings 438, Cowboys 426)
(PS Pts.—Cowboys 120, Vikings 101)
*NFC Divisional Playoff
**NFC Championship
***NFC First-Round Playoff

DALLAS vs. NEW ENGLAND
RS: Cowboys lead series, 7-1
1971—Cowboys, 44-21 (D)
1975—Cowboys, 34-31 (NE)
1978—Cowboys, 17-10 (D)
1981—Cowboys, 35-21 (NE)
1984—Cowboys, 20-17 (D)
1987—Cowboys, 23-17 (NE) OT
1996—Cowboys, 12-6 (D)
1999—Patriots, 13-6 (NE)
(RS Pts.—Cowboys 191, Patriots 136)

DALLAS vs. NEW ORLEANS
RS: Cowboys lead series, 14-5
1967—Cowboys, 14-10 (D)
    Cowboys, 27-10 (NO)
1968—Cowboys, 17-3 (NO)
1969—Cowboys, 21-17 (NO)
    Cowboys, 33-17 (D)
1971—Saints, 24-14 (NO)
1973—Cowboys, 40-3 (D)
1976—Cowboys, 24-6 (NO)
1978—Cowboys, 27-7 (D)
1982—Cowboys, 21-7 (D)
1983—Cowboys, 21-20 (D)
1984—Cowboys, 30-27 (D) OT
1988—Saints, 20-17 (NO)
1989—Saints, 28-0 (NO)
1990—Cowboys, 17-13 (D)
1991—Cowboys, 23-14 (D)
1994—Cowboys, 24-16 (NO)
1998—Saints, 22-3 (NO)
1999—Saints, 31-24 (NO)
(RS Pts.—Cowboys 397, Saints 295)

DALLAS vs. N.Y. GIANTS
RS: Cowboys lead series, 48-29-2

1960—Tie, 31-31 (NY)
1961—Giants, 31-10 (D)
    Cowboys, 17-16 (NY)
1962—Giants, 41-10 (D)
    Giants, 41-31 (NY)
1963—Giants, 37-21 (NY)
    Giants, 34-27 (D)
1964—Tie, 13-13 (NY)
    Cowboys, 31-21 (NY)
1965—Cowboys, 31-2 (D)
    Cowboys, 38-20 (NY)
1966—Cowboys, 52-7 (D)
    Cowboys, 17-7 (NY)
1967—Cowboys, 38-24 (D)
1968—Giants, 27-21 (D)
    Cowboys, 28-10 (NY)
1969—Cowboys, 25-3 (D)
1970—Cowboys, 28-10 (D)
    Giants, 23-20 (NY)
1971—Cowboys, 20-13 (D)
    Cowboys, 42-14 (NY)
1972—Cowboys, 23-14 (NY)
    Giants, 23-3 (D)
1973—Cowboys, 45-28 (D)
    Cowboys, 23-10 (New Haven)
1974—Giants, 14-6 (D)
    Cowboys, 21-7 (New Haven)
1975—Cowboys, 13-7 (NY)
    Cowboys, 14-3 (D)
1976—Cowboys, 24-14 (NY)
    Cowboys, 9-3 (D)
1977—Cowboys, 41-21 (D)
    Cowboys, 24-10 (NY)
1978—Cowboys, 34-24 (NY)
    Cowboys, 24-3 (D)
1979—Cowboys, 16-14 (NY)
    Cowboys, 28-7 (D)
1980—Cowboys, 24-3 (D)
    Giants, 38-35 (NY)
1981—Cowboys, 18-10 (D)
    Giants, 13-10 (NY) OT
1983—Cowboys, 28-13 (D)
    Cowboys, 38-20 (NY)
1984—Giants, 28-7 (NY)
    Giants, 19-7 (D)
1985—Cowboys, 30-29 (NY)
    Cowboys, 28-21 (D)
1986—Cowboys, 31-28 (D)
    Giants, 17-14 (NY)
1987—Cowboys, 16-14 (NY)
    Cowboys, 33-24 (D)
1988—Giants, 12-10 (D)
    Giants, 29-21 (NY)
1989—Giants, 30-13 (D)
    Giants, 15-0 (NY)
1990—Giants, 28-7 (D)
    Giants, 31-17 (NY)
1991—Cowboys, 21-16 (D)
    Giants, 22-9 (NY)
1992—Cowboys, 34-28 (D)
    Cowboys, 30-3 (D)
1993—Cowboys, 31-9 (D)
    Cowboys, 16-13 (NY) OT
1994—Cowboys, 38-10 (D)
    Giants, 15-10 (D)
1995—Cowboys, 35-0 (NY)
    Cowboys, 21-20 (D)
1996—Cowboys, 27-0 (D)
    Giants, 20-6 (NY)
1997—Giants, 20-17 (NY)

Giants, 20-7 (D)
1998—Cowboys, 31-7 (NY)
Cowboys, 16-6 (D)
1999—Giants, 13-10 (NY)
Cowboys, 26-18 (D)
2000—Giants, 19-14 (NY)
Giants, 17-13 (D)
2001—Giants, 27-24 (NY) OT
Cowboys, 20-13 (D)
(RS Pts.—Cowboys 1,742, Giants 1,365)

DALLAS vs. N.Y. JETS
RS: Cowboys lead series, 5-2
1971—Cowboys, 52-10 (D)
1975—Cowboys, 31-21 (NY)
1978—Cowboys, 30-7 (NY)
1987—Cowboys, 38-24 (NY)
1990—Jets, 24-9 (NY)
1993—Cowboys, 28-7 (NY)
1999—Jets, 22-21 (D)
(RS Pts.—Cowboys 209, Jets 115)

DALLAS vs. *OAKLAND
RS: Raiders lead series, 5-3
1974—Raiders, 27-23 (O)
1980—Cowboys, 19-13 (O)
1983—Raiders, 40-38 (D)
1986—Raiders, 17-13 (D)
1992—Cowboys, 28-13 (LA)
1995—Cowboys, 34-21 (O)
1998—Raiders, 13-12 (D)
2001—Raiders, 28-21 (O)
(RS Pts.—Cowboys 188, Raiders 172)
*Franchise in Los Angeles from
1982-1994*

DALLAS vs. PHILADELPHIA
RS: Cowboys lead series, 48-34
PS: Cowboys lead series, 2-1
1960—Eagles, 27-25 (D)
1961—Eagles, 43-7 (D)
Eagles, 35-13 (P)
1962—Cowboys, 41-19 (D)
Eagles, 28-14 (P)
1963—Eagles, 24-21 (P)
Cowboys, 27-20 (D)
1964—Eagles, 17-14 (D)
Eagles, 24-14 (P)
1965—Eagles, 35-24 (D)
Cowboys, 21-19 (P)
1966—Cowboys, 56-7 (D)
Eagles, 24-23 (P)
1967—Eagles, 21-14 (P)
Cowboys, 38-17 (D)
1968—Cowboys, 45-13 (P)
Cowboys, 34-14 (D)
1969—Cowboys, 38-7 (P)
Cowboys, 49-14 (D)
1970—Cowboys, 17-7 (P)
Cowboys, 21-17 (D)
1971—Cowboys, 42-7 (P)
Cowboys, 20-7 (D)
1972—Cowboys, 28-6 (D)
Cowboys, 28-7 (P)
1973—Eagles, 30-16 (P)
Cowboys, 31-10 (D)
1974—Eagles, 13-10 (P)
Cowboys, 31-24 (D)
1975—Cowboys, 20-17 (P)
Cowboys, 27-17 (D)
1976—Cowboys, 27-7 (D)
Cowboys, 26-7 (P)
1977—Cowboys, 16-10 (P)

Cowboys, 24-14 (D)
1978—Cowboys, 14-7 (D)
Cowboys, 31-13 (P)
1979—Eagles, 31-21 (D)
Cowboys, 24-17 (P)
1980—Eagles, 17-10 (P)
Cowboys, 35-27 (D)
*Eagles, 20-7 (P)
1981—Cowboys, 17-14 (P)
Cowboys, 21-10 (D)
1982—Eagles, 24-20 (D)
1983—Eagles, 37-7 (D)
Cowboys, 27-20 (P)
1984—Cowboys, 23-17 (D)
Cowboys, 26-10 (P)
1985—Eagles, 16-14 (P)
Cowboys, 34-17 (D)
1986—Cowboys, 17-14 (P)
Eagles, 23-21 (D)
1987—Cowboys, 41-22 (D)
Eagles, 37-20 (P)
1988—Eagles, 24-23 (P)
Eagles, 23-7 (D)
1989—Eagles, 27-0 (P)
Eagles, 20-10 (D)
1990—Eagles, 21-20 (P)
Eagles, 17-3 (P)
1991—Eagles, 24-0 (D)
Cowboys, 25-13 (P)
1992—Eagles, 31-7 (P)
Cowboys, 20-10 (D)
**Cowboys, 34-10 (D)
1993—Cowboys, 23-10 (P)
Cowboys, 23-17 (D)
1994—Cowboys, 24-13 (D)
Cowboys, 31-19 (P)
1995—Cowboys, 34-12 (D)
Eagles, 20-17 (P)
**Cowboys, 30-11 (D)
1996—Cowboys, 23-19 (P)
Eagles, 31-21 (D)
1997—Cowboys, 21-20 (D)
Eagles, 13-12 (P)
1998—Cowboys, 34-0 (P)
Cowboys, 13-9 (D)
1999—Eagles, 13-10 (P)
Cowboys, 20-10 (D)
2000—Eagles, 41-14 (D)
Eagles, 16-13 (P) OT
2001—Eagles, 40-18 (D)
Eagles, 36-3 (D)
(RS Pts.—Cowboys 1,824, Eagles 1,500)
(PS Pts.—Cowboys 71, Eagles 41)
*NFC Championship
**NFC Divisional Playoff*

DALLAS vs. PITTSBURGH
RS: Cowboys lead series, 14-11
PS: Steelers lead series, 2-1
1960—Steelers, 35-28 (D)
1961—Cowboys, 27-24 (D)
Steelers, 37-7 (P)
1962—Steelers, 30-28 (D)
Cowboys, 42-27 (P)
1963—Steelers, 27-21 (P)
Steelers, 24-19 (D)
1964—Steelers, 23-17 (P)
Cowboys, 17-14 (D)
1965—Steelers, 22-13 (P)
Cowboys, 24-17 (D)
1966—Cowboys, 52-21 (D)

Cowboys, 20-7 (P)
1967—Cowboys, 24-21 (P)
1968—Cowboys, 28-7 (D)
1969—Cowboys, 10-7 (P)
1972—Cowboys, 17-13 (D)
1975—*Steelers, 21-17 (Miami)
1977—Steelers, 28-13 (P)
1978—**Steelers, 35-31 (Miami)
1979—Steelers, 14-3 (P)
1982—Steelers, 36-28 (D)
1985—Cowboys, 27-13 (D)
1988—Steelers, 24-21 (P)
1991—Cowboys, 20-10 (D)
1994—Cowboys, 26-9 (P)
1995—***Cowboys, 27-17 (Tempe)
1997—Cowboys, 37-7 (P)
(RS Pts.—Cowboys 569, Steelers 497)
(PS Pts.—Cowboys 75, Steelers 73)
*Super Bowl X
**Super Bowl XIII
***Super Bowl XXX*

DALLAS vs. *ST. LOUIS
RS: Rams lead series, 9-8
PS: Series tied, 4-4
1960—Rams, 38-13 (D)
1962—Cowboys, 27-17 (LA)
1967—Rams, 35-13 (D)
1969—Rams, 24-23 (LA)
1971—Cowboys, 28-21 (D)
1973—Rams, 37-31 (LA)
**Cowboys, 27-16 (D)
1975—Cowboys, 18-7 (D)
***Cowboys, 37-7 (LA)
1976—**Rams, 14-12 (D)
1978—Rams, 27-14 (LA)
***Cowboys, 28-0 (LA)
1979—Cowboys, 30-6 (D)
**Rams, 21-19 (D)
1980—Rams, 38-14 (LA)
****Cowboys, 34-13 (D)
1981—Cowboys, 29-17 (D)
1983—****Rams, 24-17 (D)
1984—Cowboys, 20-13 (LA)
1985—**Rams, 20-0 (LA)
1986—Rams, 29-10 (LA)
1987—Cowboys, 29-21 (LA)
1989—Rams, 35-31 (D)
1990—Cowboys, 24-21 (LA)
1992—Rams, 27-23 (D)
(RS Pts.—Rams 413, Cowboys 377)
(PS Pts.—Cowboys 174, Rams 115)
*Franchise in Los Angeles prior to 1995
**NFC Divisional Playoff
***NFC Championship
****NFC First-Round Playoff*

DALLAS vs. SAN DIEGO
RS: Cowboys lead series, 5-2
1972—Cowboys, 34-28 (SD)
1980—Cowboys, 42-31 (D)
1983—Chargers, 24-23 (SD)
1986—Cowboys, 24-21 (SD)
1990—Cowboys, 17-14 (D)
1995—Cowboys, 23-9 (SD)
2001—Chargers, 32-21 (D)
(RS Pts.—Cowboys 184, Chargers 159)

DALLAS vs. SAN FRANCISCO
RS: 49ers lead series, 13-8-1
PS: Cowboys lead series, 5-2
1960—49ers, 26-14 (D)
1963—49ers, 31-24 (SF)

1965—Cowboys, 39-31 (D)
1967—49ers, 24-16 (SF)
1969—Tie, 24-24 (D)
1970—*Cowboys, 17-10 (SF)
1971—*Cowboys, 14-3 (D)
1972—49ers, 31-10 (D)
    **Cowboys, 30-28 (SF)
1974—Cowboys, 20-14 (D)
1977—Cowboys, 42-35 (SF)
1979—Cowboys, 21-13 (SF)
1980—Cowboys, 59-14 (D)
1981—49ers, 45-14 (SF)
    *49ers, 28-27 (SF)
1983—49ers, 42-17 (SF)
1985—49ers, 31-16 (SF)
1989—49ers, 31-14 (D)
1990—49ers, 24-6 (D)
1992—*Cowboys, 30-20 (SF)
1993—Cowboys, 26-17 (D)
    *Cowboys, 38-21 (D)
1994—49ers, 21-14 (SF)
    *49ers, 38-28 (SF)
1995—49ers, 38-20 (D)
1996—Cowboys, 20-17 (SF) OT
1997—49ers, 17-10 (SF)
2000—49ers, 41-24 (D)
2001—Cowboys, 27-21 (D)
(RS Pts.—49ers 588, Cowboys 477)
(PS Pts.—Cowboys 184, 49ers 148)
*NFC Championship
**NFC Divisional Playoff
DALLAS vs. SEATTLE
RS: Cowboys lead series, 5-2
1976—Cowboys, 28-13 (S)
1980—Cowboys, 51-7 (D)
1983—Cowboys, 35-10 (S)
1986—Seahawks, 31-14 (D)
1992—Cowboys, 27-0 (D)
1998—Cowboys, 30-22 (D)
2001—Seahawks, 29-3 (S)
(RS Pts.—Cowboys 188, Seahawks 112)
DALLAS vs. TAMPA BAY
RS: Cowboys lead series, 6-2
PS: Cowboys lead series, 2-0
1977—Cowboys, 23-7 (D)
1980—Cowboys, 28-17 (D)
1981—*Cowboys, 38-0 (D)
1982—Cowboys, 14-9 (D)
    **Cowboys, 30-17 (D)
1983—Cowboys, 27-24 (D) OT
1990—Cowboys, 14-10 (D)
    Cowboys, 17-13 (TB)
2000—Buccaneers, 27-7 (TB)
2001—Buccaneers, 10-6 (D)
(RS Pts.—Cowboys 136, Buccaneers 117)
(PS Pts.—Cowboys 68, Buccaneers 17)
*NFC Divisional Playoff
**NFC First-Round Playoff
DALLAS vs. *TENNESSEE
RS: Series tied, 5-5
1970—Cowboys, 52-10 (D)
1974—Cowboys, 10-0 (H)
1979—Oilers, 30-24 (D)
1982—Cowboys, 37-7 (H)
1985—Cowboys, 17-10 (H)
1988—Oilers, 25-17 (D)
1991—Oilers, 26-23 (H) OT
1994—Cowboys, 20-17 (D)
1997—Oilers, 27-14 (D)
2000—Titans, 31-0 (T)

(RS Pts.—Cowboys 214, Titans 183)
*Franchise in Houston prior to 1997;
known as Oilers prior to 1999
DALLAS vs. WASHINGTON
RS: Cowboys lead series, 49-31-2
PS: Redskins lead series, 2-0
1960—Redskins, 26-14 (W)
1961—Tie, 28-28 (D)
    Redskins, 34-24 (W)
1962—Tie, 35-35 (D)
    Cowboys, 38-10 (W)
1963—Redskins, 21-17 (W)
    Cowboys, 35-20 (D)
1964—Cowboys, 24-18 (D)
    Redskins, 28-16 (W)
1965—Cowboys, 27-7 (D)
    Redskins, 34-31 (W)
1966—Cowboys, 31-30 (W)
    Redskins, 34-31 (D)
1967—Cowboys, 17-14 (W)
    Redskins, 27-20 (D)
1968—Cowboys, 44-24 (W)
    Cowboys, 29-20 (D)
1969—Cowboys, 41-28 (W)
    Cowboys, 20-10 (D)
1970—Cowboys, 45-21 (W)
    Cowboys, 34-0 (D)
1971—Redskins, 20-16 (D)
    Cowboys, 13-0 (W)
1972—Redskins, 24-20 (W)
    Cowboys, 34-24 (D)
    *Redskins, 26-3 (W)
1973—Redskins, 14-7 (W)
    Cowboys, 27-7 (D)
1974—Redskins, 28-21 (W)
    Cowboys, 24-23 (D)
1975—Redskins, 30-24 (W) OT
    Cowboys, 31-10 (D)
1976—Cowboys, 20-7 (W)
    Redskins, 27-14 (D)
1977—Cowboys, 34-16 (D)
    Cowboys, 14-7 (W)
1978—Redskins, 9-5 (W)
    Cowboys, 37-10 (D)
1979—Redskins, 34-20 (W)
    Cowboys, 35-34 (D)
1980—Cowboys, 17-3 (W)
    Cowboys, 14-10 (D)
1981—Cowboys, 26-10 (W)
    Cowboys, 24-10 (D)
1982—Cowboys, 24-10 (W)
    *Redskins, 31-17 (W)
1983—Cowboys, 31-30 (W)
    Redskins, 31-10 (D)
1984—Redskins, 34-14 (W)
    Redskins, 30-28 (D)
1985—Cowboys, 44-14 (D)
    Cowboys, 13-7 (W)
1986—Cowboys, 30-6 (D)
    Redskins, 41-14 (W)
1987—Redskins, 13-7 (D)
    Redskins, 24-20 (W)
1988—Redskins, 35-17 (D)
    Cowboys, 24-17 (W)
1989—Redskins, 30-7 (D)
    Cowboys, 13-3 (W)
1990—Redskins, 19-15 (W)
    Cowboys, 27-17 (D)
1991—Redskins, 33-31 (D)
    Cowboys, 24-21 (W)

1992—Cowboys, 23-10 (D)
    Redskins, 20-17 (W)
1993—Redskins, 35-16 (W)
    Cowboys, 38-3 (D)
1994—Cowboys, 34-7 (W)
    Cowboys, 31-7 (D)
1995—Redskins, 27-23 (W)
    Redskins, 24-17 (D)
1996—Cowboys, 21-10 (D)
    Redskins, 37-10 (W)
1997—Redskins, 21-16 (W)
    Cowboys, 17-14 (D)
1998—Cowboys, 31-10 (W)
    Cowboys, 23-7 (D)
1999—Cowboys, 41-35 (W) OT
    Cowboys, 38-20 (D)
2000—Cowboys, 27-21 (W)
    Cowboys, 32-13 (D)
2001—Cowboys, 9-7 (D)
    Cowboys, 20-14 (W)
(RS Pts.—Cowboys 1,955, Redskins 1,583)
(PS Pts.—Redskins 57, Cowboys 20)
*NFC Championship

DENVER vs. ARIZONA
RS: Broncos lead series, 5-0-1;
See Arizona vs. Denver
DENVER vs. ATLANTA
RS: Broncos lead series, 7-3
PS: Broncos lead series, 1-0;
See Atlanta vs. Denver
DENVER vs. BALTIMORE
RS: Series tied, 1-1
PS: Ravens lead series, 1-0;
See Baltimore vs. Denver
DENVER vs. BUFFALO
RS: Bills lead series, 17-12-1
PS: Bills lead series, 1-0;
See Buffalo vs. Denver
DENVER vs. CAROLINA
RS: Broncos lead series, 1-0;
See Carolina vs. Denver
DENVER vs. CHICAGO
RS: Broncos lead series, 6-5;
See Chicago vs. Denver
DENVER vs. CINCINNATI
RS: Broncos lead series, 14-7;
See Cincinnati vs. Denver
DENVER vs. CLEVELAND
RS: Broncos lead series, 14-5
PS: Broncos lead series, 3-0;
See Cleveland vs. Denver
DENVER vs. DALLAS
RS: Series tied, 4-4
PS: Cowboys lead series, 1-0;
See Dallas vs. Denver
DENVER vs. DETROIT
RS: Broncos lead series, 5-3
1971—Lions, 24-20 (Den)
1974—Broncos, 31-27 (Det)
1978—Lions, 17-14 (Det)
1981—Broncos, 27-21 (Den)
1984—Broncos, 28-7 (Det)
1987—Broncos, 34-0 (Den)
1990—Lions, 40-27 (Det)
1999—Broncos, 17-7 (Det)
(RS Pts.—Broncos 198, Lions 143)
DENVER vs. GREEN BAY
RS: Broncos lead series, 5-3-1
PS: Broncos lead series, 1-0

1971—Packers, 34-13 (Mil)
1975—Broncos, 23-13 (D)
1978—Broncos, 16-3 (D)
1984—Broncos, 17-14 (D)
1987—Tie, 17-17 (Mil) OT
1990—Broncos, 22-13 (D)
1993—Packers, 30-27 (GB)
1996—Packers, 41-6 (GB)
1997—*Broncos, 31-24 (San Diego)
1999—Broncos, 31-10 (D)
(RS Pts.—Packers 175, Broncos 172)
(PS Pts.—Broncos 31, Packers 24)
*Super Bowl XXXII

DENVER vs. *INDIANAPOLIS
RS: Broncos lead series, 9-3
1974—Broncos, 17-6 (B)
1977—Broncos, 27-13 (D)
1978—Colts, 7-6 (B)
1981—Broncos, 28-10 (D)
1983—Broncos, 17-10 (B)
        Broncos, 21-19 (D)
1985—Broncos, 15-10 (I)
1988—Colts, 55-23 (I)
1989—Broncos, 14-3 (D)
1990—Broncos, 27-17 (I)
1993—Broncos, 35-13 (D)
2001—Colts, 29-10 (I)
(RS Pts.—Broncos 240, Colts 192)
*Franchise in Baltimore prior to 1984

DENVER vs. JACKSONVILLE
RS: Broncos lead series, 2-1
PS: Series tied, 1-1
1995—Broncos, 31-23 (D)
1996—*Jaguars, 30-27 (D)
1997—**Broncos, 42-17 (D)
1998—Broncos, 37-24 (D)
1999—Jaguars, 27-24 (J)
(RS Pts.—Broncos 92, Jaguars 74)
(PS Pts.—Broncos 69, Jaguars 47)
*AFC Divisional Playoff
**AFC First-Round Playoff

DENVER vs. *KANSAS CITY
RS: Chiefs lead series, 48-35
PS: Broncos lead series, 1-0
1960—Texans, 17-14 (D)
        Texans, 34-7 (Dal)
1961—Texans, 19-12 (D)
        Texans, 49-21 (Dal)
1962—Texans, 24-3 (D)
        Texans, 17-10 (Dal)
1963—Chiefs, 59-7 (D)
        Chiefs, 52-21 (KC)
1964—Broncos, 33-27 (D)
        Chiefs, 49-39 (KC)
1965—Chiefs, 31-23 (D)
        Chiefs, 45-35 (KC)
1966—Chiefs, 37-10 (KC)
        Chiefs, 56-10 (D)
1967—Chiefs, 52-9 (KC)
        Chiefs, 38-24 (D)
1968—Chiefs, 34-2 (KC)
        Chiefs, 30-7 (D)
1969—Chiefs, 26-13 (D)
        Chiefs, 31-17 (KC)
1970—Broncos, 26-13 (D)
        Chiefs, 16-0 (KC)
1971—Chiefs, 16-3 (D)
        Chiefs, 28-10 (KC)
1972—Chiefs, 45-24 (D)
        Chiefs, 24-21 (KC)

1973—Chiefs, 16-14 (KC)
        Broncos, 14-10 (D)
1974—Broncos, 17-14 (KC)
        Chiefs, 42-34 (D)
1975—Broncos, 37-33 (D)
        Chiefs, 26-13 (KC)
1976—Broncos, 35-26 (KC)
        Broncos, 17-16 (D)
1977—Broncos, 23-7 (D)
        Broncos, 14-7 (KC)
1978—Broncos, 23-17 (KC) OT
        Broncos, 24-3 (D)
1979—Broncos, 24-10 (KC)
        Broncos, 20-3 (D)
1980—Chiefs, 23-17 (D)
        Chiefs, 31-14 (KC)
1981—Chiefs, 28-14 (KC)
        Broncos, 16-13 (D)
1982—Chiefs, 37-16 (D)
1983—Broncos, 27-24 (D)
        Chiefs, 48-17 (KC)
1984—Broncos, 21-0 (D)
        Chiefs, 16-13 (KC)
1985—Broncos, 30-10 (KC)
        Broncos, 14-13 (D)
1986—Broncos, 38-17 (D)
        Chiefs, 37-10 (KC)
1987—Broncos, 26-17 (KC)
        Broncos, 20-17 (D)
1988—Chiefs, 20-13 (KC)
        Broncos, 17-11 (D)
1989—Broncos, 34-20 (D)
        Broncos, 16-13 (KC)
1990—Broncos, 24-23 (D)
        Chiefs, 31-20 (KC)
1991—Broncos, 19-16 (D)
        Broncos, 24-20 (KC)
1992—Broncos, 20-19 (D)
        Chiefs, 42-20 (KC)
1993—Chiefs, 15-7 (KC)
        Broncos, 27-21 (D)
1994—Chiefs, 31-28 (D)
        Broncos, 20-17 (KC) OT
1995—Chiefs, 21-7 (D)
        Chiefs, 20-17 (KC)
1996—Chiefs, 17-14 (KC)
        Broncos, 34-7 (D)
1997—Broncos, 19-3 (D)
        Chiefs, 24-22 (KC)
        **Broncos, 14-10 (KC)
1998—Broncos, 30-7 (KC)
        Broncos, 35-31 (D)
1999—Chiefs, 26-10 (KC)
        Chiefs, 16-10 (D)
2000—Chiefs, 23-22 (D)
        Chiefs, 20-7 (KC)
2001—Broncos, 20-6 (D)
        Chiefs, 26-23 (KC) OT
(RS Pts.—Chiefs 1,976, Broncos 1,562)
(PS Pts.—Broncos 14, Chiefs 10)
*Franchise in Dallas prior to 1963 and
known as Texans
**AFC Divisional Playoff

DENVER vs. MIAMI
RS: Dolphins lead series, 8-2-1
PS: Broncos lead series, 1-0
1966—Dolphins, 24-7 (M)
        Broncos, 17-7 (D)
1967—Dolphins, 35-21 (M)
1968—Broncos, 21-14 (D)

1969—Dolphins, 27-24 (M)
1971—Tie, 10-10 (D)
1975—Dolphins, 14-13 (M)
1985—Dolphins, 30-26 (D)
1998—Dolphins, 31-21 (M)
        *Broncos, 38-3 (D)
1999—Dolphins, 38-21 (D)
2001—Dolphins, 21-10 (M)
(RS Pts.—Dolphins 251, Broncos 191)
(PS Pts.—Broncos 38, Dolphins 3)
*AFC Divisional Playoff

DENVER vs. MINNESOTA
RS: Vikings lead series, 6-4
1972—Vikings, 23-20 (D)
1978—Vikings, 12-9 (M) OT
1981—Broncos, 19-17 (D)
1984—Broncos, 42-21 (D)
1987—Vikings, 34-27 (M)
1990—Vikings, 27-22 (M)
1991—Broncos, 13-6 (M)
1993—Vikings, 26-23 (D)
1996—Broncos, 21-17 (M)
1999—Vikings, 23-20 (D)
(RS Pts.—Broncos 216, Vikings 206)

DENVER vs. *NEW ENGLAND
RS: Broncos lead series, 21-14
PS: Broncos lead series, 1-0
1960—Broncos, 13-10 (B)
        Broncos, 31-24 (D)
1961—Patriots, 45-17 (B)
        Patriots, 28-24 (D)
1962—Patriots, 41-16 (B)
        Patriots, 33-29 (D)
1963—Broncos, 14-10 (D)
        Patriots, 40-21 (B)
1964—Patriots, 39-10 (D)
        Patriots, 12-7 (B)
1965—Broncos, 27-10 (B)
        Patriots, 28-20 (D)
1966—Patriots, 24-10 (D)
        Broncos, 17-10 (B)
1967—Broncos, 26-21 (D)
1968—Patriots, 20-17 (D)
        Broncos, 35-14 (B)
1969—Broncos, 35-7 (D)
1972—Broncos, 45-21 (D)
1976—Patriots, 38-14 (NE)
1979—Broncos, 45-10 (D)
1980—Patriots, 23-14 (NE)
1984—Broncos, 26-19 (D)
1986—Broncos, 27-20 (D)
        **Broncos, 22-17 (D)
1987—Broncos, 31-20 (D)
1988—Broncos, 21-10 (D)
1991—Broncos, 9-6 (NE)
        Broncos, 20-3 (D)
1995—Broncos, 37-3 (NE)
1996—Broncos, 34-8 (NE)
1997—Broncos, 34-13 (D)
1998—Broncos, 27-21 (D)
1999—Patriots, 24-23 (NE)
2000—Patriots, 28-19 (D)
2001—Broncos, 31-20 (D)
(RS Pts.—Broncos 826, Patriots 703)
(PS Pts.—Broncos 22, Patriots 17)
*Franchise in Boston prior to 1971
**AFC Divisional Playoff

DENVER vs. NEW ORLEANS
RS: Broncos lead series, 5-2
1970—Broncos, 31-6 (NO)

1974—Broncos, 33-17 (D)
1979—Broncos, 10-3 (D)
1985—Broncos, 34-23 (D)
1988—Saints, 42-0 (NO)
1994—Saints, 30-28 (D)
2000—Broncos, 38-23 (NO)
(RS Pts.—Broncos 174, Saints 144)
DENVER vs. N.Y. GIANTS
RS: Series tied, 4-4
PS: Giants lead series, 1-0
1972—Giants, 29-17 (NY)
1976—Broncos, 14-13 (D)
1980—Broncos, 14-9 (NY)
1986—Giants, 19-16 (NY)
      *Giants, 39-20 (Pasadena)
1989—Giants, 14-7 (D)
1992—Broncos, 27-13 (D)
1998—Giants, 20-16 (NY)
2001—Broncos, 31-20 (D)
(RS Pts.—Broncos 142, Giants 137)
(PS Pts.—Giants 39, Broncos 20)
*Super Bowl XXI
DENVER vs. *N.Y. JETS
RS: Broncos lead series, 14-13-1
PS: Broncos lead series, 1-0
1960—Titans, 28-24 (NY)
      Titans, 30-27 (D)
1961—Titans, 35-28 (NY)
      Broncos, 27-10 (D)
1962—Broncos, 32-10 (NY)
      Titans, 46-45 (D)
1963—Tie, 35-35 (NY)
      Jets, 14-9 (D)
1964—Jets, 30-6 (NY)
      Broncos, 20-16 (D)
1965—Broncos, 16-13 (D)
      Jets, 45-10 (NY)
1966—Jets, 16-7 (D)
1967—Jets, 38-24 (D)
      Broncos, 33-24 (NY)
1968—Broncos, 21-13 (NY)
1969—Broncos, 21-19 (D)
1973—Broncos, 40-28 (NY)
1976—Broncos, 46-3 (D)
1978—Jets, 31-28 (D)
1980—Broncos, 31-24 (D)
1986—Jets, 22-10 (NY)
1992—Broncos, 27-16 (D)
1993—Broncos, 26-20 (NY)
1994—Jets, 25-22 (NY) OT
1996—Broncos, 31-6 (D)
1998—**Broncos, 23-10 (D)
1999—Jets, 21-13 (D)
2000—Broncos, 30-23 (NY)
(RS Pts.—Broncos 689, Jets 641)
(PS Pts.—Broncos 23, Jets 10)
*Jets known as Titans prior to 1963
**AFC Championship
DENVER vs. *OAKLAND
RS: Raiders lead series, 50-31-2
PS: Series tied, 1-1
1960—Broncos, 31-14 (D)
      Raiders, 48-10 (O)
1961—Raiders, 33-19 (O)
      Broncos, 27-24 (D)
1962—Broncos, 44-7 (D)
      Broncos, 23-6 (O)
1963—Raiders, 26-10 (D)
      Raiders, 35-31 (O)
1964—Raiders, 40-7 (O)

Tie, 20-20 (D)
1965—Raiders, 28-20 (D)
      Raiders, 24-13 (O)
1966—Raiders, 17-3 (D)
      Raiders, 28-10 (O)
1967—Raiders, 51-0 (O)
      Raiders, 21-17 (D)
1968—Raiders, 43-7 (D)
      Raiders, 33-27 (O)
1969—Raiders, 24-14 (D)
      Raiders, 41-10 (O)
1970—Raiders, 35-23 (D)
      Raiders, 24-19 (O)
1971—Raiders, 27-16 (D)
      Raiders, 21-13 (O)
1972—Broncos, 30-23 (O)
      Raiders, 37-20 (D)
1973—Tie, 23-23 (D)
      Raiders, 21-17 (O)
1974—Raiders, 28-17 (D)
      Broncos, 20-17 (O)
1975—Raiders, 42-17 (D)
      Raiders, 17-10 (O)
1976—Raiders, 17-10 (D)
      Raiders, 19-6 (O)
1977—Broncos, 30-7 (O)
      Raiders, 24-14 (D)
      **Broncos, 20-17 (D)
1978—Broncos, 14-6 (D)
      Broncos, 21-6 (O)
1979—Raiders, 27-3 (O)
      Raiders, 14-10 (D)
1980—Raiders, 9-3 (O)
      Raiders, 24-21 (D)
1981—Broncos, 9-7 (D)
      Broncos, 17-0 (O)
1982—Raiders, 27-10 (LA)
1983—Raiders, 22-7 (D)
      Raiders, 22-20 (LA)
1984—Broncos, 16-13 (D)
      Broncos, 22-19 (LA) OT
1985—Raiders, 31-28 (LA) OT
      Raiders, 17-14 (D) OT
1986—Broncos, 38-36 (D)
      Broncos, 21-10 (LA)
1987—Broncos, 30-14 (D)
      Broncos, 23-17 (LA)
1988—Raiders, 30-27 (D) OT
      Raiders, 21-20 (LA)
1989—Broncos, 31-21 (D)
      Raiders, 16-13 (LA) OT
1990—Raiders, 14-9 (LA)
      Raiders, 23-20 (D)
1991—Raiders, 16-13 (LA)
      Raiders, 17-16 (D)
1992—Broncos, 17-13 (D)
      Raiders, 24-0 (LA)
1993—Raiders, 23-20 (D)
      Raiders, 33-30 (LA) OT
      ***Raiders, 42-24 (LA)
1994—Raiders, 48-16 (D)
      Raiders, 23-13 (LA)
1995—Broncos, 27-0 (D)
      Broncos, 31-28 (O)
1996—Broncos, 22-21 (O)
      Broncos, 24-19 (D)
1997—Raiders, 28-25 (O)
      Broncos, 31-3 (D)
1998—Broncos, 34-17 (O)
      Broncos, 40-14 (D)

1999—Broncos, 16-13 (O)
      Broncos, 27-21 (D) OT
2000—Broncos, 33-24 (O)
      Broncos, 27-24 (D)
2001—Raiders, 38-28 (O)
      Broncos, 23-17 (D)
(RS Pts.—Raiders 1,855, Broncos 1,588)
(PS Pts.—Raiders 59, Broncos 44)
*Franchise in Los Angeles from 1982-1994
**AFC Championship
***AFC First-Round Playoff
DENVER vs. PHILADELPHIA
RS: Eagles lead series, 6-3
1971—Eagles, 17-16 (P)
1975—Broncos, 25-10 (D)
1980—Eagles, 27-6 (P)
1983—Eagles, 13-10 (P)
1986—Broncos, 33-7 (P)
1989—Eagles, 28-24 (D)
1992—Eagles, 30-0 (P)
1995—Eagles, 31-13 (P)
1998—Broncos, 41-16 (D)
(RS Pts.—Eagles 179, Broncos 168)
DENVER vs. PITTSBURGH
RS: Broncos lead series, 10-6-1
PS: Broncos lead series, 3-2
1970—Broncos, 16-13 (D)
1971—Broncos, 22-10 (P)
1973—Broncos, 23-13 (P)
1974—Tie, 35-35 (D) OT
1975—Steelers, 20-9 (P)
1977—Broncos, 21-7 (D)
      *Broncos, 34-21 (D)
1978—Steelers, 21-17 (D)
      *Steelers, 33-10 (P)
1979—Steelers, 42-7 (P)
1983—Broncos, 14-10 (P)
1984—*Steelers, 24-17 (D)
1985—Broncos, 31-23 (P)
1986—Broncos, 21-10 (P)
1988—Steelers, 39-21 (P)
1989—Broncos, 34-7 (D)
      *Broncos, 24-23 (D)
1990—Steelers, 34-17 (D)
1991—Broncos, 20-13 (D)
1993—Broncos, 37-13 (D)
1997—Steelers, 35-24 (P)
      **Broncos, 24-21 (P)
(RS Pts.—Broncos 369, Steelers 345)
(PS Pts.—Steelers 122, Broncos 109)
*AFC Divisional Playoff
**AFC Championship
DENVER vs. *ST. LOUIS
RS: Rams lead series, 5-4
1972—Broncos, 16-10 (LA)
1974—Rams, 17-10 (D)
1979—Rams, 13-9 (D)
1982—Broncos, 27-24 (LA)
1985—Broncos, 20-16 (LA)
1988—Broncos, 35-24 (D)
1994—Rams, 27-21 (LA)
1997—Broncos, 35-14 (D)
2000—Rams, 41-36 (StL)
(RS Pts.—Broncos 205, Rams 190)
*Franchise in Los Angeles prior to 1995
DENVER vs. *SAN DIEGO
RS: Broncos lead series, 46-37-1
1960—Chargers, 23-19 (D)
      Chargers, 41-33 (LA)
1961—Chargers, 37-0 (SD)

Chargers, 19-16 (D)
1962—Broncos, 30-21 (D)
Broncos, 23-20 (SD)
1963—Broncos, 50-34 (D)
Chargers, 58-20 (SD)
1964—Chargers, 42-14 (SD)
Chargers, 31-20 (D)
1965—Chargers, 34-31 (SD)
Chargers, 33-21 (D)
1966—Chargers, 24-17 (SD)
Broncos, 20-17 (D)
1967—Chargers, 38-21 (D)
Chargers, 24-20 (SD)
1968—Chargers, 55-24 (SD)
Chargers, 47-23 (D)
1969—Broncos, 13-0 (D)
Chargers, 45-24 (SD)
1970—Chargers, 24-21 (SD)
Tie, 17-17 (D)
1971—Broncos, 20-16 (D)
Chargers, 45-17 (SD)
1972—Chargers, 37-14 (SD)
Broncos, 38-13 (D)
1973—Broncos, 30-19 (D)
Broncos, 42-28 (SD)
1974—Broncos, 27-7 (D)
Chargers, 17-0 (SD)
1975—Broncos, 27-17 (SD)
Broncos, 13-10 (D) OT
1976—Broncos, 26-0 (D)
Broncos, 17-0 (SD)
1977—Broncos, 17-14 (SD)
Broncos, 17-9 (D)
1978—Broncos, 27-14 (D)
Chargers, 23-0 (SD)
1979—Broncos, 7-0 (D)
Chargers, 17-7 (SD)
1980—Chargers, 30-13 (D)
Broncos, 20-13 (SD)
1981—Chargers, 42-24 (D)
Chargers, 34-17 (SD)
1982—Chargers, 23-3 (D)
Chargers, 30-20 (SD)
1983—Broncos, 14-6 (D)
Chargers, 31-7 (SD)
1984—Broncos, 16-13 (SD)
Broncos, 16-13 (D)
1985—Chargers, 30-10 (SD)
Broncos, 30-24 (D) OT
1986—Broncos, 31-14 (SD)
Chargers, 9-3 (D)
1987—Broncos, 31-17 (SD)
Broncos, 24-0 (D)
1988—Broncos, 34-3 (D)
Broncos, 12-0 (SD)
1989—Broncos, 16-10 (D)
Chargers, 19-16 (SD)
1990—Chargers, 19-7 (SD)
Broncos, 20-10 (D)
1991—Broncos, 27-19 (D)
Broncos, 17-14 (SD)
1992—Broncos, 21-13 (D)
Chargers, 24-21 (SD)
1993—Broncos, 34-17 (D)
Chargers, 13-10 (SD)
1994—Chargers, 37-34 (D)
Broncos, 20-15 (SD)
1995—Chargers, 17-6 (SD)
Broncos, 30-27 (D)
1996—Broncos, 28-17 (D)

Chargers, 16-10 (SD)
1997—Broncos, 38-28 (SD)
Broncos, 38-3 (D)
1998—Broncos, 27-10 (D)
Broncos, 31-16 (SD)
1999—Broncos, 33-17 (SD)
Chargers, 12-6 (D)
2000—Broncos, 21-7 (SD)
Broncos, 38-37 (D)
2001—Chargers, 27-10 (SD)
Broncos, 26-16 (D)
(RS Pts.—Broncos 1,751, Chargers 1,746)
*Franchise in Los Angeles prior to 1961
DENVER vs. SAN FRANCISCO
RS: Broncos lead series, 5-4
PS: 49ers lead series, 1-0
1970—49ers, 19-14 (SF)
1973—49ers, 36-34 (D)
1979—Broncos, 38-28 (SF)
1982—Broncos, 24-21 (D)
1985—Broncos, 17-16 (D)
1988—Broncos, 16-13 (SF) OT
1989—*49ers, 55-10 (New Orleans)
1994—49ers, 42-19 (SF)
1997—49ers, 34-17 (SF)
2000—Broncos, 38-9 (D)
(RS Pts.—49ers 218, Broncos 217)
(PS Pts.—49ers 55, Broncos 10)
*Super Bowl XXIV
DENVER vs. SEATTLE
RS: Broncos lead series, 32-17
PS: Seahawks lead series, 1-0
1977—Broncos, 24-13 (S)
1978—Broncos, 28-7 (D)
Broncos, 20-17 (S) OT
1979—Broncos, 37-34 (D)
Seahawks, 28-23 (S)
1980—Broncos, 36-20 (D)
Broncos, 25-17 (S)
1981—Seahawks, 13-10 (S)
Broncos, 23-13 (D)
1982—Seahawks, 17-10 (D)
Seahawks, 13-11 (S)
1983—Seahawks, 27-19 (S)
Broncos, 38-27 (D)
*Seahawks, 31-7 (S)
1984—Seahawks, 27-24 (D)
Broncos, 31-14 (S)
1985—Broncos, 13-10 (D) OT
Broncos, 27-24 (S)
1986—Broncos, 20-13 (D)
Seahawks, 41-16 (S)
1987—Broncos, 40-17 (D)
Seahawks, 28-21 (S)
1988—Seahawks, 21-14 (D)
Seahawks, 42-14 (S)
1989—Broncos, 24-21 (S) OT
Broncos, 41-14 (D)
1990—Broncos, 34-31 (D) OT
Seahawks, 17-12 (S)
1991—Broncos, 16-10 (D)
Seahawks, 13-10 (S)
1992—Seahawks, 16-13 (S) OT
Broncos, 10-6 (D)
1993—Broncos, 28-17 (D)
Broncos, 17-9 (S)
1994—Broncos, 16-9 (S)
Broncos, 17-10 (D)
1995—Seahawks, 27-10 (S)
Seahawks, 31-27 (D)

1996—Broncos, 30-20 (S)
Broncos, 34-7 (D)
1997—Broncos, 35-14 (S)
Broncos, 30-27 (D)
1998—Broncos, 21-16 (S)
Broncos, 28-21 (D)
1999—Seahawks, 20-17 (S)
Broncos, 36-30 (D) OT
2000—Broncos, 38-31 (S)
Broncos, 31-24 (D)
2001—Seahawks, 34-21 (S)
Broncos, 20-7 (D)
(RS Pts.—Broncos 1,140, Seahawks 965)
(PS Pts.—Seahawks 31, Broncos 7)
*AFC First-Round Playoff
DENVER vs. TAMPA BAY
RS: Broncos lead series, 3-2
1976—Broncos, 48-13 (D)
1981—Broncos, 24-7 (TB)
1993—Buccaneers, 17-10 (D)
1996—Broncos, 27-23 (D)
1999—Buccaneers, 13-10 (TB)
(RS Pts.—Broncos 119, Buccaneers 73)
DENVER vs. *TENNESSEE
RS: Titans lead series, 20-11-1
PS: Broncos lead series, 2-1
1960—Oilers, 45-25 (D)
Oilers, 20-10 (H)
1961—Oilers, 55-14 (D)
Oilers, 45-14 (H)
1962—Broncos, 20-10 (D)
Oilers, 34-17 (H)
1963—Oilers, 20-14 (H)
Oilers, 33-24 (D)
1964—Oilers, 38-17 (D)
Oilers, 34-15 (H)
1965—Broncos, 28-17 (D)
Broncos, 31-21 (H)
1966—Oilers, 45-7 (H)
Broncos, 40-38 (D)
1967—Oilers, 10-6 (H)
Oilers, 20-18 (D)
1968—Oilers, 38-17 (H)
1969—Oilers, 24-21 (H)
Tie, 20-20 (D)
1970—Oilers, 31-21 (H)
1972—Broncos, 30-17 (D)
1973—Broncos, 48-20 (H)
1974—Broncos, 37-14 (D)
1976—Oilers, 17-3 (H)
1977—Broncos, 24-14 (H)
1979—**Oilers, 13-7 (H)
1980—Oilers, 20-16 (D)
1983—Broncos, 26-14 (H)
1985—Broncos, 31-20 (D)
1987—Oilers, 40-10 (D)
***Broncos, 34-10 (D)
1991—Oilers, 42-14 (H)
***Broncos, 26-24 (D)
1992—Broncos, 27-21 (D)
1995—Oilers, 42-33 (H)
(RS Pts.—Titans 879, Broncos 678)
(PS Pts.—Broncos 67, Titans 47)
*Franchise in Houston prior to 1997;
known as the Oilers prior to 1999
**AFC First-Round Playoff
***AFC Divisional Playoff
DENVER vs. WASHINGTON
RS: Broncos lead series, 5-4
PS: Redskins lead series, 1-0

1970—Redskins, 19-3 (D)
1974—Redskins, 30-3 (W)
1980—Broncos, 20-17 (D)
1986—Broncos, 31-30 (D)
1987—*Redskins, 42-10 (San Diego)
1989—Broncos, 14-10 (W)
1992—Redskins, 34-3 (W)
1995—Broncos, 38-31 (D)
1998—Broncos, 38-16 (W)
2001—Redskins, 17-10 (D)
(RS Pts.—Redskins 204, Broncos 160)
(PS Pts.—Redskins 42, Broncos 10)
*Super Bowl XXII

DETROIT vs. ARIZONA
RS: Lions lead series, 28-20-5;
See Arizona vs. Detroit
DETROIT vs. ATLANTA
RS: Lions lead series, 21-7;
See Atlanta vs. Detroit
DETROIT vs. BALTIMORE
RS: Ravens lead series, 1-0;
See Baltimore vs. Detroit
DETROIT vs. BUFFALO
RS: Lions lead series, 3-2-1;
See Buffalo vs. Detroit
DETROIT vs. CAROLINA
RS: Lions lead series, 1-0;
See Carolina vs. Detroit
DETROIT vs. CHICAGO
RS: Bears lead series, 81-58-5;
See Chicago vs. Detroit
DETROIT vs. CINCINNATI
RS: Bengals lead series, 5-3;
See Cincinnati vs. Detroit
DETROIT vs. CLEVELAND
RS: Lions lead series, 12-4
PS: Lions lead series, 3-1;
See Cleveland vs. Detroit
DETROIT vs. DALLAS
RS: Series tied, 7-7
PS: Series tied, 1-1;
See Dallas vs. Detroit
DETROIT vs. DENVER
RS: Broncos lead series, 5-3;
See Denver vs. Detroit
***DETROIT vs. GREEN BAY**
RS: Packers lead series, 74-62-7
PS: Packers lead series, 2-0
1930—Packers, 47-13 (GB)
　　　Tie, 6-6 (P)
1932—Packers, 15-10 (GB)
　　　Spartans, 19-0 (P)
1933—Packers, 17-0 (GB)
　　　Spartans, 7-0 (P)
1934—Lions, 3-0 (GB)
　　　Packers, 3-0 (D)
1935—Packers, 13-9 (Mil)
　　　Packers, 31-7 (GB)
　　　Lions, 20-10 (D)
1936—Packers, 20-18 (GB)
　　　Packers, 26-17 (D)
1937—Packers, 26-6 (GB)
　　　Packers, 14-13 (D)
1938—Lions, 17-7 (GB)
　　　Packers, 28-7 (D)
1939—Packers, 26-7 (GB)
　　　Packers, 12-7 (D)
1940—Lions, 23-14 (GB)
　　　Packers, 50-7 (D)

1941—Packers, 23-0 (GB)
　　　Packers, 24-7 (D)
1942—Packers, 38-7 (Mil)
　　　Packers, 28-7 (D)
1943—Packers, 35-14 (GB)
　　　Packers, 27-6 (D)
1944—Packers, 27-6 (Mil)
　　　Packers, 14-0 (D)
1945—Packers, 57-21 (Mil)
　　　Lions, 14-3 (D)
1946—Packers, 10-7 (Mil)
　　　Packers, 9-0 (D)
1947—Packers, 34-17 (GB)
　　　Packers, 35-14 (D)
1948—Packers, 33-21 (GB)
　　　Lions, 24-20 (D)
1949—Packers, 16-14 (Mil)
　　　Lions, 21-7 (D)
1950—Lions, 45-7 (GB)
　　　Lions, 24-21 (D)
1951—Lions, 24-17 (GB)
　　　Lions, 52-35 (D)
1952—Lions, 52-17 (GB)
　　　Lions, 48-24 (D)
1953—Lions, 14-7 (GB)
　　　Lions, 34-15 (D)
1954—Lions, 21-17 (GB)
　　　Lions, 28-24 (D)
1955—Packers, 20-17 (GB)
　　　Lions, 24-10 (D)
1956—Lions, 20-16 (GB)
　　　Packers, 24-20 (D)
1957—Lions, 24-14 (GB)
　　　Lions, 18-6 (D)
1958—Tie, 13-13 (GB)
　　　Lions, 24-14 (D)
1959—Packers, 28-10 (GB)
　　　Packers, 24-17 (D)
1960—Packers, 28-9 (GB)
　　　Lions, 23-10 (D)
1961—Lions, 17-13 (Mil)
　　　Lions, 17-9 (D)
1962—Packers, 9-7 (GB)
　　　Lions, 26-14 (D)
1963—Packers, 31-10 (Mil)
　　　Tie, 13-13 (D)
1964—Packers, 14-10 (D)
　　　Packers, 30-7 (GB)
1965—Packers, 31-21 (D)
　　　Lions, 12-7 (GB)
1966—Packers, 23-14 (GB)
　　　Packers, 31-7 (D)
1967—Tie, 17-17 (GB)
　　　Packers, 27-17 (D)
1968—Lions, 23-17 (GB)
　　　Tie, 14-14 (D)
1969—Packers, 28-17 (D)
　　　Lions, 16-10 (GB)
1970—Lions, 40-0 (GB)
　　　Lions, 20-0 (D)
1971—Lions, 31-28 (D)
　　　Tie, 14-14 (Mil)
1972—Packers, 24-23 (D)
　　　Packers, 33-7 (GB)
1973—Tie, 13-13 (GB)
　　　Lions, 34-0 (D)
1974—Packers, 21-19 (Mil)
　　　Lions, 19-17 (D)
1975—Lions, 30-16 (Mil)
　　　Lions, 13-10 (D)

1976—Packers, 24-14 (GB)
　　　Lions, 27-6 (D)
1977—Lions, 10-6 (D)
　　　Packers, 10-9 (GB)
1978—Packers, 13-7 (D)
　　　Packers, 35-14 (Mil)
1979—Packers, 24-16 (Mil)
　　　Packers, 18-13 (D)
1980—Lions, 29-7 (Mil)
　　　Lions, 24-3 (D)
1981—Lions, 31-27 (D)
　　　Packers, 31-17 (GB)
1982—Lions, 30-10 (GB)
　　　Lions, 27-24 (D)
1983—Lions, 38-14 (D)
　　　Lions, 23-20 (Mil) OT
1984—Packers, 41-9 (GB)
　　　Lions, 31-28 (D)
1985—Packers, 43-10 (GB)
　　　Packers, 26-23 (D)
1986—Lions, 21-14 (GB)
　　　Packers, 44-40 (D)
1987—Lions, 19-16 (D) OT
　　　Packers, 34-33 (GB)
1988—Lions, 19-9 (Mil)
　　　Lions, 30-14 (D)
1989—Packers, 23-20 (Mil) OT
　　　Lions, 31-22 (D)
1990—Packers, 24-21 (D)
　　　Lions, 24-17 (GB)
1991—Lions, 23-14 (D)
　　　Lions, 21-17 (GB)
1992—Packers, 27-13 (D)
　　　Packers, 38-10 (Mil)
1993—Packers, 26-17 (Mil)
　　　Lions, 30-20 (D)
　　　**Packers, 28-24 (D)
1994—Packers, 38-30 (Mil)
　　　Lions, 34-31 (D)
　　　**Packers, 16-12 (GB)
1995—Packers, 30-21 (GB)
　　　Lions, 24-16 (D)
1996—Packers, 28-18 (GB)
　　　Packers, 31-3 (D)
1997—Lions, 26-15 (D)
　　　Packers, 20-10 (GB)
1998—Packers, 38-19 (GB)
　　　Lions, 27-20 (D)
1999—Lions, 23-15 (D)
　　　Packers, 26-17 (GB)
2000—Lions, 31-24 (D)
　　　Packers, 26-13 (GB)
2001—Packers, 28-6 (GB)
　　　Packers, 29-27 (D)
(RS Pts.—Packers 2,902, Lions 2,600)
(PS Pts.—Packers 44, Lions 36)
*Franchise in Portsmouth prior to 1934
and known as the Spartans
**NFC First-Round Playoff
DETROIT vs. *INDIANAPOLIS
RS: Series tied, 18-18-2
1953—Lions, 27-17 (B)
　　　Lions, 17-7 (D)
1954—Lions, 35-0 (D)
　　　Lions, 27-3 (B)
1955—Colts, 28-13 (B)
　　　Lions, 24-14 (D)
1956—Lions, 31-14 (D)
　　　Lions, 27-3 (D)
1957—Colts, 34-14 (B)

Lions, 31-27 (D)
1958—Colts, 28-15 (B)
Colts, 40-14 (D)
1959—Colts, 21-9 (B)
Colts, 31-24 (D)
1960—Lions, 30-17 (D)
Lions, 20-15 (B)
1961—Lions, 16-15 (B)
Colts, 17-14 (D)
1962—Lions, 29-20 (B)
Lions, 21-14 (D)
1963—Colts, 25-21 (D)
Colts, 24-21 (B)
1964—Colts, 34-0 (D)
Lions, 31-14 (B)
1965—Colts, 31-7 (B)
Tie, 24-24 (D)
1966—Colts, 45-14 (B)
Lions, 20-14 (D)
1967—Colts, 41-7 (B)
1968—Colts, 27-10 (D)
1969—Tie, 17-17 (B)
1973—Colts, 29-27 (D)
1977—Lions, 13-10 (B)
1980—Colts, 10-9 (D)
1985—Colts, 14-6 (I)
1991—Lions, 33-24 (I)
1997—Lions, 32-10 (D)
2000—Colts, 30-18 (I)
(RS Pts.—Colts 788, Lions 748)
*Franchise in Baltimore prior to 1984

DETROIT vs. JACKSONVILLE
RS: Series tied, 1-1
1995—Lions, 44-0 (D)
1998—Jaguars, 37-22 (J)
(RS Pts.—Lions 66, Jaguars 37)

DETROIT vs. KANSAS CITY
RS: Chiefs lead series, 6-3
1971—Lions, 32-21 (D)
1975—Chiefs, 24-21 (KC) OT
1980—Chiefs, 20-17 (KC)
1981—Lions, 27-10 (D)
1987—Chiefs, 27-20 (D)
1988—Lions, 7-6 (KC)
1990—Chiefs, 43-24 (KC)
1996—Chiefs, 28-24 (D)
1999—Chiefs, 31-21 (KC)
(RS Pts.—Chiefs 210, Lions 193)

DETROIT vs. MIAMI
RS: Dolphins lead series, 5-2
1973—Dolphins, 34-7 (M)
1979—Dolphins, 28-10 (D)
1985—Lions, 31-21 (D)
1991—Lions, 17-13 (D)
1994—Dolphins, 27-20 (M)
1997—Dolphins, 33-30 (M)
2000—Dolphins, 23-8 (D)
(RS Pts.—Dolphins 179, Lions 123)

DETROIT vs. MINNESOTA
RS: Vikings lead series, 50-29-2
1961—Lions, 37-10 (M)
Lions, 13-7 (D)
1962—Lions, 17-6 (M)
Lions, 37-23 (D)
1963—Lions, 28-10 (D)
Vikings, 34-31 (M)
1964—Lions, 24-20 (M)
Tie, 23-23 (D)
1965—Lions, 31-29 (M)
Vikings, 29-7 (D)

1966—Lions, 32-31 (M)
Vikings, 28-16 (D)
1967—Tie, 10-10 (M)
Lions, 14-3 (D)
1968—Vikings, 24-10 (M)
Vikings, 13-6 (D)
1969—Vikings, 24-10 (M)
Vikings, 27-0 (D)
1970—Vikings, 30-17 (D)
Vikings, 24-20 (M)
1971—Vikings, 16-13 (D)
Vikings, 29-10 (M)
1972—Vikings, 34-10 (D)
Vikings, 16-14 (M)
1973—Vikings, 23-9 (D)
Vikings, 28-7 (M)
1974—Vikings, 7-6 (D)
Lions, 20-16 (M)
1975—Vikings, 25-19 (M)
Lions, 17-10 (D)
1976—Vikings, 10-9 (D)
Vikings, 31-23 (M)
1977—Vikings, 14-7 (M)
Vikings, 30-21 (D)
1978—Vikings, 17-7 (M)
Lions, 45-14 (D)
1979—Vikings, 13-10 (D)
Vikings, 14-7 (M)
1980—Lions, 27-7 (D)
Vikings, 34-0 (M)
1981—Vikings, 26-24 (M)
Lions, 45-7 (D)
1982—Vikings, 34-31 (D)
1983—Vikings, 20-17 (M)
Lions, 13-2 (D)
1984—Vikings, 29-28 (D)
Lions, 16-14 (M)
1985—Vikings, 16-13 (M)
Lions, 41-21 (D)
1986—Lions, 13-10 (M)
Vikings, 24-10 (D)
1987—Vikings, 34-19 (M)
Vikings, 17-14 (D)
1988—Vikings, 44-17 (M)
Vikings, 23-0 (D)
1989—Vikings, 24-17 (M)
Vikings, 20-7 (D)
1990—Lions, 34-27 (M)
Vikings, 17-7 (D)
1991—Lions, 24-20 (M)
Lions, 34-14 (D)
1992—Lions, 31-17 (D)
Vikings, 31-14 (M)
1993—Lions, 30-27 (M)
Vikings, 13-0 (D)
1994—Vikings, 10-3 (M)
Lions, 41-19 (D)
1995—Vikings, 20-10 (M)
Lions, 44-38 (D)
1996—Vikings, 17-13 (M)
Vikings, 24-22 (D)
1997—Lions, 38-15 (D)
Lions, 14-13 (M)
1998—Vikings, 29-6 (M)
Vikings, 34-13 (D)
1999—Lions, 25-23 (D)
Vikings, 24-17 (M)
2000—Vikings, 31-24 (D)
Vikings, 24-17 (M)
2001—Vikings, 31-26 (M)

Lions, 27-24 (D)
(RS Pts.—Vikings 1,700, Lions 1,503)

DETROIT vs. NEW ENGLAND
RS: Lions lead series, 4-3
1971—Lions, 34-7 (NE)
1976—Lions, 30-10 (D)
1979—Patriots, 24-17 (NE)
1985—Patriots, 23-6 (NE)
1993—Lions, 19-16 (NE) OT
1994—Patriots, 23-17 (D)
2000—Lions, 34-9 (D)
(RS Pts.—Lions 157, Patriots 112)

DETROIT vs. NEW ORLEANS
RS: Saints lead series, 8-7-1
1968—Tie, 20-20 (D)
1970—Saints, 19-17 (NO)
1972—Lions, 27-14 (D)
1973—Saints, 20-13 (NO)
1974—Lions, 19-14 (D)
1976—Saints, 17-16 (NO)
1977—Lions, 23-19 (D)
1979—Saints, 17-7 (NO)
1980—Lions, 24-13 (D)
1988—Saints, 22-14 (D)
1989—Lions, 21-14 (D)
1990—Lions, 27-10 (NO)
1992—Saints, 13-7 (D)
1993—Saints, 14-3 (NO)
1997—Saints, 35-17 (NO)
2000—Lions, 14-10 (NO)
(RS Pts.—Saints 271, Lions 269)

*DETROIT vs. N.Y. GIANTS
RS: Lions lead series, 19-17-1
PS: Lions lead series, 1-0
1930—Giants, 19-6 (P)
1931—Spartans, 14-6 (P)
Giants, 14-0 (NY)
1932—Spartans, 7-0 (P)
Spartans, 6-0 (NY)
1933—Spartans, 17-7 (P)
Giants, 13-10 (NY)
1934—Lions, 9-0 (D)
1935—**Lions, 26-7 (D)
1936—Giants, 14-7 (NY)
Lions, 38-0 (D)
1937—Lions, 17-0 (NY)
1939—Lions, 18-14 (D)
1941—Giants, 20-13 (NY)
1943—Tie, 0-0 (D)
1945—Giants, 35-14 (NY)
1947—Lions, 35-7 (D)
1949—Lions, 45-21 (NY)
1953—Lions, 27-16 (NY)
1955—Giants, 24-19 (D)
1958—Giants, 19-17 (D)
1962—Giants, 17-14 (NY)
1964—Lions, 26-3 (D)
1967—Lions, 30-7 (NY)
1969—Lions, 24-0 (D)
1972—Lions, 30-16 (D)
1974—Lions, 20-19 (D)
1976—Giants, 24-10 (NY)
1982—Giants, 13-6 (D)
1983—Lions, 15-9 (D)
1988—Giants, 30-10 (NY)
Giants, 13-10 (D) OT
1989—Giants, 24-14 (NY)
1990—Giants, 20-0 (NY)
1994—Lions, 28-25 (NY) OT
1996—Giants, 35-7 (D)

1997—Giants, 26-20 (D) OT
2000—Lions, 31-21 (NY)
(RS Pts.—Lions 614, Giants 531)
(PS Pts.—Lions 26, Giants 7)
*Franchise in Portsmouth prior to 1934
and known as the Spartans
**NFL Championship
DETROIT vs. N.Y. JETS
RS: Lions lead series, 6-3
1972—Lions, 37-20 (D)
1979—Jets, 31-10 (NY)
1982—Jets, 28-13 (D)
1985—Lions, 31-20 (D)
1988—Jets, 17-10 (D)
1991—Lions, 34-20 (D)
1994—Lions, 18-7 (NY)
1997—Lions, 13-10 (D)
2000—Lions, 10-7 (NY)
(RS Pts.—Lions 176, Jets 160)
DETROIT vs. *OAKLAND
RS: Raiders lead series, 6-2
1970—Lions, 28-14 (D)
1974—Raiders, 35-13 (O)
1978—Raiders, 29-17 (O)
1981—Lions, 16-0 (D)
1984—Raiders, 24-3 (D)
1987—Raiders, 27-7 (LA)
1990—Raiders, 38-31 (D)
1996—Raiders, 37-21 (O)
(RS Pts.—Raiders 204, Lions 136)
*Franchise in Los Angeles from
1982-1994
***DETROIT vs. PHILADELPHIA**
RS: Lions lead series, 12-11-2
PS: Eagles lead series, 1-0
1933—Spartans, 25-0 (P)
1934—Lions, 10-0 (P)
1935—Lions, 35-0 (D)
1936—Lions, 23-0 (P)
1938—Eagles, 21-7 (D)
1940—Lions, 21-0 (P)
1941—Lions, 21-17 (D)
1945—Lions, 28-24 (D)
1948—Eagles, 45-21 (P)
1949—Eagles, 22-14 (D)
1951—Lions, 28-10 (P)
1954—Tie, 13-13 (D)
1957—Lions, 27-16 (P)
1960—Eagles, 28-10 (P)
1961—Eagles, 27-24 (D)
1965—Lions, 35-28 (P)
1968—Eagles, 12-0 (D)
1971—Eagles, 23-20 (D)
1974—Eagles, 28-17 (P)
1977—Lions, 17-13 (D)
1979—Eagles, 44-7 (P)
1984—Tie, 23-23 (D) OT
1986—Lions, 13-11 (P)
1995—**Eagles, 58-37 (P)
1996—Eagles, 24-17 (P)
1998—Eagles, 10-9 (P)
(RS Pts.—Lions 465, Eagles 439)
(PS Pts.—Eagles 58, Lions 37)
*Franchise in Portsmouth prior to 1934
and known as the Spartans
**NFC First-Round Playoff
DETROIT vs. *PITTSBURGH
RS: Lions lead series, 14-13-1
1934—Lions, 40-7 (D)
1936—Lions, 28-3 (D)

1937—Lions, 7-3 (D)
1938—Lions, 16-7 (D)
1940—Pirates, 10-7 (D)
1942—Steelers, 35-7 (D)
1946—Lions, 17-7 (D)
1947—Steelers, 17-10 (P)
1948—Lions, 17-14 (D)
1949—Steelers, 14-7 (P)
1950—Lions, 10-7 (D)
1952—Lions, 31-6 (P)
1953—Lions, 38-21 (D)
1955—Lions, 31-28 (D)
1956—Lions, 45-7 (D)
1959—Tie, 10-10 (P)
1962—Lions, 45-7 (D)
1966—Steelers, 17-3 (P)
1967—Steelers, 24-14 (D)
1969—Steelers, 16-13 (P)
1973—Steelers, 24-10 (P)
1983—Lions, 45-3 (D)
1986—Steelers, 27-17 (D)
1989—Steelers, 23-3 (D)
1992—Steelers, 17-14 (P)
1995—Steelers, 23-20 (P)
1998—Lions, 19-16 (D) OT
2001—Steelers, 47-14 (P)
(RS Pts.—Lions 538, Steelers 440)
*Steelers known as Pirates prior to 1941
DETROIT vs. *ST. LOUIS
RS: Rams lead series, 40-36-1
PS: Lions lead series, 1-0
1937—Lions, 28-0 (C)
       Lions, 27-7 (D)
1938—Rams, 21-17 (C)
       Lions, 6-0 (D)
1939—Lions, 15-7 (D)
       Rams, 14-3 (C)
1940—Lions, 6-0 (D)
       Rams, 24-0 (C)
1941—Lions, 17-7 (D)
       Lions, 14-0 (C)
1942—Rams, 14-0 (D)
       Rams, 27-7 (C)
1944—Rams, 20-17 (D)
       Lions, 26-14 (C)
1945—Lions, 28-21 (D)
1946—Rams, 35-14 (LA)
       Rams, 41-20 (D)
1947—Rams, 27-13 (D)
       Rams, 28-17 (LA)
1948—Rams, 44-7 (LA)
       Rams, 34-27 (D)
1949—Rams, 27-24 (LA)
       Rams, 21-10 (D)
1950—Rams, 30-28 (D)
       Rams, 65-24 (LA)
1951—Rams, 27-21 (D)
       Lions, 24-22 (LA)
1952—Lions, 17-14 (LA)
       Lions, 24-16 (D)
       **Lions, 31-21 (D)
1953—Rams, 31-19 (D)
       Rams, 37-24 (LA)
1954—Lions, 21-3 (D)
       Lions, 27-24 (LA)
1955—Rams, 17-10 (D)
       Rams, 24-13 (LA)
1956—Lions, 24-21 (D)
       Lions, 16-7 (LA)
1957—Lions, 10-7 (D)

                    Rams, 35-17 (LA)
1958—Rams, 42-28 (D)
       Lions, 41-24 (LA)
1959—Lions, 17-7 (LA)
       Lions, 23-17 (D)
1960—Rams, 48-35 (LA)
       Lions, 12-10 (D)
1961—Lions, 14-13 (D)
       Lions, 28-10 (LA)
1962—Lions, 13-10 (D)
       Lions, 12-3 (LA)
1963—Lions, 23-2 (D)
       Rams, 28-21 (D)
1964—Tie, 17-17 (LA)
       Lions, 37-17 (D)
1965—Lions, 20-0 (D)
       Lions, 31-7 (LA)
1966—Rams, 14-7 (D)
       Rams, 23-3 (LA)
1967—Rams, 31-7 (D)
1968—Rams, 10-7 (LA)
1969—Lions, 28-0 (D)
1970—Lions, 28-23 (LA)
1971—Rams, 21-13 (D)
1972—Lions, 34-17 (LA)
1974—Rams, 16-13 (LA)
1975—Lions, 20-0 (D)
1976—Rams, 20-17 (D)
1980—Lions, 41-20 (LA)
1981—Rams, 20-13 (LA)
1982—Lions, 19-14 (LA)
1983—Rams, 21-10 (LA)
1986—Rams, 14-10 (LA)
1987—Rams, 37-16 (D)
1988—Rams, 17-10 (LA)
1991—Lions, 21-10 (D)
1993—Lions, 16-13 (LA)
1999—Lions, 31-27 (D)
2001—Rams, 35-0 (D)
(RS Pts.—Rams 1,498, Lions 1,371)
(PS Pts.—Lions 31, Rams 21)
*Franchise in Los Angeles prior to 1995
and in Cleveland prior to 1946
**Conference Playoff
DETROIT vs. SAN DIEGO
RS: Chargers lead series, 4-3
1972—Lions, 34-20 (D)
1977—Lions, 20-0 (D)
1978—Lions, 31-14 (D)
1981—Chargers, 28-23 (SD)
1984—Chargers, 27-24 (SD)
1996—Chargers, 27-21 (SD)
1999—Chargers, 20-10 (D)
(RS Pts.—Lions 163, Chargers 136)
DETROIT vs. SAN FRANCISCO
RS: 49ers lead series, 30-26-1
PS: Series tied, 1-1
1950—Lions, 24-7 (D)
       49ers, 28-27 (SF)
1951—49ers, 20-10 (D)
       49ers, 21-17 (SF)
1952—49ers, 17-3 (SF)
       49ers, 28-0 (D)
1953—Lions, 24-21 (D)
       Lions, 14-10 (SF)
1954—49ers, 37-31 (SF)
       Lions, 48-7 (D)
1955—49ers, 27-24 (D)
       49ers, 38-21 (SF)
1956—Lions, 20-17 (D)

Lions, 17-13 (SF)
1957—49ers, 35-31 (SF)
Lions, 31-10 (D)
*Lions, 31-27 (SF)
1958—49ers, 24-21 (SF)
Lions, 35-21 (D)
1959—49ers, 34-13 (D)
49ers, 33-7 (SF)
1960—49ers, 14-10 (D)
Lions, 24-0 (SF)
1961—49ers, 49-0 (SF)
Tie, 20-20 (SF)
1962—Lions, 45-24 (D)
Lions, 38-24 (SF)
1963—Lions, 26-3 (D)
Lions, 45-7 (SF)
1964—Lions, 26-17 (SF)
Lions, 24-7 (D)
1965—49ers, 27-21 (D)
49ers, 17-14 (SF)
1966—49ers, 27-24 (SF)
49ers, 41-14 (D)
1967—Lions, 45-3 (SF)
1968—49ers, 14-7 (D)
1969—Lions, 26-14 (SF)
1970—Lions, 28-7 (D)
1971—49ers, 31-27 (SF)
1973—Lions, 30-20 (D)
1974—Lions, 17-13 (D)
1975—Lions, 28-17 (SF)
1977—49ers, 28-7 (SF)
1978—Lions, 33-14 (D)
1980—Lions, 17-13 (D)
1981—Lions, 24-17 (D)
1983—**49ers, 24-23 (SF)
1984—49ers, 30-27 (D)
1985—Lions, 23-21 (D)
1988—49ers, 20-13 (SF)
1991—49ers, 35-3 (SF)
1992—49ers, 24-6 (SF)
1993—49ers, 55-17 (D)
1994—49ers, 27-21 (D)
1995—Lions, 27-24 (D)
1996—49ers, 24-14 (SF)
1998—49ers, 35-13 (D)
2001—49ers, 21-13 (SF)
(RS Pts.—49ers 1,232, Lions 1,215)
(PS Pts.—Lions 54, 49ers 51)
*Conference Playoff
**NFC Divisional Playoff
DETROIT vs. SEATTLE
RS: Series tied, 4-4
1976—Lions, 41-14 (D)
1978—Seahawks, 28-16 (S)
1984—Seahawks, 38-17 (S)
1987—Seahawks, 37-14 (D)
1990—Seahawks, 30-10 (S)
1993—Lions, 30-10 (D)
1996—Lions, 17-16 (D)
1999—Lions, 28-20 (S)
(RS Pts.—Seahawks 193, Lions 173)
DETROIT vs. TAMPA BAY
RS: Lions lead series, 26-22
PS: Buccaneers lead series, 1-0
1977—Lions, 16-7 (D)
1978—Lions, 15-7 (D)
Lions, 34-23 (D)
1979—Buccaneers, 31-16 (TB)
Buccaneers, 16-14 (D)
1980—Lions, 24-10 (TB)

Lions, 27-14 (D)
1981—Buccaneers, 28-10 (TB)
Buccaneers, 20-17 (D)
1982—Buccaneers, 23-21 (TB)
1983—Lions, 11-0 (TB)
Lions, 23-20 (D)
1984—Buccaneers, 21-17 (TB)
Lions, 13-7 (D) OT
1985—Lions, 30-9 (D)
Buccaneers, 19-16 (TB) OT
1986—Buccaneers, 24-20 (D)
Lions, 38-17 (TB)
1987—Buccaneers, 31-27 (D)
Lions, 20-10 (TB)
1988—Buccaneers, 23-20 (D)
Buccaneers, 21-10 (TB)
1989—Lions, 17-16 (TB)
Lions, 33-7 (D)
1990—Buccaneers, 38-21 (D)
Buccaneers, 23-20 (TB)
1991—Lions, 31-3 (D)
Buccaneers, 30-21 (TB)
1992—Buccaneers, 27-23 (D)
Lions, 38-7 (TB)
1993—Buccaneers, 27-10 (TB)
Lions, 23-0 (D)
1994—Buccaneers, 24-14 (TB)
Lions, 14-9 (D)
1995—Lions, 27-24 (D)
Lions, 37-10 (TB)
1996—Lions, 21-6 (D)
Lions, 27-0 (TB)
1997—Buccaneers, 24-17 (D)
Lions, 27-9 (TB)
*Buccaneers, 20-10 (TB)
1998—Lions, 27-6 (D)
Lions, 28-25 (TB)
1999—Lions, 20-3 (D)
Buccaneers, 23-16 (TB)
2000—Buccaneers, 31-10 (D)
Lions, 28-14 (TB)
2001—Buccaneers, 20-17 (D)
Buccaneers, 15-12 (TB)
(RS Pts.—Lions 1,018, Buccaneers 802)
(PS Pts.—Buccaneers 20, Lions 10)
*NFC First-Round Playoff
DETROIT vs. *TENNESSEE
RS: Titans lead series, 5-3
1971—Lions, 31-7 (H)
1975—Oilers, 24-8 (H)
1983—Oilers, 27-17 (H)
1986—Lions, 24-13 (D)
1989—Oilers, 35-31 (H)
1992—Oilers, 24-21 (D)
1995—Lions, 24-17 (H)
2001—Titans, 27-24 (D)
(RS Pts.—Lions 180, Titans 174)
*Franchise in Houston prior to 1997;
known as Oilers prior to 1999
DETROIT vs. **WASHINGTON
RS: Redskins lead series, 24-10
PS: Redskins lead series, 3-0
1932—Spartans, 10-0 (P)
1933—Spartans, 13-0 (B)
1934—Lions, 24-0 (D)
1935—Lions, 17-7 (B)
Lions, 14-0 (D)
1938—Redskins, 7-5 (D)
1939—Redskins, 31-7 (W)
1940—Redskins, 20-14 (D)

1942—Redskins, 15-3 (D)
1943—Redskins, 42-20 (W)
1946—Redskins, 17-16 (W)
1947—Lions, 38-21 (D)
1948—Redskins, 46-21 (W)
1951—Lions, 35-17 (D)
1956—Redskins, 18-17 (W)
1965—Lions, 14-10 (D)
1968—Redskins, 14-3 (W)
1970—Redskins, 31-10 (W)
1973—Redskins, 20-0 (D)
1976—Redskins, 20-7 (W)
1978—Redskins, 21-19 (D)
1979—Redskins, 27-24 (D)
1981—Redskins, 33-31 (W)
1982—***Redskins, 31-7 (W)
1983—Redskins, 38-17 (W)
1984—Redskins, 28-14 (W)
1985—Redskins, 24-3 (W)
1987—Redskins, 20-13 (W)
1990—Redskins, 41-38 (D) OT
1991—Redskins, 45-0 (W)
****Redskins, 41-10 (W)
1992—Redskins, 13-10 (W)
1995—Redskins, 36-30 (W) OT
1997—Redskins, 30-7 (W)
1999—Lions, 33-17 (D)
***Redskins, 27-13 (W)
2000—Lions, 15-10 (D)
(RS Pts.—Redskins 719, Lions 542)
(PS Pts.—Redskins 99, Lions 30)
*Franchise in Portsmouth prior to 1934
and known as the Spartans.
**Franchise in Boston prior to 1937
***NFC First-Round Playoff
****NFC Championship

GREEN BAY vs. ARIZONA
RS: Packers lead series, 41-21-4
PS: Packers lead series, 1-0;
See Arizona vs. Green Bay
GREEN BAY vs. ATLANTA
RS: Series tied, 10-10
PS: Packers lead series, 1-0;
See Atlanta vs. Green Bay
GREEN BAY vs. BALTIMORE
RS: Packers lead series, 2-0;
See Baltimore vs. Green Bay
GREEN BAY vs. BUFFALO
RS: Bills lead series, 6-2;
See Buffalo vs. Green Bay
GREEN BAY vs. CAROLINA
RS: Packers lead series, 3-2
PS: Packers lead series, 1-0;
See Carolina vs. Green Bay
GREEN BAY vs. CHICAGO
RS: Bears lead series, 83-73-6
PS: Bears lead series, 1-0;
See Chicago vs. Green Bay
GREEN BAY vs. CINCINNATI
RS: Packers lead series, 5-4;
See Cincinnati vs. Green Bay
GREEN BAY vs. CLEVELAND
RS: Packers lead series, 9-6
PS: Packers lead series, 1-0;
See Cleveland vs. Green Bay
GREEN BAY vs. DALLAS
RS: Cowboys lead series, 10-9
PS: Cowboys lead series, 4-2;
See Dallas vs. Green Bay

GREEN BAY vs. DENVER
RS: Broncos lead series, 5-3-1
PS: Broncos lead series, 1-0;
See Denver vs. Green Bay

GREEN BAY vs. DETROIT
RS: Packers lead series, 74-62-7
PS: Packers lead series, 2-0;
See Detroit vs. Green Bay

GREEN BAY vs. *INDIANAPOLIS
RS: Series tied, 19-19-1
PS: Packers lead series, 1-0
1953—Packers, 37-14 (GB)
   Packers, 35-24 (B)
1954—Packers, 7-6 (B)
   Packers, 24-13 (Mil)
1955—Colts, 24-20 (Mil)
   Colts, 14-10 (B)
1956—Packers, 38-33 (Mil)
   Colts, 28-21 (B)
1957—Colts, 45-17 (Mil)
   Packers, 24-21 (B)
1958—Colts, 24-17 (Mil)
   Colts, 56-0 (B)
1959—Colts, 38-21 (B)
   Colts, 28-24 (Mil)
1960—Packers, 35-21 (GB)
   Colts, 38-24 (B)
1961—Packers, 45-7 (GB)
   Colts, 45-21 (B)
1962—Packers, 17-6 (B)
   Packers, 17-13 (GB)
1963—Packers, 31-20 (GB)
   Packers, 34-20 (B)
1964—Colts, 21-20 (GB)
   Colts, 24-21 (B)
1965—Packers, 20-17 (Mil)
   Packers, 42-27 (B)
   **Packers, 13-10 (GB) OT
1966—Packers, 24-3 (Mil)
   Packers, 14-10 (B)
1967—Colts, 13-10 (B)
1968—Colts, 16-3 (GB)
1969—Colts, 14-6 (B)
1970—Colts, 13-10 (Mil)
1974—Packers, 20-13 (B)
1982—Tie, 20-20 (B) OT
1985—Colts, 37-10 (I)
1988—Colts, 20-13 (GB)
1991—Packers, 14-10 (Mil)
1997—Colts, 41-38 (I)
2000—Packers, 26-24 (GB)
(RS Pts.—Colts 861, Packers 830)
(PS Pts.—Packers 13, Colts 10)
*Franchise in Baltimore prior to 1984
**Conference Playoff

GREEN BAY vs. JACKSONVILLE
RS: Packers lead series, 2-0
1995—Packers, 24-14 (J)
2001—Packers, 28-21 (J)
(RS Pts.—Packers 52, Jaguars 35)

GREEN BAY vs. KANSAS CITY
RS: Chiefs lead series, 5-1-1
PS: Packers lead series, 1-0
1966—*Packers, 35-10 (Los Angeles)
1973—Tie, 10-10 (Mil)
1977—Chiefs, 20-10 (KC)
1987—Packers, 23-3 (KC)
1989—Chiefs, 21-3 (GB)
1990—Chiefs, 17-3 (GB)
1993—Chiefs, 23-16 (KC)

1996—Chiefs, 27-20 (KC)
(RS Pts.—Chiefs 121, Packers 85)
(PS Pts.—Packers 35, Chiefs 10)
*Super Bowl I

GREEN BAY vs. MIAMI
RS: Dolphins lead series, 9-1
1971—Dolphins, 27-6 (Mia)
1975—Dolphins, 31-7 (GB)
1979—Dolphins, 27-7 (Mia)
1985—Dolphins, 34-24 (GB)
1988—Dolphins, 24-17 (Mia)
1989—Dolphins, 23-20 (Mia)
1991—Dolphins, 16-13 (Mia)
1994—Dolphins, 24-14 (Mil)
1997—Packers, 23-18 (GB)
2000—Dolphins, 28-20 (M)
(RS Pts.—Dolphins 252, Packers 151)

GREEN BAY vs. MINNESOTA
RS: Series tied, 40-40-1
1961—Packers, 33-7 (Minn)
   Packers, 28-10 (Mil)
1962—Packers, 34-7 (GB)
   Packers, 48-21 (Minn)
1963—Packers, 37-28 (Minn)
   Packers, 28-7 (GB)
1964—Vikings, 24-23 (GB)
   Packers, 42-13 (Minn)
1965—Packers, 38-13 (Minn)
   Packers, 24-19 (GB)
1966—Vikings, 20-17 (GB)
   Packers, 28-16 (Minn)
1967—Vikings, 10-7 (Mil)
   Packers, 30-27 (Minn)
1968—Vikings, 26-13 (Mil)
   Vikings, 14-10 (Minn)
1969—Vikings, 19-7 (Mil)
   Vikings, 9-7 (Mil)
1970—Packers, 13-10 (Mil)
   Vikings, 10-3 (Minn)
1971—Vikings, 24-13 (GB)
   Vikings, 3-0 (Minn)
1972—Vikings, 27-13 (GB)
   Packers, 23-7 (Minn)
1973—Vikings, 11-3 (Minn)
   Vikings, 31-7 (GB)
1974—Vikings, 32-17 (GB)
   Packers, 19-7 (Minn)
1975—Vikings, 28-17 (GB)
   Vikings, 24-3 (Minn)
1976—Vikings, 17-10 (Mil)
   Vikings, 20-9 (Minn)
1977—Vikings, 19-7 (Minn)
   Vikings, 13-6 (GB)
1978—Vikings, 21-7 (Minn)
   Tie, 10-10 (GB) OT
1979—Vikings, 27-21 (Minn) OT
   Packers, 19-7 (Mil)
1980—Packers, 16-3 (GB)
   Packers, 25-13 (Minn)
1981—Vikings, 30-13 (Mil)
   Packers, 35-23 (Minn)
1982—Packers, 26-7 (Mil)
1983—Vikings, 20-17 (GB) OT
   Packers, 29-21 (Minn)
1984—Packers, 45-17 (Mil)
   Packers, 38-14 (Minn)
1985—Packers, 20-17 (Mil)
   Packers, 27-17 (Minn)
1986—Vikings, 42-7 (Mil)
   Vikings, 32-6 (GB)

1987—Packers, 23-16 (Minn)
   Packers, 16-10 (Mil)
1988—Packers, 34-14 (Minn)
   Packers, 18-6 (GB)
1989—Vikings, 26-14 (Minn)
   Packers, 20-19 (Mil)
1990—Packers, 24-10 (Mil)
   Vikings, 23-7 (Minn)
1991—Vikings, 35-21 (GB)
   Packers, 27-7 (Minn)
1992—Vikings, 23-20 (GB) OT
   Vikings, 27-7 (Minn)
1993—Vikings, 15-13 (Minn)
   Vikings, 21-17 (Mil)
1994—Packers, 16-10 (GB)
   Vikings, 13-10 (M) OT
1995—Packers, 38-21 (GB)
   Vikings, 27-24 (M)
1996—Vikings, 30-21 (M)
   Packers, 38-10 (GB)
1997—Packers, 38-32 (GB)
   Packers, 27-11 (M)
1998—Vikings, 37-24 (GB)
   Vikings, 28-14 (M)
1999—Packers, 23-20 (GB)
   Vikings, 24-20 (M)
2000—Packers, 26-20 (GB) OT
   Packers, 33-28 (M)
2001—Vikings, 35-13 (M)
   Packers, 24-13 (GB)
(RS Pts.—Packers 1,628, Vikings 1,505)

GREEN BAY vs. NEW ENGLAND
RS: Series tied, 3-3
PS: Packers lead series, 1-0
1973—Patriots, 33-24 (NE)
1979—Packers, 27-14 (GB)
1985—Patriots, 26-20 (NE)
1988—Packers, 45-3 (Mil)
1994—Patriots, 17-16 (NE)
1996—*Packers, 35-21 (New Orleans)
1997—Packers, 28-10 (NE)
(RS Pts.—Packers 160, Patriots 103)
(PS Pts.—Packers 35, Patriots 21)
*Super Bowl XXXI

GREEN BAY vs. NEW ORLEANS
RS: Packers lead series, 13-4
1968—Packers, 29-7 (Mil)
1971—Saints, 29-21 (Mil)
1972—Packers, 30-20 (NO)
1973—Packers, 30-10 (Mil)
1975—Saints, 20-19 (NO)
1976—Packers, 32-27 (Mil)
1977—Packers, 24-20 (NO)
1978—Packers, 28-17 (Mil)
1979—Packers, 28-19 (Mil)
1981—Packers, 35-7 (NO)
1984—Packers, 23-13 (NO)
1985—Packers, 38-14 (NO)
1986—Saints, 24-10 (NO)
1987—Saints, 33-24 (NO)
1989—Packers, 35-34 (GB)
1993—Packers, 19-17 (NO)
1995—Packers, 34-23 (NO)
(RS Pts.—Packers 459, Saints 334)

GREEN BAY vs. N.Y. GIANTS
RS: Packers lead series, 24-20-2
PS: Packers lead series, 4-1
1928—Giants, 6-0 (GB)
   Packers, 7-0 (NY)
1929—Packers, 20-6 (NY)

1930—Packers, 14-7 (GB)
    Giants, 13-6 (NY)
1931—Packers, 27-7 (GB)
    Packers, 14-10 (NY)
1932—Packers, 13-0 (GB)
    Giants, 6-0 (NY)
1933—Giants, 10-7 (Mil)
    Giants, 17-6 (NY)
1934—Packers, 20-6 (Mil)
    Giants, 17-3 (NY)
1935—Packers, 16-7 (GB)
1936—Packers, 26-14 (NY)
1937—Giants, 10-0 (NY)
1938—Packers, 15-3 (NY)
    *Giants, 23-17 (NY)
1939—*Packers, 27-0 (Mil)
1940—Giants, 7-3 (NY)
1942—Tie, 21-21 (NY)
1943—Packers, 35-21 (NY)
1944—Giants, 24-0 (NY)
    *Packers, 14-7 (NY)
1945—Packers, 23-14 (NY)
1947—Tie, 24-24 (NY)
1948—Giants, 49-3 (Mil)
1949—Giants, 30-10 (GB)
1952—Packers, 17-3 (NY)
1957—Giants, 31-17 (GB)
1959—Giants, 20-3 (NY)
1961—Packers, 20-17 (Mil)
    *Packers, 37-0 (GB)
1962—*Packers, 16-7 (NY)
1967—Packers, 48-21 (NY)
1969—Packers, 20-10 (Mil)
1971—Giants, 42-40 (GB)
1973—Packers, 16-14 (New Haven)
1975—Packers, 40-14 (Mil)
1980—Giants, 27-21 (NY)
1981—Packers, 27-14 (NY)
    Packers, 26-24 (Mil)
1982—Packers, 27-19 (NY)
1983—Giants, 27-3 (NY)
1985—Packers, 23-20 (GB)
1986—Giants, 55-24 (NY)
1987—Giants, 20-10 (NY)
1992—Giants, 27-7 (NY)
1995—Packers, 14-6 (GB)
1998—Packers, 37-3 (NY)
2001—Packers, 34-25 (NY)
(RS Pts.—Giants 780, Packers 775)
(PS Pts.—Packers 111, Giants 37)
*NFL Championship

GREEN BAY vs. N.Y. JETS
RS: Jets lead series, 6-2
1973—Packers, 23-7 (Mil)
1979—Jets, 27-22 (GB)
1981—Jets, 28-3 (NY)
1982—Jets, 15-13 (NY)
1985—Jets, 24-3 (Mil)
1991—Jets, 19-16 (NY) OT
1994—Packers, 17-10 (GB)
2000—Jets, 20-16 (GB)
(RS Pts.—Jets 150, Packers 113)

GREEN BAY vs. *OAKLAND
RS: Raiders lead series, 5-3
PS: Packers lead series, 1-0
1967—**Packers, 33-14 (Miami)
1972—Raiders, 20-14 (GB)
1976—Raiders, 18-14 (O)
1978—Raiders, 28-3 (GB)
1984—Raiders, 28-7 (LA)

1987—Raiders, 20-0 (GB)
1990—Packers, 29-16 (LA)
1993—Packers, 28-0 (GB)
1999—Packers, 28-24 (GB)
(RS Pts.—Raiders 154, Packers 123)
(PS Pts.—Packers 33, Raiders 14)
*Franchise in Los Angeles from
1982-1994
**Super Bowl II

GREEN BAY vs. PHILADELPHIA
RS: Packers lead series, 22-9
PS: Eagles lead series, 1-0
1933—Packers, 35-9 (GB)
    Packers, 10-0 (GB)
1934—Packers, 19-6 (GB)
1935—Packers, 13-6 (P)
1937—Packers, 37-7 (Mil)
1939—Packers, 23-16 (P)
1940—Packers, 27-20 (GB)
1942—Packers, 7-0 (P)
1946—Packers, 19-7 (P)
1947—Eagles, 28-14 (P)
1951—Packers, 37-24 (GB)
1952—Packers, 12-10 (Mil)
1954—Packers, 37-14 (P)
1958—Packers, 38-35 (GB)
1960—*Eagles, 17-13 (P)
1962—Packers, 49-0 (P)
1968—Packers, 30-13 (GB)
1970—Packers, 30-17 (Mil)
1974—Eagles, 36-14 (P)
1976—Packers, 28-13 (GB)
1978—Eagles, 10-3 (P)
1979—Eagles, 21-10 (GB)
1987—Packers, 16-10 (GB) OT
1990—Eagles, 31-0 (P)
1991—Eagles, 20-3 (GB)
1992—Packers, 27-24 (Mil)
1993—Eagles, 20-17 (GB)
1994—Eagles, 13-7 (P)
1996—Packers, 39-13 (GB)
1997—Eagles, 10-9 (P)
1998—Packers, 24-16 (GB)
2000—Packers, 6-3 (GB)
(RS Pts.—Packers 640, Eagles 452)
(PS Pts.—Eagles 17, Packers 13)
*NFL Championship

GREEN BAY vs. *PITTSBURGH
RS: Packers lead series, 18-12
1933—Packers, 47-0 (GB)
1935—Packers, 27-0 (GB)
    Packers, 34-14 (P)
1936—Packers, 42-10 (Mil)
1938—Packers, 20-0 (GB)
1940—Packers, 24-3 (Mil)
1941—Packers, 54-7 (P)
1942—Packers, 24-21 (Mil)
1946—Packers, 17-7 (GB)
1947—Steelers, 18-17 (Mil)
1948—Steelers, 38-7 (P)
1949—Steelers, 30-7 (Mil)
1951—Packers, 35-33 (Mil)
    Steelers, 28-7 (P)
1953—Steelers, 31-14 (P)
1954—Steelers, 21-20 (GB)
1957—Packers, 27-10 (P)
1960—Packers, 19-13 (P)
1963—Packers, 33-14 (Mil)
1965—Packers, 41-9 (P)
1967—Steelers, 24-17 (GB)

1969—Packers, 38-34 (P)
1970—Packers, 20-12 (P)
1975—Steelers, 16-13 (Mil)
1980—Steelers, 22-20 (P)
1983—Steelers, 25-21 (GB)
1986—Steelers, 27-3 (P)
1992—Packers, 17-3 (GB)
1995—Packers, 24-19 (GB)
1998—Steelers, 27-20 (P)
(RS Pts.—Packers 709, Steelers 516)
*Steelers known as Pirates prior to 1941

GREEN BAY vs. *ST. LOUIS
RS: Rams lead series, 43-39-2
PS: Series tied, 1-1
1937—Packers, 35-10 (C)
    Packers, 35-7 (GB)
1938—Packers, 26-17 (GB)
    Packers, 28-7 (C)
1939—Rams, 27-24 (GB)
    Packers, 7-6 (C)
1940—Packers, 31-14 (GB)
    Tie, 13-13 (C)
1941—Packers, 24-7 (Mil)
    Packers, 17-14 (C)
1942—Packers, 45-28 (GB)
    Packers, 30-12 (C)
1944—Packers, 30-21 (GB)
    Packers, 42-7 (C)
1945—Rams, 27-14 (GB)
    Rams, 20-7 (C)
1946—Rams, 21-17 (Mil)
    Rams, 38-17 (LA)
1947—Packers, 17-14 (Mil)
    Packers, 30-10 (LA)
1948—Packers, 16-0 (Mil)
    Rams, 24-10 (LA)
1949—Rams, 48-7 (GB)
    Rams, 35-7 (LA)
1950—Rams, 45-14 (Mil)
    Rams, 51-14 (LA)
1951—Rams, 28-0 (Mil)
    Rams, 42-14 (LA)
1952—Rams, 30-28 (Mil)
    Rams, 45-27 (LA)
1953—Rams, 38-20 (Mil)
    Rams, 33-17 (LA)
1954—Packers, 35-17 (Mil)
    Rams, 35-27 (LA)
1955—Packers, 30-28 (Mil)
    Rams, 31-17 (LA)
1956—Packers, 42-17 (Mil)
    Rams, 49-21 (LA)
1957—Rams, 31-27 (Mil)
    Rams, 42-17 (LA)
1958—Rams, 20-7 (GB)
    Rams, 34-20 (LA)
1959—Rams, 45-6 (Mil)
    Packers, 38-20 (LA)
1960—Rams, 33-31 (Mil)
    Packers, 35-21 (LA)
1961—Packers, 35-17 (GB)
    Packers, 24-17 (LA)
1962—Packers, 41-10 (Mil)
    Packers, 20-17 (LA)
1963—Packers, 42-10 (GB)
    Packers, 31-14 (LA)
1964—Rams, 27-17 (Mil)
    Tie, 24-24 (LA)
1965—Packers, 6-3 (Mil)
    Rams, 21-10 (LA)

1966—Packers, 24-13 (GB)
  Packers, 27-23 (LA)
1967—Rams, 27-24 (LA)
  **Packers, 28-7 (Mil)
1968—Rams, 16-14 (Mil)
1969—Rams, 34-21 (LA)
1970—Rams, 31-21 (GB)
1971—Rams, 30-13 (LA)
1973—Rams, 24-7 (LA)
1974—Packers, 17-6 (Mil)
1975—Rams, 22-5 (LA)
1977—Rams, 24-6 (Mil)
1978—Rams, 31-14 (LA)
1980—Rams, 51-21 (LA)
1981—Rams, 35-23 (LA)
1982—Packers, 35-23 (Mil)
1983—Packers, 27-24 (Mil)
1984—Packers, 31-6 (Mil)
1985—Rams, 34-17 (LA)
1988—Rams, 34-7 (GB)
1989—Rams, 41-38 (LA)
1990—Packers, 36-24 (GB)
1991—Rams, 23-21 (LA)
1992—Packers, 28-13 (GB)
1993—Packers, 36-6 (Mil)
1994—Packers, 24-17 (GB)
1995—Packers, 17-14 (GB)
1996—Packers, 24-9 (StL)
1997—Packers, 17-7 (GB)
2001—***Rams, 45-17 (StL)
(RS Pts.—Rams 1,967, Packers 1,858)
(PS Pts.—Rams 52, Packers 45)
*Franchise in Los Angeles prior to 1995
and in Cleveland prior to 1946
**Conference Championship
***NFC Divisional Playoff
GREEN BAY vs. SAN DIEGO
RS: Packers lead series, 6-1
1970—Packers, 22-20 (SD)
1974—Packers, 34-0 (SD)
1978—Packers, 24-3 (SD)
1984—Chargers, 34-28 (GB)
1993—Packers, 20-13 (SD)
1996—Packers, 42-10 (GB)
1999—Packers, 31-3 (SD)
(RS Pts.—Packers 201, Chargers 83)
GREEN BAY vs. SAN FRANCISCO
RS: Series tied, 25-25-1
PS: Packers lead series, 4-1
1950—Packers, 25-21 (GB)
  49ers, 30-14 (SF)
1951—49ers, 31-19 (SF)
1952—49ers, 24-14 (SF)
1953—49ers, 37-7 (Mil)
  49ers, 48-14 (SF)
1954—49ers, 23-17 (Mil)
  49ers, 35-0 (SF)
1955—Packers, 27-21 (Mil)
  Packers, 28-7 (SF)
1956—49ers, 17-16 (GB)
  49ers, 38-20 (SF)
1957—49ers, 24-14 (Mil)
  49ers, 27-20 (SF)
1958—49ers, 33-12 (Mil)
  49ers, 48-21 (SF)
1959—Packers, 21-20 (GB)
  Packers, 36-14 (SF)
1960—Packers, 41-14 (Mil)
  Packers, 13-0 (SF)
1961—Packers, 30-10 (GB)

49ers, 22-21 (SF)
1962—Packers, 31-13 (Mil)
  Packers, 31-21 (SF)
1963—Packers, 28-10 (Mil)
  Packers, 21-17 (SF)
1964—Packers, 24-14 (Mil)
  49ers, 24-14 (SF)
1965—Packers, 27-10 (GB)
  Tie, 24-24 (SF)
1966—49ers, 21-20 (SF)
  Packers, 20-7 (Mil)
1967—Packers, 13-0 (GB)
1968—49ers, 27-20 (SF)
1969—Packers, 14-7 (Mil)
1970—49ers, 26-10 (SF)
1972—Packers, 34-24 (Mil)
1973—49ers, 20-6 (SF)
1974—49ers, 7-6 (SF)
1976—49ers, 26-14 (GB)
1977—Packers, 16-14 (Mil)
1980—Packers, 23-16 (Mil)
1981—49ers, 13-3 (Mil)
1986—49ers, 31-17 (Mil)
1987—49ers, 23-12 (GB)
1989—Packers, 21-17 (SF)
1990—49ers, 24-20 (GB)
1995—*Packers, 27-17 (SF)
1996—Packers, 23-20 (GB) OT
  *Packers, 35-14 (GB)
1997—**Packers, 23-10 (SF)
1998—Packers, 36-22 (GB)
  ***49ers, 30-27 (SF)
1999—Packers, 20-3 (SF)
2000—Packers, 31-28 (GB)
2001—***Packers, 25-15 (GB)
(RS Pts.—49ers 1,053, Packers 1,009)
(PS Pts.—Packers 137, 49ers 86)
*NFC Divisional Playoff
**NFC Championship
***NFC First-Round Playoff
GREEN BAY vs. SEATTLE
RS: Series tied, 4-4
1976—Packers, 27-20 (Mil)
1978—Packers, 45-28 (Mil)
1981—Packers, 34-24 (GB)
1984—Seahawks, 30-24 (Mil)
1987—Seahawks, 24-13 (S)
1990—Seahawks, 20-14 (Mil)
1996—Packers, 31-10 (S)
1999—Seahawks, 27-7 (GB)
(RS Pts.—Packers 195, Seahawks 183)
GREEN BAY vs. TAMPA BAY
RS: Packers lead series, 28-17-1
PS: Packers lead series, 1-0
1977—Packers, 13-0 (TB)
1978—Packers, 9-7 (GB)
  Packers, 17-7 (TB)
1979—Buccaneers, 21-10 (GB)
  Buccaneers, 21-3 (TB)
1980—Tie, 14-14 (TB) OT
  Buccaneers, 20-17 (Mil)
1981—Buccaneers, 21-10 (GB)
  Buccaneers, 37-3 (TB)
1983—Packers, 55-14 (GB)
  Packers, 12-9 (TB) OT
1984—Buccaneers, 30-27 (TB) OT
  Packers, 27-14 (GB)
1985—Packers, 21-0 (GB)
  Packers, 20-17 (TB)
1986—Packers, 31-7 (Mil)

  Packers, 21-7 (TB)
1987—Buccaneers, 23-17 (Mil)
1988—Buccaneers, 13-10 (GB)
  Buccaneers, 27-24 (TB)
1989—Buccaneers, 23-21 (GB)
  Packers, 17-16 (TB)
1990—Buccaneers, 26-14 (TB)
  Packers, 20-10 (Mil)
1991—Packers, 15-13 (GB)
  Packers, 27-0 (TB)
1992—Buccaneers, 31-3 (TB)
  Packers, 19-14 (Mil)
1993—Packers, 37-14 (TB)
  Packers, 13-10 (GB)
1994—Packers, 30-3 (GB)
  Packers, 34-19 (TB)
1995—Packers, 35-13 (GB)
  Buccaneers, 13-10 (TB) OT
1996—Packers, 34-3 (TB)
  Packers, 13-7 (GB)
1997—Packers, 21-16 (GB)
  Packers, 17-6 (TB)
  *Packers, 21-7 (GB)
1998—Packers, 23-15 (GB)
  Buccaneers, 24-22 (TB)
1999—Packers, 26-23 (GB)
  Buccaneers, 29-10 (TB)
2000—Buccaneers, 20-15 (TB)
  Packers, 17-14 (GB) OT
2001—Buccaneers, 14-10 (TB)
  Packers, 21-20 (GB)
(RS Pts.—Packers 885, Buccaneers 705)
(PS Pts.—Packers 21, Buccaneers 7)
*NFC Divisional Playoff
GREEN BAY vs. *TENNESSEE
RS: Series tied, 4-4
1972—Packers, 23-10 (H)
1977—Oilers, 16-10 (GB)
1980—Oilers, 22-3 (GB)
1983—Packers, 41-38 (H) OT
1986—Oilers, 31-3 (GB)
1992—Packers, 16-14 (H)
1998—Packers, 30-22 (GB)
2001—Titans, 26-20 (T)
(RS Pts.—Titans 179, Packers 146)
*Franchise in Houston prior to 1997;
known as Oilers prior to 1999
GREEN BAY vs. *WASHINGTON
RS: Packers lead series, 14-12-1
PS: Series tied, 1-1
1932—Packers, 21-0 (B)
1933—Tie, 7-7 (GB)
  Redskins, 20-7 (B)
1934—Packers, 10-0 (B)
1936—Packers, 31-2 (GB)
  Packers, 7-3 (B)
  **Packers, 21-6 (New York)
1937—Redskins, 14-6 (W)
1939—Packers, 24-14 (Mil)
1941—Packers, 22-17 (W)
1943—Redskins, 33-7 (Mil)
1946—Packers, 20-7 (W)
1947—Packers, 27-10 (Mil)
1948—Packers, 23-7 (Mil)
1949—Redskins, 30-0 (W)
1950—Packers, 35-21 (GB)
1952—Packers, 35-20 (Mil)
1958—Redskins, 37-21 (W)
1959—Packers, 21-0 (GB)
1968—Packers, 27-7 (W)

1972—Redskins, 21-16 (W)
***Redskins, 16-3 (W)
1974—Redskins, 17-6 (GB)
1977—Redskins, 10-9 (W)
1979—Redskins, 38-21 (W)
1983—Packers, 48-47 (GB)
1986—Redskins, 16-7 (GB)
1988—Redskins, 20-17 (Mil)
2001—Packers, 37-0 (GB)
(RS Pts.—Packers 496, Redskins 434)
(PS Pts.—Packers 24, Redskins 22)
*Franchise in Boston prior to 1937 and
known as Braves prior to 1933
**NFL Championship
***NFC Divisional Playoff

INDIANAPOLIS vs. ARIZONA
RS: Series tied, 6-6;
See Arizona vs. Indianapolis
INDIANAPOLIS vs. ATLANTA
RS: Colts lead series, 11-1;
See Atlanta vs. Indianapolis
INDIANAPOLIS vs. BALTIMORE
RS: Ravens lead series, 2-1;
See Baltimore vs. Indianapolis
INDIANAPOLIS vs. BUFFALO
RS: Bills lead series, 34-28-1;
See Buffalo vs. Indianapolis
INDIANAPOLIS vs. CAROLINA
RS: Panthers lead series, 2-0;
See Carolina vs. Indianapolis
INDIANAPOLIS vs. CHICAGO
RS: Colts lead series, 21-17;
See Chicago vs. Indianapolis
INDIANAPOLIS vs. CINCINNATI
RS: Colts lead series, 11-8
PS: Colts lead series, 1-0;
See Cincinnati vs. Indianapolis
INDIANAPOLIS vs. CLEVELAND
RS: Browns lead series, 13-8
PS: Series tied, 2-2;
See Cleveland vs. Indianapolis
INDIANAPOLIS vs. DALLAS
RS: Cowboys lead series, 7-4
PS: Colts lead series, 1-0;
See Dallas vs. Indianapolis
INDIANAPOLIS vs. DENVER
RS: Broncos lead series, 9-3;
See Denver vs. Indianapolis
INDIANAPOLIS vs. DETROIT
RS: Series tied, 18-18-2;
See Detroit vs. Indianapolis
INDIANAPOLIS vs. GREEN BAY
RS: Series tied, 19-19-1
PS: Packers lead series, 1-0;
See Green Bay vs. Indianapolis
INDIANAPOLIS vs. JACKSONVILLE
RS: Colts lead series, 2-0
1995—Colts, 41-31 (J)
2000—Colts, 43-14 (I)
(RS Pts.—Colts 84, Jaguars 45)
***INDIANAPOLIS vs. KANSAS CITY**
RS: Colts lead series, 8-6
PS: Colts lead series, 1-0
1970—Chiefs, 44-24 (B)
1972—Chiefs, 24-10 (KC)
1975—Colts, 28-14 (B)
1977—Colts, 17-6 (KC)
1979—Chiefs, 14-0 (KC)
Chiefs, 10-7 (B)

1980—Colts, 31-24 (KC)
Chiefs, 38-28 (B)
1985—Chiefs, 20-7 (KC)
1990—Colts, 23-19 (I)
1995—**Colts, 10-7 (KC)
1996—Colts, 24-19 (KC)
1999—Colts, 25-17 (I)
2000—Colts, 27-14 (KC)
2001—Colts, 35-28 (KC)
(RS Pts.—Chiefs 291, Colts 286)
(PS Pts.—Colts 10, Chiefs 7)
*Franchise in Baltimore prior to 1984
**AFC Divisional Playoff
INDIANAPOLIS vs. MIAMI
RS: Dolphins lead series, 43-21
PS: Dolphins lead series, 2-0
1970—Colts, 35-0 (B)
Dolphins, 34-17 (M)
1971—Dolphins, 17-14 (M)
Colts, 14-3 (B)
**Dolphins, 21-0 (M)
1972—Dolphins, 23-0 (B)
Dolphins, 16-0 (M)
1973—Dolphins, 44-0 (M)
Colts, 16-3 (B)
1974—Dolphins, 17-7 (M)
Dolphins, 17-16 (B)
1975—Colts, 33-17 (M)
Colts, 10-7 (B) OT
1976—Colts, 28-14 (B)
Colts, 17-16 (M)
1977—Colts, 45-28 (B)
Dolphins, 17-6 (M)
1978—Dolphins, 42-0 (B)
Dolphins, 26-8 (M)
1979—Dolphins, 19-0 (M)
Dolphins, 28-24 (B)
1980—Colts, 30-17 (M)
Dolphins, 24-14 (B)
1981—Dolphins, 31-28 (B)
Dolphins, 27-10 (M)
1982—Dolphins, 24-20 (M)
Dolphins, 34-7 (B)
1983—Dolphins, 21-7 (B)
Dolphins, 37-0 (M)
1984—Dolphins, 44-7 (M)
Dolphins, 35-17 (I)
1985—Dolphins, 30-13 (M)
Dolphins, 34-20 (I)
1986—Dolphins, 30-10 (M)
Dolphins, 17-13 (I)
1987—Dolphins, 23-10 (I)
Colts, 40-21 (M)
1988—Colts, 15-13 (I)
Colts, 31-28 (M)
1989—Dolphins, 19-13 (M)
Colts, 42-13 (I)
1990—Dolphins, 27-7 (I)
Dolphins, 23-17 (M)
1991—Dolphins, 17-6 (M)
Dolphins, 10-6 (I)
1992—Colts, 31-20 (M)
Dolphins, 28-0 (I)
1993—Dolphins, 24-20 (I)
Dolphins, 41-27 (M)
1994—Dolphins, 22-21 (M)
Colts, 10-6 (I)
1995—Colts, 27-24 (M) OT
Colts, 36-28 (I)
1996—Colts, 10-6 (I)

Dolphins, 37-13 (M)
1997—Dolphins, 16-10 (M)
Colts, 41-0 (I)
1998—Dolphins, 24-15 (I)
Dolphins, 27-14 (M)
1999—Dolphins, 34-31 (I)
Colts, 37-34 (M)
2000—Dolphins, 17-14 (I)
Colts, 20-13 (M)
***Dolphins 23-17 (M) OT
2001—Dolphins, 27-24 (I)
Dolphins, 41-6 (M)
(RS Pts.—Dolphins 1,456, Colts 1,080)
(PS Pts.—Dolphins 44, Colts 17)
*Franchise in Baltimore prior to 1984
**AFC Championship
***AFC First-Round Playoff
INDIANAPOLIS vs. MINNESOTA
RS: Colts lead series, 12-7-1
PS: Colts lead series, 1-0
1961—Colts, 34-33 (B)
Vikings, 28-20 (M)
1962—Colts, 34-7 (M)
Colts, 42-17 (B)
1963—Colts, 37-34 (M)
Colts, 41-10 (B)
1964—Vikings, 34-24 (M)
Colts, 17-14 (B)
1965—Colts, 35-16 (B)
Colts, 41-21 (M)
1966—Colts, 38-23 (M)
Colts, 20-17 (B)
1967—Tie, 20-20 (M)
1968—Colts, 21-9 (B)
**Colts, 24-14 (B)
1969—Vikings, 52-14 (M)
1971—Vikings, 10-3 (M)
1982—Vikings, 13-10 (M)
1988—Vikings, 12-3 (M)
1997—Vikings, 39-28 (M)
2000—Colts, 31-10 (I)
(RS Pts.—Colts 513, Vikings 419)
(PS Pts.—Colts 24, Vikings 14)
*Franchise in Baltimore prior to 1984
**Conference Championship
INDIANAPOLIS vs. **NEW ENGLAND
RS: Patriots lead series, 39-24
1970—Colts, 14-6 (Bos)
Colts, 27-3 (Balt)
1971—Colts, 23-3 (NE)
Patriots, 21-17 (Balt)
1972—Colts, 24-17 (NE)
Colts, 31-0 (Balt)
1973—Patriots, 24-16 (NE)
Colts, 18-13 (Balt)
1974—Patriots, 42-3 (NE)
Patriots, 27-17 (Balt)
1975—Patriots, 21-10 (NE)
Colts, 34-21 (Balt)
1976—Colts, 27-13 (NE)
Patriots, 21-14 (Balt)
1977—Patriots, 17-3 (NE)
Colts, 30-24 (Balt)
1978—Colts, 34-27 (NE)
Patriots, 35-14 (Balt)
1979—Colts, 31-26 (Balt)
Patriots, 50-21 (NE)
1980—Patriots, 37-21 (Balt)
Patriots, 47-21 (NE)
1981—Colts, 29-28 (NE)

Colts, 23-21 (Balt)
1982—Patriots, 24-13 (Balt)
1983—Colts, 29-23 (NE) OT
Colts, 12-7 (Balt)
1984—Patriots, 50-17 (I)
Patriots, 16-10 (NE)
1985—Patriots, 34-15 (NE)
Patriots, 38-31 (I)
1986—Patriots, 33-3 (NE)
Patriots, 30-21 (I)
1987—Colts, 30-16 (I)
Patriots, 24-0 (NE)
1988—Patriots, 21-17 (NE)
Colts, 24-21 (I)
1989—Patriots, 23-20 (I) OT
Patriots, 22-16 (NE)
1990—Patriots, 16-14 (I)
Colts, 13-10 (NE)
1991—Patriots, 16-7 (I)
Patriots, 23-17 (NE) OT
1992—Patriots, 37-34 (I) OT
Colts, 6-0 (NE)
1993—Colts, 9-6 (I)
Patriots, 38-0 (NE)
1994—Patriots, 12-10 (I)
Patriots, 28-13 (NE)
1995—Colts, 24-10 (NE)
Colts, 10-7 (I)
1996—Patriots, 27-9 (I)
Patriots, 27-13 (NE)
1997—Patriots, 31-6 (I)
Patriots, 20-17 (NE)
1998—Patriots, 29-6 (NE)
Patriots, 21-16 (I)
1999—Patriots, 31-28 (NE)
Colts, 20-15 (I)
2000—Patriots, 24-16 (NE)
Colts, 30-23 (I)
2001—Patriots, 44-13 (NE)
Patriots, 38-17 (I)
(RS Pts.—Patriots 1,459, Colts 1,108)
*Franchise in Baltimore prior to 1984
**Franchise in Boston prior to 1971
INDIANAPOLIS vs. NEW ORLEANS
RS: Saints lead series, 5-3
1967—Colts, 30-10 (B)
1969—Colts, 30-10 (NO)
1973—Colts, 14-10 (B)
1986—Saints, 17-14 (I)
1989—Saints, 41-6 (NO)
1995—Saints, 17-14 (NO)
1998—Saints, 19-13 (I) OT
2001—Saints, 34-20 (NO)
(RS Pts.—Saints 158, Colts 141)
*Franchise in Baltimore prior to 1984
INDIANAPOLIS vs. N.Y. GIANTS
RS: Colts lead series, 6-5
PS: Colts lead series, 2-0
1954—Colts, 20-14 (B)
1955—Giants, 17-7 (NY)
1958—Giants, 24-21 (NY)
**Colts, 23-17 (NY) OT
1959—**Colts, 31-16 (B)
1963—Giants, 37-28 (B)
1968—Colts, 26-0 (NY)
1971—Colts, 31-7 (NY)
1975—Colts, 21-0 (NY)
1979—Colts, 31-7 (NY)
1990—Giants, 24-7 (I)
1993—Giants, 20-6 (NY)

1999—Colts, 27-19 (NY)
(RS Pts.—Colts 225, Giants 169)
(PS Pts.—Colts 54, Giants 33)
*Franchise in Baltimore prior to 1984
**NFL Championship
INDIANAPOLIS vs. N.Y. JETS
RS: Colts lead series, 38-25
PS: Jets lead series, 1-0
1968—**Jets 16-7 (Miami)
1970—Colts, 29-22 (NY)
Colts, 35-20 (B)
1971—Colts, 22-0 (B)
Colts, 14-13 (NY)
1972—Jets, 44-34 (B)
Jets, 24-20 (NY)
1973—Jets, 34-10 (B)
Jets, 20-17 (NY)
1974—Colts, 35-20 (NY)
Jets, 45-38 (B)
1975—Colts, 45-28 (NY)
Colts, 52-19 (B)
1976—Colts, 20-0 (NY)
Colts, 33-16 (B)
1977—Colts, 20-12 (NY)
Colts, 33-12 (B)
1978—Jets, 33-10 (B)
Jets, 24-16 (NY)
1979—Colts, 10-8 (B)
Jets, 30-17 (NY)
1980—Colts, 17-14 (NY)
Colts, 35-21 (B)
1981—Jets, 41-14 (B)
Jets, 25-0 (NY)
1982—Jets, 37-0 (NY)
1983—Colts, 17-14 (NY)
Jets, 10-6 (B)
1984—Jets, 23-14 (I)
Colts, 9-5 (NY)
1985—Jets, 25-20 (NY)
Jets, 35-17 (I)
1986—Jets, 26-7 (I)
Jets, 31-16 (NY)
1987—Colts, 6-0 (I)
Colts, 19-14 (NY)
1988—Colts, 38-14 (I)
Jets, 34-16 (NY)
1989—Colts, 17-10 (NY)
Colts, 27-10 (I)
1990—Colts, 17-14 (I)
Colts, 29-21 (NY)
1991—Jets, 17-6 (I)
Colts, 28-27 (NY)
1992—Colts, 6-3 (I) OT
Colts, 10-6 (NY)
1993—Jets, 31-17 (I)
Colts, 9-6 (NY)
1994—Jets, 16-6 (NY)
Colts, 28-25 (I)
1995—Colts, 27-24 (NY) OT
Colts, 17-10 (I)
1996—Colts, 21-7 (NY)
Colts, 34-29 (I)
1997—Jets, 16-12 (I)
Colts, 22-14 (NY)
1998—Jets, 44-6 (NY)
Colts, 24-23 (I)
1999—Colts, 16-13 (NY)
Colts, 13-6 (I)
2000—Colts, 23-15 (I)
Jets, 27-17 (NY)

2001—Colts, 45-24 (NY)
Jets, 29-28 (I)
(RS Pts.—Colts 1,266, Jets 1,260)
(PS Pts.—Jets 16, Colts 7)
*Franchise in Baltimore prior to 1984
**Super Bowl III
INDIANAPOLIS vs **OAKLAND
RS: Raiders lead series, 7-2
PS: Series tied, 1-1
1970—***Colts, 27-17 (B)
1971—Colts, 37-14 (O)
1973—Raiders, 34-21 (B)
1975—Raiders, 31-20 (B)
1977—****Raiders, 37-31 (B) OT
1984—Raiders, 21-7 (LA)
1986—Colts, 30-24 (LA)
1991—Raiders, 16-0 (LA)
1995—Raiders, 30-17 (O)
2000—Raiders, 38-31 (I)
2001—Raiders, 23-18 (I)
(RS Pts.—Raiders 231, Colts 181)
(PS Pts.—Colts 58, Raiders 54)
*Franchise in Baltimore prior to 1984
**Franchise in Los Angeles from
1982-1994
***AFC Championship
****AFC Divisional Playoff
INDIANAPOLIS vs. PHILADELPHIA
RS: Colts lead series, 8-6
1953—Eagles, 45-14 (P)
1965—Colts, 34-24 (B)
1967—Colts, 38-6 (P)
1969—Colts, 24-20 (B)
1970—Colts, 29-10 (B)
1974—Eagles, 30-10 (P)
1978—Eagles, 17-14 (B)
1981—Eagles, 38-13 (P)
1983—Colts, 22-21 (P)
1984—Eagles, 16-7 (P)
1990—Colts, 24-23 (P)
1993—Eagles, 20-10 (I)
1996—Colts, 37-10 (I)
1999—Colts, 44-17 (P)
(RS Pts.—Colts 320, Eagles 297)
*Franchise in Baltimore prior to 1984
INDIANAPOLIS vs. PITTSBURGH
RS: Steelers lead series, 12-4
PS: Steelers lead series, 4-0
1957—Steelers, 19-13 (B)
1968—Colts, 41-7 (P)
1971—Colts, 34-21 (B)
1974—Steelers, 30-0 (P)
1975—**Steelers, 28-10 (P)
1976—**Steelers, 40-14 (B)
1977—Colts, 31-21 (B)
1978—Steelers, 35-13 (P)
1979—Steelers, 17-13 (P)
1980—Steelers, 20-17 (B)
1983—Steelers, 24-13 (B)
1984—Colts, 17-16 (I)
1985—Steelers, 45-3 (P)
1987—Steelers, 21-7 (P)
1991—Steelers, 21-3 (I)
1992—Steelers, 30-14 (P)
1994—Steelers, 31-21 (P)
1995—***Steelers, 20-16 (P)
1996—****Steelers, 42-14 (P)
1997—Steelers, 24-22 (P)
(RS Pts.—Steelers 382, Colts 262)
(PS Pts.—Steelers 130, Colts 54)

ALL-TIME TEAM VS. TEAM RESULTS

*Franchise in Baltimore prior to 1984
**AFC Divisional Playoff
***AFC Championship
****AFC First-Round Playoff

*INDIANAPOLIS vs. **ST. LOUIS
RS: Colts lead series, 21-17-2
1953—Rams, 21-13 (B)
　　　Rams, 45-2 (LA)
1954—Rams, 48-0 (B)
　　　Colts, 22-21 (LA)
1955—Tie, 17-17 (B)
　　　Rams, 20-14 (LA)
1956—Colts, 56-21 (B)
　　　Rams, 31-7 (LA)
1957—Colts, 31-14 (B)
　　　Rams, 37-21 (LA)
1958—Colts, 34-7 (B)
　　　Rams, 30-28 (LA)
1959—Colts, 35-21 (B)
　　　Colts, 45-26 (LA)
1960—Colts, 31-17 (B)
　　　Rams, 10-3 (LA)
1961—Colts, 27-24 (B)
　　　Rams, 34-17 (LA)
1962—Colts, 30-27 (B)
　　　Colts, 14-2 (LA)
1963—Rams, 17-16 (LA)
　　　Colts, 19-16 (B)
1964—Colts, 35-20 (B)
　　　Colts, 24-7 (LA)
1965—Colts, 35-20 (B)
　　　Colts, 20-17 (LA)
1966—Colts, 17-3 (LA)
　　　Rams, 23-7 (B)
1967—Tie, 24-24 (B)
　　　Rams, 34-10 (LA)
1968—Colts, 27-10 (B)
　　　Colts, 28-24 (LA)
1969—Rams, 27-20 (B)
　　　Colts, 13-7 (LA)
1971—Colts, 24-17 (B)
1975—Rams, 24-13 (LA)
1986—Rams, 24-7 (I)
1989—Rams, 31-17 (LA)
1995—Colts, 21-18 (I)
2001—Rams, 42-17 (StL)
(RS Pts.—Rams 878, Colts 841)
*Franchise in Baltimore prior to 1984
**Franchise in Los Angeles prior to 1995

*INDIANAPOLIS vs. SAN DIEGO
RS: Chargers lead series, 12-7
PS: Colts lead series, 1-0
1970—Colts, 16-14 (SD)
1972—Chargers, 23-20 (B)
1976—Colts, 37-21 (SD)
1981—Chargers, 43-14 (B)
1982—Chargers, 44-26 (SD)
1984—Chargers, 38-10 (I)
1986—Chargers, 17-3 (I)
1987—Chargers, 16-13 (I)
　　　Colts, 20-7 (SD)
1988—Colts, 16-0 (SD)
1989—Colts, 10-6 (I)
1992—Chargers, 34-14 (I)
　　　Chargers, 26-0 (SD)
1993—Chargers, 31-0 (I)
1995—Colts, 27-24 (I)
　　　**Colts, 35-20 (SD)
1996—Chargers, 26-19 (I)
1997—Chargers, 35-19 (SD)

1998—Colts, 17-12 (I)
1999—Colts, 27-19 (SD)
(RS Pts.—Chargers 439, Colts 305)
(PS Pts.—Colts 35, Chargers 20)
*Franchise in Baltimore prior to 1984
**AFC First-Round Playoff

*INDIANAPOLIS vs. SAN FRANCISCO
RS: Colts lead series, 22-18
1953—49ers, 38-21 (B)
　　　49ers, 45-14 (SF)
1954—Colts, 17-13 (B)
　　　49ers, 10-7 (SF)
1955—Colts, 26-14 (B)
　　　49ers, 35-24 (SF)
1956—49ers, 20-17 (B)
　　　49ers, 30-17 (SF)
1957—Colts, 27-21 (B)
　　　49ers, 17-13 (SF)
1958—Colts, 35-27 (B)
　　　49ers, 21-12 (SF)
1959—Colts, 45-14 (B)
　　　Colts, 34-14 (SF)
1960—49ers, 30-22 (B)
　　　49ers, 34-10 (SF)
1961—Colts, 20-17 (B)
　　　Colts, 27-24 (SF)
1962—49ers, 21-13 (B)
　　　Colts, 22-3 (SF)
1963—Colts, 20-14 (SF)
　　　Colts, 20-3 (B)
1964—Colts, 37-7 (B)
　　　Colts, 14-3 (SF)
1965—Colts, 27-24 (B)
　　　Colts, 34-28 (SF)
1966—Colts, 36-14 (B)
　　　Colts, 30-14 (SF)
1967—Colts, 41-7 (B)
　　　Colts, 26-9 (SF)
1968—Colts, 27-10 (B)
　　　Colts, 42-14 (SF)
1969—49ers, 24-21 (B)
　　　49ers, 20-17 (SF)
1972—49ers, 24-21 (B)
1986—49ers, 35-14 (SF)
1989—49ers, 30-24 (I)
1995—Colts, 18-17 (I)
1998—49ers, 34-31 (SF)
2001—49ers, 40-21 (I)
(RS Pts.—Colts 944, 49ers 819)
*Franchise in Baltimore prior to 1984

*INDIANAPOLIS vs. SEATTLE
RS: Colts lead series, 5-3
1977—Colts, 29-14 (S)
1978—Colts, 17-14 (S)
1991—Seahawks, 31-3 (S)
1994—Colts, 17-15 (I)
　　　Colts, 31-19 (S)
1997—Seahawks, 31-3 (I)
1998—Seahawks, 27-23 (S)
2000—Colts, 37-24 (S)
(RS Pts.—Seahawks 175, Colts 160)
*Franchise in Baltimore prior to 1984

*INDIANAPOLIS vs. TAMPA BAY
RS: Colts lead series, 5-4
1976—Colts, 42-17 (B)
1979—Buccaneers, 29-26 (B) OT
1985—Colts, 31-23 (TB)
1987—Colts, 24-6 (I)
1988—Colts, 35-31 (I)
1991—Buccaneers, 17-3 (TB)

1992—Colts, 24-14 (TB)
1994—Buccaneers, 24-10 (TB)
1997—Buccaneers, 31-28 (I)
(RS Pts.—Colts 223, Buccaneers 192)
*Franchise in Baltimore prior to 1984

*INDIANAPOLIS vs. **TENNESSEE
RS: Series tied, 7-7
PS: Titans lead series, 1-0
1970—Colts, 24-20 (H)
1973—Oilers, 31-27 (B)
1976—Colts, 38-14 (B)
1979—Oilers, 28-16 (B)
1980—Oilers, 21-16 (H)
1983—Colts, 20-10 (B)
1984—Colts, 35-21 (H)
1985—Colts, 34-16 (I)
1986—Oilers, 31-17 (H)
1987—Colts, 51-27 (I)
1988—Oilers, 17-14 (I) OT
1990—Oilers, 24-10 (H)
1992—Oilers, 20-10 (I)
1994—Colts, 45-21 (I)
1999—***Titans, 19-16 (I)
(RS Pts.—Colts 357, Titans 301)
(PS Pts.—Titans 19, Colts 16)
*Franchise in Baltimore prior to 1984
**Franchise in Houston prior to 1997;
known as Oilers prior to 1999
***AFC Divisional Playoff

*INDIANAPOLIS vs. WASHINGTON
RS: Colts lead series, 17-9
1953—Colts, 27-17 (B)
1954—Redskins, 24-21 (W)
1955—Redskins, 14-13 (B)
1956—Colts, 19-17 (B)
1957—Colts, 21-17 (W)
1958—Colts, 35-10 (B)
1959—Redskins, 27-24 (W)
1960—Colts, 20-0 (B)
1961—Colts, 27-6 (W)
1962—Colts, 34-21 (B)
1963—Colts, 36-20 (W)
1964—Colts, 45-17 (B)
1965—Colts, 38-7 (W)
1966—Colts, 37-10 (B)
1967—Colts, 17-13 (W)
1969—Colts, 41-17 (B)
1973—Redskins, 22-14 (W)
1977—Colts, 10-3 (B)
1978—Colts, 21-17 (B)
1981—Redskins, 38-14 (W)
1984—Redskins, 35-7 (I)
1990—Colts, 35-28 (I)
1993—Redskins, 30-24 (W)
1994—Redskins, 41-27 (I)
1996—Redskins, 31-16 (W)
1999—Colts, 24-21 (I)
(RS Pts.—Colts 647, Redskins 503)
*Franchise in Baltimore prior to 1984

JACKSONVILLE vs. ARIZONA
RS: Jaguars lead series, 1-0;
See Arizona vs. Jacksonville
JACKSONVILLE vs. ATLANTA
RS: Jaguars lead series, 2-0;
See Atlanta vs. Jacksonville
JACKSONVILLE vs. BALTIMORE
RS: Jaguars lead series, 8-4;
See Baltimore vs. Jacksonville

JACKSONVILLE vs. BUFFALO
RS: Bills lead series, 2-1
PS: Jaguars lead series, 1-0;
See Buffalo vs. Jacksonville
JACKSONVILLE vs. CAROLINA
RS: Jaguars lead series, 2-0;
See Carolina vs. Jacksonville
JACKSONVILLE vs. CHICAGO
RS: Bears lead series, 2-1;
See Chicago vs. Jacksonville
JACKSONVILLE vs. CINCINNATI
RS: Jaguars lead series, 9-5;
See Cincinnati vs. Jacksonville
JACKSONVILLE vs. CLEVELAND
RS: Jaguars lead series, 7-1;
See Cleveland vs. Jacksonville
JACKSONVILLE vs. DALLAS
RS: Series tied, 1-1;
See Dallas vs. Jacksonville
JACKSONVILLE vs. DENVER
RS: Broncos lead series, 2-1
PS: Series tied, 1-1;
See Denver vs. Jacksonville
JACKSONVILLE vs. DETROIT
RS: Series tied, 1-1;
See Detroit vs. Jacksonville
JACKSONVILLE vs. GREEN BAY
RS: Packers lead series, 2-0;
See Green Bay vs. Jacksonville
JACKSONVILLE vs. INDIANAPOLIS
RS: Colts lead series, 2-0;
See Indianapolis vs. Jacksonville
JACKSONVILLE vs. KANSAS CITY
RS: Jaguars lead series, 2-1
1997—Jaguars, 24-10 (J)
1998—Jaguars, 21-16 (J)
2001—Chiefs, 30-26 (J)
(RS Pts.—Jaguars 71, Chiefs 56)
JACKSONVILLE vs. MIAMI
RS: Jaguars lead series, 1-0
PS: Jaguars lead series, 1-0
1998—Jaguars, 28-21 (J)
1999—*Jaguars, 62-7 (J)
(RS Pts.—Jaguars 28, Dolphins 21)
(PS Pts.—Jaguars 62, Dolphins 7)
*AFC Divisional Playoff
JACKSONVILLE vs. MINNESOTA
RS: Series tied, 1-1
1998—Vikings, 50-10 (M)
2001—Jaguars, 33-3 (M)
(RS Pts.—Vikings 53, Jaguars 43)
JACKSONVILLE vs. NEW ENGLAND
RS: Patriots lead series, 2-0
PS: Series tied, 1-1
1996—Patriots, 28-25 (NE) OT
    *Patriots, 20-6 (NE)
1997—Patriots, 26-20 (J)
1998—**Jaguars, 25-10 (J)
(RS Pts.—Patriots 54, Jaguars 45)
(PS Pts.—Jaguars 31, Patriots 30)
*AFC Championship
**AFC First-Round Playoff
JACKSONVILLE vs. NEW ORLEANS
RS: Series tied, 1-1
1996—Saints, 17-13 (NO)
1999—Jaguars, 41-23 (J)
(RS Pts.—Jaguars 54, Saints 40)
JACKSONVILLE vs. N.Y. GIANTS
RS: Series tied, 1-1
1997—Jaguars, 40-13 (J)

2000—Giants, 28-25 (NY)
(RS Pts.—Jaguars 65, Giants 41)
JACKSONVILLE vs. N.Y. JETS
RS: Jaguars lead series, 2-1
PS: Jets lead series, 1-0
1995—Jets, 27-10 (NY)
1996—Jaguars, 21-17 (J)
1998—*Jets, 34-24 (NY)
1999—Jaguars, 16-6 (NY)
(RS Pts.—Jets 50, Jaguars 47)
(PS Pts.—Jets 34, Jaguars 24
*AFC Divisional Playoff
JACKSONVILLE vs. OAKLAND
RS: Series tied, 1-1
1996—Raiders, 17-3 (O)
1997—Jaguars, 20-9 (O)
(RS Pts.—Raiders 26, Jaguars 23)
JACKSONVILLE vs. PHILADELPHIA
RS: Jaguars lead series, 1-0
1997—Jaguars, 38-21 (J)
(RS Pts.—Jaguars 38, Eagles 21)
JACKSONVILLE vs. PITTSBURGH
RS: Jaguars lead series, 8-6
1995—Jaguars, 20-16 (J)
    Steelers, 24-7 (P)
1996—Jaguars, 24-9 (J)
    Steelers, 28-3 (P)
1997—Jaguars, 30-21 (J)
    Steelers, 23-17 (P) OT
1998—Steelers, 30-15 (P)
    Jaguars, 21-3 (J)
1999—Jaguars, 17-3 (P)
    Jaguars, 20-6 (J)
2000—Steelers, 24-13 (J)
    Jaguars, 34-24 (P)
2001—Jaguars, 21-3 (J)
    Steelers, 20-7 (P)
(RS Pts.—Jaguars 249, Steelers 234)
JACKSONVILLE vs. ST. LOUIS
RS: Rams lead series, 1-0
1996—Rams, 17-14 (StL)
(RS Pts.—Rams 17, Jaguars 14)
JACKSONVILLE vs. SAN FRANCISCO
RS: Jaguars lead series, 1-0
1999—Jaguars, 41-3 (J)
(RS Pts.—Jaguars 41, 49ers 3)
JACKSONVILLE vs. SEATTLE
RS: Seahawks lead series, 3-1
1995—Seahawks, 47-30 (J)
1996—Jaguars, 20-13 (J)
2000—Seahawks, 28-21 (J)
2001—Seahawks, 24-15 (S)
(RS Pts.—Seahawks 112, Jaguars 86)
JACKSONVILLE vs. TAMPA BAY
RS: Series tied, 1-1
1995—Buccaneers, 17-16 (TB)
1998—Jaguars, 29-24 (J)
(RS Pts.—Jaguars 45, Buccaneers 41)
JACKSONVILLE vs. *TENNESSEE
RS: Series tied, 7-7
PS: Titans lead, 1-0
1995—Oilers, 10-3 (J)
    Jaguars, 17-16 (H)
1996—Oilers, 34-27 (J)
    Jaguars, 23-17 (H)
1997—Jaguars, 30-24 (T)
    Jaguars, 17-9 (J)
1998—Jaguars, 27-22 (T)
    Oilers, 16-13 (J)
1999—Titans, 20-19 (J)

    Titans, 41-14 (T)
    **Titans, 33-14 (J)
2000—Titans, 27-13 (T)
    Jaguars, 16-13 (J)
2001—Jaguars, 13-6 (J)
    Titans, 28-24 (T)
(RS Pts.—Titans 283, Jaguars 256)
(PS Pts.—Titans 33, Jaguars 14)
*Franchise in Houston prior to 1997;
known as Oilers prior to 1999
**AFC Championship
JACKSONVILLE vs. WASHINGTON
RS: Redskins lead series, 2-0
1997—Redskins, 24-12 (W)
2000—Redskins, 35-16 (J)
(RS Pts.—Redskins 59, Jaguars 28)

KANSAS CITY vs. ARIZONA
RS: Chiefs lead series, 5-2-1;
See Arizona vs. Kansas City
KANSAS CITY vs. ATLANTA
RS: Chiefs lead series, 4-1;
See Atlanta vs. Kansas City
KANSAS CITY vs. BALTIMORE
RS: Chiefs lead series, 1-0;
See Baltimore vs. Kansas City
KANSAS CITY vs. BUFFALO
RS: Bills lead series, 18-14-1
PS: Bills lead series, 2-1;
See Buffalo vs. Kansas City
KANSAS CITY vs. CARLOINA
RS: Chiefs lead series, 2-0;
See Carolina vs. Kansas City
KANSAS CITY vs. CHICAGO
RS: Bears lead series, 5-3;
See Chicago vs. Kansas City
KANSAS CITY vs. CINCINNATI
RS: Chiefs lead series, 11-9;
See Cincinnati vs. Kansas City
KANSAS CITY vs. CLEVELAND
RS: Browns lead series, 8-7-2;
See Cleveland vs. Kansas City
KANSAS CITY vs. DALLAS
RS: Cowboys lead series, 4-3;
See Dallas vs. Kansas City
KANSAS CITY vs. DENVER
RS: Chiefs lead series, 48-35
PS: Broncos lead series, 1-0;
See Denver vs. Kansas City
KANSAS CITY vs. DETROIT
RS: Chiefs lead series, 6-3;
See Detroit vs. Kansas City
KANSAS CITY vs. GREEN BAY
RS: Chiefs lead series, 5-1-1
PS: Packers lead series, 1-0;
See Green Bay vs. Kansas City
KANSAS CITY vs. INDIANAPOLIS
RS: Colts lead series, 8-6
PS: Colts lead series, 1-0;
See Indianapolis vs. Kansas City
KANSAS CITY vs. JACKSONVILLE
RS: Jaguars lead series, 2-1;
See Jacksonville vs. Kansas City
KANSAS CITY vs. MIAMI
RS: Series tied, 10-10
PS: Dolphins lead series, 3-0
1966—Chiefs, 34-16 (KC)
    Chiefs, 19-18 (M)
1967—Chiefs, 24-0 (M)
    Chiefs, 41-0 (KC)

1968—Chiefs, 48-3 (M)
1969—Chiefs, 17-10 (KC)
1971—*Dolphins, 27-24 (KC) OT
1972—Dolphins, 20-10 (KC)
1974—Dolphins, 9-3 (M)
1976—Chiefs, 20-17 (M) OT
1981—Dolphins, 17-7 (KC)
1983—Dolphins, 14-6 (M)
1985—Dolphins, 31-0 (M)
1987—Dolphins, 42-0 (M)
1989—Chiefs, 26-21 (KC)
　　　Chiefs, 27-24 (M)
1990—**Dolphins, 17-16 (M)
1991—Chiefs, 42-7 (KC)
1993—Dolphins, 30-10 (M)
1994—Dolphins, 45-28 (M)
　　　**Dolphins, 27-17 (M)
1995—Dolphins, 13-6 (M)
1997—Dolphins, 17-14 (M)
(RS Pts.—Chiefs 382, Dolphins 354)
(PS Pts.—Dolphins 71, Chiefs 57)
*AFC Divisional Playoff
**AFC First-Round Playoff
KANSAS CITY vs. MINNESOTA
RS: Chiefs lead series, 4-3
PS: Chiefs lead series, 1-0
1969—*Chiefs, 23-7 (New Orleans)
1970—Vikings, 27-10 (M)
1974—Vikings, 35-15 (KC)
1981—Chiefs, 10-6 (M)
1990—Chiefs, 24-21 (KC)
1993—Vikings, 30-10 (M)
1996—Chiefs, 21-6 (M)
1999—Chiefs, 31-28 (KC)
(RS Pts.—Vikings 153, Chiefs 121)
(PS Pts.—Chiefs 23, Vikings 7)
*Super Bowl IV
*KANSAS CITY vs. **NEW ENGLAND
RS: Chiefs lead series, 15-9-3
1960—Patriots, 42-14 (B)
　　　Texans, 34-0 (D)
1961—Patriots, 18-17 (D)
　　　Patriots, 28-21 (B)
1962—Texans, 42-28 (D)
　　　Texans, 27-7 (B)
1963—Tie, 24-24 (B)
　　　Chiefs, 35-3 (KC)
1964—Patriots, 24-7 (B)
　　　Patriots, 31-24 (KC)
1965—Chiefs, 27-17 (KC)
　　　Tie, 10-10 (B)
1966—Chiefs, 43-24 (B)
　　　Tie, 27-27 (KC)
1967—Chiefs, 33-10 (B)
1968—Chiefs, 31-17 (KC)
1969—Chiefs, 31-0 (B)
1970—Chiefs, 23-10 (KC)
1973—Chiefs, 10-7 (NE)
1977—Patriots, 21-17 (NE)
1981—Patriots, 33-17 (NE)
1990—Chiefs, 37-7 (NE)
1992—Chiefs, 27-20 (KC)
1995—Chiefs, 31-26 (KC)
1998—Patriots, 40-10 (NE)
1999—Chiefs, 16-14 (KC)
2000—Patriots, 30-24 (NE)
(RS Pts.—Chiefs 659, Patriots 518)
*Franchise located in Dallas prior to 1963
and known as Texans
**Franchise in Boston prior to 1971

KANSAS CITY vs. NEW ORLEANS
RS: Chiefs lead series, 4-3
1972—Chiefs, 20-17 (NO)
1976—Saints, 27-17 (KC)
1982—Saints, 27-17 (NO)
1985—Chiefs, 47-27 (NO)
1991—Saints, 17-10 (KC)
1994—Chiefs, 30-17 (NO)
1997—Chiefs, 25-13 (KC)
(RS Pts.—Chiefs 166, Saints 145)
KANSAS CITY vs. N.Y. GIANTS
RS: Giants lead series, 8-2
1974—Giants, 33-27 (KC)
1978—Giants, 26-10 (NY)
1979—Giants, 21-17 (KC)
1983—Chiefs, 38-17 (KC)
1984—Giants, 28-27 (NY)
1988—Giants, 28-12 (NY)
1992—Giants, 35-21 (NY)
1995—Chiefs, 20-17 (KC) OT
1998—Giants, 28-7 (NY)
2001—Giants, 13-3 (KC)
(RS Pts.—Giants 246, Chiefs 182)
*KANSAS CITY vs. **N.Y. JETS
RS: Series tied, 14-14-1
PS: Series tied, 1-1
1960—Titans, 37-35 (D)
　　　Titans, 41-35 (NY)
1961—Titans, 28-7 (NY)
　　　Texans, 35-24 (D)
1962—Texans, 20-17 (D)
　　　Texans, 52-31 (NY)
1963—Jets, 17-0 (NY)
　　　Chiefs, 48-0 (KC)
1964—Jets, 27-14 (NY)
　　　Chiefs, 24-7 (KC)
1965—Chiefs, 14-10 (NY)
　　　Jets, 13-10 (KC)
1966—Chiefs, 32-24 (NY)
1967—Chiefs, 42-18 (KC)
　　　Chiefs, 21-7 (NY)
1968—Jets, 20-19 (KC)
1969—Chiefs, 34-16 (NY)
　　　***Chiefs, 13-6 (NY)
1971—Jets, 13-10 (NY)
1974—Chiefs, 24-16 (KC)
1975—Jets, 30-24 (KC)
1982—Chiefs, 37-13 (KC)
1984—Jets, 17-16 (KC)
　　　Jets, 28-7 (NY)
1986—****Jets, 35-15 (NY)
1987—Jets, 16-9 (KC)
1988—Tie, 17-17 (NY)
　　　Chiefs, 38-34 (KC)
1992—Chiefs, 23-7 (NY)
1998—Jets, 20-17 (KC)
2001—Jets, 27-7 (NY)
(RS Pts.—Chiefs 671, Jets 575)
(PS Pts.—Jets 41, Chiefs 28)
*Franchise in Dallas prior to 1963 and
known as Texans
**Jets known as Titans prior to 1963
***Inter-Divisional Playoff
****AFC First-Round Playoff
*KANSAS CITY vs. **OAKLAND
RS: Raiders lead series, 41-40-2
PS: Chiefs lead series, 2-1
1960—Texans, 34-16 (O)
　　　Raiders, 20-19 (D)
1961—Texans, 42-35 (O)

Texans, 43-11 (D)
1962—Texans, 26-16 (O)
　　　Texans, 35-7 (D)
1963—Raiders, 10-7 (O)
　　　Raiders, 22-7 (KC)
1964—Chiefs, 21-9 (O)
　　　Chiefs, 42-7 (KC)
1965—Raiders, 37-10 (O)
　　　Chiefs, 14-7 (KC)
1966—Chiefs, 32-10 (O)
　　　Raiders, 34-13 (KC)
1967—Raiders, 23-21 (O)
　　　Raiders, 44-22 (KC)
1968—Chiefs, 24-10 (KC)
　　　Raiders, 38-21 (O)
　　　***Raiders, 41-6 (O)
1969—Raiders, 27-24 (KC)
　　　Raiders, 10-6 (O)
　　　****Chiefs, 17-7 (O)
1970—Tie, 17-17 (KC)
　　　Raiders, 20-6 (O)
1971—Tie, 20-20 (O)
　　　Chiefs, 16-14 (KC)
1972—Chiefs, 27-14 (KC)
　　　Raiders, 26-3 (O)
1973—Chiefs, 16-3 (KC)
　　　Raiders, 37-7 (O)
1974—Raiders, 27-7 (O)
　　　Raiders, 7-6 (KC)
1975—Chiefs, 42-10 (KC)
　　　Raiders, 28-20 (O)
1976—Raiders, 24-21 (KC)
　　　Raiders, 21-10 (O)
1977—Raiders, 37-28 (KC)
　　　Raiders, 21-20 (O)
1978—Raiders, 28-6 (O)
　　　Raiders, 20-10 (KC)
1979—Chiefs, 35-7 (KC)
　　　Chiefs, 24-21 (O)
1980—Raiders, 27-14 (KC)
　　　Chiefs, 31-17 (O)
1981—Chiefs, 27-0 (KC)
　　　Chiefs, 28-17 (O)
1982—Raiders, 21-16 (KC)
1983—Raiders, 21-20 (LA)
　　　Raiders, 28-20 (KC)
1984—Raiders, 22-20 (KC)
　　　Raiders, 17-7 (LA)
1985—Chiefs, 36-20 (KC)
　　　Raiders, 19-10 (LA)
1986—Raiders, 24-17 (KC)
　　　Chiefs, 20-17 (LA)
1987—Raiders, 35-17 (LA)
　　　Chiefs, 16-10 (KC)
1988—Raiders, 27-17 (KC)
　　　Raiders, 17-10 (LA)
1989—Chiefs, 24-19 (KC)
　　　Raiders, 20-14 (LA)
1990—Chiefs, 9-7 (KC)
　　　Chiefs, 27-24 (LA)
1991—Chiefs, 24-21 (KC)
　　　Chiefs, 27-21 (LA)
　　　*****Chiefs, 10-6 (KC)
1992—Chiefs, 27-7 (KC)
　　　Raiders, 28-7 (LA)
1993—Chiefs, 24-9 (KC)
　　　Chiefs, 31-20 (LA)
1994—Chiefs, 13-3 (KC)
　　　Chiefs, 19-9 (LA)
1995—Chiefs, 23-17 (KC) OT

Chiefs, 29-23 (O)
1996—Chiefs, 19-3 (KC)
Raiders, 26-7 (O)
1997—Chiefs, 28-27 (O)
Chiefs, 30-0 (KC)
1998—Chiefs, 28-8 (KC)
Chiefs, 31-24 (O)
1999—Chiefs, 37-34 (O)
Raiders, 41-38 (KC) OT
2000—Raiders, 20-17 (KC)
Raiders, 49-31 (O)
2001—Raiders, 27-24 (KC)
Raiders, 28-26 (O)
(RS Pts.—Chiefs 1,744, Raiders 1,649)
(PS Pts.—Raiders 54, Chiefs 33)
*Franchise in Dallas prior to 1963 and
known as Texans
**Franchise in Los Angeles from
1982-1994
***Division Playoff
****AFL Championship
*****AFC First-Round Playoff

KANSAS CITY vs. PHILADELPHIA
RS: Series tied, 2-2
1972—Eagles, 21-20 (KC)
1992—Chiefs, 24-17 (KC)
1998—Chiefs, 24-21 (P)
2001—Eagles, 23-10 (KC)
(RS Pts.—Eagles 82, Chiefs 78)

KANSAS CITY vs. PITTSBURGH
RS: Steelers lead series, 16-7
PS: Chiefs lead series, 1-0
1970—Chiefs, 31-14 (P)
1971—Chiefs, 38-16 (KC)
1972—Steelers, 16-7 (P)
1974—Steelers, 34-24 (KC)
1975—Steelers, 28-3 (P)
1976—Steelers, 45-0 (KC)
1978—Steelers, 27-24 (P)
1979—Steelers, 30-3 (KC)
1980—Steelers, 21-16 (P)
1981—Chiefs, 37-33 (P)
1982—Steelers, 35-14 (P)
1984—Chiefs, 37-27 (P)
1985—Steelers, 36-28 (KC)
1986—Chiefs, 24-19 (P)
1987—Steelers, 17-16 (KC)
1988—Steelers, 16-10 (P)
1989—Steelers, 23-17 (P)
1992—Steelers, 27-3 (KC)
1993—*Chiefs, 27-24 (KC) OT
1996—Steelers, 17-7 (KC)
1997—Chiefs, 13-10 (P)
1998—Steelers, 20-13 (KC)
1999—Chiefs, 35-19 (KC)
2001—Steelers, 20-17 (KC)
(RS Pts.—Steelers 550, Chiefs 417)
(PS Pts.—Chiefs 27, Steelers 24)
*AFC First-Round Playoff

KANSAS CITY vs. *ST. LOUIS
RS: Rams lead series, 4-3
1973—Rams, 23-13 (KC)
1982—Rams, 20-14 (LA)
1985—Rams, 16-0 (KC)
1991—Chiefs, 27-20 (LA)
1994—Rams, 16-0 (KC)
1997—Chiefs, 28-20 (StL)
2000—Chiefs, 54-34 (KC)
(RS Pts.—Rams 149, Chiefs 136)
*Franchise in Los Angeles prior to 1995

*KANSAS CITY vs. **SAN DIEGO
RS: Chiefs lead series, 44-38-1
PS: Chargers lead series, 1-0
1960—Chargers, 21-20 (LA)
Texans, 17-0 (D)
1961—Chargers, 26-10 (D)
Chargers, 24-14 (SD)
1962—Chargers, 32-28 (SD)
Texans, 26-17 (D)
1963—Chargers, 24-10 (SD)
Chargers, 38-17 (KC)
1964—Chargers, 28-14 (KC)
Chiefs, 49-6 (SD)
1965—Tie, 10-10 (SD)
Chiefs, 31-7 (KC)
1966—Chiefs, 24-14 (KC)
Chiefs, 27-17 (SD)
1967—Chargers, 45-31 (SD)
Chargers, 17-16 (KC)
1968—Chiefs, 27-20 (KC)
Chiefs, 40-3 (SD)
1969—Chiefs, 27-9 (SD)
Chiefs, 27-3 (KC)
1970—Chiefs, 26-14 (KC)
Chargers, 31-13 (SD)
1971—Chargers, 21-14 (SD)
Chiefs, 31-10 (KC)
1972—Chiefs, 26-14 (SD)
Chargers, 27-17 (KC)
1973—Chiefs, 19-0 (SD)
Chiefs, 33-6 (KC)
1974—Chiefs, 24-14 (SD)
Chargers, 14-7 (KC)
1975—Chiefs, 12-10 (SD)
Chargers, 28-20 (KC)
1976—Chargers, 30-16 (KC)
Chiefs, 23-20 (SD)
1977—Chargers, 23-7 (KC)
Chiefs, 21-16 (SD)
1978—Chargers, 29-23 (SD) OT
Chiefs, 23-0 (KC)
1979—Chargers, 20-14 (KC)
Chargers, 28-7 (SD)
1980—Chargers, 24-7 (KC)
Chargers, 20-7 (SD)
1981—Chargers, 42-31 (KC)
Chargers, 22-20 (SD)
1982—Chiefs, 19-12 (KC)
1983—Chargers, 17-14 (KC)
Chargers, 41-38 (SD)
1984—Chiefs, 31-13 (KC)
Chiefs, 42-21 (SD)
1985—Chargers, 31-20 (SD)
Chiefs, 38-34 (KC)
1986—Chiefs, 42-41 (KC)
Chiefs, 24-23 (SD)
1987—Chiefs, 20-13 (KC)
Chargers, 42-21 (SD)
1988—Chargers, 24-23 (KC)
Chargers, 24-13 (SD)
1989—Chargers, 21-6 (SD)
Chargers, 20-13 (KC)
1990—Chiefs, 27-10 (KC)
Chiefs, 24-21 (SD)
1991—Chiefs, 14-13 (SD)
Chiefs, 20-17 (KC) OT
1992—Chiefs, 24-10 (SD)
Chiefs, 16-14 (KC)
***Chargers, 17-0 (SD)
1993—Chiefs, 17-14 (SD)

Chiefs, 28-24 (KC)
1994—Chargers, 20-6 (SD)
Chargers, 14-13 (KC)
1995—Chargers, 29-23 (KC) OT
Chiefs, 22-7 (SD)
1996—Chargers, 22-19 (SD)
Chargers, 28-14 (KC)
1997—Chiefs, 31-3 (KC)
Chiefs, 29-7 (SD)
1998—Chiefs, 23-7 (KC)
Chargers, 38-37 (SD)
1999—Chargers, 21-14 (SD)
Chiefs, 34-0 (KC)
2000—Chiefs, 42-10 (KC)
Chargers, 17-16 (SD)
2001—Chiefs, 25-20 (SD)
Chiefs, 20-17 (KC)
(RS Pts.—Chiefs 1,814, Chargers 1,578)
(PS Pts.—Chargers 17, Chiefs 0)
*Franchise in Dallas prior to 1963 and
known as Texans
**Franchise in Los Angeles prior to 1961
***AFC First-Round Playoff

KANSAS CITY vs. SAN FRANCISCO
RS: 49ers lead series, 5-3
1971—Chiefs, 26-17 (SF)
1975—49ers, 20-3 (KC)
1982—49ers, 26-13 (KC)
1985—49ers, 31-3 (SF)
1991—49ers, 28-14 (SF)
1994—Chiefs, 24-17 (KC)
1997—Chiefs, 44-9 (KC)
2000—49ers, 21-7 (SF)
(PS Pts.—49ers 169, Chiefs 134)

KANSAS CITY vs. SEATTLE
RS: Chiefs lead series, 30-17
1977—Seahawks, 34-31 (KC)
1978—Seahawks, 13-10 (KC)
Seahawks, 23-19 (S)
1979—Chiefs, 24-6 (S)
Chiefs, 37-21 (KC)
1980—Seahawks, 17-16 (KC)
Chiefs, 31-30 (S)
1981—Chiefs, 20-14 (S)
Chiefs, 40-13 (KC)
1983—Chiefs, 17-13 (KC)
Seahawks, 51-48 (S) OT
1984—Seahawks, 45-0 (S)
Chiefs, 34-7 (KC)
1985—Chiefs, 28-7 (KC)
Seahawks, 24-6 (S)
1986—Seahawks, 23-17 (S)
Chiefs, 27-7 (KC)
1987—Seahawks, 43-14 (S)
Chiefs, 41-20 (KC)
1988—Seahawks, 31-10 (S)
Chiefs, 27-24 (KC)
1989—Chiefs, 20-16 (S)
Chiefs, 20-10 (KC)
1990—Seahawks, 19-7 (S)
Seahawks, 17-16 (KC)
1991—Chiefs, 20-13 (KC)
Chiefs, 19-6 (S)
1992—Chiefs, 26-7 (KC)
Chiefs, 24-14 (S)
1993—Chiefs, 31-16 (S)
Chiefs, 34-24 (KC)
1994—Chiefs, 38-23 (KC)
Seahawks, 10-9 (S)
1995—Chiefs, 34-10 (S)

Chiefs, 26-3 (KC)
1996—Chiefs, 35-17 (S)
Chiefs, 34-16 (KC)
1997—Chiefs, 20-17 (KC) OT
Chiefs, 19-14 (S)
1998—Chiefs, 17-6 (KC)
Seahawks, 24-12 (S)
1999—Seahawks, 31-19 (KC)
Seahawks, 23-14 (S)
2000—Chiefs, 24-17 (KC)
Chiefs, 24-19 (S)
2001—Chiefs, 19-7 (KC)
Seahawks, 21-18 (S)
(RS Pts.—Chiefs 1,076, Seahawks 866)

KANSAS CITY vs. TAMPA BAY
RS: Chiefs lead series, 5-3
1976—Chiefs, 28-19 (TB)
1978—Buccaneers, 30-13 (KC)
1979—Buccaneers, 3-0 (TB)
1981—Chiefs, 19-10 (KC)
1984—Chiefs, 24-20 (KC)
1986—Chiefs, 27-20 (KC)
1993—Chiefs, 27-3 (TB)
1999—Buccaneers, 17-10 (TB)
(RS Pts.—Chiefs 148, Buccaneers 122)

*KANSAS CITY vs. **TENNESSEE
RS: Chiefs lead series, 24-18
PS: Chiefs lead series, 2-0
1960—Oilers, 20-10 (H)
Texans, 24-0 (D)
1961—Texans, 26-21 (D)
Oilers, 38-7 (H)
1962—Texans, 31-7 (H)
Oilers, 14-6 (D)
***Texans, 20-17 (H) OT
1963—Chiefs, 28-7 (KC)
Oilers, 28-7 (H)
1964—Chiefs, 28-7 (KC)
Chiefs, 28-19 (H)
1965—Chiefs, 52-21 (KC)
Oilers, 38-36 (H)
1966—Chiefs, 48-23 (H)
1967—Chiefs, 25-20 (H)
Oilers, 24-19 (KC)
1968—Chiefs, 26-21 (H)
Chiefs, 24-10 (KC)
1969—Chiefs, 24-0 (KC)
1970—Chiefs, 24-9 (KC)
1971—Chiefs, 20-16 (H)
1973—Chiefs, 38-14 (KC)
1974—Chiefs, 17-7 (H)
1975—Oilers, 17-13 (KC)
1977—Oilers, 34-20 (H)
1978—Oilers, 20-17 (KC)
1979—Oilers, 20-6 (H)
1980—Chiefs, 21-20 (KC)
1981—Chiefs, 23-10 (KC)
1983—Chiefs, 13-10 (H) OT
1984—Oilers, 17-16 (KC)
1985—Oilers, 23-20 (H)
1986—Chiefs, 27-13 (KC)
1988—Oilers, 7-6 (H)
1989—Chiefs, 34-0 (KC)
1990—Oilers, 27-10 (KC)
1991—Oilers, 17-7 (H)
1992—Oilers, 23-20 (H) OT
1993—Oilers, 30-0 (H)
****Chiefs, 28-20 (H)
1994—Chiefs, 31-9 (KC)
1995—Chiefs, 20-13 (KC)

1996—Chiefs, 20-19 (H)
2000—Titans, 17-14 (T) OT
(RS Pts.—Chiefs 886, Titans 710)
(PS Pts.—Chiefs 48, Titans 37)
Franchise in Dallas prior to 1963 and known as Texans
**Franchise in Houston prior to 1997; known as Oilers prior to 1999
***AFL Championship
****AFC Divisional Playoff

KANSAS CITY vs. WASHINGTON
RS: Chiefs lead series, 5-1
1971—Chiefs, 27-20 (KC)
1976—Chiefs, 33-30 (W)
1983—Redskins, 27-12 (W)
1992—Chiefs, 35-16 (KC)
1995—Chiefs, 24-3 (KC)
2001—Chiefs, 45-13 (W)
(RS Pts.—Chiefs 176, Redskins 109)

MIAMI vs. ARIZONA
RS: Dolphins lead series, 8-0;
See Arizona vs. Miami
MIAMI vs. ATLANTA
RS: Dolphins lead series, 7-2;
See Atlanta vs. Miami
MIAMI vs. BALTIMORE
RS: Dolphins lead series, 2-0
PS: Ravens lead series, 1-0;
See Baltimore vs. Miami
MIAMI vs. BUFFALO
RS: Dolphins lead series, 46-25-1
PS: Bills lead series, 3-1;
See Buffalo vs. Miami
MIAMI vs. CAROLINA
RS: Dolphins lead series, 2-0;
See Carolina vs. Miami
MIAMI vs. CHICAGO
RS: Dolphins lead series, 5-3;
See Chicago vs. Miami
MIAMI vs. CINCINNATI
RS: Dolphins lead series, 12-3
PS: Dolphins lead series, 1-0;
See Cincinnati vs. Miami
MIAMI vs. CLEVELAND
RS: Dolphins lead series, 6-4
PS: Dolphins lead series, 2-0;
See Cleveland vs. Miami
MIAMI vs. DALLAS
RS: Dolphins lead series, 6-3
PS: Cowboys lead series, 1-0;
See Dallas vs. Miami
MIAMI vs. DENVER
RS: Dolphins lead series, 8-2-1
PS: Broncos lead series, 1-0;
See Denver vs. Miami
MIAMI vs. DETROIT
RS: Dolphins lead series, 5-2;
See Detroit vs. Miami
MIAMI vs. GREEN BAY
RS: Dolphins lead series, 9-1;
See Green Bay vs. Miami
MIAMI vs. INDIANAPOLIS
RS: Dolphins lead series, 43-21
PS: Dolphins lead series, 2-0;
See Indianapolis vs. Miami
MIAMI vs. JACKSONVILLE
RS: Jaguars lead series, 1-0
PS: Jaguars lead series, 1-0;
See Jacksonville vs. Miami

MIAMI vs. KANSAS CITY
RS: Series tied, 10-10
PS: Dolphins lead series, 3-0;
See Kansas City vs. Miami
MIAMI vs. MINNESOTA
RS: Dolphins lead series, 4-3
PS: Dolphins lead series, 1-0
1972—Dolphins, 16-14 (Minn)
1973—*Dolphins, 24-7 (Houston)
1976—Vikings, 29-7 (Mia)
1979—Dolphins, 27-12 (Minn)
1982—Dolphins, 22-14 (Mia)
1988—Dolphins, 24-7 (Mia)
1994—Vikings, 38-35 (Minn)
2000—Vikings, 13-7 (Minn)
(RS Pts.—Dolphins 138, Vikings 127)
(PS Pts.—Dolphins 24, Vikings 7)
Super Bowl VIII
MIAMI vs. *NEW ENGLAND
RS: Dolphins lead series, 43-27
PS: Patriots lead series, 2-1
1966—Patriots, 20-14 (M)
1967—Patriots, 41-10 (B)
Dolphins, 41-32 (M)
1968—Dolphins, 34-10 (B)
Dolphins, 38-7 (M)
1969—Dolphins, 17-16 (B)
Patriots, 38-23 (Tampa)
1970—Patriots, 27-14 (B)
Dolphins, 37-20 (M)
1971—Dolphins, 41-3 (M)
Patriots, 34-13 (NE)
1972—Dolphins, 52-0 (M)
Dolphins, 37-21 (NE)
1973—Dolphins, 44-23 (M)
Dolphins, 30-14 (NE)
1974—Patriots, 34-24 (M)
Dolphins, 34-27 (M)
1975—Dolphins, 22-14 (NE)
Dolphins, 20-7 (M)
1976—Patriots, 30-14 (NE)
Dolphins, 10-3 (M)
1977—Dolphins, 17-5 (M)
Patriots, 14-10 (NE)
1978—Patriots, 33-24 (NE)
Dolphins, 23-3 (M)
1979—Patriots, 28-13 (NE)
Dolphins, 39-24 (M)
1980—Patriots, 34-0 (NE)
Dolphins, 16-13 (M) OT
1981—Dolphins, 30-27 (NE) OT
Dolphins, 24-14 (M)
1982—Patriots, 3-0 (NE)
**Dolphins, 28-13 (M)
1983—Dolphins, 34-24 (M)
Patriots, 17-6 (NE)
1984—Dolphins, 28-7 (M)
Dolphins, 44-24 (NE)
1985—Patriots, 17-13 (NE)
Dolphins, 30-27 (M)
***Patriots, 31-14 (M)
1986—Dolphins, 34-7 (NE)
Patriots, 34-27 (M)
1987—Patriots, 28-21 (NE)
Dolphins, 24-10 (M)
1988—Patriots, 21-10 (NE)
Patriots, 6-3 (M)
1989—Dolphins, 24-10 (NE)
Dolphins, 31-10 (M)
1990—Dolphins, 27-24 (NE)

Dolphins, 17-10 (M)
1991—Dolphins, 20-10 (NE)
Dolphins, 30-20 (M)
1992—Dolphins, 38-17 (M)
Dolphins, 16-13 (NE) OT
1993—Dolphins, 17-13 (M)
Patriots, 33-27 (NE) OT
1994—Dolphins, 39-35 (M)
Dolphins, 23-3 (NE)
1995—Dolphins, 20-3 (NE)
Patriots, 34-17 (M)
1996—Dolphins, 24-10 (M)
Patriots, 42-23 (NE)
1997—Patriots, 27-24 (NE)
Patriots, 14-12 (M)
**Patriots, 17-3 (NE)
1998—Dolphins, 12-9 (M) OT
Patriots, 26-23 (NE)
1999—Dolphins, 31-30 (NE)
Dolphins, 27-17 (M)
2000—Dolphins, 10-3 (M)
Dolphins, 27-24 (NE)
2001—Dolphins, 30-10 (M)
Patriots, 20-13 (NE)
(RS Pts.—Dolphins 1,600, Patriots 1,349)
(PS Pts.—Patriots 61, Dolphins 45)
*Franchise in Boston prior to 1971
**AFC First-Round Playoff
***AFC Championship
MIAMI vs. NEW ORLEANS
RS: Dolphins lead series, 5-3
1970—Dolphins, 21-10 (M)
1974—Dolphins, 21-0 (NO)
1980—Dolphins, 21-16 (M)
1983—Saints, 17-7 (NO)
1986—Dolphins, 31-27 (NO)
1992—Saints, 24-13 (NO)
1995—Saints, 33-30 (NO)
1998—Dolphins, 30-10 (M)
(RS Pts.—Dolphins 174, Saints 137)
MIAMI vs. N.Y. GIANTS
RS: Giants lead series, 3-1
1972—Dolphins, 23-13 (NY)
1990—Giants, 20-3 (NY)
1993—Giants, 19-14 (M)
1996—Giants, 17-7 (M)
(RS Pts.—Giants 69, Dolphins 47)
MIAMI vs. N.Y. JETS
RS: Jets lead series, 37-34-1
PS: Dolphins lead series, 1-0
1966—Jets, 19-14 (M)
Jets, 30-13 (NY)
1967—Jets, 29-7 (NY)
Jets, 33-14 (M)
1968—Jets, 35-17 (NY)
Jets, 31-7 (M)
1969—Jets, 34-31 (NY)
Jets, 27-9 (M)
1970—Dolphins, 20-6 (NY)
Dolphins, 16-10 (M)
1971—Jets, 14-10 (M)
Dolphins, 30-14 (NY)
1972—Dolphins, 27-17 (NY)
Dolphins, 28-24 (M)
1973—Dolphins, 31-3 (M)
Dolphins, 24-14 (NY)
1974—Dolphins, 21-17 (M)
Jets, 17-14 (NY)
1975—Dolphins, 43-0 (NY)
Dolphins, 27-7 (M)

1976—Dolphins, 16-0 (M)
Dolphins, 27-7 (NY)
1977—Dolphins, 21-17 (M)
Dolphins, 14-10 (NY)
1978—Jets, 33-20 (NY)
Jets, 24-13 (M)
1979—Jets, 33-27 (NY)
Jets, 27-24 (M)
1980—Jets, 17-14 (NY)
Jets, 24-17 (M)
1981—Tie, 28-28 (M) OT
Jets, 16-15 (NY)
1982—Dolphins, 45-28 (NY)
Dolphins, 20-19 (M)
*Dolphins, 14-0 (M)
1983—Dolphins, 32-14 (NY)
Dolphins, 34-14 (M)
1984—Dolphins, 31-17 (NY)
Dolphins, 28-17 (M)
1985—Jets, 23-7 (NY)
Dolphins, 21-17 (M)
1986—Jets, 51-45 (NY) OT
Dolphins, 45-3 (M)
1987—Jets, 37-31 (NY) OT
Dolphins, 37-28 (M)
1988—Jets, 44-30 (M)
Jets, 38-34 (NY)
1989—Jets, 40-33 (M)
Dolphins, 31-23 (NY)
1990—Dolphins, 20-16 (M)
Dolphins, 17-3 (NY)
1991—Jets, 41-23 (NY)
Jets, 23-20 (M) OT
1992—Jets, 26-14 (NY)
Dolphins, 19-17 (M)
1993—Jets, 24-14 (M)
Jets, 27-10 (NY)
1994—Dolphins, 28-14 (M)
Dolphins, 28-24 (NY)
1995—Dolphins, 52-14 (M)
Jets, 17-16 (NY)
1996—Dolphins, 36-27 (M)
Dolphins, 31-28 (NY)
1997—Dolphins, 31-20 (NY)
Dolphins, 24-17 (M)
1998—Jets, 20-9 (NY)
Jets, 21-16 (M)
1999—Jets, 28-20 (NY)
Jets, 38-31 (M)
2000—Jets, 40-37 (NY) OT
Jets, 20-3 (M)
2001—Jets, 21-17 (NY)
Jets, 24-0 (M)
(RS Pts.—Dolphins 1,659, Jets 1,580)
(PS Pts.—Dolphins 14, Jets 0)
*AFC Championship
MIAMI vs. *OAKLAND
RS: Raiders lead series, 15-9-1
PS: Raiders lead series, 3-1
1966—Raiders, 23-14 (M)
Raiders, 21-10 (O)
1967—Raiders, 31-17 (O)
1968—Raiders, 47-21 (M)
1969—Raiders, 20-17 (O)
Tie, 20-20 (M)
1970—Dolphins, 20-13 (M)
**Raiders, 21-14 (O)
1973—Raiders, 12-7 (O)
***Dolphins, 27-10 (M)
1974—**Raiders, 28-26 (O)

1975—Raiders, 31-21 (M)
1978—Dolphins, 23-6 (M)
1979—Raiders, 13-3 (O)
1980—Raiders, 16-10 (O)
1981—Raiders, 33-17 (M)
1983—Raiders, 27-14 (LA)
1984—Raiders, 45-34 (M)
1986—Raiders, 30-28 (M)
1988—Dolphins, 24-14 (LA)
1990—Raiders, 13-10 (M)
1992—Dolphins, 20-7 (M)
1994—Dolphins, 20-17 (M) OT
1996—Raiders, 17-7 (O)
1997—Dolphins, 34-16 (O)
1998—Dolphins, 27-17 (O)
1999—Dolphins, 16-9 (O)
2000—**Raiders, 27-0 (O)
2001—Dolphins, 18-15 (M)
(RS Pts.—Raiders 513, Dolphins 452)
(PS Pts.—Raiders 86, Dolphins 67)
*Franchise in Los Angeles from
1982-1994
**AFC Divisional Playoff
***AFC Championship
MIAMI vs. PHILADELPHIA
RS: Dolphins lead series, 7-3
1970—Eagles, 24-17 (P)
1975—Dolphins, 24-16 (M)
1978—Eagles, 17-3 (P)
1981—Dolphins, 13-10 (M)
1984—Dolphins, 24-23 (M)
1987—Dolphins, 28-10 (P)
1990—Dolphins, 23-20 (M) OT
1993—Dolphins, 19-14 (P)
1996—Eagles, 35-28 (P)
1999—Dolphins, 16-13 (M)
(RS Pts.—Dolphins 195, Eagles 182)
MIAMI vs. PITTSBURGH
RS: Dolphins lead series, 9-7
PS: Dolphins lead series, 2-1
1971—Dolphins, 24-21 (M)
1972—*Dolphins, 21-17 (P)
1973—Dolphins, 30-26 (M)
1976—Steelers, 14-3 (P)
1979—**Steelers, 34-14 (P)
1980—Steelers, 23-10 (P)
1981—Dolphins, 30-10 (M)
1984—Dolphins, 31-7 (P)
*Dolphins, 45-28 (M)
1985—Dolphins, 24-20 (M)
1987—Dolphins, 35-24 (M)
1988—Steelers, 40-24 (P)
1989—Steelers, 34-14 (M)
1990—Dolphins, 28-6 (P)
1993—Steelers, 21-20 (M)
1994—Steelers, 16-13 (P) OT
1995—Dolphins, 23-10 (M)
1996—Steelers, 24-17 (M)
1998—Dolphins, 21-0 (M)
(RS Pts.—Dolphins 347, Steelers 296)
(PS Pts.—Dolphins 80, Steelers 79)
*AFC Championship
**AFC Divisional Playoff
MIAMI vs. *ST. LOUIS
RS: Dolphins lead series, 7-2
1971—Dolphins, 20-14 (LA)
1976—Rams, 31-28 (M)
1980—Dolphins, 35-14 (LA)
1983—Dolphins, 30-14 (M)
1986—Dolphins, 37-31 (LA) OT

1992—Dolphins, 26-10 (M)
1995—Dolphins, 41-22 (StL)
1998—Dolphins, 14-0 (M)
2001—Rams, 42-10 (StL)
(RS Pts.—Dolphins 241, Rams 178)
*Franchise in Los Angeles prior to 1995

MIAMI vs. SAN DIEGO
RS: Chargers lead series, 10-8
PS: Series tied, 2-2
1966—Chargers, 44-10 (SD)
1967—Chargers, 24-0 (SD)
      Dolphins, 41-24 (M)
1968—Chargers, 34-28 (SD)
1969—Chargers, 21-14 (M)
1972—Dolphins, 24-10 (M)
1974—Dolphins, 28-21 (SD)
1977—Chargers, 14-13 (M)
1978—Dolphins, 28-21 (SD)
1980—Chargers, 27-24 (M) OT
1981—*Chargers, 41-38 (M) OT
1982—**Dolphins, 34-13 (M)
1984—Chargers, 34-28 (SD) OT
1986—Chargers, 50-28 (SD)
1988—Dolphins, 31-28 (SD)
1991—Chargers, 38-30 (SD)
1992—*Dolphins, 31-0 (M)
1993—Chargers, 45-20 (SD)
1994—*Chargers, 22-21 (SD)
1995—Dolphins, 24-14 (SD)
1999—Dolphins, 12-9 (M)
2000—Dolphins, 17-7 (SD)
(RS Pts.—Chargers 465, Dolphins 400)
(PS Pts.—Dolphins 124, Chargers 76)
*AFC Divisional Playoff
**AFC Second-Round Playoff

MIAMI vs. SAN FRANCISCO
RS: Series tied, 4-4
PS: 49ers lead series, 1-0
1973—Dolphins, 21-13 (M)
1977—Dolphins, 19-15 (SF)
1980—Dolphins, 17-13 (M)
1983—Dolphins, 20-17 (SF)
1984—*49ers, 38-16 (Stanford)
1986—49ers, 31-16 (M)
1992—49ers, 27-3 (SF)
1995—49ers, 44-20 (M)
2001—49ers, 21-0 (SF)
(RS Pts.—49ers 181, Dolphins 116)
(PS Pts.—49ers 38, Dolphins 16)
*Super Bowl XIX

MIAMI vs. SEATTLE
RS: Dolphins lead series, 6-2
PS: Dolphins lead series, 2-1
1977—Dolphins, 31-13 (M)
1979—Dolphins, 19-10 (M)
1983—*Seahawks, 27-20 (M)
1984—*Dolphins, 31-10 (M)
1987—Seahawks, 24-20 (S)
1990—Dolphins, 24-17 (M)
1992—Dolphins, 19-17 (S)
1996—Seahawks, 22-15 (M)
1999—**Dolphins, 20-17 (S)
2000—Dolphins, 23-0 (M)
2001—Dolphins, 24-20 (S)
(RS Pts.—Dolphins 175, Seahawks 123)
(PS Pts.—Dolphins 71, Seahawks 54)
*AFC Divisional Playoff
**AFC First-Round Playoff

MIAMI vs. TAMPA BAY
RS: Dolphins lead series, 4-3

1976—Dolphins, 23-20 (TB)
1982—Buccaneers, 23-17 (TB)
1985—Dolphins, 41-38 (M)
1988—Dolphins, 17-14 (TB)
1991—Dolphins, 33-14 (M)
1997—Buccaneers, 31-21 (TB)
2000—Buccaneers, 16-13 (M)
(RS Pts.—Dolphins 165, Buccaneers 156)

MIAMI vs. *TENNESSEE
RS: Dolphins lead series, 15-11
PS: Titans lead series, 1-0
1966—Dolphins, 20-13 (H)
      Dolphins, 29-28 (M)
1967—Oilers, 17-14 (H)
      Oilers, 41-10 (M)
1968—Oilers, 24-10 (M)
      Dolphins, 24-7 (H)
1969—Oilers, 22-10 (H)
      Oilers, 32-7 (M)
1970—Dolphins, 20-10 (H)
1972—Dolphins, 34-13 (M)
1975—Oilers, 20-19 (H)
1977—Dolphins, 27-7 (M)
1978—Oilers, 35-30 (H)
      **Oilers, 17-9 (M)
1979—Oilers, 9-6 (M)
1981—Dolphins, 16-10 (H)
1983—Dolphins, 24-17 (H)
1984—Dolphins, 28-10 (M)
1985—Oilers, 26-23 (H)
1986—Dolphins, 28-7 (M)
1989—Oilers, 39-7 (H)
1991—Oilers, 17-13 (M)
1992—Dolphins, 19-16 (M)
1996—Dolphins, 23-20 (H)
1997—Dolphins, 16-13 (M) OT
1999—Dolphins, 17-0 (M)
2001—Dolphins, 31-23 (T)
(RS Pts.—Dolphins 505, Titans 476)
(PS Pts.—Titans 17, Dolphins 9)
*Franchise in Houston prior to 1997;
known as Oilers prior to 1999
**AFC First-Round Playoff

MIAMI vs. WASHINGTON
RS: Dolphins lead series, 5-3
PS: Series tied, 1-1
1972—*Dolphins, 14-7 (Los Angeles)
1974—Redskins, 20-17 (W)
1978—Dolphins, 16-0 (W)
1981—Dolphins, 13-10 (M)
1982—**Redskins, 27-17 (Pasadena)
1984—Dolphins, 35-17 (W)
1987—Dolphins, 23-21 (M)
1990—Redskins, 42-20 (W)
1993—Dolphins, 17-10 (M)
1999—Redskins, 21-10 (W)
(RS Pts.—Dolphins 151, Redskins 141)
(PS Pts.—Redskins 34, Dolphins 31)
*Super Bowl VII
**Super Bowl XVII

MINNESOTA vs. ARIZONA
RS: Series tied, 8-8
PS: Vikings lead series, 2-0;
See Arizona vs. Minnesota

MINNESOTA vs. ATLANTA
RS: Vikings lead series, 13-6
PS: Series tied, 1-1;
See Atlanta vs. Minnesota

MINNESOTA vs. BALTIMORE
RS: Series tied, 1-1;
See Baltimore vs. Minnesota

MINNESOTA vs. BUFFALO
RS: Vikings lead series, 7-2;
See Buffalo vs. Minnesota

MINNESOTA vs. CAROLINA
RS: Vikings lead series, 3-1;
See Carolina vs. Minnesota

MINNESOTA vs. CHICAGO
RS: Vikings lead series, 44-35-2
PS: Bears lead series, 1-0;
See Chicago vs. Minnesota

MINNESOTA vs. CINCINNATI
RS: Vikings lead series, 5-4;
See Cincinnati vs. Minnesota

MINNESOTA vs. CLEVELAND
RS: Vikings lead series, 8-3
PS: Vikings lead series, 1-0;
See Cleveland vs. Minnesota

MINNESOTA vs. DALLAS
RS: Series tied, 9-9
PS: Cowboys lead series, 4-2;
See Dallas vs. Minnesota

MINNESOTA vs. DENVER
RS: Vikings lead series, 6-4;
See Denver vs. Minnesota

MINNESOTA vs. DETROIT
RS: Vikings lead series, 50-29-2;
See Detroit vs. Minnesota

MINNESOTA vs. GREEN BAY
RS: Series tied, 40-40-1;
See Green Bay vs. Minnesota

MINNESOTA vs. INDIANAPOLIS
RS: Colts lead series, 12-7-1
PS: Colts lead series, 1-0;
See Indianapolis vs. Minnesota

MINNESOTA vs. JACKSONVILLE
RS: Series tied, 1-1;
See Jacksonville vs. Minnesota

MINNESOTA vs. KANSAS CITY
RS: Chiefs lead series, 4-3
PS: Chiefs lead series, 1-0;
See Kansas City vs. Minnesota

MINNESOTA vs. MIAMI
RS: Dolphins lead series, 4-3
PS: Dolphins lead series, 1-0;
See Miami vs. Minnesota

MINNESOTA vs. *NEW ENGLAND
RS: Series tied, 4-4
1970—Vikings, 35-14 (B)
1974—Patriots, 17-14 (M)
1979—Patriots, 27-23 (NE)
1988—Vikings, 36-6 (M)
1991—Patriots, 26-23 (NE) OT
1994—Patriots, 26-20 (NE) OT
1997—Vikings, 23-18 (M)
2000—Vikings, 21-13 (NE)
(RS Pts.—Vikings 195, Patriots 147)
*Franchise in Boston prior to 1971

MINNESOTA vs. NEW ORLEANS
RS: Vikings lead series, 14-7
PS: Vikings lead series, 2-0
1968—Saints, 20-17 (NO)
1970—Vikings, 26-0 (M)
1971—Vikings, 23-10 (NO)
1972—Vikings, 37-6 (M)
1974—Vikings, 29-9 (M)
1975—Vikings, 20-7 (NO)
1976—Vikings, 40-9 (NO)

1978—Saints, 31-24 (NO)
1980—Vikings, 23-20 (NO)
1981—Vikings, 20-10 (M)
1983—Saints, 17-16 (NO)
1985—Saints, 30-23 (M)
1986—Vikings, 33-17 (M)
1987—*Vikings, 44-10 (NO)
1988—Vikings, 45-3 (M)
1990—Vikings, 32-3 (M)
1991—Saints, 26-0 (NO)
1993—Saints, 17-14 (M)
1994—Vikings, 21-20 (M)
1995—Vikings, 43-24 (M)
1998—Vikings, 31-24 (M)
2000—**Vikings, 34-16 (M)
2001—Saints, 28-15 (NO)
(RS Pts.—Vikings 532, Saints 331)
(PS Pts.—Vikings 78, Saints 26)
*NFC First-Round Playoff
**NFC Divisional Playoff

MINNESOTA vs. N.Y. GIANTS
RS: Vikings lead series, 9-5
PS: Giants lead series, 2-1
1964—Vikings, 30-21 (NY)
1965—Vikings, 40-14 (M)
1967—Vikings, 27-24 (M)
1969—Giants, 24-23 (NY)
1971—Vikings, 17-10 (NY)
1973—Vikings, 31-7 (New Haven)
1976—Vikings, 24-7 (M)
1986—Giants, 22-20 (M)
1989—Giants, 24-14 (NY)
1990—Giants, 23-15 (NY)
1993—*Giants, 17-10 (NY)
1994—Vikings, 27-10 (NY)
1996—Giants, 15-10 (NY)
1997—*Vikings, 23-22 (NY)
1999—Vikings, 34-17 (NY)
2000—**Giants, 41-0 (NY)
2001—Vikings, 28-16 (M)
(RS Pts.—Vikings 340, Giants 234)
(PS Pts.—Giants 80, Vikings 33)
*NFC First-Round Playoff
**NFC Championship

MINNESOTA vs. N.Y. JETS
RS: Jets lead series, 5-1
1970—Jets, 20-10 (NY)
1975—Vikings, 29-21 (M)
1979—Jets, 14-7 (NY)
1982—Jets, 42-14 (M)
1994—Jets, 31-21 (M)
1997—Jets, 23-21 (NY)
(RS Pts.—Jets 151, Vikings 102)

MINNESOTA vs. *OAKLAND
RS: Raiders lead series, 7-3
PS: Raiders lead series, 1-0
1973—Vikings, 24-16 (M)
1976—**Raiders, 32-14 (Pasadena)
1977—Raiders, 35-13 (O)
1978—Raiders, 27-20 (O)
1981—Raiders, 36-10 (M)
1984—Raiders, 23-20 (LA)
1987—Vikings, 31-20 (M)
1990—Raiders, 28-24 (M)
1993—Raiders, 24-7 (LA)
1996—Vikings, 16-13 (O) OT
1999—Raiders, 22-17 (M)
(RS Pts.—Raiders 244, Vikings 182)
(PS Pts.—Raiders 32, Vikings 14)
*Franchise in Los Angeles from

1982-1994
**Super Bowl XI*
MINNESOTA vs. PHILADELPHIA
RS: Vikings lead series, 11-7
PS: Eagles lead series, 1-0
1962—Vikings, 31-21 (M)
1963—Vikings, 34-13 (P)
1968—Vikings, 24-17 (P)
1971—Vikings, 13-0 (P)
1973—Vikings, 28-21 (M)
1976—Vikings, 31-12 (P)
1978—Vikings, 28-27 (M)
1980—Eagles, 42-7 (M)
    *Eagles, 31-16 (P)
1981—Vikings, 35-23 (M)
1984—Eagles, 19-17 (P)
1985—Vikings, 28-23 (P)
    Eagles, 37-35 (M)
1988—Vikings, 23-21 (M)
1989—Eagles, 10-9 (P)
1990—Eagles, 32-24 (P)
1992—Eagles, 28-17 (P)
1997—Vikings, 28-19 (M)
2001—Eagles, 48-17 (P)
(RS Pts.—Vikings 429, Eagles 413)
(PS Pts.—Eagles 31, Vikings 16)
*NFC Divisional Playoff

MINNESOTA vs. PITTSBURGH
RS: Vikings lead series, 8-5
PS: Steelers lead series, 1-0
1962—Steelers, 39-31 (P)
1964—Vikings, 30-10 (M)
1967—Vikings, 41-27 (P)
1969—Vikings, 52-14 (M)
1972—Steelers, 23-10 (P)
1974—*Steelers, 16-6 (New Orleans)
1976—Vikings, 17-6 (M)
1980—Steelers, 23-17 (M)
1983—Vikings, 17-14 (P)
1986—Vikings, 31-7 (M)
1989—Steelers, 27-14 (P)
1992—Vikings, 6-3 (P)
1995—Vikings, 44-24 (P)
2001—Steelers, 21-16 (P)
(RS Pts.—Vikings 326, Steelers 238)
(PS Pts.—Steelers 16, Vikings 6)
*Super Bowl IX

MINNESOTA vs. *ST. LOUIS
RS: Vikings lead series, 16-12-2
PS: Vikings lead series, 5-2
1961—Rams, 31-17 (LA)
    Vikings, 42-21 (M)
1962—Vikings, 38-14 (LA)
    Tie, 24-24 (M)
1963—Rams, 27-24 (LA)
    Vikings, 21-13 (M)
1964—Rams, 22-13 (LA)
    Vikings, 34-13 (M)
1965—Vikings, 38-35 (LA)
    Vikings, 24-13 (M)
1966—Vikings, 35-7 (M)
    Rams, 21-6 (LA)
1967—Rams, 39-3 (LA)
1968—Rams, 31-3 (M)
1969—Vikings, 20-13 (LA)
    **Vikings, 23-20 (M)
1970—Vikings, 13-3 (M)
1972—Vikings, 45-41 (LA)
1973—Vikings, 10-9 (M)
1974—Rams, 20-17 (LA)

    ***Vikings, 14-10 (M)
1976—Tie, 10-10 (M) OT
    ***Vikings, 24-13 (M)
1977—Rams, 35-3 (LA)
    ****Vikings, 14-7 (LA)
1978—Rams, 34-17 (M)
    ****Rams, 34-10 (LA)
1979—Rams, 27-21 (LA) OT
1985—Rams, 13-10 (LA)
1987—Vikings, 21-16 (LA)
1988—*****Vikings, 28-17 (M)
1989—Vikings, 23-21 (M) OT
1991—Vikings, 20-14 (M)
1992—Vikings, 31-17 (LA)
1998—Vikings, 38-31 (StL)
1999—****Rams, 49-37 (StL)
2000—Rams, 40-29 (StL)
(RS Pts.—Rams 655, Vikings 650)
(PS Pts.—Rams 150, Vikings 150)
*Franchise in Los Angeles prior to 1995
**Conference Championship
***NFC Championship
****NFC Divisional Playoff
*****NFC First-Round Playoff

MINNESOTA vs. SAN DIEGO
RS: Series tied, 4-4
1971—Chargers, 30-14 (SD)
1975—Vikings, 28-13 (M)
1978—Chargers, 13-7 (M)
1981—Vikings, 33-31 (SD)
1984—Chargers, 42-13 (M)
1985—Vikings, 21-17 (M)
1993—Chargers, 30-17 (M)
1999—Vikings, 35-27 (M)
(RS Pts.—Chargers 203, Vikings 168)

MINNESOTA vs. SAN FRANCISCO
RS: Series tied, 17-17-1
PS: 49ers lead series, 4-1
1961—49ers, 38-24 (M)
    49ers, 38-28 (SF)
1962—49ers, 21-7 (SF)
    49ers, 35-12 (M)
1963—Vikings, 24-20 (SF)
    Vikings, 45-14 (M)
1964—Vikings, 27-22 (SF)
    Vikings, 24-7 (M)
1965—Vikings, 42-41 (M)
    49ers, 45-24 (M)
1966—Tie, 20-20 (SF)
    Vikings, 28-3 (SF)
1967—49ers, 27-21 (M)
1968—Vikings, 30-20 (SF)
1969—Vikings, 10-7 (M)
1970—*49ers, 17-14 (M)
1971—49ers, 13-9 (M)
1972—49ers, 20-17 (SF)
1973—Vikings, 17-13 (SF)
1975—Vikings, 27-17 (M)
1976—49ers, 20-16 (M)
1977—Vikings, 28-27 (M)
1979—Vikings, 28-22 (M)
1983—49ers, 48-17 (M)
1984—49ers, 51-7 (SF)
1985—Vikings, 28-21 (M)
1986—Vikings, 27-24 (SF) OT
1987—*Vikings, 36-24 (SF)
1988—49ers, 24-21 (SF)
    *49ers, 34-9 (SF)
1989—*49ers, 41-13 (SF)
1990—49ers, 20-17 (M)

1991—Vikings, 17-14 (M)
1992—49ers, 20-17 (M)
1993—49ers, 38-19 (SF)
1994—Vikings, 21-14 (M)
1995—49ers, 37-30 (M)
1997—49ers, 28-17 (SF)
    *49ers, 38-22 (SF)
1999—Vikings, 40-16 (M)
(RS Pts.—49ers 845, Vikings 786)
(PS Pts.—49ers 154, Vikings 94)
*NFC Divisional Playoff

MINNESOTA vs. SEATTLE
RS: Seahawks lead series, 4-2
1976—Vikings, 27-21 (M)
1978—Seahawks, 29-28 (S)
1984—Seahawks, 20-12 (M)
1987—Seahawks, 28-17 (S)
1990—Vikings, 24-21 (M)
1996—Seahawks, 42-23 (S)
(RS Pts.—Seahawks 161, Vikings 131)

MINNESOTA vs. TAMPA BAY
RS: Vikings lead series, 31-17
1977—Vikings, 9-3 (TB)
1978—Buccaneers, 16-10 (M)
    Vikings, 24-7 (TB)
1979—Buccaneers, 12-10 (M)
    Vikings, 23-22 (TB)
1980—Vikings, 38-30 (M)
    Vikings, 21-10 (TB)
1981—Buccaneers, 21-13 (TB)
    Vikings, 25-10 (M)
1982—Vikings, 17-10 (M)
1983—Vikings, 19-16 (TB) OT
    Buccaneers, 17-12 (M)
1984—Buccaneers, 35-31 (M)
    Vikings, 27-24 (M)
1985—Vikings, 31-16 (TB)
    Vikings, 26-7 (M)
1986—Vikings, 23-10 (TB)
    Vikings, 45-13 (M)
1987—Buccaneers, 20-10 (TB)
    Vikings, 23-17 (M)
1988—Vikings, 14-13 (M)
    Vikings, 49-20 (TB)
1989—Vikings, 17-3 (M)
    Vikings, 24-10 (TB)
1990—Buccaneers, 23-20 (M) OT
    Buccaneers, 26-13 (TB)
1991—Vikings, 28-13 (M)
    Vikings, 26-24 (TB)
1992—Vikings, 26-20 (M)
    Vikings, 35-7 (TB)
1993—Vikings, 15-0 (M)
    Buccaneers, 23-10 (TB)
1994—Vikings, 36-13 (TB)
    Buccaneers, 20-17 (M) OT
1995—Buccaneers, 20-17 (TB) OT
    Vikings, 31-17 (M)
1996—Buccaneers, 24-13 (TB)
    Vikings, 21-10 (M)
1997—Buccaneers, 28-14 (M)
    Vikings, 10-6 (TB)
1998—Vikings, 31-7 (M)
    Buccaneers, 27-24 (TB)
1999—Vikings, 21-14 (M)
    Buccaneers, 24-17 (TB)
2000—Vikings, 30-23 (M)
    Buccaneers, 41-13 (TB)
2001—Vikings, 20-16 (M)
    Buccaneers, 41-14 (TB)

(RS Pts.—Vikings 1,043, Buccaneers 829)

MINNESOTA vs. *TENNESSEE
RS: Vikings lead series, 6-3
1974—Vikings, 51-10 (M)
1980—Oilers, 20-16 (H)
1983—Vikings, 34-14 (M)
1986—Oilers, 23-10 (H)
1989—Vikings, 38-7 (M)
1992—Oilers, 17-13 (M)
1995—Vikings, 23-17 (M) OT
1998—Vikings, 26-16 (T)
2001—Vikings, 42-24 (M)
(RS Pts.—Vikings 253, Titans 148)
*Franchise in Houston prior to 1997;
known as Oilers prior to 1999

MINNESOTA vs. WASHINGTON
RS: Redskins lead series, 6-5
PS: Redskins lead series, 3-2
1968—Vikings, 27-14 (M)
1970—Vikings, 19-10 (W)
1972—Redskins, 24-21 (M)
1973—*Vikings, 27-20 (M)
1975—Redskins, 31-30 (W)
1976—*Vikings, 35-20 (M)
1980—Vikings, 39-14 (W)
1982—**Redskins, 21-7 (W)
1984—Redskins, 31-17 (M)
1986—Redskins, 44-38 (W) OT
1987—Redskins, 27-24 (M) OT
    ***Redskins, 17-10 (W)
1992—Redskins, 15-13 (M)
    ****Redskins, 24-7 (M)
1993—Vikings, 14-9 (W)
1998—Vikings, 41-7 (M)
(RS Pts.—Vikings 283, Redskins 226)
(PS Pts.—Redskins 102, Vikings 86)
*NFC Divisional Playoff
**NFC Second-Round Playoff
***NFC Championship
****NFC First-Round Playoff

NEW ENGLAND vs. ARIZONA
RS: Cardinals lead series, 6-4;
See Arizona vs. New England
NEW ENGLAND vs. ATLANTA
RS: Falcons lead series, 6-4;
See Atlanta vs. New England
NEW ENGLAND vs. BALTIMORE
RS: Patriots lead series, 2-0;
See Baltimore vs. New England
NEW ENGLAND vs. BUFFALO
RS: Patriots lead series, 43-39-1
PS: Patriots lead series, 1-0;
See Buffalo vs. New England
NEW ENGLAND vs. CAROLINA
RS: Series tied, 1-1;
See Carolina vs. New England
NEW ENGLAND vs. CHICAGO
RS: Patriots lead series, 5-3
PS: Bears lead series, 1-0;
See Chicago vs. New England
NEW ENGLAND vs. CINCINNATI
RS: Patriots lead series, 10-8;
See Cincinnati vs. New England
NEW ENGLAND vs. CLEVELAND
RS: Browns lead series, 11-6
PS: Browns lead series, 1-0;
See Cleveland vs. New England
NEW ENGLAND vs. DALLAS
RS: Cowboys lead series, 7-1;

See Dallas vs. New England
NEW ENGLAND vs. DENVER
RS: Broncos lead series, 21-14
PS: Broncos lead series, 1-0;
See Denver vs. New England
NEW ENGLAND vs. DETROIT
RS: Lions lead series, 4-3;
See Detroit vs. New England
NEW ENGLAND vs. GREEN BAY
RS: Series tied, 3-3
PS: Packers lead series, 1-0;
See Green Bay vs. New England
NEW ENGLAND vs. INDIANAPOLIS
RS: Patriots lead series, 39-24;
See Indianapolis vs. New England
NEW ENGLAND vs. JACKSONVILLE
RS: Patriots lead series, 2-0
PS: Series tied, 1-1;
See Jacksonville vs. New England
NEW ENGLAND vs. KANSAS CITY
RS: Chiefs lead series, 15-9-3;
See Kansas City vs. New England
NEW ENGLAND vs. MIAMI
RS: Dolphins lead series, 43-27
PS: Patriots lead series, 2-1;
See Miami vs. New England
NEW ENGLAND vs. MINNESOTA
RS: Series tied, 4-4;
See Minnesota vs. New England
NEW ENGLAND vs. NEW ORLEANS
RS: Patriots lead series, 7-3
1972—Patriots, 17-10 (NO)
1976—Patriots, 27-6 (NE)
1980—Patriots, 38-27 (NO)
1983—Patriots, 7-0 (NE)
1986—Patriots, 21-20 (NO)
1989—Saints, 28-24 (NE)
1992—Saints, 31-14 (NE)
1995—Saints, 31-17 (NE)
1998—Patriots, 30-27 (NO)
2001—Patriots, 34-17 (NE)
(RS Pts.—Patriots 229, Saints 197)
***NEW ENGLAND vs. N.Y. GIANTS**
RS: Series tied, 3-3
1970—Giants, 16-0 (B)
1974—Patriots, 28-20 (New Haven)
1987—Giants, 17-10 (NY)
1990—Giants, 13-10 (NE)
1996—Patriots, 23-22 (NY)
1999—Patriots, 16-14 (NE)
(RS Pts.—Giants 102, Patriots 87)
*Franchise in Boston prior to 1971
***NEW ENGLAND vs. **N.Y. JETS**
RS: Jets lead series, 46-36-1
PS: Patriots lead series, 1-0
1960—Patriots, 28-24 (NY)
    Patriots, 38-21 (B)
1961—Titans, 21-20 (B)
    Titans, 37-30 (NY)
1962—Patriots, 43-14 (NY)
    Patriots, 24-17 (B)
1963—Patriots, 38-14 (B)
    Jets, 31-24 (NY)
1964—Patriots, 26-10 (B)
    Jets, 35-14 (NY)
1965—Jets, 30-20 (B)
    Patriots, 27-23 (NY)
1966—Tie, 24-24 (B)
    Jets, 38-28 (NY)
1967—Jets, 30-23 (NY)

Jets, 29-24 (B)
1968—Jets, 47-31 (Birmingham)
Jets, 48-14 (NY)
1969—Jets, 23-14 (B)
Jets, 23-17 (NY)
1970—Jets, 31-21 (B)
Jets, 17-3 (NY)
1971—Patriots, 20-0 (NE)
Jets, 13-6 (NY)
1972—Jets, 41-13 (NE)
Jets, 34-10 (NY)
1973—Jets, 9-7 (NE)
Jets, 33-13 (NY)
1974—Patriots, 24-0 (NY)
Jets, 21-16 (NE)
1975—Jets, 36-7 (NY)
Jets, 30-28 (NE)
1976—Patriots, 41-7 (NE)
Patriots, 38-24 (NY)
1977—Jets, 30-27 (NY)
Patriots, 24-13 (NE)
1978—Patriots, 55-21 (NE)
Patriots, 19-17 (NY)
1979—Patriots, 56-3 (NE)
Jets, 27-26 (NY)
1980—Patriots, 21-11 (NY)
Patriots, 34-21 (NE)
1981—Jets, 28-24 (NY)
Jets, 17-6 (NE)
1982—Jets, 31-7 (NE)
1983—Patriots, 23-13 (NE)
Jets, 26-3 (NY)
1984—Patriots, 28-21 (NY)
Patriots, 30-20 (NE)
1985—Patriots, 20-13 (NE)
Jets, 16-13 (NY) OT
***Patriots, 26-14 (NY)
1986—Patriots, 20-6 (NY)
Jets, 31-24 (NE)
1987—Jets, 43-24 (NY)
Patriots, 42-20 (NE)
1988—Patriots, 28-3 (NE)
Patriots, 14-13 (NY)
1989—Patriots, 27-24 (NY)
Jets, 27-26 (NE)
1990—Jets, 37-13 (NE)
Jets, 42-7 (NY)
1991—Jets, 28-21 (NY)
Patriots, 6-3 (NY)
1992—Jets, 30-21 (NY)
Patriots, 24-3 (NE)
1993—Jets, 45-7 (NY)
Jets, 6-0 (NE)
1994—Jets, 24-17 (NY)
Patriots, 24-13 (NE)
1995—Patriots, 20-7 (NY)
Patriots, 31-28 (NE)
1996—Patriots, 31-27 (NY)
Patriots, 34-10 (NE)
1997—Patriots, 27-24 (NE) OT
Jets, 24-19 (NY)
1998—Jets, 24-14 (NE)
Jets, 31-10 (NY)
1999—Patriots, 30-28 (NY)
Jets, 24-17 (NE)
2000—Jets, 20-19 (NY)
Jets, 34-17 (NE)
2001—Jets, 10-3 (NE)
Patriots, 17-16 (NY)
(RS Pts.—Jets 1,868, Patriots 1,804)

(PS Pts.—Patriots 26, Jets 14)
*Franchise in Boston prior to 1971
**Jets known as Titans prior to 1963
***AFC First-Round Playoff
NEW ENGLAND vs. **OAKLAND
RS: Raiders lead series, 13-12-1
PS: Patriots lead series, 2-1
1960—Raiders, 27-14 (O)
Patriots, 34-28 (B)
1961—Patriots, 20-17 (B)
Patriots, 35-21 (O)
1962—Patriots, 26-16 (B)
Raiders, 20-0 (O)
1963—Patriots, 20-14 (O)
Patriots, 20-14 (B)
1964—Patriots, 17-14 (O)
Tie, 43-43 (B)
1965—Raiders, 24-10 (B)
Raiders, 30-21 (O)
1966—Patriots, 24-21 (B)
1967—Raiders, 35-7 (O)
Raiders, 48-14 (B)
1968—Raiders, 41-10 (O)
1969—Raiders, 38-23 (B)
1971—Patriots, 20-6 (NE)
1974—Raiders, 41-26 (O)
1976—Patriots, 48-17 (NE)
***Raiders, 24-21 (O)
1978—Patriots, 21-14 (O)
1981—Raiders, 27-17 (O)
1985—Raiders, 35-20 (NE)
***Patriots, 27-20 (LA)
1987—Patriots, 26-23 (NE)
1989—Raiders, 24-21 (LA)
1994—Raiders, 21-17 (NE)
2001—***Patriots, 16-13 (NE) OT
(RS Pts.—Raiders 659, Patriots 554)
(PS Pts.—Patriots 64, Raiders 57)
*Franchise in Boston prior to 1971
**Franchise in Los Angeles from 1982-1994
***AFC Divisional Playoff
NEW ENGLAND vs. PHILADELPHIA
RS: Eagles lead series, 6-2
1973—Eagles, 24-23 (P)
1977—Patriots, 14-6 (NE)
1978—Patriots, 24-14 (NE)
1981—Eagles, 13-3 (P)
1984—Eagles, 27-17 (P)
1987—Eagles, 34-31 (NE) OT
1990—Eagles, 48-20 (P)
1999—Eagles, 24-9 (P)
(RS Pts.—Eagles 190, Patriots 141)
NEW ENGLAND vs. PITTSBURGH
RS: Steelers lead series, 11-4
PS: Patriots lead series, 2-1
1972—Steelers, 33-3 (P)
1974—Steelers, 21-17 (NE)
1976—Patriots, 30-27 (P)
1979—Steelers, 16-13 (NE) OT
1981—Steelers, 27-21 (P) OT
1982—Steelers, 37-14 (P)
1983—Patriots, 28-23 (P)
1986—Patriots, 34-0 (P)
1989—Steelers, 28-10 (P)
1990—Steelers, 24-3 (P)
1991—Steelers, 20-6 (P)
1993—Steelers, 17-14 (P)
1995—Steelers, 41-27 (P)
1996—*Patriots, 28-3 (NE)

1997—Steelers, 24-21 (NE) OT
*Steelers, 7-6 (P)
1998—Patriots, 23-9 (P)
2001—**Patriots, 24-17 (P)
(RS Pts.—Steelers 347, Patriots 264)
(PS Pts.—Patriots 58, Steelers 27)
*AFC Divisional Playoff
**AFC Championship
NEW ENGLAND vs. *ST. LOUIS
RS: Rams lead series, 5-3
PS: Patriots lead series, 1-0
1974—Patriots, 20-14 (NE)
1980—Rams, 17-14 (NE)
1983—Patriots, 21-7 (LA)
1986—Patriots, 30-28 (LA)
1989—Rams, 24-20 (NE)
1992—Rams, 14-0 (LA)
1998—Rams, 32-18 (StL)
2001—Patriots, 24-17 (NE)
**Patriots, 20-17 (New Orleans)
(RS Pts.—Rams 160, Patriots 140)
(PS Pts.—Patriots 20, Rams 17)
*Franchise in Los Angeles prior to 1995
**Super Bowl XXXVI
NEW ENGLAND vs. **SAN DIEGO
RS: Patriots lead series, 17-11-2
PS: Chargers lead series, 1-0
1960—Patriots, 35-0 (LA)
Chargers, 45-16 (B)
1961—Chargers, 38-27 (B)
Patriots, 41-0 (SD)
1962—Patriots, 24-20 (B)
Patriots, 20-14 (SD)
1963—Chargers, 17-13 (SD)
Chargers, 7-6 (B)
***Chargers, 51-10 (SD)
1964—Patriots, 33-28 (SD)
Chargers, 26-17 (B)
1965—Tie, 10-10 (B)
Patriots, 22-6 (SD)
1966—Chargers, 24-0 (SD)
Patriots, 35-17 (B)
1967—Chargers, 28-14 (SD)
Tie, 31-31 (SD)
1968—Chargers, 27-17 (B)
1969—Chargers, 13-10 (B)
Chargers, 28-18 (SD)
1970—Chargers, 16-14 (B)
1973—Patriots, 30-14 (NE)
1975—Patriots, 33-19 (SD)
1977—Patriots, 24-20 (SD)
1978—Patriots, 28-23 (NE)
1979—Patriots, 27-21 (NE)
1983—Patriots, 37-21 (NE)
1994—Patriots, 23-17 (NE)
1996—Patriots, 45-7 (SD)
1997—Patriots, 41-7 (NE)
2001—Patriots, 29-26 (NE) OT
(RS Pts.—Patriots 720, Chargers 570)
(PS Pts.—Chargers 51, Patriots 10)
*Franchise in Boston prior to 1971
**Franchise in Los Angeles prior to 1961
***AFL Championship
NEW ENGLAND vs. SAN FRANCISCO
RS: 49ers lead series, 7-2
1971—49ers, 27-10 (SF)
1975—Patriots, 24-16 (NE)
1980—49ers, 21-17 (SF)
1983—49ers, 33-13 (NE)
1986—49ers, 29-24 (NE)

1989—49ers, 37-20 (SF)
1992—49ers, 24-12 (NE)
1995—49ers, 28-3 (SF)
1998—Patriots, 24-21 (NE)
(RS Pts.—49ers 236, Patriots 147)
NEW ENGLAND vs. SEATTLE
RS: Seahawks lead series, 7-6
1977—Patriots, 31-0 (NE)
1980—Patriots, 37-31 (S)
1982—Patriots, 16-0 (S)
1983—Seahawks, 24-6 (S)
1984—Patriots, 38-23 (NE)
1985—Patriots, 20-13 (S)
1986—Seahawks, 38-31 (NE)
1988—Patriots, 13-7 (NE)
1989—Seahawks, 24-3 (NE)
1990—Seahawks, 33-20 (NE)
1992—Seahawks, 10-6 (NE)
1993—Seahawks, 17-14 (NE)
        Seahawks, 10-9 (S)
(RS Pts.—Patriots 244, Seahawks 230)
NEW ENGLAND vs. TAMPA BAY
RS: Patriots lead series, 3-2
1976—Patriots, 31-14 (TB)
1985—Patriots, 32-14 (TB)
1988—Patriots, 10-7 (NE) OT
1997—Buccaneers, 27-7 (TB)
2000—Buccaneers, 21-16 (NE)
(RS Pts.—Patriots 96, Buccaneers 83)
*NEW ENGLAND vs. **TENNESSEE
RS: Patriots lead series, 18-14-1
PS: Titans lead series, 1-0
1960—Oilers, 24-10 (B)
        Oilers, 37-21 (H)
1961—Tie, 31-31 (B)
        Oilers, 27-15 (H)
1962—Patriots, 34-21 (B)
        Oilers, 21-17 (H)
1963—Patriots, 45-3 (B)
        Patriots, 46-28 (H)
1964—Patriots, 25-24 (B)
        Patriots, 34-17 (H)
1965—Oilers, 31-10 (H)
        Patriots, 42-14 (B)
1966—Patriots, 27-21 (B)
        Patriots, 38-14 (H)
1967—Patriots, 18-7 (B)
        Oilers, 27-6 (H)
1968—Oilers, 16-0 (B)
        Oilers, 45-17 (H)
1969—Patriots, 24-0 (B)
        Oilers, 27-23 (H)
1971—Patriots, 28-20 (NE)
1973—Patriots, 32-0 (H)
1975—Oilers, 7-0 (NE)
1978—Oilers, 26-23 (NE)
        ***Oilers, 31-14 (NE)
1980—Oilers, 38-34 (H)
1981—Patriots, 38-10 (NE)
1982—Patriots, 29-21 (NE)
1987—Patriots, 21-7 (H)
1988—Oilers, 31-6 (H)
1989—Patriots, 23-13 (NE)
1991—Patriots, 24-20 (NE)
1993—Oilers, 28-14 (NE)
1998—Patriots, 27-16 (NE)
(RS Pts.—Patriots 782, Titans 672)
(PS Pts.—Titans 31, Patriots 14)
*Franchise in Boston prior to 1971
**Franchise in Houston prior to 1997;

known as Oilers prior to 1999
***AFC Divisional Playoff
NEW ENGLAND vs. WASHINGTON
RS: Redskins lead series, 5-1
1972—Patriots, 24-23 (NE)
1978—Redskins, 16-14 (NE)
1981—Redskins, 24-22 (W)
1984—Redskins, 26-10 (NE)
1990—Redskins, 25-10 (NE)
1996—Redskins, 27-22 (NE)
(RS Pts.—Redskins 141, Patriots 102)

NEW ORLEANS vs. ARIZONA
RS: Cardinals lead series, 12-11;
See Arizona vs. New Orleans
NEW ORLEANS vs. ATLANTA
RS: Falcons lead series, 38-27
PS: Falcons lead series, 1-0;
See Atlanta vs. New Orleans
NEW ORLEANS vs. BALTIMORE
RS: Ravens lead series, 2-0;
See Baltimore vs. New Orleans
NEW ORLEANS vs. BUFFALO
RS: Bills lead series, 4-3;
See Buffalo vs. New Orleans
NEW ORLEANS vs. CAROLINA
RS: Saints lead series, 8-6;
See Carolina vs. New Orleans
NEW ORLEANS vs. CHICAGO
RS: Bears lead series, 10-9
PS: Bears lead series, 1-0;
See Chicago vs. New Orleans
NEW ORLEANS vs. CINCINNATI
RS: Saints lead series, 5-4;
See Cincinnati vs. New Orleans
NEW ORLEANS vs. CLEVELAND
RS: Browns lead series, 10-3;
See Cleveland vs. New Orleans
NEW ORLEANS vs. DALLAS
RS: Cowboys lead series, 14-5;
See Dallas vs. New Orleans
NEW ORLEANS vs. DENVER
RS: Broncos lead series, 5-2;
See Denver vs. New Orleans
NEW ORLEANS vs. DETROIT
RS: Saints lead series, 8-7-1;
See Detroit vs. New Orleans
NEW ORLEANS vs. GREEN BAY
RS: Packers lead series, 13-4;
See Green Bay vs. New Orleans
NEW ORLEANS vs. INDIANAPOLIS
RS: Saints lead series, 5-3;
See Indianapolis vs. New Orleans
NEW ORLEANS vs. JACKSONVILLE
RS: Series tied, 1-1;
See Jacksonville vs. New Orleans
NEW ORLEANS vs. KANSAS CITY
RS: Chiefs lead series, 4-3;
See Kansas City vs. New Orleans
NEW ORLEANS vs. MIAMI
RS: Dolphins lead series, 5-3;
See Miami vs. New Orleans
NEW ORLEANS vs. MINNESOTA
RS: Vikings lead series, 14-7
PS: Vikings lead series, 2-0;
See Minnesota vs. New Orleans
NEW ORLEANS vs. NEW ENGLAND
RS: Patriots lead series, 7-3;
See New England vs. New Orleans

NEW ORLEANS vs. N.Y. GIANTS
RS: Giants lead series, 13-8
1967—Giants, 27-21 (NY)
1968—Giants, 38-21 (NY)
1969—Saints, 25-24 (NY)
1970—Saints, 14-10 (NO)
1972—Giants, 45-21 (NY)
1975—Giants, 28-14 (NY)
1978—Saints, 28-17 (NO)
1979—Saints, 24-14 (NO)
1981—Giants, 20-7 (NY)
1984—Saints, 10-3 (NY)
1985—Giants, 21-13 (NY)
1986—Giants, 20-17 (NY)
1987—Saints, 23-14 (NO)
1988—Giants, 13-12 (NO)
1993—Saints, 24-14 (NO)
1994—Saints, 27-22 (NY)
1995—Giants, 45-29 (NY)
1996—Saints 17-3 (NY)
1997—Saints, 14-9 (NY)
1999—Giants, 31-3 (NY)
2001—Giants, 21-13 (NY)
(RS Pts.—Giants 454, Saints 362)
NEW ORLEANS vs. N.Y. JETS
RS: Jets lead series, 5-4
1972—Jets, 18-17 (NY)
1977—Jets, 16-13 (NO)
1980—Saints, 21-20 (NY)
1983—Jets, 31-28 (NO)
1986—Jets, 28-23 (NY)
1989—Saints, 29-14 (NO)
1992—Saints, 20-0 (NY)
1995—Saints, 12-0 (NY)
2001—Jets, 16-9 (NO)
(RS Pts.—Saints 172, Jets 143)
NEW ORLEANS vs. *OAKLAND
RS: Raiders lead series, 5-3-1
1971—Tie, 21-21 (NO)
1975—Raiders, 48-10 (O)
1979—Raiders, 42-35 (NO)
1985—Raiders, 23-13 (LA)
1988—Saints, 20-6 (NO)
1991—Saints, 27-0 (NO)
1994—Raiders, 24-19 (LA)
1997—Saints, 13-10 (O)
2000—Raiders, 31-22 (NO)
(RS Pts.—Raiders 205, Saints 180)
**Franchise in Los Angeles from
1982-1994*
NEW ORLEANS vs. PHILADELPHIA
RS: Eagles lead series, 13-8
PS: Eagles lead series, 1-0
1967—Saints, 31-24 (NO)
        Eagles, 48-21 (P)
1968—Eagles, 29-17 (P)
1969—Eagles, 13-10 (P)
        Saints, 26-17 (NO)
1972—Saints, 21-3 (NO)
1974—Saints, 14-10 (NO)
1977—Eagles, 28-7 (P)
1978—Eagles, 24-17 (NO)
1979—Eagles, 26-14 (NO)
1980—Saints, 34-21 (NO)
1981—Eagles, 31-14 (NO)
1983—Saints, 20-17 (P) OT
1985—Saints, 23-21 (NO)
1987—Eagles, 27-17 (P)
1989—Saints, 30-20 (NO)
1991—Saints, 13-6 (P)

1992—Eagles, 15-13 (P)
   *Eagles, 36-20 (NO)
1993—Eagles, 37-26 (P)
1995—Eagles, 15-10 (NO)
2000—Eagles, 21-7 (NO)
(RS Pts.—Eagles 466, Saints 372)
(PS Pts.—Eagles 36, Saints 20)
NFC First-Round Playoff
NEW ORLEANS vs. PITTSBURGH
RS: Steelers lead series, 6-5
1967—Steelers, 14-10 (NO)
1968—Saints, 16-12 (P)
   Saints, 24-14 (NO)
1969—Saints, 27-24 (NO)
1974—Steelers, 28-7 (NO)
1978—Steelers, 20-14 (P)
1981—Steelers, 20-6 (NO)
1984—Saints, 27-24 (NO)
1987—Saints, 20-16 (P)
1990—Steelers, 9-6 (NO)
1993—Steelers, 37-14 (P)
(RS Pts.—Steelers 218, Saints 171)
NEW ORLEANS vs. *ST. LOUIS
RS: Rams lead series, 36-28
PS: Saints lead series, 1-0
1967—Rams, 27-13 (NO)
1969—Rams, 36-17 (LA)
1970—Rams, 30-17 (NO)
   Rams, 34-16 (LA)
1971—Saints, 24-20 (NO)
   Rams, 45-28 (LA)
1972—Rams, 34-14 (LA)
   Saints, 19-16 (NO)
1973—Rams, 29-7 (LA)
   Rams, 24-13 (NO)
1974—Rams, 24-0 (LA)
   Saints, 20-7 (NO)
1975—Rams, 38-14 (LA)
   Rams, 14-7 (NO)
1976—Rams, 16-10 (NO)
   Rams, 33-14 (LA)
1977—Rams, 14-7 (LA)
   Saints, 27-26 (NO)
1978—Rams, 26-20 (NO)
   Saints, 10-3 (LA)
1979—Rams, 35-17 (NO)
   Saints, 29-14 (LA)
1980—Rams, 45-31 (LA)
   Rams, 27-7 (NO)
1981—Saints, 23-17 (NO)
   Saints, 21-13 (LA)
1983—Rams, 30-27 (LA)
   Rams, 26-24 (NO)
1984—Eagles, 28-10 (NO)
   Rams, 34-21 (LA)
1985—Rams, 28-10 (LA)
   Saints, 29-3 (NO)
1986—Saints, 6-0 (NO)
   Rams, 26-13 (LA)
1987—Saints, 37-10 (NO)
   Saints, 31-14 (LA)
1988—Rams, 12-10 (NO)
   Saints, 14-10 (LA)
1989—Saints, 40-21 (LA)
   Rams, 20-17 (NO) OT
1990—Saints, 24-20 (LA)
   Saints, 20-17 (NO)
1991—Saints, 24-7 (NO)
   Saints, 24-17 (LA)
1992—Saints, 13-10 (NO)

Saints, 37-14 (LA)
1993—Saints, 37-6 (LA)
   Rams, 23-20 (NO)
1994—Saints, 37-34 (NO)
   Saints, 31-15 (LA)
1995—Rams, 17-13 (StL)
   Saints, 19-10 (NO)
1996—Rams, 26-10 (NO)
   Rams, 14-13 (StL)
1997—Rams, 38-24 (StL)
   Rams, 34-27 (NO)
1998—Saints, 24-17 (StL)
   Saints, 24-3 (NO)
1999—Rams, 43-12 (StL)
   Rams, 30-14 (NO)
2000—Saints, 31-24 (StL)
   Rams, 26-21 (NO)
   **Saints, 31-28 (NO)
2001—Saints, 34-31 (StL)
   Rams, 34-21 (NO)
(RS Pts.—Rams 1,419, Saints 1,268)
(PS Pts.—Saints 31, Rams 28)
Franchise in Los Angeles prior to 1995
**NFC First-Round Playoff
NEW ORLEANS vs. SAN DIEGO
RS: Chargers lead series, 6-2
1973—Chargers, 17-14 (SD)
1977—Chargers, 14-0 (NO)
1979—Chargers, 35-0 (NO)
1988—Saints, 23-17 (SD)
1991—Chargers, 24-21 (SD)
1994—Chargers, 36-22 (NO)
1997—Chargers, 20-6 (NO)
2000—Saints, 28-27 (SD)
(RS Pts.—Chargers 190, Saints 114)
NEW ORLEANS vs. SAN FRANCISCO
RS: 49ers lead series, 45-18-2
1967—49ers, 27-13 (SF)
1969—Saints, 43-38 (NO)
1970—Tie, 20-20 (SF)
   49ers, 38-27 (NO)
1971—49ers, 38-20 (NO)
   Saints, 26-20 (SF)
1972—49ers, 37-2 (NO)
   Tie, 20-20 (SF)
1973—49ers, 40-0 (SF)
   Saints, 16-10 (NO)
1974—49ers, 17-13 (NO)
   49ers, 35-21 (SF)
1975—49ers, 35-21 (SF)
   49ers, 16-6 (NO)
1976—49ers, 33-3 (SF)
   49ers, 27-7 (NO)
1977—49ers, 10-7 (NO) OT
   49ers, 20-17 (SF)
1978—49ers, 14-7 (SF)
   Saints, 24-13 (NO)
1979—Saints, 30-21 (SF)
   Saints, 31-20 (NO)
1980—49ers, 26-23 (NO)
   49ers, 38-35 (SF) OT
1981—49ers, 21-14 (SF)
   49ers, 21-17 (NO)
1982—Saints, 23-20 (SF)
1983—49ers, 32-13 (NO)
   49ers, 27-0 (SF)
1984—49ers, 30-20 (SF)
   49ers, 35-3 (NO)
1985—Saints, 20-17 (SF)
   49ers, 31-19 (NO)

1986—49ers, 26-17 (SF)
   Saints, 23-10 (NO)
1987—49ers, 24-22 (NO)
   Saints, 26-24 (SF)
1988—49ers, 34-33 (NO)
   49ers, 30-17 (SF)
1989—49ers, 24-20 (NO)
   49ers, 31-13 (SF)
1990—49ers, 13-12 (NO)
   Saints, 13-10 (SF)
1991—Saints, 10-3 (NO)
   49ers, 38-24 (SF)
1992—49ers, 16-10 (NO)
   49ers, 21-20 (SF)
1993—Saints, 16-13 (NO)
   49ers, 42-7 (SF)
1994—49ers, 24-13 (SF)
   49ers, 35-14 (NO)
1995—49ers, 24-22 (SF)
   Saints, 11-7 (SF)
1996—49ers, 27-11 (SF)
   49ers, 24-17 (NO)
1997—49ers, 33-7 (SF)
   49ers, 23-0 (NO)
1998—49ers, 31-0 (NO)
   49ers, 31-20 (SF)
1999—49ers, 28-21 (SF)
   Saints, 24-6 (NO)
2000—Saints, 31-15 (NO)
   Saints, 31-27 (SF)
2001—49ers, 28-27 (SF)
   49ers, 38-0 (NO)
(RS Pts.—49ers 1,600, Saints 1,100)
NEW ORLEANS vs. SEATTLE
RS: Saints lead series, 4-3
1976—Saints, 51-27 (S)
1979—Seahawks, 38-24 (S)
1985—Seahawks, 27-3 (NO)
1988—Saints, 20-19 (S)
1991—Saints, 27-24 (NO)
1997—Saints, 20-17 (NO) OT
2000—Seahawks, 20-10 (S)
(RS Pts.—Seahawks 172, Saints 155)
NEW ORLEANS vs. TAMPA BAY
RS: Saints lead series, 13-7
1977—Buccaneers, 33-14 (NO)
1978—Saints, 17-10 (TB)
1979—Saints, 42-14 (TB)
1981—Buccaneers, 31-14 (NO)
1982—Buccaneers, 13-10 (NO)
1983—Saints, 24-21 (TB)
1984—Saints, 17-13 (NO)
1985—Saints, 20-13 (NO)
1986—Saints, 38-7 (NO)
1987—Saints, 44-34 (NO)
1988—Saints, 13-9 (NO)
1989—Buccaneers, 20-10 (TB)
1990—Saints, 35-7 (NO)
1991—Saints, 23-7 (NO)
1992—Saints, 23-21 (NO)
1994—Saints, 9-7 (TB)
1996—Buccaneers, 13-7 (TB)
1998—Saints, 9-3 (NO)
1999—Buccaneers, 31-16 (NO)
2001—Buccaneers, 48-21 (TB)
(RS Pts.—Saints 406, Buccaneers 355)
NEW ORLEANS vs. *TENNESSEE
RS: Titans lead series, 5-4-1
1971—Tie, 13-13 (H)
1976—Oilers, 31-26 (NO)

1978—Oilers, 17-12 (NO)
1981—Saints, 27-24 (H)
1984—Saints, 27-10 (H)
1987—Saints, 24-10 (NO)
1990—Oilers, 23-10 (H)
1993—Saints, 33-21 (NO)
1996—Oilers, 31-14 (NO)
1999—Titans, 24-21 (NO)
(RS Pts.—Saints 207, Titans 204)
Franchise in Houston prior to 1997; known as Oilers prior to 1999
NEW ORLEANS vs. WASHINGTON
RS: Redskins lead series, 13-5
1967—Redskins, 30-10 (NO)
        Saints, 30-14 (W)
1968—Saints, 37-17 (NO)
1969—Redskins, 26-20 (NO)
        Redskins, 17-14 (W)
1971—Redskins, 24-14 (W)
1973—Saints, 19-3 (NO)
1975—Redskins, 41-3 (W)
1979—Saints, 14-10 (W)
1980—Redskins, 22-14 (W)
1982—Redskins, 27-10 (NO)
1986—Redskins, 14-6 (NO)
1988—Redskins, 27-24 (W)
1989—Redskins, 16-14 (NO)
1990—Redskins, 31-17 (W)
1992—Saints, 20-3 (NO)
1994—Redskins, 38-24 (NO)
2001—Redskins, 40-10 (NO)
(RS Pts.—Redskins 400, Saints 300)

N.Y. GIANTS vs. ARIZONA
RS: Giants lead series, 77-39-2;
See Arizona vs. N.Y. Giants
N.Y. GIANTS vs. ATLANTA
RS: Series tied, 7-7;
See Atlanta vs. N.Y. Giants
N.Y. GIANTS vs. BALTIMORE
RS: Ravens lead series, 1-0
PS: Ravens lead series, 1-0;
See Baltimore vs. N.Y. Giants
N.Y. GIANTS vs. BUFFALO
RS: Bills lead series, 5-3
PS: Giants lead series, 1-0;
See Buffalo vs. N.Y. Giants
N.Y. GIANTS vs. CAROLINA
RS: Panthers lead series, 1-0;
See Carolina vs. N.Y. Giants
N.Y. GIANTS vs. CHICAGO
RS: Bears lead series, 25-17-2
PS: Bears lead series, 5-3;
See Chicago vs. N.Y. Giants
N.Y. GIANTS vs. CINCINNATI
RS: Bengals lead series, 4-2;
See Cincinnati vs. N.Y. Giants
N.Y. GIANTS vs. CLEVELAND
RS: Browns lead series, 25-18-2
PS: Series tied, 1-1;
See Cleveland vs. N.Y. Giants
N.Y. GIANTS vs. DALLAS
RS: Cowboys lead series, 48-29-2;
See Dallas vs. N.Y. Giants
N.Y. GIANTS vs. DENVER
RS: Series tied, 4-4
PS: Giants lead series, 1-0;
See Denver vs. N.Y. Giants
N.Y. GIANTS vs. DETROIT
RS: Lions lead series, 19-17-1

PS: Lions lead series, 1-0;
See Detroit vs. N.Y. Giants
N.Y. GIANTS vs. GREEN BAY
RS: Packers lead series, 24-20-2
PS: Packers lead series, 4-1;
See Green Bay vs. N.Y. Giants
N.Y. GIANTS vs. INDIANAPOLIS
RS: Colts lead series, 6-5
PS: Colts lead series, 2-0;
See Indianapolis vs. N.Y. Giants
N.Y. GIANTS vs. JACKSONVILLE
RS: Series tied, 1-1;
See Jacksonville vs. N.Y. Giants
N.Y. GIANTS vs. KANSAS CITY
RS: Giants lead series, 8-2;
See Kansas City vs. N.Y. Giants
N.Y. GIANTS vs. MIAMI
RS: Giants lead series, 3-1;
See Miami vs. N.Y. Giants
N.Y. GIANTS vs. MINNESOTA
RS: Vikings lead series, 9-5
PS: Giants lead series, 2-1;
See Minnesota vs. N.Y. Giants
N.Y. GIANTS vs. NEW ENGLAND
RS: Series tied, 3-3;
See New England vs. N.Y. Giants
N.Y. GIANTS vs. NEW ORLEANS
RS: Giants lead series, 13-8;
See New Orleans vs. N.Y. Giants
N.Y. GIANTS vs. N.Y. JETS
RS: Giants lead series, 5-4
1970—Giants, 22-10 (NYJ)
1974—Jets, 26-20 (New Haven) OT
1981—Jets, 26-7 (NYG)
1984—Giants, 20-10 (NYJ)
1987—Giants, 20-7 (NYG)
1988—Jets, 27-21 (NYJ)
1993—Jets, 10-6 (NYG)
1996—Giants, 13-6 (NYJ)
1999—Giants, 41-28 (NYG)
(RS Pts.—Giants 170, Jets 150)
N.Y. GIANTS vs. *OAKLAND
RS: Raiders lead series, 7-2
1973—Raiders, 42-0 (O)
1980—Raiders, 33-17 (NY)
1983—Raiders, 27-12 (LA)
1986—Giants, 14-9 (LA)
1989—Giants, 34-17 (NY)
1992—Raiders, 13-10 (LA)
1995—Raiders, 17-13 (NY)
1998—Raiders, 20-17 (O)
2001—Raiders, 28-10 (NY)
(RS Pts.—Raiders 206, Giants 127)
Franchise in Los Angeles from 1982-1994
N.Y. GIANTS vs. PHILADELPHIA
RS: Giants lead series, 72-60-2
PS: Giants lead series, 2-0
1933—Giants, 56-0 (NY)
        Giants, 20-14 (P)
1934—Giants, 17-0 (NY)
        Eagles, 6-0 (P)
1935—Giants, 10-0 (NY)
        Giants, 21-14 (P)
1936—Eagles, 10-7 (P)
        Giants, 21-17 (NY)
1937—Giants, 16-7 (P)
        Giants, 21-0 (NY)
1938—Eagles, 14-10 (P)
        Giants, 17-7 (NY)

1939—Giants, 13-3 (P)
        Giants, 27-10 (NY)
1940—Giants, 20-14 (P)
        Giants, 17-7 (NY)
1941—Giants, 24-0 (P)
        Giants, 16-0 (NY)
1942—Giants, 35-17 (P)
        Giants, 14-0 (NY)
1944—Eagles, 24-17 (NY)
        Tie, 21-21 (P)
1945—Eagles, 38-17 (P)
        Giants, 28-21 (NY)
1946—Eagles, 24-14 (P)
        Giants, 45-17 (NY)
1947—Eagles, 23-0 (P)
        Eagles, 41-24 (NY)
1948—Eagles, 45-0 (P)
        Eagles, 35-14 (NY)
1949—Eagles, 24-3 (NY)
        Eagles, 17-3 (P)
1950—Giants, 7-3 (NY)
        Giants, 9-7 (P)
1951—Giants, 26-24 (NY)
        Giants, 23-7 (P)
1952—Giants, 31-7 (P)
        Eagles, 14-10 (NY)
1953—Eagles, 30-7 (P)
        Giants, 37-28 (NY)
1954—Giants, 27-14 (NY)
        Eagles, 29-14 (P)
1955—Eagles, 27-17 (P)
        Giants, 31-7 (NY)
1956—Giants, 20-3 (NY)
        Giants, 21-7 (P)
1957—Giants, 24-20 (P)
        Giants, 13-0 (NY)
1958—Eagles, 27-24 (P)
        Giants, 24-10 (NY)
1959—Eagles, 49-21 (P)
        Giants, 24-7 (NY)
1960—Eagles, 17-10 (NY)
        Eagles, 31-23 (P)
1961—Giants, 38-21 (NY)
        Giants, 28-24 (P)
1962—Giants, 29-13 (P)
        Giants, 19-14 (NY)
1963—Giants, 37-14 (P)
        Giants, 42-14 (NY)
1964—Eagles, 38-7 (P)
        Eagles, 23-17 (NY)
1965—Giants, 16-14 (P)
        Giants, 35-27 (NY)
1966—Eagles, 35-17 (P)
        Eagles, 31-3 (NY)
1967—Giants, 44-7 (NY)
1968—Giants, 34-25 (P)
        Giants, 7-6 (NY)
1969—Eagles, 23-20 (NY)
1970—Giants, 30-23 (NY)
        Eagles, 23-20 (P)
1971—Eagles, 23-7 (P)
        Eagles, 41-28 (NY)
1972—Giants, 27-12 (P)
        Giants, 62-10 (NY)
1973—Tie, 23-23 (P)
        Eagles, 20-16 (P)
1974—Eagles, 35-7 (P)
        Eagles, 20-7 (New Haven)
1975—Giants, 23-14 (P)
        Eagles, 13-10 (NY)

1976—Eagles, 20-7 (P)
    Eagles, 10-0 (NY)
1977—Eagles, 28-10 (NY)
    Eagles, 17-14 (P)
1978—Eagles, 19-17 (NY)
    Eagles, 20-3 (P)
1979—Eagles, 23-17 (P)
    Eagles, 17-13 (NY)
1980—Eagles, 35-3 (P)
    Eagles, 31-16 (NY)
1981—Eagles, 24-10 (NY)
    Giants, 20-10 (P)
    *Giants, 27-21 (P)
1982—Giants, 23-7 (NY)
    Giants, 26-24 (P)
1983—Eagles, 17-13 (NY)
    Giants, 23-0 (P)
1984—Giants, 28-27 (NY)
    Eagles, 24-10 (P)
1985—Giants, 21-0 (NY)
    Giants, 16-10 (P) OT
1986—Giants, 35-3 (NY)
    Giants, 17-14 (P)
1987—Giants, 20-17 (P)
    Giants, 23-20 (NY) OT
1988—Eagles, 24-13 (P)
    Eagles, 23-17 (NY) OT
1989—Eagles, 21-19 (P)
    Eagles, 24-17 (NY)
1990—Giants, 27-20 (NY)
    Eagles, 31-13 (P)
1991—Giants, 30-7 (P)
    Eagles, 19-14 (NY)
1992—Eagles, 47-34 (NY)
    Eagles, 20-10 (P)
1993—Giants, 21-10 (NY)
    Giants, 7-3 (P)
1994—Giants, 28-23 (NY)
    Giants, 16-13 (P)
1995—Eagles, 17-14 (NY)
    Eagles, 28-19 (P)
1996—Eagles, 19-10 (NY)
    Eagles, 24-0 (P)
1997—Giants, 31-17 (NY)
    Giants, 31-21 (P)
1998—Giants, 20-0 (NY)
    Giants, 20-10 (P)
1999—Giants, 16-15 (NY)
    Giants, 23-17 (P) OT
2000—Giants, 33-18 (P)
    Giants, 24-7 (NY)
    **Giants, 20-10 (NY)
2001—Eagles, 10-9 (NY)
    Eagles, 24-21 (P)
(RS Pts.—Giants 2,563, Eagles 2,376)
(PS Pts.—Giants 47, Eagles 31)
*NFC First-Round Playoff
**NFC Divisional Playoff
N.Y. GIANTS vs. *PITTSBURGH
RS: Giants lead series, 43-27-3
1933—Giants, 23-2 (P)
    Giants, 27-3 (NY)
1934—Giants, 14-12 (P)
    Giants, 17-7 (NY)
1935—Giants, 42-7 (P)
    Giants, 13-0 (NY)
1936—Pirates, 10-7 (P)
1937—Giants, 10-7 (P)
    Giants, 17-0 (NY)
1938—Giants, 27-14 (P)

Pirates, 13-10 (NY)
1939—Giants, 14-7 (P)
    Giants, 23-7 (NY)
1940—Tie, 10-10 (P)
    Giants, 12-0 (NY)
1941—Giants, 37-10 (P)
    Giants, 28-7 (NY)
1942—Steelers, 13-10 (P)
    Steelers, 17-9 (NY)
1945—Giants, 34-6 (P)
    Steelers, 21-7 (NY)
1946—Giants, 17-14 (P)
    Giants, 7-0 (NY)
1947—Steelers, 38-21 (NY)
    Steelers, 24-7 (P)
1948—Giants, 34-27 (NY)
    Steelers, 38-28 (P)
1949—Steelers, 28-7 (P)
    Steelers, 21-17 (NY)
1950—Giants, 18-7 (P)
    Steelers, 17-6 (NY)
1951—Tie, 13-13 (P)
    Giants, 14-0 (NY)
1952—Steelers, 63-7 (P)
1953—Steelers, 24-14 (P)
    Steelers, 14-10 (NY)
1954—Giants, 30-6 (P)
    Giants, 24-3 (NY)
1955—Steelers, 30-23 (P)
    Steelers, 19-17 (NY)
1956—Giants, 38-10 (NY)
    Giants, 17-14 (P)
1957—Giants, 35-0 (NY)
    Steelers, 21-10 (P)
1958—Giants, 17-6 (NY)
    Steelers, 31-10 (P)
1959—Giants, 21-16 (P)
    Steelers, 14-9 (NY)
1960—Giants, 19-17 (P)
    Giants, 27-24 (NY)
1961—Giants, 17-14 (P)
    Giants, 42-21 (NY)
1962—Giants, 31-27 (P)
    Steelers, 20-17 (NY)
1963—Steelers, 31-0 (P)
    Giants, 33-17 (NY)
1964—Steelers, 27-24 (P)
    Steelers, 44-17 (NY)
1965—Giants, 23-13 (P)
    Giants, 35-10 (NY)
1966—Tie, 34-34 (P)
    Steelers, 47-28 (NY)
1967—Giants, 27-24 (P)
    Giants, 28-20 (NY)
1968—Giants, 34-20 (P)
1969—Giants, 10-7 (NY)
    Giants, 21-17 (P)
1971—Steelers, 17-13 (P)
1976—Steelers, 27-0 (NY)
1985—Giants, 28-10 (NY)
1991—Giants, 23-20 (P)
1994—Steelers, 10-6 (NY)
2000—Giants, 30-10 (NY)
(RS Pts.—Giants 1,429, Steelers 1,199)
*Steelers known as Pirates prior to 1941
N.Y. GIANTS vs. *ST. LOUIS
RS: Rams lead series, 25-9
PS: Series tied, 1-1
1938—Giants, 28-0 (NY)
1940—Rams, 13-0 (NY)

1941—Giants, 49-14 (NY)
1945—Rams, 21-17 (NY)
1946—Rams, 31-21 (NY)
1947—Rams, 34-10 (LA)
1948—Rams, 52-37 (NY)
1953—Rams, 21-7 (LA)
1954—Rams, 17-16 (NY)
1959—Giants, 23-21 (LA)
1961—Giants, 24-14 (NY)
1966—Rams, 55-14 (LA)
1968—Rams, 24-21 (LA)
1970—Rams, 31-3 (NY)
1973—Rams, 40-6 (LA)
1976—Rams, 24-10 (LA)
1978—Rams, 20-17 (NY)
1979—Giants, 20-14 (LA)
1980—Rams, 28-7 (NY)
1981—Giants, 10-7 (NY)
1983—Rams, 16-6 (NY)
1984—Rams, 33-12 (LA)
    **Giants, 16-13 (LA)
1985—Giants, 24-19 (NY)
1988—Rams, 45-31 (NY)
1989—Rams, 31-10 (LA)
    ***Rams, 19-13 (NY) OT
1990—Giants, 31-7 (LA)
1991—Giants, 19-13 (NY)
1992—Rams, 38-17 (LA)
1993—Giants, 20-10 (NY)
1994—Rams, 17-10 (LA)
1997—Rams, 13-3 (StL)
1999—Rams, 31-10 (StL)
2000—Rams, 38-24 (NY)
2001—Rams, 15-14 (StL)
(RS Pts.—Rams 813, Giants 565)
(PS Pts.—Rams 32, Giants 29)
*Franchise in Los Angeles prior to 1995
and in Cleveland prior to 1946
**NFC First-Round Playoff
***NFC Divisional Playoff
N.Y. GIANTS vs. SAN DIEGO
RS: Giants lead series, 5-3
1971—Giants, 35-17 (NY)
1975—Giants, 35-24 (NY)
1980—Chargers, 44-7 (SD)
1983—Chargers, 41-34 (NY)
1986—Giants, 20-7 (NY)
1989—Giants, 20-13 (SD)
1995—Chargers, 27-17 (NY)
1998—Giants, 34-16 (SD)
(RS Pts.—Giants 202, Chargers 189)
N.Y. GIANTS vs. SAN FRANCISCO
RS: 49ers lead series, 12-11
PS: Series tied, 3-3
1952—Giants, 23-14 (NY)
1956—Giants, 38-21 (SF)
1957—49ers, 27-17 (NY)
1960—Giants, 21-19 (SF)
1963—Giants, 48-14 (NY)
1968—49ers, 26-10 (NY)
1972—Giants, 23-17 (SF)
1975—Giants, 26-23 (SF)
1977—Giants, 20-17 (NY)
1978—Giants, 27-10 (NY)
1979—Giants, 32-16 (NY)
1980—49ers, 12-0 (SF)
1981—49ers, 17-10 (SF)
    *49ers, 38-24 (SF)
1984—49ers, 31-10 (NY)
    *49ers, 21-10 (SF)

1985—**Giants, 17-3 (NY)
1986—Giants, 21-17 (SF)
    *Giants, 49-3 (NY)
1987—49ers, 41-21 (NY)
1988—49ers, 20-17 (NY)
1989—49ers, 34-24 (SF)
1990—49ers, 7-3 (SF)
    ***Giants, 15-13 (SF)
1991—Giants, 16-14 (NY)
1992—49ers, 31-14 (NY)
1993—*49ers, 44-3 (SF)
1995—49ers, 20-6 (SF)
1998—49ers, 31-7 (SF)
(RS Pts.—49ers 479, Giants 434)
(PS Pts.—49ers 122, Giants 118)
*NFC Divisional Playoff
**NFC First-Round Playoff
***NFC Championship
N.Y. GIANTS vs. SEATTLE
RS: Giants lead series, 6-3
1976—Giants, 28-16 (NY)
1980—Giants, 27-21 (S)
1981—Giants, 32-0 (S)
1983—Seahawks, 17-12 (NY)
1986—Seahawks, 17-12 (S)
1989—Giants, 15-3 (NY)
1992—Giants, 23-10 (NY)
1995—Seahawks, 30-28 (S)
2001—Giants, 27-24 (NY)
(RS Pts.—Giants 204, Seahawks 138)
N.Y. GIANTS vs. TAMPA BAY
RS: Giants lead series, 9-5
1977—Giants, 10-0 (TB)
1978—Giants, 19-13 (TB)
    Giants, 17-14 (NY)
1979—Giants, 17-14 (NY)
    Buccaneers, 31-3 (TB)
1980—Buccaneers, 30-13 (TB)
1984—Giants, 17-14 (NY)
    Buccaneers, 20-17 (TB)
1985—Giants, 22-20 (NY)
1991—Giants, 21-14 (TB)
1993—Giants, 23-7 (NY)
1997—Buccaneers, 20-8 (NY)
1998—Buccaneers, 20-3 (TB)
1999—Giants, 17-13 (TB)
(RS Pts.—Buccaneers 230, Giants 207)
N.Y. GIANTS vs. *TENNESSEE
RS: Giants lead series, 5-2
1973—Giants, 34-14 (NY)
1982—Giants, 17-14 (NY)
1985—Giants, 35-14 (H)
1991—Giants, 24-20 (NY)
1994—Giants, 13-10 (H)
1997—Oilers, 10-6 (T)
2000—Titans, 28-14 (T)
(RS Pts.—Giants 143, Titans 110)
*Franchise in Houston prior to 1997;
known as Oilers prior to 1999
N.Y. GIANTS vs. *WASHINGTON
RS: Giants lead series, 77-57-4
PS: Series tied, 1-1
1932—Braves, 14-6 (B)
    Tie, 0-0 (NY)
1933—Redskins, 21-20 (B)
    Giants, 7-0 (NY)
1934—Giants, 16-13 (B)
    Giants, 3-0 (NY)
1935—Giants, 20-12 (B)
    Giants, 17-6 (NY)

1936—Giants, 7-0 (B)
    Redskins, 14-0 (NY)
1937—Redskins, 13-3 (W)
    Redskins, 49-14 (NY)
1938—Giants, 10-7 (W)
    Giants, 36-0 (NY)
1939—Tie, 0-0 (W)
    Giants, 9-7 (NY)
1940—Redskins, 21-7 (W)
    Giants, 21-7 (NY)
1941—Giants, 17-10 (W)
    Giants, 20-13 (NY)
1942—Giants, 14-7 (W)
    Redskins, 14-7 (NY)
1943—Giants, 14-10 (NY)
    Giants, 31-7 (W)
    **Redskins, 28-0 (NY)
1944—Giants, 16-13 (W)
    Giants, 31-0 (W)
1945—Redskins, 24-14 (NY)
    Redskins, 17-0 (W)
1946—Redskins, 24-14 (W)
    Giants, 31-0 (NY)
1947—Redskins, 28-20 (W)
    Giants, 35-10 (NY)
1948—Redskins, 41-10 (W)
    Redskins, 28-21 (NY)
1949—Giants, 45-35 (W)
    Giants, 23-7 (NY)
1950—Giants, 21-17 (W)
    Giants, 24-21 (NY)
1951—Giants, 35-14 (W)
    Giants, 28-14 (NY)
1952—Giants, 14-10 (W)
    Redskins, 27-17 (NY)
1953—Redskins, 13-9 (W)
    Redskins, 24-21 (NY)
1954—Giants, 51-21 (W)
    Giants, 24-7 (NY)
1955—Giants, 35-7 (NY)
    Giants, 27-20 (W)
1956—Redskins, 33-7 (W)
    Giants, 28-14 (NY)
1957—Giants, 24-20 (W)
    Redskins, 31-14 (NY)
1958—Giants, 21-14 (W)
    Giants, 30-0 (NY)
1959—Giants, 45-14 (W)
    Giants, 24-10 (W)
1960—Tie, 24-24 (NY)
    Giants, 17-3 (W)
1961—Giants, 24-21 (W)
    Giants, 53-0 (W)
1962—Giants, 49-34 (NY)
    Giants, 42-24 (W)
1963—Giants, 24-14 (W)
    Giants, 44-14 (NY)
1964—Giants, 13-10 (W)
    Redskins, 36-21 (W)
1965—Redskins, 23-7 (NY)
    Giants, 27-10 (W)
1966—Giants, 13-10 (NY)
    Redskins, 72-41 (W)
1967—Redskins, 38-34 (W)
1968—Giants, 48-21 (NY)
    Giants, 13-10 (W)
1969—Redskins, 20-14 (W)
1970—Giants, 35-33 (W)
    Giants, 27-24 (NY)
1971—Redskins, 30-3 (NY)

    Redskins, 23-7 (W)
1972—Redskins, 23-16 (NY)
    Redskins, 27-13 (W)
1973—Redskins, 21-3 (New Haven)
    Redskins, 27-24 (W)
1974—Redskins, 13-10 (New Haven)
    Redskins, 24-3 (W)
1975—Redskins, 49-13 (W)
    Redskins, 21-13 (NY)
1976—Redskins, 19-17 (W)
    Giants, 12-9 (NY)
1977—Giants, 20-17 (NY)
    Giants, 17-6 (W)
1978—Giants, 17-6 (W)
    Redskins, 16-13 (W) OT
1979—Redskins, 27-0 (W)
    Giants, 14-6 (W)
1980—Redskins, 23-21 (NY)
    Redskins, 16-13 (W)
1981—Giants, 17-7 (W)
    Redskins, 30-27 (NY) OT
1982—Redskins, 27-17 (W)
    Redskins, 15-14 (W)
1983—Redskins, 33-17 (NY)
    Redskins, 31-22 (W)
1984—Redskins, 30-14 (W)
    Giants, 37-13 (NY)
1985—Giants, 17-3 (NY)
    Redskins, 23-21 (W)
1986—Giants, 27-20 (NY)
    Giants, 24-14 (W)
    ***Giants, 17-0 (W)
1987—Redskins, 38-12 (NY)
    Redskins, 23-19 (W)
1988—Giants, 27-20 (NY)
    Giants, 24-23 (W)
1989—Giants, 27-24 (W)
    Giants, 20-17 (NY)
1990—Giants, 24-20 (W)
    Giants, 21-10 (NY)
1991—Redskins, 17-13 (NY)
    Redskins, 34-17 (W)
1992—Giants, 24-7 (W)
    Redskins, 28-10 (NY)
1993—Giants, 41-7 (NY)
    Giants, 20-6 (NY)
1994—Giants, 31-23 (NY)
    Giants, 21-19 (W)
1995—Giants, 24-15 (NY)
    Giants, 20-13 (NY)
1996—Redskins, 31-10 (NY)
    Redskins, 31-21 (W)
1997—Tie, 7-7 (W) OT
    Giants, 30-10 (NY)
1998—Giants, 31-24 (NY)
    Redskins, 21-14 (W)
1999—Redskins, 50-21 (NY)
    Redskins, 23-13 (W)
2000—Redskins, 16-6 (W)
    Giants, 9-7 (W)
2001—Giants, 23-9 (NY)
    Redskins, 35-21 (W)
(RS Pts.—Giants 2,732, Redskins 2,501)
(PS Pts.—Redskins 28, Giants 17)
*Franchise in Boston prior to 1937 and
known as Braves prior to 1933
**Division Playoff
***NFC Championship

N.Y. JETS vs. ARIZONA
RS: Jets lead series, 3-2;
See Arizona vs. N.Y. Jets
N.Y. JETS vs. ATLANTA
RS: Series tied, 4-4;
See Atlanta vs. N.Y. Jets
N.Y. JETS vs BALTIMORE
RS: Ravens lead series, 2-1;
See Baltimore vs. N.Y. Jets
N.Y. JETS vs. BUFFALO
RS: Bills lead series, 46-36
PS: Bills lead series, 1-0;
See Buffalo vs. N.Y. Jets
N.Y. JETS vs. CAROLINA
RS: Jets lead series, 2-1;
See Carolina vs. N.Y. Jets
N.Y. JETS vs. CHICAGO
RS: Bears lead series, 4-3;
See Chicago vs. N.Y. Jets
N.Y. JETS vs. CINCINNATI
RS: Jets lead series, 11-6
PS: Jets lead series, 1-0;
See Cincinnati vs. N.Y. Jets
N.Y. JETS vs. CLEVELAND
RS: Browns lead series, 9-6
PS: Browns lead series, 1-0;
See Cleveland vs. N.Y. Jets
N.Y. JETS vs. DALLAS
RS: Cowboys lead series, 5-2;
See Dallas vs. N.Y. Jets
N.Y. JETS vs. DENVER
RS: Broncos lead series, 14-13-1
PS: Broncos lead series, 1-0;
See Denver vs. N.Y. Jets
N.Y. JETS vs. DETROIT
RS: Lions lead series, 6-3;
See Detroit vs. N.Y. Jets
N.Y. JETS vs. GREEN BAY
RS: Jets lead series, 6-2;
See Green Bay vs. N.Y. Jets
N.Y. JETS vs. INDIANAPOLIS
RS: Colts lead series, 38-25
PS: Jets lead series, 1-0;
See Indianapolis vs. N.Y. Jets
N.Y. JETS vs. JACKSONVILLE
RS: Jaguars lead series, 2-1
PS: Jets lead series, 1-0;
See Jacksonville vs. N.Y. Jets
N.Y. JETS vs. KANSAS CITY
RS: Series tied, 14-14-1
PS: Series tied, 1-1;
See Kansas City vs. N.Y. Jets
N.Y. JETS vs. MIAMI
RS: Jets lead series, 37-34-1
PS: Dolphins lead series, 1-0;
See Miami vs. N.Y. Jets
N.Y. JETS vs. MINNESOTA
RS: Jets lead series, 5-1;
See Minnesota vs. N.Y. Jets
N.Y. JETS vs. NEW ENGLAND
RS: Jets lead series, 46-36-1
PS: Patriots lead series, 1-0;
See New England vs. N.Y. Jets
N.Y. JETS vs. NEW ORLEANS
RS: Jets lead series, 5-4;
See New Orleans vs. N.Y. Jets
N.Y. JETS vs. N.Y. GIANTS
RS: Giants lead series, 5-4;
See N.Y. Giants vs. N.Y. Jets
*N.Y. JETS vs. **OAKLAND

RS: Raiders lead series, 18-11-2
PS: Jets lead series, 2-1
1960—Raiders, 28-27 (NY)
     Titans, 31-28 (O)
1961—Titans, 14-6 (O)
     Titans, 23-12 (NY)
1962—Titans, 28-17 (O)
     Titans, 31-21 (NY)
1963—Jets, 10-7 (NY)
     Raiders, 49-26 (O)
1964—Jets, 35-13 (NY)
     Raiders, 35-26 (O)
1965—Tie, 24-24 (NY)
     Raiders, 24-14 (O)
1966—Raiders, 24-21 (NY)
     Tie, 28-28 (O)
1967—Jets, 27-14 (NY)
     Raiders, 38-29 (O)
1968—Raiders, 43-32 (O)
     ***Jets, 27-23 (NY)
1969—Raiders, 27-14 (NY)
1970—Raiders, 14-13 (NY)
1972—Raiders, 24-16 (O)
1977—Raiders, 28-27 (NY)
1979—Jets, 28-19 (NY)
1982—****Jets, 17-14 (LA)
1985—Raiders, 31-0 (LA)
1989—Raiders, 14-7 (NY)
1993—Raiders, 24-20 (LA)
1995—Raiders, 47-10 (NY)
1996—Raiders, 34-13 (NY)
1997—Jets 23-22 (NY)
1999—Raiders, 24-23 (O)
2000—Raiders, 31-7 (O)
2001—Jets, 24-22 (O)
     *****Raiders, 38-24 (O)
(RS Pts.—Raiders 772, Jets 651)
(PS Pts.—Raiders 75, Jets 68)
*Jets known as Titans prior to 1963
**Franchise in Los Angeles from 1982-1994
***AFL Championship
****AFC Second-Round Playoff
*****AFC First-Round Playoff
N.Y. JETS vs. PHILADELPHIA
RS: Eagles lead series, 6-0
1973—Eagles, 24-23 (P)
1977—Eagles, 27-0 (P)
1978—Eagles, 17-9 (P)
1987—Eagles, 38-27 (NY)
1993—Eagles, 35-30 (NY)
1996—Eagles, 21-20 (NY)
(RS Pts.—Eagles 162, Jets 109)
N.Y. JETS vs. PITTSBURGH
RS: Steelers lead series, 14-1
1970—Steelers, 21-17 (P)
1973—Steelers, 26-14 (P)
1975—Steelers, 20-7 (NY)
1977—Steelers, 23-20 (NY)
1978—Steelers, 28-17 (NY)
1981—Steelers, 38-10 (P)
1983—Steelers, 34-7 (NY)
1984—Steelers, 23-17 (NY)
1986—Steelers, 45-24 (NY)
1988—Jets, 24-20 (NY)
1989—Steelers, 13-0 (NY)
1990—Steelers, 24-7 (NY)
1992—Steelers, 27-10 (P)
2000—Steelers, 20-3 (NY)
2001—Steelers, 18-7 (P)

(RS Pts.—Steelers 380, Jets 184)
N.Y. JETS vs. *ST. LOUIS
RS: Rams lead series, 8-2
1970—Jets, 31-20 (LA)
1974—Rams, 20-13 (NY)
1980—Rams, 38-13 (LA)
1983—Jets, 27-24 (NY) OT
1986—Rams, 17-3 (NY)
1989—Rams, 38-14 (LA)
1992—Rams, 18-10 (LA)
1995—Rams, 23-20 (NY)
1998—Rams, 30-10 (StL)
2001—Rams, 34-14 (NY)
(RS Pts.—Rams 262, Jets 155)
*Franchise in Los Angeles prior to 1995
*N.Y. JETS vs. **SAN DIEGO
RS: Chargers lead series, 17-9-1
1960—Chargers, 21-7 (NY)
     Chargers, 50-43 (LA)
1961—Chargers, 25-10 (NY)
     Chargers, 48-13 (SD)
1962—Chargers, 40-14 (SD)
     Titans, 23-3 (NY)
1963—Chargers, 24-20 (SD)
     Chargers, 53-7 (NY)
1964—Tie, 17-17 (NY)
     Chargers, 38-3 (SD)
1965—Chargers, 34-9 (NY)
     Chargers, 38-7 (SD)
1966—Jets, 17-16 (NY)
     Chargers, 42-27 (SD)
1967—Jets, 42-31 (SD)
1968—Jets, 23-20 (NY)
     Jets, 37-15 (SD)
1969—Chargers, 34-27 (SD)
1971—Chargers, 49-21 (SD)
1974—Jets, 27-14 (NY)
1975—Chargers, 24-16 (SD)
1983—Jets, 41-29 (SD)
1989—Jets, 20-17 (SD)
1990—Chargers, 39-3 (NY)
     Chargers, 38-17 (SD)
1991—Jets, 24-3 (NY)
1994—Chargers, 21-6 (NY)
(RS Pts.—Chargers 783, Jets 521)
*Jets known as Titans prior to 1963
**Franchise in Los Angeles prior to 1961
N.Y. JETS vs. SAN FRANCISCO
RS: 49ers lead series, 8-1
1971—49ers, 24-21 (NY)
1976—49ers, 17-6 (SF)
1980—49ers, 37-27 (NY)
1983—Jets, 27-13 (SF)
1986—49ers, 24-10 (SF)
1989—49ers, 23-10 (NY)
1992—49ers, 31-14 (NY)
1998—49ers, 36-30 (SF) OT
2001—49ers, 19-17 (NY)
(RS Pts.—49ers 224, Jets 162)
N.Y. JETS vs. SEATTLE
RS: Seahawks lead series, 8-7
1977—Seahawks, 17-0 (NY)
1978—Seahawks, 24-17 (NY)
1979—Seahawks, 30-7 (S)
1980—Seahawks, 27-17 (NY)
1981—Seahawks, 19-3 (NY)
     Seahawks, 27-23 (S)
1983—Seahawks, 17-10 (NY)
1985—Jets, 17-14 (NY)
1986—Jets, 38-7 (S)

1987—Jets, 30-14 (NY)
1991—Seahawks, 20-13 (S)
1995—Jets, 16-10 (S)
1997—Jets, 41-3 (S)
1998—Jets, 32-31 (NY)
1999—Jets, 19-9 (NY)
(RS Pts.—Jets 283, Seahawks 269)
N.Y. JETS vs. TAMPA BAY
RS: Jets lead series, 7-1
1976—Jets, 34-0 (NY)
1982—Jets, 32-17 (NY)
1984—Buccaneers, 41-21 (TB)
1985—Jets, 62-28 (NY)
1990—Jets, 16-14 (TB)
1991—Jets, 16-13 (NY)
1997—Jets, 31-0 (NY)
2000—Jets, 21-17 (TB)
(RS Pts.—Jets 233, Buccaneers 130)
*N.Y. JETS vs. **TENNESSEE
RS: Titans lead series, 20-13-1
PS: Titans lead series, 1-0
1960—Oilers, 27-21 (H)
        Oilers, 42-28 (NY)
1961—Oilers, 49-13 (H)
        Oilers, 48-21 (NY)
1962—Oilers, 56-17 (H)
        Oilers, 44-10 (NY)
1963—Jets, 24-17 (NY)
        Oilers, 31-27 (H)
1964—Jets, 24-21 (NY)
        Oilers, 33-17 (H)
1965—Oilers, 27-21 (H)
        Jets, 41-14 (NY)
1966—Jets, 52-13 (NY)
        Oilers, 24-0 (H)
1967—Tie, 28-28 (NY)
1968—Jets, 20-14 (H)
        Jets, 26-7 (NY)
1969—Oilers, 26-17 (H)
        Jets, 34-26 (H)
1972—Oilers, 26-20 (H)
1974—Oilers, 27-22 (NY)
1977—Oilers, 20-0 (H)
1979—Oilers, 27-24 (H) OT
1980—Jets, 31-28 (NY) OT
1981—Jets, 33-17 (NY)
1984—Oilers, 31-20 (H)
1988—Jets, 45-3 (NY)
1990—Jets, 17-12 (H)
1991—Oilers, 23-20 (NY)
        ***Oilers, 17-10 (H)
1993—Oilers, 24-0 (H)
1994—Oilers, 24-10 (H)
1995—Oilers, 23-6 (H)
1996—Oilers, 35-10 (NY)
1998—Jets, 24-3 (T)
(RS Pts.—Titans 861, Jets 732)
(PS Pts.—Titans 17, Jets 10)
*Jets known as Titans prior to 1963
**Franchise in Houston prior to 1997;
known as Oilers prior to 1999
***AFC First-Round Playoff
N.Y. JETS vs. WASHINGTON
RS: Redskins lead series, 6-1
1972—Redskins, 35-17 (NY)
1976—Redskins, 37-16 (NY)
1978—Redskins, 23-3 (W)
1987—Redskins, 17-16 (W)
1993—Jets, 3-0 (W)
1996—Redskins, 31-16 (W)

1999—Redskins, 27-20 (NY)
(RS Pts.—Redskins 170, Jets 91)

OAKLAND vs. ARIZONA
RS: Raiders lead series, 3-2;
See Arizona vs. Oakland
OAKLAND vs. ATLANTA
RS: Raiders lead series, 7-3;
See Atlanta vs. Oakland
OAKLAND vs. BALTIMORE
RS: Ravens lead series, 2-0
PS: Ravens lead series, 1-0;
See Baltimore vs. Oakland
OAKLAND vs. BUFFALO
RS: Raiders lead series, 16-15
PS: Bills lead series, 2-0;
See Buffalo vs. Oakland
OAKLAND vs CAROLINA
RS: Series tied, 1-1;
See Carolina vs Oakland
OAKLAND vs. CHICAGO
RS: Raiders lead series, 6-4;
See Chicago vs. Oakland
OAKLAND vs. CINCINNATI
RS: Raiders lead series, 16-7
PS: Raiders lead series, 2-0;
See Cincinnati vs. Oakland
OAKLAND vs. CLEVELAND
RS: Raiders lead series, 9-4
PS: Raiders lead series, 2-0;
See Cleveland vs. Oakland
OAKLAND vs. DALLAS
RS: Raiders lead series, 5-3;
See Dallas vs. Oakland
OAKLAND vs. DENVER
RS: Raiders lead series, 50-31-2
PS: Series tied, 1-1;
See Denver vs. Oakland
OAKLAND vs. DETROIT
RS: Raiders lead series, 6-2;
See Detroit vs. Oakland
OAKLAND vs. GREEN BAY
RS: Raiders lead series, 5-3
PS: Packers lead series, 1-0;
See Green Bay vs. Oakland
OAKLAND vs. INDIANAPOLIS
RS: Raiders lead series, 7-2
PS: Series tied, 1-1;
See Indianapolis vs. Oakland
OAKLAND vs. JACKSONVILLE
RS: Series tied, 1-1;
See Jacksonville vs. Oakland
OAKLAND vs. KANSAS CITY
RS: Raiders lead series, 41-40-2
PS: Chiefs lead series, 2-1;
See Kansas City vs. Oakland
OAKLAND vs. MIAMI
RS: Raiders lead series, 15-9-1
PS: Raiders lead series, 3-1;
See Miami vs. Oakland
OAKLAND vs. MINNESOTA
RS: Raiders lead series, 7-3
PS: Raiders lead series, 1-0;
See Minnesota vs. Oakland
OAKLAND vs. NEW ENGLAND
RS: Raiders lead series, 13-12-1
PS: Patriots lead series, 2-1;
See New England vs. Oakland
OAKLAND vs. NEW ORLEANS
RS: Raiders lead series, 5-3-1;

See New Orleans vs. Oakland
OAKLAND vs. N.Y. GIANTS
RS: Raiders lead series, 7-2;
See N.Y. Giants vs. Oakland
OAKLAND vs. N.Y. JETS
RS: Raiders lead series, 18-11-2
PS: Jets lead series, 2-1;
See N.Y. Jets vs. Oakland
*OAKLAND vs. PHILADELPHIA
RS: Series tied, 4-4
PS: Raiders lead series, 1-0
1971—Raiders, 34-10 (O)
1976—Raiders, 26-7 (P)
1980—Eagles, 10-7 (P)
        **Raiders, 27-10 (New Orleans)
1986—Eagles, 33-27 (LA) OT
1989—Eagles, 10-7 (P)
1992—Eagles, 31-10 (P)
1995—Raiders, 48-17 (O)
2001—Raiders, 20-10 (P)
(RS Pts.—Raiders 179, Eagles 128)
(PS Pts.—Raiders 27, Eagles 10)
*Franchise in Los Angeles from
1982-1994
**Super Bowl XV
*OAKLAND vs. PITTSBURGH
RS: Raiders lead series, 7-6
PS: Series tied, 3-3
1970—Raiders, 31-14 (O)
1972—Steelers, 34-28 (P)
        **Steelers, 13-7 (P)
1973—Steelers, 17-9 (O)
        **Raiders, 33-14 (O)
1974—Raiders, 17-0 (P)
        ***Steelers, 24-13 (O)
1975—***Steelers, 16-10 (P)
1976—Raiders, 31-28 (O)
        ***Raiders, 24-7 (O)
1977—Raiders, 16-7 (P)
1980—Raiders, 45-34 (P)
1981—Raiders, 30-27 (O)
1983—**Raiders, 38-10 (LA)
1984—Steelers, 13-7 (LA)
1990—Raiders, 20-3 (LA)
1994—Steelers, 21-3 (LA)
1995—Steelers, 29-10 (O)
2000—Steelers, 21-20 (P)
(RS Pts.—Raiders 267, Steelers 248)
(PS Pts.—Raiders 125, Steelers 84)
*Franchise in Los Angeles from
1982-1994
**AFC Divisional Playoff
***AFC Championship
*OAKLAND vs. **ST. LOUIS
RS: Raiders lead series, 7-2
1972—Raiders, 45-17 (O)
1977—Rams, 20-14 (LA)
1979—Raiders, 24-17 (LA)
1982—Raiders, 37-31 (LA Raiders)
1985—Raiders, 16-6 (LA Rams)
1988—Rams, 22-17 (LA Raiders)
1991—Raiders, 20-17 (LA Raiders)
1994—Raiders, 20-17 (LA Rams)
1997—Raiders, 35-17 (O)
(RS Pts.—Raiders 228, Rams 164)
*Franchise in Los Angeles from
1982-1994
**Franchise in Los Angeles prior to 1995

*OAKLAND vs. **SAN DIEGO
RS: Raiders lead series, 52-30-2
PS: Raiders lead series, 1-0
1960—Chargers, 52-28 (LA)
    Chargers, 41-17 (O)
1961—Chargers, 44-0 (SD)
    Chargers, 41-10 (O)
1962—Chargers, 42-33 (O)
    Chargers, 31-21 (SD)
1963—Chargers, 34-33 (SD)
    Raiders, 41-27 (O)
1964—Chargers, 31-17 (SD)
    Raiders, 21-20 (O)
1965—Raiders, 17-6 (O)
    Chargers, 24-14 (SD)
1966—Chargers, 29-20 (O)
    Raiders, 41-19 (SD)
1967—Raiders, 51-10 (O)
    Raiders, 41-21 (SD)
1968—Chargers, 23-14 (O)
    Raiders, 34-27 (SD)
1969—Raiders, 24-12 (SD)
    Raiders, 21-16 (O)
1970—Tie, 27-27 (SD)
    Raiders, 20-17 (O)
1971—Raiders, 34-0 (SD)
    Raiders, 34-33 (O)
1972—Tie, 17-17 (O)
    Raiders, 21-19 (SD)
1973—Raiders, 27-17 (SD)
    Raiders, 31-3 (O)
1974—Raiders, 14-10 (O)
    Raiders, 17-10 (O)
1975—Raiders, 6-0 (SD)
    Raiders, 25-0 (O)
1976—Raiders, 27-17 (SD)
    Raiders, 24-0 (O)
1977—Raiders, 24-0 (O)
    Chargers, 12-7 (SD)
1978—Raiders, 21-20 (SD)
    Chargers, 27-23 (O)
1979—Chargers, 30-10 (SD)
    Raiders, 45-22 (O)
1980—Chargers, 30-24 (SD) OT
    Raiders, 38-24 (O)
    ***Raiders, 34-27 (SD)
1981—Chargers, 55-21 (O)
    Chargers, 23-10 (SD)
1982—Raiders, 28-24 (LA)
    Raiders, 41-34 (SD)
1983—Raiders, 42-10 (SD)
    Raiders, 30-14 (LA)
1984—Raiders, 33-30 (LA)
    Raiders, 44-37 (SD)
1985—Raiders, 34-21 (LA)
    Chargers, 40-34 (SD) OT
1986—Raiders, 17-13 (LA)
    Raiders, 37-31 (SD) OT
1987—Chargers, 23-17 (LA)
    Chargers, 16-14 (SD)
1988—Raiders, 24-13 (LA)
    Raiders, 13-3 (SD)
1989—Raiders, 40-14 (LA)
    Chargers, 14-12 (SD)
1990—Raiders, 24-9 (SD)
    Raiders, 17-12 (LA)
1991—Chargers, 21-13 (LA)
    Raiders, 9-7 (SD)
1992—Chargers, 27-3 (SD)
    Chargers, 36-14 (LA)

1993—Chargers, 30-23 (LA)
    Raiders, 12-7 (SD)
1994—Chargers, 26-24 (LA)
    Raiders, 24-17 (SD)
1995—Raiders, 17-7 (O)
    Chargers, 12-6 (SD)
1996—Chargers, 40-34 (O)
    Raiders, 23-14 (SD)
1997—Chargers, 25-10 (O)
    Raiders, 38-13 (SD)
1998—Raiders, 7-6 (O)
    Raiders, 17-10 (SD)
1999—Raiders, 28-9 (O)
    Chargers, 23-20 (SD)
2000—Raiders, 9-6 (O)
    Raiders, 15-13 (SD)
2001—Raiders, 34-24 (O)
    Raiders, 13-6 (SD)
(RS Pts.—Raiders 1,929, Chargers 1,710)
(PS Pts.—Raiders 34, Chargers 27)
**Franchise in Los Angeles from
1982-1994*
**Franchise in Los Angeles prior to 1961
***AFC Championship

*OAKLAND vs. SAN FRANCISCO
RS: Raiders lead series, 6-3
1970—49ers, 38-7 (O)
1974—Raiders, 35-24 (SF)
1979—Raiders, 23-10 (O)
1982—Raiders, 23-17 (SF)
1985—49ers, 34-10 (LA)
1988—Raiders, 9-3 (SF)
1991—Raiders, 12-6 (LA)
1994—49ers, 44-14 (SF)
2000—Raiders, 34-28 (SF) OT
(RS Pts.—49ers 204, Raiders 167)
**Franchise in Los Angeles from
1982-1994*

*OAKLAND vs. SEATTLE
RS: Raiders lead series, 26-22
PS: Series tied, 1-1
1977—Raiders, 44-7 (O)
1978—Seahawks, 27-7 (S)
    Seahawks, 17-16 (O)
1979—Seahawks, 27-10 (S)
    Seahawks, 29-24 (O)
1980—Raiders, 33-14 (O)
    Raiders, 19-17 (S)
1981—Raiders, 20-10 (O)
    Raiders, 32-31 (S)
1982—Raiders, 28-23 (LA)
1983—Seahawks, 38-36 (S)
    Seahawks, 34-21 (LA)
    **Raiders, 30-14 (LA)
1984—Raiders, 28-14 (LA)
    Seahawks, 17-14 (S)
    ***Seahawks, 13-7 (S)
1985—Seahawks, 33-3 (S)
    Raiders, 13-3 (LA)
1986—Raiders, 14-10 (LA)
    Seahawks, 37-0 (S)
1987—Seahawks, 35-13 (LA)
    Raiders, 37-14 (S)
1988—Seahawks, 35-27 (S)
    Seahawks, 43-37 (LA)
1989—Seahawks, 24-20 (LA)
    Seahawks, 23-17 (S)
1990—Raiders, 17-13 (S)
    Raiders, 24-17 (LA)
1991—Raiders, 23-20 (S) OT

    Raiders, 31-7 (LA)
1992—Raiders, 19-0 (S)
    Raiders, 20-3 (LA)
1993—Raiders, 17-13 (S)
    Raiders, 27-23 (LA)
1994—Seahawks, 38-9 (LA)
    Raiders, 17-16 (S)
1995—Raiders, 34-14 (O)
    Seahawks, 44-10 (S)
1996—Raiders, 27-21 (S)
    Seahawks, 28-21 (O)
1997—Seahawks, 45-34 (S)
    Seahawks, 22-21 (O)
1998—Raiders, 31-18 (S)
    Raiders, 20-17 (O)
1999—Seahawks, 22-21 (S)
    Raiders, 30-21 (O)
2000—Raiders, 31-3 (O)
    Seahawks, 27-24 (S)
2001—Raiders, 38-14 (O)
    Seahawks, 34-27 (S)
(RS Pts.—Raiders 1,086, Seahawks 1,042)
(PS Pts.—Raiders 37, Seahawks 27)
*Franchise in Los Angeles from 1982-1994
**AFC Championship
***AFC First-Round Playoff

*OAKLAND vs. TAMPA BAY
RS: Raiders lead series, 4-1
1976—Raiders, 49-16 (O)
1981—Raiders, 18-16 (O)
1993—Raiders, 27-20 (LA)
1996—Buccaneers, 20-17 (TB) OT
1999—Raiders, 45-0 (O)
(RS Pts.—Raiders 156, Buccaneers 72)
**Franchise in Los Angeles from
1982-1994*

*OAKLAND vs. **TENNESSEE
RS: Raiders lead series, 20-16
PS: Raiders lead series, 3-0
1960—Oilers, 37-22 (H)
    Raiders, 14-13 (H)
1961—Oilers, 55-0 (H)
    Oilers, 47-16 (O)
1962—Oilers, 28-20 (O)
    Oilers, 32-17 (H)
1963—Raiders, 24-13 (H)
    Raiders, 52-49 (O)
1964—Oilers, 42-28 (H)
    Raiders, 20-10 (O)
1965—Raiders, 21-17 (O)
    Raiders, 33-21 (H)
1966—Oilers, 31-0 (H)
    Raiders, 38-23 (O)
1967—Raiders, 19-7 (H)
    ***Raiders, 40-7 (O)
1968—Raiders, 24-15 (H)
1969—Raiders, 21-17 (O)
    ****Raiders, 56-7 (O)
1971—Raiders, 41-21 (O)
1972—Raiders, 34-0 (H)
1973—Raiders, 17-6 (H)
1975—Oilers, 27-26 (O)
1976—Raiders, 14-13 (H)
1977—Raiders, 34-29 (O)
1978—Raiders, 21-17 (O)
1979—Oilers, 31-17 (H)
1980—*****Raiders, 27-7 (O)
1981—Oilers, 17-16 (H)
1983—Raiders, 20-6 (LA)
1984—Raiders, 24-14 (H)

1986—Raiders, 28-17 (H)
1988—Oilers, 38-35 (H)
1989—Oilers, 23-7 (H)
1991—Oilers, 47-17 (H)
1994—Raiders, 17-14 (LA)
1997—Oilers, 24-21 (T) OT
1999—Titans, 21-14 (T)
2001—Titans, 13-10 (O)
(RS Pts.—Titans 835, Raiders 782)
(PS Pts.—Raiders 123, Titans 21)
*Franchise in Los Angeles from
1982-1994
**Franchise in Houston prior to 1997;
known as Oilers prior to 1999
***AFL Championship
****Inter-Divisional Playoff
*****AFC First-Round Playoff
**OAKLAND vs. WASHINGTON*
RS: Raiders lead series, 6-3
PS: Raiders lead series, 1-0
1970—Raiders, 34-20 (O)
1975—Raiders, 26-23 (W) OT
1980—Raiders, 24-21 (O)
1983—Redskins, 37-35 (W)
**Raiders, 38-9 (Tampa)
1986—Redskins, 10-6 (W)
1989—Raiders, 37-24 (LA)
1992—Raiders, 21-20 (W)
1995—Raiders, 20-8 (W)
1998—Redskins, 29-19 (O)
(RS Pts.—Raiders 222, Redskins 192)
(PS Pts.—Raiders 38, Redskins 9)
*Franchise in Los Angeles from
1982-1994
**Super Bowl XVIII

PHILADELPHIA vs. ARIZONA
RS: Cardinals lead series, 52-51-5
PS: Series tied, 1-1;
See Arizona vs. Philadelphia
PHILADELPHIA vs. ATLANTA
RS: Eagles lead series, 10-9-1
PS: Falcons lead series, 1-0;
See Atlanta vs. Philadelphia
PHILADELPHIA vs. BALTIMORE
RS: Series tied, 0-0-1;
See Baltimore vs. Philadelphia
PHILADELPHIA vs. BUFFALO
RS: Bills lead series, 5-4;
See Buffalo vs. Philadelphia
PHILADELPHIA vs. CAROLINA
RS: Series tied, 1-1;
See Carolina vs. Philadelphia
PHILADELPHIA vs. CHICAGO
RS: Bears lead series, 24-6-1
PS: Eagles lead series, 2-1;
See Chicago vs. Philadelphia
PHILADELPHIA vs. CINCINNATI
RS: Bengals lead series, 6-3;
See Cincinnati vs. Philadelphia
PHILADELPHIA vs. CLEVELAND
RS: Browns lead series, 31-13-1;
See Cleveland vs. Philadelphia
PHILADELPHIA vs. DALLAS
RS: Cowboys lead series, 48-34
PS: Cowboys lead series, 2-1;
See Dallas vs. Philadelphia
PHILADELPHIA vs. DENVER
RS: Eagles lead series, 6-3;
See Denver vs. Philadelphia

PHILADELPHIA vs. DETROIT
RS: Lions lead series, 12-11-2
PS: Eagles lead series, 1-0;
See Detroit vs. Philadelphia
PHILADELPHIA vs. GREEN BAY
RS: Packers lead series, 22-9
PS: Eagles lead series, 1-0;
See Green Bay vs. Philadelphia
PHILADELPHIA vs. INDIANAPOLIS
RS: Colts lead series, 8-6;
See Indianapolis vs. Philadelphia
PHILADELPHIA vs. JACKSONVILLE
RS: Jaguars lead series, 1-0;
See Jacksonville vs. Philadelphia
PHILADELPHIA vs. KANSAS CITY
RS: Series tied, 2-2;
See Kansas City vs. Philadelphia
PHILADELPHIA vs. MIAMI
RS: Dolphins lead series, 7-3;
See Miami vs. Philadelphia
PHILADELPHIA vs. MINNESOTA
RS: Vikings lead series, 11-7
PS: Eagles lead series, 1-0;
See Minnesota vs. Philadelphia
PHILADELPHIA vs. NEW ENGLAND
RS: Eagles lead series, 6-2;
See New England vs. Philadelphia
PHILADELPHIA vs. NEW ORLEANS
RS: Eagles lead series, 13-8
PS: Eagles lead series, 1-0;
See New Orleans vs. Philadelphia
PHILADELPHIA vs. N.Y. GIANTS
RS: Giants lead series, 72-60-2
PS: Giants lead series, 2-0;
See N.Y. Giants vs. Philadelphia
PHILADELPHIA vs. N.Y. JETS
RS: Eagles lead series, 6-0;
See N.Y. Jets vs. Philadelphia
PHILADELPHIA vs. OAKLAND
RS: Series tied, 4-4
PS: Raiders lead series, 1-0;
See Oakland vs. Philadelphia
PHILADELPHIA vs. *PITTSBURGH
RS: Eagles lead series, 45-26-3
PS: Eagles lead series, 1-0
1933—Eagles, 25-6 (Phila)
1934—Eagles, 17-0 (Pitt)
Pirates, 9-7 (Phila)
1935—Pirates, 17-7 (Phila)
Eagles, 17-6 (Phila)
1936—Pirates, 17-0 (Pitt)
Pirates, 6-0 (Johnstown, Pa.)
1937—Pirates, 27-14 (Pitt)
Pirates, 16-7 (Pitt)
1938—Eagles, 27-7 (Buffalo)
Eagles, 14-7 (Charleston, W. Va.)
1939—Eagles, 17-14 (Phila)
Pirates, 24-12 (Pitt)
1940—Pirates, 7-3 (Pitt)
Eagles, 7-0 (Phila)
1941—Eagles, 10-7 (Pitt)
Tie, 7-7 (Phila)
1942—Eagles, 24-14 (Pitt)
Steelers, 14-0 (Phila)
1945—Eagles, 45-3 (Pitt)
Eagles, 30-6 (Phila)
1946—Steelers, 10-7 (Pitt)
Eagles, 10-7 (Phila)
1947—Steelers, 35-24 (Pitt)
Eagles, 21-0 (Phila)

**Eagles, 21-0 (Pitt)
1948—Eagles, 34-7 (Pitt)
Eagles, 17-0 (Phila)
1949—Eagles, 38-7 (Pitt)
Eagles, 34-17 (Phila)
1950—Eagles, 17-10 (Pitt)
Steelers, 9-7 (Phila)
1951—Eagles, 34-13 (Pitt)
Steelers, 17-13 (Phila)
1952—Eagles, 31-25 (Pitt)
Eagles, 26-21 (Phila)
1953—Eagles, 23-17 (Phila)
Eagles, 35-7 (Pitt)
1954—Eagles, 24-22 (Phila)
Steelers, 17-7 (Pitt)
1955—Steelers, 13-7 (Pitt)
Eagles, 24-0 (Phila)
1956—Eagles, 35-21 (Pitt)
Eagles, 14-7 (Phila)
1957—Steelers, 6-0 (Pitt)
Eagles, 7-6 (Phila)
1958—Steelers, 24-3 (Pitt)
Steelers, 31-24 (Phila)
1959—Eagles, 28-24 (Phila)
Steelers, 31-0 (Pitt)
1960—Eagles, 34-7 (Phila)
Steelers, 27-21 (Pitt)
1961—Eagles, 21-16 (Phila)
Eagles, 35-24 (Pitt)
1962—Steelers, 13-7 (Pitt)
Steelers, 26-17 (Phila)
1963—Tie, 21-21 (Phila)
Tie, 20-20 (Pitt)
1964—Eagles, 21-7 (Phila)
Eagles, 34-10 (Pitt)
1965—Steelers, 20-14 (Phila)
Eagles, 47-13 (Pitt)
1966—Eagles, 31-14 (Phila)
Eagles, 27-23 (Pitt)
1967—Eagles, 34-24 (Phila)
1968—Steelers, 6-3 (Pitt)
1969—Eagles, 41-27 (Phila)
1970—Eagles, 30-20 (Phila)
1974—Steelers, 27-0 (Pitt)
1979—Eagles, 17-14 (Phila)
1988—Eagles, 27-26 (Pitt)
1991—Eagles, 23-14 (Phila)
1994—Steelers, 14-3 (Phila)
1997—Eagles, 23-20 (Phila)
2000—Eagles, 26-23 (Pitt) OT
(RS Pts.—Eagles 1,411, Steelers 1,064)
(PS Pts.—Eagles 21, Steelers 0)
*Steelers known as Pirates prior to 1941
**Division Playoff
PHILADELPHIA vs. *ST. LOUIS
RS: Rams lead series, 16-14-1
PS: Rams lead series, 2-1
1937—Rams, 21-3 (P)
1939—Rams, 35-13 (Colorado Springs)
1940—Rams, 21-13 (C)
1942—Rams, 24-14 (Akron)
1944—Eagles, 26-13 (P)
1945—Eagles, 28-14 (P)
1946—Eagles, 25-14 (LA)
1947—Eagles, 14-7 (P)
1948—Tie, 28-28 (LA)
1949—Eagles, 38-14 (P)
**Eagles, 14-0 (LA)
1950—Eagles, 56-20 (P)
1955—Rams, 23-21 (P)

1956—Rams, 27-7 (LA)
1957—Rams, 17-13 (LA)
1959—Eagles, 23-20 (P)
1964—Rams, 20-10 (LA)
1967—Rams, 33-17 (LA)
1969—Rams, 23-17 (P)
1972—Rams, 34-3 (P)
1975—Rams, 42-3 (P)
1977—Rams, 20-0 (LA)
1978—Rams, 16-14 (P)
1983—Eagles, 13-9 (P)
1985—Rams, 17-6 (P)
1986—Eagles, 34-20 (P)
1988—Eagles, 30-24 (P)
1989—***Rams, 21-7 (P)
1990—Eagles, 27-21 (LA)
1995—Eagles, 20-9 (P)
1998—Eagles, 17-14 (P)
1999—Eagles, 38-31 (P)
2001—Rams, 20-17 (P) OT
　　　****Rams, 29-24 (StL)
(RS Pts.—Rams 651, Eagles 588)
(PS Pts.—Rams 50, Eagles 45)
*Franchise in Los Angeles prior to 1995
and in Cleveland prior to 1946
**NFL Championship
***NFC First-Round Playoff
****NFC Championship

PHILADELPHIA vs. SAN DIEGO
RS: Chargers lead series, 5-3
1974—Eagles, 13-7 (SD)
1980—Chargers, 22-21 (SD)
1985—Chargers, 20-14 (SD)
1986—Eagles, 23-7 (P)
1989—Chargers, 20-17 (SD)
1995—Chargers, 27-21 (P)
1998—Chargers, 13-10 (SD)
2001—Eagles, 24-14 (P)
(RS Pts.—Eagles 143, Chargers 130)
PHILADELPHIA vs. SAN FRANCISCO
RS: 49ers lead series, 15-6-1
PS: 49ers lead series, 1-0
1951—Eagles, 21-14 (P)
1953—49ers, 31-21 (SF)
1956—Tie, 10-10 (P)
1958—49ers, 30-24 (P)
1959—49ers, 24-14 (SF)
1964—49ers, 28-24 (P)
1966—Eagles, 35-34 (SF)
1967—49ers, 28-27 (P)
1969—49ers, 14-13 (SF)
1971—Eagles, 31-3 (P)
1973—49ers, 38-28 (SF)
1975—Eagles, 27-17 (P)
1983—Eagles, 22-17 (SF)
1984—49ers, 21-9 (P)
1985—49ers, 24-13 (SF)
1989—49ers, 38-28 (P)
1991—49ers, 23-7 (P)
1992—49ers, 20-14 (SF)
1993—Eagles, 37-34 (SF) OT
1994—Eagles, 40-8 (SF)
1996—*49ers, 14-0 (SF)
1997—49ers, 24-12 (P)
2001—49ers, 13-3 (SF)
(RS Pts.—49ers 521, Eagles 432)
(PS Pts.—49ers 14, Eagles 0)
*NFC First-Round Playoff
PHILADELPHIA vs. SEATTLE
RS: Eagles lead series, 5-3

1976—Eagles, 27-10 (P)
1980—Eagles, 27-20 (S)
1986—Seahawks, 24-20 (S)
1989—Eagles, 31-7 (P)
1992—Eagles, 20-17 (S) OT
1995—Seahawks, 26-14 (S)
1998—Seahawks, 38-0 (P)
2001—Eagles, 27-3 (S)
(RS Pts.—Eagles 166, Seahawks 145)
PHILADELPHIA vs. TAMPA BAY
RS: Eagles lead series, 4-3
PS: Eagles lead series, 2-1
1977—Eagles, 13-3 (P)
1979—*Buccaneers, 24-17 (TB)
1981—Eagles, 20-10 (P)
1988—Eagles, 41-14 (TB)
1991—Buccaneers, 14-13 (TB)
1995—Buccaneers, 21-6 (P)
1999—Buccaneers, 19-5 (P)
2000—**Eagles, 21-3 (P)
2001—Eagles, 17-13 (TB)
　　　**Eagles, 31-9 (P)
(RS Pts.—Eagles 115, Buccaneers 94)
(PS Pts.—Eagles 69, Buccaneers 36)
*NFC Divisional Playoff
**NFC First-Round Playoff
PHILADELPHIA vs. *TENNESSEE
RS: Eagles lead series, 6-1
1972—Eagles, 18-17 (H)
1979—Eagles, 26-20 (H)
1982—Eagles, 35-14 (P)
1988—Eagles, 32-23 (P)
1991—Eagles, 13-6 (H)
1994—Eagles, 21-6 (P)
2000—Titans, 15-13 (P)
(RS Pts.—Eagles 158, Titans 101)
*Franchise in Houston prior to 1997;
known as Oilers prior to 1999
PHILADELPHIA vs. *WASHINGTON
RS: Redskins lead series, 72-56-5
PS: Redskins lead series, 1-0
1934—Redskins, 6-0 (B)
　　　Redskins, 14-7 (P)
1935—Eagles, 7-6 (B)
1936—Redskins, 26-3 (P)
　　　Redskins, 17-7 (B)
1937—Eagles, 14-0 (W)
　　　Redskins, 10-7 (P)
1938—Redskins, 26-23 (P)
　　　Redskins, 20-14 (W)
1939—Redskins, 7-0 (P)
　　　Redskins, 7-6 (W)
1940—Redskins, 34-17 (P)
　　　Redskins, 13-6 (W)
1941—Redskins, 21-17 (P)
　　　Redskins, 20-14 (W)
1942—Redskins, 14-10 (P)
　　　Redskins, 30-27 (W)
1944—Tie, 31-31 (P)
　　　Eagles, 37-7 (W)
1945—Redskins, 24-14 (W)
　　　Eagles, 16-0 (P)
1946—Eagles, 28-24 (W)
　　　Redskins, 27-10 (P)
1947—Eagles, 45-42 (P)
　　　Eagles, 38-14 (W)
1948—Eagles, 45-0 (W)
　　　Eagles, 42-21 (P)
1949—Eagles, 49-14 (P)
　　　Eagles, 44-21 (W)

1950—Eagles, 35-3 (P)
　　　Eagles, 33-0 (W)
1951—Redskins, 27-23 (P)
　　　Eagles, 35-21 (W)
1952—Eagles, 38-20 (P)
　　　Redskins, 27-21 (W)
1953—Tie, 21-21 (P)
　　　Redskins, 10-0 (W)
1954—Eagles, 49-21 (W)
　　　Eagles, 41-33 (P)
1955—Redskins, 31-30 (P)
　　　Redskins, 34-21 (W)
1956—Eagles, 13-9 (P)
　　　Redskins, 19-17 (W)
1957—Eagles, 21-12 (P)
　　　Redskins, 42-7 (W)
1958—Redskins, 24-14 (P)
　　　Redskins, 20-0 (W)
1959—Eagles, 30-23 (P)
　　　Eagles, 34-14 (W)
1960—Eagles, 19-13 (P)
　　　Eagles, 38-28 (W)
1961—Eagles, 14-7 (P)
　　　Eagles, 27-24 (W)
1962—Redskins, 27-21 (P)
　　　Eagles, 37-14 (W)
1963—Eagles, 37-24 (W)
　　　Redskins, 13-10 (P)
1964—Redskins, 35-20 (W)
　　　Redskins, 21-10 (P)
1965—Redskins, 23-21 (W)
　　　Eagles, 21-14 (P)
1966—Redskins, 27-13 (P)
　　　Eagles, 37-28 (W)
1967—Eagles, 35-24 (P)
　　　Tie, 35-35 (W)
1968—Redskins, 17-14 (W)
　　　Redskins, 16-10 (W)
1969—Tie, 28-28 (W)
　　　Redskins, 34-29 (P)
1970—Redskins, 33-21 (P)
　　　Redskins, 24-6 (W)
1971—Tie, 7-7 (W)
　　　Redskins, 20-13 (P)
1972—Redskins, 14-0 (W)
　　　Redskins, 23-7 (P)
1973—Redskins, 28-7 (P)
　　　Redskins, 38-20 (W)
1974—Redskins, 27-20 (P)
　　　Redskins, 26-7 (W)
1975—Eagles, 26-10 (P)
　　　Eagles, 26-3 (W)
1976—Redskins, 20-17 (P) OT
　　　Redskins, 24-0 (W)
1977—Redskins, 23-17 (W)
　　　Redskins, 17-14 (P)
1978—Redskins, 35-30 (W)
　　　Eagles, 17-10 (P)
1979—Eagles, 28-17 (P)
　　　Redskins, 17-7 (W)
1980—Eagles, 24-14 (P)
　　　Eagles, 24-0 (W)
1981—Eagles, 36-13 (P)
　　　Redskins, 15-13 (W)
1982—Redskins, 37-34 (P) OT
　　　Redskins, 13-9 (P)
1983—Redskins, 23-13 (P)
　　　Redskins, 28-24 (W)
1984—Redskins, 20-0 (W)
　　　Eagles, 16-10 (P)

1985—Eagles, 19-6 (W)
    Redskins, 17-12 (P)
1986—Redskins, 41-14 (W)
    Redskins, 21-14 (P)
1987—Redskins, 34-24 (W)
    Eagles, 31-27 (P)
1988—Redskins, 17-10 (W)
    Redskins, 20-19 (P)
1989—Eagles, 42-37 (W)
    Redskins, 10-3 (P)
1990—Redskins, 13-7 (W)
    Eagles, 28-14 (P)
    **Redskins, 20-6 (P)
1991—Redskins, 23-0 (W)
    Eagles, 24-22 (P)
1992—Redskins, 16-12 (W)
    Eagles, 17-13 (P)
1993—Eagles, 34-31 (P)
    Eagles, 17-14 (W)
1994—Eagles, 21-17 (P)
    Eagles, 31-29 (W)
1995—Eagles, 37-34 (P) (OT)
    Eagles, 14-7 (W)
1996—Eagles, 17-14 (W)
    Redskins, 26-21 (P)
1997—Eagles, 24-10 (W)
    Redskins, 35-32 (W)
1998—Eagles, 17-12 (P)
    Redskins, 28-3 (W)
1999—Eagles, 35-28 (P)
    Redskins, 20-17 (W) OT
2000—Redskins, 17-14 (P)
    Eagles, 23-20 (W)
2001—Redskins, 13-3 (P)
    Eagles, 20-6 (W)
(RS Pts.—Eagles 2,676, Redskins 2,640)
(PS Pts.—Redskins 20, Eagles 6)
*Franchise in Boston prior to 1937
**NFC First-Round Playoff

PITTSBURGH vs. ARIZONA
RS: Steelers lead series, 30-22-3;
See Arizona vs. Pittsburgh
PITTSBURGH vs. ATLANTA
RS: Steelers lead series, 11-1;
See Atlanta vs. Pittsburgh
PITTSBURGH vs. BALTIMORE
RS: Steelers lead series, 8-4
PS: Steelers lead series, 1-0;
See Baltimore vs. Pittsburgh
PITTSBURGH vs. BUFFALO
RS: Steelers lead series, 9-8
PS: Steelers lead series, 2-1;
See Buffalo vs. Pittsburgh
PITTSBURGH vs. CAROLINA
RS: Series tied, 1-1;
See Carolina vs. Pittsburgh
PITTSBURGH vs. CHICAGO
RS: Bears lead series, 16-6-1;
See Chicago vs. Pittsburgh
PITTSBURGH vs. CINCINNATI
RS: Steelers lead series, 36-27;
See Cincinnati vs. Pittsburgh
PITTSBURGH vs. CLEVELAND
RS: Browns lead series, 54-44
PS: Steelers lead series, 1-0;
See Cleveland vs. Pittsburgh
PITTSBURGH vs. DALLAS
RS: Cowboys lead series, 14-11
PS: Steelers lead series, 2-1;

See Dallas vs. Pittsburgh
PITTSBURGH vs. DENVER
RS: Broncos lead series, 10-6-1
PS: Broncos lead series, 3-2;
See Denver vs. Pittsburgh
PITTSBURGH vs. DETROIT
RS: Lions lead series, 14-13-1;
See Detroit vs. Pittsburgh
PITTSBURGH vs. GREEN BAY
RS: Packers lead series, 18-12;
See Green Bay vs. Pittsburgh
PITTSBURGH vs. INDIANAPOLIS
RS: Steelers lead series, 12-4
PS: Steelers lead series, 4-0;
See Indianapolis vs. Pittsburgh
PITTSBURGH vs. JACKSONVILLE
RS: Jaguars lead series, 8-6;
See Jacksonville vs. Pittsburgh
PITTSBURGH vs. KANSAS CITY
RS: Steelers lead series, 16-7
PS: Chiefs lead series, 1-0;
See Kansas City vs. Pittsburgh
PITTSBURGH vs. MIAMI
RS: Dolphins lead series, 9-7
PS: Dolphins lead series, 2-1;
See Miami vs. Pittsburgh
PITTSBURGH vs. MINNESOTA
RS: Vikings lead series, 8-5
PS: Steelers lead series, 1-0;
See Minnesota vs. Pittsburgh
PITTSBURGH vs. NEW ENGLAND
RS: Steelers lead series, 11-4
PS: Patriots lead series, 2-1;
See New England vs. Pittsburgh
PITTSBURGH vs. NEW ORLEANS
RS: Steelers lead series, 6-5;
See New Orleans vs. Pittsburgh
PITTSBURGH vs. N.Y. GIANTS
RS: Giants lead series, 43-27-3;
See N.Y. Giants vs. Pittsburgh
PITTSBURGH vs. N.Y. JETS
RS: Steelers lead series, 14-1;
See N.Y. Jets vs. Pittsburgh
PITTSBURGH vs. OAKLAND
RS: Raiders lead series, 7-6
PS: Series tied, 3-3;
See Oakland vs. Pittsburgh
PITTSBURGH vs. PHILADELPHIA
RS: Eagles lead series, 45-26-3
PS: Eagles lead series, 1-0;
See Philadelphia vs. Pittsburgh
***PITTSBURGH vs. **ST. LOUIS**
RS: Rams lead series, 14-5-2
PS: Steelers lead series, 1-0
1938—Rams, 13-7 (New Orleans)
1939—Tie, 14-14 (C)
1941—Rams, 17-14 (Akron)
1947—Rams, 48-7 (P)
1948—Rams, 31-14 (LA)
1949—Tie, 7-7 (P)
1952—Rams, 28-14 (LA)
1955—Rams, 27-26 (LA)
1956—Steelers, 30-13 (P)
1961—Rams, 24-14 (LA)
1964—Rams, 26-14 (P)
1968—Rams, 45-10 (LA)
1971—Rams, 23-14 (P)
1975—Rams, 10-3 (LA)
1978—Rams, 10-7 (LA)
1979—***Steelers, 31-19 (Pasadena)

1981—Steelers, 24-0 (P)
1984—Steelers, 24-14 (P)
1987—Rams, 31-21 (LA)
1990—Steelers, 41-10 (P)
1993—Rams, 27-0 (LA)
1996—Steelers, 42-6 (P)
(RS Pts.—Rams 424, Steelers 347)
(PS Pts.—Steelers 31, Rams 19)
*Steelers known as Pirates prior to 1941
**Franchise in Los Angeles prior to 1995
and in Cleveland prior to 1946
***Super Bowl XIV
PITTSBURGH vs. SAN DIEGO
RS: Steelers lead series, 17-5
PS: Chargers lead series, 2-0
1971—Steelers, 21-17 (P)
1972—Steelers, 24-2 (SD)
1973—Steelers, 38-21 (P)
1975—Steelers, 37-0 (SD)
1976—Steelers, 23-0 (P)
1977—Steelers, 10-9 (SD)
1979—Chargers, 35-7 (SD)
1980—Chargers, 26-17 (SD)
1982—*Chargers, 31-28 (P)
1983—Steelers, 26-3 (P)
1984—Steelers, 52-24 (P)
1985—Chargers, 54-44 (SD)
1987—Steelers, 20-16 (SD)
1988—Chargers, 20-14 (SD)
1989—Steelers, 20-17 (P)
1990—Steelers, 36-14 (P)
1991—Steelers, 26-20 (P)
1992—Steelers, 23-6 (SD)
1993—Steelers,.16-3 (P)
1994—Chargers, 37-34 (SD)
    **Chargers, 17-13 (P)
1995—Steelers, 31-16 (P)
1996—Steelers, 16-3 (P)
2000—Steelers, 34-21 (SD)
(RS Pts.—Steelers 569, Chargers 364)
(PS Pts.—Chargers 48, Steelers 41)
*AFC First-Round Playoff
**AFC Championship
PITTSBURGH vs. SAN FRANCISCO
RS: 49ers lead series, 9-8
1951—49ers, 28-24 (P)
1952—Steelers, 24-7 (SF)
1954—49ers, 31-3 (SF)
1958—49ers, 23-20 (SF)
1961—Steelers, 20-10 (P)
1965—49ers, 27-17 (SF)
1968—49ers, 45-28 (P)
1973—Steelers, 37-14 (SF)
1977—Steelers, 27-0 (P)
1978—Steelers, 24-7 (SF)
1981—49ers, 17-14 (P)
1984—Steelers, 20-17 (SF)
1987—Steelers, 30-17 (P)
1990—49ers, 27-7 (SF)
1993—49ers, 24-13 (P)
1996—49ers, 25-15 (P)
1999—Steelers, 27-6 (SF)
(RS Pts.—Steelers 350, 49ers 325)
PITTSBURGH vs. SEATTLE
RS: Seahawks lead series, 7-6
1977—Steelers, 30-20 (P)
1978—Steelers, 21-10 (P)
1981—Seahawks, 24-21 (S)
1982—Seahawks, 16-0 (S)
1983—Steelers, 27-21 (S)

1986—Seahawks, 30-0 (S)
1987—Steelers, 13-9 (P)
1991—Seahawks, 27-7 (P)
1992—Steelers, 20-14 (P)
1993—Seahawks, 16-6 (S)
1994—Seahawks, 30-13 (S)
1998—Steelers, 13-10 (P)
1999—Seahawks, 29-10 (P)
(RS Pts.—Seahawks 256, Steelers 181)
PITTSBURGH vs. TAMPA BAY
RS: Steelers lead series, 5-1
1976—Steelers, 42-0 (P)
1980—Steelers, 24-21 (TB)
1983—Steelers, 17-12 (P)
1989—Steelers, 31-22 (TB)
1998—Buccaneers, 16-3 (TB)
2001—Steelers, 17-10 (TB)
(RS Pts.—Steelers 134, Buccaneers 81)
PITTSBURGH vs. *TENNESSEE
RS: Steelers lead series, 37-26
PS: Steelers lead series, 3-0
1970—Oilers, 19-7 (P)
    Steelers, 7-3 (H)
1971—Steelers, 23-16 (P)
    Oilers, 29-3 (H)
1972—Steelers, 24-7 (P)
    Steelers, 9-3 (H)
1973—Steelers, 36-7 (H)
    Steelers, 33-7 (P)
1974—Steelers, 13-7 (H)
    Oilers, 13-10 (P)
1975—Steelers, 24-17 (P)
    Steelers, 32-9 (H)
1976—Steelers, 32-16 (P)
    Steelers, 21-0 (H)
1977—Oilers, 27-10 (H)
    Steelers, 27-10 (P)
1978—Oilers, 24-17 (P)
    Steelers, 13-3 (H)
    **Steelers, 34-5 (P)
1979—Steelers, 38-7 (P)
    Oilers, 20-17 (H)
    **Steelers, 27-13 (P)
1980—Steelers, 31-17 (P)
    Oilers, 6-0 (H)
1981—Steelers, 26-13 (P)
    Oilers, 21-20 (H)
1982—Steelers, 24-10 (H)
1983—Steelers, 40-28 (H)
    Steelers, 17-10 (P)
1984—Steelers, 35-7 (P)
    Oilers, 23-20 (H) OT
1985—Steelers, 20-0 (P)
    Steelers, 30-7 (H)
1986—Steelers, 22-16 (H) OT
    Steelers, 21-10 (P)
1987—Oilers, 23-3 (P)
    Oilers, 24-16 (H)
1988—Oilers, 34-14 (P)
    Steelers, 37-34 (H)
1989—Oilers, 27-0 (H)
    Oilers, 23-16 (P)
    ***Steelers, 26-23 (H) OT
1990—Steelers, 20-9 (P)
    Oilers, 34-14 (H)
1991—Steelers, 26-14 (P)
    Oilers, 31-6 (H)
1992—Steelers, 29-24 (H)
    Steelers, 21-20 (P)
1993—Oilers, 23-3 (H)

Oilers, 26-17 (P)
1994—Steelers, 30-14 (P)
    Steelers, 12-9 (H) OT
1995—Steelers, 34-17 (H)
    Steelers, 21-7 (P)
1996—Steelers, 30-16 (P)
    Oilers, 23-13 (H)
1997—Steelers, 37-24 (P)
    Oilers, 16-6 (T)
1998—Steelers, 41-31 (P)
    Oilers, 23-14 (T)
1999—Titans, 16-10 (T)
    Titans, 47-36 (P)
2000—Titans, 23-20 (P)
    Titans, 9-7 (T)
2001—Steelers, 34-7 (P)
    Steelers, 34-24 (T)
(RS Pts.—Steelers 1,293, Titans 1,074)
(PS Pts.—Steelers 87, Titans 41)
*Franchise in Houston prior to 1997;
known as Oilers prior to 1999
**AFC Championship
***AFC First-Round Playoff
PITTSBURGH vs. **WASHINGTON
RS: Redskins lead series, 42-29-3
1933—Redskins, 21-6 (P)
    Pirates, 16-14 (B)
1934—Redskins, 7-0 (P)
    Redskins, 39-0 (B)
1935—Pirates, 6-0 (P)
    Redskins, 13-3 (B)
1936—Pirates, 10-0 (P)
    Redskins, 30-0 (B)
1937—Redskins, 34-20 (W)
    Pirates, 21-13 (P)
1938—Redskins, 7-0 (P)
    Redskins, 15-0 (W)
1939—Redskins, 44-14 (W)
    Redskins, 21-14 (P)
1940—Redskins, 40-10 (P)
    Redskins, 37-10 (W)
1941—Redskins, 24-20 (P)
    Redskins, 23-3 (W)
1942—Redskins, 28-14 (W)
    Redskins, 14-0 (P)
1945—Redskins, 14-0 (P)
    Redskins, 24-0 (W)
1946—Tie, 14-14 (W)
    Steelers, 14-7 (P)
1947—Redskins, 27-26 (W)
    Steelers, 21-14 (P)
1948—Redskins, 17-14 (W)
    Steelers, 10-7 (P)
1949—Redskins, 27-14 (P)
    Redskins, 27-14 (W)
1950—Steelers, 26-7 (W)
    Redskins, 24-7 (P)
1951—Redskins, 22-7 (P)
    Steelers, 20-10 (W)
1952—Redskins, 28-24 (P)
    Steelers, 24-23 (W)
1953—Redskins, 17-9 (P)
    Steelers, 14-13 (W)
1954—Steelers, 37-7 (P)
    Redskins, 17-14 (W)
1955—Redskins, 23-14 (P)
    Redskins, 28-17 (W)
1956—Steelers, 30-13 (P)
    Steelers, 23-0 (W)
1957—Steelers, 28-7 (P)

    Redskins, 10-3 (W)
1958—Steelers, 24-16 (P)
    Tie, 14-14 (W)
1959—Redskins, 23-17 (P)
    Steelers, 27-6 (W)
1960—Tie, 27-27 (W)
    Steelers, 22-10 (P)
1961—Steelers, 20-0 (P)
    Steelers, 30-14 (W)
1962—Steelers, 23-21 (P)
    Steelers, 27-24 (W)
1963—Steelers, 38-27 (P)
    Steelers, 34-28 (W)
1964—Redskins, 30-0 (P)
    Steelers, 14-7 (W)
1965—Redskins, 31-3 (P)
    Redskins, 35-14 (W)
1966—Redskins, 33-27 (P)
    Redskins, 24-10 (W)
1967—Redskins, 15-10 (P)
1968—Redskins, 16-13 (W)
1969—Redskins, 14-7 (P)
1973—Steelers, 21-16 (P)
1979—Steelers, 38-7 (P)
1985—Redskins, 30-23 (P)
1988—Redskins, 30-29 (W)
1991—Redskins, 41-14 (P)
1997—Steelers, 14-13 (P)
2000—Steelers, 24-3 (P)
(RS Pts.—Redskins 1,406, Steelers 1,155)
*Steelers known as Pirates prior to 1941
**Franchise in Boston prior to 1937

ST. LOUIS vs. ARIZONA
RS: Rams lead series, 23-21-2
PS: Rams lead series, 1-0;
See Arizona vs. St. Louis
ST. LOUIS vs. ATLANTA
RS: Rams lead series, 45-23-2;
See Atlanta vs. St. Louis
ST. LOUIS vs. BALTIMORE
RS: Series tied, 1-1;
See Baltimore vs. St. Louis
ST. LOUIS vs. BUFFALO
RS: Series tied, 4-4;
See Buffalo vs. St. Louis
ST. LOUIS vs. CAROLINA
RS: Series tied, 7-7;
See Carolina vs. St. Louis
ST. LOUIS vs. CHICAGO
RS: Bears lead series, 47-32-3
PS: Series tied, 1-1;
See Chicago vs. St. Louis
ST. LOUIS vs. CINCINNATI
RS: Bengals lead series, 5-4;
See Cincinnati vs. St. Louis
ST. LOUIS vs. CLEVELAND
RS: Series tied, 8-8
PS: Browns lead series, 2-1;
See Cleveland vs. St. Louis
ST. LOUIS vs. DALLAS
RS: Rams lead series, 9-8
PS: Series tied, 4-4;
See Dallas vs. St. Louis
ST. LOUIS vs. DENVER
RS: Rams lead series, 5-4;
See Denver vs. St. Louis
ST. LOUIS vs. DETROIT
RS: Rams lead series, 40-36-1
PS: Lions lead series, 1-0;

See Detroit vs. St. Louis
ST. LOUIS vs. GREEN BAY
RS: Rams lead series, 43-39-2
PS: Series tied, 1-1;
See Green Bay vs. St. Louis
ST. LOUIS vs. INDIANAPOLIS
RS: Colts lead series, 21-17-2;
See Indianapolis vs. St. Louis
ST. LOUIS vs. JACKSONVILLE
RS: Rams lead series, 1-0;
See Jacksonville vs. St. Louis
ST. LOUIS vs. KANSAS CITY
RS: Rams lead series, 4-3;
See Kansas City vs. St. Louis
ST. LOUIS vs. MIAMI
RS: Dolphins lead series, 7-2;
See Miami vs. St. Louis
ST. LOUIS vs. MINNESOTA
RS: Vikings lead series, 16-12-2
PS: Vikings lead series, 5-2;
See Minnesota vs. St. Louis
ST. LOUIS vs. NEW ENGLAND
RS: Rams lead series, 5-3
PS: Patriots lead series, 1-0;
See New England vs. St. Louis
ST. LOUIS vs. NEW ORLEANS
RS: Rams lead series, 36-28
PS: Saints lead series, 1-0;
See New Orleans vs. St. Louis
ST. LOUIS vs. N.Y. GIANTS
RS: Rams lead series, 25-9
PS: Series tied, 1-1;
See N.Y. Giants vs. St. Louis
ST. LOUIS vs. N.Y. JETS
RS: Rams lead series, 8-2;
See N.Y. Jets vs. St. Louis
ST. LOUIS vs. OAKLAND
RS: Raiders lead series, 7-2;
See Oakland vs. St. Louis
ST. LOUIS vs. PHILADELPHIA
RS: Rams lead series, 16-14-1
PS: Rams lead series, 2-1;
See Philadelphia vs. St. Louis
ST. LOUIS vs. PITTSBURGH
RS: Rams lead series, 14-5-2
PS: Steelers lead series, 1-0;
See Pittsburgh vs. St. Louis
*ST. LOUIS vs. SAN DIEGO
RS: Rams lead series, 4-3
1970—Rams, 37-10 (LA)
1975—Rams, 13-10 (SD) OT
1979—Chargers, 40-16 (LA)
1988—Chargers, 38-24 (LA)
1991—Rams, 30-24 (LA)
1994—Chargers, 31-17 (SD)
2000—Rams, 57-31 (StL)
(RS Pts.—Rams 194, Chargers 184)
Franchise in Los Angeles prior to 1995
*ST. LOUIS vs. SAN FRANCISCO
RS: Rams lead series, 54-48-2
PS: 49ers lead series, 1-0
1950—Rams, 35-14 (SF)
　　　Rams, 28-21 (LA)
1951—49ers, 44-17 (SF)
　　　Rams, 23-16 (LA)
1952—Rams, 35-9 (LA)
　　　Rams, 34-21 (SF)
1953—49ers, 31-30 (SF)
　　　49ers, 31-27 (LA)
1954—Tie, 24-24 (LA)

Rams, 42-34 (SF)
1955—Rams, 23-14 (SF)
　　　Rams, 27-14 (LA)
1956—49ers, 33-30 (SF)
　　　Rams, 30-6 (LA)
1957—49ers, 23-20 (SF)
　　　Rams, 37-24 (LA)
1958—Rams, 33-3 (SF)
　　　Rams, 56-7 (LA)
1959—Rams, 34-0 (SF)
　　　49ers, 24-16 (LA)
1960—49ers, 13-9 (SF)
　　　49ers, 23-7 (LA)
1961—49ers, 35-0 (SF)
　　　Rams, 17-7 (LA)
1962—49ers, 28-14 (SF)
　　　49ers, 24-17 (LA)
1963—Rams, 28-21 (LA)
　　　Rams, 21-17 (SF)
1964—Rams, 42-14 (LA)
　　　49ers, 28-7 (SF)
1965—49ers, 45-21 (LA)
　　　49ers, 30-27 (SF)
1966—Rams, 34-3 (LA)
　　　49ers, 21-13 (SF)
1967—49ers, 27-24 (LA)
　　　Rams, 17-7 (SF)
1968—Rams, 24-10 (LA)
　　　Tie, 20-20 (SF)
1969—Rams, 27-21 (SF)
　　　Rams, 41-30 (LA)
1970—49ers, 20-6 (LA)
　　　Rams, 30-13 (SF)
1971—Rams, 20-13 (SF)
　　　Rams, 17-6 (LA)
1972—Rams, 31-7 (LA)
　　　Rams, 26-16 (SF)
1973—Rams, 40-20 (SF)
　　　Rams, 31-13 (LA)
1974—Rams, 37-14 (LA)
　　　Rams, 15-13 (SF)
1975—Rams, 23-14 (SF)
　　　49ers, 24-23 (LA)
1976—Rams, 16-0 (LA)
　　　Rams, 23-3 (SF)
1977—Rams, 34-14 (LA)
　　　Rams, 23-10 (SF)
1978—Rams, 27-10 (LA)
　　　Rams, 31-28 (SF)
1979—Rams, 27-24 (LA)
　　　Rams, 26-20 (SF)
1980—Rams, 48-26 (LA)
　　　Rams, 31-17 (SF)
1981—49ers, 20-17 (SF)
　　　49ers, 33-31 (LA)
1982—49ers, 30-24 (LA)
　　　Rams, 21-20 (SF)
1983—Rams, 10-7 (SF)
　　　49ers, 45-35 (LA)
1984—49ers, 33-0 (LA)
　　　49ers, 19-16 (SF)
1985—49ers, 28-14 (LA)
　　　Rams, 27-20 (SF)
1986—Rams, 16-13 (LA)
　　　49ers, 24-14 (SF)
1987—49ers, 31-10 (LA)
　　　49ers, 48-0 (SF)
1988—49ers, 24-21 (LA)
　　　Rams, 38-16 (SF)
1989—Rams, 13-12 (SF)

49ers, 30-27 (LA)
**49ers, 30-3 (SF)
1990—Rams, 28-17 (SF)
　　　49ers, 26-10 (LA)
1991—49ers, 27-10 (SF)
　　　49ers, 33-10 (LA)
1992—49ers, 27-24 (SF)
　　　49ers, 27-10 (LA)
1993—49ers, 40-17 (SF)
　　　49ers, 35-10 (LA)
1994—49ers, 34-19 (LA)
　　　49ers, 31-27 (SF)
1995—49ers, 44-10 (StL)
　　　49ers, 41-13 (SF)
1996—49ers, 34-0 (SF)
　　　49ers, 28-11 (StL)
1997—49ers, 15-12 (StL)
　　　49ers, 30-10 (SF)
1998—49ers, 28-10 (StL)
　　　49ers, 38-19 (SF)
1999—Rams, 42-20 (StL)
　　　Rams, 23-7 (SF)
2000—Rams, 41-24 (StL)
　　　Rams, 34-24 (SF)
2001—Rams, 30-26 (SF)
　　　Rams, 27-14 (StL)
(RS Pts.—Rams 2,341, 49ers 2,301)
(PS Pts.—49ers 30, Rams 3)
Franchise in Los Angeles prior to 1995
*NFC Championship
*ST. LOUIS vs. SEATTLE
RS: Rams lead series, 5-2
1976—Rams, 45-6 (LA)
1979—Rams, 24-0 (S)
1985—Rams, 35-24 (S)
1988—Rams, 31-10 (LA)
1991—Seahawks, 23-9 (S)
1997—Seahawks, 17-9 (StL)
2000—Rams, 37-34 (Sea)
(RS Pts.—Rams 190, Seahawks 114)
Franchise in Los Angeles prior to 1995
*ST. LOUIS vs. TAMPA BAY
RS: Rams lead series, 8-5
PS: Rams lead series, 2-0
1977—Rams, 31-0 (LA)
1978—Rams, 26-23 (LA)
1979—Buccaneers, 21-6 (TB)
　　**Rams, 9-0 (TB)
1980—Buccaneers, 10-9 (TB)
1984—Rams, 34-33 (TB)
1985—Rams, 31-27 (TB)
1986—Rams, 26-20 (LA) OT
1987—Rams, 35-3 (LA)
1990—Rams, 35-14 (TB)
1992—Rams, 31-27 (TB)
1994—Buccaneers, 24-14 (TB)
1999—**Rams, 11-6 (StL)
2000—Buccaneers, 38-35 (TB)
2001—Buccaneers, 24-17 (StL)
(RS Pts.—Rams 330, Buccaneers 264)
(PS Pts.—Rams 20, Buccaneers 6)
Franchise in Los Angeles prior to 1995
**NFC Championship
*ST. LOUIS vs. **TENNESSEE
RS: Rams lead series, 5-3
PS: Rams lead series, 1-0
1973—Rams, 31-26 (H)
1978—Rams, 10-6 (H)
1981—Oilers, 27-20 (LA)
1984—Rams, 27-16 (LA)

1987—Oilers, 20-16 (H)
1990—Rams, 17-13 (LA)
1993—Rams, 28-13 (H)
1999—Titans, 24-21 (T)
   ***Rams, 23-16 (Atlanta)
(RS Pts.—Rams 170, Titans 145)
(PS Pts.—Rams 23, Titans 16)
*Franchise in Los Angeles prior to 1995
**Franchise in Houston prior to 1997;
known as Oilers prior to 1999
***Super Bowl XXXIV

*ST. LOUIS vs. WASHINGTON
RS: Redskins lead series, 18-6-1
PS: Series tied, 2-2
1937—Redskins, 16-7 (C)
1938—Redskins, 37-13 (W)
1941—Redskins, 17-13 (W)
1942—Redskins, 33-14 (W)
1944—Redskins, 14-10 (W)
1945—**Redskins, 15-14 (C)
1948—Rams, 41-13 (W)
1949—Rams, 53-27 (LA)
1951—Redskins, 31-21 (W)
1962—Redskins, 20-14 (W)
1963—Redskins, 37-14 (LA)
1967—Tie, 28-28 (LA)
1969—Rams, 24-13 (W)
1971—Redskins, 38-24 (LA)
1974—Redskins, 23-17 (LA)
   ***Rams, 19-10 (LA)
1977—Redskins, 17-14 (W)
1981—Redskins, 30-7 (LA)
1983—Redskins, 42-20 (LA)
   ***Redskins, 51-7 (W)
1986—****Redskins, 19-7 (W)
1987—Rams, 30-26 (W)
1991—Redskins, 27-6 (LA)
1993—Rams, 10-6 (LA)
1994—Redskins, 24-21 (LA)
1995—Redskins, 35-23 (StL)
1996—Redskins, 17-10 (StL)
1997—Rams, 23-20 (W)
2000—Redskins, 33-20 (StL)
(RS Pts.—Redskins 624, Rams 477)
(PS Pts.—Redskins 94, Rams 48)
*Franchise in Los Angeles prior to 1995
and in Cleveland prior to 1946
**NFL Championship
***NFC Divisional Playoff
****NFC First-Round Playoff

SAN DIEGO vs. ARIZONA
RS: Chargers lead series, 6-3;
See Arizona vs. San Diego
SAN DIEGO vs. ATLANTA
RS: Falcons lead series, 5-1;
See Atlanta vs. San Diego
SAN DIEGO vs BALTIMORE
RS: Chargers lead series, 2-1;
See Baltimore vs. San Diego
SAN DIEGO vs. BUFFALO
RS: Chargers lead series, 18-8-2
PS: Bills lead series, 2-1;
See Buffalo vs. San Diego
SAN DIEGO vs. CAROLINA
RS: Panthers lead series, 2-0;
See Carolina vs. San Diego
SAN DIEGO vs. CHICAGO
RS: Series tied, 4-4;
See Chicago vs. San Diego

SAN DIEGO vs. CINCINNATI
RS: Chargers lead series, 16-9
PS: Bengals lead series, 1-0;
See Cincinnati vs. San Diego
SAN DIEGO vs. CLEVELAND
RS: Chargers lead series, 10-7-1;
See Cleveland vs. San Diego
SAN DIEGO vs. DALLAS
RS: Cowboys lead series, 5-2;
See Dallas vs. San Diego
SAN DIEGO vs. DENVER
RS: Broncos lead series, 46-37-1;
See Denver vs. San Diego
SAN DIEGO vs. DETROIT
RS: Chargers lead series, 4-3;
See Detroit vs. San Diego
SAN DIEGO vs. GREEN BAY
RS: Packers lead series, 6-1;
See Green Bay vs. San Diego
SAN DIEGO vs. INDIANAPOLIS
RS: Chargers lead series, 12-7
PS: Colts lead series, 1-0;
See Indianapolis vs. San Diego
SAN DIEGO vs. KANSAS CITY
RS: Chiefs lead series, 44-38-1
PS: Chargers lead series, 1-0;
See Kansas City vs. San Diego
SAN DIEGO vs. MIAMI
RS: Chargers lead series, 10-8
PS: Series tied, 2-2;
See Miami vs. San Diego
SAN DIEGO vs. MINNESOTA
RS: Series tied, 4-4;
See Minnesota vs. San Diego
SAN DIEGO vs. NEW ENGLAND
RS: Patriots lead series, 17-11-2
PS: Chargers lead series, 1-0;
See New England vs. San Diego
SAN DIEGO vs. NEW ORLEANS
RS: Chargers lead series, 6-2;
See New Orleans vs. San Diego
SAN DIEGO vs. N.Y. GIANTS
RS: Giants lead series, 5-3;
See N.Y. Giants vs. San Diego
SAN DIEGO vs. N.Y. JETS
RS: Chargers lead series, 17-9-1;
See N.Y. Jets vs. San Diego
SAN DIEGO vs. OAKLAND
RS: Raiders lead series, 52-30-2
PS: Raiders lead series, 1-0;
See Oakland vs. San Diego
SAN DIEGO vs. PHILADELPHIA
RS: Chargers lead series, 5-3;
See Philadelphia vs. San Diego
SAN DIEGO vs. PITTSBURGH
RS: Steelers lead series, 17-5
PS: Chargers lead series, 2-0;
See Pittsburgh vs. San Diego
SAN DIEGO vs. ST. LOUIS
RS: Rams lead series, 4-3;
See St. Louis vs. San Diego
SAN DIEGO vs. SAN FRANCISCO
RS: 49ers lead series, 6-3
PS: 49ers lead series, 1-0
1972—49ers, 34-3 (SF)
1976—Chargers, 13-7 (SD) OT
1979—Chargers, 31-9 (SD)
1982—Chargers, 41-37 (SF)
1988—49ers, 48-10 (SD)
1991—49ers, 34-14 (SF)

1994—49ers, 38-15 (SD)
   *49ers, 49-26 (Miami)
1997—49ers, 17-10 (SF)
2000—49ers, 45-17 (SD)
(RS Pts.—49ers 269, Chargers 154)
(PS Pts.—49ers 49, Chargers 26)
*Super Bowl XXIX
SAN DIEGO vs. SEATTLE
RS: Seahawks lead series, 24-22
1977—Chargers, 30-28 (S)
1978—Chargers, 24-20 (S)
   Chargers, 37-10 (SD)
1979—Chargers, 33-16 (S)
   Chargers, 20-10 (SD)
1980—Chargers, 34-13 (S)
   Chargers, 21-14 (SD)
1981—Chargers, 24-10 (SD)
   Seahawks, 44-23 (S)
1983—Seahawks, 34-31 (S)
   Chargers, 28-21 (SD)
1984—Seahawks, 31-17 (S)
   Seahawks, 24-0 (SD)
1985—Seahawks, 49-35 (SD)
   Seahawks, 26-21 (S)
1986—Seahawks, 33-7 (S)
   Seahawks, 34-24 (SD)
1987—Seahawks, 34-3 (S)
1988—Chargers, 17-6 (SD)
   Seahawks, 17-14 (S)
1989—Seahawks, 17-16 (SD)
   Seahawks, 10-7 (S)
1990—Chargers, 31-14 (S)
   Seahawks, 13-10 (SD) OT
1991—Chargers, 20-9 (S)
   Chargers, 17-14 (SD)
1992—Chargers, 17-6 (SD)
   Chargers, 31-14 (S)
1993—Chargers, 18-12 (SD)
   Seahawks, 31-14 (S)
1994—Chargers, 24-10 (S)
   Chargers, 35-15 (SD)
1995—Chargers, 14-10 (SD)
   Chargers, 35-25 (S)
1996—Chargers, 29-7 (SD)
   Seahawks, 32-13 (S)
1997—Seahawks, 26-22 (S)
   Seahawks, 37-31 (SD)
1998—Seahawks, 27-20 (S)
   Seahawks, 38-17 (S)
1999—Chargers, 13-10 (SD)
   Chargers, 19-16 (S)
2000—Seahawks, 20-12 (SD)
   Seahawks, 17-15 (S)
2001—Seahawks, 13-10 (S) OT
   Seahawks, 25-22 (SD)
(RS Pts.—Seahawks 953, Chargers 944)
SAN DIEGO vs. TAMPA BAY
RS: Chargers lead series, 6-1
1976—Chargers, 23-0 (TB)
1981—Chargers, 24-23 (TB)
1987—Chargers, 17-13 (TB)
1990—Chargers, 41-10 (SD)
1992—Chargers, 29-14 (SD)
1993—Chargers, 32-17 (TB)
1996—Buccaneers, 25-17 (SD)
(RS Pts.—Chargers 183, Buccaneers 102)
*SAN DIEGO vs. **TENNESSEE
RS: Chargers lead series, 19-13-1
PS: Titans lead series, 3-0
1960—Oilers, 38-28 (H)

Chargers, 24-21 (LA)
***Oilers, 24-16 (H)
1961—Chargers, 34-24 (SD)
Oilers, 33-13 (H)
***Oilers, 10-3 (SD)
1962—Oilers, 42-17 (SD)
Oilers, 33-27 (H)
1963—Chargers, 27-0 (SD)
Chargers 20-14 (H)
1964—Chargers, 27-21 (SD)
Chargers, 20-17 (H)
1965—Chargers, 31-14 (SD)
Chargers, 37-26 (H)
1966—Chargers, 28-22 (H)
1967—Chargers, 13-3 (SD)
Oilers, 24-17 (H)
1968—Chargers, 30-14 (SD)
1969—Chargers, 21-17 (H)
1970—Tie, 31-31 (SD)
1971—Oilers, 49-33 (H)
1972—Chargers, 34-20 (SD)
1974—Oilers, 21-14 (H)
1975—Oilers, 33-17 (H)
1976—Chargers, 30-27 (SD)
1978—Chargers, 45-24 (H)
1979—****Oilers, 17-14 (SD)
1984—Chargers, 31-14 (SD)
1985—Oilers, 37-35 (H)
1986—Chargers, 27-0 (SD)
1987—Oilers, 33-18 (H)
1989—Chargers, 34-27 (SD)
1990—Oilers, 17-7 (SD)
1992—Oilers, 27-0 (H)
1993—Chargers, 18-17 (SD)
1998—Chargers, 13-7 (T)
(RS Pts.—Chargers 794, Titans 754)
(PS Pts.—Titans 51, Chargers 33)
*Franchise in Los Angeles prior to 1961
**Franchise in Houston prior to 1997;
known as Oilers prior to 1999
***AFL Championship
****AFC Divisional Playoff

SAN DIEGO vs. WASHINGTON
RS: Redskins lead series, 6-1
1973—Redskins, 38-0 (W)
1980—Redskins, 40-17 (W)
1983—Redskins, 27-24 (SD)
1986—Redskins, 30-27 (SD)
1989—Redskins, 26-21 (W)
1998—Redskins, 24-20 (W)
2001—Chargers, 30-3 (SD)
(RS Pts.—Redskins 188, Chargers 139)

SAN FRANCISCO vs. ARIZONA
RS: 49ers lead series, 12-9;
See Arizona vs. San Francisco
SAN FRANCISCO vs. ATLANTA
RS: 49ers lead series, 44-25-1
PS: Falcons lead series, 1-0;
See Atlanta vs. San Francisco
SAN FRANCISCO vs. BALTIMORE
RS: 49ers lead series, 1-0;
See Baltimore vs. San Francisco
SAN FRANCISCO vs. BUFFALO
RS: Series tied, 4-4;
See Buffalo vs. San Francisco
SAN FRANCISCO vs. CAROLINA
RS: Series tied, 7-7;
See Carolina vs. San Francisco

SAN FRANCISCO vs. CHICAGO
RS: Series tied, 26-26-1
PS: 49ers lead series, 3-0;
See Chicago vs. San Francisco
SAN FRANCISCO vs. CINCINNATI
RS: 49ers lead series, 7-2
PS: 49ers lead series, 2-0;
See Cincinnati vs. San Francisco
SAN FRANCISCO vs. CLEVELAND
RS: Browns lead series, 9-6;
See Cleveland vs. San Francisco
SAN FRANCISCO vs. DALLAS
RS: 49ers lead series, 13-8-1
PS: Cowboys lead series, 5-2;
See Dallas vs. San Francisco
SAN FRANCISCO vs. DENVER
RS: Broncos lead series, 5-4
PS: 49ers lead series, 1-0;
See Denver vs. San Francisco
SAN FRANCISCO vs. DETROIT
RS: 49ers lead series, 30-26-1
PS: Series tied, 1-1;
See Detroit vs. San Francisco
SAN FRANCISCO vs. GREEN BAY
RS: Series tied, 25-25-1
PS: Packers lead series, 4-1;
See Green Bay vs. San Francisco
SAN FRANCISCO vs. INDIANAPOLIS
RS: Colts lead series, 22-18;
See Indianapolis vs. San Francisco
SAN FRANCISCO vs. JACKSONVILLE
RS: Jaguars lead series, 1-0;
See Jacksonville vs. San Francisco
SAN FRANCISCO vs. KANSAS CITY
RS: 49ers lead series, 5-3;
See Kansas City vs. San Francisco
SAN FRANCISCO vs. MIAMI
RS: Series tied, 4-4
PS: 49ers lead series, 1-0;
See Miami vs. San Francisco
SAN FRANCISCO vs. MINNESOTA
RS: Series tied, 17-17-1
PS: 49ers lead series, 4-1;
See Minnesota vs. San Francisco
SAN FRANCISCO vs. NEW ENGLAND
RS: 49ers lead series, 7-2;
See New England vs. San Francisco
SAN FRANCISCO vs. NEW ORLEANS
RS: 49ers lead series, 45-18-2;
See New Orleans vs. San Francisco
SAN FRANCISCO vs. N.Y. GIANTS
RS: 49ers lead series, 12-11
PS: Series tied, 3-3;
See N.Y. Giants vs. San Francisco
SAN FRANCISCO vs. N.Y. JETS
RS: 49ers lead series, 8-1;
See N.Y. Jets vs. San Francisco
SAN FRANCISCO vs. OAKLAND
RS: Raiders lead series, 6-3;
See Oakland vs. San Francisco
SAN FRANCISCO vs. PHILADELPHIA
RS: 49ers lead series, 15-6-1
PS: 49ers lead series, 1-0;
See Philadelphia vs. San Francisco
SAN FRANCISCO vs. PITTSBURGH
RS: 49ers lead series, 9-8;
See Pittsburgh vs. San Francisco
SAN FRANCISCO vs. ST. LOUIS
RS: Rams lead series, 54-48-2
PS: 49ers lead series, 1-0;

See St. Louis vs. San Francisco
SAN FRANCISCO vs. SAN DIEGO
RS: 49ers lead series, 6-3
PS: 49ers lead series, 1-0;
See San Diego vs. San Francisco
SAN FRANCISCO vs. SEATTLE
RS: 49ers lead series, 4-2
1976—49ers, 37-21 (S)
1979—Seahawks, 35-24 (SF)
1985—49ers, 19-6 (SF)
1988—49ers, 38-7 (S)
1991—49ers, 24-22 (S)
1997—Seahawks, 38-9 (S)
(RS Pts.—49ers 151, Seahawks 129)
SAN FRANCISCO vs. TAMPA BAY
RS: 49ers lead series, 12-2
1977—49ers, 20-10 (SF)
1978—49ers, 6-3 (SF)
1979—49ers, 23-7 (SF)
1980—Buccaneers, 24-23 (SF)
1983—49ers, 35-21 (SF)
1984—49ers, 24-17 (SF)
1986—49ers, 31-7 (TB)
1987—49ers, 24-10 (TB)
1989—49ers, 20-16 (TB)
1990—49ers, 31-7 (SF)
1992—49ers, 21-14 (SF)
1993—49ers, 45-21 (TB)
1994—49ers, 41-16 (SF)
1997—Buccaneers, 13-6 (TB)
(RS Pts.—49ers 350, Buccaneers 186)
SAN FRANCISCO vs. *TENNESSEE
RS: 49ers lead series, 7-3
1970—49ers, 30-20 (H)
1975—Oilers, 27-13 (SF)
1978—Oilers, 20-19 (H)
1981—49ers, 28-6 (SF)
1984—49ers, 34-21 (H)
1987—49ers, 27-20 (SF)
1990—49ers, 24-21 (H)
1993—Oilers, 10-7 (SF)
1996—49ers, 10-9 (H)
1999—49ers, 24-22 (SF)
(RS Pts.—49ers 216, Titans 176)
*Franchise in Houston prior to 1997;
known as Oilers prior to 1999
SAN FRANCISCO vs. WASHINGTON
RS: 49ers lead series, 12-7-1
PS: 49ers lead series, 3-1
1952—49ers, 23-17 (W)
1954—49ers, 41-7 (SF)
1955—Redskins, 7-0 (W)
1961—49ers, 35-3 (SF)
1967—Redskins, 31-28 (W)
1969—Tie, 17-17 (SF)
1970—49ers, 26-17 (SF)
1971—*49ers, 24-20 (SF)
1973—Redskins, 33-9 (W)
1976—Redskins, 24-21 (SF)
1978—Redskins, 38-20 (W)
1981—49ers, 30-17 (W)
1983—**Redskins, 24-21 (W)
1984—49ers, 37-31 (SF)
1985—49ers, 35-8 (W)
1986—Redskins, 14-6 (W)
1988—49ers, 37-21 (SF)
1990—49ers, 26-13 (SF)
*49ers, 28-10 (SF)
1992—*49ers, 20-13 (SF)
1994—49ers, 37-22 (W)

1996—49ers, 19-16 (W) OT
1998—49ers, 45-10 (W)
1999—Redskins, 26-20 (SF) OT
(RS Pts.—49ers 512, Redskins 372)
(PS Pts.—49ers 93, Redskins 67)
*NFC Divisional Playoff
**NFC Championship

SEATTLE vs. ARIZONA
RS: Cardinals lead series, 5-1;
See Arizona vs. Seattle
SEATTLE vs. ATLANTA
RS: Seahawks lead series, 5-2;
See Atlanta vs. Seattle
SEATTLE vs. BALTIMORE
RS: Ravens lead series, 1-0;
See Baltimore vs. Seattle
SEATTLE vs. BUFFALO
RS: Seahawks lead series, 6-3;
See Buffalo vs. Seattle
SEATTLE vs. CAROLINA
RS: Panthers lead series, 1-0;
See Carolina vs. Seattle
SEATTLE vs. CHICAGO
RS: Seahawks lead series, 5-2;
See Chicago vs. Seattle
SEATTLE vs. CINCINNATI
RS: Seahawks lead series, 8-7
PS: Bengals lead series, 1-0;
See Cincinnati vs. Seattle
SEATTLE vs. CLEVELAND
RS: Seahawks lead series, 10-4;
See Cleveland vs. Seattle
SEATTLE vs. DALLAS
RS: Cowboys lead series, 5-2;
See Dallas vs. Seattle
SEATTLE vs. DENVER
RS: Broncos lead series, 32-17
PS: Seahawks lead series, 1-0;
See Denver vs. Seattle
SEATTLE vs. DETROIT
RS: Series tied, 4-4;
See Detroit vs. Seattle
SEATTLE vs. GREEN BAY
RS: Series tied, 4-4;
See Green Bay vs. Seattle
SEATTLE vs. INDIANAPOLIS
RS: Colts lead series, 5-3;
See Indianapolis vs. Seattle
SEATTLE vs. JACKSONVILLE
RS: Seahawks lead series, 3-1;
See Jacksonville vs. Seattle
SEATTLE vs. KANSAS CITY
RS: Chiefs lead series, 30-17;
See Kansas City vs. Seattle
SEATTLE vs. MIAMI
RS: Dolphins lead series, 6-2
PS: Dolphins lead series, 2-1;
See Miami vs. Seattle
SEATTLE vs. MINNESOTA
RS: Seahawks lead series, 4-2;
See Minnesota vs. Seattle
SEATTLE vs. NEW ENGLAND
RS: Seahawks lead series, 7-6;
See New England vs. Seattle
SEATTLE vs. NEW ORLEANS
RS: Saints lead series, 4-3;
See New Orleans vs. Seattle
SEATTLE vs. N.Y. GIANTS
RS: Giants lead series, 6-3;

See N.Y. Giants vs. Seattle
SEATTLE vs. N.Y. JETS
RS: Seahawks lead series, 8-7;
See N.Y. Jets vs. Seattle
SEATTLE vs. OAKLAND
RS: Raiders lead series, 26-22
PS: Series tied, 1-1;
See Oakland vs. Seattle
SEATTLE vs. PHILADELPHIA
RS: Eagles lead series, 5-3;
See Philadelphia vs. Seattle
SEATTLE vs. PITTSBURGH
RS: Seahawks lead series, 7-6;
See Pittsburgh vs. Seattle
SEATTLE vs. ST. LOUIS
RS: Rams lead series, 5-2;
See St. Louis vs. Seattle
SEATTLE vs. SAN DIEGO
RS: Seahawks lead series, 24-22;
See San Diego vs. Seattle
SEATTLE vs. SAN FRANCISCO
RS: 49ers lead series, 4-2;
See San Francisco vs. Seattle
SEATTLE vs. TAMPA BAY
RS: Seahawks lead series, 4-1
1976—Seahawks, 13-10 (TB)
1977—Seahawks, 30-23 (S)
1994—Seahawks, 22-21 (S)
1996—Seahawks, 17-13 (TB)
1999—Buccaneers, 16-3 (S)
(RS Pts.—Seahawks 85, Buccaneers 83)
SEATTLE vs. *TENNESSEE
RS: Seahawks lead series, 8-4
PS: Titans lead series, 1-0
1977—Oilers, 22-10 (S)
1979—Seahawks, 34-14 (S)
1980—Seahawks, 26-7 (H)
1981—Oilers, 35-17 (H)
1982—Oilers, 23-21 (H)
1987—**Oilers, 23-20 (H) OT
1988—Seahawks, 27-24 (S)
1990—Seahawks, 13-10 (S) OT
1993—Oilers, 24-14 (H)
1994—Seahawks, 16-14 (H)
1996—Seahawks, 23-16 (S)
1997—Seahawks, 16-13 (S)
1998—Seahawks, 20-18 (S)
(RS Pts.—Seahawks 237, Titans 220)
(PS Pts.—Titans 23, Seahawks 20)
*Franchise in Houston prior to 1997;
known as Oilers prior to 1999
**AFC First-Round Playoff
SEATTLE vs. WASHINGTON
RS: Redskins lead series, 6-4
1976—Redskins, 31-7 (W)
1980—Seahawks, 14-0 (W)
1983—Redskins, 27-17 (S)
1986—Redskins, 19-14 (W)
1989—Redskins, 29-0 (S)
1992—Redskins, 16-3 (S)
1994—Seahawks, 28-7 (W)
1995—Seahawks, 27-20 (W)
1998—Seahawks, 24-14 (S)
2001—Redskins, 27-14 (W)
(RS Pts.—Redskins 190, Seahawks 148)

TAMPA BAY vs. ARIZONA
RS: Series tied, 7-7;
See Arizona vs. Tampa Bay

TAMPA BAY vs. ATLANTA
RS: Buccaneers lead series, 9-8;
See Atlanta vs. Tampa Bay
TAMPA BAY vs. BALTIMORE
RS: Buccaneers lead series, 1-0;
See Baltimore vs. Tampa Bay
TAMPA BAY vs. BUFFALO
RS: Buccaneers lead series, 5-2;
See Buffalo vs. Tampa Bay
TAMPA BAY vs. CAROLINA
RS: Buccaneers lead series, 2-1;
See Carolina vs. Tampa Bay
TAMPA BAY vs. CHICAGO
RS: Bears lead series, 33-15;
See Chicago vs. Tampa Bay
TAMPA BAY vs. CINCINNATI
RS: Buccaneers lead series, 4-3;
See Cincinnati vs. Tampa Bay
TAMPA BAY vs. CLEVELAND
RS: Browns lead series, 5-0;
See Cleveland vs. Tampa Bay
TAMPA BAY vs. DALLAS
RS: Cowboys lead series, 6-2
PS: Cowboys lead series, 2-0;
See Dallas vs. Tampa Bay
TAMPA BAY vs. DENVER
RS: Broncos lead series, 3-2;
See Denver vs. Tampa Bay
TAMPA BAY vs. DETROIT
RS: Lions lead series, 26-22
PS: Buccaneers lead series, 1-0;
See Detroit vs. Tampa Bay
TAMPA BAY vs. GREEN BAY
RS: Packers lead series, 28-17-1
PS: Packers lead series, 1-0;
See Green Bay vs. Tampa Bay
TAMPA BAY vs. INDIANAPOLIS
RS: Colts lead series, 5-4;
See Indianapolis vs. Tampa Bay
TAMPA BAY vs. JACKSONVILLE
RS: Series tied, 1-1;
See Jacksonville vs. Tampa Bay
TAMPA BAY vs. KANSAS CITY
RS: Chiefs lead series, 5-3;
See Kansas City vs. Tampa Bay
TAMPA BAY vs. MIAMI
RS: Dolphins lead series, 4-3;
See Miami vs. Tampa Bay
TAMPA BAY vs. MINNESOTA
RS: Vikings lead series, 31-17;
See Minnesota vs. Tampa Bay
TAMPA BAY vs. NEW ENGLAND
RS: Patriots lead series, 3-2;
See New England vs. Tampa Bay
TAMPA BAY vs. NEW ORLEANS
RS: Saints lead series, 13-7;
See New Orleans vs. Tampa Bay
TAMPA BAY vs. N.Y. GIANTS
RS: Giants lead series, 9-5;
See N.Y. Giants vs. Tampa Bay
TAMPA BAY vs. N.Y. JETS
RS: Jets lead series, 7-1;
See N.Y. Jets vs. Tampa Bay
TAMPA BAY vs. OAKLAND
RS: Raiders lead series, 4-1;
See Oakland vs. Tampa Bay
TAMPA BAY vs. PHILADELPHIA
RS: Eagles lead series, 4-3
PS: Eagles lead series, 2-1;
See Philadelphia vs. Tampa Bay

TAMPA BAY vs. PITTSBURGH
RS: Steelers lead series, 5-1;
See Pittsburgh vs. Tampa Bay
TAMPA BAY vs. ST. LOUIS
RS: Rams lead series, 8-5
PS: Rams lead series, 2-0;
See St. Louis vs. Tampa Bay
TAMPA BAY vs. SAN DIEGO
RS: Chargers lead series, 6-1;
See San Diego vs. Tampa Bay
TAMPA BAY vs. SAN FRANCISCO
RS: 49ers lead series, 12-2;
See San Francisco vs. Tampa Bay
TAMPA BAY vs. SEATTLE
RS: Seahawks lead series, 4-1;
See Seattle vs. Tampa Bay
TAMPA BAY vs. *TENNESSEE
RS: Titans lead series, 6-1
1976—Oilers, 20-0 (H)
1980—Oilers, 20-14 (H)
1983—Buccaneers, 33-24 (TB)
1989—Oilers, 20-17 (H)
1995—Oilers, 19-7 (H)
1998—Oilers, 31-22 (TB)
2001—Titans, 31-28 (Tenn) OT
(RS Pts.—Titans 165, Buccaneers 121)
*Franchise in Houston prior to 1997;
known as Oilers prior to 1999*
TAMPA BAY vs. WASHINGTON
RS: Redskins lead series, 6-4
PS: Buccaneers lead series, 1-0;
1977—Redskins, 10-0 (TB)
1982—Redskins, 21-13 (TB)
1989—Redskins, 32-28 (W)
1993—Redskins, 23-17 (TB)
1994—Buccaneers, 26-21 (TB)
          Buccaneers, 17-14 (W)
1995—Buccaneers, 14-6 (TB)
1996—Buccaneers, 24-10 (TB)
1998—Redskins, 20-16 (W)
1999—*Buccaneers, 14-13 (TB)
2000—Redskins, 20-17 (W) OT
(RS Pts.—Redskins 177, Buccaneers 172)
(PS Pts.—Buccaneers 14, Redskins 13)
NFC Divisional Playoff

TENNESSEE VS. ARIZONA
RS: Cardinals lead series, 4-3;
See Arizona vs. Tennessee
TENNESSEE vs. ATLANTA
RS: Series tied, 5-5;
See Atlanta vs. Tennessee
TENNESSEE vs. BALTIMORE
RS: Series tied, 6-6
PS: Ravens lead series, 1-0;
See Baltimore vs. Tennessee
TENNESSEE vs. BUFFALO
RS: Titans lead series, 22-14
PS: Bills lead series, 2-1;
See Buffalo vs. Tennessee
TENNESSEE vs. CAROLINA
RS: Panthers lead series, 1-0;
See Carolina vs. Tennessee
TENNESSEE vs. CHICAGO
RS: Series tied, 4-4;
See Chicago vs. Tennessee
TENNESSEE vs. CINCINNATI
RS: Titans lead series, 36-29-1
PS: Bengals lead series, 1-0;
See Cincinnati vs. Tennessee

TENNESSEE vs. CLEVELAND
RS: Browns lead series, 31-26
PS: Titans lead series, 1-0;
See Cleveland vs. Tennessee
TENNESSEE vs. DALLAS
RS: Series tied, 5-5;
See Dallas vs. Tennessee
TENNESSEE vs. DENVER
RS: Titans lead series, 20-11-1
PS: Broncos lead series, 2-1;
See Denver vs. Tennessee
TENNESSEE vs. DETROIT
RS: Titans lead series, 5-3;
See Detroit vs. Tennessee
TENNESSEE vs. GREEN BAY
RS: Series tied, 4-4;
See Green Bay vs. Tennessee
TENNESSEE vs. INDIANAPOLIS
RS: Series tied, 7-7
PS: Titans lead series, 1-0;
See Indianapolis vs. Tennessee
TENNESSEE vs. JACKSONVILLE
RS: Series tied, 7-7
PS: Titans lead series, 1-0;
See Jacksonville vs. Tennessee
TENNESSEE vs. KANSAS CITY
RS: Chiefs lead series, 24-18
PS: Chiefs lead series, 2-0;
See Kansas City vs. Tennessee
TENNESSEE vs. MIAMI
RS: Dolphins lead series, 15-11
PS: Titans lead series, 1-0;
See Miami vs. Tennessee
TENNESSEE vs. MINNESOTA
RS: Vikings lead series, 6-3;
See Minnesota vs. Tennessee
TENNESSEE vs. NEW ENGLAND
RS: Patriots lead series, 18-14-1
PS: Titans lead series, 1-0;
See New England vs. Tennessee
TENNESSEE vs. NEW ORLEANS
RS: Titans lead series, 5-4-1;
See New Orleans vs. Tennessee
TENNESSEE vs. N.Y. GIANTS
RS: Giants lead series, 5-2;
See N.Y. Giants vs. Tennessee
TENNESSEE vs. N.Y. JETS
RS: Titans lead series, 20-13-1
PS: Titans lead series, 1-0;
See N.Y. Jets vs. Tennessee
TENNESSEE vs. OAKLAND
RS: Raiders lead series, 20-16
PS: Raiders lead series, 3-0;
See Oakland vs. Tennessee
TENNESSEE vs. PHILADELPHIA
RS: Eagles lead series, 6-1;
See Philadelphia vs. Tennessee
TENNESSEE vs. PITTSBURGH
RS: Steelers lead series, 37-26
PS: Steelers lead series, 3-0;
See Pittsburgh vs. Tennessee
TENNESSEE vs. ST. LOUIS
RS: Rams lead series, 5-3
PS: Rams lead series, 1-0;
See St. Louis vs. Tennessee
TENNESSEE vs. SAN DIEGO
RS: Chargers lead series, 19-13-1
PS: Titans lead series, 3-0;
See San Diego vs. Tennessee

TENNESSEE vs. SAN FRANCISCO
RS: 49ers lead series, 7-3;
See San Francisco vs. Tennessee
TENNESSEE vs. SEATTLE
RS: Seahawks lead series, 8-4
PS: Titans lead series, 1-0;
See Seattle vs. Tennessee
TENNESSEE vs. TAMPA BAY
RS: Titans lead series, 6-1;
See Tampa Bay vs. Tennessee
*TENNESSEE vs. WASHINGTON
RS: Titans lead series, 5-3
1971—Redskins, 22-13 (W)
1975—Oilers, 13-10 (H)
1979—Oilers, 29-27 (W)
1985—Redskins, 16-13 (W)
1988—Oilers, 41-17 (H)
1991—Redskins, 16-13 (W) OT
1997—Oilers, 28-14 (T)
2000—Titans, 27-21 (W)
(RS—Titans 177, Redskins 143)
*Franchise in Houston prior to 1997;
known as Oilers prior to 1999*

WASHINGTON vs. ARIZONA
RS: Redskins lead series, 69-44-2;
See Arizona vs. Washington
WASHINGTON vs. ATLANTA
RS: Redskins lead series, 13-4-1
PS: Redskins lead series, 1-0;
See Atlanta vs. Washington
WASHINGTON vs BALTIMORE
RS: Series tied, 1-1;
See Baltimore vs. Washington
WASHINGTON vs. BUFFALO
RS: Bills lead series, 5-4
PS: Redskins lead series, 1-0;
See Buffalo vs. Washington
WASHINGTON vs. CAROLINA
RS: Redskins lead series, 6-0;
See Carolina vs. Washington
WASHINGTON vs. CHICAGO
RS: Bears lead series, 19-15-1
PS: Redskins lead series, 4-3;
See Chicago vs. Washington
WASHINGTON vs. CINCINNATI
RS: Redskins lead series, 4-2;
See Cincinnati vs. Washington
WASHINGTON vs. CLEVELAND
RS: Browns lead series, 32-9-1;
See Cleveland vs. Washington
WASHINGTON vs. DALLAS
RS: Cowboys lead series, 49-31-2
PS: Redskins lead series, 2-0;
See Dallas vs. Washington
WASHINGTON vs. DENVER
RS: Broncos lead series, 5-4
PS: Redskins lead series, 1-0;
See Denver vs. Washington
WASHINGTON vs. DETROIT
RS: Redskins lead series, 24-10
PS: Redskins lead series, 3-0;
See Detroit vs. Washington
WASHINGTON vs. GREEN BAY
RS: Packers lead series, 14-12-1
PS: Series tied, 1-1;
See Green Bay vs. Washington
WASHINGTON vs. INDIANAPOLIS
RS: Colts lead series, 17-9;
See Indianapolis vs. Washington

WASHINGTON vs. JACKSONVILLE
RS: Redskins lead series, 2-0;
See Jacksonville vs. Washington
WASHINGTON vs. KANSAS CITY
RS: Chiefs lead series, 5-1;
See Kansas City vs. Washington
WASHINGTON vs. MIAMI
RS: Dolphins lead series, 5-3
PS: Series tied, 1-1;
See Miami vs. Washington
WASHINGTON vs. MINNESOTA
RS: Redskins lead series, 6-5
PS: Redskins lead series, 3-2;
See Minnesota vs. Washington
WASHINGTON vs. NEW ENGLAND
RS: Redskins lead series, 5-1;
See New England vs. Washington
WASHINGTON vs. NEW ORLEANS
RS: Redskins lead series, 13-5;
See New Orleans vs. Washington
WASHINGTON vs. N.Y. GIANTS
RS: Giants lead series, 77-57-4
PS: Series tied, 1-1;
See N.Y. Giants vs. Washington
WASHINGTON vs. N.Y. JETS
RS: Redskins lead series, 6-1;
See N.Y. Jets vs. Washington
WASHINGTON vs. OAKLAND
RS: Raiders lead series, 6-3
PS: Raiders lead series, 1-0;
See Oakland vs. Washington
WASHINGTON vs. PHILADELPHIA
RS: Redskins lead series, 72-56-5
PS: Redskins lead series, 1-0;
See Philadelphia vs. Washington
WASHINGTON vs. PITTSBURGH
RS: Redskins lead series, 42-29-3;
See Pittsburgh vs. Washington
WASHINGTON vs. ST. LOUIS
RS: Redskins lead series, 18-6-1
PS: Series tied, 2-2;
See St. Louis vs. Washington
WASHINGTON vs. SAN DIEGO
RS: Redskins lead series, 6-1;
See San Diego vs. Washington
WASHINGTON vs. SAN FRANCISCO
RS: 49ers lead series, 12-7-1
PS: 49ers lead series, 3-1;
See San Francisco vs. Washington
WASHINGTON vs. SEATTLE
RS: Redskins lead series, 6-4;
See Seattle vs. Washington
WASHINGTON vs. TAMPA BAY
RS: Redskins lead series, 6-4
PS: Buccaneers lead series, 1-0;
See Tampa Bay vs. Washington
WASHINGTON vs. TENNESSEE
RS: Titans lead series, 5-3;
See Tennessee vs. Washington

SUPER BOWL COMPOSITE STANDINGS

	W	L	Pct.	Pts.	OP
San Francisco 49ers	5	0	1.000	188	89
Baltimore Ravens	1	0	1.000	34	7
Chicago Bears	1	0	1.000	46	10
New York Jets	1	0	1.000	16	7
Pittsburgh Steelers	4	1	.800	120	100
Green Bay Packers	3	1	.750	127	76
Oakland/L.A. Raiders	3	1	.750	111	66
New York Giants	2	1	.667	66	73
Dallas Cowboys	5	3	.625	221	132
Washington Redskins	3	2	.600	122	103
Baltimore Colts	1	1	.500	23	29
Kansas City Chiefs	1	1	.500	33	42
Miami Dolphins	2	3	.400	74	103
Denver Broncos	2	4	.333	115	206
New England Patriots	1	2	.333	51	98
St. Louis/L.A. Rams	1	2	.333	59	67
Atlanta Falcons	0	1	.000	19	34
Philadelphia Eagles	0	1	.000	10	27
San Diego Chargers	0	1	.000	26	49
Tennessee Titans	0	1	.000	16	23
Cincinnati Bengals	0	2	.000	37	46
Buffalo Bills	0	4	.000	73	139
Minnesota Vikings	0	4	.000	34	95

SUPER BOWL MOST VALUABLE PLAYERS*

Super Bowl I	— QB Bart Starr, Green Bay
Super Bowl II	— QB Bart Starr, Green Bay
Super Bowl III	— QB Joe Namath, N.Y. Jets
Super Bowl IV	— QB Len Dawson, Kansas City
Super Bowl V	— LB Chuck Howley, Dallas
Super Bowl VI	— QB Roger Staubach, Dallas
Super Bowl VII	— S Jake Scott, Miami
Super Bowl VIII	— RB Larry Csonka, Miami
Super Bowl IX	— RB Franco Harris, Pittsburgh
Super Bowl X	— WR Lynn Swann, Pittsburgh
Super Bowl XI	— WR Fred Biletnikoff, Oakland
Super Bowl XII	— DT Randy White and
	DE Harvey Martin, Dallas
Super Bowl XIII	— QB Terry Bradshaw, Pittsburgh
Super Bowl XIV	— QB Terry Bradshaw, Pittsburgh
Super Bowl XV	— QB Jim Plunkett, Oakland
Super Bowl XVI	— QB Joe Montana, San Francisco
Super Bowl XVII	— RB John Riggins, Washington
Super Bowl XVIII	— RB Marcus Allen, L.A. Raiders
Super Bowl XIX	— QB Joe Montana, San Francisco
Super Bowl XX	— DE Richard Dent, Chicago
Super Bowl XXI	— QB Phil Simms, N.Y. Giants
Super Bowl XXII	— QB Doug Williams, Washington
Super Bowl XXIII	— WR Jerry Rice, San Francisco
Super Bowl XXIV	— QB Joe Montana, San Francisco
Super Bowl XXV	— RB Ottis Anderson, N.Y. Giants
Super Bowl XXVI	— QB Mark Rypien, Washington
Super Bowl XXVII	— QB Troy Aikman, Dallas
Super Bowl XXVIII	— RB Emmitt Smith, Dallas
Super Bowl XXIX	— QB Steve Young, San Francisco
Super Bowl XXX	— CB Larry Brown, Dallas
Super Bowl XXXI	— KR-PR Desmond Howard, Green Bay
Super Bowl XXXII	— RB Terrell Davis, Denver
Super Bowl XXXIII	— QB John Elway, Denver
Super Bowl XXXIV	— QB Kurt Warner, St. Louis
Super Bowl XXXV	— LB Ray Lewis, Baltimore
Super Bowl XXXVI	— QB Tom Brady, New England

* Award named Pete Rozelle Trophy since Super Bowl XXV.

RESULTS

Super Bowl	Date	Winner (Share)	Loser (Share)	Score	Site	Attendance
* XXXVI	2-3-02	New England ($63,000)	St. Louis ($34,500)	20-17	New Orleans	72,922
XXXV	1-28-01	Baltimore ($58,000)	N.Y. Giants ($34,500)	34-7	Tampa	71,921
* XXXIV	1-30-00	St. Louis ($58,000)	Tennessee ($33,000)	23-16	Atlanta	72,625
XXXIII	1-31-99	Denver ($53,000)	Atlanta ($32,500)	34-19	Miami	74,803
XXXII	1-25-98	Denver ($48,000)	Green Bay ($29,000)	31-24	San Diego	68,912
XXXI	1-26-97	Green Bay ($48,000)	New England ($29,000)	35-21	New Orleans	72,301
XXX	1-28-96	Dallas ($42,000)	Pittsburgh ($27,000)	27-17	Tempe	76,347
XXIX	1-29-95	San Francisco ($42,000)	San Diego ($26,000)	49-26	Miami	74,107
* XXVIII	1-30-94	Dallas ($38,000)	Buffalo ($23,500)	30-13	Atlanta	72,817
XXVII	1-31-93	Dallas ($36,000)	Buffalo ($18,000)	52-17	Pasadena	98,374
XXVI	1-26-92	Washington ($36,000)	Buffalo ($18,000)	37-24	Minneapolis	63,130
* XXV	1-27-91	N.Y. Giants ($36,000)	Buffalo ($18,000)	20-19	Tampa	73,813
XXIV	1-28-90	San Francisco ($36,000)	Denver ($18,000)	55-10	New Orleans	72,919
XXIII	1-22-89	San Francisco ($36,000)	Cincinnati ($18,000)	20-16	Miami	75,129
XXII	1-31-88	Washington ($36,000)	Denver ($18,000)	42-10	San Diego	73,302
XXI	1-25-87	N.Y. Giants ($36,000)	Denver ($18,000)	39-20	Pasadena	101,063
XX	1-26-86	Chicago ($36,000)	New England ($18,000)	46-10	New Orleans	73,818
XIX	1-20-85	San Francisco ($36,000)	Miami ($18,000)	38-16	Stanford	84,059
XVIII	1-22-84	L.A. Raiders ($36,000)	Washington ($18,000)	38-9	Tampa	72,920
* XVII	1-30-83	Washington ($36,000)	Miami ($18,000)	27-17	Pasadena	103,667
XVI	1-24-82	San Francisco ($18,000)	Cincinnati ($9,000)	26-21	Pontiac	81,270
XV	1-25-81	Oakland ($18,000)	Philadelphia ($9,000)	27-10	New Orleans	76,135
XIV	1-20-80	Pittsburgh ($18,000)	Los Angeles ($9,000)	31-19	Pasadena	103,985
XIII	1-21-79	Pittsburgh ($18,000)	Dallas ($9,000)	35-31	Miami	79,484
XII	1-15-78	Dallas ($18,000)	Denver ($9,000)	27-10	New Orleans	75,583
XI	1-9-77	Oakland ($15,000)	Minnesota ($7,500)	32-14	Pasadena	103,438
X	1-18-76	Pittsburgh ($15,000)	Dallas ($7,500)	21-17	Miami	80,187
IX	1-12-75	Pittsburgh ($15,000)	Minnesota ($7,500)	16-6	New Orleans	80,997
VIII	1-13-74	Miami ($15,000)	Minnesota ($7,500)	24-7	Houston	71,882
VII	1-14-73	Miami ($15,000)	Washington ($7,500)	14-7	Los Angeles	90,182
VI	1-16-72	Dallas ($15,000)	Miami ($7,500)	24-3	New Orleans	81,023
V	1-17-71	Baltimore ($15,000)	Dallas ($7,500)	16-13	Miami	79,204
* IV	1-11-70	Kansas City ($15,000)	Minnesota ($7,500)	23-7	New Orleans	80,562
III	1-12-69	N.Y. Jets ($15,000)	Baltimore ($7,500)	16-7	Miami	75,389
II	1-14-68	Green Bay ($15,000)	Oakland ($7,500)	33-14	Miami	75,546
I	1-15-67	Green Bay ($15,000)	Kansas City ($7,500)	35-10	Los Angeles	61,946

One week between conference championship games and Super Bowl; all others had two weeks between conference championship games and Super Bowl.

SUPER BOWL XXXVI

Louisiana Superdome, New Orleans, LA
February 3, 2002, Attendance: 72,922
NEW ENGLAND 20, ST. LOUIS 17—Adam Vinatieri's 48-yard field goal as time expired gave the New England Patriots their first Super Bowl title. The Rams outgained the Patriots 427-267 in total yards, but the Patriots forced 3 turnovers, which resulted in 17 points, while committing no turnovers. Jeff Wilkins' 50-yard field goal capped a 10-play, 48-yard drive midway through the first quarter to give the Rams a 3-0 lead. The first turnover came with 8:49 left in the second quarter, when Ty Law stepped in front of an out-pattern pass intended for Isaac Bruce and raced 47 yards untouched down the left sideline into the end zone. Late in the first half, Kurt Warner completed a 15-yard pass to Ricky Proehl to the Patriots' 40, but Antwan Harris forced Proehl to fumble and Terrell Buckley recovered. Five plays later, Tom Brady's 8-yard touchdown pass to David Patten with 21 seconds left in the quarter

gave New England a 14-3 halftime lead. Late in the third quarter, Torry Holt slipped coming off the line of scrimmage, and Otis Smith intercepted Warner's pass and returned it 30 yards to the Rams' 33 to set up Vinatieri's 37-yard field goal and a 17-3 lead. The Rams responded by driving to the Patriots' 3. On fourth-and-goal, Warner scrambled, was tackled by Roman Phifer, and fumbled. Tebucky Jones picked up the ball and raced the length of the field for an apparent touchdown, but the play was negated by Willie McGinest's holding penalty. Warner scored two plays later to trim the deficit to 17-10 with 9:31 left. The Patriots went three and out on their next two possessions, giving the Rams the ball on their 45-yard-line with 1:51 left. Warner completed an 18-yard pass to Az-Zahir Hakim and an 11-yard pass to Yo Murphy before connecting on a 26-yard touchdown pass to Proehl with 1:30 left to tie the game. Operating without any time outs, Brady completed 3 short passes to J.R. Redmond to reach the Patriots' 41 with 33

seconds left. After an incompletion, Brady completed 23- and 16-yard passes to Troy Brown and Jermaine Wiggins, respectively, to reach the Rams' 30, and then spiked the ball with 7 seconds remaining. Vinatieri drilled the 48-yard field-goal attempt, marking the first time in Super Bowl history the game had been won on the final play. Brady, who earned most valuable player honors, was 16 of 27 for 145 yards and 1 touchdown. Warner was 28 of 44 for 365 yards and 1 touchdown, with 2 interceptions.

St. Louis (17)	Offense	New Eng. (20)
Torry Holt	WR	Troy Brown
Orlando Pace	LT	Matt Light
Tom Nütten	LG	Mike Compton
Andy McCollum	C	Damien Woody
Adam Timmerman	RG	Joe Andruzzi
Ron Jones	RT	Greg Robinson-Randall
Ernie Conwell	TE	Jermaine Wiggins
Isaac Bruce	WR	David Patten
Kurt Warner	QB	Tom Brady
James Hodgins	FB	Marc Edwards

Marshall Faulk	RB	Antowain Smith
Defense		
Chidi Ahanotu	LE	Bobby Hamilton
Brian Young	LT	Brandon Mitchell
Jeff Zgonina	RT	Richard Seymour
Grant Wistrom	RE	Anthony Pleasant
Don Davis	LLB	Mike Vrabel
London Fletcher	MLB	Tedy Bruschi
Tommy Polley	RLB	Roman Phifer
Aeneas Williams	LCB	Ty Law
Dexter McCleon	RCB	Otis Smith
Adam Archuleta	SS	Lawyer Milloy
Kim Herring	FS	Tebucky Jones

SUBSTITUTIONS

ST. LOUIS—Offense: K—Jeff Wilkins. P—John Baker. RB—Trung Canidate, Robert Holcombe. WR—Az-Zahir Hakim, Yo Murphy, Ricky Proehl. TE—Brandon Manumaleuna, Jeff Robinson. G—Cameron Spikes. T—Ryan Tucker. C—Frank Garcia. Defense: DE—Leonard Little, Sean Moran. DT—Tyoka Jackson, Ryan Pickett. LB—O.J. Brigance, Mark Fields. CB—Dre' Bly, Jerametrius Butler. S—Willie Gary, Nick Sorensen. DNP: Jamie Martin. Inactive: QB—Marc Bulger. FB—Justin Watson. G—Kaulana Noa. T—John St. Clair. LB—Brian Allen, Dustin Cohen. S—Rich Coady.
NEW ENGLAND—Offense: K—Adam Vinatieri. P—Ken Walter. FB—Patrick Pass. RB—Kevin Faulk, J.R. Redmond. WR—Fred Coleman, Charles Johnson. TE—Rod Rutledge. G—Grey Ruegamer. T—Grant Williams. C—Lonie Paxton. Defense: DE—Willie McGinest. LB—Matt Chatham, Bryan Cox, Larry Izzo, Ted Johnson. CB—Terrell Buckley, Terrance Shaw. S—Je'Rod Cherry, Antwan Harris, Matt Stevens. DNP: Drew Bledsoe, Riddick Parker. Inactive: QB—Damon Huard. WR—Jimmy Farris. TE—Arther Love. G-G—Kenyatta Jones. T—Stephen Neal. DE-DT—Chris Sullivan. DT—David Nugent. CB—Leonard Myers.

OFFICIALS

Referee—Bernie Kukar. Umpire—Jeff Rice. Line Judge—Ron Phares. Side Judge—Laird Hayes. Head Linesman—Mark Hittner. Back Judge—Scott Green. Field Judge—Pete Morelli. Replay Official—Howard Slavin. Video Operator—Bud Alexander.

SCORING

St. Louis	3 0 0 14	— 17
New England	0 14 3 3	— 20

StL	—	FG Wilkins 50 (11:50)
NE	—	Law 47 interception return (Vinatieri kick) (6:11)
NE	—	Patten 8 pass from Brady (Vinatieri kick) (14:29)
NE	—	FG Vinatieri 37 (13:42)
StL	—	Warner 2 run (Wilkins kick) (5:29)
StL	—	Proehl 26 pass from Warner (Wilkins kick) (13:30)
NE	—	FG Vinatieri 48 (15:00)

TEAM STATISTICS

TEAM STATISTICS	StL	NE
Total First Downs	26	15
Rushing	7	6
Passing	16	8
Penalty	3	1
Total Net Yardage	427	267
Total Offensive Plays	69	54
Avg. Gain Per Offensive Play	6.2	4.9
Rushes	22	25
Yards Gained Rushing (Net)	90	133
Avg. Yards per Rush	4.1	5.3
Passes Attempted	44	27
Passes Completed	28	16
Had Intercepted	2	0
Tackled Attempting to Pass	3	2
Yards Lost Attempting to Pass	28	11
Yards Gained Passing (Net)	337	134
Punts	4	8
Avg. Distance	39.8	43.1
Punt Returns	3	1
Punt Return Yardage	6	4
Kickoff Returns	4	4
Kickoff Return Yardage	82	100
Interception Return Yardage	0	77
Total Return Yardage	88	181
Fumbles	2	0
Fumbles Lost	1	0
Own Fumbles Recovered	1	0
Opponent Fumbles Recovered	0	0
Penalties	6	5
Yards Penalized	39	31
Field Goals	1	2
Field Goals Attempted	2	2
Third-Down Efficiency	5/13	2/11
Fourth-Down Efficiency	0/0	0/0
Time of Possession	33:30	26:30

INDIVIDUAL STATISTICS

RUSHING: StL: M. Faulk 17-76-0, Warner 3-6-1, Hakim 1-5-0, Hodgins 1-3-0. NE: Smith 18-92-0, Patten 1-22-0, K. Faulk 2-15-0, Edwards 2-5-0, Brady 1-3-0, Redmond 1-(-4)-0.
PASSING: StL: Warner 44-28-365-1-2. NE: Brady 27-16-145-1-0.
RECEIVING: StL: Hakim 5-90-0, Bruce 5-56-0, Holt 5-49-0, M. Faulk 4-54-0, Proehl 3-71-1, Robinson 2-18-0, Conwell 2-8-0, Murphy 1-11-0, Hodgins 1-8-0. NE: Brown 6-89-0, Redmond 3-24-0, Wiggins 2-14-0, Edwards 2-7-0, Patten 1-8-1, Smith 1-4-0, K. Faulk 1-(-1)-0.
KICKOFF RETURNS: StL: Murphy 3-81-0, M. Faulk 1-1-0. NE: Pass 3-85-0, Brown 1-15-0.
PUNT RETURNS: StL: Bly 3-6-0. NE: Brown 1-4-0.
PUNTING: StL: Baker 4-159-39.8. NE: Walter 8-345-43.1.
INTERCEPTIONS: StL: none. NE: Law 1-47-1, Smith 1-30-0.
SACKS: StL: Little, Wistrom. NE: Hamilton, McGinest, Seymour.

SUPER BOWL XXXV

Raymond James Stadium, Tampa, Florida January 28, 2001, Attendance: 71,921
BALTIMORE 34, N.Y. GIANTS 7—The Ravens' defense completed a dominating

season by permitting just 152 yards, forcing 5 turnovers, recording 4 sacks, and not allowing an offensive touchdown en route to the franchise's first Super Bowl victory. Jermaine Lewis' punt return into Giants' territory midway through the first quarter was followed two plays later by Trent Dilfer's 38-yard touchdown pass to Brandon Stokley, which gave the Ravens a 7-0 lead. Early in the second quarter, Jessie Armstead intercepted a short pass by Dilfer and returned it 43 yards for a touchdown, but the play was nullified by a penalty. Dilfer's 36-yard pass to Qadry Ismail in the second quarter set up Matt Stover's 47-yard field goal with 1:48 left in the half. Tiki Barber's 27-yard run gave the Giants their deepest penetration of the game, to the Ravens' 29, but Chris McAlister intercepted Kerry Collins' pass on the next play to preserve a 10-0 lead. In the third quarter, Duane Starks stepped in front of Amani Toomer and intercepted Collins' pass. Starks returned it 49 yards untouched for a 17-0 lead. The Giants immediately cut the lead to 10 points when Ron Dixon returned the ensuing kickoff 97 yards for a touchdown. However, Jermaine Lewis then matched Dixon's kickoff return as he cut across the field and raced 84 yards for a 24-7 lead with 3:13 left in the third quarter. The 3 touchdowns in 36 seconds were a Super Bowl record. The Giants gained just 1 first down on their final four possessions. Jamal Lewis' 3-yard touchdown run midway through the fourth quarter gave Baltimore a 31-7 lead, and Robert Bailey recovered Dixon's fumble on the ensuing kickoff return to set up Stover's 34-yard field goal with 5:27 remaining to finish the scoring. Dilfer completed 12 of 25 passes for 153 yards and 1 touchdown. Jamal Lewis had 27 carries for 102 yards. Collins was 15 of 39 for 112 yards, with 4 interceptions. Ray Lewis was named Super Bowl most valuable player.

Baltimore (AFC)	7 3 14 10 — 34
N.Y. Giants (NFC)	0 0 7 0 — 7

Balt	—	Stokley 38 pass from Dilfer (Stover kick) (8:10)
Balt	—	FG Stover 47 (13:19)
Balt	—	Starks 49 interception return (Stover kick) (11:11)
NYG	—	Dixon 97 kickoff return (Daluiso kick) (11:29)
Balt	—	Je. Lewis 84 kickoff return (Stover kick) (11:47)
Balt	—	Ja. Lewis 3 run (Stover kick) (6:15)
Balt	—	FG Stover 34 (9:33)

SUPER BOWL XXXIV

Georgia Dome, Atlanta, Georgia January 30, 2000, Attendance: 72,625
ST. LOUIS 23, TENNESSEE 16—Mike Jones tackled Kevin Dyson at the 1-yard line as time expired, preserving the Rams' first-ever Super Bowl title. The Rams drove inside the Titans' 20 with each of

their first six possessions, but compiled just 3 field goals and 1 touchdown to take a 16-0 lead. Holder Mike Horan's bobbled snap averted a 35-yard field-goal attempt to conclude the Rams' first drive. The Titans responded with a 42-yard drive, their longest of the half, but Al Del Greco missed a 47-yard attempt. Jeff Wilkins added 3 field goals and missed a 34-yard attempt while the Titans did not threaten the rest of the half, giving the Rams a 9-0 lead at intermission despite outgaining the Titans in total yards (294-89). Tennessee drove 43 yards with the second half's opening kickoff, but Todd Lyght blocked Del Greco's 47-yard attempt to keep the Titans off the board. Kurt Warner's 31-yard pass to Isaac Bruce keyed the ensuing drive that was capped by Warner's 9-yard touchdown pass to Torry Holt with 7:20 left in the third quarter to give the Rams a 16-0 lead. The Titans responded with touchdown drives in excess of seven minutes on each of their next two possessions. Steve McNair's 23-yard scramble set up Eddie George's 1-yard run in the final minute of the third quarter. McNair's 2-point conversion pass to Frank Wycheck was incomplete, but the Titans' defense forced a punt and the offense drove 79 yards in 13 plays, highlighted by 21-yard passes from McNair to Isaac Byrd and Jackie Harris, and capped by George's 2-yard run to cut the deficit to 16-13 with 7:21 remaining. The Rams once again failed to get a first down, and following a punt, the Titans needed just 28 yards to set up Del Greco's game-tying 43-yard kick with 2:12 left. On the next play from scrimmage, Warner fired a deep pass down the right sideline to Bruce, who caught the ball at the Titans' 38, cut toward the inside, and outran the defense to the end zone to give the Rams a 23-16 lead with 1:54 left. The Titans drove downfield, and McNair avoided a sack and completed a 16-yard pass to Kevin Dyson at the Rams' 10 with six seconds remaining. With no timeouts, McNair attempted a quick pass to a slanting Dyson, who caught the ball in stride at the Rams' 3. However, Jones reacted quickly and stepped up to tackle Dyson at the 1-yard line as time expired. Warner, who was named the game's most valuable player, was 24 of 45 for a Super Bowl-record 414 yards and 2 touchdowns. Bruce had 6 catches for 162 yards, and Holt had 7 for 109 yards. McNair was 22 of 36 for 214 yards. The Titans were the first team in Super Bowl history to come back from a 16-point deficit.

St. Louis (NFC)	3 6 7 — 23	
Tennessee (AFC)	0 0 6 10 — 16	
StL	—	FG Wilkins 27 (12:00)
StL	—	FG Wilkins 29 (10:44)
StL	—	FG Wilkins 28 (14:45)
StL	—	Holt 9 pass from Warner (Wilkins kick) (11:01)

Tenn	—	George 1 run (pass failed) (14:46)
Tenn	—	George 2 run (Del Greco kick) (7:39)
Tenn	—	FG Del Greco 43 (12:48)
StL	—	Bruce 73 pass from Warner (Wilkins kick) (13:06)

SUPER BOWL XXXIII
Pro Player Stadium, Miami, Florida
January 31, 1999, Attendance: 74,803
DENVER 34, ATLANTA 19—John Elway, in his last game, passed for 336 yards and ran for a touchdown to earn most valuable player honors as the Broncos became the first AFC team to win consecutive Super Bowls since the Steelers won XIII and XIV. A 25-yard pass interference penalty on Ray Crockett assisted the Falcons' nine-play, 48-yard game-opening drive that was capped by Morten Andersen's 32-yard field goal. Elway's 41-yard pass to Rod Smith kept alive Denver's ensuing drive and led to Howard Griffith's 1-yard touchdown run. Ronnie Bradford's interception and return to the Broncos' 35 late in the first quarter gave Atlanta excellent field position. However, Jamal Anderson was stopped for no gain on third-and-1 and thrown for a 2-yard loss on fourth down. Denver capitalized on its defensive effort with Jason Elam's 26-yard field goal. The Falcons responded by driving to the Broncos' 8, but Andersen's 26-yard field-goal attempt sailed wide right and on the next play, Elway fired an 80-yard touchdown pass to Smith to turn a possible 10-6 game into a 17-3 Broncos lead. Andersen's 28-yard field goal and 2 misses by Elam on the Broncos' first two second-half possessions gave Atlanta an opportunity to climb back into the game. However, Darrien Gordon dashed the Falcons' hopes with interceptions on consecutive possessions inside the Broncos' 20 to stop drives and set up Broncos touchdowns. Gordon returned the first interception, on a tipped pass, 58 yards to the Falcons' 24 to set up Griffith's second touchdown five plays later, and picked the second pass off at the Broncos' 2 and returned it 50 yards. Terrell Davis turned a short pass into a 39-yard gain, and Elway scored two plays later to give Denver a 31-6 lead. Tim Dwight returned the ensuing kickoff for a touchdown, and, after a field goal by Elam, the Falcons' offense scored with 2:04 remaining on Chandler's 3-yard pass to Tony Martin. Byron Chamberlain recovered the ensuing onside kick, but Tyrone Braxton recovered Anderson's fumble at the Falcons' 33 with 1:30 remaining to ice the game. The Falcons drove inside the Broncos' 30 seven times, but tallied just 1 touchdown and 2 field goals, throwing 2 interceptions, missing 1 field goal, and turning the ball over 1 time on downs during the other possessions. Elway was 18 of 29 for 336 yards and 1 touchdown, with 1 interception. Davis had

25 carries for 102 yards. Smith had 5 receptions for 152 yards. Chandler was 19 of 35 for 219 yards and 1 touchdown, with 3 interceptions.

Denver (AFC)	7 10 0 17 — 34	
Atlanta (NFC)	3 3 0 13 — 19	
Atl	—	FG Andersen 32 (5:25)
Den	—	Griffith 1 run (Elam kick) (11:05)
Den	—	FG Elam 26 (5:43)
Den	—	R. Smith 80 pass from Elway (Elam kick) (10:06)
Atl	—	FG Andersen 28 (12:35)
Den	—	Griffith 1 run (Elam kick) (:04)
Den	—	Elway 3 run (Elam kick) (3:40)
Atl	—	Dwight 94 kickoff return (Andersen kick) (3:59)
Den	—	FG Elam 37 (7:52)
Atl	—	Mathis 3 pass from Chandler (pass failed) (12:56)

SUPER BOWL XXXII
Qualcomm Stadium, San Diego, California
January 25, 1998, Attendance: 68,912
DENVER 31, GREEN BAY 24—Terrell Davis rushed for 157 yards and a Super Bowl-record 3 touchdowns to lead the Broncos to their first NFL championship and break the NFC's streak of Super Bowl victories at 13. The defending Super Bowl champion Packers took the opening kick-off and marched 76 yards in just over four minutes, scoring the first points on Brett Favre's 22-yard touchdown pass to Antonio Freeman. The Broncos responded with a 10-play, 58-yard drive capped by Davis' 1-yard run to tie the game. Tyrone Braxton intercepted Favre two plays later, and John Elway scored on a third-and-goal play to begin the second quarter. Steve Atwater forced Favre to fumble three plays later, and Neil Smith recovered at the Packers' 33. Jason Elam converted a 51-yard field goal, the second longest in Super Bowl history, to give the Broncos a 17-7 lead with 12:21 left in the half. After an exchange of punts, the Packers produced a 17-play, 95-yard drive that consumed 7:26 and finished with Favre's 6-yard touchdown pass to Mark Chmura on third-and-5 with 12 seconds left in the half. Tyrone Williams forced and recovered Davis' fumble at the Broncos' 26 on the first play from scrimmage in the second half. However, the Broncos' defense kept the Packers out of the end zone as Ryan Longwell's 27-yard field goal tied the game with 11:59 left in the third quarter. After another exchange of punts, Elway's 36-yard pass to Ed McCaffrey keyed a 13-play, 92-yard drive capped by Davis' 1-yard touchdown run with 34 seconds left in the third quarter. Tim McKyer recovered Freeman's fumble at the Packers' 22 on the ensuing kickoff return, giving the Broncos a golden opportunity, but Eugene Robinson intercepted Elway's pass in the end zone on the next play. Sparked by Robinson's play, the Packers

took just four plays, three on passes to Freeman, to score the tying touchdown with 13:32 remaining. Each defense stiffened, forcing two punts, but the Broncos got great field position following Craig Hentrich's 39-yard punt to the Packers' 49 with 3:27 left and the score tied 24-24. Davis rushed for 2 yards on the first play, but Darrius Holland's 15-yard facemask penalty moved the ball to the Packers' 32. Elway threw a 23-yard pass to Howard Griffith two plays later, and after a holding penalty, Davis rushed 17 yards to the Packers' 1 with 1:47 left. After a timeout, Davis waltzed into the end zone to give Denver a 31-24 lead with 1:45 remaining. Freeman returned the kickoff 22 yards to the Broncos' 30, and Favre completed 22- and 13-yard screen passes to Dorsey Levens to reach the Broncos' 35 with 1:04 left. But after a 4-yard pass to Levens and incompletions to Freeman and Brooks, John Mobley knocked away Favre's pass to Chmura with 32 seconds left to give the Broncos the Vince Lombardi Trophy. Elway was 12 of 22 for 123 yards, with 1 interception. Favre was 25 of 42 for 256 yards and 1 touchdown, with 1 interception. Freeman had 9 receptions for 126 yards. Davis was named the game's most valuable player.

Green Bay (NFC)	7	7	3	7 — 24
Denver (AFC)	7	10	7	7 — 31

GB — Freeman 22 pass from Favre (Longwell kick) (4:02)
Den — Davis 1 run (Elam kick) (9:21)
Den — Elway 1 run (Elam kick) (:05)
Den — FG Elam 51 (2:39)
GB — Chmura 6 pass from Favre (Longwell kick) (14:48)
GB — FG Longwell 27 (3:01)
Den — Davis 1 run (Elam kick) (14:26)
GB — Freeman 13 pass from Favre (Longwell kick) (1:28)
Den — Davis 1 run (Elam kick) (13:15)

SUPER BOWL XXXI
Louisiana Superdome, New Orleans, LA
January 26, 1997, Attendance: 72,301
GREEN BAY 35, NEW ENGLAND 21— Desmond Howard returned a kickoff 99 yards for a touchdown and Brett Favre passed for 2 touchdowns and ran for a score as the Packers won their first Super Bowl in twenty-nine years. Howard, en route to garnering the MVP trophy, equaled a Super Bowl record with 244 total return yards. It was Favre's arm that struck first, as he hit Andre Rison for a 54-yard touchdown pass on the Packers' second play from scrimmage to take a 7-0 lead. Two plays later Doug Evans made a diving interception of Drew Bledsoe's pass at the 28-yard line, setting up Chris Jacke's field goal and giving the Packers a 10-0 lead just 6:18 into the Super Bowl. The Patriots answered with touchdowns on their next two posses-

sions. Craig Newsome's pass interference penalty set up the first touchdown and a 44-yard completion from Bledsoe to Terry Glenn preceeding Ben Coates' touchdown gave New England its first and only lead. The 24 combined first quarter points were the most in Super Bowl history. Green Bay struck again 56 seconds into the second quarter as Favre hit Antonio Freeman with a Super Bowl-record 81-yard touchdown bomb. Jacke booted his second field goal on Green Bay's next possession. After a Mike Prior interception, Favre orchestrated a 74-yard, nearly 6-minute drive that concluded with a diving Favre touching the ball against the pylon to give Green Bay a 27-14 halftime lead. Curtis Martin brought the Patriots to within a score by running in from 18 yards out with 3:27 left in the third quarter. But Howard broke the Patriots' spirit by returning the ensuing kickoff a Super Bowl-record 99 yards. Favre found Mark Chmura for the 2-point conversion to finish the scoring. Bledsoe was intercepted twice in the fourth quarter as the Patriots never crossed midfield in 4 fourth-quarter possessions. Reggie White set a Super Bowl record with 3 sacks. Favre completed 14 of 27 passes for 246 yards, with no interceptions. Bledsoe completed 11 more passes than Favre, but for just 7 more yards, and threw 4 interceptions.

New England (AFC)	14	0	7	0 — 21
Green Bay (NFC)	10	17	8	0 — 35

GB — Rison 54 pass from Favre (Jacke kick) (3:32)
GB — FG Jacke 37 (6:18)
NE — Byars 1 pass from Bledsoe (Vinatieri kick) (8:25)
NE — Coates 4 pass from Bledsoe (Vinatieri kick) (12:27)
GB — Freeman 81 pass from Favre (Jacke kick) (0:56)
GB — FG Jacke 31 (6:45)
GB — Favre 2 run (Jacke kick) (13:49)
NE — Martin 18 run (Vinatieri kick) (11:33)
GB — Howard 99 kickoff return (Chmura pass from Favre) (11:50)

SUPER BOWL XXX
Sun Devil Stadium, Tempe, Arizona
January 28, 1996, Attendance: 76,347
DALLAS 27, PITTSBURGH 17—Cornerback Larry Brown's 2 interceptions led to 14 second-half points and helped lift the Cowboys to their third Super Bowl victory in the last four seasons and their record-tying fifth title overall. Brown's interceptions foiled the comeback efforts of the Steelers, and earned him the Pete Rozelle Trophy as the game's most valuable player. Dallas scored on each of its first three possessions, taking a 13-0 lead on Troy Aikman's 3-yard touchdown pass to Jay Novacek and a pair of field goals by Chris Boniol. Neil O'Donnell's 6-yard touch-

down pass to Yancey Thigpen 13 seconds before halftime pulled Pittsburgh within 6 points, and the Steelers had the ball near midfield midway through the third quarter. But O'Donnell's third-down pass was intercepted by Brown at the Cowboys' 38-yard line, and his 44-yard return carried to Pittsburgh's 18. After Aikman's 17-yard completion to Michael Irvin, Emmitt Smith ran 1 yard for the touchdown that put Dallas ahead again by 13 points. The Steelers rallied, though, behind Norm Johnson's 46-yard field goal, a successful surprise onside kick, and Byron (Bam) Morris' 1-yard touchdown run with 6:36 to play in the game. And when they forced a punt and took possession at their own 32-yard line trailing only 20-17 with 4:15 remaining, it appeared they might have a chance to break the NFC's recent domination in the Super Bowl. But on second down, Brown struck again, intercepting O'Donnell's pass at the 39 and returning it 33 yards to the 6. Two plays later, Smith barreled over from 4 yards out for the clinching touchdown with 3:43 to go. Pittsburgh limited the Cowboys' powerful running game to only 56 yards and enjoyed a whopping 201-61 advantage in total yards in the second half, but could not overcome the 3 interceptions (another came on the game's final play) thrown by O'Donnell, the NFL's career leader for fewest interceptions per pass attempt. In all, O'Donnell completed 28 of 49 passes for 239 yards. Morris rushed for a game-high 73 yards on 19 carries. For Dallas, Aikman completed 15 of 23 pass attempts for 209 yards. The Cowboys' victory was the twelfth in a row for NFC teams over AFC teams in the Super Bowl.

Dallas (NFC)	10	3	7	7 — 27
Pittsburgh (AFC)	0	7	0	10 — 17

Dall — FG Boniol 42 (2:55)
Dall — Novacek 3 pass from Aikman (Boniol kick) (9:37)
Dall — FG Boniol 35 (8:57)
Pitt — Thigpen 6 pass from O'Donnell (N. Johnson kick) (14:47)
Dall — E. Smith 1 run (Boniol kick) (8:18)
Pitt — FG N. Johnson 46 (3:40)
Pitt — Morris 1 run (N. Johnson kick) (8:24)
Dall — E. Smith 4 run (Boniol kick) (11:17)

SUPER BOWL XXIX
Joe Robbie Stadium, Miami, Florida
January 29, 1995, Attendance: 74,107
SAN FRANCISCO 49, SAN DIEGO 26— Steve Young passed for a record 6 touchdowns, and the 49ers became the first team to win five Super Bowls when they routed the Chargers. Young, the game's most valuable player, directed an explosive offense that generated 7 touchdowns, 28 first downs, and 455 total yards. He completed 24 of 36 passes for

325 yards, and broke the record of 5 touchdown passes set by fromer 49ers quarterback Joe Montana in Super Bowl XXIV. San Francisco wasted little time scoring, taking the lead for good on Young's 44-yard touchdown pass to Jerry Rice only three plays and 1:24 into the game. The next time they had the ball, the 49ers marched 79 yards in four plays, taking a 14-0 lead when Young teamed with running back Ricky Watters on a 51-yard touchdown pass with 10:05 still to play in the opening period. San Diego then put together its most impressive posses-sion of the game, a 13-play, 78-yard drive that consumed more than 7 minutes and was capped by Natrone Means' 1-yard touchdown run, to cut its deficit to 14-7 late in the quarter. But San Francis-co countered with a 70-yard drive of its own, and Young's 5-yard touchdown pass to fullback William Floyd made it 21-7. Young's fourth touchdown pass of the half, 8 yards to Watters 4:44 before halftime, increased the advantage to 28-7, and the Chargers could get no closer than 18 points after that. Watters, who ran 9 yards for a touchdown in the third quarter, equaled the Super Bowl record with 3 touchdowns. Rice also scored 3 touch-downs (the second time in his career he'd done that in a Super Bowl) while catching 10 passes for 149 yards. He established career records for receptions, yards, and touchdowns in a Super Bowl. Young, who scrambled 21 yards and 15 yards to set up touchdowns in the first half, was the game's leading rusher with 49 yards on 5 carries. San Diego's Means, who rushed for 1,350 yards during the regular season, was limited to 33 yards on 13 attempts. Chargers quarterback Stan Humphries completed 24 of 49 passes for 275 yards. Rookie Andre Coleman became only the third player in Super Bowl history to return a kickoff for a touchdown, going 98 yards in the third quarter. The 75 points scored by the two teams established another record, breaking the previous mark of 69 set in Dallas' 52-17 victory over Buffalo in XXVII. The 49ers' victory was the eleventh straight for NFC teams over AFC teams in the Super Bowl.

San Diego (AFC)   7   3   8   8 — 26
San Francisco (NFC)   14 14 14   7 — 49

SF	—	Rice 44 pass from S. Young (Brien kick) (1:24)
SF	—	Watters 51 pass from S. Young (Brien kick) (4:55)
SD	—	Means 1 run (Carney kick) (12:16)
SF	—	Floyd 5 pass from S. Young (Brien kick) (1:58)
SF	—	Watters 8 pass from S. Young (Brien kick) (10:16)
SD	—	FG Carney 31 (13:16)
SF	—	Watters 9 run (Brien kick) (5:25)
SF	—	Rice 15 pass from S. Young (Brien kick) (11:42)

SD	—	Coleman 98 kickoff return (Seay pass from Humphries) (11:59)
SF	—	Rice 7 pass from S. Young (Brien kick) (1:11)
SD	—	Martin 30 pass from Humphries (Pupunu pass from Humphries) (12:35)

SUPER BOWL XXVIII

Georgia Dome, Atlanta, Georgia
January 30, 1994, Attendance: 72,817
DALLAS 30, BUFFALO 13—Emmitt Smith rushed for 132 yards and 2 second-half touchdowns to power the Cowboys to their second consecutive NFL title. By winning, Dallas joined San Francisco and Pittsburgh as the only franchises with four Super Bowl victories. The Bills, mean-while, extended a dubious string by losing in the Super Bowl for the fourth consec-tive year. To win, the Cowboys had to rally from a 13-6 halftime deficit. Buffalo had forged its lead on Thurman Thomas' 4-yard touchdown run and a pair of field goals by Steve Christie, including a 54-yard kick, the longest in Super Bowl histo-ry. But just 55 seconds into the second half, Thomas was stripped of the ball by Dallas defensive tackle Leon Lett. Safety James Washington recovered and weaved his way 46 yards for a touchdown to tie the game at 13-13. After forcing the Bills to punt, the Cowboys began their next possession on their 36-yard line and Smith, the game's most valuable player, took over. He carried 7 times for 61 yards on the ensuing 8-play, 64-yard drive, cap-ping the march with a 15-yard touchdown run to give Dallas the lead for good with 8:42 remaining in the third quarter. Early in the fourth quarter, Washington inter-cepted Jim Kelly's pass and returned it 12 yards to Buffalo's 34. A penalty moved the ball back to the 39, but Smith carried twice for 10 yards and caught a screen pass for 9, and quarterback Troy Aikman completed a 16-yard pass to Alvin Harper to give the Cowboys a first-and-goal at the 6. Smith took it from there, cracking the end zone on fourth-and-goal from the 1 to put Dallas ahead 27-13 with 9:50 remain-ing. Eddie Murray's third field goal, from 20 yards at 2:50 left, ended any doubt about the game's outcome. Smith had 30 carries in all, with 19 of his attempts and 92 yards coming after intermission. Washington, normally a reserve who played most of the game because the Cowboys used five defensive backs to combat the Bills' No-Huddle offense, had 11 tackles and forced another fumble by Thomas in the first quarter. Aikman com-pleted 19 of 27 passes for 207 yards. Buffalo's Kelly completed a Super Bowl-record 31 passes in 50 attempts for 260 yards. Dallas, the first team in NFL history to begin the regular season 0-2 and go on to win the Super Bowl, also became the fifth to win back-to-back titles, following

Green Bay, Miami, Pittsburgh (the Steelers did it twice), and San Francisco. Buffalo became the third team, along with Min-nesota and Denver, to lose four Super Bowls. The Cowboys' victory was the tenth in succession for the NFC over the AFC.

Dallas (NFC)   6   0 14 10 — 30
Buffalo (AFC)   3 10   0   0 — 13

Dall	—	FG Murray 41 (2:19)
Buff	—	FG Christie 54 (4:41)
Dall	—	FG Murray 24 (11:05)
Buff	—	Thomas 4 run (Christie kick) (2:34)
Buff	—	FG Christie 28 (15:00)
Dall	—	Washington 46 fumble return (Murray kick) (0:55)
Dall	—	E. Smith 15 run (Murray kick) (6:18)
Dall	—	E. Smith 1 run (Murray kick) (5:10)
Dall	—	FG Murray 20 (12:10)

SUPER BOWL XXVII

Rose Bowl, Pasadena, California
January 31, 1993, Attendance: 98,374
DALLAS 52, BUFFALO 17—Troy Aikman passed for 4 touchdowns, Emmitt Smith rushed for 108 yards, and the Cowboys converted 9 turnovers into 35 points while coasting to the victory. Dallas' win was its third in its record sixth Super Bowl appearance; the Bills became the first team to drop three in succession. Buffalo led 7-0 until the first 2 of its record num-ber of turnovers helped the Cowboys take the lead for good late in the opening quar-ter. First, Dallas safety James Washington intercepted Jim Kelly's pass and returned it 13 yards to the Bills' 47, setting up Aik-man's 23-yard touchdown pass to tight end Jay Novacek with 1:36 remaining in the period. On the next play from scrim-mage, Kelly was sacked by Charles Haley and fumbled at the Bills' 2-yard line where the Cowboys' Jimmie Jones picked up the loose ball and ran 2 yards for a touch-down. Dallas, which recovered 5 fumbles and intercepted 4 passes, struck just as quickly late in the first half, when Aikman tossed 19- and 18-yard touchdown pass-es to Michael Irvin 18 seconds apart to give the Cowboys a 28-10 lead at inter-mission. The second score was set up when Bills running back Thurman Thomas lost a fumble at his 19-yard line. Buffalo scored for the last time when backup quarterback Frank Reich, playing because Kelly was injured while attempting to pass midway through the second quarter, threw a 40-yard touchdown pass to Don Beebe on the final play of the third period to trim the deficit to 31-17. But Dallas put the game out of reach by scoring three times in a span of 2:33 of the fourth quar-ter. Aikman, the game's most valuable player, completed 22 of 30 passes for 273 yards. The victory was the ninth in suc-cession for the NFC over the AFC.

Buffalo (AFC)	7	3	7	0 — 17
Dallas (NFC)	14	14	3	21 — 52

Buff — Thomas 2 run (Christie kick) (5:00)

Dall — Novacek 23 pass from Aikman (Elliott kick) (13:24)

Dall — J. Jones 2 fumble recovery return (Elliott kick) (13:39)

Buff — FG Christie 21 (11:36)

Dall — Irvin 19 pass from Aikman (Elliott kick) (13:06)

Dall — Irvin 18 pass from Aikman (Elliott kick) (13:24)

Dall — FG Elliott 20 (6:39)

Buff — Beebe 40 pass from Reich (Christie kick) (15:00)

Dall — Harper 45 pass from Aikman (Elliott kick) (4:56)

Dall — E. Smith 10 run (Elliott kick) (6:48)

Dall — Norton 9 fumble recovery return (Elliott kick) (7:29)

SUPER BOWL XXVI

Metrodome, Minneapolis, Minnesota
January 26, 1992, Attendance: 63,130
WASHINGTON 37, BUFFALO 24—Mark Rypien passed for 292 yards and 2 touchdowns as the Redskins overwhelmed the Bills to win their third Super Bowl in the past 10 years. Rypien, the game's most valuable player, completed 18 of 33 passes, including a 10-yard scoring strike to Earnest Byner and a 30-yard touchdown to Gary Clark. The latter came late in the third quarter after Buffalo had trimmed a 24-0 deficit to 24-10, and effectively put the game out of reach. Washington went on to lead by as much as 37-10 before the Bills made it close wih a pair of touchdowns in the final six minutes. Though the Redskins struggled early, converting their first three drives inside the Bills' 20-yard line into only 3 points, they built a 17-0 halftime lead. And they made it 24-0 just 16 seconds into the second half, after Kurt Gouveia intercepted Buffalo quarterback Jim Kelly's pass on the first play of the third quarter and returned it 23 yards to the Bills' 2. One play later, Gerald Riggs scored his second touchdown of the game to make it 24-0. Kelly, forced to bring Buffalo from behind, completed 28 of a Super Bowl-record 58 passes for 275 yards and 2 touchdowns, but was intercepted 4 tImes. Bills running back Thurman Thomas, who had an AFC-high 1,407 yards rushing and an NFL-best 2,038 total yards from scrimmage during the regular season, ran for only 13 yards on 10 carries and was limited to 27 yards on 4 receptions. Clark had 7 catches for 114 yards and Art Monk added 7 for 113 for the Redskins, who amassed 417 yards of total offense while limiting the explosive Bills to 283. Washington's Joe Gibbs became only the third head coach to win three Super Bowls.

Washington (NFC)	0	17	14	6 — 37
Buffalo (AFC)	0	0	10	14 — 24

Wash — FG Lohmiller 34 (1:58)

Wash — Byner 10 pass from Rypien (Lohmiller kick) (5:06)

Wash — Riggs 1 run (Lohmiller kick) (7:43)

Wash — Riggs 2 run (Lohmiller kick) (0:16)

Buff — FG Norwood 21 (3:01)

Buff — Thomas 1 run (Norwood kick) (9:02)

Wash — Clark 30 pass from Rypien (Lohmiller kick) (13:36)

Wash — FG Lohmiller 25 (0:06)

Wash — FG Lohmiller 39 (3:24)

Buff — Metzelaars 2 pass from Kelly (Norwood kick) (9:01)

Buff — Beebe 4 pass from Kelly (Norwood kick) (11:05)

SUPER BOWL XXV

Tampa Stadium, Tampa, Florida
January 27, 1991, Attendance: 73,813
NEW YORK GIANTS 20, BUFFALO 19—The NFC champion New York Giants won their second Super Bowl in five years with a 20-19 victory over AFC titlist Buffalo. New York, employing its ball-control offense, had possession for 40 minutes, 33 seconds, a Super Bowl record. The Bills, who scored 95 points in their previous two playoff games leading to Super Bowl XXV, had the ball for less than eight minutes in the second half and just 19:27 for the game. Fourteen of New York's 73 plays came on its initial drive of the third quarter, which covered 75 yards and consumed a Super Bowl-record 9:29 before running back Ottis Anderson ran 1 yard for a touchdown. Giants quarterback Jeff Hostetler kept the long drive going by converting three third-down plays—an 11-yard pass to running back David Meggett on third-and-eight, a 14-yard toss to wide receiver Mark Ingram on third-and-13, and a 9-yard pass to Howard Cross on third-and-four—to give New York a 17-12 lead in the third quarter. Buffalo jumped to a 12-3 lead midway through the second quarter before Hostetler completed a 14-yard scoring strike to wide receiver Stephen Baker to close the score to 12-10 at halftime. Buffalo's Thurman Thomas ran 31 yards for a touchdown on the opening play of the fourth quarter to help Buffalo recapture the lead 19-17. Matt Bahr's 21-yard field goal gave the Giants a 20-19 lead, but Buffalo's Scott Norwood had a chance to win the game with seconds remaining before his 47-yard field-goal attempt sailed wide right. Hostetler completed 20 of 32 passes for 222 yards and 1 touchdown. Anderson rushed 21 times for 102 yards and 1 touchdown to capture most-valuable-player honors. Thomas totaled 190 scrimmage yards, rushing 15 times for 135 yards and catching 5 passes for 55 yards.

Buffalo (AFC)	3	9	0	7 — 19
N.Y. Giants (NFC)	3	7	7	3 — 20

NYG — FG Bahr 28 (7:46)

Buff — FG Norwood 23 (9:09)

Buff — D. Smith 1 run (Norwood kick) (2:30)

Buff — Safety, B. Smith tackled Hostetler in end zone (6:33)

NYG — Baker 14 pass from Hostetler (Bahr kick) (14:35)

NYG — Anderson 1 run (Bahr kick) (9:29)

Buff — Thomas 31 run (Norwood kick) (0:08)

NYG — FG Bahr 21 (7:40)

SUPER BOWL XXIV

Louisiana Superdome, New Orleans, LA
January 28, 1990, Attendance: 72,919
SAN FRANCISCO 55, DENVER 10—NFC titlist San Francisco won its fourth Super Bowl championship with a 55-10 victory over AFC champion Denver. The 49ers, who also won Super Bowls XVI, XIX, and XXIII, tied the Pittsburgh Steelers for most Super Bowl victories. The Steelers captured Super Bowls IX, X, XIII, and XIV. San Francisco's 55 points broke the previous Super Bowl scoring mark of 46 points by Chicago in Super Bowl XX. San Francisco scored touchdowns on four of its six first-half possessions to hold a 27-3 lead at halftime. Interceptions by Michael Walter and Chet Brooks ended the Broncos' first two possessions of the second half. San Francisco quarterback Joe Montana was named the Super Bowl most valuable player for a record third time. Montana completed 22 of 29 passes for 297 yards and a Super Bowl-record 5 touchdowns. Jerry Rice, Super Bowl XXIII most valuable player, caught 7 passes for 148 yards and 3 touchdowns. The 49ers' domination included first downs (28 to 12), net yards (461 to 167), and time of possession (39:31 to 20:29).

San Francisco (NFC)	13	14	14	14 — 55
Denver (AFC)	3	0	7	0 — 10

SF — Rice 20 pass from Montana (Cofer kick) (4:54)

Den — FG Treadwell 42 (8:13)

SF — Jones 7 pass from Montana (kick failed) (14:57)

SF — Rathman 1 run (Cofer kick) (7:45)

SF — Rice 38 pass from Montana (Cofer kick) (14:26)

SF — Rice 28 pass from Montana (Cofer kick) (2:12)

SF — Taylor 35 pass from Montana (Cofer kick) (5:16)

Den — Elway 3 run (Treadwell kick) (8:07)

SF — Rathman 3 run (Cofer kick) (0:03)

SF — Craig 1 run (Cofer kick) (1:13)

SUPER BOWL XXIII

Joe Robbie Stadium, Miami, Florida
January 22, 1989, Attendance: 75,129
SAN FRANCISCO 20, CINCINNATI 16—
NFC champion San Francisco captured its third Super Bowl of the 1980s by defeating AFC champion Cincinnati 20-16. The 49ers, who also won Super Bowls XVI and XIX, became the first NFC team to win three Super Bowls. Pittsburgh, with four Super Bowl titles (IX, X, XIII, and XIV), and the Oakland/Los Angeles Raiders, with three (XI, XV, and XVIII), lead AFC franchises. Even though San Francisco held an advantage in total net yards (453 to 229), the 49ers found themselves trailing the Bengals late in the game. With the score 13-13, Cincinnati took a 16-13 lead on Jim Breech's 40-yard field goal with 3:20 remaining. It was Breech's third field goal of the day, following earlier successes from 34 and 43 yards. The 49ers started their winning drive at their 8-yard line. Over the next 11 plays, San Francisco covered 92 yards with the decisive score coming on a 10-yard pass from quarterback Joe Montana to wide receiver John Taylor with 34 seconds remaining. At halftime, the score was 3-3, the first time in Super Bowl history the game was tied at intermission. After the teams traded third-period field goals, the Bengals jumped ahead 13-6 on Stanford Jennings' 93-yard kickoff return for a touchdown with 34 seconds remaining in the quarter. The 49ers didn't waste any time coming back as they covered 85 yards in four plays, concluding with Montana's 14-yard scoring pass to Jerry Rice 57 seconds into the final stanza. Rice was named the game's most valuable player after compiling 11 catches for a Super Bowl-record 215 yards. Montana completed 23 of 36 passes for a Super Bowl-record 357 yards and 2 touchdowns.

Cincinnati (AFC)	0	3	10	3 — 16
San Francisco (NFC)	3	0	3	14 — 20

SF	—	FG Cofer 41 (11:46)
Cin	—	FG Breech 34 (13:45)
Cin	—	FG Breech 43 (9:21)
SF	—	FG Cofer 32 (14:10)
Cin	—	Jennings 93 kickoff return (Breech kick) (14:26)
SF	—	Rice 14 pass from Montana (Cofer kick) (0:57)
Cin	—	FG Breech 40 (11:40)
SF	—	Taylor 10 pass from Montana (Cofer kick) (14:26)

SUPER BOWL XXII

San Diego Jack Murphy Stadium, San Diego, CA
January 31, 1988, Attendance: 73,302
WASHINGTON 42, DENVER 10—NFC champion Washington won Super Bowl XXII and its second NFL championship of the 1980s with a 42-10 decision over AFC champion Denver. The Redskins, who also won Super Bowl XVII, enjoyed a record-setting second quarter en route to the victory. The Broncos broke in front

10-0 when quarterback John Elway threw a 56-yard touchdown pass to wide receiver Ricky Nattiel on the Broncos' first play from scrimmage. Following a Washington punt, Denver's Rich Karlis kicked a 24-yard field goal to cap a seven-play, 61-yard scoring drive. The Redskins then erupted for 35 points on five straight possessions in the second period and coasted thereafter. The 35 points established an NFL postseason mark for most points in a period. Redskins quarterback Doug Williams led the second-period explosion by passing for a Super Bowl record-tying 4 touchdowns, including 80- and 50-yard passes to wide receiver Ricky Sanders, a 27-yard toss to wide receiver Gary Clark, and an 8-yard pass to tight end Clint Didier. Washington scored 5 touchdowns in 18 plays with total time of possession of only 5:47. Overall, Williams completed 18 of 29 passes for 340 yards and was named the game's most valuable player. His pass-yardage total eclipsed the Super Bowl record of 331 yards by Joe Montana of San Francisco in Super Bowl XIX. Sanders ended with 193 yards on 8 catches, breaking the previous Super Bowl yardage record of 161 yards by Lynn Swann of Pittsburgh in Game X. Rookie running back Timmy Smith was the game's leading rusher with 22 carries for a Super Bowl-record 204 yards, breaking the previous mark of 191 yards by Marcus Allen of the Raiders in Game XVIII. Smith also scored twice on runs of 58 and 4 yards. Washington's 6 touchdowns and 602 total yards gained also set Super Bowl records. Redskins cornerback Barry Wilburn had 2 of the team's 3 interceptions, and strong safety Alvin Walton had 2 of Washington's 5 sacks.

Washington (NFC)	0	35	0	7 — 42
Denver (AFC)	10	0	0	0 — 10

Den	—	Nattiel 56 pass from Elway (Karlis kick) (1:57)
Den	—	FG Karlis 24 (5:51)
Wash	—	Sanders 80 pass from Williams (Haji-Sheikh kick) (0:53)
Wash	—	Clark 27 pass from Williams (Haji-Sheikh kick) (4:45)
Wash	—	Smith 58 run (Haji-Sheikh kick) (8:33)
Wash	—	Sanders 50 pass from Williams (Haji-Sheikh kick) (11:18)
Wash	—	Didier 8 pass from Williams (Haji-Sheikh kick) (13:56)
Wash	—	Smith 4 run (Haji-Sheikh kick) (1:51)

SUPER BOWL XXI

Rose Bowl, Pasadena, California
January 25, 1987, Attendance: 101,063
NEW YORK GIANTS 39, DENVER 20—
The NFC champion New York Giants captured their first NFL title since 1956 when they downed the AFC champion Denver Broncos 39-20 in Super Bowl XXI. The

victory marked the NFC's fifth NFL title in the past six seasons. The Broncos, behind the passing of quarterback John Elway, who was 13 of 20 for 187 yards in the first half, held a 10-9 lead at intermission, the narrowest halftime margin in Super Bowl history. Denver's Rich Karlis opened the scoring with a Super Bowl record-tying 48-yard field goal. New York drove 78 yards in nine plays on the next series to take a 7-3 lead on quarterback Phil Simms' 6-yard touchdown pass to tight end Zeke Mowatt. The Broncos came right back with a 58-yard scoring drive on six plays capped by Elway's 4-yard touchdown run. The only scoring in the second period was the sack of Elway in the end zone by defensive end George Martin for a New York safety. The Giants produced a key defensive stand early in the second quarter when the Broncos had a first down at the New York 1-yard line, but failed to score on three running plays and Karlis' 23-yard missed field-goal attempt. The Giants took command of the game in the third period en route to a 30-point second half, the most ever scored in one half of Super Bowl play. New York took the lead for good on tight end Mark Bavaro's 13-yard touchdown catch 4:52 into the third period. The nine-play, 63-yard scoring drive included the successful conversion of a fourth-and-1 play on the New York 46-yard line. Denver was limited to only 2 net yards on 10 offensive plays in the third period. Simms set Super Bowl records for most consecutive completions (10) and highest completion percentage (88 percent on 22 completions in 25 attempts). He also passed for 268 yards and 3 touchdowns and was named the game's most valuable player. New York running back Joe Morris was the game's leading rusher with 20 carries for 67 yards. Denver wide receiver Vance Johnson led all receivers with 5 catches for 121 yards.

Denver (AFC)	10	0	0	10 — 20
N.Y. Giants (NFC)	7	2	17	13 — 39

Den	—	FG Karlis 48 (4:09)
NYG	—	Mowatt 6 pass from Simms (Allegre kick) (9:33)
Den	—	Elway 4 run (Karlis kick) (12:54)
NYG	—	Safety, Martin tackled Elway in end zone (12:14)
NYG	—	Bavaro 13 pass from Simms (Allegre kick) (4:52)
NYG	—	FG Allegre 21 (11:06)
NYG	—	Morris 1 run (Allegre kick) (14:36)
NYG	—	McConkey 6 pass from Simms (Allegre kick) (4:04)
Den	—	FG Karlis 28 (8:59)
NYG	—	Anderson 2 run (kick failed) (10:42)
Den	—	V. Johnson 47 pass from Elway (Karlis kick) (12:54)

SUPER BOWL XX

Louisiana Superdome, New Orleans, LA
January 26, 1986, Attendance: 73,818
CHICAGO 46, NEW ENGLAND 10—The NFC champion Chicago Bears, seeking their first NFL title since 1963, scored a Super Bowl-record 46 points in downing AFC champion New England 46-10 in Super Bowl XX. The previous record for most points in a Super Bowl was 38, shared by San Francisco in XIX and the Los Angeles Raiders in XVIII. The Bears' league-leading defense tied the Super Bowl record for sacks (7) and limited the Patriots to a record-low 7 rushing yards. New England took the quickest lead in Super Bowl history when Tony Franklin kicked a 36-yard field goal with 1:19 elapsed in the first period. The score came about because of Larry McGrew's fumble recovery at the Chicago 19-yard line. However, the Bears rebounded for a 23-3 first-half lead, while building a yardage advantage of 236 total yards to New England's minus 19. Running back Matt Suhey rushed 8 times for 37 yards, including an 11-yard touchdown run, and caught 1 pass for 24 yards in the first half. After the Patriot's first drive of the second half ended with a punt to the Bears' 4-yard line, Chicago marched 96 yards in nine plays with quarterback Jim McMahon's 1-yard scoring run capping the drive. McMahon became the first quarterback in Super Bowl history to rush for a pair of touchdowns. The Bears completed their scoring via a 28-yard interception return by reserve cornerback Reggie Phillips, a 1-yard run by defensive tackle/fullback William Perry, and a safety when defensive end Henry Waechter tackled Patriots quarterback Steve Grogan in the end zone. Bears defensive end Richard Dent became the fourth defender to be named the game's most valuable player after contributing 1 1/2 sacks. The Bears' victory margin of 36 points was the largest in Super Bowl history, bettering the previous mark of 29 by the Los Angeles Raiders when they topped Washington 38-9 in Game XVIII. McMahon completed 12 of 20 passes for 256 yards before leaving the game in the fourth period with a wrist injury. The NFL's all-time leading rusher, Bears running back Walter Payton, carried 22 times for 61 yards. Wide receiver Willie Gault caught 4 passes for 129 yards, the fourth-most receiving yards in a Super Bowl. Chicago coach Mike Ditka became the second man (Tom Flores of Raiders was the other) to win a Super Bowl ring as a player and a coach.

Chicago (NFC)	13 10 21 2	— 46
New England (AFC)	3 0 0 7	— 10

NE — FG Franklin 36 (1:19)
Chi — FG Butler 28 (5:40)
Chi — FG Butler 24 (13:34)
Chi — Suhey 11 run (Butler kick) (14:37)
Chi — McMahon 2 run (Butler kick) (7:36)
Chi — FG Butler 24 (15:00)
Chi — McMahon 1 run (Butler kick) (7:38)
Chi — Phillips 28 interception return (Butler kick) (8:44)
Chi — Perry 1 run (Butler kick) (11:38)
NE — Fryar 8 pass from Grogan (Franklin kick) (1:46)
Chi — Safety, Waechter tackled Grogan in end zone (9:24)

SUPER BOWL XIX

Stanford Stadium, Stanford, California
January 20, 1985, Attendance: 84,059
SAN FRANCISCO 38, MIAMI 16—The San Francisco 49ers captured their second Super Bowl title with a dominating offense and a defense that tamed Miami's explosive passing attack. The Dolphins held a 10-7 lead at the end of the first period, which represented the most points scored by two teams in an opening quarter of a Super Bowl. However, the 49ers used excellent field position in the second period to build a 28-16 halftime lead. Running back Roger Craig set a Super Bowl record by scoring 3 touchdowns on pass receptions of 8 and 16 yards and a run of 2 yards. San Francisco's Joe Montana was voted the game's most valuable player. He joined Green Bay's Bart Starr and Pittsburgh's Terry Bradshaw as the only two-time Super Bowl most valuable players. Montana completed 24 of 35 passes for a Super Bowl-record 331 yards and 3 touchdowns, and rushed 5 times for 59 yards, including a 6-yard touchdown. Craig had 58 yards on 15 carries and caught 7 passes for 77 yards. Wendell Tyler rushed 13 times for 65 yards and had 4 catches for 70 yards. Dwight Clark had 6 receptions for 77 yards, while Russ Francis had 5 for 60. San Francisco's 537 total net yards bettered the previous Super Bowl record of 429 yards by Oakland in Super Bowl XI. The 49ers also held a time of possession advantage over the Dolphins of 37:11 to 22:49.

Miami (AFC)	10 6 0 0	— 16
San Francisco (NFC)	7 21 10 0	— 38

Mia — FG von Schamann 37 (7:36)
SF — Monroe 33 pass from Montana (Wersching kick) (11:48)
Mia — D. Johnson 2 pass from Marino (von Schamann kick) (14:15)
SF — Craig 8 pass from Montana (Wersching kick) (3:26)
SF — Montana 6 run (Wersching kick) (8:02)
SF — Craig 2 run (Wersching kick) (12:55)
Mia — FG von Schamann 31 (14:48)
Mia — FG von Schamann 30 (15:00)
SF — FG Wersching 27 (4:48)
SF — Craig 16 pass from Montana (Wersching kick) (8:42)

SUPER BOWL XVIII

Tampa Stadium, Tampa, Florida
January 22, 1984, Attendance: 72,920
LOS ANGELES RAIDERS 38, WASHINGTON 9—The Los Angeles Raiders dominated the Washington Redskins from the beginning in Super Bowl XVIII and achieved the most lopsided victory in Super Bowl history, surpassing Green Bay's 35-10 win over Kansas City in Super Bowl I. The Raiders took a 7-0 lead 4:52 into the game when Derrick Jensen blocked Jeff Hayes' punt and recovered it in the end zone for a touchdown. With 9:14 remaining in the first half, Raiders quarterback Jim Plunkett fired a 12-yard touchdown pass to wide receiver Cliff Branch to complete a three-play, 65-yard drive. Washington cut the Raiders' lead to 14-3 on a 24-yard field goal by Mark Moseley. With seven seconds left in the first half, Raiders linebacker Jack Squirek intercepted Joe Theismann's pass at the Redskins' 5-yard line and ran it in for a touchdown to give Los Angeles a 21-3 halftime lead. In the third period, running back Marcus Allen, who rushed for a Super Bowl-record 191 yards on 20 carries, increased the Raiders' lead to 35-9 on touchdown runs of 5 and 74 yards, the latter erasing the Super Bowl record of 58 yards set by Baltimore's Tom Matte in Game III. Allen was named the game's most valuable player. The victory over Washington raised Raiders coach Tom Flores' playoff record to 8-1, including a 27-10 win against Philadelphia in Super Bowl XV. The 38 points scored by the Raiders were the highest total by a Super Bowl team. The previous high was 35 points by Green Bay in Game I.

Washington (NFC)	0 3 6 0	— 9
L.A. Raiders (AFC)	7 14 14 3	— 38

Raiders — Jensen recovered blocked punt in end zone (Bahr kick) (4:52)
Raiders — Branch 12 pass from Plunkett (Bahr kick) (5:46)
Wash — FG Moseley 24 (11:55)
Raiders — Squirek 5 interception return (Bahr kick) (14:53)
Wash — Riggins 1 run (kick blocked) (4:08)
Raiders — Allen 5 run (Bahr kick) (7:54)
Raiders — Allen 74 run (Bahr kick) (15:00)
Raiders — FG Bahr 21 (12:36)

SUPER BOWL XVII

Rose Bowl, Pasadena, California
January 30, 1983, Attendance: 103,667
WASHINGTON 27, MIAMI 17—Fullback John Riggins ran for a Super Bowl-record 166 yards on 38 carries to spark Washington to a 27-17 victory over AFC champion Miami. It was Riggins' fourth straight

100-yard rushing game during the play-offs, also a record. The win marked Washington's first NFL title since 1942, and was only the second time in Super Bowl history NFL/NFC teams scored consecutive victories (Green Bay did it in Super Bowls I and II and San Francisco won Super Bowl XVI). The Redskins, under second-year head coach Joe Gibbs, used a balanced offense that accounted for 400 total yards (a Super Bowl-record 276 yards rushing and 124 passing), second in Super Bowl history to 429 yards by Oakland in Super Bowl XI. The Dolphins built a 17-10 halftime lead on a 76-yard touchdown pass from quarterback David Woodley to wide receiver Jimmy Cefalo 6:49 into the first period, a 20-yard field goal by Uwe von Schamann with 6:00 left in the half, and a Super Bowl-record 98-yard kickoff return by Fulton Walker with 1:38 remaining. Washington had tied the score at 10-10 with 1:51 left on a 4-yard touchdown pass from Joe Theismann to wide receiver Alvin Garrett. Mark Moseley started the Redskins' scoring with a 31-yard field goal late in the first period, and added a 20-yard field goal midway through the third period to cut the Dolphins' lead to 17-13. Riggins, who was voted the game's most valuable player, gave Washington its first lead of the game with 10:01 left when he ran 43 yards off left tackle for a touchdown in a fourth-and-1 situation. Wide receiver Charlie Brown caught a 6-yard scoring pass from Theismann with 1:55 left to complete the scoring. The Dolphins managed only 176 yards (142 in first half). Theismann completed 15 of 23 passes for 143 yards, with 2 touchdowns and 2 interceptions. For Miami, Woodley was 4 of 14 for 97 yards, with 1 touchdown, and 1 interception. Don Strock was 0 for 3 in relief.

Miami (AFC)	7	10	0	0	— 17
Washington (NFC)	0	10	3	14	— 27

Mia — Cefalo 76 pass from Woodley (von Schamann kick) (6:49)
Wash — FG Moseley 31 (0:21)
Mia — FG von Schamann 20 (9:00)
Wash — Garrett 4 pass from Theismann (Moseley kick) (13:09)
Mia — Walker 98 kickoff return (von Schamann kick) (13:22)
Wash — FG Moseley 20 (6:51)
Wash — Riggins 43 run (Moseley kick) (4:59)
Wash — Brown 6 pass from Theismann (Moseley kick) (13:05)

SUPER BOWL XVI

Pontiac Silverdome, Pontiac, Michigan
January 24, 1982, Attendance: 81,270
SAN FRANCISCO 26, CINCINNATI 21—
Ray Wersching's Super Bowl record-tying 4 field goals and Joe Montana's controlled passing helped lift the San Francisco 49ers to their first NFL championship with a 26-21 victory over Cincinnati. The 49ers

built a game-record 20-0 halftime lead via Montana's 1-yard touchdown run, which capped an 11-play, 68-yard drive; fullback Earl Cooper's 11-yard scoring pass from Montana, which climaxed a Super Bowl record 92-yard drive on 12 plays; and Wersching's 22- and 26-yard field goals. The Bengals rebounded in the second half, closing the gap to 20-14 on quarterback Ken Anderson's 5-yard run and Dan Ross' 4-yard reception from Anderson, who established Super Bowl passing records for completions (25) and completion percentage (73.5 percent on 25 of 34). Wersching added early fourth-period field goals of 40 and 23 yards to increase the 49ers' lead to 26-14. The Bengals managed to score on an Anderson-to-Ross 3-yard pass with only 16 seconds remaining. Ross set a Super Bowl record with 11 receptions for 104 yards. Montana, the game's most valuable player, completed 14 of 22 passes for 157 yards. Cincinnati compiled 356 yards to San Francisco's 275, which marked the first time in Super Bowl history that the team that gained the most yards from scrimmage lost the game.

San Francisco (NFC)	7	13	0	6	— 26
Cincinnati (AFC)	0	0	7	14	— 21

SF — Montana 1 run (Wersching kick) (9:08)
SF — Cooper 11 pass from Montana (Wersching kick) (8:07)
SF — FG Wersching 22 (14:45)
SF — FG Wersching 26 (14:58)
Cin — Anderson 5 run (Breech kick) (3:35)
Cin — Ross 4 pass from Anderson (Breech kick) (4:54)
SF — FG Wersching 40 (9:35)
SF — FG Wersching 23 (13:03)
Cin — Ross 3 pass from Anderson (Breech kick) (14:44)

SUPER BOWL XV

Louisiana Superdome, New Orleans, LA
January 25, 1981, Attendance: 76,135
OAKLAND 27, PHILADELPHIA 10—Jim Plunkett passed for 3 touchdowns, including an 80-yard strike to Kenny King, as the Raiders became the first wild-card team to win the Super Bowl. Plunkett's touchdown bomb to King—the longest play in Super Bowl history—gave Oakland a decisive 14-0 lead with nine seconds left in the first period. Linebacker Rod Martin had set up Oakland's first touchdown, a 2-yard reception by Cliff Branch, with a 17-yard interception return to the Eagles' 30-yard line. The Eagles never recovered from that early deficit, managing only Tony Franklin's field goal (30 yards) and an 8-yard touchdown pass from Ron Jaworski to Keith Krepfle. Plunkett, who became a starter in the sixth game of the season, completed 13 of 21 for 261 yards and was named the game's most valuable player. Oakland won 9 of 11 games with Plunkett starting, but that was good

enough only for second place in the AFC West, although they tied division winner San Diego with an 11-5 record. The Raiders, who had previously won Super Bowl XI over Minnesota, had to win three playoff games to get to the championship game. Oakland defeated Houston 27-7 at home followed by road victories over Cleveland (14-12) and San Diego (34-27). Oakland's Mark van Eeghen was the game's leading rusher with 75 yards on 18 carries. Philadelphia's Wilbert Montgomery led all receivers with 6 receptions for 91 yards. Branch had 5 for 67 and Harold Carmichael of Philadelphia 5 for 83. Martin finished the game with 3 interceptions, a Super Bowl record.

Oakland (AFC)	14	0	10	3	— 27
Philadelphia (NFC)	0	3	0	7	— 10

Oak — Branch 2 pass from Plunkett (Bahr kick) (6:04)
Oak — King 80 pass from Plunkett (Bahr kick) (14:51)
Phil — FG Franklin 30 (4:32)
Oak — Branch 29 pass from Plunkett (Bahr kick) (2:36)
Oak — FG Bahr 46 (10:25)
Phil — Krepfle 8 pass from Jaworski (Franklin kick) (1:01)
Oak — FG Bahr 35 (6:31)

SUPER BOWL XIV

Rose Bowl, Pasadena, California
January 20, 1980, Attendance: 103,985
PITTSBURGH 31, LOS ANGELES 19—
Terry Bradshaw completed 14 of 21 passes for 309 yards and set two passing records as the Steelers became the first team to win four Super Bowls. Despite 3 interceptions by the Rams, Bradshaw kept his poise and brought the Steelers from behind twice in the second half. Trailing 13-10 at halftime, Pittsburgh went ahead 17-13 when Bradshaw hit Lynn Swann with a 47-yard touchdown pass after 2:48 of the third quarter. On the Rams' next possession Vince Ferragamo, who was 15 of 25 for 212 yards, responded with a 50-yard pass to Billy Waddy that moved Los Angeles from its 26 to the Steelers' 24. On the following play, Lawrence McCutcheon connected with Ron Smith on a halfback option pass that gave the Rams a 19-17 lead. On Pittsburgh's initial possession of the final period, Bradshaw lofted a 73-yard scoring pass to John Stallworth to put the Steelers in front to stay 24-19. Franco Harris scored on a 1-yard run later in the quarter to seal the verdict. A 45-yard pass from Bradshaw to Stallworth was the key play in the drive to Harris' score. Bradshaw, the game's most valuable player for the second straight year, set career Super Bowl records for most touchdown passes (9) and most passing yards (932). Larry Anderson gave the Steelers excellent field position throughout the game with 5 kickoff returns for a record 162 yards.

Los Angeles (NFC)	7	6	6	0 — 19
Pittsburgh (AFC)	3	7	7	14 — 31

Pitt — FG Bahr 41 (7:29)
LA — Bryant 1 run (Corral kick) (12:16)
Pitt — Harris 1 run (Bahr kick) (2:08)
LA — FG Corral 31 (7:39)
LA — FG Corral 45 (14:46)
Pitt — Swann 47 pass from Bradshaw (Bahr kick) (2:48)
LA — Smith 24 pass from McCutcheon (kick failed) (4:45)
Pitt — Stallworth 73 pass from Bradshaw (Bahr kick) (2:56)
Pitt — Harris 1 run (Bahr kick) (13:11)

SUPER BOWL XIII
Orange Bowl, Miami, Florida
January 21, 1979, Attendance: 79,484
PITTSBURGH 35, DALLAS 31—Terry Bradshaw passed for a record 4 touchdowns to lead the Steelers to victory. The Steelers became the first team to win three Super Bowls, mostly because of Bradshaw's accurate arm. Bradshaw, voted the game's most valuable player, completed 17 of 30 passes for 318 yards, a personal high. Four of those passes went for touchdowns—2 to John Stallworth and the third, with 26 seconds remaining in the second period, to Rocky Bleier for a 21-14 halftime lead. The Cowboys scored twice before intermission on Roger Staubach's 39-yard pass to Tony Hill and a 37-yard fumble return by linebacker Mike Hegman, who stole the ball from Bradshaw. The Steelers broke open the contest with 2 touchdowns in a span of 19 seconds midway through the final period. Franco Harris rambled 22 yards up the middle to give the Steelers a 28-17 lead with 7:10 left. Pittsburgh got the ball right back when Randy White fumbled the kickoff and Dennis Winston recovered for the Steelers. On first down, Bradshaw fired his fourth touchdown pass, an 18-yard pass to Lynn Swann to boost the Steelers' lead to 35-17 with 6:51 to play. The Cowboys refused to let the Steelers run away with the contest. Staubach connected with Billy Joe DuPree on a 7-yard scoring pass with 2:23 left. Then the Cowboys recovered an onside kick and Staubach took them in for another score, passing 4 yards to Butch Johnson with 22 seconds remaining. Bleier recovered another onside kick with 17 seconds left to seal the victory for the Steelers.

Pittsburgh (AFC)	7	14	0	14 — 35
Dallas (NFC)	7	7	3	14 — 31

Pitt — Stallworth 28 pass from Bradshaw (Gerela kick) (5:13)
Dall — Hill 39 pass from Staubach (Septien kick) (15:00)
Dall — Hegman 37 fumble recovery return (Septien kick) (2:52)
Pitt — Stallworth 75 pass from Bradshaw (Gerela kick) (4:35)

Pitt — Bleier 7 pass from Bradshaw (Gerela kick) (14:34)
Dall — FG Septien 27 (12:24)
Pitt — Harris 22 run (Gerela kick) (7:50)
Pitt — Swann 18 pass from Bradshaw (Gerela kick) (8:09)
Dall — DuPree 7 pass from Staubach (Septien kick) (12:37)
Dall — B. Johnson 4 pass from Staubach (Septien kick) (14:38)

SUPER BOWL XII
Louisiana Superdome, New Orleans, LA
January 15, 1978, Attendance: 75,583
DALLAS 27, DENVER 10—The Cowboys evened their Super Bowl record at 2-2 by defeating Denver before a sellout crowd plus 102,010,000 television viewers, largest audience ever to watch a sporting event. Dallas converted 2 interceptions into 10 points and Efren Herrera added a 35-yard field goal for a 13-0 halftime advantage. In the third period Craig Morton engineered a drive to the Cowboys' 30 and Jim Turner's 47-yard field goal made the score 13-3. After an exchange of punts, Butch Johnson made a spectacular diving catch in the end zone to complete a 45-yard pass from Roger Staubach and put the Cowboys ahead 20-3. Following Rick Upchurch's 67-yard kickoff return, Norris Weese guided the Broncos to a touchdown to cut the deficit to 20-10. Dallas clinched the victory when running back Robert Newhouse tossed a 29-yard touchdown pass to Golden Richards with 7:04 left in the game. It was the first pass thrown by Newhouse since 1975. Harvey Martin and Randy White, who were named co-most valuable players, led the Cowboys' defense, which recovered 4 fumbles and intercepted 4 passes.

Dallas (NFC)	10	3	7	7 — 27
Denver (AFC)	0	0	10	0 — 10

Dall — Dorsett 3 run (Herrera kick) (10:31)
Dall — FG Herrera 35 (13:29)
Dall — FG Herrera 43 (3:44)
Den — FG Turner 47 (2:28)
Dall — Johnson 45 pass from Staubach (Herrera kick) (8:01)
Den — Lytle 1 run (Turner kick) (9:21)
Dall — Richards 29 pass from Newhouse (Herrera kick) (7:56)

SUPER BOWL XI
Rose Bowl, Pasadena, California
January 9, 1977, Attendance: 103,438
OAKLAND 32, MINNESOTA 14—The Raiders won their first NFL championship before a record Super Bowl crowd plus 81 million television viewers, the largest audience ever to watch a sporting event. The Raiders gained a record-breaking 429 yards, including running back Clarence Davis' 137 rushing yards. Wide receiver Fred Biletnikoff made 4 key receptions,

which earned him the game's most valuable player trophy. Oakland scored on three successive possessions in the second quarter to build a 16-0 halftime lead. Errol Mann's 24-yard field goal opened the scoring, then the AFC champions put together drives of 64 and 35 yards, scoring on a 1-yard pass from Ken Stabler to Dave Casper and a 1-yard run by Pete Banaszak. The Raiders increased their lead to 19-0 on a 40-yard field goal in the third quarter, but Minnesota responded with a 12-play, 58-yard drive late in the period, with Fran Tarkenton passing 8 yards to wide receiver Sammy White to cut the deficit to 19-7. Two fourth-quarter interceptions clinched the title for the Raiders. One set up Banaszak's second touchdown run, the other resulted in cornerback Willie Brown's Super Bowl-record 75-yard interception return.

Oakland (AFC)	0	16	3	13 — 32
Minnesota (NFC)	0	0	7	7 — 14

Oak — FG Mann 24 (0:48)
Oak — Casper 1 pass from Stabler (Mann kick) (7:50)
Oak — Banaszak 1 run (kick failed) (11:27)
Oak — FG Mann 40 (9:44)
Minn — S. White 8 pass from Tarkenton (Cox kick) (14:13)
Oak — Banaszak 2 run (Mann kick) (7:21)
Oak — Brown 75 interception return (kick failed) (9:17)
Minn — Voigt 13 pass from Lee (Cox kick) (14:35)

SUPER BOWL X
Orange Bowl, Miami, Florida
January 18, 1976, Attendance: 80,187
PITTSBURGH 21, DALLAS 17—The Steelers won the Super Bowl for the second year in a row on Terry Bradshaw's 64-yard touchdown pass to Lynn Swann and an aggressive defense that snuffed out a late rally by the Cowboys with an end-zone interception on the final play of the game. In the fourth quarter, Pittsburgh ran on fourth down and gave up the ball on the Cowboys' 39 with 1:22 to play. Roger Staubach ran and passed for 2 first downs but his last desperation pass was picked off by Glen Edwards. Dallas' scoring was the result of 2 touchdown passes by Staubach, one to Drew Pearson for 29 yards and the other to Percy Howard for 34 yards. Howard's reception was the only catch of his NFL career. Toni Fritsch had a 36-yard field goal. The Steelers scored on 2 touchdown passes by Bradshaw, 1 to Randy Grossman for 7 yards and the long bomb to Swann. Roy Gerela had 36- and 18-yard field goals. Reggie Harrison blocked a punt through the end zone for a safety. Swann set a Super Bowl record by gaining 161 yards on his 4 receptions.

Dallas (NFC)	7	3	0	7	— 17
Pittsburgh (AFC)	7	0	0	14	— 21

Dall — D. Pearson 29 pass from Staubach (Fritsch kick) (4:36)
Pitt — Grossman 7 pass from Bradshaw (Gerela kick) (9:03)
Dall — FG Fritsch 36 (0:15)
Pitt — Safety, Harrison blocked Hoopes' punt through end zone (3:32)
Pitt — FG Gerela 36 (6:19)
Pitt — FG Gerela 18 (8:23)
Pitt — Swann 64 pass from Bradshaw (kick failed) (11:58)
Dall — P. Howard 34 pass from Staubach (Fritsch kick) (13:12)

SUPER BOWL IX

Tulane Stadium, New Orleans, Louisiana
January 12, 1975, Attendance: 80,997
PITTSBURGH 16, MINNESOTA 6—AFC champion Pittsburgh, in its initial Super Bowl appearance, and NFC champion Minnesota, making a third bid for its first Super Bowl title, struggled through a first half in which the only score was produced by the Steelers' defense when Dwight White downed Vikings' quarterback Fran Tarkenton in the end zone for a safety 7:49 into the second period. The Steelers forced another break and took advantage on the second-half kickoff when Minnesota's Bill Brown fumbled and Marv Kellum recovered for Pittsburgh on the Vikings' 30. After Rocky Bleier failed to gain on first down, Franco Harris carried 3 consecutive times for 24 yards, a loss of 3, and a 9-yard touchdown and a 9-0 lead. Though its offense was completely stymied by Pittsburgh's defense, Minnesota managed to move into a threatening position after 4:27 of the final period when Matt Blair blocked Bobby Walden's punt and Terry Brown recovered the ball in the end zone for a touchdown. Fred Cox's kick failed and the Steelers led 9-6. Pittsburgh wasted no time putting the victory away. The Steelers took the ensuing kickoff and marched 66 yards in 11 plays, climaxed by Terry Bradshaw's 4-yard scoring pass to Larry Brown with 3:31 left. Pittsburgh's defense permitted Minnesota only 119 yards total offense, including a Super Bowl low of 17 rushing yards. The Steelers, meanwhile, gained 333 yards, including Harris' record 158 yards on 34 carries.

Pittsburgh (AFC)	0	2	7	7	— 16
Minnesota (NFC)	0	0	0	6	— 6

Pitt — Safety, White downed Tarkenton in end zone (7:49)
Pitt — Harris 9 run (Gerela kick) (1:35)
Minn — T. Brown recovered blocked punt in end zone (kick failed) (4:27)
Pitt — L. Brown 4 pass from Bradshaw (Gerela kick) (11:29)

SUPER BOWL VIII

Rice Stadium, Houston, Texas
January 13, 1974, Attendance: 71,882
MIAMI 24, MINNESOTA 7—The defending NFL champion Dolphins, representing the AFC for the third straight year, scored the first two times they had possession on marches of 62 and 56 yards while the Miami defense limited the Vikings to only seven plays in the first period. Larry Csonka climaxed the initial 10-play drive with a 5-yard touchdown bolt through right guard after 5:27 had elapsed. Four plays later, Miami began another 10-play scoring drive, which ended with Jim Kiick bursting 1 yard through the middle for another touchdown after 13:38 of the period. Garo Yepremian added a 28-yard field goal midway in the second period for a 17-0 Miami lead. Minnesota then drove from its 20 to a second-and-2 situation on the Miami 7 yard line with 1:18 left in the half. But on two plays, Miami limited Oscar Reed to 1 yard. On fourth-and-1 from the 6, Reed went over right tackle, but Dolphins middle linebacker Nick Buoniconti jarred the ball loose and Jake Scott recovered for Miami to halt the Minnesota threat. The Vikings were unable to muster enough offense in the second half to threaten the Dolphins. Csonka rushed 33 times for a Super Bowl-record 145 yards. Bob Griese of Miami completed 6 of 7 passes for 73 yards.

Minnesota (NFC)	0	0	0	7	— 7
Miami (AFC)	14	3	7	0	— 24

Mia — Csonka 5 run (Yepremian kick) (9:33)
Mia — Kiick 1 run (Yepremian kick) (13:38)
Mia — FG Yepremian 28 (8:58)
Mia — Csonka 2 run (Yepremian kick) (6:16)
Minn — Tarkenton 4 run (Cox kick) (1:35)

SUPER BOWL VII

Memorial Coliseum, Los Angeles, CA
January 14, 1973, Attendance: 90,182
MIAMI 14, WASHINGTON 7—The Dolphins played virtually perfect football in the first half as their defense permitted the Redskins to cross midfield only once and their offense turned good field position into 2 touchdowns. On its third possession, Miami opened its first scoring drive from the Dolphins' 37 yard line. An 18-yard pass from Bob Griese to Paul Warfield preceded by three plays Griese's 28-yard touchdown pass to Howard Twilley. After Washington moved from its 17 to the Miami 48 with two minutes remaining in the first half, Dolphins linebacker Nick Buoniconti intercepted Billy Kilmer's pass at the Miami 41 and returned it to the Washington 27. Jim Kiick ran for 3 yards, Larry Csonka for 3, Griese passed to Jim Mandich for 19, and Kiick gained 1 to the 1-yard line. With 18 seconds left until intermission, Kiick scored from the 1.

Washington's only touchdown came with 2:07 left in the game and resulted from a misplayed field-goal attempt and fumble by Garo Yepremian, with the Redskins' Mike Bass picking the ball out of the air and running 49 yards for the score. Dolphins safety Jake Scott, who had 2 interceptions, including 1 in the end zone to kill a Redskins' drive, was voted the game's most valuable player.

Miami (AFC)	7	7	0	0	— 14
Washington (NFC)	0	0	7	0	— 7

Mia — Twilley 28 pass from Griese (Yepremian kick) (14:59)
Mia — Kiick 1 run (Yepremian kick) (14:42)
Wash — Bass 49 fumble recovery return (Knight kick) (12:53)

SUPER BOWL VI

Tulane Stadium, New Orleans, Louisiana
January 16, 1972, Attendance: 81,023
DALLAS 24, MIAMI 3—The Cowboys rushed for a record 252 yards and their defense limited the Dolphins to a low of 185 yards while not permitting a touchdown for the first time in Super Bowl history. Dallas converted Chuck Howley's recovery of Larry Csonka's first fumble of the season into a 3-0 advantage and led at halftime 10-3. After Dallas received the second-half kickoff, Duane Thomas led a 71-yard march in eight plays for a 17-3 margin. Howley intercepted Bob Griese's pass at the 50 and returned it to the Miami 9 early in the fourth period, and three plays later Roger Staubach passed 7 yards to Mike Ditka for the final touchdown. Thomas rushed for 95 yards and Walt Garrison gained 74. Staubach, voted the game's most valuable player, completed 12 of 19 passes for 119 yards and 2 touchdowns.

Dallas (NFC)	3	7	7	7	— 24
Miami (AFC)	0	3	0	0	— 3

Dall — FG Clark 9 (13:37)
Dall — Alworth 7 pass from Staubach (Clark kick) (13:45)
Mia — FG Yepremian 31 (14:56)
Dall — D. Thomas 3 run (Clark kick) (5:17)
Dall — Ditka 7 pass from Staubach (Clark kick) (3:18)

SUPER BOWL V

Orange Bowl, Miami, Florida
January 17, 1971, Attendance: 79,204
BALTIMORE 16, DALLAS 13—A 32-yard field goal by rookie kicker Jim O'Brien brought the Baltimore Colts a victory over the Dallas Cowboys in the final five seconds of Super Bowl V. The game between the champions of the AFC and NFC was played on artificial turf for the first time. Dallas led 13-6 at the half but interceptions by Rick Volk and Mike Curtis set up a Baltimore touchdown and O'Brien's decisive kick in the fourth period. Earl Morrall relieved an injured Johnny Unitas late in the first half, although Unitas com-

pleted the Colts' only scoring pass. It caromed off receiver Eddie Hinton's fingertips, off Dallas defensive back Mel Renfro, and finally settled into the grasp of John Mackey, who went 45 yards to score on a 75-yard play.

Baltimore (AFC)	0	6	0 10 — 16	
Dallas (NFC)	3	10	0 0 — 13	

Dall — FG Clark 14 (9:28)
Dall — FG Clark 30 (0:08)
Balt — Mackey 75 pass from Unitas (kick blocked) (0:05)
Dall — Thomas 7 pass from Morton (Clark kick) (7:07)
Balt — Nowatzke 2 run (O'Brien kick) (7:25)
Balt — FG O'Brien 32 (14:55)

SUPER BOWL IV

Tulane Stadium, New Orleans, Louisiana
January 11, 1970, Attendance: 80,562
KANSAS CITY 23, MINNESOTA 7—The AFL squared the Super Bowl at two games apiece with the NFL, building a 16-0 halftime lead behind Len Dawson's superb quarterbacking and a powerful defense. Dawson, the fourth consecutive quarterback to be chosen the Super Bowl's top player, called an almost flawless game, completing 12 of 17 passes and hitting Otis Taylor on a 46-yard play for the final Chiefs touchdown. The Kansas City defense limited Minnesota's strong rushing game to 67 yards and had 3 interceptions and 2 fumble recoveries. The crowd of 80,562 set a Super Bowl record, as did the gross receipts of $3,817,872.69.

Minnesota (NFL)	0	0	7 0 — 7	
Kansas City (AFL)	3	13	7 0 — 23	

KC — FG Stenerud 48 (8:08)
KC — FG Stenerud 32 (1:40)
KC — FG Stenerud 25 (7:08)
KC — Garrett 5 run (Stenerud kick) (9:26)
Minn — Osborn 4 run (Cox kick) (10:28)
KC — Taylor 46 pass from Dawson (Stenerud kick) (13:38)

SUPER BOWL III

Orange Bowl, Miami, Florida
January 12, 1969, Attendance: 75,389
NEW YORK JETS 16, BALTIMORE 7— Jets quarterback Joe Namath "guaranteed" victory on the Thursday before the game, then went out and led the AFL to its first Super Bowl victory over a Baltimore team that had lost only once in 16 games all season. Namath, chosen the outstanding player, completed 17 of 28 passes for 206 yards and directed a steady attack that dominated the NFL champions after the Jets' defense had intercepted Colts quarterback Earl Morrall 3 times in the first half. The Jets had 337 total yards, including 121 rushing yards by Matt Snell. Johnny Unitas, who had missed most of the season with a sore elbow, came off the bench and led Baltimore to its only

touchdown late in the fourth quarter after New York led 16-0.

New York Jets (AFL)	0	7 6 3 — 16
Baltimore (NFL)	0	0 0 7 — 7

NYJ — Snell 4 run (Turner kick) (5:57)
NYJ — FG Turner 32 (4:52)
NYJ — FG Turner 30 (11:02)
NYJ — FG Turner 9 (1:34)
Balt — Hill 1 run (Michaels kick) (11:41)

SUPER BOWL II

Orange Bowl, Miami, Florida
January 14, 1968, Attendance: 75,546
GREEN BAY 33, OAKLAND 14—Green Bay, after winning its third consecutive NFL championship, won the Super Bowl title for the second straight year, defeating the AFL champion Raiders in a game that drew the first $3-million gate in football history. Bart Starr again was chosen the game's most valuable player as he completed 13 of 24 passes for 202 yards and 1 touchdown and directed a Packers' attack that was in control all the way after building a 16-7 halftime lead. Don Chandler kicked 4 field goals and all-pro cornerback Herb Adderley capped the Green Bay scoring with a 60-yard interception return. The game marked the last for Vince Lombardi as Packers coach, ending nine years at Green Bay in which he won six Western Conference championships, five NFL championships, and two Super Bowls.

Green Bay (NFL)	3	13 10 7 — 33
Oakland (AFL)	0	7 0 7 — 14

GB — FG Chandler 39 (5:07)
GB — FG Chandler 20 (3:08)
GB — Dowler 62 pass from Starr (Chandler kick) (4:10)
Oak — Miller 23 pass from Lamonica (Blanda kick) (8:45)
GB — FG Chandler 43 (14:59)
GB — Anderson 2 run (Chandler kick) (9:06)
GB — FG Chandler 31 (14:58)
GB — Adderley 60 interception return (Chandler kick) (3:57)
Oak — Miller 23 pass from Lamonica (Blanda kick) (5:47)

SUPER BOWL I

Memorial Coliseum, Los Angeles, CA
January 15, 1967, Attendance: 61,946
GREEN BAY 35, KANSAS CITY 10—The Green Bay Packers opened the Super Bowl series by defeating the AFL champion Chiefs behind the passing of Bart Starr, the receiving of Max McGee, and a key interception by all-pro safety Willie Wood. Green Bay broke open the game with 3 second-half touchdowns, the first of which was set up by Wood's 50-yard return of an interception. McGee, filling in for ailing Boyd Dowler after having caught only 4 passes all season, caught 7 from Starr for 138 yards and 2 touchdowns. Elijah Pitts ran for 2 other scores. The

Chiefs' 10 points came in the second quarter, the only touchdown on a 7-yard pass from Len Dawson to Curtis McClinton. Starr completed 16 of 23 passes for 250 yards and 2 touchdowns and was chosen the most valuable player. The Packers collected $15,000 per man and the Chiefs $7,500—the largest single-game shares in the history of team sports.

Kansas City (AFL)	0	10 0 0 — 10
Green Bay (NFL)	7	7 14 7 — 35

GB — McGee 37 pass from Starr (Chandler kick) (8:56)
KC — McClinton 7 pass from Dawson (Mercer kick) (4:20)
GB — Taylor 14 run (Chandler kick) (10:23)
KC — FG Mercer 31 (14:06)
GB — Pitts 5 run (Chandler kick) (2:27)
GB — McGee 13 pass from Starr (Chandler kick) (14:09)
GB — Pitts 1 run (Chandler kick) (8:25)

AFC CHAMPIONSHIP GAME RESULTS
Includes AFL Championship Games (1960-69)

Season	Date	Winner (Share)	Loser (Share)	Score	Site	Attendance
2001	Jan. 27	New England ($34,500)	Pittsburgh ($34,500)	24-17	Pittsburgh	64,704
2000	Jan. 14	Baltimore ($34,500)	Oakland ($34,500)	16-3	Oakland	62,784
1999	Jan. 23	Tennessee ($33,000)	Jacksonville ($33,000)	33-14	Jacksonville	75,206
1998	Jan. 17	Denver ($32,500)	N.Y. Jets ($32,500)	23-10	Denver	75,482
1997	Jan. 11	Denver ($30,000)	Pittsburgh ($30,000)	24-21	Pittsburgh	61,382
1996	Jan. 12	New England ($29,000)	Jacksonville ($29,000)	20-6	Foxboro	60,190
1995	Jan. 14	Pittsburgh ($27,000)	Indianapolis ($27,000)	20-16	Pittsburgh	61,062
1994	Jan. 15	San Diego ($26,000)	Pittsburgh ($26,000)	17-13	Pittsburgh	61,545
1993	Jan. 23	Buffalo ($23,500)	Kansas City ($23,500)	30-13	Buffalo	76,642
1992	Jan. 17	Buffalo ($18,000)	Miami ($18,000)	29-10	Miami	72,703
1991	Jan. 12	Buffalo ($18,000)	Denver ($18,000)	10-7	Buffalo	80,272
1990	Jan. 20	Buffalo ($18,000)	L.A. Raiders ($18,000)	51-3	Buffalo	80,325
1989	Jan. 14	Denver ($18,000)	Cleveland ($18,000)	37-21	Denver	76,046
1988	Jan. 8	Cincinnati ($18,000)	Buffalo ($18,000)	21-10	Cincinnati	59,747
1987	Jan. 17	Denver ($18,000)	Cleveland ($18,000)	38-33	Denver	76,197
1986	Jan. 11	Denver ($18,000)	Cleveland ($18,000)	23-20*	Cleveland	79,973
1985	Jan. 12	New England ($18,000)	Miami ($18,000)	31-14	Miami	75,662
1984	Jan. 6	Miami ($18,000)	Pittsburgh ($18,000)	45-28	Miami	76,029
1983	Jan. 8	L.A. Raiders ($18,000)	Seattle ($18,000)	30-14	Los Angeles	91,445
1982	Jan. 23	Miami ($18,000)	N.Y. Jets ($18,000)	14-0	Miami	67,396
1981	Jan. 10	Cincinnati ($9,000)	San Diego ($9,000)	27-7	Cincinnati	46,302
1980	Jan. 11	Oakland ($9,000)	San Diego ($9,000)	34-27	San Diego	52,675
1979	Jan. 6	Pittsburgh ($9,000)	Houston ($9,000)	27-13	Pittsburgh	50,475
1978	Jan. 7	Pittsburgh ($9,000)	Houston ($9,000)	34-5	Pittsburgh	50,725
1977	Jan. 1	Denver ($9,000)	Oakland ($9,000)	20-17	Denver	75,044
1976	Dec. 26	Oakland ($8,500)	Pittsburgh ($5,500)	24-7	Oakland	53,821
1975	Jan. 4	Pittsburgh ($8,500)	Oakland ($5,500)	16-10	Pittsburgh	50,609
1974	Dec. 29	Pittsburgh ($8,500)	Oakland ($5,500)	24-13	Oakland	53,800
1973	Dec. 30	Miami ($8,500)	Oakland ($5,500)	27-10	Miami	79,325
1972	Dec. 31	Miami ($8,500)	Pittsburgh ($5,500)	21-17	Pittsburgh	50,845
1971	Jan. 2	Miami ($8,500)	Baltimore ($5,500)	21-0	Miami	76,622
1970	Jan. 3	Baltimore ($8,500)	Oakland ($5,500)	27-17	Baltimore	54,799
1969	Jan. 4	Kansas City ($7,755)	Oakland ($6,252)	17-7	Oakland	53,564
1968	Dec. 29	N.Y. Jets ($7,007)	Oakland ($5,349)	27-23	New York	62,627
1967	Dec. 31	Oakland ($6,321)	Houston ($4,996)	40-7	Oakland	53,330
1966	Jan. 1	Kansas City ($5,309)	Buffalo ($3,799)	31-7	Buffalo	42,080
1965	Dec. 26	Buffalo ($5,189)	San Diego ($3,447)	23-0	San Diego	30,361
1964	Dec. 26	Buffalo ($2,668)	San Diego ($1,738)	20-7	Buffalo	40,242
1963	Jan. 5	San Diego ($2,498)	Boston ($1,596)	51-10	San Diego	30,127
1962	Dec. 23	Dallas ($2,206)	Houston ($1,471)	20-17*	Houston	37,981
1961	Dec. 24	Houston ($1,792)	San Diego ($1,111)	10-3	San Diego	29,556
1960	Jan. 1	Houston ($1,025)	L.A. Chargers ($718)	24-16	Houston	32,183

Sudden death overtime

AFC CHAMPIONSHIP GAME COMPOSITE STANDINGS

	W	L	Pct.	Pts.	OP
Cincinnati Bengals	2	0	1.000	48	17
Baltimore Ravens	1	0	1.000	16	3
Denver Broncos	6	1	.857	172	132
Buffalo Bills	6	2	.750	180	92
Kansas City Chiefs*	3	1	.750	81	61
New England Patriots**	3	1	.750	85	88
Miami Dolphins	5	2	.714	152	115
Pittsburgh Steelers	5	6	.455	224	212
Tennessee Titans##	3	4	.429	109	154
Indianapolis Colts#	1	2	.333	43	58
New York Jets	1	2	.333	37	60
Oakland/L.A. Raiders	4	9	.308	231	280
San Diego Chargers***	2	6	.250	128	161
Seattle Seahawks	0	1	.000	14	30
Jacksonville Jaguars	0	2	.000	20	53
Cleveland Browns	0	3	.000	74	98

One game played when franchise was in Dallas (Texans) (Won 20-17)

**One game played when franchise was in Boston (Lost 51-10)*

***One game played when franchise was in Los Angeles (Lost 24-16)*

#*Two games played when franchise was in Baltimore (Won 27-17, lost 21-0)*

##*Six games played when franchise was in Houston and known as Oilers (Won 2, lost 4)*

2001 AFC CHAMPIONSHIP GAME
Heinz Field, Pittsburgh, Pennsylvania
January 27, 2002, Attendance: 64,704
NEW ENGLAND 24, PITTSBURGH 17—Troy Brown returned a punt for a touchdown, made a key play on a blocked field-goal return, and had 8 receptions for 121 yards, as the Patriots advanced to their third Super Bowl. Neither team threatened early until Brown returned a punt untouched 55 yards for a touchdown to give the Patriots a 7-0 lead. The return came one play after Troy Edwards had been penalized for not attempting to get in bounds while running downfield during punt coverage, forcing the Steelers to punt again. The Steelers responded with Kris Brown's 30-yard

field goal early in the second quarter to cut the deficit to 7-3. Late in the first half, Tom Brady injured his ankle while completing a 28-yard pass to Troy Brown. Taking over at the Steelers' 40, Drew Bledsoe completed all 3 of his pass attempts, capped by an 11-yard touchdown pass to David Patten with 58 seconds left in the half to take a 14-3 lead. The Steelers' defense stopped the Patriots on fourth-and-7 from the Steelers' 32 early in the second half, and the offense responded by driving into field-goal range. But Brandon Mitchell blocked Kris Brown's 34-yard attempt. Troy Brown scooped up the ball and ran 11 yards before lateraling to Antwan Harris, who raced the remaining 49 yards untouched for a touchdown and 21-3 lead. Pittsburgh answered with an 8-play, 79-yard drive, capped by Jerome Bettis' 1-yard run. The Steelers' defense forced a punt on the ensuing possession and Edwards returned it 28 yards to set up a 32-yard drive, culminating with Amos Zeroeoue's 11-yard scoring run, to trim the deficit to 21-17 late in the third quarter. Bledsoe responded by engineering an 11-play, 45-yard drive capped by Adam Vinatieri's 44-yard field goal with 11:12 remaining. Interceptions by Ty Law and Lawyer Milloy, the latter with 2:02 remaining, stopped the Steelers, and Antwan Smith's 19-yard run with 1:56 left allowed the Patriots to run out the clock. Brady was 12 of 18 for 115 yards, and Bledsoe was 10 of 21 for 102 yards and 1 touchdown. Stewart was 24 of 42 for 255 yards, with 3 interceptions.

New England (24)	Offense	Pittsburgh (17)
Troy Brown	WR	Plaxico Burress
Matt Light	LT	Wayne Gandy
Mike Compton	LG	Alan Faneca
Damien Woody	C	Jeff Hartings
Joe Andruzzi	RG	Rich Tylski
Greg Robinson-Randall	RT	Marvel Smith
Rod Rutledge	TE	Jerame Tuman
David Patten	WR	Hines Ward
Tom Brady	QB	Kordell Stewart
Antowain Smith	RB	Jerome Bettis
Marc Edwards	FB	Jon Witman
	Defense	
Bobby Hamilton	LE	Aaron Smith
Brandon Mitchell	LT-NT	Casey Hampton
Richard Seymour	RT-RE	Kimo von Oelhoffen
Anthony Pleasant	RE-LOLB	Jason Gildon
Mike Vrabel	LLB-LILB	Earl Holmes
Tedi Bruschi	MLB-RILB	Kendrell Bell
Roman Phifer	RLB-ROLB	Joey Porter
Ty Law	LCB	Chad Scott
Otis Smith	RCB	Dewayne Washington
Lawyer Milloy	SS	Lee Flowers
Tebucky Jones	FS	Brent Alexander

SUBSTITUTIONS
New England—Offense: T—Grant Williams. C-G—Grey Ruegamer. TE—Jermaine Wiggins. WR—Fred Coleman, Charles Johnson. FB—Patrick Pass. RB—Kevin Faulk, J.R. Redmond. QB—Damon Huard. P—Ken Walter. K—Adam Vinatieri. LS—Lonnie Paxton. Defense: DT—Riddick Parker. DE—Willie McGinest. LB—Matt Chatham, Bryan Cox, Larry Izzo, Ted Johnson. CB—Terrell Buckley, Terrance Shaw. S—Je'Rod Cherry, Antwan Harris, Matt Stevens.
Pittsburgh—Offense: G—Keydrick Vincent. T—Oliver Ross. TE—Matt Cushing. WR—Troy Edwards, Lenzie Jackson, Bobby Shaw. FB—Dan Kreider. RB—Chris Fuamatu-Ma'afala, Amos Zereoue. QB—Tee Martin. P—Josh Miller. K—Kris Brown. LS—Mike Schneck. Defense: NT—Kendrick Clancy. DE—Rodney Bailey. LB—John Fiala, Clark Haggans, Mike Jones, Justin Kurpeikis. CB—Jason Simmons, Deshea Townsend. S—Myron Bell, Mike Logan. DNP—G-C Roger Duffy, QB Tommy Maddox.
OFFICIALS
Referee—Ed Hochuli. Umpire—Ed Coukart. Line Judge—Ron Marinucci. Side Judge—Don Carlsen. Head Linesman—George Hayward. Back Judge—Kirk Dornan. Field Judge—Tom Sifferman. Replay Official—Bob Mantooth. Video Operator—Jim Pearson.

SCORING

New England	7	7	7	3	—	24
Pittsburgh	0	3	14	0	—	17

NE — T. Brown 55 punt return (Vinatieri kick)
Pitt — FG K. Brown 30
NE — Patten 11 pass from Bledsoe (Vinatieri kick)
NE — Harris 49 blocked field goal return (Vinatieri kick)
Pitt — Bettis 1 run (K. Brown kick)
Pitt — Zereoue 11 run (K. Brown kick)
NE — FG Vinatieri 44

TEAM STATISTICS	NE	Pitt
Total First Downs	15	23
Rushing	4	4
Passing	11	14
Penalty	0	5
Total Net Yardage	259	306
Total Offensive Plays	68	67
Average Gain Per Offensive Play	3.8	4.6
Rushes	25	22
Yards Gained Rushing (Net)	67	58
Average Yards per Rush	2.7	2.6
Passes Attempted	39	42
Passes Completed	22	24
Had Intercepted	0	3
Tackled Attempting to Pass	4	3
Yards Lost Attempting to Pass	25	7
Yards Gained Passing (Net)	192	248
Punts	7	6
Average Distance	39.1	43.0
Punt Returns	3	3
Punt Return Yardage	80	29
Kickoff Returns	3	5
Kickoff Return Yardage	83	86
Interception Return Yardage	30	0
Total Return Yardage	193	115
Fumbles	0	2
Fumbles Lost	0	1
Own Fumbles Recovered	0	1
Opponent Fumbles Recovered	1	1
Penalties	12	3
Yards Penalized	87	25
Field Goals	1	1
Field Goals Attempted	2	2
Third-Down Efficiency	6/17	4/14
Fourth-Down Efficiency	0/1	0/0
Time of Possession	30:55	29:05

INDIVIDUAL STATISTICS
RUSHING: NE: A. Smith 15-47-0, Redmond 3-13-0, Brady 2-3-0, Edwards 1-3-0, Bledsoe 4-1-0. PITT: Stewart 8-41-0, Zereoue 4-11-1, Bettis 9-8-1, Ward 1-(-2)-0.
PASSING: NE: Bledsoe 21-10-102-1-0, Brady 18-12-115-0-0. PITT: Stewart 42-24-255-0-3.
RECEIVING: NE: T. Brown 8-121-0, Patten 4-39-1, Edwards 4-26-0, C. Johnson 2-22-0, Wiggins 2-7-0, Redmond 2-2-0. PITT: Ward 6-64-0, Burress 5-67-0, Zereoue 4-50-0, Bettis 2-23-0, Edwards 2-16-0, Kreider 2-13-0, Cushing 1-10-0, Shaw 1-9-0, Tuman 1-3-0.
KICKOFF RETURNS: NE: Pass 3-83-0. PITT: Edwards 5-86-0.
PUNT RETURNS: NE: T. Brown 3-80-1. PITT: Edwards 3-29-0.
PUNTING: NE: Walter 7-274-39.1. PITT: Miller 6-258-43.0.
INTERCEPTIONS: NE: T. Jones 1-19-0, Milloy 1-11-0, Buckley 1-0-0. PITT: None.
SACKS: NE: McGinest, Pleasant, Bruschi 0.5, T. Johnson 0.5. PITT: Gildon 2, K. Bell, A. Smith.

NFC CHAMPIONSHIP GAME RESULTS
Includes NFL Championship Games (1933-1969)

Season	Date	Winner (Share)	Loser (Share)	Score	Site	Attendance
2001	Jan. 27	St. Louis ($34,500)	Philadelphia ($34,500)	29-24	St. Louis	66,502
2000	Jan. 14	N.Y. Giants ($34,500)	Minnesota ($34,500)	41-0	East Rutherford	79,310
1999	Jan. 23	St. Louis ($33,000)	Tampa Bay ($33,000)	11-6	St. Louis	66,396
1998	Jan. 17	Atlanta ($32,500)	Minnesota ($32,500)	30-27*	Minneapolis	64,060
1997	Jan. 11	Green Bay ($30,000)	San Francisco ($30,000)	23-10	San Francisco	68,987
1996	Jan. 12	Green Bay ($29,000)	Carolina ($29,000)	30-13	Green Bay	60,216
1995	Jan. 14	Dallas ($27,000)	Green Bay ($27,000)	38-27	Dallas	65,135
1994	Jan. 15	San Francisco ($26,000)	Dallas ($26,000)	38-28	San Francisco	69,125
1993	Jan. 23	Dallas ($23,500)	San Francisco ($23,500)	38-21	Dallas	64,902
1992	Jan. 17	Dallas ($18,000)	San Francisco ($18,000)	30-20	San Francisco	64,920
1991	Jan. 12	Washington ($18,000)	Detroit ($18,000)	41-10	Washington	55,585
1990	Jan. 20	N.Y. Giants ($18,000)	San Francisco ($18,000)	15-13	San Francisco	65,750
1989	Jan. 14	San Francisco ($18,000)	L.A. Rams ($18,000)	30-3	San Francisco	65,634
1988	Jan. 8	San Francisco ($18,000)	Chicago ($18,000)	28-3	Chicago	66,946
1987	Jan. 17	Washington ($18,000)	Minnesota ($18,000)	17-10	Washington	55,212
1986	Jan. 11	New York Giants ($18,000)	Washington ($18,000)	17-0	East Rutherford	76,891
1985	Jan. 12	Chicago ($18,000)	L.A. Rams ($18,000)	24-0	Chicago	66,030
1984	Jan. 6	San Francisco ($18,000)	Chicago ($18,000)	23-0	San Francisco	61,336
1983	Jan. 8	Washington ($18,000)	San Francisco ($18,000)	24-21	Washington	55,363
1982	Jan. 22	Washington ($18,000)	Dallas ($18,000)	31-17	Washington	55,045
1981	Jan. 10	San Francisco ($9,000)	Dallas ($9,000)	28-27	San Francisco	60,525
1980	Jan. 11	Philadelphia ($9,000)	Dallas ($9,000)	20-7	Philadelphia	71,522
1979	Jan. 6	Los Angeles ($9,000)	Tampa Bay ($9,000)	9-0	Tampa Bay	72,033
1978	Jan. 7	Dallas ($9,000)	Los Angeles ($9,000)	28-0	Los Angeles	71,086
1977	Jan. 1	Dallas ($9,000)	Minnesota ($9,000)	23-6	Dallas	64,293
1976	Dec. 26	Minnesota ($8,500)	Los Angeles ($5,500)	24-13	Minneapolis	48,379
1975	Jan. 4	Dallas ($8,500)	Los Angeles ($5,500)	37-7	Los Angeles	88,919
1974	Dec. 29	Minnesota ($8,500)	Los Angeles ($5,500)	14-10	Minneapolis	48,444
1973	Dec. 30	Minnesota ($8,500)	Dallas ($5,500)	27-10	Dallas	64,422
1972	Dec. 31	Washington ($8,500)	Dallas ($5,500)	26-3	Washington	53,129
1971	Jan. 2	Dallas ($8,500)	San Francisco ($5,500)	14-3	Dallas	63,409
1970	Jan. 3	Dallas ($8,500)	San Francisco ($5,500)	17-10	San Francisco	59,364
1969	Jan. 4	Minnesota ($7,930)	Cleveland ($5,118)	27-7	Minneapolis	46,503
1968	Dec. 29	Baltimore ($9,306)	Cleveland ($5,963)	34-0	Cleveland	78,410
1967	Dec. 31	Green Bay ($7,950)	Dallas ($5,299)	21-17	Green Bay	50,861
1966	Jan. 1	Green Bay ($9,813)	Dallas ($6,527)	34-27	Dallas	74,152
1965	Jan. 2	Green Bay ($7,819)	Cleveland ($5,288)	23-12	Green Bay	50,777
1964	Dec. 27	Cleveland ($8,052)	Baltimore ($5,571)	27-0	Cleveland	79,544
1963	Dec. 29	Chicago ($5,899)	New York ($4,218)	14-10	Chicago	45,801
1962	Dec. 30	Green Bay ($5,888)	New York ($4,166)	16-7	New York	64,892
1961	Dec. 31	Green Bay ($5,195)	New York ($3,339)	37-0	Green Bay	39,029
1960	Dec. 26	Philadelphia ($5,116)	Green Bay ($3,105)	17-13	Philadelphia	67,325
1959	Dec. 27	Baltimore ($4,674)	New York ($3,083)	31-16	Baltimore	57,545
1958	Dec. 28	Baltimore ($4,718)	New York ($3,111)	23-17*	New York	64,185
1957	Dec. 29	Detroit ($4,295)	Cleveland ($2,750)	59-14	Detroit	55,263
1956	Dec. 30	New York ($3,779)	Chi. Bears ($2,485)	47-7	New York	56,836
1955	Dec. 26	Cleveland ($3,508)	Los Angeles ($2,316)	38-14	Los Angeles	85,693
1954	Dec. 26	Cleveland ($2,478)	Detroit ($1,585)	56-10	Cleveland	43,827
1953	Dec. 27	Detroit ($2,424)	Cleveland ($1,654)	17-16	Detroit	54,577
1952	Dec. 28	Detroit ($2,274)	Cleveland ($1,712)	17-7	Cleveland	50,934
1951	Dec. 23	Los Angeles ($2,108)	Cleveland ($1,483)	24-17	Los Angeles	57,522
1950	Dec. 24	Cleveland ($1,113)	Los Angeles ($686)	30-28	Cleveland	29,751
1949	Dec. 18	Philadelphia ($1,094)	Los Angeles ($739)	14-0	Los Angeles	27,980
1948	Dec. 19	Philadelphia ($1,540)	Chi. Cardinals ($874)	7-0	Philadelphia	36,309
1947	Dec. 28	Chi. Cardinals ($1,132)	Philadelphia ($754)	28-21	Chicago	30,759
1946	Dec. 15	Chi. Bears ($1,975)	New York ($1,295)	24-14	New York	58,346
1945	Dec. 16	Cleveland ($1,469)	Washington ($902)	15-14	Cleveland	32,178
1944	Dec. 17	Green Bay ($1,449)	New York ($814)	14-7	New York	46,016
1943	Dec. 26	Chi. Bears ($1,146)	Washington ($765)	41-21	Chicago	34,320
1942	Dec. 13	Washington ($965)	Chi. Bears ($637)	14-6	Washington	36,006
1941	Dec. 21	Chi. Bears ($430)	New York ($288)	37-9	Chicago	13,341
1940	Dec. 8	Chi. Bears ($873)	Washington ($606)	73-0	Washington	36,034
1939	Dec. 10	Green Bay ($703.97)	New York ($455.57)	27-0	Milwaukee	32,279
1938	Dec. 11	New York ($504.45)	Green Bay ($368.81)	23-17	New York	48,120
1937	Dec. 12	Washington ($225.90)	Chi. Bears ($127.78)	28-21	Chicago	15,870

Season	Date	Winner (Share)	Loser (Share)	Score	Site	Attendance
1936	Dec. 13	Green Bay ($250)	Boston ($180)	21-6	New York	29,545
1935	Dec. 15	Detroit ($313.35)	New York ($200.20)	26-7	Detroit	15,000
1934	Dec. 9	New York ($621)	Chi. Bears ($414.02)	30-13	New York	35,059
1933	Dec. 17	Chi. Bears ($210.34)	New York ($140.22)	23-21	Chicago	26,000

Sudden death overtime

NFC CHAMPIONSHIP GAME COMPOSITE STANDINGS

	W	L	Pct.	Pts.	OP
Atlanta Falcons	1	0	1.000	30	27
Green Bay Packers	10	3	.769	303	177
Baltimore Colts	3	1	.750	88	60
Detroit Lions	4	2	.667	139	141
Philadelphia Eagles	4	2	.667	103	77
Washington Redskins*	7	5	.583	222	255
Chicago Bears	7	6	.538	286	245
Dallas Cowboys	8	8	.500	361	319
Minnesota Vikings	4	4	.500	135	151
Arizona Cardinals**	1	1	.500	28	28
San Francisco 49ers	5	7	.417	245	222
Cleveland Browns	4	7	.364	224	253
St. Louis Rams***	5	9	.357	163	300
New York Giants	6	11	.353	281	322
Carolina Panthers	0	1	.000	13	30
Tampa Bay Buccaneers	0	2	.000	6	20

*One game played when franchise was in Boston (Lost 21-6)
**Both games played when franchise was in Chicago (Won 28-21, lost 7-0)
***One game played when franchise was in Cleveland (Won 15-14), and 11 games when franchise was in Los Angeles (Won 2, lost 9, scored 108 points, allowed 256 points).

2001 NFC CHAMPIONSHIP GAME

Edward Jones Dome, St. Louis, Missouri
January 27, 2002, Attendance: 66,502

ST. LOUIS 29, PHILADELPHIA 24—Marshall Faulk rushed for 159 yards and 2 touchdowns as the Rams held off the Eagles to advance to their second Super Bowl in three seasons. Leonard Little forced Donovan McNabb to fumble two plays into the game, and Brian Young recovered. Kurt Warner's 5-yard touchdown pass to Isaac Bruce five plays later staked the Rams to an early 7-0 lead. After an exchange of field goals, the Rams looked to extend their seven-point lead early in the second quarter, but Jeff Wilkins' 53-yard field-goal attempt hit the right upright. The Eagles took advantage, keyed by Correll Buckhalter's 31-yard run, to tie the game on Duce Staley's 1-yard touchdown run with 6:56 left in the first half. Faulk's 31-yard run moments later set up Wilkins' 39-yard field goal, but McNabb completed 2 third-down passes on the ensuing drive to set up his 12-yard touchdown pass to Todd Pinkston with 46 seconds left in the half to take a 17-13 lead into the locker room. The Eagles had a chance to extend their lead as Yo Murphy fumbled the kickoff to open the second half, but Nick Sorensen recovered for the Rams. Warner's 21-yard third-down pass to Torry Holt keyed the ensuing 12-play drive, capped by Wilkins' third field goal, to cut the deficit to 17-16. After a three-and-out, the Rams used a 10-play, 71-yard drive to take a 22-17 lead on Faulk's 1-yard run with 1:18 left in the third quarter. After two more three-and-outs by the Eagles, Faulk's 25-yard run on third-and-1 led to his second touchdown and gave the Rams a 29-17 lead with 6:55 remaining. Brian Mitchell returned the ensuing kickoff 41 yards to give the Eagles a spark, culminating in McNabb's 3-yard touchdown run to cut the deficit to 29-24 with 2:56 to play. The Eagles' defense forced a three-and-out, but Aeneas Williams intercepted McNabb's fourth-down pass with 1:47 remaining to stop the rally. Philadephia had the ball for one last play with three seconds left, but failed to cross midfield during a lateral-pass play. Warner was 22 of 33 for 212 yards and 1 touchdown. McNabb was 18 of 30 for 171 yards and 1 touchdown, with 1 interception.

Philadelphia (24)	Offense	St. Louis (29)
Todd Pinkston	WR	Torry Holt
Tra Thomas	LT	Orlando Pace
John Welbourn	LG	Tom Nütten
Hank Fraley	C	Andy McCollum
Jermane Mayberry	RG	Adam Timmerman
Jon Runyan	RT	Rod Jones
Chad Lewis	TE-WR	Ricky Proehl
James Thrash	WR	Isaac Bruce
Donovan McNabb	QB	Kurt Warner
Duce Staley	RB	Marshall Faulk
Cecil Martin	FB-WR	Az-Zahir Hakim
	Defense	
Brandon Whiting	LE	Chidi Ahanotu
Corey Simon	LT	Brian Young
Paul Grasmanis	RT	Jeff Zgonina
Hugh Douglas	RE	Grant Wistrom
Mike Caldwell	WLB	Tommy Polley
Jeremiah Trotter	MLB	London Fletcher
Carlos Emmons	SLB	Don Davis
Troy Vincent	LCB	Aeneas Williams
Bobby Taylor	RCB	Dexter McCleon
Damon Moore	SS	Adam Archuleta
Brian Dawkins	FS	Kim Herring

SUBSTITUTIONS

Philadelphia—Offense: G—Doug Brzezinski. TE—Jeff Thomason. TE/LS—Mike Bartrum. WR—Na Brown, Dameane Douglas, Freddie Mitchell, Sean Morey. FB—Jamie Reader. RB—Correll Buckhalter. RB/KR—Brian Mitchell. QB—Koy Detmer. P—Sean Landeta. K—David Akers. Defense: DT—Darwin Walker. DE—Derrick Burgess, Ndukwe Kalu. LB—Quinton Caver, Barry Gardner. CB—William Hampton, Al Harris. S—Rashard Cook, Tim Hauck. DNP—C-G Jim Pyne.
St. Louis—Offense: T—Ryan Tucker. C—Frank Garcia. TE—Ernie Conwell, Brandon Manumaleuna, Jeff Robinson. WR—Yo Murphy. RB—Trung Canidate, James Hodgins, Robert Holcombe. P—John Baker. K—Jeff Wilkins. Defense: DT—Tyoka Jackson, Ryan Pickett. DE—Leonard Little, Sean Moran. LB—O.J. Brigance, Dustin Cohen, Mark Fields. CB—Dre' Bly, Jerametrius Butler. S—Willie Gary, Nick Sorensen. DNP—QB Jamie Martin.

OFFICIALS

Referee—Gerry Austin. Umpire—Ron Botchan. Line Judge—Ben Montgomery. Side Judge—Larry Rose. Head Linesman—Paul Weidner. Back Judge—Don Dorkowski. Field Judge—Tim Millis. Replay Official—Mark Burns. Video Operator—Ted Campbell.

SCORING

Philadelphia	3	14	0	7	—	24
St. Louis	10	3	9	7	—	29

StL — Bruce 5 pass from Warner (Wilkins kick)
Phil — FG Akers 46
StL — FG Wilkins 27
Phil — Staley 1 run (Akers kick)

StL — FG Wilkins 39
Phil — Pinkston 12 pass from McNabb (Akers kick)
StL — FG Wilkins 41
StL — Faulk 1 run (pass failed)
StL — Faulk 1 run (Wilkins kick)
Phil — McNabb 3 run (Akers kick)

TEAM STATISTICS	PHIL	STL
Total First Downs	16	22
Rushing	7	9
Passing	9	13
Penalty	0	0
Total Net Yardage	256	371
Total Offensive Plays	55	67
Average Gain Per Offensive Play	4.7	5.5
Rushes	22	33
Yards Gained Rushing (Net)	110	161
Average Yards per Rush	5.0	4.9
Passes Attempted	30	33
Passes Completed	18	22
Had Intercepted	1	0
Tackled Attempting to Pass	3	1
Yards Lost Attempting to Pass	25	2
Yards Gained Passing (Net)	146	210
Punts	4	3
Average Distance	39.3	45.0
Punt Returns	2	1
Punt Return Yardage	20	0
Kickoff Returns	7	4
Kickoff Return Yardage	148	117
Interception Return Yardage	0	0
Total Return Yardage	168	117
Fumbles	1	2
Fumbles Lost	1	0
Own Fumbles Recovered	0	2
Opponent Fumbles Recovered	0	1
Penalties	2	6
Yards Penalized	15	38
Field Goals	1	3
Field Goals Attempted	1	4
Third-Down Efficiency	5/12	7/15
Fourth-Down Efficiency	1/2	0/1
Time of Possession	24:30	35:30

INDIVIDUAL STATISTICS
RUSHING: PHIL: Buckhalter 6-50-0, Staley 11-39-1, McNabb 4-26-1, Thrash 1-(-5). STL: Faulk 31-159-2, Warner 2-2-0.
PASSING: PHIL: McNabb 30-18-171-1-1. STL: Warner 33-22-212-1-0.
RECEIVING: PHIL: Staley 8-58-0, Lewis 5-53-0, Thrash 3-46-0, Pinkston 1-12-1, F. Mitchell 1-2-0. STL: Bruce 8-84-1, Holt 5-58-0, Faulk 4-13-0, Conwell 3-33-0, Hakim 2-24-0.
KICKOFF RETURNS: PHIL: B. Mitchell 6-128-0, Douglas 1-20-0. STL: Murphy 3-95-0, Canidate 1-22-0.
PUNT RETURNS: PHIL: B. Mitchell 2-20-0. STL: Bly 1-0-0.
PUNTING: PHIL: Landeta 4-157-39.3. STL: Baker 3-135-45.0.
INTERCEPTIONS: PHIL: None. STL: A. Williams 1-0-0.
SACKS: PHIL: Burgess. STL: Little 2, Wistrom.

AFC DIVISIONAL PLAYOFFS RESULTS
Includes Second-Round Playoff Games (1982), AFC Inter-Divisional Games (1969), and special playoff games to break ties for AFL Division Championships (1963, 1968)

Season	Date	Winner (Share)	Loser (Share)	Score	Site	Attendance
2001	Jan. 20	Pittsburgh ($17,000)	Baltimore ($17,000)	27-10	Pittsburgh	63,976
	Jan. 19	New England ($17,000)	Oakland ($17,000)	16-13*	Foxboro	60,292
2000	Jan. 7	Baltimore ($16,000)	Tennessee ($16,000)	24-10	Nashville	68,527
	Jan. 6	Oakland ($16,000)	Miami ($16,000)	27-0	Oakland	61,998
1999	Jan. 16	Tennessee ($16,000)	Indianapolis ($16,000)	19-16	Indianapolis	57,097
	Jan. 15	Jacksonville ($16,000)	Miami ($16,000)	62-7	Jacksonville	75,173
1998	Jan. 10	N.Y. Jets ($15,000)	Jacksonville ($15,000)	34-24	East Rutherford	78,817
	Jan. 9	Denver ($15,000)	Miami ($15,000)	38-3	Denver	75,729
1997	Jan. 4	Denver ($15,000)	Kansas City ($15,000)	14-10	Kansas City	76,965
	Jan. 3	Pittsburgh ($15,000)	New England ($15,000)	7-6	Pittsburgh	61,228
1996	Jan. 5	New England ($14,000)	Pittsburgh ($14,000)	28-3	Foxboro	60,188
	Jan. 4	Jacksonville ($14,000)	Denver ($14,000)	30-27	Denver	75,678
1995	Jan. 7	Indianapolis ($13,000)	Kansas City ($13,000)	10-7	Kansas City	77,594
	Jan. 6	Pittsburgh ($13,000)	Buffalo ($13,000)	40-21	Pittsburgh	59,072
1994	Jan. 8	San Diego ($12,000)	Miami ($12,000)	22-21	San Diego	63,381
	Jan. 7	Pittsburgh ($12,000)	Cleveland ($12,000)	29-9	Pittsburgh	58,185
1993	Jan. 16	Kansas City ($12,000)	Houston ($12,000)	28-20	Houston	64,011
	Jan. 15	Buffalo ($12,000)	L.A. Raiders ($12,000)	29-23	Buffalo	61,923
1992	Jan. 10	Miami ($10,000)	San Diego ($10,000)	31-0	Miami	71,224
	Jan. 9	Buffalo ($10,000)	Pittsburgh ($10,000)	24-3	Pittsburgh	60,407
1991	Jan. 5	Buffalo ($10,000)	Kansas City ($10,000)	37-14	Buffalo	80,182
	Jan. 4	Denver ($10,000)	Houston ($10,000)	26-24	Denver	75,301
1990	Jan. 13	L.A. Raiders ($10,000)	Cincinnati ($10,000)	20-10	Los Angeles	92,045
	Jan. 12	Buffalo ($10,000)	Miami ($10,000)	44-34	Buffalo	77,087
1989	Jan. 7	Denver ($10,000)	Pittsburgh ($10,000)	24-23	Denver	75,477
	Jan. 6	Cleveland ($10,000)	Buffalo ($10,000)	34-30	Cleveland	78,921
1988	Jan. 1	Buffalo ($10,000)	Houston ($10,000)	17-10	Buffalo	79,532
	Dec. 31	Cincinnati ($10,000)	Seattle ($10,000)	21-13	Cincinnati	58,560
1987	Jan. 10	Denver ($10,000)	Houston ($10,000)	34-10	Denver	75,440
	Jan. 9	Cleveland ($10,000)	Indianapolis ($10,000)	38-21	Cleveland	79,372
1986	Jan. 4	Denver ($10,000)	New England ($10,000)	22-17	Denver	75,262
	Jan. 3	Cleveland ($10,000)	N.Y. Jets ($10,000)	23-20*	Cleveland	79,720
1985	Jan. 5	New England ($10,000)	L.A. Raiders ($10,000)	27-20	Los Angeles	87,163
	Jan. 4	Miami ($10,000)	Cleveland ($10,000)	24-21	Miami	74,667

1984	Dec. 30	Pittsburgh ($10,000)	Denver ($10,000)	24-17	Denver	74,981
	Dec. 29	Miami ($10,000)	Seattle ($10,000)	31-10	Miami	73,469
1983	Jan. 1	L.A. Raiders ($10,000)	Pittsburgh ($10,000)	38-10	Los Angeles	90,380
	Dec. 31	Seattle ($10,000)	Miami ($10,000)	27-20	Miami	74,136
1982	Jan. 16	Miami ($10,000)	San Diego ($10,000)	34-13	Miami	71,383
	Jan. 15	N.Y. Jets ($10,000)	L.A. Raiders ($10,000)	17-14	Los Angeles	90,038
1981	Jan. 3	Cincinnati ($5,000)	Buffalo ($5,000)	28-21	Cincinnati	55,420
	Jan. 2	San Diego ($5,000)	Miami ($5,000)	41-38*	Miami	73,735
1980	Jan. 4	Oakland ($5,000)	Cleveland ($5,000)	14-12	Cleveland	78,245
	Jan. 3	San Diego ($5,000)	Buffalo ($5,000)	20-14	San Diego	52,253
1979	Dec. 30	Pittsburgh ($5,000)	Miami ($5,000)	34-14	Pittsburgh	50,214
	Dec. 29	Houston ($5,000)	San Diego ($5,000)	17-14	San Diego	51,192
1978	Dec. 31	Houston ($5,000)	New England ($5,000)	31-14	Foxboro	60,735
	Dec. 30	Pittsburgh ($5,000)	Denver ($5,000)	33-10	Pittsburgh	50,230
1977	Dec. 24	Oakland ($5,000)	Baltimore ($5,000)	37-31*	Baltimore	59,925
	Dec. 24	Denver ($5,000)	Pittsburgh ($5,000)	34-21	Denver	75,059
1976	Dec. 19	Pittsburgh [$]	Baltimore [$]	40-14	Baltimore	59,296
	Dec. 18	Oakland [$]	New England [$]	24-21	Oakland	53,050
1975	Dec. 28	Oakland [$]	Cincinnati [$]	31-28	Oakland	53,030
	Dec. 27	Pittsburgh [$]	Baltimore [$]	28-10	Pittsburgh	49,557
1974	Dec. 22	Pittsburgh [$]	Buffalo [$]	32-14	Pittsburgh	49,841
	Dec. 21	Oakland [$]	Miami [$]	28-26	Oakland	53,023
1973	Dec. 23	Miami [$]	Cincinnati [$]	34-16	Miami	78,928
	Dec. 22	Oakland [$]	Pittsburgh [$]	33-14	Oakland	52,646
1972	Dec. 24	Miami [$]	Cleveland [$]	20-14	Miami	78,916
	Dec. 23	Pittsburgh [$]	Oakland [$]	13-7	Pittsburgh	50,327
1971	Dec. 26	Baltimore [$]	Cleveland [$]	20-3	Cleveland	70,734
	Dec. 25	Miami [$]	Kansas City [$]	27-24*	Kansas City	50,374
1970	Dec. 27	Oakland [$]	Miami [$]	21-14	Oakland	52,594
	Dec. 26	Baltimore [$]	Cincinnati [$]	17-0	Baltimore	49,694
1969	Dec. 21	Oakland [$]	Houston [$]	56-7	Oakland	53,539
	Dec. 20	Kansas City [$]	N.Y. Jets [$]	13-6	New York	62,977
1968	Dec. 22	Oakland [$]	Kansas City [$]	41-6	Oakland	53,605
1963	Dec. 28	Boston [$]	Buffalo [$]	26-8	Buffalo	33,044

Sudden death overtime.
$ Players received 1/14 of annual salary for playoff appearances.

2001 AFC DIVISIONAL PLAYOFF GAMES

Heinz Field, Pittsburgh, Pennsylvania
January 20, 2002, Attendance: 63,976

PITTSBURGH 27, BALTIMORE 10—Amos Zereoue rushed for 2 touchdowns and the Steelers' defense forced 4 turnovers, recorded 3 sacks, and permitted just 150 yards and 7 first downs en route to their fourth AFC Championship Game appearance in Bill Cowher's 10-year tenure. The Steelers played without Jerome Bettis, who had missed the season's final four games because of a groin injury, when he suffered complications from a pregame injection in his leg. Three plays into the game, Joey Porter hit Elvis Grbac as he attempted a pass downfield. Chad Scott intercepted the underthrown ball at the Ravens' 43 to set up Kris Brown's 21-yard field goal. After the Steelers' defense forced a three-and-out, Kordell Stewart completed 17- and 20-yard passes to Plaxico Burress and Hines Ward, respectively, to set up Zereoue's first touchdown with 3:49 left in the first quarter. Chris McAlister's 18-yard interception return to the Steelers' 7 late in the first quarter gave the Ravens hope, but two plays later Brent Alexander intercepted Grbac's pass in the end zone to thwart the scoring opportunity. A 27-yard punt return in the second quarter set up Zereoue's second touchdown and gave the Steelers a 17-0 lead with 5:43 left in the half. Two plays later, Terry Allen fumbled and Jason Gildon recovered, setting up Brown's second field goal of the half. The Ravens recorded their initial two first downs on the ensuing possession, capped by Matt Stover's 26-yard field goal to cut the deficit to 20-3. Jermaine Lewis's 88-yard punt return in the third quarter pulled the Ravens to within 10 points, but Stewart's 32-yard touchdown pass to Burress two plays into the fourth quarter staked the Steelers to a 27-10 lead. Alexander intercepted Grbac in the end zone

for the second time, with 4:18 left, to quell the Ravens' final scoring threat. Stewart was 12 of 22 for 154 yards and 1 touchdown, with 1 interception. Grbac was 18 of 37 for 153 yards, with 3 interceptions.

Baltimore	0	3	7	0	—	10
Pittsburgh	10	10	0	7	—	27

Pitt — FG Brown 21
Pitt — Zereoue 1 run (Brown kick)
Pitt — Zereoue 1 run (Brown kick)
Pitt — FG Brown 46
Balt — FG Stover 26
Balt — Je. Lewis 88 punt return (Stover kick)
Pitt — Burress 32 pass from Stewart (Brown kick)

Foxboro Stadium, Foxboro, Massachusetts
January 19, 2002, Attendance: 60,292

NEW ENGLAND 16, OAKLAND 13 (OT)—Adam Vinatieri's 23-yard field goal in the snow in overtime capped a 13-point rally and propelled the Patriots to victory. With the game being played in a driving snowstorm, both defenses dominated early. There was only one possession in the first half inside the opponents' 30, but the Raiders made that possession count, as James Jett caught a 13-yard touchdown pass from Rich Gannon early in the second quarter for a 7-0 lead. The clubs exchanged field goals on their first possessions of the second half, and the Raiders extended the lead to 13-3 late in the third quarter on Sebastian Janikowski's second field goal, which was set up by Gannon's 22-yard pass to Jerry Rice. With the wind at their backs for the fourth quarter, the Patriots began at their 33 with 12:29 to play. Operating without a huddle, Tom Brady completed 9 consecutive passes to begin the drive, and then scored on a 6-yard quarterback draw to cut the deficit to 13-10 with 7:52 remaining. After an exchange of punts, the Raiders were faced with third-and-1 at their 44 with 2:24 remaining, but Zack Crockett was stopped for no gain. Troy Brown returned the ensuing punt 27 yards. He fumbled at the end of his return, but Larry Izzo recovered at the Patriots' 46 with 2:06 to play and no time outs. With 1:50 remaining from the Raiders' 42, Charles Woodson blitzed and hit Brady, but after a replay review the loose ball was ruled an incomplete pass. Brady's 13-yard pass to David Patten on the next play, and a 1-yard run by Brady three plays later, set up Vinatieri's game-tying 45-yard field goal with 27 seconds remaining in regulation to force overtime. Driving into the snowstorm in overtime, Brady completed all 8 of his pass attempts, including a 6-yard pass to Patten on fourth-and-4 to the Raiders' 22, to set up Vinatieri's winning kick 8:29 into overtime. Brady was 32 of 52 for 312 yards, with 1 interception. Jermaine Wiggins had 10 receptions for 68 yards, and Patten added 8 catches for 107 yards. Gannon was 17 of 31 for 159 yards and 1 touchdown.

Oakland	0	7	6	0	0	—	13
New England	0	0	3	10	3	—	16

Oak — Jett 13 pass from Gannon (Janikowski kick)
NE — FG Vinatieri 23
Oak — FG Janikowski 38
Oak — FG Janikowski 45
NE — Brady 6 run (Vinatieri kick)
NE — FG Vinatieri 45
NE — FG Vinatieri 23

NFC DIVISIONAL PLAYOFFS RESULTS
Includes Second-Round Playoff Games (1982), NFL Conference Championship Games (1967-69), and special playoff games to break ties for NFL Division or Conference Championships (1941, 1943, 1947, 1950, 1952, 1957, 1958, 1965)

Season	Date	Winner (Share)	Loser (Share)	Score	Site	Attendance
2001	Jan. 20	St. Louis ($17,000)	Green Bay ($17,000)	45-17	St. Louis	66,338
	Jan. 19	Philadelphia ($17,000)	Chicago ($17,000)	33-19	Chicago	66,944
2000	Jan. 7	N.Y. Giants ($16,000)	Philadelphia ($16,000)	20-10	East Rutherford	78,765
	Jan. 6	Minnesota ($16,000)	New Orleans ($16,000)	34-16	Minneapolis	63,881
1999	Jan. 16	St. Louis ($16,000)	Minnesota ($16,000)	49-37	St. Louis	66,194
	Jan. 15	Tampa Bay ($16,000)	Washington ($16,000)	14-13	Tampa Bay	65,835
1998	Jan. 10	Minnesota ($15,000)	Arizona ($15,000)	41-21	Minneapolis	63,760
	Jan. 9	Atlanta ($15,000)	San Francisco ($15,000)	20-18	Atlanta	70,262
1997	Jan. 4	Green Bay ($15,000)	Tampa Bay ($15,000)	21-7	Green Bay	60,327
	Jan. 3	San Francisco ($15,000)	Minnesota ($15,000)	38-22	San Francisco	65,018
1996	Jan. 5	Carolina ($14,000)	Dallas ($14,000)	26-17	Carolina	72,808
	Jan. 4	Green Bay ($14,000)	San Francisco ($14,000)	35-14	Green Bay	60,787
1995	Jan. 7	Dallas ($13,000)	Philadelphia ($13,000)	30-11	Dallas	64,371
	Jan. 6	Green Bay ($13,000)	San Francisco ($13,000)	27-17	San Francisco	69,311
1994	Jan. 8	Dallas ($12,000)	Green Bay ($12,000)	35-9	Dallas	64,745
	Jan. 7	San Francisco ($12,000)	Chicago ($12,000)	44-15	San Francisco	64,644
1993	Jan. 16	Dallas ($12,000)	Green Bay ($12,000)	27-17	Dallas	64,790
	Jan. 15	San Francisco ($12,000)	N.Y. Giants ($12,000)	44-3	San Francisco	67,143
1992	Jan. 10	Dallas ($10,000)	Philadelphia ($10,000)	34-10	Dallas	63,721
	Jan. 9	San Francisco ($10,000)	Washington ($10,000)	20-13	San Francisco	64,991
1991	Jan. 5	Detroit ($10,000)	Dallas ($10,000)	38-6	Detroit	78,290
	Jan. 4	Washington ($10,000)	Atlanta ($10,000)	24-7	Washington	55,181
1990	Jan. 13	N.Y. Giants ($10,000)	Chicago ($10,000)	31-3	East Rutherford	77,025
	Jan. 12	San Francisco ($10,000)	Washington ($10,000)	28-10	San Francisco	65,292
1989	Jan. 7	L.A. Rams ($10,000)	N.Y. Giants ($10,000)	19-13*	East Rutherford	76,526
	Jan. 6	San Francisco ($10,000)	Minnesota ($10,000)	41-13	San Francisco	64,918
1988	Jan. 1	San Francisco ($10,000)	Minnesota ($10,000)	34-9	San Francisco	61,848
	Dec. 31	Chicago ($10,000)	Philadelphia ($10,000)	20-12	Chicago	65,534
1987	Jan. 10	Washington ($10,000)	Chicago ($10,000)	21-17	Chicago	65,268
	Jan. 9	Minnesota ($10,000)	San Francisco ($10,000)	36-24	San Francisco	63,008
1986	Jan. 4	N.Y. Giants ($10,000)	San Francisco ($10,000)	49-3	East Rutherford	75,691
	Jan. 3	Washington ($10,000)	Chicago ($10,000)	27-13	Chicago	65,524
1985	Jan. 5	Chicago ($10,000)	N.Y. Giants ($10,000)	21-0	Chicago	65,670
	Jan. 4	L.A. Rams ($10,000)	Dallas ($10,000)	20-0	Anaheim	66,581
1984	Dec. 30	Chicago ($10,000)	Washington ($10,000)	23-19	Washington	55,431
	Dec. 29	San Francisco ($10,000)	N.Y. Giants ($10,000)	21-10	San Francisco	60,303
1983	Jan. 1	Washington ($10,000)	L.A. Rams ($10,000)	51-7	Washington	54,440
	Dec. 31	San Francisco ($10,000)	Detroit ($10,000)	24-23	San Francisco	59,979
1982	Jan. 16	Dallas ($10,000)	Green Bay ($10,000)	37-26	Dallas	63,972
	Jan. 15	Washington ($10,000)	Minnesota ($10,000)	21-7	Washington	54,593
1981	Jan. 3	San Francisco ($5,000)	N.Y. Giants ($5,000)	38-24	San Francisco	58,360
	Jan. 2	Dallas ($5,000)	Tampa Bay ($5,000)	38-0	Dallas	64,848
1980	Jan. 4	Dallas ($5,000)	Atlanta ($5,000)	30-27	Atlanta	59,793
	Jan. 3	Philadelphia ($5,000)	Minnesota ($5,000)	31-16	Philadelphia	70,178
1979	Dec. 30	Los Angeles ($5,000)	Dallas ($5,000)	21-19	Dallas	64,792
	Dec. 29	Tampa Bay ($5,000)	Philadelphia ($5,000)	24-17	Tampa Bay	71,402
1978	Dec. 31	Los Angeles ($5,000)	Minnesota ($5,000)	34-10	Los Angeles	70,436
	Dec. 30	Dallas ($5,000)	Atlanta ($5,000)	27-20	Dallas	63,406

Season	Date	Winner (Share)	Loser (Share)	Score	Site	Attendance
1977	Dec. 26	Dallas ($5,000)	Chicago ($5,000)	37-7	Dallas	63,260
	Dec. 26	Minnesota ($5,000)	Los Angeles ($5,000)	14-7	Los Angeles	70,203
1976	Dec. 19	Los Angeles [$]	Dallas [$]	14-12	Dallas	63,283
	Dec. 18	Minnesota [$]	Washington [$]	35-20	Minneapolis	47,466
1975	Dec. 28	Dallas [$]	Minnesota [$]	17-14	Minneapolis	48,050
	Dec. 27	Los Angeles [$]	St. Louis [$]	35-23	Los Angeles	73,459
1974	Dec. 22	Los Angeles [$]	Washington [$]	19-10	Los Angeles	77,925
	Dec. 21	Minnesota [$]	St. Louis [$]	30-14	Minneapolis	48,150
1973	Dec. 23	Dallas [$]	Los Angeles [$]	27-16	Dallas	63,272
	Dec. 22	Minnesota [$]	Washington [$]	27-20	Minneapolis	48,040
1972	Dec. 24	Washington [$]	Green Bay [$]	16-3	Washington	52,321
	Dec. 23	Dallas [$]	San Francisco [$]	30-28	San Francisco	59,746
1971	Dec. 26	San Francisco [$]	Washington [$]	24-20	San Francisco	45,327
	Dec. 25	Dallas [$]	Minnesota [$]	20-12	Minneapolis	47,307
1970	Dec. 27	San Francisco [$]	Minnesota [$]	17-14	Minneapolis	45,103
	Dec. 26	Dallas [$]	Detroit [$]	5-0	Dallas	69,613
1969	Dec. 28	Cleveland [$]	Dallas [$]	38-14	Dallas	69,321
	Dec. 27	Minnesota [$]	Los Angeles [$]	23-20	Minneapolis	47,900
1968	Dec. 22	Baltimore [$]	Minnesota [$]	24-14	Baltimore	60,238
	Dec. 21	Cleveland [$]	Dallas [$]	31-20	Cleveland	81,497
1967	Dec. 24	Dallas [$]	Cleveland [$]	52-14	Dallas	70,786
	Dec. 23	Green Bay [$]	Los Angeles [$]	28-7	Milwaukee	49,861
1965	Dec. 26	Green Bay [$]	Baltimore [$]	13-10*	Green Bay	50,484
1958	Dec. 21	N.Y. Giants (#)	Cleveland (#)	10-0	New York	61,274
1957	Dec. 22	Detroit (#)	San Francisco (#)	31-27	San Francisco	60,118
1952	Dec. 21	Detroit (#)	Los Angeles (#)	31-21	Detroit	47,645
1950	Dec. 17	Los Angeles (#)	Chicago Bears (#)	24-14	Los Angeles	83,501
	Dec. 17	Cleveland (#)	N.Y. Giants (#)	8-3	Cleveland	33,054
1947	Dec. 21	Philadelphia (#)	Pittsburgh (#)	21-0	Pittsburgh	35,729
1943	Dec. 19	Washington (¢)	N.Y. Giants (¢)	28-0	New York	42,800
1941	Dec. 14	Chicago Bears (¢)	Green Bay (¢)	33-14	Chicago	43,425

*Sudden death overtime
Players received 1/12 of annual salary for playoff appearances.
$ Players received 1/14 of annual salary for playoff appearances.
¢ Players received 1/10 of annual salary for playoff appearances.

2001 NFC DIVISIONAL PLAYOFF GAMES

Dome at America's Center, St. Louis, Missouri
January 20, 2002, Attendance: 66,338
ST. LOUIS 45, GREEN BAY 17—Aeneas Williams set a postseason record by returning 2 interceptions for touchdowns as the Rams' defense intercepted 6 passes en route to their second NFC Championship Game appearance in three seasons. On the Packers' second possession, Brett Favre and Bill Schroeder had a miscommunication, which enabled Favre's pass to go directly to Williams, who raced 29 yards untouched for a touchdown. Darren Sharper's interception set up Favre's 22-yard touchdown pass to Antonio Freeman late in the first quarter, but the Rams responded with a 6-play, 66-yard drive, keyed by Marshall Faulk's 38-yard run, and capped by Kurt Warner's 4-yard touchdown pass to Torry Holt. Three plays later, Kim Herring's 45-yard interception return to the Packers' 4 led to Warner's 4-yard touchdown pass to James Hodgins and a 21-7 lead. Leading 24-10 early in the third quarter, Williams recovered a fumble and raced 69 yards for a touchdown, only to have the touchdown overturned, with Williams being ruled down by contact. Undaunted, the Rams drove 69 yards in four plays, highlighted by Holt's spectacular 50-yard over-the-shoulder catch, and capped by Faulk's 7-yard run. Five plays later, Favre's pass was deflected by Grant Wistrom into the hands of Tommy Polley, who returned it 34 yards for a touchdown and a 38-10 lead with 8:12 left in the third quarter. Williams capped the day with his 32-yard interception return for a touchdown midway through the final quarter. Warner was 18 of 30 for 216 yards and 2 touchdowns, with 1 interception. Favre was 26 of 44 for 281 yards and 2 touchdowns, with a postseason-tying 6 interceptions.

Green Bay	7	3	0	7	—	17
St. Louis	7	17	14	7	—	45

StL — Williams 29 interception return (Wilkins kick)
GB — Freeman 22 pass from Favre (Longwell kick)
StL — Holt 4 pass from Warner (Wilkins kick)
StL — Hodgins 4 pass from Warner (Wilkins kick)
GB — FG Longwell 28
StL — FG Wilkins 27
StL — Faulk 7 run (Wilkins kick)
StL — Polley 34 interception return (Wilkins kick)
StL — Williams 32 interception return (Wilkins kick)
GB — Freeman 8 pass from Favre (Longwell kick)

Soldier Field, Chicago, Illinois
January 19, 2002, Attendance: 66,944
PHILADELPHIA 33, CHICAGO 19—Donovan McNabb passed for 2 touchdowns and ran for another as the Eagles advanced to the NFC Championship Game for the first time since 1980. The Eagles drove 61 and 63 yards on their first two possessions to set up field goals by David Akers. Damon Moore's interception at the Eagles' 2 thwarted a Bears' drive early in the second quarter, and also ended the day for Jim Miller, who was injured during the return. Behind Shane Matthews, the Bears took the lead later in the quarter as wide receiver Ahmad Merritt ran 47 yards on a reverse for a touchdown. The Eagles responded with an 11-play, 69-yard drive, highlighted by McNabb's 9-yard pass to Jeff Thomason on fourth-and-1, and capped by his 13-yard touchdown pass to Cecil Martin with 14 seconds left in the half to give the Eagles a 13-7 lead. Jerry Azumah's 39-yard interception return early in the second half put the Bears back in front. Later in the quarter, Brad Maynard's 15-yard punt gave the Eagles the ball at the Bears' 36. The Bears forced the Eagles into a third-and-14 situation, but McNabb completed a 30-yard pass to Thomason to set up his 6-yard scoring pass to Duce Staley and give Philadelphia a 20-14 lead. The Bears answered with Paul Edinger's 38-yard field goal 44 seconds into

the fourth quarter, but the Eagles used 11 plays on the ensuing drive and took a 23-17 lead with 8:48 to play on Akers' third field goal. Quinton Caver recovered Autry Denson's fumble on the ensuing kickoff to set up Akers' fourth field goal, and Rashard Cook's 15-yard interception return to the Eagles' 20 set up McNabb's 5-yard touchdown run with 3:21 remaining to take a 33-17 lead. Sean Landeta ran out of the end zone as time expired to provide the final margin. McNabb was 26 of 40 for 262 yards and 2 touchdowns, with 1 interception. Matthews was 8 of 17 for 66 yards, with 2 interceptions, while Miller was 3 of 5 for 23 yards, with 1 interception.

Phil	— FG Akers 34
Phil	— FG Akers 23
Chi	— Merritt 47 run (Edinger kick)
Phil	— Martin 13 pass from McNabb (Akers kick)
Chi	— Azumah 39 interception return (Edinger kick)
Phil	— Staley 6 pass from McNabb (Akers kick)
Chi	— FG Edinger 38
Phil	— FG Akers 40
Phil	— FG Akers 46
Phil	— McNabb 5 run (Akers kick)
Chi	— Safety, Landeta ran out of end zone

Philadelphia	6	7	7	13	—	33
Chicago	0	7	7	5	—	19

AFC WILD CARD PLAYOFF GAMES RESULTS

Season	Date	Winner (Share)	Loser (Share)	Score	Site	Attendance
2001	Jan. 13	Baltimore ($12,500)	Miami ($12,500)	20-3	Miami	72,251
	Jan. 12	Oakland ($17,000)	N.Y. Jets ($12,500)	38-24	Oakland	61,503
2000	Dec. 31	Baltimore (12,500)	Denver ($12,500)	21-3	Baltimore	69,638
	Dec. 30	Miami ($16,000)	Indianapolis ($12,500)	23-17*	Miami	73,193
1999	Jan. 9	Miami ($10,000)	Seattle ($16,000)	20-17	Seattle	66,170
	Jan. 8	Tennessee ($10,000)	Buffalo ($10,000)	22-16	Nashville	66,672
1998	Jan. 3	Jacksonville ($15,000)	New England ($10,000)	25-10	Jacksonville	71,139
	Jan. 2	Miami ($10,000)	Buffalo ($10,000)	24-17	Miami	72,698
1997	Dec. 28	New England ($15,000)	Miami ($10,000)	17-3	Foxboro	60,041
	Dec. 27	Denver ($10,000)	Jacksonville ($10,000)	42-17	Denver	74,481
1996	Dec. 29	Pittsburgh ($14,000)	Indianapolis ($10,000)	42-14	Pittsburgh	58,078
	Dec. 28	Jacksonville ($10,000)	Buffalo ($10,000)	30-27	Buffalo	70,213
1995	Dec. 31	Indianapolis ($7,500)	San Diego ($7,500)	35-20	San Diego	61,182
	Dec. 30	Buffalo ($13,000)	Miami ($7,500)	37-22	Buffalo	73,103
1994	Jan. 1	Cleveland ($7,500)	New England ($7,500)	20-13	Cleveland	77,452
	Dec. 31	Miami ($12,000)	Kansas City ($7,500)	27-17	Miami	67,487
1993	Jan. 9	L.A. Raiders ($7,500)	Denver ($7,500)	42-24	Los Angeles	65,314
	Jan. 8	Kansas City ($12,000)	Pittsburgh ($7,500)	27-24*	Kansas City	74,515
1992	Jan. 3	Buffalo ($6,000)	Houston ($6,000)	41-38*	Buffalo	75,141
	Jan. 2	San Diego ($10,000)	Kansas City ($6,000)	17-0	San Diego	58,278
1991	Dec. 29	Houston ($10,000)	N.Y. Jets ($6,000)	17-10	Houston	61,485
	Dec. 28	Kansas City ($6,000)	L.A. Raiders ($6,000)	10-6	Kansas City	75,827
1990	Jan. 6	Cincinnati ($10,000)	Houston ($6,000)	41-14	Cincinnati	60,012
	Jan. 5	Miami ($6,000)	Kansas City ($6,000)	17-16	Miami	67,276
1989	Dec. 31	Pittsburgh ($6,000)	Houston ($6,000)	26-23*	Houston	59,406
1988	Dec. 26	Houston ($6,000)	Cleveland ($6,000)	24-23	Cleveland	75,896
1987	Jan. 3	Houston ($6,000)	Seattle ($6,000)	23-20*	Houston	50,519
1986	Dec. 28	N.Y. Jets ($6,000)	Kansas City ($6,000)	35-15	East Rutherford	75,210
1985	Dec. 28	New England ($6,000)	N.Y. Jets ($6,000)	26-14	East Rutherford	75,945
1984	Dec. 22	Seattle ($6,000)	L.A. Raiders ($6,000)	13-7	Seattle	62,049
1983	Dec. 24	Seattle ($6,000)	Denver ($6,000)	31-7	Seattle	64,275
1982	Jan. 9	N.Y. Jets ($6,000)	Cincinnati ($6,000)	44-17	Cincinnati	57,560
	Jan. 9	San Diego ($6,000)	Pittsburgh ($6,000)	31-28	Pittsburgh	53,546
	Jan. 8	L.A. Raiders ($6,000)	Cleveland ($6,000)	27-10	Los Angeles	56,555
	Jan. 8	Miami ($6,000)	New England ($6,000)	28-13	Miami	68,842
1981	Dec. 27	Buffalo ($3,000)	N.Y. Jets ($3,000)	31-27	New York	57,050
1980	Dec. 28	Oakland ($3,000)	Houston ($3,000)	27-7	Oakland	53,333
1979	Dec. 23	Houston ($3,000)	Denver ($3,000)	13-7	Houston	48,776
1978	Dec. 24	Houston ($3,000)	Miami ($3,000)	17-9	Miami	72,445

Sudden death overtime

2001 AFC WILD CARD PLAYOFF GAMES

Pro Player Stadium, Miami, Florida
January 13, 2002, Attendance: 72,251

BALTIMORE 20, MIAMI 3—The Ravens' offense rushed for 226 yards and the Ravens' defense allowed just 9 first downs, 151 total yards, and forced 3 turnovers as the Super Bowl champions won their fifth consecutive postseason game. Tommy Hendricks recovered Jermaine Lewis' fumble on the opening kickoff at the Ravens' 24, but the Dolphins could only manage Olindo Mare's 33-yard field goal. Terry Allen's 4-yard touchdown run capped an 11-play, 90-yard drive and gave the Ravens a 7-3 lead early in the second quarter. The Ravens had a chance to extend the lead just before halftime when Peter Boulware recovered Travis Minor's fumble at the Dolphins' 41, but Matt Stover's 40-yard field-goal attempt hit the left upright. Matt Turk's 44-yard punt pinned the Ravens back to their own 1-yard line midway through the third quarter, but a few nice runs by Allen, and a 45-yard pass from Elvis Grbac to Travis Taylor, set up the duo's 4-yard touchdown to give the Ravens a 14-3 lead. On the ensuing possession, Boulware sacked Jay Fiedler and forced him to fumble. Sam Adams recovered to set up Stover's 35-yard field goal, and Duane Starks' interception at the Ravens' 28 on the next drive led to Stover's 40-yard field goal with 2:01 left to finish the scoring. Grbac was 12 of 18 for 133 yards and 1 touchdown. Allen rushed 25 times for 109 yards. Fiedler was 15 of 28 for 122 yards, with 1 interception.

Baltimore	0	7	7	6	—	20
Miami	3	0	0	0	—	3

Mia — FG Mare 33
Balt — Allen 4 run (Stover kick)
Balt — Taylor 4 pass from Grbac (Stover kick)
Balt — FG Stover 35
Balt — FG Stover 40

Network Associates Coliseum, Oakland, California
January 12, 2002, Attendance: 61,503
OAKLAND 38, N.Y. JETS 24—Jerry Rice had 9 catches for 183 yards and became the oldest player to catch a postseason touchdown pass in NFL history as the Raiders fought off a late rally to defeat the Jets in the NFL's first-ever prime-time playoff game. The Raiders' first three possessions all ended with Sebastian Janikowski field goals. The Jets' first three possessions also ended with field-goal attempts, but John Hall missed a 45-yard attempt, made a 45-yard attempt, and had a 41-yard attempt blocked by Anthony Dorsett with 3:05 left in the first half. Dorsett's block, and a 29-yard run by Charlie Garner, set up Rich Gannon's 2-yard touchdown pass to Tim Brown with 22 seconds left in the first half to give the Raiders a 16-3 lead. Vinny Testaverde's 17-yard touchdown pass to Wayne Chrebet to open the second half cut the deficit to 16-10, and the Jets moved into Raiders' territory late in the third quarter. But Richie Anderson fumbled, Grady Jackson recovered, and Gannon's 47-yard pass to Rice set up Zack

Crockett's 2-yard touchdown run on the first play of the fourth quarter to give Oakland a 24-10 lead. Testaverde's 3-yard touchdown pass to Anderson cut the lead to 24-17, but the Raiders answered, keyed by Jerry Porter's 22-yard catch on third-and-8, with Gannon's 21-yard touchdown pass to Rice. At 39 years old, Rice broke the record held by Pro Football Hall of Fame tight end Jackie Smith, who was 38 years old when he caught a touchdown pass in the Cowboys' 1978 NFC Divisional Playoff Game. Testaverde's 4-yard touchdown pass to Chrebet with 1:56 left cut the lead to 31-24, and the Jets stopped the Raiders on their first two plays to set up third-and-11 from the Raiders' 20 with 1:40 left. However, Garner broke free and raced 80 yards for a game-clinching touchdown with 1:27 remaining. Gannon was 23 of 29 for 294 yards and 2 touchdowns. Garner had 15 carries for 158 yards. Testaverde was 27 of 41 for 277 yards and 3 touchdowns. Curtis Martin had 16 carries for 106 yards, and Laveranues Coles had 8 catches for 123 yards.

N.Y. Jets	0	3	7	14	—	24
Oakland	6	10	0	22	—	38

Oak — FG Janikowski 21
Oak — FG Janikowski 41
NYJ — FG Hall 45
Oak — FG Janikowski 45
Oak — Brown 2 pass from Gannon (Janikowski kick)
NYJ — Chrebet 17 pass from Testaverde (Hall kick)
Oak — Crockett 2 run (Garner run)
NYJ — Anderson 3 pass from Testaverde (Hall kick)
Oak — Rice 21 pass from Gannon (Janikowski kick)
NYJ — Chrebet 4 pass from Testaverde (Hall kick)
Oak — Garner 80 run (Janikowski kick)

NFC WILD CARD PLAYOFF GAMES RESULTS

Season	Date	Winner (Share)	Loser (Share)	Score	Site	Attendance
2001	Jan. 13	Green Bay ($12,500)	San Francisco ($12,500)	25-15	Green Bay	59,825
	Jan. 12	Philadelphia ($17,000)	Tampa Bay ($12,500)	31-9	Philadelphia	65,847
2000	Dec. 31	Philadelphia ($12,500)	Tampa Bay ($12,500)	21-3	Philadelphia	65,813
	Dec. 30	New Orleans ($16,000)	St. Louis ($12,500)	31-28	New Orleans	64,900
1999	Jan. 9	Minnesota ($10,000)	Dallas ($10,000)	27-10	Minneapolis	64,056
	Jan. 8	Washington ($10,000)	Detroit ($10,000)	27-13	Washington	79,411
1998	Jan. 3	San Francisco ($10,000)	Green Bay ($10,000)	30-27	San Francisco	66,506
	Jan. 2	Arizona ($10,000)	Dallas ($15,000)	20-7	Dallas	62,969
1997	Dec. 28	Tampa Bay ($10,000)	Detroit ($10,000)	20-10	Tampa Bay	73,361
	Dec. 27	Minnesota ($10,000)	N.Y. Giants ($15,000)	23-22	East Rutherford	77,497
1996	Dec. 29	San Francisco ($10,000)	Philadelphia ($10,000)	14-0	San Francisco	56,460
	Dec. 28	Dallas ($14,000)	Minnesota ($10,000)	40-15	Dallas	64,682
1995	Dec. 31	Green Bay ($13,000)	Atlanta ($7,500)	37-20	Green Bay	60,453
	Dec. 30	Philadelphia ($7,500)	Detroit ($7,500)	58-37	Philadelphia	66,099
1994	Jan. 1	Chicago ($7,500)	Minnesota ($12,000)	35-18	Minnesota	60,347
	Dec. 31	Green Bay ($7,500)	Detroit ($7,500)	16-12	Green Bay	58,125
1993	Jan. 9	N.Y. Giants ($7,500)	Minnesota ($7,500)	17-10	East Rutherford	75,089
	Jan. 8	Green Bay ($7,500)	Detroit ($12,000)	28-24	Detroit	68,479
1992	Jan. 3	Philadelphia ($6,000)	New Orleans ($6,000)	36-20	New Orleans	68,893
	Jan. 2	Washington ($6,000)	Minnesota ($10,000)	24-7	Minnesota	57,353
1991	Dec. 29	Dallas ($6,000)	Chicago ($6,000)	17-13	Chicago	62,594
	Dec. 28	Atlanta ($6,000)	New Orleans ($10,000)	27-20	New Orleans	68,794
1990	Jan. 6	Chicago ($10,000)	New Orleans ($6,000)	16-6	Chicago	60,767
	Jan. 5	Washington ($6,000)	Philadelphia ($6,000)	20-6	Philadelphia	65,287
1989	Dec. 31	L.A. Rams ($6,000)	Philadelphia ($6,000)	21-7	Philadelphia	65,479
1988	Dec. 26	Minnesota ($6,000)	L.A. Rams ($6,000)	28-17	Minnesota	61,204
1987	Jan. 3	Minnesota ($6,000)	New Orleans ($6,000)	44-10	New Orleans	68,546
1986	Dec. 28	Washington ($6,000)	L.A. Rams ($6,000)	19-7	Washington	54,567
1985	Dec. 29	N.Y. Giants ($6,000)	San Francisco ($6,000)	17-3	East Rutherford	75,131
1984	Dec. 23	N.Y. Giants ($6,000)	L.A. Rams ($6,000)	16-13	Anaheim	67,037
1983	Dec. 26	L.A. Rams ($6,000)	Dallas ($6,000)	24-17	Dallas	62,118
1982	Jan. 9	Dallas ($6,000)	Tampa Bay ($6,000)	30-17	Dallas	65,042
	Jan. 9	Minnesota ($6,000)	Atlanta ($6,000)	30-24	Minnesota	60,560
	Jan. 8	Green Bay ($6,000)	St. Louis ($6,000)	41-16	Green Bay	54,282

	Jan. 8	Washington ($6,000)	Detroit ($6,000)	31-7	Washington	55,045
1981	Dec. 27	N.Y. Giants ($3,000)	Philadelphia ($3,000)	27-21	Philadelphia	71,611
1980	Dec. 28	Dallas ($3,000)	Los Angeles ($3,000)	34-13	Dallas	63,052
1979	Dec. 23	Philadelphia ($3,000)	Chicago ($3,000)	27-17	Philadelphia	69,397
1978	Dec. 24	Atlanta ($3,000)	Philadelphia ($3,000)	14-13	Atlanta	59,403

2001 NFC WILD CARD PLAYOFF GAMES
Lambeau Field, Green Bay, Wisconsin
January 13, 2002, Attendance: 59,825
GREEN BAY 25, SAN FRANCISCO 15—Brett Favre set a Green Bay playoff record by completing 75.9 percent of his passes as the Packers improved to 11-0 all-time in postseason games at Lambeau Field. With the game-time temperature of 28 degrees, Favre improved to 31-0 when the temperature is 34 or below. Allen Rossum's 35-yard punt return set up Favre's 5-yard touchdown pass to Antonio Freeman. However, Dana Stubblefield blocked the extra point. Ahmed Plummer intercepted Favre late in the first quarter, but the Packers' defense forced the 49ers' into a field-goal attempt, and Cletidus Hunt blocked Jose Cortez's 34-yard attempt. The 49ers got the ball back midway through the second quarter and put together a 15-play, 86-yard drive, capped by Garrison Hearst's 2-yard touchdown run with 11 seconds left in the half to give the 49ers a 7-6 lead. Ryan Longwell's 26-yard field goal capped a 12-play drive to begin the third quarter, and Corey Bradford's 51-yard reception on the Packers' next possession set up Favre's 19-yard touchdown pass to Bubba Franks to give the Packers a 15-7 lead. Jeff Garcia's 14-yard touchdown pass to Tai Streets, and the ensuing 2-point conversion hookup by the same pair, tied the game with 12:00 left. Longwell's 45-yard field goal on the ensuing possession staked the Packers to a precarious 18-15 lead with 7:02 left. On first-and-10 from the Packers' 41 with 5:03 remaining, Terrell Owens broke open deep down the right sideline. However, Garcia's pass was slightly underthrown and Mike McKenzie hustled back to tip the pass into the hands of Tyrone Williams for an interception at the Packers' 7. Sensing an opportunity to put the game away, Favre engineered an 8-play, 93-yard drive, highlighted by a 37-yard pass to Freeman on third-and-7, and capped by Ahman Green's 9-yard scoring run with 1:55 remaining. Paul Smith fumbled the ensuing kickoff and Bradford recovered to clinch the victory. Favre was 22 of 29 for 269 yards and 2 touchdowns, with 1 interception. Garcia was 22 of 32 for 233 yards and 1 touchdown, with 1 interception.

San Francisco	0	7	0	8	—	15
Green Bay	6	0	9	10	—	25

GB — Freeman 5 pass from Favre (kick blocked)
SF — Hearst 2 run (Cortez kick)
GB — FG Longwell 26
GB — Franks 19 pass from Favre (pass failed)
SF — Streets 14 pass from Garcia (Streets pass from Garcia)
GB — FG Longwell 45
GB — Green 9 run (Longwell kick)

Veterans Stadium, Philadelphia, Pennsylvania
January 12, 2002, Attendance: 65,847
PHILADELPHIA 31, TAMPA BAY 9—Donovan McNabb passed for 2 touchdowns and the Eagles' defense recorded 4 interceptions to defeat the Buccaneers in an NFC Wild Card Game in Philadelphia for the second consecutive season. Dexter Jackson's interception and 9-yard return to the Eagles' 39 three plays into the game set up the first of three Martin Gramatica first-half field goals. A 39-yard run by McNabb on the ensuing possession led to David Akers' 26-yard field goal to tie the game, and McNabb's 41-yard pass to Todd Pinkston early in the second quarter set up Chad Lewis' 16-yard scoring catch to give the Eagles a 10-3 lead. With the Eagles leading 10-6, Mark Royals' 28-yard punt to the Buccaneers' 31 with 1:46 left in the half set up McNabb's 23-yard touchdown pass to Duce Staley. The Buccaneers answered quickly, with Brad Johnson's 46-yard pass to Keyshawn Johnson allowing Gramatica to kick his third field goal to trim the deficit to 17-9 at halftime. Correll Buckhalter's 25-yard touchdown run in the third quarter increased the Eagles' lead to 24-9. Troy Vincent's interception in the end zone stopped the Buccaneers' ensuing possession, Brian Dawkins intercepted a pass at the Eagles' 3 with 5:34 left to stop another drive, and Damon Moore's 59-yard interception return for a touchdown with 2:08 remaining iced the game. McNabb was 16 of 25 for 194 yards and 2 touchdowns, with 1 interception. Johnson was 22 of 36 for 202 yards, with 4 interceptions.

Tampa Bay	3	6	0	0	—	9
Philadelphia	3	14	7	7	—	31

TB — FG Gramatica 36
Phil — FG Akers 26
Phil — Lewis 16 pass from McNabb (Akers kick)
TB — FG Gramatica 32
Phil — Staley 23 pass from McNabb (Akers kick)
TB — FG Gramatica 27
Phil — Buckhalter 25 run (Akers kick)
Phil — Moore 59 interception return (Akers kick)

AFC-NFC PRO BOWL AT A GLANCE RESULTS (1971-2002)
Series Tied, 16-16

Year	Date	Winner (Share)	Loser (Share)	Score	Site	Attendance
2002	Feb. 9	AFC ($30,000)	NFC ($15,000)	38-30	Honolulu	50,301
2001	Feb. 4	AFC ($30,000)	NFC ($15,000)	38-17	Honolulu	50,128
2000	Feb. 6	NFC ($25,000)	AFC ($12,500)	51-31	Honolulu	50,112
1999	Feb. 7	AFC ($25,000)	NFC ($12,500)	23-10	Honolulu	50,075
1998	Feb. 1	AFC ($25,000)	NFC ($12,500)	29-24	Honolulu	49,995
1997	Feb. 2	AFC ($20,000)	NFC ($10,000)	26-23 (OT)	Honolulu	50,031
1996	Feb. 4	NFC ($20,000)	AFC ($10,000)	20-13	Honolulu	50,034
1995	Feb. 5	AFC ($20,000)	NFC ($10,000)	41-13	Honolulu	49,121
1994	Feb. 6	NFC ($20,000)	AFC ($10,000)	17-3	Honolulu	50,026
1993	Feb. 7	AFC ($10,000)	NFC ($5,000)	23-20 (OT)	Honolulu	50,007
1992	Feb. 2	NFC ($10,000)	AFC ($5,000)	21-15	Honolulu	50,209
1991	Feb. 3	AFC ($10,000)	NFC ($5,000)	23-21	Honolulu	50,345
1990	Feb. 4	NFC ($10,000)	AFC ($5,000)	27-21	Honolulu	50,445
1989	Jan. 29	NFC ($10,000)	AFC ($5,000)	34-3	Honolulu	50,113
1988	Feb. 7	AFC ($10,000)	NFC ($5,000)	15-6	Honolulu	50,113
1987	Feb. 1	AFC ($10,000)	NFC ($5,000)	10-6	Honolulu	50,101
1986	Feb. 2	NFC ($10,000)	AFC ($5,000)	28-24	Honolulu	50,101
1985	Jan. 27	AFC ($10,000)	NFC ($5,000)	22-14	Honolulu	50,385
1984	Jan. 29	NFC ($10,000)	AFC ($5,000)	45-3	Honolulu	50,445
1983	Feb. 6	NFC ($10,000)	AFC ($5,000)	20-19	Honolulu	49,883
1982	Jan. 31	AFC ($5,000)	NFC ($2,500)	16-13	Honolulu	50,402
1981	Feb. 1	NFC ($5,000)	AFC ($2,500)	21-7	Honolulu	50,360
1980	Jan. 27	NFC ($5,000)	AFC ($2,500)	37-27	Honolulu	49,800
1979	Jan. 29	NFC ($5,000)	AFC ($2,500)	13-7	Los Angeles	46,281
1978	Jan. 23	NFC ($5,000)	AFC ($2,500)	14-13	Tampa	51,337
1977	Jan. 17	AFC ($2,000)	NFC ($1,500)	24-14	Seattle	64,752
1976	Jan. 26	NFC ($2,000)	AFC ($1,500)	23-20	New Orleans	30,546
1975	Jan. 20	NFC ($2,000)	AFC ($1,500)	17-10	Miami	26,484
1974	Jan. 20	AFC ($2,000)	NFC ($1,500)	15-13	Kansas City	66,918
1973	Jan. 21	AFC ($2,000)	NFC ($1,500)	33-28	Dallas	37,091
1972	Jan. 23	AFC ($2,000)	NFC ($1,500)	26-13	Los Angeles	53,647
1971	Jan. 24	NFC ($2,000)	AFC ($1,500)	27-6	Los Angeles	48,222

2002 AFC-NFC PRO BOWL
Aloha Stadium, Honolulu, Hawaii
February 9, 2002, Attendance: 50,301

AFC 38, NFC 30—at Aloha Stadium, attendance 50,301. Rich Gannon passed for 137 yards and 2 touchdowns to become the first player to earn back-to-back Pro Bowl player of the game honors. The game had an inauspicious beginning for Gannon, who fumbled the game's first snap. Hugh Douglas recovered the fumble and returned the ball to the AFC's 2-yard line to set up Ahman Green's touchdown 27 seconds into the game. After a three-and-out series, Kurt Warner's 23-yard pass to David Boston set up David Akers' 29-yard field goal to give the NFC a 10-0 lead. Gannon responded two plays later with a 55-yard touchdown pass to Marvin Harrison. Delta O'Neal's 24-yard interception return to the NFC's 6-yard line moments later set up Curtis Martin's 4-yard touchdown run and gave the AFC a 14-10 lead. After the NFC went three-and-out, the AFC needed just five plays, keyed by Gannon's 30-yard pass to Troy Brown, and capped by Priest Holmes' 39-yard touchdown run to give the AFC its third touchdown in less than six minutes and a 21-10 lead. A 10-play NFC drive led to Akers' second field goal, but Jermaine Lewis' 54-yard kickoff return set up Gannon's 18-yard touchdown pass to Ken Dilger and gave the AFC a 28-10 lead with 12:03 left in the first half. The NFC overcame Shane Lechler's Pro Bowl-record 73-yard punt with Akers' 49-yard field goal just before halftime to cut the deficit to 28-16. Junior Seau's interception at the AFC's 5-yard line early in the fourth quarter thrwarted one NFC rally, but Champ Bailey's interception led to Dono-van McNabb's 8-yard touchdown pass to Terrell Owens to cut the deficit to 28-23 with 8:12 left. Runs of 29 and 16 yards by Corey Dillon led to Jason Elam's 38-yard field goal and, two plays later, Ty Law intercepted McNabb at the NFC 44-yard line, returned the ball to the NFC 13 before lateralling to Ray Lewis, who dragged three players into the end zone for a 38-23 lead with 2:49 remaining. McNabb's 15-yard touchdown pass to Garrison Hearst with 1:32 left cut the deficit to 38-30, but Rod Woodson recovered the ensuing onside kick to clinch the victory. Gannon was 8 of 10 for 137 yards and 2 touchdowns. Mc-Nabb was 12 of 25 for 149 yards and 2 touchdowns, with 2 interceptions, to lead the NFC. Owens had 8 receptions for 122 yards and 1 touchdown.

AFC (38)	Offense	NFC (30)
Marvin Harrison (Indianapolis)	WR	David Boston (Arizona)
Jonathan Ogden (Baltimore)	LT	James Williams (Chicago)
Alan Faneca (Pittsburgh)	LG	Ray Brown (San Francisco)
Kevin Mawae (N.Y. Jets)	C	Olin Kreutz (Chicago)
Will Shields (Kansas City)	RG	Ron Stone (N.Y. Giants)
Lincoln Kennedy (Oakland)	RT	Chris Samuels (Washington)
Shannon Sharpe (Baltimore)	TE	Bubba Franks (Green Bay)
Tim Brown (Oakland)	WR	Tim Owens (San Francisco)
Rich Gannon (Oakland)	QB	Kurt Warner (St. Louis)
Larry Centers (Buffalo)	FB	Mike Alstott (Tampa Bay)
Curtis Martin (N.Y. Jets)	RB	Marshall Faulk (St. Louis)
	Defense	
John Abraham (N.Y. Jets)	LE	Hugh Douglas (Philadelphia)
Sam Adams (Baltimore)	LT	Bryant Young (San Francisco)
John Randle (Seattle)	RT	La'Roi Glover (New Orleans)
Marcellus Wiley	RE	Michael Strahan

(San Diego)		(N.Y. Giants)
Jamir Miller	LOLB	LaVar Arrington
(Cleveland)		(Washington)
Ray Lewis	MLB	Brian Urlacher
(Baltimore)		(Chicago)
Jason Gildon	ROLB	Jessie Armstead
(Pittsburgh)		(N.Y. Giants)
Ryan McNeil	LCB	Ronde Barber
(San Diego)		(Tampa Bay)
Deltha O'Neal	RCB	Aeneas Williams
(Denver)		(St. Louis)
Rodney Harrison	SS	Sammy Knight
(San Diego)		(New Orleans)
Rod Woodson	FS	Brian Dawkins
(Baltimore)		(Philadelphia)

SUBSTITUTIONS

NFC—Offense: G—Adam Timmerman (St. Louis). T—Tra Thomas (Philadelphia). C—Jeremy Newberry (San Francisco). TE—Byron Chamberlain (Minnesota). WR—Torry Holt (St. Louis), Keyshawn Johnson (Tampa Bay). RB—Ahman Green (Green Bay), Garrison Hearst (San Francisco). QB—Jeff Garcia (San Francisco), Donovan McNabb (Philadelphia). P—Todd Sauerbrun (Carolina). K—David Akers (Philadelphia). KR—Steve Smith (Carolina). Defense: DT—Ted Washington (Chicago). DE—Robert Porcher (Detroit). LB—Keith Brooking (Atlanta), Dexter Coakley (Dallas), Jeremiah Trotter (Philadelphia). DB—Champ Bailey (Washington), John Lynch (Tampa Bay). ST—Larry Whigham (Chicago).

AFC—Offense: G—Ruben Brown (Buffalo). T—Walter Jones (Seattle). C—Bruce Matthews (Tennessee). TE—Ken Dilger (Indianapolis). WR—Troy Brown (New England), Hines Ward (Pittsburgh). RB—Corey Dillon (Cincinnati), Priest Holmes (Kansas City). QB—Tom Brady (New England), Kordell Stewart (Pittsburgh). P—Shane Lechler (Oakland). K—Jason Elam (Denver). KR—Jermaine Lewis (Baltimore). Defense: DT—Gary Walker (Jacksonville). DE—Jevon Kearse (Tennessee). LB—Kendrell Bell (Pittsburgh), Junior Seau (San Diego), Al Wilson (Denver). DB—Ty Law (New England), Lawyer Milloy (New England). ST—Ian Gold (Denver).

HEAD COACHES

AFC—Bill Cowher (Pittsburgh)
NFC—Andy Reid (Philadelphia)

OFFICIALS

Referee—Ron Blum. Umpire—Neil Gereb. Side Judge—Carl Cheffers. Head Linesman—Earnie Frantz. Back Judge—Perry Paganelli. Field Judge—Lloyd McPeters. Line Judge—Jeff Bergman.

| AFC | 21 | 7 | 0 | 10 | — | 38 |
| NFC | 13 | 3 | 0 | 14 | — | 30 |

NFC — Green 2 run (Akers kick)
NFC — FG Akers 29

AFC — Harrison 55 pass from Gannon (Elam kick)
AFC — Martin 4 run (Elam kick)
AFC — Holmes 39 run (Elam kick)
NFC — FG Akers 41
AFC — Dilger 18 pass from Gannon (Elam kick)
NFC — FG Akers 49
NFC — Owens 8 pass from McNabb (Akers kick)
AFC — FG Elam 38
AFC — R. Lewis 13 lateral from Law (Elam kick)
NFC — Hearst 15 pass from McNabb (Akers kick)

TEAM STATISTICS	AFC	NFC
Total First Downs	19	23
Rushing	10	4
Passing	9	14
Penalty	0	5
Total Net Yardage	398	346
Total Offensive Plays	60	72
Avg. Gain Per Offensive Play	6.6	4.8
Rushes	31	12
Yards Gained Rushing (Net)	201	36
Avg. Yards per Rush	6.5	3.0
Passes Attempted	28	58
Passes Completed	16	29
Had Intercepted	1	3
Tackled Attempting to Pass	1	2
Yards Lost Attempting to Pass	7	13
Yards Gained Passing (Net)	197	310
Punts	4	4
Avg. Distance	60.8	44.8
Punt Returns	1	2
Punt Return Yardage	8	65
Kickoff Returns	6	7
Kickoff Return Yardage	187	108
Interception Return Yardage	82	44
Total Return Yardage	277	217
Fumbles	1	4
Fumbles Lost	1	1
Own Fumbles Recovered	0	3
Opponent Fumbles Recovered	1	1
Penalties	7	4
Yards Penalized	91	25
Field Goals	1	3
Field Goals Attempted	3	4
Third-Down Efficiency	5/13	4/14
Fourth-Down Efficiency	0/0	1/1
Time of Possession	31:18	28:42

INDIVIDUAL STATISTICS

RUSHING: AFC: Holmes 7-77-1, Dillon 6-58-0, Martin 8-44-1, Stewart 2-20-0, Centers 3-5-0, Brady 3-(-3)-0, Gannon 1-0-0, Ward 1-0-0. NFC: Faulk 5-12-0, McNabb 1-12-0, Alstott 2-11-0, Garcia 1-1-0, Green 2-0-1, Warner 1-0-0.
PASSING: AFC: Gannon 10-8-137-2-0, Stewart 12-6-45-0-0, Brady 5-2-22-0-1, Martin 1-0-0-0-0. NFC: Warner 14-6-63-0-1, McNabb 25-12-149-2-2, Garcia 19-11-111-0-0.
RECEIVING: AFC: Harrison 4-80-1, Holmes 3-7-0, Tr. Brown 2-41-0, J. Lewis 2-27-0, Ward 2-17-0, Centers 2-14-0, Dilger 1-18-1. NFC: Owens 8-122-1, Johnson 6-50-0, Boston 3-39-0, Hearst

3-37-1, Green 3-29-0, Chamberlain 2-22-0, Faulk 2-13-0, J. Lewis 1-7-0, Alstott 1-4-0.
KICKOFF RETURNS: AFC: J. Lewis 4-133-0, Tr. Brown 2-54-0. NFC: Smith 6-93-0, Trotter 1-13-0.
PUNT RETURNS: AFC: J. Lewis 1-8-0. NFC: Smith 2-65-0.
PUNTING: AFC: Lechler 4-243-60.8. NFC: Sauerbrun 4-179-44.8.
INTERCEPTIONS: AFC: Law 1-31-0, O'Neal 1-24-0, Seau 1-14-0, R. Lewis 0-13-1. NFC: Bailey 1-44-0.
SACKS: AFC: Walker, Wiley. NFC: Douglas.

2001 AFC-NFC PRO BOWL

Aloha Stadium, Honolulu, Hawaii
February 4, 2001, Attendance: 50,128
AFC 38, NFC 17—Rich Gannon completed 12 of 14 passes for 160 yards during the game's first two possessions to win player of the game honors and lead the AFC to victory. Gannon's touchdown passes capped 87- and 90-yard drives and staked the AFC to a 14-0 lead. Gannon, who was still recovering from a separated non-throwing shoulder suffered in the AFC Championship Game, was replaced by Peyton Manning. The Colts' quarterback engineered a scoring drive, capped by Matt Stover's field goal, to give the AFC a 17-0 lead early in the second quarter. At that point, the AFC had 14 first downs and 231 yards of offense while limiting the NFC to no first downs and 6 yards. Jimmy Smith caught a 2-yard touchdown pass 54 seconds before halftime to give the AFC a 24-3 lead. Third-quarter touchdown passes by Donovan McNabb and Daunte Culpepper trimmed the AFC's lead to 31-17, but Jason Taylor batted down Culpepper's fourth-and-1 pass early in the fourth quarter, and Edgerrin James' 20-yard touchdown run a few plays later iced the game. The NFC attempted a Pro Bowl record 56 pass attempts, and the two teams combined for a Pro Bowl record 98 pass attempts. Tony Gonzalez had 6 receptions for 108 yards, all in the first half, for the AFC. Torry Holt had 7 receptions for 103 yards. Smith's touchdown reception gives him 5 for his career, an AFC-NFC Pro Bowl record.

| NFC | 0 | 3 | 14 | 0 | — | 17 |
| AFC | 14 | 10 | 7 | 7 | — | 38 |

AFC — Gonzalez 8 pass from Gannon (Stover kick)
AFC — Harrison 16 pass from Gannon (Stover kick)
AFC — FG Stover 29
NFC — FG Gramatica 48
AFC — J. Smith 2 pass from Manning (Stover kick)
NFC — Owens 17 pass from McNabb (Gramatica kick)
AFC — Harrison 24 pass from Manning (Stover kick)
NFC — Holt 20 pass from Culpepper (Gramatica kick)
AFC — James 20 run (Stover kick)

2000 AFC-NFC PRO BOWL

Aloha Stadium, Honolulu, Hawaii
February 6, 2000, Attendance: 50,112
NFC 51, AFC 31—Randy Moss earned player of the game honors by setting records with 9 receptions for 212 yards as the NFC defeated the AFC in the highest-scoring Pro Bowl ever. Aeneas Williams intercepted Peyton Manning's pass and raced 62 yards down the left sideline to give the NFC an early 7-0 lead. Kurt Warner's 48-yard pass to Moss on the NFC's first possession set up Jason Hanson's first field goal. Mike Alstott and Jimmy Smith each scored twice in the first half, and Michael Bates' 66-yard kickoff return led to Hanson's Pro Bowl-record tying 51-yard field goal as the half expired to give the NFC a 27-21 lead. Alstott's third touchdown increased the NFC's lead to 37-21, and Derrick Brooks' interception of Mark Brunell and 20-yard return staked the NFC to a 44-24 lead with 11:12 left. The AFC responded with Manning's 52-yard touchdown pass to Smith with 6:30 remaining, but Steve Beuerlein found Moss with a 25-yard scoring pass with 1:05 left to finish the scoring. Warner led the three NFC quarterbacks by completing 8 of 11 passes for 123 yards. Alstott led all rushers with 13 carries for 67 yards. The NFC forced 6 turnovers. Manning was 17 of 23 for 270 yards and 2 touchdowns, with 2 interceptions. Smith had 8 receptions for 119 yards. The previous record, 64 points, was set in 1980.

AFC	7	14	0	10	—	31
NFC	10	17	10	14	—	51

NFC	— A. Williams 62 interception return (Hanson kick)
NFC	— FG Hanson 21
AFC	— J. Smith 5 pass from Brunell (Mare kick)
NFC	— Alstott 1 run (Hanson kick)
AFC	— Gonzalez 10 pass from Gannon (Mare kick)
NFC	— Alstott 3 run (Hanson kick)
AFC	— J. Smith 21 pass from Manning (Mare kick)
NFC	— FG Hanson 51
NFC	— Alstott 1 run (Hanson kick)
NFC	— FG Hanson 23
AFC	— FG Mare 33
NFC	— Brooks 20 interception return (Hanson kick)
AFC	— J. Smith 52 pass from Manning (Mare kick)
NFC	— Moss 25 pass from Beuerlein (Hanson kick)

1999 AFC-NFC PRO BOWL

Aloha Stadium, Honolulu, Hawaii
February 7, 1999, Attendance: 50,075
AFC 23, NFC 10—John Elway, appearing in uniform on a football field for the final time, drove the AFC to its initial touchdown and then watched a strong defensive effort as the AFC won the Pro Bowl for the third consecutive season. Elway

capped a game-opening 61-yard drive with a touchdown pass to Sam Gash. The AFC led 10-3 late in the first half when Deion Sanders intercepted a Vinny Testaverde pass at the NFC's 10 and raced downfield, only to be caught by Ed McCaffrey at the AFC 3-yard line as the half expired. The NFC drove into AFC territory early in the second half, but Ty Law thwarted the NFC's spirits with a 67-yard interception return for a touchdown to give the AFC a 17-3 lead with 9:42 left in the third quarter. The NFC reached the end zone three minutes later as Emmitt Smith scored, but the AFC responded with a field goal on its ensuing possession. Jason Elam's third field goal with 1:02 remaining finished the scoring. Elway played just one drive and was 4 of 5 for 55 yards and 1 touchdown. Keyshawn Johnson had 7 catches for 87 yards and shared player of the game honors with Law. Chandler completed 9 of 25 passes for 133 yards en route to leading the NFC to its only touchdown. Randy Moss had 7 catches for 108 yards.

NFC	3	0	7	0	—	10
AFC	7	3	10	3	—	23

AFC	— Gash 3 pass from Elway (Elam kick)
NFC	— FG Anderson 23
AFC	— FG Elam 23
AFC	— Law 67 interception return (Elam kick)
NFC	— E. Smith 3 run (Anderson kick)
AFC	— FG Elam 46
AFC	— FG Elam 26

1998 AFC-NFC PRO BOWL

Aloha Stadium, Honolulu, Hawaii
February 1, 1998, Attendance: 49,995
AFC 29, NFC 24—Warren Moon guided the AFC to points on all three of his drives, including the winning touchdown from 1 yard with 1:49 left as the AFC scored the game's final 15 points to beat the NFC. Steve Young threw a 22-yard touchdown pass to Herman Moore to cap the game's opening drive and give the NFC a 7-0 lead. Late in the first quarter, Mark Brunell threw a 17-yard touchdown pass to Andre Rison to tie the game. Both touchdown passes came on third-and-8 plays. The NFC responded with a 7-play, 71-yard drive capped by Young's 36-yard touchdown pass to Rob Moore. Trent Dilfer guided the NFC to its third touchdown, keyed by a 21-yard pass to Irving Fryar and 23-yard pass to Mike Alstott, and capped by Dorsey Levens' 12-yard touchdown run with 1:36 left in the half to give the NFC a 21-7 lead. The NFC had a chance to pad its lead on its first possession of the second half, but Jason Hanson missed a 44-yard field goal. The AFC bounced back with a 10-play, 65-yard drive that culminated with Drew Bledsoe's 14-yard touchdown pass to Jimmy Smith late in the third quarter. After Hanson's

35-yard field goal gave the NFC a 24-14 lead with 13:42 left, Moon entered the game and drove the AFC into field-goal range, where Mike Hollis drilled a 48-yard attempt with 8:51 left. Attempting to grind out the clock, Warrick Dunn fumbled, and Darryl Williams recovered at the AFC's 49 with 3:03 remaining. After a holding penalty moved the AFC back 10 yards, Moon fired a 57-yard pass to Tim Brown to set up Eddie George's 4-yard run with 2:31 left. The AFC went for the lead instead of a tie, but Moon's pass to Rison fell incomplete. However, the AFC got the ball back when Chris Chandler fumbled the snap on the NFC's first play, and Michael Sinclair recovered at the NFC's 16 with 2:19 left. Three runs by George set up Moon's winning sneak with 1:49 remaining. Moon's 2-point conversion pass to Brown was incomplete, keeping the AFC's lead at 29-24. The NFC was unable to move beyond its own 31-yard line in the final moments, and the AFC prevailed. Tim Brown had 5 receptions for 129 yards. Moon, who was 4 of 8 for 89 yards, earned player of the game honors.

AFC	7	0	7	15	—	29
NFC	7	14	0	3	—	24

NFC	— H. Moore 22 pass from Young (Hanson kick)
AFC	— Rison 17 pass from Brunell (Hollis kick)
NFC	— R. Moore 36 pass from Young (Hanson kick)
NFC	— Levens 12 run (Hanson kick)
AFC	— J. Smith 14 pass from Bledsoe (Hollis kick)
NFC	— FG Hanson 35
AFC	— FG Hollis 48
AFC	— George 4 run (pass failed)
AFC	— Moon 1 run (pass failed)

1997 AFC-NFC PRO BOWL

Aloha Stadium, Honolulu, Hawaii
February 2, 1997, Attendance: 50,031
AFC 26, NFC 23 (OT)—Cary Blanchard's 37-yard field goal 8:16 into overtime gave the AFC a 26-23 victory. The field goal was an ironic ending to a game that saw Blanchard and NFC kicker John Kasay, who each broke the previous single-season record of 35 field goals, combine to miss 5 of 8 field-goal attempts. The NFC scored on its first two possessions, with Vikings guard Randall McDaniel, who lined up as a fullback, scoring his first professional touchdown to give the NFC a 9-0 lead. However, the follies of the kicking unit began as holder Matt Turk muffed the snap on the extra point attempt. Blanchard booted a 28-yard field goal with 27 seconds left in the half to cut the NFC's lead to 9-3. In the third quarter, Barry Sanders scored from 6 yards out, but Kerry Collins was sacked on the 2-point attempt. A 41-yard pass from Drew Bledsoe to Tony Martin led to Curtis Martin's 3-yard run, and after Ashley Ambrose ran an interception back 54 yards for a touch-

down 11 seconds into the fourth quarter, the AFC found itself with a 16-15 lead. The NFC drove for more than six minutes, only to have Kasay miss a 40-yard field goal attempt. After an AFC punt, Cris Carter caught a 47-yard touchdown bomb from Gus Frerotte to put the NFC ahead 23-16. After each team punted, the AFC got the ball on its own 20-yard line with 55 seconds left. Mark Brunell hit Tim Brown with an 80-yard bomb down the right sideline to tie the game with 44 seconds left. Wesley Walls caught a 33-yard pass to give the NFC a chance to win in regulation, but Kasay missed a 39-yard attempt and the game went to overtime. The AFC won the overtime toss, but Blanchard missed a 41-yard field goal attempt. The NFC had to punt after three plays, and Brunell hit Ben Coates with a 43-yard pass on the AFC's first play. After three running plays failed to gain a first down, Blanchard trotted onto the field and made the game-winning kick. The teams combined for a Pro Bowl record 962 total yards. Brunell, who completed 12 of 22 pass attempts for 236 yards, was selected as the player of the game.

AFC	0	3	7	13	3	— 26
NFC	9	0	6	8	0	— 23

NFC — FG Kasay 20
NFC — R. McDaniel 5 pass from Favre (muffed snap)
AFC — FG Blanchard 28
NFC — Sanders 6 run (pass failed)
AFC — Martin 3 run (Blanchard kick)
AFC — Ambrose 54 interception return (pass failed)
NFC — Carter 53 pass from Frerotte (Walls pass from Frerotte)
AFC — T. Brown 80 pass from Brunell (Blanchard kick)
AFC — FG Blanchard 37

1996 AFC-NFC PRO BOWL
Aloha Stadium, Honolulu, Hawaii
February 4, 1996, Attendance: 50,034
NFC 20, AFC 13—Jerry Rice had 6 receptions for 82 yards and 1 touchdown to earn player of the game honors in the NFC's victory. The 49ers' wide receiver, who was named to the Pro Bowl for the tenth consecutive year, caught a 1-yard touchdown pass from Packers quarterback Brett Favre 1:41 into the second quarter to cap an 80-yard drive and give the NFC the lead for good at 10-7. The AFC had taken a 7-0 lead 2:26 into the game when Bengals quarterback Jeff Blake connected with Steelers wide receiver Yancey Thigpen on a Pro Bowl-record 93-yard touchdown pass. The NFC increased its advantage to 20-7 at halftime on Redskins linebacker Ken Harvey's 36-yard interception return for a touchdown and Falcons kicker Morten Andersen's 24-yard field goal. The AFC trimmed its deficit to 20-13 when Colts quarterback Jim Harbaugh teamed with Patriots running back Curtis Martin on a 17-yard

touchdown pass in the final minute of the third quarter, but its bid to win or tie was rebuffed twice in the final minutes of the fourth quarter. First, 49ers safety Tim McDonald intercepted Harbaugh's pass in the end zone with 1:50 remaining. Then, after the AFC forced a punt and got the ball back near midfield, Harbaugh drove his team to the NFC's 9-yard line in the closing seconds. But he spiked the ball once to stop the clock and threw 3 consecutive incompletions as time ran out. The AFC outgained the NFC 390 total yards to 287, but its quarterbacks suffered 4 interceptions, including 3 off Harbaugh, the NFL's leading passer during the regular season. The NFC raised its edge to 15-11 in Pro Bowl games since the AFL-NFL merger in 1970.

NFC	3	17	0	0	— 20
AFC	7	0	6	0	— 13

AFC — Thigpen 93 pass from Blake (Elam kick)
NFC — FG Andersen 36
NFC — Rice 1 pass from Favre (Andersen kick)
NFC — Harvey 36 interception return (Andersen kick)
NFC — FG Andersen 24
AFC — Martin 17 pass from Harbaugh (kick failed)

1995 AFC-NFC PRO BOWL
Aloha Stadium, Honolulu, Hawaii
February 5, 1995, Attendance: 49,121
AFC 41, NFC 13—Colts rookie Marshall Faulk rushed for a Pro Bowl-record 180 yards to key the AFC's rout of the NFC. Faulk, who earned the Dan McGuire Trophy as the player of the game, averaged nearly 14 yards on his 13 carries and shattered the previous rushing mark of 112 yards set by O.J. Simpson in the 1973 game. Faulk's 49-yard touchdown run from punt formation in the fourth quarter was the longest in Pro Bowl history. The Seahawks' Chris Warren added 127 yards on 14 carries as the AFC amassed records for rushing yards (400) and total yards (552). Steelers tight end Eric Green caught 2 touchdown passes for the victors. The NFC managed only 196 total yards, a large chunk coming when 49ers quarterback Steve Young and Vikings wide receiver Cris Carter teamed on a 51-yard touchdown pass in the first quarter. That gave the NFC a 10-0 advantage, but the AFC rallied in the second quarter and took the lead for good when the Browns' Leroy Hoard scored on a 4-yard touchdown run 2:07 before halftime.

AFC	0	17	3	21	— 41
NFC	10	0	3	0	— 13

NFC — FG Reveiz 28
NFC — Carter 51 pass from Young (Reveiz kick)
AFC — Green 22 pass from Elway (Carney kick)
AFC — FG Carney 22
AFC — Hoard 4 run (Carney kick)

NFC — FG Reveiz 49
AFC — FG Carney 23
AFC — Warren 11 run (Carney kick)
AFC — Green 16 pass from Hostetler (Carney kick)
AFC — Faulk 49 run (Carney kick)

1994 AFC-NFC PRO BOWL
Aloha Stadium, Honolulu, Hawaii
February 6, 1994, Attendance: 50,026
NFC 17, AFC 3—The NFC converted a blocked punt and a fumble recovery into touchdowns just 2:20 apart in the second half of its victory over the AFC. With the score tied 3-3 late in the third quarter, Saints linebacker Renaldo Turnbull deflected a punt by the Oilers' Greg Montgomery, and the NFC took possession at the AFC's 48-yard line. A 32-yard pass from Bobby Hebert to Falcons teammate Andre Rison positioned Rams running back Jerome Bettis for a 4-yard touchdown run with 1:27 left in the third quarter. Moments later, Rams defensive tackle Sean Gilbert recovered a fumble by Oilers quarterback Warren Moon at the AFC's 19. Hebert then teamed with the Vikings' Cris Carter on a 15-yard touchdown pass 53 seconds into the fourth period. The NFC kept the AFC out of the end zone by maintaining possession for more than 38 minutes and forcing 6 turnovers. Rison earned the Dan McGuire Trophy as the player of the game by catching 6 passes for 86 yards. The victory was the fourth in the last six years for the NFC, which leads the series 14-10.

NFC	3	0	7	7	— 17
AFC	0	3	0	0	— 3

NFC — FG Johnson 35
AFC — FG Anderson 25
NFC — Bettis 4 run (Johnson kick)
NFC — Carter 15 pass from Hebert (Johnson kick)

1993 AFC-NFC PRO BOWL
Aloha Stadium, Honolulu, Hawaii
February 7, 1993, Attendance: 50,007
AFC 23, NFC 20—Nick Lowery's 33-yard field goal 4:09 into overtime gave the American Conference all-stars an unlikely 23-20 victory over the National Conference. Despite being overwhelmed by the NFC in first downs (30-9), and total yards (471-114), the AFC won because it forced 6 turnovers, blocked a pair of field goals (1 of which was returned for a touchdown), and returned an interception for a score. Special-teams star Steve Tasker of the Bills earned the Dan McGuire Trophy as the player of the game for making 4 tackles, forcing a fumble, and blocking a field goal. The block came with eight minutes left in regulation and the game tied at 13-13. The Raiders' Terry McDaniel picked up the loose ball and ran 28 yards for a touchdown and a 20-13 AFC lead. The NFC rallied behind 49ers quarterback Steve Young, whose fourth-down, 23-yard touchdown pass to Giants running

back Rodney Hampton tied the game at 20-20 with 10 seconds left in regulation. Young completed 18 of 32 passes for 196 yards but was intercepted 3 times and lost a fumble when sacked in overtime. Raiders defensive end Howie Long fell on that fumble at the NFC 28-yard line, and five plays later, Lowery converted the winning field goal.

AFC	0	10	3	7	3	—	23
NFC	3	10	0	7	0	—	20

NFC — FG Andersen 27
AFC — Seau 31 interception return (Lowery kick)
NFC — FG Andersen 37
NFC — Irvin 9 pass from Aikman (Andersen kick)
AFC — FG Lowery 42
AFC — FG Lowery 29
AFC — McDaniel 28 blocked field goal return (Lowery kick)
NFC — Hampton 23 pass from Young (Andersen kick)
AFC — FG Lowery 33

1992 AFC-NFC PRO BOWL
Aloha Stadium, Honolulu, Hawaii
February 2, 1992, Attendance: 50,209
NFC 21, AFC 15—Atlanta's Chris Miller threw an 11-yard touchdown pass to San Francisco's Jerry Rice with 4:04 remaining in the game to lift the NFC over the AFC. It was the NFC's thirteenth win in the 22-game series. The AFC had taken a 15-14 lead when the Raiders' Jeff Jaeger kicked a 27-yard field goal 1:49 into the fourth quarter. But the NFC, aided by a key roughing-the-passer penalty on a third-down incompletion from the AFC 24-yard line, drove 85 yards for the winning score. The Cowboys' Michael Irvin, playing in his first Pro Bowl, caught 8 passes for 125 yards, including a 13-yard touchdown in the first quarter, and was named the player of the game. Rice had 7 catches for 77 yards. Mark Rypien of Washington, the Super Bowl most valuable player one week earlier, completed 11 of 18 passes for 165 yards and 2 touchdowns for the NFC, including a 35-yard pass to Redskins teammate Gary Clark just 26 seconds before halftime. Miller completed 7 of his 10 attempts for 85 yards.

NFC	7	7	0	7	—	21
AFC	7	5	0	3	—	15

AFC — Clayton 4 pass from Kelly (Jaeger kick)
NFC — Irvin 13 pass from Rypien (Lohmiller kick)
AFC — Safety, Townsend tackled Byner in end zone
AFC — FG Jaeger 48
NFC — Clark 35 pass from Rypien (Lohmiller kick)
AFC — FG Jaeger 27
NFC — Rice 11 pass from Miller (Lohmiller kick)

1991 AFC-NFC PRO BOWL
Aloha Stadium, Honolulu, Hawaii
February 3, 1991, Attendance: 50,345
AFC 23, NFC 21—Buffalo's Jim Kelly and Houston's Ernest Givins combined for a 13-yard scoring pass late in the fourth quarter to rally the AFC over the NFC. Phoenix rookie Johnny Johnson scored on runs of 1 and 9 yards to put the NFC ahead 14-3 in the third quarter. Buffalo's Andre Reed, who led all receivers with 4 catches for 80 yards, caught a 20-yard scoring reception from Kelly early in the fourth quarter to move the AFC to within 1 point. Barry Sanders ran 22 yards for a touchdown to increase the NFC's lead to 21-13. Miami's Jeff Cross blocked a 46-yard field-goal attempt by New Orleans' Morten Andersen with seven seconds remaining to preserve the win. Buffalo's Bruce Smith recorded 3 sacks and also had a blocked field goal. Kelly, who completed 13 of 19 passes for 210 yards and 2 touchdowns, was presented the Dan McGuire Award as player of the game. The AFC's victory narrowed the NFC's Pro Bowl series lead to 12-9.

AFC	3	0	3	17	—	23
NFC	0	7	7	7	—	21

AFC — FG Lowery 26
NFC — J. Johnson 1 run (Andersen kick)
AFC — FG Lowery 43
NFC — J. Johnson 9 run (Andersen kick)
AFC — Reed 20 pass from Kelly (Lowery kick)
NFC — Sanders 22 run (Andersen kick)
AFC — FG Lowery 34
AFC — Givins 13 pass from Kelly (Lowery kick)

1990 AFC-NFC PRO BOWL
Aloha Stadium, Honolulu, Hawaii
February 4, 1990, Attendance: 50,445
NFC 27, AFC 21—The NFC captured its second straight Pro Bowl as the defense accounted for a pair of touchdowns and forced 5 turnovers before the eleventh consecutive sellout crowd at Aloha Stadium. The AFC held a 7-6 halftime edge on a 1-yard scoring run by Christian Okoye of the Chiefs. The NFC then rallied with 21 unanswered points in the third quarter. David Meggett of the Giants began the comeback with an 11-yard touchdown reception from Philadelphia's Randall Cunningham. The Rams' Jerry Gray followed with a 51-yard interception return for a score and the Vikings' Keith Millard added an 8-yard fumble return for a touchdown four minutes later to give the NFC a commanding 27-7 lead. Seattle's Dave Krieg rallied the AFC with a 5-yard touchdown pass to Miami's Ferrell Edmunds. Cleveland's Mike Johnson then returned an interception 22 yards for a score to pull the AFC to within 27-21. Gray, who was credited with 7 tackles,

was given the Dan McGuire Award as player of the game. Krieg led all quarterbacks by completing 15 of 23 for 148 yards and 1 touchdown. Buffalo's Thurman Thomas topped all receivers with 5 catches for 47 yards, while Indianapolis' Eric Dickerson led all rushers with 46 yards on 15 carries. The win gave the NFC a 12-8 advantage in Pro Bowl games since 1971.

NFC	3	3	21	0	—	27
AFC	0	7	0	14	—	21

NFC — FG Murray 23
NFC — FG Murray 41
AFC — Okoye 1 run (Treadwell kick)
NFC — Meggett 11 pass from Cunningham (Murray kick)
NFC — Gray 51 interception return (Murray kick)
NFC — Millard 8 fumble recovery return (Murray kick)
AFC — Edmunds 5 pass from Krieg (Treadwell kick)
AFC — M. Johnson 22 interception return (Treadwell kick)

1989 AFC-NFC PRO BOWL
Aloha Stadium, Honolulu, Hawaii
January 29, 1989, Attendance: 50,113
NFC 34, AFC 3—The NFC scored 34 unanswered points to snap a two-game losing streak to the AFC before the tenth straight sellout crowd in Honolulu's Aloha Stadium. Bills kicker Scott Norwood provided the AFC's only points on a 38-yard field goal 6:23 into the game. Touchdown runs by Dallas' Herschel Walker (4 yards) and Atlanta's John Settle (1) brought the NFC a 14-3 halftime lead. Walker added a 7-yard scoring run, the Saints' Morten Andersen kicked field goals of 27 and 51 yards, and Los Angeles Rams' wide receiver Henry Ellard caught an 8-yard scoring pass from Minnesota quarterback Wade Wilson in the second half to complete the scoring. Chicago running back Neal Anderson and Philadelphia quarterback Randall Cunningham, who were both appearing in their first Pro Bowl, also played major roles in the NFC's victory. Anderson rushed 13 times for 85 yards and had 2 receptions for 17. Cunningham, who was voted the game's outstanding player, completed 10 of 14 passes for 63 yards and rushed for 49 yards. The NFC, which had 5 takeaways, outgained the AFC 355 yards to 167 and held a time-of-possession advantage of 35:18 to 24:42. Houston quarterback Warren Moon completed 13 of 20 passes for 134 yards for the AFC. The win gave the NFC an 11-8 advantage in Pro Bowl games.

AFC	3	0	0	0	—	3
NFC	7	7	10	10	—	34

AFC — FG Norwood 38
NFC — Walker 4 run (Andersen kick)
NFC — Settle 1 run (Andersen kick)
NFC — FG Andersen 27
NFC — Walker 7 run (Andersen kick)
NFC — FG Andersen 51

NFC — Ellard 8 pass from Wilson
(Andersen kick)

1988 AFC-NFC PRO BOWL
Aloha Stadium, Honolulu, Hawaii
February 7, 1988, Attendance: 50,113
AFC 15, NFC 6—Led by a tenacious pass rush, the AFC defeated the NFC for the second consecutive year before the ninth straight sellout crowd in Honolulu's Aloha Stadium. Buffalo quarterback Jim Kelly scored the game's lone touchdown on a 1-yard run for a 7-6 halftime lead. Colts kicker Dean Biasucci added field goals from 37 and 30 yards to complete the AFC's scoring. Saints kicker Morten Andersen had 25- and 36-yard field goals to account for the NFC's points. AFC defenders held the NFC to 213 yards and recorded 8 sacks. Bills defensive end Bruce Smith, who had 2 sacks among his 5 tackles, was voted the game's outstanding player. Oilers running back Mike Rozier led all rushers with 49 yards on 9 carries. Jets wide receiver Al Toon had 5 receptions for 75 yards. The AFC generated 341 yards total offense and held a time-of-possession advantage of 34:14 to 25:46. By winning, the AFC cut the NFC's lead in the Pro Bowl series to 10-8.

NFC	0	6	0	0 —	6
AFC	0	7	6	2 —	15

NFC — FG Andersen 25
AFC — Kelly 1 run (Biasucci kick)
NFC — FG Andersen 36
AFC — FG Biasucci 37
AFC — FG Biasucci 30
AFC — Safety, Montana forced out of end zone

1987 AFC-NFC PRO BOWL
Aloha Stadium, Honolulu, Hawaii
February 1, 1987, Attendance: 50,101
AFC 10, NFC 6—The AFC defeated the NFC in the lowest-scoring game in AFC-NFC Pro Bowl history. The AFC took a 10-0 halftime lead on Broncos quarterback John Elway's 10-yard touchdown pass to Raiders tight end Todd Christensen and Patriots kicker Tony Franklin's 26-yard field goal. The AFC defense made the lead stand by forcing the NFC to settle for a pair of field goals from 38 and 19 yards by Saints kicker Morten Andersen after the NFC had first downs at the AFC 31-, 7-, 16-, 15-, 5-, and 7-yard lines. Both AFC scores were set up by fumble recoveries by Seahawks linebacker Fredd Young and Dolphins linebacker John Offerdahl, respectively. Eagles defensive end Reggie White, who tied a Pro Bowl record with 4 sacks among his 7 solo tackles, was voted the game's outstanding player. The AFC victory cut the NFC's lead in the Pro Bowl series to 10-7.

AFC	7	3	0	0 —	10
NFC	0	0	3	3 —	6

AFC — Christensen 10 pass from Elway (Franklin kick)
AFC — FG Franklin 26

NFC — FG Andersen 38
NFC — FG Andersen 19

1986 AFC-NFC PRO BOWL
Aloha Stadium, Honolulu, Hawaii
February 2, 1986, Attendance: 50,101
NFC 28, AFC 24—New York Giants quarterback Phil Simms brought the NFC back from a 24-7 halftime deficit to defeat the AFC. Simms, who completed 15 of 27 passes for 212 yards and 3 touchdowns, was named the most valuable player of the game. The AFC had taken its first-half lead behind a 2-yard run by Los Angeles Raiders running back Marcus Allen, who also threw a 51-yard scoring pass to San Diego wide receiver Wes Chandler, an 11-yard touchdown catch by Pittsburgh wide receiver Louis Lipps, and a 34-yard field goal by Steelers kicker Gary Anderson. Minnesota's Joey Browner accounted for the NFC's only score before halftime on a 48-yard interception return. After intermission, the NFC blanked the AFC while scoring 3 touchdowns via a 15-yard catch by Washington wide receiver Art Monk, a 2-yard reception by Dallas tight end Doug Cosbie, and a 15-yard catch by Tampa Bay tight end Jimmie Giles with 2:47 remaining in the game. The victory gave the NFC a 10-6 Pro Bowl record against the AFC.

NFC	0	7	7	14 —	28
AFC	7	17	0	0 —	24

AFC — Allen 2 run (Anderson kick)
NFC — Browner 48 interception return (Andersen kick)
AFC — Chandler 51 pass from Allen (Anderson kick)
AFC — FG Anderson 34
AFC — Lipps 11 pass from O'Brien (Anderson kick)
NFC — Monk 15 pass from Simms (Andersen kick)
NFC — Cosbie 2 pass from Simms (Andersen kick)
NFC — Giles 15 pass from Simms (Andersen kick)

1985 AFC-NFC PRO BOWL
Aloha Stadium, Honolulu, Hawaii
January 27, 1985, Attendance: 50,385
AFC 22, NFC 14—Defensive end Art Still of the Kansas City Chiefs recovered a fumble and returned it 83 yards for a touchdown to clinch the AFC's victory over the NFC. Still's touchdown came in the fourth period with the AFC trailing 14-12 and was one of several outstanding defensive plays in a Pro Bowl dominated by two record-breaking defenses. The teams combined for a Pro Bowl-record 17 sacks, including 4 by New York Jets defensive end Mark Gastineau, who was named the game's outstanding player. The AFC's first score came on a safety when Gastineau tackled running back Eric Dickerson of the Los Angeles Rams in the end zone. The AFC's second score, a 6-yard pass from Miami's Dan Marino to Los

---

Angeles Raiders running back Marcus Allen, was set up by a partial block of a punt by Seahawks linebacker Fredd Young. The NFC leads the series 9-6.

AFC	0	9	0	13 —	22
NFC	0	0	7	7 —	14

AFC — Safety, Gastineau tackled Dickerson in end zone
AFC — Allen 6 pass from Marino (Johnson kick)
NFC — Lofton 13 pass from Montana (Stenerud kick)
NFC — Payton 1 run (Stenerud kick)
AFC — FG Johnson 33
AFC — Still 83 fumble recovery return (Johnson kick)
AFC — FG Johnson 22

1984 AFC-NFC PRO BOWL
Aloha Stadium, Honolulu, Hawaii
January 29, 1984, Attendance: 50,445
NFC 45, AFC 3—The NFC won its sixth Pro Bowl in the last seven seasons by routing the AFC. The NFC was led by the passing of most valuable player Joe Theismann of Washington, who completed 21 of 27 passes for 242 yards and 3 touchdowns. Theismann set Pro Bowl records for completions and touchdown passes. The NFC established Pro Bowl marks for most points scored and fewest points allowed. Running back William Andrews of Atlanta had 6 carries for 43 yards and caught 4 passes for 49 yards, including scoring receptions of 16 and 2 yards. Los Angeles Rams rookie Eric Dickerson gained 46 yards on 11 carries, including a 14-yard touchdown run, and had 45 yards on 5 catches. Rams safety Nolan Cromwell had a 44-yard interception return for a touchdown early in the third period to give the NFC a commanding 24-3 lead. Green Bay wide receiver James Lofton caught an 8-yard touchdown pass, while tight end teammate Paul Coffman had a 6-yard scoring catch.

NFC	3	14	14	14 —	45
AFC	0	3	0	0 —	3

NFC — FG Haji-Sheikh 23
NFC — Andrews 16 pass from Theismann (Haji-Sheikh kick)
NFC — Andrews 2 pass from Montana (Haji-Sheikh kick)
AFC — FG Anderson 43
NFC — Cromwell 44 interception return (Haji-Sheikh kick)
NFC — Lofton 8 pass from Theismann (Haji-Sheikh kick)
NFC — Coffman 6 pass from Theismann (Haji-Sheikh kick)
NFC — Dickerson 14 run (Haji-Sheikh kick)

1983 AFC-NFC PRO BOWL
Aloha Stadium, Honolulu, Hawaii
February 6, 1983, Attendance: 49,883
NFC 20, AFC 19—Dallas' Danny White threw an 11-yard touchdown pass to the Packers' John Jefferson with 35 seconds remaining to rally the NFC over the AFC.

White, who completed 14 of 26 passes for 162 yards, kept the winning 65-yard drive alive with a 14-yard completion to Jefferson on a fourth-and-7 play at the AFC 25. The AFC was ahead 12-10 at halftime and increased the lead to 19-10 in the third period, when Marcus Allen scored on a 1-yard run. San Diego's Dan Fouts, who attempted 30 passes, set Pro Bowl records for most completions (17) and yards (274). Pittsburgh's John Stallworth was the AFC's leading receiver with 7 catches for 67 yards. William Andrews topped the NFC with 5 receptions for 48 yards. Fouts and Jefferson were co-winners of the player of the game award.

AFC	9	3	7	0	—	19
NFC	0	10	0	10	—	20

AFC — Walker 34 pass from Fouts (Benirschke kick)
AFC — Safety, Still tackled Theismann in end zone
NFC — Andrews 3 run (Moseley kick)
NFC — FG Moseley 35
AFC — FG Benirschke 29
AFC — Allen 1 run (Benirschke kick)
NFC — FG Moseley 41
NFC — Jefferson 11 pass from D. White (Moseley kick)

1982 AFC-NFC PRO BOWL
Aloha Stadium, Honolulu, Hawaii
January 31, 1982, Attendance: 50,402
AFC 16, NFC 13—Nick Lowery of Kansas City kicked a 23-yard field goal with three seconds remaining to give the AFC a last-second victory over the NFC. Lowery's kick climaxed a 69-yard drive directed by quarterback Dan Fouts. The NFC gained a 13-13 tie with 2:43 to go when Dallas' Tony Dorsett ran 4 yards for a touchdown. In the drive to the winning field goal, Fouts completed 3 passes, including a 23-yard toss to San Diego teammate Kellen Winslow that put the ball on the NFC's 5-yard line. Two plays later, Lowery kicked the field goal. Winslow, who caught 6 passes for 86 yards, was named co-player of the game along with Tampa Bay defensive end Lee Roy Selmon.

NFC	0	6	0	7	—	13
AFC	0	13	0	3	—	16

NFC — Giles 4 pass from Montana (kick blocked)
AFC — Muncie 2 run (kick failed)
AFC — Campbell 1 run (Lowery kick)
NFC — Dorsett 4 run (Septien kick)
AFC — FG Lowery 23

1981 AFC-NFC PRO BOWL
Aloha Stadium, Honolulu, Hawaii
February 1, 1981, Attendance: 50,360
NFC 21, AFC 7—Eddie Murray kicked 4 field goals and Steve Bartkowski fired a 55-yard scoring pass to Alfred Jenkins to lead the NFC to its fourth straight victory over the AFC and a 7-4 edge in the series. Murray was named the game's most valuable player and missed tying Garo Yepremian's Pro Bowl record of 5 field

goals when a 37-yard attempt hit the crossbar with 22 seconds left. The AFC's only score came on a 9-yard pass from Brian Sipe to Stanley Morgan. Bartkowski completed 9 of 21 passes for 173 yards, while Sipe connected on 10 of 15 for 142 yards. Ottis Anderson led all rushers with 70 yards on 10 carries. Earl Campbell, the NFL's leading rusher in 1980, was limited to 24 yards on 8 attempts.

AFC	0	7	0	0	—	7
NFC	3	6	0	12	—	21

NFC — FG Murray 31
AFC — Morgan 9 pass from Sipe (J. Smith kick)
NFC — FG Murray 31
NFC — FG Murray 34
NFC — Jenkins 55 pass from Bartkowski (Murray kick)
NFC — FG Murray 36
NFC — Safety, Shell called for holding in end zone

1980 AFC-NFC PRO BOWL
Aloha Stadium, Honolulu, Hawaii
January 27, 1980, Attendance: 49,800
NFC 37, AFC 27—Chuck Muncie ran for 2 touchdowns and threw a 25-yard option pass for another score to give the NFC its third consecutive victory over the AFC. The Saints' Muncie, who was selected the game's most valuable player, snapped a 3-3 tie on a 1-yard touchdown run at 1:41 of the second quarter, then scored on an 11-yard run in the fourth quarter for the NFC's final touchdown. Two scoring records were set in the game—37 points by the NFC, eclipsing the 33 by the AFC in 1973, and the 64 points by both teams, surpassing the 61 scored in 1973.

NFC	3	20	7	7	—	37
AFC	3	7	10	7	—	27

NFC — FG Moseley 37
AFC — FG Fritsch 19
NFC — Muncie 1 run (Moseley kick)
AFC — Pruitt 1 pass from Bradshaw (Fritsch kick)
NFC — D. Hill 13 pass from Manning (kick failed)
NFC — T. Hill 25 pass from Muncie (Moseley kick)
NFC — Henry 86 punt return (Moseley kick)
AFC — Campbell 2 run (Fritsch kick)
AFC — FG Fritsch 29
NFC — Muncie 11 run (Moseley kick)
AFC — Campbell 1 run (Fritsch kick)

1979 AFC-NFC PRO BOWL
Memorial Coliseum, Los Angeles, CA
January 29, 1979, Attendance: 46,281
NFC 13, AFC 7—Roger Staubach completed 9 of 15 passes for 173 yards, including the winning touchdown on a 19-yard strike to Dallas Cowboys teammate Tony Hill in the third period. The winning drive began at the AFC's 45-yard line after a shanked punt. Staubach hit Ahmad Rashad with passes of 15 and 17 yards to set up Hill's decisive catch. The victory

gave the NFC a 5-4 advantage in Pro Bowl games. Rashad, who accounted for 89 yards on 5 receptions, was named the player of the game. The AFC led 7-6 at halftime on Bob Griese's 8-yard scoring toss to Steve Largent late in the second quarter. Largent had 5 receptions for 75 yards. The NFC scored first as Archie Manning marched his team 70 yards in 11 plays, capped by Wilbert Montgomery's 2-yard touchdown run. The AFC's Earl Campbell was the game's leading rusher with 66 yards on 12 carries.

AFC	0	7	0	0	—	7
NFC	0	6	7	0	—	13

NFC — Montgomery 2 run (kick failed)
AFC — Largent 8 pass from Griese (Yepremian kick)
NFC — T. Hill 19 pass from Staubach (Corral kick)

1978 AFC-NFC PRO BOWL
Tampa Stadium, Tampa, Florida
January 23, 1978, Attendance: 51,337
NFC 14, AFC 13—Walter Payton, the NFL's leading rusher in 1977, sparked a second-half comeback to give the NFC the win and tie the series between the two conferences at four victories each. Payton, who was the game's most valuable player, gained 77 yards on 13 carries and scored the tying touchdown on a 1-yard burst with 7:37 left in the game. Efren Herrera kicked the winning extra point. The AFC dominated the first half of the game, taking a 13-0 lead on field goals of 21 and 39 yards by Toni Linhart and a 10-yard touchdown pass from Ken Stabler to Oakland teammate Cliff Branch. On the NFC's first possession of the second half, Pat Haden put together the first touchdown drive after Eddie Brown returned a punt to the AFC 46-yard line. Haden connected on all 4 of his passes on that drive, finally hitting Terry Metcalf with a 4-yard scoring toss. The NFC continued to rally and, with Jim Hart at quarterback, moved 63 yards in 12 plays for the go-ahead score. During the winning drive, Hart completed 5 of 6 passes for 38 yards and Payton picked up 20 more on the ground.

AFC	3	10	0	0	—	13
NFC	0	0	7	7	—	14

AFC — FG Linhart 21
AFC — Branch 10 pass from Stabler (Linhart kick)
AFC — FG Linhart 39
NFC — Metcalf 4 pass from Haden (Herrera kick)
NFC — Payton 1 run (Herrera kick)

1977 AFC-NFC PRO BOWL
Kingdome, Seattle, Washington
January 17, 1977, Attendance: 64,752
AFC 24, NFC 14—O.J. Simpson's 3-yard touchdown burst at 7:03 of the first quarter gave the AFC a lead it would not surrender, breaking a two-game NFC win streak and giving the AFC stars a 4-3

series lead. The AFC took a 17-7 lead midway through the second period on the first of 2 Ken Anderson touchdown passes, a 12-yard toss to Charlie Joiner. But the NFC mounted a 73-yard drive capped by Lawrence McCutcheon's 1-yard touchdown plunge to pull within 17-14 at the half. Following a scoreless third quarter, player of the game Mel Blount thwarted a possible NFC score when he intercepted Jim Hart's pass in the end zone. Less than three minutes later, Blount again picked off a Hart pass. That set up Anderson's 27-yard touchdown strike to Cliff Branch for the final score.

NFC	0	14	0	0	—	14
AFC	10	7	0	7	—	24

AFC — Simpson 3 run (Linhart kick)
AFC — FG Linhart 31
NFC — Thomas 15 run (Bakken kick)
AFC — Joiner 12 pass from Anderson (Linhart kick)
NFC — McCutcheon 1 run (Bakken kick)
AFC — Branch 27 pass from Anderson (Linhart kick)

1976 AFC-NFC PRO BOWL
Superdome, New Orleans, Louisiana
January 26, 1976, Attendance: 30,546
NFC 23, AFC 20—Mike Boryla, a late substitute who did not enter the game until 5:39 remained, lifted the National Football Conference to the victory over the American Football Conference with 2 touchdown passes in the final minutes. It was the second straight NFC win, squaring the series at 3-3. Until Boryla started firing the ball the AFC was in control, leading 13-0 at the half. Boryla entered the game after Billy Johnson had raced 90 yards with a punt to give the AFC a 20-9 lead. He floated a 14-yard touchdown pass to Terry Metcalf and later fired an 8-yard scoring pass to Mel Gray for the winner.

AFC	0	13	0	7	—	20
NFC	0	0	9	14	—	23

AFC — FG Stenerud 20
AFC — FG Stenerud 35
AFC — Burrough 64 pass from Pastorini (Stenerud kick)
NFC — FG Bakken 42
NFC — Foreman 4 pass from Hart (kick blocked)
AFC — Johnson 90 punt return (Stenerud kick)
NFC — Metcalf 14 pass from Boryla (Bakken kick)
NFC — Gray 8 pass from Boryla (Bakken kick)

1975 AFC-NFC PRO BOWL
Orange Bowl, Miami, Florida
January 20, 1975, Attendance: 26,484
NFC 17, AFC 10—Los Angeles quarterback James Harris, who took over the NFC offense after Jim Hart of St. Louis suffered a laceration above his right eye in the second period, threw 2 touchdown passes early in the fourth period to pace

the NFC to its second victory in the five-game Pro Bowl series. The NFC win snapped a three-game AFC victory string. Harris, who was named the player of the game, connected with St. Louis' Mel Gray for an 8-yard touchdown 2:03 into the final period. One minute and 24 seconds later, following a fumble recovery by Washington's Ken Houston, Harris tossed another 8-yard scoring pass to Washington's Charley Taylor for the decisive points.

NFC	0	3	0	14	—	17
AFC	0	0	10	0	—	10

NFC — FG Marcol 33
AFC — Warfield 32 pass from Griese (Gerela kick)
AFC — FG Gerela 33
NFC — Gray 8 pass from J. Harris (Marcol kick)
NFC — Taylor 8 pass from J. Harris (Marcol kick)

1974 AFC-NFC PRO BOWL
Arrowhead Stadium, Kansas City, MO
January 20, 1974, Attendance: 66,918
AFC 15, NFC 13—Miami's Garo Yepremian's fifth field goal—a 42-yard kick with 21 seconds remaining—gave the AFC its third straight victory since the NFC won the inaugural game following the 1970 season. The field goal by Yepremian, who was voted the game's outstanding player, offset a 21-yard field goal by Atlanta's Nick Mike-Mayer that had given the NFC a 13-12 advantage with 1:41 remaining. The only touchdown in the game was scored by the NFC on a 14-yard pass from Philadelphia's Roman Gabriel to the Rams' Lawrence McCutcheon.

NFC	0	10	0	3	—	13
AFC	3	3	3	6	—	15

AFC — FG Yepremian 16
NFC — FG Mike-Mayer 27
NFC — McCutcheon 14 pass from Gabriel (Mike-Mayer kick)
AFC — FG Yepremian 37
NFC — FG Yepremian 27
AFC — FG Yepremian 41
NFC — FG Mike-Mayer 21
AFC — FG Yepremian 42

1973 AFC-NFC PRO BOWL
Texas Stadium, Irving, Texas
January 21, 1973, Attendance: 37,091
AFC 33, NFC 28—Paced by the rushing and receiving of player of the game O.J. Simpson, the AFC erased a 14-0 first period deficit and built a commanding 33-14 lead midway through the fourth period before the NFC managed 2 touchdowns in the final minute of play. Simpson rushed for 112 yards and caught 3 passes for 58 more to gain unanimous recognition in the balloting for player of the game. Green Bay Packers running back John Brockington scored 3 touchdowns for the NFC.

AFC	0	10	10	13	—	33
NFC	14	0	0	14	—	28

NFC — Brockington 1 run (Marcol kick)
NFC — Brockington 3 pass from Kilmer (Marcol kick)
AFC — Simpson 7 run (Gerela kick)
AFC — FG Gerela 18
AFC — FG Gerela 22
AFC — Hubbard 11 run (Gerela kick)
AFC — O. Taylor 5 pass from Lamonica (kick failed)
AFC — Bell 12 interception return (Gerela kick)
NFC — Brockington 1 run (Marcol kick)
NFC — Kwalick 12 pass from Snead (Marcol kick)

1972 AFC-NFC PRO BOWL
Memorial Coliseum, Los Angeles, CA
January 23, 1972, Attendance: 53,647
AFC 26, NFC 13—Kansas City's Jan Stenerud kicked 4 field goals to lead the AFC from a 6-0 deficit to victory. The AFC defense picked off 3 passes. Stenerud was selected as the outstanding offensive player and his Kansas City teammate, linebacker Willie Lanier, was the game's outstanding defensive player.

AFC	0	3	13	10	—	26
NFC	0	6	0	7	—	13

NFC — Grim 50 pass from Landry (kick failed)
AFC — FG Stenerud 25
AFC — FG Stenerud 23
AFC — FG Stenerud 48
AFC — Morin 5 pass from Dawson (Stenerud kick)
AFC — FG Stenerud 42
NFC — V. Washington 2 run (Knight kick)
AFC — F. Little 6 run (Stenerud kick)

1971 AFC-NFC PRO BOWL
Memorial Coliseum, Los Angeles, CA
January 24, 1971, Attendance: 48,222
NFC 27, AFC 6—Mel Renfro of Dallas broke open the first meeting between the American Football Conference and National Football Conference all-star teams as he returned a pair of punts 82 and 56 yards for touchdowns in the final period to clinch the NFC victory over the AFC. Renfro was voted the game's outstanding back and linebacker Fred Carr of Green Bay the outstanding lineman.

AFC	0	3	3	0	—	6
NFC	0	3	10	14	—	27

AFC — FG Stenerud 37
NFC — FG Cox 13
NFC — Osborn 23 pass from Brodie (Cox kick)
NFC — FG Cox 35
AFC — FG Stenerud 16
NFC — Renfro 82 punt return (Cox kick)
NFC — Renfro 56 punt return (Cox kick)

Date	Result/Honored players	Site (attendance)
Jan. 15, 1939	New York Giants 13, Pro All-Stars 10	Wrigley Field, Los Angeles (20,000)
Jan. 14, 1940	Green Bay 16, NFL All-Stars 7	Gilmore Stadium, Los Angeles (18,000)
Dec. 29, 1940	Chicago Bears 28, NFL All-Stars 14	Gilmore Stadium, Los Angeles (21,624)
Jan. 4, 1942	Chicago Bears 35, NFL All-Stars 24	Polo Grounds, New York (17,725)
Dec. 27, 1942	NFL All-Stars 17, Washington 14	Shibe Park, Philadelphia (18,671)
Jan. 14, 1951	American Conf. 28, National Conf. 27	Los Angeles Memorial Coliseum (53,676)
	Otto Graham, Cleveland, player of the game	
Jan. 12, 1952	National Conf. 30, American Conf. 13	Los Angeles Memorial Coliseum (19,400)
	Dan Towler, Los Angeles, player of the game	
Jan. 10, 1953	National Conf. 27, American Conf. 7	Los Angeles Memorial Coliseum (34,208)
	Don Doll, Detroit, player of the game	
Jan. 17, 1954	East 20, West 9	Los Angeles Memorial Coliseum (44,214)
	Chuck Bednarik, Philadelphia, player of the game	
Jan. 16, 1955	West 26, East 19	Los Angeles Memorial Coliseum (43,972)
	Billy Wilson, San Francisco, player of the game	
Jan. 15, 1956	East 31, West 30	Los Angeles Memorial Coliseum (37,867)
	Ollie Matson, Chi. Cardinals, player of the game	
Jan. 13, 1957	West 19, East 10	Los Angeles Memorial Coliseum (44,177)
	Bert Rechichar, Baltimore, outstanding back	
	Ernie Stautner, Pittsburgh, outstanding lineman	
Jan. 12, 1958	West 26, East 7	Los Angeles Memorial Coliseum (66,634)
	Hugh McElhenny, San Francisco, outstanding back	
	Gene Brito, Washington, outstanding lineman	
Jan. 11, 1959	East 28, West 21	Los Angeles Memorial Coliseum (72,250)
	Frank Gifford, N.Y. Giants, outstanding back	
	Doug Atkins, Chi. Bears, outstanding lineman	
Jan. 17, 1960	West 38, East 21	Los Angeles Memorial Coliseum (56,876)
	Johnny Unitas, Baltimore, outstanding back	
	Gene (Big Daddy) Lipscomb, Baltimore, outstanding lineman	
Jan. 15, 1961	West 35, East 31	Los Angeles Memorial Coliseum (62,971)
	Johnny Unitas, Baltimore, outstanding back	
	Sam Huff, N.Y. Giants, outstanding lineman	
Jan. 7, 1962	AFL West 47, East 27	Balboa Stadium, San Diego (20,973)
	Cotton Davidson, Dallas Texans, player of the game	
Jan. 14, 1962	NFL West 31, East 30	Los Angeles Memorial Coliseum (57,409)
	Jim Brown, Cleveland, outstanding back	
	Henry Jordan, Green Bay, outstanding lineman	
Jan. 13, 1963	AFL West 21, East 14	Balboa Stadium, San Diego (27,641)
	Curtis McClinton, Dallas Texans, outstanding offensive player	
	Earl Faison, San Diego, outstanding defensive player	
Jan. 13, 1963	NFL East 30, West 20	Los Angeles Memorial Coliseum (61,374)
	Jim Brown, Cleveland, outstanding back	
	Gene (Big Daddy) Lipscomb, Pittsburgh, outstanding lineman	
Jan. 12, 1964	NFL West 31, East 17	Los Angeles Memorial Coliseum (67,242)
	Johnny Unitas, Baltimore, player of the game	
	Gino Marchetti, Baltimore, outstanding lineman	
Jan. 19, 1964	AFL West 27, East 24	Balboa Stadium, San Diego (20,016)
	Keith Lincoln, San Diego, outstanding offensive player	
	Archie Matsos, Oakland, outstanding defensive player	
Jan. 10, 1965	NFL West 34, East 14	Los Angeles Memorial Coliseum (60,598)
	Fran Tarkenton, Minnesota, outstanding back	
	Terry Barr, Detroit, outstanding lineman	
Jan. 16, 1965	AFL West 38, East 14	Jeppesen Stadium, Houston (15,446)
	Keith Lincoln, San Diego, outstanding offensive player	
	Willie Brown, Denver, outstanding defensive player	
Jan. 15, 1966	AFL All-Stars 30, Buffalo 19	Rice Stadium, Houston (35,572)
	Joe Namath, N.Y. Jets, most valuable player, offense	
	Frank Buncom, San Diego, most valuable player, defense	
Jan. 15, 1966	NFL East 36, West 7	Los Angeles Memorial Coliseum (60,124)
	Jim Brown, Cleveland, outstanding back	
	Dale Meinert, St. Louis, outstanding lineman	
Jan. 21, 1967	AFL East 30, West 23	Oakland-Alameda County Coliseum (18,876)
	Babe Parilli, Boston, outstanding offensive player	
	Verlon Biggs, N.Y. Jets, outstanding defensive player	
Jan. 22, 1967	NFL East 20, West 10	Los Angeles Memorial Coliseum (15,062)
	Gale Sayers, Chicago, outstanding back	
	Floyd Peters, Philadelphia, outstanding lineman	

Jan. 21, 1968   AFL East 25, West 24 ....Gator Bowl, Jacksonville, Fla. (40,103)
                 Joe Namath and Don Maynard, N.Y. Jets, out. off. players
                 Leslie (Speedy) Duncan, San Diego, out. def. player
Jan. 21, 1968   NFL West 38, East 20 ....Los Angeles Memorial Coliseum (53,289)
                 Gale Sayers, Chicago, outstanding back
                 Dave Robinson, Green Bay, outstanding lineman
Jan. 19, 1969   AFL West 38, East 25 ....Gator Bowl, Jacksonville, Fla. (41,058)
                 Len Dawson, Kansas City, outstanding offensive player
                 George Webster, Houston, outstanding defensive player
Jan. 19, 1969   NFL West 10, East 7 ....Los Angeles Memorial Coliseum (32,050)
                 Roman Gabriel, Los Angeles, outstanding back
                 Merlin Olsen, Los Angeles, outstanding lineman
Jan. 17, 1970   AFL West 26, East 3 ....Astrodome, Houston (30,170)
                 John Hadl, San Diego, player of the game
Jan. 18, 1970   NFL West 16, East 13 ....Los Angeles Memorial Coliseum (57,786)
                 Gale Sayers, Chicago, outstanding back
                 George Andrie, Dallas, outstanding lineman
Jan. 24, 1971   NFC 27, AFC 6 ....Los Angeles Memorial Coliseum (48,222)
                 Mel Renfro, Dallas, outstanding back
                 Fred Carr, Green Bay, outstanding lineman
Jan. 23, 1972   AFC 26, NFC 13 ....Los Angeles Memorial Coliseum (53,647)
                 Jan Stenerud, Kansas City, outstanding offensive player
                 Willie Lanier, Kansas City, outstanding defensive player
Jan. 21, 1973   AFC 33, NFC 28 ....Texas Stadium, Irving (37,091)
                 O.J. Simpson, Buffalo, player of the game
Jan. 20, 1974   AFC 15, NFC 13 ....Arrowhead Stadium, Kansas City (66,918)
                 Garo Yepremian, Miami, player of the game
Jan. 20, 1975   NFC 17, AFC 10 ....Orange Bowl, Miami (26,484)
                 James Harris, Los Angeles, player of the game
Jan. 26, 1976   NFC 23, AFC 20 ....Louisiana Superdome, New Orleans (30,546)
                 Billy Johnson, Houston, player of the game
Jan. 17, 1977   AFC 24, NFC 14 ....Kingdome, Seattle (64,752)
                 Mel Blount, Pittsburgh, player of the game
Jan. 23, 1978   NFC 14, AFC 13 ....Tampa Stadium (51,337)
                 Walter Payton, Chicago, player of the game
Jan. 29, 1979   NFC 13, AFC 7 ....Los Angeles Memorial Coliseum (46,281)
                 Ahmad Rashad, Minnesota, player of the game
Jan. 27, 1980   NFC 37, AFC 27 ....Aloha Stadium, Honolulu (49,800)
                 Chuck Muncie, New Orleans, player of the game
Feb. 1, 1981   NFC 21, AFC 7 ....Aloha Stadium, Honolulu (50,360)
                 Eddie Murray, Detroit, player of the game
Jan. 31, 1982   AFC 16, NFC 13 ....Aloha Stadium, Honolulu (50,402)
                 Kellen Winslow, San Diego, and Lee Roy Selmon, Tampa Bay, players of the game
Feb. 6, 1983   NFC 20, AFC 19 ....Aloha Stadium, Honolulu (49,883)
                 Dan Fouts, San Diego, and John Jefferson, Green Bay, players of the game
Jan. 29, 1984   NFC 45, AFC 3 ....Aloha Stadium, Honolulu (50,445)
                 Joe Theismann, Washington, player of the game
Jan. 27, 1985   AFC 22, NFC 14 ....Aloha Stadium, Honolulu (50,385)
                 Mark Gastineau, N.Y. Jets, player of the game
Feb. 2, 1986   NFC 28, AFC 24 ....Aloha Stadium, Honolulu (50,101)
                 Phil Simms, N.Y. Giants, player of the game
Feb. 1, 1987   AFC 10, NFC 6 ....Aloha Stadium, Honolulu (50,101)
                 Reggie White, Philadelphia, player of the game
Feb. 7, 1988   AFC 15, NFC 6 ....Aloha Stadium, Honolulu (50,113)
                 Bruce Smith, Buffalo, player of the game
Jan. 29, 1989   NFC 34, AFC 3 ....Aloha Stadium, Honolulu (50,113)
                 Randall Cunningham, Philadelphia, player of the game
Feb. 4, 1990   NFC 27, AFC 21 ....Aloha Stadium, Honolulu (50,445)
                 Jerry Gray, L.A. Rams, player of the game
Feb. 3, 1991   AFC 23, NFC 21 ....Aloha Stadium, Honolulu (50,345)
                 Jim Kelly, Buffalo, player of the game
Feb. 2, 1992   NFC 21, AFC 15 ....Aloha Stadium, Honolulu (50,209)
                 Michael Irvin, Dallas, player of the game
Feb. 7, 1993   AFC 23, NFC 20 (OT) ....Aloha Stadium, Honolulu (50,007)
                 Steve Tasker, Buffalo, player of the game
Feb. 6, 1994   NFC 17, AFC 3 ....Aloha Stadium, Honolulu (50,026)
                 Andre Rison, Atlanta, player of the game
Feb. 5, 1995   AFC 41, NFC 13 ....Aloha Stadium, Honolulu (49,121)
                 Marshall Faulk, Indianapolis, player of the game

| Feb. 4, 1996 | NFC 20, AFC 13 | Aloha Stadium, Honolulu (50,034) |

Jerry Rice, San Francisco, player of the game

| Feb. 2, 1997 | AFC 26, NFC 23 (OT) | Aloha Stadium, Honolulu (50,031) |

Mark Brunell, Jacksonville, player of the game

| Feb. 1, 1998 | AFC 29, NFC 24 | Aloha Stadium, Honolulu (49,995) |

Warren Moon, Seattle, player of the game

| Feb. 7, 1999 | AFC 23, NFC 10 | Aloha Stadium, Honolulu (50,075) |

Keyshawn Johnson, N.Y. Jets and Ty Law, New England, co-players of the game

| Feb. 6, 2000 | NFC 51, AFC 31 | Aloha Stadium, Honolulu (50,112) |

Randy Moss, Minnesota, player of the game

| Feb. 4, 2001 | AFC 38, NFC 17 | Aloha Stadium, Honolulu (50,128) |

Rich Gannon, Oakland, player of the game

| Feb. 9, 2002 | AFC 38, NFC 30 | Aloha Stadium, Honolulu (50,301) |

Rich Gannon, Oakland, player of the game

AFC VS. NFC (REGULAR SEASON), 1970-2001

	Balt	Buff	Cin	Cle	Den	Ind	Jax	KC	Mia
1970		0-3	1-2	0-3	2-2	3-0		0-2-1	2-1
1971		0-3	1-2	2-1	1-3	2-1		2-1	3-0
1972		2-0-1	2-1	1-2	1-3	0-3		2-1	3-0
1973		2-1	2-1	1-2	0-3-1	2-1		1-1-1	3-0
1974		2-1	2-1	1-2	2-2	1-2		1-2	2-1
1975		1-2	3-0	1-3	2-1	2-1		2-1	3-0
1976		0-2	2-0	2-0	2-0	0-2		1-1	0-2
1977		1-1	2-1	1-1	1-1	1-1		1-1	2-0
1978		1-1	2-2	4-0	2-2	2-2		0-2	3-1
1979		2-2	2-2	3-1	3-1	1-1		0-2	4-0
1980		3-1	2-2	3-1	3-1	1-1		2-0	4-0
1981		1-3	2-2	3-1	3-1	0-4		2-2	3-1
1982		1-2	1-0	0-2	2-1	0-1-1		0-3	1-1
1983		1-3	3-1	2-2	0-2	2-0		2-2	3-1
1984		1-3	2-2	1-3	3-1	0-4		1-1	4-0
1985		0-2	2-2	1-3	3-1	3-1		2-2	3-1
1986		1-1	3-1	2-2	3-1	1-3		1-1	2-2
1987		1-2	1-2	2-2	2-1-1	1-0		1-2	3-0
1988		2-2	4-0	4-0	3-1	2-2		0-2	3-1
1989		1-3	2-2	3-1	2-2	1-3		2-0	2-0
1990		3-1	1-3	1-3	1-3	2-2		4-0	2-2
1991		3-1	1-3	0-4	2-0	0-4		2-2	3-1
1992		4-0	1-3	2-2	1-3	2-0		2-2	2-2
1993		4-0	2-2	3-1	1-3	0-4		2-2	3-1
1994		1-3	1-3	3-1	1-3	0-2		3-1	2-2
1995		3-1	2-2	1-3	2-2	2-2	0-4	3-1	2-2
1996	2-2	4-0	2-2		3-1	3-1	2-2	4-0	1-3
1997	2-1-1	1-3	2-2		3-1	1-3	2-2	4-0	1-3
1998	1-3	3-1	1-3		3-1	0-4	3-1	3-1	3-1
1999	2-1	3-1	1-2	1-2	2-2	4-0	4-0	2-2	2-2
2000	2-1	2-2	1-2	0-3	3-1	2-2	2-2	2-2	2-2
2001	2-2	1-3	1-2	1-2	3-1	1-3	1-2	1-3	2-2
Total	**11-10-1**	**55-54-1**	**57-55**	**49-53**	**65-51-2**	**42-60-1**	**14-13**	**55-45-2**	**78-35**

	NE	NYJ	Oak	Pitt	SD	Sea	Tenn	TB	TOTALS
1970	0-3	2-1	1-2	0-3	1-2		0-3		12-27-1
1971	0-3	0-3	1-1-1	1-2	2-1		0-2-1		15-23-2
1972	3-0	1-2	3-0	2-1	0-3		0-3		20-19-1
1973	2-1	0-3	2-1	3-0	1-2		0-3		19-19-2
1974	3-0	2-1	3-0	3-0	1-2		0-3		23-17
1975	1-2	0-3	3-0	2-1	0-3		3-0		23-17
1976	1-1	0-2	3-0	1-1	2-0		2-0	0-1	16-12
1977	2-0	1-1	1-1	2-0	1-1	1-0	2-0		19-9
1978	2-2	1-3	4-0	3-1	2-2	3-1	2-2		31-21
1979	3-1	3-1	4-0	3-1	3-1	3-1	2-2		36-16
1980	1-3	1-3	2-2	4-0	2-2	1-3	4-0		33-19
1981	0-4	2-0	2-2	3-1	2-2	0-2	1-3		24-28
1982	0-1	4-0	3-0	1-0	1-0	1-0	0-3		15-14-1
1983	2-2	3-1	2-2	2-2	2-2	1-3	1-3		26-26
1984	0-4	0-2	3-1	3-1	4-0	4-0	0-4		26-26
1985	3-1	2-2	3-1	1-3	1-1	2-2	1-3		27-25
1986	3-1	2-2	1-3	2-2	0-4	3-1	2-2		26-26
1987	0-3	0-4	2-2	2-2	2-0	4-0	2-2		23-22-1
1988	2-2	2-0	1-3	1-3	2-2	1-3	3-1		30-22
1989	0-4	1-3	2-2	3-1	2-2	0-4	3-1		24-28
1990	0-4	2-0	3-1	3-1	1-1	2-2	1-3		26-26
1991	1-1	2-2	2-2	0-4	1-3	1-3	1-3		19-33
1992	0-4	0-4	2-2	1-3	2-0	0-4	3-1		22-30
1993	1-1	2-2	3-1	2-2	2-2	0-2	2-2		27-25
1994	4-0	1-3	3-1	2-2	2-2	2-0	0-4		25-27
1995	0-4	0-4	3-1	2-2	3-1	3-1	1-3		27-33
1996	2-2	1-3	1-3	2-2	1-3	2-2	2-2		32-28
1997	1-3	3-1	2-2	2-2	1-3	2-2	4-0		31-28-1
1998	2-2	2-2	3-1	2-2	1-3	3-1	1-3		31-29
1999	3-1	2-2	3-1	3-0	1-3	2-2	3-1		38-22
2000	0-4	3-1	4-0	1-2	0-4	2-2	4-0		30-30
2001	3-1	2-2	3-1	3-0	2-2	1-3	3-1		30-30
Total	**45-65**	**47-63**	**78-39-1**	**65-47**	**48-59**	**44-44**	**53-63-1**	**0-1**	**806-757-9**

NFC VS. AFC (REGULAR SEASON), 1970-2001

	Ariz	Atl	Car	Chi	Dall	Det	GB	Minn	NO
1970	2-0-1	1-2		1-2	3-0	3-0	2-1	2-1	0-3
1971	2-1	3-0		1-2	3-0	4-0	2-1	2-1	0-1-2
1972	1-2	2-2		1-2	3-0	2-0-1	2-1	1-2	0-3
1973	0-2-1	2-1		2-2	2-1	0-3	1-1-1	2-1	1-2
1974	2-1	0-3		0-3	2-1	1-2	2-1	2-1	0-3
1975	2-1	1-2		0-3	2-1	1-2	0-3	4-0	0-3
1976	1-1	0-2		0-2	2-0	2-0	0-2	2-0	1-2
1977	0-2	0-2		1-1	1-1	2-0	0-3	1-1	0-2
1978	0-4	1-3		0-4	3-1	2-2	2-2	1-3	1-3
1979	1-3	1-3		2-2	1-3	0-4	1-3	1-3	0-4
1980	1-1	2-2		0-4	3-1	0-2	1-3	1-3	1-3
1981	3-1	1-3		4-0	4-0	2-2	1-1	1-3	2-2
1982		1-1		1-1	2-1	0-1	1-1-1	1-3	1-0
1983	3-1	3-1		1-1	2-2	1-3	2-2	4-0	1-3
1984	3-1	1-3		2-2	2-2	0-4	0-4	0-4	3-1
1985	2-2	0-4		3-1	3-1	2-2	0-4	2-0	0-4
1986	1-1	1-3		4-0	1-3	1-3	1-3	1-3	1-3
1987	0-1	0-4		2-2	2-1	0-4	1-2-1	2-1	4-0
1988	1-3	1-3		3-1	0-4	1-1	1-3	2-2	4-0
1989	1-3	2-2		2-2	0-2	1-3	0-2	2-2	4-0
1990	2-2	2-2		2-2	1-1	1-3	1-3	2-2	2-2
1991	1-1	3-1		2-2	3-1	4-0	1-3	0-2	3-1
1992	0-2	2-2		1-3	4-0	2-2	3-1	3-1	3-1
1993	1-1	1-3		2-2	2-2	2-0	3-1	2-2	2-2
1994	3-1	1-3		3-1	3-1	2-2	1-3	2-2	1-3
1995	1-3	2-2	3-1	2-2	4-0	3-1	4-0	3-1	4-0
1996	0-4	0-4	3-1	2-2	2-2	1-3	3-1	1-3	1-3
1997	1-3	2-2	2-2	2-2	2-2	2-2	3-1	3-1	2-2
1998	1-3	3-1	1-3	2-2	1-3	1-3	3-1	4-0	1-3
1999	0-4	0-4	2-2	2-2	1-3	1-3	2-2	2-2	0-4
2000	1-3	1-3	2-2	2-2	1-3	2-2	1-3	3-1	1-3
2001	3-1	1-3	0-4	3-1	0-4	0-4	3-1	1-3	2-2
Total	**40-59-2**	**41-76**	**13-15**	**55-60**	**65-47**	**46-63-1**	**48-63-3**	**60-54**	**46-68-2**

	NYG	Phil	StL	SF	Sea	TB	Wash	TOTALS
1970	3-0	2-1	2-1	4-0			2-1	27-12-1
1971	1-2	1-2	1-2	2-1			1-2	23-15-2
1972	1-2	2-1	1-2	2-1			1-2	19-20-1
1973	1-2	2-1	3-0	1-2			2-1	19-19-2
1974	1-2	2-1	3-1	0-3			2-1	17-23
1975	2-1	0-3	3-0	1-2			1-2	17-23
1976	0-2	0-2	1-1	1-1	1-0		1-1	12-16
1977	0-2	1-1	2-0	0-2		0-1	1-1	9-19
1978	1-1	3-1	2-2	1-3		2-0	2-2	21-31
1979	1-1	2-2	2-2	0-4		2-0	2-2	16-36
1980	1-3	3-1	2-2	2-2		1-3	1-3	19-33
1981	1-1	3-1	1-3	3-1		0-4	2-2	28-24
1982	1-0	2-1	1-2	1-3		2-1		14-15-1
1983	0-4	1-1	1-3	2-2		1-3	4-0	26-26
1984	2-0	3-1	3-1	3-1		1-1	3-1	26-26
1985	2-2	1-1	3-1	3-1		0-4	4-0	25-27
1986	3-1	2-2	2-2	4-0		1-1	3-1	26-26
1987	2-1	3-1	1-2	3-1		0-2	2-1	22-23-1
1988	1-1	2-2	2-2	2-2		1-3	1-3	22-30
1989	4-0	3-1	3-1	4-0		0-4	2-2	28-24
1990	3-1	1-3	2-2	4-0		0-2	3-1	26-26
1991	3-1	4-0	1-3	3-1		1-3	4-0	33-19
1992	2-2	3-1	2-2	3-1		0-2	2-2	30-22
1993	2-2	2-2	2-2	2-2		1-3	1-3	25-27
1994	3-1	1-3	2-2	3-1		1-1	1-1	27-25
1995	0-4	1-3	1-3	3-1		2-2	0-4	33-27
1996	2-2	2-2	2-2	4-0		2-2	3-1	28-32
1997	1-3	2-1-1	0-4	2-2		3-1	1-3	28-31-1
1998	3-1	0-4	3-1	2-2		2-2	2-2	29-31
1999	2-2	1-3	3-1	1-3		3-1	2-2	22-38
2000	3-1	3-1	3-1	2-2		3-1	2-2	30-30
2001	2-2	3-1	4-0	4-0		2-2	2-2	30-30
Total	**54-50**	**61-51-1**	**64-53**	**72-47**	**1-0**	**31-49**	**60-51**	**757-806-9**

2001 INTERCONFERENCE GAMES
(Home Team in capital letters)

AFC 30, NFC 30

AFC Victories
BALTIMORE 17, Chicago 6
SAN DIEGO 30, Washington 3
DENVER 31, New York Giants 20
CLEVELAND 24, Detroit 14
San Diego 32, DALLAS 21
Denver 38, ARIZONA 17
Kansas City 45, WASHINGTON 13
OAKLAND 28, Dallas 21
TENNESSEE 31, Tampa Bay 28 (OT)
Pittsburgh 17, TAMPA BAY 10
Tennessee 27, DETROIT 24
Cincinnati 31, DETROIT 27
New York Jets 13, CAROLINA 12
Oakland 20, PHILADELPHIA 10
MIAMI 23, Carolina 6
New England 24, ATLANTA 10
New York Jets 16, NEW ORLEANS 9
Denver 26, DALLAS 24
NEW ENGLAND 34, New Orleans 17
Oakland 28, NEW YORK GIANTS 10
PITTSBURGH 21, Minnesota 16
BUFFALO 25, Carolina 24
INDIANAPOLIS 41, Atlanta 27
SEATTLE 29, Dallas 3
TENNESSEE 26, Green Bay 20
PITTSBURGH 47, Detroit 14
Jacksonville 33, MINNESOTA 3
MIAMI 21, Atlanta 14
New England 38, CAROLINA 6
BALTIMORE 19, Minnesota 3

NFC Victories
New Orleans 24, BUFFALO 6
New York Giants 13, KANSAS CITY 3
Philadelphia 27, SEATTLE 3
ST. LOUIS 42, Miami 10
San Francisco 19, NEW YORK JETS 17
GREEN BAY 31, Baltimore 23
Chicago 24, CINCINNATI 0
ARIZONA 24, Kansas City 16
St. Louis 34, NEW YORK JETS 14
CHICAGO 27, Cleveland 21 (OT)
WASHINGTON 27, Seattle 14
NEW ORLEANS 34, Indianapolis 20
Washington 17, DENVER 10
St. Louis 24, NEW ENGLAND 17
Arizona 20, SAN DIEGO 17
San Francisco 40, INDIANAPOLIS 21
Philadelphia 23, KANSAS CITY 10
Arizona 34, OAKLAND 31 (OT)
Tampa Bay 16, CINCINNATI 13 (OT)
SAN FRANCISCO 35, Buffalo 0
Green Bay 28, JACKSONVILLE 21
PHILADELPHIA 24, San Diego 14
MINNESOTA 42, Tennessee 24
SAN FRANCISCO 21, Miami 0
ATLANTA 33, Buffalo 30
GREEN BAY 30, Cleveland 7
NEW YORK GIANTS 27, Seattle 24
TAMPA BAY 22, Baltimore 10
ST. LOUIS 42, Indianapolis 17
CHICAGO 33, Jacksonville 13

REGULAR SEASON INTERCONFERENCE RECORDS, 1970-2001

AMERICAN FOOTBALL CONFERENCE

East	W	L	T	Pct.
Miami	78	35	0	.690
Buffalo	55	54	1	.505
New York Jets	47	63	0	.427
New England	45	65	0	.409
North	**W**	**L**	**T**	**Pct.**
Pittsburgh	65	47	0	.580
Baltimore	11	10	1	.523
Cincinnati	57	55	0	.509
Cleveland	49	53	0	.480
South	**W**	**L**	**T**	**Pct.**
Jacksonville	14	13	0	.519
Tennessee	53	63	1	.457
Indianapolis	42	60	1	.413
Houston	0	0	0	—
West	**W**	**L**	**T**	**Pct.**
Oakland	78	39	1	.665
Denver	65	51	2	.559
Kansas City	55	45	2	.549
San Diego	48	59	0	.449

NATIONAL FOOTBALL CONFERENCE

East	W	L	T	Pct.
Dallas	65	47	0	.580
Philadelphia	61	51	1	.544
Washington	60	51	0	.541
New York Giants	54	50	0	.519
North	**W**	**L**	**T**	**Pct.**
Minnesota	60	54	0	.526
Chicago	55	60	0	.478
Green Bay	48	63	3	.434
Detroit	46	63	1	.423
South	**W**	**L**	**T**	**Pct.**
Carolina	13	15	0	.464
New Orleans	46	68	2	.405
Tampa Bay*	31	50	0	.383
Atlanta	41	76	0	.350
West	**W**	**L**	**T**	**Pct.**
San Francisco	72	47	0	.605
St. Louis	64	53	0	.547
Seattle* #	45	44	0	.506
Arizona	40	59	2	.406

*   *Records include one game played between Seattle and Tampa Bay, won by the Seahawks 13-10, during their inaugural season (1976) when Seattle competed in the NFC and Tampa Bay in the AFC.*

Seattle was a member of the AFC from 1977-2001.

RECORDS AFTER BYE WEEKS, 1990-2001

AMERICAN FOOTBALL CONFERENCE

	W-L
Baltimore	2-4
Buffalo	10-3
Cincinnati	3-10
Cleveland	2-6
Denver	10-3
Indianapolis	5-8
Jacksonville	4-3
Kansas City	9-4
Miami	9-4
New England	5-8
N.Y. Jets	5-8
Oakland	8-5
Pittsburgh	7-6
San Diego	5-7
Tennessee	7-6

NATIONAL FOOTBALL CONFERENCE

	W-L
Arizona	5-8
Atlanta	7-6
Carolina	2-5
Chicago	10-3
Dallas	10-3
Detroit	6-7
Green Bay	6-7
Minnesota	10-3
New Orleans	6-7
N.Y. Giants	3-10
Philadelphia	9-4
St. Louis	7-6
San Francisco	6-7
Seattle	3-10
Tampa Bay	4-9
Washington	7-6

INTERCONFERENCE GAMES

INTERCONFERENCE VICTORIES, 1970-2001

REGULAR SEASON	AFC	NFC	Tie	PRESEASON	AFC	NFC	Tie
1970	12	27	1	1970	21	28	1
1971	15	23	2	1971	28	28	3
1972	20	19	1	1972	27	25	4
1973	19	19	2	1973	23	35	2
1974	23	17	0	1974	35	25	0
1975	23	17	0	1975	30	26	1
1976	16	12	0	1976	30	31	0
1977	19	9	0	1977	38	25	0
1978	31	21	0	1978	20	19	0
1979	36	16	0	1979	25	18	0
1980	33	19	0	1980	22	20	1
1981	24	28	0	1981	18	19	0
1982	15	14	1	1982	25	16	0
1983	26	26	0	1983	15	24	0
1984	26	26	0	1984	16	19	0
1985	27	25	0	1985	10	22	1
1986	26	26	0	1986	22	17	0
1987	23	22	1	1987	22	22	0
1988	30	22	0	1988	23	16	1
1989	24	28	0	1989	16	27	0
1990	26	26	0	1990	15	29	0
1991	19	33	0	1991	19	27	0
1992	22	30	0	1992	30	22	0
1993	27	25	0	1993	17	22	0
1994	25	27	0	1994	22	16	0
1995	27	33	0	1995	19	26	0
1996	32	28	0	1996	27	19	0
1997	31	28	1	1997	26	17	0
1998	31	29	0	1998	34	16	0
1999	38	22	0	1999	22	25	0
2000	30	30	0	2000	34	17	0
2001	30	30	0	2001	28	23	0
Total	806	757	9	Total	759	721	14

PRO FOOTBALL HALL OF FAME GAME (39)

1962	New York Giants 21, St. Louis Cardinals 21
1963	Pittsburgh Steelers 16, Cleveland Browns 7
1964	Baltimore Colts 48, Pittsburgh Steelers 17
1965	Washington Redskins 20, Detroit Lions 3
1966	No game
1967	Philadelphia Eagles 28, Cleveland Browns 13
1968	Chicago Bears 30, Dallas Cowboys 24
1969	Green Bay Packers 38, Atlanta Falcons 24
1970	New Orleans Saints 14, Minnesota Vikings 13
1971	Los Angeles Rams (NFC) 17, Houston Oilers (AFC) 6
1972	Kansas City Chiefs (AFC) 23, New York Giants (NFC) 17
1973	San Francisco 49ers (NFC) 20, New England Patriots (AFC) 7
1974	St. Louis Cardinals (NFC) 21, Buffalo Bills (AFC) 13
1975	Washington Redskins (NFC) 17, Cincinnati Bengals (AFC) 9
1976	Denver Broncos (AFC) 10, Detroit Lions (NFC) 7
1977	Chicago Bears (NFC) 20, New York Jets (AFC) 6
1978	Philadelphia Eagles (NFC) 17, Miami Dolphins (AFC) 3
1979	Oakland Raiders (AFC) 20, Dallas Cowboys (NFC) 13
1980*	San Diego Chargers (AFC) 0, Green Bay Packers (NFC) 0
1981	Cleveland Browns (AFC) 24, Atlanta Falcons (NFC) 10
1982	Minnesota Vikings (NFC) 30, Baltimore Colts (AFC) 14
1983	Pittsburgh Steelers (AFC) 27, New Orleans Saints (NFC) 14
1984	Seattle Seahawks (AFC) 38, Tampa Bay Buccaneers (NFC) 0
1985	New York Giants (NFC) 21, Houston Oilers (AFC) 20
1986	New England Patriots (AFC) 21, St. Louis Cardinals (NFC) 16
1987	San Francisco 49ers (NFC) 20, Kansas City Chiefs (AFC) 7
1988	Cincinnati Bengals (AFC) 14, Los Angeles Rams (NFC) 7
1989	Washington Redskins (NFC) 31, Buffalo Bills (AFC) 6
1990	Chicago Bears (NFC) 13, Cleveland Browns (AFC) 0
1991	Detroit Lions (NFC) 14, Denver Broncos (AFC) 3
1992	New York Jets (AFC) 41, Philadelphia Eagles (NFC) 14
1993	Los Angeles Raiders (AFC) 19, Green Bay Packers (NFC) 3
1994	Atlanta Falcons (NFC) 21, San Diego Chargers (AFC) 17
1995	Carolina Panthers (NFC) 20, Jacksonville Jaguars (AFC) 14
1996	Indianapolis Colts (AFC) 10, New Orleans Saints (NFC) 3
1997	Minnesota Vikings (NFC) 28, Seattle Seahawks (AFC) 26
1998	Tampa Bay Buccaneers (NFC) 30, Pittsburgh Steelers (AFC) 6
1999	Cleveland Browns (AFC) 20, Dallas Cowboys (NFC) 17 (OT)
2000	New England Patriots (AFC) 20, San Francisco 49ers (NFC) 0
2001	St. Louis Rams (NFC) 17, Miami Dolphins (AFC) 10

Game called with 5:29 remaining because of severe thunder and lightning.

NFL INTERNATIONAL GAMES (53)

Date	Site	Teams
Aug. 12, 1950	Ottawa, Canada	N.Y. Giants 27, Ottawa Rough Riders 6
Aug. 11, 1951	Ottawa, Canada	N.Y. Giants 41, Ottawa Rough Riders 18
Aug. 5, 1959	Toronto, Canada	Chi. Cardinals 55, Tor. Argonauts 26
Aug. 3, 1960	Toronto, Canada	Pittsburgh 43, Toronto Argonauts 16
Aug. 15, 1960	Toronto, Canada	Chicago 16, N.Y. Giants 7
Aug. 2, 1961	Toronto, Canada	St. Louis 36, Toronto Argonauts 7
Aug. 5, 1961	Montreal, Canada	Chicago 34, Montreal Allouettes 16
Aug. 8, 1961	Hamilton, Canada	Hamilton Tiger-Cats 38, Buffalo 21
Sept. 11, 1969	Montreal, Canada	Pittsburgh 17, N.Y. Giants 13
Aug. 25, 1969	Montreal, Canada	Detroit 22, Boston 9
Aug. 16, 1976	Tokyo, Japan	St. Louis 20, San Diego 10
Aug. 5, 1978	Mexico City, Mexico	New Orleans 14, Philadelphia 7
Aug. 6, 1983	London, England	Minnesota 28, St. Louis 10
* Aug. 3, 1986	London, England	Chicago 17, Dallas 6
* Aug. 9, 1987	London, England	L.A. Rams 28, Denver 27
* July 31, 1988	London, England	Miami 27, San Francisco 21
Aug. 14, 1988	Goteborg, Sweden	Minnesota 28, Chicago 21
Aug. 18, 1988	Montreal, Canada	N.Y. Jets 11, Cleveland 7
* Aug. 5, 1989	Tokyo, Japan	L.A. Rams 16, San Francisco 13 (OT)
* Aug. 6, 1989	London, England	Philadelphia 17, Cleveland 13
* Aug. 4, 1990	Tokyo, Japan	Denver 10, Seattle 7
* Aug. 5, 1990	London, England	New Orleans 17, L.A. Raiders 10
* Aug. 9, 1990	Montreal, Canada	Pittsburgh 30, New England 14
* Aug. 11, 1990	Berlin, Germany	L.A. Rams 19, Kansas City 3
* July 28, 1991	London, England	Buffalo 17, Philadelphia 13
* Aug. 3, 1991	Berlin, Germany	San Francisco 21, Chicago 7
* Aug. 3, 1991	Tokyo, Japan	Miami 19, L.A. Raiders 17
* Aug. 1, 1992	Tokyo, Japan	Houston 34, Dallas 23
* Aug. 15, 1992	Berlin, Germany	Miami 31, Denver 27
* Aug. 16, 1992	London, England	San Francisco 17, Washington 15
* July 31, 1993	Tokyo, Japan	New Orleans 28, Philadelphia 16
* Aug. 1, 1993	Barcelona, Spain	San Francisco 21, Pittsburgh 14
* Aug. 7, 1993	Berlin, Germany	Minnesota 20, Buffalo 6
* Aug. 8, 1993	London, England	Dallas 13, Detroit 13 (OT)
Aug. 14, 1993	Toronto, Canada	Cleveland 12, New England 9
* July 31, 1994	Barcelona, Spain	L.A. Raiders 25, Denver 22
* Aug. 6, 1994	Tokyo, Japan	Minnesota 17, Kansas City 9
* Aug. 13, 1994	Berlin, Germany	N.Y. Giants 28, San Diego 20
* Aug. 15, 1994	Mexico City, Mexico	Houston 6, Dallas 0
* Aug. 5, 1995	Tokyo, Japan	Denver 24, San Francisco 10
* Aug. 12, 1995	Toronto, Canada	Buffalo 9, Dallas 7
* July 27, 1996	Tokyo, Japan	San Diego 20, Pittsburgh 10
* Aug. 5, 1996	Monterrey, Mexico	Kansas City 32, Dallas 6
* July 27, 1997	Dublin, Ireland	Pittsburgh 30, Chicago 17
* Aug. 4, 1997	Mexico City, Mexico	Miami 38, Denver 19
* Aug. 16, 1997	Toronto, Canada	Green Bay 35, Buffalo 3
* Aug. 1, 1998	Tokyo, Japan	Green Bay 27, Kansas City 24 (OT)
* Aug. 15, 1998	Vancouver, Canada	San Francisco 24, Seattle 21
* Aug. 17, 1998	Mexico City, Mexico	New England 21, Dallas 3
* Aug. 7, 1999	Sydney, Australia	Denver 20, San Diego 17
* Aug. 5, 2000	Tokyo, Japan	Atlanta 20, Dallas 9
* Aug. 19, 2000	Mexico City, Mexico	Indianapolis 24, Pittsburgh 23
* Aug. 27, 2001	Mexico City, Mexico	Dallas 21, Oakland 6

*American Bowl Game

CHICAGO ALL-STAR GAME

Pro teams won 31, lost 9, and tied 2. The game was discontinued after 1976.

Year	Date	Winner	Loser	Attendance
1976*	July 23	Pittsburgh 24	All-Stars 0	52,895
1975	Aug. 1	Pittsburgh 21	All-Stars 14	54,103
1974		No game was played		
1973	July 27	Miami 14	All-Stars 3	54,103
1972	July 28	Dallas 20	All-Stars 7	54,162
1971	July 30	Baltimore 24	All-Stars 17	52,289
1970	July 31	Kansas City 24	All-Stars 3	69,940
1969	Aug. 1	N.Y. Jets 26	All-Stars 24	74,208
1968	Aug. 2	Green Bay 34	All-Stars 17	69,917
1967	Aug. 4	Green Bay 27	All-Stars 0	70,934
1966	Aug. 5	Green Bay 38	All-Stars 0	72,000
1965	Aug. 6	Cleveland 24	All-Stars 16	68,000
1964	Aug. 7	Chicago 28	All-Stars 17	65,000
1963	Aug. 2	All-Stars 20	Green Bay 17	65,000
1962	Aug. 3	Green Bay 42	All-Stars 20	65,000
1961	Aug. 4	Philadelphia 28	All-Stars 14	66,000
1960	Aug. 12	Baltimore 32	All-Stars 7	70,000
1959	Aug. 14	Baltimore 29	All-Stars 0	70,000
1958	Aug. 15	All-Stars 35	Detroit 19	70,000
1957	Aug. 9	N.Y. Giants 22	All-Stars 12	75,000
1956	Aug. 10	Cleveland 26	All-Stars 0	75,000
1955	Aug. 12	All-Stars 30	Cleveland 27	75,000
1954	Aug. 13	Detroit 31	All-Stars 6	93,470
1953	Aug. 14	Detroit 24	All-Stars 10	93,818
1952	Aug. 15	Los Angeles 10	All-Stars 7	88,316
1951	Aug. 17	Cleveland 33	All-Stars 0	92,180
1950	Aug. 11	All-Stars 17	Philadelphia 7	88,885
1949	Aug. 12	Philadelphia 38	All-Stars 0	93,780
1948	Aug. 20	Chi. Cardinals 28	All-Stars 0	101,220
1947	Aug. 22	All-Stars 16	Chi. Bears 0	105,840
1946	Aug. 23	All-Stars 16	Los Angeles 0	97,380
1945	Aug. 30	Green Bay 19	All-Stars 7	92,753
1944	Aug. 30	Chi. Bears 24	All-Stars 21	48,769
1943	Aug. 25	All-Stars 27	Washington 7	48,471
1942	Aug. 28	Chi. Bears 21	All-Stars 0	101,100
1941	Aug. 28	Chi. Bears 37	All-Stars 13	98,203
1940	Aug. 29	Green Bay 45	All-Stars 28	84,567
1939	Aug. 30	N.Y. Giants 9	All-Stars 0	81,456
1938	Aug. 31	All-Stars 28	Washington 16	74,250
1937	Sept. 1	All-Stars 6	Green Bay 0	84,560
1936	Sept. 3	Detroit 7	All-Stars 7 (tie)	76,000
1935	Aug. 29	Chi. Bears 5	All-Stars 0	77,450
1934	Aug. 31	Chi. Bears 0	All-Stars 0 (tie)	79,432

*Game shortened because of thunderstorms.

NFL PLAYOFF BOWL

Consolation game that matched conference runners-up.
Western Conference won 8, Eastern Conference won 2.
All games played at Miami's Orange Bowl.

1970   Los Angeles Rams 31, Dallas Cowboys 0
1969   Dallas Cowboys 17, Minnesota Vikings 13
1968   Los Angeles Rams 30, Cleveland Browns 6
1967   Baltimore Colts 20, Philadelphia Eagles 14
1966   Baltimore Colts 35, Dallas Cowboys 3
1965   St. Louis Cardinals 24, Green Bay Packers 17
1964   Green Bay Packers 40, Cleveland Browns 23
1963   Detroit Lions 17, Pittsburgh Steelers 10
1962   Detroit Lions 28, Philadelphia Eagles 10
1961   Detroit Lions 17, Cleveland Browns 16

Compiled by Elias Sports Bureau
*Tied NFL all-time record.

MONDAY NIGHT RECORDS

SCORING
TOUCHDOWNS
Most Touchdowns, Game
- 4   Ron Johnson, N.Y. Giants at Philadelphia, Oct. 2, 1972
  Earl Campbell, Houston vs. Miami, Nov. 20, 1978
  Marcus Allen, L.A. Raiders vs. San Diego, Sept. 24, 1984
  Eric Dickerson, Indianapolis vs. Denver, Oct. 31, 1988
  Emmitt Smith, Dallas at N.Y. Giants, Sept. 4, 1995
  Marshall Faulk, St. Louis at Tampa Bay, Dec. 18, 2000

FIELD GOALS
Most Field Goals, Game
- 7   Chris Boniol, Dallas vs. Green Bay, Nov. 18, 1996*
- 5   Tim Mazzetti, Atlanta vs. Los Angeles, Oct. 30, 1978
  Roger Ruzek, Dallas at L.A. Rams, Dec. 21, 1987
  Rich Karlis, Minnesota vs. Cincinnati, Dec. 25, 1989
  Nick Lowery, Kansas City vs. Denver, Sept. 20, 1993
  Chris Jacke, Green Bay vs. San Francisco, Oct. 14, 1996 (OT)
  Richie Cunningham, Dallas vs. Philadelphia, Sept. 15, 1997

RUSHING
YARDS GAINED
Most Yards Rushing, Game
- 221   Bo Jackson, L.A. Raiders at Seattle, Nov. 30, 1987
- 214   Thurman Thomas, Buffalo at N.Y. Jets, Sept. 24, 1990
- 199   Earl Campbell, Houston vs. Miami, Nov. 20, 1978

Longest Run From Scrimage, Game
- 99   Tony Dorsett, Dallas at Minnesota, Jan. 3, 1983 (TD)*
- 91   Bo Jackson, L.A. Raiders at Seattle, Nov. 30, 1987 (TD)
- 83   James Lofton, Green Bay at N.Y. Giants, Sept. 20, 1982 (TD)

TOUCHDOWNS
Most Rushing Touchdowns, Game
- 4   Earl Campbell, Houston vs. Miami, Nov. 20, 1978
  Eric Dickerson, Indianapolis vs. Denver, Oct. 31, 1988
  Emmitt Smith, Dallas at N.Y. Giants, Sept. 4, 1995

PASSING
YARDS GAINED
Most Yards Passing, Game
- 458   Joe Montana, San Francisco at L.A. Rams, Dec. 11, 1989
- 447   Ken Anderson, Cincinnati vs. Buffalo, Nov. 17, 1975
- 445   Charley Johnson, Denver vs. Kansas City, Nov. 18, 1974

Longest Pass Play
- 99   Brett Favre to Robert Brooks, Green Bay at Chicago, Sept. 11, 1995 (TD)*
- 97   Bernie Kosar to Webster Slaughter, Cleveland vs. Chicago, Oct. 23, 1989 (TD)
- 95   Joe Montana to John Taylor, San Francisco at L.A. Rams, Dec. 11, 1989 (TD)

TOUCHDOWNS
Most Touchdown Passes, Game
- 5   Dave Krieg, Seattle vs. L.A. Raiders, Nov. 28, 1988
  Jim Kelly, Buffalo vs. Cincinnati, Oct. 21, 1991
  Vinny Testaverde, N.Y. Jets vs. Miami, Oct. 23, 2000 (OT)

PASS RECEIVING
RECEPTIONS
Most Pass Receptions, Game
- 14   Herman Moore, Detroit vs. Chicago, Dec. 4, 1995

Jerry Rice, San Francisco vs. Minnesota, Dec. 18, 1995
- 13   Andre Reed, Buffalo vs. Denver, Sept. 18, 1989

YARDS GAINED
Most Yards on Pass Receptions, Game
- 289   Jerry Rice, San Francisco vs. Minnesota, Dec. 18, 1995
- 286   John Taylor, San Francisco at L.A. Rams, Dec. 11, 1989
- 260   Wes Chandler, San Diego vs. Cincinnati, Dec. 20, 1982

TOUCHDOWNS
Most Touchdown Pass Receptions, Game
- 3   Ron Johnson, N.Y. Giants at Philadelphia, Oct. 2, 1972
  Wesley Walker, N.Y. Jets at Detroit, Dec. 6, 1982
  Steve Largent, Seattle at San Diego, Oct. 29, 1984
  Mark Clayton, Miami vs. Dallas, Dec. 17, 1984
  Jerry Rice, San Francisco vs. Chicago, Dec. 14, 1987
  Jerry Rice, San Francisco vs. Minnesota, Dec. 18, 1995
  Lamar Thomas, Miami vs. Denver, Dec. 21, 1998
  Ed McCaffrey, Denver vs. Miami, Sept. 13, 1999

INTERCEPTIONS BY
Most Interceptions, Game
- 4   Dick Anderson, Miami vs. Pittsburgh, Dec. 3, 1973*
- 3   Johnny Robinson, Kansas City at Baltimore, Sept. 28, 1970
  Charlie Babb, Miami vs. Oakland, Sept. 22, 1975
  Charles Phillips, Oakland vs. Denver, Dec. 8, 1975
  Mark Murphy, Washington at San Diego, Oct. 31, 1983
  Ken Easley, Seattle at San Diego, Oct. 29, 1984
  Dwayne Harper, San Diego vs. Oakland, Nov. 27, 1995
  Marcus Coleman, N.Y. Jets vs. Miami, Oct. 23, 2000 (OT)

Longest Interception Return
- 102   Eddie Anderson, L.A. Raiders at Miami, Dec. 14, 1992 (TD)
- 98   Marcus Coleman, N.Y. Jets vs. Miami, Dec. 27, 1999 (TD)
- 94   Nolan Cromwell, L.A. Rams vs. Atlanta, Dec. 14, 1981
  Walker Lee Ashley, Minnesota vs. Chicago, Dec. 19, 1988 (TD)

PUNTING
Longest Punt
- 83   Bryan Barker, Jacksonville vs. N.Y. Jets, Oct. 11, 1999
- 74   Craig Colquitt, Pittsburgh vs. Oakland, Dec. 7, 1981
- 73   Tom Tupa, New England at Denver, Oct. 6, 1997

PUNT RETURNS
Longest Punt Return
- 95   John Taylor, San Francisco vs. Washington, Nov. 21, 1988 (TD)
- 94   Dennis McKinnon, Chicago vs. N.Y. Giants, Sept. 14, 1987 (TD)
- 91   JoJo Townsell, N.Y. Jets vs. Seattle, Nov. 9, 1987 (TD)

KICKOFF RETURNS
Longest Kickoff Return
- 105   Terry Fair, Detroit vs. Tampa Bay, Sept. 28, 1998 (TD)
- 102   Harold Hart, Oakland at Miami, Sept. 22, 1975 (TD)
- 101   Roell Preston, Green Bay vs. Minnesota, Oct. 5, 1998 (TD)

FUMBLES
Longest Fumble Return
- 99   Don Griffin, San Francisco vs. Chicago, Dec. 23, 1991 (TD)
- 96   Joe Lavender, Philadelphia vs. Dallas, Sept. 23, 1974 (TD)
- 88   Keith McKenzie, Pittsburgh vs. Green Bay, Nov. 9, 1998 (TD)

MONDAY NIGHT FOOTBALL,
1970-2001
(Home Team in capitals, games listed in chronological order.)

2001
DENVER 31, N.Y. Giants 20
GREEN BAY 37, Washington 0
San Francisco 19, N.Y. JETS 17
St. Louis 35, DETROIT 0
DALLAS 9, Washington 7
Philadelphia 10, N.Y. GIANTS 9
PITTSBURGH 34, Tennessee 7
OAKLAND 38, Denver 28
Baltimore 16, TENNESSEE 10
MINNESOTA 28, N.Y. Giants 16
Tampa Bay 24, ST. LOUIS 17
Green Bay 28, JACKSONVILLE 21
MIAMI 41, Indianapolis 6
St. Louis 34, NEW ORLEANS 21
Tennessee 13, OAKLAND 10 (Sat.)
TAMPA BAY 22, Baltimore 10 (Sat.)
BALTIMORE 19, Minnesota 3

2000
ST. LOUIS 41, Denver 36
N.Y. JETS 20, New England 19
Dallas 27, WASHINGTON 21
INDIANAPOLIS 43, Jacksonville 14
KANSAS CITY 24, Seattle 17
MINNESOTA 30, Tampa Bay 23
TENNESSEE 27, Jacksonville 13
N.Y. JETS 40, Miami 37 (OT)
Tennessee 27, WASHINGTON 21
GREEN BAY 26, Minnesota 20 (OT)
DENVER 27, Oakland 24
Washington 33, ST. LOUIS 20
CAROLINA 31, Green Bay 14
NEW ENGLAND 30, Kansas City 24
INDIANAPOLIS 44, Buffalo 20
TAMPA BAY 38, St. Louis 35
TENNESSEE 31, Dallas 0

1999
Miami 38, DENVER 21
DALLAS 24, Atlanta 7
San Francisco 24, ARIZONA 10
Buffalo 23, MIAMI 18
Jacksonville 16, N.Y. JETS 6
N.Y. GIANTS 13, Dallas 10
PITTSBURGH 13, Atlanta 9
Seattle 27, GREEN BAY 7
MINNESOTA 27, Dallas 17
N.Y. Jets 24, NEW ENGLAND 17
DENVER 27, Oakland 21 (OT)
Green Bay 20, SAN FRANCISCO 3
TAMPA BAY 24, Minnesota 17
JACKSONVILLE 27, Denver 24
MINNESOTA 24, Green Bay 20
N.Y. Jets 38, MIAMI 31
ATLANTA 34, San Francisco 29

1998
DENVER 27, New England 21
San Francisco 45, WASHINGTON 10
Dallas 31, N.Y. GIANTS 7
DETROIT 27, Tampa Bay 6
Minnesota 37, GREEN BAY 24
JACKSONVILLE 28, Miami 21
N.Y. Jets 24, NEW ENGLAND 14
Pittsburgh 20, KANSAS CITY 13
Dallas 34, PHILADELPHIA 0
PITTSBURGH 27, Green Bay 20
Denver 30, KANSAS CITY 7
NEW ENGLAND 26, Miami 23
SAN FRANCISCO 31, N.Y. Giants 7
TAMPA BAY 24, Green Bay 22
SAN FRANCISCO 35, Detroit 13
MIAMI 31, Denver 21
JACKSONVILLE 21, Pittsburgh 3

1997
GREEN BAY 38, Chicago 24
Kansas City 28, OAKLAND 27
DALLAS 21, Philadelphia 20
JACKSONVILLE 30, Pittsburgh 21
San Francisco 34, CAROLINA 21
DENVER 34, New England 13
WASHINGTON 21, Dallas 16
Buffalo 9, INDIANAPOLIS 6
Green Bay 28, NEW ENGLAND 10
Chicago 36, MIAMI 33 (OT)
KANSAS CITY 13, Pittsburgh 10
San Francisco 24, PHILADELPHIA 12
MIAMI 30, Buffalo 13
DENVER 31, Oakland 3
Green Bay 27, MINNESOTA 11
Carolina 23, DALLAS 13
SAN FRANCISCO 34, Denver 17
New England 14, MIAMI 12

1996
CHICAGO 22, Dallas 6
GREEN BAY 39, Philadelphia 13
PITTSBURGH 24, Buffalo 6
INDIANAPOLIS 10, Miami 6
Dallas 23, PHILADELPHIA 19
Pittsburgh 17, KANSAS CITY 7
GREEN BAY 23, San Francisco 20 (OT)
Oakland 23, SAN DIEGO 14
Chicago 15, MINNESOTA 13
Denver 22, OAKLAND 21
SAN DIEGO 27, Detroit 21
DALLAS 21, Green Bay 6
Pittsburgh 24, MIAMI 17
San Francisco 34, ATLANTA 10
OAKLAND 26, Kansas City 7
MIAMI 16, Buffalo 14
SAN FRANCISCO 24, Detroit 14

1995
Dallas 35, N.Y. GIANTS 0
Green Bay 27, CHICAGO 24
MIAMI 23, Pittsburgh 10
DETROIT 27, San Francisco 24
Buffalo 22, CLEVELAND 19
KANSAS CITY 29, San Diego 23 (OT)
DENVER 27, Oakland 0
NEW ENGLAND 27, Buffalo 14
Chicago 14, MINNESOTA 6
DALLAS 34, Philadelphia 12
PITTSBURGH 20, Cleveland 3
San Francisco 44, MIAMI 20
SAN DIEGO 12, Oakland 6
DETROIT 27, Chicago 7
MIAMI 13, Kansas City 6
SAN FRANCISCO 37, Minnesota 30
Dallas 37, ARIZONA 13

1994
SAN FRANCISCO 44, L.A. Raiders 14
PHILADELPHIA 30, Chicago 22
Detroit 20, DALLAS 17 (OT)
BUFFALO 27, Denver 20
PITTSBURGH 30, Houston 14
Minnesota 27, N.Y. GIANTS 10
Kansas City 31, DENVER 28
PHILADELPHIA 21, Houston 6
Green Bay 33, CHICAGO 6
DALLAS 38, N.Y. Giants 10
PITTSBURGH 23, Buffalo 10
N.Y. Giants 13, HOUSTON 10
San Francisco 35, NEW ORLEANS 14
L.A. Raiders 24, SAN DIEGO 17
MIAMI 45, Kansas City 28
Dallas 24, NEW ORLEANS 16
MINNESOTA 21, San Francisco 14

1993
WASHINGTON 35, Dallas 16
CLEVELAND 23, San Francisco 13
KANSAS CITY 15, Denver 7
Pittsburgh 45, ATLANTA 17
MIAMI 17, Washington 10
BUFFALO 35, Houston 7
L.A. Raiders 23, DENVER 20
Minnesota 19, CHICAGO 12
BUFFALO 24, Washington 10
KANSAS CITY 23, Green Bay 16
PITTSBURGH 23, Buffalo 0
SAN FRANCISCO 42, New Orleans 7
San Diego 31, INDIANAPOLIS 0
DALLAS 23, Philadelphia 17
Pittsburgh 21, MIAMI 20
N.Y. Giants 24, NEW ORLEANS 14
SAN DIEGO 45, Miami 20
Philadelphia 37, SAN FRANCISCO 34 (OT)

1992
DALLAS 23, Washington 10
Miami 27, CLEVELAND 23
N.Y. Giants 27, CHICAGO 14
KANSAS CITY 27, L.A. Raiders 7
PHILADELPHIA 31, Dallas 7
WASHINGTON 34, Denver 3
PITTSBURGH 20, Cincinnati 0
Buffalo 24, N.Y. JETS 20
Minnesota 38, CHICAGO 10
San Francisco 41, ATLANTA 3
Buffalo 26, MIAMI 20
NEW ORLEANS 20, Washington 3
SEATTLE 16, Denver 13 (OT)
HOUSTON 24, Chicago 7
MIAMI 20, L.A. Raiders 7
Dallas 41, ATLANTA 17
SAN FRANCISCO 24, Detroit 6

1991
N.Y. GIANTS 16, San Francisco 14
Washington 33, DALLAS 31
HOUSTON 17, Kansas City 7
CHICAGO 19, N.Y. Jets 13 (OT)
WASHINGTON 23, Philadelphia 0
KANSAS CITY 33, Buffalo 6
N.Y. Giants 23, PITTSBURGH 20
BUFFALO 35, Cincinnati 10
KANSAS CITY 24, L.A. Raiders 21
PHILADELPHIA 30, N.Y. Giants 7
Chicago 34, MINNESOTA 17
Buffalo 41, MIAMI 27
San Francisco 33, L.A. RAMS 10
Philadelphia 13, HOUSTON 6
MIAMI 37, Cincinnati 13
NEW ORLEANS 27, L.A. Raiders 0
SAN FRANCISCO 52, Chicago 14

1990
San Francisco 13, NEW ORLEANS 12
DENVER 24, Kansas City 23
Buffalo 30, N.Y. JETS 7
SEATTLE 31, Cincinnati 16
Cleveland 30, DENVER 29
PHILADELPHIA 32, Minnesota 24
Cincinnati 34, CLEVELAND 13
PITTSBURGH 41, L.A. Rams 10
N.Y. Giants 24, INDIANAPOLIS 7
PHILADELPHIA 28, Washington 14
L.A. Raiders 13, MIAMI 10
HOUSTON 27, Buffalo 24
SAN FRANCISCO 7, N.Y. Giants 3
L.A. Raiders 38, DETROIT 31
San Francisco 26, L.A. RAMS 10
NEW ORLEANS 20, L.A. Rams 17

1989
N.Y. Giants 27, WASHINGTON 24
Denver 28, BUFFALO 14
CINCINNATI 21, Cleveland 14
CHICAGO 27, Philadelphia 13
L.A. Raiders 14, N.Y. JETS 7
BUFFALO 23, L.A. Rams 20
CLEVELAND 27, Chicago 7
N.Y. GIANTS 24, Minnesota 14
SAN FRANCISCO 31, New Orleans 13
HOUSTON 26, Cincinnati 24
Denver 14, WASHINGTON 10
SAN FRANCISCO 34, N.Y. Giants 24
SEATTLE 17, Buffalo 16
San Francisco 30, L.A. RAMS 27
NEW ORLEANS 30, Philadelphia 20
MINNESOTA 29, Cincinnati 21

1988
N.Y. GIANTS 27, Washington 20
Dallas 17, PHOENIX 14
CLEVELAND 23, Indianapolis 17
L.A. Raiders 30, DENVER 27 (OT)
NEW ORLEANS 20, Dallas 17
PHILADELPHIA 24, N.Y. Giants 13
Buffalo 37, N.Y. JETS 14
CHICAGO 10, San Francisco 9
INDIANAPOLIS 55, Denver 23
HOUSTON 24, Cleveland 17
Buffalo 31, MIAMI 6
SAN FRANCISCO 37, Washington 21
SEATTLE 35, L.A. Raiders 27
L.A. RAMS 23, Chicago 3
MIAMI 38, Cleveland 31
MINNESOTA 28, Chicago 27

1987
CHICAGO 34, N.Y. Giants 19
N.Y. JETS 43, New England 24
San Francisco 41, N.Y. GIANTS 21
DENVER 30, L.A. Raiders 14
Washington 13, DALLAS 7
CLEVELAND 30, L.A. Rams 17
MINNESOTA 34, Denver 27
DALLAS 33, N.Y. Giants 24
N.Y. JETS 30, Seattle 14
DENVER 31, Chicago 29
L.A. Rams 30, WASHINGTON 26
L.A. Raiders 37, SEATTLE 14
MIAMI 37, N.Y. Jets 28
SAN FRANCISCO 41, Chicago 0
Dallas 29, L.A. RAMS 21
New England 24, MIAMI 10

1986
DALLAS 31, N.Y. Giants 28
Denver 21, PITTSBURGH 10
Chicago 25, GREEN BAY 12
Dallas 31, ST. LOUIS 7
SEATTLE 33, San Diego 7
CINCINNATI 24, Pittsburgh 22
N.Y. JETS 22, Denver 10
N.Y. GIANTS 27, Washington 20
L.A. Rams 20, CHICAGO 17
CLEVELAND 26, Miami 16
WASHINGTON 14, San Francisco 6
MIAMI 45, N.Y. Jets 3
N.Y. Giants 21, SAN FRANCISCO 17
SEATTLE 37, L.A. Raiders 0
Chicago 16, DETROIT 13
New England 34, MIAMI 27

1985
DALLAS 44, Washington 14
CLEVELAND 17, Pittsburgh 7
L.A. Rams 35, SEATTLE 24
Cincinnati 37, PITTSBURGH 24
WASHINGTON 27, St. Louis 10
N.Y. JETS 23, Miami 7
CHICAGO 23, Green Bay 7
L.A. RAIDERS 34, San Diego 21
ST. LOUIS 21, Dallas 10
DENVER 17, San Francisco 16
WASHINGTON 23, N.Y. Giants 21
SAN FRANCISCO 19, Seattle 6
MIAMI 38, Chicago 24
L.A. Rams 27, SAN FRANCISCO 20
MIAMI 30, New England 27
L.A. Raiders 16, L.A. RAMS 6

1984
Dallas 20, L.A. RAMS 13
SAN FRANCISCO 37, Washington 31
Miami 21, BUFFALO 17
L.A. RAIDERS 33, San Diego 30
PITTSBURGH 38, Cincinnati 17
San Francisco 31, N.Y. GIANTS 10
DENVER 17, Green Bay 14
L.A. Rams 24, ATLANTA 10
Seattle 24, SAN DIEGO 0
WASHINGTON 27, Atlanta 14
SEATTLE 17, L.A. Raiders 14
NEW ORLEANS 27, Pittsburgh 24
MIAMI 28, N.Y. Jets 17
SAN DIEGO 20, Chicago 7
L.A. Raiders 24, DETROIT 3
MIAMI 28, Dallas 21

1983
Dallas 31, WASHINGTON 30
San Diego 17, KANSAS CITY 14
L.A. RAIDERS 27, Miami 14
N.Y. GIANTS 27, Green Bay 3
N.Y. Jets 34, BUFFALO 10
Pittsburgh 24, CINCINNATI 14
GREEN BAY 48, Washington 47
ST. LOUIS 20, N.Y. Giants 20 (OT)
Washington 27, SAN DIEGO 24
DETROIT 15, N.Y. Giants 9
L.A. Rams 36, ATLANTA 13
N.Y. Jets 31, NEW ORLEANS 28
MIAMI 38, Cincinnati 14
DETROIT 13, Minnesota 2
Green Bay 12, TAMPA BAY 9 (OT)
SAN FRANCISCO 42, Dallas 17

1982
Pittsburgh 36, DALLAS 28
Green Bay 27, N.Y. GIANTS 19
L.A. RAIDERS 28, San Diego 24
TAMPA BAY 23, Miami 17
N.Y. Jets 28, DETROIT 13
Dallas 37, HOUSTON 7
SAN DIEGO 50, Cincinnati 34
MIAMI 27, Buffalo 10
MINNESOTA 31, Dallas 27

1981
San Diego 44, CLEVELAND 14
Oakland 36, MINNESOTA 10
Dallas 35, NEW ENGLAND 21
Los Angeles 24, CHICAGO 7
PHILADELPHIA 16, Atlanta 13
BUFFALO 31, Miami 21
DETROIT 48, Chicago 17
PITTSBURGH 26, Houston 13
DENVER 19, Minnesota 17
DALLAS 27, Buffalo 14
SEATTLE 44, San Diego 23
ATLANTA 31, Minnesota 30
MIAMI 13, Philadelphia 10
OAKLAND 30, Pittsburgh 27
LOS ANGELES 21, Atlanta 16
SAN DIEGO 23, Oakland 10

1980
Dallas 17, WASHINGTON 3
Houston 16, CLEVELAND 7
PHILADELPHIA 35, N.Y. Giants 3
NEW ENGLAND 23, Denver 14
CHICAGO 23, Tampa Bay 0
DENVER 20, Washington 17
Oakland 45, PITTSBURGH 34
N.Y. JETS 17, Miami 14
CLEVELAND 27, Chicago 21
HOUSTON 38, New England 34
Oakland 19, SEATTLE 17
Los Angeles 27, NEW ORLEANS 7
OAKLAND 9, Denver 3
MIAMI 16, New England 13 (OT)
LOS ANGELES 38, Dallas 14
SAN DIEGO 26, Pittsburgh 17

1979
Pittsburgh 16, NEW ENGLAND 13 (OT)
Atlanta 14, PHILADELPHIA 10
WASHINGTON 27, N.Y. Giants 0
CLEVELAND 26, Dallas 7
GREEN BAY 27, New England 14
OAKLAND 13, Miami 3
N.Y. JETS 14, Minnesota 7
PITTSBURGH 42, Denver 7
Seattle 31, ATLANTA 28
Houston 9, MIAMI 6
Philadelphia 31, DALLAS 21
LOS ANGELES 20, Atlanta 14
SEATTLE 30, N.Y. Jets 7
Oakland 42, NEW ORLEANS 35
HOUSTON 20, Pittsburgh 17
SAN DIEGO 17, Denver 7

1978
DALLAS 38, Baltimore 0
MINNESOTA 12, Denver 9 (OT)
Baltimore 34, NEW ENGLAND 27
Minnesota 24, CHICAGO 20
WASHINGTON 9, Dallas 5
MIAMI 21, Cincinnati 0
DENVER 16, Chicago 7
Houston 24, PITTSBURGH 17
ATLANTA 15, Los Angeles 7
BALTIMORE 21, Washington 17
Oakland 34, CINCINNATI 21
HOUSTON 35, Miami 30
Pittsburgh 24, SAN FRANCISCO 7
SAN DIEGO 40, Chicago 7
Cincinnati 20, LOS ANGELES 19
MIAMI 23, New England 3

1977
PITTSBURGH 27, San Francisco 0
CLEVELAND 30, New England 27 (OT)
Oakland 37, KANSAS CITY 28
CHICAGO 24, Los Angeles 23
PITTSBURGH 20, Cincinnati 14
LOS ANGELES 35, Minnesota 3
ST. LOUIS 28, N.Y. Giants 0
BALTIMORE 10, Washington 3
St. Louis 24, DALLAS 17
WASHINGTON 10, Green Bay 9
OAKLAND 34, Buffalo 13
MIAMI 17, Baltimore 6
Dallas 42, SAN FRANCISCO 35

1976
Miami 30, BUFFALO 21
Oakland 24, KANSAS CITY 21
Washington 20, PHILADELPHIA 17 (OT)
MINNESOTA 17, Pittsburgh 6
San Francisco 16, LOS ANGELES 0
NEW ENGLAND 41, N.Y. Jets 7
WASHINGTON 20, St. Louis 10
BALTIMORE 38, Houston 14
CINCINNATI 20, Los Angeles 12
DALLAS 17, Buffalo 10
Baltimore 17, MIAMI 16
SAN FRANCISCO 20, Minnesota 16
OAKLAND 35, Cincinnati 20

1975
Oakland 31, MIAMI 21
DENVER 23, Green Bay 13
Dallas 36, DETROIT 10
WASHINGTON 27, St. Louis 17
N.Y. Giants 17, BUFFALO 14
Minnesota 13, CHICAGO 9
Los Angeles 42, PHILADELPHIA 3
Kansas City 34, DALLAS 31
CINCINNATI 33, Buffalo 24
Pittsburgh 32, HOUSTON 9
MIAMI 20, New England 7
OAKLAND 17, Denver 10
SAN DIEGO 24, N.Y. Jets 16

1974
BUFFALO 21, Oakland 20
PHILADELPHIA 13, Dallas 10
WASHINGTON 30, Denver 3
MIAMI 21, N.Y. Jets 17
DETROIT 17, San Francisco 13
CHICAGO 10, Green Bay 9
PITTSBURGH 24, Atlanta 17
Los Angeles 15, SAN FRANCISCO 13
Minnesota 24, ST. LOUIS 24
Kansas City 42, DENVER 34
Pittsburgh 28, NEW ORLEANS 7
MIAMI 24, Cincinnati 3
Washington 23, LOS ANGELES 17

1973
GREEN BAY 23, N.Y. Jets 7
DALLAS 40, New Orleans 3
DETROIT 31, Atlanta 6
WASHINGTON 14, Dallas 7
Miami 17, CLEVELAND 9
DENVER 23, Oakland 23
BUFFALO 23, Kansas City 14
PITTSBURGH 21, Washington 16
KANSAS CITY 19, Chicago 7
ATLANTA 20, Minnesota 14
SAN FRANCISCO 20, Green Bay 6
MIAMI 30, Pittsburgh 26
LOS ANGELES 40, N.Y. Giants 6

1972
Washington 24, MINNESOTA 21
Kansas City 20, NEW ORLEANS 17
N.Y. Giants 27, PHILADELPHIA 12
Oakland 34, HOUSTON 0
Green Bay 24, DETROIT 23
CHICAGO 13, Minnesota 10
DALLAS 28, Detroit 24
Baltimore 24, NEW ENGLAND 17
Cleveland 21, SAN DIEGO 17
WASHINGTON 24, Atlanta 13
MIAMI 31, St. Louis 10
Los Angeles 26, SAN FRANCISCO 16
OAKLAND 24, N.Y. Jets 16

1971
Minnesota 16, DETROIT 13
ST. LOUIS 17, N.Y. Jets 10
Oakland 34, CLEVELAND 20
DALLAS 20, N.Y. Giants 13
KANSAS CITY 38, Pittsburgh 16
MINNESOTA 10, Baltimore 3
GREEN BAY 14, Detroit 14
BALTIMORE 24, Los Angeles 17
SAN DIEGO 20, St. Louis 17
ATLANTA 28, Green Bay 21
MIAMI 34, Chicago 3
Kansas City 26, SAN FRANCISCO 17
Washington 38, LOS ANGELES 24

1970
CLEVELAND 31, N.Y. Jets 21
Kansas City 44, BALTIMORE 24
DETROIT 28, Chicago 14
Green Bay 22, SAN DIEGO 20
OAKLAND 34, Washington 20
MINNESOTA 13, Los Angeles 3
PITTSBURGH 21, Cincinnati 10
Baltimore 13, GREEN BAY 10
St. Louis 38, DALLAS 0
PHILADELPHIA 23, N.Y. Giants 20
Miami 20, ATLANTA 7
Cleveland 21, HOUSTON 10
Detroit 28, LOS ANGELES 23

MONDAY NIGHT WON-LOST RECORDS, 1970-2001
AMERICAN FOOTBALL CONFERENCE

	Balt.	Buff.	Cin.	Cle.	Den.	Hou.	Ind.	Jax.	K.C.	Mia.	N.E.	N.Y.J.	Oak.	Pitt.	S.D.	Tenn.
Total	2-1	17-20	7-16	13-11	21-25-1	0-0	12-9	5-3	17-13	36-29	8-18	14-18	34-19-1	29-18	14-12	15-13
2001	2-1			1-1			0-1	0-1		1-0		0-1	1-1	1-0		1-2
2000		0-1		1-1			2-0	0-2	1-1	0-1	1-1	2-0	0-1			3-0
1999		1-0		1-2				2-0		1-2	0-1	2-1	0-1	1-0		
1998				2-1				2-0	0-2	1-2	1-2	1-0		2-1		
1997		1-1		2-1				0-1	1-0	2-0	1-2	1-2		0-2	0-2	
1996		0-2		1-0			1-0		0-2	1-2			2-1	3-0	1-1	
1995		1-1	0-2	1-0					1-1	2-1	1-0		0-2	1-1	1-1	
1994		1-1		0-2					1-1	1-0			1-1	2-0	0-1	0-3
1993		2-1	1-0	0-2			0-1		2-0	1-2			1-0	3-0	2-0	0-1
1992		2-0	0-1	0-1	0-2				1-0	2-1		0-1	0-2	1-0		1-0
1991		2-1	0-2						2-1	1-1		0-1	0-2	0-1		1-1
1990		1-1	1-1	1-1	1-1		0-1		0-1	0-1		0-1	2-0	1-0		1-0
1989		1-2	1-2	1-1	2-0							0-1	1-0			1-0
1988		2-0		1-2	0-2		1-1			1-1		0-1	1-1			1-0
1987				1-0	2-1					1-1	1-1	2-1	1-1			
1986			1-0	1-0	1-1					1-2	1-0	1-1		0-2	0-1	
1985			1-0	1-0	1-0					2-1	0-1	1-0	2-0	0-2	0-1	
1984		0-1	0-1		1-0					3-0		0-1	2-1	1-1	1-2	
1983		0-1	0-2						0-1	1-1	2-0		1-0	1-0	1-1	
1982		0-1	0-1	0-1						1-1		1-0	1-0	1-0	1-1	0-1
1981		1-1	0-1	1-0						1-1	0-1		2-1	1-1	2-1	0-1
1980			1-1	1-2						1-1	1-2	1-0	3-0	0-2	1-0	2-0
1979			1-0	0-2						0-2	1-2		2-0	2-1	1-0	2-0
1978		1-2		1-1			2-1			2-1	0-2		1-0	1-1	1-0	2-0
1977		0-1	0-1	1-0			1-1		0-1	1-0	0-1		2-0	2-0		
1976		0-2	1-1				2-0		0-1	1-1	1-0	0-1	2-0	0-1		0-1
1975		0-2	1-0	1-1					1-0	1-1	0-1	0-1	2-0	1-0	1-0	0-1
1974		1-0	0-1	0-2					1-0	2-0		0-1	0-1	2-0		
1973		1-0	0-1	0-0-1					1-1	2-0		0-1	0-0-1	1-1		
1972			1-0				1-0		1-0	1-0	0-1	0-1	2-0		0-1	0-1
1971			0-1						1-1	2-0	1-0	0-1	1-0	0-1	1-0	
1970			0-1	2-0					1-1	1-0	1-0	0-1	1-0	1-0	0-1	0-1

MONDAY NIGHT WON-LOST RECORDS, 1970-2001
NATIONAL FOOTBALL CONFERENCE

	Ariz.	Atl.	Car.	Chi.	Dall.	Det.	G.B.	Minn.	N.O.	N.Y.G.	Phil.	St.L.	S.F.	Sea.	T.B.	Wash.
Total	5-10-1	6-17	2-1	16-28	35-26	11-13-1	18-18-1	21-20	6-13	15-26-1	15-15	20-23	35-20	12-6	6-4	24-26
2001				1-0	0-1		2-0	1-1	0-1	0-3	1-0	2-1	1-0		2-0	0-2
2000			1-0	1-1				1-1	1-1			1-2		0-1	1-1	1-2
1999	0-1	1-2		1-2				1-2	2-1	1-0			1-2	1-0	1-0	
1998				2-0	1-1		0-3	1-0		0-2	0-1		3-0		1-1	0-1
1997			1-1	1-1	1-2			3-0	0-1		0-2		3-0			1-0
1996		0-1	2-0	2-1		0-2	2-1	0-1			0-2		2-1			
1995	0-1		1-2	3-0	2-0		1-0	0-2		0-1	0-1		2-1			
1994			0-2	2-1	1-0		1-0	2-0	0-2	1-2	2-0		2-1			
1993		0-1	0-1	1-1			0-1	1-0	0-2	1-0	1-1		1-2			1-2
1992		0-2	0-3	2-1	0-1			1-0	1-0	1-0	1-0		2-0	1-0		1-2
1991			2-1	0-1				0-1	1-0	2-1	2-1	0-1	2-1			2-0
1990				0-1				0-1	1-1	1-1	2-0	0-3	3-0	1-0		0-1
1989			1-1					1-1	1-1	2-1	0-2	0-2	3-0	1-0		0-2
1988	0-1		1-2	1-1				1-0	1-0	1-1	1-0	1-0	1-1	1-0		0-2
1987			1-2	2-1				1-0		0-3		1-2	2-0	0-2		1-1
1986	0-1		2-1	2-0	0-1	0-1				2-1		1-0	0-2	2-0		1-1
1985	1-1		1-1	1-1		0-1				0-1		2-1	1-2	0-2		2-1
1984		0-2	0-1	1-1	0-1	0-1			1-0	0-1		1-1	2-0	2-0		1-1
1983	0-0-1	0-1		1-1	2-0	2-1	0-1	0-1	1-1-1			1-0	1-0		0-1	1-2
1982				1-2	0-1	1-0	1-0			0-1					1-0	
1981		1-2	0-2	2-0	1-0			0-3				1-1	2-0		1-0	
1980			1-1	1-1					0-1	0-1	1-0	2-0		0-1	0-1	0-2
1979		1-2		0-2			1-0	0-1	0-1	0-1	1-1	1-0		2-0		1-0
1978		1-0	0-3	1-1				2-0				0-2	0-1			1-1
1977	2-0		1-0	1-1		0-1		0-1		0-1		1-1	0-2			1-1
1976	0-1			1-0				1-1			0-1	0-2	2-0			2-0
1975	0-1		0-1		0-1	0-1	1-0			1-0	0-1	1-0				1-0
1974	0-1	0-1	1-0	0-1	1-0	0-1	1-0	0-1				1-0	1-1	0-2		2-0
1973		1-1	0-1	1-1	1-0	1-1	0-1	0-1		0-1		1-0	1-0			1-1
1972	0-1	0-1	1-0	1-0	0-2	1-0	0-2	0-1		1-0	0-1	1-0	0-1			2-0
1971	1-1	1-0	0-1	1-0	0-1-1	0-1-1	2-0			0-1			0-2	0-1		1-0
1970	1-0	0-1		0-1	0-1	2-0	1-1	1-0		0-1	1-0	0-2				0-1

THURSDAY-SUNDAY NIGHT FOOTBALL, 1974-2001
(Home Team in capitals, games listed in chronological order.)

2001
Miami 31, TENNESSEE 23 (Sun.)
Denver 38, ARIZONA 17 (Sun.)
PHILADELPHIA 40, Dallas 18 (Sun.)
SAN FRANCISCO 24, Carolina 14 (Sun.)
Oakland 23, INDIANAPOLIS 18 (Sun.)
Buffalo 13, JACKSONVILLE 10 (Thurs.)
Indianapolis 35, KANSAS CITY 28 (Thurs.)
New York Jets 16, NEW ORLEANS 9 (Sun.)
SEATTLE 34, Oakland 27 (Sun.)
St. Louis 24, NEW ENGLAND 17 (Sun.)
Chicago 13, MINNESOTA 6 (Sun.)
SAN FRANCISCO 35, Buffalo 0 (Sun.)
DENVER 20, Seattle 7 (Sun.)
Pittsburgh 26, BALTIMORE 21 (Sun.)
New York Jets 29, INDIANAPOLIS 28 (Sun.)
Washington 40, NEW ORLEANS 10 (Sun.)
Philadelphia 17, TAMPA BAY 13 (Sun.)

2000
BUFFALO 16, Tennessee 13 (Sun.)
ARIZONA 32, Dallas 31 (Sun.)
MIAMI 19, Baltimore 6 (Sun.)
Washington 16, NEW YORK GIANTS 6 (Sun.)
PHILADELPHIA 38, Atlanta 10 (Sun.)
Baltimore 15, JACKSONVILLE 10 (Sun.)
Minnesota 28, CHICAGO 16 (Sun.)
Detroit 28, TAMPA BAY 14 (Thurs.)
Oakland 15, SAN DIEGO 13 (Sun.)
Carolina 27, ST. LOUIS 24 (Sun.)
INDIANAPOLIS 23, New York Jets 15 (Sun.)
Jacksonville 34, PITTSBURGH 24 (Sun.)
New York Giants 31, ARIZONA 7 (Sun.)
MINNESOTA 24, Detroit 17 (Thurs.)
Green Bay 28, CHICAGO 6 (Sun.)
OAKLAND 31, New York Jets 7 (Sun.)
New York Giants 17, DALLAS 13 (Sun.)
Buffalo 42, SEATTLE 23 (Sat.)

1999
Pittsburgh 43, CLEVELAND 0 (Sun.)
BUFFALO 17, N.Y. Jets 3 (Sun.)
NEW ENGLAND 16, N.Y. Giants 14 (Sun.)
SEATTLE 22, Oakland 21 (Sun.)
GREEN BAY 26, Tampa Bay 23 (Sun.)
Washington 24, ARIZONA 10 (Sun.)
Kansas City 35, BALTIMORE 8 (Thurs.)
DETROIT 20, Tampa Bay 3 (Sun.)
MIAMI 17, Tennessee 0 (Sun.)
SEATTLE 20, Denver 17 (Sun.)
JACKSONVILLE 41, New Orleans 23 (Sun.)
CAROLINA 34, Atlanta 28 (Sun.)
JACKSONVILLE 20, Pittsburgh 6 (Thurs.)
NEW ENGLAND 13, Dallas 6 (Sun.)
TENNESSEE 21, Oakland 14 (Thurs.)
KANSAS CITY 31, Minnesota 28 (Sun.)
Buffalo 31, ARIZONA 21 (Sun.)
Washington 26, SAN FRANCISCO 20 (OT) (Sun.)

1998
KANSAS CITY 28, Oakland 8 (Sun.)
NEW ENGLAND 29, Indianapolis 6 (Sun.)
ARIZONA 17, Philadelphia 3 (Sun.)
BALTIMORE 31, Cincinnati 24 (Sun.)
KANSAS CITY 17, Seattle 6 (Sun.)
Atlanta 34, NEW YORK GIANTS 20 (Sun.)
DETROIT 27, Green Bay 20 (Thurs.)
Buffalo 30, CAROLINA 14 (Sun.)
Oakland 31, SEATTLE 18 (Sun.)
Tennessee 31, TAMPA BAY 22 (Sun.)
DETROIT 26, Chicago 3 (Sun.)
SAN FRANCISCO 31, New Orleans 20 (Sun.)
Denver 31, SAN DIEGO 16 (Sun.)
PHILADELPHIA 17, St. Louis 14 (Thurs.)
MINNESOTA 48, Chicago 22 (Sun.)
New York Jets 21, MIAMI 16 (Sun.)
MINNESOTA 50, Jacksonville 10 (Sun.)
Dallas 23, WASHINGTON 7 (Sun.)

1997
Washington 24, CAROLINA 10 (Sun.)
ARIZONA 25, Dallas 22 (OT) (Sun.)
NEW ENGLAND 27, New York Jets 24 (OT) (Sun.)
TAMPA BAY 31, Miami 21 (Sun.)
MINNESOTA 28, Philadelphia 19 (Sun.)
New Orleans 20, CHICAGO 17 (Sun.)
PITTSBURGH 24, Indianapolis 22 (Sun.)
KANSAS CITY 31, San Diego 3 (Thurs.)
CAROLINA 21, Atlanta 12 (Sun.)
GREEN BAY 20, Detroit 10 (Sun.)
PITTSBURGH 37, Baltimore 0 (Sun.)
Oakland 38, SAN DIEGO 13 (Sun.)
WASHINGTON 7, New York Giants 7 (OT) (Sun.)
Denver 38, SAN DIEGO 28 (Sun.)
CINCINNATI 41, Tennessee 14 (Thurs.)
MIAMI 33, Detroit 30 (Sun.)
Chicago 13, ST. LOUIS 10 (Sun.)
SEATTLE 38, San Francisco 9 (Sun.)

1996
Buffalo 23, NEW YORK GIANTS 20 (OT) (Sun.)
Miami 38, ARIZONA 10 (Sun.)
DENVER 27, Tampa Bay 23 (Sun.)
Philadelphia 33, ATLANTA 18 (Sun.)
WASHINGTON 31, New York Jets 16 (Sun.)
Houston 30, CINCINNATI 27 (OT) (Sun.)
INDIANAPOLIS 26, Baltimore 21 (Sun.)
KANSAS CITY 34, Seattle 16 (Sun.)
NEW ENGLAND 28, Buffalo 25 (Sun.)
San Francisco 24, NEW ORLEANS 17 (Sun.)
CAROLINA 27, New York Giants 17 (Sun.)
Minnesota 16, OAKLAND 13 (OT) (Sun.)
Green Bay 24, ST. LOUIS 9 (Sun.)
New England 45, SAN DIEGO 7 (Sun.)
INDIANAPOLIS 37, Philadelphia 10 (Thurs.)
Minnesota 24, DETROIT 22 (Sun.)
JACKSONVILLE 20, Seattle 13 (Sun.)
SAN DIEGO 16, Denver 10 (Sun.)

1995
DENVER 22, Buffalo 7 (Sun.)
Philadelphia 31, ARIZONA 19 (Sun.)
Dallas 23, MINNESOTA 17 (OT) (Sun.)
Green Bay 24, JACKSONVILLE 14 (Sun.)
Oakland 47, NEW YORK JETS 10 (Sun.)
Denver 37, NEW ENGLAND 3 (Sun.)
ST. LOUIS 21, Atlanta 19 (Thurs.)
Cincinnati 27, PITTSBURGH 9 (Thurs.)
New York Giants 24, WASHINGTON 15 (Sun.)
Miami 24, SAN DIEGO 14 (Sun.)
PHILADELPHIA 31, Denver 13 (Sun.)
KANSAS CITY 20, Houston 13 (Sun.)
NEW ORLEANS 34, Carolina 26 (Sun.)
New York Giants 10, ARIZONA 6 (Thurs.)
SAN FRANCISCO 27, Buffalo 17 (Sun.)
TAMPA BAY 13, Green Bay 10 (OT) (Sun.)
SEATTLE 44, Oakland 10 (Sun.)
INDIANAPOLIS 10, New England 7 (Sat.)

1994
San Diego 17, DENVER 34 (Sun.)
New York Giants 20, ARIZONA 17 (Sun.)
Kansas City 30, ATLANTA 10 (Sun.)
Chicago 19, NEW YORK JETS 7 (Sun.)
Miami 23, CINCINNATI 7 (Sun.)
PHILADELPHIA 21, Washington 17 (Sun.)
Cleveland 11, HOUSTON 8 (Thurs.)
MINNESOTA 13, Green Bay 10 (OT) (Thurs.)
ARIZONA 20, Pittsburgh 17 (OT) (Sun.)
KANSAS CITY 13, Los Angeles Raiders 3 (Sun.)
DETROIT 14, Tampa Bay 9 (Sun.)
SAN FRANCISCO 31, Los Angeles Rams 27 (Sun.)
New England 12, INDIANAPOLIS 10 (Sun.)
MINNESOTA 33, Chicago 27 (OT) (Thurs.)
Buffalo 42, MIAMI 31 (Sun.)
New Orleans 29, ATLANTA 20 (Sun.)
Los Angeles Raiders 17, SEATTLE 16 (Sun.)
MIAMI 27, Detroit 20 (Sun.)

1993
NEW ORLEANS 33, Houston 21 (Sun.)
Los Angeles Raiders 17, SEATTLE 13 (Sun.)
Dallas 17, PHOENIX 10 (Sun.)
NEW YORK JETS 45, New England 7 (Sun.)
BUFFALO 17, New York Giants 14 (Sun.)
GREEN BAY 30, Denver 27 (Sun.)
ATLANTA 30, Los Angeles Rams 24 (Thurs.)
MIAMI 41, Indianapolis 27 (Sun.)
Detroit 30, MINNESOTA 27 (Sun.)
WASHINGTON 30, Indianapolis 24 (Sun.)
Chicago 16, SAN DIEGO 13 (Sun.)
TAMPA BAY 23, Minnesota 10 (Sun.)
HOUSTON 23, Pittsburgh 3 (Sun.)
SAN FRANCISCO 21, Cincinnati 8 (Sun.)
Green Bay 20, SAN DIEGO 13 (Sun.)
Philadelphia 20, INDIANAPOLIS 10 (Sun.)
MINNESOTA 30, Kansas City 10 (Sun.)
HOUSTON 24, New York Jets 0 (Sun.)

1992
DENVER 17, Los Angeles Raiders 13 (Sun.)
Philadelphia 31, PHOENIX 14 (Sun.)
BUFFALO 38, Indianapolis 0 (Sun.)
San Francisco 16, NEW ORLEANS 10 (Sun.)
NEW YORK JETS 30, New England 21 (Sun.)
NEW ORLEANS 13, Los Angeles Rams 10 (Sun.)
MINNESOTA 31, Detroit 14 (Thurs.)
Pittsburgh 27, KANSAS CITY 3 (Sun.)
New York Giants 24, WASHINGTON 7 (Sun.)
Cincinnati 31, CHICAGO 28 (OT) (Sun.)
DENVER 27, New York Giants 13 (Sun.)
Kansas City 24, SEATTLE 14 (Sun.)
SAN DIEGO 27, Los Angeles Raiders 3 (Sun.)
NEW ORLEANS 22, Atlanta 14 (Thurs.)
Los Angeles Rams 31, TAMPA BAY 27 (Sun.)
Green Bay 16, HOUSTON 14 (Sun.)
MIAMI 19, New York Jets 17 (Sun.)
HOUSTON 27, Buffalo 3 (Sun.)

1991
WASHINGTON 45, Detroit 0 (Sun.)
Houston 30, CINCINNATI 7 (Sun.)
NEW ORLEANS 24, Los Angeles Rams 7 (Sun.)
Dallas 17, PHOENIX 9 (Sun.)
Denver 13, MINNESOTA 6 (Sun.)
Pittsburgh 21, INDIANAPOLIS 3 (Sun.)
Los Angeles Raiders 23, SEATTLE 20 (Sun.)
Chicago 10, GREEN BAY 0 (Thurs.)
Washington 17, NEW YORK GIANTS 13 (Sun.)
DENVER 20, Pittsburgh 13 (Sun.)
MIAMI 30, New England 20 (Sun.)
HOUSTON 28, Cleveland 24 (Sun.)
Atlanta 23, NEW ORLEANS 20 (OT) (Sun.)
Los Angeles Raiders 9, SAN DIEGO 7 (Sun.)
Minnesota 26, TAMPA BAY 24 (Sun.)
Buffalo 35, INDIANAPOLIS 7 (Sun.)
SEATTLE 23, Los Angeles Rams 9 (Sun.)

1990
NEW YORK GIANTS 27, Philadelphia 20 (Sun.)
PITTSBURGH 20, Houston 9 (Sun.)
TAMPA BAY 23, Detroit 20 (Sun.)
Washington 38, PHOENIX 10 (Sun.)
BUFFALO 38, Los Angeles Raiders 24 (Sun.)
CHICAGO 38, Los Angeles Rams 9 (Sun.)
MIAMI 17, New England 10 (Thurs.)
ATLANTA 38, Cincinnati 17 (Sun.)
MINNESOTA 27, Denver 22 (Sun.)
San Francisco 24, DALLAS 6 (Sun.)
CINCINNATI 27, Pittsburgh 3 (Sun.)
Seattle 13, SAN DIEGO 10 (Sun.)
MINNESOTA 23, Green Bay 7 (Sun.)
MIAMI 23, Philadelphia 20 (Sun.)
DETROIT 38, Chicago 21 (Sun.)
INDIANAPOLIS 35, Washington 28 (Sat.)
SEATTLE 17, Denver 12 (Sun.)
HOUSTON 34, Pittsburgh 14 (Sun.)

1989
Dallas 13, WASHINGTON 3 (Sun.)
SAN DIEGO 14, Los Angeles Raiders 12 (Sun.)
INDIANAPOLIS 27, New York Jets 10 (Sun.)
Los Angeles Rams 20, NEW ORLEANS 17 (Sun.)
MINNESOTA 27, Chicago 16 (Sun.)
MIAMI 31, New England 10 (Sun.)
SEATTLE 23, Los Angeles Raiders 17 (Sun.)
Cleveland 24, HOUSTON 20 (Sat.)

1988
HOUSTON 41, Washington 17 (Sun.)
Los Angeles Raiders 13, SAN DIEGO 3 (Sun.)
Minnesota 43, DALLAS 3 (Sun.)
New England 6, MIAMI 3 (Sun.)
New York Giants 13, NEW ORLEANS 12 (Sun.)
Pittsburgh 37, HOUSTON 34 (Sun.)
SEATTLE 42, Denver 14 (Sun.)
Los Angeles Rams 38, SAN FRANCISCO 16 (Sun.)

1987
NEW YORK GIANTS 17, New England 10 (Sun.)
SAN DIEGO 16, Los Angeles Raiders 14 (Sun.)
Miami 20, DALLAS 14 (Sun.)
SAN FRANCISCO 38, Cleveland 24 (Sun.)
Chicago 30, MINNESOTA 24 (Sun.)
SEATTLE 28, Denver 21 (Sun.)
MIAMI 23, Washington 21 (Sun.)
SAN FRANCISCO 48, Los Angeles Rams 0 (Sun.)

1986
New England 20, NEW YORK JETS 6 (Thurs.)
Cincinnati 30, CLEVELAND 13 (Thurs.)
Los Angeles Raiders 37, SAN DIEGO 31 (OT) (Thurs.)
LOS ANGELES RAMS 29, Dallas 10 (Sun.)
SAN FRANCISCO 24, Los Angeles Rams 14 (Fri.)

1985
KANSAS CITY 36, Los Angeles Raiders 20 (Thurs.)
Chicago 33, MINNESOTA 24 (Thurs.)
Dallas 30, NEW YORK GIANTS 29 (Sun.)
SAN DIEGO 54, Pittsburgh 44 (Sun.)
Denver 27, SEATTLE 24 (Fri.)

1984
Pittsburgh 23, NEW YORK JETS 17 (Thurs.)
Denver 24, CLEVELAND 14 (Sun.)
DALLAS 30, New Orleans 27 (Sun.)
Washington 31, MINNESOTA 17 (Thurs.)
SAN FRANCISCO 19, Los Angeles Rams 16 (Fri.)

1983
San Francisco 48, MINNESOTA 17 (Thurs.)
CLEVELAND 17, Cincinnati 7 (Thurs.)
Los Angeles Raiders 40, DALLAS 38 (Sun.)
Los Angeles Raiders 42, SAN DIEGO 10 (Thurs.)
MIAMI 34, New York Jets 14 (Fri.)

1982
BUFFALO 23, Minnesota 22 (Thurs.)
SAN FRANCISCO 30, Los Angeles Rams 24 (Thurs.)
ATLANTA 17, San Francisco 7 (Sun.)

1981
MIAMI 30, Pittsburgh 10 (Thurs.)
Philadelphia 20, BUFFALO 14 (Thurs.)
DALLAS 29, Los Angeles 17 (Sun.)
HOUSTON 17, Cleveland 13 (Thurs.)

1980
TAMPA BAY 10, Los Angeles 9 (Thurs.)
DALLAS 42, San Diego 31 (Sun.)
San Diego 27, MIAMI 24 (OT) (Thurs.)
HOUSTON 6, Pittsburgh 0 (Thurs.)

1979
Los Angeles 13, DENVER 9 (Thurs.)
DALLAS 30, Los Angeles 6 (Sun.)
OAKLAND 45, San Diego 22 (Thurs.)
MIAMI 39, New England 24 (Thurs.)

1978
New England 21, OAKLAND 14 (Sun.)
Minnesota 21, DALLAS 10 (Thurs.)
LOS ANGELES 10, Pittsburgh 7 (Sun.)
Denver 21, OAKLAND 6 (Sun.)

1977
Minnesota 30, DETROIT 21 (Sat.)

1976
Los Angeles 20, DETROIT 17 (Sat.)

1975
LOS ANGELES 10, Pittsburgh 3 (Sat.)

1974
OAKLAND 27, Dallas 23 (Sat.)

THANKSGIVING DAY FOOTBALL, 1920-2001

(Home Team in capitals, games listed in chronological order.)

(AFL)-American Football League, 1960-69.

Nov. 25, 1920	AKRON PROS 7, Canton Bulldogs 0 Decatur Staleys 6, CHICAGO TIGERS 0 ELYRIA (OH) ATHLETICS* 0, Columbus Panhandles 0 DAYTON TRIANGLES 28, Detroit Heralds 0 CHICAGO BOOSTERS* 27, Hammond Pros 0 All-Tonawanda (NY) 14, ROCHESTER JEFFERSONS 3 * Non league team. Games between league teams and non league teams counted in standings in 1920.
Nov. 24, 1921	Canton Bulldogs 14, AKRON PROS 0 Buffalo All-Americans 7, CHICAGO STALEYS 6
Nov. 30, 1922	Buffalo All-Americans 21, ROCHESTER JEFFERSONS 0 CHICAGO CARDINALS 6, Chicago Bears 0 RACINE LEGION 3, Milwaukee Badgers 0 Oorang Indians 18, COLUMBUS PANHANDLES 6 CANTON BULLDOGS 14, Akron Pros 0
Nov. 29, 1923	CANTON BULLDOGS 28, Toledo Maroons 0 CHICAGO BEARS 3, Chicago Cardinals 0 GREEN BAY PACKERS 19, Hammond Pros 0 Milwaukee Badgers 16, RACINE LEGION 0 AKRON PROS 2, Buffalo All-Americans 0
Nov. 27, 1924	AKRON PROS 22, Buffalo Bisons 0 Chicago Bears 21, CHICAGO CARDINALS 0 FRANKFORD YELLOWJACKETS 32, Dayton Triangles 7 CLEVELAND BULLDOGS 53, Milwaukee Badgers 10 (at Canton, Ohio) Green Bay Packers 17, KANSAS CITY BLUES 6
Nov. 26, 1925	CHICAGO BEARS 0, Chicago Cardinals 0 Kansas City Cowboys 17, CLEVELAND BULLDOGS 0 (at Hartford, Connecticut) Rock Island Independents 6, DETROIT PANTHERS 3 POTTSVILLE MAROONS 31, Green Bay Packers 0
Nov. 25, 1926	New York Giants 17, BROOKLYN LIONS 0 Los Angeles Buccaneers 9, DETROIT PANTHERS 6 CHICAGO BEARS 0, Chicago Cardinals 0 FRANKFORD YELLOWJACKETS 20, Green Bay Packers 14 POTTSVILLE MAROONS 8, Providence Steam Roller 0 CANTON BULLDOGS 0, Akron Pros 0
Nov. 24, 1927	Chicago Cardinals 3, CHICAGO BEARS 0 POTTSVILLE MAROONS 6, Providence Steam Roller 0 Green Bay Packers 17, FRANKFORD YELLOWJACKETS 9 Cleveland Bulldogs 30, NEW YORK YANKEES 19
Nov. 29, 1928	Providence Steam Roller 7, POTTSVILLE MAROONS 0 DETROIT WOLVERINES 33, Dayton Triangles 0 FRANKFORD YELLOWJACKETS 2, Green Bay Packers 0 CHICAGO BEARS 34, Chicago Cardinals 0
Nov. 28, 1929	New York Giants 21, STATEN ISLAND STAPLETONS 7 FRANKFORD YELLOWJACKETS 0, Green Bay Packers 0 Chicago Cardinals 40, CHICAGO BEARS 6
Nov. 27, 1930	STATEN ISLAND STAPLETONS 7, New York Giants 6 BROOKLYN DODGERS 33, Providence Steam Roller 12 Green Bay Packers 25, FRANKFORD YELLOWJACKETS 7 CHICAGO BEARS 6, Chicago Cardinals 0
Nov. 26, 1931	Green Bay Packers 38, PROVIDENCE STEAM ROLLER 7 STATEN ISLAND STAPLETONS 9, New York Giants 6 CHICAGO BEARS 18, Chicago Cardinals 7
Nov. 24, 1932	CHICAGO BEARS 24, Chicago Cardinals 0 Green Bay Packers 7, BROOKLYN DODGERS 0 STATEN ISLAND STAPLETONS 13, New York Giants 13

Nov. 30, 1933	Chicago Bears 22, CHICAGO CARDINALS 6 New York Giants 10, BROOKLYN DODGERS 0
Nov. 29, 1934	CHICAGO CARDINALS 6, Green Bay Packers 0 Chicago Bears 19, DETROIT LIONS 16 New York Giants 27, BROOKLYN DODGERS 0
Nov. 28, 1935	New York Giants 21, BROOKLYN DODGERS 0 CHICAGO CARDINALS 9, Green Bay Packers 7 DETROIT LIONS 14, Chicago Bears 2
Nov. 26, 1936	DETROIT LIONS 13, Chicago Bears 7 New York Giants 14, BROOKLYN DODGERS 0
Nov. 25, 1937	Chicago Bears 13, DETROIT LIONS 0 BROOKLYN DODGERS 13, New York Giants 13
Nov. 24, 1938	DETROIT LIONS 14, Chicago Bears 7 BROOKLYN DODGERS 7, New York Giants 7
Nov. 23, 1939#	PHILADELPHIA EAGLES 17, Pittsburgh Steelers 14
Nov. 28, 1940#	Pittsburgh Steelers 7, PHILADELPHIA EAGLES 0

In 1939 and 1940, President Roosevelt moved Thanksgiving one week earlier. Various states celebrated on the date declared by the President, while other states recognized the traditional fourth Thursday of the month. In 1941, Thanksgiving was sanctioned by Congress to be celebrated on the fourth Thursday of November, which it has been ever since.

Nov. 22, 1945	Cleveland Rams 28, DETROIT LIONS 21
Nov. 28, 1946	Boston Yanks 34, DETROIT LIONS 10
Nov. 27, 1947	Chicago Bears 34, DETROIT LIONS 14
Nov. 25, 1948	Chicago Cardinals 28, DETROIT LIONS 14
Nov. 24, 1949	Chicago Bears 28, DETROIT LIONS 7
Nov. 23, 1950	DETROIT LIONS 49, New York Yanks 14 Pittsburgh Steelers 28, CHICAGO CARDINALS 17
Nov. 22, 1951	DETROIT LIONS 52, Green Bay Packers 35
Nov. 27, 1952	DETROIT LIONS 48, Green Bay Packers 24 DALLAS TEXANS 27, Chicago Bears 23 (at Akron, Ohio)
Nov. 26, 1953	DETROIT LIONS 34, Green Bay Packers 15
Nov. 25, 1954	DETROIT LIONS 28, Green Bay Packers 24
Nov. 24, 1955	DETROIT LIONS 24, Green Bay Packers 10
Nov. 22, 1956	Green Bay Packers 24, DETROIT LIONS 20
Nov. 28, 1957	DETROIT LIONS 18, Green Bay Packers 6
Nov. 27, 1958	DETROIT LIONS 24, Green Bay Packers 14
Nov. 26, 1959	Green Bay Packers 24, DETROIT LIONS 17
Nov. 24, 1960	DETROIT LIONS 23, Green Bay Packers 10 (AFL) - NEW YORK TITANS 41, Dallas Texans 35
Nov. 23, 1961	Green Bay Packers 17, DETROIT LIONS 9 (AFL) - NEW YORK TITANS 21, Buffalo Bills 14
Nov. 22, 1962	DETROIT LIONS 26, Green Bay Packers 14 (AFL) - New York Titans 46, DENVER BRONCOS 45
Nov. 28, 1963	DETROIT LIONS 13, Green Bay Packers 13 (AFL) - Oakland Raiders 26, DENVER BRONCOS 10
Nov. 26, 1964	Chicago Bears 27, DETROIT LIONS 24 (AFL) - Buffalo Bills 27, SAN DIEGO CHARGERS 24
Nov. 25, 1965	DETROIT LIONS 24, Baltimore Colts 24 (AFL) - SAN DIEGO CHARGERS 20, Buffalo Bills 20

Nov. 24, 1966	San Francisco 49ers 41, DETROIT LIONS 14 DALLAS COWBOYS 26, Cleveland Browns 14 (AFL) - Buffalo Bills 31, OAKLAND RAIDERS 10
Nov. 23, 1967	Los Angeles Rams 31, DETROIT LIONS 7 DALLAS COWBOYS 46, St. Louis Cardinals 21 (AFL) - Oakland Raiders 44, KANSAS CITY CHIEFS 22 (AFL) - SAN DIEGO CHARGERS 24, Denver Broncos 20
Nov. 28, 1968	Philadelphia Eagles 12, DETROIT LIONS 0 DALLAS COWBOYS 29, Washington Redskins 20 (AFL) - OAKLAND RAIDERS 13, Buffalo Bills 10 (AFL) - KANSAS CITY CHIEFS 24, Houston Oilers 10
Nov. 27, 1969	Minnesota Vikings 27, DETROIT LIONS 0 DALLAS COWBOYS 24, San Francisco 49ers 24 (AFL) - KANSAS CITY CHIEFS 31, Denver Broncos 17 (AFL) - San Diego Chargers 21, HOUSTON OILERS 17
Nov. 26, 1970	DETROIT LIONS 28, Oakland Raiders 14 DALLAS COWBOYS 16, Green Bay Packers 3
Nov. 25, 1971	DETROIT LIONS 32, Kansas City Chiefs 21 DALLAS COWBOYS 28, Los Angeles Rams 21
Nov. 23, 1972	DETROIT LIONS 37, New York Jets 20 San Francisco 49ers 31, DALLAS COWBOYS 10
Nov. 22, 1973	Washington Redskins 20, DETROIT LIONS 0 Miami Dolphins 14, DALLAS COWBOYS 7
Nov. 28, 1974	Denver Broncos 31, DETROIT LIONS 27 DALLAS COWBOYS 24, Washington Redskins 23
Nov. 27, 1975	Los Angeles Rams 20, DETROIT LIONS 0 Buffalo Bills 32, ST. LOUIS CARDINALS 14
Nov. 25, 1976	DETROIT LIONS 27, Buffalo Bills 14 DALLAS COWBOYS 19, St. Louis Cardinals 14
Nov. 24, 1977	Chicago Bears 31, DETROIT LIONS 14 Miami Dolphins 55, ST. LOUIS CARDINALS 14
Nov. 23, 1978	DETROIT LIONS 17, Denver Broncos 14 DALLAS COWBOYS 37, Washington Redskins 10
Nov. 22, 1979	DETROIT LIONS 20, Chicago Bears 0 Houston Oilers 30, DALLAS COWBOYS 24
Nov. 27, 1980	Chicago Bears 23, DETROIT LIONS 17 (OT) DALLAS COWBOYS 51, Seattle Seahawks 7
Nov. 26, 1981	DETROIT LIONS 27, Kansas City Chiefs 10 DALLAS COWBOYS 10, Chicago Bears 9
Nov. 25, 1982	New York Giants 13, DETROIT LIONS 6 DALLAS COWBOYS 31, Cleveland Browns 14
Nov. 24, 1983	DETROIT LIONS 45, Pittsburgh Steelers 3 DALLAS COWBOYS 35, St. Louis Cardinals 17
Nov. 22, 1984	DETROIT LIONS 31, Green Bay Packers 28 DALLAS COWBOYS 20, New England Patriots 17
Nov. 28, 1985	DETROIT LIONS 31, New York Jets 20 DALLAS COWBOYS 35, St. Louis Cardinals 17
Nov. 27, 1986	Green Bay Packers 44, DETROIT LIONS 40 Seattle Seahawks 31, DALLAS COWBOYS 14
Nov. 26, 1987	Kansas City Chiefs 27, DETROIT LIONS 20 Minnesota Vikings 44, DALLAS COWBOYS 38 (OT)
Nov. 24, 1988	Minnesota Vikings 23, DETROIT LIONS 0 Houston Oilers 25, DALLAS COWBOYS 17

Nov. 23, 1989	DETROIT LIONS 13, Cleveland Browns 10 Philadelphia Eagles 27, DALLAS COWBOYS 0
Nov. 22, 1990	DETROIT LIONS 40, Denver Broncos 27 DALLAS COWBOYS 27, Washington Redskins 17
Nov. 28, 1991	DETROIT LIONS 16, Chicago Bears 6 DALLAS COWBOYS 20, Pittsburgh Steelers 10
Nov. 26, 1992	Houston Oilers 24, DETROIT LIONS 21 DALLAS COWBOYS 30, New York Giants 3
Nov. 25, 1993	Chicago Bears 10, DETROIT LIONS 6 Miami Dolphins 16, DALLAS COWBOYS 14
Nov. 24, 1994	DETROIT LIONS 35, Buffalo Bills 21 DALLAS COWBOYS 42, Green Bay Packers 31
Nov. 23, 1995	DETROIT LIONS 44, Minnesota Vikings 38 DALLAS COWBOYS 24, Kansas City Chiefs 12
Nov. 28, 1996	Kansas City Chiefs 28, DETROIT LIONS 24 DALLAS COWBOYS 21, Washington Redskins 10
Nov. 27, 1997	DETROIT LIONS 55, Chicago Bears 20 Tennessee Titans 27, DALLAS COWBOYS 14
Nov. 26, 1998	DETROIT LIONS 19, Pittsburgh Steelers 16 (OT) Minnesota Vikings 46, DALLAS COWBOYS 36
Nov. 25, 1999	DETROIT LIONS 21, Chicago Bears 17 DALLAS COWBOYS 20, Miami Dolphins 0
Nov. 23, 2000	DETROIT LIONS 34, New England Patriots 9 Minnesota Vikings 27, DALLAS COWBOYS 15
Nov. 22, 2001	Green Bay Packers 29, DETROIT LIONS 27 Denver Broncos 26, DALLAS COWBOYS 24

THANKSGIVING DAY RECORDS
Compiled by Elias Sports Bureau
*Set NFL all-time record.

SCORING
Most Touchdowns, Game
6   Ernie Nevers, Chi. Cardinals vs. Chi. Bears, Nov. 28, 1929*
4   Sterling Sharpe, Green Bay at Dallas, Nov. 24, 1994
3   By many players

RUSHING
Most Yards Rushing, Game
273   O.J. Simpson, Buffalo at Detroit, Nov. 25, 1976
198   Bob Hoernschemeyer, Detroit vs. N.Y. Yankees, Nov. 23, 1950
195   Earl Campbell, Houston at Dallas, Nov. 22, 1979

PASSING
Most Yards Passing, Game
455   Troy Aikman, Dallas vs. Minnesota, Nov. 26, 1998
410   Scott Mitchell, Detroit vs. Minnesota, Nov. 23, 1995
384   Warren Moon, Minnesota at Detroit, Nov. 23, 1995

PASS RECEIVING
RECEPTIONS
Most Pass Receptions, Game
12   Brett Perriman, Detroit vs. Minnesota, Nov. 23, 1995
11   Daryl Johnston, Dallas vs. Miami, Nov. 25, 1993
     Michael Irvin, Dallas vs Kansas City, Nov. 23, 1995
YARDS GAINED
Most Yards on Pass Receptions, Game
303   Jim Benton, Cleveland at Detroit, Nov. 22, 1945
185   Lance Alworth, San Diego vs. Buffalo, Nov. 26, 1964
184   Anthony Carter, Minnesota at Dallas, Nov. 26, 1987 (OT)

HISTORY OF OVERTIME GAMES
PRESEASON

Aug. 28, 1955	Los Angeles 23, New York Giants 17, at Portland, Oregon
Aug. 24, 1962	Denver 27, Dallas Texans 24, at Fort Worth, Texas
Aug. 10, 1974	San Diego 20, New York Jets 14, at San Diego
Aug. 17, 1974	Pittsburgh 33, Philadelphia 30, at Philadelphia
Aug. 17, 1974	Dallas 19, Houston 13, at Dallas
Aug. 17, 1974	Cincinnati 13, Atlanta 7, at Atlanta
Sept. 6, 1974	Buffalo 23, New York Giants 17, at Buffalo
Aug. 9, 1975	Baltimore 23, Denver 20, at Denver
Aug. 30, 1975	New England 20, Green Bay 17, at Milwaukee
Sept. 13, 1975	Minnesota 14, San Diego 14, at San Diego
Aug. 1, 1976	New England 13, New York Giants 7, at New England
Aug. 2, 1976	Kansas City 9, Houston 3, at Kansas City
Aug. 20, 1976	New Orleans 26, Baltimore 20, at Baltimore
Sept. 4, 1976	Dallas 26, Houston 20, at Dallas
Aug. 13, 1977	Seattle 23, Dallas 17, at Seattle
Aug. 28, 1977	New England 13, Pittsburgh 10, at New England
Aug. 28, 1977	New York Giants 24, Buffalo 21, at East Rutherford, N.J.
Aug. 2, 1979	Seattle 12, Minnesota 9, at Minnesota
Aug. 4, 1979	Los Angeles 20, Oakland 14, at Los Angeles
Aug. 24, 1979	Denver 20, New England 17, at Denver
Aug. 23, 1980	Tampa Bay 20, Cincinnati 14, at Tampa Bay
Aug. 5, 1981	San Francisco 27, Seattle 24, at Seattle
Aug. 29, 1981	New Orleans 20, Detroit 17, at New Orleans
Aug. 28, 1982	Miami 17, Kansas City 17, at Kansas City
Sept. 3, 1982	Miami 16, New York Giants 13, at Miami
Aug. 6, 1983	L.A. Raiders 26, San Francisco 23, at Los Angeles
Aug. 6, 1983	Atlanta 13, Washington 10, at Atlanta
Aug. 13, 1983	St. Louis 27, Chicago 24, at St. Louis
Aug. 18, 1983	New York Jets 20, Cincinnati 17, at Cincinnati
Aug. 27, 1983	Chicago 20, Kansas City 17, at Chicago
Aug. 11, 1984	Pittsburgh 20, Philadelphia 17, at Pittsburgh
Aug. 9, 1985	Buffalo 10, Detroit 10, at Pontiac, Mich.
Aug. 10, 1985	Minnesota 16, Miami 13, at Miami
Aug. 17, 1985	Dallas 27, San Diego 24, at San Diego
Aug. 24, 1985	N.Y. Giants 34, N.Y. Jets 31, at East Rutherford, N.J.
Aug. 15, 1986	Washington 27, Pittsburgh 24, at Washington
Aug. 15, 1986	Detroit 30, Seattle 27, at Detroit
Aug. 23, 1986	Los Angeles Rams 20, San Diego 17, at Anaheim
Aug. 30, 1986	Minnesota 23, Indianapolis 20, at Indianapolis
Aug. 23, 1987	Philadelphia 19, New England 13, at New England
Sept. 5, 1987	Cleveland 30, Green Bay 24, at Milwaukee
Sept. 6, 1987	Kansas City 13, St. Louis 10, at Memphis, Tenn.
Aug. 11, 1988	Seattle 16, Detroit 13, at Detroit
Aug. 19, 1988	Miami 16, Denver 13, at Miami
Aug. 19, 1988	Green Bay 21, Kansas City 21, at Milwaukee
Aug. 20, 1988	Houston 20, Los Angeles Rams 17, at Anaheim
Aug. 21, 1988	Minnesota 19, Phoenix 16, at Phoenix
Aug. 5, 1989	Los Angeles Rams 16, San Francisco 13, at Tokyo, Japan
Aug. 26, 1989	Denver 24, Dallas 21, at Denver
Sept. 1, 1989	N.Y. Jets 15, Kansas City 13, at Kansas City
Aug. 24, 1990	Cincinnati 13, New England 10, at New England
Aug. 16, 1991	Cleveland 24, Washington 21, at Washington
Aug. 17, 1991	Cincinnati 27, Minnesota 24, at Cincinnati
Aug. 23, 1991	Dallas 20, Atlanta 17, at Dallas
Aug. 24, 1991	Cincinnati 19, Green Bay 16, at Green Bay
Aug. 22, 1992	Los Angeles Rams 16, Green Bay 13, at Anaheim
Aug. 8, 1993	Dallas 13, Detroit 13, at London, England
Aug. 12, 1995	Washington 16, Houston 13, at Knoxville, Tenn.
Aug. 19, 1995	Indianapolis 20, Green Bay 17, at Green Bay
Aug. 3, 1996	Minnesota 23, San Diego 20, at Minnesota
Aug. 10, 1996	San Francisco 16, San Diego 13, at San Francisco
Aug. 1, 1998	Green Bay 27, Kansas City 24, at Tokyo, Japan
Aug. 7, 1998	Detroit 13, Arizona 10, at Pontiac, Mich.
Aug. 22, 1998	Minnesota 25, Carolina 22, at Charlotte, N.C.
Aug. 9, 1999	Cleveland 20, Dallas 17, at Canton, Ohio
Aug. 4, 2001	Chicago 16, Cincinnati 13, at Chicago
Aug. 18, 2001	San Diego 23, Miami 20, at Miami
Aug. 18, 2001	Arizona 16, Seattle 13, at Seattle
Aug. 25, 2001	San Diego 13, St. Louis 10, at San Diego

OVERTIME GAMES

REGULAR SEASON

Sept. 22, 1974—Pittsburgh 35, Denver 35, at Denver; Steelers win toss. Gilliam's pass intercepted and returned by Rowser to Denver's 42. Turner misses 41-yard field goal. Walden punts and Greer returns to Broncos' 39. Van Heusen punts and Edwards returns to Steelers' 16. Game ends with Steelers on own 26.

Nov. 10, 1974—New York Jets 26, New York Giants 20, at New Haven, Conn.; Giants win toss. Gogolak misses 42-yard field goal. Namath passes to Boozer for five yards and touchdown at 6:53.

Sept. 28, 1975—Dallas 37, St. Louis 31, at Dallas; Cardinals win toss. Hart's pass intercepted and returned by Jordan to Cardinals' 37. Staubach passes to DuPree for three yards and touchdown at 7:53.

Oct. 12, 1975—Los Angeles 13, San Diego 10, at San Diego; Chargers win toss. Partee punts to Rams' 14. Dempsey kicks 22-yard field goal at 9:27.

Nov. 2, 1975—Washington 30, Dallas 24, at Washington; Cowboys win toss. Staubach's pass intercepted and returned by Houston to Cowboys' 35. Kilmer runs one yard for touchdown at 6:34.

Nov. 16, 1975—St. Louis 20, Washington 17, at St. Louis; Cardinals win toss. Bakken kicks 37-yard field goal at 7:00.

Nov. 23, 1975—Kansas City 24, Detroit 21, at Kansas City; Lions win toss. Chiefs take over on downs at own 38. Stenerud kicks 26-yard field goal at 6:44.

Nov. 23, 1975—Oakland 26, Washington 23, at Washington; Redskins win toss. Bragg punts to Raiders' 42. Blanda kicks 27-yard field goal at 7:13.

Nov. 30, 1975—Denver 13, San Diego 10, at Denver; Broncos win toss. Turner kicks 25-yard field goal at 4:13.

Nov. 30, 1975—Oakland 37, Atlanta 34, at Oakland; Falcons win toss. James punts to Raiders' 16. Guy punts and Herron returns to Falcons' 41. Nick Mike-Mayer misses 45-yard field goal. Guy punts into Falcons' end zone. James punts to Raiders' 39. Blanda kicks 36-yard field goal at 15:00.

Dec. 14, 1975—Baltimore 10, Miami 7, at Baltimore; Dolphins win toss. Seiple punts to Colts' 4. Linhart kicks 31-yard field goal at 12:44.

Sept. 19, 1976—Minnesota 10, Los Angeles 10, at Minnesota; Vikings win toss. Tarkenton's pass intercepted by Monte Jackson and returned to Minnesota 16. Allen blocks Dempsey's 30-yard field goal attempt, ball rolls into end zone for touchback. Clabo punts and Scribner returns to Rams' 20. Rusty Jackson punts to Vikings' 35. Tarkenton's pass intercepted by Kay at Rams' 1, no return. Game ends with Rams on own 3.

* **Sept. 27, 1976—Washington 20, Philadelphia 17,** at Philadelphia; Eagles win toss. Jones punts and E. Brown loses one yard on return to Redskins' 40. Bragg punts 51 yards into end zone for touchback. Jones punts and E. Brown returns to Redskins' 42. Bragg punts and Marshall returns to Eagles' 41. Boryla's pass intercepted by Dusek at Redskins' 37, no return. Bragg punts and Bradley returns. Philadelphia holding penalty moves ball back to Eagles' 8. Boryla pass intercepted by E. Brown and returned to Eagles' 22. Moseley kicks 29-yard field goal at 12:49.

Oct. 17, 1976—Kansas City 20, Miami 17, at Miami; Chiefs win toss. Wilson punts into end zone for touchback. Bulaich fumbles into Kansas City end zone, Collier recovers for touchback. Stenerud kicks 34-yard field goal at 14:48.

Oct. 31, 1976—St. Louis 23, San Francisco 20, at St. Louis; Cardinals win toss. Joyce punts and Leonard fumbles on return, Jones recovers at 49ers' 43. Bakken kicks 21-yard field goal at 6:42.

Dec. 5, 1976—San Diego 13, San Francisco 7, at San Diego; Chargers win toss. Morris runs 13 yards for touchdown at 5:12.

Sept. 18, 1977—Dallas 16, Minnesota 10, at Minnesota;

Vikings win toss. Dallas starts on Vikings' 47 after a punt early in the overtime period. Staubach scores seven plays later on a four-yard run at 6:14.

* **Sept. 26, 1977—Cleveland 30, New England 27,** at Cleveland; Browns win toss. Sipe throws a 22-yard pass to Logan at Patriots' 19. Cockroft kicks 35-yard field goal at 4:45.

Oct. 16, 1977—Minnesota 22, Chicago 16, at Minnesota; Bears win toss. Parsons punts 53 yards to Vikings' 18. Minnesota drives to Bears' 11. On a first-and-10, Vikings fake a field goal and holder Krause hits Voigt with a touchdown pass at 6:45.

Oct. 30, 1977—Cincinnati 13, Houston 10, at Cincinnati; Bengals win toss. Bahr kicks a 22-yard field goal at 5:51.

Nov. 13, 1977—San Francisco 10, New Orleans 7, at New Orleans; Saints win toss. Saints fail to move ball and Blanchard punts to 49ers' 41. Wersching kicks a 33-yard field goal at 6:33.

Dec. 18, 1977—Chicago 12, New York Giants 9, at East Rutherford, N.J.; Giants win toss. Ball changes hands eight times before Thomas kicks a 28-yard field goal at 14:51.

Sept. 10, 1978—Cleveland 13, Cincinnati 10, at Cleveland; Browns win toss. Collins returns kickoff 41 yards to Browns' 47. Cockroft kicks 27-yard field goal at 4:30.

* **Sept. 11, 1978—Minnesota 12, Denver 9,** at Minnesota; Vikings win toss. Danmeier kicks 44-yard field goal at 2:56.

Sept. 24, 1978—Pittsburgh 15, Cleveland 9, at Pittsburgh; Steelers win toss. Cunningham scores on a 37-yard "gadget" pass from Bradshaw at 3:43. Steelers start winning drive on their 21.

Sept. 24, 1978—Denver 23, Kansas City 17, at Kansas City; Broncos win toss. Dilts punts to Kansas City. Chiefs advance to Broncos' 40 where Reed fails to make first down on fourth-and-one situation. Broncos march downfield. Preston scores two-yard touchdown at 10:28.

Oct. 1, 1978—Oakland 25, Chicago 19, at Chicago; Bears win toss. Both teams punt on first possession. On Chicago's second offensive series, Colzie intercepts Avellini's pass and returns it to Bears' 3. Three plays later, Whittington runs two yards for a touchdown at 5:19.

Oct. 15, 1978—Dallas 24, St. Louis 21, at St. Louis; Cowboys win toss. Dallas drives from its 23 into field goal range. Septien kicks 27-yard field goal at 3:28.

Oct. 29, 1978—Denver 20, Seattle 17, at Seattle; Broncos win toss. Ball changes hands four times before Turner kicks 18-yard field goal at 12:59.

Nov. 12, 1978—San Diego 29, Kansas City 23, at San Diego; Chiefs win toss. Fouts hits Jefferson for decisive 14-yard touchdown pass on the last play (15:00) of overtime period.

Nov. 12, 1978—Washington 16, New York Giants 13, at Washington; Redskins win toss. Moseley kicks winning 45-yard field goal at 8:32 after missing first down field goal attempt of 35 yards at 4:50.

Nov. 26, 1978—Green Bay 10, Minnesota 10, at Green Bay; Packers win toss. Both teams have possession of the ball four times.

Dec. 9, 1978—Cleveland 37, New York Jets 34, at Cleveland; Browns win toss. Cockroft kicks 22-yard field goal at 3:07.

Sept. 2, 1979—Atlanta 40, New Orleans 34, at New Orleans; Falcons win toss. Bartkowski's pass intercepted by Myers and returned to Falcons' 46. Erxleben punts to Falcons' 4. James punts to Chandler on Saints' 43. Erxleben punts and Ryckman returns to Falcons' 28. James punts and Chandler returns to Saints' 36. Erxleben retrieves punt snap on Saints' 1 and attempts pass. Mayberry intercepts and returns six yards for touchdown at 8:22.

Sept. 2, 1979—Cleveland 25, New York Jets 22, at New York; Jets win toss. Leahy's 43-yard field goal attempt goes wide right at 4:41. Evans's punt blocked by Dykes is recovered by Newton. Ramsey punts into end zone for touchback. Evans punts and Harper returns to Jets' 24. Robinson's pass intercepted by Davis and returned 33 yards to Jets' 31. Cockroft kicks 27-yard field goal at 14:45.

* **Sept. 3, 1979—Pittsburgh 16, New England 13,** at Foxboro; Patriots win toss. Hare punts to Swann at Steelers' 31. Bahr kicks 41-yard field goal at 5:10.

Sept. 9, 1979—Tampa Bay 29, Baltimore 26, at Baltimore; Colts win toss. Landry fumbles, recovered by Kollar at Colts' 14. O'Donoghue kicks 31-yard, first-down field goal at 1:41.

Sept. 16, 1979—Denver 20, Atlanta 17, at Atlanta; Broncos win toss. Broncos march 65 yards to Falcons' 7. Turner kicks 24-yard field goal at 6:15.

Sept. 23, 1979—Houston 30, Cincinnati 27, at Cincinnati; Oilers win toss. Parsley punts and Lusby returns to Bengals' 33. Bahr's 32-yard field goal attempt is wide right at 8:05. Parsley's punt downed on Bengals' 5. McInally punts and Ellender returns to Bengals' 42. Fritsch's third down, 29-yard field goal attempt hits left upright and bounces through at 14:28.

Sept. 23, 1979—Minnesota 27, Green Bay 21, at Minnesota; Vikings win toss. Kramer throws 50-yard touchdown pass to Rashad at 3:18.

Oct. 28, 1979—Houston 27, New York Jets 24, at Houston; Oilers win toss. Oilers march 58 yards to Jets' 18. Fritsch kicks 35-yard field goal at 5:10.

Nov. 18, 1979—Cleveland 30, Miami 24, at Cleveland; Browns win toss. Sipe passes 39 yards to Rucker for touchdown at 1:59.

Nov. 25, 1979—Pittsburgh 33, Cleveland 30, at Pittsburgh; Browns win toss. Sipe's pass intercepted by Blount on Steelers' 4. Bradshaw pass intercepted by Bolton on Browns' 12. Evans punts and Bell returns to Steelers' 17. Bahr kicks 37-yard field goal at 14:51.

Nov. 25, 1979—Buffalo 16, New England 13, at Foxboro; Patriots win toss. Hare's punt downed on Bills' 38. Jackson punts and Morgan returns to Patriots' 20. Grogan's pass intercepted by Haslett and returned to Bills' 42. Ferguson's 51-yard pass to Butler sets up N. Mike-Mayer's 29-yard field goal at 9:15.

Dec. 2, 1979—Los Angeles 27, Minnesota 21, at Los Angeles; Rams win toss. Clark punts and Miller returns to Vikings' 25. Kramer's pass intercepted by Brown and returned to Rams' 40. Cromwell, holding for 22-yard field goal attempt, runs around left end untouched for winning score at 6:53.

Sept. 7, 1980—Green Bay 12, Chicago 6, at Green Bay; Bears win toss. Parsons punts and Nixon returns 16 yards. Five plays later, Marcol returns own blocked field goal attempt 24 yards for touchdown at 6:00.

Sept. 14, 1980—San Diego 30, Oakland 24, at San Diego; Raiders win toss. Pastorini's first-down pass intercepted by Edwards. Millen intercepts Fouts' first-down pass and returns to San Diego 46. Bahr's 50-yard field goal attempt partially blocked by Williams and recovered on Chargers' 32. Eight plays later, Fouts throws 24-yard touchdown pass to Jefferson at 8:09.

Sept. 14, 1980—San Francisco 24, St. Louis 21, at San Francisco; Cardinals win toss. Swider punts and Robinson returns to 49ers' 32. San Francisco drives 52 yards to St. Louis 16, where Wersching kicks 33-yard field goal at 4:12.

Oct. 12, 1980—Green Bay 14, Tampa Bay 14, at Tampa Bay; Packers win toss. Teams trade punts twice. Lee returns second Tampa Bay punt to Green Bay 42. Dickey completes three passes to Buccaneers' 18, where Birney's 36-yard field goal attempt is wide right as time expires.

Nov. 9, 1980—Atlanta 33, St. Louis 27, at St. Louis; Falcons win toss. Strong runs 21 yards for touchdown at 4:20.

\# **Nov. 20, 1980—San Diego 27, Miami 24,** at Miami; Chargers win toss. Partridge punts into end zone, Dolphins take over on their own 20. Woodley's pass for Nathan intercepted by Lowe and returned 28 yards to Dolphins' 12. Benirschke kicks 28-yard field goal at 7:14.

Nov. 23, 1980—New York Jets 31, Houston 28, at New York;

Jets win toss. Leahy kicks 38-yard field goal at 3:58.

Nov. 27, 1980—Chicago 23, Detroit 17, at Detroit; Bears win toss. Williams returns kickoff 95 yards for touchdown at 0:21.

Dec. 7, 1980—Buffalo 10, Los Angeles 7, at Buffalo; Rams win toss. Corral punts and Hooks returns to Bills' 34. Ferguson's 30-yard pass to Lewis sets up N. Mike-Mayer's 30-yard field goal at 5:14.

Dec. 7, 1980—San Francisco 38, New Orleans 35, at San Francisco; Saints win toss. Erxleben's punt downed by Hardy on 49ers' 27. Wersching kicks 36-yard field goal at 7:40.

* **Dec. 8, 1980—Miami 16, New England 13,** at Miami; Dolphins win toss. Von Schamann kicks 23-yard field goal at 3:20.

Dec. 14, 1980—Cincinnati 17, Chicago 14, at Chicago; Bengals win toss. Breech kicks 28-yard field goal at 4:23.

Dec. 21, 1980—Los Angeles 20, Atlanta 17, at Los Angeles; Rams win toss. Corral's punt downed at Rams' 37. James punts into end zone for touchback. Corral's punt downed on Falcons' 17. Bartkowski fumbles when hit by Harris, recovered by Delaney. Corral kicks 23-yard field goal on first play of possession at 7:00.

Sept. 27, 1981—Cincinnati 27, Buffalo 24, at Cincinnati; Bills win toss. Cater punts into end zone for touchback. Bengals drive to the Bills' 10 where Breech kicks 28-yard field goal at 9:33.

Sept. 27, 1981—Pittsburgh 27, New England 21, at Pittsburgh; Patriots win toss. Hubach punts and Smith returns five yards to midfield. Four plays later Bradshaw throws 24-yard touchdown pass to Swann at 3:19.

Oct. 4, 1981—Miami 28, New York Jets 28, at Miami; Jets win toss. Teams trade punts twice. Leahy's 48-yard field goal attempt is wide right as time expires.

Oct. 25, 1981—New York Giants 27, Atlanta 24, at Atlanta; Giants win toss. Jennings' punt goes out of bounds at New York 47. Bright returns Atlanta punt to Giants' 14. Woerner fair catches punt at own 28. Andrews fumbles on first play, recovered by Van Pelt. Danelo kicks 40-yard field goal four plays later at 9:20.

Oct. 25, 1981—Chicago 20, San Diego 17, at Chicago; Bears win toss. Teams trade punts. Bears' second punt returned by Brooks to Chargers' 33. Fouts pass intercepted by Fencik and returned 32 yards to San Diego 27. Roveto kicks 27-yard field goal seven plays later at 9:30.

Nov. 8, 1981—Chicago 16, Kansas City 13, at Kansas City; Bears win toss. Teams trade punts. Kansas City takes over on downs on its own 38. Fuller's fumble recovered by Harris on Chicago 36. Roveto's 37-yard field goal wide, but Chiefs penalized for leverage. Roveto's 22-yard field goal attempt three plays later is good at 13:07.

Nov. 8, 1981—Denver 23, Cleveland 20, at Denver; Browns win toss. D. Smith recovers Hill's fumble at Denver 48. Morton's 33-yard pass to Upchurch and 6-yard run by Preston set up Steinfort's 30-yard field goal at 4:10.

Nov. 8, 1981—Miami 30, New England 27, at New England; Dolphins win toss. Orosz punts and Morgan returns six yards to New England 26. Grogan's pass intercepted by Brudzinski who returns 19 yards to Patriots' 26. Von Schamann kicks 30-yard field goal on first down at 7:09.

Nov. 15, 1981—Washington 30, New York Giants 27, at New York; Giants win toss. Nelms returns Giants' punt 26 yards to New York 47. Five plays later Moseley kicks 48-yard field goal at 3:44.

Dec. 20, 1981—New York Giants 13, Dallas 10, at New York; Cowboys win toss and kick off. Jennings punts to Dallas 40. Taylor recovers Dorsett's fumble on second down. Danelo's 33-yard field goal attempt hits right upright and bounces back. White's pass for Pearson intercepted by Hunt and returned seven yards to Dallas 24. Four plays later Danelo kicks 35-yard field goal at 6:19.

Sept. 12, 1982—Washington 37, Philadelphia 34, at Philadelphia; Redskins win toss. Theismann completes five passes for 63 yards to set up Moseley's 26-yard field goal at 4:47.

Sept. 19, 1982—Pittsburgh 26, Cincinnati 20, at Pittsburgh; Bengals win toss. Anderson's pass intended for Kreider intercepted by Woodruff and returned 30 yards to Cincinnati 2. Bradshaw completes two-yard touchdown pass to Stallworth on first down at 1:08.

Dec. 19, 1982—Baltimore 20, Green Bay 20, at Baltimore; Packers win toss. K. Anderson intercepts Dickey's first-down pass and returns to Packers' 42. Miller's 44-yard field goal attempt blocked by G. Lewis. Teams trade punts before Stenerud's 47-yard field goal attempt is wide right. Teams trade punts again before time expires in Colts possession.

Jan. 2, 1983—Tampa Bay 26, Chicago 23, at Tampa; Bears win toss. Parsons punts to T. Bell at Buccaneers' 40. Capece kicks 33-yard field goal at 3:14.

Sept. 4, 1983—Baltimore 29, New England 23, at New England; Patriots win toss. Cooks runs 52 yards with fumble recovery three plays into overtime at 0:30.

Sept. 4, 1983—Green Bay 41, Houston 38, at Houston; Packers win toss. Stenerud kicks 42-yard field goal at 5:55.

Sept. 11, 1983—New York Giants 16, Atlanta 13, at Atlanta; Giants win toss. Dennis returns kickoff 54 yards to Atlanta 41. Haji-Sheikh kicks 30-yard field goal at 3:38.

Sept. 18, 1983—New Orleans 34, Chicago 31, at New Orleans; Bears win toss. Parsons punts and Groth returns five yards to New Orleans 34. Stabler pass intercepted by Schmidt at Chicago 47. Parsons punt downed by Gentry at New Orleans 2. Stabler gains 36 yards in four passes; Wilson 38 on six carries. Andersen kicks 41-yard field goal at 10:57.

Sept. 18, 1983—Minnesota 19, Tampa Bay 16, at Tampa; Vikings win toss. Coleman punts and Bell returns eight yards to Tampa Bay 47. Capece's 33-yard field goal attempt sails wide at 7:26. Dils and Young combine for 48-yard gain to Tampa Bay 27. Ricardo kicks 34-yard field goal at 9:27.

Sept. 25, 1983—Baltimore 22, Chicago 19, at Baltimore; Colts win toss. Allegre kicks 33-yard field goal nine plays later at 4:51.

Sept. 25, 1983—Cleveland 30, San Diego 24, at San Diego; Browns win toss. Walker returns kickoff 33 yards to Cleveland 37. Sipe completes 48-yard touchdown pass to Holt four plays later at 1:53.

Sept. 25, 1983—New York Jets 27, Los Angeles Rams 24, at New York; Jets win toss. Ramsey punts to Irvin who returns to 25 but penalty puts Rams on own 13. Holmes 30-yard interception return sets up Leahy's 26-yard field goal at 3:22.

Oct. 9, 1983—Buffalo 38, Miami 35, at Miami; Dolphins win toss. Von Schamann's 52-yard field goal attempt goes wide at 12:36. Cater punts to Clayton who loses 11 to own 13. Von Schamann's 43-yard field goal attempt sails wide at 5:15. Danelo kicks 36-yard field goal nine plays later at 13:58.

Oct. 9, 1983—Dallas 27, Tampa Bay 24, at Dallas; Cowboys win toss. Septien's 51-yard field-goal attempt goes wide but Buccaneers penalized for roughing kicker. Septien kicks 42-yard field goal at 4:38.

Oct. 23, 1983—Kansas City 13, Houston 10, at Houston; Chiefs win toss. Lowery kicks 41-yard field goal 13 plays later at 7:41.

Oct. 23, 1983—Minnesota 20, Green Bay 17, at Green Bay; Packers win toss. Scribner's punt downed on Vikings' 42. Ricardo kicks 32-yard field goal eight plays later at 5:05.

* **Oct. 24, 1983—New York Giants 20, St. Louis 20,** at St. Louis; Cardinals win toss. Teams trade punts before O'Donoghue's 44-yard field goal attempt is wide left. Jennings' punt returned by Bird to St. Louis 21. Lomax pass intercepted by Haynes who loses six yards to New York 33. Jennings' punt downed on St. Louis 17. O'Donoghue's 19-yard field goal attempt is wide right. Rutledge's pass intercepted by L. Washington who returns 25 yards to New York 25. O'Donoghue's 42-yard field goal attempt is wide right. Rutledge's pass inter-

cepted by W. Smith at St. Louis 33 to end game.

Oct. 30, 1983—Cleveland 25, Houston 19, at Cleveland; Oilers win toss. Teams trade punts. Nielsen's pass intercepted by Whitwell who returns to Houston 20. Green runs 20 yards for touchdown on first down at 6:34.

Nov. 20, 1983—Detroit 23, Green Bay 20, at Milwaukee; Packers win toss. Scribner punts and Jenkins returns 14 yards to Green Bay 45. Murray's 33-yard field goal attempt is wide left at 9:32. Whitehurst's pass intercepted by Watkins and returned to Green Bay 27. Murray kicks 37-yard field goal four plays later at 8:30.

Nov. 27, 1983—Atlanta 47, Green Bay 41, at Atlanta; Packers win toss. K. Johnson returns interception 31 yards for touchdown at 2:13.

Nov. 27, 1983—Seattle 51, Kansas City 48, at Seattle; Seahawks win toss. Dixon's 47-yard kickoff return sets up N. Johnson's 42-yard field goal at 1:36.

Dec. 11, 1983—New Orleans 20, Philadelphia 17, at Philadelphia; Eagles win toss. Runager punts to Groth who fair catches on New Orleans 32. Stabler completes two passes for 36 yards to Goodlow to set up Andersen's 50-yard field goal at 5:30.

* **Dec. 12, 1983—Green Bay 12, Tampa Bay 9,** at Tampa; Packers win toss. Stenerud kicks 23-yard field goal 11 plays later at 4:07.

Sept. 9, 1984—Detroit 27, Atlanta 24, at Atlanta; Lions win toss. Murray kicks 48-yard field goal nine plays later at 5:06.

Sept. 30, 1984—Tampa Bay 30, Green Bay 27, at Tampa; Packers win toss. Scribner punts 44 yards to Tampa Bay 2. Epps returns Garcia's punt three yards to Green Bay 27. Scribner's punt downed on Buccaneers' 33. Ariri kicks 46-yard field goal 11 plays later at 10:32.

Oct. 14, 1984—Detroit 13, Tampa Bay 7, at Detroit; Buccaneers win toss. Tampa Bay drives to Lions' 39 before Wilder fumbles. Five plays later Danielson hits Thompson with 37-yard touchdown pass at 4:34.

Oct. 21, 1984—Dallas 30, New Orleans 27, at Dallas; Cowboys win toss. Septien kicks 41-yard field goal eight plays later at 3:42.

Oct. 28, 1984—Denver 22, Los Angeles Raiders 19, at Los Angeles; Raiders win toss. Hawkins fumble recovered by Foley at Denver 7. Teams trade punts. Karlis's 42-yard field goal attempt is wide left. Teams trade punts. Wilson pass intercepted by R. Jackson at Los Angeles 45, returned 23 yards to Los Angeles 22. Karlis kicks 35-yard field goal two plays later at 15:00.

Nov. 4, 1984—Philadelphia 23, Detroit 23, at Detroit; Lions win toss. Lions drive to Eagles' 3 in eight plays. Murray's 21-yard field goal attempt hits right upright and bounces bad. Jaworski's pass intercepted by Watkins at Detroit 5. Teams trade punts. Cooper returns Black's punt five yards to Eagles' 14. Time expires four plays later with Eagles on own 21.

Nov. 18, 1984—San Diego 34, Miami 28, at San Diego; Chargers win toss. McGee scores eight plays later on a 25-yard run at 3:17.

Dec. 2, 1984—Cincinnati 20, Cleveland 17, at Cleveland; Browns win toss. Simmons returns Cox's punt 30 yards to Cleveland 35. Breech kicks 35-yard field goal seven plays later at 4:34.

Dec. 2, 1984—Houston 23, Pittsburgh 20, at Houston; Oilers win toss. Cooper kicks 30-yard field goal 16 plays later at 5:53.

Sept. 8, 1985—St. Louis 27, Cleveland 24, at Cleveland; Cardinals win toss. O'Donoghue kicks 35-yard field goal nine plays later at 5:27.

Sept. 29, 1985—New York Giants 16, Philadelphia 10, at Philadelphia; Eagles win toss. Jaworski's pass tipped by Quick and intercepted by Patterson who returns 29 yards for touchdown at 0:55.

Oct. 20, 1985—Denver 13, Seattle 10, at Denver; Seahawks win toss. Teams trade punts twice. Krieg's pass intercepted by Hunter and returned to Seahawks' 15. Karlis kicks 24-yard field goal four plays later at 9:19.

Nov. 10, 1985—Philadelphia 23, Atlanta 17, at Philadelphia; Falcons win toss. Donnelly's 62-yard punt goes out of bounds at Eagles' 1. Jaworski completes 99-yard touchdown pass to Quick two plays later at 1:49.

Nov. 10, 1985—San Diego 40, Los Angeles Raiders 34, at San Diego; Chargers win toss. James scores on 17-yard run seven plays later at 3:44.

Nov. 17, 1985—Denver 30, San Diego 24, at Denver; Chargers win toss. Thomas' 40-yard field goal attempt is blocked by Smith and returned 60 yards by Wright for touchdown at 4:45.

Nov. 24, 1985—New York Jets 16, New England 13, at New York; Jets win toss. Teams trade punts twice. Patriots' second punt returned 46 yards by Sohn to Patriots' 15. Leahy kicks 32-yard field goal one play later at 10:05.

Nov. 24, 1985—Tampa Bay 19, Detroit 16, at Tampa; Lions win toss. Teams trade punts. Lions' punt downed on Buccaneers' 38. Igwebuike kicks 24-yard field goal 11 plays later at 12:31.

Nov. 24, 1985—Los Angeles Raiders 31, Denver 28, at Los Angeles; Raiders win toss. Bahr kicks 32-yard field goal six plays later at 2:42.

Dec. 8, 1985—Los Angeles Raiders 17, Denver 14, at Denver; Broncos win toss. Teams trade punts twice. Elway's fumble recovered by Townsend at Broncos' 8. Bahr kicks 26-yard field goal one play later at 4:55.

Sept. 14, 1986—Chicago 13, Philadelphia 10, at Chicago; Eagles win toss. Crawford's fumble of kickoff recovered by Jackson at Eagles' 35. Butler kicks 23-yard field goal 10 plays later at 5:56.

Sept. 14, 1986—Cincinnati 36, Buffalo 33, at Cincinnati; Bills win toss. Zander intercepts Kelly's first-down pass and returns it to Bills' 17. Breech kicks 20-yard field goal two plays later at 0:56.

Sept. 21, 1986—New York Jets 51, Miami 45, at New York; Jets win toss. O'Brien completes 43-yard touchdown pass to Walker five plays later at 2:35.

Sept. 28, 1986—Pittsburgh 22, Houston 16, at Houston; Oilers win toss. Johnson's punt returned 41 yards by Woods to Oilers' 15. Abercrombie scores on three-yard run three plays later at 2:35.

Sept. 28, 1986—Atlanta 23, Tampa Bay 20, at Tampa; Falcons win toss. Teams trade punts. Luckhurst kicks 34-yard field goal 10 plays later at 12:35.

Oct. 5, 1986—Los Angeles Rams 26, Tampa Bay 20, at Anaheim; Rams win toss. Dickerson scores four plays later on 42-yard run at 2:16.

Oct. 12, 1986—Minnesota 27, San Francisco 24, at San Francisco; Vikings win toss. C. Nelson kicks 28-yard field goal nine plays later at 4:27.

Oct. 19, 1986—San Francisco 10, Atlanta 10, at Atlanta; Falcons win toss. Teams trade punts twice. Donnelly punts to 49ers' 27. The following play Wilson recovers Rice's fumble at 49ers' 46 as time expires.

Nov. 2, 1986—Washington 44, Minnesota 38, at Washington; Redskins win toss. Schroeder completes 38-yard touchdown pass to Clark four plays later at 1:46.

Nov. 20, 1986—Los Angeles Raiders 37, San Diego 31, at San Diego; Raiders win toss. Teams trade punts. Allen scores five plays later on 28-yard run at 8:33.

Nov. 23, 1986—Cleveland 37, Pittsburgh 31, at Cleveland; Browns win toss. Teams trade punts. Six plays later Kosar hits Slaughter with 36-yard touchdown pass at 6:37.

Nov. 30, 1986—Chicago 13, Pittsburgh 10, at Chicago; Bears win toss and kick off. Newsome's punt returned by Barnes to Chicago 49. Butler kicks 42-yard field goal five plays later at 3:55.

Nov. 30, 1986—Philadelphia 33, Los Angeles Raiders 27, at Los Angeles; Eagles win toss. Teams trade punts. Long recovers Cunningham's fumble at Philadelphia 42. Waters returns

Allen's fumble 81 yards to Los Angeles 4. Cunningham scores on one-yard run two plays later at 6:53.

Nov. 30, 1986—Cleveland 13, Houston 10, at Cleveland; Oilers win toss and kick off. Gossett punts to Houston 39. Luck's pass intercepted by Minnifield at Cleveland 21. Gossett punts to Houston 34. Luck's pass intercepted by Minnifield at Cleveland 43 who returns 20 yards to Houston 37. Moseley kicks 29-yard field goal nine plays later at 14:44.

Dec. 7, 1986—St. Louis 10, Philadelphia 10, at Philadelphia; Cardinals win toss. White blocks Schubert's 40-yard field goal attempt. Teams trade punts. McFadden's 43-yard field goal attempt is wide left. Schubert's 37-yard field goal attempt is wide right. Cavanaugh's pass intercepted by Carter and returned to Eagles' 48 to end game.

Dec. 14, 1986—Miami 37, Los Angeles Rams 31, at Anaheim; Dolphins win toss. Marino completes 20-yard touchdown pass to Duper six plays later at 3:04.

Sept. 20, 1987—Denver 17, Green Bay 17, at Milwaukee; Packers win toss. Del Greco's 47-yard field goal attempt is short. Teams trade punts. Elway intercepted by Noble who returns 10 yards to Green Bay 34. Davis fumbles on next play and Smith recovers. Two plays later, Karlis' 40-yard field goal attempt is wide left. Time expires two plays later with Packers on own 23.

Oct. 11, 1987—Detroit 19, Green Bay 16, at Green Bay; Lions win toss. Prindle's 42-yard field goal attempt is wide left. Packers punt downed on Detroit 17. Prindle kicks 31-yard field goal 16 plays later at 12:26.

Oct. 18, 1987—New York Jets 37, Miami 31, at New York; Jets win toss. Teams trade punts. Ryan intercepted by Hooper at Jets' 47 who returns 11 yards. Mackey intercepted by Haslett at Jets' 37 who returns 9 yards. Jets punt. Mackey intercepted by Radachowsky who returns 45 yards to Miami 24. Ryan completes eight-yard touchdown pass to Hunter five plays later at 14:26.

Oct. 18, 1987—Green Bay 16, Philadelphia 10, at Green Bay; Packers win toss. Hargrove scores on seven-yard run 10 plays later at 5:04.

Oct. 18, 1987—Buffalo 6, New York Giants 3, at Buffalo; Bills win toss. Schlopy's 28-yard field goal attempt is wide left. Teams trade punts. Rutledge intercepted by Clark who returns 23 yards to Buffalo 40. Schlopy kicks 27-yard field goal nine plays later at 14:41.

Oct. 25, 1987—Buffalo 34, Miami 31, at Miami; Bills win toss. Norwood kicks 27-yard field goal seven plays later at 4:12.

Nov. 1, 1987—San Diego 27, Cleveland 24, at San Diego; Browns win toss. Kosar intercepted by Glenn who returns 20 yards to Browns' 25. Abbott kicks 33-yard field goal three plays later at 2:16.

Nov. 15, 1987—Dallas 23, New England 17, at New England; Cowboys win toss. Walker scores on 60-yard run four plays later at 1:50.

Nov. 26, 1987—Minnesota 44, Dallas 38, at Dallas; Vikings win toss. Coleman's punt downed by Hilton at Cowboys' 37. White intercepted by Studwell who returns 12 yards to Vikings' 37. D. Nelson scores on 24-yard run seven plays later at 7:51.

Nov. 29, 1987—Philadelphia 34, New England 31, at New England; Patriots win toss. Ramsey intercepted by Joyner who returns 29 yards to Eagles' 13. Fryar fair catches Teltschik's punt at Patriots' 13. Franklin's 46-yard field-goal attempt is short. McFadden's 39-yard field goal attempt is wide left. Tatupu fumbles on next play and Cobb recovers. McFadden kicks 38-yard field goal four plays later at 12:16.

Dec. 6, 1987—New York Giants 23, Philadelphia 20, at New York; Giants win toss and kick off. Teams trade punts twice. Teltschik's punt is returned 16 yards by McConkey to Eagles' 33. Three plays later, Allegre's 50-yard field goal attempt is blocked by Joyner and returned 25 yards by Hoage to Eagles' 30. McConkey returns Teltschik's punt four yards to Giants' 44.

Allegre kicks 28-yard field goal four plays later at 10:42.

Dec. 6, 1987—Cincinnati 30, Kansas City 27, at Cincinnati; Bengals win toss. Teams trade punts. Breech kicks 32-yard field goal 16 plays later at 9:44.

Dec. 26, 1987—Washington 27, Minnesota 24, at Minnesota; Redskins win toss. Haji-Sheikh kicks 26-yard field goal six plays later at 2:09.

Sept. 4, 1988—Houston 17, Indianapolis 14, at Indianapolis; Colts win toss. Dickerson fumble recovered by Lyles who returns six yards to Colts' 42. Zendejas kicks 35-yard field goal six plays later at 3:51.

* **Sept. 26, 1988—Los Angeles Raiders 30, Denver 27,** at Denver; Broncos win toss. Teams trade punts twice. Elway intercepted by Lee who returns 20 yards to Broncos' 31. Bahr kicks 35-yard field goal four plays later at 12:35.

Oct. 2, 1988—New York Jets 17, Kansas City 17, at New York; Chiefs win toss. Chiefs punt goes into end zone for touchback. Leahy's 44-yard field goal attempt is wide right. Chiefs punt is returned by Townsell to Jets' 26. Burruss recovers McNeil's fumble at Chiefs' 11. DeBerg intercepted by Humphery at Jets' 49. Three plays later, time expires.

Oct. 9, 1988—Denver 16, San Francisco 13, at San Francisco; Broncos win toss and kick off. Young intercepted by Haynes at Broncos' 32. Denver punt downed at 49ers' 5. Young intercepted by Wilson who returns seven yards to 49ers' 5. Karlis kicks 22-yard field goal two plays later at 8:11.

Oct. 30, 1988—New York Giants 13, Detroit 10, at Detroit; Lions win toss. James's fumble recovered by Taylor at Lions' 22. Three plays later, McFadden kicks 33-yard field goal at 1:13.

Nov. 20, 1988—Buffalo 9, New York Jets 6, at Buffalo; Jets win toss. Vick's fumble recovered by Bennett at Bills' 32. Norwood kicks 30-yard field goal five plays later at 3:47.

Nov. 20, 1988—Philadelphia 23, New York Giants 17, at New York; Eagles win toss. Philadelphia's punt goes into end zone for touchback. Hostetler intercepted by Hoage who returns 11 yards to Giants' 41. Six plays later, Zendejas's 30-yard field-goal attempt is blocked and ball is recovered behind line of scrimmage by Eagles' Simmons, who runs 15 yards for touchdown at 3:09.

Dec. 11, 1988—New England 10, Tampa Bay 7, at New England; Buccaneers win toss and kick off. Staurovsky kicks 27-yard field goal six plays later at 3:08.

Dec. 17, 1988—Cincinnati 20, Washington 17, at Cincinnati; Bengals win toss. Cincinnati's punt returned by Oliphant to Redskins' 16. Grant recovers Williams's fumble at Redskins' 17. Breech kicks 20-yard field goal three plays later at 7:01.

Sept. 24, 1989—Buffalo 47, Houston 41, at Houston; Oilers win toss. Johnson returns Brady's kickoff 17 yards to Oilers' 19. Oilers drive to Buffalo 25, Zendejas's 37-yard field goal blocked, but Bills offsides and Zendejas's second attempt is wide left. Bills' ball and Kelly completes series of passes, including 28-yard game-winner to Andre Reed, at 8:42.

Oct. 8, 1989—Miami 13, Cleveland 10, at Miami; Browns win toss. Metcalf returns Stoyanovich's kickoff 20 yards to Browns' 28. Browns drive ball 46 yards in eight plays; Bahr wide left on 44-yard field goal attempt. Dolphins ball. Browns called for pass interference on Marino pass to Banks at Cleveland 47. Two plays later, Banks's 20-yard reception at Browns' 23 sets up winning 35-yard field goal by Stoyanovich at 6:23.

Oct. 22, 1989—Denver 24, Seattle 21, at Seattle; Seahawks win toss. Treadwell's 56-yard kickoff returned 18 yards by Jefferson to Seahawks' 27. Seahawks drive to Broncos' 22 in 10 plays, but Johnson's 40-yard field goal attempt wide left. Smith intercepts a Krieg pass and returns it 28 yards to Seahawks' 10. Treadwell kicks winning 27-yard field goal at 7:46.

Oct. 29, 1989—New England 23, Indianapolis 20, at Indianapolis; Patriots win toss. Biasucci kickoff returned 13 yards to Patriots' 23 by Martin. Holding penalty brings ball back to Patriots' 13. After six plays, Feagles punt returned 11 yards by Verdin to Colts' 28. Six plays later, Colts punt to Martin at Patriots' 12.

Grogan completes three straight passes to Patriots' 44. Five consecutive runs put New England on Colts' 33. Davis kicks a 51-yard winning field goal for Patriots at 9:46.

Oct. 29, 1989—Green Bay 23, Detroit 20, at Milwaukee; Lions win toss. Sanders touchback on Jacke kickoff. On first play, Murphy intercepts Lions' Peete and returns it three yards to Lions' 26. Fullwood gains five yards on three plays to set up Jacke's 38-yard field goal at 2:14.

Nov. 5, 1989—Minnesota 23, Los Angeles Rams 21, at Minneapolis; Rams win toss. Karlis's kick returned 18 yards by Delpino to Rams' 19. Drive stops at Rams' 28. Merriweather blocks Hatcher's punt at 12. Ball rolls out of end zone for safety.

Nov. 19, 1989—Cleveland 10, Kansas City 10, at Cleveland; Browns win toss. Browns punt three times; Chiefs twice; before Kansas City's Lowery misses 47-yard field goal with 17 seconds remaining in overtime. Kosar's pass intercepted as time expired.

Nov. 26, 1989—Los Angeles Rams 20, New Orleans 17, at New Orleans; Saints win toss. Lansford's kickoff returned 27 yards to Saints' 30. After four plays, Barnhardt punts to Rams' 15. Saints penalized 35 yards for interference to Rams' 43. Three plays later, Everett hits Anderson with 14-yard pass to Saints' 40, then 26-yarder to put Rams in field goal position. Lansford kicks 31-yard field goal at 6:38.

Dec. 3, 1989—Los Angeles Raiders 16, Denver 13, at Los Angeles; Broncos win toss. Bell returns Jaeger kickoff 14 yards to Broncos' 18. Broncos' penalized for illegal block to Broncos' 9. Elway completes three passes for two first downs. On third and eight Elway sacked for 10-yard loss. Horan punts, Adams calls for fair catch at Raiders' 29. Dyal's 26-yard reception moves Raiders to Denver 43. Raiders move ball 34 yards in three plays to set up Jaeger's 26-yard field goal at 7:02.

Dec. 10, 1989—Indianapolis 23, Cleveland 17, at Indianapolis; Browns win toss. Teams trade punts. McNeil returns Colts' punt 42 yards to 42. Seven plays later, Bahr misses 35-yard field goal attempt. Three plays later, Stark punts and McNeil returns ball to 50-yard line. Two plays later, Prior intercepts Kosar's pass at Colts' 42 and returns it 58 yards for touchdown at 10:54.

Dec. 17, 1989—Cleveland 23, Minnesota 17, at Cleveland; Browns win toss. Browns punt to Vikings' 18. Six plays later, Vikings punt to Browns' 22. Nine plays later, Bahr lines up to attempt 31-yard field goal. Holder Pagel takes snap and passes 14 yards to Waiters for touchdown at 9:30.

Sept. 23, 1990—Denver 34, Seattle 31, at Denver; Seahawks win toss. Loville returns kickoff 19 yards to Seahawks' 27. Seahawks drive to Broncos' 26, where Johnson misses 44-yard field goal wide right. Broncos take over and Elway completes series of passes to set up Treadwell's 25-yard field goal at 9:14.

Sept. 30, 1990—Tampa Bay 23, Minnesota 20, at Minnesota; Vikings win toss. Vikings drive to Buccaneers' 31; Igwebuike's 48-yard field goal attempt wide left. Buccaneers drive to Vikings' 43 and punt. Gannon's pass is intercepted at Vikings' 26 by Wayne Haddix. Buccaneers drive to Vikings' 19 to set up Christie's 36-yard field goal at 9:11.

Oct. 7, 1990—Cincinnati 34, Los Angeles Rams 31, at Anaheim; Rams win toss. Berry returns kickoff to Rams' 21. After 3 plays, English punts and Green downs ball at Bengals' 25. After 3 plays, Johnson punts and Sutton downs ball at Rams' 29-yard line. After 3 plays, English punts and Price signals fair catch at Bengals' 47. Esiason completes series of passes to 26-yard line to set up Breech's 44-yard field goal at 11:56.

Nov. 4, 1990—Washington 41, Detroit 38, at Detroit; Redskins win toss. Howard downs kickoff on Redskins' 15. After 3 plays, Mojsiejenko punts to Redskins' 45. After 3 plays, Arnold punts to Redskins' 10. Rutledge completes series of passes to set up Lohmiller's 34-yard field goal at 9:10.

Nov. 18, 1990—Chicago 16, Denver 13, at Denver; Broncos win toss. Ezor returns kickoff to Broncos' 12. Both teams have ball twice and have to punt after each possession. Broncos punt after third possession of overtime and Bailey returns 20 yards to Broncos' 34. Harbaugh completes 10-yard pass to Thornton to set up Butler's 44-yard field goal at 13:14.

Nov. 25, 1990—Seattle 13, San Diego 10, at San Diego; Chargers win toss. Lewis returns kickoff to Chargers' 22. After 2 plays, Cox fumbles and ball is recovered by Porter at Chargers' 23. After two plays, Johnson kicks 40-yard field goal at 3:01.

Dec. 2, 1990—Chicago 23, Detroit 17, at Chicago; Lions win toss. Gray returns kickoff to Detroit 35. After 10 plays, Murray misses 35-yard field goal. Bears take possession at Chicago 20. Harbaugh completes 50-yard game-winning pass to Anderson at 10:57.

Dec. 2, 1990—Seattle 13, Houston 10, at Seattle; Seahawks win toss. Warren returns kickoff to Seahawks' 13. After 5 plays, Donnelly punts to Oilers' 23-yard line. Ford's fumble recovered by Wyman. Seahawks take possession at Oilers' 27. After 2 plays, Johnson kicks 42-yard field goal at 4:25.

Dec. 9, 1990—Miami 23, Philadelphia 20, at Miami; Eagles win toss. After 11 plays, Feagles punts to Dolphins' 26. After 6 plays, Roby punts to Eagles' 14 and Harris returns to 25. After 3 plays, Feagles punts to Dolphins' 43. Marino completes series of passes to Eagles' 22. Stoyanovich kicks 39-yard field goal at 12:32.

Dec. 9, 1990—San Francisco 20, Cincinnati 17, at Cincinnati; 49ers win toss. Carter returns kickoff to 49ers' 19. After 10 plays, Cofer kicks 23-yard field goal at 6:12.

Sept. 23, 1991—Chicago 19, New York Jets 13, at Chicago; Jets win toss. Mathis returns kickoff seven yards to New York's 12. Jets drive to New York 26; Bailey returns punt to Chicago 39. Bears drive to Jets' 44-yard line and punt into the end zone. Jets drive to Bears' 11 where Leahy's 28-yard field goal attempt is wide left. Bears drive from 20 to Jets' 1 where Harbaugh runs for touchdown at 14:42.

Oct. 13, 1991—Los Angeles Raiders 23, Seattle 20, at Seattle; Seahawks win toss. Seahawks begin on 20. After 5 plays, Tuten punts and Brown signals fair catch at Raiders' 24. After 3 plays, Gossett punts and Land downs ball at Seattle 9. After 1 play, Lott intercepts at Seahawks' 19 to set up Jaeger's game-winning 37-yard field goal at 6:37.

Oct. 20, 1991—Cleveland 30, San Diego 24, at San Diego; Chargers win toss. After kickoff, Chargers drive to Browns' 45 and punt to Browns' 6 where Hendrickson downs ball. Browns drive to 38 and punt; Taylor fair catches on Chargers' 14. After 3 plays, Brandon intercepts at Chargers' 30 and scores at 5:58.

Oct. 20, 1991—New England 26, Minnesota 23, at New England; Patriots win toss. Martin returns kickoff 18 yards to New England 22. Patriots drive to Minnesota 19. Staurovsky's 36-yard field goal attempt is wide left. Minnesota drives to the 50 where Newsome punts into end zone. On first play, McMillian intercepts at the 40 for Minnesota. After 2 plays, Marion causes Jordan fumble and Pool recovers at New England 20. New England drives to Minnesota 24 where Staurovsky kicks 42-yard field goal as time expires.

Nov. 3, 1991—New York Jets 19, Green Bay 16, at New York; Packers win toss. Thompson returns kickoff 30 yards to Packers' 39. Green Bay drives to New York 24 where Jacke's 42-yard field-goal attempt is wide right. Jets drive to 50. Aguiar's punt is fumbled by Sikahema and recovered by New York at Packers' 23. After 2 plays, Leahy kicks 37-yard field goal at 9:40.

Nov. 3, 1991—Washington 16, Houston 13, at Washington; Redskins win toss. Mitchell returns kickoff 9 yards to Washington 14. After 4 plays, Goodburn punts and Givins returns to Houston 31. After 1 play, Moon's pass is intercepted by Green at Oilers' 35. After 3 plays, Lohmiller kicks 41-yard field goal at 4:01.

Nov. 10, 1991—Houston 26, Dallas 23, at Houston; Oilers win toss. Pinkett returns kickoff 20 yards to Houston 24. After 6 plays, Montgomery punts and Martin returns to Dallas 24. Cowboys drive to Oilers' 24 where Smith fumbles and McDowell

recovers at Oilers' 15. Houston drives to Dallas 5 where Del Greco kicks 23-yard field goal at 14:31.

Nov. 10, 1991—Pittsburgh 33, Cincinnati 27, at Cincinnati; Steelers wins toss. Woodson downs kickoff for touchback. After 3 plays, Stryzinski punts and Barber returns 7 yards to Cincinnati 38. Bengals drive to Pittsburgh 37 where Woods fumbles and Lloyd returns recovery to Cincinnati 44. After 2 plays, O'Donnell passes to Green for 26-yard touchdown at 6:32.

Nov. 24, 1991—Atlanta 23, New Orleans 20, at New Orleans; Falcons win toss. Falcons begin at 20. After 3 plays, Fulhage punts and Fenerty signals fair catch at New Orleans 43. After 3 plays, Barnhardt punts and Thompson downs ball at Atlanta 23. After 3 plays, Fulhage punts and Fenerty fair catches at New Orleans 25. Saints drive to Atlanta 38 where Andersen misses 55-yard field-goal attempt. After 1 play, Rozier fumbles and Martin recovers on 50. Saints drive to Atlanta 38 where Barnhardt punts to Falcons' 2. Atlanta drives to New Orleans 33 where Johnson kicks 50-yard field goal at 13:03.

Nov. 24, 1991—Miami 16, Chicago 13, at Chicago; Dolphins wins toss. Butler kicks to Miami 20 where Paige returns kickoff 15 yards to 35. Miami drives to Chicago 9 where Stoyanovich kicks 27-yard field goal at 4:11.

Dec. 8, 1991—Buffalo 30, Los Angeles Raiders 27, at Los Angeles; Raiders win toss. Daluiso kicks into end zone for touchback. On third play, Kelso intercepts for Buffalo and returns ball to Bills' 36. Bills drive to Los Angeles 24 where Norwood kicks 42-yard field goal at 2:34.

Dec. 8, 1991—Kansas City 20, San Diego 17, at Kansas City; Chiefs win toss. Carney kicks to Kansas City 10 where Stradford returns 23 yards to 33. After 3 plays, Barker punts to San Diego 4. Chargers drive to 40 where Kidd punts 60 yards into end zone for touchback. Kansas City drives to San Diego 39 where Barker punts 38 yards to 1. After 3 plays, Kidd punts 41 yards to San Diego 42 where Stradford returns 12 yards to 30. Chiefs drive to San Diego 1 where Lowery kicks 18-yard field goal at 11:26.

Dec. 8, 1991—New England 23, Indianapolis 17, at New England; Colts wins toss. Baumann kicks off to Indianapolis 2 where Martin returns 23 yards to 25. After 3 downs, Stark punts to New England 17 where Henderson returns 8 yards to 25. New England drives to 50 where McCarthy punts and Prior signals fair catch at Indianapolis 15. After 3 plays, Stark punts to New England 40 where Henderson returns 7 yards to 47. After 2 plays, Millen passes to Timpson for 45-yard touchdown at 8:55.

Dec. 22, 1991—Detroit 17, Buffalo 14, at Buffalo; Lions wins toss. Daluiso kicks off to Detroit 20 where Dozier returns 15 yards to Lions 35. Lions drive to Bills' 3 where Murray kicks 21-yard field goal at 4:23.

Dec. 22, 1991—New York Jets 23, Miami 20, at Miami; Jets win toss. Aguiar kicks to Miami's 30 where Logan returns 3 yards to the 33. After 4 downs, Stoyanovich punts to Jets' 15 where Baty returns 8 yards to 23. Jets drive to Miami 12 where Allegre kicks 30-yard field goal at 6:33.

Sept. 6, 1992—Minnesota 23, Green Bay 20, at Green Bay; Vikings win toss. Nelson returns kickoff 14 yards to the Minnesota 23. After 5 plays, Newsome punts 49 yards to Green Bay 21 where Brooks returns 12 yards to the 33. After 2 plays, Glenn intercepts pass at the Vikings' 48. On first play, Allen fumbles and Billups recovers at Green Bay 35. After 3 plays, McJulien punts 33 yards to Vikings' 35. Vikings drive to Minnesota 48; Newsome punts 52 yards for touchback. After 3 plays, McJulien punts and Parker returns 10 yards to Green Bay 48. Vikings drive to Packers' 9 where Reveiz kicks 26-yard field goal at 10:20.

Sept. 13, 1992—Cincinnati 24, Los Angeles Raiders 21, at Cincinnati; Raiders win toss. Land returns kickoff 13 yards but fumbles at Los Angeles's 20; ball recovered by Bengals' Bennett at Raiders' 21. After 1 play, Breech kicks 34-yard field goal at 1:01.

Sept. 20, 1992—Houston 23, Kansas City 20, at Houston; Chiefs win toss. Carter returns kickoff 25 yards to Kansas City

28. On third play of drive, Birden fumbles at Kansas City 34; ball recovered by Houston's D. Smith at Chiefs' 23. After one play, Del Greco kicks 39-yard field goal at 1:55.

Oct. 11, 1992—Indianapolis 6, New York Jets 3, at Indianapolis; Colts win toss. Verdin returns kickoff 33 yards to Colts' 36. Colts drive to Jets' 30 where Biasucci kicks 47-yard field goal at 3:01.

Nov. 8, 1992—Cincinnati 31, Chicago 28, at Chicago; Bears win toss. Lewis returns kickoff 22 yards to Chicago's 29. Bears drive to Chicago's 46 where Gardocki punts; fair catch by Wright at the Cincinnati 17. Bengals drive to Bears' 18 where Breech kicks 36-yard field goal at 8:39.

Nov. 15, 1992—New England 37, Indianapolis 34, at Indianapolis; Colts win toss. Verdin returns kickoff 10 yards to Colts' 20; holding penalty brings ball back to Colts' 10. After two plays, Henderson intercepts pass at Colts' 38 and returns it 9 yards to the 29. In three plays, Patriots drive to 1 where Baumann kicks 18-yard field goal at 3:25.

Nov. 29, 1992—Indianapolis 16, Buffalo 13, at Indianapolis; Colts win toss. Verdin returns kickoff 24 yards to Colts' 22. Colts drive to Buffalo 22 where Biasucci kicks 40-yard field goal at 3:51.

* **Nov. 30, 1992—Seattle 16, Denver 13,** at Seattle; Seahawks win toss. Daluiso kicks through end zone for touchback. After three plays, Tuten punts 53 yards to Denver 18 where Marshall returns for no gain. After three plays, Rodriguez punts 29 yards to Seattle 45 where Warren signals fair catch. Seahawks drive to Denver 15 where Kasay's 33-yard field goal attempt misses. Broncos take over at Denver 20. After three plays, Rodriguez punts 43 yards to Seattle 38 where Warren signals for fair catch. After four plays, Tuten punts 39 yards to Denver 4 where Daniels downs punt. After three plays, Rodriguez punts 46 yards to Denver 48 where Warren returns 10 yards to the 38. Seahawks drive to Denver 14 where Kasay kicks 32-yard field goal at 11:10.

Dec. 13, 1992—Philadelphia 20, Seattle 17, at Seattle; Eagles win toss. Sydner returns kick 12 yards to Eagles' 16; illegal block penalty brings ball back to 8. Eagles drive to Philadelphia 45 where Feagles punts for a touchback. After 6 plays, Tuten punts 45 yards to Philadelphia 22 where Sydner returns 7 yards to 29. After 6 plays, Feagles punts 44 yards to Seattle 26 where Warren returns 5 yards to 31. After 5 plays, Tuten punts 32 yards to Philadelphia 20 where Sydner signals for fair catch. Eagles drive to Seattle 27 where Ruzek kicks 44-yard field goal with no time remaining.

Dec. 27, 1992—Miami 16, New England 13, at New England; Patriots win toss. Lockwood returns kickoff 15 yards to Patriots' 21. After three plays, McCarthy punts 39 yards to Miami 33 where Miller returns 2 yards to the 35. Miami drives to New England 18 where Stoyanovich kicks 35-yard field goal at 8:17.

Sept. 12, 1993—Detroit 19, New England 16, at New England; Patriots win toss. Patriots begin at 20. After 3 plays, Saxon punts 42 yards to Detroit 29 where Gray returns 12 yards to the 41. After 3 plays, Arnold punts 41 yards to New England 12 where Brown returns 16 yards to the 28. Patriots drive to Detroit 44 where Saxon punts into the end zone for a touchback. Detroit drives to New England 20 where Hanson kicks 38-yard field goal at 11:04.

Nov. 7, 1993—Buffalo 13, New England 10, at New England; Patriots win toss. T. Brown returns kickoff 27 yards to Patriots 30. Patriots drive to Buffalo 48 where Bills take over on downs. Bills drive to New England 25 where Metzelaars fumbles, and C. Brown recovers. After 3 plays, Saxon punts 46 yards to Buffalo 24 where Copeland returns 11 yards to the 35. Bills drive to New England 14 where Christie kicks 32-yard field goal at 9:22.

Dec. 19, 1993—Phoenix 30, Seattle 27, at Seattle; Cardinals win toss. Bailey returns kickoff 14 yards to Cardinals 20. Cardinals drive to Seattle 23 where Davis kicks 41-yard field goal at 6:45.

Jan. 2, 1994—Dallas 16, New York Giants 13, at New York; Giants win toss. Meggett returns kickoff 19 yards to Giants 19.

After 6 plays, Horan punts 45 yards to Cowboys 25 where Widmer downs punt. Cowboys drive to Giants' 23 where Murray kicks 41-yard field goal at 10:44.

Jan. 2, 1994—New England 33, Miami 27, at New England; Dolphins win toss. McDuffie returns kickoff 21 yards to Miami 27. After 3 plays, Hatcher punts 43 yards to New England 29 where Harris returns 6 yards to the 35. After 2 plays, Brown intercepts pass from Bledsoe and returns 3 yards to Miami 49. After 3 plays, Hatcher punts 37 yards to New England 14 where Harris returns 18 yards to the 32. After 2 plays, Bledsoe passes 36 yards to Timpson for touchdown at 4:44.

Jan. 2, 1994—Los Angeles Raiders 33, Denver 30, at Los Angeles; Broncos win toss. Delpino returns kickoff 12 yards to Denver 25. Broncos drive to Los Angeles 22 where Elam's 40-yard field goal attempt is wide left. Raiders drive to Denver 29 where Jaeger kicks 47-yard field goal at 7:10.

* **Jan. 3, 1994—Philadelphia 37, San Francisco 34,** at San Francisco; 49ers win toss. Walker returns kickoff, 19 yards to San Francisco 27. 49ers drive to Philadelphia 14 where Cofer misses 32-yard field goal. Eagles start at their 20-yard line, and, after 3 plays, Feagles punts 48 yards to San Francisco 36 where Carter fumbles and 49ers recover. After 7 plays, Wilmsmeyer punts 57 yards to Philadelphia 6 where Sikahema returns 16 yards to the 22. Eagles drive to San Francisco 10 where Ruzek kicks 28-yard field goal with no time remaining.

Sept. 4, 1994—Detroit 31, Atlanta 28, at Detroit; Falcons win toss. Falcons start at their own 14 after holding penalty on kickoff. After 3 plays, Alexander punts 41 yards to Detroit 39 where Clay returns 12 yards to Atlanta 49. Detroit drives to Atlanta 20 where Hanson kicks 37-yard field goal at 5:14.

Sept. 11, 1994—New York Jets 25, Denver 22, at New York; Jets win toss. Murrell returns kickoff 24 yards to New York 33. Jets drive to Denver 22 where Lowery kicks 39-yard field goal at 3:57.

* **Sept. 19, 1994—Detroit 20, Dallas 17,** at Dallas; Lions win toss. Gray returns kickoff 24 yards to Detroit 32. Lions drive to Dallas 34 where Hanson's 51-yard field-goal attempt is blocked by Lett. Cowboys take possession at Dallas 42. Cowboys drive to Detroit 37 where Kennard fumbles and Swilling recovers. Lions take possession at Detroit 45. After 6 plays, Montgomery punts 31 yards to Dallas 16. Cowboys drive to Dallas 49 where Aikman fumbles and Thomas recovers at Dallas 43. Lions drive to Dallas 26 where Hanson kicks 44-yard field goal at 14:33.

Oct. 16, 1994—Arizona 19, Washington 16, at Washington; Redskins win toss. Mitchell returns kickoff 27 yards to Washington 41. Redskins drive to Arizona 34 where Lohmiller's 51-yard field-goal attempt is blocked by Joyner and recovered by Williams who returns it to the Washington 37. After 5 plays, Peterson's 45-yard field-goal attempt is wide right. Redskins take possession at the Washington 36. After 3 plays, Roby punts 36 yards to the Arizona 37 where Robinson returns 3 yards to the 40. After 3 plays, Feagles punts 51 yards for a touchback. After 1 play, Shuler's pass is intercepted by Hoage who returns it to the Washington 12. Peterson kicks 29-yard field goal at 10:00.

Oct. 16, 1994—Miami 20, Los Angeles Raiders 17, at Miami; Dolphins win toss. McDuffie returns kickoff 19 yards to Miami 23. Dolphins drive to Los Angeles 12 where Stoyanovich kicks 29-yard field goal at 5:46.

\# **Oct. 20, 1994—Minnesota 13, Green Bay 10,** at Minnesota; Vikings win toss. Ismail returns kickoff 22 yards to Minnesota 29. Vikings drive to Green Bay 9 where Fuad Reveiz kicks 27-yard field goal at 4:26.

Oct. 30, 1994—Detroit 28, New York Giants 25, at New York; Giants win toss. Lewis returns kickoff 16 yards to New York 27. After 3 plays, Horan punts 42 yards to Detroit 24 where Gray calls for fair catch. Detroit drives to New York 6 where Hanson kicks 24-yard field goal at 6:43.

Oct. 30, 1994—Arizona 20, Pittsburgh 17, at Arizona; Steelers win toss. Johnson returns kickoff 24 yards to Pittsburgh 30 where he fumbles and Arizona's Merritt recovers at Pittsburgh 32. After 3 plays, Davis kicks 51-yard field goal at 1:40.

Nov. 6, 1994—Cincinnati 20, Seattle 17, at Seattle; Seahawks win toss. Warren returns kickoff 32 yards to Seattle 33. After 3 plays, Tuten punts 37 yards to Cincinnati 28 where Sawyer calls for fair catch. After 3 plays, Johnson punts 64 yards to Seattle 2 where Truitt downs ball. Seahawks drive to Seattle 38 where Tuten punts 50 yards to Cincinnati 12 and Sawyer returns 5 yards to 17. Blake passes to Scott for 76 yards to Seattle 7. Pelfrey kicks 26-yard field goal at 8:14.

Nov. 6, 1994—Pittsburgh 12, Houston 9, at Houston; Steelers win toss. Stone returns kickoff 15 yards to Pittsburgh 28. After 3 plays, Royals punts 53 yards to Houston 13 where Givins downs ball. After 3 plays, Camarillo punts 57 yards to Pittsburgh 31 where Woodson returns 20 yards to Houston 49. After 3 plays, Royals punts 43 yards to Houston 15 where Coleman returns 3 yards to 18. After 5 plays, Camarillo punts 57 yards to Pittsburgh 12 where Hastings returns 12 yards to 24. Steelers drive to Houston 41 where Royals punts 29 yards to Houston 12, and Coleman calls for fair catch. Brown fumbles on first play and Jones recovers at Houston 22. After 1 play, Anderson kicks 40-yard field goal at 11:24.

Nov. 13, 1994—New England 26, Minnesota 20, at New England; Patriots win toss. Thompson returns kickoff 27 yards to New England 33. Patriots drive to Minnesota 14 where Bledsoe passes 14 yards to Turner for touchdown at 4:10.

Nov. 20, 1994—Pittsburgh 16, Miami 13, at Pittsburgh; Steelers win toss. Stone returns kickoff 15 yards to Pittsburgh 16. Steelers drive to Miami 39 where they lose possession on downs. Dolphins drive to Pittsburgh 47 where Arnold punts 35 yards to Pittsburgh 12 and Oliver downs ball. Steelers drive to Miami 21 where Anderson kicks 39-yard field goal at 10:19.

Nov. 27, 1994—Chicago 19, Arizona 16, at Arizona; Cardinals win toss. Levy returns kickoff 31 yards to Arizona 45. After 5 plays, Feagles punts 38 yards to the end zone for a touchback. Bears drive to Arizona 10 where Butler kicks 27-yard field goal at 8:11.

Nov. 27, 1994—Tampa Bay 20, Minnesota 17, at Minnesota; Buccaneers win toss. Harris returns kickoff 12 yards to Tampa Bay 38. After 6 plays, Stryzinski punts 40 yards to Minnesota 4 where Guliford muffs punt and Buccaneers' Brady recovers. Husted kicks 22-yard field goal at 2:08.

 # Dec. 1, 1994—Minnesota 33, Chicago 27, at Minnesota; Bears win toss. Lewis returns kickoff 23 yards to Chicago 33. Bears drive to Minnesota 22 where Butler's 40-yard field goal attempt is wide left. After 1 play, Moon passes 65 yards to Carter for touchdown at 5:46.

Dec. 4, 1994—Denver 20, Kansas City 17, at Kansas City; Broncos win toss. Milburn returns kickoff 24 yards to Denver 29. After 3 plays, Millen fumbles and Phillips recovers at Denver 35. After 4 plays, Allen fumbles and Smith recovers at Denver 27. After 6 plays, Rouen punts 45 yards to Kansas City 25 where Hughes calls for fair catch. After 3 plays, Aguiar punts 33 yards to Denver 42 where Chiefs down ball. Broncos drive to Kansas City 17 where Elam kicks 34-yard field goal at 12:12.

Sept. 3, 1995—Cincinnati 24, Indianapolis 21, at Indianapolis; Bengals win toss. Dunn returns kickoff 35 yards to Bengals' 17. Cincinnati drives to Indianapolis 29 where Pelfrey kicks 47-yard field goal at 2:36.

Sept. 3, 1995—Atlanta 23, Carolina 20, at Atlanta; Panthers win toss. Baldwin downs kickoff for touchback. Panthers drive to Carolina 42 where Reich fumbles and ball is recovered by Archambeau at Carolina 31. Falcons drive to Panthers' 16 where Andersen kicks 35-yard field goal at 6:17.

Sept. 10, 1995—Indianapolis 27, New York Jets 24, at New York; Jets win toss. Carter downs kickoff for touchback. Jets punt downed at Colts' 37. Colts drive to Jets' 35 where Cofer kicks 52-yard field goal at 4:27.

Sept. 10, 1995—Kansas City 20, New York Giants 17, at Kansas City; Chiefs win toss. Vanover returns kickoff 30 yards to Chiefs' 28. Aguiar punts to Giants' 3. Horan punts to Chiefs' 49. Chiefs drive to Giants' 6 where Elliott kicks 23-yard field goal at 7:49.

Sept. 17, 1995—Dallas 23, Minnesota 17, at Minnesota; Cowboys win toss. K. Williams returns kickoff 23 yards to Cowboys' 27. E. Smith scores on 31-yard run at 2:26.

Sept. 17, 1995—Kansas City 23, Oakland 17, at Kansas City; Chiefs win toss. Vanover returns kickoff 28 yards to Chiefs' 41. M. Allen fumbles, ball recovered by Robbins at Raiders' 38. Hasty intercepts pass at Chiefs' 36 and returns it 64 yards for touchdown at 4:27.

Sept. 17, 1995—Atlanta 27, New Orleans 24, at Atlanta; Saints win toss. Hughes returns kickoff 21 yards to Saints' 17. Metcalf returns Wilmsmeyer's punt 18 yards to Saints' 39. Stryzinski punts, fair catch by Hughes at Saints' 14. Wilmsmeyer punt downed at Falcons' 6. Falcons drive to Saints' 3 where Andersen kicks 21-yard field goal at 7:58.

Oct. 8, 1995—Indianapolis 27, Miami 24, at Miami; Colts win toss. Warren returns kickoff 25 yards to Colts' 33. Colts drive to Dolphins' 10 where Blanchard kicks 27-yard field goal at 4:58.

Oct. 8, 1995—New York Giants 27, Arizona 21, at New York; Cardinals win toss. Terry returns kickoff 20 yards to Cardinals' 23. Hamilton recovers Krieg's fumble at Cardinals' 36. Lynch recovers Brown's fumble at Cardinals' 38. Armstead intercepts pass at Giants' 42 and returns it 58 yards for touchdown at 4:05.

Oct. 8, 1995—Minnesota 23, Houston 17, at Minnesota; Vikings win toss. Palmer returns kickoff 10 yards to Vikings' 15. Saxon's punt downed at Oilers' 8. Washington intercepts pass at Vikings' 47 and returns it 25 yards to Oilers' 28. R. Smith scores on 20-yard run at 7:10.

Oct. 8, 1995—Philadelphia 37, Washington 34, at Philadelphia; Redskins win toss. Redskins take possession at their 20 after touchback. Turk punt out of bounds at Eagles' 9. Eagles drive to Redskins' 18 where Anderson kicks 35-yard field goal at 10:06.

* Oct. 9, 1995—Kansas City 29, San Diego 23, at Kansas City; Chargers win toss. Coleman returns kickoff 24 yards to Chargers' 28. Vanover makes fair catch of Bennett's punt at Chiefs' 15. Coleman makes fair catch of Aguiar's punt at Chargers' 43. Vanover returns Bennett's punt 86 yards for a touchdown at 7:27.

Oct. 15, 1995—Tampa Bay 20, Minnesota 17, at Tampa Bay; Buccaneers win toss. Edmonds returns kickoff 19 yards to Buccaneers' 22. A. Lee returns Roby's punt to Vikings' 48. Vikings drive to Tampa Bays' 35 where Reveiz's 53-yard field-goal attempt is wide right. Buccaneers take over at own 43 and drive to Vikings' 33 where Husted kicks 51-yard field goal at 6:23.

Oct. 22, 1995—Washington 36, Detroit 30, at Washington; Redskins win toss. B. Mitchell returns kickoff 16 yards to Redskins' 27. Turk's punt downed at Lions' 4. D. Green intercepts S. Mitchell's pass and returns it 7 yards for touchdown at 3:41.

Oct. 29, 1995—Carolina 20, New England 17, at New England; Panthers win toss. Baldwin returns kickoff 22 yards to Panthers' 25. Meggett makes fair catch of Barnhardt's punt at Patriots' 9. Guliford returns O'Neill's punt 9 yards to Panthers' 32. Panthers drive to Patriots' 12 where Kasay kicks 29-yard field goal at 7:08.

Oct. 29, 1995—Cleveland 29, Cincinnati 26, at Cincinnati; Browns win toss. Hunter returns kickoff 31 yards to Browns' 31. Bieniemy returns Tupa's punt 9 yards to Bengals' 37. McCardell makes fair catch of Johnson's punt at Browns' 12. Bieniemy returns Tupa's punt 0 yards to Bengals' 38. Hall intercepts Blake's pass and returns it 5 yards to Bengals' 45. Browns drive to Bengals' 11 where Stover kicks 28-yard field goal at 6:30.

Oct. 29, 1995—Arizona 20, Seattle 14, at Arizona; Cardinals win toss. Dowdell returns kickoff 16 yards to Cardinals' 25. Cardinals drive to Seahawks' 10 where G. Davis' 27-yard field goal attempt is blocked. L. Lynch intercepts Friesz's pass at Cardinals' 28 and returns it 72 yards for a touchdown at 11:16.

Nov. 5, 1995—Pittsburgh 37, Chicago 34, at Chicago; Bears win toss. Timpson returns kickoff 23 yards to Bears' 33. Hastings returns Sauerbrun's punt 2 yards to Steelers' 31. Steelers drive to Bears' 6 where N. Johnson kicks 24-yard field goal at 8:19.

Nov. 12, 1995—Minnesota 30, Arizona 24, at Arizona; Vikings win toss. A. Lee returns kickoff 20 yards to Vikings' 25. Moon throws 50-yard touchdown pass to Ismail at 2:16.

Nov. 26, 1995—Arizona 40, Atlanta 37, at Arizona; Falcons win toss. J. Anderson returns kickoff 20 yards to Falcons' 20. Stryzinski fumbles punt snap. Recovered by England at Falcons' 10 where G. Davis kicks 28-yard field goal at 1:43.

Dec. 10, 1995—Tampa Bay 13, Green Bay 10, at Tampa Bay; Buccaneers win toss. Edmonds returns kickoff 24 yards to Buccaneers' 23. Tampa Bay drives to Packers' 29 where Husted kicks 47-yard field goal at 3:46.

Sept. 1, 1996—Buffalo 23, New York Giants 20, at New York; Bills win toss. Daluiso kick is a touchback. Bills drive to Buffalo 46. Toomer returns Mohr's punt to Giants' 16. Dave Brown's fumble recovered by Spielman at Giants' 33. Bills drive to Giants' 16 where Christie kicks 34-yard field goal at 9:08.

Sept. 22, 1996—New England 28, Jacksonville 25, at New England; Patriots win toss. T. Brown returns kickoff 18 yards to Patriots' 29. Patriots drive to Jaguars' 22 where Vinatieri kicks 40-yard field goal at 2:36.

Sept. 29, 1996—Arizona 31, St. Louis 28, at Arizona; Cardinals win toss. Lohmiller kick is a touchback. Cardinals drive to Rams' 7 where G. Davis kicks 24-yard field goal at 1:54.

Oct. 6, 1996—Buffalo 16, Indianapolis 13, at Buffalo; Colts win toss. Christie kick is a touchback. Colts drive to Indianapolis 32. Burris returns Gardocki's punt to Bills' 35. Bills drive to Colts' 48. Mohr punts out of bounds at Colts' 14. Colts drive to Indianapolis 9. Burris returns Gardocki's punt to Colts' 48. Bills drive to Colts' 22 where Christie kicks 39-yard field goal at 9:22.

Oct. 6, 1996—Houston 30, Cincinnati 27, at Cincinnati; Bengals win toss. Dunn returns kickoff 34 yards to Bengals' 34. Bengals drive to Cincinnati 36. Floyd returns L. Johnson's punt to Oilers' 18. Oilers drive to Bengals' 31 where Del Greco kicks 49-yard field goal at 7:07.

* **Oct. 14, 1996—Green Bay 23, San Francisco 20,** at Green Bay; 49ers win toss. D. Carter returns kickoff 23 yards to 49ers' 22. 49ers' drive to San Francisco 25. Howard makes fair catch of Thompson's punt at Packers' 44. Packers drive to 49ers' 35 where Jacke kicks 53-yard field goal at 3:41.

Oct. 27, 1996—Baltimore 37, St. Louis 31, at Baltimore; Rams win toss. J. Thomas returns kickoff 17 yard to Rams' 17. Rams drive to Ravens' 15. F. Miller fumble in field goal formation recovered by S. Moore at Ravens' 17. Ravens drive to Baltimore 49 and turn ball over on downs. Rams drive to Ravens' 40 and turn ball over on downs. Testaverde throws 22-yard scoring pass to M. Jackson at 14:50.

Nov. 10, 1996—Dallas 20, San Francisco 17, at San Francisco; Cowboys win toss. H. Walker returns kickoff 10 yards to Cowboys' 23. Cowboys drive to 49ers' 11 where Boniol kicks 29-yard field goal at 6:17.

Nov. 10, 1996—Arizona 37, Washington 34, at Washington; Cardinals win toss. Blanton's kickoff is a touchback. Cardinals drive to Redskins' 15 where Butler misses 32-yard field goal. Redskins drive to Cardinals' 43 where Turk punts for touchback. L. Johnson fumble returned by Morrison to Cardinals' 27. Redskins drive to Cardinals' 31 where Blanton misses 48-yard field goal. Cardinals drive to Redskins' 15 where Butler kicks 32-yard field goal at 14:27.

Nov. 10, 1996—Tampa Bay 20, Oakland 17, at Tampa Bay; Buccaneers win toss. M. Marshall returns kickoff 15 yards to Bucs' 17. Bucs drive to Tampa Bay 36. T. Brown returns Barnhardt's punt four yards to Raiders' 22. Raiders drive to Oakland 25. M. Marshall returns Gossett's punt nine yards to Bucs' 39. Bucs drive to Raiders' 4 where Husted kicks 23-yard field goal at 11:56.

Nov. 17, 1996—Minnesota 16, Oakland 13, at Oakland; Raiders win toss. Kaufman returns kickoff 32 yards to Raiders' 27. Raiders drive to Oakland 46 where Gossett punts to Vikings' 17. Vikings drive to Raiders' 12 where Sisson kicks 31-yard field goal at 11:53.

Nov. 24, 1996—Jacksonville 28, Baltimore 25, at Baltimore; Jaguars win toss. Jordon returns kickoff 16 yards to Jaguars' 30. Jaguars drive to Jacksonville 37. Barker's punt is downed at Ravens' 6. Ravens drive to Jaguars' 37 where Pritchett recovers Byner's fumble. Jaguars drive to Ravens' 15 where Hollis kicks 34-yard field goal at 9:06.

Nov. 24, 1996—San Francisco 19, Washington 16, at Washington; 49ers win toss. D. Carter returns kickoff 20 yards to 49ers' 32. 49ers drive to Redskins' 20 where Wilkins kicks 38-yard field goal at 3:24.

Dec. 1, 1996—Indianapolis 13, Buffalo 10, at Indianapolis; Bills win toss. Moulds returns kickoff 26 yards to Bills' 25. Bills drive to Buffalo 49. Stock returns Mohr's punt one yard to Colts' 16. Colts drive to Bills' 32 where Blanchard kicks 49-yard field goal at 10:46.

Aug. 31, 1997—Tennessee 24, Oakland 21, at Tennessee; Oilers win toss. Gray returns kickoff 32 yards to Tennessee 33. Oilers drive to Tennessee 38. Roby's punt is downed at the Oakland 33. Raiders drive to Oakland 33. Gray returns Araguz punt to Tennessee 35. Oilers drive to Oakland 15 where Del Greco kicks 33-yard field goal at 6:57.

Sept. 7, 1997—Miami 16, Tennessee 13, at Miami; Dolphins win toss. Spikes returns kickoff 48 yards to Tennessee 45. Dolphins drive to Tennessee 11 where Mare kicks 29-yard field goal at 2:15.

Sept. 7, 1997— Arizona 25, Dallas 22, at Arizona; Cowboys win toss. Walker returns kickoff 21 yards to Dallas 25. Cowboys drive to Arizona 43. Gowin punts 43 yards for a touchback. Cardinals drive to Dallas 44. Graham fumbles. Cowboys drive to Arizona 42. Williams fumbles. Cardinals drive to Dallas 3 where Butler kicks 20-yard field goal at 8:30.

Sept. 14, 1997—Washington 19, Arizona 13, at Washington; Cardinals win toss. K. Williams returns kickoff 27 yards to Arizona 34. Cardinals drive to Arizona 40. McElroy fumbles. Redskins drive to Arizona 40. Westbrook catches 40-yard touchdown pass from Frerotte at 1:36.

Sept. 14, 1997—New England 27, New York Jets 24, at New England; Patriots win toss. Hall's kickoff is a touchback. Patriots drive to New England 15. Bledsoe pass intercepted by O. Smith. Jets drive to New York 15. Hansen punts 47 yards. Meggett returns to New England 21. Patriots drive to New York 17 where Vinatieri kicks 34-yard field goal at 8:03.

Sept. 28, 1997—Kansas City 20, Seattle 17, at Kansas City; Seahawks win toss. Broussard returns kickoff 12 yards to Seattle 14. Seahawks drive to Seattle 17. Vanover returns Tuten punt 8 yards to Kansas City 26. Chiefs drive to Seattle 44. Aguiar punt downed at Seattle 11. Seahawks drive to Seattle 26. Moon pass intercepted by Woods and returned 13 yards to 50. Chiefs drive to Seattle 23 where Stoyanovich kicks 41-yard field goal at 13:04.

Oct. 19, 1997—Philadelphia 13, Arizona 10, at Philadelphia; Cardinals win toss. K. Williams returns kickoff 28 yards to Arizona 42. Cardinals drive to Philadelphia 48. Feagles punts 48 yards for touchback. Eagles drive to Arizona 7 where Boniol kicks 24-yard field goal at 4:02.

Oct. 19, 1997—New York Giants 26, Detroit 20, at Detroit; Giants win toss. Pegram returns kickoff 16 yards to New York 18. Giants drive to New York 32. Calloway catches 68-yard touchdown pass from Kanell at 1:40.

Oct. 26, 1997—Denver 23, Buffalo 20, at Buffalo; Broncos win toss and elects to kickoff. Holmes returns kickoff 20 yards to Buffalo 25. Bills drive to Buffalo 23. Mohr punt downed at Denver 40. Broncos drive to Buffalo 48. Rouen punt downed at Buffalo 1. Bills drive to Buffalo 20. Gordon returns Mohr punt to Denver 42. Broncos drive to Buffalo 15 where Elam kicks

33-yard field goal at 13:04.

Oct. 26, 1997—Pittsburgh 23, Jacksonville 17, at Pittsburgh; Steelers win toss. Coleman returns kickoff 23 yards to Pittsburgh 23. Steelers drive to Jacksonville 17. Bettis catches 17-yard touchdown pass from Stewart at 3:47.

Oct. 27, 1997—Chicago 36, Miami 33, at Miami; Dolphins win toss. McPhail returns kickoff 23 yards to Miami 27. Dolphins drive to Miami 36. Kidd punts out of bounds at Chicago 10. Bears drive to the Chicago 39. Sauerbrun punt out of bounds at Miami 27. Reeves recovers Marino fumble at Miami 17. Bears drive to Miami 17 where Jaeger kicks 35-yard field goal at 9:25.

Nov. 2, 1997—New York Jets 19, Baltimore 16, at New York; Jets win toss. Stover's kickoff is a touchback. Jets drive to Baltimore 20 where Hall kicks 37-yard field goal at 4:58.

Nov. 16, 1997—Philadelphia 10, Baltimore 10, at Baltimore; Eagles win toss. Stover's kickoff is a touchback. Eagles drive to Philadelphia 19. Hutton punts 36 yards to Baltimore 45. Ravens drive to Baltimore 36 where Eagles take over on downs. Eagles drive to Baltimore 33 where Ravens take over on downs. Ravens drive to Baltimore 37. Montgomery punts 55 yards, and Solomon returns to Philadelphia 22. Eagles drive to Philadelphia 16. Hutton punts 41 yards, and Roe returns to Baltimore 46. Ravens drive to Philadelphia 35 where Stover's 53-yard field-goal attempt is no good. Eagles drive to Baltimore 22 where Boniol's 40-yard field-goal is no good as time expires.

Nov. 16, 1997—New Orleans 20, Seattle 17, at New Orleans; Seahawks win toss. Brien's kickoff is a touchback. Seahawks start at Seattle 20 where Moon's pass intercepted by Tubbs who returns 15 yards to Seattle 20. Saints Brien kicks 38-yard field goal at 17 seconds.

Nov. 23, 1997—New York Giants 7, Washington 7, at Washington; Redskins win toss. Davis returns kickoff 28 yards to Washington 39. Redskins drive to Washington 36 where Hostetler's pass intercepted by Sehorn who returns minus–2 yards before lateralling to Wooten who returns 5 yards to New York 41. Giants drive to New York 26 where Maynard punts 37 yards to Washington 37. Redskins drive to New York 39 where Hostetler fumble is recovered by Harris at New York 40. Giants drive to New York 43 where Maynard punts 57 yards for a touchback. Washington drives to New York 41. Giants take over on downs at New York 40. Giants drive to Washington 36 where Daluiso's 54-yard field-goal attempt is no good. Redskins drive to Washington 45 where Hostetler's pass intercepted by Sparks at New York 49. Giants drive to Washington 36 where Maynard punts 36 yards for a touchback. Redskins drive to New York 36 where Blanton's 54-yard field-goal attempt is no good. Giants drive to New York 45 where Kanell's pass intercepted by Patton who laterals to Pounds who returns 11 yards to Washington 24 as time expires.

Nov. 30, 1997—Pittsburgh 24, Arizona 20, at Arizona; Cardinals win toss. K. Williams returns kickoff 11 yards to Arizona 23. Cardinals drive to Arizona 18 where Feagles punts 43 yards. Hawkins returns punt 9 yards to Pittsburgh 48. Steelers drive to Arizona 10 where Bettis scores on a 10-yard touchdown run at 5:34.

Dec. 13, 1997—Pittsburgh 24, New England 21, at New England; Steelers win toss. Coleman returns kickoff 19 yards to Pittsburgh 26. Steelers drive to New England 13 where Johnson kicks a 31-yard field goal at 4:43.

Sept. 6, 1998—San Francisco 36, New York Jets 30, at San Francisco; Jets win toss. Richey's kickoff is a touchback. Jets drive to New York 11. Gallery punts 48 yards. McQuarters returns to New York 43. 49ers drive to New York 44. Howard punts 23 yards to New York 21. Johnson calls fair catch. Jets drive to New York 47. Gallery's 49-yard punt downed at San Francisco 4. Hearst runs for a 96-yard touchdown at 4:08.

Sept. 13, 1998—Cincinnati 34, Detroit 28, at Detroit; Lions win toss. Johnson's kickoff is a touchback. Lions drive to

Detroit 47 where Mitchell's pass is intercepted by Sawyer and returned for a 58-yard touchdown at 2:06.

Sept. 27, 1998—New Orleans 19, Indianapolis 13, at Indianapolis; Saints win toss. Gardocki's kickoff is returned by Ismail to New Orleans 28. Saints drive to New Orleans 30. Royals punts 64 yards. Poole returns to Indianapolis 12. Colts drive to Indianapolis 20. Gardocki punts 58 yards. Hastings returns to New Orleans 29. Saints drive to New Orleans 32. Royals punts 59 yards. Punt downed at Indianapolis 9. Colts drive to Indianapolis 44 where Manning's pass is intercepted by Drakeford and returned to Indianapolis 36. Saints drive to Indianapolis 33. Wuerffel throws 33-yard touchdown pass to Cleeland at 6:10.

Oct. 25, 1998—Miami 12, New England 9, at Miami; Dolphins win toss. Vinatieri's kickoff is returned by Avery to Miami 15. Dolphins drive to New England 26 where Mare kicks 43-yard field goal at 4:36.

Nov. 26, 1998—Detroit 19, Pittsburgh 16, at Detroit; Lions win toss. Johnson's kickoff is returned by Fair to Detroit 35. Lions drive to Pittsburgh 24 where Hanson kicks 42-yard field goal at 2:52.

Dec. 6, 1998—San Francisco 31, Carolina 28, at Carolina; Panthers win toss. Richey's kickoff is returned by Floyd to Carolina 36. Panthers drive to Carolina 38 where Beuerlein's fumble is recovered by Doleman at Carolina 30. 49ers drive to Carolina 5 where Richey kicks 23-yard field goal at 4:16.

Dec. 13, 1998—Arizona 20, Philadelphia 17, at Philadelphia; Cardinals win toss. Boniol's kickoff is returned by Metcalf to Arizona 28. Cardinals drive to Philadelphia 15 where Jacke kicks 32-yard field goal at 4:30.

Sept. 12, 1999—Dallas 41, Washington 35, at Washington; Redskins win toss. Gowin's kickoff is returned by B. Mitchell to Washington 24. Redskins drive to Washington 47. M. Turk punts 48 yards. Punt downed at Dallas 5. Cowboys drive to Dallas 24. Aikman passes 76-yard touchdown to R. Ismail at 4:09.

Oct. 3, 1999—Baltimore 19, Atlanta 13, at Atlanta; Falcons win toss. Stover's kickoff is returned by Oliver to Atlanta 18. Falcons drive to Atlanta 23. Stryzinski punts 41 yards, out of bounds at Baltimore 36. Baltimore drive to Baltimore 46. Case passes 54-yard touchdown to Armour at 2:29.

Oct. 31, 1999—New York Giants 23, Philadelphia 17, at Philadelphia; Giants win toss. Akers' kickoff is returned by Levingston to New York 27. New York drives to Giants 31. Maynard punts 43 yards to Philadelphia 26. Rossum returns to Eagles 28. Pederson drives to New York 45. Pederson's pass is intercepted by Strahan at Philadelphia 44. Giants' Peter batted ball up in the air as Pederson backpedaled. Strahan for 44 yards and touchdown at 4:24.

Nov. 14, 1999—Minnesota 27, Chicago 24, at Chicago; Vikings win toss. Boniol kicks to Minnesota 2, Williams touchback. Minnesota starts from own 20. George's pass is intercepted by Harris at Minnesota 29 for -1 yard. Chicago starts at Minnesota 29 and moves to Minnesota 23. Boniol's 41-yard field goal is no good. Minnesota starts from own 31 and drives to Chicago 20. Anderson kicks 38-yard field goal at 9:02.

Nov. 21, 1999—Chicago 23, San Diego 20, at San Diego; Bears win toss. Chicago starts from own 22. Miller completes four consecutive passes and Bears drive to San Diego 22. Enis rushes twice to San Diego 19. Boniol kicks 36-yard field goal at 4:58.

* **Nov. 22, 1999—Denver 27, Oakland 21,** at Denver; Broncos win toss. Denver starts from own 33 and drives to Broncos' 35. Rouen punts 46 yards to Oakland 19. Oakland starts at own 19 and drives to Raiders' 25. Gannon fumbles and Broncos' Pryce recovers at Oakland 25. Denver running back Gary scores on 24-yard run at 2:40.

Nov. 28, 1999—Washington 20, Philadelphia 17, at Washington; Redskins win toss. Akers' kickoff is returned by Thrash for 48 yards to Philadelphia 46. Johnson completes 20-yard pass to Connell to Philadelphia 26. Johnson completes 9-yard pass to Mitchell to Philadelphia 9. Mitchell runs for seven yards to Philadelphia 2. On third down, Washington attempts field goal from Philadelphia 2. Johnson fumbles and recovers at Philadelphia 9. Conway kicks 27-yard field goal at 4:34.

Dec. 19, 1999—Denver 36, Seattle 30, at Denver; Broncos win toss. Peterson kicks to Denver 8. Watson returns kick to Denver 27 for 19 yards. Broncos do not convert a first down. Rouen punts 46 yards, out of bounds at Seattle 25. Kitna passes to Dawkins for 17 yards at Seattle 47. Watters runs for 6 yards to Denver 47. Kitna sacked for 11-yard loss by Crockett. Kitna fumbles, forced by Crockett, recovered by Cadrez at Seattle 37. Cadrez for 37 yards and touchdown at 2:34.

Dec. 26, 1999—Washington 26, San Francisco 20, at San Francisco; Redskins win toss. Richey kicks to Washington 9, Thrash returns 13 yards to Washington 22. Johnson passes to Hicks for 25 yards to Washington 47. Centers runs for 12 yards to San Francisco 33. Johnson passes to Centers for 33 yards and touchdown at 2:00.

Dec. 26, 1999—Buffalo 13, New England 10, at New England; Patriots win toss. New England's Vinatieri misses 44-yard field goal from Buffalo 26. Buffalo takes over at Bills 34. Flutie passes to Moulds to New England 21 for 17 yards. Moulds fumbles, recovered by Bruschi at Patriots 21. New England drives to own 34. Johnson punts from New England 34 to Buffalo 42. Flutie passes to Price for 7 yards to New England 44. Flutie passes to Moulds for 11 yards to New England 27. Thomas runs for 9 yards to New England 6. Christie kicks 23-yard field goal at 13:12.

Jan. 2, 2000—Oakland 41, Kansas City 38, at Kansas City; Raiders win toss. Baker kicks 69 yards from Kansas City 30 to Oakland 1 and out of bounds. Oakland starts at Raiders 40. Gannon passes to Dudley for 21 yards to Kansas City 40. Gannon passes to Brown at Kansas City 16 for 24 yards. Crockett runs to Kansas City 15 for 1 yard. Nedney kicks 33-yard field goal at 3:13.

Sept. 10, 2000—Tennessee 17, Kansas City 14, at Tennessee; Titans win toss. Mason returns kickoff 28 yards to Tennessee 29. Face-mask penalty on Kansas City, 5 yards, enforced at 29. Titans drive to Kansas City 18 where Del Greco kicks 36-yard field goal at 2:58.

Oct. 1, 2000—Dallas 16, Carolina 13, at Carolina; Cowboys win toss. Tucker returns kickoff 20 yards to Dallas 26. Dallas drives to Carolina 6 where Seder kicks 24-yard field goal at 3:52.

Oct. 1, 2000—Washington 20, Tampa Bay 17, at Washington; Redskins win toss. Thrash returns kickoff 32 yards to Washington 30. Washington gains five yards where Barnhardt punts 52 yards to Tampa Bay 13. Green returns for one yard to Tampa Bay 14. Buccaneers gain one yard to Tampa Bay 15 where Royals punts 50 yards to Washington 35. Sanders returns punt 57 yards to Tampa Bay 8. Davis rushes three times and gets to Tampa Bay 2 where Husted kicks 20-yard field goal at 4:09.

Oct. 8, 2000—Oakland 34, San Francisco 28, at San Francisco; Raiders win toss. Dunn returns kickoff 20 yards to Oakland 19. Raiders drive to San Francisco 17 where Janikowski misses 35-yard field-goal attempt wide right. San Francisco drives to Oakland 11 where Richey's 29-yard field-goal attempt is blocked by Dorsett. Raiders recover at Oakland 16. Oakland drives to San Francisco 31 where Gannon passes to Brown for 31-yard touchdown at 10:15.

Oct. 15, 2000—Buffalo 27, San Diego 24, at Buffalo; Bills win toss. Bills drive to Buffalo 47. Mohr punts 42 yards to San Diego 11. Chargers drive to San Diego 38 where Harbaugh is intercepted at Buffalo 41. Flutie in for injured Johnson. Bills drive to San Diego 28. Christie kicks 46-yard field goal at 8:26.

* **Oct. 23, 2000—New York Jets 40, Miami 37,** at New York; Dolphins win toss. Marion returns kickoff 31 yards to Miami 37. Fielder is intercepted at Miami 46 by Coleman, who returns

ball to 39 where he fumbles. Gadsden recovers ball for Dolphins and runs out of bounds at Miami 34. Dolphins drive to New York 43 where Fiedler is intercepted again by Coleman at the Jets 34. Jets drive to Miami 23 where Hall kicks 40-yard field goal at 6:47.

Oct. 29, 2000—Jacksonville 23, Dallas 17, at Dallas; Jaguars win toss. Stith returns kickoff 24 yards to Jacksonville 34. Jaguars drive to Dallas 37 where Brunell passes to Whitted for a 37-yard touchdown at 3:02.

Nov. 5, 2000—Buffalo 16, New England 13, at New England; Patriots win toss. Faulk returns kickoff 38 yards to New England 43. Penalty on New England for offensive holding, 10 yards, enforced at New England 33. Patriots lose one yard on three plays. Johnson punts 43 yards to Buffalo 35. Bills drive to New England 13 where Christie kicks 32-yard field goal at 4:21.

Nov. 5, 2000—Philadelphia 16, Dallas 13, at Philadelphia; Eagles win toss. Mitchell returns kickoff 30 yards to Philadelphia 34. Eagles drive to Dallas 36 where McNabb is intercepted by Wortham at Dallas 30. Wortham returns interception to Dallas 31. Cowboys drive to Dallas 48 where Thomas fumbles. Recovered by Hauck at Dallas 48. Eagles drive to Dallas 13 where Akers kicks 32-yard field goal at 7:52.

* **Nov. 6, 2000—Green Bay 26, Minnesota 20,** at Green Bay; Packers win toss. Rossum returns kickoff 13 yards to Green Bay 18. Packers drive to Minnesota 43 where Favre passes to Freeman for a 43-yard touchdown at 3:27.

Nov. 12, 2000—Philadelphia 26, Pittsburgh 23, at Pittsburgh; Eagles win toss. Mitchell returns kickoff 24 yards to Philadelphia 37. Eagles drive to Pittsburgh 24 where Akers kicks 42-yard field goal at 4:09.

Dec. 17, 2000—New England 13, Buffalo 10, at Buffalo; Bills win toss and elect to defend the South goal. Patriots elect to receive. Jackson returns kickoff 38 yards to New England 48. Patriots drive to Buffalo 31 where they turn the ball over on downs. Bills drive to New England 12 where Christie's 30-yard field goal attempt is blocked by Eaton. Patriots recover at New England 11. Patriots drive to Buffalo 6 where Vinatieri kicks 24-yard field goal at 14:37.

Dec. 24, 2000—Green Bay 17, Tampa Bay 14, at Green Bay; Packers win toss. Rossum returns kickoff 29 yards to Green Bay 38. Packers drive to Tampa Bay 4 where Longwell kicks 22-yard field goal at 6:28.

Sept. 9, 2001—St. Louis 20, Philadelphia 17, at Philadelphia; Eagles win toss. Wilkins' kickoff is a touchback. Eagles drive to Philadelphia 30. Landeta punts 34 yards to St. Louis 36. Rams drive to Philadelphia 8. Wilkins kicks 26-yard field goal at 7:56.

Sept. 9, 2001—San Francisco 16, Atlanta 13, at San Francisco; 49ers win toss. Feely's kickoff is a touchback. 49ers drive to Atlanta 6. Cortez kicks 24-yard field goal at 4:04.

Oct. 14, 2001—New England 29, San Diego 26, at New England; Chargers win toss. Jenkins returns kickoff 39 yards to San Diego 40. Chargers drive to San Diego 45. Bennett punts 32 yards to New England 23. Patriots drive to San Diego 26. Vinatieri kicks 44-yard field goal at 4:00.

Oct. 14, 2001—San Francisco 37, Atlanta 31, at Atlanta; 49ers win toss. Sutherland returns kickoff 24 yards to San Francisco 24. 49ers drive to Atlanta 14. Garcia fumbles, Hall recovers at Atlanta 16. Falcons drive to Atlanta 23. Mohr punts 44 yards to San Francisco 33. Garcia throws 52-yard touchdown to Owens at 8:34.

Oct. 14, 2001—Tennessee 31, Tampa Bay 28, at Tennessee; Buccaneers win toss. D. Smith returns kickoff 17 yards to Tampa Bay 18. Buccaneers forced back to Tampa Bay 9. Royals punts 45 yards to Tennessee 46. Titans drive to Tampa Bay 32. Nedney kicks 49-yard field goal at 1:52.

Oct. 21, 2001—Washington 17, Carolina 14, at Washington; Redskins win toss. Bates returns kickoff 17 yards to Washington 14. Redskins drive to Carolina 5. Conway kicks 23-yard field goal at 1:47.

Oct. 28, 2001—Chicago 37, San Francisco 31, at Chicago; 49ers win toss. Edinger's kickoff is a touchback. M. Brown intercepts Garcia pass and returns it 33 yards for touchdown at 16 seconds.

Nov. 4, 2001—Chicago 27, Cleveland 21, at Chicago; Bears win toss. L. Johnson returns kickoff 31 yards to Chicago 32. Bears drive to Chicago 40. Maynard punts 52 yards to Cleveland 8. M. Brown intercepts Couch pass and returns it 16 yards for touchdown at 2:50.

Nov. 4, 2001—New York Giants 27, Dallas 24, at New York; Cowboys win toss. Swinton returns kickoff 21 yards to Dallas 29. Cowboys drive to New York 48. Knorr punts 33 yards to New York 15. Giants drive to Dallas 24. Andersen kicks 42-yard field goal at 7:12.

Nov. 11, 2001—Pittsburgh 15, Cleveland 12, at Cleveland; Steelers win toss. T. Edwards returns kickoff 21 yards to Pittsburgh 28. Steelers drive to Cleveland 14. Brown kicks 32-yard field goal at 5:22.

Nov. 18, 2001—San Francisco 25, Carolina 22, at Carolina; 49ers win toss. Sutherland returns kickoff 24 yards to San Francisco 26. 49ers drive to Carolina 8. Cortez kicks 26-yard field goal at 4:41.

Dec. 2, 2001—Arizona 34, Oakland 31, at Oakland; Raiders win toss. Gramatica's kickoff is a touchback. Raiders drive to Oakland 40. Lechler punts 37 yards to Arizona 23. Cardinals drive to Arizona 48. Stanley punts 29 yards to Oakland 23. Woods recovers Dunn fumble on Oakland 25. Arizona drives to Oakland 18. Gramatica kicks 36-yard field goal at 7:29.

Dec. 2, 2001—Seattle 13, San Diego 10, at Seattle; Seahawks win toss. Rogers returns kickoff 33 yards to Seattle 32. Seahawks drive to San Diego 6. Lindell kicks 24-yard field goal at 6:23.

Dec. 2, 2001—Tampa Bay 16, Cincinnati 13, at Cincinnati; Buccaneers win toss. F. Murphy returns kickoff 20 yards to Tampa Bay 38. Buccaneers drive to Cincinnati 35. Royals punts 31 yards to Cincinnati 4. Lynch recovers Dillon fumble on Cincinnati 3. Gramatica kicks 21-yard field goal at 5:06.

Dec. 16, 2001—Kansas City 26, Denver 23, at Kansas City; Broncos win toss. Carter returns kickoff 24 yards to Denver 41. Broncos drive to Denver 35. Rouen punts 35 yards to Kansas City 30. Chiefs drive to Denver 23. T. Peterson misses 41-yard field-goal attempt. Broncos drive to Denver 32. Rouen punts 38 yards to Kansas City 30. Chiefs drive to Denver 14. T. Peterson misses 32-yard field goal at 9:04.

Dec. 16, 2001—New England 12, Buffalo 9, at Buffalo; Bills win toss. Bryson returns kickoff 23 yards to Buffalo 28. Bills drive to Buffalo 48. Moorman punts 52 yards to end zone. Patriots drive to Buffalo 5. Vinatieri kicks 23-yard field goal at 5:45.

Dec. 30, 2001—Cincinnati 26, Pittsburgh 23, at Cincinnati; Steelers win toss. Geason returns kickoff and laterals to Logan who carries ball 9 yards to Pittsburgh 38. Steelers drive to Cincinnati 39. Miller punts 38 yards to Cincinnati 1. Bengals drive to Pittsburgh 13. Rackers kicks 31-yard field goal at 10:52.

* indicates Monday night game
 # indicates Thursday night game

POSTSEASON

Dec. 28, 1958—Baltimore 23, New York Giants 17, at New York in NFL Championship Game; Giants win toss. Maynard returns kickoff to Giants' 20. Chandler punts and Taseff returns one yard to Colts' 20. Colts win at 8:15 on a 1-yard run by Ameche.

Dec. 23, 1962—Dallas Texans 20, Houston Oilers 17, at Houston in AFL Championship Game; Texans win toss and kick off. Jancik returns kickoff to Oilers' 33. Norton punts and Jackson makes fair catch on Texans' 22. Wilson punts and Jancik makes fair catch on Oilers' 45. Robinson intercepts Blanda's pass and returns 13 yards to Oilers' 47. Wilson's punt rolls dead at Oilers' 12. Hull intercepts Blanda's pass and returns 23 yards to midfield. Texans win at 17:54 on a 25-yard field goal by Brooker.

Dec. 26, 1965—Green Bay 13, Baltimore 10, at Green Bay in NFL Divisional Playoff Game; Packers win toss. Moore returns kickoff to Packers' 22. Chandler punts and Haymond returns nine yards to Colts' 41. Gilburg punts and Wood makes fair catch at Packers' 21. Chandler punts and Haymond returns one yard to Colts' 41. Michaels misses 47-yard field goal. Packers win at 13:39 on 25-yard field goal by Chandler.

Dec. 25, 1971—Miami 27, Kansas City 24, at Kansas City in AFC Divisional Playoff Game; Chiefs win toss. Podolak, after a lateral from Buchanan, returns kickoff to Chiefs' 46. Stenerud's 42-yard field goal is blocked. Seiple punts and Podolak makes fair catch at Chiefs' 17. Wilson punts and Scott returns 18 yards to Dolphins' 39. Yepremian misses 62-yard field goal. Scott intercepts Dawson's pass and returns 13 yards to Dolphins' 46. Seiple punts and Podolak loses one yard to Chiefs' 15. Wilson punts and Scott makes fair catch on Dolphins' 30. Dolphins win at 22:40 on a 37-yard field goal by Yepremian.

Dec. 24, 1977—Oakland 37, Baltimore 31, at Baltimore in AFC Divisional Playoff Game; Colts win toss. Raiders start on own 42 following a punt late in the first overtime. Oakland works way into field-goal range on Stabler's 19-yard pass to Branch at Colts' 26. Four plays later, on the second play of the second overtime, Stabler hits Casper with a 10-yard touchdown pass at 15:43.

Jan. 2, 1982—San Diego 41, Miami 38, at Miami in AFC Divisional Playoff Game; Chargers win toss. San Diego drives from its 13 to Miami 8. On second-and-goal, Benirschke misses 27-yard field goal attempt wide left at 9:15. Miami has the ball twice and San Diego twice more before the Dolphins get their third possession. Miami drives from the San Diego 46 to Chargers' 17 and on fourth-and-two, von Schamann's 34-yard field goal attempt is blocked by San Diego's Winslow after 11:27. Fouts then completes four of five passes, including a 39-yarder to Joiner that puts the ball on Dolphins' 10. On first down, Benirschke kicks a 29-yard field goal at 13:52. San Diego's winning drive covered 74 yards in six plays.

Jan. 3, 1987—Cleveland 23, New York Jets 20, at Cleveland in AFC Divisional Playoff Game; Jets win toss. Jets' punt downed at Browns' 26. Moseley's 23-yard field goal attempt is wide right. Teams trade punts. Jets' second punt downed at Browns' 31. First overtime period expires eight plays later with Browns in possession at Jets' 42. Moseley kicks 27-yard field goal four plays into second overtime at 17:02.

Jan. 11, 1987—Denver 23, Cleveland 20, at Cleveland in AFC Championship Game; Browns win toss. Broncos hold Browns on four downs. Browns' punt returned four yards to Denver's 25. Elway completes 22- and 28-yard passes to set up Karlis's 33-yard field goal nine plays into drive at 5:38.

Jan. 3, 1988—Houston 23, Seattle 20, at Houston in AFC Wild Card Game; Seahawks win toss. Rodriguez punts to K. Johnson who returns one yard to Houston 15. Zendejas kicks 32-yard field goal 12 plays later at 8:05.

Dec. 31, 1989—Pittsburgh 26, Houston 23, at Houston in AFC Wild Card Playoff Game; Steelers win toss. Steelers punt to Oilers. Oilers' fumble recovered by Woodson and returned three yards. Four plays and 13 yards later, Anderson kicks a 50-yard field goal at 3:26.

Jan. 7, 1990—Los Angeles Rams 19, New York Giants 13, at New York in NFC Divisional Game; Rams win toss. Everett completes two passes to move ball to Giants' 48. White called for pass interference; ball spotted on Giants' 25. Everett hits Anderson with a 30-yard touchdown pass at 1:06.

Jan. 3, 1993—Buffalo 41, Houston 38, at Buffalo in AFC Wild Card Game; Oilers win toss. Oilers begin at 20. After 2 plays, Moon's pass is intercepted by Odomes who returns ball 2 yards to Houston 35. After 2 plays, Christie kicks 32-yard field goal at 3:06.

Jan. 8, 1994—Kansas City 27, Pittsburgh 24, at Kansas City in AFC Wild Card Game; Cheifs win toss. Hughes returns kickoff 20 yards to Kansas City 25. After 3 plays, Barker punts 48 yards to Pittsburgh 18 where Woodson returns 8 yards to the 26. After 6 plays, Royals punts 30 yards to Kansas City 20. Kansas City drives to Pittsburgh 14 where Lowery kicks 32-yard field goal at 11:03.

Jan. 17, 1999—Atlanta 30, Minnesota 27, at Minnesota in NFC Championship Game; Vikings win toss. Palmer returns kickoff 30 yards to Minnesota 29. After four plays, Berger punts 51 yards to Atlanta 7 where Dwight returns 8 yards to Atlanta 15. Falcons drive to Atlanta 36. Stryzinski punts 37 yards to Vikings' 27. Palmer calls fair catch. Vikings drive to Minnesota 39. Berger punts 52 yards to Atlanta 9. Downed by Vikings. Atlanta drives to Minnesota 21 where Andersen kicks 38-yard field goal at 11:52.

Dec. 30, 2000—Miami 23, Indianapolis 17, at Miami in AFC Wild Card Game; Dolphins win toss. Williams returns kickoff 18 yards to Miami 20. Offensive holding penalty on Freeman, 10 yards, ball spotted on Miami 10. Dolphins drive to Miami 29 where Turk punts 53 yards to Indianapolis 18. Colts drive to Miami 31 where Vanderjagt misses 49-yard field-goal attempt wide right. Dolphins drive to Indianapolis 17 where Smith rushes for a 17-yard touchdown at 11:16.

Jan. 19, 2002—New England 16, Oakland 13, at New England; Patriots win toss. Pass returns kickoff 24 yards to New England 34. Patriots drive to Oakland 5. Vinatieri kicks 23-yard field goal at 8:29.

NFL POSTSEASON OVERTIME GAMES
(BY LENGTH OF GAME)

Date	Game	Time
Dec. 25, 1971	Miami 27, KANSAS CITY 24	82:40
Dec. 23, 1962	Dallas Texans 20, HOUSTON 17	77:54
Jan. 3, 1987	CLEVELAND 23, New York Jets 20	77:02
Dec. 24, 1977	Oakland 37, BALTIMORE 31	75:43
Jan. 2, 1982	San Diego 41, MIAMI 38	73:52
Dec. 26, 1965	GREEN BAY 13, Baltimore 10	73:39
Jan. 17, 1999	Atlanta 30, MINNESOTA 27	71:52
Dec. 30, 2000	MIAMI 23, Indianapolis 17	71:16
Jan. 8, 1994	KANSAS CITY 27, Pittsburgh 24	71:03
Jan. 19, 2002	NEW ENGLAND 16, Oakland 13	68:29
Dec. 28, 1958	Baltimore 23, N.Y. GIANTS 17	68:15
Jan. 3, 1988	HOUSTON 23, Seattle 20	68:05
Jan. 11, 1987	Denver 23, CLEVELAND 20	65:38
Dec. 31, 1989	Pittsburgh 26, HOUSTON 23	63:26
Jan. 3, 1993	BUFFALO 41, Houston 38	63:06
Jan. 7, 1990	Los Angeles Rams 19, N.Y. GIANTS 13	61:06

Home team in CAPS

There have been 16 overtime postseason games dating back to 1958. In 14 cases, both teams had at least one possession. Last time: 12/30/00, MIAMI 23, Indianapolis 17.

OVERTIME WON-LOST RECORDS, 1974-2001
(REGULAR SEASON)

Team	Win	Loss	Tie	Pct.
AFC				
Baltimore	2	2	1	.500
Buffalo	14	8	0	.636
Cincinnati	14	8	0	.636
Cleveland	12	10	1	.543
Denver	15	10	2	.593
Indianapolis	9	8	1	.528
Jacksonville	2	2	0	.500
Kansas City	9	9	2	.500
Miami	10	15	1	.404
New England	12	18	0	.400
New York Jets	11	9	2	.545
Oakland	12	13	0	.480
Pittsburgh	14	7	1	.659
San Diego	7	14	0	.333
Tennessee	10	13	0	.435
NFC				
Arizona	13	10	2	.560
Atlanta	7	12	1	.375
Carolina	1	5	0	.167
Chicago	14	12	0	.538
Dallas	11	9	0	.550
Detroit	10	10	1	.500
Green Bay	8	10	4	.455
Minnesota	14	13	2	.517
New Orleans	4	7	0	.364
New York Giants	10	10	2	.500
Philadelphia	10	12	3	.460
St. Louis	7	7	1	.500
San Francisco	10	10	1	.500
Seattle	5	12	0	.294
Tampa Bay	10	10	1	.500
Washington	15	8	1	.646

OVERTIME GAMES BY YEAR
(REGULAR SEASON)

2001-17	1994-16	1987-13	1980-13
2000-13	1993-7	1986-16	1979-12
1999-11	1992-10	1985-10	1978-11
1998-7	1991-15	1984- 9	1977-6
1997-17	1990-10	1983-19	1976-5
1996-14	1989-11	1982- 4	1975-9
1995-21	1988- 9	1981-10	1974-2

OVERTIME GAME SUMMARY—1974-2001

There have been 317 overtime games in regular season play since the rule was adopted in 1974 (17 in 2001 season). Breakdown follows:

- 230(12) times both teams had at least one possession (73%)
- 163 (9) times the team which won the toss won the game (51%)
- 139 (8) times the team which lost the toss won the game (44%)
- 15 (0) games ended tied (5%). Last time: Nov. 23, 1997, N.Y. Giants 7, at Washington 7.
- 87 (5) times the team which won the toss drove for winning score (62 FG, 25 TD) (27%)
- 8 (0) times the team which won the toss elected to kick off (4 wins) (3%)
- 219(14) games were decided by a field goal (69%)
- 82 (3) games were decided by a touchdown (26%)
- 1 (0) games were decided by a safety (0.3%)

Note: The number in parentheses represents 2001 Season Total in each category.

MOST OVERTIME GAMES, SEASON

5	Green Bay Packers, 1983
4	Denver Broncos, 1985
	Cleveland Browns, 1989
	Minnesota Vikings, 1994
	Arizona Cardinals, 1995
	Minnesota Vikings, 1995
	Arizona Cardinals, 1997
	San Francisco, 2001
3	By many teams, last time: Buffalo, 2000

LONGEST CONSECUTIVE GAME STREAKS
WITHOUT OVERTIME (Current)

61   New Orleans Saints (Last OT Game, 9/27/98 at Indianapolis)

(Record: 110, St. Louis/Phoenix Cardinals, 12/7/86-12/19/93)

SHORTEST OVERTIME GAMES

0:16	Chicago 37, San Francisco 31; 10/28/01
0:17	New Orleans 20, Seattle 17; 11/16/97
0:21	Chicago 23, Detroit 17; 11/27/80—only kickoff return for TD
0:30	Baltimore 29, New England 23; 9/4/83
0:55	New York Giants 16, Philadelphia 10; 9/29/85

LONGEST OVERTIME GAMES
(ALL POSTSEASON GAMES)

22:40	Miami 27, Kansas City 24; 12/25/71
17:54	Dallas Texans 20, Houston 17; 12/23/62
17:02	Cleveland 23, New York Jets 20; 1/3/87
15:43	Oakland 37, Balitmore 31; 12/24/77

OVERTIME SCORING SUMMARY

219	were decided by a field goal
37	were decided by a touchdown pass
22	were decided by a touchdown run
13	were decided by interceptions (Atlanta 40, New Orleans 34, 9/2/79; Atlanta 47, Green Bay 41, 11/27/83; New York Giants 16, Philadelphia 10, 9/29/85; Indianapolis 23, Cleveland 17, 12/10/89; Cleveland 30, San Diego 24, 10/20/91; Kansas City 23, Oakland 17, 9/17/95; New York Giants 27, Arizona 21, 10/8/95; Washington 36, Detroit 30, 10/22/95; Arizona 20, Seattle 14, 10/29/95; Cincinnati 34, Detroit 28, 9/13/98; New York Giants 23, Philadelphia 17, 10/31/99; Chicago 37, San Francisco 31, 10/28/01; Chicago 27, Cleveland 21, 11/4/01)
2	were decided on a fake field goal/touchdown pass (Minnesota 22, Chicago 16, 10/16/77; Cleveland 23, Minnesota 17, 12/17/89)
2	were decided by a fumble recovery (Baltimore 29, New England 23, 9/4/83; Denver 36, Seattle 30, 12/19/99)
1	was decided by a kickoff return (Chicago 23, Detroit 17, 11/27/80)
1	was decided by a punt return (Kansas City 29, San Diego 23, 10/9/95)
1	was decided on a fake field goal/touchdown run (Los Angeles Rams 27, Minnesota 21, 12/2/79)
1	was decided on a blocked field goal (Denver 30, San Diego 24, 11/17/85)
1	was decided on a blocked field goal/recovery by kicker (Green Bay 12, Chicago 6, 9/7/80)
1	was decided on a blocked field goal/recovery by kicking team (Philadelphia 23, New York Giants 17, 11/20/88)
1	was decided by a safety (Minnesota 23, Los Angeles Rams 21, 11/5/89)
15	ended tied

OVERTIME RECORDS

Longest Touchdown Pass

99 Yards — Ron Jaworski to Mike Quick, Philadelphia 23, Atlanta 17 (11/10/85)

76 Yards — Troy Aikman to Raghib Ismail, Dallas 41, Washington 35 (9/12/99)

68 Yards — Danny Kanell to Chris Calloway, New York Giants 26, Detroit 20 (10/19/97)

Longest Touchdown Run

96 Yards — Garrison Hearst, San Francisco 36, N.Y. Jets 30 (9/6/98)

60 Yards — Herschel Walker, Dallas 23, New England 17 (11/15/87)

42 Yards — Eric Dickerson, Los Angeles Rams 26, Tampa Bay 20 (10/5/86)

Longest Field Goal

53 Yards — Chris Jacke, Green Bay 23, San Francisco 20 (10/4/96)

52 Yards — Mike Cofer, Indianapolis 27, N.Y. Jets 24 (9/10/95)

51 Yards — Greg Davis, New England 23, Indianapolis 20 (10/29/89) Greg Davis, Arizona 20, Pittsburgh 17 (10/30/94) Michael Husted, Tampa Bay 20, Minnesota 17 (10/15/95)

Longest Touchdown Plays

99 Yards — (Pass) Ron Jaworski to Mike Quick, Philadelphia 23, Atlanta 17 (11/10/85)

96 Yards — (Run) Garrison Hearst, San Francisco 36, N.Y. Jets 30 (9/6/98)

95 Yards — (Kickoff return) Dave Williams, Chicago 23, Detroit 17 (11/27/80)

86 Yards — (Punt return) Tamarick Vanover, Kansas City 29, San Diego 23 (10/9/95)

76 Yards — (Pass) Troy Aikman to Raghib Ismail, Dallas 41, Washington 35 (9/12/99)

FIRST-ROUND SELECTIONS
If club had no first-round selection, first player drafted is listed with round in parentheses.

ARIZONA CARDINALS
Year Player, College, Position
1936 Jim Lawrence, Texas Christian, B
1937 Ray Buivid, Marquette, B
1938 Jack Robbins, Arkansas, B
1939 Charles (Ki) Aldrich, TCU, C
1940 George Cafego, Tennessee, B
1941 John Kimbrough, Texas A&M, B
1942 Steve Lach, Duke, B
1943 Glenn Dobbs, Tulsa, B
1944 Pat Harder, Wisconsin, B
1945 Charley Trippi, Georgia, B
1946 Dub Jones, Louisiana State, B
1947 DeWitt (Tex) Coulter, Army, T
1948 Jim Spavital, Oklahoma A&M, B
1949 Bill Fischer, Notre Dame, G
1950 Jack Jennings, Ohio State, T (2)
1951 Jerry Groom, Notre Dame, C
1952 Ollie Matson, San Francisco, B
1953 Johnny Olszewski, California, B
1954 Lamar McHan, Arkansas, B
1955 Max Boydston, Oklahoma, E
1956 Joe Childress, Auburn, B
1957 Jerry Tubbs, Oklahoma, C
1958 King Hill, Rice, B
      John David Crow, Texas A&M, B
1959 Bill Stacy, Mississippi State, B
1960 George Izo, Notre Dame, QB
1961 Ken Rice, Auburn, T
1962 Fate Echols, Northwestern, DT
      Irv Goode, Kentucky, C
1963 Jerry Stovall, Louisiana State, S
      Don Brumm, Purdue, DE
1964 Ken Kortas, Louisville, DT
1965 Joe Namath, Alabama, QB
1966 Carl McAdams, Oklahoma, LB
1967 Dave Williams, Washington, WR
1968 MacArthur Lane, Utah State, RB
1969 Roger Wehrli, Missouri, DB
1970 Larry Stegent, Texas A&M, RB
1971 Norm Thompson, Utah, CB
1972 Bobby Moore, Oregon, RB-WR
1973 Dave Butz, Purdue, DT
1974 J.V. Cain, Colorado, TE
1975 Tim Gray, Texas A&M, DB
1976 Mike Dawson, Arizona, DT
1977 Steve Pisarkiewicz, Missouri, QB
1978 Steve Little, Arkansas, K
      Ken Greene, Washington State, DB
1979 Ottis Anderson, Miami, RB
1980 Curtis Greer, Michigan, DE
1981 E.J. Junior, Alabama, LB
1982 Luis Sharpe, UCLA, T
1983 Leonard Smith, McNeese St., DB
1984 Clyde Duncan, Tennessee, WR
1985 Freddie Joe Nunn, Mississippi, LB
1986 Anthony Bell, Michigan State, LB
1987 Kelly Stouffer, Colorado State, QB
1988 Ken Harvey, California, LB
1989 Eric Hill, Louisiana State, LB
      Joe Wolf, Boston College, G
1990 Anthony Thompson, Indiana, RB (2)
1991 Eric Swann, No College, DE
1992 Tony Sacca, Penn State, QB (2)

1993 Garrison Hearst, Georgia, RB
      Ernest Dye, South Carolina, T
1994 Jamir Miller, UCLA, LB
1995 Frank Sanders, Auburn, WR (2)
1996 Simeon Rice, Illinois, DE
1997 Tom Knight, Iowa, DB
1998 Andre Wadsworth, Florida St., DE
1999 David Boston, Ohio State, WR
      L.J. Shelton, Eastern Michigan, T
2000 Thomas Jones, Virginia, RB
2001 Leonard Davis, Texas, T
2002 Wendell Bryant, Wisconsin, DT

ATLANTA FALCONS
Year Player, College, Position
1966 Tommy Nobis, Texas, LB
      Randy Johnson, Texas A&I, QB
1967 Leo Carroll, San Diego St., DE (2)
1968 Claude Humphrey, Tennessee St., DE
1969 George Kunz, Notre Dame, T
1970 John Small, Citadel, LB
1971 Joe Profit, Northeast Louisiana, RB
1972 Clarence Ellis, Notre Dame, DB
1973 Greg Marx, Notre Dame, DT (2)
1974 Gerald Tinker, Kent State, WR (2)
1975 Steve Bartkowski, California, QB
1976 Bubba Bean, Texas A&M, RB
1977 Warren Bryant, Kentucky, T
      Wilson Faumuina, San Jose St., DT
1978 Mike Kenn, Michigan, T
1979 Don Smith, Miami, DE
1980 Junior Miller, Nebraska, TE
1981 Bobby Butler, Florida State, DB
1982 Gerald Riggs, Arizona State, RB
1983 Mike Pitts, Alabama, DE
1984 Rick Bryan, Oklahoma, DT
1985 Bill Fralic, Pittsburgh, T
1986 Tony Casillas, Oklahoma, NT
      Tim Green, Syracuse, LB
1987 Chris Miller, Oregon, QB
1988 Aundray Bruce, Auburn, LB
1989 Deion Sanders, Florida State, DB
      Shawn Collins, No. Arizona, WR
1990 Steve Broussard, Washington St., RB
1991 Bruce Pickens, Nebraska, DB
      Mike Pritchard, Colorado, WR
1992 Bob Whitfield, Stanford, T
      Tony Smith, So. Mississippi, RB
1993 Lincoln Kennedy, Washington, T
1994 Bert Emanuel, Rice, WR (2)
1995 Devin Bush, Florida State, DB
1996 Shannon Brown, Alabama, DT (3)
1997 Michael Booker, Nebraska, DB
1998 Keith Brooking, Georgia Tech, LB
1999 Patrick Kerney, Virginia, DE
2000 Travis Claridge, So. California, T (2)
2001 Michael Vick, Virginia Tech, QB
2002 T.J. Duckett, Michigan State, RB

BALTIMORE RAVENS
Year Player, College, Position
1996 Jonathan Ogden, UCLA, T
      Ray Lewis, Miami, LB
1997 Peter Boulware, Florida State, DE
1998 Duane Starks, Miami, DB
1999 Chris McAlister, Arizona, DB
2000 Jamal Lewis, Tennessee, RB
      Travis Taylor, Florida, WR
2001 Todd Heap, Arizona State, TE
2002 Ed Reed, Miami, DB

BUFFALO BILLS
Year Player, College, Position
1960 Richie Lucas, Penn State, QB
1961 Ken Rice, Auburn, T
1962 Ernie Davis, Syracuse, RB
1963 Dave Behrman, Michigan State, C
1964 Carl Eller, Minnesota, DE
1965 Jim Davidson, Ohio State, T
1966 Mike Dennis, Mississippi, RB
1967 John Pitts, Arizona State, S
1968 Haven Moses, San Diego St., WR
1969 O.J. Simpson, So. California, RB
1970 Al Cowlings, So. California, DE
1971 J.D. Hill, Arizona State, WR
1972 Walt Patulski, Notre Dame, DE
1973 Paul Seymour, Michigan, TE
      Joe DeLamielleure, Michigan St., G
1974 Reuben Gant, Oklahoma State, TE
1975 Tom Ruud, Nebraska, LB
1976 Mario Clark, Oregon, DB
1977 Phil Dokes, Oklahoma State, DT
1978 Terry Miller, Oklahoma State, RB
1979 Tom Cousineau, Ohio State, LB
      Jerry Butler, Clemson, WR
1980 Jim Ritcher, North Carolina St., C
1981 Booker Moore, Penn State, RB
1982 Perry Tuttle, Clemson, WR
1983 Tony Hunter, Notre Dame, TE
      Jim Kelly, Miami, QB
1984 Greg Bell, Notre Dame, RB
1985 Bruce Smith, Virginia Tech, DE
      Derrick Burroughs, Memphis St., DB
1986 Ronnie Harmon, Iowa, RB
      Will Wolford, Vanderbilt, T
1987 Shane Conlan, Penn State, LB
1988 Thurman Thomas, Oklahoma St., RB (2)
1989 Don Beebe, Chadron, Neb., WR (3)
1990 James Williams, Fresno State, DB
1991 Henry Jones, Illinois, DB
1992 John Fina, Arizona, T
1993 Thomas Smith, North Carolina, DB
1994 Jeff Burris, Notre Dame, DB
1995 Ruben Brown, Pittsburgh, G
1996 Eric Moulds, Mississippi St., WR
1997 Antowain Smith, Houston, RB
1998 Sam Cowart, Florida State, LB (2)
1999 Antoine Winfield, Ohio State, DB
2000 Erik Flowers, Arizona State, DE
2001 Nate Clements, Ohio State, DB
2002 Mike Williams, Texas, T

CAROLINA PANTHERS
Year Player, College, Position
1995 Kerry Collins, Penn State, QB
      Tyrone Poole, Ft. Valley State, DB
      Blake Brockermeyer, Texas, T
1996 Tim Biakabutuka, Michigan, RB
1997 Rae Carruth, Colorado, WR
1998 Jason Peter, Nebraska, DT
1999 Chris Terry, Georgia, T (2)
2000 Rashard Anderson, Jackson St., DB
2001 Dan Morgan, Miami, LB
2002 Julius Peppers, North Carolina, DE

CHICAGO BEARS
Year Player, College, Position
1936 Joe Stydahar, West Virginia, T
1937 Les McDonald, Nebraska, E
1938 Joe Gray, Oregon State, B
1939 Sid Luckman, Columbia, QB

Bill Osmanski, Holy Cross, B
1940 Clyde (Bulldog) Turner, Hardin-Simmons, C
1941 Tom Harmon, Michigan, B
Norm Standlee, Stanford, B
Don Scott, Ohio State, B
1942 Frankie Albert, Stanford, B
1943 Bob Steber, Missouri, B
1944 Ray Evans, Kansas, B
1945 Don Lund, Michigan, B
1946 Johnny Lujack, Notre Dame, QB
1947 Bob Fenimore, Oklahoma State, B
Don Kindt, Wisconsin, B
1948 Bobby Layne, Texas, QB
Max Bumgardner, Texas, E
1949 Dick Harris, Texas, C
1950 Chuck Hunsinger, Florida, B
Fred Morrison, Ohio State, B
1951 Bob Williams, Notre Dame, B
Billy Stone, Bradley, B
Gene Schroeder, Virginia, E
1952 Jim Dooley, Miami, B
1953 Billy Anderson, Compton (Calif.) J.C., B
1954 Stan Wallace, Illinois, B
1955 Ron Drzewiecki, Marquette, B
1956 Menan (Tex) Schriewer, Texas, E
1957 Earl Leggett, Louisiana State, T
1958 Chuck Howley, West Virginia, G
1959 Don Clark, Ohio State, B
1960 Roger Davis, Syracuse, G
1961 Mike Ditka, Pittsburgh, E
1962 Ronnie Bull, Baylor, RB
1963 Dave Behrman, Michigan State, C
1964 Dick Evey, Tennessee, DT
1965 Dick Butkus, Illinois, LB
Gale Sayers, Kansas, RB
Steve DeLong, Tennessee, T
1966 George Rice, Louisiana State, DT
1967 Loyd Phillips, Arkansas, DE
1968 Mike Hull, Southern California, RB
1969 Rufus Mayes, Ohio State, T
1970 George Farmer, UCLA, WR (3)
1971 Joe Moore, Missouri, RB
1972 Lionel Antoine, Southern Illinois, T
Craig Clemons, Iowa, DB
1973 Wally Chambers, Eastern Kentucky, DE
1974 Waymond Bryant, Tennessee St., LB
Dave Gallagher, Michigan, DT
1975 Walter Payton, Jackson State, RB
1976 Dennis Lick, Wisconsin, T
1977 Ted Albrecht, California, T
1978 Brad Shearer, Texas, DT (3)
1979 Dan Hampton, Arkansas, DT
Al Harris, Arizona State, DE
1980 Otis Wilson, Louisville, LB
1981 Keith Van Horne, So. California, T
1982 Jim McMahon, Brigham Young, QB
1983 Jim Covert, Pittsburgh, T
Willie Gault, Tennessee, WR
1984 Wilber Marshall, Florida, LB
1985 William Perry, Clemson, DT
1986 Neal Anderson, Florida, RB
1987 Jim Harbaugh, Michigan, QB
1988 Brad Muster, Stanford, RB
Wendell Davis, Louisiana St., WR
1989 Donnell Woolford, Clemson, DB
Trace Armstrong, Florida, DE
1990 Mark Carrier, So. California, DB
1991 Stan Thomas, Texas, T
1992 Alonzo Spellman, Ohio State, DE
1993 Curtis Conway, So. California, WR

1994 John Thierry, Alcorn State, DE
1995 Rashaan Salaam, Colorado, RB
1996 Walt Harris, Mississippi State, DB
1997 John Allred, So. California, TE (2)
1998 Curtis Enis, Penn State, RB
1999 Cade McNown, UCLA, QB
2000 Brian Urlacher, New Mexico, LB
2001 David Terrell, Michigan, WR
2002 Marc Colombo, Boston College, T

CINCINNATI BENGALS

Year	Player, College, Position
1968	Bob Johnson, Tennessee, C
1969	Greg Cook, Cincinnati, QB
1970	Mike Reid, Penn State, DT
1971	Vernon Holland, Tennessee St., T
1972	Sherman White, California, DE
1973	Isaac Curtis, San Diego State, WR
1974	Bill Kollar, Montana State, DT
1975	Glenn Cameron, Florida, LB
1976	Billy Brooks, Oklahoma, WR
	Archie Griffin, Ohio State, RB
1977	Eddie Edwards, Miami, DT
	Wilson Whitley, Houston, DT
	Mike Cobb, Michigan State, TE
1978	Ross Browner, Notre Dame, DT
	Blair Bush, Washington, C
1979	Jack Thompson, Washington St., QB
	Charles Alexander, Louisiana St., RB
1980	Anthony Muñoz, So. California, T
1981	David Verser, Kansas, WR
1982	Glen Collins, Mississippi State, DE
1983	Dave Rimington, Nebraska, C
1984	Ricky Hunley, Arizona, LB
	Pete Koch, Maryland, DE
	Brian Blados, North Carolina, T
1985	Eddie Brown, Miami, WR
	Emanuel King, Alabama, LB
1986	Joe Kelly, Washington, LB
	Tim McGee, Tennessee, WR
1987	Jason Buck, Brigham Young, DE
1988	Rickey Dixon, Oklahoma, DB
1989	Eric Ball, UCLA, RB (2)
1990	James Francis, Baylor, LB
1991	Alfred Williams, Colorado, LB
1992	David Klingler, Houston, QB
	Darryl Williams, Miami, DB
1993	John Copeland, Alabama, DE
1994	Dan Wilkinson, Ohio State, DT
1995	Ki-Jana Carter, Penn State, RB
1996	Willie Anderson, Auburn, T
1997	Reinard Wilson, Florida State, LB
1998	Takeo Spikes, Auburn, LB
	Brian Simmons, North Carolina, LB
1999	Akili Smith, Oregon, QB
2000	Peter Warrick, Florida State, WR
2001	Justin Smith, Missouri, DE
2002	Levi Jones, Arizona State, T

CLEVELAND BROWNS

Year	Player, College, Position
1950	Ken Carpenter, Oregon State, B
1951	Ken Konz, Louisiana State, B
1952	Bert Rechichar, Tennessee, DB
	Harry Agganis, Boston U., QB
1953	Doug Atkins, Tennessee, DE
1954	Bobby Garrett, Stanford, QB
	John Bauer, Illinois, G
1955	Kurt Burris, Oklahoma, C
1956	Preston Carpenter, Arkansas, B

1957 Jim Brown, Syracuse, RB
1958 Jim Shofner, Texas Christian, DB
1959 Rich Kreitling, Illinois, DE
1960 Jim Houston, Ohio State, DE
1961 Bobby Crespino, Mississippi, TE
1962 Gary Collins, Maryland, WR
Leroy Jackson, Western Illinois, RB
1963 Tom Hutchinson, Kentucky, WR
1964 Paul Warfield, Ohio State, WR
1965 James Garcia, Purdue, T (2)
1966 Milt Morin, Massachusetts, TE
1967 Bob Matheson, Duke, LB
1968 Marvin Upshaw, Trinity, Tex., DT-DE
1969 Ron Johnson, Michigan, RB
1970 Mike Phipps, Purdue, QB
Bob McKay, Texas, T
1971 Clarence Scott, Kansas State, CB
1972 Thom Darden, Michigan, DB
1973 Steve Holden, Arizona State, WR
Pete Adams, Southern California, T
1974 Billy Corbett, Johnson C. Smith, T (2)
1975 Mack Mitchell, Houston, DE
1976 Mike Pruitt, Purdue, RB
1977 Robert Jackson, Texas A&M, LB
1978 Clay Matthews, So. California, LB
Ozzie Newsome, Alabama, TE
1979 Willis Adams, Houston, WR
1980 Charles White, So. California, RB
1981 Hanford Dixon, So. Mississippi, DB
1982 Chip Banks, So. California, LB
1983 Ron Brown, Arizona State, WR (2)
1984 Don Rogers, UCLA, DB
1985 Greg Allen, Florida State, RB (2)
1986 Webster Slaughter, San Diego St., WR (2)
1987 Mike Junkin, Duke, LB
1988 Clifford Charlton, Florida, LB
1989 Eric Metcalf, Texas, RB
1990 Leroy Hoard, Michigan, RB (2)
1991 Eric Turner, UCLA, DB
1992 Tommy Vardell, Stanford, RB
1993 Steve Everitt, Michigan, C
1994 Antonio Langham, Alabama, DB
Derrick Alexander, Michigan, WR
1995 Craig Powell, Ohio State, LB
1999 Tim Couch, Kentucky, QB
2000 Courtney Brown, Penn State, DE
2001 Gerard Warren, Florida, DT
2002 William Green, Boston College, RB

DALLAS COWBOYS

Year	Player, College, Position
1960	None
1961	Bob Lilly, Texas Christian, DT
1962	Sonny Gibbs, TCU, QB (2)
1963	Lee Roy Jordan, Alabama, LB
1964	Scott Appleton, Texas, DT
1965	Craig Morton, California, QB
1966	John Niland, Iowa, G
1967	Phil Clark, Northwestern, DB (3)
1968	Dennis Homan, Alabama, WR
1969	Calvin Hill, Yale, RB
1970	Duane Thomas, West Texas St., RB
1971	Tody Smith, So. California, DE
1972	Bill Thomas, Boston College, RB
1973	Billy Joe DuPree, Michigan St., TE
1974	Ed (Too Tall) Jones, Tennessee St., DE
	Charley Young, North Carolina St., RB
1975	Randy White, Maryland, DT
	Thomas Henderson, Langston, LB
1976	Aaron Kyle, Wyoming, DB

1977 Tony Dorsett, Pittsburgh, RB
1978 Larry Bethea, Michigan State, DE
1979 Robert Shaw, Tennessee, C
1980 Bill Roe, Colorado, LB (3)
1981 Howard Richards, Missouri, T
1982 Rod Hill, Kentucky State, DB
1983 Jim Jeffcoat, Arizona State, DE
1984 Billy Cannon, Jr., Texas A&M, LB
1985 Kevin Brooks, Michigan, DE
1986 Mike Sherrard, UCLA, WR
1987 Danny Noonan, Nebraska, DT
1988 Michael Irvin, Miami, WR
1989 Troy Aikman, UCLA, QB
1990 Emmitt Smith, Florida, RB
1991 Russell Maryland, Miami, DT
     Alvin Harper, Tennessee, WR
     Kelvin Pritchett, Mississippi, DT
1992 Kevin Smith, Texas A&M, DB
     Robert Jones, East Carolina, LB
1993 Kevin Williams, Miami, WR (2)
1994 Shante Carver, Arizona State, DE
1995 Sherman Williams, Alabama, RB (2)
1996 Kavika Pittman, McNeese St., DE (2)
1997 David LaFleur, Louisiana State, TE
1998 Greg Ellis, North Carolina, DE
1999 Ebenezer Ekuban, North Carolina, DE
2000 Dwayne Goodrich, Tennessee, DB (2)
2001 Quincy Carter, Georgia, QB (2)
2002 Roy Williams, Oklahoma, DB

DENVER BRONCOS
Year Player, College, Position
1960 Roger LeClerc, Trinity, Conn., C
1961 Bob Gaiters, New Mexico St., RB
1962 Merlin Olsen, Utah State, DT
1963 Kermit Alexander, UCLA, CB
1964 Bob Brown, Nebraska, T
1965 Dick Butkus, Illinois, LB (2)
1966 Jerry Shay, Purdue, DT
1967 Floyd Little, Syracuse, RB
1968 Curley Culp, Arizona State, DE (2)
1969 Grady Cavness, Texas-El Paso, DB (2)
1970 Bob Anderson, Colorado, RB
1971 Marv Montgomery, So. California, T
1972 Riley Odoms, Houston, TE
1973 Otis Armstrong, Purdue, RB
1974 Randy Gradishar, Ohio State, LB
1975 Louis Wright, San Jose State, DB
1976 Tom Glassic, Virginia, G
1977 Steve Schindler, Boston College, G
1978 Don Latimer, Miami, DT
1979 Kelvin Clark, Nebraska, T
1980 Rulon Jones, Utah State, DE (2)
1981 Dennis Smith, So. California, DB
1982 Gerald Willhite, San Jose St., RB
1983 Chris Hinton, Northwestern, G
1984 Andre Townsend, Mississippi, DE (2)
1985 Steve Sewell, Oklahoma, RB
1986 Jim Juriga, Illinois, T (4)
1987 Ricky Nattiel, Florida, WR
1988 Ted Gregory, Syracuse, NT
1989 Steve Atwater, Arkansas, DB
1990 Alton Montgomery, Houston, DB (2)
1991 Mike Croel, Nebraska, LB
1992 Tommy Maddox, UCLA, QB
1993 Dan Williams, Toledo, DE
1994 Allen Aldridge, Houston, LB (2)
1995 Jamie Brown, Florida A&M, T (4)
1996 John Mobley, Kutztown, LB
1997 Trevor Pryce, Clemson, DT

1998 Marcus Nash, Tennessee, WR
1999 Al Wilson, Tennessee, LB
2000 Deltha O'Neal, California, DB
2001 Willie Middlebrooks, Minnesota, DB
2002 Ashley Lelie, Hawaii, WR

DETROIT LIONS
Year Player, College, Position
1936 Sid Wagner, Michigan State, G
1937 Lloyd Cardwell, Nebraska, B
1938 Alex Wojciechowicz, Fordham, C
1939 John Pingel, Michigan State, B
1940 Doyle Nave, Southern California, B
1941 Jim Thomason, Texas A&M, B
1942 Bob Westfall, Michigan, B
1943 Frank Sinkwich, Georgia, B
1944 Otto Graham, Northwestern, B
1945 Frank Szymanski, Notre Dame, C
1946 Bill Dellastatious, Missouri, B
1947 Glenn Davis, Army, B
1948 Y.A. Tittle, Louisiana State, B
1949 John Rauch, Georgia, B
1950 Leon Hart, Notre Dame, E
     Joe Watson, Rice, C
1951 Dick Stanfel, San Francisco, G (2)
1952 Yale Lary, Texas A&M, B (3)
1953 Harley Sewell, Texas, G
1954 Dick Chapman, Rice, T
1955 Dave Middleton, Auburn, B
1956 Hopalong Cassady, Ohio State, B
1957 Bill Glass, Baylor, G
1958 Alex Karras, Iowa, T
1959 Nick Pietrosante, Notre Dame, B
1960 John Robinson, Louisiana State, S
1961 Danny LaRose, Missouri, T (2)
1962 John Hadl, Kansas, QB
1963 Daryl Sanders, Ohio State, T
1964 Pete Beathard, So. California, QB
1965 Tom Nowatzke, Indiana, RB
1966 Nick Eddy, Notre Dame, RB (2)
1967 Mel Farr, UCLA, RB
1968 Greg Landry, Massachusetts, QB
     Earl McCullouch, So. California, WR
1969 Altie Taylor, Utah State, RB (2)
1970 Steve Owens, Oklahoma, RB
1971 Bob Bell, Cincinnati, DT
1972 Herb Orvis, Colorado, DE
1973 Ernie Price, Texas A&I, DE
1974 Ed O'Neil, Penn State, LB
1975 Lynn Boden, South Dakota St., G
1976 James Hunter, Grambling, DB
     Lawrence Gaines, Wyoming, RB
1977 Walt Williams, New Mexico St., DB (2)
1978 Luther Bradley, Notre Dame, DB
1979 Keith Dorney, Penn State, T
1980 Billy Sims, Oklahoma, RB
1981 Mark Nichols, San Jose State, WR
1982 Jimmy Williams, Nebraska, LB
1983 James Jones, Florida, RB
1984 David Lewis, California, TE
1985 Lomas Brown, Florida, T
1986 Chuck Long, Iowa, QB
1987 Reggie Rogers, Washington, DE
1988 Bennie Blades, Miami, DB
1989 Barry Sanders, Oklahoma St., RB
1990 Andre Ware, Houston, QB
1991 Herman Moore, Virginia, WR
1992 Robert Porcher, South Carolina St., DE
1993 Ryan McNeil, Miami, DB (2)
1994 Johnnie Morton, So. California, WR

1995 Luther Elliss, Utah, DT
1996 Reggie Brown, Texas A&M, LB
     Jeff Hartings, Penn State, G
1997 Bryant Westbrook, Texas, DB
1998 Terry Fair, Tennessee, DB
1999 Chris Claiborne, So. California, LB
     Aaron Gibson, Wisconsin, T
2000 Stockar McDougle, Oklahoma, T
2001 Jeff Backus, Michigan, T
2002 Joey Harrington, Oregon, QB

GREEN BAY PACKERS
Year Player, College, Position
1936 Russ Letlow, San Francisco, G
1937 Eddie Jankowski, Wisconsin, B
1938 Cecil Isbell, Purdue, B
1939 Larry Buhler, Minnesota, B
1940 Harold Van Every, Minnesota, B
1941 George Paskvan, Wisconsin, B
1942 Urban Odson, Minnesota, T
1943 Dick Wildung, Minnesota, T
1944 Merv Pregulman, Michigan, G
1945 Walt Schlinkman, Texas Tech, B
1946 Johnny Strzykalski, Marquette, B
1947 Ernie Case, UCLA, B
1948 Earl (Jug) Girard, Wisconsin, B
1949 Stan Heath, Nevada, B
1950 Clayton Tonnemaker, Minnesota, C
1951 Bob Gain, Kentucky, T
1952 Babe Parilli, Kentucky, QB
1953 Al Carmichael, So. California, B
1954 Art Hunter, Notre Dame, T
     Veryl Switzer, Kansas State, B
1955 Tom Bettis, Purdue, G
1956 Jack Losch, Miami, B
1957 Paul Hornung, Notre Dame, B
     Ron Kramer, Michigan, E
1958 Dan Currie, Michigan State, C
1959 Randy Duncan, Iowa, B
1960 Tom Moore, Vanderbilt, RB
1961 Herb Adderley, Michigan State, CB
1962 Earl Gros, Louisiana State, RB
1963 Dave Robinson, Penn State, LB
1964 Lloyd Voss, Nebraska, DT
1965 Donny Anderson, Texas Tech, RB
     Lawrence Elkins, Baylor, E
1966 Jim Grabowski, Illinois, RB
     Gale Gillingham, Minnesota, T
1967 Bob Hyland, Boston College, C
     Don Horn, San Diego State, QB
1968 Fred Carr, Texas-El Paso, LB
     Bill Lueck, Arizona, G
1969 Rich Moore, Villanova, DT
1970 Mike McCoy, Notre Dame, DT
     Rich McGeorge, Elon, TE
1971 John Brockington, Ohio State, RB
1972 Willie Buchanon, San Diego St., DB
     Jerry Tagge, Nebraska, QB
1973 Barry Smith, Florida State, WR
1974 Barty Smith, Richmond, RB
1975 Bill Bain, So. California, G (2)
1976 Mark Koncar, Colorado, T
1977 Mike Butler, Kansas, DE
     Ezra Johnson, Morris Brown, DE
1978 James Lofton, Stanford, WR
     John Anderson, Michigan, LB
1979 Eddie Lee Ivery, Georgia Tech, RB
1980 Bruce Clark, Penn State, DE
     George Cumby, Oklahoma, LB
1981 Rich Campbell, California, QB

1982 Ron Hallstrom, Iowa, G
1983 Tim Lewis, Pittsburgh, DB
1984 Alphonso Carreker, Florida St., DE
1985 Ken Ruettgers, So. California, T
1986 Kenneth Davis, TCU, RB (2)
1987 Brent Fullwood, Auburn, RB
1988 Sterling Sharpe, South Carolina, WR
1989 Tony Mandarich, Michigan State, T
1990 Tony Bennett, Mississippi, LB
Darrell Thompson, Minnesota, RB
1991 Vinnie Clark, Ohio State, DB
1992 Terrell Buckley, Florida State, DB
1993 Wayne Simmons, Clemson, LB
George Teague, Alabama, DB
1994 Aaron Taylor, Notre Dame, T
1995 Craig Newsome, Arizona State, DB
1996 John Michels, Southern California, T
1997 Ross Verba, Iowa, T
1998 Vonnie Holliday, North Carolina, DT
1999 Antuan Edwards, Clemson, DB
2000 Bubba Franks, Miami, TE
2001 Jamal Reynolds, Florida State, DE
2002 Javon Walker, Florida State, WR

HOUSTON TEXANS
Year Player, College, Position
2002 David Carr, Fresno State, QB

INDIANAPOLIS COLTS
Year Player, College, Position
1953 Billy Vessels, Oklahoma, B
1954 Cotton Davidson, Baylor, B
1955 George Shaw, Oregon, B
Alan Ameche, Wisconsin, FB
1956 Lenny Moore, Penn State, B
1957 Jim Parker, Ohio State, G
1958 Lenny Lyles, Louisville, B
1959 Jackie Burkett, Auburn, C
1960 Ron Mix, Southern California, T
1961 Tom Matte, Ohio State, RB
1962 Wendell Harris, Louisiana State, S
1963 Bob Vogel, Ohio State, T
1964 Marv Woodson, Indiana, CB
1965 Mike Curtis, Duke, LB
1966 Sam Ball, Kentucky, T
1967 Bubba Smith, Michigan State, DT
Jim Detwiler, Michigan, RB
1968 John Williams, Minnesota, G
1969 Eddie Hinton, Oklahoma, WR
1970 Norman Bulaich, Texas Christian, RB
1971 Don McCauley, North Carolina, RB
Leonard Dunlap, North Texas St., DB
1972 Tom Drougas, Oregon, T
1973 Bert Jones, Louisiana State, QB
Joe Ehrmann, Syracuse, DT
1974 John Dutton, Nebraska, DE
Roger Carr, Louisiana Tech, WR
1975 Ken Huff, North Carolina, G
1976 Ken Novak, Purdue, DT
1977 Randy Burke, Kentucky, WR
1978 Reese McCall, Auburn, TE
1979 Barry Krauss, Alabama, LB
1980 Curtis Dickey, Texas A&M, RB
Derrick Hatchett, Texas, DB
1981 Randy McMillan, Pittsburgh, RB
Donnell Thompson, North Carolina, DT
1982 Johnie Cooks, Mississippi St., LB
Art Schlichter, Ohio State, QB
1983 John Elway, Stanford, QB
1984 Leonard Coleman, Vanderbilt, DB

Ron Solt, Maryland, G
1985 Duane Bickett, So. California, LB
1986 Jon Hand, Alabama, DE
1987 Cornelius Bennett, Alabama, LB
1988 Chris Chandler, Washington, QB (3)
1989 Andre Rison, Michigan State, WR
1990 Jeff George, Illinois, QB
1991 Shane Curry, Miami, DE (2)
1992 Steve Emtman, Washington, DT
Quentin Coryatt, Texas A&M, LB
1993 Sean Dawkins, California, WR
1994 Marshall Faulk, San Diego St., RB
Trev Alberts, Nebraska, LB
1995 Ellis Johnson, Florida, DT
1996 Marvin Harrison, Syracuse, WR
1997 Tarik Glenn, California, T
1998 Peyton Manning, Tennessee, QB
1999 Edgerrin James, Miami, RB
2000 Rob Morris, Brigham Young, LB
2001 Reggie Wayne, Miami, WR
2002 Dwight Freeney, Syracuse, DE

JACKSONVILLE JAGUARS
Year Player, College, Position
1995 Tony Boselli, Southern California, T
James Stewart, Tennessee, RB
1996 Kevin Hardy, Illinois, LB
1997 Renaldo Wynn, Notre Dame, DT
1998 Fred Taylor, Florida, RB
Donovin Darius, Syracuse, DB
1999 Fernando Bryant, Alabama, DB
2000 R. Jay Soward, So. California, WR
2001 Marcus Stroud, Georgia, DT
2002 John Henderson, Tennessee, DT

KANSAS CITY CHIEFS
Year Player, College, Position
1960 Don Meredith, So. Methodist, QB
1961 E.J. Holub, Texas Tech, C
1962 Ronnie Bull, Baylor, RB
1963 Buck Buchanan, Grambling, DT
Ed Budde, Michigan State, G
1964 Pete Beathard, So. California, QB
1965 Gale Sayers, Kansas, RB
1966 Aaron Brown, Minnesota, DE
1967 Gene Trosch, Miami, DE-DT
1968 Mo Moorman, Texas A&M, G
George Daney, Texas-El Paso, G
1969 Jim Marsalis, Tennessee State, CB
1970 Sid Smith, Southern California, T
1971 Elmo Wright, Houston, WR
1972 Jeff Kinney, Nebraska, RB
1973 Gary Butler, Rice, TE (2)
1974 Woody Green, Arizona State, RB
1975 Elmore Stephens, Kentucky, TE (2)
1976 Rod Walters, Iowa, G
1977 Gary Green, Baylor, DB
1978 Art Still, Kentucky, DE
1979 Mike Bell, Colorado State, DE
Steve Fuller, Clemson, QB
1980 Brad Budde, Southern California, G
1981 Willie Scott, South Carolina, TE
1982 Anthony Hancock, Tennessee, WR
1983 Todd Blackledge, Penn State, QB
1984 Bill Maas, Pittsburgh, DT
John Alt, Iowa, T
1985 Ethan Horton, North Carolina, RB
1986 Brian Jozwiak, West Virginia, T
1987 Paul Palmer, Temple, RB
1988 Neil Smith, Nebraska, DE

1989 Derrick Thomas, Alabama, LB
1990 Percy Snow, Michigan State, LB
1991 Harvey Williams, Louisiana St., RB
1992 Dale Carter, Tennessee, DB
1993 Will Shields, Nebraska, G (3)
1994 Greg Hill, Texas A&M, RB
1995 Trezelle Jenkins, Michigan, T
1996 Jerome Woods, Memphis, DB
1997 Tony Gonzalez, California, TE
1998 Victor Riley, Auburn, T
1999 John Tait, Brigham Young, T
2000 Sylvester Morris, Jackson St., WR
2001 Eric Downing, Syracuse, DT (3)
2002 Ryan Sims, North Carolina, DT

MIAMI DOLPHINS
Year Player, College, Position
1966 Jim Grabowski, Illinois, RB
Rick Norton, Kentucky, QB
1967 Bob Griese, Purdue, QB
1968 Larry Csonka, Syracuse, RB
Doug Crusan, Indiana, T
1969 Bill Stanfill, Georgia, DE
1970 Jim Mandich, Michigan, TE (2)
1971 Otto Stowe, Iowa State, WR (2)
1972 Mike Kadish, Notre Dame, DT
1973 Chuck Bradley, Oregon, C (2)
1974 Donald Reese, Jackson State, DE
1975 Darryl Carlton, Tampa, T
1976 Larry Gordon, Arizona State, LB
Kim Bokamper, San Jose State, LB
1977 A.J. Duhe, Louisiana State, DT
1978 Guy Benjamin, Stanford, QB (2)
1979 Jon Giesler, Michigan, T
1980 Don McNeal, Alabama, DB
1981 David Overstreet, Oklahoma, RB
1982 Roy Foster, Southern California, G
1983 Dan Marino, Pittsburgh, QB
1984 Jackie Shipp, Oklahoma, LB
1985 Lorenzo Hampton, Florida, RB
1986 John Offerdahl, Western Michigan, LB (2)
1987 John Bosa, Boston College, DE
1988 Eric Kumerow, Ohio State, DE
1989 Sammie Smith, Florida State, RB
Louis Oliver, Florida, DB
1990 Richmond Webb, Texas A&M, T
1991 Randal Hill, Miami, WR
1992 Troy Vincent, Wisconsin, DB
Marco Coleman, Georgia Tech, LB
1993 O.J. McDuffie, Penn State, WR
1994 Tim Bowens, Mississippi, DT
1995 Billy Milner, Houston, T
1996 Daryl Gardener, Baylor, DT
1997 Yatil Green, Miami, WR
1998 John Avery, Mississippi, RB
1999 J.J. Johnson, Mississippi St., RB (2)
2000 Todd Wade, Mississippi, T (2)
2001 Jamar Fletcher, Wisconsin, DB
2002 Seth McKinney, Texas A&M, C (3)

MINNESOTA VIKINGS
Year Player, College, Position
1961 Tommy Mason, Tulane, RB
1962 Bill Miller, Miami, WR (3)
1963 Jim Dunaway, Mississippi, T
1964 Carl Eller, Minnesota, DE
1965 Jack Snow, Notre Dame, WR
1966 Jerry Shay, Purdue, DT

1967 Clint Jones, Michigan State, RB	1980 Roland James, Tennessee, DB	2002 Donte' Stallworth, Tennessee, WR
Gene Washington, Michigan St., WR	Vagas Ferguson, Notre Dame, RB	Charles Grant, Georgia, DE
Alan Page, Notre Dame, DT	1981 Brian Holloway, Stanford, T	
1968 Ron Yary, Southern California, T	1982 Kenneth Sims, Texas, DT	**NEW YORK GIANTS**
1969 Ed White, California, G (2)	Lester Williams, Miami, DT	**Year Player, College, Position**
1970 John Ward, Oklahoma State, DT	1983 Tony Eason, Illinois, QB	1936 Art Lewis, Ohio U., T
1971 Leo Hayden, Ohio State, RB	1984 Irving Fryar, Nebraska, WR	1937 Ed Widseth, Minnesota, T
1972 Jeff Siemon, Stanford, LB	1985 Trevor Matich, Brigham Young, C	1938 George Karamatic, Gonzaga, B
1973 Chuck Foreman, Miami, RB	1986 Reggie Dupard, So. Methodist, RB	1939 Walt Neilson, Arizona, B
1974 Fred McNeill, UCLA, LB	1987 Bruce Armstrong, Louisville, T	1940 Grenville Lansdell, So. California, B
Steve Riley, Southern California, T	1988 John Stephens, Northwestern St., La., RB	1941 George Franck, Minnesota, B
1975 Mark Mullaney, Colorado State, DE	1989 Hart Lee Dykes, Oklahoma St., WR	1942 Merle Hapes, Mississippi, B
1976 James White, Oklahoma State, DT	1990 Chris Singleton, Arizona, LB	1943 Steve Filipowicz, Fordham, B
1977 Tommy Kramer, Rice, QB	Ray Agnew, North Carolina St., DE	1944 Billy Hillenbrand, Indiana, B
1978 Randy Holloway, Pittsburgh, DE	1991 Pat Harlow, Southern California, T	1945 Elmer Barbour, Wake Forest, B
1979 Ted Brown, North Carolina St., RB	Leonard Russell, Arizona St., RB	1946 George Connor, Notre Dame, T
1980 Doug Martin, Washington, DT	1992 Eugene Chung, Virginia Tech, T	1947 Vic Schwall, Northwestern, B
1981 Mardye McDole, Mississippi St., WR (2)	1993 Drew Bledsoe, Washington St., QB	1948 Tony Minisi, Pennsylvania, B
1982 Darrin Nelson, Stanford, RB	1994 Willie McGinest, So. California, DE	1949 Paul Page, Southern Methodist, B
1983 Joey Browner, So. California, DB	1995 Ty Law, Michigan, DB	1950 Travis Tidwell, Auburn, B
1984 Keith Millard, Washington St., DE	1996 Terry Glenn, Ohio State, WR	1951 Kyle Rote, Southern Methodist, B
1985 Chris Doleman, Pittsburgh, LB	1997 Chris Canty, Kansas State, DB	Jim Spavital, Oklahoma A&M, B
1986 Gerald Robinson, Auburn, DE	1998 Robert Edwards, Georgia, RB	1952 Frank Gifford, Southern California, B
1987 D.J. Dozier, Penn State, RB	Tebucky Jones, Syracuse, DB	1953 Bobby Marlow, Alabama, B
1988 Randall McDaniel, Arizona State, G	1999 Damien Woody, Boston College, C	1954 Ken Buck, Pacific, C (2)
1989 David Braxton, Wake Forest, LB (2)	Andy Katzenmoyer, Ohio State, LB	1955 Joe Heap, Notre Dame, B
1990 Mike Jones, Texas A&M, TE (3)	2000 Adrian Klemm, Hawaii, T (2)	1956 Henry Moore, Arkansas, B (2)
1991 Carlos Jenkins, Michigan St., LB (3)	2001 Richard Seymour, Georgia, DT	1957 Sam DeLuca, South Carolina, T (2)
1992 Robert Harris, Southern Univ., DE (2)	2002 Daniel Graham, Colorado, TE	1958 Phil King, Vanderbilt, B
1993 Robert Smith, Ohio State, RB		1959 Lee Grosscup, Utah, B
1994 DeWayne Washington, N. Carolina St., DB	**NEW ORLEANS SAINTS**	1960 Lou Cordileone, Clemson, G
Todd Steussie, California, T	**Year Player, College, Position**	1961 Bruce Tarbox, Syracuse, G (2)
1995 Derrick Alexander, Florida St., DE	1967 Les Kelley, Alabama, RB	1962 Jerry Hillebrand, Colorado, LB
Korey Stringer, Ohio State, T	1968 Kevin Hardy, Notre Dame, DE	1963 Frank Lasky, Florida, T (2)
1996 Duane Clemons, California, DE	1969 John Shinners, Xavier, G	1964 Joe Don Looney, Oklahoma, RB
1997 Dwayne Rudd, Alabama, LB	1970 Ken Burrough, Texas Southern, WR	1965 Tucker Frederickson, Auburn, RB
1998 Randy Moss, Marshall, WR	1971 Archie Manning, Mississippi, QB	1966 Francis Peay, Missouri, T
1999 Daunte Culpepper, Central Florida, QB	1972 Royce Smith, Georgia, G	1967 Louis Thompson, Alabama, DT (4)
Dimitrius Underwood, Michigan St., DE	1973 Derland Moore, Oklahoma, DE (2)	1968 Dick Buzin, Penn State, T (2)
2000 Chris Hovan, Boston College, DT	1974 Rick Middleton, Ohio State, LB	1969 Fred Dryer, San Diego State, DE
2001 Michael Bennett, Wisconsin, RB	1975 Larry Burton, Purdue, WR	1970 Jim Files, Oklahoma, LB
2002 Bryant McKinnie, Miami, T	Kurt Schumacher, Ohio State, T	1971 Rocky Thompson, West Texas St., WR
	1976 Chuck Muncie, California, RB	1972 Eldridge Small, Texas A&I, DB
NEW ENGLAND PATRIOTS	1977 Joe Campbell, Maryland, DE	Larry Jacobson, Nebraska, DE
Year Player, College, Position	1978 Wes Chandler, Florida, WR	1973 Brad Van Pelt, Michigan St., LB (2)
1960 Ron Burton, Northwestern, RB	1979 Russell Erxleben, Texas, P-K	1974 John Hicks, Ohio State, G
1961 Tommy Mason, Tulane, RB	1980 Stan Brock, Colorado, T	1975 Al Simpson, Colorado State, T (2)
1962 Gary Collins, Maryland, WR	1981 George Rogers, South Carolina, RB	1976 Troy Archer, Colorado, DE
1963 Art Graham, Boston College, WR	1982 Lindsay Scott, Georgia, WR	1977 Gary Jeter, Southern California, DT
1964 Jack Concannon, Boston College, QB	1983 Steve Korte, Arkansas, G (2)	1978 Gordon King, Stanford, T
1965 Jerry Rush, Michigan State, DE	1984 James Geathers, Wichita State, DE	1979 Phil Simms, Morehead State, QB
1966 Karl Singer, Purdue, T	1985 Alvin Toles, Tennessee, LB	1980 Mark Haynes, Colorado, DB
1967 John Charles, Purdue, S	1986 Jim Dombrowski, Virginia, T	1981 Lawrence Taylor, North Carolina, LB
1968 Dennis Byrd, North Carolina St., DE	1987 Shawn Knight, Brigham Young, DT	1982 Butch Woolfolk, Michigan, RB
1969 Ron Sellers, Florida State, WR	1988 Craig Heyward, Pittsburgh, RB	1983 Terry Kinard, Clemson, DB
1970 Phil Olsen, Utah State, DE	1989 Wayne Martin, Arkansas, DE	1984 Carl Banks, Michigan State, LB
1971 Jim Plunkett, Stanford, QB	1990 Renaldo Turnbull, West Virginia, DE	William Roberts, Ohio State, T
1972 Tom Reynolds, San Diego St., WR (2)	1991 Wesley Carroll, Miami, WR (2)	1985 George Adams, Kentucky, RB
1973 John Hannah, Alabama, G	1992 Vaughn Dunbar, Indiana, RB	1986 Eric Dorsey, Notre Dame, DE
Sam Cunningham, So. California, RB	1993 Willie Roaf, Louisiana Tech, T	1987 Mark Ingram, Michigan State, WR
Darryl Stingley, Purdue, WR	Irv Smith, Notre Dame, TE	1988 Eric Moore, Indiana, T
1974 Steve Corbett, Boston College, G (2)	1994 Joe Johnson, Louisville, DE	1989 Brian Williams, Minnesota, C-G
1975 Russ Francis, Oregon, TE	1995 Mark Fields, Washington State, LB	1990 Rodney Hampton, Georgia, RB
1976 Mike Haynes, Arizona State, DB	1996 Alex Molden, Oregon, DB	1991 Jarrod Bunch, Michigan, RB
Pete Brock, Colorado, C	1997 Chris Naeole, Colorado, G	1992 Derek Brown, Notre Dame, TE
Tim Fox, Ohio State, DB	1998 Kyle Turley, San Diego State, T	1993 Michael Strahan, Texas Southern, DE (2)
1977 Raymond Clayborn, Texas, DB	1999 Ricky Williams, Texas, RB	1994 Thomas Lewis, Indiana, WR
Stanley Morgan, Tennessee, WR	2000 Darren Howard, Kansas St., DE (2)	1995 Tyrone Wheatley, Michigan, RB
1978 Bob Cryder, Alabama, G	2001 Deuce McAllister, Mississippi, RB	1996 Cedric Jones, Oklahoma, DE
1979 Rick Sanford, South Carolina, DB		1997 Ike Hilliard, Florida, WR

1998 Shaun Williams, UCLA, DB
1999 Luke Petitgout, Notre Dame, T
2000 Ron Dayne, Wisconsin, RB
2001 Will Allen, Syracuse, DB
2002 Jeremy Shockey, Miami, TE

NEW YORK JETS
Year Player, College, Position
1960 George Izo, Notre Dame, QB
1961 Tom Brown, Minnesota, G
1962 Sandy Stephens, Minnesota, QB
1963 Jerry Stovall, Louisiana State, S
1964 Matt Snell, Ohio State, RB
1965 Joe Namath, Alabama, QB
     Tom Nowatzke, Indiana, RB
1966 Bill Yearby, Michigan, DT
1967 Paul Seiler, Notre Dame, T
1968 Lee White, Weber State, RB
1969 Dave Foley, Ohio State, T
1970 Steve Tannen, Florida, CB
1971 John Riggins, Kansas, RB
1972 Jerome Barkum, Jackson St., WR
     Mike Taylor, Michigan, LB
1973 Burgess Owens, Miami, DB
1974 Carl Barzilauskas, Indiana, DT
1975 Anthony Davis, So. California, RB (2)
1976 Richard Todd, Alabama, QB
1977 Marvin Powell, So. California, T
1978 Chris Ward, Ohio State, T
1979 Marty Lyons, Alabama, DE
1980 Johnny (Lam) Jones, Texas, WR
1981 Freeman McNeil, UCLA, RB
1982 Bob Crable, Notre Dame, LB
1983 Ken O'Brien, Cal-Davis, QB
1984 Russell Carter, So. Methodist, DB
     Ron Faurot, Arkansas, DE
1985 Al Toon, Wisconsin, WR
1986 Mike Haight, Iowa, T
1987 Roger Vick, Texas A&M, RB
1988 Dave Cadigan, So. California, T
1989 Jeff Lageman, Virginia, LB
1990 Blair Thomas, Penn State, RB
1991 Browning Nagle, Louisville, QB (2)
1992 Johnny Mitchell, Nebraska, TE
1993 Marvin Jones, Florida State, LB
1994 Aaron Glenn, Texas A&M, DB
1995 Kyle Brady, Penn State, TE
     Hugh Douglas, Central St., Ohio, DE
1996 Keyshawn Johnson, So. California, WR
1997 James Farrior, Virginia, LB
1998 Dorian Boose, Washington St., DE (2)
1999 Randy Thomas, Mississippi St., G (2)
2000 Shaun Ellis, Tennessee, DE
     John Abraham, South Carolina, LB
     Chad Pennington, Marshall, QB
     Anthony Becht, West Virginia, TE
2001 Santana Moss, Miami, WR
2002 Bryan Thomas, Ala.-Birmingham, DE

OAKLAND RAIDERS
Year Player, College, Position
1960 Dale Hackbart, Wisconsin, CB
1961 Joe Rutgens, Illinois, DT
1962 Roman Gabriel, North Carolina St., QB
1963 George Wilson, Alabama, RB (6)
1964 Tony Lorick, Arizona State, RB
1965 Harry Schuh, Memphis State, T
1966 Rodger Bird, Kentucky, S
1967 Gene Upshaw, Texas A&I, G
1968 Eldridge Dickey, Tennessee St., QB

1969 Art Thoms, Syracuse, DT
1970 Raymond Chester, Morgan St., TE
1971 Jack Tatum, Ohio State, S
1972 Mike Siani, Villanova, WR
1973 Ray Guy, Southern Mississippi, P
1974 Henry Lawrence, Florida A&M, T
1975 Neal Colzie, Ohio State, DB
1976 Charles Philyaw, Texas Southern, DT (2)
1977 Mike Davis, Colorado, DB (2)
1978 Dave Browning, Washington, DE (2)
1979 Willie Jones, Florida State, DE (2)
1980 Marc Wilson, Brigham Young, QB
1981 Ted Watts, Texas Tech, DB
     Curt Marsh, Washington, T
1982 Marcus Allen, So. California, RB
1983 Don Mosebar, So. California, T
1984 Sean Jones, Northeastern, DE (2)
1985 Jessie Hester, Florida State, WR
1986 Bob Buczkowski, Pittsburgh, DE
1987 John Clay, Missouri, T
1988 Tim Brown, Notre Dame, WR
     Terry McDaniel, Tennessee, DB
     Scott Davis, Illinois, DE
1989 Jeff Francis, Tennessee, QB (6)
1990 Anthony Smith, Arizona, DE
1991 Todd Marinovich, So. California, QB
1992 Chester McGlockton, Clemson, DE
1993 Patrick Bates, Texas A&M, DB
1994 Rob Fredrickson, Michigan St., LB
1995 Napoleon Kaufman, Washington, RB
1996 Rickey Dudley, Ohio State, TE
1997 Darrell Russell, Southern
     California, DT
1998 Charles Woodson, Michigan, DB
     Mo Collins, Florida, T
1999 Matt Stinchcomb, Georgia, T
2000 Sebastian Janikowski, Florida St., K
2001 Derrick Gibson, Florida State, DB
2002 Phillip Buchanon, Miami, DB
     Napoleon Harris, Northwestern, LB

PHILADELPHIA EAGLES
Year Player, College, Position
1936 Jay Berwanger, Chicago, B
1937 Sam Francis, Nebraska, B
1938 Jim McDonald, Ohio State, B
1939 Davey O'Brien, Texas Christian, B
1940 George McAfee, Duke, B
1941 Art Jones, Richmond, B (2)
1942 Pete Kmetovic, Stanford, B
1943 Joe Muha, Virginia Military, B
1944 Steve Van Buren, Louisiana St., B
1945 John Yonaker, Notre Dame, E
1946 Leo Riggs, Southern California, B
1947 Neill Armstrong, Oklahoma A&M, E
1948 Clyde (Smackover) Scott, Arkansas, B
1949 Chuck Bednarik, Pennsylvania, C
     Frank Tripucka, Notre Dame, B
1950 Harry (Bud) Grant, Minnesota, E
1951 Ebert Van Buren, Louisiana St., B
     Chet Mutryn, Xavier, B
1952 Johnny Bright, Drake, B
1953 Al Conway, Army, B (2)
1954 Neil Worden, Notre Dame, B
1955 Dick Bielski, Maryland, B
1956 Bob Pellegrini, Maryland, C
1957 Clarence Peaks, Michigan State, B
1958 Walt Kowalczyk, Michigan State, B
1959 J.D. Smith, Rice, T (2)
1960 Ron Burton, Northwestern, RB

1961 Art Baker, Syracuse, RB
1962 Pete Case, Georgia, G (2)
1963 Ed Budde, Michigan State, G
1964 Bob Brown, Nebraska, T
1965 Ray Rissmiller, Georgia, T (2)
1966 Randy Beisler, Indiana, DE
1967 Harry Jones, Arkansas, RB
1968 Tim Rossovich, So. California, DE
1969 Leroy Keyes, Purdue, RB
1970 Steve Zabel, Oklahoma, TE
1971 Richard Harris, Grambling, DE
1972 John Reaves, Florida, QB
1973 Jerry Sisemore, Texas, T
     Charle Young, So. California, TE
1974 Mitch Sutton, Kansas, DT (3)
1975 Bill Capraun, Miami, T (7)
1976 Mike Smith, Florida, DE (4)
1977 Skip Sharp, Kansas, DB (5)
1978 Reggie Wilkes, Georgia Tech, LB (3)
1979 Jerry Robinson, UCLA, LB
1980 Roynell Young, Alcorn State, DB
1981 Leonard Mitchell, Houston, DE
1982 Mike Quick, North Carolina St., WR
1983 Michael Haddix, Mississippi St., RB
1984 Kenny Jackson, Penn State, WR
1985 Kevin Allen, Indiana, T
1986 Keith Byars, Ohio State, RB
1987 Jerome Brown, Miami, DT
1988 Keith Jackson, Oklahoma, TE
1989 Jessie Small, Eastern Kentucky, LB (2)
1990 Ben Smith, Georgia, DB
1991 Antone Davis, Tennessee, T
1992 Siran Stacy, Alabama, RB (2)
1993 Lester Holmes, Jackson State, T
     Leonard Renfro, Colorado, DT
1994 Bernard Williams, Georgia, T
1995 Mike Mamula, Boston College, DE
1996 Jermane Mayberry, Texas A&M-Kingsville, T
1997 Jon Harris, Virginia, DE
1998 Tra Thomas, Florida State, T
1999 Donovan McNabb, Syracuse, QB
2000 Corey Simon, Florida State, DT
2001 Freddie Mitchell, UCLA, WR
2002 Lito Sheppard, Florida, DB

PITTSBURGH STEELERS
Year Player, College, Position
1936 Bill Shakespeare, Notre Dame, B
1937 Mike Basrak, Duquesne, C
1938 Byron (Whizzer) White, Colorado, B
1939 Bill Patterson, Baylor, B (3)
1940 Kay Eakin, Arkansas, B
1941 Chet Gladchuk, Boston College, C (2)
1942 Bill Dudley, Virginia, B
1943 Bill Daley, Minnesota, B
1944 Johnny Podesto, St. Mary's, Calif., B
1945 Paul Duhart, Florida, B
1946 Felix (Doc) Blanchard, Army, B
1947 Hub Bechtol, Texas, E
1948 Dan Edwards, Georgia, E
1949 Bobby Gage, Clemson, B
1950 Lynn Chandnois, Michigan St., B
1951 Butch Avinger, Alabama, B
1952 Ed Modzelewski, Maryland, B
1953 Ted Marchibroda, St. Bonaventure, B
1954 Johnny Lattner, Notre Dame, B
1955 Frank Varrichione, Notre Dame, T
1956 Gary Glick, Colorado A&M, B
     Art Davis, Mississippi State, B
1957 Len Dawson, Purdue, B

1958	Larry Krutko, West Virginia, B (2)	
1959	Tom Barnett, Purdue, B (8)	
1960	Jack Spikes, Texas Christian, RB	
1961	Myron Pottios, Notre Dame, LB (2)	
1962	Bob Ferguson, Ohio State, RB	
1963	Frank Atkinson, Stanford, T (8)	
1964	Paul Martha, Pittsburgh, S	
1965	Roy Jefferson, Utah, WR (2)	
1966	Dick Leftridge, West Virginia, RB	
1967	Don Shy, San Diego State, RB (2)	
1968	Mike Taylor, Southern California, T	
1969	Joe Greene, North Texas State, DT	
1970	Terry Bradshaw, Louisiana Tech, QB	
1971	Frank Lewis, Grambling, WR	
1972	Franco Harris, Penn State, RB	
1973	J.T. Thomas, Florida State, DB	
1974	Lynn Swann, So. California, WR	
1975	Dave Brown, Michigan, DB	
1976	Bennie Cunningham, Clemson, TE	
1977	Robin Cole, New Mexico, LB	
1978	Ron Johnson, Eastern Michigan, DB	
1979	Greg Hawthorne, Baylor, RB	
1980	Mark Malone, Arizona State, QB	
1981	Keith Gary, Oklahoma, DE	
1982	Walter Abercrombie, Baylor, RB	
1983	Gabriel Rivera, Texas Tech, DT	
1984	Louis Lipps, So. Mississippi, WR	
1985	Darryl Sims, Wisconsin, DE	
1986	John Rienstra, Temple, G	
1987	Rod Woodson, Purdue, DB	
1988	Aaron Jones, Eastern Kentucky, DE	
1989	Tim Worley, Georgia, RB	
	Tom Ricketts, Pittsburgh, T	
1990	Eric Green, Liberty, TE	
1991	Huey Richardson, Florida, DE	
1992	Leon Searcy, Miami, T	
1993	Deon Figures, Colorado, DB	
1994	Charles Johnson, Colorado, WR	
1995	Mark Bruener, Washington, TE	
1996	Jamain Stephens, North Carolina A&T, T	
1997	Chad Scott, Maryland, DB	
1998	Alan Faneca, Louisiana State, G	
1999	Troy Edwards, Lousiana Tech, WR	
2000	Plaxico Burress, Michigan St., WR	
2001	Casey Hampton, Texas, DT	
2002	Kendall Simmons, Auburn, G	

ST. LOUIS RAMS

Year	Player, College, Position
1937	Johnny Drake, Purdue, B
1938	Corbett Davis, Indiana, B
1939	Parker Hall, Mississippi, B
1940	Ollie Cordill, Rice, B
1941	Rudy Mucha, Washington, C
1942	Jack Wilson, Baylor, B
1943	Mike Holovak, Boston College, B
1944	Tony Butkovich, Illinois, B
1945	Elroy (Crazylegs) Hirsch, Wisconsin, B
1946	Emil Sitko, Notre Dame, B
1947	Herman Wedemeyer, St. Mary's, Calif., B
1948	Tom Keane, West Virginia, B (2)
1949	Bobby Thomason, Virginia Military, B
1950	Ralph Pasquariello, Villanova, B
	Stan West, Oklahoma, G
1951	Bud McFadin, Texas, G
1952	Bill Wade, Vanderbilt, QB
	Bob Carey, Michigan State, E
1953	Donn Moomaw, UCLA, C
	Ed Barker, Washington State, E
1954	Ed Beatty, Cincinnati, C

1955	Larry Morris, Georgia Tech, C
1956	Joe Marconi, West Virginia, B
	Charles Horton, Vanderbilt, B
1957	Jon Arnett, Southern California, B
	Del Shofner, Baylor, E
1958	Lou Michaels, Kentucky, T
	Jim Phillips, Auburn, E
1959	Dick Bass, Pacific, B
	Paul Dickson, Baylor, T
1960	Billy Cannon, Louisiana State, RB
1961	Marlin McKeever, So. California, E-LB
1962	Roman Gabriel, North Carolina St., QB
	Merlin Olsen, Utah State, DT
1963	Terry Baker, Oregon State, QB
	Rufus Guthrie, Georgia Tech, G
1964	Bill Munson, Utah State, QB
1965	Clancy Williams, Washington St., CB
1966	Tom Mack, Michigan, G
1967	Willie Ellison, Texas Southern, RB (2)
1968	Gary Beban, UCLA, QB (2)
1969	Larry Smith, Florida, RB
	Jim Seymour, Notre Dame, WR
	Bob Klein, Southern California, TE
1970	Jack Reynolds, Tennessee, LB
1971	Isiah Robertson, Southern, LB
	Jack Youngblood, Florida, DE
1972	Jim Bertelsen, Texas, RB (2)
1973	Cullen Bryant, Colorado, DB (2)
1974	John Cappelletti, Penn State, RB
1975	Mike Fanning, Notre Dame, DT
	Dennis Harrah, Miami, T
	Doug France, Ohio State, T
1976	Kevin McLain, Colorado State, LB
1977	Bob Brudzinski, Ohio State, LB
1978	Elvis Peacock, Oklahoma, RB
1979	George Andrews, Nebraska, LB
	Kent Hill, Georgia Tech, T
1980	Johnnie Johnson, Texas, DB
1981	Mel Owens, Michigan, LB
1982	Barry Redden, Richmond, RB
1983	Eric Dickerson, So. Methodist, RB
1984	Hal Stephens, East Carolina, DE (5)
1985	Jerry Gray, Texas, DB
1986	Mike Schad, Queen's Univ., Canada, T
1987	Donald Evans, Winston-Salem, DE (2)
1988	Gaston Green, UCLA, RB
	Aaron Cox, Arizona State, WR
1989	Bill Hawkins, Miami, DE
	Cleveland Gary, Miami, RB
1990	Bern Brostek, Washington, C
1991	Todd Lyght, Notre Dame, DB
1992	Sean Gilbert, Pittsburgh, DE
1993	Jerome Bettis, Notre Dame, RB
1994	Wayne Gandy, Auburn, T
1995	Kevin Carter, Florida, DE
1996	Lawrence Phillips, Nebraska, RB
	Eddie Kennison, Louisiana St., WR
1997	Orlando Pace, Ohio State, T
1998	Grant Wistrom, Nebraska, DE
1999	Torry Holt, North Carolina St., WR
2000	Trung Canidate, Arizona, RB
2001	Damione Lewis, Miami, DT
	Adam Archuleta, Arizona State, DB
	Ryan Pickett, Ohio State, DT
2002	Robert Thomas, UCLA, LB

SAN DIEGO CHARGERS

Year	Player, College, Position
1960	Monty Stickles, Notre Dame, E
1961	Earl Faison, Indiana, DE

1962	Bob Ferguson, Ohio State, RB
1963	Walt Sweeney, Syracuse, G
1964	Ted Davis, Georgia Tech, LB
1965	Steve DeLong, Tennessee, DE
1966	Don Davis, Cal St.-Los Angeles, DT
1967	Ron Billingsley, Wyoming, DE
1968	Russ Washington, Missouri, DT
	Jimmy Hill, Texas A&I, DB
1969	Marty Domres, Columbia, QB
	Bob Babich, Miami, Ohio, LB
1970	Walker Gillette, Richmond, WR
1971	Leon Burns, Long Beach State, RB
1972	Pete Lazetich, Stanford, DE (2)
1973	Johnny Rodgers, Nebraska, WR
1974	Bo Matthews, Colorado, RB
	Don Goode, Kansas, LB
1975	Gary Johnson, Grambling, DT
	Mike Williams, Louisiana State, DB
1976	Joe Washington, Oklahoma, RB
1977	Bob Rush, Memphis State, C
1978	John Jefferson, Arizona State, WR
1979	Kellen Winslow, Missouri, TE
1980	Ed Luther, San Jose State, QB (4)
1981	James Brooks, Auburn, RB
1982	Hollis Hall, Clemson, DB (7)
1983	Billy Ray Smith, Arkansas, LB
	Gary Anderson, Arkansas, WR
	Gill Byrd, San Jose State, DB
1984	Mossy Cade, Texas, DB
1985	Jim Lachey, Ohio State, G
1986	Leslie O'Neal, Oklahoma State, DE
	James FitzPatrick, So. California, T
1987	Rod Bernstine, Texas A&M, TE
1988	Anthony Miller, Tennessee, WR
1989	Burt Grossman, Pittsburgh, DE
1990	Junior Seau, So. California, LB
1991	Stanley Richard, Texas, DB
1992	Chris Mims, Tennessee, DE
1993	Darrien Gordon, Stanford, DB
1994	Isaac Davis, Arkansas, G (2)
1995	Terrance Shaw, Stephen F. Austin, DB (2)
1996	Bryan Still, Virginia Tech, WR (2)
1997	Freddie Jones, North Carolina, TE (2)
1998	Ryan Leaf, Washington State, QB
1999	Jermaine Fazande, Oklahoma, RB (2)
2000	Rogers Beckett, Marshall, DB (2)
2001	LaDainian Tomlinson, TCU, RB
2002	Quentin Jammer, Texas, DB

SAN FRANCISCO 49ERS

Year	Player, College, Position
1950	Leo Nomellini, Minnesota, T
1951	Y.A. Tittle, Louisiana State, B
1952	Hugh McElhenny, Washington, B
1953	Harry Babcock, Georgia, E
	Tom Stolhandske, Texas, E
1954	Bernie Faloney, Maryland, B
1955	Dickie Moegle, Rice, B
1956	Earl Morrall, Michigan State, B
1957	John Brodie, Stanford, B
1958	Jim Pace, Michigan, B
	Charlie Krueger, Texas A&M, T
1959	Dave Baker, Oklahoma, B
	Dan James, Ohio State, C
1960	Monty Stickles, Notre Dame, E
1961	Jimmy Johnson, UCLA, CB
	Bernie Casey, Bowling Green, WR
	Bill Kilmer, UCLA, QB
1962	Lance Alworth, Arkansas, WR
1963	Kermit Alexander, UCLA, CB

1964 Dave Parks, Texas Tech, WR
1965 Ken Willard, North Carolina, RB
George Donnelly, Illinois, DB
1966 Stan Hindman, Mississippi, DE
1967 Steve Spurrier, Florida, QB
Cas Banaszek, Northwestern, T
1968 Forrest Blue, Auburn, C
1969 Ted Kwalick, Penn State, TE
Gene Washington, Stanford, WR
1970 Cedrick Hardman, North Texas St., DE
Bruce Taylor, Boston U., DB
1971 Tim Anderson, Ohio State, DB
1972 Terry Beasley, Auburn, WR
1973 Mike Holmes, Texas Southern, DB
1974 Wilbur Jackson, Alabama, RB
Bill Sandifer, UCLA, DT
1975 Jimmy Webb, Mississippi St., DT
1976 Randy Cross, UCLA, C (2)
1977 Elmo Boyd, Eastern Kentucky, WR (3)
1978 Ken MacAfee, Notre Dame, TE
Dan Bunz, Cal St.-Long Beach, LB
1979 James Owens, UCLA, WR (2)
1980 Earl Cooper, Rice, RB
Jim Stuckey, Clemson, DT
1981 Ronnie Lott, So. California, DB
1982 Bubba Paris, Michigan, T (2)
1983 Roger Craig, Nebraska, RB (2)
1984 Todd Shell, Brigham Young, LB
1985 Jerry Rice, Mississippi Valley St., WR
1986 Larry Roberts, Alabama, DE (2)
1987 Harris Barton, North Carolina, T
Terrence Flagler, Clemson, RB
1988 Danny Stubbs, Miami, DE (2)
1989 Keith DeLong, Tennessee, LB
1990 Dexter Carter, Florida State, RB
1991 Ted Washington, Louisville, DT
1992 Dana Hall, Washington, DB
1993 Dana Stubblefield, Kansas, DT
Todd Kelly, Tennessee, DE
1994 Bryant Young, Notre Dame, DT
William Floyd, Florida State, RB
1995 J.J. Stokes, UCLA, WR
1996 Israel Ifeanyi, So.California, DE (2)
1997 Jim Druckenmiller, Virginia Tech, QB
1998 R.W. McQuarters, Oklahoma St., DB
1999 Reggie McGrew, Florida, DT
2000 Julian Peterson, Michigan St., LB
Ahmed Plummer, Ohio State, DB
2001 Andre Carter, California, DE
2002 Mike Rumph, Miami, DB

SEATTLE SEAHAWKS
Year Player, College, Position
1976 Steve Niehaus, Notre Dame, DT
1977 Steve August, Tulsa, G
1978 Keith Simpson, Memphis St., DB
1979 Manu Tuiasosopo, UCLA, DT
1980 Jacob Green, Texas A&M, DE
1981 Ken Easley, UCLA, DB
1982 Jeff Bryant, Clemson, DE
1983 Curt Warner, Penn State, RB
1984 Terry Taylor, Southern Illinois, DB
1985 Owen Gill, Iowa, RB (2)
1986 John L. Williams, Florida, RB
1987 Tony Woods, Pittsburgh, LB
1988 Brian Blades, Miami, WR (2)
1989 Andy Heck, Notre Dame, T
1990 Cortez Kennedy, Miami, DT
1991 Dan McGwire, San Diego St., QB
1992 Ray Roberts, Virginia, T

1993 Rick Mirer, Notre Dame, QB
1994 Sam Adams, Texas A&M, DT
1995 Joey Galloway, Ohio State, WR
1996 Pete Kendall, Boston College, T
1997 Shawn Springs, Ohio State, DB
Walter Jones, Florida State, T
1998 Anthony Simmons, Clemson, LB
1999 Lamar King, Saginaw Valley St., DE
2000 Shaun Alexander, Alabama, RB
Chris McIntosh, Wisconsin, T
2001 Koren Robinson, North Carolina St., WR
Steve Hutchinson, Michigan, G
2002 Jerramy Stevens, Washington, TE

TAMPA BAY BUCCANEERS
Year Player, College, Position
1976 Lee Roy Selmon, Oklahoma, DT
1977 Ricky Bell, Southern California, RB
1978 Doug Williams, Grambling, QB
1979 Greg Roberts, Oklahoma, G (2)
1980 Ray Snell, Wisconsin, G
1981 Hugh Green, Pittsburgh, LB
1982 Sean Farrell, Penn State, G
1983 Randy Grimes, Baylor, C (2)
1984 Keith Browner, So. California, LB (2)
1985 Ron Holmes, Washington, DE
1986 Bo Jackson, Auburn, RB
Roderick Jones, So. Methodist, DB
1987 Vinny Testaverde, Miami, QB
1988 Paul Gruber, Wisconsin, T
1989 Broderick Thomas, Nebraska, LB
1990 Keith McCants, Alabama, LB
1991 Charles McRae, Tennessee, T
1992 Courtney Hawkins, Michigan St., WR (2)
1993 Eric Curry, Alabama, DE
1994 Trent Dilfer, Fresno State, QB
1995 Warren Sapp, Miami, DT
Derrick Brooks, Florida State, LB
1996 Regan Upshaw, California, DE
Marcus Jones, North Carolina, DT
1997 Warrick Dunn, Florida State, RB
Reidel Anthony, Florida, WR
1998 Jacquez Green, Florida, WR (2)
1999 Anthony McFarland, Louisiana St., DT
2000 Cosey Coleman, Tennessee, G (2)
2001 Kenyatta Walker, Florida, T
2002 Marquise Walker, Michigan, WR (3)

TENNESSEE TITANS
Year Player, College, Position
1960 Billy Cannon, Louisiana State, RB
1961 Mike Ditka, Pittsburgh, E
1962 Ray Jacobs, Howard Payne, DT
1963 Danny Brabham, Arkansas, LB
1964 Scott Appleton, Texas, DT
1965 Lawrence Elkins, Baylor, WR
1966 Tommy Nobis, Texas, LB
1967 George Webster, Michigan St., LB
Tom Regner, Notre Dame, G
1968 Mac Haik, Mississippi, WR (2)
1969 Ron Pritchard, Arizona State, LB
1970 Doug Wilkerson, N. Carolina Central, G
1971 Dan Pastorini, Santa Clara, QB
1972 Greg Sampson, Stanford, DE
1973 John Matuszak, Tampa, DE
George Amundson, Iowa State, RB
1974 Steve Manstedt, Nebraska, LB (4)
1975 Robert Brazile, Jackson State, LB
Don Hardeman, Texas A&I, RB
1976 Mike Barber, Louisiana Tech, TE (2)

1977 Morris Towns, Missouri, T
1978 Earl Campbell, Texas, RB
1979 Mike Stensrud, Iowa State, DE (2)
1980 Angelo Fields, Michigan St., T (2)
1981 Michael Holston, Morgan St., WR (3)
1982 Mike Munchak, Penn State, G
1983 Bruce Matthews, So. California, T
1984 Dean Steinkuhler, Nebraska, T
1985 Ray Childress, Texas A&M, DE
Richard Johnson, Wisconsin, DB
1986 Jim Everett, Purdue, QB
1987 Alonzo Highsmith, Miami, RB
Haywood Jeffires, North Carolina St., WR
1988 Lorenzo White, Michigan State, RB
1989 David Williams, Florida, T
1990 Lamar Lathon, Houston, LB
1991 Mike Dumas, Indiana, DB (2)
1992 Eddie Robinson, Alabama St., LB (2)
1993 Brad Hopkins, Illinois, T
1994 Henry Ford, Arkansas, DE
1995 Steve McNair, Alcorn State, QB
1996 Eddie George, Ohio State, RB
1997 Kenny Holmes, Miami, DE
1998 Kevin Dyson, Utah, WR
1999 Jevon Kearse, Florida, DE
2000 Keith Bulluck, Syracuse, LB
2001 Andre Dyson, Utah, DB (2)
2002 Albert Haynesworth, Tennessee, DT

WASHINGTON REDSKINS
Year Player, College, Position
1936 Riley Smith, Alabama, B
1937 Sammy Baugh, Texas Christian, B
1938 Andy Farkas, Detroit, B
1939 I.B. Hale, Texas Christian, T
1940 Ed Boell, New York U., B
1941 Forest Evashevski, Michigan, B
1942 Orban (Spec) Sanders, Texas, B
1943 Jack Jenkins, Missouri, B
1944 Mike Micka, Colgate, B
1945 Jim Hardy, Southern California, B
1946 Cal Rossi, UCLA, B*
1947 Cal Rossi, UCLA, B
1948 Harry Gilmer, Alabama, B
Lowell Tew, Alabama, B
1949 Rob Goode, Texas A&M, B
1950 George Thomas, Oklahoma, B
1951 Leon Heath, Oklahoma, B
1952 Larry Isbell, Baylor, B
1953 Jack Scarbath, Maryland, B
1954 Steve Meilinger, Kentucky, E
1955 Ralph Guglielmi, Notre Dame, B
1956 Ed Vereb, Maryland, B
1957 Don Bosseler, Miami, B
1958 Mike Sommer, George
Washington, B (2)
1959 Don Allard, Boston College, B
1960 Richie Lucas, Penn State, QB
1961 Norman Snead, Wake Forest, QB
Joe Rutgens, Illinois, DT
1962 Ernie Davis, Syracuse, RB
1963 Pat Richter, Wisconsin, TE
1964 Charley Taylor, Arizona St., RB-WR
1965 Bob Breitenstein, Tulsa, T (2)
1966 Charlie Gogolak, Princeton, K
1967 Ray McDonald, Idaho, RB
1968 Jim Smith, Oregon, DB
1969 Eugene Epps, Texas-El Paso, DB (2)
1970 Bill Bundige, Colorado, DT (2)
1971 Cotton Speyrer, Texas, WR (2)

1972 Moses Denson, Maryland St., RB (8)
1973 Charles Cantrell, Lamar, G (5)
1974 Jon Keyworth, Colorado, TE (6)
1975 Mike Thomas, Nevada-Las Vegas, RB (6)
1976 Mike Hughes, Baylor, G (5)
1977 Duncan McColl, Stanford, DE (4)
1978 Tony Green, Florida, RB (6)
1979 Don Warren, San Diego St., TE (4)
1980 Art Monk, Syracuse, WR
1981 Mark May, Pittsburgh, T
1982 Vernon Dean, San Diego St., DB (2)
1983 Darrell Green, Texas A&I, DB
1984 Bob Slater, Oklahoma, DT (2)
1985 Tory Nixon, San Diego St., DB (2)
1986 Markus Koch, Boise State, DE (2)
1987 Brian Davis, Nebraska, DB (2)
1988 Chip Lohmiller, Minnesota, K (2)
1989 Tracy Rocker, Auburn, DT (3)
1990 Andre Collins, Penn State, LB (2)
1991 Bobby Wilson, Michigan State, DT
1992 Desmond Howard, Michigan, WR
1993 Tom Carter, Notre Dame, DB
1994 Heath Shuler, Tennessee, QB
1995 Michael Westbrook, Colorado, WR
1996 Andre Johnson, Penn State, T
1997 Kenard Lang, Miami, DE
1998 Stephen Alexander, Oklahoma, TE (2)
1999 Champ Bailey, Georgia, DB
2000 LaVar Arrington, Penn State, LB
     Chris Samuels, Alabama, T
2001 Rod Gardner, Clemson, WR
2002 Patrick Ramsey, Tulane, QB
Choice lost because of ineligibility

NUMBER-ONE DRAFT CHOICES

Season	Date	Team	Player	Position	College
2002	April 20-21	Houston	David Carr	QB	Fresno State
2001	April 21-22	Atlanta	Michael Vick	QB	Virginia Tech
2000	April 15-16	Cleveland	Courtney Brown	DE	Penn State
1999	April 17-18	Cleveland	Tim Couch	QB	Kentucky
1998	April 18-19	Indianapolis	Peyton Manning	QB	Tennessee
1997	April 19-20	St. Louis	Orlando Pace	T	Ohio State
1996	April 20-21	New York Jets	Keyshawn Johnson	WR	Southern California
1995	April 22-23	Cincinnati	Ki-Jana Carter	RB	Penn State
1994	April 24-25	Cincinnati	Dan Wilkinson	DT	Ohio State
1993	April 25-26	New England	Drew Bledsoe	QB	Washington State
1992	April 26-27	Indianapolis	Steve Emtman	DT	Washington
1991	April 21-22	Dallas	Russell Maryland	DT	Miami
1990	April 22-23	Indianapolis	Jeff George	QB	Illinois
1989	April 23-24	Dallas	Troy Aikman	QB	UCLA
1988	April 24-25	Atlanta	Aundray Bruce	LB	Auburn
1987	April 28-29	Tampa Bay	Vinny Testaverde	QB	Miami
1986	April 29-30	Tampa Bay	Bo Jackson	RB	Auburn
1985	April 30-May 1	Buffalo	Bruce Smith	DE	Virginia Tech
1984	May 1-2	New England	Irving Fryar	WR	Nebraska
1983	April 26-27	Baltimore	John Elway	QB	Stanford
1982	April 27-28	New England	Kenneth Sims	DT	Texas
1981	April 28-29	New Orleans	George Rogers	RB	South Carolina
1980	April 29-30	Detroit	Billy Sims	RB	Oklahoma
1979	May 3-4	Buffalo	Tom Cousineau	LB	Ohio State
1978	May 2-3	Houston	Earl Campbell	RB	Texas
1977	May 3-4	Tampa Bay	Ricky Bell	RB	Southern California
1976	April 8-9	Tampa Bay	Lee Roy Selmon	DE	Oklahoma
1975	January 28-29	Atlanta	Steve Bartkowski	QB	California
1974	January 29-30	Dallas	Ed Jones	DE	Tennessee State
1973	January 30-31	Houston	John Matuszak	DE	Tampa
1972	February 1-2	Buffalo	Walt Patulski	DE	Notre Dame
1971	January 28-29	New England	Jim Plunkett	QB	Stanford
1970	January 27-28	Pittsburgh	Terry Bradshaw	QB	Louisiana Tech
1969	January 28-29	Buffalo (AFL)	O.J. Simpson	RB	Southern California
1968	January 30-31	Minnesota	Ron Yary	T	Southern California
1967	March 14	Baltimore	Bubba Smith	DT	Michigan State
1966	November 27, 1965	Atlanta	Tommy Nobis	LB	Texas
	November 28, 1965	Miami (AFL)	Jim Grabowski	RB	Illinois
1965	November 28, 1964	New York Giants	Tucker Frederickson	RB	Auburn
	November 28, 1964	Houston (AFL)	Lawrence Elkins	E	Baylor
1964	December 2, 1963	San Francisco	Dave Parks	E	Texas Tech
	November 30, 1963	Boston (AFL)	Jack Concannon	QB	Boston College
1963	December 3, 1962	Los Angeles	Terry Baker	QB	Oregon State
	December 1, 1962	Kansas City (AFL)	Buck Buchanan	DT	Grambling
1962	December 4, 1961	Washington	Ernie Davis	RB	Syracuse
	December 2, 1961	Oakland (AFL)	Roman Gabriel	QB	North Carolina State
1961	December 27-28, 1960	Minnesota	Tommy Mason	RB	Tulane
	November 23, 1960	Buffalo (AFL)	Ken Rice	G	Auburn
1960	Secret Draft	Los Angeles	Billy Cannon	RB	Louisiana State
	November 22, December 2, 1959	(AFL had no formal first pick)			
1959	December 2, 1958	Green Bay	Randy Duncan	QB	Iowa
1958	December 2, 1957	Chicago Cardinals	King Hill	QB	Rice
1957	November 27, 1956	Green Bay	Paul Hornung	HB	Notre Dame
1956	November 29, 1955	Pittsburgh	Gary Glick	DB	Colorado A&M
1955	January 27-28	Baltimore	George Shaw	QB	Oregon
1954	January 28	Cleveland	Bobby Garrett	QB	Stanford
1953	January 22	San Francisco	Harry Babcock	E	Georgia
1952	January 17	Los Angeles	Bill Wade	QB	Vanderbilt
1951	January 18-19	New York Giants	Kyle Rote	HB	Southern Methodist
1950	January 21-22	Detroit	Leon Hart	E	Notre Dame
1949	December 21, 1948	Philadelphia	Chuck Bednarik	C	Pennsylvania

1948	December 19, 1947	Washington	Harry Gilmer	QB	Alabama
1947	December 16, 1946	Chicago Bears	Bob Fenimore	HB	Oklahoma A&M
1946	January 14	Boston	Frank Dancewicz	QB	Notre Dame
1945	April 6	Chicago Cardinals	Charley Trippi	HB	Georgia
1944	April 19	Boston	Angelo Bertelli	QB	Notre Dame
1943	April 8	Detroit	Frank Sinkwich	HB	Georgia
1942	December 22, 1941	Pittsburgh	Bill Dudley	HB	Virginia
1941	December 10, 1940	Chicago Bears	Tom Harmon	HB	Michigan
1940	December 9, 1939	Chicago Cardinals	George Cafego	HB	Tennessee
1939	December 8, 1938	Chicago Cardinals	Ki Aldrich	C	Texas Christian
1938	December 12, 1937	Cleveland	Corbett Davis	FB	Indiana
1937	December 12, 1936	Philadelphia	Sam Francis	FB	Nebraska
1936	February 8	Philadelphia	Jay Berwanger	HB	Chicago

Note: From 1947 through 1958, the first selection in the draft was a Bonus pick, awarded to the winner of a random draw. That club, in turn, forfeited its last-round draft choice. The winner of the Bonus choice was eliminated from future draws. The system was abolished after 1958, by which time all clubs had received a Bonus choice.

NFL MOST VALUABLE PLAYERS NAMED BY *ASSOCIATED PRESS* IN BALLOTING BY A NATIONWIDE PANEL OF MEDIA:

YEAR	PLAYER	POS.	TEAM	ACCOMPLISHMENTS
1957	Jim Brown	RB	Cleveland Browns	Rushed for league-leading 942 yards and added 9 TDs as a rookie.
1958	Gino Marchetti	DE	Baltimore Colts	Leader of defense that permitted league-low 1,291 rushing yards and division-low 203 points.
1959	Charley Conerly	QB	New York Giants	Passed for 14 TDs vs. 4 interceptions. Led offense to division-leading 284 points.
1960*	Norm Van Brocklin	QB	Philadelphia Eagles	Guided Eagles to first division title since 1949. Passed for 2,471 yards and 24 TDs.
	Joe Schmidt	LB	Detroit Lions	Team went 7-2 after 0-3 start when he returned from injury. Scored 2 defensive TDs.
1961	Paul Hornung	RB	Green Bay Packers	Led league in scoring for second straight season with 146 points (10 TD, 15 FG, 41 PAT).
1962	Jim Taylor	RB	Green Bay Packers	League rushing champion with 1,474 yards. Scored then all-time record 19 touchdowns.
1963	Y.A. Tittle	QB	New York Giants	Set then all-time season record with 36 TD passes. Guided league's top offense (5,024 yards).
1964	Johnny Unitas	QB	Baltimore Colts	Guided Colts to NFL's best record (12-2) and league's top offensive attack (4,779 yards).
1965	Jim Brown	RB	Cleveland Browns	Leader of NFL's top rushing attack. Led league with 1,544 yards, added 21 total TDs.
1966	Bart Starr	QB	Green Bay Packers	Passed for 14 touchdowns vs. 3 interceptions. Led Packers to league-best 12-2 record.
1967	Johnny Unitas	QB	Baltimore Colts	Passed for 3,428 yards and 20 touchdowns. Led Colts to 11-1-2 record.
1968	Earl Morrall	QB	Baltimore Colts	Guided Colts to NFL-best 13-1 record. Led league with 26 touchdown passes.
1969	Roman Gabriel	QB	Los Angeles Rams	Led NFL with 24 touchdown passes. Guided Rams to 11-3 record.
1970	John Brodie	QB	San Francisco 49ers	Took 49ers to first-ever division title. Threw NFL-best 24 TD passes.
1971	Alan Page	DT	Minnesota Vikings	Led defense that allowed NFL-low 139 points. Vikings won fourth straight NFC Central title.
1972	Larry Brown	RB	Washington Redskins	Led conference with 1,216 rushing yards. Redskins had NFC-best 11-3 record.
1973	O.J. Simpson	RB	Buffalo Bills	Rushed for then all-time record 2,003 yards, including three 200-yard performances.
1974	Ken Stabler	QB	Oakland Raiders	Led league with 26 touchdown passes vs. 12 interceptions. Raiders had NFL-best 12-2 record.
1975	Fran Tarkenton	QB	Minnesota Vikings	Tied for league-best 12-2 record. Led NFC with 91.7 passer rating.
1976	Bert Jones	QB	Baltimore Colts	Threw 24 touchdowns vs. 9 interceptions for 102.5 passer rating.
1977	Walter Payton	RB	Chicago Bears	Rushed for league-leading 1,852 yards and 16 total touchdowns.
1978	Terry Bradshaw	QB	Pittsburgh Steelers	Led Steelers to league-leading 14-2 mark. Set team record with 28 TD passes.
1979	Earl Campbell	RB	Houston Oilers	Led league with 1,697 rushing yards and 19 touchdowns.
1980	Brian Sipe	QB	Cleveland Browns	NFL-best 91.4 passer rating. Set Browns' records with 30 TD passes and 4,132 yards.
1981	Ken Anderson	QB	Cincinnati Bengals	Led Bengals to first division title since 1973. NFL-high 98.5 passer rating.
1982	Mark Moseley	K	Washington Redskins	Converted 20 of 21 FGs. Set then consecutive field-goal record at 23 (including last three in '81).
1983	Joe Theismann	QB	Washington Redskins	Leader of offense that scored then-NFL record 541 points. Redskins had NFL-best 14-2 mark.
1984	Dan Marino	QB	Miami Dolphins	Set NFL records with 5,084 yards and 48 TD passes. Led Dolphins to AFC-best 14-2 mark.
1985	Marcus Allen	RB	Los Angeles Raiders	Rushed for league-leading 1,759 yards. Tied for AFC lead with 11 rushing touchdowns.
1986	Lawrence Taylor	LB	New York Giants	Recorded league-high 20.5 sacks, and led Giants' second-ranked defense (297.3).
1987	John Elway	QB	Denver Broncos	In 12 games, passed for 19 TDs and 3,198 yards, including four 300-yard games.
1988	Boomer Esiason	QB	Cincinnati Bengals	Led NFL with 97.4 passer rating. Tied for AFC lead with 28 TD passes.
1989	Joe Montana	QB	San Francisco 49ers	Set then-NFL record with 112.4 passer rating, including 70.2 completion percentage.
1990	Joe Montana	QB	San Francisco 49ers	Led 49ers to league-best 14-2 record. Completed NFC-high 61.7 percent of passes.
1991	Thurman Thomas	RB	Buffalo Bills	Recorded league-high 2,038 yards from scrimmage (1,407 rushing, 631 receiving).
1992	Steve Young	QB	San Francisco 49ers	NFL's top passer with 107.0 rating. Led 49ers to league-best 14-2 record.

1993	Emmitt Smith	RB	Dallas Cowboys	Led league in rushing (1,486 yards) for third straight year despite missing first two games.
1994	Steve Young	QB	San Francisco 49ers	Compiled NFL all-time best 112.8 passer rating. Completed more than 70 percent of his passes.
1995	Brett Favre	QB	Green Bay Packers	Led league with 38 touchdown passes and NFC with 99.5 passer rating.
1996	Brett Favre	QB	Green Bay Packers	Led Packers to top conference record (13-3). Threw NFL-best 39 TD passes.
1997*	Brett Favre	QB	Green Bay Packers	Led league with 35 touchdown passes. Led NFC with 3,867 passing yards.
	Barry Sanders	RB	Detroit Lions	Rushed for all-time second-best 2,053 yards, including record 14 straight 100-yard games.
1998	Terrell Davis	RB	Denver Broncos	Rushed for 2,008 yards and scored league-best 23 total touchdowns.
1999	Kurt Warner	QB	St. Louis Rams	Became the second QB in history to have 40 touchdown passes in a season (41).
2000	Marshall Faulk	RB	St. Louis Rams	Set NFL record with 26 touchdowns and led NFC with 2,189 yards from scrimmage.
2001	Kurt Warner	QB	St. Louis Rams	Led NFL with 4,830 passing yards, 36 touchdowns, 68.7 completion percentage, and 101.4 passer rating.

Total *Associated Press* **NFL MVPs:** 47
Two-time Winners: Jim Brown, Brett Favre (3), Joe Montana, Johnny Unitas, Kurt Warner, Steve Young
* The award was shared in 1960 and 1997.

ASSOCIATED PRESS MVPs WHO WON SUPER BOWL/ NFL CHAMPIONSHIP IN SAME SEASON: 15

1958	Gino Marchetti	Baltimore Colts
1960	Norm Van Brocklin	Philadelphia Eagles
1961	Paul Hornung	Green Bay Packers
1962	Jim Taylor	Green Bay Packers
1966	Bart Starr	Green Bay Packers
1968	Earl Morrall	Baltimore Colts
1978	Terry Bradshaw	Pittsburgh Steelers
1982	Mark Moseley	Washington Redskins
1986	Lawrence Taylor	New York Giants
1989	Joe Montana	San Francisco 49ers
1993	Emmitt Smith	Dallas Cowboys
1994	Steve Young	San Francisco 49ers
1996	Brett Favre	Green Bay Packers
1998	Terrell Davis	Denver Broncos
1999	Kurt Warner	St. Louis Rams

ASSOCIATED PRESS MVPs BY TEAM

6	Green Bay Packers	1	Chicago Bears
			Dallas Cowboys
5	Baltimore Colts		Houston Oilers
	San Francisco 49ers		Miami Dolphins
			Philadelphia Eagles
4	St. Louis/Los Angeles Rams		Pittsburgh Steelers
3	Cleveland Browns		
	New York Giants		
	Washington Redskins		
2	Buffalo Bills		
	Cincinnati Bengals		
	Denver Broncos		
	Detroit Lions		
	Minnesota Vikings		
	Oakland/Los Angeles Raiders		

ASSOCIATED PRESS NFL MVP BY POSITION

Quarterback:	28	Defensive End:	1
Running Back:	14	Defensive Tackle:	1
Linebacker:	2	Kicker:	1

MILLER LITE PLAYERS OF THE YEAR

YEAR	PLAYER	POS.	TEAM
1989	Joe Montana	QB	San Francisco 49ers
1990	Joe Montana	QB	San Francisco 49ers
1991	Thurman Thomas	RB	Buffalo Bills
1992	Steve Young	QB	San Francisco 49ers
1993	Emmitt Smith	RB	Dallas Cowboys
1994	Steve Young	QB	San Francisco 49ers
1995	Brett Favre	QB	Green Bay Packers
1996	Brett Favre	QB	Green Bay Packers
1997	Barry Sanders	RB	Detroit Lions
1998	Randall Cunningham	QB	Minnesota Vikings
1999	Kurt Warner	QB	St. Louis Rams
2000	Marshall Faulk	RB	St. Louis Rams
2001	Marshall Faulk	RB	St. Louis Rams

NFL'S 10 HIGHEST SCORING WEEKENDS

Point Total	Date	Weekend
762	November 10-11, 1996	11th
761	October 16-17, 1983	7th
740	November 29-30, 1998	13th
739	November 23, 26-27, 1995	13th
736	October 25-26, 1987	7th
734	November 19-20, 1995	12th
732	November 9-10, 1980	10th
725	November 24, 27-28, 1983	13th
719	November 27, 30-December 1, 1997	14th
714	September 17-18, 1989	2nd

TOP 10 TELEVISED SPORTS EVENTS OF ALL-TIME
(Based on A.C. Nielsen Figures)

Program	Date	Network	Share	Rating
Super Bowl XVI	1/24/82	CBS	73%	49.1
Super Bowl XVII	1/30/83	NBC	69%	48.6
Winter Olympics	2/23/94	CBS	64%	48.5
Super Bowl XX	1/26/86	NBC	70%	48.3
Super Bowl XII	1/15/78	CBS	67%	47.2
Super Bowl XIII	1/21/79	NBC	74%	47.1
Super Bowl XI	1/22/84	CBS	71%	46.4
Super Bowl XIX	1/20/85	ABC	63%	46.4
Super Bowl XIV	1/20/80	CBS	67%	46.3
Super Bowl XXX	1/28/96	NBC	68%	46.0

TEN MOST WATCHED TV PROGRAMS & ESTIMATED TOTAL NUMBER OF VIEWERS
(Based on A.C. Nielsen Figures)

Program	Date	Network	*Total Viewers
Super Bowl XXX	Jan. 28, 1996	NBC	138,488,000
Super Bowl XXVIII	Jan. 30, 1994	NBC	134,800,000
Super Bowl XXXII	Jan. 25, 1998	NBC	133,400,000
Super Bowl XXVII	Jan. 31, 1993	NBC	133,400,000
Super Bowl XXXVI	Feb. 3, 2002	FOX	131,700,000
Super Bowl XXXV	Jan. 28, 2001	CBS	131,200,000
Super Bowl XXXIV	Jan. 30, 2000	ABC	130,744,800
Super Bowl XXXI	Jan. 26, 1997	FOX	128,900,000
Super Bowl XXXIII	Jan. 31, 1999	FOX	127,500,000
Super Bowl XX	Jan. 26, 1986	NBC	127,000,000

*Watched some portion of the broadcast

NFL'S TOP FIVE PAID ATTENDANCE TOTALS FOR ALL GAMES

Year	Preseason	Regular Season	Postseason	All Games
2000	3,757,231	16,387,289	809,132	20,953,652
1999	3,762,331	16,206,640	793,759	20,762,730
2001	3,656,928	16,166,258	766,905	20,590,091
1998	3,553,735	15,364,873	822,885	19,741,493
1995	3,368,289	15,043,562	790,906	19,202,757

TEN HIGHEST-RATED ABC *NFL MONDAY NIGHT FOOTBALL* GAMES OF ALL-TIME
(Based on A.C. Nielsen Figures)

Game	Date	Share	Rating
Chicago at Miami	12/2/85	46%	29.6
N.Y. Giants at San Francisco	12/3/90	42%	26.9
Dallas at Washington	10/2/78	43%	26.8
Pittsburgh at San Diego	12/22/80	40%	25.3
Philadelphia at Miami	11/30/81	40%	25.3
Pittsburgh at Houston	12/10/79	40%	25.1
Dallas at Miami	12/17/84	40%	25.1
Pittsburgh at Dallas	9/13/82	42%	24.9
Cincinnati at Oakland	12/6/76	40%	24.7
Dallas at Washington	10/8/73	40%	24.6
Minnesota at Atlanta	11/19/73	40%	24.6

NFL'S 10 BIGGEST SINGLE-GAME ATTENDANCE TOTALS

Date	Site	Game	Teams	Attendance
August 15, 1994	Azteca Stadium	American Bowl (Mexico City)	Cowboys vs. Oilers	112,376
August 17, 1998	Azteca Stadium	American Bowl (Mexico City)	Cowboys vs. Patriots	106,424
August 22, 1947	Soldier Field	College All-Star	Bears vs. All-Stars	105,840
August 4, 1997	Estadio Guillermo Canedo	American Bowl (Mexico City)	Broncos vs. Dolphins	104,629
January 20, 1980	Rose Bowl	Super Bowl XIV	Steelers vs. Rams	103,985
January 30, 1983	Rose Bowl	Super Bowl XVII	Redskins vs. Dolphins	103,667
January 9, 1977	Rose Bowl	Super Bowl XI	Raiders vs. Vikings	103,438
November 10, 1957	L.A. Coliseum	Regular Season	49ers at Rams	102,368
January 25, 1987	Rose Bowl	Super Bowl XXI	Giants vs. Broncos	101,643
August 20, 1948	Soldier Field	College All-Star	Cardinals vs. All-Stars	101,220
August 28, 1942	Soldier Field	College All-Star	Bears vs. All-Stars	101,100

NFL'S TOP 10 PAID ATTENDANCE WEEKENDS

Weekend	Games	Attendance
November 21-22, 1999	15	1,027,861
December 15-17, 2001	15	1,023,788
November 12-13, 2000	15	1,013,519
November 22-26, 2001	15	1,012,296
November 19-20, 2000	15	1,011,224
September 19-20, 1999	15	1,010,820
December 29-30, 2001	15	1,010,439
December 10-11, 2000	15	1,009,732
January 6-7, 2002	15	1,009,010
September 10-11, 2000	15	1,005,960

NFL'S TOP 10 TEAM SINGLE-SEASON HOME PAID ATTENDANCE TOTALS

Year	Club	Games	Attendance
2001	Washington Redskins	8	661,970
2000	Washington Redskins	8	656,599
1980	Detroit Lions	8	634,204
1988	Buffalo Bills	8	631,818
1991	Buffalo Bills	8	631,786
1992	Buffalo Bills	8	630,978
1997	Kansas City Chiefs	8	629,763
1999	Kansas City Chiefs	8	629,569
1998	Kansas City Chiefs	8	629,209
1999	Washington Redskins	8	628,535

NFL PAID ATTENDANCE

For detailed 2001 attendance, see page 334.

Year	Regular Season		Average	Postseason	Total
2001	16,166,258	(248 games)	65,187	766,905 (12)	16,933,163
2000	#16,387,289	(248 games)	#66,078	809,132 (12)	#17,196,421
1999	16,206,640	(248 games)	65,349	793,759 (12)	17,000,399
1998	15,364,873	(240 games)	64,020	822,885 (12)	16,187,758
1997	14,967,314	(240 games)	62,364	801,879 (12)	15,769,193
1996	14,612,417	(240 games)	60,885	769,310 (12)	15,381,727
1995	15,043,562	(240 games)	62,682	790,906 (12)	15,834,468
1994	14,030,435	(224 games)	62,636	779,738 (12)	14,810,173
1993	13,966,843	(224 games)	62,352	814,607 (12)	14,781,450
1992	13,828,887	(224 games)	61,736	815,910 (12)	14,644,797
1991	13,841,459	(224 games)	61,792	813,247 (12)	14,654,706
1990	13,959,896	(224 games)	62,321	847,543 (12)	14,807,439
1989	13,625,662	(224 games)	60,829	685,771 (10)	14,311,433
1988	13,539,848	(224 games)	60,446	658,317 (10)	14,198,165
1987	*11,406,166	(210 games)	54,315	656,977 (10)	12,063,143
1986	13,588,551	(224 games)	60,663	734,002 (10)	14,322,553
1985	13,345,047	(224 games)	59,567	710,768 (10)	14,055,815
1984	13,398,112	(224 games)	59,813	665,194 (10)	14,063,306
1983	13,277,222	(224 games)	59,273	675,513 (10)	13,952,735
1982	**7,367,438	(126 games)	58,472	1,033,153 (16)	8,400,591
1981	13,606,990	(224 games)	60,745	637,763 (10)	14,244,753
1980	13,392,230	(224 games)	59,787	624,430 (10)	14,016,660
1979	13,182,039	(224 games)	58,848	630,326 (10)	13,812,365
1978	12,771,800	(224 games)	57,017	624,388 (10)	13,396,188
1977	11,018,632	(196 games)	56,218	534,925 (8)	11,553,557
1976	11,070,543	(196 games)	56,482	492,884 (8)	11,563,427
1975	10,213,193	(182 games)	56,116	475,919 (8)	10,689,112
1974	10,236,322	(182 games)	56,244	438,664 (8)	10,674,986
1973	10,730,933	(182 games)	58,961	525,433 (8)	11,256,366
1972	10,445,827	(182 games)	57,395	483,345 (8)	10,929,172
1971	10,076,035	(182 games)	55,363	483,891 (8)	10,559,926
1970	9,533,333	(182 games)	52,381	458,493 (8)	9,991,826
1969	6,096,127	(112 games) NFL	54,430	162,279 (3)	6,258,406
	2,843,373	(70 games) AFL	40,620	167,088 (3)	3,010,461
1968	5,882,313	(112 games) NFL	52,521	215,902 (3)	6,098,215
	2,635,004	(70 games) AFL	37,643	114,438 (2)	2,749,442
1967	5,938,924	(112 games) NFL	53,026	166,208 (3)	6,105,132
	2,295,697	(63 games) AFL	36,439	53,330 (1)	2,349,027
1966	5,337,044	(105 games) NFL	50,829	74,152 (1)	5,411,196
	2,160,369	(63 games) AFL	34,291	42,080 (1)	2,202,449
1965	4,634,021	(98 games) NFL	47,286	100,304 (2)	4,734,325
	1,782,384	(56 games) AFL	31,828	30,361 (1)	1,812,745
1964	4,563,049	(98 games) NFL	46,562	79,544 (1)	4,642,593
	1,447,875	(56 games) AFL	25,855	40,242 (1)	1,488,117
1963	4,163,643	(98 games) NFL	42,486	45,801 (1)	4,209,444
	1,208,697	(56 games) AFL	21,584	63,171 (2)	1,271,868
1962	4,003,421	(98 games) NFL	40,851	64,892 (1)	4,068,313
	1,147,302	(56 games) AFL	20,487	37,981 (1)	1,185,283
1961	3,986,159	(98 games) NFL	40,675	39,029 (1)	4,025,188
	1,002,657	(56 games) AFL	17,904	29,556 (1)	1,032,213
1960	3,128,296	(78 games) NFL	40,106	67,325 (1)	3,195,621
	926,156	(56 games) AFL	16,538	32,183 (1)	958,339
1959	3,140,000	(72 games)	43,617	57,545 (1)	3,197,545

Year	Total		Avg	Other	Total
1958	3,006,124	(72 games)	41,752	123,659 (2)	3,129,783
1957	2,836,318	(72 games)	39,393	119,579 (2)	2,955,897
1956	2,551,263	(72 games)	35,434	56,836 (1)	2,608,099
1955	2,521,836	(72 games)	35,026	85,693 (1)	2,607,529
1954	2,190,571	(72 games)	30,425	43,827 (1)	2,234,398
1953	2,164,585	(72 games)	30,064	54,577 (1)	2,219,162
1952	2,052,126	(72 games)	28,502	97,507 (2)	2,149,633
1951	1,913,019	(72 games)	26,570	57,522 (1)	1,970,541
1950	1,977,753	(78 games)	25,356	136,647 (3)	2,114,400
1949	1,391,735	(60 games)	23,196	27,980 (1)	1,419,715
1948	1,525,243	(60 games)	25,421	36,309 (1)	1,561,552
1947	1,837,437	(60 games)	30,624	66,268 (2)	1,903,705
1946	1,732,135	(55 games)	31,493	58,346 (1)	1,790,481
1945	1,270,401	(50 games)	25,408	32,178 (1)	1,302,579
1944	1,019,649	(50 games)	20,393	46,016 (1)	1,065,665
1943	969,128	(40 games)	24,228	71,315 (2)	1,040,443
1942	887,920	(55 games)	16,144	36,006 (1)	923,926
1941	1,108,615	(55 games)	20,157	55,870 (2)	1,164,485
1940	1,063,025	(55 games)	19,328	36,034 (1)	1,099,059
1939	1,071,200	(55 games)	19,476	32,279 (1)	1,103,479
1938	937,197	(55 games)	17,040	48,120 (1)	985,317
1937	963,039	(55 games)	17,510	15,878 (1)	978,917
1936	816,007	(54 games)	15,111	29,545 (1)	845,552
1935	638,178	(53 games)	12,041	15,000 (1)	653,178
1934	492,684	(60 games)	8,211	35,059 (1)	527,743

Record

*Players' 24-day strike reduced 224-game schedule to 210 games.
**Players' 57-day strike reduced 224-game schedule to 126 games.

75TH ANNIVERSARY ALL-TIME TEAM

Chosen by a selection committee of media and league personnel in 1994.

Position	Name	Team(s)	Ht.	Wt.	College
OFFENSE					
QB	Sammy Baugh	Washington Redskins (1937-52)	6-2	180	Texas Christian
QB	Otto Graham	Cleveland Browns (1946-55)	6-1	195	Northwestern
QB	Joe Montana	San Francisco 49ers (1979-92), Kansas City Chiefs (1993-94)	6-2	195	Notre Dame
QB	Johnny Unitas	Baltimore Colts (1956-72), San Diego Chargers (1973)	6-1	195	Louisville
RB	Jim Brown	Cleveland Browns (1957-65)	6-2	232	Syracuse
RB	Marion Motley	Cleveland Browns (1946-53), Pittsburgh Steelers (1955)	6-1	238	Nevada-Reno
RB	Bronko Nagurski	Chicago Bears (1930-37, 1943)	6-2	225	Minnesota
RB	Walter Payton	Chicago Bears (1975-87)	5-10	202	Jackson State
RB	Gale Sayers	Chicago Bears (1965-71)	6-0	200	Kansas
RB	O.J. Simpson	Buffalo Bills (1969-77), San Francisco 49ers (1978-79)	6-1	212	Southern California
RB	Steve Van Buren	Philadelphia Eagles (1944-51)	6-1	200	Louisiana State
WR	Lance Alworth	San Diego Chargers (1962-70), Dallas Cowboys (1971-72)	6-0	184	Arkansas
WR	Raymond Berry	Baltimore Colts (1955-67)	6-2	187	Southern Methodist
WR	Don Hutson	Green Bay Packers (1935-45)	6-1	180	Alabama
WR	Jerry Rice	San Francisco 49ers (1985-present)	6-2	200	Miss. Valley State
TE	Mike Ditka	Chicago Bears (1961-66), Philadelphia Eagles (1967-68), Dallas Cowboys (1969-72)	6-3	225	Pittsburgh
TE	Kellen Winslow	San Diego Chargers (1979-87)	6-5	250	Missouri
T	Roosevelt Brown	New York Giants (1953-65)	6-3	255	Morgan State
T	Forrest Gregg	Green Bay Packers (1956, 1958-70)	6-4	250	Southern Methodist
T	Anthony Muñoz	Cincinnati Bengals (1980-92)	6-6	285	Southern California
G	John Hannah	New England Patriots (1973-85)	6-3	265	Alabama
G	Jim Parker	Baltimore Colts (1957-67)	6-3	273	Ohio State
G	Gene Upshaw	Oakland Raiders (1967-81)	6-5	255	Texas A&I
C	Mel Hein	New York Giants (1931-45)	6-2	225	Washington State
C	Mike Webster	Pittsburgh Steelers (1974-88), Kansas City Chiefs (1989-90)	6-2	250	Wisconsin
DEFENSE					
DE	David (Deacon) Jones	Los Angeles Rams (1961-71), San Diego Chargers (1972-73), Washington Redskins (1974)	6-5	250	Miss. Vocational-South Carolina St.
DE	Gino Marchetti	Dallas Texans (1952), Baltimore Colts (1953-64,1966)	6-4	245	San Francisco
DE	Reggie White	Philadelphia Eagles (1985-95), Green Bay Packers (1993-present)	6-5	290	Tennessee
DT	Joe Greene	Pittsburgh Steelers (1969-81)	6-4	260	North Texas State
DT	Bob Lilly	Dallas Cowboys (1961-74)	6-5	260	Texas Christian
DT	Merlin Olsen	Los Angeles Rams (1962-76)	6-5	270	Utah State
LB	Dick Butkus	Chicago Bears (1965-73)	6-3	245	Illinois
LB	Jack Ham	Pittsburgh Steelers (1971-82)	6-1	225	Penn State
LB	Ted Hendricks	Baltimore Colts (1969-73), Green Bay Packers (1974), Oakland/L.A. Raiders (1975-83)	6-7	235	Miami
LB	Jack Lambert	Pittsburgh Steelers (1974-84)	6-4	220	Kent State
LB	Willie Lanier	Kansas City Chiefs (1967-77)	6-1	245	Morgan State
LB	Ray Nitschke	Green Bay Packers (1958-72)	6-3	235	Illinois
LB	Lawrence Taylor	New York Giants (1981-93)	6-3	243	North Carolina
CB	Mel Blount	Pittsburgh Steelers (1970-83)	6-3	205	Southern
CB	Mike Haynes	New England Patriots (1976-82), Los Angeles Raiders (1983-89)	6-2	190	Arizona State
CB	Dick (Night Train) Lane	Los Angeles Rams (1952-53), Chicago Cardinals (1954-59), Detroit Lions (1960-65)	6-2	210	Scottsbluff JC
CB	Rod Woodson	Pittsburgh Steelers (1987-96), San Francisco 49ers (1997)	6-0	200	Purdue
S	Ken Houston	Houston Oilers (1967-72), Washington Redskins (1973-80)	6-3	198	Prairie View A&M
S	Ronnie Lott	San Francisco 49ers (1981-90), Los Angeles Raiders (1991-92), New York Jets (1993-94)	6-0	200	Southern California-
S	Larry Wilson	St. Louis Cardinals (1960-72)	6-0	190	Utah
SPECIAL TEAMS					
P	Ray Guy	Oakland/L.A. Raiders (1973-86)	6-3	190	Southern Miss.
K	Jan Stenerud	Kansas City Chiefs (1967-79), Green Bay Packers (1980-83), Minnesota Vikings (1984-85)	6-2	190	Montana State
PR	Billy (White Shoes) Johnson	Houston Oilers (1974-80), Atlanta Falcons (1982-87), Washington Redskins (1988)	5-9	170	Widener
KR	Gale Sayers	Chicago Bears (1965-71)	6-0	200	Kansas

75TH ANNIVERSARY ALL-TWO-WAY TEAM
Positions

Position	Player
Quarterback, Defensive Halfback, Punter	Sammy Baugh
Center, Linebacker	Chuck Bednarik
Quarterback, Defensive Halfback, Punter	Earl (Dutch) Clark
Tackle, Defensive Tackle	George Connor
Guard, Defensive Tackle	Danny Fortmann
Center, Defensive Tackle	Mel Hein
Tackle, Defensive Tackle, Punter	Wilbur (Pete) Henry
Back, Defensive Halfback	Bill Hewitt
Fullback, Linebacker, Kicker	Clarke Hinkle
Tackle, Defensive Tackle	Cal Hubbard
End, Defensive Halfback	Don Hutson
Back, Defensive Back	George McAfee
Fullback, Linebacker	Marion Motley
Guard-Tackle, Defensive Tackle	George Musso
Fullback, Linebacker	Bronko Nagurski
Halfback, Defensive Halfback	Ernie Nevers
End, Defensive Back	Pete Pihos
Tackle, Defensive Tackle	Joe Stydahar
Running Back, Defensive Back	Steve Van Buren

50TH ANNIVERSARY TEAM
Chosen by the Hall of Fame Selection Committee in 1969.
Offense

Position	Player
Split End	Don Hutson
Tight End	John Mackey
Tackle	Cal Hubbard
Guard	Jerry Kramer
Center	Chuck Bednarik
Flanker	Elroy Hirsch
Quarterback	Johnny Unitas
Halfback	Jim Thorpe
Halfback	Gale Sayers
Fullback	Jim Brown
Kicker	Lou Groza

Defense

Position	Player
End	Gino Marchetti
Tackle	Leo Nomellini
Linebacker	Ray Nitschke
Cornerback	Dick (Night Train) Lane
Safety	Emlen Tunnell

SUPER BOWL SILVER ANNIVERSARY TEAM
Chosen by the fans in 1990 prior to Super Bowl XXV.

Position	Player
Head Coach	Vince Lombardi

Offense

Position	Player
Quarterback	Joe Montana
Running Back	Franco Harris
Running Back	Larry Csonka
Wide Receiver	Lynn Swann
Wide Receiver	Jerry Rice
Tight End	Dave Casper
Tackle	Art Shell
Tackle	Forrest Gregg
Guard	Gene Upshaw
Guard	Jerry Kramer
Center	Mike Webster

Defense

Position	Player
Defensive End	L.C. Greenwood
Defensive End	Ed (Too Tall) Jones
Defensive Tackle	Joe Greene
Defensive Tackle	Randy White
Inside Linebacker	Jack Lambert
Inside Linebacker	Mike Singletary
Outside Linebacker	Jack Ham
Outside Linebacker	Ted Hendricks
Cornerback	Ronnie Lott
Cornerback	Mel Blount
Safety	Donnie Shell
Safety	Willie Wood

Special Teams

Position	Player
Punter	Ray Guy
Kicker	Jan Stenerud
Kick Returner	John Taylor

All-Decade teams chosen by the Hall of Fame Selection Committee members.

1920s ALL-DECADE TEAM

End	Guy Chamberlin
End	Lavern Dilweg
End	George Halas
Tackle	Ed Healey
Tackle	Wilbur (Pete) Henry
Tackle	Cal Hubbard
Tackle	Steve Owen
Guard	Hunk Anderson
Guard	Walt Kiesling
Guard	Mike Michalske
Center	George Trafton
Quarterback	Jimmy Conzelman
Quarterback	John (Paddy) Driscoll
Halfback	Harold (Red) Grange
Halfback	Joe Guyon
Halfback	Earl (Curly) Lambeau
Halfback	Jim Thorpe
Fullback	Ernie Nevers

1930s ALL-DECADE TEAM

End	Bill Hewitt
End	Don Hutson
End	Wayne Millner
End	Gaynell Tinsley
Tackle	George Christensen
Tackle	Frank Cope
Tackle	Glen (Turk) Edwards
Tackle	Bill Lee
Guard	Joe Stydahar
Guard	Grover (Ox) Emerson
Guard	Dan Fortmann
Guard	Charles (Buckets) Goldenberg
Guard	Russ Letlow
Center	Mel Hein
Center	George Svendsen
Quarterback	Earl (Dutch) Clark
Quarterback	Arnie Herber
Quarterback	Cecil Isbell
Halfback	Cliff Battles
Halfback	Johnny (Blood) McNally
Halfback	Beattie Feathers
Halfback	Alphonse (Tuffy) Leemans
Halfback	Ken Strong
Fullback	Clarke Hinkle
Fullback	Bronko Nagurski

1940s ALL-DECADE TEAM

End	Jim Benton
End	Jack Ferrante
End	Ken Kavanaugh
End	Dante Lavelli
End	Pete Pihos
End	Mac Speedie
End	Ed Sprinkle
Tackle	Al Blozis
Tackle	George Connor
Tackle	Frank (Bucko) Kilroy
Tackle	Buford (Baby) Ray
Tackle	Vic Sears
Tackle	Al Wistert
Guard	Bruno Banducci
Guard	Bill Edwards
Guard	Garrard (Buster) Ramsey
Guard	Bill Willis
Guard	Len Younce
Center	Charley Brock
Center	Clyde (Bulldog) Turner
Center	Alex Wojciechowicz
Quarterback	Sammy Baugh
Quarterback	Sid Luckman
Quarterback	Bob Waterfield
Halfback	Tony Canadeo
Halfback	Bill Dudley
Halfback	George McAfee
Halfback	Charley Trippi
Halfback	Steve Van Buren
Halfback	Byron (Whizzer) White
Fullback	Pat Harder
Fullback	Marion Motley
Fullback	Bill Osmanski

1950s ALL-DECADE TEAM

Offense

End	Raymond Berry
End	Tom Fears
End	Bobby Walston
Halfback-End	Elroy (Crazylegs) Hirsch
Tackle	Roosevelt Brown
Tackle	Bob St. Clair
Guard	Dick Barwegan
Guard	Jim Parker
Guard	Dick Stanfel
Center	Chuck Bednarik
Quarterback	Otto Graham
Quarterback	Bobby Layne
Quarterback	Norm Van Brocklin
Halfback	Frank Gifford
Halfback	Ollie Matson
Halfback	Hugh McElhenny
Halfback	Lenny Moore
Fullback	Alan Ameche
Fullback	Joe Perry
Kicker	Lou Groza

Defense

End	Len Ford
End	Gino Marchetti
Tackle	Art Donovan
Tackle	Leo Nomellini
Tackle	Ernie Stautner
Linebacker	Joe Fortunato
Linebacker	Bill George
Linebacker	Sam Huff
Linebacker	Joe Schmidt
Halfback	Jack Butler

Halfback	Dick (Night Train) Lane
Safety	Jack Christiansen
Safety	Yale Lary
Safety	Emlen Tunnell

1960s ALL-DECADE TEAM

Offense

Split End	Del Shofner
Split End	Charley Taylor
Flanker	Gary Collins
Flanker	Boyd Dowler
Tight End	John Mackey
Tackle	Bob Brown
Tackle	Forrest Gregg
Tackle	Ralph Neely
Guard	Gene Hickerson
Guard	Jerry Kramer
Guard	Howard Mudd
Center	Jim Ringo
Quarterback	Sonny Jurgensen
Quarterback	Bart Starr
Quarterback	Johnny Unitas
Halfback	John David Crow
Halfback	Paul Hornung
Halfback	Leroy Kelly
Halfback	Gale Sayers
Fullback	Jim Brown
Fullback	Jim Taylor
Kicker	Jim Bakken

Defense

End	Doug Atkins
End	Willie Davis
End	David (Deacon) Jones
Tackle	Alex Karras
Tackle	Bob Lilly
Tackle	Merlin Olsen
Linebacker	Dick Butkus
Linebacker	Larry Morris
Linebacker	Ray Nitschke
Linebacker	Tommy Nobis
Linebacker	Dave Robinson
Cornerback	Herb Adderley
Cornerback	Lem Barney
Cornerback	Bobby Boyd
Safety	Eddie Meador
Safety	Larry Wilson
Safety	Willie Wood
Punter	Don Chandler

1970s ALL-DECADE TEAM
Offense
Position	Player
Wide Receiver	Harold Carmichael
Wide Receiver	Drew Pearson
Wide Receiver	Lynn Swann
Wide Receiver	Paul Warfield
Tight End	Dave Casper
Tight End	Charlie Sanders
Tackle	Dan Dierdorf
Tackle	Art Shell
Tackle	Rayfield Wright
Tackle	Ron Yary
Guard	Joe DeLamielleure
Guard	John Hannah
Guard	Larry Little
Guard	Gene Upshaw
Center	Jim Langer
Center	Mike Webster
Quarterback	Terry Bradshaw
Quarterback	Ken Stabler
Quarterback	Roger Staubach
Running Back	Earl Campbell
Running Back	Franco Harris
Running Back	Walter Payton
Running Back	O.J. Simpson
Kicker	Garo Yepremian

Defense
Position	Player
End	Carl Eller
End	L.C. Greenwood
End	Harvey Martin
End	Jack Youngblood
Tackle	Joe Greene
Tackle	Bob Lilly
Tackle	Merlin Olsen
Tackle	Alan Page
Linebacker	Bobby Bell
Linebacker	Robert Brazile
Linebacker	Dick Butkus
Linebacker	Jack Ham
Linebacker	Ted Hendricks
Linebacker	Jack Lambert
Cornerback	Willie Brown
Cornerback	Jimmy Johnson
Cornerback	Roger Wehrli
Cornerback	Louis Wright
Safety	Dick Anderson
Safety	Cliff Harris
Safety	Ken Houston
Safety	Larry Wilson
Punter	Ray Guy

1980s ALL-DECADE TEAM
Offense
Position	Player
Wide Receiver	Jerry Rice
Wide Receiver	Steve Largent
Wide Receiver	James Lofton
Wide Receiver	Art Monk
Tight End	Kellen Winslow
Tight End	Ozzie Newsome
Tackle	Anthony Munoz
Tackle	Jim Covert
Tackle	Gary Zimmerman
Tackle	Joe Jacoby
Guard	John Hannah
Guard	Russ Grimm
Guard	Bill Fralic
Guard	Mike Munchak
Center	Dwight Stephenson
Center	Mike Webster
Quarterback	Joe Montana
Quarterback	Dan Fouts
Running Back	Walter Payton
Running Back	Eric Dickerson
Running Back	Roger Craig
Running Back	John Riggins

Defense
Position	Player
End	Reggie White
End	Howie Long
End	Lee Roy Selmon
End	Bruce Smith
Tackle	Randy White
Tackle	Dan Hampton
Tackle	Keith Millard
Tackle	Dave Butz
Linebacker	Mike Singletary
Linebacker	Lawrence Taylor
Linebacker	Ted Hendricks
Linebacker	Jack Lambert
Linebacker	Andre Tippett
Linebacker	John Anderson
Linebacker	Carl Banks
Cornerback	Mike Haynes
Cornerback	Mel Blount
Cornerback	Frank Minnifield
Cornerback	Lester Hayes
Safety	Ronnie Lott
Safety	Kenny Easley
Safety	Deron Cherry
Safety	Joey Browner
Safety	Nolan Cromwell

Specialists
Punter	Sean Landeta
Punter	Reggie Roby
Kicker	Morten Andersen
Kicker	Gary Anderson
Kicker	Eddie Murray
Punt Returner	Billy (White Shoes) Johnson
Punt Returner	John Taylor
Kick Returner	Mike Nelms
Kick Returner	Rick Upchurch
Coach	Bill Walsh
Coach	Chuck Noll

1990s ALL-DECADE TEAM
Offense
Position	Player
Wide Receiver	Cris Carter
Wide Receiver	Jerry Rice
Wide Receiver	Tim Brown
Wide Receiver	Michael Irvin
Tight End	Shannon Sharpe
Tight End	Ben Coates
Tackle	William Roaf
Tackle	Gary Zimmerman
Tackle	Tony Boselli
Tackle	Richmond Webb
Guard	Bruce Matthews
Guard	Randall McDaniel
Guard	Larry Allen
Guard	Steve Wisniewski
Center	Dermontti Dawson
Center	Mark Stepnoski
Quarterback	John Elway
Quarterback	Brett Favre
Running Back	Barry Sanders
Running Back	Emmitt Smith
Running Back	Terrell Davis
Running Back	Thurman Thomas

Defense
Position	Player
End	Bruce Smith
End	Reggie White
End	Chris Doleman
End	Neil Smith
Tackle	Cortez Kennedy
Tackle	John Randle
Tackle	Warren Sapp
Tackle	Bryant Young
Linebacker	Kevin Greene
Linebacker	Junior Seau
Linebacker	Derrick Thomas
Linebacker	Cornelius Bennett
Linebacker	Hardy Nickerson
Linebacker	Levon Kirkland
Cornerback	Deion Sanders
Cornerback	Rod Woodson
Cornerback	Darrell Green
Cornerback	Aeneas Williams
Safety	Steve Atwater
Safety	LeRoy Butler
Safety	Carnell Lake
Safety	Ronnie Lott

Specialists
Position	Player
Punter	Darren Bennett
Punter	Sean Landeta
Kicker	Morten Andersen
Kicker	Gary Anderson
Punt Returner	Deion Sanders
Punt Returner	Mel Gray
Kick Returner	Michael Bates
Kick Returner	Mel Gray
Coach	Bill Parcells
Coach	Marv Levy

ALL-TIME AFL TEAM
Chosen by 1969 AFL Hall of Fame Selection Committee members.

Offense

Flanker	Lance Alworth
End	Don Maynard
Tight End	Fred Arbanas
Tackle	Ron Mix
Tackle	Jim Tyrer
Guard	Ed Budde
Guard	Billy Shaw
Center	Jim Otto
Quarterback	Joe Namath
Running Back	Clem Daniels
Running Back	Paul Lowe

Defense

End	Jerry Mays
End	Gerry Philbin
Tackle	Houston Antwine
Tackle	Tom Sestak
Linebacker	Bobby Bell
Linebacker	George Webster
Linebacker	Nick Buoniconti
Cornerback	Willie Brown
Cornerback	Dave Grayson
Safety	Johnny Robinson
Safety	George Saimes

Special Teams

Kicker	George Blanda
Punter	Jerrel Wilson

ALL-TIME NFL TEAM
Chosen by members of the Hall of Fame Selection Committee in 2000 for the book NFL's Greatest.

Offense

Wide Receiver	Don Hutson
Wide Receiver	Jerry Rice
Tight End	John Mackey
Tackle	Roosevelt Brown
Tackle	Anthony Muñoz
Guard	John Hannah
Guard	Jim Parker
Center	Mike Webster
Quarterback	Johnny Unitas
Running Back	Jim Brown
Running Back	Walter Payton

Defense

End	Deacon Jones
End	Reggie White
Tackle	Joe Greene
Tackle	Bob Lilly
Middle Linebacker	Dick Butkus
Outside Linebacker	Jack Ham
Outside Linebacker	Lawrence Taylor
Cornerback	Mel Blount
Cornerback	Dick (Night Train) Lane
Safety	Ronnie Lott
Safety	Larry Wilson

Special Teams

Kicker	Jan Stenerud
Punter	Ray Guy
Kick Returner	Gale Sayers
Punt Returner	Deion Sanders
Special Teams	Steve Tasker

AFL-NFL 1960-1984 ALL-STAR TEAM
Chosen by the Hall of Fame Selection Committee in 1985.

Offense

Quarterback	Johnny Unitas
Running Back	Jim Brown
Running Back	O.J. Simpson
Wide Receiver	Lance Alworth
Wide Receiver	Raymond Berry
Tight End	Kellen Winslow
Tight End	Forrest Gregg
Tight End	Ron Mix
Guard	Jim Parker
Guard	John Hannah
Center	Jim Otto

Defense

End	Gino Marchetti
End	Willie Davis
Tackle	Bob Lilly
Tackle	Merlin Olsen
Linebacker	Dick Butkus
Linebacker	Jack Lambert
Linebacker	Ray Nitschke
Cornerback	Willie Brown
Cornerback	Dick (Night Train) Lane
Safety	Larry Wilson
Safety	Yale Lary

Special Teams

Punter	Ray Guy
Kicker	Jan Stenerud
Kick Returner	Gale Sayers
Kick Returner	Rick Upchurch
Coach	Don Shula
Coach	Vince Lombardi

Records

Compiled by Elias Sports Bureau
The following records reflect all available official information on the National Football League from its formation in 1920 to date. Also included are all applicable records from the American Football League, 1960-69.

Individuals eligible for Rookie records are players who were in their first season of professional football and had not been on the roster of another professional football team, including teams in other leagues, for any regular-season or postseason games in a previous season. Eligible players, therefore, include those who were under contract to a National Football League club for a previous season but were terminated prior to their club's first regular-season game and not re-signed, or who were placed on Reserve/Injured (or another category of the Reserve List) prior to their club's first regular-season game and were not activated during the rest of the regular season or postseason.

INDIVIDUAL RECORDS

SERVICE
Most Seasons
- 26 George Blanda, Chi. Bears, 1949, 1950-58; Baltimore, 1950; Houston, 1960-66; Oakland, 1967-1975
- 21 Earl Morrall, San Francisco, 1956; Pittsburgh, 1957-58; Detroit, 1958-1964; N.Y. Giants, 1965-67; Baltimore, 1968-1971; Miami, 1972-76
- 20 Jim Marshall, Cleveland, 1960; Minnesota, 1961-1979
     Jackie Slater, L.A. Rams, 1976-1994; St. Louis, 1995
     Morten Andersen, New Orleans, 1982-1994; Atlanta, 1995-2000; N.Y. Giants, 2001
     Gary Anderson, Pittsburgh, 1982-1994; Philadelphia, 1995-96; San Francisco, 1997; Minnesota, 1998-2001

Most Seasons, One Club
- 20 Jackie Slater, L.A. Rams, 1976-1994; St. Louis, 1995
- 19 Jim Marshall, Minnesota, 1961-1979
     Darrell Green, Washington, 1983-2001
     Bruce Matthews, Houston, 1983-1996; Tennessee, 1997-2001
- 18 Jim Hart, St. Louis, 1966-1983
     Jeff Van Note, Atlanta, 1969-1986
     Pat Leahy, N.Y. Jets, 1974-1991

Most Games Played, Career
- 340 George Blanda, Chi. Bears, 1949, 1950-58; Baltimore, 1950; Houston, 1960-66; Oakland, 1967-1975
- 309 Gary Anderson, Pittsburgh, 1982-1994; Philadelphia, 1995-96; San Francisco, 1997; Minnesota, 1998-2001
- 308 Morten Andersen, New Orleans, 1982-1994; Atlanta, 1995-2000; N.Y. Giants, 2001

Most Consecutive Games Played, Career
- 282 Jim Marshall, Cleveland, 1960; Minnesota, 1961-1979
- 240 Mick Tingelhoff, Minnesota, 1962-1978
- 234 Jim Bakken, St. Louis, 1962-1978
     Morten Andersen, New Orleans, 1987-1994; Atlanta, 1995-2000; N.Y. Giants, 2001 (current)
     Gary Anderson, Pittsburgh, 1987-1994; Philadelphia, 1995-96; San Francisco, 1997; Minnesota, 1998-2001 (current)

SCORING
Most Seasons Leading League
- 5 Don Hutson, Green Bay, 1940-44
     Gino Cappelletti, Boston, 1961, 1963-66
- 3 Earl (Dutch) Clark, Portsmouth, 1932; Detroit, 1935-36
     Pat Harder, Chi. Cardinals, 1947-49
     Paul Hornung, Green Bay, 1959-1961
- 2 Jack Manders, Chi. Bears, 1934, 1937
     Gordy Soltau, San Francisco, 1952-53

Doak Walker, Detroit, 1950, 1955
Gene Mingo, Denver, 1960, 1962
Jim Turner, N.Y. Jets, 1968-69
Fred Cox, Minnesota, 1969-1970
Chester Marcol, Green Bay, 1972, 1974
John Smith, New England, 1979-1980
Marshall Faulk, St. Louis, 2000-01

Most Consecutive Seasons Leading League
- 5 Don Hutson, Green Bay, 1940-44
- 4 Gino Cappelletti, Boston, 1963-66
- 3 Pat Harder, Chi. Cardinals, 1947-49
     Paul Hornung, Green Bay, 1959-1961

POINTS
Most Points, Career
- 2,133 Gary Anderson, Pittsburgh, 1982-1994; Philadelphia, 1995-96; San Francisco, 1997; Minnesota, 1998-2001 (705-pat, 476-fg)
- 2,036 Morten Andersen, New Orleans, 1982-1994; Atlanta, 1995-2000; N.Y. Giants, 2001 (644-pat, 464-fg)
- 2,002 George Blanda, Chi. Bears, 1949, 1950-58; Baltimore, 1950; Houston, 1960-66; Oakland, 1967-1975 (9-td, 943-pat, 335-fg)

Most Points, Season
- 176 Paul Hornung, Green Bay, 1960 (15-td, 41-pat, 15-fg)
- 164 Gary Anderson, Minnesota, 1998 (59-pat, 35-fg)
- 161 Mark Moseley, Washington, 1983 (62-pat, 33-fg)

Most Points, No Touchdowns, Season
- 164 Gary Anderson, Minnesota, 1998 (59-pat, 35-fg)
- 161 Mark Moseley, Washington, 1983 (62-pat, 33-fg)
- 149 Chip Lohmiller, Washington, 1991 (56-pat, 31-fg)

Most Seasons, 100 or More Points
- 13 Gary Anderson, Pittsburgh, 1983-85, 1988, 1991-94; Philadelphia, 1996; San Francisco, 1997; Minnesota, 1998-2000
- 12 Morten Andersen, New Orleans, 1985-89, 1991-94; Atlanta, 1995, 1997-98
- 11 Nick Lowery, Kansas City, 1981, 1983-86, 1988-1993

Most Points, Rookie, Season
- 144 Kevin Butler, Chicago, 1985 (51-pat, 31-fg)
- 132 Gale Sayers, Chicago, 1965 (22-td)
- 128 Doak Walker, Detroit, 1950 (11-td, 38-pat, 8-fg)
     Chester Marcol, Green Bay, 1972 (29-pat, 33-fg)

Most Points, Game
- 40 Ernie Nevers, Chi. Cardinals vs. Chi. Bears, Nov. 28, 1929 (6-td, 4-pat)
- 36 Dub Jones, Cleveland vs. Chi. Bears, Nov. 25, 1951 (6-td)
     Gale Sayers, Chicago vs. San Francisco, Dec. 12, 1965 (6-td)
- 33 Paul Hornung, Green Bay vs. Baltimore, Oct. 8, 1961 (4-td, 6-pat, 1-fg)

Most Consecutive Games Scoring
- 286 Morten Andersen, New Orleans, 1982-1994; Atlanta, 1995-2000; N.Y. Giants, 2001 (current)
- 186 Jim Breech, Oakland, 1979; Cincinnati, 1980-1992
- 155 Ray Wersching, San Francisco, 1977-1987

TOUCHDOWNS
Most Seasons Leading League
- 8 Don Hutson, Green Bay, 1935-38, 1941-44
- 3 Jim Brown, Cleveland, 1958-59, 1963
     Lance Alworth, San Diego, 1964-66
     Emmitt Smith, Dallas, 1992, 1994-95
- 2 By many players

Most Consecutive Seasons Leading League
- 4 Don Hutson, Green Bay, 1935-38, 1941-44
- 3 Lance Alworth, San Diego, 1964-66
- 2 By many players

Most Touchdowns, Career
- 196 Jerry Rice, San Francisco, 1985-2000; Oakland, 2001 (10-r, 185-p, 1-ret)
- 159 Emmitt Smith, Dallas, 1990-2001 (148-r, 11-p)
- 145 Marcus Allen, L.A. Raiders, 1982-1992; Kansas City, 1993-97 (123-r, 21-p, 1-ret)

Most Touchdowns, Season
- 26 Marshall Faulk, St. Louis, 2000 (18-r, 8-p)
- 25 Emmitt Smith, Dallas, 1995 (25-r)
- 24 John Riggins, Washington, 1983 (24-r)

Most Touchdowns, Rookie, Season
- 22 Gale Sayers, Chicago, 1965 (14-r, 6-p, 2-ret)
- 20 Eric Dickerson, L.A. Rams, 1983 (18-r, 2-p)
- 17 Randy Moss, Minnesota, 1998 (17-p)
-     Fred Taylor, Jacksonville, 1998 (14-r, 3-p)
-     Edgerrin James, Indianapolis, 1999 (13-r, 4-p)

Most Touchdowns, Game
- 6 Ernie Nevers, Chi. Cardinals vs. Chi. Bears, Nov. 28, 1929 (6-r)
-    Dub Jones, Cleveland vs. Chi. Bears, Nov. 25, 1951 (4-r, 2-p)
-    Gale Sayers, Chicago vs. San Francisco, Dec. 12, 1965 (4-r, 1-p, 1-ret)
- 5 Bob Shaw, Chi. Cardinals vs. Baltimore, Oct. 2, 1950 (5-p)
-    Jim Brown, Cleveland vs. Baltimore, Nov. 1, 1959 (5-r)
-    Abner Haynes, Dall. Texans vs. Oakland, Nov. 26, 1961 (4-r, 1-p)
-    Billy Cannon, Houston vs. N.Y. Titans, Dec. 10, 1961 (3-r, 2-p)
-    Cookie Gilchrist, Buffalo vs. N.Y. Jets, Dec. 8, 1963 (5-r)
-    Paul Hornung, Green Bay vs. Baltimore, Dec. 12, 1965 (3-r, 2-p)
-    Kellen Winslow, San Diego vs. Oakland, Nov. 22, 1981 (5-p)
-    Jerry Rice, San Francisco vs. Atlanta, Oct. 14, 1990 (5-p)
-    James Stewart, Jacksonville vs. Philadelphia, Oct. 12, 1997 (5-r)
- 4 By many players. Last time: Marshall Faulk, St. Louis vs. Indianapolis, Dec. 30, 2001 (3-r, 1-p)

Most Consecutive Games Scoring Touchdowns
- 18 Lenny Moore, Baltimore, 1963-65
- 14 O.J. Simpson, Buffalo, 1975
- 13 John Riggins, Washington, 1982-83
-    George Rogers, Washington, 1985-86
-    Jerry Rice, San Francisco, 1986-87

POINTS AFTER TOUCHDOWN
Most Seasons Leading League
- 8 George Blanda, Chi. Bears, 1956; Houston, 1961-62; Oakland, 1967-69, 1972, 1974
- 4 Bob Waterfield, Cleveland, 1945; Los Angeles, 1946, 1950, 1952
- 3 Earl (Dutch) Clark, Portsmouth, 1932; Detroit, 1935-36 Jack Manders, Chi. Bears, 1933-35
-    Don Hutson, Green Bay, 1941-42, 1945

Most (Kicking) Points After Touchdown Attempted, Career
- 959 George Blanda, Chi. Bears, 1949, 1950-58; Baltimore, 1950; Houston, 1960-66; Oakland, 1967-1975
- 711 Gary Anderson, Pittsburgh, 1982-1994; Philadelphia, 1995-96; San Francisco, 1997; Minnesota, 1998-2001
- 657 Lou Groza, Cleveland, 1950-59, 1961-67

Most (Kicking) Points After Touchdown Attempted, Season
- 70 Uwe von Schamann, Miami, 1984
- 65 George Blanda, Houston, 1961

- 64 Jeff Wilkins, St. Louis, 1999

Most (Kicking) Points After Touchdown Attempted, Game
- 10 Charlie Gogolak, Washington vs. N.Y. Giants, Nov. 27, 1966
- 9 Pat Harder, Chi. Cardinals vs. N.Y. Giants, Oct. 17, 1948; vs. N.Y. Bulldogs, Nov. 13, 1949
-    Bob Waterfield, Los Angeles vs. Baltimore, Oct. 22, 1950
-    Bob Thomas, Chicago vs. Green Bay, Dec. 7, 1980
- 8 By many players

Most (One-Point) Points After Touchdown, Career
- 943 George Blanda, Chi. Bears, 1949, 1950-58; Baltimore, 1950; Houston, 1960-66; Oakland, 1967-1975
- 705 Gary Anderson, Pittsburgh, 1982-1994; Philadelphia, 1995-96; San Francisco, 1997; Minnesota, 1998-2001
- 644 Morten Andersen, New Orleans, 1982-1994; Atlanta, 1995-2000; N.Y. Giants, 2001

Most (One-Point) Points After Touchdown, Season
- 66 Uwe von Schamann, Miami, 1984
- 64 George Blanda, Houston, 1961
-    Jeff Wilkins, St. Louis, 1999
- 62 Mark Moseley, Washington, 1983

Most (One-Point) Points After Touchdown, Game
- 9 Pat Harder, Chi. Cardinals vs. N.Y. Giants, Oct. 17, 1948
-    Bob Waterfield, Los Angeles vs. Baltimore, Oct. 22, 1950
-    Charlie Gogolak, Washington vs. N.Y. Giants, Nov. 27, 1966
- 8 By many players

Most Consecutive (Kicking) Points After Touchdown
- 344 Jason Elam, Denver, 1993-2001 (current)
- 301 Norm Johnson, Atlanta, 1991-94; Pittsburgh, 1995-98; Philadelphia, 1999
- 250 Eddie Murray, Detroit, 1988-1991; Kansas City, 1992; Tampa Bay, 1992; Dallas, 1993; Philadelphia, 1994; Washington, 1995; Minnesota, 1997

Highest (Kicking) Points After Touchdown Percentage, Career (200 points after touchdown)
- 99.73 Jason Elam, Denver, 1993-2001 (369-368)
- 99.57 Todd Peterson, Arizona, 1994; Seattle, 1995-99; Kansas City, 2000-01 (234-233)
- 99.43 Tommy Davis, San Francisco, 1959-1969 (350-348)

Most (Kicking) Points After Touchdown, No Misses, Season
- 64 Jeff Wilkins, St. Louis, 1999
- 59 Gary Anderson, Minnesota, 1998
- 58 Jason Elam, Denver, 1998
-    Jeff Wilkins, St. Louis, 2001

Most (Kicking) Points After Touchdown, No Misses, Game
- 9 Pat Harder, Chi. Cardinals vs. N.Y. Giants, Oct. 17, 1948
-    Bob Waterfield, Los Angeles vs. Baltimore, Oct. 22, 1950
- 8 By many players

Most Two-Point Conversions, Career
Two-point conversions include AFL (1960-69) and NFL (since 1994).
- 6 Terance Mathis, Atlanta, 1994-2001
- 5 Cris Carter, Minnesota, 1994-2001
-    Rob Moore, N.Y. Jets, 1994; Arizona, 1995-99
-    Willie Jackson, Jacksonville, 1995-97; Cincinnati, 1998-99; New Orleans, 2000-01
-    Keenan McCardell, Cleveland, 1994-95; Jacksonville, 1996-2001
- 4 Gino Cappelletti, Boston, 1960-69
-    Jerry Rice, San Francisco, 1994-2000; Oakland, 2001
-    Lamar Smith, Seattle, 1994-97; New Orleans, 1998-99; Miami, 2000-01

Floyd Turner, Indianapolis, 1994-95; Baltimore,
1996, 1998
Marvin Harrison, Indianapolis, 1996-2001
Jackie Harris, Tampa Bay, 1994-97; Tennessee,
1998-99; Dallas, 2000-01
Marcus Pollard, Indianapolis, 1995-2001
Marshall Faulk, Indianapolis, 1994-98; St. Louis,
1999-2001

Most Two-Point Conversions, Season
3   Gino Cappelletti, Boston, 1960
Richie Lucas, Buffalo, 1961
Ronnie Harmon, San Diego, 1994
Haywood Jeffires, Houston, 1994
Tom Tupa, Cleveland, 1994
Terance Mathis, Atlanta, 1995
Lamar Smith, Seattle, 1996
Cris Carter, Minnesota, 1997
Terrell Davis, Denver, 1997
James Stewart, Detroit, 2000
2   By many players

Most Two-Point Conversions, Game
2   Brett Perriman, Detroit vs. Green Bay, Nov. 6, 1994
Michael Jackson, Baltimore vs. New England,
Oct. 6, 1996
Terrell Davis, Denver vs. Atlanta, Sept. 28, 1997
Charles Johnson, Pittsburgh vs. Tennessee,
Nov. 1, 1998
Marshall Faulk, St. Louis vs. Atlanta, Oct. 15, 2000

FIELD GOALS

Most Seasons Leading League
5   Lou Groza, Cleveland, 1950, 1952-54, 1957
4   Jack Manders, Chi. Bears, 1933-34, 1936-37
Ward Cuff, N.Y. Giants, 1938-39, 1943; Green Bay,
1947
Mark Moseley, Washington, 1976-77, 1979, 1982
3   Bob Waterfield, Los Angeles, 1947, 1949, 1951
Gino Cappelletti, Boston, 1961, 1963-64
Fred Cox, Minnesota, 1965, 1969-1970
Jan Stenerud, Kansas City, 1967, 1970, 1975

Most Consecutive Seasons Leading League
3   Lou Groza, Cleveland, 1952-54
2   Jack Manders, Chi. Bears, 1933-34
Armand Niccolai, Pittsburgh, 1935-36
Jack Manders, Chi. Bears, 1936-37
Ward Cuff, N.Y. Giants, 1938-39
Clark Hinkle, Green Bay, 1940-41
Cliff Patton, Philadelphia, 1948-49
Gino Cappelletti, Boston, 1963-64
Jim Turner, N.Y. Jets, 1968-69
Fred Cox, Minnesota, 1969-1970
Mark Moseley, Washington, 1976-77
Chip Lohmiller, Washington, 1991-92
Pete Stoyanovich, Miami, 1991-92

Most Field Goals Attempted, Career
637   George Blanda, Chi. Bears, 1949, 1950-58; Baltimore,
1950; Houston, 1960-66; Oakland, 1967-1975
596   Gary Anderson, Pittsburgh, 1982-1994; Philadelphia,
1995-96; San Francisco, 1997; Minnesota,
1998-2001
590   Morten Andersen, New Orleans, 1982-1994; Atlanta,
1995-2000; N.Y. Giants, 2001

Most Field Goals Attempted, Season
49   Bruce Gossett, Los Angeles, 1966
Curt Knight, Washington, 1971
48   Chester Marcol, Green Bay, 1972
47   Jim Turner, N.Y. Jets, 1969
David Ray, Los Angeles, 1973
Mark Moseley, Washington, 1983

Most Field Goals Attempted, Game
9   Jim Bakken, St. Louis vs. Pittsburgh, Sept. 24, 1967
8   Lou Michaels, Pittsburgh vs. St. Louis, Dec. 2, 1962
Garo Yepremian, Detroit vs. Minnesota, Nov. 13, 1966
Jim Turner, N.Y. Jets vs. Buffalo, Nov. 3, 1968
7   By many players

Most Field Goals, Career
476   Gary Anderson, Pittsburgh, 1982-1994; Philadelphia,
1995-96; San Francisco, 1997; Minnesota,
1998-2001
464   Morten Andersen, New Orleans, 1982-1994; Atlanta,
1995-2000; N.Y. Giants, 2001
383   Nick Lowery, New England, 1978; Kansas City,
1980-1993; N.Y. Jets, 1994-1996

Most Field Goals, Season
39   Olindo Mare, Miami, 1999
37   John Kasay, Carolina, 1996
36   Cary Blanchard, Indianapolis, 1996
Al Del Greco, Tennessee, 1998

Most Field Goals, Rookie, Season
35   Ali Haji-Sheikh, N.Y. Giants, 1983
34   Richie Cunningham, Dallas, 1997
33   Chester Marcol, Green Bay, 1972

Most Field Goals, Game
7   Jim Bakken, St. Louis vs. Pittsburgh, Sept. 24, 1967
Rich Karlis, Minnesota vs. L.A. Rams, Nov. 5, 1989
(OT)
Chris Boniol, Dallas vs. Green Bay, Nov. 18, 1996
6   Gino Cappelletti, Boston vs. Denver, Oct. 4, 1964
Garo Yepremian, Detroit vs. Minnesota, Nov. 13,
1966
Jim Turner, N.Y. Jets vs. Buffalo, Nov. 3, 1968
Tom Dempsey, Philadelphia vs. Houston,
Nov. 12, 1972
Bobby Howfield, N.Y. Jets vs. New Orleans,
Dec. 3, 1972
Jim Bakken, St. Louis vs. Atlanta, Dec. 9, 1973
Joe Danelo, N.Y. Giants vs. Seattle, Oct. 18, 1981
Ray Wersching, San Francisco vs. New Orleans,
Oct. 16, 1983
Gary Anderson, Pittsburgh vs. Denver, Oct. 23, 1988
John Carney, San Diego vs. Seattle, Sept. 5, 1993
John Carney, San Diego vs. Houston, Sept. 19, 1993
Doug Pelfrey, Cincinnati vs. Seattle, Nov. 6, 1994 (OT)
Norm Johnson, Atlanta vs. New Orleans,
Nov. 13, 1994
Jeff Wilkins, San Francisco vs. Atlanta,
Sept. 29, 1996
Steve Christie, Buffalo vs. N.Y. Jets, Oct. 20, 1996
Greg Davis, San Diego vs. Oakland, Oct. 5, 1997
Gary Anderson, Minnesota vs. Baltimore,
Dec. 13, 1998
Olindo Mare, Miami vs. New England, Oct. 17, 1999
Jason Hanson, Detroit vs. Minnesota, Oct. 17, 1999
5   By many players

Most Field Goals, One Quarter
4   Garo Yepremian, Detroit vs. Minnesota, Nov. 13, 1966
(second quarter)
Curt Knight, Washington vs. N.Y. Giants, Nov. 15, 1970
(second quarter)
Roger Ruzek, Dallas vs. N.Y. Giants, Nov. 2, 1987
(fourth quarter)
Cary Blanchard, Indianapolis vs. Buffalo,
Sept. 21 1997 (second quarter)
3   By many players

Most Consecutive Games Scoring Field Goals
38   Matt Stover, Baltimore, 1999-2001
31   Fred Cox, Minnesota, 1968-1970
28   Jim Turner, N.Y. Jets, 1970; Denver, 1971-72
Chip Lohmiller, Washington, 1988-1990

Most Consecutive Field Goals
- 40 Gary Anderson, San Francisco, 1997; Minnesota, 1998
- 31 Fuad Reveiz, Minnesota, 1994-95
- 30 Jeff Wilkins, St. Louis, 1999-2001

Longest Field Goal
- 63 Tom Dempsey, New Orleans vs. Detroit, Nov. 8, 1970
  Jason Elam, Denver vs. Jacksonville, Oct. 25, 1998
- 60 Steve Cox, Cleveland vs. Cincinnati, Oct. 21, 1984
  Morten Andersen, New Orleans vs. Chicago, Oct. 27, 1991
- 59 Tony Franklin, Philadelphia vs. Dallas, Nov. 12, 1979
  Pete Stoyanovich, Miami vs. N.Y. Jets, Nov. 12, 1989
  Steve Christie, Buffalo vs. Miami, Sept. 26, 1993
  Morten Andersen, Atlanta vs. San Francisco, Dec. 24, 1995

Highest Field Goal Percentage, Career (100 field goals)
- 87.69 Mike Vanderjagt, Indianapolis, 1998-2001 (130-114)
- 84.47 Olindo Mare, Miami, 1997-2001 (161-136)
- 81.46 John Carney, Tampa Bay, 1988-89; L.A. Rams, 1990; San Diego, 1990-2000; New Orleans, 2001 (356-290)

Highest Field Goal Percentage, Season (Qualifiers)
- 100.00 Tony Zendejas, L.A. Rams, 1991 (17-17)
  Gary Anderson, Minnesota, 1998 (35-35)
  Jeff Wilkins, St. Louis, 2000 (17-17)
- 96.43 Chris Boniol, Dallas, 1995 (28-27)
- 96.30 Norm Johnson, Atlanta, 1993 (27-26)
  Pete Stoyanovich, Kansas City, 1997 (27-26)

Most Field Goals, No Misses, Game
- 7 Rich Karlis, Minnesota vs. L.A. Rams, Nov. 5, 1989 (OT)
  Chris Boniol, Dallas vs. Green Bay, Nov. 18, 1996
- 6 Gino Cappelletti, Boston vs. Denver, Oct. 4, 1964
  Joe Danelo, N.Y. Giants vs. Seattle, Oct. 18, 1981
  Ray Wersching, San Francisco vs. New Orleans, Oct. 16, 1983
  Gary Anderson, Pittsburgh vs. Denver, Oct. 23, 1988
  John Carney, San Diego vs. Seattle, Sept. 5, 1993
  John Carney, San Diego vs. Houston, Sept. 19, 1993
  Doug Pelfrey, Cincinnati vs. Seattle, Nov. 6, 1994 (OT)
  Norm Johnson, Atlanta vs. New Orleans, Nov. 13, 1994
  Jeff Wilkins, San Francisco vs. Atlanta, Sept. 29, 1996
  Greg Davis, San Diego vs. Oakland, Oct. 5, 1997
  Gary Anderson, Minnesota vs. Baltimore, Dec. 13, 1998
  Olindo Mare, Miami vs. New England, Oct. 17, 1999
- 5 By many players

Most Field Goals, 50 or More Yards, Career
- 39 Morten Andersen, New Orleans, 1982-1994; Atlanta, 1995-2000; N.Y. Giants, 2001
- 25 Jason Elam, Denver, 1993-2001
- 22 Nick Lowery, New England, 1978; Kansas City, 1980-1993; N.Y. Jets, 1994-96

Most Field Goals, 50 or More Yards, Season
- 8 Morten Andersen, Atlanta, 1995
- 6 Dean Biasucci, Indianapolis, 1988
  Chris Jacke, Green Bay, 1993
  Tony Zendejas, L.A. Rams, 1993
  Mike Vanderjagt, Indianapolis, 1998
- 5 Fred Steinfort, Denver, 1980
  Norm Johnson, Seattle, 1986
  Kevin Butler, Chicago, 1993
  Jason Elam, Denver, 1995
  Cary Blanchard, Indianapolis, 1996
  Jason Elam, Denver, 1999
  Martin Gramatica, Tampa Bay, 2000

Most Field Goals, 50 or More Yards, Game
- 3 Morten Andersen, Atlanta vs. New Orleans, Dec. 10, 1995
- 2 By many players. Last time: Paul Edinger, Chicago vs. Detroit, Dec. 24, 2000

SAFETIES

Most Safeties, Career
- 4 Ted Hendricks, Baltimore, 1969-1973; Green Bay, 1974; Oakland, 1975-1981; L.A. Raiders, 1982-83
  Doug English, Detroit, 1975-79, 1981-85
- 3 Bill McPeak, Pittsburgh, 1949-1957
  Charlie Krueger, San Francisco, 1959-1973
  Ernie Stautner, Pittsburgh, 1950-1963
  Jim Katcavage, N.Y. Giants, 1956-1968
  Roger Brown, Detroit, 1960-66; Los Angeles, 1967-69
  Bruce Maher, Detroit, 1960-67; N.Y. Giants, 1968-69
  Ron McDole, St. Louis, 1961; Houston, 1962; Buffalo, 1963-1970; Washington, 1971-78
  Alan Page, Minnesota, 1967-1978; Chicago, 1979-1981
  Lyle Alzado, Denver, 1971-78; Cleveland, 1979-1981; L.A. Raiders, 1982-85
  Rulon Jones, Denver, 1980-88
  Steve McMichael, New England, 1980; Chicago, 1981-1993; Green Bay, 1994
  Kevin Greene, L.A. Rams, 1985-1992; Pittsburgh, 1993-95; Carolina, 1996, 1998-99; San Francisco, 1997
  Burt Grossman, San Diego, 1989-1993; Philadelphia, 1994
  Eric Swann, Phoenix, 1991-93; Arizona, 1994-99; Carolina, 2000
  Dan Saleaumua, Detroit, 1987-88; Kansas City, 1989-1996; Seattle, 1997-98
  Derrick Thomas, Kansas City, 1989-1999
  Bryant Young, San Francisco, 1994-2001
- 2 By many players

Most Safeties, Season
- 2 Tom Nash, Green Bay, 1932
  Roger Brown, Detroit, 1962
  Ron McDole, Buffalo, 1964
  Alan Page, Minnesota, 1971
  Fred Dryer, Los Angeles, 1973
  Benny Barnes, Dallas, 1973
  James Young, Houston, 1977
  Doug English, Detroit, 1983
  Don Blackmon, New England, 1985
  Tim Harris, Green Bay, 1988
  Brian Jordan, Atlanta, 1991
  Burt Grossman, San Diego, 1992
  Rod Stephens, Seattle, 1993
  Bryant Young, San Francisco, 1996

Most Safeties, Game
- 2 Fred Dryer, Los Angeles vs. Green Bay, Oct. 21, 1973

RUSHING

Most Seasons Leading League
- 8 Jim Brown, Cleveland, 1957-1961, 1963-65
- 4 Steve Van Buren, Philadelphia, 1945, 1947-49
  O.J. Simpson, Buffalo, 1972-73, 1975-76
  Eric Dickerson, L.A. Rams, 1983-84, 1986; Indianapolis, 1988
  Emmitt Smith, Dallas, 1991-93, 1995
  Barry Sanders, Detroit, 1990, 1994, 1996-97
- 3 Earl Campbell, Houston, 1978-1980

Most Consecutive Seasons Leading League
- 5 Jim Brown, Cleveland, 1957-1961

3 Steve Van Buren, Philadelphia, 1947-49
Jim Brown, Cleveland, 1963-65
Earl Campbell, Houston, 1978-1980
Emmitt Smith, Dallas, 1991-93
2 Bill Paschal, N.Y. Giants, 1943-44
Joe Perry, San Francisco, 1953-54
Jim Nance, Boston, 1966-67
Leroy Kelly, Cleveland, 1967-68
O.J. Simpson, Buffalo, 1972-73; 1975-76
Eric Dickerson, L.A. Rams, 1983-84
Barry Sanders, Detroit, 1996-97
Edgerrin James, Indianapolis, 1999-2000

ATTEMPTS

Most Seasons Leading League
6 Jim Brown, Cleveland, 1958-59, 1961, 1963-65
4 Steve Van Buren, Philadelphia, 1947-1950
Walter Payton, Chicago, 1976-79
3 Cookie Gilchrist, Buffalo, 1963-64; Denver, 1965
Jim Nance, Boston, 1966-67, 1969
O.J. Simpson, Buffalo, 1973-75
Eric Dickerson, L.A. Rams, 1983, 1986;
Indianapolis, 1988
Emmitt Smith, Dallas, 1991, 1994-95

Most Consecutive Seasons Leading League
4 Steve Van Buren, Philadelphia, 1947-1950
Walter Payton, Chicago, 1976-79
3 Jim Brown, Cleveland, 1963-65
Cookie Gilchrist, Buffalo, 1963-64; Denver, 1965
O.J. Simpson, Buffalo, 1973-75
2 By many players

Most Attempts, Career
3,838 Walter Payton, Chicago, 1975-1987
3,798 Emmitt Smith, Dallas, 1990-2001
3,062 Barry Sanders, Detroit, 1989-1998

Most Attempts, Season
410 Jamal Anderson, Atlanta, 1998
407 James Wilder, Tampa Bay, 1984
404 Eric Dickerson, L.A. Rams, 1986

Most Attempts, Rookie, Season
390 Eric Dickerson, L.A. Rams, 1983
378 George Rogers, New Orleans, 1981
369 Edgerrin James, Indianapolis, 1999

Most Attempts, Game
45 Jamie Morris, Washington vs. Cincinnati,
Dec. 17, 1988 (OT)
43 Butch Woolfolk, N.Y. Giants vs. Philadelphia,
Nov. 20, 1983
James Wilder, Tampa Bay vs. Green Bay,
Sept. 30, 1984 (OT)
42 James Wilder, Tampa Bay vs. Pittsburgh,
Oct. 30, 1983
Terrell Davis, Denver vs. Buffalo, Oct. 26, 1997 (OT)

YARDS GAINED

Most Yards Gained, Career
16,726 Walter Payton, Chicago, 1975-1987
16,187 Emmitt Smith, Dallas, 1990-2001
15,269 Barry Sanders, Detroit, 1989-1998

Most Seasons, 1,000 or More Yards Rushing
11 Emmitt Smith, Dallas, 1991-2001
10 Walter Payton, Chicago, 1976-1981, 1983-86
Barry Sanders, Detroit, 1989-1998
8 Franco Harris, Pittsburgh, 1972, 1974-79, 1983
Tony Dorsett, Dallas, 1977-1981, 1983-85
Thurman Thomas, Buffalo, 1989-1996
Jerome Bettis, L.A. Rams, 1993-94; Pittsburgh,
1996-2001
7 Jim Brown, Cleveland, 1958-1961, 1963-65

Eric Dickerson, L.A. Rams, 1983-86; L.A. Rams-
Indianapolis, 1987; Indianapolis, 1988-89
Ricky Watters, San Francisco, 1992; Philadelphia
1995-97; Seattle, 1998-2000
Marshall Faulk, Indianapolis, 1994-95, 1997-98;
St. Louis, 1999-2001
Curtis Martin, New England, 1995-97; N.Y. Jets,
1998-2001

Most Consecutive Seasons, 1,000 or More Yards Rushing
11 Emmitt Smith, Dallas, 1991-2001 (current)
10 Barry Sanders, Detroit, 1989-1998
8 Thurman Thomas, Buffalo, 1989-1996

Most Yards Gained, Season
2,105 Eric Dickerson, L.A. Rams, 1984
2,053 Barry Sanders, Detroit, 1997
2,008 Terrell Davis, Denver, 1998

Most Yards Gained, Rookie, Season
1,808 Eric Dickerson, L.A. Rams, 1983
1,674 George Rogers, New Orleans, 1981
1,605 Ottis Anderson, St. Louis, 1979

Most Yards Gained, Game
278 Corey Dillon, Cincinnati vs. Denver, Oct. 22, 2000
275 Walter Payton, Chicago vs. Minnesota,
Nov. 20, 1977
273 O.J. Simpson, Buffalo vs. Detroit, Nov. 25, 1976

Most Games, 200 or More Yards Rushing, Career
6 O.J. Simpson, Buffalo, 1969-1977; San Francisco,
1978-79
4 Jim Brown, Cleveland, 1957-1965
Earl Campbell, Houston, 1978-1984; New Orleans,
1984-85
Barry Sanders, Detroit, 1989-1998
3 Eric Dickerson, L.A. Rams, 1983-87; Indianapolis,
1987-1991; L.A. Raiders, 1992; Atlanta, 1993
Greg Bell, Buffalo, 1984-87; L.A. Rams, 1987-89;
L.A. Raiders, 1990
Terrell Davis, Denver, 1995-2001
Corey Dillon, Cincinnati, 1997-2001
Marshall Faulk, Indianapolis, 1994-98; St. Louis,
1999-2001

Most Games, 200 or More Yards Rushing, Season
4 Earl Campbell, Houston, 1980
3 O.J. Simpson, Buffalo, 1973
2 Jim Brown, Cleveland, 1963
O.J. Simpson, Buffalo, 1976
Walter Payton, Chicago, 1977
Eric Dickerson, L.A. Rams, 1984
Greg Bell, L.A. Rams, 1989
Terrell Davis, Denver, 1997
Barry Sanders, Detroit, 1997
Corey Dillon, Cincinnati, 2000
Marshall Faulk, St. Louis, 2000

Most Consecutive Games, 200 or More Yards Rushing
2 O.J. Simpson, Buffalo, 1973, 1976
Earl Campbell, Houston, 1980

Most Games, 100 or More Yards Rushing, Career
77 Walter Payton, Chicago, 1975-1987
76 Barry Sanders, Detroit, 1989-1998
74 Emmitt Smith, Dallas, 1990-2001

Most Games, 100 or More Yards Rushing, Season
14 Barry Sanders, Detroit, 1997
12 Eric Dickerson, L.A. Rams, 1984
Barry Foster, Pittsburgh, 1992
Jamal Anderson, Atlanta, 1998
11 O.J. Simpson, Buffalo, 1973
Earl Campbell, Houston, 1979
Marcus Allen, L.A. Raiders, 1985
Eric Dickerson, L.A. Rams, 1986
Emmitt Smith, Dallas, 1995
Terrell Davis, Denver, 1998

Most Consecutive Games, 100 or More Yards Rushing
- 14 Barry Sanders, Detroit, 1997
- 11 Marcus Allen, L.A. Raiders, 1985-86
- 9 Walter Payton, Chicago, 1985
   Fred Taylor, Jacksonville, 2000

Longest Run From Scrimmage
- 99 Tony Dorsett, Dallas vs. Minnesota, Jan. 3, 1983 (TD)
- 97 Andy Uram, Green Bay vs. Chi. Cardinals, Oct. 8, 1939 (TD)
   Bob Gage, Pittsburgh vs. Chi. Bears, Dec. 4, 1949 (TD)
- 96 Jim Spavital, Baltimore vs. Green Bay, Nov. 5, 1950 (TD)
   Bob Hoernschemeyer, Detroit vs. N.Y. Yanks, Nov. 23, 1950 (TD)
   Garrison Hearst, San Francisco vs. N.Y. Jets, Sept. 6, 1998 (TD)
   Corey Dillon, Cincinnati vs. Detroit, Oct. 28, 2001 (TD)

AVERAGE GAIN
Highest Average Gain, Career (750 attempts)
- 6.36 Randall Cunningham, Philadelphia, 1985-1995; Minnesota, 1997-99; Dallas, 2000; Baltimore, 2001 (775-4,928)
- 5.22 Jim Brown, Cleveland, 1957-1965 (2,359-12,312)
- 5.14 Eugene (Mercury) Morris, Miami, 1969-1975; San Diego, 1976 (804-4,133)

Highest Average Gain, Season (Qualifiers)
- 8.44 Beattie Feathers, Chi. Bears, 1934 (119-1,004)
- 7.98 Randall Cunningham, Philadelphia 1990 (118-942)
- 6.87 Bobby Douglass, Chicago, 1972 (141-968)

Highest Average Gain, Game (10 attempts)
- 17.09 Marion Motley, Cleveland vs. Pittsburgh, Oct. 29, 1950 (11-188)
- 16.70 Bill Grimes, Green Bay vs. N.Y. Yanks, Oct. 8, 1950 (10-167)
- 16.57 Bobby Mitchell, Cleveland vs. Washington, Nov. 15, 1959 (14-232)

TOUCHDOWNS
Most Seasons Leading League
- 5 Jim Brown, Cleveland, 1957-59, 1963, 1965
- 4 Steve Van Buren, Philadelphia, 1945, 1947-49
- 3 Abner Haynes, Dall. Texans, 1960-62
   Cookie Gilchrist, Buffalo, 1962-64
   Paul Lowe, L.A. Chargers, 1960; San Diego, 1961, 1965
   Leroy Kelly, Cleveland, 1966-68
   Emmitt Smith, Dallas, 1992, 1994-95

Most Consecutive Seasons Leading League
- 3 Steve Van Buren, Philadelphia, 1947-49
   Jim Brown, Cleveland, 1957-59
   Abner Haynes, Dall. Texans, 1960-62
   Cookie Gilchrist, Buffalo, 1962-64
   Leroy Kelly, Cleveland, 1966-68

Most Touchdowns, Career
- 148 Emmitt Smith, Dallas, 1990-2001
- 123 Marcus Allen, L.A. Raiders, 1982-1992; Kansas City, 1993-97
- 110 Walter Payton, Chicago, 1975-1987

Most Touchdowns, Season
- 25 Emmitt Smith, Dallas, 1995
- 24 John Riggins, Washington, 1983
- 21 Joe Morris, N.Y. Giants, 1985
   Emmitt Smith, Dallas, 1994
   Terry Allen, Washington, 1996
   Terrell Davis, Denver, 1998

Most Touchdowns, Rookie, Season
- 18 Eric Dickerson, L.A. Rams, 1983
- 15 Ickey Woods, Cincinnati, 1988
   Mike Anderson, Denver, 2000
- 14 Gale Sayers, Chicago, 1965
   Barry Sanders, Detroit, 1989
   Curtis Martin, New England, 1995
   Fred Taylor, Jacksonville, 1998

Most Touchdowns, Game
- 6 Ernie Nevers, Chi. Cardinals vs. Chi. Bears, Nov. 28, 1929
- 5 Jim Brown, Cleveland vs. Baltimore, Nov. 1, 1959
   Cookie Gilchrist, Buffalo vs. N.Y. Jets, Dec. 8, 1963
   James Stewart, Jacksonville vs. Philadelphia, Oct. 12, 1997
- 4 By many players

Most Consecutive Games Rushing for Touchdowns
- 13 John Riggins, Washington, 1982-83
   George Rogers, Washington, 1985-86
- 11 Lenny Moore, Baltimore, 1963-64
   Emmitt Smith, Dallas, 1994-95
   Emmitt Smith, Dallas, 1995
- 10 Greg Bell, L.A. Rams, 1988-89
   Terry Allen, Washington, 1995-96

PASSING
Most Seasons Leading League
- 6 Sammy Baugh, Washington, 1937, 1940, 1943, 1945, 1947, 1949
   Steve Young San Francisco, 1991-94, 1996-97
- 4 Len Dawson, Dall. Texans; 1962; Kansas City, 1964, 1966, 1968
   Roger Staubach, Dallas, 1971, 1973, 1978-79
   Ken Anderson, Cincinnati, 1974-75, 1981-82
- 3 Arnie Herber, Green Bay, 1932, 1934, 1936
   Norm Van Brocklin, Los Angeles, 1950, 1952, 1954
   Bart Starr, Green Bay, 1962, 1964, 1966

Most Consecutive Seasons Leading League
- 4 Steve Young, San Francisco, 1991-94
- 2 Cecil Isbell, Green Bay, 1941-42
   Milt Plum, Cleveland, 1960-61
   Ken Anderson, Cincinnati, 1974-75, 1981-82
   Roger Staubach, Dallas, 1978-79
   Steve Young, San Francisco, 1996-97

PASSER RATING
Highest Passer Rating, Career (1,500 attempts)
- 96.8 Steve Young, Tampa Bay, 1985-86; San Francisco, 1987-1999
- 92.3 Joe Montana, San Francisco, 1979-1990, 1992; Kansas City, 1993-94
- 86.8 Brett Favre, Atlanta, 1991; Green Bay, 1992-2001

Highest Passer Rating, Season (Qualifiers)
- 112.8 Steve Young, San Francisco, 1994
- 112.4 Joe Montana, San Francisco, 1989
- 110.4 Milt Plum, Cleveland, 1960

Highest Passer Rating, Rookie, Season (Qualifiers)
- 96.0 Dan Marino, Miami, 1983
- 88.2 Greg Cook, Cincinnati, 1969
- 84.0 Charlie Conerly, N.Y. Giants, 1948

ATTEMPTS
Most Seasons Leading League
- 5 Dan Marino, Miami, 1984, 1986, 1988, 1992, 1997
- 4 Sammy Baugh, Washington, 1937, 1943, 1947-48
   Johnny Unitas, Baltimore, 1957, 1959-1961
   George Blanda, Chi. Bears, 1953; Houston, 1963-65
- 3 Arnie Herber, Green Bay, 1932, 1934, 1936
   Sonny Jurgensen, Washington, 1966-67, 1969
   Drew Bledsoe, New England, 1994-96

Most Consecutive Seasons Leading League
- 3 Johnny Unitas, Baltimore, 1959-1961
  George Blanda, Houston, 1963-65
  Drew Bledsoe, New England, 1994-96
- 2 By many players

Most Passes Attempted, Career
- 8,358 Dan Marino, Miami, 1983-1999
- 7,250 John Elway, Denver, 1983-1998
- 6,823 Warren Moon, Houston, 1984-1993; Minnesota, 1994-96; Seattle, 1997-98; Kansas City, 1999-2000

Most Passes Attempted, Season
- 691 Drew Bledsoe, New England, 1994
- 655 Warren Moon, Houston, 1991
- 636 Drew Bledsoe, New England, 1995

Most Passes Attempted, Rookie, Season
- 575 Peyton Manning, Indianapolis, 1998
- 540 Chris Weinke, Carolina, 2001
- 486 Rick Mirer, Seattle, 1993

Most Passes Attempted, Game
- 70 Drew Bledsoe, New England vs. Minnesota, Nov. 13, 1994 (OT)
- 69 Vinny Testaverde, N.Y. Jets vs. Baltimore, Dec. 24, 2000
- 68 George Blanda, Houston vs. Buffalo, Nov. 1, 1964
  Jon Kitna, Cincinnati vs. Pittsburgh, Dec. 30, 2001 (OT)

COMPLETIONS
Most Seasons Leading League
- 6 Dan Marino, Miami, 1984-86, 1988, 1992, 1997
- 5 Sammy Baugh, Washington, 1937, 1943, 1945, 1947-48
- 4 George Blanda, Chi. Bears, 1953; Houston, 1963-65
  Sonny Jurgensen, Philadelphia, 1961; Washington, 1966-67, 1969

Most Consecutive Seasons Leading League
- 3 George Blanda, Houston, 1963-65
  Dan Marino, Miami, 1984-86
- 2 By many players

Most Passes Completed, Career
- 4,967 Dan Marino, Miami, 1983-1999
- 4,123 John Elway, Denver, 1983-1998
- 3,988 Warren Moon, Houston, 1984-1993; Minnesota, 1994-96; Seattle, 1997-98; Kansas City, 1999-2000

Most Passes Completed, Season
- 404 Warren Moon, Houston, 1991
- 400 Drew Bledsoe, New England, 1994
- 385 Dan Marino, Miami, 1994

Most Passes Completed, Rookie, Season
- 326 Peyton Manning, Indianapolis, 1998
- 293 Chris Weinke, Carolina, 2001
- 274 Rick Mirer, Seattle, 1993

Most Passes Completed, Game
- 45 Drew Bledsoe, New England vs. Minnesota, Nov. 13, 1994 (OT)
- 42 Richard Todd, N.Y. Jets vs. San Francisco, Sept. 21, 1980
  Vinny Testaverde, N.Y. Jets vs. Seattle, Dec. 6, 1998
- 41 Warren Moon, Houston vs. Dallas, Nov. 10, 1991 (OT)

Most Consecutive Passes Completed
- 22 Joe Montana, San Francisco vs. Cleveland (5), Nov. 29, 1987; vs. Green Bay (17), Dec. 6, 1987
- 20 Ken Anderson, Cincinnati vs. Houston, Jan. 2, 1983
  Hugh Millen, Denver vs. L.A. Raiders (7), Dec. 11, 1994; vs. San Francisco (13), Dec. 17, 1994

Steve Young, San Francisco vs. Washington, Nov. 24, 1996
- 18 Steve DeBerg, Denver vs. L.A. Rams (17), Dec. 12, 1982; vs. Kansas City (1), Dec. 19, 1982
  Lynn Dickey, Green Bay vs. Houston, Sept. 4, 1983
  Joe Montana, San Francisco vs. L.A. Rams (13), Oct. 28, 1984; vs. Cincinnati (5), Nov. 4, 1984
  Don Majkowski, Green Bay vs. New Orleans, Sept. 18, 1989
  Boomer Esiason, N.Y. Jets vs. Miami (5), Sept. 12, 1993; vs. New England (13), Sept. 26, 1993

COMPLETION PERCENTAGE
Most Seasons Leading League
- 8 Len Dawson, Dall. Texans, 1962; Kansas City, 1964-69, 1975
- 7 Sammy Baugh, Washington, 1940, 1942-43, 1945, 1947-49
- 5 Joe Montana, San Francisco, 1980-81, 1985, 1987, 1989
  Steve Young, San Francisco, 1992, 1994-97

Most Consecutive Seasons Leading League
- 6 Len Dawson, Kansas City, 1964-69
- 4 Steve Young, San Francisco, 1994-97
- 3 Sammy Baugh, Washington, 1947-49
  Otto Graham, Cleveland, 1953-55
  Milt Plum, Cleveland, 1959-1961
  Kurt Warner, St. Louis, 1999-2001

Highest Completion Percentage, Career (1,500 attempts)
- 64.28 Steve Young, Tampa Bay, 1985-86; San Francisco, 1987-1999 (4,149-2,667)
- 63.24 Joe Montana, San Francisco, 1979-1990, 1992; Kansas City, 1993-94 (5,391-3,409)
- 61.60 Brad Johnson, Minnesota, 1994-98; Washington, 1999-2000; Tampa Bay, 2001 (2,380-1,466)

Highest Completion Percentage, Season (Qualifiers)
- 70.55 Ken Anderson, Cincinnati, 1982 (309-218)
- 70.33 Sammy Baugh, Washington, 1945 (182-128)
- 70.28 Steve Young, San Francisco, 1994 (461-324)

Highest Completion Percentage, Rookie, Season (Qualifiers)
- 58.45 Dan Marino, Miami, 1983 (296-173)
- 57.14 Jim McMahon, Chicago, 1982 (210-120)
- 57.10 Charlie Batch, Detroit, 1998 (303-173)

Highest Completion Percentage, Game (20 attempts)
- 91.30 Vinny Testaverde, Cleveland vs. L.A. Rams, Dec. 26, 1993 (23-21)
- 90.91 Ken Anderson, Cincinnati vs. Pittsburgh, Nov. 10, 1974 (22-20)
- 90.48 Lynn Dickey, Green Bay vs. New Orleans, Dec. 13, 1981 (21-19)

YARDS GAINED
Most Seasons Leading League
- 5 Sonny Jurgensen, Philadelphia, 1961-62; Washington, 1966-67, 1969
  Dan Marino, Miami, 1984-86, 1988, 1992
- 4 Sammy Baugh, Washington, 1937, 1940, 1947-48
  Johnny Unitas, Baltimore, 1957, 1959-1960, 1963
  Dan Fouts, San Diego, 1979-1982
- 3 Arnie Herber, Green Bay, 1932, 1934, 1936
  Sid Luckman, Chi. Bears, 1943, 1945-46
  John Brodie, San Francisco, 1965, 1968, 1970
  John Hadl, San Diego, 1965, 1968, 1971
  Joe Namath, N.Y. Jets, 1966-67, 1972

Most Consecutive Seasons Leading League
- 4 Dan Fouts, San Diego, 1979-1982
- 3 Dan Marino, Miami, 1984-86
- 2 By many players

Most Yards Gained, Career
- 61,361   Dan Marino, Miami, 1983-1999
- 51,475   John Elway, Denver, 1983-1998
- 49,325   Warren Moon, Houston, 1984-1993; Minnesota, 1994-96; Seattle, 1997-98; Kansas City, 1999-2000

Most Seasons, 3,000 or More Yards Passing
- 13   Dan Marino, Miami, 1984-1992, 1994-95, 1997-98
- 12   John Elway, Denver, 1985-1991, 1993-97
- 10   Brett Favre, Green Bay, 1992-2001

Most Yards Gained, Season
- 5,084   Dan Marino, Miami, 1984
- 4,830   Kurt Warner, St. Louis, 2001
- 4,802   Dan Fouts, San Diego, 1981

Most Yards Gained, Rookie, Season
- 3,739   Peyton Manning, Indianapolis, 1998
- 2,931   Chris Weinke, Carolina, 2001
- 2,833   Rick Mirer, Seattle, 1993

Most Yards Gained, Game
- 554   Norm Van Brocklin, Los Angeles vs. N.Y. Yanks, Sept. 28, 1951
- 527   Warren Moon, Houston vs. Kansas City, Dec. 16, 1990
- 522   Boomer Esiason, Arizona vs. Washington, Nov. 10, 1996

Most Games, 400 or More Yards Passing, Career
- 13   Dan Marino, Miami, 1983-1999
- 7   Joe Montana, San Francisco, 1979-1990, 1992; Kansas City, 1993-94
-    Warren Moon, Houston, 1984-1993; Minnesota, 1994-96; Seattle, 1997-98; Kansas City, 1999-2000
- 6   Dan Fouts, San Diego, 1973-1987

Most Games, 400 or More Yards Passing, Season
- 4   Dan Marino, Miami, 1984
- 3   Dan Marino, Miami, 1986
- 2   By many players

Most Consecutive Games, 400 or More Yards Passing
- 2   Dan Fouts, San Diego, 1982
-    Dan Marino, Miami, 1984
-    Phil Simms, N.Y. Giants, 1985

Most Games, 300 or More Yards Passing, Career
- 63   Dan Marino, Miami, 1983-1999
- 51   Dan Fouts, San Diego, 1973-1987
- 49   Warren Moon, Houston, 1984-1993; Minnesota, 1994-96; Seattle, 1997-98; Kansas City, 1999-2000

Most Games, 300 or More Yards Passing, Season
- 9   Dan Marino, Miami, 1984
-    Warren Moon, Houston, 1990
-    Kurt Warner, St. Louis, 1999
-    Kurt Warner, St. Louis, 2001
- 8   Dan Fouts, San Diego, 1980
-    Kurt Warner, St. Louis, 2000
- 7   Dan Fouts, San Diego, 1981
-    Bill Kenney, Kansas City, 1983
-    Neil Lomax, St. Louis, 1984
-    Dan Fouts, San Diego, 1985
-    Brett Favre, Green Bay, 1995
-    Steve Young, San Francisco, 1998

Most Consecutive Games, 300 or More Yards Passing
- 6   Steve Young, San Francisco, 1998
-    Kurt Warner, St. Louis, 2000
- 5   Joe Montana, San Francisco, 1982
- 4   Dan Fouts, San Diego, 1979
-    Dan Fouts, San Diego, 1980-81
-    Bill Kenney, Kansas City, 1983
-    Joe Montana, San Francisco, 1985-86
-    Joe Montana, San Francisco, 1990
-    Warren Moon, Houston, 1990

   Drew Bledsoe, New England, 1993-94
   Kurt Warner, St. Louis, 1999

Longest Pass Completion (All TDs except as noted)
- 99   Frank Filchock (to Farkas), Washington vs. Pittsburgh, Oct. 15, 1939
-    George Izo (to Mitchell), Washington vs. Cleveland, Sept. 15, 1963
-    Karl Sweetan (to Studstill), Detroit vs. Baltimore, Oct. 16, 1966
-    Sonny Jurgensen (to Allen), Washington vs. Chicago, Sept. 15, 1968
-    Jim Plunkett (to Branch), L.A. Raiders vs. Washington, Oct. 2, 1983
-    Ron Jaworski (to Quick), Philadelphia vs. Atlanta, Nov. 10, 1985
-    Stan Humphries (to Martin), San Diego vs. Seattle, Sept. 18, 1994
-    Brett Favre (to Brooks), Green Bay vs. Chicago, Sept. 11, 1995
- 98   Doug Russell (to Tinsley), Chi. Cardinals vs. Cleveland, Nov. 27, 1938
-    Ogden Compton (to Lane), Chi. Cardinals vs. Green Bay, Nov. 13, 1955
-    Bill Wade (to Farrington), Chicago Bears vs. Detroit, Oct. 8, 1961
-    Jacky Lee (to Dewveall), Houston vs. San Diego, Nov. 25, 1962
-    Earl Morrall (to Jones), N.Y. Giants vs. Pittsburgh, Sept. 11, 1966
-    Jim Hart (to Moore), St. Louis vs. Los Angeles, Dec. 10, 1972 (no TD)
-    Bobby Hebert (to Haynes), Atlanta vs. New Orleans, Sept. 12, 1993
-    Charlie Batch (to Morton), Detroit vs. Chicago, Oct. 4, 1998
- 97   Pat Coffee (to Tinsley), Chi. Cardinals vs. Chi. Bears, Dec. 5, 1937
-    Bobby Layne (to Box), Detroit vs. Green Bay, Nov. 26, 1953
-    George Shaw (to Tarr), Denver vs. Boston, Sept. 21, 1962
-    Bernie Kosar (to Slaughter), Cleveland vs. Chicago, Oct. 23, 1989
-    Steve Young (to Taylor), San Francisco vs. Atlanta, Nov. 3, 1991

AVERAGE GAIN

Most Seasons Leading League
- 7   Sid Luckman, Chi. Bears, 1939-1943, 1946-47
- 5   Steve Young, San Francisco, 1991-94, 1997
- 3   Arnie Herber, Green Bay, 1932, 1934, 1936
-    Norm Van Brocklin, Los Angeles, 1950, 1952, 1954
-    Len Dawson, Dall. Texans, 1962; Kansas City, 1966, 1968
-    Bart Starr, Green Bay, 1966-68
-    Kurt Warner, St. Louis, 1999-2001

Most Consecutive Seasons Leading League
- 5   Sid Luckman, Chi. Bears, 1939-1943
- 4   Steve Young, San Francisco, 1991-94
- 3   Bart Starr, Green Bay, 1966-68
-    Kurt Warner, St. Louis, 1999-2001

Highest Average Gain, Career (1,500 attempts)
- 8.63   Otto Graham, Cleveland, 1950-55 (1,565-13,499)
- 8.42   Sid Luckman, Chi. Bears, 1939-1950 (1,744-14,686)
- 8.16   Norm Van Brocklin, Los Angeles, 1949-1957; Philadelphia, 1958-1960 (2,895-23,611)

Highest Average Gain, Season (Qualifiers)
- 11.17   Tommy O'Connell, Cleveland, 1957 (110-1,229)
- 10.86   Sid Luckman, Chi. Bears, 1943 (202-2,194)

10.55   Otto Graham, Cleveland, 1953 (258-2,722)

Highest Average Gain, Rookie, Season (Qualifiers)
9.411   Greg Cook, Cincinnati, 1969 (197-1,854)
9.409   Bob Waterfield, Cleveland, 1945 (171-1,609)
8.36   Zeke Bratkowski, Chi. Bears, 1954 (130-1,087)

Highest Average Gain, Game (20 attempts)
18.58   Sammy Baugh, Washington vs. Boston,
        Oct. 31, 1948 (24-446)
18.50   Johnny Unitas, Baltimore vs. Atlanta, Nov. 12, 1967
        (20-370)
17.71   Joe Namath, N.Y. Jets vs. Baltimore, Sept. 24, 1972
        (28-496)

TOUCHDOWNS

Most Seasons Leading League
4   Johnny Unitas, Baltimore, 1957-1960
    Len Dawson, Dall. Texans, 1962; Kansas City, 1963,
    1965-66
    Steve Young, San Francisco, 1992-94, 1998
3   Arnie Herber, Green Bay, 1932, 1934, 1936
    Sid Luckman, Chi. Bears, 1943, 1945-46
    Y.A. Tittle, San Francisco, 1955; N.Y. Giants, 1962-63
    Dan Marino, Miami, 1984-86
    Brett Favre, Green Bay, 1995-97
2   By many players

Most Consecutive Seasons Leading League
4   Johnny Unitas, Baltimore, 1957-1960
3   Dan Marino, Miami, 1984-86
    Steve Young, San Francisco, 1992-94
    Brett Favre, Green Bay, 1995-97
2   By many players

Most Touchdown Passes, Career
420   Dan Marino, Miami, 1983-1999
342   Fran Tarkenton, Minnesota, 1961-66, 1972-78;
     N.Y. Giants, 1967-1971
300   John Elway, Denver, 1983-1998

Most Touchdown Passes, Season
48   Dan Marino, Miami, 1984
44   Dan Marino, Miami, 1986
41   Kurt Warner, St. Louis, 1999

Most Touchdown Passes, Rookie, Season
26   Peyton Manning, Indianapolis, 1998
22   Charlie Conerly, N.Y. Giants, 1948
20   Dan Marino, Miami, 1983

Most Touchdown Passes, Game
7   Sid Luckman, Chi. Bears vs. N.Y. Giants,
    Nov. 14, 1943
    Adrian Burk, Philadelphia vs. Washington,
    Oct. 17, 1954
    George Blanda, Houston vs. N.Y. Titans,
    Nov. 19, 1961
    Y.A. Tittle, N.Y. Giants vs. Washington, Oct. 28, 1962
    Joe Kapp, Minnesota vs. Baltimore, Sept. 28, 1969
6   By many players. Last time:
    Mark Rypien, Washington vs. Atlanta, Nov. 10, 1991

Most Games, Four or More Touchdown Passes, Career
21   Dan Marino, Miami, 1983-1999
17   Johnny Unitas, Baltimore, 1956-1972; San Diego,
     1973
14   Brett Favre, Atlanta, 1991; Green Bay, 1992-2001

Most Games, Four or More Touchdown Passes, Season
6   Dan Marino, Miami, 1984
5   Dan Marino, Miami, 1986
    Brett Favre, Green Bay, 1996
4   George Blanda, Houston, 1961
    Vince Ferragamo, Los Angeles, 1980
    Steve Young, San Francisco, 1994
    Randall Cunningham, Minnesota, 1998

Most Consecutive Games, Four or More Touchdown Passes
4   Dan Marino, Miami, 1984
2   By many players

Most Consecutive Games, Touchdown Passes
47   Johnny Unitas, Baltimore, 1956-1960
30   Dan Marino, Miami, 1985-87
28   Dave Krieg, Seattle, 1983-85

HAD INTERCEPTED

Most Consecutive Passes Attempted, None Intercepted
308   Bernie Kosar, Cleveland, 1990-91
294   Bart Starr, Green Bay, 1964-65
279   Jeff George, Indianapolis, 1993; Atlanta, 1994

Most Passes Had Intercepted, Career
277   George Blanda, Chi. Bears, 1949, 1950-58; Baltimore,
     1950; Houston, 1960-66; Oakland, 1967-1975
268   John Hadl, San Diego, 1962-1972; Los Angeles,
     1973-74; Green Bay, 1974-75; Houston, 1976-77
266   Fran Tarkenton, Minnesota, 1961-66, 1972-78;
     N.Y. Giants, 1967-1971

Most Passes Had Intercepted, Season
42   George Blanda, Houston, 1962
35   Vinny Testaverde, Tampa Bay, 1988
34   Frank Tripucka, Denver, 1960

Most Passes Had Intercepted, Game
8   Jim Hardy, Chi. Cardinals vs. Philadelphia,
    Sept. 24, 1950
7   Parker Hall, Cleveland vs. Green Bay, Nov. 8, 1942
    Frank Sinkwich, Detroit vs. Green Bay, Oct. 24, 1943
    Bob Waterfield, Los Angeles vs. Green Bay,
    Oct. 17, 1948
    Zeke Bratkowski, Chicago vs. Baltimore,
    Oct. 2, 1960
    Tommy Wade, Pittsburgh vs. Philadelphia,
    Dec. 12, 1965
    Ken Stabler, Oakland vs. Denver, Oct. 16, 1977
    Steve DeBerg, Tampa Bay vs. San Francisco,
    Sept. 7, 1986
    Ty Detmer, Detroit vs. Cleveland, Sept. 23, 2001
6   By many players

Most Attempts, No Interceptions, Game
70   Drew Bledsoe, New England vs. Minnesota,
    Nov. 13, 1994 (OT)
63   Rich Gannon, Minnesota vs. New England,
    Oct. 20, 1991 (OT)
60   Davey O'Brien, Philadelphia vs. Washington,
    Dec. 1, 1940

LOWEST PERCENTAGE, PASSES HAD INTERCEPTED

Most Seasons Leading League, Lowest Percentage, Passes Had Intercepted
5   Sammy Baugh, Washington, 1940, 1942, 1944-45,
    1947
3   Charlie Conerly, N.Y. Giants, 1950, 1956, 1959
    Bart Starr, Green Bay, 1962, 1964, 1966
    Roger Staubach, Dallas, 1971, 1977, 1979
    Ken Anderson, Cincinnati, 1972, 1981-82
    Ken O'Brien, N.Y. Jets, 1985, 1987-88
2   By many players

Lowest Percentage, Passes Had Intercepted, Career
(1,500 attempts)
2.10   Neil O'Donnell, Pittsburgh, 1991-95; N.Y. Jets,
     1996-97; Cincinnati, 1998; Tennessee,
     1999-2001 (3,197-67)
2.47   Steve Bono, Minnesota, 1985-86; Pittsburgh,
     1987-88; San Francisco, 1989, 1991-93;
     Kansas City, 1994-96; Green Bay, 1997;
     St. Louis, 1998; Carolina, 1999 (1,701-42)
2.51   Mark Brunell, Green Bay, 1994; Jacksonville,
     1995-2001 (3,145-79)

Lowest Percentage, Passes Had Intercepted, Season (Qualifiers)
- 0.66   Joe Ferguson, Buffalo, 1976 (151-1)
- 0.90   Steve DeBerg, Kansas City, 1990 (444-4)
- 1.16   Steve Bartkowski, Atlanta, 1983 (432-5)

Lowest Percentage, Passes Had Intercepted, Rookie, Season (Qualifiers)
- 1.98   Charlie Batch, Detroit, 1998 (303-6)
- 2.03   Dan Marino, Miami, 1983 (296-6)
- 2.10   Gary Wood, N.Y. Giants, 1964 (143-3)

TIMES SACKED

Times Sacked has been compiled since 1963.

Most Times Sacked, Career
- 516   John Elway, Denver, 1983-1998
- 494   Dave Krieg, Seattle, 1980-1991; Kansas City, 1992-93; Detroit, 1994; Arizona, 1995; Chicago, 1996; Tennessee, 1997-98
- 484   Randall Cunningham, Philadelphia, 1985-1995; Minnesota, 1997-99; Dallas, 2000; Baltimore, 2001

Most Times Sacked, Season
- 72   Randall Cunningham, Philadelphia, 1986
- 62   Ken O'Brien, N.Y. Jets, 1985
-      Steve Beuerlein, Carolina, 2000
- 61   Neil Lomax, St. Louis, 1985

Most Times Sacked, Game
- 12   Bert Jones, Baltimore vs. St. Louis, Oct. 26, 1980
-      Warren Moon, Houston vs. Dallas, Sept. 29, 1985
- 11   Charley Johnson, St. Louis vs. N.Y. Giants, Nov. 1, 1964
-      Bart Starr, Green Bay vs. Detroit, Nov. 7, 1965
-      Jack Kemp, Buffalo vs. Oakland, Oct. 15, 1967
-      Bob Berry, Atlanta vs. St. Louis, Nov. 24, 1968
-      Greg Landry, Detroit vs. Dallas, Oct. 6, 1975
-      Ron Jaworski, Philadelphia vs. St. Louis, Dec. 18, 1983
-      Paul McDonald, Cleveland vs. Kansas City, Sept. 30, 1984
-      Archie Manning, Minnesota vs. Chicago, Oct. 28, 1984
-      Steve Pelluer, Dallas vs. San Diego, Nov. 16, 1986
-      Randall Cunningham, Philadelphia vs. L.A. Raiders, Nov. 30, 1986 (OT)
-      David Norrie, N.Y. Jets vs. Dallas, Oct. 4, 1987
-      Troy Aikman, Dallas vs. Philadelphia, Sept. 15, 1991
-      Bernie Kosar, Cleveland vs. Indianapolis, Sept. 6, 1992
- 10   By many players

RECEIVING

Most Seasons Leading League
- 8   Don Hutson, Green Bay, 1936-37, 1939, 1941-45
- 5   Lionel Taylor, Denver, 1960-63, 1965
- 3   Tom Fears, Los Angeles, 1948-1950
-     Pete Pihos, Philadelphia, 1953-55
-     Billy Wilson, San Francisco, 1954, 1956-57
-     Raymond Berry, Baltimore, 1958-1960
-     Lance Alworth, San Diego, 1966, 1968-69
-     Sterling Sharpe, Green Bay, 1989, 1992-93

Most Consecutive Seasons Leading League
- 5   Don Hutson, Green Bay, 1941-45
- 4   Lionel Taylor, Denver, 1960-63
- 3   Tom Fears, Los Angeles, 1948-1950
-     Pete Pihos, Philadelphia, 1953-55
-     Raymond Berry, Baltimore, 1958-1960

Most Pass Receptions, Career
- 1,364   Jerry Rice, San Francisco, 1985-2000; Oakland 2001
- 1,093   Cris Carter, Philadelphia, 1987-89; Minnesota, 1990-2001

- 951   Andre Reed, Buffalo, 1985-1999; Washington 2000

Most Seasons, 50 or More Pass Receptions
- 15   Jerry Rice, San Francisco, 1986-1996, 1998-2000; Oakland, 2001
- 13   Andre Reed, Buffalo, 1986-1994, 1996-99
- 11   Cris Carter, Minnesota, 1991-2001

Most Pass Receptions, Season
- 123   Herman Moore, Detroit, 1995
- 122   Cris Carter, Minnesota, 1994
-     Cris Carter, Minnesota, 1995
-     Jerry Rice, San Francisco, 1995
- 119   Isaac Bruce, St. Louis, 1995

Most Pass Receptions, Rookie, Season
- 90   Terry Glenn, New England, 1996
- 83   Earl Cooper, San Francisco, 1980
- 81   Keith Jackson, Philadelphia, 1988

Most Pass Receptions, Game
- 20   Terrell Owens, San Francisco vs. Chicago, Dec. 17, 2000
- 18   Tom Fears, Los Angeles vs. Green Bay, Dec. 3, 1950
- 17   Clark Gaines, N.Y. Jets vs. San Francisco, Sept. 21, 1980

Most Consecutive Games, Pass Receptions
- 241   Jerry Rice, San Francisco, 1985-2000; Oakland, 2001 (current)
- 183   Art Monk, Washington, 1983-1993; N.Y. Jets, 1994; Philadelphia, 1995
- 177   Steve Largent, Seattle, 1977-1989

YARDS GAINED

Most Seasons Leading League
- 7   Don Hutson, Green Bay, 1936, 1938-39, 1941-44
- 6   Jerry Rice, San Francisco, 1986, 1989-1990, 1993-95
- 3   Raymond Berry, Baltimore, 1957, 1959-1960
-     Lance Alworth, San Diego, 1965-66, 1968

Most Consecutive Seasons Leading League
- 4   Don Hutson, Green Bay, 1941-44
- 3   Jerry Rice, San Francisco, 1993-95
- 2   By many players

Most Yards Gained, Career
- 20,386   Jerry Rice, San Francisco, 1985-2000; Oakland, 2001
- 14,004   James Lofton, Green Bay, 1978-1986; L.A. Raiders, 1987-88; Buffalo, 1989-1992; L.A. Rams, 1993; Philadelphia, 1993
- 13,833   Cris Carter, Philadelphia, 1987-89; Minnesota, 1990-2001

Most Seasons, 1,000 or More Yards, Pass Receiving
- 13   Jerry Rice, San Francisco, 1986-1996, 1998; Oakland, 2001
- 9   Tim Brown, L.A. Raiders, 1993-94; Oakland, 1995-2001
- 8   Steve Largent, Seattle, 1978-1981, 1983-86
-     Cris Carter, Minnesota, 1993-2000

Most Yards Gained, Season
- 1,848   Jerry Rice, San Francisco, 1995
- 1,781   Isaac Bruce, St. Louis, 1995
- 1,746   Charley Hennigan, Houston, 1961

Most Yards Gained, Rookie, Season
- 1,473   Bill Groman, Houston, 1960
- 1,313   Randy Moss, Minnesota, 1998
- 1,231   Bill Howton, Green Bay, 1952

Most Yards Gained, Game
- 336   Willie Anderson, L.A. Rams vs. New Orleans, Nov. 26, 1989 (OT)
- 309   Stephone Paige, Kansas City vs. San Diego, Dec. 22, 1985
- 303   Jim Benton, Cleveland vs. Detroit, Nov. 22, 1945

Most Games, 200 or More Yards Pass Receiving, Career
- 5 Lance Alworth, San Diego, 1962-1970; Dallas, 1971-72
- 4 Don Hutson, Green Bay, 1935-45
  - Charley Hennigan, Houston, 1960-66
  - Jerry Rice, San Francisco, 1985-2000; Oakland, 2001
- 3 Don Maynard, N.Y. Giants, 1958; N.Y. Jets, 1960-1972; St. Louis, 1973
  - Wes Chandler, New Orleans, 1978-1981; San Diego, 1981-87; San Francisco, 1988
  - Isaac Bruce, L.A. Rams, 1994; St. Louis, 1995-2001

Most Games, 200 or More Yards Pass Receiving, Season
- 3 Charley Hennigan, Houston, 1961
- 2 Don Hutson, Green Bay, 1942
  - Gene Roberts, N.Y. Giants, 1949
  - Lance Alworth, San Diego, 1963
  - Don Maynard, N.Y. Jets, 1968

Most Games, 100 or More Yards Pass Receiving, Career
- 68 Jerry Rice, San Francisco, 1985-2000; Oakland, 2001
- 50 Don Maynard, N.Y. Giants, 1958; N.Y. Jets, 1960-1972; St. Louis, 1973
- 47 Michael Irvin, Dallas, 1988-1999

Most Games, 100 or More Yards Pass Receiving, Season
- 11 Michael Irvin, Dallas, 1995
- 10 Charley Hennigan, Houston, 1961
  - Herman Moore, Detroit, 1995
- 9 Elroy (Crazylegs) Hirsch, Los Angeles, 1951
  - Bill Groman, Houston, 1960
  - Lance Alworth, San Diego, 1965
  - Don Maynard, N.Y. Jets, 1967
  - Stanley Morgan, New England, 1986
  - Mark Carrier, Tampa Bay, 1989
  - Robert Brooks, Green Bay, 1995
  - Isaac Bruce, St. Louis, 1995
  - Jerry Rice, San Francisco, 1995
  - Marvin Harrison, Indianapolis, 1999
  - Jimmy Smith, Jacksonville, 1999
  - David Boston, Arizona, 2001

Most Consecutive Games, 100 or More Yards Pass Receiving
- 7 Charley Hennigan, Houston, 1961
  - Michael Irvin, Dallas, 1995
- 6 Raymond Berry, Baltimore, 1960
  - Bill Groman, Houston, 1961
  - Pat Studstill, Detroit, 1966
  - Isaac Bruce, St. Louis, 1995
- 5 Elroy (Crazylegs) Hirsch, Los Angeles, 1951
  - Bob Boyd, Los Angeles, 1954
  - Terry Barr, Detroit, 1963
  - Lance Alworth, San Diego, 1966
  - Don Maynard, N.Y. Jets, 1968-69
  - Harold Jackson, Philadelphia, 1971-72
  - Patrick Jeffers, Carolina, 1999

Longest Pass Reception (All TDs except as noted)
- 99 Andy Farkas (from Filchock), Washington vs. Pittsburgh, Oct. 15, 1939
  - Bobby Mitchell (from Izo), Washington vs. Cleveland, Sept. 15, 1963
  - Pat Studstill (from Sweetan), Detroit vs. Baltimore, Oct. 16, 1966
  - Gerry Allen (from Jurgensen), Washington vs. Chicago, Sept. 15, 1968
  - Cliff Branch (from Plunkett), L.A. Raiders vs. Washington, Oct. 2, 1983
  - Mike Quick (from Jaworski), Philadelphia vs. Atlanta, Nov. 10, 1985
  - Tony Martin (from Humphries), San Diego vs. Seattle, Sept. 18, 1994
  - Robert Brooks (from Favre), Green Bay vs. Chicago, Sept. 11, 1995

- 98 Gaynell Tinsley (from Russell), Chi. Cardinals vs. Cleveland, Nov. 17, 1938
  - Dick (Night Train) Lane (from Compton), Chi. Cardinals vs. Green Bay, Nov. 13, 1955
  - John Farrington (from Wade), Chicago vs. Detroit, Oct. 8, 1961
  - Willard Dewveall (from Lee), Houston vs. San Diego, Nov. 25, 1962
  - Homer Jones (from Morrall), N.Y. Giants vs. Pittsburgh, Sept. 11, 1966
  - Bobby Moore (from Hart), St. Louis vs. Los Angeles, Dec. 10, 1972 (no TD)
  - Michael Haynes (from Hebert), Atlanta vs. New Orleans, Sept. 12, 1993
  - Johnnie Morton (from Batch), Detroit vs. Chicago, Oct. 4, 1998
- 97 Gaynell Tinsley (from Coffee), Chi. Cardinals vs. Chi. Bears, Dec. 5, 1937
  - Cloyce Box (from Layne), Detroit vs. Green Bay, Nov. 26, 1953
  - Jerry Tarr (from Shaw), Denver vs. Boston, Sept. 21, 1962
  - Webster Slaughter (from Kosar), Cleveland vs. Chicago, Oct. 23, 1989
  - John Taylor (from Young), San Francisco vs. Atlanta, Nov. 3, 1991

AVERAGE GAIN
Highest Average Gain, Career (200 receptions)
- 22.26 Homer Jones, N.Y. Giants, 1964-69; Cleveland, 1970 (224-4,986)
- 20.83 Buddy Dial, Pittsburgh, 1959-1963; Dallas, 1964-66 (261-5,436)
- 20.24 Harlon Hill, Chi. Bears, 1954-1961; Pittsburgh, 1962; Detroit, 1962 (233-4,717)

Highest Average Gain, Season (24 receptions)
- 32.58 Don Currivan, Boston, 1947 (24-782)
- 31.44 Bucky Pope, Los Angeles, 1964 (25-786)
- 28.60 Bobby Duckworth, San Diego, 1984 (25-715)

Highest Average Gain, Game (3 receptions)
- 63.00 Torry Holt, St. Louis vs. Atlanta, Sept. 24, 2000 (3-189)
- 60.67 Bill Groman, Houston vs. Denver, Nov. 20, 1960 (3-182)
  - Homer Jones, N.Y. Giants vs. Washington, Dec. 12, 1965 (3-182)
- 60.33 Don Currivan, Boston vs. Washington, Nov. 30, 1947 (3-181)

TOUCHDOWNS
Most Seasons Leading League
- 9 Don Hutson, Green Bay, 1935-38, 1940-44
- 6 Jerry Rice, San Francisco, 1986-87, 1989-1991, 1993
- 3 Lance Alworth, San Diego, 1964-66
  - Cris Carter, Minnesota, 1995, 1997, 1999

Most Consecutive Seasons Leading League
- 5 Don Hutson, Green Bay, 1940-44
- 4 Don Hutson, Green Bay, 1935-38
- 3 Lance Alworth, San Diego, 1964-66
  - Jerry Rice, San Francisco, 1989-1991

Most Touchdowns, Career
- 185 Jerry Rice, San Francisco, 1985-2000; Oakland, 2001
- 129 Cris Carter, Philadelphia, 1987-89; Minnesota, 1990-2001
- 100 Steve Largent, Seattle, 1976-1989

Most Touchdowns, Season
- 22 Jerry Rice, San Francisco, 1987
- 18 Mark Clayton, Miami, 1984
  - Sterling Sharpe, Green Bay, 1994

RECEIVING-YARDS FROM SCRIMMAGE-INTERCEPTIONS   ALL-TIME RECORDS

17 Don Hutson, Green Bay, 1942
    Elroy (Crazylegs) Hirsch, Los Angeles, 1951
    Bill Groman, Houston, 1961
    Jerry Rice, San Francisco, 1989
    Cris Carter, Minnesota, 1995
    Carl Pickens, Cincinnati, 1995
    Randy Moss, Minnesota, 1998

Most Touchdowns, Rookie, Season
17 Randy Moss, Minnesota, 1998
13 Bill Howton, Green Bay, 1952
    John Jefferson, San Diego, 1978
12 Harlon Hill, Chi. Bears, 1954
    Bill Groman, Houston, 1960
    Mike Ditka, Chicago, 1961
    Bob Hayes, Dallas, 1965

Most Touchdowns, Game
5   Bob Shaw, Chi. Cardinals vs. Baltimore, Oct. 2, 1950
    Kellen Winslow, San Diego vs. Oakland, Nov. 22, 1981
    Jerry Rice, San Francisco vs. Atlanta, Oct. 14, 1990
4   By many players. Last time: Isaac Bruce, St. Louis
    vs. San Francisco, Oct. 10, 1999

Most Consecutive Games, Touchdowns
13 Jerry Rice, San Francisco, 1986-87
11 Elroy (Crazylegs) Hirsch, Los Angeles, 1950-51
    Buddy Dial, Pittsburgh, 1959-1960
10 Carl Pickens, Cincinnati, 1994-95

YARDS FROM SCRIMMAGE
Most Scrimmage Yards, Career
21,264 Walter Payton, Chicago, 1975-1987
21,011 Jerry Rice, San Francisco 1985-2000; Oakland 2001
19,110 Emmitt Smith, Dallas, 1990-2001

Most Scrimmage Yards, Season
2,429 Marshall Faulk, St. Louis, 1999 (1,381 rush., 1,048 rec.)
2,358 Barry Sanders, Detroit, 1997 (2,053 rush., 305 rec.)
2,314 Marcus Allen, L.A. Raiders, 1985 (1,759 rush., 555 rec.)

Most Scrimmage Yards, Rookie, Season
2,212 Eric Dickerson, L.A. Rams, 1983 (1,808 rush., 404 rec.)
2,139 Edgerrin James, Indianapolis, 1999 (1,553 rush., 586 rec.)
1,924 Billy Sims, Detroit, 1980 (1,303 rush., 621 rec.)

Most Scrimmage Yards, Game
336 Flipper Anderson, L.A. Rams vs. New Orleans, Nov. 26, 1989 (OT) (336 rec.)
330 Billy Cannon, Houston vs. N.Y. Titans, Dec. 10, 1961 (216 rush., 114 rec.)
309 Stephone Paige, Kansas City vs. San Diego, Dec. 22, 1985 (309 rec.)

INTERCEPTIONS BY
Most Seasons Leading League
3   Everson Walls, Dallas, 1981-82, 1985
2   Dick (Night Train) Lane, Los Angeles, 1952; Chi. Cardinals, 1954
    Jack Christiansen, Detroit, 1953, 1957
    Milt Davis, Baltimore, 1957, 1959
    Dick Lynch, N.Y. Giants, 1961, 1963
    Johnny Robinson, Kansas City, 1966, 1970
    Bill Bradley, Philadelphia, 1971-72
    Emmitt Thomas, Kansas City, 1969, 1974
    Ronnie Lott, San Francisco, 1986; L.A. Raiders, 1991

Most Interceptions By, Career
81 Paul Krause, Washington, 1964-67; Minnesota, 1968-1979
79 Emlen Tunnell, N.Y. Giants, 1948-1958; Green Bay, 1959-1961

68 Dick (Night Train) Lane, Los Angeles, 1952-53; Chi. Cardinals, 1954-59; Detroit, 1960-65

Most Interceptions By, Season
14 Dick (Night Train) Lane, Los Angeles, 1952
13 Dan Sandifer, Washington, 1948
    Orban (Spec) Sanders, N.Y. Yanks, 1950
    Lester Hayes, Oakland, 1980
12 By nine players

Most Interceptions By, Rookie, Season
14 Dick (Night Train) Lane, Los Angeles, 1952
13 Dan Sandifer, Washington, 1948
12 Woodley Lewis, Los Angeles, 1950
    Paul Krause, Washington, 1964

Most Interceptions By, Game
4   Sammy Baugh, Washington vs. Detroit, Nov. 14, 1943
    Dan Sandifer, Washington vs. Boston, Oct. 31, 1948
    Don Doll, Detroit vs. Chi. Cardinals, Oct. 23, 1949
    Bob Nussbaumer, Chi. Cardinals vs. N.Y. Bulldogs, Nov. 13, 1949
    Russ Craft, Philadelphia vs. Chi. Cardinals, Sept. 24, 1950
    Bobby Dillon, Green Bay vs. Detroit, Nov. 26, 1953
    Jack Butler, Pittsburgh vs. Washington, Dec. 13, 1953
    Austin (Goose) Gonsoulin, Denver vs. Buffalo, Sept. 18, 1960
    Jerry Norton, St. Louis vs. Washington, Nov. 20, 1960; vs. Pittsburgh, Nov. 26, 1961
    Dave Baker, San Francisco vs. L.A. Rams, Dec. 4, 1960
    Bobby Ply, Dall. Texans vs. San Diego, Dec. 16, 1962
    Bobby Hunt, Kansas City vs. Houston, Oct. 4, 1964
    Willie Brown, Denver vs. N.Y. Jets, Nov. 15, 1964
    Dick Anderson, Miami vs. Pittsburgh, Dec. 3, 1973
    Willie Buchanon, Green Bay vs. San Diego, Sept. 24, 1978
    Deron Cherry, Kansas City vs. Seattle, Sept. 29, 1985
    Kwamie Lassiter, Arizona vs. San Diego, Dec. 27, 1998
    Deltha O'Neal, Denver vs. Kansas City, Oct. 7, 2001

Most Consecutive Games, Passes Intercepted By
8   Tom Morrow, Oakland, 1962-63
7   Tom Landry, N.Y. Giants, 1950-51
    Paul Krause, Washington, 1964
    Larry Wilson, St. Louis, 1966
    Ben Davis, Cleveland, 1968
6   By many players. Last time: Doug Evans, Carolina, 2001

YARDS GAINED
Most Seasons Leading League
2   Dick (Night Train) Lane, Los Angeles, 1952; Chi. Cardinals, 1954
    Herb Adderley, Green Bay, 1965, 1969
    Dick Anderson, Miami, 1968, 1970

Most Yards Gained, Career
1,282 Emlen Tunnell, N.Y. Giants, 1948-1958; Green Bay, 1959-1961
1,240 Rod Woodson, Pittsburgh, 1987-1996; San Francisco, 1997; Baltimore, 1998-2001
1,207 Dick (Night Train) Lane, Los Angeles, 1952-53; Chi. Cardinals, 1954-59; Detroit, 1960-65

Most Yards Gained, Season
349 Charlie McNeil, San Diego, 1961
303 Deion Sanders, San Francisco, 1994
301 Don Doll, Detroit, 1949

Most Yards Gained, Rookie, Season
301 Don Doll, Detroit, 1949
298 Dick (Night Train) Lane, Los Angeles, 1952
275 Woodley Lewis, Los Angeles, 1950

Most Yards Gained, Game
177   Charlie McNeil, San Diego vs. Houston,
     Sept. 24, 1961
170   Louis Oliver, Miami vs. Buffalo, Oct. 4, 1992
167   Dick Jauron, Detroit vs. Chicago, Nov. 18, 1973

Longest Return (All TDs)
103   Vencie Glenn, San Diego vs. Denver, Nov. 29, 1987
     Louis Oliver, Miami vs. Buffalo, Oct. 4, 1992
102   Bob Smith, Detroit vs. Chi. Bears, Nov. 24, 1949
     Erich Barnes, N.Y. Giants vs. Dall. Cowboys,
     Oct. 15, 1961
     Gary Barbaro, Kansas City vs. Seattle, Dec. 11, 1977
     Louis Breeden, Cincinnati vs. San Diego, Nov. 8, 1981
     Eddie Anderson, L.A. Raiders vs. Miami,
     Dec. 14, 1992
     Donald Frank, San Diego vs. L.A. Raiders,
     Oct. 31, 1993
101   Richie Petitbon, Chicago vs Los Angeles,
     Dec. 9, 1962
     Henry Carr, N.Y. Giants vs. Los Angeles,
     Nov. 13, 1966
     Tony Greene, Buffalo vs. Kansas City, Oct. 3, 1976
     Tom Pridemore, Atlanta vs. San Francisco,
     Sept. 20, 1981
     Bryant Westbrook, Detroit vs. New England,
     Nov. 23, 2000

TOUCHDOWNS

Most Touchdowns, Career
10   Rod Woodson, Pittsburgh, 1987-1996;
     San Francisco, 1997; Baltimore, 1998-2001
9   Ken Houston, Houston, 1967-1972; Washington,
     1973-1980
8   Deion Sanders, Atlanta, 1989-1993; San Francisco,
     1994; Dallas, 1995-99; Washington, 2000
     Eric Allen, Philadelphia, 1988-1994; New Orleans,
     1995-97; Oakland, 1998-2001
     Aeneas Williams, Phoenix, 1991-93; Arizona,
     1994-2000; St. Louis, 2001

Most Touchdowns, Season
4   Ken Houston, Houston, 1971
     Jim Kearney, Kansas City, 1972
     Eric Allen, Philadelphia, 1993
3   Dick Harris, San Diego, 1961
     Dick Lynch, N.Y. Giants, 1963
     Herb Adderley, Green Bay, 1965
     Lem Barney, Detroit, 1967
     Miller Farr, Houston, 1967
     Monte Jackson, Los Angeles, 1976
     Rod Perry, Los Angeles, 1978
     Ronnie Lott, San Francisco, 1981
     Lloyd Burruss, Kansas City, 1986
     Wayne Haddix, Tampa Bay, 1990
     Robert Massey, Phoenix, 1992
     Ray Buchanan, Indianapolis, 1994
     Deion Sanders, San Francisco, 1994
     Mark McMillian, Kansas City, 1997
     Otis Smith, N.Y. Jets, 1997
     Jimmy Hitchcock, Minnesota, 1998
     Eric Allen, Oakland, 2000
2   By many players

Most Touchdowns, Rookie, Season
3   Lem Barney, Detroit, 1967
     Ronnie Lott, San Francisco, 1981
2   By many players

Most Touchdowns, Game
2   Bill Blackburn, Chi. Cardinals vs. Boston,
     Oct. 24, 1948
     Dan Sandifer, Washington vs. Boston, Oct. 31, 1948

     Bob Franklin, Cleveland vs. Chicago, Dec. 11, 1960
     Bill Stacy, St. Louis vs. Dall. Cowboys, Nov. 5, 1961
     Jerry Norton, St. Louis vs. Pittsburgh, Nov. 26, 1961
     Miller Farr, Houston vs. Buffalo, Dec. 7, 1968
     Ken Houston, Houston vs. San Diego, Dec. 19, 1971
     Jim Kearney, Kansas City vs. Denver, Oct. 1, 1972
     Lemar Parrish, Cincinnati vs. Houston, Dec. 17, 1972
     Dick Anderson, Miami vs. Pittsburgh, Dec. 3, 1973
     Prentice McCray, New England vs. N.Y. Jets,
     Nov. 21, 1976
     Kenny Johnson, Atlanta vs. Green Bay,
     Nov. 27, 1983 (OT)
     Mike Kozlowski, Miami vs. N.Y. Jets, Dec. 16, 1983
     Dave Brown, Seattle vs. Kansas City, Nov. 4, 1984
     Lloyd Burruss, Kansas City vs. San Diego,
     Oct. 19, 1986
     Henry Jones, Buffalo vs. Indianapolis, Sept. 20, 1992
     Robert Massey, Phoenix vs. Washington, Oct. 4, 1992
     Eric Allen, Philadelphia vs. New Orleans,
     Dec. 26, 1993
     Ken Norton, San Francisco vs. St. Louis,
     Oct. 22, 1995
     Otis Smith, N.Y. Jets vs. Tampa Bay, Dec. 14, 1997
     Dewayne Washington, Pittsburgh vs. Jacksonville,
     Nov. 22, 1998

PUNTING

Most Seasons Leading League
4   Sammy Baugh, Washington, 1940-43
     Jerrel Wilson, Kansas City, 1965, 1968, 1972-73
3   Yale Lary, Detroit, 1959, 1961, 1963
     Jim Fraser, Denver, 1962-64
     Ray Guy, Oakland, 1974-75, 1977
     Rohn Stark, Baltimore, 1983; Indianapolis, 1985-86
2   By many players

Most Consecutive Seasons Leading League
4   Sammy Baugh, Washington, 1940-43
3   Jim Fraser, Denver, 1962-64
2   By many players

PUNTS

Most Punts, Career
1,216   Sean Landeta, N.Y. Giants, 1985-1993; L.A. Rams,
     1993-94; St. Louis, 1995-96; Tampa Bay, 1997;
     Green Bay, 1998; Philadelphia, 1999-2001
1,212   Lee Johnson, Houston, 1985-87; Cleveland,
     1987-88; Cincinnati, 1988-1998; New England,
     1999-2001; Minnesota, 2001
1,154   Dave Jennings, N.Y. Giants, 1974-1984; N.Y. Jets,
     1985-87

Most Punts, Season
114   Bob Parsons, Chicago, 1981
111   Brad Maynard, N.Y. Giants, 1997
109   John James, Atlanta, 1978

Most Punts, Rookie, Season
111   Brad Maynard, N.Y. Giants, 1997
108   John Teltschik, Philadelphia, 1986
101   Daniel Pope, Kansas City, 1999

Most Punts, Game
16   Leo Araguz, Oakland vs. San Diego, Oct. 11, 1998
15   John Teltschik, Philadelphia vs. N.Y. Giants,
     Dec. 6, 1987 (OT)
14   Dick Nesbitt, Chi. Cardinals vs. Chi. Bears,
     Nov. 30, 1933
     Keith Molesworth, Chi. Bears vs. Green Bay,
     Dec. 10, 1933
     Sammy Baugh, Washington vs. Philadelphia,
     Nov. 5, 1939
     Carl Kinscherf, N.Y. Giants vs. Detroit, Nov. 7, 1943

George Taliaferro, N.Y. Yanks vs. Los Angeles,
Sept. 28, 1951

Longest Punt
- 98   Steve O'Neal, N.Y. Jets vs. Denver, Sept. 21, 1969
- 94   Joe Lintzenich, Chi. Bears vs. N.Y. Giants,
Nov. 16, 1931
- 93   Shawn McCarthy, New England vs. Buffalo,
Nov. 3, 1991

AVERAGE YARDAGE
Highest Average, Punting, Career (250 punts)
- 45.10   Sammy Baugh, Washington, 1937-1952
(338-15,245)
- 44.68   Tommy Davis, San Francisco, 1959-1969
(511-22,833)
- 44.52   Darren Bennett, San Diego, 1995-2001
(602-26,800)

Highest Average, Punting, Season (Qualifiers)
- 51.40   Sammy Baugh, Washington, 1940 (35-1,799)
- 48.94   Yale Lary, Detroit, 1963 (35-1,713)
- 48.73   Sammy Baugh, Washington, 1941 (30-1,462)

Highest Average, Punting, Rookie, Season (Qualifiers)
- 45.92   Frank Sinkwich, Detroit, 1943 (12-551)
- 45.91   Shane Lechler, Oakland, 2000 (65-2,984)
- 45.66   Tommy Davis, San Francisco, 1959 (59-2,694)

Highest Average, Punting, Game (4 punts)
- 61.75   Bob Cifers, Detroit vs. Chi. Bears, Nov. 24, 1946
(4-247)
- 61.60   Roy McKay, Green Bay vs. Chi. Cardinals,
Oct. 28, 1945 (5-308)
- 59.50   Darren Bennett, San Diego vs. Pittsburgh,
Oct. 1, 1995 (4-238)

PUNTS HAD BLOCKED
Most Consecutive Punts, None Blocked
- 825   Chris Gardocki, Chicago, 1992-94; Indianapolis,
1995-98; Cleveland, 1999-2001 (current)
- 630   Bryan Barker, Kansas City, 1993; Philadelphia, 1994;
Jacksonville, 1995-2000; Washington, 2001
- 623   Dave Jennings, N.Y. Giants, 1976-1983

Most Punts Had Blocked, Career
- 14   Herman Weaver, Detroit, 1970-76; Seattle, 1977-1980
Harry Newsome, Pittsburgh, 1985-89; Minnesota,
1990-93
- 12   Jerrel Wilson, Kansas City, 1963-1977;
New England, 1978
Tom Blanchard, N.Y. Giants, 1971-73; New Orleans,
1974-78; Tampa Bay, 1979-1981
- 11   David Lee, Baltimore, 1966-1978

Most Punts Had Blocked, Season
- 6   Harry Newsome, Pittsburgh, 1988
- 4   Bryan Wagner, Cleveland, 1990
- 3   By many players

PUNTS INSIDE THE 20
Punts Inside the 20 have been compiled since 1976.

Most Punts Inside the 20, Career
- 354   Jeff Feagles, New England, 1988-89; Philadelphia,
1990-93; Arizona, 1994-97; Seattle, 1998-2001
- 332   Sean Landeta, N.Y. Giants, 1985-1993; L.A. Rams,
1993-94; St. Louis, 1995-96; Tampa Bay, 1997;
Green Bay, 1998; Philadelphia, 1999-2001
- 314   Lee Johnson, Houston, 1985-87; Cleveland,
1987-88; Cincinnati, 1988-1998; New England,
1999-2001; Minnesota, 2001

Most Punts Inside the 20, Season
- 39   Kyle Richardson, Baltimore, 1999
- 36   Brad Maynard, Chicago, 2001
- 35   Rich Camarillo, Houston, 1994
      Mark Royals, Pittsburgh, 1994

Craig Hentrich, Tennessee, 1999
Kyle Richardson, Baltimore, 2000
Todd Sauerbrun, Carolina, 2001

Most Punts Inside the 20, Game
- 8   Mark Royals, Pittsburgh vs. Houston, Nov. 6, 1994
(OT)
    Bryan Barker, Jacksonville vs. Baltimore,
Nov. 14, 1999
- 7   Josh Miller, Pittsburgh vs. Cincinnati, Dec. 20, 1998
- 6   By many players

PUNT RETURNS
Most Seasons Leading League
- 3   Les (Speedy) Duncan, San Diego, 1965-66;
Washington, 1971
    Rick Upchurch, Denver, 1976, 1978, 1982
- 2   Dick Christy, N.Y. Titans, 1961-62
    Claude Gibson, Oakland, 1963-64
    Billy (White Shoes) Johnson, Houston, 1975, 1977
    Mel Gray, New Orleans, 1987; Detroit, 1991
    Jermaine Lewis, Baltimore, 1997, 2000

PUNT RETURNS
Most Punt Returns, Career
- 388   Brian Mitchell, Washington, 1990-99; Philadelphia,
2000-01
- 349   David Meggett, N.Y. Giants, 1989-1994;
New England, 1995-97; N.Y. Jets, 1998
- 348   Eric Metcalf, Cleveland, 1989-1994; Atlanta, 1995-
96; San Diego, 1997; Arizona, 1998; Carolina,
1999; Washington, 2001

Most Punt Returns, Season
- 70   Danny Reece, Tampa Bay, 1979
- 62   Fulton Walker, Miami-L.A. Raiders, 1985
- 58   J.T. Smith, Kansas City, 1979
    Greg Pruitt, L.A. Raiders, 1983
    Leo Lewis, Minnesota, 1988
    Desmond Howard, Green Bay, 1996

Most Punt Returns, Rookie, Season
- 57   Lew Barnes, Chicago, 1986
- 54   James Jones, Dallas, 1980
- 53   Louis Lipps, Pittsburgh, 1984

Most Punt Returns, Game
- 11   Eddie Brown, Washington vs. Tampa Bay,
Oct. 9, 1977
- 10   Theo Bell, Pittsburgh vs. Buffalo, Dec. 16, 1979
    Mike Nelms, Washington vs. New Orleans,
Dec. 26, 1982
    Ronnie Harris, New England vs. Pittsburgh,
Dec. 5, 1993
- 9   Rodger Bird, Oakland vs. Denver, Sept. 10, 1967
    Ralph McGill, San Francisco vs. Atlanta,
Oct. 29, 1972
    Ed Podolak, Kansas City vs. San Diego,
Nov. 10, 1974
    Anthony Leonard, San Francisco vs. New Orleans,
Oct. 17, 1976
    Butch Johnson, Dallas vs. Buffalo, Nov. 15, 1976
    Larry Marshall, Philadelphia vs. Tampa Bay,
Sept. 18, 1977
    Nesby Glasgow, Baltimore vs. Kansas City,
Sept. 2, 1979
    Mike Nelms, Washington vs. St. Louis, Dec. 21, 1980
    Leon Bright, N.Y. Giants vs. Philadelphia,
Dec. 11, 1982
    Pete Shaw, N.Y. Giants vs. Philadelphia,
Nov. 20, 1983
    Cleotha Montgomery, L.A. Raiders vs. Detroit,
Dec. 10, 1984

Phil McConkey, N.Y. Giants vs. Philadelphia,
Dec. 6, 1987 (OT)
Andre Hastings, Pittsburgh vs. Cleveland,
Nov. 13, 1995

FAIR CATCHES
Most Fair Catches, Career
206 Brian Mitchell, Washington, 1990-99; Philadelphia,
2000-01
144 Glyn Milburn, Denver, 1993-95; Detroit, 1996-97;
Chicago, 1998-2001; San Diego, 2001
133 Tim Brown, L.A. Raiders, 1988-1994; Oakland,
1995-2001
Most Fair Catches, Season
33 Brian Mitchell, Philadelphia, 2000
27 Leo Lewis, Minnesota, 1989
26 Eric Guliford, New Orleans, 1997
Glyn Milburn, Detroit, 1997
Glyn Milburn, Chicago, 2000
Most Fair Catches, Game
7 Lem Barney, Detroit vs. Chicago, Nov. 21, 1976
Bobby Morse, Philadelphia vs. Buffalo, Dec. 27, 1987
6 Jake Scott, Miami vs. Buffalo, Dec. 20, 1970
Greg Pruitt, L.A. Raiders vs. Seattle, Oct. 7, 1984
Phil McConkey, San Diego vs. Kansas City,
Dec. 17, 1989
Gerald McNeil, Houston vs. Pittsburgh,
Sept. 16, 1990
Bobby Engram, Chicago vs. Minnesota,
Sept. 15, 1996
Eddie Kennison, New Orleans vs. Baltimore,
Dec. 19, 1999
5 By many players

YARDS GAINED
Most Seasons Leading League
3 Alvin Haymond, Baltimore, 1965-66; Los Angeles,
1969
2 Bill Dudley, Pittsburgh, 1942, 1946
Emlen Tunnell, N.Y. Giants, 1951-52
Dick Christy, N.Y. Titans, 1961-62
Claude Gibson, Oakland, 1963-64
Rodger Bird, Oakland, 1966-67
J.T. Smith, Kansas City, 1979-1980
Vai Sikahema, St. Louis, 1986-87
David Meggett, N.Y. Giants, 1989-1990
Tamarick Vanover, Kansas City, 1995, 1999
Most Yards Gained, Career
4,278 Brian Mitchell, Washington, 1990-99; Philadelphia,
2000-01
3,708 David Meggett, N.Y. Giants, 1989-1994;
New England, 1995-97; N.Y. Jets, 1998
3,454 Eric Metcalf, Cleveland, 1989-1994; Atlanta,
1995-96; San Diego, 1997; Arizona, 1998;
Carolina, 1999; Washington, 2001
Most Yards Gained, Season
875 Desmond Howard, Green Bay, 1996
692 Fulton Walker, Miami-L.A. Raiders, 1985
666 Greg Pruitt, L.A. Raiders, 1983
Most Yards Gained, Rookie, Season
656 Louis Lipps, Pittsburgh, 1984
655 Neal Colzie, Oakland, 1975
619 Leon Johnson, N.Y. Jets, 1997
Most Yards Gained, Game
207 LeRoy Irvin, Los Angeles vs. Atlanta, Oct. 11, 1981
205 George Atkinson, Oakland vs. Buffalo, Sept. 15, 1968
184 Tom Watkins, Detroit vs. San Francisco, Oct. 6, 1963
Jermaine Lewis, Baltimore vs. Seattle, Dec. 7, 1997

Longest Punt Return (All TDs)
103 Robert Bailey, L.A. Rams vs. New Orleans,
Oct. 23, 1994
98 Gil LeFebvre, Cincinnati vs. Brooklyn, Dec. 3, 1933
Charlie West, Minnesota vs. Washington, Nov. 3, 1968
Dennis Morgan, Dallas vs. St. Louis, Oct. 13, 1974
Terance Mathis, N.Y. Jets vs. Dallas, Nov. 4, 1990
97 Greg Pruitt, L.A. Raiders vs. Washington,
Oct. 2, 1983

AVERAGE YARDAGE
Highest Average, Career (75 returns)
12.78 George McAfee, Chi. Bears, 1940-41, 1945-1950
(112-1,431)
12.75 Jack Christiansen, Detroit, 1951-58 (85-1,084)
12.55 Claude Gibson, San Diego, 1961-62; Oakland,
1963-65 (110-1,381)
Highest Average, Season (Qualifiers)
23.00 Herb Rich, Baltimore, 1950 (12-276)
21.47 Jack Christiansen, Detroit, 1952 (15-322)
21.28 Dick Christy, N.Y. Titans, 1961 (18-383)
Highest Average, Rookie, Season (Qualifiers)
23.00 Herb Rich, Baltimore, 1950 (12-276)
20.88 Jerry Davis, Chi. Cardinals, 1948 (16-334)
20.73 Frank Sinkwich, Detroit, 1943 (11-228)
Highest Average, Game (3 returns)
47.67 Chuck Latourette, St. Louis vs. New Orleans,
Sept. 29, 1968 (3-143)
47.33 Johnny Roland, St. Louis vs. Philadelphia,
Oct. 2, 1966 (3-142)
46.33 Darrien Gordon, Atlanta vs. Dallas, Nov. 11, 2001
(3-139)

TOUCHDOWNS
Most Touchdowns, Career
10 Eric Metcalf, Cleveland, 1989-1994; Atlanta,
1995-96; San Diego, 1997; Arizona, 1998;
Carolina, 1999; Washington, 2001
8 Jack Christiansen, Detroit, 1951-58
Rick Upchurch, Denver, 1975-1983
Desmond Howard, Washington, 1992-94;
Jacksonville, 1995; Green Bay, 1996, 1999;
Oakland, 1997-98; Detroit, 1999-2001
Brian Mitchell, Washington, 1990-99; Philadelphia
2000-01
7 David Meggett, N.Y. Giants, 1989-1994;
New England, 1995-97; N.Y. Jets, 1998
Most Touchdowns, Season
4 Jack Christiansen, Detroit, 1951
Rick Upchurch, Denver, 1976
3 Emlen Tunnell, N.Y. Giants, 1951
Billy (White Shoes) Johnson, Houston, 1975
LeRoy Irvin, Los Angeles, 1981
Desmond Howard, Green Bay, 1996
Darrien Gordon, Denver, 1997
Eric Metcalf, San Diego, 1997
2 By many players
Most Touchdowns, Rookie, Season
4 Jack Christiansen, Detroit, 1951
2 By many players
Most Touchdowns, Game
2 Jack Christiansen, Detroit vs. Los Angeles,
Oct. 14, 1951; vs. Green Bay, Nov. 22, 1951
Dick Christy, N.Y. Titans vs. Denver, Sept. 24, 1961
Rick Upchurch, Denver vs. Cleveland, Sept. 26, 1976
LeRoy Irvin, Los Angeles vs. Atlanta, Oct. 11, 1981
Vai Sikahema, St. Louis vs. Tampa Bay,
Dec. 21, 1986
Todd Kinchen, L.A. Rams vs. Atlanta, Dec. 27, 1992
Eric Metcalf, Cleveland vs. Pittsburgh, Oct. 24, 1993;

San Diego vs. Cincinnati, Nov. 2, 1997
Darrien Gordon, Denver vs. Carolina, Nov. 9, 1997
Jermaine Lewis, Baltimore vs. Seattle, Dec. 7, 1997;
    Baltimore vs. N.Y. Jets, Dec. 24, 2000

KICKOFF RETURNS
Most Seasons Leading League
- 3   Abe Woodson, San Francisco, 1959, 1962-63
- 2   Lynn Chandnois, Pittsburgh, 1951-52
      Bobby Jancik, Houston, 1962-63
      Travis Williams, Green Bay, 1967; Los Angeles, 1971
      Mel Gray, Detroit, 1991, 1994
      Michael Bates, Carolina, 1996-97

KICKOFF RETURNS
Most Kickoff Returns, Career
- 509   Brian Mitchell, Washington, 1990-99; Philadelphia 2000-01
- 421   Mel Gray, New Orleans, 1986-88; Detroit, 1989-1994; Houston, 1995-96; Tennessee, 1997; Philadelphia, 1997
- 407   Glyn Milburn, Denver, 1993-95; Detroit, 1996-97; Chicago, 1998-2001; San Diego, 2001

Most Kickoff Returns, Season
- 82   MarTay Jenkins, Arizona, 2000
- 70   Tyrone Hughes, New Orleans, 1996
- 67   Ronney Jenkins, San Diego, 2000

Most Kickoff Returns, Rookie, Season
- 67   Ronney Jenkins, San Diego, 2000
- 56   Tony Horne, St. Louis, 1998
      Steve Smith, Carolina, 2001
- 55   Stump Mitchell, St. Louis, 1981

Most Kickoff Returns, Game
- 10   Desmond Howard, Oakland vs. Seattle, Oct. 26, 1997
- 9   Noland Smith, Kansas City vs. Oakland, Nov. 23, 1967
      Dino Hall, Cleveland vs. Pittsburgh, Oct. 7, 1979
      Paul Palmer, Kansas City vs. Seattle, Sept. 20, 1987
      Eric Metcalf, Atlanta vs. San Francisco,
        Sept. 29, 1996; vs. St. Louis, Nov. 10, 1996
      Michael Bates, Carolina vs. Atlanta, Oct. 4, 1998
      Nate Jacquet, Minnesota vs. Philadelphia,
        Nov. 11, 2001
- 8   By many players

YARDS GAINED
Most Seasons Leading League
- 3   Bruce Harper, N.Y. Jets, 1977-79
      Tyrone Hughes, New Orleans, 1994-96
- 2   Marshall Goldberg, Chi. Cardinals, 1941-42
      Woodley Lewis, Los Angeles, 1953-54
      Al Carmichael, Green Bay, 1956-57
      Timmy Brown, Philadelphia, 1961, 1963
      Bobby Jancik, Houston, 1963, 1966
      Ron Smith, Atlanta, 1966-67

Most Yards Gained, Career
- 11,735   Brian Mitchell, Washington, 1990-99; Philadelphia, 2000-01
- 10,250   Mel Gray, New Orleans, 1986-88; Detroit, 1989-1994; Houston, 1995-96; Tennessee, 1997; Philadelphia, 1997
- 9,788   Glyn Milburn, Denver, 1993-95; Detroit, 1996-97; Chicago, 1998-2001; San Diego, 2001

Most Yards Gained, Season
- 2,186   MarTay Jenkins, Arizona, 2000
- 1,791   Tyrone Hughes, New Orleans, 1996
- 1,629   Charlie Rogers, Seattle, 2000

Most Yards Gained, Rookie, Season
- 1,531   Ronney Jenkins, San Diego, 2000
- 1,431   Steve Smith, Carolina, 2001
- 1,428   Terry Fair, Detroit, 1998

Most Yards Gained, Game
- 304   Tyrone Hughes, New Orleans vs. L.A. Rams, Oct. 23, 1994
- 294   Wally Triplett, Detroit vs. Los Angeles, Oct. 29, 1950
- 267   Tony Horne, St. Louis vs. Kansas City, Oct. 22, 2000

Longest Kickoff Return (All TDs)
- 106   Al Carmichael, Green Bay vs. Chi. Bears, Oct. 7, 1956
      Noland Smith, Kansas City vs. Denver, Dec. 17, 1967
      Roy Green, St. Louis vs. Dallas, Oct. 21, 1979
- 105   Frank Seno, Chi. Cardinals vs. N.Y. Giants, Oct. 20, 1946
      Ollie Matson, Chi. Cardinals vs. Washington, Oct. 14, 1956
      Abe Woodson, San Francisco vs. Los Angeles, Nov. 8, 1959
      Timmy Brown, Philadelphia vs. Cleveland, Sept. 17, 1961
      Jon Arnett, Los Angeles vs. Detroit, Oct. 29, 1961
      Eugene (Mercury) Morris, Miami vs. Cincinnati, Sept. 14, 1969
      Travis Williams, Los Angeles vs. New Orleans, Dec. 5, 1971
      Terry Fair, Detroit vs. Tampa Bay, Sept. 28, 1998
- 104   By many players

AVERAGE YARDAGE
Highest Average, Career (75 returns)
- 30.56   Gale Sayers, Chicago, 1965-1971 (91-2,781)
- 29.57   Lynn Chandnois, Pittsburgh, 1950-56 (92-2,720)
- 28.69   Abe Woodson, San Francisco, 1958-1964; St. Louis, 1965-66 (193-5,538)

Highest Average, Season (Qualifiers)
- 41.06   Travis Williams, Green Bay, 1967 (18-739)
- 37.69   Gale Sayers, Chicago, 1967 (16-603)
- 35.50   Ollie Matson, Chi. Cardinals, 1958 (14-497)

Highest Average, Rookie, Season (Qualifiers)
- 41.06   Travis Williams, Green Bay, 1967 (18-739)
- 33.08   Tom Moore, Green Bay, 1960 (12-397)
- 32.88   Duriel Harris, Miami, 1976 (17-559)

Highest Average, Game (3 returns)
- 73.50   Wally Triplett, Detroit vs. Los Angeles, Oct. 29, 1950 (4-294)
- 67.33   Lenny Lyles, San Francisco vs. Baltimore, Dec. 18, 1960 (3-202)
- 65.33   Ken Hall, Houston vs. N.Y. Titans, Oct. 23, 1960 (3-196)

TOUCHDOWNS
Most Touchdowns, Career
- 6   Ollie Matson, Chi. Cardinals, 1952, 1954-58; L.A. Rams, 1959-1962; Detroit, 1963; Philadelphia, 1964
      Gale Sayers, Chicago, 1965-1971
      Travis Williams, Green Bay, 1967-1970; Los Angeles, 1971
      Mel Gray, New Orleans, 1986-88; Detroit, 1989-1994; Houston, 1995-96; Tennessee, 1997; Philadelphia, 1997
- 5   Bobby Mitchell, Cleveland, 1958-1961; Washington, 1962-68
      Abe Woodson, San Francisco, 1958-1964; St. Louis, 1965-66
      Timmy Brown, Green Bay, 1959; Philadelphia, 1960-67; Baltimore, 1968
      Michael Bates, Seattle, 1993-94; Cleveland, 1995; Carolina, 1996-2000; Washington, 2001
- 4   Cecil Turner, Chicago, 1968-1973
      Ron Brown, L.A. Rams, 1984-89, 1991; L.A. Raiders, 1990

Jon Vaughn, New England, 1991-92; Seattle,
1993-94; Kansas City, 1994
Andre Coleman, San Diego, 1994-96; Seattle, 1997;
Pittsburgh, 1997-98
Tamarick Vanover, Kansas City, 1995-99
Tony Horne, St. Louis, 1998-2000
Brian Mitchell, Washington, 1990-99; Philadelphia,
2000-01
Darrick Vaughn, Atlanta, 2000-01

Most Touchdowns, Season

4   Travis Williams, Green Bay, 1967
    Cecil Turner, Chicago, 1970
3   Verda (Vitamin T) Smith, Los Angeles, 1950
    Abe Woodson, San Francisco, 1963
    Gale Sayers, Chicago, 1967
    Raymond Clayborn, New England, 1977
    Ron Brown, L.A. Rams, 1985
    Mel Gray, Detroit, 1994
    Darrick Vaughn, Atlanta, 2000
2   By many players

Most Touchdowns, Rookie, Season

4   Travis Williams, Green Bay, 1967
3   Raymond Clayborn, New England, 1977
    Darrick Vaughn, Atlanta, 2000
2   By many players

Most Touchdowns, Game

2   Timmy Brown, Philadelphia vs. Dallas, Nov. 6, 1966
    Travis Williams, Green Bay vs. Cleveland,
    Nov. 12, 1967
    Ron Brown, L.A. Rams vs. Green Bay, Nov. 24, 1985
    Tyrone Hughes, New Orleans vs. L.A. Rams,
    Oct. 23, 1994

COMBINED KICK RETURNS

Most Combined Kick Returns, Career

897   Brian Mitchell, Washington, 1990-99; Philadelphia,
    2000-01 (p-388, k-509)
711   Glyn Milburn, Denver, 1993-95; Detroit, 1996-97;
    Chicago, 1998-2001; San Diego, 2001 (p-304,
    k-407)
673   Mel Gray, New Orleans, 1986-88; Detroit,
    1989-1994; Houston, 1995-96; Tennessee,
    1997; Philadelphia, 1997 (p-252, k-421)

Most Combined Kick Returns, Season

103   Brian Mitchell, Washington, 1998 (p-44; k-59)
102   Glyn Milburn, Detroit, 1997 (p-47, k-55)
101   Roell Preston, Green Bay, 1998 (p-44; k-57)

Most Combined Kick Returns, Game

13   Stump Mitchell, St. Louis vs. Atlanta, Oct. 18, 1981
    (p-6, k-7)
    Ronnie Harris, New England vs. Pittsburgh,
    Dec. 5, 1993 (p-10, k-3)
12   Mel Renfro, Dallas vs. Green Bay, Nov. 29, 1964
    (p-4, k-8)
    Larry Jones, Washington vs. Dallas, Dec. 13, 1975
    (p-6, k-6)
    Eddie Brown, Washington vs. Tampa Bay,
    Oct. 9, 1977 (p-11, k-1)
    Nesby Glasgow, Baltimore vs. Denver, Sept. 2, 1979
    (p-9, k-3)
    Tim Dwight, Atlanta vs. Detroit, Nov. 12, 2000
    (p-8, k-4)
11   By many players

YARDS GAINED

Most Yards Returned, Career

16,013   Brian Mitchell, Washington, 1990-99; Philadelphia,
    2000-01 (p-4,278; k-11,735)

13,003   Mel Gray, New Orleans, 1986-88; Detroit,
    1989-1994; Houston, 1995-96; Tennessee,
    1997; Philadelphia, 1997 (p-2,753; k-10,250)
12,772   Glyn Milburn, Denver, 1993-95; Detroit, 1996-97;
    Chicago, 1998-2001; San Diego, 2001
    (p-2,984; k-9,788)

Most Yards Returned, Season

2,187   MarTay Jenkins, Arizona, 2000 (p-1, k-2,186)
1,992   Charlie Rogers, Seattle, 2000 (p-363, k-1,629)
1,943   Tyrone Hughes, New Orleans, 1996 (p-152, k-1,791)

Most Yards Returned, Game

347   Tyrone Hughes, New Orleans vs. L.A. Rams,
    Oct. 23, 1994 (p-43, k-304)
294   Wally Triplett, Detroit vs. Los Angeles, Oct. 29, 1950
    (k-294)
    Woodley Lewis, Los Angeles vs. Detroit,
    Oct. 18, 1953 (p-120, k-174)
289   Eddie Payton, Detroit vs. Minnesota, Dec. 17, 1977
    (p-105, k-184)

TOUCHDOWNS

Most Touchdowns, Career

12   Eric Metcalf, Cleveland, 1989-1994; Atlanta,
    1995-96; San Diego, 1997; Arizona, 1998;
    Carolina, 1999; Washington, 2001 (p-10, k-2)
    Brian Mitchell, Washington, 1990-99; Philadelphia,
    2000-01 (p-8, k-4)
9   Ollie Matson, Chi. Cardinals, 1952, 1954-58;
    Los Angeles, 1959-1962; Detroit, 1963;
    Philadelphia, 1964-66 (p-3, k-6)
    Mel Gray, New Orleans, 1986-88; Detroit,
    1989-1994; Houston, 1995-96; Tennessee,
    1997; Philadelphia, 1997 (p-3, k-6)
    Deion Sanders, Atlanta, 1989-1993; San Francisco,
    1994; Dallas, 1995-99; Washington, 2000
    (p-6, k-3)
8   Jack Christiansen, Detroit, 1951-58 (p-8)
    Bobby Mitchell, Cleveland, 1958-1961; Washington,
    1962-68 (p-3, k-5)
    Gale Sayers, Chicago, 1965-1971 (p-2, k-6)
    Rick Upchurch, Denver, 1975-1983 (p-8)
    Billy (White Shoes) Johnson, Houston, 1974-1980;
    Atlanta, 1982-87; Washington, 1988 (p-6, k-2)
    David Meggett, N.Y. Giants, 1989-1994;
    New England, 1995-97; N.Y. Jets, 1998 (p-7, k-1)
    Tamarick Vanover, Kansas City, 1995-99 (p-4, k-4)
    Desmond Howard, Washington, 1992-94;
    Jacksonville, 1995; Green Bay, 1996, 1999;
    Oakland, 1997-98; Detroit, 1999-2001 (p-8)

Most Touchdowns, Season

4   Jack Christiansen, Detroit, 1951 (p-4)
    Emlen Tunnell, N.Y. Giants, 1951 (p-3, k-1)
    Gale Sayers, Chicago, 1967 (p-1, k-3)
    Travis Williams, Green Bay, 1967 (k-4)
    Cecil Turner, Chicago, 1970 (k-4)
    Billy Johnson, Houston, 1975 (p-3, k-1)
    Rick Upchurch, Denver, 1976 (p-4)
3   Verda (Vitamin T) Smith, Los Angeles, 1950 (k-3)
    Abe Woodson, San Francisco, 1963 (k-3)
    Raymond Clayborn, New England, 1977 (k-3)
    Billy Johnson, Houston, 1977 (p-2, k-1)
    LeRoy Irvin, Los Angeles, 1981 (p-3)
    Ron Brown, L.A. Rams, 1985 (k-3)
    Tyrone Hughes, New Orleans, 1993 (p-2, k-1)
    Mel Gray, Detroit, 1994 (k-3)
    Andre Coleman, San Diego, 1995 (p-2; k-1)
    Tamarick Vanover, Kansas City, 1995 (p-1, k-2)
    Desmond Howard, Green Bay, 1996 (p-3)
    Darrien Gordon, Denver, 1997 (p-3)
    Eric Metcalf, San Diego, 1997 (p-3)

Glyn Milburn, Chicago, 1998 (p-2, k-1)
Roell Preston, Green Bay, 1998 (p-2, k-1)
Darrick Vaughn, Atlanta, 2000 (k-3)
Steve Smith, Carolina, 2001 (p-1, k-2)
2 By many players

Most Touchdowns, Game
2 Jack Christiansen, Detroit vs. Los Angeles,
    Oct. 14, 1951 (p-2); vs. Green Bay,
    Nov. 22, 1951 (p-2)
    Jim Patton, N.Y. Giants vs. Washington,
    Oct. 30, 1955 (p-1, k-1)
    Bobby Mitchell, Cleveland vs. Philadelphia,
    Nov. 23, 1958 (p-1, k-1)
    Dick Christy, N.Y. Titans vs. Denver, Sept. 24, 1961
    (p-2)
    Al Frazier, Denver vs. Boston, Dec. 3, 1961 (p-1, k-1)
    Timmy Brown, Philadelphia vs. Dallas, Nov. 6, 1966
    (k-2)
    Travis Williams, Green Bay vs. Cleveland,
    Nov. 12, 1967 (k-2); vs. Pittsburgh,
    Nov. 2, 1969 (p-1, k-1)
    Gale Sayers, Chicago vs. San Francisco,
    Dec. 3, 1967 (p-1, k-1)
    Rick Upchurch, Denver vs. Cleveland,
    Sept. 26, 1976 (p-2)
    Eddie Payton, Detroit vs. Minnesota, Dec. 17, 1977
    (p-1, k-1)
    LeRoy Irvin, Los Angeles vs. Atlanta, Oct. 11, 1981
    (p-2)
    Ron Brown, L.A. Rams vs. Green Bay,
    Nov. 24, 1985 (k-2)
    Vai Sikahema, St. Louis vs. Tampa Bay,
    Dec. 21, 1986 (p-2)
    Todd Kinchen, L.A. Rams vs. Atlanta, Dec. 27, 1992
    (p-2)
    Eric Metcalf, Cleveland vs. Pittsburgh, Oct. 24, 1993
    (p-2); San Diego vs. Cincinnati, Nov. 2, 1997
    (p-2)
    Tyrone Hughes, New Orleans vs. L.A. Rams,
    Oct. 23, 1994 (k-2)
    Darrien Gordon, Denver vs. Carolina, Nov. 9, 1997
    (p-2)
    Jermaine Lewis, Baltimore vs. Seattle, Dec. 7, 1997
    (p-2); Baltimore vs. N.Y. Jets, Dec. 24, 2000
    (p-2)

FUMBLES
Most Fumbles, Career
161 Warren Moon, Houston, 1984-1993; Minnesota,
     1994-96; Seattle, 1997-98; Kansas City,
     1999-2000
153 Dave Krieg, Seattle, 1980-1991; Kansas City,
     1992-93; Detroit, 1994; Arizona, 1995;
     Chicago, 1996; Tennessee, 1997-98
137 John Elway, Denver, 1983-1998

Most Fumbles, Season
23 Kerry Collins, N.Y. Giants, 2001
21 Tony Banks, St. Louis, 1996
18 Dave Krieg, Seattle, 1989
    Warren Moon, Houston, 1990

Most Fumbles, Game
7 Len Dawson, Kansas City vs. San Diego,
    Nov. 15, 1964
6 Sam Etcheverry, St. Louis vs. N.Y. Giants,
    Sept, 17, 1961
    Dave Krieg, Seattle vs. Kansas City, Nov. 5, 1989
    Brett Favre, Green Bay vs. Tampa Bay, Dec. 7, 1998
5 Paul Christman, Chi. Cardinals vs. Green Bay,
    Nov. 10, 1946

Charlie Conerly, N.Y. Giants vs. San Francisco,
    Dec. 1, 1957
Jack Kemp, Buffalo vs. Houston, Oct. 29, 1967
Roman Gabriel, Philadelphia vs. Oakland,
    Nov. 21, 1976
Randall Cunningham, Philadelphia vs. L.A. Raiders,
    Nov. 30, 1986 (OT)
Willie Totten, Buffalo vs. Indianapolis, Oct. 4, 1987
Dave Walter, Cincinnati vs. Seattle, Oct. 11, 1987
Dave Krieg, Seattle vs. San Diego, Nov. 25, 1990 (OT)
Andre Ware, Detroit vs. Green Bay, Dec. 6, 1992
Steve Beuerlein, Carolina vs. San Francisco,
    Nov. 8, 1998

FUMBLES RECOVERED
Most Fumbles Recovered, Career, Own and Opponents'
56 Warren Moon, Houston, 1984-1993; Minnesota,
    1994-96; Seattle, 1997-98; Kansas City,
    1999-2000 (56 own)
47 Dave Krieg, Seattle, 1980-1991; Kansas City,
    1992-93; Detroit, 1994; Arizona, 1995; Chica-
    go, 1996; Tennessee, 1997-98 (47 own)
45 Boomer Esiason, Cincinnati, 1984-1992, 1997;
    N.Y. Jets, 1993-95; Arizona, 1996 (45 own)

Most Fumbles Recovered, Season, Own and Opponents'
9 Don Hultz, Minnesota, 1963 (9 opp)
    Dave Krieg, Seattle, 1989 (9 own)
    Brian Griese, Denver, 1999 (9 own)
    Jon Kitna, Seattle, 2000 (9 own)
8 Paul Christman, Chi. Cardinals, 1945 (8 own)
    Joe Schmidt, Detroit, 1955 (8 opp)
    Bill Butler, Minnesota, 1963 (8 own)
    Kermit Alexander, San Francisco, 1965
    (4 own, 4 opp)
    Jack Lambert, Pittsburgh, 1976 (1 own, 7 opp)
    Danny White, Dallas, 1981 (8 own)
    Dan Marino, Miami, 1988 (7 own, 1 opp)
    Tony Banks, St. Louis, 1998 (8 own)
7 By many players

Most Fumbles Recovered, Game, Own and Opponents'
4 Otto Graham, Cleveland vs. N.Y. Giants,
    Oct. 25, 1953 (4 own)
    Sam Etcheverry, St. Louis vs. N.Y. Giants,
    Sept. 17, 1961 (4 own)
    Roman Gabriel, Los Angeles vs. San Francisco,
    Oct. 12, 1969 (4 own)
    Joe Ferguson, Buffalo vs. Miami, Sept. 18, 1977
    (4 own)
    Randall Cunningham, Philadelphia vs. L.A. Raiders,
    Nov. 30, 1986 (OT) (4 own)
3 By many players

OWN FUMBLES RECOVERED
Most Own Fumbles Recovered, Career
56 Warren Moon, Houston, 1984-1993; Minnesota,
    1994-96; Seattle, 1997-98; Kansas City,
    1999-2000
47 Dave Krieg, Seattle, 1980-1991; Kansas City,
    1992-93; Detroit, 1994; Arizona, 1995;
    Chicago, 1996; Tennessee, 1997-98
45 Boomer Esiason, Cincinnati, 1984-1992, 1997;
    N.Y. Jets, 1993-95; Arizona, 1996

Most Own Fumbles Recovered, Season
9 Dave Krieg, Seattle, 1989
    Brian Griese, Denver, 1999
    Jon Kitna, Seattle, 2000
8 Paul Christman, Chi. Cardinals, 1945
    Bill Butler, Minnesota, 1963
    Danny White, Dallas, 1981
    Tony Banks, St. Louis, 1998

7   By many players

Most Own Fumbles Recovered, Game
4   Otto Graham, Cleveland vs. N.Y. Giants, Oct. 25, 1953
     Sam Etcheverry, St. Louis vs. N.Y. Giants,
       Sept. 17, 1961
     Roman Gabriel, Los Angeles vs. San Francisco,
       Oct. 12, 1969
     Joe Ferguson, Buffalo vs. Miami, Sept. 18, 1977
     Randall Cunningham, Philadelphia vs. L.A. Raiders,
       Nov. 30, 1986 (OT)
3   By many players

OPPONENTS' FUMBLES RECOVERED
Most Opponents' Fumbles Recovered, Career
29   Jim Marshall, Cleveland, 1960; Minnesota, 1961-1979
28   Rickey Jackson, New Orleans, 1981-1993;
      San Francisco, 1994-95
26   Kevin Greene, L.A. Rams, 1985-1992; Pittsburgh,
      1993-95; Carolina, 1996, 1998-99;
      San Francisco, 1997
      Cornelius Bennett, Buffalo, 1987-1995; Atlanta,
      1996-98; Indianapolis, 1999-2000
Most Opponents' Fumbles Recovered, Season
9   Don Hultz, Minnesota, 1963
8   Joe Schmidt, Detroit, 1955
7   Alan Page, Minnesota, 1970
     Jack Lambert, Pittsburgh, 1976
     Ray Childress, Houston, 1988
     Rickey Jackson, New Orleans, 1990
Most Opponents' Fumbles Recovered, Game
3   Corwin Clatt, Chi. Cardinals vs. Detroit, Nov. 6, 1949
     Vic Sears, Philadelphia vs. Green Bay, Nov. 2, 1952
     Ed Beatty, San Francisco vs. Los Angeles,
       Oct. 7, 1956
     Ron Carroll, Houston vs. Cincinnati, Oct. 27, 1974
     Maurice Spencer, New Orleans vs. Atlanta,
       Oct. 10, 1976
     Steve Nelson, New England vs. Philadelphia,
       Oct. 8, 1978
     Charles Jackson, Kansas City vs. Pittsburgh,
       Sept. 6, 1981
     Willie Buchanon, San Diego vs. Denver,
       Sept. 27, 1981
     Joey Browner, Minnesota vs. San Francisco,
       Sept. 8, 1985
     Ray Childress, Houston vs. Washington, Oct. 30, 1988
     John Thierry, Chicago vs. Houston, Oct. 22, 1995
     Stephen Boyd, Detroit vs. Chicago, Oct. 4, 1998
     Darryl Williams, Seattle vs. Kansas City, Oct. 4, 1998
2   By many players

YARDS RETURNING FUMBLES
Longest Fumble Run (All TDs)
104   Jack Tatum, Oakland vs. Green Bay, Sept. 24, 1972
       Aeneas Williams, Arizona vs. Washington,
       Nov. 5, 2000
102   Travis Davis, Pittsburgh vs. Carolina, Dec. 26, 1999
100   Chris Martin, Kansas City vs. Miami, Oct. 13, 1991

TOUCHDOWNS
Most Touchdowns, Career (Total)
5   Jessie Tuggle, Atlanta, 1987-2000
4   Bill Thompson, Denver, 1969-1981
     Derrick Thomas, Kansas City, 1989-1999
3   By many players
Most Touchdowns, Season (Total)
2   Harold McPhail, Boston, 1934
     Harry Ebding, Detroit, 1937
     John Morelli, Boston, 1944
     Frank Maznicki, Boston, 1947

     Fred (Dippy) Evans, Chi. Bears, 1948
     Ralph Heywood, Boston, 1948
     Art Tait, N.Y. Yanks, 1951
     John Dwyer, Los Angeles, 1952
     Leo Sugar, Chi. Cardinals, 1957
     Doug Cline, Houston, 1961
     Jim Bradshaw, Pittsburgh, 1964
     Royce Berry, Cincinnati, 1970
     Ahmad Rashad, Buffalo, 1974
     Tim Gray, Kansas City, 1977
     Charles Phillips, Oakland, 1978
     Kenny Johnson, Atlanta, 1981
     George Martin, N.Y. Giants, 1981
     Del Rodgers, Green Bay, 1982
     Mike Douglass, Green Bay, 1983
     Shelton Robinson, Seattle, 1983
     Erik McMillan, N.Y. Jets, 1989
     Les Miller, San Diego, 1990
     Seth Joyner, Philadelphia, 1991
     Robert Goff, New Orleans, 1992
     Willie Clay, Detroit, 1993
     Tyrone Hughes, New Orleans, 1994
     Chad Brown, Seattle, 1997
     Marcus Robertson, Tennessee, 1997
     Dwayne Rudd, Minnesota, 1998
     Keith McKenzie, Green Bay, 1999
Most Touchdowns, Career (Own recovered)
2   Ken Kavanaugh, Chi. Bears, 1940-41, 1945-1950
     Mike Ditka, Chicago, 1961-66; Philadelphia,
       1967-68; Dallas, 1969-1972
     Gail Cogdill, Detroit, 1960-68; Baltimore, 1968;
       Atlanta, 1969-1970
     Ahmad Rashad, St. Louis, 1972-73; Buffalo, 1974;
       Minnesota, 1976-1982
     Jim Mitchell, Atlanta, 1969-1979
     Drew Pearson, Dallas, 1973-1983
     Del Rodgers, Green Bay, 1982, 1984; San Francisco,
       1987-88
Most Touchdowns, Season (Own recovered)
2   Ahmad Rashad, Buffalo, 1974
     Del Rodgers, Green Bay, 1982
1   By many players
Most Touchdowns, Career (Opponents' recovered)
5   Jessie Tuggle, Atlanta, 1987-2000
4   Derrick Thomas, Kansas City, 1989-1999
3   By many players
Most Touchdowns, Season (Opponents' recovered)
2   Harold McPhail, Boston, 1934
     Harry Ebding, Detroit, 1937
     John Morelli, Boston, 1944
     Frank Maznicki, Boston, 1947
     Fred (Dippy) Evans, Chi. Bears, 1948
     Ralph Heywood, Boston, 1948
     Art Tait, N.Y. Yanks, 1951
     John Dwyer, Los Angeles, 1952
     Leo Sugar, Chi. Cardinals, 1957
     Doug Cline, Houston, 1961
     Jim Bradshaw, Pittsburgh, 1964
     Royce Berry, Cincinnati, 1970
     Tim Gray, Kansas City, 1977
     Charles Phillips, Oakland, 1978
     Kenny Johnson, Atlanta, 1981
     George Martin, N.Y. Giants, 1981
     Mike Douglass, Green Bay, 1983
     Shelton Robinson, Seattle, 1983
     Erik McMillan, N.Y. Jets, 1989
     Les Miller, San Diego, 1990
     Seth Joyner, Philadelphia, 1991
     Robert Goff, New Orleans, 1992
     Willie Clay, Detroit, 1993

Tyrone Hughes, New Orleans, 1994
Chad Brown, Seattle, 1997
Marcus Robertson, Tennessee, 1997
Dwayne Rudd, Minnesota, 1998
Keith McKenzie, Green Bay, 1999

Most Touchdowns, Game (Opponents' recovered)
2 Fred (Dippy) Evans, Chi. Bears vs. Washington, Nov. 28, 1948

COMBINED NET YARDS GAINED
Rushing, receiving, interception returns, punt returns, kickoff returns, and fumble returns

Most Seasons Leading League
5 Jim Brown, Cleveland, 1958-1961, 1964
4 Brian Mitchell, Washington, 1994-96, 1998
3 Cliff Battles, Boston, 1932-33; Washington, 1937
   Gale Sayers, Chicago, 1965-67
   Eric Dickerson, L.A. Rams, 1983-84, 1986
   Thurman Thomas, Buffalo, 1989, 1991-92

Most Consecutive Seasons Leading League
4 Jim Brown, Cleveland, 1958-1961
3 Gale Sayers, Chicago, 1965-67
   Brian Mitchell, Washington, 1994-96
2 Cliff Battles, Boston, 1932-33
   Charley Trippi, Chi. Cardinals, 1948-49
   Timmy Brown, Philadelphia, 1962-63
   Floyd Little, Denver, 1967-68
   James Brooks, San Diego, 1981-82
   Eric Dickerson, L.A. Rams, 1983-84
   Thurman Thomas, Buffalo, 1991-92

ATTEMPTS
Most Attempts, Career
4,368 Walter Payton, Chicago, 1975-1987
4,279 Emmitt Smith, Dallas, 1990-2001
3,624 Marcus Allen, L.A. Raiders, 1982-1992; Kansas City, 1993-97

Most Attempts, Season
496 James Wilder, Tampa Bay, 1984
455 Eddie George, Tennessee, 2000
450 Edgerrin James, Indianapolis, 2000

Most Attempts, Rookie, Season
442 Eric Dickerson, L.A. Rams, 1983
433 Edgerrin James, Indianapolis, 1999
401 Curtis Martin, New England, 1995

Most Attempts, Game
48 James Wilder, Tampa Bay vs. Pittsburgh, Oct. 30, 1983
47 James Wilder, Tampa Bay vs. Green Bay, Sept. 30, 1984 (OT)
    Terrell Davis, Denver vs. Buffalo, Oct. 26, 1997 (OT)
46 Gerald Riggs, Atlanta vs. L.A. Rams, Nov. 17, 1985

YARDS GAINED
Most Yards Gained, Career
21,803 Walter Payton, Chicago, 1975-1987
21,017 Jerry Rice, San Francisco, 1985-2000; Oakland, 2001
20,263 Brian Mitchell, Washington, 1990-99; Philadelphia, 2000-01

Most Yards Gained, Season
2,690 Derrick Mason, Tennessee, 2000
2,535 Lionel James, San Diego, 1985
2,477 Brian Mitchell, Washington, 1994

Most Yards Gained, Rookie, Season
2,317 Tim Brown, L.A. Raiders, 1988
2,272 Gale Sayers, Chicago, 1965
2,212 Eric Dickerson, L.A. Rams, 1983

Most Yards Gained, Game
404 Glyn Milburn, Denver vs. Seattle, Dec. 10, 1995
373 Billy Cannon, Houston vs. N.Y. Titans, Dec. 10, 1961

347 Tyrone Hughes, New Orleans vs. L.A. Rams, Oct. 23, 1994

SACKS
Sacks have been compiled since 1982.

Most Seasons Leading League
2 Mark Gastineau, N.Y. Jets, 1983-84
   Reggie White, Philadelphia, 1987-88
   Kevin Greene, Pittsburgh, 1994; Carolina, 1996

Most Sacks, Career
198.0 Reggie White, Philadelphia, 1985-1992; Green Bay, 1993-98; Carolina, 2000
186.0 Bruce Smith, Buffalo, 1985-1999; Washington, 2000-01
160.0 Kevin Greene, L.A. Rams, 1985-1992; Pittsburgh, 1993-95; Carolina, 1996, 1998-99; San Francisco, 1997

Most Sacks, Season
22.5 Michael Strahan, N.Y. Giants, 2001
22.0 Mark Gastineau, N.Y. Jets, 1984
21.0 Reggie White, Philadelphia, 1987
      Chris Doleman, Minnesota, 1989

Most Sacks, Rookie, Season
14.5 Jevon Kearse, Tennessee, 1999
12.5 Leslie O'Neal, San Diego, 1986
      Simeon Rice, Arizona, 1996
12.0 Charles Haley, San Francisco, 1986

Most Sacks, Game
7.0 Derrick Thomas, Kansas City vs. Seattle, Nov. 11, 1990
6.0 Fred Dean, San Francisco vs. New Orleans, Nov. 13, 1983
     Derrick Thomas, Kansas City vs. Oakland, Sept. 6, 1998
5.5 William Gay, Detroit vs. Tampa Bay, Sept. 4, 1983

Most Seasons, 10 or More Sacks
13 Bruce Smith, Buffalo, 1986-1990, 1992-98; Washington, 2000
12 Reggie White, Philadelphia, 1985-1992; Green Bay, 1993, 1995, 1997-98
10 Kevin Greene, L.A. Rams, 1988-1990, 1992; Pittsburgh, 1993-94; Carolina, 1996, 1998-99; San Francisco, 1997

Most Consecutive Seasons, 10 or More Sacks
9 Reggie White, Philadelphia, 1985-1992; Green Bay, 1993
8 John Randle, Minnesota, 1992-99
7 Lawrence Taylor, N.Y. Giants, 1984-1990
   Bruce Smith, Buffalo, 1992-98

Most Consecutive Games, Sack
10 Simon Fletcher, Denver, Nov. 15, 1992-Sept. 20, 1993
9   Bruce Smith, Buffalo, Nov. 16, 1986-Oct. 25, 1987
    Kevin Greene, San Francisco-Carolina, Dec. 7, 1997-Oct. 18, 1998
8   By many players

MISCELLANEOUS
Longest Return of Missed Field Goal (All TDs)
104 Aaron Glenn, N.Y. Jets vs. Indianapolis, Nov. 15, 1998
101 Al Nelson, Philadelphia vs. Dallas, Sept. 26, 1971
100 Al Nelson, Philadelphia vs. Cleveland, Dec. 11, 1966
     Ken Ellis, Green Bay vs. N.Y. Giants, Sept. 19, 1971

TEAM RECORDS

CHAMPIONSHIPS
Most Seasons League Champion
12 Green Bay, 1929-1931, 1936, 1939, 1944, 1961-62, 1965-67, 1996

  9 Chi. Bears, 1921, 1932-33, 1940-41, 1943, 1946, 1963, 1985
  6 N.Y. Giants, 1927, 1934, 1938, 1956, 1986, 1990

Most Consecutive Seasons League Champion
  3 Green Bay, 1929-1931
     Green Bay, 1965-67
  2 Canton, 1922-23
     Chi. Bears, 1932-33
     Chi. Bears, 1940-41
     Philadelphia, 1948-49
     Detroit, 1952-53
     Cleveland, 1954-55
     Baltimore, 1958-59
     Houston, 1960-61
     Green Bay, 1961-62
     Buffalo, 1964-65
     Miami, 1972-73
     Pittsburgh, 1974-75
     Pittsburgh, 1978-79
     San Francisco, 1988-89
     Dallas, 1992-93
     Denver, 1997-98

Most Times Finishing First, Regular Season
 20 N.Y. Giants, 1927, 1933-35, 1938-39, 1941, 1944, 1946, 1956, 1958-59, 1961-63, 1986, 1989-1990, 1997, 2000
 19 Dallas, 1966-1971, 1973, 1976-79, 1981, 1985, 1992-96, 1998
     Chi. Bears, 1921, 1932-34, 1937, 1940-43, 1946, 1956, 1963, 1984-88, 1990, 2001
 18 Cle. Browns, 1950-55, 1957, 1964-65, 1967-69, 1971, 1980, 1985-87, 1989

Most Consecutive Times Finishing First, Regular Season
  7 Los Angeles, 1973-79
  6 Cleveland, 1950-55
     Dallas, 1966-1971
     Minnesota, 1973-78
     Pittsburgh, 1974-79
  5 Oakland, 1972-76
     Chicago, 1984-88
     San Francisco, 1986-1990
     Dallas, 1992-96

GAMES WON

Most Consecutive Games Won
 17 Chi. Bears, 1933-34
 16 Chi. Bears, 1941-42
     Miami, 1971-73
     Miami, 1983-84
 15 L.A. Chargers/San Diego, 1960-61
     San Francisco, 1989-1990

Most Consecutive Games Without Defeat
 25 Canton, 1921-23 (won 22, tied 3)
 24 Chi. Bears, 1941-43 (won 23, tied 1)
 23 Green Bay, 1928-1930 (won 21, tied 2)

Most Games Won, Season
 15 San Francisco, 1984
     Chicago, 1985
     Minnesota, 1998
 14 Frankford, 1926
     Miami, 1972
     Pittsburgh, 1978
     Washington, 1983
     Miami, 1984
     Chicago, 1986
     N.Y. Giants, 1986
     San Francisco, 1989
     San Francisco, 1990
     Washington, 1991
     San Francisco, 1992

     Atlanta, 1998
     Denver, 1998
     Jacksonville, 1999
     St. Louis, 2001
 13 By many teams

Most Consecutive Games Won, Season
 14 Miami, 1972
 13 Chi. Bears, 1934
     Denver, 1998
 12 Minnesota, 1969
     Chicago, 1985

Most Consecutive Games Won, Start of Season
 14 Miami, 1972, entire season
 13 Chi. Bears, 1934, entire season
     Denver, 1998
 12 Chicago, 1985

Most Consecutive Games Won, End of Season
 14 Miami, 1972, entire season
 13 Chi. Bears, 1934, entire season
 11 Chi. Bears, 1942, entire season
     Cleveland, 1951
     Houston, 1993

Most Consecutive Games Without Defeat, Season
 14 Miami, 1972 (won 14)
 13 Chi. Bears, 1926 (won 11, tied 2)
     Green Bay, 1929 (won 12, tied 1)
     Chi. Bears, 1934 (won 13)
     Baltimore, 1967 (won 11, tied 2)
     Denver, 1998 (won 13)
 12 Canton, 1922 (won 10, tied 2)
     Canton, 1923 (won 11, tied 1)
     Minnesota, 1969 (won 12)
     Chicago, 1985 (won 12)

Most Consecutive Games Without Defeat, Start of Season
 14 Miami, 1972 (won 14), entire season
 13 Chi. Bears, 1926 (won 11, tied 2)
     Green Bay, 1929 (won 12, tied 1), entire season
     Chi. Bears, 1934 (won 13), entire season
     Baltimore, 1967 (won 11, tied 2)
     Denver, 1998 (won 13)
 12 Canton, 1922 (won 10, tied 2), entire season
     Chicago, 1985 (won 12)

Most Consecutive Games Without Defeat, End of Season
 14 Miami, 1972 (won 14), entire season
 13 Green Bay, 1929 (won 12, tied 1), entire season
     Chi. Bears, 1934 (won 13), entire season
 12 Canton, 1922 (won 10, tied 2), entire season
     Canton, 1923 (won 11, tied 1), entire season

Most Consecutive Home Games Won
 27 Miami, 1971-74
 25 Green Bay, 1995-98
 24 Denver, 1996-98

Most Consecutive Home Games Without Defeat
 30 Green Bay, 1928-1933 (won 27, tied 3)
 27 Miami, 1971-74 (won 27)
 25 Chi. Bears, 1923-25 (won 19, tied 6)
     Green Bay, 1995-98 (won 25)

Most Consecutive Road Games Won
 18 San Francisco, 1988-1990
 11 L.A. Chargers/San Diego, 1960-61
     San Francisco, 1987-88
 10 Chi. Bears, 1941-42
     Dallas, 1968-69
     New Orleans, 1987-88

Most Consecutive Road Games Without Defeat
 18 San Francisco, 1988-1990 (won 18)
 13 Chi. Bears, 1941-43 (won 12, tied 1)
 12 Green Bay, 1928-1930 (won 10, tied 2)

Most Shutout Games Won or Tied, Season
- 10 Pottsville, 1926 (won 9, tied 1)
  N.Y. Giants, 1927 (won 9, tied 1)
- 9 Akron, 1921 (won 8, tied 1)
  Canton, 1922 (won 7, tied 2)
  Frankford, 1926 (won 9)
  Frankford, 1929 (won 6, tied 3)
- 8 By many teams

Most Consecutive Shutout Games Won or Tied
- 13 Akron, 1920-21 (won 10, tied 3)
- 7 Pottsville, 1926 (won 6, tied 1)
  Detroit, 1934 (won 7)
- 6 Buffalo, 1920-21 (won 5, tied 1)
  Frankford, 1926 (won 6)
  Detroit, 1926 (won 4, tied 2)
  N.Y. Giants, 1926-27 (won 5, tied 1)

GAMES LOST
Most Consecutive Games Lost
- 26 Tampa Bay, 1976-1977
- 19 Chi. Cardinals, 1942-43, 1945
  Oakland, 1961-62
- 18 Houston, 1972-73

Most Consecutive Games Without Victory
- 26 Tampa Bay, 1976-77 (lost 26)
- 23 Rochester, 1922-25 (lost 21, tied 2)
  Washington, 1960-61 (lost 20, tied 3)
- 19 Dayton, 1927-29 (lost 18, tied 1)
  Chi. Cardinals, 1942-43, 1945 (lost 19)
  Oakland, 1961-62 (lost 19)

Most Games Lost, Season
- 15 New Orleans, 1980
  Dallas, 1989
  New England, 1990
  Indianapolis, 1991
  N.Y. Jets, 1996
  San Diego, 2000
  Carolina, 2001
- 14 By many teams

Most Consecutive Games Lost, Season
- 15 Carolina, 2001
- 14 Tampa Bay, 1976
  New Orleans, 1980
  Baltimore, 1981
  New England, 1990
- 13 Oakland, 1962
  Pittsburgh, 1969
  Indianapolis, 1986

Most Consecutive Games Lost, Start of Season
- 14 Tampa Bay, 1976, entire season
  New Orleans, 1980
- 13 Oakland, 1962
  Indianapolis, 1986
- 12 Tampa Bay, 1977
  Detroit, 2001

Most Consecutive Games Lost, End of Season
- 15 Carolina, 2001
- 14 Tampa Bay, 1976, entire season
  New England, 1990
- 13 Pittsburgh, 1969

Most Consecutive Games Without Victory, Season
- 15 Carolina, 2001 (lost 15)
- 14 Tampa Bay, 1976 (lost 14), entire season
  New Orleans, 1980 (lost 14)
  Baltimore, 1981 (lost 14)
  New England, 1990 (lost 14)
- 13 Washington, 1961 (lost 12, tied 1)
  Oakland, 1962 (lost 13)
  Pittsburgh, 1969 (lost 13)
  Indianapolis, 1986 (lost 13)

Most Consecutive Games Without Victory, Start of Season
- 14 Tampa Bay, 1976 (lost 14), entire season
  New Orleans, 1980 (lost 14)
- 13 Washington, 1961 (lost 12, tied 1)
  Oakland, 1962 (lost 13)
  Indianapolis, 1986 (lost 13)
- 12 Dall. Cowboys, 1960 (lost 11, tied 1), entire season
  Tampa Bay, 1977 (lost 12)
  Detroit, 2001 (lost 12)

Most Consecutive Games Without Victory, End of Season
- 15 Carolina, 2001
- 14 Tampa Bay, 1976, (lost 14), entire season
  New England, 1990 (lost 14)
- 13 Pittsburgh, 1969 (lost 13)

Most Consecutive Home Games Lost
- 14 Dallas, 1988-89
- 13 Houston, 1972-73
  Tampa Bay, 1976-77
  N.Y. Jets, 1995-97
- 11 Oakland, 1961-62
  Los Angeles, 1961-63
  Cincinnati, 1998-99

Most Consecutive Home Games Without Victory
- 14 Dallas, 1988-89 (lost 14)
- 13 Houston, 1972-73 (lost 13)
  Tampa Bay, 1976-77 (lost 13)
  N.Y. Jets, 1995-97 (lost 13)
- 12 Philadelphia, 1936-38 (lost 11, tied 1)

Most Consecutive Road Games Lost
- 23 Houston, 1981-84
- 22 Buffalo, 1983-86
- 19 Tampa Bay, 1983-85
  Atlanta, 1988-1991

Most Consecutive Road Games Without Victory
- 23 Houston, 1981-84 (lost 23)
- 22 Buffalo, 1983-86 (lost 22)
- 19 Tampa Bay, 1983-85 (lost 19)
  Atlanta, 1988-1991 (lost 19)

Most Shutout Games Lost or Tied, Season
- 8 Frankford, 1927 (lost 6, tied 2)
  Brooklyn, 1931 (lost 8)
- 7 Dayton, 1925 (lost 6, tied 1)
  Orange, 1929 (lost 4, tied 3)
  Frankford, 1931 (lost 6, tied 1)
- 6 By many teams

Most Consecutive Shutout Games Lost or Tied
- 8 Rochester, 1922-24 (lost 8)
- 7 Hammond, 1922-23 (lost 6, tied 1)
- 6 Providence, 1926-27 (lost 5, tied 1)
  Brooklyn, 1942-43 (lost 6)

TIE GAMES
Most Tie Games, Season
- 6 Chi. Bears, 1932
- 5 Frankford, 1929
- 4 Chi. Bears, 1924
  Orange, 1929
  Portsmouth, 1932

Most Consecutive Tie Games
- 3 Chi. Bears, 1932
- 2 By many teams

SCORING
Most Seasons Leading League
- 10 Chi. Bears, 1932, 1934-35, 1939, 1941-43,
     1946-47, 1956
- 9 San Francisco, 1953, 1965, 1970, 1987, 1989,
     1992-95
  L.A./St. Louis Rams, 1950-52, 1957, 1967, 1973,
     1999-2001

7   Green Bay, 1931, 1936-38, 1961-62, 1996

Most Consecutive Seasons Leading League
4   San Francisco, 1992-1995
3   Green Bay, 1936-38
    Chi. Bears, 1941-43
    Los Angeles, 1950-52
    Oakland, 1967-69
    St. Louis, 1999-2001
2   By many teams

POINTS

Most Points, Season
556   Minnesota, 1998
541   Washington, 1983
540   St. Louis, 2000

Fewest Points, Season (Since 1932)
37   Cincinnati/St. Louis, 1934
38   Cincinnati, 1933
     Detroit, 1942
51   Pittsburgh, 1934
     Philadelphia, 1936

Most Points, Game
72   Washington vs. N.Y. Giants, Nov. 27, 1966
70   Los Angeles vs. Baltimore, Oct. 22, 1950
65   Chi. Cardinals vs. N.Y. Bulldogs, Nov. 13, 1949
     Los Angeles vs. Detroit, Oct. 29, 1950

Most Points, Both Teams, Game
113   Washington (72) vs. N.Y. Giants (41), Nov. 27, 1966
101   Oakland (52) vs. Houston (49), Dec. 22, 1963
99   Seattle (51) vs. Kansas City (48), Nov. 27, 1983 (OT)

Fewest Points, Both Teams, Game
0   In many games. Last time: N.Y. Giants vs. Detroit,
    Nov. 7, 1943

Most Points, Shutout Victory, Game
64   Philadelphia vs. Cincinnati, Nov. 6, 1934
62   Akron vs. Oorang, Oct. 29, 1922
60   Rock Island vs. Evansville, Oct. 15, 1922
     Chi. Cardinals vs. Rochester, Oct. 7, 1923

Fewest Points, Shutout Victory, Game
2   Green Bay vs. Chi. Bears, Oct. 16, 1932
    Chi. Bears vs. Green Bay, Sept. 18, 1938

Most Points Overcome to Win Game
28   San Francisco vs. New Orleans, Dec. 7, 1980 (OT)
     (trailed 7-35, won 38-35)
26   Buffalo vs. Indianapolis, Sept., 21, 1997
     (trailed 0-26, won 37-35)
25   St. Louis vs. Tampa Bay, Nov. 8, 1987
     (trailed 3-28, won 31-28)

Most Points Overcome to Tie Game
31   Denver vs. Buffalo, Nov. 27, 1960
     (trailed 7-38, tied 38-38)
28   Los Angeles vs. Philadelphia, Oct. 3, 1948
     (trailed 0-28, tied 28-28)

Most Points, Each Half
1st: 49   Green Bay vs. Tampa Bay, Oct. 2, 1983
       48   Buffalo vs. Miami, Sept. 18, 1966
       45   Green Bay vs. Cleveland, Nov. 12, 1967
            Indianapolis vs. Denver, Oct. 31, 1988
            Houston vs. Cleveland, Dec. 9, 1990
2nd: 49   Chi. Bears vs. Philadelphia, Nov. 30, 1941
       48   Chi. Cardinals vs. Baltimore, Oct. 2, 1950
            N.Y. Giants vs. Baltimore, Nov. 19, 1950
       45   Cincinnati vs. Houston, Dec. 17, 1972

Most Points, Both Teams, Each Half
1st: 70   Houston (35) vs. Oakland (35), Dec. 22, 1963
       62   N.Y. Jets (41) vs. Tampa Bay (21), Nov. 17, 1985
       59   St. Louis (31) vs. Philadelphia (28), Dec. 16, 1962
2nd: 65   Washington (38) vs. N.Y. Giants (27), Nov. 27, 1966
       62   L.A. Raiders (31) vs. San Diego (31), Jan. 2, 1983
       58   New England (37) vs. Baltimore (21), Nov. 23, 1980

N.Y. Jets (37) vs. New England (21), Sept. 21, 1987

Most Points, One Quarter
41   Green Bay vs. Detroit, Oct. 7, 1945 (second quarter)
     Los Angeles vs. Detroit, Oct. 29, 1950
     (third quarter)
37   Los Angeles vs. Green Bay, Sept. 21, 1980
     (second quarter)
35   Chi. Cardinals vs. Boston, Oct. 24, 1948
     (third quarter)
     Green Bay vs. Cleveland, Nov. 12, 1967
     (first quarter)
     Green Bay vs. Tampa Bay, Oct. 2, 1983
     (second quarter)

Most Points, Both Teams, One Quarter
49   Oakland (28) vs. Houston (21), Dec. 22, 1963
     (second quarter)
48   Green Bay (41) vs. Detroit (7), Oct. 7, 1945
     (second quarter)
     Los Angeles (41) vs. Detroit (7), Oct. 29, 1950
     (third quarter)
47   St. Louis (27) vs. Philadelphia (20), Dec. 13, 1964
     (second quarter)

Most Points, Each Quarter
1st: 35   Green Bay vs. Cleveland, Nov. 12, 1967
       31   Buffalo vs. Kansas City, Sept. 13, 1964
       28   By eight teams
2nd: 41   Green Bay vs. Detroit, Oct. 7, 1945
       37   Los Angeles vs. Green Bay, Sept. 21, 1980
       35   Green Bay vs. Tampa Bay, Oct. 2, 1983
3rd: 41   Los Angeles vs. Detroit, Oct. 29, 1950
       35   Chi. Cardinals vs. Boston, Oct. 24, 1948
       28   By 10 teams
4th: 31   Oakland vs. Denver, Dec. 17, 1960
            Oakland vs. San Diego, Dec. 8, 1963
            Atlanta vs. Green Bay, Sept. 13, 1981
       30   N.Y. Jets vs. Miami, Oct. 23, 2000
       28   By many teams

Most Points, Both Teams, Each Quarter
1st: 42   Green Bay (35) vs. Cleveland (7), Nov. 12, 1967
       35   Dall. Texans (21) vs. N.Y. Titans (14), Nov. 11, 1962
            Dallas (28) vs. Philadelphia (7), Oct. 19, 1969
            Kansas City (21) vs. Seattle (14), Dec. 11, 1977
            Detroit (21) vs. L.A. Raiders (14), Dec. 10, 1990
            Dallas (21) vs. Atlanta (14), Dec. 22, 1991
       34   Los Angeles (21) vs. Baltimore (13), Oct. 22, 1950
            Oakland (21) vs. Atlanta (13), Nov. 30, 1975
2nd: 49   Oakland (28) vs. Houston (21), Dec. 22, 1963
       48   Green Bay (41) vs. Detroit (7), Oct. 7, 1945
       47   St. Louis (27) vs. Philadelphia (20), Dec. 13, 1964
3rd: 48   Los Angeles (41) vs. Detroit (7), Oct. 29, 1950
       42   Washington (28) vs. Philadelphia (14), Oct. 1, 1955
       41   Green Bay (21) vs. N.Y. Yanks (20), Oct. 8, 1950
4th: 42   Chi. Cardinals (28) vs. Philadelphia (14), Dec. 7, 1947
            Green Bay (28) vs. Chi. Bears (14), Nov. 6, 1955
            N.Y. Jets (28) vs. Boston (14), Oct. 27, 1968
            Pittsburgh (21) vs. Cleveland (21), Oct. 18, 1969
       41   Baltimore (27) vs. New England (14), Sept. 18, 1978
            New England (27) vs. Baltimore (14), Nov. 23, 1980
       40   Chicago (21) vs. Tampa Bay (19), Nov. 19, 1989

Most Consecutive Games Scoring
386   San Francisco, 1977-2001 (current)
274   Cleveland, 1950-1971
218   Dallas, 1970-1985

TOUCHDOWNS

Most Seasons Leading League, Touchdowns
13   Chi. Bears, 1932, 1934-35, 1939, 1941-44,
     1946-48, 1956, 1965
7   Dallas, 1966, 1968, 1971, 1973, 1977-78, 1980

San Francisco, 1953, 1970, 1987, 1992-95
L.A./St. Louis Rams, 1949-1952, 1999-2001
6 Oakland, 1967-69, 1972, 1974, 1977
   San Diego, 1963, 1965, 1979, 1981-82, 1985
   Green Bay, 1932, 1937-38, 1961-62, 1996

Most Consecutive Seasons Leading League, Touchdowns
4 Chi. Bears, 1941-44
   Los Angeles, 1949-1952
   San Francisco, 1992-95
3 Chi. Bears, 1946-48
   Baltimore, 1957-59
   Oakland, 1967-69
   St. Louis, 1999-2001 (current)
2 By many teams

Most Touchdowns, Season
70 Miami, 1984
67 St. Louis, 2000
66 Houston, 1961
    San Francisco, 1994
    St. Louis, 1999

Fewest Touchdowns, Season (Since 1932)
3 Cincinnati, 1933
4 Cincinnati/St. Louis, 1934
5 Detroit, 1942

Most Touchdowns, Game
10 Philadelphia vs. Cincinnati, Nov. 6, 1934
    Los Angeles vs. Baltimore, Oct. 22, 1950
    Washington vs. N.Y. Giants, Nov. 27, 1966
9 Chi. Cardinals vs. Rochester, Oct. 7, 1923
   Chi. Cardinals vs. N.Y. Giants, Oct. 17, 1948
   Chi. Cardinals vs. N.Y. Bulldogs, Nov. 13, 1949
   Los Angeles vs. Detroit, Oct. 29, 1950
   Pittsburgh vs. N.Y. Giants, Nov. 30, 1952
   Chicago vs. San Francisco, Dec. 12, 1965
   Chicago vs. Green Bay, Dec. 7, 1980
8 By many teams

Most Touchdowns, Both Teams, Game
16 Washington (10) vs. N.Y. Giants (6), Nov. 27, 1966
14 Chi. Cardinals (9) vs. N.Y. Giants (5), Oct. 17, 1948
    Los Angeles (10) vs. Baltimore (4), Oct. 22, 1950
    Houston (7) vs. Oakland (7), Dec. 22, 1963
13 New Orleans (7) vs. St. Louis (6), Nov. 2, 1969
    Kansas City (7) vs. Seattle (6), Nov. 27, 1983 (OT)
    San Diego (8) vs. Pittsburgh (5), Dec. 8, 1985
    N.Y. Jets (7) vs. Miami (6), Sept. 21, 1986 (OT)

Most Consecutive Games Scoring Touchdowns
166 Cleveland, 1957-1969
97 Oakland, 1966-1973
    Minnesota, 1995-2001
96 Kansas City, 1963-1970

POINTS AFTER TOUCHDOWN
Most (One-Point) Points After Touchdown, Season
66 Miami, 1984
65 Houston, 1961
64 St. Louis, 1999

Fewest (One-Point) Points After Touchdown, Season
2 Chi. Cardinals, 1933
3 Cincinnati, 1933
   Pittsburgh, 1934
4 Cincinnati/St. Louis, 1934

Most (One-Point) Points After Touchdown, Game
10 Los Angeles vs. Baltimore, Oct. 22, 1950
9 Chi. Cardinals vs. N.Y. Giants, Oct. 17, 1948
   Pittsburgh vs. N.Y. Giants, Nov. 30, 1952
   Washington vs. N.Y. Giants, Nov. 27, 1966
8 By many teams

Most (One-Point) Points After Touchdown, Both Teams, Game
14 Chi. Cardinals (9) vs. N.Y. Giants (5), Oct. 17, 1948
    Houston (7) vs. Oakland (7), Dec. 22, 1963

Washington (9) vs. N.Y. Giants (5), Nov. 27, 1966
13 Los Angeles (10) vs. Baltimore (3), Oct. 22, 1950
12 In many games

Most Two-Point Conversions, Season
6 Miami, 1994
   Minnesota, 1997
5 Arizona, 1995
   Baltimore, 1996
   Jacksonville, 1996
   Chicago, 1997
   San Francisco, 1998
4 By many teams

Most Two-Point Conversions, Game
4 St. Louis vs. Atlanta, Oct. 15, 2000
3 Baltimore vs. New England, Oct. 6, 1996
   Pittsburgh vs. Tennessee, Nov. 1, 1998
2 By many teams

Most Two-Point Conversions, Both Teams, Game
5 Baltimore (3) vs. New England (2), Oct. 6, 1996
   St. Louis (4) vs. Atlanta (1), Oct. 15, 2000
3 Seattle (2) vs. Kansas City (1), Oct. 23, 1994
   Minnesota (2) vs. Seattle (1), Nov. 10, 1996
   Pittsburgh (3) vs. Tennessee (0), Nov. 1, 1998
2 In many games

FIELD GOALS
Most Seasons Leading League, Field Goals
11 Green Bay, 1935-36, 1940-43, 1946-47, 1955,
    1972, 1974
8 Washington, 1945, 1956, 1971, 1976-77, 1979,
   1982, 1992
7 N.Y. Giants, 1933, 1937, 1939, 1941, 1944, 1959,
   1983

Most Consecutive Seasons Leading League, Field Goals
4 Green Bay, 1940-43
3 Cleveland, 1952-54
2 By many teams

Most Field Goals Attempted, Season
49 Los Angeles, 1966
    Washington, 1971
48 Green Bay, 1972
47 N.Y. Jets, 1969
    Los Angeles, 1973
    Washington, 1983

Fewest Field Goals Attempted, Season (Since 1938)
0 Chi. Bears, 1944
2 Cleveland, 1939
   Card-Pitt, 1944
   Boston, 1946
   Chi. Bears, 1947
3 Chi. Bears, 1945
   Cleveland, 1945

Most Field Goals Attempted, Game
9 St. Louis vs. Pittsburgh, Sept. 24, 1967
8 Pittsburgh vs. St. Louis, Dec. 2, 1962
   Detroit vs. Minnesota, Nov. 13, 1966
   N.Y. Jets vs. Buffalo, Nov. 3, 1968
7 By many teams

Most Field Goals Attempted, Both Teams, Game
11 St. Louis (6) vs. Pittsburgh (5), Nov. 13, 1966
    Washington (6) vs. Chicago (5), Nov. 14, 1971
    Green Bay (6) vs. Detroit (5), Sept. 29, 1974
    Washington (6) vs. N.Y. Giants (5), Nov. 14, 1976
10 In many games

Most Field Goals, Season
39 Miami, 1999
37 Carolina, 1996
36 Indianapolis, 1996
    Tennessee, 1998

Fewest Field Goals, Season (Since 1932)

0	Boston, 1932, 1935
	Chi. Cardinals, 1932, 1945
	Green Bay, 1932, 1944
	N.Y. Giants, 1932
	Brooklyn, 1944
	Card-Pitt, 1944
	Chi. Bears, 1944, 1947
	Boston, 1946
	Baltimore, 1950
	Dallas, 1952

Most Field Goals, Game

7	St. Louis vs. Pittsburgh, Sept. 24, 1967
	Minnesota vs. L.A. Rams, Nov. 5, 1989 (OT)
	Dallas vs. Green Bay, Nov. 18, 1996
6	Boston vs. Denver, Oct. 4, 1964
	Detroit vs. Minnesota, Nov. 13, 1966
	N.Y. Jets vs. Buffalo, Nov. 3, 1968
	Philadelphia vs. Houston, Nov. 12, 1972
	N.Y. Jets vs. New Orleans, Dec. 3, 1972
	St. Louis vs. Atlanta, Dec. 9, 1973
	N.Y. Giants vs. Seattle, Oct. 18, 1981
	San Francisco vs. New Orleans, Oct. 16, 1983
	Pittsburgh vs. Denver, Oct. 23, 1988
	San Diego vs. Seattle, Sept. 5, 1993
	San Diego vs. Houston, Sept. 19, 1993
	Cincinnati vs. Seattle, Nov. 6, 1994
	Atlanta vs. New Orleans, Nov. 13, 1994
	San Francisco vs. Atlanta, Sept. 29, 1996
	Buffalo vs. N.Y. Jets, Oct. 20, 1996
	San Diego vs. Oakland, Oct. 5, 1997
	Minnesota vs. Baltimore, Dec. 13, 1998
	Detroit vs. Minnesota, Oct. 17, 1999
	Miami vs. New England, Oct. 17, 1999
5	By many teams

Most Field Goals, Both Teams, Game

9	San Diego (5) vs. Kansas City (4), Sept. 29, 1996
	Miami (6) vs. New England (3), Oct. 17, 1999
8	Cleveland (4) vs. St. Louis (4), Sept. 20, 1964
	Chicago (5) vs. Philadelphia (3), Oct. 20, 1968
	Washington (5) vs. Chicago (3), Nov. 14, 1971
	Kansas City (5) vs. Buffalo (3), Dec. 19, 1971
	Detroit (4) vs. Green Bay (4), Sept. 29, 1974
	Cleveland (5) vs. Denver (3), Oct. 19, 1975
	New England (4) vs. San Diego (4), Nov. 9, 1975
	San Francisco (6) vs. New Orleans (2), Oct. 16, 1983
	Seattle (5) vs. L.A. Raiders (3), Dec. 18, 1988
	Atlanta (6) vs. New Orleans (2), Nov. 13, 1994
	Indianapolis (4) vs. San Diego (4), Nov. 3, 1996
7	In many games

Most Consecutive Games Scoring Field Goals

38	Baltimore, 1999-2001
31	Minnesota, 1968-1970
28	Washington, 1988-1990

SAFETIES

Most Safeties, Season

4	Cleveland, 1927
	Detroit, 1962
	Seattle, 1993
	San Francisco, 1996
	Tennessee, 1999
3	By many teams

Most Safeties, Game

3	L.A. Rams vs. N.Y. Giants, Sept. 30, 1984
2	N.Y. Giants vs. Pottsville, Oct. 30, 1927
	Chi. Bears vs. Pottsville, Nov. 13, 1927
	Detroit vs. Brooklyn, Dec. 1, 1935
	N.Y. Giants vs. Pittsburgh, Sept. 17, 1950
	N.Y. Giants vs. Washington, Nov. 5, 1961

	Chicago vs. Pittsburgh, Nov. 9, 1969
	Dallas vs. Philadelphia, Nov. 19, 1972
	Los Angeles vs. Green Bay, Oct. 21, 1973
	Oakland vs. San Diego, Oct. 26, 1975
	Denver vs. Seattle, Jan. 2, 1983
	New Orleans vs. Cleveland, Sept. 13, 1987
	Buffalo vs. Denver, Nov. 8, 1987
	San Francisco vs. St. Louis, Sept. 8, 1996
	Jacksonville vs. Pittsburgh, Oct. 3, 1999

Most Safeties, Both Teams, Game

3	L.A. Rams (3) vs. N.Y. Giants (0), Sept. 30, 1984
2	Chi. Cardinals (1) vs. Frankford (1), Nov. 19, 1927
	Chi. Cardinals (1) vs. Cincinnati (1), Nov. 12, 1933
	Chi. Bears (1) vs. San Francisco (1), Oct. 19, 1952
	Cincinnati (1) vs. Los Angeles (1), Oct. 22, 1972
	Chi. Bears (1) vs. San Francisco (1), Sept. 19, 1976
	Baltimore (1) vs. Miami (1), Oct. 29, 1978
	Atlanta (1) vs. Detroit (1), Oct. 5, 1980
	Houston (1) vs. Philadelphia (1), Oct. 2, 1988
	Cleveland (1) vs. Seattle (1), Nov. 14, 1993
	Arizona (1) vs. Houston (1), Dec. 4, 1994
	(Also see previous record)

FIRST DOWNS

Most Seasons Leading League

9	Chi. Bears, 1935, 1939, 1941, 1943, 1945, 1947-49, 1955
7	San Diego, 1965, 1969, 1980-83, 1985
	L.A./St. Louis Rams, 1946, 1950-51, 1954, 1957, 1973, 2001
6	San Francisco, 1965, 1987, 1989, 1993-94, 1998

Most Consecutive Seasons Leading League

4	San Diego, 1980-83
3	Chi. Bears, 1947-49
2	By many teams

Most First Downs, Season

387	Miami, 1984
383	Denver, 2000
381	San Francisco, 1998

Fewest First Downs, Season

51	Cincinnati, 1933
64	Pittsburgh, 1935
67	Philadelphia, 1937

Most First Downs, Game

39	N.Y. Jets vs. Miami, Nov. 27, 1988
	Washington vs. Detroit, Nov. 4, 1990 (OT)
38	Los Angeles vs. N.Y. Giants, Nov. 13, 1966
37	Green Bay vs. Philadelphia, Nov. 11, 1962

Fewest First Downs, Game

0	N.Y. Giants vs. Green Bay, Oct. 1, 1933
	Pittsburgh vs. Boston, Oct. 29, 1933
	Philadelphia vs. Detroit, Sept. 20, 1935
	N.Y. Giants vs. Washington, Sept. 27, 1942
	Denver vs. Houston, Sept. 3, 1966

Most First Downs, Both Teams, Game

62	San Diego (32) vs. Seattle (30), Sept. 15, 1985
	Oakland (31) vs. Kansas City (31), Nov. 5, 2000
59	Miami (31) vs. Buffalo (28), Oct. 9, 1983 (OT)
	Seattle (33) vs. Kansas City (26), Nov. 27, 1983 (OT)
	N.Y. Jets (32) vs. Miami (27), Sept. 21, 1986 (OT)
	N.Y. Jets (39) vs. Miami (20), Nov. 27, 1988
	Oakland (31) vs. San Francisco (28), Oct. 8, 2000 (OT)
58	Los Angeles (30) vs. Chi. Bears (28), Oct. 24, 1954
	Denver (34) vs. Kansas City (24), Nov. 18, 1974
	Atlanta (35) vs. New Orleans (23), Sept. 2, 1979 (OT)
	Pittsburgh (36) vs. Cleveland (22), Nov. 25, 1979 (OT)
	San Diego (34) vs. Miami (24), Nov. 18, 1984 (OT)
	Cincinnati (32) vs. San Diego (26), Sept. 22, 1985

Fewest First Downs, Both Teams, Game
- 7 Chi. Cardinals (2) vs. Detroit (5), Sept. 15, 1940
- 9 Pittsburgh (1) vs. Boston (8), Oct. 27, 1935
  Boston (4) vs. Brooklyn (5), Nov. 24, 1935
  N.Y. Giants (3) vs. Detroit (6), Nov. 7, 1943
  Pittsburgh (4) vs. Chi. Cardinals (5), Nov. 11, 1945
  N.Y. Bulldogs (1) vs. Philadelphia (8), Sept. 22, 1949
- 10 N.Y. Giants (4) vs. Washington (6), Dec. 11, 1960

Most First Downs, Rushing, Season
- 181 New England, 1978
- 177 Los Angeles, 1973
- 176 Chicago, 1985

Fewest First Downs, Rushing, Season
- 36 Cleveland, 1942
  Boston, 1944
- 39 Brooklyn, 1943
- 40 Philadelphia, 1940
  Detroit, 1945

Most First Downs, Rushing, Game
- 25 Philadelphia vs. Washington, Dec. 2, 1951
- 23 St. Louis vs. New Orleans, Oct. 5, 1980
- 21 Cleveland vs. Philadelphia, Dec. 13, 1959
  Green Bay vs. Philadelphia, Nov. 11, 1962
  Los Angeles vs. New Orleans, Nov. 25, 1973
  Pittsburgh vs. Kansas City, Nov. 7, 1976
  New England vs. Denver, Nov. 28, 1976
  Oakland vs. Green Bay, Sept. 17, 1978
  Buffalo vs. Washington, Nov. 3, 1996
  San Francisco vs. Detroit, Dec. 14, 1998

Fewest First Downs, Rushing, Game
- 0 By many teams. Last time: Carolina vs. San Diego, Dec. 17, 2000

Most First Downs, Rushing, Both Teams, Game
- 36 Philadelphia (25) vs. Washington (11), Dec. 2, 1951
- 31 Detroit (18) vs. Washington (13), Sept. 30, 1951
- 30 Los Angeles (17) vs. Minnesota (13), Nov. 5, 1961
  New Orleans (17) vs. Green Bay (13), Sept. 9, 1979
  New Orleans (16) vs. San Francisco (14), Nov. 11, 1979
  New England (16) vs. Kansas City (14), Oct. 4, 1981

Fewest First Downs, Rushing, Both Teams, Game
- 2 Houston (0) vs. Denver (2), Dec. 2, 1962
  N.Y. Jets, (1) vs. St. Louis (1), Dec. 3, 1995
  Miami (1) vs. San Diego (1), Dec. 19, 1999
  New Orleans (0) vs. Baltimore (2), Dec. 19, 1999
- 3 Philadelphia (1) vs. Pittsburgh (2), Oct. 27, 1957
  Boston (1) vs. Buffalo (2), Nov. 15, 1964
  Los Angeles (0) vs. San Francisco (3), Dec. 6, 1964
  Pittsburgh (1) vs. St. Louis (2), Nov. 13, 1966
  Seattle (1) vs. New Orleans (2), Sept. 1, 1991
  New Orleans (0) vs. N.Y. Jets (3), Dec. 24, 1995
  Philadelphia (1) vs. Carolina (2), Oct. 27, 1996
  San Diego (1) vs. New Orleans (2), Sept. 7, 1997
  New Orleans (1) vs. Tampa Bay (2), Oct, 25, 1998
  New England (1) vs. Miami (2), Oct. 25, 1998 (OT)
  Miami (1) vs. New England (2), Nov. 23, 1998
  San Diego (1) vs. Seattle (2), Dec. 30, 2001
- 4 In many games

Most First Downs, Passing, Season
- 259 San Diego, 1985
- 251 Houston, 1990
- 250 Miami, 1986

Fewest First Downs, Passing, Season
- 18 Pittsburgh, 1941
- 23 Brooklyn, 1942
  N.Y. Giants, 1944
- 24 N.Y. Giants, 1943

Most First Downs, Passing, Game
- 29 N.Y. Giants vs. Cincinnati, Oct. 13, 1985
- 27 San Diego vs. Seattle, Sept. 15, 1985

- 26 Miami vs. Cleveland, Dec. 12, 1988

Fewest First Downs, Passing, Game
- 0 By many teams. Last time: Cleveland vs. Jacksonville, Dec. 3, 2000

Most First Downs, Passing, Both Teams, Game
- 43 San Diego (23) vs. Cincinnati (20), Dec. 20, 1982
  Miami (24) vs. N.Y. Jets (19), Sept. 21, 1986 (OT)
- 42 San Francisco (22) vs. San Diego (20), Dec. 11, 1982
- 41 San Diego (27) vs. Seattle (14), Sept. 15, 1985
  Miami (26) vs. Cleveland (15), Dec. 12, 1988
  Kansas City (23) vs. Oakland (18), Nov. 5, 2000

Fewest First Downs, Passing, Both Teams, Game
- 0 Brooklyn vs. Pittsburgh, Nov. 29, 1942
- 1 Green Bay (0) vs. Cleveland (1), Sept. 21, 1941
  Pittsburgh (0) vs. Brooklyn (1), Oct. 11, 1942
  N.Y. Giants (0) vs. Detroit (1), Nov. 7, 1943
  Pittsburgh (0) vs. Chi. Cardinals (1), Nov. 11, 1945
  N.Y. Bulldogs (0) vs. Philadelphia (1), Sept. 22, 1949
  Chicago (0) vs. Buffalo (1), Oct. 7, 1979
- 2 In many games

Most First Downs, Penalty, Season
- 43 Denver, 1994
- 42 Chicago, 1987
- 41 Denver, 1986

Fewest First Downs, Penalty, Season
- 2 Brooklyn, 1940
- 4 Chi. Cardinals, 1940
  N.Y. Giants, 1942, 1944
  Washington, 1944
  Cleveland, 1952
  Kansas City, 1969
- 5 Brooklyn, 1939
  Chi. Bears, 1939
  Detroit, 1953
  Los Angeles, 1953
  Houston, 1982

Most First Downs, Penalty, Game
- 11 Denver vs. Houston, Oct. 6, 1985
- 9 Chi. Bears vs. Cleveland, Nov. 25, 1951
  Baltimore vs. Pittsburgh, Oct. 30, 1977
  N.Y. Jets vs. Houston, Sept. 18, 1988
- 8 Philadelphia vs. Detroit, Dec. 2, 1979
  Cincinnati vs. N.Y. Jets, Oct. 6, 1985
  Buffalo vs. Houston, Sept. 20, 1987
  Houston vs. Atlanta, Sept. 9, 1990
  Kansas City vs. L.A. Raiders, Oct. 3, 1993
  San Francisco vs. New Orleans, Oct. 11, 1998
  Oakland vs. San Francisco, Oct. 8, 2000 (OT)

Most First Downs, Penalty, Both Teams, Game
- 12 Buffalo (7) vs. San Francisco (5), Oct. 4, 1998
- 11 Chi. Bears (9) vs. Cleveland (2), Nov. 25, 1951
  Cincinnati (8) vs. N.Y. Jets (3), Oct. 6, 1985
  Denver (11) vs. Houston (0), Oct. 6, 1985
  Detroit (6) vs. Dallas (5), Nov. 8, 1987
  N.Y. Jets (9) vs. Houston (2), Sept. 18, 1988
  Kansas City (8) vs. L.A. Raiders (3), Oct. 3, 1993
  Detroit (6) vs. San Diego (5), Nov. 11, 1996
- 10 In many games

NET YARDS GAINED RUSHING AND PASSING
Most Seasons Leading League
- 12 Chi. Bears, 1932, 1934-35, 1939, 1941-44, 1947, 1949, 1955-56
- 9 L.A./St. Louis Rams, 1946, 1950-51, 1954, 1957, 1973, 1999-2001
- 7 San Diego, 1963, 1965, 1980-83, 1985

Most Consecutive Seasons Leading League
- 4 Chi. Bears, 1941-44
  San Diego, 1980-83

3   Baltimore, 1958-1960
      Houston, 1960-62
      Oakland, 1968-1970
      St. Louis, 1999-2001 (current)
2   By many teams

Most Yards Gained, Season
7,075   St. Louis, 2000
6,936   Miami, 1984
6,800   San Francisco, 1998

Fewest Yards Gained, Season
1,150   Cincinnati, 1933
1,443   Chi. Cardinals, 1934
1,486   Chi. Cardinals, 1933

Most Yards Gained, Game
735   Los Angeles vs. N.Y. Yanks, Sept. 28, 1951
683   Pittsburgh vs. Chi. Cardinals, Dec. 13, 1958
682   Chi. Bears vs. N.Y. Giants, Nov. 14, 1943

Fewest Yards Gained, Game
−7   Seattle vs. Los Angeles, Nov. 4, 1979
−5   Denver vs. Oakland, Sept. 10, 1967
14   Chi. Cardinals vs. Detroit, Sept. 15, 1940

Most Yards Gained, Both Teams, Game
1,133   Los Angeles (636) vs. N.Y. Yanks (497), Nov. 19, 1950
1,102   San Diego (661) vs. Cincinnati (441), Dec. 20, 1982
1,087   St. Louis (589) vs. Philadelphia (498), Dec. 16, 1962

Fewest Yards Gained, Both Teams, Game
30   Chi. Cardinals (14) vs. Detroit (16), Sept. 15, 1940
136   Chi. Cardinals (50) vs. Green Bay (86), Nov. 18, 1934
154   N.Y. Giants (51) vs. Washington (103), Dec. 11, 1960

Most Consecutive Games, 400 or More Yards Gained
11   San Diego, 1982-83
8   St. Louis, 1999-2000
6   Houston, 1961-62
    San Diego, 1981
    San Francisco, 1987

Most Consecutive Games, 300 or More Yards Gained
30   Minnesota, 1999-2000
29   Los Angeles, 1949-1951
26   Miami, 1983-85

RUSHING

Most Seasons Leading League
16   Chi. Bears, 1932, 1934-35, 1939-1942, 1951, 1955-56, 1968, 1977, 1983-86
7   Buffalo, 1962, 1964, 1973, 1975, 1982, 1991-92
6   Cleveland, 1958-59, 1963, 1965-67
    San Francisco, 1952-54, 1987, 1998-99

Most Consecutive Seasons Leading League
4   Chi. Bears, 1939-1942
    Chi. Bears, 1983-86
3   Detroit, 1936-38
    San Francisco, 1952-54
    Cleveland, 1965-67
2   By many teams

ATTEMPTS

Most Rushing Attempts, Season
681   Oakland, 1977
674   Chicago, 1984
671   New England, 1978

Fewest Rushing Attempts, Season
211   Philadelphia, 1982
219   San Francisco, 1982
225   Houston, 1982

Most Rushing Attempts, Game
72   Chi. Bears vs. Brooklyn, Oct. 20, 1935
70   Chi. Cardinals vs. Green Bay, Dec. 5, 1948
69   Chi. Cardinals vs. Green Bay, Dec. 6, 1936
    Kansas City vs. Cincinnati, Sept. 3, 1978

Fewest Rushing Attempts, Game
6   Chi. Cardinals vs. Boston, Oct. 29, 1933
7   Oakland vs. Buffalo, Oct. 15, 1963
    Houston vs. N.Y. Giants, Dec. 8, 1985
    Seattle vs. L.A. Raiders, Nov. 17, 1991
    Green Bay vs. Miami, Sept. 11, 1994
8   Denver vs. Oakland, Dec. 17, 1960
    Buffalo vs. St. Louis, Sept. 9, 1984
    Detroit vs. San Francisco, Oct. 20, 1991
    Atlanta vs. Detroit, Sept. 5, 1993

Most Rushing Attempts, Both Teams, Game
108   Chi. Cardinals (70) vs. Green Bay (38), Dec. 5, 1948
105   Oakland (62) vs. Atlanta (43), Nov. 30, 1975 (OT)
104   Chi. Bears (64) vs. Pittsburgh (40), Oct. 18, 1936

Fewest Rushing Attempts, Both Teams, Game
34   Atlanta (12) vs. Houston (22), Dec. 5, 1993
    Atlanta (15) vs. San Francisco (19), Dec. 24, 1995
35   Seattle (15) vs. New Orleans (20), Sept. 1, 1991
36   Houston (15) vs. N.Y. Jets (21), Oct. 13, 1991
    St. Louis (16) vs. Detroit (20), Nov. 7, 1999
    Detroit (15) vs. Washington (21), Dec. 5, 1999
    Tennessee (14) vs. Baltimore (22), Dec. 5, 1999

YARDS GAINED

Most Yards Gained Rushing, Season
3,165   New England, 1978
3,088   Buffalo, 1973
2,986   Kansas City, 1978

Fewest Yards Gained Rushing, Season
298   Philadelphia, 1940
467   Detroit, 1946
471   Boston, 1944

Most Yards Gained Rushing, Game
426   Detroit vs. Pittsburgh, Nov. 4, 1934
423   N.Y. Giants vs. Baltimore, Nov. 19, 1950
420   Boston vs. N.Y. Giants, Oct. 8, 1933

Fewest Yards Gained Rushing, Game
−53   Detroit vs. Chi. Cardinals, Oct. 17, 1943
−36   Philadelphia vs. Chi. Bears, Nov. 19, 1939
−33   Phil-Pitt vs. Brooklyn, Oct. 2, 1943

Most Yards Gained Rushing, Both Teams, Game
595   Los Angeles (371) vs. N.Y. Yanks (224), Nov. 18, 1951
574   Chi. Bears (396) vs. Pittsburgh (178), Oct. 10, 1934
558   Boston (420) vs. N.Y. Giants (138), Oct. 8, 1933

Fewest Yards Gained Rushing, Both Teams, Game
−15   Detroit (−53) vs. Chi. Cardinals (38), Oct. 17, 1943
4   Detroit (−10) vs. Chi. Cardinals (14), Sept. 15, 1940
62   L.A. Rams (15) vs. San Francisco (47), Dec. 6, 1964

AVERAGE GAIN

Highest Average Gain, Rushing, Season
5.74   Cleveland, 1963
5.65   San Francisco, 1954
5.56   San Diego, 1963

Lowest Average Gain, Rushing, Season
0.94   Philadelphia, 1940
1.45   Boston, 1944
1.55   Pittsburgh, 1935

TOUCHDOWNS

Most Touchdowns, Rushing, Season
36   Green Bay, 1962
33   Pittsburgh, 1976
30   Chi. Bears, 1941
    New England, 1978
    Washington, 1983

Fewest Touchdowns, Rushing, Season
1   Brooklyn, 1934
2   Chi. Cardinals, 1933

Cincinnati, 1933
Pittsburgh, 1934
Philadelphia, 1935
Philadelphia, 1936
Philadelphia, 1937
Philadelphia, 1938
Pittsburgh, 1940
Philadelphia, 1972
N.Y. Jets, 1995
3 By many teams

Most Touchdowns, Rushing, Game
7 Los Angeles vs. Atlanta, Dec. 4, 1976
6 By many teams

Most Touchdowns, Rushing, Both Teams, Game
8 Los Angeles (6) vs. N.Y. Yanks (2), Nov. 18, 1951
Chi. Bears (5) vs. Green Bay (3), Nov. 6, 1955
Cleveland (6) vs. Los Angeles (2), Nov. 24, 1957
7 In many games

PASSING
ATTEMPTS
Most Passes Attempted, Season
709 Minnesota, 1981
699 New England, 1994
686 New England, 1995

Fewest Passes Attempted, Season
102 Cincinnati, 1933
106 Boston, 1933
120 Detroit, 1937

Most Passes Attempted, Game
70 New England vs. Minnesota, Nov. 13, 1994 (OT)
69 N.Y. Jets vs. Baltimore, Dec. 24, 2000
68 Houston vs. Buffalo, Nov 1, 1964

Fewest Passes Attempted, Game
0 Green Bay vs. Portsmouth, Oct. 8, 1933
Detroit vs. Cleveland, Sept. 10, 1937
Pittsburgh vs. Brooklyn, Nov. 16, 1941
Pittsburgh vs. Los Angeles, Nov. 13, 1949
Cleveland vs. Philadelphia, Dec. 3, 1950

Most Passes Attempted, Both Teams, Game
112 New England (70) vs. Minnesota (42), Nov. 13, 1994
104 Miami (55) vs. N.Y. Jets (49), Oct. 18, 1987 (OT)
N.Y. Jets (58) vs. San Francisco (46),
Sept. 6, 1998 (OT)
103 Cincinnati (68) vs. Pittsburgh (35), Dec. 30, 2001 (OT)

Fewest Passes Attempted, Both Teams, Game
4 Chi. Cardinals (1) vs. Detroit (3), Nov. 3, 1935
Detroit (0) vs. Cleveland (4), Sept. 10, 1937
6 Chi. Cardinals (2) vs. Detroit (4), Sept. 15, 1940
8 Brooklyn (2) vs. Philadelphia (6), Oct. 1, 1939

COMPLETIONS
Most Passes Completed, Season
432 San Francisco, 1995
411 Houston, 1991
409 Minnesota, 1994

Fewest Passes Completed, Season
25 Cincinnati, 1933
33 Boston, 1933
34 Chi. Cardinals, 1934
Detroit, 1934

Most Passes Completed, Game
45 New England vs. Minnesota, Nov. 13, 1994 (OT)
43 Washington vs. Detroit, Nov. 4, 1990 (OT)
42 N.Y. Jets vs. San Francisco, Sept. 21, 1980
N.Y. Jets vs. Seattle, Dec. 6, 1998

Fewest Passes Completed, Game
0 By many teams. Last time: Buffalo vs. N.Y. Jets,
Sept. 29, 1974

Most Passes Completed, Both Teams, Game
71 New England (45) vs. Minnesota (26), Nov. 13, 1994
68 San Francisco (37) vs. Atlanta (31), Oct. 6, 1985
66 Cincinnati (40) vs. San Diego (26), Dec. 20, 1982

Fewest Passes Completed, Both Teams, Game
1 Chi. Cardinals (0) vs. Philadelphia (1), Nov. 8, 1936
Detroit (0) vs. Cleveland (1), Sept. 10, 1937
Chi. Cardinals (0) vs. Detroit (1), Sept. 15, 1940
Brooklyn (0) vs. Pittsburgh (1), Nov. 29, 1942
2 Chi. Cardinals (0) vs. Detroit (2), Nov. 3, 1935
Buffalo (0) vs. N.Y. Jets (2), Sept. 29, 1974
Chi. Cardinals (0) vs. Green Bay (2), Nov. 18, 1934
3 In seven games

YARDS GAINED
Most Seasons Leading League, Passing Yardage
10 San Diego, 1965, 1968, 1971, 1978-1983, 1985
8 Chi. Bears, 1932, 1939, 1941, 1943, 1945, 1949,
1954, 1964
Washington, 1938, 1940, 1944, 1947-48, 1967,
1974, 1989
7 Houston, 1960-61, 1963-64, 1990-92
L.A./St. Louis Rams, 1946, 1950-51, 1956,
1999-2001

Most Consecutive Seasons Leading League, Passing Yardage
6 San Diego, 1978-1983
4 Green Bay, 1934-37
3 Miami, 1986-88
Houston, 1990-92
St. Louis, 1999-2001 (current)

Most Yards Gained, Passing, Season
5,232 St. Louis, 2000
5,018 Miami, 1984
4,870 San Diego, 1985

Fewest Yards Gained, Passing, Season
302 Chi. Cardinals, 1934
357 Cincinnati, 1933
459 Boston, 1934

Most Yards Gained, Passing, Game
554 Los Angeles vs. N.Y. Yanks, Sept. 28, 1951
530 Minnesota vs. Baltimore, Sept. 28, 1969
521 Miami vs. N.Y. Jets, Oct. 23, 1988

Fewest Yards Gained, Passing, Game
–53 Denver vs. Oakland, Sept. 10, 1967
–52 Cincinnati vs. Houston, Oct. 31, 1971
–39 Atlanta vs. San Francisco, Oct. 23, 1976

Most Yards Gained, Passing, Both Teams, Game
884 N.Y. Jets (449) vs. Miami (435), Sept. 21, 1986 (OT)
883 San Diego (486) vs. Cincinnati (397), Dec. 20, 1982
874 Miami (456) vs. New England (418), Sept. 4, 1994

Fewest Yards Gained, Passing, Both Teams, Game
–11 Green Bay (–10) vs. Dallas (–1), Oct. 24, 1965
1 Chi. Cardinals (0) vs. Philadelphia (1), Nov. 8, 1936
7 Brooklyn (0) vs. Pittsburgh (7), Nov. 29, 1942

TIMES SACKED
Most Seasons Leading League, Fewest Times Sacked
10 Miami, 1973, 1982-1990
5 N.Y. Jets, 1965-66, 1968, 1993, 2000
4 San Diego, 1963-64, 1967-68
San Francisco, 1964-65, 1970-71

Most Consecutive Seasons Leading League, Fewest Times Sacked
9 Miami, 1982-1990
3 St. Louis, 1974-76
2 By many teams

Most Times Sacked, Season
104 Philadelphia, 1986
78 Arizona, 1997
72 Philadelphia, 1987

Fewest Times Sacked, Season
  7 Miami, 1988
  8 San Francisco, 1970
     St. Louis, 1975
  9 N.Y. Jets, 1966
     Washington, 1991

Most Times Sacked, Game
  12 Pittsburgh vs. Dallas, Nov. 20, 1966
      Baltimore vs. St. Louis, Oct. 26, 1980
      Detroit vs. Chicago, Dec. 16, 1984
      Houston vs. Dallas, Sept. 29, 1985
  11 St. Louis vs. N.Y. Giants, Nov. 1, 1964
      Los Angeles vs. Baltimore, Nov. 22, 1964
      Denver vs. Buffalo, Dec. 13, 1964
      Green Bay vs. Detroit, Nov. 7, 1965
      Buffalo vs. Oakland, Oct. 15, 1967
      Denver vs. Oakland, Nov. 5, 1967
      Atlanta vs. St. Louis, Nov. 24, 1968
      Detroit vs. Dallas, Oct. 6, 1975
      Philadelphia vs. St. Louis, Dec. 18, 1983
      Cleveland vs. Kansas City, Sept. 30, 1984
      Minnesota vs. Chicago, Oct. 28, 1984
      Atlanta vs. Cleveland, Nov. 18, 1984
      Dallas vs. San Diego, Nov. 16, 1986
      Philadelphia vs. Detroit, Nov. 16, 1986
      Philadelphia vs. L.A. Raiders, Nov. 30, 1986 (OT)
      L.A. Raiders vs. Seattle, Dec. 8, 1986
      N.Y. Jets vs. Dallas, Oct. 4, 1987
      Philadelphia vs. Chicago, Oct. 4, 1987
      Dallas vs. Philadelphia, Sept. 15, 1991
      Cleveland vs. Indianapolis, Sept. 6, 1992
  10 By many teams

Most Times Sacked, Both Teams, Game
  18 Green Bay (10) vs. San Diego (8), Sept. 24, 1978
  17 Buffalo (10) vs. N.Y. Titans (7), Nov. 23, 1961
      Pittsburgh (12) vs. Dallas (5), Nov. 20, 1966
      Atlanta (9) vs. Philadelphia (8), Dec. 16, 1984
      Philadelphia (11) vs. L.A. Raiders (6),
         Nov. 30, 1986 (OT)
  16 Los Angeles (11) vs. Baltimore (5), Nov. 22, 1964
      Buffalo (11) vs. Oakland (5), Oct. 15, 1967

COMPLETION PERCENTAGE

Most Seasons Leading League, Completion Percentage
  14 San Francisco, 1952, 1957-58, 1965, 1981, 1983,
      1987, 1989, 1992-97
  11 Washington, 1937, 1939-1940, 1942-45, 1947-48,
      1969-1970
    8 Green Bay, 1936, 1941, 1961-62, 1964, 1966,
      1968, 1998

Most Consecutive Seasons Leading League,
Completion Percentage
    6 San Francisco, 1992-97
    4 Washington, 1942-45
      Kansas City, 1966-69
    3 Cleveland, 1953-55
      St. Louis, 1999-2001 (current)

Highest Completion Percentage, Season
  70.65 Cincinnati, 1982 (310-219)
  70.25 San Francisco, 1994 (511-359)
  70.19 San Francisco, 1989 (483-339)

Lowest Completion Percentage, Season
  22.9 Philadelphia, 1936 (170-39)
  24.5 Cincinnati, 1933 (102-25)
  25.0 Pittsburgh, 1941 (168-42)

TOUCHDOWNS

Most Touchdowns, Passing, Season
  49 Miami, 1984
  48 Houston, 1961

  46 Miami, 1986

Fewest Touchdowns, Passing, Season
    0 Cincinnati, 1933
      Pittsburgh, 1945
    1 Boston, 1932
      Boston, 1933
      Chi. Cardinals, 1934
      Cincinnati/St. Louis, 1934
      Detroit, 1942
    2 Chi. Cardinals, 1932
      Stapleton, 1932
      Chi. Cardinals, 1935
      Brooklyn, 1936
      Pittsburgh, 1942

Most Touchdowns, Passing, Game
    7 Chi. Bears vs. N.Y. Giants, Nov. 14, 1943
      Philadelphia vs. Washington, Oct. 17, 1954
      Houston vs. N.Y. Titans, Nov. 19, 1961
      Houston vs. N.Y. Titans, Oct. 14, 1962
      N.Y. Giants vs. Washington, Oct. 28, 1962
      Minnesota vs. Baltimore, Sept. 28, 1969
      San Diego vs. Oakland, Nov. 22, 1981
    6 By many teams

Most Touchdowns, Passing, Both Teams, Game
  12 New Orleans (6) vs. St. Louis (6), Nov. 2, 1969
  11 N.Y. Giants (7) vs. Washington (4), Oct. 28, 1962
      Oakland (6) vs. Houston (5), Dec. 22, 1963
  10 San Diego (5) vs. Seattle (5), Sept. 15, 1985
      Miami (6) vs. N.Y. Jets (4), Sept. 21, 1986 (OT)
      San Francisco (6) vs. Atlanta (4), Oct. 14, 1990

PASSES HAD INTERCEPTED

Most Passes Had Intercepted, Season
  48 Houston, 1962
  45 Denver, 1961
  41 Card-Pitt, 1944

Fewest Passes Had Intercepted, Season
    5 Cleveland, 1960
      Green Bay, 1966
      Kansas City, 1990
      N.Y. Giants, 1990
    6 Green Bay, 1964
      St. Louis, 1982
      Dallas, 1993
    7 Los Angeles, 1969

Most Passes Had Intercepted, Game
    9 Detroit vs. Green Bay, Oct. 24, 1943
      Pittsburgh vs. Philadelphia, Dec. 12, 1965
    8 Green Bay vs. N.Y. Giants, Nov. 21, 1948
      Chi. Cardinals vs. Philadelphia, Sept. 24, 1950
      N.Y. Yanks vs. N.Y. Giants, Dec. 16, 1951
      Denver vs. Houston, Dec. 2, 1962
      Chi. Bears vs. Detroit, Sept. 22, 1968
      Baltimore vs. N.Y. Jets, Sept. 23, 1973
    7 By many teams. Last time: Detroit vs. Cleveland,
      Sept. 23, 2001

Most Passes Had Intercepted, Both Teams, Game
  13 Denver (8) vs. Houston (5), Dec. 2, 1962
  11 Philadelphia (7) vs. Boston (4), Nov. 3, 1935
      Boston (6) vs. Pittsburgh (5), Dec. 1, 1935
      Cleveland (7) vs. Green Bay (4), Oct. 30, 1938
      Green Bay (7) vs. Detroit (4), Oct. 20, 1940
      Detroit (7) vs. Chi. Bears (4), Nov. 22, 1942
      Detroit (7) vs. Cleveland (4), Nov. 26, 1944
      Chi. Cardinals (8) vs. Philadelphia (3), Sept. 24, 1950
      Washington (7) vs. N.Y. Giants (4), Dec. 8, 1963
      Pittsburgh (9) vs. Philadelphia (2), Dec 12, 1965
  10 In many games

PUNTING

Most Seasons Leading League (Average Distance)
- 7 Denver 1962-64, 1966-67, 1982, 1999
- 6 Washington, 1940-43, 1945, 1958
  Kansas City, 1968, 1971-73, 1979, 1984
- 5 L.A. Rams, 1946, 1949, 1955-56, 1994

Most Consecutive Seasons Leading League (Average Distance)
- 4 Washington, 1940-43
- 3 Cleveland, 1950-52
  Denver, 1962-64
  Kansas City, 1971-73

Most Punts, Season
- 114 Chicago, 1981
- 113 Boston, 1934
  Brooklyn, 1934
- 112 Boston, 1935
  N.Y. Giants, 1997

Fewest Punts, Season
- 23 San Diego, 1982
- 31 Cincinnati, 1982
- 32 Chi. Bears, 1941

Most Punts, Game
- 17 Chi. Bears vs. Green Bay, Oct. 22, 1933
  Cincinnati vs. Pittsburgh, Oct. 22, 1933
- 16 Cincinnati vs. Portsmouth, Sept. 17, 1933
  Chi. Cardinals vs. Chi. Bears, Nov. 30, 1933
  Chi. Cardinals vs. Detroit, Sept. 15, 1940
  Oakland vs. San Diego, Oct. 11, 1998
- 15 N.Y. Giants vs. Chi. Bears, Nov. 17, 1935
  Philadelphia vs. N.Y. Giants, Dec. 6, 1987 (OT)

Fewest Punts, Game
- 0 By many teams. Last time:
  Indianapolis vs. Buffalo, Sept. 23, 2001

Most Punts, Both Teams, Game
- 31 Chi. Bears (17) vs. Green Bay (14), Oct. 22, 1933
  Cincinnati (17), vs. Pittsburgh (14), Oct. 22, 1933
- 29 Chi. Cardinals (15) vs. Cincinnati (14), Nov. 12, 1933
  Chi. Cardinals (16) vs. Chi. Bears (13), Nov. 30, 1933
  Chi. Cardinals (16) vs. Detroit (13), Sept. 15, 1940
- 28 Philadelphia (14) vs. Washington (14), Nov. 5, 1939

Fewest Punts, Both Teams, Game
- 0 Buffalo vs. San Francisco, Sept. 13, 1992
- 1 Baltimore (0) vs. Cleveland (1), Nov. 1, 1959
  Dall. Cowboys (0) vs. Cleveland (1), Dec. 3, 1961
  Chicago (0) vs. Detroit (1), Oct. 1, 1972
  San Francisco (0) vs. N.Y. Giants (1), Oct. 15, 1972
  Green Bay (0) vs. Buffalo (1), Dec. 5, 1982
  Miami (0) vs. Buffalo (1), Oct. 12, 1986
  Green Bay (0) vs. Chicago (1), Dec. 17, 1989
  Oakland (0) vs. Seattle (1), Dec. 5, 1999
  Tampa Bay (0) vs. Minnesota (1), Oct. 29, 2000
- 2 In many games

AVERAGE YARDAGE

Highest Average Distance, Punting, Season
- 47.6 Detroit, 1961 (56-2,664)
- 47.5 Carolina, 2001 (93-4,419)
- 47.2 Tennessee, 1998 (69-3,258)

Lowest Average Distance, Punting, Season
- 32.7 Card-Pitt, 1944 (60-1,964)
- 33.8 Cincinnati, 1986 (59-1,996)
- 33.9 Detroit, 1969 (74-2,510)

PUNT RETURNS

Most Seasons Leading League (Average Return)
- 9 Detroit, 1943-45, 1951-52, 1962, 1966, 1969, 1991
- 7 Chi. Cardinals/St. Louis, 1948-49, 1955-56, 1959, 1986-87
- 6 Green Bay, 1950, 1953-54, 1961, 1972, 1996

Most Consecutive Seasons Leading League (Average Return)
- 3 Detroit, 1943-45
- 2 By many teams

Most Punt Returns, Season
- 71 Pittsburgh, 1976
  Tampa Bay, 1979
  L.A. Raiders, 1985
- 67 Pittsburgh, 1974
  Los Angeles, 1978
  L.A. Raiders, 1984
- 65 San Francisco, 1976

Fewest Punt Returns, Season
- 12 Baltimore, 1981
  San Diego, 1982
- 14 Los Angeles, 1961
  Philadelphia, 1962
  Baltimore, 1982
- 15 Houston, 1960
  Washington, 1960
  Oakland, 1961
  N.Y. Giants, 1969
  Philadelphia, 1973
  Kansas City, 1982

Most Punt Returns, Game
- 12 Philadelphia vs. Cleveland, Dec. 3, 1950
- 11 Chi. Bears vs. Chi. Cardinals, Oct. 8, 1950
  Washington vs. Tampa Bay, Oct. 9, 1977
- 10 Philadelphia vs. N.Y. Giants, Nov. 26, 1950
  Philadelphia vs. Tampa Bay, Sept. 18, 1977
  Pittsburgh vs. Buffalo, Dec. 16, 1979
  Washington vs. New Orleans, Dec. 26, 1982
  Philadelphia vs. Seattle, Dec. 13, 1992 (OT)
  New England vs. Pittsburgh, Dec. 5, 1993

Most Punt Returns, Both Teams, Game
- 17 Philadelphia (12) vs. Cleveland (5), Dec. 3, 1950
- 16 N.Y. Giants (9) vs. Philadelphia (7), Dec. 12, 1954
  Washington (11) vs. Tampa Bay (5), Oct. 9, 1977
  Oakland (8) vs. San Diego (8), Oct. 11, 1998
- 15 Detroit (8) vs. Cleveland (7), Sept. 27, 1942
  Los Angeles (8) vs. Baltimore (7), Nov. 27, 1966
  Pittsburgh (8) vs. Houston (7), Dec. 1, 1974
  Philadelphia (10) vs. Tampa Bay (5), Sept. 18, 1977
  Baltimore (9) vs. Kansas City (6), Sept. 2, 1979
  Washington (10) vs. New Orleans (5), Dec. 26, 1982
  L.A. Raiders (8) vs. Cleveland (7), Nov. 16, 1986

FAIR CATCHES

Most Fair Catches, Season
- 34 Baltimore, 1971
- 33 Philadelphia, 2000
- 32 San Diego, 1969
  Oakland, 2001

Fewest Fair Catches, Season
- 0 San Diego, 1975
  New England, 1976
  Tampa Bay, 1976
  Pittsburgh, 1977
  Dallas, 1982
- 1 Cleveland, 1974
  San Francisco, 1975
  Kansas City, 1976
  St. Louis, 1976
  San Diego, 1976
  L.A. Rams, 1982
  St. Louis, 1982
  Tampa Bay, 1982
  Arizona, 2001
- 2 By many teams

Most Fair Catches, Game
- 7 Minnesota vs. Dallas, Sept. 25, 1966

Detroit vs. Chicago, Nov. 21, 1976
Philadelphia vs. Buffalo, Dec. 27, 1987
8 By many teams

YARDS GAINED
Most Yards, Punt Returns, Season
875 Green Bay, 1996
785 L.A. Raiders, 1985
781 Chi. Bears, 1948
Fewest Yards, Punt Returns, Season
27 St. Louis, 1965
35 N.Y. Giants, 1965
37 New England, 1972
Most Yards, Punt Returns, Game
231 Detroit vs. San Francisco, Oct. 6, 1963
225 Oakland vs. Buffalo, Sept. 15, 1968
219 Los Angeles vs. Atlanta, Oct. 11, 1981
Fewest Yards, Punt Returns, Game
-28 Washington vs. Dallas, Dec. 11, 1966
-23 N.Y. Giants vs. Buffalo, Oct. 20, 1975
    Pittsburgh vs. Houston, Sept. 20, 1970
-20 New Orleans vs. Pittsburgh, Oct. 20, 1968
Most Yards, Punt Returns, Both Teams, Game
282 Los Angeles (219) vs. Atlanta (63), Oct. 11, 1981
245 Detroit (231) vs. San Francisco (14), Oct. 6, 1963
244 Oakland (225) vs. Buffalo (19), Sept. 15, 1968
Fewest Yards, Punt Returns, Both Teams, Game
-18 Buffalo (-18) vs. Pittsburgh (0), Oct. 29, 1972
-14 Miami (-14) vs. Boston (0), Nov. 30, 1969
-13 N.Y. Giants (-13) vs. Cleveland (0), Nov. 14, 1965

AVERAGE YARDS RETURNING PUNTS
Highest Average, Punt Returns, Season
20.2 Chi. Bears, 1941 (27-546)
19.1 Chi. Cardinals, 1948 (35-669)
18.2 Chi. Cardinals, 1949 (30-546)
Lowest Average, Punt Returns, Season
1.2 St. Louis, 1965 (23-27)
1.5 N.Y. Giants, 1965 (24-35)
1.7 Washington, 1970 (27-45)

TOUCHDOWNS RETURNING PUNTS
Most Touchdowns, Punt Returns, Season
5 Chi. Cardinals, 1959
4 Chi. Cardinals, 1948
  Detroit, 1951
  N.Y. Giants, 1951
  Denver, 1976
3 Washington, 1941
  Detroit, 1952
  Pittsburgh, 1952
  Houston, 1975
  Los Angeles, 1981
  Cleveland, 1993
  Green Bay, 1996
  Denver, 1997
  San Diego, 1997
Most Touchdowns, Punt Returns, Game
2 Detroit vs. Los Angeles, Oct. 14, 1951
  Detroit vs. Green Bay, Nov. 22, 1951
  Chi. Cardinals vs. Pittsburgh, Nov. 1, 1959
  Chi. Cardinals vs. N.Y. Giants, Nov. 22, 1959
  N.Y. Titans vs. Denver, Sept. 24, 1961
  Denver vs. Cleveland, Sept. 26, 1976
  Los Angeles vs. Atlanta, Oct. 11, 1981
  St. Louis vs. Tampa Bay, Dec. 21, 1986
  L.A. Rams vs. Atlanta, Dec. 27, 1992
  Cleveland vs. Pittsburgh, Oct. 24, 1993
  San Diego vs. Cincinnati, Nov. 2, 1997
  Denver vs. Carolina, Nov. 9, 1997

Baltimore vs. Seattle, Dec. 7, 1997
Baltimore vs. N.Y. Jets, Dec. 24, 2000
Most Touchdowns, Punt Returns, Both Teams, Game
2 Philadelphia (1) vs. Washington (1), Nov. 9, 1952
  Kansas City (1) vs. Buffalo (1), Sept. 11, 1966
  Baltimore (1) vs. New England (1), Nov. 18, 1979
  L.A. Raiders (1) vs. Philadelphia (1),
    Nov. 30, 1986 (OT)
  Cincinnati (1) vs. Green Bay (1), Sept. 20, 1992
  Oakland (1) vs. Seattle (1), Nov. 15, 1998
(Also see previous record)

KICKOFF RETURNS
Most Seasons Leading League (Average Return)
8 Washington, 1942, 1947, 1962-63, 1973-74, 1981,
  1995
6 Chicago Bears, 1943, 1948, 1958, 1966, 1972, 1985
5 N.Y. Giants, 1944, 1946, 1949, 1951, 1953
Most Consecutive Seasons Leading League (Average Return)
3 Denver, 1965-67
2 By many teams
Most Kickoff Returns, Season
89 Cleveland, 1999
88 New Orleans, 1980
87 Atlanta, 1996
  New Orleans, 2001
Fewest Kickoff Returns, Season
17 N.Y. Giants, 1944
20 N.Y. Giants, 1941, 1943
  Chi. Bears, 1942
23 Washington, 1942
Most Kickoff Returns, Game
12 N.Y. Giants vs. Washington, Nov. 27, 1966
10 By many teams
Most Kickoff Returns, Both Teams, Game
19 N.Y. Giants (12) vs. Washington (7), Nov. 27, 1966
18 Houston (10) vs. Oakland (8), Dec. 22, 1963
17 Washington (9) vs. Green Bay (8), Oct. 17, 1983
  San Diego (9) vs. Pittsburgh (8), Dec. 8, 1985
  Detroit (9) vs. Green Bay (8), Nov. 27, 1986
  L.A. Raiders (9) vs. Seattle (8), Dec. 18, 1988
  Oakland (10) vs. Seattle (7), Oct. 26, 1997

YARDS GAINED
Most Yards, Kickoff Returns, Season
2,296 Arizona, 2000
2,027 New Orleans, 2001
2,020 Cincinnati, 1999
Fewest Yards, Kickoff Returns, Season
282 N.Y. Giants, 1940
381 Green Bay, 1940
424 Chicago, 1963
Most Yards, Kickoff Returns, Game
367 Baltimore vs. Minnesota, Dec. 13, 1998
362 Detroit vs. Los Angeles, Oct. 29, 1950
304 Chi. Bears vs. Green Bay, Nov. 9, 1952
  New Orleans vs. L.A. Rams, Oct. 23, 1994
Most Yards, Kickoff Returns, Both Teams, Game
560 Detroit (362) vs. Los Angeles (198), Oct. 29, 1950
511 Baltimore (367) vs. Minnesota (144), Dec. 13, 1998
501 New Orleans (304) vs. L.A. Rams (197),
  Oct. 23, 1994

AVERAGE YARDAGE
Highest Average, Kickoff Returns, Season
29.4 Chicago, 1972 (52-1,528)
28.9 Pittsburgh, 1952 (39-1,128)
28.2 Washington, 1962 (61-1,720)
Lowest Average, Kickoff Returns, Season
14.7 N.Y. Jets, 1993 (46-675)

15.8   N.Y. Giants, 1993 (32-507)
15.9   Tampa Bay, 1993 (58-922)

TOUCHDOWNS
Most Touchdowns, Kickoff Returns, Season
- 4   Green Bay, 1967
-    Chicago, 1970
-    Detroit, 1994
- 3   Los Angeles, 1950
-    Chi. Cardinals, 1954
-    San Francisco, 1963
-    Denver, 1966
-    Chicago, 1967
-    New England, 1977
-    L.A. Rams, 1985
-    Atlanta, 2000
- 2   By many teams

Most Touchdowns, Kickoff Returns, Game
- 2   Chi. Bears vs. Green Bay, Sept. 22, 1940
-    Chi. Bears vs. Green Bay, Nov. 9, 1952
-    Philadelphia vs. Dallas, Nov. 6, 1966
-    Green Bay vs. Cleveland, Nov. 12, 1967
-    L.A. Rams vs. Green Bay, Nov. 24, 1985
-    New Orleans vs. L.A. Rams, Oct. 23, 1994
-    Baltimore vs. Minnesota, Dec. 13, 1998

Most Touchdowns, Kickoff Returns, Both Teams, Game
- 3   Baltimore (2) vs. Minnesota (1), Dec. 13, 1998
- 2   In many games

FUMBLES
Most Fumbles, Season
- 56   Chi. Bears, 1938
-     San Francisco, 1978
- 54   Philadelphia, 1946
- 51   New England, 1973

Fewest Fumbles, Season
- 8   Cleveland, 1959
- 10   Indianapolis, 1998
-     Minnesota, 1998
- 11   Green Bay, 1944

Most Fumbles, Game
- 10   Phil-Pitt vs. N.Y. Giants, Oct. 9, 1943
-     Detroit vs. Minnesota, Nov. 12, 1967
-     Kansas City vs. Houston, Oct. 12, 1969
-     San Francisco vs. Detroit, Dec. 17, 1978
- 9   Philadelphia vs. Green Bay, Oct. 13, 1946
-    Kansas City vs. San Diego, Nov. 15, 1964
-    N.Y. Giants vs. Buffalo, Oct. 20, 1975
-    St. Louis vs. Washington, Oct. 25, 1976
-    San Diego vs. Green Bay, Sept. 24, 1978
-    Pittsburgh vs. Cincinnati, Oct. 14, 1979
-    Cleveland vs. Seattle, Dec. 20, 1981
-    Cleveland vs. Pittsburgh, Dec. 23, 1990
-    Oakland vs. Seattle, Dec. 22, 1996
- 8   By many teams

Most Fumbles, Both Teams, Game
- 14   Washington (8) vs. Pittsburgh (6), Nov. 14, 1937
-     Chi. Bears (7) vs. Cleveland (7), Nov. 24, 1940
-     St. Louis (8) vs. N.Y. Giants (6), Sept. 17, 1961
-     Kansas City (10) vs. Houston (4), Oct. 12, 1969
- 13   Washington (8) vs. Pittsburgh (5), Nov. 14, 1937
-     Philadelphia (7) vs. Boston (6), Dec. 8, 1946
-     N.Y. Giants (7) vs. Washington (6), Nov. 5, 1950
-     Kansas City (9) vs. San Diego (4), Nov. 15, 1964
-     Buffalo (7) vs. Denver (6), Dec. 13, 1964
-     N.Y. Jets (7) vs. Houston (6), Sept. 12, 1965
-     Cleveland (7) vs. New Orleans (6), Dec. 12, 1971
-     Houston (8) vs. Pittsburgh (5), Dec. 9, 1973
-     St. Louis (9) vs. Washington (4), Oct. 25, 1976
-     Cleveland (9) vs. Seattle (4), Dec. 20, 1981

Green Bay (7) vs. Detroit (6), Oct. 6, 1985
12   In many games

FUMBLES LOST
Most Fumbles Lost, Season
- 36   Chi. Cardinals, 1959
- 31   Green Bay, 1952
- 29   Chi. Cardinals, 1946
-     Pittsburgh, 1950
-     Cleveland, 1978

Fewest Fumbles Lost, Season
- 3   Philadelphia, 1938
-    Minnesota, 1980
- 4   San Francisco, 1960
-    Kansas City, 1982
-    Minnesota, 1998
- 5   Chi. Cardinals, 1943
-    Detroit, 1943
-    N.Y. Giants, 1943
-    Cleveland, 1959
-    Minnesota, 1982
-    San Diego, 1993
-    Detroit, 1996
-    Indianapolis, 1998

Most Fumbles Lost, Game
- 8   St. Louis vs. Washington, Oct. 25, 1976
-    Cleveland vs. Pittsburgh, Dec. 23, 1990
- 7   Cincinnati vs. Buffalo, Nov. 30, 1969
-    Pittsburgh vs. Cincinnati, Oct. 14, 1979
-    Cleveland vs. Seattle, Dec. 20, 1981
- 6   By many teams

FUMBLES RECOVERED
Most Fumbles Recovered, Season, Own and Opponents'
- 58   Minnesota, 1963 (27 own, 31 opp)
- 51   Chi. Bears, 1938 (37 own, 14 opp)
-     San Francisco, 1978 (24 own, 27 opp)
- 50   Philadelphia, 1987 (23 own, 27 opp)

Fewest Fumbles Recovered, Season, Own and Opponents'
- 9   San Francisco, 1982 (5 own, 4 opp)
- 11   Cincinnati, 1982 (5 own, 6 opp)
- 12   Washington, 1994 (6 own, 6 opp)
-     Arizona, 1997 (7 own, 5 opp)

Most Fumbles Recovered, Game, Own and Opponents'
- 10   Denver vs. Buffalo, Dec. 13, 1964 (5 own, 5 opp)
-     Pittsburgh vs. Houston, Dec. 9, 1973 (5 own, 5 opp)
-     Washington vs. St. Louis, Oct. 25, 1976
-     (2 own, 8 opp)
- 9   St. Louis vs. N.Y. Giants, Sept. 17, 1961
-    (6 own, 3 opp)
-    Houston vs. Cincinnati, Oct. 27, 1974 (4 own, 5 opp)
-    Kansas City vs. Dallas, Nov. 10, 1975 (4 own, 5 opp)
-    Green Bay vs. Detroit, Oct. 6, 1985 (5 own, 4 opp)
-    Pittsburgh vs. Cleveland, Dec. 23, 1990 (1 own, 8 opp)
- 8   By many teams

Most Own Fumbles Recovered, Season
- 37   Chi. Bears, 1938
- 28   Pittsburgh, 1987
- 27   Philadelphia, 1946
-     Minnesota, 1963

Fewest Own Fumbles Recovered, Season
- 2   Washington, 1958
-    Miami, 2000
- 3   Detroit, 1956
-    Cleveland, 1959
-    Houston, 1982
- 4   By many teams

Most Opponents' Fumbles Recovered, Season
- 31   Minnesota, 1963

29 Cleveland, 1951
28 Green Bay, 1946
      Houston, 1977
      Seattle, 1983

Fewest Opponents' Fumbles Recovered, Season
3 Los Angeles, 1974
   Green Bay, 1995
4 Philadelphia, 1944
   San Francisco, 1982
5 Baltimore, 1982
   Arizona, 1997
   Baltimore, 1998

Most Opponents' Fumbles Recovered, Game
8 Washington vs. St. Louis, Oct. 25, 1976
   Pittsburgh vs. Cleveland, Dec. 23, 1990
7 Buffalo vs. Cincinnati, Nov. 30, 1969
   Cincinnati vs. Pittsburgh, Oct. 14, 1979
   Seattle vs. Cleveland, Dec. 20, 1981
6 By many teams

TOUCHDOWNS

Most Touchdowns, Fumbles Recovered, Season, Own and Opponents'
5 Chi. Bears, 1942 (1 own, 4 opp)
   Los Angeles, 1952 (1 own, 4 opp)
   San Francisco, 1965 (1 own, 4 opp)
   Oakland, 1978 (2 own, 3 opp)
4 Chi. Bears, 1948 (1 own, 3 opp)
   Boston, 1948 (4 opp)
   Denver, 1979 (1 own, 3 opp)
   Atlanta, 1981 (1 own, 3 opp)
   Denver, 1984 (4 opp)
   St. Louis, 1987 (4 opp)
   Minnesota, 1989 (4 opp)
   Atlanta, 1991 (4 opp)
   Philadelphia, 1995 (4 opp)
   Atlanta, 1998 (4 opp)
   New Orleans, 1998 (4 opp)
   Kansas City, 1999 (4 opp)
3 By many teams

Most Touchdowns, Own Fumbles Recovered, Season
2 Chi. Bears, 1953
   New England, 1973
   Buffalo, 1974
   Denver, 1975
   Oakland, 1978
   Green Bay, 1982
   New Orleans, 1983
   Cleveland, 1986
   Green Bay, 1989
   Miami, 1996
   Buffalo, 2000

Most Touchdowns, Opponents' Fumbles Recovered, Season
4 Detroit, 1937
   Chi. Bears, 1942
   Boston, 1948
   Los Angeles, 1952
   San Francisco, 1965
   Denver, 1984
   St. Louis, 1987
   Minnesota, 1989
   Atlanta, 1991
   Philadelphia, 1995
   Atlanta, 1998
   New Orleans, 1998
   Kansas City, 1999
3 By many teams

Most Touchdowns, Fumbles Recovered, Game, Own and Opponents'
2 By many teams

Most Touchdowns, Fumbles Recovered, Game, Both Teams, Own and Opponents'
3 Detroit (2) vs. Minnesota (1), Dec. 9, 1962
    (2 own, 1 opp)
   Green Bay (2) vs. Dallas (1), Nov. 29, 1964 (3 opp)
   Oakland (2) vs. Buffalo (1), Dec. 24, 1967 (3 opp)
   Oakland (2) vs. Philadelphia (1), Sept. 24, 1995
    (3 opp)
   Tennessee (2) vs. Pittsburgh (1), Jan. 2, 2000
    (3 opp)

Most Touchdowns, Own Fumbles Recovered, Game
2 Miami vs. New England, Sept.1, 1996

Most Touchdowns, Opponents' Fumbles Recovered, Game
2 Many times. Last time:
     N.Y. Jets vs. Buffalo, Oct. 7, 2001

Most Touchdowns, Opponents' Fumbles Recovered, Game, Both Teams
3 Green Bay (2) vs. Dallas (1), Nov. 29, 1964
   Oakland (2) vs. Buffalo (1), Dec. 24, 1967
   Oakland (2) vs. Philadelphia (1), Sept. 24, 1995
   Tennessee (2) vs. Pittsburgh (1), Jan. 2, 2000

TURNOVERS
(Number of times losing the ball on interceptions and fumbles.)
Most Turnovers, Season
63 San Francisco, 1978
58 Chi. Bears, 1947
    Pittsburgh, 1950
    N.Y. Giants, 1983
57 Green Bay, 1950
    Houston, 1962, 1963
    Pittsburgh, 1965

Fewest Turnovers, Season
12 Kansas City, 1982
14 N.Y. Giants, 1943
    Cleveland, 1959
    N.Y. Giants, 1990
15 Dallas, 1998

Most Turnovers, Game
12 Detroit vs. Chi. Bears, Nov. 22, 1942
    Chi. Cardinals vs. Philadelphia, Sept. 24, 1950
    Pittsburgh vs. Philadelphia, Dec. 12, 1965
11 San Diego vs. Green Bay, Sept. 24, 1978
10 Washington vs. N.Y. Giants, Dec. 4, 1938
    Pittsburgh vs. Green Bay, Nov. 23, 1941
    Detroit vs. Green Bay, Oct. 24, 1943
    Chi. Cardinals vs. Green Bay, Nov. 10, 1946
    Chi. Cardinals vs. N.Y. Giants, Nov. 2, 1952
    Minnesota vs. Detroit, Dec. 9, 1962
    Houston vs. Oakland, Sept. 7, 1963
    Washington vs. N.Y. Giants, Dec. 8, 1963
    Chicago vs. Detroit, Sept. 22, 1968
    St. Louis vs. Washington, Oct. 25, 1976
    N.Y. Jets vs. New England, Nov. 21, 1976
    San Francisco vs. Dallas, Oct. 12, 1980
    Cleveland vs. Seattle, Dec. 20, 1981
    Detroit vs. Denver, Oct. 7, 1984

Most Turnovers, Both Teams, Game
17 Detroit (12) vs. Chi. Bears (5), Nov. 22, 1942
    Boston (9) vs. Philadelphia (8), Dec. 8, 1946
16 Chi. Cardinals (12) vs. Philadelphia (4),
     Sept. 24, 1950
    Chi. Cardinals (8) vs. Chi. Bears (8), Dec. 7, 1958
    Minnesota (10) vs. Detroit (6), Dec. 9, 1962
    Houston (9) vs. Kansas City (7), Oct. 12, 1969
15 Philadelphia (8) vs. Chi. Cardinals (7), Oct. 3, 1954
    Denver (9) vs. Houston (6), Dec. 2, 1962
    Washington (10) vs. N.Y. Giants (5), Dec. 8, 1963
    St. Louis (9) vs. Kansas City (6), Oct. 2, 1983

PENALTIES

Most Seasons Leading League, Fewest Penalties
- 13   Miami, 1968, 1976-1984, 1986, 1990-91
- 9   Pittsburgh, 1946-47, 1950-52, 1954, 1963, 1965, 1968
- 7   Boston/New England, 1962, 1964-65, 1973, 1987, 1989, 1993

Most Consecutive Seasons Leading League, Fewest Penalties
- 9   Miami, 1976-1984
- 3   Pittsburgh, 1950-52
- 2   By many teams

Most Seasons Leading League, Most Penalties
- 16   Chi. Bears, 1941-44, 1946-49, 1951, 1959-1961, 1963, 1965, 1968, 1976
- 12   Oakland/L.A. Raiders, 1963, 1966, 1968-69, 1975, 1982, 1984, 1991, 1993-96
- 7   L.A./St. Louis Rams, 1950, 1952, 1962, 1969, 1978, 1980, 1997

Most Consecutive Seasons Leading League, Most Penalties
- 4   Chi. Bears, 1941-44, 1946-49
   Oakland/L.A. Raiders, 1993-96
- 3   Chi. Cardinals, 1954-56
   Chi. Bears, 1959-1961

Fewest Penalties, Season
- 19   Detroit, 1937
- 21   Boston, 1935
- 24   Philadelphia, 1936

Most Penalties, Season
- 158   Kansas City, 1998
- 156   L.A. Raiders, 1994
   Oakland, 1996
- 149   Houston, 1989

Fewest Penalties, Game
- 0   By many teams. Last time:
   San Francisco vs. New Orleans, Jan. 6, 2002

Most Penalties, Game
- 22   Brooklyn vs. Green Bay, Sept. 17, 1944
   Chi. Bears vs. Philadelphia, Nov. 26, 1944
   San Francisco vs. Buffalo, Oct. 4, 1998
- 21   Cleveland vs. Chi. Bears, Nov. 25, 1951
- 20   Tampa Bay vs. Seattle, Oct. 17, 1976
   Oakland vs. Denver, Dec. 15, 1996

Fewest Penalties, Both Teams, Game
- 0   Brooklyn vs. Pittsburgh, Oct. 28, 1934
   Brooklyn vs. Boston, Sept. 28, 1936
   Cleveland vs. Chi. Bears, Oct. 9, 1938
   Pittsburgh vs. Philadelphia, Nov. 10, 1940

Most Penalties, Both Teams, Game
- 37   Cleveland (21) vs. Chi. Bears (16), Nov. 25, 1951
- 35   Tampa Bay (20) vs. Seattle (15), Oct. 17, 1976
- 34   San Francisco (22) vs. Buffalo (12), Oct. 4, 1998

YARDS PENALIZED

Most Seasons Leading League, Fewest Yards Penalized
- 13   Miami, 1967-68, 1973, 1977-1984, 1990-91
- 10   Boston/Washington, 1935, 1953-54, 1956-58, 1970, 1985, 1995, 1997
- 7   Pittsburgh, 1946-47, 1950, 1952, 1962, 1965, 1968
   Boston/New England, 1962, 1964-66, 1987, 1989, 1993

Most Consecutive Seasons Leading League, Fewest Yards Penalized
- 8   Miami, 1977-1984
- 3   Washington, 1956-58
   Boston, 1964-66
- 2   By many teams

Most Seasons Leading League, Most Yards Penalized
- 15   Chi. Bears, 1935, 1937, 1939-1944, 1946-47, 1949, 1951, 1961-62, 1968

- 11   Oakland/L.A. Raiders, 1963-64, 1968-69, 1975, 1982, 1984, 1991, 1993-94, 1996
- 6   Buffalo, 1962, 1967, 1970, 1972, 1981, 1983
   Houston, 1961, 1985-86, 1988-1990

Most Consecutive Seasons Leading League, Most Yards Penalized
- 6   Chi. Bears, 1939-1944
- 3   Houston, 1988-1990
- 2   By many teams

Fewest Yards Penalized, Season
- 139   Detroit, 1937
- 146   Philadelphia, 1937
- 159   Philadelphia, 1936

Most Yards Penalized, Season
- 1,304   Kansas City, 1998
- 1,274   Oakland, 1969
- 1,266   Oakland, 1996

Fewest Yards Penalized, Game
- 0   By many teams. Last time:
   San Francisco vs. New Orleans, Jan. 6, 2002

Most Yards Penalized, Game
- 212   Tennessee vs. Baltimore, Oct. 10, 1999
- 209   Cleveland vs. Chi. Bears, Nov. 25, 1951
- 191   Philadelphia vs. Seattle, Dec. 13, 1992 (OT)

Fewest Yards Penalized, Both Teams, Game
- 0   Brooklyn vs. Pittsburgh, Oct. 28, 1934
   Brooklyn vs. Boston, Sept. 28, 1936
   Cleveland vs. Chi. Bears, Oct. 9, 1938
   Pittsburgh vs. Philadelphia, Nov. 10, 1940

Most Yards Penalized, Both Teams, Game
- 374   Cleveland (209) vs. Chi. Bears (165), Nov. 25, 1951
- 310   Tampa Bay (190) vs. Seattle (120), Oct. 17, 1976
- 309   Green Bay (184) vs. Boston (125), Oct. 21, 1945

DEFENSE

SCORING

Most Seasons Leading League, Fewest Points Allowed
- 11   N.Y. Giants, 1927, 1935, 1938-39, 1941, 1944, 1958-59, 1961, 1990, 1993
- 10   Chi. Bears, 1932, 1936-37, 1942, 1948, 1963, 1985-86, 1988, 2001
- 7   Cleveland, 1951, 1953-57, 1994
   Green Bay, 1929, 1935, 1947, 1962, 1965-66, 1996

Most Consecutive Seasons Leading League, Fewest Points Allowed
- 5   Cleveland, 1953-57
- 3   Buffalo, 1964-66
   Minnesota, 1969-1971
- 2   By many teams

Fewest Points Allowed, Season (Since 1932)
- 44   Chi. Bears, 1932
- 54   Brooklyn, 1933
- 59   Detroit, 1934

Most Points Allowed, Season
- 533   Baltimore, 1981
- 501   N.Y. Giants, 1966
- 487   New Orleans, 1980

Fewest Touchdowns Allowed, Season (Since 1932)
- 6   Chi. Bears, 1932
   Brooklyn, 1933
- 7   Detroit, 1934
- 8   Green Bay, 1932

Most Touchdowns Allowed, Season
- 68   Baltimore, 1981
- 66   N.Y. Giants, 1966
- 63   Baltimore, 1950

FIRST DOWNS

Fewest First Downs Allowed Season
77 Detroit, 1935
79 Boston, 1935
82 Washington, 1937

Most First Downs Allowed, Season
406 Baltimore, 1981
371 Seattle, 1981
368 Cleveland, 1999

Fewest First Downs Allowed, Rushing, Season
35 Chi. Bears, 1942
40 Green Bay, 1939
41 Brooklyn, 1944

Most First Downs Allowed, Rushing, Season
179 Detroit, 1985
178 New Orleans, 1980
175 Seattle, 1981

Fewest First Downs Allowed, Passing, Season
33 Chi. Bears, 1943
34 Pittsburgh, 1941
   Washington, 1943
35 Detroit, 1940
   Philadelphia, 1940, 1944

Most First Downs Allowed, Passing, Season
230 Atlanta, 1995
218 San Diego, 1985
216 San Diego, 1981
    N.Y. Jets, 1986

Fewest First Downs Allowed, Penalty, Season
1 Boston, 1944
3 Philadelphia, 1940
  Pittsburgh, 1945
  Washington, 1957
4 Cleveland, 1940
  Green Bay, 1943
  N.Y. Giants, 1943

Most First Downs Allowed, Penalty, Season
56 Kansas City, 1998
48 Houston, 1985
46 Houston, 1986

NET YARDS ALLOWED RUSHING AND PASSING

Most Seasons Leading League, Fewest Yards Allowed
8 Chi. Bears, 1942-43, 1948, 1958, 1963, 1984-86
6 N.Y. Giants, 1938, 1940-41, 1951, 1956, 1959
  Philadelphia, 1944-45, 1949, 1953, 1981, 1991
  Minnesota, 1969-1970, 1975, 1988-89, 1993
5 Boston/Washington, 1935-37, 1939, 1946

Most Consecutive Seasons Leading League, Fewest Yards Allowed
3 Boston/Washington, 1935-37
  Chicago, 1984-86
2 By many teams

Fewest Yards Allowed, Season
1,539 Chi. Cardinals, 1934
1,703 Chi. Bears, 1942
1,789 Brooklyn, 1933

Most Yards Allowed, Season
6,793 Baltimore, 1981
6,403 Green Bay, 1983
6,391 Seattle, 2000

RUSHING

Most Seasons Leading League, Fewest Yards Allowed
10 Chi. Bears, 1937, 1939, 1942, 1946, 1949, 1963, 1984-85, 1987-88
7 Detroit, 1938, 1950, 1952, 1962, 1970, 1980-81
  Philadelphia, 1944-45, 1947-48, 1953, 1990-91
  Dallas, 1966-69, 1972, 1978, 1992

5 N.Y. Giants, 1940, 1951, 1956, 1959, 1986
  L.A./St. Louis Rams, 1964-65, 1973-74, 1999
  Pittsburgh, 1961, 1976, 1982, 1997, 2001

Most Consecutive Seasons Leading League, Fewest Yards Allowed
4 Dallas, 1966-69
2 By many teams

Fewest Yards Allowed, Rushing, Season
519 Chi. Bears, 1942
558 Philadelphia, 1944
762 Pittsburgh, 1982

Most Yards Allowed, Rushing, Season
3,228 Buffalo, 1978
3,106 New Orleans, 1980
3,010 Baltimore, 1978

Fewest Touchdowns Allowed, Rushing, Season
2 Detroit, 1934
  Dallas, 1968
  Minnesota, 1971
3 By many teams

Most Touchdowns Allowed, Rushing, Season
36 Oakland, 1961
31 N.Y. Giants, 1980
   Tampa Bay, 1986
30 Baltimore, 1981

PASSING

Most Seasons Leading League, Fewest Yards Allowed
9 Green Bay, 1947-48, 1962, 1964-68, 1996
7 Washington, 1939, 1942, 1945, 1952-53, 1980, 1985
  Philadelphia 1934, 1936, 1940, 1949, 1981, 1991, 1998
6 Chi. Bears, 1938, 1943-44, 1958, 1960, 1963
  Minnesota, 1969-1970, 1972, 1975-76, 1989
  Pittsburgh, 1941, 1946, 1951, 1955, 1974, 1990

Most Consecutive Seasons Leading League, Fewest Yards Allowed
5 Green Bay, 1964-68
2 By many teams

Fewest Yards Allowed, Passing, Season
545 Philadelphia, 1934
558 Portsmouth, 1933
585 Chi. Cardinals, 1934

Most Yards Allowed, Passing, Season
4,541 Atlanta, 1995
4,389 N.Y. Jets, 1986
4,311 San Diego, 1981

Fewest Touchdowns Allowed, Passing, Season
1 Portsmouth, 1932
  Philadelphia, 1934
2 Brooklyn, 1933
  Chi. Bears, 1934
3 Chi. Bears, 1932
  Green Bay, 1932
  Green Bay, 1934
  Chi. Bears, 1936
  New York, 1939
  New York, 1944

Most Touchdowns Allowed, Passing, Season
40 Denver, 1963
38 St. Louis, 1969
37 Washington, 1961
   Baltimore, 1981

SACKS

Most Seasons Leading League
5 Oakland/L.A. Raiders, 1966-68, 1982, 1986
4 New England/Boston, 1961, 1963, 1977, 1979
  Dallas, 1966, 1968-69, 1978
  Dallas/Kansas City, 1960, 1965, 1969, 1990

L.A./St. Louis Rams, 1968, 1970, 1988, 1999
3 San Francisco, 1967, 1972, 1976
   N.Y. Giants, 1963, 1985, 1998
   New Orleans, 1992, 1997, 2000
   Pittsburgh, 1974, 1994, 2001

Most Consecutive Seasons Leading League
3 Oakland, 1966-68
2 Dallas, 1968-69

Most Sacks, Season
72 Chicago, 1984
71 Minnesota, 1989
70 Chicago, 1987

Fewest Sacks, Season
11 Baltimore, 1982
12 Buffalo, 1982
13 Baltimore, 1981

Most Sacks, Game
12 Dallas vs. Pittsburgh, Nov. 20, 1966
    St. Louis vs. Baltimore, Oct. 26, 1980
    Chicago vs. Detroit, Dec. 16, 1984
    Dallas vs. Houston, Sept. 29, 1985
11 N.Y. Giants vs. St. Louis, Nov. 1, 1964
    Baltimore vs. Los Angeles, Nov. 22, 1964
    Buffalo vs. Denver, Dec. 13, 1964
    Detroit vs. Green Bay, Nov. 7, 1965
    Oakland vs. Buffalo, Oct. 15, 1967
    Oakland vs. Denver, Nov. 5, 1967
    St. Louis vs. Atlanta, Nov. 24, 1968
    Dallas vs. Detroit, Oct. 6, 1975
    St. Louis vs. Philadelphia, Dec. 18, 1983
    Kansas City vs. Cleveland, Sept. 30, 1984
    Chicago vs. Minnesota, Oct. 28, 1984
    Cleveland vs. Atlanta, Nov. 18, 1984
    Detroit vs. Philadelphia, Nov. 16, 1986
    San Diego vs. Dallas, Nov. 16, 1986
    L.A. Raiders vs. Philadelphia, Nov. 30, 1986 (OT)
    Seattle vs. L.A. Raiders, Dec. 8, 1986
    Chicago vs. Philadelphia, Oct. 4, 1987
    Dallas vs. N.Y. Jets, Oct. 4, 1987
    Philadelphia vs. Dallas, Sept. 15, 1991
    Indianapolis vs. Cleveland, Sept. 6, 1992
10 By many teams

Most Opponents Yards Lost Attempting to Pass, Season
666 Oakland, 1967
583 Chicago, 1984
573 San Francisco, 1976

Fewest Opponents Yards Lost Attempting to Pass, Season
72 Jacksonville, 1995
75 Green Bay, 1956
77 N.Y. Bulldogs, 1949

INTERCEPTIONS BY

Most Seasons Leading League
10 N.Y. Giants, 1933, 1937-39, 1944, 1948, 1951,
     1954, 1961, 1997
8 Green Bay, 1940, 1942-43, 1947, 1955, 1957,
     1962, 1965
    Chi. Bears, 1935-36, 1941-42, 1946, 1963, 1985,
     1990
6 Kansas City, 1966-1970, 1974

Most Consecutive Seasons Leading League
5 Kansas City, 1966-1970
3 N.Y. Giants, 1937-39
2 By many teams

Most Passes Intercepted By, Season
49 San Diego, 1961
42 Green Bay, 1943
41 N.Y. Giants, 1951

Fewest Passes Intercepted By, Season
3 Houston, 1982

5 Baltimore, 1982
6 Houston, 1972
   St. Louis, 1982
   Atlanta, 1996

Most Passes Intercepted By, Game
9 Green Bay vs. Detroit, Oct. 24, 1943
   Philadelphia vs. Pittsburgh, Dec. 12, 1965
8 N.Y. Giants vs. Green Bay, Nov. 21, 1948
   Philadelphia vs. Chi. Cardinals, Sept. 24, 1950
   N.Y. Giants vs. N.Y. Yanks, Dec. 16, 1951
   Houston vs. Denver, Dec. 2, 1962
   Detroit vs. Chicago, Sept. 22, 1968
   N.Y. Jets vs. Baltimore, Sept. 23, 1973
7 By many teams. Last time:
     Cleveland vs. Detroit, Sept. 23, 2001

Most Consecutive Games, One or More Interceptions By
46 L.A. Chargers/San Diego, 1960-63
37 Detroit, 1960-63
36 Boston, 1944-47

Most Yards Returning Interceptions, Season
929 San Diego, 1961
712 Los Angeles, 1952
697 Seattle, 1984

Fewest Yards Returning Interceptions, Season
5 Los Angeles, 1959
37 Dallas, 1989
41 Atlanta, 1996

Most Yards Returning Interceptions, Game
325 Seattle vs. Kansas City, Nov. 4, 1984
314 Los Angeles vs. San Francisco, Oct. 18, 1964
245 Houston vs. N.Y. Jets, Oct. 15, 1967

Most Yards Returning Interceptions, Both Teams, Game
356 Seattle (325) vs. Kansas City (31), Nov. 4, 1984
338 Los Angeles (314) vs. San Francisco (24),
     Oct. 18, 1964
308 Dallas (182) vs. Los Angeles (126), Nov. 2, 1952

Most Touchdowns, Returning Interceptions, Season
9 San Diego, 1961
8 Seattle, 1998
7 Seattle, 1984
   St. Louis, 1999

Most Touchdowns Returning Interceptions, Game
4 Seattle vs. Kansas City, Nov. 4, 1984
3 Baltimore vs. Green Bay, Nov. 5, 1950
   Cleveland vs. Chicago, Dec. 11, 1960
   Philadelphia vs. Pittsburgh, Dec. 12, 1965
   Baltimore vs. Pittsburgh, Sept. 29, 1968
   Buffalo vs. N.Y. Jets, Sept. 29, 1968
   Houston vs. San Diego, Dec. 19, 1971
   Cincinnati vs. Houston, Dec. 17, 1972
   Tampa Bay vs. New Orleans, Dec. 11, 1977
2 By many teams

Most Touchdown Returning Interceptions, Both Teams, Game
4 Philadelphia (3) vs. Pittsburgh (1), Dec. 12, 1965
   Seattle (4) vs. Kansas City (0), Nov. 4, 1984
3 Los Angeles (2) vs. Detroit (1), Nov. 1, 1953
   Cleveland (2) vs. N.Y. Giants (1), Dec. 18, 1960
   Pittsburgh (2) vs. Cincinnati (1), Oct. 10, 1983
   Kansas City (2) vs. San Diego (1), Oct. 19, 1986
   (Also see previous record)

PUNT RETURNS

Fewest Opponents Punt Returns, Season
7 Washington, 1962
   San Diego, 1982
10 Buffalo, 1982+
11 Boston, 1962

Most Opponents Punt Returns, Season
71 Tampa Bay, 1976, 1977
69 N.Y. Giants, 1953

Cleveland, 2000
68 Cleveland, 1974
Cleveland, 1999

Fewest Yards Allowed, Punt Returns, Season
22 Green Bay, 1967
30 Buffalo, 1982
34 Washington, 1962

Most Yards Allowed, Punt Returns, Season
932 Green Bay, 1949
913 Boston, 1947
906 New Orleans, 1974

Lowest Average Allowed, Punt Returns, Season
1.20 Chi. Cardinals, 1954 (46-55)
1.22 Cleveland, 1959 (32-39)
1.55 Chi. Cardinals, 1953 (44-68)

Highest Average Allowed, Punt Returns, Season
18.6 Green Bay, 1949 (50-932)
18.0 Cleveland, 1977 (31-558)
17.9 Boston, 1960 (20-357)

Most Touchdowns Allowed, Punt Returns, Season
4 New York, 1959
   Atlanta, 1992
3 Green Bay, 1949
   Chi. Cardinals, 1951
   L.A. Rams, 1951, 1994
   Washington, 1952
   Dallas, 1952
   Pittsburgh, 1959, 1993
   N.Y. Jets, 1968
   Cleveland, 1977
   Atlanta, 1986
   Tampa Bay, 1986
2 By many teams

KICKOFF RETURNS
Fewest Opponents Kickoff Returns, Season
10 Brooklyn, 1943
13 Denver, 1992
15 Detroit, 1942
   Brooklyn, 1944

Most Opponents Kickoff Returns, Season
91 Washington, 1983
90 Denver, 2000
89 New England, 1980
   San Francisco, 1994
   Denver, 1997
   Denver, 1998

Fewest Yards Allowed, Kickoff Returns, Season
225 Brooklyn, 1943
254 Denver, 1992
293 Brooklyn, 1944

Most Yards Allowed, Kickoff Returns, Season
2,194 St. Louis, 2001
2,115 St. Louis, 1999
2,045 Kansas City, 1966

Lowest Average Allowed, Kickoff Returns, Season
14.3 Cleveland, 1980 (71-1,018)
14.9 Indianapolis, 1993 (37-551)
15.0 Seattle, 1982 (24-361)

Highest Average Allowed, Kickoff Returns, Season
29.5 N.Y. Jets, 1972 (47-1,386)
29.4 Los Angeles, 1950 (48-1,411)
29.1 New England, 1971 (49-1,427)

Most Touchdowns Allowed, Kickoff Returns, Season
4 Minnesota, 1998
3 Minnesota, 1963, 1970
   Dallas, 1966
   Detroit, 1980
   Pittsburgh, 1986
   Buffalo, 1997

Atlanta, 2000
2 By many teams

FUMBLES
Fewest Opponents Fumbles, Season
11 Cleveland, 1956
   Baltimore, 1982
   Tennessee, 1998
12 Green Bay, 1995
   Cincinnati, 1998
13 Los Angeles, 1956
   Chicago, 1960
   Cleveland, 1963
   Cleveland, 1965
   Detroit, 1967
   San Diego, 1969

Most Opponents Fumbles, Season
50 Minnesota, 1963
   San Francisco, 1978
48 N.Y. Giants, 1980
   N.Y. Jets, 1986
47 N.Y. Giants, 1977
   Seattle, 1984

TURNOVERS
(Number of times losing the ball on interceptions and fumbles.)
Fewest Opponents Turnovers, Season
11 Baltimore, 1982
13 San Francisco, 1982
15 St. Louis, 1982

Most Opponents Turnovers, Season
66 San Diego, 1961
63 Seattle, 1984
61 Washington, 1983

Most Opponents Turnovers, Game
12 Chi. Bears vs. Detroit, Nov. 22, 1942
   Philadelphia vs. Chi. Cardinals, Sept. 24, 1950
   Philadelphia vs. Pittsburgh, Dec. 12, 1965
11 Green Bay vs. San Diego, Sept. 24, 1978
10 By 14 teams

1,000 YARDS RUSHING IN A SEASON

Year	Player, Team	Att.	Yards	Avg.	Long	TD
2001	Priest Holmes, Kansas City[2]	327	1,555	4.8	41	8
	Curtis Martin, N.Y. Jets[7]	333	1,513	4.5	47	10
	Stephen Davis, Washington[3]	356	1,432	4.0	32	5
	Ahman Green, Green Bay[2]	304	1,387	4.6	83	9
	Marshall Faulk, St. Louis[7]	260	1,382	5.3	71	12
	Shaun Alexander, Seattle	309	1,318	4.3	88	14
	Corey Dillon, Cincinnati[5]	340	1,315	3.9	96	10
	Ricky Williams, New Orleans[2]	313	1,245	4.0	46	6
	*LaDainian Tomlinson, San Diego	339	1,236	3.6	54	10
	Garrison Hearst, San Francisco[4]	252	1,206	4.8	43	4
	*Anthony Thomas, Chicago	278	1,183	4.3	46	7
	Antowain Smith, New England[2]	287	1,157	4.0	44	12
	*Dominic Rhodes, Indianapolis	233	1,104	4.7	77	9
	Jerome Bettis, Pittsburgh[8]	225	1,072	4.8	48	4
	Emmitt Smith, Dallas[11]	261	1,021	3.9	44	3
2000	Edgerrin James, Indianapolis[2]	387	1,709	4.4	30	13
	Robert Smith, Minnesota[4]	295	1,521	5.2	72	7
	Eddie George, Tennessee[5]	403	1,509	3.7	35	14
	*Mike Anderson, Denver	297	1,487	5.0	80	15
	Corey Dillon, Cincinnati[4]	315	1,435	4.6	80	7
	Fred Taylor, Jacksonville[2]	292	1,399	4.8	71	12
	*Jamal Lewis, Baltimore	309	1,364	4.4	45	6
	Marshall Faulk, St. Louis[6]	253	1,359	5.4	36	18
	Jerome Bettis, Pittsburgh[7]	355	1,341	3.8	30	8
	Stephen Davis, Washington[2]	332	1,318	4.0	50	11
	Ricky Watters, Seattle[7]	278	1,242	4.5	55	7
	Curtis Martin, N.Y. Jets[6]	316	1,204	3.8	55	9
	Emmitt Smith, Dallas[10]	294	1,203	4.1	52	9
	James Stewart, Detroit	339	1,184	3.5	34	10
	Ahman Green, Green Bay	263	1,175	4.5	39	10
	Charlie Garner, San Francisco[2]	258	1,142	4.4	42	7
	Lamar Smith, Miami	309	1,139	3.7	68	14
	Warrick Dunn, Tampa Bay[2]	248	1,133	4.6	70	8
	James Allen, Chicago	290	1,120	3.9	29	2
	Tyrone Wheatley, Oakland	232	1,046	4.5	80	9
	Jamal Anderson, Atlanta[4]	282	1,024	3.6	42	6
	Tiki Barber, N.Y. Giants	213	1,006	4.7	78	8
	Ricky Williams, New Orleans	248	1,000	4.0	26	8
1999	*Edgerrin James, Indianapolis	369	1,553	4.2	72	13
	Curtis Martin, N.Y. Jets[5]	367	1,464	4.0	50	5
	Stephen Davis, Washington	290	1,405	4.8	76	17
	Emmitt Smith, Dallas[9]	329	1,397	4.3	63	11
	Marshall Faulk, St. Louis[5]	253	1,381	5.5	58	7
	Eddie George, Tennessee[4]	320	1,304	4.1	40	9
	Duce Staley, Philadelphia[2]	325	1,273	3.9	29	4
	Charlie Garner, San Francisco	241	1,229	5.1	53	4
	Ricky Watters, Seattle[6]	325	1,210	3.7	45	5
	Corey Dillon, Cincinnati[3]	263	1,200	4.6	50	5
	*Olandis Gary, Denver	276	1,159	4.2	71	7
	Jerome Bettis, Pittsburgh[6]	299	1,091	3.7	35	7
	Dorsey Levens, Green Bay[2]	279	1,034	3.7	36	9
	Robert Smith, Minnesota[3]	221	1,015	4.6	70	2
1998	Terrell Davis, Denver[4]	392	2,008	5.1	70	21
	Jamal Anderson, Atlanta[3]	410	1,846	4.5	48	14
	Garrison Hearst, San Francisco[3]	310	1,570	5.1	96	7
	Barry Sanders, Detroit[10]	343	1,491	4.3	73	4
	Emmitt Smith, Dallas[8]	319	1,332	4.2	32	13
	Marshall Faulk, Indianapolis[4]	324	1,319	4.1	68	6
	Eddie George, Tennessee[3]	348	1,294	3.7	37	5
	Curtis Martin, N.Y. Jets[4]	369	1,287	3.5	60	8
	Ricky Watters, Seattle[5]	319	1,239	3.9	39	9
	*Fred Taylor, Jacksonville	264	1,223	4.6	77	14
	Robert Smith, Minnesota[2]	249	1,187	4.8	74	6
	Jerome Bettis, Pittsburgh[5]	316	1,185	3.8	42	3
	Corey Dillon, Cincinnati[2]	262	1,130	4.3	66	4
	Antowain Smith, Buffalo	300	1,124	3.7	30	8
	*Robert Edwards, New England	291	1,115	3.8	53	9
	Duce Staley, Philadelphia	258	1,065	4.1	64	5

Year	Player	Att	Yards	Avg	Long	TD
	Gary Brown, N.Y. Giants[2]	247	1,063	4.3	45	5
	Adrian Murrell, Arizona[3]	274	1,042	3.8	32	8
	Warrick Dunn, Tampa Bay	245	1,026	4.2	50	2
	Priest Holmes, Baltimore	233	1,008	4.3	56	7
1997	Barry Sanders, Detroit[9]	335	2,053	6.1	82	11
	Terrell Davis, Denver[3]	369	1,750	4.7	50	15
	Jerome Bettis, Pittsburgh[4]	375	1,665	4.4	34	7
	Dorsey Levens, Green Bay	329	1,435	4.4	52	7
	Eddie George, Tennessee[2]	357	1,399	3.9	30	6
	Napoleon Kaufman, Oakland	272	1,294	4.8	83	6
	Robert Smith, Minnesota	232	1,266	5.5	78	6
	Curtis Martin, New England[9]	274	1,160	4.2	70	4
	*Corey Dillon, Cincinnati	233	1,129	4.8	71	10
	Ricky Watters, Philadelphia[4]	285	1,110	3.9	28	7
	Adrian Murrell, N.Y. Jets[2]	300	1,086	3.6	43	7
	Emmitt Smith, Dallas[7]	261	1,074	4.1	44	4
	Marshall Faulk, Indianapolis[3]	264	1,054	4.0	45	7
	Raymont Harris, Chicago	275	1,033	3.8	68	10
	Garrison Hearst, San Francisco[2]	234	1,019	4.4	51	4
	Jamal Anderson, Atlanta[2]	290	1,002	3.5	39	7
1996	Barry Sanders, Detroit[8]	307	1,553	5.1	54	11
	Terrell Davis, Denver[2]	345	1,538	4.5	71	13
	Jerome Bettis, Pittsburgh[3]	320	1,431	4.5	50	11
	Ricky Watters, Philadelphia[3]	353	1,411	4.0	56	13
	*Eddie George, Houston	335	1,368	4.1	76	8
	Terry Allen, Washington[4]	347	1,353	3.9	49	21
	Adrian Murrell, N.Y. Jets	301	1,249	4.1	78	6
	Emmitt Smith, Dallas[6]	327	1,204	3.7	42	12
	Curtis Martin, New England[2]	316	1,152	3.6	57	14
	Anthony Johnson, Carolina	300	1,120	3.7	29	6
	*Karim Abdul-Jabbar, Miami	307	1,116	3.6	29	11
	Jamal Anderson, Atlanta	232	1,055	4.5	32	5
	Thurman Thomas, Buffalo[8]	281	1,033	3.7	36	8
1995	Emmitt Smith, Dallas[5]	377	1,773	4.7	60	25
	Barry Sanders, Detroit[7]	314	1,500	4.8	75	11
	*Curtis Martin, New England	368	1,487	4.0	49	14
	Chris Warren, Seattle[4]	310	1,346	4.3	52	15
	Terry Allen, Washington[3]	338	1,309	3.9	28	10
	Ricky Watters, Philadelphia[2]	337	1,273	3.8	57	11
	Errict Rhett, Tampa Bay[2]	332	1,207	3.6	21	11
	Rodney Hampton, N.Y. Giants[5]	306	1,182	3.9	32	10
	*Terrell Davis, Denver	237	1,117	4.7	60	7
	Harvey Williams, Oakland	255	1,114	4.4	60	9
	Craig Heyward, Atlanta	236	1,083	4.6	31	6
	Marshall Faulk, Indianapolis[2]	289	1,078	3.7	40	11
	*Rashaan Salaam, Chicago	296	1,074	3.6	42	10
	Garrison Hearst, Arizona	284	1,070	3.8	38	1
	Edgar Bennett, Green Bay	316	1,067	3.4	23	3
	Thurman Thomas, Buffalo[7]	267	1,005	3.8	49	6
1994	Barry Sanders, Detroit[6]	331	1,883	5.7	85	7
	Chris Warren, Seattle[3]	333	1,545	4.6	41	9
	Emmitt Smith, Dallas[4]	368	1,484	4.0	46	21
	Natrone Means, San Diego	343	1,350	3.9	25	12
	*Marshall Faulk, Indianapolis[8]	314	1,282	4.1	52	11
	Thurman Thomas, Buffalo[6]	287	1,093	3.8	29	7
	Rodney Hampton, N.Y. Giants[4]	327	1,075	3.3	27	6
	Terry Allen, Minnesota[2]	255	1,031	4.0	45	8
	Jerome Bettis, L.A. Rams[2]	319	1,025	3.2	19	3
	*Errict Rhett, Tampa Bay	284	1,011	3.6	27	7
1993	Emmitt Smith, Dallas[3]	283	1,486	5.3	62	9
	*Jerome Bettis, L.A. Rams	294	1,429	4.9	71	7
	Thurman Thomas, Buffalo[5]	355	1,315	3.7	27	6
	Eric Pegram, Atlanta	292	1,185	4.1	29	3
	Barry Sanders, Detroit[5]	243	1,115	4.6	42	3
	Leonard Russell, New England	300	1,088	3.6	21	7
	Rodney Hampton, N.Y. Giants[3]	292	1,077	3.7	20	5
	Chris Warren, Seattle[2]	273	1,072	3.9	45	7
	*Reggie Brooks, Washington	223	1,063	4.8	85	3
	*Ron Moore, Phoenix	263	1,018	3.9	20	9
	Gary Brown, Houston	195	1,002	5.1	26	6

Year	Player	Att	Yards	Avg	Long	TD
1992	Emmitt Smith, Dallas[2]	373	1,713	4.6	68	18
	Barry Foster, Pittsburgh	390	1,690	4.3	69	11
	Thurman Thomas, Buffalo[4]	312	1,487	4.8	44	9
	Barry Sanders, Detroit[4]	312	1,352	4.3	55	9
	Lorenzo White, Houston	265	1,226	4.6	44	7
	Terry Allen, Minnesota	266	1,201	4.5	51	13
	Reggie Cobb, Tampa Bay	310	1,171	3.8	25	9
	Harold Green, Cincinnati	265	1,170	4.4	53	2
	Rodney Hampton, N.Y. Giants[2]	257	1,141	4.4	63	14
	Cleveland Gary, L.A. Rams	279	1,125	4.0	63	7
	Herschel Walker, Philadelphia[2]	267	1,070	4.0	38	8
	Chris Warren, Seattle	223	1,017	4.6	52	3
	Ricky Watters, San Francisco	206	1,013	4.9	43	9
1991	Emmitt Smith, Dallas	365	1,563	4.3	75	12
	Barry Sanders, Detroit[3]	342	1,548	4.5	69	16
	Thurman Thomas, Buffalo[3]	288	1,407	4.9	33	7
	Rodney Hampton, N.Y. Giants	256	1,059	4.1	44	10
	Earnest Byner, Washington[3]	274	1,048	3.8	32	5
	Gaston Green, Denver	261	1,037	4.0	63	4
	Christian Okoye, Kansas City[2]	225	1,031	4.6	48	9
1990	Barry Sanders, Detroit[2]	255	1,304	5.1	45	13
	Thurman Thomas, Buffalo[2]	271	1,297	4.8	80	11
	Marion Butts, San Diego	265	1,225	4.6	52	8
	Earnest Byner, Washington[2]	297	1,219	4.1	22	6
	Bobby Humphrey, Denver[2]	288	1,202	4.2	37	7
	Neal Anderson, Chicago[3]	260	1,078	4.1	52	10
	Barry Word, Kansas City	204	1,015	5.0	53	4
	James Brooks, Cincinnati[3]	195	1,004	5.1	56	5
1989	Christian Okoye, Kansas City	370	1,480	4.0	59	12
	*Barry Sanders, Detroit	280	1,470	5.3	34	14
	Eric Dickerson, Indianapolis[7]	314	1,311	4.2	21	7
	Neal Anderson, Chicago[2]	274	1,275	4.7	73	11
	Dalton Hilliard, New Orleans	344	1,262	3.7	40	13
	Thurman Thomas, Buffalo	298	1,244	4.2	38	6
	James Brooks, Cincinnati[2]	221	1,239	5.6	65	7
	*Bobby Humphrey, Denver	294	1,151	3.9	40	7
	Greg Bell, L.A. Rams[3]	272	1,137	4.2	47	15
	Roger Craig, San Francisco[3]	271	1,054	3.9	27	6
	Ottis Anderson, N.Y. Giants[6]	325	1,023	3.1	36	14
1988	Eric Dickerson, Indianapolis[6]	388	1,659	4.3	41	14
	Herschel Walker, Dallas	361	1,514	4.2	38	5
	Roger Craig, San Francisco[2]	310	1,502	4.8	46	9
	Greg Bell, L.A. Rams[2]	288	1,212	4.2	44	16
	*John Stephens, New England	297	1,168	3.9	52	4
	Gary Anderson, San Diego	225	1,119	5.0	36	3
	Neal Anderson, Chicago	249	1,106	4.4	80	12
	Joe Morris, N.Y. Giants[3]	307	1,083	3.5	27	5
	*Ickey Woods, Cincinnati	203	1,066	5.3	56	15
	Curt Warner, Seattle[4]	266	1,025	3.9	29	10
	John Settle, Atlanta	232	1,024	4.4	62	7
	Mike Rozier, Houston	251	1,002	4.0	28	10
1987	Charles White, L.A. Rams	324	1,374	4.2	58	11
	Eric Dickerson, L.A. Rams-Indianapolis[5]	283	1,288	4.6	57	6
1986	Eric Dickerson, L.A. Rams[4]	404	1,821	4.5	42	11
	Joe Morris, N.Y. Giants[2]	341	1,516	4.4	54	14
	Curt Warner, Seattle[3]	319	1,481	4.6	60	13
	*Rueben Mayes, New Orleans	286	1,353	4.7	50	8
	Walter Payton, Chicago[10]	321	1,333	4.2	41	8
	Gerald Riggs, Atlanta[3]	343	1,327	3.9	31	9
	George Rogers, Washington[4]	303	1,203	4.0	42	18
	James Brooks, Cincinnati	205	1,087	5.3	56	5
1985	Marcus Allen, L.A. Raiders[3]	380	1,759	4.6	61	11
	Gerald Riggs, Atlanta[2]	397	1,719	4.3	50	10
	Walter Payton, Chicago[9]	324	1,551	4.8	40	9
	Joe Morris, N.Y. Giants	294	1,336	4.5	65	21
	Freeman McNeil, N.Y. Jets[2]	294	1,331	4.5	69	3
	Tony Dorsett, Dallas[8]	305	1,307	4.3	60	7
	James Wilder, Tampa Bay[2]	365	1,300	3.6	28	10
	Eric Dickerson, L.A. Rams[3]	292	1,234	4.2	43	12
	Craig James, New England	263	1,227	4.7	65	5

Year	Player	Att	Yards	Avg	Long	TD
	Kevin Mack, Cleveland	222	1,104	5.0	61	7
	Curt Warner, Seattle[2]	291	1,094	3.8	38	8
	George Rogers, Washington[3]	231	1,093	4.7	35	7
	Roger Craig, San Francisco	214	1,050	4.9	62	9
	Earnest Jackson, Philadelphia[2]	282	1,028	3.6	59	5
	Stump Mitchell, St. Louis	183	1,006	5.5	64	7
	Earnest Byner, Cleveland	244	1,002	4.1	36	8
1984	Eric Dickerson, L.A. Rams[2]	379	2,105	5.6	66	14
	Walter Payton, Chicago[8]	381	1,684	4.4	72	11
	James Wilder, Tampa Bay	407	1,544	3.8	37	13
	Gerald Riggs, Atlanta	353	1,486	4.2	57	13
	Wendell Tyler, San Francisco[3]	246	1,262	5.1	40	7
	John Riggins, Washington[5]	327	1,239	3.8	24	14
	Tony Dorsett, Dallas[7]	302	1,189	3.9	31	6
	Earnest Jackson, San Diego	296	1,179	4.0	32	8
	Ottis Anderson, St. Louis[5]	289	1,174	4.1	24	6
	Marcus Allen, L.A. Raiders[2]	275	1,168	4.2	52	13
	Sammy Winder, Denver	296	1,153	3.9	24	4
	*Greg Bell, Buffalo	262	1,100	4.2	85	7
	Freeman McNeil, N.Y. Jets	229	1,070	4.7	53	5
1983	*Eric Dickerson, L.A. Rams	390	1,808	4.6	85	18
	William Andrews, Atlanta[4]	331	1,567	4.7	27	7
	*Curt Warner, Seattle	335	1,449	4.3	60	13
	Walter Payton, Chicago[7]	314	1,421	4.5	49	6
	John Riggins, Washington[4]	375	1,347	3.6	44	24
	Tony Dorsett, Dallas[6]	289	1,321	4.6	77	8
	Earl Campbell, Houston[5]	322	1,301	4.0	42	12
	Ottis Anderson, St. Louis[4]	296	1,270	4.3	43	5
	Mike Pruitt, Cleveland[4]	293	1,184	4.0	27	10
	George Rogers, New Orleans[2]	256	1,144	4.5	76	5
	Joe Cribbs, Buffalo[3]	263	1,131	4.3	45	3
	Curtis Dickey, Baltimore	254	1,122	4.4	56	4
	Tony Collins, New England	219	1,049	4.8	50	10
	Billy Sims, Detroit[3]	220	1,040	4.7	41	7
	Marcus Allen, L.A. Raiders	266	1,014	3.8	19	9
	Franco Harris, Pittsburgh[8]	279	1,007	3.6	19	5
1981	*George Rogers, New Orleans	378	1,674	4.4	79	13
	Tony Dorsett, Dallas[5]	342	1,646	4.8	75	4
	Billy Sims, Detroit[2]	296	1,437	4.9	51	13
	Wilbert Montgomery, Philadelphia[3]	286	1,402	4.9	41	8
	Ottis Anderson, St. Louis[3]	328	1,376	4.2	28	9
	Earl Campbell, Houston[4]	361	1,376	3.8	43	10
	William Andrews, Atlanta[3]	289	1,301	4.5	29	10
	Walter Payton, Chicago[6]	339	1,222	3.6	39	6
	Chuck Muncie, San Diego[2]	251	1,144	4.6	73	19
	*Joe Delaney, Kansas City	234	1,121	4.8	82	3
	Mike Pruitt, Cleveland[3]	247	1,103	4.5	21	7
	Joe Cribbs, Buffalo[2]	257	1,097	4.3	35	3
	Pete Johnson, Cincinnati	274	1,077	3.9	39	12
	Wendell Tyler, Los Angeles[2]	260	1,074	4.1	69	12
	Ted Brown, Minnesota	274	1,063	3.9	34	6
1980	Earl Campbell, Houston[3]	373	1,934	5.2	55	13
	Walter Payton, Chicago[5]	317	1,460	4.6	69	6
	Ottis Anderson, St. Louis[2]	301	1,352	4.5	52	9
	William Andrews, Atlanta[2]	265	1,308	4.9	33	4
	*Billy Sims, Detroit	313	1,303	4.2	52	13
	Tony Dorsett, Dallas[4]	278	1,185	4.3	56	11
	*Joe Cribbs, Buffalo	306	1,185	3.9	48	11
	Mike Pruitt, Cleveland[2]	249	1,034	4.2	56	6
1979	Earl Campbell, Houston[2]	368	1,697	4.6	61	19
	Walter Payton, Chicago[4]	369	1,610	4.4	43	14
	*Ottis Anderson, St. Louis	331	1,605	4.8	76	8
	Wilbert Montgomery, Philadelphia[2]	338	1,512	4.5	62	9
	Mike Pruitt, Cleveland	264	1,294	4.9	77	9
	Ricky Bell, Tampa Bay	283	1,263	4.5	49	7
	Chuck Muncie, New Orleans	238	1,198	5.0	69	11
	Franco Harris, Pittsburgh[7]	267	1,186	4.4	71	11
	John Riggins, Washington[3]	260	1,153	4.4	66	9
	Wendell Tyler, Los Angeles	218	1,109	5.1	63	9
	Tony Dorsett, Dallas[3]	250	1,107	4.4	41	6

Year	Player	Att	Yards	Avg	Long	TD
	*William Andrews, Atlanta	239	1,023	4.3	23	3
1978	*Earl Campbell, Houston	302	1,450	4.8	81	13
	Walter Payton, Chicago[3]	333	1,395	4.2	76	11
	Tony Dorsett, Dallas[2]	290	1,325	4.6	63	7
	Delvin Williams, Miami[2]	272	1,258	4.6	58	8
	Wilbert Montgomery, Philadelphia	259	1,220	4.7	47	9
	Terdell Middleton, Green Bay	284	1,116	3.9	76	11
	Franco Harris, Pittsburgh[6]	310	1,082	3.5	37	8
	Mark van Eeghen, Oakland[3]	270	1,080	4.0	34	9
	*Terry Miller, Buffalo	238	1,060	4.5	60	7
	Tony Reed, Kansas City	206	1,053	5.1	62	5
	John Riggins, Washington[2]	248	1,014	4.1	31	5
1977	Walter Payton, Chicago[2]	339	1,852	5.5	73	14
	Mark van Eeghen, Oakland[2]	324	1,273	3.9	27	7
	Lawrence McCutcheon, Los Angeles[4]	294	1,238	4.2	48	7
	Franco Harris, Pittsburgh[5]	300	1,162	3.9	61	11
	Lydell Mitchell, Baltimore[3]	301	1,159	3.9	64	3
	Chuck Foreman, Minnesota[3]	270	1,112	4.1	51	6
	Greg Pruitt, Cleveland[3]	236	1,086	4.6	78	3
	Sam Cunningham, New England	270	1,015	3.8	31	4
	*Tony Dorsett, Dallas	208	1,007	4.8	84	12
1976	O.J. Simpson, Buffalo[5]	290	1,503	5.2	75	8
	Walter Payton, Chicago	311	1,390	4.5	60	13
	Delvin Williams, San Francisco	248	1,203	4.9	80	7
	Lydell Mitchell, Baltimore[2]	289	1,200	4.2	43	5
	Lawrence McCutcheon, Los Angeles[3]	291	1,168	4.0	40	9
	Chuck Foreman, Minnesota[2]	278	1,155	4.2	46	13
	Franco Harris, Pittsburgh[4]	289	1,128	3.9	30	14
	Mike Thomas, Washington	254	1,101	4.3	28	5
	Rocky Bleier, Pittsburgh	220	1,036	4.7	28	5
	Mark van Eeghen, Oakland	233	1,012	4.3	21	3
	Otis Armstrong, Denver[2]	247	1,008	4.1	31	5
	Greg Pruitt, Cleveland[2]	209	1,000	4.8	64	4
1975	O.J. Simpson, Buffalo[4]	329	1,817	5.5	88	16
	Franco Harris, Pittsburgh[3]	262	1,246	4.8	36	10
	Lydell Mitchell, Baltimore	289	1,193	4.1	70	11
	Jim Otis, St. Louis	269	1,076	4.0	30	5
	Chuck Foreman, Minnesota	280	1,070	3.8	31	13
	Greg Pruitt, Cleveland	217	1,067	4.9	50	8
	John Riggins, N.Y. Jets	238	1,005	4.2	42	8
	Dave Hampton, Atlanta	250	1,002	4.0	22	5
1974	Otis Armstrong, Denver	263	1,407	5.3	43	9
	*Don Woods, San Diego	227	1,162	5.1	56	7
	O.J. Simpson, Buffalo[3]	270	1,125	4.2	41	3
	Lawrence McCutcheon, Los Angeles[2]	236	1,109	4.7	23	3
	Franco Harris, Pittsburgh[2]	208	1,006	4.8	54	5
1973	O.J. Simpson, Buffalo[2]	332	2,003	6.0	80	12
	John Brockington, Green Bay[3]	265	1,144	4.3	53	3
	Calvin Hill, Dallas[2]	273	1,142	4.2	21	6
	Lawrence McCutcheon, Los Angeles	210	1,097	5.2	37	2
	Larry Csonka, Miami[3]	219	1,003	4.6	25	5
1972	O.J. Simpson, Buffalo	292	1,251	4.3	94	6
	Larry Brown, Washington[2]	285	1,216	4.3	38	8
	Ron Johnson, N.Y. Giants[2]	298	1,182	4.0	35	9
	Larry Csonka, Miami[2]	213	1,117	5.2	45	6
	Marv Hubbard, Oakland	219	1,100	5.0	39	4
	*Franco Harris, Pittsburgh	188	1,055	5.6	75	10
	Calvin Hill, Dallas	245	1,036	4.2	26	6
	Mike Garrett, San Diego[2]	272	1,031	3.8	41	6
	John Brockington, Green Bay[2]	274	1,027	3.7	30	8
	Eugene (Mercury) Morris, Miami	190	1,000	5.3	33	12
1971	Floyd Little, Denver	284	1,133	4.0	40	6
	*John Brockington, Green Bay	216	1,105	5.1	52	4
	Larry Csonka, Miami	195	1,051	5.4	28	7
	Steve Owens, Detroit	246	1,035	4.2	23	8
	Willie Ellison, Los Angeles	211	1,000	4.7	80	4
1970	Larry Brown, Washington	237	1,125	4.7	75	5
	Ron Johnson, N.Y. Giants	263	1,027	3.9	68	8
1969	Gale Sayers, Chicago[2]	236	1,032	4.4	28	8
1968	Leroy Kelly, Cleveland[3]	248	1,239	5.0	65	16

Year	Player, Team	Att.	Yards	Avg.	Long	TD
	*Paul Robinson, Cincinnati	238	1,023	4.3	87	8
1967	Jim Nance, Boston[2]	269	1,216	4.5	53	7
	Leroy Kelly, Cleveland[2]	235	1,205	5.1	42	11
	Hoyle Granger, Houston	236	1,194	5.1	67	6
	Mike Garrett, Kansas City	236	1,087	4.6	58	9
1966	Jim Nance, Boston	299	1,458	4.9	65	11
	Gale Sayers, Chicago	229	1,231	5.4	58	8
	Leroy Kelly, Cleveland	209	1,141	5.5	70	15
	Dick Bass, Los Angeles[2]	248	1,090	4.4	50	8
1965	Jim Brown, Cleveland[7]	289	1,544	5.3	67	17
	Paul Lowe, San Diego[2]	222	1,121	5.0	59	7
1964	Jim Brown, Cleveland[6]	280	1,446	5.2	71	7
	Jim Taylor, Green Bay[5]	235	1,169	5.0	84	12
	John Henry Johnson, Pittsburgh[2]	235	1,048	4.5	45	7
1963	Jim Brown, Cleveland[5]	291	1,863	6.4	80	12
	Clem Daniels, Oakland	215	1,099	5.1	74	3
	Jim Taylor, Green Bay[4]	248	1,018	4.1	40	9
	Paul Lowe, San Diego	177	1,010	5.7	66	8
1962	Jim Taylor, Green Bay[3]	272	1,474	5.4	51	19
	John Henry Johnson, Pittsburgh	251	1,141	4.5	40	7
	Cookie Gilchrist, Buffalo	214	1,096	5.1	44	13
	Abner Haynes, Dall. Texans	221	1,049	4.7	71	13
	Dick Bass, Los Angeles	196	1,033	5.3	57	6
	Charlie Tolar, Houston	244	1,012	4.1	25	7
1961	Jim Brown, Cleveland[4]	305	1,408	4.6	38	8
	Jim Taylor, Green Bay[2]	243	1,307	5.4	53	15
1960	Jim Brown, Cleveland[3]	215	1,257	5.8	71	9
	Jim Taylor, Green Bay	230	1,101	4.8	32	11
	John David Crow, St. Louis	183	1,071	5.9	57	6
1959	Jim Brown, Cleveland[2]	290	1,329	4.6	70	14
	J.D. Smith, San Francisco	207	1,036	5.0	73	10
1958	Jim Brown, Cleveland	257	1,527	5.9	65	17
1956	Rick Casares, Chi. Bears	234	1,126	4.8	68	12
1954	Joe Perry, San Francisco[2]	173	1,049	6.1	58	8
1953	Joe Perry, San Francisco	192	1,018	5.3	51	10
1949	Steve Van Buren, Philadelphia[2]	263	1,146	4.4	41	11
	Tony Canadeo, Green Bay	208	1,052	5.1	54	4
1947	Steve Van Buren, Philadelphia	217	1,008	4.6	45	13
1934	*Beattie Feathers, Chi. Bears	119	1,004	8.4	82	8

First season of professional football.

200 YARDS RUSHING IN A GAME

Date	Player, Team, Opponent	Att.	Yards	TD
Dec. 23, 2001	Marshall Faulk, St. Louis vs. Carolina	30	202	2
Nov. 11, 2001	Shaun Alexander, Seattle vs. Oakland	35	266	3
Dec. 24, 2000	Marshall Faulk, St. Louis vs. New Orleans	32	220	2
Dec. 3, 2000	Corey Dillon, Cincinnati vs. Arizona	35	216	1
Dec. 3, 2000	Warrick Dunn, Tampa Bay vs. Dallas	22	210	2
Dec. 3, 2000	*Mike Anderson, Denver vs. New Orleans	37	251	4
Dec. 3, 2000	Curtis Martin, N.Y. Jets vs. Indianapolis	30	203	1
Nov. 19, 2000	Fred Taylor, Jacksonville vs. Pittsburgh	30	234	3
Oct. 22, 2000	Corey Dillon, Cincinnati vs. Denver	22	278	2
Oct. 15, 2000	Marshall Faulk, St. Louis vs. Atlanta	25	208	1
Oct. 15, 2000	Edgerrin James, Indianapolis vs. Seattle	38	219	3
Sept. 24, 2000	Charlie Garner, San Francisco vs. Dallas	36	201	1
Sept. 3, 2000	Duce Staley, Philadelphia vs. Dallas	26	201	1
Nov. 22, 1998	Priest Holmes, Baltimore vs. Cincinnati	36	227	1
Oct. 11, 1998	Terrell Davis, Denver vs Seattle	30	208	1
Dec. 4, 1997	*Corey Dillon, Cincinnati vs. Tennessee	39	246	4
Nov. 23, 1997	Barry Sanders, Detroit vs. Indianapolis	24	216	2
Oct. 26, 1997	Terrell Davis, Denver vs. Buffalo (OT)	42	207	1
Oct. 19, 1997	Napoleon Kaufman, Oakland vs. Denver	28	227	1
Oct. 12, 1997	Barry Sanders, Detroit vs. Tampa Bay	24	215	2
Sept. 21, 1997	Terrell Davis, Denver vs. Cincinnati	27	215	1
Aug. 31, 1997	Eddie George, Tennessee vs. Oakland (OT)	35	216	1
Sept. 22, 1996	LeShon Johnson, Arizona vs. New Orleans	21	214	2
Nov. 13, 1994	Barry Sanders, Detroit vs. Tampa Bay	26	237	0
Dec. 12, 1993	*Jerome Bettis, L.A. Rams vs. New Orleans	28	212	1
Oct. 31, 1993	Emmitt Smith, Dallas vs. Philadelphia	30	237	1
Nov. 24, 1991	Barry Sanders, Detroit vs. Minnesota	23	220	4

Date	Player, Team	Att.	Yards	TD
Dec. 23, 1990	James Brooks, Cincinnati vs. Houston	20	201	1
Oct. 14, 1990	Barry Word, Kansas City vs. Detroit	18	200	2
Sept. 24, 1990	Thurman Thomas, Buffalo vs. N.Y. Jets	18	214	0
Dec. 24, 1989	Greg Bell, L.A. Rams vs. New England	26	210	1
Sept. 24, 1989	Greg Bell, L.A. Rams vs. Green Bay	28	221	2
Sept. 17, 1989	Gerald Riggs, Washington vs. Philadelphia	29	221	1
Dec. 18, 1988	Gary Anderson, San Diego vs. Kansas City	34	217	1
Nov. 30, 1987	*Bo Jackson, L.A. Raiders vs. Seattle	18	221	2
Nov. 15, 1987	Charles White, L.A. Rams vs. St. Louis	34	213	1
Dec. 7, 1986	Rueben Mayes, New Orleans vs. Miami	28	203	2
Oct. 5, 1986	Eric Dickerson, L.A. Rams vs. Tampa Bay (OT)	30	207	2
Dec. 21, 1985	George Rogers, Washington vs. St. Louis	34	206	1
Dec. 21, 1985	Joe Morris, N.Y. Giants vs. Pittsburgh	36	202	3
Dec. 9, 1984	Eric Dickerson, L.A. Rams vs. Houston	27	215	2
Nov. 18, 1984	*Greg Bell, Buffalo vs. Dallas	27	206	1
Nov. 4, 1984	Eric Dickerson, L.A. Rams vs. St. Louis	21	208	0
Sept. 2, 1984	Gerald Riggs, Atlanta vs. New Orleans	35	202	2
Nov. 27, 1983	*Curt Warner, Seattle vs. Kansas City (OT)	32	207	3
Nov. 6, 1983	James Wilder, Tampa Bay vs. Minnesota	31	219	1
Sept. 18, 1983	Tony Collins, New England vs. N.Y. Jets	23	212	3
Sept. 4, 1983	George Rogers, New Orleans vs. St. Louis	24	206	2
Dec. 21, 1980	Earl Campbell, Houston vs. Minnesota	29	203	1
Nov. 16, 1980	Earl Campbell, Houston vs. Chicago	31	206	0
Oct. 26, 1980	Earl Campbell, Houston vs. Cincinnati	27	202	2
Oct. 19, 1980	Earl Campbell, Houston vs. Tampa Bay	33	203	0
Nov. 26, 1978	*Terry Miller, Buffalo vs. N.Y. Giants	21	208	2
Dec. 4, 1977	*Tony Dorsett, Dallas vs. Philadelphia	23	206	2
Nov. 20, 1977	Walter Payton, Chicago vs. Minnesota	40	275	1
Oct. 30, 1977	Walter Payton, Chicago vs. Green Bay	23	205	2
Dec. 5, 1976	O.J. Simpson, Buffalo vs. Miami	24	203	1
Nov. 25, 1976	O.J. Simpson, Buffalo vs. Detroit	29	273	2
Oct. 24, 1976	Chuck Foreman, Minnesota vs. Philadelphia	28	200	2
Dec. 14, 1975	Greg Pruitt, Cleveland vs. Kansas City	26	214	3
Sept. 28, 1975	O.J. Simpson, Buffalo vs. Pittsburgh	28	227	1
Dec. 16, 1973	O.J. Simpson, Buffalo vs. N.Y. Jets	34	200	1
Dec. 9, 1973	O.J. Simpson, Buffalo vs. New England	22	219	1
Sept. 16, 1973	O.J. Simpson, Buffalo vs. New England	29	250	2
Dec. 5, 1971	Willie Ellison, Los Angeles vs. New Orleans	26	247	1
Dec. 20, 1970	John (Frenchy) Fuqua, Pittsburgh vs. Philadelphia	20	218	2
Nov. 3, 1968	Gale Sayers, Chicago vs. Green Bay	24	205	0
Oct. 30, 1966	Jim Nance, Boston vs. Oakland	38	208	2
Oct. 10, 1964	John Henry Johnson, Pittsburgh vs. Cleveland	30	200	3
Dec. 8, 1963	Cookie Gilchrist, Buffalo vs. N.Y. Jets	36	243	5
Nov. 3, 1963	Jim Brown, Cleveland vs. Philadelphia	28	223	1
Oct. 20, 1963	Clem Daniels, Oakland vs. N.Y. Jets	27	200	2
Sept. 22, 1963	Jim Brown, Cleveland vs. Dallas	20	232	2
Dec. 10, 1961	Billy Cannon, Houston vs. N.Y. Titans	25	216	3
Nov. 19, 1961	Jim Brown, Cleveland vs. Philadelphia	34	237	4
Dec. 18, 1960	John David Crow, St. Louis vs. Pittsburgh	24	203	0
Nov. 15, 1959	Bobby Mitchell, Cleveland vs. Washington	14	232	3
Nov. 24, 1957	*Jim Brown, Cleveland vs. Los Angeles	31	237	4
Dec. 16, 1956	*Tom Wilson, Los Angeles vs. Green Bay	23	223	0
Nov. 22, 1953	Dan Towler, Los Angeles vs. Baltimore	14	205	1
Nov. 12, 1950	Gene Roberts, N.Y. Giants vs. Chi. Cardinals	26	218	2
Nov. 27, 1949	Steve Van Buren, Philadelphia vs. Pittsburgh	27	205	0
Oct. 8, 1933	Cliff Battles, Boston vs. N.Y. Giants	16	215	1

*First season of professional football.

TIMES 200 OR MORE

83 times by 56 players...Simpson 6; Brown, Campbell, Sanders 4; Bell, Davis, Dickerson, Dillon, Faulk 3; Payton, Riggs, Rogers 2.

4,000 YARDS PASSING IN A SEASON

Year	Player, Team	Att.	Comp.	Pct.	Yards	TD	Int.
2001	Kurt Warner, St. Louis[2]	546	375	68.7	4,830	36	22
	Peyton Manning, Indianapolis[3]	547	343	62.7	4,131	26	23
2000	Peyton Manning, Indianapolis[2]	571	357	62.5	4,413	33	15
	Jeff Garcia, San Francisco	561	355	63.3	4,278	31	10

Year	Player, Team	Att	Comp	Pct	Yards	TD	Int
	Elvis Grbac, Kansas City	547	326	59.6	4,169	28	14
1999	Steve Beuerlein, Carolina	571	343	60.1	4,436	36	15
	Kurt Warner, St. Louis	499	325	65.1	4,353	41	13
	Peyton Manning, Indianapolis	533	331	62.1	4,135	26	15
	Brett Favre, Green Bay[3]	595	341	57.3	4,091	22	23
	Brad Johnson, Washington	519	316	60.9	4,005	24	13
1998	Brett Favre, Green Bay[2]	551	347	63.0	4,212	31	23
	Steve Young, San Francisco[2]	517	322	62.3	4,170	36	12
1996	Mark Brunell, Jacksonville	557	353	63.4	4,367	19	20
	Vinny Testaverde, Baltimore	549	325	59.2	4,177	33	19
	Drew Bledsoe, New England[2]	623	373	59.9	4,086	27	15
1995	Brett Favre, Green Bay	570	359	63.0	4,413	38	13
	Scott Mitchell, Detroit	583	346	59.3	4,338	32	12
	Warren Moon, Minnesota[4]	606	377	62.2	4,228	33	14
	Jeff George, Atlanta	557	336	60.3	4,143	24	11
1994	Drew Bledsoe, New England[6]	691	400	57.9	4,555	25	27
	Dan Marino, Miami[6]	615	385	62.6	4,453	30	17
	Warren Moon, Minnesota[3]	601	371	61.7	4,264	18	19
1993	John Elway, Denver	551	348	63.2	4,030	25	10
	Steve Young, San Francisco	462	314	68.0	4,023	29	16
1992	Dan Marino, Miami[5]	554	330	59.6	4,116	24	16
1991	Warren Moon, Houston[2]	655	404	61.7	4,690	23	21
1990	Warren Moon, Houston	584	362	62.0	4,689	33	13
1989	Don Majkowski, Green Bay	599	353	58.9	4,318	27	20
	Jim Everett, L.A. Rams	518	304	58.7	4,310	29	17
1988	Dan Marino, Miami[4]	606	354	58.4	4,434	28	23
1986	Dan Marino, Miami[3]	623	378	60.7	4,746	44	23
	Jay Schroeder, Washington	541	276	51.0	4,109	22	22
1985	Dan Marino, Miami[2]	567	336	59.3	4,137	30	21
1984	Dan Marino, Miami	564	362	64.2	5,084	48	17
	Neil Lomax, St. Louis	560	345	61.6	4,614	28	16
	Phil Simms, N.Y. Giants	533	286	53.7	4,044	22	18
1983	Lynn Dickey, Green Bay	484	289	59.7	4,458	32	29
	Bill Kenney, Kansas City	603	346	57.4	4,348	24	18
1981	Dan Fouts, San Diego[3]	609	360	59.1	4,802	33	17
1980	Dan Fouts, San Diego[2]	589	348	59.1	4,715	30	24
	Brian Sipe, Cleveland	554	337	60.8	4,132	30	14
1979	Dan Fouts, San Diego	530	332	62.6	4,082	24	24
1967	Joe Namath, N.Y. Jets	491	258	52.5	4,007	26	28

400 YARDS PASSING IN A GAME

Date	Player, Team, Opponent	Att.	Comp.	Yards	TD
Dec. 30, 2001	Jon Kitna, Cincinnati vs. Pittsburgh	68	35	411	2
Dec. 23, 2001	Chris Chandler, Atlanta vs. Buffalo	40	28	431	2
Nov. 18, 2001	Charlie Batch, Detroit vs. Arizona	62	36	436	3
Nov. 18, 2001	Kurt Warner, St. Louis vs. New England	42	30	401	3
Sept. 23, 2001	Peyton Manning, Indianapolis vs. Buffalo	29	23	421	4
Dec. 24, 2000	Vinny Testaverde, N.Y. Jets vs. Baltimore	69	36	481	2
Dec. 17, 2000	Jeff Garcia, San Francisco vs. Chicago	44	36	402	2
Dec. 3, 2000	Aaron Brooks, New Orleans vs. Denver	48	30	441	2
Nov. 19, 2000	Gus Frerotte, Denver vs. San Diego	58	36	462	5
Nov. 5, 2000	Elvis Grbac, Kansas City vs. Oakland	53	39	504	2
Nov. 5, 2000	Trent Green, St. Louis vs. Carolina	42	29	431	2
Sept. 25, 2000	Peyton Manning, Indianapolis vs. Jacksonville	36	23	440	4
Sept. 4, 2000	Kurt Warner, St. Louis vs. Denver	35	25	441	3
Dec. 26, 1999	Brad Johnson, Washington vs. San Francisco (OT)	47	32	471	2
Dec. 5, 1999	Jeff Garcia, San Francisco vs. Cincinnati	49	33	437	3
Nov. 28, 1999	Jim Harbaugh, San Diego vs. Minnesota	39	25	404	1
Nov. 14, 1999	Jim Miller, Chicago vs. Minnesota (OT)	48	34	422	3
Sept. 26, 1999	Peyton Manning, Indianapolis vs. San Diego	54	29	404	2
Dec. 6, 1998	Vinny Testaverde, N.Y. Jets vs. Seattle	63	42	418	2
Dec. 6, 1998	John Elway, Denver vs. Kansas City	32	22	400	2
Nov. 26, 1998	Troy Aikman, Dallas vs. Minnesota	57	34	455	1
Nov. 23, 1998	Drew Bledsoe, New England vs. Miami	54	28	423	2
Nov. 15, 1998	Jake Plummer, Arizona vs. Dallas	56	31	465	3
Oct. 5, 1998	Randall Cunningham, Minnesota vs. Green Bay	32	20	442	4
Sept. 6, 1998	Glenn Foley, N.Y. Jets vs. San Francisco (OT)	58	30	455	1
Nov. 2, 1997	Tony Banks, St. Louis vs. Atlanta	34	23	401	2
Oct. 26, 1997	Warren Moon, Seattle vs. Oakland	44	28	409	5
Nov. 10, 1996	Boomer Esiason, Arizona vs. Washington (OT)	59	35	522	3

Date	Player, Team vs. Opponent	Att	Comp	Yards	TD
Nov. 3, 1996	Drew Bledsoe, New England vs. Miami	41	30	419	3
Oct. 27, 1996	Vinny Testaverde, Baltimore vs. St. Louis (OT)	51	31	429	3
Oct. 20, 1996	Mark Brunell, Jacksonville vs. St. Louis	52	37	421	0
Sept. 22, 1996	Mark Brunell, Jacksonville vs. New England (OT)	39	23	432	3
Dec. 18, 1995	Steve Young, San Francisco vs. Minnesota	49	30	425	3
Nov. 26, 1995	Dave Krieg, Arizona vs. Atlanta (OT)	43	27	413	4
Nov. 23, 1995	Scott Mitchell, Detroit vs. Minnesota	45	30	410	4
Oct. 1, 1995	Dan Marino, Miami vs. Cincinnati	48	33	450	2
Nov. 20, 1994	Warren Moon, Minnesota vs. N.Y. Jets	50	33	400	2
Nov. 13, 1994	Drew Bledsoe, New England vs. Minnesota (OT)	70	45	426	3
Nov. 6, 1994	Warren Moon, Minnesota vs. New Orleans	57	33	420	3
Sept. 25, 1994	Dan Marino, Miami vs. Minnesota	54	29	431	3
Sept. 4, 1994	Dan Marino, Miami vs. New England (OT)	42	23	473	5
Sept. 4, 1994	Drew Bledsoe, New England vs. Miami (OT)	51	32	421	4
Dec. 19, 1993	Steve Beuerlein, Phoenix vs. Seattle	53	34	431	3
Dec. 5, 1993	Brett Favre, Green Bay vs. Chicago	54	36	402	2
Nov. 28, 1993	Steve Young, San Francisco vs. L.A. Rams	32	26	462	4
Oct. 31, 1993	Jeff Hostetler, L.A. Raiders vs. San Diego	32	20	424	2
Sept. 13, 1992	Steve Young, San Francisco vs. Buffalo	37	26	449	3
Sept. 13, 1992	Jim Kelly, Buffalo vs. San Francisco	33	22	403	3
Nov. 10, 1991	Warren Moon, Houston vs. Dallas (OT)	56	41	432	0
Nov. 10, 1991	Mark Rypien, Washington vs. Atlanta	31	16	442	6
Oct. 13, 1991	Warren Moon, Houston vs. N.Y. Jets	50	35	423	2
Dec. 16, 1990	Warren Moon, Houston vs. Kansas City	45	27	527	3
Nov. 4, 1990	Joe Montana, San Francisco vs. Green Bay	40	25	411	3
Oct. 14, 1990	Joe Montana, San Francisco vs. Atlanta	49	32	476	6
Oct. 7, 1990	Boomer Esiason, Cincinnati vs. L.A. Rams (OT)	45	31	490	3
Dec. 23, 1989	Warren Moon, Houston vs. Cleveland	51	32	414	2
Dec. 11, 1989	Joe Montana, San Francisco vs. L.A. Rams	42	30	458	3
Nov. 26, 1989	Jim Everett, L.A. Rams vs. New Orleans (OT)	51	29	454	1
Nov. 26, 1989	Mark Rypien, Washington vs. Chicago	47	30	401	4
Oct. 2, 1989	Randall Cunningham, Philadelphia vs. Chicago	62	32	401	1
Sept. 24, 1989	Joe Montana, San Francisco vs. Philadelphia	34	25	428	5
Sept. 24, 1989	Dan Marino, Miami vs. N.Y. Jets	55	33	427	3
Sept. 17, 1989	Randall Cunningham, Phil. vs. Washington	46	34	447	5
Dec. 18, 1988	Dave Krieg, Seattle vs. L.A. Raiders	32	19	410	4
Dec. 12, 1988	Dan Marino, Miami vs. Cleveland	50	30	404	4
Oct. 23, 1988	Dan Marino, Miami vs. N.Y. Jets	60	35	521	3
Oct. 16, 1988	Vinny Testaverde, Tampa Bay vs. Indianapolis	42	25	469	2
Sept. 11, 1988	Doug Williams, Washington vs. Pittsburgh	52	30	430	2
Nov. 29, 1987	Tom Ramsey, New England vs. Philadelphia	53	34	402	3
Nov. 22, 1987	Boomer Esiason, Cincinnati vs. Pittsburgh	53	30	409	0
Sept. 20, 1987	Neil Lomax, St. Louis vs. San Diego	61	32	457	3
Dec. 21, 1986	Boomer Esiason, Cincinnati vs. N.Y. Jets	30	23	425	5
Dec. 14, 1986	Dan Marino, Miami vs. L.A. Rams (OT)	46	29	403	5
Nov. 23, 1986	Bernie Kosar, Cleveland vs. Pittsburgh (OT)	46	28	414	2
Nov. 17, 1986	Joe Montana, San Francisco vs. Washington	60	33	441	0
Nov. 16, 1986	Dan Marino, Miami vs. Buffalo	54	39	404	4
Nov. 10, 1986	Bernie Kosar, Cleveland vs. Miami	50	32	401	0
Nov. 2, 1986	Tommy Kramer, Minnesota vs. Washington (OT)	35	20	490	4
Nov. 2, 1986	Ken O'Brien, N.Y. Jets vs. Seattle	32	26	431	4
Oct. 27, 1986	Jay Schroeder, Washington vs. N.Y. Giants	40	22	420	1
Oct. 12, 1986	Steve Grogan, New England vs. N.Y. Jets	42	23	401	3
Sept. 21, 1986	Ken O'Brien, N.Y. Jets vs. Miami (OT)	43	29	479	4
Sept. 21, 1986	Dan Marino, Miami vs. N.Y. Jets (OT)	50	30	448	6
Sept. 21, 1986	Tony Eason, New England vs. Seattle	45	26	414	3
Dec. 20, 1985	John Elway, Denver vs. Seattle	42	24	432	1
Nov. 10, 1985	Dan Fouts, San Diego vs. L.A. Raiders (OT)	41	26	436	4
Oct. 13, 1985	Phil Simms, N.Y. Giants vs. Cincinnati	62	40	513	1
Oct. 13, 1985	Dave Krieg, Seattle vs. Atlanta	51	33	405	4
Oct. 6, 1985	Phil Simms, N.Y. Giants vs. Dallas	36	18	432	3
Oct. 6, 1985	Joe Montana, San Francisco vs. Atlanta	57	37	429	5
Sept. 19, 1985	Tommy Kramer, Minnesota vs. Chicago	55	28	436	4
Sept. 15, 1985	Dan Fouts, San Diego vs. Seattle	43	29	440	4
Dec. 16, 1984	Neil Lomax, St. Louis vs. Washington	46	37	468	2
Dec. 9, 1984	Dan Marino, Miami vs. Indianapolis	41	29	404	4
Dec. 2, 1984	Dan Marino, Miami vs. L.A. Raiders	57	35	470	4
Nov. 25, 1984	Dave Krieg, Seattle vs. Denver	44	30	406	3
Nov. 4, 1984	Dan Marino, Miami vs. N.Y. Jets	42	23	422	2
Oct. 21, 1984	Dan Fouts, San Diego vs. L.A. Raiders	45	24	410	3

Date	Player	Att	Comp	Yds	TD
Sept. 30, 1984	Dan Marino, Miami vs. St. Louis	36	24	429	3
Sept. 2, 1984	Phil Simms, N.Y. Giants vs. Philadelphia	30	23	409	4
Dec. 11, 1983	Bill Kenney, Kansas City vs. San Diego	41	31	411	4
Nov. 20, 1983	Dave Krieg, Seattle vs. Denver	42	31	418	3
Oct. 9, 1983	Joe Ferguson, Buffalo vs. Miami (OT)	55	38	419	5
Oct. 2, 1983	Joe Theismann, Washington vs. L.A. Raiders	39	23	417	3
Sept. 25, 1983	Richard Todd, N.Y. Jets vs. L.A. Rams (OT)	50	37	446	2
Dec. 26, 1982	Vince Ferragamo, L.A. Rams vs. Chicago	46	30	509	3
Dec. 20, 1982	Dan Fouts, San Diego vs. Cincinnati	40	25	435	1
Dec. 20, 1982	Ken Anderson, Cincinnati vs. San Diego	56	40	416	2
Dec. 11, 1982	Dan Fouts, San Diego vs. San Francisco	48	33	444	5
Nov. 21, 1982	Joe Montana, San Francisco vs. St. Louis	39	26	408	3
Nov. 15, 1981	Steve Bartkowski, Atlanta vs. Pittsburgh	50	33	416	2
Oct. 25, 1981	Brian Sipe, Cleveland vs. Baltimore	41	30	444	4
Oct. 25, 1981	David Woodley, Miami vs. Dallas	37	21	408	3
Oct. 11, 1981	Tommy Kramer, Minnesota vs. San Diego	43	27	444	4
Dec. 14, 1980	Tommy Kramer, Minnesota vs. Cleveland	49	38	456	4
Nov. 16, 1980	Doug Williams, Tampa Bay vs. Minnesota	55	30	486	4
Oct. 19, 1980	Dan Fouts, San Diego vs. N.Y. Giants	41	26	444	3
Oct. 12, 1980	Lynn Dickey, Green Bay vs. Tampa Bay (OT)	51	35	418	1
Sept. 21, 1980	Richard Todd, N.Y. Jets vs. San Francisco	60	42	447	3
Oct. 3, 1976	James Harris, Los Angeles vs. Miami	29	17	436	2
Nov. 17, 1975	Ken Anderson, Cincinnati vs. Buffalo	46	30	447	2
Nov. 18, 1974	Charley Johnson, Denver vs. Kansas City	42	28	445	2
Dec. 11, 1972	Joe Namath, N.Y. Jets vs. Oakland	46	25	403	1
Sept. 24, 1972	Joe Namath, N.Y. Jets vs. Baltimore	28	15	496	6
Dec. 21, 1969	Don Horn, Green Bay vs. St. Louis	31	22	410	5
Sept. 28, 1969	Joe Kapp, Minnesota vs. Baltimore	43	28	449	7
Sept. 9, 1968	Pete Beathard, Houston vs. Kansas City	48	23	413	2
Nov. 26, 1967	Sonny Jurgensen, Washington vs. Cleveland	50	32	418	3
Oct. 1, 1967	Joe Namath, N.Y. Jets vs. Miami	39	23	415	3
Sept. 17, 1967	Johnny Unitas, Baltimore vs. Atlanta	32	22	401	2
Nov. 13, 1966	Don Meredith, Dallas vs. Washington	29	21	406	2
Nov. 28, 1965	Sonny Jurgensen, Washington vs. Dallas	43	26	411	3
Oct. 24, 1965	Fran Tarkenton, Minnesota vs. San Francisco	35	21	407	3
Nov. 1, 1964	Len Dawson, Kansas City vs. Denver	38	23	435	6
Oct. 25, 1964	Cotton Davidson, Oakland vs. Denver	36	23	427	5
Oct. 16, 1964	Babe Parilli, Boston vs. Oakland	47	25	422	4
Dec. 22, 1963	Tom Flores, Oakland vs. Houston	29	17	407	6
Nov. 17, 1963	Norm Snead, Washington vs. Pittsburgh	40	23	424	2
Nov. 10, 1963	Don Meredith, Dallas vs. San Francisco	48	30	460	3
Oct. 13, 1963	Charley Johnson, St. Louis vs. Pittsburgh	41	20	428	2
Dec. 16, 1962	Sonny Jurgensen, Philadelphia vs. St. Louis	34	15	419	5
Nov. 18, 1962	Bill Wade, Chicago vs. Dall. Cowboys	46	28	466	2
Oct. 28, 1962	Y.A. Tittle, N.Y. Giants vs. Washington	39	27	505	7
Sept. 15, 1962	Frank Tripucka, Denver vs. Buffalo	56	29	447	2
Dec. 17, 1961	Sonny Jurgensen, Philadelphia vs. Detroit	42	27	403	3
Nov. 19, 1961	George Blanda, Houston vs. N.Y. Titans	32	20	418	7
Oct. 29, 1961	George Blanda, Houston vs. Buffalo	32	18	464	4
Oct. 29, 1961	Sonny Jurgensen, Philadelphia vs. Washington	41	27	436	3
Oct. 13, 1961	Jacky Lee, Houston vs. Boston	41	27	457	2
Dec. 13, 1958	Bobby Layne, Pittsburgh vs. Chi. Cardinals	49	23	409	2
Nov. 8, 1953	Bobby Thomason, Philadelphia vs. N.Y. Giants	44	22	437	4
Oct. 4, 1952	Otto Graham, Cleveland vs. Pittsburgh	49	21	401	3
Sept. 28, 1951	Norm Van Brocklin, Los Angeles vs. N.Y. Yanks	41	27	554	5
Dec. 11, 1949	Johnny Lujack, Chi. Bears vs. Chi. Cardinals	39	24	468	6
Oct. 31, 1948	Sammy Baugh, Washington vs. Boston	24	17	446	4
Oct. 31, 1948	Jim Hardy, Los Angeles vs. Chi. Cardinals	53	28	406	3
Nov. 14, 1943	Sid Luckman, Chi. Bears vs. N.Y. Giants	32	21	433	7

TIMES 400 OR MORE

157 times by 84 players. . .Marino 13; Montana, Moon 7; Fouts 6; Jurgensen, Krieg 5; Bledsoe, Esiason, Kramer, Testaverde 4; Cunningham, Manning, Namath, Simms, Young 3; Anderson, Blanda, Brunell, Elway, Garcia, Johnson, Kosar, Lomax, Meredith, O'Brien, Rypien, Todd, Warner, Williams 2.

100 PASS RECEPTIONS IN A SEASON

Year	Player, Team	No.	Yards	Avg.	Long	TD
2001	Rod Smith, Denver[2]	113	1,343	11.9	65	11
	Jimmy Smith, Jacksonville[2]	112	1,373	12.3	35	8
	Marvin Harrison, Indianapolis[3]	109	1,524	14.0	68	15
	Keyshawn Johnson, Tampa Bay	106	1,266	11.9	47	1
	Troy Brown, New England	101	1,199	11.9	60	5
	Marty Booker, Chicago	100	1,071	10.7	66	8
2000	Marvin Harrison, Indianapolis[2]	102	1,413	13.9	78	14
	Muhsin Muhammad, Carolina	102	1,183	11.6	36	6
	Ed McCaffrey, Denver	101	1,317	13.0	61	9
	Rod Smith, Denver	100	1,602	16.0	49	8
1999	Jimmy Smith, Jacksonville	116	1,636	14.1	62	6
	Marvin Harrison, Indianapolis	115	1,663	14.5	57	12
1997	Tim Brown, Oakland	104	1,408	13.5	59	5
	Herman Moore, Detroit[3]	104	1,293	12.4	79	8
1996	Jerry Rice, San Francisco[4]	108	1,254	11.6	39	8
	Herman Moore, Detroit[2]	106	1,296	12.2	50	9
	Carl Pickens, Cincinnati	100	1,180	11.8	61	12
1995	Herman Moore, Detroit	123	1,686	13.7	69	14
	Jerry Rice, San Francisco[3]	122	1,848	15.1	81	15
	Cris Carter, Minnesota[2]	122	1,371	11.2	60	17
	Isaac Bruce, St. Louis	119	1,781	15.0	72	13
	Michael Irvin, Dallas	111	1,603	14.4	50	10
	Brett Perriman, Detroit	108	1,488	13.8	91	9
	Eric Metcalf, Atlanta	104	1,189	11.4	62	8
	Robert Brooks, Green Bay	102	1,497	14.7	99	13
	Larry Centers, Arizona	101	962	9.5	32	2
1994	Cris Carter, Minnesota	122	1,256	10.3	65	7
	Jerry Rice, San Francisco[2]	112	1,499	13.4	69	13
	Terance Mathis, Atlanta	111	1,342	12.1	81	11
1993	Sterling Sharpe, Green Bay[2]	112	1,274	11.4	54	11
1992	Sterling Sharpe, Green Bay	108	1,461	13.5	76	13
1991	Haywood Jeffires, Houston	100	1,181	11.8	44	7
1990	Jerry Rice, San Francisco	100	1,502	15.0	64	13
1984	Art Monk, Washington	106	1,372	12.9	72	7
1964	Charley Hennigan, Houston	101	1,546	15.3	53	8
1961	Lionel Taylor, Denver	100	1,176	11.8	52	4

1,000 YARDS PASS RECEIVING IN A SEASON

Year	Player, Team	No.	Yards	Avg.	Long	TD
2001	David Boston, Arizona[2]	98	1,598	16.3	61	8
	Marvin Harrison, Indianapolis[3]	109	1,524	14.0	68	15
	Terrell Owens, San Francisco[3]	93	1,412	15.2	60	16
	Jimmy Smith, Jacksonville[6]	112	1,373	12.3	35	8
	Torry Holt, St. Louis[2]	81	1,363	16.8	51	7
	Rod Smith, Denver[5]	113	1,343	11.9	65	11
	Keyshawn Johnson, Tampa Bay[3]	106	1,266	11.9	47	1
	Joe Horn, New Orleans[2]	83	1,265	15.2	56	9
	Randy Moss, Minnesota[4]	82	1,233	15.0	73	10
	Troy Brown, New England	101	1,199	11.9	60	5
	Tim Brown, Oakland[9]	91	1,165	12.8	46	9
	Johnnie Morton, Detroit[4]	77	1,154	15.0	76	4
	Jerry Rice, Oakland[13]	83	1,139	13.7	40	9
	Derrick Mason, Tennessee	73	1,128	15.5	71	9
	Curtis Conway, San Diego[3]	71	1,125	15.8	72	6
	Keenan McCardell, Jacksonville[4]	93	1,110	11.9	45	6
	Isaac Bruce, St. Louis[5]	64	1,106	17.3	51	6
	Kevin Johnson, Cleveland	84	1,097	13.1	55	9
	Darrell Jackson, Seattle	70	1,081	15.4	64	8
	Marty Booker, Chicago	100	1,071	10.7	66	8
	Qadry Ismail, Baltimore[2]	74	1,059	14.3	77	7
	Amani Toomer, N.Y. Giants[3]	72	1,054	14.6	60	5
	Willie Jackson, New Orleans	81	1,046	12.9	63	5
	Plaxico Burress, Pittsburgh	66	1,008	15.3	43	6
	Hines Ward, Pittsburgh	94	1,003	10.7	34	4
2000	Torry Holt, St. Louis	82	1,635	19.9	85	6
	Rod Smith, Denver[4]	100	1,602	16.0	49	8
	Isaac Bruce, St. Louis[4]	87	1,471	16.9	78	9
	Terrell Owens, San Francisco[2]	97	1,451	15.0	69	13

Year	Player	Rec	Yds	Avg	Long	TD
	Randy Moss, Minnesota[3]	77	1,437	18.7	78	15
	Marvin Harrison, Indianapolis[2]	102	1,413	13.9	78	14
	Derrick Alexander, Kansas City[3]	78	1,391	17.8	81	10
	Joe Horn, New Orleans	94	1,340	14.3	52	8
	Eric Moulds, Buffalo[2]	94	1,326	14.1	52	5
	Ed McCaffrey, Denver[3]	101	1,317	13.0	61	9
	Cris Carter, Minnesota[8]	96	1,274	13.3	53	9
	Jimmy Smith, Jacksonville[5]	91	1,213	13.3	65	8
	Keenan McCardell, Jacksonville[3]	94	1,207	12.8	67	5
	Tony Gonzalez, Kansas City	93	1,203	12.9	39	9
	Muhsin Muhammad, Carolina[2]	102	1,183	11.6	36	6
	David Boston, Arizona	71	1,156	16.3	70	7
	Tim Brown, Oakland[8]	76	1,128	14.8	45	11
	Amani Toomer, N.Y. Giants[2]	78	1,094	14.0	54	7
1999	Marvin Harrison, Indianapolis	115	1,663	14.5	57	12
	Jimmy Smith, Jacksonville[4]	116	1,636	14.1	62	6
	Randy Moss, Minnesota[2]	80	1,413	17.7	67	11
	Marcus Robinson, Chicago	84	1,400	16.7	80	9
	Tim Brown, Oakland[7]	90	1,344	14.9	47	6
	Germane Crowell, Detroit	81	1,338	16.5	77	7
	Muhsin Muhammad, Carolina	96	1,253	13.1	60	8
	Cris Carter, Minnesota[7]	90	1,241	13.8	68	13
	Michael Westbrook, Washington	65	1,191	18.3	65	9
	Amani Toomer, N.Y. Giants	79	1,183	15.0	80	6
	Keyshawn Johnson, N.Y. Jets[2]	89	1,170	13.2	65	8
	Isaac Bruce, St. Louis[3]	77	1,165	15.1	60	12
	Terry Glenn, New England[2]	69	1,147	16.6	67	4
	Albert Connell, Washington	62	1,132	18.3	62	7
	Johnnie Morton, Detroit[3]	80	1,129	14.1	48	5
	Qadry Ismail, Baltimore	68	1,105	16.3	76	6
	Raghib Ismail, Dallas[2]	80	1,097	13.7	76	6
	Patrick Jeffers, Carolina	63	1,082	17.2	88	12
	Antonio Freeman, Green Bay[3]	74	1,074	14.5	51	6
	Bill Schroeder, Green Bay	74	1,051	14.2	51	5
	Marshall Faulk, St. Louis	87	1,048	12.1	57	5
	Tony Martin, Miami[4]	67	1,037	15.5	69	5
	Darnay Scott, Cincinnati	68	1,022	15.0	76	7
	Rod Smith, Denver[3]	79	1,020	12.9	71	4
	Ed McCaffrey, Denver[2]	71	1,018	14.3	78	7
	Terance Mathis, Atlanta[4]	81	1,016	12.5	52	6
1998	Antonio Freeman, Green Bay[2]	84	1,424	17.0	84	14
	Eric Moulds, Buffalo	67	1,368	20.4	84	9
	*Randy Moss, Minnesota	69	1,313	19.0	61	17
	Rod Smith, Denver[2]	86	1,222	14.2	58	6
	Jimmy Smith, Jacksonville[3]	78	1,182	15.2	72	8
	Tony Martin, Atlanta[3]	66	1,181	17.9	62	6
	Jerry Rice, San Francisco[12]	82	1,157	14.1	75	9
	Frank Sanders, Arizona[2]	89	1,145	12.9	42	3
	Terance Mathis, Atlanta[3]	64	1,136	17.8	78	11
	Keyshawn Johnson, N.Y. Jets	83	1,131	13.6	41	10
	Terrell Owens, San Francisco	67	1,097	16.4	79	14
	Wayne Chrebet, N.Y. Jets	75	1,083	14.4	63	8
	Michael Irvin, Dallas[7]	74	1,057	14.3	51	1
	Ed McCaffrey, Denver	64	1,053	16.5	48	10
	O.J. McDuffie, Miami	90	1,050	11.7	61	7
	Joey Galloway, Seattle[3]	65	1,047	16.1	81	10
	Johnnie Morton, Detroit[2]	69	1,028	14.9	98	2
	Raghib Ismail, Carolina	69	1,024	14.8	62	8
	Carl Pickens, Cincinnati[4]	82	1,023	12.5	67	5
	Tim Brown, Oakland[6]	81	1,012	12.5	49	9
	Cris Carter, Minnesota[6]	78	1,011	13.0	54	12
1997	Rob Moore, Arizona[3]	97	1,584	16.3	47	8
	Tim Brown, Oakland[5]	104	1,408	13.5	59	5
	Yancey Thigpen, Pittsburgh[2]	79	1,398	17.7	69	7
	Jimmy Smith, Jacksonville[2]	82	1,324	16.1	75	4
	Irving Fryar, Philadelphia[5]	86	1,316	15.3	72	6
	Herman Moore, Detroit[4]	104	1,293	12.4	79	8
	Antonio Freeman, Green Bay	81	1,243	15.3	58	12
	Michael Irvin, Dallas[6]	75	1,180	15.7	55	9
	Rod Smith, Denver	70	1,180	16.9	78	12

Year	Player	Rec	Yards	Avg	Long	TD
	Keenan McCardell, Jacksonville[2]	85	1,164	13.7	60	5
	Jake Reed, Minnesota[4]	68	1,138	16.7	56	6
	Shannon Sharpe, Denver[3]	72	1,107	15.4	68	3
	Andre Rison, Kansas City[6]	72	1,092	15.2	45	7
	Cris Carter, Minnesota[5]	89	1,069	12.0	43	13
	Johnnie Morton, Detroit	80	1,057	13.2	73	6
	Joey Galloway, Seattle[2]	72	1,049	14.6	53	12
	Frank Sanders, Arizona	75	1,017	13.6	70	4
	Robert Brooks, Green Bay[2]	60	1,010	16.8	48	7
	Derrick Alexander, Baltimore[2]	65	1,009	15.5	92	9
1996	Isaac Bruce, St. Louis[2]	84	1,338	15.9	70	7
	Jake Reed, Minnesota[3]	72	1,320	18.3	82	7
	Herman Moore, Detroit[3]	106	1,296	12.2	50	9
	Jerry Rice, San Francisco[11]	108	1,254	11.6	39	8
	Jimmy Smith, Jacksonville	83	1,244	15.0	62	7
	Michael Jackson, Baltimore	76	1,201	15.8	86	14
	Irving Fryar, Philadelphia[4]	88	1,195	13.6	42	11
	Carl Pickens, Cincinnati[3]	100	1,180	11.8	61	12
	Tony Martin, San Diego[2]	85	1,171	13.8	55	14
	Cris Carter, Minnesota[4]	96	1,163	12.1	43	10
	*Terry Glenn, New England	90	1,132	12.6	37	6
	Keenan McCardell, Jacksonville	85	1,129	13.3	52	3
	Tim Brown, Oakland[4]	90	1,104	12.3	42	9
	Derrick Alexander, Baltimore	62	1,099	17.7	64	9
	Shannon Sharpe, Denver[2]	80	1,062	13.3	51	10
	Curtis Conway, Chicago[2]	81	1,049	13.0	58	7
	Andre Reed, Buffalo[4]	66	1,036	15.7	67	6
	Brett Perriman, Detroit[2]	94	1,021	10.9	44	5
	Rob Moore, Arizona[2]	58	1,016	17.5	69	4
	Henry Ellard, Washington[7]	52	1,014	19.5	51	2
	Charles Johnson, Pittsburgh	60	1,008	16.8	70	3
1995	Jerry Rice, San Francisco[10]	122	1,848	15.1	81	15
	Isaac Bruce, St. Louis	119	1,781	15.0	72	13
	Herman Moore, Detroit[2]	123	1,686	13.7	69	14
	Michael Irvin, Dallas[5]	111	1,603	14.4	50	10
	Robert Brooks, Green Bay	102	1,497	14.7	99	13
	Brett Perriman, Detroit	108	1,488	13.8	91	9
	Cris Carter, Minnesota[3]	122	1,371	11.2	60	17
	Tim Brown, Oakland[3]	89	1,342	15.1	80	10
	Yancey Thigpen, Pittsburgh	85	1,307	15.4	43	5
	Jeff Graham, Chicago	82	1,301	15.9	51	4
	Carl Pickens, Cincinnati[2]	99	1,234	12.5	68	17
	Tony Martin, San Diego	90	1,224	13.6	51	6
	Eric Metcalf, Atlanta	104	1,189	11.4	62	8
	Jake Reed, Minnesota[2]	72	1,167	16.2	55	9
	Quinn Early, New Orleans	81	1,087	13.4	70	8
	Anthony Miller, Denver[6]	59	1,079	18.3	62	14
	Bert Emanuel, Atlanta	74	1,039	14.0	52	5
	*Joey Galloway, Seattle	67	1,039	15.5	59	7
	Terance Mathis, Atlanta[2]	78	1,039	13.3	54	9
	Curtis Conway, Chicago	62	1,037	16.7	76	12
	Henry Ellard, Washington[6]	56	1,005	17.9	59	5
	Mark Carrier, Carolina[2]	66	1,002	15.2	66	3
	Brian Blades, Seattle[4]	77	1,001	13.0	49	4
1994	Jerry Rice, San Francisco[9]	112	1,499	13.4	69	13
	Henry Ellard, Washington[5]	74	1,397	18.9	73	6
	Terance Mathis, Atlanta	111	1,342	12.1	81	11
	Tim Brown, L.A. Raiders[2]	89	1,309	14.7	77	9
	Andre Reed, Buffalo[2]	90	1,303	14.5	83	8
	Irving Fryar, Miami[3]	73	1,270	17.4	54	7
	Cris Carter, Minnesota[2]	122	1,256	10.3	65	7
	Michael Irvin, Dallas[4]	79	1,241	15.7	65	6
	Jake Reed, Minnesota	85	1,175	13.8	59	4
	Ben Coates, New England	96	1,174	12.2	62	7
	Herman Moore, Detroit	72	1,173	16.3	51	11
	Fred Barnett, Philadelphia[2]	78	1,127	14.4	54	5
	Carl Pickens, Cincinnati	71	1,127	15.9	70	11
	Sterling Sharpe, Green Bay[4]	94	1,119	11.9	49	18
	Anthony Miller, Denver[4]	60	1,107	18.5	76	5
	Andre Rison, Atlanta[3]	81	1,088	13.4	69	8

	Brian Blades, Seattle[3]	81	1,088	13.4	45	4
	Rob Moore, N.Y. Jets	78	1,010	12.9	41	6
	Shannon Sharpe, Denver	87	1,010	11.6	44	4
1993	Jerry Rice, San Francisco[8]	98	1,503	15.3	80	15
	Michael Irvin, Dallas[3]	88	1,330	15.1	61	7
	Sterling Sharpe, Green Bay[4]	112	1,274	11.4	54	11
	Andre Rison, Atlanta[3]	86	1,242	14.4	53	15
	Tim Brown, L.A. Raiders	80	1,180	14.8	71	7
	Anthony Miller, San Diego[3]	84	1,162	13.8	66	7
	Cris Carter, Minnesota	86	1,071	12.5	58	9
	Reggie Langhorne, Indianapolis	85	1,038	12.2	72	3
	Irving Fryar, Miami[2]	64	1,010	15.8	65	5
1992	Sterling Sharpe, Green Bay[3]	108	1,461	13.5	76	13
	Michael Irvin, Dallas[2]	78	1,396	17.9	87	7
	Jerry Rice, San Francisco[7]	84	1,201	14.3	80	10
	Andre Rison, Atlanta[2]	93	1,119	12.0	71	11
	Fred Barnett, Philadelphia	67	1,083	16.2	71	6
	Anthony Miller, San Diego[2]	72	1,060	14.7	67	7
	Eric Martin, New Orleans[3]	68	1,041	15.3	52	5
1991	Michael Irvin, Dallas	93	1,523	16.4	66	8
	Gary Clark, Washington[5]	70	1,340	19.1	82	10
	Jerry Rice, San Francisco[6]	80	1,206	15.1	73	14
	Haywood Jeffires, Houston[2]	100	1,181	11.8	44	7
	Michael Haynes, Atlanta	50	1,122	22.4	80	11
	Andre Reed, Buffalo[2]	81	1,113	13.7	55	10
	Drew Hill, Houston[5]	90	1,109	12.3	61	4
	Mark Duper, Miami[4]	70	1,085	15.5	43	5
	James Lofton, Buffalo[6]	57	1,072	18.8	77	8
	Mark Clayton, Miami[5]	70	1,053	15.0	43	12
	Henry Ellard, L.A. Rams[4]	64	1,052	16.4	38	3
	Art Monk, Washington[5]	71	1,049	14.8	64	8
	Irving Fryar, New England	68	1,014	14.9	56	3
	John Taylor, San Francisco[2]	64	1,011	15.8	97	9
	Brian Blades, Seattle[2]	70	1,003	14.3	52	2
1990	Jerry Rice, San Francisco[5]	100	1,502	15.0	64	13
	Henry Ellard, L.A. Rams[3]	76	1,294	17.0	50	4
	Andre Rison, Atlanta	82	1,208	14.7	75	10
	Gary Clark, Washington[4]	75	1,112	14.8	53	8
	Sterling Sharpe, Green Bay[2]	67	1,105	16.5	76	6
	Willie Anderson, L.A. Rams[2]	51	1,097	21.5	55	4
	Haywood Jeffires, Houston	74	1,048	14.2	87	8
	Stephone Paige, Kansas City	65	1,021	15.7	86	5
	Drew Hill, Houston[4]	74	1,019	13.8	57	5
	Anthony Carter, Minnesota[3]	70	1,008	14.4	56	8
1989	Jerry Rice, San Francisco[4]	82	1,483	18.1	68	17
	Sterling Sharpe, Green Bay	90	1,423	15.8	79	12
	Mark Carrier, Tampa Bay	86	1,422	16.5	78	9
	Henry Ellard, L.A. Rams[2]	70	1,382	19.7	53	8
	Andre Reed, Buffalo	88	1,312	14.9	78	9
	Anthony Miller, San Diego	75	1,252	16.7	69	10
	Webster Slaughter, Cleveland	65	1,236	19.0	97	6
	Gary Clark, Washington[3]	79	1,229	15.6	80	9
	Tim McGee, Cincinnati	65	1,211	18.6	74	8
	Art Monk, Washington[4]	86	1,186	13.8	60	8
	Willie Anderson, L.A. Rams	44	1,146	26.0	78	5
	Ricky Sanders, Washington[2]	80	1,138	14.2	68	4
	Vance Johnson, Denver	76	1,095	14.4	69	7
	Richard Johnson, Detroit	70	1,091	15.6	75	8
	Eric Martin, New Orleans[2]	68	1,090	16.0	53	8
	John Taylor, San Francisco	60	1,077	18.0	95	10
	Mervyn Fernandez, L.A. Raiders	57	1,069	18.8	75	9
	Anthony Carter, Minnesota[2]	65	1,066	16.4	50	4
	Brian Blades, Seattle	77	1,063	13.8	60	5
	Mark Clayton, Miami[4]	64	1,011	15.8	78	9
1988	Henry Ellard, L.A. Rams	86	1,414	16.4	68	10
	Jerry Rice, San Francisco[3]	64	1,306	20.4	96	9
	Eddie Brown, Cincinnati	53	1,273	24.0	86	9
	Anthony Carter, Minnesota	72	1,225	17.0	67	6
	Ricky Sanders, Washington	73	1,148	15.7	55	12
	Drew Hill, Houston[3]	72	1,141	15.8	57	10

Year	Player					
	Mark Clayton, Miami[3]	86	1,129	13.1	45	14
	Roy Green, Phoenix[3]	68	1,097	16.1	52	7
	Eric Martin, New Orleans	85	1,083	12.7	40	7
	Al Toon, N.Y. Jets[2]	93	1,067	11.5	42	5
	Bruce Hill, Tampa Bay	58	1,040	17.9	42	9
	Lionel Manuel, N.Y. Giants	65	1,029	15.8	46	4
1987	J.T. Smith, St. Louis[2]	91	1,117	12.3	38	8
	Jerry Rice, San Francisco[2]	65	1,078	16.6	57	22
	Gary Clark, Washington[2]	56	1,066	19.0	84	7
	Carlos Carson, Kansas City[3]	55	1,044	19.0	81	7
1986	Jerry Rice, San Francisco	86	1,570	18.3	66	15
	Stanley Morgan, New England[3]	84	1,491	17.8	44	10
	Mark Duper, Miami[3]	67	1,313	19.6	85	11
	Gary Clark, Washington	74	1,265	17.1	55	7
	Al Toon, N.Y. Jets	85	1,176	13.8	62	8
	Todd Christensen, L.A. Raiders[3]	95	1,153	12.1	35	8
	Mark Clayton, Miami[2]	60	1,150	19.2	68	10
	*Bill Brooks, Indianapolis	65	1,131	17.4	84	8
	Drew Hill, Houston[2]	65	1,112	17.1	81	5
	Steve Largent, Seattle[8]	70	1,070	15.3	38	9
	Art Monk, Washington[3]	73	1,068	14.6	69	4
	*Ernest Givins, Houston	61	1,062	17.4	60	3
	Cris Collinsworth, Cincinnati[4]	62	1,024	16.5	46	10
	Wesley Walker, N.Y. Jets[2]	49	1,016	20.7	83	12
	J.T. Smith, St. Louis	80	1,014	12.7	45	6
	Mark Bavaro, N.Y. Giants	66	1,001	15.2	41	4
1985	Steve Largent, Seattle[7]	79	1,287	16.3	43	6
	Mike Quick, Philadelphia[3]	73	1,247	17.1	99	11
	Art Monk, Washington[2]	91	1,226	13.5	53	2
	Wes Chandler, San Diego[4]	67	1,199	17.9	75	10
	Drew Hill, Houston	64	1,169	18.3	57	9
	James Lofton, Green Bay[5]	69	1,153	16.7	56	4
	Louis Lipps, Pittsburgh	59	1,134	19.2	51	12
	Cris Collinsworth, Cincinnati[3]	65	1,125	17.3	71	5
	Tony Hill, Dallas[3]	74	1,113	15.0	53	7
	Lionel James, San Diego	86	1,027	11.9	67	6
	Roger Craig, San Francisco	92	1,016	11.0	73	6
1984	Roy Green, St. Louis[2]	78	1,555	19.9	83	12
	John Stallworth, Pittsburgh[3]	80	1,395	17.4	51	11
	Mark Clayton, Miami	73	1,389	19.0	65	18
	Art Monk, Washington	106	1,372	12.9	72	7
	James Lofton, Green Bay[4]	62	1,361	22.0	79	7
	Mark Duper, Miami[2]	71	1,306	18.4	80	8
	Steve Watson, Denver[3]	69	1,170	17.0	73	7
	Steve Largent, Seattle[6]	74	1,164	15.7	65	12
	Tim Smith, Houston[2]	69	1,141	16.5	75	4
	Stacey Bailey, Atlanta	67	1,138	17.0	61	6
	Carlos Carson, Kansas City[2]	57	1,078	18.9	57	4
	Mike Quick, Philadelphia[2]	61	1,052	17.2	90	9
	Todd Christensen, L.A. Raiders[2]	80	1,007	12.6	38	7
	Kevin House, Tampa Bay[2]	76	1,005	13.2	55	5
	Ozzie Newsome, Cleveland[2]	89	1,001	11.2	52	5
1983	Mike Quick, Philadelphia	69	1,409	20.4	83	13
	Carlos Carson, Kansas City	80	1,351	16.9	50	7
	James Lofton, Green Bay[3]	58	1,300	22.4	74	8
	Todd Christensen, L.A. Raiders	92	1,247	13.6	45	12
	Roy Green, St. Louis	78	1,227	15.7	71	14
	Charlie Brown, Washington	78	1,225	15.7	75	8
	Tim Smith, Houston	83	1,176	14.2	47	6
	Kellen Winslow, San Diego[3]	88	1,172	13.3	46	8
	Earnest Gray, N.Y. Giants	78	1,139	14.6	62	5
	Steve Watson, Denver[2]	59	1,133	19.2	78	5
	Cris Collinsworth, Cincinnati[2]	66	1,130	17.1	63	5
	Steve Largent, Seattle[5]	72	1,074	14.9	46	11
	Mark Duper, Miami	51	1,003	19.7	85	10
1982	Wes Chandler, San Diego[3]	49	1,032	21.1	66	9
1981	Alfred Jenkins, Atlanta[2]	70	1,358	19.4	67	13
	James Lofton, Green Bay[2]	71	1,294	18.2	75	8
	Steve Watson, Denver	60	1,244	20.7	95	13
	Frank Lewis, Buffalo[2]	70	1,244	17.8	33	4

Year	Player	Rec	Yards	Avg	Long	TD
	Steve Largent, Seattle[4]	75	1,224	16.3	57	9
	Charlie Joiner, San Diego[4]	70	1,188	17.0	57	7
	Kevin House, Tampa Bay	56	1,176	21.0	84	9
	Wes Chandler, N.O.-San Diego[2]	69	1,142	16.6	51	6
	Dwight Clark, San Francisco	85	1,105	13.0	78	4
	John Stallworth, Pittsburgh[2]	63	1,098	17.4	55	5
	Kellen Winslow, San Diego[2]	88	1,075	12.2	67	10
	Pat Tilley, St. Louis	66	1,040	15.8	75	3
	Stanley Morgan, New England[2]	44	1,029	23.4	76	6
	Harold Carmichael, Philadelphia[3]	61	1,028	16.9	85	6
	Freddie Scott, Detroit	53	1,022	19.3	48	5
	*Cris Collinsworth, Cincinnati	67	1,009	15.1	74	8
	Joe Senser, Minnesota	79	1,004	12.7	53	8
	Ozzie Newsome, Cleveland	69	1,002	14.5	62	6
	Sammy White, Minnesota	66	1,001	15.2	53	3
1980	John Jefferson, San Diego[3]	82	1,340	16.3	58	13
	Kellen Winslow, San Diego	89	1,290	14.5	65	9
	James Lofton, Green Bay	71	1,226	17.3	47	4
	Charlie Joiner, San Diego[3]	71	1,132	15.9	51	4
	Ahmad Rashad, Minnesota[2]	69	1,095	15.9	76	5
	Steve Largent, Seattle[3]	66	1,064	16.1	67	6
	Tony Hill, Dallas[2]	60	1,055	17.6	58	8
	Alfred Jenkins, Atlanta	57	1,026	18.0	57	6
1979	Steve Largent, Seattle[2]	66	1,237	18.7	55	9
	John Stallworth, Pittsburgh	70	1,183	16.9	65	8
	Ahmad Rashad, Minnesota	80	1,156	14.5	52	9
	John Jefferson, San Diego[2]	61	1,090	17.9	65	10
	Frank Lewis, Buffalo	54	1,082	20.0	55	2
	Wes Chandler, New Orleans	65	1,069	16.4	85	6
	Tony Hill, Dallas	60	1,062	17.7	75	10
	Drew Pearson, Dallas[2]	55	1,026	18.7	56	8
	Wallace Francis, Atlanta	74	1,013	13.7	42	8
	Harold Jackson, New England[3]	45	1,013	22.5	59	7
	Charlie Joiner, San Diego[2]	72	1,008	14.0	39	4
	Stanley Morgan, New England	44	1,002	22.8	63	12
1978	Wesley Walker, N.Y. Jets	48	1,169	24.4	77	8
	Steve Largent, Seattle	71	1,168	16.5	57	8
	Harold Carmichael, Philadelphia[2]	55	1,072	19.5	56	8
	*John Jefferson, San Diego	56	1,001	17.9	46	13
1976	Roger Carr, Baltimore	43	1,112	25.9	79	11
	Cliff Branch, Oakland[2]	46	1,111	24.2	88	12
	Charlie Joiner, San Diego	50	1,056	21.1	81	7
1975	Ken Burrough, Houston	53	1,063	20.1	77	8
1974	Cliff Branch, Oakland	60	1,092	18.2	67	13
	Drew Pearson, Dallas	62	1,087	17.5	50	2
1973	Harold Carmichael, Philadelphia	67	1,116	16.7	73	9
1972	Harold Jackson, Philadelphia[2]	62	1,048	16.9	77	4
	John Gilliam, Minnesota	47	1,035	22.0	66	7
1971	Otis Taylor, Kansas City[2]	57	1,110	19.5	82	7
1970	Gene Washington, San Francisco	53	1,100	20.8	79	12
	Marlin Briscoe, Buffalo	57	1,036	18.2	48	8
	Dick Gordon, Chicago	71	1,026	14.5	69	13
	Gary Garrison, San Diego[2]	44	1,006	22.9	67	12
1969	Warren Wells, Oakland[2]	47	1,260	26.8	80	14
	Harold Jackson, Philadelphia	65	1,116	17.2	65	9
	Roy Jefferson, Pittsburgh[2]	67	1,079	16.1	63	9
	Dan Abramowicz, New Orleans	73	1,015	13.9	49	7
	Lance Alworth, San Diego[7]	64	1,003	15.7	76	4
1968	Lance Alworth, San Diego[6]	68	1,312	19.3	80	10
	Don Maynard, N.Y. Jets[5]	57	1,297	22.8	87	10
	George Sauer, N.Y. Jets[3]	66	1,141	17.3	43	3
	Warren Wells, Oakland	53	1,137	21.5	94	11
	Gary Garrison, San Diego	52	1,103	21.2	84	10
	Roy Jefferson, Pittsburgh	58	1,074	18.5	62	11
	Paul Warfield, Cleveland	50	1,067	21.3	65	12
	Homer Jones, N.Y. Giants[3]	45	1,057	23.5	84	7
	Fred Biletnikoff, Oakland	61	1,037	17.0	82	6
	Lance Rentzel, Dallas	54	1,009	18.7	65	6
1967	Don Maynard, N.Y. Jets[4]	71	1,434	20.2	75	10
	Ben Hawkins, Philadelphia	59	1,265	21.4	87	10

	Homer Jones, N.Y. Giants[2]	49	1,209	24.7	70	13
	Jackie Smith, St. Louis	56	1,205	21.5	76	9
	George Sauer, N.Y. Jets[2]	75	1,189	15.9	61	6
	Lance Alworth, San Diego[5]	52	1,010	19.4	71	9
1966	Lance Alworth, San Diego[4]	73	1,383	18.9	78	13
	Otis Taylor, Kansas City	58	1,297	22.4	89	8
	Pat Studstill, Detroit	67	1,266	18.9	99	5
	Bob Hayes, Dallas[2]	64	1,232	19.3	95	13
	Charlie Frazier, Houston	57	1,129	19.8	79	12
	Charley Taylor, Washington	72	1,119	15.5	86	12
	George Sauer, N.Y. Jets	63	1,081	17.2	77	5
	Homer Jones, N.Y. Giants	48	1,044	21.8	98	8
	Art Powell, Oakland[5]	53	1,026	19.4	46	11
1965	Lance Alworth, San Diego[3]	69	1,602	23.2	85	14
	Dave Parks, San Francisco	80	1,344	16.8	53	12
	Don Maynard, N.Y. Jets[3]	68	1,218	17.9	56	14
	Pete Retzlaff, Philadelphia	66	1,190	18.0	78	10
	Lionel Taylor, Denver[4]	85	1,131	13.3	63	6
	Tommy McDonald, Los Angeles[3]	67	1,036	15.5	51	9
	*Bob Hayes, Dallas	46	1,003	21.8	82	12
1964	Charley Hennigan, Houston[3]	101	1,546	15.3	53	8
	Art Powell, Oakland[4]	76	1,361	17.9	77	11
	Lance Alworth, San Diego[2]	61	1,235	20.2	82	13
	Johnny Morris, Chicago	93	1,200	12.9	63	10
	Elbert Dubenion, Buffalo	42	1,139	27.1	72	10
	Terry Barr, Detroit[2]	57	1,030	18.1	58	9
1963	Bobby Mitchell, Washington[2]	69	1,436	20.8	99	7
	Art Powell, Oakland[3]	73	1,304	17.9	85	16
	Buddy Dial, Pittsburgh[2]	60	1,295	21.6	83	9
	Lance Alworth, San Diego	61	1,205	19.8	85	11
	Del Shofner, N.Y. Giants[4]	64	1,181	18.5	70	9
	Lionel Taylor, Denver[3]	78	1,101	14.1	72	10
	Terry Barr, Detroit	66	1,086	16.5	75	13
	Charley Hennigan, Houston[2]	61	1,051	17.2	83	10
	Sonny Randle, St. Louis[2]	51	1,014	19.9	68	12
	Bake Turner, N.Y. Jets	71	1,009	14.2	53	6
1962	Bobby Mitchell, Washington	72	1,384	19.2	81	11
	Sonny Randle, St. Louis	63	1,158	18.4	86	7
	Tommy McDonald, Philadelphia[2]	58	1,146	19.8	60	10
	Del Shofner, N.Y. Giants[3]	53	1,133	21.4	69	12
	Art Powell, N.Y. Titans[2]	64	1,130	17.7	80	8
	Frank Clarke, Dall. Cowboys	47	1,043	22.2	66	14
	Don Maynard, N.Y. Titans[2]	56	1,041	18.6	86	8
1961	Charley Hennigan, Houston	82	1,746	21.3	80	12
	Lionel Taylor, Denver[2]	100	1,176	11.8	52	4
	Bill Groman, Houston[2]	50	1,175	23.5	80	17
	Tommy McDonald, Philadelphia	64	1,144	17.9	66	13
	Del Shofner, N.Y. Giants[2]	68	1,125	16.5	46	11
	Jim Phillips, Los Angeles	78	1,092	14.0	69	5
	*Mike Ditka, Chicago	56	1,076	19.2	76	12
	Dave Kocourek, San Diego	55	1,055	19.2	76	4
	Buddy Dial, Pittsburgh	53	1,047	19.8	88	12
	R.C. Owens, San Francisco	55	1,032	18.8	54	5
1960	*Bill Groman, Houston	72	1,473	20.5	92	12
	Raymond Berry, Baltimore	74	1,298	17.5	70	10
	Don Maynard, N.Y. Titans	72	1,265	17.6	65	6
	Lionel Taylor, Denver	92	1,235	13.4	80	12
	Art Powell, N.Y. Titans	69	1,167	16.9	76	14
1958	Del Shofner, Los Angeles	51	1,097	21.5	92	8
1956	Bill Howton, Green Bay[2]	55	1,188	21.6	66	12
	Harlon Hill, Chi. Bears[2]	47	1,128	24.0	79	11
1954	Bob Boyd, Los Angeles	53	1,212	22.9	80	6
	*Harlon Hill, Chi. Bears	45	1,124	25.0	76	12
1953	Pete Pihos, Philadelphia	63	1,049	16.7	59	10
1952	*Bill Howton, Green Bay	53	1,231	23.2	90	13
1951	Elroy (Crazylegs) Hirsch, Los Angeles	66	1,495	22.7	91	17
1950	Tom Fears, Los Angeles[2]	84	1,116	13.3	53	7
	Cloyce Box, Detroit	50	1,009	20.2	82	11
1949	Bob Mann, Detroit	66	1,014	15.4	64	4
	Tom Fears, Los Angeles	77	1,013	13.2	51	9

1945	Jim Benton, Cleveland..45	1,067	23.7	84	8
1942	Don Hutson, Green Bay..74	1,211	16.4	73	17

*First season of professional football.

250 YARDS PASS RECEIVING IN A GAME

Date	Player, Team, Opponent	No.	Yards	TD
Dec. 17, 2000	Terrell Owens, San Francisco vs. Chicago............................20		283	1
Sept. 10, 2000	Jimmy Smith, Jacksonville vs. Baltimore 15		291	3
Dec. 12, 1999	Qadry Ismail, Baltimore vs. Pittsburgh 6		258	3
Dec. 18, 1995	Jerry Rice, San Francisco vs. Minnesota 14		289	3
Dec. 11, 1989	John Taylor, San Francisco vs. L.A. Rams.........................11		286	2
Nov. 26, 1989	Willie Anderson, L.A. Rams vs. New Orleans (OT)..............15		336	1
Oct. 18, 1987	Steve Largent, Seattle vs. Detroit 15		261	3
Oct. 4, 1987	Anthony Allen, Washington vs. St. Louis.................................7		255	3
Dec. 22, 1985	Stephone Paige, Kansas City vs. San Diego 8		309	2
Dec. 20, 1982	Wes Chandler, San Diego vs. Cincinnati...............................10		260	1
Sept. 23, 1979	*Jerry Butler, Buffalo vs. N.Y. Jets....................................10		255	4
Nov. 4, 1962	Sonny Randle, St. Louis vs. N.Y. Giants..............................16		256	1
Oct. 28, 1962	Del Shofner, N.Y. Giants vs. Washington.............................11		269	1
Oct. 13, 1961	Charley Hennigan, Houston vs. Boston 13		272	1
Oct. 21, 1956	Billy Howton, Green Bay vs. Los Angeles...............................7		257	2
Dec. 3, 1950	Cloyce Box, Detroit vs. Baltimore 12		302	4
Nov. 22, 1945	Jim Benton, Cleveland vs. Detroit..10		303	1

*First season of professional football.

2,000 COMBINED NET YARDS GAINED IN A SEASON

Year	Player, Team	Rushing Att.-Yds.	Pass Rec.	Punt Ret.	Kickoff Ret.	Fum. Ret.	Total Yds.
2001	Priest Holmes, Kansas City.........................327-1,555	62-614	0-0	0-0	0-0	389-2,169
	Marshall Faulk, St. Louis.............................260-1,382	83-765	0-0	0-0	2-0	345-2,147
	Derrick Mason, Tennessee..................................0-0	73-1,128	20-128	34-748	1-0	128-2,004
2000	Derrick Mason, Tennessee...................................1-1	63-895	51-662	42-1,132	1-0	158-2,690
	MarTay Jenkins, Arizona ....1-(-4)	17-219	1-1	82-2,186	0-0	101-2,402
	Edgerrin James, Indianapolis 387-1,709	63-594	0-0	0-0	0-0	450-2,303
	Marshall Faulk, St. Louis...............................253-1,359	81-830	0-0	1-18	2-0	337-2,207
	Tiki Barber, N.Y. Giants................................213-1,006	70-719	39-332	1-28	5-0	328-2,085
1999	Marshall Faulk, St. Louis...............................253-1,381	87-1,048	0-0	0-0	0-0	340-2,429
	*Edgerrin James, Indianapolis 369-1,553	62-586	0-0	0-0	2-0	433-2,139
	*Terrence Wilkins, Indianapolis...........................1-2	42-565	41-388	51-1,134	1-0	136-2,089
	Glyn Milburn, Chicago 16-102	20-151	30-346	61-1,426	2-0	129-2,025
1998	Brian Mitchell, Washington 39-208	44-306	44-506	59-1,337	0-0	186-2,357
	Marshall Faulk, Indianapolis 324-1,319	86-908	0-0	0-0	2-13	412-2,240
	Terrell Davis, Denver....................................392-2,008	25-217	0-0	0-0	1-0	418-2,225
	Jamal Anderson, Atlanta................................410-1,846	27-319	0-0	0-0	1-0	438-2,165
	Garrison Hearst, San Francisco 310-1,570	39-535	0-0	0-0	1-0	350-2,105
1997	Barry Sanders, Detroit 335-2,053	33-305	0-0	0-0	1-0	369-2,358
	Kevin Williams, Arizona ....1-(-2)	20-273	40-462	59-1,458	1-0	121-2,191
	Brian Mitchell, Wash. 23-107	36-438	38-442	47-1,094	0-0	144-2,081
	Terrell Davis, Denver....................................369-1,750	42-287	0-0	0-0	2-(-7)	413-2,030
	Jermaine Lewis, Balt. 3-35	42-648	28-437	41-905	2-0	116-2,025
1995	Brian Mitchell, Wash. 46-301	38-324	25-315	55-1,408	0-0	164-2,348
	Emmitt Smith, Dallas 377-1,773	62-375	0-0	0-0	0-0	439-2,148
	Glyn Milburn, Denver..49-266	22-191	31-354	47-1,269	0-0	149-2,080
	Ernie Mills, Pittsburgh...5-39	39-679	0-0	54-1,306	0-0	98-2,024
1994	Brian Mitchell, Wash. 78-311	26-236	32-452	58-1,478	0-0	194-2,477
	Barry Sanders, Detroit 331-1,883	44-283	0-0	0-0	0-0	375-2,166
1992	Thurman Thomas, Buffalo 312-1,487	58-626	0-0	0-0	1-0	371-2,113
	Emmitt Smith, Dallas 373-1,713	59-335	0-0	0-0	1-0	433-2,048
	Barry Foster, Pittsburgh 390-1,690	36-344	0-0	0-0	2-(-20)	428-2,014
1991	Thurman Thomas, Buffalo 288-1,407	62-631	0-0	0-0	0-0	350-2,038
1990	Herschel Walker, Minnesota...........................184-770	35-315	0-0	44-966	4-0	267-2,051
1988	*Tim Brown, L.A. Raiders...................................14-50	43-725	49-444	41-1,098	7-0	154-2,317
	Roger Craig, San Fran. 310-1,502	76-534	0-0	2-32	2-0	390-2,068
	Eric Dickerson, Indianapolis 388-1,659	36-377	0-0	0-0	1-0	425-2,036
	Herschel Walker, Dallas 361-1,514	53-505	0-0	0-0	3-0	417-2,019
1986	Eric Dickerson, L.A. Rams..............................404-1,821	26-205	0-0	0-0	2-0	432-2,026
	Gary Anderson, San Diego 127-442	80-871	25-227	24-482	2-0	258-2,022
1985	Lionel James, San Diego 105-516	86-1,027	25-213	36-779	1-0	253-2,535
	Marcus Allen, L.A. Raiders 380-1,759	67-555	0-0	0-0	2-(-6)	449-2,308
	Roger Craig, San Fran. 214-1,050	92-1,016	0-0	0-0	0-0	306-2,066

Year	Player, Team						
	Walter Payton, Chicago	324-1,551	49-483	0-0	0-0	1-0	374-2,034
1984	Eric Dickerson, L.A. Rams	379-2,105	21-139	0-0	0-0	4-15	404-2,259
	James Wilder, Tampa Bay	407-1,544	85-685	0-0	0-0	4-0	496-2,229
	Walter Payton, Chicago	381-1,684	45-368	0-0	0-0	1-0	427-2,052
1983	*Eric Dickerson, L.A. Rams	390-1,808	51-404	0-0	0-0	1-0	442-2,212
	William Andrews, Atlanta	331-1,567	59-609	0-0	0-0	2-0	392-2,176
	Walter Payton, Chicago	314-1,421	53-607	0-0	0-0	2-0	369-2,028
1981	*James Brooks, San Diego	109-525	46-329	22-290	40-949	2-0	219-2,093
	William Andrews, Atlanta	289-1,301	81-735	0-0	0-0	0-0	370-2,036
1980	Bruce Harper, N.Y. Jets	45-126	50-634	28-242	49-1,070	3-0	175-2,072
1979	Wilbert Montgomery, Phil.	338-1,512	41-494	0-0	1-6	2-0	382-2,012
1978	Bruce Harper, N.Y. Jets	58-303	13-196	30-378	55-1,280	1-0	157-2,157
1977	Walter Payton, Chicago	339-1,852	27-269	0-0	2-95	5-0	373-2,216
	Terry Metcalf, St. Louis	149-739	34-403	14-108	32-772	1-0	230-2,022
1975	Terry Metcalf, St. Louis	165-816	43-378	23-285	35-960	2-23	268-2,462
	O.J. Simpson, Buffalo	329-1,817	28-426	0-0	0-0	1-0	358-2,243
1974	Mack Herron, New England	231-824	38-474	35-517	28-629	3-0	335-2,444
	Otis Armstrong, Denver	263-1,407	38-405	0-0	16-386	1-0	318-2,198
	Terry Metcalf, St. Louis	152-718	50-377	26-340	20-623	7-0	255-2,058
1973	O.J. Simpson, Buffalo	332-2,003	6-70	0-0	0-0	0-0	338-2,073
1966	Gale Sayers, Chicago	229-1,231	34-447	6-44	23-718	3-0	295-2,440
	Leroy Kelly, Cleveland	209-1,141	32-366	13-104	19-403	0-0	273-2,014
1965	*Gale Sayers, Chicago	166-867	29-507	16-238	21-660	4-0	236-2,272
1963	Timmy Brown, Philadelphia	192-841	36-487	16-152	33-945	2-3	279-2,428
	Jim Brown, Cleveland	291-1,863	24-268	0-0	0-0	0-0	315-2,131
1962	Timmy Brown, Philadelphia	137-545	52-849	6-81	30-831	4-0	229-2,306
	Dick Christy, N.Y. Titans	114-535	62-538	15-250	38-824	2-0	231-2,147
1961	Billy Cannon, Houston	200-948	43-586	9-70	18-439	2-0	272-2,043
1960	*Abner Haynes, Dall. Texans	156-875	55-576	14-215	19-434	4-0	248-2,100

*First season of professional football.

300 COMBINED NET YARDS GAINED IN A GAME

Date	Player, Team, Opponent	No.	Yards	TD
Dec. 24, 1999	Jason Tucker, Dallas vs. New Orleans	13	331	1
Dec. 7, 1997	Jermaine Lewis, Baltimore vs. Seattle	10	308	3
Dec. 25, 1995	Kevin Williams, Dallas vs. Arizona	16	307	2
Dec. 10, 1995	Glyn Milburn, Denver vs. Seattle	33	404	0
Oct. 23, 1994	Tyrone Hughes, New Orleans vs. L.A. Rams	11	347	2
Dec. 11, 1989	John Taylor, San Francisco vs. L.A. Rams	14	321	2
Nov. 26, 1989	Willie Anderson, L.A. Rams vs. New Orleans (OT)	15	336	1
Nov. 28, 1988	*Tim Brown, L.A. Raiders vs. Seattle	12	308	1
Dec. 22, 1985	Stephone Paige, Kansas City vs. San Diego	8	309	2
Nov. 10, 1985	Lionel James, San Diego vs. L.A. Raiders (OT)	23	345	0
Sept. 22, 1985	Lionel James, San Diego vs. Cincinnati	20	316	2
Dec. 21, 1975	*Walter Payton, Chicago vs. New Orleans	32	300	1
Nov. 23, 1975	Greg Pruitt, Cleveland vs. Cincinnati	28	304	2
Nov. 1, 1970	Eugene (Mercury) Morris, Miami vs. Baltimore	17	302	0
Oct. 4, 1970	O.J. Simpson, Buffalo vs. N.Y. Jets	26	303	2
Dec. 6, 1969	Jerry LeVias, Houston vs. N.Y. Jets	18	329	1
Nov. 2, 1969	Travis Williams, Green Bay vs. Pittsburgh	11	314	3
Dec. 18, 1966	Gale Sayers, Chicago vs. Minnesota	20	339	2
Dec. 12, 1965	*Gale Sayers, Chicago vs. San Francisco	17	336	6
Nov. 17, 1963	Gary Ballman, Pittsburgh vs. Washington	12	320	2
Dec. 16, 1962	Timmy Brown, Philadelphia vs. St. Louis	19	341	2
Dec. 10, 1961	Billy Cannon, Houston vs. N.Y. Titans	32	373	5
Nov. 19, 1961	Jim Brown, Cleveland vs. Philadelphia	38	313	4
Dec. 3, 1950	Cloyce Box, Detroit vs. Baltimore	13	302	4
Oct. 29, 1950	Wally Triplett, Detroit vs. Los Angeles	11	331	1
Nov. 22, 1945	Jim Benton, Cleveland vs. Detroit	10	303	1

*First season of professional football.

2,000 SCRIMMAGE YARDS GAINED IN A SEASON

Year	Player, Team	Att.	Rushing Yards	Receptions	Receiving Yards	Scrimm. Yards
2001	Priest Holmes, Kansas City	327	1,555	62	614	2,169
	Marshall Faulk, St. Louis	260	1,382	83	765	2,147
2000	Edgerrin James, Indianapolis	387	1,709	63	594	2,303
	Marshall Faulk, St. Louis	253	1,359	81	830	2,189
1999	Marshall Faulk, St. Louis	253	1,381	87	1,048	2,429
	*Edgerrin James, Indianapolis	369	1,553	62	586	2,139

1998	Marshall Faulk, Indianapolis	324	1,319	86	908	2,227
	Terrell Davis, Denver	392	2,008	25	217	2,225
	Jamal Anderson, Atlanta	410	1,846	27	319	2,165
	Garrison Hearst, San Francisco	310	1,570	39	535	2,105
1997	Barry Sanders, Detroit	335	2,053	33	305	2,358
	Terrell Davis, Denver	369	1,750	42	287	2,037
1995	Emmitt Smith, Dallas	377	1,773	62	375	2,148
1994	Barry Sanders, Detroit	331	1,883	44	283	2,166
1992	Thurman Thomas, Buffalo	312	1,487	58	626	2,113
	Emmitt Smith, Dallas	373	1,713	59	335	2,048
	Barry Foster, Pittsburgh	390	1,690	36	344	2,034
1991	Thurman Thomas, Buffalo	288	1,407	62	631	2,038
1988	Roger Craig, San Francisco	310	1,502	76	534	2,036
	Eric Dickerson, Indianapolis	388	1,659	36	377	2,036
	Herschel Walker, Dallas	361	1,514	53	505	2,019
1986	Eric Dickerson, L.A. Rams	404	1,821	26	205	2,026
1985	Marcus Allen, L.A. Raiders	380	1,759	67	555	2,314
	Roger Craig, San Francisco	214	1,050	92	1,016	2,066
	Walter Payton, Chicago	324	1,551	49	483	2,034
1984	Eric Dickerson, L. A. Rams	379	2,105	21	139	2,244
	James Wilder, Tampa Bay	407	1,544	85	685	2,229
	Walter Payton, Chicago	381	1,684	45	368	2,052
1983	*Eric Dickerson, L.A. Rams	390	1,808	51	404	2,212
	William Andrews, Atlanta	331	1,567	59	609	2,176
	Walter Payton, Chicago	314	1,421	53	607	2,028
1981	William Andrews, Atlanta	289	1,301	81	735	2,036
1979	Wilbert Montgomery, Philadelphia	338	1,512	41	494	2,006
1977	Walter Payton, Chicago	339	1,852	27	269	2,121
1975	O.J. Simpson, Buffalo	329	1,817	28	426	2,243
1973	O.J. Simpson, Buffalo	332	2,003	6	70	2,073
1963	Jim Brown, Cleveland	91	1,863	24	268	2,131

*First season of professional football.

300 COMBINED SCRIMMAGE YARDS GAINED IN A GAME

Date	Player, Team, Opponent	Att.	Yards	TD
Nov. 26, 1989	Flipper Anderson, L.A. Rams vs. New Orleans (OT)	15	336	1
Dec. 22, 1985	Stephone Paige, Kansas City vs. San Diego	8	309	2
Dec. 10, 1961	Billy Cannon, Houston vs. N.Y. Titans	30	330	5
Dec. 3, 1950	Cloyce Box, Detroit vs. Baltimore	12	302	4
Nov. 22, 1945	Jim Benton, Cleveland vs. Detroit	10	303	1

TOP 20 SCORERS

Player	Years	TD	FG	PAT	TP
Gary Anderson	20	0	476	705	2,133
Morten Andersen	20	0	464	644	2,036
George Blanda	26	9	335	942	2,002
Norm Johnson	18	0	366	638	1,736
Nick Lowery	18	0	383	562	1,711
Jan Stenerud	19	0	373	580	1,699
Eddie Murray	19	0	352	538	1,594
Al Del Greco	17	0	347	543	1,584
Pat Leahy	18	0	304	558	1,470
Jim Turner	16	1	304	521	1,439
Matt Bahr	17	0	300	522	1,422
Mark Moseley	16	0	300	482	1,382
Jim Bakken	17	0	282	534	1,380
Fred Cox	15	0	282	519	1,365
Lou Groza	17	1	234	641	1,349
Jim Breech	14	0	243	517	1,246
Pete Stoyanovich	12	0	272	420	1,236
Chris Bahr	14	0	241	490	1,213
Kevin Butler	13	0	265	413	1,208
Steve Christie	12	0	281	364	1,207

TOP 20 TOUCHDOWN SCORERS

Player	Years	Rush	Rec.	Total Returns	TD
Jerry Rice	17	10	185	1	196
Emmitt Smith	12	148	11	0	159
Marcus Allen	16	123	21	1	145

Cris Carter	15	0	129	1	130
Jim Brown	9	106	20	0	126
Walter Payton	13	110	15	0	125
John Riggins	14	104	12	0	116
Lenny Moore	12	63	48	2	113
Marshall Faulk	8	79	31	0	110
Barry Sanders	10	99	10	0	109
Don Hutson	11	3	99	3	105
Steve Largent	14	1	100	0	101
Tim Brown	14	1	95	4	100
Franco Harris	13	91	9	0	100
Eric Dickerson	11	90	6	0	96
Jim Taylor	10	83	10	0	93
Tony Dorsett	12	77	13	1	91
Bobby Mitchell	11	18	65	8	91
Ricky Watters	10	78	13	0	91
Leroy Kelly	10	74	13	3	90
Charley Taylor	13	11	79	0	90

TOP 20 RUSHERS

Player	Years	Att.	Yards	Avg.	Long	TD
Walter Payton	13	3,838	16,726	4.4	76	110
Emmitt Smith	12	3,798	16,187	4.3	75	148
Barry Sanders	10	3,062	15,269	5.0	85	99
Eric Dickerson	11	2,996	13,259	4.4	85	90
Tony Dorsett	12	2,936	12,739	4.3	99	77
Jim Brown	9	2,359	12,312	5.2	80	106
Marcus Allen	16	3,022	12,243	4.1	61	123
Franco Harris	13	2,949	12,120	4.1	75	91
Thurman Thomas	13	2,877	12,074	4.2	80	65
John Riggins	14	2,916	11,352	3.9	66	104
O.J. Simpson	11	2,404	11,236	4.7	94	61
Jerome Bettis	9	2,686	10,876	4.0	71	53
Ricky Watters	10	2,622	10,643	4.1	57	78
Ottis Anderson	14	2,562	10,273	4.0	76	81
Marshall Faulk	8	2,155	9,442	4.4	71	79
Earl Campbell	8	2,187	9,407	4.3	81	74
Curtis Martin	7	2,343	9,267	4.0	70	64
Terry Allen	10	2,152	8,614	4.0	55	73
Jim Taylor	10	1,941	8,597	4.4	84	83
Joe Perry	14	1,737	8,378	4.8	78	53

TOP 20 COMBINED YARDS GAINED

	Years	Tot.	Rush.	Rec.	Int. Ret.	Punt Ret.	Kickoff Ret.	Fumble Ret.
Walter Payton	13	21,803	16,726	4,538	0	0	539	0
Jerry Rice	17	21,017	625	20,386	0	0	6	0
Brian Mitchell	12	20,263	1,947	2,298	0	4,278	11,735	5
Emmitt Smith	12	19,110	16,187	2,923	0	0	0	0
Barry Sanders	10	18,308	15,269	2,921	0	0	118	0
Herschel Walker	12	18,168	8,225	4,859	0	0	5,084	0
Tim Brown	14	17,863	171	13,237	0	3,217	1,235	3
Marcus Allen	16	17,648	12,243	5,411	0	0	0	-6
Eric Metcalf	12	17,183	2,385	5,572	0	3,454	5,772	0
Thurman Thomas	13	16,532	12,074	4,458	0	0	0	0
Tony Dorsett	12	16,326	12,739	3,554	0	0	0	33
Henry Ellard	16	15,718	50	13,777	0	1,527	364	0
Irving Fryar	17	15,594	242	12,785	0	2,055	505	7
Jim Brown	9	15,459	12,312	2,499	0	0	648	0
Eric Dickerson	11	15,411	13,259	2,137	0	0	0	15
Marshall Faulk	8	14,920	9,442	5,447	0	0	18	13
Glyn Milburn	9	14,911	817	1,322	0	2,984	9,788	0
James Brooks	12	14,910	7,962	3,621	0	565	2,762	0
Ricky Watters	10	14,891	10,643	4,248	0	0	0	-18
Franco Harris	13	14,622	12,120	2,287	0	0	233	0

TOP 20 YARDS FROM SCRIMMAGE

	Years	Scrimmage Yards	Rushing Yards	Receiving Yards
Walter Payton	13	21,264	16,726	4,538
Jerry Rice	17	21,011	625	20,386

Emmitt Smith	12	19,110	16,187	2,923
Barry Sanders	10	18,190	15,269	2,921
Marcus Allen	16	17,654	12,243	5,411
Thurman Thomas	13	16,532	12,074	4,458
Tony Dorsett	12	16,293	12,739	3,554
Eric Dickerson	11	15,396	13,259	2,137
Ricky Watters	10	14,891	10,643	4,248
Marshall Faulk	8	14,889	9,442	5,447
Jim Brown	9	14,811	12,312	2,499
Franco Harris	13	14,407	12,120	2,287
James Lofton	16	14,250	246	14,004
Cris Carter	15	13,874	41	13,833
Henry Ellard	16	13,827	50	13,777
Andre Reed	16	13,698	500	13,198
John Riggins	14	13,442	11,352	2,090
Tim Brown	14	13,408	171	13,237
O.J. Simpson	11	13,378	11,236	2,142
Ottis Anderson	14	13,335	10,273	3,062

TOP 20 PASSERS

Player	Years	Att.	Comp.	Pct. Comp.	Yards	Avg. Gain	TD	Pct. TD	Int.	Pct. Int.	Rating
Steve Young	15	4,149	2,667	64.3	33,124	7.98	232	5.6	107	2.6	96.8
Joe Montana	15	5,391	3,409	63.2	40,551	7.52	273	5.1	139	2.6	92.3
Brett Favre	11	5,442	3,311	60.8	38,627	7.10	287	5.3	172	3.2	86.8
Dan Marino	17	8,358	4,967	59.4	61,361	7.34	420	5.0	252	3.0	86.4
Peyton Manning	4	2,226	1,357	61.0	16,418	7.38	111	5.0	81	3.6	85.1
Mark Brunell	8	3,145	1,897	60.3	22,521	7.16	125	4.0	79	2.5	85.0
Jim Kelly	11	4,779	2,874	60.1	35,467	7.42	237	5.0	175	3.7	84.4
Roger Staubach	11	2,958	1,685	57.0	22,700	7.67	153	5.2	109	3.7	83.4
Brad Johnson	8	2,380	1,466	61.6	16,379	6.88	92	3.9	68	2.9	83.1
Rich Gannon	13	3,295	1,949	59.2	22,256	6.75	145	4.4	88	2.7	83.1
Neil Lomax	8	3,153	1,817	57.6	22,771	7.22	136	4.3	90	2.9	82.7
Sonny Jurgensen	18	4,262	2,433	57.1	32,224	7.56	255	6.0	189	4.4	82.6
Len Dawson	19	3,741	2,136	57.1	28,711	7.67	239	6.4	183	4.9	82.6
Ken Anderson	16	4,475	2,654	59.3	32,838	7.34	197	4.4	160	3.6	81.9
Bernie Kosar	12	3,365	1,994	59.3	23,301	6.92	124	3.7	87	2.6	81.8
Danny White	13	2,950	1,761	59.7	21,959	7.44	155	5.3	132	4.5	81.7
Neil O'Donnell	12	3,197	1,844	57.7	21,434	6.70	118	3.7	67	2.1	81.7
Troy Aikman	12	4,715	2,898	61.5	32,942	6.99	165	3.5	141	3.0	81.6
Dave Krieg	19	5,311	3,105	58.5	38,147	7.18	261	4.9	199	3.7	81.5
Randall Cunningham	16	4,289	2,429	56.6	29,979	6.99	207	4.8	134	3.1	81.5

1,500 or more attempts. The passing ratings are based on performance standards established for completion percentage, interception percentage, touchdown percentage, and average gain. Please consult page 15 for more information.

TOP 20 LEADERS IN PASSES COMPLETED

Dan Marino	4,967
John Elway	4,123
Warren Moon	3,988
Fran Tarkenton	3,686
Joe Montana	3,409
Brett Favre	3,311
Dan Fouts	3,297
Vinny Testaverde	3,157
Dave Krieg	3,105
Boomer Esiason	2,969
Troy Aikman	2,898
Steve DeBerg	2,874
Jim Kelly	2,874
Jim Everett	2,841
Johnny Unitas	2,830
Steve Young	2,667
Ken Anderson	2,654
Jim Hart	2,593
Phil Simms	2,576
Drew Bledsoe	2,544

TOP 20 LEADERS IN PASSING YARDS

Dan Marino	61,361
John Elway	51,475
Warren Moon	49,325
Fran Tarkenton	47,003
Dan Fouts	43,040
Joe Montana	40,551
Johnny Unitas	40,239
Vinny Testaverde	39,059
Brett Favre	38,627
Dave Krieg	38,147
Boomer Esiason	37,920
Jim Kelly	35,467
Jim Everett	34,837
Jim Hart	34,665
Steve DeBerg	34,241
John Hadl	33,503
Phil Simms	33,462
Steve Young	33,124
Troy Aikman	32,942
Ken Anderson	32,838

TOP 20 LEADERS IN TOUCHDOWN PASSES

Dan Marino	420
Fran Tarkenton	342
John Elway	300
Warren Moon	291
Johnny Unitas	290
Brett Favre	287
Joe Montana	273
Dave Krieg	261
Sonny Jurgensen	255
Dan Fouts	254
Boomer Esiason	247
John Hadl	244
Vinny Testaverde	241
Len Dawson	239
Jim Kelly	237
George Blanda	236
Steve Young	232
John Brodie	214
Terry Bradshaw	212
Y.A. Tittle	212

TOP 20 LEADERS IN RECEPTION YARDS

Jerry Rice	20,386
James Lofton	14,004
Cris Carter	13,833
Henry Ellard	13,777
Tim Brown	13,237
Andre Reed	13,198
Steve Largent	13,089
Irving Fryar	12,785
Art Monk	12,721
Charlie Joiner	12,146
Michael Irvin	11,904
Don Maynard	11,834
Gary Clark	10,856
Stanley Morgan	10,716
Harold Jackson	10,372
Lance Alworth	10,266
Andre Rison	10,205
Drew Hill	9,831
Rob Moore	9,368
Raymond Berry	9,275

TOP 20 PASS RECEIVERS

Player	Years	No.	Yards	Avg.	Long	TD
Jerry Rice	17	1,364	20,386	14.9	96	185
Cris Carter	15	1,093	13,833	12.7	80	129
Andre Reed	16	951	13,198	13.9	83	87
Art Monk	16	940	12,721	13.5	79	68
Tim Brown	14	937	13,237	14.1	80	95
Irving Fryar	17	851	12,785	15.0	80	84
Steve Largent	14	819	13,089	16.0	74	100
Henry Ellard	16	814	13,777	16.9	81	65
Larry Centers	12	765	6,303	8.2	54	27
James Lofton	16	764	14,004	18.3	80	75
Michael Irvin	12	750	11,904	15.9	87	65
Charlie Joiner	18	750	12,146	16.2	87	65
Andre Rison	12	743	10,205	13.7	80	84
Gary Clark	11	699	10,856	15.5	84	65
Shannon Sharpe	12	692	8,604	12.4	68	51
Herman Moore	11	670	9,174	13.7	93	62
Terance Mathis	12	666	8,591	12.9	81	61
Ozzie Newsome	13	662	7,980	12.1	74	47
Charley Taylor	13	649	9,110	14.0	88	79
Drew Hill	14	634	9,831	15.5	81	60

TOP 20 INTERCEPTORS

Player	Years	No.	Yards	Avg.	Long	TD
Paul Krause	16	81	1,185	14.6	81	3
Emlen Tunnell	14	79	1,282	16.2	55	4
Dick (Night Train) Lane	14	68	1,207	17.8	80	5
Ken Riley	15	65	596	9.2	66	5
Ronnie Lott	14	63	730	11.6	83	5
Dick LeBeau	14	62	762	12.3	70	3
Dave Brown	15	62	698	11.3	90	5
Rod Woodson	15	61	1,240	20.3	66	10
Emmitt Thomas	13	58	937	16.2	73	5
Bobby Boyd	9	57	994	17.4	74	4
Eugene Robinson	16	57	762	13.4	49	1
Johnny Robinson	12	57	741	13.0	57	1
Mel Blount	14	57	736	12.9	52	2
Everson Walls	13	57	504	8.8	40	1
Lem Barney	11	56	1,077	19.2	71	7
Pat Fischer	17	56	941	16.8	69	4
Eric Allen	14	54	826	15.3	94	8
Darrell Green	19	54	621	11.5	83	6
Willie Brown	16	54	472	8.7	45	2
Bobby Dillon	8	52	976	18.8	61	5
Jack Butler	9	52	827	15.9	52	4
Larry Wilson	13	52	800	15.4	96	5
Jimmy Patton	12	52	712	13.7	51	2
Mel Renfro	14	52	626	12.0	90	3

TOP 20 PUNTERS

Player	Years	No.	Yards	Avg.	Long	Blk.
Sammy Baugh	16	338	15,245	45.1	85	9
Tommy Davis	11	511	22,833	44.7	82	2
Darren Bennett	7	602	26,800	44.5	66	1
Yale Lary	11	503	22,279	44.3	74	4
Tom Rouen	9	612	26,907	44.0	76	5
Bob Scarpitto	8	283	12,408	43.8	87	4
Horace Gillom	7	385	16,872	43.8	80	5
Jerry Norton	11	358	15,671	43.8	78	2
Dave Lewis	4	285	12,447	43.7	63	0
Todd Sauerbrun	7	503	21,924	43.6	73	1
Greg Montgomery	9	524	22,831	43.6	77	8
Don Chandler	12	660	28,678	43.5	90	4
Rick Tuten	11	741	32,190	43.4	73	2
Sean Landeta	17	1,216	52,737	43.4	74	6
Rohn Stark	16	1,141	49,471	43.4	72	7
Tom Tupa	13	597	25,872	43.3	73	1
Josh Miller	6	433	18,759	43.3	75	2
Reggie Roby	16	992	42,951	43.3	77	5
Mitch Berger	7	411	17,746	43.2	75	2
Chris Gardocki	11	825	35,560	43.1	72	0

250 or more punts.

TOP 20 PUNT RETURNERS

Player	Years	No.	Yards	Avg.	Long	TD
George McAfee	8	112	1,431	12.8	74	2
Jack Christiansen	8	85	1,084	12.8	89	8
Claude Gibson	5	110	1,381	12.6	85	3
Darrien Gordon	8	279	3,421	12.3	94	6
Bill Dudley	9	124	1,515	12.2	96	3
Rick Upchurch	9	248	3,008	12.1	92	8
Desmond Howard	10	235	2,847	12.1	95	8
Jermaine Lewis	6	231	2,730	11.8	89	6
Billy Johnson	14	282	3,317	11.8	87	6
Mack Herron	3	84	982	11.7	66	0
Billy Thompson	13	157	1,814	11.6	60	0
Troy Brown	9	172	1,973	11.5	85	3
Az-Zahir Hakim	4	112	1,280	11.4	86	2
Karl Williams	6	155	1,759	11.3	88	4
Henry Ellard	16	135	1,527	11.3	83	4
Rodger Bird	3	94	1,063	11.3	78	0
Bosh Pritchard	6	95	1,072	11.3	81	2
Terry Metcalf	6	84	936	11.1	69	1

Bob Hayes	11	104	1,158	11.1	90	3
Brian Mitchell	12	388	4,278	11.0	84	8

75 or more returns.

TOP 20 KICKOFF RETURNERS

Player	Years	No.	Yards	Avg.	Long	TD
Gale Sayers	7	91	2,781	30.6	103	6
Lynn Chandnois	7	92	2,720	29.6	93	3
Abe Woodson	9	193	5,538	28.7	105	5
Buddy Young	6	90	2,514	27.9	104	2
Travis Williams	5	102	2,801	27.5	105	6
Joe Arenas	7	139	3,798	27.3	96	1
Clarence Davis	8	79	2,140	27.1	76	0
Steve Van Buren	8	76	2,030	26.7	98	3
Lenny Lyles	12	81	2,161	26.7	103	3
Mercury Morris	8	111	2,947	26.5	105	3
Bobby Jancik	6	158	4,185	26.5	61	0
Mel Renfro	14	85	2,246	26.4	100	2
Bobby Mitchell	14	102	2,690	26.4	98	5
Ollie Matson	14	143	3,746	26.2	105	6
Alvin Haymond	10	170	4,438	26.1	98	2
Noland Smith	3	82	2,137	26.1	106	1
Al Nelson	9	101	2,625	26.0	78	0
Timmy Brown	11	184	4,781	26.0	105	5
Vic Washington	6	129	3,341	25.9	98	1
Dave Hampton	8	113	2,923	25.9	101	3

75 or more returns.

TOP 20 LEADERS IN SACKS

Player	*Years	No.
Reggie White	15	198.0
Bruce Smith	17	186.0
Kevin Greene	15	160.0
Chris Doleman	15	150.5
Richard Dent	15	137.5
Leslie O'Neal	13	132.5
Lawrence Taylor	12	132.5
Rickey Jackson	14	128.0
Derrick Thomas	11	126.5
John Randle	12	125.0
Clyde Simmons	15	121.5
Sean Jones	13	113.0
Greg Townsend	13	109.5
Pat Swilling	12	107.5
Neil Smith	13	104.5
Jim Jeffcoat	15	102.5
William Fuller	13	100.5
Charles Haley	12	100.5
Andre Tippett	11	100.0
Trace Armstrong	13	99.0

*Years played since 1982 when sacks became an official statistic.

POSTSEASON LEADERS
TOP 10 RUSHERS

Player	Att.	Yards	Avg.	Long	TD
Emmitt Smith	349	1,586	4.5	65	19
Franco Harris	400	1,556	3.9	50	16
Thurman Thomas	339	1,442	4.3	40	16
Tony Dorsett	302	1,383	4.6	53	9
Marcus Allen	267	1,347	5.0	74	11
Terrell Davis	204	1,140	5.6	62	12
John Riggins	251	996	4.0	43	12
Larry Csonka	225	891	4.0	49	9
Chuck Foreman	229	860	3.8	62	7
Roger Craig	208	841	4.0	80	7

OUTSTANDING PERFORMERS

TOP 10 POSTSEASON PASSERS

Player	Att.	Comp.	Pct. Comp.	Yards	Avg. Gain	TD	Pct. TD	Int.	Pct. Int.	Rating
Bart Starr	213	130	61.0	1,753	8.23	15	7.0	3	1.4	104.8
Joe Montana	734	460	62.7	5,772	7.86	45	6.1	21	2.9	95.6
Ken Anderson	166	110	66.3	1,321	7.96	9	5.4	6	3.6	93.5
Kurt Warner	268	169	63.1	2,221	8.29	15	5.6	10	3.7	92.3
Joe Theismann	211	128	60.7	1,782	8.45	11	5.2	7	3.3	91.4
Troy Aikman	502	320	63.7	3,849	7.67	23	4.6	17	3.4	88.3
Brett Favre	522	318	60.9	3,940	7.55	29	5.6	19	3.6	87.7
Steve Young	471	292	62.0	3,326	7.06	20	4.2	13	2.8	85.8
Warren Moon	403	259	64.3	2,870	7.12	17	4.2	14	3.5	84.9
Ken Stabler	351	203	57.8	2,641	7.52	19	5.4	13	3.7	84.2

150 or more attempts. The passer ratings are based on performance standards established for completion percentage, interception percentage, touchdown percentage, and average gain. Please consult page 15 for more information.

TOP 10 POSTSEASON PASS RECEIVERS

Player	No.	Yards	Avg.	Long	TD
Jerry Rice	137	2,042	14.9	72	20
Micahel Irvin	87	1,315	15.1	53	8
Andre Reed	85	1,229	14.5	72	9
Thurman Thomas	76	672	8.8	27	5
Cliff Branch	73	1,289	17.7	72	5
Fred Biletnikoff	70	1,167	16.7	57	10
Art Monk	69	1,062	15.4	48	7
Drew Pearson	67	1,105	16.5	83	8
Tony Nathan	65	649	10.0	39	2
Cris Carter	63	870	13.8	66	8
Roger Craig	63	606	9.6	40	2

TOP 10 POSTSEASON INTERCEPTION LEADERS

Player	Interceptions
Ronnie Lott	9
Bill Simpson	9
Charlie Waters	9
Lester Hayes	8
Willie Brown	7
Dennis Thurman	7
Bobby Bryant	6
Eric Davis	6
Glen Edwards	6
Darrell Green	6
Cliff Harris	6
Vernon Perry	6
Aeneas Williams	6

TOP 10 POSTSEASON SACK LEADERS

Player	Sacks
Bruce Smith	14.5
Reggie White	12.0
Charles Haley	11.0
Richard Dent	10.5
Trace Armstrong	10.0
Charles Mann	10.0
Tony Tolbert	10.0
Neil Smith	9.5
Jeff Wright	9.0
Kevin Greene	8.5

ANNUAL SCORING LEADERS

Year	Player, Team	TD	FG	PAT	TP
2001	Marshall Faulk, St. Louis, NFC	21	0	0	#128
	Mike Vanderjagt, Indianapolis, AFC	0	28	41	125
2000	Marshall Faulk, St. Louis, NFC	26	0	0	##160
	Matt Stover, Baltimore, AFC	0	35	30	135
1999	Mike Vanderjagt, Indianapolis, AFC	0	34	43	145
	Jeff Wilkins, St. Louis, NFC	0	20	64	124
1998	Gary Anderson, Minnesota, NFC	0	35	59	164
	Steve Christie, Buffalo, AFC	0	33	41	140
1997	Mike Hollis, Jacksonville, AFC	0	31	41	134
	Richie Cunningham, Dallas, NFC	0	34	24	126
1996	John Kasay, Carolina, NFC	0	37	34	145
	Cary Blanchard, Indianapolis, AFC	0	36	27	135
1995	Emmitt Smith, Dallas, NFC	25	0	0	150
	Norm Johnson, Pittsburgh, AFC	0	34	39	141
1994	John Carney, San Diego, AFC	0	34	33	135
	Fuad Reveiz, Minnesota, NFC	0	34	30	132
1993	Jeff Jaeger, L.A. Raiders, AFC	0	35	27	132
	Jason Hanson, Detroit, NFC	0	34	28	130
1992	Pete Stoyanovich, Miami, AFC	0	30	34	124
	Morten Andersen, New Orleans, NFC	0	29	33	120
	Chip Lohmiller, Washington, NFC	0	30	30	120
1991	Chip Lohmiller, Washington, NFC	0	31	56	149
	Pete Stoyanovich, Miami, AFC	0	31	28	121
1990	Nick Lowery, Kansas City, AFC	0	34	37	139
	Chip Lohmiller, Washington, NFC	0	30	41	131
1989	Mike Cofer, San Francisco, NFC	0	29	49	136
	*David Treadwell, Denver, AFC	0	27	39	120
1988	Scott Norwood, Buffalo, AFC	0	32	33	129
	Mike Cofer, San Francisco, NFC	0	27	40	121
1987	Jerry Rice, San Francisco, NFC	23	0	0	138
	Jim Breech, Cincinnati, AFC	0	24	25	97
1986	Tony Franklin, New England, AFC	0	32	44	140
	Kevin Butler, Chicago, NFC	0	28	36	120
1985	*Kevin Butler, Chicago, NFC	0	31	51	144
	Gary Anderson, Pittsburgh, AFC	0	33	40	139
1984	Ray Wersching, San Francisco, NFC	0	25	56	131
	Gary Anderson, Pittsburgh, AFC	0	24	45	117
1983	Mark Moseley, Washington, NFC	0	33	62	161
	Gary Anderson, Pittsburgh, AFC	0	27	38	119
1982	*Marcus Allen, L.A. Raiders, AFC	14	0	0	84
	Wendell Tyler, L.A. Rams, NFC	13	0	0	78
1981	Ed Murray, Detroit, NFC	0	25	46	121
	Rafael Septien, Dallas, NFC	0	27	40	121
	Jim Breech, Cincinnati, AFC	0	22	49	115
	Nick Lowery, Kansas City, AFC	0	26	37	115
1980	John Smith, New England, AFC	0	26	51	129
	*Ed Murray, Detroit, NFC	0	27	35	116
1979	John Smith, New England, AFC	0	23	46	115
	Mark Moseley, Washington, NFC	0	25	39	114
1978	*Frank Corral, Los Angeles, NFC	0	29	31	118
	Pat Leahy, N.Y. Jets, AFC	0	22	41	107
1977	Errol Mann, Oakland, AFC	0	20	39	99
	Walter Payton, Chicago, NFC	16	0	0	96
1976	Toni Linhart, Baltimore, AFC	0	20	49	109
	Mark Moseley, Washington, NFC	0	22	31	97
1975	O.J. Simpson, Buffalo, AFC	23	0	0	138
	Chuck Foreman, Minnesota, NFC	22	0	0	132
1974	Chester Marcol, Green Bay, NFC	0	25	19	94
	Roy Gerela, Pittsburgh, AFC	0	20	33	93
1973	David Ray, Los Angeles, NFC	0	30	40	130
	Roy Gerela, Pittsburgh, AFC	0	29	36	123
1972	*Chester Marcol, Green Bay, NFC	0	33	29	128
	Bobby Howfield, N.Y. Jets, AFC	0	27	40	121
1971	Garo Yepremian, Miami, AFC	0	28	33	117
	Curt Knight, Washington, NFC	0	29	27	114
1970	Fred Cox, Minnesota, NFC	0	30	35	125
	Jan Stenerud, Kansas City, AFC	0	30	26	116
1969	Jim Turner, N.Y. Jets, AFL	0	32	33	129

	Fred Cox, Minnesota, NFL...0	26	43	121
1968	Jim Turner, N.Y. Jets, AFL 0	34	43	145
	Leroy Kelly, Cleveland, NFL...20	0	0	120
1967	Jim Bakken, St. Louis, NFL...0	27	36	117
	George Blanda, Oakland, AFL 0	20	56	116
1966	Gino Cappelletti, Boston, AFL 6	16	35	119
	Bruce Gossett, Los Angeles, NFL 0	28	29	113
1965	*Gale Sayers, Chicago, NFL 22	0	0	132
	Gino Cappelletti, Boston, AFL 9	17	27	132
1964	Gino Cappelletti, Boston, AFL 7	25	36	#155
	Lenny Moore, Baltimore, NFL.......................................20	0	0	120
1963	Gino Cappelletti, Boston, AFL 2	22	35	113
	Don Chandler, N.Y. Giants, NFL 0	18	52	106
1962	Gene Mingo, Denver, AFL 4	27	32	137
	Jim Taylor, Green Bay, NFL..19	0	0	114
1961	Gino Cappelletti, Boston, AFL 8	17	48	147
	Paul Hornung, Green Bay, NFL....................................10	15	41	146
1960	Paul Hornung, Green Bay, NFL....................................15	15	41	176
	*Gene Mingo, Denver, AFL 6	18	33	123
1959	Paul Hornung, Green Bay 7	7	31	94
1958	Jim Brown, Cleveland..18	0	0	108
1957	Sam Baker, Washington..1	14	29	77
	Lou Groza, Cleveland...0	15	32	77
1956	Bobby Layne, Detroit..5	12	33	99
1955	Doak Walker, Detroit...7	9	27	96
1954	Bobby Walston, Philadelphia..11	4	36	114
1953	Gordy Soltau, San Francisco 6	10	48	114
1952	Gordy Soltau, San Francisco 7	6	34	94
1951	Elroy (Crazylegs) Hirsch, Los Angeles 17	0	0	102
1950	*Doak Walker, Detroit..11	8	38	128
1949	Pat Harder, Chi. Cardinals..8	3	45	102
	Gene Roberts, N.Y. Giants 17	0	0	102
1948	Pat Harder, Chi. Cardinals..6	7	53	110
1947	Pat Harder, Chi. Cardinals..7	7	39	102
1946	Ted Fritsch, Green Bay..10	9	13	100
1945	Steve Van Buren, Philadelphia......................................18	0	2	110
1944	Don Hutson, Green Bay 9	0	31	85
1943	Don Hutson, Green Bay 12	3	36	117
1942	Don Hutson, Green Bay 17	1	33	138
1941	Don Hutson, Green Bay 12	1	20	95
1940	Don Hutson, Green Bay 7	0	15	57
1939	Andy Farkas, Washington..11	0	2	68
1938	Clarke Hinkle, Green Bay 7	3	7	58
1937	Jack Manders, Chi. Bears...5	8	15	69
1936	Earl (Dutch) Clark, Detroit...7	4	19	73
1935	Earl (Dutch) Clark, Detroit...6	1	16	55
1934	Jack Manders, Chi. Bears...3	10	31	79
1933	Ken Strong, N.Y. Giants..6	5	13	64
	Glenn Presnell, Portsmouth..6	6	10	64
1932	Earl (Dutch) Clark, Portsmouth 6	3	10	55

*First season of professional football.
#Cappelletti's total and Faulk's total in 2001 include a two-point conversion.
##Faulk's total in 2000 includes 2 two-point conversions.

ANNUAL TOUCHDOWN LEADERS

Year	Player, Team	TD	Rush	Pass	Ret.
2001	Marshall Faulk, St. Louis, NFC 21		12	9	0
	Shaun Alexander, Seattle, AFC 16		14	2	0
2000	Marshall Faulk, St. Louis, NFC 26		18	8	0
	Edgerrin James, Indianapolis, AFC................................18		13	5	0
1999	Stephen Davis, Washington, NFC..................................17		17	0	0
	*Edgerrin James, Indianapolis, AFC...............................17		13	4	0
1998	Terrell Davis, Denver, AFC..23		21	2	0
	*Randy Moss, Minnesota, NFC......................................17		0	17	0
1997	Karim Abdul-Jabbar, Miami, AFC 16		15	1	0
	Barry Sanders, Detroit, NFC..14		11	3	0
1996	Terry Allen, Washington, NFC..21		21	0	0
	Curtis Martin, New England, AFC...................................17		14	3	0
1995	Emmitt Smith, Dallas, NFC..25		25	0	0
	Carl Pickens, Cincinnati, AFC..17		0	17	0

Year	Player				
1994	Emmitt Smith, Dallas, NFC	22	21	1	0
	*Marshall Faulk, Indianapolis, AFC	12	11	1	0
	Natrone Means, San Diego, AFC	12	12	0	0
1993	Jerry Rice, San Francisco, NFC	16	1	15	0
	Marcus Allen, Kansas City, AFC	15	12	3	0
1992	Emmitt Smith, Dallas, NFC	19	18	1	0
	Thurman Thomas, Buffalo, AFC	12	9	3	0
1991	Barry Sanders, Detroit, NFC	17	16	1	0
	Mark Clayton, Miami, AFC	12	0	12	0
	Thurman Thomas, Buffalo, AFC	12	7	5	0
1990	Barry Sanders, Detroit, NFC	16	13	3	0
	Derrick Fenner, Seattle, AFC	15	14	1	0
1989	Dalton Hilliard, New Orleans, NFC	18	13	5	0
	Christian Okoye, Kansas City, AFC	12	12	0	0
	Thurman Thomas, Buffalo, AFC	12	6	6	0
1988	Greg Bell, L.A. Rams, NFC	18	16	2	0
	Eric Dickerson, Indianapolis, AFC	15	14	1	0
	*Ickey Woods, Cincinnati, AFC	15	15	0	0
1987	Jerry Rice, San Francisco, NFC	23	1	22	0
	Johnny Hector, N.Y. Jets, AFC	11	11	0	0
1986	George Rogers, Washington, NFC	18	18	0	0
	Sammy Winder, Denver, AFC	14	9	5	0
1985	Joe Morris, N.Y. Giants, NFC	21	21	0	2
	Louis Lipps, Pittsburgh, AFC	15	1	12	0
1984	Marcus Allen, L.A. Raiders, AFC	18	13	5	0
	Mark Clayton, Miami, AFC	18	0	18	0
	Eric Dickerson, L.A. Rams, NFC	14	14	0	0
	John Riggins, Washington, NFC	14	14	0	0
1983	John Riggins, Washington, NFC	24	24	0	0
	Pete Johnson, Cincinnati, AFC	14	14	0	0
	*Curt Warner, Seattle, AFC	14	13	1	0
1982	*Marcus Allen, L.A. Raiders, AFC	14	11	3	0
	Wendell Tyler, L.A. Rams, NFC	13	9	4	0
1981	Chuck Muncie, San Diego, AFC	19	19	0	0
	Wendell Tyler, Los Angeles, NFC	17	12	5	0
1980	*Billy Sims, Detroit, NFC	16	13	3	0
	Earl Campbell, Houston, AFC	13	13	0	0
	*Curtis Dickey, Baltimore, AFC	13	11	2	0
	John Jefferson, San Diego, AFC	13	0	13	0
1979	Earl Campbell, Houston, AFC	19	19	0	0
	Walter Payton, Chicago, NFC	16	14	2	0
1978	David Sims, Seattle, AFC	15	14	1	0
	Terdell Middleton, Green Bay, NFC	12	11	1	0
1977	Walter Payton, Chicago, NFC	16	14	2	0
	Nat Moore, Miami, AFC	13	1	12	0
1976	Chuck Foreman, Minnesota, NFC	14	13	1	0
	Franco Harris, Pittsburgh, AFC	14	14	0	0
1975	O.J. Simpson, Buffalo, AFC	23	16	7	0
	Chuck Foreman, Minnesota, NFC	22	13	9	0
1974	Chuck Foreman, Minnesota, NFC	15	9	6	0
	Cliff Branch, Oakland, AFC	13	0	13	0
1973	Larry Brown, Washington, NFC	14	8	6	0
	Floyd Little, Denver, AFC	13	12	1	0
1972	Emerson Boozer, N.Y. Jets, AFC	14	11	3	0
	Ron Johnson, N.Y. Giants, NFC	14	9	5	0
1971	Duane Thomas, Dallas, NFC	13	11	2	0
	Leroy Kelly, Cleveland, AFC	12	10	2	0
1970	Dick Gordon, Chicago, NFC	13	0	13	0
	MacArthur Lane, St. Louis, NFC	13	11	2	0
	Gary Garrison, San Diego, AFC	12	0	12	0
1969	Warren Wells, Oakland, AFL	14	0	14	0
	Tom Matte, Baltimore, NFL	13	11	2	0
	Lance Rentzel, Dallas, NFL	13	0	12	1
1968	Leroy Kelly, Cleveland, NFL	20	16	4	0
	Warren Wells, Oakland, AFL	12	1	11	0
1967	Homer Jones, N.Y. Giants, NFL	14	1	13	0
	Emerson Boozer, N.Y. Jets, AFL	13	10	3	0
1966	Leroy Kelly, Cleveland, NFL	16	15	1	0
	Dan Reeves, Dallas, NFL	16	8	8	0
	Lance Alworth, San Diego, AFL	13	0	13	0

Year	Player, Team	Total			
1965	*Gale Sayers, Chicago, NFL	22	14	6	2
	Lance Alworth, San Diego, AFL	14	0	14	0
	Don Maynard, N.Y. Jets, AFL	14	0	14	0
1964	Lenny Moore, Baltimore, NFL	20	16	3	1
	Lance Alworth, San Diego, AFL	15	2	13	0
1963	Art Powell, Oakland, AFL	16	0	16	0
	Jim Brown, Cleveland, NFL	15	12	3	0
1962	Abner Haynes, Dallas, AFL	19	13	6	0
	Jim Taylor, Green Bay, NFL	19	19	0	0
1961	Bill Groman, Houston, AFL	18	1	17	0
	Jim Taylor, Green Bay, NFL	16	15	1	0
1960	Paul Hornung, Green Bay, NFL	15	13	2	0
	Sonny Randle, St. Louis, NFL	15	0	15	0
	Art Powell, N.Y. Titans, AFL	14	0	14	0
1959	Raymond Berry, Baltimore	14	0	14	0
	Jim Brown, Cleveland	14	14	0	0
1958	Jim Brown, Cleveland	18	17	1	0
1957	Lenny Moore, Baltimore	11	3	7	1
1956	Rick Casares, Chi. Bears	14	12	2	0
1955	*Alan Ameche, Baltimore	9	9	0	0
	Harlon Hill, Chi. Bears	9	0	9	0
1954	*Harlon Hill, Chi. Bears	12	0	12	0
1953	Joseph Perry, San Francisco	13	10	3	0
1952	Cloyce Box, Detroit	15	0	15	0
1951	Elroy (Crazylegs) Hirsch, Los Angeles	17	0	17	0
1950	Bob Shaw, Chi. Cardinals	12	0	12	0
1949	Gene Roberts, N.Y. Giants	17	9	8	0
1948	Mal Kutner, Chi. Cardinals	15	1	14	0
1947	Steve Van Buren, Philadelphia	14	13	0	1
1946	Ted Fritsch, Green Bay	10	9	1	0
1945	Steve Van Buren, Philadelphia	18	15	2	1
1944	Don Hutson, Green Bay	9	0	9	0
	Bill Paschal, N.Y. Giants	9	9	0	0
1943	Don Hutson, Green Bay	12	0	11	1
	*Bill Paschal, N.Y. Giants	12	10	2	0
1942	Don Hutson, Green Bay	17	0	17	0
1941	Don Hutson, Green Bay	12	2	10	0
	George McAfee, Chi. Bears	12	6	3	3
1940	John Drake, Cleveland	9	9	0	0
	Richard Todd, Washington	9	4	4	1
1939	Andrew Farkas, Washington	11	5	5	1
1938	Don Hutson, Green Bay	9	0	9	0
1937	Cliff Battles, Washington	7	5	1	1
	Clarke Hinkle, Green Bay	7	5	2	0
	Don Hutson, Green Bay	7	0	7	0
1936	Don Hutson, Green Bay	9	0	8	1
1935	*Don Hutson, Green Bay	7	0	6	1
1934	*Beattie Feathers, Chi. Bears	9	8	1	0
1933	*Charlie (Buckets) Goldenberg, Green Bay	7	4	1	2
	John (Shipwreck) Kelly, Brooklyn	7	2	3	2
	*Elvin (Kink) Richards, N.Y. Giants	7	4	3	0
1932	Earl (Dutch) Clark, Portsmouth	6	3	3	0
	Red Grange, Chi. Bears	6	3	3	0

First season of professional football.

ANNUAL LEADERS—MOST FIELD GOALS MADE

Year	Player, Team	Att.	Made	Pct.
2001	Jason Elam, Denver, AFC	36	31	86.1
	*Jay Feely, Atlanta, NFC	37	29	78.4
2000	Matt Stover, Baltimore, AFC	39	35	89.7
	Ryan Longwell, Green Bay, NFC	38	33	86.8
1999	Olindo Mare, Miami, AFC	46	39	84.8
	*Martin Gramatica, Tampa Bay, NFC	32	27	84.4
1998	Al Del Greco, Tennessee, AFC	39	36	92.3
	Gary Anderson, Minnesota, NFC	35	35	100.0
1997	Richie Cunningham, Dallas, NFC	37	34	91.9
	Cary Blanchard, Indianapolis, AFC	41	32	78.1
1996	John Kasay, Carolina, NFC	45	37	82.2
	Cary Blanchard, Indianapolis, AFC	40	36	90.0
1995	Norm Johnson, Pittsburgh, AFC	41	34	82.9

	Morten Andersen, Atlanta, NFC	37	31	83.8
1994	John Carney, San Diego, AFC	38	34	89.5
	Fuad Reveiz, Minnesota, NFC	39	34	87.2
1993	Jeff Jaeger, L.A. Raiders, AFC	44	35	79.5
	Jason Hanson, Detroit, NFC	43	34	79.1
1992	Pete Stoyanovich, Miami, AFC	37	30	81.1
	Chip Lohmiller, Washington, NFC	40	30	75.0
1991	Pete Stoyanovich, Miami, AFC	37	31	83.8
	Chip Lohmiller, Washington, NFC	43	31	72.1
1990	Nick Lowery, Kansas City, AFC	37	34	91.9
	Chip Lohmiller, Washington, NFC	40	30	75.0
1989	Rich Karlis, Minnesota, NFC	39	31	79.5
	*David Treadwell, Denver, AFC	33	27	81.8
1988	Scott Norwood, Buffalo, AFC	37	32	86.5
	Mike Cofer, San Francisco, NFC	38	27	71.1
1987	Morten Andersen, New Orleans, NFC	36	28	77.8
	Dean Biasucci, Indianpolis, AFC	27	24	88.9
	Jim Breech, Cincinnati, AFC	30	24	80.0
1986	Tony Franklin, New England, AFC	41	32	78.0
	Kevin Butler, Chicago, NFC	41	28	68.3
1985	Gary Anderson, Pittsburgh, AFC	42	33	78.6
	Morten Andersen, New Orleans, NFC	35	31	88.6
	*Kevin Butler, Chicago, NFC	37	31	83.8
1984	*Paul McFadden, Philadelphia, NFC	37	30	81.1
	Gary Anderson, Pittsburgh, AFC	32	24	75.0
	Matt Bahr, Cleveland, AFC	32	24	75.0
1983	*Ali-Haji-Sheikh, N.Y. Giants, NFC	42	35	83.3
	*Raul Allegre, Baltimore, AFC	35	30	85.7
1982	Mark Moseley, Washington, NFC	21	20	95.2
	Nick Lowery, Kansas City, AFC	24	19	79.2
1981	Rafael Septien, Dallas, NFC	35	27	77.1
	Nick Lowery, Kansas City, AFC	36	26	72.2
1980	*Ed Murray, Detroit, NFC	42	27	64.3
	John Smith, New England, AFC	34	26	76.5
	Fred Steinfort, Denver, AFC	34	26	76.5
1979	Mark Moseley, Washington, NFC	33	25	75.8
	John Smith, New England, AFC	33	23	69.7
1978	*Frank Corral, Los Angeles, NFC	43	29	67.4
	Pat Leahy, N.Y. Jets, AFC	30	22	73.3
1977	Mark Moseley, Washington, NFC	37	21	56.8
	Errol Mann, Oakland, AFC	28	20	71.4
1976	Mark Moseley, Washington, NFC	34	22	64.7
	Jan Stenerud, Kansas City, AFC	38	21	55.3
1975	Jan Stenerud, Kansas City, AFC	32	22	68.8
	Toni Fritsch, Dallas, NFC	35	22	62.9
1974	Chester Marcol, Green Bay, NFC	39	25	64.1
	Roy Gerela, Pittsburgh, AFC	29	20	69.0
1973	David Ray, Los Angeles, NFC	47	30	63.8
	Roy Gerela, Pittsburgh, AFC	43	29	67.4
1972	*Chester Marcol, Green Bay, NFC	48	33	68.8
	Roy Gerela, Pittsburgh, AFC	41	28	68.3
1971	Curt Knight, Washington, NFC	49	29	59.2
	Garo Yepremian, Miami, AFC	40	28	70.0
1970	Jan Stenerud, Kansas City, AFC	42	30	71.4
	Fred Cox, Minnesota, NFC	46	30	65.2
1969	Jim Turner, N.Y. Jets, AFL	47	32	68.1
	Fred Cox, Minnesota, NFL	37	26	70.3
1968	Jim Turner, N.Y. Jets, AFL	46	34	73.9
	Mac Percival, Chicago, NFL	36	25	69.4
1967	Jim Bakken, St. Louis, NFL	39	27	69.2
	Jan Stenerud, Kansas City, AFL	36	21	58.3
1966	Bruce Gossett, Los Angeles, NFL	49	28	57.1
	Mike Mercer, Oakland-Kansas City, AFL	30	21	70.0
1965	Pete Gogolak, Buffalo, AFL	46	28	60.9
	Fred Cox, Minnesota, NFL	35	23	65.7
1964	Jim Bakken, St. Louis, NFL	38	25	65.8
	Gino Cappelletti, Boston, AFL	39	25	64.1
1963	Jim Martin, Baltimore, NFL	39	24	61.5
	Gino Cappelletti, Boston, AFL	38	22	57.9

Year	Player, Team			
1962	Gene Mingo, Denver, AFL	39	27	69.2
	Lou Michaels, Pittsburgh, NFL	42	26	61.9
1961	Steve Myhra, Baltimore, NFL	39	21	53.8
	Gino Cappelletti, Boston, AFL	32	17	53.1
1960	Tommy Davis, San Francisco, NFL	32	19	59.4
	*Gene Mingo, Denver, AFL	28	18	64.3
1959	Pat Summerall, N.Y. Giants	29	20	69.0
1958	Paige Cothren, Los Angeles	25	14	56.0
	*Tom Miner, Pittsburgh	28	14	50.0
1957	Lou Groza, Cleveland	22	15	68.2
1956	Sam Baker, Washington	25	17	68.0
1955	Fred Cone, Green Bay	24	16	66.7
1954	Lou Groza, Cleveland	24	16	66.7
1953	Lou Groza, Cleveland	26	23	88.5
1952	Lou Groza, Cleveland	33	19	57.6
1951	Bob Waterfield, Los Angeles	23	13	56.5
1950	Lou Groza, Cleveland	19	13	68.4
1949	Cliff Patton, Philadelphia	18	9	50.0
	Bob Waterfield, Los Angeles	16	9	56.3
1948	Cliff Patton, Philadelphia	12	8	66.7
1947	Ward Cuff, Green Bay	16	7	43.8
	Pat Harder, Chi. Cardinals	10	7	70.0
	Bob Waterfield, Los Angeles	16	7	43.8
1946	Ted Fritsch, Green Bay	17	9	52.9
1945	Joe Aguirre, Washington	13	7	53.8
1944	Ken Strong, N.Y. Giants	12	6	50.0
1943	Ward Cuff, N.Y. Giants	9	3	33.3
	Don Hutson, Green Bay	5	3	60.0
1942	Bill Daddio, Chi. Cardinals	10	5	50.0
1941	Clarke Hinkle, Green Bay	14	6	42.9
1940	Clarke Hinkle, Green Bay	14	9	64.3
1939	Ward Cuff, N.Y. Giants	16	7	43.8
1938	Ward Cuff, N.Y. Giants	9	5	55.6
	Ralph Kercheval, Brooklyn	13	5	38.5
1937	Jack Manders, Chi. Bears		8	
1936	Jack Manders, Chi. Bears		7	
	Armand Niccolai, Pittsburgh		7	
1935	Armand Niccolai, Pittsburgh		6	
	Bill Smith, Chi. Cardinals		6	
1934	Jack Manders, Chi. Bears		10	
1933	*Jack Manders, Chi. Bears		6	
	Glenn Presnell, Portsmouth		6	
1932	Earl (Dutch) Clark, Portsmouth		3	

*First season of professional football.

ANNUAL RUSHING LEADERS

Year	Player, Team	Att.	Yards	Avg.	TD
2001	Priest Holmes, Kansas City, AFC	327	1,555	4.8	8
	Stephen Davis, Washington, NFC	356	1,432	4.0	5
2000	Edgerrin James, Indianapolis, AFC	387	1,709	4.4	13
	Robert Smith, Minnesota, NFC	295	1,521	5.2	7
1999	*Edgerrin James, Indianapolis, AFC	369	1,553	4.2	13
	Stephen Davis, Washington, NFC	290	1,405	4.8	17
1998	Terrell Davis, Denver, AFC	392	2,008	5.1	21
	Jamal Anderson, Atlanta, NFC	410	1,846	4.5	14
1997	Barry Sanders, Detroit, NFC	335	2,053	6.1	11
	Terrell Davis, Denver, AFC	369	1,750	4.7	15
1996	Barry Sanders, Detroit, NFC	307	1,553	5.1	11
	Terrell Davis, Denver, AFC	345	1,538	4.5	13
1995	Emmitt Smith, Dallas, NFC	377	1,773	4.7	25
	*Curtis Martin, New England, AFC	368	1,487	4.0	14
1994	Barry Sanders, Detroit, NFC	331	1,883	5.7	7
	Chris Warren, Seattle, AFC	333	1,545	4.6	9
1993	Emmitt Smith, Dallas, NFC	283	1,486	5.3	9
	Thurman Thomas, Buffalo, AFC	355	1,315	3.7	6
1992	Emmitt Smith, Dallas, NFC	373	1,713	4.6	18
	Barry Foster, Pittsburgh, AFC	390	1,690	4.3	11
1991	Emmitt Smith, Dallas, NFC	365	1,563	4.3	12
	Thurman Thomas, Buffalo, AFC	288	1,407	4.9	7
1990	Barry Sanders, Detroit, NFC	255	1,304	5.1	13

Year	Player	Att	Yards	Avg	TD
	Thurman Thomas, Buffalo, AFC	271	1,297	4.8	11
1989	Christian Okoye, Kansas City, AFC	370	1,480	4.0	12
	*Barry Sanders, Detroit, NFC	280	1,470	5.3	14
1988	Eric Dickerson, Indianapolis, AFC	388	1,659	4.3	14
	Herschel Walker, Dallas, NFC	361	1,514	4.2	5
1987	Charles White, L.A. Rams, NFC	324	1,374	4.2	11
	Eric Dickerson, Indianapolis, AFC	223	1,011	4.5	5
1986	Eric Dickerson, L.A. Rams, NFC	404	1,821	4.5	11
	Curt Warner, Seattle, AFC	319	1,481	4.6	13
1985	Marcus Allen, L.A. Raiders, AFC	380	1,759	4.6	11
	Gerald Riggs, Atlanta, NFC	397	1,719	4.3	10
1984	Eric Dickerson, L.A. Rams, NFC	379	2,105	5.6	14
	Earnest Jackson, San Diego, AFC	296	1,179	4.0	8
1983	*Eric Dickerson, L.A. Rams, NFC	390	1,808	4.6	18
	*Curt Warner, Seattle, AFC	335	1,449	4.3	13
1982	Freeman McNeil, N.Y. Jets, AFC	151	786	5.2	6
	Tony Dorsett, Dallas, NFC	177	745	4.2	5
1981	*George Rogers, New Orleans, NFC	378	1,674	4.4	13
	Earl Campbell, Houston, AFC	361	1,376	3.8	10
1980	Earl Campbell, Houston, AFC	373	1,934	5.2	13
	Walter Payton, Chicago, NFC	317	1,460	4.6	6
1979	Earl Campbell, Houston, AFC	368	1,697	4.6	19
	Walter Payton, Chicago, NFC	369	1,610	4.4	14
1978	*Earl Campbell, Houston, AFC	302	1,450	4.8	13
	Walter Payton, Chicago, NFC	333	1,395	4.2	11
1977	Walter Payton, Chicago, NFC	339	1,852	5.5	14
	Mark van Eeghen, Oakland, AFC	324	1,273	3.9	7
1976	O.J. Simpson, Buffalo, AFC	290	1,503	5.2	8
	Walter Payton, Chicago, NFC	311	1,390	4.5	13
1975	O.J. Simpson, Buffalo, AFC	329	1,817	5.5	16
	Jim Otis, St. Louis, NFC	269	1,076	4.0	5
1974	Otis Armstrong, Denver, AFC	263	1,407	5.3	9
	Lawrence McCutcheon, Los Angeles, NFC	236	1,109	4.7	3
1973	O.J. Simpson, Buffalo, AFC	332	2,003	6.0	12
	John Brockington, Green Bay, NFC	265	1,144	4.3	3
1972	O.J. Simpson, Buffalo, AFC	292	1,251	4.3	6
	Larry Brown, Washington, NFC	285	1,216	4.3	8
1971	Floyd Little, Denver, AFC	284	1,133	4.0	6
	*John Brockington, Green Bay, NFC	216	1,105	5.1	4
1970	Larry Brown, Washington, NFC	237	1,125	4.7	5
	Floyd Little, Denver, AFC	209	901	4.3	3
1969	Gale Sayers, Chicago, NFL	236	1,032	4.4	8
	Dickie Post, San Diego, AFL	182	873	4.8	6
1968	Leroy Kelly, Cleveland, NFL	248	1,239	5.0	16
	*Paul Robinson, Cincinnati, AFL	238	1,023	4.3	8
1967	Jim Nance, Boston, AFL	269	1,216	4.5	7
	Leroy Kelly, Cleveland, NFL	235	1,205	5.1	11
1966	Jim Nance, Boston, AFL	299	1,458	4.9	11
	Gale Sayers, Chicago, NFL	229	1,231	5.4	8
1965	Jim Brown, Cleveland, NFL	289	1,544	5.3	17
	Paul Lowe, San Diego, AFL	222	1,121	5.0	7
1964	Jim Brown, Cleveland, NFL	280	1,446	5.2	7
	Cookie Gilchrist, Buffalo, AFL	230	981	4.3	6
1963	Jim Brown, Cleveland, NFL	291	1,863	6.4	12
	Clem Daniels, Oakland, AFL	215	1,099	5.1	3
1962	Jim Taylor, Green Bay, NFL	272	1,474	5.4	19
	Cookie Gilchrist, Buffalo, AFL	214	1,096	5.1	13
1961	Jim Brown, Cleveland, NFL	305	1,408	4.6	8
	Billy Cannon, Houston, AFL	200	948	4.7	6
1960	Jim Brown, Cleveland, NFL	215	1,257	5.8	9
	*Abner Haynes, Dall. Texans, AFL	156	875	5.6	9
1959	Jim Brown, Cleveland	290	1,329	4.6	14
1958	Jim Brown, Cleveland	257	1,527	5.9	17
1957	*Jim Brown, Cleveland	202	942	4.7	9
1956	Rick Casares, Chi. Bears	234	1,126	4.8	12
1955	*Alan Ameche, Baltimore	213	961	4.5	9
1954	Joe Perry, San Francisco	173	1,049	6.1	8
1953	Joe Perry, San Francisco	192	1,018	5.3	10
1952	Dan Towler, Los Angeles	156	894	5.7	10
1951	Eddie Price, N.Y. Giants	271	971	3.6	7

Year	Player, Team	Att.	Yards	Avg.	TD
1950	Marion Motley, Cleveland	140	810	5.8	3
1949	Steve Van Buren, Philadelphia	263	1,146	4.4	11
1948	Steve Van Buren, Philadelphia	201	945	4.7	10
1947	Steve Van Buren, Philadelphia	217	1,008	4.6	13
1946	Bill Dudley, Pittsburgh	146	604	4.1	3
1945	Steve Van Buren, Philadelphia	143	832	5.8	15
1944	Bill Paschal, N.Y. Giants	196	737	3.8	9
1943	*Bill Paschal, N.Y. Giants	147	572	3.9	10
1942	*Bill Dudley, Pittsburgh	162	696	4.3	5
1941	Clarence (Pug) Manders, Brooklyn	111	486	4.4	5
1940	Byron (Whizzer) White, Detroit	146	514	3.5	5
1939	*Bill Osmanski, Chicago	121	699	5.8	7
1938	*Byron (Whizzer) White, Pittsburgh	152	567	3.7	4
1937	Cliff Battles, Washington	216	874	4.0	5
1936	*Alphonse (Tuffy) Leemans, N.Y. Giants	206	830	4.0	2
1935	Doug Russell, Chi. Cardinals	140	499	3.6	0
1934	*Beattie Feathers, Chi. Bears	119	1,004	8.4	8
1933	Jim Musick, Boston	173	809	4.7	5
1932	*Cliff Battles, Boston	148	576	3.9	3

*First season of professional football.

ANNUAL PASSING LEADERS
(Current rating system implemented in 1973)

Year	Player, Team	Att.	Comp.	Yards	TD	Int.	Rating
2001	Kurt Warner, St. Louis, NFC	546	375	4,830	36	22	101.4
	Rich Gannon, Oakland, AFC	549	361	3,828	27	9	95.5
2000	Brian Griese, Denver, AFC	336	216	2,688	19	4	102.9
	Trent Green, St. Louis, NFC	240	145	2,063	16	5	101.8
1999	Kurt Warner, St. Louis, NFC	499	325	4,353	41	13	109.2
	Peyton Manning, Indianapolis, AFC	533	331	4,135	26	15	90.7
1998	Randall Cunningham, Minnesota, NFC	425	259	3,704	34	10	106.0
	Vinny Testaverde, N.Y. Jets, AFC	421	259	3,256	29	7	101.6
1997	Steve Young, San Francisco, NFC	356	241	3,029	19	6	104.7
	Mark Brunell, Jacksonville, AFC	435	264	3,281	18	7	91.2
1996	Steve Young, San Francisco NFC	316	214	2,410	14	6	97.2
	John Elway, Denver, AFC	466	287	3,328	26	14	89.2
1995	Jim Harbaugh, Indianapolis, AFC	314	200	2,575	17	5	100.7
	Brett Favre, Green Bay, NFC	570	359	4,413	38	13	99.5
1994	Steve Young, San Francisco, NFC	461	324	3,969	35	10	112.8
	Dan Marino, Miami, AFC	615	385	4,453	30	17	89.2
1993	Steve Young, San Francisco, NFC	462	314	4,023	29	16	101.5
	John Elway, Denver, AFC	551	348	4,030	25	10	92.8
1992	Steve Young, San Francisco, NFC	402	268	3,465	25	7	107.0
	Warren Moon, Houston, AFC	346	224	2,521	18	12	89.3
1991	Steve Young, San Francisco, NFC	279	180	2,517	17	8	101.8
	Jim Kelly, Buffalo, AFC	474	304	3,844	33	17	97.6
1990	Jim Kelly, Buffalo, AFC	346	219	2,829	24	9	101.2
	Phil Simms, N.Y. Giants, NFC	311	184	2,284	15	4	92.7
1989	Joe Montana, San Francisco, NFC	386	271	3,521	26	8	112.4
	Boomer Esiason, Cincinnati, AFC	455	258	3,525	28	11	92.1
1988	Boomer Esiason, Cincinnati, AFC	388	223	3,572	28	14	97.4
	Wade Wilson, Minnesota, NFC	332	204	2,746	15	9	91.5
1987	Joe Montana, San Francisco, NFC	398	266	3,054	31	13	102.1
	Bernie Kosar, Cleveland, AFC	389	241	3,033	22	9	95.4
1986	Tommy Kramer, Minnesota, NFC	372	208	3,000	24	10	92.6
	Dan Marino, Miami, AFC	623	378	4,746	44	23	92.5
1985	Ken O'Brien, N.Y. Jets, AFC	488	297	3,888	25	8	96.2
	Joe Montana, San Francisco, NFC	494	303	3,653	27	13	91.3
1984	Dan Marino, Miami, AFC	564	362	5,084	48	17	108.9
	Joe Montana, San Francisco, NFC	432	279	3,630	28	10	102.9
1983	Steve Bartkowski, Atlanta, NFC	432	274	3,167	22	5	97.6
	*Dan Marino, Miami, AFC	296	173	2,210	20	6	96.0
1982	Ken Anderson, Cincinnati, AFC	309	218	2,495	12	9	95.3
	Joe Theismann, Washington, NFC	252	161	2,033	13	9	91.3
1981	Ken Anderson, Cincinnati, AFC	479	300	3,754	29	10	98.4
	Joe Montana, San Francisco, NFC	488	311	3,565	19	12	88.4
1980	Brian Sipe, Cleveland, AFC	554	337	4,132	30	14	91.4
	Ron Jaworski, Philadelphia, NFC	451	257	3,529	27	12	91.0
1979	Roger Staubach, Dallas, NFC	461	267	3,586	27	11	92.3
	Dan Fouts, San Diego, AFC	530	332	4,082	24	24	82.6

Year	Player, Team, Conf	Att	Comp	Yards	TD	Int	Rating
1978	Roger Staubach, Dallas, NFC	413	231	3,190	25	16	84.9
	Terry Bradshaw, Pittsburgh, AFC	368	207	2,915	28	20	84.7
1977	Bob Griese, Miami, AFC	307	180	2,252	22	13	87.8
	Roger Staubach, Dallas, NFC	361	210	2,620	18	9	87.0
1976	Ken Stabler, Oakland, AFC	291	194	2,737	27	17	103.4
	James Harris, Los Angeles, NFC	158	91	1,460	8	6	89.6
1975	Ken Anderson, Cincinnati, AFC	377	228	3,169	21	11	93.9
	Fran Tarkenton, Minnesota, NFC	425	273	2,994	25	13	91.8
1974	Ken Anderson, Cincinnati, AFC	328	213	2,667	18	10	95.7
	Sonny Jurgensen, Washington, NFC	167	107	1,185	11	5	94.5
1973	Roger Staubach, Dallas, NFC	286	179	2,428	23	15	94.6
	Ken Stabler, Oakland, AFC	260	163	1,997	14	10	88.3
1972	Norm Snead, N.Y. Giants, NFC	325	196	2,307	17	12	
	Earl Morrall, Miami, AFC	150	83	1,360	11	7	
1971	Roger Staubach, Dallas, NFC	211	126	1,882	15	4	
	Bob Griese, Miami, AFC	263	145	2,089	19	9	
1970	John Brodie, San Francisco, NFC	378	223	2,941	24	10	
	Daryle Lamonica, Oakland, AFC	356	179	2,516	22	15	
1969	Sonny Jurgensen, Washington, NFL	442	274	3,102	22	15	
	*Greg Cook, Cincinnati, AFL	197	106	1,854	15	11	
1968	Len Dawson, Kansas City, AFL	224	131	2,109	17	9	
	Earl Morrall, Baltimore, NFL	317	182	2,909	26	17	
1967	Sonny Jurgensen, Washington, NFL	508	288	3,747	31	16	
	Daryle Lamonica, Oakland, AFL	425	220	3,228	30	20	
1966	Bart Starr, Green Bay, NFL	251	156	2,257	14	3	
	Len Dawson, Kansas City, AFL	284	159	2,527	26	10	
1965	Rudy Bukich, Chicago, NFL	312	176	2,641	20	9	
	John Hadl, San Diego, AFL	348	174	2,798	20	21	
1964	Len Dawson, Kansas City, AFL	354	199	2,879	30	18	
	Bart Starr, Green Bay, NFL	272	163	2,144	15	4	
1963	Y.A. Tittle, N.Y. Giants, NFL	367	221	3,145	36	14	
	Tobin Rote, San Diego, AFL	286	170	2,510	20	17	
1962	Len Dawson, Dallas Texans, AFL	310	189	2,759	29	17	
	Bart Starr, Green Bay, NFL	285	178	2,438	12	9	
1961	George Blanda, Houston, AFL	362	187	3,330	36	22	
	Milt Plum, Cleveland, NFL	302	177	2,416	18	10	
1960	Milt Plum, Cleveland, NFL	250	151	2,297	21	5	
	Jack Kemp, L.A. Chargers, AFL	406	211	3,018	20	25	
1959	Charlie Conerly, N.Y. Giants	194	113	1,706	14	4	
1958	Eddie LeBaron, Washington	145	79	1,365	11	10	
1957	Tommy O'Connell, Cleveland	110	63	1,229	9	8	
1956	Ed Brown, Chicago Bears	168	96	1,667	11	12	
1955	Otto Graham, Cleveland	185	98	1,721	15	8	
1954	Norm Van Brocklin, Los Angeles	260	139	2,637	13	21	
1953	Otto Graham, Cleveland	258	167	2,722	11	9	
1952	Norm Van Brocklin, Los Angeles	205	113	1,736	14	17	
1951	Bob Waterfield, Los Angeles	176	88	1,566	13	10	
1950	Norm Van Brocklin, Los Angeles	233	127	2,061	18	14	
1949	Sammy Baugh, Washington	255	145	1,903	18	14	
1948	Tommy Thompson, Philadelphia	246	141	1,965	25	11	
1947	Sammy Baugh, Washington	354	210	2,938	25	15	
1946	Bob Waterfield, Los Angeles	251	127	1,747	18	17	
1945	Sammy Baugh, Washington	182	128	1,669	11	4	
	Sid Luckman, Chicago Bears	217	117	1,725	14	10	
1944	Frank Filchock, Washington	147	84	1,139	13	9	
1943	Sammy Baugh, Washington	239	133	1,754	23	19	
1942	Cecil Isbell, Green Bay	268	146	2,021	24	14	
1941	Cecil Isbell, Green Bay	206	117	1,479	15	11	
1940	Sammy Baugh, Washington	177	111	1,367	12	10	
1939	*Parker Hall, Cleveland	208	106	1,227	9	13	
1938	Ed Danowski, N.Y. Giants	129	70	848	7	8	
1937	*Sammy Baugh, Washington	171	81	1,127	8	14	
1936	Arnie Herber, Green Bay	173	77	1,239	11	13	
1935	Ed Danowski, N.Y. Giants	113	57	794	10	9	
1934	Arnie Herber, Green Bay	115	42	799	8	12	
1933	*Harry Newman, N.Y. Giants	136	53	973	11	17	
1932	Arnie Herber, Green Bay	101	37	639	9	9	

*First season of professional football.

ANNUAL PASSING TOUCHDOWN LEADERS

Year	Player, Team	TD
2001	Kurt Warner, St. Louis, NFC	36
	Rich Gannon, Oakland, AFC	27
2000	Daunte Culpepper, Minnesota, NFC	33
	Peyton Manning, Indianapolis, AFC	33
1999	Kurt Warner, St. Louis, NFC	41
	Peyton Manning, Indianapolis, AFC	26
1998	Steve Young, San Francisco, NFC	36
	Vinny Testaverde, N.Y. Jets, AFC	29
1997	Brett Favre, Green Bay, NFC	35
	Jeff George, Oakland, AFC	29
1996	Brett Favre, Green Bay, NFC	39
	Vinny Testaverde, Baltimore, AFC	33
1995	Brett Favre, Green Bay, NFC	38
	Jeff Blake, Cincinnati, AFC	28
1994	Steve Young, San Francisco, NFC	35
	Dan Marino, Miami, AFC	30
1993	Steve Young, San Francisco, NFC	29
	John Elway, Denver, AFC	25
1992	Steve Young, San Francisco, NFC	25
	Dan Marino, Miami, AFC	24
1991	Jim Kelly, Buffalo, AFC	33
	Mark Rypien, Washington, NFC	28
1990	Warren Moon, Houston, AFC	33
	Randall Cunningham, Philadelphia, NFC	30
1989	Jim Everett, L.A. Rams, NFC	29
	Boomer Esiason, Cincinnati, AFC	28
1988	Jim Everett, L.A. Rams, NFC	31
	Boomer Esiason, Cincinnati, AFC	28
	Dan Marino, Miami, AFC	28
1987	Joe Montana, San Francisco, NFC	31
	Dan Marino, Miami, AFC	26
1986	Dan Marino, Miami, AFC	44
	Tommy Kramer, Minnesota, NFC	24
1985	Dan Marino, Miami, AFC	30
	Joe Montana, San Francisco, NFC	27
1984	Dan Marino, Miami, AFC	48
	Neil Lomax, St. Louis, NFC	28
	Joe Montana, San Francisco, NFC	28
1983	Lynn Dickey, Green Bay, NFC	32
	Joe Ferguson, Buffalo, AFC	26
	Brian Sipe, Cleveland, AFC	26
1982	Terry Bradshaw, Pittsburgh, AFC	17
	Dan Fouts, San Diego, AFC	17
	Joe Montana, San Francisco, NFC	17
1981	Dan Fouts, San Diego, AFC	33
	Steve Bartkowski, Atlanta, NFC	30
1980	Steve Bartkowski, Atlanta, NFC	31
	Dan Fouts, San Diego, AFC	30
	Brian Sipe, Cleveland, AFC	30
1979	Steve Grogan, New England, AFC	28
	Brian Sipe, Cleveland, AFC	28
	Roger Staubach, Dallas, NFC	27
1978	Terry Bradshaw, Pittsburgh, AFC	28
	Roger Staubach, Dallas, NFC	25
	Fran Tarkenton, Minnesota, NFC	25
1977	Bob Griese, Miami, AFC	22
	Ron Jaworski, Philadelphia, NFC	18
	Roger Staubach, Dallas, NFC	18
1976	Ken Stabler, Oakland, AFC	27
	Jim Hart, St. Louis, NFC	18
1975	Joe Ferguson, Buffalo, AFC	25
	Fran Tarkenton, Minnesota, NFC	25
1974	Ken Stabler, Oakland, AFC	26
	Jim Hart, St. Louis, NFC	20
1973	Roman Gabriel, Philadelphia, NFC	23
	Roger Staubach, Dallas, NFC	23
	Charley Johnson, Denver, AFC	20
1972	Billy Kilmer, Washington, NFC	19
	Joe Namath, N.Y. Jets, AFC	19
1971	John Hadl, San Diego, AFC	21
	John Brodie, San Francisco, NFC	18
1970	John Brodie, San Francisco, NFC	24
	John Hadl, San Diego, AFC	22
	Daryle Lamonica, Oakland, AFC	22
1969	Daryle Lamonica, Oakland, AFL	34
	Roman Gabriel, Los Angeles, NFL	24
1968	John Hadl, San Diego, AFL	27
	Earl Morrall, Baltimore, NFL	26
1967	Sonny Jurgensen, Washington, NFL	31
	Daryle Lamonica, Oakland, AFL	30
1966	Frank Ryan, Cleveland, NFL	29
	Len Dawson, Kansas City, AFL	26
1965	John Brodie, San Francisco, NFL	30
	Len Dawson, Kansas City, AFL	21
1964	Babe Parilli, Boston, AFL	31
	Frank Ryan, Cleveland, NFL	25
1963	Y.A. Tittle, N.Y. Giants, NFL	36
	Len Dawson, Kansas City, AFL	26
1962	Y.A. Tittle, N.Y. Giants, NFL	33
	Len Dawson, Dallas, AFL	29
1961	George Blanda, Houston, AFL	36
	Sonny Jurgensen, Philadelphia, NFL	32
1960	Al Dorow, N.Y. Titans, AFL	26
	Johnny Unitas, Baltimore, NFL	25
1959	Johnny Unitas, Baltimore	32
1958	Johnny Unitas, Baltimore	19
1957	Johnny Unitas, Baltimore	24
1956	Tobin Rote, Green Bay	18
1955	Tobin Rote, Green Bay	17
	Y.A. Tittle, San Francisco	17
1954	Adrian Burk, Philadelphia	23
1953	Robert Thomason, Philadelphia	21
1952	Jim Finks, Pittsburgh	20
	Otto Graham, Cleveland	20
1951	Bobby Layne, Detroit	26
1950	George Ratterman, N.Y. Yanks	22
1949	Johnny Lujack, Chi. Bears	23
1948	Tommy Thompson, Philadelphia	25
1947	Sammy Baugh, Washington	25
1946	Sid Luckman, Chi. Bears	17
	Bob Waterfield, Los Angeles	17
1945	Sid Luckman, Chi. Bears	14
	*Bob Waterfield, Cleveland	14
1944	Frank Filchock, Washington	13
1943	Sid Luckman, Chi. Bears	28
1942	Cecil Isbell, Green Bay	24
1941	Cecil Isbell, Green Bay	15
1940	Sammy Baugh, Washington	12
1939	Frank Filchock, Washington	11
1938	Bob Monnett, Green Bay	9
1937	Bernie Masterson, Chi. Bears	9
1936	Arnie Herber, Green Bay	11
1935	Ed Danowski, N.Y. Giants	10
1934	Arnie Herber, Green Bay	8
1933	*Harry Newman, N.Y. Giants	11
1932	Arnie Herber, Green Bay	9

*First season of professional football.

ANNUAL PASS RECEIVING LEADERS

Year	Player, Team	No.	Yards	Avg.	TD
2001	Rod Smith, Denver, AFC	113	1,343	11.9	11
	Keyshawn Johnson, Tampa Bay, NFC	106	1,266	11.9	1
2000	Marvin Harrison, Indianapolis, AFC	102	1,413	13.9	14
	Muhsin Muhammad, Carolina, NFC	102	1,183	11.6	6
1999	Jimmy Smith, Jacksonville, AFC	116	1,636	14.1	6
	Muhsin Muhammad, Carolina, NFC	96	1,253	13.1	8
1998	O.J. McDuffie, Miami, AFC	90	1,050	11.7	7
	Frank Sanders, Arizona, NFC	89	1,145	12.9	3
1997	Tim Brown, Oakland, AFC	104	1,408	13.5	5
	Herman Moore, Detroit, NFC	104	1,293	12.4	8
1996	Jerry Rice, San Francisco, NFC	108	1,254	11.6	8
	Carl Pickens, Cincinnati, AFC	100	1,180	11.8	12
1995	Herman Moore, Detroit, NFC	123	1,686	13.7	14
	Carl Pickens, Cincinnati, AFC	99	1,234	12.5	17
1994	Cris Carter, Minnesota, NFC	122	1,256	10.3	7
	Ben Coates, New England, AFC	96	1,174	12.2	7
1993	Sterling Sharpe, Green Bay, NFC	112	1,274	11.4	11
	Reggie Langhorne, Indianapolis, AFC	85	1,038	12.2	3
1992	Sterling Sharpe, Green Bay, NFC	108	1,461	13.5	13
	Haywood Jeffires, Houston, AFC	90	913	10.1	9
1991	Haywood Jeffires, Houston, AFC	100	1,181	11.8	7
	Michael Irvin, Dallas, NFC	93	1,523	16.4	8
1990	Jerry Rice, San Francisco, NFC	100	1,502	15.0	13
	Haywood Jeffires, Houston, AFC	74	1,048	14.2	8
	Drew Hill, Houston, AFC	74	1,019	13.8	5
1989	Sterling Sharpe, Green Bay, NFC	90	1,423	15.8	12
	Andre Reed, Buffalo, AFC	88	1,312	14.9	9
1988	Al Toon, N.Y. Jets, AFC	93	1,067	11.5	5
	Henry Ellard, L.A. Rams, NFC	86	1,414	16.4	10
1987	J.T. Smith, St. Louis, NFC	91	1,117	12.3	8
	Al Toon, N.Y. Jets, AFC	68	976	14.4	5
1986	Todd Christensen, L.A. Raiders, AFC	95	1,153	12.1	8
	Jerry Rice, San Francisco, NFC	86	1,570	18.3	15
1985	Roger Craig, San Francisco, NFC	92	1,016	11.0	6
	Lionel James, San Diego, AFC	86	1,027	11.9	6
1984	Art Monk, Washington, NFC	106	1,372	12.9	7
	Ozzie Newsome, Cleveland, AFC	89	1,001	11.2	5
1983	Todd Christensen, L.A. Raiders, AFC	92	1,247	13.6	12
	Roy Green, St. Louis, NFC	78	1,227	15.7	14
	Charlie Brown, Washington, NFC	78	1,225	15.7	8
	Earnest Gray, N.Y. Giants, NFC	78	1,139	14.6	5
1982	Dwight Clark, San Francisco, NFC	60	913	15.2	5
	Kellen Winslow, San Diego, AFC	54	721	13.4	6
1981	Kellen Winslow, San Diego, AFC	88	1,075	12.2	10
	Dwight Clark, San Francisco, NFC	85	1,105	13.0	4
1980	Kellen Winslow, San Diego, AFC	89	1,290	14.5	9
	*Earl Cooper, San Francisco, NFC	83	567	6.8	4
1979	Joe Washington, Baltimore, AFC	82	750	9.1	3
	Ahmad Rashad, Minnesota, NFC	80	1,156	14.5	9
1978	Rickey Young, Minnesota, NFC	88	704	8.0	5
	Steve Largent, Seattle, AFC	71	1,168	16.5	8
1977	Lydell Mitchell, Baltimore, AFC	71	620	8.7	4
	Ahmad Rashad, Minnesota, NFC	51	681	13.4	2
1976	MacArthur Lane, Kansas City, AFC	66	686	10.4	1
	Drew Pearson, Dallas, NFC	58	806	13.9	6
1975	Chuck Foreman, Minnesota, NFC	73	691	9.5	9
	Reggie Rucker, Cleveland, AFC	60	770	12.8	3
	Lydell Mitchell, Baltimore, AFC	60	544	9.1	4
1974	Lydell Mitchell, Baltimore, AFC	72	544	7.6	2
	Charles Young, Philadelphia, NFC	63	696	11.0	3
1973	Harold Carmichael, Philadelphia, NFC	67	1,116	16.7	9
	Fred Willis, Houston, AFC	57	371	6.5	1
1972	Harold Jackson, Philadelphia, NFC	62	1,048	16.9	4
	Fred Biletnikoff, Oakland, AFC	58	802	13.8	7
1971	Fred Biletnikoff, Oakland, AFC	61	929	15.2	9
	Bob Tucker, N.Y. Giants, NFC	59	791	13.4	4
1970	Dick Gordon, Chicago, NFC	71	1,026	14.5	13
	Marlin Briscoe, Buffalo, AFC	57	1,036	18.2	8

Year	Player, Team	No.	Yards	Avg.	TD
1969	Dan Abramowicz, New Orleans, NFL	73	1,015	13.9	7
	Lance Alworth, San Diego, AFL	64	1,003	15.7	4
1968	Clifton McNeil, San Francisco, NFL	71	994	14.0	7
	Lance Alworth, San Diego, AFL	68	1,312	19.3	10
1967	George Sauer, N.Y. Jets, AFL	75	1,189	15.9	6
	Charley Taylor, Washington, NFL	70	990	14.1	9
1966	Lance Alworth, San Diego, AFL	73	1,383	18.9	13
	Charley Taylor, Washington, NFL	72	1,119	15.5	12
1965	Lionel Taylor, Denver, AFL	85	1,131	13.3	6
	Dave Parks, San Francisco, NFL	80	1,344	16.8	12
1964	Charley Hennigan, Houston, AFL	101	1,546	15.3	8
	Johnny Morris, Chicago, NFL	93	1,200	12.9	10
1963	Lionel Taylor, Denver, AFL	78	1,101	14.1	10
	Bobby Joe Conrad, St. Louis, NFL	73	967	13.2	10
1962	Lionel Taylor, Denver, AFL	77	908	11.8	4
	Bobby Mitchell, Washington, NFL	72	1,384	19.2	11
1961	Lionel Taylor, Denver, AFL	100	1,176	11.8	4
	Jim (Red) Phillips, Los Angeles, NFL	78	1,092	14.0	5
1960	Lionel Taylor, Denver, AFL	92	1,235	13.4	12
	Raymond Berry, Baltimore, NFL	74	1,298	17.5	10
1959	Raymond Berry, Baltimore	66	959	14.5	14
1958	Raymond Berry, Baltimore	56	794	14.2	9
	Pete Retzlaff, Philadelphia	56	766	13.7	2
1957	Billy Wilson, San Francisco	52	757	14.6	6
1956	Billy Wilson, San Francisco	60	889	14.8	5
1955	Pete Pihos, Philadelphia	62	864	13.9	7
1954	Pete Pihos, Philadelphia	60	872	14.5	10
	Billy Wilson, San Francisco	60	830	13.8	5
1953	Pete Pihos, Philadelphia	63	1,049	16.7	10
1952	Mac Speedie, Cleveland	62	911	14.7	5
1951	Elroy (Crazylegs) Hirsch, Los Angeles	66	1,495	22.7	17
1950	Tom Fears, Los Angeles	84	1,116	13.3	7
1949	Tom Fears, Los Angeles	77	1,013	13.2	9
1948	*Tom Fears, Los Angeles	51	698	13.7	4
1947	Jim Keane, Chi. Bears	64	910	14.2	10
1946	Jim Benton, Los Angeles	63	981	15.6	6
1945	Don Hutson, Green Bay	47	834	17.7	9
1944	Don Hutson, Green Bay	58	866	14.9	9
1943	Don Hutson, Green Bay	47	776	16.5	11
1942	Don Hutson, Green Bay	74	1,211	16.4	17
1941	Don Hutson, Green Bay	58	738	12.7	10
1940	*Don Looney, Philadelphia	58	707	12.2	4
1939	Don Hutson, Green Bay	34	846	24.9	6
1938	Gaynell Tinsley, Chi. Cardinals	41	516	12.6	1
1937	Don Hutson, Green Bay	41	552	13.5	7
1936	Don Hutson, Green Bay	34	536	15.8	8
1935	*Tod Goodwin, N.Y. Giants	26	432	16.6	4
1934	Joe Carter, Philadelphia	16	238	14.9	4
	Morris (Red) Badgro, N.Y. Giants	16	206	12.9	1
1933	John (Shipwreck) Kelly, Brooklyn	22	246	11.2	3
1932	Ray Flaherty, N.Y. Giants	21	350	16.7	3

*First season of professional football.

ANNUAL PASS RECEIVING LEADERS (YARDS)

Year	Player, Team	No.	Yards	Avg.	TD
2001	David Boston, Arizona, NFC	98	1,598	16.3	8
	Marvin Harrison, Indianapolis, AFC	109	1,524	14.0	15
2000	Torry Holt, St. Louis, NFC	82	1,635	19.9	6
	Rod Smith, Denver, AFC	100	1,602	16.0	8
1999	Marvin Harrison, Indianapolis, AFC	115	1,663	14.5	12
	Randy Moss, Minnesota, NFC	80	1,413	17.7	11
1998	Antonio Freeman, Green Bay, NFC	84	1,424	17.0	14
	Eric Moulds, Buffalo, AFC	67	1,368	20.4	9
1997	Rob Moore, Arizona, NFC	97	1,584	16.3	8
	Tim Brown, Oakland, AFC	104	1,408	13.5	5
1996	Isaac Bruce, St. Louis, NFC	84	1,338	15.9	7
	Jimmy Smith, Jacksonville, AFC	83	1,244	15.0	7
1995	Jerry Rice, San Francisco, NFC	122	1,848	15.1	15
	Tim Brown, Oakland, AFC	89	1,342	15.1	10
1994	Jerry Rice, San Francisco, NFC	112	1,499	13.4	13

Year	Player, Team, Conf	No.	Yards	Avg.	TD
	Tim Brown, L.A. Raiders, AFC	89	1,309	14.7	9
1993	Jerry Rice, San Francisco, NFC	98	1,503	15.3	15
	Tim Brown, L.A. Raiders, AFC	80	1,180	14.8	7
1992	Sterling Sharpe, Green Bay, NFC	108	1,461	13.5	13
	Anthony Miller, San Diego, AFC	72	1,060	14.7	7
1991	Michael Irvin, Dallas, NFC	93	1,523	16.4	8
	Haywood Jeffires, Houston, AFC	100	1,181	11.8	7
1990	Jerry Rice, San Francisco, NFC	100	1,502	15.0	13
	Haywood Jeffires, Houston, AFC	74	1,048	14.2	8
1989	Jerry Rice, San Francisco, NFC	82	1,483	18.1	17
	Andre Reed, Buffalo, AFC	88	1,312	14.9	9
1988	Henry Ellard, L.A. Rams, NFC	86	1,414	16.4	10
	Eddie Brown, Cincinnati, AFC	53	1,273	24.0	9
1987	J.T. Smith, St. Louis, NFC	91	1,117	12.3	8
	Carlos Carson, Kansas City, AFC	55	1,044	19.0	7
1986	Jerry Rice, San Francisco, NFC	86	1,570	18.3	15
	Stanley Morgan, New England, AFC	84	1,491	17.8	10
1985	Steve Largent, Seattle, AFC	79	1,287	16.3	6
	Mike Quick, Philadelphia, NFC	73	1,247	17.1	11
1984	Roy Green, St. Louis, NFC	78	1,555	19.9	12
	John Stallworth, Pittsburgh, AFC	80	1,395	17.4	11
1983	Mike Quick, Philadelphia, NFC	69	1,409	20.4	13
	Carlos Carson, Kansas City, AFC	80	1,351	16.9	7
1982	Wes Chandler, San Diego, AFC	49	1,032	21.1	9
	Dwight Clark, San Francisco, NFC	60	913	15.2	5
1981	Alfred Jenkins, Atlanta, NFC	70	1,358	19.4	13
	Frank Lewis, Buffalo, AFC	70	1,244	17.8	4
	Steve Watson, Denver, AFC	60	1,244	20.7	13
1980	John Jefferson, San Diego, AFC	82	1,340	16.3	13
	James Lofton, Green Bay, NFC	71	1,226	17.3	4
1979	Steve Largent, Seattle, AFC	66	1,237	18.7	9
	Ahmad Rashad, Minnesota, NFC	80	1,156	14.5	9
1978	Wesley Walker, N.Y. Jets, AFC	48	1,169	24.4	8
	Harold Carmichael, Philadelphia, NFC	55	1,072	19.5	8
1977	Drew Pearson, Dallas, NFC	48	870	18.1	2
	Ken Burrough, Houston, AFC	43	816	19.0	8
1976	Roger Carr, Baltimore, AFC	43	1,112	25.9	11
	*Sammy White, Minnesota, NFC	51	906	17.8	10
1975	Ken Burrough, Houston, AFC	53	1,063	20.1	8
	Mel Gray, St. Louis, NFC	48	926	19.3	11
1974	Cliff Branch, Oakland, AFC	60	1,092	18.2	13
	Drew Pearson, Dallas, NFC	62	1,087	17.5	2
1973	Harold Carmichael, Philadelphia, NFC	67	1,116	16.7	9
	*Isaac Curtis, Cincinnati, AFC	45	843	18.7	9
1972	Harold Jackson, Philadelphia, NFC	62	1,048	16.9	4
	Rich Caster, N.Y. Jets, AFC	39	833	21.4	10
1971	Otis Taylor, Kansas City, AFC	57	1,110	19.5	7
	Gene Washington, San Francisco, NFC	46	884	19.2	4
1970	Gene Washington, San Francisco, NFC	53	1,100	20.8	12
	Marlin Briscoe, Buffalo, AFC	57	1,036	18.2	8
1969	Warren Wells, Oakland, AFL	47	1,260	26.8	14
	Harold Jackson, Philadelphia, NFL	65	1,116	17.2	9
1968	Lance Alworth, San Diego, AFL	68	1,312	19.3	10
	Roy Jefferson, Pittsburgh, NFL	58	1,074	18.5	11
1967	Don Maynard, N.Y. Jets, AFL	71	1,434	20.3	10
	Ben Hawkins, Philadelphia, NFL	59	1,265	21.4	10
1966	Lance Alworth, San Diego, AFL	73	1,383	18.9	13
	Pat Studstill, Detroit, NFL	67	1,266	18.9	5
1965	Lance Alworth, San Diego, AFL	69	1,602	23.2	14
	Dave Parks, San Francisco, NFL	80	1,344	16.8	12
1964	Charley Hennigan, Houston, AFL	101	1,546	15.3	8
	Johnny Morris, Chicago, NFL	93	1,200	12.9	10
1963	Bobby Mitchell, Washington, NFL	69	1,436	20.8	7
	Art Powell, Oakland, AFL	73	1,304	17.8	16
1962	Bobby Mitchel, Washington, NFL	72	1,384	19.2	11
	Art Powell, N.Y. Titans, AFL	64	1,130	17.6	8
1961	Charley Hennigan, Houston, AFL	82	1,746	21.3	12
	Tommy McDonald, Philadelphia, NFL	64	1,144	17.9	13
1960	*Bill Groman, Houston, AFL	72	1,473	20.5	12
	Raymond Berry, Baltimore, NFL	74	1,298	17.5	10

Year	Player, Team	No.	Yards	Avg.	TD
1959	Raymond Berry, Baltimore	66	959	14.5	14
1958	Del Shofner, Los Angeles	51	1,097	21.5	8
1957	Raymond Berry, Baltimore	47	800	17.0	6
1956	Billy Howton, Green Bay	55	1,188	21.6	12
1955	Pete Pihos, Philadelphia	62	864	13.9	7
1954	Bob Boyd, Los Angeles	53	1,212	22.9	6
1953	Pete Pihos, Philadelphia	63	1,049	16.7	10
1952	*Bill Howton, Green Bay	53	1,231	23.2	13
1951	Elroy (Crazylegs) Hirsch, Los Angeles	66	1,495	22.7	17
1950	Tom Fears, Los Angeles	84	1,116	13.3	7
1949	Bob Mann, Detroit	66	1,014	15.4	4
1948	Mal Kutner, Chi. Cardinals	41	943	23.0	14
1947	Mal Kutner, Chi. Cardinals	43	944	21.9	7
1946	Jim Benton, Los Angeles	63	981	15.5	6
1945	Jim Benton, Cleveland	45	1,067	23.7	8
1944	Don Hutson, Green Bay	58	866	14.6	9
1943	Don Hutson, Green Bay	47	776	16.5	11
1942	Don Hutson, Green Bay	74	1,211	16.4	17
1941	Don Hutson, Green Bay	58	738	12.7	10
1940	*Don Looney, Philadelphia	58	707	12.2	4
1939	Don Hutson, Green Bay	34	846	24.9	6
1938	Don Hutson, Green Bay	32	548	17.1	9
1937	*Gaynell Tinsley, Chi. Cardinals	36	675	18.8	5
1936	Don Hutson, Green Bay	34	526	15.5	8
1935	Charley Malone, Boston	22	433	19.7	2
1934	Harry Ebding, Detroit	9	257	28.6	2
1933	*Paul Moss, Pittsburgh	18	383	21.3	2
1932	Johnny (Blood) McNally, Green Bay	19	326	17.2	3

*First season of professional football.

ANNUAL INTERCEPTION LEADERS

Year	Player, Team	No.	Yards	TD
2001	*Anthony Henry, Cleveland, AFC	10	177	1
	Ronde Barber, Tampa Bay, NFC	10	86	1
2000	Darren Sharper, Green Bay, NFC	9	109	0
	Samari Rolle, Tennessee, AFC	7	140	1
	Brian Walker, Miami, AFC	7	80	0
1999	Rod Woodson, Baltimore, AFC	7	195	2
	Sam Madison, Miami, AFC	7	164	1
	James Hasty, Kansas City, AFC	7	98	2
	Donnie Abraham, Tampa Bay, NFC	7	115	2
	Troy Vincent, Philadelphia, NFC	7	91	0
1998	Ty Law, New England, AFC	9	133	1
	Kwamie Lassiter, Arizona, NFC	8	80	0
1997	Ryan McNeil, St. Louis, NFC	9	127	1
	Mark McMillian, Kansas City, AFC	8	274	3
	Darryl Williams, Seattle, AFC	8	172	1
1996	Tyrone Braxton, Denver, AFC	9	128	1
	Keith Lyle, St. Louis, NFC	9	152	0
1995	*Orlando Thomas, Minnesota, NFC	9	108	1
	Willie Williams, Pittsburgh, AFC	7	122	1
1994	Eric Turner, Cleveland, AFC	9	199	1
	Aeneas Williams, Arizona, NFC	9	89	0
1993	Eugene Robinson, Seattle, AFC	9	80	0
	Nate Odomes, Buffalo, AFC	9	65	0
	Deion Sanders, Atlanta, NFC	7	91	0
1992	Henry Jones, Buffalo, AFC	8	263	2
	Audray McMillian, Minnesota, NFC	8	157	2
1991	Ronnie Lott, L.A. Raiders, AFC	8	52	0
	Ray Crockett, Detroit, NFC	6	141	1
	Deion Sanders, Atlanta, NFC	6	119	1
	*Aeneas Williams, Phoenix, NFC	6	60	0
	Tim McKyer, Atlanta, NFC	6	24	0
1990	*Mark Carrier, Chicago, NFC	10	39	0
	Richard Johnson, Houston, AFC	8	100	1
1989	Felix Wright, Cleveland, AFC	9	91	1
	Eric Allen, Philadelphia, NFC	8	38	0
1988	Scott Case, Atlanta, NFC	10	47	0
	Erik McMillan, N.Y. Jets, AFC	8	168	2
1987	Barry Wilburn, Washington, NFC	9	135	1
	Mike Prior, Indianapolis, AFC	6	57	0
	Mark Kelso, Buffalo, AFC	6	25	0
	Keith Bostic, Houston, AFC	6	-14	0
1986	Ronnie Lott, San Francisco, NFC	10	134	1
	Deron Cherry, Kansas City, AFC	9	150	0
1985	Everson Walls, Dallas, NFC	9	31	0
	Albert Lewis, Kansas City, AFC	8	59	0
	Eugene Daniel, Indianapolis, AFC	8	53	0
1984	Ken Easley, Seattle, AFC	10	126	2
	*Tom Flynn, Green Bay, NFC	9	106	0
1983	Mark Murphy, Washington, NFC	9	127	0
	Ken Riley, Cincinnati, AFC	8	89	2
	Vann McElroy, L.A. Raiders, AFC	8	68	0
1982	Everson Walls, Dallas, NFC	7	61	0
	Ken Riley, Cincinnati, AFC	5	88	1
	Bobby Jackson, N.Y. Jets, AFC	5	84	1
	Dwayne Woodruff, Pittsburgh, AFC	5	53	0
	Donnie Shell, Pittsburgh, AFC	5	27	0
1981	*Everson Walls, Dallas, NFC	11	133	0
	John Harris, Seattle, AFC	10	155	2
1980	Lester Hayes, Oakland, AFC	13	273	1
	Nolan Cromwell, Los Angeles, NFC	8	140	1
1979	Mike Reinfeldt, Houston, AFC	12	205	0
	Lemar Parrish, Washiongton, NFC	9	65	0
1978	Thom Darden, Cleveland, AFC	10	200	0
	Ken Stone, St. Louis, NFC	9	139	0
	Willie Buchanon, Green Bay, NFC	9	93	1
1977	Lyle Blackwood, Baltimore, AFC	10	163	0
	Rolland Lawrence, Atlanta, NFC	7	138	0
1976	Monte Jackson, Los Angeles, NFC	10	173	3
	Ken Riley, Cincinnati, AFC	9	141	1
1975	Mel Blount, Pittsburgh, AFC	11	121	0
	Paul Krause, Minnesota, NFC	10	201	0
1974	Emmitt Thomas, Kansas City, AFC	12	214	2
	Ray Brown, Atlanta, NFC	8	164	1
1973	Dick Anderson, Miami, AFC	8	163	2
	Mike Wagner, Pittsburgh, AFC	8	134	0
	Bobby Bryant, Minnesota, NFC	7	105	1
1972	Bill Bradley, Philadelphia, NFC	9	73	0
	Mike Sensibaugh, Kansas City, AFC	8	65	0
1971	Bill Bradley, Philadelphia, NFC	11	248	0
	Ken Houston, Houston, AFC	9	220	4
1970	Johnny Robinson, Kansas City, AFC	10	155	0
	Dick LeBeau, Detroit, NFC	9	96	0
1969	Mel Renfro, Dallas, NFL	10	118	0
	Emmitt Thomas, Kansas City, AFL	9	146	1
1968	Dave Grayson, Oakland, AFL	10	195	1
	Willie Williams, N.Y. Giants, NFL	10	103	0
1967	Miller Farr, Houston, AFL	10	264	3
	*Lem Barney, Detroit, NFL	10	232	3
	Tom Janik, Buffalo, AFL	10	222	2
	Dave Whitsell, New Orleans, NFL	10	178	2
	Dick Westmoreland, Miami, AFL	10	127	1
1966	Larry Wilson, St. Louis, NFL	10	180	2
	Johnny Robinson, Kansas City, AFL	10	136	1
	Bobby Hunt, Kansas City, AFL	10	113	0
1965	W.K. Hicks, Houston, AFL	9	156	0
	Bobby Boyd, Baltimore, NFL	9	78	1
1964	Dainard Paulson, N.Y. Jets, AFL	12	157	1
	*Paul Krause, Washington, NFL	12	140	1
1963	Fred Glick, Houston, AFL	12	180	1
	Dick Lynch, N.Y. Giants, NFL	9	251	3
	Roosevelt Taylor, Chicago, NFL	9	172	1
1962	Lee Riley, N.Y. Titans, AFL	11	122	0
	Willie Wood, Green Bay, NFL	9	132	0
1961	Billy Atkins, Buffalo, AFL	10	158	0
	Dick Lynch, N.Y. Giants, NFL	9	60	0
1960	*Austin (Goose) Gonsoulin, Denver, AFL	11	98	0
	Dave Baker, San Francisco, NFL	10	96	0
	Jerry Norton, St. Louis, NFL	10	96	0
1959	Dean Derby, Pittsburgh	7	127	0
	Milt Davis, Baltimore	7	119	1
	Don Shinnick, Baltimore	7	70	0
1958	Jim Patton, N.Y. Giants	11	183	0
1957	Milt Davis, Baltimore	10	219	2
	Jack Christiansen, Detroit	10	137	1
	Jack Butler, Pittsburgh	10	85	0
1956	Linden Crow, Chi. Cardinals	11	170	0
1955	Will Sherman, Los Angeles	11	101	0
1954	Dick (Night Train) Lane, Chi. Cardinals	10	181	0
1953	Jack Christiansen, Detroit	12	238	1
1952	*Dick (Night Train) Lane, Los Angeles	14	298	2
1951	Otto Schnellbacher, N.Y. Giants	11	194	2
1950	Orban (Spec) Sanders, N.Y. Yanks	13	199	0
1949	Bob Nussbaumer, Chi. Cardinals	12	157	0
1948	*Dan Sandifer, Washington	13	258	2
1947	Frank Reagan, N.Y. Giants	10	203	0
	Frank Seno, Boston	10	100	0
1946	Bill Dudley, Pittsburgh	10	242	1
1945	Roy Zimmerman, Philadelphia	7	90	0
1944	*Howard Livingston, N.Y. Giants	9	172	1
1943	Sammy Baugh, Washington	11	112	0
1942	Clyde (Bulldog) Turner, Chi. Bears	8	96	1
1941	Marshall Goldberg, Chi. Cardinals	7	54	0
	*Art Jones, Pittsburgh	7	35	0
1940	Clarence (Ace) Parker, Brooklyn	6	146	1
	Kent Ryan, Detroit	6	65	0
	Don Hutson, Green Bay	6	24	0

First season of professional football.

YEARLY STATISTICAL LEADERS

ANNUAL PUNTING LEADERS

Year	Player, Team	No.	Avg.	Long
2001	Todd Sauerbrun, Carolina, NFC	93	47.5	73
	Shane Lechler, Oakland, AFC	73	46.2	65
2000	Darren Bennett, San Diego, AFC	92	46.2	66
	Mitch Berger, Minnesota, NFC	62	44.7	60
1999	Tom Rouen, Denver, AFC	84	46.5	65
	Mitch Berger, Minnesota, NFC	61	45.4	75
1998	Craig Hentrich, Tennessee, AFC	69	47.2	71
	Mark Royals, New Orleans, NFC	88	45.6	64
1997	Mark Royals, New Orleans, NFC	88	45.9	66
	Tom Tupa, New England, AFC	78	45.8	73
1996	John Kidd, Miami, AFC	78	46.3	63
	Matt Turk, Washington, NFC	75	45.1	63
1995	Rick Tuten, Seattle, AFC	83	45.0	73
	Sean Landeta, St. Louis, NFC	83	44.3	63
1994	Sean Landeta, L.A. Rams, NFC	78	44.8	62
	Jeff Gossett, L.A. Raiders, AFC	77	43.9	65
1993	Greg Montgomery, Houston, AFC	54	45.6	77
	Jim Arnold, Detroit, NFC	72	44.5	68
1992	Greg Montgomery, Houston, AFC	53	46.9	66
	Harry Newsome, Minnesota, NFC	72	45.0	84
1991	Reggie Roby, Miami, AFC	54	45.7	64
	Harry Newsome, Minnesota, AFC	68	45.5	65
1990	Mike Horan, Denver, AFC	58	44.4	67
	Sean Landeta, N.Y. Giants, NFC	75	44.1	67
1989	Rich Camarillo, Phoenix, NFC	76	43.4	58
	Greg Montgomery, Houston, AFC	56	43.3	63
1988	Harry Newsome, Pittsburgh, AFC	65	45.4	62
	Jim Arnold, Detroit, NFC	97	42.4	69
1987	Rick Donnelly, Atlanta, NFC	61	44.0	62
	Ralf Mojsiejenko, San Diego, AFC	67	42.9	57
1986	Rohn Stark, Indianapolis, AFC	76	45.2	63
	Sean Landeta, N.Y. Giants, NFC	79	44.8	61
1985	Rohn Stark, Indianapolis, AFC	78	45.9	68
	*Rick Donnelly, Atlanta, NFC	59	43.6	68
1984	Jim Arnold, Kansas City, AFC	98	44.9	63
	*Brian Hansen, New Orleans, NFC	69	43.8	66
1983	Rohn Stark, Baltimore, AFC	91	45.3	68
	Frank Garcia, Tampa Bay, NFC	95	42.2	64
1982	Luke Prestridge, Denver, AFC	45	45.0	65
	Carl Birdsong, St. Louis, NFC	54	43.8	65
1981	Pat McInally, Cincinnati, AFC	72	45.4	62
	Tom Skladany, Detroit, NFC	64	43.5	74
1980	Dave Jennings, N.Y. Giants, NFC	94	44.8	63
	Luke Prestridge, Denver, AFC	70	43.9	57
1979	*Bob Grupp, Kansas City, AFC	89	43.6	74
	Dave Jennings, N.Y. Giants, NFC	104	42.7	72
1978	Pat McInally, Cincinnati, AFC	91	43.1	65
	*Tom Skladany, Detroit, NFC	86	42.5	63
1977	Ray Guy, Oakland, AFC	59	43.3	74
	Tom Blanchard, New Orleans, NFC	82	42.4	66
1976	Marv Bateman, Buffalo, AFC	86	42.8	78
	John James, Atlanta, NFC	101	42.1	67
1975	Ray Guy, Oakland, AFC	68	43.8	64
	Herman Weaver, Detroit, NFC	80	42.0	61
1974	Ray Guy, Oakland, AFC	74	42.2	66
	Tom Blanchard, New Orleans, NFC	88	42.1	71
1973	Jerrel Wilson, Kansas City, AFC	80	45.5	68
	*Tom Wittum, San Francisco, NFC	79	43.7	62
1972	Jerrel Wilson, Kansas City, AFC	66	44.8	69
	Dave Chapple, Los Angeles, NFC	53	44.2	70
1971	Dave Lewis, Cincinnati, AFC	72	44.8	56

Year	Player, Team	No.	Avg.	Long
	Tom McNeill, Philadelphia, NFC	73	42.0	64
1970	Dave Lewis, Cincinnati, AFC	79	46.2	63
	*Julian Fagan, New Orleans, NFC	77	42.5	64
1969	David Lee, Baltimore, NFL	57	45.3	66
	Dennis Partee, San Diego, AFL	71	44.6	62
1968	Jerrel Wilson, Kansas City, AFL	63	45.1	70
	Billy Lothridge, Atlanta, NFL	75	44.3	70
1967	Bob Scarpitto, Denver, AFL	105	44.9	73
	Billy Lothridge, Atlanta, NFL	87	43.7	62
1966	Bob Scarpitto, Denver, AFL	76	45.8	70
	*David Lee, Baltimore, NFL	49	45.6	64
1965	Gary Collins, Cleveland, NFL	65	46.7	71
	Jerrel Wilson, Kansas City, AFL	69	45.4	64
1964	Bobby Walden, Minnesota, NFL	72	46.4	73
	Jim Fraser, Denver, AFL	73	44.2	67
1963	Yale Lary, Detroit, NFL	35	48.9	73
	Jim Fraser, Denver, AFL	81	44.4	66
1962	Tommy Davis, San Francisco, NFL	48	45.6	82
	Jim Fraser, Denver, AFL	55	43.6	75
1961	Yale Lary, Detroit, NFL	52	48.4	71
	Billy Atkins, Buffalo, AFL	85	44.5	70
1960	Jerry Norton, St. Louis, NFL	39	45.6	62
	*Paul Maguire, L.A. Chargers, AFL	43	40.5	61
1959	Yale Lary, Detroit	45	47.1	67
1958	Sam Baker, Washington	48	45.4	64
1957	Don Chandler, N.Y. Giants	60	44.6	61
1956	Norm Van Brocklin, Los Angeles	48	43.1	72
1955	Norm Van Brocklin, Los Angeles	60	44.6	61
1954	Pat Brady, Pittsburgh	66	43.2	72
1953	Pat Brady, Pittsburgh	80	46.9	64
1952	Horace Gillom, Cleveland	61	45.7	73
1951	Horace Gillom, Cleveland	73	45.5	66
1950	*Fred (Curly) Morrison, Chi. Bears	57	43.3	65
1949	*Mike Boyda, N.Y. Bulldogs	56	44.2	61
1948	Joe Muha, Philadelphia	57	47.3	82
1947	Jack Jacobs, Green Bay	57	43.5	74
1946	Roy McKay, Green Bay	64	42.7	64
1945	Roy McKay, Green Bay	44	41.2	73
1944	Frank Sinkwich, Detroit	45	41.0	73
1943	Sammy Baugh, Washington	50	45.9	81
1942	Sammy Baugh, Washington	37	48.2	74
1941	Sammy Baugh, Washington	30	48.7	75
1940	Sammy Baugh, Washington	35	51.4	85
1939	*Parker Hall, Cleveland	58	40.8	80

First season of professional football.

ANNUAL PUNT RETURN LEADERS

Year	Player, Team	No.	Yards	Avg.	Long	TD
2001	Troy Brown, New England, AFC	29	413	14.2	85	2
	Darrien Gordon, Atlanta, NFC	31	437	14.1	74	0
2000	Jermaine Lewis, Baltimore, AFC	36	578	16.1	89	2
	Az-Zahir Hakim, St. Louis, NFC	32	489	15.3	86	1
1999	*Charlie Rogers, Seattle, AFC	22	318	14.5	94	1
	*Mac Cody, Arizona, NFC	32	373	11.7	31	0
1998	Deion Sanders, Dallas, NFC	24	375	15.6	69	2
	Reggie Barlow, Jacksonville, AFC	43	555	12.9	85	1
1997	Jermaine Lewis, Baltimore, AFC	28	437	15.6	89	2
	David Palmer, Minnesota, NFC	34	444	13.1	57	0
1996	Desmond Howard, Green Bay, NFC	58	875	15.1	92	3
	Darrien Gordon, San Diego, AFC	36	537	14.9	81	1
1995	David Palmer, Minnesota, NFC	26	342	13.2	74	1
	Andre Coleman, San Diego, AFC	28	326	11.6	88	1
1994	Brian Mitchell, Washington, NFC	32	452	14.1	78	2
	Darrien Gordon, San Diego, AFC	36	475	13.2	90	2
1993	*Tyrone Hughes, New Orleans, NFC	37	503	13.6	83	2
	Eric Metcalf, Cleveland, AFC	36	464	12.9	91	2
1992	Johnny Bailey, Phoenix, NFC	20	263	13.2	65	0
	Rod Woodson, Pittsburgh, AFC	32	364	11.4	80	1
1991	Mel Gray, Detroit, NFC	25	385	15.4	78	1
	Rod Woodson, Pittsburgh, AFC	28	320	11.4	40	0
1990	Clarence Verdin, Indianapolis, AFC	31	396	12.8	36	0
	*Johnny Bailey, Chicago, NFC	36	399	11.1	95	1
1989	Walter Stanley, Detroit, NFC	36	496	13.8	74	0
	Clarence Verdin, Indianapolis, AFC	23	296	12.9	49	1
1988	John Taylor, San Francisco, NFC	44	556	12.6	95	2
	JoJo Townsell, N.Y. Jets, AFC	35	409	11.7	59	1
1987	Mel Gray, New Orleans, NFC	24	352	14.7	80	0
	Bobby Joe Edmonds, Seattle, AFC	20	251	12.6	40	0
1986	*Bobby Joe Edmonds, Seattle, AFC	34	419	12.3	75	1
	*Vai Sikahema, St. Louis, NFC	43	522	12.1	71	2
1985	Irving Fryar, New England, AFC	37	520	14.1	85	2
	Henry Ellard, L.A. Rams, NFC	37	501	13.5	80	1
1984	Mike Martin, Cincinnati, AFC	24	376	15.7	55	0
	Henry Ellard, L.A. Rams, NFC	30	403	13.4	83	2
1983	*Henry Ellard, L.A. Rams, NFC	16	217	13.6	72	1
	Kirk Springs, N.Y. Jets, AFC	23	287	12.5	76	1
1982	Rick Upchurch, Denver, AFC	15	242	16.1	78	0
	Billy Johnson, Atlanta, NFC	24	273	11.4	71	0
1981	LeRoy Irvin, Los Angeles, NFC	46	615	13.4	84	3
	*James Brooks, San Diego, AFC	22	290	13.2	42	0
1980	J.T. Smith, Kansas City, AFC	40	581	14.5	75	2
	*Kenny Johnson, Atlanta, NFC	23	281	12.2	56	0
1979	John Sciarra, Philadelphia, NFC	16	182	11.4	38	0
	*Tony Nathan, Miami, AFC	28	306	10.9	86	1
1978	Rick Upchurch, Denver, AFC	36	493	13.7	75	1
	Jackie Wallace, Los Angeles, NFC	52	618	11.9	58	0
1977	Billy Johnson, Houston, AFC	35	539	15.4	87	2
	Larry Marshall, Philadelphia, NFC	46	489	10.6	48	0
1976	Rick Upchurch, Denver, AFC	39	536	13.7	92	4
	Eddie Brown, Washington, NFC	48	646	13.5	71	1
1975	Billy Johnson, Houston, AFC	40	612	15.3	83	3
	Terry Metcalf, St. Louis, NFC	23	285	12.4	69	1
1974	Lemar Parrish, Cincinnati, AFC	18	338	18.8	90	2
	Dick Jauron, Detroit, NFC	17	286	16.8	58	0
1973	Bruce Taylor, San Francisco, NFC	15	207	13.8	61	0
	Ron Smith, San Diego, AFC	27	352	13.0	84	2
1972	Ken Ellis, Green Bay, NFC	14	215	15.4	80	1
	Chris Farasopoulos, N.Y. Jets, AFC	17	179	10.5	65	1
1971	Les (Speedy) Duncan, Washington, NFC	22	233	10.6	33	0

Year	Player, Team	No.	Yards	Avg.	Long	TD
	Leroy Kelly, Cleveland, AFC	30	292	9.7	74	0
1970	Ed Podolak, Kansas City, AFC	23	311	13.5	60	0
	*Bruce Taylor, San Francisco, NFC	43	516	12.0	76	0
1969	Alvin Haymond, Los Angeles, NFL	33	435	13.2	52	0
	*Bill Thompson, Denver, AFL	25	288	11.5	40	0
1968	Bob Hayes, Dallas, NFL	15	312	20.8	90	2
	Noland Smith, Kansas City, AFL	18	270	15.0	80	1
1967	Floyd Little, Denver, AFL	16	270	16.9	72	1
	Ben Davis, Cleveland, NFL	18	229	12.7	52	1
1966	Les (Speedy) Duncan, San Diego, AFL	18	238	13.2	81	1
	Johnny Roland, St. Louis, NFL	20	221	11.1	86	1
1965	Leroy Kelly, Cleveland, NFL	17	265	15.6	67	2
	Les (Speedy) Duncan, San Diego, AFL	30	464	15.5	66	2
1964	Bobby Jancik, Houston, AFL	12	220	18.3	82	1
	Tommy Watkins, Detroit, NFL	16	238	14.9	68	2
1963	Dick James, Washington, NFL	16	214	13.4	39	0
	Claude (Hoot) Gibson, Oakland, AFL	26	307	11.8	85	2
1962	Dick Christy, N.Y. Titans, AFL	15	250	16.7	73	2
	Pat Studstill, Detroit, NFL	29	457	15.8	44	0
1961	Dick Christy, N.Y. Titans, AFL	18	383	21.3	70	2
	Willie Wood, Green Bay, NFL	14	225	16.1	72	2
1960	*Abner Haynes, Dall. Texans, AFL	14	215	15.4	46	0
	Abe Woodson, San Francisco, NFL	13	174	13.4	48	0
1959	Johnny Morris, Chi. Bears	14	171	12.2	78	1
1958	Jon Arnett, Los Angeles	18	223	12.4	58	0
1957	Bert Zagers, Washington	14	217	15.5	76	2
1956	Ken Konz, Cleveland	13	187	14.4	65	1
1955	Ollie Matson, Chi. Cardinals	13	245	18.8	78	2
1954	*Veryl Switzer, Green Bay	24	306	12.8	93	1
1953	Charley Trippi, Chi. Cardinals	21	239	11.4	38	0
1952	Jack Christiansen, Detroit	15	322	21.5	79	2
1951	Claude (Buddy) Young, N.Y. Yanks	12	231	19.3	79	1
1950	*Herb Rich, Baltimore	12	276	23.0	86	1
1949	Verda (Vitamin T) Smith, Los Angeles	27	427	15.8	85	1
1948	George McAfee, Chi. Bears	30	417	13.9	60	1
1947	*Walt Slater, Pittsburgh	28	435	15.5	33	0
1946	Bill Dudley, Pittsburgh	27	385	14.3	52	0
1945	*Dave Ryan, Detroit	15	220	14.7	56	0
1944	*Steve Van Buren, Philadelphia	15	230	15.3	55	1
1943	Andy Farkas, Washington	15	168	11.2	33	0
1942	Merlyn Condit, Brooklyn	21	210	10.0	23	0
1941	Byron (Whizzer) White, Detroit	19	262	13.8	64	0

*First season of professional football.

ANNUAL KICKOFF RETURN LEADERS

Year	Player, Team	No.	Yards	Avg.	Long	TD
2001	Ronney Jenkins, San Diego, AFC	58	1,541	26.6	93	2
	*Steve Smith, Carolina, NFC	56	1,431	25.6	99	2
2000	*Darrick Vaughn, Atlanta, NFC	39	1,082	27.7	100	3
	Derrick Mason, Tennessee, AFC	42	1,132	27.0	66	0
1999	Tony Horne, St. Louis, NFC	30	892	29.7	101	2
	Tremain Mack, Cincinnati, AFC	51	1,382	27.1	99	1
1998	*Terry Fair, Detroit, NFC	51	1,428	28.0	105	2
	Corey Harris, Baltimore, AFC	35	965	27.6	95	1
1997	Michael Bates, Carolina, NFC	47	1,281	27.3	56	0
	Aaron Glenn, N.Y. Jets, AFC	28	741	26.5	96	1
1996	Michael Bates, Carolina, NFC	33	998	30.2	93	1
	Tamarick Vanover, Kansas City, AFC	33	854	25.9	97	1
1995	Ron Carpenter, N.Y. Jets, AFC	20	553	27.7	58	0
	Brian Mitchell, Washington, NFC	55	1,408	25.6	59	0
1994	Mel Gray, Detroit, NFC	45	1,276	28.4	102	3
	Randy Baldwin, Cleveland, AFC	28	753	26.9	85	1
1993	Robert Brooks, Green Bay, NFC	23	611	26.6	95	1

	*Raghib Ismail, L.A. Raiders, AFC	25	605	24.2	66	0
1992	Jon Vaughn, New England, AFC	20	564	28.2	100	1
	Deion Sanders, Atlanta, NFC	40	1,067	26.7	99	2
1991	Mel Gray, Detroit, NFC	36	929	25.8	71	0
	Nate Lewis, San Diego, AFC	23	578	25.1	95	1
1990	Kevin Clark, Denver, AFC	20	505	25.3	75	0
	David Meggett, N.Y. Giants, NFC	21	492	23.4	58	0
1989	Rod Woodson, Pittsburgh, AFC	36	982	27.3	84	1
	Mel Gray, Detroit, NFC	24	640	26.7	57	0
1988	*Tim Brown, L.A. Raiders, AFC	41	1,098	26.8	97	1
	Donnie Elder, Tampa Bay, NFC	34	772	22.7	51	0
1987	Sylvester Stamps, Atlanta, NFC	24	660	27.5	97	1
	Paul Palmer, Kansas City, AFC	38	923	24.3	95	2
1986	Dennis Gentry, Chicago, NFC	20	576	28.8	91	1
	Lupe Sanchez, Pittsburgh, AFC	25	591	23.6	64	0
1985	Ron Brown, L.A. Rams, NFC	28	918	32.8	98	3
	Glen Young, Cleveland, AFC	35	898	25.7	63	0
1984	*Bobby Humphery, N.Y. Jets, AFC	22	675	30.7	97	1
	Barry Redden, L.A. Rams, NFC	23	530	23.0	40	0
1983	Fulton Walker, Miami, AFC	36	962	26.7	78	0
	Darrin Nelson, Minnesota, NFC	18	445	24.7	50	0
1982	*Mike Mosley, Buffalo, AFC	18	487	27.1	66	0
	Alvin Hall, Detroit, NFC	16	426	26.6	96	1
1981	Mike Nelms, Washington, NFC	37	1,099	29.7	84	0
	Carl Roaches, Houston, AFC	28	769	27.5	96	1
1980	Horace Ivory, New England, AFC	36	992	27.6	98	1
	Rich Mauti, New Orleans, NFC	31	798	25.7	52	0
1979	Larry Brunson, Oakland, AFC	17	441	25.9	89	0
	Jimmy Edwards, Minnesota, NFC	44	1,103	25.1	83	0
1978	Steve Odom, Green Bay, NFC	25	677	27.1	95	1
	*Keith Wright, Cleveland, AFC	30	789	26.3	86	0
1977	*Raymond Clayborn, New England, AFC	28	869	31.0	101	3
	*Wilbert Montgomery, Philadelphia, NFC	23	619	26.9	99	1
1976	*Duriel Harris, Miami, AFC	17	559	32.9	69	0
	Cullen Bryant, Los Angeles, NFC	16	459	28.7	90	1
1975	*Walter Payton, Chicago, NFC	14	444	31.7	70	0
	Harold Hart, Oakland, AFC	17	518	30.5	102	1
1974	Terry Metcalf, St. Louis, NFC	20	623	31.2	94	1
	Greg Pruitt, Cleveland, AFC	22	606	27.5	88	1
1973	Carl Garrett, Chicago, NFC	16	486	30.4	67	0
	*Wallace Francis, Buffalo, AFC	23	687	29.9	101	2
1972	Ron Smith, Chicago, NFC	30	924	30.8	94	1
	*Bruce Laird, Baltimore, AFC	29	843	29.1	73	0
1971	Travis Williams, Los Angeles, NFC	25	743	29.7	105	1
	Eugene (Mercury) Morris, Miami, AFC	15	423	28.2	94	1
1970	Jim Duncan, Baltimore, AFC	20	707	35.4	99	1
	Cecil Turner, Chicago, NFC	23	752	32.7	96	4
1969	Bobby Williams, Detroit, NFL	17	563	33.1	96	1
	*Bill Thompson, Denver, AFL	18	513	28.5	63	0
1968	Preston Pearson, Baltimore, NFL	15	527	35.1	102	2
	*George Atkinson, Oakland, AFL	32	802	25.1	60	0
1967	*Travis Williams, Green Bay, NFL	18	739	41.1	104	4
	*Zeke Moore, Houston, AFL	14	405	28.9	92	1
1966	Gale Sayers, Chicago, NFL	23	718	31.2	93	2
	*Goldie Sellers, Denver, AFL	19	541	28.5	100	2
1965	Tommy Watkins, Detroit, NFL	17	584	34.4	94	0
	Abner Haynes, Denver, AFL	34	901	26.5	60	0
1964	*Clarence Childs, N.Y. Giants, NFL	34	987	29.0	100	1
	Bo Roberson, Oakland, AFL	36	975	27.1	59	0
1963	Abe Woodson, San Francisco, NFL	29	935	32.2	103	3
	Bobby Jancik, Houston, AFL	45	1,317	29.3	53	0
1962	Abe Woodson, San Francisco, NFL	37	1,157	31.3	79	0
	*Bobby Jancik, Houston, AFL	24	826	30.3	61	0

Year	Player	Value				
1961	Dick Bass, Los Angeles, NFL	23	698	30.3	64	0
	*Dave Grayson, Dall. Texans, AFL	16	453	28.3	73	0
1960	*Tom Moore, Green Bay, NFL	12	397	33.1	84	0
	Ken Hall, Houston, AFL	19	594	31.3	104	1
1959	Abe Woodson, San Francisco	13	382	29.4	105	1
1958	Ollie Matson, Chi. Cardinals	14	497	35.5	101	2
1957	*Jon Arnett, Los Angeles	18	504	28.0	98	1
1956	*Tom Wilson, Los Angeles	15	477	31.8	103	1
1955	Al Carmichael, Green Bay	14	418	29.9	100	1
1954	Billy Reynolds, Cleveland	14	413	29.5	51	0
1953	Joe Arenas, San Francisco	16	551	34.4	82	0
1952	Lynn Chandnois, Pittsburgh	17	599	35.2	93	2
1951	Lynn Chandnois, Pittsburgh	12	390	32.5	55	0
1950	Verda (Vitamin T) Smith, Los Angeles	22	742	33.7	97	3
1949	*Don Doll, Detroit	21	536	25.5	56	0
1948	*Joe Scott, N.Y. Giants	20	569	28.5	99	1
1947	Eddie Saenz, Washington	29	797	27.5	94	2
1946	Abe Karnofsky, Boston	21	599	28.5	97	1
1945	Steve Van Buren, Philadelphia	13	373	28.7	98	1
1944	Bob Thurbon, Card.-Pitt.	12	291	24.3	55	0
1943	Ken Heineman, Brooklyn	16	444	27.8	69	0
1942	Marshall Goldberg, Chi. Cardinals	15	393	26.2	95	1
1941	Marshall Goldberg, Chi. Cardinals	12	290	24.2	41	0

*First season of professional football.

ANNUAL LEADERS IN SACKS (SINCE 1982)

Year	Player, Team	Sacks
2001	Michael Strahan, N.Y. Giants, NFC	22.5
	Peter Boulware, Baltimore, AFC	15.0
2000	La'Roi Glover, New Orleans, NFC	17.0
	Trace Armstrong, Miami, AFC	16.5
1999	Kevin Carter, St. Louis, NFC	17.0
	*Jevon Kearse, Tennessee, AFC	14.5
1998	Michael Sinclair, Seattle, AFC	16.5
	Reggie White, Green Bay, NFC	16.0
1997	John Randle, Minnesota, NFC	15.5
	Bruce Smith, Buffalo, AFC	14.0
1996	Kevin Greene, Carolina, NFC	14.5
	Michael McCrary, Seattle, AFC	13.5
	Bruce Smith, Buffalo, AFC	13.5
1995	Bryce Paup, Buffalo, AFC	17.5
	William Fuller, Philadelphia, NFC	13.0
	Wayne Martin, New Orleans, NFC	13.0
1994	Kevin Greene, Pittsburgh, AFC	14.0
	Ken Harvey, Washington, NFC	13.5
	John Randle, Minnesota, NFC	13.5
1993	Neil Smith, Kansas City, AFC	15.0
	Renaldo Turnbull, New Orleans, NFC	13.0
	Reggie White, Green Bay, NFC	13.0
1992	Clyde Simmons, Philadelphia, NFC	19.0
	Leslie O'Neal, San Diego, AFC	17.0
1991	Pat Swilling, New Orleans, NFC	17.0
	William Fuller, Houston, AFC	15.0
1990	Derrick Thomas, Kansas City, AFC	20.0
	Charles Haley, San Francisco, NFC	16.0
1989	Chris Doleman, Minnesota, NFC	21.0
	Lee Williams, San Diego, AFC	14.0
1988	Reggie White, Philadelphia, NFC	18.0
	Greg Townsend, L.A. Raiders, AFC	11.5
1987	Reggie White, Philadelphia, NFC	21.0
	Andre Tippett, New England, AFC	12.5
1986	Lawrence Taylor, N.Y. Giants, NFC	20.5
	Sean Jones, L.A. Raiders, AFC	15.5
1985	Richard Dent, Chicago, NFC	17.0
	Andre Tippett, New England, AFC	16.5
1984	Mark Gastineau, N.Y. Jets, AFC	22.0
	Richard Dent, Chicago, NFC	17.5
1983	Mark Gastineau, N.Y. Jets, AFC	19.0
	Fred Dean, San Francisco, NFC	17.5
1982	Doug Martin, Minnesota, NFC	11.5
	Jesse Baker, Houston, AFC	7.5

*First season of professional football.

POINTS SCORED

Year	Team	Points
2001	St. Louis, NFC	503
	Indianapolis, AFC	413
2000	St. Louis, NFC	540
	Denver, AFC	485
1999	St. Louis, NFC	526
	Indianapolis, AFC	423
1998	Minnesota, NFC	556
	Denver, AFC	501
1997	Denver, AFC	472
	Green Bay, NFC	422
1996	Green Bay, NFC	456
	New England, AFC	418
1995	San Francisco, NFC	457
	Pittsburgh, AFC	407
1994	San Francisco, NFC	505
	Miami, AFC	389
1993	San Francisco, NFC	473
	Denver, AFC	373
1992	San Francisco, NFC	431
	Buffalo, AFC	381
1991	Washington, NFC	485
	Buffalo, AFC	458
1990	Buffalo, AFC	428
	Philadelphia, NFC	396
1989	San Francisco, NFC	442
	Buffalo, AFC	409
1988	Cincinnati, AFC	448
	L.A. Rams, NFC	407
1987	San Francisco, NFC	459
	Cleveland, AFC	390
1986	Miami, AFC	430
	Minnesota, NFC	398
1985	San Diego, AFC	467
	Chicago, NFC	456
1984	Miami, AFC	513
	San Francisco, NFC	475
1983	Washington, NFC	541
	L.A. Raiders, AFC	442
1982	San Diego, AFC	288
	Dallas, NFC	226
	Green Bay, NFC	226
1981	San Diego, AFC	478
	Atlanta, NFC	426
1980	Dallas, NFC	454
	New England, AFC	441
1979	Pittsburgh, AFC	416
	Dallas, NFC	371
1978	Dallas, NFC	384
	Miami, AFC	372
1977	Oakland, AFC	351
	Dallas, NFC	345
1976	Baltimore, AFC	417
	Los Angeles, NFC	351
1975	Buffalo, AFC	420
	Minnesota, NFC	377
1974	Oakland, AFC	355
	Washington, NFC	320
1973	Los Angeles, NFC	388
	Denver, AFC	354
1972	Miami, AFC	385
	San Francisco, NFC	353
1971	Dallas, NFC	406
	Oakland, AFC	344
1970	San Francisco, NFC	352
	Baltimore, AFC	321
1969	Minnesota, NFL	379
	Oakland, AFL	377
1968	Oakland, AFL	453
	Dallas, NFL	431
1967	Oakland, AFL	468
	Los Angeles, NFL	398
1966	Kansas City, AFL	448
	Dallas, NFL	445
1965	San Francisco, NFL	421
	San Diego, AFL	340
1964	Baltimore, NFL	428
	Buffalo, AFL	400
1963	N.Y. Giants, NFL	448
	San Diego, AFL	399
1962	Green Bay, NFL	415
	Dall. Texans, AFL	389
1961	Houston, AFL	513
	Green Bay, NFL	391
1960	N.Y. Titans, AFL	382
	Cleveland, NFL	362
1959	Baltimore	374
1958	Baltimore	381
1957	Los Angeles	307
1956	Chi. Bears	363
1955	Cleveland	349
1954	Detroit	337
1953	San Francisco	372
1952	Los Angeles	349
1951	Los Angeles	392
1950	Los Angeles	466
1949	Philadelphia	364
1948	Chi. Cardinals	395
1947	Chi. Bears	363
1946	Chi. Bears	289
1945	Philadelphia	272
1944	Philadelphia	267
1943	Chi. Bears	303
1942	Chi. Bears	376
1941	Chi. Bears	396
1940	Washington	245
1939	Chi. Bears	298
1938	Green Bay	223
1937	Green Bay	220
1936	Green Bay	248
1935	Chi. Bears	192
1934	Chi. Bears	286
1933	N.Y. Giants	244
1932	Chicago Bears	160

TOTAL YARDS GAINED

Year	Team	Yards
2001	St. Louis, NFC	6,690
	Indianapolis, AFC	5,955
2000	St. Louis, NFC	7,075
	Denver, AFC	6,554
1999	St. Louis, NFC	6,412
	Indianapolis, AFC	5,726
1998	San Francisco, NFC	6,800
	Denver, AFC	6,092
1997	Denver, AFC	5,872
	Detroit, NFC	5,798
1996	Denver, AFC	5,791
	Philadelphia, NFC	5,627
1995	Detroit, NFC	6,113
	Denver, AFC	6,040
1994	Miami, AFC	6,078
	San Francisco, NFC	6,060
1993	San Francisco, NFC	6,435
	Miami, AFC	5,812
1992	San Francisco, NFC	6,195
	Buffalo, AFC	5,893
1991	Buffalo, AFC	6,252
	San Francisco, NFC	5,858

1990	Houston, AFC	6,222
	San Francisco, NFC	5,895
1989	San Francisco, NFC	6,268
	Cincinnati, AFC	6,101
1988	Cincinnati, AFC	6,057
	San Francisco, NFC	5,900
1987	San Francisco, NFC	5,987
	Denver, AFC	5,624
1986	Cincinnati, AFC	6,490
	San Francisco, NFC	6,082
1985	San Diego, AFC	6,535
	San Francisco, NFC	5,920
1984	Miami, AFC	6,936
	San Francisco, NFC	6,366
1983	San Diego, AFC	6,197
	Green Bay, NFC	6,172
1982	San Diego, AFC	4,048
	San Francisco, NFC	3,242
1981	San Diego, AFC	6,744
	Detroit, NFC	5,933
1980	San Diego, AFC	6,410
	Los Angeles, NFC	6,006
1979	Pittsburgh, AFC	6,258
	Dallas, NFC	5,968
1978	New England, AFC	5,965
	Dallas, NFC	5,959
1977	Dallas, NFC	4,812
	Oakland, AFC	4,736
1976	Baltimore, AFC	5,236
	St. Louis, NFC	5,136
1975	Buffalo, AFC	5,467
	Dallas, NFC	5,025
1974	Dallas, NFC	4,983
	Oakland, AFC	4,718
1973	Los Angeles, NFC	4,906
	Oakland, AFC	4,773
1972	Miami, AFC	5,036
	N.Y. Giants, NFC	4,483
1971	Dallas, NFC	5,035
	San Diego, AFC	4,738
1970	Oakland, AFC	4,829
	San Francisco, NFC	4,503
1969	Dallas, NFL	5,122
	Oakland, AFL	5,036
1968	Oakland, AFL	5,696
	Dallas, NFL	5,117
1967	N.Y. Jets, AFL	5,152
	Baltimore, NFL	5,008
1966	Dallas, NFL	5,145
	Kansas City, AFL	5,114
1965	San Francisco, NFL	5,270
	San Diego, AFL	5,188
1964	Buffalo, AFL	5,206
	Baltimore, NFL	4,779
1963	San Diego, AFL	5,153
	N.Y. Giants, NFL	5,024
1962	N.Y. Giants, NFL	5,005
	Houston, AFL	4,971
1961	Houston, AFL	6,288
	Philadelphia, NFL	5,112
1960	Houston, AFL	4,936
	Baltimore, NFL	4,245
1959	Baltimore	4,458
1958	Baltimore	4,539
1957	Los Angeles	4,143
1956	Chi. Bears	4,537
1955	Chi. Bears	4,316
1954	Los Angeles	5,187
1953	Philadelphia	4,811
1952	Cleveland	4,352

1951	Los Angeles	5,506
1950	Los Angeles	5,420
1949	Chi. Bears	4,873
1948	Chi. Cardinals	4,705
1947	Chi. Bears	5,053
1946	Los Angeles	3,793
1945	Washington	3,549
1944	Chi. Bears	3,239
1943	Chi. Bears	4,045
1942	Chi. Bears	3,900
1941	Chi. Bears	4,265
1940	Green Bay	3,400
1939	Chi. Bears	3,988
1938	Green Bay	3,037
1937	Green Bay	3,201
1936	Detroit	3,703
1935	Chi. Bears	3,454
1934	Chi. Bears	3,900
1933	N.Y. Giants	2,973
1932	Chi. Bears	2,755

YARDS RUSHING

Year	Team	Yards
2001	Pittsburgh, AFC	2,774
	San Francisco, NFC	2,244
2000	Oakland, AFC	2,470
	Minnesota, NFC	2,129
1999	San Francisco, NFC	2,095
	Jacksonville, AFC	2,091
1998	San Francisco, NFC	2,544
	Denver, AFC	2,468
1997	Pittsburgh, AFC	2,479
	Detroit, NFC	2,464
1996	Denver, AFC	2,362
	Washington, NFC	1,910
1995	Kansas City, AFC	2,222
	Dallas, NFC	2,201
1994	Pittsburgh, AFC	2,180
	Detroit, NFC	2,080
1993	N.Y. Giants, NFC	2,210
	Seattle, AFC	2,015
1992	Buffalo, AFC	2,436
	Philadelphia, NFC	2,388
1991	Buffalo, AFC	2,381
	Minnesota, NFC	2,201
1990	Philadelphia, NFC	2,556
	San Diego, AFC	2,257
1989	Cincinnati, AFC	2,483
	Chicago, NFC	2,287
1988	Cincinnati, AFC	2,710
	San Francisco, NFC	2,523
1987	San Francisco, NFC	2,237
	L.A. Raiders, AFC	2,197
1986	Chicago, NFC	2,700
	Cincinnati, AFC	2,533
1985	Chicago, NFC	2,761
	Indianapolis, AFC	2,439
1984	Chicago, NFC	2,974
	N.Y. Jets, AFC	2,189
1983	Chicago, NFC	2,727
	Baltimore, AFC	2,695
1982	Buffalo, AFC	1,371
	Dallas, NFC	1,313
1981	Detroit, NFC	2,795
	Kansas City, AFC	2,633
1980	Los Angeles, NFC	2,799
	Houston, AFC	2,635
1979	N.Y. Jets, AFC	2,646
	St. Louis, NFC	2,582
1978	New England, AFC	3,165
	Dallas, NFC	2,783
1977	Chicago, NFC	2,811
	Oakland, AFC	2,627
1976	Pittsburgh, AFC	2,971
	Los Angeles, NFC	2,528
1975	Buffalo, AFC	2,974
	Dallas, NFC	2,432
1974	Dallas, NFC	2,454
	Pittsburgh, AFC	2,417
1973	Buffalo, AFC	3,088
	Los Angeles, NFC	2,925
1972	Miami, AFC	2,960
	Chicago, NFC	2,360
1971	Miami, AFC	2,429
	Detroit, NFC	2,376
1970	Dallas, NFC	2,300
	Miami, AFC	2,082
1969	Dallas, NFL	2,276
	Kansas City, AFL	2,220
1968	Chicago, NFL	2,377
	Kansas City, AFL	2,227
1967	Cleveland, NFL	2,139
	Houston, AFL	2,122
1966	Kansas City, AFL	2,274
	Cleveland, NFL	2,166
1965	Cleveland, NFL	2,331
	San Diego, AFL	2,085
1964	Green Bay, NFL	2,276
	Buffalo, AFL	2,040
1963	Cleveland, NFL	2,639
	San Diego, AFL	2,203
1962	Buffalo, AFL	2,480
	Green Bay, NFL	2,460
1961	Green Bay, NFL	2,350
	Dall. Texans, AFL	2,189
1960	St. Louis, NFL	2,356
	Oakland, AFL	2,056
1959	Cleveland	2,149
1958	Cleveland	2,526
1957	Los Angeles	2,142
1956	Chi. Bears	2,468
1955	Chi. Bears	2,388
1954	San Francisco	2,498
1953	San Francisco	2,230
1952	San Francisco	1,905
1951	Chi. Bears	2,408
1950	N.Y. Giants	2,336
1949	Philadelphia	2,607
1948	Chi. Cardinals	2,560
1947	Los Angeles	2,171
1946	Green Bay	1,765
1945	Cleveland	1,714
1944	Philadelphia	1,661
1943	Phil-Pitt	1,730
1942	Chi. Bears	1,881
1941	Chi. Bears	2,263
1940	Chi. Bears	1,818
1939	Chi. Bears	2,043
1938	Detroit	1,893
1937	Detroit	2,074
1936	Detroit	2,885
1935	Chi. Bears	2,096
1934	Chi. Bears	2,847
1933	Boston	2,260
1932	Chi. Bears	1,770

YARDS PASSING

Leadership in this category has been based on net yards since 1952.

Year	Team	Yards
2001	St. Louis, NFC	4,663
	Indianapolis, AFC	3,989
2000	St. Louis, NFC	5,232
	Indianapolis, AFC	4,282
1999	St. Louis, NFC	4,353
	Indianapolis, AFC	4,066
1998	Minnesota, NFC	4,328
	N.Y. Jets, AFC	3,836
1997	Seattle, AFC	3,959
	Green Bay, NFC	3,705
1996	Jacksonville, AFC	4,110
	Philadelphia, NFC	3,745
1995	San Francisco, NFC	4,608
	Miami, AFC	4,210
1994	New England, AFC	4,444
	Minnesota, NFC	4,324
1993	Miami, AFC	4,353
	San Francisco, NFC	4,302
1992	Houston, AFC	4,029
	San Francisco, NFC	3,880
1991	Houston, AFC	4,621

	San Francisco, NFC	3,997
1990	Houston, AFC	4,805
	San Francisco, NFC	4,177
1989	Washington, NFC	4,349
	Miami, AFC	4,216
1988	Miami, AFC	4,516
	Washington, NFC	4,136
1987	Miami, AFC	3,876
	San Francisco, NFC	3,750
1986	Miami, AFC	4,779
	San Francisco, NFC	4,096
1985	San Diego, AFC	4,870
	Dallas, NFC	3,861
1984	Miami, AFC	5,018
	St. Louis, NFC	4,257
1983	San Diego, AFC	4,661
	Green Bay, NFC	4,365
1982	San Diego, AFC	2,927
	San Francisco, NFC	2,502
1981	San Diego, AFC	4,739
	Minnesota, NFC	4,333
1980	San Diego, AFC	4,531
	Minnesota, NFC	3,688
1979	San Diego, AFC	3,915
	San Francisco, NFC	3,641
1978	San Diego, AFC	3,375
	Minnesota, NFC	3,243
1977	Buffalo, AFC	2,530
	St. Louis, NFC	2,499
1976	Baltimore, AFC	2,933
	Minnesota, NFC	2,855
1975	Cincinnati, AFC	3,241
	Washington, NFC	2,917
1974	Washington, NFC	2,978
	Cincinnati, AFC	2,804
1973	Philadelphia, NFC	2,998
	Denver, AFC	2,519
1972	N.Y. Jets, AFC	2,777
	San Francisco, NFC	2,735
1971	San Diego, AFC	3,134
	Dallas, NFC	2,786
1970	San Francisco, NFC	2,923
	Oakland, AFC	2,865
1969	Oakland, AFL	3,271
	San Francisco, NFL	3,158
1968	San Diego, AFL	3,623
	Dallas, NFL	3,026
1967	N.Y. Jets, AFL	3,845
	Washington, NFL	3,730
1966	N.Y. Jets, AFL	3,464
	Dallas, NFL	3,023
1965	San Francisco, NFL	3,487
	San Diego, AFL	3,103
1964	Houston, AFL	3,527
	Chicago, NFL	2,841
1963	Baltimore, NFL	3,296
	Houston, AFL	3,222
1962	Denver, AFL	3,404
	Philadelphia, NFL	3,385
1961	Houston, AFL	4,392
	Philadelphia, NFL	3,605
1960	Houston, AFL	3,203
	Baltimore, NFL	2,956
1959	Baltimore	2,753
1958	Pittsburgh	2,752
1957	Baltimore	2,388
1956	Los Angeles	2,419
1955	Philadelphia	2,472
1954	Chi. Bears	3,104
1953	Philadelphia	3,089

1952	Cleveland	2,566
1951	Los Angeles	3,296
1950	Los Angeles	3,709
1949	Chi. Bears	3,055
1948	Washington	2,861
1947	Washington	3,336
1946	Los Angeles	2,080
1945	Chi. Bears	1,857
1944	Washington	2,021
1943	Chi. Bears	2,310
1942	Green Bay	2,407
1941	Chi. Bears	2,002
1940	Washington	1,887
1939	Chi. Bears	1,965
1938	Washington	1,536
1937	Green Bay	1,398
1936	Green Bay	1,629
1935	Green Bay	1,449
1934	Green Bay	1,165
1933	N.Y. Giants	1,348
1932	Chi. Bears	1,013

FEWEST POINTS ALLOWED

Year	Team	Points
2001	Chicago, NFC	203
	Pittsburgh, AFC	212
2000	Baltimore, AFC	165
	Philadelphia, NFC	245
1999	Jacksonville, AFC	217
	Tampa Bay, NFC	235
1998	Miami, AFC	265
	Dallas, NFC	275
1997	Kansas City, AFC	232
	Tampa Bay, NFC	263
1996	Green Bay, NFC	210
	Pittsburgh, AFC	257
1995	Kansas City, AFC	241
	San Francisco, NFC	258
1994	Cleveland, AFC	204
	Dallas, NFC	248
1993	N.Y. Giants, NFC	205
	Houston, AFC	238
1992	New Orleans, NFC	202
	Pittsburgh, AFC	225
1991	New Orleans, NFC	211
	Denver, AFC	235
1990	N.Y. Giants, NFC	211
	Pittsburgh, AFC	240
1989	Denver, AFC	226
	N.Y. Giants, NFC	252
1988	Chicago, NFC	215
	Buffalo, AFC	237
1987	Indianapolis, AFC	238
	San Francisco, NFC	253
1986	Chicago, NFC	187
	Seattle, AFC	293
1985	Chicago, NFC	198
	N.Y. Jets, AFC	264
1984	San Francisco, NFC	227
	Denver, AFC	241
1983	Miami, AFC	250
	Detroit, NFC	286
1982	Washington, NFC	128
	Miami, AFC	131
1981	Philadelphia, NFC	221
	Miami, AFC	275
1980	Philadelphia, NFC	222
	Houston, AFC	251
1979	Tampa Bay, NFC	237
	San Diego, AFC	246

1978	Pittsburgh, AFC	195
	Dallas, NFC	208
1977	Atlanta, NFC	129
	Denver, AFC	148
1976	Pittsburgh, AFC	138
	Minnesota, NFC	176
1975	Los Angeles, NFC	135
	Pittsburgh, AFC	162
1974	Los Angeles, NFC	181
	Pittsburgh, AFC	189
1973	Miami, AFC	150
	Minnesota, NFC	168
1972	Miami, AFC	171
	Washington, NFC	218
1971	Minnesota, NFC	139
	Baltimore, AFC	140
1970	Minnesota, NFC	143
	Miami, AFC	228
1969	Minnesota, NFL	133
	Kansas City, AFL	177
1968	Baltimore, NFL	144
	Kansas City, AFL	170
1967	Los Angeles, NFL	196
	Houston, AFL	199
1966	Green Bay, NFL	163
	Buffalo, AFL	255
1965	Green Bay, NFL	224
	Buffalo, AFL	226
1964	Baltimore, NFL	225
	Buffalo, AFL	242
1963	Chicago, NFL	144
	San Diego, AFL	255
1962	Green Bay, NFL	148
	Dall. Texans, AFL	233
1961	San Diego, AFL	219
	N.Y. Giants, NFL	220
1960	San Francisco, NFL	205
	Dall. Texans, AFL	253
1959	N.Y. Giants	170
1958	N.Y. Giants	183
1957	Cleveland	172
1956	Cleveland	177
1955	Cleveland	218
1954	Cleveland	162
1953	Cleveland	162
1952	Detroit	192
1951	Cleveland	152
1950	Philadelphia	141
1949	Philadelphia	134
1948	Chi. Bears	151
1947	Green Bay	210
1946	Pittsburgh	117
1945	Washington	121
1944	N.Y. Giants	75
1943	Washington	137
1942	Chi. Bears	84
1941	N.Y. Giants	114
1940	Brooklyn	120
1939	N.Y. Giants	85
1938	N.Y. Giants	79
1937	Chi. Bears	100
1936	Chi. Bears	94
1935	Green Bay	96
	N.Y. Giants	96
1934	Detroit	59
1933	Brooklyn	54
1932	Chi. Bears	44

FEWEST TOTAL YARDS ALLOWED

Year	Team	Yards
2001	Pittsburgh, AFC	4,137
	St. Louis, NFC	4,471
2000	Tennessee, AFC	3,813
	Washington, NFC	4,474
1999	Buffalo, AFC	4,045
	Tampa Bay, NFC	4,280
1998	San Diego, AFC	4,208
	Tampa Bay, NFC	4,345
1997	San Francisco, NFC	4,013
	Denver, AFC	4,671
1996	Green Bay, NFC	4,156
	Pittsburgh, AFC	4,362
1995	San Francisco, NFC	4,398
	Kansas City, AFC	4,549
1994	Dallas, NFC	4,313
	Pittsburgh, AFC	4,326
1993	Minnesota, NFC	4,406
	Pittsburgh, AFC	4,531
1992	Dallas, NFC	3,931
	Houston, AFC	4,211
1991	Philadelphia, NFC	3,549
	Denver, AFC	4,549
1990	Pittsburgh, AFC	4,115
	N.Y. Giants, NFC	4,206
1989	Minnesota, NFC	4,184
	Kansas City, AFC	4,293
1988	Minnesota, NFC	4,091
	Buffalo, AFC	4,578
1987	San Francisco, NFC	4,095
	Cleveland, AFC	4,264
1986	Chicago, NFC	4,130
	L.A. Raiders, AFC	4,804
1985	Chicago, NFC	4,135
	L.A. Raiders, AFC	4,603
1984	Chicago, NFC	3,863
	Cleveland, AFC	4,641
1983	Cincinnati, AFC	4,327
	New Orleans, NFC	4,691
1982	Miami, AFC	2,312
	Tampa Bay, NFC	2,442
1981	Philadelphia, NFC	4,447
	N.Y. Jets, AFC	4,871
1980	Buffalo, AFC	4,101
	Philadelphia, NFC	4,443
1979	Tampa Bay, NFC	3,949
	Pittsburgh, AFC	4,270
1978	Los Angeles, NFC	3,893
	Pittsburgh, AFC	4,168
1977	Dallas, NFC	3,213
	New England, AFC	3,638
1976	Pittsburgh, AFC	3,323
	San Francisco, NFC	3,562
1975	Minnesota, NFC	3,153
	Oakland, AFC	3,629
1974	Pittsburgh, AFC	3,074
	Washington, NFC	3,285
1973	Los Angeles, NFC	2,951
	Oakland, AFC	3,160
1972	Miami, AFC	3,297
	Green Bay, NFC	3,474
1971	Baltimore, AFC	2,852
	Minnesota, NFC	3,406
1970	Minnesota, NFC	2,803
	N.Y. Jets, AFC	3,655
1969	Minnesota, NFL	2,720
	Kansas City, AFL	3,163
1968	Los Angeles, NFL	3,118
	N.Y. Jets, AFL	3,363

1967	Oakland, AFL	3,294
	Green Bay, NFL	3,300
1966	St. Louis, NFL	3,492
	Oakland, AFL	3,910
1965	San Diego, AFL	3,262
	Detroit, NFL	3,557
1964	Green Bay, NFL	3,179
	Buffalo, AFL	3,878
1963	Chicago, NFL	3,176
	Boston, AFL	3,834
1962	Detroit, NFL	3,217
	Dall. Texans, AFL	3,951
1961	San Diego, AFL	3,726
	Baltimore, NFL	3,782
1960	St. Louis, NFL	3,029
	Buffalo, AFL	3,866
1959	N.Y. Giants	2,843
1958	Chi. Bears	3,066
1957	Pittsburgh	2,791
1956	N.Y. Giants	3,081
1955	Cleveland	2,841
1954	Cleveland	2,658
1953	Philadelphia	2,998
1952	Cleveland	3,075
1951	N.Y. Giants	3,250
1950	Cleveland	3,154
1949	Philadelphia	2,831
1948	Chi. Bears	2,931
1947	Green Bay	3,396
1946	Washington	2,451
1945	Philadelphia	2,073
1944	Philadelphia	1,943
1943	Chi. Bears	2,262
1942	Chi. Bears	1,703
1941	N.Y. Giants	2,368
1940	N.Y. Giants	2,219
1939	Washington	2,116
1938	N.Y. Giants	2,029
1937	Washington	2,123
1936	Boston	2,181
1935	Boston	1,996
1934	Chi. Cardinals	1,539
1933	Brooklyn	1,789

FEWEST RUSHING YARDS ALLOWED

Year	Team	Yards
2001	Pittsburgh, AFC	1,195
	Chicago, NFC	1,313
2000	Baltimore, AFC	970
	N.Y. Giants, NFC	1,156
1999	St. Louis, NFC	1,189
	Baltimore, AFC	1,231
1998	San Diego, AFC	1,140
	Atlanta, NFC	1,203
1997	Pittsburgh, AFC	1,318
	San Francisco, NFC	1,366
1996	Denver, AFC	1,331
	Green Bay, NFC	1,416
1995	San Francisco, NFC	1,061
	Pittsburgh, AFC	1,321
1994	Minnesota, NFC	1,090
	San Diego, AFC	1,404
1993	Houston, AFC	1,273
	Minnesota, NFC	1,536
1992	Dallas, NFC	1,244
	Buffalo, AFC	1,395
	San Diego, AFC	1,395
1991	Philadelphia, NFC	1,136
	N.Y. Jets, AFC	1,442
1990	Philadelphia, NFC	1,169

	San Diego, AFC	1,515
1989	New Orleans, NFC	1,326
	Denver, AFC	1,580
1988	Chicago, NFC	1,326
	Houston, AFC	1,592
1987	Chicago, NFC	1,413
	Cleveland, AFC	1,433
1986	N.Y. Giants, NFC	1,284
	Denver, AFC	1,651
1985	Chicago, NFC	1,319
	N.Y. Jets, AFC	1,516
1984	Chicago, NFC	1,377
	Pittsburgh, AFC	1,617
1983	Washington, NFC	1,289
	Cincinnati, AFC	1,499
1982	Pittsburgh, AFC	762
	Detroit, NFC	854
1981	Detroit, NFC	1,623
	Kansas City, AFC	1,747
1980	Detroit, NFC	1,599
	Cincinnati, AFC	1,680
1979	Denver, AFC	1,693
	Tampa Bay, NFC	1,873
1978	Dallas, NFC	1,721
	Pittsburgh, AFC	1,774
1977	Denver, AFC	1,531
	Dallas, NFC	1,651
1976	Pittsburgh, AFC	1,457
	Los Angeles, NFC	1,564
1975	Minnesota, NFC	1,532
	Houston, AFC	1,680
1974	Los Angeles, NFC	1,302
	New England, AFC	1,587
1973	Los Angeles, NFC	1,270
	Oakland, AFC	1,470
1972	Dallas, NFC	1,515
	Miami, AFC	1,548
1971	Baltimore, AFC	1,113
	Dallas, NFC	1,144
1970	Detroit, NFC	1,152
	N.Y. Jets, AFC	1,283
1969	Dallas, NFL	1,050
	Kansas City, AFL	1,091
1968	Dallas, NFL	1,195
	N.Y. Jets, AFL	1,195
1967	Dallas, NFL	1,081
	Oakland, AFL	1,129
1966	Buffalo, AFL	1,051
	Dallas, NFL	1,176
1965	San Diego, AFL	1,094
	Los Angeles, NFL	1,409
1964	Buffalo, AFL	913
	Los Angeles, NFL	1,501
1963	Boston, AFL	1,107
	Chicago, NFL	1,442
1962	Detroit, NFL	1,231
	Dall. Texans, AFL	1,250
1961	Boston, AFL	1,041
	Pittsburgh, NFL	1,463
1960	St. Louis, NFL	1,212
	Dall. Texans, AFL	1,338
1959	N.Y. Giants	1,261
1958	Baltimore	1,291
1957	Baltimore	1,174
1956	N.Y. Giants	1,443
1955	Cleveland	1,189
1954	Cleveland	1,050
1953	Philadelphia	1,117
1952	Detroit	1,145
1951	N.Y. Giants	913

1950	Detroit	1,367
1949	Chi. Bears	1,196
1948	Philadelphia	1,209
1947	Philadelphia	1,329
1946	Chi. Bears	1,060
1945	Philadelphia	817
1944	Philadelphia	558
1943	Phil-Pitt	793
1942	Chi. Bears	519
1941	Washington	1,042
1940	N.Y. Giants	977
1939	Chi. Bears	812
1938	Detroit	1,081
1937	Chi. Bears	933
1936	Boston	1,148
1935	Boston	998
1934	Chi. Cardinals	954
1933	Brooklyn	964

FEWEST PASSING YARDS ALLOWED

Leadership in this category has been based on net yards since 1952.

Year	Team	Yards
2001	Miami, AFC	2,829
	Philadelphia, NFC	2,864
2000	Tennessee, AFC	2,423
	Washington, NFC	2,621
1999	Buffalo, AFC	2,675
	Tampa Bay, NFC	2,873
1998	Philadelphia, NFC	2,720
	Oakland, AFC	2,876
1997	Dallas, NFC	2,522
	Indianapolis, AFC	2,820
1996	Green Bay, NFC	2,740
	Pittsburgh, AFC	2,947
1995	N.Y. Jets, AFC	2,740
	Philadelphia, NFC	2,816
1994	Dallas, NFC	2,752
	Houston, AFC	2,795
1993	New Orleans, NFC	2,606
	Cincinnati, AFC	2,798
1992	New Orleans, NFC	2,470
	Kansas City, AFC	2,537
1991	Philadelphia, NFC	2,413
	Denver, AFC	2,755
1990	Pittsburgh, AFC	2,500
	Dallas, NFC	2,639
1989	Minnesota, NFC	2,501
	Kansas City, AFC	2,527
1988	Kansas City, AFC	2,434
	Minnesota, NFC	2,489
1987	San Francisco, NFC	2,484
	L.A. Raiders, AFC	2,727
1986	St. Louis, NFC	2,637
	New England, AFC	2,978
1985	Washington, NFC	2,746
	Pittsburgh, AFC	2,783
1984	New Orleans, NFC	2,453
	Cleveland, AFC	2,696
1983	New Orleans, NFC	2,691
	Cincinnati, AFC	2,828
1982	Miami, AFC	1,027
	Tampa Bay, NFC	1,384
1981	Philadelphia, NFC	2,696
	Buffalo, AFC	2,870
1980	Washington, NFC	2,171
	Buffalo, AFC	2,282
1979	Tampa Bay, NFC	2,076
	Buffalo, AFC	2,530
1978	Buffalo, AFC	1,960

	Los Angeles, NFC	2,048
1977	Atlanta, NFC	1,384
	San Diego, AFC	1,725
1976	Minnesota, NFC	1,575
	Cincinnati, AFC	1,758
1975	Minnesota, NFC	1,621
	Cincinnati, AFC	1,729
1974	Pittsburgh, AFC	1,466
	Atlanta, NFC	1,572
1973	Miami, AFC	1,290
	Atlanta, NFC	1,430
1972	Minnesota, NFC	1,699
	Cleveland, AFC	1,736
1971	Atlanta, NFC	1,638
	Baltimore, AFC	1,739
1970	Minnesota, NFC	1,438
	Kansas City, AFC	2,010
1969	Minnesota, NFL	1,631
	Kansas City, AFL	2,072
1968	Houston, AFL	1,671
	Green Bay, NFL	1,796
1967	Green Bay, NFL	1,377
	Buffalo, AFL	1,825
1966	Green Bay, NFL	1,959
	Oakland, AFL	2,118
1965	Green Bay, NFL	1,981
	San Diego, AFL	2,168
1964	Green Bay, NFL	1,647
	San Diego, AFL	2,518
1963	Chicago, NFL	1,734
	Oakland, AFL	2,589
1962	Green Bay, NFL	1,746
	Oakland, AFL	2,306
1961	Baltimore, NFL	1,913
	San Diego, AFL	2,363
1960	Chicago, NFL	1,388
	Buffalo, AFL	2,124
1959	N.Y. Giants	1,582
1958	Chi. Bears	1,769
1957	Cleveland	1,300
1956	Cleveland	1,103
1955	Pittsburgh	1,295
1954	Cleveland	1,608
1953	Washington	1,751
1952	Washington	1,580
1951	Pittsburgh	1,687
1950	Cleveland	1,581
1949	Philadelphia	1,607
1948	Green Bay	1,626
1947	Green Bay	1,790
1946	Pittsburgh	939
1945	Washington	1,121
1944	Chi. Bears	1,052
1943	Chi. Bears	980
1942	Washington	1,093
1941	Pittsburgh	1,168
1940	Philadelphia	1,012
1939	Washington	1,116
1938	Chi. Bears	897
1937	Detroit	804
1936	Philadelphia	853
1935	Chi. Cardinals	793
1934	Philadelphia	545
1933	Portsmouth	558

SUPER BOWL RECORDS

Compiled by Elias Sports Bureau

Super Bowl I, 1/15/67	Super Bowl XIX, 1/20/85
Super Bowl II, 1/14/68	Super Bowl XX, 1/26/86
Super Bowl III, 1/12/69	Super Bowl XXI, 1/25/87
Super Bowl IV, 1/11/70	Super Bowl XXII, 1/31/88
Super Bowl V, 1/17/71	Super Bowl XXIII, 1/22/89
Super Bowl VI, 1/16/72	Super Bowl XXIV, 1/28/90
Super Bowl VII, 1/14/73	Super Bowl XXV, 1/27/91
Super Bowl VIII, 1/13/74	Super Bowl XXVI, 1/26/92
Super Bowl IX, 1/12/75	Super Bowl XXVII, 1/31/93
Super Bowl X, 1/18/76	Super Bowl XXVIII, 1/30/94
Super Bowl XI, 1/9/77	Super Bowl XXIX, 1/29/95
Super Bowl XII, 1/15/78	Super Bowl XXX, 1/28/96
Super Bowl XIII, 1/21/79	Super Bowl XXXI, 1/26/97
Super Bowl XIV, 1/20/80	Super Bowl XXXII, 1/25/98
Super Bowl XV, 1/25/81	Super Bowl XXXIII, 1/31/99
Super Bowl XVI, 1/24/82	Super Bowl XXXIV, 1/30/00
Super Bowl XVII, 1/30/83	Super Bowl XXXV, 1/28/01
Super Bowl XVIII, 1/22/84	Super Bowl XXXVI, 2/3/02

INDIVIDUAL RECORDS

SERVICE

Most Games

- 6 Mike Lodish, Buffalo, XXV-XXVIII; Denver, XXXII-XXXIII
- 5 Marv Fleming, Green Bay, I-II; Miami, VI-VIII
  Larry Cole, Dallas, V-VI, X, XII-XIII
  Cliff Harris, Dallas, V-VI, X, XII-XIII
  Charles Haley, San Francisco, XXIII-XXIV; Dallas, XXVII-XXVIII, XXX
  D.D. Lewis, Dallas, V-VI, X, XII-XIII
  Preston Pearson, Baltimore, III; Pittsburgh, IX; Dallas, X, XII-XIII
  Charlie Waters, Dallas, V-VI, X, XII-XIII
  Rayfield Wright, Dallas, V-VI, X, XII-XIII
  Cornelius Bennett, Buffalo, XXV-XXVIII; Atlanta, XXXIII
  John Elway, Denver, XXI-XXII, XXIV, XXXII-XXXIII
  Glenn Parker, Buffalo, XXV-XXVIII; N.Y. Giants, XXXV
- 4 By many players

Most Games, Winning Team

- 5 Charles Haley, San Francisco, XXIII-XXIV; Dallas, XXVII-XXVIII, XXX
- 4 By many players

Most Games, Coach

- 6 Don Shula, Baltimore, III; Miami, VI-VIII, XVII, XIX
- 5 Tom Landry, Dallas, V-VI, X, XII-XIII
- 4 Bud Grant, Minnesota, IV, VIII-IX, XI
  Chuck Noll, Pittsburgh, IX-X, XIII-XIV
  Joe Gibbs, Washington, XVII-XVIII, XXII, XXVI
  Marv Levy, Buffalo, XXV-XXVIII
  Dan Reeves, Denver, XXI-XXII, XXIV; Atlanta, XXXIII

Most Games, Winning Team, Coach

- 4 Chuck Noll, Pittsburgh, IX-X, XIII-XIV
- 3 Bill Walsh, San Francisco, XVI, XIX, XXIII
  Joe Gibbs, Washington, XVII, XXII, XXVI
- 2 Vince Lombardi, Green Bay, I-II
  Tom Landry, Dallas, VI, XII
  Don Shula, Miami, VII-VIII
  Tom Flores, Oakland, XV; L.A. Raiders, XVIII
  Bill Parcells, N.Y. Giants, XXI, XXV
  Jimmy Johnson, Dallas, XXVII-XXVIII
  George Seifert, San Francisco, XXIV, XXIX
  Mike Shanahan, Denver, XXXII-XXXIII

Most Games, Losing Team, Coach

- 4 Bud Grant, Minnesota, IV, VIII-IX, XI
  Don Shula, Baltimore, III; Miami, VI, XVII, XIX
  Marv Levy, Buffalo, XXV-XXVIII
  Dan Reeves, Denver, XXI-XXII, XXIV; Atlanta, XXXIII
- 3 Tom Landry, Dallas, V, X, XIII

SCORING

POINTS

Most Points, Career

- 42 Jerry Rice, San Francisco, 3 games (7-td)
- 30 Emmitt Smith, Dallas, 3 games (5-td)
- 24 Franco Harris, Pittsburgh, 4 games (4-td)
  Roger Craig, San Francisco, 3 games (4-td)
  Thurman Thomas, Buffalo, 4 games (4-td)
  John Elway, Denver, 5 games (4-td)

Most Points, Game

- 18 Roger Craig, San Francisco vs. Miami, XIX (3-td)
  Jerry Rice, San Francisco vs. Denver, XXIV (3-td); vs. San Diego, XXIX (3-td)
  Ricky Watters, San Francisco vs. San Diego, XXIX (3-td)
  Terrell Davis, Denver vs. Green Bay, XXXII (3-td)
- 15 Don Chandler, Green Bay vs. Oakland, II (3-pat, 4-fg)
- 14 Ray Wersching, San Francisco vs. Cincinnati, XVI (2-pat, 4-fg)
  Kevin Butler, Chicago vs. New England, XX (5-pat, 3-fg)

TOUCHDOWNS

Most Touchdowns, Career

- 7 Jerry Rice, San Francisco, 3 games (7-p)
- 5 Emmitt Smith, Dallas, 3 games (5-r)
- 4 Franco Harris, Pittsburgh, 4 games (4-r)
  Roger Craig, San Francisco, 3 games (2-r, 2-p)
  Thurman Thomas, Buffalo, 4 games (4-r)
  John Elway, Denver, 5 games (4-r)

Most Touchdowns, Game

- 3 Roger Craig, San Francisco vs. Miami, XIX (1-r, 2-p)
  Jerry Rice, San Francisco vs. Denver, XXIV (3-p); vs. San Diego, XXIX (3-p)
  Ricky Watters, San Francisco vs. San Diego, XXIX (1-r, 2-p)
  Terrell Davis, Denver vs. Green Bay, XXXII (3-r)
- 2 Max McGee, Green Bay vs. Kansas City, I (2-p)
  Elijah Pitts, Green Bay vs. Kansas City, I (2-r)
  Bill Miller, Oakland vs. Green Bay, II (2-p)
  Larry Csonka, Miami vs. Minnesota, VIII (2-r)
  Pete Banaszak, Oakland vs. Minnesota, XI (2-r)
  John Stallworth, Pittsburgh vs. Dallas, XIII (2-p)
  Franco Harris, Pittsburgh vs. Los Angeles, XIV (2-r)
  Cliff Branch, Oakland vs. Philadelphia, XV (2-p)
  Dan Ross, Cincinnati vs. San Francisco, XVI (2-p)
  Marcus Allen, L.A. Raiders vs. Washington, XVIII (2-r)
  Jim McMahon, Chicago vs. New England, XX (2-r)
  Ricky Sanders, Washington vs. Denver, XXII (2-p)
  Timmy Smith, Washington vs. Denver, XXII (2-r)
  Tom Rathman, San Francisco vs. Denver, XXIV (2-r)
  Gerald Riggs, Washington vs. Buffalo, XXVI (2-r)
  Michael Irvin, Dallas vs. Buffalo, XXVII (2-p)
  Emmitt Smith, Dallas vs. Buffalo, XXVIII (2-r)
  Emmitt Smith, Dallas vs. Pittsburgh, XXX (2-r)
  Antonio Freeman, Green Bay vs. Denver, XXXII (2-p)
  Howard Griffith, Denver vs. Atlanta, XXXIII (2-r)
  Eddie George, Tennessee vs. St. Louis, XXXIV (2-r)

POINTS AFTER TOUCHDOWN

Most (One-Point) Points After Touchdown, Career

- 9 Mike Cofer, San Francisco, 2 games (10 att)
- 8 Don Chandler, Green Bay, 2 games (8 att)
  Roy Gerela, Pittsburgh, 3 games (9 att)
  Chris Bahr, Oakland-L.A. Raiders, 2 games (8 att)
  Jason Elam, Denver, 2 games (8 att)
- 7 Ray Wersching, San Francisco, 2 games (7 att)
  Lin Elliott, Dallas, 1 game (7 att)
  Doug Brien, San Francisco, 1 game (7 att)

Most (One-Point) Points After Touchdown, Game
- 7 Mike Cofer, San Francisco vs. Denver, XXIV (8 att)
  Lin Elliott, Dallas vs. Buffalo, XXVII (7 att)
  Doug Brien, San Francisco vs. San Diego, XXIX (7 att)
- 6 Ali Haji-Sheikh, Washington vs. Denver, XXII (6 att)
- 5 Don Chandler, Green Bay vs. Kansas City, I (5 att)
  Roy Gerela, Pittsburgh vs. Dallas, XIII (5 att)
  Chris Bahr, L.A. Raiders vs. Washington, XVIII (5 att)
  Ray Wersching, San Francisco vs. Miami, XIX (5 att)
  Kevin Butler, Chicago vs. New England, XX (5 att)

Most Two-Point Conversions, Game
- 1 Mark Seay, San Diego vs. San Francisco, XXIX
  Alfred Pupunu, San Diego vs. San Francisco, XXIX
  Mark Chmura, Green Bay vs. New England, XXXI

FIELD GOALS
Field Goals Attempted, Career
- 6 Jim Turner, N.Y. Jets-Denver, 2 games
  Roy Gerela, Pittsburgh, 3 games
  Rich Karlis, Denver, 2 games
  Jeff Wilkins, St. Louis, 2 games
- 5 Efren Herrera, Dallas, 1 game
  Ray Wersching, San Francisco, 2 games
  Jason Elam, Denver, 2 games

Most Field Goals Attempted, Game
- 5 Jim Turner, N.Y. Jets vs. Baltimore, III
  Efren Herrera, Dallas vs. Denver, XII
- 4 Don Chandler, Green Bay vs. Oakland, II
  Roy Gerela, Pittsburgh vs. Dallas, X
  Ray Wersching, San Francisco vs. Cincinnati, XVI
  Rich Karlis, Denver vs. N.Y. Giants, XXI
  Mike Cofer, San Francisco vs. Cincinnati, XXIII
  Jason Elam, Denver vs. Atlanta, XXXIII
  Jeff Wilkins, St. Louis vs. Tennessee, XXXIV

Most Field Goals, Career
- 5 Ray Wersching, San Francisco, 2 games (5 att)
- 4 Don Chandler, Green Bay, 2 games (4 att)
  Jim Turner, N.Y. Jets-Denver, 2 games (6 att)
  Uwe von Schamann, Miami, 2 games (4 att)
  Jeff Wilkins, St. Louis, 2 games (6 att)
- 3 Mike Clark, Dallas, 2 games (3 att)
  Jan Stenerud, Kansas City, 1 game (3 att)
  Chris Bahr, Oakland-L.A. Raiders, 2 games (4 att)
  Mark Moseley, Washington, 2 games (4 att)
  Kevin Butler, Chicago, 1 game (3 att)
  Rich Karlis, Denver, 2 games (6 att)
  Jim Breech, Cincinnati, 2 games (3 att)
  Matt Bahr, Pittsburgh-N.Y. Giants, 2 games (3 att)
  Chip Lohmiller, Washington, 1 game (3 att)
  Steve Christie, Buffalo, 2 games (3 att)
  Eddie Murray, Dallas, 1 game (3 att)
  Jason Elam, Denver, 2 games (5 att)

Most Field Goals, Game
- 4 Don Chandler, Green Bay vs. Oakland, II
  Ray Wersching, San Francisco vs. Cincinnati, XVI
- 3 Jim Turner, N.Y. Jets vs. Baltimore, III
  Jan Stenerud, Kansas City vs. Minnesota, IV
  Uwe von Schamann, Miami vs. San Francisco, XIX
  Kevin Butler, Chicago vs. New England, XX
  Jim Breech, Cincinnati vs. San Francisco, XXIII
  Chip Lohmiller, Washington vs. Buffalo, XXVI
  Eddie Murray, Dallas vs. Buffalo, XXVIII
  Jeff Wilkins, St. Louis vs. Tennessee, XXXIV

Longest Field Goal
- 54 Steve Christie, Buffalo vs. Dallas, XXVIII
- 51 Jason Elam, Denver vs. Green Bay, XXXII
- 50 Jeff Wilkins, St. Louis vs. New England, XXXVI

SAFETIES
Most Safeties, Game
- 1 Dwight White, Pittsburgh vs. Minnesota, IX
  Reggie Harrison, Pittsburgh vs. Dallas, X
  Henry Waechter, Chicago vs. New England, XX
  George Martin, N.Y. Giants vs. Denver, XXI
  Bruce Smith, Buffalo vs. N.Y. Giants, XXV

RUSHING
ATTEMPTS
Most Attempts, Career
- 101 Franco Harris, Pittsburgh, 4 games
- 70 Emmitt Smith, Dallas, 3 games
- 64 John Riggins, Washington, 2 games

Most Attempts, Game
- 38 John Riggins, Washington vs. Miami, 1983
- 34 Franco Harris, Pittsburgh vs. Minnesota, 1975
- 33 Larry Csonka, Miami vs. Minnesota, 1974

YARDS GAINED
Most Yards Gained, Career
- 354 Franco Harris, Pittsburgh, 4 games
- 297 Larry Csonka, Miami, 3 games
- 289 Emmitt Smith, Dallas, 3 games

Most Yards Gained, Game
- 204 Timmy Smith, Washington vs. Denver, XXII
- 191 Marcus Allen, L.A. Raiders vs. Washington, XVIII
- 166 John Riggins, Washington vs. Miami, XVII

Longest Run From Scrimmage
- 74 Marcus Allen, L.A. Raiders vs. Washington, XVIII (TD)
- 58 Tom Matte, Baltimore vs. N.Y. Jets, III
  Timmy Smith, Washington vs. Denver, XXII (TD)
- 49 Larry Csonka, Miami vs. Washington, VII

AVERAGE GAIN
Highest Average Gain, Career (20 attempts)
- 9.6 Marcus Allen, L.A. Raiders, 1 game (20-191)
- 9.3 Timmy Smith, Washington, 1 game (22-204)
- 5.3 Walt Garrison, Dallas, 2 games (26-139)

Highest Average Gain, Game (10 attempts)
- 10.5 Tom Matte, Baltimore vs. N.Y. Jets, III (11-116)
- 9.6 Marcus Allen, L.A. Raiders vs. Washington, XVIII (20-191)
- 9.3 Timmy Smith, Washington vs. Denver, XXII (22-204)

TOUCHDOWNS
Most Touchdowns, Career
- 5 Emmitt Smith, Dallas, 3 games
- 4 Franco Harris, Pittsburgh, 4 games
  Thurman Thomas, Buffalo, 4 games
  John Elway, Denver, 5 games
- 3 Terrell Davis, Denver, 2 games

Most Touchdowns, Game
- 3 Terrell Davis, Denver vs. Green Bay, XXXII
- 2 Elijah Pitts, Green Bay vs. Kansas City, I
  Larry Csonka, Miami vs. Minnesota, VIII
  Pete Banaszak, Oakland vs. Minnesota, XI
  Franco Harris, Pittsburgh vs. Los Angeles, XIV
  Marcus Allen, L.A. Raiders vs. Washington, XVIII
  Jim McMahon, Chicago vs. New England, XX
  Timmy Smith, Washington vs. Denver, XXII
  Tom Rathman, San Francisco vs. Denver, XXIV
  Gerald Riggs, Washington vs. Buffalo, XXVI
  Emmitt Smith, Dallas vs. Buffalo, XXVIII
  Emmitt Smith, Dallas vs. Pittsburgh, XXX
  Howard Griffith, Denver vs. Atlanta, XXXIII
  Eddie George, Tennessee vs. St. Louis, XXXIV

SUPER BOWL RECORDS

PASSING

PASSER RATING

Highest Passer Rating, Career (40 attempts)
- 127.8   Joe Montana, San Francisco, 4 games
- 122.8   Jim Plunkett, Oakland-L.A. Raiders, 2 games
- 112.8   Terry Bradshaw, Pittsburgh, 4 games

ATTEMPTS

Most Passes Attempted, Career
- 152   John Elway, Denver, 5 games
- 145   Jim Kelly, Buffalo, 4 games
- 122   Joe Montana, San Francisco, 4 games

Most Passes Attempted, Game
- 58   Jim Kelly, Buffalo vs. Washington, XXVI
- 50   Dan Marino, Miami vs. San Francisco, XIX
-       Jim Kelly, Buffalo vs. Dallas, XXVIII
- 49   Stan Humphries, San Diego vs. San Francisco, XXIX
-       Neil O'Donnell, Pittsburgh vs. Dallas, XXX

COMPLETIONS

Most Passes Completed, Career
- 83   Joe Montana, San Francisco, 4 games
- 81   Jim Kelly, Buffalo, 4 games
- 76   John Elway, Denver, 5 games

Most Passes Completed, Game
- 31   Jim Kelly, Buffalo vs. Dallas, XXVIII
- 29   Dan Marino, Miami vs. San Francisco, XIX
- 28   Jim Kelly, Buffalo vs. Washington, XXVI
-       Neil O'Donnell, Pittsburgh vs. Dallas, XXX
-       Kurt Warner, St. Louis vs. New England, XXXVI

Most Consecutive Completions, Game
- 13   Joe Montana, San Francisco vs. Denver, XXIV
- 10   Phil Simms, N.Y. Giants vs. Denver, XXI
-       Troy Aikman, Dallas vs. Pittsburgh, XXX
- 9   Jim Kelly, Buffalo vs. Dallas, XXVIII
-     Neil O'Donnell, Pittsburgh vs. Dallas, XXX
-     Steve McNair, Tennessee vs. St. Louis, XXXIV

COMPLETION PERCENTAGE

Highest Completion Percentage, Career (40 attempts)
- 70.0   Troy Aikman, Dallas, 3 games, (80-56)
- 68.0   Joe Montana, San Francisco, 4 games (122-83)
- 63.6   Len Dawson, Kansas City, 2 games (44-28)

Highest Completion Percentage, Game (20 attempts)
- 88.0   Phil Simms, N.Y. Giants vs. Denver, XXI (25-22)
- 75.9   Joe Montana, San Francisco vs. Denver, XXIV (29-22)
- 73.5   Ken Anderson, Cincinnati vs. San Francisco, XVI (34-25)

YARDS GAINED

Most Yards Gained, Career
- 1,142   Joe Montana, San Francisco, 4 games
- 1,128   John Elway, Denver, 5 games
- 932   Terry Bradshaw, Pittsburgh, 4 games

Most Yards Gained, Game
- 414   Kurt Warner, St. Louis vs. Tennessee, XXXIV
- 365   Kurt Warner, St. Louis vs. New England, XXXVI
- 357   Joe Montana, San Francisco vs. Cincinnati, XXIII

Longest Pass Completion
- 81   Brett Favre (to Freeman), Green Bay vs. New England, XXXI (TD)
- 80   Jim Plunkett (to King), Oakland vs. Philadelphia, XV (TD)
-       Doug Williams (to Sanders), Washington vs. Denver, XXII (TD)
-       John Elway (to R. Smith), Denver vs. Atlanta, XXXIII (TD)
- 76   David Woodley (to Cefalo), Miami vs. Washington, XVII (TD)

AVERAGE GAIN

Highest Average Gain, Career (40 attempts)
- 11.10   Terry Bradshaw, Pittsburgh, 4 games (84-932)
- 9.62   Bart Starr, Green Bay, 2 games (47-452)
- 9.41   Jim Plunkett, Oakland-L.A. Raiders, 2 games (46-433)

Highest Average Gain, Game (20 attempts)
- 14.71   Terry Bradshaw, Pittsburgh vs. Los Angeles, XIV (21-309)
- 12.80   Jim McMahon, Chicago vs. New England, XX (20-256)
- 12.43   Jim Plunkett, Oakland vs. Philadelphia, XV (21-261)

TOUCHDOWNS

Most Touchdown Passes, Career
- 11   Joe Montana, San Francisco, 4 games
- 9   Terry Bradshaw, Pittsburgh, 4 games
- 8   Roger Staubach, Dallas, 4 games

Most Touchdown Passes, Game
- 6   Steve Young, San Francisco vs. San Diego, XXIX
- 5   Joe Montana, San Francisco vs. Denver, XXIV
- 4   Terry Bradshaw, Pittsburgh vs. Dallas, XIII
-     Doug Williams, Washington vs. Denver, XXII
-     Troy Aikman, Dallas vs. Buffalo, XXVII

HAD INTERCEPTED

Lowest Percentage, Passes Had Intercepted, Career (40 attempts)
- 0.00   Jim Plunkett, Oakland-L.A. Raiders, 2 games (46-0)
-       Joe Montana, San Francisco, 4 games (122-0)
- 1.25   Troy Aikman, Dallas, 3 games (80-1)
- 1.45   Brett Favre, Green Bay, 2 games (69-1)

Most Attempts, Without Interception, Game
- 45   Kurt Warner, St. Louis vs. Tennessee, XXXIV
- 36   Joe Montana, San Francisco vs. Cincinnati, XXIII
-     Steve Young, San Francisco vs. San Diego, XXIX
-     Steve McNair, Tennessee vs. St. Louis, XXXIV
- 35   Joe Montana, San Francisco vs. Miami, XIX

Most Passes Had Intercepted, Career
- 8   John Elway, Denver, 5 games
- 7   Craig Morton, Dallas-Denver, 2 games
-    Jim Kelly, Buffalo, 4 games
- 6   Fran Tarkenton, Minnesota, 3 games

Most Passes Had Intercepted, Game
- 4   Craig Morton, Denver vs. Dallas, XII
-     Jim Kelly, Buffalo vs. Washington, XXVI
-     Drew Bledsoe, New England vs. Green Bay, XXXI
-     Kerry Collins, N.Y. Giants vs. Baltimore, XXXV
- 3   By ten players

PASS RECEIVING

RECEPTIONS

Most Receptions, Career
- 28   Jerry Rice, San Francisco, 3 games
- 27   Andre Reed, Buffalo, 4 games
- 20   Roger Craig, San Francisco, 3 games
-     Thurman Thomas, Buffalo, 4 games

Most Receptions, Game
- 11   Dan Ross, Cincinnati vs. San Francisco, XVI
-     Jerry Rice, San Francisco vs. Cincinnati, XXIII
- 10   Tony Nathan, Miami vs. San Francisco, XIX
-     Jerry Rice, San Francisco vs. San Diego, XXIX
-     Andre Hastings, Pittsburgh vs. Dallas, XXX
- 9   Ricky Sanders, Washington vs. Denver, XXII
-    Antonio Freeman, Green Bay vs. Denver, XXXII

YARDS GAINED

Most Yards Gained, Career
- 512   Jerry Rice, San Francisco, 3 games
- 364   Lynn Swann, Pittsburgh, 4 games
- 323   Andre Reed, Buffalo, 4 games

Most Yards Gained, Game
- 215   Jerry Rice, San Francisco vs. Cincinnati, XXIII

193   Ricky Sanders, Washington vs. Denver, XXII
162   Isaac Bruce, St. Louis vs. Tennessee, XXXIV

Longest Reception
81   Antonio Freeman (from Favre), Green Bay vs. New England, XXXI (TD)
80   Kenny King (from Plunkett), Oakland vs. Philadelphia, XV (TD)
    Ricky Sanders (from Williams), Washington vs. Denver, XXII (TD)
    Rod Smith (from Elway), Denver vs. Atlanta, XXXIII
76   Jimmy Cefalo (from Woodley), Miami vs. Washington, XVII (TD)

AVERAGE GAIN
Highest Average Gain, Career (8 receptions)
24.4   John Stallworth, Pittsburgh, 4 games (11-268)
23.4   Ricky Sanders, Washington, 2 games (10-234)
22.8   Lynn Swann, Pittsburgh, 4 games (16-364)
Highest Average Gain, Game (3 receptions)
40.33   John Stallworth, Pittsburgh vs. Los Angeles, XIV (3-121)
40.25   Lynn Swann, Pittsburgh vs. Dallas, X (4-161)
38.33   John Stallworth, Pittsburgh vs. Dallas, XIII (3-115)

TOUCHDOWNS
Most Touchdowns, Career
7   Jerry Rice, San Francisco, 3 games
3   John Stallworth, Pittsburgh, 4 games
   Lynn Swann, Pittsburgh, 4 games
   Cliff Branch, Oakland-L.A. Raiders, 3 games
   Antonio Freeman, Green Bay, 2 games
2   Max McGee, Green Bay, 2 games
   Bill Miller, Oakland, 1 game
   Butch Johnson, Dallas, 2 games
   Dan Ross, Cincinnati, 1 game
   Roger Craig, San Francisco, 3 games
   Ricky Sanders, Washington, 2 games
   John Taylor, San Francisco, 3 games
   Gary Clark, Washington, 2 games
   Don Beebe, Buffalo-Green Bay, 4 games
   Michael Irvin, Dallas, 3 games
   Ricky Watters, San Francisco, 1 game
   Jay Novacek, Dallas, 3 games
Most Touchdowns, Game
3   Jerry Rice, San Francisco vs. Denver, XXIV; vs. San Diego, XXIX
2   Max McGee, Green Bay vs. Kansas City, I
   Bill Miller, Oakland vs. Green Bay, II
   John Stallworth, Pittsburgh vs. Dallas, XIII
   Cliff Branch, Oakland vs. Philadelphia, XV
   Dan Ross, Cincinnati vs. San Francisco, XVI
   Roger Craig, San Francisco vs. Miami, XIX
   Ricky Sanders, Washington vs. Denver, XXII
   Michael Irvin, Dallas vs. Buffalo, XXVII
   Ricky Watters, San Francisco vs. San Diego, XXIX
   Antonio Freeman, Green Bay vs. Denver, XXXII

INTERCEPTIONS BY
Most Interceptions By, Career
3   Chuck Howley, Dallas, 2 games
   Rod Martin, Oakland-L.A. Raiders, 2 games
   Larry Brown, Dallas, 3 games
2   Randy Beverly, N.Y. Jets, 1 game
   Jake Scott, Miami, 3 games
   Mike Wagner, Pittsburgh, 3 games
   Mel Blount, Pittsburgh, 4 games
   Eric Wright, San Francisco, 4 games
   Barry Wilburn, Washington, 1 game
   Brad Edwards, Washington, 1 game
   Thomas Everett, Dallas, 2 games

   James Washington, Dallas, 2 games
   Darrien Gordon, San Diego-Denver, 3 games
Most Interceptions By, Game
3   Rod Martin, Oakland vs. Philadelphia, XV
2   Randy Beverly, N.Y. Jets vs. Baltimore, III
   Chuck Howley, Dallas vs. Baltimore, V
   Jake Scott, Miami vs. Washington, VII
   Barry Wilburn, Washington vs. Denver, XXII
   Brad Edwards, Washington vs. Buffalo, XXVI
   Thomas Everett, Dallas vs. Buffalo, XXVII
   Larry Brown, Dallas vs. Pittsburgh, XXX
   Darrien Gordon, Denver vs. Atlanta, XXXIII

YARDS GAINED
Most Yards Gained, Career
108   Darrien Gordon, San Diego-Denver, 3 games
77   Larry Brown, Dallas, 3 games
75   Willie Brown, Oakland, 2 games
Most Yards Gained, Game
108   Darrien Gordon, Denver vs. Atlanta, XXXIII
77   Larry Brown, Dallas vs. Pittsburgh, XXX
75   Willie Brown, Oakland vs. Minnesota, XI
Longest Return
75   Willie Brown, Oakland vs. Minnesota, XI (TD)
60   Herb Adderley, Green Bay vs. Oakland, II (TD)
58   Darrien Gordon, Denver vs. Atlanta, XXXIII

TOUCHDOWNS
Most Touchdowns, Game
1   Herb Adderley, Green Bay vs. Oakland, II
   Willie Brown, Oakland vs. Minnesota, XI
   Jack Squirek, L.A. Raiders vs. Washington, XVIII
   Reggie Phillips, Chicago vs. New England, XX
   Duane Starks, Baltimore vs. N.Y. Giants, XXXV
   Ty Law, New England vs. St. Louis, XXXVI

PUNTING
Most Punts, Career
17   Mike Eischeid, Oakland-Minnesota, 3 games
   Mike Horan, Denver-St. Louis, 4 games
15   Larry Seiple, Miami, 3 games
14   Ron Widby, Dallas, 2 games
   Ray Guy, Oakland-L.A. Raiders, 3 games
   Chris Mohr, Buffalo, 3 games
   Craig Hentrich, Green Bay-Tennessee, 3 games
Most Punts, Game
11   Brad Maynard, N.Y. Giants vs. Baltimore, XXXV
10   Kyle Richardson, Baltimore vs. N.Y. Giants, XXXV
9   Ron Widby, Dallas vs. Baltimore, V
Longest Punt
63   Lee Johnson, Cincinnati vs. San Francisco, XXIII
62   Rich Camarillo, New England vs. Chicago, XX
61   Jerrel Wilson, Kansas City vs. Green Bay, I

AVERAGE YARDAGE
Highest Average, Punting, Career (10 punts)
46.5   Jerrel Wilson, Kansas City, 2 games (11-511)
43.0   Kyle Richardson, Baltimore, 1 game (10-430)
41.9   Ray Guy, Oakland-L.A. Raiders, 3 games (14-587)
Highest Average, Punting, Game (4 punts)
48.8   Bryan Wagner, San Diego vs. San Francisco, XXIX (4-195)
48.5   Jerrel Wilson, Kansas City vs. Minnesota, IV (4-194)
46.3   Jim Miller, San Francisco vs. Cincinnati, XVI (4-185)

PUNT RETURNS
Most Punt Returns, Career
6   Willie Wood, Green Bay, 2 games
   Jake Scott, Miami, 3 games
   Theo Bell, Pittsburgh, 2 games

Mike Nelms, Washington, 1 game
John Taylor, San Francisco, 3 games
Desmond Howard, Green Bay, 1 game
David Meggett, N.Y. Giants-New England, 2 games
5 Dana McLemore, San Francisco, 1 game
4 By eight players

Most Punt Returns, Game

6 Mike Nelms, Washington vs. Miami, XVII
Desmond Howard, Green Bay vs. New England, XXXI
5 Willie Wood, Green Bay vs. Oakland, II
Dana McLemore, San Francisco vs. Miami, XIX
4 By seven players

Most Fair Catches, Game

4 Jermaine Lewis, Baltimore vs. N.Y. Giants, XXXV
3 Ron Gardin, Baltimore vs. Dallas, V
Golden Richards, Dallas vs. Pittsburgh, X
Greg Pruitt, L.A. Raiders vs. Washington, XVIII
Al Edwards, Buffalo vs. N.Y. Giants, XXV
David Meggett, N.Y. Giants vs. Buffalo, XXV

YARDS GAINED

Most Yards Gained, Career

94 John Taylor, San Francisco, 3 games
90 Desmond Howard, Green Bay, 1 game
67 David Meggett, N.Y. Giants-New England, 2 games

Most Yards Gained, Game

90 Desmond Howard, Green Bay vs. New England, XXXI
56 John Taylor, San Francisco vs. Cincinnati, XXIII
52 Mike Nelms, Washington vs. Miami, XXII

Longest Return

45 John Taylor, San Francisco vs. Cincinnati, XXIII
34 Darrell Green, Washington vs. L.A. Raiders, XVIII
Desmond Howard, Green Bay vs. New England, XXXI
Jermaine Lewis, Baltimore vs. N.Y. Giants, XXXV
32 Desmond Howard, Green Bay vs. New England, XXXI

AVERAGE YARDAGE

Highest Average, Career (4 returns)

15.7 John Taylor, San Francisco, 3 games (6-94)
15.0 Desmond Howard, Green Bay, 1 game (6-90)
11.2 David Meggett, N.Y. Giants-New England, 2 games (6-67)

Highest Average, Game (3 returns)

18.7 John Taylor, San Francisco vs. Cincinnati, XXIII (3-56)
15.0 Desmond Howard, Green Bay vs. New England, XXXI (6-90)
12.7 John Taylor, San Francisco vs. Denver, XXIV (3-38)

TOUCHDOWNS

Most Touchdowns, Game

None

KICKOFF RETURNS

Most Kickoff Returns, Career

10 Ken Bell, Denver, 3 games
8 Larry Anderson, Pittsburgh, 2 games
Fulton Walker, Miami, 2 games
Andre Coleman, San Diego, 1 game
7 Preston Pearson, Baltimore-Pittsburgh-Dallas, 5 games
Stephen Starring, New England, 1 game
David Meggett, N.Y. Giants-New England, 2 games

Most Kickoff Returns, Game

8 Andre Coleman, San Diego vs. San Francisco, XXIX
7 Stephen Starring, New England vs. Chicago, XX
6 Darren Carrington, Denver vs. San Francisco, XXIV
Antonio Freeman, Green Bay vs. Denver, XXXII
Ron Dixon, N.Y. Giants vs. Baltimore, XXXV

YARDS GAINED

Most Yards Gained, Career

283 Fulton Walker, Miami, 2 games
244 Andre Coleman, San Diego, 1 game
210 Tim Dwight, Atlanta, 1 game

Most Yards Gained, Game

244 Andre Coleman, San Diego vs. San Francisco, XXIX
210 Tim Dwight, Atlanta vs. Denver, XXXIII
190 Fulton Walker, Miami vs. Washington, XVII

Longest Return

99 Desmond Howard, Green Bay vs. New England, XXXI (TD)
98 Fulton Walker, Miami vs. Washington, XVII (TD)
Andre Coleman, San Diego vs. San Francisco, XXIX (TD)
97 Ron Dixon, N.Y. Giants vs. Baltimore, XXXV (TD)

AVERAGE YARDAGE

Highest Average, Career (4 returns)

42.0 Tim Dwight, Atlanta, 1 game (5-210)
38.5 Desmond Howard, Green Bay, 1 game (4-154)
35.4 Fulton Walker, Miami, 2 games (8-283)

Highest Average, Game (3 returns)

47.5 Fulton Walker, Miami vs. Washington, XVII (4-190)
42.0 Tim Dwight, Atlanta vs. Denver, XXXIII (5-210)
38.5 Desmond Howard, Green Bay vs. New England, XXXI (4-154)

TOUCHDOWNS

Most Touchdowns, Game

1 Fulton Walker, Miami vs. Washington, XVII
Stanford Jennings, Cincinnati vs. San Francisco, XXIII
Andre Coleman, San Diego vs. San Francisco, XXIX
Desmond Howard, Green Bay vs. New England, XXXI
Tim Dwight, Atlanta vs. Denver, XXXIII
Ron Dixon, N.Y. Giants vs. Baltimore, XXXV
Jermaine Lewis, Baltimore vs. N.Y. Giants, XXXV

FUMBLES

Most Fumbles, Career

5 Roger Staubach, Dallas, 4 games
4 Jim Kelly, Buffalo, 4 games
3 Franco Harris, Pittsburgh, 4 games
Terry Bradshaw, Pittsburgh, 4 games
John Elway, Denver, 5 games
Frank Reich, Buffalo, 4 games
Thurman Thomas, Buffalo, 4 games

Most Fumbles, Game

3 Roger Staubach, Dallas vs. Pittsburgh, X
Jim Kelly, Buffalo vs. Washington, XXVI
Frank Reich, Buffalo vs. Dallas, XXVII
2 Franco Harris, Pittsburgh vs. Minnesota, IX
Butch Johnson, Dallas vs. Denver, XII
Terry Bradshaw, Pittsburgh vs. Dallas, XIII
Joe Montana, San Francisco vs. Cincinnati, XXIII
John Elway, Denver vs. San Francisco, XXIV
Thurman Thomas, Buffalo vs. Dallas, XXVIII

RECOVERIES

Most Fumbles Recovered, Career

2 Jake Scott, Miami, 3 games (1 own, 1 opp)
Fran Tarkenton, Minnesota, 3 games (2 own)
Franco Harris, Pittsburgh, 4 games (2 own)
Roger Staubach, Dallas, 4 games (2 own)
Bobby Walden, Pittsburgh, 2 games (2 own)
John Fitzgerald, Dallas, 4 games (2 own)
Randy Hughes, Dallas, 3 games (2 opp)
Butch Johnson, Dallas, 2 games (2 own)
Mike Singletary, Chicago, 1 game (2 opp)
John Elway, Denver, 5 games (2 own)

Jimmie Jones, Dallas, 2 games (2 opp)
Kenneth Davis, Buffalo, 4 games (2 own)
Kurt Warner, St. Louis, 2 games (2 own)
Most Fumbles Recovered, Game
2   Jake Scott, Miami vs. Minnesota, VIII (1 own, 1 opp)
    Roger Staubach, Dallas vs. Pittsburgh, X (2 own)
    Randy Hughes, Dallas vs. Denver, XII (2 own)
    Butch Johnson, Dallas vs. Denver, XII (2 own)
    Mike Singletary, Chicago vs. New England, XX (2 opp)
    Jimmie Jones, Dallas vs. Buffalo, XXVII (2 opp)

YARDS GAINED
Most Yards Gained, Game
64 Leon Lett, Dallas vs. Buffalo, XXVII (opp)
49 Mike Bass, Washington vs. Miami, VII (opp)
46 James Washington, Dallas vs. Buffalo, XXVIII (opp)
Longest Return
64 Leon Lett, Dallas vs. Buffalo, XXVII
49 Mike Bass, Washington vs. Miami, VII (TD)
46 James Washington, Dallas vs. Buffalo, XXVIII (TD)

TOUCHDOWNS
Most Touchdowns, Game
1   Mike Bass, Washington vs. Miami, VII (opp 49 yds)
    Mike Hegman, Dallas vs. Pittsburgh, XIII (opp 37 yds)
    Jimmie Jones, Dallas vs. Buffalo, XXVII (opp 2 yds)
    Ken Norton, Dallas vs. Buffalo, XXVII (opp 9 yds)
    James Washington, Dallas vs. Buffalo, XXVIII
    (opp 46 yds)

COMBINED NET YARDS GAINED
(Rushing, receiving, interception returns, punt returns, kickoff returns, and fumble returns)
ATTEMPTS
Most Attempts, Career
108 Franco Harris, Pittsburgh, 4 games
81 Emmitt Smith, Dallas, 3 games
72 Roger Craig, San Francisco, 3 games
    Thurman Thomas, Buffalo, 4 games
Most Attempts, Game
39 John Riggins, Washington vs. Miami, XVII
35 Franco Harris, Pittsburgh vs. Minnesota, IX
34 Matt Snell, N.Y. Jets vs. Baltimore, III
    Emmitt Smith, Dallas vs. Buffalo, XXVIII

YARDS GAINED
Most Yards Gained, Career
527 Jerry Rice, San Francisco, 3 games
468 Franco Harris, Pittsburgh, 4 games
410 Roger Craig, San Francisco, 3 games
Most Yards Gained, Game
244 Andre Coleman, San Diego vs. San Francisco, XXIX
    Desmond Howard, Green Bay vs. New England, XXXI
235 Ricky Sanders, Washington vs. Denver, XXII
230 Antonio Freeman, Green Bay vs. Denver, XXXII

SACKS
Sacks have been compiled since XVII.
Most Sacks, Career
4.5 Charles Haley, San Francisco-Dallas, 5 games
3.0 Danny Stubbs, San Francisco, 2 games
    Leonard Marshall, N.Y. Giants, 2 games
    Jeff Wright, Buffalo, 4 games
    Reggie White, Green Bay, 2 games
2.5 Dexter Manley, Washington, 3 games
Most Sacks, Game
3.0 Reggie White, Green Bay vs. New England, XXXI
2.0 Dwaine Board, San Francisco vs. Miami, XIX
    Dennis Owens, New England vs. Chicago, XX
    Otis Wilson, Chicago vs. New England, XX

Leonard Marshall, N.Y. Giants vs. Denver, XXI
Alvin Walton, Washington vs. Denver, XXII
Charles Haley, San Francisco vs. Cincinnati, XXIII
Danny Stubbs, San Francisco vs. Denver, XXIV
Jeff Wright, Buffalo vs. Dallas, XXVIII
Raylee Johnson, San Diego vs. San Francisco, XXIX
Chad Hennings, Dallas vs. Pittsburgh, XXX
Tedy Bruschi, New England vs. Green Bay, XXXI
Michael McCrary, Baltimore vs. N.Y. Giants, XXXV

TEAM RECORDS

GAMES, VICTORIES, DEFEATS
Most Games
8   Dallas, V-VI, X, XII-XIII, XXVII-XXVIII, XXX
6   Denver, XII, XXI-XXII, XXIV, XXXII-XXXIII
5   Miami, VI-VIII, XVII, XIX
    Washington, VII, XVII-XVIII, XXII, XXVI
    San Francisco, XVI, XIX, XXIII-XXIV, XXIX
    Pittsburgh, IX-X, XIII-XIV, XXX
Most Consecutive Games
4   Buffalo, XXV-XXVIII
3   Miami, VI-VIII
2   Green Bay, I-II; XXXI-XXXII
    Dallas, V-VI; XII-XIII; XXVII-XXVIII
    Minnesota, VIII-IX
    Pittsburgh, IX-X; XIII-XIV
    Washington, XVII-XVIII
    Denver, XXI-XXII; XXXII-XXXIII
    San Francisco XXIII-XXIV
Most Games Won
5   San Francisco, XVI, XIX, XXIII-XXIV, XXIX
    Dallas, VI, XII, XXVII-XXVIII, XXX
4   Pittsburgh, IX-X, XIII-XIV
3   Oakland/L.A. Raiders, XI, XV, XVIII
    Washington, XVII, XXII, XXVI
    Green Bay, I-II, XXXI
Most Consecutive Games Won
2   Green Bay, I-II
    Miami, VII-VIII
    Pittsburgh, IX-X, XIII-XIV
    San Francisco, XXIII-XXIV
    Dallas, XXVII-XXVIII
    Denver, XXXII-XXXIII
Most Games Lost
4   Minnesota, IV, VIII-IX, XI
    Denver, XII, XXI-XXII, XXIV
    Buffalo, XXV-XXVIII
3   Dallas, V, X, XIII
    Miami, VI, XVII, XIX
2   Washington, VII, XVIII
    Cincinnati, XVI, XXIII
    New England, XX, XXXI
    L.A./St. Louis Rams, XIV, XXXVI
Most Consecutive Games Lost
4   Buffalo, XXV-XXVIII
2   Minnesota, VIII-IX
    Denver, XXI-XXII

SCORING
Most Points, Game
55 San Francisco vs. Denver, XXIV
52 Dallas vs. Buffalo, XXVII
49 San Francisco vs. San Diego, XXIX
Fewest Points, Game
3   Miami vs. Dallas, VI
6   Minnesota vs. Pittsburgh, IX
7   By five teams
Most Points, Both Teams, Game
75 San Francisco (49) vs. San Diego (26), XXIX

69 Dallas (52) vs. Buffalo (17), XXVII
66 Pittsburgh (35) vs. Dallas (31), XIII
Fewest Points, Both Teams, Game
21 Washington (7) vs. Miami (14), VII
22 Minnesota (6) vs. Pittsburgh (16), IX
23 Baltimore (7) vs. N.Y. Jets (16), III
Largest Margin of Victory, Game
45 San Francisco vs. Denver, XXIV (55-10)
36 Chicago vs. New England, XX (46-10)
35 Dallas vs. Buffalo, XXVII (52-17)
Most Points, Each Half
1st: 35 Washington vs. Denver, XXII
2nd: 30 N.Y. Giants vs. Denver, XXI
Most Points, Each Quarter
1st: 14 Miami vs. Minnesota, VIII
        Oakland vs. Philadelphia, XV
        Dallas vs. Buffalo, XXVII
        San Francisco vs. San Diego, XXIX
        New England vs. Green Bay, XXXI
2nd: 35 Washington vs. Denver, XXII
3rd: 21 Chicago vs. New England, XX
4th: 21 Dallas vs. Buffalo, XXVII
Most Points, Both Teams, Each Half
1st: 45 Washington (35) vs. Denver (10), XXII
2nd: 44 Buffalo (24) vs. Washington (20), XXVI
Fewest Points, Both Teams, Each Half
1st: 2 Minnesota (0) vs. Pittsburgh (2), IX
2nd: 7 Miami (0) vs. Washington (7), VII
        Denver (0) vs. Washington (7), XXII
Most Points, Both Teams, Each Quarter
1st: 24 New England (14) vs. Green Bay (10), XXXI
2nd: 35 Washington (35) vs. Denver (0), XXII
3rd: 24 Washington (14) vs. Buffalo (10), XXVI
4th: 30 Denver (17) vs. Atlanta (13), XXXIII

TOUCHDOWNS
Most Touchdowns, Game
8 San Francisco vs. Denver, XXIV
7 Dallas vs. Buffalo, XXVII
    San Francisco vs. San Diego, XXIX
6 Washington vs. Denver, XXII
Fewest Touchdowns, Game
0 Miami vs. Dallas, VI
1 By 18 teams
Most Touchdowns, Both Teams, Game
10 San Francisco (7) vs. San Diego (3), XXIX
9 Pittsburgh (5) vs. Dallas (4), XIII
    San Francisco (8) vs. Denver (1), XXIV
    Dallas (7) vs. Buffalo (2), XXVII
7 N.Y. Giants (5) vs. Denver (2), XXI
    Washington (6) vs. Denver (1), XXII
    Washington (4) vs. Buffalo (3), XXVI
    Green Bay (4) vs. New England (3), XXXI
    Denver (4) vs. Green Bay (3), XXXII
Fewest Touchdowns, Both Teams, Game
2 Baltimore (1) vs. N.Y. Jets (1), III
3 In six games

POINTS AFTER TOUCHDOWN
Most (One-Point) Points After Touchdown, Game
7 San Francisco vs. Denver, XXIV
    Dallas vs. Buffalo, XXVII
    San Francisco vs. San Diego, XXIX
6 Washington vs. Denver, XXII
5 Green Bay vs. Kansas City, I
    Pittsburgh vs. Dallas, XIII
    L.A. Raiders vs. Washington, XVIII
    San Francisco vs. Miami, XIX
    Chicago vs. New England, XX

Most (One-Point) Points After Touchdown, Both Teams, Game
9 Pittsburgh (5) vs. Dallas (4), XIII
    Dallas (7) vs. Buffalo (2), XXVII
8 San Francisco (7) vs. Denver (1), XXIV
    San Francisco (7) vs. San Diego (1), XXIX
7 Washington (6) vs. Denver (1), XXII
    Washington (4) vs. Buffalo (3), XXVI
    Denver (4) vs. Green Bay (3), XXXII
Fewest (One-Point) Points After Touchdown, Both Teams, Game
2 Baltimore (1) vs. N.Y. Jets (1), III
    Baltimore (1) vs. Dallas (1), V
    Minnesota (0) vs. Pittsburgh (2), IX
Most Two-Point Conversions, Game
2 San Diego vs. San Francisco, XXIX
Most Two-Point Conversions, Both Teams, Game
2 San Diego (2) vs. San Francisco (0), XXIX

FIELD GOALS
Most Field Goals Attempted, Game
5 N.Y. Jets vs. Baltimore, III
    Dallas vs. Denver, XII
4 Green Bay vs. Oakland, II
    Pittsburgh vs. Dallas, XX
    San Francisco vs. Cincinnati, XVI; XXIII
    Denver vs. N.Y. Giants, XXI
    Denver vs. Atlanta, XXXIII
    St. Louis vs. Tennessee, XXXIV
Most Field Goals Attempted, Both Teams, Game
7 N.Y. Jets (5) vs. Baltimore (2), III
    San Francisco (4) vs. Cincinnati (3), XXIII
    St. Louis (4) vs. Tennessee (3), XXXIV
    Denver (4) vs. Atlanta (3), XXXIII
6 Dallas (5) vs. Denver (1), XII
5 Green Bay (4) vs. Oakland (1), II
    Pittsburgh (4) vs. Dallas (1), X
    Oakland (3) vs. Philadelphia (2), XV
    Denver (4) vs. N.Y. Giants (1), XXI
    Dallas (3) vs. Buffalo (2), XXVIII
Fewest Field Goals Attempted, Both Teams, Game
1 Minnesota (0) vs. Miami (1), VIII
    San Francisco (0) vs. Denver (1), XXIV
2 Green Bay (0) vs. Kansas City (2), I
    Miami (1) vs. Washington (1), VII
    Minnesota (1) vs. Pittsburgh (1), IX
    Dallas (1) vs. Pittsburgh (1), XIII
    Dallas (1) vs. Buffalo (1), XXVII
    San Diego (1) vs. San Francisco (1), XXIX
    Denver (1) vs. Green Bay (1), XXXII
Most Field Goals, Game
4 Green Bay vs. Oakland, II
    San Francisco vs. Cincinnati, XVI
3 N.Y. Jets vs. Baltimore, III
    Kansas City vs. Minnesota, IV
    Miami vs. San Francisco, XIX
    Chicago vs. New England, XX
    Cincinnati vs. San Francisco, XXIII
    Washington vs. Buffalo, XXVI
    Dallas vs. Buffalo, XXVIII
    St. Louis vs. Tennessee, XXXIV
Most Field Goals, Both Teams, Game
5 Cincinnati (3) vs. San Francisco (2), XXIII
    Dallas (3) vs. Buffalo (2), XXVIII
4 Green Bay (4) vs. Oakland (0), II
    San Francisco (4) vs. Cincinnati (0), XVI
    Miami (3) vs. San Francisco (1), XIX
    Chicago (3) vs. New England (1), XX
    Washington (3) vs. Buffalo (1), XXVI
    Atlanta (2) vs. Denver (2), XXXIII
    St. Louis (3) vs. Tennessee (1), XXXIV
3 In 12 games

Fewest Field Goals, Both Teams, Game
- 0   Miami vs. Washington, VII
  - Pittsburgh vs. Minnesota, IX
- 1   Green Bay (0) vs. Kansas City (1), I
  - Minnesota (0) vs. Miami (1), VIII
  - Pittsburgh (0) vs. Dallas (1), XIII
  - Washington (0) vs. Denver (1), XXII
  - San Francisco (0) vs. Denver (1), XXIV
  - San Francisco (0) vs. San Diego (1), XXIX

SAFETIES
Most Safeties, Game
- 1   Pittsburgh vs. Minnesota, IX; vs. Dallas, X
  - Chicago vs. New England, XX
  - N.Y. Giants vs. Denver, XXI
  - Buffalo vs. N.Y. Giants, XXV

FIRST DOWNS
Most First Downs, Game
- 31   San Francisco vs. Miami, XIX
- 28   San Francisco vs. Denver, XXIV
  - San Francisco vs. San Diego, XXIX
- 27   Tennessee vs. St. Louis, XXXIV

Fewest First Downs, Game
- 9   Minnesota vs. Pittsburgh, IX
  - Miami vs. Washington, XVII
- 10   Dallas vs. Baltimore, V
  - Miami vs. Dallas, VI
- 11   Denver vs. Dallas, XII
  - N.Y. Giants vs. Baltimore, XXXV

Most First Downs, Both Teams, Game
- 50   San Francisco (31) vs. Miami (19), XIX
  - Tennessee (27) vs. St. Louis (23), XXXIV
- 49   Buffalo (25) vs. Washington (24), XXVI
- 48   San Francisco (28) vs. San Diego (20), XXIX

Fewest First Downs, Both Teams, Game
- 24   Dallas (10) vs. Baltimore (14), V
  - N.Y. Giants (11) vs. Baltimore (13), XXXV
- 26   Minnesota (9) vs. Pittsburgh (17), IX
- 27   Pittsburgh (13) vs. Dallas (14), X

RUSHING
Most First Downs, Rushing, Game
- 16   San Francisco vs. Miami, XIX
- 15   Dallas vs. Miami, VI
- 14   Washington vs. Miami, XVII
  - San Francisco vs. Denver, XXIV
  - Denver vs. Green Bay, XXXII

Fewest First Downs, Rushing, Game
- 1   New England vs. Chicago, XX
  - St. Louis vs. Tennessee, XXXIV
- 2   Minnesota vs. Kansas City, IV; vs. Pittsburgh, IX;
  -       vs. Oakland, XI
  - Pittsburgh vs. Dallas, XIII
  - Miami vs. San Francisco, XIX
  - N.Y. Giants vs. Baltimore, XXXV
- 3   Miami vs. Dallas, VI
  - Philadelphia vs. Oakland, XV
  - New England vs. Green Bay, XXXI

Most First Downs, Rushing, Both Teams, Game
- 21   Washington (14) vs. Miami (7), XVII
- 19   Washington (13) vs. Denver (6), XXIV
  - San Francisco (14) vs. Denver (5), XXIV
- 18   Dallas (15) vs. Miami (3), VI
  - Miami (13) vs. Minnesota (5), VIII
  - San Francisco (16) vs. Miami (2), XIX
  - N.Y. Giants (10) vs. Buffalo (8), XXV
  - Denver (14) vs. Green Bay (4), XXXII

Fewest First Downs, Rushing, Both Teams, Game
- 8   Baltimore (4) vs. Dallas (4), V

-     Pittsburgh (2) vs. Dallas (6), XIII
  - N.Y. Giants (2) vs. Baltimore (6), XXXV
- 9   Philadelphia (3) vs. Oakland (6), XV
- 10   Minnesota (2) vs. Kansas City (8), IV

PASSING
Most First Downs, Passing, Game
- 18   Buffalo vs. Washington, XXVI
  - St. Louis vs. Tennessee, XXXIV
- 17   Miami vs. San Francisco, XIX
  - San Francisco vs. San Diego, XXIX
- 16   Denver vs. N.Y. Giants, XXI
  - San Francisco vs. Cincinnati, XXIII
  - St. Louis vs. New England, XXXVI

Fewest First Downs, Passing, Game
- 1   Denver vs. Dallas, XII
- 2   Miami vs. Washington, XVII
- 4   Miami vs. Minnesota, VIII

Most First Downs, Passing, Both Teams, Game
- 32   Miami (17) vs. San Francisco (15), XIX
- 31   San Francisco (17) vs. San Diego (14), XXIX
  - St. Louis (18) vs. Tennessee (13), XXXIV
- 30   Buffalo (18) vs. Washington (12), XXVI

Fewest First Downs, Passing, Both Teams, Game
- 9   Denver (1) vs. Dallas (8), XII
- 10   Minnesota (5) vs. Pittsburgh (5), IX
- 11   Dallas (5) vs. Baltimore (6), V
  - Miami (2) vs. Washington (9), XVII

PENALTY
Most First Downs, Penalty, Game
- 4   Baltimore vs. Dallas, V
  - Miami vs. Minnesota, VIII
  - Cincinnati vs. San Francisco, XVI
  - Buffalo vs. Dallas, XXVII
  - St. Louis vs. Tennessee, XXXIV
- 3   Kansas City vs. Minnesota, IV
  - Minnesota vs. Oakland, XI
  - Buffalo vs. Washington, XXVI
  - Green Bay vs. Denver, XXXII
  - N.Y. Giants vs. Baltimore, XXXV
  - St. Louis vs. New England, XXXVI

Most First Downs, Penalty, Both Teams, Game
- 6   Cincinnati (4) vs. San Francisco (2), XVI
  - St. Louis (4) vs. Tennessee (2), XXXIV
- 5   Baltimore (4) vs. Dallas (1), V
  - Miami (4) vs. Minnesota (1), VIII
  - Buffalo (3) vs. Washington (2), XXVI
  - Green Bay (3) vs. Denver (2), XXXII
- 4   Kansas City (3) vs. Minnesota (1), IV
  - Buffalo (4) vs. Dallas (0), XXVII
  - N.Y. Giants (3) vs. Baltimore (1), XXXV
  - St. Louis (3) vs. New England (1), XXXVI

Fewest First Downs, Penalty, Both Teams, Game
- 0   Dallas vs. Miami, VI
  - Miami vs. Washington, VII
  - Dallas vs. Pittsburgh, X
  - Miami vs. San Francisco, XIX
- 1   Green Bay (0) vs. Kansas City (1), I
  - Miami (0) vs. Washington (1), XVII
  - Cincinnati (0) vs. San Francisco (1), XXIII
  - San Francisco (0) vs. Denver (1), XXIV
  - Dallas (0) vs. Buffalo (1), XXVIII
  - Dallas (0) vs. Pittsburgh (1), XXX
  - Denver (0) vs. Atlanta (1), XXXIII

NET YARDS GAINED RUSHING AND PASSING
Most Yards Gained, Game
- 602   Washington vs. Denver, XXII
- 537   San Francisco vs. Miami, XIX

461 San Francisco vs. Denver, XXIV

Fewest Yards Gained, Game

119 Minnesota vs. Pittsburgh, IX
123 New England vs. Chicago, XX
152 N.Y. Giants vs. Baltimore, XXXV

Most Yards Gained, Both Teams, Game

929 Washington (602) vs. Denver (327), XXII
851 San Francisco (537) vs. Miami (314), XIX
809 San Francisco (455) vs. San Diego (354), XXIX

Fewest Yards Gained, Both Teams, Game

396 N.Y. Giants (152) vs. Baltimore (244), XXXV
452 Minnesota (119) vs. Pittsburgh (333), IX
481 Washington (228) vs. Miami (253), VII
    Denver (156) vs. Dallas (325), XII

RUSHING
ATTEMPTS

Most Attempts, Game

57 Pittsburgh vs. Minnesota, IX
53 Miami vs. Minnesota, VIII
52 Oakland vs. Minnesota, XI
   Washington vs. Miami, XVII

Fewest Attempts, Game

9 Miami vs. San Francisco, XIX
11 New England vs. Chicago, XX
13 New England vs. Green Bay, XXXI
   St. Louis vs. Tennessee, XXXIV

Most Attempts, Both Teams, Game

81 Washington (52) vs. Miami (29), XVII
78 Pittsburgh (57) vs. Minnesota (21), IX
   Oakland (52) vs. Minnesota (26), XI
77 Miami (53) vs. Minnesota (24), VIII
   Pittsburgh (46) vs. Dallas (31), X

Fewest Attempts, Both Teams, Game

47 St. Louis (22) vs. New England (25), XXXVI
49 Miami (9) vs. San Francisco (40), XIX
   New England (13) vs. Green Bay (36), XXXI
   St. Louis (13) vs. Tennessee (36), XXXIV
   N.Y. Giants (16) vs. Baltimore (33), XXXV
51 San Diego (19) vs. San Francisco (32), XXIX

YARDS GAINED

Most Yards Gained, Game

280 Washington vs. Denver, XXII
276 Washington vs. Miami, XVII
266 Oakland vs. Minnesota, XI

Fewest Yards Gained, Game

7 New England vs. Chicago, XX
17 Minnesota vs. Pittsburgh, IX
25 Miami vs. San Francisco, XIX

Most Yards Gained, Both Teams, Game

377 Washington (280) vs. Denver (97), XXII
372 Washington (276) vs. Miami (96), XVII
338 N.Y. Giants (172) vs. Buffalo (166), XXV

Fewest Yards Gained, Both Teams, Game

158 New England (43) vs. Green Bay (115), XXXI
159 Dallas (56) vs. Pittsburgh (103), XXX
168 Buffalo (43) vs. Washington (125), XXVI

AVERAGE GAIN

Highest Average Gain, Game

7.00 L.A. Raiders vs. Washington, XVIII (33-231)
     Washington vs. Denver, XXII (40-280)
6.64 Buffalo vs. N.Y. Giants, XXV (25-166)
6.22 Baltimore vs. N.Y. Jets, III (23-143)

Lowest Average Gain, Game

0.64 New England vs. Chicago, XX (11-7)
0.81 Minnesota vs. Pittsburgh, IX (21-17)
2.23 Baltimore vs. Dallas, V (31-69)

TOUCHDOWNS

Most Touchdowns, Game

4 Chicago vs. New England, XX
  Denver vs. Green Bay, XXXII
3 Green Bay vs. Kansas City, I
  Miami vs. Minnesota, VIII
  San Francisco vs. Denver, XXIV
  Denver vs. Atlanta, XXXIII
2 Oakland vs. Minnesota, XI
  Pittsburgh vs. Los Angeles, XIV
  L.A. Raiders vs. Washington, XVIII
  San Francisco vs. Miami, XIX
  N.Y. Giants vs. Denver, XXI
  Washington vs. Denver, XXII; vs. Buffalo, XXVI
  Buffalo vs. N.Y. Giants, XXV
  Dallas vs. Buffalo, XXVIII; vs. Pittsburgh, XXX
  Tennessee vs. St. Louis, XXXIV

Fewest Touchdowns, Game

0 By 23 teams

Most Touchdowns, Both Teams, Game

4 Miami (3) vs. Minnesota (1), VIII
  Chicago (4) vs. New England (0), XX
  San Francisco (3) vs. Denver (1), XXIV
  Denver (4) vs. Green Bay (0), XXXII
3 In nine games

Fewest Touchdowns, Both Teams, Game

0 Pittsburgh vs. Dallas, X
  Oakland vs. Philadelphia, XV
  Cincinnati vs. San Francisco, XXIII
1 In nine games

PASSING
ATTEMPTS

Most Passes Attempted, Game

59 Buffalo vs. Washington, XXVI
55 San Diego vs. San Francisco, XXIX
50 Miami vs. San Francisco, XIX
   Buffalo vs. Dallas, XXVIII

Fewest Passes Attempted, Game

7 Miami vs. Minnesota, VIII
11 Miami vs. Washington, VII
14 Pittsburgh vs. Minnesota, IX

Most Passes Attempted, Both Teams, Game

93 San Diego (55) vs. San Francisco (38), XXIX
92 Buffalo (59) vs. Washington (33), XXVI
85 Miami (50) vs. San Francisco (35), XIX

Fewest Passes Attempted, Both Teams, Game

35 Miami (7) vs. Minnesota (28), VIII
39 Miami (11) vs. Washington (28), VII
40 Pittsburgh (14) vs. Minnesota (26), IX
   Miami (17) vs. Washington (23), XVII

COMPLETIONS

Most Passes Completed, Game

31 Buffalo vs. Dallas, XXVIII
29 Miami vs. San Francisco, XIX
   Buffalo vs. Washington, XXVI
28 Pittsburgh vs. Dallas, XXX
   St. Louis vs. New England, XXXVI

Fewest Passes Completed, Game

4 Miami vs. Washington, XVII
6 Miami vs. Minnesota, VIII
8 Miami vs. Washington, VII
  Denver vs. Dallas, XII

Most Passes Completed, Both Teams, Game

53 Miami (29) vs. San Francisco (24), XIX
52 San Diego (27) vs. San Francisco (25), XXIX
50 Buffalo (31) vs. Dallas (19), XXVIII

Fewest Passes Completed, Both Teams, Game
- 19 Miami (4) vs. Washington (15), XVII
- 20 Pittsburgh (9) vs. Minnesota (11), IX
- 22 Miami (8) vs. Washington (14), VII

COMPLETION PERCENTAGE
Highest Completion Percentage, Game (20 attempts)
- 88.0 N.Y. Giants vs. Denver, XXI (25-22)
- 75.0 San Francisco vs. Denver, XXIV (32-24)
- 73.5 Cincinnati vs. San Francisco, XVI (34-25)

Lowest Completion Percentage, Game (20 attempts)
- 32.0 Denver vs. Dallas, XII (25-8)
- 37.9 Denver vs. San Francisco, XXIV (29-11)
- 38.5 Denver vs. Washington, XXII (39-15)
- N.Y. Giants vs. Baltimore, XXXV (39-15)

YARDS GAINED
Most Yards Gained, Game
- 407 St. Louis vs. Tennessee, XXXIV
- 341 San Francisco vs. Cincinnati, XXIII
- 337 St. Louis vs. New England, XXXVI

Fewest Yards Gained, Game
- 35 Denver vs. Dallas, XII
- 63 Miami vs. Minnesota, VIII
- 69 Miami vs. Washington, VII

Most Yards Gained, Both Teams, Game
- 615 San Francisco (326) vs. Miami (289), XIX
- St. Louis (407) vs. Tennessee (208), XXXIV
- 603 San Francisco (316) vs. San Diego (287), XXIX
- 583 Denver (320) vs. N.Y. Giants (263), XXI

Fewest Yards Gained, Both Teams, Game
- 156 Miami (69) vs. Washington (87), VII
- 186 Pittsburgh (84) vs. Minnesota (102), IX
- 204 Miami (80) vs. Washington (124), XVII

TIMES SACKED
Most Times Sacked, Game
- 7 Dallas vs. Pittsburgh, X
- New England vs. Chicago, XX
- 6 Kansas City vs. Green Bay, I
- Washington vs. L.A. Raiders, XVIII
- Denver vs. San Francisco, XXIV
- 5 Dallas vs. Denver, XII; vs. Pittsburgh, XIII
- Cincinnati vs. San Francisco, XVI; XXIII
- Denver vs. Washington, XXII
- Buffalo vs. Washington, XXVI
- Green Bay vs. New England, XXXI
- New England vs. Green Bay, XXXI

Fewest Times Sacked, Game
- 0 Baltimore vs. N.Y. Jets, III; vs. Dallas, V
- Minnesota vs. Pittsburgh, IX
- Pittsburgh vs. Los Angeles, XIV
- Philadelphia vs. Oakland, XV
- Washington vs. Buffalo, XXVI
- Denver vs. Green Bay, XXXII; vs. Atlanta, XXXIII
- 1 By 13 teams

Most Times Sacked, Both Teams, Game
- 10 New England (7) vs. Chicago (3), XX
- Green Bay (5) vs. New England (5), XXXI
- 9 Kansas City (6) vs. Green Bay (3), I
- Dallas (7) vs. Pittsburgh (2), X
- Dallas (5) vs. Denver (4), XII
- Dallas (5) vs. Pittsburgh (4), XIII
- Cincinnati (5) vs. San Francisco (4), XXIII
- 8 Washington (6) vs. L.A. Raiders (2), XVIII

Fewest Times Sacked, Both Teams, Game
- 1 Philadelphia (0) vs. Oakland (1), XV
- Denver (0) vs. Green Bay (1), XXXII

- 2 Baltimore (0) vs. N.Y. Jets (2), III
- Baltimore (0) vs. Dallas (2), V
- Minnesota (0) vs. Pittsburgh (2), IX
- Denver (0) vs. Atlanta (2), XXXIII
- 3 In five games

TOUCHDOWNS
Most Touchdowns, Game
- 6 San Francisco vs. San Diego, XXIX
- 5 San Francisco vs. Denver, XXIV
- 4 Pittsburgh vs. Dallas, XIII
- Washington vs. Denver, XXII
- Dallas vs. Buffalo, XXVII

Fewest Touchdowns, Game
- 0 By 19 teams

Most Touchdowns, Both Teams, Game
- 7 Pittsburgh (4) vs. Dallas (3), XIII
- San Francisco (6) vs. San Diego (1), XXIX
- 5 Washington (4) vs. Denver (1), XXII
- San Francisco (5) vs. Denver (0), XXIV
- Dallas (4) vs. Buffalo (1), XXVII
- 4 Dallas (2) vs. Pittsburgh (2), X
- Oakland (3) vs. Philadelphia (1), XV
- San Francisco (3) vs. Miami (1), XIX
- N.Y. Giants (3) vs. Denver (1), XXI
- Washington (2) vs. Buffalo (2), XXVI
- Green Bay (2) vs. New England (2), XXXI

Fewest Touchdowns, Both Teams, Game
- 0 N.Y. Jets vs. Baltimore, III
- Miami vs. Minnesota, VIII
- Buffalo vs. Dallas, XXVIII
- 1 In seven games

INTERCEPTIONS BY
Most Interceptions By, Game
- 4 N.Y. Jets vs. Baltimore, III
- Dallas vs. Denver, XII
- Washington vs. Buffalo, XXVI
- Dallas vs. Buffalo, XXVII
- Green Bay vs. New England, XXXI
- Baltimore vs. N.Y. Giants, XXXV
- 3 By 12 teams

Most Interceptions By, Both Teams, Game
- 6 Baltimore (3) vs. Dallas (3), V
- 5 Washington (4) vs. Buffalo (1), XXVI
- 4 In 10 games

Fewest Interceptions By, Both Teams, Game
- 0 Buffalo vs. N.Y. Giants, XXV
- St. Louis vs. Tennessee, XXXIV
- 1 Oakland (0) vs. Green Bay (1), II
- Miami (0) vs. Dallas (1), VI
- Minnesota (0) vs. Miami (1), VIII
- N.Y. Giants (0) vs. Denver (1), XXI
- Cincinnati (0) vs. San Francisco (1), XXIII

YARDS GAINED
Most Yards Gained, Game
- 136 Denver vs. Atlanta, XXXIII
- 95 Miami vs. Washington, VII
- 91 Oakland vs. Minnesota, XI

Most Yards Gained, Both Teams, Game
- 137 Denver (136) vs. Atlanta (1), XXXIII
- 95 Miami (95) vs. Washington (0), VII
- 91 Oakland (91) vs. Minnesota (0), XI

TOUCHDOWNS

Most Touchdowns, Game

 1 Green Bay vs. Oakland, II
    Oakland vs. Minnesota, XI
    L.A. Raiders vs. Washington, XVIII
    Chicago vs. New England, XX
    Baltimore vs. N.Y. Giants, XXXV
    New England vs. St. Louis, XXXVI

PUNTING

Most Punts, Game

 11 N.Y. Giants vs. Baltimore, XXXV
 10 Baltimore vs. N.Y. Giants, XXXV
  9 Dallas vs. Baltimore, V

Fewest Punts, Game

  1 Atlanta vs. Denver, XXXIII
     Denver vs. Atlanta, XXXIII
  2 Pittsburgh vs. Los Angeles, XIV
     Denver vs. N.Y. Giants, XXI
     St. Louis vs. Tennessee, XXXIV
  3 By 11 teams

Most Punts, Both Teams, Game

 21 N.Y. Giants (11) vs. Baltimore (10), XXXV
 15 Washington (8) vs. L.A. Raiders (7), XVIII
     New England (8) vs. Green Bay (7), XXXI
 13 Dallas (9) vs. Baltimore (4), V
     Pittsburgh (7) vs. Minnesota (6), IX

Fewest Punts, Both Teams, Game

  2 Atlanta (1) vs. Denver (1), XXXIII
  5 Denver (2) vs. N.Y. Giants (3), XXI
     St. Louis (2) vs. Tennessee (3), XXXIV
  6 Oakland (3) vs. Philadelphia (3), XV

AVERAGE YARDAGE

Highest Average, Game (4 punts)

 48.75 San Diego vs. San Francisco, XXIX (4-195)
 48.50 Kansas City vs. Minnesota, IV (4-194)
 46.25 San Francisco vs. Cincinnati, XVI (4-185)

Lowest Average, Game (4 punts)

 31.20 Washington vs. Miami, VII (5-156)
 32.38 Washington vs. L.A. Raiders, XVIII (8-259)
 32.40 Oakland vs. Minnesota, XI (5-162)

PUNT RETURNS

Most Punt Returns, Game

  6 Washington vs. Miami, XVII
     Green Bay vs. New England, XXXI
  5 By six teams

Fewest Punt Returns, Game

  0 Minnesota vs. Miami, VIII
     Buffalo vs. N.Y. Giants, XXV
     Washington vs. Buffalo, XXVI
     Denver vs. Green Bay, XXXII
     Green Bay vs. Denver, XXXII
     Atlanta vs. Denver, XXXIII
     Denver vs. Atlanta, XXXIII
  1 By 17 teams

Most Punt Returns, Both Teams, Game

 10 Green Bay (6) vs. New England (4), XXXI
  9 Pittsburgh (5) vs. Minnesota (4), IX
  8 Green Bay (5) vs. Oakland (3), II
     Baltimore (5) vs. Dallas (3), V
     Washington (6) vs. Miami (2), XVII
     N.Y. Giants (5) vs. Baltimore (3), XXXV

Fewest Punt Returns, Both Teams, Game

  0 Denver vs. Green Bay, XXXII
     Atlanta vs. Denver, XXXIII
  2 Dallas (1) vs. Miami (1), VI
     Denver (1) vs. N.Y. Giants (1), XXI

     Buffalo (0) vs. N.Y. Giants (2), XXV
     Buffalo (1) vs. Dallas (1), XXVIII
  3 Kansas City (1) vs. Minnesota (2), IV
     Minnesota (0) vs. Miami (3), VIII
     Washington (1) vs. Denver (2), XXII
     Washington (0) vs. Buffalo (3), XXVI
     Dallas (1) vs. Pittsburgh (2), XXX
     Tennessee (1) vs. St. Louis (2), XXXIV

YARDS GAINED

Most Yards Gained, Game

 90 Green Bay vs. New England, XXXI
 56 San Francisco vs. Cincinnati, XXIII
 52 Washington vs. Miami, XVII

Fewest Yards Gained, Game

 −1 Dallas vs. Miami, VI
     Tennessee vs. St. Louis, XXXIV
  0 By 12 teams

Most Yards Gained, Both Teams, Game

 120 Green Bay (90) vs. New England (30), XXXI
  80 N.Y. Giants (46) vs. Baltimore (34), XXXV
  74 Washington (52) vs. Miami (22), XVII

Fewest Yards Gained, Both Teams, Game

  0 Denver vs. Green Bay, XXXII
     Atlanta vs. Denver, XXXIII
  7 Tennessee (-1) vs. St. Louis (8), XXXIV
  9 Washington (0) vs. Bufffalo (9), XXVI

AVERAGE RETURN

Highest Average, Game (3 returns)

 18.7 San Francisco vs. Cincinnati, XXIII (3-56)
 15.0 Green Bay vs. New England, XXXI (6-90)
 12.7 San Francisco vs. Denver, XXIV (3-38)

TOUCHDOWNS

Most Touchdowns, Game

     None

KICKOFF RETURNS

Most Kickoff Returns, Game

  9 Denver vs. San Francisco, XXIV
  8 San Diego vs. San Francisco, XXIX
  7 By eight teams

Fewest Kickoff Returns, Game

  1 N.Y. Jets vs. Baltimore, III
     L.A. Raiders vs. Washington, XVIII
     Washington vs. Buffalo, XXVI
  2 By eight teams

Most Kickoff Returns, Both Teams, Game

 12 Denver (9) vs. San Francisco (3), XXIV
     San Diego (8) vs. San Francisco (4), XXIX
 11 Los Angeles (6) vs. Pittsburgh (5), XIV
     Miami (7) vs. San Francisco (4), XIX
     New England (7) vs. Chicago (4), XX
     Green Bay (6) vs. Denver (5), XXXII
 10 Oakland (7) vs. Green Bay (3), II
     New England (6) vs. Green Bay (4), XXXI
     Atlanta (7) vs. Denver (3), XXXIII

Fewest Kickoff Returns, Both Teams, Game

  5 N.Y. Jets (1) vs. Baltimore (4), III
     Miami (2) vs. Washington (3), VII
     Washington (1) vs. Buffalo (4), XXVI
  6 In three games

YARDS GAINED

Most Yards Gained, Game

 244 San Diego vs. San Francisco, XXIX
 227 Atlanta vs. Denver, XXXIII
 222 Miami vs. Washington, XVII

Fewest Yards Gained, Game
- 16   Washington vs. Buffalo, XXVI
- 17   L.A. Raiders vs. Washington, XVIII
- 25   N.Y. Jets vs. Baltimore, III

Most Yards Gained, Both Teams, Game
- 292   San Diego (244) vs. San Francisco (48), XXIX
- 289   Green Bay (154) vs. New England (135), XXXI
- 281   N.Y. Giants (170) vs. Baltimore (111), XXXV

Fewest Yards Gained, Both Teams, Game
- 78   Miami (33) vs. Washington (45), VII
- 82   Pittsburgh (32) vs. Minnesota (50), IX
- 92   San Francisco (40) vs. Cincinnati (52), XVI

AVERAGE GAIN
Highest Average, Game (3 returns)
- 44.0   Cincinnati vs. San Francisco, XXIII (3-132)
- 38.5   Green Bay vs. New England, XXXI (4-154)
- 37.0   Miami vs. Washington, XVII (6-222)

TOUCHDOWNS
Most Touchdowns, Game
- 1   Miami vs. Washington, XVII
     Cincinnati vs. San Francisco, XXIII
     San Diego vs. San Francisco, XXIX
     Green Bay vs. New England, XXXI
     Atlanta vs. Denver, XXXIII
     Baltimore vs. N.Y. Giants, XXXV
     N.Y. Giants vs. Baltimore, XXXV

Most Touchdowns, Both Teams, Game
- 2   Baltimore (1) vs. N.Y. Giants (1), XXXV

PENALTIES
Most Penalties, Game
- 12   Dallas vs. Denver, XII
- 10   Dallas vs. Baltimore, V
- 9   Dallas vs. Pittsburgh, XIII
     Green Bay vs. Denver, XXXII
     Baltimore vs. N.Y. Giants, XXXV

Fewest Penalties, Game
- 0   Miami vs. Dallas, VI
     Pittsburgh vs. Dallas, X
     Denver vs. San Francisco, XXIV
     Atlanta vs. Denver, XXXIII
- 1   Green Bay vs. Oakland, II
     Miami vs. Minnesota, VIII; vs. San Francisco, XIX
     Buffalo vs. Dallas, XXVIII
- 2   By six teams

Most Penalties, Both Teams, Game
- 20   Dallas (12) vs. Denver (8), XII
- 16   Cincinnati (8) vs. San Francisco (8), XVI
     Green Bay (9) vs. Denver (7), XXXII
- 15   St. Louis (8) vs. Tennessee (7), XXXIV
     Baltimore (9) vs. N.Y. Giants (6), XXXV

Fewest Penalties, Both Teams, Game
- 2   Pittsburgh (0) vs. Dallas (2), X
- 3   Miami (0) vs. Dallas (3), VI
     Miami (1) vs. San Francisco (2), XIX
- 4   Denver (0) vs. San Francisco (4), XXIV
     Atlanta (0) vs. Denver (4), XXXIII

YARDS PENALIZED
Most Yards Penalized, Game
- 133   Dallas vs. Baltimore, X
- 122   Pittsburgh vs. Minnesota, IX
- 94   Dallas vs. Denver, XII

Fewest Yards Penalized, Game
- 0   Miami vs. Dallas, VI
     Pittsburgh vs. Dallas, X
     Denver vs. San Francisco, XXIV
     Atlanta vs. Denver, XXXIII

- 4   Miami vs. Minnesota, VIII
- 10   Miami vs. San Francisco, XIX
     San Francisco vs. Miami, XIX
     Buffalo vs. Dallas, XXVIII

Most Yards Penalized, Both Teams, Game
- 164   Dallas (133) vs. Baltimore (31), V
- 154   Dallas (94) vs. Denver (60), XII
- 140   Pittsburgh (122) vs. Minnesota (18), IX

Fewest Yards Penalized, Both Teams, Game
- 15   Miami (0) vs. Dallas (15), VI
- 20   Pittsburgh (0) vs. Dallas (20), X
     Miami (10) vs. San Francisco (10), XIX
- 38   Denver (0) vs. San Francisco (38), XXIV

FUMBLES
Most Fumbles, Game
- 8   Buffalo vs. Dallas, XXVII
- 6   Dallas vs. Denver, XII
     Buffalo vs. Washington, XXVI
- 5   Baltimore vs. Dallas, V

Fewest Fumbles, Game
- 0   By 17 teams

Most Fumbles, Both Teams, Game
- 12   Buffalo (8) vs. Dallas (4), XXVII
- 10   Dallas (6) vs. Denver (4), XII
- 8   Dallas (4) vs. Pittsburgh (4), X

Fewest Fumbles, Both Teams, Game
- 0   Los Angeles vs. Pittsburgh, XIV
     Green Bay vs. New England, XXXI
- 1   Oakland (0) vs. Minnesota (1), XI
     Oakland (0) vs. Philadelphia (1), XV
     Denver (0) vs. Washington (1), XXII
     N.Y. Giants (0) vs. Buffalo (1), XXV
     Denver (0) vs. Atlanta (1), XXXIII
- 2   In six games

Most Fumbles Lost, Game
- 5   Buffalo vs. Dallas, XXVII
- 4   Baltimore vs. Dallas, V
     Denver vs. Dallas, XII
     New England vs. Chicago, XX
- 2   In many games

Most Fumbles Lost, Both Teams, Game
- 7   Buffalo (5) vs. Dallas (2), XXVII
- 6   Denver (4) vs. Dallas (2), XII
     New England (4) vs. Chicago (2), XX
- 5   Baltimore (4) vs. Dallas (1), V

Fewest Fumbles Lost, Both Teams, Game
- 0   Green Bay vs. Kansas City, I
     Dallas vs. Pittsburgh, X
     Los Angeles vs. Pittsburgh, XIV
     Denver vs. N.Y. Giants, XXI; vs. Washington, XXII
     Buffalo vs. N.Y. Giants, XXV
     San Diego vs. San Francisco, XXIX
     Dallas vs. Pittsburgh, XXX
     Green Bay vs. New England, XXXI
     St. Louis vs. Tennessee, XXXIV

Most Fumbles Recovered, Game
- 8   Dallas vs. Denver, XII (4 own, 4 opp.)
- 6   Dallas vs. Buffalo, XXVII (1 own, 5 opp.)
- 5   Chicago vs. New England, XX (1 own, 4 opp.)

TURNOVERS
(Number of times losing the ball on interceptions and fumbles.)
Most Turnovers, Game
- 9   Buffalo vs. Dallas, XXVII
- 8   Denver vs. Dallas, XII
- 7   Baltimore vs. Dallas, V

Fewest Turnovers, Game
- 0 Green Bay vs. Oakland, II
  Miami vs. Minnesota, VIII
  Pittsburgh vs. Dallas, X
  Oakland vs. Minnesota, XI; vs. Philadelphia, XV
  N.Y. Giants vs. Denver, XXI; vs. Buffalo, XXV
  San Francisco vs. Denver, XXIV; vs. San Diego, XXIX
  Buffalo vs. N.Y. Giants, XXV
  Dallas vs. Pittsburgh, XXX
  Green Bay vs. New England, XXXI
  St. Louis vs. Tennessee, XXXIV
  Tennessee vs. St. Louis, XXXIV
  Baltimore vs. N.Y. Giants, XXXV
  New England vs. St. Louis, XXXVI
- 1 By many teams

Most Turnovers, Both Teams, Game
- 11 Baltimore (7) vs. Dallas (4), V
  Buffalo (9) vs. Dallas (2), XXVII
- 10 Denver (8) vs. Dallas (2), XII
- 8 New England (6) vs. Chicago (2), XX

Fewest Turnovers, Both Teams, Game
- 0 Buffalo vs. N.Y. Giants, XXV
  St. Louis vs. Tennessee, XXXIV
- 1 N.Y. Giants (0) vs. Denver (1), XXI
- 2 Green Bay (1) vs. Kansas City (1), I
  Miami (0) vs. Minnesota (2), VIII
  Cincinnati (1) vs. San Francisco (1), XXIII

Compiled by Elias Sports Bureau

Throughout this all-time postseason record section, the following abbreviations are used to indicate various levels of postseason games:

SB	Super Bowl (1966 to date)
AFC	AFC Championship Game (1970 to date) or AFL Championship Game (1960-69)
NFC	NFC Championship Game (1970 to date) or NFL Championship Game (1933-69)
AFC-D	AFC Divisional Playoff Game (1970 to date), AFC Second-Round Playoff Game (1982), AFL Inter-Divisional Playoff Game (1969), or special playoff game to break tie for AFL Division Championship (1963, 1968)
NFC-D	NFC Divisional Playoff Game (1970 to date), NFC Second-Round Playoff Game (1982), NFL Conference Championship Game (1967-69), or special playoff game to break tie for NFL Division or Conference Championship (1941, 1943, 1947, 1950, 1952, 1957, 1958, 1965)
AFC-FR	AFC First-Round Playoff Game (1978 to date)
NFC-FR	NFC First-Round Playoff Game (1978 to date)

Year indicates season in which game took place and does not necessarily reflect calendar year.

POSTSEASON GAME COMPOSITE STANDINGS

	W	L	PCT.	PTS.	OP
Baltimore Ravens	5	1	.833	125	53
Green Bay Packers	23	11	.676	814	618
Dallas Cowboys	32	21	.604	1,271	979
San Francisco 49ers	24	16	.600	999	784
Washington Redskins*	22	15	.595	778	642
Pittsburgh Steelers	22	16	.579	845	741
Oakland Raiders**	23	17	.575	936	715
Denver Broncos	16	12	.571	616	657
Miami Dolphins	20	19	.513	780	848
Carolina Panthers	1	1	.500	39	47
Jacksonville Jaguars	4	4	.500	208	200
New England Patriots#	10	10	.500	370	404
Buffalo Bills	14	15	.483	681	658
Chicago Bears	14	15	.483	598	585
Philadelphia Eagles	12	13	.480	478	449
Indianapolis Colts***	10	12	.455	393	431
St. Louis Rams††	18	22	.450	703	848
New York Giants	16	20	.444	609	660
Tennessee Titans†	12	15	.444	471	626
New York Jets	6	8	.429	284	285
Minnesota Vikings	17	23	.425	779	913
Kansas City Chiefs****	8	11	.421	301	384
Cincinnati Bengals	5	7	.417	246	257
Detroit Lions	7	10	.412	365	404
Atlanta Falcons	4	6	.400	208	260
San Diego Chargers†††	7	11	.389	332	428
Seattle Seahawks	3	5	.375	145	159
Cleveland Browns	11	19	.367	596	692
Tampa Bay Buccaneers	3	7	.300	100	201
Arizona Cardinals††††	2	5	.286	122	182
New Orleans Saints	1	5	.167	103	185

*	One game played when franchise was in Boston (lost 21-6).
**	12 games played when franchise was in Los Angeles (won 6, lost 6, 268 points scored, 224 points allowed).
***	15 games played when franchise was in Baltimore (won 8, lost 7, 264 points scored, 262 points allowed).
****	One game played when franchise was Dallas Texans (won 20-17).
#	Two games played when franchise was in Boston (won 26-8, lost 51-10).
†	22 games played when franchise was in Houston and known as the Oilers (won 9, lost 13, 371 points scored, 533 points allowed).
††	One game played when franchise was in Cleveland (won 15-14), 32 games played when franchise was in Los Angeles (won 12, lost 20, 486 points scored, 683 points allowed).
†††	One game played when franchise was in Los Angeles (lost 24-16).
††††	Two games played when franchise was in Chicago (won 28-21, lost 7-0), three games played when franchise was in St. Louis (lost 30-14, lost 35-23, lost 41-16).

INDIVIDUAL RECORDS

SERVICE

Most Games, Career

27 D.D. Lewis, Dallas (SB 5, NFC 9, NFC-D 12, NFC-FR 1)
26 Larry Cole, Dallas (SB 5, NFC 8, NFC-D 12, NFC-FR 1)
25 Charlie Waters, Dallas (SB 5, NFC 9, NFC-D 10, NFC-FR 1)
  Jerry Rice, San Francisco-Oakland (SB 3, NFC 6, NFC-D 11, AFC-D 1, NFC-FR 3, AFC-FR 1)

Most Games, Head Coach

36 Tom Landry, Dallas
  Don Shula, Baltimore-Miami
24 Chuck Noll, Pittsburgh
22 Bud Grant, Minnesota

Most Games Won, Head Coach

20 Tom Landry, Dallas
19 Don Shula, Baltimore-Miami
16 Chuck Noll, Pittsburgh
  Joe Gibbs, Washington

Most Games Lost, Head Coach

17 Don Shula, Baltimore-Miami
16 Tom Landry, Dallas
12 Bud Grant, Minnesota

SCORING

POINTS

Most Points, Career

143 Gary Anderson, Pittsburgh-Philadelphia-San Francisco-Minnesota, 20 games (53-pat, 30-fg)
126 Thurman Thomas, Buffalo, 21 games (21-td)
  Emmitt Smith, Dallas, 17 games (21-td)
120 Jerry Rice, San Francisco-Oakland, 25 games (20-td)

Most Points, Game

30 Ricky Watters, NFC-D:San Francisco vs. N.Y. Giants, 1993 (5-td)
19 Pat Harder, NFC-D: Detroit vs. Los Angeles, 1952 (2-td, 4-pat, 1-fg)
  Paul Hornung, NFC: Green Bay vs. N.Y. Giants, 1961 (1-td, 4-pat, 3-fg)
18 By many players

Most Consecutive Games Scoring

19 George Blanda, Chi. Bears-Houston-Oakland, 1956-1975
16 Norm Johnson, Seattle-Atlanta-Pittsburgh, 1983-1997
15 Roy Gerela, Houston-Pittsburgh, 1969-1978

TOUCHDOWNS

Most Touchdowns, Career

21 Thurman Thomas, Buffalo, 21 games (16-r, 5-p)
  Emmitt Smith, Dallas, 17 games (19-r, 2-p)
20 Jerry Rice, San Francisco-Oakland, 25 games (0-r, 20-p)
17 Franco Harris, Pittsburgh, 19 games (16-r, 1-p)

Most Touchdowns, Game

5 Ricky Watters, NFC-D:San Francisco vs. N.Y. Giants, 1993 (5-r)
3 Andy Farkas, NFC-D: Washington vs. N.Y. Giants, 1943 (3-r)
  Tom Fears, NFC-D: Los Angeles vs. Chi. Bears, 1950 (3-r)
  Otto Graham, NFC: Cleveland vs. Detroit, 1954 (3-r)
  Gary Collins, NFC: Cleveland vs. Baltimore, 1964 (3-p)
  Craig Baynham, NFC-D: Dallas vs. Cleveland, 1967 (2-r, 1-p)
  Fred Biletnikoff, AFC-D: Oakland vs. Kansas City, 1968 (3-p)

Tom Matte, NFC: Baltimore vs. Cleveland, 1968 (3-r)
Larry Schreiber, NFC-D: San Francisco vs. Dallas, 1972 (3-r)
Larry Csonka, AFC: Miami vs. Oakland, 1973 (3-r)
Franco Harris, AFC-D: Pittsburgh vs. Buffalo, 1974 (3-r)
Preston Pearson, NFC: Dallas vs. Los Angeles, 1975 (3-p)
Dave Casper, AFC-D: Oakland vs. Baltimore, 1977 (OT) (3-p)
Alvin Garrett, NFC-FR: Washington vs. Detroit, 1982 (3-p)
John Riggins, NFC-D: Washington vs. L.A. Rams, 1983 (3-r)
Roger Craig, SB: San Francisco vs. Miami, 1984 (1-r, 2-p)
Jerry Rice, NFC-D: San Francisco vs. Minnesota, 1988 (3-p)
Jerry Rice, SB: San Francisco vs. Denver, 1989 (3-p)
Kenneth Davis, AFC: Buffalo vs. L.A. Raiders, 1990 (3-r)
Andre Reed, AFC-FR: Buffalo vs. Houston, 1992 (OT) (3-p)
Sterling Sharpe, NFC-FR: Green Bay vs. Detroit, 1993 (3-p)
Napoleon McCallum, AFC-FR: L.A. Raiders vs. Denver, 1993 (3-r)
Thurman Thomas, AFC: Buffalo vs. Kansas City, 1993 (3-r)
William Floyd, NFC-D: San Francisco vs. Chicago, 1994 (3-r)
Ricky Watters, SB: San Francisco vs. San Diego, 1994 (1-r, 2-p)
Jerry Rice, SB: San Francisco vs. San Diego, 1994 (3-p)
Emmitt Smith, NFC: Dallas vs. Green Bay, 1995 (3-r)
Curtis Martin, AFC-D: New England vs. Pittsburgh, 1996 (3-r)
Terrell Davis, SB: Denver vs. Green Bay, 1997 (3-r)
Mario Bates, NFC-D: Arizona vs. Minnesota, 1998 (3-r)
Leroy Hoard, NFC-D: Minnesota vs. Arizona, 1998 (2-r, 1-p)
Willie Jackson, NFC-FR: New Orleans vs. St. Louis, 2000 (3-p)

Most Consecutive Games Scoring Touchdowns
9 Thurman Thomas, Buffalo, 1992-98
8 John Stallworth, Pittsburgh, 1978-1983
   Emmitt Smith, Dallas, 1993-96
7 John Riggins, Washington, 1982-84
   Marcus Allen, L.A. Raiders, 1982-85
   Terrell Davis, Denver, 1996-98

POINTS AFTER TOUCHDOWN
Most (One-Point) Points After Touchdown, Career
53 Gary Anderson, Pittsburgh-Philadelphia-San Francisco-Minnesota, 20 games (53 att)
49 George Blanda, Chi. Bears-Houston-Oakland, 19 games (49 att)
42 Mike Cofer, San Francisco, 12 games (46 att)

Most (One-Point) Points After Touchdown, Game
8 Lou Groza, NFC: Cleveland vs. Detroit, 1954 (8 att)
   Jim Martin, NFC: Detroit vs. Cleveland, 1957 (8 att)
   George Blanda, AFC-D: Oakland vs. Houston, 1969 (8 att)
   Mike Hollis, AFC-D: Jacksonville vs. Miami, 1999 (8 att)
7 Danny Villanueva, NFC-D: Dallas vs. Cleveland, 1967 (7 att)
   Raul Allegre, NFC-D: N.Y. Giants vs. San Francisco, 1986 (7 att)
   Mike Cofer, SB: San Francisco vs. Denver, 1989 (8 att)
   Lin Elliott, SB: Dallas vs. Buffalo, 1992 (7 att)
   Doug Brien, SB: San Francisco vs. San Diego, 1994 (7 att)
   Gary Anderson, NFC-FR: Philadelphia vs. Detroit, 1995 (7 att)
   Jeff Wilkins, NFC-D: St. Louis vs. Minnesota, 1999 (7 att)
6 George Blair, AFC: San Diego vs. Boston, 1963 (6 att)
   Mark Moseley, NFC-D: Washington vs. L.A. Rams, 1983 (6 att)
   Uwe von Schamann, AFC: Miami vs. Pittsburgh, 1984 (6 att)
   Ali Haji-Sheikh, SB: Washington vs. Denver, 1987 (6 att)
   Scott Norwood, AFC: Buffalo vs. L.A. Raiders, 1990 (7 att)
   Jeff Jaeger, AFC-FR: L.A. Raiders vs. Denver, 1993 (6 att)
   Jason Elam, AFC-FR: Denver vs. Jacksonville, 1997 (6 att)
   Jeff Wilkins, NFC-D: St. Louis vs. Green Bay, 2001 (6 att)

Most (Kicking) Points After Touchdown, No Misses, Career
53 Gary Anderson, Pittsburgh-Philadelphia-San Francisco-Minnesota, 20 games
49 George Blanda, Chi. Bears-Houston-Oakland, 19 games
41 Rafael Septien, L.A. Rams-Dallas, 15 games

Most Two-Point Conversions, Career
1 By many players
Most Two-Point Conversions, Game
1 By many players

FIELD GOALS
Most Field Goals Attempted, Career
39 George Blanda, Chi. Bears-Houston-Oakland, 19 games
37 Gary Anderson, Pittsburgh-Philadelphia-San Francisco-Minnesota, 20 games
31 Mark Moseley, Washington-Cleveland, 11 games
Most Field Goals Attempted, Game
6 George Blanda, AFC: Oakland vs. Houston, 1967
   David Ray, NFC-D: Los Angeles vs. Dallas, 1973
   Mark Moseley, AFC-D: Cleveland vs. N.Y. Jets, 1986 (OT)
   Matt Bahr, NFC: N.Y. Giants vs. San Francisco, 1990
   Steve Christie, AFC: Buffalo vs. Miami, 1992
5 By many players
Most Field Goals, Career
30 Gary Anderson, Pittsburgh-Philadelphia-San Francisco-Minnesota, 20 games
22 George Blanda, Chi. Bears-Houston-Oakland, 19 games
    Steve Christie, Buffalo, 12 games
21 Matt Bahr, Pittsburgh-Cleveland-N.Y. Giants-New England, 14 games
Most Field Goals, Game
5 Chuck Nelson, NFC-D: Minnesota vs. San Francisco, 1987
   Matt Bahr, NFC: N.Y. Giants vs. San Francisco, 1990
   Steve Christie, AFC: Buffalo vs. Miami, 1992
   Brad Daluiso, NFC-FR: N.Y. Giants vs. Minnesota, 1997
4 Gino Cappelletti, AFC-D: Boston vs. Buffalo, 1963
   George Blanda, AFC: Oakland vs. Houston, 1967
   Don Chandler, SB: Green Bay vs. Oakland, 1967
   Curt Knight, NFC: Washington vs. Dallas, 1972
   George Blanda, AFC-D: Oakland vs. Pittsburgh, 1973
   Ray Wersching, SB: San Francisco vs. Cincinnati, 1981
   Tony Franklin, AFC-FR: New England vs. N.Y. Jets, 1985
   Jess Atkinson, NFC-FR: Washington vs. L.A. Rams, 1986
   Luis Zendejas, NFC-D: Philadelphia vs. Chicago, 1988
   Gary Anderson, AFC-FR: Pittsburgh vs. Houston, 1989 (OT)
   Norm Johnson, AFC-D: Pittsburgh vs. Buffalo, 1995
   Chris Boniol, NFC-FR: Dallas vs. Minnesota, 1996
   John Kasay, NFC-D: Carolina vs. Dallas, 1996
   Mike Hollis, AFC-D: Jacksonville vs. New England, 1998
   Al Del Greco, AFC-D: Tennessee vs. Indianapolis, 1999
   David Akers, NFC-D: Philadelphia vs. Chicago, 2001
3 By many players
Most Consecutive Games Scoring Field Goals
13 Toni Fritsch, Dallas-Houston, 1972-79
9 Kevin Butler, Chicago, 1985-1991
   Scott Norwood, Buffalo, 1988-1991
   Al Del Greco, Houston-Tennessee, 1991-2000
8 Mark Moseley, Washington-Cleveland, 1982-86
   Rich Karlis, Denver-Minnesota, 1984-89
   Steve Christie, SB: Buffalo vs. Dallas, 1993
   Gary Anderson, Pittsburgh-Philadelphia, 1989-1995
   Morten Andersen, New Orleans-Atlanta, 1987-1998 (current)
Most Consecutive Field Goals
16 Gary Anderson, Pittsburgh-Philadelphia, 1989-1995
15 Rafael Septien, Dallas, 1978-1982
14 Mike Hollis, Jacksonville, 1996-99
Longest Field Goal
58 Pete Stoyanovich, AFC-FR: Miami vs. Kansas City, 1990
54 Ed Murray, NFC-D: Detroit vs. San Francisco, 1983
    Steve Christie, SB: Buffalo vs. Dallas, 1993
    John Carney, AFC-FR: San Diego vs. Indianapolis, 1995
53 Al Del Greco, AFC-FR: Houston vs. N.Y. Jets, 1991
Highest Field Goal Percentage, Career (10 field goals)
90.9 Chuck Nelson, L.A. Rams-Minnesota, 6 games (11-10)
88.9 Mike Hollis, Jacksonville, 8 games (18-16)

88.0   Steve Christie, Buffalo, 12 games (25-22)

SAFETIES
Most Safeties, Game
1   Bill Willis, NFC-D: Cleveland vs. N.Y. Giants, 1950
   Carl Eller, NFC-D: Minnesota vs. Los Angeles, 1969
   George Andrie, NFC-D: Dallas vs. Detroit, 1970
   Alan Page, NFC-D: Minnesota vs. Dallas, 1971
   Dwight White, SB: Pittsburgh vs. Minnesota, 1974
   Reggie Harrison, SB: Pittsburgh vs. Dallas, 1975
   Jim Jensen, NFC-D: Dallas vs. Los Angeles, 1976
   Ted Washington, AFC: Houston vs. Pittsburgh, 1978
   Randy White, NFC-D: Dallas vs. Los Angeles, 1979
   Henry Waechter, SB: Chicago vs. New England, 1985
   Rulon Jones, AFC-FR: Denver vs. New England, 1986
   George Martin, SB: N.Y. Giants vs. Denver, 1986
   D.D. Hoggard, AFC: Cleveland vs. Denver, 1987
   Bruce Smith, SB: Buffalo vs. N.Y. Giants, 1990
   Reggie White, NFC-FR: Philadelphia vs. New Orleans, 1992
   Willie Clay, NFC-D: Detroit vs. Green Bay, 1994
   Carnell Lake, AFC-D: Pittsburgh vs. Cleveland, 1994
   Reuben Davis, AFC-D: San Diego vs. Miami, 1994
   Jevon Kearse, AFC-FR: Tennessee vs. Buffalo, 1999

RUSHING
ATTEMPTS
Most Attempts, Career
400   Franco Harris, Pittsburgh, 19 games
349   Emmitt Smith, Dallas, 17 games
339   Thurman Thomas, Buffalo, 21 games

Most Attempts, Game
40   Lamar Smith, AFC-FR: Miami vs. Indianapolis, 2000 (OT)
38   Ricky Bell, NFC-D: Tampa Bay vs. Philadelphia, 1979
   John Riggins, SB: Washington vs. Miami, 1982
37   Lawrence McCutcheon, NFC-D: Los Angeles vs. St. Louis, 1975
   John Riggins, NFC-D: Washington vs. Minnesota, 1982

YARDS GAINED
Most Yards Gained, Career
1,586   Emmitt Smith, Dallas, 17 games
1,556   Franco Harris, Pittsburgh, 19 games
1,442   Thurman Thomas, Buffalo, 21 games

Most Yards Gained, Game
248   Eric Dickerson, NFC-D: L.A. Rams vs. Dallas, 1985
209   Lamar Smith, AFC-FR: Miami vs. Indianapolis, 2000 (OT)
206   Keith Lincoln, AFC: San Diego vs. Boston, 1963

Most Games, 100 or More Yards Rushing, Career
7   Emmitt Smith, Dallas, 17 games
   Terrell Davis, Denver, 8 games
6   John Riggins, Washington, 9 games
   Thurman Thomas, Buffalo, 21 games
5   Franco Harris, Pittsburgh, 19 games
   Marcus Allen, L.A. Raiders-Kansas City, 16 games

Most Consecutive Games, 100 or More Yards Rushing
7   Terrell Davis, Denver, 1997-98 (current)
6   John Riggins, Washington, 1982-83
4   Thurman Thomas, Buffalo, 1990-91

Longest Run From Scrimmage
90   Fred Taylor, AFC-D: Jacksonville vs. Miami, 1999 (TD)
80   Roger Craig, NFC-D: San Francisco vs. Minnesota, 1988 (TD)
   Charlie Garner, AFC-FR: Oakland vs. N.Y. Jets, 2001 (TD)
78   Curtis Martin, AFC-D: New England vs. Pittsburgh, 1996 (TD)

AVERAGE GAIN
Highest Average Gain, Career (100 attempts)
5.59   Terrell Davis, Denver, 8 games (204-1,140)
5.04   Marcus Allen, L.A. Raiders-Kansas City, 16 games (267-1,347)
4.89   Eric Dickerson, L.A. Rams-Indianapolis, 7 games (148-724)

Highest Average Gain, Game (10 attempts)
15.90   Elmer Angsman, NFC: Chi. Cardinals vs. Philadelphia, 1947 (10-159)
15.85   Keith Lincoln, AFC: San Diego vs. Boston, 1963 (13-206)
11.31   Zack Crockett, AFC-FR: Indianapolis vs. San Diego, 1995 (13-147)

TOUCHDOWNS
Most Touchdowns, Career
19   Emmitt Smith, Dallas, 17 games
16   Franco Harris, Pittsburgh, 19 games
   Thurman Thomas, Buffalo, 21 games
12   John Riggins, Washington, 9 games
   Terrell Davis, Denver, 8 games

Most Touchdowns, Game
5   Ricky Watters, NFC-D: San Francisco vs. N.Y. Giants, 1993
3   Andy Farkas, NFC-D: Washington vs. N.Y. Giants, 1943
   Otto Graham, NFC: Cleveland vs. Detroit, 1954
   Tom Matte, NFC: Baltimore vs. Cleveland, 1968
   Larry Schreiber, NFC-D: San Francisco vs. Dallas, 1972
   Larry Csonka, AFC: Miami vs. Oakland, 1973
   Franco Harris, AFC-D: Pittsburgh vs. Buffalo, 1974
   John Riggins, NFC-D: Washington vs. L.A. Rams, 1983
   Kenneth Davis, AFC: Buffalo vs. L.A. Raiders, 1990
   Napoleon McCallum, AFC-FR: L.A. Raiders vs. Denver, 1993
   Thurman Thomas, AFC: Buffalo vs. Kansas City, 1993
   William Floyd, NFC-D: San Francisco vs. Chicago, 1994
   Emmitt Smith, NFC: Dallas vs. Green Bay, 1995
   Curtis Martin, AFC-D: New England vs. Pittsburgh, 1996
   Terrell Davis, SB: Denver vs. Green Bay, 1997
   Mario Bates, NFC-D: Arizona vs. Minnesota, 1998

Most Consecutive Games Rushing for Touchdowns
8   Emmitt Smith, Dallas, 1993-96
   Thurman Thomas, Buffalo, 1992-98
7   John Riggins, Washington, 1982-84
   Terrell Davis, Denver, 1996-98
5   Franco Harris, Pittsburgh, 1974-75
   Franco Harris, Pittsburgh, 1977-79
   Curtis Martin, New England-N.Y. Jets, 1996-98

PASSING
PASSER RATING
Highest Passer Rating, Career (150 attempts)
104.8   Bart Starr, Green Bay, 10 games
95.6   Joe Montana, San Francisco-Kansas City, 23 games
93.5   Ken Anderson, Cincinnati, 6 games

ATTEMPTS
Most Passes Attempted, Career
734   Joe Montana, San Francisco-Kansas City, 23 games
687   Dan Marino, Miami, 18 games
651   John Elway, Denver, 22 games

Most Passes Attempted, Game
65   Steve Young, NFC-D: San Francisco vs. Green Bay, 1995
64   Bernie Kosar, AFC-D: Cleveland vs. N.Y. Jets, 1986 (OT)
   Dan Marino, AFC-FR: Miami vs. Buffalo, 1995
58   Jim Kelly, SB: Buffalo vs. Washington, 1991

COMPLETIONS
Most Passes Completed, Career
460   Joe Montana, San Francisco-Kansas City, 23 games
385   Dan Marino, Miami, 18 games
355   John Elway, Denver, 22 games

Most Passes Completed, Game
36   Warren Moon, AFC-FR: Houston vs. Buffalo, 1992 (OT)
33   Dan Fouts, AFC-D: San Diego vs. Miami, 1981 (OT)
   Bernie Kosar, AFC-D: Cleveland vs. N.Y. Jets, 1986 (OT)
   Dan Marino, AFC-FR: Miami vs. Buffalo, 1995
32   Neil Lomax, NFC-FR: St. Louis vs. Green Bay, 1982
   Danny White, NFC-FR: Dallas vs. L.A. Rams, 1983

Warren Moon, AFC-D: Houston vs. Kansas City, 1993
Neil O'Donnell, AFC: Pittsburgh vs. San Diego, 1994
Steve Young, NFC-D: San Francisco vs. Green Bay, 1995
Tom Brady, AFC-D: New England vs. Oakland, 2001 (OT)

COMPLETION PERCENTAGE
Highest Completion Percentage, Career (150 attempts)
66.3 Ken Anderson, Cincinnati, 6 games (166-110)
64.3 Warren Moon, Houston-Minnesota, 10 games (403-259)
63.8 Troy Aikman, Dallas, 16 games (502-320)
Highest Completion Percentage, Game (15 completions)
88.0 Phil Simms, SB: N.Y. Giants vs. Denver, 1986 (25-22)
86.7 Joe Montana, NFC: San Francisco vs. L.A. Rams, 1989 (30-26)
84.2 David Woodley, AFC-FR: Miami vs. New England, 1982 (19-16)

YARDS GAINED
Most Yards Gained, Career
5,772 Joe Montana, San Francisco-Kansas City, 23 games
4,964 John Elway, Denver, 22 games
4,510 Dan Marino, Miami, 18 games
Most Yards Gained, Game
489 Bernie Kosar, AFC-D: Cleveland vs. N.Y. Jets, 1986 (OT)
433 Dan Fouts, AFC: San Diego vs. Miami, 1981 (OT)
423 Jeff George, NFC-D: Minnesota vs. St. Louis, 1999
Most Games, 300 or More Yards Passing, Career
6 Joe Montana, San Francisco-Kansas City, 23 games
5 Dan Fouts, San Diego, 7 games
4 Warren Moon, Houston-Minnesota, 10 games
  Troy Aikman, Dallas, 16 games
  Dan Marino, Miami, 18 games
  John Elway, Denver, 22 games
  Kurt Warner, St. Louis, 7 games
Most Consecutive Games, 300 or More Yards Passing
4 Dan Fouts, San Diego, 1979-1981
3 Jim Kelly, Buffalo, 1989-1990
  Warren Moon, Houston, 1991-93
2 Daryle Lamonica, Oakland, 1968
  Ken Anderson, Cincinnati, 1981-82
  Terry Bradshaw, Pittsburgh, 1979-1982
  Joe Montana, San Francisco, 1983-84
  Dan Marino, Miami, 1984
  Troy Aikman, Dallas, 1994
  Steve Young, San Francisco, 1994-95
  Kurt Warner, St. Louis, 1999-2000
Longest Pass Completion
96 Trent Dilfer (to Sharpe), AFC: Baltimore vs. Oakland, 2000 (TD)
94 Troy Aikman (to Harper), NFC-D: Dallas vs. Green Bay, 1994 (TD)
93 Daryle Lamonica (to Dubenion), AFC-D: Buffalo vs. Boston, 1963 (TD)

AVERAGE GAIN
Highest Average Gain, Career (150 attempts)
8.45 Joe Theismann, Washington, 10 games (211-1,782)
8.43 Jim Plunkett, Oakland/L.A.Raiders, 10 games (272-2,293)
8.41 Terry Bradshaw, Pittsburgh, 19 games (456-3,833)
Highest Average Gain, Game (20 attempts)
14.71 Terry Bradshaw, SB: Pittsburgh vs. Los Angeles, 1979 (21-309)
13.33 Bob Waterfield, NFC-D: Los Angeles vs. Chi. Bears, 1950 (21-280)
13.16 Dan Marino, AFC: Miami vs. Pittsburgh, 1984 (32-421)

TOUCHDOWNS
Most Touchdown Passes, Career
45 Joe Montana, San Francisco-Kansas City, 23 games
32 Dan Marino, Miami, 18 games
30 Terry Bradshaw, Pittsburgh, 19 games
Most Touchdown Passes, Game
6 Daryle Lamonica, AFC-D: Oakland vs. Houston, 1969

Steve Young, SB: San Francisco vs. San Diego, 1994
5 Sid Luckman, NFC: Chi. Bears vs. Washington, 1943
  Daryle Lamonica, AFC-D: Oakland vs. Kansas City, 1968
  Joe Montana, SB: San Francisco vs. Denver, 1989
  Kurt Warner, NFC-D: St. Louis vs. Minnesota, 1999
  Kerry Collins, NFC: N.Y. Giants vs. Minnesota, 2000
4 Otto Graham, NFC: Cleveland vs. Los Angeles, 1950
  Tobin Rote, NFC: Detroit vs. Cleveland, 1957
  Bart Starr, NFC: Green Bay vs. Dallas, 1966
  Ken Stabler, AFC-D: Oakland vs. Miami, 1974
  Roger Staubach, NFC: Dallas vs. Los Angeles, 1975
  Terry Bradshaw, SB: Pittsburgh vs. Dallas, 1978
  Don Strock, AFC-D: Miami vs. San Diego, 1981 (OT)
  Lynn Dickey, NFC-FR: Green Bay vs. St. Louis, 1982
  Dan Marino, AFC: Miami vs. Pittsburgh, 1984
  Phil Simms, NFC-D: N.Y. Giants vs. San Francisco, 1986
  Doug Williams, SB: Washington vs. Denver, 1987
  Jim Kelly, AFC-D: Buffalo vs. Cleveland, 1989
  Joe Montana, NFC-D: San Francisco vs. Minnesota, 1989
  Warren Moon, AFC-FR: Houston vs. Buffalo, 1992 (OT)
  Frank Reich, AFC-FR: Buffalo vs. Houston, 1992 (OT)
  Troy Aikman, SB: Dallas vs. Buffalo, 1992
  Jeff George, NFC-D: Minnesota vs. St. Louis, 1999
  Aaron Brooks, NFC-FR: New Orleans vs. St. Louis, 2000
Most Consecutive Games, Touchdown Passes
13 Dan Marino, Miami, 1983-1995
12 Brett Favre, Green Bay, 1995-2001 (current)
10 Ken Stabler, Oakland, 1973-77
  Joe Montana, San Francisco-Kansas City, 1988-1993

HAD INTERCEPTED
Lowest Percentage, Passes Had Intercepted, Career (150 attempts)
1.41 Bart Starr, Green Bay, 10 games (213-3)
1.96 Steve McNair, Tennessee, 5 games (153-3)
2.15 Phil Simms, N.Y. Giants, 10 games (279-6)
Most Attempts Without Interception, Game
54 Neil O'Donnell, AFC: Pittsburgh vs. San Diego, 1994
48 Warren Moon, AFC-FR: Houston vs. Pittsburgh, 1989 (OT)
  Randall Cunningham, NFC: Minnesota vs. Atlanta, 1998 (OT)
47 Daryle Lamonica, AFC: Oakland vs. N.Y. Jets, 1968
Most Passes Had Intercepted, Career
28 Jim Kelly, Buffalo, 17 games
26 Terry Bradshaw, Pittsburgh, 19 games
24 Dan Marino, Miami, 18 games
Most Passes Had Intercepted, Game
6 Frank Filchock, NFC: N.Y. Giants vs. Chi. Bears, 1946
  Bobby Layne, NFC: Detroit vs. Cleveland, 1954
  Norm Van Brocklin, NFC: Los Angeles vs. Cleveland, 1955
  Brett Favre, NFC-D: Green Bay vs. St. Louis, 2001
5 Frank Filchock, NFC: Washington vs. Chi. Bears, 1940
  George Blanda, AFC: Houston vs. San Diego, 1961
  George Blanda, AFC: Houston vs. Dall. Texans, 1962 (OT)
  Y.A. Tittle, NFC: N.Y. Giants vs. Chicago, 1963
  Mike Phipps, AFC-D: Cleveland vs. Miami, 1972
  Dan Pastorini, AFC: Houston vs. Pittsburgh, 1978
  Dan Fouts, AFC-D: San Diego vs. Houston, 1979
  Tommy Kramer, NFC-D: Minnesota vs. Philadelphia, 1980
  Dan Fouts, AFC-D: San Diego vs. Miami, 1982
  Richard Todd, AFC: N.Y. Jets vs Miami, 1982
  Gary Danielson, NFC-D: Detroit vs. San Francisco, 1983
  Jay Schroeder, AFC: L.A. Raiders vs. Buffalo, 1990
4 By many players

PASS RECEIVING
RECEPTIONS
Most Receptions, Career
137 Jerry Rice, San Francisco-Oakland, 25 games
87 Michael Irvin, Dallas, 16 games
85 Andre Reed, Buffalo, 21 games

Most Receptions, Game
13 Kellen Winslow, AFC-D: San Diego vs. Miami, 1981 (OT)
    Thurman Thomas, AFC-D: Buffalo vs. Cleveland, 1989
    Shannon Sharpe, AFC-FR: Denver vs. L.A. Raiders, 1993
    Chad Morton, NFC-D: New Orleans vs. Minnesota, 2000
12 Raymond Berry, NFC: Baltimore vs. N.Y. Giants, 1958
    Michael Irvin, NFC: Dallas vs. San Francisco, 1994
11 Dante Lavelli, NFC: Cleveland vs. Los Angeles, 1950
    Dan Ross, SB: Cincinnati vs. San Francisco, 1981
    Franco Harris, AFC-FR: Pittsburgh vs. San Diego, 1982
    Steve Watson, AFC-D: Denver vs. Pittsburgh, 1984
    John L. Williams, AFC-D: Seattle vs. Cincinnati, 1988
    Jerry Rice, SB: San Francisco vs. Cincinnati, 1988
    Ernest Givins, AFC-FR: Houston vs. Pittsburgh, 1989 (OT)
    Amp Lee, NFC-D: Minnesota vs. Chicago, 1994
    Jay Novacek, NFC-D: Dallas vs. Green Bay, 1994
    O.J. McDuffie, AFC-FR: Miami vs. Buffalo, 1995
    Jerry Rice, NFC-C: San Francisco vs. Green Bay, 1995

Most Consecutive Games, Pass Receptions
25 Jerry Rice, San Francisco-Oakland, 1985-2001 (current)
22 Drew Pearson, Dallas, 1973-1983
18 Paul Warfield, Cleveland-Miami, 1964-1974
    Cliff Branch, Oakland/L.A. Raiders, 1974-1983
    Thurman Thomas, Buffalo, 1989-1998

YARDS GAINED
Most Yards Gained, Career
2,042 Jerry Rice, San Francisco-Oakland, 25 games
1,315 Michael Irvin, Dallas, 16 games
1,289 Cliff Branch, Oakland/L.A. Raiders, 22 games
Most Yards Gained, Game
240 Eric Moulds, AFC-FR: Buffalo vs. Miami, 1998
227 Anthony Carter, NFC-D: Minnesota vs. San Francisco, 1987
215 Jerry Rice, SB: San Francisco vs. Cincinnati, 1988
Most Games, 100 or More Yards Receiving, Career
8 Jerry Rice, San Francisco-Oakland, 25 games
6 Michael Irvin, Dallas, 16 games
5 John Stallworth, Pittsburgh, 18 games
   Andre Reed, Buffalo, 21 games
Most Consecutive Games, 100 or More Yards Receiving, Career
3 Tom Fears, Los Angeles, 1950-51
   Jerry Rice, San Francisco, 1988-89
   Randy Moss, Minnesota, 1999-2000
2 By many players
Longest Reception
96 Shannon Sharpe (from Dilfer), AFC: Baltimore vs. Oakland, 2000 (TD)
94 Alvin Harper (from Aikman), NFC-D: Dallas vs. Green Bay, 1994 (TD)
93 Elbert Dubenion (from Lamonica), AFC-D: Buffalo vs. Boston, 1963 (TD)

AVERAGE GAIN
Highest Average Gain, Career (20 receptions)
27.3 Alvin Harper, Dallas, 10 games (24-655)
23.7 Willie Gault, Chicago-L.A. Raiders, 12 games (21-497)
22.8 Harold Jackson, L.A. Rams-New England-Minnesota-Seattle, 14 games (24-548)
Highest Average Gain, Game (3 receptions)
46.3 Harold Jackson, NFC: Los Angeles vs. Minnesota, 1974 (3-139)
42.7 Billy Cannon, AFC: Houston vs. L.A. Chargers, 1960 (3-128)
42.0 Lenny Moore, NFC: Baltimore vs. N.Y. Giants, 1959 (3-126)

TOUCHDOWNS
Most Touchdowns, Career
20 Jerry Rice, San Francisco-Oakland, 25 games
12 John Stallworth, Pittsburgh, 18 games
10 Fred Biletnikoff, Oakland, 19 games
    Antonio Freeman, Green Bay, 12 games

Most Touchdowns, Game
3 Tom Fears, NFC-D: Los Angeles vs. Chi. Bears, 1950
   Gary Collins, NFC: Cleveland vs. Baltimore, 1964
   Fred Biletnikoff, AFC-D: Oakland vs. Kansas City, 1968
   Preston Pearson, NFC: Dallas vs. Los Angeles, 1975
   Dave Casper, AFC-D: Oakland vs. Baltimore, 1977 (OT)
   Alvin Garrett, NFC-FR: Washington vs. Detroit, 1982
   Jerry Rice, NFC-D: San Francisco vs. Minnesota, 1988
   Jerry Rice, SB: San Francisco vs. Denver, 1989
   Andre Reed, AFC-FR: Buffalo vs. Houston, 1992 (OT)
   Sterling Sharpe, NFC-FR: Green Bay vs. Detroit, 1993
   Jerry Rice, SB: San Francisco vs. San Diego, 1994
   Willie Jackson, NFC-FR: New Orleans vs. St. Louis, 2000

Most Consecutive Games, Touchdown Passes Caught
8 John Stallworth, Pittsburgh, 1978-1983
5 James Lofton, Green Bay-Buffalo, 1982-1990
   Randy Moss, Minnesota, 1998-2000
   Antonio Freeman, Green Bay, 1997-2001 (current)
4 Lynn Swann, Pittsburgh, 1978-79
   Harold Carmichael, Philadelphia, 1978-1980
   Fred Solomon, San Francisco, 1983-84
   Jerry Rice, San Francisco, 1988-89
   John Taylor, San Francisco, 1988-89

INTERCEPTIONS BY
Most Interceptions, Career
9 Charlie Waters, Dallas, 25 games
   Bill Simpson, Los Angeles-Buffalo, 11 games
   Ronnie Lott, San Francisco-L.A. Raiders, 20 games
8 Lester Hayes, Oakland/L.A. Raiders, 13 games
7 Willie Brown, Oakland, 17 games
   Dennis Thurman, Dallas, 14 games
Most Interceptions, Game
4 Vernon Perry, AFC-D: Houston vs. San Diego, 1979
3 Joe Laws, NFC: Green Bay vs. N.Y. Giants, 1944
   Charlie Waters, NFC-D: Dallas vs. Chicago, 1977
   Rod Martin, SB: Oakland vs. Philadelphia, 1980
   Dennis Thurman, NFC-D: Dallas vs. Green Bay, 1982
   A.J. Duhe, AFC: Miami vs. N.Y. Jets, 1982
2 By many players
Most Consecutive Games, Interceptions
4 Aeneas Williams, Arizona-St. Louis, 1998-2001
3 By many players. Last time:
   Duane Starks, Baltimore, 2000-01

YARDS GAINED
Most Yards Gained, Career
196 Willie Brown, Oakland, 17 games
187 Ronnie Lott, San Francisco-L.A.-Raiders, 20 games
160 George Teague, Green Bay-Dallas-Miami-Dallas, 12 games
Most Yards Gained, Game
108 Darrien Gordon, SB: Denver vs. Atlanta, 1998
101 George Teague, NFC-FR: Green Bay vs. Detroit, 1993
98 Darrol Ray, AFC-FR: N.Y. Jets vs. Cincinnati, 1982
    Tory James, AFC-D: Oakland vs. Miami, 2000
Longest Return
101 George Teague, NFC-FR: Green Bay vs. Detroit, 1993 (TD)
98 Darrol Ray, AFC-FR: N.Y. Jets vs. Cincinnati, 1982 (TD)
94 LeRoy Irvin, NFC-FR: L.A. Rams vs. Dallas, 1983

TOUCHDOWNS
Most Touchdowns, Career
3 Willie Brown, Oakland, 17 games
2 Lester Hayes, Oakland/L.A. Raiders, 13 games
   Ronnie Lott, San Francisco-L.A. Raiders, 20 games
   Darrell Green, Washington, 18 games
   Melvin Jenkins, Seattle-Detroit, 5 games
   George Teague, Green Bay-Dallas-Miami-Dallas, 12 games
   Aeneas Williams, Arizona-St. Louis, 5 games

POSTSEASON RECORDS

Most Touchdowns, Game
2 Aeneas Williams, NFC-D: St. Louis vs. Green Bay, 2001
1 By many players

PUNTING
Most Punts, Career
111 Ray Guy, Oakland/L.A. Raiders, 22 games
84 Danny White, Dallas, 18 games
83 Sean Landeta, N.Y. Giants-Tampa Bay-Green Bay-Philadelphia, 17 games
Most Punts, Game
14 Dave Jennings, AFC-D: N.Y. Jets vs. Cleveland, 1986 (OT)
12 David Lee, AFC-D: Baltimore vs. Oakland, 1977 (OT)
11 Ken Strong, NFC: N.Y. Giants vs. Chi. Bears, 1933
    Jim Norton, AFC: Houston vs. Oakland, 1967
    Ode Burrell, AFC-D: Houston vs. Oakland, 1969
    Dale Hatcher, NFC: L.A. Rams vs. Chicago, 1985
    Brad Maynard, SB: N.Y. Giants vs. Baltimore, 2000
Longest Punt
76 Ed Danowski, NFC: N.Y. Giants vs. Detroit, 1935
    Mike Horan, AFC: Denver vs. Buffalo, 1991
72 Charlie Conerly, NFC-D: N.Y. Giants vs. Cleveland, 1950
    Yale Lary, NFC: Detroit vs. Cleveland, 1953
71 Ray Guy: Oakland vs. San Diego, 1980

AVERAGE YARDAGE
Highest Average, Career (25 punts)
44.5 Rich Camarillo, New England, 6 games (35-1,559)
44.4 Lee Johnson, Cleveland-Cincinnati, 7 games (28-1,244)
44.3 Jeff Feagles, Philadelphia-Seattle, 4 games (26-1,151)
Highest Average, Game (4 punts)
56.0 Ray Guy, AFC: Oakland vs. San Diego, 1980 (4-224)
52.5 Sammy Baugh, NFC: Washington vs. Chi. Bears, 1942 (6-315)
52.0 Craig Hentrich, AFC-D: Tennessee vs. Indianapolis, 1999 (5-260)

PUNT RETURNS
Most Punt Returns, Career
34 David Meggett, N.Y. Giants-New England-N.Y. Jets, 13 games
28 Brian Mitchell, Washington-Philadelphia, 14 games
25 Theo Bell, Pittsburgh-Tampa Bay, 10 games
Most Punt Returns, Game
7 Ron Gardin, AFC-D: Baltimore vs. Cincinnati, 1970
   Carl Roaches, AFC-FR: Houston vs. Oakland, 1980
   Gerald McNeil, AFC-D: Cleveland vs. N.Y. Jets, 1986 (OT)
   Phil McConkey, NFC-D: N.Y. Giants vs. San Francisco, 1986
   David Meggett, AFC-D: New England vs. Pittsburgh, 1996
   Reggie Barlow, AFC-FR: Jacksonville vs. New England, 1998
6 George McAfee, NFC-D: Chi. Bears vs. Los Angeles, 1950
   Eddie Brown, NFC-D: Washington vs. Minnesota, 1976
   Theo Bell, AFC: Pittsburgh vs. Houston, 1978
   Eddie Brown, NFC: Los Angeles vs. Tampa Bay, 1979
   John Sciarra, NFC: Philadelphia vs. Dallas, 1980
   Kurt Sohn, AFC: N.Y. Jets vs. Miami, 1982
   Mike Nelms, SB: Washington vs. Miami, 1982
   Anthony Carter, NFC-FR: Minnesota vs. New Orleans, 1987
   Desmond Howard, SB: Green Bay vs. New England, 1996
   Nate Jacquet, AFC-FR: Miami vs. Seattle, 1999
5 By many players

YARDS GAINED
Most Yards Gained, Career
312 David Meggett, N.Y. Giants-New England-N.Y. Jets, 13 games
301 Brian Mitchell, Washington-Philadelphia, 14 games

259 Anthony Carter, Minnesota-Detroit, 9 games
Most Yards Gained, Game
143 Anthony Carter, NFC-FR: Minnesota vs. New Orleans, 1987
141 Bob Hayes, NFC-D: Dallas vs. Cleveland, 1967
117 Desmond Howard, NFC-D: Green Bay vs. San Francisco, 1996
Longest Return
88 Jermaine Lewis, AFC-D: Baltimore vs. Pittsburgh, 2001 (TD)
84 Anthony Carter, NFC-FR: Minnesota vs. New Orleans, 1987 (TD)
81 Hugh Gallarneau, NFC-D: Chi. Bears vs. Green Bay, 1941 (TD)

AVERAGE YARDAGE
Highest Average, Career (10 returns)
15.3 Robert Brooks, Green Bay, 11 games (14-214)
15.2 Anthony Carter, Minnesota-Detroit, 9 games (17-259)
14.3 Antonio Freeman, Green Bay, 12 games (10-143)
Highest Average Gain, Game (3 returns)
47.0 Bob Hayes, NFC-D: Dallas vs. Cleveland, 1967 (3-141)
33.0 Jermaine Lewis, AFC-D: Baltimore vs. Pittsburgh, 2001 (3-99)
29.0 George (Butch) Byrd, AFC: Buffalo vs. San Diego, 1965 (3-87)

TOUCHDOWNS
Most Touchdowns
1 Hugh Gallarneau, NFC-D: Chicago Bears vs. Green Bay, 1941
   Bosh Pritchard, NFC-D: Philadelphia vs. Pittsburgh, 1947
   Charley Trippi, NFC: Chicago Cardinals vs. Philadelphia, 1947
   Verda (Vitamin T) Smith, NFC-D: Los Angeles vs. Detroit, 1952
   George (Butch) Byrd, AFC: Buffalo vs. San Diego, 1965
   Golden Richards, NFC: Dallas vs. Minnesota, 1973
   Wes Chandler, AFC-D: San Diego vs. Miami, 1981 (OT)
   Shaun Gayle, NFC-D: Chicago vs. N.Y. Giants, 1985
   Anthony Carter, NFC-FR: Minnesota vs. New Orleans, 1987
   Darrell Green, NFC-D: Washington vs. Chicago, 1987
   Antonio Freeman, NFC-FR: Green Bay vs. Atlanta, 1995
   Desmond Howard, NFC-D: Green Bay vs. San Francisco, 1996
   Jermaine Lewis, AFC-D: Baltimore vs. Pittsburgh, 2001
   Troy Brown, AFC: New England vs. Pittsburgh, 2001

KICKOFF RETURNS
Most Kickoff Returns, Career
31 Kevin Williams, Dallas-Buffalo, 12 games
    Brian Mitchell, Washington-Philadelphia, 14 games
29 Fulton Walker, Miami-L.A. Raiders, 10 games
25 David Meggett, N.Y. Giants-New England-N.Y. Jets, 13 games
    Eric Metcalf, Cleveland-Atlanta-Arizona, 7 games
Most Kickoff Returns, Game
8 Marc Logan, AFC-D: Miami vs. Buffalo, 1990
   Andre Coleman, SB: San Diego vs. San Francisco, 1994
7 Don Bingham, NFC: Chi. Bears vs. N.Y. Giants, 1956
   Reggie Brown, NFC-FR: Atlanta vs. Minnesota, 1982
   David Verser, AFC-FR: Cincinnati vs. N.Y. Jets, 1982
   Del Rodgers, NFC-D: Green Bay vs. Dallas, 1982
   Henry Ellard, NFC: L.A. Rams vs. Washington, 1983
   Stephen Starring, SB: New England vs. Chicago, 1985
   Darick Holmes, AFC-D: Buffalo vs. Pittsburgh, 1995
   Antonio Freeman, NFC: Green Bay vs. Dallas, 1995
   Roell Preston, NFC-FR: Green Bay vs. San Francisco, 1998

Robert Tate, NFC-D: Minnesota vs. St. Louis, 1999
Fred McAfee, NFC-D: New Orleans vs. Minnesota, 2000
6   By many players

YARDS GAINED
Most Yards Gained, Career
741   Brian Mitchell, Washington-Philadelphia, 14 games
677   Fulton Walker, Miami-L.A. Raiders, 10 games
632   Kevin Williams, Dallas-Buffalo, 12 games
Most Yards Gained, Game
244   Andre Coleman, SB: San Diego vs. San Francisco, 1994
210   Tim Dwight, SB: Atlanta vs. Denver, 1998
194   Roell Preston, NFC-FR: Green Bay vs. San Francisco, 1998

Longest Return
100   Brian Mitchell, NFC-D: Washington vs. Tampa Bay, 1999 (TD)
99   Desmond Howard, SB: Green Bay vs. New England, 1996 (TD)
98   Fulton Walker, SB: Miami vs. Washington, 1982 (TD)
Andre Coleman, SB: San Diego vs. San Francisco, 1994 (TD)

AVERAGE YARDAGE
Highest Average, Career (10 returns)
34.3   Tim Dwight, Atlanta, 3 games (10-343)
30.1   Carl Garrett, Oakland, 5 games (16-481)
30.0   Reggie Barlow, Jacksonville, 8 games (12-360)
Highest Average, Game (3 returns)
56.7   Les (Speedy) Duncan, NFC-D: Washington vs. San Francisco, 1971 (3-170)
51.3   Ed Podolak, AFC-D: Kansas City vs. Miami, 1971 (OT) (3-154)
49.0   Les (Speedy) Duncan, AFC: San Diego vs. Buffalo, 1964 (3-147)

TOUCHDOWNS
Most Touchdowns, Career
2   Ron Dixon, N.Y. Giants, 3 games
1   By many players
Most Touchdowns, Game
1   Vic Washington, NFC-D: San Francisco vs. Dallas, 1972
Nat Moore, AFC-D: Miami vs. Oakland, 1974
Marshall Johnson, AFC-D: Baltimore vs. Oakland, 1977 (OT)
Fulton Walker, SB: Miami vs. Washington, 1982
Stanford Jennings, SB: Cincinnati vs. San Francisco, 1988
Eric Metcalf, AFC-D: Cleveland vs. Buffalo, 1989
Andre Coleman, SB: San Diego vs. San Francisco, 1994
Desmond Howard, SB: Green Bay vs. New England, 1996
Chuck Levy, NFC: San Franisco vs. Green Bay, 1997
Tim Dwight, SB: Atlanta vs. Denver, 1998
Kevin Dyson, AFC-FR: Tennessee vs. Buffalo, 1999
Charlie Rogers, AFC-FR: Seattle vs. Miami, 1999
Brian Mitchell, NFC-D: Washington vs. Tampa Bay, 1999
Tony Horne, NFC-D: St. Louis vs. Minnesota, 1999
Derrick Mason, AFC: Tennessee vs. Jacksonville, 1999
Ron Dixon, NFC-D: N.Y. Giants vs. Philadelphia, 2000; SB: N.Y. Giants vs. Baltimore, 2000
Jermaine Lewis, SB: Baltimore vs. N.Y. Giants, 2000

FUMBLES
Most Fumbles, Career
16   Warren Moon, Houston-Minnesota, 10 games
14   John Elway, Denver, 22 games
13   Tony Dorsett, Dallas, 17 games
Most Fumbles, Game
5   Warren Moon, AFC-D: Houston vs. Kansas City, 1993
4   Brian Sipe, AFC-D: Cleveland vs. Oakland, 1980

Randall Cunningham, NFC-FR: Minnesota vs. N.Y. Giants, 1997
3   By many players

RECOVERIES
Most Own Fumbles Recovered, Career
8   Warren Moon, Houston-Minnesota, 10 games
7   John Elway, Denver, 22 games
6   Jim Kelly, Buffalo, 17 games
Most Opponents' Fumbles Recovered, Career
4   Cliff Harris, Dallas, 21 games
Harvey Martin, Dallas, 22 games
Ted Hendricks, Baltimore-Oakland/L.A. Raiders, 21 games
Alvin Walton, Washington, 9 games
Monte Coleman, Washington, 21 games
Dave Thomas, Dallas-Jacksonville-N.Y. Giants, 13 games
3   Paul Krause, Minnesota, 19 games
Jack Lambert, Pittsburgh, 18 games
Fred Dryer, Los Angeles, 14 games
Charlie Waters, Dallas, 25 games
Jack Ham, Pittsburgh, 16 games
Mike Hegman, Dallas, 18 games
Tom Jackson, Denver, 10 games
Rich Milot, Washington, 13 games
Mike Singletary, Chicago, 12 games
Darryl Grant, Washington, 16 games
Wes Hopkins, Philadelphia, 3 games
Wilber Marshall, Chicago-Washington, 15 games
Tyrone Braxton, Denver-Miami-Denver, 19 games
Neil Smith, Kansas City-Denver, 16 games
Tony Brackens, Jacksonville, 7 games
Phil Hansen, Buffalo, 14 games
Carnell Lake, Pittsburgh-Jacksonville-Baltimore, 17 games
Jason Gildon, Pittsburgh, 11 games
2   By many players
Most Fumbles Recovered, Game, Own and Opponents'
3   Jack Lambert, AFC: Pittsburgh vs. Oakland, 1975 (3 opp)
Ron Jaworski, NFC-FR: Philadelphia vs. N.Y. Giants, 1981 (3 own)
2   By many players

YARDS GAINED
Longest Return
93   Andy Russell, AFC-D: Pittsburgh vs. Baltimore, 1975 (opp, TD)
79   Neil Smith, AFC-D: Denver vs. Miami, 1998 (opp, TD)
64   Leon Lett, SB: Dallas vs. Buffalo, 1992 (opp)

TOUCHDOWNS
Most Touchdowns
1   By many players

COMBINED NET YARDS GAINED
Rushing, receiving, interception returns, punt returns, kickoff returns, and fumble returns.
ATTEMPTS
Most Attempts, Career
454   Franco Harris, Pittsburgh, 19 games
417   Thurman Thomas, Buffalo, 21 games
397   Emmitt Smith, Dallas, 17 games
Most Attempts, Game
43   Lamar Smith, AFC-FR: Miami vs. Indianapolis, 2000 (OT)
42   Curtis Martin, AFC-D: N.Y. Jets vs. Jacksonville, 1998
40   Lawrence McCutcheon, NFC-D: Los Angeles vs. St. Louis, 1975

YARDS GAINED
Most Yards Gained, Career
2,124   Thurman Thomas, Buffalo, 21 games
2,086   Jerry Rice, San Francisco-Oakland, 25 games

2,060   Franco Harris, Pittsburgh, 19 games
Most Yards Gained, Game
350   Ed Podolak, AFC-D: Kansas City vs. Miami, 1971 (OT)
329   Keith Lincoln, AFC: San Diego vs. Boston, 1963
285   Bob Hayes, NFC-D: Dallas vs. Cleveland, 1967

SACKS
Sacks have been compiled since 1982.
Most Sacks, Career
14.5   Bruce Smith, Buffalo, 20 games
12.0   Reggie White, Philadelphia-Green Bay, 19 games
11.0   Charles Haley, San Francisco-Dallas-San Francisco, 21 games
Most Sacks, Game
3.5   Rich Milot, NFC-D: Washington vs. Chicago, 1984
      Richard Dent, NFC-D: Chicago vs. N.Y. Giants, 1985
3.0   Richard Dent, NFC-D: Chicago vs. Washington, 1984
      Garin Veris, AFC-FR: New England vs. N.Y. Jets, 1985
      Gary Jeter, NFC-D: L.A. Rams vs. Dallas, 1985
      Carl Hairston, AFC-D: Cleveland vs. N.Y. Jets, 1986 (OT)
      Charles Mann, NFC-D: Washington vs. Chicago, 1987
      Kevin Greene, NFC-FR: L.A. Rams vs. Minnesota, 1988
      Greg Townsend, AFC-D: L.A. Raiders vs. Cincinnati, 1990
      Wilber Marshall, NFC: Washington vs. Detroit, 1991
      Fred Stokes, NFC-FR: Washington vs. Minnesota, 1992
      Pierce Holt, NFC-D: San Francisco vs. Washington, 1992
      Tony Casillas, NFC: Dallas vs. San Francisco, 1992
      Gerald Williams, AFC-FR: Pittsburgh vs. Kansas City, 1993
      Chad Brown, AFC-FR: Pittsburgh vs. Indianapolis, 1996
      Reggie White, SB: Green Bay vs. New England, 1996
      Warren Sapp, NFC-D: Tampa Bay vs. Green Bay, 1997
      Trace Armstrong, AFC-FR: Miami vs. Seattle, 1999
      Michael McCrary, AFC-FR: Baltimore vs. Denver, 2000
2.5   Lyle Alzado, AFC-D: L.A. Raiders vs. Pittsburgh, 1983
      Jacob Green, AFC-FR: Seattle vs. L.A. Raiders, 1984
      Larry Roberts, NFC-D: San Francisco vs. Minnesota, 1988
      Leslie O'Neal, AFC-FR: San Diego vs. Kansas City, 1992
      Bruce Smith, AFC-FR: Buffalo vs. Tennessee, 1999

TEAM RECORDS

GAMES, VICTORIES, DEFEATS
Most Seasons Participating in Postseason Games
26   Dallas, 1966-1973, 1975-1983, 1985, 1991-96, 1998-99
25   N.Y. Giants, 1933-35, 1938-39, 1941, 1943-44, 1946,
     1950, 1956, 1958-59, 1961-63, 1981, 1984-86,
     1989-1990, 1993, 1997, 2000
     Cleveland/L.A./St. Louis Rams, 1945, 1949-1952, 1955,
     1967, 1969, 1973-1980, 1983-86, 1988-89,
     1999-2001
23   Cleveland, 1950-55, 1957-58, 1964-65, 1967-69,
     1971-72, 1980, 1982, 1985-89, 1994
     Minnesota, 1968-1971, 1973-78, 1980, 1982, 1987-89,
     1992-94, 1996-2000
Most Consecutive Seasons Participating in Postseason Games
9   Dallas, 1975-1983
8   Dallas, 1966-1973
    Pittsburgh, 1972-79
    Los Angeles, 1973-1980
    San Francisco, 1983-1990
7   Houston, 1987-1993
    San Francisco, 1992-98
Most Games
53   Dallas, 1966-1973, 1975-1983, 1985, 1991-96, 1998-99
40   Minnesota, 1968-1971, 1973-78, 1980, 1982, 1987-89,
     1992-94, 1996-2000
     San Francisco, 1957, 1970-72, 1981, 1983-1990,
     1992-98, 2001

Cleveland/L.A./St. Louis Rams, 1945, 1949-1952, 1955,
     1967, 1969, 1973-1980, 1983-86, 1988-89,
     1999-2001
     Oakland/L.A. Raiders, 1967-1970, 1972-77, 1980,
     1982-85, 1990-91, 1993, 2000-01
39   Miami, 1970-74, 1978-79, 1981-85, 1990, 1992,
     1994-95, 1997-2001
Most Games Won
32   Dallas, 1967, 1970-73, 1975, 1977-78, 1980-82,
     1991-96
24   San Francisco, 1970-71, 1981, 1983-84, 1988-1990,
     1992-94, 1996-98
23   Green Bay, 1936, 1939, 1944, 1961-62, 1965-67, 1982,
     1993-97, 2001
     Oakland/L.A. Raiders, 1967-1970, 1973-77, 1980,
     1982-83, 1990, 1993, 2000-01
Most Consecutive Games Won
9   Green Bay, 1961-62, 1965-67
7   Pittsburgh, 1974-76
    San Francisco, 1988-1990
    Dallas, 1992-94
    Denver, 1997-98
6   Miami, 1972-73
    Pittsburgh, 1978-79
    Washington, 1982-83
Most Games Lost
23   Minnesota, 1968-1971, 1973-78, 1980, 1982, 1987-89,
     1992-94, 1996-2000
22   L.A./St. Louis Rams, 1949-1950, 1952, 1955, 1967,
     1969, 1973-1980, 1983-86, 1988-89, 2000-01
21   Dallas, 1966-1970, 1972-73, 1975-76, 1978-1983, 1985,
     1991, 1994, 1996, 1998-99
Most Consecutive Games Lost
6   N.Y. Giants, 1939, 1941, 1943-44, 1946, 1950
    Cleveland, 1969, 1971-72, 1980, 1982, 1985
    Minnesota, 1988-89, 1992-94, 1996
    Detroit, 1991, 1993-95, 1997, 1999 (current)
5   N.Y. Giants, 1958-59, 1961-63
    Los Angeles, 1952, 1955, 1967, 1969, 1973
    Denver, 1977-79, 1983-84
    Baltimore/Indianapolis, 1971, 1975-77, 1987
    Philadelphia, 1980-81, 1988-1990
4   Washington, 1972-74, 1976
    Miami, 1974, 1978-79, 1981
    Chi. Cardinals/St. Louis, 1948, 1974-75, 1982
    Boston/New England, 1963, 1976, 1978, 1982
    New Orleans, 1987, 1990-92
    Kansas City, 1993-95, 1997 (current)
    Seattle, 1984, 1987-88, 1999 (current)
    Buffalo, 1995-96, 1998-99 (current)
    Indianapolis, 1995-96, 1999-2000 (current)

SCORING
Most Points, Game
73   NFC: Chi. Bears vs. Washington, 1940
62   AFC-D: Jacksonville vs. Miami, 1999
59   NFC: Detroit vs. Cleveland, 1957
Most Points, Both Teams, Game
95   NFC-FR: Philadelphia (58) vs. Detroit (37), 1995
86   NFC-D: St. Louis (49) vs. Minnesota (37), 1999
79   AFC-D: San Diego (41) vs. Miami (38), 1981 (OT)
     AFC-FR: Buffalo (41) vs. Houston (38), 1992 (OT)
Fewest Points, Both Teams, Game
5   NFC-D: Detroit (0) vs. Dallas (5), 1970
7   NFC: Chi. Cardinals (0) vs. Philadelphia (7), 1948
9   NFC: Tampa Bay (0) vs. Los Angeles (9), 1979
Largest Margin of Victory, Game
73   NFC: Chi. Bears vs. Washington, 1940 (73-0)
55   AFC-D: Jacksonville vs. Miami, 1999 (62-7)
49   AFC-D: Oakland vs. Houston, 1969 (56-7)

Most Points, Shutout Victory, Game
73 NFC: Chi. Bears vs. Washington, 1940
41 NFC: N.Y. Giants vs. Minnesota, 2000
38 NFC-D: Dallas vs. Tampa Bay, 1981

Most Points Overcome to Win Game
32 AFC-FR: Buffalo vs. Houston, 1992 (trailed 3-35, won 41-38) (OT)
20 NFC-D: Detroit vs. San Francisco, 1957 (trailed 7-27, won 31-27)
18 NFC-D: Dallas vs. San Francisco, 1972 (trailed 3-21, won 30-28)
    AFC-D: Miami vs. Cleveland, 1985 (trailed 3-21, won 24-21)

Most Points, Each Half
1st: 41 AFC: Buffalo vs. L.A. Raiders, 1990
        AFC: Jacksonville vs. Miami, 1999
     38 NFC-D: Washington vs. L.A. Rams, 1983
        NFC-FR: Philadelphia vs. Detroit, 1995
     35 NFC: Cleveland vs. Detroit, 1954
        AFC-D: Oakland vs. Houston, 1969
        SB: Washington vs. Denver, 1987
2nd: 45 NFC: Chi. Bears vs. Washington, 1940
     35 AFC-FR: Buffalo vs. Houston, 1992
        NFC-D: St. Louis vs. Minnesota, 1999
     30 SB: N.Y. Giants vs. Denver, 1986
        AFC: Cleveland vs. Denver, 1987
        NFC-FR: Detroit vs. Philadelphia, 1995

Most Points, Each Quarter
1st: 28 AFC-D: Oakland vs. Houston, 1969
     24 AFC-D: San Diego vs. Miami, 1981
        AFC-D: Jacksonville vs. Miami, 1999
     21 NFC: Chi. Bears vs. Washington, 1940
        AFC: San Diego vs. Boston, 1963
        AFC-D: Oakland vs. Kansas City, 1968
        AFC: Oakland vs. San Diego, 1980
        AFC: Buffalo vs. L.A. Raiders, 1990
        NFC: San Francisco vs. Dallas, 1994
2nd: 35 SB: Washington vs. Denver, 1987
     31 NFC-FR: Philadelphia vs. Detroit, 1995
     26 AFC-D: Pittsburgh vs. Buffalo, 1974
3rd: 28 AFC-FR: Buffalo vs. Houston, 1992
     26 NFC: Chi. Bears vs. Washington, 1940
     21 NFC-D: Dallas vs. Cleveland, 1967
        NFC-D: Dallas vs. Tampa Bay, 1981
        AFC-D: L.A. Raiders vs. Pittsburgh, 1983
        SB: Chicago vs. New England, 1985
        NFC-D: N.Y. Giants vs. San Francisco, 1986
        AFC: Cleveland vs. Denver, 1987
        AFC: Cleveland vs. Denver, 1989
        NFC-D: St. Louis vs. Minnesota, 1999
4th: 27 NFC: N.Y. Giants vs. Chi. Bears, 1934
     26 NFC-FR: Philadelphia vs. New Orleans, 1992
     24 NFC: Baltimore vs. N.Y. Giants, 1959
OT: 6 NFC: Baltimore vs. N.Y. Giants, 1958
        AFC-D: Oakland vs. Baltimore, 1977
        NFC-D: L.A. Rams vs. N.Y. Giants, 1989
        AFC-FR: Miami vs. Indianapolis, 2000

TOUCHDOWNS
Most Touchdowns, Game
11 NFC: Chi. Bears vs. Washington, 1940
8 NFC: Cleveland vs. Detroit, 1954
   NFC: Detroit vs. Cleveland, 1957
   AFC-D: Oakland vs. Houston, 1969
   SB: San Francisco vs. Denver, 1989
   AFC-D: Jacksonville vs. Miami, 1999
7 AFC: San Diego vs. Boston, 1963
   NFC-D: Dallas vs. Cleveland, 1967
   NFC-D: N.Y. Giants vs. San Francisco, 1986
   AFC: Buffalo vs. L.A. Raiders, 1990

SB: Dallas vs. Buffalo, 1992
SB: San Francisco vs. San Diego, 1994
NFC-FR: Philadelphia vs. Detroit, 1995
NFC-D: St. Louis vs. Minnesota, 1999

Most Touchdowns, Both Teams, Game
12 NFC-FR: Philadelphia (7) vs. Detroit (5), 1995
   NFC-D: St. Louis (7) vs. Minnesota (5), 1999
11 NFC: Chi. Bears (11) vs. Washington (0), 1940
10 NFC: Detroit (8) vs. Cleveland (2), 1957
   AFC-D: Miami (5) vs. San Diego (5), 1981 (OT)
   AFC: Miami (6) vs. Pittsburgh (4), 1984
   AFC-FR: Buffalo (5) vs. Houston (5), 1992 (OT)
   SB: San Francisco (7) vs. San Diego (3), 1994

Fewest Touchdowns, Both Teams, Game
0 NFC-D: N.Y. Giants vs. Cleveland, 1950
   NFC-D: Dallas vs. Detroit, 1970
   NFC: Los Angeles vs. Tampa Bay, 1979
1 NFC: Chi. Cardinals (0) vs. Philadelphia (1), 1948
   NFC-D: Cleveland (0) vs. N.Y. Giants (1), 1958
   AFC: San Diego (0) vs. Houston (1), 1961
   AFC-D: N.Y. Jets (0) vs. Kansas City (1), 1969
   NFC: Green Bay (0) vs. Washington (1), 1972
   NFC-FR: New Orleans (0) vs. Chicago (1), 1990
   NFC: N.Y. Giants (0) vs. San Francisco (1), 1990
   AFC-FR: L.A. Raiders (0) vs. Kansas City (1), 1991
   AFC-D: New England (0) vs. Pittsburgh (1), 1997
   NFC: Tampa Bay (0) vs. St. Louis (1), 1999
   AFC: Oakland (0) vs. Baltimore (1), 2000
2 In many games

POINTS AFTER TOUCHDOWN
Most (One-Point) Points After Touchdown, Game
8 NFC: Cleveland vs. Detroit, 1954
   NFC: Detroit vs. Cleveland, 1957
   AFC-D: Oakland vs. Houston, 1969
   AFC-D: Jacksonville vs. Miami, 1999
7 NFC: Chi. Bears vs. Washington, 1940
   NFC-D: Dallas vs. Cleveland, 1967
   NFC-D: N.Y. Giants vs. San Francisco, 1986
   SB: San Francisco vs. Denver, 1989
   SB: Dallas vs. Buffalo, 1992
   SB: San Francisco vs. San Diego, 1994
   NFC-FR: Philadelphia vs. Detroit, 1995
   NFC-D: St. Louis vs. Minnesota, 1999
6 AFC: San Diego vs. Boston, 1963
   NFC-D: Washington vs. L.A. Rams, 1983
   AFC: Miami vs. Pittsburgh, 1984
   SB: Washington vs. Denver, 1987
   AFC: Buffalo vs. L.A. Raiders, 1990
   AFC-FR: L.A. Raiders vs. Denver, 1993
   AFC-FR: Denver vs. Jacksonville, 1997
   NFC-D: St. Louis vs. Green Bay, 2001

Most (One-Point) Points After Touchdown, Both Teams, Game
10 NFC: Detroit (8) vs. Cleveland (2), 1957
   AFC-D: Miami (5) vs. San Diego (5), 1981 (OT)
   AFC: Miami (6) vs. Pittsburgh (4), 1984
   AFC-FR: Buffalo (5) vs. Houston (5), 1992 (OT)
   NFC-FR: Philadelphia (7) vs. Detroit (3), 1995
9 In many games

Fewest (One-Point) Points After Touchdown, Both Teams, Game
0 NFC-D: N.Y. Giants vs. Cleveland, 1950
   NFC-D: Dallas vs. Detroit, 1970
   NFC: Los Angeles vs. Tampa Bay, 1979
   NFC: St. Louis vs. Tampa Bay, 1999

Most Two-Point Conversions, Game
2 SB: San Diego vs. San Francisco, 1994
   NFC-FR: Detroit vs. Philadelphia, 1995
1 By many teams

FIELD GOALS
Most Field Goals, Game
- 5 NFC-D: Minnesota vs. San Francisco, 1987
  NFC: N.Y. Giants vs. San Francisco, 1990
  AFC: Buffalo vs. Miami, 1992
  NFC-FR: N.Y. Giants vs. Minnesota, 1997
- 4 AFC-D: Boston vs. Buffalo, 1963
  AFC: Oakland vs. Houston, 1967
  SB: Green Bay vs. Oakland, 1967
  NFC: Washington vs. Dallas, 1972
  AFC-D: Oakland vs. Pittsburgh, 1973
  SB: San Francisco vs. Cincinnati, 1981
  AFC-FR: New England vs. N.Y. Jets, 1985
  NFC-FR: Washington vs. L.A. Rams, 1986
  NFC-D: Philadelphia vs. Chicago, 1988
  AFC-FR: Pittsburgh vs. Houston, 1989 (OT)
  AFC-D: Pittsburgh vs. Buffalo, 1995
  NFC-FR: Dallas vs. Minnesota, 1996
  NFC-D: Carolina vs. Dallas, 1996
  AFC-FR: Jacksonville vs. New England, 1998
  AFC-D: Tennessee vs. Indianapolis, 1999
  NFC-D: Philadelphia vs. Chicago, 2001
- 3 By many teams

Most Field Goals, Both Teams, Game
- 8 NFC-FR: N.Y. Giants (5) vs. Minnesota (3), 1997
- 7 AFC-FR: Pittsburgh (4) vs. Houston (3), 1989 (OT)
  NFC: N.Y. Giants (5) vs. San Francisco (2), 1990
  NFC-D: Carolina (4) vs. Dallas (3), 1996
  AFC-D: Tennessee (4) vs. Indianapolis (3), 1999
- 6 NFC-D: Minnesota (5) vs. San Francisco (1), 1987
  NFC-D: Philadelphia (4) vs. Chicago (2), 1988
  AFC: Buffalo (5) vs. Miami (1), 1992

Most Field Goals Attempted, Game
- 6 AFC: Oakland vs. Houston, 1967
  NFC-D: Los Angeles vs. Dallas, 1973
  AFC-D: Cleveland vs. N.Y. Jets, 1986 (OT)
  NFC: N.Y. Giants vs. San Francisco, 1990
  AFC: Buffalo vs. Miami, 1992
- 5 By many teams

Most Field Goals Attempted, Both Teams, Game
- 9 NFC-D: Philadelphia (5) vs. Chicago (4), 1988
  NFC-FR: N.Y. Giants (5) vs. Minnesota (4), 1997
- 8 NFC-D: Los Angeles (6) vs. Dallas (2), 1973
  NFC-D: Detroit (5) vs. San Francisco (3), 1983
  AFC-D: Cleveland (6) vs. N.Y. Jets (2), 1986 (OT)
  NFC-D: Minnesota (5) vs. San Francisco (3), 1987
  AFC-FR: Houston (4) vs. Pittsburgh (4), 1989 (OT)
  NFC-FR: Chicago (4) vs. New Orleans (4), 1990
  NFC: N.Y. Giants (6) vs. San Francisco (2), 1990
- 7 In many games

SAFETIES
Most Safeties, Game
- 1 By many teams
Most Safeties, Both Teams, Game
- 1 In many games

FIRST DOWNS
Most First Downs, Game
- 34 AFC-D: San Diego vs. Miami, 1981 (OT)
- 33 AFC-D: Cleveland vs. N.Y. Jets, 1986 (OT)
- 31 SB: San Francisco vs. Miami, 1984
  NFC-D: San Francisco vs. Minnesota, 1997
  NFC: N.Y. Giants vs. Minnesota, 2000

Fewest First Downs, Game
- 6 NFC: N.Y. Giants vs. Green Bay, 1961
  AFC-D: Baltimore vs. Tennessee, 2000
- 7 NFC: Green Bay vs. Boston, 1936
  NFC-D: Pittsburgh vs. Philadelphia, 1947
  NFC: Chi. Cardinals vs. Philadelphia, 1948

NFC: Los Angeles vs. Philadelphia, 1949
NFC-D: Cleveland vs. N.Y. Giants, 1958
AFC-D: Cincinnati vs. Baltimore, 1970
NFC-D: Detroit vs. Dallas, 1970
NFC: Tampa Bay vs. Los Angeles, 1979
AFC-D: Baltimore vs. Pittsburgh, 2001
- 8 By many teams

Most First Downs, Both Teams, Game
- 59 AFC-D: San Diego (34) vs. Miami (25), 1981 (OT)
- 55 AFC-FR: San Diego (29) vs. Pittsburgh (26), 1982
- 54 AFC-FR: Buffalo (28) vs. Miami (26), 1995

Fewest First Downs, Both Teams, Game
- 15 NFC: Green Bay (7) vs. Boston (8), 1936
- 19 NFC: N.Y. Giants (9) vs. Green Bay (10), 1939
  NFC: Washington (9) vs. Chi. Bears (10), 1942
- 20 NFC-D: Cleveland (9) vs. N.Y. Giants (11), 1950

RUSHING
Most First Downs, Rushing, Game
- 19 NFC-FR: Dallas vs. Los Angeles, 1980
- 18 AFC-D: Miami vs. Cincinnati, 1973
  AFC: Miami vs. Oakland, 1973
  AFC-D: Pittsburgh vs. Buffalo, 1974
  AFC-FR: Buffalo vs. Miami, 1995
  AFC-FR: Denver vs. Jacksonville, 1997
- 17 AFC-D: Cincinnati vs. Seattle, 1988
  AFC: Buffalo vs. Kansas City, 1993

Fewest First Downs, Rushing, Game
- 0 NFC: Los Angeles vs. Philadelphia, 1949
  AFC-D: Buffalo vs. Boston, 1963
  AFC: Oakland vs. Pittsburgh, 1974
  NFC-FR: New Orleans vs. Minnesota, 1987
  NFC: L.A. Rams vs. San Francisco, 1989
  NFC-D: Chicago vs. N.Y. Giants, 1990
  AFC-FR: Indianapolis vs. Pittsburgh, 1996
  AFC-FR: Seattle vs. Miami, 1999
  AFC-D: Miami vs. Jacksonville, 1999
  AFC-D: Miami vs. Oakland, 2000
  AFC-D: Baltimore vs. Pittsburgh, 2001
- 1 By many teams

Most First Downs, Rushing, Both Teams, Game
- 26 AFC: Buffalo (14) vs. L.A. Raiders (12), 1990
- 25 NFC-FR: Dallas (19) vs. Los Angeles (6), 1980
- 23 NFC: Cleveland (15) vs. Detroit (8), 1952
  AFC-D: Miami (18) vs. Cincinnati (5), 1973
  AFC-D: Pittsburgh (18) vs. Buffalo (5), 1974
  AFC-FR: Buffalo (18) vs. Miami (5), 1995

Fewest First Downs, Rushing, Both Teams, Game
- 2 NFC-FR: New Orleans (1) vs. St. Louis (1), 2000
- 5 AFC-D: Buffalo (0) vs. Boston (5), 1963
  NFC-D: Washington (1) vs. Tampa Bay (4), 1999
- 6 NFC: Green Bay (2) vs. Boston (4), 1936
  NFC-D: Baltimore (2) vs. Minnesota (4), 1968
  AFC: Houston (1) vs. Oakland (5), 1969
  AFC-FR: N.Y. Jets (1) vs. Houston (5), 1991
  AFC-FR: Denver (1) vs. Baltimore (5), 2000

PASSING
Most First Downs, Passing, Game
- 21 AFC-D: Miami vs. San Diego, 1981 (OT)
  AFC-D: San Diego vs. Miami, 1981 (OT)
  AFC-D: Cleveland vs. N.Y. Jets, 1986 (OT)
  NFC-D: Philadelphia vs. Chicago, 1988
- 20 NFC-FR: Dallas vs. L.A. Rams, 1983
  AFC-D: Buffalo vs. Cleveland, 1989
  AFC-FR: Miami vs. Buffalo, 1995
  NFC-FR: Detroit vs. Philadelphia, 1995
  AFC-FR: San Diego vs. Indianapolis, 1995
  NFC-D: Minnesota vs. St. Louis, 1999
- 19 NFC-FR: St. Louis vs. Green Bay, 1982

NFC-FR: Dallas vs. Tampa Bay, 1982
AFC-FR: Pittsburgh vs. San Diego, 1982
AFC-FR: San Diego vs. Pittsburgh, 1982
NFC: Dallas vs. Washington, 1982
NFC-D: Detroit vs. Dallas, 1991
AFC-FR: Kansas City vs. Pittsburgh, 1993 (OT)
NFC: Minnesota vs. Atlanta, 1998 (OT)
NFC: N.Y. Giants vs. Minnesota, 2000

Fewest First Downs, Passing, Game
0 NFC: Philadelphia vs. Chi. Cardinals, 1948
1 NFC-D: N.Y. Giants vs. Washington, 1943
   NFC: Cleveland vs. Detroit, 1953
   SB: Denver vs. Dallas, 1977
2 By many teams

Most First Downs, Passing, Both Teams, Game
42 AFC-D: Miami (21) vs. San Diego (21), 1981 (OT)
38 AFC-FR: Pittsburgh (19) vs. San Diego (19), 1982
   NFC-D: Minnesota (20) vs. St. Louis (18), 1999
36 NFC: Minnesota (19) vs. Atlanta (17), 1998 (OT)

Fewest First Downs, Passing, Both Teams, Game
2 NFC: Philadelphia (0) vs. Chi. Cardinals (2), 1948
4 NFC-D: Cleveland (2) vs. N.Y. Giants (2), 1950
5 NFC: Detroit (2) vs. N.Y. Giants (3), 1935
   NFC: Green Bay (2) vs. N.Y. Giants (3), 1939

PENALTY
Most First Downs, Penalty, Game
7 AFC-D: New England vs. Oakland, 1976
6 AFC-D: Cleveland vs. N.Y. Jets, 1986 (OT)
5 AFC-FR: Cleveland vs. L. A. Raiders, 1982
   NFC-D: San Francisco vs. Minnesota, 1997
   AFC-FR: Miami vs. Buffalo, 1998
   NFC-D: Arizona vs. Minnesota, 1998
   AFC: Pittsburgh vs. New England, 2001

Most First Downs, Penalty, Both Teams, Game
9 AFC-D: New England (7) vs. Oakland (2), 1976
8 NFC-FR: Atlanta (4) vs. Minnesota (4), 1982
   AFC-FR: Miami (5) vs. Buffalo (3), 1998
7 AFC-D: Baltimore (4) vs. Oakland (3), 1977 (OT)
   AFC-FR: Denver (4) vs. L.A. Raiders (3), 1993
   NFC-D: Dallas (4) vs. Carolina (3), 1996
   AFC-D: Kansas City (4) vs. Denver (3), 1997

NET YARDS GAINED RUSHING AND PASSING
Most Yards Gained, Game
610 AFC: San Diego vs. Boston, 1963
602 SB: Washington vs. Denver, 1987
569 AFC: Miami vs. Pittsburgh, 1984

Fewest Yards Gained, Game
86 NFC-D: Cleveland vs. N.Y. Giants, 1958
99 NFC: Chi. Cardinals vs. Philadelphia, 1948
114 NFC-D: N.Y. Giants vs. Washington, 1943
   NFC: Minnesota vs. N.Y. Giants, 2000

Most Yards Gained, Both Teams, Game
1,038 AFC-FR: Buffalo (536) vs. Miami (502), 1995
1,036 AFC-D: San Diego (564) vs. Miami (472), 1981 (OT)
1,024 AFC: Miami (569) vs. Pittsburgh (455), 1984

Fewest Yards Gained, Both Teams, Game
331 NFC: Chi. Cardinals (99) vs. Philadelphia (232), 1948
332 NFC-D: N.Y. Giants (150) vs. Cleveland (182), 1950
336 NFC: Boston (116) vs. Green Bay (220), 1936

RUSHING
ATTEMPTS
Most Attempts, Game
65 NFC: Detroit vs. N.Y. Giants, 1935
61 NFC: Philadelphia vs. Los Angeles, 1949
59 AFC: New England vs. Miami, 1985

Fewest Attempts, Game
8 AFC-D: Miami vs. San Diego, 1994

9 SB: Miami vs. San Francisco, 1984
   NFC: Minnesota vs. N.Y. Giants, 2000
10 NFC: L.A. Rams vs. San Francisco, 1989
   NFC-FR: Atlanta vs. Green Bay, 1995
   NFC-FR: Detroit vs. Washington, 1999

Most Attempts, Both Teams, Game
109 NFC: Detroit (65) vs. N.Y. Giants (44), 1935
97 AFC-D: Baltimore (50) vs. Oakland (47), 1977 (OT)
91 NFC: Philadelphia (57) vs. Chi. Cardinals (34), 1948

Fewest Attempts, Both Teams, Game
32 AFC-D: Houston (14) vs. Kansas City (18), 1993
38 NFC-D: Detroit (16) vs. Dallas (22), 1991
39 NFC-FR: Atlanta (10) vs. Green Bay (29), 1995

YARDS GAINED
Most Yards Gained, Game
382 NFC: Chi. Bears vs. Washington, 1940
341 AFC-FR: Buffalo vs. Miami, 1995
338 NFC-FR: Dallas vs. Los Angeles, 1980

Fewest Yards Gained, Game
– 4 NFC-FR: Detroit vs. Green Bay, 1994
7 AFC-D: Buffalo vs. Boston, 1963
   SB: New England vs. Chicago, 1985
14 AFC-D: Miami vs. Denver, 1998
   AFC: N.Y. Jets vs. Denver, 1998

Most Yards Gained, Both Teams, Game
430 NFC-FR: Dallas (338) vs. Los Angeles (92), 1980
426 NFC: Cleveland (227) vs. Detroit (199), 1952
411 AFC-FR: Buffalo (341) vs. Miami (70), 1995

Fewest Yards Gained, Both Teams, Game
77 NFC-FR: Detroit (–4) vs. Green Bay (81), 1994
84 NFC-FR: St. Louis (34) vs. New Orleans (50), 2000
90 AFC-D: Buffalo (7) vs. Boston (83), 1963
   NFC-D: Tampa Bay (44) vs. Washington (46), 1999

AVERAGE GAIN
Highest Average Gain, Game
9.94 AFC: San Diego vs. Boston, 1963 (32-318)
9.29 NFC-D: Green Bay vs. Dallas, 1982 (17-158)
7.35 NFC: Dallas vs. Los Angeles, 1980 (46-338)

Lowest Average Gain, Game
– 0.27 NFC-FR: Detroit vs. Green Bay, 1994 (15-(– 4))
0.58 AFC-D: Buffalo vs. Boston, 1963 (12-7)
0.64 SB: New England vs. Chicago, 1985 (11-7)

TOUCHDOWNS
Most Touchdowns, Game
7 NFC: Chi. Bears vs. Washington, 1940
6 NFC-D: San Francisco vs. N.Y. Giants, 1993
5 NFC: Cleveland vs. Detroit, 1954
   NFC-D: San Francisco vs. Chicago, 1994
   AFC-FR: Pittsburgh vs. Indianapolis, 1996
   AFC-FR: Denver vs. Jacksonville, 1997

Most Touchdowns, Both Teams, Game
7 NFC: Chi. Bears (7) vs. Washington (0), 1940
6 NFC: Cleveland (5) vs. Detroit (1), 1954
   NFC-D: San Francisco (6) vs. N.Y. Giants (0), 1993
   NFC-D: San Francisco (5) vs. Chicago (1), 1994
   AFC-FR: Denver (5) vs. Jacksonville (1), 1997
5 NFC: Chi. Cardinals (3) vs. Philadelphia (2), 1947
   AFC: San Diego (4) vs. Boston (1), 1963
   AFC-D: Cincinnati (3) vs. Buffalo (2), 1981
   AFC-FR: Pittsburgh (5) vs. Indianapolis (0), 1996
   NFC-D: Arizona (3) vs. Minnesota (2), 1998

PASSING
ATTEMPTS
Most Attempts, Game
66 AFC-FR: Miami vs. Buffalo, 1995
65 AFC-D: Cleveland vs. N.Y. Jets, 1986 (OT)

NFC-D: San Francisco vs. Green Bay, 1995
61 NFC-FR: Minnesota vs. Chicago, 1994

Fewest Attempts, Game
5 NFC: Detroit vs. N.Y. Giants, 1935
6 AFC: Miami vs. Oakland, 1973
7 SB: Miami vs. Minnesota, 1973

Most Attempts, Both Teams, Game
102 AFC-D: San Diego (54) vs. Miami (48), 1981 (OT)
96 AFC: N.Y. Jets (49) vs. Oakland (47), 1968
95 AFC-D: Cleveland (65) vs. N.Y. Jets (30), 1986 (OT)

Fewest Attempts, Both Teams, Game
18 NFC: Detroit (5) vs. N.Y. Giants (13), 1935
23 NFC: Chi. Cardinals (11) vs. Philadelphia (12), 1948
24 NFC-D: Cleveland (9) vs. N.Y. Giants (15), 1950

COMPLETIONS

Most Completions, Game
36 AFC-FR: Houston vs. Buffalo, 1992 (OT)
34 AFC-D: Cleveland vs. N.Y. Jets, 1986 (OT)
   AFC-FR: Miami vs. Buffalo, 1995
33 AFC-D: San Diego vs. Miami, 1981 (OT)
   NFC-FR: Minnesota vs. Chicago, 1994

Fewest Completions, Game
2 NFC: Detroit vs. N.Y. Giants, 1935
   NFC: Philadelphia vs. Chi. Cardinals, 1948
3 NFC: N.Y. Giants vs. Chi. Bears, 1941
   NFC: Green Bay vs. N.Y. Giants, 1944
   NFC: Chi. Cardinals vs. Philadelphia, 1947
   NFC: Chi. Cardinals vs. Philadelphia, 1948
   NFC-D: Cleveland vs. N.Y. Giants, 1950
   NFC-D: N.Y. Giants vs. Cleveland, 1950
   NFC: Cleveland vs. Detroit, 1953
   AFC: Miami vs. Oakland, 1973
4 NFC: N.Y. Giants vs. Detroit, 1935
   NFC-D: N.Y. Giants vs. Washington, 1943
   NFC-D: Pittsburgh vs. Philadelphia, 1947
   NFC-D: Dallas vs. Detroit, 1970
   AFC: Miami vs. Baltimore, 1971
   SB: Miami vs. Washington, 1982
   AFC-FR: Seattle vs. L.A. Raiders, 1984

Most Completions, Both Teams, Game
64 AFC-D: San Diego (33) vs. Miami (31), 1981 (OT)
57 AFC-FR: Houston (36) vs. Buffalo (21), 1992 (OT)
56 NFC-D: Dallas (28) vs. Green Bay (28), 1993
   NFC: Minnesota (29) vs. Atlanta (27), 1998 (OT)
   NFC-D: Minnesota (29) vs. St. Louis (27), 1999

Fewest Completions, Both Teams, Game
5 NFC: Philadelphia (2) vs. Chi. Cardinals (3), 1948
6 NFC: Detroit (2) vs. N.Y. Giants (4), 1935
   NFC-D: Cleveland (3) vs. N.Y. Giants (3), 1950
11 NFC: Green Bay (3) vs. N.Y. Giants (8), 1944
   NFC-D: Dallas (4) vs. Detroit (7), 1970

COMPLETION PERCENTAGE

Highest Completion Percentage, Game (20 attempts)
88.0 SB: N.Y. Giants vs. Denver, 1986 (25-22)
87.1 NFC: San Francisco vs. L.A. Rams, 1989 (31-27)
81.8 NFC-D: St. Louis vs. Minnesota, 1999 (33-27)

Lowest Completion Percentage, Game (20 attempts)
18.5 NFC: Tampa Bay vs. Los Angeles, 1979 (27-5)
20.0 NFC-D: N.Y. Giants vs. Washington, 1943 (20-4)
25.8 NFC: Chi. Bears vs. Washington, 1937 (31-8)

YARDS GAINED

Most Yards Gained, Game
483 AFC-D: Cleveland vs. N.Y. Jets, 1986 (OT)
435 AFC: Miami vs. Pittsburgh, 1984
432 AFC-FR: Miami vs. Buffalo, 1995

Fewest Yards Gained, Game
3 NFC: Chi. Cardinals vs. Philadelphia, 1948

7 NFC: Philadelphia vs. Chi. Cardinals, 1948
9 NFC-D: N.Y. Giants vs. Cleveland, 1950
   NFC: Cleveland vs. Detroit, 1953

Most Yards Gained, Both Teams, Game
809 AFC-D: San Diego (415) vs. Miami (394), 1981 (OT)
762 NFC-D: Minnesota (388) vs. St. Louis (374), 1999
747 AFC: Miami (435) vs. Pittsburgh (312), 1984

Fewest Yards Gained, Both Teams, Game
10 NFC: Chi. Cardinals (3) vs. Philadelphia (7), 1948
38 NFC-D: N.Y. Giants (9) vs. Cleveland (29), 1950
102 NFC-D: Dallas (22) vs. Detroit (80), 1970

TIMES SACKED

Most Times Sacked, Game
9 AFC: Kansas City vs. Buffalo, 1966
   NFC: Chicago vs. San Francisco, 1984
   AFC-D: N.Y. Jets vs. Cleveland, 1986 (OT)
   AFC-D: Houston vs. Kansas City, 1993
8 NFC: Green Bay vs. Dallas, 1967
   NFC: Minnesota vs. Washington, 1987
7 NFC-D: Dallas vs. Los Angeles, 1973
   SB: Dallas vs. Pittsburgh, 1975
   AFC-FR: Houston vs. Oakland, 1980
   NFC-D: Washington vs. Chicago, 1984
   SB: New England vs. Chicago, 1985
   AFC-FR: Kansas City vs. San Diego, 1992
   AFC-D: Pittsburgh vs. Buffalo, 1992

Most Times Sacked, Both Teams, Game
13 AFC: Kansas City (9) vs. Buffalo (4), 1966
   AFC-D: N.Y. Jets (9) vs. Cleveland (4), 1986 (OT)
12 NFC-D: Dallas (7) vs. Los Angeles (5), 1973
   NFC-D: Washington (7) vs. Chicago (5), 1984
   NFC: Chicago (9) vs. San Francisco (3), 1984
   AFC-FR: Kansas City (7) vs. San Diego (5), 1992
11 AFC-D: Houston (9) vs. Kansas City (2), 1993

Fewest Times Sacked, Both Teams, Game
0 AFC-D: Buffalo vs. Pittsburgh, 1974
   AFC-FR: Pittsburgh vs. San Diego, 1982
   AFC: Miami vs. Pittsburgh, 1984
   AFC-D: Buffalo vs. Miami, 1990
   AFC-D: Denver vs. Houston, 1991
   AFC-FR: Buffalo vs. Miami, 1995
   AFC-D: Indianapolis vs. Tennessee, 1999
1 In many games

TOUCHDOWNS

Most Touchdowns, Game
6 AFC-D: Oakland vs. Houston, 1969
   SB: San Francisco vs. San Diego, 1994
5 NFC: Chi. Bears vs. Washington, 1943
   NFC: Detroit vs. Cleveland, 1957
   AFC-D: Oakland vs. Kansas City, 1968
   SB: San Francisco vs. Denver, 1989
   NFC-D: St. Louis vs. Minnesota, 1999
   NFC: N.Y. Giants vs. Minnesota, 2000
4 By many teams

Most Touchdowns, Both Teams, Game
9 NFC-D: St. Louis (5) vs. Minnesota (4), 1999
8 AFC-FR: Buffalo (4) vs. Houston (4), 1992 (OT)
7 NFC: Chi. Bears (5) vs. Washington (2), 1943
   AFC-D: Oakland (6) vs. Houston (1), 1969
   SB: Pittsburgh (4) vs. Dallas (3), 1978
   AFC-D: Miami (4) vs. San Diego (3), 1981 (OT)
   AFC: Miami (4) vs. Pittsburgh (3), 1984
   AFC-D: Buffalo (4) vs. Cleveland (3), 1989
   SB: San Francisco (6) vs. San Diego (1), 1994
   NFC-FR: Detroit (4) vs. Philadelphia (3), 1995
   NFC-FR: New Orleans (4) vs. St. Louis (3), 2000

INTERCEPTIONS BY
Most Interceptions By, Game
- 8 NFC: Chi. Bears vs. Washington, 1940
- 7 NFC: Cleveland vs. Los Angeles, 1955
- 6 NFC: Green Bay vs. N.Y. Giants, 1939
- NFC: Chi. Bears vs. N.Y. Giants, 1946
- NFC: Cleveland vs. Detroit, 1954
- AFC: San Diego vs. Houston, 1961
- AFC: Buffalo vs. L.A. Raiders, 1990
- NFC-FR: Philadelphia vs. Detroit, 1995
- NFC-D: St. Louis vs. Green Bay, 2001

Most Interceptions By, Both Teams, Game
- 10 NFC: Cleveland (7) vs. Los Angeles (3), 1955
- AFC: San Diego (6) vs. Houston (4), 1961
- 9 NFC: Green Bay (6) vs. N.Y. Giants (3), 1939
- 8 NFC: Chi. Bears (8) vs. Washington (0), 1940
- NFC: Chi. Bears (6) vs. N.Y. Giants (2), 1946
- NFC: Cleveland (6) vs. Detroit (2), 1954
- AFC-FR: Buffalo (4) vs. N.Y. Jets (4), 1981
- AFC: Miami (5) vs. N.Y. Jets (3), 1982

YARDS GAINED
Most Yards Gained, Game
- 161 NFC-D: St. Louis vs. Green Bay, 2001
- 138 AFC-FR: N.Y. Jets vs. Cincinnati, 1982
- 136 AFC: Dall. Texans vs. Houston, 1962 (OT)
- SB: Denver vs. Atlanta, 1998

Most Yards Gained, Both Teams, Game
- 161 NFC-D: St. Louis (161) vs. Green Bay (0), 2001
- 156 NFC: Green Bay (123) vs. N.Y. Giants (33), 1939
- 149 NFC: Cleveland (103) vs. Los Angeles (46), 1955

TOUCHDOWNS
Most Touchdowns, Game
- 3 NFC: Chi. Bears vs. Washington, 1940
- NFC-D: St. Louis vs. Green Bay, 2001
- 2 NFC-D: Los Angeles vs. St. Louis, 1975
- NFC-FR: Philadelphia vs. Detroit, 1995
- 1 In many games

Most Touchdowns, Both Teams, Game
- 3 NFC: Chi. Bears (3) vs. Washington (0), 1940
- NFC-D: St. Louis (3) vs. Green Bay (0), 2001
- 2 NFC-D: Los Angeles (2) vs. St. Louis (0), 1975
- NFC-D: Dallas (1) vs. Green Bay (1), 1982
- NFC-D: Minnesota (1) vs. San Francisco (1), 1987
- NFC-FR: Detroit (1) vs. Green Bay (1), 1993
- NFC-FR: Philadelphia (2) vs. Detroit (0), 1995
- AFC-FR: Buffalo (1) vs. Jacksonville (1), 1996
- 1 In many games

PUNTING
Most Punts, Game
- 14 AFC-D: N.Y. Jets vs. Cleveland, 1986 (OT)
- 13 NFC: N.Y. Giants vs. Chi. Bears, 1933
- AFC-D: Baltimore vs. Oakland, 1977 (OT)
- 11 AFC: Houston vs. Oakland, 1967
- AFC-D: Houston vs. Oakland, 1969
- NFC: L.A. Rams vs. Chicago, 1985
- SB: N.Y. Giants vs. Baltimore, 2000

Fewest Punts, Game
- 0 NFC-FR: St. Louis vs. Green Bay, 1982
- AFC-FR: N.Y. Jets vs. Cincinnati, 1982
- 1 By many teams

Most Punts, Both Teams, Game
- 23 NFC: N.Y. Giants (13) vs. Chi. Bears (10), 1933
- 22 AFC-D: N.Y. Jets (14) vs. Cleveland (8), 1986 (OT)
- 21 AFC-D: Baltimore (13) vs. Oakland (8), 1977 (OT)
- NFC: L.A. Rams (11) vs. Chicago (10), 1985
- SB: N.Y. Giants (11) vs. Baltimore (10), 2000

Fewest Punts, Both Teams, Game
- 1 NFC-FR: St. Louis (0) vs. Green Bay (1), 1982
- 2 AFC-FR: N.Y. Jets (0) vs. Cincinnati (2), 1982
- SB: Atlanta (1) vs. Denver (1), 1998
- 3 AFC: Miami (1) vs. Oakland (2), 1973
- AFC-FR: San Diego (1) vs. Pittsburgh (2), 1982
- AFC-D: Buffalo (1) vs. Miami (2), 1990
- AFC-FR: L.A. Raiders (1) vs. Kansas City (2), 1991
- AFC-D: Houston (1) vs. Denver (2), 1991
- NFC-FR: Dallas (1) vs. Minnesota (2), 1996
- AFC-FR: Miami (1) vs. Buffalo (2), 1998
- NFC: Minnesota (1) vs. Arizona (2), 1998
- AFC-FR: N.Y. Jets (1) vs. Oakland (2), 2001

AVERAGE YARDAGE
Highest Average, Punting, Game (4 punts)
- 56.0 AFC: Oakland vs. San Diego, 1980
- 52.5 NFC: Washington vs. Chi. Bears, 1942
- 52.0 AFC-D: Tennessee vs. Indianapolis, 1999

Lowest Average, Punting, Game (4 punts)
- 24.9 NFC: Washington vs. Chi. Bears, 1937
- 25.3 AFC-FR: Pittsburgh vs. Houston, 1989
- 25.5 NFC: Green Bay vs. N.Y. Giants, 1962

PUNT RETURNS
Most Punt Returns, Game
- 8 NFC: Green Bay vs. N.Y. Giants, 1944
- 7 By many teams

Most Punt Returns, Both Teams, Game
- 13 AFC-FR: Houston (7) vs. Oakland (6), 1980
- 12 AFC-D: New England (7) vs. Pittsburgh (5), 1996
- 11 NFC: Green Bay (8) vs. N.Y. Giants (3), 1944
- NFC-D: Green Bay (6) vs. Baltimore (5), 1965
- AFC-FR: Jacksonville (7) vs. New England (4), 1998

Fewest Punt Returns, Both Teams, Game
- 0 NFC: Chi. Bears vs. N.Y. Giants, 1941
- AFC: Boston vs. San Diego, 1963
- NFC-FR: Green Bay vs. St. Louis, 1982
- AFC-FR: Houston vs. N.Y. Jets, 1991
- AFC-D: Denver vs. Houston, 1991
- NFC-D: San Francisco vs. Washington, 1992
- SB: Denver vs. Green Bay, 1997
- SB: Atlanta vs. Denver, 1998
- AFC-FR: Oakland vs. N.Y. Jets, 2001
- 1 In many games

YARDS GAINED
Most Yards Gained, Game
- 155 NFC-D: Dallas vs. Cleveland, 1967
- 150 NFC: Chi. Cardinals vs. Philadelphia, 1947
- 143 NFC-FR: Minnesota vs. New Orleans, 1987

Fewest Yards Gained, Game
- −10 NFC: Green Bay vs. Cleveland, 1965
- −9 NFC: Dallas vs. Green Bay, 1966
- AFC-D: Kansas City vs. Oakland, 1968
- −7 NFC-D: San Francisco vs. Atlanta, 1998

Most Yards Gained, Both Teams, Game
- 166 NFC-D: Dallas (155) vs. Cleveland (11), 1967
- AFC-D: Baltimore (99) vs. Pittsburgh (67), 2001
- 160 NFC: Chi. Cardinals (150) vs. Philadelphia (10), 1947
- 146 NFC-D: Philadelphia (112) vs. Pittsburgh (34), 1947

Fewest Yards Gained, Both Teams, Game
- −9 NFC: Dallas (−9) vs. Green Bay (0), 1966
- −6 AFC-D: Miami (−5) vs. Oakland (−1), 1970
- −3 NFC-D: San Francisco (−5) vs. Dallas (2), 1972

TOUCHDOWNS
Most Touchdowns, Game
- 1 By 14 teams

KICKOFF RETURNS
Most Kickoff Returns, Game
- 10 NFC-D: L.A. Rams vs. Washington, 1983
  - NFC-FR: Detroit vs. Philadelphia, 1995
- 9 NFC: Chi. Bears vs. N.Y. Giants, 1956
  - AFC: Boston vs. San Diego, 1963
  - AFC: Houston vs. Oakland, 1967
  - SB: Denver vs. San Francisco, 1989
  - AFC-D: Miami vs. Buffalo, 1990
  - AFC: L.A. Raiders vs. Buffalo, 1990
  - AFC-D: Miami vs. Jacksonville, 1999
- 8 By many teams

Most Kickoff Returns, Both Teams, Game
- 15 AFC-D: Miami (9) vs. Buffalo (6), 1990
- 14 NFC-FR: Detroit (10) vs. Philadelphia (4), 1995
- 13 NFC-D: Green Bay (7) vs. Dallas (6), 1982
  - NFC-FR: Green Bay (7) vs. San Francisco (6), 1998
  - AFC-FR: N.Y. Jets (8) vs. Oakland (5), 2001

Fewest Kickoff Returns, Both Teams, Game
- 1 NFC: Green Bay (0) vs. Boston (1), 1936
  - AFC-FR: San Diego (0) vs. Kansas City (1), 1992
- 2 NFC-D: Los Angeles (0) vs. Chi. Bears (2), 1950
  - AFC: Houston (0) vs. San Diego (2), 1961
  - AFC-D: Oakland (1) vs. Pittsburgh (1), 1972
  - AFC-D: N.Y. Jets (0) vs. L.A. Raiders (2), 1982
  - AFC: Miami (1) vs. N.Y. Jets (1), 1982
  - NFC: N.Y. Giants (0) vs. Washington (2), 1986
- 3 In many games

YARDS GAINED
Most Yards Gained, Game
- 244 SB: San Diego vs. San Francisco, 1994
- 227 SB: Atlanta vs. Denver, 1998
- 225 NFC: Washington vs. Chi. Bears, 1940

Most Yards Gained, Both Teams, Game
- 379 AFC-D: Baltimore (193) vs. Oakland (186), 1977 (OT)
- 348 NFC-D: Minnesota (174) vs. St. Louis (174), 1999
- 322 NFC-D: Green Bay (194) vs. San Francisco (128), 1998

Fewest Yards Gained, Both Teams, Game
- 5 AFC-FR: San Diego (0) vs. Kansas City (5), 1992
- 15 NFC: N.Y. Giants (0) vs. Washington (15), 1986
- 31 NFC-D: Los Angeles (0) vs. Chi. Bears (31), 1950

TOUCHDOWNS
Most Touchdowns, Game
- 1 NFC-D: San Francisco vs. Dallas, 1972
  - AFC-D: Miami vs. Oakland, 1974
  - AFC-D: Baltimore vs. Oakland, 1977 (OT)
  - SB: Miami vs. Washington, 1982
  - SB: Cincinnati vs. San Francisco, 1988
  - AFC-D: Cleveland vs. Buffalo, 1989
  - SB: San Diego vs. San Francisco, 1994
  - SB: Green Bay vs. New England, 1996
  - NFC: San Francisco vs. Green Bay, 1997
  - SB: Atlanta vs. Denver, 1998
  - AFC-FR: Tennessee vs. Buffalo, 1999
  - AFC-FR: Seattle vs. Miami, 1999
  - NFC-D: Washington vs. Tampa Bay, 1999
  - NFC-D: St. Louis vs. Minnesota, 1999
  - AFC: Tennessee vs. Jacksonville, 1999
  - NFC-D: N.Y. Giants vs. Philadelphia, 2000
  - SB: Baltimore vs. N.Y. Giants, 2000
  - SB: N.Y. Giants vs. Baltimore, 2000

Most Touchdowns, Both Teams, Game
- 2 SB: Baltimore (1) vs. N.Y. Giants (1), 2000

PENALTIES
Most Penalties, Game
- 17 AFC-FR: L.A. Raiders vs. Denver, 1993

- 14 AFC-FR: Oakland vs. Houston, 1980
  - NFC-D: San Francisco vs. N.Y. Giants, 1981
- 13 AFC-FR: Houston vs. Cleveland, 1988
  - AFC-D: Houston vs. Denver, 1991
  - NFC-D: Arizona vs. Minnesota, 1998

Fewest Penalties, Game
- 0 NFC: Philadelphia vs. Green Bay, 1960
  - NFC-D: Detroit vs. Dallas, 1970
  - AFC-D: Miami vs. Oakland, 1970
  - SB: Miami vs. Dallas, 1971
  - NFC-D: Washington vs. Minnesota, 1973
  - SB: Pittsburgh vs. Dallas, 1975
  - NFC: San Francisco vs. Chicago, 1988
  - SB: Denver vs. San Francisco, 1989
  - AFC-D: L.A. Raiders vs. Cincinnati, 1990
  - AFC-D: Miami vs. San Diego, 1992
  - SB: Atlanta vs. Denver, 1998
  - AFC-FR: N.Y. Jets vs. Oakland, 2001
- 1 By many teams

Most Penalties, Both Teams, Game
- 27 AFC-FR: L.A. Raiders (17) vs. Denver (10), 1993
- 22 AFC-FR: Oakland (14) vs. Houston (8), 1980
  - NFC-D: San Francisco (14) vs. N.Y. Giants (8), 1981
  - AFC-FR: Houston (13) vs. Cleveland (9), 1988
  - NFC-D: Arizona (13) vs. Minnesota (9), 1998
- 21 AFC-D: Oakland (11) vs. New England (10), 1976

Fewest Penalties, Both Teams, Game
- 1 AFC-D: L.A. Raiders (0) vs. Cincinnati (1), 1990
- 2 NFC: Washington (1) vs. Chi. Bears (1), 1937
  - NFC-D: Washington (0) vs. Minnesota (2), 1973
  - SB: Pittsburgh (0) vs. Dallas (2), 1975
- 3 AFC: Miami (1) vs. Baltimore (2), 1971
  - NFC: San Francisco (1) vs. Dallas (2), 1971
  - SB: Miami (0) vs. Dallas (3), 1971
  - AFC-D: Pittsburgh (1) vs. Oakland (2), 1972
  - AFC-D: Miami (1) vs. Cincinnati (2), 1973
  - SB: Miami (1) vs. San Francisco (2), 1984
  - NFC: San Francisco (0) vs. Chicago (3), 1988

YARDS PENALIZED
Most Yards Penalized, Game
- 145 NFC-D: San Francisco vs. N.Y. Giants, 1981
- 133 SB: Dallas vs. Baltimore, 1970
- 130 AFC-FR: L.A. Raiders vs. Denver, 1993

Fewest Yards Penalized, Game
- 0 By 12 teams

Most Yards Penalized, Both Teams, Game
- 227 AFC-FR: L.A. Raiders (130) vs. Denver (97), 1993
- 206 NFC-D: San Francisco (145) vs. N.Y. Giants (61), 1981
- 201 NFC-FR: Detroit (126) vs. Washington (75), 1999

Fewest Yards Penalized, Both Teams, Game
- 5 AFC-D: L.A. Raiders (0) vs. Cincinnati (5), 1990
- 9 NFC-D: Washington (0) vs. Minnesota (9), 1973
- 15 SB: Miami (0) vs. Dallas (15), 1971

FUMBLES
Most Fumbles, Game
- 8 SB: Buffalo vs. Dallas, 1992
- 7 AFC-D: Houston vs. Kansas City, 1993
- 6 By 12 teams

Most Fumbles, Both Teams, Game
- 12 AFC: Houston (6) vs. Pittsburgh (6), 1978
  - SB: Buffalo (8) vs. Dallas (4), 1992
- 10 NFC: Chi. Bears (5) vs. N.Y. Giants (5), 1934
  - SB: Dallas (6) vs. Denver (4), 1977
  - AFC: Jacksonville (5) vs. Tennessee (5), 1999
- 9 NFC-D: San Francisco (6) vs. Detroit (3), 1957
  - NFC-D: San Francisco (5) vs. Dallas (4), 1972
  - NFC: Dallas (5) vs. Philadelphia (4), 1980

Most Fumbles Lost, Game
- 5 SB: Buffalo vs. Dallas, 1992
  AFC-D: Miami vs. Jacksonville, 1999
- 4 NFC: N.Y. Giants vs. Baltimore, 1958 (OT)
  AFC: Kansas City vs. Oakland, 1969
  SB: Baltimore vs. Dallas, 1970
  AFC: Pittsburgh vs. Oakland, 1975
  SB: Denver vs. Dallas, 1977
  AFC: Houston vs. Pittsburgh, 1978
  AFC: Miami vs. New England, 1985
  SB: New England vs. Chicago, 1985
  NFC-FR: L.A. Rams vs. Washington, 1986
  NFC-FR: Minnesota vs. Dallas, 1996
  AFC-FR: Buffalo vs. Miami, 1998
  AFC: N.Y. Jets vs. Denver, 1998
  AFC: Jacksonville vs. Tennessee, 1999
- 3 By many teams

Fewest Fumbles, Both Teams, Game
- 0 NFC: Green Bay vs. Cleveland, 1965
  AFC-D: Houston vs. San Diego, 1979
  NFC-D: Dallas vs. Los Angeles, 1979
  SB: Los Angeles vs. Pittsburgh, 1979
  AFC-D: Buffalo vs. Cincinnati, 1981
  NFC: Minnesota vs. Washington, 1987
  NFC-D: San Francisco vs. Washington, 1990
  NFC: Dallas vs. Green Bay, 1995
  AFC-D: New England vs. Pittsburgh, 1996
  SB: Green Bay vs. New England, 1996
  AFC-FR: Miami vs. Seattle, 1999
  AFC-FR: Miami vs. Indianapolis, 2000 (OT)
  AFC-D: Baltimore vs. Tennessee, 2000
- 1 In many games

RECOVERIES

Most Total Fumbles Recovered, Game
- 8 SB: Dallas vs. Denver, 1977 (4 own, 4 opp)
- 7 NFC: Chi. Bears vs. N.Y. Giants, 1934 (5 own, 2 opp)
  NFC-D: San Francisco vs. Detroit, 1957 (4 own, 3 opp)
  NFC-D: San Francisco vs. Dallas, 1972 (4 own, 3 opp)
  AFC: Pittsburgh vs. Houston, 1978 (3 own, 4 opp)
- 6 AFC: Houston vs. San Diego, 1961 (4 own, 2 opp)
  AFC-D: Cleveland vs. Baltimore, 1971 (4 own, 2 opp)
  AFC-D: Cleveland vs. Oakland, 1980 (5 own, 1 opp)
  NFC: Philadelphia vs. Dallas, 1980 (3 own, 3 opp)
  SB: Dallas vs. Buffalo, 1992 (1 own, 5 opp)
  NFC-D: Green Bay vs. San Francisco, 1996
    (4 own, 2 opp)
  AFC: Denver vs. N.Y. Jets, 1998 (2 own, 4 opp)
  AFC: Tennessee vs. Jacksonville, 1999 (2 own, 4 opp)

Most Own Fumbles Recovered, Game
- 5 NFC: Chi. Bears vs. N.Y. Giants, 1934
  AFC-D: Cleveland vs. Oakland, 1980
- 4 By many teams

TOUCHDOWNS

Most Touchdowns, Game
- 2 SB: Dallas vs. Buffalo, 1992

TURNOVERS

Numbers of times losing the ball on interceptions and fumbles.

Most Turnovers, Game
- 9 NFC: Washington vs. Chi. Bears, 1940
  NFC: Detroit vs. Cleveland, 1954
  AFC: Houston vs. Pittsburgh, 1978
  SB: Buffalo vs. Dallas, 1992
- 8 NFC: N.Y. Giants vs. Chi. Bears, 1946
  NFC: Los Angeles vs. Cleveland, 1955
  NFC: Cleveland vs. Detroit, 1957
  SB: Denver vs. Dallas, 1977
  NFC-D: Minnesota vs. Philadelphia, 1980

NFC-D: Green Bay vs. St. Louis, 2001
- 7 In many games

Fewest Turnovers, Game
- 0 By many teams

Most Turnovers, Both Teams, Game
- 14 AFC: Houston (9) vs. Pittsburgh (5), 1978
- 13 NFC: Detroit (9) vs. Cleveland (4), 1954
  AFC: Houston (7) vs. San Diego (6), 1961
- 12 AFC: Pittsburgh (7) vs. Oakland (5), 1975

Fewest Turnovers, Both Teams, Game
- 0 SB: Buffalo vs. N.Y. Giants, 1990
  AFC-FR: Kansas City vs. Pittsburgh, 1993 (OT)
  NFC-FR: Detroit vs. Green Bay, 1994
  AFC-FR: Denver vs. Jacksonville, 1996
  SB: St. Louis vs. Tennessee, 1999
- 1 AFC-D: Baltimore (0) vs. Cincinnati (1), 1970
  AFC-D: Pittsburgh (0) vs. Buffalo (1), 1974
  AFC: Oakland (0) vs. Pittsburgh (1), 1976
  NFC-D: Minnesota (0) vs. Washington (1), 1982
  NFC-D: Chicago (0) vs. N.Y. Giants (1), 1985
  SB: N.Y. Giants (0) vs. Denver (1), 1986
  NFC: Washington (0) vs. Minnesota (1), 1987
  AFC-D: Cincinnati (0) vs. L.A. Raiders (1), 1990
  NFC: N.Y. Giants (0) vs. San Francisco (1), 1990
  NFC-FR: N.Y. Giants (0) vs. Minnesota (1), 1993
  AFC-FR: L.A. Raiders (0) vs. Denver (1), 1993
  NFC: Dallas (0) vs. San Francisco (1), 1993
  AFC: Indianapolis (0) vs. Pittsburgh (1), 1995
  NFC-D: San Francisco (0) vs. Minnesota (1), 1997
  AFC-D: Indianapolis (0) vs. Tennessee (1), 1999
  AFC-FR: Baltimore (0) vs. Denver (1), 2000
  AFC-D: Baltimore (0) vs. Tennessee (1), 2000
  AFC-D: Oakland (0) vs. New England (1), 2001
- 2 In many games

Includes records of AFC-NFC Pro Bowls, 1971-2002
Compiled by Elias Sports Bureau

INDIVIDUAL RECORDS

SERVICE
Most Games
- 12 Randall McDaniel, Minnesota 1990-2000; Tampa Bay 2001
- 11 *Reggie White, Philadelphia, 1987-1993; Green Bay, 1994, 1996-97, 1999
  Junior Seau, San Diego, 1992-2002
- 10 Lawrence Taylor, N.Y. Giants, 1982-1991
  Ronnie Lott, San Francisco, 1982-85, 1987-1991; L.A. Raiders 1992
  Mike Singletary, Chicago, 1984-1993
  **Bruce Matthews, Houston, 1989-1995, 1997; Tennessee, 2000, 2002
  Rod Woodson, Pittsburgh, 1990-95, 1997; Baltimore, 2000-02

*Also selected, but did not play, in two additional games
**Also selected, but did not play, in four additional games

SCORING
POINTS
Most Points, Career
- 45 Morten Andersen, New Orleans, 1986-89, 1991, 1993; Atlanta, 1996 (15-pat, 10-fg)
- 30 Jan Stenerud, Kansas City, 1971-72, 1976; Minnesota, 1985 (6-pat, 8-fg)
  Jimmy Smith, Jacksonville, 1998-2001 (5-td)
- 26 Nick Lowery, Kansas City, 1982, 1991, 1993 (5 pat, 7 fg)

Most Points, Game
- 18 John Brockington, Green Bay, 1973 (3-td)
  Mike Alstott, Tampa Bay, 2000 (3-td)
  Jimmy Smith, Jacksonville, 2000 (3-td)
- 15 Garo Yepremian, Miami, 1974 (5-fg)
  Jason Hanson, Detroit, 2000 (6-pat, 3-fg)
- 14 Jan Stenerud, Kansas City, 1972 (2-pat, 4-fg)

TOUCHDOWNS
Most Touchdowns, Career
- 5 Jimmy Smith, Jacksonville, 1998-2001 (5-p)
- 3 John Brockington, Green Bay, 1972-74 (2-r, 1-p)
  Earl Campbell, Houston, 1979-1982, 1984 (3-r)
  Chuck Muncie, New Orleans, 1980; San Diego, 1982-83 (3-r)
  William Andrews, Atlanta, 1981-84 (1-r, 2-p)
  Marcus Allen, L.A. Raiders, 1983, 1985-86, 1988; Kansas City, 1994 (2-r, 1-p)
  Cris Carter, Minnesota, 1994-2001 (3-p)
  Mike Alstott, Tampa Bay, 1998-2002 (3-r)
  Curtis Martin, New England, 1996-97; N.Y. Jets, 1999, 2002 (2-r, 1-p)
  Marvin Harrison, Indianapolis, 2000-02 (3-p)
- 2 By 18 players

Most Touchdowns, Game
- 3 John Brockington, Green Bay, 1973 (2-r, 1-p)
  Mike Alstott, Tampa Bay, 2000 (3-r)
  Jimmy Smith, Jacksonville, 2000 (3-p)
- 2 Mel Renfro, Dallas, 1971 (2-ret)
  Earl Campbell, Houston, 1980 (2-r)
  Chuck Muncie, New Orleans, 1980 (2-r)
  William Andrews, Atlanta, 1984 (2-p)
  Herschel Walker, Dallas, 1989 (2-r)
  Johnny Johnson, Phoenix, 1991 (2-r)
  Eric Green, Pittsburgh, 1995 (2-p)
  Marvin Harrison, Indianapolis, 2001 (2-p)

POINTS AFTER TOUCHDOWN
Most Points After Touchdown, Career
- 15 Morten Andersen, New Orleans, 1986-89, 1991, 1993; Atlanta, 1996 (15 att)
- 9 Jason Hanson, Detroit, 1998, 2000 (9 att)
- 8 Jason Elam, Denver, 1996, 1999, 2002 (9 att)

Most Points After Touchdown, Game
- 6 Ali Haji-Sheikh, N.Y. Giants, 1984 (6 att)
  Jason Hanson, Detroit, 2000 (6 att)
- 5 John Carney, San Diego, 1995 (5 att)
  Matt Stover, Baltimore, 2001 (5 att)
  Jason Elam, Denver, 2002 (5 att)
- 4 Chester Marcol, Green Bay, 1973 (4 att)
  Mark Moseley, Washington, 1980 (5 att)
  Morten Andersen, New Orleans, 1986 (4 att), 1989 (4 att)
  Olindo Mare, Miami, 2000 (4 att)

FIELD GOALS
Most Field Goals Attempted, Career
- 18 Morten Andersen, New Orleans, 1986-89, 1991, 1993; Atlanta, 1996
- 15 Jan Stenerud, Kansas City, 1971-72, 1976; Minnesota, 1985
- 10 Nick Lowery, Kansas City, 1982, 1991, 1993

Most Field Goals Attempted, Game
- 6 Jan Stenerud, Kansas City, 1972
  Eddie Murray, Detroit, 1981
  Mark Moseley, Washington, 1983
- 5 Garo Yepremian, Miami, 1974
- 4 Jan Stenerud, Kansas City, 1976
  Nick Lowery, Kansas City, 1991, 1993
  Morten Andersen, New Orleans, 1993
  Cary Blanchard, Indianapolis, 1997
  John Kasay, Carolina, 1997
  David Akers, Philadelphia, 2002

Most Field Goals, Career
- 10 Morten Andersen, New Orleans, 1986-89, 1991, 1993; Atlanta, 1996
- 8 Jan Stenerud, Kansas City, 1971-72, 1976; Minnesota, 1985
- 7 Nick Lowery, Kansas City, 1982, 1991, 1993

Most Field Goals, Game
- 5 Garo Yepremian, Miami, 1974 (5 att)
- 4 Jan Stenerud, Kansas City, 1972 (6 att)
  Eddie Murray, Detroit, 1981 (6 att)
- 3 Nick Lowery, Kansas City, 1991 (4 att)
  Nick Lowery, Kansas City, 1993 (4 att)
  Jason Elam, Denver, 1999 (3 att)
  Jason Hanson, Detroit, 2000 (3 att)
  David Akers, Philadelphia, 2002 (4 att)

Longest Field Goal
- 51 Morten Andersen, New Orleans, 1989
  Jason Hanson, Detroit, 2000
- 49 Fuad Reveiz, Minnesota, 1995
  David Akers, Philadelphia, 2002
- 48 Jan Stenerud, Kansas City, 1972
  Jeff Jaeger, L.A. Raiders, 1992
  Mike Hollis, Jacksonville, 1998
  Martin Gramatica, Tampa Bay, 2001

SAFETIES
Most Safeties, Game
- 1 Art Still, Kansas City, 1983
  Mark Gastineau, N.Y. Jets, 1985
  Greg Townsend, L.A. Raiders, 1992

RUSHING
ATTEMPTS
Most Attempts, Career
- 81 Walter Payton, Chicago, 1977-1981, 1984-87
- 68 O.J. Simpson, Buffalo, 1973-77
- 66 Barry Sanders, Detroit, 1990-93, 1995-98

Most Attempts, Game
- 19 O.J. Simpson, Buffalo, 1974
- 17 Marv Hubbard, Oakland, 1974
- 16 O.J. Simpson, Buffalo, 1973
- Marcus Allen, L.A. Raiders, 1986

YARDS GAINED
Most Yards Gained, Career
- 368 Walter Payton, Chicago, 1977-1981, 1984-87
- 356 O.J. Simpson, Buffalo, 1973-77
- 264 Marshall Faulk, Indianapolis, 1995-96, 1999; St. Louis, 2000, 2002

Most Yards Gained, Game
- 180 Marshall Faulk, Indianapolis, 1995
- 127 Chris Warren, Seattle, 1995
- 112 O. J. Simpson, Buffalo, 1973

Longest Run From Scrimmage
- 49 Marshall Faulk, Indianapolis, 1995 (TD)
- 41 Lawrence McCutcheon, Los Angeles, 1976
- Natrone Means, San Diego, 1995
- Marshall Faulk, Indianapolis, 1995
- 39 Chris Warren, Seattle, 1994
- Priest Holmes, Kansas City, 2002

AVERAGE GAIN
Highest Average Gain, Career (20 attempts)
- 9.36 Chris Warren, Seattle, 1994-96, (25-234)
- 6.95 Marshall Faulk, Indianapolis, 1995-96, 1999; St. Louis, 2000, 2002 (38-264)
- 5.81 Marv Hubbard, Oakland, 1972-74 (36-209)

Highest Average Gain, Game (10 attempts)
- 13.85 Marshall Faulk, Indianapolis, 1995 (13-180)
- 9.07 Chris Warren, Seattle, 1995 (14-127)
- 7.00 O.J. Simpson, Buffalo, 1973 (16-112)
- Ottis Anderson, St. Louis, 1981 (10-70)

TOUCHDOWNS
Most Touchdowns, Career
- 3 Earl Campbell, Houston, 1979-1982, 1984
- Chuck Muncie, New Orleans, 1980; San Diego, 1982-83
- Mike Alstott, Tampa Bay, 1998-2002
- 2 John Brockington, Green Bay, 1972-74
- O.J. Simpson, Buffalo, 1973-77
- Walter Payton, Chicago, 1977-1981, 1984-87
- Marcus Allen, L.A. Raiders, 1983, 1985-86, 1988; Kansas City, 1994
- Herschel Walker, Dallas, 1988-89
- Johnny Johnson, Phoenix, 1991
- Barry Sanders, Detroit, 1990-93, 1995-98
- Curtis Martin, New England, 1996-97; N.Y. Jets, 1999, 2002

Most Touchdowns, Game
- 3 Mike Alstott, Tampa Bay, 2000
- 2 John Brockington, Green Bay, 1973
- Earl Campbell, Houston, 1980
- Chuck Muncie, New Orleans, 1980
- Herschel Walker, Dallas, 1989
- Johnny Johnson, Phoenix, 1991

PASSING
ATTEMPTS
Most Attempts, Career
- 120 Dan Fouts, San Diego, 1980-84, 1986
- 101 Steve Young, San Francisco, 1993-96, 1998-99
- 90 Warren Moon, Houston, 1989-1994; Minnesota, 1995-96; Seattle 1998

Most Attempts, Game
- 32 Bill Kenney, Kansas City, 1984
- Steve Young, San Francisco, 1993
- 30 Dan Fouts, San Diego, 1983
- 28 Jim Hart, St. Louis, 1976
- Jeff Garcia, San Francisco, 2001

COMPLETIONS
Most Completions, Career
- 63 Dan Fouts, San Diego, 1980-84, 1986
- 48 Steve Young, San Francisco, 1993-96, 1998-99
- 45 Warren Moon, Houston, 1989-1994; Minnesota, 1995-96; Seattle 1998

Most Completions, Game
- 21 Joe Theismann, Washington, 1984
- 18 Steve Young, San Francisco, 1993
- 17 Dan Fouts, San Diego, 1983
- Peyton Manning, Indianapolis, 2000

COMPLETION PERCENTAGE
Highest Completion Percentage, Career (40 attempts)
- 71.7 Peyton Manning, Indianapolis, 2000-01 (46-33)
- 68.9 Joe Theismann, Washington, 1983-84 (45-31)
- 64.4 Jim Kelly, Buffalo, 1988, 1991-92 (45-29)

Highest Completion Percentage, Game (10 attempts)
- 90.0 Archie Manning, New Orleans, 1980 (10-9)
- 85.7 Rich Gannon, Oakland, 2001 (14-12)
- 80.0 Rich Gannon, Oakland, 2002 (10-8)

YARDS GAINED
Most Yards Gained, Career
- 890 Dan Fouts, San Diego, 1980-84, 1986
- 614 Steve Young, San Francisco, 1993-96, 1998-99
- 554 Bob Griese, Miami, 1971-72, 1974-75, 1977, 1979

Most Yards Gained, Game
- 274 Dan Fouts, San Diego, 1983
- 270 Peyton Manning, Indianapolis, 2000
- 242 Joe Theismann, Washington, 1984

Longest Completion
- 93 Jeff Blake, Cincinnati (to Thigpen, Pittsburgh), 1996 (TD)
- 80 Mark Brunell, Jacksonville (to Brown, Oakland), 1997 (TD)
- 64 Dan Pastorini, Houston (to Burrough, Houston), 1976 (TD)

AVERAGE GAIN
Highest Average Gain, Career (40 attempts)
- 9.13 Peyton Manning, Indianapolis, 2000-01 (46-420)
- 8.12 Brett Favre, Green Bay, 1993-94, 1996-97 (57-463)
- 8.06 Randall Cunningham, Philadelphia, 1989-1991; Minnesota, 1999 (52-419)

Highest Average Gain, Game (10 attempts)
- 15.27 Randall Cunningham, Philadelphia, 1991 (11-168)
- 13.70 Rich Gannon, Oakland, 2002 (10-137)
- 13.00 Brett Favre, Green Bay, 1997 (11-143)

TOUCHDOWNS
Most Touchdowns, Career
- 5 Rich Gannon, Oakland, 2000-02
- 4 Steve Young, San Francisco, 1993-96, 1998-99
- Peyton Manning, Indianapolis, 2000-01

3   Joe Theismann, Washington, 1983-84
    Joe Montana, San Francisco, 1982, 1984-85, 1988
    Phil Simms, N.Y. Giants, 1986
    Jim Kelly, Buffalo, 1988, 1991-92
    John Elway, Denver, 1987-88, 1994-95, 1999
    Mark Brunell, Jacksonville, 1997-98, 2000
    Donovan McNabb, Philadelphia, 2001-02

Most Touchdowns, Game

3   Joe Theismann, Washington, 1984
    Phil Simms, N.Y. Giants, 1986
2   James Harris, Los Angeles, 1975
    Mike Boryla, Philadelphia, 1976
    Ken Anderson, Cincinnati, 1977
    Jim Kelly, Buffalo, 1991
    Mark Rypien, Washington, 1992
    Steve Young, San Francisco, 1998
    Peyton Manning, Indianapolis, 2000
    Rich Gannon, Oakland, 2001
    Peyton Manning, Indianapolis, 2001
    Rich Gannon, Oakland, 2002
    Donovan McNabb, Philadelphia, 2002

HAD INTERCEPTED
Most Passes Had Intercepted, Career

8   Dan Fouts, San Diego, 1980-84, 1986
6   Jim Hart, St. Louis, 1975-78
5   Ken Stabler, Oakland, 1974-75, 1978

Most Passes Had Intercepted, Game

5   Jim Hart, St. Louis, 1977
4   Ken Stabler, Oakland, 1974
3   Dan Fouts, San Diego, 1986
    Mark Rypien, Washington, 1990
    Steve Young, San Francisco, 1993
    Jim Harbaugh, Indianapolis, 1996
    Vinny Testaverde, N.Y. Jets, 1999

Most Attempts, Without Interception, Game

27 Joe Theismann, Washington, 1984
    Phil Simms, N.Y. Giants, 1986
26 John Brodie, San Francisco, 1971
    Danny White, Dallas, 1983
23 Dave Krieg, Seattle, 1990

PERCENTAGE, PASSES HAD INTERCEPTED
Lowest Percentage, Passes Had Intercepted, Career (40 attempts)

0.00 Joe Theismann, Washington, 1983-84 (45-0)
2.13 Dave Krieg, Seattle, 1985, 1989-1990 (47-1)
      Jeff Garcia, San Francisco, 2001-02 (47-1)
2.22 Jim Kelly, Buffalo, 1988, 1991-92 (45-1)

PASS RECEIVING
RECEPTIONS
Most Receptions, Career

33 Jerry Rice, San Francisco, 1987-88, 1990-94, 1996, 1999
27 Cris Carter, Minnesota, 1994-2001
23 Tim Brown, L.A. Raiders, 1989, 1992, 1994-95; Oakland 1996-98, 2002

Most Receptions, Game

9   Randy Moss, Minnesota, 2000
8   Steve Largent, Seattle, 1986
    Michael Irvin, Dallas, 1992
    Andre Rison, Atlanta, 1993
    Jimmy Smith, Jacksonville, 2000
    Marvin Harrison, Indianapolis, 2001
    Terrell Owens, San Francisco, 2002
7   John Stallworth, Pittsburgh, 1983
    Jerry Rice, San Francisco, 1992
    Isaac Bruce, St. Louis, 1997
    Keyshawn Johnson, N.Y. Jets, 1999

Randy Moss, Minnesota, 1999
Warrick Dunn, Tampa Bay, 2001
Torry Holt, St. Louis, 2001

YARDS GAINED
Most Yards Gained, Career

459 Jerry Rice, San Francisco, 1987-88, 1990-94, 1996, 1999
408 Tim Brown, L.A. Raiders, 1989, 1992, 1994-95; Oakland, 1996-98, 2002
335 Cris Carter, Minnesota, 1994-2001

Most Yards Gained, Game

212 Randy Moss, Minnesota, 2000
137 Tim Brown, Oakland, 1997
129 Tim Brown, Oakland, 1998

Longest Reception

93 Yancey Thigpen, Pittsburgh (from Blake, Cincinnati), 1996 (TD)
80 Tim Brown, Oakland (from Brunell, Jacksonville), 1997 (TD)
64 Ken Burrough, Houston (from Pastorini, Houston), 1976 (TD)

TOUCHDOWNS
Most Touchdowns, Career

5   Jimmy Smith, Jacksonville, 1998-2001
3   Cris Carter, Minnesota, 1994-2001
    Marvin Harrison, Indianapolis, 2000-02
2   Mel Gray, St. Louis, 1975-78
    Cliff Branch, Oakland, 1975-78
    Terry Metcalf, St. Louis, 1975-76, 1978
    Tony Hill, Dallas, 1979-1980, 1986
    William Andrews, Atlanta, 1981-84
    James Lofton, Green Bay, 1979, 1981-86; Buffalo 1992
    Jimmie Giles, Tampa Bay, 1981-83, 1986
    Michael Irvin, Dallas, 1992-95
    Eric Green, Pittsburgh, 1994-95
    Jerry Rice, San Francisco, 1987-88, 1990-94, 1996, 1999
    Tony Gonzalez, Kansas City, 2000-01
    Terrell Owens, San Francisco, 2001-02

Most Touchdowns, Game

3   Jimmy Smith, Jacksonville, 2000
2   William Andrews, Atlanta, 1984
    Eric Green, Pittsburgh, 1995
    Marvin Harrison, Indianapolis, 2001

INTERCEPTIONS BY
Most Interceptions By, Career

4   Everson Walls, Dallas, 1982-84, 1986
    Deion Sanders, Atlanta, 1992-94; San Francisco, 1995; Dallas, 1999
3   Ken Houston, Houston, 1971-73; Washington, 1974-79
    Jack Lambert, Pittsburgh, 1976-1984
    Ted Hendricks, Baltimore, 1972-74; Green Bay, 1975; Oakland, 1981-82; L.A. Raiders, 1983-84
    Mike Haynes, New England, 1978-1981, 1983; L.A. Raiders, 1985-87
2   By 16 players

Most Interceptions By, Game

2   Mel Blount, Pittsburgh, 1977
    Everson Walls, Dallas, 1982, 1983
    LeRoy Irvin, L.A. Rams, 1986
    David Fulcher, Cincinnati, 1990
    Brian Dawkins, Philadelphia, 2000

YARDS GAINED

Most Yards Gained, Career
103 Deion Sanders, Atlanta, 1992-94; San Francisco, 1995; Dallas, 1999
98 Ty Law, New England, 1999, 2002
77 Ted Hendricks, Baltimore, 1972-74; Green Bay, 1975; Oakland, 1981-82; L.A. Raiders, 1983-84

Most Yards Gained, Game
87 Deion Sanders, Dallas, 1999
73 Rod Woodson, Pittsburgh, 1994
67 Ty Law, New England, 1999

Longest Gain
87 Deion Sanders, Dallas, 1999
73 Rod Woodson, Pittsburgh, 1994 (lateral)
67 Ty Law, New England, 1999 (TD)

TOUCHDOWNS

Most Touchdowns, Game
1 Bobby Bell, Kansas City, 1973
Nolan Cromwell, L.A. Rams, 1984
Joey Browner, Minnesota, 1986
Jerry Gray, L.A. Rams, 1990
Mike Johnson, Cleveland, 1990
Junior Seau, San Diego, 1993
Ken Harvey, Washington, 1996
Ashley Ambrose, Cincinnati, 1997
Ty Law, New England, 1999
Derrick Brooks, Tampa Bay, 2000
Aeneas Williams, Arizona, 2000
Ray Lewis, Baltimore, 2002

PUNTING

Most Punts, Career
33 Ray Guy, Oakland, 1974-79, 1981
23 Rohn Stark, Indianapolis, 1986-87, 1991, 1993
22 Reggie Roby, Miami, 1985, 1990; Washington, 1995

Most Punts, Game
10 Reggie Roby, Miami, 1985
9 Tom Wittum, San Francisco, 1974
Rohn Stark, Indianapolis, 1987
8 Jerrel Wilson, Kansas City, 1971
Tom Skladany, Detroit, 1982
Reggie Roby, Washington, 1995

Longest Punt
73 Shane Lechler, Oakland, 2002
70 Shane Lechler, Oakland, 2002
64 Tom Wittum, San Francisco, 1974
Darren Bennett, San Diego, 1996

AVERAGE YARDAGE

Highest Average, Career (10 punts)
46.73 Reggie Roby, Miami, 1985, 1990; Washington, 1995 (22-1,028)
45.27 Matt Turk, Washington, 1997-99 (15-679)
45.25 Jerrel Wilson, Kansas City, 1971-73 (16-724)

Highest Average, Game (4 punts)
60.75 Shane Lechler, Oakland, 2002 (4-243)
55.50 Darren Bennett, San Diego, 1996 (4-222)
52.00 Matt Turk, Washington, 1999 (4-208)

PUNT RETURNS

Most Punt Returns, Career
13 Rick Upchurch, Denver, 1977, 1979-1980, 1983
11 Vai Sikahema, St. Louis, 1987-88
Eric Metcalf, Cleveland 1994-95; San Diego 1998
10 Mike Nelms, Washington, 1981-83

Most Punt Returns, Game
7 Vai Sikahema, St. Louis, 1987
6 Henry Ellard, L.A. Rams, 1985
Gerald McNeil, Cleveland, 1988

Eric Metcalf, Cleveland, 1995
5 Rick Upchurch, Denver, 1980
Mike Nelms, Washington, 1981
Carl Roaches, Houston, 1982
Johnny Bailey, Phoenix, 1993

Most Fair Catches, Game
2 Jerry Logan, Baltimore, 1971
Dick Anderson, Miami, 1974
Henry Ellard, L.A. Rams, 1985
Isaac Bruce, St. Louis, 1997
Desmond Howard, Detroit, 2001

YARDS GAINED

Most Yards Gained, Career
183 Billy Johnson, Houston, 1976, 1978; Atlanta, 1984
138 Mel Renfro, Dallas, 1971-72, 1974
Rick Upchurch, Denver, 1977, 1979-1980, 1983
135 Eric Metcalf, Cleveland, 1994-95; San Diego 1998

Most Yards Gained, Game
159 Billy Johnson, Houston, 1976
138 Mel Renfro, Dallas, 1971
117 Wally Henry, Philadelphia, 1980

Longest Punt Return
90 Billy Johnson, Houston, 1976 (TD)
86 Wally Henry, Philadelphia, 1980 (TD)
82 Mel Renfro, Dallas, 1971 (TD)

AVERAGE YARDAGE

Highest Average, Career (4 returns)
22.88 Billy Johnson, Houston, 1976, 1978; Atlanta, 1984 (8-183)
21.50 Tony Green, Washington, 1979 (4-86)
15.67 David Meggett, N.Y. Giants, 1990; New England, 1997

Highest Average, Game (3 returns)
39.75 Billy Johnson, Houston, 1976 (4-159)
39.00 Wally Henry, Philadelphia, 1980 (3-117)
21.50 Tony Green, Washington, 1979 (4-86)

TOUCHDOWNS

Most Touchdowns, Game
2 Mel Renfro, Dallas, 1971
1 Billy Johnson, Houston, 1976
Wally Henry, Philadelphia, 1980

KICKOFF RETURNS

Most Kickoff Returns, Career
17 Michael Bates, Carolina, 1997-2001
14 Mel Gray, Detroit, 1991-92, 1995
11 Eric Metcalf, Cleveland, 1994-95; San Diego, 1998

Most Kickoff Returns, Game
7 Mel Gray, Detroit, 1995
6 Greg Pruitt, L.A. Raiders, 1984
David Meggett, New England, 1997
Michael Bates, Carolina, 1998
Steve Smith, Carolina, 2002
5 By seven players

YARDS GAINED

Most Yards Gained, Career
488 Michael Bates, Carolina, 1997-2001
309 Greg Pruitt, Cleveland, 1974-75, 1977-78; L.A. Raiders, 1984
294 Mel Gray, Detroit, 1991-92, 1995

Most Yards Gained, Game
192 Greg Pruitt, L.A. Raiders, 1984
175 Les (Speedy) Duncan, Washington, 1972
173 David Meggett, New England, 1997

Longest Kickoff Return
66 Michael Bates, Carolina, 2000
62 Greg Pruitt, L.A. Raiders, 1984

61   Eugene (Mercury) Morris, Miami, 1972

AVERAGE YARDAGE
Highest Average, Career (4 returns)
35.00   Les (Speedy) Duncan, Washington, 1972 (5-175)
31.25   Eugene (Mercury) Morris, Miami, 1972-73 (4-125)
30.90   Greg Pruitt, Cleveland, 1974-75, 1977-78;
          L.A. Raiders, 1984 (10-309)
Highest Average, Game (3 returns)
42.00   Michael Bates, Carolina, 2000 (4-168)
35.00   Les (Speedy) Duncan, Washington, 1972 (5-175)
33.33   Jermaine Lewis, Baltimore, 2002 (4-133)

TOUCHDOWNS
Most Touchdowns, Game
None

FUMBLES
Most Fumbles, Career
6   Dan Fouts, San Diego, 1980-84, 1986
4   Lawrence McCutcheon, Los Angeles, 1974-78
     Franco Harris, Pittsburgh, 1973-76, 1978-1981
     Jay Schroeder, Washington, 1987
     Vai Sikahema, St. Louis, 1987-88
3   O.J. Simpson, Buffalo, 1973-77
     William Andrews, Atlanta, 1981-84
     Joe Montana, San Francisco, 1982, 1984-85, 1988
     Walter Payton, Chicago, 1977-1981, 1984-87
     Neil Lomax, St. Louis, 1985, 1988
     Jim Kelly, Buffalo, 1988, 1991-92
     Chris Chandler, Atlanta, 1998-99
Most Fumbles, Game
4   Jay Schroeder, Washington, 1987
3   Dan Fouts, San Diego, 1982
     Vai Sikahema, St. Louis, 1987
2   By 14 players

RECOVERIES
Most Fumbles Recovered, Career
3   Harold Jackson, Philadelphia, 1973; Los Angeles,
     1974, 1976, 1978 (3-own)
     Dan Fouts, San Diego, 1980-84, 1986 (3-own)
     Randy White, Dallas, 1978, 1980-86 (3-opp)
2   By many players
Most Fumbles Recovered, Game
2   Dick Anderson, Miami, 1974 (1-own, 1-opp)
     Harold Jackson, Los Angeles, 1974 (2-own)
     Dan Fouts, San Diego, 1982 (2-own)
     Joey Browner, Minnesota, 1990 (2-opp)
     Jessie Armstead, N.Y. Giants, 1999 (1-own, 1-opp)
     Steve Beuerlein, Carolina, 2000 (2-own)

YARDAGE
Longest Fumble Return
83   Art Still, Kansas City, 1985 (TD, opp)
51   Phil Villapiano, Oakland, 1974 (opp)
37   Sam Mills, New Orleans, 1988 (opp)

TOUCHDOWNS
Most Touchdowns, Game
1   Art Still, Kansas City, 1985
     Keith Millard, Minnesota, 1990

SACKS
Sacks have been compiled since 1983.
Most Sacks, Career
9.5   Reggie White, Philadelphia, 1987-1993; Green Bay,
        1994, 1996-97, 1999
9.0   Howie Long, L.A. Raiders, 1984-88, 1990, 1993-1994
7.5   Bruce Smith, Buffalo, 1988-1991, 1995-96, 1998-99

Most Sacks, Game
4   Mark Gastineau, N.Y. Jets, 1985
     Reggie White, Philadelphia, 1987
3   Richard Dent, Chicago, 1985
     Bruce Smith, Buffalo, 1991
2.5   Bruce Smith, Buffalo, 1998

TEAM RECORDS

SCORING
Most Points, Game
51   NFC, 2000
Fewest Points, Game
3   AFC, 1984, 1989, 1994
Most Points, Both Teams, Game
82   NFC (51) vs. AFC (31), 2000
Fewest Points, Both Teams, Game
16   NFC (6) vs. AFC (10), 1987

TOUCHDOWNS
Most Touchdowns, Game
6   NFC, 1984, 2000
Fewest Touchdowns, Game
0   AFC, 1971, 1974, 1984, 1989, 1994
     NFC, 1987, 1988
Most Touchdowns, Both Teams, Game
10   NFC (6) vs. AFC (4), 2000
Fewest Touchdowns, Both Teams, Game
1   AFC (0) vs. NFC (1), 1974
     NFC (0) vs. AFC (1), 1987
     NFC (0) vs. AFC (1), 1988

POINTS AFTER TOUCHDOWN
Most Points After Touchdown, Game
6   NFC, 1984, 2000
Most Points After Touchdown, Both Teams, Game
10   NFC (6) vs. AFC (4), 2000

FIELD GOALS
Most Field Goals Attempted, Game
6   AFC, 1972
     NFC, 1981, 1983
Most Field Goals Attempted, Both Teams, Game
9   NFC (6) vs. AFC (3), 1983
Most Field Goals, Game
5   AFC, 1974
Most Field Goals, Both Teams, Game
7   AFC (5) vs. NFC (2), 1974

NET YARDS GAINED RUSHING AND PASSING
Most Yards Gained, Game
552   AFC, 1995
Fewest Yards Gained, Game
114   AFC, 1993
Most Yards Gained, Both Teams, Game
962   NFC (496) vs. AFC (466), 1997
Fewest Yards Gained, Both Teams, Game
424   AFC (202) vs. NFC (222), 1987

RUSHING
ATTEMPTS
Most Attempts, Game
50   AFC, 1974
Fewest Attempts, Game
9   NFC, 2001
Most Attempts, Both Teams, Game
80   AFC (50) vs. NFC (30), 1974

Fewest Attempts, Both Teams, Game
  32   NFC (9) vs. AFC (23), 2001

YARDS GAINED
Most Yards Gained, Game
  400   AFC, 1995
Fewest Yards Gained, Game
  28   NFC, 1992
Most Yards Gained, Both Teams, Game
  441   AFC (400) vs. NFC (41), 1995
Fewest Yards Gained, Both Teams, Game
  119   NFC (36) vs. AFC (83), 2001

TOUCHDOWNS
Most Touchdowns, Game
  3   NFC, 1989, 1991, 2000
      AFC, 1995
Most Touchdowns, Both Teams, Game
  4   AFC (2) vs. NFC (2), 1973
      AFC (2) vs. NFC (2), 1980

PASSING
ATTEMPTS
Most Attempts, Game
  58   NFC, 2002
Fewest Attempts, Game
  17   NFC, 1972
Most Attempts, Both Teams, Game
  98   NFC (56) vs. AFC (42), 2001
Fewest Attempts, Both Teams, Game
  42   NFC (17) vs. AFC (25), 1972

COMPLETIONS
Most Completions, Game
  32   NFC, 1993
      AFC, 2001
Fewest Completions, Game
  7   NFC, 1972, 1982
Most Completions, Both Teams, Game
  60   AFC (32) vs. NFC (28), 2001
Fewest Completions, Both Teams, Game
  18   NFC (7) vs. AFC (11), 1972

YARDS GAINED
Most Yards Gained, Game
  387   AFC, 1983
Fewest Yards Gained, Game
  42   NFC, 1982
Most Yards Gained, Both Teams, Game
  735   AFC (369) vs. NFC (366), 1997
Fewest Yards Gained, Both Teams, Game
  215   NFC (89) vs. AFC (126), 1972

TIMES SACKED
Most Times Sacked, Game
  9   NFC, 1985
Fewest Times Sacked, Game
  0   AFC, 1998, 1999, 2000
      NFC, 1971, 1997, 2001
Most Times Sacked, Both Teams, Game
  17   NFC (9) vs. AFC (8), 1985
Fewest Times Sacked, Both Teams, Game
  1   NFC (0) vs. AFC (1), 1997

TOUCHDOWNS
Most Touchdowns, Game
  4   NFC, 1984
      AFC, 2000, 2001

Most Touchdowns, Both Teams, Game
  6   AFC (4) vs. NFC (2), 2001

INTERCEPTIONS BY
Most Interceptions By, Game
  6   AFC, 1977
Most Interceptions By, Both Teams, Game
  7   AFC (6) vs. NFC (1), 1977

YARDS GAINED
Most Yards Gained, Game
  103   AFC, 1994
Most Yards Gained, Both Teams, Game
  172   NFC (102) vs. AFC (70), 1999

TOUCHDOWNS
Most Touchdowns, Game
  2   NFC, 2000

PUNTING
Most Punts, Game
  10   AFC, 1985
Fewest Punts, Game
  0   NFC, 1989
Most Punts, Both Teams, Game
  16   AFC (10) vs. NFC (6), 1985
Fewest Punts, Both Teams, Game
  4   NFC (1) vs. AFC (3), 1992

PUNT RETURNS
Most Punt Returns, Game
  7   NFC, 1985, 1987
      AFC, 1995
Fewest Punt Returns, Game
  0   AFC, 1984, 1989
Most Punt Returns, Both Teams, Game
  11   NFC (7) vs. AFC (4), 1985
Fewest Punt Returns, Both Teams, Game
  2   AFC (1) vs. NFC (1), 1996

YARDS GAINED
Most Yards Gained, Game
  177   AFC, 1976
Fewest Yards Gained, Game
  –1   NFC, 1991
Most Yards Gained, Both Teams, Game
  263   AFC (177) vs. NFC (86), 1976
Fewest Yards Gained, Both Teams, Game
  16   AFC (0) vs. NFC (16), 1984

TOUCHDOWNS
Most Touchdowns, Game
  2   NFC, 1971

KICKOFF RETURNS
Most Kickoff Returns, Game
  8   NFC, 1995
Fewest Kickoff Returns, Game
  1   NFC, 1971, 1984, 1994
      AFC, 1988, 1991
Most Kickoff Returns, Both Teams, Game
  13   AFC (7) vs. NFC (6), 2000
       NFC (7) vs. AFC (6), 2002
Fewest Kickoff Returns, Both Teams, Game
  5   NFC (2) vs. AFC (3), 1979
      AFC (1) vs. NFC (4), 1988
      NFC (2) vs. AFC (3), 1992
      NFC (1) vs. AFC (4), 1994

YARDS GAINED
Most Yards Gained, Game
   232 NFC, 2000
Fewest Yards Gained, Game
     6 NFC, 1971
Most Yards Gained, Both Teams, Game
   436 NFC (232) vs. AFC (204), 2000
Fewest Yards Gained, Both Teams, Game
    99 NFC (48) vs. AFC (51), 1987

TOUCHDOWNS
Most Touchdowns, Game
  None

FUMBLES
Most Fumbles, Game
   10 NFC, 1974
Most Fumbles, Both Teams, Game
    15 NFC (10) vs. AFC (5), 1974

RECOVERIES
Most Fumbles Recovered, Game
    10 NFC, 1974 (6 own, 4 opp)
Most Fumbles Lost, Game
    4 AFC, 1974, 1988
       NFC, 1974

YARDS GAINED
Most Yards Gained, Game
   87 AFC, 1985

TOUCHDOWNS
Most Touchdowns, Game
    1 AFC, 1985
      NFC, 1990

TURNOVERS
(Number of times losing the ball on interceptions and fumbles.)
Most Turnovers, Game
    8 AFC, 1974
Fewest Turnovers, Game
    0 AFC, 1991, 1997
       NFC, 1991, 1995, 1996, 2001
Most Turnovers, Both Teams, Game
   12 AFC (8) vs. NFC (4), 1974
Fewest Turnovers, Both Teams, Game
    0 AFC vs. NFC, 1991

Rules

2002 NFL ROSTER OF OFFICIALS

Mike Pereira, Director of Officiating
Larry Upson, Director of Officiating Operations
Al Hynes, Supervisor of Officials

Jim Daopoulos, Supervisor of Officials
Ron Baynes, Supervisor of Officials
Neely Dunn, Supervisor of Officials

No.	Name	Position	College
81	Anderson, Dave	Line Judge	Salem College
66	Anderson, Walt	Line Judge	Texas
108	Arthur, Gary	Line Judge	Wright State
34	Austin, Gerald	Referee	Western Carolina
48	Balliet, Brian	Umpire	Lehigh
26	Baltz, Mark	Head Linesman	Ohio University
72	Banks, Michael	Side Judge	Illinois State
55	Barnes, Tom	Line Judge	Minnesota
32	Bergman, Jeff	Line Judge	Robert Morris
91	Bergman, Jerry	Head Linesman	Robert Morris
7	Blum, Ron	Referee	Marin College
18	Boston, Byron	Line Judge	Austin
31	Brown, Chad	Umpire	East Texas State
134	Camp, Ed	Head Linesman	William Paterson
126	Carey, Don	Back Judge	UC-Riverside
94	Carey, Mike	Referee	Santa Clara
39	Carlsen, Don	Side Judge	Cal State-Chico
63	Carollo, Bill	Referee	Wisconsin-Milwaukee
11	Carroll, Duke	Field Judge	Ithaca
41	Cheek, Boris	Field Judge	Morgan State
51	Cheffers, Carl	Side Judge	UC-Irvine
65	Coleman, Walt	Referee	Arkansas
99	Corrente, Tony	Referee	Cal State-Fullerton
71	Coukart, Ed	Umpire	Northwestern
70	Dawson, Scott	Umpire	Virginia Tech
53	DeFelice, Garth	Umpire	San Diego State
113	Dorkowski, Don	Back Judge	Cal State-Los Angeles
6	Dornan, Kirk	Back Judge	Central Washington
74	Duke, James	Umpire	Howard
3	Edwards, Scott	Field Judge	Alabama
61	Ferguson, Keith	Back Judge	San Diego State
47	Fincken, Tom	Side Judge	Kansas State
133	Freeman, Steve	Back Judge	Mississippi State
80	Gautreaux, Greg	Field Judge	Southwestern Louisiana
19	Green, Scott	Back Judge	Delaware
23	Grier, Johnny	Referee	University of D.C.
40	Hannah, Butch	Umpire	Middle Tennessee State
105	Hantak, Dick	Referee	Southeast Missouri
125	Hayes, Laird	Side Judge	Princeton
54	Hayward, George	Head Linesman	Missouri Western
97	Hill, Tom	Side Judge	Carson-Newman
28	Hittner, Mark	Head Linesman	Pittsburg State
85	Hochuli, Ed	Referee	Texas-El Paso
82	Horton, Buddy	Back Judge	Oregon State
37	Howey, Jim	Back Judge	Erskine College
76	Jenkins, Darrell	Umpire	San Jose State
101	Johnson, Carl	Line Judge	Nicholls State
114	Johnson, Tom	Head Linesman	Miami, Ohio
106	Jury, Al	Field Judge	San Bernardino Valley
86	Kukar, Bernie	Referee	St. John's
103	Lamberth, Jeff	Field Judge	Texas A&M
17	Lawing, Bob	Back Judge	North Carolina State
127	Leavy, Bill	Referee	San Jose State
130	Lewis, Darryll	Line Judge	Dartmouth
49	Look, Dean	Side Judge	Michigan State
98	Lovett, Bill	Field Judge	Maryland
59	Luckett, Phil	Back Judge	Texas-El Paso
92	Madsen, Carl	Umpire	Washington
107	Marinucci, Ron	Line Judge	Glassboro State
77	McAulay, Terry	Referee	Louisiana State
95	McElwee, Bob	Referee	Navy
120	McGrath, John	Head Linesman	Kentucky
110	McKinnely, Phil	Head Linesman	UCLA
64	McPeters, Lloyd	Field Judge	Oklahoma State
78	Meyer, Greg	Field Judge	Texas Christian
115	Michalek, Tony	Umpire	Indiana
117	Montgomery, Ben	Line Judge	Morehouse
60	Moore, Tommy	Side Judge	Stephen F. Austin
135	Morelli, Peter	Field Judge	St. Mary's College
20	Nemmers, Larry	Referee	Upper Iowa
124	Paganelli, Carl	Umpire	Michigan State
46	Paganelli, Perry	Back Judge	Hope College
132	Parry, John	Side Judge	Purdue
15	Patterson, Rick	Side Judge	Wofford
9	Perlman, Mark	Line Judge	Salem
10	Phares, Ron	Line Judge	Virginia Tech
79	Pointer, Aaron	Head Linesman	Pacific Lutheran
38	Powers, Eddy	Field Judge	Tennessee
5	Quirk, Jim	Umpire	Delaware
83	Reels, Richard	Back Judge	Chicago State
44	Rice, Jeff	Umpire	Northwestern
121	Rivers, Sanford	Head Linesman	Youngstown State
128	Rose, Larry	Side Judge	Florida
67	Rosenbaum, Doug	Side Judge	Illinois Wesleyan
58	Saracino, Jim	Field Judge	Northern Colorado
21	Schleyer, John	Head Linesman	Millersville
122	Schmitz, Bill	Back Judge	Colorado State
129	Schuster, Bill	Umpire	Alfred
45	Seeman, Jeff	Line Judge	Minnesota
118	Sifferman, Tom	Field Judge	Seattle
30	Slaughter, Gary	Head Linesman	East Texas State
2	Smith, Billy	Back Judge	East Carolina
90	Spanier, Michael	Line Judge	St. Cloud State
119	Spitler, Ron	Back Judge	Panhandle State
12	Spyksma, Bill	Side Judge	South Dakota
24	Stabile, Tom	Head Linesman	Slippery Rock
88	Steenson, Scott	Field Judge	North Texas
84	Steinkerchner, Mark	Line Judge	Akron
68	Stephan, Tom	Line Judge	Pittsburg State
112	Steratore, Anthony	Back Judge	California (Penn.)
62	Stewart, Charles	Line Judge	Long Beach State
4	Toole, Doug	Side Judge	Utah State
42	Triplette, Jeff	Referee	Wake Forest
36	Veteri, Tony	Head Linesman	Manhattan College
52	Vinovich, Bill	Side Judge	San Diego
25	Waggoner, Bob	Back Judge	Juniata College
100	Wagner, Bob	Umpire	Penn State
27	Warden, David	Field Judge	Oklahoma State
96	Wash, Undrey	Umpire	Texas-Arlington
116	Weatherford, Mike	Side Judge	Oklahoma State
87	Weidner, Paul	Head Linesman	Cincinnati
50	Weir, Mike	Field Judge	Missouri
123	White, Tom	Referee	Temple
8	Williams, Dale	Head Linesman	Cal State-Northridge
43	Wilson, James	Head Linesman	Eastern Kentucky
29	Wilson, Steve	Umpire	Whitworth College
14	Winter, Ron	Referee	Michigan State
16	Wyant, David	Side Judge	Virginia
33	Zimmer, Steve	Field Judge	Hofstra

NUMERICAL ROSTER

No.	Name	Position
2	Billy Smith	BJ
3	Scott Edwards	FJ
4	Doug Toole	SJ
5	Jim Quirk	U
6	Kirk Dornan	BJ
7	Ron Blum	R
8	Dale Williams	HL
9	Mark Perlman	LJ
10	Ron Phares	LJ
11	Duke Carroll	FJ
12	Bill Spyksma	SJ
14	Ron Winter	R
15	Rick Patterson	SJ
16	David Wyant	SJ
17	Bob Lawing	BJ
18	Byron Boston	LJ
19	Scott Green	BJ
20	Larry Nemmers	R
21	John Schleyer	HL
23	Johnny Grier	R
24	Tom Stabile	HL
25	Bob Waggoner	BJ
26	Mark Baltz	HL
27	David Warden	FJ
28	Mark Hittner	HL
29	Steve Wilson	U
30	Gary Slaughter	HL
31	Chad Brown	U
32	Jeff Bergman	LJ
33	Steve Zimmer	FJ
34	Gerry Austin	R
36	Tony Veteri	HL
37	Jim Howey	BJ
38	Eddy Powers	FJ
39	Don Carlsen	SJ
40	Butch Hannah	U
41	Boris Cheek	FJ
42	Jeff Triplette	R
43	James Wilson	HL
44	Jeff Rice	U
45	Jeff Seeman	LJ
46	Perry Paganelli	BJ
47	Tom Fincken	SJ
48	Brian Balliet	U
49	Dean Look	SJ
50	Mike Weir	FJ
51	Carl Cheffers	SJ
52	Bill Vinovich	SJ
53	Garth DeFelice	U
54	George Hayward	HL
55	Tom Barnes	LJ
58	Jim Saracino	FJ
59	Phil Luckett	BJ
60	Tommy Moore	SJ
61	Keith Ferguson	BJ
62	Charles Stewart	LJ
63	Bill Carollo	R
64	Lloyd McPeters	FJ
65	Walt Coleman	R
66	Walt Anderson	LJ
67	Doug Rosenbaum	SJ
68	Tom Stephan	LJ
70	Scott Dawson	U
71	Ed Coukart	U
72	Michael Banks	SJ
74	James Duke	U
76	Darrell Jenkins	U
77	Terry McAulay	R
78	Greg Meyer	FJ
79	Aaron Pointer	HL
80	Greg Gautreaux	FJ
81	Dave Anderson	LJ
82	Buddy Horton	BJ
83	Richard Reels	BJ
84	Mark Steinkerchner	LJ
85	Ed Hochuli	R
86	Bernie Kukar	R
87	Paul Weidner	HL
88	Scott Steenson	FJ
90	Michael Spanier	LJ
91	Jerry Bergman	HL
92	Carl Madsen	U
94	Mike Carey	R
95	Bob McElwee	R
96	Undrey Wash	U
97	Tom Hill	SJ
98	Bill Lovett	FJ
99	Tony Corrente	R
100	Bob Wagner	U
101	Carl Johnson	LJ
103	Jeff Lamberth	FJ
105	Dick Hantak	R
106	Al Jury	FJ
107	Ron Marinucci	LJ
108	Gary Arthur	LJ
110	Phil McKinnely	HL
112	Anthony Steratore	BJ
113	Don Dorkowski	BJ
114	Tom Johnson	HL
115	Tony Michalek	U
116	Mike Weatherford	SJ
117	Ben Montgomery	LJ
118	Tom Sifferman	FJ
119	Ron Spitler	BJ
120	John McGrath	HL
121	Sanford Rivers	HL
122	Bill Schmitz	BJ
123	Tom White	R
124	Carl Paganelli	U
125	Laird Hayes	SJ
126	Don Carey	BJ
127	Bill Leavy	R
128	Larry Rose	SJ
129	Bill Schuster	U
130	Darryll Lewis	LJ
132	John Parry	SJ
133	Steve Freeman	BJ
134	Ed Camp	HL
135	Peter Morelli	FJ

2002 OFFICIALS AT A GLANCE
REFEREES
Gerry Austin, No. **34,** Western Carolina, president, leadership development group, 21st year.
Ron Blum, No. **7,** Marin College, professional golfer, 18th year.
Mike Carey, No. **94,** Santa Clara, owner, skiing accessories, 13th year.
Bill Carollo, No. **63,** Wisconsin-Milwaukee, marketing executive, 14th year.
Walt Coleman, No. **65,** Arkansas, manager, dairy processor, 14th year.
Tony Corrente, No. **99,** Cal State-Fullerton, educator, 8th year.
Johnny Grier, No. **23,** University of D.C., planning engineer, 22nd year.
Dick Hantak, No. **105,** Southeast Missouri, educator, 25th year.
Ed Hochuli, No. **85,** Texas-El Paso, attorney, 13th year.
Bernie Kukar, No. **86,** St. John's, sales representative, employees benefit plan, 19th year.
Bill Leavy, No. **127,** San Jose State, supervisor of officials, retired firefighter, 8th year.
Terry McAulay, No. **77,** Louisiana State, senior computer scientist, 5th year.
Bob McElwee, No. **95,** Navy, owner, heavy construction firm, 27th year.
Larry Nemmers, No. **20,** Upper Iowa, motivational speaker, 18th year.
Jeff Triplette, No. **42,** Wake Forest, vice president, world-wide energy company, 7th year.
Tom White, No. **123,** Temple, president, athletic sportswear, 14th year.
Ron Winter, No. **14,** Michigan State, university professor, 8th year.

UMPIRES
Brian Balliet, No. **48,** Lehigh, industrial manufacturing distrbution, 6th year.
Chad Brown, No. **31,** East Texas State, manager, intramural/sports clubs, 11th year.
Ed Coukart, No. **71,** Northwestern, vice-president, commercial bank, 14th year.
Scott Dawson, No. **70,** Virginia Tech, president/owner, commercial construction company, 8th year.
Garth DeFelice, No. **53,** San Diego State, director of distributing, beverage company, 5th year.
James Duke, No. **74,** Howard, director of volunteer resources boys and girls clubs, 10th year.
Butch Hannah, No. **40,** Middle Tennessee State, federal probation officer, 4th year.
Darrell Jenkins, No. **76,** San Jose State, retired, 1st year.
Carl Madsen, No. **92,** Washington, vice president of operations, 5th year.
Tony Michalek, No. **115,** Indiana, Futures Trader, 1st year.
Carl Paganelli, No. **124,** Michigan State, federal probation officer, 4th year.
Jim Quirk, No. **5,** Delaware, consultant, 15th year.
Jeff Rice, No. **44,** Northwestern, attorney, 8th year.
Bill Schuster, No. **129,** Alfred College, insurance broker, 3rd year.
Bob Wagner, No. **100,** Penn State, executive director, cardiovascular institute, 18th year.
Undrey Wash, No. **96,** Texas-Arlington, claims manager, 3rd year.
Steve Wilson, No. **29,** Whitworth College, church administrator, 4th year.

HEAD LINESMEN
Mark Baltz, No. **26,** Ohio University, sales consultant, 14th year.
Jerry Bergman, No. **91,** Robert Morris, sales executive, 1st year.
Ed Camp, No. **134,** William Paterson, teacher, 3rd year.
George Hayward, No. **54,** Missouri Western, vice-president and manager, warehouse company, 12th year.
Mark Hittner, No. **28,** Pittsburg State, insurance sales, 6th year.
Tom Johnson, No. **114,** Miami, Ohio, retired educator, president/owner, security company, 21st year.
John McGrath, No. **120,** Kentucky, senior account executive, 1st year.
Phil McKinnely, No. **110,** UCLA, inventory control, 1st year.
Aaron Pointer, No. **79,** Pacific Lutheran, park department administrator, 15th year.
Sanford Rivers, No. **121,** Youngstown State, university vice-president, 14th year.
John Schleyer, No. **21,** Millersville, medical sales, 13th year.
Gary Slaughter, No. **30,** East Texas State, general manager, 7th year.
Tom Stabile, No. **24,** Slippery Rock, secondary educational administrator, 8th year.
Tony Veteri, No. **36,** Manhattan, director of athletics, 11th year.
Paul Weidner, No. **87,** Cincinnati, marketing manager, 17th year.
Dale Williams, No. **8,** Cal State-Northridge, sports official, 23rd year.
James Wilson, No. **43,** Eastern Kentucky, area sales manager, 5th year.

LINE JUDGES
Dave Anderson, No. **81,** Salem, insurance executive, 19th year.
Walt Anderson, No. **66,** Texas, dentist, orthodontics, 7th year.
Gary Arthur, No. **108,** Wright State, president, commercial printing sales, 6th year.
Tom Barnes, No. **55,** Minnesota, manufacturing representative, 17th year.
Jeff Bergman, No. **32,** Robert Morris, president and chief executive officer, medical services, 11th year.
Byron Boston, No. **18,** Austin, tax consultant, 8th year.
Carl Johnson, No. **101,** Nicholls State, district sales manager, 2nd year.
Darryll Lewis, No. **130,** Dartmouth, associate professor, 4th year.
Ron Marinucci, No. **107,** Glassboro State, vice president, novelty cone company, 6th year.
Ben Montgomery, No. **117,** Morehouse, school administrator, 21st year.
Mark Perlman, No. **9,** Salem, teacher, 3rd year.
Ron Phares, No. **10,** Virginia Tech, president, construction company, 18th year.
Jeff Seeman, No. **45,** Minnesota, brokerage sales, 1st year.
Michael Spanier, No. **90,** St. Cloud State, middle-school principal, 4th year.
Mark Steinkerchner, No. **84,** Akron, president, plastics company, 9th year.
Tom Stephan, No. **68,** Pittsburg State, business broker, 4th year.
Charles Stewart, No. **62,** Long Beach State, human services administrator, 11th year.

FIELD JUDGES

Duke Carroll, No. **11,** Ithaca, chairman of the board, insurance agency, 8th year.

Boris Cheek, No. **41,** Morgan State, director of operations and management, 7th year.

Scott Edwards, No. **3,** Alabama, environmental engineer, 4th year.

Greg Gautreaux, No. **80,** Southwestern Louisiana, athletic programs manager, 1st year.

Al Jury, No. **106,** San Bernardino Valley, state traffic officer, 25th year.

Jeff Lamberth, No. **103,** Texas A&M, attorney, 1st year.

Bill Lovett, No. **98,** Maryland, managing partner, financial sales, 13th year.

Lloyd McPeters, No. **64,** Oklahoma State, business insurance sales, 10th year.

Greg Meyer, No. **78,** Texas Christian, banker, 1st year.

Peter Morelli, No. **135,** St. Mary's, high school principal, 6th year.

Eddy Powers, No. **38,** Tennessee, sales/design office supply, 1st year.

Jim Saracino, No. **58,** Northern Colorado, secondary educator, 8th year.

Tom Sifferman, No. **118,** Seattle, manufacturer's representative, 17th year.

Scott Steenson, No. **88,** North Texas, commercial real estate broker, 12th year.

David Warden, No. **27,** Oklahoma State, dentist, 5th year.

Mike Weir, No. **50,** Missouri, owner, sporting goods store, 1st year.

Steve Zimmer, No. **33,** Hofstra, attorney, 6th year.

SIDE JUDGES

Michael Banks, No. **72,** Illinos State, carpenter foremen, 1st year.

Don Carlsen, No. **39,** Cal State-Chico, assistant superintendent, county school, 14th year.

Carl Cheffers, No. **51,** UC-Irvine, national sales manager, 3rd year.

Tom Fincken, No. **47,** Emporia State, retired educational administrator, 19th year.

Laird Hayes, No. **125,** Princeton, professor, physical education & athletics, 8th year.

Tom Hill, No. **97,** Carson-Newman, teacher, 4th year.

Dean Look, No. **49,** Michigan State, consultant, medical manufacturing, former AFL player, 30th year.

Tommy Moore, No. **60,** Stephen F. Austin, marketing, manufacturing representative, 11th year.

John Parry, No. **132,** Purdue, corporate pilot, 3rd year.

Rick Patterson, No. **15,** Wofford, banker, 7th year.

Larry Rose, No. **128,** Florida, financial planner, 6th year.

Doug Rosenbaum, No. **67,** Illinois Wesleyan, financial consultant, 2ndt year.

Bill Spyksma, No. **12,** South Dakota, commercial real estate, construction sales, 8th year.

Doug Toole, No. **4,** Utah State, physical therapist, 15th year.

Bill Vinovich, No. **52,** San Diego, certified public accountant, 2nd year.

Mike Weatherford, No. **116,** Oklahoma State, energy trader, 1st year.

David Wyant, No. **16,** Virginia, consulting engineer, 12th year.

BACK JUDGES

Don Carey, No. **126,** UC-Riverside, contract manager, 8th year.

Don Dorkowski, No. **113,** Cal State-Los Angeles, pump manufacturer, 17th year.

Kirk Dornan, No. **6,** Central Washington, purchasing manager, 9th year.

Keith Ferguson, No. **61,** San Jose State, sales, 3rd year.

Steve Freeman, No. **133,** Mississippi State, custom home builder, 2nd year.

Scott Green, No. **19,** Delaware, vice-president, government relations, 12th year.

Buddy Horton, No. **82,** Oregon State, water service worker, 4th year.

Jim Howey, No. **37,** Erskine College, director of adult education, 4th year.

Bob Lawing, No. **17,** North Carolina State, real estate management, 6th year.

Phil Luckett, No. **59,** Texas-El Paso, computer program analyst, federal civil services, 12th year.

Perry Paganelli, No. **46,** Hope College, high school administrator, 5th year.

Richard Reels, No. **83,** Chicago State, director of security, court services, 10th year.

Bill Schmitz, No. **122,** Colorado State, general sales manager, 14th year.

Billy Smith, No. **2,** East Carolina, federal government, 9th year.

Ron Spitler, No. **119,** Panhandle State, owner, service center, 21st year.

Anthony Steratore, No. **112,** California (Penn.), president, sanitary supply company, 3rd year.

Bob Waggoner, No. **25,** Juniata College, probation officer, 6th year.

1

TOUCHDOWN, FIELD GOAL, or SUCCESSFUL TRY
Both arms extended above head.

2

SAFETY
Palms together above head.

3

FIRST DOWN
Arm pointed toward defensive team's goal.

4

CROWD NOISE, DEAD BALL, or NEUTRAL ZONE ESTABLISHED
One arm above head with an open hand.
With fist closed: **Fourth Down.**

5

BALL ILLEGALLY TOUCHED, KICKED, or BATTED
Fingertips tap both shoulders.

6

TIME OUT
Hands crisscrossed above head.
Same signal followed by placing one hand on top of cap: **Referee's Time Out.**
Same signal followed by arm swung at side: **Touchback.**

7

**NO TIME OUT or
TIME IN WITH WHISTLE**
Full arm circled to
simulate moving clock.

8

**DELAY OF GAME
or EXCESS TIME OUT**
Folded arms.

9

**FALSE START,
ILLEGAL FORMATION, or
KICKOFF or SAFETY KICK
OUT OF BOUNDS or
KICKING TEAM PLAYER
VOLUNTARILY OUT OF BOUNDS
DURING A PUNT**
Forearms rotated over and over
in front of body.

10

PERSONAL FOUL
One wrist striking the other above head.
Same signal followed by swinging leg:
Roughing the Kicker.
Same signal followed by raised arm
swinging forward:
Roughing the Passer.
Same signal followed by grasping
face mask: **Major Face Mask.**

11

HOLDING
Grasping one wrist,
the fist clenched,
in front of chest.

12

**ILLEGAL USE OF HANDS,
ARMS, or BODY**
Grasping one wrist,
the hand open and facing
forward, in front of chest.

13

PENALTY REFUSED, INCOMPLETE PASS, PLAY OVER, or MISSED FIELD GOAL or EXTRA POINT
Hands shifted in horizontal plane.

14

PASS JUGGLED INBOUNDS AND CAUGHT OUT OF BOUNDS
Hands up and down in front of chest (following incomplete pass signal).

15

ILLEGAL FORWARD PASS
One hand waved behind back followed by loss of down signal (23), when appropriate.

16

INTENTIONAL GROUNDING OF PASS
Parallel arms waved in a diagonal plane across body. Followed by loss of down signal (23).

17

INTERFERENCE WITH FORWARD PASS or FAIR CATCH
Hands open and extended forward from shoulders with hands vertical.

18

INVALID FAIR-CATCH SIGNAL
One hand waved above head.

19

**INELIGIBLE RECEIVER
or INELIGIBLE
MEMBER OF KICKING TEAM
DOWNFIELD**
Right hand touching top of cap.

20

ILLEGAL CONTACT
One open hand extended forward.

21

**OFFSIDE, ENCROACHMENT, or
NEUTRAL ZONE INFRACTION**
Hands on hips.

22

ILLEGAL MOTION AT SNAP
Horizontal arc with one hand.

23

LOSS OF DOWN
Both hands held behind head.

24

**INTERLOCKING
INTERFERENCE, PUSHING, or
HELPING RUNNER**
Pushing movement of hands
to front with arms downward.

25

**TOUCHING A FORWARD
PASS or SCRIMMAGE KICK**
Diagonal motion of
one hand across another.

26

**UNSPORTSMANLIKE
CONDUCT**
Arms outstretched,
palms down.

27

ILLEGAL CUT
Hand striking front of thigh.
ILLEGAL BLOCK BELOW THE WAIST
One hand striking front of thigh
preceded by personal-foul signal (10).
CHOP BLOCK
Both hands striking side of thighs
preceded by personal-foul signal (10).
CLIPPING
One hand striking back of calf
preceded by personal-foul signal (10).

28

ILLEGAL CRACKBACK
Strike of an
open right hand
against the right mid-thigh
preceded by personal foul
signal (10).

29

PLAYER DISQUALIFIED
Ejection signal.

30

TRIPPING
Repeated action of right foot
in back of left heel.

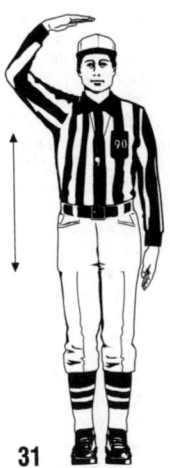

31

UNCATCHABLE FORWARD PASS
Palm of right hand held parallel to ground above head and moved back and forth.

32

TWELVE MEN IN OFFENSIVE HUDDLE or TOO MANY MEN ON THE FIELD
Both hands on top of head.

33

FACE MASK
Grasping face mask with one hand.

34

ILLEGAL SHIFT
Horizontal arcs with two hands.

35

RESET PLAY CLOCK– 25 SECONDS
Pump one arm vertically.

36

RESET PLAY CLOCK– 40 SECONDS
Pump two arms vertically.

NFL DIGEST OF RULES

This Digest of Rules of the National Football League has been prepared to aid players, fans, and members of the press, radio, and television media in their understanding of the game.

It is not meant to be a substitute for the official rule book. In any case of conflict between these explanations and the official rules, the rules always have precedence.

In order to make it easier to coordinate the information in this digest, the topics discussed generally follow the order of the rule book.

OFFICIALS' JURISDICTIONS, POSITIONS, AND DUTIES

Referee—General oversight and control of game. Gives signals for all fouls and is final authority for rule interpretations. Takes a position in backfield 10 to 12 yards behind line of scrimmage, favors right side (if quarterback is right-handed passer). Determines legality of snap, observes deep back(s) for legal motion. On running play, observes quarterback during and after handoff, remains with him until action has cleared away, then proceeds downfield, checking on runner and contact behind him. When runner is downed, Referee determines forward progress from wing official and, if necessary, adjusts final position of ball.

On pass plays, drops back as quarterback begins to fade back, picks up legality of blocks by near linemen. Changes to complete concentration on quarterback as defenders approach. Primarily responsible to rule on possible roughing action on passer and if ball becomes loose, rules whether ball is free on a fumble or dead on an incomplete pass.

During kicking situations, Referee has primary responsibility to rule on kicker's actions and whether or not any subsequent contact by a defender is legal. The Referee stays wide and parallel on punts and will announce on the microphone when each period has ended.

Umpire—Primary responsibility to rule on players' equipment, as well as their conduct and actions on scrimmage line. Lines up approximately four to five yards downfield, varying position in front of weakside tackle to strongside guard. Looks for possible false start by offensive linemen. Observes legality of contact by both offensive linemen while blocking and by defensive players while they attempt to ward off blockers. Is prepared to call rule infractions if they occur on offense or defense. Moves forward to line of scrimmage when pass play develops in order to insure that interior linemen do not move illegally downfield. If offensive linemen indicate screen pass is to be attempted, Umpire shifts his attention toward screen side, picks up potential receiver in order to insure that he will legally be permitted to run his pattern and continues to rule on action of blockers. Umpire is to assist in ruling on incomplete or trapped passes when ball is thrown overhead or short. On punt plays, Umpire positions himself opposite Referee in offensive backfield—5 yards from kicker and one yard behind.

Head Linesman—Primarily responsible for ruling on offside, encroachment, and actions pertaining to scrimmage line prior to or at snap. Generally, keys on closest setback on his side of the field. On pass plays, Linesman is responsible to clear his receiver approximately seven yards downfield as he moves to a point five yards beyond the line. Linesman's secondary responsibility is to rule on any illegal action taken by defenders on any delay receiver moving downfield. Has full responsibility for ruling on sideline plays on his side, e.g., pass receiver or runner in or out of bounds. Together with Referee, Linesman is responsible for keeping track of number of downs and is in charge of mechanics of his chain crew in connection with its duties.

Linesman must be prepared to assist in determining forward progress by a runner on play directed toward middle or into his side zone. He, in turn, is to signal Referee or Umpire what forward point ball has reached. Linesman is also responsible to rule on legality of action involving any receiver who approaches his side zone. He is to call pass interference when the infraction occurs and is to rule on legality of blockers and defenders on plays involving ball carriers, whether it is entirely a running play, a combination pass and run, or a play involving a kick. Also assists referee with intentional grounding.

Line Judge—Straddles line of scrimmage on side of field opposite Linesman. Keeps time of game as a backup for clock operator. Along with Linesman is responsible for offside, encroachment, and actions pertaining to scrimmage line prior to or at snap. Line Judge keys on closest setback on his side of field. Line Judge is to observe his receiver until he moves at least seven yards downfield. He then moves toward backfield side, being especially alert to rule on any back in motion and on flight of ball when pass is made (he must rule whether forward or backward). Line Judge has primary responsibility to rule whether or not passer is behind or beyond line of scrimmage when pass is made. He also assists in observing actions by blockers and defenders when pass is made. After pass is thrown, Line Judge directs attention toward activities that occur in back of Umpire. During punting situations, Line Judge remains at line of scrimmage to be sure that only the end men move downfield until kick has been made. He also rules whether or not the kick crossed line and then observes action by members of the kicking team who are moving downfield to cover the kick. The Line Judge will advise the Referee when time has expired at the end of each period. Also assists referee with intentional grounding and determines whether pass is forward or backward.

Field Judge—Operates on same side of field as Line Judge, 20 yards deep. Keys on wide receiver on his side. Concentrates on path of end or back, observing legality of his potential block(s) or of actions taken against him. Is prepared to rule from deep position on holding or illegal use of hands by end or back or on defensive infractions committed by player guarding him. Has primary responsibility to make decisions involving sideline on his side of field, e.g., pass receiver or runner in or out of bounds.

Field Judge makes decisions involving catching, recovery, or illegal touching of a loose ball beyond line of scrimmage; rules on plays involving pass receiver, including legality of catch or pass interference; assists in covering actions of runner, including blocks by teammates and that of defenders; calls clipping on punt returns; and, together with Back Judge, rules whether or not field goal attempts are successful.

Side Judge—Operates on same side of field as Linesman, 20 yards deep. Keys on wide receiver on his side. Concentrates on path of end or back, observing legality of his potential block(s) or of actions taken against him. Is prepared to rule from deep position on holding or illegal use of hands by end or back or on defensive infractions committed by player guarding him. Has primary responsibility to make decisions involving sideline on his side of field, e.g., pass receiver or runner in or out of bounds.

Side Judge makes decisions involving catching, recovery, or illegal touching of a loose ball beyond line of scrimmage; rules on plays involving pass receiver, including legality of catch or pass interference; assists in covering actions of runner, including blocks by teammates and that of defenders; and calls clipping on punt returns. On field goals and point after touchdown attempts, he becomes a double umpire.

Back Judge—Takes a position 25 yards downfield. In general, favors the tight end's side of field. Keys on tight end, concentrates on his path and observes legality of tight end's potential block(s) or of actions taken against him. Is prepared to rule from deep position on holding or illegal use of hands by end or back or on defensive infractions committed by player guarding him.

Back Judge times interval between plays on 40/25-second clock plus intermission between two periods of each half; makes decisions involving catching, recovery, or illegal touching of a loose ball beyond line of scrimmage; is responsible to rule on plays involving end line; calls pass interference, fair catch infractions, and clipping on kick returns; together with Field Judge, rules whether or not field goals and conversions are successful; and stays with ball on punts.

DEFINITIONS

1. **Chucking:** Warding off an opponent who is in front of a defender by contacting him with a quick extension of arm or arms, followed by the return of arm(s) to a flexed position, thereby breaking the original contact.
2. **Clipping:** Throwing the body across the back of an opponent's leg or hitting him from the back below the waist while moving up from behind unless the opponent is a runner or the action is in close line play.
3. **Close Line Play:** The area between the positions normally occupied by the offensive tackles, extending three yards on each side of the line of scrimmage. It is legal to clip above the knee.
4. **Crackback:** Eligible receivers who take or move to a position more than two yards outside the tackle may not block an opponent below the waist if they then move back inside to block.
5. **Dead Ball:** Ball not in play.
6. **Double Foul:** A foul by each team during the same down.
7. **Down:** The period of action that starts when the ball is put in play and ends when it is dead.
8. **Encroachment:** When a player enters the neutral zone and makes <u>contact</u> with an opponent before the ball is snapped.
9. **Fair Catch:** An unhindered catch of a kick by a member of the receiving team who must raise one arm a full length above his head and wave his arm from side to side while the kick is in flight.
10. **Foul:** Any violation of a playing rule.
11. **Free Kick:** A kickoff or safety kick. It may be a placekick, dropkick, or punt, except a punt may <u>not</u> be used on a kickoff following a touchdown, successful field goal, or to begin each half or overtime period. A tee cannot be used on a fair-catch or safety kick.
12. **Fumble:** The loss of possession of the ball.
13. **Game Clock:** Scoreboard game clock.
14. **Impetus:** The action of a player that gives momentum to the ball.
15. **Live Ball:** A ball legally free kicked or snapped. It continues in play until the down ends.
16. **Loose Ball:** A live ball not in possession of any player.
17. **Muff:** The touching of a loose ball by a player in an <u>unsuccessful</u> attempt to obtain possession.
18. **Neutral Zone:** The space the length of a ball between the two scrimmage lines. The offensive team and defensive team must remain behind their end of the ball.
    Exception: The offensive player who snaps the ball.
19. **Offside:** A player is offside when any part of his body is beyond his scrimmage or free kick line <u>when the ball is snapped or kicked.</u>
20. **Own Goal:** The goal a team is guarding.
21. **Play Clock:** 40/25 second clock.
22. **Pocket Area:** Applies from a point two yards outside of either offensive tackle and includes the tight end if he drops off the line of scrimmage to pass protect. Pocket extends longitudinally behind the line back to offensive team's own end line.
23. **Possession:** When a player controls the ball throughout the act of <u>clearly</u> touching both feet, or any other part of his body other than his hand(s), to the ground inbounds.
24. **Post-Possession Foul:** A foul by the receiving team that occurs after a ball is legally kicked from scrimmage prior to possession changing. The ball must cross the line of scrimmage and the receiving team must retain possession of the kicked ball.
25. **Punt:** A kick made when a player drops the ball and kicks it while it is in flight.
26. **Safety:** The situation in which the ball is dead on or behind a team's own goal if the <u>impetus</u> comes from a player on that team. Two points are scored for the opposing team.
27. **Shift:** The movement of two or more offensive players at the same time before the snap.
28. **Striking:** The act of swinging, clubbing, or propelling the arm or forearm in contacting an opponent.
29. **Sudden Death:** The continuation of a tied game into sudden death overtime in which the team scoring first (by safety, field goal, or touchdown) wins.
30. **Touchback:** When a ball is dead on or behind a team's own goal line, provided the impetus came from an opponent and provided it is not a touchdown or a missed field goal.
31. **Touchdown:** When any part of the ball, legally in possession of a player inbounds, breaks the plane of the opponent's goal line, provided it is not a touchback.
32. **Unsportsmanlike Conduct:** Any act contrary to the generally understood principles of sportsmanship.

SUMMARY OF PENALTIES
Automatic First Down
1. Awarded to offensive team on all <u>defensive fouls</u> with these exceptions:
   (a) Offside.
   (b) Encroachment.
   (c) Delay of game.
   (d) Illegal substitution.
   (e) Excessive time out(s).
   (f) Incidental grasp of facemask.
   (g) Neutral zone infraction.
   (h) Running into the kicker.
   (i) More than 11 players on the field at the snap.

Five Yards
1. Defensive holding or illegal use of hands (automatic first down).
2. Delay of game on offense or defense.
3. Delay of kickoff.
4. Encroachment.
5. Excessive time out(s).
6. False start.
7. Illegal formation.
8. Illegal shift.
9. Illegal motion.
10. Illegal substitution.
11. First onside kickoff out of bounds between goal lines and untouched or last touched by kicker.
12. Invalid fair catch signal.
13. More than 11 players on the field at snap for either team.
14. Less than seven men on offensive line at snap.
15. Offside.
16. Failure to pause one second after shift or huddle.
17. Running into kicker.
18. More than one man in motion at snap.
19. Grasping facemask of the ball carrier or quarterback.
20. Player out of bounds at snap.
21. Ineligible member(s) of kicking team going beyond line of scrimmage before ball is kicked.
22. Illegal return.
23. Failure to report change of eligibility.
24. Neutral zone infraction.
25. Loss of team time out(s) or five-yard penalty on the defense for excessive crowd noise.
26. Ineligible player downfield during passing down.
27. Second forward pass <u>behind</u> the line.
28. Forward pass is first touched by eligible receiver who has gone out of bounds and returned.
29. Forward pass touches or is caught by an ineligible receiver on or behind line.
30. Forward pass thrown from behind line of scrimmage after ball once crossed the line.
31. Kicking team player voluntarily out of bounds during a punt.
32. Twelve (12) men in the huddle.

10 Yards
1. Offensive pass interference.
2. Holding, illegal use of hands, arms, or body by offense.
3. Tripping by a member of either team.
4. Helping the runner.
5. Deliberately batting or punching a loose ball.
6. Deliberately kicking a loose ball.
7. Illegal block above the waist.

15 Yards
1. Chop block.
2. Clipping below the waist.
3. Fair catch interference.
4. Illegal crackback block by offense.
5. Piling on.
6. Roughing the kicker.
7. Roughing the passer.
8. Twisting, turning, or pulling an opponent by the facemask.
9. Unnecessary roughness.
10. Unsportsmanlike conduct.
11. Delay of game at start of either half.
12. Illegal low block.
13. A tackler using his helmet to butt, spear, or ram an opponent.
14. Any player who uses the top of his helmet unnecessarily.
15. A punter, placekicker, or holder who simulates being roughed by a defensive player.
16. Leaping.
17. Leverage.
18. Any player who removes his helmet after a play while on the field.
19. Taunting.

Five Yards and Loss of Down (Combination Penalty)
1. Forward pass thrown from beyond line of scrimmage.

10 Yards and Loss of Down (Combination Penalty)
1. Intentional grounding of forward pass (safety if passer is in own end zone). If foul occurs more than 10 yards behind line, play results in loss of down at spot of foul.

15 Yards and Loss of Coin Toss Option
1. Team's late arrival on the field prior to scheduled kickoff.
2. Captains not appearing for coin toss.

15 Yards (and disqualification if flagrant)
1. Striking opponent with fist.
2. Kicking or kneeing opponent.
3. Striking opponent on head or neck with forearm, elbow, or hands whether or not the initial contact is made below the neck area.
4. Roughing kicker.
5. Roughing passer.
6. Malicious unnecessary roughness.
7. Unsportsmanlike conduct.
8. Palpably unfair act. (Distance penalty determined by the Referee after consultation with other officials.)

15 Yards and Automatic Disqualification
1. Using a helmet (not worn) as a weapon.
2. Striking or purposely shoving a game official.

Suspension From Game For One Down
1. Illegal equipment. (Player may return after one down when legally equipped.)

Touchdown Awarded (Palpably Unfair Act)
1. When Referee determines a palpably unfair act deprived a team of a touchdown. (Example: Player comes off bench and tackles runner apparently en route to touchdown.)

FIELD
1. Sidelines and end lines are out of bounds. The goal line is actually in the end zone. A player with the ball in his possession scores a touchdown when the ball is on, above, or over the goal line.
2. The field is rimmed by a white border, six feet wide, along the sidelines. All of this is out of bounds.

3. The hashmarks (inbound lines) are 70 feet, 9 inches from each sideline.
4. Goal posts must be single-standard type, offset from the end line and painted bright gold. The goal posts must be 18 feet, 6 inches wide and the top face of the crossbar must be 10 feet above the ground. Vertical posts extend at least 30 feet above the crossbar. A ribbon 4 inches by 42 inches long is to be attached to the top of each post. The actual goal is the plane extending indefinitely above the crossbar and between the outer edges of the posts.
5. The field is 360 feet long and 160 feet wide. The end zones are 30 feet deep. The line used in try-for-point plays is two yards out from the goal line.
6. Chain crew members and ball boys must be uniformly identifiable.
7. All clubs must use standardized sideline markers. Pylons must be used for goal line and end line markings.
8. End zone markings and club identification at 50 yard line must be approved by the Commissioner to avoid any confusion as to delineation of goal lines, sidelines, and end lines.

BALL
1. The home club shall have 36 balls for outdoor games and 24 for indoor games available for testing with a pressure gauge by the referee two hours prior to the starting time of the game to meet with League requirements. Twelve (12) new footballs, sealed in a special box and shipped by the manufacturer, will be opened in the officials' locker room two hours prior to the starting time of the game. These balls are to be specially marked with the letter "k" and used exclusively for the kicking game.

COIN TOSS
1. The toss of coin will take place within three minutes of kickoff in center of field. The toss will be called by the visiting captain before the coin is flipped. The winner may choose one of two privileges and the loser gets the other:
   (a) Receive or kick
   (b) Goal his team will defend
2. Immediately prior to the start of the second half, the captains of both teams must inform the officials of their respective choices. The loser of the original coin toss gets first choice.

TIMING
1. The stadium game clock is official. In case it stops or is operating incorrectly, the Line Judge takes over the official timing on the field.
2. Each period is 15 minutes. The intermission between the periods is two minutes. Halftime is 12 minutes, unless otherwise specified.
3. On charged team time outs, the Field Judge starts watch and blows whistle after 1 minute 50 seconds, unless television does not utilize the time for commercial. In this case the length of the time out is reduced to 30 seconds.
4. The Referee will allow necessary time to attend to an injured player, or repair a legal player's equipment.
5. Each team is allowed three time outs each half.
6. Time between plays will be 40 seconds from the end of a given play until the snap of the ball for the next play, or a 25-second interval after certain administrative stoppages and game delays.
7. Clock will start running when ball is snapped following all changes of team possession.
8. With the exception of the last two minutes of the first half and the last five minutes of the second half, the game clock will be restarted following a player going out of bounds on a play from scrimmage, or after declined penalties when appropriate on the referee's signal.

9. Consecutive team time outs can be taken by opposing teams but the length of the second time out will be reduced to 30 seconds.
10. When, in the judgment of the Referee, the level of crowd noise prevents the offense from hearing its signals, he can institute a series of procedures which can result in a loss of team time outs or a five-yard penalty against the defensive team.
11. On kickoff, clock does not start until the ball has been legally touched by player of either team in the field of play.

SUDDEN DEATH
1. The sudden death system of determining the winner shall prevail when score is tied at the end of the regulation playing time of all NFL games. The team scoring first during overtime play shall be the winner and the game automatically ends upon any score (by safety, field goal, or touchdown) or when a score is awarded by Referee for a palpably unfair act.
2. At the end of regulation time the Referee will immediately toss coin at center of field in accordance with rules pertaining to the usual pregame toss. The captain of the visiting team will call the toss prior to the coin being flipped.
3. Following a three-minute intermission after the end of the regulation game, play will be continued in 15-minute periods or until there is a score. There is a two-minute intermission between subsequent periods. The teams change goals at the start of each period. Each team has three time outs per half and all general timing provisions apply as during a regular game. Disqualified players are not allowed to return.
Exception: In preseason and regular season games there shall be a maximum of 15 minutes of sudden death with two time outs instead of three. General provisions that apply for the fourth quarter will prevail. Try not attempted if touchdown scored.

TIMING IN FINAL TWO MINUTES OF EACH HALF
1. A team cannot buy an excess time out for a penalty. However, a fourth time out is allowed without penalty for an injured player, who must be removed immediately. A fifth time out or more is allowed for an injury and a five-yard penalty is assessed if the clock was running. Additionally, if the clock was running and the score is tied or the team in possession is losing, the ball cannot be put in play for at least 10 seconds on the fourth or more time out. The half or game can end while those 10 seconds are run off on the clock.
2. If the defensive team is behind in the score and commits a foul when it has no time outs left in the final 40 seconds of either half, the offensive team can decline the penalty for the foul and have the time on the clock expire.
3. Fouls that occur in the last five minutes of the fourth quarter as well as the last two minutes of the first half will result in the clock starting on the snap.

TRY
1. After a touchdown, the scoring team is allowed a try during one scrimmage down. The ball may be spotted anywhere between the inbounds lines, two or more yards from the goal line. The successful conversion counts one point by kick; two points for a successful conversion by touchdown; or one point for a safety.
2. The defensive team never can score on a try. As soon as defense gets possession or the kick is blocked or a touchdown is not scored, the try is over.
3. Any distance penalty for fouls committed by the defense that prevent the try from being attempted can be enforced on the succeeding try or succeeding kickoff. Any foul committed on a successful try will result in a distance penalty being assessed on the ensuing kickoff.
4. Only the fumbling player can recover and advance a fumble during a try.

PLAYERS-SUBSTITUTIONS
1. Each team is permitted 11 men on the field at the snap.
2. Unlimited substitution is permitted. However, players may enter the field only when the ball is dead. Players who have been substituted for are not permitted to linger on the field. Such lingering will be interpreted as unsportsmanlike conduct.
3. Players leaving the game must be out of bounds on their own side, clearing the field between the end lines, before a snap or free kick. If player crosses end line leaving field, it is delay of game (five-yard penalty).
4. Offensive substitutes who remain in the game must move onto the field as far as the inside of the field numerals before moving to a wide position.
5. With the exception of the last two minutes of either half, the offensive team, while in the process of substitution or simulated substitution, is prohibited from rushing quickly to the line and snapping the ball with the obvious attempt to cause a defensive foul; i.e., too many men on the field.
6. There never can be 12 or more players in the offensive huddle.

KICKOFF
1. The kickoff shall be from the kicking team's 30-yard line at the start of each half and after a field goal and try. A kickoff is one type of free kick.
2. A one-inch tee may be used (no tee permitted for field goal, safety kick, or try attempt) on a kickoff. The ball is put in play by a placekick.
3. A kickoff may not score a field goal.
4. A kickoff is illegal unless it travels 10 yards OR is touched by the receiving team. Once the ball is touched by the receiving team or has gone 10 yards, it is a free ball. Receivers may recover and advance. Kicking team may recover but NOT advance UNLESS receiver had possession and lost the ball.
5. When a kickoff goes out of bounds between the goal lines without being touched by the receiving team, the ball belongs to the receivers 30 yards from the spot of the kick or at the out-of-bounds spot unless the ball went out-of-bounds the first time an onside kick was attempted. In this case, the kicking team is penalized five yards and the ball must be kicked again.
6. When a kickoff goes out of bounds between the goal lines and is touched last by receiving team, it is receiver's ball at out-of-bounds spot.
7. If the kicking team either illegally kicks off out of bounds or is guilty of a short free kick on two or more consecutive onside kicks, receivers may take possession of the ball at the dead ball spot, out-of-bounds spot, or spot of illegal touch.

SAFETY
1. In addition to a kickoff, the other free kick is a kick after a safety (safety kick). A punt may be used (a punt may not be used on a kickoff).
2. On a safety kick, the team scored upon puts ball in play by a punt, dropkick, or placekick without tee. No score can be made on a free kick following a safety, even if a series of penalties places team in position. (A field goal can be scored only on a play from scrimmage or a free kick after a fair catch.)

FAIR CATCH KICK
1. After a fair catch, the receiving team has the option to put the ball in play by a snap or a fair catch kick (field goal attempt), with fair catch kick lines established ten yards apart. All general rules apply as for a field goal attempt from scrimmage. The clock starts when the ball is kicked. (No tee permitted.)

FIELD GOAL

1. All field goals attempted (kicker) and missed from beyond the 20-yard line will result in the defensive team taking possession of the ball at the spot of the kick. On any field goal attempted and missed where the spot of the kick is on or inside the 20-yard line, ball will revert to defensive team at the 20-yard line.

SAFETY

1. The important factor in a safety is impetus. Two points are scored for the opposing team when the ball is dead on or behind a team's own goal line if the impetus came from a player on that team.

Examples of Safety:

(a) Blocked punt goes out of kicking team's end zone. Impetus was provided by punting team. The block only changes direction of ball, not impetus.

(b) Ball carrier retreats from field of play into his own end zone and is downed. Ball carrier provides impetus.

(c) Offensive team commits a foul and spot of enforcement is behind its own goal line.

(d) Player on receiving team muffs punt and, trying to get ball, forces or illegally kicks (creating new impetus) it into end zone where it goes out of the end zone or is recovered by a member of the receiving team in the end zone.

Examples of Non-Safety:

(a) Player intercepts a pass with both feet inbounds in the field of play and his momentum carries him into his own end zone. Ball is put in play at spot of interception.

(b) Player intercepts a pass in his own end zone and is downed in the end zone, even after recovering in the end zone. Impetus came from passing team, not from defense. (Touchback)

(c) Player passes from behind his own goal line. Opponent bats down ball in end zone. (Incomplete pass)

MEASURING

1. The forward point of the ball is used when measuring.

POSITION OF PLAYERS AT SNAP

1. Offensive team must have at least seven players on line.

2. Offensive players, not on line, must be at least one yard back at snap.
(**Exception:** player who takes snap.)

3. No interior lineman may move abruptly after taking or simulating a three-point stance.

4. No player of either team may enter neutral zone before snap.

5. No player of offensive team may charge or move abruptly, after assuming set position, in such manner as to lead defense to believe snap has started. No player of the defensive team within one yard of the line of scrimmage may make an abrupt movement in an attempt to cause the offense to false start.

6. If a player changes his eligibility, the Referee must alert the defensive captain after player has reported to him.

7. All players of offensive team must be stationary at snap, except one back who may be in motion parallel to scrimmage line or backward (not forward).

8. After a shift or huddle all players on offensive team must come to an absolute stop for at least one second with no movement of hands, feet, head, or swaying of body.

9. Quarterbacks can be called for a false start penalty (five yards) if their actions are judged to be an obvious attempt to draw an opponent offside.

10. Offensive linemen are permitted to interlock legs.

USE OF HANDS, ARMS, AND BODY

1. No player on offense may assist a runner except by blocking for him. There shall be no interlocking interference.

2. A runner may ward off opponents with his hands and arms but no other player on offense may use hands or arms to obstruct an opponent by grasping with hands, pushing, or encircling any part of his body during a block. Hands (open or closed) can be thrust forward to initially contact an opponent on or outside the opponent's frame, but the blocker immediately must work to bring his hands on or inside the frame.
Note: Pass blocking: Hand(s) thrust forward that slip outside the body of the defender will be legal if blocker immediately worked to bring them back inside. Hand(s) or arm(s) that encircle a defender—i.e., hook an opponent—are to be considered illegal and officials are to call a foul for holding. Blocker cannot use his hands or arms to push from behind, hang onto, or encircle an opponent in a manner that restricts his movement as the play develops.

3. Hands cannot be thrust forward above the frame to contact an opponent on the neck, face or head.
Note: The frame is defined as the part of the opponent's body below the neck that is presented to the blocker.

4. A defensive player may not tackle or hold an opponent other than a runner. Otherwise, he may use his hands, arms, or body only:

(a) To defend or protect himself against an obstructing opponent.
Exception: An eligible receiver is considered to be an obstructing opponent ONLY to a point five yards beyond the line of scrimmage unless the player who receives the snap clearly demonstrates no further intention to pass the ball. Within this five-yard zone, a defensive player may chuck an eligible player in front of him. A defensive player is allowed to maintain continuous and unbroken contact within the five-yard zone until a point when the receiver is even with the defender. The defensive player cannot use his hands or arms to push from behind, hang onto, or encircle an eligible receiver in a manner that restricts movement as the play develops. Beyond this five-yard limitation, a defender may use his hands or arms ONLY to defend or protect himself against impending contact caused by a receiver. In such reaction, the defender may not contact a receiver who attempts to take a path to evade him.

(b) To push or pull opponent out of the way on line of scrimmage.

(c) In actual attempt to get at or tackle runner.

(d) To push or pull opponent out of the way in a legal attempt to recover a loose ball.

(e) During a legal block on an opponent who is not an eligible pass receiver.

(f) When legally blocking an eligible pass receiver above the waist.
Exception: Eligible receivers lined up within two yards of the tackle, whether on or immediately behind the line, may be blocked below the waist at or behind the line of scrimmage. NO eligible receiver may be blocked below the waist after he goes beyond the line. (Illegal cut)
Note: Once the quarterback hands off or pitches the ball to a back, or if the quarterback leaves the pocket area, the restrictions (illegal chuck, illegal cut) on the defensive team relative to the offensive receivers will end, provided the ball is not in the air.

5. A defensive player may not contact an opponent above the shoulders with the palm of his hand except to ward him off on the line. This exception is permitted only if it is not a repeated act against the same opponent during any one contact. In all other cases the palms may be used on head, neck, or face only to ward off or push an opponent in legal attempt to get at the ball.

6. Any offensive player who pretends to possess the ball or to whom a teammate pretends to give the ball may be tackled

provided he is <u>crossing</u> his scrimmage line between the ends of a normal tight offensive line.

7. An offensive player who lines up more than two yards outside his own tackle or a player who, at the snap, is in a backfield position and subsequently takes a position more than two yards outside a tackle may not clip an opponent anywhere nor may he contact an opponent below the waist if the blocker is moving toward the ball and if contact is made within an area five yards on either side of the line. (crackback)

8. A player of either team may block at any time provided it is not pass interference, fair catch interference, or unnecessary roughness.

9. A player may not bat or punch:
   (a) A loose ball (in field of play) <u>toward</u> his opponent's goal line or in any direction in either end zone.
   (b) A ball in player possession.
      Note: If there is any question as to whether a defender is stripping or batting a ball in player possession, the official(s) will rule the action as a legal act (stripping the ball).
      Exception: A forward or backward pass may be batted, tipped, or deflected in any direction at any time by either the offense or the defense.
      Note: A pass in flight that is controlled or caught may only be thrown backward, if it is thrown forward it is considered an illegal bat.

10. No player may deliberately kick any ball except as a punt, dropkick, or placekick.

FORWARD PASS

1. A forward pass may be touched or caught by any eligible receiver. All members of the defensive team are eligible. Eligible receivers on the offensive team are players on either end of line (other than center, guard, or tackle) or players at least one yard behind the line at the snap. A T-formation quarterback is <u>not</u> eligible to receive a forward pass during a play from scrimmage.
   Exception: T-formation quarterback becomes eligible if pass is previously touched by an eligible receiver.

2. An offensive team may make only <u>one</u> forward pass during each play from scrimmage (Loss of 5 yards).

3. The passer must be behind his line of scrimmage (Loss of down and five yards, enforced from the spot of pass).

4. Any eligible offensive player may catch a forward pass. If a pass is touched by one eligible offensive player and touched or caught by a second offensive player, pass completion is legal. Further, all offensive players become eligible once a pass is touched by an eligible receiver or any defensive player.

5. The rules concerning a forward pass and ineligible receivers:
   (a) If ball is touched <u>accidentally</u> by an ineligible receiver on or <u>behind his line</u>: loss of five yards.
   (b) If ineligible receiver is illegally downfield: loss of five yards.
   (c) If touched or caught (intentionally or accidentally) by ineligible receiver <u>beyond</u> the line: loss of 5 yards.

6. The player who first controls and continues to maintain control of a pass will be awarded the ball even though his opponent later establishes joint control of the ball.

7. Any forward pass becomes incomplete and ball is dead if:
   (a) Pass hits the ground or goes out of bounds.
   (b) Pass hits the goal post or the crossbar of either team.

8. A forward pass is complete when a receiver clearly possesses the pass and touches the ground with <u>both feet</u> inbounds while in <u>possession</u> of the ball. If a receiver would have landed inbounds with both feet but is carried or pushed out of bounds while maintaining possession of the ball, pass is complete at the out-of-bounds spot.

9. On a <u>fourth down</u> pass an incomplete pass results in a loss of down at the line of scrimmage.

10. If a personal foul is committed by the <u>defense prior</u> to the completion of a pass, the penalty is 15 yards from the spot where ball becomes dead.

11. If a personal foul is committed by the <u>offense prior</u> to the completion of a pass, the penalty is 15 yards from the previous line of scrimmage.

INTENTIONAL GROUNDING OF FORWARD PASS

1. Intentional grounding of a forward pass is a foul: loss of down and 10 yards from previous spot if passer is in the field of play or loss of down at the spot of the foul if it occurs more than 10 yards behind the line or safety if passer is in his own end zone when ball is released.

2. Intentional grounding will be called when a passer, facing an imminent loss of yardage due to pressure from the defense, throws a forward pass without a realistic chance of completion.

3. Intentional grounding will not be called when a passer, while out of the pocket and facing an imminent loss of yardage, throws a pass that lands at or beyond the line of scrimmage, even if no offensive player(s) have a realistic chance to catch the ball (including if the ball lands out of bounds over the sideline or end line).

PROTECTION OF PASSER

1. By interpretation, a pass begins when the passer—with possession of ball—starts to bring his hand forward. If ball strikes ground after this action has begun, play is ruled an incomplete pass. If passer loses control of ball prior to his bringing his hand forward, play is ruled a fumble.

2. When a passer is holding the ball to pass it forward, any intentional movement forward of his arm starts a forward pass. If a defensive player contacts the passer or the ball after forward movement begins, and the ball leaves the passer's hand, a forward pass is ruled, regardless of where the ball strikes the ground or a player.

3. No defensive player may run into a passer of a legal forward pass after the ball has left his hand (15 yards). The Referee must determine whether opponent had a <u>reasonable chance to stop his momentum</u> during an attempt to block the pass or tackle the passer while he still had the ball.

4. No defensive player who has an unrestricted path to the quarterback may hit him flagrantly in the area of the knee(s) or below when approaching in any direction.

5. Officials are to blow the play dead as soon as the quarterback is <u>clearly</u> in the grasp and control of any tackler, and his safety is in jeopardy.

6. No defensive player may hit the quarterback in the head, face, or neck.

PASS INTERFERENCE

1. There shall be no interference with a forward pass thrown from behind the line. The restriction for the <u>passing team</u> starts <u>with the snap</u>. The restriction on the <u>defensive team</u> starts <u>when the ball leaves the passer's hand</u>. Both restrictions <u>end when the ball is touched by anyone</u>.

2. The penalty for <u>defensive</u> pass interference is an automatic first down at the spot of the foul. If interference is in the end zone, it is first down for the offense on the defense's 1-yard line. If previous spot was inside the defense's 1-yard line, penalty is half the distance to the goal line.

3. The penalty for <u>offensive</u> pass interference is 10 yards from the previous spot.

4. It is pass interference by either team when any player movement beyond the line of scrimmage significantly hinders the progress of an eligible player of such player's opportunity to catch the ball. Offensive pass interference rules apply from the time the ball is snapped until the ball is touched. Defensive pass interference rules apply from the time the ball is thrown until the ball is touched.

Actions that constitute defensive pass interference include but are not limited to:

(a) Contact by a defender who is not playing the ball and such contact restricts the receiver's opportunity to make the catch.

(b) Playing through the back of a receiver in an attempt to make a play on the ball.

(c) Grabbing a receiver's arm(s) in such a manner that restricts his opportunity to catch a pass.

(d) Extending an arm across the body of a receiver thus restricting his ability to catch a pass, regardless of whether the defender is playing the ball.

(e) Cutting off the path of a receiver by making contact with him without playing the ball.

(f) Hooking a receiver in an attempt to get to the ball in such a manner that it causes the receiver's body to turn prior to the ball arriving.

Actions that do not constitute pass interference include but are not limited to:

(a) Incidental contact by a defender's hands, arms, or body when both players are competing for the ball, or neither player is looking for the ball. If there is any question whether contact is incidental, the ruling shall be no interference.

(b) Inadvertent tangling of feet when both players are playing the ball or neither player is playing the ball.

(c) Contact that would normally be considered pass interference, but the pass is clearly uncatchable by the involved players.

(d) Laying a hand on a receiver that does not restrict the receiver in an attempt to make a play on the ball.

(e) Contact by a defender who has gained position on a receiver in an attempt to catch the ball.

Actions that constitute offensive pass interference include but are not limited to:

(a) Blocking downfield by an offensive player prior to the ball being touched.

(b) Initiating contact with a defender by shoving or pushing off thus creating a separation in an attempt to catch a pass.

(c) Driving through a defender who has established a position on the field.

Actions that do not constitute offensive pass interference include but are not limited to:

(a) Incidental contact by a receiver's hands, arms, or body when both players are competing for the ball or neither player is looking for the ball.

(b) Inadvertent touching of feet when both players are playing the ball or neither player is playing the ball.

(c) Contact that would normally be considered pass interference, but the ball is *clearly* uncatchable by involved players.

Note 1: If there is any question whether player contact is incidental, the ruling is no interference.

Note 2: Defensive players have as much right to the path of the ball as eligible offensive players.

Note 3: Pass interference for both teams ends when the pass is touched.

Note 4: There can be no pass interference at or behind the line of scrimmage, but defensive actions such as tackling a receiver can still result in a 5-yard penalty for defensive holding, if accepted.

Note 5: Whenever a team presents an apparent punting formation, defensive pass interference is not to be called for action on the end man on the line of scrimmage, or an eligible receiver behind the line of scrimmage who is aligned or in motion more than one yard outside the end man on the line. Defensive holding, such as tackling a receiver, still can be called and result in a 5-yard penalty and automatic first down from the previous spot, if

accepted. Offensive pass interference rules still apply.

BACKWARD PASS

1. Any pass not forward is regarded as a backward pass. A pass parallel to the line is a backward pass. A runner may pass backward at any time.

2. A backward pass that strikes the ground can be recovered and advanced by either team.

3. A backward pass caught in the air can be advanced by either team.

4. A backward pass in flight may not be batted forward by an offensive player.

FUMBLE

1. The distinction between a fumble and a muff should be kept in mind in considering rules about fumbles. A fumble is the loss of player possession of the ball. A muff is the touching of a loose ball by a player in an unsuccessful attempt to obtain possession.

2. A fumble may be advanced by any player on either team regardless of whether recovered before or after ball hits the ground.

3. A fumble that goes forward and out of bounds will return to the fumbling team at the spot of the fumble unless the ball goes out of bounds in the opponent's end zone. In this case, it is a touchback.

4. On a play from scrimmage, if an offensive player fumbles anywhere on the field during fourth down, only the fumbling player is permitted to recover and/or advance the ball. If any player fumbles after the two-minute warning in a half, only the fumbling player is permitted to recover and/or advance the ball. If recovered by any other offensive player, the ball is dead at the spot of the fumble unless it is recovered behind the spot of the fumble. In that case, the ball is dead at the spot of recovery. Any defensive player may recover and/or advance any fumble at any time.

5. A muffed hand-to-hand snap from center is treated as a fumble.

KICKS FROM SCRIMMAGE

1. Any kick from scrimmage must be made from behind the line to be legal.

2. Any punt or missed field goal that touches a goal post is dead.

3. During a kick from scrimmage, only the end men, as eligible receivers on the line of scrimmage at the time of the snap, are permitted to go beyond the line before the ball is kicked.
   Exception: An eligible receiver who, at the snap, is aligned or in motion behind the line and more than one yard outside the end man on his side of the line, clearly making him the outside receiver, replaces that end man as the player eligible to go downfield after the snap. All other members of the kicking team must remain at the line of scrimmage until the ball has been kicked.

4. Any punt that is blocked and does not cross the line of scrimmage can be recovered and advanced by either team. However, if offensive team recovers it must make the yardage necessary for its first down to retain possession if punt was on fourth down.

5. The kicking team may never advance its own kick even though legal recovery is made beyond the line of scrimmage. Possession only.

6. A member of the receiving team may not run into or rough a kicker who kicks from behind his line unless contact is:

   (a) Incidental to and after he had touched ball in flight.

   (b) Caused by kicker's own motions.

   (c) Occurs during a quick kick, or a kick made after a run behind the line, or after kicker recovers a loose ball on the ground. Ball is loose when kicker muffs snap or snap hits ground.

(d) Defender is blocked into kicker.

The penalty for <u>running</u> into the kicker is 5 yards. For <u>roughing</u> the kicker: 15 yards, an automatic first down and disqualification if flagrant.

7. If a member of the kicking team attempting to down the ball on or inside opponent's 5-yard line carries the ball into the end zone, it is a touchback.

8. Fouls during a punt are enforced from the previous spot (line of scrimmage).

Exception: Illegal touching, fair-catch interference, invalid fair-catch signal, or personal foul (blocking after a fair-catch signal).

9. While the ball is in the air or rolling on the ground following a punt or field-goal attempt and receiving team commits a foul only before or after gaining possession, receiving team will retain possession and will be penalized for its foul.

10. It will be illegal for a defensive player to jump or stand on any player, or be picked up by a teammate or to use a hand or hands on a teammate to gain additional height in an attempt to block a kick (Penalty: 15 yards, unsportsmanlike conduct).

11. A punted ball remains a kicked ball until it is declared dead or in possession of either team.

12. Any member of the punting team may <u>down</u> the ball anywhere in the field of play. However, it is <u>illegal touching</u> (Official's time out and receiver's ball at spot of illegal touching). This foul does <u>not</u> offset any foul by receivers during the down.

13. Defensive team may advance all kicks from scrimmage (including unsuccessful field goal) whether or not ball crosses defensive team's goal line. Rules pertaining to kicks from scrimmage apply until defensive team gains possession.

14. When a team presents a punt formation, defensive pass interference is not to be called for actions on the widest player eligible to go beyond line. Defensive holding may be called.

FAIR CATCH

1. The member of the receiving team must raise one arm a full length above his head and wave it from side to side while kick is in flight. (Failure to give proper sign: receivers' ball five yards behind spot of signal.) **Note:** It is legal for the receiver to shield his eyes from the sun by raising one hand no higher than the helmet.

2. No opponent may interfere with the fair catcher, the ball, or his path to the ball. Penalty: 15 yards from spot of foul and fair catch is awarded.

3. A player who signals for a fair catch is <u>not</u> required to catch the ball. However, if a player signals for a fair catch, he may not block or initiate contact with any player on the kicking team <u>until the ball touches a player. Penalty: snap 15 yards.</u>

4. If ball hits ground or is touched by member of kicking team in flight, fair catch signal is off and all rules for a kicked ball apply.

5. Any <u>undue advance</u> by a fair catch receiver is delay of game. No specific distance is specified for undue advance as ball is dead at spot of catch. If player comes to a reasonable stop, no penalty. For penalty, five yards.

6. If time expires while ball is in play and a fair catch is awarded, receiving team may choose to extend the period with one fair catch kick down. However, placekicker may <u>not</u> use tee.

FOUL ON LAST PLAY OF HALF OR GAME

1. On a foul by <u>defense</u> on last play of half or game, the <u>down is replayed</u> if penalty is accepted.

2. On a foul by the offense on last play of half or game, the down is not <u>replayed</u> and the play in which the foul is committed is nullified.

Exception: Fair catch interference, foul following change of possession, illegal touching. <u>No score by offense counts.</u>

SPOT OF ENFORCEMENT OF FOUL

1. There are four basic spots at which a penalty for a foul is enforced:

(a) Spot of foul: The spot where the foul is committed.

(b) Previous spot: The spot where the ball was put in play.

(c) Spot of snap, backward pass or fumble: The spot where the foul occurred or the spot where the penalty is to be enforced.

(d) Succeeding spot: The spot where the ball next would be put in play if no distance penalty were to be enforced.

Exception: If foul occurs after a touchdown and before the whistle for a try, succeeding spot is spot of next kickoff.

2. All fouls committed by <u>offensive</u> team <u>behind</u> the line of scrimmage (except in the end zone) shall be penalized from the <u>previous spot</u>. If the foul is in the end zone, it is a safety.

3. When spot of enforcement for fouls involving defensive holding or illegal use of hands by the defense is behind the line of scrimmage, any penalty yardage to be assessed on that play shall be measured from the line if the foul occurred beyond the line.

DOUBLE FOUL

1. If there is a double foul <u>during</u> a down in which there is a change of possession, the team last gaining possession may keep the ball unless its foul was committed prior to the change of possession.

2. If double foul occurs <u>after</u> a change of possession, the defensive team retains the ball at the spot of its foul or dead ball spot.

3. If one of the fouls of a double foul involves disqualification, that player must be removed, but no penalty yardage is to be assessed.

4. If the kickers foul during a kickoff, punt, safety kick, or field-goal attempt before possession changes, the receivers will have the option of replaying the down at the previous spot (offsetting fouls), or keeping the ball after enforcement for its fouls.

PENALTY ENFORCED ON FOLLOWING KICKOFF

1. When a team scores by touchdown, field goal, extra point, or safety and either team commits a personal foul, unsportsmanlike conduct, or obvious unfair act during the down, the penalty will be assessed on the following kickoff.

EMERGENCIES AND UNFAIR ACTS
Emergencies—Policy

The National Football League requires all League personnel, including game officials, League office employees, players, coaches, and other club employees to use best effort to see that each game—preseason, regular season, and postseason—is played to its conclusion. The League recognizes, however, that emergencies may arise that make a game's completion impossible or inadvisable. Such circumstances may include, but are not limited to, severely inclement weather, natural or manmade disaster, power failure, and spectator interference. Games should be suspended, cancelled, postponed, or terminated when circumstances exist such that commencement or continuation of play would pose a threat to the safety of participants or spectators.

Authority of Commissioner's Office

1. Authority to cancel, postpone, or terminate games is vested only in the Commissioner and the League President (other League office representatives and referees may suspend play temporarily; see point No. 3 under this section and point No. 1 under "Authority of Referee" below). The following definitions apply:

• **Cancel.** To cancel a game is to nullify it either before or after it begins and to make no provision for rescheduling it or for including its score or other performance statistics in League records.

- **Postpone.** To postpone a game is (a) to defer its starting time to a later date, or (b) to suspend it after play has begun and to make provision to resume at a later date with all scores and other performance statistics up to the point of postponement added to those achieved in the resumed portion of the game.
- **Terminate.** To terminate a game is to end it short of a full 60 minutes of play, to record it officially as a completed game, and to make no provision to resume it at a later date. The Commissioner or League President may terminate a game in an emergency if, in his opinion, it is reasonable to project that its resumption (a) would not change its ultimate result or (b) would not adversely affect any other interteam competitive issue.
- **Forfeit.** The Commissioner, (except in cases of disciplinary action; see last section on "Removing Team from Field"), League President, and their representatives, including referees, are not authorized unilaterally to declare forfeits. A forfeit occurs only when a game is not played because of the failure or refusal of *one* team to participate. In that event, the other team, if ready and willing to play, is the winner by a score of 2-0.

2. If an emergency arises that may require cancellation, postponement, or termination (see above), the highest ranking representative from the Commissioner's office working the game in a "control" capacity will consult with the Commissioner, League President, or game-day duty officer designated by the League (by telephone, if that person is not in attendance) concerning such decision. If circumstances warrant, the League representative should also attempt to consult with the weather bureau and with appropriate security personnel of the League, club, stadium, and local authorities. If no representative from the Commissioner's office is working the game in a "control" capacity, the referee will be in charge (see "Authority of Referee" below).

3. In circumstances where safety is of immediate concern, the Commissioner's office representative may, after consulting with the referee, authorize a temporary suspension in play and, if warranted, removal of the participants from the playing field. The representative should be mindful of the safety of spectators, players, game officials, nonplayer personnel in the bench areas, and other field-level personnel such as photographers and cheerleaders.

4. If possible, the League-office representative should consult with authorized representatives of the two participating clubs before any decision involving cancellation, postponement, or termination is made by the Commissioner or League President.

5. If the Commissioner or League President decides to cancel, postpone, or terminate a game, his representative at the game or the game-day duty officer will then determine the method(s) for announcing such decision, e.g., by public-address announcement over referee's wireless microphone, by public-address announcement by home club, or by communication to radio, television, and other news media.

Authority of Referee

1. If a referee determines that an emergency warrants immediate removal of participants from the playing field for safety reasons, he may do so on his own authority. If, however, circumstances allow him the time, he must reach the highest ranking full-time League office representative working at the game in a "control" capacity or the game-day duty officer designated by the League (by telephone, if that person is not in attendance) and discuss the actual or potential emergency with such representative or duty officer. That representative or duty officer then will make the final decision on removal of participants from the field or obtain a decision from the Commissioner or League President.

2. If a referee removes participants from the playing field under No. 1 above, he may order them to their respective bench areas or to their locker rooms, whichever is appropriate in the circumstances.

3. After appropriate consultation under No. 1 above, the referee must advise the two participating head coaches of the nature of the emergency and the action contemplated (if the decision has not yet been reached) or of the final decision.

4. The referee must *not*, before a decision is reached, make an announcement on his microphone concerning the possibility of a cancellation, postponement, or termination unless instructed to do so by an appropriate representative of the Commissioner's office.

5. The referee must *not* discuss a forfeit with head coaches or club personnel and must *not* use that term over the referee's microphone (see definition of *forfeit* under No. 1 of "Authority of Commissioner's Office" above).

6. The referee must *not* assess an unsportsmanlike-conduct penalty on the home team for actions of fans that cause or contribute to an emergency.

7. The referee should be mindful of the safety of not only players and officials, but also of the spectators and other nonparticipants.

8. If an emergency involves spectator interference (for example, nonparticipants on the field or thrown objects), the referee immediately should contact the appropriate club or League representative for additional security assistance, including, if applicable, involvement of the League's security representative(s) assigned to the game.

9. The referee may order the resumption of play when he deems conditions safe for all concerned and, if circumstances warrant, after consultation with appropriate representatives of the Commissioner's office.

10. Under no circumstances is the referee authorized to cancel, postpone, terminate, or declare forfeiture of a game unilaterally.

Procedures for Starting and Resuming Games

Subject to the points of authority listed above, League personnel and referees will be guided by the following procedures for starting and resuming games that are affected by emergencies.

1. If, because of an emergency, a regular-season or postseason game is not started at its scheduled time and cannot be played at any later time that same day, the game nevertheless must be played on a subsequent date to be determined by the Commissioner.

2. If an emergency threatens to occur during the playing of a game (for example, an incoming tropical storm), the starting time of the game will not be moved to an earlier time unless there is clearly sufficient time to make an orderly change.

3. All games that are suspended temporarily and resumed on the same day, and all suspended games that are postponed to a later date, will be resumed at the point of suspension. On suspension, the referee will call timeout and make a record of the following: team possessing the ball, direction in which its offense was headed, position of the ball on the field, down, distance, period, time remaining in the period, and any other pertinent information required for an orderly and equitable resumption of play.

4. For regular-season postponements, the Commissioner will make every effort to set the game for no later than two days after its originally scheduled date and at the same site. If unable to schedule at the same site, he will select an appropriate alternative site. If it is impossible to schedule the game within two days after its original date, the Commissioner will attempt to schedule it on the Tuesday of the next calendar week. The Commissioner will keep in mind the potential for competitive inequities if one or both of the involved clubs has already been scheduled for a game close to the Tuesday of that week (for example, a Thursday game).

5. For postseason postponements, the Commissioner will make every effort to set the game as soon as possible after its originally scheduled date and at the same site. If unable to

schedule at the same site, he will select an appropriate alternative site.

6. Whenever postponement is attributable to negligence by a club, the negligent club is responsible for all home club costs and expenses, including, subject to approval by the Commissioner, gate receipts and television-contract income. [See Section 19.11 (C) of the NFL Constitution and Bylaws.]

7. Each home club is strictly responsible for having the playing surface of its stadium well maintained and suitable for NFL play.

UNFAIR ACTS

Commissioner's Authority

The Commissioner has sole authority to investigate and to take appropriate disciplinary or corrective measures if any club action, nonparticipant interference, or emergency occurs in an NFL game which he deems so unfair or outside the accepted tactics encountered in professional football that such action has a major effect on the result of a game.

No Club Protests

The authority and measures provided for in this section (UNFAIR ACTS) do not constitute a protest machinery for NFL clubs to dispute the result of a game. The Commissioner will conduct an investigation under this section only to review an act or occurrence that he deems so unfair that the result of the game in question may be inequitable to one of the participating teams. The Commissioner will not apply his authority under this section when a club registers a complaint concerning judgmental errors or routine errors of omission by game officials. Games involving such complaints will continue to stand as completed.

Penalties for Unfair Acts

The Commissioner's powers under this section (UNFAIR ACTS) include the imposition of monetary fines and draft choice forfeitures, suspension of persons involved, and, if appropriate, the reversal of a game's result or the rescheduling of a game, either from the beginning or from the point at which the extraordinary act occurred. In the event of rescheduling a game, the Commissioner will be guided by the procedures specified above ("Procedures for Starting and Resuming Games" under EMERGENCIES). In all cases, the Commissioner will conduct a full investigation, including the opportunity for hearings, use of game videotape, and any other procedures he deems appropriate.

REMOVING TEAM FROM FIELD

No player, coach, or other person affiliated with a club may remove that club's team from the field during the playing of any game, including preseason, except at the direction of the referee. Any club violating this rule will be subject to disciplinary action by the Commissioner, including possible game forfeiture and sole liability for financial losses suffered by the opposing club and any other affected member clubs of the League. [See Section 9.1 (E) of the NFL Constitution and Bylaws.]

280 Park Avenue, New York, New York 10017 (212) 450-2000

NFL Internet Network: www.NFL.com

Commissioner: Paul Tagliabue

Executive Vice President/Chief Operating Officer: Roger Goodell

Executive Vice President/Chief Administrative Officer-Counsel: Jeff Pash

Executive Vice President of Labor Relations/Chairman NFLMC: Harold Henderson

Executive Vice President of Communications and Public Affairs: Joe Browne

Chief Financial Officer: Barbara Kaczynski

Holy Bible

From the Ancient Eastern Text

Holy Bible

FROM THE ANCIENT
EASTERN TEXT

George M. Lamsa's Translations
From the Aramaic of the
Peshitta

1817

Harper & Row, Publishers, San Francisco
Cambridge, Hagerstown, New York, Philadelphia
London, Mexico City, São Paulo, Singapore, Sydney

Library of Congress Catalog Card Number 84-48225
ISBN 0-06-064922
ISBN 0-06-064923-2 (pbk.)

85 86 87 88 89 10 9 8 7 6 5 4 3 2 1

PREFACE

The favorable reception accorded the Lamsa translation of the Gospels, later of the New Testament and of the Psalms, has prompted us to publish a complete translation of The Holy Bible from the Peshitta, the authorized Bible of the Church of the East. This translation of the Old and New Testaments into English is based on Peshitta manuscripts which have comprised the accepted Bible of all of those Christians who have used Syriac as their language of prayer and worship for many centuries. It is appropriate that as we have translations based on the Greek Septuagint of the Old Testament and on the Latin Bible of Jerome, so also should there be available to the modern reader that form of the text which was translated anciently into a branch of the Aramaic language which has been used by Christians from earliest times.

In the long history of the Aramaic language, there are three periods of special interest to us. From the sixth to the fourth century before Christ, it was a language of empire extending from the borders of Persia to those of Europe, and down the Nile through the length of Egypt. It was in those days spoken and written by the Jewish people at least equally with Hebrew; and so we have parts of Ezra and Daniel, and one verse in Jeremiah (10:11), that were composed in Aramaic and preserved in that ancient form of the language in the midst of the Hebrew Old Testament.

In the first century, Jesus and his earliest followers certainly spoke Aramaic for the most part, although they also knew Hebrew. Therefore the Gospel message was first preached in the Aramaic of the Jews of Palestine. Modern scholarship tells us that the originals of the Four Gospels and of other parts of the New Testament were written in Greek; this is disputed by the Church of the East and by some noted Western scholars. Regardless of which view one may accept, Aramaic speech is an underlying factor and it is unquestionably true that documents written in Aramaic were drawn on by writers of the New Testament, the basic inspired form of the Christian message.

Aramaic was the language of the Church that spread east, almost from the beginning of Christianity, from Antioch and Jerusalem, beyond the confines of the Roman Empire. This differed from the language of Palestine in choice of words and grammatical forms rather more extensively than does American English from British English and in written form these differences became regular and standardized. The Jews and Christians used the literary dialect of Aramaic that we call Syriac almost at the same time to propagate their translations of the sacred books brought from Palestine and the West, reaching into Syria and Mesopotamia and the nearby mountains, quite early into India, and into China in the course of time. Modern scholarship believes that as happened in other parts of the Church, the earliest copies of the sacred books in Syriac were revised again and again to bring them closer to the standard of the Hebrew and Greek texts from which they were drawn; this view, too, is not accepted by the Church of the East. Under any conditions by the fifth century A.D. the Peshitta version in its present form held the field by universal acclaim.

i

Preface

The fixed stand of the Church of the East with respect to some of the points mentioned above can best be understood by reference to the following letter, which we are authorized to quote, from the Patriarch and Head of that Church:

Patriarchate of the East, Modesto, California, April 5, 1957
"With reference to your letter concerning Lamsa's translation of the Aramaic Bible, and the originality of the Peshitta text, as the Patriarch and Head of the Holy Apostolic and Catholic Church of the East we wish to state, that the Church of the East received the scriptures from the hands of the blessed Apostles themselves in the Aramaic original, the language spoken by our Lord Jesus Christ himself, and that the Peshitta is the text of the Church of the East which has come down from the Biblical times without any change or revision."

Mar Eshai Shimun
by Grace, Catholicos Patriarch
of the East

From the Mediterranean east into India the Peshitta is still the Bible of preference among Christians, though today nearly all who use it speak Arabic, or one of the tongues of South India. West of the Euphrates, spoken Aramaic as a mother-tongue survives today only in two mountain villages northwest of Damascus, differing as much from the speech of Jesus' day as French from its parent Latin. East of the Euphrates, in the Kurdish mountains, and near Lake Urmia, perhaps a hundred thousand people (Christian, Jew and Muslim) speak another form of it, strangely mixed with borrowed words from the various languages of their polyglot neighbors, but still basically akin to the Aramaic (Syriac) of olden times.

George M. Lamsa, B.A., F.R.S.A., the translator of this work is uniquely fitted for the task to which he has devoted the major part of his life. He is an Assyrian and a native of ancient Biblical lands, where he lived until World War I. Until that time, isolated from the rest of Christendom, his people retained Biblical customs and Semitic culture which had perished everywhere else. This background, together with his knowledge of the Aramaic (Syriac) language, has enabled him to recover much of the meaning that has been lost in other translations of the Scriptures.

Manuscripts used in making this translation were the Codex Ambrosianus for the Old Testament and the so-called Mortimer-McCawley manuscript for the New Testament; the former is in the Ambrosian Library at Milan, Italy, and has been identified as fifth century A.D.; the latter was used for our previous translation of the New Testament, of which this edition is a revision, and has been variously identified as sixth or seventh century A.D. Comparisons have been had with Peshitta manuscripts in the Morgan Library, New York, N. Y., with manuscripts in the Freer Collection, Washington, D. C., with the Urumiah edition, and with a manuscript of the Peshitta Old Testament in the British Museum, the oldest *dated* Biblical manuscript in existence. Our translator states that comparisons show no differences in text between these various manuscripts, and that he has filled in the few missing portions of Chronicles from other authentic Peshitta sources, as noted in his Introduction.

We hope that this translation will be of aid to Bible readers and students in obtaining a more thorough and complete understanding of the Scriptures.

THE PUBLISHER

INTRODUCTION

North of the Garden of Eden in the basin of the river Tigris, in the mountain fastnesses of what is known today as Kurdistan, there lived an ancient people, the descendants of the Assyrians, the founders of the great Assyrian empire and culture in Bible days, the originators of the alphabet and many sciences which contributed so generously to the Semitic culture from which sprang our Bible. These people, the Assyrians, played an important part in the history of the Near East, of the Bible, and of religion in general.

When Nineveh was destroyed in 612 B.C., many of the princes and noblemen of this once vast empire fled northward into inaccessible mountains where they remained secluded and cut off until the dawn of the twentieth century. Nahum says: "Thy shepherds slumber, O king of Assyria: thy nobles shall dwell in the dust: thy people is scattered upon the mountains, and no man gathereth them." Nah. 3:18.

Some descendants of the Assyrians and some of the descendants of the ten tribes who were taken captive by the Assyrian kings in 721 B.C., and settled in Assyria, Babylon, Persia and other places east of the river Euphrates, were among the first converts to Christianity.

When Jesus sent seventy of his disciples to preach the gospel, he instructed them not to go in the way of the Gentiles or into any city of the Samaritans but to go to the lost sheep of the house of Israel, meaning the ten tribes who were lost from the house of Israel. Some of the descendants of these Hebrew tribes are still living in Iraq, Iran, and Turkey, and most of them still converse in Aramaic. Jesus' command was carried out. The gospel was preached to the Jews first. "Now those who had been dispersed by the persecution which occurred on account of Stephen traveled as far as Phoenicia and even to the land of Cyprus and to Antioch, preaching the word to none but to the Jews only." Acts 11:19.

The Assyrians remained dormant during the Persian, Greek, Roman and Arab conquests. Being isolated and surrounded by their enemies, they remained secluded throughout the centuries, thus preserving the Aramaic language, which was the language of the Near East, and perpetuating the ancient Biblical customs and manners which were common to all races and peoples in this part of the ancient world. Not until the Turkish reign did these isolated Assyrian tribes recognize any government or pay any taxes. During the centuries of Arab and Turkish reigns, the Assyrians retained their cultural independence, later recognizing the sympathetic Turkish rule which permitted the continuation of their institutions and their religion. Under magnanimous Turks they were ruled by their patriarchs and chiefs, paying a nominal tax to the Turkish government.

The Assyrian church, or as it is known, the ancient Apostolic and Catholic Church of the East, was one of the strongest Christian churches in the world and was noted for its missions in the Middle East, India, and China. Its missionaries carried the Christian gospel as far as China and Mongolia, Indonesia, Japan and other parts of the world. Not until the 14th century was this church rivaled by any other church in the world. It was the most powerful branch of Christen-

Introduction

dom in the Near East, Palestine, Arabia, Lebanon, Iran, India and elsewhere.

All the literature of this church was written in literary Aramaic, the lingua franca of that time. This is corroborated by Dr. Arnold J. Toynbee in his *A Study of History* wherein he writes: " . . . Darius the Great's account of his own acts on the rock of Behistan, overhanging the Empire's great north-east road, was transcribed in triplicate in three different adaptations of the cuneiform script conveying the three imperial capitals: Elamite for Susa, Medo-Persian for Ecbatana, and Akkadian for Babylon. But the winning language within this universal state was none of the three thus officially honoured; it was Aramaic, with its handier alphabetic script. The sequel showed that commerce and culture may be more important than politics in making a language's fortune; for the speakers of Aramaic were politically of no account in the Achaemenian Empire . . . " *

The Persians used the Aramaic language because this tongue was the language of the two Semitic empires, the empire of Assyria and the empire of Babylon. Aramaic was so firmly established as the lingua franca that no government could dispense with its use as a vehicle of expression in a far-flung empire, especially in the western provinces. Moreover, without schools and other modern facilities, Aramaic could not be replaced by the speech of conquering nations. Conquerors were not interested in imposing their languages and cultures on subjugated peoples. What they wanted was taxes, spoils, and other levies.

The transition from Aramaic [1] into Arabic, a sister tongue, took place after the conquest of the Near East by the Moslem armies in the 7th century, A.D. Nevertheless, Aramaic lingered for many centuries and still is spoken in Lebanon, Syria, Iraq, and northwestern Iran, as well as among the Christian Arab tribes in northern Arabia. Its alphabet was borrowed by the Hebrews, Arabs, Iranians, and Mongols.

Dr. Philip K. Hitti, noted historian and Professor of Semitic languages at Princeton University, in his book *The History of the Arabs*, uses the terms *Aramaic* and *Syriac* interchangeably and states that Aramaic is still a living language. He says, "In country places and on their farms these dhimmis clung to their ancient cultural patterns and preserved their native languages: Aramaic and Syriac in Syria and Al-'Iraq, Iranian in Persia and Coptic in Egypt." And again, "In Al-'Iraq and Syria the transition from one Semitic tongue, the Aramaic, to another, the Arabic, was of course easier. In the out-of-the-way places, however, such as the Lebanons with their preponderant Christian population, the native Syriac put up a desperate fight and has lingered until modern times. Indeed Syriac is still spoken in Ma'lula and two other villages in Anti-Lebanon. With its disappearance, Aramaic has left in the colloquial Arabic unmistakable traces noticeable in vocabulary, accent and grammatical structure." **

The late Dr. W. A. Wigram in *The Assyrians and Their Neighbours* wrote: "One thing is certain, that the Assyrians boast with justice that they alone of all Christian nations still keep as their spoken language what is acknowledged to be the language of Palestine in the first century . . . " ***

Quoting Dr. Toynbee again from *A Study of History*: " . . . As for the Aramaic alphabet, it achieved far wider conquests. In 1599 A.D., it was adopted for the conveyance of the Manchu language on the eve of the Manchu conquest of China. The higher religions sped it on its way by taking it into their service. In its 'Square Hebrew' variant it became the vehicle of the Jewish Scriptures and liturgy; in an Arabic adaptation it became the alphabet of Islam . . . " *

As a miracle of miracles, Aramaic and most of the ancient Biblical customs which were common to Semitic people have survived in northern Iraq until today. Aramaic is still spoken in Iraq and in northwestern Iran by remnants of the Assyrian people and the Jews of the exile, and the literary Aramaic remains the same today as it was of yore. Some of the Aramaic words which are still retained in all Bible versions are still used in the Aramaic language spoken today: for

---

[1] The Greeks called it *Syriac* (derived from Sur, Tyre).
* By permission of Oxford University Press, Publishers, and D. C. Somervell.
** By permission of the author, the book, Macmillan & Co., Ltd. and St. Martin's Press.
*** By permission of G. Bell & Sons, Publishers, London.

Introduction

example, *Raca, Ethpatakh, Rabbuli, Lemana, Shabakthani, Talitha Koomi, Maran Etha, Manna, Khakal-Dema.*

As we have said, the survival of this small remnant of this segment of the ancient Semitic culture was due to the isolation, tenacity, and warlike character of the Assyrian people who were living isolated, now under the Parthian Empire, now under the Persian Empire, now under the Arabian Empire and now under the Turkish Empire. And because of this isolation, these ancient Christians had hardly any contact with Christians in the West. Only one of their bishops and a deacon participated in the Nicene Council in 325 A.D.

After the conversion of Emperor Constantine to Christianity in 318 A.D., Christians in the Persian Empire who hitherto had been tolerated and looked upon as the enemies of Rome, the persecutor of Christianity, now were looked upon as the friends of the Christian emperor, Constantine, and the enemies of the Persian government. Persecution of these Christians did not begin until the 4th century A.D., and lasted until the Arab conquest of Persia, 632 A.D. This is why this ancient Church was unable to establish contacts with Western Christianity.

The Scriptures in the Church of the East, from the inception of Christianity to the present day, are in Aramaic and have never been tampered with or revised, as attested by the present Patriarch of the Church of the East. The Biblical manuscripts were carefully and zealously handed down from one generation to another and kept in the massive stone walls of the ancient churches and in caves. They were written on parchment and many of them survive to the present day. When these texts were copied by expert scribes, they were carefully examined for accuracy before they were dedicated and permitted to be read in churches. Even one missing letter would render the text void. Easterners still adhere to God's commandment not to add to or omit a word from the Scriptures. The Holy Scripture condemns any addition or subtraction or modification of the Word of God.

"You shall not add to the commandment which I command you, neither shall you take from it, but you must keep the commandments of the LORD your God which I command you." Deut. 4:2.

"Everything that I command you, that you must be careful to do; you shall not add nor take from it." Deut. 12:32.

"Do not add to his words; lest he reprove you, and you be found a liar." Prov. 30:6.

"And if any man shall take away from the words of the book of this prophecy, God shall take away his portion from the tree of life and from the holy city and from the things which are written in this book." Rev. 22:19.

It is also true of the Jews and Moslems that they would not dare to alter a word of the Torah or Koran. Easterners are afraid that they may incur the curse if they make a change in the Word of God.

Some of these ancient manuscripts go back to the 5th century A.D. The oldest dated Biblical manuscript in the world is that of the four Books of Moses, 464 A.D., which now lies in the British Museum. Another one is the Codex Ambrosianus. Some of it goes back to the 7th century, some of it to the 5th century, and some of it might be earlier. This Codex is not the work of one man. Apparently some portions were written before the vowel system was invented and that would put it prior to the 5th century. The Pentateuch of the British Museum must have been written before the vowel system was invented. Aramaic documents of the 5th century and later use the vowel system, some of them fully and some in part. It is interesting to know that this vowel system was adopted by the Jews and was begun about the 5th century, A.D. In some portions of the above texts, the old Aramaic original consonantal spelling without apparatus of vowel points is well preserved. This is also true of some of the New Testament texts in the Pierpont Morgan Library, New York City.

Unfortunately many ancient and valuable Aramaic texts were lost during World War I. But printed copies of them, carefully made by American missionaries under the help and guidance of competent native scholars, are available. Moreover, a number of ancient New Testament texts, some of them going back to the 5th century A.D. are in various libraries. The New Testament texts in the Pierpont Morgan Library are among the oldest in existence.

Introduction

The translator of this work has access to the existing texts; he has spent many years comparing them in the course of translating the Bible.

Astonishingly enough, all the Peshitta texts in Aramaic agree. There is one thing of which the Eastern scribes can boast: they copied their holy books diligently, faithfully, and meticulously. Sir Frederick Kenyon, Curator of the British Museum, in his book *Textual Criticism of the New Testament,* speaks highly of the accuracy of copying and of the antiquity of Peshitta MSS.

The versions translated from Semitic languages into Greek and Latin were subject to constant revisions. Learned men who copied them introduced changes, trying to simplify obscurities and ambiguities which were due to the work of the first translators. Present translators and Bible revisers do the same when translating the Bible, treaties, and documents from one language to another. The American Constitution, written in English, will always remain the same when new copies are made, but translations into other languages will be subject to revision. Therefore, a copy of the United States Constitution published ten years ago is far more valuable than a translation made two hundred years ago. Translations are always subject to revisions and disputes over exact meaning because words and terms of speech in one language cannot be translated easily into another without loss. This is one reason why we have so many translations and revisions of the King James version.

As said before, Aramaic was the language of Semitic culture, the language of the Hebrew patriarchs and, in the older days, the lingua franca of the Fertile Crescent. The term "Hebrew" is derived from the Aramaic word *Abar* or *Habar* which means "to cross over." This name was given to the Hebrew people simply because Abraham and the people who were with him crossed the river Euphrates and went to Palestine. Therefore, they were known by those who lived east of the river Euphrates as Hebrews, that is, "the people across the river." All branches of the great Semitic people had a common speech. How could the people of Nineveh have understood Jonah, a Hebrew prophet, had the Biblical Hebrew tongue been different from Aramaic? There were some differences similar to the differences we have in English spoken in Tennessee and that spoken in New York.

This small pastoral Hebrew tribe through which God chose to reveal himself to mankind, for several generations continued to keep its paternal and racial relations with the people who lived in Padan-Aram (Mesopotamia), and preserved customs and manners which they brought with them from Padan-Aram, and the language which their fathers spoke. Jacob changed the name of Luz to Beth-el (Aramaic—the house of God). Abraham instructed his servant not to let his son, Isaac, marry a Palestinian maid but to go to Padan-Aram to his own kindred from whence to bring a maid to his son. Years later, Jacob, the grandson of Abraham, went to Padan-Aram and married his uncle's two daughters and their handmaids and lived in Haran about twenty years. Eleven of his sons were born in Padan-Aram. The first generation of the children of Jacob went to Egypt. Their sojourn in Palestine was so brief that there was no possibility of linguistic change. That is why they spoke the language which they had learned in Padan-Aram. While in Egypt, living by themselves, they continued to use names of Aramaic derivation such as Manasseh, Ephraim, Bar-Nun, Miriam, etc.

After the captivity, Aramaic became the vernacular of the Jewish people and is still used by them in their worship. Both of the Jewish Talmuds, namely, the Babylonian and Palestinian, were written in Aramaic. The later findings, especially of Jewish-Aramaic papyri which were found in Egypt in 1900, have produced many passages in Biblical Aramaic. The discovery of the Commentary on the Book of Habakkuk in the caves of Qumran in Jordan proves that Aramaic has been in constant use from early times to the present day.

It is evident that during the exile and post-exile the Hebrew writers used Aramaic. Some of the portions of their works were put into Hebrew. Daniel and Ezra were born during the captivity. Hebrew was no longer spoken and the official language of writing in Babylon was southern Aramaic and the Jewish community had already parted with their Hebrew.[1] Thus, the captivity produced the transition from Hebrew, a sister language, into Aramaic.

[1] The two languages were so close that Hebrew could not be retained in Babylon.

Introduction

Biblical Hebrew and Aramaic were very closely related, like American English and English spoken in England. Whether the Hebrew prophets wrote in Hebrew or Aramaic would make little difference. The differences would be like those between several Arabic dialects which are spoken in Arabia. Even though the vernacular speech differs because of local color and idioms, the norm of the written language remains the same. This is true today with written Arabic when compared with spoken Arabic. And such was the case with Attic Greek when compared with other Greek dialects. The grammar, verbs, nouns and other parts of speech are practically the same in the basic ancient Biblical Hebrew language and Aramaic. The structure of a sentence, in point of grammar and syntax of Biblical Hebrew and Aramaic, is the same. But this is not the case when translating from Hebrew or Aramaic into a totally alien tongue such as Greek, Latin, or English. Moreover, the alphabet in Hebrew and Aramaic is exactly the same and all letters are pronounced alike.

The Jewish Encyclopedia, Vol. II, tells us:
"In Palestinian Aramaic the dialect of Galilee was different from that of Judea, and as a result of the religious separation of the Jews and the Samaritans, a special Samaritan dialect was evolved, but its literature cannot be considered Jewish. To the eastern Aramaic, whose most distinctive point of difference is "n" in place of "y" as the prefix for the third person masculine of the imperfect tense of the verb, belong the idioms of the Babylonian Talmud, which most closely agree with the language of the Mandaean writings." *

The strongest points in ascertaining the originality of a text are the style of writing, the idioms, and the internal evidence. Words which make sense and are easily understood in one language, when translated literally into another tongue, may lose their meaning. One can offer many instances where scores of Aramaic words, some with several meanings and others with close resemblance to other words, were confused and thus mistranslated.

This is why in Jeremiah 4:10, we read in the King James:
". . . Ah, LORD God! surely thou hast greatly deceived this people . . ."
The Aramaic reads:
". . . Ah, LORD God! I have greatly deceived this people . . . " The translator's confusion is due to the position of a dot, for the position of a dot frequently determines the meaning of a word.
In Isaiah 43:28, the King James version reads:
"Therefore, I have profaned the princes of the sanctuary . . ."
The Aramaic reads:
". . . Your princes have profaned my sanctuary . . . " This error was caused by misunderstanding of a passive plural verb. The same error occurs in John 12:40, which in the Eastern Text reads:
'. . . Their eyes have become blind . . ." instead of ". . . He hath blinded their eyes . . ."
In Isaiah 14:12, the Aramaic word *ailel,* to howl, is confused by the Hebrew word *helel,* light. The reference here is to the king of Babylon and not to Lucifer.
In Psalm 22:29, King James version, we read:
"All they that be fat upon earth shall eat and worship . . . and none can keep alive his own soul."
The Aramaic text reads:
"All those who are hungry (for truth) shall eat and worship . . . my soul is alive to him." The error in this instance is due to the confusion of the Aramaic words which have some resemblance. Some of these words when written by hand resemble one another. A list of words, their meanings and how they were confused one with the other will be found in this Introduction.

THE ARAMAIC PESHITTA TEXT

The term Peshitta means straight, simple, sincere and true, that is, the original. This name was given to this ancient and authoritative text to distinguish it from

---

* By special permission of Funk and Wagnalls, copyright owners, New York and London.

Introduction

other Bible revisions and translations which were introduced into some of the Churches of the East (Monophysites) after the division at Ephesus and Chalcedon in 431 and 451 A.D., respectively. This ancient Peshitta is still the only authoritative text of the Old and New Testament of all Eastern Christians in the Near East and India, the Church of the East, the Roman Catholic Church in the East, the Monophysites, and Indian Christians. This is because this text was in use for 400 years before the Christian Church was divided into several sects.

The Peshitta Old Testament contains what is known as the Books of the Apocrypha, which have been handed down in the Peshitta manuscripts together with the Books of the Law and the Books of the Prophets, and since these Apocryphal books are included in the text they are looked upon as a sacred literature, even though they are not as commonly used as the others. Moreover this ancient New Testament text omits the story of the woman taken in adultery, 2 Peter, 2 and 3 John, Jude, and Revelation. (But these books are included in later Aramaic texts.) The Peshitta canon was set before the discovery of these books.

Amid persecutions, the ancient Church of the East, through God's help and protection, was able to keep these sacred writings of the Old and New Testaments in the Biblical lands in Persia and India just as the Roman Catholic Church preserved them in the West. Christianity also owes a debt to the Jewish people who preserved the Word of God amid persecution and suffering.

Therefore, Peshitta should not be confused with the 5th century Bible revisions in Aramaic and new versions which were made from Greek. None of these new revisions and versions made by the Monophysite bishops in the 5th century has ever been accepted by the Church of the East. Moreover, these bishops who left their church and joined the Greek church and produced these versions for theological reasons so that their doctrine might agree with the doctrine of the Byzantine Church, which was the powerful imperial sect, were expelled by the Patriarch of the East and their works were condemned. However, in some provinces, owing to the pressure exerted by the Byzantine emperors, these new revisions were introduced. But when the territory was occupied by the Persian government, they were destroyed.

Had the Peshitta been made by order of one of the rival churches, the others would have rejected it. But since all Christians, even the Moslems, in the Middle East accept and revere the Peshitta text, it proves beyond a doubt that it was in use many centuries before the division of the Church.

The originality of the Peshitta text is strongly supported by early evidence. Aphraates quoted it. St. Ephraim wrote a commentary on it and the doctrine of Addi placed it at the apostolic times.

According to the Peshitta text, the Semitic names of people and towns and localities, in both the New and Old Testaments, agree. The names which end with "s" are retained for the western reader. In the Peshitta text, Barnabas is Barnba, Abbas is Abba, Peter is Kepa. Then again, some of the names of localities are different but older than those in other texts. For example, Rakim is used instead of Kadesh, Mathnin instead of Bashan, Amorah for Gomorah; the error in this instance is due to close similarity between *gamel* and *ain*. A town near the city of Gomorah is called Amoriah. No doubt, the pre-exile Hebrew texts used these older names.

The late Mar-Yacob (Jacob) Eugene Manna, Chaldean Roman Catholic Metropolitan of Armenia, a distinguished Aramaic scholar whose writings are in Aramaic, says that the text which is called Peshitta is without dispute even earlier than the writings which came down from the works of Bar-Dasan, who was living in the latter part of the second century. He also states that the Aramaic speech in Mesopotamia was richer and purer than the Aramaic speech of other regions. It was the richness and the beauty of this language which was used as the lingua franca by the three great empires in the Near East and Middle East which enriched the English language. The Greek and Latin translators made literal translations of the Scriptures, keeping the Semitic rhythm and sentence structure.

Indeed, the translation of the Scriptures into the English language facilitated the work of later English writers. The style of Shakespeare, Milton, and Browning could not have been what it is without the beauty of the King James translation which was inherited from Semitic languages. This is true also of all languages into which the Bible has been translated.

The Septuagint is based on early Hebrew manuscripts and not on the later ones known as the Massoretic, which were made in the 6th to the 9th centuries. In other words, there are many similarities between the Septuagint and the Peshitta text but the former contains inevitable mistranslations which were due to difficulties in transmitting Hebrew or Aramaic thought and mannerisms of speech into a totally alien tongue like Greek. But as has been said, such was not the case between Biblical Aramaic and Biblical Hebrew which are of the same origin. Josephus used Aramaic and Hebrew words indiscriminately. Thus, the term "translating" from Hebrew into Aramaic or vice versa is incorrect. It would be like one stating as having translated the United States Constitution from the Pennsylvania language into the English language or from lower German to higher German. Even before the first captivity, 721 B.C., Jewish kings, scribes, and learned men understood Aramaic. 2 Kings 18:26.

The Israelites never wrote their sacred literature in any language but Aramaic and Hebrew, which are sister languages. The Septuagint was made in the 3rd century, B.C., for the Alexandrian Jews. This version was never officially read by the Jews in Palestine who spoke Aramaic and read Hebrew. Instead, the Jewish authorities condemned the work and declared a period of mourning because of the defects in the version. Evidently Jesus and his disciples used a text which came from an older Hebrew original. This is apparent because Jesus' quotations from the Old Testament agree with the Peshitta text but do not agree with the Greek text. For example, in John 12:40, the Peshitta Old Testament and New Testament agree. This is not all. Jesus and his disciples not only could not converse in Greek but they never heard it spoken.

We believe that the Scriptures were conceived and inspired by the Holy Spirit and written by Hebrew prophets who spoke and wrote, as the Holy Spirit moved them, to the people in their days, using idioms, similes, parables and metaphors in order to convey their messages. Moreover, these men of God sacrificed their lives that the Word of God might live. The Jewish race treasured these sacred writings as a priceless possession.

Writing was prevalent from the earliest days. The Israelites made more extensive use of the instrument of writing than neighboring nations such as the Ammonites, Moabites, and other kindred people round about them. Moses wrote the Ten Commandments; Joshua wrote on an altar which he built west of Jordan. The Israelites were admonished to fasten the commandments to their foreheads and necks and to write them on their doorsteps. Everything was written at the time it was revealed. God said to Moses,

"Now therefore write this song for them, and teach it to the children of Israel; and put it into their mouths; this song will be a witness for me against the children of Israel." Deut. 31:19.

"And the Lord answered me and said, Write the vision, and make it plain upon tablets, that he who reads it may understand it clearly." Hab. 2:2. Thus, the Old Testament Scriptures were written very early.

This is also true of the Gospels. They were written a few years after the resurrection and some of the portions were written by Matthew while Jesus was preaching. They were not handed down orally and then written after the Pauline Epistles, as some western scholars say; they were written many years before those Epistles. Other contemporary Jewish literature was produced at the same time the Gospels were in circulation. The Gospels, as well as the Epistles, were written in Aramaic, the language of the Jewish people, both in Palestine and in the Greco-Roman Empire.

Greek was never the language of Palestine. Josephus' book on the Jewish Wars was written in Aramaic. Josephus states that even though a number of Jews had tried to learn the language of the Greeks, hardly any of them succeeded.

Josephus wrote (42 A.D.): "I have also taken a great deal of pains to obtain the learning of the Greeks, and understand the elements of the Greek language; although I have so accustomed myself to speak our own tongue, that I cannot pronounce Greek with sufficient exactness. For our nation does not encourage

Introduction

those that learn the language of many nations. On this account, as there have been many who have done their endeavors, with great patience, to obtain this Greek learning, there have yet hardly been two or three that have succeeded herein, who were immediately rewarded for their pains." *Antiquities XX, XI 2.*

Indeed, the teaching of Greek was forbidden by Jewish rabbis. It was said that it was better for a man to give his child meat of swine than to teach him the language of the Greeks.

When the King James translation was made, western scholars had no access to the East as we have today. In the 16th century, A.D., the Turkish empire had extended its borders as far as Vienna. One European country after another was falling under the impact of the valiant Turkish army. Europe was almost conquered. This is not all. The reformations and controversies in the Western Church had destroyed Christian unity. Moreover, the Scriptures in Aramaic were unknown in Europe. The only recourse scholars had was to Latin and to a few portions of Greek manuscripts. This is clearly seen from the works of Erasmus. Besides, the knowledge of Greek was almost lost at this time and Christians were just emerging from the Dark Ages.

Many people have asked why the King James' translators did not use the Peshitta text from Aramaic or the Scriptures used in the East. The answer is: there were no contacts between East and West until after the conquest of India by Great Britain and the rise of the imperial power of Britain in the Near East, Middle East, and the Far East. It is a miracle that the King James' translators were able to produce such a remarkable translation from sources available in this dark period of European history. Even fifty years ago, the knowledge of Western scholars relative to the Eastern Scriptures in Aramaic and the Christian Church in the East was conjectural. Moreover, these scholars knew very little of the Eastern customs and manners in which the Biblical literature was nurtured. Thank God, today new discoveries have been made; new facts have come to light; new democratic institutions and governments have been established in the East. What in the 16th and 17th centuries was viewed at a long distance now can be seen face to face. Today, not only scholars, ministers, and Bible teachers walk on Palestinian soil but also thousands of men and women visit Biblical lands every year.

For centuries translations from Semitic languages have been subject to revision. They are, even now, subject to revision. This is why there are so many Bible versions varying each from the other. Let us just take one instance which I consider very important. In the King James version, we read in Numbers 25:4:

"And the LORD said unto Moses, Take all the heads of the people, and hang them up before the LORD against the sun, that the fierce anger of the LORD may be turned away from Israel."

The Aramaic reads:

"And the LORD said to Moses, Take all the chiefs of the people and expose them before the LORD in the daylight that the fierce anger of the LORD may be turned away from the children of Israel."

Some noted Greek scholars in recent translations have changed the word hang to execute, but this is not what the original writer said. God could not have told Moses to behead or execute all Israelites. The Lord was angry at the princes of Israel because of the sin of Baal-peor. They had been lax in enforcing the law and also guilty in joining the sensual Baal worship.

And in 1 Corinthians 7:36 and 38, King James, we read:

"But if any man think that he behaveth himself uncomely toward his virgin, if she pass the flower of her age, and needs so require, let him do what he will, he sinneth not: let them marry." "So then he that giveth her in marriage doeth well; but he that giveth her not in marriage doeth better."

The Aramaic reads:

"If any man thinks that he is shamed by the behavior of his virgin daughter because she has passed the marriage age and he has not given her in marriage and that he should give her, let him do what he will and he does not sin. Let her be married." "So then he who gives his virgin daughter in marriage does well; and he who does not give his virgin daughter in marriage does even better." Some of

Introduction

the scholars use "betrothed" instead of "virgin daughter." The American Standard Version of 1901 correctly used the term "virgin daughter." Certainly the King James' translators would have known the difference between "virgin daughter" and "betrothed." Paul, in this instance, is referring to a virgin's vow. Num. 30:16.

These discrepancies between various versions have been the cause of contentions and divisions among sincere men and women who are earnestly seeking to understand the Word of God. At times, they do not know what to believe and what not to believe. They cannot understand why the Scripture in one place says, "Love your father and mother" and in another place admonishes, "Hate your father and mother." Moreover, they are bewildered when told that Jesus on the cross cried out, "My God, my God, why hast thou forsaken me?" The King James says in John 16:32, "Behold, the hour cometh, yea, is now come, that ye shall be scattered, every man to his own, and shall leave me alone: and yet I am not alone, because the Father is with me." Then again, the Old Testament in many instances states that God does not forsake the righteous nor those who trust in him. Jesus was the son of God and entrusted his spirit to God. Jesus could not have contradicted himself.

The Peshitta text reads: "My God, my God, for this I was spared!"

After all the Bible is an Eastern Book, written primarily for the Israelites, and then for the Gentile world.

When we come to the New Testament, the new Covenant, we must not forget that Christianity grew out of Judaism. The Christian gospel was another of God's messages, first to the Jewish people and then to the Gentile world. For several centuries, the Christian movement was directed and guided by the Jews. All of the apostles and the evangelists were Jewish. These facts are strongly supported by the gospels and history.

The Pauline Epistles were letters written by Paul to small Christian congregations in Asia Minor, Greece, and Rome. These early Christians were mostly Jews of the dispersion, men and women of Hebrew origin who had been looking for the coming of the promised Messiah whose coming was predicted by the Hebrew prophets who had hailed him as a deliverer.

At the outset, the Romans were the masters of the world and the Greeks were not looking for a deliverer to rise up from among a people whom they hated and had crushed. Paul, on his journeys, always spoke in the Jewish synagogues. His first converts were Hebrews. Then came Arameans, the kindred of the Hebrews, as in the case of Timothy and Titus. Their fathers were Aramean and their mothers were Jewish.

Jesus and his disciples spoke the Galilean dialect of Aramaic, the language which the early Galileans had brought from the other side of the river Euphrates. 2 Kings 17:22-25. Mark tells us in his Gospel, 14:70 that Peter was exposed by his Galilean Aramaic speech.

Paul, in all of his Epistles, emphasizes Hebrew law, Jewish ordinances and temple rituals. He refers to Abraham, Isaac, and Jacob as "our fathers." In his letters and teaching he appeals to the Jewish people to accept Jesus as the promised Messiah. Paul's mission was first to his own people. When they refused to listen to him, he shook his garment and went out among the Gentiles. Acts 18:6. Paul preached the Christian gospel written in Aramaic. His Epistles were written years later when Christianity had spread into Syria and parts of the Near East and India. In other words, the Pauline Epistles were letters addressed to the Christian churches already established. Moreover, Paul, in nearly all of his Epistles, speaks of the Hebrew fathers, subjugation in Egypt, crossing the Red Sea, eating manna, and wandering in the desert. This proves beyond a doubt that these letters were written to members of the Hebrew race and not to the Gentile world who knew nothing of Hebrew history and divine promises made to them. The Greeks had not been persecuted in Egypt nor did they cross the Red Sea, nor did they eat manna in the desert.

Paul was educated in Jewish law in Jerusalem. He was a member of the Jewish Council. His native language was western Aramaic but he acquired his education through Hebrew and Chaldean or Palestinian Aramaic, the language spoken in

Introduction

Judea. He defended himself when on trial in his own tongue and not in Greek. Acts 22:2. Paul was converted, healed, and baptized in Damascus in Syria. Acts 9:17,18.

The Epistles were translated into Greek for the use of converts who spoke Greek. Later they were translated into Latin and other tongues.

I believe that this translation of the Bible based on the Eastern text of the Scriptures, written in a Semitic tongue which for many centuries was the lingua franca of the Near East and Palestine, will throw considerable light on many obscure passages and that it will elucidate many other passages which have lost their meaning because of mistranslations.

Many church authorities in the Near East, India, and other parts of Asia have been looking for a long time for a translation of their venerable Aramaic text of the Scriptures into the English language. Many of them, despite their religious differences, have prayed for the translation and publication of this work so that thousands of educated men and women whose second language is English might read the Word of God translated from their own ancient text rather than made from secondary sources. This is also true of thousands of educated Moslems who revere the Peshitta and look upon it as the authentic text of the Scriptures.

All the English speaking people in Asia will welcome a translation based on what they believe to be the pure original sources which have been carefully kept all these centuries without the slightest modification or revision. I firmly believe that this work will strengthen the faith in Jesus Christ of many Christians in the Near East and Far East and enhance missionary efforts in spreading the Word of God to millions of people in Asia. These were the facts which motivated me when I undertook this task, to which I have devoted my life.

Since World War I, when the Aramaic speaking people were brought to the attention of the Western world and some of their ancient books brought to America, more facts from the ancient past have come to light. *The National Geographic Magazine,* as well as British and American newspapers have touched on the question of the Aramaic speaking people. *The National Geographic Magazine* in an article on Syria and Lebanon, December, 1946, speaks of Assyrian nurses, newly trained in Christian healing, who could have understood The Sermon on the Mount as it left Jesus' lips nearly two thousand years ago. The article also mentions *The Four Gospels According to the Eastern Version,* translated by George M. Lamsa, an Assyrian, from Aramaic into English, and states that Aramaic is the still living language which Jesus spoke.

The translator wishes to express his sincerest and deepest gratitude to Dr. Walter D. Ferguson of Temple University for editorial work, for his sincere interest in this translation, for his rich knowledge and understanding of the Biblical background, and also for his inspiration and enthusiasm. I am also indebted to many others for consultation, among them my countrymen, Archdeacon Saul Neesan and the Rev. Isaac Rehana; also to a number of Jewish scholars.

The translator is also grateful to the men and women of many denominations whose generous interest and financial help enabled me to complete this work. God only can reward them for their generous part in this work.

I wish also to state that I firmly believe in the Bible as the inspired Word of God. I believe in the miracles and wonders which God wrought in the past and which are still demonstrated today. May the Holy Word of God give us faith, wisdom, and understanding to grasp the inner meaning of God's Holy Word and to make us partakers in His Kingdom. May the blessings of God rest upon the readers and students of this translation. May God's richest blessings be upon this country without whose freedom and democratic institutions, this translation could not have been made.

"Thy word is a lamp to my feet and a light to my path." Psalm 119:105.

GEORGE M. LAMSA

WORDS RESEMBLING ONE ANOTHER

The following list of Aramaic words further illustrates the difficulties of the early translators from the Aramaic into Greek, at a time when questions of punctuation, accentuation and paragraphing were unknown. This is especially true of Aramaic, which is the richest and most expressive language of the Semitic group, but having a small vocabulary when compared with the Greek and Latin. This limitation of words made necessary the use of the same words with various shades of meanings. This is because Aramaic is one of the world's most ancient languages.

Translators are well aware of these grammatical difficulties, particularly in a language like Aramaic where a single dot above or under a letter radically changes the meaning of a word. These tiny dots are made by scribes, who are not authors but mere copyists, hired for this purpose by rich and by learned men. But owing to the humidity of the climate and the nature of the ink, blots appear on the pages when pressed against each other. Again because of exposure of a manuscript and its careless handling, flies alight on the pages and leave marks. Furthermore as the lines are crowded for lack of space, a dot placed above one letter may read as though it were placed under a letter in the previous line. For example, the only difference in the words *learned man* and *stupid man* is a dot, over or under the word, respectively.

Some Aramaic words are written and pronounced alike, but their meaning differs according to the context. In other cases the differences are indicated by dots which alter the pronunciation. In yet other instances, if the translator does not speak the language from which he translates the meaning and usage of some words must be left to his knowledge and judgment.

Moreover, some Aramaic letters resemble one another especially in manuscripts. For instance, *Nun, Aey, Lamed* and *Yoth* are very close to one another when placed in certain positions. *Shilometha*, a Shilomite, in other translations reads Shunammite. 1 Kings 1:3. 2 Kings 4:12. *Gamel* is confused with *Aey*, especially when falling in the beginning of the verse. And *Nun* and *Yoth* are hard to distinguish when in the middle of a word. Some of the most important mistranslations were due to the confusion of letters and words.

The following list of words will clearly show the similarity of words and letters and how some of the mistranslations were handed down from one language into another. The confusion of letters, no doubt, was caused when the Israelites, during the time of Ezra, made a new Bible after the ancient Hebrew text was lost. See 2 Esdras, Apocrypha. The Peshitta is the only text through which we can ascertain the ancient Bible text. Dr. Joshua Block, an eminent scholar of Semitic languages, formerly head of the Department of Semitic Languages and Literature of New York University says in an article in the *American Journal of Semitic Languages*, April, 1919:

" . . . Owing to its great antiquity, (the Peshitta) is one of the most valuable documents in ascertaining the original text of the Bible. In fact, in point of age, the Peshitta takes precedence of every other Oriental version; and such has been the high esteem in which it has been held by men of great eminence . . . "*

* By permission of the University of Chicago Press.

Words Resembling One Another

PESHITTA TEXT	KING JAMES VERSION

Genesis 30:8 ܐܬܟܫܦܬ *ethkashpeth*, pleaded

ܐܬܟܬܫܬ *ethkathsheth*, wrestled

8 And Rachel said, I have besought the LORD, and pleaded with my sister . . .

8 And Rachel said, With great wrestlings have I wrestled with my sister . . .

Numbers 25:4 ܪܫܝ *reshey*, chiefs

ܪܫܝ *reshey*, heads

4 And the LORD said to Moses, Take all the chiefs of the people and expose them before the LORD in the daylight . . .

4 And the LORD said unto Moses, Take all the heads of the people, and hang them up before the LORD against the sun . . .

Deuteronomy 27:16 ܕܢܙܟܝ *danzakhey*, to revile

ܙܡܟܐ *zimkha*, radiance

16 Cursed be he who reviles his father or his mother. . . .

16 Cursed be he that setteth light by his father or his mother . . .

Deuteronomy 32:33 ܚܡܬܐ *khimtha*, venom

ܚܡܪܐ *khamra*, wine

33 Their venom is the venom of dragons, and the cruel venom of asps.

33 Their wine is the poison of dragons, and the cruel venom of asps.

2 Samuel 4:6 ܚܛܐ *kheta*, sinful

ܚܛܝ *khetey*, wheat

6 And behold, they came into the midst of the house; then those sons of wickedness took and smote him in his abdomen . . .

6 And they came thither into the midst of the house, as though they would have fetched wheat; and they smote him under the fifth rib . . .

2 Kings 4:28 ܬܫܐܠ *tishal*, to ask

ܬܫܕܠ *teshadal*, to entice

28 Then she said, Did I ask a son of my lord? Did I not say to you, Do not ask a son for me?

28 Then she said, Did I desire a son of my lord, did I not say, Do not deceive me?

Job 19:18 ܥܘܠܝ *awaley*, ungodly

ܥܘܠܝ *eweley*, babies

18 Yea, even the wicked despise me; when I rise, they speak against me.

18 Yea, young children despised me; I arose, and they spake against me.

xiv

Job 29:18

ܩܢܝܐ *kanya,* reed

ܩܢܐ *kina,* nest

18 Then I said, I shall become straight like a reed, I shall deliver the poor and multiply my days like the sand of the seas.

18 Then I said, I shall die in my nest, and I shall multiply *my* days as the sand.

Psalm 144: 7,11

ܥܘܠܝ *awaley,* ungodly

ܥܘܠܝ *eweley,* babies

7 Stretch forth thy hand from above; deliver me out of great waters, from the hand of the ungodly,

7 Send thine hand from above; rid me, and deliver me out of great waters, from the hand of strange children;

11 Deliver me from the hand of the wicked, whose mouths speak vanity, and their right hand is a right hand of falsehood,

11 Rid me, and deliver me from the hand of strange children, whose mouth speaketh vanity, and their right hand *is* a right hand of falsehood:

Proverbs 11:14

ܡܕܒܪܢܐ *medabrana,* leader

ܡܠܟܢܐ *melkana,* counsellor

14 A people who have no leader shall fall; but in the multitude of counsels there is deliverance.

14 Where no counsel *is,* the people fall: but in the multitude of counselors *there is* safety.

Ecclesiastes 2:4

ܥܒܕܝ *abdey,* servants

ܥܒܕܝ *abadey,* works

4 I multiplied my servants . . .

4 I made me great works . . .

Ecclesiastes 11:5

ܪܘܚܐ *rokha,* wind

ܪܘܚܐ *rokha,* spirit

5 As you do not know the path of the wind, and the manner of a woman who is with child . . .

5 As thou knowest not what *is* the way of the spirit, *nor* how the bones *do grow* in the womb of her that is with child . . .

Isaiah 7:14

ܒܬܘܠܬܐ *betholta,* virgin

14 Therefore the LORD himself shall give you a sign; behold, a virgin shall conceive and bear a son, and shall call his name Immanuel.

14 Therefore the Lord himself shall give you a sign; Behold, a virgin shall conceive, and bear a son, and shall call his name Immanuel.

Isaiah 10:27

ܡܘܫܟܐ *moshkha,* bull

ܡܫܟܐ *mishkha,* oil

27 . . . and the yoke shall be destroyed from your neck because of your strength.

27 . . . and the yoke shall be destroyed because of the anointing.

PESHITTA TEXT	KING JAMES VERSION

Isaiah 29:15

ܡܬܗܦܟܝܢ *mithakmin,* to act crookedly

ܡܬܥܡܩܝܢ *mithamkin,* to dig deep

15 Woe to them who act perversely to hide their counsel from the LORD; and their works are in the dark, and they say, Who sees us? And, Who knows what we do corruptly?

15 Woe unto them that seek deep to hide their counsel from the LORD, and their works are in the dark, and they say, Who seeth us? and who knoweth us?

Jeremiah 4:10

ܐܛܥܝܬ *ataeth,* I have deceived

ܐܛܥܝܬ *ataith,* You have deceived

10 Then I said, I beseech thee, O LORD God, surely I have greatly deceived this people and Jerusalem; for I have said . . .

10 Then said I, Ah, Lord GOD! surely thou hast greatly deceived this people and Jerusalem, saying . . .

Ezekiel 32:5

ܪܡܬܐ *rimtha,* dust

ܪܡܬܐ *ramtha,* height

5 And I will scatter your flesh upon the mountains, and fill the valleys with your dust;

5 And I will lay thy flesh upon the mountains, and fill the valleys with thy height.

Obadiah 1:21

ܦܪܝܩܐ *preekey,* saved

ܦܪܘܩܐ *parokey,* saviours

21 And those who are saved shall come up to mount Zion to judge mount Esau . . .

21 And saviours shall come up on mount Zion to judge the mount of Esau . . .

Micah 1:12

ܡܪܕܬ *mirdath,* rebellious

ܡܪܘܬ *maroth,* bitter

12 For the rebellious inhabitant is sick of waiting for good; for disaster is come down from the LORD to the gate of Jerusalem.

12 For the inhabitant of Maroth waited carefully for good: but evil came down from the LORD unto the gate of Jerusalem.

Habakkuk 3:4

ܩܪܝܬܐ *keritha,* town

ܩܪܢܬܐ *karnatha,* horns

4 And his brightness was as the light; in the city which his hands had established shall he store his power.

4 And *his* brightness was as the light; he had horns *coming* out of his hand: and there *was* the hiding of his power.

St. Matthew 19:24

ܓܡܠܐ *gamla,* rope

ܓܡܠܐ *gamla,* camel

24 Again I say to you, it is easier for a rope to go through the eye of a needle . . .

24 And again I say unto you, It is easier for a camel to go through the eye of a needle . . .

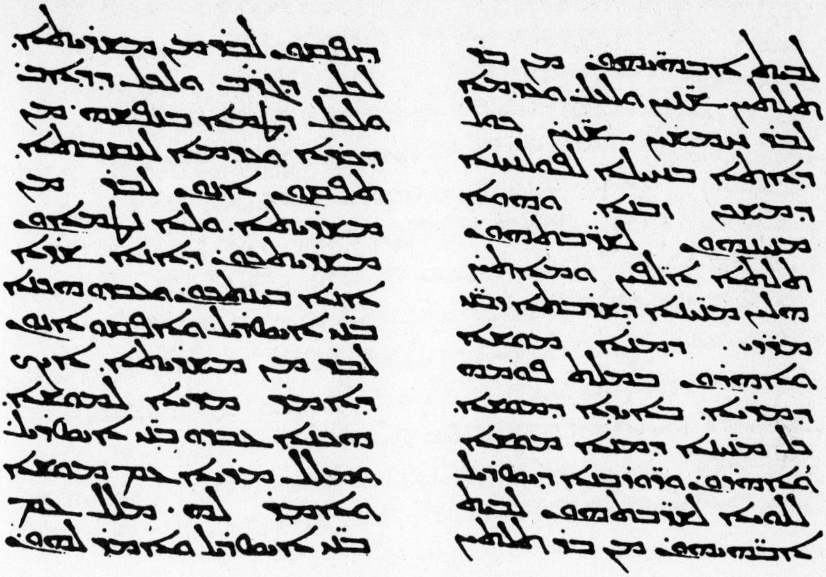

PLATE I

CODEX AMBROSIANUS — 5TH CENTURY
(Ambrosian Library, Milan, Italy.)

Punctuation, accents and breathings by original scribe.

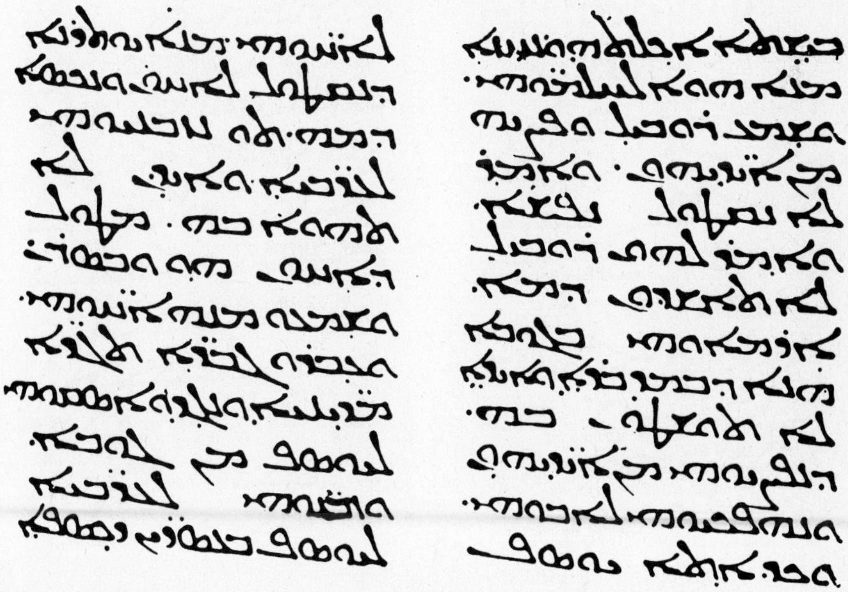

PLATE II

SYRIAC (ARAMAIC) OLD TESTAMENT MS. — A.D. 464.
(British Museum, Add. MS. 14,425.)

Oldest *dated* Biblical manuscript in existence.

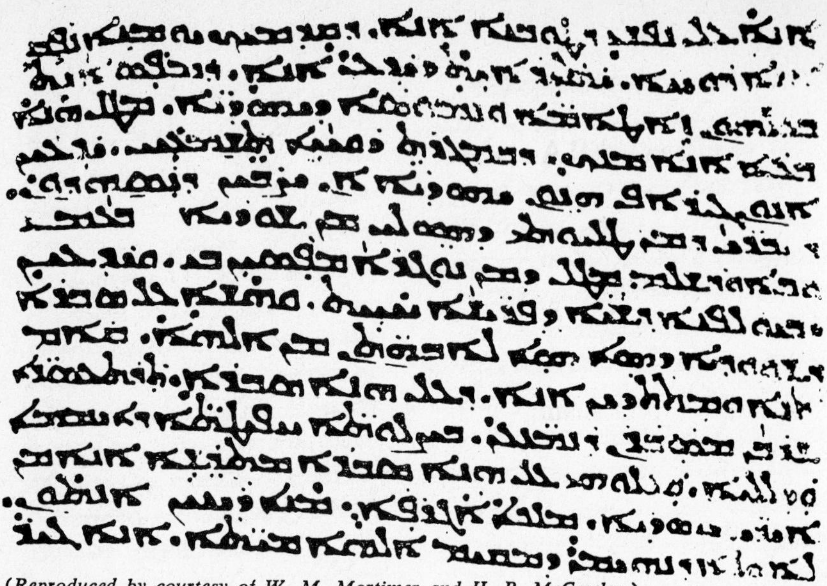

PLATE III

ARAMAIC (SYRIAC) NEW TESTAMENT MS.
Variously identified as 6th or 7th Century.

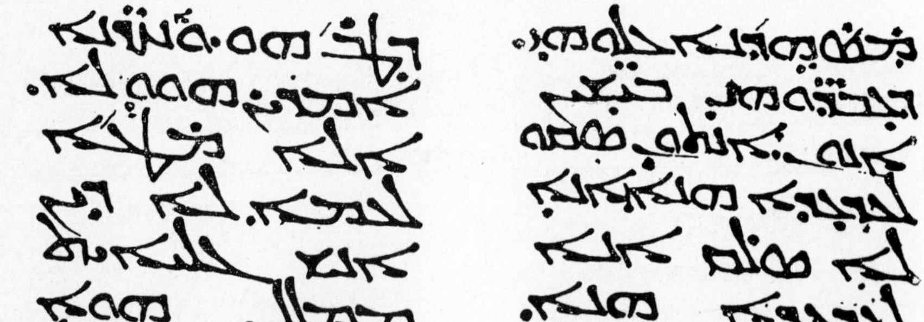

PLATE IV

ARAMAIC (SYRIAC) LECTIONARY — ABOUT A.D. 550.
(*Pierpont Morgan Library, New York, N. Y.*)

ENGLISH NAMES AND THEIR ARAMAIC EQUIVALENTS

THE DEITY

God . . . Alaha

Lord . . . Mariah

Jesus . . . Eshoo

Messiah . . . Meshikhah

Spirit (Ghost) . . . Rohka

PATRIARCHS

Abraham . . . Oraham

Isaac . . . Eskhak

Jacob . . . Yacob

SONS OF JACOB

Reuben . . . Rubel

Simon . . . Shimun

Levi . . . Levi

Judah . . . Ehodah

Zebulun . . . Zebolun

Issachar . . . Esakhar

Dan . . . Dan

Gad . . . Gad

Asher . . . Asher

Naphtali . . . Naphtali

Joseph . . . Yosep

Benjamin . . . Benyamin

HEBREW LEADERS

Aaron . . . Ahron

Joshua . . . Eshoo Barnun

Samson . . . Shimshon

Saul . . . Shawol

David . . . Dawid

Solomon . . . Shlemon

PROPHETS

Moses . . . Moshey

Samuel . . . Shmowel

Isaiah . . . Eshaya

Jeremiah . . . Eramiah

Ezekiel . . . Khazkiel

Daniel . . . Daniel

Hosea . . . Hoshah

Joel . . . Yoel

Amos . . . Amos

Obadiah . . . Aobadiah

Jonah . . . Yonan

Micah . . . Mikha

Nahum . . . Nakhom

Habakkuk . . . Khabakuk

Zephaniah . . . Zepaniah

Haggai . . . Khagi

Zechariah . . . Zekhariah

Malachi . . . Malakhi

APOSTLES

Simon . . . Shimun Kepa

Andrew . . . Andreaos

James . . . Yacob

John . . . Yokhannan

Philip . . . Pilipus

Bartholomew . . . Bartolmi

Thomas . . . Tooma

Matthew . . . Mattai

James . . . Yacob Bar-Khalpai

Lebbaeus . . . Labai or Taddai

Simon . . . Shimun Kananaya or Tanana

Judas . . . Ehodah Scariota

xix

THE NAMES AND ORDER

OF ALL THE

BOOKS OF THE OLD AND NEW TESTAMENT

WITH THE NUMBER OF THEIR CHAPTERS

THE BOOKS OF THE OLD TESTAMENT

THE BOOKS OF THE NEW TESTAMENT

THE
Old Testament

THE FIRST BOOK OF MOSES, CALLED

GENESIS

CHAPTER 1

GOD created the heavens and the earth in the very beginning.

2 And the earth was without form, and void; and darkness was upon the face of the deep. And the Spirit of God moved upon the face of the water.

3 And God said, Let there be light; and there was light.

4 And God saw that the light was good; and God separated the light from the darkness.

5 And God called the light Day, and the darkness he called Night. And there was evening and there was morning, the first day.

6 ¶And God said, Let there be a firmament in the midst of the waters, and let it divide the waters from the waters.

7 And God made the firmament, and divided the waters that were under the firmament from the waters that were above the firmament; and it was so.

8 And God called the firmament Sky. And there was evening and there was morning, the second day.

9 ¶And God said, Let the waters that are under the sky be gathered together in one place, and let the dry land appear; and it was so.

10 And God called the dry land Earth; and the gathering together of the waters he called Seas; and God saw that it was good.

11 And God said, Let the earth bring forth vegetation, the herb yielding seed after its kind, and the fruit tree yielding fruit after its kind, wherein is their seed, upon the earth; and it was so.

12 And the earth brought forth vegetation, the herb yielding seed after its kind, and the tree bearing fruit, wherein is its seed, after its kind; and God saw that it was good.

13 And there was evening and there was morning, the third day.

14 ¶Then God said, Let there be lights in the firmament of the heaven to separate the day from the night; and let them be for signs, and for seasons, and for days, and years.

15 And let them be for lights in the firmament of the heaven to give light upon the earth; and it was so.

16 And God made two great lights, the greater light to rule the day, and the smaller light to rule the night; and the stars also.

17 And God set them in the firmament of the heavens to give light upon the earth,

18 And to rule over the day and over the night, and to separate the light from the darkness; and God saw that it was good.

19 And there was evening and there was morning, the fourth day.

20 And God said, Let the waters bring forth swarms of living creatures, and let fowl fly above the earth in the open firmament of the heaven.

21 And God created great sea monsters, and every living creature that moves, which the waters brought forth abundantly after their kind, and every winged fowl after its kind; and God saw that it was good.

22 And God blessed them, saying, Be fruitful and multiply, and fill the

waters in the seas, and let fowl multiply on the earth.

23 And there was evening and there was morning, the fifth day.

24 ¶Then God said, Let the earth bring forth living creatures after their kind, cattle, and creeping things, and beasts of the earth after their kind; and it was so.

25 And God made the beasts of the earth after their kind, and the cattle after their kind, and everything that creeps upon the earth after its kind; and God saw that it was good.

26 ¶Then God said, Let us make man in our image, after our likeness; and let them have dominion over the fish of the sea, and over the fowl of the air, and over the cattle, and over all the wild beasts of the earth, and over every creeping thing that creeps upon the earth.

27 So God created man in his own image, in the image of God he created him; male and female he created them.

28 And God blessed them, and God said to them, Be fruitful, and multiply, and fill the earth, and subdue it; and have dominion over the fish of the sea, and over the fowl of the air, and over the cattle, and over all the wild beasts that move upon the earth.

29 ¶And God said, Behold, I have given you every herb yielding seed, which is upon the face of all the earth, and every tree which bears fruit yielding seed; to you it shall be for food.

30 And to every beast of the earth, and to every fowl of the air, and to everything that creeps upon the earth, wherein there is life, I have given every green herb for food; and it was so.

31 And God saw everything that he had made, and, behold, it was very good. And there was evening and there was morning, the sixth day.

CHAPTER 2

THUS the heavens and the earth were finished, and all the host of them.

2 And on the sixth day God finished his works which he had made;

and he rested on the seventh day from all his works which he had made.

3 So God blessed the seventh day, and sanctified it; because in it he had rested from all his works which God created and made.

4 ¶These are the generations of the heavens and of the earth when they were created, in the day that the LORD God made the heavens and the earth.

5 And all the trees of the field were not yet in the ground, and every herb of the field had not yet sprung up; for the LORD God had not caused it to rain upon the earth, and there was no man to till the ground.

6 But a powerful spring gushed out of the earth, and watered all the face of the ground.

7 And the LORD God formed Adam out of the soil of the earth, and breathed into his nostrils the breath of life; and man became a living being.

8 ¶And the LORD God planted a garden eastward in Eden; and there he put the man whom he had formed.

9 And out of the ground the LORD God made to grow every tree that is pleasant to the sight and good for food; the tree of life also in the midst of the garden, and the tree of the knowledge of good and evil.

10 And a river flowed out of Eden to water the garden; and from thence it divided and became into four heads.

11 The name of the first is Pishon; it is the one which encircles the whole land of Havilah, where there is gold;

12 And the gold of that land is good; there is also beryllium and the onyx stone.

13 And the name of the second river is Gihon, the one which encircles the whole land of Ethiopia.

14 And the name of the third river is Deklat (Tigris); it is the one which flows east of Assyria. And the fourth river is the Euphrates.

15 And the LORD God took the man, and put him in the garden of Eden to till it and to keep it.

16 And the LORD God commanded the man, saying, Of every tree of the garden you may freely eat;

17 But of the tree of the knowledge of good and evil, you shall not eat; for in the day that you eat of it you shall surely die.

18 ¶Then the LORD God said, It is not good that the man should be alone; I will make him a helper who is like him.

19 And out of the ground the LORD God formed every beast of the field, and every fowl of the air; and brought them to Adam to see what he would call them; and whatever Adam called every living creature, that was its name.

20 And Adam gave names to all cattle, and to all fowl of the air, and to all wild beasts; but for Adam there was not found a helper who was equal to him.

21 So the LORD God caused a deep sleep to fall upon Adam, and he slept; and he took one of his ribs, and closed up the place with flesh in its stead;

22 And of the rib which the LORD God had taken from Adam he made a woman, and brought her to Adam.

23 And Adam said, This is now bone of my bones, and flesh of my flesh; she shall be called Woman, because she was taken out of Man.

24 Therefore shall a man leave his father and his mother, and shall cleave unto his wife, and they shall be one flesh.

25 And they were both naked, Adam and his wife, and were not ashamed.

CHAPTER 3

NOW the serpent was more subtle than all the wild beasts that the LORD God had made. And the serpent said to the woman, Truly has God said that you shall not eat of any tree of the garden?

2 And the woman said to the serpent, We may eat of the fruit of all the trees of the garden;

3 But of the fruit of the tree which is in the midst of the garden, God has said, You shall not eat of it, neither shall you touch it, lest you die.

4 And the serpent said to the woman, You shall not surely die;

5 For God knows that in the day you eat of it, your eyes shall be opened, and you shall be like gods, knowing good and evil.

6 So when the woman saw that the tree was good for food, and that it was pleasant to the eyes, and that the tree was delightful to look at, she took of the fruit thereof, and did eat, and she also gave to her husband with her; and he did eat.

7 Then the eyes of them both were opened, and they knew that they were naked; and they sewed fig leaves together, and made themselves aprons.

8 And they heard the voice of the LORD God walking in the garden in the cool of the day; and Adam and his wife hid themselves from the presence of the LORD God among the trees of the garden.

9 And the LORD God called to Adam, and said to him, Where are you, Adam?

10 And he said, I heard thy voice in the garden, and when I saw that I was naked, I hid myself.

11 And the LORD God said to him, Who told you that you were naked? Have you eaten of the tree of which I commanded you that you should not eat?

12 And Adam said, The woman whom thou gavest to be with me, she gave me of the fruit of the tree, and I did eat.

13 And the LORD God said to the woman, What is this that you have done? And the woman said, The serpent beguiled me, and I did eat.

14 And the LORD God said to the serpent, Because you have done this thing, cursed are you above all cattle, and above all beasts of the field; on your belly shall you go, and dust shall you eat all the days of your life;

15 And I will put enmity between you and the woman, and between your posterity and her posterity; her posterity shall tread your head under foot, and you shall strike him in his heel.

16 To the woman he said, I will greatly multiply your pain and your conception; in pain you shall bring forth children, and you shall be de'

pendent on your husband, and he shall rule over you.

17 And to Adam he said, Because you have listened to the voice of your wife, and have eaten of the tree of which I commanded you, saying, You shall not eat of it, cursed is the ground for your sake; in sorrow shall you eat the fruits of it all the days of your life;

18 Thorns also and thistles shall it bring forth to you; and you shall eat the herb of the field;

19 In the sweat of your face shall you eat bread, until you return to the ground; out of it you were taken; for dust you are, and to dust shall you return.

20 So Adam called his wife's name Eve because she was the mother of all living.

21 And the LORD God made for Adam and for his wife coats of skin, and clothed them.

22 ¶Then the LORD God said, Behold, the man has become like one of us, to know good and evil; and now, lest he put forth his hand, and take also of the tree of life, and eat, and live forever;

23 Therefore the LORD God sent him forth from the garden of Eden, to till the ground from whence he was taken.

24 So the LORD God drove out the man; and he placed at the east of the garden of Eden Cherubim, and a flaming sword which turned every way, to guard the path to the tree of life.

CHAPTER 4

AND Adam knew Eve his wife; and she conceived, and bore Cain, and said, I have gotten a man for the LORD.

2 And she again bore his brother Abel. And Abel was a keeper of sheep, but Cain was a tiller of the ground.

3 And in the course of time it came to pass that Cain brought of the fruit of the ground an offering to the LORD.

4 And Abel also brought of the first-born of his flock and of the fatlings thereof. And the LORD was pleased with Abel and with his offering;

5 But with Cain and with his offering he was not pleased. So Cain was exceedingly displeased, and his countenance was sad.

6 And the LORD said to Cain, Why are you displeased? and why is your countenance sad?

7 Behold, if you do well, shall you not be accepted? and if you do not well, sin lies at the door. You should return to your brother, and he shall be subject to you.

8 And Cain said to Abel his brother, Let us go to the plain; and it came to pass, when they were in the field, that Cain rose up against Abel his brother, and slew him.

9 ¶And the LORD said to Cain, Where is Abel your brother? And he said, I do not know. Am I my brother's keeper?

10 And the LORD said, What have you done? The voice of your brother's blood cries to me from the ground.

11 And from henceforth, you are cursed from the earth, which has opened its mouth to receive your brother's blood from your hand;

12 When you till the ground, it shall no more yield to you its strength; a fugitive and a wanderer shall you be on the earth.

13 And Cain said to the LORD, My transgression is too great to be forgiven.

14 Behold, thou hast driven me out this day from the face of the land; and from thy face shall I be hidden; and I shall be a fugitive and a wanderer on the earth; and it shall come to pass, that whoever finds me shall slay me.

15 And the LORD said to him, It shall not be so; whoever slays Cain, vengeance shall be taken on him sevenfold. And the LORD set a mark upon Cain, so that anyone who may find him may not kill him.

16 ¶And Cain went out from the presence of the LORD, and dwelt in the land of Nod, on the east of Eden.

17 And Cain knew his wife; and she conceived, and bore Enoch; and he started to build a village, and named

the village after the name of his son, Enoch.

18 And to Enoch was born Irad; and Irad begot Mehujael; and Mehujael begot Methusael: and Methusael begot Lamech.

19 ¶And Lamech took two wives: the name of the one was Adah, and the name of the other Zillah.

20 And Adah bore Jabal, who was the father of those who dwell in tents, and are owners of cattle.

21 And his brother's name was Jubal; he was the father of all those who play the guitar and harp.

22 And Zillah also bore Tubal-cain, a craftsman in every work of brass and iron; and the sister of Tubal-cain was Naamah.

23 And Lamech said to his wives, Adah and Zillah, Hear my voice; you wives of Lamech, hearken to my speech; for I have killed a man by wounding him, and a boy by beating him.

24 For if Cain is to be avenged sevenfold, then Lamech seventy and sevenfold.

25 ¶And Adam knew his wife Eve again; and she conceived and bore a son, and called his name Seth; For God, she said, has given me another offspring instead of Abel, whom Cain slew.

26 And to Seth also there was born a son; and he called his name Enosh. Then men began to call upon the name of the LORD.

CHAPTER 5

THIS is the book of the generations of Adam. In the day that God created man, in the likeness of God created he him;

2 Male and female he created them; and God blessed them, and called their name Adam, in the day when they were created.

3 ¶And Adam lived a hundred and thirty years, and begot a son in his own likeness, after his image; and called his name Seth;

4 And Adam lived after he had begotten Seth eight hundred years; and he begot sons and daughters.

5 Thus all the days that Adam lived were nine hundred and thirty years, and he died.

6 And Seth lived a hundred and five years, and begot Enosh;

7 And Seth lived after he begot Enosh eight hundred and seven years, and begot sons and daughters;

8 And all the days of Seth were nine hundred and twelve years, and he died.

9 ¶And Enosh lived ninety years, and begot Cainan;

10 And Enosh lived after he begot Cainan eight hundred and fifteen years, and begot sons and daughters;

11 And all the days of Enosh were nine hundred and five years, and he died.

12 ¶And Cainan lived seventy years, and begot Mahlalael;

13 And Cainan lived after he begot Mahlalael eight hundred and forty years, and begot sons and daughters;

14 And all the days of Cainan were nine hundred and ten years, and he died.

15 ¶And Mahlalael lived sixty and five years, and begot Jared;

16 And Mahlalael lived after he begot Jared eight hundred and thirty years, and begot sons and daughters.

17 And all the days of Mahlalael were eight hundred ninety and five years, and he died.

18 ¶And Jared lived a hundred sixty and two years, and he begot Enoch:

19 And Jared lived after he begot Enoch eight hundred years, and begot sons and daughters;

20 And all the days of Jared were nine hundred sixty and two years, and he died.

21 ¶And Enoch lived sixty and five years, and begot Methuselah;

22 And Enoch found favor in the presence of God three hundred years after he begot Methuselah, and begot sons and daughters;

23 And all the days of Enoch were three hundred sixty-five years;

24 And Enoch found favor in the presence of God, and disappeared; for God took him away.

25 And Methuselah lived a hundred eighty-seven years, and begot Lamech;

26 And Methuselah lived after he begot Lamech seven hundred and eighty-two years, and begot sons and daughters;

27 And all the days of Methuselah were nine hundred sixty-nine years, and he died.

28 ¶And Lamech lived a hundred eighty-two years, and begot a son;

29 And he called his name Noah, saying, This one shall comfort us concerning our work and the toil of our hands, because of the ground which the LORD has cursed.

30 And Lamech lived after he begot Noah five hundred ninety-five years, and begot sons and daughters.

31 Thus all the days of Lamech were seven hundred seventy-seven years, and he died.

32 And Noah was five hundred years old, and Noah begot Shem, Ham, and Japheth.

CHAPTER 6

AND it came to pass, when men began to multiply on the face of the earth and daughters were born to them,

2 That the sons of God saw that the daughters of men were fair; so they took them wives of all whom they chose.

3 Then the LORD said, My spirit shall not dwell in man forever, because he is flesh; let his days be a hundred and twenty years.

4 There were giants on the earth in those days; and also after that, for the sons of God came in unto the daughters of men, and they bore children to them, and they became giants who in the olden days were mighty men of renown.

5 ¶And the LORD saw that the wickedness of man was great in the earth, and that every imagination of the thoughts of his heart was evil continually.

6 And the LORD was sorry that he had made man on the earth, and it grieved him in his heart.

7 So the LORD said, I will destroy men whom I have created from the face of the earth; both men and animals, and the creeping things, and the fowls of the air; I am sorry that I have made them.

8 But Noah found mercy in the eyes of the LORD.

9 ¶These are the generations of Noah: Noah was a just man and innocent in his days, and God was pleased with Noah.

10 And Noah begot three sons, Shem, Ham, and Japheth.

11 The earth was corrupt in the presence of God, and the earth was filled with wickedness.

12 And God saw that the earth was corrupt; for all flesh had corrupted its way upon the earth.

13 So God said to Noah, The end of all flesh is come before me; for the earth is full of wickedness through men; and, behold, I will destroy them with the earth.

14 ¶Make yourself an ark of gopher wood; make rooms in the ark and daub it without and within with pitch.

15 And this is how you shall make it: the length of the ark shall be three hundred cubits, the breadth of it fifty cubits, and the height of it thirty cubits.

16 And you shall make a window in the ark, and to the width of a cubit shall you finish it above; and the door of the ark you shall make in its side; with lower, second, and third decks you shall make it.

17 And, behold, I will bring a flood of waters upon the earth, to destroy all flesh that has the breath of life in it from under heaven; and everything that is on the earth shall die.

18 But I will establish my covenant with you; and you shall enter into the ark, you, and your sons, and your wife, and your sons' wives with you.

19 And of every living thing of all flesh, two of every kind bring into the ark, to keep them alive with you; they shall be male and female.

20 Of fowls after their kind, and of animals after their kind, and of every creeping thing of the earth after its kind, two of every kind shall enter with you, that they may live.

21 And you must take a supply of all food that is eaten, and you shall

store it by you; and it shall be for food for you and for them.

22 Thus did Noah; according to all that God commanded him, so did he.

CHAPTER 7

THEN God said to Noah, Enter into the ark; you and all your household, for you alone have I seen righteous before me in this generation.

2 Of all clean animals you shall take with you seven pairs, both males and females; and of the beasts that are not clean two pairs, males and females.

3 Likewise, of the fowls of the air that are clean seven pairs, both males and the females; to keep their posterity alive upon the face of the earth.

4 For in seven days I will cause it to rain upon the earth forty days and forty nights; and every living thing that I have made will I destroy from off the face of the earth.

5 And Noah did according to all that the LORD commanded him.

6 And Noah was six hundred years old when the flood of waters came upon the earth.

7 ¶And Noah, with his sons and his wife and his sons' wives, went into the ark because of the waters of the flood.

8 Of clean animals, and of unclean animals, and of fowls, and of everything that creeps upon the earth,

9 There went in two and two with Noah into the ark, the males and the females, as God had commanded Noah.

10 And it came to pass after seven days that the waters of the flood came upon the earth.

11 ¶In the six hundredth year of Noah's life, in the second month, the seventeenth day of the month, on that very day all the fountains of the great deep burst forth and the windows of heaven were opened.

12 And the rain fell upon the earth for forty days and forty nights.

13 On that same day entered Noah and Shem and Ham and Japheth, the sons of Noah, and Noah's wife, and the three wives of his sons with him, into the ark;

14 They and every beast after its kind and all the cattle after their kind and every creeping thing that creeps upon the earth after its kind and every fowl after its kind, every bird of every sort.

15 They went with Noah into the ark, two and two of all flesh in which there is the breath of life.

16 And they that entered, males and females of every living thing went in, as God had commanded him. Then the LORD shut him in.

17 And the flood lasted forty days upon the earth; and the waters increased and bore up the ark so that it was lifted up above the earth.

18 And the waters prevailed and rose higher upon the earth; and the ark floated on the face of the waters.

19 And the waters prevailed exceedingly upon the earth; so that all the high mountains under the whole heaven were covered.

20 Fifteen cubits above the mountains did the waters prevail; and the mountains were covered.

21 And all flesh died that moved upon the earth, both of fowl and of cattle and of wild beast and of every creeping thing that creeps upon the earth and every man:

22 Everything in whose nostrils was the breath of life, of all that was on the dry land, died.

23 And every living thing was destroyed that was upon the face of the ground, both man and animals and the creeping things and the fowl of the air; they were destroyed from the earth; and Noah only remained, and those who were with him in the ark.

24 And the waters prevailed upon the earth a hundred and fifty days.

CHAPTER 8

AND God remembered Noah and every living thing and all the animals and all the fowls that were with him in the ark; and God made a wind to blow over the earth, and the waters became calm;

2 The fountains of the deep and the

windows of heaven were closed, and the rain from the sky was restrained;

3 And the waters receded from the earth gradually; and after the end of a hundred and fifty days the waters abated.

4 And in the seventh month, on the seventeenth day of the month, the ark rested upon the mountains of Kardo.[1]

5 And the waters decreased gradually until the tenth month; on the first day of the tenth month, the tops of the mountains were seen.

6 ¶And it came to pass at the end of forty days that Noah opened the window of the ark which he had made;

7 And he sent forth a raven which went to and fro, but did not return until the waters were dried up from the face of the earth.

8 Then he sent forth a dove from the ark, to see if the waters had abated from the face of the ground;

9 But the dove found no resting place for her foot, and she returned to him in the ark, for the waters were still on the face of the whole earth. Then he put forth his hand, and took her, and brought her into the ark with him.

10 And he waited yet another seven days; and again he sent forth the dove out of the ark;

11 And the dove came back to him in the evening; and, lo, in her mouth was an olive leaf plucked off; so Noah knew that the waters had subsided from off the earth.

12 And he waited yet another seven days, and sent forth the dove; but the dove did not return again to him any more.

13 ¶And it came to pass in the six hundred and first year, in the first month, the first day of the month, the waters were dried up from off the earth; and Noah removed the covering of the ark, and looked, and, behold, the face of the ground was dry.

14 And in the second month, on the twenty-seventh day of the month, the earth was dry.

[1] A chain of mountains in northern Iraq.

15 ¶And God spoke to Noah, saying,

16 Go forth out of the ark, you and your wife and your sons and your sons' wives with you.

17 Bring forth with you every beast of every kind that is with you, both fowl and cattle and every creeping thing that creeps on the earth; that they may breed abundantly on the earth and be fruitful and multiply upon the face of the earth.

18 So Noah went forth, and his sons and his wife and his sons' wives with him;

19 Every beast, every domestic animal, and every fowl, and whatever creeps upon the earth, after their kinds, went forth out of the ark.

20 ¶Then Noah built an altar to the LORD; and took of every clean animal and of every clean fowl, and offered burnt offerings on the altar.

21 And the LORD smelled the sweet savour; and the LORD said in his heart, I will not again curse the ground any more for man's sake; for the inclination of man's heart is evil from his youth; neither will I again destroy any more every living thing, as I have done.

22 From henceforth, while the earth remains, seedtime and harvest, and cold and heat, and summer and winter, and day and night shall not cease.

CHAPTER 9

AND God blessed Noah and his sons, and said to them, Be fruitful, and multiply, and replenish the earth.

2 And the fear of you and the dread of you shall be upon every beast of the earth, and upon every fowl of the air, upon all that moves upon the earth, and all the fish of the sea; into your hand they are delivered.

3 Every moving thing that is alive shall be food for you; even as the green herb have I given you all things.

4 Only flesh with the life thereof,

that is, the blood thereof, you shall not eat.

5 And surely your lifeblood will I avenge; of every beast will I avenge it, and at the hand of man; and at the hand of a man and his brother will I avenge the life of man.

6 Whoever sheds the blood of men, by men shall his blood be shed; for man was made in the image of God.

7 As for you, be fruitful, and multiply; bring forth abundantly on the earth, and multiply in it.

8 ¶And God spoke to Noah, and to his sons with him, saying,

9 As for me, behold, I will establish my covenant with you and with your descendants after you;

10 And with every living creature that is with you, the fowl, the cattle, and every wild beast of the earth with you; with all that come out of the ark, and with every beast of the earth.

11 And I will establish my covenant with you; so that never again shall all flesh perish by the waters of a flood; neither shall there any more be a flood to destroy the earth.

12 And God said to Noah, This is the sign of the covenant which I make between me and you and every living creature that is with you, for perpetual generations:

13 I set my bow in the clouds, and it shall be for a sign of a covenant between me and the earth.

14 And it shall come to pass, when I bring clouds over the earth, that the bow shall be seen in the clouds;

15 And I will remember my covenant, which is between me and you and every living creature that is with you of all flesh; and the waters shall no more become a flood to destroy all flesh.

16 And the bow shall be in the clouds; and I will look upon it as a remembrance of the everlasting covenant between God and every living creature of all flesh that is upon the earth.

17 And God said to Noah, This is the sign of the covenant which I have established between me and all the flesh that is upon the earth.

18 ¶The sons of Noah who went forth out of the ark were Shem and Ham and Japheth; and Ham is the father of Canaan.

19 These three were the sons of Noah; and from them the people spread throughout the earth.

20 And Noah began to till the ground; and he planted a vineyard;

21 And he drank of its wine, and became drunken; and he was uncovered within his tent.

22 And Ham, the father of Canaan, saw the nakedness of his father, and he told his two brothers outside.

23 And Shem and Japheth took a mantle and laid it upon both their shoulders and walked backward and covered the nakedness of their father; and their faces were backward and they did not see their father's nakedness.

24 When Noah awoke from his wine and knew what his younger son had done to him,

25 He said, Cursed be Canaan; a servant of servants shall he be to his brothers.

26 Then he said, Blessed be the LORD God of Shem; and let Canaan be his servant.

27 God shall enrich Japheth, and he shall dwell in the tents of Shem; and Canaan shall be their servant.

28 ¶And Noah lived after the flood three hundred and fifty years.

29 And all the days of Noah were nine hundred and fifty years, and he died.

CHAPTER 10

NOW these are the descendants of the sons of Noah, Shem, Ham, and Japheth: and to them were sons born after the flood.

2 The sons of Japheth were Gomer, Mongolia, Madai, Javan, Tubal, Meshech, and Tiras.

3 And the sons of Gomer: Ashkenaz, Diphar, and Togarmah.

4 And the sons of Javan: Elishah, Tarshish, China, and Doranim.

5 It was from these that the people were divided into the Islands of the Gentiles and their main lands; every one after his language, after their families, in their nations.

6 ¶And the sons of Ham: Cush, Mizraim, Put, and Canaan.

7 And the sons of Cush: Sheba, Havilah, Sabtah, Raamah, and Sabtechah. And the sons of Raamah: Sheba, and Daran.

8 And Cush begot Nimrod; he began to be a mighty one on the earth.

9 He was a mighty hunter before the LORD; wherefore it is said, Even as Nimrod was a mighty hunter before the LORD.

10 And the beginning of his kingdom was Babylon, Erech, Akhar, and Caliah, in the land of Sinar.

11 Out of Sinar went forth the Assyrian and built Nineveh, and the city of Rehoboth, and Calah,

12 And Resen which lies between Nineveh and Calah; the same is a great city.

13 And Mizraim begot Ludim and Anamim and Lehabim and Naphtuhim

14 And Pathrusim and Casluhim (out of whom came the Philistines) and Caphtorim.

15 ¶And Canaan begot Sidon, his first-born, and Heth,

16 And the Jebusite, the Amorite, the Girgasite,

17 And the Havite, the Arkite, the Sinite,

18 And the Arvadite, the Zemarite, and the Hamathite; and afterward the families of the Canaanites spread abroad.

19 And the border of the Canaanites extended from Sidon, which is at the entrance of Gadar, as far as Gaza; which is at the entrance of Sodom, Gomorrah,[1] Admah, and Zeboim, as far as Lasha.

20 These are the sons of Ham, after their families and their languages, in their lands and in their nations.

21 ¶To Shem also, the father of all the children of Eber, the elder brother of Japheth, even to him were children born.

22 The sons of Shem: Elam, Asshur, Arphakhashar, Lud and Aram.

23 And the children of Aram: Uz, Hul, Gether, and Mash.

1 Aramaic Amorrah.

24 And Arphakhashar begot Shalah; and Shalah begot Eber.

25 And to Eber were born two sons: the name of the one was Peleg; for in his days the earth was divided; and his brother's name was Joktan.

26 And Joktan begot Almodad, Sheleph, Hazarmaveth, Jerah,

27 Hadoram, Uzal, Diklah,

28 Obal, Abimael, and Sheba,

29 Ophir, Havilah, and Jobab; all these were sons of Joktan.

30 The lands which they inhabited extended from Mesha, which is at the entrance of Sepharvim, a mount in the east.

31 These are the sons of Shem, after their families, their languages, in their lands, after their nations.

32 These are the descendants of the sons of Noah, according to their families, in their nations: and from these the people spread abroad on the earth after the flood.

CHAPTER 11

NOW the whole earth spoke one language and with one manner of speech.

2 And it came to pass, as men journeyed from the east, they found a plain in the land of Sinar; and they settled there.

3 And they said one to another, Come, let us make bricks and burn them with fire. And they had bricks for stone, and slime for mortar.

4 Then they said, Come, let us build ourselves a city, and a tower whose top may reach to heaven; and let us make a name for ourselves, lest we be scattered abroad upon the face of the whole earth.

5 And the LORD came down to see the city and the tower which men were building.

6 And the LORD said, Behold, they are one people, and they have all one language; and they have reasoned to do this thing; and now nothing will prevent them from doing that which they have imagined to do.

7 Come, let us go down, and there

divide their language so that they may not understand one another's speech.

8 So the LORD scattered them abroad from there upon the face of all the earth; and they ceased from building the city.

9 Therefore they called the name of it Babel; because it was there that the LORD confounded the language of all the earth; and from there the LORD scattered them upon the face of all the earth.

10 ¶These are the descendants of Shem: Shem was a hundred years old, and begot Arphakhashar, two years after the flood;

11 And Shem lived after he begot Arphakhashar five hundred years, and begot sons and daughters.

12 And Arphakhashar lived thirty-five years, and begot Shalah;

13 And Arphakhashar lived after he begot Shalah four hundred and three years, and begot sons and daughters.

14 And Shalah lived thirty years, and begot Eber;

15 And Shalah lived after he begot Eber four hundred and three years, and begot sons and daughters.

16 And Eber lived thirty-four years, and begot Peleg;

17 And Eber lived after he begot Peleg four hundred and thirty years, and begot sons and daughters.

18 And Peleg lived thirty years, and begot Rau;

19 And Peleg lived after he begot Rau two hundred and nine years, and begot sons and daughters.

20 And Rau lived thirty-two years, and begot Serug;

21 And Rau lived after he begot Serug two hundred and seven years, and begot sons and daughters.

22 And Serug lived thirty years, and begot Nahor;

23 And Serug lived after he begot Nahor two hundred years, and begot sons and daughters.

24 And Nahor lived twenty-nine years, and begot Terah;

25 And Nahor lived after he begot Terah one hundred and nineteen years, and begot sons and daughters.

26 And Terah lived seventy-five years, and begot Abram, Nahor, and Haran.

27 ¶Now these are the descendants of Terah: Terah begot Abram, Nahor, and Haran; and Haran begot Lot.

28 And Haran died before his father Terah in his native land, in Ur of the Çhaldeans.

29 And Abram and Nahor took wives for themselves; the name of Abram's wife was Sarai; and the name of Nahor's wife, Milcah, the daughter of Haran, the father of Milcah and Iscah.

30 But Sarai was barren; she had no child.

31 And Terah took Abram his son, and Lot the son of Haran, his grandson, and Sarai his daughter-in-law, his son Abram's wife; and they went forth with them from Ur of the Chaldeans to go to the land of Canaan; and they came as far as Haran, and they settled there.

32 And the days of Terah were two hundred and five years; and Terah died in Haran.

CHAPTER 12

NOW the LORD said to Abram, Depart from your country, and from the place of your nativity, and from your father's house, to a land that I will show you;

2 And I will make of you a great people, and I will bless you, and make your name great; and you shall be a blessing;

3 And I will bless those who bless you, and curse those who curse you; and in you shall all the families of the earth be blessed.

4 So Abram did as the LORD had spoken to him; and Lot went with him; and Abram was seventy-five years old when he departed from Haran.

5 And Abram took Sarai his wife and Lot his brother's son and all their possessions which they had gained and the persons that they had gotten in Haran, and they went on their way to the land of Canaan, and to the land of Canaan they came.

6 ¶And Abram passed through the land as far as the country of Shechem,

and as far as the oak of Mamre. And the Canaanites were settled then in the land.

7 Then the Lord appeared to Abram and said to him, To your descendants will I give this land; and Abram built there an altar to the Lord, for he had appeared to him.

8 And from thence he removed to a mountain on the east of Beth-el, and pitched his tent, having Beth-el on the west, and Ai on the east; and there he built an altar to the Lord and called upon the name of the Lord.

9 And Abram journeyed, going on still toward the south.

10 ¶Now there was a famine in the land; so Abram went down to Egypt to sojourn there; for the famine was severe in the land.

11 And it came to pass when he was about to enter into Egypt, he said to Sarai his wife, Behold now, I know that you are a woman beautiful to look upon;

12 And it shall come to pass, when the Egyptians see you, they will say, This is his wife; and they will kill me, but they will spare you.

13 Say, therefore, that you are my sister because I will be treated well for your sake; and my life shall be spared because of you.

14 ¶And it came to pass when Abram entered Egypt, the Egyptians saw that his wife was very beautiful.

15 The princes of Pharaoh also saw her and praised her before Pharaoh; and the woman was taken into Pharaoh's house.

16 And Abram was well treated for her sake; and he became the owner of sheep, oxen, he asses, menservants, maidservants, she asses, and camels.

17 And the Lord afflicted Pharaoh and his household with great plagues because of Sarai, Abram's wife.

18 So Pharaoh called Abram, and said to him, What is this that you have done to me? Why did you not tell me that she was your wife?

19 Why did you say, She is my sister, so that I took her for my wife? Now, therefore, here is your wife, take her, and leave the country.

20 And Pharaoh charged his men concerning him; and sent him away together with his wife, and all that he had.

CHAPTER 13

AND Abram went up from Egypt, he and his wife and all that he had, and Lot with him, into the south.

2 And Abram was very rich in cattle, in silver, and in gold.

3 And he went on his journey from the south as far as Beth-el, to the place where he had pitched his tent at first, between Beth-el and Ai;

4 To the place of the altar which he had built there at the first; and there Abram had called upon the name of the Lord.

5 ¶And Lot also, who went with Abram, had large flocks, herds, and tents.

6 And the land was not able to support them, that they might dwell together; for their herds were so large that they could not dwell together.

7 And there was a strife between the herdsmen of Abram's cattle and the herdsmen of Lot's cattle; and the Canaanites and the Perizzites dwelt then in the land.

8 And Abram said to Lot, Let there be no strife between me and you, and between my shepherds and your shepherds; for we are brethren.

9 Behold the whole land is before you, separate yourself from me; if you choose the left hand, then I will choose the right hand; or if you depart to the right hand, then I will go to the left.

10 And Lot lifted up his eyes, and saw all the land of Jordan, that it was well watered everywhere, before the Lord destroyed Sodom and Gomorrah, like the garden of God, like the land of Egypt at the entrance of Zoan.

11 Then Lot chose for himself all the land of Jordan; and Lot journeyed east; thus they separated one brother from the other.

12 Abram dwelt in the land of Canaan, and Lot dwelt in the villages of the plain, thus possessing the land as far as Sodom.

13 Now the men of Sodom were wicked and sinners in the presence of the LORD exceedingly.

14 ¶And the LORD said to Abram, after Lot had separated from him, Lift up now your eyes, and look from the place where you are, northward and southward and eastward and westward;

15 For all the land which you see, to you will I give it, and to your descendants forever.

16 And I will make your descendants like the dust of the earth; so that if you can number the dust of the earth, then shall your descendants also be numbered.

17 Arise, walk through the land in the length of it and in the breadth of it; for I will give it to you.

18 Then Abram removed his tent and came and dwelt by the oak of Mamre which is in Hebron, and built there an altar to the LORD.

CHAPTER 14

AND it came to pass in the days of Amarphel king of Sinar, Arioch king of Dalasar, Cardlaamar king of Elam, and Tarael king of Gelites

2 That these made war with Bera king of Sodom, Birsha king of Gomorrah, Shinab king of Admah, Shemer king of Zeboim, and the king of Bela, that is, Zoar.

3 All of these joined together in the valley of Siddim, which is the Salt Sea.

4 Twelve years they served Cardlaamar, and in the thirteenth year they rebelled.

5 And in the fourteenth year came Cardlaamar, and the kings that were with him, and smote the mighty men who were in Ashteroth Karnaim and the valiant men who were in the city, and the Emins in Shaveh Koriathaim,

6 And the Horites in the mountains of Seir, as far as the oak of Paran, which is in the wilderness.

7 And they returned, and came to En-dina, which is Rakim (Kadesh) and they smote all the princes of the Amalekites and also the Amorites who dwelt in En-gad.

8 And there went out the king of Sodom, the king of Gomorrah, the king of Admah, the king of Zeboim, and the king of Bela (that is, Zoar); all of these made war in the valley of Siddim,

9 With Cardlaamar, the king of Elam, Tarael the king of Gelites, Amarphel king of Sinar, and Arioch king of Dalasar; four kings against five.

10 And the valley of Siddim was full of bitumen pits; and the kings of Sodom and Gomorrah fled, and fell there; and those who survived fled to the mountain.

11 And the raiders took all the goods of Sodom and Gomorrah, and all their provisions, and went their way.

12 And they carried away Lot, Abram's brother's son, who dwelt in Sodom, and his goods, and departed.

13 ¶And there came one who escaped, and told Abram the Hebrew, who dwelt by the oak of Mamre, which belonged to the Amorite, brother of Aner and brother of Eshcol, who were allies of Abram.

14 And when Abram heard that his nephew had been taken captive, he armed his young men, born in his own house, three hundred and eighteen, and pursued the raiders as far as Dan.

15 And he divided his forces against them by night, he and his servants, and defeated them, and pursued them as far as Hobah, which is on the left hand of Damascus.

16 And he brought back all the goods, and also brought back Lot, his nephew, and his goods, and the women also, and the people.

17 ¶And the king of Sodom went out to greet him, after his return from the destruction of the forces of Cardlaamar, and the kings who were with him, at the valley of Shaveh, that is, the king's valley.

18 And Melchizedek king of Salem brought out bread and wine; he was the priest of the Most High God.

19 And he blessed him, saying, Blessed be Abram to God Most High, possessor of heaven and earth;

20 And blessed be the Most High God, who has delivered your enemies into your hands. And Abram gave him tithes of everything.

21 And the king of Sodom said to Abram, Give me the people, and take the goods for yourself.

22 And Abram said to the king of Sodom, I have lifted up my hands to the God Most High, the possessor of heaven and earth,

23 That I will not take of anything that belongs to you, from a thread to a shoestring, lest you should say, I have made Abram rich;

24 Save that which the young men have eaten and the portions of the men who went with me, Aner, Eshcol, and Mamre; let them take their portions.

CHAPTER 15

AFTER these things the word of the LORD came to Abram in a vision, saying, Fear not, Abram; I am your shield, and your reward is exceedingly great.

2 And Abram said, O LORD God, what will thou give me, for I will die childless, and Eliezer of Damascus, one of my household, will be my heir?

3 And Abram said, Behold, thou hast given me no son; and, behold, one of the members of my household will be my heir.

4 Then the LORD said to him, This man shall not be your heir; but your own son that shall come out of your own loins shall be your heir.

5 And he brought him outside, and said to him, Look now toward heaven and number the stars, if you are able to number them; and he said to him, So shall your descendants be.

6 And Abram believed in the LORD; and it was counted to him for righteousness.

7 And he said to him, I am the LORD, who brought you out of Ur of the Chaldeans, to give you this land to inherit it.

8 And Abram said, O LORD God, whereby shall I know that I shall inherit it?

9 And he said to him, Take for yourself a heifer, three years old, a three year old ram, a three year old she-goat, a pigeon, and a young dove.

10 And he took to himself all these, and cut them in two, and laid each piece against another; but the birds he did not divide.

11 And when the birds of prey came down upon the carcasses, Abram drove them away.

12 And when the sun was going down, a deep sleep fell on Abram; and, lo, fear and a great darkness fell upon him.

13 And the LORD said to Abram, Know of a surety that your descendants shall be strangers in a land that is not theirs, and shall be in servitude; and they shall afflict them for four hundred years;

14 But I will judge the nation which they shall serve; and afterward they shall come out with great wealth.

15 And you shall depart from this life and go to your fathers in peace; and you shall be buried at a good old age.

16 And after four centuries, they shall return here; for the iniquities of the Amorites are not yet full.

17 And it came to pass that when the sun had set and it was dark, behold there appeared a smoking furnace and a burning torch that passed between those pieces.

18 On that day the LORD made a covenant with Abram, saying, To your descendants have I given this land, from the river of Egypt to the great river, the river Euphrates:

19 The land of the Kenites, Kenizzites, and the Kadmonites,

20 The Hittites, the Perizzites, the Giants,

21 The Amorites, the Canaanites, the Girgashites, and the Jebusites.

CHAPTER 16

NOW Sarai, Abram's wife, bore him no children; and she had an Egyptian handmaid, whose name was Hagar.

2 And Sarai said to Abram, Behold now, the LORD has restrained me from bearing children; therefore go in unto my maid; it may be that I may be

consoled by her. And Abram hearkened to the voice of Sarai.

3 And Sarai, Abram's wife, took Hagar her Egyptian maid, and gave her to her husband Abram to be his wife. This happened after Abram had dwelt ten years in the land of Canaan.

4 ¶And he went in unto Hagar, and she conceived: and when she saw that she had conceived, her mistress was despised in her eyes.

5 And Sarai said to Abram, My wrong be upon you; I gave my maid into your bosom; and when she saw that she had conceived, I was despised in her eyes; may the LORD judge between me and you.

6 But Abram said to Sarai his wife, Behold your maid is at your disposal; do to her as it pleases you. And when Sarai dealt harshly with her, she fled from her.

7 ¶And the angel of the LORD found her by a fountain of water in the wilderness, by the fountain on the road to Gadar.

8 And he said to her, Hagar, maid of Sarai, where have you come from, and where are you going? And she said, I flee from the presence of my mistress Sarai.

9 And the angel of the LORD said to her, Return to your mistress, and submit yourself under her hands.

10 And again the angel of the LORD said to her, I will greatly multiply your descendants, that they can not be numbered because of their multitude.

11 And the angel of the LORD said to her, Behold, you are with child, and shall bear a son, and you shall call his name Ishmael; because the LORD has heard of your afflictions.

12 And he will be like a wild ass among men; with his hand against every man, and every man's hand against him, and he shall dwell on the borders of all his brethren.

13 And she called the name of the LORD who spoke to her, and said, Thou art God whom I saw; for she said, Behold, I have also seen a vision after he had seen me.

14 Therefore she called the well, Beer-di-khaya-khizan (which means, the well of the Living One who saw me). Behold, it is between Rakim and Gadar.

15 ¶And Hagar bore Abram a son; and Abram called his son's name, whom Hagar bore, Ishmael.

16 And Abram was eighty-six years old when Hagar bore Ishmael to him.

CHAPTER 17

WHEN Abram was ninety-nine years old, the LORD appeared to him, and said to him, I am the Almighty God; walk well before me, and be faultless.

2 And I will make my covenant between me and you and will multiply you exceedingly.

3 And Abram fell on his face; and God talked with him, saying,

4 As for me, behold, I am establishing my covenant with you, and you shall be a father of many peoples.

5 Neither shall your name any more be called Abram, but your name shall be Abraham; for I have made you a father of many peoples.

6 And I will make you fruitful, and multiply you exceedingly; and I will make you father of many nations, and kings shall come out of your loins.

7 And I will establish my covenant between me and you and your descendants after you throughout their generations for an everlasting covenant, and I will be God to you and to your descendants after you.

8 And I will give to you, and your descendants after you, the land in which you sojourn, all the land of Canaan, for an everlasting inheritance; and I will be their God.

9 ¶And God said to Abraham, You shall keep my covenant, you, and your descendants after you throughout their generations.

10 This is my covenant, which you shall keep between me and you and your descendants after you: Every male among you shall be circumcised.

11 And you shall circumcise the flesh of your foreskin; and it shall be a token of the covenant between me and you.

12 And he that is eight days old

shall be circumcised among you, every male throughout your generations, he that is born in the house, or bought with money of any stranger, who is not of your descendants.

13 He that is born in your house, and he that is bought with your money, shall be circumcised; and my covenant shall be in your flesh for an everlasting covenant.

14 And the uncircumcised male who is not circumcised in the flesh of his foreskin, that person shall be cut off from his people; for he has broken my covenant.

15 ¶Then God said to Abraham, As for Sarai your wife, you shall not call her name Sarai, for Sarah is her name.

16 And I will bless her, and also I will give you a son by her; yea, I will bless him and make nations of him; and the kings of the people shall come from him.

17 Then Abraham fell on his face and laughed and said in his heart, Shall a son be born to him who is a hundred years old? Or shall Sarah, who is ninety years old, bear a child?

18 And Abraham said to God, O that Ishmael might live in thy presence!

19 And God said to Abraham, Truly, Sarah your wife shall bear you a son; and you shall call his name Isaac; and I will establish my covenant with him for an everlasting covenant, and with his descendants after him.

20 And as for Ishmael, I have heard you; behold, I have blessed him, and will multiply him, and will make him exceedingly great; twelve princes shall he beget, and I will make him a great nation.

21 But I will establish my covenant with Isaac, whom Sarah shall bear to you at this set time next year.

22 And when God was through talking with him, he went up from Abraham.

23 ¶And Abraham took Ishmael his son and all of those that were born in his house and all of those that were bought with his money, every male among the men of Abraham's house-

hold, and circumcised the flesh of their foreskin in that very day, as God had said unto him.

24 And Abraham was ninety-nine years old when he was circumcised in the flesh of his foreskin.

25 And Ishmael his son was thirteen years old when he was circumcised in the flesh of his foreskin.

26 In that very day was Abraham circumcised and Ishmael his son

27 And all the men of his household, both born in the house and bought with money. He also circumcised some of the strangers with him.

CHAPTER 18

AND the LORD revealed himself to him by the oak of Mamre, as he was sitting at the door of the tent in the heat of the day;

2 And he lifted up his eyes and looked, and, behold, three men stood at a distance from him; and when he saw them, he ran from the door of the tent to meet them and bowed himself to the ground,

3 And said, O LORD, if now I have found mercy in thy sight, do not pass away from thy servant;

4 Let me bring a little water and wash your feet and rest yourselves under the tree;

5 And take a morsel of bread and sustain your hearts; after that you shall go on your way, since you have come to your servant. And they said, So do as you have said.

6 So Abraham hastened into the tent to Sarah, and said, Make ready quickly three measures of fine flour, knead it, and make cakes on a griddle.

7 And Abraham ran to the herd, and took a calf fat and good, and gave it to a servant, and he hastened to prepare it.

8 And he took butter and milk and the calf which he had prepared, and set them before them; and he stood by them under the tree, and they ate.

9 ¶And they said to him, Where is Sarah your wife? And he said, Behold, she is in the tent.

10 And the LORD said, I will cer-

tainly return to you at this time next year, and lo, Sarah your wife shall be with child, and shall have a son. And Sarah heard it in the tent door which was behind her.

11 Now Abraham and Sarah were old and well advanced in years; and Sarah was beyond the age of child-bearing.

12 Therefore Sarah laughed within herself, saying, After I am grown old, shall I renew my youth, my lord being old also?

13 And the LORD said to Abraham, Why did Sarah laugh, saying, Shall I truly bear a child, when I am so old?

14 Is anything too hard for the LORD? I will return to you at this season, and Sarah your wife shall be with child, and shall have a son.

15 Then Sarah denied, saying, I did not laugh; because she was afraid. And he said, No; but you did laugh.

16 ¶And the men rose up from there and looked toward Sodom; and Abraham went with them to see them off.

17 And the LORD said, Shall I hide from my servant Abraham the thing which I am going to do,

18 Seeing that Abraham shall surely become a great and mighty nation, and all the nations of the earth shall be blessed through him?

19 For I know him well, and that he will command his children and his household after him, to keep the ways of the LORD, to do justice and right-eousness; for the LORD shall fulfil for Abraham the thing that he has spoken concerning him.

20 And the LORD said, Because the cry of Sodom and Gomorrah has come before me and their sins are very grievous,

21 I will go down now and see whether they have done altogether according to their cry which has come before me; and if not, I will know.

22 So the men turned from there and went toward Sodom; but Abra-ham stood yet before the LORD.

23 ¶And Abraham drew near and said, Wilt thou in thine anger destroy the righteous with the sinners?

24 Suppose there are fifty righteous within the city; wilt thou in thine anger destroy it, and not spare the place for the sake of the fifty right-eous that are in it?

25 Far be it from thee to do such a thing as this, to slay the innocent with the guilty, far be it from thee, O thou Judge of the whole earth! Such a judgment should never be carried out.

26 And the LORD said, If I find in Sodom fifty righteous within the city, then I will spare the whole country for their sake.

27 And Abraham answered and said, Behold, I have ventured to speak before the LORD, and yet I am but dust and ashes;

28 Suppose there shall lack five of the fifty righteous; wilt thou destroy the whole city for the lack of five men? And he said, If I find there forty-five, I will not destroy it.

29 And Abraham spoke to him and said, Suppose there shall be forty found there? And he said, I will not destroy it, if I find there forty.

30 Then Abraham said, Oh let not the LORD be displeased and I will speak: Suppose there shall thirty be found there? And he said, I will not destroy it, if I find thirty there.

31 And he said, Behold, I have ven-tured to speak before the LORD; sup-pose there shall be twenty found there? And he said, I will not destroy it for the sake of twenty.

32 And he said, Oh, let not the LORD be displeased, and I will speak only once more; suppose ten shall be found there? And he said, I will not destroy it for the sake of ten.

33 And the LORD went his way when he had finished communing with Abraham; and Abraham re-turned to his place.

CHAPTER 19

AND there came two angels [1] to Sodom in the evening; and Lot was sitting at the gate of Sodom; and

---

[1] Aramaic: also *messengers, ministers.*

Lot saw them and rose up to meet them; and he bowed himself with his face toward the ground;

2 And he said, My lords, turn aside, I pray you, into your servant's house and spend the night and wash your feet; then rise up early in the morning and go on your way. And they said, No, we will spend the night in the street.

3 But Lot urged them greatly; and they turned in to him and entered into his house; and he made them a feast and baked unleavened cakes and they ate.

4 ¶But before they lay down, the men of the city, that is, the men of Sodom, surrounded the house, both young and old, all the people of the town;

5 And they called to Lot and said to him, Where are the men who came to you tonight? Bring them out to us that we may know them.

6 And Lot went out at the door to them; and he shut the door after him.

7 And Lot said to them, I pray you, my brethren, do not so wickedly.

8 Behold now, I have two daughters who have not known man; let me bring them out to you, and do to them whatever you please; only to these men do nothing; for they have come under the protection of my roof.

9 And they said, Get away. And they said again, This fellow came to sojourn among us, and now he tries to judge us; and they said to Lot, Now we will deal worse with you than with them. Then Lot fought desperately with them, and they drew near to break the door.

10 But the men put forth their hands and pulled Lot into the house to them and locked the door.

11 And they smote the men that were at the door of the house with blindness, from the least to the greatest, so that they became tired trying in vain to find the door.

12 ¶And the men said to Lot, What are you doing in this place? Now, your sons-in-law, your sons, your daughters, and whatsoever you have in this city, take them out of this place;

13 For we will destroy this place, because the cry of the oppressed has come before the LORD; and the LORD has sent us to destroy it.

14 Then Lot went out and spoke to his sons-in-law who married his daughters, and said, Arise, get out of this place; for the LORD will destroy it. But his sons-in-law thought he was joking.

15 ¶And when the morning dawned, the angels urged Lot, saying, Arise, take your wife and your two daughters who are not given in marriage, lest you be engulfed in the sins of the city.

16 But Lot lingered; then the angels held his hand, the hand of his wife, and the hands of his two daughters, because the LORD pitied him; and they took him out and set him outside the city.

17 ¶And it came to pass when they had brought them out of the city, they said to Lot: Now escape for your life; do not look back nor stop anywhere in the plain, but flee to the mountain lest you be consumed.

18 And Lot said to them, I beseech you, my lords,

19 Behold now, your servant has found mercy in your sight, and great is the favor which you have shown to me in saving my life; but I cannot escape to the mountain, lest evil overtake me and I die;

20 Behold now, this town is near to flee to, and it is a little one. Oh, let me escape there, and behold, because it is a little one my life will be spared.

21 And he said to him, See, I have granted you this thing also that I will not overthrow the city of which you have spoken.

22 Make haste and escape there; for I cannot do anything till you enter into it. Therefore the name of the city was called Zoar.

23 ¶The sun was risen upon the earth when Lot entered into Zoar.

24 Then the LORD rained upon Sodom and upon Gomorrah brimstone and fire from the presence of the LORD out of heaven;

25 And he overthrew those cities and all the plain and all the inhabi-

tants of the region and that which grew on the ground.

26 ¶But his wife looked back from behind him and she became a pillar of salt. [1]

27 ¶And Abraham rose up early in the morning and went to the place where he had stood before the LORD;

28 And he looked toward Sodom and Gomorrah and toward all the region of the plain, and beheld, lo, the smoke of the country went up like the smoke of a furnace.

29 ¶And it came to pass when God destroyed the cities of the plain that God remembered Abraham and sent Lot out of the midst of the devastated region, when he overthrew the cities wherein Lot dwelt.

30 ¶And Lot went up out of Zoar and dwelt in the mountain, and his two daughters were with him; for he was afraid to live in Zoar; and he dwelt in a cave, both he and his two daughters.

31 And the first-born said to the younger, Behold our father is old and there is not a man in the land to take us for wives after the manner of all the earth:

32 Come, let us make our father drink wine and we will lie with him so that we may raise an offspring from our father.

33 And they made their father drink wine that night; and the first-born went in and lay with her father; and he did not know when she lay down, nor when she arose.

34 And it came to pass on the next day, the first-born said to the younger, Behold, I lay last night with my father; let us make him drink wine tonight also; and then you go in and lie with him so that we may raise offspring from our father.

35 So they made their father drink wine that night also; and the younger went in and lay with him; and he did not know when she lay down, nor when she arose.

36 Thus were both the daughters of Lot with child by their father.

37 And the first-born bore a son and called his name Moab; he is the father of the Moabites to this day.

38 And the younger also bore a son and called his name Bar-ammi; he is the father of the Ammonites to this day.

CHAPTER 20

AND Abraham journeyed from thence toward the south country, and settled between Rakim and Gadar, and Abraham sojourned in Gadar.

2 And Abraham said of Sarah his wife, She is my sister; and Abimeleck king of Gadar sent and took Sarah.

3 But God came to Abimeleck in a dream by night and said to him, Behold, you will die on account of the woman whom you have taken; for she is another man's wife.

4 But Abimeleck had not touched her; and he said, O LORD, wilt thou slay an innocent people?

5 Behold, he said, She is my sister; and she herself also said, He is my brother; in the innocence of my heart and purity of my hands have I done this.

6 And God said to him in a dream, Yea, I know that you have done this in the innocence of your heart; for I also restrained you from sinning against me; therefore I did not permit you to touch her.

7 Now therefore restore the man's wife, for he is a prophet, and he shall pray for you, and you shall live; but if you do not restore her, then know that you will surely die, you, and all your family.

8 Therefore Abimeleck rose early in the morning and called all of his servants and told them all these words; and the men were exceedingly afraid.

9 Then Abimeleck called Abraham and said to him, What have I done to you? and what crime have I committed against you, that you have brought on me and on my kingdom such a great sin? You have done to me things that ought not to be done.

10 And Abimeleck said to Abra-

---

[1] Aramaic: *Pillar of salt* means that she became petrified with fear and died.

ham, What induced you to do this thing?

11 And Abraham said, Because I thought, perhaps there is no fear of God in this country; and they will slay me for my wife's sake.

12 And yet truly she is my sister; she is the daughter of my father, but not the daughter of my mother; and she became my wife.

13 And it came to pass when God brought me forth out of my father's house, I said to her, This is the favor which you shall do to me; at every place whither we shall go, say of me, He is my brother.

14 And Abimeleck took sheep and oxen and male and female servants and gave them to Abraham and restored to him Sarah his wife.

15 Then Abimeleck said to Abraham, Behold, my land is before you; dwell wherever you please.

16 And to Sarah he said, Behold, I have given a thousand pieces of silver to your brother; behold, it is given for you, because you have been humbled in the eyes of my people, and because of the other things for which I have reproved you.

17 ¶So Abraham prayed to God and God healed Abimeleck and his wife and his maidservants, and they bore children.

18 For the LORD had fast closed up the wombs of all women in the household of Abimeleck because of Sarah, Abraham's wife.

CHAPTER 21

AND the LORD remembered Sarah, as he had said, and the LORD did to Sarah as he had spoken.

2 For Sarah conceived and bore Abraham a son in his old age, at the set time of which God had spoken to him.

3 And Abraham called the name of his son that was born to him, whom Sarah bore to him, Isaac.

4 And Abraham circumcised his son Isaac when he was eight days old, as God had commanded him.

5 And Abraham was a hundred years old when his son Isaac was born to him.

6 ¶And Sarah said, God has made me to rejoice today exceedingly; everyone that hears the news will rejoice with me.

7 And she said, Who would have said to Abraham that Sarah would give suck to children? For I have borne him a son in his old age.

8 And the child grew and was weaned; and Abraham made a great feast on the day that Isaac was weaned.

9 ¶And Sarah saw the son of Hagar, the Egyptian, whom she had borne to Abraham, mocking.

10 Therefore she said to Abraham, Expel this maidservant and her son; for the son of this maidservant shall not be heir with my son Isaac.

11 And the thing was very grievous in Abraham's sight because of his son.

12 ¶And God said to Abraham, Let it not be grievous in your sight because of the boy and because of your maidservant; whatever Sarah tells you, hearken to her voice; for your descendants shall come through Isaac.

13 And also of the son of the maidservant will I make a great nation because he is your offspring.

14 And Abraham rose up early in the morning and took bread and a skin containing water and gave them to Hagar, putting them on her shoulder, and the boy; and sent her away. And she departed, and lost her way in the wilderness of Beer-sheba.

15 And the water in the skin was spent, and she cast the boy under one of the shrubs.

16 And she went and sat down opposite him about the distance of a bowshot; for she said, Let me not see the death of the boy. And she sat down opposite him and lifted up her voice and wept.

17 And the LORD heard the voice of the boy; and the angel of God called to Hagar from heaven, and said to her, What troubles you, Hagar? Fear not; for God has heard the voice of the boy where he is.

18 Arise, take up the boy, and hold him fast in your arms; for I will make him a great nation.

19 Then God opened her eyes and

she saw a well of water; and she went and filled the skin with water and gave the boy a drink.

20 And God was with the boy; and he grew up and dwelt in the wilderness of Paran and learned to become an archer in the wilderness of Paran.

21 And his mother took him a wife out of the land of Egypt.

22 ¶And it came to pass at that time that Abimeleck and Phichol, the general of his army, said to Abraham, God is with you in all that you do;

23 Now therefore swear to me by God in this place that you will never deal falsely with me, nor with my family, nor with my descendants; but according to the kindness that I have done to you, you shall do to me and to the land wherein you have sojourned.

24 And Abraham said, I will swear.

25 And Abraham reproved Abimeleck because of a well which Abraham's servants had dug and which Abimeleck's servants had seized.

26 And Abimeleck said, I do not know who has done this thing; neither did you tell me, nor have I heard of it until today.

27 And Abraham took sheep and oxen and gave them to Abimeleck; and both of them made a covenant.

28 And Abraham set seven ewe lambs of the flock by themselves.

29 And Abimeleck said to Abraham, What is the meaning of these seven ewe lambs of the flock which you have set by themselves?

30 And he said, For these seven ewe lambs you shall take of my hands that they may be a witness for me that I have digged this well.

31 Therefore he called that place Beer-sheba, because there they swore both of them.

32 Thus they made a covenant at Beer-sheba; then Abimeleck and Phichol, the general of the army, rose up and returned to the land of the Philistines.

33 ¶And Abraham planted a grove in Beer-sheba and called there on the name of the LORD Everlasting.

34 And Abraham sojourned in the land of the Philistines for a long time.

CHAPTER 22

AND it came to pass after these things that God tested Abraham and said to him, Abraham. And he said, Behold, here I am.

2 And he said, Take now your son, your only son Isaac, whom you love, and go to the land of the Amorites; and offer him there for a burnt offering upon one of the mountains of which I will tell you.

3 ¶And Abraham rose up early in the morning and saddled his ass and took two of his young men with him and Isaac his son, and cut wood for the burnt offering and rose up and went to the place of which God had told him.

4 And on the third day Abraham lifted up his eyes and saw the place afar off.

5 And he said to his young men, You stay here with the ass, and I and the boy will go yonder to worship and return to you.

6 And Abraham took the wood for the burnt offering and laid it upon Isaac his son, and he took the fire in a container and a knife in his hand, and they went both of them together.

7 And Isaac spoke to Abraham his father and said, My father. And he answered, Here I am, my son. And Isaac said, Behold the fire and the wood: but where is the lamb for a burnt offering?

8 And Abraham said, God will provide himself the lamb for a burnt offering, my son. So they went both of them together.

9 And they came to the place of which God had told him; and Abraham built an altar there and laid the wood in order and bound Isaac his son and laid him on the altar upon the wood.

10 Then Abraham stretched forth his hand and took the knife to slay his son.

11 And the angel of the LORD called to him from heaven and said, Abraham! Abraham! And he said, Here am I.

12 And he said to him, Do not lay your hand on the boy, neither shall

you harm him; for now I know that you are a man who reveres God, seeing that you have not withheld your son, your only son, from me.

13 And Abraham lifted up his eyes and looked, and behold a ram caught in a thicket by his horns; and Abraham went and took the ram and offered it up for a burnt offering instead of his son.

14 And Abraham called the name of that place Mariah-nekhzey, that is, the LORD will provide, as it is said to this day on this mountain, The LORD shall provide.

15 ¶And the angel of the LORD called to Abraham from heaven a second time

16 And said, I have sworn by myself, says the LORD, for because you have done this thing and have not withheld your son, your only son, from me,

17 I will surely bless you, and I will surely multiply your descendants as the stars of the heaven, and as the sand which is on the sea shore; and your descendants shall inherit the lands of their enemies;

18 And by your seed [1] shall all the nations of the earth be blessed because you have obeyed my voice.

19 So Abraham returned to his young men and they rose up and went together to Beer-sheba, and Abraham dwelt in Beer-sheba.

20 ¶And it came to pass after these things that it was told Abraham, saying, Behold, Milcah has also borne children to your brother Nahor:

21 Uz his first-born, Buz his brother, and Kemuel the father of Aram,

22 And Khasar, Hazo, Pilrash, Jarlaph, and Bethuel.

23 And Bethuel begot Rebekah; these eight Milcah did bear to Nahor, Abraham's brother.

24 And his concubine, whose name was Romah, also bore Tebah, Gaham, Thahash, and Maachah.

CHAPTER 23

AND Sarah was a hundred and twenty-seven years old; these were the years of the life of Sarah.

[1] *Seed* in Aramaic also means teaching.

2 And Sarah died at Koriath Gabarey (the Town of the Giants); that is Hebron in the land of Canaan; and Abraham came to mourn for Sarah and to weep for her.

3 ¶And Abraham rose up from before the bier of his dead and spoke to the sons of Heth, saying,

4 I am a stranger and a sojourner with you; give me the possession of a burial ground with you that I may bury my dead out of my sight.

5 And the sons of Heth answered and said to Abraham,

6 Hear us, our lord; you are a prince of God among us; bury your dead in the choicest of our sepulchres; none of us will withhold from you his sepulchre for the burial of your dead.

7 And Abraham stood up and bowed himself to the people of the land, that is, to the Hittites.

8 And he discussed the matter with them and said to them, If you consent that I may bury my dead out of my sight, hear me and entreat for me to Ephron the son of Zohar,

9 That he may give me the double cave which belongs to him, which is by the side of his field; let him give it to me for a full price as a possession for a burial ground among you.

10 And Ephron dwelt among the Hittites; and Ephron the Hittite answered Abraham in the presence of the Hittites and in the presence of all that went in at the gate of his city, saying,

11 No, my lord, listen to me; I will give you the field and the cave which is in it, I will give it to you; in the presence of my people I give it to you; bury your dead.

12 And Abraham bowed down before the people of the land,

13 Then he said to Ephron in the presence of the people of the land, If you are willing, then hearken to me; I will give you money for the price of the field; take it from me, and I will bury my dead there.

14 And Ephron answered Abraham and said,

15 My lord, hearken to me; the land is worth four hundred shekels of sil-

ver; what is that between me and you? You may bury your dead.

16 And Abraham hearkened to Ephron; and Abraham weighed to Ephron the sum of money which he had named in the presence of the Hittites, four hundred shekels of silver, legal tender with the merchants.

17 ¶Thus the field of Ephron, which was by the side of the double cave which was before Mamre, that is, the Field of the Cave and the cave which was in it and all the trees that were in the field that were on its borders round about were made sure

18 And sold to Abraham in the presence of the Hittites and in the presence of all that went in at the gate of his city.

19 And after this, Abraham buried Sarah his wife in the double cave which is in the field before Mamre; the same is Hebron in the land of Canaan.

20 Thus the field and the cave that is in it were deeded to Abraham for a possession of a burial ground by the Hittites.

CHAPTER 24

NOW Abraham was old and well advanced in years; and the LORD had blessed him in all things.

2 And Abraham called his eldest servant, the steward of his house, who was in charge of everything that he had; and he said to him, Put your hand under my girdle;

3 And I will make you swear by the LORD, the God of heaven and the God of the earth, that you shall not take to my son a wife of the daughters of the Canaanites, among whom I dwell;

4 But that you will go to my country and to my kindred, and take a wife for my son Isaac.

5 And the servant said to him, Suppose the woman will not be willing to follow me to this land; must I then take your son back to the land from whence you came?

6 And Abraham said to him, Beware that you do not take my son thither again.

7 ¶The LORD God of heaven, who took me from thence, from my father's household and from the land of my kindred, and who spoke to me, and who made a covenant with me, saying, To your descendants will I give this land; he shall send his angel before you, and you shall take a wife to my son from there.

8 And if the woman will not be willing to follow you, then you shall be clear from this my oath; only you must not take my son there again.

9 So the servant put his hand under the girdle of Abraham his master, and swore to him concerning this matter.

10 ¶And the servant took ten camels of the camels of his master, and departed, carrying with him all kinds of choice things of his master; and he arose, and went to Aram-nahrin (Mesopotamia), to the city of Nahor.

11 And he made his camels to kneel down outside the city by a well of water in the evening, the very time when women go out to draw water.

12 And he prayed, saying, O LORD God of my master Abraham, prosper my journey, and show kindness to my master Abraham.

13 Behold, I stand here by the well of water; and the daughters of the men of the city are coming out to draw water.

14 Let it come to pass that the damsel to whom I shall say, Let down your pitcher, that I may drink; and she shall say to me, Drink, and I will water your camels also; let the same be she that thou hast selected for thy servant Isaac; and by this token shall I know that thou hast shown kindness and faithfulness to my master.

15 ¶And it came to pass, before he had finished speaking, that, behold, Rebekah came out, who was born to Bethuel, son of Milcah, the wife of Nahor, Abraham's brother, with her pitcher on her shoulder.

16 And the damsel was very beautiful to look upon, a virgin whom no man had known; and she went down to the well and filled her pitcher and came up.

17 And the servant ran to meet her and said, Let me drink a little water from your pitcher.

18 And she said, Drink, my lord; and she hastened and let down the pitcher upon her hands and gave him a drink.

19 And when she had finished giving him a drink, she said, I will draw water for your camels also, until they are all watered.

20 So she hastened and emptied her pitcher into the trough and ran again to the well to draw water, and she drew water for all his camels.

21 And as the man watered his camels he scrutinized her, and waited to know whether the LORD had made his journey prosperous or not.

22 And it came to pass, when the camels were through drinking, the man took golden earrings weighing a shekel and two bracelets for her wrists weighing ten shekels of gold,

23 And said to her, Whose daughter are you? tell me, is there room in your father's house for us to lodge?

24 And she said to him, I am the daughter of Bethuel the son of Milcah, whom she bore to Nahor.

25 And she said moreover to him, We have plenty of straw and hay, and room to lodge in.

26 And the man knelt on the ground and worshipped the LORD.

27 And he said, Blessed be the LORD God of my master Abraham, who has not withheld his grace and his truth from my master; while I was on the road, the LORD led me to the house of my master's brother, to take his brother's daughter to his son.

28 Then the damsel ran, and related these things to her father's household.

29 ¶And Rebekah had a brother, and his name was Laban; so Laban ran out to the man, to the well.

30 And it came to pass, when he saw the earrings and the bracelets on his sister's hands and when he heard the words of Rebekah his sister, saying, Thus spoke the man to me, he came to the man; and, behold, he was standing by the camels at the well.

31 And he said to him, Come in, you blessed of the LORD; why do you stand in the street? For I have prepared the house and a place for the camels.

32 ¶So the man came into the house and ungirded the camels and gave straw and hay for the camels, and was given water to wash his feet and the feet of the men who were with him.

33 And there was set food before them to eat; but Abraham's steward said, I will not eat until I have told my errand. And they said, Speak on.

34 And he said, I am Abraham's servant.

35 And the LORD has blessed my master greatly, so that he has become great; and he has given him flocks and herds, silver and gold, menservants and maidservants, and camels and asses.

36 And Sarah my master's wife bore a son to my master when she was old; and to him he has given all that he has.

37 And my master made me swear, saying, You must not take a wife to my son of the daughters of the Canaanites, in whose land I dwell;

38 But you shall go to my father's house and to my kindred, and take a wife to my son.

39 And I said to my master, Suppose the woman will be unwilling to follow me?

40 And he said to me, The LORD before whom I worship will send his angel with you, and prosper your way; and you shall take a wife for my son of my kindred and of my father's house;

41 Then you shall be clear from my oath, when you go to my kindred; and if they do not give you a bride, you shall be clear from my oath.

42 And I came today to the well, and said, O LORD God of my master Abraham, if now thou do prosper my mission for which I came,

43 Behold, I am standing by the well of water, and it shall come to pass that when the damsel comes forth to draw water, and I say to her, Let me drink a little water from your pitcher,

44 And she say to me, Drink, and

I will also draw for your camels, let the same be the woman whom the LORD has appointed for my master's son.

45 And before I was through speaking in my heart, behold, Rebekah came forth with her pitcher on her shoulder; and she went down to the fountain, and drew water; and I said to her, Let me drink a little water from your pitcher.

46 And she hastened, and let down her pitcher from her shoulder, and said, Drink, and I will water your camels also; so I drank, and she watered my camels also.

47 Then I asked her, and said, Whose daughter are you? And she said, The daughter of Bethuel, the son of Nahor, whom Milcah bore to him; and I put the earrings on her ears and the bracelets on her hands.

48 And I knelt and worshipped the LORD, and blessed the LORD God of my master Abraham, who had led me in the right way to the house of my master's brother to take my master's brother's daughter to his son.

49 And now if you will deal kindly and truly with my master, tell me; and if not, tell me; so that I may know what to do.

50 Then Laban and Bethuel answered and said, The thing proceeded from the LORD; we cannot say anything to you good or bad.

51 Behold, Rebekah is before you; take her and go, and let her become the wife of your master's son, as the LORD has spoken.

52 And it came to pass that, when Abraham's servant heard their words, he worshipped the LORD, bowing himself to the earth.

53 And the servant brought forth jewels of gold and jewels of silver and raiment, and gave them to Rebekah; he also gave gifts to her brother and to her mother.

54 And he and the men who were with him ate and drank, and spent the night there; and the servant rose up in the morning, and said to them, Send me away to my master.

55 And her brother and her mother said to him, Let the damsel stay with us a month, or at least a few days; and then she shall go.

56 And he said to them, Do not delay me, seeing the LORD has prospered my errand; send me away that I may go to my master.

57 And they said, We will call the damsel, and ask her.

58 So they called Rebekah, and said to her, Will you go with this man? And she said, I will go.

59 And they sent away Rebekah their sister and her nurse and Abraham's servant and his men.

60 And they blessed Rebekah their sister, and said to her, You are our sister, be the mother of thousands and of millions, and let your descendants inherit the lands of their enemies.

61 ¶Then Rebekah arose with her maids, and they rode upon the camels, and followed the man; and the servant took Rebekah and went his way.

62 And Isaac had returned from the well of Khaya-khezan; for he dwelt in the south country.

63 Now Isaac strolled in the field in the evening; and he lifted up his eyes and saw, and behold, the camels were coming.

64 And Rebekah lifted up her eyes, and when she saw Isaac, she leaned over the camel,

65 And she said to the servant, Who is this man who is walking in the field to meet us? And the servant said, It is my master; therefore she took a veil and covered herself.

66 And the servant told Isaac all the things that she had done.

67 And Isaac brought her into his mother Sarah's tent, and took Rebekah, and she became his wife; and he loved her; and Isaac was comforted after his mother's death.

CHAPTER 25

THEN again Abraham took another wife, and her name was Kenturah.

2 And she bore him Zimran, Jokshan, Medan, Midian, Ishbak, and Shuah.

3 And Jokshan begot Sheba and

Daran. And the sons of Daran were Asshurim, Letushim, and Ammim.

4 And the sons of Midian were Ephah, Haphar, Hanoch, Abidah, and Eldaah. All these were the children of Kenturah.

5 ¶And Abraham gave everything that he had to Isaac.

6 But to the sons of his concubine, Abraham gave gifts, and sent them away from Isaac, his son, eastward to the east country, while he was still alive.

7 And these are the days of the years of Abraham's life which he lived, a hundred and seventy-five years.

8 Then Abraham became sick, and died in a good old age, an old man satisfied with his days; and was gathered to his people.

9 And his sons Isaac and Ishmael buried him in the double cave, (Machpelah) which is in the field of Ephron the son of Zohar the Hittite, which is before Mamre;

10 The field which Abraham purchased from the sons of Heth, as a possession for a burial ground. There was Abraham buried, and Sarah his wife.

11 ¶And it came to pass after the death of Abraham that God blessed his son Isaac; and Isaac dwelt by the well of Khaya-khezan (The Well of The Living One who saw me).

12 ¶Now these are the generations of Ishmael, Abraham's son, whom Hagar the Egyptian, Sarah's maid, bore to Abraham;

13 And these are the names of the sons of Ishmael, by their names, according to their generations: the firstborn of Ishmael, Nebioth, and Kedar, Arbal, and Mibsam,

14 Mishma, Romah, Massa,

15 Hadar, Tema, Nator, Naphish, and Kedem.

16 These are the sons of Ishmael, and these are their names by their villages and by their sheepfolds, twelve princes according to their nations.

17 And these are the years of the life of Ishmael, a hundred and thirty-seven years; and he became sick and died; and was gathered to his people.

18 And they dwelt from Havilah as far as Shud, which extends from the border of Egypt to the gateway of Assyria; he dwelt adjacent to the lands of all his brethren.

19 ¶These are the generations of Isaac, Abraham's son: Abraham begot Isaac;

20 And Isaac was forty years old when he took Rebekah to wife, the daughter of Bethuel the Aramean of Padan-aram, the sister of Laban, the Aramean (Syrian).

21 And Isaac prayed before the LORD for his wife, because she was barren; and the LORD answered him, and Rebekah his wife conceived.

22 And the children struggled together within her womb; and she said, If it is to be like this, why do I live? So she went to enquire of the LORD.

23 And the LORD said to her, Two peoples are in your womb, and two nations shall be separated from your body; and the one nation shall be stronger than the other nation; and the elder shall serve the younger.

24 ¶And when her days to be delivered were fulfilled, behold, there were twins in her womb.

25 And the first came out red, all covered with ringlets of hair; and they called his name Esau.

26 And after him his brother came forth, and his hand held Esau's heel; and his name was called Jacob; [1] and Isaac was sixty years old when Rebekah bore them.

27 And the boys grew up; and Esau became an expert hunter, a man of outdoor life; but Jacob was a simple man, living in a tent.

28 And Isaac was fond of Esau, because he ate of Esau's game; but Rebekah was fond of Jacob.

29 ¶And Jacob cooked pottage,[2] and behold, his brother Esau came in from the field, and he was very hungry;

30 And Esau said to Jacob, Give me some of that pottage, for I am

---

[1] Heel holder.   [2] Lentil stew.

famished; that is why he was called Edom.

31 And Jacob said, Sell me this day your birthright.

32 And Esau said, Behold, I am at the point of death; and what profit shall a birthright be to me?

33 And Jacob said to him, Swear to me this day; and he swore to him; and he sold his birthright to Jacob.

34 Then Jacob gave Esau bread and pottage; and he ate, and drank, and rose up and went his way; thus Esau despised his birthright.

CHAPTER 26

AND there was a famine in the land, besides the first famine that was in the days of Abraham. And Isaac went to Gadar, to Abimeleck king of the Philistines.

2 And the LORD appeared to him, and said, Do not go down to Egypt; dwell in the land of which I shall tell you;

3 Sojourn in this land, and I will be with you and will bless you; for to you and to your descendants I will give all these kingdoms, and I will perform the oath which I swore to Abraham your father;

4 And I will make your descendants to multiply as the stars of heaven, and will give to your descendants all these lands; and by your descendants shall all the nations of the earth be blessed;

5 Because that Abraham obeyed my voice, and kept my charge, my commandments, my statutes, and my laws.

6 ¶And Isaac dwelt in Gadar;

7 And the men of the place asked him concerning his wife; and he said, She is my sister; for he was afraid to say, She is my wife; lest the men of the place should kill him on account of Rebekah, because she was fair to look upon.

8 And it came to pass when he had been there a long time that Abimeleck king of the Philistines looked out of a window and saw Isaac fondling Rebekah his wife.

9 So Abimeleck called Isaac, and said, Behold, she is your wife; how then did you say, She is my sister? And Isaac said to him, Because I said, Lest I may die on account of her.

10 And Abimeleck said to him, What is this thing that you have done to us? One of the people might easily have lain with your wife, and you would have brought sin upon us.

11 And Abimeleck charged all the people, saying, Whoever harms this man or his wife shall surely be put to death.

12 Then Isaac sowed in that land, and received in the same year a hundredfold; and the LORD blessed him.

13 And the man became great, and went forward and grew until he became very great;

14 And he had possessions of flocks and possessions of herds and much wealth, so that the Philistines envied him.

15 For all the wells which his father's servants had dug in the days of Abraham his father, the Philistines had polluted them and filled them with earth.

16 And Abimeleck said to Isaac, Go away from among us; for you are much mightier than we.

17 ¶So Isaac departed from thence, and encamped in the valley of Gadar, and dwelt there.

18 And Isaac digged again the wells of water which had been dug by the servants of his father in the days of Abraham his father; for the Philistines had polluted them after the death of Abraham; and he called their names after the names by which his father had called them.

19 And Isaac's servants dug in the valley, and found there a well of living water.

20 And the herdsmen of Gadar quarreled with Isaac's herdsmen, saying, The water is ours; and he called the name of the well Aska (difficulty); because they disputed with him.

21 And they dug another well, and they quarreled over that also; and he called the name of it Satana (the adversary).

22 Then he moved from there, and

dug another well; but over that they did not quarrel; and he called the name of it Rehoboth (to enlarge); and he said, For now the LORD has made room for us, and we shall multiply in the land.

23 And he went up from thence to Beer-sheba.

24 And the LORD appeared to him the same night, and said, I am the God of Abraham your father; fear not, for I am with you, and I will bless you, and multiply your descendants for my servant Abraham's sake.

25 And he built an altar there, and called upon the name of the LORD, and pitched his tent there; and there Isaac's servants dug a well.

26 ¶Then Abimeleck went to him from Gadar, and Ahuzzath one of his friends, and Phichol the general of his army.

27 And Isaac said to them, Why have you come to me, seeing that you hate me, and have sent me away from you?

28 And they said, We saw certainly that the LORD is with you; so we said, Let there be now an oath between us and you, and let us make a covenant with you,

29 That you will do us no evil, just as we have not hurt you, and as we have done nothing but good to you, and have sent you away in peace; you are now the blessed of the LORD.

30 And he made them a feast, and they did eat and drink.

31 And they rose up in the early morning, and took oaths one with another; and Isaac sent them away, and they departed from him in peace.

32 And it came to pass the same day that Isaac's servants came, and spoke to him concerning the well which they had dug, and said to him, We have found water.

33 And he called it Sheba; therefore the name of the town is called Beer-sheba to this day.

34 ¶And Esau was forty years old when he took to wife Judith the daughter of Beeri the Hittite, and Bismath the daughter of Elon the Hivite;

35 And they made life miserable for Isaac and Rebekah.

CHAPTER 27

AND it came to pass, when Isaac was old and his eyes were dim so that he could not see, he called Esau his eldest son, and said to him, My son; and he said to him, Behold, here I am.

2 And Isaac said to him, Behold now, I am old, and I do not know the day of my death;

3 Now therefore take your weapons, your sword and your bow, and go out into the field and hunt game;

4 And make me stewed meat, such as I like, and bring it to me, that I may eat, that my soul may bless you before I die.

5 And Rebekah heard when Isaac spoke to Esau his son. So Esau went to the field to hunt game and to bring it.

6 ¶Then Rebekah said to Jacob her son, Behold, I heard your father say to Esau your brother,

7 Bring me game, and make me stewed meat, that I may eat and bless you in the presence of the LORD before I die.

8 Now therefore, my son, listen to me according to that which I command you.

9 Go now to the flock, and bring me from there two kids of the goats; and I will make from them stew for your father, such as he likes;

10 And you shall bring it to your father, that he may eat, and that he may bless you in the presence of the LORD before his death.

11 And Jacob said to Rebekah his mother, Behold, Esau my brother is a hairy man and I am a smooth man;

12 Perhaps my father will feel me, and I shall seem to him as a mocker; and I shall bring a curse upon myself, and not a blessing.

13 And his mother said to him, Let your curses be upon me, my son; only listen to me, and go and fetch them to me.

14 So he went and picked them up, and brought them to his mother; and his mother made a stew, such as his father liked.

15 And Rebekah took the best

clothes of her elder son Esau, which were with her in the house, and put them upon Jacob her younger son;

16 And she put the skins of the kids of the goats upon his hands, and upon the back of his neck;

17 And she gave the stew and the bread which she had prepared into the hand of her son Jacob.

18 ¶And he brought them in to his father, and said, My father; and he said, Here am I. Then he said, Who are you, my son?

19 And Jacob said to his father, I am Esau, your first-born; I have done as you told me; now arise and sit up and eat of my game, that your soul may bless me.

20 And Isaac said to his son, How is it that you have found it so quickly, my son? And he said, Because the LORD your God brought it my way.

21 Then Isaac said to Jacob his son, Come near me, that I may feel you, my son, to know whether you are my son Esau or not.

22 And Jacob drew near to Isaac his father; and he felt him, and said, The voice is Jacob's voice, but the hands are Esau's.

23 But he did not recognize him, because his hands were hairy, like his brother Esau's hands; so he blessed him.

24 And he said, Are you my very son Esau? And Jacob said, I am.

25 And he said, Bring the stew near to me, and I will eat of my son's game, that my soul may bless you. And he brought it near to him, and he did eat; and he brought him wine, and he drank.

26 And his father Isaac said to him, Come near now, and kiss me, my son; so he drew near and kissed him;

27 And he came near, and kissed him; and he smelled the smell of his garments, and blessed him, and said, See, the smell of my son is like the smell of a field which the LORD has blessed;

28 Therefore may God give you of the dew of heaven and the richness of the earth, and the abundance of wheat and wine;

29 Let people serve you, and na-

tions bow down to you; be a prince over your brethren, and let your mother's sons bow down to you; cursed be they who curse you, and blessed be they who bless you.

30 ¶And it came to pass when Isaac had finished blessing Jacob and Jacob had gone out from the presence of Isaac his father, behold, Esau his brother came in from his hunting.

31 And he also made stew, and brought it to his father, and said to his father, Let my father arise, and eat of his son's game, that your soul may bless me.

32 And Isaac his father said to him, Who are you? And he said, I am your son, your first-born, Esau.

33 And Isaac was greatly alarmed, and said, Who was it then that hunted game and brought it to me? I have eaten of everything before you came, and I have blessed him, yea, and he shall be blessed.

34 And when Esau heard the words of his father, he cried out bitterly, and said to his father, Bless me, even me also, O my father.

35 But his father said, Your brother came with deceit, and has already received your blessing.

36 And Esau said, Is he not rightly named Jacob? For he has acted treacherously toward me twice: he took away my birthright; and, behold, now he has taken away my blessing. And Esau said to his father, Have you not reserved a blessing for me?

37 And Isaac answered and said to Esau, Behold, I have made him a prince over you, and all his brethren have I given to him for servants; and with wheat and wine have I sustained him; and what shall I do now for you, my son?

38 And Esau said to his father, Have you only one blessing, my father? Bless me, even me also, O my father. And Esau lifted up his voice and wept.

39 And Isaac his father answered and said to him, Behold, your dwelling shall be in the fertile places of the earth, and the dew of heaven shall fall upon you from above;

40 And by your sword you shall

live, and you shall serve your brother; but if you shall repent, his yoke shall pass away from off your neck.

41 ¶And Esau hated Jacob because of the blessings with which his father had blessed him; and Esau said in his heart, After the days of mourning for my father are over, then I will slay my brother Jacob.

42 And the words of Esau her elder son were told to Rebekah; so she sent and called her younger son Jacob, and said to him, Behold, your brother Esau is threatening to kill you.

43 Now therefore, my son, hearken to me; and arise, and go to Laban my brother, to Haran;

44 And stay there a few days, until your brother's fury is spent;

45 Until your brother's anger turns away from you, and he forgets what you have done to him; then I will send messengers, and bring you back from there; lest I be deprived also of both of you in one day.

46 Then Rebekah said to Isaac, I am weary of my life because of the daughters of Heth; if Jacob takes a wife of the daughters of Heth, such as these which are of the daughters of the land, what good will my life be to me?

CHAPTER 28

THEN Isaac called Jacob, and blessed him, and charged him, and said to him, You shall not take a wife of the daughters of Canaan.

2 Arise, go to Padan-aram, to the house of Bethuel your mother's father; and take for yourself a wife from there of the daughters of Laban your mother's brother.

3 May God Almighty bless you and make you fruitful and multiply you, that you may become a multitude of peoples;

4 And give the blessings of Abraham to you and to your descendants with you, that you may inherit the land in which you dwell, which God gave to Abraham.

5 And Isaac sent away Jacob; and he went to Padan-aram, to Laban, the son of Bethuel, the Aramean, the brother of Rebekah, Jacob's and Esau's mother.

6 ¶When Esau saw that Isaac had blessed his brother Jacob and sent him away to Padan-aram to take for himself a wife from there, and that as he blessed him, he charged him, saying, You shall not take a wife of the daughters of Canaan;

7 And Jacob obeyed his father and his mother, and went to Padan-aram;

8 And Esau saw that Isaac his father despised the daughters of Canaan;

9 Then Esau went to Ishmael, Abraham's son, and took Bismath, the daughter of Ishmael, Abraham's son, the sister of Nebioth, to be his wife, in addition to his other wives.

10 ¶And Jacob went out from Beer-sheba, on his way to Haran.

11 And he arrived at a certain place, and spent the night there, because the sun was set; and he took of the stones of the place, and put them for his pillows, and lay down in that place to sleep.

12 And he dreamed, and behold a ladder was set upon the earth, and the top of it reached to heaven; and behold the angels of God were ascending and descending on it.

13 And, behold, the LORD stood above it and said, I am the LORD God of Abraham your father, and the God of Isaac; the land whereon you are lying, I will give to you and to your descendants;

14 And your descendants shall be as numerous as the dust of the earth, and you shall spread abroad to the east and to the west and to the north and to the south; and in you and through your descendants shall all the families of the earth be blessed.

15 And, behold, I am with you, and will keep you wherever you go, and will bring you back to this land; for I will not leave you until I have done the thing of which I have spoken to you.

16 ¶And Jacob awoke from his sleep, and he said, Surely the LORD is in this place; and I did not know it.

17 And Jacob was exceedingly fearful, and he said, How sacred is this place today! This is none other but

the house of God, and this is the gate of heaven.

18 And Jacob rose up early in the morning, and took the stone which he had put for his pillow, and set it up for a pillar, and poured oil on the top of it.

19 Then Jacob called the name of that place Beth-el (the house of God); but at the first the name of that place was called Luz.

20 And Jacob vowed a vow, saying, If God will be with me and will protect me in this way that I go, and will give me food to eat and clothing to wear

21 So that I may return to my father's house in peace, then the LORD shall be my God;

22 And this stone which I have set up for a pillar shall be God's house; and of all that thou shalt give me I will give the tenth to thee.

CHAPTER 29

THEN Jacob hastened on his journey, and came to the land of the people of the east.

2 And he looked, and beheld a well in the field, and, lo, there were three flocks of sheep lying by it; for out of that well they watered the flocks; and a large stone was upon the well's mouth.

3 And all the flocks were gathered there; and the shepherds rolled the stone from the well's mouth, and watered the sheep, and then put the stone back in its place upon the well's mouth.

4 And Jacob said to them, My brethren, where do you come from? And they said, We are from Haran.

5 And he said to them, Do you know Laban the son of Nahor? And they said, We do know him.

6 And he said to them, Is he well? And they said, He is well; and, behold, Rachel his daughter is coming with the sheep.

7 And Jacob said, Lo, the sun is still high, it is not yet time that the cattle should be gathered together; water the sheep, and go and feed them.

8 And they said, We cannot until all the flocks are gathered together and the shepherds roll the stone from the well's mouth; then we water the sheep.

9 ¶And while he was still conversing with them, Rachel came with her father's sheep; for she was a shepherdess.

10 And it came to pass, when Jacob saw Rachel the daughter of Laban his mother's brother and the sheep of Laban his mother's brother, that Jacob drew near and rolled the stone from the well's mouth and watered the sheep of Laban his mother's brother.

11 And Jacob kissed Rachel, and lifted up his voice, and wept.

12 And Jacob told Rachel that he was her father's kinsman and that he was Rebekah's son; and she ran and told her father.

13 And it came to pass when Laban heard the tidings of Jacob his sister's son, he ran to meet him and embraced him and kissed him and brought him to his house. And Jacob related to Laban all these things.

14 And Laban said to him, Surely you are my bone and my flesh. And he stayed with him for a month.

15 ¶And Laban said to Jacob, Because you are my kinsman, should you therefore work for me for nothing? Tell me, what shall your wages be?

16 And Laban had two daughters: the name of the older was Leah, and the name of the younger Rachel.

17 And Leah had attractive eyes; but Rachel was beautiful and well favored.

18 And Jacob loved Rachel; and he said, I will serve you seven years for Rachel, your younger daughter.

19 And Laban said to him, It is better that I give her to you than that I should give her to another man; abide with me.

20 Thus Jacob served seven years for Rachel; and they seemed to him but a few days because he was in love with her.

21 ¶And Jacob said to Laban, Give me my wife, for my days are fulfilled, that I may go in unto her.

22 And so Laban gathered together all the men of the place and made a feast.

23 And it came to pass in the evening, he took Leah his daughter, and brought her to him; and Jacob went in unto her.

24 And Laban gave Zilpah his maid to his daughter Leah for a servant.

25 And it came to pass in the morning, behold, it was Leah; and Jacob said to Laban, What is this thing that you have done to me? Did not I serve with you for Rachel? Why then have you deceived me?

26 Then Laban said to Jacob, It is not so done in our country, to give the younger in marriage before the elder.

27 Finish the wedding feast [1] for this one, and then I will give you the other also for the service which you shall serve with me yet another seven years.

28 And Jacob did so, and finished her wedding feast; and Laban gave him his daughter Rachel to wife.

29 And Laban gave Bilhah his maid to Rachel his daughter to be her maid.

30 And he went in unto Rachel also, and he loved Rachel also more than Leah, and served with Laban another seven years.

31 ¶And when the LORD saw that Leah was hated, he opened her womb; but Rachel was barren.

32 And Leah conceived, and bore a son, and she called his name Reuben; for she said, Because the LORD has seen my affliction, now therefore my husband will love me.

33 And she conceived again, and bore a son; and said, Because the LORD has heard that I am hated, he has therefore given me this son also; so she called his name Simeon.

34 And she conceived again, and bore a son; and said, Now this time my husband will surely love me, because I have born him three sons; therefore she called his name Levi.

35 And she conceived again, and bore a son; and she said, This time I will praise the LORD; therefore she

¹ Three days or seven days according to social standing.

called his name Judah; and then she ceased bearing.

CHAPTER 30

AND when Rachel saw that she was not bearing children to Jacob, she envied her sister; and said to Jacob, Give me children, or else I die.

2 And Jacob's anger was kindled against Rachel; and he said to her, Am I in the place of God, that I have prevented you from having a child?

3 Then she said to him, Behold my maid Bilhah, go in unto her; and she shall bear upon my knees, that I may also be comforted by her.

4 And she gave him her maid Bilhah to wife; and Jacob went in unto her.

5 And Bilhah conceived, and bore Jacob a son.

6 And Rachel said, God has judged me, and has also heard my voice, and has given me a son; therefore she called his name Dan.

7 And Bilhah, Rachel's maid, conceived again, and bore Jacob a second son.

8 And Rachel said, I have besought the LORD, and pleaded with my sister, and I have attained my desire; and she called his name Naphtali.

9 When Leah saw that she had ceased bearing children, she took her maid Zilpah, and gave her to Jacob to wife.

10 And Zilpah, Leah's maid, bore Jacob a son.

11 And Leah said, My fortune has come; so she called his name Gad.

12 And Zilpah, Leah's maid, bore Jacob a second son.

13 And Leah said, The girls will sing my praise, so she called his name Asher.

14 ¶And Reuben went at the time of the wheat harvest and found mandrakes in the field and brought them to his mother Leah. Then Rachel said to Leah, Give me some of your son's mandrakes.

15 But Leah said to her, Is it not enough for you that you have taken

away my husband? And would you take away my son's mandrakes also? And Rachel said, He may lie with you tonight for your son's mandrakes.

16 And when Jacob came home from the field in the evening, Leah went out to meet him, and said, You must come in unto me; for surely I have hired you with my son's mandrakes. And he lay with her that night.

17 And God hearkened to Leah, and she conceived, and bore Jacob the fifth son.

18 And Leah said, God has rewarded me, because I have given my maid to my husband; so she called his name Issachar.

19 And Leah conceived again, and bore Jacob the sixth son.

20 And Leah said, God has enriched me exceedingly; now my husband will surely have more affection for me, because I have borne him six sons; so she called his name Zebulun.

21 And afterwards she bore a daughter, and called her name Dinah.

22 ¶And God remembered Rachel, and God hearkened to her and opened her womb.

23 And she conceived, and bore a son; and said, God has taken away my reproach;

24 And she called his name Joseph; and said, The LORD shall add to me another son.

25 ¶And it came to pass, when Rachel had borne Joseph, that Jacob said to Laban, Send me away, that I may go to my own place, and to my land.

26 Give me my wives and my children, for whom I have served you, and let me go; for you know the service which I have rendered you.

27 And Laban said to Jacob, If I have found favor in your eyes, I have proven by experience that the LORD has blessed me for your sake.

28 Then he said, Specify your wages, and I will give them.

29 And Jacob said to him, You yourself know the service which I have given you, and how your cattle have prospered with me.

30 For it was little which you had before I came, and now it has increased abundantly; and the LORD has blessed you for my sake; and now what shall I do in order to provide for my own household also?

31 And Laban said, What shall I give you? And Jacob said, You shall not give me anything; if you will do for me the thing which I will tell you, I will go back to feed and keep your flock.

32 I will pass through all your flock today, and select for myself from it every speckled and spotted lamb, and every brown lamb, and the spotted and speckled among the goats; and of such shall be my wages.

33 Just as my innocence is evident today, so it will be in the future when my wages are brought before your presence; every one that is not speckled and spotted among the goats and brown among the white sheep, that shall be counted stolen by me.

34 Laban said to him, Yes, let it be according to your word.

35 And he removed that day the he goats that were speckled and spotted, and all the she goats that were speckled and spotted, and every one that had some white on it, and all the brown among the white sheep, and entrusted them to his sons.

36 And he set three days journey between himself and Jacob; and Jacob fed the rest of Laban's flocks.

37 ¶And Jacob took some fresh white rods of almond and poplar trees; and peeled white streaks in them, and made the white appear which was in the rods.

38 And he set the rods which he had peeled before the flocks in the running water, in the watering troughs where the flocks came to drink; and they conceived when they came to drink.

39 And the flocks conceived before the rods, and brought forth lambs that were speckled and spotted.

40 And Jacob separated the lambs, and set the faces of the flocks toward the speckled and spotted, and all the brown in the flock of Laban; and he put his own flocks by themselves, and

did not mix them with Laban's flock.

41 And it came to pass, whenever the stronger of the flock did conceive, Jacob laid the rods in front of the sheep in the troughs, that they might conceive by the means of the rods.

42 But when the sheep were feeble, he did not put the rods in; so the feebler were Laban's and the stronger Jacob's.

43 And the man grew exceedingly rich, and had large flocks, menservants, maidservants, and she asses, camels, and he asses.

CHAPTER 31

AND Jacob heard the words of Laban's sons, saying, Jacob has taken away all that was our father's; and of that which was our father's has he acquired all of this wealth.

2 And Jacob saw that Laban's countenance toward him was not as it had been yesterday and the day before.

3 And the LORD said to Jacob, Return to the land of your fathers, and to your kindred; and I will be with you.

4 So Jacob sent and called Rachel and Leah to the field to his flock,

5 And said to them, I see that your father's countenance toward me is not as it has been yesterday and the day before; but the God of my father has been with me.

6 And you know that I have worked for your father with all my strength.

7 And yet your father has deceived me, and changed my wages ten times; but God has not permitted him to hurt me.

8 If he said thus, The speckled shall be your wages, then all the flock bore speckled; and if he said thus, The spotted shall be your wages; then all the flock bore spotted.

9 Thus God has selected some of your father's cattle, and given them to me.

10 And it came to pass at the time when the sheep conceive, I lifted up my eyes and saw in a dream, and, behold, the rams that leaped upon the sheep were speckled, spotted, and striped.

11 And the angel of God said to me in a dream, Jacob; and I said, Here am I.

12 Then he said, Lift up now your eyes, and see; all the rams that leap upon the sheep are speckled, spotted, and ringstreaked; for I have seen all that Laban has done to you.

13 I am the God of Beth-el, the place where you anointed a pillar to me, and where you vowed a vow to me; now arise, get out from this land, and return to the land of your kindred.

14 And Rachel and Leah answered and said to him, We have no portion or inheritance in our father's house.

15 Behold, we are counted by him as strangers, for he has sold us, and has squandered also our money.

16 For all the riches which God has selected from our father belong to us and our children; now then, whatever God has said to you, do it.

17 ¶Then Jacob rose up and set his sons and his wives on camels;

18 And he carried away all his cattle and all his wealth which he had gained in Padan-aram, to go to Isaac his father in the land of Canaan.

19 Now Laban went to shear his sheep; and Rachel stole the images that belonged to her father.

20 And Jacob deceived Laban, the Aramean, in that he did not tell him that he was going.

21 So he fled with all that he had; and he rose up, and crossed the river, and set his face toward mount Gilead.

22 And it was told Laban on the third day that Jacob had fled.

23 And he took his brethren with him, and pursued after him seven days journey; and they overtook him on mount Gilead.

24 And God came to Laban, the Aramean, in a dream by night, and said to him, Take heed that you speak not to Jacob either good or bad.

25 ¶Then Laban overtook Jacob. Now Jacob had pitched his tent on the mount; and Laban with his brethren encamped on mount Gilead.

26 And Laban said to Jacob, What have I done to you, that you have deceived me and carried away my

daughters as though they were captives taken with the sword?

27 Why did you flee secretly, and deceive me; and did not tell me, for I would have sent you away with joy and songs, and with harp and tambourine?

28 And you did not permit me to give a farewell kiss to my sons and my daughters? Now you have done foolishly in so doing.

29 I could have done you harm, but the God of your fathers said to me last evening, Take heed that you speak not to Jacob either good or bad.

30 And now you are on your way, because you longed for your father's house; yet why did you steal my gods?

31 And Jacob answered and said to Laban, Because I was afraid; for I said, Perhaps you would take your daughters from me by force.

32 With whomsoever you find your gods, he shall not live; moreover, in the presence of our brethren point out whatever I have that belongs to you, and take it for yourself. For Jacob did not know that Rachel had stolen them.

33 And Laban went into Jacob's tent and into Leah's tent and into the tent of the two maidservants; but he did not find the gods. So he went out of Leah's tent into Rachel's tent.

34 Now Rachel had taken the images, and put them in the camel's saddle bag, and sat upon them. And Laban had searched all the tent, but did not find them.

35 And Rachel said to her father, Let it not displease my lord that I cannot rise up before you; for I am with child. Nevertheless he searched, but did not find the images.

36 And Jacob was displeased, and argued with Laban; and Jacob answered and said to Laban, What is my trespass? and what is my fault, that you have hotly pursued after me?

37 Behold you have searched all my baggage, and what have you found of all your household articles? Put it here before my brethren and your brethren, that they may judge between us both.

38 Behold, I have been with you for the past twenty years; your ewes and your she goats have not cast their young, and I have not eaten of the rams of your flock.

39 That which was torn by wild beasts I never brought to you; I bore the loss of it; of my hand you did require it; likewise that which was stolen by the day or by the night.

40 Thus by day I was scorched by the heat, and at night suffered from cold; and my sleep departed from my eyes.

41 Behold, I have been twenty years in your house; I served you fourteen years for your two daughters, and six years for your flock; and you have changed my wages ten times.

42 And if it had not been for the God of my father, the God of Abraham, and your regard for Isaac, which have been on my side, surely you would have sent me away now empty. God saw my toil and the labor of my hands, and rebuked you last evening.

43 ¶Then Laban answered and said to Jacob, These daughters are my daughters, and these children are my children, and the flocks are my flocks, and all that you see is mine; and what can I do this day for these my daughters, or for their children whom they have borne?

44 Now therefore come then, let us make a covenant, I and you; and let it be for a witness between me and you.

45 So Jacob took a stone and set it up for a pillar.

46 And Jacob said to his brethren, Gather stones; and they took stones, and made a heap; and they did eat there upon the heap.

47 And Laban called it Jegar-saha-dutha (the Pillar of Witness); but Jacob called it Galead (Gilead).

48 And Laban said, This heap is a witness between me and you this day. Therefore he called its name Galead,

49 And a watchtower; for he said, Let the LORD watch between me and you, because we are parting one from another.

50 If you despise my daughters, or

if you shall take other wives besides my daughters, now no man is with us; see, God only is witness between me and you.

51 And Laban said to Jacob, Behold this heap, and behold this pillar, which I have set between me and you;

52 This heap is a witness, and this pillar is a witness, that I will not pass over this pillar against you, and that you also shall not pass over this pillar against me or this heap for harm.

53 The God of Abraham and the God of Nahor and the God of our forefathers judge between us. And Jacob swore by the reverence of his father Isaac.

54 Then Jacob offered a sacrifice on the mountain, and invited his brethren to eat bread; and they did eat food, and spent the night on the mountain.

55 And early in the morning Laban rose up and kissed his grandsons and his daughters, and blessed them; then Laban returned and went to his country.

CHAPTER 32

AND Jacob also went on his journey, and the angels of God met him.

2 And when Jacob saw them, he said, This is God's host; so he called the name of that place Mahanaim.

3 And Jacob sent messengers before him to Esau his brother to the land of Seir, the country of Edom.

4 And he commanded them, saying, Thus shall you speak to my lord Esau; Thus says your servant Jacob, I have sojourned with Laban, and stayed there until now;

5 I have oxen, asses, flocks, menservants, and maidservants; and I have sent to tell my lord, that I may find mercy in your sight.

6 ¶And the messengers returned to Jacob, saying, We came to your brother Esau, and behold he also is coming to meet you, and four hundred men with him.

7 Then Jacob was afraid and greatly distressed; and he divided the people that were with him, and the flocks and herds and camels, into two groups;

8 And Jacob said, If my brother Esau should come against one group and destroy it, then the group which is left shall escape.

9 ¶And Jacob prayed, and said, O God of my father Abraham, and God of my father Isaac, the LORD who didst say to me, Return to the land of your fathers and to your kindred, and I will deal well with you;

10 I am not worthy of the least of all thy favors, and of all the truth that thou hast shown to thy servant; for alone with my staff I crossed over this Jordan; and now I have become two companies.

11 Deliver me, I pray thee, from the hands of my brother Esau; for I am afraid of him, lest he will come to smite me, and the mothers with their children.

12 And thou didst say, I will surely do you good, and make your descendants numerous as the sand of the sea which cannot be numbered for multitude.

13 ¶And he spent that night there; and took of that which he had with him as a present for his brother Esau;

14 Two hundred she goats, and twenty he goats, two hundred ewes, and twenty rams,

15 Thirty milch camels with their colts, forty cows, and ten bulls, twenty she asses, and ten foals.

16 And he entrusted them to his servants, every drove by itself; and said to his servants, Pass over before me, and keep a distance between drove and drove.

17 And he commanded the leader of the first drove, and said to him, When Esau my brother meets you, and asks you, saying, Who are you? and where are you going? and whose are these that are before you?

18 Then you shall say to him, They belong to your servant Jacob; they are a present which he has sent to my lord Esau; and, behold, also he is coming behind us.

19 And so he commanded the second and the third and all who followed with the droves, saying, In this

manner you shall speak to Esau, when you find him.

20 And you shall say to him, moreover, Behold, your servant Jacob also is behind us. For he said, I may appease him with the present that goes before me, and afterward I will see his face; and perhaps he will accept me.

21 So the present went over before him; and he himself lodged that night in the encampment.

22 And he rose up in the night, and took his two wives and his two maidservants and his eleven sons, and led them to the desert of Jabbok.

23 And he took them, and brought them over the brook, and then he brought across everything that he had.

24 ¶And Jacob was left alone; and there a man wrestled with him until daybreak.

25 And when the man saw that he did not prevail against him, he touched the hollow of his thigh; and the hollow of Jacob's thigh was out of joint, as he wrestled with him.

26 And the man said to him, Let me go, for day is breaking. And he said, I will not let you go unless you bless me.

27 And he said to him, What is your name? And he said, Jacob.

28 And he said to him, Your name shall no more be called Jacob, but Israel (the Prince of God); for you have proved your strength wrestling with an angel and with man, and have prevailed.

29 And Jacob asked him, and said, Tell me your name. And he said, Why is it that you ask my name? And the angel blessed him there.

30 And Jacob called the name of that place Peniel; for he said, I have seen an angel face to face, and my life is preserved.

31 The sun rose upon him just as he left Peniel, and he limped because of his thigh.

32 That is why the children of Israel do not eat of the sinew of the hip, which is on the hollow of the thigh, to this day; because the angel touched the hollow of Jacob's thigh on the sinew of the thigh.

CHAPTER 33

AND Jacob raised his eyes, and looked, and, behold, Esau was coming, and with him four hundred men. And he divided the children among Leah, Rachel, and the two maids.

2 Then he brought the maids and their children to the front, and Leah and her children next, and kept Rachel and Joseph in the rear.

3 And he himself went on before them, and bowed himself to the ground seven times, until he came near to his brother.

4 And Esau ran to meet him, and embraced him, and fell on his neck and kissed him; and they wept.

5 Then Esau raised his eyes and saw the women and the children, and said, Where did you get these? And Jacob said to him, They are the children whom God has graciously given your servant.

6 Then the maids drew near, they and their children, and they bowed themselves.

7 And Leah also with her children drew near, and bowed themselves; and afterwards came Rachel and Joseph who also drew near, and bowed themselves.

8 And Esau said to Jacob, Where did you get all this company which I met? And Jacob said to him, Because I have found favor in the sight of my lord.

9 Then Esau said to him, I have plenty, my brother; keep what you have to yourself.

10 But Jacob said to him, If now I have found mercy in your sight, then receive my present from my hands; because now I have seen your face, as I saw the face of an angel, and you were pleased with me.

11 Now accept my blessings that I have brought to you; because God has dealt graciously with me, and because I have enough. And Jacob urged him, and he did accept them.

12 Then Esau said to him, Let us depart, and go, and I will go before you.

13 But Jacob said, My lord knows

that the children are too young, and that the flocks and herds with young are with me; and if I should overdrive them one day, all the flock will die.

14 Let my lord pass before his servant, and I will travel slowly, according to the pace of the cattle which are before me and according to the pace of the children, until I come to my lord to Seir.

15 And Esau said to him, Let me leave with you some of the men that are with me. But Jacob said, What need have I for them? Let me find mercy in the sight of my lord.

16 ¶So Esau returned that day on his way to Seir.

17 And Jacob journeyed to Succoth, and built himself a house, and made sheepfolds for his cattle; therefore he called the name of the place Succoth.

18 ¶And Jacob came to Shalem, a city of Shechem, which is in the land of Canaan, when he came forth from Padan-aram; and encamped before the city.

19 And he bought a parcel of a field from the children of Hamor, father of Shechem, for a hundred ewes.

20 And he pitched his tent there, and erected an altar, and called it El-Alaha di Israel (God, the God of Israel).

CHAPTER 34

AND Dinah the daughter of Leah, whom she had borne to Jacob, went out to see the native girls.

2 And when Shechem the son of Hamor the Hivite, prince of the country, saw her, he took her and lay with her, and defiled her.

3 And his soul longed for Dinah the daughter of Jacob, and he loved the girl, and spoke kindly to the girl, and won her heart.

4 And Shechem spoke to his father Hamor, saying, Get me this girl to wife.

5 And Jacob heard that Dinah his daughter had been defiled; now his sons were with the cattle in the field; so Jacob held his peace until they came.

6 ¶And Hamor the father of Shechem went out to Jacob to speak with him.

7 And the sons of Jacob came from the field, and when they heard the news, they were grieved; and they were very indignant, because they had wrought folly in Israel in the disgracing of Jacob's daughter, which thing ought not to be done.

8 And Hamor spoke with them, saying, The soul of my son Shechem longs for your daughter; give her to him in marriage.

9 Intermarry with us, and give your daughters to us in marriage, and take our daughters to you,

10 And dwell with us; behold, the land is before you; dwell and trade in it and inherit in it.

11 And Shechem said to her father and to her brothers, Let me find mercy in your presence, and whatever you shall ask of me I will give.

12 Ask me as much as you wish, both dowry and gifts, and I will give you according as you shall say to me; but give me this girl to wife.

13 And the sons of Jacob answered Shechem and Hamor his father deceitfully, because they had defiled Dinah their sister,

14 And they said to them, We cannot do this thing, to give our sister to a man who is uncircumcised; for that would be a reproach to us;

15 But on this condition will we consent to you: that you will become like us, and circumcise every male as we are circumcised;

16 Then we will give our daughters to you in marriage, and take your daughters to us in marriage, and we will dwell with you, and we will become one people.

17 But if you will not hearken to us, to be circumcised, then we will take our daughter and we will be gone.

18 And their words pleased Hamor, and Shechem, Hamor's son.

19 And the young man did not delay to do the thing, because he was delighted with Jacob's daughter and he was honored above all the household of his father.

20 ¶Then Hamor and Shechem his son came to the gate of their town and spoke to the men of their town, saying,

21 These men are peaceable with us; therefore let them dwell in the land, and trade in it, for the land is large enough before them; let us take their daughters to us for wives, and let us give them our daughters.

22 But only on this condition will the men consent to dwell with us, to become one people, when every male among us is circumcised, as they are circumcised.

23 Behold, their wealth, their possessions, and all their cattle will eventually be ours; only let us consent to their proposals, and they will dwell with us.

24 And when all the adults of the town had heard from Shechem and from his father Hamor, they circumcised every male, those that went out of the gate [1] of his town.

25 ¶And it came to pass on the third day, when the men were sore, two sons of Jacob, Simeon and Levi, Dinah's brothers, took each man his sword, and came against the town quietly, and slew every male.

26 And they slew Hamor and Shechem his son with the edge of the sword, and took Dinah out of Shechem's house, and went out.

27 Then the sons of Jacob came back to the slain, and plundered the town, because they had defiled their sister.

28 They took their sheep and their oxen and their asses and whatever was in the town and in the field.

29 And all their wealth and all their little ones; and their wives they carried captive, and plundered everything that was in the town.

30 Then Jacob said to Simeon and Levi, You have done me a great harm, for you have hurt my reputation among the inhabitants of the land, among the Canaanites and the Perizzites; and I being few in numbers, they may gather themselves together against me, and attack me;

I shall be destroyed, both I and my household.

31 But they said, Our sister has been treated like a harlot.

CHAPTER 35

AND God said to Jacob, Arise, go up to Beth-el, and dwell there; and build there an altar to God, who appeared to you when you fled from the presence of your brother Esau.

2 Then Jacob said to his household and to all who were with him, Put away the strange gods that are among you, and cleanse yourselves, and change your garments;

3 And let us arise and go up to Beth-el; and I will build there an altar to God, who answered me in the day of my distress, and was with me in the journey that I took.

4 So they gave to Jacob all the strange gods that were in their possession, and the earrings that were in their ears; and Jacob buried them under the oak which was by Shechem.

5 And they journeyed; and the fear of God fell upon the towns that were round about them, and they did not pursue after Jacob and his sons.

6 ¶So Jacob came to Luz, that is Beth-el, which is in the land of Canaan, he and all the people that were with him.

7 And he built there an altar, and called the place Beth-el (the house of God), because there God appeared to him when he fled from the presence of his brother Esau.

8 Then Deborah Rebekah's nurse died, and she was buried below Bethel under an oak; so the name of the oak was called Betemtha dabkhatha (the oak of weeping).

9 ¶And God appeared to Jacob again, when he came from Padanaram, and blessed him.

10 And God said to him, Your name shall no longer be called Jacob, but Israel shall be your name; so he called his name Israel.

11 And God said to him, I am God Almighty; be fruitful and multiply; a people and a multitude of peoples

---

[1] *went out of the gate* is an idiom which means *grown up*

shall come from you, and kings shall come out of your loins;

12 And the land which I gave to Abraham and Isaac, I will give to you, and to your descendants after you will I give the land.

13 And God went up from him in the place where he talked with him.

14 And Jacob set up a pillar in the place where he had talked with him, a pillar of stone, and he poured out a drink offering on it, and he poured oil on it.

15 And Jacob called the name of the place where God spoke with him, Beth-el.

16 ¶And they journeyed from Beth-el, and continued until they came within the distance of a mile from the entrance to Ephrath; and Rachel travailed, and she had hard labor while she was being delivered.

17 And it came to pass, when she was in hard labor, the midwife said to her, Fear not; for this one also is a son for you.

18 And it came to pass, as her soul was departing and she was dying, she called the child's name Bar-kebai (the Son of My Sorrow); but his father called him Benjamin (the Son of My Right Hand).

19 And Rachel died, and was buried on the way to Ephrath, which is Beth-lehem.

20 And Jacob set up a pillar upon the grave of Rachel; that is the pillar of Rachel's grave to this day.

21 ¶And Israel journeyed, and pitched his tent beyond the tower of Gadar.

22 And it came to pass, when Israel dwelt in that land, that Reuben went and lay with Bilhah, his father's concubine; and Israel heard of it. Now the sons of Jacob were twelve:

23 The sons of Leah: Reuben, Jacob's first-born, Simeon, Levi, Judah, Issachar, and Zebulun.

24 And the sons of Rachel: Joseph, and Benjamin.

25 And the sons of Bilhah, Rachel's maid: Dan, and Naphtali.

26 And the sons of Zilpah, Leah's maid: Gad, and Asher. These are the sons of Jacob that were born to him in Padan-aram.

27 ¶And Jacob came to his father Isaac to Mamre, to Koriath Gabarey, which is Hebron, where Abraham and Isaac had sojourned.

28 And the days of Isaac were a hundred and eighty years.

29 Then Isaac grew weak and died; and he was gathered to his people, being very old and full of days; and his sons Esau and Jacob buried him in the burial ground which his father Abraham had purchased.

CHAPTER 36

NOW these are the generations of Esau, who is Edom.

2 Esau took his wives from among the daughters of Canaan: Adah the daughter of Elon the Hittite, Aholibamah the daughter of Anah, the son of Zibeon the Hivite;

3 And Bismath, Ishmael's daughter, sister of Nebioth.

4 And Adah bore to Esau Eliphaz; and Bismath bore Reuel;

5 And Aholibamah bore Jeush, Jaalan, and Korah; these are the sons of Esau that were born to him in the land of Canaan.

6 And Esau took his wives, his sons, his daughters, and all the persons of his household, and all his cattle, and all the wealth which he had acquired in the land of Canaan; and went to the land of Seir from the presence of his brother Jacob.

7 For their wealth was too great for them to dwell together; and the land in which they sojourned could not sustain them because of their cattle.

8 Thus Esau dwelt in mount Seir; Esau is Edom.

9 ¶And these are the generations of Esau the father of the Edomites in mount Seir;

10 These are the names of Esau's sons: Eliphaz the son of Adah the wife of Esau, Reuel the son of Bismath the wife of Esau.

11 And the sons of Eliphaz were Teman, Omar, Zepho, Gatham, and Kenaz.

12 And Timna was a concubine of

Eliphaz, Esau's son; and she bore to Eliphaz Amalek. These were the sons of Adah, Esau's wife.

13 And these are the sons of Reuel: Nahath, Zerah, Shammah, and Mizzah; these were the sons of Bismath, Esau's wife.

14 ¶These are the sons of Aholibamah, the daughter of Anah the son of Zibeon, Esau's wife; and she bore to Esau Jeush, Jaalan, and Korah.

15 ¶These are the chiefs of the sons of Esau, the sons of Eliphaz the firstborn of Esau: chief Teman, chief Omar, chief Zepho, chief Kenaz,

16 Chief Gatham, chief Korah, and chief Amalek; these are the chiefs that came of Eliphaz in the land of Edom; these were the sons of Adah.

17 ¶And these are the sons of Reuel, Esau's son: chief Nahath, chief Zerah, chief Shammah, and chief Mizzah; these are the chiefs that came of Reuel in the land of Edom; these are the sons of Bismath, Esau's wife.

18 ¶These are the sons of Aholibamah, Esau's wife: chief Jeush, chief Jaalan, and chief Korah; these were the sons of Aholibamah, the daughter of Anah, Esau's wife.

19 These are the sons of Esau, who is Edom, and these are their chiefs.

20 ¶These are the sons of Seir the Horite, the inhabitants of the land: Lotan, Shobal, Zibeon, Anah,

21 Dishon, Ezer, and Dishan; these are the chiefs of the Horites, the children of Seir in the land of Edom.

22 And the sons of Lotan were Hori and Heman; and Lotan's sister was Timna.

23 These are the sons of Shobal: Alvan, Manahath, Ebal, Shapar, and Oiam.

24 And these are the sons of Zibeon: Ana and Anah; he is the Anah who discovered water in the desert while he was feeding the asses of Zibeon his father.

25 These are the children of Anah: Dishon and Aholibamah, the daughter of Anah.

26 These are the sons of Dishon: Hemran, Eshban, Ithran, and Cheran.

27 These are the sons of Ezer: Bilhan, Zaavan, and Akan.

28 These are the sons of Dishan: Uz and Aran.

29 These are the chiefs of the Horites: chief Lotan, chief Shobal, chief Zibeon, chief Anah,

30 Chief Dishon, chief Ezer, and chief Dishan; these are the chiefs of the Horites, according to their chiefs in the land of Seir.

31 ¶And these are the kings who reigned in the land of Edom, before there reigned any king over the children of Israel:

32 Bela, the son of Beor, reigned in Edom; and the name of his city was Dihab.

33 And Bela died, and Jobab the son of Zerah of Bozrah reigned in his stead.

34 And Jobab died, and Husham of the land of Teman reigned in his stead.

35 And Husham died, and Hadad, the son of Bedad, who smote the Midianites in the fields of Moab, reigned in his stead; and the name of his city was Gevith.

36 And Hadad died, and Samlah of Masrekah reigned in his stead.

37 And Samlah died, and Saul of Rehoboth by the river reigned in his stead.

38 And Saul died, and Baal-hanan, the son of Abcor, reigned in his stead.

39 And Baal-hanan, the son of Abcor died, and Hadad reigned in his stead; and the name of his city was Pau; and his wife's name was Mehetabel, the daughter of Matred, the daughter of Mezahab.

40 And these are the names of the chiefs of Esau, according to their families, and according to their generations, by their names: chief Timnah, chief Anvah, chief Jetheth,

41 Chief Aholibamah, chief Elah, chief Pinon,

42 Chief Kenaz, chief Teman, chief Mibzar,

43 Chief Magdiel, chief Giram; these are the chiefs of the Edomites, according to their habitations in the land of their possession; Edom is Esau the father of the Edomites.

CHAPTER 37

AND Jacob dwelt in the land wherein his father was a sojourner, in the land of Canaan.

2 These are the generations of Jacob. Joseph, being seventeen years old, was feeding the flock with his brothers; and the lad was reared with the sons of Zilpah, and with the sons of Bilhah, his father's wives; and Joseph brought an evil report of them to their father.

3 Now Israel loved Joseph more than all his other sons, because he was the son of his old age; and he had made him a rich robe with long sleeves.

4 And when his brothers saw that their father loved him more than all his brothers, they hated him, and could not speak peaceably to him.

5 ¶And Joseph dreamed a dream, and he told it to his brothers; and they hated him yet the more.

6 And he said to them, Listen to this dream which I have dreamed:

7 Behold, we were binding sheaves in the field, and, lo, my sheaf arose and stood upright; and, behold, your sheaves stood round about and bowed down to my sheaf.

8 And his brothers said to him, Are you indeed going to reign over us? Or are you going to have dominion over us? And they hated him yet the more for his dreams, and for his words.

9 ¶And he dreamed another dream, and told it to his brothers, and said, Behold, I have dreamed another dream; and, behold, the sun and the moon and the eleven stars bowed down to me.

10 And when he told it to his father and to his brothers, his father rebuked him, and said to him, What is this dream that you have dreamed? Shall I and your mother and your brothers indeed come to bow down ourselves to the ground to you?

11 And his brothers envied him; but his father observed the sayings.

12 ¶And Joseph's brothers went to feed their father's flock in Shechem.

13 And Israel said to Joseph, Behold, your brothers are feeding the flocks in Shechem; come, I will send you to them. And he said to him, Here am I.

14 Then his father said to him, Go, see whether it is well with your brothers and well with the flocks; and bring me word again. So Jacob sent him from the valley of Hebron, and he came to Shechem.

15 And a certain man found him while he was wandering in the field; and the man asked him, and said to him, What are you seeking?

16 And he said, I am seeking my brothers; do tell me where they are feeding their flocks.

17 And the man said, They have departed from here; for I heard them say, Let us go to Dothan. So Joseph went after his brothers, and found them in Dothan.

18 And they saw him from afar, and before he came near to them, they conspired against him to kill him.

19 And they said to one another, Behold, here comes the dreamer.

20 Come now therefore, and let us slay him, and throw him into one of the pits; and then we will say that a wild beast has devoured him, and we shall see what will become of his dreams.

21 And Reuben heard it, and he delivered him out of their hands; and he said to them, Let us not kill him.

22 And Reuben said to them, Shed no blood; throw him into this pit that is in the wilderness, but do not harm him; that he might deliver him from their hands, and bring him back to his father.

23 ¶And it came to pass, when Joseph was come to his brothers, they stripped him of the rich robe that he was wearing;

24 And they took him, and threw him into a pit; and the pit was empty, there was no water in it.

25 And they sat down to eat bread; and they lifted up their eyes and looked, and, behold, a caravan of Arabians coming from Gilead, with their camels bearing gum, balm and myrrh, and they were on their way to carry it down to Egypt.

26 And Judah said to his brothers, What profit is it if we slay our brother, and conceal his blood?

27 Come, let us sell him to the Arabians, and let us not harm him; for he is our brother and our flesh. And his brothers listened to him.

28 Then some Midianite merchants passed by; and they drew and lifted up Joseph out of the pit, and sold Joseph to the Arabians for twenty pieces of silver; and they brought him into Egypt.

29 ¶And then Reuben returned to the pit, and, behold, Joseph was not in the pit; and he tore his clothes.

30 And he returned to his brothers, and said to them, Where is the boy; and as for me, where shall I go?

31 And they took Joseph's robe, and killed a kid of the goats, and dipped the robe in the blood;

32 And they sent the robe with long sleeves, and they brought it to their father; and said, This we have found: know now whether it be your son's coat or not.

33 And he recognized it, and said, It is my son's coat; a wild beast has devoured him; my son Joseph is surely torn to pieces.

34 Then Jacob tore his clothes, and put sackcloth upon his loins, and mourned for his son many days.

35 And all his sons and all his daughters made an effort to comfort him; but he refused to be comforted; and he said, I will go down to Sheol, to my son mourning. Thus his father wept for him.

36 And the Midianites sold Joseph in Egypt to Potiphar, one of Pharaoh's officers, the commander of the guard.

CHAPTER 38

AND it came to pass at that time that Judah went down from his brothers, and turned in to a certain Arlemite, whose name was Hirah.

2 And Judah saw there the daughter of a certain Canaanite, whose name was Shuah; and he took her, and went in unto her.

3 And she conceived, and bore a son; and he called his name Er.

4 And she conceived again, and bore a son; and he called his name Onan.

5 And she conceived again, and bore a son; and he called his name Shelah; and after she bore him she stopped bearing.

6 And Judah took a wife for Er, his first-born, whose name was Tamar.

7 And Er, Judah's first-born, was wicked in the sight of the LORD; and the LORD slew him.

8 And Judah said to Onan, Go in to your brother's wife, and perform the duty of a brother-in-law to her, and raise up an offspring to your brother.

9 And Onan knew that the offspring would not be his; and it came to pass when he went in unto his brother's wife that he spilled the semen on the ground, lest that he should raise an offspring to his brother.

10 And the thing which he did was displeasing in the sight of the LORD; wherefore he slew him also.

11 Then said Judah to Tamar, his daughter-in-law, Remain a widow in your father's house, until my son Shelah grows up; for he said, Lest he die also, as his brothers did. And Tamar went and dwelt in her father's house.

12 ¶And in the course of time Shuah's daughter, the wife of Judah, died; and Judah was comforted, and went up to his sheepshearers to Timnath, he and his friend Hirah the Arlemite.

13 And it was told Tamar, saying, Behold your father-in-law is going up to Timnath to shear his sheep.

14 And she put off her widow's dress, and adorned herself, and covered her face with a veil, and sat down at the parting of the road to Timnath; for she saw that Shelah was grown up, and she was not given to him to wife.

15 When Judah saw her, he thought her to be a harlot; because she had covered her face.

16 And he turned to her by the way and said to her, Come, let me come in unto you (for he did not know

that she was his daughter-in-law).
And she said, What will you give me
that you may come in unto me?

17 And he said, I will send you a
kid from the flock. And she said,
Will you give me a pledge until you
send it?

18 And he said, What kind of a
pledge shall I give you? And she said,
Your ring and your robe and the staff
that is in your hand. So he gave them
to her, and then went in unto her,
and she conceived by him.

19 And she arose and went away
and took off her veil from her and
put on the garments of her widowhood.

20 And Judah sent the kid by the
hand of his friend the Arlemite, to
receive the pledge from the woman's
hand; but he could not find her.

21 Then he asked the men of the
place, saying, Where is the harlot
who sat at the parting of the road?
And they said, There is no harlot
here.

22 And he returned to Judah, and
said, I cannot find her; and also the
men of the place said, No harlot has
been here.

23 And Judah said, Let her keep
the pledge, lest I be laughed at; behold, I sent this kid, but you could
not find her.

24 ¶And it came to pass, about
three months later, that it was told
Judah, saying, Tamar, your daughter-
in-law, has played the harlot; and
moreover, she is with child because
of her harlotry. And Judah said,
Bring her out, and let her be burned.

25 When they brought her out, she
sent to her father-in-law, saying, By
the man to whom these articles belong, I am with child; and she said,
Determine whose they are, the ring,
the robe, and the staff.

26 And Judah recognized them, and
said, She is more righteous than I;
because I did not give her in marriage
to Shelah my son. And he knew her
again no more.

27 ¶And it came to pass in the time
of her travail that, behold, there were
twins in her womb.

28 And it came to pass, when she

travailed, that one of the babes put
out his hand; and the midwife took
and bound upon his hand a scarlet
thread, saying, This came out first.

29 And it came to pass, as he drew
back his hand, behold, his brother
came out; and she said, What a breach
has been made for you! Therefore his
name was called Pharez.

30 And afterward came out his
brother, who had the scarlet thread
on his hand; and she called his name
Zarah.

CHAPTER 39

AND Joseph was brought down to
Egypt; and Potiphar, an officer
of Pharaoh, commander of the guard,
an Egyptian, bought him from the
Arabians who had brought him down
there.

2 And the LORD was with Joseph,
and he became a prosperous man in
the house of his master, the Egyptian.

3 And his master saw that the LORD
was with him, and that the LORD
made all that he did to prosper under
his hands.

4 And Joseph found favor in his
sight, and served him; and he made
him steward of his house, and all that
he had he put in his charge.

5 And it came to pass from the
time that he had made him steward
of his house, and over all that he had,
that the LORD blessed the Egyptian's
house for Joseph's sake; and the
blessing of the LORD was upon all that
he had both in the house and in the
field.

6 And he left all that he had in
Joseph's charge; and he did not know
what he had, except the food that
he ate. And Joseph was very handsome and pleasant to look at.

7 ¶And it came to pass after these
things that his master's wife cast her
eyes upon Joseph; and she said to
him, Lie with me.

8 But he refused, and said to his
master's wife, Behold, my master
does not know what he has in the
house, and he has put everything that
he has in my charge;

9 There is no one greater in this
house than I; neither has he kept back

anything from me except yourself, because you are his wife; how then can I do this great wickedness, and sin against God?

10 And it came to pass, as she spoke to him daily, he did not listen to her, to lie with her, or to be with her.

11 And it came to pass one day that Joseph went in to the house to do his work; and none of the men of the household were there in the house.

12 And she caught him by his garment, and said to him, Lie with me; but he left the garment in her hands, and fled, and got out to the street.

13 And it came to pass, when she saw that he had left his garment in her hands, and had fled out to the street,

14 She called to the men of her household, and said to them, See, he has brought in a Hebrew servant to us to disgrace us; he came in to me to lie with me, and I cried out with a loud voice;

15 And when he heard that I lifted up my voice and cried aloud, he left his garment in my hands, and fled, and got out to the street.

16 And she laid up his garment by her, until his master came home.

17 And she spoke to him according to these words, saying, The Hebrew servant whom you brought to us, came in to disgrace me;

18 But as I lifted up my voice and cried aloud, he left his garment in my hands, and fled, and got out to the street.

19 And when the master heard the words of his wife, which she spoke to him, saying, After this manner did your servant to me; his wrath was kindled.

20 And Joseph's master took him, and put him into the prison, a place where the king's prisoners were confined; and he remained there in the prison.

21 ¶But the LORD was with Joseph, and showed him mercy, and gave him favor in the sight of the keeper of the prison.

22 And the keeper of the prison intrusted to Joseph's care all the prisoners who were in the prison; and he was in charge of whatever they did there.

23 The keeper of the prison did not look to anything that was in Joseph's charge, because the LORD was with him, and whatever he did, the LORD made it to prosper.

CHAPTER 40

AND it came to pass after these things that the chief butler of the king of Egypt and the chief baker had offended their lord the king of Egypt.

2 And Pharaoh was wroth against two of his officers, against the chief of the butlers, and against the chief of the bakers.

3 And he put them into the prison in the house of the commander of the guard, in the ward where Joseph was bound.

4 And the commander of the guard charged Joseph with them, and he served them; and they remained for some time in the prison.

5 ¶And they both dreamed, each man his own dream in the same night, each man according to the interpretation of his dream, the butler and the baker of the king of Egypt, who were bound in the prison.

6 And Joseph came in to them in the morning, and saw them, and behold, they were sad.

7 So he asked Pharaoh's officers who were with him in the prison of his master's house, saying, Why do you look so sad today?

8 And they said to him, We have dreamed a dream, and there is no one to interpret it. And Joseph said to them, Behold, the interpretations belong to God; tell them to me.

9 Then the chief butler told his dream to Joseph, and said to him, In my dream, behold, a vine was before me;

10 And in the vine were three branches; and when it budded, its blossoms shot forth; and the clusters thereof brought forth ripe grapes;

11 And Pharaoh's cup was in my hand; and I took the grapes, and pressed them into Pharaoh's cup, and I gave the cup into Pharaoh's hands.

12 And Joseph said to him, This is the interpretation of your dream: The three branches are three days;

13 After three days Pharaoh shall remember you and restore you to your position; and you shall give Pharaoh's cup into his hand, as you did before when you were his butler.

14 But remember me when it shall be well with you, and do me a favor and justice, and make mention of me in the presence of Pharaoh, and bring me out of this prison house;

15 For indeed I was stolen away out of the land of the Hebrews; and here also I have done nothing that they should put me into the prison.

16 When the chief baker saw that the interpretation was good, he said to Joseph, I also saw in my dream, and, behold, I had three baskets containing white bread on my head;

17 And in the uppermost basket there was of every kind of food for Pharaoh, prepared by a baker; and the birds of prey were eating it out of the basket on my head.

18 And Joseph answered and said to him, This is the interpretation of your dream: The three baskets are three days;

19 After three days Pharaoh shall have you beheaded, and then shall crucify you on a tree, and the birds of prey shall eat your flesh from off you.

20 ¶And it came to pass on the third day, which was Pharaoh's birthday, that he made a banquet for all his servants; and he remembered the chief butler and the chief baker among his servants.

21 And he restored the chief butler to his position; and he gave the cup into Pharaoh's hands:

22 But he crucified the chief baker, as Joseph had interpreted to them.

23 Yet the chief butler did not remember Joseph, but forgot him.

CHAPTER 41

AND it came to pass, two years later, Pharaoh dreamed; and he was standing by the river.

2 And, behold, there came up out of the river seven beautiful and fat cows; and they fed in a meadow.

3 And, behold, seven other cows came up after them out of the river, ill-favored and lean; and stood beside the other cows on the bank of the river.

4 And the ill-favored and lean cows ate up the seven beautiful and fat cows. So Pharaoh awoke.

5 And he slept and dreamed a second time; and, behold, seven ears of grain were growing on a single stalk, rank and good.

6 And, behold, seven thin ears blasted by the east wind, sprang up after them.

7 And the seven thin ears devoured the seven rank and full ears. And Pharaoh awoke, and, behold, it was a dream.

8 And it came to pass in the morning that his spirit was troubled; so he sent and called for all the magicians and all the wise men of Egypt; and Pharaoh told them his dreams; but there was no man who could interpret them to Pharaoh.

9 ¶Then the chief butler spoke in the presence of Pharaoh, and said, I will mention my offense today;

10 Pharaoh was angry with his servants, and put me in the prison in the commander of the guard's house, both me and the chief baker;

11 And we dreamed dreams in the same night, I and he; we dreamed each man according to the interpretation of his dream.

12 And there was with us a young man, a Hebrew, a servant of the commander of the guard; and we told him our dreams, and he interpreted to us our dreams; to each man according to his dream he did interpret.

13 And it came to pass, as he interpreted to us, so it was; I was restored to my position, and he was crucified.

14 ¶Then Pharaoh sent and called Joseph, and they brought him hastily out of the dungeon; and he shaved himself, and changed his clothes, and came in before Pharaoh.

15 And Pharaoh said to Joseph, I have dreamed a dream, and there is

none that can interpret it; and I have heard concerning you, that when you hear a dream you can interpret it.

16 And Joseph answered and said to Pharaoh, Do you think, perhaps, that without God I am able to give Pharaoh an answer that everything will be well?

17 Then Pharaoh said to Joseph, In my dream I was standing on the bank of the river;

18 And, behold, there came up out of the river seven fat and beautiful cows; and they fed in a meadow;

19 And, behold, seven other cows came up after them, poor and ill-favored and lean. I had never seen such ill-favored cows in all the land of Egypt.

20 And the lean and ill-favored cows ate up the first seven fat cows;

21 And when they had eaten them up, it could not be known that they had eaten them; for they were still ill-favored, as at the beginning. Then I awoke.

22 And again, I saw in my dream, and, behold, seven ears of grain growing on one stalk, full and good;

23 And, behold, seven other ears, thin and blasted by the east wind, sprang up after them;

24 And the thin ears devoured the seven good ears; and I told this to the magicians; but there was no one who could interpret these dreams to me.

25 ¶And Joseph said to Pharaoh, The dream of Pharaoh is one; God has shown Pharaoh what he is about to do.

26 The seven good cows are seven years; and the seven good ears are seven years; the dream is one.

27 And the seven lean and ill-favored cows that came up after them are seven years; and the seven thin ears blasted by the east wind shall be seven years of famine.

28 It is the thing which I told Pharaoh; what God is about to do he has shown to Pharaoh.

29 Behold, there are coming seven years of great plenty throughout all the land of Egypt;

30 And there shall arise after them seven years of famine; and all the plenty shall be forgotten in the land of Egypt; and the famine shall consume the land;

31 And the plenty shall not be remembered in the land because of the famine which shall follow; for it shall be very severe.

32 And as for that the dream was repeated to Pharaoh twice; it is because the thing is already prepared by God, and God will hasten to bring it to pass.

33 Now therefore let Pharaoh find a discreet and wise man, and appoint him an overseer over the land of Egypt.

34 Let Pharaoh do this, and let him appoint officers over the land of Egypt to take the fifth part of the produce of the land of Egypt during the seven plenteous years.

35 And let them gather all the wheat of these good years that are coming, and store up the grain under the authority of Pharaoh, and let them keep the grain in the towns.

36 And let the grain be kept for the land against the seven years of famine which shall come in the land of Egypt; so that the land may not perish through the famine.

37 ¶And the thing was good in the eyes of Pharaoh, and in the eyes of all his servants.

38 And Pharaoh said to his servants, Can we find such a man as this, in whom the Spirit of God is?

39 Then Pharaoh said to Joseph, Forasmuch as God has shown you all this, there is none so wise and discreet as you are;

40 You shall be over my household, and according to your word shall all my people be ruled; only on the throne will I be greater than you.

41 And Pharaoh said to Joseph, See, I have made you governor over all the land of Egypt.

42 Then Pharaoh took off his ring from his hand, and put it on Joseph's hand, and arrayed him in robes of fine linen, and put a gold chain about his neck;

43 And he made him to ride in another chariot which belonged to him;

and they cried before him, Father and governor! Thus he made him governor over all the land of Egypt.

44 And Pharaoh said to Joseph, I Pharaoh have commanded that without your orders no man shall undertake anything in all the land of Egypt.

45 Then Pharaoh called Joseph's name Zaphnath-paaneah (because the hidden things were revealed to him); and he gave him to wife Asiath the daughter of Potipherah priest of On. And Joseph went throughout all the land of Egypt.

46 ¶And Joseph was thirty years old when he stood before Pharaoh king of Egypt. And Joseph went out from the presence of Pharaoh, and went throughout all the land of Egypt.

47 And in the seven plenteous years the land brought forth abundantly.

48 And he gathered up all the grain of the seven plenteous years which were in the land of Egypt, and stored up the grain in towns; the grain of the fields which was round about every town he stored in the same.

49 And Joseph stored up grain as the sand of the sea, very much, until he was tired of numbering it; for it was without number.

50 And to Joseph were born two sons before the years of famine came, whom Asiath the daughter of Potipherah priest of On bore to him.

51 And Joseph called the name of his first-born Manasseh; For God, said he, has made me forget all my troubles, and all my father's house.

52 And the name of the second he called Ephraim; For God has made me to be fruitful in the land of my affliction.

53 ¶And the seven years of plenty that were in the land of Egypt came to an end.

54 And the seven years of famine began to come, according as Joseph had said; and there was famine in all lands; and in all the land of Egypt there was no bread.

55 And when all the land of Egypt was famished, the people complained against Pharaoh because of the lack of bread; and Pharaoh said to all the Egyptians, Go to Joseph; and what he says to you, do.

56 And the famine was over all the face of the land, and Joseph opened all the storehouses, and sold to the Egyptians;

57 And the famine was severe in the land of Egypt. And the people from all lands came to Egypt to Joseph to buy grain; because the famine was severe in all lands.

CHAPTER 42

NOW when Jacob saw that there was grain in Egypt, Jacob said to his sons, Fear not.

2 Behold, I have heard that there is grain in Egypt; go down there, and buy for us from there; that we may live, and not die.

3 ¶And so Joseph's ten brothers went down to buy grain in Egypt.

4 But Benjamin, Joseph's brother, Jacob did not send with his brothers; for he said, Lest some misfortune might befall him.

5 And the sons of Israel came to buy grain with those that came; for the famine was severe in the land of Canaan.

6 Now Joseph was the governor over the land, and he it was who sold the grain to all the people of the land; and Joseph's brothers came, and bowed down themselves before him with their faces to the ground.

7 And Joseph saw his brothers and recognized them, but he deceived them and spoke harshly to them; and he said to them, Where have you come from? And they said, We came from the land of Canaan to buy grain.

8 And Joseph recognized his brothers, but they did not recognize him.

9 Then Joseph remembered the dreams which he had dreamed about them, and said to them, You are spies; you have come to get a report about the land.

10 And they said to him, No, our lord, but to buy grain your servants have come.

11 We are all one man's sons; we are pious men; your servants are not spies.

12 And Joseph said to them, It is not so, but to get a report about the land you have come.

13 And they said to him, Your servants are twelve brothers, the sons of one man in the land of Canaan; and, behold, the youngest is this day with our father, and one is dead.

14 And Joseph said to them, It is just as I said to you, you are spies:

15 By this you shall be proved; by the life of Pharaoh you shall not go forth from this place, except your younger brother comes here.

16 Send one of you, and let him bring your brother, and you shall be bound in prison, so that your words may be proved, to see if your statements are true; and if they are not true, by the life of Pharaoh, surely you are spies.

17 And he put them all together in prison for three days.

18 And on the third day Joseph said to them, Do this, and live; for I worship God;

19 If you are pious men, let one of your brothers be bound in your prison; and the rest of you, go and carry grain for the famished who are in your household;

20 But bring your youngest brother to me; so shall your words be verified, and you shall not die. And they did so.

21 ¶And they said one to another, Truly we are guilty concerning our brother, for we saw the anguish of his soul when he pleaded with us, and we would not listen to him; therefore is this distress come upon us.

22 And Reuben answered and said to them, Did I not tell you, Do not sin against the boy; but you did not listen? So now his blood is required.

23 And they did not know that Joseph understood them; for he spoke to them by an interpreter.

24 And he turned aside from them and wept; and he returned to them again, and conversed with them, and took Simeon from them, and bound him before their eyes.

25 ¶Then Joseph commanded the servants to fill their sacks with wheat, and to restore every man's money into his sack, and to give them provisions for the journey; and they did so for them.

26 And they loaded their asses with their wheat, and departed thence.

27 And as one of them opened his sack to give his ass provender in the inn, he saw his money in the mouth of his sack.

28 And he said to his brothers, My money has been returned; and, lo, it is in the mouth of my sack; and their hearts failed them, and they were amazed, staring at one another, saying, What is this that God has done to us?

29 ¶And they came to Jacob their father to the land of Canaan, and told him all that had befallen them, saying,

30 The man who is the lord of the land spoke roughly to us, and took us for spies of the land.

31 But we said to him, We are pious men; we are not spies;

32 We are twelve brothers, sons of our father; and one is dead, and the youngest is this day with our father in the land of Canaan.

33 And the man, the lord of the land, said to us, By this shall I know that you are pious men; leave one of your brothers here with me, and take wheat for the famished who are in your households, and go your way;

34 And bring your youngest brother to me; then shall I know that you are not spies, but that you are pious men; so I will deliver your brother to you, and you shall trade in the land.

35 ¶And it came to pass as they emptied their sacks, behold, every man's bag of money was in his sack; and when both they and their father saw the bags of money, they were afraid.

36 And Jacob their father said to them, You have bereaved me of my children: Joseph is dead, and Simeon is missing, and now you will take Benjamin away; all these things are against me.

37 Then Reuben said to his father, Put to death my two sons if I do not bring him back to you; intrust him to me, and I will bring him back to you.

38 And he said, My son shall not go down with you; for his brother is dead, and he alone is left to his mother: if misfortune should befall him by the way in which you go, then you shall bring down my gray hairs with sorrow to Sheol.

CHAPTER 43

THE famine was very severe in the land.

2 And when they had finished eating the wheat which they had brought from Egypt, their father Jacob said to them, Go down to Egypt, and buy us a little grain.

3 And Judah said to him, The man did solemnly charge us, saying, You shall not see my face except your brother is with you.

4 If you will send our brother with us, we will go down and buy grain for ourselves;

5 But if you will not send him, we will not go down; for the man said to us, You shall not see my face except your brother is with you.

6 Then their father Israel said to them, Why did you cause me this displeasure, as to tell the man whether you had another brother?

7 And they said, The man asked us straitly about ourselves and our kindred, saying, Is your father still alive? Have you another brother? And we told him simply because of these words; could we have known in advance that he would say to us that we should bring our brother down?

8 And Judah said to Israel his father, Send the lad with us, and we will arise and go; that we may live, and not die, both we, and you, and also our little ones.

9 And I will be surety for him; of my hands shall you require him; if I do not bring him back to you, and set him before you, then I shall be guilty before my father forever;

10 For if we had not delayed, perhaps we would have now returned a second time.

11 And their father Israel said to them, If it must be so now, then do this: take some of the best fruits of the land in your sacks, and carry down the man a present, a little balm, and a little honey, gum, and myrrh, pistachio nuts, and almonds;

12 And take double money with you; and the money that was brought back in the mouth of your sacks, take it again with you; perhaps it was an oversight;

13 Take also your brother, and arise, and go again to the man;

14 And may God Almighty give you mercy before the man, that he may send away your other brother, and Benjamin with you. And as for me, if I am bereaved of my children, I am bereaved.

15 ¶So the men took the present, and they took double money with them, and Benjamin; and rose up and went down to Egypt and stood before Joseph.

16 And when Joseph saw Benjamin with them, he said to the steward of his house, Bring these men into the house, and kill a sheep, and make ready; for these men shall dine with me at noon.

17 And the servant did as Joseph had told him; and brought the men into Joseph's house.

18 And they were afraid, when they brought them into Joseph's house; and they said, It is because of the money that was returned in our sacks at the first time that we are brought in; so that he may seek occasion against us, and conspire against us, that they may make us slaves, and take away our asses.

19 So they came near to the steward of Joseph's house and spoke with him at the door of the house,

20 And said, We beseech you, O our lord, we truly came down at the first time to buy grain;

21 And it came to pass when we came to the inn that we opened our sacks, and, behold, every man's money was in the mouth of his sack, our money in full weight; and we have brought it back again with us.

22 And we have brought other money down with us to buy grain; we did not know who put our money in our sacks.

23 He said to them, Peace be to

you, fear not; your God, and the God of your father, has put a treasure in your sacks; I had your money. And he brought Simeon out to them.

24 Then the servant brought the men into Joseph's house and gave them water, and they washed their feet; and he put fodder before their asses.

25 And the men made ready the present before Joseph came at noon; for they heard that they should eat bread there.

26 ¶And when Joseph came home, they brought him the present which they had in their hands into the house, and bowed themselves to him to the ground.

27 And he asked them of their welfare, and said to them, Is your father well, the old man of whom you spoke to me? Is he still alive?

28 And they answered, Your servant our father is well, he is still alive. And they bowed down their heads and made obeisance.

29 And he raised up his eyes and saw his brother Benjamin, his mother's son, and said to them, Is this your youngest brother, of whom you spoke to me? And he said, May God be gracious to you, my son.

30 And Joseph made haste; for his heart did yearn for his brother; and he sought where to weep; and he entered into his chamber and wept there.

31 Then he washed his face and went out and controlled his emotions and said, Let us eat.

32 And they served Joseph by himself, and them by themselves, and the Egyptians, who did eat with him, by themselves; because the Egyptians could not eat bread with the Hebrews; for that is an abomination to the Egyptians.

33 And they sat before him, the firstborn according to his birthright, and the youngest according to his youth; and the men looked at one another and marveled.

34 And the servants took portions to them from before Joseph; but Benjamin's portion was five times as much as any of theirs. And they drank and were merry with him.

CHAPTER 44

AND he commanded the steward of his house, saying, Fill the men's sacks with wheat, as much as they can carry, and put every man's money in his sack's mouth.

2 And take my cup, the silver cup, and put it in the sack's mouth of the youngest, with his money for the wheat. And the servant did according to the word that Joseph had spoken.

3 As soon as the morning was light, the men started on their way, together with their asses.

4 And when they were gone out of the city, but not yet far off, Joseph said to the steward, Arise, pursue the men; and when you overtake them, say to them, Why have you returned evil for good?

5 This is the cup from which my lord drinks, and by which indeed he divines. You have done evil in so doing.

6 ¶And he overtook them, and he spoke to them these same words.

7 They said to him, Let not our lord speak such words. Far be it from your servants that they should do such a thing;

8 Behold, the money which we found in our sacks' mouths we brought back to you from the land of Canaan; how then should we steal from your master's house gold or silver?

9 With whomsoever of your servants it be found, both let him die, and we also will be to our lord servants.

10 And he said to them, Now also let it be according to your words; he with whom it is found shall be my servant; and the rest of you shall be blameless.

11 Then they speedily took down every man his sack to the ground, and opened every man his sack.

12 And they searched, beginning with the eldest and ending with the youngest; and the cup was found in Benjamin's sack.

13 And they tore their clothes, and loaded every man his ass, and returned to the town.

14 ¶And Judah and his brothers came to Joseph's house; for he was still there; and they fell before him on the ground.

15 And Joseph said to them, What deed is this that you have done? Did you not know that such a man as I can certainly divine?

16 And Judah said, What shall we say to my lord? What shall we speak? Or how shall we clear ourselves? God has found out the iniquity of your servants; behold, we are my lord's servants, both we, and he also with whom the cup is found.

17 And he said to them, Far be it from me that I should do such a thing; only the man with whom the cup has been found, he shall be my servant; and as for you, go up in peace to your father.

18 ¶Then Judah came near to him and said, I beg you, O my lord, let your servant speak a few words in my lord's presence, and let not your anger burn against your servant; for you are even like Pharaoh.

19 My lord asked his servants, saying, Have you a father, or a brother?

20 And we said to my lord, We have a father, an old man, and he has a young son, the child of his old age; and his brother is dead, and he alone is left of his mother, and his father loves him.

21 Then you said to your servants, Bring him down to me, that I may set my eyes upon him.

22 And we said to my lord, The lad cannot leave his father; for if he should leave his father, his father would die.

23 And you said to your servants, Unless your youngest brother comes down with you, you shall see my face no more.

24 And when we came up to your servant our father, we told him the words of my lord.

25 And your servant our father said to us, Go back again and buy us a little grain.

26 And we said to our father, We cannot go down; if our youngest brother goes down with us, then we will go down; for we cannot see the man's face unless our youngest brother is with us.

27 Then your servant our father said to us, You know that my wife bore me two sons;

28 And the one of them left me, and I said, Surely he has been killed; and I have never seen him since;

29 And now you want to take this one also from me, and if misfortune should befall him, you will bring down my gray hairs with sorrow to Sheol.

30 Now therefore when we come to your servant our father, and the lad is not with us; seeing that his life is dear to him like his own life;

31 It shall come to pass when he sees that the lad is not with us, he will die; and your servants shall bring down the gray hairs of your servant our father with sorrow to Sheol.

32 For your servant became surety for the lad to our father, saying, If I do not bring him back to you, then I shall be guilty before my father forever.

33 Now therefore, let your servant stay here instead of the lad as a servant to my lord; and let the lad go up with his brothers.

34 For how can I go up to my father, if the lad is not with me? Lest I see the misfortune which will come on my father.

CHAPTER 45

THEN Joseph could no longer control his emotions before all those who stood in his presence; and he said, Cause everyone to go out from me. And there remained no one with him when Joseph made himself known to his brothers.

2 And he wept aloud; and the Egyptians and the household of Pharaoh heard it.

3 And Joseph said to his brothers, I am Joseph your brother; is my father still alive? But his brothers could not answer him because they were afraid at his presence.

4 And Joseph said to his brothers, Come near to me; and they came near. And he said to them, I am

Joseph your brother, whom you sold to the Egyptians.

5 Now do not be grieved, nor displeased with yourselves, that you sold me here; for it was to provide for you that God sent me before you.

6 For behold the famine has been in the land for two years; and yet there are five years, in which there will be no one that sows or that reaps.

7 And God sent me before you to preserve you a remnant on the earth, and to save your lives by a great deliverance.

8 So now it was not you who sent me here, but God; and he has made me a father to Pharaoh, and lord over all his house, and a ruler throughout all the land of Egypt.

9 Hasten, and go up to my father, and say to him, Thus says your son Joseph, God has made me lord over all Egypt; come down to me, do not delay;

10 And you shall dwell in the land of Goshen, and you shall be near me, you and your children and your children's children and your flocks and your herds and all that you have;

11 And there I will provide for you; for the famine will yet last five years more; lest you, your household, and all that you have perish.

12 And, behold, your eyes see, and the eyes of my brother Benjamin, that it is my mouth that speaks to you.

13 And you must tell my father of all my glory in Egypt and of all that you have seen; and you shall hasten and bring down my father here.

14 Then he fell upon his brother Benjamin's neck and wept; and Benjamin wept upon his neck.

15 Moreover he kissed all his brothers and wept upon them; and after that, his brothers talked with him.

16 ¶And the news of their meeting was reported in Pharaoh's house, saying, Joseph's brothers are come; and the news pleased Pharaoh well, and his servants.

17 And Pharaoh said to Joseph, Say to your brothers, Do this: load your beasts with wheat, and go, and carry it to the land of Canaan;

18 And take your father and your households, and come to me; and I will give you the best of the land of Egypt, and you shall eat of the fat of the land.

19 Behold, you are the governor; say to your brothers, Do this: take wagons from the land of Egypt for your wives and for your little ones, and bring your father, and come.

20 And do not regard your stuff which you leave behind; for the choicest of all the land of Egypt is yours.

21 And the sons of Israel did so; and Joseph gave them wagons, according to the command of Pharaoh, and gave them provisions for the journey.

22 To all of them he gave each man two pairs of garments; but to Benjamin he gave three hundred pieces of silver and five pairs of garments.

23 And to his father he sent after this manner: ten asses laden with the good things of Egypt, and ten she-asses laden with wheat, wine, and provisions for his father's journey.

24 So he sent his brothers away, and they departed; and he said to them, Quarrel not on the journey.

25 ¶And they went up out of Egypt, and came to the land of Canaan to their father Jacob.

26 And they told him, saying, Joseph is still alive, and he is governor over all the land of Egypt. But Jacob disregarded their story, for he did not believe them.

27 And they told him all the words which Joseph had said to them; and when he saw the wagons which Joseph had sent to carry him, their father Jacob was content.

28 And he said, This is great news for me, for my son Joseph is still alive; I will go and see him before I die.

CHAPTER 46

AND Israel journeyed with all that he had, and came to Beer-sheba, and offered sacrifices to the God of his father Isaac.

2 And God spoke to Israel in a vision of the night, and said, Jacob, Jacob. And he said, Here am I.

3 Then he said to him, I am El, the God of your father; fear not to go down to Egypt; for I will there make of you a great people;

4 I will go down with you into Egypt; and I will also surely bring you up again; and Joseph shall close your eyes when you die.

5 And Jacob rose up from Beer-sheba; and the sons of Israel carried Jacob their father, their little ones, and their wives in the wagons which Pharaoh had sent to carry him.

6 And they took their cattle and their goods which they had gotten in the land of Canaan, and came into Egypt, Jacob and all his offspring with him;

7 His sons and his grandsons, his daughters and his sons' daughters, and all his offspring he brought with him into Egypt.

8 ¶And these are the names of the children of Israel, who came into Egypt, Jacob and his sons: Reuben, Jacob's first-born.

9 And the sons of Reuben: Hanoch, Pallu, Hezron, and Carmi.

10 ¶The sons of Simeon: Jemuel, Jamin, Ohar, Jachin, Zohar, and Shaul the son of a Canaanitish woman.

11 ¶The sons of Levi: Gershon, Ko-hath, and Merari.

12 ¶The sons of Judah: Er, Onan, Shelah, Pharez, and Zarah; but Er and Onan died in the land of Canaan. And the sons of Pharez were Hezron and Hamul.

13 ¶The sons of Issachar: Tola, Phuvah, Job, and Shimron.

14 ¶The sons of Zebulun: Seder, Elon, and Nahlael.

15 These are the sons of Leah, whom she bore to Jacob in Padan-aram, together with his daughter Dinah; the number of persons, his sons and his daughters being thirty-three in all.

16 ¶The sons of Gad: Ziphion, Hag-gi, Shuni, Ezbon, Adi, Arod, and Adri.

17 ¶And the sons of Asher: Jim-nah, Ishuah, Isui, and Beriah, and Serah their sister; and the sons of Beriah: Heber, and Malchiel.

18 These are the sons of Zilpah, whom Laban gave to Leah his daughter, and these she bore to Jacob, sixteen persons.

19 The sons of Rachel Jacob's wife: Joseph, and Benjamin.

20 ¶And to Joseph in the land of Egypt were born Manasseh and Ephraim, whom Asiath the daughter of Potipherah priest of On bore to him.

21 ¶The sons of Benjamin: Belah, Akbar, Ashkel, Gera, Naaman, Ehi, Arosh, Muppim, Huppim, and Ard.

22 These are the sons of Rachel, whom she bore to Jacob, fourteen persons in all.

23 ¶The son of Dan: Hushim.

24 ¶And the sons of Naphtali: Nahzael, Guni, Jezer, and Shillem.

25 These are the sons of Bilhah, whom Laban gave to Rachel, his daughter, and she bore these to Jacob, seven persons in all.

26 All the persons that came with Jacob into Egypt, who came out of his loins, besides Jacob's sons' wives, were sixty-six persons in all;

27 And the sons of Joseph who were born to him in Egypt were two persons; thus all the persons of the house of Jacob who came into Egypt were seventy.

28 ¶And he sent Judah before him to Joseph to present himself before him in Goshen; and they came into the land of Goshen.

29 And Joseph made ready his chariots, and went up to meet Israel his father in Goshen, and he pre-sented himself to him, and fell on his neck, and wept on his neck for a while.

30 And Israel said to Joseph, Now let me die, since I have seen your face, my son, because you are still alive.

31 And Joseph said to his brothers and to his father's household, I will go up and inform Pharaoh, and say to him, My brothers and my father's household, who were in the land of Canaan, have come to me;

32 And the men are shepherds, for they are cattle raisers; and they have brought their flocks and their herds and all that they have.

33 And it shall come to pass, when Pharaoh shall call you and shall say to you, What is your occupation?

34 You shall say to him, Your servants are cattle raisers from their youth even until now, both we and also our fathers; that you may dwell in the land of Goshen; for the Egyptians despise all those who feed sheep.

CHAPTER 47

THEN Joseph came and informed Pharaoh, and said to him, My father and my brothers and their flocks and their herds and all that they have, are come from the land of Canaan; and, behold, they are now settled in the land of Goshen.

2 And he took from among his brothers five men and presented them to Pharaoh.

3 And Pharaoh said to Joseph's brothers, What is your occupation? And they said to Pharaoh, Your servants are shepherds, both we and also our fathers, from our youth.

4 They said moreover to Pharaoh, We have come to sojourn in the land; for there is no pasture for your servants' flocks; for the famine is severe in the land of Canaan; now, therefore, let your servants dwell in the land of Goshen.

5 And Pharaoh said to Joseph, Your father and your brothers have come to you;

6 The land of Egypt is before you; settle your father and your brothers in the best of the land; let them dwell in the land of Goshen; and if you know of any able men among them, make them overseers over all my cattle.

7 And Joseph brought in Jacob his father and presented him to Pharaoh; and Jacob blessed Pharaoh.

8 And Pharaoh said to Jacob, How old are you?

9 And Jacob said to Pharaoh, The days of the years of my pilgrimage are a hundred and thirty years; few and difficult have been the years of my life, and I have not attained to the days of the years of the life of my fathers in the days of their pilgrimage.

10 And Jacob blessed Pharaoh and went out from before Pharaoh.

11 ¶Then Joseph settled his father and his brothers, and gave them a possession in the land of Egypt in the best of the land, in the land of Rameses, as Pharaoh had commanded.

12 And Joseph supplied his father and his brothers and all his father's household with wheat according to their families.

13 ¶And there was no grain in all the land; for the famine was very severe, so that the land of Egypt and the land of Canaan were desolate by reason of the famine.

14 And Joseph gathered up all the money that was to be found in the land of Egypt and in the land of Canaan for the grain which they bought; and Joseph brought the money into Pharaoh's house.

15 And when the money was spent from the land of Egypt and from the land of Canaan, all the Egyptians came to Joseph and said to him, Give us wheat that we may live, and not die in your presence; for the money is spent.

16 And Joseph said to them, Give me your cattle, and I will give you grain for your cattle, if your money is spent.

17 So they brought their cattle to Joseph; and Joseph gave them grain in exchange for horses and for flocks and for herds and for asses; and he supplied them with food in exchange for all their herds that year.

18 When that year was ended, they came to him the second year, and said to him, We will not hide it from our lord, for the money is spent; and our lord also has all the herds and cattle; there is nothing left in the sight of our lord but our persons and our lands;

19 Why should we die before your eyes, both we and our lands? Buy us and our lands for bread, and we and our lands will be servants to Pharaoh; and give us seed, that we may live, and not die and that the land be not desolate.

20 And Joseph bought all the land

of Egypt for Pharaoh; for the Egyptians sold every man his field, because the famine prevailed over them; so the land became Pharaoh's.

21 And as for the people, he removed them from town to town from one end of the borders of Egypt to the other end thereof.

22 Only the land of the priests he did not buy; for the priests had a grant from Pharaoh, and did eat their portion which Pharaoh gave them; therefore they did not sell their lands.

23 Then Joseph said to the people, Behold, I have bought you this day and your lands for Pharaoh; lo, here is seed for you, and you shall sow the land.

24 And it shall come to pass when the crops are gathered in, you shall give the fifth part to Pharaoh, and four parts shall be your own, for seed of the field and for your food and for food for your household and for food for your little ones.

25 And they said, You have saved our lives; let us find mercy in the sight of our lord, and we will be Pharaoh's servants.

26 And Joseph made it a law over the land of Egypt to this day that Pharaoh should have the fifth part, except the land of the priests only, for it did not belong to Pharaoh.

27 ¶And Israel dwelt in the land of Egypt in the region of Goshen; and they became powerful in it, and grew, and multiplied exceedingly.

28 And Jacob lived in the land of Egypt seventeen years; so the whole age of Jacob was a hundred and forty-seven years.

29 And when the time drew near that Israel must die, he called his son Joseph, and said to him, If now I have found grace in your sight, put your hand under my girdle, and I will make you to swear by the Lord that you will deal graciously and truly with me; do not bury me in Egypt;

30 But when I sleep with my fathers, you shall carry me out of Egypt and bury me in their burial place. And Joseph said, I will do as you have said.

31 And he said, Swear to me. And he swore to him. And Israel bowed himself upon the head of his staff.

CHAPTER 48

AND it came to pass after these things that Joseph was told, Behold, your father is sick; and he took with him his two sons, Manasseh and Ephraim.

2 And they informed Jacob, and said to him, Behold, your son Joseph has come to you; and Israel strengthened himself, and sat up on the bed.

3 And Jacob said to Joseph, God Almighty appeared to me at Luz in the land of Canaan and blessed me,

4 And he said to me, Behold, I will bless you, and multiply you, and I will make of you a multitude of peoples; and I will give this land to your descendants after you for an everlasting possession.

5 ¶And now your two sons, Ephraim and Manasseh, who were born to you in the land of Egypt before I came to you into the land of Egypt, are mine; as Reuben and Simeon, they shall be mine.

6 But the children that you begot after them shall be yours, and shall be called after the name of their brothers when they come into their inheritance.

7 And as for me, when I was coming from Padan-aram, Rachel died at my side in the land of Canaan on the way, within the distance of three or four miles from the entrance to Ephrath; and I buried her there on the road to Ephrath; the same is Bethlehem.

8 And when Israel saw Joseph's sons, he said to him, Who are these?

9 And Joseph said to his father, They are my sons whom God has given me in this place. And he said, Bring them near me, and I will bless them.

10 Now the eyes of Israel were dim because of age, so that he could not see well. And Joseph brought them near to him; and he kissed them and embraced them.

11 And Israel said to Joseph, I had not thought to see your face; and, lo, God has shown me your children also.

12 And Joseph removed them from before his knees, and they bowed themselves before him with their faces to the ground.

13 Then Joseph took both of his sons, Ephraim in his right hand toward Israel's left hand, and Manasseh in his left hand toward Israel's right hand, and brought them near to him.

14 And Israel stretched out his right hand, and laid it upon Ephraim's head, who was the younger, and his left hand upon Manasseh's head; he changed the position of his hands [1] wittingly, even though Manasseh was the first-born.

15 ¶And Jacob blessed Joseph his son, saying, The God before whom my fathers Abraham and Isaac walked righteously, the God who has supplied my needs from my youth to this day,

16 The angel who has delivered me from all evil, bless the lads; and let them bear my name and the names of my fathers, Abraham and Isaac; and let them grow and multiply in the midst of the earth.

17 And when Joseph saw that his father laid his right hand upon the head of Ephraim, it displeased him; and he held up his father's hand, to remove it from Ephraim's head to Manasseh's head.

18 And Joseph said to his father, Not so, my father; for this is the first-born; put your right hand upon his head.

19 But his father refused, and said, I know it, my son, I know it; he also shall become a people, and he also shall be great: but his younger brother shall be greater than he, and his descendants shall become a multitude of peoples.

20 And he blessed them that day, saying, By you shall Israel bless, and they shall say, May God make you as Ephraim and as Manasseh; and thus he set Ephraim before Manasseh.

21 Then Israel said to Joseph, Behold, I am dying, but God shall be with you, and bring you again to the land of your fathers.

22 Moreover I have given to you one portion of the land more than your brothers, which I took from the hand of the Amorites with my sword and with my bow.

CHAPTER 49

THEN Jacob called his sons and said to them, Gather yourselves together that I may tell you that which shall befall you in the last days.

2 Gather yourselves together and listen, O sons of Jacob; and hearken to Israel your father.

3 ¶Reuben, you are my first-born, my might, and the beginning of my strength, and the excellency of dignity, and the excellency of power:

4 You went astray like water, you shall not excel; because you went up to your father's bed; truly, you have defiled my bed by going up into it.

5 ¶Simeon and Levi are brothers; instruments of anger are in their nature.

6 I never agreed to their counsels; nor did I lower myself to sit in their assembly; for in their anger they slew men and in their rage they destroyed a town wall.

7 Cursed be their anger, for it is raging; and their wrath, for it is fierce; I will divide them in Jacob, and scatter them in Israel.

8 ¶Judah, your brothers shall praise you; your hand shall be on the neck of your enemies; your father's sons shall bow down before you.

9 Judah is a lion's whelp; from the prey, my son, you are gone up; he stooped down, he crouched as a lion, and as a young lion; who shall rouse him up?

10 The sceptre shall not depart from Judah, nor a lawgiver from between his feet, until the coming of the One to whom the sceptre belongs,[2] to whom the Gentiles shall look forward.

11 He shall tie up his foal to the vine, and his ass's colt to a branch; he shall bleach his garments with wine, and his robe with the juices of the grape;

12 His eyes shall be radiant with

---

[1] Departed from custom.　　[2] Messiah.

wine, and his teeth white with milk.[1]

13 ¶Zebulun shall dwell at the shore of the seas; and he shall be a haven for ships; and his border shall extend as far as Zidon.

14 ¶Issachar is a mighty man couching by the highways;

15 And he saw that his dwelling place was good, and his land fertile; and he bowed his shoulder to servitude, and became a servant to tribute.

16 ¶Dan shall judge his people as if the tribes of Israel were one.

17 Dan shall be a serpent by the way, an adder in the paths, that bites the horse's heel and causes its rider to fall backward.

18 I have waited for thy salvation, O LORD.

19 ¶Gad shall go out to raid, and shall pursue at the heels of his enemies.

20 ¶As for Asher, his land is good, and he shall supply kings with food.

21 ¶Naphtali is a swift messenger; he gives goodly words.

22 ¶Joseph is a disciplined son, an educated son; a fruitful bough by a spring, whose branches run over the wall.

23 A company of men quarreled with him, and being great in numbers, envied him;

24 But in strength he bent his bow, and his arms were made strong by the hands of the mighty One of Jacob; (by the name of the Shepherd, the Strength of Israel:)

25 May the God of your father help you and the Almighty bless you with the blessings of heaven above, blessings of the deep beneath, blessings of the breasts, and of the womb;

26 The blessings of your father have prevailed above the blessings of my forbears to the utmost bound of the everlasting hills; they shall be on the head of Joseph, on the crown of the head of him who is the prince of his brothers.

27 ¶Benjamin is a plundering wolf; in the morning he shall devour the prey, and in the evening he shall divide the spoil.

28 ¶All these are the twelve tribes of Israel; and this is what their father Jacob said to them; he addressed them, then he blessed them, according to his blessing, he blessed every one of them.

29 Then their father blessed them, and charged them, and said to them, I am to be gathered to my people; bury me with my fathers in the cave that is in the field of Ephron the Hittite,

30 In the cave which is in the field of Ephron the Hittite, in the double cave which is in the field, before Mamre, in the land of Canaan, the field which Abraham bought from Ephron the Hittite as a possession for a burial ground.

31 There they buried Abraham and Sarah his wife; there they buried Isaac and Rebekah his wife; and there I buried Leah.

32 The field and the cave which is in it were purchased from the children of Heth.

33 And when Jacob had finished charging his sons, he stretched his feet on his bed, and grew weak, and died, and was gathered to his people.

CHAPTER 50

AND Joseph fell upon his father's face, and wept over him, and kissed him.

2 Then Joseph commanded his servants the physicians to embalm his father; and the physicians embalmed Israel.

3 And forty days were fulfilled for him; for so are fulfilled the days of those who are embalmed; and the Egyptians mourned for him seventy days.

4 And when the days of his mourning were past, Joseph spoke to the household of Pharaoh, saying, If now I have found mercy in your eyes, speak in the presence of Pharaoh, saying,

5 My father made me swear, saying, Behold I am dying; in my grave which I bought for myself in the land of Canaan, there you shall bury me. Now therefore let me go up and

[1] An Aramaic idiom meaning *abundance of wine and milk.*

bury my father, and I will come back again.

6 And Pharaoh said, Go up and bury your father, according as he made you swear.

7 ¶So Joseph went up to bury his father; and with him went up all the servants of Pharaoh, the elders of his household, and all the elders of the land of Egypt,

8 And all the household of Joseph, his brothers, and his father's household; only their little ones, their flocks, and their herds, they left in the land of Goshen.

9 And there went up with him both chariots and horsemen; and it was a very great company.

10 And they came to the threshing floor of Atar, which is beyond the Jordan, and there they mourned with a great and very sore lamentation; and Joseph made a mourning for his father seven days.

11 And when the inhabitants of the land, the Canaanites, saw the mourning in the threshing floor of Atar, they said, This is a grievous mourning to the Egyptians; therefore the name of it was called Abel-mizrin, which is beyond Jordan.

12 And his sons did to Jacob just as he had commanded them;

13 For they carried him into the land of Canaan, and buried him in the double cave, which is in the field, which Abraham purchased with the field for a possession for a burial ground from Ephron, the Hittite, before Mamre.

14 ¶And Joseph returned to Egypt, he and his brothers, and all who went up with him to bury his father, after he had buried his father.

15 ¶And when Joseph's brothers saw that their father was dead, they were afraid, saying, It may be Joseph will harm us, and perhaps he will requite us all the evil which we did to him.

16 So they came to Joseph and said to him, Your father did command before he died, saying,

17 Thus shall you say to Joseph, Forgive, we pray you now, the trespass of your brothers and their sins; for they did evil to you; and now forgive the trespass of the servants of the God of your father. And Joseph wept when they spoke to him.

18 And his brothers also went and fell down before him; and they said, Behold, we are your servants.

19 But Joseph said to them, Fear not; for I am a servant of God.

20 But as for you, you thought evil against me; but God meant it for good, to do as he has done this day, to save many lives.

21 Now therefore do not be afraid; I will provide for you and your little ones. And he comforted them, and spoke kindly to them.

22 ¶And Joseph dwelt in Egypt, he, and all his father's house; and Joseph lived a hundred and ten years.

23 And Joseph saw Ephraim's children of the third generation; the children also of Machir the son of Manasseh were brought up upon Joseph's knees.

24 And Joseph said to his brothers, I am dying; and God will surely remember you, and bring you up out of this land to the land which he swore to Abraham, to Isaac, and to Jacob.

25 And Joseph took an oath of the children of Israel, saying, God will surely remember you, and you shall carry up my bones from here with you.

26 So Joseph died, being a hundred and ten years old; and they embalmed him and put him in a coffin in Egypt.

THE SECOND BOOK OF MOSES, CALLED

EXODUS

CHAPTER 1

THESE are the names of the children of Israel, who came into Egypt; every man and his household came with Jacob:

2 Reuben, Simeon, Levi, and Judah,

3 Issachar, Zebulun, and Benjamin,

4 Dan, and Naphtali, Gad, and Asher.

5 And all the persons that came out of the loins of Jacob were seventy persons; for Joseph was in Egypt already.

6 And Joseph died, and all his brothers, and all that generation.

7 ¶And the children of Israel were fruitful and increased abundantly, and multiplied and grew exceedingly strong; and the land was filled with them.

8 Now there rose up a new king over Egypt who knew not Joseph.

9 And he said to his people, Behold, the people of the children of Israel are more numerous and stronger than we;

10 Come, let us deal wisely with them, before they multiply, lest when we chance to be at war, they will be added also to our enemies, and fight against us, and so drive us out of the land.

11 Therefore they appointed over them cruel taskmasters to afflict them with their burdens. And they built for Pharaoh cities with storehouses, Pithom and Raamses.

12 But the more they oppressed them, the more they multiplied and became strong. And the Egyptians were grieved because of the children of Israel.

13 So the Egyptians oppressed the children of Israel severely;

14 And they made their lives bitter with hard labor, in mortar and in bricks and in all manner of work in the field; all their service wherein they made them serve was with rigor.

15 ¶And the king of Egypt spoke to the Hebrew midwives, of whom the name of the one was Puah and the name of the other Shoprah;

16 And he said to them, When you do perform your duties as midwives to the Hebrew women, look out when they kneel to deliver; if it is a male, then you must kill him; but if it is a female, then let her live.

17 But the midwives feared God, and did not do as the king of Egypt commanded them, but let the boys live.

18 So the king of Egypt called for the midwives and said to them, Why have you done this thing, and let the boys live?

19 And the midwives said to Pharaoh, The Hebrew women are not like the Egyptian women; for they themselves are midwives, and are delivered before a midwife comes in to them.

20 Therefore God dealt well with the midwives, because they spared the males; and the people multiplied, and grew exceedingly strong.

21 And it came to pass, because the midwives feared God, he blessed them with families.

22 And Pharaoh charged all the people, saying, Every son that is born you shall cast into the river, and every daughter you shall save alive.

CHAPTER 2

AND there went a man from the house of Levi, and took to wife a daughter of the house of Levi.

2 And the woman conceived and bore a son; and when she saw that he was a handsome boy, she hid him for three months

3 And when she could no longer hide him, she took for herself an ark made of acacia wood, and daubed it with slime and with pitch, and put the child into it; and laid it among the reeds by the river's bank.

4 And his sister stood afar off, to know what would be done to him.

5 ¶And the daughter of Pharaoh came down to bathe in the river; and her maidens walked along by the river's side; and when she saw the ark among the reeds, she sent her maidens to fetch it.

6 And when she had opened it, she saw the child; and, behold, the babe was weeping. And she had compassion on him, and said, This is one of the Hebrews' children.

7 Then his sister said to Pharaoh's daughter, Shall I go and call for you a nurse of the Hebrew women, that she may nurse this child for you?

8 And Pharaoh's daughter said to her, Go. And the girl went and called the child's mother.

9 And Pharaoh's daughter said to her, Take this child away and nurse him for me, and I will give you your wages. So the woman took the child and nursed him.

10 And the child grew, and she brought him to Pharaoh's daughter, and he became her son. And she called his name Moses; for she said, I drew him out of the water.

11 ¶And it came to pass in those days, when Moses was grown up, that he went out among his brethren, and saw their oppression; and he saw an Egyptian beating a Hebrew, one of his brethren of the children of Israel.

12 And he looked this way and that way, and when he saw that there was no man watching, he slew the Egyptian and hid him in the sand.

13 And when he went out the second day, he looked, and behold, two Hebrew men were quarreling together; and he said to him that did the wrong, Why do you beat your fellow?

14 And he replied, Who made you a prince and a judge over us? Do you intend to kill me, as you killed the Egyptian yesterday? And Moses was afraid, and said, Surely this thing is known.

15 Now when Pharaoh heard this thing, he sought to slay Moses. But Moses fled from the presence of Pharaoh, and went to the land of Midian; and he sat down by a well.

16 Now the priest of Midian had seven daughters; and they came and drew water, and filled the troughs to water their father's flock.

17 And the shepherds came and drove them away; but Moses rose up and rescued them, and watered their flock.

18 And when they came to Reuel their father, he said to them, How is it that you have watered the flock so soon today?

19 And they said to him, An Egyptian delivered us out of the hands of the shepherds and also drew water for us and watered our flock.

20 And he said to his daughters, And where is he? Why is it that you have left the man? Go, invite him, that he may eat bread.

21 And Moses was content to dwell with the man; and he gave Moses Zipporah his daughter.

22 And she bore a son, and he called his name Gershon; for Moses said, I have been a stranger in a strange land. And she bore again, the second son to Moses, and he called his name Eleazar, saying, For the God of my fathers has helped me and has delivered me from the sword of Pharaoh.

23 ¶And it came to pass after a long time that the king of Egypt died; and the children of Israel groaned because of severe oppression, and they prayed, and their cry came up to God because of severe oppression.

24 And God heard their groaning, and God remembered his covenant with Abraham, with Isaac, and with Jacob.

25 And God looked upon the children of Israel, and God noticed their oppression.

CHAPTER 3

NOW Moses was feeding the flock of Jethro [1] his father-in-law, the priest of Midian; and he led the flock to the desert and came to the mountain of God, even to Horeb.

2 And the angel of the LORD appeared to him in a flame of fire out of the midst of a bush; and he looked, and, behold, the bush was on fire, and the bush was not consumed.

3 And Moses said, I will now turn aside and see this great sight, why the bush is not burned.

4 And when the LORD saw that he turned aside to see, God called to him out of the midst of the bush, and said, Moses, Moses. And he said, Here am I.

5 And he said, Do not draw near; take your shoes from off your feet, for the place whereon you are standing is holy ground.

6 Moreover he said, I am the God of your father, the God of Abraham, the God of Isaac, and the God of Jacob. And Moses hid his face; for he was afraid to look at God.

7 ¶And the LORD said, I have surely seen the affliction of my people who are in Egypt, and I have heard their cry because of their taskmasters; for I know their sorrows;

8 And I have come down to deliver them out of the hand of the Egyptians, and to bring them up out of that land to a good and large land, to a land flowing with milk and honey; to the land of the Canaanites, the Hittites, the Amorites, the Perizzites, the Hivites, and the Jebusites.

9 Now therefore, behold, the cry of the children of Israel is come to me; and I have also seen the oppression wherewith the Egyptians oppress them.

10 Come now, therefore, and I will send you to Pharaoh, that you may bring forth my people, the children of Israel, out of Egypt.

11 ¶And Moses said to God, Who am I that I should go to Pharaoh, and that I should bring the children of Israel out of Egypt?

12 And God said to him, I will be with you; and this shall be a sign to you that I have sent you: when you have brought forth the people out of Egypt, you shall worship God upon this mountain.

13 And Moses said to God, Behold, when I go to the children of Israel and say to them, The God of your fathers has sent me to you; and they shall say to me, What is his name? what shall I say to them?

14 And God said to Moses, I am AHIAH ASHAR HIGH (that is, THE LIVING GOD); and he said, Thus you shall say to the children of Israel: AHIAH has sent me to you.

15 And God said moreover to Moses, Thus shall you say to the children of Israel: The LORD God of your fathers, the God of Abraham, the God of Isaac, and the God of Jacob, has sent me to you; this is my name for ever, and this is my memorial to all generations.

16 Go and gather the elders of Israel together, and say to them, The LORD God of your fathers, the God of Abraham, of Isaac, and of Jacob, appeared to me, saying, I have surely remembered you and seen that which is done to you in Egypt;

17 And I have said, I will bring you up out of the affliction of the Egyptians to the land of the Canaanites, the Hittites, the Amorites, the Perizzites, the Hivites, and the Jebusites, to a land flowing with milk and honey.

18 And they shall hearken to your voice; and you and the elders of Israel shall go to the king of Egypt, and you shall say to him, The LORD God of the Hebrews has appeared to us; and now let us go three days' journey into the wilderness that we may sacrifice to the LORD our God.

19 ¶And I know that the king of Egypt will not let you go, except by force.

20 And I will stretch out my hand and smite the Egyptians with all kinds of wonders which I will do among them; and after that Pharaoh will let you go.

[1] A priestly title, meaning *His Excellency,* or *Reverend,* applied to Reuel.

21 And I will give this people favor in the sight of the Egyptians; and it shall come to pass that, when you go, you shall not go empty-handed;

22 But every woman shall borrow of her neighbor and of her that sojourns in her house, jewels of silver and jewels of gold and clothes; and you shall put them on your sons, and on your daughters; and you shall despoil the Egyptians.

CHAPTER 4

AND Moses answered and said, But, behold, they will not believe me, nor listen to my voice; for they will say, The LORD has not appeared to you.

2 And the LORD said to him, What is that in your hand? He said, A staff.

3 And the LORD said, Cast it on the ground. And he cast it on the ground, and it became a serpent; and Moses fled from before it.

4 And the LORD said to Moses, Put forth your hand and take it by the tail. And he put forth his hand and caught it, and it became a staff in his hand;

5 This is done that they may believe that the LORD God of their fathers, the God of Abraham, the God of Isaac, and the God of Jacob, has appeared to you.

6 ¶And the LORD said furthermore to him, again, Put now your hand into your bosom. And he put his hand into his bosom; and when he took it out, behold, his hand was leprous, as white as snow.

7 Then the LORD said to him, Put your hand back into your bosom again. And he put his hand back into his bosom; and when he took it out of his bosom, behold, it was clean like his other flesh.

8 And if they will not believe you, neither hearken to the voice of the first sign, they will believe the voice of the latter sign.

9 And if they will not believe also these two signs, neither listen to your voice, you shall take some of the water of the river and pour it upon the dry land; and the water which you take from the river shall become blood upon the dry land.

10 ¶And Moses said to the LORD, I beseech thee, O my LORD, I am not eloquent, neither heretofore nor since thou has spoken to thy servant; for I am a stutterer and slow of speech.

11 The LORD said to him, Who has made man's mouth? or who makes the dumb, or the deaf, or the seeing, or the blind? Is it not I the LORD?

12 Now therefore go, and I will be with your mouth and teach you what you shall speak.

13 And Moses said to him, O my LORD, send I beseech thee, by the hand of whomsoever thou wilt send.

14 And the anger of the LORD kindled against Moses, and he said to him, Behold, Aaron, your brother, the Levite. I know that he is a good speaker, and also, behold, he will come forth to meet you, and when he sees you, he will be glad in his heart.

15 And you shall speak to him and put my words in his mouth; and I will be with your mouth and with his mouth, and will teach you what you shall do.

16 And he shall be your spokesman to the people; and he shall be an interpreter for you, and you shall be to him instead of God.

17 And you shall take this staff in your hand, with which you shall do signs.

18 ¶And Moses returned, and went to Jethro his father-in-law, and said to him, Let me go and return to my brethren who are in Egypt and see whether they are still alive. And Jethro said to Moses, Go in peace.

19 And the LORD said to Moses in Midian, Go, return to Egypt; for all the men who sought your life are dead.

20 And Moses took his wife and his sons, and set them upon an ass, and started on his way back to Egypt; and he took the staff of God in his hand.

21 And the LORD said to Moses, When you return to Egypt, see that you perform all the wonders before Pharaoh which I have performed by your hand, but I will harden his heart

so that he will not let the people go.

22 And you shall say to Pharaoh, Thus says the Lord, Israel is my first-born son;

23 And I say to you, Let my son go, that he may serve me; and if you refuse to let him go, behold, I will slay your first-born son.

24 ¶And it came to pass when Moses was on his way to the inn that the Lord met him and sought to kill him.

25 Then Zipporah took a flint and cut off the foreskin of her son, and she fell down at the feet of the Lord and said, I have a bloody husband.

26 So the Lord let him go. Then she said, You are a bloody husband, because of the circumcision.

27 ¶And the Lord said to Aaron, Go into the wilderness to meet Moses. And he went and met him in the mountain of God, Horeb, and kissed him.

28 And Moses told Aaron all the words of the Lord, who had sent him, and all the signs which he had commanded him to perform.

29 ¶Then Moses and Aaron went and gathered together all the elders of the children of Israel;

30 And Aaron spoke all the words which the Lord had said to Moses, and performed the signs in the presence of the people.

31 And the people believed; and when they heard that the Lord had remembered the children of Israel, and that he had seen their affliction, then they knelt down and worshipped before the Lord.

CHAPTER 5

AND afterward Moses and Aaron went into the palace and told Pharaoh, Thus says the Lord God of Israel, Let my people go that they may hold a feast to me in the wilderness.

2 And Pharaoh said, Who is the Lord, that I should obey his voice to let Israel go? I do not know the Lord, neither will I let Israel go.

3 And they said, The Lord God of the Hebrews has appeared to us; now let us go three days' journey into the wilderness that we may sacrifice to the Lord our God; lest he fall upon us with the sword or with pestilence.

4 And the king of Egypt said to them, Wherefore do you, Moses and Aaron, cause the people to stop from their work? Go back to your tasks.

5 And Pharaoh said to them, Behold, the people of the land now are many, and you cause them to stop from their work.

6 And Pharaoh commanded the same day the taskmasters of the people and their scribes, saying,

7 You shall no more give the people straw to make bricks, as heretofore; let them go and gather straw for themselves.

8 But the number of bricks which they did make heretofore, you shall lay upon them; you shall not reduce the number thereof; for they are idle; that is why they cry, saying, Let us go and sacrifice to our God.

9 Let more work be assigned to the men, that they may be occupied, so that they may not think to engage in vain conversations.

10 ¶And the taskmasters of the people and their scribes went out and said to the people, Thus says Pharaoh, I will not give you straw.

11 Go, get straw for yourselves wherever you can find it; but your work shall not be reduced.

12 So the people were scattered throughout all the land of Egypt to gather the stubble.

13 And the taskmasters pressed them, saying, Complete your work as you have always done, as when straw was given to you.

14 And the scribes of the children of Israel, whom Pharaoh's taskmasters had appointed over them, were beaten, and demanded, Why have you not completed your quota of bricks both yesterday and today, as heretofore?

15 ¶Then the scribes of the children of Israel came and complained to Pharaoh, saying, Why are your servants treated in this manner?

16 There is no straw given to your servants, and yet they say to us, Make bricks: and, behold, your servants are

beaten; and you sin against your people.

17 But Pharaoh said to them, You are surely idle; therefore you say, Let us go and sacrifice to the LORD.

18 Go therefore now and work; and straw shall not be given you, yet you shall deliver the number of bricks.

19 And the scribes of the children of Israel saw that they were in a bad situation, for it was said to them, You must not reduce the number of your bricks, of your daily task.

20 ¶And they met Moses and Aaron standing opposite them, as they came out from the presence of Pharaoh;

21 And they said to them, May the LORD look upon you and judge; because you have made us to be in disfavor in the eyes of Pharaoh and in the eyes of his servants, to put a sword in their hands to kill us.

22 And Moses returned to the LORD and said, O my LORD, Why hast thou caused this people to be ill-treated? And why didst thou send me here?

23 For since the hour I came to Pharaoh to speak in thy name, he has ill-treated this people; and thou hast not delivered thy people at all.

CHAPTER 6

THEN the LORD said to Moses, Now you shall see what I will do to Pharaoh; for with a strong hand shall he let them go, and by a mighty arm shall he drive them out of his land.

2 And God spoke to Moses and said to him, I am the LORD,

3 Who appeared to Abraham, to Isaac, and to Jacob, by the name of God Almighty; but my name the LORD I did not make known to them.

4 And I have also established my covenant with them, to give them the land of Canaan, the land of their pilgrimage, wherein they dwelt.

5 And I have also heard the groaning of the children of Israel, whom the Egyptians keep in bondage; and I have remembered my covenant.

6 Therefore say to the children of Israel, I am the LORD your God, and I will bring you out from under the burdens of the Egyptians, and I will deliver you from their bondage, and I will save you by a strong hand and by a mighty arm and with great judgments;

7 And I will take you to me for a people, and I will be to you a God; and you shall know that I am the LORD your God, who brings you out from under the burdens of the Egyptians.

8 And I will bring you into the land concerning which I swore to give it to Abraham, to Isaac, and to Jacob; and I will give it to you for an inheritance; I am the LORD.

9 ¶And Moses spoke so to the children of Israel; but they did not listen to him, because of their misery and because of bondage.

10 And the LORD spoke to Moses, saying,

11 Go in, and speak to Pharaoh king of Egypt that he let the children of Israel go out of his land.

12 But Moses said to the LORD, Behold, the children of Israel have not hearkened to me; how then shall Pharaoh listen to me, for I am a stutterer?

13 And the LORD spoke to Moses and to Aaron and gave them a charge to the children of Israel and to Pharaoh king of Egypt to bring the children of Israel out of the land of Egypt.

14 ¶These are the heads of their fathers' houses: the sons of Reuben the first-born of Israel; Hanoch, and Pallu, Hezron, and Carmi; these are the families of Reuben.

15 And the sons of Simeon: Jemuel, Jamin, Ohar, Jachin, Zohar, and Shaul, the son of a Canaanitish woman; these are the families of Simeon.

16 ¶And these are the names of the sons of Levi according to their generations: Gershon, Kohath, and Merari; and the years of the life of Levi were a hundred and thirty-seven years.

17 The sons of Gershon: Libni, and Shimi, according to their families.

18 And the sons of Kohath: Amram, Izhar, Hebron, and Uzziel; and

the years of the life of Kohath were a hundred and thirty-three years.

19 The sons of Merari: Mahali and Mushi; these are the families of the Levites according to their generations.

20 And Amram took his uncle's daughter Jokhaber, and she bore him Aaron, Moses, and Miriam; and the years of the life of Amram were a hundred and thirty-seven years.

21 ¶And the sons of Izhar: Korah, Nepheg, and Zichri.

22 And the sons of Uzziel: Minshael, Elizphan, and Zithri.

23 And Aaron took to wife Elisabeth, the daughter of Amminadab, sister of Nehshon, and she bore him Nadab, Abihu, Eleazar, and Ithamar.

24 And the sons of Korah: Assir, Hilkanah, and Akensap; these are the families of the Korhites.

25 And Eleazar, Aaron's son, took him one of the daughters of Puntiel to wife; and she bore him Phinehas; these are the heads of the families of the Levites according to their tribes.

26 These are Moses and Aaron, to whom the LORD said, Bring out the children of Israel from the land of Egypt with all of their armies.

27 It was they who spoke to Pharaoh king of Egypt, to bring out the children of Israel from the land of Egypt: Moses and Aaron.

28 ¶And it came to pass on the day when the LORD spoke to Moses in the land of Egypt,

29 That the LORD spoke to Moses, and said to him, I am the LORD; speak to Pharaoh king of Egypt all that I say to you.

30 And Moses said to the LORD, My tongue stutters; how shall Pharaoh hearken to me?

CHAPTER 7

AND the LORD said to Moses, See, I have made you a god to Pharaoh;[1] and Aaron your brother shall be your prophet.

2 You shall speak all that I command you; and Aaron your brother shall speak to Pharaoh that he send the children of Israel out of his land.

3 And I will harden Pharaoh's heart, and multiply my signs and my wonders in the land of Egypt.

4 But Pharaoh will not hearken to you, that I may smite Egypt, and bring forth my hosts and my people the children of Israel out of the land of Egypt by great judgments.

5 And the Egyptians shall know that I am the LORD, when I lift up my hand against Egypt and bring out the children of Israel from among them.

6 And Moses and Aaron did as the LORD commanded them, so did they.

7 And Moses was eighty years old and Aaron eighty-three when they spoke to Pharaoh.

8 ¶And the LORD spoke to Moses and to Aaron, saying,

9 If Pharaoh should say to you, Show me a sign; then you shall say to Aaron, Take your staff and cast it down before Pharaoh, and it shall become a serpent.

10 ¶So Moses and Aaron went to Pharaoh, and they did as the LORD had commanded; and Aaron cast down his staff before Pharaoh and before his noblemen, and it became a serpent.

11 Then Pharaoh called the wise men and the magicians; now the magicians of Egypt, they also did the same with their magic.

12 For they cast down every man his staff and they became serpents; but Aaron's staff swallowed up their staffs.

13 However Pharaoh's heart was hardened, and would not let them go, as the LORD had said.

14 ¶Then the LORD said to Moses, Pharaoh's heart is hardened, he refuses to let the people go.

15 Go to Pharaoh in the morning; behold, he goes out to his daily duty; and you stand toward him by the river's brink and wait; and take in your hand the staff which was turned into a serpent.

16 And you shall say to him, The LORD God of the Hebrews has sent me to you, saying, Let my people go that they may serve me in the wilder-

[1] Given you power over Pharaoh.

ness; and, behold, hitherto you have not listened.

17 Thus says the LORD, By this you shall know that I am the LORD: behold, with the staff that is in my hand I will strike upon the waters of the river, and they shall be turned to blood.

18 And the fish that are in the river shall die, and the river shall stink; and the Egyptians shall loathe to drink of the water of the river.

19 ¶And the LORD said to Moses, Say to Aaron, Take your staff and lift up your hand upon the waters of Egypt, upon their rivers, upon their ponds, and upon all their pools of water, and upon the streams, and they shall become blood; and there shall be blood throughout all the land of Egypt, in both vessels of wood and vessels of stone.

20 And Moses and Aaron did as the LORD had commanded them; and Aaron lifted up the staff which was in his hand and smote the waters of the river, in the sight of Pharaoh and in the sight of his servants; and all the waters that were in the river were turned into blood.

21 And the fish that were in the river died; and the river stank, and the Egyptians could not drink the water of the river; and there was blood throughout all the land of Egypt.

22 And the magicians of Egypt did the same by their enchantments; but Pharaoh's heart was hardened and he did not listen to them, as the LORD had said.

23 And Pharaoh turned and went into his house, and he did not take to heart even this sign.

24 And all the Egyptians dug round about the river for water to drink; for they could not drink of the water of the river.

25 And seven days passed after the LORD had smitten the river.

CHAPTER 8

THEN the LORD said to Moses, Go to Pharaoh and say to him, Thus says the LORD, Let my people go that they may serve me.

2 And if you refuse to let them go, behold, I will smite all your borders with frogs;

3 And the river shall swarm with frogs, which shall come up and enter into your house and into your bedchamber and into your bed and into the houses of your servants and of your people and into your inner chambers and into your kneading troughs;

4 And the frogs shall come up both on you and on all your people.

5 ¶And the LORD said to Moses, Say to Aaron your brother, Lift up your hand with your staff over the rivers and over the streams and over the ponds, and cause frogs to come up upon the land of Egypt.

6 So Aaron lifted up his hand over the waters of Egypt; and the frogs came up and covered the land of Egypt.

7 And the magicians did the same with their enchantments, and brought up frogs upon the land of Egypt.

8 ¶Then Pharaoh called for Moses and Aaron and said to them, Pray to the LORD, that he may take away the frogs from me and from my people; and I will let the people go that they may sacrifice to the LORD.

9 And Moses said to Pharaoh, Appoint a time; when shall I pray for you and for your servants and for your people, to destroy the frogs from you and your house?

10 And he said to him, Tomorrow. And Moses said, Be it according to your word, that you may know that there is none like the LORD our God.

11 And the frogs shall depart from you and from your house and from your servants and from your people; they shall remain in the river only.

12 And Moses and Aaron went out from the presence of Pharaoh; and Moses prayed before the LORD because of the frogs which he had brought against Pharaoh.

13 And the LORD did according to the word of Moses; and the frogs died that were in the houses and in the courtyards and in the fields.

14 And they gathered them together in heaps; and the land stank.

15 And when Pharaoh saw that there was respite, he hardened his heart and would not listen to them, as the LORD had said to Moses.

16 ¶And the LORD said to Moses, Say to Aaron, Lift up your staff and smite the dust of the earth, that it may become lice throughout all the land of Egypt.

17 And he did so; and Aaron lifted up his hand with his staff and smote the dust of the earth, and it became lice on men and on cattle; all the dust of the land became lice throughout all the land of Egypt.

18 And the magicians did the same by means of their magic to bring forth lice, but they could not get rid of the lice; so there were lice on men and on cattle.

19 Then the magicians said to Pharaoh, This is the finger of God; and Pharaoh's heart was hardened, and he did not listen to them, as the LORD had said.

20 ¶And the LORD said to Moses, Rise up early in the morning and stand before Pharaoh; lo, he goes out again to his daily duty; and say to him, Thus says the LORD, Let my people go that they may serve me.

21 Else, if you will not let my people go, behold, I will send swarms of flies upon you and upon your people and upon your house; and the houses of the Egyptians shall be filled with swarms of flies, like a field when it is covered with them.

22 And I will set apart on that day the land of Goshen, in which my people dwell, that no swarms of flies shall be there, to the end that you may know that I am the LORD in the midst of the earth.

23 And I will put a division between my people and your people; tomorrow shall this sign be.

24 And the LORD did so; and he brought great swarms of flies into the house of Pharaoh and into his servants' houses and into all the land of Egypt; and the land was ruined by reason of the swarms of flies.

25 ¶Then Pharaoh called for Moses and for Aaron, and said to them, Go, sacrifice to your God within the land.

26 And Moses said, It is not proper to do so; for we shall sacrifice to the LORD our God some of the animals that are an abomination to the Egyptians. And if we should sacrifice animals that are idols before Egyptian eyes, they would stone us.

27 We will go three days' journey into the wilderness and sacrifice to the LORD our God, as he has commanded us.

28 And Pharaoh said, I will let you go that you may sacrifice to the LORD your God in the wilderness; only you shall not go very far away, and you must pray for me also.

29 And Moses said, Behold, I go out from your presence and I will pray before the LORD and he will cause the swarms of flies to depart from Pharaoh, from his servants, and from his people, tomorrow; but let not Pharaoh deal deceitfully any more by refusing to allow the people to go to sacrifice to the LORD.

30 So Moses went out from the presence of Pharaoh and prayed before the LORD.

31 And the LORD did according to the word of Moses; and he removed the swarms of flies from Pharaoh and from his servants and from his people; there remained not one.

32 And Pharaoh hardened his heart at this time also and did not let the people go.

CHAPTER 9

THEN the LORD said to Moses, Go to Pharaoh and say to him, Thus says the LORD God of the Hebrews, Let my people go that they may serve me.

2 For if you refuse to let them go (and until now you have withheld them),

3 Behold, the LORD will smite your cattle which are in the desert, the horses, the asses, the camels, the oxen, and the sheep; there shall be a very severe plague.

4 And the LORD will discriminate between the cattle of Israel and the cattle of the Egyptians, so that none of the cattle that belong to the children of Israel shall die, not even one.

5 And the LORD appointed a set time, saying, Tomorrow the LORD shall do this thing in the land.

6 And the LORD did that thing the next day, and all the cattle of the Egyptians died; but of the cattle of the children of Israel not one died.

7 And Pharaoh sent, and, behold, there was not one of the cattle of the Israelites dead. And the heart of Pharaoh was hardened and he did not let the people go.

8 ¶And the LORD said to Moses and to Aaron, Take two handfuls of the ashes of the furnace and let Moses scatter it toward the heaven in the sight of Pharaoh.

9 And it shall become fine dust in all the land of Egypt, and there shall be boils breaking forth with sores upon men, and upon cattle, throughout all the land of Egypt.

10 So they took ashes of the furnace and stood before Pharaoh; and Moses scattered it toward the heaven in the sight of Pharaoh; and it became blistering boils, breaking out with sores upon men, and upon cattle.

11 And the magicians could not stand before Moses because of the boils; for the boils had spread among the magicians and throughout all the land of Egypt.

12 And the LORD hardened the heart of Pharaoh and he did not listen to them, as the LORD had said to Moses.

13 ¶And the LORD said to Moses, Arise early in the morning, and stand before Pharaoh, and say to him, Thus says the LORD God of the Hebrews, Let my people go that they may serve me.

14 For this time I will send my plague on your heart and on your servants and on your people, that you may know that there is none like me in all the earth.

15 For now I will stretch out my hand that I may strike you and your people with pestilence; and you shall perish from the earth.

16 But for this cause have I raised you to the throne, to show you my power, and that my name may be declared throughout all the earth.

17 As yet you are continuing to detain this people and refusing to let them go.

18 Behold, tomorrow about this time I will cause a severe storm of hail, such as there has not been in Egypt from the day that it was founded even until now.

19 Send therefore now, and gather your cattle, and all that you have in the field; for upon every man and the cattle which be found in the field, and shall not be brought home, the hail shall come down upon them, and they shall die.

20 He who feared the word of the LORD among the servants of Pharaoh brought his servants and his cattle into the house.

21 But he who regarded not the word of the LORD left his servants and his cattle in the field.

22 ¶And the LORD said to Moses, Lift up your hand toward heaven that there may be hail in all the land of Egypt, upon men and upon cattle and upon all the grass in the field, throughout the land of Egypt.

23 And Moses lifted up his staff toward heaven; and the LORD sent thunder and hail, and lightning ran along on the ground; and the LORD showered hail upon the land of Egypt.

24 So there was hail, and flaming fire mingled with the hail, very grievous, such as had never been in all the land of Egypt since it became a nation.

25 And the hail smote throughout all the land of Egypt all that was in the field, both man and cattle; and the hail destroyed all the herbs of the field and broke every tree of the field.

26 Only in the land of Goshen, where the children of Israel dwelt, was there no hail.

27 ¶Then Pharaoh sent and called for Moses and Aaron, and said to them, I have sinned this time; the LORD is righteous, and I and my people are wicked.

28 Pray before the LORD, for there is yet a chance for forgiveness in his presence that there be no more mighty thunderings and hail; and I will let you go, and you shall stay no longer.

29 And Moses said to him, As soon as I am gone out of the city, I will stretch forth my hands to the LORD; and the thunder shall cease and there shall be no more hail, that you may know that the earth belongs to the LORD.

30 But as for you and your servants, I know that you have not yet feared the LORD God.

31 And the flax and the barley were lost; for the barley was in the ear and the flax was bolled.

32 But the wheat and the rye were not lost; for they were sown late.

33 And Moses went out of the city from the presence of Pharaoh, and spread out his hands to the LORD; and the thunders and hail ceased, and the rain was not poured upon the earth.

34 And when Pharaoh saw that the rain and the hail and the thunders had ceased, he sinned yet more, and his heart was hardened, and the heart of his servants.

35 And the heart of Pharaoh was hardened and he did not let the children of Israel go, as the LORD had sent word to him by Moses.

CHAPTER 10

AND the LORD said to Moses, Go in to Pharaoh; for I have hardened his heart and the hearts of his servants, that I may perform these signs among them,

2 That you may relate in the presence of your son and of your son's son the things which I have done to the Egyptians and the signs which I have performed among them, that you may know that I am the LORD.

3 And Moses and Aaron came to Pharaoh, and said to him, Thus says the LORD God of the Hebrews, How long will you refuse to fear me? Let my people go that they may serve me.

4 Else, if you refuse to let my people go, behold, tomorrow I will bring locusts upon all your domain;

5 And they shall cover the face of the land so that men cannot see the ground; and they shall eat the residue of that which is left to you from the hail and shall eat all the trees which

have budded for you in the field;

6 And they shall fill your houses and the houses of your servants and the houses of all the Egyptians such as neither your fathers nor your grandfathers have seen, from the day that they were upon the earth even to this day. And they turned, and went out from the presence of Pharaoh.

7 And Pharaoh's servants said to him, How long shall we suffer this disaster? Let the men go that they may serve the LORD their God; do you not yet know that Egypt is destroyed?

8 So Moses and Aaron were brought again to Pharaoh; and he said to them, Go, serve before the LORD your God; but who are they that are going?

9 And Moses said to him, We will go with our young and with our old, with our sons and with our daughters; with our flocks and with our herds will we go, for it is a festival of the LORD for all of us.

10 And Pharaoh said to them, Let the LORD be with you, but when I let you and your little ones go, look to it; perhaps you have evil intent.

11 Let it not be so; go now, the older men, and serve before the LORD; for it is the rest that you desire. And they were driven out from Pharaoh's presence.

12 ¶And the LORD said to Moses, Lift up your hand over the land of Egypt for the locusts, that they may come up upon the land of Egypt and eat the herbs of the land, even all that the hail has left.

13 And Moses lifted up his staff over the land of Egypt, and the LORD brought an east wind upon the land all that day and all that night; and when it was morning, the east wind brought the locusts.

14 And the locusts went up over all the land of Egypt and rested in all the domain of the Egyptians; it was a great swarm; before them there were no such swarms of locusts as they, neither after them shall be such.

15 For they covered the face of the whole earth so that the land was darkened; and they did eat all the herbs of the land and all the fruit of

the trees which the hail had left; and there remained no leaf on the trees, neither grass in the field, through all the land of Egypt.

16 ¶Then Pharaoh called for Moses and Aaron in haste; and he said to them, I have sinned against the LORD your God and against you.

17 Now therefore, forgive me my fault this time also, and pray before the LORD your God that he may remove from me this death.

18 And Moses went out from the presence of Pharaoh and prayed before the LORD.

19 And the LORD turned a mighty strong west wind, which took away the locusts and cast them into the Red Sea; there remained not one locust in all the domain of Egypt.

20 But the LORD hardened Pharaoh's heart so that he would not let the children of Israel go.

21 ¶Then the LORD said to Moses, Lift up your hand toward the heaven that there may be darkness over the land of Egypt, even thick darkness.

22 And Moses lifted up his hand toward heaven; and there was a thick darkness in all the land of Egypt three days;

23 They did not see one another, nor rose any from his place for three days; but all the children of Israel had light in their dwellings.

24 ¶And Pharaoh called to Moses and said to him, Go, serve before the LORD your God; only let your flocks and herds remain here; let your little ones also go with you.

25 Then Moses said to Pharaoh, You must give us also sacrifices and burnt offerings that we may sacrifice to the LORD our God.

26 Our cattle also shall go with us; there shall not an hoof be left behind; for thereof must we take to serve before the LORD our God; and we do not know what else we must offer to the LORD until we come there.

27 ¶But the LORD hardened Pharaoh's heart and he would not let them go.

28 And Pharaoh said to Moses, Get away from here, take heed to yourself, do not try to see my face again, for in the day that you see my face you shall die.

29 And Moses said, You have spoken well, I will not try to see your face any more.

CHAPTER 11

AND the LORD said to Moses, Yet will I bring one plague more upon Pharaoh, and upon the Egyptians; then I will let you go from here; when he shall let you go, then you must get out altogether.

2 Speak now in the presence of the people that they ask every man of his neighbor, and every woman of her neighbor, jewels of silver and jewels of gold.

3 And the LORD gave the people favor in the sight of the Egyptians. Moreover the man Moses was well honored in the land of Egypt in the sight of Pharaoh's servants and in the sight of the people.

4 And Moses said, Thus says the LORD, About midnight I will go forth into the midst of Egypt;

5 And all the first-born in the land of Egypt shall die, from the first-born of Pharaoh who sits on his throne even to the first-born of the maidservant who sits behind the mill; and all the first-born of the animals.

6 And there shall be a great wailing throughout all the land of Egypt, such as there was none like it, nor shall there be any like it any more.

7 But of the children of Israel no one shall be harmed, not even a dog shall bark against man or animals; that you may know that the LORD distinguishes between the Egyptians and Israel.

8 And all these your servants shall come down to me and bow down themselves to me, saying, Get out, both you and all the people that are with you; and after that I will go out. And Moses departed from the presence of Pharaoh in a great anger.

9 And the LORD said to Moses, Pharaoh shall not listen to you; that my wonders may be multiplied in the land of Egypt.

10 And Moses and Aaron did all

these wonders before Pharaoh; but the LORD hardened Pharaoh's heart so that he would not let the children of Israel go out of his land.

CHAPTER 12

THEN the LORD spoke to Moses and Aaron in the land of Egypt, saying,

2 This month shall be to you the beginning of months; it shall be the first month of the year to you.

3 ¶Speak to all the congregation of Israel, saying, On the tenth day of this month they shall take to themselves every man a lamb for his own household, and a lamb for his father's household;

4 And if the household is too little for the lamb, let him and his neighbor next to his house take it according to the number of the persons; every man according to the portion of his eating shall make your count for the lamb.

5 The lamb shall be without blemish, a male of the first year; you shall take it from the lambs or from the kids:

6 And you shall keep it until the fourteenth day of this same month; and the whole assembly of the congregation of Israel shall kill it at sunset.

7 And they shall take some of the blood thereof and sprinkle it on the two door posts and on the lintel and on the houses wherein they shall eat it.

8 And they shall eat the meat in that night, roasted with fire, with unleavened bread; and with bitter herbs they shall eat it.

9 You shall not eat any of it raw, nor cooked with water, but roasted with fire; its head with its legs, and the entrails thereof.

10 And you shall leave none of it remaining until morning; and that which remains of it until the morning you shall burn with fire.

11 ¶And thus you shall eat it; with your loins girded, your shoes on your feet, and your staff in your hand; and you shall eat it in haste; for it is the LORD's passover.

12 For I will pass through the land of Egypt this night, and all the firstborn of the land of Egypt shall die, both man and beast; and against all the idols of Egypt I will execute judgment; I am the LORD.

13 And the blood shall be to you for a sign upon the houses where you are; and when I see the blood, I will make you glad, and the plague shall not be among you to destroy you when I smite the land of Egypt.

14 And this day shall be to you for a memorial; and you shall keep it a feast to the LORD, a festival throughout your generations; you shall keep it a feast by an ordinance for ever.

15 Seven days you shall eat unleavened bread; and from the first day you shall put away leaven out of your houses; for whosoever eats leavened bread from your houses from the first day until the seventh day, that person shall perish from Israel.

16 On the first day there shall be a holy convocation and on the seventh day there shall be a holy convocation to you; no manner of work shall be done in them; except that which every man must eat, that only may be prepared by you.

17 And you shall observe the feast of unleavened bread; for on this very day have I brought your hosts out of the land of Egypt; therefore you shall observe this day throughout your generations by an ordinance for ever.

18 ¶In the first month, on the fourteenth day of the month at evening, you shall eat unleavened bread until the twenty-first day of the month at evening.

19 Seven days there shall be no leaven found in your houses; for whoever eats that which is leavened, that person shall perish from the congregation of Israel, whether he is a stranger or a native of the land.

20 You shall eat nothing leavened; in all your habitations you shall eat unleavened bread.

21 ¶Then Moses called all the elders of the children of Israel and said to them, Hasten, take lambs for your-

selves according to your families and kill the passover lamb.

22 And you shall take a bunch of hyssop and dip it in the blood of the lamb and sprinkle the lintel and the two side posts with the blood that is in the basin; and none of you shall go out of the door of his house until the morning.

23 For the LORD will pass through to smite the Egyptians; and when he sees the blood upon the lintel and on the two side posts, the LORD will bring joy to the doors and will not suffer the destroyer to come into your houses to smite you.

24 And you shall observe this rite and this ordinance for yourselves and your sons for ever.

25 And it shall come to pass, when you come to the land which the LORD will give you, as he has promised, you shall observe this service.

26 And it shall come to pass when your children shall say to you, What is the meaning of this service?

27 You shall say, It is the sacrifice of the LORD'S passover, who brought joy to the house of the children of Israel in Egypt when he smote the Egyptians and delivered our houses. Then the people bowed their heads and worshipped the LORD.

28 And the children of Israel went away and did as the LORD had commanded Moses and Aaron; so did they.

29 ¶And it came to pass that at midnight the LORD slew all the first-born in the land of Egypt, from the first-born of Pharaoh who sits on his throne to the first-born of the captive who was in the prison; and all the first-born of cattle.

30 And Pharaoh rose up in the night, he and all his servants and all the Egyptians; and there was a great wailing in the land of Egypt; for there was not a house where there was not one dead.

31 ¶And Pharaoh called Moses and Aaron that night, and said to them, Rise up and get out from among my people, both you and the children of Israel; and go, serve the LORD, as you have said.

32 Also take your flocks and your herds, as you have said, and be gone; and bless me also.

33 And the Egyptians urged the people, that they might get them out of the land of Egypt in haste; for they said, We shall all die.

34 And the people took their kneading dough before it was leavened and their cold kneading dough wrapped up in their mantles upon their shoulders.

35 And the children of Israel did according to the word of Moses; and they borrowed of the Egyptians jewels of silver and jewels of gold and clothing;

36 And the LORD gave the people favor in the sight of the Egyptians, so that they lent to them whatever they asked. And thus they stripped the Egyptians.

37 ¶Then the children of Israel journeyed from Rameses to Succoth, about six hundred thousand men on foot, besides the little ones.

38 And a mixed multitude went up also with them; and their flocks, and herds, and many cattle.

39 And they baked on a griddle unleavened bread of the dough which they had brought forth out of the land of Egypt, for it was not leavened; because the Egyptians drove them out, and they could not make it into flat loaves, neither had they prepared for themselves any provisions for the journey.

40 ¶Now the sojourning of the children of Israel, who dwelt in Egypt, was four hundred and thirty years.

41 And it came to pass at the end of the four hundred and thirty years, on this very day that all the hosts of the LORD went out from the land of Egypt.

42 It was a night to be observed to the LORD for bringing them out of the land of Egypt; therefore, this very night is to be observed to the LORD by all the children of Israel throughout their generations.

43 ¶Then the LORD said to Moses and Aaron, This is the ordinance of the passover; no foreigner shall eat of it;

44 But every man's servant who is bought for money, when you have circumcised him, then shall he eat of it.

45 An alien and a hired servant shall not eat thereof.

46 In one house shall it be eaten; you shall not take any of the meat outside of the house; neither shall you break a bone thereof.

47 All the congregation of Israel shall keep the feast.

48 And when a stranger shall sojourn with you who would keep the passover to the LORD, when he has circumcised every male in his household, then he may draw near to take part in it; and he shall be considered as a native of the land; for no uncircumcised person shall eat thereof.

49 There shall be one law for the natives and for the strangers who sojourn among you.

50 Thus did all the children of Israel; as the LORD had commanded Moses and Aaron, so did they.

51 And it came to pass on that very day that the LORD brought the children of Israel out of the land of Egypt with all their hosts.

CHAPTER 13

AND the LORD spoke to Moses, saying,

2 Sanctify to me every first-born that opens the womb among the children of Israel, both of men and of animals; for they are mine.

3 ¶And Moses said to the people, Remember this day in which you came out from Egypt, out of the house of bondage; for by a strong hand the LORD brought you out from this place; there shall no leavened bread be eaten on this day.

4 In this day you are going forth in the month of Abib.

5 ¶And it shall be when the LORD shall bring you into the land of the Canaanites, the Hittites, the Amorites, the Hivites, the Jebusites, and the Perizzites, which he swore to your fathers to give you, a land flowing with milk and honey, therefore you shall keep this service in this month.

6 Seven days you shall eat unleavened bread, and on the seventh day there shall be a festival to the LORD.

7 Unleavened bread shall you eat for seven days; and there shall no leavened bread be seen with you throughout all your territory.

8 ¶And you shall tell your son on that day, This is done because of what my God did for me when I came forth out of Egypt.

9 And it shall be to you for a sign, a token of remembrance upon your hand, and for a memorial between your eyes, so that the law of the LORD may be in your mouth; for with a strong hand has the LORD brought you out of Egypt.

10 You must therefore keep this ordinance and this law at its appointed time from year to year.

11 ¶And it shall be when the LORD brings you into the land of the Canaanites, as he swore to you and to your fathers, and shall give it to you,

12 You shall set apart to the LORD every first-born that opens the womb and every firstling that comes of the animals that you have; the males shall be the LORD's.

13 And every firstling male of the cattle you shall redeem with a lamb; but if you do not wish to. redeem it, then you must kill it: and every first-born of men among your sons you shall redeem.

14 ¶And it shall be when your son asks you in time to come, saying, What is this? You shall say to him, By a strong hand the LORD brought us out of Egypt from the house of bondage;

15 And it came to pass, when Pharaoh was stubborn, and would not let us go, the LORD slew all the first-born in the land of Egypt, from the first-born of man to the first-born of animals; that is why I sacrifice to the LORD all that open the womb, being males; but all the first-born of my sons I redeem.

16 And it shall be as a token on your hand and as a memorial between your eyes; for by a strong hand the LORD brought you out of Egypt.

17 ¶And it came to pass when Pharaoh had let the people go, God did

not lead them by the way of the land of the Philistines, although that was near; for God said, Lest the people be afraid when they see war, and return to Egypt:

18 But God led the people by the way of the wilderness by the Red Sea; and the children of Israel went up armed out of the land of Egypt.

19 And Moses took the bones of Joseph with him; for he had solemnly made the children of Israel to swear, saying, God will surely remember you; and you must carry up my bones from here with you.

20 ¶And they journeyed from Succoth and encamped at Etham, on the edge of the wilderness.

21 And the LORD went before them by day in a pillar of cloud, to lead them on the way; and by night in a pillar of fire, to give them light; so that they might travel by day and by night;

22 The pillar of cloud by day and the pillar of fire by night never failed to go before the people.

CHAPTER 14

THEN the LORD spoke to Moses, saying,

2 Speak to the children of Israel that they turn back and encamp by the inlet of Kheritha,[1] between Migdol and the sea, in front of Baal-zephon; opposite it shall you encamp by the sea.

3 For Pharaoh will say of the children of Israel, They are strangers in the land, the wilderness has shut them in.

4 And the LORD said to Moses, I will harden Pharaoh's heart, and he will pursue them; and I will triumph over Pharaoh, and over all his army; and the Egyptians shall know that I am the LORD. And they did so.

5 ¶And it was told the king of Egypt that the people had gone away; and the heart of Pharaoh and of his servants changed against the people, and they said, What have we done that we have let Israel go from serving us?

6 And he made ready his chariots and took his people with him:

7 And he took six hundred chosen chariots and all chariots of the Egyptians and warriors over every one of them.

8 And the LORD hardened the heart of Pharaoh, king of Egypt and he pursued the children of Israel; but the children of Israel had gone out victoriously.

9 And the Egyptians pursued after them, all the horses and chariots of Pharaoh, and his horsemen and his army, and overtook them encamping by the inlet of Kheritha, before Baal-zephon.

10 ¶And when Pharaoh drew near, the children of Israel lifted up their eyes and saw the Egyptians marching after them; and they were terribly afraid; and the children of Israel prayed before the LORD.

11 And they said to Moses, Is it because there were no graves in Egypt that you have taken us away to die in the wilderness? Why have you dealt thus with us, and brought us out of Egypt?

12 Is not this the word that we told you in Egypt, saying, Let us alone that we may serve the Egyptians? For it would have been better for us to serve the Egyptians than to die in this wilderness.

13 ¶And Moses said to the people, Fear not, wait, and see the salvation of the LORD, which he will perform for you today; for the Egyptians whom you have seen today, you shall see them again no more for ever.

14 The LORD will fight for you, and you shall hold your peace.

15 ¶And the LORD said to Moses, Why do you pray before me? Tell the children of Israel to go forward;

16 And as for you, lift up your staff and stretch out your hand over the sea and divide it; and the children of Israel shall go on dry ground through the sea.

17 And, behold, I will harden the hearts of the Egyptians, so that they shall follow them; and I will triumph

1 Dry at low tide.

over Pharaoh and over all his army, his chariots, and his horsemen.

18 And the Egyptians shall know that I am the LORD, when I have been triumphant over Pharaoh, over all his army, his chariots, and his horsemen.

19 ¶And the angel of God, who went before the camp of Israel, moved and went behind them; and the pillar of the cloud moved from before them and stood behind them:

20 And it came between the army of the Egyptians and the camp of Israel; and it was cloudy and dark all the night, but it gave light all the night to the children of Israel, so that they could not draw near one to another all the night.

21 And Moses lifted up his hand over the sea; and the LORD caused the sea to go back by a strong east wind all that night and made the sea dry land, and the waters were divided.

22 And the children of Israel went into the midst of the sea on the dry ground; and the waters were like a wall to them on their right hand and on their left.

23 ¶And the Egyptians pursued and went into the sea after them, all of Pharaoh's horses, his chariots, and his horsemen.

24 And it came to pass that in the morning watch the LORD appeared to the Egyptian army in a pillar of fire and of cloud, and threw the Egyptian army into confusion,

25 Thus clogging their chariot wheels that they drew heavily, so that the Egyptians said, Let us flee from before the house of Israel; for the LORD fights for them against Egypt.

26 ¶And the LORD said to Moses, Stretch out your hand over the sea that the waters may come back upon the Egyptians, upon their chariots and upon their horsemen.

27 And Moses lifted up his hand over the sea, and the sea returned to its place when the morning appeared; and the Egyptians fled against it; and the LORD overthrew the Egyptians in the midst of the sea.

28 And the waters returned, and covered the chariots and the horse-

men and all the host of Pharaoh that came into the sea after them; there remained not a single one of them.

29 But the children of Israel walked through the sea as if they were walking on the dry land; and the waters were like a wall to them on their right hand and on their left.

30 Thus the LORD saved Israel that day out of the hand of the Egyptians; and Israel saw the Egyptians lying dead upon the seashore.

31 And Israel saw that great work which the LORD did against the Egyptians; and the people feared the LORD, and believed the LORD and his servant Moses.

CHAPTER 15

THEN Moses and the children of Israel sang this song to the LORD, saying, I will sing to the LORD, for he has triumphed gloriously; the horse and his rider he has thrown into the sea.

2 He is mighty and glorious, The LORD JEHOVAH has become our Saviour; he is our God, and we will praise him; our father's God, and we will exalt him.

3 The LORD is a mighty warrior: the LORD is his name.

4 Pharaoh's chariots and his host he cast into the sea; his valiant men also are drowned in the Red Sea.

5 The depths have covered them; they sank to the bottom like stones.

6 Thy right hand, O LORD, has become glorious in power; thy right hand, O LORD, has defeated thy enemies.

7 And in the greatness of thy might thou hast overthrown them that hate thee; thou sentest thy wrath, and it consumed them like stubble.

8 And with the blast of thy nostrils the waters piled up, the floods stood up as if it were in sheepskins; the waves gathered in heaps in the heart of the sea.

9 The enemy said, I will pursue, I will overtake, I will divide the spoil; my soul will devour them; I will draw my sword, my hand shall destroy them.

10 Thou didst blow with thy wind,

the sea covered them; they sank as lead in the mighty waters.

11 Who is like unto thee, O LORD? Who is like unto thee, glorious in his holiness, revered and praised, doing wonders?

12 Thou didst lift up thy right hand, the earth swallowed them.

13 Thou in thy mercy hast led forth this people whom thou hast saved; thou hast guided them in thy strength to thy holy habitation.

14 The people heard and they trembled; fear took hold on the inhabitants of Philistia.

15 Then the princes of Edom were afraid; the mighty men of Moab, trembling seized them; all the inhabitants of Canaan were heartbroken.

16 Fear and dread shall fall upon them; by the greatness of thine arm they shall sink as stones, till thy people, O LORD, pass over; till this people whom thou hast saved pass over.

17 Thou shalt bring them in and plant them on the mountain of thine inheritance, in the place, O LORD, which thou hast made for thee to dwell in; even thy sanctuary, O LORD; establish it by thy hands.

18 The LORD shall reign for ever and ever.

19 For the horses of Pharaoh, with his chariots and his horsemen, went through the sea, and the LORD brought back the waters of the sea upon them; but the children of Israel walked on the dry land in the midst of the sea.

20 ¶Then Miriam the prophetess, the sister of Aaron, took a timbrel in her hand; and all the women went out after her with tambourines and with timbrels.

21 And Miriam answered them, Sing to the LORD, for he has triumphed gloriously; the horse and his rider he has thrown into the sea.

22 So Moses brought Israel from the Red Sea, and they went out into the wilderness of Shud; and they went three days in the wilderness, and found no water.

23 ¶And when they came to Morath,[1] they could not drink the waters of Morath, for they were bit-

ter; therefore the name of the place was called Morath.

24 And the people murmured against Moses, saying, What shall we drink?

25 And Moses prayed before the LORD; and the LORD showed him a tree, and when he cast it into the water, the water became sweet; there the LORD taught him laws and ordinances, and there he tested him,

26 And said to him, If you will diligently hearken to the voice of the LORD your God and will do that which is right in his sight and will obey his commandments and keep all his statutes, I will bring none of these plagues upon you which I have brought upon the Egyptians; for I am the LORD your Healer.

27 ¶And they came to Elim, where there were twelve springs of water and seventy palm trees; and they encamped there by the water.

CHAPTER 16

AND they journeyed from Elim, and the whole congregation of the children of Israel came to the wilderness of Seen, which is between Elim and Sinai, on the fifteenth day of the second month after their departure from the land of Egypt.

2 And the whole congregation of the children of Israel murmured against Moses and Aaron in the wilderness;

3 And the children of Israel said to them, Would that we had died by the hand of the LORD in the land of Egypt, when we sat by the pots of meat, and when we did eat bread to the full; for you have brought us forth into this wilderness to destroy the whole assembly of Israel with hunger.

4 ¶Then the LORD said to Moses, Behold, I will rain bread from heaven for you; and the people shall go out and gather sufficient food, day by day, for I will prove them, whether they will keep my laws or not.

5 And it shall come to pass that on the sixth day they shall prepare that which they bring in; and it shall be twice as much as they gather daily.

6 And Moses and Aaron said to all

[1] Bitter.

the children of Israel, At evening, then you shall know that the LORD has brought you out from the land of Egypt;

7 And in the morning, then you shall see the glory of the LORD; for your murmuring has been heard before the LORD; but as for us, what are we that you should murmur against us?

8 And Moses said, When the LORD shall give you in the evening meat to eat and in the morning bread to the full, then the LORD has heard your murmuring which you murmured against him; but as for us, what are we? Your murmurings are not against us but against the LORD.

9 ¶And Moses said to Aaron, Say to all the congregation of the children of Israel, Come near before the LORD; for he has heard your murmurings.

10 And it came to pass, as Aaron spoke to the whole congregation of the children of Israel, they turned their faces toward the wilderness, and, behold, the glory of the LORD appeared in the cloud.

11 ¶Then the LORD spoke to Moses, saying,

12 I have heard the murmurings of the children of Israel; say to them, At evening you shall eat meat, and in the morning you shall be filled with bread; and you shall know that I am the LORD your God.

13 And it came to pass that at evening the quails came up and covered the camp; and in the morning the dew lay round about the camp.

14 And when the dew that lay was gone up, behold, upon the face of the wilderness there lay a thin round crust, like the hoar frost on the ground.

15 And when the children of Israel saw it, they said one to another, Manna-ho? (What is it?) For they did not know what it was. And Moses said to them, This is the bread which the LORD has given you to eat.

16 ¶This is the thing which the LORD has commanded, Gather of it every man according to his eating, an omer for every man, according to the number of your persons; each man shall take it for those in his tent.

17 And the children of Israel did so, and gathered, some more, some less.

18 And when they measured it with an omer, he that gathered much had nothing over, and he that gathered little had no lack; they gathered every man according to his eating.

19 And Moses said to them, Let no man leave of it till the morning.

20 Notwithstanding they listened not to Moses; but some of them left of it until the morning, and it bred worms and stank; and Moses was angry with them.

21 And they gathered it every morning, every man according to his eating; and when the sun grew hot, it melted.

22 ¶And it came to pass that on the sixth day they gathered twice as much bread, two omers for one person; and all the elders of the congregation came and told Moses.

23 Moses said to them, This is what the LORD has said, Tomorrow is a day of holy rest, a sabbath to the LORD; bake that which you will bake today, and cook what you will cook; and that which is left over, keep it cold for yourselves until the morning.

24 So they left over some of it till the morning, as Moses had commanded them; and it did not stink, neither was there any worm in it.

25 And Moses said to them, Eat it today; for today is a sabbath to the LORD; today you shall not find it in the field.

26 Six days you shall gather it; but on the seventh day, which is the sabbath, in it there shall be none.

27 ¶And it came to pass that there went out some of the people on the seventh day to gather, and they found none.

28 And the LORD said to Moses, How long will you refuse to keep my commandments and my laws?

29 See, for the LORD has given you the sabbath, therefore he gives you on the sixth day bread for two days; abide every man in his place; let no man go out of his house on the seventh day.

30 So the people rested on the seventh day.

31 And the children of Israel called the name thereof manna; and it was like coriander seed, white; and the taste of it was like honeycomb.

32 ¶And Moses said, This is the thing which the LORD has commanded, Fill an omer to be kept for your generations, that they may see the bread with which I have fed you in the wilderness when I brought you forth from the land of Egypt.

33 And Moses said to Aaron, Take a pot, and put an omer full of manna therein, and lay it before the LORD, to be kept for your generations.

34 As the LORD commanded Moses, so Aaron laid it up as a testimony, to be kept.

35 And the children of Israel did eat manna for forty years until they came to an inhabited land; they did eat manna until they reached the border of the land of Canaan.

36 Now an omer is the tenth of an ephah.

CHAPTER 17

AND the whole congregation of the children of Israel journeyed from the wilderness of Seen, after their journeys, according to the command of the LORD, and camped at Rephidim; and there was no water for the people to drink.

2 Wherefore the people quarreled with Moses, and said to him, Give us water that we may drink. And Moses said to them, Why do you quarrel with me? Why do you tempt the LORD?

3 And the people thirsted there for water; and they murmured against Moses, and said to him, Why did you bring us up out of Egypt, to kill us and our children and our cattle with thirst?

4 And Moses prayed to the LORD, saying, What shall I do with this people? They were almost ready to stone me.

5 And the LORD said to Moses, Go on before the people and take with you some of the elders of Israel; and your staff with which you smote the river, take it in your hand and go.

6 Behold, I will stand before you there on the flinty rock at Horeb, and you shall strike the flinty rock, and there shall gush water out of it, that the people may drink. And Moses did so in the sight of the elders of Israel.

7 And he called the name of the place Nassah and Meribah, because of the quarreling of the children of Israel, and because they tested the LORD, saying, Let us see if the LORD is among us or not?

8 ¶Then came Amalek to fight with Israel at Rephidim.

9 And Moses said to Joshua, Choose for yourself men, and go out, fight with Amalek tomorrow; and I will stand on the top of the hill with the staff of God in my hand.

10 So Joshua did as Moses had said to him, and he went to fight with Amalek; and Moses, Aaron, and Hur went up to the top of the hill.

11 And it came to pass, when Moses lifted up his hand, Israel prevailed; and when he let down his hands, Amalek prevailed.

12 But Moses' hands became tired; so they took a stone and put it under him, and he sat upon it; and Aaron and Hur supported his hands, the one on one side, and the other on the other side; and his hands were steady until the going down of the sun.

13 And Joshua defeated Amalek with the edge of the sword.

14 Then the LORD said to Moses, Write this for a memorial in a book and place it before Joshua; for I will utterly blot out the remembrance of Amalek from under heaven.

15 And Moses built an altar, and called the name of it Jehovah-nasi:

16 For he said, Behold, as the LORD has sworn, the LORD will fight with Amalek from generation to generation.

CHAPTER 18

AND Jethro, the priest of Midian, Moses' father-in-law, heard of all that God had done for Moses and for

Israel his people, and that the LORD had brought the children of Israel out of Egypt;

2 Then Jethro, Moses' father-in-law, took his daughter Zipporah, Moses' wife, after he had sent her back,

3 And her two sons; of whom the name of the one was Gershon; for he said, I have been an alien in a foreign land;

4 And the name of the other was Eliezer; For the God of my fathers, said he, was my help, and delivered me from the sword of Pharaoh;

5 And Jethro, Moses' father-in-law, came with his sons and his wife to Moses in the wilderness, where he encamped at the mountain of God;

6 And Moses was told, Behold, your father-in-law Jethro has come to you with your wife and your two sons accompanying him,

7 ¶And Moses went out to meet his father-in-law, and did obeisance and kissed him, and they asked each other of their welfare; and they went into the tent.

8 And Moses told his father-in-law all that the LORD had done to Pharaoh and the Egyptians for Israel's sake, and all the travail that they had suffered on the journey, and how the LORD had delivered them.

9 And Jethro rejoiced for all the goodness which the LORD had done to Israel, because he had delivered them out of the hand of the Egyptians and out of the hand of Pharaoh.

10 And Jethro said, Blessed be the LORD, who has delivered you out of the hand of the Egyptians and out of the hand of Pharaoh, for he has delivered his people from under the rule of the Egyptians.

11 Now I know that the LORD is greater than all gods; for despite the counsel which the Egyptians had devised against them, he triumphed over them.

12 And Jethro, Moses' father-in-law, offered burnt offerings and sacrifices to the LORD; and Aaron came, and all the elders of Israel, to eat bread with Moses' father-in-law before God.

13 ¶And it came to pass the next day that Moses sat to judge the peo-ple; and the people stood by Moses from morning to evening.

14 And when Moses' father-in-law saw all that he did for the people, he said to him, What is this thing that you are doing for the people? Why do you sit in judgment all alone, and all the people stand by you from morning to evening?

15 And Moses said to his father-in-law, Because the people come to me to inquire of God;

16 And when they have a controversy, they come to me; and I judge between one and another, and I make them know the statutes of God and his laws.

17 And Moses' father-in-law said to him, The thing that you are doing is not good.

18 You will surely wear yourself out, both you, and all this people that is with you; for this thing is too heavy for you; you are not able to do it alone.

19 Listen now to my voice, I will give you counsel, and God shall be with you; you must become a teacher from God to the people, to bring their disputes before God;

20 And you shall warn them to keep the ordinances and laws that you may show them how to conduct themselves and the works that they must do.

21 Moreover you shall provide out of all the people able men who fear God, truthful men who hate bribes and deceit; and appoint such over them to be officers of thousands, of hundreds, of fifties, and of tens.

22 Let them judge the people at all times; and when they have an important matter, let them come to you; but every small matter they shall judge for themselves; so it shall be easier for you, and they shall bear the burden with you.

23 If you shall do this thing, and God commands you so, then you shall be able to endure, and all this people shall also go each one to his own house in peace.

24 So Moses listened to the voice of his father-in-law, and did all that he had told him.

25 And Moses chose able men out of all Israel, and appointed them officers over the people, officers of thousands, of hundreds, of fifties, and of tens.

26 And they judged the people at all times; the hard cases they brought to Moses, but every small matter they judged themselves.

27 ¶Then Moses let his father-in-law depart, and he went to his own land.

CHAPTER 19

IN the third month after the departure of the children of Israel out of the land of Egypt, on the same day they came to the wilderness of Seen.

2 Then they journeyed from Rephidim and came to the wilderness of Sinai, and they encamped in the wilderness; and there Israel camped before the mountain.

3 And Moses went up to God, and God called to him out of the mountain and said to him, Thus shall you say to the house of Jacob, and tell the children of Israel,

4 You have seen what I did to the Egyptians, and how I bore you as though you were on eagles' wings and brought you to myself.

5 Now therefore, if you will obey my voice indeed and keep my covenant, then you shall be my beloved ones above all peoples, for all the earth is mine;

6 And you shall be to me a kingdom and priests and an holy people. These are the words which you shall speak to the children of Israel.

7 ¶And Moses came and called for the elders of the people, and said in their presence all these words which the LORD commanded him.

8 And all the people answered together and said, All that the LORD has spoken we will do. And Moses returned the words of the people to the LORD.

9 And the LORD said to Moses, Lo, I am coming to you in a thick cloud, that the people may hear when I speak with you and also believe you for ever. And Moses told the words of the people before the LORD.

10 ¶And the LORD said to Moses, Go to the people and sanctify them today and tomorrow, and let them wash their clothes,

11 And be ready by the third day; for on the third day the LORD will come down in the sight of all the people upon mount Sinai.

12 And you shall publish a warning among the people, saying, Take heed to yourselves, neither go up into the mountain, nor draw near to the border of it; whoever draws near to the mountain shall be put to death:

13 No hand shall touch it, but he shall surely be stoned and hurled down; whether it be beast or man, it shall not live; when the trumpet is silent, then you are permitted to ascend the mountain.

14 ¶And Moses went down from the mountain to the people and sanctified the people; and they washed their clothes.

15 And he said to the people, Be ready on the third day; do not touch your wives.

16 ¶And it came to pass on the third day in the morning that there were thunders and lightnings and a thick cloud appeared upon the mountain and the sound of the trumpet exceedingly loud; so that all the people that were in the camp trembled.

17 Then Moses brought forth the people out of the camp to meet God; and they stood at the base of the mountain.

18 And the whole mountain of Sinai was smoking because the LORD descended upon it in fire; and the smoke thereof ascended like the smoke of a furnace, and the whole mountain quaked greatly.

19 And when the blast of the trumpet sounded long and grew louder and louder, Moses spoke, and God answered him by a voice.

20 And the LORD came down upon mount Sinai, to the very top of the mountain; and the LORD called Moses up to the top of the mountain; and Moses went up.

21 And the LORD said to Moses, Go

down, warn the people, lest they break through to the LORD to gaze, and many of them perish.

22 And let the priests also who come near to the LORD sanctify themselves, lest the LORD break forth upon them.

23 And Moses said to the LORD, The people cannot come up to mount Sinai; for thou didst warn us, saying, Set bounds about the mountain and sanctify it.

24 And the LORD said to him, Hasten, go down, and then come up, you, and Aaron your brother with you; but let not the priests and the people break through to come up before the LORD, lest he kill them.

25 So Moses went down to the people and told them.

CHAPTER 20

AND God spoke all these words, saying,

2 I am the LORD your God, who brought you out of the land of Egypt, out of the house of bondage.

3 You shall have no other gods except me.

4 You shall not make for yourself any graven image, or any likeness of anything that is in heaven above or that is in the earth beneath or that is in the water under the earth;

5 You shall not worship them nor serve them; for I the LORD your God am a zealous God, visiting the offenses of the fathers upon their children to the third and fourth generations of those who hate me;

6 And showing mercy to thousands of generations of those who love me and keep my commandments.

7 You shall not take a false oath in the name of the LORD your God; for the LORD will not declare him innocent who takes an oath in his name falsely.

8 Remember the sabbath day to keep it holy.

9 Six days shall you labor and do all your work;

10 But the seventh day is a sabbath to the LORD your God; in it you shall not do any work, you, nor your son, nor your daughter, nor your manservant, nor your maidservant, nor your cattle, nor the sojourner who dwells in your towns;

11 For in six days the LORD made heaven and earth, the seas, and all things that are in them, and rested on the seventh day; therefore the LORD blessed the sabbath day and sanctified it.

12 ¶Honor your father and your mother, that your days may be long upon the land which the LORD your God gives you.

13 You shall not kill.

14 You shall not commit adultery.

15 You shall not steal.

16 You shall not bear false witness against your neighbor.

17 You shall not covet your neighbor's house, you shall not covet your neighbor's wife, nor his manservant, nor his maidservant, nor his ox, nor his ass, nor anything that is your neighbor's.

18 ¶And all the people observed the thunderings and the lightning flashes and the sound of the trumpet and the mountain smoking; and when the people saw all of this, they were afraid and they stood afar off.

19 And they said to Moses, You speak to us, and we will listen; but let not God speak with us, lest we die.

20 And Moses said to the people, Fear not; for God is come to prove you, that his worship may be before your faces, and that you may not sin.

21 And the people stood afar off, and Moses drew near to the thick darkness where God was.

22 ¶And the LORD said to Moses, Thus you shall say to the children of Israel, You have seen that I have talked with you from heaven.

23 You shall not make for yourselves gods of gold to be worshipped along with me, neither shall you make for yourselves gods of silver.

24 ¶An altar of earth shall you make to me, and you shall sacrifice on it your burnt offerings and your peace offerings, your sheep and your oxen; in every place where I shall make a memorial to my name I will come to you and I will bless you.

25 And if you make me a stone altar, you shall not build it of hewn stones; for if you lift a tool of iron upon it, you will have polluted it.
26 Neither shall you go up by steps to my altar, that your nakedness be not exposed [1] on it.

CHAPTER 21

NOW these are the judgments which you shall set before them.
2 When you buy a Hebrew servant, six years he shall serve you; and in the seventh year he shall go out free from your house without price.
3 If he came in single, he shall go out single; if he were married, then his wife shall go out with him.
4 If his master has given him a wife and she has borne him sons or daughters, the wife and her children shall be his master's and he shall go out alone.
5 And if the servant shall say, I love my master, my wife, and my children; I will not go out free;
6 Then his master shall bring him to the judges; he shall also bring him to the door, or to the door post; and his master shall bore his ear through with an awl; and he shall serve him for ever.
7 ¶And when a man sells his daughter to be a maidservant, she shall not go out free as the menservants do.
8 If her master hates her, so that he will not take her to himself as a wife, then he shall let her be redeemed; he shall have no authority to sell her to a foreign people, because he has dealt deceitfully with her.
9 And if he takes her for wife to his son, then he shall deal with her after the manner of daughters.
10 If he takes to himself another wife, he shall not diminish her food, her clothes, and her conjugal rights.
11 And if he does not these three things to her, then she shall go out free without price.
12 ¶He who strikes a man so that he dies shall surely be put to death.
13 But if he did not lie in wait for him, but God delivered him into his hand, then I will appoint for you a place to which he may flee.
14 But if a man ventures to attack his neighbor and slay him treacherously, you shall take him even from my altar to put him to death.
15 ¶He who strikes his father or his mother shall surely be put to death.
16 ¶He who steals a person and sells him, or he is found in his possession, he shall surely be put to death.
17 ¶He who curses his father or his mother shall surely be put to death.
18 ¶And if two men quarrel, and one strikes another with a stone or with his fist, and he does not die but is put to bed from the injury:
19 If he rises again and walks in the street with his staff, then the one who struck him shall be acquitted, except that he shall pay for the loss of his time and the physician's fee.
20 ¶And if a man strikes his servant, or his maid with a staff, and dies under his hand, he shall surely be punished.
21 But if the victim is well after a day or two, he shall not be punished; for he is his property.
22 ¶If two men quarrel, and strike a woman with child so that she miscarries, and yet no mischief follow; he shall surely pay a fine such as the woman's husband will lay upon him; and he shall pay as the judges determine.
23 But if any mischief follow, then you shall give life for life,
24 Eye for eye, tooth for tooth, hand for hand, foot for foot,
25 Burning for burning, wound for wound, slap for slap.
26 ¶And if a man strike the eye of his servant or the eye of his maid, and injure it, he shall let him go free for his eye's sake.
27 And if he knocks out the tooth of his manservant or the tooth of his maidservant, he must let him go free for his tooth's sake.
28 ¶If an ox gores a man or a woman that he or she die; then the ox shall be surely stoned and its meat shall not be eaten; but the owner of the ox shall be blameless.

[1] Undergarments, such as we have today, were not worn then.

29 But if the ox were known to be in the habit of goring in the past, and its owner has been warned, and he has not kept it in, and it kills a man or a woman; the ox shall be stoned, and its owner also shall be put to death.

30 But if a sum of money is imposed on him, then he shall give for the ransom of his life whatever they ask from him.

31 Whether the ox has gored a son or a daughter, according to this judgment it shall be done to him.

32 If the ox gores a manservant or a maidservant, the owner shall give to their master thirty shekels of silver and the ox shall be stoned.

33 ¶And if a man shall open a wheat pit or a man shall dig a well, and not cover them, and an ox or an ass fall into it;

34 The owner of the pit shall pay money to the owner of the animal, and the dead animal shall be his.

35 ¶And if one man's ox gores another man's ox so that it dies; then they shall sell the live ox and divide the money; and the dead ox also they shall divide.

36 But if it be known that the ox has been in the habit of goring, and his owner has not kept it in; he shall surely pay ox for ox; and the dead animal shall belong to him.

CHAPTER 22

IF a man shall steal an ox or a ewe, and kill it, or sell it; he shall restore five oxen for an ox and four ewes for a ewe.

2 ¶If a thief is found breaking into a house and is wounded so that he dies, there is no penalty for bloodshed.

3 But if the sun be risen upon him, there shall be blood penalty for him; and he should make full restitution; if he has nothing, then he shall be sold for his theft.

4 If the animal is found in his possession alive, whether it is an ox or an ass, or a ewe, he shall restore double.

5 ¶If a man shall cause a field or a vineyard to be eaten, and shall let his cattle loose to feed in another man's field, of the best of his own field and of the best of his own vineyard, he shall make restitution.

6 ¶If fire breaks out and catches in the thorns so that the shocks of grain or the standing wheat or the field is consumed, he who kindled the fire shall surely make restitution.

7 ¶If a man shall deliver to his neighbor money or stuff to keep and it is stolen out of the man's house, if the thief is found, let him pay double.

8 If the thief is not found, then the master of the house shall be brought to the judges to see whether he had a hand in the theft of his neighbor's goods.

9 For all manner of trespass, whether it be for an ox for an ass for a lamb for clothing or for any manner of lost thing which another man claims to be his, the case of both parties shall come before the judges; and whomever the judges shall convict, he shall make two-fold restitution to his neighbor.

10 If a man delivers to his neighbor an ass or an ox or a lamb or any kind of animal to keep; and it dies or is hurt or taken away in plunder and no man saw it;

11 Then there shall be an oath of the Lord between them both, that he had no hand in the theft of his neighbor's property; and the owner of it shall accept the oaths and he shall not make restitution.

12 But if it is stolen from him, he shall make restitution to the owner thereof.

13 If it is torn in pieces, then let him bring it as evidence, and he shall not make good that which was torn.

14 ¶And if a man borrow of his neighbor an animal, and it dies or it is injured, the owner thereof not being with it, he shall surely make restitution.

15 But if the owner thereof is with it, he shall not make restitution; and if it was hired, it came for its hire.

16 ¶And if a man entices a virgin who is not betrothed, and lies with her, he shall surely marry her.

17 If her father refuses to give her to him, he shall pay money according to the dowry of a virgin.

18 ¶You shall not suffer a witch to live.

19 ¶Whoever lies with an animal shall surely be put to death.

20 ¶He who sacrifices to idols shall be utterly destroyed; but to the LORD alone shall he sacrifice.

21 ¶You shall neither harm a stranger nor oppress him; for you were strangers in the land of Egypt.

22 ¶You shall not harm any widow or orphan.

23 If you harm them, and they pray before me, I will surely hear their prayer;

24 And my wrath shall kindle, and I will kill you with the sword; and your wives shall become widows and your children fatherless.

25 ¶If you lend money to any of my people who are the poor among you, you shall not be to him as an usurer, neither shall you take any usury from him.

26 If you at all take your neighbor's clothes as a pledge, you must give them back to him by sunset;

27 For they are his only covering, it is his raiment for his body; with what shall he sleep? And if he prays before me, I will hear him; for I am compassionate.

28 ¶You shall not revile the judge nor curse the ruler of your people.

29 ¶You shall not delay to offer the first fruits of the harvest of your threshing floor, and of your wine press; the first-born of your sons you shall give to me.

30 Likewise you shall do with your oxen and with your sheep: seven days it shall be with its dam; on the eighth day you shall give it to me.

31 ¶And you shall be holy men to me; neither shall you eat any flesh that has been torn by beasts in the field; you shall throw it to the dogs.

CHAPTER 23

YOU shall not confirm a false report; do not stretch out your hand taking oaths with the guilty to become a false witness for him.

2 ¶You shall not follow a multitude to do evil; neither shall you testify in a lawsuit so as to pervert justice, in order to side with a multitude which deviates from justice.

3 ¶Neither shall you be partial to a poor man in his lawsuit.

4 ¶If you meet your enemy's ox or his ass going astray, you shall surely bring it back to him again.

5 If you should see the ass of your enemy lying under its burden, and you are unwilling to help him lift it up, you should surely help him to lift it up nevertheless.

6 You shall not pervert the justice due to a poor man in his lawsuit.

7 Keep far from a false matter; and the innocent and righteous you shall not slay; for I will not justify the wicked.

8 ¶And you shall take no bribe; for a bribe blinds the eyes of the wise in judgment and perverts the words of the righteous.

9 ¶You shall not oppress strangers; for you know the life of a stranger; you were strangers in the land of Egypt.

10 For six years you shall sow your land and shall gather in the crops thereof:

11 But the seventh year you shall leave it fallow, so that the poor of your people may eat of the fruits of it; and what is left the wild beasts may eat. You shall do in like manner with your vineyard and with your olive yard.

12 Six days you shall do your work, and on the seventh day you shall rest, that your ox and your ass may rest and the son of your handmaid; and that the stranger in your towns may be refreshed.

13 Take heed of all things that I have said to you; and make no mention of the name of false idols, neither think of them.

14 ¶Three times in the year you shall celebrate a festival for me.

15 You shall keep the festival of the unleavened bread (you shall eat unleavened bread for seven days, as I commanded you, at the time appointed of the month of Abib; for in

the month of Abib you came out of the land of Egypt; you shall not appear before me without a gift offering:)

16 And the festival of the harvest, the first fruits of your grain which you sow in the field; and the festival of the ingathering, which is at the end of the year, when you have gathered your crop from the field.

17 Three times in the year all your gift offerings shall appear before the LORD your God.

18 You shall not offer the blood of a sacrifice with leavened bread; neither shall the fat of the festival sacrifices remain until morning.

19 The best of the first fruits of your land you shall bring into the house of the LORD your God. You shall not cook the meat of a kid in its mother's milk.

20 ¶Behold, I send an angel before you to guard you on the way and to bring you into the land which I have prepared.

21 Heed him and obey his voice; do not strive against him; perhaps he will not pardon your transgressions; for my name is upon him.

22 But if you shall indeed obey his voice and do all that he says to you, then I will hate those who hate you and oppress your enemies.

23 For my angel shall go before you and bring you against the Amorites and the Hittites and the Perizzites and the Canaanites and the Hivites and the Jebusites; and I will destroy them.

24 You shall not worship their gods nor serve them nor do after their works; but you shall utterly overthrow them and break down their statues.

25 And you shall serve the LORD your God, and he shall bless your bread and your water; and I will take sickness away from your houses.

26 ¶There shall nothing cast their young nor be barren in your land; the number of your days I will fulfil.

27 I will send my fear before you and will destroy all the peoples against whom you shall go to war, and I will make all your enemies flee from you.

28 And I will send fierce armies before you, and will destroy the Canaanites and the Hittites from before you.

29 I will not destroy them from before you in one year, lest the land become desolate and the wild beasts multiply against you.

30 Little by little I will destroy them before you, till you become strong and inherit the land.

31 And I will set your boundaries from the Red Sea as far as the sea of the Philistines, and from the desert to the river Euphrates; for I will deliver the inhabitants of the land into your hands; and you shall destroy them.

32 You shall make no covenant with them, nor with their idols.

33 They shall not dwell in your land, lest they make you sin before me; you shall not serve their gods, lest they be a stumbling block to you.

CHAPTER 24

AND he said to Moses, Come up to the LORD, you and Aaron, Nadab and Abihu, and seventy of the elders of Israel; and you shall worship afar off.

2 And Moses alone shall come near the LORD; but they shall not draw near; neither shall the people come up with him.

3 ¶And Moses came and told the people all the words of the LORD and all the ordinances; and all the people answered with one voice, and said, Everything which the LORD has said we will do.

4 And Moses wrote all the words of the LORD, and rose up early in the morning and built an altar at the foot of the mountain, and twelve pillars, according to the twelve tribes of Israel.

5 And he sent young men of the children of Israel, who offered burnt offerings and sacrificed peace offerings of oxen to the LORD.

6 And Moses took half of the blood, and put it into basins; and half of the blood he sprinkled on the altar.

7 And he took the book of the covenant and read it in the presence of the people; and they said, All that

the LORD has said we will obey and do.

8 And Moses took the blood and sprinkled it on the people and said, This is the blood of the covenant which the LORD has made with you concerning all these words.

9 ¶Then Moses and Aaron, Nadab and Abihu, and seventy of the elders of Israel went up;

10 And they saw the God of Israel; and there was under his feet as it were a paved work of sapphire stone, clear as the color of the sky.

11 And he did not harm the elders of the children of Israel; and they saw God, and ate and drank.

12 ¶And the LORD said to Moses, Come up to me to the mountain, and present yourself there; and I will give you tablets of stone, and the laws and commandments which I have written; that you may teach them.

13 And Moses rose up and his minister Joshua; and Moses went up to the mountain of God.

14 And he said to the elders, You wait here for us until we return to you; and, behold, Aaron and Hur are with you; whoever has a problem, let him come to them.

15 And Moses went up to the mountain, and a cloud covered the mountain.

16 And the glory of the LORD rested upon mount Sinai, and the cloud covered it for six days; and on the seventh day the LORD called to Moses out of the midst of the cloud.

17 And in the sight of all the children of Israel he saw the glory of the LORD like a burning fire on the top of the mountain.

18 And Moses went into the midst of the cloud and went up to the mountain; and Moses was in the mountain forty days and forty nights.

CHAPTER 25

AND the LORD spoke to Moses, saying,

2 Speak to the Israelites to set aside an offering for me; of every man that gives it willingly with his heart you shall take an offering.

3 And this is the offering which you shall take of them: gold, silver, and brass,

4 Blue, purple, and scarlet, fine linen, and goats' hair,

5 And rams' skins dyed red, skins dyed with vermilion, and shittim wood,

6 Oil for the lamps, spices for anointing oil, and for sweet incense,

7 Onyx stones, and precious stones to be set in the ephod and in the breastplate.

8 And let them make me a sanctuary, that I may dwell among them.

9 According to all that I show you, after the pattern of the tabernacle and the pattern of all the vessels thereof, even so shall you make it.

10 ¶And they shall make an ark of shittim wood, two and a half cubits long, and a cubit and a half broad, and a cubit and a half high.

11 And you shall overlay it with pure gold, without and within shall you overlay it, and shall make upon it a crown of gold round about.

12 And you shall cast four rings of gold for it, and put them in the four corners thereof; and two rings on the one side of it, and two rings on the other side of it.

13 And you shall make poles of shittim wood, and overlay them with gold.

14 And you shall put the poles into the rings by the sides of the ark, that the ark may be borne with them.

15 The poles shall remain in the rings of the ark; they shall never be taken out of them.

16 And you shall put into the ark the testimony which I shall give you.

17 And you shall make a mercy seat of pure gold, two and a half cubits long, and a cubit and a half broad.

18 And you shall make two cherubim of gold, of cast work shall you make them, on the two sides of the mercy seat.

19 And make one cherub on the one side, and the other cherub on the other side of the mercy seat; thus you shall make two cherubim on the two sides thereof.

20 And the cherubim shall spread

forth their wings on high, covering the mercy seat with their wings, and their faces shall look one to another; toward the mercy seat shall the faces of the cherubim be.

21 And you shall put the mercy seat on top of the ark; and in the ark you shall put the testimony that I shall give you.

22 And there I will meet you, and I will commune with you from above the mercy seat, from between the two cherubim which are upon the ark of the testimony, of all things which I will command you concerning the children of Israel.

23 ¶You shall also make a table of shittim wood, two cubits long, a cubit broad, and a cubit and a half high.

24 And you shall overlay it with pure gold, and make for it a crown of gold round about.

25 And you shall make for it a border of a handbreadth round about, and you shall make a golden crown for the border thereof round about.

26 And you shall make for it four rings of gold, and put the rings in the four corners that are on the four feet thereof.

27 The rings shall be put toward the border to be places for the poles to carry the table.

28 You shall make the poles of shittim wood, and overlay them with gold, that the table may be borne with them.

29 You shall make dishes, spoons, jars, and bowls to pour out wine with them; of pure gold you shall make them.

30 And you shall set shewbread on the table before me always.

31 ¶And you shall make a candlestick of pure gold; of cast work shall the candlestick be made; its shaft, its branches, its bowls, its buds, and its flowers shall be of one piece.

32 And six branches shall come out of the sides of it; three branches of the candlestick out of the one side, and three branches of the candlestick out of the other side;

33 Three bowls shall be fastened on one shaft, with buds and flowers on one branch; and three bowls shall be fastened on another shaft, with buds and flowers on the other branch; so on all the six branches that come out of the candlestick.

34 And on the candlestick shall be four bowls made like almonds, with their buds and flowers.

35 And there shall be a bud under two branches of the same, and a bud under two branches of the same, and a bud under two branches of the same, likewise for the six branches that come out of the candlestick.

36 Their buds and their branches shall be of one piece; all of it shall be of one piece cast of pure gold.

37 And you shall make the seven lamps thereof; and they shall light the lamps thereof, that they may give light over against it.

38 And you shall make snuffers thereof, and snuff dishes thereof of pure gold.

39 Of a talent of pure gold shall you make it, with all these vessels.

40 And see that you make them after the same pattern which I have shown you on the mountain.

CHAPTER 26

MOREOVER you shall make the tabernacle with ten curtains of fine twined linen, and blue and purple and scarlet material; with cherubim, the workmanship of a craftsman shall you make them.

2 The length of each curtain shall be twenty-eight cubits, and the breadth of each curtain four cubits; all the curtains shall be of the same measure.

3 Five curtains shall be coupled one to another; and the other five curtains shall be coupled one to another.

4 And you shall make loops of blue on the edge of the one curtain from the selvedge in the coupling; and likewise shall you make loops on the edge of the other curtain from the selvedge in the coupling of the second.

5 Fifty loops shall you make on the edge of one curtain, and fifty loops shall you make on the edge of the other curtain that is in the coupling of the second; and the loops shall be directly opposite one another.

6 And you shall make fifty taches of gold, and couple the curtains together with the taches; and it shall be one tabernacle.

7 ¶And you shall make curtains of goats' hair for a covering of the tabernacle; eleven curtains shall you make.

8 The length of each curtain shall be thirty cubits, and the breadth of each curtain four cubits; all the eleven curtains shall be of the same measure.

9 And you shall couple five curtains by themselves, and six curtains by themselves, and shall double the sixth curtain in the forefront of the tabernacle.

10 And you shall make fifty loops on the edge of the curtain that is outermost in the coupling, and fifty loops on the edge of the curtain which couples the second.

11 And you shall make fifty taches of brass, and put the taches into the loops, and couple the tent together that it may be one.

12 And what is left over of the curtains of the tent, the half curtain that remains, shall hang over the back of the tabernacle.

13 And a cubit on the one side and a cubit on the other side of that which is left over in the length of the curtains of the tent shall hang over the sides of the tabernacle on this side and on that side to cover it.

14 And you shall make a covering for the tent of rams' skins dyed red and a covering of rams' skins dyed with vermilion.

15 ¶You shall make boards for the tabernacle of shittim wood standing up.

16 Ten cubits shall be the length of each board; and a cubit and a half, the breadth of each board.

17 There shall be two tenons to each board, set in order, one opposite the other; thus shall you make all the boards of the tabernacle.

18 And you shall make the boards for the tabernacle, twenty boards on the south side.

19 And you shall make forty sockets of silver under the twenty boards; two sockets under one board for its two tenons, and two sockets under another board for its two tenons.

20 And for the other side of the tabernacle on the north side there shall be twenty boards,

21 And their forty sockets of silver; two sockets under one board and two sockets under another board.

22 And for the sides of the tabernacle westward you shall make six boards.

23 And two boards shall you make for the corners of the tabernacle on the two sides.

24 And they shall be even at the bottom, and shall be coupled together above the head of it to one ring; thus it shall be for both sockets; they shall be for the two corners.

25 And there shall be eight boards, and their sockets of silver, sixteen sockets; two sockets under one board and two sockets under another board.

26 ¶And you shall make bars of shittim wood; five for the boards of the one side of the tabernacle,

27 And five bars for the boards of the other side of the tabernacle, and five bars for the boards at the westward side of the tabernacle.

28 And the middle bar in the midst of the boards shall reach from end to end.

29 And you shall overlay the boards with gold, and make their rings of gold for places for the bars; and you shall overlay the bars with gold.

30 And you shall erect the tabernacle according to the right pattern thereof which I have shown you on the mountain.

31 ¶And you shall make a veil of blue, purple, and scarlet material, and fine twined linen, the work of a craftsman; with cherubim shall it be made;

32 And you shall hang it upon four pillars of shittim wood overlaid with gold; with their hooks of gold, upon the four sockets of silver.

33 ¶And you shall hang up the veil under the taches, and then bring in thither within the veil the ark of the testimony; and you shall spread the veil between the holy place and the most holy.

34 And you shall put the mercy seat upon the ark of the testimony in the most holy place.

35 And you shall set the table outside the veil, and the candlestick opposite the table on the side of the tabernacle toward the south; and you shall put the table on the north side.

36 And you shall make a curtain for the door of the tent, of blue, and purple, and scarlet material and fine twined linen made of embroidered work.

37 And you shall make for the curtain five pillars of shittim wood, and overlay them with gold, and their hooks shall be of gold; and you shall make five sockets of brass for them.

CHAPTER 27

AND you shall make an altar of shittim wood, five cubits long and five cubits broad; the altar shall be foursquare; and the height thereof three cubits.

2 And you shall make the horns of it on the four corners thereof; its horns shall be of the same; and you shall overlay it with brass.

3 And you shall make pots for the use thereof; and its cauldrons and its shovels and its fleshhooks and censers, all the vessels thereof you shall make of brass.

4 You shall make for it a grating of network of brass; and upon the grating you shall make four rings of brass at its four corners.

5 And you shall put it under the ledge of the altar, that the grate may reach to the midst of the altar.

6 And you shall make poles for the altar, poles of shittim wood, and overlay them with brass.

7 And the poles shall be put into the rings, and they shall be on both sides of the altar, when they carry it.

8 Hollow with boards shall you make it; as I have shown you on the mountain, so shall they make it.

9 ¶And you shall make the court of the tabernacle; on the south side, there shall be hangings for the court of fine twined linen a hundred cubits long for one side;

10 And the twenty pillars thereof and their twenty sockets shall be of brass; the hooks of the pillars and their fillets shall be of silver.

11 And likewise for the north side there shall be hangings a hundred cubits long, and its twenty pillars and their twenty sockets shall be of brass; the hooks of the pillars and their fillets of silver.

12 ¶And for the breadth of the court on the west side there shall be hangings of fifty cubits, their pillars ten and their sockets ten.

13 And the breadth of the court on the east side shall be fifty cubits.

14 The hangings for one side of the gate shall be fifteen cubits, their pillars three and their sockets three.

15 And on the other side shall be fifteen hangings, their pillars three and their sockets three.

16 ¶And for the gate of the court there shall be a hanging of twenty cubits of blue and purple and scarlet material and fine twined linen made of embroidered work; and their pillars shall be four and their sockets four.

17 All the pillars round about the court shall be filleted with silver; their hooks shall be of silver and their sockets of brass.

18 ¶The length of the court shall be a hundred cubits, the breadth fifty everywhere, and the height five cubits of fine twined linen and their sockets of brass.

19 All the vessels of the tabernacle in all the service thereof and all the pins thereof and all the tent-pins of the court shall be of brass.

20 ¶And you shall command the children of Israel that they bring you pure olive oil from beaten olives for the light, so that the lamps may burn always.

21 In the tabernacle of the congregation outside the veil which is before the testimony, Aaron and his sons shall set them in order burning from evening to morning before the LORD; it shall be a statute for ever to your generations from the children of Israel.

CHAPTER 28

AND bring to you Aaron your brother, and his sons with him, from among the children of Israel, that they may minister to me in the priest's office, even Aaron, Nadab, and Abihu, Eleazar and Ithamar, Aaron's sons.

2 And you shall make holy vestments for Aaron your brother for glory and for beauty.

3 And you shall speak to all who are wise hearted, whom I have filled with the spirit of wisdom, that they may make holy vestments for Aaron to consecrate him that he may minister to me in the priest's office.

4 And these are the vestments which they shall make for them: a breastplate and an ephod and a robe and an embroidered coat and a mitre and a girdle; and they shall make holy vestments for Aaron your brother and his sons that they may minister to me in the priest's office.

5 And they shall take gold and blue and purple and scarlet material and fine twined linen.

6 ¶And they shall make the ephod of gold, of blue and purple and scarlet material and fine twined linen, the work of a craftsman.

7 It shall have the two shoulder-pieces thereof joined at the two edges; so it shall be joined together,

8 And the embroidered girdle of the ephod which is upon it shall be of the same, according to the work thereof; of gold, of blue and purple and scarlet material and fine twined linen.

9 And you shall take two onyx stones, and engrave on them the names of the sons of Israel;

10 Six of their names on one stone, and the other remaining six on the other stone, according to their birth;

11 With the work of an engraver in stones, like the engravings of a signet, you shall engrave the two stones with the names of the sons of Israel; and you shall mount them on the settings of gold.

12 And you shall put the two stones upon the shoulders of the ephod for stones of memorial to the children of Israel; and Aaron shall bear their names before the LORD upon his two shoulders for a memorial.

13 ¶And you shall make settings of gold;

14 And two chains of pure gold, of braided work you shall make; twine, and fasten the two chains of braided work to the settings.

15 ¶And you shall make the breastplate of judgment with the work of a craftsman; like the work of the ephod you shall make it; of gold, of blue and of purple and of scarlet material and fine twined linen.

16 It shall be foursquare being doubled; a span is its length and a span its width.

17 And you shall set in it settings of stones, four rows of stones; the first row shall be a sardius, a topaz, and an emerald:

18 And the second row a carbuncle, a sapphire, and a jasper.

19 And the third row a jacinth (zircon), carnelian, and an amethyst.

20 And the fourth row a beryl, an onyx, and a jasper; they shall be set in gold in their enclosings.

21 And the stones shall be engraved with the names of the sons of Israel, twelve, according to their names, like the engravings of a signet; every one shall be engraved with his name according to the number of the twelve tribes.

22 ¶And you shall make upon the breastplate twin chains, braided work of pure gold.

23 And you shall make upon the breastplate two rings of pure gold, and shall put the two rings on the two ends of the breastplate.

24 And you shall fasten the two braided chains of gold on the two rings which are on the ends of the breastplate.

25 And the other two ends of the braided chains you shall fasten in the two settings, and put them on the shoulder-pieces of the ephod in front of it.

26 ¶And you shall make two rings of gold, and you shall put them upon the two ends of the breastplate on the

border thereof which is in the side of the ephod from within.

27 And you shall make two rings of gold, and shall put them on the two shoulder-pieces of the ephod underneath, toward the forepart thereof, over against the joining thereof, above the embroidered girdle of the ephod.

28 And they shall bind the breastplate by its rings to the rings of the ephod with a lace of blue that it may rest upon the embroidered girdle of the ephod, so that the breastplate may not come loose from the ephod.

29 And Aaron shall bear the names of the sons of Israel in the breastplate of judgment upon his heart, when he enters the holy place, for a continual memorial before the LORD.

30 ¶And you shall put in the breastplate of judgment the Urim and the Thummim; and they shall be upon Aaron's heart when he enters before the LORD; and Aaron shall bear the judgments of the children of Israel upon his heart before the LORD continually.

31 ¶And you shall make the robe of the ephod all of blue.

32 And there shall be an opening in the top of it, in the midst thereof; and it shall have a binding of woven work round about the opening of it, hemmed on the edge so that it may not be torn.

33 ¶And on the hem of it you shall make pomegranates of blue and of purple and of scarlet round about the hem thereof; and bells of gold shall be between them round about:

34 A golden bell and a pomegranate, a golden bell and a pomegranate, on the hem of the robe round about.

35 And it shall be upon Aaron when he ministers; and its sound shall be heard when he enters the holy place before the LORD and when he comes out, that he may not die.

36 ¶And you shall make a crown of pure gold, and engrave upon it, like the engravings of a signet, HOLINESS TO THE LORD.

37 And you shall put it on blue lace, that it may be upon the mitre;

upon the forefront of the mitre it shall be.

38 And it shall be upon Aaron's forehead, and Aaron shall bear the sins of the children of Israel when they shall offer holy sacrifices and all their holy gifts; and the mitre shall be always upon his forehead, that they may be accepted before the LORD.

39 ¶And you shall make the coat of fine linen, and you shall also make the mitre of fine linen and a girdle of embroidered work.

40 ¶And for Aaron's sons you shall make coats, and you shall make for them girdles, and bonnets you shall make for them, for glory and for beauty.

41 And you shall put them upon Aaron your brother, and upon his sons with him; and shall anoint them and consecrate them and sanctify them, that they may minister to me in the priest's office.

42 And you shall make them breeches of fine linen to cover their nakedness; from their loins to their thighs they shall reach;

43 And they shall be upon Aaron and upon his sons when they enter the tabernacle of the congregation or when they come near to the altar to minister in the holy place; that they may not bear iniquity and die; it shall be a statute for ever to Aaron and to his descendants after him.

CHAPTER 29

AND this is the thing that you shall do to them to consecrate them, to minister to me in the priest's office: take one young bullock and two rams without blemish

2 And unleavened bread and unleavened cakes mixed with oil and unleavened wafers mixed with oil; of fine wheat flour shall you make them.

3 And you shall put them in one basket and bring them in the basket with the bullock and the two rams.

4 And Aaron and his sons you shall bring to the door of the tabernacle of the congregation, and you shall wash them with water.

5 And you shall take the vestments and put upon Aaron the coat and the robe of the mitre, the ephod, and the breastplate, and gird him with the embroidered girdle of the ephod;

6 And you shall put the mitre on his head, and put the holy crown upon the mitre.

7 Then you shall take the anointing oil, and pour it upon his head, and anoint him.

8 And you shall bring his sons and put coats upon them.

9 And you shall gird them with girdles, Aaron and his sons, and put the bonnets on them; and the priest's office shall be theirs for a perpetual statute; and thus you shall consecrate Aaron and his sons.

10 And you shall bring a bullock before the tabernacle of the congregation; and Aaron and his sons shall put their hands on the head of the bullock.

11 And you shall slaughter the bullock before the LORD at the door of the tabernacle of the congregation.

12 And you shall take some of the blood of the bullock and sprinkle it upon the horns of the altar with your finger and pour all the rest of the blood at the bottom of the altar.

13 And you shall take all the fat that covers the entrails, and the caul that is above the liver, and the two kidneys and the fat that is on them and burn them upon the altar.

14 But the flesh of the bullock and its skin and its dung you shall burn with fire outside the camp; it is a sin offering.

15 ¶You shall also take one ram; and Aaron and his sons shall put their hands on the head of the ram.

16 And you shall slaughter the ram; and you must take some of its blood and sprinkle it round about upon the altar.

17 And then you shall cut the ram into pieces, and wash its entrails and its legs, and put them over its pieces and over its head.

18 And you shall burn the whole ram upon the altar; it is a burnt offering to the LORD; it is a sweet savour, an offering made by fire to the LORD.

19 ¶And you shall take the other ram; and Aaron and his sons shall put their hands upon the head of the ram.

20 Then you shall slaughter the ram, and take some of its blood, and sprinkle it upon the tip of the right ear of Aaron and upon the tips of the right ears of his sons and upon the thumbs of their right hands and upon the great toes of their right feet, and sprinkle the blood upon the altar round about.

21 And you shall take some of the blood that is on the altar and some of the anointing oil, and sprinkle it upon Aaron and upon his vestments and upon his sons and upon the vestments of his sons with him; and he shall be consecrated and his vestments and his sons and his sons' vestments with him.

22 And you shall take of the fat and the rump, and the fat that covers the entrails, the caul of the liver, the two kidneys, and the fat that is on them and the right shoulder; for it is a ram of consecration;

23 And you shall take one loaf of bread and one loaf of bread baked with oil and a cake baked with flour and oil out of the basket of the unleavened bread that is before the LORD;

24 And you shall put all of these in the hands of Aaron and in the hands of his sons; and you shall wave them for a wave offering before the LORD.

25 And you shall receive them from their hands, and burn the breast of the ram upon the altar for a burnt offering, for a sweet savour before the LORD; it is an offering made by fire to the LORD.

26 And you shall take the breast of the ram of Aaron's consecration and wave it for a wave offering before the LORD; and it shall become your share.

27 And you shall sanctify the breast of the wave offering and the thigh of the heave offering which is waved and which is placed upon the altar from the ram of the consecration,

even of that which is for Aaron, and of that which is for his sons;

28 And it shall belong to Aaron and his sons by a statute for ever from the children of Israel; for it is a heave offering; and it shall be a heave offering from the children of Israel from their peace offerings, an oblation to the LORD.

29 ¶And the holy vestments of Aaron shall belong to his sons after him, to be anointed in them and to be consecrated in them.

30 And one of his sons who is to become priest in his stead shall put them on seven days, when he enters into the tabernacle of the congregation to minister in the holy place.

31 ¶And you shall take the ram of the consecration and cook its meat in the holy place.

32 And Aaron and his sons shall eat the meat of the ram and the bread that is in the basket at the door of the tabernacle of the congregation.

33 And they shall eat of those things with which the atonement was made, to consecrate and to sanctify them; but a stranger shall not eat of them because they are holy.

34 And if any of the meat of the consecration, or of the bread, remain unto the morning, then you shall burn what is left over with fire; it shall not be eaten because it is holy.

35 And thus shall you do to Aaron and to his sons, just as I have commanded you; seven days shall you consecrate them.

36 And you shall offer every day a bullock for a sin offering for atonement; and you shall sprinkle blood on the altar, when you make an atonement for it, and you shall anoint it to sanctify it.

37 Seven days you shall make an atonement for the altar and sanctify it; and the altar shall be most holy; whatever touches the altar shall be holy.

38 ¶Now this is what you shall offer upon the altar: two lambs of the first year day by day continually.

39 One lamb you shall offer in the morning and the other lamb you shall offer in the evening;

40 And with the one lamb you shall offer a tenth part of an ephah of fine flour mixed with a fourth part of a hin of beaten oil, and a fourth part of a hin of wine for a drink offering.

41 And the other lamb you shall offer in the evening, and shall do to it according to the meat offering of the morning and according to the drink offering thereof for a sweet savour, an offering made by fire to the LORD.

42 It shall be a continual burnt offering throughout your generations at the door of the tabernacle of the congregation before the LORD, where I will meet you, to speak there to you.

43 And there I will meet with the children of Israel, and the people shall be sanctified by my glory.

44 And I will sanctify the tabernacle of the congregation and the altar; I will also sanctify both Aaron and his sons to minister to me in the priest's office.

45 ¶And I will dwell among the children of Israel and will be their God.

46 And they shall know that I am the LORD their God who brought them forth out of the land of Egypt that I may dwell among them; I am the LORD their God.

CHAPTER 30

YOU shall make an altar to burn incense upon; of shittim wood shall you make it.

2 A cubit long, and a cubit wide; foursquare shall it be; and its height shall be two cubits; the horns thereof shall be of one piece of the same material.

3 And you shall overlay it with pure gold, the top thereof, and the sides thereof round about, and the horns thereof; and you shall make for it a crown of gold round about.

4 And two golden rings you shall make for it under the crown of it, on the two corners thereof, upon the two sides of it shall you make it; and they shall be for places for the poles to carry it with them.

5 And you shall make the poles of shittim wood and overlay them with gold.

6 And you shall put it before the veil that is by the ark of the testimony, before the mercy seat that is over the testimony, where I will meet with you.

7 And Aaron shall burn upon it sweet incense every morning; when he prepares the lamps, he shall burn incense upon it.

8 And when Aaron lights the lamps in the evening, he shall burn incense upon it, a perpetual incense before the LORD throughout your generations.

9 You shall not offer strange incense thereon, nor burnt offering, nor meat offering; neither shall you pour drink offering thereon.

10 And Aaron shall make an atonement upon the horns of it once in a year with the blood of the sin offering of atonement; once in a year shall he make atonement upon it throughout your generations; it is most holy to the LORD.

11 ¶And the LORD spoke to Moses, saying,

12 When you receive the sum of the children of Israel after their number, then every man shall give a ransom for himself to the LORD, when you have numbered the people; that there be no plague among them, when you number them.

13 This is what everyone who is included in the number shall give, half a shekel according to the shekel of the sanctuary (a shekel is twenty gerahs); half a shekel shall be the offering to the LORD.

14 Every one among them who is included in the number from twenty years old and upward shall give an offering to the LORD.

15 The rich shall not give more, and the poor shall not give less than half a shekel, when they give an offering to the LORD to make an atonement for your souls.

16 And you shall take the atonement money from the children of Israel, and shall give it for the work of the tabernacle of the congregation; that it may be a memorial to the children of Israel before the LORD, to make an atonement for your souls.

17 ¶And the LORD spoke to Moses, saying,

18 You shall also make a laver of brass, and its base of brass, for washing; and you shall put it between the tabernacle of the congregation and the altar, and you shall put water into it.

19 And Aaron and his sons shall wash their hands and their feet thereat;

20 When they enter into the tabernacle of the congregation, they shall wash with water, that they die not; or when they draw near to the altar to minister, and to burn incense, and to offer an offering to the LORD.

21 So they shall wash their hands and their feet, that they die not; and it shall be a statute for ever to them, even to him and to his descendants throughout their generations.

22 ¶Moreover the LORD spoke to Moses, saying,

23 Take the choicest spices, of pure myrrh five hundred shekels and of sweet cinnamon half so much, that is, two hundred and fifty shekels, and of sweet calamus two hundred and fifty shekels,

24 And of cassia five hundred shekels, by the weight of the sanctuary, and of olive oil a hin:

25 And you shall make it an oil of holy ointment, an ointment compounded after the art of the perfumer; it shall be a holy anointing oil.

26 And you shall anoint the tabernacle of the congregation with it, and the ark of the testimony,

27 And the table and all its vessels, and the candlestick and its vessels, and the altar of incense,

28 And the altar of the burnt offering with all its vessels, and the laver and its base.

29 And you shall sanctify them, and they shall become most holy; whatsoever touches them shall be holy.

30 And you shall anoint Aaron and his sons, and consecrate them that they may minister to me in the priest's office.

31 And you shall speak to the children of Israel, saying, This shall be

a holy anointing oil to me throughout your generations.

32 Upon men's bodies shall it not be rubbed, neither shall you make any other oil like it, after the composition of it; because it is holy, and it shall be holy to you.

33 Whosoever compounds any like it or whosoever shall give any of it to a stranger shall be cut off from his people.

34 ¶And the LORD said to Moses, Take sweet spices, stacte and onycha and galbanum; sweet spices, with pure frankincense; of each shall there be equal weight;

35 And you shall make it a perfume, a compound made by the work of the perfumer, tempered together, pure and holy;

36 And you shall beat some of it very fine, and put of it before the testimony in the tabernacle of the congregation, where I will meet with you; it shall be to you most holy.

37 And as for the perfume which you shall make, you shall not make to yourselves according to its composition; it shall be to you holy for the LORD.

38 Whosoever shall make any like it, to anoint with it, shall be cut off from his people.

CHAPTER 31

THE LORD spoke to Moses, saying, 2 See, I have called by name Bezaliel the son of Uri, the son of Hur, of the tribe of Judah;

3 And I have filled him with the Spirit of God, in wisdom and in understanding, and in knowledge and in all manner of workmanship,

4 To teach cunning works, to do work in gold and in silver and in brass

5 And in the art of cutting of stones to be set and in the carving of timber and in all manner of workmanship.

6 And I, behold, have appointed with him Elihab, the son of Ahisamakh, of the tribe of Dan; and I have put wisdom in the heart of every skillful man that he may make all things which I have commanded you:

7 The tabernacle of the congregation, and the ark of the testimony, and the mercy seat that is thereupon, and all the vessels of the tabernacle,

8 And the table and all its vessels, and the pure candlestick with all its instruments, and the altar of incense,

9 And the altar of burnt offering with all its vessels, and the laver and its base,

10 And the vestments for the service, and the holy vestments for Aaron the priest, and the vestments for his sons, to minister to me in the priest's office,

11 And the anointing oil, and the sweet incense for the holy place; according to all that I have commanded you, shall they do.

12 ¶And the LORD spoke to Moses, saying,

13 Speak to the children of Israel, saying, My sabbaths you must keep; for it is a sign between me and you throughout your generations; that you may know that I am the LORD your God who sanctifies you.

14 You shall keep the sabbath; for it is holy to you; every one who defiles it shall surely be put to death; and whoever shall do any work on it, that soul shall surely be cut off from among his people.

15 Six days you shall do work; but the seventh day is the sabbath of rest, holy to the LORD; whosoever does any work on the sabbath day shall surely be put to death.

16 Wherefore the children of Israel shall keep the sabbath to the LORD to observe the sabbath throughout all their generations for a perpetual covenant.

17 It is a sign between me and the children of Israel for ever; for in six days the LORD made heaven and earth and the seas and all that are therein, and on the seventh day he ceased from work and rested.

18 ¶And he gave to Moses, when he had made an end of talking with him on mount Sinai, two tablets of testimony, the stone tablets written by the finger of God.

CHAPTER 32

WHEN the people saw that Moses delayed to come down from the mountain, they gathered themselves together unto Aaron and said to him, Arise, make us gods that they may go before us; as for this man Moses who brought us up out of the land of Egypt, we do not know what has become of him.

2 And Aaron said to them, Remove the golden earrings which are in the ears of your wives, of your sons, and of your daughters, and bring them to me.

3 So all the people removed the golden earrings which were in their ears, and brought them to Aaron.

4 And he received them, and drew a design, and made it a molten calf; and they said, This is your god, O Israel, who brought you up out of the land of Egypt.

5 And Aaron was afraid, and he built an altar before it; then Aaron made a proclamation, and said, To-morrow is a feast to the LORD.

6 And they rose up early on the morrow and offered burnt offerings and brought peace offerings; and the people sat down to eat and to drink, and rose up to play and to quarrel.

7 ¶And the LORD said to Moses, Go down, get away from here; for your people whom you have brought out of the land of Egypt have corrupted themselves;

8 They have turned aside quickly from the way which I commanded them; they have made for themselves a molten calf, and have worshipped it, and have sacrificed to it, and said, This is your god, O Israel, who has brought you out of the land of Egypt.

9 And the LORD said to Moses, I have seen this people, and, behold it is a stiff-necked people;

10 Now therefore let me alone, that my wrath may be kindled against them and that I may destroy them; and I will make of you a great nation.

11 But Moses prayed before the LORD his God and said, Not so, O LORD, let not thy wrath kindle against thy people whom thou hast brought forth out of the land of Egypt with great power and with a mighty hand.

12 Why should the Egyptians say, It was for their injury he did bring them out to slay them in the mountains and to consume them from the face of the earth? Rest from thy fierce anger and be reconciled concerning the evil deed of thy people.

13 Remember Abraham, Isaac, and Israel, thy servants, to whom thou didst swear by thine own self and didst say to them, I will multiply your descendants as the stars in heaven, and all the land that I have spoken of I will give to thy descendants, and they shall inherit it for ever.

14 And the LORD was reconciled concerning the evil which he had purposed to do to his people.

15 ¶And Moses turned and went down from the mountain, and the two stone tablets of the testimony were in his hand, the tablets that were written on both sides; on the one side and on the other were they written.

16 The tablets were the work of God, and the writing was the writing of God, engraved upon the tablets.

17 And when Joshua heard the noise of the people fighting, he said to Moses, There is a noise of war in the camp.

18 Moses said to him, It is not the sound of the cry of mighty men, neither is it the sound of the cry of weak men; but it is the sound of sin that I hear.

19 ¶And it came to pass as soon as they came near to the camp, he saw the calf and the cymbals; and Moses' anger raged, and he threw the tablets out of his hand and broke them at the foot of the mountain.

20 And he took the calf which they had made, and burned it in the fire, and filed it with a file until it was ground into dust, and he scattered it upon the water, and made the children of Israel drink of it.

21 And Moses said to Aaron, What has this people done to you that you have brought so great a sin upon them?

22 And Aaron said, Let not the anger of my lord rage; you yourself know this people, that they are bad.

23 For they said to me, Make us gods that they shall go before us; as for this Moses who brought us up out of the land of Egypt, we do not know what has become of him.

24 And I said to them, Whosoever has any gold bring it to me. So they brought it to me; then I cast it into the fire, and it became this calf.

25 ¶And when Moses saw that the people had sinned; (for Aaron had caused them to sin, and to leave a bad name behind them);

26 Then Moses stood in the gate of the camp and said, Who is on the LORD's side? Let him come to me. And all the Levites gathered themselves together to him.

27 And Moses said to them, Thus says the LORD God of Israel: Put every man his sword by his side, and go in and out from door to door throughout the camp, and slay every man his brother, his friend, and his neighbor.

28 And the Levites did according to the word of Moses; and there fell of the people that day about three thousand men.

29 And Moses said to them, Strengthen yourselves today before the LORD, every man with his son and with his brother; for a blessing shall come upon you today.

30 ¶And it came to pass on the next day, Moses said to the people, You have sinned this great sin; and now I will go up to the LORD; perhaps he may forgive your transgressions.

31 So Moses returned to the LORD and said, I beseech thee, O LORD God, truly this people have sinned a great sin and have made for themselves gods of gold.

32 But now, if thou wilt, forgive their sins; and if not, blot me, I pray thee, out of thy book which thou hast written.

33 And the LORD said to Moses, Whosoever has sinned against me, him will I blot out of my book.

34 Therefore now go, lead the people to the place where I tell you; behold, my angel shall go before you; nevertheless in the day when I punish I will visit their sins upon them.

35 And the LORD smote the people because they worshipped the calf which Aaron made.

CHAPTER 33

AND the LORD said to Moses, Depart, and go up hence, you and the people whom you have brought up out of the land of Egypt, to the land which I swore to Abraham, Isaac, and Jacob, saying, To your descendants will I give it;

2 And I will send an angel before you; and he will destroy the Canaanites, the Amorites, the Hittites, the Perizzites, the Hivites, and the Jebusites;

3 Go to a land flowing with milk and honey; for I will not go up among you; for you are a stiff-necked people; lest I consume you on the way.

4 ¶And when the people heard this bad news, they mourned; and no man did put on him his armor.

5 Then the LORD said to Moses, Say to the children of Israel, You are a stiff-necked people; I will come up among you in a moment, and consume you; therefore now put off your armor from you, that I may know what to do to you.

6 And the children of Israel stripped themselves of their armor by mount Horeb.

7 And Moses took his tent and pitched it outside the camp, afar off from the camp, and called it the tabernacle of the congregation. And it came to pass that every one who sought to inquire of the LORD went out to the tabernacle of the congregation, which was outside the camp.

8 And it came to pass when Moses went out to the tabernacle that all the people rose up and stood every man at his tent door and looked after Moses until he entered the tabernacle.

9 And it came to pass as Moses entered into the tabernacle the pillar of cloud descended and stood at the door of the tabernacle and the LORD talked with Moses.

10 And all the people saw the pillar

of cloud standing at the door of the tabernacle; and all the people rose up and worshipped, every man in his tent door.

11 And the Lord spoke to Moses face to face, as a man speaks to his friend. And he returned to the camp; but his servant Joshua, the son of Nun, a young man, departed not from the tabernacle.

12 ¶And Moses said to the Lord, See, thou sayest to me, Bring up this people; and thou hast not let me know whom thou wilt send with me. Yet thou hast said, I know you by name, and thou hast also found favor in my sight.

13 Now therefore, if I have found favor in thy sight, show me now the way that I may know thee, that I may find favor in thy sight; and consider that this thy people is a great nation.

14 And the Lord said to Moses, Go ahead of me, and I will give you rest.

15 And he said to him, If thou thyself will not go with us, let us not leave this place.

16 For wherein shall it be known here that I and thy people have found mercy in thy sight? Is it not in that thou goest with us? So that we be distinguished, I and thy people, from all the people that are upon the face of the earth.

17 And the Lord said to Moses, I will do this thing also that you have spoken; for you have found grace in my sight, and I know you by your name.

18 And Moses said, Show me thy glory.

19 And he said, I will make all my goodness pass before you, and I will proclaim the name of the Lord before you; and I will be gracious to whom I will be gracious, and will show mercy on whom I will show mercy.

20 And he said, You cannot see my face; for no man can see me and live.

21 And the Lord said to Moses, Behold, there is a place in front of me, and you shall stand upon the rock;

22 And it shall come to pass when my glory passes by that I will put you in a cave of the rock and will rest my hand upon you till I pass by;

23 And I will take away my hand, and you shall see my back; but my face shall not be seen.

CHAPTER 34

AND the Lord said to Moses, Hew two tablets of stone like the first ones; and write upon the tablets the words that were on the first tablets, which you broke.

2 And be ready in the morning, and come up in the morning to mount Sinai, and present yourself there to me on the top of the mountain.

3 And no man shall come up with you, neither shall any man be seen throughout all the mountain; neither let the flocks nor herds feed opposite that mountain.

4 ¶And Moses hewed two tablets of stone like the first ones; and he arose early in the morning and went up to the top of mount Sinai, as the Lord had commanded him, and took in his hand the two stone tablets.

5 And the Lord descended in the cloud and stood with him there and announced the name of the Lord.

6 And the Lord passed by before him, and proclaimed, The Lord, The Lord, The God merciful and compassionate, longsuffering, and abundant in goodness and truth,

7 Keeping mercy for thousands of generations, forgiving sins and transgressions, who by no means justifies the guilty; visiting the iniquity of the fathers upon the children, and upon the children's children, to the third and fourth generation.

8 And Moses made haste and fell on the ground and worshipped.

9 And he said, If now I have found mercy in thy sight, O my Lord, let now my Lord go with us; for it is a stiff-necked people; and pardon our offenses and our sins and our guilty conscience.

10 ¶And the Lord said, Behold, I will make a covenant before all your people; I will do marvels such as have not been done in all the earth, nor in any of the nations; and all this people

among whom you are shall see the work of the LORD; for it is a terrible thing that I will do with you.

11 Observe the things which I command you this day; behold, I will destroy from before you the Canaanites, the Amorites, the Hittites, the Perizzites, the Hivites, and the Jebusites.

12 Take heed to yourself lest you make a covenant with the inhabitants of the land whither you go, lest they become a stumbling block to you.

13 But you must destroy their altars, break their images, and cut down their idols.

14 For you shall worship no other god; for the LORD whose name is zealous,[1] is a zealous God.

15 You shall not make a covenant with the inhabitants of the land, so that the people may not go astray after their idols and sacrifice to their gods, and they shall invite you, and you shall eat of their sacrifices;

16 And you shall take of their daughters to your sons, and give your daughters to their sons; and your daughters shall go astray after their gods, and their daughters cause your sons to go astray after their gods.

17 You shall make to yourself no molten gods.

18 ¶The feast of unleavened bread you shall keep. Seven days you shall eat unleavened bread, as I commanded you, in the time of the month of Abib; for in the month of Abib you came out from Egypt.

19 All that opens the womb is mine; and every firstling among your cattle, both of the oxen and of the lambs.

20 And all the firstlings of the cattle you shall redeem with a lamb; but if you shall not redeem it, then you shall kill it. All the first-born of your sons you shall redeem. And none shall appear before me empty-handed.

21 ¶Six days you shall work, but on the seventh day you shall rest; in the time of ploughing and during harvest you shall rest.

22 ¶And you shall observe the feast of weeks, the feast of the firstfruits of wheat harvest, and the feast of ingathering at the year's end.

23 ¶Three times a year shall all your memorial offerings be brought before the LORD, the God of Israel.

24 For I will destroy the nations from before you, and enlarge your borders; neither shall any man covet your land when you shall go up to appear before the LORD your God three times in a year.

25 You shall not offer the blood of a sacrifice with leavened bread; neither shall the sacrifice of the feast of the passover be left over to the morning.

26 The first of the firstfruits of your land you shall bring to the house of the LORD your God. You shall not cook a kid in its mother's milk.

27 And the LORD said to Moses, Write these words; for by these words I have made a covenant with you and with all Israel.

28 And he was there with the LORD forty days and forty nights; he neither ate bread nor drank water. And he wrote upon the tablets the words of the covenant, the ten commandments.

29 ¶And it came to pass, when Moses came down from mount Sinai with the two tablets of testimony in his hand, when he came down from the mountain, Moses knew not that the skin of his face shone while the LORD talked with him.

30 And when Aaron and all the children of Israel saw Moses' face, behold, the skin of Moses' face shone; and they were afraid to come near to him.

31 So Moses called to them; and Aaron and all the leaders of the congregation returned to him; and Moses talked with them.

32 And afterward all the children of Israel came near to him; and he gave them in commandment all that the LORD had spoken with him in mount Sinai.

33 And when Moses had finished speaking with them, he put a veil on his face.

34 But when Moses went in before

---

[1] In Aramaic the same word may mean either zealous or jealous. God was not jealous of idols, but was zealous to keep his people from worshipping idols.

the LORD to speak with him, he took the veil off until he came out. And he came out and spoke to the children of Israel that which he was commanded.

35 And the children of Israel saw the face of Moses, that the skin of Moses' face shone; and Moses took off the veil from his face when he went in to speak with the LORD.

CHAPTER 35

AND Moses gathered all the congregation of the children of Israel together and said to them, These are the things which the LORD has commanded to be done.

2 Six days shall work be done, but the seventh day shall be holy to you, a sabbath of rest to the LORD; whosoever does any work on it shall be put to death.

3 You shall kindle no fire throughout your habitations on the sabbath day.

4 ¶And Moses spoke to all the congregation of the children of Israel, saying, This is the thing which the LORD has commanded to be done:

5 Take from among you an offering for the LORD; whosoever is of a willing heart, let him bring an offering to the LORD, gold, silver, and brass,

6 Blue, purple, and scarlet material, and fine linen, and goats' hair,

7 And rams' skins dyed red, and dark blue skins, and shittim wood,

8 And oil for the light, and spices for anointing oil and for the sweet incense,

9 And onyx stones, and precious stones for the ephod, and for the breastplate,

10 And every wisehearted one among you shall come, and make all that the LORD has commanded;

11 The tabernacle, its tent, and its covering, its taches, and its boards, its bars, its pillars, and its sockets,

12 The ark, and its poles, the mercy seat, and the veil of the covering,

13 The table, and its poles, and all its vessels, and the shewbread,

14 The candlestick for the light, and its instruments and its lamps, and the oil for the light,

15 And the incense altar, and its poles, and the anointing oil, and the sweet incense, and the hanging for the door at the entrance of the tabernacle,

16 The altar of burnt offering, with its bronze grate, its poles, and all its vessels, the laver, and its base,

17 The hangings of the court, its pillars, and their sockets, and the hanging for the door of the court,

18 The pins of the tabernacle, and the pins of the court, and their cords,

19 The vestments of service, to minister in the holy place, the holy vestments for Aaron the priest, and the vestments for his sons, to minister in the priest's office.

20 ¶And the whole congregation of the children of Israel departed from the presence of Moses.

21 And they came, every one who was willing in his heart and every one whose spirit made him willing, and they brought offerings for the LORD, to the work of the tabernacle of the congregation, and for all its service, and for the holy vestments.

22 And they came, both men and women, as many as were willinghearted, and brought bracelets and earrings and rings and necklaces and all sorts of jewels of gold; and every man that had set aside an offering of gold brought it to the LORD.

23 And every man with whom was found blue, and purple, and scarlet material, and fine linen, and goats' hair, and red skins of rams, and dark blue skins, brought them.

24 Every one who had set aside an offering of silver and brass brought it as an offering for the LORD; and every man with whom was found shittim wood for any work of the service brought it.

25 And all the women who were skillful did spin with their hands, and brought that which they had spun, both of blue, and of purple, and of scarlet material, and of fine linen.

26 And all the women who were willing skillfully spun goats' hair.

27 And the princes brought onyx stones and precious stones for the ephod and for the breastplate,

28 And spices, and oil for the light,

and for the anointing oil, and for the sweet incense.

29 The children of Israel brought a willing offering to the LORD, every man and woman who were willing-hearted to bring material for all manner of work which the LORD had commanded to be done by Moses.

30 ¶Then Moses said to the children of Israel, See, the LORD has called by name Bezaliel the son of Uri, the son of Hur, of the tribe of Judah;

31 And he has filled him with the Spirit of God, with wisdom and with understanding, and with knowledge, and with all manner of workmanship,

32 To devise artistic works, to work in gold, and in silver, and in brass,

33 And in the cutting of stones to be set, and in the carving of wood to make any manner of art work.

34 And he has inspired him to teach, both he and Elihab, the son of Ahisa-makh, of the tribe of Dan.

35 Both of them he has filled with wisdom and inspiration to do all manner of work of the carpenter and of the workman of art and of the embroiderer in blue, and in purple, in fine linen, and in scarlet material, and in weaving, and of those who do any kind of work, and of those who devise skillful work.

CHAPTER 36

THEN Bezaliel and Elihab and every wise man to whom the LORD gave wisdom and understanding to know how to work all manner of work for the service of the sanctuary did everything, according to all that the LORD had commanded.

2 And Moses called Bezaliel and Elihab and every skillful man in whose heart the LORD had put wisdom, every one whose heart stirred him up to come to do the work.

3 And they received of Moses all the offering which the children of Israel had brought for the service of the tabernacle of the congregation, with which to make it. And they brought yet to him free offerings every morning.

4 And all the skillful men who did the work of the sanctuary brought in every man some of his work which he made;

5 ¶And they said to Moses, The people bring much more than is necessary for the service of the work which the LORD commanded to make.

6 And Moses gave command, which the heralds proclaimed throughout the camp, saying, Let neither man nor woman make any more work for the offering of the sanctuary. So the people were restrained.

7 For the stuff they had was sufficient for all the things they had to make, and some was left over.

8 ¶And all the skillful men among those who did the work of the tabernacle made ten curtains of fine twined linen and blue and purple and scarlet material; with cherubim artistically wrought they made them.

9 The length of each curtain was twenty-eight cubits, and the breadth of each curtain four cubits; the curtains were all of one size.

10 And they coupled the five curtains one to another; and the other five curtains they coupled one to another.

11 And they made loops of blue on the edge of each curtain from the selvedge in the coupling; likewise they wrought on the other edge of the curtain, on the coupling of the second.

12 They made fifty loops on the one curtain and fifty loops on the edge of the curtain which was in the coupling of the second; the loops were opposite each other.

13 And they made fifty clasps of gold, and coupled the curtains one to another with the clasps so that it became one tabernacle.

14 ¶And they made curtains of goats' hair for the tent over the tabernacle; they made eleven curtains.

15 The length of each curtain was thirty cubits, and the breadth of each curtain four cubits; the eleven curtains were of one size.

16 And they coupled five curtains by themselves, and six curtains by themselves.

17 And they made fifty loops on the edge of the curtain in the coupling,

and fifty loops on the edge of the curtain which coupled the second.

18 And they made fifty clasps of brass to couple the tent together, that it might be one.

19 And they made a covering for the tent of rams' skins dyed red and a covering of badgers' skins above that.

20 ¶And they made boards for the tabernacle of shittim wood, standing up.

21 The length of each board was ten cubits, and the breadth of each board one cubit and a half.

22 Each board had two sockets, one exactly opposite the other; thus did they make all the boards of the tabernacle.

23 And they made boards for the tabernacle; twenty boards for the south side:

24 And forty sockets of silver they made under the twenty boards; two sockets under one board for its two tenons, and two sockets under another board for its two tenons.

25 And for the other side of the tabernacle, which is toward the north side, they made twenty boards,

26 And their forty sockets of silver; two sockets under one board, and two sockets under another board.

27 And for the side of the tabernacle westward they made six boards.

28 And two boards made they for the corners of the tabernacle on the two sides.

29 And they were coupled beneath, and coupled together at the top thereof, to one ring; thus they made both of them in both the corners.

30 And there were eight boards; and their sockets were sixteen sockets of silver, under every board two sockets.

31 ¶And they made bars of shittim wood; five bars for the boards of the one side of the tabernacle,

32 And five bars for the boards of the other side of the tabernacle, and five bars for the boards of the tabernacle for the side westward.

33 And they made the middle bar to pass through the boards from the one end to the other.

34 And they overlaid the boards with gold, and made their rings of gold to be places for the bars, and overlaid the bars with gold.

35 ¶And they made a veil of blue and purple and scarlet material and fine twined linen; with cherubim made they it of the work of an artist.

36 And they made for it four pillars of shittim wood, and overlaid them with gold; their hooks were of gold; and they cast for them four sockets of silver.

37 ¶And they made a hanging for the door of the tabernacle, of blue and purple and scarlet material and fine twined linen of needlework;

38 And they made the five pillars of it with their hooks; and they overlaid their capitals and their fillets with gold; but their five sockets were of brass.

CHAPTER 37

THEN Bezaliel made the ark of shittim wood; two cubits and a half was the length of it, and a cubit and a half the breadth of it, and a cubit and a half the height of it:

2 And he overlaid it with pure gold within and without, and made a crown of gold for it round about.

3 And he cast for it four rings of gold to be set on its four corners; two rings on one side of it and two rings on the other side of it.

4 And he made poles of shittim wood, and overlaid them with gold.

5 And he put the poles into the rings by the sides of the ark to carry the ark.

6 ¶And he made the mercy seat of pure gold; two cubits and a half was its length and one cubit and a half its breadth.

7 And he made two cherubim of gold; of casting work he made them, on the two ends of the mercy seat;

8 One cherub on one side and the other cherub on the other side; above the mercy seat made he the cherubim on its two ends.

9 And the cherubim spread out their wings on high, covering the mercy seat with their wings, with their faces

9

one to another; over the mercy seat were the faces of the cherubim.

10 ¶And he made the table of shittim wood; two cubits was its length and a cubit its breadth and a cubit and a half its height;

11 And he overlaid it with pure gold, and made for it a crown of gold round about.

12 Also he made for it a border of a handbreadth round about; and made a crown of gold for the border thereof round about.

13 And he cast for it four rings of gold, and fastened the rings on the four corners that were in the four feet thereof.

14 Over against the border were the rings, the places for the poles to carry the table.

15 And he made the poles of shittim wood, and overlaid them with gold to carry the table with them.

16 And he made the vessels which were upon the table, its flagons, its spoons, its cups, and its bowls, wherein the drink offering is poured out, of pure gold.

17 ¶And he made the candlestick of pure gold; of cast work made he the candlestick; its shaft, its branches, its bowls, its buds, and its flowers were of the same;

18 And six branches went out of its sides; three branches of the candlestick went out of the one side of it and three branches of the candlestick out of the other side of it;

19 Three bowls were fastened on one shaft with their buds and flowers; and three bowls were fastened on another shaft with their buds and flowers; so, throughout the six branches going out of the candlestick.

20 And in the candlestick were four bowls fastened to it with their buds and flowers;

21 And a bud under two branches of the same, and a bud under two branches of the same, and a bud under two branches of the same; likewise for the six branches going out of the candlestick.

22 Their buds and branches were of the same; all of it was one piece of molten work of pure gold.

23 And he made its seven lamps and its snuffers and its snuff dishes of pure gold.

24 Of a talent of pure gold he made it, and all its vessels.

25 ¶And he made the incense altar of shittim wood; the length of it was a cubit and the breadth of it a cubit; it was foursquare; and two cubits was the height of it; and its horns were of the same.

26 And he overlaid it with pure gold, both the top of it and its sides round about, and the horns of it; and he made for it a crown of gold round about.

27 And he made two rings of gold for it under its crown, by the two corners of it, upon the two sides thereof, as places for the poles to carry it with them.

28 And he made the poles of shittim wood, and overlaid them with gold.

29 ¶And he made the holy anointing oil and the pure incense of sweet spices, according to the work of a perfumer.

CHAPTER 38

AND he made the altar of burnt offering of shittim wood; five cubits was its length and five cubits its breadth; it was foursquare; and three cubits were the height thereof.

2 And he made its horns on the four corners of it; its horns were of the same; and he overlaid it with brass.

3 And he made all the vessels of the altar, the pots, the cauldrons, the hanging pots, the fleshhooks, the shovels, the censers; all its vessels he made of brass.

4 And he made for the altar a bronze grate of network halfway under the base of it.

5 And he cast four rings for the four corners of the grate of brass to be places for the poles.

6 And he made the poles of shittim wood, and overlaid them with brass.

7 And put the poles into the rings on the sides of the altar to carry it with them; he made the altar hollow with boards.

8 ¶And he placed the laver of brass

and its base of brass at the assembly house, for the women who came to pray at the door of the tabernacle of the congregation.

9 ¶And he made the court: for the south side southward the hangings of the court were of fine twined linen, a hundred cubits;

10 Their pillars were twenty, and their bronze sockets twenty; the hooks of the pillars and their fillets were of silver.

11 And for the north side the hangings were a hundred cubits, their pillars were twenty, and their sockets of brass twenty; the hooks of the pillars and their fillets were of silver.

12 And for the west side were hangings of fifty cubits, their pillars ten, and their sockets ten; the hooks of the pillars and their fillets were of silver.

13 And for the east side eastward fifty cubits.

14 The hangings of the one side of the gate were fifteen cubits; their pillars three, and their sockets three.

15 And for the other side, on this hand and that of the gate of the court, were hangings of fifteen cubits for each side; their pillars three, and their sockets three.

16 All the hangings of the court round about were of fine twined linen.

17 And the sockets of the pillars were of brass; the hooks of the pillars and their fillets were of silver; and the overlaying of their capitals of silver; and all the pillars of the court were overlaid with silver.

18 And the hanging for the gate of the court was needlework, of blue, and purple, and scarlet material, and fine twined linen; and twenty cubits long, and the height and the width were five cubits, opposite the hangings of the court.

19 And their pillars were four, and their sockets of brass four; their hooks of silver, and the overlaying of their capitals and their fillets of silver.

20 And all the pins of the tabernacle, and of the court round about, were of brass.

21 ¶This is the sum of the tabernacle, even of the tabernacle of the testimony, as it was counted, according to the commandment of Moses, and the work of the Levites, under the supervision of Ithamar, the son of Aaron, the priest.

22 And Bezaliel the son of Uri, the son of Hur, of the tribe of Judah, made all that the LORD commanded Moses.

23 And with him was Elihab, the son of Ahisamakh, of the tribe of Dan, a carpenter, and a craftsman, and an embroiderer in blue, and in purple, and in scarlet material, and in fine linen.

24 All the gold that was used for the work in all the work of the holy place, even the gold of the offering, was twenty-nine talents, and four hundred and thirty shekels, by the weight of the sanctuary.

25 And the silver of those who were numbered of the congregation was a hundred talents, and a thousand seven hundred and seventy-five shekels, by the shekel of the sanctuary:

26 A shekel for every head, that is half a shekel, by the weight of the sanctuary, for every one who was included in the number, from twenty years old and upward, for six hundred thousand and three thousand and five hundred and fifty men.

27 And the total sum was one hundred talents of silver, for the casting of the sockets of the sanctuary, and the sockets of the veil; a hundred sockets were made from a hundred talents, a talent for a socket.

28 And of the thousand seven hundred and seventy-five shekels he made hooks for the pillars, and overlaid their capitals, and overlaid the hooks with silver.

29 And the total sum of the brass of the offering was seventy talents, and two thousand and four hundred shekels.

30 And with it he made the sockets of the door of the tabernacle of the congregation, and the bronze altar, and the bronze grate for it, and all the vessels of the altar,

31 And the sockets of the court round about, and the sockets of the

court gate, and all the pins of the tabernacle, and all the pins of the court round about.

CHAPTER 39

AND of the blue and purple and scarlet material, they made vestments for the service, to minister in the sanctuary, and made the holy vestments for Aaron, as the LORD commanded Moses.

2 And they made the ephod of gold, blue, and purple, and scarlet, and fine twined linen.

3 And they did beat the gold into thin plates, and cut it into wires, to be worked in the blue, and in the purple, and in the scarlet material, and in the fine linen, with artistic workmanship.

4 They made shoulder-pieces for it, to join it together; by the two edges was it joined together.

5 And the embroidered girdle of the ephod that was upon it was of the same material, according to the work thereof; of gold, blue, and purple, and scarlet material, and fine twined linen; as the LORD commanded Moses.

6 ¶And they made the onyx stones inclosed and set in work of gold, engraved, as signets are engraved, with the names of the sons of Israel.

7 And they put them on the shoulder-pieces of the ephod, that they should be stones for a memorial for the sons of Israel; as the LORD commanded Moses.

8 ¶And they made the breastplate, the work of an artist, like the work of the ephod; of gold, blue, and purple, and scarlet material, and fine twined linen.

9 It was foursquare; they made the breastplate double; a span was its length and a span its breadth, being doubled.

10 And they set it in four rows of stones; the first row was a sardius, a topaz, and an emerald; this was the first row.

11 And the second row, a carbuncle, a sapphire, and a jasper.

12 And the third row, a jacinth, a carnelian, and an amethyst.

13 And the fourth row, a beryl, an onyx, and a jasper; they were inclosed and set in the work of gold in their inclosings.

14 And the stones were according to the names of the sons of Israel, twelve, according to their names, engraved like the engravings of signets, everyone with his name, according to the twelve tribes.

15 And they made upon the breastplate chains at the two ends, of braided work of pure gold.

16 And they made two settings of gold and two gold rings; and put the two rings on the two ends of the breastplate.

17 And they fastened the two braided chains of gold to the two rings on the ends of the breastplate.

18 And the two ends of the two braided chains they fastened to the two settings, and put them on the shoulder-pieces of the ephod, in the front of it.

19 And they made two rings of gold, and put them on the two ends of the breastplate, on the border of it, which was on the side of the ephod from within.

20 And they made two other golden rings, and put them on the two shoulder-pieces of the ephod from within, toward the front of it, over against the other coupling thereof, above the embroidered girdle of the ephod.

21 And they did bind the breastplate by its rings to the rings of the ephod with a cord of blue, that it might be above the embroidered girdle of the ephod and that the breastplate might not be loosed from the ephod; as the LORD commanded Moses.

22 ¶And they made the robe of the ephod of fine woven work, all of blue.

23 And the opening of the robe was within it, as the hole of a coat of mail, with a binding round about the opening, that it might not be torn.

24 And they made on the hems of the robe pomegranates of blue and purple and scarlet material and fine twined linen.

25 And they made bells of pure gold, and fastened the bells between the pomegranates on the hem of the

robe, round about between the pomegranates;

26 A bell of gold and a pomegranate, and a bell of gold and a pomegranate, round about the hem of the robe to minister in; as the LORD commanded Moses.

27 ¶And they made coats of fine linen of woven work for Aaron and for his sons,

28 And a mitre of fine linen, and goodly bonnets of fine linen, and breeches of fine linen,

29 And a girdle of fine twined linen, and blue and purple and scarlet needlework; as the LORD commanded Moses,

30 ¶And they made the plate of the holy crown of pure gold, and wrote upon it an inscription like to the engraving of a signet, HOLINESS TO THE LORD.

31 And they tied to it a cord of blue to fasten it over the mitre; as the LORD commanded Moses.

32 ¶Thus all the work of the tabernacle of the congregation was finished; and the children of Israel did according to all that the LORD commanded Moses, so did they.

33 ¶And they brought the tabernacle to Moses, the tent and all its vessels, its rings, its clasps, its boards, its pins, its bars, its pillars, and its sockets,

34 And the covering of rams' skins dyed red, and the covering of badgers' skins, and the veil for the covering of the door,

35 The ark of the testimony, and its poles, and the mercy seat,

36 The table, and all its vessels, and the shewbread,

37 The pure candlestick, with its lamps, and with the lamps to be set in order, and all its vessels, and the oil for light,

38 And the golden altar, and the anointing oil, and the sweet incense, and the hanging for the tabernacle door,

39 The altar of brass, and its grate of brass, its poles, and all its vessels, the laver and its base,

40 The hangings of the court, its pillars, its sockets, and the hanging for the court gate, its cords, its pins, and all the vessels of the service of the tabernacle of the congregation,

41 The vestments of the service to minister in the holy place, and the holy vestments for Aaron the priest, and vestments for his sons, to minister in the priest's office.

42 According to all that the LORD commanded Moses, so the children of Israel made all the work.

43 And Moses looked upon all the work, and, behold, they had done it as the LORD had commanded Moses, even so had they done it; and Moses blessed them.

CHAPTER 40

AND the LORD said to Moses, 2 On the first day of the first month you shall set up the tabernacle of the congregation.

3 And you shall put in it the ark of the testimony, and cover the ark with the veil.

4 And you shall bring in the table, and set in order the things that are to be placed upon it; and you shall bring in the candlestick and light the lamps thereof.

5 And you shall set the altar of gold for the incense before the ark of the testimony, and fasten the hanging to the entry of the tabernacle.

6 And you shall set the altar of the burnt offering in front of the door of the tabernacle of the congregation.

7 And you shall set the laver between the tent of the congregation and the altar, and shall put water in it.

8 And you shall set up the court round about, and hang up the hanging at the court gate.

9 And you shall take the anointing oil, and anoint the tabernacle and all that is in it, and shall sanctify it and all its vessels; and it shall be holy.

10 And you shall anoint the altar of the burnt offering and all its vessels, and sanctify the altar; and it shall be an altar most holy.

11 And you shall anoint the laver and its base, and sanctify it.

12 Then you shall bring Aaron and his sons to the door of the tabernacle

of the congregation, and wash them with water.

13 And you shall put upon Aaron the holy vestments and anoint him and sanctify him; that he may minister to me in the priest's office.

14 Then you shall bring his sons and clothe them with coats;

15 And you shall anoint them, as you did anoint Aaron your brother, that they may minister to me in the priest's office; for their anointing shall surely be an everlasting priesthood throughout their generations.

16 Thus did Moses according to all that the LORD commanded him; so did he.

17 ¶And it came to pass in the first month in the second year, on the first day of the week, that the tabernacle was set up.

18 And Moses set up the tabernacle and fastened its pegs and set up its boards and put in its bars and raised up its pillars.

19 And he spread the covering over the tabernacle and put the covering of skins over it; as the LORD commanded Moses.

20 ¶And he took the testimony and put it into the ark and set the poles on the ark and put the mercy seat above upon the ark:

21 And he brought the ark into the tabernacle and set up the veil of the covering of the door and covered the ark of the testimony; as the LORD commanded Moses.

22 ¶And he put the table in the tent of the congregation on the side of the tabernacle northward, outside the veil.

23 And he set the bread in order upon it before the LORD; as the LORD had commanded Moses.

24 ¶And he put the candlestick in the tabernacle of the congregation, over against the table on the side of the tabernacle southward.

25 And he lighted the lamps before the LORD; as the LORD commanded Moses.

26 ¶And he put the golden altar in the tabernacle of the congregation in front of the veil;

27 And he burnt sweet incense upon it; as the LORD commanded Moses.

28 ¶And he set up the hanging at the door of the tabernacle.

29 And he put the altar of burnt offering at the door of the tabernacle of the congregation, and offered upon it the burnt offering and the meal offering; as the LORD commanded Moses.

30 ¶And he set the laver between the tent of the congregation and the altar, and put water there to wash with it.

31 And Moses and Aaron and his sons washed their hands and their feet at it;

32 When they went into the tent of the congregation, and when they came near to the altar, they washed; as the LORD commanded Moses.

33 And he set up the court round about the tabernacle and the altar, and set up the hanging of the court gate. So Moses finished the work.

34 ¶Then a cloud covered the tent of the congregation, and the glory of the LORD filled the tabernacle.

35 And Moses was not able to enter into the tent of the congregation, because the cloud abode upon it, and the glory of the LORD filled the tabernacle.

36 And when the cloud was lifted up from over the tabernacle, the children of Israel started onward in all their journeys;

37 But if the cloud was not lifted up, then they did not journey till the day that it was lifted up.

38 For the cloud of the LORD was upon the tabernacle by day, and fire was on it by night in the sight of all the house of Israel throughout all their journeys.

THE THIRD BOOK OF MOSES, CALLED

LEVITICUS

CHAPTER 1

AND the LORD called to Moses and spoke to him from the tabernacle of the congregation, saying,

2 Speak to the children of Israel and say to them, When any man of you brings an offering to the LORD, you shall bring your offerings of the cattle, even of the herd and of the flock.

3 If his offering be a burnt sacrifice of the herd, let him offer a male without blemish; he shall offer it at the door of the tabernacle of the congregation to make reconciliation for himself before the LORD.

4 And he shall put his hand upon the head of his burnt offering; and it shall be accepted for him to make atonement for him.

5 And he shall kill the bullock before the LORD; and the priests, Aaron's sons, shall bring the blood and sprinkle the blood round about upon the altar that is by the door of the tabernacle of the congregation.

6 And he shall flay the burnt offering and cut it into pieces.

7 And the priests, Aaron's sons, shall put fire upon the altar and lay the wood in order upon the fire;

8 And the priests, Aaron's sons, shall lay the parts, the head and the fat, in order upon the wood that is on the fire which is upon the altar;

9 But its entrails and its legs he shall wash with water; and the priest shall burn all on the altar; it is a burnt offering, an offering of a sweet savour made by fire to the LORD.

10 ¶And if his offering be of the flocks, of the sheep or of the goats, for a burnt sacrifice, he shall offer a male without blemish.

11 And he shall kill it on the north side of the altar before the LORD; and the priests, Aaron's sons, shall sprinkle its blood round about upon the altar.

12 And he shall cut it into pieces, with its head and its fat; and the priest shall lay them in order on the wood, that is on the fire, which is upon the altar;

13 But he shall wash the entrails and the legs with water; and the priest shall offer it all and burn it upon the altar; it is a burnt sacrifice, an offering made by fire, a sweet savour to the LORD.

14 ¶And if the burnt sacrifice for his offering to the LORD be of fowls, then he shall bring his offering of turtledoves or of young pigeons.

15 And the priest shall bring it to the altar, and wring off its head and burn it on the altar; and its blood shall be wrung out at the side of the altar round about;

16 And he shall pluck away its crop with its feathers, and cast it beside the altar on the east side in the place of the ashes;

17 And he shall cleave it between its wings, but shall not divide it asunder; and the priest shall burn it upon the altar, upon the wood that is upon the fire; it is a burnt sacrifice, an offering made by fire, a sweet savour to the LORD.

CHAPTER 2

WHEN any person shall offer a meal offering to the LORD, his offering shall be of fine flour; and he shall pour oil upon it and put frankincense thereon;

2 And he shall bring it to Aaron's sons, the priests; and he shall take from it his handful of the fine flour,

and from the oil, with all the frankincense thereof; and the priest shall burn his memorial offering upon the altar to be an offering made by fire, a sweet savour to the LORD.

3 And the remnant of the meal offering shall be for Aaron and his sons; it is a thing most holy of the offerings of the LORD made by fire.

4 ¶And when you offer a meal offering baked in the oven, it shall be unleavened cakes of fine flour mixed with oil or unleavened wafers mixed with oil.

5 ¶And if your offering be a meal offering baked on a griddle, it shall be of fine unleavened flour mixed with oil.

6 You shall part it in pieces and pour oil upon the meal offering.

7 ¶And if your offering is a meal offering baked in a pan, it shall be made of fine flour with oil.

8 And you shall bring the meal offering that is made of these things to the LORD; and you shall present it to the priest and he shall place it upon the altar to the LORD.

9 And the priest shall take from the meal offering a memorial thereof and shall burn it upon the altar; it is an offering made by fire, a sweet savour to the LORD.

10 And what is left of the meal offering shall be for Aaron and his sons; it is a thing most holy of the offerings of the LORD made by fire.

11 Every meal offering which you shall offer to the LORD shall be made without leaven, for you shall burn no leaven nor any honey in any offering of the LORD made by fire.

12 ¶As for the offerings of the firstfruits, you shall offer them to the LORD; but they shall not be burnt on the altar for a sweet savour.

13 And every offering of your meal offering you shall season with salt; neither shall you let the salt of the covenant of your God to be lacking from your meal offering; with all your offerings you shall offer salt.

14 And if you offer a meal offering of the first-fruits to the LORD, you shall offer for the meal offering a handful of pure ears of wheat parched by fire; wheat beaten out of full ears, pure, you shall offer of your firstfruits.

15 And you shall put oil upon it and lay frankincense thereon; for it is a meal offering.

16 And the priest shall burn the memorial offering of it, part of the beaten wheat and part of the oil with all the frankincense thereof; it is an offering made by fire to the LORD.

CHAPTER 3

IF his offering is a sacrifice of peace offering, if he offer it of the herd, whether it be a male or a female, he shall offer it without blemish before the LORD.

2 And he shall lay his hand upon the head of his offering and kill it at the door of the tabernacle of the congregation and Aaron's sons, the priests, shall sprinkle the blood upon the altar round about.

3 And he shall offer of the sacrifice of the peace offering an offering made by fire to the LORD, the fat that covers the entrails, and all the fat that is on the entrails

4 And the two kidneys, and the fat that is on them which is by the flanks, and the caul above the liver, with the kidneys, he shall take away.

5 And Aaron's sons shall burn it on the altar upon the burnt sacrifice which is upon the wood that is on the fire; it is an offering made by fire, a sweet savour to the LORD.

6 ¶And if his offering for a sacrifice of peace offering to the LORD be of the flock, male or female, he shall offer it without blemish.

7 If he offer a lamb for his offering, then shall he offer it before the LORD.

8 And he shall lay his hand upon the head of his offering and kill it before the LORD at the door of the tabernacle of the congregation and Aaron's sons shall sprinkle its blood round about upon the altar.

9 And he shall offer of the sacrifice of the peace offering an offering made by fire to the LORD; its fat and the whole rump shall he remove close to the backbone, and the fat that

covers the entrails, and all the fat that is upon the entrails,

10 And the two kidneys, and the fat that is upon them which is by the flanks, and the caul above the liver, with the kidneys, shall he remove.

11 And the priest shall burn it upon the altar; it is a food offering made by fire to the LORD.

12 ¶And if his offering be of the goats, then he shall offer it before the LORD.

13 And he shall lay his hand upon the head of it and kill it before the tabernacle of the congregation; and the sons of Aaron shall sprinkle its blood upon the altar round about.

14 And he shall offer part of it as his offering made by fire to the LORD; the fat that covers the entrails, and all the fat that is upon the entrails

15 And the two kidneys, and the fat that is upon them which is by the flanks, and the caul above the liver, with the kidneys, shall he remove.

16 And the priest shall burn them upon the altar; it is a food offering made by fire for a sweet savour; all the fat is the LORD's.

17 It shall be a perpetual statute for your generations throughout all your dwellings that you eat neither fat nor blood.

CHAPTER 4

AND the LORD spoke unto Moses, saying,

2 Speak to the children of Israel, saying, If a person shall sin through ignorance against any of the commandments of the LORD concerning things which ought not to be done, and shall do any one of them;

3 If the priest that is anointed do sin according to the sins of the people; then let him offer for the sin which he has committed a young bullock without blemish to the LORD for his sin offering.

4 And he shall bring the bullock to the door of the tabernacle of the congregation before the LORD; and he shall lay his hand upon the bullock's head and kill the bullock before the LORD.

5 And the anointed priest shall take of the blood of the bullock and bring it to the tabernacle of the congregation;

6 And the priest shall dip his finger in the blood and sprinkle of the blood seven times before the LORD before the veil of the sanctuary.

7 And the priest shall put some of the blood upon the horns of the altar of sweet incense before the LORD, which is in the tabernacle of the congregation; and he shall pour all the rest of the blood of the bullock at the bottom of the altar of the burnt offering, which is at the door of the tabernacle of the congregation.

8 And he shall take off from it all the fat of the bullock for the sin offering, the fat that covers the entrails, and all the fat that is on the entrails,

9 And the two kidneys, and the fat that is on them which is by the flanks, and the caul above the liver, with the kidneys, it he shall take away,

10 Just as it was taken off from the bullock of the sacrifice of peace offering; and the priest shall burn them upon the altar of the burnt offering.

11 And the skin of the bullock and all its flesh, with its dung, its head, its legs, and its entrails,

12 The whole bullock he shall carry forth outside the camp to a clean place where the ashes are poured out and shall burn it on the wood which is upon the fire; where the ashes are poured out it shall be burnt.

13 ¶And if the whole congregation of Israel go wrong, and the thing is hidden from the eyes of the assembly, and they have done somewhat against any of the commandments of the LORD concerning things which should not be done and are guilty;

14 When the sin which they have committed against it is known, then the whole congregation shall offer a young bullock for the sin and bring it before the tabernacle of the congregation.

15 And the elders of the congregation shall lay their hands upon the head of the bullock before the LORD

and the bullock shall be killed before the LORD.

16 And the priest that is anointed shall bring of the blood of the bullock to the tabernacle of the congregation;

17 And the priest shall dip his finger in the blood and sprinkle it seven times before the LORD in front of the veil.

18 And he shall put some of the blood upon the horns of the altar which is before the LORD, in the tabernacle of the congregation, and shall pour out all the blood at the bottom of the altar of the burnt offering, which is at the door of the tabernacle of the congregation.

19 And he shall take all its fat from it and burn it upon the altar.

20 And he shall do with the bullock just as he did with the bullock for a sin offering, so shall he do with this; and the priest shall make an atonement for them and it shall be forgiven them.

21 And they shall carry forth the bullock outside the camp and burn it as he burned the first bullock; it is a sin offering for the congregation.

22 ¶When a ruler shall sin and shall do something through ignorance against any of the commandments of the LORD his God concerning things which should not be done, and is guilty;

23 Or if his sin which he has committed is made known to him, he shall bring as his offering a kid of the goats, a male without blemish;

24 And he shall lay his hand upon the head of the goat and kill it in the place where they kill the burnt offering before the LORD; it is a sin offering.

25 And the priest shall take some of the blood of the sin offering with his finger and put it upon the horns of the altar of burnt offering and pour out the rest of the blood at the bottom of the altar of burnt offering.

26 And he shall burn all its fat upon the altar as the fat of the sacrifice of peace offerings; and the priest shall make an atonement for him for his sin and it shall be forgiven him.

27 ¶And if any one of the common people of the land sin through ignorance, while he does something against any of the commandments of the LORD concerning things which ought not to be done, and be guilty;

28 Or if his sin which he has committed is made known to him; then he shall bring as his offering a kid of the goats, a female without blemish, for his sin which he has committed.

29 And he shall lay his hand upon the head of the sin offering and slay the sin offering in the place where the burnt offering is killed.

30 And the priest shall take some of the blood with his finger and sprinkle it upon the horns of the altar of burnt offering and the rest of the blood he shall pour out at the bottom of the altar.

31 And he shall take away all the fat thereof, as the fat is taken away from the sacrifice of peace offerings; and the priest shall burn it upon the altar for a sweet savour to the LORD; and the priest shall make an atonement for him and it shall be forgiven him.

32 And if he bring of the lambs for his sin offering, then he shall bring a female without blemish.

33 And he shall lay his hand upon the head of the sin offering and slay it for a sin offering at the place where burnt offering victims are killed.

34 And the priest shall take some of the blood of the sin offering with his finger and sprinkle it upon the horns of the altar of burnt offering and the rest of the blood he shall pour out at the bottom of the altar;

35 And he shall take away all its fat, as the fat of the lamb is taken away from the sacrifice of the peace offerings; and the priest shall burn them upon the altar according to the offerings made by fire to the LORD; and the priest shall make an atonement for his sin that he has committed and it shall be forgiven him.

CHAPTER 5

WHEN a person sins and hears the voice of swearing and is a witness, whether he has seen or known of it, if he do not tell it, then he shall suffer for his iniquity.

2 Or if any person touches any unclean thing, whether it be a carcass of an unclean beast or a carcass of unclean cattle or the carcass of unclean creeping things, and disregards it, he also is unclean and guilty.

3 Or if he touches the uncleanness of man, whatever uncleanness it be that a man shall be defiled with, and disregards it, and he knows that he has sinned;

4 Or if any person swears with his lips to do evil or to do good, in whatever decision a man has sworn by an oath, and he disregards it, and yet he knows that he has sinned in one of these things,

5 And it shall be when he shall be guilty in one of these things that he shall confess that he has sinned in that thing;

6 And he shall bring as his trespass offering to the LORD for his sin that he has committed, a female from the flock, a lamb or a female kid of the goats, for a sin offering; and the priest shall make an atonement for him concerning his sin;

7 And if he cannot afford to bring a she lamb, then he shall bring for his sin offering two turtledoves or two young pigeons, one for a sin offering and the other for a burnt offering.

8 And he shall bring them to the priest, who shall offer that which is for the sin offering first, and he shall wring off its head from its neck, but shall not sever it;

9 And he shall sprinkle some of the blood of the sin offering upon the side of the altar; and the rest of the blood shall be wrung out at the bottom of the altar; it is a sin offering.

10 And he shall offer the second for a burnt offering, according to the ritual; and the priest shall make an atonement for him for his sin which he has committed and it shall be forgiven him.

11 ¶But if he cannot afford two turtledoves or two young pigeons, then he shall bring for his offering for the sin which he has committed the tenth part of an ephah of fine flour for a sin offering; he shall put no oil upon it, neither shall he put any frankincense thereon; for it is a sin offering.

12 Then he shall bring it to the priest, and the priest shall take his handful of it as a memorial thereof and burn it on the altar according to the offerings made by fire to the LORD; it is a sin offering.

13 And the priest shall make an atonement for him for the sin which he has committed in any one of these things, and it shall be forgiven him; and the rest shall be the priest's as a meal offering.

14 ¶And the LORD spoke to Moses, saying,

15 If any person commits a trespass and sins through ignorance in the holy things of the LORD; then he shall bring for his trespass offering to the LORD a ram without blemish out of the flocks, valued in money at two shekels of silver, according to the shekel of the sanctuary, for a trespass offering;

16 And the sinner shall make amends for the harm that he has done in the holy thing, and shall add a fifth part to it and give it to the priest; and the priest shall make an atonement for him with the ram of the trespass offering and it shall be forgiven him.

17 ¶And if any person sins and commits any of these things which are forbidden to be done by the commandments of the LORD; though he does not know that he has sinned, yet he is guilty and shall suffer for his iniquity.

18 And he shall bring to the priest a ram of value without blemish out of the flocks for a trespass offering; and the priest shall make an atonement for him for his ignorance in erring, even though he knew it not, and it shall be forgiven him.

19 It is a trespass offering; he certainly shall bring an offering to the LORD.

CHAPTER 6

AND the LORD spoke to Moses, saying,

2 If any person sins and commits an

iniquity against the LORD or lies to his neighbor over a pledge or partnership or takes away a thing by violence or has defrauded his neighbor

3 Or has found that which was lost, and lies about it, and swears falsely; in any of these things that a man does, sinning therein;

4 Then it shall be, because he has sinned and is guilty, he shall restore what he took violently or what he got deceitfully or the pledge which was delivered to him to keep or the lost thing which he found

5 Or anything about which he has sworn falsely; he shall restore it in the principal and shall add a fifth part more to it and give it to him to whom it belongs on the day of his trespass offering.

6 And he shall bring his trespass offering to the LORD, a ram of value without blemish out of the flocks for a trespass offering to the priest;

7 And the priest shall make an atonement for him before the LORD; and it shall be forgiven him for any of the things that he has done in trespassing therein.

8 ¶And the LORD spoke to Moses, saying,

9 Command Aaron and his sons, saying, This is the law of the burnt offering: It is the burnt offering because of the burning upon the altar all night unto the morning, and the fire of the altar shall be kept burning in it.

10 And the priest shall put on his linen garment, and his linen breeches shall be put upon his body, and he shall remove the ashes which the fire has consumed with the burnt offering on the altar, and he shall put them beside the altar.

11 Then he shall put off his garments and put on other garments and carry forth the ashes outside the camp to a clean place.

12 And the fire upon the altar shall be kept burning on it; it shall not be put out; and the priest shall pile up wood on it from morning to morning and lay the burnt offering in order upon it; and he shall burn on it the fat of the peace offerings.

13 The fire shall be kept burning upon the altar continually; it shall never go out.

14 ¶This is the law of the meal offering: the sons of Aaron shall offer it before the LORD, before the altar.

15 And the priest shall take of it his handful of the fine flour of the meal offering and of the oil thereof and all the frankincense which is upon the meal offering, and shall burn it upon the altar for a sweet savour, as a memorial to the LORD.

16 And the remainder of it shall Aaron and his sons eat; with unleavened bread shall it be eaten in a holy place; in the court of the tabernacle of the congregation shall they eat it.

17 It shall not be baked with leaven. I have given it to them for their portion of my offerings made by fire; it is most holy, as is the sin offering and as is the trespass offering.

18 All the males among the children of Aaron shall eat of it. It shall be a statute for ever throughout your generations out of the offerings of the LORD made by fire; every one that touches them shall be holy.

19 ¶And the LORD spoke to Moses, saying,

20 This is the offering of Aaron and of his sons which they shall offer to the LORD on the day when he is anointed: a tenth part of an ephah of fine flour for a perpetual meal offering, half of it in the morning and half of it in the evening, continually.

21 On a griddle it shall be made with oil; he shall bake it soft, and the baked pieces of the meal offering you shall offer for a sweet savour to the LORD.

22 And the priest of his sons who is anointed in his stead shall offer it; it is a statute for ever to the LORD; it shall be wholly burned.

23 For every meal offering for the priest shall be wholly burned; it shall not be eaten.

24 ¶And the LORD spoke to Moses, saying,

25 Speak to Aaron and to his sons, saying, This is the law of the sin offering: In the place where the burnt offering is killed shall the sin offering

be killed before the LORD; it is most holy.

26 The priest who offers it for sin shall eat it; in a holy place shall it be eaten, in the court of the tabernacle of the congregation.

27 Whosoever shall touch the meat thereof shall be holy; and when there is sprinkled of its blood upon any garment, you shall wash that whereon it was sprinkled in a holy place.

28 But the earthen vessel in which it was cooked shall be broken; and if it is cooked in a bronze vessel, it shall be both scoured, and rinsed in water.

29 All the priests among Aaron's sons shall eat of it; it is most holy.

30 And no sin offering whereof any of the blood is brought into the tabernacle of the congregation to make atonement in the holy place shall be eaten; it shall be burned in the fire.

CHAPTER 7

THIS is the law of the trespass offering; it is most holy.

2 In the place where they kill the burnt offering they shall kill the trespass offering; and its blood shall they sprinkle round about upon the altar.

3 Then he shall offer of it all its fat; the rump, and the fat that covers the entrails,

4 And the two kidneys, and the fat that is on them which is by the flanks, and the caul above the liver, with the kidneys, it he shall take away;

5 And the priest shall burn them upon the altar for an offering made by fire to the LORD; it is a trespass offering.

6 Every male among the children of Aaron shall eat of it; it shall be eaten in the holy place; it is most holy.

7 As the sin offering is, so is the trespass offering; there is one law for them: the priest who makes atonement with it shall have it.

8 And the priest who offers any man's burnt offering, even the priest shall have to himself the skin of the burnt offering which he has offered.

9 And all the meal offering that is baked in the oven and all that is baked on the griddle and in the pan shall belong to the priest who offers it.

10 And every meal offering, mixed with oil or dry, shall belong to all the sons of Aaron, every one according to his portion.

11 And this is the law of the sacrifice of peace offering, which is offered to the LORD.

12 If he offers it for a thanksgiving, then he shall offer with the sacrifice of thanksgiving unleavened cakes mixed with oil and unleavened wafers anointed with oil and soft baked cakes of fine flour mixed with oil.

13 Besides the cakes, he shall offer for his offering leavened bread with the sacrifice of thanksgiving of his peace offerings.

14 And of it he shall offer one cake out of the whole offering as an offering to the LORD, and it shall be the portion of the priest who sprinkles the blood of the peace offering.

15 And the meat of the sacrifice of his peace offerings for his thanksgiving shall be eaten the same day that it is offered; nothing of it shall be left over until the morning.

16 But if the sacrifice of his offering is a vow or a gift offering, it shall be eaten on the same day that he offers his sacrifice; and on the morrow also the remainder of it shall be eaten;

17 But what is left over of the meat of the sacrifice on the third day shall be burned with fire.

18 And if any of the meat of the sacrifice of the peace offering be eaten at all on the third day, it shall not be accepted, neither shall it be imputed to him that offers it; it shall be an abomination, and the person who eats of it shall suffer for his iniquity.

19 And the meat that touches any unclean thing shall not be eaten; it shall be burned with fire; and as for the meat, all who are clean shall eat of it.

20 But the person who eats of the meat of the sacrifice of the peace offering that pertains to the LORD, having his uncleanness upon him, that person shall be cut off from his people.

21 Moreover the person that shall

touch any unclean thing, such as the uncleanness of man or any unclean beast or any unclean creeping thing, and eat of the meat of the sacrifice of peace offerings which pertain to the LORD, that person shall be cut off from his people.

22 ¶And the LORD spoke to Moses, saying,

23 Speak to the children of Israel, saying, You shall eat no manner of fat, of oxen or of lambs or of goats.

24 And the fat of the beast that dies of itself, and the fat of that which is torn by wild beasts, may be used in any other use; but you shall in no wise eat of it.

25 For whosoever eats the fat of the animal of which men offer an offering made by fire to the LORD, the person that eats it shall be cut off from his people.

26 Moreover you shall eat no manner of blood, whether it be of fowl or of beast, in any of your dwellings.

27 Whosoever eats any manner of blood, that person shall be cut off from his people.

28 ¶And the LORD spoke to Moses, saying,

29 Speak to the children of Israel, saying, He that offers the sacrifice of his peace offerings to the LORD shall bring his offering to the LORD from the sacrifice of his burnt offering.

30 His own hands shall bring his offering for the LORD made by fire; he shall bring the fat which is upon the breast, that the breast may be waved for a wave offering before the LORD.

31 And the priest shall burn the fat upon the altar; but the breast shall be for Aaron and his sons.

32 And the right shoulder shall you give to the LORD for an offering of the sacrifices of your peace offerings.

33 He among the sons of Aaron who offers the blood and the fat of the peace offering shall have the right shoulder for his part.

34 For the wave breast and the shoulder offering have I taken from the children of Israel from off the sacrifices of their peace offerings, and have given them to Aaron the priest

and to his sons by a statute for ever from among the children of Israel.

35 ¶This is the portion of the anointing of Aaron and of the anointing of his sons from the offerings of the LORD made by fire, on the day when they are presented to minister to the LORD in the priest's office;

36 That which the LORD commanded to be given them of the children of Israel, on the day that he anointed them, by a statute for ever throughout their generations.

37 This is the law of the burnt offering, of the meal offering, of the sin offering, of the trespass offering, of the consecration, and of the sacrifice of the peace offerings,

38 Which the LORD commanded Moses on mount Sinai on the day that he commanded him concerning the children of Israel to offer their offerings to the LORD in the wilderness of Sinai.

CHAPTER 8

AND the LORD spoke to Moses, saying,

2 Take Aaron and his sons with him, and take the vestments and the anointing oil and a bullock for the sin offering and two rams and a basket of unleavened bread,

3 And gather all the congregation together at the door of the tabernacle of the congregation.

4 And Moses did as the LORD commanded him; and the assembly was gathered together at the door of the tabernacle of the congregation.

5 And Moses said to the congregation, This is the commandment which the LORD has commanded to be done.

6 And Moses brought Aaron and his sons, and washed them with water;

7 And put upon him the coat and girded him with the girdle and clothed him with the robe and bound the loin cloth on his loins and put the ephod upon him and girded him with the embroidered girdle of the ephod.

8 And he put the breastplate upon him; and he put on the breastplate the Urim and the Thummin.

9 And he put the mitre upon his

head; and upon the mitre upon his forefront, he put the golden plate, the holy crown; as the LORD commanded Moses.

10 Then Moses took the anointing oil and anointed the tabernacle and all that was in it and sanctified them.

11 And he sprinkled of it upon the altar seven times and anointed the altar and all its vessels and the laver and its base and sanctified them.

12 And he poured some of the anointing oil upon Aaron's head and anointed him and sanctified him.

13 And Moses brought Aaron's sons and put linen vestments upon them and girded them with girdles and put mitres upon them; as the LORD commanded Moses.

14 And he brought the bullock for the sin offering, and Aaron and his sons laid their hands upon the head of the bullock for the sin offering.

15 And he killed it; and Moses took some of the blood with his finger and sprinkled it upon the horns of the altar round about and purified the altar, and the rest of the blood he poured at the base of the altar and sanctified it to make atonement for it.

16 And he took all the fat that was upon the entrails, and the caul above the liver, and the two kidneys, and their fat, and Moses burned it upon the altar.

17 But the bullock and its hide and its meat and its dung he burned with fire outside the camp; as the LORD commanded Moses.

18 ¶And he brought the ram for the burnt offering; and Aaron and his sons laid their hands upon the head of the ram.

19 And he killed it; and Moses sprinkled the blood upon the altar round about.

20 And he cut the ram into pieces; and Moses burned the head and the pieces and the fat.

21 And he washed the entrails and the legs in water; and Moses burned the whole ram upon the altar; it was a burnt sacrifice for a sweet savour, an offering to the LORD; as the LORD commanded Moses.

22 ¶And he brought the other ram, the ram of consecration; and Aaron and his sons laid their hands upon the head of the ram.

23 And Moses killed it; and he took some of the blood of it, and sprinkled it on the tip of Aaron's right ear and upon the thumb of his right hand and upon the great toe of his right foot.

24 And he brought Aaron's sons, and Moses sprinkled some of the blood on the tips of their right ears and on the thumbs of their right hands and on the great toes of their right feet; and Moses sprinkled the blood upon the altar round about.

25 And he took the fat and the rump and all the fat that was upon the entrails and the caul above the liver and the two kidneys, and their fat, and the right shoulder;

26 And out of the basket of unleavened bread that was before the LORD, he took one unleavened cake and a cake of bread with oil and one wafer, and put them on the fat and upon the right shoulder;

27 And he put all upon Aaron's hands, and upon his sons' hands, and waved them for a wave offering before the LORD.

28 And Moses took them from off their hands, and burned them on the altar as a burnt offering; they were consecration offerings for a sweet savour, an offering made by fire to the LORD.

29 And Moses took the breast and waved it for a wave offering before the LORD; for of the ram of consecration it was Moses' portion; as the LORD commanded Moses.

30 And Moses took some of the anointing oil and of the blood which was upon the altar, and sprinkled it upon Aaron and upon his garments and upon his sons and upon his sons' garments with him, and sanctified Aaron and his garments and his sons and his sons' garments with him.

31 ¶And Moses said to Aaron and to his sons, Cook the meat at the door of the tabernacle of the congregation, and there eat it with the bread that is in the basket of consecration, as I

commanded, saying, Aaron and his sons shall eat it.

32 And that which remains of the meat and of the bread you shall burn with fire.

33 And you shall not go out of the door of the tabernacle of the congregation for seven days, until the days of your consecration are at an end; for your consecration will be completed in seven days.

34 Just as I have done this day, so the LORD has commanded to do to make an atonement for you.

35 Therefore you shall remain at the door of the tabernacle of the congregation day and night for seven days and keep the charge of the LORD's observance, that you die not; for so I am commanded.

36 So Aaron and his sons did all things which the LORD commanded by the hand of Moses.

CHAPTER 9

AND it came to pass on the eighth day, Moses called Aaron and his sons and the elders of Israel;

2 And he said to Aaron, Take for yourself a young calf for a sin offering and a ram for a burnt offering, both without blemish, and offer them before the LORD.

3 And he said to the children of Israel, Take for yourselves a kid of the goats for a sin offering, and a calf and a lamb, both of the first year, without blemish, for a burnt offering;

4 Also a bullock and a ram for a peace offering, to sacrifice before the LORD; and a meal offering mixed with oil; for today the LORD will appear to you.

5 ¶And they brought everything that Moses had commanded before the tabernacle of the congregation; and all the congregation drew near and stood before the LORD.

6 And Moses said, This is the thing which the LORD commanded that you should do, and the glory of the LORD shall appear to you.

7 And Moses said to Aaron, Draw near to the altar, and offer your sin offering and your burnt offering, and make an atonement for yourself and for the people; and offer the offering of the people, and make an atonement for them; as the LORD commanded.

8 ¶Aaron therefore drew near to the altar, and killed the calf of the sin offering, which was for himself.

9 And the sons of Aaron brought the blood to him; and he dipped his finger in the blood and sprinkled it upon the horns of the altar, and poured out the blood at the bottom of the altar;

10 But the fat and the kidneys and the caul above the liver of the sin offering he burned upon the altar; as the LORD commanded Moses.

11 And the meat and the hide he burned with fire outside the camp.

12 And he slew the burnt offering; and Aaron's sons presented to him the blood, and he sprinkled it round about upon the altar.

13 And they presented the burnt offering to him, and he cut it into pieces and burned the head upon the altar.

14 And he washed the entrails and the legs, and burned them for a burnt offering upon the altar.

15 ¶And he brought the people's offering, and took the goat which was for the sin offering for the people, and killed it and washed it and offered it for sin, as the first.

16 And he brought the burnt offering, and offered it according to the ritual.

17 And he brought the meal offering and filled his hand from it and burned it upon the altar beside the burnt sacrifice of the morning.

18 Then he killed the bullock also and the ram for a sacrifice of peace offering which was for the people; and Aaron's sons presented to him the blood, which he sprinkled upon the altar round about,

19 And the fat of the bullock and of the ram, the rump, the fat that covers the entrails, and the kidneys, and the caul above the liver;

20 And they put the fat upon the breasts, and he burned the fat upon the altar;

21 And the breasts and the right

shoulder Aaron waved for a wave offering before the LORD; as Moses commanded.

22 And Aaron lifted up his hand toward the people and blessed them, and came down from offering of the sin offering and the burnt offering and the peace offering.

23 And Moses and Aaron went into the tabernacle of the congregation, and came out and blessed the people; and the glory of the LORD appeared in the presence of all the people.

24 And there came a fire out from before the LORD and consumed the burnt offering and the fat upon the altar, which all the people saw; they gave praise and fell on their faces.

CHAPTER 10

AND Nadab and Abihu, the sons of Aaron, each took his censer and put fire therein and laid incense on it and offered strange fire before the LORD, not at its appointed time, and not as he had commanded them.

2 And there went out fire from before the LORD and devoured them, and they died before the LORD.

3 Then Moses said to Aaron, This is what the LORD has spoken, saying, I will be sanctified by those that come near me, and before all the people I will be glorified. And Aaron held his peace.

4 And Moses called Manshael and Elizphan, the sons of Uzziel the uncle of Aaron, and said to them, Come near, carry your brethren from before the sanctuary out of the camp.

5 So they drew near and carried them in their vestments out of the camp; as Moses had said.

6 Then Moses said to Aaron, and to Eleazar and to Ithamar, his sons who were left to him, Do not shave your heads, neither rend your clothes, lest you die, and lest wrath come upon all the people; but let all your brethren, the whole house of Israel, bewail over the victims, whom the LORD burned.

7 And you shall not go out from the door of the tabernacle of the congregation, lest you die; for the anointing oil of the LORD is upon you. And they did according to the word of Moses.

8 ¶And the LORD spoke to Aaron, saying,

9 Do not drink wine nor strong drink, you, nor your sons with you, when you go into the tabernacle of the congregation, lest you die; it shall be a statute for ever throughout your generations;

10 That you may make a distinction between holy and unholy, and between clean and unclean;

11 And that you may teach the children of Israel all the statutes which the LORD has spoken to them by the hand of Moses.

12 ¶And Moses spoke to Aaron, and to Eleazar and to Ithamar, his sons that were left, Take the meal offering that remains of the offerings of the LORD made by fire, and eat it without leaven beside the altar; for it is most holy:

13 And you shall eat it in the holy place because it is your due and your sons' due from the offerings of the LORD made by fire; for so was I commanded.

14 And the wave breast and shoulder offering you shall eat in a clean place; you and your sons and your daughters with you; for they are your due and your sons' due which are given out of the sacrifices of peace offerings of the children of Israel.

15 The shoulder offering and the wave breast they shall bring with the offerings of the fat, made by fire, to wave it as a wave offering before the LORD; and it shall be yours and your sons with you by a statute for ever; as the LORD has commanded, that Aaron and his sons shall eat it.

16 ¶And Moses diligently sought the goat of the sin offering, and, behold, it was burned; and he was angry with Eleazar and Ithamar, the sons of Aaron that were left, and he said to them,

17 Why have you not eaten the sin offering in the holy place, seeing it is most holy, and I have given it to you to bear the iniquity of the congregation, to make atonement for them before the LORD?

18 Behold, the blood of it was not brought in within the sanctuary; you should indeed have eaten it in the holy place, as I was commanded, that Aaron and his sons shall eat it.

19 And Aaron said to Moses, Behold, this day they have offered their sin offerings and their burnt offerings before the LORD; and such things have befallen me; and if I had eaten the sin offering today, should it have been better accepted in the presence of the LORD?

20 And when Moses heard that, he was content.

CHAPTER 11

AND the LORD spoke to Moses and Aaron, and said to them,

2 Speak to the children of Israel and say to them, These are the beasts which you shall eat among all the beasts that are on the earth:

3 Whatever parts the hoof and is cloven-footed and chews the cud among the beasts, that you may eat.

4 Nevertheless these you shall not eat of: those that chew the cud, or those that divide the hoof, as the camel, because it chews the cud but does not divide the hoof; it is unclean to you.

5 And the coney, because it chews the cud but does not divide the hoof; it is unclean to you.

6 And the hare, because it chews the cud but it does not divide the hoof; it is unclean to you.

7 And the swine, though it divide the hoof and is cloven-footed, yet it does not chew the cud; it is unclean to you.

8 Of their flesh you shall not eat, and their carcass you shall not touch; they are unclean to you.

9 ¶These shall you eat of all that are in the waters; whatever has fins and scales in the waters, in the seas, and in the rivers, you shall eat.

10 But all that have not fins and scales in the seas and in the rivers, of all that move in the waters, and of any living thing that is in the waters, they are unclean to you;

11 You shall not eat of their flesh, and their carcasses you shall declare unclean.

12 Whatever has no fins nor scales in the waters is unclean to you.

13 ¶And these you shall abhor among the birds; they shall not be eaten, because they are unclean: the eagle and the vulture

14 And the raven after its kind;

15 And the ostrich and the night hawk after its kind;

16 And the little owl and the pelican, the great owl, the cuckoo, and the hawk after its kind;

17 And the stork, the bee eater,

18 And the swan and the hoopoe after their kind,

19 And the heron and the peacock.

20 All species that creep, going upon all fours, are unclean to you.

21 Yet these things you may eat of every flying insect that goes upon all fours, which have legs above their feet with which to leap on the earth;

22 Of these you may eat: the locust after its kind and the large winged locust after its kind,

23 But all other flying insects which have four feet are unclean to you.

24 And by these you shall be unclean; whosoever touches their carcasses shall be unclean until the evening.

25 And whosoever carries of their carcasses shall wash his clothes and be unclean until the evening.

26 The carcasses of every beast which divides the hoof and is not cloven-footed, nor chews the cud, are unclean to you; every one who touches them shall be unclean until the evening.

27 And whatever goes upon his paws, among all manner of beasts that go on all fours, are unclean to you; whosoever touches their carcasses shall be unclean until the evening.

28 And he who carries their carcasses shall wash his clothes and be unclean until the evening, because they are unclean to you.

29 ¶These also are unclean to you among all the creeping things that creep upon the earth: the weasel, and the mouse, the lizard after its kind,

30 And the ferret, and the mole, the

yellow lizard, and the chameleon, and the snail.

31 These are unclean to you among all that creep; whosoever touches them, when they are dead, shall be unclean until the evening.

32 And upon whatever thing any of them falls when they are dead, that thing shall be unclean; whether it be any vessel of wood or a garment or a skin or a sack or whatever vessel it be wherein any work is done, it must be put into water and it shall be unclean until the evening; so it shall be cleansed.

33 And every earthen vessel into which any of them falls, whatever is in it shall be unclean; and you shall break it.

34 Of all food which may be eaten, that on which such water falls shall be unclean; and all drink that may be drunk in every such vessel shall be unclean.

35 And everything upon which any part of their carcasses falls shall be unclean; whether it be oven or bakehouse, they shall be broken down: for they are unclean, and shall be unclean to you.

36 Nevertheless a fountain or a cistern and the pools of water shall be clean; but whosoever touches their carcasses shall be unclean.

37 And if any part of their carcasses falls upon any sowing seed which is to be sown, it shall be clean.

38 But if any water be put upon the seed and any part of their carcasses falls on it, it shall be unclean to you.

39 And if any animal of which you may eat dies, he who touches the carcass thereof shall be unclean until the evening.

40 And he who eats of its carcass shall wash his clothes and shall be unclean until the evening; he also that carries the carcass of it shall wash his clothes and be unclean until the evening.

41 And every creeping thing that creeps upon the earth is unclean to you; it shall not be eaten.

42 Whatever goes upon its belly and whatever goes upon all fours or whatever has many feet among all creeping things that creep upon the earth, you shall not eat of them; for they are unclean.

43 You shall not make yourselves unclean with any creeping thing that creeps upon the earth, lest you become unclean with them; defile not yourselves with them.

44 For I am the LORD your God; you shall therefore sanctify yourselves, and you shall be holy; for I am holy; neither shall you defile yourselves with any manner of creeping thing that creeps upon the earth.

45 For I am the LORD your God who brought you up out of the land of Egypt to be your God; you shall therefore be holy, for I am holy.

46 This is the law of beast and of fowl and of every living creature that moves in the water and of every creature that creeps upon the earth;

47 To make a distinction between the unclean and the clean and between the beast that may be eaten and the beast that may not be eaten.

CHAPTER 12

AND the LORD spoke to Moses and said to him,

2 Speak to the children of Israel, saying, If a woman have conceived and bear a male child, then she shall be unclean seven days; according to the days of her menstruation she shall be unclean.

3 And on the eighth day the flesh of his foreskin shall be circumcised.

4 And she shall continue for thirty-three days in the blood of her purifying; she shall touch no hallowed thing, nor come into the sanctuary, until the days of her purifying be fulfilled.

5 But if she bears a female child, then she shall be unclean two weeks, as in her menstruation; and she shall continue in the blood of her purifying for sixty-six days.

6 And when the days of her purifying are fulfilled for a son or for a daughter, she shall bring a lamb of the first year for a burnt offering and a young pigeon or a turtledove for a sin offering to the door of the taber-

nacle of the congregation, to the priest;

7 And he shall offer it before the LORD and make an atonement for her; and she shall be cleansed from the issue of her blood. This is the law for her who has borne a male child or a female.

8 And if she cannot afford a lamb, then she shall bring two pigeons or two young turtledoves; the one for the sin offering and the other for the burnt offering; and the priest shall make an atonement for her and she shall be clean.

CHAPTER 13

AND the LORD spoke to Moses and Aaron, saying,

2 When a man shall have a sore on the skin of his body, or a scab or a shiny spot, and it be on the skin of his body like the plague of leprosy, then he shall be brought to Aaron the priest or to one of his sons the priests;

3 And the priest shall look on the disease on the skin of his body; and if the hair in the sore is turned white and the appearance of the plague is deeper than the skin of his body, it is a plague of leprosy; and the priest shall look on it and pronounce him unclean.

4 And if the shiny spot be white on the skin of his body, but does not appear to be deeper than the skin, and the hair in it has not turned white; then the priest shall observe the disease for seven days;

5 And the priest shall look on him on the seventh day, and if the disease has remained in its place and has not spread in the skin, then the priest shall observe it seven days more.

6 And the priest shall look on him after seven days, and if the disease has been checked and has not spread in the skin, the priest shall pronounce him clean; because it is only a scab, and he shall wash his clothes and be clean.

7 But if the scab spreads much in the skin after that the priest has seen it and cleaned it, he shall show it to the priest again;

8 And if the priest shall see that the scab has spread in the skin, then the priest shall pronounce him unclean because it is leprosy.

9 ¶When the plague of leprosy is in a man, then he shall be brought to the priest;

10 And the priest shall see him, and if there is a white swelling in the skin and it has turned the hair white and the indication of the flesh is raw in the swelling,

11 It is an old leprosy in the skin of his body, and the priest shall pronounce him unclean and shall not shut him up; for he is unclean.

12 And if the leprosy breaks out all over his skin, so that the leprosy covers all of the skin of him who has the plague from his head to his feet, wherever the priest looks,

13 Then the priest shall consider; and, behold, if the leprosy has covered all his body, he shall pronounce him clean of the plague; for it has all turned white; he is clean.

14 But on the day when raw flesh appears on him, he shall become unclean.

15 And the priest shall see the raw flesh, and pronounce the raw flesh unclean; for it is unclean; it is leprosy.

16 Or if the raw flesh turns again, and is changed to white, then he shall be brought to the priest;

17 And the priest shall see him; and if the plague has turned white, then the priest shall pronounce him clean that has the plague; he is clean.

18 ¶The flesh also, if there is in the skin thereof a boil and it is healed,

19 And in the place of the boil there be a white swelling or a shiny spot, white or reddish, it shall be shown to the priest;

20 And when the priest sees it, if it appears deeper than the skin and its hair has turned white, then the priest shall pronounce him unclean; for it is a plague of leprosy broken out of the boil.

21 But if the priest look on it, and, behold, there is no white hair in it and if it is not deeper than the skin but is even with the skin, then the priest shall observe it seven days;

22 And if it spreads much in the

skin, then the priest shall pronounce him unclean; because it is the plague of leprosy.

23 But if the shiny spot stays in its place and spreads not, it is a scar of the boil, and the priest shall pronounce him clean.

24 ¶Or if a person's body has a burn on its skin, and the quick flesh of the burn has a shiny spot, somewhat white or reddish,

25 Then the priest shall look on it, and if the hair in the shiny spot has turned white, and it appears to be deeper than the skin, it is a leprosy broken out in the burn; wherefore the priest shall pronounce him unclean; because it is the plague of leprosy.

26 But if the priest look on it, and there is no white hair in the shiny spot and it is no deeper than the skin, but is even; then the priest shall observe it seven days;

27 And the priest shall look upon him the seventh day; and if it has spread in the skin, then the priest shall pronounce him unclean; because it is the plague of leprosy.

28 And if the shiny spot stays in its place and does not spread in the skin and is somewhat even, it is a scab of the burn, and the priest shall pronounce him clean; because it is the scab of the burn.

29 ¶If a man or woman has a disease on the head or the beard;

30 Then the priest shall see the disease; and, if it appears deeper than the skin, and there be in it yellow thin hair, then the priest shall pronounce him unclean; because it is the disease of leprosy of the head or beard.

31 And if the priest look on the disease, and it does not appear deeper than the skin and there is no black hair in it; then the priest shall observe it seven days;

32 And on the seventh day the priest shall look on the disease; and if the disease has not spread, and if there is no yellow hair in it and the appearance of the disease is not deeper than the skin,

33 Then he shall shave the sides of the sore, but the sore he shall not shave; and the priest shall observe the disease seven days more;

34 And on the seventh day the priest shall look on the disease; and if the disease has not spread in the skin and does not appear deeper than the skin, then the priest shall pronounce him clean, and he shall wash his clothes and be clean.

35 But if the disease spreads much in the skin after his cleansing,

36 Then the priest shall look on him; and if the disease has spread in the skin, the priest shall not look for yellow hair; he is unclean.

37 But if the disease remains in its place and there is black hair grown up in it; the disease is healed, he is clean; and the priest shall pronounce him clean.

38 ¶If a man or a woman have in the skin of the body shiny spots, bright or white spots,

39 Then the priest shall look; and if the shiny spots in the skin of the body are darkish white or reddish, it is a scab that has grown on the skin; he is clean.

40 And the man whose hair is fallen off his head, he is bald; yet he is clean.

41 And he whose hair has fallen off from the part of his head toward his face, he is forehead bald; yet he is clean.

42 And if there is on his bald head or bald forehead a white or reddish sore, it is leprosy breaking out on his bald head or his bald forehead.

43 Then the priest shall look on the swelling of the sore; and if the sore is white or reddish on his bald head or on his bald forehead like the appearance of leprosy in the skin of the body,

44 He is a leprous man, he is unclean; the priest shall pronounce him utterly unclean; for the disease is on his head.

45 And he who has the plague, his clothes shall be rent and his head shaved, and he shall cover his lips and call himself unclean.

46 All the days wherein the plague is on him he shall be defiled; for he is unclean; he shall dwell alone; out-

side the camp shall his habitation be.

47 ¶If a garment has leprous disease in it, whether it be a woolen garment or a linen garment,

48 Whether it be in the warp or woof, of linen or of woolen, in a skin or in anything made of skin,

49 And if the plague is greenish or reddish in the garment or in the skin, either in the warp or in the woof or in anything of skin, it is a plague of leprosy and shall be shown to the priest;

50 And the priest shall look upon the plague and observe it seven days;

51 And the priest shall look on the plague on the seventh day; if the disease has spread in the garment, either in the warp or in the woof or in a skin or in any article that is made of skin, the plague is a malignant leprosy; it is unclean.

52 He shall therefore burn the garment, whether warp or woof, in woolen or in linen, or anything of skin in which is the plague; for it is a malignant leprosy; it shall be burned in the fire.

53 And if the priest shall look, and the plague has not spread in the garment, either in the warp or in the woof or in anything of skin,

54 Then the priest shall command that they wash the thing in which is the plague and he shall observe it seven days more;

55 And the priest shall look on the plague after it is washed; and if the plague has not changed its appearance and the disease has not changed its color and the plague has not spread, it is unclean; you shall burn it in the fire; it has been diseased when it was new or when old.

56 And if the priest sees that the disease has diminished after being washed, then he shall rend it out of the garment or out of the skin or out of the warp or out of the woof;

57 And if it appears still in the garment, either in the warp or in the woof or in anything of skin, they shall burn it with fire, for the plague has spread in it.

58 And the garment, either warp or woof or anything of skin which has been washed, if the disease departs from them, then it shall be washed the second time and shall be clean.

59 This is the law of the plague of leprosy in a garment of woolen or linen, either in the warp or woof or anything of skin, to pronounce it clean or to pronounce it unclean.

CHAPTER 14

AND the LORD spoke to Moses, saying,

2 This shall be the law for the leper in the day of his cleansing: He shall be brought to the priest;

3 And the priest shall go forth out of the camp; and the priest shall look, and if the plague of leprosy is healed in the leper,

4 Then the priest shall command to take for him who is to be cleansed two birds alive and clean and cedar wood and scarlet material and hyssop;

5 And the priest shall command that one of the birds be killed in an earthen vessel over running water;

6 Then he shall take the living bird and the cedar wood and the scarlet dye and the hyssop, and shall dip them and the living bird in the blood of the bird that was killed over the running water;

7 And he shall sprinkle upon him who is to be cleansed from the leprosy seven times, and shall pronounce him clean, and shall let the living bird fly into the open field.

8 And he who is to be cleansed shall wash his clothes and shave off all his hair and bathe himself in water, that he may be clean; and after that he shall come into the camp but shall tarry outside his tent seven days.

9 And on the seventh day he shall shave all the hair off his head and his beard and his eyebrows, even all his hair he shall shave off; and he shall wash his clothes and bathe his body in water, and he shall be clean.

10 And on the eighth day he shall take two male lambs without blemish and one ewe lamb of the first year without blemish and three tenth deals of fine flour, for a meal offering mixed with oil, and one half pint of oil.

11 And the priest who does the cleansing shall present the man who is to be cleansed and those things before the LORD at the door of the tabernacle of the congregation;

12 And the priest shall take one male lamb and offer it for a trespass offering, and the half pint of oil, and wave them for a wave offering before the LORD;

13 And he shall kill the male lamb in the place where he kills the sin offering and the burnt offering, in the holy place; for as the sin offering belongs to the priest, so does the trespass offering; it is most holy;

14 And the priest shall take some of the blood of the trespass offering, and the priest shall sprinkle it on the tip of the right ear of him who is to be cleansed and on the thumb of his right hand and on the great toe of his right foot;

15 And the priest shall take some of the oil, and pour it into the palm of his own left hand;

16 Then the priest shall dip his right finger in the oil that is in his left hand and shall sprinkle some of the oil with his finger seven times before the LORD;

17 And of the rest of the oil that is in his hand the priest shall sprinkle it upon the tip of the right ear of him who is to be cleansed and upon the thumb of his right hand and upon the great toe of his right foot, upon the place of the blood of the trespass offering;

18 And the rest of the oil that is in the priest's hand he shall pour upon the head of him who is to be cleansed; and the priest shall make an atonement for him before the LORD.

19 And the priest shall offer the sin offering and make an atonement for the man who is to be cleansed from his uncleanness; and afterward he shall kill the burnt offering;

20 And the priest shall offer the burnt offering and the meal offering upon the altar; and the priest shall make an atonement for him and he shall be clean.

21 And if he is poor and cannot afford so much, then he shall take one lamb for a trespass offering to be waved, to make an atonement for him, and one tenth of an ephah of fine flour mixed with oil for a meal offering, and a half pint of oil,

22 And two turtledoves or two young pigeons such as he can afford; and the one shall be a sin offering and the other a burnt offering.

23 And he shall bring them on the eighth day for his cleansing to the priest, to the door of the tabernacle of the congregation, before the LORD.

24 And the priest shall take one lamb and the half pint of oil, and the priest shall wave them for a wave offering before the LORD;

25 Then he shall kill the lamb of the trespass offering, and the priest shall take some of the blood of the trespass offering, and sprinkle it upon the tip of the right ear of him who is to be cleansed and upon the thumb of his right hand and upon the great toe of his right foot;

26 And the priest shall pour some of the oil into the palm of his own left hand;

27 And the priest shall sprinkle with his right finger some of the oil that is in his left hand seven times before the LORD;

28 And the priest shall sprinkle some of the oil that is in his hand upon the tip of the right ear of him who is to be cleansed and upon the thumb of his right hand and upon the great toe of his right foot, in the place of the blood of the trespass offering;

29 And the rest of the oil that is in the priest's hand he shall sprinkle upon the head of him who is to be cleansed, to make an atonement for him before the LORD.

30 And he shall offer one of the turtledoves or of the young pigeons such as he can afford;

31 One shall be for a sin offering and the other for a burnt offering, with the meal offering; and the priest shall make an atonement for him who is to be cleansed before the LORD.

32 This is the law of him in whom is the plague of leprosy who cannot

afford the regular offerings for his cleansing.

33 ¶And the Lord spoke to Moses and Aaron, saying,

34 Speak to the children of Israel and say to them, When you come into the land of Canaan which I give to you for a possession, and I put the plague of leprosy in a house of the land of your possession,

35 The owner of the house shall come and tell the priest, saying, It seems to me that there is a plague of leprosy in the house.

36 Then the priest shall command that they empty the house before the priest shall go into it to see the plague, that all that is in the house may not be made unclean; and afterward the priest shall go in to see the house;

37 And he shall look on the plague, and, behold, if the plague be in the walls of the house with greenish or reddish scales, and appear to be deeper than the wall;

38 Then the priest shall go out of the house and stand at the door and observe the house seven days;

39 And the priest shall come back again on the seventh day and shall see if the plague has spread in the walls of the house;

40 Then the priest shall command that they take away the stones in which the plague of leprosy is, and they shall cast them into an unclean place outside the city;

41 And they shall scrape the house within round about, and they shall throw out the dust that they scrape off outside the city into an unclean place;

42 And they shall take other stones and put them in the place of those stones; and they shall take other mortar and plaster the house.

43 And if the plague spreads and breaks out in the house after the stones have been taken away and after the house has been scraped and plastered,

44 Then the priest shall go in and look, and if the plague has spread in the house, it is a malignant leprosy in the house; it is unclean.

45 And they shall demolish the house, its stones and its timber and all the mortar of the house; and they shall carry them forth out of the town into an unclean place and burn it with fire.

46 Moreover, he who enters the house while it is shut up shall be unclean until the evening.

47 And he who lies in the house shall wash his clothes; and he who eats in the house shall wash his clothes.

48 And if the priest shall come in and look upon it, and, behold, the plague has not spread in the house after the house was plastered, then the priest shall pronounce the house clean, because the plague has been healed.

49 And he shall take to cleanse the house two birds alive and clean and cedar wood and hyssop and scarlet material;

50 And the priest shall command and they shall kill one of the birds in an earthen vessel over running water;

51 And he shall take the other living bird, the cedar wood, and the hyssop, and the scarlet material and dip them in the blood of the bird that was killed and in the running water, and sprinkle the house seven times;

52 And he shall cleanse the house with the blood of the bird and with the running water and with the live bird and with the cedar wood and with hyssop and with the scarlet material;

53 But he shall let the live bird fly out of the town into the open field and make an atonement for the house; and it shall be clean.

54 This law shall be for all manner of plagues of leprosy

55 And for the plague of leprosy in a garment and of a house

56 And for a swelling and for a scab and for a shiny spot;

57 To distinguish between clean, and unclean; this is the law of leprosy.

CHAPTER 15

THE Lord spoke to Moses and to Aaron, saying,

2 Speak to the children of Israel

and say to them, When any man has a seminal discharge from his body, his discharge is unclean,

3 And this shall be his uncleanness in his discharge: whether his body runs with its discharge or his body has stopped from its discharge, it is his uncleanness.

4 Every bed on which he who has the discharge lies shall be unclean, and everything on which he sits shall be unclean.

5 And any man who touches his bed shall wash his clothes and bathe himself in water and be unclean until the evening.

6 And he who sits on anything on which sat he who has the discharge shall wash his clothes and bathe himself in water and be unclean until the evening.

7 And he who touches the body of him who has the discharge shall wash his clothes and bathe himself in water and be unclean until the evening.

8 And if he who has the discharge spits on him who is clean, then he shall wash his clothes and bathe himself in water and be unclean until the evening.

9 And anything on which he rides who has the discharge shall be unclean,

10 And whosoever touches anything that has been under him shall be unclean until the evening; and he who carries any of those things shall wash his clothes and bathe himself in water and be unclean until the evening.

11 And any one who touches him who has the discharge, and has not washed his hands in water, he shall wash his clothes and bathe himself in water and be unclean until the evening.

12 And the earthen vessel which he touched who has the discharge shall be broken; and every vessel of wood or of brass shall be washed in water.

13 And when he who has a discharge is cleansed of his discharge, then he shall number to himself seven days for his cleansing, and wash his clothes and bathe his body in running water and shall be clean.

14 And on the eighth day he shall take two turtledoves or two young pigeons and bring them before the LORD at the door of the tabernacle of the congregation and give them to the priest,

15 And the priest shall offer them, the one for a sin offering and the other for a burnt offering; and the priest shall make an atonement for him before the LORD for his discharge.

16 And if any man has an emission of semen, then he shall bathe all his body in water and be unclean until the evening.

17 And every garment or bed on which the semen has fallen shall be washed with water and be unclean until the evening.

18 If a woman also lie with a man having an emission of semen, they shall both bathe themselves in water and be unclean until the evening.

19 ¶And if a woman has a discharge of blood, and her discharge is in her body, she shall be put apart for seven days in her menstruation, and whosoever touches her shall be unclean until the evening.

20 And everything upon which she lies during her menstruous discharge shall be unclean; and everything also that she sits upon shall be unclean.

21 And whosoever touches her bed shall wash his clothes and bathe himself in water and be unclean until the evening.

22 And whosoever touches anything that she sits upon shall wash his clothes and bathe himself in water and be unclean until the evening.

23 And if it be on the bed or on anything on which she sits, when he touches it, he shall be unclean until the evening.

24 And if any man lies with her and some of her menstruous discharge falls on him, he shall be unclean for seven days; and every bed on which he lies shall be unclean.

25 And if a woman has a menstruous discharge of blood for many days, not at the time of her menstruation, or if she has a menstruous discharge beyond the time of her menstruation,

all the days of the discharge of her uncleanness shall be as the days of her menstruation; she shall be unclean.

26 Every bed on which she lies all the days of her discharge shall be to her as the bed of her menstruation; and everything upon which she sits shall be unclean, as the uncleanness of her menstruation.

27 And whosoever touches those things shall be unclean and shall wash his clothes and bathe himself in water and be unclean until the evening.

28 But if she is cleansed of her discharge, then she shall number for herself seven days, and after that she shall be clean.

29 And on the eighth day she shall take to herself two turtledoves or two young pigeons and bring them to the priest, to the door of the tabernacle of the congregation.

30 And the priest shall offer them, the one for a sin offering and the other for a burnt offering; and the priest shall make an atonement for her before the LORD for the discharge of her uncleanness.

31 Thus shall you admonish the children of Israel concerning their uncleanness, that they may not die in their uncleanness and that they may not defile my tabernacle that is among them.

32 This law shall be for him who has a discharge and for him who has an emission of semen and is defiled therewith;

33 And for her who has monthly course and for him who has a discharge, male or female, and for the man who lies with a woman who is unclean.

CHAPTER 16

AND the LORD spoke to Moses after the death of the two sons of Aaron, when they offered strange fire before the LORD and died;

2 And the LORD said to Moses, Speak to Aaron your brother that he come not at all times into the holy place within the veil before the mercy seat which is upon the ark, that he die not; for I will appear in the cloud upon the mercy seat.

3 Thus shall Aaron come into the holy place: with a young bullock for a sin offering and a ram for a burnt offering.

4 He shall put on the holy linen coat and he shall have linen breeches upon his body and shall be girded with a linen girdle and shall put a linen mitre upon his head; because these are the vestments of the sanctuary; therefore he shall bathe his body in water, and then put them on.

5 And he shall take from the congregation of the children of Israel two kids of the goats for a sin offering and one ram for a burnt offering.

6 And Aaron shall offer the bullock of the sin offering, which is for himself, and make an atonement for himself and for his house.

7 And he shall take the two goats and present them alive before the LORD at the door of the tabernacle of the congregation.

8 And Aaron shall cast lots upon the two goats, one lot for the LORD and the other lot for Azazael.

9 And Aaron shall bring the goat upon which the LORD's lot fell and offer it for a sin offering.

10 But the goat on which the lot of Azazael fell shall be presented alive before the LORD to make an atonement with it and to send it away to Azazael into the wilderness.

11 And Aaron shall bring the bullock of the sin offering which is for himself, and shall make an atonement for himself and for his house; and shall kill the bullock of the sin offering;

12 And he shall take a censer full of burning coals of fire from the altar before the LORD and his hands full of sweet incense beaten small, and enter within the veil;

13 And he shall put the incense on the fire before the LORD, that the cloud of the incense may cover the mercy seat that is upon the testimony, that he die not;

14 And he shall take some of the blood of the bullock and sprinkle it with his finger upon the mercy seat

eastward; before the mercy seat shall he sprinkle of the blood with his finger seven times.

15 ¶Then he shall kill the goat of the sin offering which is for the people and bring its blood within the veil, and do with its blood as he did with the blood of the bullock, and sprinkle it upon the mercy seat and before the mercy seat;

16 And he shall make an atonement for the holy place, because of the uncleanness of the children of Israel and because of their transgressions in all their sins; and so shall he do for the tabernacle of the congregation which remains among them in the midst of their uncleanness.

17 And there shall be no man in the tabernacle of the congregation when he goes in to make an atonement in the holy place, until he comes out and has made an atonement for himself and for his household and for all the congregation of Israel.

18 And he shall go out to the altar that is before the LORD and make an atonement for it; and shall take some of the blood of the bullock and some of the blood of the goat, and sprinkle it upon the horns of the altar round about.

19 And he shall sprinkle some of the blood upon it with his finger seven times, and cleanse it and hallow it from the uncleanness of the children of Israel.

20 ¶And when he has made an end of atoning for the holy place and the tabernacle of the congregation and the altar, he shall bring the live goat;

21 And Aaron shall lay both his hands upon the head of the live goat and confess over it all the iniquities of the children of Israel and all their transgressions and all their sins, putting them upon the head of the goat, and shall send it away by the hand of a fit man into the wilderness;

22 And the goat shall bear upon him all their iniquities to a barren land; and he shall leave the goat in the wilderness.

23 And Aaron shall come into the tabernacle of the congregation, and shall put off the linen vestments which he put on when he went into the holy place, and shall leave them there;

24 And he shall bathe his body in water in the holy place and put on his garments, and come forth and offer his burnt offering and the burnt offering of the people, and make an atonement for himself and for the people.

25 And the fat of the sin offering he shall burn upon the altar.

26 And he who let go the goat for Azazael shall wash his clothes and bathe his body in water and afterward shall come into the camp.

27 And the bullock for the sin offering and the goat for the sin offering, some of whose blood was brought in to make atonement in the holy place, they shall carry forth outside the camp; and they shall burn in the fire their skins and their meat and their dung.

28 And he who burns them shall wash his clothes and bathe his body in water and afterward he shall come into the camp.

29 ¶And this shall be a statute for ever to you: that in the seventh month, on the tenth day of the month, you shall humble yourselves and do no work at all, both you and the proselytes who sojourn among you;

30 For on this day shall the priest make an atonement for you, that you may be clean from all your sins and that you may be clean before the LORD.

31 It shall be a sabbath and a rest to you, and you shall humble yourselves; it is a statute for ever.

32 And the priest who shall be anointed and who is consecrated to minister in the priest's office in his father's stead shall make the atonement and shall put on the linen clothes, even the holy garments;

33 And he shall make an atonement for the holy sanctuary, and he shall make an atonement for the tabernacle of the congregation and for the altar, and he shall make an atonement for the priests and for all the people of the congregation.

34 And this shall be an everlasting statute for you, to make an atonement

for the children of Israel for all their sins once a year. And he did as the LORD commanded Moses.

CHAPTER 17

AND the LORD spoke to Moses, saying,

2 Speak to Aaron and to his sons and to all the children of Israel, and say to them, This is the thing which the LORD has commanded, saying,

3 Any man whosoever be of the house of Israel, who kills an ox or a lamb or a goat in the camp, or who kills it outside the camp,

4 And does not bring it to the door of the tabernacle of the congregation to offer it as an offering to the LORD before the tabernacle of the LORD, blood shall be imputed to that man because he has shed blood; and that man shall be cut off from among his people,

5 To the end that the children of Israel may bring their sacrifices which they offer in the open field, that they may bring them before the LORD to the door of the tabernacle of the congregation, to the priest, and offer them for peace offerings to the LORD.

6 And the priest shall sprinkle the blood upon the altar of the LORD at the door of the tabernacle of the congregation and burn the fat for a sweet savour to the LORD.

7 And they shall no more offer their sacrifices to the demons after whom they have gone astray. This shall be a statute for ever to them throughout their generations.

8 ¶And you shall say to them, Any man of the house of Israel or of the proselytes who sojourn among you who offers a burnt offering or a sacrifice

9 And does not bring it to the door of the tabernacle of the congregation to offer it to the LORD, that man shall be cut off from among his people.

10 ¶And if any man of the children of Israel or of the proselytes who sojourn among you eats any manner of blood, I will pour out my anger against that person who eats blood, and will cut him off from among his people.

11 For the life of the flesh is in the blood; and I have given it to you upon the altar to make an atonement for yourselves; for it is the blood that makes an atonement for the soul.

12 Therefore I have said to the children of Israel, No person among you shall eat blood, neither shall the proselytes who sojourn among you eat blood.

13 And any man of the children of Israel or of the proselytes who sojourn among you who hunts and catches any beast or fowl that may be eaten, he shall pour out its blood and cover it with dust.

14 For the life of all flesh is the blood thereof; therefore I said to the children of Israel, You shall not eat the blood of any flesh, for the life of all flesh is the blood thereof; whosoever eats it shall be cut off.

15 And every person who eats that which died of itself or that which was torn by wild beasts, whether it be one of you or one of the proselytes who sojourn among you, he shall both wash his clothes and bathe himself in water and be unclean until the evening; then shall he be clean.

16 But if he does not wash them nor bathe his body, then he shall suffer for his iniquity.

CHAPTER 18

AND the LORD spoke to Moses, saying,

2 Speak to the children of Israel and say to them, I am the LORD your God.

3 You shall not do according to the doings of the land of Egypt wherein you dwelt, neither shall you do according to the doings of the land of Canaan whither I bring you; neither shall you walk in their ordinances.

4 But you shall do my judgments and keep my commandments and walk in them; I am the LORD your God.

5 You shall therefore keep my commandments and my judgments, which if a man do, he shall live in them; I am the LORD.

6 ¶None of you shall be intimate with any that is near of kin to him

to uncover her nakedness; I am the LORD.

7 You shall not shame your father by approaching your mother; she is your mother, you shall not uncover her nakedness.

8 You shall not approach your father's wife; it is your father's nakedness.

9 You shall not approach your sister, the daughter of your father or the daughter of your mother, whether she is begotten of your father or of another man.

10 You shall not approach your son's daughter or your daughter's daughter, because they are your own kin.

11 You shall not approach your father's wife's daughter, begotten of your father, she is your sister; you shall not uncover her nakedness.

12 You shall not approach your father's sister, she is your father's near kinswoman.

13 You shall not approach your mother's sister, for she is your mother's near kinswoman.

14 You shall not put to shame your father's brother; you shall not approach his wife: for she is your aunt, you shall not uncover her nakedness.

15 You shall not approach your daughter-in-law; for she is your son's wife; you shall not uncover her nakedness.

16 You shall not approach your brother's wife; it is your brother's nakedness.

17 You shall not approach a woman and her daughter; neither shall you take her son's daughter or her daughter's daughter to uncover nakedness; for they are her near kinswomen; it is wickedness.

18 And you shall not take to wife a sister of your wife, to distress her, to uncover her nakedness, beside the other in her life time.

19 You shall not be intimate with a woman while she is unclean during her menstruation.

20 Moreover you shall not lie carnally with your neighbor's wife to defile yourself with her.

21 You shall not let any of your semen be cast into a strange woman to cause her to be pregnant; neither shall you profane the name of your God; I am the LORD.

22 You shall not lie with a male as with a woman; because it is an abomination.

23 Neither shall you lie with any beast to defile yourself with it; neither shall any woman stand before a beast to lie with it; because it is an abomination.

24 Do not defile yourselves in any of these things; for it was in all these that the nations are defiled which I am casting out before you;

25 And the land is defiled; therefore I do visit the iniquity thereof upon it so that the land is bereaved of its inhabitants.

26 You shall therefore keep my statutes and my judgments, and shall not commit any of these abominations; neither you nor any proselytes who sojourn among you

27 (For all these sins have the men of the land done who were before you, and the land is defiled);

28 Do not defile the land, lest it cast you out as it cast out the nations that were before you.

29 For whosoever shall commit any of these abominations, even the persons who commit them shall be cut off from among their people.

30 Therefore you shall keep my ordinance, and you shall not commit any of these abominable customs which were committed before you, and you shall not defile yourselves by them; I am the LORD your God.

CHAPTER 19

AND the LORD spoke to Moses, saying,

2 Speak to all the congregation of the children of Israel and say to them, You shall be holy; for I the LORD your God am holy.

3 ¶You must revere every man his father and his mother, and keep my commandments; for I am the LORD your God.

4 ¶You shall not turn to idols nor make to yourselves molten gods; I am the LORD your God.

5 ¶And if you offer a sacrifice of peace offering to the LORD, you shall offer the ones which are acceptable.

6 It shall be eaten the same day you offer it and on the morrow; and what is left over until the third day, it shall be burned in the fire and shall not be eaten.

7 And if it is eaten at all on the third day, it is abominable; and it shall not be accepted.

8 Therefore every one who eats of it shall suffer for his iniquity, because he has profaned the hallowed thing of the LORD; and that person shall be cut off from among his people.

9 ¶And when you reap the harvest of your land, you shall not reap your field to the very corners, neither shall you gather the gleanings of your harvest.

10 And you shall not glean your vineyards, neither shall you gather that which is fallen from your olive trees, but you shall leave them for the poor and the proselytes; for I am the LORD your God.

11 ¶You shall not steal; you shall not deal falsely; neither shall you lie to one another.

12 ¶You shall not swear by my name falsely and so profane the name of your God; I am the LORD.

13 ¶You shall not oppress your neighbor, neither carry him away by force; the wages of him who is hired shall not remain with you all night until the morning.

14 ¶You shall not curse the deaf, nor put a stumbling block before the blind, but you shall revere your God; I am the LORD.

15 ¶You shall do no injustice in judgment; you shall not be partial to the poor, nor respect the person of the mighty; but in righteousness shall you judge your neighbor.

16 ¶You shall not accuse your own people neither shall you stand against the blood of your neighbor; I am the LORD.

17 ¶You shall not hate your brother in your heart; but you shall in any wise rebuke your neighbor, lest you incur sin because of him.

18 ¶You shall not bear any enmity against the children of your own people, but you shall love your neighbor as yourself; I am the LORD.

19 ¶You shall keep my statutes. You shall not let your cattle breed with a diverse kind; you shall not sow your field with mixed seed; neither shall you wear a mantle made of mixed materials.

20 ¶And whosoever lies carnally with a woman who is his bondmaid betrothed to a husband, and not yet redeemed nor given her freedom, an inquiry shall be made into their case; and they shall not be put to death, because she was not free.

21 And he shall bring his trespass offering to the LORD, to the door of the tabernacle of the congregation, a ram for a trespass offering.

22 And the priest shall make an atonement for him with the ram of the trespass offering before the LORD for his sin which he has committed; and the sin which he has committed shall be forgiven him.

23 ¶And when you shall come into the land and shall have planted all kinds of trees for food, then you shall leave them for three years, and you shall not eat of their fruit.

24 And in the fourth year all their fruit shall be holy to praise the LORD withal.

25 And in the fifth year you shall eat of the fruit thereof, that it may yield to you the increase thereof; I am the LORD your God.

26 ¶You shall not eat blood; you shall not practice divination with birds, nor shall you consult an oracle.

27 You shall not let the hair of your heads grow, neither shall you trim the corners of your beard.

28 You shall not make any cuttings in your flesh for the dead, nor inscribe any marks upon you; I am the LORD.

29 ¶You shall not permit your daughter to become a whore, lest the land fall to whoredom and the land become full of wickedness.

30 ¶You shall keep my commandments and reverence my sanctuary; I am the LORD.

31 ¶You shall not go after diviners,

neither after the soothsayers, nor shall you consult them to be defiled by them; I am the LORD your God.

32 ¶You shall rise up before an elder and honor the person who is older than you and revere your God; I am the LORD your God.

33 ¶And when a proselyte sojourns with you in your land, you shall not wrong him;

34 But let him be among you as one of you; and the proselytes who sojourn among you, you must love them as yourselves; for you also were sojourners in the land of Egypt; I am the LORD your God.

35 ¶You shall do no injustices in judgment, in balances, in weight, or in measure.

36 You shall have just balances, just weights, a just ephah, and a just hin; I am the LORD your God who brought you out of the land of Egypt.

37 Therefore you shall keep all my commandments and all my judgments, and do them; I am the LORD.

CHAPTER 20

AND the LORD spoke to Moses, saying,

2 Say to the children of Israel, Any man of the children of Israel or of the proselytes who sojourn in Israel who shall cast any of his semen into an alien woman, he shall surely be put to death; the people of the land shall stone him with stones.

3 And I will pour out my anger against that man and will cut him off from among his people; because he has cast his semen into an alien woman to defile my sanctuary and to profane my holy name.

4 And if the people of the land do in any way ignore the offense of the man who has cast of his semen into an alien woman, that they may not kill him,

5 Then I will set my anger against that man and against his family, and will cut him off and all who go astray after him, because they go astray after alien women from among their people.

6 ¶And the person that goes after diviners and soothsayers to go astray after them, I will pour out my anger against that person and will cut him off from among his people.

7 ¶Sanctify yourselves, therefore, and be holy; for I am the LORD your God.

8 You shall keep my commandments and do them; I am the LORD who sanctifies you.

9 ¶And he who curses his father or his mother shall be surely put to death; he has cursed his father or his mother; his blood shall be upon him.

10 ¶And the man who commits adultery with another man's wife, even he who commits adultery with his neighbor's wife, both the adulterer and the adulteress shall surely be put to death.

11 And the man who lies with his father's wife has uncovered his father's nakedness; both of them shall surely be put to death; their blood shall be upon them.

12 And if a man lies with his daughter-in-law, both of them shall surely be put to death, because they have committed a sin; their blood shall be upon them.

13 If a man lies with a male as he lies with a woman, both of them have committed an abomination; they shall surely be put to death; their blood shall be upon them.

14 And if a man takes a wife and her mother, it is wickedness; they shall be burned with fire, both he and they, that there may be no wickedness among you.

15 And if a man lies with a beast, he shall surely be put to death and the beast shall be stoned.

16 And if a woman approaches any beast and lies with it, you shall kill the woman and the beast; they shall surely be put to death; their blood shall be upon them.

17 And if a man shall take his sister, his father's daughter or his mother's daughter, and be intimate with her and she be intimate with him, it is a shameful thing; and they shall be cut off in the sight of their people; he has uncovered his sister's

nakedness; they shall suffer for their iniquity.

18 And if a man shall lie with a woman having her menstruation and shall be intimate with her, he has uncovered her fountain and she has uncovered the fountain of her blood; and both of them shall be cut off from among their people.

19 And you shall not be intimate with your mother's sister nor your father's sister; for he uncovers the nakedness of his near kin; they shall suffer for their iniquity.

20 And if a man shall lie with his uncle's wife, he has uncovered his uncle's nakedness; they shall suffer for their sin; they shall die childless.

21 And if a man shall take his brother's wife, it is an iniquity, for he has uncovered his brother's nakedness; they shall be childless.

22 ¶You shall therefore keep all my commandments and all my judgments and do them, that the land whither I bring you to dwell therein may not be bereaved of you.

23 And you shall not walk in the manners of the nations which I am casting out before you; for they committed all these things, and therefore I was grieved by them.

24 But I have said to you, You shall inherit their land and I will give it to you to possess it, a land flowing with milk and honey; I am the LORD your God who have separated you from other peoples.

25 You shall therefore make a distinction between clean beasts and unclean, and between clean fowls and unclean; and you shall not make yourselves abominable by beast or by fowl or by any manner of living thing that creeps on the ground, which I have separated from you as unclean.

26 And you shall be holy to me; for I the LORD am holy and have separated you from other peoples, that you should be mine.

27 ¶A man or a woman who is a diviner, or soothsayer shall surely be put to death; they shall stone them with stones; their blood shall be upon them.

¹ The dead were considered unclean.

CHAPTER 21

THE LORD said to Moses, Speak to the priests the sons of Aaron and say to them, There shall none of you defile himself by mourning for the dead among his people,¹

2 Except for his kin who is near to him, that is, for his father and for his mother and for his son and for his daughter and for his brother,

3 And for his virgin sister, who is near to him, who had no husband; for her he may defile himself.

4 But he shall not defile himself for the prince of his people, lest he profane himself.

5 They shall not make baldness upon their head, neither shall they shave off the corner of their beard, nor make any cuttings in their flesh.

6 But they shall be holy to their God, and not profane the name of their God; for the offerings of the LORD made by fire and the bread of their God they do offer; therefore they shall be holy.

7 They shall not marry a harlot or an unclean woman; neither shall they marry a woman who has been put away from her husband; for he is holy to his God.

8 You shall sanctify him therefore; for he offers the bread of your God; he shall be holy to you; for he is holy, because I am the LORD who sanctifies you.

9 ¶And the daughter of any priest, when she starts playing the whore, she profanes her father; she shall be burned with fire.

10 And the priest who is the high priest among his brethren, upon whose head the anointing oil was poured, and who is consecrated to put on the vestments, shall not shave his head nor rend his clothes;

11 Neither shall he go near any dead body, nor defile himself by mourning for his father or for his mother;

12 Neither shall he go out of the sanctuary nor profane the sanctuary of his God; for the crown of the

anointing oil of his God is upon him; I am the LORD.

13 And he shall take a wife in her virginity.

14 A widow or a woman who is put away or one who is defiled by whoredom, these he shall not take; but he shall take a virgin of his own people to wife.

15 Neither shall he profane his descendants among his people; for I am the LORD who sanctifies him.

16 ¶And the LORD spoke to Moses, saying,

17 Speak to Aaron and say to him, Whosoever he be of your descendants throughout their generations who has any blemish, let him not approach to offer the bread of his God.

18 For any man who has a blemish, he shall not approach: a lame man or a blind man or one whose nose is cut off or one who is deprived of ears

19 Or a man who has a broken foot or broken hand

20 Or crooked back or is a dwarf or whose eyebrows have fallen or whose eyes are dimmed or has cataract in his eyes or has leprosy or a hunchback or has one testicle;

21 No man of the descendants of Aaron the priest who has a blemish shall come near to offer the offerings of the LORD made by fire; for he has a blemish; he shall not come near to offer the bread of his God.

22 He shall eat the bread of his God, both of the most holy and of the holy.

23 But he shall not go in to the veil nor come near to the altar, because he has a blemish, that he may not profane my sanctuary; for I am the LORD who sanctifies them.

24 So Moses told it to Aaron and to his sons and to all the children of Israel.

CHAPTER 22

AND the LORD spoke to Moses, saying,

2 Say to Aaron and to his sons, that they may keep themselves separate from the holy things of the children of Israel and that they may not profane my holy name in those things which they hallow to me; I am the LORD.

3 Say to them, Whosoever he be of all your descendants throughout your generations who approaches to the holy things which the children of Israel hallow to the LORD while he is unclean, that person shall be cut off from my presence; I am the LORD.

4 Any man of the descendants of Aaron who is a leper or has a discharge, he shall not eat of the holy things until he is clean. And whosoever touches anything that is unclean through contact with the dead or a man who has an emission of semen,

5 Or whoever touches any creeping thing whereby he may be made unclean, or a man of whom he may take uncleanness, whatever uncleanness he has,

6 Any person who touches him shall be unclean until evening and shall not eat of the holy things unless he has bathed his body in water.

7 And when the sun is down, he shall be clean and shall afterward eat of the holy things, because it is his food.

8 That which has been torn by wild beasts, he shall not eat that he may not defile himself by it; I am the LORD.

9 They shall therefore keep my ordinances, lest they bear sins for it and die because of them, if they had profaned themselves; I am the LORD who sanctifies them.

10 There shall no alien eat of the holy things; a sojourner of the priest, or a hired servant, shall not eat of the holy thing.

11 But if a priest buys any person with his money, he shall eat of his food, and those that are born in his house shall eat of his food.

12 If a priest's daughter is married to a stranger,[1] she also may not eat of an offering of the holy things.

13 But if a priest's daughter has become a widow or is divorced, and has no children, and shall return to her father's house as in her youth, she

---

[1] Not of the priestly tribe.

shall eat of her father's food; but no stranger shall ever eat of it.

14 ¶And if a man eats of the holy thing unwittingly, then he shall add a fifth part thereof to it and shall give it to the priest with the holy thing.

15 And the children of Israel shall not profane the holy things which they offer to the LORD;

16 And thus shall suffer for the iniquity and sins, when they eat of their holy things; for I am the LORD who sanctifies them.

17 ¶And the LORD spoke to Moses, saying,

18 Speak to Aaron and to his sons and to all the children of Israel, and say to them, Any one of the house of Israel and of the proselytes who dwell in Israel that will offer his offering for all their vows and for all their freewill offerings which they offer to the LORD for a burnt offering,

19 You shall offer acceptable ones, a male without blemish, of the herds or of the lambs or of the goats.

20 But whatsoever has a blemish, that you shall not offer; for it shall not be acceptable for you.

21 And whosoever offers a sacrifice of peace offering to the LORD to fulfill his vow or a freewill offering from oxen or from goats, it shall be perfect to be accepted; there shall be no blemish in it.

22 Any blind animal or broken or scabbed or maimed or scurvy, you shall not offer to the LORD nor make an offering by fire of them upon the altar to the LORD.

23 A bullock or a lamb which has the ear or the tail cut off you may offer for a freewill offering; but for a vow it shall not be accepted.

24 You shall not offer to the LORD that which is bruised, cut off, or broken; neither shall you make such offerings in your land.

25 Neither from a stranger's hand shall you offer the bread of your God of any of these; because they are corrupt and there is blemish in them; they shall not be accepted from you.

26 ¶And the LORD spoke to Moses, saying,

27 When a bullock or a lamb or a goat is born, it shall remain seven days with its dam; and from the eighth day on it shall be accepted for an offering made by fire to the LORD.

28 And whether it be a cow or a sheep, you shall not slaughter it and its young both in one day.

29 And when you will offer a sacrifice of thanksgiving to the LORD, you shall offer it in an acceptable manner.

30 On the same day it shall be eaten up; you shall leave none of it until morning; I am the LORD.

31 Therefore you shall keep my commandments and do them; I am the LORD.

32 Neither shall you profane my holy name, which is holy among the children of Israel; I am the LORD who sanctifies you,

33 Who brought you out of the land of Egypt to be your God; I am the LORD.

CHAPTER 23

AND the LORD spoke to Moses, saying,

2 Speak to the children of Israel and say to them, Concerning the feasts of the LORD which you shall proclaim to be holy convocations, these are my feasts.

3 Six days you shall do work; but the seventh day is the sabbath of rest, it shall be holy to the LORD; you shall do no work thereon; it is the sabbath to the LORD in all your dwellings.

4 ¶These are the feasts of the LORD, even the holy convocations which you shall proclaim in their seasons:

5 On the fourteenth day of the first month at evening is the LORD's passover.

6 And on the fifteenth day of the same month is the feast of the unleavened bread to the LORD; for seven days you must eat unleavened bread.

7 On the first day you shall have a holy convocation; you shall do no manner of work thereon.

8 But you shall offer an offering made by fire to the LORD seven days; on the seventh day is a holy convocation; you shall do no manner of work thereon.

9 ¶And the LORD spoke to Moses, saying,

10 Speak to the children of Israel and say to them, When you come into the land which I give to you and shall reap the harvest thereof, then you shall bring a sheaf of the first fruits of your harvest to the priest;

11 And he shall wave the sheaf before the LORD to be accepted for you; on the morrow the priest shall wave it.

12 You shall offer that day when you wave the sheaf a male lamb of the first year without blemish for a burnt offering to the LORD.

13 And its meal offering shall be two tenths of an ephah of fine flour mixed with oil, an offering made by fire to the LORD for a sweet savour; and the drink offering thereof shall be of wine, a fourth part of a hin.

14 And you shall eat neither bread nor parched wheat nor green ears until that same day, until the day when you have brought an offering to your God; it shall be a statute for ever throughout your generations in all your dwellings.

15 ¶And you shall count to you from the morrow, that is, from the day that you brought the sheaf of the wave offering; seven sabbaths shall be complete;

16 Even to the morrow after the seventh sabbath you shall count fifty days; and you shall offer a meal offering of new wheat to the LORD.

17 You shall bring out of your dwellings two wave loaves of two tenths of an ephah; they shall be of fine flour; they shall be baked with leaven; they are the firstfruits to the LORD.

18 And you shall offer with the bread seven lambs without blemish of the first year and one young bullock and two rams; they shall be for a burnt offering to the LORD, with their meal offering and their drink offering made by fire, an offering for a sweet savour to the LORD.

19 Then you shall sacrifice one kid of the goats for a sin offering and two lambs of the first year for a sacrifice of peace offering.

20 And the priest shall wave them with the bread of the firstfruits for a wave offering before the LORD, with the two lambs; they shall be holy before the LORD for the priest.

21 And you shall proclaim on the same day, that it may be a holy convocation to you; you shall do no manner of work thereon; it shall be a statute for ever in all your dwellings throughout your generations.

22 ¶And when you reap the harvest of your land, you shall not reap your fields to their very corners, neither shall you gather any gleaning of your harvest; but you shall leave them to the poor and to the proselytes; I am the LORD your God.

23 ¶And the LORD spoke to Moses, saying,

24 Speak to the children of Israel and say to them, The seventh month on the first day of the month shall be to you a day of rest, and a memorial of blowing of trumpets, a holy convocation.

25 You shall do no manner of work thereon; but you shall offer an offering by fire to the LORD.

26 ¶And the LORD spoke to Moses, saying,

27 Speak to the children of Israel and say to them, Also the tenth day of this seventh month is the day of atonement; it shall be a holy convocation to you; and you shall humble yourselves and offer an offering made by fire to the LORD.

28 And you shall do no work on this same day; for it is a day of atonement, to make an atonement for you before the LORD your God.

29 For whatever person it be who does not humble himself on this same day, he shall be cut off from among his people.

30 And whatever person it be who does any work on this same day, the same person will I destroy from among his people.

31 You shall do no manner of work; it shall be a statute for ever throughout your generations in all your dwellings.

32 It is the sabbath of sabbaths to you, and you shall humble yourselves;

on the ninth day of the month at evening, from evening to evening, shall you keep your sabbaths.

33 ¶And the LORD spoke to Moses, saying,

34 Speak to the children of Israel and say to them, On the fifteenth day of this seventh month you shall keep the feast of tabernacles for seven days to the LORD.

35 The first day shall be a holy convocation to you; you shall do no manner of work thereon.

36 Seven days you shall offer an offering made by fire to the LORD; the eighth day shall be a holy convocation to you; and you shall offer an offering made by fire to the LORD; and you shall be assembled together; and you shall do no manner of work thereon.

37 These are the feasts of the LORD, which you shall proclaim to be holy convocations, to offer on them offerings made by fire to the LORD, burnt offerings and a meal offering and drink offerings and sacrifices, as it is due on each day;

38 Besides the sabbaths of the LORD, and besides your offerings, and besides your gifts, and besides all your vows, and besides all your freewill offerings, which you give to the LORD.

39 But on the fifteenth day of the seventh month, when you have gathered in the produce of the land, you shall celebrate a feast to the LORD for seven days; on the first day shall be suspension of labor, and on the eighth day shall be a solemn rest.

40 And you shall take for yourselves on the first day the fruits of goodly trees, citron, branches of palm trees, myrtle, and willows of the brook; and you shall rejoice before the LORD your God seven days, all the people of the house of Israel.

41 And you shall keep this feast to the LORD seven days in the year. It is a statute for ever throughout your generations; you shall celebrate it in the seventh month.

42 You shall dwell in huts seven days; all the house of Israel shall dwell in huts,

43 That your generations may know that I made the children of Israel to dwell in huts when I brought them out of the land of Egypt; I am the LORD your God.

44 And Moses declared to the children of Israel the feasts of the LORD.

CHAPTER 24

AND the LORD spoke to Moses, saying,

2 Command the children of Israel to bring to you pure olive oil, beaten, to cause the lamps to burn continually.

3 Outside the veil of the testimony, in the tabernacle of the congregation, shall Aaron set them in order from the evening to the morning before the LORD continually; it is a statute for ever throughout your generations.

4 He shall set the lamps in order upon the large candlestick before the LORD continually.

5 ¶And you shall take fine flour, and bake twelve cakes of it; two tenths of an ephah shall be in each cake.

6 And you shall set them in order in two rows, six in a row, upon the pure table before the LORD.

7 And you shall put pure frankincense upon each row before the LORD, that it may be on the bread for a memorial, even an offering made by fire to the LORD.

8 On the sabbath day Aaron shall set them in order before the LORD continually, as a gift from the children of Israel for an everlasting covenant.

9 And it shall be Aaron's and his sons'; and they shall eat it in a holy place; for it is a most holy to him of the offerings of the LORD made by fire by a perpetual statute.

10 ¶And the son of an Israelite woman, whose father was an Egyptian, went out among the children of Israel; and this son of the Israelite woman and a man of Israel quarreled in the camp;

11 And the Israelite woman's son blasphemed the name of the LORD and cursed it. And they brought him to Moses (and his mother's name was Shelomith, the daughter of Dibri, of the tribe of Dan),

12 And they put him in prison, till the LORD's decision might be made known to them.

13 And the LORD spoke to Moses and said to him,

14 Bring outside the camp him who has cursed; and let all who heard him lay their hands upon his head, and let all the congregation stone him.

15 And you shall speak to the children of Israel, saying, Whosoever curses his God shall suffer for his sin.

16 And he who blasphemes the name of the LORD shall surely be put to death, and all the congregation shall surely stone him; the proselyte as well as the Israelite, when he blasphemes my name, shall be put to death.

17 ¶And he who kills any man shall surely be put to death.

18 And he who kills a beast shall make it good; beast for beast.

19 And if a man causes a blemish in his neighbor, as he has done, so shall it be done to him;

20 Wound for wound, eye for eye, tooth for tooth; as he has caused a blemish in his neighbor, so shall it be done to him.

21 And he who kills a beast shall restore it; and he who kills a man shall be put to death.

22 You shall have one manner of justice; as for a proselyte, so for an Israelite; for I am the LORD your God.

23 ¶And Moses spoke to the children of Israel, and they brought forth him who had cursed outside the camp, and stoned him with stones and he died. And the children of Israel did as the LORD commanded Moses.

CHAPTER 25

AND the LORD spoke to Moses on mount Sinai, saying,

2 Speak to the children of Israel and say to them, When you come into the land which I give you for an inheritance, then shall the land keep a sabbath to the LORD.

3 Six years you shall sow your fields and six years you shall prune your vineyards and six years you shall gather in your produce;

4 But the seventh year shall be a sabbath of rest to the land, and it shall be to you a sabbath for the LORD; you shall neither sow your fields nor prune your vineyards.

5 That which grows of itself of your harvest you shall not reap, neither gather the grapes of your undressed vine; for it is the year of rest to the land.

6 And the sabbath of the land shall be food for you, for yourself and for your servants and for your maids and for your hired laborers and for the stranger that sojourns with you

7 And for your cattle and for the beasts that are in your land shall all its increase be for food to you.

8 ¶And you shall count seven sabbaths of years to you, seven times seven years; and the space of the seven sabbaths of years shall be to you forty-nine years.

9 Then you shall cause the trumpet of the jubilee to sound on the tenth day of the seventh month; on the day of atonement shall you sound the trumpet throughout all your land.

10 And you shall hallow the fiftieth year and proclaim liberty throughout all the land to all the inhabitants thereof; it shall be a jubilee to you; and you shall return every man to his own possession, and you shall return every man to his family.

11 A jubilee shall that fiftieth year be to you; you shall not sow, neither reap that which grows of itself in it, nor gather the grapes from the undressed vine.

12 For it is the jubilee; it shall be holy to you; you shall eat the produce out of the field.

13 In this year of jubilee you shall return every man to his own possession.

14 And if you sell to your neighbor or buy from your neighbor, you shall not defraud one another:

15 According to the number of years after the jubilee you shall buy from your neighbor, and according to the number of years of the produce he shall sell to you;

16 In proportion to the multitude

of years you shall increase the price thereof, and in proportion to the fewness of years you shall decrease the price of it; for according to the number of the years of produce does he sell to you.

17 You shall not therefore defraud one another; but you shall fear your God; for I am the LORD your God.

18 ¶Wherefore you shall do my commandments and keep my judgments and do them; and you shall dwell in the land in safety.

19 And the land shall yield its fruit, and you shall eat your fill and dwell therein in safety.

20 And if you shall say, What shall we eat in the seventh year? For we shall not sow, nor gather in the produce thereof;

21 Then I will send my blessings upon you in the sixth year, and it shall bring forth fruit for three years.

22 And you shall sow in the eighth year, and eat yet of old produce until the ninth year; until the new produce comes in, you shall eat of the old produce.

23 ¶Surely the land shall not be sold outright; for the land is mine; you are strangers and sojourners with me.

24 And in all the land of your possession you shall grant a redemption for the land.

25 ¶If your brother becomes poor and sells some of his possession, then his nearest kin shall come and redeem that which his brother has sold.

26 And if the man has no one to redeem it, and himself has sufficient means and is able to redeem it,

27 Then let him count the years of the sale thereof and refund the overplus to the man to whom he sold it, that he may return to his possession.

28 But if he cannot afford to pay him back, then that which he sold shall remain secure in the hand of him who has bought it until the year of jubilee; and in the jubilee it shall be released, and he shall return to his possession.

29 If a man sells a dwelling house in a walled city, then he may redeem it within a whole year after it is sold; within a full year he may redeem it.

30 And if it is not redeemed within a full year, then the house that is in the walled city shall be confirmed for ever to him who bought it throughout his generations; it shall not be released in the jubilee.

31 But the houses of the villages which have no walls round about them shall be counted as the fields of the country; they may be redeemed, and they shall be released in the jubilee.

32 Notwithstanding the cities of the Levites, and the houses which are in the cities of their possession, the Levites shall have the right to redeem for ever.

33 And if a man purchases of the Levites, then the house that was sold, and the city of his possession, shall be released in the year of jubilee; for the houses in the cities of the Levites are their possessions among the children of Israel.

34 But the field of the suburbs of their cities may not be sold; for it is their perpetual possession.

35 ¶And if your brother becomes poor and stretches out his hand for help, you shall not look upon him as a stranger or a sojourner; he shall live with you.

36 You shall not take a discount of him or usury; but fear your God, that your brother may live with you.

37 You shall not lend him your money with a discount nor give him your food with usury.

38 I am the LORD your God, who brought you forth out of the land of Egypt to give you the land of Canaan and to be your God.

39 ¶And if your brother becomes poor and be sold to you, you shall not compel him to serve as a bondservant;

40 But as a hired laborer, and as a sojourner, he shall be with you, and shall serve you until the year of jubilee;

41 And then he shall depart from you, both he and his children with him, and shall return to his own family, and to the possession of his fathers shall he return.

42 For they are my servants whom I brought forth out of the land of

Egypt; they shall not be sold as bondmen.

43 You shall not compel them to do hard work; but shall fear your God.

44 But as for your male servants and your female servants whom you may have from among the people that are round about you, of them shall you buy bondmen and bondwomen.

45 Moreover of the children of the strangers who have sojourned among you, of them shall you buy, and of their families that are with you, who have been born in your land; and they shall be your possession.

46 And you shall bequeath them to your children after you, to inherit them as a possession; you may make slaves of them for ever; but as for your brethren the children of Israel, you shall not compel them to do hard work.

47 ¶And if a sojourner or stranger who dwells with you becomes rich, and your brother who dwells with him becomes poor and is sold to the stranger or sojourner who dwells with you or to a native born of the stranger's family who dwells with you,

48 After that he is sold he may be redeemed again; one of his brethren may redeem him;

49 Either his uncle or his uncle's son may redeem him, or any of his near kin belonging to his family may redeem him; or if he can afford it, he may redeem himself.

50 He shall reckon with him who bought him from the year that he was sold him to the year of jubilee; and the price of his sale shall be according to the number of years, according to the time of a hired servant shall it be with him.

51 If there are still many years remaining, according to them he shall give again the price of his redemption out of the money that he was bought for.

52 And if there remain but a few years to the year of jubilee, then he shall count with him, and according to his years shall he give him again the price of his redemption.

53 As a yearly hired servant shall he be with him; and he shall not subject him to hard labor in your sight.

54 And if he is not redeemed in any of these ways, then he shall go out in the year of jubilee, both he and his children with him.

55 For to me the children of Israel are servants; they are my servants whom I brought forth out of the land of Egypt; I am the LORD your God.

CHAPTER 26

YOU shall make for yourselves no idols nor graven images, neither shall you erect obelisks for yourselves, nor shall you set up any image of stones in your land to bow down to them or worship them; for I am the LORD your God.

2 ¶You shall keep my commandments and reverence my sanctuary; I am the LORD.

3 ¶If you walk in my statutes and keep my commandments and do them,

4 Then I will give you rain in due season, and the land shall yield its increase, and the trees of the field shall yield their fruit.

5 And your threshing shall last to the time of vintage, and the vintage shall last to the sowing time; and you shall eat your bread to the full and dwell in your land safely.

6 And I will give peace in your land, and you shall lie down and none shall make you afraid; and I will rid vicious beasts out of the land, neither shall the sword go through your land.

7 And you shall chase your enemies, and they shall fall before you by the sword.

8 And five of you shall chase a hundred, and a hundred of you shall pursue ten thousand; and your enemies shall fall before you by the sword.

9 For I will return to you and make you great and multiply you and establish my covenant with you.

10 And you shall eat grain which has been stored, and bring forth the old grain before the new.

11 And I will set my tabernacle among you; and my soul shall not abhor you.

12 And I will walk among you and

will be your God, and you shall be my people.

13 I am the LORD your God, who brought you forth out of the land of Egypt that you should not be their bondmen; and I have broken the bands of your yoke and made you walk upright.

14 ¶But if you will not hearken to me and will not do all these commandments,

15 And if you despise my laws, or if your soul abhor my judgments so that you will not do all my commandments, and make my covenant of no effect;

16 I also will do this to you: I will visit you with terror, leprosy, scab, and the burning ague, that shall consume the eyes and cause life to waste away; and you shall sow your seed in vain, for your enemies shall eat it.

17 And I will pour out my anger against you, and you shall be defeated before your enemies; they that hate you shall reign over you; and you shall flee when none pursue you.

18 And if you will not yet for all these things hearken to me, then I will punish you seven times more for your sins.

19 And I will break the pride of your power; and I will make your heaven like iron and your earth like brass;

20 And your strength shall be spent in vain; for your land shall not yield its increase, neither shall the trees of the land yield their fruits.

21 ¶And if you walk contrary to me and will not hearken to me, I will bring seven times more plagues upon you according to your sins.

22 I will also send wild beasts against you, which shall bereave you of your children and destroy your cattle and make you few in number; and your highways shall be desolate.

23 And if by these things you shall not be disciplined, but continue to walk contrary to me;

24 Then I also will walk contrary to you and will punish you yet seven times for your sins.

25 And I will bring a sword upon you, which shall avenge the breaking of the covenant; and you shall flee to your cities; I will send pestilence among you; and you shall be delivered into the hand of the enemy.

26 And when I have broken the staff of your grain, ten women shall bake your bread in one oven, and they shall deliver your bread by weight; and you shall eat and not be satisfied.

27 And if you will not for all these things hearken to me, but walk contrary to me;

28 Then I will also walk contrary to you in fury; and I, even I, will chastise you seven times for your sins.

29 And you shall eat the flesh of your sons, and the flesh of your daughters shall you eat.

30 And I will destroy your high places and break your idols and cast your carcasses upon the carcasses of your idols, and my soul shall abhor you.

31 And I will make your cities waste and reduce your sanctuaries to desolation, and I will not smell the savour of your sweet odors.

32 And I will bring the land into desolation; and your enemies who dwell therein shall be astonished at it.

33 I will scatter you among the Gentiles, and will draw out a sword against you; and your land shall be desolate, and your cities waste.

34 Then shall the land enjoy its sabbaths as long as it lies desolate, while you are in your enemies' land; even then shall the land rest and enjoy its sabbaths.

35 As long as it lies desolate it shall rest; because it did not rest in your sabbaths when you dwelt upon it.

36 And as for those who are left among you, I will send a faintness into their hearts in the lands of their enemies; and the sound of a shaken leaf shall chase them; and they shall flee as fleeing from the sword; and they shall fall when none pursues them.

37 And they shall stumble one after another, as it were from the sword, when none pursues them; and they shall have no power to stand before their enemies.

38 And you shall perish among the Gentiles, and the land of your enemies shall devour you.

39 And those of you who are left shall pine away in their iniquity in their enemies' lands; and also in the iniquity of their fathers shall they pine away with them.

40 If they shall confess their iniquity and the iniquity of their fathers, with their wickedness with which they transgressed against me, and also that they have walked contrary to me;

41 And that I also walked contrary to them, and brought them into the land of their enemies; and if then their uncircumcised heart shall be humbled, and they then shall accept the punishment of their iniquity;

42 Then I will remember my covenant with Jacob, and also my covenant with Isaac, and my covenant with Abraham will I remember; and I will remember the land.

43 The land also shall be left by them, and shall enjoy its sabbaths while it lies desolate without them; and they shall accept the punishment of their iniquity because they have despised my judgments and because their soul abhorred my statutes.

44 And yet for all that, when they are in the land of their enemies I will not abhor them, neither will I cast them away to destroy them utterly, nor have I nullified my covenant with them; for I am the LORD their God.

45 But I will for their sakes remember the covenant of their ancestors whom I brought forth out of the land of Egypt in the sight of the nations, and I became their God; I am the LORD.

46 These are the commandments and laws and judgments which the LORD made between him and the children of Israel in mount Sinai by the hand of Moses.

CHAPTER 27

AND the LORD spoke to Moses, saying,

2 Speak to the children of Israel and say to them, When a man makes a special vow with the price of persons to the LORD,

3 Then the valuation of a male from twenty years old up to sixty years old shall be fifty shekels of silver, after the shekel of the sanctuary.

4 And if it is a female, then her valuation shall be thirty shekels.

5 And if it is from five years old up to twenty years old, then the valuation of the male shall be twenty shekels, and for the female ten shekels.

6 And if it is from a month old up to five years old, then the valuation of males shall be for the male five shekels of silver, and for the female three shekels of silver.

7 And if it is from sixty years old and up, if it is a male, his valuation shall be fifteen shekels, and for the female ten shekels.

8 But if he is poorer than the valuation, then he shall present himself before the priest, and the priest shall value him; according to the ability of the person who vowed shall the priest value him.

9 And if it is an animal whereof men bring an offering to the LORD, all that any man gives of such to the LORD shall be holy.

10 He shall not exchange it, a good for a bad, or a bad for a good; and if he shall at all exchange an animal for an animal, then both it and the one exchanged for it shall be holy to the LORD.

11 And if it is an unclean animal of which they do not offer a sacrifice to the LORD, then he shall present the animal before the priest;

12 And the priest shall value it, whether it be good or bad; and as the priest values it, so shall it be.

13 But if he wishes to redeem it, then he shall add a fifth part to its valuation.

14 ¶And when a man shall sanctify his house to be holy to the LORD, then the priest shall value it, whether it be good or bad, and as the priest shall estimate it, so shall it stand.

15 And if he who sanctified it will redeem his house, then he shall add a fifth of the money of its estimation to it, and it shall be his.

16 And if a man shall sanctify to

the LORD some part of a field of his possession, then its valuation shall be according to the seed thereof; about ten ephahs of barley seed shall be valued at fifty shekels of silver.

17 If he sanctifies his field from the year of jubilee, according to its estimation so it shall stand.

18 But if he sanctify his field after the jubilee, then the priest shall reckon to him the money according to the years that remain until the year of jubilee, and he shall deduct from its valuation.

19 And if the man who sanctifies the field wishes to redeem it, then he shall add a fifth of the money of the valuation to it, and it shall be his.

20 And if he will not redeem the field, or if he sell it to another man, it shall not be redeemed any more.

21 But the field, when it is released in the jubilee, shall be holy to the LORD, as a field devoted; its possession shall be the priest's.

22 And if a man sanctifies to the LORD a field which he has bought, which was not a field of his inheritance,

23 Then the priest shall reckon the valuation thereof until the year of jubilee; and he shall give the price of the valuation thereof in that day as a holy thing to the LORD.

24 In the year of the jubilee the field shall return to him from whom it was bought, even to him to whom the inheritance of the land did belong.

25 And all the valuations thereof shall be according to the shekel of the sanctuary; twenty gerahs shall be the shekel.

26 ¶But the firstling of an animal, which should be the LORD's firstling, no man shall sanctify it; whether it be ox or sheep, it is the LORD's.

27 And if it is of an unclean beast, then he shall redeem it according to its valuation, and shall add a fifth part to it; or if it is not redeemed, then it shall be sold according to its valuation.

28 But every devoted thing that a man shall devote to the LORD of all that he has, both of man and beast and of the field of his inheritance, shall not be sold or redeemed; every devoted thing is most holy to the LORD.

29 Every devoted thing which shall be devoted by men shall not be redeemed, but shall surely be put to death.

30 And all the tithe of the land, whether of the seed of the land or of the fruit of the trees, is the LORD's; it is holy to the LORD.

31 And if a man wishes to redeem some of his tithes, he shall add to it a fifth part thereof.

32 And all the tithe of the herd or of the flock, even of whatever passes under the shepherd's staff, the tenth shall be holy to the LORD.

33 He shall not inquire whether it is good or bad, neither shall he exchange it; and if he exchanges it at all, then both it and the exchange thereof shall be holy; it shall not be redeemed.

34 These are the commandments which the LORD commanded Moses for the children of Israel in mount Sinai.

THE FOURTH BOOK OF MOSES, CALLED

NUMBERS

CHAPTER 1

AND the LORD spoke to Moses in the wilderness of Sinai, in the tabernacle of the congregation, on the first day of the second month, in the second year after the children of Israel were come out of the land of Egypt, saying,

2 Take the census of all the congregation of the children of Israel, by their families, by the house of their fathers, with the number of their names, every male by their polls;

3 From twenty years old and upward, all who are able to go forth to war in Israel; you and Aaron your brother shall number them by their armies.

4 And with you there shall be a man of every tribe; every one the head of the house of his fathers.

5 ¶And these are the names of the men who shall help you: of the tribe of Reuben, Elizur the son of Shedeur.

6 Of Simeon, Shelmuiel the son of Zurishaddai.

7 Of Judah, Nahshon the son of Amminadab.

8 Of Issachar, Nethanael the son of Zuar.

9 Of Zebulun, Eliab the son of Helon.

10 Of the sons of Joseph, of Ephraim, Elishama the son of Ammihud; of Manasseh, Gamaliel the son of Perzur.

11 Of Benjamin, Abidan the son of Gideoni.

12 Of Dan, Ahiezer the son of Ammishaddai.

13 Of Asher, Pagiel the son of Ocran.

14 Of Gad, Eliasaph the son of Reuel.

15 Of Naphtali, Ahida the son of Enan.

16 These were the renowned of the congregation, princes of the tribes of their fathers, heads of thousands of the army of Israel.

17 ¶And Moses and Aaron took these men who were chosen by their names;

18 And they assembled all the congregation together on the first day of the second month, and they were numbered after their families, by the house of their fathers, according to the number of their names from twenty years old and upward, by their polls.

19 As the LORD commanded Moses, so he numbered them in the wilderness of Sinai.

20 And the children of Reuben, Israel's first-born, by their generations, after their families, by the house of their fathers, according to the number of the names, by their polls, every male from twenty years old and upward, all who were able to go forth to war in Israel;

21 The number of the tribe of Reuben was forty-six thousand and five hundred.

22 ¶Of the children of Simeon, by their generations, after their families, by the house of their fathers, those that were numbered of them, according to the number of the names, by their polls, every male from twenty years old and upward, all who were able to go forth to war in Israel;

23 The number of the tribe of Simeon was fifty-nine thousand and three hundred.

24 ¶Of the children of Gad, by their generations, after their families, by the house of their fathers, according

to the number of the names, by their polls, every male from twenty years old and upward, all who were able to go forth to war in Israel;

25 The number of the tribe of Gad was forty-five thousand and six hundred and fifty.

26 ¶Of the children of Judah, by their generations, after their families, according to the number of the names, from twenty years old and upward, all who were able to go forth to war in Israel;

27 The number of the tribe of Judah was seventy-four thousand and six hundred.

28 ¶Of the children of Issachar, by their generations, after their families, by the house of their fathers, according to the number of the names, from twenty years old and upward, all who were able to go forth to war in Israel;

29 The number of the tribe of Issachar was fifty-four thousand and four hundred.

30 ¶Of the children of Zebulun, by their generations, after their families, by the house of their fathers, according to the number of the names, from twenty years old and upward, all who were able to go forth to war in Israel;

31 The number of the tribe of Zebulun was fifty-seven thousand and four hundred.

32 ¶Of the children of Joseph, namely, of the children of Ephraim, by their generations, after their families, by the house of their fathers, according to the number of the names, from twenty years old and upward, all who were able to go forth to war in Israel;

33 The number of the tribe of Ephraim was forty thousand and five hundred.

34 ¶Of the children of Manasseh, by their generations, after their families, by the house of their fathers, according to the number of the names, from twenty years old and upward, all who were able to go forth to war in Israel;

35 The number of the tribe of Manasseh was thirty-two thousand and two hundred.

36 ¶Of the children of Benjamin, by their generations, after their families, by the house of their fathers, according to the number of the names, from twenty years old and upward, all who were able to go forth to war in Israel;

37 The number of the tribe of Benjamin was thirty-five thousand and four hundred.

38 ¶Of the children of Dan, by their generations, after their families, by the house of their fathers, according to the number of the names, from twenty years old and upward, all who were able to go forth to war in Israel;

39 The number of the tribe of Dan was sixty-two thousand and seven hundred.

40 ¶Of the children of Asher, by their generations, after their families, by the house of their fathers, according to the number of the names, from twenty years old and upward, all who were able to go forth to war in Israel;

41 The number of the tribe of Asher was forty-one thousand and five hundred.

42 ¶Of the children of Naphtali, by their generations, after their families, by the house of their fathers, according to the number of the names, from twenty years old and upward, all who were able to go forth to war in Israel;

43 The number of the tribe of Naphtali was fifty-three thousand and four hundred.

44 These are those who were numbered, whom Moses and Aaron numbered, and the princes of Israel, being twelve men; each one was from the house of his fathers.

45 So were all those that were numbered of the children of Israel, by the house of their fathers, from twenty years old and upward, all who were able to go forth to war in Israel;

46 The total number of the children of Israel was six hundred and three thousand and five hundred and fifty.

47 ¶But the Levites and the tribe of their fathers were not numbered among them.

48 Because the LORD had spoken to Moses, saying,

49 You shall not number the tribe

of Levi, neither take the sum of them among the children of Israel;

50 But you shall appoint the Levites over the tabernacle of the testimony and over all its vessels and over all that belongs to it; they shall carry the tabernacle and all its vessels; and they shall minister to it, and shall encamp round about the tabernacle.

51 And when the tabernacle shall set forward, the Levites shall take it down; and when the tabernacle is to be pitched, the Levites shall set it up; and the stranger who comes near shall be put to death.

52 And the children of Israel shall pitch their tents, every man by his own camp and every man by his own standard, throughout their hosts.

53 But the Levites shall pitch round about the tabernacle of the testimony, that there be no wrath against the congregation of the children of Israel; and the Levites shall keep the charge of the tabernacle of the testimony.

54 And the children of Israel did according to all that the LORD commanded Moses, so did they.

CHAPTER 2

AND the LORD spoke to Moses and to Aaron, saying,

2 Every man of the children of Israel shall encamp by his own standard, at the places of their father's house; far off round about the tabernacle of the congregation shall they encamp.

3 Those who encamp first toward the east shall be of the standard of the camp of Judah throughout their armies; and Nahshon the son of Amminadab shall be chief of the children of Judah.

4 And the number of his host was seventy-four thousand and six hundred.

5 And those who encamp next to him shall be the tribe of Issachar; and Nethanael the son of Zuar shall be chief of the children of Issachar.

6 And the number of his host was fifty-four thousand and four hundred.

7 Then shall encamp the tribe of Zebulun; and Eliab the son of Helon shall be chief of the children of Zebulun.

8 And the number of his host was fifty-seven thousand and four hundred.

9 The total number of the camp of Judah was one hundred and eighty-six thousand and four hundred, throughout their armies. They shall march first.

10 ¶On the south side shall be the standard of the camp of Reuben according to their armies; and the chief of the children of Reuben shall be Elizur the son of Shedeur.

11 And the number of his host was forty-six thousand and five hundred.

12 And those who encamp by him shall be the tribe of Simeon; and the chief of the children of Simeon shall be Shelmuiel the son of Zurishaddai.

13 And the number of his host was fifty-nine thousand and three hundred.

14 Then shall encamp the tribe of Gad; and the chief of the sons of Gad shall be Eliasaph the son of Reuel.

15 And the number of his host was forty-five thousand six hundred and fifty.

16 The total number of the camp of Reuben was one hundred and fifty-one thousand four hundred and fifty, throughout their armies. They shall march in the second place.

17 ¶Then the tabernacle of the congregation shall march with the camp of the Levites in the midst of the camps; as they encamped so shall they march, every man by his standard throughout their armies.

18 ¶On the west side shall be the standard of the camp of Ephraim according to their armies; and the chief of the children of Ephraim shall be Elishama the son of Ammihud.

19 And the number of his host was forty thousand and five hundred.

20 And those who encamp by him shall be the tribe of Manasseh; and the chief of the children of Manasseh shall be Gamaliel the son of Perzur.

21 And the number of his host was thirty-two thousand and two hundred.

22 Then shall encamp the tribe of Benjamin; and the chief of the sons of Benjamin shall be Abidan the son of Gideoni.

23 And the number of his host was

thirty-five thousand and four hundred.

24 The total number of the camp of Ephraim was an hundred and eight thousand and one hundred, throughout their armies. They shall march in the third place.

25 ¶The standard of the camp of Dan shall be on the north side by their armies; and the chief of the children of Dan shall be Ahiezer the son of Ammishaddai.

26 And the number of his host was sixty-two thousand and seven hundred.

27 And those that encamp by him shall be the tribe of Asher; and the chief of the children of Asher shall be Pagiel the son of Ocran.

28 And the number of his host was forty-one thousand and five hundred.

29 ¶Then shall encamp the tribe of Naphtali; and the chief of the children of Naphtali shall be Ahida the son of Enan.

30 And the number of his host was fifty-three thousand and four hundred.

31 The total number of the camp of Dan was a hundred and fifty-seven thousand and six hundred. They shall march last with their standards.

32 ¶These are the numbers of the children of Israel by the house of their fathers; all those who were numbered of the camps throughout their hosts were six hundred and three thousand and five hundred and fifty.

33 But the Levites and the tribe of their fathers were not numbered among the children of Israel; as the LORD commanded Moses.

34 And the children of Israel did according to all that the LORD commanded Moses; so they marched by their standards, and so they encamped, every man in his camp, according to the house of his fathers.

CHAPTER 3

THESE are the generations of Aaron and Moses in the day that the LORD spoke with Moses on mount Sinai.

2 And these are the names of the sons of Aaron: Nadab, his first-born, and Abihu, Eleazar, and Ithamar.

3 These are the names of the sons of Aaron the priest, who were anointed and consecrated to minister in the priest's office.

4 But Nadab and Abihu died before the LORD when they offered strange fire before the LORD in the wilderness of Sinai, and they had no children; and Eleazar and Ithamar ministered in the priest's office during the lifetime of Aaron their father.

5 ¶And the LORD spoke to Moses, saying,

6 Bring the tribe of Levi near, and present them before Aaron the priest, that they may minister to him.

7 And they shall keep his charge and the charge of the whole congregation in the presence of the LORD before the tabernacle of the congregation, to do the service of the tabernacle.

8 And they shall keep all the instruments of the tabernacle of the congregation and the charge of the children of Israel, to do the service of the tabernacle.

9 And you shall give the Levites to Aaron and to his sons; they are wholly given to him as a gift out of the children of Israel.

10 And you shall appoint Aaron and his sons, and they shall wait on their priest's office; and the stranger that comes near shall be put to death.

11 And the LORD spoke to Moses, saying,

12 Behold I have taken the Levites from among the children of Israel instead of all the first-born that open the womb among the children of Israel; therefore the Levites shall be mine;

13 Because all the first-born are mine; for on the day that I smote all the first-born in the land of Egypt, I consecrated to me all the first-born in Israel, both man and beast; they shall be mine; I am the LORD.

14 ¶And the LORD spoke to Moses in the wilderness of Sinai, saying,

15 Number the children of Levi after the house of their fathers, by their families; every male from a

month old and upward, you shall number them.

16 So Moses numbered them according to the word of the LORD, as he was commanded.

17 These were the sons of Levi by their names: Gershon and Kohath and Merari.

18 And these are the names of the sons of Gershon by their families: Libni and Shimei.

19 And the sons of Kohath by their families: Amram and Izhar, Hebron and Uzziel.

20 And the sons of Merari by their families: Mahali and Mushi. These are the families of the Levites according to the house of their fathers.

21 Of Gershon was the family of the Libnites and the family of the Shimites; these are the families of the Gershonites.

22 Their number, according to the number of all the males from a month old and upward was seven thousand and five hundred.

23 The families of the Gershonites shall encamp behind the tabernacle westward.

24 And the chief of the house of the fathers of the Gershonites shall be Eliasaph the son of Eliab.

25 And the charge of the sons of Gershon in the tabernacle of the congregation shall be the tabernacle and the tent, its covering and the curtains for the door of the tabernacle of the congregation

26 And the curtains of the court and the covering for the door of the court which is by the tabernacle and by the altar round about, and the cords of it, and all the instruments thereof.

27 ¶And of Kohath was the family of the Amramites and the family of the Izeharites and the family of the Hebronites and the family of the Uzzielites; these are the families of the Kohathites.

28 Their number according to the number of all the males, from a month old and upward, was eight thousand and six hundred, looking after the sanctuary.

29 The families of the sons of Ko-hath shall encamp on the side of the tabernacle southward.

30 And the chief of the house of the fathers of the families of the Ko-hathites shall be Elizphan the son of Uzziel.

31 And their charge shall be the ark and the table and the candlestick and the altars and the vessels of the sanctuary with which they minister and the curtain of the door and all the service thereof.

32 And Eleazar the son of Aaron the priest shall be the chief over the chiefs of the Levites and have the oversight over those who have charge of the sanctuary.

33 ¶Of Merari was the family of the Mahlites and the family of the Mushites; these are the families of Merari.

34 Their number according to the number of all the males, from a month old and upward, was six thousand and two hundred.

35 And the chief of the house of the fathers of the families of Merari was Zuriel the son of Abihail; they shall encamp on the side of the tabernacle northward.

36 And under the custody and charge of the sons of Merari shall be the boards of the tabernacle and its bars and its pillars and its sockets and all the vessels thereof and all that pertains to it

37 And the pillars of the court round about and their sockets and their pins and their cords.

38 ¶But those that encamp before the tabernacle toward the east, even before the tabernacle of the congregation eastward, shall be Moses and Aaron and his sons, keeping the charge of the sanctuary in addition to the charge of the children of Israel; and the stranger who comes near shall be put to death.

39 All who were numbered of the Levites, whom Moses numbered at the commandment of the LORD, by their families, all the males from a month old and upward, were twenty and two thousand.

40 ¶And the LORD said to Moses, Number all the first-born of the

males of the children of Israel from a month old and upward, and take the number of their names.

41 And you shall present the Levites for me (I am the LORD) instead of all the first-born among the children of Israel; and the cattle of the Levites instead of all the firstlings among the cattle of the children of Israel.

42 And Moses numbered, as the LORD commanded him, all the first-born among the children of Israel,

43 And all the first-born males by the number of names, from a month old and upward, and their number was twenty-two thousand two hundred and seventy-three.

44 ¶And the LORD spoke to Moses, saying,

45 Present the Levites instead of all the first-born among the children of Israel, and the cattle of the Levites instead of their cattle; and the Levites shall be mine; I am the LORD.

46 And for the redemption of the two hundred and seventy-three of the first-born of the children of Israel, that are above the number of the Levites,

47 You shall take five shekels apiece by the poll, by the shekel of the sanctuary shall you take them (the shekel is twenty gerahs).

48 And you shall give the money wherewith the excess number of them is to be redeemed to Aaron and to his sons.

49 So Moses took the redemption money from those who were over and above them that were redeemed by the Levites;

50 From the first-born of the children of Israel he took the money, one thousand three hundred and sixty-five shekels, by the shekel of the sanctuary:

51 And Moses gave the redemption money to Aaron and to his sons, according to the word of the LORD, as the LORD commanded Moses.

CHAPTER 4

AND the LORD spoke to Moses and to Aaron, saying,

2 Take the sum of the sons of Kohath from among the sons of Levi, after their families, by the house of their fathers,

3 From thirty years old and upward to fifty years old, all who can enter into the host to do the work in the tabernacle of the congregation.

4 This is the service of the sons of Kohath in the tabernacle of the congregation concerning the most holy things;

5 ¶And when the camp marches forward, Aaron and his sons shall come in, and they shall take down the covering veil and cover the ark of testimony with it,

6 And shall put on it the covering of badgers' skins, and shall spread over it a cloth all of blue, and shall put in the poles thereof.

7 And upon the table of shewbread they shall spread a cloth of blue, and put upon it the dishes, the spoons, the bowls, the flagons for drink offering; and the continual shewbread shall be on it;

8 And they shall spread thereon a cloth of scarlet, and cover the same with a covering of badgers' skins, and shall put in the poles thereof.

9 And they shall take a cloth of blue, and cover the candlestick of the light and its lamps and its tongs and its snuffdishes and all the oil vessels thereof with which they minister to it;

10 And they shall put it and all its vessels within a covering of badgers' skins, and shall put it upon its poles.

11 And upon the golden altar they shall spread a cloth of blue, and cover it with a covering of badgers' skins, and shall put it upon its poles;

12 And they shall take all the vessels of the ministry wherewith they minister in the sanctuary, and put them in a cloth of blue, and cover them with a covering of badgers' skins, and shall put them on poles;

13 And they shall take apart the altar, and spread a purple cloth over it;

14 And they shall put with it all the vessels thereof, with which they minister upon it, the censers, the meathooks and the shovels and the basins and all the vessels of the altar;

and they shall spread upon it a covering of badgers' skins, and put in its poles.

15 And when Aaron and his sons have finished covering the sanctuary and all the vessels of the sanctuary, as the camp is to march after that, the sons of Kohath shall come in to bear it, that they may not touch any holy thing, lest they die. These things are to be borne by the sons of Kohath in the service of the tabernacle of the congregation.

16 ¶And to the office of Eleazar the son of Aaron the priest pertains the charge of the oil for the light and the sweet incense and the daily meal offering and the anointing oil and the oversight of all the tabernacle and of all the things that are in it and of the sanctuary and its vessels.

17 ¶And the LORD spoke to Moses and to Aaron, saying,

18 You shall not destroy the tribe of the families of the Kohathites from among the Levites;

19 But do this to them, that they may live, and not die, when they enter into the most holy place; Aaron and his sons shall go in and appoint them every one to his service and to his burden;

20 But they shall not go in to observe when the holy things are covered, lest they die.

21 ¶And the LORD spoke to Moses, saying,

22 Take also the sum of the sons of Gershon, throughout the houses of their fathers, by their families:

23 From thirty years old and up until fifty years old you shall number them; all who are able-bodied to perform the service, to do the work in the tabernacle of the congregation.

24 This is the service of the families of the Gershonites, to serve, and to bear burdens;

25 They shall carry the curtains of the tabernacle, and the tabernacle of the congregation itself, the veil of the door thereof, and the covering of the badgers' skins that is upon it, and the hangings of the door of the tabernacle of the congregation,

26 And the hangings of the court, and the hanging for the entrance of the door of the court which is by the tabernacle and by the altar round about, and the cords thereof, and all the instruments of their service, and all that they do and serve.

27 At the command of Aaron and his sons shall be all the service of the sons of Gershon, in all their burdens and in all their service; and you shall appoint unto them in charge all their burdens.

28 This is the service of the families of the sons of Gershon in the tabernacle of the congregation; and their charge shall be under the hand of Ithamar the son of Aaron the priest.

29 ¶As for the sons of Merari, you shall number them after their families, by the house of their fathers;

30 From thirty years old and upward to fifty years old you shall number them, every able man, to do the work of the tabernacle of the congregation.

31 And this is the charge of their burden, and of all their service in the tabernacle of the congregation; the boards of the tabernacle, its bars and its pillars and its sockets

32 And the pillars of the court round about and their sockets, their pins and their cords, with all their instruments and with all their service; and by name you shall count the instruments included in their burden.

33 This is the service of the families of the sons of Merari, and all their service in the tabernacle of the congregation, under the hand of Ithamar the son of Aaron the priest.

34 ¶And Moses and Aaron and the chiefs of the congregation numbered the sons of the Kohathites after their families, by the house of their fathers,

35 From thirty years old and upward to fifty years old, every able man, for the work of the tabernacle of the congregation;

36 And their number by their families was two thousand and seven hundred and fifty.

37 These were the numbers of the

families of Kohath, all that might do service in the tabernacle of the congregation, whom Moses and Aaron numbered according to the commandment of the LORD by Moses.

38 And the number of the sons of Gershon by their families, and by the house of their fathers,

39 From thirty years old and upward to fifty years old, every able man, for the work in the tabernacle of the congregation,

40 And their number by their families and by the house of their fathers was two thousand and six hundred and thirty.

41 These were the numbers of the family of the sons of Gershon, all who served in the tabernacle of the congregation, whom Moses and Aaron numbered according to the commandment of the LORD.

42 ¶And the number of the families of the sons of Merari by their families, by the house of their fathers,

43 From thirty years old and upward to fifty years old, every able man, for the work in the tabernacle of the congregation,

44 And their number by their families was three thousand and two hundred.

45 These are the numbers of the sons of Merari, whom Moses and Aaron numbered according to the commandment of the LORD by the hand of Moses.

46 All those who were numbered of the Levites, whom Moses and Aaron and the chiefs of Israel numbered, after their families and by the house of their fathers,

47 From thirty years old and upward to fifty years old, all able men, to do the service of the ministry and the work of the burden in the tabernacle of the congregation,

48 Their number was eight thousand and five hundred and eighty.

49 According to the commandment of the LORD they were numbered by the hand of Moses, every one according to his service and according to his burden; thus they were numbered as the LORD commanded Moses.

CHAPTER 5

THE LORD spoke to Moses, saying,

2 Command the children of Israel that they put out of the camp every leper and every one who has a discharge and whosoever has defiled himself;

3 Both male and female shall you put outside the camp, that they may not defile your camps, for I dwell among you.

4 And the children of Israel did so, and put them outside the camp; as the LORD had said to Moses, so did the children of Israel.

5 ¶And the LORD spoke to Moses, saying,

6 Say to the children of Israel, When a man or a woman shall commit any sin that men commit, to do wrong in the sight of the LORD, and that person shall be guilty,

7 Then he shall confess his sins which he has committed; and his guilt shall return upon his own head; and he shall add a fifth part thereof, and give it to him whom he had wronged.

8 And if the person has no kinsman to whom to recompense the trespass, let the trespass offering which they bring on his behalf before the LORD be given to the priest in addition to the ram of the atonement with which an atonement is made for him.

9 And every offering of all the holy things of the children of Israel which they bring to the priest shall be his.

10 And every man's hallowed things shall be his; and whatever any man gives to the priest, shall be his.

11 ¶And the LORD spoke to Moses, saying,

12 Speak to the children of Israel and say to them, If any man's wife does wrong, and commits a trespass against him,

13 And a man lies with her carnally and it is hidden from the eyes of her husband and the act is kept secret and she is defiled and there is no witness against her, neither is she caught in the act,

14 And the temper of jealousy

comes upon him and he be jealous of his wife and she is defiled; or if the temper of jealousy comes upon him and he becomes jealous of his wife and she is not defiled,

15 Then the man shall bring his wife to the priest, and he shall bring as his offering a tenth part of an ephah of barley flour; and he shall pour no oil upon it, nor put frankincense upon it; for it is a meal offering of jealousy, a meal offering for a memorial, bringing iniquity to remembrance.

16 And the priest shall bring her near, and she shall stand before the LORD;

17 And the priest shall take holy water in an earthen vessel; and some of the dust that is in the base of the altar of the tabernacle the priest shall take and put it into the water;

18 And the priest shall set the woman before the LORD and shave the woman's head and put the offering of memorial in her hands, which is the jealousy offering; and the priest shall have in his hand the bitter water of testing;

19 And the priest shall charge the woman by an oath, and say to her, If no man has lain with you besides your husband, and if you have not done wrong and become unclean, be absolved from these charges by this bitter water of testing;

20 But if you have done wrong by having lain with another man besides your husband, and if you have defiled yourself, and some other man has lain with you besides your husband;

21 Then the priest shall adjure the woman with the oaths of cursing, and the priest shall say to the woman, The LORD make you a curse and an oath among your people, when the LORD makes your thigh to rot and your belly to swell;

22 And this water of testing shall go into your belly and make your belly to swell and your thighs to rot; and the woman shall say, Amen, amen.

23 And the priest shall write these curses in a book, and he shall blot out the writing in the water of testing;

24 And he shall make the woman drink the bitter water of testing; and the water of testing shall enter into her, to try her.

25 Then the priest shall take the jealousy meal offering out of the woman's hand, and shall wave the meal offering before the LORD, and offer it upon the altar;

26 And the priest shall take some of the meal offering as the memorial thereof, and burn it upon the altar, and afterward shall make the woman drink the water.

27 And when he has made her drink the water, if she has defiled herself and has committed iniquity against her husband, the water of testing shall enter into her, and shall try her, and if her belly shall swell and her thighs shall rot, then that woman shall be a curse among her people.

28 But if the woman has not defiled herself, but is pure, then she shall be absolved, and shall bear a male child.

29 This is the law of jealousy when a woman does wrong by having lain with another man besides her husband and defiles herself,

30 Or when the temper of jealousy comes upon a man and he is jealous over his wife and shall set the woman before the LORD, and the priest shall execute upon her all this law;

31 Then the man shall be blameless from guilt, but the woman shall bear her iniquity.

CHAPTER 6

THE LORD spoke to Moses, saying, 2 Speak to the children of Israel and say to them, When a man or woman shall separate himself to vow a vow of a Nazarite, to separate himself to the LORD,

3 He shall abstain from wine and strong drink, and shall drink no vinegar of wine or vinegar of strong drink, neither shall he drink any juice of grapes, or eat grapes or raisins;

4 All the days of his separation he shall eat nothing that is made of the grapevine, from the skins even to the stones of raisins.

5 All the days of the vow of his

separation there shall no razor come upon his head; until the days are fulfilled for which he separated himself to the LORD, he shall be holy and shall let the locks of the hair of his head grow.

6 All the days that he separates himself to the LORD he shall not come near a dead body.

7 He shall not defile himself for his father or for his mother, for his brother or for his sister when they die; because the crown of consecration of his God is upon his head.

8 All the days of his separation he is holy unto the LORD.

9 And if any man dies very suddenly by him, he has defiled the crown of his separation; then he shall shave his head on the day of his cleansing, on the seventh day shall he shave it.

10 And on the eighth day he shall bring two turtledoves or two young pigeons to the priest, to the door of the tabernacle of the congregation;

11 And the priest shall offer the one for a sin offering and the other for a burnt offering, and make an atonement for him, for the sin that he sinned by the dead body; and shall sanctify his head that same day.

12 And he shall consecrate to the LORD the days of his separation, and he shall bring a lamb of the first year for a trespass offering; but the previous days of his separation shall be void, because his separation was defiled.

13 ¶This is the law of the Nazarite when the days of his separation are fulfilled: he shall be brought to the door of the tabernacle of the congregation,

14 And he shall offer his offering to the LORD, one male lamb of the first year without blemish for a burnt offering and one ewe lamb without blemish for a sin offering and one ram without blemish for a peace offering

15 And a basket of unleavened bread, cakes of fine flour mixed with oil and wafers of unleavened bread mixed with oil and their meal offering and their drink offering.

16 And the priest shall bring them

before the LORD, and shall offer his sin offering and his burnt offering:

17 And he shall offer the ram for a sacrifice of peace offering to the LORD, with the basket of unleavened bread; the priest shall offer also his meal offering and his drink offering.

18 And the Nazarite shall shave his head as a sign of his separation at the door of the tabernacle of the congregation, and shall take the hair of the head of his separation and put it in the fire which is under the sacrifice of the peace offering.

19 And the priest shall take the cooked shoulder of the ram and one unleavened cake from the basket and one unleavened wafer, and shall put them in the hands of the Nazarite after he has shaved his hair as a sign of his separation;

20 And the priest shall wave them for a wave offering before the LORD: this is holy for the priest, with the wave breast and the shoulder; and after that the Nazarite may drink wine.

21 This is the law of the Nazarite who has made a vow, and of his offering to the LORD for his separation, excepting what he can afford in addition; according to the vow which he has vowed, so shall he do after the law of his separation.

22 ¶And the LORD spoke to Moses, saying,

23 Speak to Aaron and to his sons and say to them, Thus you shall bless the children of Israel, saying to them,

24 The LORD bless you and keep you;

25 The LORD make his face shine upon you and give you life;

26 The LORD lift up his countenance upon you and give you peace.

27 And they shall put my name upon the children of Israel, and I will bless them.

CHAPTER 7

AND it came to pass on the day that Moses had finished setting up the tabernacle and had anointed it and sanctified it and all the instruments thereof, both the altar and all its vessels, and had anointed them and sanctified them;

2 That the princes of Israel, heads of the house of their fathers who were the princes of the tribes and were over those who were numbered,

3 Brought their offerings before the LORD, six excellently constructed wagons and twelve oxen, a wagon for two of the princes, and for each one an ox; and they brought them before the tabernacle.

4 And the LORD said to Moses,

5 Take the offerings from them, that they may be used to do the service of the tabernacle of the congregation, and give them to the Levites, to every man according to his service.

6 And Moses took the oxen and the wagons, and gave them to the Levites.

7 Two wagons and four oxen he gave to the sons of Gershon, according to their service;

8 And four wagons and eight oxen he gave to the sons of Merari, according to their service, under the hand of Ithamar, the son of Aaron the priest.

9 But to the sons of Kohath he gave none, because the service of the sanctuary assigned to them was that they should carry upon their shoulders.

10 ¶And the princes offered offerings for the dedication of the altar on the day that it was anointed; and the princes offered their offerings before the LORD.

11 And the LORD said to Moses, They shall offer each their offerings, each prince on his day, for the dedication of the altar.

12 ¶And he who offered his offering on the first day was Nahshon the son of Amminadab, the prince of the tribe of Judah;

13 And his offering was one silver plate, weighing a hundred and thirty shekels, one silver bowl of seventy shekels, according to the shekel of the sanctuary; both of them were full of fine flour mixed with oil for a meal offering;

14 One spoon of gold of ten shekels, full of incense;

15 One young bullock, one ram, one lamb of the first year, for a burnt offering;

16 One kid of the goats for a sin offering;

17 And for a sacrifice of peace offering, two oxen, five rams, five kids of the goats, five lambs of the first year; this was the offering of Nahshon the son of Amminadab.

18 ¶On the second day, Nethanael the son of Zuar, prince of Issachar, did offer.

19 He offered for his offering one silver plate, weighing a hundred and thirty shekels, one silver bowl of seventy shekels, according to the shekel of the sanctuary; both of them were full of fine flour mixed with oil for a meal offering;

20 One spoon of gold of ten shekels, full of incense;

21 One young bullock, one ram, one lamb of the first year, for a burnt offering;

22 One kid of the goats for a sin offering;

23 And for a sacrifice of peace offering, two oxen, five rams, five kids of the goats, and five lambs of the first year; this was the offering of Nethanael the son of Zuar.

24 ¶On the third day Eliab the son of Helon, prince of the tribe of Zebulun, did offer.

25 His offering was one silver plate, weighing a hundred and thirty shekels, one silver bowl of seventy shekels, according to the shekel of the sanctuary; both of them were full of fine flour mixed with oil for a meal offering;

26 One golden spoon of ten shekels, full of incense;

27 One young bullock, one ram, one lamb of the first year, for a burnt offering;

28 One kid of the goats for a sin offering;

29 And for a sacrifice of peace offering, two oxen, five rams, five kids of the goats, five lambs of the first year; this was the offering of Eliab the son of Helon.

30 ¶On the fourth day Elizur the son of Shedeur, the prince of the tribe of Reuben, did offer.

31 His offering was one silver plate, weighing a hundred and thirty shekels, one silver bowl of seventy shekels, according to the shekel of the sanctuary; both of them were full of fine flour mixed with oil for a meal offering;

32 One golden spoon of ten shekels, full of incense;

33 One young bullock, one ram, one lamb of the first year, for a burnt offering;

34 One kid of the goats for a sin offering;

35 And for a sacrifice of peace offering, two oxen, five rams, five kids of the goats, five lambs of the first year; this was the offering of Elizur the son of Shedeur.

36 ¶On the fifth day Shelumiel the son of Zurishaddai, prince of the tribe of Simeon, did offer.

37 His offering was one silver plate, weighing a hundred and thirty shekels, one silver bowl of seventy shekels, according to the shekel of the sanctuary; both of them were full of fine flour mixed with oil for a meal offering;

38 One golden spoon of ten shekels, full of incense;

39 One young bullock, one ram, one lamb of the first year, for a burnt offering;

40 One kid of the goats for a sin offering;

41 And for the sacrifice of peace offering, two oxen, five rams, five kids of the goats, and five lambs of the first year; this was the offering of Shelumiel the son of Zurishaddai.

42 ¶On the sixth day Eliasaph the son of Reuel, prince of the tribe of Gad, did offer.

43 His offering was one silver plate, weighing a hundred and thirty shekels, one silver bowl of seventy shekels, according to the shekel of the sanctuary; both of them were full of fine flour mixed with oil for a meal offering;

44 One golden spoon of ten shekels, full of incense;

45 One young bullock, one ram, one lamb of the first year, for a burnt offering;

46 One kid of the goats for a sin offering:

47 And for a sacrifice of peace offering, two oxen, five rams, five kids of the goats, five lambs of the first year; this was the offering of Eliasaph the son of Reuel.

48 ¶On the seventh day Elishama the son of Ammihud, prince of the tribe of Ephraim, offered.

49 His offering was one silver plate, weighing a hundred and thirty shekels, one silver bowl of seventy shekels, according to the shekel of the sanctuary; both of them were full of fine flour mixed with oil for a meal offering;

50 One golden spoon of ten shekels, full of incense;

51 One young bullock, one ram, one lamb of the first year, for a burnt offering;

52 One kid of the goats for a sin offering;

53 And for a sacrifice of peace offering, two oxen, five rams, five kids of the goats, five lambs of the first year; this was the offering of Elishama the son of Ammihud.

54 ¶On the eighth day Gamaliel the son of Perzur, prince of the tribe of Manasseh, offered.

55 His offering was one silver plate, weighing a hundred and thirty shekels, one silver bowl of seventy shekels, according to the shekel of the sanctuary; both of them were full of fine flour mixed with oil for a meal offering;

56 One golden spoon of ten shekels, full of incense;

57 One young bullock, one ram, one lamb of the first year, for a burnt offering;

58 One kid of the goats for a sin offering;

59 And for a sacrifice of peace offering, two oxen, five rams, five kids of the goats, five lambs of the first year; this was the offering of Gamaliel the son of Perzur.

60 ¶On the ninth day Abidan the son of Gideoni, prince of the tribe of Benjamin, offered.

61 His offering was one silver plate, weighing a hundred and thirty shekels, one silver bowl of seventy shekels, according to the shekel of the sanctuary; both of them were full of fine

flour mixed with oil for a meal offering;

62 One golden spoon of ten shekels, full of incense;

63 One young bullock, one ram, one lamb of the first year, for a burnt offering;

64 One kid of the goats for a sin offering;

65 And for a sacrifice of peace offering, two oxen, five rams, five kids of the goats, and five lambs of the first year; this was the offering of Abidan the son of Gideoni.

66 ¶On the tenth day Ahiezer the son of Ammishaddai, prince of the tribe of Dan, offered.

67 His offering was one silver plate, weighing a hundred and thirty shekels, one silver bowl of seventy shekels, according to the shekel of the sanctuary; both of them were full of fine flour mixed with oil for a meal offering;

68 One golden spoon of ten shekels, full of incense;

69 One young bullock, one ram, one lamb of the first year, for a burnt offering;

70 One kid of the goats for a sin offering;

71 And for a sacrifice of peace offering, two oxen, five rams, five kids of the goats, five lambs of the first year; this was the offering of Ahiezer the son of Ammishaddai.

72 ¶On the eleventh day Pagiel the son of Ocran, prince of the tribe of Asher, offered.

73 His offering was one silver plate, weighing a hundred and thirty shekels, one silver bowl of seventy shekels, according to the shekel of the sanctuary; both of them were full of fine flour mixed with oil for a meal offering;

74 One golden spoon of ten shekels, full of incense;

75 One young bullock, one ram, one lamb of the first year, for a burnt offering;

76 One kid of the goats for a sin offering;

77 And for a sacrifice of peace offering, two oxen, five rams, five kids of the goats, five lambs of the first

year; this was the offering of Pagiel the son of Ocran.

78 ¶On the twelfth day Ahida the son of Enan, prince of the tribe of Naphtali, offered.

79 His offering was one silver plate, weighing a hundred and thirty shekels, one silver bowl of seventy shekels, according to the shekel of the sanctuary; both of them were full of fine flour mixed with oil for a meal offering;

80 One golden spoon of ten shekels, full of incense;

81 One young bullock, one ram, one lamb of the first year, for a burnt offering;

82 One kid of the goats for a sin offering;

83 And for a sacrifice of peace offering, two oxen, five rams, five kids of the goats, and five lambs of the first year; this was the offering of Ahida the son of Enan.

84 This was the dedication offering from the princes of Israel for the altar, on the day that it was anointed: twelve plates of silver, twelve silver bowls, twelve spoons of gold,

85 Each plate of silver weighing a hundred and thirty shekels, and each bowl seventy. All the silver of the vessels weighed two thousand and four hundred shekels, according to the shekel of the sanctuary.

86 The golden spoons were twelve, full of incense, weighing ten shekels apiece, according to the shekel of the sanctuary; all the gold of the spoons was a hundred and twenty shekels.

87 All the oxen for the burnt offering were twelve bullocks, the rams twelve, the lambs of the first year twelve, with their meal offering; and the kids of the goats for sin offering twelve;

88 And all the oxen for the sacrifice of the peace offering twenty and four bullocks, the rams sixty, the kids of the goats sixty, the lambs of the first year sixty; this was the dedication offering for the altar, after it was anointed.

89 And when Moses entered into the tabernacle of the congregation, he heard a voice speaking to him from

off the mercy seat that was upon the ark of the testimony, from between the two cherubim; and he spoke to him.

CHAPTER 8

THE Lord spoke to Moses, saying, 2 Speak to Aaron and say to him, When you light the lamps, the seven lamps shall give light in front of the candlestick.

3 And Aaron did so; he lighted the seven lamps thereof in front of the candlestick, as the Lord commanded Moses.

4 And the work of the candlestick was of molten gold; from its base to its flower was of cast work; according to the pattern which the Lord had shown to Moses, so he made the candlestick.

5 ¶And the Lord spoke to Moses, saying,

6 Take the Levites from among the children of Israel, and cleanse them.

7 And thus you shall do to them to cleanse them: Sprinkle purifying water upon them, and let them shave all the body, and let them wash their clothes, and so make themselves clean.

8 Then let them take a young bullock with its meal offering, a dish full of fine flour mixed with oil, and another young bullock shall you offer for a sin offering.

9 And you shall bring the Levites before the tabernacle of the congregation; and you shall gather the whole assembly of the children of Israel together;

10 Then you shall bring the Levites before the Lord; and the children of Israel shall put their hands upon the Levites;

11 And Aaron shall offer the Levites before the Lord for an offering from the children of Israel, that they may perform the service of the Lord.

12 And the Levites shall lay their hands upon the heads of the bullocks, and you shall offer the one for a sin offering and the other for a burnt offering to the Lord, to make an atonement for the Levites.

13 And you shall make the Levites stand before Aaron and before his sons, and offer them for an offering to the Lord.

14 Thus shall you separate the Levites from among the children of Israel; and the Levites shall be mine.

15 And after that the Levites shall go in to do the service of the tabernacle of the congregation; and you shall cleanse them, and offer them for an offering before the Lord.

16 For they are wholly given to me as a gift from among the children of Israel; instead of all that open the womb, even instead of the first-born of all the children of Israel, have I taken them to me.

17 For all the first-born of the children of Israel are mine, both man and beast; on the day that I smote every first-born in the land of Egypt I sanctified them for myself.

18 And I have taken the Levites for all the first-born of the children of Israel.

19 And I have given the Levites as a gift to Aaron and to his sons from among the children of Israel, to do the service of the children of Israel in the tabernacle of the congregation and to make an atonement for the children of Israel, that there be no plague among the children of Israel when they come near to the sanctuary.

20 And Moses and Aaron and all the congregation of the children of Israel did to the Levites according to all that the Lord had commanded Moses concerning the Levites; so did the children of Israel to them.

21 And the Levites were purified, and they washed their clothes; and Aaron offered them as an offering before the Lord; and Aaron made an atonement for them and cleansed them.

22 And after that the Levites went in to do their service in the tabernacle of the congregation before Aaron and before his sons; as the Lord had commanded Moses concerning the Levites, so did unto them the children of Israel.

23 ¶And the Lord spoke to Moses, saying,

24 This shall be the law for the Levites: from twenty-five years old

and upward they shall go in to do the work of the tabernacle of the congregation;

25 And from the age of fifty years they shall cease from the service and shall serve no more,

26 But shall minister with their brethren in the tabernacle of the congregation to keep guard, and shall do no service. Thus shall you do to the Levites concerning their charge.

CHAPTER 9

THE LORD spoke to Moses in the wilderness of Sinai in the first month of the second year after the children of Israel had come out of the land of Egypt, saying,

2 Let the children of Israel keep the passover at its appointed time.

3 On the fourteenth day of this month, in the evening, you shall keep it at its appointed time; according to all its rites, and according to all its ceremonies, shall you keep it.

4 And Moses told the children of Israel that they should keep the passover.

5 And they kept the passover on the fourteenth day of the first month, at evening, in the wilderness of Sinai; according to all that the LORD commanded Moses, so did the children of Israel.

6 ¶And there were certain men who were defiled by touching the dead body of a man so that they could not keep the passover on that day; and they came before Moses and before Aaron on that day.

7 And those men said unto them, We are defiled by touching the dead body of a man; why are we kept back from offering the offering of the LORD at the appointed time among the children of Israel?

8 And Moses said to them, Stay where you are, and I will hear what the LORD will command concerning you.

9 ¶And the LORD spoke to Moses, saying,

10 Speak to the children of Israel and say to them, If any man of you or of your posterity shall be unclean by touching a dead body, or is on a jour-

ney afar off, yet he shall keep the passover to the LORD.

11 On the fourteenth day of the second month at the evening they shall keep it, and shall eat it with unleavened bread and bitter herbs.

12 They shall leave none of it to the morning, nor break any bone of it; according to all the ordinances of the passover they shall keep it.

13 But the man who is clean, and is not on a journey, and yet fails to keep the passover, at its appointed time, that person shall be cut off from among his people; because he brought not the offering of the LORD at its appointed time, that man shall suffer for his sin.

14 And if a proselyte shall sojourn among you and will keep the passover to the LORD, according to the ordinance of the passover and according to its statutes, so shall he do; you shall have one ordinance, both for the proselyte and for the native of the land.

15 ¶And on the day that the tabernacle was set up, the cloud covered the tabernacle of the congregation; in front of the door of the tent of the testimony at evening there was upon the tabernacle as it were the appearance of fire, until the morning.

16 So it was always: the cloud covered it by day, and the appearance of fire by night;

17 And when the cloud was taken up from the tabernacle, after that the children of Israel journeyed and at the place where the cloud abode, there the children of Israel encamped.

18 At the commandment of the LORD the children of Israel journeyed, and at the commandment of the LORD they encamped; all the days that the cloud abode upon the tabernacle they remained in their tents.

19 And when the cloud tarried long upon the tabernacle many days, then the children of Israel kept the charge of the LORD and journeyed not.

20 Sometimes the cloud was a few days upon the tabernacle; then according to the commandment of the LORD they remained in their tents, and according to the commandment of the LORD they journeyed.

21 And sometimes the cloud was upon the tabernacle from evening to morning; and when the cloud was taken up in the morning, then they journeyed; whether it was by day or by night that the cloud was taken up, they journeyed.

22 And whether it was a few days or months or a year, as long as the cloud tarried upon the tabernacle, resting thereon, the children of Israel remained in their tents and journeyed not; but when the cloud was taken up, they journeyed.

23 At the commandment of the LORD they encamped, and at the commandment of the LORD they journeyed; they kept the ordinances of the LORD, at the commandment of the LORD by the hand of Moses.

CHAPTER 10

THE LORD spoke to Moses, saying, 2 Make two trumpets of silver; of casting work shall you make them, that you may use them for the calling of the assembly and for the journeying of the camps.

3 And when they shall blow with them, all the people shall assemble themselves to you at the door of the tabernacle of the congregation.

4 And if they blow but with one trumpet, the princes and the heads of the thousands of Israel shall gather themselves to you.

5 When they blow the trumpet, the camps that lie on the east side shall take their journey.

6 And when they blow with the second trumpet, the camps that lie on the south side shall take their journey; they shall blow a trumpet for their journeys.

7 But when the congregation is to be gathered together, you shall blow, but you shall not make a joyful noise.

8 And the sons of Aaron the priest shall blow with the trumpets; and they shall be to you for an ordinance for ever throughout your generations.

9 And if you go to war in your land against the enemies that oppress you, you shall blow with the trumpets; and you shall be remembered before the LORD your God, and you shall be delivered from your enemies.

10 Also in the day of your gladness and in your solemn days and in the beginning of your months you shall blow with the trumpets over your burnt offerings and over the sacrifices of your peace offerings, that they may be to you for a memorial before your God; I am the LORD your God.

11 ¶And it came to pass on the twentieth day of the second month, in the second year, the cloud was taken up from over the tabernacle of the testimony.

12 And the children of Israel took their journeys from the wilderness of Sinai; and the cloud rested in the wilderness of Paran.

13 And they took their journey for the first time according to the commandment of the LORD by the hand of Moses.

14 ¶In the first place went the standard of the camp of the children of Judah according to their armies; and over their host was Nahshon the son of Amminadab.

15 And over the host of the tribe of the children of Issachar was Nethanael the son of Zuar.

16 And over the host of the tribe of the children of Zebulun was Eliab the son of Helon.

17 And the tabernacle was taken down; and the sons of Gershon and the sons of Merari set forward, carrying the tabernacle.

18 ¶And then the standard of the camp of Reuben set forward according to their armies; and over their host was Elizur the son of Shedeur.

19 And over the host of the tribe of the children of Simeon was Shelmuiel the son of Zurishaddai.

20 And over the tribe of the children of Gad was Eliasaph the son of Reuel.

21 Then the Kohathites set forward, carrying the sanctuary; and they set up the tabernacle before the people came.

22 ¶And the standard of the camp of the children of Ephraim set forward according to their armies; and

over their host was Elishama the son of Ammihud.

23 And over the host of the tribe of the children of Manasseh was Gamaliel the son of Perzur.

24 And over the host of the tribe of the children of Benjamin was Abidan the son of Gideoni.

25 ¶And the standard of the children of Dan set forward, which was at the end of all the camps throughout their hosts; and over the host of the tribe of the children of Dan was Ahiezer the son of Ammishaddai.

26 And over the host of the tribe of the children of Asher was Pagiel the son of Ocran.

27 And over the host of the tribe of Naphtali was Ahida the son of Enan.

28 Thus was the order of the journeyings of the children of Israel according to their hosts.

29 ¶And Moses said to Hobab, the son of Reuel the Midianite, Moses' father-in-law, We are journeying to the place of which the LORD said, I will give it to you. Come with us, and we will do you good; for the LORD has spoken good concerning Israel.

30 But he said to him, I will not go; but I will depart to my own land, where I was born.

31 And Moses said to him, Do not leave us, for you know how we are to encamp in the wilderness, and you will serve as a guide for us.

32 And if you shall go with us, it shall be that whatever goodness the LORD shall do to us, the same will we do to you.

33 ¶And they departed from the mount of God three days' journey; and the ark of the covenant of the LORD went before them a day's journey to prepare a resting place for them.

34 And the cloud of the LORD was upon them by day, when they went out of the camp.

35 And it came to pass, when the ark set forward, Moses said, Arise, O LORD, and let them that hate thee be scattered; and let thy enemies flee before thee.

36 And when it rested, he said, Return, O LORD, to the many thousands of Israel.

CHAPTER 11

AND when the people complained, it displeased the LORD; and the LORD heard it, and his anger was kindled; and the fire of the LORD burned among them and consumed in the uttermost parts of the camp.

2 And the people cried to Moses; and Moses prayed to the LORD, and the fire was quenched.

3 And he called the name of that place Yakdana (a burning), because the fire of the LORD burned among them.

4 ¶And the mixed multitude that was among them had a strong craving; and they went about and caused the children of Israel to weep, saying, Who shall give us meat to eat?

5 We remember the fish that we used to eat in Egypt freely, the cucumbers, the melons, the leeks, the onions, and the garlic;

6 But now our soul is dried up; there is nothing at all, besides this manna, before our eyes.

7 And the manna was like coriander seed, and its color as the color of beryllium.

8 And the people went about and gathered it and ground it in a mill or beat it in a mortar and baked it in pans and made cakes of it; and the taste of it was as the taste of bread kneaded with oil.

9 And when the dew came down upon the camp in the night, the manna fell upon it.

10 ¶Then Moses heard the people weeping throughout their families, every man in the door of his tent; and the anger of the LORD was kindled greatly; Moses also was displeased.

11 And Moses said to the LORD, My LORD, why hast thou caused displeasure to thy servant? And why have I not found favor in thy sight, that thou layest the burden of all this people upon me?

12 Have I conceived all this people? Or have I begotten them, that thou

shouldest say to me, Carry them in your bosom, as a nursing father carries the suckling child, to the land which thou swearest to their fathers?

13 Where can I find meat to give to all this people? For they weep protesting to me, saying, Give us meat, that we may eat.

14 I am not able to bear all this people alone, because the burden is too heavy for me.

15 And if thou deal thus with me, kill me right away, if I have found favor in thy sight; and let me not see my wretchedness.

16 ¶And the LORD said to Moses, Gather to me seventy men of the elders of Israel, whom you know to be chiefs of the people and its scribes; and bring them to the tabernacle of the congregation, that they may be ready there with you.

17 And I will come down and talk with you there; and I will take some of the spirit which is upon you, and will put it upon them; and they shall bear the burden of the people with you, that you may not bear it yourself alone.

18 And Moses said to the people, Sanctify yourselves for tomorrow and you shall eat meat: for you have wept before the LORD, saying, Who shall give us meat to eat? For it was well with us in Egypt; therefore the LORD will give you meat, and you shall eat.

19 You shall not eat one day, nor two days, nor five days, neither ten days, nor twenty days;

20 But you shall eat it for a whole month, till it comes out of your nostrils and it become loathsome to you, because you have despised the LORD who is among you and have wept before him, saying, Why did we come forth out of Egypt?

21 Then Moses said before the LORD, The people, among whom I am, are six hundred thousand footmen, and thou hast said, I will give them meat, that they may eat a whole month.

22 Shall the flocks and the herds be slaughtered for them, to suffice them? Or shall all the fish of the sea be caught for them, to suffice them?

23 And the LORD said to Moses, The LORD's hand is full; now you shall see whether my word shall come true to you or not.

24 ¶And Moses went out and told the people the words of the LORD, and gathered the seventy men of the elders of the people, and made them stand round about the tabernacle.

25 And the LORD came down in a cloud and spoke to him, and took of the spirit that was upon him and gave it to the seventy elders; and it came to pass that, when the spirit rested upon them, they prophesied, and then they ceased to complain.

26 But there remained two men in the camp, the name of the one was Eldad, and the name of the other Medad; and the spirit rested upon them; and they were among those who were registered, but they went not out to the tabernacle; and they prophesied in the camp.

27 And there ran a young man, and told Moses, and said, Eldad and Medad are prophesying in the camp.

28 And Joshua the son of Nun, who had ministered to Moses from his youth, answered and said, My lord Moses, forbid them.

29 But Moses said to him, Are you jealous for my sake? Would God that all the LORD's people were prophets, and that the LORD would put his spirit upon them!

30 Then Moses came into the camp, he and the elders of Israel.

31 ¶And there went forth a wind from before the LORD, and brought quails from the sea, and let them fall by the camp, about a day's journey on this side and about a day's journey on the other side, round about the camp, and about two cubits high upon the face of the earth.

32 And the people rose all that day and all that night and all the next day, and they gathered the quails; he that gathered least gathered ten homers; and they spread them out in the sun for themselves round about the camp.

33 And while the meat was yet between their teeth, before it was chewed, the wrath of the LORD was kindled against the people, and the

LORD smote the people with a very great plague.

34 And he called the name of that place Kabrey di Rigta (the graves of craving); because it was there that they buried the people who craved meat.

35 And the people journeyed from Kabrey di Rigta to Hazeroth, and abode at Hazeroth.

CHAPTER 12

AND Miriam and Aaron spoke against Moses because of the Ethiopian woman whom he had married; for he had married an Ethiopian woman.

2 And they said, Has the LORD indeed spoken only by Moses? Has he not spoken by us also? And the LORD heard it.

3 (Now the man Moses was very meek, above all the men that were upon the face of the earth.)

4 And the LORD spoke suddenly to Moses and to Aaron and to Miriam, Come out, you three, to the tabernacle of the congregation. And the three of them came out.

5 And the LORD came down in a pillar of cloud and stood in the door of the tabernacle and called Aaron and Miriam; and they both came forth.

6 And the LORD said to them, Hear now my words: If you are prophets, I the LORD will reveal myself to you in a vision and will speak to you in a dream.

7 Not so with my servant Moses, who is faithful in all my house.

8 With him I will speak mouth to mouth, in a vision, and not in similes; and the glory of the LORD has he seen: why then were you not afraid to speak against my servant Moses?

9 And the anger of the LORD was kindled against them; and he departed.

10 And the cloud departed from off the tabernacle; and, behold, Miriam became leprous, white as snow; and when Aaron turn d toward Miriam, behold, she was leprous;

11 Then Aaron said to Moses, Oh,

my lord, I beseech you, do not lay the sin upon us, wherein we have done foolishly and wherein we have sinned.

12 Let her not be as one dead, of whom the flesh is half consumed when he comes out of his mother's womb.

13 And Moses cried to the LORD, saying, Heal her now, O God, I beseech thee.

14 ¶And the LORD said to Moses, If her father had but spit in her face, should she not be ashamed seven days? Let her be shut out from the camp seven days, and after that let her come in again.

15 And Miriam was shut out from the camp seven days; and the people did not journey till Miriam came in again.

16 And after that the people journeyed from Hazeroth, and encamped in the wilderness of Paran.

CHAPTER 13

THE LORD spoke to Moses, saying, 2 Send men that they may spy out the land of Canaan, which I give to the children of Israel; of every tribe of their fathers shall you send a man, every one a chief among them.

3 And Moses sent them from the wilderness of Paran by the commandment of the LORD; all of those men were chieftains of the children of Israel.

4 And these were their names: from the tribe of Reuben, Shammua the son of Zaccur.

5 From the tribe of Simeon, Shaphat the son of Hadi.

6 From the tribe of Judah, Caleb the son of Jophaniah.

7 From the tribe of Issachar, Negail the son of Joseph.

8 From the tribe of Ephraim, Hosea the son of Nun.

9 From the tribe of Benjamin, Palti the son of Daphu.

10 From the tribe of Zebulun, Gaddi the son of Sori.

11 From the tribe of Joseph, namely, of the tribe of Manasseh, Gaddi the son of Susi.

12 From the tribe of Dan, Gamaliel the son of Gamli.

13 From the tribe of Asher, Sethur the son of Michael.

14 From the tribe of Naphtali, Nahbi the son of Vophsi.

15 From the tribe of Gad, Geuel the son of Machir.

16 These are the names of the men whom Moses sent to spy out the land. And Moses called Hosea, the son of Nun, Joshua.

17 ¶And Moses sent them to spy out the land of Canaan, and said to them, Go up this way into the south,[1] and go up on the mountain

18 And see what the land is, and the people who dwell in it, whether they are strong or weak, few or many;

19 And what the land is, in which they dwell, whether it is fertile, or poor, or whether it has trees in it or not.

20 Be of good courage, and bring some of the fruit of the land. Now the time was the season of the first ripe grapes.

21 ¶So they went up and spied out the land from the wilderness of Zin to Rehob, which is at the entrance of Hamath.

22 And they went up into the south, and came as far as Hebron, where Ahiman, Sheshai, and Tolmai, the sons of giants were. (Now Hebron was built seven years before Zoan in Egypt.)

23 And they came as far as the valley of Segola,[2] and cut down from there a branch with one bunch of grapes, and they carried it between two of them on a pole; and they brought some pomegranates and some figs.

24 That place was called the valley of Segola, because of the bunch of grapes which the children of Israel cut down from there.

25 And they returned from spying out the land after forty days.

26 ¶And they came to Moses and Aaron and to all the congregation of the children of Israel, to the wilderness of Paran, to Rakim; and they brought back word to them and to all the congregation, and showed them the fruit of the land.

27 And they related to Moses, and said, We went to the land to which you sent us, and surely it flows with milk and honey; and this is the fruit of it.

28 Nevertheless the people who dwell in the land are strong, and the cities are fortified and very great: and moreover we saw the sons of giants there.

29 The Amalekites dwell in the land of the south; and the Hittites and the Jebusites and the Amorites dwell in the mountains; and the Canaanites dwell by the sea and by the banks of Jordan.

30 Then Caleb stilled the people before Moses and said, Let us go up at once, and possess it; for we are well able to overcome it.

31 But the men who went up with him said, We are not able to go up against the people; for they are stronger than we.

32 And they brought up to the children of Israel an evil report of the land which they had spied out, saying, The land through which we have gone to spy out is a land that devours its inhabitants; and all the people that we saw in it are men of a great stature.

33 There we saw giants, the sons of giants, the descendants of giants; and we were in their sight like grasshoppers, and so we were in their eyes.

CHAPTER 14

THEN all the congregation was in commotion, and lifted up their voices and cried; and the people wept that night.

2 And all the children of Israel murmured against Moses and against Aaron; and the whole congregation said to them, Would God we had died in the land of Egypt! Or would God that we had died in this wilderness!

3 Why has the LORD brought us into this land, to fall by the sword, that our wives and children should

---

1 Negeb.　　　2 A bunch of grapes.

be a prey? We were better off when we dwelt in Egypt.

4 And they said one to another, Let us appoint a leader, and let us return to Egypt.

5 Then Moses and Aaron fell on their faces before all the assembly of the congregation of the children of Israel.

6 ¶And Joshua the son of Nun, and Caleb the son of Jophaniah, who were of those who had spied out the land, rent their clothes;

7 And they said to all the congregation of the children of Israel, The land through which we passed to spy it out is an exceedingly good land.

8 If the LORD delights in us, he will bring us into this land and give it to us, a land which flows indeed with milk and honey.

9 Only do not rebel against the LORD, neither be afraid of the people of the land; for their conquest will be as easy as eating bread;[1] their strength has left them, and the LORD is with us; fear them not.

10 But the whole congregation said to stone them with stones. And the glory of the LORD appeared in the cloud in the tabernacle of the congregation before all the children of Israel.

11 ¶And the LORD said to Moses, How long will this people provoke me? And how long will they not believe me, for all the signs which I have done among them?

12 I will smite them with pestilence, and destroy them, and I will make of you a nation which is greater and mightier than they.

13 ¶And Moses said to the LORD, Then the Egyptians shall hear it (for thou didst bring up this people in thy might from among them),

14 And they will tell it to the inhabitants of this land; for they have heard that thou LORD art in the midst of this people, that thou LORD art seen face to face, and that thy cloud stands over them, and that thou goest before them in a pillar of cloud by day and in a pillar of fire by night.

15 ¶And if thou shalt kill all this people as one man, then the nations who have heard the fame of thee will say,

16 Because the LORD was not able to bring this people into the land which he swore to them, therefore he has slain them in the wilderness.

17 And now, let thy power, O LORD, be great according as thou hast spoken, saying,

18 The LORD is longsuffering and of great mercy, and thou forgivest iniquity and transgression, by no means clearing the guilty, but visiting the iniquity of the fathers upon the children and upon their children's children to the third and fourth generation.

19 Pardon the iniquity of this people according to the greatness of thy mercy, and as thou hast forgiven them from Egypt even until now.

20 And the LORD said to Moses, I have forgiven them according to your word;

21 But as truly as I live, the whole earth shall be filled with the glory of the LORD.

22 And yet all the men who have seen my glory and the signs which I did in Egypt and in the wilderness have tempted me, behold now, these ten times, and have not hearkened to my voice;

23 Surely they shall not see the land which I swore to their fathers, neither shall any one of those who provoked me see it;

24 But my servant Caleb, because he has my spirit with him and has followed me fully, I will bring into the land into which he went; and his descendants shall possess it.

25 (Now the Amalekites and the Canaanites dwelt in the mountains.) Tomorrow turn and set out for the wilderness by the way of the Red Sea.

26 ¶And the LORD spoke to Moses and to Aaron, saying,

27 How long shall this wicked congregation murmur in my presence? I have heard the complaints of the children of Israel which they murmur in my presence.

[1] In Aramaic when a task is simple or easy, it is said, *It is like eating bread.*

28 Say to them, As I live, says the LORD, as you have spoken in my presence, so will I do to you;

29 Your corpses shall fall in this wilderness; and all that were numbered of you, according to your whole number, from twenty years old and upward, because you have murmured against me.

30 You shall not come into the land concerning which I swore to make you dwell therein, except Caleb the son of Jophaniah, and Joshua the son of Nun.

31 But your little ones, who you said would become the prey, and your sons who today do not know good and evil, they shall enter into the land, and I will bring them there, and they shall know the land which you have despised.

32 But as for you, your corpses shall fall in this wilderness.

33 And your sons shall be shepherds forty years in this wilderness, and shall suffer for your whoredom until your corpses are consumed in this wilderness.

34 According to the number of the days in which you spied out the land, even forty days, a year for each day, shall you suffer for your iniquities, forty years; then you shall know that it is because you have murmured before me.

35 I the LORD have said, I will surely do it to all this evil congregation that are gathered together before me; in this wilderness they shall be consumed, and there they shall die.

36 And the men whom Moses sent to spy out the land, who returned and made all the congregation murmur against him by publishing an evil report concerning the land,

37 These men who published an evil report of the land died by a sudden plague before the LORD.

38 But Joshua the son of Nun, and Caleb the son of Jophaniah, who were of the men who went to spy out the land, still lived.

39 And Moses told these sayings to all the children of Israel; and the people mourned greatly.

40 ¶And they rose up early in the morning and went up to the top of the mountain, saying, Behold, we will go up to the place which the LORD has promised us; for we have sinned.

41 And Moses said to them, Why now do you transgress the commandment of the LORD? Therefore you shall not succeed.

42 Do not go up, for the LORD is not with you; lest you be defeated before your enemies.

43 For the Canaanites and the Amalekites are there before you, and you shall fall by the sword; because you are turned away from following the LORD, therefore the LORD will not be with you.

44 Yet they started to go up to the top of the mountain; but neither the ark of the covenant of the LORD nor Moses departed out of the camp.

45 Then the Amalekites and the Canaanites who dwelt in that mountain came down and smote them and pursued them as far as Hirmah.

CHAPTER 15

A ND the LORD spoke to Moses, saying,

2 Speak to the children of Israel and say to them, When you come into the land of your habitation, which I give to you for an inheritance,

3 You shall offer an offering to the LORD, a burnt offering or a sacrifice in performing a vow, or in a freewill offering, or in your solemn feasts, to make a sweet savour to the LORD, of the herd, or of the flock;

4 Then shall he who offers his offering to the LORD bring a meal offering of a tenth part of an ephah of fine flour mixed with a fourth part of a hin of oil.

5 And a fourth part of a hin of wine for a drink offering shall you offer with the burnt offering or sacrifice, for one lamb.

6 Or for a ram, you shall prepare for a meal offering two tenths of an ephah of fine flour mixed with a third part of a hin of oil.

7 And for a drink offering you shall offer a third part of a hin of wine, for a sweet savour to the LORD.

8 And when you offer a bullock for

a burnt offering, or for a sacrifice in performing a vow, or as a peace offering to the LORD;

9 Then you shall offer with the bullock a meal offering of three tenths of an ephah of fine flour mixed with half a hin of oil.

10 And you shall bring for a drink offering half a hin of wine, for an offering made by fire, of a sweet savour to the LORD.

11 Thus shall you do for one bullock, or for one ram, or for a lamb, or a kid of the goats.

12 According to the number that you shall prepare, so shall you do to every one according to their number.

13 All the house of Israel shall do these things after this manner, and shall offer an offering made by fire, of a sweet savour to the LORD.

14 And if a proselyte sojourn with you, or whoever is among you throughout your generations, and will offer an offering made by fire, of a sweet savour to the LORD; as you do, so shall he do.

15 One ordinance shall be both for you and for the proselyte who sojourns with you, an ordinance for ever throughout your generations; the proselyte shall be like you before the LORD.

16 One law and one ordinance shall be for you and for the proselyte who sojourns with you.

17 ¶The LORD spoke to Moses, saying,

18 Speak to the children of Israel and say to them, When you come into the land whither I will bring you,

19 Then it shall be that when you eat of the bread of the land, you shall offer up a heave offering to the LORD.

20 You shall offer up a cake of the first of your dough as an offering to the LORD; as you make the offering of the threshing floor, so shall you offer it.

21 Of the first of your dough you shall give to the LORD a heave offering throughout your generations.

22 ¶And if you err, and do not observe all these commandments which the LORD has spoken to Moses,

23 Even all that the LORD has commanded you by the hand of Moses from the day that the LORD commanded Moses and henceforward throughout your generations;

24 Then it shall be, if the error was committed in the presence of the congregation, all the congregation shall offer one young bullock for a burnt offering, for a sweet savour to the LORD, with its meal offering and its drink offering, according to the ordinance thereof, and one kid of the goats for a sin offering.

25 And the priest shall make atonement for the whole congregation of the children of Israel, and it shall be forgiven them; for it was an error; and they shall bring their offering, a sacrifice made by fire to the LORD, and their sin offering to the LORD for their folly;

26 And it shall be forgiven all the congregation of the children of Israel and the proselyte who sojourns among them, because all the people had erred.

27 ¶And if any person sins through an error, then he shall offer a she-goat of the first year for a sin offering.

28 And the priest shall make atonement for the person who sins, when he sins by an error before the LORD, to make an atonement for him; and it shall be forgiven him.

29 You shall have one law for him who does anything through ignorance, both for the children of Israel and for the proselytes who sojourn among you.

30 ¶But the person who commits sin wittingly, whether he be of you or of the proselytes, the same blasphemes before the LORD; and that person shall be cut off from among his people.

31 Because he has despised the word of the LORD and has broken his commandments, that person shall utterly be cut off; his iniquity shall be upon him.

32 ¶And while the children of Israel were in the wilderness, they found a man gathering sticks on the sabbath day.

33 And those who found him gathering sticks brought him to Moses

and Aaron, and to all the congregation.

34 And they put him in prison, because it had not been declared what should be done to him.

35 And the LORD said to Moses, The man shall be surely put to death; all the congregation shall stone him with stones outside the camp.

36 And all the congregation brought him outside the camp, and stoned him with stones, and he died; as the LORD commanded Moses.

37 ¶And the LORD spoke to Moses, saying,

38 Speak to the children of Israel and bid them that they make fringes on the borders of their mantles throughout their generations, and that they put upon the fringes of the borders a ribbon of blue;

39 And it shall be to you for a fringe, that you may look upon it and remember all the commandments of the LORD your God and do them; and that you may not go astray, seeking after your own hearts and your own mind, after which you used to go astray;

40 That you may remember, and do all my commandments, and be holy to your God.

41 I am the LORD your God, who brought you out of the land of Egypt, to be your God; I am the LORD your God.

CHAPTER 16

NOW Korah, the son of Izhar, the son of Kohath, the son of Levi, and Dathan and Abiram, the sons of Eliab, and On, the son of Peleth, sons of Reuben, started a faction;

2 And they rose up before Moses with certain of the children of Israel, two hundred and fifty chiefs of the assembly, who at that time were men of renown;

3 And they gathered themselves together against Moses and against Aaron and said to them, Is it not enough for you, seeing all the congregation are holy, every one of them, and the LORD is among them; wherefore then do you lift up yourselves above the whole congregation of the LORD?

4 And when Moses heard it, he fell upon his face;

5 And he spoke to Korah and to all his company and said to them, In the morning the LORD will show who are his, and who are holy; and he will cause them to come near to him; and those whom he has chosen will he cause to come near to him.

6 This do: Take for yourselves censers, you Korah, and all your company;

7 And put fire into them, and put incense into them before the LORD tomorrow; and it shall be that the man whom the LORD chooses, he shall be holy; this is enough for you, O you sons of Levi.

8 And Moses said to Korah, Hear again, O you sons of Levi;

9 Is it not enough for you that the God of Israel has separated you from the whole congregation of Israel and brought you near to himself to do the service of the tabernacle of the LORD and to stand before the congregation to minister to them?

10 And he has brought you near to him, and all your brethren the sons of Levi with you; and do you seek the priesthood also?

11 Therefore both you and all your company gather yourselves together before the LORD tomorrow; and what is Aaron, that you should murmur against him?

12 ¶And Moses sent to call Dathan and Abiram, the sons of Eliab; but they said, We will not come up;

13 Is it not enough for you that you have brought us out of a land that flows with milk and honey, to kill us in the wilderness, but that you should also make yourselves princes over us?

14 Moreover you have not brought us into a land that flows with milk and honey, nor given us inheritance of fields and vineyards; even if you should put out our eyes, we will not come up.

15 And Moses was greatly displeased, and said to the LORD, Respect not thou their offerings, because I have not taken an ass from one of

them, neither have I hurt one of them.

16 And Moses said to Korah, Present yourselves, you and all your company before the LORD, you and they and Aaron, tomorrow;

17 And take every man his censer, and put fire into it, and put incense into it, and bring before the LORD every man his censer, two hundred and fifty censers; you also and Aaron, each of you his censer.

18 So they took every man his censer, and put fire into it, and laid incense upon it, and stood in the door of the tabernacle of the congregation with Moses and Aaron.

19 And Korah gathered all the congregation against them at the door of the tabernacle of the congregation; and the glory of the LORD appeared to all the congregation.

20 And the LORD spoke to Moses and to Aaron, saying,

21 Separate yourselves from the midst of this congregation, that I may destroy them in a moment.

22 And they fell upon their faces and said, O God, the God of the spirits of all flesh, shall one man sin, and shall the wrath come upon all the congregation?

23 ¶And the LORD spoke to Moses, saying,

24 Speak to all the congregation, saying, Keep away from about the tents of Korah, Dathan, and Abiram.

25 And Moses rose up and went to Dathan and Abiram; and the elders of Israel followed him.

26 And he spoke to all the congregation and said to them, Depart from the tents of these sinful men and touch nothing of theirs, lest you be consumed in their sins.

27 So they withdrew from the tents of Korah, Dathan, and Abiram; and Dathan and Abiram came out, and stood in the door of their tents with their wives and their sons and their little ones.

28 And Moses said, Hereby you shall know that the LORD has sent me to do all these works; for I have not done them of my own mind.

29 If these men die the common death of all men or if they be visited after the visitation of all men, then the LORD has not sent me.

30 But if the LORD make a new thing, and the earth opens its mouth and swallows them up with all things that belong to them, and they go down alive with all that belongs to them into Sheol, then you shall know that these men have provoked the LORD.

31 ¶And when Moses had finished speaking these words, the ground split asunder under them;

32 And the earth opened its mouth and swallowed them up with their households and all the men who were with Korah and all their goods.

33 They, and all that belonged to them went down alive into Sheol, and the earth closed upon them, and they perished from among the congregation.

34 And all Israel that were round about them fled at the cry of them, saying, Lest the earth swallow us up also.

35 And there came out a fire from before the LORD and consumed the two hundred and fifty men that offered incense.

36 ¶And the LORD spoke to Moses, saying,

37 Speak to Eleazar the son of Aaron the priest, to take up the censers from among the burned men and scatter the fire yonder; for they are sanctified.

38 The censers of these who sinned against their own souls, make them thin plates for a covering of the altar; for they offered them before the LORD, therefore they are holy; and they shall be a sign to the children of Israel.

39 So Eleazar the priest took the bronze censers, with which they who were burned had offered incense, and they were made thin plates for a covering of the altar,

40 To be a memorial to the children of Israel, so that no stranger, who is not of the descendants of Aaron, come near to offer incense before the LORD; that he be not as Korah and all his company, whom the earth opened its mouth and swallowed, just as the LORD had spoken by the hand of Moses.

41 ¶But on the morrow all the con-

gregation of the children of Israel murmured against Moses and Aaron, saying, You have killed the people of the LORD.

42 And when all the congregation was gathered against Moses and against Aaron, they turned toward the tabernacle of the congregation; and, behold, the cloud covered it, and the glory of the LORD appeared.

43 And Moses and Aaron came before the tabernacle of the congregation.

44 ¶And the LORD spoke to Moses and to Aaron, saying,

45 Get you away from the midst of this congregation, that I may destroy them in a moment. And they fell upon their faces.

46 ¶And Moses said to Aaron, Take a censer, and put fire therein from off the altar, and put on incense, and carry it quickly to the congregation, and make an atonement for them; for wrath has gone out from before the LORD; the plague has already begun among the people.

47 And Aaron took it as Moses commanded, and ran into the midst of the congregation; and, behold, the plague had already begun among the people; and he put on incense, and made atonement for the people.

48 And he stood between the dead and the living; and the plague ceased.

49 Now those who died in the plague were fourteen thousand and seven hundred, besides those who died in the sedition of Korah.

50 And Aaron returned to Moses at the door of the tabernacle of the congregation; and the plague had ceased.

CHAPTER 17

AND the LORD spoke to Moses, saying,

2 Speak to the children of Israel, and take from every one of them a rod according to the house of their fathers, from all their princes according to the house of their fathers, twelve rods; write each man's name upon his rod.

3 And you shall write Aaron's name upon the rod of Levi; for one rod shall be for the head of the tribe of their fathers.

4 And you shall put them in the tabernacle of the congregation before the testimony, where I will meet with you.

5 And it shall come to pass, that the rod of the man with whom I am pleased shall bud; thus I will make to cease from me the murmurings of the children of Israel, whereby they murmur against you.

6 ¶And Moses spoke to the children of Israel, and every one of their princes gave him a rod apiece, for each prince one, according to their fathers' houses, twelve rods; and the rod of Aaron was in the midst of their rods.

7 And Moses placed the rods before the LORD in the tabernacle of the testimony.

8 And on the morrow Moses went into the tabernacle of the testimony; and, behold, the rod of Aaron for the house of Levi was budded, and blossomed, and yielded ripe almonds.

9 And Moses brought out all the rods from before the LORD to all the children of Israel; and they looked, and took every man his rod.

10 ¶And the LORD said to Moses, Bring Aaron's rod back before the testimony, to be kept as a token for the rebellious children; so that their murmurings may cease from me, that they die not.

11 And Moses did so; as the LORD commanded him, so did he.

12 And the children of Israel said to Moses, Behold, we perish and are lost, we all perish.

13 Whosoever comes near to the tabernacle of the LORD shall die; and, behold, we also are near to perish.

CHAPTER 18

AND the LORD said to Aaron, You and your sons and your father's house with you shall bear any guilt in connection with the sanctuary; and you and your sons with you shall bear any guilt in connection with your priesthood.

2 And your brethren also of the

tribe of Levi, the tribe of your father, you shall bring with you, that they may accompany you and minister to you; but you and your sons with you shall minister before the tabernacle of the testimony.

3 And they shall keep your charge and the charge of all the tabernacle; but they shall not come near the vessels of the sanctuary and the vessels of the altar, that neither they, nor you also, die.

4 And they shall accompany you, and keep the charge of the tabernacle of the congregation for all the service of the tabernacle; and a stranger shall not come near you.

5 And you shall have charge of the sanctuary, and charge of the altar, that there be no wrath any more upon the children of Israel.

6 And I, behold, I have taken your brethren the Levites from among the children of Israel; they are given as a gift for the LORD, to do the service of the tabernacle of the congregation.

7 Therefore you and your sons with you shall keep your priest's office for everything of the altar and within the veil; and you shall serve; I have given your priest's office as a gift; and the stranger who comes near shall be put to death.

8 ¶And the LORD said to Aaron, Behold, I also have given you the charge of my gift offerings and all the hallowed things of the children of Israel; I have given them to you by reason of the anointing, and to your sons by an ordinance for ever.

9 This shall be yours of the most holy things from offerings made by fire: every offering of theirs, every meal offering of theirs, and every sin offering of theirs, and all the offerings of theirs which they shall offer to me shall be most holy for you and for your sons.

10 In the most holy place shall you eat it; every male shall eat it; it shall be holy to you.

11 And this is the offering of your gifts, with all the wave offerings of the children of Israel; I have given them to you and to your sons and to your daughters with you, by a statute for ever; every one who is clean in your household shall eat of it.

12 All the best of the oil and all the best of the wheat and of the wine, the firstfruits of them that they shall give to the LORD, I have given them to you.

13 The first ripe fruits of all that is in their land which they shall bring to the LORD shall be yours; every one who is clean in your household shall eat of it.

14 Everything dedicated in Israel shall be yours.

15 Everything that opens the womb of all flesh which they offer to the LORD, whether it be of man or beasts, shall be yours; nevertheless the firstborn of man shall you surely redeem, and the firstling of unclean beasts shall you redeem.

16 And those that are to be redeemed from a month old and upward shall you redeem, for a price of money of fifty shekels, after the shekel of the sanctuary, which is twenty gerahs.

17 But the firstlings of the cattle or the firstlings of the sheep or the firstlings of the goats, you shall not redeem, because they are holy; you shall sprinkle their blood upon the altar and shall burn their fat for an offering made by fire, for a sweet savour to the LORD.

18 But their meat shall be yours, as the wave breast and as the right shoulder are yours.

19 All the gift offerings of the holy things which the children of Israel offer to the LORD have I given to you and to your sons and your daughters with you, by a statute for ever; it is a covenant of salt [1] for ever before the LORD to you and to your descendants with you.

20 ¶And the LORD said to Aaron, You shall have no inheritance in their land, neither shall you have any portion among them; but your portion and your inheritance among the chil-

[1] Salt is considered sacred, and is a token of loyalty and true friendship. When people make covenants they break bread and eat salt together.

dren of Israel shall be the gift offerings and the holy things of the LORD.

21 And, behold, I have given to the children of Levi all the tithes of the children of Israel for an inheritance, for their service which they serve, even the service of the tabernacle of the congregation.

22 Neither shall the children of Israel henceforth come near the tabernacle of the congregation, lest they bear sin and die.

23 But the Levites shall do the service of the tabernacle of the congregation, and they shall bear their iniquity; it shall be a statute for ever throughout their generations, that among the children of Israel they have no inheritance.

24 For the tithes of the children of Israel which they offer to the LORD I have given to the Levites for an inheritance; therefore I have said to them, Among the children of Israel they shall have no inheritance.

25 ¶The LORD spoke to Moses, saying,

26 Speak to the Levites and say to them, When you take from the children of Israel the tithes which I have given you from them for your inheritance, then you shall offer some of them as a gift offering to the LORD, a tenth part of the tithe.

27 And this your gift offering shall be reckoned to you, as though it were the grain from the threshing floor, and as the gift offering of the wine press.

28 Thus you also shall offer a gift offering to the LORD of all your tithes which you receive from the children of Israel; and you shall give from it the LORD's gift offering to Aaron the priest and to his sons.

29 Out of all your gifts you shall offer every gift offering to the LORD, of all the best of them and the hallowed of them.

30 Therefore you shall say to them, When you have set apart the best thereof from it, then it shall be counted to the Levites as the produce of the threshing floor, and as the produce of the wine press.

31 And you shall eat it in any place, you and your households; for it is your wages for your service in the tabernacle of the congregation.

32 And you shall bear no sin by reason of it, when you have offered the best of it; neither shall you pollute the holy things of the children of Israel, lest you die.

CHAPTER 19

AND the LORD spoke to Moses and to Aaron, saying,

2 This is the ordinance of the law which the LORD has commanded, saying, Speak to the children of Israel, that they bring you a red heifer, perfect, in which there is no blemish, and upon which never came yoke;

3 And you shall give her to Eleazar the priest, that he may bring her forth outside the camp, and one shall slaughter her in his sight;

4 And Eleazar the priest shall take some of her blood with his finger, and sprinkle of her blood towards the front of the tabernacle of the congregation seven times;

5 And one shall burn the heifer in his sight; her skin and her blood and her flesh, with her dung, shall he burn;

6 And the priest shall take cedar wood and hyssop and scarlet material, and cast them into the midst of the burning of the heifer.

7 Then the priest shall wash his clothes, and he shall bathe his body in water, and afterward he shall come into the camp; and the priest shall be unclean until the evening.

8 And he who burns the heifer shall wash his clothes and bathe his body in water; and he shall be unclean until the evening.

9 And a man who is clean shall gather up the ashes of the heifer and lay them outside the camp in a clean place, and it shall be kept for all the congregation of the children of Israel for the water of sprinkling, because it is a purification for sin.

10 And he who gathers the ashes of the heifer shall wash his clothes and be unclean until the evening; and it shall be to the children of Israel

and to the proselytes who sojourn among them for a statute for ever.

11 ¶He who touches the dead body of any man shall be unclean seven days.

12 He shall purify himself by sprinkling with the water on the third day, and on the seventh day he shall be clean; but if he does not purify himself by sprinkling on the third day, then on the seventh day he shall not be clean.

13 Whosoever touches the body of any man who is dead, and does not purify himself by sprinkling, defiles the tabernacle of the LORD; and that person shall be cut off from Israel, because the water of purification was not sprinkled upon him, he shall be unclean; his uncleanness is yet with him.

14 This is the law when a man dies in a tent: all who come into the tent and every one who is in the tent shall be unclean for seven days.

15 And every open vessel which is not covered is unclean.

16 And whosoever in the open field touches one who is slain with a sword, or a dead body or a bone of a man or a grave shall be unclean seven days.

17 And for an unclean person they shall take some of the ashes of the burnt sin offering and shall pour running water into it in a vessel;

18 And a clean person shall take hyssop and dip it in the water and sprinkle it upon the tent and upon all the vessels and upon the persons who were there and upon him who touched a bone or a slain person or one dead or a grave;

19 And the clean person shall sprinkle upon the unclean on the third day and on the seventh day; and on the seventh day he shall wash his clothes and bathe himself in water, and shall be clean in the evening.

20 But the man who shall be unclean and shall not purify himself, that soul shall be cut off from among the congregation, because he has defiled the sanctuary of the LORD; the water of sprinkling has not been sprinkled upon him; he is unclean.

21 And it shall be a perpetual statute to you that he who sprinkles the water of purification shall wash his clothes; and he who touches the water of sprinkling shall be unclean until evening.

22 And whatever the unclean person touches shall be unclean; and the person who touches it shall be unclean until evening.

CHAPTER 20

THEN came the children of Israel, the whole congregation, into the wilderness of Zin in the first month; and the people abode in Rakim; and Miriam died there, and was buried there.

2 And there was no water for the people to drink; and they gathered themselves together against Moses and against Aaron.

3 And the people quarreled with Moses and with Aaron, saying, Would God that we had died with the death with which our brethren died before the LORD!

4 Why have you brought the congregation of the LORD into this wilderness, that we and our cattle should die here?

5 And why have you made us to come up out of Egypt, and have brought us to this evil place? It is no place for grain, or for wine or figs or pomegranates; neither is there any water to drink.

6 Then Moses and Aaron went from the presence of the assembly to the door of the tabernacle of the congregation, and they fell upon their faces; and the glory of the LORD appeared to them.

7 ¶And the LORD spoke to Moses, saying,

8 Take the rod, and gather the assembly together, you and Aaron your brother, and speak over the rock before their eyes; and it shall give forth its water, and you shall bring forth to them water out of the rock, so that you shall give the congregation and their cattle drink.

9 And Moses took the rod from be-

fore the Lord, as he commanded him.

10 And Moses and Aaron gathered the congregation together before the rock, and he said to them, Hear now, you rebels; out of this rock we will bring forth water for you.

11 And Moses lifted up his hand and struck the rock with his rod twice; and the water came out abundantly, and the people drank and all their cattle also.

12 ¶And the Lord said to Moses and Aaron, Because you did not believe in me, to sanctify me in the presence of the children of Israel, therefore you shall not bring this congregation into the land which I have given them.

13 These are the waters of Mesotha (contention); because the children of Israel strove before the Lord, and he was sanctified among them.

14 ¶And Moses sent messengers from Rakim to the king of Edom, saying, Thus says your brother Israel: You know all the trouble that has befallen us,

15 How our fathers went down into Egypt, and we have dwelt in Egypt a long time; and the Egyptians oppressed us and our fathers;

16 And when we prayed before the Lord, he heard our voice and sent an angel, and has brought us forth out of Egypt; and, behold, we are in Rakim, a town in the uttermost of your border;

17 Now let us pass through your land; we will not pass through the fields, nor through the vineyards, neither will we drink the water of the wells; but we will go by the king's highway, we will not turn to the right hand nor to the left until we have passed your borders.

18 But Edom said to him, You shall not pass through my border, lest I come out against you with the sword.

19 And the children of Israel said to him, We will go up by the highway; and if we and our cattle drink of your water, then we will pay for it; we will only pass through it on foot.

20 But Edom said, You shall not pass through. And Edom came out against them with a strong force, and with a strong hand.

21 Thus Edom refused to give Israel passage through his border; wherefore Israel turned away from him.

22 ¶And the children of Israel, the whole congregation, journeyed from Rakim, and came to mount Hor.

23 And the Lord said to Moses and Aaron at mount Hor by the border of the land of Edom,

24 Aaron shall be gathered to his people for he shall not enter into the land which I have given to the children of Israel, because you rebelled against my word at the water of Mesotha, and did not sanctify me at the water in their presence.

25 Take Aaron and Eleazar his son, and bring them up to mount Hor;

26 And strip Aaron of his garments, and put them upon Eleazar his son; and Aaron shall be gathered unto his people and shall die there.

27 And Moses did as the Lord commanded him; and they went up into mount Hor in the sight of all the congregation.

28 And Moses stripped Aaron of his garments, and put them upon Eleazar his son; and Aaron died there on mount Hor; and Moses and Eleazar came down from the mountain.

29 And when all the congregation saw that Aaron was dead, they mourned for Aaron thirty days, all the house of Israel.

CHAPTER 21

WHEN the Canaanite, the king of Gadar who dwelled in the south, heard that Israel came by the way of the spies, then he fought against Israel and took some of them prisoners.

2 And Israel vowed a vow to the Lord and said, If thou wilt surely deliver this people into our hands, then we will utterly destroy their cities.

3 And the Lord hearkened to the voice of Israel, and delivered up the Canaanites into their hands; and they utterly destroyed them and their cities;

and they called the name of that place Hirmah.

4 ¶And they journeyed from mount Hor by the way of the Red Sea, to go around the land of Edom; and the people were much distressed because of the way.

5 And the people murmured against God and against Moses, saying, Why have you brought us up out of Egypt to die in the wilderness? For neither is there bread, nor water; and our soul is wearied with this inferior bread (manna).

6 And the LORD sent fiery serpents against the people, and they bit the people, so that many people of Israel died.

7 ¶Therefore the people came to Moses and said to him, We have sinned, for we have murmured against the LORD and against you; pray before the LORD, that he take the serpents away from us. And Moses prayed for the people.

8 And the LORD said to Moses, Make a fiery serpent of brass, and set it upon a pole; and it shall come to pass that every one who is bitten by a serpent, when he looks upon it, shall live.

9 So Moses made a serpent of brass, and put it upon a pole, and it came to pass that if a serpent had bitten any man, when he beheld the serpent of brass, he lived.

10 ¶And the children of Israel journeyed, and encamped in Aboth.

11 And they journeyed from Aboth, and encamped at the Een di Ebraye (the spring of the Hebrews), in the wilderness which is before Moab, to the east toward the sunrise.

12 ¶From thence they journeyed, and encamped in the valley of Zared.

13 From thence they journeyed, and encamped on the other side of Arnon, which is in the wilderness that extends from the border of the Amorites; for Arnon is the border of Moab, between Moab and the Amorites.

14 Wherefore it is said in the book of the wars of the LORD, A flame of fire is in the whirlwind and in the river of Arnon,

15 And he made straight the slope of the valleys which extended to the site of Ad, which lies over the border of Moab.

16 And there is the Bera; that is, the well of which the LORD said to Moses, Gather the people together and I will give them water.

17 ¶Then Israel sang this song, Spring up, O well; sing ye to it:

18 The well which the princes dug, which the nobles of the people uncovered and searched out with their staves. And from the wilderness they went to Mattanah;

19 And from Mattanah to Nahaliel; and from Nahaliel to Bamoth;

20 And from Bamoth in the valley, which is in the country of Moab, to the top of the hill which looks toward Ashimon (the desert).

21 ¶And Israel sent messengers to Sihon, king of the Amorites, saying,

22 Let us pass through your land; we will not turn aside into the fields or into the vineyards; we will not drink water from the wells; but we will go along by the king's highway until we have passed through your borders.

23 And Sihon would not let Israel pass through his borders; but Sihon gathered all his army together, and went out against Israel into the wilderness; and he came to Jahaz and fought against Israel.

24 And Israel smote him with the edge of the sword, and possessed his land from Arnon to Jabbok, and as far as the border of the children of Ammon; for the border of the children of Ammon was fortified.

25 And Israel took all those cities; and Israel settled in all the cities of the Amorites, in Heshbon and in all the villages thereof.

26 For Heshbon was the capital city of Sihon the king of the Amorites, who had fought against the former king of Moab and taken all his land out of his hand as far as Arnon.

27 Wherefore they say in the proverbs, Come into Heshbon, let the city of Sihon be built and prepared;

28 For a fire has gone out of Heshbon, a flame from the city of Sihon. It has consumed Ad of Moab, and

the worshippers of the high places of Arnon.

29 Woe to you, O Arnon! Woe to you, O Moab! You are destroyed, O people of Chemosh; he has given his sons hostages, and his daughters into captivity to Sihon king of the Amorites.

30 The fields of Heshbon have perished as far as Ribon, and have been laid waste as far as Lanhakh, which is in the wilderness.

31 ¶Thus Israel dwelt in the land of the Amorites.

32 And Moses sent to spy out Jaazer, and they captured its villages, and destroyed the Amorites that were there.

33 ¶And they turned and went up to the land of Mathnin; and Og the king of Mathnin went out against them, he and all his people, to the battle at Ardai.

34 And the LORD said to Moses, Fear him not; for I will deliver him into your hands, and all his people and his country; and you shall do to him as you did to Sihon king of the Amorites, who dwelt in Heshbon.

35 So they smote him and his sons and all his people until there was not a survivor left to him; and they possessed his land.

CHAPTER 22

AND the children of Israel journeyed, and encamped in the plains of Moab on this side of Jordan by Jericho.

2 ¶And Balak the son of Zippor saw all that Israel had done to the Amorites.

3 And the Moabites were in great fear of the people because they were many; and Moab was distressed at the presence of the children of Israel.

4 And Moab said to the elders of Midian, Now this multitude is licking up all that are around about us, as the ox licks up the grass of the field. And Balak the son of Zippor was king of the Moabites at that time.

5 So he sent messengers to Balaam the son of Beor, an interpreter of dreams, who dwelt by the river of the land of the children of Ammon, to call him, saying, Behold, there is a people come out from Egypt; they cover the face of the land, and they are settled over against me.

6 Come now therefore and curse this people for me, for they are too mighty for me; perhaps I shall be able to defeat some of them and destroy them out of the land; for I know that he whom you bless is blessed and he whom you curse is cursed.

7 And the elders of Moab and the elders of Midian departed with gifts for divination in their hands; and they came to Balaam and told him the words of Balak.

8 And he said to them, Lodge here this night and I will give you an answer as the LORD shall speak to me; and the princes of Moab stayed with Balaam.

9 And God came to Balaam and said to him, Who are these men that are with you?

10 And Balaam said to God, Balak the son of Zippor, king of Moab, has sent to me, saying,

11 Behold, there is a people come out of Egypt who cover the face of the earth; come now, and curse them for me; perhaps I shall be able to fight against them and destroy them.

12 And God said to Balaam, You shall not go with them; and you shall not curse the people; for they are blessed.

13 And Balaam rose up in the morning and said to the princes of Balak, Go to your land; for the LORD refuses to permit me to go with you.

14 So the princes of Moab rose up and went to Balak, and said to him, Balaam refused to come with us.

15 ¶And again Balak sent messengers who were greater and more honorable than they.

16 And they came to Balaam and said to him, Thus says Balak the son of Zippor, Let nothing hinder you from coming to me;

17 For I will surely honor you exceedingly, and I will do for you whatever you say to me; come therefore, curse this people for me.

18 And Balaam answered and said

to the servants of Balak, If Balak would give me his house full of silver and gold, I could not transgress against the word of the LORD my God, neither concerning a small matter nor concerning a great matter.

19 Now, therefore, tarry you also here this night, that I may know what more the LORD will say to me.

20 And God came to Balaam at night and said to him, If these men have come to call you, rise up and go with them; but only the word which I shall say to you, that shall you do.

21 So Balaam rose up in the morning and saddled his ass and went with the princes of Balak.

22 ¶And God's anger was kindled against him because he went; and the angel of the LORD stood in the way for an adversary against him. Now as he was riding on his she-ass, and his two servants with him,

23 The she-ass saw the angel of the LORD standing in the way, and his sword drawn and held in his hand; and the she-ass turned aside out of the way and went into the field; and Balaam struck the she-ass to turn her into the way.

24 But the angel of the LORD stood in a path of the vineyard, a wall being on this side and a wall on that side.

25 And when the she-ass saw the angel of the LORD, she thrust herself against the wall and pressed Balaam's foot against the wall; and he struck her again.

26 And the angel of the LORD went further, and stood in a narrow place where there was no way to turn either to the right or to the left.

27 And when the she-ass saw the angel of the LORD, she lay down under Balaam; and Balaam's anger was kindled, and he struck the she-ass with a staff.

28 And the LORD opened the mouth of the she-ass and she said to Balaam, What have I done to you that you have struck me these three times?

29 And Balaam said to the she-ass, Because you have mocked me; I would there were a sword in my hands, for now would I kill you.

30 And the she-ass said to Balaam, Am I not your she-ass upon which you have ridden from your youth even to this day? Have I ever behaved in this manner toward you? And he said to her, No.

31 Then the LORD opened the eyes of Balaam and he saw the angel of the LORD standing in the way with his sword drawn and held in his hand; and he bowed down his head and worshipped on his face.

32 And the angel of the LORD said to him, Why have you struck your she-ass these three times? Behold, I went out to be an adversary against you, because you have directed your course contrary to me;

33 And the she-ass saw me and turned aside from me these three times; and if she had not turned aside from me, surely now I would have slain you, and saved her alive.

34 And Balaam said to the angel of the LORD, I have sinned; for I did not know that thou didst stand in the way against me; now therefore, if my mission is evil in thy eyes, I will turn back again.

35 And the angel of the LORD said to Balaam, Go with the men; but only the command that I shall speak to you, that shall you do. So Balaam went with the princes of Balak.

36 ¶And when Balak heard that Balaam was come, he went out to meet him in a town of Moab, which is in the border of Arnon at the uttermost end of the border.

37 And Balak said to Balaam, Did I not earnestly send messengers to you to call you? Why did you not come to me? Perhaps you were saying that I am not able to honor you?

38 And Balaam said to Balak, Lo, I have come to you; have I now any power at all to say anything? The word that God puts in my mouth, that shall I speak.

39 And Balaam went with Balak, and they came to Koriath-Hizroth.

40 And Balak slaughtered oxen and sheep, and sent to Balaam and to the princes who were with him.

41 And in the morning Balak took Balaam and brought him to a high place of Baal, and from there he saw

the uttermost part of the people of Israel.

CHAPTER 23

AND Balaam said to Balak, Build me here seven altars, and prepare me here seven oxen and seven rams.

2 And Balak did as Balaam had told him; and Balak and Balaam offered on every altar a bullock and a ram.

3 And Balaam said to Balak, Stand here by your burnt offerings, and I will go. Perhaps the LORD will come to meet me; and whatever he shows me I will tell you. So he went away quietly.

4 And God appeared to Balaam and said to him, You have prepared seven altars, and have offered upon every altar a bullock and a ram.

5 Then the LORD put a word in Balaam's mouth and said to him, Return to Balak, and thus you shall speak.

6 And he returned to him, and, lo, he stood by his burnt offerings, he and all the princes of Moab.

7 And he took up his parable and said, Balak the king of the Moabites has brought me from Aram,[1] from the mountains of the east, saying, Come, curse Jacob for me, and come, destroy Israel for me.

8 How can I curse whom God has not cursed? How can I destroy whom the LORD has not destroyed?

9 For from the top of the mountains I see him, and from the hills I behold him; lo, the people are dwelling alone and are not reckoned among the nations.

10 Who can count the multitude of the descendants of Jacob, and the number of the fourth part of Israel? Let me die the death of the righteous, and let my end be like theirs!

11 And Balak said to Balaam, What have you done to me? I called you to curse my enemies, and, behold, you have surely blessed them.

12 And Balaam answered and said, Behold, whatever the LORD puts in my mouth that thing will I speak.

13 And Balak said to him, Come with me to another place, from which you may see them; but you shall see the utmost part of them, and shall not see them all; and curse them for me from thence.

14 ¶And he brought him to the field of watchmen, to the top of the hill, and built seven altars, and offered a bullock and a ram on every altar.

15 And Balaam said to Balak, Stand here by your burnt offerings while I go yonder.

16 And the LORD appeared to Balaam and put a word in his mouth and said to him, Go again to Balak and say thus.

17 And when he came to him, he was standing by his burnt offerings, and the princes of Moab with him. And Balak said to him, What has the LORD spoken?

18 And he took up his parable and said, Rise up, Balak, and hear; and give ear to my testimony, O son of Zippor;

19 God is not a man that he should lie; neither the son of man that he should be given counsel; he speaks and he shall do it, and his word abides for ever.

20 Behold, I was brought here to bless; and I cannot reverse the blessing.

21 I do not behold iniquity in Jacob, neither have I seen malice in Israel; the LORD his God is with him, and the glory of his King is among them.

22 God brought them out of Egypt with his might and excellency.

23 For there is no augury in Jacob, neither is there any divination in Israel; according to this time it shall be said of Jacob and of Israel, What has God wrought!

24 Behold, the people shall rise up as a lion and march like a lion; he shall not lie down until he eats the prey and drinks the blood of the slain.

25 ¶Then Balak said to Balaam, Neither curse them at all, nor bless them at all.

26 But Balaam answered and said to Balak, Did I not tell you, All that

---

[1] Mesopotamia.

the LORD speaks to me, that very thing I must do?

27 ¶And Balak said to Balaam, Come, I will take you to another place; perhaps it will please God that you may curse them for me from there.

28 Then Balak took Balaam to the top of Peor, that looks toward Ashimon.

29 And Balaam said to Balak, Build me here seven altars and prepare me seven bullocks and seven rams.

30 And Balak did as Balaam had said, and offered a bullock and a ram on every altar.

CHAPTER 24

AND when Balaam saw that it pleased the LORD to bless Israel, he did not go, as at other times, to seek divination; but set his face toward the wilderness.

2 And Balaam lifted up his eyes, and he saw Israel encamping, tribe by tribe; and the spirit of God came upon him.

3 And he took up his parable, and said, Balaam the son of Beor has said, and the man whose eyes are open has said;

4 He has said, who heard the word of God, who saw the vision of God, falling into a trance but having his eyes open:

5 How beautiful are your tents, O Jacob, and your tabernacles, O Israel!

6 Like the valleys that flow, like gardens by the river's side, like the tabernacle which the LORD has pitched, and like cedar trees beside the waters.

7 A man shall rise up from among his sons, and his offspring shall dwell by many waters; he shall be greater than Agag, and his kingdom shall be exalted.

8 The God who brought them forth out of Egypt with his might and excellency, he shall devour the nations that are their enemies, and shall break their bones in pieces, and cut off their loins.

9 He couched, he lay down as a lion, and as a young lion; who shall rouse him up? Blessed are they who bless you, and cursed are they who curse you.

10 ¶And Balak's anger was kindled against Balaam, and he struck his hands together; and Balak said to Balaam, I called you to curse my enemies, and, behold, you have surely blessed them these three times.

11 Therefore, now get you out and go to your own country; for I had said, I will surely honor you but, lo, the LORD has deprived you of my honors.

12 And Balaam answered and said to Balak, Did I not say to your messengers whom you sent to me,

13 If Balak would give me his house full of silver and gold, I would not transgress the commandment of the LORD to do either good or bad of my own mind; but what the LORD says, that will I speak.

14 And now, behold, I am going to my land; come, therefore, and I will give you counsel what this people shall do to your people in the latter days.

15 ¶And he took up his parable and said, Balaam the son of Beor has said, and the man whose eyes are open has said;

16 He has said, who heard the words of God and knew the knowledge of the Most High, who saw the vision of God, falling into a trance but having his eyes open;

17 I have seen him, but not clearly enough; I beheld him, but he was not nigh; there shall come a Star out of Jacob, and a Prince shall rise out of Israel, and shall destroy the mighty men of Moab and subdue all the children of Sheth.

18 And Edom shall be his possession; Seir, also the possession of his enemies, shall be his; and Israel shall gain strength.

19 Out of Jacob shall come he that shall have dominion, and shall destroy him who has survived out of the city.

20 ¶And when he looked on Amalek, he took up his parable and said, Amalek is the chief of the nations; but in the end he shall perish for ever.

21 And he looked on the Kenites and took up his parable and said,

Strong is your dwelling place, and your nest is set in a rock.

22 Nevertheless the Kenite shall be wasted until Assyria shall carry you away captive.

23 And he took up his parable and said, Alas, who shall live when God does this!

24 And legions shall come from the land of China,[1] and shall conquer Assyria, and shall subdue the Hebrews, and they also shall perish for ever.

25 Then Balaam rose up and returned to his country; and Balak also went his way.

CHAPTER 25

AND Israel abode in Shittim, and the people began to commit whoredom with the daughters of Moab.

2 And they invited the people to the sacrifices offered to their gods; and the people did eat, and worshipped their gods.

3 And Israel joined himself to Baal-peor; and the anger of the LORD was kindled against the children of Israel.

4 And the LORD said to Moses, Take all the chiefs of the people and expose them before the LORD in the daylight that the fierce anger of the LORD may be turned away from the children of Israel.

5 And Moses said to the judges of Israel, Slay every one of you his men who have joined themselves to Baal-peor.

6 ¶And, behold, one of the men of the children of Israel came to his brethren, and then he went in to a Midianite woman in the sight of Moses and in the sight of all the congregation of the children of Israel while they were weeping at the door of the tabernacle of the congregation.

7 And when Phinehas, the son of Eleazar, the son of Aaron the priest, saw it, he rose up from the midst of the congregation and took a spear in his hand;

8 And he went in after the man of Israel into the private chamber and thrust both of them through, the man of Israel and the woman through her belly. So the plague was stayed from the children of Israel.

9 And those that died in the plague were twenty-four thousand.

10 ¶Then the LORD spoke to Moses and said to him.

11 Phinehas, the son of Eleazar, the son of Aaron the priest, has turned my wrath away from the children of Israel because he was moved with my zeal among them that I did not consume the children of Israel in my anger.

12 Therefore I said, Behold, I will give to him my covenant of peace;

13 And he shall have it and his sons after him, the covenant of an everlasting priesthood, because he was zealous for his God and made atonement for the children of Israel.

14 Now the name of the Israelite who was slain with the Midianite woman was Zimri, the son of Salu, a chief of a father's house of the tribe of Simeon.

15 And the name of the Midianite woman was Cozbi, the daughter of Zur; he was the chief of the people of his father's house in Midian.

16 ¶And the LORD spoke to Moses, saying,

17 Harass the Midianites and destroy them;

18 For they have distressed you with their treachery, wherewith they have plotted against you in the matter of Peor and in the matter of Cozbi, the daughter of a prince of Midian, their sister, who was slain in the day of the plague in the matter of Peor.

CHAPTER 26

AND it came to pass after the plague that the LORD said to Moses and to Eleazar the son of Aaron the priest,

2 Take a census of all the congregation of the children of Israel, from twenty years old and upward, throughout their fathers' houses, all that are able to go to war in Israel.

3 And Moses and Eleazar the priest talked with the people in the plains of Moab by the Jordan at Jericho.

4 And Moses numbered them from

1 Cathay.

twenty years old and upward, as the LORD commanded Moses and the children of Israel who went forth out of the land of Egypt.

5 ¶Reuben, the first-born of Israel; the sons of Reuben, Hanoch, the family of the Hanochites; of Pallu, the family of the Palluites;

6 Of Hezron, the family of the Hezronites; of Carmi, the family of the Carmites.

7 These are the families of the Reubenites; and their number was forty-three thousand and seven hundred and thirty.

8 And the son of Pallu, Eliab.

9 And the sons of Eliab, Nebuel, and Dathan, and Abiram, the prominent men of the congregation who strove against Moses and against Aaron in the company of Korah when they strove against the LORD;

10 And the earth opened its mouth and swallowed them up together with Korah when that company died, when the fire devoured two hundred and fifty men; and they became an example.

11 Notwithstanding, the children of Korah did not die.

12 ¶The sons of Simeon after their families: of Jemuel, the family of the Jemuelites; of Jamin, the family of the Jaminites; of Jachin, the family of the Jachinites;

13 Of Zerah, the family of the Zarhites; of Shaul, the family of the Shaulites.

14 These are the families of the Simeonites, twenty-two thousand and two hundred.

15 ¶The sons of Gad after their families: of Zephon, the family of the Zephonites; of Haggi, the family of the Haggites; of Shuni, the family of the Shunites.

16 Of Ozni, the family of the Oznites; of Edi, the family of the Edites;

17 Of Arod, the family of the Arodites; of Adel, the family of the Adelites;

18 These are the families of the sons of Gad according to those that were numbered of them, forty thousand and five hundred.

19 ¶The sons of Judah were Er and Onan; and Er and Onan died in the land of Canaan.

20 And the sons of Judah after their families were: of Shelah, the family of the Shelanites; of Pharez, the family of the Pharzites; of Zerah, the family of the Zarhites.

21 And the sons of Pharez were: of Hezron, the family of the Hezronites; of Hamul, the family of the Hamulites.

22 These are the families of Judah according to those that were numbered of them, seventy-six thousand and five hundred.

23 ¶The sons of Issachar after their families: of Tola, the family of the Tolaites; of Pua, the family of the Puaites;

24 Of Jashub, the family of the Jashubites; of Shimron, the family of the Shimronites.

25 These are the families of Issachar according to those that were numbered of them, sixty-four thousand and three hundred.

26 ¶The sons of Zebulun after their families: of Seder, the family of the Sadrites; of Elon, the family of the Elonites; of Nahlael, the family of the Nahlaites.

27 These are the families of the Zebulunites according to those that were numbered of them, sixty thousand and five hundred.

28 ¶The sons of Joseph after their families were Manasseh and Ephraim:

29 Of the sons of Manasseh: of Machir, the family of the Machirites; and Machir begat Gilead; of Gilead comes the family of the Gileadites.

30 These are the sons of Gilead: of Jeezer, the family of the Jeezerites; of Helek, the family of the Helekites;

31 And of Ashdael, the family of the Ashdaelites; and of Shechem, the family of the Shechemites;

32 And of Shemida, the family of the Shemidaites; and of Hepher, the family of the Hepherites.

33 ¶And Zelophehad the son of Hepher had no sons, but daughters; and the names of the daughters of Zelophehad were Mahlah, Joah, Hoglah, Milcah, and Tirzah.

34 These are the families of Manas-

seh and those that were numbered of them, fifty-two thousand and seven hundred.

35 ¶These are the sons of Ephraim after their families: of Shuthelah, the family of the Shuthalhites; of Becher, the family of the Bachrites; of Tahan, the family of the Tahanites.

36 And these are the sons of Shuthelah: of Edan, the family of the Edanites.

37 These are the families of the sons of Ephraim according to those that were numbered of them, thirty-two thousand and five hundred. These are the sons of Joseph after their families.

38 ¶The sons of Benjamin after their families: of Bela, the family of the Belaites; of Ashbel, the family of the Ashbelites; of Ahiram, the family of the Ahiramites;

39 Of Shupham, the family of the Shuphamites; of Hupham, the family of the Huphamites.

40 And the sons of Bela were Ard and Naaman: of Ard, the family of the Ardites; and of Naaman, the family of the Naamites.

41 These are the sons of Benjamin after their families; and those that were numbered of them were forty-five thousand and six hundred.

42 ¶These are the sons of Dan after their families: of Shuham, the family of the Shuhamites. These are the families of Dan after their families.

43 All the families of the Shuhamites, according to those that were numbered of them, were sixty-four thousand and four hundred.

44 ¶The sons of Asher by their families: of Jimna, the family of the Jimnites; of Jesui, the family of the Jesuites; of Beriah, the family of the Berites.

45 The sons of Beriah: of Heber, the family of the Heberites; of Malchiel, the family of the Malchielites.

46 And the name of the daughter of Asher was Sarah.

47 These are the families of the sons of Asher according to those that were numbered of them; fifty-three thousand and four hundred.

48 ¶The sons of Naphtali after their families: Nahzeel, the family of the Nahzeelites; of Guni, the family of the Gunites;

49 Of Jezer, the family of the Jezerites; of Shillem, the family of the Shillemites.

50 These are the families of Naphtali according to their families; and they that were numbered of them were forty-five thousand and four hundred.

51 These were the numbers of the children of Israel, six hundred and one thousand, seven hundred and thirty.

52 ¶And the LORD spoke to Moses, saying,

53 To these the land shall be divided for an inheritance according to the number of names.

54 To a large family you shall give a large inheritance and to a small family you shall give a small inheritance; every one shall receive his inheritance according to those that were numbered of him.

55 Notwithstanding the land shall be divided by lots; according to the names of the tribes of their fathers they shall inherit.

56 According to the lots shall their inheritance be divided between the larger families and the smaller families.

57 ¶These are they that were numbered of the Levites after their families: of Gershon, the family of the Gershonites; of Kohath, the family of the Kohathites; of Merari, the family of the Merarites.

58 These are the families of the Levites: the family of the Libnites, the family of the Hebronites, the family of the Mahlites, the family of the Mushites, the family of the Korathites. And Kohath begat Amram.

59 And the name of Amram's wife was Jochaber, the daughter of Levi, who was born to Levi in Egypt; and she bore to Amram, Aaron and Moses and their sister Miriam.

60 And to Aaron were born Nadab, Abihu, Eleazar, and Ithamar.

61 But Nadab and Abihu died when they offered strange fire before the LORD.

62 And those that were numbered of them were twenty-three thousand, all males from a month old and upward; for they were not numbered among the children of Israel, because there was no inheritance given them among the children of Israel.

63 ¶These are those that were numbered by Moses and Eleazar the priest, who numbered the children of Israel in the plains of Moab by the Jordan near Jericho.

64 But among these there was not a man of those whom Moses and Aaron the priest numbered, when they numbered the children of Israel in the wilderness of Sinai.

65 For the LORD had said of them, They shall surely die in the wilderness. And there was not left a man of them except Caleb the son of Jophaniah and Joshua the son of Nun.

CHAPTER 27

THEN came the daughters of Zelophehad, the son of Hepher, the son of Gilead, the son of Machir, the son of Manasseh, of the families of Manasseh the son of Joseph; and these are the names of his daughters: Mahlah, Joah, and Hogla, and Milcah, and Tirzah.

2 And they stood before Moses and before Eleazar the priest and before the princes and all the congregation at the door of the tabernacle of the congregation, saying,

3 Our father died in the wilderness, and he was not in the company of those who revolted before the LORD in the company of Korah; but he died in his own sins and had no sons.

4 Why should the name of our father be lost from among his family because he had no son? Give to us therefore a possession among the brothers of our father.

5 And Moses brought their cause before the LORD.

6 ¶And the LORD said to Moses,

7 The daughters of Zelophehad speak right, you shall surely give them a possession of an inheritance among their father's brothers; and you shall cause the inheritance of their father to pass to them.

8 And you shall say to the children of Israel, If a man dies and has no son, then you shall cause his inheritance to pass to his daughter.

9 And if he has no daughter, then you shall give his inheritance to his brothers.

10 And if he has no brothers, then you shall give his inheritance to his father's brothers.

11 And if his father has no brothers, then you shall give his inheritance to his kinsman that is next to him of his family, and he shall possess it; and it shall be to the children of Israel a statute of judgment, as the LORD commanded Moses.

12 ¶And the LORD said to Moses, Go up into this mountain of the Hebrews and see the land which I have given to the children of Israel.

13 And when you have seen it, you also shall be gathered to your people, as Aaron your brother was gathered.

14 Because you rebelled against my commandment in the wilderness of Zin, in the strife of the congregation, and you did not sanctify me before their eyes; that is, the waters of Mesotha, at Rakim in the wilderness of Zin.

15 ¶And Moses spoke to the LORD, saying,

16 Let the LORD, the God of the spirits of all flesh, appoint a man over the congregation

17 Who may go out before them and who may come in before them, and who may lead them out and bring them in; that the congregation of the LORD may not be as sheep which have no shepherd.

18 And the LORD said to Moses, Take Joshua the son of Nun, a man in whom is the spirit, and lay your hand upon him;

19 And make him to stand before Eleazar the priest and before all the congregation; and put him in charge in their sight.

20 And you shall put some of your honor upon him that all the congregation of the children of Israel may obey him.

21 And he shall stand before Eleazar the priest, who shall ask for him after the ordinance of the law before the LORD; at his word they shall go out and at his word they shall come in, both he and all the children of Israel with him, the whole congregation.

22 And Moses did as the LORD commanded him; and he took Joshua and made him stand before Eleazar the priest and before all the congregation;

23 And he laid his hands upon him, and gave him authority, as the LORD commanded by the hand of Moses.

CHAPTER 28

AND the LORD spoke to Moses and said to him,

2 Command the children of Israel and say to them, My offerings and the bread of my offerings made by fire for a sweet savour to me they shall observe, to offer to me in their due season.

3 And you shall say to them, This is the offering made by fire which you shall offer to the LORD: two lambs of the first year without blemish day by day for a continual burnt offering.

4 The one lamb you shall offer in the morning and the other lamb you shall offer at evening;

5 And a tenth part of an ephah of fine flour for a meal offering, mixed with a fourth part of a hin of beaten oil.

6 It is a continual burnt offering which was ordained in mount Sinai for a sweet savour, a sacrifice made by fire to the LORD.

7 And the drink offering thereof shall be a fourth of a hin for the one lamb; in the holy place you shall pour out the old wine before the LORD for a drink offering.

8 And the other lamb you shall offer at evening; as the meat offering of the morning and as its drink offering you shall offer it, a sacrifice made by fire for a sweet savour to the LORD.

9 ¶And on the sabbath day two lambs of the first year without blemish and two tenths of an ephah of fine flour mixed with oil for a meal offering with its drink offering;

10 This is the burnt offering of every sabbath, besides the continual burnt offering and its drink offering.

11 ¶And in the beginning of your months you shall offer burnt offerings to the LORD: two young bullocks, and one ram, seven lambs of the first year without blemish;

12 And three tenths of an ephah of fine flour mixed with oil for a meal offering, for one bullock; and two tenths of an ephah of fine flour mixed with oil, for a meal offering, for one ram;

13 And a tenth of an ephah of fine flour mixed with oil for a meal offering for one lamb; for a burnt offering of a sweet savour, a sacrifice made by fire to the LORD.

14 And their drink offerings shall be half a hin of wine to a bullock and a third part of a hin to a ram and a fourth part of a hin to a lamb; this is the burnt offering of the beginning of every month throughout the months of the year.

15 And one kid of the goats for a sin offering to the LORD shall be offered, besides the continual burnt offering and its drink offering.

16 And on the fourteenth day of the first month is the passover of the LORD.

17 And on the fifteenth day of this month is the feast; seven days shall unleavened bread be eaten.

18 On the first day shall be a holy convocation; you shall do no manner of hard work;

19 But you shall offer sacrifices made by fire for burnt offerings to the LORD; two young bullocks and one ram and seven lambs of the first year: they shall be to you without blemish:

20 And their meal offering shall be of fine flour mixed with oil; three tenths of an ephah shall you offer for a bullock, and two tenths of an ephah for a ram;

21 And a tenth of an ephah you shall offer for every lamb; thus you shall do for every one of the seven lambs.

22 And one yearling goat for a sin offering to make atonement for you.

23 You shall offer these besides the burnt offering of the morning, which is for a continual burnt offering.

24 After this manner you shall offer daily for seven days the bread of the sacrifice made by fire for a sweet savour to the LORD; it shall be offered besides the continual burnt offering and its drink offering.

25 And on the seventh day you shall have a holy convocation; you shall do no manner of work.

26 ¶Also on the day of first fruits, when you offer a meal offering of new wheat to the LORD at your feast of weeks, you shall have a holy convocation; you shall do no manner of hard work;

27 But you shall offer the burnt offerings for a sweet savour to the LORD; two young bullocks, one ram, seven lambs of the first year;

28 And their meal offering of fine flour mixed with oil, three tenths of an ephah for each bullock, two tenths of an ephah for one ram,

29 And a tenth of an ephah for each lamb, likewise for each of the seven lambs;

30 And one kid of the goats to make atonement for you.

31 You shall offer them besides the continual burnt offering and its meal offering; you shall offer them without blemish, and their drink offerings.

CHAPTER 29

AND on the first day of the seventh month you shall have a holy convocation; you shall do no manner of hard work; it is a day of blowing trumpets to you.

2 And you shall offer burnt offerings for a sweet savour to the LORD; one young bullock, one ram, and seven lambs of the first year without blemish;

3 And their meal offering shall be of fine flour mixed with oil, three tenths of an ephah for a bullock and two tenths of an ephah for a ram,

4 And one tenth of an ephah for each lamb, likewise for each of the seven lambs;

5 And one kid of the goats for a sin offering, to make atonement for you;

6 Besides the burnt offering of the beginning of the month and its meal offering and the daily burnt offering and their meal offering and their drink offering, according to their manner, for a sweet savour, a sacrifice made by fire to the LORD.

7 ¶And you shall have on the tenth day of this seventh month a holy convocation; and you shall do no manner of hard work;

8 But you shall offer burnt offerings to the LORD for a sweet savour: one young bullock, one ram, and seven lambs of the first year without blemish;

9 And their meal offering shall be of fine flour mixed with oil, three tenths of an ephah for the bullock and two tenths of an ephah for the one ram,

10 And a tenth of an ephah for one lamb, likewise for each of the seven lambs;

11 One kid of the goats for a sin offering; besides the sin offering of atonement and the continual burnt offering and the meal offering of it and their drink offerings.

12 ¶And on the fifteenth day of this seventh month you shall have a holy convocation; you shall do no manner of hard work, and you shall keep a feast to the LORD for seven days;

13 And you shall offer burnt offerings, a sacrifice made by fire, a sweet savour to the LORD; thirteen young bullocks, two rams, and fourteen lambs of the first year; they shall be without blemish:

14 And their meal offering shall be of fine flour mixed with oil, three tenths of an ephah for every bullock of the thirteen bullocks, two tenths of an ephah for each of the two rams,

15 And a tenth of an ephah for each lamb of the fourteen lambs,

16 And one kid of the goats for a sin offering; besides the continual burnt offering, its meal offering, and its drink offering.

17 ¶And on the second day you shall offer twelve young bullocks,

two rams, and fourteen lambs of the first year without blemish;

18 And their meal offering and their drink offerings for the bullocks, for the rams, and for the lambs, shall be according to their number, after the ritual;

19 And one kid of the goats for a sin offering; besides the continual burnt offering, and its meal offering, and their drink offering.

20 ¶And on the third day eleven bullocks, two rams, and fourteen lambs of the first year without blemish;

21 And their meal offering and their drink offering for the bullocks, for the rams, and for the lambs, according to their number, according to the ritual;

22 And one kid of the goats for a sin offering; besides the continual burnt offering and its meal offering and its drink offering.

23 ¶And on the fourth day ten bullocks, two rams, and fourteen lambs of the first year without blemish;

24 Their meal offering and their drink offering for the bullocks, for the rams, and for the lambs, according to their number, according to the ritual;

25 And one kid of the goats for a sin offering; besides the continual burnt offering, its meal offering, and its drink offering.

26 ¶And on the fifth day nine bullocks, two rams, and fourteen lambs of the first year without blemish;

27 And their meal offering and their drink offering for the bullocks, for the rams, and for the lambs, according to their number, according to the ritual;

28 And one goat of the first year for a sin offering; besides the continual burnt offering and its meal offering and its drink offering.

29 ¶And on the sixth day eight bullocks, two rams, and fourteen lambs of the first year without blemish;

30 And their meal offering and their drink offering for the bullocks, for the rams, and for the lambs, according to their number, according to the ritual;

31 And one goat of the first year for a sin offering; besides the continual burnt offering, its meal offering, and its drink offering.

32 ¶And on the seventh day seven bullocks, two rams, and fourteen lambs of the first year without blemish;

33 And their meal offering and their drink offerings for the bullocks, for the rams and for the lambs, according to their number, according to the ritual;

34 And one he-goat of the first year for a sin offering; besides the continual burnt offering, its meal offering, and its drink offering.

35 ¶On the eighth day you shall have a solemn assembly; you shall do no manner of hard work;

36 But you shall offer burnt offerings, a sacrifice made by fire, of a sweet savour to the Lord: one bullock, one ram, and four lambs of the first year without blemish;

37 Their meal offering and their drink offering for the bullock, for the ram, and for the lambs, according to their number, according to the ritual;

38 And one goat of the first year for a sin offering; besides the continual burnt offering and its meal offering and its drink offering.

39 These things you shall do to the Lord at the time of your feasts, besides your vows and your freewill offerings and your burnt offerings and your meal offerings and your drink offerings.

40 And Moses told the children of Israel according to all that the Lord commanded Moses.

CHAPTER 30

AND Moses spoke to the chiefs of the tribes of the children of Israel and said to them, This is the thing which the Lord has commanded:

2 When a man vows a vow to the Lord and swears an oath to bind himself by a bond, he shall not break his word; he shall do according to all that proceeds out of his mouth.

3 If a woman also vows a vow to

the LORD and binds herself by a bond while she is in her father's house in her youth,

4 And her father hears of her vows and the bonds wherewith she has bound herself, and her father shall keep silent toward her; then all her vows shall stand and every bond wherewith she has bound herself shall stand.

5 But if her father shall make them void in the day that he hears of all the vows and all the bonds by which she has bound herself, then they shall not stand; and the LORD shall forgive her because her father had declared them void.

6 And if she is given in marriage to a husband, and her vows are upon her or she has uttered anything out of her lips by which she bound herself,

7 And her husband hears of it and keeps silent in the day that he hears it; then all her vows shall stand and her bonds by which she has bound herself shall stand.

8 But if her husband makes them void on the day that he hears of it, then shall her vows be void and that which she uttered with her lips, and the gifts which she has promised, by which she bound herself, shall be of none effect; and the LORD shall forgive her.

9 But as to the vow of a widow or a deserted woman, everything by which she has bound herself shall stand against her.

10 And if she vowed in her husband's house or bound herself with an oath,

11 And her husband heard it but kept silent toward her and did not nullify it; then her vow shall stand, and the bond by which she has bound herself shall stand.

12 But if her husband has utterly made her vows void on the day when he heard them; then whatsoever proceeded out of her lips concerning her vows or concerning the bonds by which she bound herself shall not stand, because her husband has made them void; and the LORD shall forgive her.

13 Every vow and every binding oath to afflict the soul, her husband may establish or her husband may make it void.

14 But if her husband should remain silent toward her from day to day; then he confirms all her vows and all her bonds which are upon her; he confirms them because he kept silent toward her on the day that he heard them.

15 But if he shall make them void after he has heard them, then he shall bear her iniquity.

16 These are the statutes, which the LORD commanded Moses, between a man and his wife, between a father and his daughter while she is still in her youth in her father's house.

CHAPTER 31

AND the LORD spoke to Moses, saying,

2 Avenge the children of Israel against the Midianites; afterward you shall be gathered to your people.

3 And Moses said to the people, Arm some of the men from among you for the host, and let them go against the Midianites to avenge the LORD against Midian.

4 Of every tribe, a thousand from each tribe, throughout all the tribes of Israel, you shall send into the army.

5 So there were selected out of the tribes of Israel a thousand men from each tribe, twelve thousand armed for war.

6 Then Moses sent them to war, a thousand from each tribe, twelve thousand armed men, them and Phinehas the son of Eleazar the priest, to the army, with the holy vessels of the sanctuary and with trumpets to blow in his hand.

7 And they warred against Midian, as the LORD commanded Moses; and they slew all the males.

8 And they slew the kings of Midian with the rest of those that were slain; namely, Evi, Rakim, Zur, Hur, and Reba, the five kings of Midian; Balaam also, the son of Beor, they slew with the sword.

9 And the children of Israel took all the women of Midian captives; and their little ones and all their

cattle and all their flocks and all their wealth they plundered.

10 And they burned all the cities wherein they dwelt and all their unwalled villages with fire.

11 And they carried away all the spoil and all the booty, both of men and of beasts.

12 And they brought the captives, the booty, and the spoil, to Moses and to Eleazar the priest and to the congregation of the children of Israel, to the camp at the plains of Moab which are by the Jordan near Jericho.

13 ¶And Moses and Eleazar the priest and all the princes of the congregation went forth to meet them outside the camp.

14 And Moses was wroth with the officers of the army, the commanders of thousands and captains over hundreds who had come from the battle.

15 And Moses said to them, Why have you let all the women live?

16 For it was they who caused the children of Israel, through the counsel of Balaam, to commit trespass against the LORD in the matter of Peor, and there was a plague in the congregation of the LORD.

17 Now therefore kill every male among the little ones and kill every woman who has known man by lying with him.

18 But all the female children, who have not known a man by lying with him, keep alive for yourselves.

19 And as for you, you shall abide outside the camp seven days; whosoever has killed any person and whosoever has touched any slain purify both yourselves and your captives on the third day and on the seventh day,

20 And purify all your garments and all that is made of skin and all the work of goats' hair and all things made of wood.

21 ¶And Eleazar the priest said to the men of war who had returned from the battle, This is the ordinance of the law which the LORD commanded Moses:

22 Only the gold, and the silver, the brass, the iron, the tin, and the lead,

23 Everything that may abide the fire, you shall make it to go through the fire and it shall be clean; nevertheless it shall be purified with the water which is used for cleansing; and all that cannot abide the fire, you shall make pass through the water.

24 And you must wash your clothes on the seventh day, and you shall be clean, and afterward you shall come into the camp.

25 ¶And the LORD spoke to Moses, saying,

26 Take the count of the prey that was taken and of the captives, both of man and of beast, you and Eleazar the priest and the chiefs of the fathers of the congregation;

27 And divide the booty into two parts; between the men of war who went out to battle and between all the congregation;

28 And levy a tribute for the LORD from the men of war who went out to battle; out of all the congregation, one person of every five hundred, both of the persons and of the oxen and of the asses and of the sheep;

29 Take it from their half and give it to Eleazar the priest as an offering to the LORD.

30 And from the children of Israel's half, you shall take one out of every fifty, of the persons, of the oxen, of the asses, and of the flocks, and of all the beasts, and give them to the Levites, who have charge of the tabernacle of the LORD.

31 And Moses and Eleazar the priest did as the LORD commanded Moses.

32 And the booty and the captives which the men of war had plundered was six hundred and seventy-five thousand sheep,

33 And seventy-two thousand oxen,

34 And sixty-one thousand asses,

35 And thirty-two thousand persons in all, of women who had not known man by lying with him.

36 And the half, which was the portion of those who went out to war was in number three hundred and thirty-seven thousand and five hundred sheep;

37 And the LORD's tribute of the sheep was six thousand and seven hundred and fifty.

38 And the oxen were thirty-six thousand; of which the LORD's tribute was seven hundred and twenty.

39 And the asses were thirty thousand and five hundred; of which the LORD's tribute was six hundred and ten.

40 And the persons were sixteen thousand; of which the LORD's tribute was three hundred and twenty persons.

41 And Moses gave the tribute, which was the LORD's gift offering, to Eleazar the priest, as the LORD commanded Moses.

42 And of the children of Israel's half, which Moses divided from the men who had gone out to war,

43 (Now the half that pertained to the congregation was three hundred and thirty-seven thousand and five hundred sheep,

44 And thirty-six thousand oxen,

45 And thirty thousand and five hundred asses,

46 And sixteen thousand persons),

47 Even of the children of Israel's half, Moses took one portion of every fifty, both of man and of beasts, and gave them to the Levites, who have charge of the tabernacle of the LORD; as the LORD commanded Moses.

48 ¶And the officers who were over thousands of the host, the commanders of thousands and the captains of hundreds came near to Moses;

49 And they said to Moses, Your servants have taken the sum of the men of war who are under our charge and there lacks not one man of us.

50 We have therefore brought as an offering for the LORD what every man has found, articles of gold, ankle chains, and bracelets, rings, earrings, and necklaces, to make atonement for our souls before the LORD.

51 And Moses and Eleazar the priest took the gold from them, all wrought jewels.

52 And all the gold of the gift offering that they offered to the LORD, from the commanders of thousands and from the captains of hundreds, was sixteen thousand seven hundred and fifty shekels.

53 (For the men of war had plundered every man for himself.)

54 And Moses and Eleazar the priest took the gold from commanders of thousands and from captains of hundreds and brought it into the tabernacle of the congregation for a memorial for the children of Israel before the LORD.

CHAPTER 32

NOW the children of Reuben and the children of Gad had a very great multitude of cattle; and when they saw the land of Jazer and the land of Gilead, behold, the place was a place for cattle;

2 The children of Reuben and the children of Gad came and said to Moses and to Eleazar the priest and to the princes of the congregation,

3 Ataroth, Ribon, Jazer, Nimrah, Heshbon, Elealeh, Sheba, Nebo, and Beon,

4 The land which the LORD smote before the children of Israel is a land for cattle, and your servants have cattle;

5 Wherefore, they said, if we have found mercy in your sight, let this land be given to your servants for a possession, and bring us not across the Jordan.

6 ¶And Moses said to the children of Reuben and to the children of Gad, Shall your brethren go to war, while you settle here?

7 Why do you discourage the heart of the children of Israel from going over into the land which the LORD has given them?

8 Thus did your fathers, when I sent them from Rakim-gia to spy out the land.

9 For when they went up as far as the valley of Segola, and spied out the land, they discouraged the heart of the children of Israel that they should not go into the land which the LORD had given them.

10 And the LORD's anger was kindled against them on that day, and he swore, saying,

11 Surely none of the men who came up out of the land of Egypt, from twenty years old and upward,

shall see the land which I swore to Abraham, to Isaac, and to Jacob; because they have not wholly followed me;

12 Except Caleb the son of Jophaniah the Kenezite and Joshua the son of Nun; for they have wholly followed the LORD.

13 And the LORD's anger was kindled against Israel, and he made them wander in the wilderness forty years until all the generation that had done evil in the sight of the LORD was consumed.

14 And, behold, you also are risen up in your father's stead, a generation of sinful men, to augment still the fierce anger of the LORD against Israel.

15 For if you turn away from after the LORD, he will again make you wander in the wilderness; and you shall destroy all this people.

16 ¶Then they came near to him and said, We will build sheepfolds here for our cattle and cities for our little ones;

17 But we ourselves will arm and go before the children of Israel, until we have brought them to their place; and our little ones shall dwell in fortified cities because of the inhabitants of the land.

18 We will not return to our houses until the children of Israel have inherited every man his inheritance;

19 For we will not inherit with them on the other side of the Jordan or beyond; because we have already received our inheritance on this side of the Jordan eastward.

20 ¶And Moses said to them, If you will do this thing and arm yourselves before the LORD for war,

21 And will go all of you armed across the Jordan before the LORD, to war, until he has destroyed his enemies from before his presence,

22 And the land is subdued before the LORD; then after that you shall return and be guiltless before the LORD and before Israel; and this land shall be your possession before the LORD.

23 But if you will not do so, behold, you will be sinning against the LORD;

and be sure your sins will overtake you.

24 Build cities for your little ones and folds for your sheep; and do that which you have promised.

25 And the children of Reuben and the children of Gad said to Moses, Your servants will do as our lord commands.

26 Our little ones, our wives, our flocks, and all our cattle shall remain there in the cities of Gilead;

27 But your servants will pass over, every man armed for war, before the LORD for battle, as our lord said.

28 So concerning all of them Moses commanded Eleazar the priest and Joshua the son of Nun and the chiefs of the fathers of the tribes of the children of Israel;

29 And Moses said to them, If the children of Reuben and the children of Gad will cross with you over the Jordan, every man armed for battle before the LORD, and the land shall be subdued before you, then you shall give them the land of Gilead for a possession;

30 But if they will not cross over with you armed, they shall have possessions among you in the land of Canaan.

31 And the children of Reuben and the children of Gad answered, saying, As the LORD has said to your servants, so will we do.

32 We will pass over armed before the LORD into the land of Canaan to war, that the possession of our inheritance on this side of the Jordan may be ours.

33 And Moses gave to them, to the children of Reuben and to the children of Gad and to half of the tribe of Manasseh the son of Joseph, the kingdom of Sihon king of the Amorites and the kingdom of Og king of Mathnin, all the land with its cities throughout its territories and the towns of the country round about it.

34 ¶And the children of Gad built Ribon and Ataroth and Adoer

35 And Atroth, Shopham and Jazer and Jogbehah,

36 Beth-nimrah and Beth-hauran, fenced cities and folds for sheep.

37 And the children of Reuben built Heshbon, Elealeh, Koriathaim,

38 Nebo, and Baal-meon (their names being changed), and Sibmah; and gave other names to the cities which they built.

39 And the children of Machir the son of Manasseh went to Gilead and took it, and destroyed the Amorites who were in it.

40 And Moses gave Gilead to Machir the son of Manasseh; and he dwelt therein.

41 And Jair the son of Manasseh went and took their villages, and called them Caproney Jair (hamlets of Jair, to this day).

42 And Nocah went and took Keeth and its villages, and called it Nocah, after his own name.

CHAPTER 33

THESE are the journeys of the children of Israel when they went forth out of the land of Egypt with their armies under the command of Moses and Aaron.

2 And Moses wrote down their goings out and their journeys by the commandment of the LORD; and these are their journeys according to their goings out.

3 They departed from Rameses in the first month, on the fifteenth day of the first month; on the morrow after the passover the children of Israel went out with a mighty hand in the sight of all the Egyptians,

4 While the Egyptians were burying all their first-born whom the LORD had slain among them; upon their gods also the LORD executed judgments.

5 And the children of Israel departed from Rameses and encamped in Succoth.

6 And they departed from Succoth and encamped in Etham, which is on the edge of the wilderness.

7 And they departed from Etham and encamped at the entrance of Heritha, the canal, which is before Baal-sephon; and they encamped before Migdol.

8 And they departed from the entrance of Heritha and passed through the midst of the sea into the wilderness, and went three days' journey in the wilderness of Etham and encamped in Morath.

9 And they departed from Morath and came to Elim; and in Elim were twelve fountains of water and seventy palm trees; and they encamped there by the water.

10 And they departed from Elim and encamped by the Red Sea.

11 And they departed from the Red Sea and encamped in the wilderness of Seen.

12 And they departed from the wilderness of Seen, and encamped at Raphka.

13 And they departed from Raphka and encamped in Alush.

14 And they departed from Alush and encamped at Rephidim, where there was no water for the people to drink.

15 And they departed from Rephidim and encamped in the wilderness of Sinai.

16 And they departed from the wilderness of Sinai, and encamped at Kabrey di ragrigtha.[1]

17 And they departed from Kabrey di ragrigtha, and encamped at Hazeroth.

18 And they departed from Hazeroth, and encamped at Rithmah.

19 And they departed from Rithmah, and encamped at Rimmon-parez.

20 And they departed from Rimmon-parez, and encamped at Libnah.

21 And they departed from Libnah, and encamped at Rissah.

22 And they departed from Rissah, and encamped at Kehlat.

23 And they departed from Kehlat, and encamped at mount Shapher.

24 And they departed from mount Shapher, and encamped at Haradah.

25 And they departed from Haradah, and encamped at Makheloth.

26 And they departed from Makheloth, and encamped at Tahath.

27 And they departed from Tahath, and encamped at Tarah.

28 And they departed from Tarah, and encamped at Mithcah.

[1] Graves of lust.

29 And they departed from Mithcah, and encamped at Hashmonah.

30 And they departed from Hashmonah, and encamped at Moseroth.

31 And they departed from Moseroth, and encamped at Bene-jaakan.

32 And they departed from Bene-jaakan, and encamped at Had-gadgad.

33 And they departed from Hadgadgad, and encamped at Jotbath.

34 And they departed from Jotbath, and encamped at Acronah.

35 And they departed from Acronah, and encamped at Ezion-gaber.

36 And they departed from Eziongaber, and encamped in the wilderness of Zin, which is Kadesh.

37 And they departed from Kadesh, and encamped at mount Hor on the edge of the land of Edom.

38 And Aaron the priest went up on mount Hor at the commandment of the LORD, and died there, in the fortieth year after the children of Israel were come out of the land of Egypt, on the first day of the first month.

39 And Aaron was a hundred and twenty-three years old when he died on mount Hor.

40 And the king of Gadar the Canaanite, who dwelt in the south in the land of Canaan, heard of the coming of the children of Israel.

41 And they departed from mount Hor, and encamped at Zalmonah.

42 And they departed from Zalmonah, and encamped at Punon.

43 And they departed from Punon, and encamped in Aboth.

44 And they departed from Aboth, and encamped at Een-Ebraye, in the border of Moab.

45 And they departed from Een-Ebraye, and encamped at Ribon-gad.

46 And they journeyed from Ribongad, and encamped at Almon-diblathaim.

47 And they journeyed from Almon-diblathaim, and encamped at the mountain of Hebrews, which is before Nebo.

48 And they departed from the mountain of the Hebrews, and encamped in the plains of Moab by the Jordan near Jericho.

49 And they encamped by the Jordan from Beth-ashimon as far as Abel-shittim in the plains of Moab.

50 ¶And the LORD said to Moses in the plains of Moab by the Jordan near Jericho,

51 Speak to the children of Israel and say to them, When you cross the Jordan into the land of Canaan;

52 Then you shall destroy all the inhabitants of the land from before you and destroy all their idols and destroy all their molten images and demolish all their high places;

53 And you shall possess the land and dwell therein; for I have given you the land to possess it.

54 And you shall divide the land by lot for an inheritance among your families; and to the large families you shall give a large inheritance, and to the small families you shall give a small inheritance; every man's inheritance shall be in the place where his lot falls; according to the tribes of their fathers they shall inherit.

55 But if you will not destroy the inhabitants of the land from before you, then it shall come to pass, that those who are left of them shall be splinters in your eyes, and spears in your sides, and shall trouble you in the land wherein you dwell.

56 And as I thought to do to them, I shall do to you.

CHAPTER 34

AND the LORD spoke to Moses, saying,

2 Command the children of Israel and say to them, When you enter the land of Canaan (this is the land which shall be divided to you for an inheritance, even the land of Canaan with its territories),

3 Then your south boundary shall be from the wilderness of Zin along by the border of Edom, and your southern border shall be from the end of the salt sea eastward;

4 And your boundary shall turn from the south to the ascent of Sepharvim, and pass on to Zin; and the limits thereof shall be from the south of Rakim-gia, and shall go on to Hazar-addar, and pass on to Azmon;

5 And the boundary shall turn from Azmon to the river of Egypt, and the limits thereof shall be at the sea.

6 And as for the western border, you shall have the Great Sea and its coasts; this shall be your western border.

7 And this shall be your northern border: from the Great Sea you shall mark out for you a boundary to mount Hor;

8 From mount Hor you shall mark out the boundary to the entrance of Hamath; and the limits of the border shall be at Zedad;

9 ¶And the border shall go on to Ziphron, and its end shall be at Hazar-enan; these shall be your northern boundaries.

10 And you shall mark out your eastern boundary from Hazar-enan to Shepham;

11 And the boundary shall go down from Shepham to Diblath, on the east side of Ain; and the boundary shall descend and shall reach to the side of the sea of Chinnereth eastward;

12 And the border shall go down to the Jordan, and its limits shall be at the salt sea; this shall be your land with the borders thereof round about.

13 And Moses commanded the children of Israel, saying, This is the land which you shall divide by lots, which the LORD has commanded to give to the nine tribes, and to the half tribe;

14 For the tribe of the children of Reuben according to the house of their fathers, and the tribe of the children of Gad according to the house of their fathers, and the half tribe of Manasseh, have received their inheritance;

15 The two tribes and the half tribe have received their inheritance on this side of the Jordan near Jericho eastward, toward the sunrise.

16 And the LORD spoke to Moses, saying,

17 These are the names of the men who shall divide the land to you for an inheritance: Eleazar the priest and Joshua the son of Nun.

18 And you shall take one prince of every tribe to divide the land to you.

19 And these are the names of the chiefs: of the tribe of Judah, Caleb the son of Jophaniah.

20 Of the tribe of Simeon, Shelmuel the son of Ammihud.

21 Of the tribe of Benjamin, Eldad the son of Chislon.

22 Of the tribe of Dan, Bakki the son of Jogli.

23 Of the tribe of Joseph, of the tribe of Manasseh, Nahlael the son of Ephod.

24 Of the tribe of Ephraim, Kemuel the son of Shiptan.

25 Of the tribe of Zebulun, Elizaphan the son of Parnach.

26 Of the tribe of Issachar, Petael the son of Azzor.

27 Of the tribe of Asher, Ahihud the son of Shelomi.

28 Of the tribe of Naphtali, Pedahel the son of Ammihud.

29 These are they whom the LORD commanded to divide the inheritance to the children of Israel in the land of Canaan.

CHAPTER 35

THE LORD spoke to Moses in the plains of Moab by the Jordan near Jericho, saying,

2 Command the children of Israel that they give to the Levites of the inheritance of their possession cities to dwell in; and they shall give also to the Levites the suburbs of the cities round about them.

3 And the cities they shall have to dwell in; and their suburbs shall be for their cattle and for their herds and for all their beasts.

4 And the suburbs of the cities which you shall give to the Levites shall reach from the wall of the city and outward a thousand cubits round about.

5 And you shall measure from outside the city on the east side two thousand cubits, and on the south side two thousand cubits, and on the west side two thousand cubits, and on the north side two thousand cubits; and the city shall be in the midst; this shall be to them the suburbs of the cities.

6 And among the cities which you shall give to the Levites, six cities

shall be set aside for you for refuge, that the manslayer who had slain his neighbor without intent may flee thither; and to them you shall add forty-two other cities.

7 So all the cities which you shall give to the Levites shall be forty-eight cities in all, together with their suburbs.

8 And with regard to the cities which you shall give of the inheritance of the children of Israel: from those that have many you shall take many; but from those that have few you shall take few; every one shall give of his cities to the Levites in proportion to the inheritance which he inherits.

9 ¶And the LORD spoke to Moses, saying,

10 Speak to the children of Israel and say to them, When you cross the Jordan into the land of Canaan,

11 Then you shall select for yourselves cities to be cities of refuge for you; that the person who kills someone unawares may flee there.

12 And they shall be to you cities for refuge from the avenger, that the manslayer may not be killed until he stand before the congregation in judgment.

13 And of these cities which you shall give, six cities shall you have for refuge.

14 You shall give three cities on this side of the Jordan, and three cities you shall give in the land of Canaan, which shall be cities of refuge.

15 These six cities shall be for refuge, both for the children of Israel and for the proselytes and for the sojourner among them; that every one who kills any person unawares may flee there.

16 But if he struck him with an instrument of iron, so that he might die, and he did die, he is a murderer; the murderer shall surely be put to death.

17 And if he struck him with a stone in the hand, so that he might die, and he did die, he is a murderer; the murderer shall surely be put to death.

18 Or if he struck him with an instrument of wood by hand, so that

he might die, and he did die, he is a murderer; the murderer shall surely be put to death.

19 The avenger of blood himself shall slay the murderer when he meets him.

20 But if he wound him because of hatred, or shoot an arrow at him by lying in wait, that he might die, he is a murderer;

21 Or in enmity smite him with his hand, that he might die, and he did die, the murderer shall surely be put to death; the avenger of the blood himself shall slay the murderer when he meets him.

22 But if he thrust him suddenly without enmity, or have cast upon him anything without lying in wait,

23 Or with any stone with which a man may die, without seeing him when he cast it upon him, and he died, and was not his enemy, neither sought his harm;

24 Then the congregation shall judge between the slayer and the avenger of the blood according to these judgments;

25 And the congregation shall deliver the slayer from the hand of the avenger of blood, and the congregation shall send him to the city of refuge, to which he had fled; and he shall dwell in it until the death of the high priest, who was anointed with the holy oil.

26 But if the slayer shall at any time go outside the bounds of the city of his refuge, to which he has fled;

27 And the avenger of the blood find him outside the bounds of the city of his refuge, and the avenger of the blood kill the slayer; he shall not be guilty of blood;

28 Because he should have remained in the city of his refuge until the death of the high priest; but after the death of the high priest the slayer shall return to the land of his possession.

29 So these things shall be for a statute of judgment to you throughout your generations in all of your dwellings.

30 Whosoever kills any person, the

murderer shall be put to death on the testimony of witnesses; but just one witness shall not testify against any person that he may be put to death.

31 Moreover you shall not accept a bribe for the life of a slayer, who is guilty of death; but he shall be surely put to death.

32 And you shall not take a bribe that he may flee to the city of refuge, that he should come again to dwell in the land, until the death of the high priest.

33 So you shall not pollute the land in which you live; for blood defiles the land; and the land in which blood is shed cannot be cleansed except by the shedding of the blood of him who shed it.

34 Defile not therefore the land in which you dwell, and wherein I dwell; for I the LORD dwell among the children of Israel.

CHAPTER 36

THEN the chief fathers of the families of the children of Gilead, the son of Machir, the son of Manasseh, the son of Joseph, came near, and spoke before Moses and before Eleazar the priest and before the princes of the congregation, the chief fathers of the children of Israel;

2 And they said, The LORD commanded our lord to give the land for an inheritance by lot to the children of Israel: and our lord was commanded by the LORD to give the inheritance of Zelophehad our brother to his daughters.

3 And if they be married to any of the sons of the other tribes of the children of Israel, then shall their inheritance be taken from the inheritance of their fathers, and shall be added to the inheritance of the tribe into which they married; so shall it be taken from the lot of our inheritance.

4 And when the jubilee year of the children of Israel shall come, then shall their inheritance be added to the inheritance of the tribes into which they married; so shall their inheritance be taken away from the inheritance of the tribe of their fathers.

5 And Moses commanded the children of Israel according to the word of the LORD, saying, The tribe of the sons of Joseph has said well.

6 This is the thing which the LORD has commanded concerning the daughters of Zelophehad, saying, Let them marry whom they think best; but only within the family of the tribe of their father shall they marry,

7 So that no inheritance of the children of Israel shall be transferred from one tribe to another tribe; for every one of the children of Israel shall cleave to the inheritance of the tribe of his father.

8 And every daughter who possesses an inheritance in any tribe of the children of Israel shall be wife to one of the family of the tribe of her father, that the children of Israel may inherit every man the inheritance of his fathers.

9 Neither shall the inheritance be transferred from one tribe to another; but every one of the tribes of the children of Israel shall cleave to his own inheritance.

10 Just as the LORD had commanded Moses, so did the daughters of Zelophehad;

11 For Mahlah, Tirzah, Hagla, Milcah, and Joah, the daughters of Zelophehad, were married to the sons of their father's brothers;

12 And they were married into the families of the sons of Manasseh the son of Joseph; and their inheritance remained in the tribe of the family of their father.

13 These are the commandments and the judgments which the LORD commanded by the hand of Moses concerning the children of Israel in the plains of Moab by the Jordan near Jericho.

DEUTERONOMY

CHAPTER 1

THESE are the words which Moses spoke to all Israel beyond the Jordan in the wilderness, in the low desert plain opposite the Red Sea, between Paran and Tophel and Lebanon and Hazeroth and Dizahab.

2 (There are eleven days' journey from Horeb to mount Seir to Rakimgia.)

3 And it came to pass in the fortieth year, in the eleventh month, on the first day of the month, that Moses spoke to the children of Israel according to all that the LORD had given him in commandment concerning them;

4 After he had slain Sihon the king of the Amorites, who dwelt in Heshbon, and Og the king of Mathnin, who dwelt in Astaroth and in Erdei,

5 Beyond the Jordan, in the land of Moab; Moses began to explain this law, saying,

6 The LORD our God said to us in Horeb, You have dwelt long enough in this mountain;

7 Turn and set out on your journey, and go to the mountain of the Amorites, and to all the places round about it, in the low desert plain, in the mountain, in the lowland and in the south and by the sea side, to the land of the Canaanites, and to Lebanon, as far as the great river, the river Euphrates.

8 Behold, I have given you the land before you; go in and possess the land which the LORD swore to your fathers, Abraham, Isaac, and Jacob, to give to them and to their descendants after them.

9 ¶And I said to you at that time, I am not able to bear you myself alone;

10 The LORD your God has multiplied you, and behold, you are this day as the stars of heaven in multitude.

11 (May the LORD God of your fathers make you a thousand times as many more as you are, and bless you, as he has promised you!)

12 How can I myself bear alone your encumbrance and your burden and your strife?

13 Choose for yourselves wise men, who have understanding and are renowned among your tribes, and I will make them chiefs over you.

14 And you answered and said to me, The thing that you have spoken is good for us to do.

15 So I took the chiefs of your tribes, wise men and renowned, and made them chieftains over you, commanders over thousands and captains over hundreds and officers over fifty and officers over ten and scribes for your tribes.

16 And I charged your judges at that time, saying, Hear the causes between your brethren, and judge righteously between a man and his brother, and the stranger that is with him.

17 You shall not be partial to persons in judgment; but you shall hear the small as well as the great; you shall not be afraid of the face of man, for the judgment is God's; and the cause that is too hard for you, bring it to me, and I will hear it.

18 And I commanded you at that time all the things that you should do.

19 ¶And when we journeyed from Horeb, we went through all that great and terrible wilderness, which you saw by the way of the mountain of

the Amorites, as the Lord our God commanded us; and we came as far as Rakim-gia.

20 And I said to you, You have come to the mountain of the Amorites, which the Lord our God has given us.

21 Behold, the Lord your God has given the land before you; go up and possess it, as the Lord God of your fathers has said to you; fear not, neither be terrified.

22 ¶Then all of you came near to me and said, Let us send men before us, and they shall spy out the land for us, and bring us word again and show us the way by which we must go up and the cities into which we shall come.

23 And the saying pleased me well; and I took twelve men of you, one man of each tribe;

24 And they turned and went up into the mountain, and came as far as the valley of Segola, and spied out the land.

25 And they took some of the fruit of the land in their hands, and brought it down to us, and they brought us word again and said to us, It is a good land which the Lord our God does give to us.

26 But in spite of this, you would not go up, but rebelled against the commandment of the Lord your God;

27 And you murmured in your tents and said, It is because the Lord hated us that he has brought us forth out of the land of Egypt, to deliver us into the hand of the Amorites, to destroy us.

28 Whither shall we go up? Our brethren have discouraged our heart, ᴣying, The people are greater and taller than we; the cities are great and walled up to heaven; and moreover we have seen the sons of giants there.

29 Then I said to you, Fear not, neither tremble of them.

30 The Lord your God, who goes before you, shall fight for you, just as he did for you in Egypt before your eyes;

31 And in the wilderness, where you saw how the Lord your God nourished you, just as a man nourishes his son, in all the way that you went, until you came to this place.

32 Yet in this thing you did not believe the Lord your God,

33 Who went in the way before you to prepare a place for you to encamp in it, in fire by night to show you by what way you should go, and in a cloud by day.

34 And the Lord heard the voice of your complaining, and was angry, and swore, saying,

35 Surely there shall not one of these men of this evil generation see the good land which I swore to give to your fathers,

36 Except Caleb the son of Jophaniah; he shall see it, and to him will I give the land upon which he has trodden, and to his children, because he has wholly followed the Lord.

37 Also the Lord was angry with me on your account, saying, You also shall not go in thither.

38 But Joshua the son of Nun, who stands before you, he shall go in there; encourage him; for he shall cause Israel to inherit it.

39 Moreover your little ones, who you said would be a prey, and your children, who in that day had no knowledge between good and evil, shall go in there, and to them will I give it, and they shall possess it.

40 But as for you, turn you and take your journey into the wilderness by the way of the Red Sea.

41 Then you answered and said to me, We have sinned against the Lord our God, we will go up and fight, just as the Lord our God commanded us. And when you had girded on every man his weapons of war, you were stirred up to go up into the mountain.

42 And the Lord said to me, Say to them, You shall not go up, neither fight; for I am not among you; lest you be defeated before your enemies.

43 So I spoke to you; and you would not listen, and you rebelled against the commandment of the Lord, and went presumptuously up into the mountain.

44 And the Amorites, who dwelt in that mountain, came out against you

and chased you as smoked-out bees do, and drove you away from Seir, as far as Hirmah.

45 Then you sat down and wept before the Lord; but the Lord would not hearken to your voice nor give ear to you.

46 So you remained in Rakim many days, according to the days that you remained there.

CHAPTER 2

THEN we turned, and journeyed into the wilderness by the way of the Red Sea, as the Lord spoke to me; and we circled mount Seir for many days.

2 And the Lord spoke to me, saying,

3 You have circled this mountain long enough; turn northward.

4 And command the people, saying, You are going to pass through the territory of your brethren the children of Esau, who dwell in Seir; and they shall be afraid of you; take heed to yourselves therefore;

5 Do not provoke them; for I will not give you a possession of their land, no, not so much as the breadth of a foot to tread on, because I have given mount Seir to Esau for a possession.

6 You may buy grain from them for money, that you may eat; and you may also buy water from them for money, that you may drink.

7 For the Lord your God has blessed you in all the work of your hand; he knows how to lead you through this great wilderness; behold, these forty years the Lord your God has been with you; you have lacked nothing.

8 And when we passed by from our brethren the children of Esau, who dwelt in Seir, and from the way of the desert plain, from Elath and from Ezion-gaber we turned and passed by the way of the wilderness of Moab.

9 And the Lord said to me, Do not distress the Moabites, neither provoke them to battle; for I will not give you of their land for a possession; because I have given it to the children of Lot for an inheritance.

10 The Amney dwelt in it formerly, a people great and many and tall, like giants;

11 For they were giants, and also were accounted as giants; but the Moabites call them Amney.

12 The Horites also dwelt formerly in Seir; but the children of Esau possessed them and destroyed them from before them and settled in their land, as Israel did to the land of his possession, which the Lord gave to them.

13 Now rise up and go over the brook Zered. So we went over the brook Zered.

14 And the time in which we journeyed from Rakim-gia until we crossed the brook Zered was thirty-eight years; until all the generation of the men of war had perished from the midst of the camp, as the Lord had sworn to them.

15 For indeed the hand of the Lord was also against them, to destroy them from the midst of the camp until they were consumed.

16 ¶So it came to pass, when all the men of war were consumed and dead from among the people,

17 The Lord spoke to me, saying,

18 You are to pass over through the border of Moab and Ad this day;

19 And when you come near the territory of the children of Ammon, do not oppress them nor provoke them; for I will not give you of the land of the children of Ammon any possession, because I have given it to the children of Lot for a possession.

20 (That also was accounted a land of giants; giants dwelt in it formerly; and the Ammonites call them Zamzumins;

21 A people great and many and tall, like giants; but the Lord destroyed them from before them; and they succeeded them, and dwelt in their land,

22 As the children of Esau did, who dwelt in Seir when they destroyed the Horites from before them, and they succeeded them and settled in their land even to this day;

23 And the Avites who dwelt in Hazerim, as far as Azzah, the Caphedokian, who came out of Caphedoki,

destroyed them and dwelt in their land.)

24 ¶Rise up, take your journey, and cross over the river Arnon; behold, I have delivered into your hand Sihon the king of Heshbon, the Amorite, and his land; begin to destroy him, and provoke him to battle.

25 This day I will begin to put the dread of you and the fear of you upon the peoples that are under the whole heaven, who shall hear report of you, and shall tremble and be in anguish because of you.

26 ¶And I sent messengers from the wilderness of Kermoth to Sihon king of Heshbon with words of peace, saying,

27 Let me pass through your land; I will go along by the highway; I will neither turn to the right hand nor to the left.

28 You shall sell me grain for money, that I may eat; and sell me water for money, that I may drink; only let me pass through on foot;

29 Just as the children of Esau who dwell in Seir and the Moabites who dwell in Ad did for me; until I shall cross the Jordan into the land which the LORD our God gives us.

30 But Sihon king of Heshbon would not let us pass through his territory; for the LORD your God hardened his spirit and made his heart obstinate, that he might deliver him into your hands, as it is this day.

31 And the LORD said to me, Behold, I have begun to deliver Sihon and his land into your hands; begin to destroy him, and to possess his land.

32 Then Sihon came out against us, he and all his people, to fight at Jahaz.

33 And the LORD our God delivered him to us; and we smote him and his sons and all his people.

34 And we conquered all his cities at that time, and utterly destroyed all the towns; even the women and the little ones, we left none to remain;

35 Only the cattle we took for a prey to ourselves, and the spoil of the cities which we conquered.

36 From Adoer, which is by the brink of the river Arnon, and from the city that is in the valley, as far as Gilead, there was not one city too strong for us; the LORD our God delivered all to us;

37 Only to the land of the children of Ammon we did not draw near, nor to all that is by the river Jabbok, nor to the cities that are in the mountains, nor to whatever the LORD our God forbade us.

CHAPTER 3

THEN we turned and went up the way to Mathnin; and Og the king of Mathnin came out against us, he and all his people, to battle at Erdei.

2 And the LORD said to me, Do not fear him; for I have delivered him, and all his people and his land into your hand; and you shall do to him as you did to Sihon king of the Amorites, who dwelt in Heshbon.

3 So the LORD our God delivered into our hand Og also, the king of Mathnin, and all his people; and we smote him until none was left to him surviving.

4 And we captured all his cities at that time, and we left not a city which we did not take from them, sixty cities, all the region of Argob, the kingdom of Og in Mathnin.

5 All these cities were fenced with high walls, gates, and bars; besides the suburban towns a great many.

6 And we utterly destroyed them, as we did to Sihon the king of Heshbon, for we utterly destroyed all his cities, even the women and the little ones.

7 But all the cattle and the spoil of the cities, we took for a prey to ourselves.

8 And we took at that time out of the hand of the two kings of the Amorites the land that was on this side of the Jordan, from the river Arnon to mount Hermon

9 (The Sidonians call Hermon Sirion, and the Amorites call it Senir),

10 All the cities of the plain and all Gilead and all Mathnin as far as Salcah and Erdei, all the cities of the kingdom of Og in Mathnin.

11 For only Og the king of Mathnin

remained of the remnant of the giants; behold, his bedstead was a bedstead of iron; and behold, it is in Rabbath of the children of Ammon, nine cubits long and four cubits broad, according to the measure of the cubit of giants.

12 And this land we possessed at that time, from Adoer, which is by the river of Arnon; and half of mount Gilead, and its cities, I gave to the Reubenites and to the Gadites.

13 And the rest of Gilead, and all Mathnin, being the kingdom of Og, I gave to the half tribe of Manasseh; all the region of Argob, with all Mathnin, which is called the land of giants.

14 Jair the son of Manasseh took for himself all the region of Argob as far as the border of Geshur and Maachath; and called them after his own name, Mathnin and Caproney Jair, to this day.

15 To Machir I gave Gilead.

16 And to the Reubenites and to the Gadites I gave the region from Gilead as far as the valley of Arnon, and the inside of the valley, and its border as far as the river Jabbok, which is the border of the children of Ammon;

17 Along with the desert plain, and the Jordan, and the territory thereof, from Chinnereth as far as the sea of Arabah, the Salt Sea, which lies at the foot of Ashdod and Pisgah which is in the hilly country eastward.

18 ¶And I commanded you at that time, saying, The LORD your God has given you this land to possess it; you shall pass over armed before your brethren the children of Israel, all of you who are valiant men of war.

19 But your wives and your little ones and your cattle (for I know that you have much cattle) shall remain in your cities which I have given you

20 Until the LORD have given rest to your brethren, as he has given to you, and until they also possess the land which the LORD your God is giving them beyond the Jordan; and then shall you return every man to the possession which I have given you.

21 ¶And I commanded Joshua at that time, saying, Your eyes have seen

all that the LORD your God has done to these two kings; so shall the LORD do to all these kingdoms through which you are going.

22 You shall not fear them; for it is the LORD your God who is fighting for you.

23 And I besought the LORD at that time, saying,

24 I beseech thee O LORD God, thou who hast begun to show thy servant thy greatness, and thy mighty hand, and thy outstretched arm (for what god is there in heaven or on earth who can do according to thy works and according to thy mighty deeds?),

25 I pray thee, let me now go over and see the good land that is beyond the Jordan, that goodly mountain, and Lebanon.

26 But the LORD was wroth with me on your account, and would not hearken to me; and the LORD said to me, Let it suffice for you; speak no more before me of this matter.

27 Go up to the top of the hill (Pisgah) and lift up your eyes eastward and westward and northward and southward, and behold it with your eyes; for you shall not cross this Jordan.

28 But charge Joshua, and encourage him, and strengthen him; for he shall go over before this people, and he shall cause them to inherit the land which you shall see.

29 So we dwelt in the valley opposite Beth-peor.

CHAPTER 4

NOW therefore hearken, O Israel, to the law and to the judgments which I teach you this day, to do them, that you may live and go in and possess the land which the LORD the God of your fathers gives you.

2 You shall not add to the commandment which I command you, neither shall you take from it, but you must keep the commandments of the LORD your God which I command you.

3 Your eyes have seen what the LORD did because of Baal-peor; for

every man who followed Baal-peor, the LORD your God has destroyed him from among you.

4 But you who did cleave to the LORD your God are all alive this day.

5 Behold, I have taught you statutes and judgments, as the LORD my God has commanded me, that you should do them in the land which you are entering, to possess it.

6 And you shall keep them, therefore, and do them; for this is your wisdom and your understanding in the sight of the nations which shall hear all these statutes, and will say, Surely this great nation is a wise and understanding people.

7 For what nation is there so great, whose god is so near to it as the LORD our God is in all things that we call upon him for?

8 And what nation is there so great, that has laws and judgments so righteous as all this law which I set before you this day?

9 Only take heed for yourselves, and keep your soul diligently, lest you forget the things which your eyes have seen, and lest they depart from your heart all the days of your life; but declare them to your children and your children's children.

10 The day that you stood before the LORD your God in Horeb, when the LORD said to me, Gather the people together before me, and I will make them hear my words, that they may learn to worship me all the days that they shall live upon the earth, and that they may teach their children.

11 And you came near and stood at the foot of the mountain; and the mountain burned with fire to the midst of heaven, with darkness, clouds, and thick darkness.

12 And the LORD spoke to you on the mountain out of the midst of the fire; you heard the sound of the words, but saw no form; there was only a voice.

13 And he declared to you his covenant, which he commanded you to perform, even ten commandments; and he wrote them upon two tablets of stone.

14 ¶And the LORD commanded me at that time to teach you statutes and judgments, that you might do them in the land into which you are going to possess it.

15 Take therefore good heed to yourselves; for you saw no manner of form on the day that the LORD spoke to you at Horeb out of the midst of the fire;

16 Lest you corrupt yourselves, and make for yourselves images and the forms of any figure, the likeness of male or female,

17 The likeness of any beast that is on the earth, the likeness of any winged fowl that flies in the air,

18 The likeness of anything that creeps on the ground, the likeness of any fish that is in the waters beneath the earth;

19 And lest you lift up your eyes to heaven, and when you see the sun and the moon, and the stars and all the host of heaven, should go astray and worship them and serve those things which the LORD your God has provided for all the peoples under heaven.

20 But the LORD has taken you, and brought you forth out of the iron furnace, even out of Egypt, to be to him a people and an inheritance, as you are this day.

21 Furthermore the LORD was angry with me on your account, and swore that I should not cross this Jordan, and that I should not enter the good land which the LORD your God gives you for an inheritance;

22 Because I must die in this land, I must not cross this Jordan; but you shall cross it and possess that good land.

23 Take heed to yourselves, lest you forget the covenant of the LORD your God, which he made with you, and corrupt yourselves, and make for yourselves images, or the likeness of anything, which the LORD your God has forbidden you.

24 For the LORD your God is a consuming fire, a zealous God.

25 ¶When you shall beget children and children's children, and you shall have remained long in the land, and

shall corrupt yourselves and make images or the likeness of any thing, and shall do evil in the sight of the LORD your God and provoke him to anger;

26 I call heaven and earth to witness against you this day, that you shall soon utterly perish from off the land which you are going across the Jordan to possess; you shall not live long upon it, but shall utterly be destroyed.

27 And the LORD shall scatter you among the nations, and you shall be left few in number among the nations where the LORD your God shall scatter you.

28 And there you shall serve gods, the work of men's hands, of wood and stone, which neither see nor hear nor eat nor smell.

29 But if from there you shall seek the LORD your God, you shall find him, if you search for him with all your heart and with all your soul.

30 When you are in tribulation, and all these things are come upon you in the latter days, if you return to the LORD your God and shall be obedient to his voice

31 (For the LORD your God is a merciful God), he will not destroy you, neither forsake you, nor forget the covenant which he swore to your fathers.

32 For ask now about the days that are past, which were before you, since the day that God created man upon the earth, and ask from one end of heaven to the other whether there has been any such thing as this great thing is, or has been heard like it.

33 Did any other people ever hear the voice of God speaking out of the midst of the fire, as you have heard, and live?

34 Or have they tried out the God who went forth and took for himself a nation from the midst of another nation, by trials, by signs and by wonders and by war and by a mighty hand and by a stretched out arm and by great visions, according to all that the LORD your God did to the Egyptians before your eyes?

35 You saw and knew that the LORD is God; there is none else besides him.

36 Out of heaven he made you to hear his voice, that he might teach you; and upon earth he showed you his great fire; he made you to hear his words out of the midst of the fire.

37 And because he loved your fathers, therefore he chose their descendants after them, and brought you out of Egypt with his own person, with a mighty power;

38 To destroy nations from before you, who are greater and mightier than you are, to bring you in, to give you their land for an inheritance, as it is this day.

39 Know therefore this day, and cause your heart to repent, for it is the LORD who is God in heaven above and upon the earth beneath; there is none else besides him.

40 You must keep therefore his statutes and his commandments, which I command you this day, that it may be well with you and with your children after you, and that you may prolong your days in the land which the LORD your God gives you for ever.

41 ¶Then Moses set apart three cities on this side of the Jordan toward the rising sun;

42 That the slayer might flee there, who might kill his neighbor unintentionally, and hated him not in time past; and that by fleeing to one of these cities he might live;

43 Namely, Bezer in the wilderness, in the plain country, of the Reubenites; and Ramath in Gilead, of the Gadites; and Golan in Mathnin, of the Manassites.

44 ¶This is the law which Moses set before the children of Israel;

45 These are the testimonies, the statutes, and the judgments which Moses spoke to the children of Israel after they came forth out of Egypt,

46 On this side of the Jordan, in the valley over against Beth-peor, in the land of Sihon king of the Amorites, who dwelt in Heshbon, whom Moses and the children of Israel slew when they came out of Egypt;

47 And they possessed his land, and the land of Og king of Mathnin, two

kings of the Amorites, who were on this side of Jordan toward the rising sun;

48 From Adoer, which is on the edge of the river Arnon, as far as mount Serion, which is Hermon,

49 And all the low desert on this side of Jordan eastward, as far as the sea of the plain which is at the foot of Ashdod and Pisgah.

CHAPTER 5

AND Moses called all Israel, and said to them, Hear, O Israel, the statutes and judgments which I speak in your presence this day, that you may learn them, and keep and do them.

2 The LORD our God made a covenant with us in Horeb.

3 It was not with our fathers that the LORD made this covenant, but with us, even us, who are all of us here alive this day.

4 The LORD talked with you face to face in the mountain out of the midst of the fire,

5 (I stood between the LORD and you at that time, to declare to you the words of the LORD your God; for you were afraid because of the fire, and did not go up into the mountain), saying,

6 ¶I am the LORD your God, who brought you out of the land of Egypt, from the house of bondage.

7 You shall have no other gods besides me.

8 You shall not make for yourself any graven image or any likeness of anything that is in heaven above, or that is on the earth beneath, or that is in the waters under the earth;

9 You shall not worship them, nor serve them; for I the LORD your God am a zealous God, visiting the iniquities of the fathers upon the children to the third and fourth generation of those who hate me,

10 But showing mercy to thousands of generations of those who love me and keep my commandments.

11 You shall not take an oath by the name of the LORD your God in vain; for the LORD will not hold him guiltless who takes an oath by his name in vain.

12 Keep the sabbath day and sanctify it, as the LORD your God has commanded you.

13 Six days you shall labor, and do all your work;

14 But the seventh day is the sabbath to the LORD your God; in it you shall not do any work, you, nor your son, nor your daughter, nor your manservant, nor your maidservant, nor your ox, nor your ass, nor any of your cattle, nor the sojourner that is in your towns; that your manservant and your maidservant may rest as well as you.

15 And remember that you were a servant in the land of Egypt, and that the LORD your God brought you out thence by a mighty hand and by a stretched out arm; therefore the LORD your God has commanded you to keep the sabbath day.

16 ¶Honor your father and your mother, as the LORD your God has commanded you; that your days may be prolonged, and that it may go well with you, in the land which the LORD your God gives you.

17 You shall not kill.

18 You shall not commit adultery.

19 You shall not steal.

20 You shall not bear false witness against your neighbor.

21 You shall not covet your neighbor's wife, neither shall you covet your neighbor's house, nor his field, nor his vineyard, nor his manservant, nor his maidservant, nor his ox, nor his ass, nor anything that is your neighbor's.

22 ¶These words the LORD spoke to all the assembly on the mountain out of the midst of the fire, in the cloud and in the thick darkness, with a loud voice which cannot be measured. And he wrote them upon two tablets of stone, and gave them to me.

23 And when you heard the voice out of the midst of the darkness and saw the mountain burning with fire, you came near to me, all the heads of your tribes and your elders;

24 And you said, Behold, the LORD our God has shown us his glory and

his greatness, and we have heard his voice out of the midst of the fire; have seen this day that God does talk with man, and that he lives.

25 Now therefore why should we die? For this great fire will consume us; if we hear the voice of the LORD our God any more, then we shall die.

26 For who is there of all flesh, that has heard the voice of the living God speaking out of the midst of the fire, as we have, and lived?

27 Go near and hear all that the LORD our God shall say; and speak to us all that the LORD our God shall speak to you; and we will hear it and do it.

28 And the LORD heard the voice of your words, when you spoke to me; and the LORD said to me, I have heard the voice of the people and the words which they have spoken to you; they have well said all that they have spoken.

29 O that there were such a heart in them, to worship, and keep all my commandments always, that it might be well with them and with their children for ever!

30 Go and say to them, Return to your tents.

31 But as for you, stand here before me, and I will tell you all my commandments and my statutes and my judgments, which you shall teach them, that they may do them in the land which I give them to possess.

32 You must observe and do therefore as the LORD your God has commanded you; you shall not turn aside to the right hand or to the left.

33 You shall walk in all the ways which the LORD your God has commanded you, that you may live, and that it may be well with you, and that you may prolong your days in the land which you shall possess.

CHAPTER 6

NOW these are the commandments, the statutes, and the judgments which the LORD your God commanded me to teach you, that you shall do them in the land into which you are going to possess it;

2 That you may fear the LORD your God, to keep all his commandments and his statutes and his judgments, which I commanded you, this day, you and your son and your son's son, all the days of your life; and that your days may be prolonged;

3 ¶Hear therefore, O Israel, and observe and do them; that it may be well with you, and that you may increase greatly; for the LORD God of your fathers has promised you that he will give you a land that flows with milk and honey.

4 Hear, O Israel: the LORD our God is one LORD;

5 And you shall love the LORD your God with all your heart and with all your soul and with all your might.

6 And these words which I command you this day shall be in your heart:

7 And you shall repeat them diligently to your children, and shall talk of them when you sit in your house and when you walk by the way and when you lie down and when you rise up.

8 And you shall bind them for a sign upon your hand, and they shall be as a token between your eyes.

9 And you shall write them upon the doorposts of your house and on your gates.

10 And it shall be, when the LORD your God shall have brought you into the land which he swore to your fathers, to Abraham, to Isaac, and to Jacob, to give you great and goodly cities, which you did not build,

11 And houses full of all good things, which you did not fill, and cisterns digged, which you did not dig, and vineyards and olive trees, which you did not plant; when you shall eat and be full;

12 Then take heed lest you forget the LORD your God, who brought you forth out of the land of Egypt, from the house of bondage.

13 You shall reverence the LORD your God, and serve him, and shall swear by his name.

14 You shall not go after other gods, the gods of the people who are round about you,

15 (For the LORD your God is a

zealous God among you) lest the anger of the LORD your God be kindled against you, and he destroy you from off the face of the earth.

16 ¶You shall not tempt the LORD your God, as you tempted him with temptations.

17 You shall diligently keep the commandments of the LORD your God and his testimonies and his statutes, which he has commanded you.

18 And you shall do that which is good and right in the sight of the LORD; that it may be well with you, and that you may go in and possess the good land which the LORD swore to your fathers,

19 And defeat all your enemies from before you, as the LORD has spoken.

20 And when your son asks you in time to come, saying, What mean the testimonies and the statutes and the judgments which the LORD our God has commanded you?

21 Then you shall say to your son, We were Pharaoh's slaves in Egypt; and the LORD brought us out of Egypt with a mighty hand;

22 And the LORD wrought signs and great wonders, and plagues in Egypt against Pharaoh and against all his army, before our eyes;

23 And the LORD brought us out from there, that he might bring us in and give us the land which he swore to our fathers.

24 And the LORD commanded us to do all these statutes, to revere the LORD our God, for our good always, that he might preserve us alive, as it is at this day.

25 And it shall be our righteousness, if we observe and do all these commandments before the LORD our God, as he has commanded us.

CHAPTER 7

WHEN the LORD your God shall bring you into the land which you are entering to possess, and has destroyed many nations before you, the Hittites, the Girgasites, the Amorites, the Canaanites, the Perizzites, the Hivites, and the Jebusites, seven nations greater and mightier than yourselves;

2 And when the LORD your God shall deliver them before you, and you shall defeat them; then you shall utterly destroy them; you shall make no covenant with them, nor show mercy to them;

3 Neither shall you make marriages with them; you shall not give your daughters to their sons, nor take their daughters for your sons,

4 That they may not turn away your sons from following me, and serve other gods; and then the anger of the LORD would kindle against you and destroy you quickly.

5 But thus shall you deal with them: you shall destroy their altars and break down their statues and cut down their ornaments and burn their graven images with fire.

6 For you are a holy people to the LORD your God; the LORD your God has chosen you to be a beloved people to himself, above all people that are upon the face of the earth.

7 It was not because you were more in number than any other peoples that the LORD was delighted in you and chose you, for you were the fewest of all peoples;

8 But it was because the LORD loved you, and because he would keep the oaths which he had sworn to your fathers, that the LORD brought you out with a mighty hand, and delivered you out of the house of bondage from the hand of Pharaoh king of Egypt,

9 That you may know therefore that the LORD your God, he is God, the faithful God, who keeps covenant and mercy with those that love him and keep his commandments to a thousand generations,

10 And repays those that hate him during their lifetime; he requites them that he may destroy them; he shall not be slack to those that hate him, but he repays them during their lifetime.

11 You shall therefore keep the commandments and the statutes and the judgments which I command you this day, and do them.

12 ¶Wherefore if you hearken to these judgments, and keep them and do them, the LORD your God shall keep with you the covenant and the mercy which he swore to your fathers;

13 And he will love you and bless you and multiply you; he will also bless the fruit of your womb and the fruit of your land, your grain and your wine and your oil, the increase of your cattle and the flocks of your sheep, in the land which he swore to your fathers to give you.

14 You shall be blessed above all peoples; there shall not be male or female barren among you or among your cattle.

15 And the LORD will take away from you all sickness; and all evil diseases of the Egyptians, which you know, he will not bring upon you; but will bring them upon your enemies.

16 And you shall consume all the peoples that the LORD your God shall deliver to you; your eye shall have no pity upon them; neither shall you serve their gods; for they are a snare to you.

17 If you shall say in your heart, These nations are greater than I; how will I be able to destroy them?

18 You shall not be afraid of them; but you shall remember what the LORD your God did to Pharaoh and to all Egypt;

19 The great trials which your eyes saw, the signs, the wonders, the mighty hand, and the outstretched arm, whereby the LORD your God brought you out; so shall the LORD your God do to all the peoples of whom you are afraid.

20 Moreover the LORD your God will send raiders among them, until they that are left and hide themselves from you, are destroyed.

21 You shall not be afraid of them, for the LORD your God is among you, a great and terrible God.

22 And the LORD your God will destroy those nations from before you little by little; you will not be able to destroy them quickly, lest the wild beasts increase upon you.

23 But the LORD your God shall deliver them to you, and shall smite them with a great destruction, until they are destroyed.

24 And he shall deliver their kings into your hands, and you shall destroy their name from under heaven; there shall no man be able to stand before you, until you have destroyed them.

25 The graven images of their gods you shall burn with fire; you shall not covet the silver or the gold that is on them, nor take it for yourselves, lest you become unclean with it; for it is an abomination before the LORD your God.

26 Neither shall you bring an abomination into your house, lest you be a cursed thing like it; but you shall utterly detest it, and you shall utterly abhor it; for it is a cursed thing.

CHAPTER 8

ALL the commandments which I command you this day you shall observe to do, that you may live and multiply, and go in and possess the land which the LORD swore to your fathers.

2 And you shall remember all the way which the LORD your God led you these forty years in the wilderness, that he might humble you, and prove you, to know what is in your heart, whether you would keep his commandments or not.

3 And he humbled you and suffered you to hunger and fed you with manna, which you did not know, neither did your fathers know; that he might make you to understand that man does not live by bread alone; but by everything that proceeds out of the mouth of the LORD does man live.

4 Your clothes did not wear out upon you, neither did your feet go bare during these forty years.

5 You must know in your heart that, as a man disciplines his son, so the LORD your God disciplines you.

6 Therefore you must keep the commandments of the LORD your God, to walk in his ways and fear him.

7 For the LORD your God brings you into a good land, a land of

brooks of water, of fountains and depths that spring out of valleys and mountains;

8 A land of wheat and barley, and of vines and fig trees and pomegranates; a land of olive trees, and of oil and honey;

9 A land wherein you shall eat bread without scarcity, you shall not lack anything in it; a land whose stones are iron, and out of whose mountains you may dig brass.

10 You shall eat and be full, and then you shall bless the LORD your God for the good land which he has given you.

11 Take heed, lest you forget the LORD your God, in not keeping his commandments and his judgments and his statutes, which I command you this day;

12 Lest when you have eaten and are full, and have built beautiful houses, and dwell in them;

13 And when your flocks and herds multiply, and your silver and gold are multiplied, and all that you have is multiplied;

14 Then your heart be lifted up, and you forget the LORD your God, who brought you forth out of the land of Egypt, from the house of bondage;

15 Who led you through the great and terrible wilderness, a place of fiery serpents and scorpions and droughts, a place where there was no water; who brought you forth water out of the flinty rock;

16 Who fed you in the wilderness with manna, which your fathers did not know, that he might humble you, and that he might prove you, to do you good at the end;

17 And you say in your heart, My power and the might of my hand have gotten me this wealth.

18 But you shall remember the LORD your God; for it is he who gives you power to get wealth, that he may establish his covenant which he swore to your fathers, as it is this day.

19 And if you do forget the LORD your God, and walk after other gods and serve them and worship them, I have testified against you this day that you shall surely perish.

20 As the nations which the LORD destroyed before you, so shall you perish if you are not obedient to the voice of the LORD your God.

CHAPTER 9

HEAR, O Israel: You are to cross the Jordan this day, to go in to destroy nations greater and mightier than yourselves, cities great and fenced up to heaven,

2 A people great and tall, the sons of giants, whom you know, and of whom you have heard it said, No man can stand up before the giants!

3 And that you may know therefore this day that the LORD your God is he who will go over before you; as a consuming fire he shall destroy them, and he shall defeat them before you; so that you shall rout them, and destroy them quickly, as the LORD has said to you.

4 Do not say in your heart, after the LORD your God has defeated them from before you, It is because of my righteousness that the LORD has brought me in to possess this land; but it is because of the wickedness of these nations that the LORD is destroying them from before you.

5 It is not because of your righteousness, or for the uprightness of your heart, that you are going in to possess their land; but it is because of the sins of these nations the LORD your God is destroying them from before you, and that he may perform the word which he swore to your fathers, Abraham, Isaac, and Jacob.

6 Know therefore, that it is not because of your righteousness that the LORD your God is giving you this good land to possess it; for you are a stiffnecked people.

7 ¶Remember, and forget not, how you provoked the LORD your God to wrath in the wilderness; from the day that you came out of Egypt until you came to this place, you have been rebellious against the LORD.

8 Also in Horeb you provoked the LORD to wrath, so the LORD was angry enough with you to have destroyed you.

9 When I went up on the mountain to receive the tablets of stone, the tablets of the covenant which the LORD made with you, and I abode on the mountain forty days and forty nights, I neither did eat bread nor drink water;

10 And the LORD gave me two tablets of stone, written with the finger of God; and on them were written all the words which the LORD had spoken with you in the mountain out of the midst of the fire on the day of the assembly.

11 And at the end of forty days and forty nights, the LORD gave me two tablets of stone, the tablets of the covenant.

12 And the LORD said to me, Arise and go down quickly from here; for your people whom you have brought forth out of Egypt have corrupted themselves; they have quickly turned aside out of the way which I commanded them; and they have made themselves a molten image.

13 Furthermore the LORD said to me, I have seen this people, and behold, it is a stiffnecked people:

14 Now let me alone, that I may destroy them, and blot out their name from under heaven; and I will make of you a nation mightier and greater than they.

15 So I turned and came down from the mountain, and the mountain was burning with fire and the two tablets of the covenant were in my two hands.

16 And I looked, and behold, you had sinned against the LORD your God, and had made to yourselves a molten calf; and you had turned aside quickly out of the way which the LORD your God had commanded you.

17 And I took the two tablets, and cast them out of my two hands, and broke them before your eyes.

18 Then I prayed before the LORD, as at the first, forty days and forty nights; I did neither eat bread nor drink water, because of all your sins which you sinned, in doing evil in the presence of the LORD, to provoke him to anger.

19 For I was afraid of the wrath and the anger wherewith the LORD was angry against you to destroy you. But the LORD hearkened to me at that time also.

20 And the LORD was angry enough with Aaron to have destroyed him; and I prayed for Aaron also the same time.

21 And I took the calf by which you sinned, which you had made, and burned it with fire, and ground it very small, until it was as fine as dust; and I threw the dust of it into the brook that flowed down out of the mountain.

22 And in heat, and in trials, and at the Kabrey di ragrigtha the people lusted for meat; you provoked the LORD to anger.

23 Likewise when the LORD sent you from Rakim-gia, and said to you, Go up and possess the land which I have given you; then you rebelled against the commandment of the LORD your God, and you did not believe him, nor hearken to his voice.

24 You have been rebellious against the LORD from the day that I knew you.

25 Thus I prayed before the LORD forty days and forty nights, because the LORD had said he would destroy you.

26 I prayed therefore before the LORD, and said, O LORD God, destroy not thy people and thy inheritance, whom thou hast saved through thy greatness, whom thou hast brought forth out of Egypt with a mighty hand.

27 But remember thy servants, Abraham, Isaac and Jacob; look not to the stubbornness of this people, nor to their wickedness, nor to their sins;

28 Lest the inhabitants of the land out of which thou didst bring them say, Because the LORD was not able to bring them into the land which he promised them, and because he hated them, he has brought them out to slay them in the wilderness.

29 Yet they are thy people and thy inheritance, whom thou broughtest out by thy mighty power and by thy outstretched arm.

CHAPTER 10

AT that time the LORD said to me, Hew two tablets of stone like the first, and come up to me on the mountain, and make yourself an ark of wood.

2 And I will write on the tablets the words that were on the first tablets which you broke, and you shall put them in the ark.

3 So I made an ark of shittim wood, and hewed two tablets of stone like the first, and went up on the mountain, having the two tablets in my hands.

4 And he wrote on the tablets, according to the first writing, the ten commandments, which the LORD spoke to you on the mountain out of the midst of the fire in the day of the assembly; and the LORD gave them to me.

5 And I turned and came down from the mountain, and put the tablets in the ark which I had made; and I left them in it, as the LORD commanded me.

6 ¶And the children of Israel took their journey from Beeroth of the children of Jaakan to Mosera; there Aaron died, and there he was buried, and Eleazar his son ministered in the priest's office in his stead.

7 From thence they journeyed to Gadgad; and from Gadgad to Jotbath, a land of brooks of waters.

8 ¶At that time the LORD set apart the tribe of Levi, to carry the ark of the covenant of the LORD, to stand before the LORD to minister to him, and to bless the name of the LORD, to this day.

9 Therefore Levi has no portion nor inheritance with his brethren; because the LORD is his inheritance, according as the LORD your God promised him.

10 And I stayed before the LORD on the mountain according to the first time, forty days and forty nights; and the LORD hearkened to me at that time also, and the LORD would not destroy you.

11 And the LORD said to me, Arise, take your journey before the people, that they may go in and possess the land which I swore to their fathers to give to them.

12 ¶And now, Israel, what does the LORD your God require of you, but to revere the LORD your God, to walk in his ways, and to love him, and to serve the LORD your God with all your heart and with all your soul,

13 To keep the commandments of the LORD your God, and his statutes, which I command you this day for your good?

14 Behold, the heaven and the heaven of heavens belongs to the LORD your God, the earth also, with all that therein is.

15 Only the LORD had a delight in your fathers and he loved them, and he chose their descendants after them, even you above all peoples, as it is this day.

16 Circumcise therefore the foreskin of your heart,[1] and be no more stiff-necked.

17 For the LORD your God is he who is the God of gods, and the LORD of lords, a great God, a mighty and a terrible, who is never partial, nor takes bribes;

18 He does execute justice for the fatherless and the widows, and loves him who turns to him, and gives him food and clothing.

19 Love therefore those who turn to him; for you were sojourners in the land of Egypt.

20 You shall revere the LORD your God; him shall you serve, and to him shall you cleave, and swear by his name.

21 For he is your praise, and he is your God, who has done for you these great and wonderful things which your eyes have seen.

22 Your fathers went down to Egypt seventy persons; and now the LORD your God has made you as the stars of heaven in multitude.

CHAPTER 11

THEREFORE you shall love the LORD your God, and keep his precepts, his statutes, his judgments, and his commandments, always.

[1] Surrender your heart.

2 And know this day that I do not speak to your children who have not known and who have not seen the discipline of the LORD your God, his greatness, his mighty hand, and his outstretched arm,

3 And his signs, and his deeds, which he did in Egypt to Pharaoh the king of Egypt, and to all his land;

4 And what he did to the army of the Egyptians, to their horses and to their chariots and to their horsemen; how he made the water of the Red Sea to overflow them as they pursued after you, and how the LORD has destroyed them to this day;

5 And what he did to you in the wilderness, until you came into this place;

6 And what he did to Dathan and Abiram, the sons of Eliab, the son of Reuben; how the earth opened its mouth, and swallowed them up, and their children and their tents and everything which they had, as they stood on their feet in the midst of all Israel;

7 But it is your eyes that have seen all the great acts of the LORD which he did.

8 Therefore you shall keep all the commandments which I command you this day, that you may be strong and go in and possess the land which you are going over to possess;

9 And that you may prolong your days in the land which the LORD swore to your fathers to give to them and to their descendants, a land that flows with milk and honey.

10 ¶For the land into which you are entering to possess it is not like the land of Egypt, from which you came out, where you sowed your seed and watered it with your feet, like a vegetable garden;

11 But the land which you are going over to possess is a land of mountains and valleys, that drinks water of the rain from heaven;

12 A land which the LORD your God cares for always; the eyes of the LORD your God are upon it, from the beginning of the year to the end of the year.

13 ¶And if you shall hearken diligently to the commandments which I command you this day, to love the LORD your God, and to serve him with all your heart and with all your soul,

14 He will give you the rain of your land in its due season, the early rain and the latter rain, and you shall gather in your grain and your wine and your oil.

15 And he will make grass to grow in your fields for your cattle, that you shall eat and be full.

16 Take heed to yourselves, lest your heart be enticed, and you turn aside and serve other gods and worship them;

17 And then the LORD's anger be kindled against you, and he shut up the heaven, that there be no rain and that the land may not produce its fruit, and that you perish quickly from off the good land which the LORD your God gives you.

18 ¶Therefore you shall lay up these commandments in your heart and in your soul, and bind them for a sign upon your hands, that they may be a token between your eyes.

19 And you shall teach them to your children, that they may talk of them when you sit in your house, and when you walk by the way, when you lie down, and when you rise up.

20 And you shall write them on the doorposts of your houses, and upon your gates;

21 That your days and the days of your children, may be multiplied in the land which the LORD your God swore to your fathers to give them, as the days of heaven upon earth.

22 ¶For if you shall diligently keep all these commandments which I command you this day, and do them, and love the LORD your God, and walk in all his ways, and cleave to him;

23 Then the LORD will destroy all these nations from before you, and you shall possess nations greater and mightier than yourselves.

24 Every place whereon the sole of your foot treads shall be yours; from the wilderness and Lebanon, from the river, the great river Euphrates, to

the uttermost sea shall your territory be.

25 There shall no man be able to stand before you; for the LORD your God shall lay the fear of you and the dread of you upon all the land that you shall tread, as he has said to you.

26 ¶Behold, I set before you this day blessings and curses;

27 Blessings, if you obey the commandments of the LORD your God which I am commanding you this day:

28 And curses, if you will not obey the commandments of the LORD your God, and if you turn aside from the way which I command you this day, to go after other gods, which you have not known.

29 And it shall come to pass, when the LORD your God has brought you into the land whither you are entering to possess it, you shall put the blessings upon mount Gerizim, and the curses upon mount Gebel.

30 Behold, they are on the other side of the Jordan, behind the way, toward the setting of the sun, in the land of the Canaanites, who dwell in the low desert over against Gilgal, towards the house of the oak of Mamre.

31 For you are to cross the Jordan to go in to possess the land which the LORD your God gives you, and you shall possess it and dwell therein.

32 And you shall observe to do all the statutes and judgments which I set before you this day.

CHAPTER 12

THESE are the statutes and judgments which you shall observe to do in the land which the LORD God of your fathers gives you to possess all the days that you live upon the earth.

2 You must destroy all the places wherein the nations whom you are to possess worshipped, and all their gods upon high mountains and upon the hills and under every green tree;

3 And you shall tear down their altars and break their statues and burn their graven images with fire; and break the graven images of their gods, and destroy the names of them out of that place.

4 You shall not do so to the LORD your God.

5 But to the place which the LORD your God shall choose out of all your tribes to put his name there, his habitation shall you seek, and thither you shall go;

6 And thither you shall bring your burnt offerings and your sacrifices and your tithes and your gift offerings of your hands and your vows and your freewill offerings and the firstlings of your herds and of your flocks;

7 And there you shall eat before the LORD your God, and you shall rejoice in all that you put your hand to, you and your households, in which the LORD your God has blessed you.

8 You shall not do according to all the things that we are doing here this day, every man whatever is right in his own eyes.

9 For you are not as yet come to the dwelling place and to the inheritance which the LORD your God gives you.

10 But when you cross the Jordan and dwell in the land which the LORD your God gives you to inherit, and when he gives you rest from all your enemies round about you, so that you shall dwell in safety;

11 Then to the place which the LORD your God shall choose to cause his name to dwell there, thither you shall bring all the things that I command you, your burnt offerings and your sacrifices, your tithes and the gift offerings of your hands and all your choice things of your vows which you vow to the LORD.

12 And you shall rejoice before the LORD your God, you and your sons and your daughters and your menservants and your maidservants and the Levites that are living within your towns; because they have no portion nor inheritance with you.

13 Take heed to yourselves that you do not offer your burnt offerings in every place that you please;

14 But in the place which the LORD shall choose in one of your tribes, there you shall offer your burnt offer-

ings, and there you shall do all that I command you.

15 Notwithstanding you may slaughter and eat meat in all your towns, whatever your soul may desire, according to the blessing of the LORD your God which he has given you; the unclean and the clean may be eaten, such as of the gazelle, and as of the hart.

16 Only you shall not eat the blood; you shall pour it out upon the earth like water.

17 ¶It is unlawful to eat within your towns the tithes of your grain, or of your wine, or of your oil, or the firstlings of your herds, or of your flock, or any of things which you vow, nor your freewill offerings, nor gift offerings of your hands;

18 But you must eat them before the LORD your God yearly at the place which the LORD your God shall choose, you and your son and your daughter and your manservant and your maidservant and the Levite that is within your towns; and you shall rejoice before the LORD your God in all that you put your hand to.

19 Take heed to yourselves that you do not forsake the Levites as long as you live upon the earth.

20 ¶When the LORD your God shall enlarge your territory, as he has promised you, and you shall say, I will eat meat, because your soul longs to eat meat; you shall eat meat, whatever your soul may desire.

21 And if the place where the LORD your God shall choose to put his name is too far from you, then you may slaughter of your herds and of your flocks, which the LORD your God has given you, as I have commanded you, and you shall eat in your towns whatever your soul may desire.

22 But as the gazelle and the hart is eaten, so you shall eat of it, the clean and the unclean, you shall eat of it alike.

23 Only be sure that you do not eat the blood; for the blood is the life; and you shall not eat the life with the flesh.

24 You shall not eat it; but you must pour it out on the earth like water.

25 You shall not eat it; that it may go well with you, and with your children after you, when you shall do that which is right in the sight of the LORD your God.

26 Only the holy things which you have, and your votive offerings you shall take and go to the place which the LORD shall choose;

27 And you shall offer your burnt offerings, the flesh and the blood, upon the altar of the LORD your God; and the blood of your sacrifices shall be poured out upon the altar of the LORD your God, and you shall eat the meat.

28 Observe and hear all these commandments which I command you this day, that it may go well with you and with your children after you for ever, when you do that which is good and right in the sight of the LORD your God.

29 ¶When the LORD your God shall destroy the nations against whom you are going, and shall cut them off from before you, and you shall possess them and dwell in their land;

30 Take heed to yourselves that you may not go astray by following them, after the LORD has destroyed them from before you; and that you do not inquire after their gods, saying, How did these nations serve their gods? Even so I may do likewise.

31 You shall not do so to the LORD your God; for every thing abominable to the LORD, which he hates, they have done to their gods; even their sons and their daughters they have burnt in the fire to their gods.

32 Everything that I command you, that you must be careful to do; you shall not add nor take from it.

CHAPTER 13

IF there arise among you a prophet, or a dreamer of dreams, and give you a sign or a wonder,

2 And the sign or the wonder of which he speaks to you come to pass, and then he shall say to you, Come, let us go after other gods, which you have not known, and let us serve them;

3 You shall not listen to the words of that prophet, or that dreamer of dreams; for the LORD your God is proving you, to know whether you love the LORD your God with all your heart and with all your soul.

4 You shall walk after the LORD your God, and reverence him and keep his commandments and obey him, and you shall serve him and cleave to him.

5 And that prophet, or that dreamer of dreams, shall be put to death; because he has spoken iniquity before the LORD your God, who brought you out of the land of Egypt and delivered you out of the house of bondage, to cause you to go astray from the way in which the LORD your God commanded you to walk. So you shall put the evil away from the midst of you.

6 ¶If your brother, the son of your mother, or your son, or your daughter, or your lawful wife, or your friend, who is as your own soul, entices you secretly, saying, Let us go and serve other gods, which you have not known, you nor your fathers;

7 Namely, of the gods of the peoples who are round about you, who are near you, or far off from you, from the one end of the earth to the other end of the earth;

8 You shall not consent to him, nor listen to him; neither shall your eye pity him, neither shall you have mercy upon him, neither shall you conceal him;

9 But you shall surely kill him; your own hand shall start first to put him to death, and afterwards the hand of all the people.

10 And you shall stone him with stones, that he die; because he has sought to cause you to go astray from the LORD your God, who brought you out of the land of Egypt, from the house of bondage.

11 And all Israel shall hear and be afraid, and shall do no more any such an evil thing as this among you.

12 ¶When you shall hear, in one of your cities which the LORD your God gives you to dwell in, one saying,

13 Certain wicked men have gone out from among you, and have led astray the inhabitants of their cities, saying, Let us go and serve other gods, whom you have not known;

14 Then you shall inquire, and make search, and ask diligently; and behold, if the thing be true, that such an abomination has been done among you;

15 You shall surely smite the inhabitants of that city with the edge of the sword, destroying it utterly, and all that is therein, and its cattle, with the edge of the sword.

16 And you shall gather all the spoil of it into the midst of an open space beyond the walls thereof, and burn the city with fire, and all its spoil every bit, before the LORD your God; and it shall be a heap for ever; it shall not be built again.

17 And there shall not cleave to your hand anything of the cursed spoil; that the LORD may turn from the fierceness of his anger and show you mercy and have compassion upon you and multiply you, as he has sworn to your fathers;

18 When you shall hearken to the voice of the LORD your God, and keep all his commandments which I command you this day, you shall do that which is right in the sight of the LORD your God.

CHAPTER 14

YOU are the children of the LORD your God; you shall not make tattooed patterns in the skin, nor any baldness between your eyes for the dead.

2 For you are a holy people to the LORD your God, and the LORD has chosen you to be a beloved people to himself, above all the peoples that are on the face of the earth.

3 ¶You shall not eat any abominable thing.

4 These are the beasts which you shall eat: the ox, the sheep, the goat,

5 The hart, the gazelle, the roebuck, the wild goat, the buffalo, the rockgoat, the mountain goat.

6 Every animal that parts the hoof and has the hoof divided into two

parts and chews the cud among the animals, that you shall eat.

7 Nevertheless you shall not eat of these that chew the cud, or of these that have the hoof divided, such as the camel, the hare, and the coney; for they chew the cud, but their hoofs are not divided; therefore they are unclean for you.

8 And the swine, because it divides the hoof, but does not chew the cud, is unclean for you; you shall not eat of their meat, nor touch their dead carcasses.

9 ¶These you shall eat of all that are in the waters: all that have fins and scales you shall eat:

10 And whatever does not have fins and scales, you shall not eat; it is unclean for you.

11 ¶Of all clean birds you shall eat.

12 But these are the ones of which you shall not eat: the eagle, the vulture, and the raven after its kind,

13 The ostrich, and the hawk after its kind,

14 The owl, the pelican, the crow,

15 The little owl, the night hawk, and the bee eater,

16 The stork, the hoopoe after its kind,

17 The desert cock, and the peacock,

18 And all the brood of these birds is unclean for you, you shall not eat them.

19 But of all clean birds you shall eat.

20 ¶You shall not eat of anything that is unclean, but you shall give it to the stranger who is in your towns, that he may eat it.

21 Or you may sell it to an alien; for you are a holy people to the LORD your God. You shall not cook a kid in its mother's milk.

22 You shall truly tithe all the increase of your seed that the field brings forth year by year.

23 And you shall eat before the LORD your God, in the place where he shall choose to set his name, the tithes of your grain, of your wine and of your oil and of the firstlings of your herds and of your flocks; that you may learn to revere the LORD your God always.

24 And if the way is too long for you, so that you are not able to carry it; because the place where the LORD your God chooses to set his name is too far from you, when the LORD your God has blessed you;

25 Then you shall turn them into money, and bind up the money in a cloth and keep it in your possession, and go to the place which the LORD your God chooses;

26 And you shall buy with that money whatever you desire, oxen or sheep or wine or strong drink or whatever you may desire; and you shall eat there before the LORD your God, and you shall rejoice, you and your household,

27 And the Levite who is within your towns; you shall not forsake him; for he has no portion nor inheritance with you.

28 ¶At the end of three years you shall bring forth all the tithes of your crops the same year, and you shall lay it up within your towns;

29 And the Levite, who has no portion nor inheritance with you, and the proselyte and the orphan and the widow who are within your towns shall come, and shall eat and be satisfied; that the LORD your God may bless you in all the work of your hand which you shall do.

CHAPTER 15

AT the end of every seven years you shall make a release.

2 And this is the manner of the release: every creditor shall release any debt which his neighbor owes him; he shall not exact it of his neighbor, or of his brother; because it is called the year of the LORD's release.

3 Of a foreigner you may exact it again; but that which you have with your brother (kindred) you shall release,

4 So that there will be no poor among you; for the LORD your God shall greatly bless you in the land which the LORD your God gives you for an inheritance to possess,

5 If you hearken to the voice of the LORD your God, to observe to do all

these commandments which I command you this day.

6 For the LORD your God shall bless you, as he promised you; and you shall lend to many nations, but you shall not borrow; and you shall rule over many nations, but they shall not rule over you.

7 ¶If there is among you a poor person of one of your brethren within any of your towns in the land which the LORD your God gives you, you shall not harden your heart, nor shut your hand from your poor brother:

8 But you shall open your hand wide to him, and shall surely lend him whatsoever he lacks.

9 Beware that there be not a wicked thought in your heart, and you say, The seventh year, the year of release, is near; and your eye be evil toward your poor brother, and you give him nothing; and he cry to the LORD against you, and it be sin to you.

10 You shall surely give to him, and your heart shall not be displeased when you give to him; because for this thing the LORD your God shall bless you in all your works and in all things that you undertake.

11 For the poor shall never cease out of the land; therefore I command you, saying, You shall open your hand wide to your poor brother and to the needy in your land.

12 ¶And if your brother, a Hebrew man or a Hebrew woman, is sold to you, and he shall serve you six years, then in the seventh year you shall let him go free from you.

13 And when you let him go free from you, you shall not let him go away empty-handed;

14 But you shall set aside and give to him out of your flocks and out of your oxen and out of your threshing floor and out of your wine press; out of everything which the LORD your God gives you, you shall give to him.

15 And you shall remember that you were a bondman in Egypt, and the LORD your God delivered you; therefore I command you this thing today.

16 But if he says to you, I will not go away from you, because I love you and your household, and because it is better for me to be with you,

17 Then you must take an awl, and thrust it through his ear to the door, and he shall be your servant for ever. You shall do likewise to your maidservant.

18 You shall not show displeasure when you let him go free from you; for he has served you double according to the wages of a hired servant, in serving you six years; and the LORD your God shall bless you in all that you do.

19 ¶All the firstling males that are born of your herds and of your flock you shall sanctify to the LORD your God; you shall do no work with the firstlings of your oxen, nor shear the firstlings of your sheep.

20 You shall eat a firstling before the LORD your God year by year in the place which the LORD shall choose, you and your household;

21 And if there is any blemish in it, or it is lame or blind, or have any ill blemish, you shall not sacrifice it to the LORD your God.

22 But you shall eat it within your towns; the unclean and the clean shall eat of it alike, as a gazelle, and as the hart.

23 Only you shall not eat the blood; but you must pour it out on the ground like water.

CHAPTER 16

OBSERVE the month of Abib[1] and keep the passover to the LORD your God; because in the month of Abib the LORD your God brought you out of Egypt by night.

2 You shall therefore sacrifice the passover to the LORD, of the flock and the herd, at the place where the LORD your God shall choose to set his name.

3 You shall eat no leavened bread with it; but seven days you shall eat unleavened bread with it, even the bread of affliction; for you came forth out of Egypt in haste; that you may remember the day when you came forth out of Egypt all the days of your life.

4 And there shall no leavened bread

[1] Aramaic *Hababey* (blossoms, that is, April).

be seen with you in all your territory for seven days; neither shall there anything of the meat, which you sacrifice on the evening of the first day, remain all night until the morning.

5 It is unlawful for you to sacrifice the passover within any of your towns which the LORD your God gives you:

6 But at the place where the LORD your God shall choose to set his name, there you shall sacrifice the passover in the evening at the going down of the sun, at the time that you came out of Egypt.

7 And you shall cook it and eat it in the place which the LORD your God shall choose; and you shall turn in the morning and go to your tents.

8 For six days you shall eat unleavened bread; and on the seventh day there shall be a solemn assembly to the LORD your God; you shall do no work therein.

9 ¶You shall count seven weeks to yourselves; begin to count the seven weeks from the time you begin to put the sickle to the standing grain.

10 And then you shall keep the feast of weeks to the LORD your God with sufficient of freewill offering of your hand, which you shall set aside as the LORD your God has blessed you;

11 And you shall rejoice before the LORD your God, you and your son and your daughter and your manservant and your maidservant and the Levite who is within your towns and the sojourner and the fatherless and the widow who is among you, at the place where the LORD your God has chosen to place his name.

12 And you must remember that you were a bondman in Egypt; so you shall observe and do these statutes.

13 ¶You shall observe the feast of tabernacles seven days, after you have gathered in from your threshing floor and from your wine press;

14 And you shall rejoice in your feast, you and your son and your daughter and your manservant and your maidservant and the Levite, the sojourner, the orphan, and the widow who is within your towns.

15 For seven days you shall keep a solemn feast to the LORD your God in the place which the Lord chooses; because the LORD your God shall bless you in all your increase and in all the works of your hand, and you shall rejoice.

16 ¶Three times in a year shall all your memorial gifts be brought before the LORD your God in the place which he shall choose; in the feast of unleavened bread, and in the feast of weeks, and in the feast of the tabernacles; and you shall not appear before the LORD your God emptyhanded;

17 But every man shall give as he is able, according to the blessing of the LORD your God which he has given you.

18 ¶You shall appoint to yourselves judges and scribes in all your cities, which the LORD your God gives you, throughout your tribes; and they shall judge the people with just judgment.

19 You shall not pervert judgment; you shall not be partial, neither take a bribe; for a bribe blinds the eyes of the wise men in judgment, and perverts the cause of the innocent.

20 But you must judge your neighbor righteously, that you may live and go in and inherit the land which the LORD your God gives you.

21 ¶You shall not plant for yourselves a grove of any trees near the altar of the LORD your God, which you shall make for yourselves.

22 Neither shall you set up for yourselves any statue, which the LORD your God hates.

CHAPTER 17

YOU shall not sacrifice to the LORD your God an ox or a lamb wherein is blemish, or anything impious; for that is an abomination in the sight of the LORD your God.

2 ¶If there is found among you, within any of your towns which the LORD your God gives you, a man or a woman who shall do evil in the sight of the LORD your God and transgress his covenant,

3 And shall go and serve other gods and worship them, either the sun, or the moon, or any of the host of

heaven, which I have not commanded;
4 And it is told you, and you shall hear of it, you shall inquire diligently, and if it is true that such an abomination has been committed in Israel;
5 Then you shall bring forth that man or that woman who has committed that wicked thing within your towns, whether he is a man or a woman; and you shall stone him with stones, till he die.
6 On the testimony of two witnesses or three witnesses shall he that is worthy of death be put to death; but on the testimony of one witness he shall not be put to death.
7 And the hand of the witnesses shall be the first against him to put him to death, and afterward the hands of all the people. So you shall destroy the evildoers from among you.
8 ¶If there arise a matter which is too difficult for you to judge, between murder and murder, between lawsuit and lawsuit, and between a sore of leprosy and a sore of leprosy, any matters of controversy within your towns; then you shall arise and go to the place which the LORD your God shall choose for himself;
9 And you shall come to the priest, or the Levite, or to the judge who shall be in those days, and inquire; and they shall show you the sentence of judgment;
10 And you shall do according to the decision which they of that place shall show you, as the LORD has commanded; and you shall observe to do according to all that they teach you;
11 According to the sentence of the law which they shall declare to you, and according to the judgment which they shall tell you, you shall do; you shall not swerve from the sentence which they shall show you, neither to the right hand nor to the left.
12 And the man who will do presumptuously, and will not hearken to the priest who stands to minister there before the LORD your God, or to the judge, that man shall be put to death; you shall destroy the evildoers from Israel.
13 And all the people shall hear, and fear, and do no more presumptuously.
14 ¶When you shall come to the land which the LORD your God gives you, and you shall possess it and dwell therein, and shall say, I will set a king over me, like as all the nations that are about me;
15 You shall in any wise set a king over you whom the LORD your God shall choose; one from among your brethren you shall set king over you; it is unlawful for you to set a foreigner over you, who is not from among your brethren.
16 But he shall not multiply horses to himself, that he may not cause the people to return to Egypt, when his horses have multiplied; since the LORD has said to you, You shall never return that way again.
17 Neither shall he multiply wives to himself, that they may not cause his heart to turn away; neither shall he greatly multiply to himself silver and gold.
18 And when he sits upon the throne of his kingdom, he shall write for himself a copy of this law in a book out of that which is before the priests and the Levites;
19 And it shall be with him, and he shall read therein all the days of his life; that he may learn to fear the LORD his God, to keep all the words of this law, and these commandments, to do them;
20 That his heart may not be lifted up above his brethren, and that he may not turn aside from the commandments, neither to the right hand nor to the left; so that he may prolong his days in his kingdom, he and his children, in the midst of Israel.

CHAPTER 18

THE priests and the Levites, shall have neither portion nor inheritance among the children of Israel; but they shall eat sacrifices offered to the LORD, and his inheritance.
2 Therefore they shall have no inheritance among their brethren; the LORD is their inheritance, as he has said to them.
3 ¶And this shall be the priest's due from the people: from those who offer

a sacrifice, whether it be an ox or a lamb, they shall give to the priest the shoulder and the two cheeks and the maw.

4 The first fruits also of your grain, of your wine, and of your oil, and the first of the fleece of your sheep, you shall give him.

5 For the LORD your God has chosen him out of all your tribes, to stand to minister in the name of the LORD your God, him and his sons for ever.

6 ¶And if a Levite come from any of the towns of your brethren out of all Israel, where he sojourned, and come with all the desire of his soul to the place which the LORD shall choose;

7 Then he shall minister in the name of the LORD his God, as do all his brethren the Levites, who stand there before the LORD.

8 They shall have equal portion to eat, besides that which comes of the sale of his patrimony.

9 ¶When you come into the land which the LORD your God gives you, you shall not learn to do after the abominations of those nations.

10 There shall not be found among you any one who makes his son or his daughter pass through the fire, or who practices divination or black magic, or is an enchanter or a witch

11 Or a charmer or a consulter with familiar spirits or a sorcerer or a necromancer.

12 For whoever does these things is an abomination in the sight of the LORD your God; and because of these abominations the LORD your God is destroying them from before you.

13 You shall be innocent before the LORD your God.

14 For these nations which you are to possess hearken to men with familiar spirits and diviners; but as for you, the LORD your God has not allowed you to do so.

15 ¶The LORD your God will raise up to you a prophet like me from the midst of you, of your brethren; to him you shall hearken.

16 Just as you asked of the LORD your God at Horeb on the day of the assembly, saying, Let me not hear any more the voice of the LORD my God, neither let me see this great fire any more, that I die not.

17 And the LORD said to me, They have well spoken that which they have spoken.

18 I will raise up for them a prophet like you from among their brethren, and will put my words in his mouth; and he shall speak to them all that I shall command him.

19 Whosoever will not hearken to my words which he shall speak in my name, I will require it of him.

20 But the prophet who shall presume to speak a word in my name which I have not commanded him to speak, or who shall speak in the name of other gods, that prophet shall be put to death.

21 And if you say in your heart, How shall we know the word which the LORD has not spoken?

22 When a prophet speaks in the name of the LORD, and the thing does not come to pass, nor follow; that is the thing which the LORD has not spoken, but the prophet has spoken it presumptuously; you shall not be afraid of him.

CHAPTER 19

WHEN the LORD your God has destroyed the nations whose land the LORD your God gives you, and you shall possess them and dwell in their cities, and in their houses;

2 You shall set apart for you three cities in the midst of your land which the LORD your God gives you as an inheritance.

3 You shall prepare for you a highway, and divide into three parts the land which the LORD your God gives you to inherit, that any slayer may flee thither.

4 ¶And this is the law in the case of the slayer who kills his neighbor and flees there that he may live, whosoever kills his neighbor unintentionally, whom he hated not in time past;

5 And when a man goes into the forest with his neighbor to cut wood, and as he lifts up his hand with the axe to cut down a tree, the iron head slips from the helve and strikes his

neighbor so that he dies; he shall flee to one of these cities, and live;

6 Lest the avenger of the blood pursue the slayer, while his anger is hot, and overtake him, because the way is long, and slay him; though he was not worthy of death, because he hated him not in time past.

7 Therefore I command you, saying, You shall set apart three cities for you.

8 And when the LORD your God shall enlarge your territory, as he has sworn to your fathers, and gives you all the land which he promised to give to your fathers;

9 If you shall keep all these commandments to do them, which I command you this day, to love the LORD your God, and to walk in his ways always; then you shall add three cities more for you besides these three;

10 That innocent blood may not be shed in the land which the LORD your God gives you, and that the guilt of innocent blood not be upon you.

11 ¶But if any man hate his neighbor, and lie in wait for him, and attack him, and smite him mortally so that he dies, and he flees to one of these cities;

12 Then the elders of his city shall send and fetch him from there, and deliver him into the hand of the avenger of blood, and he shall slay him.

13 Your eyes shall not pity him, but you shall kill him, and thus purge the guilt of innocent blood from Israel, that it may go well with you.

14 ¶You shall not remove your neighbor's landmark, which they of old time have set in your inheritance, which you shall inherit in the land that the LORD your God gives you to possess.

15 ¶A single witness shall not rise up against a man for any offense, or for any crime, in whatever offense or crime he may commit; on the testimony of two witnesses, or on the testimony of three witnesses, shall a charge be established.

16 ¶If a false witness rise up against any man, and testify against him that which is wrong;

17 Then both the men between whom the controversy is, shall stand before the LORD, before the priests and the judges who shall be in those days;

18 And the judges shall investigate the case diligently; and, behold, if the witness has deliberately testified falsely against his brother;

19 Then you shall do to him as he had thought to do to his brother; so shall you put the evil away from among you.

20 And those who remain shall hear, and fear, and shall never again commit any such an evil thing among you.

21 And your eye shall not pity; but life shall be for life, eye for eye, tooth for tooth, hand for hand, foot for foot.

CHAPTER 20

WHEN you go out to battle against your enemies, and see horses and chariots and a people more than you, you shall not be afraid of them; for the LORD your God is with you, who brought you up out of the land of Egypt.

2 And when you come near to the battle, the priest shall appproach and speak to the people,

3 And shall say to them, Hear, O Israel, you approach this day to the battle with your enemies; let not your heart faint, fear not, and do not tremble, neither be terrified because of them;

4 For the LORD your God is he that goes with you, who brought you out of the land of Egypt, and it is he who shall fight for you with your enemies, and he shall save you.

5 ¶Then the scribes shall speak to the people, saying, What man is there who has built a new house, and has not dedicated it? Let him return and go to his house, lest he die in the battle, and another man dedicate it.

6 And what man is there who has planted a vineyard, and has not yet trod the grapes of it? Let him return and go to his house, lest he die in the battle, and another man tread its grapes.

7 And what man is there who has

betrothed a wife, and has not taken her? Let him return and go to his house, lest he die in the battle, and another man take her.

8 And the scribes shall speak further to the people, and they shall say, What man is there who is fearful and fainthearted? Let him return and go to his house, lest his brethren's heart faint as well as his heart.

9 And when the scribes have made an end of speaking to the people, the commanders of the army shall stand at the head of the people.

10 ¶When you come near to a city to fight against it, then proclaim peace to it.

11 And if the city give you answer of peace, and it open to you, then all the people who are found in it shall be servants and tributaries to you, and they shall serve you.

12 But if it will not surrender to you, but will make war with you, then you shall besiege it;

13 And when the LORD your God has delivered it into your hands, you shall slay all its males with the edge of the sword;

14 But the women and the little ones and the cattle and all that is in the city, even all its spoil, you shall plunder for yourselves; and you shall eat of the spoil of your enemies, which the LORD your God gives you.

15 Thus shall you do to all the cities which are very far off from you, which are not of the cities of these nations.

16 But of the cities of these people which the LORD your God gives you for an inheritance, you shall save alive nothing that breathes;

17 But you shall utterly destroy them; namely, the Hittites, and the Amorites, the Canaanites, and the Perizzites, the Hivites, and the Jebusites; as the LORD your God has commanded you;

18 That they may not teach you to do after all their abominations, which they have done in worshipping their gods; so you should sin in the sight of the LORD your God.

19 ¶When you shall besiege a city a long time, in making war against it to capture it, you shall not destroy

its trees, nor wield an axe against them; because you may eat of them, and you shall not cut them down (for the trees of the field are not like men to flee from before you at the time of the siege).

20 Only the trees which you know are not trees for food you may destroy and cut down that you may build bulwarks against the city that makes war with you, until it is captured.

CHAPTER 21

IF a person is found slain in the land which the LORD your God gives you to possess, lying in the field, and it is not known who has slain him;

2 Then your elders and your judges shall come forth, and they shall measure the distance to the cities which are round about him that is slain;

3 And the elders of the city which is nearest to the slain man shall take a heifer which has never been used for work nor has pulled in the yoke,

4 And the elders of that city shall bring down the heifer to a barren valley which has never been ploughed nor sown, and shall slaughter the heifer there in the valley;

5 And the priests the sons of Levi shall come near, for them the LORD your God has chosen to minister to him, and to bless in the name of the LORD; and by their word shall every lawsuit and every attack be tried;

6 And all the elders of that city which is nearest to the slain man shall wash their hands over the heifer which is slaughtered in the valley;

7 And they shall answer and say, Our hands have not shed this blood, neither have our eyes seen the victim.

8 Pardon, O LORD, thy people Israel, whom thou hast saved, and lay not innocent blood upon thy people Israel. And the guilt of blood shall be forgiven them.

9 So shall you put away the guilt of innocent blood from among you, when you shall do that which is right in the sight of the LORD.

10 ¶When you go forth to war against your enemies, and the LORD

your God delivers them into your hands, and you take them captive,

11 And see among the captives a beautiful woman, and you desire her, and would have her for yourself as a wife;

12 Then you shall bring her home to your house; and she shall shave her head and pare her nails;

13 And she shall put off the clothes of her captivity and shall remain in your house, and mourn for her father and her mother a full month; and after that you shall go in unto her, and be her husband, and she shall be your wife.

14 And it shall be, if you have no delight in her, then you shall let her go where she will; but you shall not sell her at all for money; you shall not make a harlot of her, for sake of a gain, because you have humbled her.

15 ¶If a man has two wives, one beloved and the other hated, and they have borne him children, both the beloved and the hated; and if the first-born son be hers that is hated;

16 Then it shall be, when he makes his sons to inherit his property, it is unlawful for him to make the son of the beloved wife first-born before the son of the hated;

17 But the first-born, the son of the hated, he must receive double portion of all that he has; for he is the first of his children; and the right of the first-born is his.

18 ¶If a man has a stubborn and rebellious son, who will not obey the voice of his father or the voice of his mother, and who, when they have chastised him, will not hearken to them;

19 Then his father and his mother shall lay hold on him, and bring him out to the elders of the city, at the gate of his place;

20 And they shall say to the elders of his city, This our son is stubborn and rebellious, he does not obey our voice; he is a glutton and a drunkard.

21 Then all the men of his city shall stone him with stones, that he die; so shall you put evil away fom among you; and all Israel shall hear, and fear.

22 ¶And if any man has committed a sin worthy of death, and he is crucified on a tree, and thus put to death;

23 His body shall not remain all night upon the tree, but you shall bury him the same day (for he who shall revile God shall be crucified), and you shall not defile your land, which the LORD your God gives you for an inheritance.

CHAPTER 22

YOU shall not see your brother's ox or his sheep go astray, and disregard them; but you shall surely bring them back to your brother.

2 And if your brother is not near you, or if you do not know him, then you shall bring it to your own house, and it shall be with you until your brother seeks after it, and you shall restore it to him again.

3 In like manner shall you do with his ox and with his ass, and so with his garment; and so shall you do with anything which your brother has lost, and you have found; it is unlawful for you to delay in restoring it.

4 ¶You shall not see your enemy's ass or his ox fallen down by the way, and turn away your eyes from them; but you shall surely help him to lift them up again.

5 ¶A woman shall not wear any garment that pertains to a man, neither shall a man put on a woman's garments; for whosoever does these things is an abomination in the sight of the LORD your God.

6 ¶When you chance to find a bird's nest before you in the way in any tree, or on the ground, with young ones or eggs and the mother sitting upon the young or upon the eggs, you shall not take the mother with her young;

7 But you shall surely let the mother go, and take the young for yourself; that it may be well with you, and that you may live long.

8 ¶When you build a new house, you must make a parapet for your roof, that no man may fall from it, and bring blood upon your house.

9 ¶You shall not sow your furrow

with mixed seeds, lest the produce of the seed which you have sown and the produce of your vineyard be seized for the sanctuary.

10 ¶You shall not plow with an ox and an ass together.

11 ¶You shall not wear a garment woven of different sorts of wool and cotton together.

12 ¶You shall make for yourself fringes on the four corners of your cloak, with which you cover yourself.

13 ¶If any man take a wife, and go in unto her, and then hate her,

14 And give an occasion of speech against her, charging her with adultery, and bring an evil name upon her, and say, I took this woman, and when I lay with her, I found her not a virgin;

15 Then shall the father of the damsel, and her mother, take and bring forth the tokens of the damsel's virginity to the elders of the city at the gate;

16 And the damsel's father shall say to the elders, I gave my daughter to this man to wife, and he hates her;

17 And, lo, he has given occasion of speech against her, charging her with whoredom, saying, I found not your daughter a virgin; and yet these are the tokens of my daughter's virginity. And they shall spread the cloth before the elders of the city.

18 And the elders of that city shall take that man and chastise him;

19 And they shall fine him a hundred shekels of silver, and give it to the father of the damsel, because he has brought an evil name upon a virgin daughter of Israel; and she shall be his wife; he has no right to put her away all his days.

20 But if this thing is true, and the tokens of virginity are not found for the damsel;

21 Then they shall bring out the damsel to the door of her father's house, and the men of the city shall stone her with stones that she die; because she has committed a shameful act in Israel, to play the whore in her father's house; so you shall put away evil from among you.

22 ¶If a man is found lying with another man's wife, then both of them shall surely die, the man who lay with the woman, and the woman; so shall you put away evil from Israel.

23 ¶If there is a damsel who is a virgin and who is betrothed to a man, and another man find her in the city and lie with her;

24 Then you shall bring them both out to the gate of that city, and you shall stone them with stones, that they die; the damsel, because she did not cry for help, being in the city; and the man, because he has treated shamefully his neighbor's wife; so shall you put away evil from among you.

25 ¶But if a man find a betrothed damsel in the field, and seize her by force, and lie with her; then the man only who lay with her shall die:

26 But to the damsel you shall do nothing; because there is in the damsel no sin worthy of death; for as when a man rises against his neighbor and slays him, even so is this case.

27 For he found her in the field, and the betrothed damsel cried for help, and there was no one to save her.

28 ¶If a man finds a damsel who is a virgin who is not betrothed, and seizes her, and lies with her, and they are found;

29 Then the man who lay with her shall give to the damsel's father fifty shekels of silver, and she shall be his wife; because he has humbled her, he has no right to put her away all his days.

30 ¶A man shall not take his father's wife, nor uncover the skirt of his father's wife.

CHAPTER 23

NO adulterer shall enter into the assembly of the LORD.

2 Neither shall a bastard enter into the assembly of the LORD; even to the tenth generation, his descendants shall not enter into the assembly of the LORD.

3 An Ammonite or Moabite shall not enter into the congregation of the LORD; even to the tenth generation, his descendants shall not enter into

the assembly of the LORD for ever;

4 Because they did not meet you with bread and with water on the way, when you came forth out of Egypt; and because they hired against you Balaam the son of Beor from Pethor of Aram-nahrin (Mesopotamia) to curse you.

5 Nevertheless the LORD your God would not hearken to Balaam; but the LORD your God turned his curses into blessings to you, because the LORD your God loved you.

6 You shall not seek their peace nor their prosperity all the days of your life for ever.

7 ¶You shall not drive away an Edomite, for he is your brother; you shall not drive away an Egyptian, because you were a sojourner in his land.

8 The children that are born to them shall enter into the assembly of the LORD in their third generation.

9 ¶When you go forth into the camp against your enemies, you shall beware of every wicked thing.

10 ¶If there is among you any man who is not clean by reason of an emission at night, then he shall go outside the camp, he shall not come within the camp;

11 But when the evening comes on, he shall bathe himself with water; and when the sun is down, he shall come into the camp again.

12 ¶You shall have a latrine outside the camp, to which you shall go to relieve yourself.

13 And you shall have a peg upon your weapon; and it shall be, when you relieve yourself, you shall dig with it, and then you shall cover your dung;

14 For the LORD your God walks in the midst of your camp, to deliver you and to subdue your enemies before you; therefore shall your camp be holy, that he may not see anything unclean in your camp, and turn away from you.

15 ¶You shall not deliver to his master a servant who has escaped from his master to you;

16 But he shall dwell with you in the place which he shall choose in one of your towns, where it pleases him best; you shall not oppress him.

17 ¶There shall be no whore of the daughters of Israel, also there shall be no sodomite of the sons of Israel.

18 You shall not bring the hire of a whore or the price of a dog into the house of the LORD your God for any vow; for both of these are an abomination before the LORD your God.

19 ¶You shall not lend with interest to your brother: interest of money, interest of grain, and the interest of anything that is lent with interest;

20 To a foreigner you may lend with interest; but to your brother you shall not lend with interest, that the LORD your God may bless you in all that you set your hand to in the land which you shall go in to possess.

21 ¶When you shall vow a vow to the LORD your God, you shall not be slack to pay it; for the LORD your God will surely require it of you; and it would be a sin in you.

22 But if you are unwilling to make a vow, then it shall be no sin in you.

23 That which is gone out of your lips you shall keep and perform; just as you have vowed a freewill offering to the LORD your God, which you have promised with your mouth.

24 ¶When you come into your neighbor's vineyard, then you may eat grapes, your fill at your own pleasure; but you shall not put any into your vessel.

25 When you come into the standing wheat of your neighbor, you may pluck the ears with your hand; but you shall not put a sickle to your neighbor's standing grain.

CHAPTER 24

IF a man takes a wife, and lies with her, and if she finds no favor in his eyes, because he has found some evidence of open prostitution in her; then let him write her a bill of divorcement, and give it to her, and send her out of his house.

2 And when she has left his house, and if she goes and becomes another man's wife,

3 And if that husband hates her,

and writes her a bill of divorcement, and gives it to her, and sends her out of his house, or if that husband who took her to be his wife dies;

4 Then her former husband, who sent her away, has no right to take her again to be his wife, after she has been defiled; for that is an abomination before the LORD; and you shall not cause the land to sin, which the LORD your God gives you for an inheritance.

5 ¶When a man takes a new wife, he shall not go out with the army, neither shall he be charged with any business; but he shall be free at his home for one year, and shall rejoice with his wife whom he has taken.

6 ¶No man shall take the nether or the upper millstone as a pledge; for he takes a man's life to pledge.

7 ¶If a man of the children of Israel is found stealing any of his brethren of the children of Israel, to make merchandise of him, or sell him; then that thief shall surely die; and you shall put evil away from among you.

8 ¶Take heed in the plague of leprosy, and be exceedingly careful, and do according to all that the priests and the Levites shall teach you; as I commanded them, so you shall be careful to do.

9 Remember what the LORD your God did to Miriam on the way, after you came forth out of Egypt.

10 If your neighbor owes you a debt, you shall not go into his house to fetch his pledge.

11 But you shall wait in the street, and the man who is your debtor shall bring out the pledge to you.

12 And if the man is poor, you shall not sleep with his mantle.[1]

13 But you shall return to him his mantle again when the sun goes down, that he may sleep in his own mantle, and bless you; and it shall be righteousness to you before the LORD your God.

14 ¶You shall not cheat the wages of a hired laborer who is poor and needy, whether he is of your brethren or of the strangers who are in your cities;

15 But you shall pay him his wages on the same day, neither shall the sun go down upon it; for he is poor, and it is because of his wages that he places himself at your disposal; lest he cry against you to the LORD, and it be sin against you.

16 The fathers shall not be put to death for their children, neither shall the children be put to death for their fathers; but every man shall be put to death for his own sin.

17 ¶You shall not pervert the justice due to the stranger, nor to the orphan; nor take a widow's garment as a pledge;

18 But you shall remember that you were a bondman in Egypt, and the LORD your God delivered you from there; therefore I command you to do this thing:

19 ¶When you reap the harvest in your field, and have forgotten a sheaf in the field, you shall not return to fetch it; it shall be for the stranger, for the fatherless, and for the widow, that the LORD your God may bless you in all the works of your hands.

20 When you beat your olive trees, you shall not go over the boughs again; it shall be for the stranger, for the orphan, and for the widow.

21 When you gather the grapes of your vineyard, you shall not glean it afterward; it shall be for the stranger, for the fatherless, and for the widow.

22 And you shall remember that you were a bondman in Egypt; therefore I command you to do this thing.

CHAPTER 25

IF there is a lawsuit between a man and his neighbor, they shall come before the judges, and the judges shall judge them; and they shall acquit the innocent, and condemn the guilty.

2 And it shall be, if the guilty man deserves punishment, the judge shall cause him to lie down, and have him flogged in his presence, according to

[1] In the East clothing and other garments are taken as a pledge, especially in places where poverty prevails and money is scarce.

his offense, with a certain number of stripes.

3 Forty stripes he may give him, but not more; lest, if he should exceed, and scourge him above this number of stripes, then your brother would be hurt severely before your eyes.

4 ¶You shall not muzzle an ox when it treads out the grain.

5 ¶When brothers dwell together, and one of them dies, and has no son, the wife of the dead shall not marry to a stranger; but her husband's brother shall take her, and she shall become his wife, and he shall perform the duty of a brother-in-law to her.

6 And it shall be, that the first-born which she bears shall be named after the name of his brother who is dead, that his name may not be forgotten in Israel.

7 And if the man refuses to take his brother's wife, then let his brother's wife go up to the gate to the elders, and say, My brother-in-law refuses to raise up to his brother a name in Israel, and is unwilling to take me as a wife.

8 Then the elders of his city shall call him, and speak to him; and if he should rise up and say, I will not take her;

9 Then his sister-in-law shall come to him in the presence of the elders, and loose his shoe from off his foot, and spit in his face, and say, So shall it be done to the man who will not raise a family to his brother.

10 And his name shall be called in Israel, the house of him that has his shoe loosed.

11 ¶When two brothers are fighting, and the wife of one draws near to deliver her husband out of the hands of his adversary, and puts forth her hand, and seizes him by the private parts;

12 Then you shall cut off her hand; your eye shall not pity her.

13 ¶You shall not have in your bag different weights, a large and a small.

14 You shall not have in your house different measures, a large and a small.

15 But you shall have a perfect and just weight; a perfect and a just measure shall you have, that your days may be prolonged in the land which the LORD your God gives you.

16 For all who do such things and all who act wickedly are an abomination before the LORD your God.

17 ¶Remember all that Amalek did to you by the way, when you came forth out of Egypt;

18 How he met you with the sword, and smote all of those who were left behind you, when you were faint and weary, and he feared not the LORD your God.

19 Therefore when the LORD your God has given you rest from all your enemies round about, in the land which the LORD your God gives you as an inheritance, you shall blot out the remembrance of Amalek from under heaven; you shall not forget it.

CHAPTER 26

AND when you come into the land which the LORD your God gives you as an inheritance, and possess it, and dwell in it;

2 You shall take some of the first of all the fruit of the land, which you shall bring in from the land which the LORD your God gives you, and shall put it in a basket, and you shall arise and go to the place where the LORD your God chooses to place his name.

3 And you shall go to the priest who shall be in those days, and say to him, I profess this day to the LORD your God that I have come into the land which the LORD swore to our fathers to give us.

4 And the priest shall take the basket from your hand, and set it down before the LORD your God.

5 And you shall speak and say before the LORD your God, My father was led to Aram and he went down into Egypt, and sojourned there for a short time, and there he became a nation, great, mighty, and populous;

6 And the Egyptians mistreated us and afflicted us and laid upon us hard work;

7 And when we cried to the LORD

God of our fathers, the LORD heard our voice and saw our affliction, our labor, and our oppression;

8 And the LORD brought us forth out of Egypt with a mighty hand and with an outstretched arm and with a great revelation and with signs and with wonders;

9 And we came to this place, and the LORD has given us this land, a land flowing with milk and honey.

10 And now, behold, I have brought the firstfruits of the land, which thou, O LORD, hast given me; and you shall set it down before the LORD your God, and worship there before the LORD your God;

11 And you shall rejoice in every good thing which the LORD your God has given to you and to your house, you and the Levite and the sojourner that is among you.

12 ¶When you have finished tithing all the tithes of your produce in the third year, which is the year of tithing, then you shall give to the Levite, the sojourner, the fatherless, and the widow, that they may eat within your towns and be filled;

13 Then you shall say before the LORD your God, I have brought all the hallowed things out of my house, and also have given them to the Levite, to the sojourner, to the fatherless, and to the widow, according to all thy commandments which thou hast commanded me; I have not transgressed thy commandments, neither have I forgotten them;

14 I have not eaten of them in my mourning, neither have I touched them while I was unclean, nor used any of them for funerals;[1] but I have hearkened to the voice of the LORD my God, and have done according to all that thou hast commanded me.

15 Look down from thy holy habitation, from heaven, and bless thy people Israel and the land which thou hast given us, as thou didst swear to our fathers, a land that flows with milk and honey.

16 ¶This day the LORD your God has commanded you to do these statutes and judgments; you shall therefore keep and do them with all your heart and with all your soul.

17 You have confessed the LORD this day to be your God, and promised to walk in his ways and to keep his statutes and his judgments and his commandments, and to hearken to his voice;

18 And the LORD has promised you again this day to be his beloved people, as he had promised you, that you shall keep and do all his commandments;

19 And that he shall exalt you above all nations which he has made, in praise, in name, and in honor; and that you may be a holy people to the LORD your God, as he has spoken.

CHAPTER 27

AND Moses and the elders of Israel commanded the people, saying, Keep all the commandments which I command you this day.

2 And it shall be on the day that you cross the Jordan into the land which the LORD your God gives you, you shall set up large stones, and cover them with plaster;

3 And you shall write upon them all the words of this law, when you have crossed the Jordan, that you may go into the land which the LORD your God gives you, a land flowing with milk and honey, as the LORD God of your fathers has promised you.

4 Therefore when you have crossed the Jordan, you shall set up these stones, which I command you this day, on mount Gebel,[2] and you shall cover them with plaster.

5 And there you shall build an altar to the LORD your God, an altar of stones; you shall not lift up any iron tool upon them.

6 You shall build the altar of the LORD your God of undressed stones, and you shall offer burnt offerings on it to the LORD your God:

7 And you shall offer peace offerings, and shall eat there and rejoice before the LORD your God.

[1] In the East the nearest relatives of the dead, after the burial, feed the mourners and the poor.
[2] Other versions, *Ebal.*

8 And you shall write upon the stones all the words of this law very plainly.

9 ¶And Moses and the priests and the Levites said to all Israel, Give ear and hearken, O Israel; this day you have become the people of the Lord your God.

10 You shall therefore obey the voice of the Lord your God, and do his commandments and his statutes which I command you this day.

11 ¶And Moses charged the people that same day, saying,

12 These tribes shall stand upon mount Gerizim to bless the people when you have crossed the Jordan: Simeon, Levi, Judah, Issachar, Joseph and Benjamin;

13 And these tribes shall stand upon Gebel to curse: Reuben, Gad, Asher, Zebulun, Dan, and Naphtali.

14 ¶And the Levites shall speak and say to all the people of Israel with a loud voice,

15 Cursed be the man who makes any graven or molten images, for they are an abomination before the Lord, the work of the hands of the craftsman, and puts them in a secret place. And all the people shall answer and say, Amen.

16 Cursed be he who reviles his father or his mother. And all the people shall say, Amen.

17 Cursed be he who removes his neighbor's landmark. And all the people shall say, Amen.

18 Cursed be he who causes a blind man to wander out of the way. And all the people shall say, Amen.

19 Cursed be he who perverts the judgment of the stranger, the fatherless, and the widow. And all the people shall say, Amen.

20 Cursed be he who lies with his father's wife; and thus uncovers his father's skirt. And all the people shall say, Amen.

21 Cursed be he who lies with any kind of beast. And all the people shall say, Amen.

22 Cursed be he who lies with his sister, the daughter of his father, or the daughter of his mother. And all the people shall say, Amen.

23 Cursed be he who lies with his mother-in-law. And all the people shall say, Amen.

24 Cursed be he who smites his neighbor secretly. And all the people shall say, Amen.

25 Cursed be he who takes a bribe to slay an innocent person. And all the people shall say, Amen.

26 Cursed be he who does not confirm all the words of this law to do them. And all the people shall say, Amen.

CHAPTER 28

AND if you shall hearken diligently to the voice of the Lord your God, to observe and to do all his commandments which I command you this day, the Lord your God will set you on high above all the nations of the earth;

2 And all these blessings shall come on you, and overtake you, if you shall hearken to the voice of the Lord your God.

3 Blessed shall you be in the city, and blessed shall you be in the field.

4 Blessed shall be the fruit of your body and the fruit of your ground, the bearing of your cattle, the increase of your herds, and the flocks of your sheep.

5 Blessed shall be your breadbasket and your dough.

6 Blessed shall you be when you come in, and blessed shall you be when you go out.

7 The Lord shall cause your enemies who rise up against you to surrender defeated before you; they shall come out against you by one way, and flee before you by seven ways.

8 The Lord shall command blessings upon you in your storehouses, and in all that you put your hand to; and he shall bless you in the land which the Lord your God gives you.

9 The Lord shall establish you a holy people to himself, as he has sworn to you, if you shall keep all the commandments of the Lord your God and walk in his ways.

10 And all the people of the earth shall see that you are called by the

name of the LORD, and they shall be afraid of you.

11 And the LORD shall enrich you in good things, in the fruit of your body and in the bearing of your cattle and in the fruit of your ground, in the land which the LORD swore to your fathers to give you.

12 The LORD shall open to you his good storehouse, the heaven, to give you rain to your land in its season; and he will bless all the works of your hands; and you shall lend to many nations, but you shall not borrow; and you shall rule over many nations, but they shall not rule over you.

13 And the LORD shall make you the head, and not the tail; [1] and you shall be on top only, and you shall not be beneath; if you will hearken to the commandments of the LORD your God which I command you this day, to observe and to do them.

14 And you shall not turn aside from any of the commandments which I command you this day, to the right hand, or to the left, and you shall not go after the Gentile gods, nor serve them.

15 ¶But if you will not hearken to the voice of the LORD your God, and do not observe and do all his commandments and his statutes which I command you this day, then all these curses shall come upon you and overtake you.

16 Cursed shall you be in the city, and cursed shall you be in the field.

17 Cursed shall be your breadbasket and your dough.

18 Cursed shall be the fruit of your body and the fruit of your land, the herds of your oxen and the flocks of your sheep.

19 Cursed shall you be when you come in, and cursed shall you be when you go out.

20 The LORD shall send upon you ruin, confusion, and rebuke in all that you set your hand to do, until you are destroyed, and until you perish quickly; because of your evil doings, because you have forsaken me.

21 The LORD shall send pestilence upon you, until he has consumed you from off the land which you are entering to possess.

22 The LORD shall afflict you with confusion and with skin disease and with an inflammation and with burning fever and with the sword and with blasting and with mildew; and they shall pursue you until you perish.

23 And the heaven that is over your head shall be brass, and the earth that is under you shall be iron.

24 The LORD shall make the rain of your land powder and dust; from heaven shall they come down upon you, until you are destroyed.

25 The LORD shall cause you to be routed before your enemies; you shall go out one way against them, but you shall flee seven ways before them; and you shall be a horror to all the kingdoms of the earth.

26 And your carcass shall be food for the fowls of the air and the beasts of the earth, and there shall be no one to drive them off.

27 The LORD will smite you with the boils of Egypt and with hemorrhoids and with leprosy and with the itch, and thereof you cannot be healed.

28 The LORD shall smite you with madness and blindness and dumbness of heart;

29 And you shall grope at noonday, as the blind grope in darkness, and you shall not prosper in your ways; and you shall be carried away violently, and oppressed and wronged all your days, and no man shall save you.

30 You shall betroth a wife, and another man shall take her; you shall build a house, and you shall not dwell in it; you shall plant a vineyard, and you shall not press grapes of it.

31 Your ox shall be slaughtered before your eyes, and you shall not eat of it; your ass shall be violently taken away from you, and shall not be restored to you; your sheep shall be given to your enemies, and you shall have none to rescue them.

32 Your sons and your daughters

---

[1] Idiom meaning *greatest, not least*

shall be given to another people, and your eyes shall look on, and you shall grieve over them all the day long; and there shall be no might in your hand to do anything.

33 The fruit of your land and all your labors shall a nation which you know not eat up; and you shall be only wronged and oppressed always;

34 So that you shall be blinded of the sight with which your eyes shall see.

35 The Lord shall smite you in your knees and in your legs with malignant boils that cannot be healed, from the sole of your foot to the top of your head.

36 The Lord shall drive you away, and your king whom you have set over you, to a nation that neither you nor your fathers have known; and there you shall serve other gods, of wood and stone.

37 And you shall become a horror, a proverb, and a byword, among all nations where the Lord your God shall drive you.

38 You shall carry much seed into your field, and you shall gather but little in; for the locust shall consume it.

39 You shall plant a vineyard and dress it, but you shall neither drink of the wine nor gather the grapes, because the worms shall eat it.

40 You shall have olive trees throughout all your territory, but you shall not anoint yourself with the oil; for your olives shall drop off.

41 You shall beget sons and daughters, but they shall not remain yours; for they shall go into captivity.

42 All your trees and fruits of your land shall the locust consume.

43 The stranger who is in your midst shall rise up above you very high; and you shall come down very low.

44 He shall lend to you, and you shall not lend to him; he shall be the head, and you shall be the tail.

45 Moreover all these curses shall come upon you and shall pursue you and overtake you, until you are destroyed; because you did not hearken to the voice of the Lord your God,

and did not keep his commandments and his statutes which he commanded you;

46 And they shall be upon you for signs and wonders, and upon your descendants for ever.

47 Because you did not serve the Lord your God with joyfulness and with gladness of heart, for the abundance of all things;

48 Therefore you shall serve your enemies whom the Lord shall send against you, in hunger and in thirst and in nakedness and in want of all things; and he shall put a yoke of iron upon your neck, until he has destroyed you.

49 The Lord shall bring a nation against you from afar, from the ends of the earth, as swift as the eagle that flies; a nation whose language you do not understand;

50 A people of fierce countenance, who shall not regard the person of the old, nor show mercy to the young;

51 And they shall eat the young of your cattle and the fruit of your land, until they destroy you; they also shall not leave you either grain or wine or oil or herds of oxen or flocks of sheep, until they have destroyed you.

52 And they shall besiege you in all your cities, until your high and fortified walls in which you trust are taken throughout all your land; and they shall besiege you in all your cities throughout all your land, which the Lord your God has given you.

53 And you shall eat the fruit of your own body, the flesh of your sons and of your daughters, whom the Lord your God has given you; and you shall eat them in the siege and in the distress with which your enemies shall harass you;

54 So that the man who abounds in delights among you and lives a luxurious life, his eye shall be evil toward his brother and toward his lawful wife and toward the remnant of his children that are left;

55 So that he will not give to any of them of the flesh of his children whom he shall eat; because he has nothing left him in the siege and in the distress with which your enemies

shall harass you in all your cities.

56 The woman who abounds in delights, who lives a luxurious life among you, who would not venture to set the sole of her foot upon the ground because of her delicacy and tenderness, her eye shall be evil toward her husband and toward her son and toward her daughter

57 And toward the afterbirth that comes out from between her feet and toward her child whom she shall bear, when she eats them for want of all things in the siege and distress with which your enemy shall harass you in all your cities.

58 If you will not observe and do all the words of this law that are written in this book, that you may fear the glorious and wonderful name of the LORD your God;

59 Then the LORD will send your plagues and the plagues of your descendants, even great plagues of long duration, and sore sicknesses of long duration.

60 Moreover he will bring upon you all the diseases of Egypt, of which you were afraid; and they shall cleave to you.

61 Also all kinds of sickness and all plagues which are not written in this book of the law, then will the LORD bring upon you, until you are destroyed.

62 And you shall be left few in number, whereas you were as the stars of the heaven for multitude; because you would not obey the voice of the LORD your God.

63 And as the LORD rejoiced over you to do you good and to multiply you; so the LORD will rejoice over you to destroy you and exterminate you; and you shall be carried away from the land which you are entering to possess.

64 And the LORD shall scatter you among all peoples, from one end of the earth to the other; and there you shall serve other gods, of wood and stone, which neither you nor your fathers have known.

65 And among these nations you shall find no ease, neither shall the sole of your foot have rest; but the LORD shall give you there a trembling heart and failing of eyes and sorrow of the soul;

66 And your life shall be uncertain before you; and you shall fear day and night, and shall have no assurance of your life;

67 In the morning you shall say, Would God it were evening! and in the evening you shall say, Would God it were morning! because of the fear of your heart with which you shall fear, and because of the hardships which you shall see with your eyes.

68 And the LORD shall bring you back into Egypt with ships, by the way whereof he said to you, You shall see it no more again; and there you shall be sold to your enemies as bondmen and bondwomen, but there shall be no one to buy you.

CHAPTER 29

THESE are the words of the covenant which the LORD commanded Moses to make with the children of Israel in the land of Moab, besides the covenant which he made with them in Horeb.

2 ¶And Moses called to all Israel, and said to them, You have seen all that the LORD did to Pharaoh before your eyes in the land of Egypt and to all his servants and to all his army and to all his land;

3 The great trials which your eyes have seen, the signs, and those great marvels which you saw;

4 Yet to this day the LORD has not given you a heart to understand and eyes to see and ears to hear.

5 And I have led you forty years in the wilderness; your clothes are not worn out upon you and your shoes are not worn out upon your feet.

6 You have not eaten bread, neither have you drunk wine or strong drink, that you might know that I am the LORD your God.

7 And when you came to this place, Sihon the king of Heshbon and Og the king of Mathnin came out against us to battle, and we slew them;

8 And we took their land and gave it for an inheritance to the Reubenites

and to the Gadites and to the half tribe of Manasseh.

9 Keep therefore the words of this covenant and do them, that you may prosper in all that you do.

10 ¶You stand this day before the LORD your God, all the heads of your tribes, your elders and your scribes, all the men of Israel,

11 Your little ones, your wives, and the stranger who is in your camp, from the gatherer of your wood to the drawer of your water;

12 That you may not transgress the covenant of the LORD your God, and the oath of the LORD your God, which he made with you this day;

13 Because he will establish you this day a people to himself, and he will be to you the God, as he has promised you, and as he has sworn to your fathers, to Abraham, to Isaac, and to Jacob.

14 Neither is it with you only that I do make this covenant and this oath;

15 But with all who stand here with us this day before the LORD our God, and also with him who is not here with us this day

16 (For you know how we have sojourned in the land of Egypt; and how we came through the nations which you passed by;

17 And you have seen their abominations and their idols of wood and stone, overlaid with silver and gold).

18 Perhaps there is among you a man or woman or family or tribe whose heart turns away this day from the LORD our God, to go and serve the gods of these nations; or perhaps there is among you a root that springs up and bears poison and wormwood;

19 And when he hears the words of this oath, he shall reason in his heart, saying, I shall have peace, though I walk in the imagination of my heart, to add drunkenness to thirst;

20 The LORD would not forgive him, but then the anger of the LORD and his zealousness would be grievous against that man, and all the curses that are written in this book shall lie upon him, and the LORD shall blot out his name from under the heaven.

21 And the LORD shall single him out to misfortune from all the tribes of Israel, according to all the curses of the covenant that are written in this book of the law.

22 So that the generation to come, your children that shall rise up after you and the strangers that shall come from a far land, shall say, when they see the plagues of that land and the sicknesses which the LORD has brought upon it;

23 Laying it waste with brimstone and with scorched salt, that the whole land is not sown, nor any grass grows in it, like the overthrow of Sodom and Gomorrah, Admah and Zeboim, which the LORD overthrew in his anger and in his wrath;

24 And all the nations shall say, Why has the LORD done thus to this land? And why has his anger kindled so much?

25 Then men shall say, Because they have forsaken the covenant of the LORD God of their fathers, which he made with them when he brought them forth out of the land of Egypt;

26 And they went and served other gods, and worshipped them, gods whom they had not known, nor had they divided spoils among them;

27 Therefore the anger of the LORD was kindled against this land, to bring upon it all the curses that are written in this book;

28 And the LORD uprooted them from their land in anger and in wrath and in great indignation, and cast them into another land, as it is this day.

29 The secret things belong to the LORD our God; but those things that are revealed belong to us and to our children for ever, that we may keep and do all the words of this law.

CHAPTER 30

AND it shall come to pass, when all these are come upon you, the blessings and the curses which I have set before you, and you shall call them to mind among all the nations where the LORD your God has driven you,

2 And shall return to the LORD your

God and shall obey his voice according to all that I command you this day, you and your children, with all your heart and with all your soul;

3 Then the LORD your God will bring back again your captivity, and have compassion upon you, and will return and gather you from all the nations where the LORD your God has driven you.

4 If your scattered ones are in the outmost parts of heaven, O Israel, from thence will the LORD your God gather you, and from thence will he fetch you;

5 And the LORD your God will bring you into the land which your fathers possessed, and you shall possess it; and he will do you good, and multiply you more than your fathers.

6 And the LORD your God will circumcise your heart and the heart of your descendants, and then you will love the LORD your God with all your heart and with all your soul, because he will give you rest.

7 And the LORD your God will put all these curses upon your enemies, and on those who hate you, who persecuted you.

8 And you shall return and obey the voice of the LORD your God, and do all his commandments which I command you this day.

9 And the LORD your God will make you plenteous in every work of your hand, in the fruit of your body and in the bearing of your cattle and in the fruit of your land, for good; for the LORD will again rejoice over you for good, as he rejoiced over your fathers;

10 If you will obey the voice of the LORD your God, and keep his commandments and his statutes which are written in this book of the law, and if you turn to the LORD your God with all your heart and with all your soul.

11 ¶For this commandment which I command you this day is not hidden from you, neither is it far off.

12 It is not in heaven, that you should say, Who shall go up for us to heaven and bring it to us, that we may hear it and do it?

13 Neither is it beyond the sea, that you should say, Who shall go over the sea for us and bring it to us, that we may hear it and do it?

14 But the word is very near you, in your mouth and in your heart, that you may do it.

15 ¶See, I have set before you this day life and good, and death and misfortunes;

16 In that I command you this day to love the LORD your God, to walk in his ways, and to keep his commandments and his statutes and his judgments; then you shall live; and multiply exceedingly; and the LORD your God shall bless you in the land which you are entering to possess.

17 But if your heart turns away, so that you will not hear, but shall go astray, and worship other gods and serve them;

18 I declare to you this day that you shall surely perish, and that you shall not live long in the land which you are crossing over the Jordan to possess.

19 I call heaven and earth to bear witness against you this day, that I have set before you life and death, blessings and cursings; therefore choose life, that both you and your descendants may live;

20 That you may love the LORD your God, and that you may obey his voice, and that you may cleave to him; for he is your life and the length of your days; that you may dwell in the land which the LORD swore to your fathers, to Abraham, to Isaac, and to Jacob, to give to you.

CHAPTER 31

AND Moses went and spoke all these words to all Israel.

2 And he said to them, I am a hundred and twenty years old this day; I can no longer go out and come in; and the LORD has said to me, You shall not cross the Jordan.

3 The LORD your God, he will go over before you, and he will destroy these nations from before you, and you shall possess them; and Joshua shall go over before you, as the LORD has said.

4 And the LORD shall do to them as he did to Sihon and to Og, the kings of the Amorites, and to their lands, which he destroyed.

5 And the LORD shall deliver them also before you, and you shall do to them according to all the commandments which I have commanded you.

6 Be strong and of good courage, fear not, nor tremble before them; for it is the LORD your God who goes with you; he will not fail you, nor forsake you.

7 ¶Then Moses called Joshua, and said to him in the sight of all Israel, Be strong and of good courage; for you shall bring this people into the land which the LORD has sworn to their fathers to give them; and you shall cause them to inherit it.

8 And it is the LORD who goes before you; he will be with you, he will not fail you, nor forsake you; fear not, neither tremble, nor be dismayed.

9 ¶And Moses wrote this law, and gave it to the priests, the sons of Levi, who carried the ark of the covenant of the LORD, and to all the elders of Israel.

10 And Moses commanded them, saying, At the end of every seven years, at the time of the year of release, at the feast of tabernacles,

11 When all Israel comes to appear before the LORD your God in the place which he shall choose, you shall read this law before all Israel in their hearing.

12 Gather the people together, men and women and children and the stranger who is within your cities, that they may hear, and that they may learn and revere the LORD your God and observe and do all the words of this law;

13 And that their children, who have not known anything, may hear and learn to fear the LORD your God, as long as you live in the land which you are crossing the Jordan to possess.

14 ¶And the LORD said to Moses, Behold, the day is coming when you must die; call Joshua, and present yourselves in the tabernacle of the congregation, that I may give him a charge. And Moses and Joshua went, and presented themselves in the tabernacle of the congregation.

15 And the LORD appeared in the tabernacle in a pillar of cloud; and the pillar of cloud stood over the door of the tabernacle.

16 ¶And the LORD said to Moses, Behold, you shall sleep with your fathers; and this people will rise up and go astray after strange gods of the land where they go to dwell among them, and will forsake me and break my covenant which I have made with them.

17 Then my anger shall be kindled against them in that day, and I will forsake them, and I will turn away my face from them, and they shall be devoured, and many evils and troubles shall befall them; so that they will say in that day, Are not these evils come upon us because our God is not in our midst?

18 And I will surely turn away from them in that day for all the evils which they have done, in that they have gone astray after other gods.

19 Now therefore write this song for them, and teach it to the children of Israel; and put it into their mouths; this song will be a witness for me against the children of Israel.

20 For I will bring them into the land which I swore to their fathers, a land that flows with milk and honey; and when they have eaten and are full, and live in luxury, then they will go astray after other gods and serve them, and provoke me, and break my covenant.

21 And when many evils and troubles are befallen them, then this song shall be read before them as a witness; for it shall not be forgotten out of the mouths of their descendants; for I know their inclination and all that they do here this day, before I have brought them into the land which I swore to their fathers.

22 ¶Moses therefore wrote this song the same day, and taught it to the children of Israel.

23 And he gave Joshua the son of Nun a charge, and said to him, Be

strong and of good courage; for you shall bring the children of Israel into the land which I swore to their fathers; and I will be with you.

24 ¶And when Moses had made an end of writing the words of this law in a book, and they were finished,

25 He commanded the Levites who carried the ark of the covenant of the LORD, saying,

26 Take this book of the law, and put it in the side of the ark of the covenant of the LORD your God, that it may be there as a witness against you.

27 For I know how rebellious and stiffnecked you are; behold, while I am yet alive with you this day, you have been rebellious against the LORD; and how much more after my death?

28 ¶Gather to me all the elders of your tribes and your scribes, that I may speak these words to you, and call heaven and earth to witness against you.

29 For I know that after my death you will surely become corrupt and turn aside from the way which I have commanded you; and evil will befall you in the latter days; when you have done evil in the sight of the LORD and have provoked him to anger through the work of your hands.

30 And Moses spoke the words of this song before all the congregation of the children of Israel, until they were ended.

CHAPTER 32

GIVE ear, O heavens, and I will speak; and let the earth hear the words of my mouth.

2 My word shall drop as rain, my speech shall fall as dew, as the gentle wind upon the tender herbs, and as the showers upon the grass;

3 For I will call upon the name of the LORD; ascribe majesty to our God, the Mighty One.

4 For his works are perfect; and all his ways are just; he is a faithful God and without iniquity, just and upright is he.

5 They have corrupted themselves, and they are not his children because of blemish; they are a perverse and crooked generation.

6 Are these the things that you return unto the LORD, O foolish and unwise people? Is he not your father who has redeemed you? Has he not made you and established you?

7 ¶Remember the days of old, consider the years of many generations; ask your father, and he will show you; your elders, and they will tell you.

8 When the Most High divided the nations, when he separated mankind, he set the bounds of the people according to the number of the children of Israel.

9 For the LORD's portion is his people; Jacob is the lot of his inheritance.

10 He found him in a desert land, and in the waste and howling wilderness; he made him to settle down, he loved him, he kept him as the apple of his eye.

11 As an eagle encircles his nest, fluttering over his young, spreading out its wings, taking them, bearing them on the strength of his wings;

12 So the LORD alone did lead Israel, and there was no strange god with him.

13 He made him to dwell in a fertile land, and fed him with the produce of the field; and he made him to suck honey out of the rock and oil out of the flinty rock;

14 And gave him butter of cows and milk of sheep, with fat of fatlings and rams of the breed of rock-goats and goats, with the fat and the best wheat; and he gave him wine to drink, and of the juices of grapes.

15 ¶And Israel grew fat and kicked; he became rich and mighty, he gained wealth; then he forsook God who made him, and reviled the Mighty One who had saved him.

16 They provoked him to zealousness with strange gods, they made him angry with idols.

17 They sacrificed to demons that were not gods; to gods whom they knew not, to new gods that were just made, whom your fathers had never worshipped.

18 But you forsook the Mighty One

who bore you, and you forgot the God who made you glorious.

19 And the LORD saw it, and was angry, because his sons and daughters provoked him.

20 And he said, I will turn away my face from them, I will see what their end will be; for they are a perverse generation, children in whom is no faith.

21 They have provoked me to zealousness with that which is not God; they have provoked me to anger with their idols; so I will move them to jealousy with those that are not my people; I will provoke them to anger with a foolish nation.

22 For a fire is kindled in my anger, and shall burn to the lowest parts of Sheol, and shall consume the earth and its increase, and set on fire the foundations of the mountains.

23 I will heap mischiefs upon them; I will spend my arrows upon them.

24 They shall be disabled with hunger, and I will deliver them to evil spirits, and I will deliver them to vultures; I will also stir up wild beasts upon them, with the poison of serpents which creep in the dust.

25 Outside the sword shall bereave, and terror in inner chambers shall destroy both the young men and the virgins, the suckling also with the men of gray hairs.

26 And I said, Where are they? I would blot out the memory of them from among men.

27 Had it not been for the wrath of the enemy, who had become strong, and had it not been for the boasting of the adversary, who would say, It is our hand that has prevailed, and the LORD has not done all this, I would have blotted them out.

28 For they are a nation void of counsel, neither is there any understanding in them.

29 O that they were wise, that they understood this, that they would consider their latter end!

30 How should one chase a thousand, and two put ten thousand to flight, except their Mighty One had delivered them to their enemies, and the LORD had hemmed them in?

31 For their strength is not as our strength, even our enemies themselves being judges.

32 For their vine is of the vine of Sodom, and of the fields of Gomorrah; their grapes are bitter grapes, the clusters are gall to them;

33 Their venom is the venom of dragons, and the cruel venom of asps.

34 Is not this laid up in store with me, and sealed up in my treasures?

35 To me belongs vengeance, and I will recompense them at the time when their foot shall slip; for the day of their destruction is at hand, and the misfortune that shall come upon them makes haste.

36 For the LORD shall judge his people, and be consoled for his servants, because he will see that their power is gone, and there is none to help or sustain.

37 And he shall say, Where are their mighty gods, those in whom they trusted,

38 Who ate the fat of their sacrifices, and drank the wine of their drink offerings? Let them now rise up and help you, let them be your protection.

39 See now that I, even I, am he, and there is no god besides me; I cause men to die, and I make alive; I wound, and I heal; and there is none that can escape out of my hands.

40 For I lift up my hand to heaven and say, I live for ever.

41 I will whet my glittering sword as the lightning, and my hand shall take hold of judgment; I will render vengeance on those that hate me, and cause my enemies to surrender.

42 I will make my arrows drunk with blood, and my sword shall devour flesh, with the blood of the slain and of the captives, from the crown of the head of the enemy.

43 Therefore praise his people, O you nations; for the blood of his servants shall be avenged, and he will take vengeance upon his adversaries, and will give absolution to his land and to his people.

44 ¶And Moses came and recited all the words of this song before the

people, he and Joshua the son of Nun.

45 And when Moses had finished reciting all these words to all Israel,

46 He said to them, Set your hearts to all the words which I testify among you this day, which you shall command your children to do, all the words of this law.

47 For it is not a vain thing for you, because it is your life; and through this thing you shall prolong your days in the land which you are crossing the Jordan to possess.

48 And the LORD spoke to Moses that same day, saying,

49 Go up into this mountain of the Abraye,[1] into mount Nebo, which is in the land of Moab, that is over toward Jericho; and view the land of Canaan, which I give to the children of Israel as a possession:

50 And die on the mountain which you ascend, and be gathered to your people; as Aaron your brother died on mount Hor, and was gathered to his people:

51 Because you transgressed against me among the children of Israel at the waters of Mesotha which is at Rakim, in the wilderness of Zin; because you did not sanctify me in the midst of the children of Israel.

52 Yet you shall see the land before you, which I give to the children of Israel; but you shall not enter there.

CHAPTER 33

AND this is the blessing, wherewith Moses the servant of God blessed the children of Israel before his death.

2 And he said, The LORD came from Sinai, and shined upon us from Seir; he rose up from mount Paran; he came with ten thousands of saints at his right hand.

3 Yea, he supplied their needs; he also made them to be beloved by the nations; he blessed all his saints; and they followed closely after his feet, every one receiving one of his words.

4 Moses delivered to us a law, and he gave it as an inheritance to the congregation of Jacob.

5 And there shall be a king in Is-rael, when the heads of the people and the tribes of Israel are gathered together.

6 ¶Let Reuben live, and not die; and let his people be numerous.

7 ¶And this is the blessing of Judah: Hear, O LORD, the voice of Judah, and bring him close to his people; let his hands contend for him, and be thou a help to him from his oppressors.

8 ¶And of Levi he said, Let your consecration and your light be upon the just one whom thou didst prove in trials and whom thou didst test at the waters of Mesotha;

9 Who said of his father and of his mother, I have not seen them; neither did he recognize his brothers nor know his own children; for they have observed thy word and kept thy covenant.

10 They shall teach Jacob thy judgments, and Israel thy law; they shall put incense before thee when thou art angry, and whole burnt sacrifice upon thy altar.

11 Bless, O LORD, his substance, and accept the work of his hands; smite the loins of his adversaries, and of his enemies, that they rise not again.

12 ¶And of Benjamin he said, The beloved of the LORD shall dwell in safety; and the LORD shall have compassion on him all the day long, and he shall dwell in his bosom.

13 ¶And of Joseph he said, Blessed of the LORD be his land and its fruit, with the dew of heaven from above, with the deep that couches beneath,

14 With the fruit of the earth brought forth by the sun, with the products brought forth by the moon,

15 With the best fruits of the eastern mountains, with the fruit of the eternal hills,

16 With the precious things of the earth and the fulness thereof, and with the good will of him who dwelt in the bush; let blessing come upon the head of Joseph, and upon the crown of the head of his brothers.

17 His glory is like the firstlings of the bullocks, and his horns are like

[1] The Ammonites and the Moabites were known as Abraye, Hebrews, people who had crossed the river Euphrates. They were the descendants of Lot, the nephew of Abraham.

the horns of unicorns; with them he shall push the peoples together to the ends of the earth; and they are the ten thousands of Ephraim, and they are the thousands of Manasseh.

18 ¶And of Zebulun he said, Rejoice, O Zebulun, in your going out; and Issachar, in your tents.

19 They shall call the people to the mountain; there they shall offer sacrifices of righteousness; for they shall suck of the abundance of the sea, and of the treasures which lie hidden in ships on the beaches.

20 ¶And of Gad he said, Blessed be he who enlarges Gad; he dwells like a lion, and tears the arm together with the head.

21 And he provided the first part of the spoil for himself, out of which he set aside the portion of the lawgiver; he went out at the head of the people; he executed the justice of the LORD and his judgments with Israel.

22 ¶And of Dan he said, Dan is a lion's whelp, who sucks milk from Mathnin.

23 ¶And of Naphtali he said, O Naphtali, satisfied with abundance, and filled with the blessing of the LORD; he shall possess the west and the south.

24 ¶And of Asher he said, Let Asher be blessed with children; let him be acceptable to his brethren, and let him have abundance of oil.

25 Your shoes shall be iron and brass; and as to your days, so shall your strength be.

26 ¶There is none like the God of Israel, who rides through the heaven to your help, and in his excellency on the sky.

27 In the heaven of heavens is the dwelling of our God from everlasting, and below he creates men; and he shall destroy your enemies from before you; for he said, Destroy them.

28 Israel then shall dwell in safety alone; the fountain of Jacob shall be in a land of grain and wine and oil; also the heavens shall drop down dew.

29 Happy are you, O Israel; who is like you, a people whose salvation is sustained by the LORD, God is your

¹ Pisgah.

help, and your pride is not in the sword; your enemies shall deal treacherously with you; but you shall tread upon their necks.

CHAPTER 34

AND Moses went up from the plains of Moab to the mountain of Nebo. to the top of the hill ¹ which is opposite Jericho. And the LORD showed him all the land of Gilead as far as Dan,

2 And all Naphtali, and the land of Ephraim, and Manasseh, and all the land of Judah as far as the Mediterranean Sea,

3 And the south, and the plain of the valley of Jericho, the city of palm trees, as far as Zoar.

4 And the LORD said to him, This is the land which I swore to Abraham, to Isaac, and to Jacob, saying, I will give it to your descendants; I have permitted you to see it with your eyes, but you shall not go over to it.

5 ¶So Moses the servant of the LORD died there in the land of Moab, according to the word of the LORD.

6 And he buried him in a valley in the land of Moab, over against Bethpeor; but no man knows of his sepulchre to this day.

7 ¶And Moses was a hundred and twenty years old when he died; but his eye was not dim, nor the skin of his cheeks wrinkled.

8 ¶And the children of Israel wept for Moses in the plains of Moab thirty days; so the days of weeping and mourning for Moses were ended.

9 ¶And Joshua the son of Nun was full of the spirit of wisdom; for Moses had laid his hands upon him; and the children of Israel obeyed him, and did as the LORD commanded Moses.

10 ¶And there arose not a prophet since in Israel like Moses, whom the LORD knew face to face,

11 In all the signs and the wonders, which the LORD sent him to do in the land of Egypt to Pharaoh and to all his servants and to all his land,

12 And in all that mighty power, and in all the great signs which Moses wrought in the sight of all Israel.

THE BOOK OF

JOSHUA

CHAPTER 1

AFTER the death of Moses the servant of the LORD, the LORD said to Joshua the son of Nun, Moses' minister,

2 Moses my servant is dead; now therefore arise, cross this Jordan, you and all this people, into the land which I am giving to them, even to the children of Israel.

3 Every place that the sole of your foot shall tread upon, it shall be yours, as I promised Moses.

4 From the wilderness and this Lebanon even to the great river, the river Euphrates, all the land of the Hittites, as far as the Great Sea toward the going down of the sun shall be your boundaries.

5 No man shall be able to resist you all the days of your life; as I was with Moses, so I will be with you; I will not fail you, nor forsake you.

6 Be strong and of good courage; for you shall cause this people to inherit the land which I swore to their fathers to give them.

7 Only be strong and very courageous, that you may observe to do according to all the laws which Moses my servant has commanded you; turn not from it to the right hand or to the left, that you may succeed wherever you go.

8 This book of the law shall not depart out of your mouth; but you shall meditate thereon day and night, that you may observe to do according to all that is written therein; for then you shall succeed and prosper.

9 Behold, I have commanded you. Be strong and of good courage; fear not, neither be dismayed; for the LORD your God is with you wherever you go.

10 ¶Then Joshua commanded the officers of the people and their scribes, saying,

11 Pass through the camp, and command the people, saying, Prepare for yourselves provisions for a journey; for within three days you are to cross this Jordan, to go in to possess the land which the LORD your God gives you.

12 ¶And to the Reubenites and to the Gadites and to the half tribe of Manasseh, Joshua said,

13 Remember the word which Moses the servant of the LORD commanded you, saying, The LORD your God has given you rest, and has given you this land.

14 Your wives, your little ones, and your cattle shall remain in the land which Moses gave you on this side of the Jordan; but you shall cross armed before your brethren, all of you who are mighty men of valor, and help them;

15 Until the LORD gives rest to your brethren, as he has given you, and they also have possessed the land which the LORD your God gives them; then you shall return to the land of your possession, and shall inherit it, the land which Moses the servant of the LORD gave you on this side of the Jordan toward the sunrising.

16 ¶And the Reubenites, the Gadites, and the Manassites answered and said to Joshua, All that you have commanded us we will do, and wherever you send us, we will go.

17 Just as we obeyed Moses in all things, so will we obey you; only the LORD your God be with you, as he was with Moses.

18 Anyone who shall quarrel with you and will not obey your word in all that you command him, he shall be put to death; only be strong and of good courage.

CHAPTER 2

AND Joshua the son of Nun sent out from Shittim two men who were familiar with the land, and said to them, Go view the land of Jericho. And they went, and came into the house of a woman who was a harlot, named Rahab, and lodged there.

2 And it was told the king of Jericho, saying, Behold, there came certain men here tonight from the children of Israel to spy in the country.

3 So the king of Jericho sent to Rahab, saying, Bring forth the men that have entered into your house at night; for they have come to spy in the country.

4 And the woman took the two men, and hid them, and said, Truly, the men came to me, but I did not know where they came from;

5 And it came to pass about the time of the shutting of the gate, when it was dark, they went out; and I did not know where they went. Pursue them quickly; for you will overtake them.

6 But she had brought them up to the roof of the house, and hid them beneath the stalks of flax which she had piled up on the roof.

7 And the men pursued after them by the way of the Jordan to the fords; and after the pursuers were gone out after the spies, they shut the gate.

8 ¶And before they lay down, she came up to them upon the roof;

9 And she said to the men, I know that the LORD has given you the land, and that your terror has fallen upon us, and that also all the inhabitants of the land are terrified because of you.

10 For we have heard how the LORD dried up the waters of the Red Sea before you, when you came out of Egypt; and what you did to the two kings of the Amorites, to Sihon and Og, whom you utterly destroyed.

11 And when we heard these things, our hearts trembled, neither did there remain any more courage in any one of us, because of you; for the LORD your God, is he who is God in heaven above and on earth beneath.

12 Now therefore, swear to me by the LORD, because I have showed you kindness, that you also will show kindness to me and to my father's household, and give me a true sign;

13 And that you will save alive my father, my mother, my brothers, and my sisters, and all that belongs to us, and deliver our lives from death.

14 And the men said to her, We will give our lives to death instead of you, if you will not disclose this affair. And it shall be, when the LORD has given us this land, then we will deal kindly and truly with you.

15 Then she let them down by a rope through the window; for her house was joined to the city wall, and she dwelt upon the wall.

16 And she said to them, Go by way of the mountain, lest the pursuers meet you; and hide yourselves there three days, until the pursuers have returned, and then you shall go on your way.

17 And the men said to her, We will be blameless of this oath which you have made us swear.

18 Behold, when we come into the land, you must bind this cord of scarlet thread in the window through which you let us down; and you shall bring your father and your mother and your brothers and all your father's household home to you.

19 And it shall be, that whosoever shall go out of the door of your house into the street, his blood shall be on his head, and we will be guiltless; and whosoever shall be with you in the house, his blood shall be on our heads, and we are guilty if any man should harm him.

20 And if you disclose this affair, then we will be absolved from this oath which you have made us swear.

21 And she said, According to your words, so be it. And she sent them away, and they departed; and she bound the scarlet cord in the window.

22 And they went to the mountain,

and stayed there three days, until the pursuers were returned; and the pursuers sought them throughout all the way, and when they failed to find them, they returned.

23 ¶So the two spies came down from the mountain, and passed over and came to Joshua the son of Nun, and told him all that had befallen them.

24 And they said to Joshua, The LORD has delivered all the land into our hands; for the inhabitants of the land are afraid of us.

CHAPTER 3

AND Joshua rose early in the morning; and they journeyed from Shittim, and came to the Jordan, he and all the people of Israel, and lodged there and did not cross over.

2 And it came to pass after three days the officers went through the camp;

3 And they commanded the people, saying, When you see the ark of the covenant of the LORD your God, and the priests and the Levites carrying it, then you must proceed from your place, and go after it.

4 And there shall be a space between you and the ark, about two thousand cubits by measure; you shall not come near to it, that you may know the way by which you shall go; for you have not passed this way before.

5 And Joshua said to the people, Sanctify yourselves; for tomorrow the LORD will do wonders among you.

6 And Joshua said to the priests, Take up the ark of the covenant, and pass over before the people. And they took up the ark of the covenant, and went before the people.

7 ¶And the LORD said to Joshua, From this day I will begin to exalt you in the sight of all Israel, that they may know that as I was with Moses, so I will be with you.

8 And you shall command the priests who carry the ark of the covenant of the LORD, saying, When you are come to the brink of the waters of the Jordan, you shall stand still in the Jordan.

9 ¶And Joshua said to the children of Israel, Come hither, and hear the words of the LORD your God.

10 And Joshua said, Hereby you shall know that the living God is among you, and that he will destroy from before you the Hittites, the Canaanites, the Hivites, the Perizzites, the Girgashites, the Amorites, and the Jebusites.

11 Behold, the ark of the covenant of the LORD of all the earth is passing over before you in the Jordan.

12 Now therefore take twelve men from all the tribes of Israel, a man out of each tribe.

13 And when the soles of the feet of the priests who bear the ark of the covenant of the LORD, the LORD of all the earth, shall rest in the waters of the Jordan, the waters of the Jordan shall be divided, the waters that are flowing down from above shall pile up as though they were in sheepskins, one beside the other.

14 ¶And it came to pass, when the people set out from their tents to cross the Jordan and the priests who were bearing the ark of the covenant went before the people;

15 And as soon as those that bore the ark reached the Jordan, and the feet of the priests who were bearing the ark were dipped in the brim of the water (for the Jordan overflows its banks all the time of harvest);

16 That the waters that flowed down from above piled up as though they were in sheepskins, one beside the other; and extended for a long distance from the town of Aram, that is beside Zaretan; and those that flowed down toward the sea of the plain, the Salt Sea, failed to flow, and were divided; and the people passed over opposite Jericho.

17 And the priests who bore the ark of the covenant of the LORD stood on dry ground in the midst of the Jordan, and all the Israelites passed over on dry ground until all the people finished passing over the Jordan.

CHAPTER 4

AND when all the people had finished passing over the Jordan, the LORD said to Joshua.

2 Take twelve men from the people, a man out of every tribe,

3 And command them, saying, Take from here out of the midst of the Jordan, out of the place where the priests' feet stood, twelve stones, and you shall carry them over with you, and lay them in the lodging place where you lodge this night.

4 Then Joshua called the twelve men who were selected from the children of Israel, out of each tribe a man;

5 And Joshua said to them, Pass over before the ark of the LORD your God into the midst of the Jordan, and take up every man of you a stone upon his shoulder, according to the number of the tribes of the children of Israel;

6 That this may be a sign among you, that when your children ask you in time to come, saying, What is the meaning of these stones?

7 Then you shall tell them, The waters of the Jordan were divided before the ark of the covenant of the LORD; when we passed over the Jordan, the waters of the Jordan were divided; and these stones shall be for a memorial to the children of Israel for ever.

8 And the children of Israel did as Joshua commanded them, and took up twelve stones out of the midst of the Jordan, as the LORD had said to Joshua, according to the number of the tribes of the children of Israel, and carried them over with them to the place where they lodged, and laid them down there.

9 And they set up the twelve stones which they had taken out of the midst of the Jordan, where stood the feet of the priests who were bearing the ark of the covenant; and they are there to this day.

10 ¶And the priests who bore the ark stood in the midst of the Jordan until everything was finished that the LORD commanded Joshua to tell to the people, according to all that Moses had commanded Joshua; and the people made haste and passed over.

11 And when all the people had finished passing over, the ark of the LORD and the priests passed over before the people.

12 Then the Reubenites, the Gadites, and the half tribe of Manasseh, passed over armed before the children of Israel, as Moses had told them;

13 About forty thousand men armed for war passed over before the LORD to battle, to the plains of Jericho.

14 ¶On that very day the LORD exalted Joshua in the sight of all Israel; and they feared him, as they had feared Moses, all the days of his life.

15 And the LORD said to Joshua,

16 Command the priests who bear the ark of the testimony to come up out of the Jordan.

17 Joshua therefore commanded the priests, saying, Come up out of the Jordan.

18 And when the priests who bore the ark of the covenant of the LORD had come up out of the midst of the Jordan, and the soles of the priests' feet rested firm on the dry land, the waters of the Jordan rushed to their place, and overflowed all its banks, as they did before.

19 ¶And the people came up out of the Jordan on the tenth day of the first month, and encamped in Gilgal, on the east border of Jericho.

20 And those twelve stones which they took out of the Jordan, Joshua set up at Gilgal.

21 And he said to the children of Israel, When your children shall ask you in time to come, saying, What is the meaning of these stones?

22 Then you shall explain them to your children, and say to them, The children of Israel crossed this Jordan on dry land.

23 For the LORD your God dried up the waters of the Jordan from before them, until they passed over, as the LORD your God did to the Red Sea, which he dried up from before us until we passed over;

24 So that all the peoples of the earth might know that the hand of the LORD is mighty, and that you may worship the LORD your God for ever.

CHAPTER 5

AND when all the kings of the Amorites, who were beyond the Jordan westward, and all the kings of the Canaanites, who were by the sea, heard that the LORD had dried up the waters of the Jordan from before the children of Israel, until they had passed over, their hearts trembled, and there was no strength left in them, because of the children of Israel.

2 ¶At that time the LORD said to Joshua, Make for yourself a flint knife, and circumcise again the children of Israel the second time.

3 So Joshua made a flint knife for himself, and circumcised the children of Israel the second time at the Hill of the Uncircumcised.

4 And these are the men whom Joshua did circumcise: every male child who had been born after they had come out of Egypt, because all the men of war had died in the wilderness on the journey, after they came out of Egypt.

5 Because all the people who came out had been circumcised; but all the people that were born in the wilderness during the journey after they came out of Egypt had not been circumcised.

6 For the children of Israel journeyed forty years in the wilderness, until all the people who were men of war and came out of Egypt had perished, because they did not obey the voice of their LORD; to whom the LORD had sworn that he would not show them the land which he had sworn to their fathers that he would give them, a land that flows with milk and honey.

7 And it was their children who came after them that Joshua circumcised; for they were uncircumcised, because they had not been circumcised on the journey.

8 And when all the people were circumcised, they remained in their places in the camp till they were healed.

9 And the LORD said to Joshua, This day I have taken away the reproach of the Egyptians from you. Wherefore the name of that place is called Gilgal to this day.

10 ¶And the children of Israel encamped in Gilgal, and kept the passover on the fourteenth day of the month at evening in the plain of Jericho.

11 And they ate from the grain of the land on the morrow after the passover, unleavened bread and parched wheat did they eat on that very day.

12 ¶And the manna ceased on the morrow after they had eaten of the grain of the land; neither had the children of Israel manna any more; but they did eat of the produce of the land of Canaan that year.

13 ¶And it came to pass, when Joshua was in the plain of Jericho, he lifted up his eyes and looked, and, behold, there stood a man opposite him with his sword drawn in his hand; and Joshua went to him, and said to him, Are you of us or of our enemies?

14 And he said to him, I am the commander of the host of the LORD, and now I have come here. And Joshua fell on his face to the earth, and worshipped, and said, What hath my LORD to say to his servant?

15 And the commander of the LORD's host said to Joshua, Take your shoes from off your feet; for the place whereon you stand is holy. And Joshua did so.

CHAPTER 6

NOW Jericho was shut up because of the presence of the children of Israel; none went out and none came in.

2 And the LORD said to Joshua, See, I have delivered Jericho into your hands, with its king and all its armed forces.

3 And you shall encircle the city, all the men of war, and you shall go round about the city once a day. Thus shall you do for six days.

4 And seven priests shall bear trumpets, and blow before the ark; and on the seventh day you shall go around the city seven times, and the priests shall blow with the trumpets.

5 And it shall come to pass that when they blow the trumpets and

when you hear the sound of the trumpet, then all the people shall shout with a great shout; and the wall of the city shall fall down flat, and the people shall go up every man straight before him.

6 ¶And Joshua the son of Nun called the priests, and said to them, Take up the ark of the covenant of the LORD, and let seven priests bear seven trumpets and blow them before the ark of the LORD.

7 And he said to the people, Pass on, and encircle the city, and let those who are armed march on before the the ark of the LORD.

8 ¶And as Joshua had spoken to the people, the seven priests bearing seven trumpets passed on before the ark of the LORD, blowing on the trumpets; and the ark of the covenant of the LORD followed them.

9 ¶And the armed men went before the priests who blew on the trumpets, and the rest of the people who were gathered went after the ark, and they marched on blowing the trumpets.

10 But Joshua had commanded the people, saying, You shall not shout, nor let your voice be heard, neither shall any word come out of your mouth, until the day that I bid you to shout; then shall you shout.

11 So the ark of the LORD made a circuit of the city, going about it once; and they came into the camp, and lodged in the camp.

12 ¶And Joshua rose early in the morning, and the priests took up the ark of the LORD.

13 And seven priests bearing seven trumpets went before the ark of the LORD; they went on continually, and blew with the trumpets; and the armed men went before them; and the rest of the multitude went after the ark of the LORD, while the priests were blowing with trumpets.

14 And the second day they compassed the city once, and returned to the camp; so they did for six days.

15 And on the seventh day, they rose in the morning, and compassed the city after the same manner seven times; it was on that day only that they compassed the city seven times.

16 At the seventh time, when the priests blew the trumpets, Joshua said to the people, Shout; for the LORD has delivered the city to you.

17 ¶And this city and all that is therein, is to be devoted to the LORD; only Rahab the harlot you shall spare, she and all who are with her in the house, because she hid the spies that we sent.

18 And as for you, you are to be careful of the devoted things, lest you defile yourselves by taking some of the devoted things, and make the camp of Israel a curse, and trouble it.

19 But all the silver and gold and vessels of brass and iron are consecrated to the LORD; they shall come into the treasury of the LORD.

20 So the people shouted and the priests blew the trumpets; and it came to pass, when the people heard the sound of the trumpets, they shouted with a great shout, and the wall fell down flat, so that the people went up into the city, every man straight before him, and they took the city.

21 And they utterly destroyed all that were in the city, both men and women, young and old and oxen and sheep and asses, with the edge of the sword.

22 But Joshua said to the two men who had spied out the country, Go into the harlot's house, and bring out from there the woman and all that she has, as you swore to her.

23 And the spies went in, and brought out Rahab and her father and her mother and her brothers and all that she had; and they brought out all her kindred, and placed them outside the camp of Israel.

24 And they burned the city with fire, and all that was therein; only the silver and the gold and the vessels of brass and of iron, they brought into the treasury of the house of the LORD.

25 But Rahab the harlot and her father's household and all that she had, Joshua saved alive; and she dwelt among the children of Israel even to this day; because she hid the spies

whom Joshua sent to spy out Jericho.

26 ¶And Joshua swore at that time, saying, Cursed before the LORD be the man that rises up and rebuilds this city, Jericho; with the death of his first-born shall he build it, and with the death of his youngest son shall he set up its gates.

27 So the LORD was with Joshua; and his fame spread throughout all the land.

CHAPTER 7

BUT the children of Israel committed a trespass in the devoted things; for Achar, the son of Carmi, the son of Zabdi, the son of Zerah, of the tribe of Judah, took some of the devoted things, and hid them; and the anger of the LORD was kindled against the children of Israel.

2 And Joshua sent men from Jericho to Ai, which is beside Beth-aon, on the east side of Beth-el, and said to them, Go up and spy out the land. And the men went up and spied out Ai.

3 And they returned to Joshua, and said to him, Let not all the people go up; but let about two or three thousand men go up, and destroy Ai; and do not send all the people there, for the men of Ai are but few.

4 So there went up about three thousand men; and they fled before the men of Ai.

5 And the men of Ai smote thirty-six of the Israelites; and they chased them from before the gate until they were defeated, and they smote them with a great slaughter; wherefore the hearts of the people melted, and became as water.

6 ¶And Joshua rent his clothes, and fell to the earth upon his face before the ark of the LORD until the evening, he and the elders of Israel, and put dust upon their heads.

7 And Joshua said, Alas, O LORD God, why hast thou brought this people over the Jordan, to deliver us into the hands of the Amorites? Would to God we had been content, and dwelt on the other side of the Jordan!

8 Now, what shall I say, when Israel has turned their backs before their enemies!

9 For the Canaanites and all the inhabitants of the land shall hear of it, and shall gather together against us, and cut off our name from the face of the earth; and what wilt thou do to thy great name?

10 ¶And the LORD said to Joshua, Get up; why do you lie upon your face on the earth?

11 Israel has sinned, and they have also transgressed the commandment which I commanded them; for they have even taken some of the devoted things, and have also stolen, and lied, and they have hidden them among their own stuff.

12 Therefore the children of Israel cannot stand again before their enemies, but they shall turn their backs before their enemies, because they are accursed; neither will I be with you any more, unless you remove the curse from among you.

13 Up, summon this people, and say, Be ready tomorrow; for thus says the LORD God of Israel, There is an accursed thing in the midst of you, O Israel; you cannot stand before your enemies any more until you remove the accursed thing from among you.

14 In the morning therefore you shall be brought near according to your tribes; and it shall be that the tribe which the LORD takes shall come by families; and the family which the LORD shall take shall come by households; and the household which the LORD shall take shall come man by man.

15 And it shall be that he who is taken with the devoted thing shall be burned with fire, he and all that he has; because he has transgressed the commandment of the LORD, and because he has done wickedness in Israel.

16 ¶So Joshua rose up early in the morning, and brought forward Israel by tribes; and the tribe of Judah was taken;

17 And he brought the tribe of Judah by families; and the family of the Zarhites was taken; and he

brought the family of the Zarhites man by man; and Zabdi was taken.

18 Then he brought his household man by man; and Achar, the son of Carmi, the son of Zabdi, the son of Zerah, of the tribe of Judah, was taken.

19 And Joshua said to Achar, Give glory to the LORD God of Israel, and give praise to him; and tell me now what you have done; and do not hide it from me.

20 Achar answered Joshua, and said, Truly I have sinned against the LORD God of Israel, and this is what I did:

21 When I saw among the spoils a beautiful Babylonian tapestry and two hundred shekels of silver and a wedge of gold weighing fifty shekels, then I coveted them and took them; and, behold, they are hidden in the earth inside of my tent, and the silver under it.

22 ¶So Joshua sent messengers, and they ran to his tent, and, behold, it was hidden in his tent, and the silver under it.

23 And they took them out of his tent, and brought them to Joshua and to all the people of Israel, and laid them out before the LORD.

24 And Joshua and all Israel with him took Achar the son of Zerah and the silver and the tapestry and the wedge of gold and his sons and his daughters and his oxen and his asses and his sheep and his tent and all that he had; and they brought them to the valley of Achar.

25 And Joshua said to him, Why have you troubled us? The LORD shall trouble you this day. And all Israel stoned him with stones, both him and all that he had, and burned them with fire.

26 And they raised over him a great heap of stones which remain to this day. So the LORD turned from his fierce anger. Therefore the name of that place is called the Valley of Achar, to this day.

CHAPTER 8

AND the LORD said to Joshua, Fear not, neither be dismayed; take all the men of war with you, and arise and go up to Ai; because I have delivered into your hands the king of Ai and his people, his city and his land;

2 And you shall do to Ai and its king as you did to Jericho and its king; only the spoil and the cattle shall you take as a prey for yourselves; lay an ambush against the city, from behind it.

3 ¶So Joshua arose, and all the men of war, to go up against Ai; and Joshua chose three thousand mighty men of valor, and sent them away by night.

4 And he commanded them, saying, Behold, when you shall lie in wait against the city, from behind it, do not go very far from the city, but all of you be ready;

5 And I and the men that are with me will approach the city; and it shall come to pass, when they first come out against us, we will flee before them;

6 For they will come out after us, and drive us away from the city, and they will say, They are fleeing before us, as at first; and behold, as we flee before them,

7 Then you shall rise up from your ambush, and seize upon the city; for the LORD your God will deliver it into your hands.

8 And it shall be, when you have taken the city, you shall set it on fire; according to the commandment of the LORD you shall do. See, I have commanded you.

9 ¶So Joshua sent them forth; and they went to the place of ambush, and lay between Beth-el and Ai, on the west side of Ai; but Joshua spent that night among the people.

10 And Joshua rose up early in the morning, and counted the people, and went up, he and the elders of Israel, before the people to Ai.

11 And all the men of war that were with him went up and drew near to the city, and encamped on the north side of Ai. Now there was a valley between them and Ai;

12 And Joshua took five thousand men, and set them in ambush between Beth-el and Ai, on the west side of the city;

13 And when he had set his men and all his host on the north side of the city, and the rear guard on the west of the city, Joshua went that night among the people.

14 ¶And when the king of Ai saw it, he hastened, and the men of the city rose up, and went out against Israel to battle; so all the people of Ai were in the plain; and they did not know that there was an ambush against them from behind the city.

15 And Joshua and all Israel scattered before them to flee by way of the wilderness.

16 And all the people of Ai shouted as they pursued them; and they followed Joshua, and were drawn out of the city.

17 And there was not a man left in Ai or Beth-el who did not go out after Israel; and they left the city open, and pursued Israel.

18 And the LORD said to Joshua, Stretch out the spear that is in your hand toward Ai; for I have delivered it into your hands. And Joshua stretched out the spear that was in his hand toward the city.

19 And the men in ambush arose quickly from their places, and they ran as soon as he had stretched out his hand; and they entered into the city and took it, and hasted and set the city on fire.

20 And when the men of Ai looked behind them, they saw the smoke of their city going up to heaven, and they had no power to flee this way or that way; and the people of Israel that fled to the wilderness turned back upon their pursuers.

21 And when Joshua and all Israel saw that the ambush had taken the city, and that the city was going up in smoke, then they turned back and slew the men of Ai.

22 And the others went out of the city to meet them; so the men of Ai were caught in the midst of Israel, some on this side and some on that side; and they smote them, so that they let none of them remain or escape.

23 And they took the king of Ai alive, and brought him to Joshua.

24 And when Israel had finished slaying all the inhabitants of Ai in the fields and in the wilderness where they pursued them, and when all of them had fallen by the edge of the sword until they were consumed, then all Israel returned to Ai and smote it with the edge of the sword.

25 And so it was, that twelve thousand men and women, all the inhabitants of Ai, fell that day.

26 For Joshua did not draw his hand back, wherewith he stretched out the spear until he had utterly destroyed all the inhabitants of Ai.

27 Only the cattle and the spoil of that city Israel took for a prey for themselves, according to the word of the LORD which he commanded Joshua.

28 And Joshua burned Ai, and made it a heap of ruins for ever to this day.

29 And the king of Ai he hanged on a tree until the evening; and when the sun was set, Joshua commanded, and they took his corpse down from the tree and cast it at the entrance of the gate of the city, and raised over it a heap of large stones that remains to this day.

30 ¶Then Joshua built an altar to the LORD God of Israel in mount Gebal,[1]

31 As Moses the servant of the LORD had commanded the children of Israel, as it is written in the book of the law of Moses, an altar of unhewn stones upon which no man has lifted up any iron instrument; and they offered thereon burnt offerings to the LORD, and sacrificed peace offerings.

32 ¶And he wrote there upon the stones of the altar a copy of the law of Moses, which he wrote in the presence of the children of Israel.

33 And all Israel and their elders and their scribes and their judges stood on this side of the ark, and on that side the priests and the Levites who carried the ark of the covenant of the LORD, the natives as well as the

[1] Ebal.

sojourners; half of them toward mount Gerizim, and half of them toward mount Gebal, as Moses the servant of the LORD had commanded, that they should bless the people of Israel as before.

34 And afterward Joshua read all the words of the law, the blessings and the cursings, according to all that is written in the book of the law.

35 There was not a word of all that Moses commanded which Joshua did not read before all the congregation of Israel and before the women and the little ones and sojourners who were among them.

CHAPTER 9

AND when all the kings who were on this side of the Jordan, in the mountains and in the valleys, and on all the coasts of the Great Sea toward Lebanon, the Hittites, the Amorites, the Canaanites, the Perizzites, the Hivites, and the Jebusites, heard of it;

2 And they gathered themselves together, with one accord, to fight with Joshua and with Israel.

3 ¶And when the inhabitants of Gibeon heard what Joshua had done to Jericho and to Ai,

4 They worked subtly, and prepared provisions, and laid old sacks upon their asses, and wine skins, old, torn, and patched;

5 They put on old shoes, or bound their feet with sandals, and dressed in old garments; and all the bread of their provision was dry and mouldy.

6 And they went to Joshua to the camp at Gilgal, and said to him and to the men of Israel, We have come from a far country; now therefore make a treaty with us.

7 And the men of Israel said to the Hivites, If you dwell among us, why then should you have a treaty?

8 And they said to Joshua, We are your servants. And Joshua said to them, Who are you? And where do you come from?

9 And they said to him, From a very far country your servants have come because of the name of the LORD your God; for we have heard the fame of him, and all that he did in Egypt.

10 And all that he did to the two kings of the Amorites, who were beyond the Jordan, to Sihon king of Heshbon, and to Og king of Mathnin, who lived at Astaroth.

11 Wherefore our elders and all the inhabitants of our country said to us, Take provisions with you for the journey, and go to meet them, and say to them, We are your servants; therefore now make a treaty with us.

12 Moreover, they also said to Joshua, This bread we took hot out of our houses for our provisions on the day we came forth to go to you; but now, behold, it is dry, and is mouldy.

13 And these wine skins, which we filled, were new; and, behold, they are worn out; and these our garments and our shoes were new when we put them on us, and, behold, now they are old because the journey was very long.

14 And the men took of their provisions and went away, and the Israelites did not ask counsel from the LORD.

15 And Joshua made peace with them, and he made a treaty with them to let them live; and the princes of the congregation swore to them.

16 ¶And at the end of three days after they had made the treaty with them, they heard that they were their neighbors, and that they dwelt among them.

17 And the children of Israel journeyed, and came to their cities on the third day. Now the names of their cities were Gibeon, Chephirah, Aeerooth and Koriath-naarin.

18 And the children of Israel did not kill them, because the princes of the congregation had sworn to them by the LORD God of Israel. And the whole congregation murmured and were in an uproar against the princes.

19 But the princes said to the congregation, We have sworn to them by the LORD God of Israel; now therefore we cannot harm them.

20 This we will do to them: we will let them live, lest wrath be upon us, because of the oaths which we swore to them.

21 And the princes said to the children of Israel, Let them live; but let them become gatherers of wood and drawers of water to all the congregation; so they became gatherers of wood and drawers of water to all the congregation of the land; as the princes had promised them.

22 ¶And Joshua called for them, and he said to them, Why have you deceived us, saying, We are very far from you, when you dwell among us?

23 Now therefore you are cursed, and there shall none of you be freed from being gatherers of wood and drawers of water for the house of God.

24 And they answered and said to Joshua, Because it was certainly told your servants that the LORD your God commanded Moses his servant to give you all the land and to destroy all the inhabitants of the land from before you, therefore we were exceedingly afraid for our lives because of you, and have done this thing.

25 And now, behold, we are in your hands; do to us as it seems good in your sight.

26 And so Joshua did unto them, and delivered them out of the hand of the Israelites, and they did not slay them.

27 And Joshua made them that day gatherers of wood and drawers of water for the congregation and for the altar of the LORD, even to this day, in the place which he should choose.

CHAPTER 10

WHEN Adoni-zedek king of Jerusalem heard how Joshua had captured Ai and had utterly destroyed it (as he had done to Jericho and its king, so he had done to Ai and its king) and how the inhabitants of Gibeon had made peace with Israel, and were among them;

2 He feared greatly, because Gibeon was a large city, like one of the royal cities, and it was larger than Ai, and all its men were mighty.

3 Wherefore Adoni-zedek king of Jerusalem sent to Hoham king of Hebron and to Baran king of Jarmuth and to Napia king of Lachish and to Debir king of Eglon, saying,

4 Come up to me and help me, and let us fight against Gibeon; for it has made peace with Joshua and with the children of Israel.

5 Therefore the five kings of the Amorites, the king of Jerusalem, the king of Hebron, the king of Jarmuth, the king of Lachish, and the king of Eglon, gathered themselves together, and came up, they and all their armies, and encamped before Gibeon and made war against it.

6 ¶And the men of Gibeon sent to Joshua in the camp at Gilgal, saying, Do not withhold your hands from your servants; because all the kings of the Amorites that dwell in the mountains are gathered together against us.

7 So Joshua went up from Gilgal, he, and all the men of war that were with him, and all the mighty men of valor.

8 ¶And the LORD said to Joshua, Fear them not; for I have delivered them into your hands; and there shall not a man of them stand before you.

9 Joshua therefore came to them suddenly, going up all night from Gilgal.

10 And the LORD discomfited them before Israel, and they smote them with great slaughter at Gibeon, and chased them along the way that goes up to Beth-hauran, and smote them as far as Akkar, and on to Makkar.

11 And as they fled from before Israel, and were going down in the descent of Beth-hauran, the LORD cast down great hailstones from heaven upon them as far as Akkar, and they died; and there were more that died from the hailstones than the children of Israel slew with the sword.

12 ¶Then spoke Joshua to the LORD on the day when the LORD delivered the Amorites to the children of Israel, and Joshua said in the sight of the children of Israel, Sun, stand thou still over Gibeon; and thou Moon, in the valley over Ajalon.

13 And the sun stood still, and the moon stayed, until the people had avenged themselves upon their en-

emies. And, behold, it is written in the Book of the Songs, So the sun stood still in the midst of heaven, and hasted not to go down, about a whole day.

14 And there was no day like that before it or after it, when the LORD hearkened to the voice of a man; for the LORD fought for Israel.

15 ¶Then Joshua returned, and all Israel with him, to the camp at Gilgal.

16 But these five kings fled, and hid themselves in the cave of Makkar.

17 And Joshua was told, The five kings have been found hidden in the cave of Makkar.

18 And Joshua said, Roll great stones, and put them upon the mouth of the cave, and leave men there to guard them.

19 Do not stay yourselves, but pursue your enemies and overtake them; and do not let them enter the city; for the LORD your God has delivered them into your hands.

20 When Joshua and the children of Israel had finished slaying them with a very great slaughter, till they were annihilated and no survivor was left of them; then they brought the men of Gibeon who had revolted against the kings into their walled cities.

21 And all the people returned in peace to the camp to Joshua at Makkar; and no man moved his tongue against any of the children of Israel.

22 Then said Joshua, Open the mouth of the cave, and bring out those five kings to me.

23 And they did as Joshua had commanded them, and they brought to him those five kings out of the cave, the king of Jerusalem, the king of Hebron, the king of Jarmuth, the king of Lachish, and the king of Eglon.

24 And when they brought out those kings to Joshua, Joshua called for all the commanders of the armed forces who went with him, and said to them, Come near, and put your feet upon the necks of these kings. And they came near, and put their feet upon the necks of the kings.

25 And Joshua said to them, Fear not, nor be dismayed; be strong and of good courage; for thus shall the LORD do to all your enemies against whom you fight.

26 And after that Joshua slew them, and hanged them on five trees; and they remained hung on the trees until the evening.

27 And at the time of the going down of the sun, Joshua commanded, and they took them down from the trees, and cast them into the cave where they had hidden themselves, and laid large stones at the mouth of the cave, which remain to this very day.

28 ¶And the same day Joshua captured Makkar, and smote it with the edge of the sword, and he slew the king thereof and all the persons that were in it; he left none remaining; and he did to the king of Makkar as he had done to the king of Jericho.

29 Then Joshua passed from Makkar, and all Israel with him, to Libnah, and they fought against Libnah;

30 And the LORD delivered it also into the hand of Israel, and they smote it and its king with the edge of the sword, and all the persons that were in it; he left none remaining in it; but Joshua did to its king as he had done to the king of Jericho.

31 ¶And Joshua passed from Libnah, and all Israel with him, to Lachish, and encamped against it, and fought against it;

32 And the LORD delivered Lachish into the hand of Israel, and he captured it on the second day, and smote it with the edge of the sword, and all the persons that were in it, as he had done to Libnah.

33 ¶Then Harmon the king of Gezer came up to help Lachish; and Joshua smote him and his people with the edge of the sword until he had left him none remaining.

34 ¶And Joshua passed from Lachish, and all Israel with him to Eglon, and they encamped against it and fought against it;

35 And they took it on that day, and smote it with the edge of the sword, and all the persons that were in it, as he had done to Lachish.

36 And Joshua went up from Eg-

lon and all Israel with him, to Hebron; and they fought against it;

37 And they captured it, and smote it with the edge of the sword, and its king and all its towns and all the persons that were in it; he left none remaining, as he had done to Eglon; but destroyed it utterly, and all the persons that were in it.

38 ¶Then Joshua returned, and all Israel with him, to Debir; and fought against it;

39 And he captured it and its king and all its towns; and they smote them with the edge of the sword and utterly destroyed all the persons that were in it; and he left none remaining; as he had done to Hebron, so he did to Debir and to its king; as he had done to Libnah and to its king.

40 ¶So Joshua smote all the land, the mountain region, the southern region, the plain, and Ashdod, and all their kings; he left none remaining, but utterly destroyed all their armies, as the LORD God of Israel had commanded him.

41 So Joshua smote them from Rakim-gia as far as Gaza, and all the country of Goshen as far as Gibeon.

42 And Joshua conquered all these kings and their countries at one time; because the LORD God of Israel was with him, and it was he who fought for Israel.

43 [1]And Joshua returned, and all Israel with him, to the camp at Gilgal.

CHAPTER 11

AND when Nabin king of Hazur heard of these things, he sent to Jobab king of Meron, and to the king of Shamrin, and to the king of Achshaph,

2 And to the kings that were north of him in the mountains, and to the south, and in the plain of Chinnereth, and in the valleys and in Napotdor on the west,

3 And to the Canaanites on the east and on the west, and to the Amorites and the Hittites and the Perizzites and the Jebusites in the mountains, and to the Hivites below mount Hermon in the land of Mizpeh.

4 And they came out with all their hosts, many people, as the sand that is upon the sea shore in multitude, with many horses and chariots.

5 And when all these kings were met together, they came and encamped together at the waters of Meron, and prepared to fight against Israel.

6 ¶And the LORD said to Joshua, Do not be afraid of them; for tomorrow about this time I will cause them to be routed before Israel; and I will annihilate their horses and burn their chariots with fire.

7 So Joshua came suddenly to the waters of Meron, he and all the people of war who were with him; and they fell upon them.

8 And the LORD delivered them into the hand of Israel, who smote them and pursued them as far as great Zidon, and to the lake, and as far as the valley of Mizpeh eastward; and they smote them, and they left none remaining.

9 And Joshua did to them as the LORD had told him: he utterly destroyed their horses and burned their chariots with fire.

10 ¶And Joshua at that time turned back and took Hazor, and slew its king with the sword; for Hazor before had been the head of all those kingdoms.

11 And they smote with the edge of the sword all the people that were in it, utterly destroying them; there was not a soul left among them; and he burned Hazor with fire.

12 And all the cities of those kings, and all their kings, Joshua took and smote them with the edge of the sword, and utterly destroyed them, as Moses the servant of the LORD had commanded him.

13 And all the towns that stood on the hills did Israel burn, and Joshua burned Hazor.

14 And all the spoil of these cities and the cattle, the children of Israel took for themselves; but every man they smote with the edge of the sword

---

[1] Verse 43 is not found in the Peshitta.

until they had annihilated them, and they did not leave a soul among them.

15 ¶Just as the LORD had commanded Moses his servant, so did Moses command Joshua, and so did Joshua; he left nothing undone of all that the LORD had commanded Moses.

16 So Joshua took all that land, the mountain country and all the south country and all the land of the plain and all the mountains and their lowlands;

17 From mount Paleg that goes up to Seir, as far as Gadgad in the valley of Lebanon below mount Hermon; and all their kings Joshua took and slew.

18 Joshua made war for a long time with all those kings.

19 There was not a city that was not delivered up to the children of Israel, and they destroyed it, except the Hivites who dwell in Gibeon, whom Joshua allowed to live, and work for Israel. Now all these kingdoms are seven in number, and Joshua destroyed them all.

20 For it was of the LORD to encourage their hearts, that they should come against Israel in battle, that they might destroy them utterly, and that they might not have compassion upon them, but that they might destroy them, as the LORD had commanded Moses.

21 ¶And at that time came Joshua and smote the giants who were in the mountains, from Hebron, from Debir, from Gebal and from all the mountains of Judah and from all the mountains of Israel; Joshua destroyed them utterly with their cities.

22 There was none of the giants left remaining in the land of the children of Israel; only in Gaza, in Gath, and in Ashdod, did any remain.

23 So Joshua took the whole land, according to all that the LORD had spoken to Moses; and Joshua gave it as an inheritance to Israel according to their divisions by their tribes. And the land rested from war.

CHAPTER 12

NOW these are the kings of the land whom the children of Israel smote, and whose lands they possessed beyond the Jordan toward the rising of the sun, from the river Arnon as far as mount Hermon, and all the plain on the east:

2 Sihon king of the Amorites, who dwelt in Heshbon and ruled from Adoer, which is on the bank of the river Arnon, and ruled the middle of the valley, and half of Gilead, as far as the river of Jabbok, which is the border of the children of Ammon;

3 And ruled from the plain to the sea of Chinnereth on the east, and to the sea of the plain, the Salt Sea on the east, the way of Beth-Ashimon; and from Teman, which is below the hill of Ashdoth;

4 ¶And the territory of Og king of Bashan, who was of the family of giants, who dwelt at Ashtaroth and at Erdei,

5 And ruled in mount Ashimon, and in Salcah, and in all Bashan, to the border of En-dor and of Maacath, and half Gilead, the border of Sihon king of Heshbon,

6 Whom Moses the servant of the LORD slew, and gave his land for a possession to the Reubenites and the Gadites and the half tribe of Manasseh.

7 ¶And these are the kings of the land whom Joshua and the children of Israel slew on this side of Jordan on the west, and from Gilgal which is in the valley of Lebanon as far as the mount of Paleg, that goes up to Seir; whose lands Joshua gave to the tribes of Israel as a possession according to their divisions;

8 In the mountains and in the valleys, in the low plain, in Ashdod, in the desert, and in the south country; the Hittites, the Amorites, the Canaanites, the Perizzites, the Hivites, and the Jebusites;

9 ¶These are the kings of the land whom Joshua slew: The king of Jericho, one; the king of Ai, which is beside Beth-el, one;

10 The king of Jerusalem, one; the king of Hebron, one;

11 The king of Jarmuth, one; the king of Lachish, one;

12 The king of Eglon, one; the king of Gezer, one;

13 The king of Debir, one; the king of Hirmah, one;

14 The king of Gadar, one; the king of Arad, one;

15 The king of Libnah, one; the king of Arlam, one;

16 The king of Makkar, one; the king of Beth-el, one;

17 The king of Tappuah, one; the king of Hepher, one;

18 The king of Aphik, one; the king of Nishron, one;

19 The king of Madon, one; the king of Hazor, one;

20 The king of Shamrin and Meron, one; the king of Achshaph, one;

21 The king of Taanach, one; the king of Megiddo, one;

22 The king of Rakim, one; the king of Nokneam and Carmel, one;

23 The king of Dor and of Napodor, one; the king of the low country and of Gilgal, one;

24 The king of Tirzah, one; all the kings whom Joshua slew were thirty-one.

CHAPTER 13

NOW Joshua was old and advanced in years; and the LORD said to him, Behold, you are old and advanced in years, and there remains yet very much land to be possessed.

2 This is the land that yet remains in all regions of the Philistines and in all the country of En-dor,

3 From Sihor, which is before Egypt, as far as the border of Ekron northward, which is counted to the Canaanites; five lords of the Philistines; the Gazathites, the Ashdothites, the Eshkalonites, the Gittites, and the Ekronites; and also the Avites to the south;

4 And all the land of the Canaanites, and Maarthah which belongs to the Sidonians, as far as Aphik, to the border of the Amorites;

5 And the land of Gebal, and all Lebanon, toward the sunrising, from Gilead below mount Hermon to the entrance of Hamath.

6 All the inhabitants of the mountains from Lebanon to the place of hot waters, and all the Sidonians, will I the LORD drive out from before the children of Israel; only divide the land by lot to the Israelites as I have commanded you.

7 Now therefore divide this land as an inheritance to the nine tribes, and the half tribe of Manasseh along with them,

8 Because the Reubenites and the Gadites and the half of the tribe of Manasseh have received their inheritance which Moses gave them beyond the Jordan eastward, as my servant Moses gave them;

9 From Adoer, which is on the bank of the river Arnon, and the city which is in the middle of the valley, and all the plain which is westward as far as Ribon;

10 And all the towns of Sihon king of the Amorites, who reigned in Heshbon, to the border of the children of Ammon;

11 And Gilead, and the territory of En-dor and of Koros, and all mount Hermon, and all Mathnin to Salcah;

12 All the kingdom of Og in Mathnin, who reigned in Ashtaroth and in Erdei, who was left of the remnant of the giants, whom Moses slew, and Israel possessed their land.

13 Nevertheless the children of Israel did not destroy the people of En-dor and Koros; so the En-dorites and the Korosites dwell among the children of Israel until this day.

14 Only to the tribe of Levi he gave no inheritance, because the offerings of the LORD God of Israel are their inheritance, as Moses had said.

15 ¶And Moses gave an inheritance to the tribe of the Reubenites according to their families.

16 And their territory was from Adoer, which is on the bank of the river Arnon, and the town which is in the middle of the valley, and all the plain as far as Riba;

17 And Heshbon, and all the towns which are in the plain; Ribon and Math-Baal and Beth-beni-ammon

18 And Jahaz and Kermoth and Aenath

19 And Koriathaim and Shammah and Jazreth and Seir on the mount of the valley

20 And Beth-peor and Ashtaroth

and Pisgah and Beth-jeshimoth

21 And all the cities of the plain and all the kingdom of Sihon king of the Amorites, who reigned in Heshbon, whom Moses and the children of Israel slew in Midian, both him and his princes, Evi, Rakim, and Zur, and Hur, and Reba, the five princes of Sihon, who dwelt in the land.

22 ¶Balaam also, the son of Beor, the soothsayer, did the children of Israel slay with the sword along with the rest of them that were slain by them.

23 And the border of the Reubenites was the region of the Jordan. This is the inheritance of the Reubenites according to their families, the cities and the villages thereof.

24 And Moses gave an inheritance to the tribe of Gad, according to their families.

25 And their territory was Jazer and all the cities of Gilead and half the land of the children of Ammon to Adoer which is before Rabbath;

26 And from Heshbon to Ramath-mizpah, and Betonin; and from Mahanaim to the border of Debir;

27 And in the valley, Beth-atim and Beth-nimrah and Succoth and the region northward and the rest of the kingdom of Sihon king of Heshbon, and their borders extended as far as the Jordan, and to the edge of the sea of Chinnereth beyond the Jordan eastward.

28 This is the inheritance of the Gadites by their families, the cities and their villages.

29 ¶And Moses gave an inheritance to the half tribe of Manasseh; and this was the possession of the half tribe of Manasshites by their families.

30 And their territory was from Mahanaim, all Mathnin, all the kingdom of Og king of Mathnin, and all the villages of Jair, which are in Mathnin, sixty towns;

31 And half Gilead, and Ashtaroth and Edrei, cities of the kingdom of Og in Mathnin. These cities and their villages Moses gave to the children of Machir the son of Manasseh, to the half of the children of Machir by their families.

32 These two tribes and the half of the tribe of Manasseh Moses gave an inheritance in the plains of Moab, beyond the Jordan, eastward.

33 But to the tribe of Levi Moses gave no inheritance; because, as he said to them, the LORD God of Israel was their inheritance.

CHAPTER 14

AND these are the countries which the children of Israel inherited in the land of Canaan, which Eleazar the priest and Joshua the son of Nun and the heads of the fathers of the tribes of the children of Israel distributed as inheritance to them.

2 By lot was their inheritance divided, as the LORD had commanded by the hand of Moses, to be given to the nine tribes and to the half tribe.

3 For Moses had given the inheritance of two tribes and a half tribe beyond the Jordan; but to the Levites he gave no inheritance.

4 For the children of Joseph were two tribes, Manasseh and Ephraim; therefore he gave no portion to the Levites in the land, save cities to dwell in, with their suburbs for their cattle and for their substance.

5 As the LORD commanded Moses, so did the children of Israel, and they divided the land.

6 ¶Then the children of Judah came to Joshua in Gilgal; and Caleb the son of Jophaniah the Kenezite said to Joshua, You know the thing that the LORD spoke to Moses his servant concerning me and you at Rakim-gia.

7 I was forty years old when Moses the servant of the LORD sent me from Rakim-gia to spy out the land; and I brought him word again as it was in my heart.

8 Nevertheless our brethren who went up with us made the heart of the people quake; but I wholly followed the LORD my God.

9 And Moses swore at that time, saying, Surely the land on which your foot has trodden shall be your inheritance, and your children's forever, because you have wholly followed the LORD God.

10 And now, behold, the LORD has

given us rest, as he said; behold, it is forty-five years since the LORD spoke this word to Moses, while Israel wandered in the wilderness; and now, lo, I am this day eighty-five years old,

11 And today I am as strong as the day when Moses sent me; as my strength was then, so is my strength now, for war, both to go out and to come in.

12 Now therefore give me this mountain, of which the LORD spoke on that day; for you have heard on that day how the giants were there, and that the cities were great and fortified; perhaps the LORD will be with me, and I shall destroy them, as the LORD said.

13 And Joshua blessed Caleb the son of Jophaniah, and gave him Hebron and its environs as an inheritance.

14 Hebron therefore and its environs became the inheritance of Caleb the son of Jophaniah the Kenezite to this day, because he wholly followed the LORD God of Israel.

15 And the name of Hebron and its environs before was Koriath-arba, which belonged to the giants. And the land rested from war.

CHAPTER 15

THIS then was the lot of the tribe of the children of Judah by their families; it extended to the border of Edom, to the wilderness of Zin, to the uttermost of the southern border.

2 And their south border was from the southern end of the Salt Sea, and from thence went up to the bay that faces southward;

3 And it went out toward the ascent of Akrakam, and passed along to Zin, then went up on the south side of Rakim-gia, and passed along to Hezroth, and went up to Adar, and circled Karka;

4 Then it passed along to Azmon, and went out to the river of Egypt; and the limits of the border were at the sea; this shall be your south boundary.

5 And the east boundary was from the farthest end of the Salt Sea, as far as the mouth of the Jordan. And the border on the north side was from the bay of the Sea at the mouth of the Jordan;

6 And the border went up to Leban, which belongs to the descendants of Reuben,

7 And then the border went up toward Debir from the valley of Achar and so northward, turning toward Galilee, which is opposite the slope of Ramin, which is on the south side of the river; and the border passed toward the En-shemesh, and the limits of the border were at En-dogel;

8 And the border went up to the valley of the son of Hinnom to the south side of the Jebusite city, which is Jerusalem; and the boundary went up to the top of the mountain that lies before the valley of the son of Hinnom westward, which is at the end of the valley of the Giants:

9 And the border ran from the top of the mountain to the fountain of the waters of Nephtoah, and thence to the tip of mount Ebron; then the border ran to Baalah, which is Koriath-narin;

10 And the border continued from Baalah westward to mount Seir, and passed along to the side of mount Narim, that is Chesalon, on the north side, and went down to Beth-shemesh, and passed along to the south;

11 And the border went out to the side of Ekron northward; and the border was drawn to Shicron, and passed along to mount Baalah, and went out to Jahbael; and the limits of the border were at the Great Sea.

12 And the west border was extended to the Great Sea, and the coast thereof. This is the boundary of the descendants of Judah according to their families.

13 ¶And to Caleb the son of Jophaniah Joshua gave a portion among the children of Judah, according to the commandment of the LORD. And Caleb said to Joshua, Give me this Koriath-arba which belongs to the father of giants; and Joshua gave to Caleb Koriath-arba, that is, Hebron.

14 And Caleb slew there the three descendants of giants, Sheshai and Ahiman and Tholmai, the descendants of the giants.

15 And he went up thence against the inhabitants of Debir; and the name of Debir before was Koriath-sepra.

16 ¶And Caleb said, Whoever takes Koriath-sepra and destroys it, to him will I give Achsah my daughter to wife.

17 And Othniel the son of Kenaz, the brother of Caleb, took it; and he gave him Achsah his daughter to wife.

18 And it came to pass, when she became his wife, she desired from her father a field as an inheritance; and she alighted from her ass; and Caleb said to her, What troubles you, my daughter?

19 She said to him, Give me a blessing; because you have given me a heritage in the south land; give me also this pool of water. And Caleb gave her the upper pool and the lower pool.

20 This is the inheritance of the tribe of the descendants of Judah by their families.

21 And the uttermost cities of the tribe of the descendants of Judah extended toward the border of Edom southward. These are the names of the cities of the descendants of Judah: Kabzeel, Eder, Jagur,

22 Kinah, Jarmonah, Gadgada,

23 Kedesh, Hazor, Nathnin,

24 Zib, Atlam, Bealoth,

25 Hazor, Hadattah, Koriath-hezron,

26 Amam, Ashma, Moladah,

27 Hazar-ada, Heshmon, Beth-palet,

28 Darath-taaley, Beer-sheba, Beerjothanah,

29 Baalah, Alian, Azem,

30 Altlam, Achsin, Hirmah,

31 Zinklag, Marmanah, Samsalah,

32 Lebaoth, Shaloh, and Airmon, all the cities are thirty-six with their villages;

33 And in the valley, Eshtaol, Zedaa, Ashtnah,

34 Khokh, En-gahom, Patoh, Eliam,

35 Jarmuth, Arlam, Socoh, Azekah,

36 Shatin, Azilthaim, Gathar, Gethronin; fifteen cities with their villages;

37 Zalan, Harshah, Migdal-gad,

38 Dilban, Kaspa, Nakthael,

39 Lachish, Ezkat, Eglon,

40 Cebshon, Lahmish, Kithlish,

41 Gederoth, Beth-dagon, Naamah, Nakdah; sixteen cities with their villages;

42 Libnah, Ether, Naphtah,

43 Ashan, Ashia, Zinklag,

44 Keilah, Achzib, and Mareshah; nine cities with their villages;

45 Ekron, with its towns and its villages westward;

46 And all the land of Ashdod with its villages;

47 And Ashdod with its villages and farm lands, Gaza with its towns and farm lands, to the river of Egypt, and the Great Sea, with its coast;

48 ¶And in the mountains, Shamir, Jattir, and Socoh,

49 Rannah, Koriath-sepra, that is, Debir,

50 Ganab, Eshtemoa, Elian,

51 Eshian, Holon, and Giloh; eleven towns with their villages;

52 Jab, Romah,[1] Ashan,

53 Jalom, Beth-tappuah, Aphekah,

54 Humta, Koriath-arba, that is, Hebron, and Zebaon; nine cities with their villages;

55 Maon, Carmel, Zib, Atna,

56 Jezreel, Nekemaam, Zaloh,

57 Cain, Gibeah, and Timnah; ten cities with their villages;

58 Halhul, Beth-zur, Gedar,

59 Maarath, Beth-anoth, and Lathkin; six cities with their villages:

60 Rabbath, and Koriath-baal, that is, Koriath-narin; two cities with their villages;

61 In the wilderness, Beth-arabah, Midian, Secasah,

62 Jashan, Air-mehel, and En-gad; six cities with their villages.

63 ¶As for the Jebusites, the inhabitants of Jerusalem, the descendants of Judah could not destroy them; so the Jebusites dwell among the descendants of Judah at Jerusalem to this day.

CHAPTER 16

AND the lot of the descendants of Joseph fell from the Jordan by Jericho to the waters of Jericho on the

---

[1] Rome, hills.

east, into the wilderness that goes up from Jericho to mount Beth-el,

2 And goes out from Beth-el to Luz, and then passes along to the border of Ebra and Ataroth,

3 And goes down westward to the border of Palta, as far as the border of Beth-hauran, the lower, then to Gadar; and its limits extended to the sea.

4 So the descendants of Joseph, Manasseh and Ephraim, received their inheritance.

5 ¶And the border of the descendants of Ephraim according to their families was thus: the boundary of their inheritance was Ataroth and Addar, as far as Beth-hauran, the upper;

6 Then the border went westward to the northern portion; after which the border turned eastward below Shiloh, and passed by it on the east of Jaloh;

7 And it went down from Jaloh to Ataroth and Jagrath and Pagar, and came to Jericho, and went out of Tappuah to the Jordan;

8 And the border went out westward to the river Kabah; and the limits thereof were at the sea. This is the inheritance of the tribe of the descendants of Ephraim by their families.

9 And the cities which were set apart for the descendants of Ephraim were within the inheritance of the children of Manasseh, all the cities with their villages.

10 And they did not destroy the Canaanites that dwelt in Gadar; so the Canaanites dwell among the Ephraimites to this day, but they were brought into subjection, and they pay tribute.

CHAPTER 17

AND Gilead became the lot for the tribe of Manasseh; for he was the first-born of Joseph; to Machir the first-born of Manasseh, the father of Gilead; because he was the first-born and a man of war, therefore he had Gilead and Mathnin.

2 And became also the portion for the rest of the children of Manasseh by their families; for the descendants of Abiezer and for the descendants of He-lek and for the descendants of Neshrael and for the descendants of Shopam and for the descendants of Hepher and for the descendants of Shemida; these were the male children of Manasseh the son of Joseph by their families.

3 ¶But Zelophehad, the son of Hepher, the son of Gilead, the son of Machir, the son of Manasseh, had no sons, but daughters; and these are the names of his daughters, Mahlah, and Joah, Hoglah, Milcah and Tirzah.

4 And they came near before Eleazar the priest, and before Joshua the son of Nun, and before the princes of Israel, saying, The LORD commanded Moses to give us an inheritance among our brethren; so he gave us according to the command of the LORD, among the brothers of our father. Now therefore give us an inheritance among the brethren of our father. So Joshua gave them an inheritance among the brethren of their father.

5 And there fell ten portions to Manasseh, besides the land of Gilead and Mathnin, which were on the other side of the Jordan;

6 Because the daughters of Manasseh received an inheritance among his sons; and the land of Gilead fell to the lot of the rest of the sons of Manasseh.

7 ¶And the border of Manasseh was from the boundary of Maacath, which lies on the right hand of the inhabitants of En-tappuah.

8 Thus their land was in the region of Tappuah and Patah, which became the boundary to the descendants of Manasseh the son of Joseph, and to the Ephraimites;

9 And the boundary went down to the river of the Sea, to the south of the river of the cities which belong to Ephraim among the cities of Manasseh; and the border of Manasseh ran on the north side of the river, and the outgoings thereof reached to the sea;

10 The land to the south went to Ephraim, and that to the north to Manasseh, and the sea as their border;

and they met together in Asher on the north, and in Issachar on the east.

11 And Manasseh had opposite Issachar and Asher, Beth-shean and its towns, and Neb-leam and its towns, and En-dor and its towns, and Taanach and its towns, and Megiddo and its towns, three districts.

12 Yet the Israelites could not destroy these cities, because the Canaanites took refuge and dwelt in them.

13 But when the children of Israel became strong, they subdued the Canaanites and made them pay tribute; but did not utterly destroy them.

14 And the descendants of Joseph spoke to Joshua, saying, Why have you given us but one portion to inherit, seeing we are a numerous people, forasmuch as the LORD has blessed us hitherto?

15 Joshua said to them, If you are a numerous people, then go up on the side of the mountain, and choose for yourselves a portion in the land of the Perizzites and of the giants, if mount Ephraim is too narrow for you.

16 And the descendants of Joseph said, The mountain and the cities of the Perizzites are not enough for us; for the Canaanites still dwell in the land of the valley, and in Beth-shean and its towns, and in the valley of Jezreel.

17 Then Joshua spoke to the house of Joseph, even to Ephraim and Manasseh, saying, You are a numerous people, and have a great power; if one portion is not enough for you,

18 Then choose for yourselves the mountain, and it will be enough for you, and the slopes of the mountain and its limits shall be yours; and you shall destroy the Canaanites and the Perizzites, though they have great iron chariots, and though they are strong.

CHAPTER 18

THEN the whole congregation of the children of Israel assembled together at Shiloh, and set up the tabernacle of the congregation there. And the land was subdued before them.

2 And there remained among the children of Israel seven tribes which had not yet received their inheritance.

3 And Joshua said to the children of Israel, How long will you be backward about going in and possessing the land which the LORD God of your fathers has given you?

4 Choose for yourselves three men from each tribe; and I will send them, and they shall rise and go through the land, and survey and describe it according to their inheritance; and they shall come again to me.

5 And they shall divide the land into seven parts; Judah shall remain in their territory on the south, and the house of Joseph shall remain in their territory on the north.

6 And you shall therefore map out the land into seven parts, and then bring the map here, and I will cast lots for you here before the LORD our God.

7 But the Levites have no part among you; for the priesthood of the LORD is their inheritance; and Gad and Reuben and half the tribe of Manasseh have received their inheritance beyond the Jordan to the east, which Moses the servant of the LORD gave them.

8 ¶And the men arose and went away; and Joshua charged those who went to map the land, saying, Go and walk through the land, and map it, and come again here to me, that I may cast lots for you before the LORD in Shiloh.

9 And the men went and passed through the land, and mapped it by towns into seven parts on a scroll, and came again to Joshua at the city of Shiloh.

10 ¶And Joshua cast lots for them in Shiloh before the LORD; and there Joshua divided the land to the children of Israel into districts.

11 ¶And the lot of the tribe of Benjamin came up according to their families; and the territory of their inheritance came forth between the children of Judah and the children of Joseph.

12 And their border on the north side was from the Jordan; and the

border went up to the side of Jericho on the north side, and went up through the mountain westward; and the extreme limits thereof were at the wilderness of Beth-aon.

13 And the border went over from thence toward Luz, to the side of Luz, that is Beth-el, southward; then the border descended to Ataroth-adar, upon the mountain that lies south of lower Beth-hauran.

14 And the border extended to the side of the sea southward, from the mountain that lies before Beth-hauran southward; and the limits thereof were at Koriath-baal, which is Koriath-narin, a city of the children of Judah: this is the sea side.

15 And the southern boundary was from the end of Koriath-narin, and the border went out to the sea, and went out to the fountain of waters of Naphtali:

16 Then the border descended to the end of the mountain that lies before the valley of the son of Hinnom, which is in the valley of the Giants on the north, and went down to the valley of the son of Hinnom, to the side of the Jebusites on the south, then descended to En-dogel,

17 And was drawn from the north, and went to the En-shemesh, and thence towards Galilee, which is opposite the ascent of Ramin, then descended to Leban, and Bohan which belonged to the son of Reuben,

18 And passed along towards the side which is opposite the plain northward, and went down to the plain;

19 Then the border passed along to the side of Beth-hoglah northward; and the limits of the border were at the northern bay of the Salt Sea at the side of the Jordan southward; this was the south border.

20 And the Jordan was its border on the east side. This was the inheritance of the children of Benjamin, by the borders thereof round about, according to their families.

21 Now the cities of the tribe of the children of Benjamin according to their families were Jericho, Beth-hoglah, Amak, and Keziz,

22 Beth-arabah, Zemaraim, Beth-el,

23 Avin, Parah, Ophrah,

24 Chephar-aomka, Ophli, and Gaba; fourteen cities with their villages;

25 Gibeon, Ramtha, Beeroth,

26 Mizpah, Chepirah, Mozah,

27 Rakim, Repeel, Taralah,

28 Zelah, Geberah, and Jebusi, that is, Jerusalem, Gibeath, and Koriath-aim; fourteen cities with their villages. This is the inheritance of the children of Benjamin according to their families.

CHAPTER 19

AND the second lot came forth for the tribe of the children of Simeon according to their families; and their inheritance was within the inheritance of the children of Judah.

2 And they had in their inheritance Beer-sheba, Sheba, Moladah,

3 Darath-taley, Balah, and Azem,

4 Eltolad, Beth-el, Hirmah,

5 Zinklag, Beth-marcaboth, Hazar-susah,

6 Beth-lebaoth, and Sharwenan; fourteen cities and their villages;

7 Ain, Remmon, Gather, and Ashan; four cities and their villages;

8 And all the villages that were round about these cities as far as Labath, Beth-ramtha of the south. This is the inheritance of the tribe of the children of Simeon according to their families.

9 Out of the portion of the children of Judah was the inheritance of the children of Simeon; because the portion of the children of Judah was too much for them; therefore the children of Simeon inherited some of their inheritance.

10 ¶And the third lot came up for the children of Zebulun according to their families; and the border of their inheritance extended as far as Ashdod;

11 And their border went up westward, and to Ramath-taley, and reached to Debbashet, then reached to the river that is before Nekemaam;

12 Then turned from Ashdod eastward toward the sunrise to the border of Chisloth and Bethor, and then ex-

tended to Rabbath, and went up to Naphia,

13 And from thence passed along eastward to Gath, to Hepher, to Attah, and to Kazin, and then went out to Remmon, and Mathwa, and Awa;

14 And the border turned around the north side of Haditon; and the limits thereof ended at the Valley of Chiphtanael;

15 And Kattath, Jahallal, Shamrin, Aralah and Beth-lehem; twelve cities with their villages.

16 This is the inheritance of the children of Zebulun according to their families.

17 ¶And the fourth lot came out to the children of Issachar, according to their families.

18 And their border included Jezreel, Chesulloth, Shunem,

19 Haphraim, Shinan, Ahtar,

20 Deblath, Kishon, Apaz,

21 Ramath-en, Einjan, En-hadah, and Beth-pizian;

22 And the border reached to Tabor, Shahazimah, and Beth-shemesh; and the limits of their border were at the Jordan; thirteen cities with their villages.

23 This is the inheritance of the tribe of the children of Issachar according to their families, the cities and their villages.

24 ¶And the fifth lot came out for the tribe of the children of Asher according to their families.

25 And their border was Haklath, Hali, Batan, Achshaph,

26 Amlekh, Amcar and Amshael; and reached to Carmel westward, and to Shihor, and to Labeth;

27 And then it turned toward the sunrise to Beth-dagon, and reached to Zebulun, and to the valley of Niphtahael toward the north side, and to Beth-aomka, and Neil, and it went out northward to Cobel,

28 And Ebron, Rehob, Hammon, and Kaah, as far as great Zidon;

29 And then the border turned to Ramtha, as far as the strong city of Tyre; the border then turned to Has; and the limits thereof reached to the west of the valley of Achzib;

30 Umkah also Aphik, and Rehob;

twenty-two cities with their villages.

31 This is the inheritance of the tribe of the children of Asher according to their families, these cities with their villages.

32 ¶And the sixth lot went to the children of Naphtali, according to their families.

33 And their border was from Halpa, from Allon, and from Zinaam, Adama, Nekeb, and Nakbael, to Lakum; and the limits thereof were at the Jordan;

34 And then the boundary turned westward to Aznoth-boz, and went out from there to Hakik, and reached to Zebulun on the south side, and reached to Asher on the west side, and to Judah at the Jordan toward the sunrise.

35 And the great cities were Tyre, Zidon, Hammath, Karath, Chinnereth,

36 Adamah, Damah, Hazor,

37 Kedesh, Edrei, En-zur,

38 Dion, Migdal-el, Hadon, Bethanoth, and Beth-shemesh; nineteen cities with their villages.

39 This is the inheritance of the tribe of Naphtali according to their families, the cities and their villages.

40 ¶And the seventh lot went to the tribe of Dan according to their families.

41 And the border of their inheritance was Zidah, Eshtaol, Kerith-shemish,

42 Shaalabbin, Ajalon, Nethlah,

43 Elon, Timmnah, Ekron,

44 Elkath, Gibbethon, Baalath,

45 Jehudith, Beldabak, Gath-rimmon,

46 Mehrikon, and Carkon, as far as the territory which is opposite Elath.

47 And the territory of the children of Dan was not sufficient for them; therefore the Danites went up and fought against Eino, and captured it, and smote it with the edge of the sword, and possessed it, and dwelt in it, and called Eino, Dan, after the name of Dan their father.

48 This is the inheritance of the tribe of Dan according to their families, these cities with their villages.

49 ¶When they had finished dividing the land as their inheritance and de-

lineating its boundaries, the children of Israel gave an inheritance to Joshua the son of Nun among them;

50 According to the word of the LORD they gave him the city which he asked, Timnath-serah on mount Ephraim; and he built the city and dwelt in it.

51 These are the inheritances which Eleazar the priest and Joshua the son of Nun and the heads of the fathers of the tribes of Israel divided by lot at Shiloh before the LORD, at the door of the tabernacle of the congregation. So they completed the division of the land.

CHAPTER 20

THEN the LORD said to Joshua,
2 Speak to the children of Israel, saying, Reserve for you cities of refuge, of which I spoke to you through my servant Moses;

3 That the slayer who kills any person suddenly and unwittingly may flee there; and they shall be your refuge from the avenger of blood.

4 And when he that shall flee to one of these cities shall stand at the entrance of the gate of the city, and shall speak to the elders of that city and explain his case, they shall take him into the city with them and give him a place, that he may dwell among them.

5 And when the avenger of blood pursues him, then they shall not deliver the slayer into his hand; because he slew his neighbor unwittingly, and did not hate him beforehand.

6 And he shall dwell in that city until he stand before the congregation for judgment, and until the death of the high priest that shall be in those days; then the slayer shall return, and come to his own city and to his own house, to the city from which he fled.

7 ¶So they set apart these cities for the places of refuge: Rakim in Galilee in mount Naphtali, and Shechem in mount Ephraim, and Koriath-arba, which is Hebron, in the mountain of Judah.

8 And on the other side of the Jordan, east of Jericho, they assigned Bozer in the wilderness, which is situated upon the plain, from the tribe of Reuben, and Ramoth in Gilead, from the tribe of Gad, and Golan in Mathnin, from the tribe of Manasseh.

9 These were the cities set apart for all the children of Israel and for the strangers that sojourned among them, that any one who killed a person unawares might flee there, and not be delivered into the hand of the avenger of blood, until he had stood before the congregation.

CHAPTER 21

THEN the chiefs of the priests and the Levites came near to Eleazar the priest and to Joshua the son of Nun and to the heads of the fathers of the tribes of Israel,

2 And they said to them at Shiloh in the land of Canaan, The LORD commanded by the hand of Moses to give us cities to dwell in, with their suburbs for our cattle.

3 And the children of Israel gave to the Levites out of their inheritance, at the commandment of the LORD, these cities and their suburbs.

4 And lots were drawn for the families of the Kohathites; and the children of Aaron the priest, who were of the Levites, had by lot from the tribe of Judah, from the tribe of Simeon, and from the tribe of Benjamin, thirteen cities.

5 And the rest of the Kohathites had by lot from the tribe of Ephraim, from the tribe of Dan, and from the half tribe of Manasseh, ten cities.

6 And the Gershonites had by lot from the tribe of Issachar, from the tribe of Asher, from the tribe of Naphtali, and from the half tribe of Manasseh in Mathnin, thirteen cities.

7 And the descendants of Merari by their families had from the tribe of Reuben, from the tribe of Gad, and from the tribe of Zebulun, twelve cities.

8 And the children of Israel gave by lot to the Levites these cities with their suburbs, as the LORD had commanded Moses.

9 ¶These are the names of the cities

which they gave out of the tribe of Judah, and out of the tribe of Simeon, each city mentioned by its name.

10 They became the property of the descendants of Aaron, being of the family of the Kohathites, who were the children of Levi, for theirs was the first lot.

11 And they gave them Koriath-arba, which belonged to the father of giants, that is, Hebron, on the mountain of Judah, with its suburbs round about it.

12 But the fields of the city, with its villages, they gave to Caleb the son of Jophaniah for his possession.

13 ¶Thus they gave to the children of Aaron the priest, Hebron, the city of refuge for the slayers, with its suburbs, and Libnah with its suburbs,

14 And Jarath with its suburbs, and Eshtemoa with its suburbs,

15 Halol with its suburbs, Debir with its suburbs,

16 Ain with its suburbs, Aata with its suburbs, and Beth-shemesh with its suburbs; nine cities out of the tribes of Judah and Simeon.

17 And out of the tribe of Benjamin, Gibeon with its suburbs, Geba with its suburbs,

18 Anathoth with its suburbs, and Almon with its suburbs; four cities.

19 All the cities of the children of Aaron, the priest, were thirteen cities with their suburbs.

20 ¶And for the families of the Kohathites, the Levites, that remained of the children of Kohath, they had the cities of their lot out of the tribe of Ephraim.

21 For they gave them Shechem, the city of refuge for the slayers, with its suburbs, on mount Ephraim, Gedar with its suburbs,

22 Kibzaim with its suburbs, and Beth-hauran with its suburbs; four cities.

23 And out of the tribe of Dan, Ethleka with its suburbs, Gibethon with its suburbs,

24 Aijalon with its suburbs, and Gath-rimmon with its suburbs; four cities with their suburbs.

25 And out of the half tribe of Ma-nasseh, Tanach with its suburbs, and Gath-rimmon with its suburbs; two cities with their suburbs.

26 All the towns and the cities were ten with their suburbs which went for the remaining families of the Kohathites.

27 ¶And the Gershonites, of the families of the Levites, had their cities out of the half tribe of Manasseh, Golan in Mathnin, the city of refuge for the slayer, with its suburbs, and Ashteroth with its suburbs; two cities with their suburbs.

28 And out of the tribe of Issachar, Kishian with its suburbs, Rabbath with its suburbs,

29 Jarmuth with its suburbs, En-gad with its suburbs; four cities with their suburbs.

30 And out of the tribe of Asher, Mishal with its suburbs, Acron with its suburbs,

31 Helkath with its suburbs, and Rehob with its suburbs; four cities with their suburbs.

32 And out of the tribe of Naphtali, Rakim in Galilee [1] with its suburbs, the city of refuge for the slayer, Ham-moth-dor with its suburbs, and Kartan with its suburbs; three cities with their suburbs.

33 All the cities of the families of the Gershonites were thirteen cities with their suburbs.

34 ¶And the children of Merari, the rest of the Levites, received their cities out of the tribe of Reuben, Jahaz with its suburbs, Kermoth with its suburbs, Kiriathim with its suburbs,

35 And Ahshemoth with its suburbs, four cities with their suburbs.

36 And out of the tribe of Zebulun, Nacah with its suburbs, Karthan with its suburbs,

37 Ramin with its suburbs, and Jah-lah with its suburbs, four cities with their suburbs.

38 And out of the tribe of Gad, Ramoth in Gilead with its suburbs, the city of refuge for the slayer, and Mahanaim with its suburbs,

39 Heshbon with its suburbs, and Jazer with its suburbs; four cities with their suburbs.

[1] Later called Kedesh.

40 So all the cities for the children of Merari by their families, who were remaining of the families of the Levites, were by their lot twelve cities with their suburbs.

41 All the cities of the Levites within the possession of the children of Israel were forty-eight cities with their suburbs.

42 These cities with their towns were situated thus, each town with its suburbs round about it; thus were all these towns with their cities.

43 ¶And the LORD gave to Israel all the land which he had sworn to give to their fathers; and they possessed it, and dwelt therein.

44 And the LORD gave them rest round about, according to all that he swore to their fathers; and there stood not a man of their enemies before them, but the LORD delivered all their enemies into their hands.

45 There failed not one of the good things which the LORD has spoken to the house of Israel; all came to pass.

CHAPTER 22

THEN Joshua called the Reubenites and the Gadites and the half tribe of Manasseh,

2 And said to them, You have kept all that Moses the servant of the LORD commanded you, and have obeyed my voice in all that I have commanded you;

3 You have not deserted your brethren these many days even to this time, but have kept the commandments of the LORD your God.

4 And now the LORD your God has given rest to your brethren, as he promised them; therefore now return, and go to your towns and to the land of your possession, which Moses the servant of the LORD gave you on the other side of the Jordan to the east.

5 But only take diligent heed to observe the commandments and the laws which Moses the servant of the LORD charged you, to love the LORD your God, to keep his commandments, and to cleave to him, and to serve him with all your heart and with all your soul.

6 So Joshua blessed them and sent them away; and they went to their towns.

7 ¶Now to the half of the tribe of Manasseh Moses had given an inheritance in Mathnin; but to the other half thereof Joshua had given an inheritance among their brethren on this side of the Jordan to the west. And when Joshua sent them away to their towns, he blessed them;

8 And he spoke to them, saying, Return to your towns and to the land of your inheritance with much wealth and with very many cattle, with silver, with gold, with brass, with iron, and with very much clothing; divide the spoil of your enemies with your brethren.

9 ¶So the Reubenites and the Gadites and the half tribe of Manasseh returned, and departed from the children of Israel out of Shiloh, which is in the land of Canaan, to go to the land of Gilead, to the land of their possessions, in which they were given an inheritance, according to the word of the LORD by the hand of Moses.

10 ¶And when they came to Gilgal, which is by the side of the Jordan in the land of Canaan, the Reubenites, the Gadites, and the half tribe of Manasseh built there an altar by the Jordan, a large and remarkable altar.

11 ¶And the children of Israel heard it said, Behold, the Reubenites and the Gadites and the half tribe of Manasseh have built an altar at the border of the land of Canaan, in Gilgal which is by the side of the Jordan, in the land of the children of Israel.

12 Then the whole congregation of the children of Israel gathered themselves together at Shiloh to go to war against them.

13 And the children of Israel sent to the Reubenites and to the Gadites and to the half tribe of Manasseh, into the land of Gilead, Phinehas the son of Eleazar the priest,

14 And with him ten princes, one prince from every tribe of Israel; and these men were chiefs of the armies of Israel.

15 ¶And they came to the Reubenites and to the Gadites and to the half

tribe of Manasseh, in the land of Gilead, and they spoke with them, saying,

16 Thus says the whole congregation of the LORD, What treachery is this which you have committed against the God of Israel, in turning away from following the LORD, in that you have builded yourselves an altar, that you might abandon the worship of the LORD?

17 Is the iniquity of Peor not enough for us, from which we are not cleansed until this day, although there was a plague in the congregation of the LORD?

18 And as for you, when you turned away this day from the worship of the LORD, tomorrow the anger will be against the whole congregation of Israel.

19 If, however, the land of your possession is unclean, then pass over to the land of the possession of the LORD, where the LORD's tabernacle dwells, and inherit land among us; but do not disdain the worship of the LORD, nor rebel against us by building for yourselves an altar beside the altar of the LORD the God of Israel.

20 Did you not see that when Achar the son of Carmi coveted and took the devoted things, wrath fell upon the whole congregation of Israel? He was but one man, yet he devoured us all in his iniquity.

21 ¶Then the Reubenites the Gadites and the half tribe of Manasseh answered and said to Phinehas the son of Eleazar the priest and to the heads of the armies of Israel,

22 The LORD is the God of gods, the God of gods is the LORD, and he is our God, and he knows Israel and he knows us also; if we shall depart from him, or if we shall transgress against the worship of the LORD in doing this thing, then let him not save us this day.

23 And if we have built us an altar to turn from the worship of the LORD, or to offer upon it burnt offerings, or use it for any other service, let the LORD himself seek vengeance against us;

24 And if we have not rather done this thing because of reverence to him, so that in time to come your children might not say to our children, What have you to do with the LORD God of Israel, O you Reubenites and Gadites?

25 For the LORD has made the Jordan a boundary between us and you; now therefore you have no part in the LORD; so in time to come shall your children make our children cease from worshipping the LORD.

26 Therefore we said, Let us now prepare to build us an altar, not for burnt offering, nor for sacrifice;

27 But that it may be a witness between us and you, and between our generations after us, and between ourselves and our generations after us, that we might do the service of the LORD before him with our burnt offerings and with our sacrifices and with our peace offerings, in the place where the LORD chooses to dwell; so that your children may not say to our children in time to come, You have no part in the LORD.

28 Therefore we said that it shall be, if they should ever speak to us or to our generations in time to come, then we may say to them, Behold the pattern of the altar of the LORD which our fathers made not for burnt offerings, nor for sacrifices; but to be a witness between us and you.

29 God forbid that we should reject the worship of the LORD, and turn away from revering him, and build for ourselves an altar for burnt offerings, for gift offerings, or for sacrifices, besides the altar of the LORD God of Israel that is before his tabernacle.

30 ¶And when Phinehas the son of Eleazar the priest and the princes of the congregation and the heads of the armies of Israel who were with him heard the words that the Reubenites and the Gadites and the half tribe of Manasseh spoke, it pleased them.

31 And Phinehas the son of Eleazar the priest said to the Reubenites and to the Gadites and to the half tribe of Manasseh, This day we know that the LORD is among us, because you have not committed this trespass against the LORD; now you have de-

livered the children of Israel, that the hand of the LORD might not be against them with wrath.

32 ¶Then Phinehas the son of Eleazar the priest, and the princes who were with him, returned from the Reubenites and from the Gadites and the Manashites, out of the land of Gilead, to the land of Canaan, to the children of Israel, and brought them an answer.

33 And the answer pleased the children of Israel; and the children of Israel blessed God, and decided not to go up against them to battle to destroy the land wherein the Reubenites and the Gadites and the Manashites dwelt.

34 And the Reubenites and the Gadites and the Manashites called the altar which they had made, The Altar of Testimony, for it is a witness between us that the LORD is the only God.

CHAPTER 23

AND it came to pass after a long time, when the LORD had given rest to Israel from all their enemies round about, that Joshua was old, and well advanced in years.

2 And Joshua summoned all Israel, their elders, their heads, their judges, and their scribes, and said to them, I am old and well advanced in years;

3 And you have seen all that the LORD your God has done to all these nations, which he destroyed from before you; for it is the LORD your God who has fought for you.

4 Behold, I have not divided to you the land of these nations that remain, in the inheritance of your tribes; but from the Jordan, all the nations that I have destroyed, even to the Great Sea westward, have I divided among you.

5 The LORD your God will defeat them, and destroy them from before you; and you shall possess their land, as the LORD your God has promised you.

6 Only be strong to keep and do all that is written in the book of the law of Moses, the servant of God, and not turn aside from it, neither to the right hand nor to the left;

7 And you shall not mix with these nations that remain among you; neither make mention of the names of their gods, nor swear by them, neither serve them, nor worship them;

8 But cleave to the LORD your God, as you have done even to this day.

9 For the LORD has destroyed from before you great and strong nations; and no man has been able to stand against you to this day.

10 One man of you shall chase a thousand; for the LORD your God is with you, he it is who fights for you, as he has promised you.

11 Take good heed therefore to yourselves, to revere the LORD your God.

12 For if you ever turn back and join the remnant of these nations that remain among you and make marriages with them and mix with them and they with you;

13 Then know for sure that the LORD your God will no more destroy these nations from before you; but they shall be snares and traps to you, and spears in your sides and fishhooks in your eyes, until you perish from off this good land which the LORD your God has given you.

14 And as for me, I am now going the way of all the earth; and you know in all your hearts and in all your souls that not one thing has failed of all the good promises which the LORD your God spoke concerning you; all have come to pass to you, and not one thing has failed.

15 Therefore, just as all the good things have come upon you which the LORD your God promised, so shall come upon you all the curses, until he have destroyed you from off this good land which the LORD your God has given you;

16 If you should transgress against the covenant of the LORD your God and against the commandments which he commanded you, and go and serve other gods and worship them; then shall the anger of the LORD be kindled against you, and you shall perish

quickly from off the good land which he has given you.

CHAPTER 24

AND Joshua gathered all the tribes of Israel to Shechem, and called for the elders of Israel, their heads, their judges, and their scribes; and they presented themselves before God in front of the tabernacle of the congregation.

2 And Joshua said to all the people, Thus says the LORD God of Israel, Your fathers dwelt on the other side of the river Euphrates in olden times, even Terah, the father of Abraham and of Nachor; and they served there other gods.

3 And I took your father Abraham from the other side of the river Euphrates, and led him throughout all the land of Canaan, and multiplied his offspring, and I gave him Isaac,

4 And I gave to Isaac, Jacob and Esau; and I gave to Esau mount Seir for a possession; but Jacob and his children went down to Egypt.

5 I sent Moses and Aaron, and I plagued Egypt, and performed wonders among them; and afterward I brought you out.

6 And I brought your fathers out of Egypt; and I brought them to the sea; and the Egyptians pursued your fathers with chariots and horsemen to the Red Sea.

7 And when your fathers cried to the LORD, he put darkness between you and the Egyptians, and then the LORD divided the Red Sea, and brought your fathers through the midst thereof; then he brought the sea upon the Egyptians, and covered them; and your eyes have seen what I did to the Egyptians; and I brought you to the wilderness, and you dwelt in the wilderness a long time.

8 And I brought you to the land of the Amorites, who dwelt on the other side of the Jordan; and they fought with you; and I delivered them into your hands, and I destroyed them from before you and you possessed their land.

9 Then Balak the son of Zippor, king of Moabites, arose and fought against Israel, and sent and called Balaam the son of Beor to curse you;

10 But I would not hearken to Balaam; therefore he blessed you still; so I delivered you from his hands.

11 And you crossed the Jordan, and came to Jericho; and the men of Jericho fought against you, the Amorites, the Canaanites, the Perizzites, the Hittites, the Girgasites, the Hivites, and the Jebusites; and I delivered them into your hands.

12 And I sent raiders before you, and I destroyed from before you the two kings of the Amorites; but not with your swords, nor with your bows.

13 And I have given you a land for which you did not labor, and cities which you did not build, and you dwell in them; and behold, you eat of vineyards and olive yards which you did not plant.

14 ¶Now therefore fear the LORD, and serve him in sincerity and in truth; and put away out of your heart the strange gods which your fathers served on the other side of the river Euphrates, and in Egypt; and serve the LORD.

15 And if it seems evil to you to serve the LORD, choose you this day whom you will serve; whether the gods which your fathers served on the other side of the river Euphrates, or the gods of the Amorites in whose land you dwell; but as for me and my house, we will serve the LORD.

16 And the people answered and said, God forbid that we should forsake the LORD to serve other gods;

17 For it is the LORD our God who has brought us up out of the land of Egypt, from the house of bondage, and who performed those great signs in our sight, and preserved us in all the way wherein we went, and among all the peoples through whom we passed;

18 And the LORD destroyed from before us all these peoples, the Amorites in whose land we dwell; the LORD destroyed them from before us; therefore we will serve the LORD; for he is the only God, and he is our God.

19 And Joshua said to the people, Behold, but it may be you cannot serve the LORD faithfully; for he is a holy God and a zealous God; he may not forgive your transgressions nor your sins.

20 If you forsake the LORD and serve strange gods of the land, then the LORD will turn and do you harm, and consume you after having been good to you.

21 And the people said to Joshua, Nay, we will not serve any other, but we will serve the LORD God.

22 And Joshua said to the people, You are witnesses against yourselves that you have chosen the LORD, to serve him. And they said, We are witnesses.

23 Then Joshua said to them, Now therefore put away the strange gods which are among you, and incline your hearts to the LORD God of Israel.

24 And the people said to Joshua, The LORD our God will we serve, and his voice will we obey.

25 So Joshua made a covenant with the people that day, and taught them the commandments and the ordinances in Shechem.

26 ¶And Joshua wrote these words in the book of the law of God, and took a great stone, and set it up there under an oak that was by the sanctuary of the LORD.

27 And Joshua said to all the people, Behold, this stone shall be a witness against us; for it has heard all the words of the LORD which he spoke to us; it shall be therefore a witness against you, lest you deal treacherously with the LORD your God.

28 And after Joshua had charged the people, he sent them away, every man to his inheritance.

29 ¶And it came to pass after these things, Joshua the son of Nun, the servant of the LORD, died, being a hundred and ten years old.

30 And they buried him in the border of his inheritance in Timnathserah, which is on mount Ephraim, on the north side of mount Gaash.

31 And Israel served the LORD all the days of Joshua and all the days of the elders that outlived Joshua, and who had known all the works of the LORD that he had done for Israel.

32 ¶And the bones of Joseph, which the children of Israel brought up from Egypt, they buried in Shechem in a parcel of ground which Jacob bought from the sons of Hamor the father of Shechem for a hundred ewes; and it became the inheritance of the descendants of Joseph.

33 And Eleazar the priest, the son of Aaron the priest, died; and they buried him at Gibaatha that belongs to Phinehas his son, which was given him on mount Ephraim.

THE BOOK OF

JUDGES

CHAPTER 1

NOW after the death of Joshua, the servant of the LORD, the children of Israel inquired of the LORD, saying, Who shall go up for us against the Canaanites first, to fight against them?

2 And the LORD said, Judah shall go up; behold, I have delivered the land into his hands.

3 And Judah said to Simeon his

brother, Come up with me into my inheritance, that we may fight against the Canaanites; and I likewise will go up with you into your inheritance. So Simeon went with him.

4 And Judah went up; and the LORD delivered the Canaanites and the Perizzites into their hands; and they slew ten thousand of them in Bezek.

5 And they found the lord of Bezek in Bezek; and they fought against him, and they slew the Canaanites and the Perizzites.

6 But the lord of Bezek fled; and they pursued him and caught him, and cut off his thumbs and his great toes.

7 And the lord of Bezek said, Seventy kings, with their thumbs and great toes cut off, used to pick up bread under my table; as I have done, so God has requited me. And they brought him to Jerusalem, and there he died.

8 And the children of Judah fought against Jerusalem, and took it and smote it with the edge of the sword and set the villages thereof on fire.

9 ¶And afterwards the children of Judah went down to fight against the Canaanites, who dwelt in the mountain and in the south and in the plain.

10 And Judah went against the Canaanites who dwelt in Hebron (now the name of Hebron before was Koriath-arba); and they slew Sheshai and Ahiman and Talmai, the sons of the giants.

11 And from thence they went against the inhabitants of Debir; and the name of Debir before was Koriath-sephra;

12 And Caleb said, He who takes Koriath-sephra, and destroys it, I will give him Achsah my daughter to wife.

13 And Othniel the son of Kenaz, Caleb's younger brother, took it; and he gave him Achsah his daughter to wife.

14 And it came to pass, when she entered the city, she desired to ask of her father a field; and she alighted from her ass; and Caleb said to her, What troubles you, my daughter?

15 And she said to him, Give me a blessing; for you have given me a south land; give me also pools of water; and Caleb gave her the upper pools and the lower pools.

16 ¶And the children of the Kenite, Moses' father-in-law, went up from the city of palm trees with the children of Judah into the wilderness of Judah, which lies in the south of Adar; and they went and dwelt among the people.

17 And Simeon went with Judah his brother, and they slew the Canaanites that inhabited Zephath, and utterly destroyed it. And they called the name of the city Khirma.

18 Judah also took Gaza with its territory, and Ashkelon with its territory, and Ekron with its territory.

19 And the LORD was with Judah; and they possessed the mountain; but they could not destroy the inhabitants of the valley, because they had chariots of iron.

20 And they gave Hebron to Caleb, as Moses had said; and he destroyed from thence the three sons of giants.

21 But the children of Benjamin did not destroy the Jebusites who inhabited Jerusalem; but the Jebusites dwell with the children of Benjamin in Jerusalem to this day.

22 ¶The house of Joseph also went out against Beth-el; and the LORD was with them.

23 And the house of Joseph spied on Beth-el. (Now the name of the city before was Luz.)

24 And the spies saw a man coming out of the city, and they said to him, Show us the entrance into the city, and we will have mercy on you.

25 And when he had shown them the entrance into the city, they smote the city with the edge of the sword; but they spared the man and all his family.

26 And the man went to the land of the Hittites, and built a village and called its name Luz, which is its name to this day.

27 ¶Neither did Manasseh destroy the inhabitants of Beth-shean and its villages, nor Taanach and its villages, nor the inhabitants of Dor and its villages, nor the inhabitants of Abinaam and its villages, nor the inhabit-

ants of Megiddo and its villages; but the Canaanites that inhabited the land could not be subdued.

28 And it came to pass, when Israel was strong, they made the Canaanites pay tribute but did not utterly destroy them.

29 ¶Neither did Ephraim destroy the Canaanites who dwelt in Gezer; but the Canaanites dwelt in Gezer among them.

30 ¶Neither did Zebulun destroy the inhabitants of Kitron, nor the inhabitants of Jahlel; but the Canaanites dwelt among them, and paid tribute.

31 ¶Neither did Asher destroy the inhabitants of Accho nor the inhabitants of Zidon nor of Lahbel nor of Jezebel nor of Helbah nor of Aphik nor of Rehob;

32 But the Asherites dwelt among the Canaanites, the inhabitants of the land; for they did not destroy them.

33 ¶Neither did Naphtali destroy the inhabitants of Beth-shemesh nor the inhabitants of Beth-anoth; but he dwelt among the Canaanites, the inhabitants of the land; nevertheless the inhabitants of Beth-shemesh and of Beth-anoth paid tribute to them.

34 And the Amorites forced the children of Dan into the mountain; for they would not let them come down to the valley;

35 The Amorites sought refuge in the land of Hedas in the mountain and in Aijalon and in Shaalbim; but the hand of the house of Joseph prevailed against them, and they paid tribute.

36 And the border of the Amorites was from the ascent of Ekron, from the rock and upward.

CHAPTER 2

AND the angel of the LORD came up from Gilgal to Bikhian, and said to the children of Israel, Thus says the LORD, I have brought you up from the land of Egypt, and have brought you into the land which I swore to your fathers; and I said, I will never break my covenant with you.

2 And you shall make no league with the inhabitants of this land; you shall destroy their altars; but you have not obeyed my voice. Why have you done this?

3 Wherefore I also said, I will not destroy them from before you; but they shall become vanity, and their gods shall be a stumbling block to you.

4 And when the angel of the LORD spoke these words to the children of Israel, all the people lifted up their voices and wept.

5 And the people called the name of that place Bikhian; and they sacrificed there to the LORD.

6 ¶And when Joshua had dismissed the people, the children of Israel went away every man to his inheritance to possess the land.

7 And the people served the LORD all the days of Joshua and all the days of the elders who outlived Joshua, who had seen all the works of the LORD and the great things which he had done for Israel.

8 And Joshua the son of Nun, the servant of the LORD, died at the age of one hundred and ten years.

9 And they buried him in the land of his inheritance at Timnath-serah on the mount of Ephraim, on the north side of mount Gaash.

10 And all that generation were gathered to their fathers; and there arose another generation after them, who did not know the LORD nor the works which he had done for Israel.

11 ¶And the children of Israel did evil in the sight of the LORD, and served Baal;

12 And they forsook the LORD God of their fathers, who had brought them up out of the land of Egypt, and followed other gods, gods of the peoples who were round about them, and they worshipped them, and provoked the LORD to anger.

13 So they forsook the LORD and served Baal and Ashtaroth.

14 ¶And the anger of the LORD was kindled against Israel, and he delivered them into the hands of spoilers, and they plundered them, and he delivered them into the hands of their enemies round about them, so that they could no longer stand before their enemies.

15 Wherever they went, the hand of the LORD was against them for evil, as the LORD had said, and as the LORD had sworn to them; and they were greatly distressed.

16 ¶Then the LORD raised up judges among the Israelites, and they delivered them out of the hand of those who plundered them.

17 And yet they would not hearken to their judges, because they had gone astray after other gods and worshipped them; they turned aside quickly from the way in which their fathers walked, who had listened to the commandments of the LORD, but they did not do so.

18 And when the LORD raised up judges for them, then the LORD was with the judges, and delivered them out of the hand of their enemies all the days of the judges; the LORD would hear their groaning because of their oppressors and those that drove them away.

19 And it came to pass, when the judges were dead, they returned and became more corrupt than their fathers, in following other gods to serve and to worship them; they did not cease from their wickedness, nor from their evil ways.

20 ¶And the anger of the LORD was kindled against Israel; and he said, Because this people have transgressed my covenant which I commanded their fathers, and have not hearkened to my voice;

21 I also will no longer destroy any man from before them of the nations which Joshua left when he died;

22 That through them I may prove Israel whether they will keep the way of the LORD, and whether they will walk in it, as their fathers did keep it, or not.

23 Therefore the LORD left these nations, and did not destroy them hastily; neither had he delivered them into the hand of Joshua.

CHAPTER 3

NOW these are the nations which the LORD left, to test Israel by them, even the Israelites who had not experienced all the wars of Canaan.

2 Only that the generations of the children of Israel might learn warfare, at least such as had not experienced it before;

3 Namely, the five lords of the Philistines, and all the Canaanites, and the Sidonians, and the Hivites who dwelt on mount Lebanon, from the mount of the people of mount Hermon as far as the entrance to Hamath.

4 And they were to prove Israel by them, to know whether they would obey the commandments of the LORD, which he commanded their fathers by the hand of Moses.

5 ¶So the children of Israel dwelt among the Canaanites, Hivites, Amorites, Perizzites, Hittites, and Jebusites;

6 And they took their daughters to be their wives, and gave their daughters to their sons, and served their gods.

7 And the children of Israel did evil in the sight of the LORD, and forgot the LORD their God, and served Baal and Ashtaroth.

8 ¶Therefore the anger of the LORD kindled against Israel, and he delivered them into the hand of Cushan the Wicked, king of Aram-nahrin (Mesopotamia); and the children of Israel served Cushan the Wicked eight years.

9 And when the children of Israel cried to the LORD, the LORD raised up a deliverer for the children of Israel, and they were delivered by Othniel, the son of Kenaz, Caleb's younger brother.

10 And the hand of the LORD was with him, and he judged Israel, and went out to war; and the LORD delivered Cushan the Wicked, king of Aram-nahrin, into his hands; and his hand prevailed against Cushan the Wicked.

11 And the land had rest forty years. Then Othniel the son of Kenaz died.

12 ¶And the children of Israel again did evil in the sight of the LORD; and the LORD strengthened Eglon the king of Moab against Is-

rael, because they had done evil in the sight of the LORD.

13 And he mobilized the children of Ammon and Amalek against them, and went and smote Israel, and possessed the city of palm trees.

14 So the children of Israel served Eglon the king of Moab eighteen years.

15 But when the children of Israel cried to the LORD, the LORD raised up for them a deliverer, Ehur the son of Gera, of the tribe of Benjamin, a man whose right hand was crippled, and the children of Israel sent a present by him to Eglon the king of Moab.

16 So Ehur made for himself a two edged dagger, and he made it short; and he girded it under his garment on his right thigh.

17 And he brought the present to Eglon king of Moab; and King Eglon was a simple-minded man.

18 And when Ehur had finished offering the present, he sent away the people that bore the present.

19 But he himself turned back from the quarries that were by Gilgal, and said, I have a secret message to impart to you, O king; and the king said to those who were present, Get away from here. And all that stood by him went out.

20 And Ehur came to him; and he was sitting alone in the upper room which was made for him. And Ehur said to him, I have a message from God to impart to you. So Eglon arose from his seat.

21 And Ehur put forth his left hand, and took the sword from his right thigh, and thrust it into his belly;

22 And the haft also went in after the blade; and the fat closed upon the blade, because he did not draw the sword out of his belly; and he went out hastily.

23 Then Ehur went out into the porch, and shut the doors of the upper room upon him, locked them, and left.

24 When he had gone out, the king's servants came in; and when they saw that the doors of the upper chamber were locked, they said, Perhaps he has gone to the toilet in the closet of the upper chamber.

25 And they waited for a long time; and seeing that he did not open the doors of the upper chamber, they took keys and opened them; and, behold, their lord was fallen down dead on the floor.

26 And while they were in confusion, Ehur passed beyond the quarries, and escaped to Seirath.

27 And it came to pass, when he had returned, he sounded the trumpet on the mountain of Ephraim, and the children of Israel went down with him from the mountain, and he went before them.

28 And he said to them, Follow after me; for the LORD has delivered your enemies the Moabites into your hands. And they went down after him, and seized the fords of the Jordan on the side of Moab, and allowed not a man to pass over.

29 And they slew of the Moabites at that time about ten thousand men, all great and valiant men; and there escaped not a man.

30 So the Moabites were subdued at that time under the hand of Israel. And the land had rest for eighty years.

31 ¶And after him was Shamgar the son of Anath, who slew six hundred of the Philistines with an ox goad; and he also delivered Israel.

CHAPTER 4

AND the children of Israel again did evil in the sight of the LORD, after Ehur was dead.

2 And the LORD delivered them into the hand of Nabin king of Canaan, who reigned in Hazor; the general of whose army was Sisera, who dwelt in Harosheth of the Gentiles.

3 And the children of Israel cried to the LORD; for he had nine hundred chariots of iron, and oppressed the children of Israel for twenty years.

4 ¶And Deborah, a prophetess, the wife of Lapithor, judged Israel at that time.

5 And Deborah dwelt under the

palm tree between Ramtha and Beth-el on mount Ephraim; and the children of Israel came up to her for judgment.

6 And she sent and called Barak the son of Abinoam from Rakim of Naphtali, and said to him, Has not the LORD God of Israel commanded you, saying, Go and dwell on mount Tabor, and take with you ten thousand men from the children of Naphtali and from the children of Zebulun?

7 And let them come with you to the river Kishon against Sisera, the general of Nabin's army, and against his chariots, and against his forces; and I will deliver him into your hands.

8 And Barak said to her, If you will go with me, then I will go; but if you will not go with me, then I will not go.

9 And she said, I will surely go with you; nevertheless you shall not glory on account of the journey which you are taking; for the LORD shall deliver Sisera into the hands of a woman. And Deborah arose and went with Barak to Rakim.

10 ¶And Barak mobilized Zebulun and Naphtali to Rakim; and ten thousand men went up with him; and Deborah also went up with him.

11 Now Heber the Kenite had left the Kenites, the descendants of Hobab the father-in-law of Moses, and had pitched his tent as far as the oak which is in Zaanaim, which is by Rakim.

12 And they told Sisera that Barak the son of Abinoam had gone up to mount Tabor.

13 And Sisera gathered together all of his chariots, nine hundred chariots of iron, and all the people that were with him, from Harosheth of the Gentiles as far as the river of Kishon.

14 And Deborah said to Barak, Arise, for this is the day in which the LORD has delivered Sisera into your hands; behold, the LORD is going out before you. So Barak went down from mount Tabor, and ten thousand men with him.

15 And the LORD defeated Sisera and all his chariots and all his army, with the edge of the sword before Barak; so that Sisera alighted from his chariot and fled on foot.

16 But Barak pursued his chariots and his army as far as Harosheth of the Gentiles; and all the army of Sisera fell by the edge of the sword; and not a man escaped.

17 However, Sisera fled on foot, and entered the tent of Anael the wife of Heber the Kenite, because there was peace between Nabin the king of Hazor and the house of Heber the Kenite.

18 ¶And Anael went out to meet Sisera, and said to him, Turn in, my lord, turn in to me; fear not. And he went in to her into the tent, and she covered him with a rug.

19 And he said to her, Give me a little water to drink; for I am thirsty. And she untied the milkskin and gave him a drink and covered him.

20 Again he said to her, Stand at the door of the tent, and if any man does come and ask you, and say, Is there any man here? You shall say to him, No.

21 Then Anael, Heber's wife, got a tent peg, and took a hammer in her hand and went to him as he was sleeping, and drove the peg into his temples, and pounded it into the ground while he was fast asleep, and he shivered and died.

22 And, behold, as Barak pursued Sisera, Anael went out to meet him and said to him, Come, and I will show you the man whom you seek. And he went into her tent, and, behold, Sisera lay dead, and the peg was through his temples.

23 So on that day God defeated Nabin the king of Canaan before the children of Israel.

24 And the hand of the children of Israel prospered and prevailed against Nabin the king of Canaan until they slew Nabin king of Canaan.

CHAPTER 5

THEN sang Deborah and Barak the son of Abinoam on that day, saying,

2 With requital has Israel been

avenged; praise the LORD with a song for avenging Israel.

3 Hear, O kings; give ear, O princes; I will sing to the LORD; I will sing praise to the LORD God of Israel.

4 LORD, when thou wentest out of Seir, when thou marchedst in the fields of Edom, the earth trembled and the heavens dropped, the clouds also dropped water.

5 The mountains melted from before the LORD, even this Sinai from the presence of the LORD the Holy One of Israel.

6 In the days of Shamgar the son of Anath, in the days of Anael, the highways were cut off, and the travellers who once walked on main roads, had to go through the crooked byways.

7 The little villages ceased in Israel; they ceased, until I Deborah arose, I arose as a mother in Israel.

8 The LORD will choose new things; then the barley bread,[1] and a sword or a spear shall not be seen among forty thousand in Israel.

9 My heart said to the lawgiver of Israel, They that are chosen among the people bless the LORD.

10 O you who ride on white asses, you who dwell in houses, and you who travel on the highways,

11 Meditate on the words of the inquirers, who are among the teachers; they shall execute the righteousness of the LORD, even his righteousness which he has multiplied in Israel; then shall the people of the LORD march to the gates.

12 Awake, awake, Deborah; awake, utter a song; arise, Barak, and lead away your captives, O son of Abinoam.

13 Then the deliverer went down to sing praise before the LORD; thou hast given me victory by the hand of a man out of Ephraim.

14 And Barak's works are known in Amalek; after you marched Benjamin with affection for you; out of Machir came forth a seer, and out of Zebulun those who write with the pen of a scribe.

15 And the princes of Issachar were with Deborah; even Issachar is like Barak among the peoples; he was sent on foot to a portion of Reuben; great are those who give oracles to comfort the heart.

16 Why abodest thou on the highways to hear the bleatings of the wild asses? For the divisions of Reuben there were great searchings of heart.

17 Gad abode beyond the Jordan; and Dan brought ships to the harbor; Asher dwelt on the sea shore, and remained in its harbors.

18 Zebulun and Naphtali were peoples who jeopardized their lives on the high places of his field.

19 The kings came and fought; then fought the kings of Canaan; they fought in Taanach by the waters of Megiddo; they took no goods nor money.

20 The stars fought from their courses; they fought from heaven against Sisera by the river Kishon.

21 The river Kishon and the river Karmin swept them away. O my soul, you have defeated an army!

22 Then the hoofs of his horses fell down, were broken because of the prancing of his mighty ones.

23 Curse ye Meroz, said the angel of the LORD, curse it, and curse the inhabitants thereof, because they came not with men to the help of the LORD.

24 Blessed above women shall Anael the wife of Heber the Kenite be, blessed shall she be above women in the tent.

25 He asked water, and she gave him milk; she brought forth butter in a giant bowl.

26 She put her hand to the peg and her right hand to the carpenter's hammer, and with the hammer she struck Sisera and crushed his head, when she had struck and pierced his temples.

27 At her feet he bowed, he fell, he lay down; at the place where he bowed, there he fell down dead, the plunderer.

28 The mother of Sisera looked out of the window and cried through

---

[1] Barley bread is symbolical of poverty.

the lattice, Why are the chariots of my son so long in coming? Why tarries the clatter of his chariots?

29 Her wise ladies answered her, saying,

30 Perhaps he went and found great spoil, dividing the prey, giving to every man a mule and great booty, and to Sisera a prey of diverse colors of needlework and divers colors of embroidered work, meet for the necks of them that take the spoil.

31 So let all thine enemies perish, O LORD; but let them that love thee be like the sun when he goeth forth in his might. And the land had rest for forty years.

CHAPTER 6

AND the children of Israel did evil in the sight of the LORD; and the LORD delivered them into the hand of the Midianites seven years.

2 And the hand of the Midianites prevailed against Israel, in that they fled from before the Midianites; and the children of Israel made for themselves dens in the mountains, and caves, and sheepfolds.

3 And whenever Israel had sown, the Midianites and the Amalekites and the Rakimites came up and encamped against them;

4 And they destroyed the produce of the whole land as far as the entrance of Gaza, and left no food for Israel to raise either oxen or sheep or asses.

5 For they came up with their cattle and their tents, and they came like locusts in multitude; for both they and their camels were without number; and they entered into the land to destroy it.

6 And Israel trembled exceedingly from before the Midianites;

7 ¶And the children of Israel cried to the LORD because of the Midianites,

8 And the LORD sent a prophet to the children of Israel, and he said to them, Thus says the LORD God of Israel, I brought you up out of the land of Egypt, and brought you forth out of the house of bondage;

9 And I delivered you from the hand of the Egyptians and from the hand of all your oppressors, and destroyed them from before you and gave you their land;

10 And I said to you, I am the LORD your God; you shall not worship the gods of the Amorites in whose land you dwell; but you have not obeyed my voice.

11 ¶And there came an angel of the LORD, and sat under an oak which was at Ophrah, the town of Joash the father of Azri; and his son Gideon was beating out wheat by the winepress, to hide it from the Midianites.

12 And the angel of the LORD appeared and said to him, The LORD is with you, you mighty man of valor.

13 And Gideon said to him, I beseech you, O my lord, if the LORD be with us, why then have all these misfortunes befallen us? And where are all his wonders of which our fathers have told us, saying, Did not the LORD bring us up from Egypt? But now the LORD has forsaken us and delivered us into the hand of the Midianites.

14 And the LORD turned to him, and said, Go with this might of yours, and you shall save Israel from the hand of the Midianites; behold, I have sent you.

15 And he said to him, I beseech thee, O my LORD, with what shall I save Israel? Behold, my family is the least in Manasseh, and I am the youngest in my father's family.

16 And the LORD said to him, I will be with you, and you shall smite the Midianites as one man.

17 And he said to him, If now I have found mercy in thy sight, then show me a sign that I may know that thou speakest with me.

18 Do not depart from here until I come to thee and bring out my meal and set it before thee. And he said, I will tarry until you come again.

19 ¶So Gideon went in and prepared a kid and unleavened cakes of an ephah of flour; the meat he put in a basket, and he put the broth in a pot, and brought it out to him under the oak and presented it.

20 And the angel of the LORD said to him, Take the meat and the unleavened cakes, and lay them on the rock, and pour out the broth over it. And he did so.

21 ¶Then the angel of the LORD put forth the end of the staff that was in his hand, and touched the meat and the unleavened cakes; and there rose up fire out of the rock, and consumed the meat and the unleavened cakes. Then the angel of the LORD vanished from his sight.

22 And when Gideon perceived that he was an angel of the LORD, Gideon said, Alas, O LORD God! for I have seen the angel of the LORD face to face.

23 And the LORD said to him, Peace be unto you; fear not; you shall not die.

24 Then Gideon built an altar there to the LORD, and called it Mariah-shalama; and to this day it still stands in Ophrah, the town of the father of Azri.

25 ¶And it came to pass on that day, the LORD said to him, Take your father's bullock, and the second bullock seven years old, and pull down the altar of Baal, the idol of your father, and cut down the grove that is by it;

26 And build an altar to the LORD your God upon the top of this rock, in an orderly manner, and take the second bullock, and offer it upon it as a burnt offering with the wood of the grove which you shall cut down.

27 Then Gideon took ten men of his servants, and did as the LORD had said to him; and because he was afraid of doing it by day, because of his father's household and the men of the town, he did it by night.

28 ¶And when the men of the town arose early in the morning, behold, the altar of Baal was pulled down and the grove which was beside it was destroyed and the second bullock was offered upon another altar which had been built.

29 And they said one to another, Who has done this thing? And when they had asked and enquired, they said, Gideon the son of Joash has done this thing.

30 Then the men of the town said to Joash, Bring out your son, that he may die; because he has pulled down the altar of Baal and has cut down the grove that was by it.

31 And Joash said to all who stood against him, Will you plead for Baal? Or will you try to save him? Whosoever pleads for him shall be put to death while it is yet morning; if he is a god, let him plead for himself, because his altar has been thrown down.

32 Therefore on that day he called Gideon Nedo-baal, saying, Let Baal judge him, because he has thrown down his altar.

33 ¶Then all the Midianites and the Amalekites and the Rakimites were gathered together, and went over and encamped in the valley of Jezreel.

34 But the Spirit of the LORD came upon Gideon, and he blew a trumpet; and Jezreel shouted his approval.

35 And he sent his messengers throughout all Manasseh; and they also blew trumpets and followed him; and he sent his messengers to Asher and to Zebulun and to Naphtali; and they came up to meet them.

36 ¶And Gideon said to God, If thou wilt save Israel by my hand, as thou hast said,

37 Behold, I will put a fleece of wool on the threshing floor; and if there is dew on the fleece only, and it is dry on all the ground, then I shall know that thou wilt save Israel by my hand, as thou hast said.

38 And it was so; and he rose early the next day and pressed the fleece and wrung the dew out of the fleece, a bowlful of water.

39 And Gideon said to God, Let not thy anger kindle against me, and I will speak but this once; let me prove thee again but this once with the fleece; let now only the fleece be dry, and upon all the ground let there be dew.

40 And God did so that night; for only the fleece was dry, and there was dew on all the ground.

CHAPTER 7

THEN Nedo-baal, who is Gideon, and all the people who were with him, rose up early, and encamped beside the spring of Hadar; and the camp of Midian was north of the hill of Gibath, in the valley.

2 And the LORD said to Gideon, The people that are with you are too many for me to deliver the Midianites into their hands, lest Israel should glory in themselves, saying, My own hand has made me victorious.

3 Now therefore proclaim in the ears of the people, saying, Whoever is fearful and trembling, let him stay behind and return from mount Gilead. And there returned of the people twenty-two thousand; and there remained ten thousand.

4 And the LORD said to Gideon, The people are still too many; bring them down to the water, and I will try them for you there; and it shall be that he of whom I say to you, This one shall go with you, the same shall go with you; and of whomsoever I say to you, This one shall not go with you, the same shall not go.

5 So he brought down the people to the water; and the LORD said to Gideon, All who lap of the water with their tongues, as a dog laps, you shall make them stand together; likewise all who kneel down upon their knees to drink, you shall make them stand together.

6 And the number of those that lapped, putting the hand to the mouth, was three hundred men; but all the rest of the people knelt down upon their knees to drink water.

7 And the LORD said to Gideon, By the three hundred men that lapped I will save you and deliver the Midianites into your hands; and let all the other people go, every man to his place.

8 So the people took their provisions in their hands and their trumpets; and he dismissed all the children of Israel every man to his possession and to his tent, and he relied upon those three hundred men; and the camp of Midian was beneath him in the valley.

9 ¶And it came to pass the same night, that the LORD said to him, Arise, go down to the camp, for I have delivered it into your hands.

10 But if you fear to go down, go down with Pera your servant to the army camp;

11 And you shall hear what they say; and afterwards your hands shall be strengthened. So he went down with Pera his servant to a detachment of the armed men that were in the army camp.

12 And the Midianites and the Amalekites and all the Rakimites lay along the valley like locusts in multitude; and their camels were without number, as the sand by the seashore in multitude.

13 And when Gideon was come, behold, a man was relating a dream to his fellow, and he said to him, Behold, I dreamed a dream, and, lo, a cake of barley bread tumbled into the camp of Midian, and came as far as a tent, and struck it on the top, and the tent fell down.

14 And his fellow answered and said, This is nothing else but the sword of Gideon the son of Joash, the mighty man of Israel; for into his hand has God delivered the camp of Midian.

15 ¶Now when Gideon heard the telling of the dream and its interpretation, he worshipped and returned to the camp of Israel, and said, Arise, for the LORD has delivered the camp of Midian into your hands.

16 And he divided the three hundred men into three companies, and he put a trumpet in every man's hand, with empty pitchers, and torches inside the pitchers.

17 And he said to them, Watch me and do as I do; and, behold, when I come to the outside of the camp, as I do, so shall you do.

18 When I blow a trumpet, I and all the people who are with me, then you blow with trumpets also on every side of the camp, and say, The sword of the LORD, and of Gideon.

19 ¶So Gideon and the hundred

men that were with him, came to the outside of the camp at the beginning of the middle watch; and they had but newly set the watch; and they blew the trumpets, and broke the pitchers.

20 And the three companies blew their trumpets, and broke the pitchers, and held the torches in their left hands, and the trumpets in their right hands; and they cried, The sword of the LORD, and of Gideon.

21 And they stood every man in his place round about the camp; and all the host ran, and they blew a trumpet, and fled.

22 And when the three hundred blew the trumpets, the LORD set every man's sword against his fellow, even throughout all the army; and the whole army fled as far as Beth-shab-tey and Zeddath, and as far as the border of Abel-meholah, which is by Jatbath.

23 And the men of Israel gathered themselves together from Naphtali and from Asher and from all Manasseh, and pursued the Midianites.

24 ¶And Gideon sent messengers throughout all mount Ephraim, saying, Come down against the Midianites and seize the waters as far as Beth-barah, which is by the Jordan. Then all the men of Ephraim gathered themselves together and seized the waters as far as Beth-barah by the Jordan.

25 And they captured two princes of Midian, Oreb and Zeeb; and they slew Oreb at Tyre, and Zeeb they slew at Beth-kabrab; and they pursued Midian, and they brought the heads of Oreb and Zeeb to Gideon on the other side of the Jordan.

CHAPTER 8

THEN the men of Ephraim said to him, Why have you done thus, that you never called us when you went to fight with the Midianites? And they quarreled with him violently.

2 And he said to them, What have I done now in comparison to you? Is not the gleaning of the grapes of Ephraim better than the vintage of Jezreel?

3 For in Jezreel God has delivered into your hands the two princes of Midian, Oreb and Zeeb; and what was I able to do in comparison to you? Then their anger was abated toward him, when he had said that.

4 ¶And Gideon came to the Jordan and passed over, he and the three hundred men who were with him, pursuing, yet faint from hunger.

5 And he said to the men of Succoth, Give a few loaves of bread to the people who are with me; for they are faint from hunger, and, behold, I am pursuing Zebah and Zalmunna, kings of Midian.

6 ¶And the princes of Succoth said to him, Are the hands of Zebah and Zalmunna now in your hands, that we should give bread to your army?

7 And Gideon said to them, Therefore when the LORD has delivered Zebah and Zalmunna into my hands, then I will tear your flesh with the thorns of the wilderness and with briers.

8 ¶And he went up from there to Penuel, and the men of Penuel answered him as the men of Succoth had answered him.

9 And he said also to the men of Penuel, When I come again in peace, I will break down this tower.

10 ¶Now Zebah and Zalmunna were staying at Karkab, and their armies with them, about fifteen thousand men, all that were left of all the armies of the people of the east; for there fell a hundred and twenty thousand men that drew sword.

11 ¶And Gideon went up by the way of them who dwell in tents on the east of Necah and Jogbehah, and attacked the army camp; for the army was not on guard.

12 And Zebah and Zalmunna fled, and he pursued them, and captured the two kings of Midian, Zebah and Zalmunna, and threw the whole army into confusion.

13 ¶And Gideon the son of Joash returned from the battle at the slope of Hadas.

14 And he captured a young man

of the men of Succoth, and questioned him; and he wrote down for him a description of the princes of Succoth and its elders, seventy-seven men.

15 And he came to the men of Succoth and said to them, Behold Zebah and Zalmunna, about whom you upbraided me, saying, Are the hands of Zebah and Zalmunna now in your hands, that we should give bread to your servants who are faint from hunger?

16 And he dragged the elders of the city over the briers and thorns of the wilderness, and thus inflicted tortures on the men of Succoth.

17 And he broke down the tower of Penuel, and slew the men of the city.

18 ¶Then he said to Zebah and Zalmunna, What manner of men were they whom you slew at Tabor? They said to him, They were like yourself, they resembled the sons of kings.

19 And he said, They were my brothers, the sons of my mother; as the LORD lives, if you had saved them alive, I would not slay you.

20 And he said to Jether his firstborn, Arise and slay them. But the youth did not draw his sword; for he was afraid, because he was still a youth.

21 Then Zebah and Zalmunna said, Rise yourself, and fall upon us; for as the man is, so is his might. And Gideon arose and slew Zebah and Zalmunna, and took away the ornaments that were on their camels' necks.

22 ¶Then the men of Israel said to Gideon, Rule over us, both you and your son and your son's son also; for you have delivered us from the hand of Midian.

23 And Gideon said to them, I will not rule over you, neither shall my son rule over you; the LORD shall rule over you.

24 ¶And Gideon said to them, I would like to make a request of you: give me every man of you an earring of his spoil. (For they had golden earrings, since the enemies were Arabians.)

25 And they said to him, We will gladly give it. And they spread a mantle, and every man threw onto it one earring from his spoil.

26 And the weight of the golden earrings that he requested was one thousand seven hundred shekels of gold; besides ornaments, neck chains, and purple raiment that were worn by the kings of Midian, and besides the chains that were about their camels' necks.

27 And Gideon took some of them and made a little idol, and set it up in his town, Ophrah; and all Israel went astray after it there; and it became a stumbling block to Gideon and to all his household.

28 ¶Thus the Midianites were defeated before the children of Israel, so that they lifted up their heads no more. And the land was tranquil forty years in the days of Gideon.

29 ¶Then Nedo-baal the son of Joash went and dwelt in his own house.

30 And Gideon had seventy sons who were begotten by him; for he had many wives.

31 And his concubine who was in Shechem also bore him a son, whose name he called Abimeleck.

32 ¶And Gideon the son of Joash died at a good old age, and was buried in the town of his father Joash, in Ophrah of the father of Azri.

33 And it came to pass, as soon as Gideon was dead, the children of Israel turned again and went astray after Baal, and made Baal-kiama their god.

34 And the children of Israel did not remember the LORD their God, who had delivered them from the hand of all their enemies on every side;

35 Neither did they show kindness to the house of Nedo-baal, that is, Gideon, according to all the goodness that he had done to Israel.

CHAPTER 9

AND Abimeleck the son of Nedo-baal went to Shechem to his mother's brothers, and spoke to them and to all the family of the house of his mother's father, saying,

2 Speak, before all the lords of Shechem, Which is better for you, that all the seventy men, the sons of Nedo-baal, rule over you, or that one man rule over you? Remember also that I am your bone and your flesh.

3 And his mother's brothers spoke of him before all the lords of Shechem all these words; and their hearts inclined to follow Abimeleck; for they said, He is our brother.

4 And they gave him seventy pieces of silver from the house of Baal-kiama, with which Abimeleck hired vain and wanton persons, who followed him.

5 And he went to his father's house at Ophrah, and slew his brothers, the sons of Nedo-baal, seventy men, upon one stone; but Jotham the youngest son of Nedo-baal was left; for he hid himself.

6 And all the lords of Shechem gathered together, and all the people of Beth-millo, and went and made Abimeleck king over them, by the oak of Mazpiah which is in Shechem.

7 ¶And when they told it to Jotham, he went and stood on the top of mount Gerizim, and lifted up his voice and cried, and said to them, Hearken to me, O lords of Shechem, that God may hearken to you.

8 Once upon a time the trees went forth to anoint a king over them; and they said to the olive tree, Reign over us.

9 But the olive tree said to them, Should I leave my fertility, by which gods and men are honored, to be abominated for reigning over the trees?

10 And the trees said to the fig tree, Come you, and reign over us.

11 But the fig tree said to them, I am not going to leave my sweetness and my good fruit, to be abominated for reigning over the trees.

12 Then the trees said to the vine, Come you, and reign over us.

13 But the vine said to them, I am not going to leave my wine which cheers the hearts of gods and men, to be abominated for reigning over the trees.

14 Then all the trees said to the bramble, Come you, and reign over us.

15 And the bramble said to the trees, If in truth you anoint me king over you, then come and take refuge in my shade; and if not, let fire come out of the bramble and devour the cedars of Lebanon.

16 Now therefore, if you have done truly and sincerely, in that you have made Abimeleck king, and if you have dealt well with Nedo-baal and his household, and have rewarded him according to the deeds of his hands;

17 (For my father fought for you, and ventured his life afar, and delivered you from the hand of Midian;

18 And you have risen up against my father's house this day, and have slain his sons, seventy men, upon one stone, and have made Abimeleck, the son of his maidservant, king over the lords of Shechem, because he is your brother;)

19 If you then have dealt truly and sincerely with Nedo-baal and with his house this day, then rejoice in Abimeleck, and let him also rejoice in you;

20 But if not, let fire come out from Abimeleck, and devour the lords of Shechem and the lords of Millo; and let fire come out from the lords of Shechem and from the lords of Millo, and devour Abimeleck.

21 And Jotham ran away and escaped, and went to Debir, and dwelt there, the place where Abimeleck had lived before.

22 ¶When Abimeleck had reigned over Israel three years,

23 Then God sent an evil spirit upon Abimeleck and upon the lords of Shechem; and the lords of Shechem dealt treacherously with Abimeleck,

24 That the cruelty done to the seventy sons of Nedo-baal might come, and their blood be laid upon Abimeleck their brother, who slew them; and upon the lords of Shechem,

who strengthened his hands in the killing of his brothers.

25 And the men of Shechem laid an ambush against him on the top of the mountain, and they robbed all who passed by them along that way; and it was told Abimeleck.

26 And Gaal the son of Epar came with his brothers, and went over to Shechem; and the lords of Shechem put their confidence in him.

27 And they went out into the fields, and gathered their vineyards and trod the grapes, and they made a banquet and went into the house of their gods and did eat and drink, and reviled Abimeleck.

28 And Gaal the son of Epar said, Who is Abimeleck and who is Shechem that we would serve him? Is he not the son of Nedo-baal? And Zebul because he changed his allegiance served the men of Hamor the father of Shechem; why then should we serve him?

29 And would to God this people were under my command! Then I would remove Abimeleck. And he said to Abimeleck, Increase your army, and come out.

30 ¶And when Zebul the governor of the city heard the words of Gaal the son of Epar, his anger was kindled.

31 And he sent messengers to Abimeleck deceitfully, saying, Behold, Gaal the son of Epar and his brothers have come to Shechem; and, behold, they fortify the city against you.

32 Now therefore arise by night, you and the people that are with you, and lie in wait in the field;

33 And in the morning as soon as the sun is up, you must rise early, and march upon the city; and, behold, when he and the people that are with him come out against you, you may do to them as you are able to do.

34 ¶And Abimeleck and all the people that were with him rose up by night, and they laid in ambush against Shechem in four companies.

35 And Gaal the son of Epar went out and stood in the entrance of the gate of the city; and Abimeleck and the people that were with him rose up from ambush.

36 And when Gaal saw the people, he said to Zebul, Behold, there are people coming down from the top of the mountains. And Zebul said to him, You see the shadows of the mountains that look like men.

37 And Gaal spoke again and said, Behold, there are people coming down from the center of the land, and one company is coming along from the way of the house of the oak of Meaonin.

38 Then Zebul said to him, Where is now your mouth with which you said, Who is Abimeleck that we should serve him? Are not these the people whom you have despised? Go out now and fight with them.

39 And Gaal went out before the lords of Shechem and fought with Abimeleck.

40 And Abimeleck chased him, and he fled before him, and many people fell slain, even to the entrance of the gate.

41 And Abimeleck dwelt at Adomah; and Zebul expelled Gaal and his brethren, that they should not dwell in Shechem.

42 And it came to pass on the next day, that the people went out into the fields, and they told Abimeleck.

43 And he took the people and divided them into three companies, and lay in wait in the fields, and he looked, and, behold, the people were coming forth out of the city; and he rose up against them and slew them.

44 And Abimeleck and the company that was with him rushed forward, and stood in the entrance of the gate of the city; and the two other companies rushed against all the people who were in the fields, and slew them.

45 And Abimeleck fought in the city all that day; and he took the city, and he slew all the people that were in it, and he destroyed the city, and sowed it with salt.[1]

46 ¶And when all the lords of the

[1] To make the land barren.

tower of Shechem heard of it, they came to take refuge in the house of the god of the covenant.

47 And it was told Abimeleck that all the lords of the tower of Shechem were gathered together.

48 And Abimeleck went up to mount Zalmon, he and all the people that were with him; and Abimeleck took an axe in his hand and cut down a branch from the trees, and took it and laid it on his shoulder, and said to the people that were with him, What you have seen me do, make haste and do as I have done.

49 So every man cut down his branch and followed Abimeleck, and they piled them up, and then set the city on fire, so that all the men that were in the tower of Shechem died in fire, about a thousand men and women.

50 ¶Then Abimeleck went to Thebez, and encamped against Thebez and took it.

51 But there was a strong tower within the city, and thither fled all the men and women and all the lords of the city, and shut it behind themselves, and went to the top of the tower.

52 And Abimeleck advanced as far as the tower, and fought against it, and drew near to the door of the tower to set it on fire.

53 And a certain woman threw a piece of an upper millstone upon Abimeleck's head and broke his skull.

54 Then he called hastily to his young armorbearer, and said to him, Draw your sword and slay me with it, that men may not say of me, A woman slew him. So the young man thrust him through, and he died.

55 And when the men of Israel saw that Abimeleck was dead, they departed every man to his place.

56 ¶Thus God requited the wickedness of Abimeleck, which he did to his father, in slaying his seventy brothers;

57 And all the wickedness of the men of Shechem did God bring upon their heads; and upon them came the curse of Jotham the son of Nedobaal.

CHAPTER 10

AFTER Abimeleck there arose to save Israel Tola the son of Puah, the son of his uncle, a man of Issachar; and he dwelt in Shamir on mount Ephraim.

2 And he judged Israel twenty-three years, and he died and was buried in Shamir.

3 ¶And after him arose Jair, the Gileadite, and he judged Israel for twenty-two years.

4 And he had thirty sons who rode on thirty ass colts, and they had thirty towns, which are called villages of Jair to this day, which are in the land of Gilead.

5 And Jair died and was buried in Camon.

6 ¶And the children of Israel did evil again in the sight of the Lord, and served Baal and Ashtaroth and the gods of Edom, the gods of Zidon, the gods of Moab, the gods of the children of Ammon, the gods of the Philistines, and the gods of the rest of the nations, and they forsook the Lord and did not serve him.

7 And the anger of the Lord was kindled against Israel, and he delivered them into the hands of the Philistines and into the hands of the children of Ammon.

8 And from that year they vexed and oppressed the children of Israel, eighteen years, all the children of Israel who were on the other side of the Jordan in the land of the Amorites, which is in Gilead.

9 Moreover the children of Ammon crossed the Jordan to fight against Judah and also against the house of Ephraim and against Benjamin; so that Israel was exceedingly distressed.

10 ¶And the children of Israel cried to the Lord, saying, We have sinned against thee, because we have forsaken our God and have served Baal.

11 And the Lord said to the children of Israel, Did not the Egyptians, the Moabites, the children of Ammon, the Philistines,

12 The Zidonians, the Amalekites, and the Amorites oppress you; and

you cried to me, and I delivered you from their hands?

13 Yet you have forsaken me and served other gods; therefore I will save you no more.

14 Go and pray to the gods with whom you are pleased; let them become your saviors in the time of your distress.

15 ¶And the children of Israel said to the LORD, We have sinned; do thou to us whatever seems good to thee; only deliver us this day.

16 And the children of Israel put away the strange gods from among them and served the LORD; for the soul of Israel was grieved.

17 Then the children of Ammon were gathered together and encamped in Gilead. And the children of Israel assembled themselves together and encamped in Mizpeh.

18 And the people and princes of Gilead said one to another, Whosoever shall first start to fight against the children of Ammon, he shall be prince over all the inhabitants of Gilead.

CHAPTER 11

NOW Jephthah the Gileadite was a mighty man of valor, but he was the son of a harlot; and Gilead begat Jephthah.

2 And Gilead's wife bore him sons; and when his wife's sons grew up, they expelled Jephthah, saying, He shall not inherit in our father's house, because he is the son of another woman.

3 Then Jephthah fled from his brothers, and dwelt in the land of Tobtha; and there were gathered worthless men to Jephthah, and they went raiding with him.

4 ¶And it came to pass after a time, the children of Ammon made war against Israel.

5 And when the children of Ammon made war against the children of Israel, the elders of Gilead went to bring Jephthah from the land of Tobtha;

6 And they said to Jephthah, Come and be our leader, that we may fight with the children of Ammon.

7 And Jephthah said to the elders of Gilead, Did you not hate me and expel me from my father's house? And why have you come to me now when you are in distress?

8 And the elders of Gilead said to Jephthah, That is why we have come to you now, that you may go with us and fight against the children of Ammon and be the leader over all the inhabitants of Gilead.

9 And Jephthah said to the elders of Gilead, If you bring me back to fight against the children of Ammon, and the LORD deliver them before me, shall I be your chief?

10 And the elders of Gilead said to him, The LORD shall be witness between us, if we do not so according to your words.

11 Then Jephthah went with the elders of Gilead, and the people made him chief and ruler over them; and Jephthah uttered all his words before the LORD in Mizpeh.

12 ¶And Jephthah sent messengers to the king of the children of Ammon, saying, What have we against each other, that you have come against me to fight in my land?

13 And the king of the children of Ammon said to the messengers of Jephthah, Because the children of Israel took away my land when they came up out of the land of Egypt from Arnon even to Jabbok and to the Jordan, now therefore restore these lands to me peaceably.

14 And Jephthah sent letters and messengers again to the king of the children of Ammon;

15 And said to him, Thus says Jephthah, Israel did not take away the land of Moab nor the land of the children of Ammon;

16 Because when the children of Israel came up from Egypt, Israel journeyed through the wilderness as far as the Red Sea, and came to Rakim;

17 Then Israel sent messengers to the king of Edom, saying, Let me pass through your land; but the king of Edom would not listen. And they sent also to the king of Moab; but he would not consent; so Israel stayed in Rakim.

18 Then they journeyed through the wilderness, and went around the land of Edom and the land of Moab, and they encamped on the other side of Arnon, but they did not enter the territory of Moab; for Arnon was the border of Moab.

19 And Israel sent messengers to Sihon king of the Amorites, the king of Heshbon; and Israel said to him, Let us pass through your land until we come to our land.

20 But Sihon did not trust Israel to pass through his territory; so Sihon gathered all his people together and encamped at Jahaz and fought against Israel.

21 And the LORD our God delivered Sihon and all his people into the hand of Israel, and Israel destroyed the land of the Amorites.

22 And they possessed all their territory, from Arnon as far as Jabbok, and from the wilderness even to the Jordan.

23 So now after the LORD God of Israel has destroyed the Amorites from before his people Israel, are you to possess their land?

24 Will you not possess that which Chemosh your god gives you to possess? So whomever the LORD our God has destroyed from before us, their land will we possess.

25 And now are you any better than Balak the son of Zippor, king of Moab? Did he ever strive against Israel? Or did he ever fight against them?

26 While Israel dwelt in Heshbon and its villages, and in Adoer and its villages, and in all the cities that are along the banks of Arnon, three hundred years? Why did you not recover them within that time?

27 Now therefore I have not sinned against you, but you do me wrong to make war against me; let the LORD judge this day between the children of Israel and the children of Ammon.

28 But the king of the children of Ammon did not listen to the words of Jephthah which he sent him.

29 ¶Then the Spirit of the LORD came upon Jephthah, and he passed over Gilead and Manasseh, and passed over Mizpeh of Gilead; and from Mizpeh of Gilead hē passed over to the children of Ammon.

30 And Jephthah vowed a vow to the LORD, and said, If thou wilt surely deliver the children of Ammon into my hands,

31 Then whosoever comes forth of the door of my house to meet me when I return in peace from the children of Ammon shall be the LORD's, and I will offer him up for a burnt offering.

32 So Jephthah passed over to the children of Ammon to fight against them; and the LORD delivered them into his hands.

33 And he smote them from Adoer, as far as the entrance of Machir, twenty cities, and as far as Abel Karmin, the plain of vineyards, with a very great slaughter. Thus the children of Ammon were defeated before the children of Israel.

34 ¶Then Jephthah came to Mizpeh to his house, and, behold, his daughter came out to meet him with timbrels and with dances; and she was his only child; besides her he had neither son nor daughter.

35 And when he saw her, he rent his clothes, and said, Alas, my daughter! You have brought me very low, and you have become today one of those that ruin me; for I have made a promise to God, and I cannot go back on it.

36 And his daughter said to him, My father, if you have made a promise to God, do to me according to that which has proceeded out of your mouth; since the LORD has taken vengeance for you on your enemies, even of the children of Ammon.

37 And she said to her father, Grant me this thing only: let me alone two months that I may go and wander on the mountains and bewail my virginity, I and my companions.

38 And he said, Go. And he sent her away for two months; and she went with her companions, and bewailed her virginity on the mountains.

39 And at the end of two months,

she returned to her father, who did with her according to his vow; and she knew no man. And it became a custom among the children of Israel,

40 That the daughters of Israel went yearly to weep and lament over the daughter of Jephthah the Gileadite four days in a year.

CHAPTER 12

THEN the men of Ephraim gathered themselves together, and went northward, and said to Jephthah, Why did you cross over to fight against the children of Ammon, and did not call us to go with you? We will burn your house over you with fire.

2 And Jephthah said to them, O men! I and my people had strife with the children of Ammon; and when I called you, you did not deliver me from their hands.

3 And when I saw that there was no one to deliver me, I risked my life, and crossed over against the children of Ammon, and the LORD delivered them into my hands; now why have you come up against me this day, to fight with me?

4 Then Jephthah gathered together all the men of Gilead and fought with Ephraim; and the men of Gilead smote the men of Ephraim, because they said, The Ephraimites dominate Ephraim and Manasseh.

5 And the Gileadites took the fords of the Jordan which belonged to Ephraim; and when any of the fugitives of Ephraim tried to cross over the passage, the men of Gilead said to him, Are you an Ephraimite? If he said, No;

6 Then they said to him, Say now Shibboleth; and he said Sibboleth; for he could not pronounce it so. Then they took him and slew him at the fords of the Jordan; and there fell at that time forty-two thousand of the Ephraimites.

7 And Jephthah judged Israel six years. Then Jephthah the Gileadite died and was buried in his city in Gilead.

8 ¶And after him Ibzan of Bethlehem judged Israel.

9 And he had thirty sons, and thirty daughters, and his thirty daughters he gave in marriage outside of his tribe, and brought in thirty daughters-in-law from outside. And he judged Israel seven years.

10 Then Ibzan died and was buried in Beth-lehem.

11 ¶And after him Elon, a Zebulunite, judged Israel; and he judged Israel ten years.

12 And Elon the Zebulunite died and was buried in Aijalon in the land of Zebulun.

13 ¶And after him Acran the son of Hillian, the Aprathonite, judged Israel.

14 And he had forty sons and thirty grandsons, who rode on seventy ass colts; and he judged Israel eight years.

15 Then Acran the son of Hillian, the Aprathonite died, and was buried in Aprathon in the land of Ephraim on the mount of the Amalekites.

CHAPTER 13

AND the children of Israel did evil again in the sight of the LORD; and the LORD delivered them into the hand of the Philistines for forty years.

2 ¶And there was a certain man of Zedah, of the family of the Danites, whose name was Manoah; and his wife was barren, and never had children.

3 And the angel of the LORD appeared to the woman and said to her, Behold, you are barren, and have borne no children; but now you shall conceive, and bear a son.

4 Now therefore beware, lest you drink wine or strong drink; and you shall not eat anything unclean.

5 For lo, you have conceived and will bear a son; and no razor shall come on his head; for the child shall be a Nazarite to God from the womb; and he will begin to deliver Israel out of the hand of the Philistines.

6 ¶Then the woman came and told her husband, saying, A man of God came to me, and his countenance was like the countenance of an angel of God, and I trembled exceedingly, and I did not ask him whence he was, nor did he tell me his name;

7 But he said to me, Behold, you have conceived, and you will bear a son; and from henceforth drink no wine nor strong drink, neither eat any unclean thing; for the child shall be a Nazarite to God from the womb to the day of his death.

8 ¶Then Manoah entreated the LORD and said, I beseech thee, O LORD, let the man of God whom thou didst send come again to us and teach us what we shall do to the child that shall be born.

9 And the LORD hearkened to the voice of Manoah; and the angel of the LORD came again to the woman as she sat in the field; but Manoah her husband was not with her.

10 And the woman made haste and ran, and told her husband and said to him, Behold, the man has appeared to me, who came to me the other day.

11 And Manoah arose and went with his wife, and came to the man and said to him, Are you the man who spoke to this woman? And he said, I am.

12 And Manoah said, Now let your words come to pass. But tell me, what is the manner by which the child is to be brought up, and what shall we do to him?

13 And the angel of the LORD said to Manoah, Of all that I said to the woman let her beware.

14 She must not eat of anything that comes of the vine, neither shall she drink wine or strong drink, nor eat any unclean thing; all that I have commanded her let her observe.

15 ¶Then Manoah said to the angel of the LORD, Let us detain you, and make ready a kid for you.

16 And the angel of the LORD said to Manoah, Though you detain me, I will not eat of your food; and if you will offer a burnt offering, you must offer it to the LORD. For Manoah did not know that he was the angel of the LORD.

17 And Manoah said to the angel of the LORD, What is your name, that when your sayings come to pass we may invoke your name?

18 And the angel of the LORD said to him, Why do you ask my name, seeing it is Glorious?

19 So Manoah took a kid with the meal offering, and offered it upon a rock to the LORD; and the angel praised the LORD; and Manoah and his wife looked on.

20 And when a flame went up toward heaven from off the rock, the angel of the LORD ascended in the flame of the altar. And Manoah and his wife looked on it, and fell on their faces to the ground and worshipped.

21 The angel of the LORD did no more appear to Manoah and to his wife. Then Manoah and his wife knew that he was an angel of the LORD.

22 And Manoah said to his wife, We shall surely die, because we have seen God.

23 But his wife said to him, If God were pleased to kill us, he would not have received a burnt offering and a meal offering from us, neither would he have showed us all these things at this time, nor would he have told such things as these.

24 ¶And the woman bore a son, and called his name Samson; and the child grew, and the LORD blessed him.

25 And the Spirit of the LORD began to make Samson to travel with the host of Dan between Zedah and Eshtoal.

CHAPTER 14

AND Samson went down to Timnath, and saw a woman in Timnath of the daughters of the Philistines.

2 And he came up, and told his father and his mother, and said, I have seen a woman in Timnath of the daughters of the Philistines; now therefore get her for me to wife.

3 Then his father and mother said to him, Is there not a woman here among the daughters of the kinsmen of your father, or among all your people, that you are going to take a wife of the uncircumcised Philistines? And Samson said to his father, Get her for me; for she pleased me well.

4 But his father and his mother did

not know that it was of the LORD, that he might seek vengeance against the Philistines; for at that time the Philistines had dominion over Israel.

5 ¶Then Samson went down with his father and mother to Timnath, and they came to the vineyards of Timnath; and, behold, a young lion roared at him.

6 And the Spirit of the LORD came mightily upon him, and he tore the lion as one tears a kid, and he had nothing in his hand; but he did not tell his father or his mother what he had done.

7 And they went down and talked with the woman; and she pleased Samson well.

8 ¶And after a time he returned to take her, and he turned aside to see the carcass of the lion; and, behold, there was a swarm of bees in the carcass of the lion, and the honey ran out on his hands as he walked.

9 And he went to his father and mother, and gave some honey to them, and they did eat; but he did not tell them that the honey came from the carcass of the lion.

10 ¶So his father went down to the woman; and Samson made there a wedding feast for seven days; for so the young men used to do.

11 And when they saw him, there came thirty men and became his groomsmen.

12 ¶And Samson said to them, I will now put forth a riddle to you; if you can interpret it to me within the seven days of the feast and find it out, then I will give you thirty overcoats made of felt and thirty changes of garments;

13 But if you cannot interpret it to me, then you shall give me thirty overcoats made of felt and thirty changes of garments. And they said to him, Put forth your riddle, that we may hear it.

14 And he said to them, Out of the eater came forth something to eat, and out of the bitter came forth something sweet. And for three days they could not interpret the riddle.

15 But on the fourth day, they said to Samson's wife, Entice your hus-band, that he may declare to us his riddle, lest we burn you and your father's house with fire and take over his possessions.

16 And Samson's wife wept and said to him, You truly hate me and do not love me; you have put forth a riddle to my countrymen, and you have never told it to me. And he said to her, I have not told it to my father nor to my mother, and shall I tell it to you?

17 And she wept the seven days, while the feast lasted; and it came to pass on the seventh day, that he told her, because she distressed him; and she told the riddle to her country-men.

18 And the men of the city said to him on the seventh day before the banquet, What is sweeter than honey? And what is stronger than a lion? And Samson said to them, If you had not enticed my heifer, you would not have interpreted my riddle.

19 ¶And the Spirit of the LORD came upon him, and he went down to Ashkelon, and he seized thirty of their men, and he slew them and took their garments and gave them to those who had interpreted his riddle. And his anger was kindled, and he went up to his father's house.

20 And Samson's wife, whom he loved, was given to one of his grooms-men.

CHAPTER 15

BUT it came to pass after a while, in the time of the wheat harvest, Samson visited his wife with a kid as a present; and he said, I will go in to my wife in the chamber. But her father would not let him go in.

2 And her father said, I surely thought that you had utterly hated her; therefore I gave her to your groomsman; behold, her younger sister, who is fairer than she, take her to wife instead.

3 ¶And Samson said to them, Now I shall be more blameless than the Philistines, although I am going to do them mischief.

4 So Samson went and caught three hundred foxes, and took torches and

tied tail to tail, two foxes together; and he tied a torch between each pair of foxes, between two tails.

5 And when he had set the torches on fire, he let the foxes go into the standing grain of the Philistines, and burned up both the shocks and the standing grain, and also the vineyards and olives.

6 ¶Then the Philistines said, Who has done this? And they said, Samson, the son-in-law of the Timnite, because he had taken his wife and given her to his groomsman. And the Philistines came up and burned her and her father's family with fire.

7 ¶And Samson said to them, Because you have done this, I will be avenged of you, and after that I will cease.

8 And he smote them hip and thigh with a great slaughter; and he went down and dwelt in a cave of the rock of Atmin.

9 ¶Then the Philistines went up and encamped in Judah.

10 And the men of Judah said, Why have you come up against us? And they answered, We have come up to bind Samson, to do to him as he has done to us.

11 Then three thousand men of Judah went down to the cave of the rock of Atmin, and said to Samson, Do you not know that the Philistines are rulers over us? What is this you have done to us? And he said to them, As they did to me, so have I done to them.

12 And they said to him, We have come down to bind you, that we may deliver you into the hand of the Philistines. And Samson said to them, Swear to me that you will not harm me yourselves.

13 And they said to him, No; but we will bind you and deliver you into their hands; but surely we will not kill you. So they bound him with two new chains and brought him up from the rock.

14 ¶And when he came to Lehi, the Philistines rose up to kill him; and the Spirit of the LORD came mightily upon him, and the chains that were on his arms became like flax that has caught fire, and his bands loosed from off his hands.

15 And he found a hard jawbone of an ass, and put forth his hand and took it, and slew a thousand men with it.

16 And Samson said, With the jawbone of an ass I have made heaps upon heaps, with the jawbone of an ass I have slain a thousand men.

17 And it came to pass, when he had finished speaking, he threw away the jawbone out of his hand, and called the name of that place, the Bloody Jawbone.

18 ¶And he was very thirsty, so he called on the LORD, and said, Thou hast given this great victory into the hand of thy servant; and now shall I die of thirst and fall into the hand of the uncircumcised?

19 And the LORD God opened the hollow place that was in the jawbone of the ass, and there came water from it; and when he had drunk, his spirit returned and he revived; therefore he called the name of that place En-karna di paka di khmara, to this day.

20 And he judged Israel twenty years in the days of the Philistines.

CHAPTER 16

THEN Samson went to Gaza, and saw there a harlot, and he went in unto her.

2 And it was told the Gazites, saying, Samson has come here. And they lay in wait for him all night in the gate of the city, and were whispering all night, saying, When the morning dawns, we shall kill him.

3 But Samson slept till midnight, and arose at midnight, and took the two door-posts of the gate of the city, and lifted them up, together with the bars thereof, and put them on his shoulder and carried them to the mountain that is before Hebron.

4 ¶And it came to pass after this, he loved a woman in the valley of Sarok, whose name was Delilah.

5 And the lords of the Philistines came up to her and said to her, Entice him, and see wherein his great strength lies, and by what means we

may prevail against him, that we may bind him to disgrace him; and we will give you every one of us thirteen hundred pieces of silver.

6 ¶And Delilah said to Samson, Tell me wherein your great strength lies, and with what you might be bound, and how that you may become weak.

7 And Samson said to her, If they bind me with seven fresh bowstrings that were never dried, then I shall become weak and be like any other man.

8 Then the lords of the Philistines brought up to her seven fresh bowstrings that had never been dried, and she bound him with them.

9 Now there were men lying in wait in her inner chamber. And she said to him, The Philistines have come upon you, Samson. And he broke the bowstrings as a thread of tow is broken when it touches the fire. So his strength was not disturbed.

10 And Delilah said to Samson, Behold, you have deceived me and told me lies; now tell me with what you might be bound.

11 And he said to her, If they bind me fast with new chains that never were used, then shall I be weak and be like any other man.

12 So Delilah took new chains and bound him with them, and said to him, The Philistines have come upon you, Samson. And the men were lying in wait in the inner chamber. And he broke them from off his arms like a thread.

13 And Delilah said to Samson, Behold you have deceived me and told me lies; tell me with what you might be bound. And he said to her, If you weave the seven locks of my head into a web.

14 And she wove it with the weaver's web, and said, The Philistines have come upon you, Samson. And he awoke from his sleep, and pulled away both the weaver's loom and the web.

15 ¶And she said to him, How can you say to me, I love you, when your heart is not with me? For behold, you have deceived me these three times,

and you have not told me wherein your great strength lies.

16 And it came to pass, when she had pressed him daily with her words and urged him, his soul was vexed to death;

17 So he told her all his heart, and said to her, There has never come a razor upon my head; for I have been a Nazarite to God from my mother's womb; if I be shaven, then my strength will depart from me, and I shall become weak and be like any other man.

18 And when Delilah saw that he had told her all his heart, she sent and called for the lords of the Philistines, saying, Come up now, for he has told me all his heart. Then the lords of the Philistines came up to her, and brought the money with them.

19 And she made him sleep upon her knees; and she called for the barber, and had him shave off the seven locks of his head; and she began to overpower him, and his strength had departed from him.

20 And she said to him, The Philistines have come upon you, Samson. And he awoke from his sleep, and said, I will go out as at other times before, and I will torment them. And he did not know that the LORD had departed from him.

21 ¶And the Philistines seized him, and put out his eyes and bound him with fetters and brought him down to Gaza, and he did grind wheat in the prison house.

22 But the hair of his head began to grow again after he was shaven.

23 Then the lords of the Philistines assembled to offer a great sacrifice to Dagon their god, and to rejoice; for they said, Our god has delivered Samson our enemy into our hand.

24 And when the people saw him, they praised their god; for they said, Our god has delivered into our hands our enemy and the destroyer of our country, who slew many of us.

25 And it came to pass when their hearts were merry, they said, Call for Samson that he may make sport before us. And they called Samson out of the prison house; and he made

sport before them; and they set him between the pillars.

26 And Samson said to the lad who held him by the hand, Let me feel the pillars on which the house stands, that I may lean against them.

27 Now the house was full of men and women; and all the lords of the Philistines were there; and there were upon the roof about three thousand men and women, looking on while Samson made sport.

28 Then Samson called to the Lord, and said, O Lord God, remember me, I pray thee, and strengthen me only this once, O God, that I may be avenged of the Philistines for my two eyes.

29 And Samson took hold of the two middle pillars upon which the house stood, and he leaned against them, grasping one with his right hand and the other with his left.

30 And Samson said, Let me die with the Philistines. Then he pulled with all his might; and the house fell upon the lords and upon all the people that were therein. So the dead whom Samson slew at his death were more than those whom he slew during his life.

31 Then his brothers and all the house of his father came down and took him, and brought him up and buried him between Zedah and Eshtaol in the burying place of Menoah his father. And he had judged Israel twenty years.

CHAPTER 17

AND there was a man from mount Ephraim, whose name was Micah.

2 And he said to his mother, The eleven hundred shekels of silver which were taken from you, which you swore about, and spoke of also in my ears, behold, it was I who took the silver. And his mother said, Blessed of the Lord is my son.

3 And when he had restored the eleven hundred shekels of silver to his mother, his mother said, I have wholly consecrated the silver to the Lord from the hands of my son, to make a graven image and a molten image; now therefore restore it to me.

4 So he restored the money to his mother; and his mother took two hundred shekels of silver and gave it to the silversmith, who made it into a graven image and a molten image; and they were kept in the house of Micah.

5 And the man Micah had a house of gods, and he made an ephod and a teraphim, and consecrated one of his sons, who became his priest.

6 In those days there was no king in Israel, but every man did that which was right in his own eyes.

7 ¶Now there was a young man from Beth-lehem of Judah, whose name was Levi, and he sojourned there.

8 And the man had left the city of Beth-lehem of Judah to dwell wherever he could find a place; and he came to mount Ephraim, to the house of Micah, to obtain provisions for his journey.

9 And Micah said to him, Whence do you come? And he replied, I am a Levite of Beth-lehem of Judah, and I go to sojourn where I may find a place.

10 And Micah said to him, Dwell with me, and be to me as a father and a priest, and I will give you ten shekels of silver yearly, and your clothes and your food. So the Levite went in.

11 And the Levite was content to dwell with the man; and the young man was to him as one of his sons.

12 And Micah consecrated the Levite; and he became his priest, and was in the house of Micah.

13 Then said Micah, Now I know that the Lord will do me good, seeing that the Levite has become my priest.

CHAPTER 18

IN those days there was no king in Israel; and in those days the tribe of Dan sought for itself an inheritance to dwell in; for until that day no inheritance had fallen to them among the tribes of Israel.

2 And the Danites sent of their families five men from Zedah and from Eshtaol, to spy out the land, and to explore it; and they said to them, Go

and explore the land. And they came to mount Ephraim, to the house of Micah, and they lodged there.

3 When they were at the house of Micah, they recognized the voice of the young man, the Levite, and they turned aside there and said to him, Why did you come here? And what are you doing here?

4 And he said to them, Thus and thus has Micah dealt with me, and has hired me, and I have become his priest.

5 And they said to him, Inquire for us of God, that we may know whether the errand for which we go shall prosper.

6 And the priest said to them, Go in peace; and may the LORD prosper the errand on which you go.

7 ¶Then the five men departed and came to Laish, and saw the people who were in it, how they dwelt in tranquillity after the manner of the Zidonians, peaceful and quiet; and there was no one to do harm in the land, neither was there anyone to harass and to oppress; and they were far from the Zidonians, and had no business with any man.

8 And they came back to their brethren at Zedah and Eshtaol; and their brethren said to them, Whence did you come?

9 They said to them, Even from Laish. Now arise, let us go up against them; for we have seen the land, and, behold, it is very good; and do not hesitate, nor tarry to go and to take possession of the land.

10 When you go, you shall come against a rich people, and an extensive and arable land is before you; for the LORD has delivered it into your hands, a place where there is no lack of anything that is on the earth.

11 ¶And there went from thence of the family of the Danites, from Zedah and from Eshtaol, six hundred men armed with weapons of war.

12 And they went up and encamped at Koriath-narin, in Judah; wherefore they called that place the Camp of Dan to this day; behold, it is behind Koriath-narin.

13 And they passed on from there to mount Ephraim, and went to the house of Micah.

14 ¶Then answered the five men who had gone to spy out the land of Laish, and said to their brethren, Do you know that there is on these hills an ephod and teraphim and a graven image and a molten image? Now therefore you must consider what you have to do.

15 So they turned aside, and came to the house of the young man, Levi, even to the house of Micah, and saluted him.

16 And the six hundred men armed with weapons of war, who were Danites, stood by the entrance of the gate.

17 And the five men who had gone to spy out the land went up and entered there, and took the graven image and the ephod and the teraphim and the molten image, while the priest stood at the entrance of the gate with the six hundred men armed with weapons of war.

18 And they entered into Micah's house, and took the image, the ephod, and the teraphim, and the molten image. Then the priest said to them, What are you doing?

19 And they said to him, Hold your peace, stop talking, and come with us, and be to us a father and a priest. Which is better for you, to be a priest for one man's household, or to be a priest to a family and a tribe of Israel?

20 And the priest's heart was glad, and he took the graven image, the ephod, and the teraphim, and went with the people.

21 So they turned and departed, and put the sheep and the goods and the cattle in front of them.

22 ¶And when they were at a distance from the house of Micah, a man who was in the house beside Micah's house cried out and pursued the Danites.

23 And he shouted to the Danites, and they turned and said to Micah, What ails you, that you shout?

24 And he said to them, You have taken away the god which I made,

and also the priest, and you have gone away; and what have I left? And what is this that you say to me, What ails you?

25 And the Danites said to him, Let not your voice be heard among us, lest some angry fellows attack you, and you lose your life and the lives of your sons.

26 Then the Danites went their way; and when Micah saw that they were too strong for him, he turned and went back to his house.

27 And they took the things which Micah had made and the priest that he had, and came to Laish against the people who were rich and quiet; and they smote them with the edge of the sword, and burned the city with fire.

28 And there was no one to rescue them, because it was far from Zidon, and they had no business with any man; and the city was situated in the valley of Beth-rehob. And they rebuilt the city and dwelt in it.

29 And they called the name of the city Dan, after the name of Dan their father, who was born to Israel; but the name of the city was Laish at first.

30 ¶And the Danites set up the graven image; and Jonathan, the son of Gershon, the son of Manasseh, he and his sons were priests to the tribe of Dan until the day of the captivity of the land.

31 And they set up for themselves Micah's graven image, which he had made, all the time that the house of God was in Shiloh.

CHAPTER 19

AND it came to pass in those days, when there was no king in Israel, there was a certain Levite sojourning on the side of mount Ephraim, who took to himself a concubine from Beth-lehem of Judah.

2 And his concubine played the whore against him, and then arose and went away from him to her father's house to Beth-lehem of Judah, and remained there four whole months.

3 And her husband arose and went after her to speak lovingly to her and to bring her back, taking with him his servant and a couple of asses; and she brought him into her father's house; and when the father of the damsel saw him, he rejoiced to meet him.

4 And his father-in-law, the damsel's father, detained him; and he stayed with him three days; so they did eat and drink and lodged there.

5 ¶And on the fourth day, they rose early in the morning to depart; and the damsel's father said to his son-in-law, Strengthen yourself with a piece of bread; and after that rise and go.

6 So they sat down and did eat and drink, both of them together; and the damsel's father said to his son-in-law, If you wish you may spend the night and it will do you good.

7 And when the man rose up to depart, his father-in-law urged him to stay; and he spent the night there again.

8 And he arose early in the morning on the fifth day to depart; and the damsel's father said to him, Strengthen your heart, refresh yourself, and tarry until afternoon. And they did eat and drink both of them.

9 And when the man rose up to depart, he and his concubine and his servant, his father-in-law, the damsel's father, said to him, Behold, now the day is spent, tarry all night here; and it will do you good; and tomorrow, rise up early and go to your home.

10 But the man would not tarry that night, but he rose up and departed, and came opposite Jebus, which is Jerusalem; and there were with him two asses with burdens, and his concubine also was with him.

11 And when they were near Jebus, the day was far spent; and the servant said to his master, Come, let us turn aside to this city of the Jebusites and spend the night in it.

12 And his master said to him, We will not turn aside into a strange city that does not belong to the house of Israel; but we will pass on to Gibeah.

13 And he said to his servant, Come, let us draw near to one of

these places to lodge the night in Gibeah, or in Ramtha.

14 So they passed on and went their way; and the sun went down upon them when they were near Gibeah, which belongs to Benjamin.

15 And they turned aside there to spend the night; and they went to Gibeah, and sat down in a street of the city; for there was no man to take them into his house to spend the night.

16 ¶And, behold, there came an old man from his work out of the field at evening, and the man was also of mount Ephraim; and he sojourned in Gibeah, which belongs to Benjamin, but the men of the place were Benjamites whose deeds were exceedingly bad.

17 And the old man lifted up his eyes and saw the wayfarer in the street of the city; and the old man said to him, Where are you going? And whence do you come?

18 And he said to him, We are travelling from Beth-lehem of Judah toward the side of mount Ephraim; from thence am I; and I went as far as Beth-lehem of Judah, but now I am going to the house of the LORD, but there is no man to take us into his house.

19 And yet there is both straw and fodder for our asses; and there is bread and wine also for me and for your maidservant and for the young man, your servant; there is no lack of anything.

20 And the old man said to him, Peace be with you; anything that you may lack I will provide for you; only do not spend the night in the street.

21 So he brought him into his house, and gave fodder to his asses; and they washed their feet, and did eat and drink.

22 ¶Now as they were making their hearts merry, behold, the men of the city, certain wicked men, beset the house round about, and they beat at the door and spoke to the master of the house, the old man, saying, Bring out the man who came into your house, that we may know him.

23 And the old man, the master of the house, went out to them and said to them, No, my brethren, no, do not be so wicked; seeing that this man has come into my house, do not commit this shameful act.

24 Behold, here is my daughter, a virgin, and his concubine; I will bring them out for you, and you may humble them, and do with them what seems good to you; but to this man you shall not do any shameful thing.

25 But the men would not listen to him; so the man took his concubine and brought her outside to them; and they raped her and abused her all the night until the morning; and when dawn began to break, they let her go.

26 Then as the day was dawning, the woman came and fell down at the door of the man's house where her master was, till it was light.

27 And her master rose up in the morning and opened the door of the house and went out to go his way; and he saw his concubine lying at the door of the house, with her hands upon the threshold.

28 And he said to her, Get up, let us go. But she did not answer. Then he put her upon the ass, and the man rose up and went on to his own home.

29 ¶And when he had come to his house, he took a knife and cut his concubine in pieces, and divided her into twelve portions, and distributed them throughout all the tribes of Israel.

30 And all who saw it said, There has never been, nor seen, such a deed from the day that the children of Israel came up out of the land of Egypt until this day. So they considered it, and took counsel, and spoke out.

CHAPTER 20

THEN all the children of Israel went out, and the congregation gathered together as one man from Dan to Beer-sheba, to the land of Gilead, to the LORD in Mizpeh.

2 And the chiefs of all the families of all the people, even of all the tribes of Israel, presented themselves in the assembly of the people of God, four

hundred thousand footmen who could draw sword.

3 (Now the Benjamites heard that the children of Israel were gone up to Mizpeh.) Then said the children of Israel, Tell us, how did this wickedness happen?

4 And the Levite, the husband of the woman who was killed, answered and said to them, I came into Gibeah, that belongs to Benjamin, I and my concubine, to spend the night.

5 And the men of Gibeah rose against me, and beset me in the house during the night, and they sought to kill me; and they raped my concubine, and she died.

6 And I took my concubine, and cut her in pieces, and sent them throughout all the country of the inheritance of Israel; for they had committed sin and wickedness in Israel.

7 Behold, you are all here, O children of Israel, give an answer and counsel concerning this crime.

8 ¶And all the people arose as one man, saying, We will not any of us go to our tents, neither shall any one of us turn aside to go to his house.

9 But now this will be the thing which we shall do to Gibeah; we will draw lots against it;

10 We will take ten men of a hundred throughout all the tribes of Israel, and a hundred of a thousand, and a thousand out of ten thousand, to take provisions for the people, who cross over against Gibeah of Benjamin, to do to it according to all the wickedness which they have committed in Israel.

11 So all the men of Israel were gathered against the city, agreeing together as one man.

12 ¶And the tribes of Israel sent men through all the tribe of Benjamin, saying, What wickedness is this that has been done among you?

13 Now therefore deliver up the wicked men, who are in Gibeah, that we may put them to death, and put away evil from Israel. But the Benjamites would not listen to the voice of their brethren, the children of Israel;

14 But all the Benjamites gathered themselves together in Gibeah from their cities, to go out to battle against the children of Israel.

15 And the Benjamites were numbered in that day out of the cities twenty-six thousand men that drew sword, besides the inhabitants of Gibeah, who were numbered seven hundred chosen men.

16 Among all these people there were seven hundred chosen men who were lefthanded; every one of them could sling stones at an hairbreadth, and not miss.

17 And the men of Israel, as compared with the Benjamites, were numbered four hundred thousand men that drew sword; all these were men of war.

18 ¶And the children of Israel arose and went up to Beth-el, and inquired of God, and said, Which of us shall go up first to battle against the Benjamites? And the LORD said, Judah shall go first.

19 And the children of Israel rose up in the morning and encamped against Gibeah.

20 And the Benjamites went out of Gibeah to battle against Israel, and arrayed themselves against Israel; and the men of Israel put themselves in array to fight against them at Gibeah.

21 And the Benjamites came forth out of Gibeah, and put themselves in array against Israel, and left dead on the ground that day twenty-two thousand men of the children of Israel.

22 But the children of Israel rallied themselves, and once more set themselves in array in the same place where they had put themselves in array the first day.

23 And the children of Israel went up to Beth-el, and wept before the LORD until evening, and they asked counsel of the LORD, saying, Shall we go up again to battle against our brethren the Benjamites? And the LORD said, Go up against them.

24 And the children of Israel drew near to battle against the Benjamites on the second day.

25 And the Benjamites went out against them from Gibeah the second

day, and left dead on the ground eighteen thousand men of the children of Israel; all of these men who drew the sword.

26 ¶Then all the children of Israel, and all the people, went up and came to Beth-el, and wept and sat there before the LORD, and fasted that day until evening, and offered burnt offerings and peace offerings before the LORD.

27 And the children of Israel inquired of the LORD (for the ark of the covenant of the LORD was there in those days;

28 And Phinehas, the son of Eleazar, the son of Aaron the priest, ministered before it in those days), saying, Shall we yet again go out to battle against our brethren the Benjamites, or shall we cease? And the LORD said, Go up; for tomorrow I will deliver them into your hands.

29 So Israel set ambushes round about Gibeah.

30 Then the children of Israel went up against the Benjamites on the third day, and put themselves in array against Gibeah, as at other times.

31 And the Benjamites went out against the people, and were drawn away from the city; and they began to smite the people, and kill, as at other times, in the highways, one of which goes up to Gibeah, and the other to Beth-el through the field, about thirty men of Israel.

32 And the Benjamites said, They are defeated before us, as at first. But the children of Israel said, Let us flee, and draw them away from the city to the highways.

33 And all the men of Israel rose up out of their places, and put themselves in array at Baal-tamar; and those Israelites in ambush came forth out of their places from the cave which is in Gibeah.

34 And there came toward Gibeah ten thousand chosen men out of all Israel, and the battle was hard fought; but they did not know that disaster was near them.

35 And the LORD defeated Benjamin before Israel; and the children of Israel destroyed of the Benjamites that day twenty-five thousand, one hundred men; all of those who drew the sword.

36 So the Benjamites saw that they were defeated; and the children of Israel gave ground to the Benjamites, because they trusted in the ambushes that they had set against Gibeah.

37 And the men who were in ambush quietly made an attack against Gibeah; then the men in ambush moved forward and smote all the city with the edge of the sword.

38 Now there was an appointed signal between the men of Israel and the men in ambush, which was that they should make a great flame with smoke rise up out of the city.

39 And when the men of Israel retreated in the battle, the Benjamites killed of the men of Israel about thirty men; for they said, Surely they are defeated before us, as in the first battle.

40 But when the smoke began to rise out of the city like a pillar, the Benjamites looked behind them, and, behold, the flames of the city ascended up to heaven.

41 And when the men of Israel turned against them, the Benjamites were terrified; for they saw that disaster was upon them.

42 Therefore they fled before the men of Israel on their way to the wilderness; but the battle overtook them; and those who came out of the city first were trapped in the midst of them.

43 Thus they pursued the Benjamites and drove them away, and smote them with ease, to the east beyond Gibeah.

44 And there fell of the Benjamites eighteen thousand men; all these were men of valor.

45 And they turned and fled toward the wilderness to the rock of Rimmon; and five thousand of them fell in the highway; all men that drew the sword; and they pursued hard after them as far as Gibeon, and slew two thousand men of them.

46 So all who fell that day of Benjamin were twenty-five thousand men

that drew the sword; all these were men of valor.

47 But six hundred men turned and fled to the wilderness to the rock of Rimmon, and abode in the rock of Rimmon four months.

48 And the men of Israel turned again upon the Benjamites, and smote them with the edge of the sword, and consumed them out of the cities, both men and beasts and all that they found; also they set on fire all the cities which they found.

CHAPTER 21

NOW the men of Israel had sworn at Mizpeh, saying, None of us shall give his daughter in marriage to the Benjamites.

2 And the people came to Beth-el, and abode there till evening before God, and lifted up their voices and wept bitterly;

3 And said, O LORD God of Israel, why has this disaster come to pass in Israel, that there should be today one tribe missing from Israel?

4 And on the morrow the people rose early and built there an altar, and offered burnt offerings and peace offerings.

5 And the children of Israel said, Who is there among all the tribes of Israel that did not come up in the assembly before the LORD? For they had made a great oath concerning him who did not come up to Mizpeh before the LORD, saying, He shall surely be put to death.

6 Then the children of Israel were sorry for the Benjamites their brethren, and said, One tribe has disappeared from Israel this day.

7 And they said, What shall we do for those who are left without wives, seeing we have sworn by the LORD that we will not give them our daughters to wife?

8 ¶And they said, Which one is there of the tribes of Israel that did not come up to Mizpeh before the LORD? And, behold, there had come none to the camp from the inhabitants of Jabesh-gilead to the assembly.

9 For the people were numbered there, and behold, not one man of the inhabitants of Jabesh-gilead was found there.

10 And the people sent thither twelve thousand of the bravest men, and commanded them, saying, Go and smite the inhabitants of Jabesh-gilead with the edge of the sword, including the women and the children.

11 And this is the thing that you must do, You must utterly destroy every male and every woman that has lain with a man.

12 And they found among the inhabitants of Jabesh-gilead four hundred young virgins that had known no man by lying with him; and they brought them to the camp at Shiloh, which is in the land of Canaan.

13 Then the whole congregation sent messengers to speak to the Benjamites that were in the rock of Rimmon, and to proclaim peace to them.

14 And Benjamin came back at that time, and they gave them the women whom they had saved alive of the women of Jabesh-gilead; but there were not enough for them.

15 And the people were sorry for Benjamin, because the LORD had made a breach in the tribes of Israel.

16 ¶Then the elders of the people said, What shall we do for wives for those that remain, for all the Benjamite women have perished?

17 And they said, The remnant of Benjamin must be spared, that a tribe may not be missing from Israel.

18 Howbeit we cannot give them wives of our daughters; for the children of Israel have sworn, saying, Cursed be he who gives a wife to Benjamin.

19 Then they said, Behold, there is a feast of the LORD in Shiloh yearly in a place which is on the north side of Beth-el, on the east side of the highway that goes up from Beth-el to Shechem, south of Lebonah.

20 So they commanded the Benjamites, saying, Go and lie in wait in the vineyards;

21 And when you shall see the daughters of Shiloh come out to dance with tambourines, then come out of the vineyards and catch you every man his wife of the daughters of

Shiloh, and go to the land of Benjamin.

22 And if their parents or their brothers should come to complain before us, we will say to them, Have compassion upon them, because they did not take each man his wife with him in the war; and it is not you who gave them to them, that you should be guilty.

23 And the Benjamites did so, and they took them wives from all of those who played tambourines, whom they caught; and they returned and went to their inheritance, and rebuilt the towns, and dwelt in them.

24 And the children of Israel departed thence at that time, every man to his tribe and to his family, and they went out from thence every man to his inheritance.

25 In those days there was no king in Israel; every man did that which seemed right in his own eyes.

THE BOOK OF

RUTH

CHAPTER 1

NOW it came to pass in the days when the judges ruled, there was a famine in the land. And a certain man from Beth-lehem of Judah went to sojourn in the land of Moab, he and his wife and his two sons.

2 And the name of the man was Elimeleck, and the name of his wife Naomi, and the names of his two sons Malion and Calion, Ephrathites from Beth-lehem of Judah. And they came to the land of Moab to sojourn there.

3 And Elimeleck the husband of Naomi died; and she was left with her two sons.

4 And they took them wives of the Moabite women; the name of the one was Orpah, and the name of the other Ruth; and they dwelt there about ten years.

5 And Malion and Calion, her two sons, died; and the woman was bereft of her husband and her two sons.

6 ¶Then she started with her daughters-in-law to return from the land of Moab; for she had heard in the land of Moab that the LORD had visited his people in giving them food.

7 So she went forth out of the place where they sojourned, along with her two daughters-in-law, to return and go to the land of Judah.

8 And Naomi said to her two daughters-in-law, Return, go back to your own country and to the house of your kinsmen; may the LORD deal kindly with you, as you have dealt with me and with both of my sons who now are dead.

9 The LORD grant you favor so that you may find rest in the house of your parents. Then she kissed them; and they lifted up their voices and wept.

10 And they said to her, No, we will return with you to your land and to your people.

11 But Naomi said to them, Turn back, my daughters; why will you go with me? Will I bear sons again that they may be your husbands?

12 Turn back, my daughters, go your way; for I am too old to have a husband. If I should say, I have hope, and even if I should have a husband, and should also bear sons;

13 Would you wait for them till they were grown? Would you stay for

them from having husbands? No, my daughters; for I am greatly grieved for your sakes, and it grieves me more than it does you, because the hand of the LORD is gone forth against me.

14 And they lifted up their voices again and wept; and Orpah kissed her mother-in-law, and turned back and went away; but Ruth clung to her.

15 And her mother-in-law said to her, Behold, your sister-in-law has gone back to her people and to her kinsmen; return also after your sister-in-law.

16 And Ruth said to her, Far be it from me to return from following after you, and to leave you; for where you go, I will go; and where you dwell, I will dwell; your people shall be my people, and your God my God:

17 Where you die, I will die, and there will I be buried; may the LORD do so to me, and more also, if even death can separate me from you.

18 When Naomi saw that she was determined to go with her, then she ceased from urging her to go back.

19 ¶So they went together until they came to Beth-lehem of Judah. And it came to pass, when they were come to Beth-lehem, the whole city rejoiced over them, and they said, Is this Naomi?

20 And she said to them, Do not call me Naomi, but call me Bitter of Soul; for the Almighty has dealt bitterly with me.

21 For I went forth from here full, and the LORD has brought me back empty; why then call me Naomi, seeing the LORD has humbled me, and has sorely afflicted me?

22 So Naomi returned, and Ruth the Moabitess, her daughter-in-law, with her, for she was wholeheartedly willing to return with her, and they came from the land of Moab at the beginning of the barley harvest.

CHAPTER 2

AND Naomi had a kinsman of her husband's, a well-known man of wealth, of the family of Elimeleck, whose name was Boaz.

2 And Ruth the Moabitess said to her mother-in-law Naomi, Let me now go to the field and glean ears of wheat after the reapers in whose sight I may find favor. And her mother-in-law said to her, Go, my daughter.

3 So Ruth went to glean ears of wheat after the reapers; and it happened that she came upon a portion of the field belonging to Boaz, who was of the kindred of Elimeleck.

4 ¶And, behold, Boaz came from Beth-lehem, and said to the reapers, Peace be with you. And they answered him, The LORD bless you.

5 Then Boaz said to the young man who was in charge of the reapers, Whose damsel is this?

6 And the young man answered and said to him, It is the Moabite woman who came back with Naomi from the land of Moab;

7 And she said, Let me glean the ears of wheat after the reapers; so she has been gleaning from the morning until the time of rest.

8 Then Boaz said to Ruth, My daughter, have you not heard the saying, Do not glean in a field which is not yours? Now therefore stay here, and spend the night with my maidens.

9 Look at the field where they are reaping, and follow them; behold, I have charged the young men that no man shall harm you; and when you get thirsty, go and drink from the vessels which the young men have drawn.

10 Then she fell on her face to the ground, and made obeisance to him, and said, Is it because I have found grace in your eyes, that you should recognize me, seeing that I am a stranger?

11 And Boaz said to her, I have been fully informed of all that you have done for your mother-in-law after the death of your husband; and how you have left your father and mother and your family, and come to a people that you did not know before.

12 May the LORD God of Israel reward you, and may the One under whose wings you have come to take shelter recompense you.

13 Then she said to him, Because I have found favor in your sight, my

lord, and you have comforted me and have spoken kindly to your handmaid, let me become like one of your maidservants.

14 And Boaz said to her at mealtime, Come near and eat of the bread; and he set her beside the reapers, and gave her barley-meal, and dipped bread in milk; then he gave her parched wheat, and she did eat and was satisfied, and she had some left over.

15 And when she was risen up to glean, Boaz commanded his servants, saying, Let her glean even among the sheaves, and do not harm her;

16 And they let her glean between the sheaves, and they did not harm her.

17 So she gleaned in the field until evening, and beat out what she had gleaned; and it was about an ephah of barley.

18 ¶And she took it up and went into the city; and she showed her mother-in-law what she had gleaned; and she gave her of the food which was left over after she had eaten and was satisfied.

19 And her mother-in-law said to her, Where did you glean today? Blessed be the place in which you were and the man in whose eyes you have found favor. And she told her mother-in-law where she had been, and said, The man's name in whose field I gleaned today is Boaz.

20 And Naomi said to her daughter-in-law, Blessed is the LORD, because he has not caused his kindness to cease from the living nor from the dead. And Naomi said to her, The man is near of kin to us, he is one of our nearest kinsmen.

21 And Ruth said to her mother-in-law, He said to me also, You shall keep close by my servants until all the harvest is finished.

22 And Naomi said to Ruth her daughter-in-law, Happy are you, my daughter, for you have kept close to his maidens, and no man harmed you in the field, whose owner you did not know!

23 So she kept close by the maidservants of Boaz to glean until the end of the barley harvest and of the wheat harvest; and Ruth dwelt with her mother-in-law.

CHAPTER 3

THEN Naomi said to her, My daughter, shall I not seek rest for you, that it may be well with you?

2 And, behold, Boaz is our kinsman, with whose maidens you were; and behold, he is going to winnow barley tonight in the threshing floor.

3 Wash yourself therefore, and anoint yourself, and put on your best garments, and go down to the threshing floor; but do not show yourself to him until he has finished eating and drinking.

4 And it shall be, when he lies down, that you shall remember the place where he lies, and you shall draw near and lie down near his feet; and he will tell you what you shall do.

5 And she said to her, All that you say to me I will do.

6 ¶So she went down to the threshing floor, and did according to all that her mother-in-law had told her.

7 And when Boaz had eaten and drunk, and his heart was merry, he went and lay at the side of the threshing floor; and while he was in deep sleep in the threshing floor, she came secretly and lifted the end of his robe and lay down near his feet.

8 ¶And it came to pass at midnight that the man woke up and was startled when he saw a woman lying at his feet.

9 And he said to her, Who are you? And she answered, I am Ruth, your handmaid; cover therefore your maidservant with the end of your robe, for you are a near kinsman.

10 And Boaz said to her, Blessed be you of the LORD, my daughter; for you have shown more kindness in the latter days than at the beginning of your life in that you have not gone after young men, whether rich or poor.

11 And now, my daughter, fear not; for I will do for you all that you ask of me; for all the family of our

people know that you are a virtuous woman.

12 And now it is true that I am a near kinsman; however, there is another kinsman nearer than I.

13 Now, tarry this night and lodge here till dawn, and it shall be in the morning, if he will perform to you the part of a kinsman, well, let him do it; but if he is unwilling to do the part of a kinsman to you, then, as the LORD lives, if he does not do the part of a next of kin to you, I will do the part of a kinsman to you; then he said to her, Lie down until the morning.

14 ¶So she lay at his feet until dawn; and she rose up early in the morning while it was dark, before one could recognize another. And she said to him, Let it not be known that I came down to you to the threshing floor.

15 And Boaz said to her, Spread your mantle; and she spread it, and he measured six measures of barley, lifted it up, and laid it on her back; and she went into the city.

16 And when she came to her mother-in-law, she said to her, Who are you, my daughter? And she answered, I am Ruth, and she told her all that Boaz had done for her;

17 And how he had given her six measures of barley, and had said to her, Go not empty-handed to your mother-in-law.

18 Then her mother-in-law said to her, Sit still, my daughter, until you know the outcome; for the man will not rest until he brings the case to judgment today.

CHAPTER 4

THEN Boaz went up to the city gate and sat down there; and behold, the near kinsman of whom Boaz had spoken was passing by; and Boaz said to him, Come, sit down here. And the man said to him, What do you wish? And he sat down by him.

2 And Boaz selected ten men of the elders of the city, and seated them by him.

3 And he said to the near kinsman, Naomi is selling to me the parcel of land which belonged to our brother Elimeleck;

4 And I thought to let you know, and say to you, Buy it in the presence of those who are seated, for I am ready to speak and to purchase it in the presence of the elders of my people who are seated. And now, if you will redeem it, redeem it; but if you will not redeem it, then tell me, that I may know that you will not redeem it; then I will redeem it. And he said, I will redeem it.

5 Then Boaz said, On the day you buy the field from Naomi and from Ruth, the Moabitess, the widow of the dead, you must buy it with the intention of raising the name of the dead upon his inheritance.

6 ¶And the near kinsman said, I cannot redeem it for myself, lest I damage my own inheritance; you can redeem it yourself; because of my lack of confidence in this transaction I cannot redeem it.

7 Now this was the custom in former time in Israel concerning redeeming and the exchanging of rights to redeem which confirmed transactions: a man pulled off his shoe and gave it to another; and this was the testimonial ceremony in Israel.

8 Therefore the near kinsman said to Boaz, Buy it for yourself. And he took off his shoe.

9 ¶And Boaz said to the elders and to all the people, You are witnesses this day, that I have bought all that belonged to Elimeleck, and all that belonged to Malion and Calion, from the hand of Naomi.

10 Moreover, Ruth the Moabitess, the wife of Malion, have I taken to be my wife, to raise up the name of the dead upon his inheritance, so that the name of the dead may not be cut off and his remembrance may not be forgotten among his brethren and his family; you are witnesses this day.

11 And all the people and the elders that were at the city gate, answered, saying, We are witnesses. And they blessed him, and said to him, May the LORD make this woman who is

in your presence like Rachel and like Leah, for both of them built up the house of Israel; and may you do worthily in Ephratah, and call its name Beth-lehem.

12 And let your house be like the house of Pharez, whom Tamar bore to Judah, and may the LORD give you an offspring from this woman.

13 ¶So Boaz took Ruth, and she became his wife; and when he went in unto her, the LORD gave her conception, and she bore a son.

14 And the women said to Naomi, Blessed be the LORD, who has not left you this day without a kinsman, that his name may be famous in Israel.

15 And he shall be to you a comforter of your soul and a nourisher to your city; for your daughter-in-law, who loves you and is better to you than seven sons, has borne him.

16 And Naomi took the child, and laid him in her bosom, and became nurse to him.

17 And the women who were her neighbors said, A son has been born to Naomi; and they called his name Obed; he is the father of Jesse, the father of David.

18 ¶Now these are the generations of Pharez: Pharez begat Hezron,

19 And Hezron begat Aram, and Aram begat Amminadab,

20 And Amminadab begat Nahshon, and Nahshon begat Shelah,

21 And Shelah begat Boaz, and Boaz begat Obed,

22 And Obed begat Jesse, and Jesse begat King David.

THE FIRST BOOK OF

SAMUEL

otherwise called

THE FIRST BOOK OF THE KINGS

CHAPTER 1

NOW there was a certain man of Ramath-dokey, of mount Ephraim, and his name was Hilkanah, the son of Jeroham, the son of Elihu, the son of Tohu, the son of Zuph, an Ephrathite;

2 And he had two wives; the name of the one was Hannah, and the name of the other Pannah; and Pannah had children, but Hannah had no children.

3 And this man used to go up out of his town yearly to worship and to sacrifice to the LORD of hosts in Shiloh. And the two sons of Eli, Hophni and Phinehas, the priests of the LORD, were there.

4 ¶And when the time came, Hilkanah sacrificed, and he gave to Pannah his wife, and to all her sons and her daughters, portions;

5 But to Hannah he gave a double portion; for he loved Hannah; but the LORD had shut up her womb.

6 And her rival also taunted her sorely to make her fret because the LORD had shut up her womb.

7 And Pannah did this year by year when she went up to the house of the LORD, and thus she provoked her; therefore Hannah wept and did not eat.

8 Then Hilkanah her husband said to her, Why do you weep? And why do you not eat? And why is your heart grieved? Behold, am I not better to you than ten sons?

9 ¶So Hannah rose up after she had

eaten and drunk in Shiloh, and she went up to the house of the LORD. Now Eli the priest was sitting upon a seat by the post of the temple of the LORD.

10 And she was bitter of soul, and she prayed before the LORD and wept bitterly.

11 And she made a vow, and said, O LORD of hosts, if thou wilt indeed look upon the affliction of thy maidservant, and remember me, and not forget thy handmaid, but wilt give to thy maidservant a son, then I will give him to the LORD all the days of his life, and there shall no razor come upon his head.

12 And it came to pass, as she continued praying before the LORD, that Eli watched her mouth.

13 Now Hannah spoke in her heart only, and her lips moved, but her voice was not heard; therefore Eli thought her to be drunk.

14 And Eli said to her, How long will you be drunk? Put away your wine from you.

15 Hannah answered and said to him, No, my lord, I am a woman full of grief; I have drunk neither wine nor strong drink, but have poured out my soul before the LORD.

16 Count not your maidservant in your presence a wicked woman; for out of the abundance of my sorrow and grief have I spoken hitherto.

17 Then Eli answered and said to her, Go in peace; and the God of Israel grant you the petition that you have asked of him.

18 And she said, Let your maidservant find grace in your sight. So the woman went her way, and her countenance was no more sad.

19 ¶And they rose up early in the morning and worshipped before the LORD, and returned and came to their house at Ramtha; and Hilkanah knew Hannah his wife; and the LORD remembered her.

20 And it came to pass, in due time Hannah conceived and bore a son, and called his name Samuel, saying, Because I have asked him of the LORD.

21 And the man Hilkanah and all his household went up to offer to the LORD the yearly sacrifices of his vow.

22 But Hannah did not go up; for she said to her husband, I will wait until the child is weaned, and then I will bring him, that he may appear before the LORD, and there abide forever.

23 And Hilkanah her husband said to her, Do what seems good to you; wait until you have weaned him; may the LORD establish your word. So the woman waited, and nursed her son until she weaned him.

24 ¶And when she had weaned him, she took him up with her, with a three-year old bullock and an ephah of flour and a skin of wine, and brought him to the house of the LORD in Shiloh; and the boy was very young.

25 And they slew the bullock, and brought the child to Eli.

26 Then Hannah said to Eli, I beseech you, my lord, as your soul lives, my lord, I am the woman that stood by you here, praying to the LORD for this boy.

27 I prayed and the LORD has granted me my petition which I asked of him;

28 Therefore also I have promised him to the LORD as long as he lives; for I petitioned him of the LORD. And they worshipped the LORD there.

CHAPTER 2

AND Hannah prayed and said, My heart is magnified in the LORD, my horn is exalted in my God; my mouth utters words against my enemies, because thou hast caused me to rejoice in thy salvation.

2 There is none holy like the LORD; for there is none besides thee; and there is none powerful like our God.

3 Talk no more so exceeding proudly; let not arrogancy come out of your mouths; for the LORD is a God of knowledge, and no devices can stand before him.

4 The bows of the mighty men are broken, and they that are weak are girded with strength.

5 Those who were full have hired out themselves for bread; and those who were hungry have food left over; the barren has given birth and

is satisfied; and she who has many children is lonely.

6 It is the LORD who makes men to die and makes alive; he brings down to Sheol and brings up.

7 The LORD makes poor and makes rich; he brings low and he also exalts.

8 He raises up the poor out of the dust and lifts up the needy from the dung-hill, to set them with the princes and to make them inherit the throne of glory; for the depths of the earth are protected by the LORD, and he has set the world upon them.

9 He will guard the feet of his saints, and the wicked shall be silent in darkness; for not by his own strength shall a mighty man prevail.

10 The LORD shall defeat his adversaries; out of heaven shall he thunder against them; the LORD shall judge the ends of the earth; and he shall give strength to his king and exalt the horn of his anointed.

11 And Hilkanah and his wife Hannah returned to Ramtha to his house. And the boy Samuel ministered to the LORD before Eli the priest.

12 ¶Now the sons of Eli were wicked men; they did not know the LORD.

13 They took the dues of the priests from the people, of every man who offered a sacrifice; and they made for themselves meat-forks with three prongs, and the priest's servant came, while the meat was boiling, with the three-pronged fork in his hand,

14 And he thrust it into the pot or caldron or pan or kettle; all that the meat-fork brought up the priest took for himself. Thus they did to all the Israelites who came thither to Shiloh.

15 Also before they burnt the sacrifices, the priest's servant came and said to the man who was sacrificing, Give meat to roast for the priest; for I will not accept boiled meat from you, but only raw.

16 And if the man said to him, They will surely offer sacrifices today, and then take for yourself as much as you wish; then he would say, No; you shall give it now; and if not, I will take it by force.

17 Wherefore the sin of the young men was very great before the LORD; because they offended the men who offered before the LORD.

18 ¶But the boy Samuel ministered before the LORD, and he wore a linen ephod.

19 And his mother made him a little mantle, and brought it to him from year to year when she came up with her husband to offer the yearly sacrifices of his vow.

20 ¶And Eli blessed Hilkanah and his wife, and said, The LORD give you another offspring from this woman for the child which she has dedicated to the LORD. And they went to their own home.

21 And the LORD blessed Hannah, and she conceived and bore three sons and two daughters. And the boy Samuel grew before the LORD.

22 ¶Now Eli was very old, and heard all that his sons were doing to all Israel; and how they reviled the women who prayed in the tabernacle of the congregation.

23 And he said to them, Why do you do such things? For I hear evil reports about you from all this people.

24 No, my sons; for it is not a good report that I hear; for you drive away the people of the LORD.

25 If a man sin against a man, he will seek forgiveness before the LORD; but if a man sin against the LORD, from whom shall he seek forgiveness? But they did not hearken to the voice of their father, because it was the LORD's will that they should be slain.

26 And the boy Samuel grew up, and was in favor both with the LORD and also with men.

27 ¶And there came a man of the LORD to Eli, and said to him, Thus says the LORD, I did surely reveal myself to the house of your father when they were in Egypt in the house of Pharaoh;

28 And I chose him out of all the tribes of Israel to be my priest, to offer upon my altar, to burn incense before me, and to wear an ephod; and I gave to the house of your father all the offerings made by fire of the children of Israel.

29 Why then do you deal wrongly with my sacrifices and my offerings, which I have commanded in the wilderness; and honor your sons above me, to choose the choicest of all the offerings of Israel my people?

30 Therefore thus says the LORD God of Israel, I said indeed that your house and the house of your father should minister before me for ever; but now the LORD says, Far be this from me; for those that honor me I will honor, and those that despise me shall be despised.

31 Behold, the days are coming when I will cut off your offspring and the offspring of your father, that there shall not be an old man in your house,

32 Nor him that bears rule in your habitation, in all the prosperity which God shall bring in Israel; and there shall not be an old man in your house for ever.

33 And a man of you whom I shall not cut off from my altar shall be spared to sadden you and to grieve your heart; and all the increase of your house shall die in the flower of their age.

34 And this shall be a sign to you that shall come upon your two sons, upon Hophni and upon Phinehas; both of them shall die on the same day.

35 And I will raise me up a faithful priest, according to the choice of my heart, who shall do according to that which is in my heart and in my mind; and I will build him a sure house; and he shall walk before my anointed for ever.

36 And it shall come to pass that every one who is left in your house shall come to bow down to him for a piece of silver and a loaf of bread, and shall say, Send me to one of the priests, that I may eat a piece of bread.

CHAPTER 3

AND the boy Samuel was ministering to the LORD, assisting Eli the priest. And the word of the LORD was precious in those days; there was no open vision.

2 And it came to pass at that time, when Eli was lying down in his bed, and his eyes had begun to grow dim so that he could not see;

3 And the lamp of the LORD was not yet put out, and Samuel was lying down to sleep in the temple of the LORD, where the ark of God was.

4 And the LORD called Samuel; and he answered, Here I am.

5 And he ran to Eli and said, Here I am; for you called me. And he said, I did not call; go back and lie down. And he went and lay down.

6 And the LORD called again, Samuel. And Samuel arose and went to Eli, and said, Here I am; for you did call me. And he answered, I did not call, my son; go back and lie down.

7 Now Samuel did not yet know the LORD, neither was the word of the LORD revealed to him.

8 And the LORD called Samuel again the third time. And Samuel arose and went to Eli, and said, Here I am; for you did call me. Then Eli perceived that the LORD had called the boy.

9 Therefore Eli said to Samuel, Go back and lie down; and it shall be, if he calls you, you shall say, Speak, LORD; for thy servant hears. So Samuel went back and lay down in his place.

10 And the LORD came and stood and called twice, Samuel, Samuel. Then Samuel said, Speak, LORD; for thy servant hears.

11 ¶And the LORD said to Samuel, Behold, I will do such a thing in Israel that whoever shall hear of it, shall give heed.

12 In that day I will perform against Eli all things which I have spoken concerning his house, from beginning to end.

13 And I will show him that I will judge his house for ever for the iniquity which he knew when his sons reviled the people and he did not rebuke them.

14 Therefore I have sworn to the house of Eli that the iniquity of Eli's household shall not be purged with sacrifices nor offerings for ever.

15 ¶And Samuel lay until the morn-

ing; then he opened the doors of the house of the LORD. And Samuel feared to tell the vision to Eli.

16 Then Eli called Samuel, and said, Samuel, my son. And he answered, Here am I.

17 And he said to him, What is the thing that the LORD has said to you? Do not be afraid of me. May God do so to you, and more also, if you hide anything from me of all the things that the LORD said to you.

18 And Samuel told him everything, and hid nothing from him. And Eli said, It is the LORD; let him do what is good in his sight.

19 ¶And Samuel knew that the LORD was with him, and he did not ignore any of his words.

20 And all Israel from Dan to Beersheba knew that Samuel was to be a prophet of the LORD.

21 And the LORD continued to reveal himself by his words in Shiloh; and Samuel's words were declared throughout all Israel.

CHAPTER 4

AND the word of Samuel came to all Israel. Now Israel went out against the Philistines to battle, and encamped by the Rock of Help; and the Philistines encamped at Aphek.

2 And the Philistines put themselves in array against Israel; and when they fought, Israel was defeated before the Philistines; and there were slain on the battlefield about four thousand men.

3 ¶And when the people were come to the camp, the elders of Israel said, Why has the LORD smitten us today before the Philistines? Let us bring the ark of the covenant of the LORD of hosts out of Shiloh to us, that it may go with us and save us from our enemies.

4 So the people sent to Shiloh, and they brought from thence the ark of the covenant of the LORD of hosts, who dwells upon the cherubim; and the two sons of Eli, Hophni and Phinehas, were there with the ark of the covenant of the LORD.

5 And it came to pass, when the ark of the covenant of the LORD came into camp, all Israel shouted with a great shout, so that it re-echoed.

6 And when the Philistines heard the noise, they said, What is this noise of shouting in the camp of the Hebrews? And they learned that the ark of the LORD had come into the camp.

7 And the Philistines were afraid, for they said, God is come into the camp. And they said, Woe to us! For there has not been such a thing before.

8 Woe to us! who shall deliver us from the hands of the mighty God? This is the God who smote the whole of Egypt with all sorts of plagues and performed wonders in the wilderness.

9 Be strong, and conduct yourselves like men, O Philistines, lest you become servants to the Hebrews, as they have served you; be strong and fight with them.

10 ¶And the Philistines fought with Israel, and Israel was defeated, and they fled every man to his tent; and there was a very great slaughter in Israel; for there fell of Israel in that day thirty thousand footmen.

11 And the ark of God was taken; and the two sons of Eli, Hophni and Phinehas, were slain.

12 ¶And there ran a man of Benjamin from the battle line, and came to Shiloh the same day with his clothes rent and with earth upon his head.

13 And Eli was sitting upon a seat by the wayside watching; for his heart trembled for the ark of God. And when the man came into the city to tell of the disaster, all the city cried out.

14 And when Eli heard the noise of crying, he said, What is this noise of tumult? And the man came in hastily and told Eli.

15 Now Eli was seventy-eight years old; and his eyes were dim so that he could not see.

16 And the man said to Eli, I am he who came from the battle line, and I fled today from the battle line. And he said to him, What is the news, my son?

17 And the messenger answered and said, Israel has fled before the Philistines, and there has been also a great slaughter among the people, and your two sons also, Hophni and Phinehas, are dead, and the ark of God has been taken.

18 And it came to pass, when Eli thought of the ark of God, he fell from off the seat backward by the side of the gate, and his neck broke, and he died; for he was an old man, and heavy. And he had judged Israel forty years.

19 ¶And his daughter-in-law, Phinehas' wife, was with child; and was near to be delivered; and when she heard the news that the ark of God was taken and that her father-in-law and her husband were dead, she bowed down and travailed; for her pains came upon her.

20 And about the time of her death, the women that stood by her said to her, Fear not; for you have borne a son. But she neither answered nor did she pay attention to it.

21 And she named the child Jochabar, saying, The glory is departed from Israel; because the ark of God was taken, and because of her father-in-law and her husband.

22 And she said, The glory is departed from Israel; for the ark of God is taken.

CHAPTER 5

AND the Philistines took the ark of God, and brought it from the Rock of Help to Ashdod.

2 Then the Philistines took the ark of God, and brought it into the house of Dagon and set it by the side of Dagon.

3 ¶And when the inhabitants of Ashdod arose early the next morning, they found Dagon was fallen upon his face on the ground before the ark of the LORD. And they took Dagon and set him in his place again.

4 And when they arose early the next morning, behold, Dagon was fallen upon his face on the ground before the ark of the LORD; and the head of Dagon and both of his hands were cut off upon the threshold; only the trunk of Dagon was left.

5 Therefore neither the priests of Dagon nor any that enter Dagon's house cross the threshold of Dagon in Ashdod to this day.

6 But the hand of the LORD was heavy upon the inhabitants of Ashdod, and he destroyed them and afflicted them with boils, both Ashdod and the territory thereof.

7 And when the men of Ashdod saw that it was so, they said, The ark of the God of Israel shall not stay with us; for his hand is heavy upon us and upon Dagon our god.

8 They sent therefore and gathered all the lords of the Philistines to them, and said, What shall we do with the ark of the God of Israel? And they answered, Let the ark of the God of Israel be returned to Gath. So they took back the ark of the God of Israel there.

9 And after they took it back, the hand of the LORD was against the city with a very great destruction; and he smote the men of the city, both small and great, and they were covered with boils.

10 ¶Therefore they sent the ark of God to Ekron. And when the ark of God came to Ekron, the Ekronites cried out, saying, They have brought the ark of the God of Israel to us, to slay us and our people.

11 So they sent and gathered together all the lords of the Philistines, and said, Send away the ark of the God of Israel, and let it return to its own place, that it may not slay us and our people. For the fear of death caused a panic that spread throughout all the city; the hand of God was very heavy there.

12 And the men who did not die were smitten with the boils; and the cry of the city went up to heaven.

CHAPTER 6

AND the ark of the LORD was in the country of the Philistines seven months.

2 And the Philistines called for the priests and the lords, saying, What shall we do with the ark of the

LORD? Tell us by what means shall we send it to its place.

3 And they said, If you send away the ark of the LORD God of Israel, do not send it away empty; but you must surely bring trespass offerings to it; then you shall be healed, and it shall be known to you why his hand is not removed from you.

4 And they said, What sort of offerings shall we bring to it? They answered, Five golden boils and five golden mice, according to the number of the lords of the Philistines; for one plague was upon you all and upon your lords.

5 Wherefore you shall make likenesses of your boils and images of the mice that are destroying the land; and you shall give glory to the God of Israel; perhaps he will remove his hand from you and from your god and from your land.

6 And you shall not harden your hearts, as the Egyptians and Pharaoh hardened their hearts, and as they mocked the Israelites and did not send them nor let them go.

7 Now therefore make a new cart, and take two milch cows upon which there has come no yoke, and tie the cows to the cart, and bring their calves home from them;

8 And take the ark of the LORD, and lay it upon the cart; and put the vessels of gold which you have brought for it as offerings, in a box by its side; and send it away, that it may go on its way.

9 And watch, for if it goes up by the way of the border which goes up to Beth-shemesh, then it is the LORD who has done us this great evil; but if not, then we shall know that it is not his hand that afflicted us, but it has happened to us by chance.

10 ¶And the men did so; and took two milch cows and tied them to the cart and shut up their calves at home;

11 And they laid the ark of God upon the cart, and the box with the mice of gold and the images of their boils.

12 And they sent out the cows by the way which is by the border of Beth-shemesh, and they went along the highway, lowing as they went, and turned not aside to the right hand nor to the left; and the lords of the Philistines went after them as far as the border of Beth-shemesh.

13 And the men of the town of Beth-shemesh were reaping their wheat harvest in the valley; and they lifted up their eyes and saw the ark, and rejoiced when they saw it.

14 And the cart came into the field of Joshua, a Beth-shemeshite, and stopped where there was a great stone; and they split the wood of the cart, and offered the cows as a burnt offering to the LORD.

15 And the Levites took down the ark of the LORD and the box that was with it in which were the vessels of gold, and put them on the great stone; and the men of Beth-shemesh offered burnt offerings and sacrifices on that day to the LORD.

16 And when the five lords of the Philistines had seen it, they returned to Ekron the same day.

17 And these are the golden boils which the Philistines had brought as offerings to God: for Ashdod one, for Gaza one, for Ashkelon one, for Gath one, for Ekron one;

18 And the golden mice, according to the number of all the cities of the Philistines, belonging to the five lords, both of the five fortified cities and of the country villages of the Perrizites, and as far as the great stone of Abel, whereon they set down the ark of the LORD, which to this day is in the field of Joshua, the Beth-shemeshite.

19 ¶And the LORD smote the men of Beth-shemesh because they worshipped the ark of the LORD, and the LORD smote five thousand and seventy men of the people; and the people mourned because the LORD had smitten many of the people with a great slaughter.

20 And the men of Beth-shemesh said, Who is able to stand before this holy LORD God? And who shall carry up from us the ark?

21 ¶So they sent messengers to the

inhabitants of Koriath-narin, saying, The Philistines have brought back the ark of the LORD; come down and take it up to you.

CHAPTER 7

AND the men of Koriath-narin came, and took up the ark of the LORD, and brought it into the house of Abinadab on the hill, and Abinadab consecrated Eleazar his son, who kept the ark of the LORD.

2 And it came to pass, from the day that the ark abode in Koriath-narin, that the time was long; for it was about twenty years; and all the house of Israel yearned after the LORD.

3 ¶Then Samuel said to all the house of Israel, If you return with all your heart to the LORD, then put away the strange gods and Ashtaroth from among you, and prepare your heart unto the LORD, and serve him only; and he will deliver you out of the hand of the Philistines.

4 So the children of Israel put away Baal and Ashtaroth, and served the LORD only.

5 And Samuel said, Gather all Israel at Mizpeh, and I will pray for you to the LORD.

6 And they gathered together at Mizpeh, and drew water and poured it out before the LORD, and fasted on that day, and said, We have sinned against the LORD. And Samuel judged the children of Israel at Mizpeh.

7 And when the Philistines heard that the children of Israel were gathered together at Mizpeh, the lords of the Philistines went up against Israel. And when the children of Israel heard it, they were afraid of the Philistines.

8 And the children of Israel said to Samuel, Do not cease to pray before the LORD our God for us, that he may save us from the hand of the Philistines.

9 ¶And Samuel took a suckling lamb and offered it for a burnt offering wholly to the LORD; and Samuel prayed before the LORD for the children of Israel; and the LORD answered him.

10 And as Samuel was offering up the burnt offering, the Philistines drew near to battle against Israel; but the LORD thundered with a great thunder on that day against the Philistines, and threw them into confusion; and they were defeated before Israel.

11 And the men of Israel went out of Mizpeh and pursued the Philistines and smote them as far as below Beth-jashan.

12 Then Samuel took a stone and set it between Mizpeh and Beth-jashan, and called its name Rock of Help, and he said, Hitherto the LORD has helped us.

13 ¶So the Philistines were defeated, and they came no more into the territory of Israel; and the hand of the LORD was against the Philistines all the days of Samuel.

14 And the cities which the Philistines had taken from Israel were restored to Israel from Ekron even to Gath, and the boundaries thereof. Thus the LORD delivered Israel from the hand of the Philistines. And there was peace between Israel and the Amorites.

15 And Samuel judged Israel all the days of his life.

16 And he went from year to year in circuit to Beth-el and Gilgal and Mizpeh, and judged Israel in all those places.

17 And he always returned to Ramtha; for there was his house, and there he judged Israel, and there he built an altar to the LORD.

CHAPTER 8

AND it came to pass, when Samuel was old, he made his sons judges over Israel.

2 Now the name of his first-born son was Joel; and the name of his second, Abiah; they were judges in Beer-sheba.

3 But his sons did not walk in his ways, but turned aside after lucre, and took bribes and perverted judgment.

4 Then all the elders of Israel gathered themselves together and came to Samuel to Ramtha,

5 And they said to him, Behold, you are old, and your sons do not walk in your ways; now give us a king to judge us like all the nations.

6 ¶But the thing displeased Samuel, when they said to him, Give us a king to judge us like all the nations. And Samuel prayed before the LORD.

7 And the LORD said to Samuel, Hearken to the voice of the people in all that they say to you; for they have not rejected you, but they have rejected me, that I should not reign over them.

8 According to all the works which they have done since the day that I brought them up out of the land of Egypt even to this day, as they have forsaken me and served other gods, so do they also to you.

9 Now therefore hearken to their voice; but testify solemnly to them, and show them the law of the king who shall reign over them.

10 ¶And Samuel told all the words of the LORD to the people who asked of him a king.

11 Then he said, This will be the law of the king who will reign over you: he will take your sons and appoint them for himself for his chariots, and to be his horsemen; and they shall run before his chariots.

12 And he will appoint for himself officers of thousands and officers of hundreds and officers of fifties and officers of tens. And they shall plow his ground and reap his harvest and make his implements of war and instruments for his chariots.

13 And he will take your daughters to be weavers and grinders and bakers.

14 And he will take the best of your fields and your vineyards and your oliveyards, and give them to his servants.

15 And he will take the tenth of your crops and of your vineyards, and give to his officers and to his servants.

16 And he will take your menservants and your maidservants, and your goodly young men and your asses, and put them to his work.

17 He will take the tenth of your sheep; and you shall be his servants.

18 And you shall cry for help in that day because of your king whom you shall have chosen for yourselves; and the LORD will not answer you on that day.

19 ¶Nevertheless the people refused to obey the voice of Samuel; and they said to him, No; but we will have a king over us,

20 That we also may be like all the nations, and that our king may judge us and go out before us and fight our battles.

21 And Samuel heard all the words of the people, and he repeated them before the LORD.

22 And the LORD said to Samuel, Hearken to their voice, and make them a king. And Samuel said to the men of Israel, Go every man to his city.

CHAPTER 9

NOW there was a man from Benjamin, whose name was Kish, the son of Abiel, the son of Zerod, the son of Bechorath, the son of Aphiah, a Benjamite, a mighty man of power.

2 And he had a son whose name was Saul, a choice young man and a goodly; and there was not among the children of Israel a more attractive person than he; he was head and shoulders higher than any of the people.

3 And the asses of Kish, Saul's father, were lost. And Kish said to Saul his son, Take now one of the servants with you, and arise, go seek the asses. And Saul arose and went, and took one of the servants with him, and they went to seek the asses of his father.

4 And they passed through mount Ephraim and through the land of Gomrey, but they did not find them; then they passed through the land of Taley, and they were not there; and they passed through the land of Benjamin, but they did not find them.

5 And when they came to the land of Sur, Saul said to the servant who was with him, Come, let us return, lest my father cease to be anxious

about the asses and begin to be concerned about us.

6 But his servant said to him, Behold, there is a man of God in this city, and he is an honorable man in the eyes of the people; all that he says comes surely to pass; now let us go there; perhaps he can tell us about the errand for which we have come.

7 Then Saul said to his servant, Behold, if we go, what shall we bring to the man of God? For the bread is spent in our bags and there are no provisions to bring a present to the man of God, because we have nothing.

8 And the servant answered his master again, and said, Behold, I have here at hand the fourth part of a shekel of silver; let us give it to the man of God, that he may tell us about our errand.

9 (Because formerly in Israel, when a man went to inquire of God, thus he said, Come, let us go to the seer; for he who is now called a prophet, before was called a seer.)

10 Then Saul said to his servant, Well said; come, let us go. So they went to the city where the man of God was.

11 ¶And as they went up the hill to the city, they found young maidens going out to draw water, and Saul said to them, Is there a seer here?

12 And they answered him and said, There is; behold, he is ahead of you; go up now quickly, for he came today to the city; for there is a sacrifice of the people today on the high place;

13 As soon as you enter the city, you shall straightway find him, before he goes up to the high place to eat; for the people will not eat until he comes, because he blesses the sacrifices; and afterwards those who are invited, eat. Now therefore go up; for today you shall find him.

14 And they went up to the city; and just as they were entering the city gate, behold, Samuel was coming out toward them to go up to the high place.

15 Now the LORD had told Samuel a day before Saul came, saying,

16 Tomorrow about this time I will send you a man from the land of Benjamin, and you shall anoint him to be a ruler over my people Israel, and he shall save my people from the hand of the Philistines; for I have seen the oppression of my people, and their cry has come to me.

17 And when Samuel saw Saul, whom the LORD had chosen, then the LORD said to Samuel, Behold the man of whom I spoke to you! This man shall reign over my people.

18 Then Saul drew near to Samuel at the gate, and said, Tell me, where is the house of the seer?

19 And Samuel answered Saul, and said, I am the seer; go up before me to the high place; for you shall eat with me today, and in the morning I will let you go, and will tell you all that is in your heart.

20 And as for your asses that were lost three days ago, do not be anxious about them, for they have been found. And on whom is all the hope of the house of Israel? Is it not on you and on your father's house?

21 And Saul answered and said to Samuel, Behold, I am a Benjamite, of the smallest of the tribes of Israel, and my family is the least of all the families of the tribe of Benjamin. Why then have you spoken thus to me?

22 And Samuel took Saul and his servant, and brought them into the house, and gave them a place at the head of those who were invited, who were about thirty persons.

23 And Samuel said to the cook, Bring the portion which I gave you, of which I said to you, Set it apart.

24 And the cook took up the shoulder and the thigh, and set them before Saul. And Samuel said, Behold that which is left! Set it before you and eat; because it has been kept for you for some time. So Saul ate with Samuel that day.

25 ¶And when they were come down from the high place into the city, Samuel conversed with Saul upon the roof.

26 And they arose at dawn, and Samuel called to Saul upon the roof,

saying, Up, that I may send you away. And Saul arose, and they went out both of them, he and Samuel.

27 And as they were going down to the end of the city, Samuel said to Saul, Tell the servant to pass on before us, but you stop where you are, that I may tell you the word of God.

CHAPTER 10

THEN Samuel took a vial of oil, and poured it upon his head and kissed him, and said to him, Behold, the LORD has anointed you to be a ruler over his inheritance.

2 When you depart from me today, behold, you will find two men at Rachel's sepulchre in the territory of Benjamin at Zelzah; and they will say to you, The asses which you went to seek are found; and, lo, your father has ceased worrying about the asses, and is concerned about you, saying, What shall I do for my son?

3 Then when you shall go on from there and you shall come to the oak of Tabor, behold, you will find there three men going up to God to Beth-el, one carrying three kids and another carrying three loaves of bread and another carrying a skin of wine;

4 And they will salute you, and give you two loaves of bread, which you shall receive from their hands.

5 After that you shall come to the hill of God where there is a garrison of the Philistines; and it shall come to pass when you arrive there at the city, behold, you will meet a company of prophets coming down from the high place with psalteries and tabrets and tambourines and timbrels before them; and they will be prophesying;

6 And the Spirit of the LORD will come upon you, and you shall prophesy with them, and you shall be changed into another man.

7 And it shall be when these signs are come to you, that you shall do whatever you wish, for the LORD is with you.

8 And you shall go down before me to Gilgal; and, behold, I will come down to you to offer burnt offerings and to make sacrifices of peace offerings; seven days you shall wait, till I come to you, and show you what you shall do.

9 ¶And it came to pass when he had turned his back to go from Samuel, God gave him another heart; and all those signs came to pass that day.

10 And when they came to Ramtha, behold, a company of prophets met him; and the Spirit of God came upon him, and he prophesied among them.

11 And it came to pass when all that knew him beforetime saw that, behold, he prophesied among the prophets, then the people said one to another, What is this that has come to the son of Kish? Is Saul also among the prophets?

12 And a man of the same place answered and said, But who is his father? Therefore it became a by-word, Is Saul also among the prophets?

13 And when he had finished prophesying, he left the high place, and came home.

14 ¶And Saul's uncle said to him and to his servant, Where did you go? And they said, To seek the asses; and when we found them nowhere, we went to Samuel.

15 And Saul's uncle said to him, Tell me what Samuel said to you.

16 And Saul said to his uncle, He told us plainly that the asses were found. But of the matter of the kingdom of which Samuel had spoken, he did not tell him.

17 ¶And Samuel called the people together before the LORD at Mizpeh;

18 And he said to the children of Israel, Thus says the LORD God of Israel, I brought up Israel out of the land of Egypt and later delivered you from the hand of the Philistines and from the hand of all the kingdoms that oppressed you;

19 But you have this day rejected your God, who himself saved you from all your calamities and your tribulations; and you have said, Not so, but set a king over us. Now therefore present yourselves before the

LORD by your tribes and by your thousands.

20 And when Samuel had caused all the tribes of Israel to come near, the tribe of Benjamin was taken by lot.

21 Then when he caused the tribe of Benjamin to come near by their families, the family of Matri was taken by lot, and Saul the son of Kish was taken by lot. But when they sought him, he could not be found.

22 Therefore Samuel inquired further of the LORD, saying, Where is this man? And the LORD said to Samuel, Behold, he has hidden himself among the baggage.

23 And they ran and brought him from there; and when he stood among the people, he was head and shoulders higher than any of the people.

24 And Samuel said to all the people, Now have you seen him whom the LORD has chosen, because there is none like him among all the people? And the people shouted and said, Long live the king!

25 Then Samuel told the people the law governing the king, and wrote it in a book and laid it before the LORD. And Samuel sent all the people away, and they went every man to his house.

26 ¶And Saul also went to his house at Ramtha; [1] and there went with him a band of men whose hearts God had touched.

27 But some of the wicked men said, How shall this man save us? And they despised him and brought him no presents. But he held his peace.

CHAPTER 11

THEN Nahash the Ammonite came up and encamped against Jabesh-Gilead; and all the men of Jabesh said to Nahash, Make a treaty with us and we will serve you.

2 But Nahash the Ammonite said to them, On th condition will I make a treaty with you, when you thrust out all your right eyes, that I may make you a reproach upon all Israel.

3 And the elders of Jabesh said to him, Give us seven days respite, that we may send messengers throughout all the territory of Israel; and when we see if we have a savior or not, then we will come out to you.

4 ¶Then the messengers came to Ramtha of Saul, and told these words before the people; and all the people lifted up their voices and wept.

5 And, behold, Saul was coming behind the oxen from the field; and Saul said, What ails the people that they are weeping? And they told him the words of the men of Jabesh.

6 And the Spirit of God came upon Saul when he heard these words, and his anger was kindled greatly.

7 And he took a yoke of oxen and cut them in pieces and sent them throughout all the territory of Israel by the hand of messengers, saying, Whosoever does not follow after Saul and after Samuel, so shall it be done to his oxen. And the fear of the LORD fell on the people, and they all came out as one man.

8 And when he numbered them in Bezek, the children of Israel were three hundred thousand and the men of Judah thirty thousand.

9 And they said to the messengers who had come from Jabesh, Thus shall you say to the men of Jabesh and of Gilead, Tomorrow, by the time the sun is hot, you shall be delivered. And the messengers came and told the men of Jabesh; and they were glad.

10 Therefore the men of Jabesh said, Tomorrow we will come out to you, and you shall do to us whatever seems good to you.

11 And it came to pass, on the next day, Saul divided the people in three companies; and they came into the midst of the camp in the morning watch, and slew the Ammonites until the heat of the day; and those who remained were scattered, so that no two of them were left together.

12 ¶Then the people said to Samuel, Who is he that said, Shall Saul reign over us? Bring the men that we may put them to death.

13 And Saul said, There shall not a man be put to death this day; for to-

[1] Gibeah.

day the LORD has wrought salvation in Israel.

14 Then Samuel said to the people, Come, let us go to Gilgal and renew the kingdom there.

15 And all the people went to Gilgal; and there they made Saul king before the LORD in Gilgal; and there they made sacrifices of peace offerings before the LORD; and there Saul and all the men of Israel rejoiced greatly.

CHAPTER 12

AND Samuel said to all Israel, Behold, I have hearkened to your voice in all that you said to me, and have made a king over you.

2 And now, behold, the king is before you; and I am old and grayheaded; and, behold, my sons are with you; and I have walked before you from my childhood to this day.

3 Behold, I am standing before you; testify against me before the LORD and before his anointed; whose ox have I taken? Or whose ass have I taken? Or whom have I defrauded? Or whom have I oppressed? Or of whose hand have I taken a bribe to look upon him with favor? Tell me, and I will restore it to you.

4 And they said to him, You have not defrauded us nor oppressed us, neither have you taken anything from any one of us.

5 And he said to them, The LORD is witness against you, and his anointed is witness this day, that you have not found anything wrong with me. And they said, He is witness.

6 ¶And Samuel said to the people, The LORD is the only God, who advanced Moses and Aaron and who brought your fathers up out of the land of Egypt.

7 Now therefore stand still that I may judge you before the LORD in all his righteous acts which he did to you and to your fathers.

8 When Jacob went into Egypt and your fathers prayed before the LORD, then the LORD sent Moses and Aaron, who brought your fathers out of the land of Egypt and made them dwell in this place.

9 And when they forgot the LORD their God, he delivered them into the hand of Sisera, general of the army of Hazor, and into the hand of the Philistines, and into the hand of the king of Moab, and they fought against them.

10 And they prayed before the LORD, and said, We have sinned, because we have forsaken the LORD our God and have served Baal and Ashtaroth; but now deliver us out of the hand of our enemies and we will serve thee.

11 And the LORD sent Deborah and Barak and Gideon and Jephthah and Samson, and delivered you out of the hand of your enemies round about you, and you dwelt in safety.

12 And when you saw that Nahash the king of the children of Ammon came against you, you said to me, No; but a king shall reign over us; yet the LORD your God was your king.

13 Now therefore behold the king whom you have chosen, and whom you have requested! And, behold, the LORD has given you a king.

14 If you will fear the LORD and serve him and obey his voice and not provoke him, then shall both you and also the king who reigns over you continue following the LORD your God.

15 But if you will not obey the voice of the LORD your God, but provoke him, then shall the hand of the LORD be against you as it was against your fathers.

16 ¶Now therefore be ready, and see this great thing which the LORD will do for you.

17 Behold, it is wheat harvest today; I will call to the LORD, and he shall send thunder and rain; and you shall know and see that your wickedness is great, in that you have asked for yourselves a king.

18 Then Samuel called to the LORD; and the LORD sent thunder and rain on that place; and all the people greatly feared the LORD and Samuel.

19 And all the people said to Samuel, Pray for your servants before the LORD your God, that we may not

die; for we have added to all our sins a great evil, in that we have asked for ourselves a king.

20 ¶And Samuel said to the people, Fear not; you have done all this wickedness; yet do not turn aside from following the LORD, but serve him with all your heart;

21 And do not turn aside after vain things which cannot deliver you; that you may not die, for they are vain things.

22 For the LORD will not forsake his people for his great name's sake; because he is pleased to make you his people.

23 Moreover as for me, far be it from me that I should sin against the LORD in ceasing to pray for you; but I will teach you the good and the right way;

24 Only revere the LORD, and serve him in truth with all your heart and with all your soul; for consider what great things he has done for you.

25 But if you shall continue to do wickedly, you shall die, both you and your king.

CHAPTER 13

AND when Saul had reigned one or two years in his kingdom over Israel,

2 He then chose for himself three thousand men of Israel; two thousand were with him in Michmash and in mount Beth-el, and a thousand were with Jonathan his son in Ramtha of Benjamin; and the rest of the people he sent every man to his house.

3 And Jonathan smote the garrison of the Philistines that was in Geba, and the Philistines heard of it. And Saul blew the trumpet throughout all the land, saying, Let the Hebrews and all Israel hear the news

4 That Saul has smitten the garrison of the Philistines and that Israel has prevailed over the Philistines. And the people were called together after Saul to Gilgal.

5 ¶And the Philistines gathered themselves together to fight with Israel, three thousand chariots, and six thousand horsemen, and people as the sand which is on the seashore in multitude; and they came up and encamped in Michmash, east of Beth-el.

6 And when the men of Israel saw them, they were afraid; so they hid themselves in caves and in holes and in rocks and in clefts and in pits.

7 And some of the Hebrews went over the Jordan to the land of Gad and Gilead. But Saul was still in Gilgal, and all the people were with him.

8 ¶And he waited seven days, according to the set time appointed by Samuel; but Samuel did not come to Gilgal; and the people were deserting Saul.

9 And Saul said, Bring here a burnt offering to me, and he offered peace offerings and burnt offerings.

10 And as soon as he had finished making the burnt offering, behold, Samuel came; and Saul went out to meet him, that he might bless him.

11 ¶And Samuel said, What have you done? And Saul said, When I saw that the people were deserting me and that you did not come within the time appointed and that the Philistines gathered themselves together at Michmash;

12 Therefore I said, The Philistines might come down against me at Gilgal, and I have not inquired of the LORD, so I ventured to offer a burnt offering.

13 And Samuel said to Saul, You have done foolishly; for you have not kept the commandment of the LORD your God, which he commanded you; for now would the LORD have established your kingdom over Israel, as he had said, I will establish you for ever.

14 But now your kingdom shall not continue; for the LORD has chosen for himself a man after his own heart, and the LORD has commanded him to be a ruler over his people, because you have not kept all the commandments that the LORD your God gave you.

15 And Samuel arose and went up from Gilgal to Ramtha of Benjamin. And Saul numbered the people that

were present with him, about six hundred men.

16 And Saul and Jonathan his son dwelt in Gibeah of Benjamin; but the Philistines encamped in Michmash.

17 ¶And raiders came out of the camp of the Philistines in three companies; one went toward the way of Ophrah to attack the land of Shual;

18 And another went toward the way of Beth-hauran; and another turned toward the way of the border that looks toward the valley of Zebaon and to the wilderness.

19 ¶Now there was no smith found throughout all the land of Israel; for the Philistines said, We do not want the Hebrews to make swords and spears;

20 But all the Israelites went down to the Philistines to sharpen every man his sickle and his ploughshare and his axe and his mattock.

21 And there was a broad file for the sickle and for the ploughshare and for mattocks and for the axe and to sharpen the goads.

22 So in the day of the battle, there was neither sword nor spear found in the hand of any of the people who were with Saul and Jonathan; but Saul and Jonathan his son had them.

23 And the garrison of the Philistines went out to the passage of Michmash.

CHAPTER 14

NOW it came to pass one day, Jonathan the son of Saul said to the young man who bore his armor, Come, let us go over to the Philistine garrison that is on the other side yonder. But he did not tell his father.

2 And Saul was staying in the outskirts of Ramtha under the pomegranate tree which is in Gibeon; and the people who were with him were about six hundred men;

3 And Ahiah, the son of Ahitub, Jochebar's brother, the son of Phinehas, the son of Eli, the LORD's priest in Shiloh, was wearing an ephod. And the people did not know that Jonathan was gone to the crossing place.

4 ¶And as he sought to cross over to the Philistine garrison, behold, there was a steep rock on one side and a steep rock on the other side; and the name of the one was Bozez, and the name of the other Siaa.

5 One crag stood out northward over against Michmash and the other southward over against Gibeah.

6 And Jonathan said to the young man who bore his armor, Come, let us cross over to the garrison of these uncircumcised; it may be that the LORD will help us; for nothing will prevent the LORD from saving by many or by few.

7 And his armorbearer said to him, Do all that is in your heart; turn aside, and go; behold, I am with you; do whatever is in your heart.

8 Then Jonathan said to him, Behold, we will cross over against these men, and we will show ourselves to them.

9 If they say to us, Stop until we come to you; then we will stand still in our place, and will not go up against them.

10 But if they say to us thus, Come up to us; then we will go up; for the LORD our God has delivered them into our hand; and this shall be a sign to us.

11 So both of them showed themselves to the garrison of the Philistines; and the Philistines said, Behold, the Hebrews are coming forth out of the holes where they had hid themselves.

12 And the men of the garrison answered Jonathan and his armorbearer, and said, Come up to us, and we will show you something. And Jonathan said to his armorbearer, Come up after me; for the LORD has delivered them into the hand of Israel.

13 And Jonathan climbed up on his hands and on his feet, and his armorbearer followed after him; and the Philistine garrison retreated before Jonathan; and his armorbearer slew with him.

14 And the first slaughter which Jonathan and his armorbearer made

was about twenty men; they cut them to pieces like stone-cutters and like men who plough a field.

15 And there was trembling in the camp, in the field, and among all the people that stood by; and the raiders also trembled and the earth quaked; and the fear of the LORD fell upon them.

16 And the watchmen of Saul in Gibeah of Benjamin looked; and, behold, the Philistine army was in confusion, going away defeated.

17 Then Saul said to the people that were with him, Take a count and see who is gone from us. And when they had mustered, behold, Jonathan and his armorbearer were not there.

18 And Saul said to Ahiah, Bring here the ark of God. For the ark of God was at that time with the children of Israel.

19 ¶And it came to pass, while Saul was talking to the priest, that the noise in the camp of the Philistines went on and increased; and Saul said to the priest, Withdraw your hand.

20 Then Saul and all the people who were with him shouted together, and they came to the battle; and, behold, every man's sword was against his fellow, and there was a very great confusion.

21 Moreover the Hebrews who were with the Philistines before that time, who had gone up with them to the camp, even they also turned to be with the Israelites and with Saul and Jonathan.

22 Likewise all the men of Israel who had hid themselves in mount Ephraim, when they heard that the Philistines fled before the Israelites, even they armed themselves and followed hard after them in the battle.

23 So the LORD saved Israel that day; then the men of Israel passed over to Beth-aon to battle.

24 ¶And Saul drew near that day and said to the people, Cursed be the man who eats food until evening, until I am avenged on my enemies. So none of the people tasted any food.

25 And they went throughout all the land and came into a forest; and,

behold, there was honey in the forest on the ground.

26 And when the people were come into the forest, behold, the honey was dropping; but no one put his hand to his mouth; for the people feared the oath.

27 But Jonathan had not heard when his father adjured the people; so he put forth the end of the staff that was in his hand, and dipped it in a honeycomb, and put his hand to his mouth; and his eyes brightened.

28 Then one of the men of the people spoke and said to Jonathan, Your father has surely adjured the people, saying, Cursed be the man who eats food this day. And the people were faint with hunger.

29 Then Jonathan said, My father has troubled the land; see, how my eyes have been brightened because I tasted a little of this honey.

30 Moreover, because the people had not eaten today of the spoil of their enemies which they found, therefore there was not a greater slaughter of the Philistines.

31 We have smitten the Philistines today from Michmash to Aijalon; and the people are very faint with hunger.

32 Then the people rushed greedily on the spoil, and took sheep and oxen and calves, and slew them on the ground; and the people ate them with the blood.

33 ¶Then they told Saul, saying, Behold, the people have sinned against the LORD in eating flesh with blood. And Saul said, You have transgressed; roll a great stone to me this day.

34 And Saul said, Go round about among the people and say to them, Bring every man his ox, and every man his sheep, and slay them here, and do not sin against the LORD in eating flesh with the blood. So all the people brought every man his ox with him that night, and slew them there.

35 And Saul built there an altar to the LORD; thus he began to build his first altar to the LORD.

36 ¶And Saul said, Let us go down after the Philistines by night, and

plunder them until the morning, and let us not leave a man of them. And they said, Do whatever seems good to you.

37 And Saul said to God, Shall I go down after the Philistines? Wilt thou deliver them into the hands of Israel? But the LORD did not answer him that day.

38 And Saul said, Bring here all the families of the people; and know and see wherein this sin has been committed this day.

39 For, as the LORD lives, who saved Israel, though it be in Jonathan my son, he shall surely die. But there was no one of all the people that answered him.

40 Then Saul said to all Israel, Be you on one side, and I and Jonathan my son will be on the other side. And the people said to Saul, Do whatever seems good to you.

41 Therefore Saul said, O LORD God of Israel, give a perfect lot. And Saul and Jonathan were taken; but the people were not taken.

42 And Saul said, Cast lots between me and Jonathan my son. And Jonathan was taken.

43 Then Saul said to Jonathan, Tell me what you have done. And Jonathan told him, and said, I did taste a little honey with the end of the staff that was in my hand, and on account of that must I die?

44 And Saul said, God do so to me and more also, unless you shall surely die, Jonathan.

45 And the people said to Saul, Shall Jonathan die, who has wrought this great salvation in Israel? God forbid; as the LORD lives, there shall not a hair of his head fall to the ground; for he has saved the people of God this day. So the people delivered Jonathan and he did not die.

46 Then Saul returned from following the Philistines; and the Philistines went to their own country.

47 ¶And Saul took the kingship over Israel, and he fought against all his enemies on every side, against Moab and against the children of Ammon and against Edom and against the kingdom of Zobah and against the Philistines; and wherever he turned he was victorious.

48 And he mobilized an army and smote the Amalekites, and delivered Israel out of the hand of those who plundered them.

49 Now these were the sons of Saul: Jonathan, Ishui, Melchi-shua, and Ashbashul; and the names of his two daughters were these: the name of the elder Nadab, and the name of the younger Malchel;

50 And the name of Saul's wife was Ahinoam, the daughter of Ahimaaz; and the name of the general of his army was Abner, the son of Ner, Saul's uncle.

51 And Kish was the father of Saul; and Ner, the father of Abner, was the son of Abiel.

52 And there was severe war against the Philistines all the days of Saul; and when Saul saw any valiant man or any strong man, he took him to himself.

CHAPTER 15

SAMUEL said to Saul, The LORD sent me to anoint you to be king over his people Israel. Now therefore hearken to the voice of the words of the LORD.

2 Thus says the LORD of hosts, I remember what Amalek did to Israel on their journey when they were coming up out of Egypt.

3 Now go and smite the Amalekites, and utterly destroy all that they have, and spare them not; but slay both men and women, young people and infants, oxen and sheep, camels and asses.

4 And Saul summoned the people to war, and he numbered them in Telaye, two hundred thousand footmen and ten thousand men of Judah.

5 And Saul came to a city of the Amalekites, and issued a directive in the valley.

6 ¶And Saul said to the Kenites, Turn aside, depart, get you down from among the Amalekites, lest I destroy you with them; for you showed kindness to all the children

of Israel when they came up out of Egypt. So the Kenites departed from among the Amalekites.

7 And Saul smote the Amalekites from Havilah as far as Shur, which is over near Egypt.

8 And he took Agag the king of the Amalekites alive, and utterly destroyed all the people with the edge of the sword.

9 But Saul and the people spared King Agag and the best of the sheep and of the oxen and of the fatlings and the stall-fed beasts and all that was good, and would not utterly destroy them; but everything that was vile and despised in their sight, that they destroyed utterly.

10 ¶Then the word of the LORD came to Samuel, saying,

11 I regret that I have made Saul king; for he has turned back from following me, and has not performed my commandments. And it grieved Samuel; and he prayed before the LORD all night.

12 And when Samuel rose early to meet Saul in the morning, it was told Samuel, saying, Saul has come to Carmel, and, behold, he has set up a dwelling place for himself, and has turned and passed on and gone down to Gilgal.

13 And Samuel came to Saul; and Saul said to him, Blessed be the LORD, who has performed his commandment.

14 And Samuel said, What then is this bleating of the sheep in my ears and the lowing of the oxen that I hear?

15 And Saul said, They have brought them from the Amalekites; for the people spared the best of the sheep and of the oxen, and brought them to sacrifice to the LORD your God; and the rest we have utterly destroyed.

16 Then Samuel said to Saul, Be still, and I will tell you what the LORD has said to me this night. And Saul said to him, Say on.

17 And Samuel said to Saul, Behold, even though you were little in your own eyes; nevertheless you were made the head of the tribes of Israel,

and the LORD anointed you king over Israel.

18 And the LORD sent you on a mission, and said, Go and utterly destroy the sinners, the Amalekites, and fight against them until they are consumed.

19 Why then did you not obey the voice of the LORD, but have spared the plunder, and have done evil in the sight of the LORD?

20 And Saul said to Samuel, I have obeyed the voice of the LORD, and have gone on the mission on which the LORD sent me, and have brought Agag the king of the Amalekites, and have utterly destroyed the Amalekites.

21 But the people took some of the spoil, sheep and oxen, the best of the things which should have been utterly destroyed, to sacrifice to the LORD your God in Gilgal.

22 And Samuel said, The LORD is not as well pleased with burnt offerings and sacrifices as with one who obeys his voice. Behold, to obey is better than sacrifices, and to hearken, than the fat of rams.

23 For divination is a rebellion, and divination is a grievous iniquity. Because you have rejected the word of the LORD, he has also rejected you from being king.

24 ¶And Saul said to Samuel, I have sinned; for I have transgressed the commandment of the LORD and your words, because I feared the people and obeyed their voice.

25 Now therefore, pardon my sin, and return with me, that I may worship the LORD.

26 And Samuel said to Saul, I will not return home with you; for you have rejected the word of the LORD, and the LORD has rejected you from being king over Israel.

27 And as Samuel turned about to go away, Saul laid hold upon the skirt of his mantle, and it tore.

28 And Samuel said to him, The LORD has torn the kingdom of Israel from you this day, and has given it to a neighbor of yours, who is better than you.

29 And also his Excellency the LORD

of Israel will not lie nor seek counsel; for he is not a human being, that he should seek counsel.

30 Then Saul said, I have sinned; yet honor me now before the elders of my people and before Israel, and return again with me, that I may worship the LORD your God.

31 So Samuel returned again with Saul, and Saul worshipped the LORD.

32 ¶Then said Samuel, Bring Agag the king of the Amalekites here to me. And Agag said, Surely death is bitter.

33 And Samuel said, As your sword has made women childless, so shall your mother be childless among women. And Samuel cut King Agag in pieces before the LORD in Gilgal.

34 ¶Then Samuel went to Ramtha; and Saul went up to his house to Ramtha of Saul.

35 And Samuel saw Saul no more until the day of his death; nevertheless, Samuel grieved for Saul; and the LORD regretted that he had made Saul king over Israel.

CHAPTER 16

AND the LORD said to Samuel, How long will you mourn for Saul, seeing I have rejected him from reigning over Israel? Fill your horn with oil, and come; I will send you to Jesse the Beth-lehemite; for I have found for myself a king among his sons.

2 And Samuel said, How can I go? If Saul hear it, he will kill me. And the LORD said to Samuel, Take a heifer with you, and say, I have come to sacrifice to the LORD.

3 And invite Jesse to the sacrifice, and I will show you what you shall do; and you shall anoint to me him whom I name unto you.

4 And Samuel did as the LORD had commanded him, and came to Bethlehem of Judah. And the elders of the town went out to meet him, and said, Is your coming peaceable?

5 And he said, Peaceably; I have come to sacrifice to the LORD; sanctify yourselves, and come with me to the sacrifice. And he sanctified Jesse

and his sons, and invited them to the sacrifice.

6 ¶And when they were come, he looked to Eliab, and said, Surely the LORD's anointed is like him.

7 But the LORD said to Samuel, Do not look on his appearance or on the height of his stature; because I have rejected him; for I do not see as man sees; for man looks on the outward appearance, but the LORD looks on the heart.

8 Then Jesse called Abinadab, and made him pass before Samuel. And he said, Neither has the LORD chosen this one.

9 Then Jesse made Shammah pass by. And he said, Neither has the LORD chosen this one.

10 And Jesse made seven of his sons pass before Samuel. And Samuel said to Jesse, The LORD has not chosen these.

11 And Samuel said to Jesse, Are these all the sons you have? And he said to him, There remains yet the youngest, and, behold, he is tending the sheep. And Samuel said to Jesse, Send and bring him here; for I will not leave till he comes here.

12 And he sent and brought him in. Now he was ruddy, with beautiful eyes, and very handsome. And the LORD said to Samuel, Arise, anoint him; for this is he.

13 Then Samuel took the horn of oil and anointed him in the midst of his brothers; and the Spirit of the LORD came upon David from that day forward. Then Samuel rose up and went to Ramtha to his house.

14 ¶But the Spirit of the LORD departed from Saul, and an evil spirit from before the LORD troubled him.

15 And Saul's servants said to him, Behold, your servants are before you;

16 Let them seek out a man who can play well on the harp; and when the evil spirit is upon you, he will play with his hands, and you shall be well.

17 And Saul said to his servants, Provide me now a man who can play well, and bring him to me.

18 Then one of the young men an-

swered and said, Behold, I have seen a son of Jesse the Beth-lehemite, who is skilful in playing and a mighty valiant man, a man of war and prudent in speech, a handsome man, and the LORD is with him.

19 ¶Wherefore King Saul sent messengers to Jesse and said, Send me David your son; he will be useful to me.

20 And Jesse took an ass laden with bread and a skin of wine and a kid of goats, and sent them by David his son to Saul.

21 And David came to Saul, and stood before him; and he loved him greatly; and he became his armor-bearer.

22 And Saul sent to Jesse, saying, Let David attend me; for he has found favor in my sight.

23 And whenever the evil spirit from the LORD was upon Saul, David took a harp, and played on it; so Saul was refreshed and was well, and the evil spirit departed from him.

CHAPTER 17

NOW the Philistines gathered together their armies for battle, and were massed at the border of Judah, and they encamped between the border and Arka in Epher-samin.

2 And Saul and the men of Israel were gathered together, and encamped in the valley of Terebinth, and they set the army in array to fight against the Philistines.

3 And the Philistines stood on a mountain on the one side and Israel stood on a mountain on the other side, and the valley was between them.

4 ¶And there went out a mighty man from the camp of the Philistines, named Goliath of Gath, whose height was six cubits and a span.

5 And he had a helmet of brass upon his head, and he was armed with a coat of mail, and the weight of his coat of mail was five thousand shekels of brass.

6 And he had greaves of brass upon his legs, and a cuirass of mail between his shoulders.

7 And the staff of his spear was like a weaver's beam, and his spear's head weighed six hundred shekels of iron; and his shieldbearer went before him.

8 And he stood and cried to the armies of Israel, and said to them, Why have you come out to set your battle in array? Am I not a Philistine, and you the servants of Saul? Choose a man for yourselves, that he may come out against me.

9 If he is able to fight with me and kill me, then we will be your servants; but if I prevail against him and kill him, then you shall be our servants and serve us.

10 And the Philistine said, I have defied the armies of Israel this day; give me a man, that we may fight together.

11 When Saul and all Israel heard the words of the Philistine, they were dismayed and greatly afraid.

12 ¶Now David was the son of an Ephrathite of Beth-lehem of Judah, whose name was Jesse; and he had eight sons; and the man was old and advanced in years in the days of Saul.

13 And the three older sons of Jesse went and followed Saul to the battle; and their names were Eliab the first-born, and next to him Abinadab, and the third Shammah.

14 And David was the youngest;

15 Now David had returned from Saul, and was gone to tend his father's sheep at Beth-lehem.

16 And the Philistine drew near morning and evening, and presented himself for forty days.

17 And Jesse said to David his son, Take now for your brothers an ephah of parched wheat and ten loaves of bread, and run to the camp to your brothers;

18 And carry these ten cheeses to the commander of their thousand and inquire into the welfare of your brothers and bring the news of them to me.

19 Now Saul and all the men of Israel were in the valley of Terebinth fighting with the Philistines.

20 ¶And David rose up early in the morning and left the sheep with the keeper, and took and went as Jesse had commanded him; and he came to

the camp in the valley which goes up to the battle array, and the army shouted for the battle.

21 Then Israel and the Philistines put themselves in battle array, army against army.

22 And David put off his provisions by the side of the baggage, and ran into the army ranks, and came and saluted his brothers.

23 And while he was talking with them, behold, there came up the champion, the Philistine of Gath, Goliath by name, out of the armies of the Philistines, and spoke the same words; and David heard them.

24 And all the men of Israel, when they saw the mighty man, were afraid and fled from him.

25 And the men of Israel said, Have you seen this man who has come up? Surely to defy Israel he has come up; and it shall be that the man who kills him, the king will enrich him with great riches and will give him his daughter and make his father's house free in Israel.

26 And David said to the men who stood by him, What shall be done for the man who kills this uncircumcised Philistine and takes away the reproach from Israel? For who is this uncircumcised Philistine that he should defy the armies of the living God?

27 And the people told him the king's promises, saying, So shall it be done to the man who kills him.

28 ¶And Eliab his eldest brother heard him when he spoke to the men; and Eliab's anger was kindled against David, and he said to him, Why have you come down here? And with whom have you left those few sheep in the wilderness? I know your boldness and the evil of your heart; for you have come down to see the battle.

29 And David said, What have I done now? Behold, I was just talking.

30 ¶And he turned from him to the other side, and spoke in the same manner; and the people answered him again as they had done before.

31 And when the words which David spoke were reported to Saul, he sent for him.

32 ¶And David said to Saul, Let no man's heart fail because of him; your servant will go and fight with this Philistine.

33 And Saul said to David, You are not able to go against this Philistine to fight with him; for you are but a boy, and he has been a man of war from his youth.

34 And David said to Saul, Your servant was tending his father's sheep, and there came a lion and a bear, and took a lamb from the flock;

35 And I went out after the lion and smote him, and delivered it out of his mouth; and he growled at me, and I caught him by his beard, and I smote him and slew him.

36 Your servant slew both the lion and the bear; and this uncircumcised Philistine shall be as one of them, seeing he has defied the armies of the living God.

37 David said moreover, The LORD who delivered me from the paw of the lion and from the paw of the bear will deliver me out of the hands of the Philistine. And Saul said to David, Go, and the LORD be with you.

38 ¶And Saul armed David with his own armor and put a helmet of brass upon his head; and armed him with a coat of mail.

39 And David girded his sword upon his armor, but he was unwilling to go; for he had not tried them out. So David took them off.

40 And he took his staff in his hand, and chose five smooth stones out of the gravel, and put them into his shepherd's bag, even into his wallet, and his sling was in his hand; and he drew near to the Philistine.

41 And behold, the Philistine came and drew near to David; and his shieldbearer went before him.

42 And when the Philistine looked about and saw David, he disdained him; for he was but a youth, and ruddy, and of a fair countenance.

43 And the Philistine said to David, Am I a dog, that you come to me with a staff? And the Philistine cursed David by his gods.

44 And the Philistine said to David,

Come to me, and I will give your flesh to the fowls of the air and to the beasts of the field.

45 Then David said to the Philistine, You come against me with a sword and with a spear and with a shield; but I come against you in the name of the LORD of hosts, the God of the armies of Israel, whom you have defied.

46 This day the LORD will deliver you into my hands; and I will slay you and take your head from you; and I will give the carcasses of the host of the Philistines this day to the wild beasts of the earth and to the fowls of the air, that all the earth may know that there is a God in Israel.

47 And all this assembly shall know that the LORD saves not with sword and spear; for the battle is the LORD's, and he will deliver you into our hands.

48 And, behold, when the Philistine came and drew near to meet David, David hastened and ran to the battle line to meet the Philistine.

49 And David put his hand in his bag and took thence a stone, and slung it and struck the Philistine in his forehead, and the stone sunk into his forehead; and he fell upon his face to the earth.

50 So David prevailed over the Philistine with a sling and with a stone, and smote the Philistine and slew him; but there was no sword in the hand of David.

51 Therefore David ran and stood over the Philistine, and took his sword and drew it out of its sheath, and slew him and cut off his head. And when the Philistines saw that their champion was dead, they fled.

52 And the men of Israel and of Judah arose and shouted, and pursued the Philistines as far as the entrance of the valley and as far as the valley of Ekron. And the slain of the Philistines fell by the way of Shaarain, even to Gath and to Ekron.

53 And the children of Israel returned from chasing the Philistines, and plundered their camps.

54 And David took the head of the Philistine and brought it to Jerusalem; but he put his armor in his tent.

55 ¶And when Saul saw David go forth against the Philistine, he said to Abner, the commander of his army, Whose son is this youth? And Abner said, As your soul lives, O king, I do not know.

56 And the king said, Inquire whose son this young man is.

57 And when David returned after he had slain the Philistine, Abner took him and brought him before Saul with the head of the Philistine in his hand.

58 And Saul said to him, Whose son are you, young man? And David said to him, I am the son of your servant Jesse the Beth-lehemite.

CHAPTER 18

WHEN David had finished speaking to Saul, the soul of Jonathan was knit to the soul of David, and Jonathan loved him as his own soul.

2 And Saul took him that day, and would not let him return to his father's house.

3 Then Jonathan and David made a covenant, because Jonathan loved David as his own soul.

4 And Jonathan stripped himself of the robe that was upon him and gave it to David, and his garments, even to his sword and his bow and his girdle.

5 ¶And David went out wherever Saul sent him and was victorious; so that Saul appointed him over the men of war, and he found favor in the sight of all the people and also in the sight of Saul's servants.

6 And it came to pass as they returned, when David came back from the slaughter of the Philistines, the women came out of all the cities of Israel, singing and dancing, to meet King Saul with tambourines, and with cymbals, and were rejoicing.

7 And the women sang as they played, and laughed, saying, Saul has slain by thousands, and David by tens of thousands.

8 And Saul was very wroth, and this

saying displeased him; and he said, They have ascribed to David ten thousands, and to me they have ascribed but thousands; and what more can he have but the kingdom?

9 And Saul began to envy David from that day forward.

10 ¶And it came to pass after some days that an evil spirit from God came upon Saul, and he prophesied in the midst of his house, and David was playing music in his presence, as at other times; and there was a javelin in Saul's hand.

11 And Saul threw the javelin; for he said, I will pin David to the wall. But David evaded it twice.

12 ¶And Saul was afraid of David, because the LORD was with him, and had departed from Saul.

13 Therefore Saul removed him from his presence, and made him a commander over a thousand; and he went out to war and came in before the people.

14 And David was a man of understanding in all his ways; and the LORD was with him.

15 And when Saul saw that he was exceedingly wise, he was afraid of him.

16 But all Israel and Judah loved David, because he went out to war and came in before them.

17 ¶And Saul said to David, Behold my elder daughter Nadab, I will give her to you to wife, but you must become a commander-in-chief for me and fight the LORD's battles. For Saul said, Let not my hand be against him, but let the hand of the Philistines be against him.

18 And David said to Saul, Who am I? And what have I done, or what is my life or my father's family in Israel, that I should be son-in-law to the king?

19 But it came to pass at the time when Nadab, Saul's daughter should have been given to David, she was given to Azriel the Meholathite to wife.

20 And Malchel Saul's daughter loved David; and they told Saul, and the thing pleased him.

21 And Saul said, I will give her to him, that she may be a hindrance to him and that the hand of the Philistines may be against him. Wherefore Saul said to David, You shall this day be my son-in-law in doing one of two things.

22 ¶And Saul commanded his servants to speak to David the son of Jesse, saying, Behold the king has delight in you, and all his servants love you; now therefore be the king's son-in-law.

23 And Saul's servants spoke these words to David. And David said, Seems it to you a light thing to be a king's son-in-law, seeing that I am a poor man and despised?

24 And the servants of Saul told him, saying, These are the words which David spoke.

25 And Saul said, Thus shall you say to David, The king does not desire any dowry, but two hundred foreskins of the Philistines, to be avenged of his enemies. But King Saul thought to make David fall by the hand of the Philistines.

26 And when the servants of Saul told David these words, it pleased David well to be the king's son-in-law; but the time had not come.

27 Wherefore David arose and went out, he and his men, and slew two hundred men of the Philistines; and David brought their foreskins and gave them to the king, that he might be the king's son-in-law. And Saul gave him Malchel his daughter to wife.

28 ¶And Saul saw and knew that the LORD was with David and that Malchel Saul's daughter loved David exceedingly.

29 And Saul was still the more afraid of David; and Saul became David's enemy thenceforth.

30 Then the princes of the Philistines went forth raiding; and it came to pass at the time they went forth raiding, David was more successful than all the servants of Saul; so that his name was highly honored.

CHAPTER 19

AND Saul told Jonathan his son and all his servants that they should kill David.

2 But Jonathan, Saul's son, was delighted much in David; and Jonathan spoke to David, saying, Saul my father seeks to kill you; now therefore take heed to yourself, and sit in a secret place and hide yourself;

3 And I will go out and stand beside my father in the field where you are, and I will speak to my father concerning you; and I will see what is on his mind, and I will tell you.

4 ¶And Jonathan spoke good of David to Saul his father, and said to him, Let not the king sin against his servant David; for he has not sinned against you, and his works are sufficient proof of his loyalty to you;

5 For he put his life at your disposal, and slew the Philistine, and the LORD wrought a great salvation for all Israel by his hand; you saw it and rejoiced; and now, why then will you sin against innocent blood, to slay David without a cause?

6 And Saul listened to the voice of Jonathan his son; and Saul swore, saying, As the LORD lives, he shall not be put to death.

7 Then Jonathan called David and told him all these things. And Jonathan brought David to Saul, and he was with him as in times past.

8 ¶And there was war again; and David went out and fought with the Philistines, and slew them with a great slaughter; and they fled before him.

9 And an evil spirit from the LORD came upon Saul as he sat in his house with his javelin in his hand; and David played the harp in his presence.

10 And Saul sought to pin David to the wall with the javelin; but he fled from Saul's presence, and Saul stuck the javelin into the wall; and David fled, and escaped that night.

11 Saul then sent messengers to David's house to watch him and to slay him in the morning; but Malchel, David's wife, told him, saying, If you do not save yourself tonight, tomorrow you will be put to death.

12 ¶So Malchel let David down through a window; and he fled and escaped.

13 And Malchel took an idol, and laid it in the bed, and put a pillow of goat's skin at the head of it, and covered it with a bedcover.

14 And when Saul sent messengers to take David, she said, He is sick.

15 And Saul sent the messengers again to see David, saying, Bring him up to me in the bed, that I may kill him.

16 And when the messengers came in, behold, there was an idol in the bed, with a pillow of goat's skin at its head.

17 And they told Saul, and Saul said to Malchel, Why have you deceived me so, and let my enemy depart, so that he has escaped? And Malchel said to Saul, He said to me, Let me go; or else I will kill you.

18 ¶So David fled and escaped, and came to Samuel at Ramtha and told him all that Saul had done to him. And he and Samuel went and dwelt in Jonath which is in Ramtha.

19 And it was told Saul, saying, Behold, David is at Jonath which is in Ramtha.

20 And Saul sent messengers to take David; and when they saw the company of the prophets prophesying and Samuel standing as a leader over them, the Spirit of God came upon the messengers of Saul, and they also prophesied.

21 And when it was told Saul, he sent other messengers, and they also prophesied. And Saul sent messengers again the third time, and they prophesied also.

22 Then he himself went to Ramtha, and came as far as the great cistern which is at the end of the town; and Saul said, Where are Samuel and David? And they said to him, Behold, they are at Jonath which is in Ramtha.

23 And he went toward Jonath in Ramtha; and the Spirit of God came upon him also; and he went on, and prophesied, until he came to Jonath in Ramtha.

24 And he stripped off his clothes and prophesied before Samuel, and lay down naked all that day and all that night. Wherefore they say, Behold, is Saul also among the prophets?

CHAPTER 20

AND David fled from Jonath, which is in Ramtha, and came and said to Jonathan, What have I done? And what is my offence? And what is my crime before your father that he seeks my life?

2 And Jonathan said to him, God forbid; you shall not die; behold, my father does nothing either great or small which he does not reveal to me; and why should my father hide this thing from me? It is not so.

3 And David swore moreover, and said, It is because your father knows that I have found favor in your eyes; therefore he has said, Let not Jonathan know this, lest he be grieved; but truly as the LORD lives, and as your soul lives, there is but a step between me and death.

4 Then Jonathan said to David, Whatever you desire, I will do for you.

5 And David said to Jonathan, Behold, tomorrow is the new moon, and I should not fail to sit in the presence of your father to eat; but let me go that I may hide myself in the field until the third day at evening.

6 If your father should miss me, then say to him, David earnestly asked leave of me that he might go to Beth-lehem his city; for there is a yearly sacrifice there for all the family.

7 If he says thus, It is well; then your servant shall have peace; but if he is displeased, then be sure that evil is determined by him.

8 Therefore you shall deal kindly with your servant; for you have brought your servant into a covenant of the LORD with you; but if there is folly in me, slay me yourself; why should you bring me to your father?

9 And Jonathan said, God forbid; for if I knew of a certainty that evil were determined by my father to come upon you, then I would come to you and tell you.

10 Then David said to Jonathan, Who shall report to me, if your father answers you roughly?

11 ¶And Jonathan said to David, Come, and let us go out into the field. So they both went out into the field.

12 And Jonathan said to David, The LORD God of Israel be a witness that I will sound my father about this time tomorrow, the third hour; and behold, if he feels good toward you, then I will send to you, and disclose it to you;

13 The LORD do so and much more to Jonathan; but if it please my father to do you harm, then I will disclose it to you, and send you away that you may go in peace; and the LORD be with you as he has been with my father.

14 And if only you will show me the kindness of God while I live, before I die;

15 And also you shall not cut off your kindness from my house for ever, when the LORD destroys the enemies of David from the face of the earth;

16 So Jonathan's house shall flourish with the house of David; and may the LORD take vengeance on David's enemies.

17 And Jonathan caused David to swear again, because he loved him; for he loved him as he loved his own soul.

18 Then Jonathan said to him, Tomorrow is the new moon; and you shall be missed, because your seat will be empty.

19 And when at the third hour you will be wanted very much, then you shall come tomorrow to the place where you hid yourself, and you shall sit down beside the same stone.

20 And I will shoot three arrows to the side of it, as though I shot at a mark.

21 And, behold, I will send a lad to go to gather up the arrows. And if I should say to the lad, The arrows are on this side of you, take them and come; then you will know and see that there is peace to you, there is no danger, as the LORD liveth.

22 But if I say thus to the lad, Behold, the arrows are beyond you; then go your way; for the LORD has sent you away.

23 And as for the matter of which you and I have spoken, behold, the LORD is between you and me forever.

24 ¶So David hid himself in the field; and when the new moon came, the king sat down to dine.

25 And the king sat upon his seat by the wall as at other times; and Jonathan went and sat upon a seat, and Abner sat by Saul's side, but David's place was empty.

26 Nevertheless Saul did not say anything that day; for he thought, Something has happened to him, or perhaps he is unclean,[1] or perhaps he has not purified himself.

27 And it came to pass on the morrow, the second day of the new moon, David's place was still empty; and Saul said to Jonathan his son, Why has not the son of Jesse come to eat, either yesterday or today?

28 And Jonathan answered and said to Saul his father, David earnestly asked leave of me to go to Bethlehem;

29 And he said, Let me go, for our family has a sacrifice in the city; and my brother has commanded me to be there; and now, if I have found favor in your eyes, let me get away and see my brothers. That is the reason he has not come to the king's table.

30 Then Saul's anger was kindled against Jonathan, and he said to him, O you rebellious son, do I not know that you are delighted in the son of Jesse to your own shame and to the shame of your mother's nakedness?

31 For as long as the son of Jesse lives upon the earth, you shall not be established, nor your kingdom. Therefore, now I will send and have him brought to me, for he shall surely die.

32 And Jonathan answered and said to Saul his father, Why should he be put to death? What has he done?

33 And Saul lifted up a javelin to smite him; whereby Jonathan knew that his father was determined to slay David.

34 So Jonathan arose from the table in fierce anger, and did not eat food the second day of the month; for he was grieved for David, because his father had determined evil against him.

35 ¶And it came to pass in the morning, Jonathan went out into the field to meet David, and a little lad was with him.

36 And he said to his lad, Run, gather up the arrows which I shoot. And as the lad ran, he shot an arrow beyond him.

37 And when the lad came to the place where Jonathan had shot the arrow, Jonathan called after the lad and said, Behold, the arrow is beyond you.

38 And Jonathan called again after the lad, saying, Make haste, quick, stay not. And Jonathan's lad gathered up the arrows and brought them to his master.

39 But the lad knew not anything; only Jonathan and David knew the matter.

40 And Jonathan gave his weapons to his lad, and said to him, Go, carry them to the city.

41 ¶And as soon as the lad was gone, David arose from beside the stone and came to Jonathan and fell on his face to the ground and bowed himself three times; and they kissed each other, and wept over each other; but David wept more.

42 Then Jonathan said to David, Go in peace, inasmuch as we have sworn both of us in the name of the LORD, saying, The LORD be between me and you and between my descendants and your descendants forever. Then Jonathan arose and went into the city.

CHAPTER 21

THEN David came to Noh, to Ahimeleck the priest; and Ahimeleck was afraid at meeting David, and said to him, Why have you come alone, and no man with you?

2 And David said to Ahimeleck the priest, The king has entrusted me with a matter, and has said to me,

---

[1] When a person had been defiled by breaking certain ordinances he was required to purify himself before a feast. See 21:4.

Let no man know the thing for which I send you, and what I have commanded you; and I have stationed my servants at hidden and obscure places.

3 Now therefore what provisions have you in your possession? Give me five loaves of bread in my hand, or whatever can be found.

4 And the priest answered David and said to him, There is no common bread in my possession, but there is hallowed bread; you may have it if the young men have kept themselves from touching unclean things.

5 And David answered the priest and said to him, The hallowed bread has been lawful for us since yesterday and the day before, when we left, and behold, the clothes of the young men are holy, and the bread is now practically common, even though it were sanctified this day in the vessels.

6 So the priest gave him hallowed bread; for there was no bread there but the shewbread that was taken from before the Lord to be replaced by hot bread on the day when it was taken away.

7 Now a certain man of the servants of Saul was there that day, detained before the Lord; and his name was Doeg, an Edomite, the chief of the herdsmen that belonged to Saul.

8 ¶And David said to Ahimeleck, Is there not here in your possession a sword or a spear? For I have brought neither my sword nor my javelin with me, because the king's business required haste.

9 And the priest said, The sword of Goliath the Philistine, whom you slew in the valley of Terebinth, behold, it is here wrapped in a cloth behind the ephod; if you wish to take that, take it, for there is no other but that here. And David said, There is none like that; give it to me.

10 ¶And David arose and fled that day from fear of Saul, and went to Achish the king of Gath.

11 And the servants of Achish said to him, Is not this David, the king of the land of Israel? Did not the daughters of Israel sing to one another of him in dances, saying, Saul has slain his thousands, and David his tens of thousands?

12 And David laid up these words in his heart, and was exceedingly afraid of Achish, the king of Gath.

13 So he changed his behavior in his presence, and disguised himself in their sight, and he sat at the doorpost and let his spittle fall down upon his beard.

14 Then Achish said to his servants, Lo, you see the man is mad; why then have you brought him to me?

15 Do I lack good manners, that you have brought this fellow who misbehaves in my presence? Shall this fellow come into my house?

CHAPTER 22

DAVID therefore departed thence, and escaped to the cave of Arlam; and when his brothers and all his father's household heard it, they went down there to him.

2 And there gathered to him every man who was in distress and every man who was in debt and every man who was discontented, and he became chief over them; and there were with him about four hundred men.

3 ¶And David went thence to Mizpeh of Moab; and he said to the king of Moab, Let my father and my mother dwell with you, till I know what God will do with me.

4 And he left them with the king of Moab; and they dwelt with him all the time that David was in Mizpeh.

5 ¶And the prophet Gad said to David, Do not abide in Mizpeh; depart and go into the land of Judah. Then David departed and came into the forest of Hiziuth.

6 ¶And when Saul heard that David was located, and the men who were with him (now Saul was staying in Gibeah under the almond tree in Ramtha, with his spear in his hand, and all his servants were standing about him);

7 Then Saul said to his servants who stood about him, Hear now, you Benjamites, will the son of Jesse give every one of you fields and vineyards, and make you all commanders of thousands and captains of hundreds;

8 And have all of you conspired against me, so that there is none to tell me about the covenant of my son with the son of Jesse; and is there none that discloses to me that my son has made a league with the son of Jesse, and is there none of you who is sorry for me, or discloses to me that my son has stirred up my servants against me to lie in wait as at this day?

9 ¶Then answered Doeg the Edomite, who was set over the servants of Saul, and said, I saw David when he came to Noh, to Ahimeleck, the son of Ahitub the priest.

10 And he inquired of God for him and gave him weapons and provisions and gave him the sword of Goliath the Philistine.

11 Then the king summoned Ahimeleck the priest, the son of Ahitub, and all his father's house, the priests that were in Noh; and all of them came to the king.

12 And Saul said, Hear now, I beseech you, son of Ahitub. And he answered, Here I am, my lord.

13 Then Saul said to him, Why have you conspired against me, you and the son of Jesse, in that you have given him bread and a sword, and have inquired of God for him, that he should rise against me to lie in wait as at this day?

14 And Ahimeleck the priest answered the king and said, And who among all your servants is so faithful as David, who is the king's son-in-law, and heeds your commands and is honored in your house?

15 Did I begin today to inquire of God for him? Far be it from me; let not the king impute anything to his servant, nor to all the house of my father; for your servant knew nothing of all this matter, less or more.

16 And the king said, You shall surely die, Ahimeleck, you and all your father's house.

17 ¶Then the king said to the guards who stood about him, Turn, and slay the priests of God; because their hand also is with David and because they knew that he fled, and

did not reveal it to me. But the servants of the king would not put forth their hands and harm the priests of God.

18 And the king said to Doeg, Turn and fall upon the priests. And Doeg fell upon the priests and slew on that day eighty-five persons who wore the linen ephod.

19 And Noh, the city of the priests, smote he with the edge of the sword, both men and women, young men and children and oxen and asses and sheep, with the edge of the sword.

20 ¶But one of the sons of Ahimeleck, the son of Ahitub, named Abiathar, escaped and fled after David.

21 And Abiathar told David that Saul had slain the priests of God.

22 And David said to Abiathar, I knew it that day when Doeg the Edomite was there that he would surely tell Saul; I myself am guilty for the death of all the persons of your father's house.

23 Abide with me; fear not; for he that seeks my life seeks your life also, but with me you shall be protected.

CHAPTER 23

THEN they told David, saying, Behold, the Philistines are fighting against Keilah and are robbing the threshing floors.

2 And David inquired of the LORD, saying, Shall I go and smite these Philistines? And the LORD said to him, Go and smite the Philistines and save Keilah.

3 And David's men said to him, We are afraid here in Judea, how much more then if we go to Keilah against the armies of the Philistines?

4 Then David inquired of the LORD again. And the LORD answered him and said, Arise, go down to Keilah; for I will deliver the Philistines into your hand.

5 So David and his men went to Keilah and fought with the Philistines and brought away their cattle and smote them with a great slaughter. So David saved the inhabitants of Keilah.

6 And it came to pass, when Abia-

thar the son of Ahimeleck fled to David to Keilah, he came down with an ephod in his hand.

7 ¶And it was told Saul that David was come to Keilah. And Saul said, God has delivered him into my hands; for he has shut himself up by entering a town that has gates and bars.

8 And Saul called all the people together to war to go down to Keilah to besiege David and his men.

9 ¶And David knew that Saul was plotting mischief against him; and he said to Abiathar the priest, Bring the ephod to me.

10 Then David said, O LORD God of Israel, thy servant has heard for certain that Saul seeks to come to Keilah to destroy the city on my account.

11 Will the men of the city deliver me and the men who are with me into the hand of Saul?

12 And the LORD said, They will deliver you; arise and go out of the city.

13 ¶Then David and his men, who were about six hundred, arose and departed from Keilah and went wherever they could go. And it was told Saul that David had fled from Keilah; and he forbore to go forth.

14 And David abode in the wilderness of Misroth, and remained in a mountain in the wilderness of Ziph. And Saul sought him every day, but God did not deliver him into his hand.

15 And David saw that Saul was come out to seek his life; and David was in the wilderness of Ziph in a forest.

16 ¶And Jonathan, Saul's son, arose and went to David in the forest, and strengthened his hands in God.

17 And he said to him, Fear not; for the hand of Saul my father shall not find you; and you shall be king over Israel, and I shall be with you, and you shall live; and even Saul my father knows that it is so.

18 And they two made a covenant in the valley before the LORD (who sits upon the cherubim). And Jonathan went to his house.

19 ¶Then the Ziphites came up to Saul at Gibeah, saying, Behold, David is hiding himself with us in Mizroth,

in the forest in Gibaoth, in the valley which is on the right side of the desert.

20 Now therefore, come down against us according to all the desire of your soul, and we shall deliver him into the king's hand.

21 And Saul said to them, Blessed be you of the LORD; for you have compassion on me.

22 Return and search and find the place where his haunt is and learn who has seen him there; for I am told that he is very subtle.

23 Know therefore and learn of all the lurking places where he hides himself, and return to me, to inform me with certainty, and I will go with you; and if he is in the land, I will search him out throughout all the thousands of Judah.

24 So they arose and went to Ziph before Saul; but David and his men were in the wilderness of Maon, in the plain by the side of the desert.

25 And Saul and his men went to seek David. And they told David; therefore he came down to Selah and abode in the wilderness of Maon. And when Saul heard that, he pursued David in the wilderness of Maon.

26 And Saul went on one side of the mountain and David and his men on the other side of the mountain; and David made haste to flee from Saul; for Saul and his men surrounded David and his men to take them.

27 ¶But there came a messenger to Saul, saying, Make haste and come; for the Philistines have invaded the land.

28 Wherefore Saul returned from pursuing David, and went against the Philistines; therefore they called that land the Division of Sinar.

29 ¶And David went up from thence, and dwelt in Mizroth, which is in Gibaoth.

CHAPTER 24

AND it came to pass when Saul returned from pursuing the Philistines that it was told him, saying, Behold, David is in Mizroth, which is in Gibaoth.

2 Then Saul took three thousand chosen men out of all Israel, and went to seek David and his men upon the mountains of the wild goats.

3 And he came to the sheepfolds on the way where there was a cave; and Saul went into the cave and lay down there; and David and his men were staying on the slope of the cave.

4 And the men of David said to him, Behold, this is the day of which the LORD said to you, Behold, I will deliver your enemy into your hands, that you may do to him as shall seem good in your sight. Then David arose and cut off the skirt of Saul's robe stealthily.

5 But afterward David regretted that he had cut off the skirt of Saul's robe.

6 And David said to the men who were with him, The LORD forbid that I should do this thing to my master, the LORD's anointed, to stretch forth my hand against him, because he is the anointed of the LORD.

7 So David restrained the men who were with him with these words, and did not permit them to rise against Saul. And Saul rose up out of the cave and went on his way.

8 David also arose afterward and went out of the cave and cried after Saul, saying, My lord the king. And when Saul looked behind him, David bowed with his face to the earth and did him obeisance.

9 ¶And David said to Saul, You must not listen to the words of the men who say, Behold, David seeks your hurt.

10 Behold, this day your eyes have seen how the LORD had delivered you today into my hand in the cave; and the men who were with me bade me kill you, but I had pity on you, and I said, I will not put forth my hand against my lord; for he is the LORD's anointed.

11 Moreover, turn back, and see that even the skirt of your robe is in my hand; because when I cut off the skirt of your robe I did not kill you; now you should know and see that there is neither evil nor fault in my

hand, and I have not sinned against you; yet you hunt me to take my life.

12 May the LORD judge between me and you, and the LORD avenge me of you; but my hand shall not be against you.

13 As it is said in the proverb of the ancients, Out of the wicked proceeds wickedness: but my hand shall not be against you.

14 After whom have you come out, O king of Israel? After whom do you pursue? After a dead dog,[1] and after a flea?

15 The LORD therefore shall be judge, and judge between me and you, and see, and plead my cause, and deliver me from your hands.

16 ¶And when David had finished speaking these words to Saul, Saul said to him, Is this your voice, my son David? And Saul lifted up his voice and wept.

17 And he said to David, You are more righteous than I; for you have rewarded me with good, whereas I have rewarded you with evil.

18 And you have showed this day how you have dealt well with me, in that the LORD had delivered me into your hands, and you did not kill me.

19 For when a man finds his enemy, and lets him go free, the LORD will reward him with good; wherefore the LORD reward you with good for what you have done to me this day.

20 And now, behold, I know well that you shall surely be king, and that the kingdom of Israel shall be established in your hand.

21 Swear now therefore to me by the LORD that you will not cut off my descendants after me and that you will not destroy my name out of my father's house.

22 So David swore to Saul. And Saul went to his home; but David and the men who were with him went up to Mizpeh.

CHAPTER 25

AND Samuel died; and all the Israelites were gathered together and mourned for him, and buried him in his grave at Ramtha. And David

---

[1] A man of no account.

arose and went down to the wilderness of Paran.

2 And there was a man in Maon whose possessions were in Carmel; and the man was very wealthy; he had three thousand sheep and a thousand goats; and it came to pass, that he sheared his sheep in Carmel.

3 Now the name of the man was Nabal; and the name of his wife was Abigail; and she was a beautiful woman, and of a beautiful countenance; but the man Nabal was harsh and evil in his doings, and like a dog.

4 ¶And David heard in the wilderness that Nabal was shearing his sheep.

5 And David sent out ten young men, and said to the young men, Go up to Carmel, and go to Nabal and greet him in my name;

6 And thus shall you say to him who lives in prosperity, Peace be both to you and to your house.

7 Your shepherds were with us and we did not harm them, and they did not miss anything all the time they were in Carmel.

8 Ask your servants, and they will tell you. Now therefore let the young men find favor in your eyes; for we have come on a good day;[1] give whatever you wish to your servants and to your son David.

9 And when David's young men came, they spoke to Nabal according to all those words in the name of David.

10 ¶And Nabal answered David's servants, and said, Who is David? And who is the son of Jesse? There are many servants today who have broken away every man from his master.

11 Shall I then take my bread and my water and my meat that I have killed for my shearers, and give it to men whom I know not whence they are?

12 So David's young men turned about and came back and told David all these words.

13 And David said to the men who were with him, Gird you on every man his sword. And they girded on every man his sword; and David also girded on his sword; and there went up after David about four hundred men; and two hundred remained with the baggage.

14 ¶But one of the young men told Abigail, Nabal's wife, saying, Behold, David sent messengers out of the wilderness to bless our master; and he railed at them.

15 But the men were very good to us and did not hurt us, and neither have they caused us to miss anything all the time that we went with them;

16 And when we were in the wilderness, they were a wall to us both by night and day, and all the time we were with them tending the sheep.

17 Now therefore know and consider what you will do; for evil is determined against our master and against all his household; and Nabal was with the shepherds.

18 ¶Then Abigail made haste, and took two hundred loaves of bread and two skins of wine and five sheep ready dressed and five measures of parched wheat and one hundred cheeses and two hundred bunches of raisins, and laid them on asses.

19 And she said to the servants, Go on before me; behold, I come after you. But she did not tell her husband Nabal.

20 And as she was riding on the ass and coming down by the covert of the mountain, behold, David and his men were coming up in her direction; and she met them.

21 Now David had said, Surely in vain have we guarded all that this fellow has in the wilderness, so that nothing was missing of all that belonged to him; and he has rewarded us evil for good.

22 The LORD do so and more also to his servant David, if I leave of all that belongs to him by morning any mature male.

23 And when Abigail saw David, she hastened and alighted from the ass, and fell before David on her

[1] When sheep are shorn, the owner prepares a banquet, and strangers and wayfarers come to eat.

face and bowed herself to the ground,

24 And fell at his feet, and said, I beseech you, my lord, let this iniquity be upon me, my lord; and let your handmaid speak before you concerning this man Nabal.

25 For as his name is, so is he; Nabal is his name, and his folly is with him; but I, your handmaid, did not see the young men whom my lord sent.

26 Now therefore, my lord, as the LORD lives, and as your soul lives, my lord, seeing the LORD has withholden you from coming to shed blood, now, my lord, let your enemies and those who seek to do evil to you be as Nabal.

27 And now this present which your handmaid has brought to my lord, let it be given to the young men that follow my lord.

28 Forgive this trespass of your handmaid; for the LORD will certainly make for my lord a sure house; because my lord is fighting the battles of the LORD, and evil has not been found in you all your days.

29 Yet a man is resolved to pursue you and to seek your life; but the life of my lord is bound in the bundle of life with the LORD your God; but the lives of your enemies the LORD shall throw out of a sling.

30 And it shall come to pass, when the LORD shall have done to my lord according to all the good that he has spoken concerning you, and shall have appointed you ruler over Israel,

31 That this shall not be a grief to you, nor an offence in your heart, to shed blood without cause; and when the LORD shall have dealt well with you, then remember your handmaid.

32 ¶And David said to Abigail, Blessed be the LORD God of Israel who sent you this day to meet me;

33 And blessed be your advice, and blessed be you, who have kept me this day from coming to shed blood, and spared my hands this day from shedding blood.

34 For indeed, as the LORD God of Israel lives, who has restrained me from hurting you, if you had not made haste and come to meet me, surely there would not have been left to Nabal by the morning any mature male.

35 So David received of her hands that which she had brought, and said to her, Go up in peace to your house; see, I have hearkened to your voice and have accepted your person.

36 ¶And Abigail came to Nabal; and, behold, he held a feast in his house, like the feast of a king; and Nabal's heart was merry within him, for he was very drunk; wherefore she told him nothing, less or more, until the morning.

37 But it came to pass in the morning, when he had shaken off the effects of wine, that his wife told him these things, and his heart died within him and he became paralyzed.

38 And it came to pass about ten days after, the LORD smote Nabal and he died.

39 ¶And when David heard that Nabal was dead, he said, Blessed be the LORD, who has pleaded the cause of my reproach from the hands of Nabal, and has kept his servant from evil; for the LORD has returned the wickedness of Nabal upon his own head. And David sent and communed with Abigail, to take her to him to wife.

40 And when the servants of David came to Abigail at Carmel, they spoke to her, saying, David has sent us to you, to take you to him to wife.

41 And she arose and bowed herself on her face to the earth, and said, Behold, let your handmaid be a servant to wash the feet of the servants of my lord.

42 And Abigail hastened and arose, and rode upon an ass with five of her maidens who went after her; and she went with the messengers of David and became his wife.

43 David also took Ahinoam of Jezreel; and both of them became his wives.

44 ¶But Saul had given Malchel his daughter, David's wife, to Phalti the son of Laish, who was of Gallim.

CHAPTER 26

THEN the Ziphites came to Saul at Gibeah, saying, Behold, David is hiding himself in Gibaoth-hawilah, which is before the wilderness.

2 Then Saul arose and went down to the wilderness of Ziph, having three thousand chosen men of Israel with him, to seek David in the wilderness of Ziph.

3 And Saul encamped in Gibaoth-hawilah, which is before the wilderness by the wayside. But David abode in the wilderness, and he saw that Saul came after him in the wilderness.

4 David therefore sent out spies, and learned that Saul had come after him.

5 ¶And David arose and came to the place where Saul was encamped; and David saw the place where Saul lay, and Abner the son of Ner, the commander of Saul's army, was lying in the path, and the people were encamped round about him.

6 Then David said to Ahimeleck the Hittite and to Abishai the son of Zoriah, Joab's brother, saying, Who will go down with me to Saul's camp? And Abishai said, I will go down with you.

7 So David and Abishai came to the people by night; and, behold, Saul lay asleep in the path, with his spear lying on the ground by his bedside; and Abner and the people lay round about him.

8 Then said Abishai to David, Your God has delivered your enemy into your hands this day; now therefore let me smite him just once with this spear which is on the ground, and I will not smite him the second time.

9 But David said to Abishai, Destroy him not; for who can stretch forth his hand against the LORD's anointed, and be guiltless?

10 David said furthermore, As the LORD lives, the LORD shall smite him; or the day of his death shall come; or he will be smitten in battle and perish.

11 The LORD forbid that I should stretch forth my hand against the LORD's anointed; but now take the spear that is by his bedside, and the jug of water, and let us go.

12 So David took the spear and the jug of water from Saul's bedside; and they went away, and no man saw it nor knew it, neither awaked, for they were all asleep; because a deep sleep from the LORD had fallen upon them.

13 ¶Then David went over to the other side from Saul, and stood on the top of a hill afar off, a great space being between them;

14 And David called to the king and to Abner the son of Ner, saying, Will you not answer, Abner? Then Abner answered and said, Who are you that calls to the king?

15 And David said to Abner, Are you not a valiant man? And who is like you in all Israel? Why then have you not guarded your lord the king? For there came in one of the people today to destroy your lord the king.

16 This thing that you have done is not good. As the LORD lives, you are worthy to die, because you have not guarded your master, the LORD's anointed. And now see where the king's spear is, and the jug of water that was at his bedside.

17 And Saul heard David's voice, and said to him, Is this your voice, my son David? And David said, It is my voice, my lord, O king.

18 Then David said, Why does my lord pursue after his servant? For what have I done? Or what evil is in my hands?

19 Now therefore, let my lord the king hear the words of his servant. If the LORD has stirred you up against me, let us make an offering; but if it be of men, cursed be they before the LORD; for they have driven me out, that I should have no shelter in the inheritance of the LORD, saying, Go, serve other gods.

20 Now therefore, let not my blood fall to the earth far off from the face of the LORD; for the king of Israel has come out to seek a flea, as one who pursues a partridge in the mountain.

21 ¶Then Saul said to David, I have sinned; return, my son David; for I will no more do you harm, be-

cause my life was precious in your eyes this day; behold, I have played the fool, and have erred exceedingly.

22 And David answered and said, Behold the king's spear! Let one of the young men come over and take it.

23 The LORD renders to every man his righteousness and his faithfulness; for the LORD delivered you into my hands today, but I would not stretch forth my hand against the LORD's anointed.

24 And, behold, as your life was highly esteemed this day in my sight, so my life shall be highly esteemed in the sight of the LORD.

25 Then Saul said to David, Blessed be you, my son; you have surely done great things, and also you have surely prevailed. So David went on his way, and Saul also returned to his house.

CHAPTER 27

AND David said in his heart, Now if I should fall some day into the hands of Saul, it would not be good for me, but it is better for me that I should escape to the land of the Philistines; and Saul shall despair of seeking me any more in the territory of Israel; so I shall escape out of his hands.

2 So David arose and went over, he and the six hundred men who were with him, to Achish, the son of Maachah, king of Gath.

3 And David dwelt with Achish at Gath, he and his men and the household of David and his two wives, Ahinoam the Jezreelitess, and Abigail the Carmelitess, Nabal's wife.

4 And it was told Saul that David had fled to Gath; and he sought no more after him.

5 ¶And David said to Achish, If I have now found grace in your eyes, let the people give me a place in one of the towns in the desert, that I may dwell there; so that your servant may not dwell in the royal city with you.

6 Then Achish gave him Zinklag that day; therefore Zinklag belongs to the kings of Judah to this day.

7 And the time that David dwelt in the land of the Philistines was a full year and four months.

8 ¶And David and his men went up and made raids upon the Geshurites and the Gadolites and the Amalekites; for these nations were of old the inhabitants of the land, and they raided Geshur as far as the land of Egypt.

9 And David smote the land and left neither man nor woman alive, and he took away the sheep and the oxen and the asses and the camels and the apparel; then David returned and came to Achish.

10 And Achish said to David, Where have you made a raid today? And David said, Against the south of Judah and against the south of Jerahmel and against the south of Kailah.

11 And David spared neither man nor woman alive, to bring tidings to Gath, saying, Lest they should tell on us, saying, Thus David has done, and such was his custom all the while he dwelt in the land of the Philistines.

12 And Achish believed David, saying, He has surely displeased his people Israel; therefore he has become my servant for ever.

CHAPTER 28

AND it came to pass in those days, the Philistines gathered their armies together in the valley for war to fight with Israel. And Achish said to David, Know assuredly that you shall go out with me to the host, you and your men.

2 And David said to Achish, Surely you shall know what your servant can do. And Achish said to David, Therefore I will make you my bodyguard forever.

3 ¶Now Samuel was dead, and all Israel had mourned over him and buried him in Ramtha in his own sepulchre. And Saul had put away the diviners and the wizards out of the land.

4 And the Philistines gathered themselves together, and came and encamped in Shechem; and Saul gathered all Israel together, and they encamped in Gilgal.

5 And when Saul saw the army of the Philistines, he was afraid, and his heart greatly trembled.

6 And when Saul inquired of the LORD, he did not answer him, either by dreams or by fire or by prophets.

7 ¶Then Saul said to his servants, Seek me a woman who has a familiar spirit, that I may go to her and inquire of her. And his servants said to him, Behold, there is a woman who has a familiar spirit at En-dor.

8 And Saul disguised himself and put on other raiment, and he went and two men with him, and they came to the woman by night; and Saul said to her, Divine for me by the familiar spirit, and bring up for me him whom I shall tell you.

9 And the woman said to him, Behold, you know what Saul has done, how he has removed those who have familiar spirits and the wizards out of the land. Why then are you laying a snare for my life to cause me to be put to death?

10 And Saul swore to her by the LORD, saying, As the LORD lives, there shall no harm come upon you for this thing.

11 Then the woman said, Whom shall I bring up to you? And he said, Bring me up Samuel.

12 And when the woman saw Samuel, she cried out with a loud voice; and she said to Saul, Why have you deceived me? For you are Saul.

13 And the king said to her, Fear not; what do you see? And the woman said to Saul, I saw gods ascending out of the earth.

14 And he said to her, What is their appearance? And she said to him, An old man is coming up; and he is covered with a mantle. And Saul perceived that it was Samuel, and he bowed with his face to the ground and made obeisance.

15 ¶And Samuel said to Saul, Why have you disturbed me to bring me up? And Saul answered, I am sore distressed; for the Philistines are making war against me, and God has departed from me, and answers me no more although I have inquired by the prophets and also by dreams; therefore I have called you, that you may tell me what I shall do.

16 Then Samuel said to Saul, Why do you ask of me, seeing the LORD has departed from you, and now he is with your neighbor David?

17 And the LORD has done to him, as he spoke by me; for he has rent asunder the kingdom out of your hand and given it to your neighbor David;

18 Because you did not obey the voice of the LORD and did not execute his fierce wrath upon Amalek, therefore the LORD has done this thing to you this day.

19 Moreover the LORD will also deliver Israel with you into the hand of the Philistines; and tomorrow you and your sons shall be with me; the LORD also shall deliver the army of Israel into the hand of the Philistines.

20 Then Saul fell straightway upon his face on the ground, and was exceedingly afraid because of the words of Samuel; and there was no strength in him; for he had eaten no bread all that day, nor all that night.

21 ¶And the woman came to Saul, and saw that he was exceedingly afraid, and said to him, Behold, your handmaid has obeyed your voice, and I have put my life in your hand, and have listened to the words which you spoke to me.

22 Now therefore, listen also to the voice of your handmaid, and let me set a morsel of bread before you; and eat, that you may have strength, because you are going on a journey.

23 But he refused, and said, I will not eat. But his servants, together with the woman, begged him; and he hearkened to their voice. So he arose from the ground and sat upon the bed.

24 Now the woman had a fatted calf in the house; and she made haste and killed it, and took flour and kneaded it and baked unleavened bread;

25 And she brought it before Saul and before his servants; and they ate. Then they rose up and went away that night.

CHAPTER 29

NOW the Philistines gathered together all their armies at Aphek; and the Israelites were encamped by the fountain which is in Jezreel.

2 And the lords of the Philistines were passing in review by hundreds and by thousands; but David and his men marched in the rear with Achish.

3 Then the princes of the Philistines said to Achish, Why are these men marching here? And Achish said to the princes of the Philistines, This is David, the servant of Saul, the king of Israel, who has been with us a year and some months, and I have found no fault in him from the day he came to me until this day.

4 But the princes of the Philistines were angry with him; and they said to him, Drive this fellow out of the camp, that he may return to his place which you have assigned him; and let him not go with us to the battle, lest he be an adversary to us there; for how could this man reconcile himself to his lord, except with our heads?

5 Is not this David, of whom the daughters of Israel sang one to another with timbrels, saying, Saul has slain his thousands, and David his tens of thousands?

6 ¶Then Achish called David and said to him, As the LORD lives, you have been upright, and your coming in and your going out with me in the battle is good in my sight; for I have not found evil in you since the day of your coming to us to this day; nevertheless you are not good in the sight of the lords.

7 Wherefore now return, and go in peace, that you may not displease the lords of the Philistines.

8 ¶And David said to Achish, But what have I done? And what have you found in your servant from the day that I have come to you until this day, that I may not go and fight against the enemies of my lord the king?

9 And Achish answered and said to David, I know that you are as good in my sight as an angel of God; but the princes of the Philistines have said, He shall not go with us to the battle.

10 Now therefore rise up early in the morning with your master's servants who came with you; and at daybreak, go on your way.

11 So David and his men rose up early in the morning to return to the land of the Philistines. And the Philistines went up to Jezreel.

CHAPTER 30

AND when David and his men were come to Zinklag on the third day, the Amalekites had raided the Negeb and Zinklag, and burned them with fire;

2 And had taken captive all the people who were in them, both the small and the great; and they put to death the men of war; and they took the spoil and went on their way.

3 ¶And David and his men came to the city, and, behold, it was burned with fire; and their wives and their sons and their daughters were taken captives.

4 Then David and the people who were with him lifted up their voices and wept until they had no more strength to weep.

5 And David's two wives were taken captive, Ahinoam the Jezreelitess and Abigail the wife of Nabal the Carmelite.

6 And David was greatly distressed; for the people spoke of stoning him, because the soul of all the people was grieved, every man for his sons and for his daughters; but David strengthened himself in the LORD his God.

7 And David said to Abiathar the priest, Ahimeleck's son, Bring me here the ephod. And Abiathar brought the ephod to David.

8 And David inquired of the LORD, saying, Shall I pursue these raiders? Shall I overtake them? And he answered him, Pursue; for you shall surely overtake them soon and deliver the captives.

9 So David went, he and the six hundred men who were with him,

and they came to the brook of Besor, and David left two hundred men there.

10 And David continued the pursuit with four hundred men; then the two hundred men who were left behind rose up and kept guard, that the raiders might not cross the brook of Besor.

11 ¶And they found an Egyptian in a field, and brought him to David, and gave him bread, and he did eat; and they gave him water to drink;

12 And they gave him two cakes of figs, and when he had eaten, his spirit revived; for he had not eaten bread nor drunk water for three days and three nights.

13 And David said to him, To whom do you belong? And where do you come from? And the young man said, I am an Egyptian, a servant of an Amalekite; and my master left me because I have been sick for three days,

14 After we returned from raiding the Negeb of Judah and the Negeb of Caleb and from Zinklag, and we burned the towns with fire.

15 And David said to him, Will you bring me down to this band of robbers? And he said to him, Swear to me by the LORD that you will neither kill me nor deliver me into the hand of my master, and I will show you this band of robbers.

16 ¶And David swore to him, and when he had brought him down, behold, they were scattered upon the ground, eating and drinking and rejoicing because of all the great spoil that they had taken from the land of the Philistines and from the land of Judah.

17 And David smote them from the morning until evening from the rear; and there escaped not a man of them, except four hundred men who rode upon camels and fled.

18 And David recovered all that the Amalekites had taken captive, and he rescued his two wives that day.

19 And they lost nothing, for David recovered all.

20 And David took all the flocks and the herds, and an abundance of other things in addition; and they said, This is David's spoil.

21 ¶And David came to the two hundred men who were left behind to guard the baggage, whom he had placed there to guard the road to Besor; and they went out to meet David and to meet the people who were with him; and when David and the people drew near, they exchanged greetings.

22 Then answered some of David's men who were evil and wicked, and said, Because they did not go with us, we will not give them any portion of the spoil which we have recovered, save that every man may take his wife and his children.

23 But David said, You shall not do thus, my brethren, with that which the LORD has given us, he who has preserved us and delivered into our hands the raiders that came against us.

24 For who will hearken to you in this matter? For as his portion is who goes down to battle, so shall his portion be who tarries by the baggage: they shall divide alike.

25 And it was so from that day forward that David made it a statute and an ordinance for Israel even to this day.

26 ¶And when David came to Zinklag, he sent some of the spoil to the elders of Judah and to their neighbors, saying, Here is a blessing for you from the spoil of the enemies of the LORD;

27 Moreover, he sent of the spoil to those who were in Beth-el and to those who were in Ramoth of the Negeb and to those who were in Ai

28 And to those who were in Adoer and those who were in Siphmoth and to those who were in Eshtemoa

29 And to those who were in Rachal and to those who were in the cities of the Jerahmeelites and to those who were in the cities of the Kenites

30 And to those who were in Hirmah and to those who were in Barbeshan and to those who were in Tanach

31 And to those who were in Hebron and to all the places in which David and his men had traveled.

CHAPTER 31

NOW the Philistines fought against Israel; and the men of Israel fled from before the Philistines, and many fell dead on mount Gilboa.

2 And the Philistines overtook Saul and his sons; and the Philistines slew Jonathan and Jeshui and Melchishua, Saul's sons.

3 And the battle was intense against Saul, and the archers overtook him with bows, and he was exceedingly afraid of the archers.

4 Then Saul said to his armorbearer, Draw your sword and thrust me through with it, lest these uncircumcised come and slay me and abuse me. But his armorbearer would not; for he was exceedingly afraid. Thereupon Saul took his sword and fell upon it.

5 And when his armorbearer saw that Saul was dead, he fell likewise upon his sword, and died with him.

6 So Saul died, and his three sons and his armorbearer and also all his servants, that same day together.

7 ¶And when the men of Israel who were on the other side of the valley of the Jordan saw that the men of Israel fled and that Saul and his sons were slain, they abandoned the cities and fled; and the Philistines came and dwelt in them.

8 And on the morrow, when the Philistines came to strip the slain, they found Saul and his three sons fallen on mount Gilboa.

9 And they cut off his head and stripped off his armor, and sent messengers to publish the news in the land of the Philistines and among the people and in the house of their idols.

10 And they put his armor in the house of Ashtaroth; and they fastened his body to the wall of Beth-jashan.

11 ¶Now when the inhabitants of Jabesh-gilead heard of that which the Philistines had done to Saul and to his sons,

12 All the valiant men arose and marched all night, and took the body of Saul and the bodies of his sons from the wall of Beth-jashan, and brought them to Jabesh and burnt them there.

13 And they took their bones and buried them under the almond tree at Jabesh, and fasted seven days.

THE SECOND BOOK OF

SAMUEL

otherwise called

THE SECOND BOOK OF THE KINGS

CHAPTER 1

NOW it came to pass after the death of Saul, when David had returned from the slaughter of the Amalekites and had abode two days in Zinklag;

2 It came to pass on the third day, that, behold, a man came out of the camp from Saul with his clothes torn and earth upon his head; and so it was that when he came to David, he fell to the earth and did obeisance.

3 And David said to him, Where do you come from? And he replied, Out of the camp of Israel have I escaped.

4 And David said to him, What is

the news? Tell me. And he answered,
The people fled from the battle, and
many of them also have fallen; and
Saul and Jonathan his son are also
dead.

5 And David said to the young man,
Tell me, how did Saul and Jonathan
his son die?

6 And the young man said to him,
I happened by chance to be on mount
Gilboa, and behold, Saul was leaning upon his spear; and lo, the chariots and horsemen overtook him.

7 And when he looked behind him,
he saw me and called to me. And I
answered, Here am I.

8 And he said to me, Who are you?
And I answered him, I am an Amalekite.

9 Then he said to me, Stand over
me and slay me; for anguish has
seized me because my life is still
whole in me.

10 So I stood over him and slew
him, because I knew that he could
not live after he had fallen; and I
took the crown that was upon his
head and the bracelet that was on his
arm, and I have brought them here
to my lord.

11 Then David took hold of his
clothes and tore them; and likewise
all the men who were with him;

12 And they mourned and wept and
fasted until evening for Saul and
for Jonathan his son and for the
people of the LORD and for the house
of Israel, because they had fallen by
the sword.

13 ¶Then David said to the young
man who told him, Where do you
come from? And he answered, I am
the son of a proselyte, an Amalekite.

14 And David said to him, How
was it that you were not afraid to
stretch forth your hand to destroy
the LORD's anointed?

15 And David called one of the
young men and said to him, Go near
and fall upon him. And he drew near
and fell upon him, and he smote him
so that he died.

16 And David said to him, Your
blood be upon your head; for your
mouth has testified against you, for

you have said, I have slain the LORD's
anointed.

17 ¶And David lamented with this
song of mourning over Saul and over
Jonathan his son

18 (Also he commanded them to
teach the children of Judah the use
of the bow; behold, it is written in
the book of Asher):

19 Israel was swift like a gazelle,
and is slain upon her proud hills!
How are the mighty fallen!

20 Tell it not in Gath, publish it
not in the streets of Ashkelon; lest
the daughters of the Philistines rejoice, lest the daughters of the uncircumcised exult.

21 O you mountains of Gilboa, let
there be no dew, neither let there be
rain upon you, nor upon the choicest
fields; for there the shield of the
mighty was broken, the shield of
Saul, who was anointed with oil.

22 From the blood of the slain,
from the fat of the mighty, the bow
of Jonathan turned not back and
the sword of Saul returned not empty.

23 Saul and Jonathan were lovely
and pleasant in their lives, and in
their death they were not divided;
they were swifter than eagles, stronger
than lions.

24 O daughters of Israel, weep over
Saul, who clothed you in scarlet and
dyed garments, who put ornaments
of gold upon your apparel.

25 How are the mighty fallen in the
midst of the battle! O Jonathan, upon
her high places are many slain.

26 I am distressed for you, my
brother Jonathan; you were very dear
to me; your love to me was wonderful, passing the love of women.

27 How are the mighty fallen and
the weapons of war perished!

CHAPTER 2

AND it came to pass after this,
that David inquired of the LORD,
saying, Shall I go up to one of the
cities of Judah? And the LORD said
to him, Go up. And David said,
Whither shall I go up? And he said,
To Hebron.

2 So David went up there, and his

two wives also, Ahinoam the Jezreelitess, and Abigail, Nabal's wife, the Carmelite.

3 And David and his men who were with him went up together, every man with his household; and they dwelt in Hebron.

4 And the men of Judah came, and there they anointed David king over the house of Judah. And they told David, saying, It was the men of Jabesh-gilead who buried Saul.

5 ¶And David sent messengers to the men of Jabesh-gilead and said to them, Blessed be you of the LORD, that you have shown this kindness to your lord, even to Saul, and have buried him.

6 And now may the LORD show kindness and truth to you; and I also will requite you this kindness, because you have done this thing.

7 Therefore now let your hands be strengthened and be valiant; for your master Saul is dead, and the house of Judah have anointed me king over them.

8 ¶But Abner the son of Ner, commander of Saul's army, took Ashbashul, the son of Saul, and brought him over to Mahanaim;

9 And made him king over Gilead and over Geshur and over Jezreel and over Ephraim and over Benjamin and over all Israel.

10 Ashbashul Saul's son was forty years old when he began to reign over Israel, and he reigned two years. But the house of Judah followed David.

11 And the time that David was king in Hebron over the house of Judah was seven years and six months.

12 ¶And Abner the son of Ner and the servants of Ashbashul the son of Saul went out from Mahanaim to Gibeon.

13 And Joab the son of Zoriah and the men of David went out and met the young men together in Gibeon; and they sat down, these young men on the one side and the other young men on the other.

14 And Abner said to Joab, Let the young men now arise and play before us. And Joab said, Let them arise.

15 Then there arose and went over by number twelve of the men of Benjamin, who belonged to Ashbashul the son of Saul and twelve of the men of David.

16 And every man caught his fellow by the head, and thrust his sword in the other's side; so they fell down together; therefore they called that place Haklath-zadan, which is in Gibeon.

17 And there was a very fierce battle that day; and Abner was defeated, and the men of Israel, before the servants of David.

18 ¶And there were three sons of Zoriah there, Joab, Abishai, and Ashael; and Ashael was as swift of foot as a desert gazelle.

19 And Ashael pursued Abner; and he turned not to the right hand nor to the left as he followed Abner.

20 Then Abner looked behind him and said, Is that you, Ashael? And he answered, It is I.

21 And Abner said to him, Turn aside to your right hand or to your left, and seize one of the young men and take for yourself his armor. But Ashael would not turn aside from following him.

22 And Abner spoke again to Ashael, to turn from following him, saying, Turn from following me, lest I smite you and throw you on the ground; how then could I lift up my face and look at Joab your brother.

23 But he refused to turn; therefore Abner smote him with the end of the spear upon his breast, and the spear came out at his back; and he fell down there and died in the same place; and all who came to the place where Ashael fell down and died stood still.

24 Then Joab and Abishai arose and pursued Abner; and the sun went down when they came to lake Giboath which lies before Giah by the way of the wilderness of Gibeon.

25 ¶And the Benjamites gathered themselves together behind Abner, and became one company, and stood on the top of a hill.

26 Then Abner called to Joab and said, Shall the sword devour forever? Do you not know that there will be bitterness in the end? How long will it be then before you bid the people return from following their brethren?

27 And Joab said, As the LORD lives, unless you had spoken, surely in the morning I would have let the people give up every one from pursuing his brother.

28 So Joab blew the trumpet, and all the people stood still and pursued Israel no more, neither did they fight any more.

29 And Abner and his men walked all that night in the desert, and crossed the Jordan, and went toward Geshur, and they came to Mahanaim.

30 And Joab returned from following Abner; and when he had gathered all the people together and they were numbered, there were twelve wounded of David's men, and Ashael was dead.

31 But the men of David had slain of Benjamin and of Abner, three hundred and sixty men.

32 ¶And they took Ashael and buried him in the sepulchre of his father in Beth-lehem. And Joab and his men marched all night, and the day dawned upon them at Hebron.

CHAPTER 3

NOW there was a long war between the house of Saul and the house of David; but David grew stronger and stronger, and the house of Saul became weaker and impoverished.

2 ¶And sons were born to David in Hebron; and his first-born was Amnon, of Ahinoam the Jezreelitess;

3 And his second, Caleb, of Abigail the wife of Nabal the Carmelite; and the third, Absalom, the son of Maacah the daughter of Talmai king of Geshur;

4 And the fourth, Adonijah, the son of Haggith; and the fifth, Shephatiah, the son of Abital;

5 And the sixth, Ithream, by David's wife Eglah. These were born to David in Hebron.

6 ¶And it came to pass, while there was war between the house of Saul and the house of David, Abner made himself strong for the house of Saul.

7 And Saul had a concubine, whose name was Rizpah, the daughter of Ana; and Ashbashul said to Abner, Why are you going in unto my father's concubine?

8 Then Abner was exceedingly displeased at the words of Ashbashul, and Abner said, Am I the leader of vicious men in Judah? This day I show kindness to the house of Saul your father, to his brothers and to his friends, and have not delivered you into the hand of David, and yet you charge me today with this iniquity concerning a woman?

9 So do God to Abner, and more also, if I do not perform what the LORD has spoken to David, even so will I do,

10 To transfer the kingdom from the house of Saul and to establish the throne of David over Israel and over Judah from Dan to Beer-sheba.

11 And Ashbashul could not reply to Abner, because he feared him.

12 ¶And Abner sent messengers to David, saying, Whose is the land? Now make your covenant with me, and, behold, my hand shall be with you, to bring all Israel to you.

13 ¶And David said, Well, I will make a covenant with you; but one thing I require of you, you shall not see my face, unless you first bring Malchel, Saul's daughter with you.

14 Then David sent messengers to Ashbashul Saul's son, saying, Deliver to me my wife, Malchel, whom I espoused for two hundred foreskins of the Philistines.

15 And Ashbashul sent, and took her from her husband, Palti, the son of Laish of Gallim.

16 And her husband went along with her weeping as far as Bethhurim. Then Abner said to him, Return. And he returned.

17 ¶And Abner had communication with the elders of Israel, saying, You have sought for David in times past to be king over you;

18 Now then do so; for the LORD has spoken of David, saying, By the hand of my servant David I will save

my people Israel from the hand of the Philistines and out of the hand of all their enemies.

19 And Abner also spoke in the presence of the Benjamites; and Abner went also to speak in the presence of David in Hebron. And when it seemed good in the sight of all Israel and in the sight of the whole house of Benjamin,

20 Then Abner came to David at Hebron, and twenty men with him. And David made Abner and the men who were with him a great feast.

21 And Abner said to David, I will arise and go, and will gather all Israel to my lord the king, that they may make a covenant with you and that you may reign over all that your soul desires. And David sent Abner away; and he went in peace.

22 ¶And behold, the men of David and Joab came from a raid and brought a great spoil with them; but Abner was not with David in Hebron; for he had sent him away, and he was gone in peace.

23 When Joab and all the people who were with him were come, they told Joab, saying, Abner the son of Ner came to King David, and he has sent him away and he has gone in peace.

24 Then Joab came to King David, and said to him, What have you done? Behold, Abner came to you; why have you sent him away, and he is gone from you?

25 Do you not know that Abner the son of Ner came to deceive you and to know your going out and your coming in and to know all that you are doing?

26 And when Joab was come out from the presence of David, he sent messengers after Abner, and they brought him back from the well of Sirah; but David knew it not.

27 And when Abner was returned to Hebron, Joab took him aside to a secret place within the gate to speak with him quietly, and he smote him there in his abdomen, and he died, for the blood of Ashael his brother.

28 ¶And afterward when David heard it, he said, I and my kingdom are guiltless before the LORD for ever from the blood of Abner the son of Ner;

29 Let it rest on the head of Joab and on the head of all his father's house; and let there never fail to be in the house of Joab one who has a discharge or who is a leper or who is a beggar holding a bowl or who falls by the sword or who lacks bread.

30 So Joab and Abishai his brother slew Abner because he had slain their brother Ashael at Gibeon in the battle.

31 ¶And David said to Joab and to all the people who were with him, Rend your clothes and gird yourselves with sackcloth and mourn for Abner. And King David himself and all the people followed the bier.

32 And they buried Abner in Hebron; and the king lifted up his voice and wept at the grave of Abner; and all the people wept.

33 And the king lamented over Abner and said, Abner died like Nabal.

34 Your hands were not bound nor were your feet put into fetters; as one falls before the wicked men, so have you fallen. And all the people wept again over him.

35 And all the people tried to persuade David to eat food while it was still day, but David swore, saying, So do God to me, and more also, if I taste bread or anything else till the sun goes down.

36 And all the people took notice of it, and it pleased them; whatever the king did pleased all the people;

37 For all the people and all Israel understood that day that the king had no hand in the slaying of Abner, the son of Ner.

38 And the king said to the people, Do you not know that there is a great prince fallen this day in Israel?

39 And I am this day troubled, and as king I see that the sons of Zoriah are too hard for me; the LORD shall reward the evil doer according to his wickedness.

CHAPTER 4

WHEN Ashbashul Saul's son heard that Abner was dead in Hebron, he trembled, and all Israel was troubled.

2 And Saul's son had two men who were captains of raiding bands; the name of the one was Baana, and the name of the other Rechab, the sons of Rimmon a Beerothite of the children of Benjamin (for Beeroth also is reckoned to the Benjamites;

3 And the Beerothites fled to Gittaim and are sojourners there until this day).

4 And Jonathan, Saul's son, had a son who was lame in his feet. He was five years old when the news about Saul and Jonathan came from Jezreel, and his nurse took him up and fled; and, as she made haste to flee, he fell and became lame. And his name was Mephibosheth.

5 And the sons of Rimmon the Beerothite, Rechab and Baana, went, and came about the heat of the day to the house of Ashbashul as he was taking his noontide rest.

6 And behold, they came into the midst of the house; then those sons of wickedness took and smote him in his abdomen; and Rechab and Banna his brother escaped.

7 For when they came into the house, he was lying on his bed in his bedchamber, and they smote him and slew him and beheaded him, and took his head and fled by the way of the plain all night.

8 And they brought the head of Ashbashul to David at Hebron, and said to King David, Behold the head of Ashbashul the son of Saul your enemy, who sought your life; and the LORD has avenged our lord the king this day of Saul and of his offspring.

9 ¶And David answered Rechab and Baana his brother, the sons of Rimmon the Beerothite, and said to them, As the LORD lives, who has saved my life out of every adversity,

10 When one told me, saying, Behold, Saul is dead, thinking to have brought me good tidings, I seized him and slew him in Zinklag, instead of giving him a reward for his tidings;

11 How much more, when wicked men have slain a man in his own house upon his bed? Now I will avenge his blood at your hands and destroy you from the earth.

12 And David commanded his young men, and they slew them, and cut off their hands and their feet, and hanged them on the hill in Hebron. But they took the head of Ashbashul and buried it in the sepulchre of Abner in Hebron.

CHAPTER 5

THEN all the tribes of Israel came to David at Hebron and said to him, Behold, we are your flesh and your bone.

2 Also in time past, when Saul was king over us, it was you who led out and brought in Israel; and the LORD said to you, You shall feed my people Israel, and you shall be a ruler over my people Israel.

3 So all the elders of Israel came to the king at Hebron; and King David made a covenant with them in Hebron before the LORD; and they anointed David king over Israel.

4 ¶David was thirty years old when he began to reign, and he reigned forty years.

5 In Hebron he reigned over Judah seven years and six months; and in Jerusalem he reigned thirty-three years over all Israel and Judah.

6 ¶And King David and his men went to Jerusalem against the Jebusites, the inhabitants of the land, who spoke to David, saying, You shall not come in here, except you destroy both the blind and the lame; [1] and they said, David cannot come in here.

7 Nevertheless David took the stronghold of Zion; the same is the city of David.

8 And David said on that day, Whosoever smites a Jebusite and whosoever strikes with a weapon the blind and the lame, he is a hater of David's soul. Therefore they say, The blind and the lame shall not come into the temple.

9 So David dwelt in the fort, that is, Zion; and he called it the city of David. And David built round about the fort from within.

10 And David continued to become

[1] Idiomatic: we will fight to the last man.

greater, and the LORD God of hosts was with him.

11 ¶And Hiram king of Tyre sent messengers to David, and cedar trees and carpenters and masons; and they built David a house.

12 And David perceived that the LORD had established him king over Israel, and that he had exalted his kingdom for the sake of his people Israel.

13 ¶And David took more concubines and wives from Jerusalem, after he was come from Hebron; and there were more sons and daughters born to David.

14 And these are the names of the sons who were born to him in Jerusalem: Shammuah, Shachab, Nathan, Solomon,

15 Jocabar, Elisha, Nepheg, Naphia,

16 Elishama, Eliada, and Eliphalet.

17 ¶But when the Philistines heard that they had anointed David king over Israel, all the Philistines came up to seek David; and David heard of it, and went down to the fort.

18 The Philistines also came and encamped in the Valley of Giants.

19 And David inquired of the LORD, saying, Shall I go up against the Philistines? Wilt thou deliver them into my hands? And the LORD said to David, Go up; for I will deliver them into your hands.

20 And David came to Baal-perazim, and David defeated them there, and David said, The LORD has made a breach through my enemies before me, like the breach of waters. Therefore he called the name of that place Baal-perazim.

21 And they left their idols there, and David and his men carried them away.

22 ¶And the Philistines came up yet again and encamped in the Valley of the Giants.

23 And when David inquired of the LORD, the LORD said to him, You shall not go up; but circle behind them, and come upon them opposite Bachim.

24 And when you hear the sound of marching on the top of the moun-

tain of Bachim, then you shall become strong; for then shall the LORD go out before you to smite the army of the Philistines.

25 And David did as the LORD had commanded him; and he smote the Philistines from Geba to the entrance of Gadar.

CHAPTER 6

AGAIN David gathered together all the young men of Israel, thirty thousand.

2 And David arose with all the people who were with him of the men of Judah and went to Geba to bring up from thence the ark of God, for at that place was invoked the name of the LORD of hosts, who dwells upon the cherubim.

3 And they set the ark of God upon a new cart, and brought it out of the house of Abinadab that was in Gibeah; and Uzzah and Ahia, the sons of Abinadab, drove the cart, walking behind it.

4 And they brought the ark of God out of the house of Abinadab which was in Gibeah, and Ahia went before the ark.

5 And David and all the house of Israel danced before the LORD waving branches of cedar trees and cypress, and played upon harps and lyres and timbrels and cornets and cymbals.

6 ¶And when they came to the threshing floors, Uzzah put forth his hand to the ark of the LORD, and took hold of it; for the oxen broke loose from the harness.

7 And the anger of the LORD was kindled against Uzzah; and the LORD smote him there because he put forth his hand to the ark; and he died there beside the ark of God.

8 And David was displeased because the LORD had stricken Uzzah; and he called the name of that place Toraetha-uzzah, and so it is called even to this day.

9 And David was afraid of the LORD that day, and he said, How shall I bring in the ark of the LORD to me?

10 So David was unwilling to bring

the ark of God with him into the city of David; but David took it aside into the house of Ober-edom the Gittite.

11 And the ark of the LORD remained in the house of Ober-edom the Gittite three months; and the LORD blessed Ober-edom the Gittite, and all his household because of the ark of the LORD.

12 ¶And it was told King David, saying, The LORD has blessed Ober-edom and all that belongs to him, because of the ark of the LORD. So David went and brought up the ark of the LORD from the house of Ober-edom into the city of David with gladness.

13 And it was so that when those who bore the ark of the LORD had gone six paces, David sacrificed fat oxen.

14 And David sang praises before the LORD with all his might; and David was girded with a linen ephod.

15 So David and all the house of Israel brought up the ark of the LORD with shouting and with the sound of the trumpet.

16 And as the ark of the LORD came past the house of David, Malchel Saul's daughter looked through a window and saw King David rejoicing and dancing before the ark of the LORD; and she despised him in her heart.

17 ¶And they brought in the ark of the LORD, and set it in the midst of the tent that David had pitched for it; and David offered burnt offerings and peace offerings before the LORD.

18 And when David had finished offering the burnt offerings and peace offerings to the LORD, he blessed the people in the name of the LORD of hosts.

19 And he distributed among all the people, even among the whole multitude of Israel, both men and women, to everyone a loaf of bread and a portion of meat and a fine white loaf of bread. So all the people departed everyone to his house.

20 ¶Then David returned to go to his house. And Malchel the daughter of Saul came out to meet David, and said, How glorious was the king of Israel today, for he appeared publicly before the eyes of the handmaids of his servants, for he surely conducted himself as a vain man!

21 And David said to Malchel, It was before the LORD, who chose me rather than your father and rather than all his house, and appointed me to be a ruler over the people of the LORD, over Israel; it was because of him that I danced before the LORD.

22 And I will abase myself still more than this, and will humble myself in my own eyes; and the maidservants of whom you have spoken shall yet honor me.

23 Therefore Malchel the daughter of Saul had no child to the day of her death.

CHAPTER 7

WHEN the king dwelt in his house, and the LORD had given him rest from all his enemies,

2 The king said to Nathan the prophet, See now, I dwell in a house of cedar, but the ark of God dwells within curtains.

3 And Nathan said to the king, Go, do all that is in your heart; for the LORD is with you.

4 ¶And it came to pass that very night, the word of the LORD came to Nathan, the prophet, saying,

5 Go and tell my servant David, Thus says the LORD, You shall not build me a house for me to dwell in;

6 Because I have not dwelt in a house since the day that I brought up the children of Israel out of Egypt, to this day, but I have moved in tents.

7 In all the places where I have walked with all the children of Israel, have I spoken to any of those whom I commanded to feed my people Israel, saying, Why have you not built me a house of cedar?

8 Now therefore shall you say to my servant David, Thus says the LORD of hosts: I took you from the sheepfold, from following the sheep, to be the ruler over my people Israel;

9 And I have been with you wherever you went, and I have destroyed

all your enemies from before you, and I will make for you a great name, like the name of the great men that are on the earth.

10 Moreover I will appoint a place for my people Israel, and will plant them and make them to dwell in their own place in peace and be disturbed no more; neither shall wicked men enslave them any more, as formerly.

11 From the day that I commanded you to be a judge over my people Israel, I have given you rest from all your enemies. Also the LORD declares to you that he will make you a house.

12 ¶And when your days are fulfilled and you shall sleep with your fathers, I will raise up your offspring after you, who shall come out of your loins, and I will establish his kingdom.

13 He shall build a house for my name, and I will establish the throne of his kingdom for ever.

14 I will be like a father to him and he shall be like a son to me. If he commit folly, I will chasten him with the rod of men and with the stripes of the children of men;

15 But my mercy I will not take from him, as I took it from Saul who was king before you, and whom I put away from before me.

16 And your house and your kingdom shall be established for ever before me; your throne shall be established for ever.

17 According to all these words and according to all this vision, so did Nathan the prophet speak to David.

18 ¶Then King David went in and sat before the LORD, and he said, Who am I, O LORD God? And what is my house, that thou hast elevated me to this place?

19 And is this yet a small thing in thy sight, O LORD God, that thou hast spoken also concerning thy servant's descendants for a great while to come? Is this for the guidance of men, O LORD God?

20 And what more can thy servant David say to thee? For thou knowest thy servant, O LORD God.

21 For thy word's sake and according to thine own heart hast thou done all these great things, to make thy servant know them.

22 Therefore thou art great, O LORD God; for there is none like thee, neither is there any God besides thee, according to all that we have heard with our ears.

23 And is there a nation on the earth like thy people Israel, whom God saved to be a people for himself and to make him a name and to do for him great and notable deeds upon the earth, as he had done in former days for thy people whom thou savedst for thyself out of Egypt, a people whose God thou art?

24 For thou hast established for thyself thy people Israel to be a people to thee for ever; and thou, O LORD, hast become their God.

25 And now, O LORD God, the word that thou hast spoken concerning thy servant and concerning his house, confirm it for ever, and do as thou hast said.

26 And let thy name be magnified for ever, and let everything be as thou hast said, O LORD of hosts, the God of Israel; and let the house of thy servant David be established before thee for ever.

27 For thou, O LORD of hosts, God of Israel, hast revealed to thy servant, saying, I will build you a house; therefore thy servant has purposed in his heart to pray this prayer before thee.

28 And now, O LORD God, thou art God and thy words are true, for thou hast promised this goodness unto thy servant;

29 Therefore now let it please thee to bless the house of thy servant, that it may continue for ever before thee; for thou, O LORD God, hast spoken it; and with thy blessing let the house of thy servant be blessed for ever.

CHAPTER 8

AND it came to pass after this that David smote the Philistines and defeated them; and David took Ramath-gema from the Philistines.

2 And he defeated the Moabites, making them lie down on the ground, and measured them with a line; and

he measured two lines to be put to death and one full line to keep alive. And so the Moabites became David's servants and brought tribute.

3 ¶Then David defeated Hadarezer, the son of Rehob, king of Zobah, as he went to have dominion at the river Euphrates.

4 And David took from him one thousand and seven hundred chariots and twenty thousand footmen; and David destroyed all the chariots, but reserved of them one hundred chariots.

5 And when the Edomites and the Arameans of Damascus came to help Hadarezer king of Zobah, David slew of the Edomites twenty-two thousand men.

6 Then David put governors in Edom and in Damascus; and the Edomites became servants to David and brought tribute. And the LORD preserved David wherever he went.

7 And David took the shields of gold that were on the servants of Hadarezer;

8 And from Tebah and from Berothai, cities of Hadarezer, King David took a great quantity of brass and brought it to Jerusalem.

9 ¶And when Toa king of Hamath heard that David had defeated all the army of Hadarezer,

10 Then Toa sent Joram his son to King David to salute him and to bless him, because he had fought against Hadarezer and defeated him; for Hadarezer was a warlike man. And Joram the son of Toa took with him vessels of silver and vessels of gold and vessels of brass; and brought them to David;

11 These also King David dedicated to the LORD, with the silver and gold that he had dedicated from all the nations which he had subdued,

12 From Edom, Moab, the Ammonites, the Philistines, the Amalekites, and from the dominion of Hadarezer, son of Rehob, king of Zobah.

13 And David fought there when he returned, after he had defeated Edom in the Valley of Salt, killing eighteen thousand men.

14 ¶And David appointed governors throughout all Edom, and all the Edomites became David's servants. And the LORD preserved David wherever he went.

15 And David reigned over all Israel, and executed judgment and justice to all his people.

16 And Joab the son of Zoriah was over the army; and Jehoshaphat the son of Ahilud was recorder;

17 And Zadok the son of Ahitub, the Gelionite, and Abiathar the son of Ahimeleck were priests, and Seraiah was the scribe;

18 And Benaiah the son of Jehoiada was over both the nobles and the laborers, and David's sons were princes.

CHAPTER 9

AND David said, Is there yet any one left of the house of Saul, that I may show kindness to him for Jonathan's sake?

2 Now there was of the house of Saul a servant whose name was Ziba. And they called him to David, and the king said to him, Are you Ziba? And he said, I am your servant.

3 And the king said to him, Is there any one still left of the house of Saul, that I may show kindness to him for the sake of God? And Ziba said to the king, There is yet a son left to Jonathan, who is lame in his feet.

4 And the king said to him, Where is he? And Ziba said to the king, Behold, he is in the house of Machir, the son of Gammir, in Lo-debar.

5 ¶Then King David sent and took him from the house of Machir, the son of Gammir, from Lo-debar.

6 Now when Mephibosheth, the son of Jonathan, the son of Saul, was come to David, he fell on his face and did obeisance. And David said to him, Mephibosheth. And he answered, Behold your servant!

7 ¶And David said to him, Fear not; for I will surely show you kindness for Jonathan your father's sake, and I will restore to you all the land of Saul your father; and you shall eat bread at my table continually.

8 And he bowed himself and said,

What is your servant, that you should look upon me? For I am like a dead dog.

9 ¶Then the king called to Ziba and said to him, All that belonged to Saul and to all his house I have given to your master's son.

10 You therefore and your sons and your servants shall till the land for him, and you shall bring in food for your master's son, that he may eat; but Mephibosheth your master's son shall eat bread always at my table. Now Ziba had fifteen sons and twenty servants.

11 Then Ziba said to the king, Whatever my lord the king commands his servant, so shall your servant do. So Mephibosheth ate bread at the king's table, as one of the king's sons.

12 And Mephibosheth had a little son, whose name was Micha. And all who dwelt in the house of Ziba were servants to Mephibosheth.

13 So Mephibosheth dwelt in Jerusalem; for he ate continually at the king's table; and he was lame in both his feet.

CHAPTER 10

AFTER this the king of the Ammonites died, and Hanun his son reigned in his stead.

2 Then said David, I will show kindness to Hanun the son of Nahash, as his father showed kindness to me. So David sent by his servants to comfort him for his father. And David's servants came to the land of the Ammonites.

3 And the princes of the Ammonites said to Hanun their lord, Do you think that David is honoring your father, that he has sent comforters to you? Has not David rather sent his servants to you to spy out the city and to explore it and to overthrow it?

4 Wherefore Hanun took David's servants and shaved off the one-half of their beards and cut off their garments in the middle as far as their buttocks, and sent them away.

5 When they told it to David, he sent to meet them, because the men were greatly ashamed; and the king said to them, Tarry at Jericho until your beards have grown and then return.

6 ¶And when the Ammonites saw that they had acted foolishly toward David, the Ammonites sent and hired the Arameans of the son of Rehob and the Arameans of the son of Zobah, twenty thousand footmen, and of the king of Maacah a thousand men and of Ish-tob twelve thousand footmen.

7 And when David heard of it, he sent Joab and all the host of the mighty men.

8 And the Ammonites came out and set their men in battle array at the entrance of the gate of Edom the son of Rehob; and the forces of Aram the son of Zobah and Ish-tob and Maacah were by themselves in the field.

9 When Joab saw that the battle was set against him both in the front and in the rear, he selected the choice men of Israel and put them in array against Aram;

10 And the rest of the people he placed in the charge of Abishai his brother, and he put them in array against the Ammonites.

11 And he said to Abishai his brother, If the Arameans prove too strong for me, then you shall help me; but if the Ammonites prove too strong for you, then I will come and help you.

12 Be of good courage, and let us fight for the sake of our people and for the sake of the cities of our God: and the LORD will do what is good in his sight.

13 And Joab and the people who were with him drew near to battle against the Arameans, and they fled before him.

14 And when the Ammonites saw that the Arameans had fled, then they fled also before Abishai and entered into the city. So Joab returned from fighting against the Ammonites and came to Jerusalem.

15 ¶And when the Arameans saw that they were defeated before Israel, they gathered themselves together.

16 And Hadarezer sent and brought out the Arameans that were beyond

the river Euphrates; and they came to Helam; and Shobach the general of Hadarezer's army went before them.

17 And when it was told David, he gathered all Israel together and crossed the Jordan and came to Helam. And the Arameans set themselves in array against David, and David fought against them.

18 And the Arameans fled before Israel; and David destroyed one thousand and seven hundred chariots of the Arameans and slew four thousand horsemen and a great many of the people, and he smote Shobach the general of their army, who died there.

19 And when all the kings who were servants of Hadarezer saw that they were defeated before Israel, they made peace with Israel and served them. So the Arameans feared to help the Ammonites any more.

CHAPTER 11

AFTER the year expired, at the time when the king leaves the palace, David sent Joab and his servants with him and all Israel; and they besieged Rabbath. But David remained in Jerusalem.

2 ¶And it came to pass in the evening that David arose from his bed and walked upon the roof of the king's house; and he saw a woman bathing; and the woman was very beautiful to look upon.

3 And David sent and inquired about the woman. And one said, She is Bathsheba, the daughter of Ahinam, the wife of Uriah the Hittite.

4 So David sent a messenger and took her; and she came in to him and he lay with her; and that very day she had cleansed herself after her menstruation; and she returned and went to her house.

5 And the woman conceived, and sent and told David and said to him, I am with child.

6 ¶And David sent to Joab, saying, Send me Uriah the Hittite. And Joab sent Uriah to David.

7 And when Uriah came to him,

David asked of Uriah about Joab and about the people and about the war.

8 Then David said to Uriah, Go down to your house and wash your feet. And Uriah went out of the king's house, and there followed him a present from the king.

9 But Uriah slept at the door of the king's house beside all the servants of his lord, and did not go down to his house.

10 And when they told David that Uriah did not go down to his house, David said to Uriah, Behold, you have come from a journey, why then did you not go down to your house?

11 And Uriah said to David, The ark of the covenant of the LORD, and Israel, and Judah dwell in tents, and my lord Joab and the servants of my lord are encamped in the open fields; shall I then go to my house, to eat and to drink and to lie with my wife? No. As you live and as your soul lives, I will not do this thing.

12 And David said to Uriah, Remain here today also, and tomorrow I will send you away. So Uriah remained in Jerusalem that day.

13 And the next day David called him and ate before him, and he did drink, and got drunk; and in the evening he went out and slept beside the servants of his lord, but he did not go down to his house.

14 ¶And in the morning, David wrote a letter to Joab, and sent it by the hand of Uriah.

15 And he wrote in the letter, Set Uriah in the forefront of the battle, and then retire from him that he may be smitten and die.

16 So when Joab besieged the city, he assigned Uriah to a place where he knew that valiant men were.

17 And the men of the city went out and fought with Joab; and there fell some of the people of the servants of David; and Uriah the Hittite died also.

18 ¶Then Joab sent and told David all that took place in the battle;

19 And Joab charged the messenger, saying, When you have finished telling everything which took place in the battle to the king,

20 And if the king's wrath rise and he say to you, Why did you approach so near to the city to fight against it? Did you not know that they would shoot from the wall?

21 Who killed Abimeleck the son of Nedo-baal? Did not a woman cast a piece of a millstone upon him from the wall, that he died? Why did you go near the wall? Now if he should say these things to you, then you shall say to him, Your servant Uriah the Hittite is dead also.

22 ¶So the messenger went and came and told David all that Joab had charged him to say.

23 And the messenger said to David, The men prevailed against us and came out against us into the field, and we chased them back to the entrance of the city.

24 And the archers shot from the wall; and some of your servants died, O king! And your servant Uriah the Hittite is dead also.

25 Then David said to the messenger, Thus shall you say to Joab, Let not this thing displease you, for things happen this way or that way in the battle; make the battle more vigorous against the city, and take it and destroy it.

26 ¶And when the wife of Uriah the Hittite heard that her husband was dead, she mourned for her husband.

27 And when the days of her mourning were over, David sent and brought her to his house, and she became his wife and bore him a son. But the thing that David had done displeased the LORD.

CHAPTER 12

AND the LORD sent Nathan the prophet to David. And he came to him and said to him, There were two men in a certain city, the one rich and the other poor.

2 The rich man had exceedingly many flocks and herds;

3 But the poor man had nothing but one little ewe lamb which he had bought; and it lived together with him and with his children; it did eat of his food and drink from his cup and lie in his bosom, and it was to him like a daughter.

4 And there came a guest to the rich man, and he refused to take of his own herds or flocks to make a banquet for the guest who had come to him, but he took the poor man's ewe lamb and prepared it for the guest who had come to him.

5 And David's anger was greatly kindled against the man; and he said, As the LORD lives, the man who has done this thing is worthy of death;

6 And he shall restore the ewe lamb fourfold because he did this thing and because he had no pity.

7 ¶And Nathan said to David, You are the man. Thus says the LORD God of Israel, I anointed you king over my people Israel and I delivered you out of the hands of Saul,

8 And I gave you your master's daughters and your master's wives into your bosom, and I also gave you the daughters of Israel and of Judah; and if they were too few you should have told me, and I would have added to you twice that many.

9 Why have you despised the commandment of the LORD and have done that which is evil in the sight of the LORD? You have killed Uriah the Hittite with the sword and have taken his wife to be your wife and have slain him with the sword of the Ammonites.

10 Now therefore the sword shall not depart from your house for ever; because you have despised me and have taken the wife of Uriah the Hittite to be your wife.

11 Thus says the LORD, Behold, I will raise up evil against you out of your own house, and I will take your wives before your eyes and give them to your neighbor, and he shall lie with them in the broad daylight.

12 For you did it secretly; but I will do this thing in the sight of all Israel, in the daytime.

13 And David said to Nathan, I have sinned against the LORD. And Nathan said to David, The LORD also has put away your transgression; you shall not die.

14 Nevertheless, because by this deed you have made the enemies of the LORD to boast, the son also that is born to you shall surely die.

15 ¶Then Nathan went to his house. And the LORD struck the child that the wife of Uriah the Hittite bore to David, and it was very sick.

16 David therefore besought God for the child; and David fasted and went in and lay all night on the ground.

17 And the elders of his household arose and tried to raise him up from the ground, but he would not, neither did he eat bread with them.

18 And it came to pass on the seventh day that the child died. And the servants of David feared to tell him that the child was dead; for they said, Behold, while the child was yet alive, we spoke to him, and he would not listen to us; how then shall we tell him now that the child is dead? He may react violently.

19 But when David saw that his servants were whispering, David perceived that the child was dead; therefore he said to his servants, Is the child dead? And they said, He is dead.

20 Then David arose from the earth, and washed and anointed himself, and changed his garments and went into the house of the LORD and worshipped; then he came to his own house and asked for food, and they set it before him and he did eat.

21 Then his servants said to him, What is this that you have done? While the child was still alive, you were fasting and praying, but when he was dead, you did rise up and eat food.

22 David said to them, While the child was still alive, I fasted and prayed; for I said, Who knows whether God will be gracious to me, and let the child live?

23 But now he is dead, why should I fast? Can I bring him back again? I shall go to him, but he cannot return to me.

24 ¶And David comforted Bathsheba his wife, and went in to her and lay with her; and she bore a son, and she called his name Solomon; and the LORD loved the child.

25 Then he sent for Nathan the prophet; and he named the child Jedidah because the LORD loved him.

26 ¶And Joab fought against Rabbath of the children of Ammon, and took the royal city.

27 And Joab sent messengers to David and said, I have fought against Rabbath and I have also taken the royal city.

28 Now therefore gather the rest of the people together, and come and encamp against the city and take it; lest I take the city, and it shall be called after my name.

29 So David gathered all the people together and went against Rabbath, and fought against it and took it.

30 And he took their king's crown from off his head; the weight of it was a talent of gold, and in it were precious stones; and it was set on David's head. And he brought forth the spoil of the city in great abundance.

31 And he brought forth the people who were in it, and put them in iron bands and in chains, and made them pass through the measuring line; and thus did he to all the cities of the Ammonites. Then David and all the people returned to Jerusalem.

CHAPTER 13

AND it came to pass after this, that Absalom the son of David had a sister whose name was Tamar; and Amnon the son of David loved her.

2 And Amnon was much grieved on account of his sister Tamar; for she was a virgin; and Amnon felt unable to say anything to her.

3 But Amnon had a friend whose name was Jonadab, the son of Shimeah David's brother; and Jonadab was a very wise man.

4 And he said to Amnon, O son of the king why are you so losing weight from day to day? Will you not tell me? And Amnon said to him, I love Tamar, my brother Absalom's sister.

5 And Jonadab said to him, Lie down on your bed and pretend that you are sick; and when your father

comes to see you, say to him, Let my sister Tamar come and give me food to eat and make me a couple of cakes in my sight, that I may see it and eat it from her hand.

6 ¶So Amnon lay down and pretended to be sick; and when the king came to see him, Amnon said to the king, Let Tamar my sister come and make me a couple of cakes in my sight that I may eat from her hand.

7 Then David sent for Tamar, and said to her, Go now to your brother Amnon's house and prepare food for him.

8 So Tamar went to her brother Amnon's house; and he was lying down. And she took dough and kneaded it and baked cakes.

9 And she took the cakes and placed them before him; but he refused to eat. And Amnon said, Let every one go out from the house. And they went out every man from the house.

10 And Amnon said to Tamar, Bring the food into the chamber that I may eat from your hands. And Tamar took the cakes which she had made and brought them into the chamber to Amnon her brother.

11 And when she had brought them to him to eat, he took hold of her and said to her, Come lie with me, my sister.

12 And she answered him, No, my brother, do not treat me shamefully; for no such folly ought to be done in Israel;

13 And as for me, where shall I carry my shame? And as for you, you would be reckoned as one of the fools in Israel. Now therefore, speak to the king; for he will not withhold me from you.

14 But he would not listen to her; but, being stronger than she, he forced her and lay with her and disgraced her.

15 ¶Then Amnon hated her exceedingly; so that the hatred with which he hated her was greater than the love with which he had loved her. And Amnon said to her, Arise, be gone.

16 And she said to him, So now, since you have done this great evil to me, you send me away? But he would not listen to her.

17 Then he called his servant who ministered to him, and said to him, Put now this woman out of my house, and bolt the door after her.

18 And Tamar took ashes and put them on her head,

19 And she tore the embroidered garment which she wore; then she laid her hands on her head, and went away crying mournfully.

20 And Absalom her brother said to her, Has Amnon your brother lain with you? But hold now your peace, my sister; he is your brother; do not take this deed to your heart. So Tamar remained horrified in the house of Absalom her brother.

21 ¶But when King David heard all these things, he was exceedingly displeased.

22 And Absalom spoke to his brother Amnon neither good nor bad; for Absalom hated Amnon because he had forced his sister Tamar.

23 ¶Now from season to season, Absalom had sheepshearers in Baalhazor, which is near Ephraim; and Absalom invited all the king's sons.

24 And Absalom came to the king and said to him, Behold now your servant has sheepshearers; let the king and his servants go with your servant.

25 And the king said to him, No, my son, let us not all now go lest we be burdensome to you. And he pressed him, but he would not go with him, but he blessed him.

26 Then said Absalom, Why should not my brother Amnon go with me? The king said to him, Why should he go with you?

27 But Absalom pressed him that he should let Amnon and all the king's sons go with him.

28 ¶Then Absalom commanded his servants, saying, Mark when Amnon's heart is merry with wine, and when I say to you, Smite Amnon and kill him, fear not; have I not commanded you? Be courageous and be valiant.

29 So the servants of Absalom did to Amnon as Absalom had commanded them. Then all the king's

sons arose, and every man mounted his mule and fled.

30 ¶And while they were on the way, the news came to David that Absalom had murdered all the king's sons and there was not one of them left.

31 Then the king arose and tore his garments and lay on the earth; and all his servants stood by with their clothes rent.

32 And Jonadab, the son of Shimeah David's brother, said to him, Let not my lord the king think that all the king's sons are dead; for Amnon alone is dead; for Absalom had been determined to do this from the day that Amnon forced his sister Tamar.

33 Now therefore let not my lord the king think that all the king's sons are dead; for Amnon alone is dead.

34 But Absalom fled. And the watchman lifted up his eyes and looked, and behold, many people were coming by the way on the side of the mountain.

35 And Jonadab said to the king, Behold, the king's sons come; as your servant said, so it is.

36 And as soon as he had finished speaking, behold, the king's sons came and lifted up their voices and wept; and the king and all his servants also wept bitterly.

37 ¶But Absalom fled, and went to Talmai, the son of Ammihud, the king of Geshur. And David mourned for his son many days.

38 So Absalom fled and went to Geshur, and was there three years.

39 And King David longed to go forth after Absalom; for he was comforted concerning Amnon, seeing he was dead.

CHAPTER 14

NOW Joab the son of Zoriah perceived that the king's heart was reconciled toward Absalom.

2 And Joab sent to Tekoah, and fetched from thence a wise woman and said to her, Pretend to be a mourner and put on mourning apparel, and do not anoint yourself with oil, but be as a woman who has been mourning many days for the dead;

3 And come to the king and speak in this manner to him. So Joab prepared the words and put them in her mouth.

4 ¶And when the woman of Tekoah came to the king, she fell on her face to the ground, and did obeisance and said, Deliver me, O my lord the king.

5 And the king said to her, What ails you? And she answered, I am indeed a widow, my husband is dead.

6 And your handmaid had two sons, and they two quarrelled together in the field, and there was none to part them, and one was stronger than the other and slew him.

7 And behold, the whole family is risen against your handmaid, and they say, Deliver to us the man who slew his brother that we may kill him for the life of his brother whom he slew; so they want to destroy the heir also; moreover they want to quench the spark of life which is left for me, that they may not leave to his father either name or family upon the earth.

8 And the king said to her, Go to your house, and I will give orders concerning you.

9 But the woman of Tekoah said to the king, My lord, O king, let this iniquity be on me and on my father's house; and the king and his throne be guiltless.

10 And the king said to her, Whosoever says anything to you, bring him to me and he shall not touch you any more.

11 Then she said, Let my lord the king remember that the LORD your God would not suffer the avengers of blood to destroy any more, wherefore let them not destroy my son. And the king said to her, As the LORD God lives, there shall not one hair of your son fall to the earth.

12 Then the woman said, Let your handmaid speak a word to the king, and he said to her, Speak.

13 And the woman said to him, Why then have you thought such a thing against the people of God? And why do you speak, O king, as one who is guilty, in that, O king, you do not bring back your lost one?

14 For we will all surely die, and we are as water that is poured upon the ground, which cannot be gathered up again; neither does God destroy a soul, but devises means that no man should go astray from him.

15 Now therefore if I have spoken this thing to my lord the king, it is because the people have made me afraid; and your handmaid said, I will now speak to the king; it may be that the king will deliver his handmaid from the hand of men,

16 That they may not destroy me and my son together from the heritage of God.

17 Then your handmaid said, The word of my lord the king shall now be confirmed and shall be like an offering; for as an angel of God, so is my lord the king to discern good and evil; therefore the LORD your God will be with you.

18 Then the king answered and said to the woman, Do not hide from me anything that I ask you. And the woman said to him, Let my lord the king now speak.

19 And the king said, Is not the hand of Joab with you in all this? And the woman answered and said to him, As your soul lives, my lord the king, I have not turned to the right hand or to the left from all that my lord the king has spoken; for it was your servant Joab who bade me, and he put all these words in the mouth of your handmaid,

20 Because he wanted to do it through me, that is why your servant Joab has done this thing; and my lord is wise, according to the wisdom of an angel of God, to know all things that are on the earth.

21 ¶And the king said to Joab, Behold now, I have done as you have said; go therefore, bring me the young man Absalom again.

22 And Joab fell on his face to the ground and did obeisance and blessed the king: and Joab said, Today your servant knows that I have found grace in your sight, my lord, O king, in that the king has fulfilled the request of his servant.

23 So Joab arose and went to Geshur and brought Absalom to Jerusalem.

24 And the king said, Let him go to his own house, but let him not be seen in my presence. So Absalom went to his own house and did not see the king's face.

25 ¶Now in all Israel there was no man so much praised for his beauty as Absalom; from the sole of his foot to the crown of his head there was no blemish in him.

26 And when he had his hair shorn (he used to cut it once a year because it was heavy on him, therefore he cut it), the hair of his head weighed two hundred shekels by the king's weight.

27 And there were born to Absalom three sons and one daughter, whose name was Tamar; she was a beautiful woman.

28 ¶So Absalom dwelt two years in Jerusalem, and saw not the king's face.

29 Therefore Absalom summoned Joab to send him to the king; but he would not come to him; and he sent a second time, but he would not come.

30 Then Absalom said to his servants, See, there is a field belonging to Joab near mine; whether it be of wheat or barley, go and set it on fire. And Absalom's servants set Joab's field on fire.

31 Then Joab arose and came to Absalom's house and said to Absalom, Why have your servants set my field on fire?

32 And Absalom answered Joab, Behold, I sent to you, saying, Come here, that I may send you to the king, to ask why I have come from Geshur. It was better for me while I was there; now I want to appear before the king and if there is any iniquity in me, let him kill me.

33 So Joab came to the king and told him the words of Absalom; and he called for Absalom, and Absalom came in before the king and bowed himself on his face to the ground before the king; and the king kissed Absalom.

CHAPTER 15

AND after this, Absalom prepared for himself chariots and horsemen, and fifty men to run before him.

2 And Absalom rose up early and stood beside the king's gate; and it was so that when any man had a case to be tried before the king, then Absalom called him to him, and said, Of what city are you? And he said, Your servant is of one of the tribes of Israel.

3 And Absalom said to him, I see your arguments are good and just; but there is no man deputed by the king to hear you.

4 Absalom said moreover, Oh that I were made a judge in the land, that every man who has a lawsuit or a cause might come to me, and I would do him justice!

5 And whenever a man arose to do him obeisance, he held him by his hand and kissed him.

6 And in this manner did Absalom to all the Israelites who came to the king for judgment; so Absalom stole the hearts of the men of Israel.

7 ¶And it came to pass after four years Absalom said to the king, Let me go and fulfil my vow which I have vowed to the Lord, in Hebron;

8 For your servant made a vow while I abode at Geshur and in Aram, saying, If the Lord will bring me again indeed to Jerusalem, then I will serve the Lord.

9 And the king said to him, Go in peace. So he arose and went to Hebron.

10 ¶But Absalom sent spies throughout all the tribes of Israel, saying, As soon as you hear the sound of the trumpet, then you shall say, Absalom reigns in Hebron.

11 And with Absalom went two hundred men from Jerusalem, but they went innocently, not knowing anything of the plot.

12 And Absalom sent for Ahithophel the Gilonite, David's counsellor, and brought him from his city, from Giloh, while he was offering sacrifices. And the conspiracy grew strong; and the people increased continually on the side of Absalom.

13 ¶And there came a messenger to David, saying, The hearts of the men of Israel are with Absalom.

14 And David said to all his servants who were with him at Jerusalem, Arise and let us flee; for we shall not else escape from Absalom; make haste to depart, lest he overtake us suddenly and bring evil upon us and smite the city with the edge of the sword.

15 And the king's servants said to the king, Behold, your servants are ready to do whatever our lord the king wants to do.

16 So the king went forth and all his household after him. And the king left ten women who were concubines to keep his house.

17 And the king went forth and all the people after him, and they halted in a place at a distance from the city.

18 And all his servants passed on beside him; and all his noblemen and all his army and all the Gittites who had followed him from Gath passed on before the king.

19 ¶Then said the king to Ittai the Gittite, Why do you also go with us? Depart from the king; for you are a stranger, and also you were brought captive from your country.

20 You came but yesterday, and shall I trouble you today to go with us, seeing I go wherever I may? Return, and make your brethren to settle down; it will be well with you.

21 But Ittai answered the king and said, As the Lord lives and as the king lives, wherever my lord the king shall be, whether in death or life, even there will your servant be also.

22 And David said to Ittai, Go and pass over. So Ittai the Gittite passed over, and all his men and all the little ones that were with him.

23 And all the country wept with a loud voice, and all the people passed over; then the king also passed over the brook Kidron, and all the people passed over toward the way of the wilderness.

24 ¶And behold, Zadok the priest

went also and all the Levites who were with him, bearing the ark of God; and Abiathar went up and stood until all the people had finished passing over from the city.

25 Then the king said to Zadok, Carry back the ark of God into the city; perhaps I shall find favor in the eyes of the LORD, and he will bring me back again and show me both it and his habitation;

26 But if he shall say, I have no delight in you; behold, here I am, let him do to me as seems good in his sight.

27 The king said also to Zadok the priest, Return, go to the city in peace, you and your sons with you, Ahimaaz your son and Nathan the son of Abiathar.

28 See, I will wait in the plain of the wilderness until there come a man from you to inform me.

29 Zadok therefore and Abiathar carried the ark of God back to Jerusalem; and they remained there.

30 ¶And David went up by the ascent of mount Olivet and wept as he went up and had his head covered and all the people who were with him also covered their heads, and they went up on foot, weeping as they went.

31 ¶And they told David, saying, Ahithophel has conspired with Absalom. And David said, O LORD, I pray thee, nullify the counsel of Ahithophel.

32 ¶And when David came to a place where he used to worship God, behold, Hushai the Archite came to meet him with his coat torn and earth upon his head;

33 And David said to him, If you pass on with me, then you will be a burden to me;

34 But if you return to the city, say to Absalom, I am your servant, O king, as I was your father's servant hitherto. And now, I the king, want you to go and defeat the counsel of Ahithophel.

35 Behold, there are with you in the city Zadok and Abiathar the priests. Therefore it shall be that every word you hear from the king's house, you shall tell to Zadok and Abiathar the priests.

36 Behold, they have there with them their two sons Ahimaaz Zadok's son and Nathan Abiathar's son; and by them you shall send to me everything that you can hear.

37 So Hushai, David's friend, came to the city, just as Absalom entered Jerusalem.

CHAPTER 16

AND when David had passed a little beyond the place where he used to worship, behold, Ziba the servant of Mephibosheth came to meet him, with a couple of asses, laden with two hundred loaves of bread and a hundred bunches of raisins and a hundred cakes of figs and a skin of wine.

2 And the king said to Ziba, Where did you get these? Ziba said to him, The asses are to carry the burden of the king's household; and the bread and fig cakes are for the young men to eat, and the wine, that those who faint in the wilderness may drink.

3 And the king said to him, Where is your master's son? Ziba said to him, Behold he remains at Jerusalem; for he said, Today shall the house of Israel restore to me the kingdom of Saul my father.

4 Then David said to Ziba, Behold, all that belonged to Mephibosheth is given to you. And Ziba said to him, I have plenty, and I have found grace in your sight, my lord, O king.

5 ¶And when King David came to Beth-hurim, behold, there came out from there a man of the family of the house of Saul, whose name was Shimei, the son of Gera; he came forth and cursed David;

6 And he threw stones at him and at all his servants and at all his people and at all his servants who were on his right hand and on his left.

7 And thus said Shimei to David when he cursed him, Get out, get out, you bloody man, you wicked man;

8 The LORD has requited upon you

all the blood of the house of Saul, in whose stead you have reigned; and the LORD has delivered the kingdom into the hand of Absalom your son; and, behold, you have been requited for your evil, because you are a bloody man.

9 ¶Then Abishai the son of Zoriah said to David, Why should this dead dog curse my lord the king? Let me go over and take off his head.

10 And King David said to him, What is it to me and to you, O sons of Zoriah? Let him curse, it is the LORD who has told him to curse David. Therefore who can say to me, Why has this happened?

11 And David said to Abishai and to all his servants, Behold, my own son, who came forth from my loins, seeks my life; so now let this Benjamite alone, let him curse; for God has bidden him.

12 It may be the LORD will look on my affliction and requite me good for his cursing this day.

13 And as David and his servants went on the way, Shimei walked along the mountain side opposite him and cursed him as he went and threw stones at him and cast dust at him.

14 And the king and all the people who were with him arrived at their destination weary, and they refreshed themselves there.

15 ¶And Absalom and all the people who were with him and all Israel came to Jerusalem, and Ahithophel with him.

16 And when Hushai the Archite, David's friend, came to Absalom, Hushai said to Absalom, Long live the king! long live the king!

17 And Absalom said to Hushai, Is this your kindness to your friend? Why did you not go with your friend?

18 And Hushai said to Absalom, No; but whom the LORD and this people and all Israel have chosen, with him will I dwell, and his will I be.

19 And again, whom should I serve? I have no choice. As I have served in your father's presence, so will I serve before you.

20 ¶Then Absalom said to Ahitho-phel, Give me counsel, as to what we shall do.

21 And Ahithophel said to Absalom, Go in to your father's concubines, whom he has left to keep his house; and when all Israel shall hear that you have gone in to your father's concubines, then shall the hands of all who are with you be strengthened.

22 So they pitched a tent for Absalom upon the roof; and Absalom went in to his father's concubines in the sight of all Israel.

23 And the counsel of Ahithophel which he gave in those days was as if a man had inquired at the oracle of God; so was all the counsel of Ahithophel both with David and with Absalom.

CHAPTER 17

MOREOVER Ahithophel said to Absalom, Let me now choose twelve thousand men, and I will arise and pursue David this night;

2 And I will overtake him while he is weary and weak, and I will throw him into a panic, and all the people who are with him shall flee, and I will kill the king only;

3 And I will bring back all the people to you, just as those whom you sought have come back; so all the people shall be in peace.

4 And the saying pleased Absalom well, and all the elders of Israel.

5 Then Absalom said, Call now Hushai the Archite also, and let us likewise hear what he has to say.

6 And when Hushai came to Absalom, Absalom said to him, Ahithophel has spoken after this manner; shall we do what he has said? If not, you speak.

7 And Hushai said to Absalom, The counsel that Ahithophel has given is not good at this time.

8 For said Hushai to Absalom, You know well that your father and his servants are mighty men, and they are furious as a bear that devours the prey in the field; moreover, your father is a man of war, and will not spend the night with the people.

9 Behold now, he has hidden in one of the countries or in some other place; and when we attack them according to the first counsel, then the rumor will spread that there has been a great slaughter among the people who follow Absalom.

10 Even though he is valiant and his heart is as the heart of a lion, he shall utterly melt; for all Israel knows that your father is a mighty man and that those who are with him are valiant men.

11 Therefore I counsel that when all Israel is gathered to you from Dan to Beer-sheba, then you yourself march in their midst.

12 So we shall go against him in some place where he shall be found, and we will light upon him as the dew falls on the ground; and of him and of all the men who are with him there shall not be left even one.

13 Moreover, if he should enter into a city, then all Israel shall cast ropes on it, and we will drag it into the valley, and they shall leave there not even a cricket.

14 And Absalom and all the men of Israel said, The counsel of Hushai the Archite is better than the counsel of Ahithophel. For the LORD had decreed to defeat the good counsel of Ahithophel so that the LORD might bring evil upon Absalom.

15 ¶Then Hushai said to Zadok and to Abiathar the priests, Thus and thus did Ahithophel counsel Absalom and all the men of Israel; and thus and thus have I counseled.

16 Now therefore send quickly and tell David, saying, Do not spend the night in the plain of the wilderness, but pass over, lest you and all the people who are with you be destroyed.

17 Now Nathan and Ahimaaz were standing by the side of the fountain of the palace, so they might not be seen to enter the city; and a maidservant went and told them; and they went and told King David.

18 Nevertheless a lad saw them, and told Absalom; but they both went away, and came into the house of a man of Beth-hurim who had a well in his courtyard; and they went down into it.

19 And the woman took and spread a covering over the well's mouth, and put barley upon it; and the thing was not known.

20 And when Absalom's servants came to the woman at the house, they said, Where are Ahimaaz and Nathan? And the woman said to them, They have gone from here, for they wanted water; but when they could not find any, they returned to Jerusalem.

21 And after Absalom's servants had gone, they came up out of the well and went and told King David, and said to him, Arise and cross quickly over the water; for thus has Ahithophel counselled against you.

22 Then David arose and all the people who were with him and they crossed the Jordan; by early morning there was not one left who had not crossed the Jordan.

23 ¶And when Ahithophel saw that his counsel was not followed, he saddled his ass and arose and went home to his city; and he put his household in order and hanged himself and died and was buried in the sepulchre of his father.

24 And David came to Mahanaim. And Absalom crossed the Jordan, he and all the men of Israel with him.

25 ¶And Absalom had appointed Amasa over the army instead of Joab. Amasa was the son of an Israelite whose name was Ithra, who went in to Abigail the daughter of Nahash, sister of Zoriah Joab's mother.

26 So Israel and Absalom encamped in the land of Gilead.

27 ¶When David came to Mahanaim, Abishai, the son of Nahash of Rabbath of the children of Ammon, and Machir the son of Gamil of Lodebar, and Barzillai the Gileadite of Dobelin

28 Brought beds and carpets and earthen vessels and wheat and barley and parched wheat and flour and beans and lentils

29 And honey and butter and sheep and cheese of cows, and offered them to David, and to the people who were

with him, to eat; for they said, The people are hungry and weary and thirsty in the wilderness.

CHAPTER 18

AND David numbered the people who were with him, and set over them commanders of thousands and captains of hundreds.

2 And David placed a third part of the people under the command of Joab, and a third part under the command of Abishai the son of Zoriah, Joab's brother, and a third part under the command of Ittai the Gittite.

3 And the king said to the people, If we surely should flee, the enemy will not care about us; now therefore ten thousand men are enough for us; for it is better for us to receive help from the cities.

4 And the servants of David said to him, We will go forth quickly to fight against them. And the king said to them, Whatever seems good to you, do it. Then the king stood by the side of the gate, and all the people went out by hundreds and by thousands.

5 And the king commanded Joab and Abishai and Ittai, saying, Capture for me the young man Absalom alive. And all the people heard when the king gave orders to all commanders concerning Absalom.

6 ¶So the people went out into the field against Israel;

7 And there was a battle, and the people of Israel were defeated there before the servants of David, and there was a great slaughter on that day of twenty thousand men.

8 For there was a great battle which spread over the face of the country; and the wild beasts of the forest devoured more people that day than the sword devoured.

9 ¶And it happened that Absalom met the servants of David. And Absalom was riding upon a mule, and the mule went under the thick boughs of a great oak, and Absalom's head caught fast in the great oak, and he was hanging between the heaven and the earth; and the mule that was under him went away.

10 And a certain man saw it and told Joab and said, Behold, I saw Absalom hanging in an oak.

11 And Joab said to the man who told him, When you saw him, why then did you not smite him there and throw him to the ground? And I would have given you ten shekels of silver and a garment.

12 And the man said to Joab, Though you should count to me a thousand shekels of silver, I would not put forth my hand against the king's son; for in our hearing the king charged you and Abishai and Ittai, saying, Be careful not to harm the young man Absalom for my sake.

13 And if I should have done it, then I would have been guilty; and nothing would have been hidden from the king, and you yourself would have stood against me.

14 Then Joab said to him, That is not true, I will do it now myself. Then Joab took three darts in his hand and thrust them through the heart of Absalom while he was still alive and hanging from the oak.

15 And ten young men who bore Joab's armor circled about and smote Absalom and slew him.

16 And Joab blew the trumpet, and the people returned from pursuing Israel; for Joab had held back the people.

17 And they took Absalom's body and cast it into a great pit, and raised over it a great heap of large stones; and all Israel fled every man to his tent.

18 ¶Now Absalom in his lifetime had taken and set up for himself a monument in the valley of the kings; for he said, I have no son to keep my name in remembrance; and he called the monument by his own name; and it is called the work of Absalom to this day.

19 ¶Then said Ahimaaz the son of Zadok, Let me now run and bring the good tidings to the king, how the LORD has avenged him of his enemies.

20 And Joab said to him, It is not proper that you bear tidings this day,

but you may bear tidings another day; this day you shall bear no tidings because the king's son is dead.

21 Then Joab said to Cushi, Go tell the king what you have seen; and he ran.

22 Then Ahimaaz the son of Zadok said again to Joab, Why should not I too run after Cushi? And Joab said to him, Why will you run, my son, seeing no one will give you a reward for the tidings?

23 He said to him, What is the difference? Let me run. And he said to him, Run. Then Ahimaaz ran by the way of the plain, and passed Cushi.

24 Now David was sitting between the two gates; and the watchman went up to the roof over the gate to the wall, and he lifted up his eyes and looked, and saw a man running alone.

25 And the watchman called out and told the king. And the king said, If he is alone, there are tidings in his mouth. And he came apace, and drew near.

26 And the watchman drew near toward the gate, and said, Behold, another man is running alone;

27 Moreover the watchman said, I see the running of the first is like the running of Ahimaaz the son of Zadok. And the king said, He is a good man and comes with good tidings.

28 And the king called to Ahimaaz, and said to him, Have you come in peace? And he bowed before the king with his face to the earth, and said, Blessed be the LORD your God, who delivered up the men who lifted their hands against my lord the king.

29 Then the king said, Is the young man Absalom safe? And Ahimaaz answered, I saw a great army arrayed against Joab the servant of my lord the king, but I your servant knew not what was the outcome.

30 And the king said to him, Turn aside and stand here. And he turned aside and stood still.

31 And, behold, Cushi came; and he said, Tidings, my lord the king! for the LORD has avenged you this day from the hand of all those who rose up against you.

32 And the king said to Cushi, Is the young man Absalom safe? And Cushi answered, Let your enemies, my lord the king, and all who rise up against you for evil be as that young man is.

33 ¶And the king was overcome, and went up to his bedchamber and wept; and as he wept, he said, O my son Absalom, my son, my son Absalom! Would that I had died instead of you, O Absalom, my son!

CHAPTER 19

AND it was told Joab, Behold, the king is weeping and mourning for Absalom.

2 And there was mourning that day among all the people; for the people heard that day how the king was grieved for his son.

3 And the people concealed themselves as they entered into the city that day, as people who are ashamed steal away when they flee from battle.

4 But the king covered his face, and cried with a loud voice, saying, O my son Absalom, O Absalom, my son, my son!

5 And Joab came into the king's house and said to him, You have shamed this day the faces of all your servants who this day have saved your life and the lives of all your sons and your daughters and the lives of your wives and the lives of your concubines,

6 Because you have loved your enemies and hated your friends. For you have declared this day that you have neither noblemen nor servants; for this day I perceive that if Absalom were alive and all of us were dead, it would have pleased you better.

7 Now therefore arise, go out and speak comfortingly to your servants; for I swear by the LORD, if you do not go out, not a man will remain with you this night; and this will be worse for you than all the evils that have befallen you from your youth until now.

8 Then the king arose and sat in the gate. And they told all the people, saying, Behold, the king is sitting in

the gate. And all the people came before the king; for Israel had fled every man to his tent.

9 ¶And all the people were thinking in all the tribes of Israel and saying, The king delivered us from the hand of all our enemies and rescued us from the hand of the Philistines; so now let us flee from the land and from following Absalom.

10 And Absalom, whom we anointed and made king over us, is dead in battle. And they said every man to his neighbor, Why therefore hesitate to go back with the king?

11 ¶Come, therefore, let us bring him back to his house. And the words of the Israelites came to the king.

12 And the king said to them, You are my brethren and my flesh and my bones, why then are you the last to return to the king?

13 And he said to Amasa, Behold, you are my flesh and my bone. God do so to me, and more also, if you are not commander of my army permanently instead of Joab.

14 And he swayed the heart of all the men of Judah as one man; so that they sent word to the king, saying, Return you and all your servants.

15 So the king returned and came to the Jordan. And Judah came to Gilgal to meet the king and bring the king over the Jordan.

16 ¶And Shimei the son of Gera, a Benjamite, made haste and came down with the men of Judah to meet King David.

17 And Ziba the servant of Saul and his fifteen sons and his twenty servants with him crossed over and constructed a bridge over the Jordan before the king.

18 And they constructed rafts to bring over the king's household and to do whatever was good in his sight. And Shimei the son of Gera fell down before the king as he was crossing the Jordan;

19 And said to the king, Let not my lord impute iniquity to me, neither remember that which your servant did perversely the day that my lord the king went out of Jeru-salem; let not my lord the king take it to his heart.

20 For your servant does know that I have sinned; therefore, behold, I have come this day the first of all the house of Joseph to go down to meet my lord the king.

21 But Abishai the son of Zoriah answered and said, Shall not Shimei be put to death for this, because he cursed the LORD's anointed?

22 And David said, What is it to me and to you, you sons of Zoriah, that you should this day be deceivers to me? Shall any man be put to death this day in Israel? For do I not know that I am this day king over Israel?

23 Then the king said to Shimei, You shall not die. And the king swore to him.

24 ¶And Mephibosheth the son of Jonathan, the son of Saul, came down to meet the king, and he had neither trimmed his beard nor changed his clothes, from the day the king departed until the day the king came again in peace.

25 And it came to pass, when he came to Jerusalem to meet the king, the king said to him, Mephibosheth, why did you not go with me?

26 Mephibosheth answered, My lord, O king, my servant deceived me; for I said to him, Saddle me an ass that I may ride upon it and go with my lord the king; because your servant is lame.

27 And my servant has lied about me, O my lord the king; but you, my lord the king, you are as an angel of God; do therefore what is good in your eyes.

28 For all of my father's house were worthy of death before my lord the king; yet you counted your servant among those who eat at your table. Now therefore I cannot justify myself, neither speak before my lord the king.

29 And the king said to him, You have spoken more than enough, I have already commanded that you and Ziba shall divide the fields.

30 And Mephibosheth said to the king, Yea, let him take all the produce also forasmuch as my lord the

king has come again in peace to his own house.

31 ¶Now Barzillai the Gileadite came down from Dobelin and went with the king to conduct him over the Jordan.

32 Now Barzillai was a very aged man, eighty years old; and he had provided the king with food while he remained at Mahanaim; for he was a very wealthy man.

33 And the king said to Barzillai, Come along with me, and I will feed you with me in Jerusalem.

34 And Barzillai said to the king, How many years have I to live, that I should go up with the king to Jerusalem?

35 I am this day eighty years old; and I cannot discern between luxury and simple living; neither can your servant taste what he eats or what he drinks. Nor can I hear any more the voice of singing men and singing women. Why then should your servant be a burden to my lord the king?

36 Your servant can hardly cross the Jordan with my lord the king; let not my lord the king recompense me with such a reward.

37 Let your servant turn back again, that I may die in my own city and be buried beside the grave of my father and my mother. But behold here is with you your servant Bimham my son; let him go over with my lord the king, and do you to him what seems good in your sight.

38 And the king said, Bimham shall go over with me and I will do ·to him that which seems good to you; and whatever you shall ask of me, that will I do for you.

39 And when all the people had crossed the Jordan and the king had crossed also, the king kissed Barzillai and blessed him; and he returned to his own place.

40 Then the king went on to Gilgal, and Bimham went on with him; and all the people of Judah went on with the king, and also half the people of Israel.

41 ¶And, behold, the men of Israel came to the king and said to him, Why have our brethren the men of Judah stolen you away and have brought you over the Jordan and all your household and all men of Judah with you?

42 And all the men of Judah answered and said to the men of Israel, Because the king is near of kin to us; why then are you displeased over this matter? Have we eaten at all at the king's cost? Or has he given us any gifts?

43 And the men of Israel answered the men of Judah, and said, We have ten parts in the king, and we have also more right in David than you; why then did you go ahead of us? We should have been the first to bring back the king. And the words of the men of Judah were fiercer than the words of the men of Israel.

CHAPTER 20

AND there happened to be there a wicked man, whose name was Shamoa, the son of Bichri, a Benjamite; and he blew a trumpet and said, We have no portion in David, neither have we an inheritance with the son of Jesse; every man to his tents, O Israel!

2 So all the men of Israel ceased from following David, and followed Shamoa, the son of Bichri; but the men of Judah remained loyal to the king from the Jordan to Jerusalem.

3 ¶And David came to his house at Jerusalem; and the king took the ten women his concubines whom he had left to keep his house and put them in custody and fed them, but did not go in unto them. So they were shut up to the day of their death, and were like widows.

4 ¶Then said the king to Amasa, Assemble me the men of Judah within three days, and you yourself be present.

5 So Amasa went to assemble the men of Judah; but he tarried longer than the set time which had been appointed.

6 And David said to Joab, Now Shamoa the son of Bichri will do us more harm than did Absalom; take your lord's servants and pursue him,

lest he find him fortified cities, and stay in them and incite a revolt against us.

7 And there went out after him Joab's men, the noblemen and the army and all the mighty men; and they went out from Jerusalem to pursue Shamoa, the son of Bichri.

8 When they were at the great stone which is in Gibeon, Amasa came before them. And Joab was wearing armor, and upon it was a girdle with a sword fastened upon his loins in its sheath; and as Amasa appeared, Joab placed his hand upon his sword.

9 And Joab said to Amasa, Peace be with you, my brother. And Joab took Amasa by the beard with his hand to kiss him.

10 But Amasa took no notice of the sword that was in Joab's hand; so Joab smote him with it in the middle of his body, and let out his bowels to the ground, and struck him not again; and he died. So Joab and Abishai his brother pursued Shamoa, the son of Bichri.

11 And one of Joab's men went and stood by Amasa, and said to those who passed by, To whom do you belong? Are you of the men of David who are after Joab?

12 And Amasa wallowed in his blood, lying in the highway. And when the man saw that all the people stopped to look at him, he dragged Amasa out of the highway and threw him into a field and cast a garment over him, when he saw that every one who came by him stopped.

13 When he was dragged out of the highway, all the people went on after Joab, to pursue Shamoa, the son of Bichri.

14 ¶And they went through all the tribes of Israel to Abel and to Beth-maachah and to Berin; and they went after him.

15 And they came and besieged him in Abel and in Beth-maachah, and they set ambushes against the city, and the city was in distress; and all the people who were with Joab battered the wall to throw it down.

16 ¶Then a wise woman cried out from the wall, saying, Hear, hear, and say to Joab, Come near, that I may speak to you.

17 And when he was come near to her, she said to him, Are you Joab? And he answered, I am he. Then she said to him, Hear the words of your maidservant. And he answered, I do hear.

18 Then she said, They used to say in old time, They first inquire of the prophets, then they destroy.

19 I am of those who have suffered the pangs of childbirth in Israel; you seek to destroy a child and his mother in Israel; why will you swallow up the heritage of the LORD?

20 And Joab answered and said to her, Far be it from me that I should swallow up or destroy.

21 The matter is not so; but a man of mount Ephraim, Shamoa, the son of Bichri by name, has lifted up his hand against King David; deliver him alive to me and I will depart from the city. And the woman said to Joab, Now his head shall be thrown to you over the wall.

22 Then the woman went to all the people in her wisdom. And they cut off the head of Shamoa, the son of Bichri, and threw it out over the wall to Joab. And Joab blew the trumpet, and they withdrew from the city and departed every man to his tent. And Joab returned to Jerusalem to the king.

23 ¶Now Joab was in command of all the army of Israel; and Benaiah the son of Jehoiada was in command of the freedmen and the laborers,

24 And Adoniram was in charge of the tribute, and Jehoshaphat the son of Ahilud was the recorder,

25 And Sheriah was the scribe, and Zadok and Abiathar were the priests,

26 And also Aza of Jathir was a priest to David.

CHAPTER 21

THEN there was a famine in the days of David for three years, year after year; and David inquired of the LORD. And the LORD answered, It is because of Saul and because of his bloody house, because he slew the Gibeonites.

2 So the king called the Gibeonites and said to them (now the Gibeonites were not of the children of Israel, but of the remnant of the Amorites; and the children of Israel had sworn to them, and Saul had sought to slay them in his zeal to cause the children of Israel and Judah to sin),

3 Wherefore David said to the Gibeonites, What shall I do for you? And with what shall I make an atonement to you, that you may bless the heritage of the LORD?

4 And the Gibeonites said to him, It is not silver and gold that Saul and his house owe us; neither do we wish to kill any one in Israel. And he said to them, Whatever you shall say, that will I do for you.

5 And they said to the king, The man who consumed us and planned to destroy us so that we should not remain in all the territory of Israel,

6 Let seven of his sons be delivered to us, and we will sacrifice them before the LORD in Gibeah of Saul. And the king said, I will give them.

7 But the king spared Mephibosheth, the son of Jonathan the son of Saul, because of the LORD's oath that was between them, between David and Jonathan the son of Saul.

8 But the king took the two sons of Rizpah the daughter of Ana, whom she bore to Saul, Armoni and Mephibosheth; and the five sons of Nadab the daughter of Saul, whom she bore to Azriel, the son of Barzillai the Meholathite;

9 And he delivered them to the Gibeonites, and they sacrificed them in the mountain before the LORD; and they fell all seven together, and were slain in the first days of harvest, in the beginning of barley harvest.

10 ¶And Rizpah the daughter of Ana took sackcloth and spread it under her upon the rock, from the beginning of the harvest until water dropped upon them from the heaven, and she did not let the birds of the air rest upon the bodies by day nor the wild beasts of the field by night.

11 And it was told David what Rizpah the daughter of Ana, the concubine of Saul, had done.

12 ¶And David went and took the bones of Saul and the bones of Jonathan his son from the men of Jabeshgilead, who had stolen them from Rehab of Beth-shan, where the Philistines had hanged them, on the day the Philistines slew Saul in the mountain of Gilboa;

13 And he brought up from thence the bones of Saul and the bones of Jonathan his son; and they gathered the bones of those who were slain;

14 And they buried the bones of Saul and of Jonathan his son in the land of Benjamin in Zelzah, in the sepulchre of Kish his father; and they did all that the king commanded. And after that God was reconciled toward the land.

15 ¶Moreover the Philistines were again at war with Israel; and David went down and his servants with him to fight against the Philistines;

16 But David, Joab, and Abishai were afraid of a giant, the weight of whose breastplate was three hundred shekels of brass, and who was girded with a new sword, and had threatened to slay David.

17 But Abishai the son of Zoriah succored him and smote the Philistine and killed him. Then the servants of David swore to him, saying, You shall go out no more with us to battle, that you may not quench the lamp of Israel.

18 And it came to pass after this, that there was again war with the Philistines at Gath; then Sibbechai the Hushathite slew Saphar, who was of the sons of the giants.

19 And there was again war between Israel and the Philistines, and Elhanan the son of Malap a weaver, a Beth-lehemite, slew a brother of [1] Goliath the Philistine, the staff of whose spear was like a weaver's beam.

20 And there was again war in Gath, where there was a man of great stature, who had on each hand six fingers and on each foot six toes,

---

[1] *Brother* inserted for clarity. There might have been another Goliath.

twenty-four in number; and he also was born to the giants.

21 And when he had defied Israel, Jonathan the son of Shimeah the brother of David slew him.

22 These four were born to the giants in Gath, and fell by the hand of David and by the hand of his servants.

CHAPTER 22

AND David spoke to the LORD the words of this song on the day that the LORD had delivered him out of the hand of all his enemies and out of the hand of Saul;

2 And he said: I will love thee, O LORD my strength and my trust; the LORD is my strength and my fortress and my deliverer,

3 The mighty God in whom I trust; he is my succor and the horn of my salvation, my refuge who delivered me from the wicked men, my glorious Saviour.

4 I will call upon the LORD, and I shall be saved from my enemies.

5 For the pangs of death have compassed me, the torrents of ungodly men made me afraid;

6 The pangs of Sheol compassed me about; the snares of death lay ahead of me;

7 In my distress I called upon the LORD and cried to my God; and he did hear my voice out of his temple, and my cry did enter into his ears.

8 Then the earth shook and trembled; the foundations of the mountains quaked and burst asunder, because he was angry at them.

9 There went up a smoke because of his anger, and fire kindled out of his face; and coals were kindled by it.

10 He bowed the heavens and came down; and darkness was under his feet.

11 And he rode upon a cherub, and did fly; he flew mightily upon the wings of the wind.

12 And he made darkness his pavilion round about him, the dark waters and thick clouds of the skies.

13 Out of the brightness of his shelter he made his clouds hail and coals of fire.

14 The LORD thundered from heaven, and the most High uttered his voice, hail and coals of fire.

15 And he sent out his arrows and scattered them; he increased his lightning and discomfited them.

16 Then the channels of the sea appeared, the foundations of the world were uncovered, at thy rebuke, O LORD, at the blast of the breath of thine anger.

17 He sent from above and took me; he drew me out of many waters;

18 He delivered me from my strong enemies and from them that hated me; for they were too strong for me.

19 They fell upon me in the day of my affliction; but the LORD became my succor.

20 He relieved me from my distress; he delivered me, because he delighted in me.

21 The LORD rewarded me according to my righteousness; according to the cleanness of my hands has he recompensed me.

22 For I have kept the ways of the LORD and have not rebelled against my God.

23 For all his judgments were before me; and his statutes I have not put away from me.

24 I was blameless before him, and have kept myself from my sin.

25 Therefore the LORD has recompensed me according to my righteousness, according to the cleanness of my hands in his sight.

26 With the good man thou wilt show thyself good, with the upright man thou wilt show thyself upright.

27 With the pure thou wilt show thyself pure; and with the perverse thou wilt show thyself perverse.

28 For thou wilt save the afflicted people; and the proud ones thou wilt bring down.

29 For thou wilt light my lamp; O LORD my God, lighten my darkness.

30 For by thee I can run against a band of robbers; by the help of my God I have leaped over a wall.

31 As for God, his way is perfect; the word of the LORD is tried; he succors all who trust in him.

32 For there is no God except the LORD. And there is no one who is mighty but our God.

33 The God who has girded me with strength makes my way perfect.

34 He makes my feet like hart's feet, and makes me stand upon my high places.

35 He teaches my hands to war, and strengthens my arms like a bow of brass.

36 Thou hast also given me the shield of thy salvation, and thy right hand has helped me; thy gentleness has made me great.

37 Thou hast enlarged my steps under me, so that my feet did not slip.

38 I will pursue my enemies and will overtake them, and will not turn back until I have consumed them.

39 I will strike them that they may not arise; yea, they shall fall under my feet.

40 Thou hast girded me with strength for the battle; thou hast made them that rise up against me to be subdued under me.

41 Thou hast also made mine enemies to bend their necks to me, that I might silence those that hate me.

42 They shall cry to the LORD, but there shall be none to save them; they shall seek the LORD, but he shall not answer them.

43 I shall beat them as small as the dust which is carried by the wind; I shall tread upon them as the mire of the streets.

44 Thou hast delivered me from the strivings of the people, thou hast made me the head of the nations; a people whom I have not known shall serve me.

45 Those who give ear shall hearken to me; the sons of strangers shall be obedient to me.

46 Strangers shall halt and be restrained from their ways.

47 The LORD lives; blessed be he who gives me strength; and exalted be God my Saviour.

48 Thou art the God who has given me vengeance and hast brought down the peoples under me

49 And hast delivered me from my enemies; thou also hast exalted me over those who rose up against me; thou hast delivered me from wicked men.

50 Therefore I will give thanks unto thee, O LORD, among the nations, and I will sing praises to thy name.

51 He gives great salvation to his king and shows mercy to his anointed, to David and to his descendants for ever.

CHAPTER 23

NOW these are the last words of David. David the son of Jesse, the anointed one whose rule has been established, the one whom the God of Jacob has made the sweet psalmist of Israel said,

2 The Spirit of the LORD spoke by me and his word is upon my tongue.

3 The God of Israel said, the Mighty One of Israel spoke to me: He who governs men must be righteous, ruling over those who revere God.

4 He is like the light of the morning when the sun rises, even a morning without clouds, before dawn, a morning free from rain which makes the grass to spring up.

5 Is not my house so with God? For he has made with me an everlasting covenant, ordered in all things and sure; for it is he who fulfils all my desire and all my decrees.

6 ¶But the ungodly are all like hard thorns, for they cannot be gathered with hands;

7 But when a man comes near them, he gathers them with the handle of an axe and with iron; and they are utterly burned with fire in the same place.

8 ¶These are the names of the mighty men whom David had: seated in the first seat, in the third rank, his name was Gadho, a man who went down and slew eight hundred men in one hour.

9 Next to him was Eleazar, the cousin of Gadho, who went down with David and three other men when

the Philistines defied them and were gathered there to battle; and when the men of Israel withdrew,

10 He arose, and smote the Philistines until his hand was weary, and his hand clave to his sword; and the LORD wrought a great victory that day; and the people returned with him only to strip the slain.

11 And next to him was Shammah, the son of Agee, from the king's mountain. When the Philistines were gathered together to plunder cattle where there was a piece of ground full of lentils and the people fled from the Philistines,

12 He stood in the midst of the field and delivered the cattle and slew the Philistines; and the LORD wrought a great victory by his hand.

13 And three of the valiant men went down and came to David in the harvest time to the cave of Arlam; and the Philistines' cattle were grazing in the Plain of Giants.

14 And David was then staying in the stronghold, and the princes of the Philistines were encamped in Bethlehem.

15 And David longed for water and said, O that one would give me a drink of water from the great well which is in the city of Beth-lehem!

16 So the three valiant men broke through the camp of the Philistines and drew water out of the great well which is in the city of Beth-lehem, and took it and brought it to David; but he would not drink of it, but poured it out before the LORD.

17 And he said, Far be it from me, on account of the LORD, that I should do this; because these men went at the risk of their lives. Therefore he would not drink it. These things did these three valiant men.

18 And Abishai, the brother of Joab, the son of Zoriah, was chief of thirty men. And he lifted up his spear against three hundred and slew them.

19 And he was honored above the thirty men; therefore he became their chief and performed heroic deeds equal to thirty men.

20 And Benaiah the son of Jehoiada was a mighty man of Kabzeel who had performed good acts; he slew two mighty men of Moab and went down also and slew a lion in the midst of a forest in time of snow;

21 And he slew an Egyptian, a handsome man; and the Egyptian had a spear in his hand; but he went down against him with a staff, and seized the spear out of the Egyptian's hand and slew him with his own spear.

22 These things did Benaiah the son of Jehoiada, and he was renowned among the thirty men.

23 He performed heroic deeds equal to thirty men. And David set him over his guard.

24 Ashael, the brother of Joab, was one of the thirty;

25 Also Shammah of the king's mountain,

26 And Helez the Paltite, Ira the son of Ikkesh the Tekoite,

27 Abiezer the Anethothite, Mebunai the Hushathite,

28 Zalmon of the mount House, Mahar of Netophath,

29 Heleb the son of Baana a Netophathite, Ittai the son of Ribai of Ramtha of the children of Benjamin,

30 Benaiah the son of Pirathon of Gibeah, Hiddai of the Brooks of Gaash,

31 Abi the son of Abialemon the Gileadite, Arboth of Horim,

32 Alhana the Shaalbonite, Jonathan of the house of Nashor,

33 Shammah of the mount of Olives, Ahiam the son of Ashdad of Edri,

34 Eliphelet the son of Ahasbai the Maachathite, Eliam the son of Ahithophel the Gilonite,

35 Hezrai the Carmelite, Gadai the Arbite,

36 Negael the son of Nathan of Zobah, Baana the Gadite,

37 Zelek the Ammonite, Nahari the Beerothite, the armorbearer of Joab the son of Zoriah,

38 Hira the Ithrite, Arab of Lachish,

39 And Uriah the Hittite: the serv-

ants of David were thirty-seven in all.

CHAPTER 24

AND again the anger of the LORD was kindled against Israel, and he incited David against them and said to him, Go, number Israel and Judah.

2 So the king said to Joab the commander of the army who was with him, Go now through all the tribes of Israel, from Dan to Beer-sheba and number the people, and bring to me the sum of the number of the people.

3 And Joab said to the king, May the LORD your God add to the people a hundredfold, howsoever many they be, so that the eyes of my lord the king may see it; but why does my lord the king delight in this thing?

4 Notwithstanding the king's word prevailed against Joab and against the commanders of the army. And Joab and the commanders of the army went out from the presence of the king to number the people of Israel.

5 ¶And they crossed the Jordan and came to Sharob, which is on the right side of the city that lies in the midst of the valley of Gad and toward Eleazer;

6 Then they came to Tyre and Zidon, to the land of the Canaanites and the land of the Hittites and the land of the Jebusites,

7 And when they had gone through the whole land, they came to the land of Judah in thirty-eight days. Then they came to Dan, and circled Zidon.

8 And when they had gone through all the land, they came to Jerusalem at the end of nine months and twenty days.

9 And Joab brought the sum of the number of the people to the king; and there were in Israel eight hundred thousand valiant men who drew the sword; and the men of Judah were five hundred thousand men.

10 ¶But David's heart smote him after he had numbered the people. And David said to the LORD, I have sinned greatly in what I have done; and now, I beseech thee, O LORD, for I have done very foolishly.

11 When David arose in the morning, the word of the LORD came to the prophet Gad, saying,

12 Go and say to David, Thus says the LORD: I will bring upon you one of three calamities; choose one of them, that I may do it to you.

13 So the prophet Gad came to David and said to him, These are the calamities which may come upon you: there shall seven years of famine come in your land, or you shall flee three months before your enemies while they pursue you, or there shall be three days of pestilence in your land. Now therefore say what answer I shall return to him who sent me to you.

14 Then David answered and said to the prophet Gad, I am greatly distressed; it is better for me to be punished by the hand of the LORD our God; for his mercies are great: let us not be punished by the hand of men.

15 ¶So the LORD sent a pestilence upon Israel from the morning until the evening; and there died of the people from Dan to Beer-sheba seventy thousand men.

16 And when the angel stretched out his hand toward Jerusalem to destroy it, the LORD restrained the angel of death who was destroying the people, and said to him, You have destroyed enough, stay now your hand. And the angel of the LORD was standing by the threshing floor of Aran the Jebusite.

17 Then David spoke to the LORD when he saw the angel who smote the people, and said to the angel, I have sinned and I have given provocation; but these innocent sheep, what have they done? Let thy hand be against me, and against my father's house.

18 ¶And Gad the prophet came that day to David and said to him, Go up and build an altar to the LORD in the threshing floor of Aran the Jebusite.

19 And David went up, according to the word of Gad, as the LORD had commanded him.

20 And when Aran the Jebusite turned back and saw the king and his servants coming toward him, Aran fell down and did obeisance to the king with his face to the ground.

21 And Aran said, Why has my lord the king come to his servant? And David said to him, To buy the threshing floor from you, to build an altar to the LORD, that the plague may be stayed from the people.

22 Then Aran said to David, Let my lord the king take what seems good to him; behold, here are the oxen for the burnt offering, and the ploughshare and the yokes for fuel.

23 All these things did Aran give to King David. And Aran said to the king, May the LORD your God bless you.

24 And the king said to Aran, No, but I will surely buy it from you for a price; and I will not offer burnt offerings to the LORD my God of that which cost me nothing. So David bought the threshing floor by the garden and the oxen for fifty shekels of silver.

25 And David built there an altar to the LORD, and offered burnt offerings and peace offerings. So the LORD was entreated for the land, and the plague was stayed from Israel.

THE FIRST BOOK OF THE

KINGS

commonly called

THE THIRD BOOK OF THE KINGS

CHAPTER 1

NOW King David was old and well advanced in years; and they covered him with clothes, but he could not get warm.

2 Wherefore his servants said to him, Behold, your servants are before you, let them seek for our lord the king a young virgin; and let her wait upon the king, and let her minister to him, and let her lie in your bosom, that our lord the king may get warm.

3 So they sought for a beautiful maiden throughout all the territory of Israel, and found Abishag a Shilommite, and brought her to the king.

4 And the maiden was very beautiful, and she became the king's attendant and ministered to him; but the king knew her not.

5 ¶Then Adonijah the son of Haggith exalted himself, saying, I will be king; and he prepared for himself chariots and horsemen, and fifty men to run before him.

6 And his father had never rebuked him at any time by saying, Why have you done so? And he also was a very handsome man; and his mother bore him after Absalom.

7 And he conferred with Joab the son of Zoriah and with Abiathar the priest; and they followed Adonijah and helped him.

8 But Zadok the priest and Benaiah the son of Jehoiada and Nathan the prophet and Shimei and Rei and the mighty men who belonged to David were not with Adonijah.

9 And Adonijah sacrificed sheep and oxen and fat cattle by the great stone which is by En-kasra, and he invited

all his brothers, the king's sons, and all the men of Judah and the king's servants;

10 But he did not invite Nathan the prophet; and Benaiah, the son of Jehoiada; and David's mighty men; and Solomon his brother;

11 ¶Wherefore Nathan the prophet said to Bath-sheba the mother of Solomon, Have you not heard that Adonijah has become king, and David our lord does not know it?

12 Now therefore come, let me give you counsel, that you may save your own life and the life of your son Solomon.

13 Go and get you in to the King David and say to him, Did you not my lord, O king, swear to your handmaid, saying, Solomon your son shall reign after me, and he shall sit upon my throne? Why then does Adonijah reign?

14 And, while you are still speaking there in the presence of the king, I also will come in after you and confirm your words.

15 ¶So Bath-sheba went in to King David into the chamber; and the king was very old; and Abishag the Shilommite ministered to the king.

16 And Bath-sheba bowed and did obeisance to the king. And the king said to her, What troubles you, Bathsheba?

17 She said to him, My lord the king, you swore by the Lord your God to your handmaid, saying, Solomon your son shall reign after me and he shall sit upon my throne.

18 And now, behold, Adonijah reigns; and you, my lord the king, do not know it;

19 And he has sacrificed oxen and fat cattle and sheep in abundance, and has invited all the sons of the king and Abiathar the priest and Joab the general of the army; but Nathan the prophet; Benaiah, the son of Jehoiada; and Solomon your servant he has not invited.

20 And you, my lord, O king, the eyes of all Israel are upon you, that you should tell them who shall sit on the throne of my lord the king after him.

21 Otherwise it shall come to pass, when my lord the king shall sleep with his fathers in peace, I and my son Solomon shall be counted offenders.

22 ¶And, while she was still speaking there before the king, Nathan the prophet also came in.

23 And they told the king, saying, Behold Nathan the prophet has come. And when he was come in before the king, he bowed himself before the king with his face to the ground and did obeisance.

24 And Nathan said, My lord, O king, have you said, Adonijah shall reign after me and he shall sit upon my throne?

25 For he has gone down this day and has sacrificed oxen and fat cattle and sheep in abundance, and has invited all the king's sons and the commanders of the army and Abiathar the priest; and, behold, they are eating and drinking before him and saying, Long live King Adonijah!

26 But me, even me your servant, and Zadok the priest; and Benaiah, the son of Jehoiada; and your servant Solomon he has not invited.

27 Has this thing been done by the order of my lord the king, and you have not told your servants who should sit on the throne of my lord the king after him?

28 ¶Then King David answered and said, Call me Bath-sheba. And she came into the king's presence and stood before him.

29 And the king swore to her, and said, As the Lord lives, who has saved my soul out of all distress,

30 Even as I swore to you by the Lord God of Israel, saying, Solomon your son shall reign after me and he shall sit upon my throne, even so will I do this day.

31 Then Bath-sheba bowed with her face to the earth and did obeisance to the king, and said, Let my lord King David live for ever.

32 ¶And King David said, Call me Zadok the priest; and Nathan the prophet; and Benaiah, the son of Jehoiada. And they came before the king.

33 And the king said to them, Arise, take with you the servants of your lord, and cause Solomon my son to ride upon my own mule, and take him down to Shilokha;

34 And let Zadok the priest and Nathan the prophet anoint him there king over Israel; and blow with the trumpet, and say, Long live King Solomon.

35 Then you shall come after him, and he shall sit upon my throne; for he shall be king in my stead; I have appointed him to be king over Israel and over Judah.

36 And Benaiah the son of Jehoiada answered and said before the king, Amen; so may the LORD your God do.

37 As the LORD has been with my lord the king, even so may he be with Solomon, and make his throne greater than the throne of my lord King David.

38 So Zadok the priest and Nathan the prophet and Benaiah, the son of Jehoiada and the archers and the slingers went down and caused Solomon to ride upon King David's mule, and took him to Shilokha.

39 Then Zadok the priest and Nathan the prophet took a horn of oil out of the tabernacle and anointed Solomon. And they blew the trumpet; and all the people said, Long live King Solomon.

40 And all the people came up after him, and the people played on tambourines and rejoiced with great joy, so that the earth was shaken with their noise.

41 ¶And Adonijah and all the guests who were with him heard it as they finished eating. And when Joab heard the sound of the trumpet, he said, What is this noise of the city being in an uproar?

42 And while he was still speaking, behold, Nathan the son of Abiathar the priest came; and Adonijah said to him, Come in; for you are a valiant man, and you bring good tidings.

43 And Nathan answered and said to Adonijah, Truly our lord King David has made Solomon king.

44 And the king has sent with him Zadok the priest; and Nathan the prophet; and Benaiah, the son of Jehoiada; and the archers; and the slingers, and they have caused Solomon to ride upon the king's mule;

45 And Zadok the priest and Nathan the prophet have anointed him king in Shilokha; and they are come up from there rejoicing, so that the whole city is rejoicing. This is the noise that you have heard.

46 And also Solomon sits on the throne of the kingdom.

47 And moreover the king's servants came to bless our lord King David, saying, May the LORD your God make the name of Solomon better than your name, and make his throne greater than your throne. And the king bowed himself upon his bed.

48 And also thus said the king, Blessed be the LORD God of Israel, who has given me a son to sit upon my throne this day, my own eyes seeing it.

49 Then all the guests who were invited by Adonijah were afraid, and rose up and went every man his way.

50 ¶And Adonijah feared because of Solomon, and arose and went and took hold of the horns of the altar.

51 And it was told King Solomon, saying, Behold, Adonijah is afraid because of you, and, lo, has taken refuge on the horns of the altar, saying, Let King Solomon swear to me this day that he will not slay his servant with the sword.

52 And Solomon said, If he will show himself to be a worthy man, there shall not a hair of his head fall to the earth; but if wickedness shall be found in him, he shall die.

53 So King Solomon sent, and they brought him down from the altar. And he came and did obeisance to King Solomon; and Solomon said to him, Go to your house.

CHAPTER 2

NOW the days of David to die drew near; and he charged Solomon his son, saying,

2 I go the way of all the earth; be

strong therefore, and show yourself a man;

3 And keep the charge of the LORD your God, and walk in his ways and keep his statutes, his commandments, his judgments, and his testimonies, as it is written in the law of Moses, that you may prosper in all that you do and succeed wherever you go;

4 That the LORD may establish his word which he spoke concerning me, saying, If your children take heed to their ways, to walk before me in truth with all their heart and with all their soul, there shall not fail you a man on the throne of Israel.

5 Now, you know also what Joab the son of Zoriah did to me, and what he did to the two commanders of the armies of Israel, to Abner the son of Ner and to Amasa the son of Jether, whom he slew and considered them as though they were in the battle, and shed their blood with the sword that was about his loins and trampled upon it with the shoes that were on his feet.

6 Do to him therefore according to your wisdom, and let not his hoary head go down to the grave in peace.

7 But show kindness to the sons of Barzillai the Gileadite, and let them be of those who eat at your table; for so they ministered to me in everything when I fled from Absalom your brother.

8 And, behold, you have with you Shimei the son of Gera, of the tribe of Benjamin, of the house of Horim, who cursed me with grievous curses on the day when I went to Mahanaim; but he came down to meet me at the Jordan and I swore to him by the LORD, saying, I will not put you to death with the sword.

9 Now therefore hold him not guiltless; for you are a wise man, and know what you ought to do to him; and bring his folly on his head; and you shall bring down his hoary head with blood to Sheol.

10 So David slept with his fathers and was buried in the city of David.

11 And the time that David reigned over Israel was forty years; seven years he reigned in Hebron, and thirty-three years he reigned in Jerusalem.

12 ¶Then Solomon sat upon the throne of David his father; and his kingdom was firmly established.

13 ¶And Adonijah the son of Haggith came to Bath-sheba the mother of Solomon. And she said to him, Have you come in peace? And he said, In peace.

14 Then he said to her, I have something to say to you. And she said to him, Say on.

15 And he said to her, You know that the kingdom rightly was mine, and that all Israel were looking forward to me to be king over them; but the kingdom was taken from me and is become my brother's; for it was his from the LORD.

16 And now I make one petition of you, do not refuse me. And she said to him, Say on.

17 And he said to her, Speak to King Solomon (for he will not refuse you) that he give me Abishag the Shilommite to wife.

18 And Bath-sheba said, Very well; I will speak for you to the king.

19 ¶Bath-sheba therefore went to King Solomon to speak to him for Adonijah. And the king rose up to meet her and bowed himself to her and then sat on his throne, and they brought a chair for the king's mother; and she sat on his right hand.

20 Then she said, I desire one small petition of you; do not refuse me. And the king said to her, Ask on, my mother; for I will not refuse you.

21 And she said to him, Let Abishag the Shilommite be given to Adonijah your brother to wife.

22 And King Solomon answered and said to his mother, Why do you ask Abishag the Shilommite for Adonijah? Ask for him the kingdom also; for he is my elder brother; ask even for him and for Abiathar the priest and for Joab the son of Zoriah.

23 Then King Solomon swore by the LORD, saying, God do so to me, and more also, if Adonijah have not spoken this word against his own life.

24 Now therefore, as the LORD lives, who has established me and set me on the throne of David my father, and who has made me a house as he promised, Adonijah shall be put to death this day.

25 And King Solomon sent Benaiah the son of Jehoiada, and he attacked him and slew him.

26 And to Abiathar the priest the king said, Go to Anathoth, to your own fields; for you are worthy of death; but I will not at this time put you to death because you bore the ark of the LORD before David my father and because you have been afflicted in all wherein my father was afflicted.

27 So Solomon expelled Abiathar from being priest to the LORD; that the word of the LORD might be fulfilled which he spoke concerning the house of Eli in Shiloh.

28 ¶Now when the news reached Joab that Adonijah had been slain (for Joab had been leaning toward Adonijah and he was not leaning toward Solomon), Joab fled to the tabernacle of the LORD and took refuge on the horns of the altar.

29 And it was told King Solomon that Joab had fled to the tabernacle of the LORD and had taken refuge on the horns of the altar. Then Solomon sent Benaiah the son of Jehoiada, saying, Go and attack him.

30 And Benaiah came to the tabernacle of the LORD and said to him, Thus says the king, Come forth. But he said, No, I will not go out; but I will die here. And Benaiah brought the king word, saying, Thus said Joab, and thus he answered me.

31 And the king said to him, Do to him as he has said, and attack him and kill him, that you may take away the innocent blood, which Joab shed, from me and from the house of my father.

32 And the LORD shall return his blood upon his own head, because he attacked two men more righteous and better than he and slew them with the sword, my father David not knowing of it; namely, Abner the son of Ner, commander of the army of Israel;

and Amasa the son of Jether, commander of the army of Judah.

33 Their blood shall therefore return upon the head of Joab and upon the head of his descendants for ever; but to David and to his descendants and to his house and to his throne shall there be peace for ever from the LORD.

34 So Benaiah the son of Jehoiada went up and attacked him and slew him; and he was buried in his own sepulchre in the wilderness.

35 ¶Then King Solomon appointed Benaiah the son of Jehoiada in his stead over the army; and Zadok the priest the king appointed in the place of Abiathar.

36 ¶And the king sent and called for Shimei, and said to him, Build yourself a house in Jerusalem and dwell there, and do not go forth from there hither and thither.

37 For on the day that you go out and cross the brook Kidron, you shall know for certain that you shall surely die; your blood shall be upon your own head.

38 And Shimei said to the king, The saying is good; as my lord the king has said, so will your servant do. So Shimei dwelt in Jerusalem many days.

39 And it came to pass at the end of three years that two of the servants of Shimei ran away to Achish the son of Maachah king of Gath. And they told Shimei, saying, Behold, your servants are in Gath.

40 And Shimei arose and saddled his ass, and went to Gath to Achish to seek his servants; and Shimei went and brought his servants from Gath.

41 And it was told King Solomon that Shimei had gone from Jerusalem to Gath and had returned.

42 And the king sent and called for Shimei, and said to him, Did I not make you to swear by the LORD, and witnessed against you, saying, Know for certain, on the day that you go out of Jerusalem and cross the brook Kidron, you shall surely die? And you said to me, The saying is good, so will I do.

43 Why then have you not kept the

oath of the LORD and the commandment that I have charged you with?

44 The king said moreover to
Shimei, You know all the evil of
which your heart is conscious that
you did to David my father; therefore the LORD shall return your
wickedness upon your own head;

45 And King Solomon shall be
blessed, and the throne of David shall
be established before the LORD for
ever.

46 So the king commanded Benaiah
the son of Jehoiada; and he went out
and attacked him so that he died.
And the kingdom was established in
the hand of Solomon.

CHAPTER 3

AND Solomon became the son-in-
law to Pharaoh king of Egypt,
and took Pharaoh's daughter and
brought her into the city of David,
until he had finished building his own
house and the house of the LORD and
the wall of Jerusalem round about.

2 The people sacrificed only in
high places, because there was no
house yet built to the name of the
LORD, until those days.

3 And Solomon loved the LORD,
walking in the statutes of David his
father; only he sacrificed and burned
incense on the high places.

4 And the king went to Gibeon to
sacrifice there; for that was the great
high place; a thousand burnt offerings
did Solomon offer upon the altar
which was in Gibeon.

5 ¶Then the LORD appeared to
Solomon in a vision by night; and
God said to him, Ask that which I
should give you.

6 And Solomon said, Thou hast
shown to thy servant David my
father great mercy, according as he
walked before thee in truth and in
faithfulness and in uprightness of
heart with thee; and thou hast kept
for him this great kindness that thou
hast given him a son to sit on his
throne as it is this day.

7 And now, O LORD God, thou hast
made thy servant king in place of
David my father; and I am but a little child; I know not how to go out

or come in among thy people, whom
thou hast chosen,

8 A great people that cannot be
numbered nor counted for multitude.

9 Give therefore to thy servant an
understanding heart to judge thy people and to discern between good and
bad; for who is able to judge this thy
so great a people?

10 And it pleased the LORD because Solomon had asked this thing.

11 And the LORD said to Solomon,
Because you have asked this thing
and have not asked for yourself
riches, neither have you asked the
lives of your enemies nor have you
asked for yourself long life, but have
asked for yourself wisdom to discern
judgment;

12 Behold, I have done according
to your words; lo, I have given you
a wise and understanding heart, so
that there has been none like you
before you, neither shall any arise
after you like you.

13 And I have also given you that
which you have not asked, both
riches and honor, so that there shall
not be any among the kings like
you all your days.

14 And if you will walk in my
ways, to keep my statutes and my
commandments, as your father David
did walk, then I will lengthen your
days.

15 And Solomon awoke; and, behold, it was a dream. And he came
to Jerusalem and stood before the
ark of the covenant of the LORD and
offered up burnt offerings and peace
offerings, and made a feast for all
his servants.

16 ¶Then came there two women
who were harlots to plead before
King Solomon.

17 And one of them said, I beseech
you, O my lord, I and this woman
dwelt in one house; and I was delivered of a child with her in the house.

18 And on the third day after I
was delivered, this woman was delivered also; and we were together in
the house; there was no stranger with
us, only we two in the house.

19 And this woman's child died in
the night because she lay on it.

20 And she arose at midnight and took my son from beside me while your handmaid slept, and laid it in her bosom, and laid her dead son in my bosom.

21 And when I rose in the morning to nurse my son, behold, it was dead; but when I had examined it in the morning, behold, it was not my son which I had borne.

22 And the other woman said, It is not so; but the living is my son, and the dead is your son. And this one said, It is not so; the dead is your son, and the living is my son.

23 And the other woman said, It is not so, the living is my son and the dead is your son. Thus they argued before the king.

24 Then the king said, Bring me a sword. And they brought a sword before the king.

25 And the king said, Divide the living child in two, and give half to the one and half to the other.

26 Then the woman whose child was alive said to the king, because her affections yearned for her son, I beseech you, O my lord, give her the child alive, and in no wise slay it. But the other said, Let it be neither mine nor yours, but divide it in two.

27 Then the king answered and said, Give the child alive to the first woman and in no wise slay it; she is the mother thereof.

28 And all Israel heard of the judgment which the king had judged; and they feared the king; for they saw that the wisdom of God was in him, to do justice.

CHAPTER 4

SO Solomon was king over all Israel.

2 And these were the princes whom he had: Azariah the son of Zadok the priest;

3 Elihoreph and Ahiah, the sons of Shisha, scribes; Jehoshaphat the son of Ahilud, the recorder.

4 And Benaiah the son of Jehoiada was over the army; and Zadok and Abiathar were priests;

5 And Azariah the son of Nathan was over the governors; and Zabur, the son of Nathan, the priest, was the king's friend;

6 And Abinshar was over the household; and Adoniram the son of Abda was over the tribute.

7 ¶And Solomon had twelve governors over all Israel, who provided food for the king and his household and for the army; each month of the year it fell on one of them to supply provisions.

8 And these are their names: the son of Hur, who ruled in mount Ephraim;

9 The son of Dekar, in Makaz, and in Shaalbim, and Beth-shemesh, and Elon-beth-hanan;

10 The son of Hesed, in Raboth; to him belonged Socoth, and all the land of Hepher;

11 The son of Abinadab, in Naphatdor, who had Taphath the daughter of Solomon to wife;

12 Baana the son of Ahilud, who ruled in Taanach and Megiddo, and in all Beth-shean, which is beside Zartan, below Jezreel, from Bethshean to Abel-meholah, as far as the other side of Nekemaam;

13 The son of Geber, in Ramothgilead; to him belonged the towns of Jair the son of Manasseh; to him also belonged the region of Argob, which is in Bashan, sixty great cities with walls and bronze bars;

14 Ahinadab the son of Iddo, in Mahanaim;

15 Ahimaaz was in Naphtali; he also took Basmath the daughter of Solomon to wife;

16 Baana the son of Hushai was in Asher and in Aloth;

17 Jehoshaphat the son of Paroh, in Issachar;

18 Shimei the son of Elah, in Benjamin;

19 Geber the son of Uri was in the land of Gilead, the country of Sihon king of the Amorites and of Og king of Bashan; and the governors ruled in the land.

20 ¶Judah and Israel were as many in multitude as the sand which is by the sea; they ate and drank and made merry.

21 And Solomon ruled over all the kingdoms from the river which is in the land of the Philistines as far as the border of Egypt; and his subjects brought presents and served Solomon all the days of his life.

22 ¶And Solomon's provision for one day was thirty measures of fine flour and sixty measures of meal,

23 Ten fat oxen and twenty oxen out of the pastures and a hundred sheep, besides harts and gazelles and roebucks and fatted fowls.

24 For he had dominion over all the region on this side of the river, from Tiphsah even to Azzah,[1] over all the kings on this side of the river; and he had peace on all sides round about him.

25 And Judah and Israel dwelt safely, every man under his vine and under his fig tree, from Dan even to Beer-sheba, all the days of Solomon.

26 ¶And Solomon had forty thousand stalls of horses for his chariots and twelve thousand horsemen.

27 And those governors supplied provisions for King Solomon and for all who came to King Solomon's table, every man in his month; they lacked nothing.

28 Barley also and straw for the horses and the dromedaries they brought to the place where the officers were, every man as it was his due.

29 ¶And God gave Solomon wisdom and understanding exceeding much, and largeness of heart,

30 So that Solomon's wisdom excelled the wisdom of all the people of the east and all the wisdom of the Egyptians.

31 For he was wiser than all men; than Ethan the Easterner, and Heman, and Calcol and Darda, the sons of Mahol; and his fame was in all the nations round about.

32 And he spoke three thousand proverbs; and his songs were a thousand and five.

33 And he spoke of trees, from the cedar tree that is in Lebanon even to the hyssop that springs out of the wall; he spoke also of beasts and of fowl and of creeping things and of fishes.

34 And there came men from all nations to hear the wisdom of Solomon, from all kings of the earth; and he received presents from all kings of the earth who had heard of his wisdom.

CHAPTER 5

AND Hiram king of Tyre sent his servants to Solomon; for he had heard that they had anointed him king in place of his father; for Hiram was always a lover of David.

2 And Hiram sent to Solomon and blessed him. And Solomon sent to Hiram, saying,

3 You know how David my father could not build a house to the name of the LORD his God because of the wars which were about him on every side, until the LORD put his enemies under the soles of his feet.

4 But now the LORD my God has given me rest on every side, so that there is neither adversary nor evil occurrence.

5 And, behold, I purpose to build a house to the name of the LORD my God, as the LORD spoke to David my father, saying, Your son, whom I will set upon your throne in your place, shall build a house to my name.

6 Now therefore command that they cut for me cedar trees out of Lebanon; and my servants shall be with your servants; and I will give you wages for your servants according to all that you shall ask; for you know that there is no one among us who has the skill to cut timber like the Zidonians.

7 ¶And when Hiram heard the words of Solomon, he rejoiced greatly, and said, Blessed be the LORD this day, who has given to David a wise son over this great people.

8 And Hiram sent to Solomon, saying, I have heard the things for which you have sent to me; and I will do all your desire concerning timber of cedar and timber of fir.

9 My servants shall bring them down from Lebanon to the sea, and

---

[1] Or Gaza.

I will convey them by sea in floats to the place that you shall appoint me, and I will cause them to be discharged there, and you shall receive them from there; and you shall also accomplish my desire in giving food for my household.

10 So Hiram gave Solomon cedar trees and fir trees according to his desire.

11 And Solomon gave Hiram twenty thousand measures of wheat for food for his household and twenty thousand measures of pure oil; thus gave Solomon to Hiram year by year.

12 And the LORD gave Solomon wisdom, as he promised him; and there was peace between Hiram and Solomon always, and they two made a league together.

13 ¶And King Solomon raised a levy out of all Israel; and the levy was thirty thousand men.

14 And he sent them to Lebanon, ten thousand a month by turns; a month they were in Lebanon and two months at home; and Adoniram was in charge of the levy.

15 And Solomon had seventy thousand men who bore burdens and eighty thousand hewers of stone in the mountain,

16 Besides the chiefs of Solomon's officers who were set over the work, three thousand and three hundred, who were in charge of the people doing the work.

17 And the king commanded and they brought great stones, costly stones, and hewed stones to complete the house.

18 And Solomon's builders and Hiram's builders and the stonemasons did hew them; so they prepared stones and timber for the building of the house.

CHAPTER 6

AND it came to pass in the four hundred and eightieth year after the children of Israel were come out of the land of Egypt, in the fourth year of Solomon's reign over Israel, in the month of May, which is the second month, that he began to build the house of the LORD.

2 And the house which Solomon built for the LORD was in length sixty cubits and in breadth twenty cubits and in height thirty cubits.

3 And the porch in front of the door of the temple was twenty cubits long, the same as the breadth of the house; and ten cubits was the depth before the length of the house.

4 And for the house he made windows of narrow lights.

5 ¶And against the wall of the house he built rooms encircling the wall of the house, both of the temple and of the Holy of Holies; and he made side rooms round about.

6 The lowest chamber was five cubits broad, and the middle was six cubits broad, and the third was seven cubits broad; for outside in the wall of the house he made narrowed copings round about in order that the walls should be fastened together.

7 And the house, when it was building, was made of stones hewn before they were brought thither; so that there was neither hammer nor axe nor any tool of iron heard in the house while it was building.

8 The door of the middle chamber was on the south side of the house; and it went up with winding stairs into the middle chamber, and out of the middle into the third.

9 So he built the house and finished it; and roofed the house with beams and boards of cedar.

10 And then he built additional rooms against the whole house, five cubits high, and they were fastened to the house with timbers of cedar.

11 ¶And the word of the LORD came to Solomon, saying,

12 Concerning this house which you are building, if you will walk in my statutes and execute my judgments and keep all my commandments to walk in them, then I will perform my word with you, which I spoke to David your father;

13 And I will dwell among the children of Israel, and I will not forsake my people Israel.

14 So Solomon built the house and finished it.

15 And he covered the walls of the

house within with boards of cedar, from the floor of the house, to the rafters of the ceiling; and he covered them on the inside with wood, and he covered the floor of the house with boards of cypress.

16 And Solomon built twenty cubits in extent on the sides of the house, both the floor and the walls with boards of cedar; and he built within it the Holy of Holies.

17 And the house, that is, the inner sanctuary, was forty cubits long.

18 And the house was covered within with cedar, which was carved with buds and open flowers; all was cedar; there was no stone seen in it.

19 And the holy place he made in the inner part of the house, to set there the ark of the covenant of the LORD.

20 And the length of the holy place was twenty cubits, and the breadth was twenty cubits, and the height was twenty cubits; and he overlaid it with pure gold; and he covered the altar with gold.

21 And Solomon overlaid the house within with pure gold; and he made a doorpost in front of the sanctuary, and overlaid it with gold.

22 And the whole house he overlaid with gold, until all the house was finished; also the whole altar that was in the sanctuary he overlaid with gold.

23 ¶And within the sanctuary he made two cherubim of olive wood, each ten cubits high.

24 And five cubits was the one wing of the cherub, and five cubits the other wing of the cherub, ten cubits from the tip of the one wing to the tip of the other.

25 And the other cherub was ten cubits; both cherubim were of the same measure and the same size.

26 The height of the one cherub was ten cubits, and so was it of the other cherub.

27 And he set the cherubim within the inner house; and the wings of the cherubim were stretched forth so that the wing of one touched the one wall, and the wing of the other cherub touched the other wall; and

their wings touched each other in the middle of the house.

28 And he overlaid the cherubim with pure gold.

29 And he carved all the walls of the house round about with ornaments; and he fashioned carved ornaments and cherubim and palm trees and open flowers, within and without.

30 And the floor of the house he overlaid with gold, within and without.

31 ¶And for the entrance of the sanctuary he made doors of olive wood; the lintel and the doorposts were strongly fastened.

32 The two doors also were of olive wood; and he carved upon them figures of cherubim, and carved ornaments and palm trees and open flowers; and he overlaid them with gold, and spread gold upon the cherubim and upon the palm trees.

33 So also he made for the door of the temple, posts of olive wood, plain and square.

34 And the two doors were of fir wood; the two leaves of the one door were ornamented, and the two leaves of the other door were ornamented.

35 And he carved on them cherubim and palm trees and open flowers, and covered them with gold overlaid upon the carved work.

36 ¶And he built the inner court with three rows of hewn stone and a row of cedar beams.

37 ¶In the fourth year was the foundation of the house of the LORD laid, in the month of May;

38 And in the eleventh year, in the month Tishrin, which is the eighth month, was the house finished throughout all its parts, and according to all the fashion of it. So he was seven years in building it.

CHAPTER 7

BUT Solomon took thirteen years to build his own house and to finish it.

2 ¶He built also the house of the forest of Lebanon; its length was a hundred cubits and its breadth fifty cubits and its height thirty cubits,

upon four rows of cedar pillars, with cedar beams upon the pillars.

3 And it was covered with cedar above upon beams that lay upon forty-five pillars, fifteen in a row.

4 And there were balconies in three rows set one against another in three tiers.

5 And all the doors and posts were square, set one against another in three tiers.

6 ¶And he made a porch of pillars; its length was fifty cubits, its breadth thirty cubits; and the porch was upon the pillars, with a court in front.

7 ¶Then he made a porch for the throne where he might judge, even the porch of judgment; and covered it with cedar from the floor to the ceiling.

8 ¶And his own house where he dwelt was in another court within the porch, and was of like workmanship. Solomon also made a house like this in workmanship for Pharaoh's daughter, whom he had taken to wife.

9 All these were of costly stones, according to the measures of hewn stones, sawed with saws within and without, even from the foundation to the coping, and from the outside to the court of the temple.

10 And the foundation was of great and costly stones, some of ten cubits and some of eight cubits.

11 And above were costly stones, after the measures of hewn stones, and cedars.

12 And the great court round about was made with three rows of hewn stones and a row of cedar beams, both for the inner court of the house of the LORD and for the porch of the house.

13 ¶And King Solomon sent and brought Hiram from Tyre.

14 He was a widow's son of the tribe of Naphtali, and his father was an artist and a worker in brass; and he was filled with wisdom and understanding and cunning knowledge to fashion any work in brass. And he came to King Solomon and did all his work.

15 He cast two pillars of brass; the height of each pillar was eighteen cubits and the circumference was twelve cubits.

16 And he made two capitals of molten brass to set upon the tops of the pillars; the height of one capital was five cubits, and the height of the other wa, five cubits;

17 And he made carved ornaments of network and wreaths of chain work for the capitals which were upon the top of the pillars; seven for one capital and seven for the other.

18 And he made the pillars, and two rows of buds round about upon one network, to cover the capitals that were upon the top of the pillars; and he did so to the other pillar.

19 And the capitals that were upon the top of the pillars were of lily work in the porch, four cubits.

20 And the capitals that were upon the two pillars had pomegranates also above, and over against the side which was by the network; and the pomegranates were two hundred in rows round about upon the one capital; and in like manner the other capital.

21 And he made the pillars of the porch of the temple; and he set up the pillar on the right hand, and called its name Jachin; and he set up the pillar on the left hand, and called its name Boaz.

22 And upon the top of the pillars was lily work; so was the work of the pillars finished.

23 ¶Then he made a molten sea,[1] ten cubits in diameter; it was round about, and its height was five cubits and its circumference thirty cubits.

24 And under the brim of it round about there were buds encircling it, ten in a cubit, enclosing the sea; the buds were formed in two rows when it was cast.

25 It stood upon twelve oxen, three looking toward the north, three looking toward the west, three looking toward the south, and three looking toward the east; and the sea was set upon them, and their hinder parts were inward.

26 And its thickness was a hand-

[1] A large basin used for ceremonial washing.

breadth, and its brim was made like the brim of a cup, with lilies; it contained two thousand baths.[1]

27 ¶And he made ten bases of brass; four cubits was the length of one base, and four cubits its breadth, and three cubits the height of it.

28 And the work of the bases was in this manner: they had borders between panels;

29 And on the borders that were between the panels were lions, oxen, and cherubim; and upon the panels was the same, both above and below, lions and oxen; the appearance of the work was beautiful.

30 And every base had four bronze wheels and axles of brass; and the four corners thereof had a framework under the laver joined to it, framework molten, beautiful work.

31 And the opening of the base within was a cubit; and its opening was round like the work of the base, a cubit and a half; and also upon the opening of it were engravings with borders foursquare, not round.

32 And under each border were four wheels; and the axletrees of the wheels were joined to the base; and the height of a wheel was a cubit and a half.

33 And the work of the wheels was like the work of a chariot wheel; their axletrees and their spokes and their rims and their hubs were all cast.

34 And there were four supports at the four corners of one base; and the supports were part of the very base itself.

35 The supports and the frame of the base were half a cubit; and on the top of the base there was a rim; and the top of the base, its axletrees, and its borders were of the same.

36 And on the plates of the axletrees and on its borders he engraved cherubim, lions, and palm trees round about.

37 After this manner he made the ten bases: all of them were of one casting, one measure, and one size.

38 ¶Then he made ten lavers of brass; one laver held forty baths; and every laver was four cubits; and upon every one of the ten bases one laver.

39 And he put five bases on the right side of the house and five on the left side of the house; and he set the sea on the right side of the house, toward the south.

40 ¶And Hiram made the lavers and the pots and the cauldrons and the large hanging pots. So Hiram finished all the work that King Solomon made in the house of the LORD;

41 The two pillars, and the two bowls of the capitals that were on the top of the two pillars; and the two networks to cover the two bowls of the capitals which were upon the top of the pillars;

42 And four hundred pomegranates for the two networks, two rows of pomegranates for each network to cover the two bowls of the capitals that were upon the pillars;

43 And the ten bases and the ten lavers upon the bases;

44 And the one sea and the twelve oxen under the sea;

45 And the pots and the cauldrons and the hanging pots; and all the vessels of ministration which Hiram made for King Solomon for the house of the LORD were of Corinthian brass.

46 In Kakar which is in the plain of Jericho by the side of the Jordan did the king cast them, in the clay ground between Succoth and Zarthan.

47 And Solomon made all sorts of vessels, exceeding many; there was no limit to the weighing of the brass which King Solomon used for the house of the LORD;

48 And he made all the vessels that pertained to the house of the LORD: the altar of gold, and the table of gold whereupon the shewbread was,

49 And the candlesticks of pure gold, five on the right side and five on the left before the sanctuary, the snuffers, and the lamps, and the tongs of gold,

50 And the bowls, and the saucers, and the basons, and the spoons, and the censers of pure gold; and the hinges of pure gold, both for the

---

[1] A *bath* is about ten gallons.

doors of the inner house, the most holy place, and for the doors of the house of the temple.

51 Thus was ended all the work that King Solomon made in the house of the LORD. And Solomon brought in the things which David his father had dedicated; the silver and the gold and the vessels, and placed them among the treasures of the house of the LORD.

CHAPTER 8

THEN Solomon assembled all the tribes of Israel, all the heads of the tribes, and the chiefs of the fathers, to him in Jerusalem to bring up the ark of the covenant of the LORD out of the city of David, which is Zion.

2 And all the men of Israel assembled themselves to King Solomon at the feast in the month of the harvest, which is the seventh month.

3 And all the tribes of Israel came, and the priests took up the ark of the LORD.

4 And they brought it up to the temple of the LORD, and brought the tabernacle of the congregation and all the holy vessels that were in the tabernacle, and the priests and the Levites of Israel went up with them.

5 And King Solomon and all the congregation of Israel that were assembled to him were with him before the ark, sacrificing sheep and oxen that could not be counted or numbered for multitude.

6 And the priests brought in the ark of the covenant of the LORD to its place, into the temple, to the inner house, the Holy of Holies, under the wings of the cherubim.

7 For the cherubim spread forth their wings over the holy place, and the cherubim covered the ark and its staves above.

8 And the staves were so long that the ends of them were seen from the holy place before the inner house, but they were not seen outside; and there they are to this day.

9 There was nothing in the ark except the two tablets of stone, which Moses had put there at Horeb when the LORD made a covenant with the children of Israel when they came out of the land of Egypt.

10 And when the priests came out of the holy place, a cloud filled the house of the LORD,

11 So that the priests could not stand to minister because of the cloud; for the glory of the LORD had filled the house of the LORD.

12 ¶Then Solomon said, O LORD, thou hast said that thou wouldst dwell in the thick darkness.

13 And I have surely built thee a house to dwell in, a settled place for thee to abide in for ever.

14 Then the king turned his face about and blessed all the congregation of Israel; and all the congregation of Israel stood;

15 And he said, Blessed be the LORD God of Israel, who spoke with his mouth to David my father, and has with his hands fulfilled his promise, saying,

16 Since the day that I brought forth my people Israel out of Egypt, I chose no city out of all the tribes of Israel to build a house, that my name might be therein; but I chose David to be over my people Israel.

17 And it was in the heart of David my father to build a house for the name of the LORD God of Israel.

18 But the LORD said to David my father, Whereas it was in your heart to build a house to my name, you did well that it was in your heart.

19 Nevertheless you shall not build the house to my name; but your son who shall come forth out of your loins, he shall build the house to my name.

20 Now the LORD has performed the word that he spoke, and I have risen up in the place of David my father and sit on the throne of Israel, as the LORD promised, and have built a house to the name of the LORD God of Israel.

21 And I have set there the ark of the covenant of the LORD, which he made with our fathers when he brought them out of the land of Egypt.

22 ¶And Solomon stood before the altar of the LORD in the presence of all the congregation of Israel, and spread forth his hands toward heaven and prayed;

23 And he said, O LORD God of Israel, there is no one like thee in heaven above or on earth beneath, who keepeth covenant and mercy with thy servants who walk before thee in truth with all their heart and with all their soul;

24 Who hast kept with thy servant David my father what thou didst promise him; thou didst speak with thy mouth, and hast fulfilled it with thy hand, as it is this day.

25 Therefore, now, O LORD God of Israel, keep with thy servant David my father what thou didst promise him, saying, There shall not fail you a man in my sight to sit on the throne of Israel; if only your sons take heed to their way, to walk before me in truth as you have walked before me.

26 And now, O LORD God of Israel, let thy word be confirmed, which thou hast sworn to thy servant David my father.

27 But will God indeed dwell on the earth? Behold, the heaven and the heaven of heavens cannot contain thee; how much less this house that I have built?

28 But turn toward the prayer of thy servant, and to his supplication, O LORD my God, to hearken to the supplication and to the prayer which thy servant prays before thee this day;

29 That thine eyes may be open upon this house day and night, even toward this place of which thou hast said, My name shall be there; that thou mayest hearken to the prayer which thy servant prays before thee for this place.

30 And hearken thou to the supplication of thy servant and of thy people Israel, when they pray before thee in this place; and hear thou, O our God, from thy dwelling place in heaven, and forgive.

31 ¶If any man sins against his neighbor and an oath be laid upon him to cause him to swear and he comes and swears before thine altar in this house;

32 Then hear thou in heaven, and do, and judge thy servants, condemning the wicked, and bring his transgressions upon his head, and vindicating the righteous to reward him according to his innocence.

33 ¶When thy people Israel are defeated in the battle before the enemy because they have sinned before thee, and shall turn again to thee and confess thy name and pray and make supplication to thee in this house;

34 Then hear thou in heaven and forgive the sin of thy servants and of thy people Israel, and bring them back to the land which thou gavest to their fathers.

35 ¶When the heavens are shut up and there is no rain because they have sinned against thee; and they shall come and pray in this place and confess thy name and turn from their sins, when thou dost afflict them;

36 Then hear thou in heaven and forgive the sins of thy servants and of thy people Israel, when thou teach them the good way wherein they should walk, and give thy rain upon the land which thou hast given to thy people for an inheritance.

37 ¶And when there is famine in the land, if there is pestilence, blasting, mildew, locust, or when there are caterpillars; or when their enemy besieges them in one of their cities; whatsoever sickness, or whatsoever plague may be;

38 Whatsoever prayer and whatsoever supplication be made by any man or by all thy people Israel, who shall know every man the trouble of his own heart, and shall spread forth his hands before thee in this house;

39 Then hear thou in heaven thy dwelling place, and forgive, and do, and give to every man according to his ways, whose heart thou knowest (for thou, even thou only, knowest the hearts of all the children of men);

40 That they may reverence thee all the days that they live on the face of the land which thou gavest to their fathers.

41 Moreover concerning a stranger

who is not of thy people Israel, but comes from a far country for thy name's sake

42 (When they shall hear of thy great name and of thy strong hand and of thy stretched out arm), when he shall come before thee and pray in this house;

43 Hear thou in heaven thy dwelling place, and do according to all that the stranger calls to thee for; that all the peoples of the earth may know thy name, to worship thee, as do thy people Israel; and that they may know that this house which I have built is called by thy name.

44 ¶When thy people go out to battle against their enemies, by whatever way thou shalt send them, and shall pray to the LORD toward the city which thou hast chosen and toward the house that I have built for thy name;

45 Then hear thou in heaven their prayer and their supplication, and maintain their cause.

46 When they sin against thee (for there is no man who does not sin), and thou be angry with them and deliver them to the enemy so that they carry them away captives to the land of their enemies, far or near;

47 Yet if they shall reckon it in their heart in the land to which they have been carried captives, and repent and make supplication to thee in the land of their captivity, saying, We have sinned and have done perversely, we have committed wickedness;

48 And so return to thee with all their heart and with all their soul, in the land of their enemies who carried them away captive, and pray to thee according to the religion of their own land, which thou gavest to their fathers, the city which thou hast chosen and the house which I have built for thy name;

49 Then hear thou in heaven, thy dwelling place, their prayer and their supplication, and maintain their cause,

50 And forgive thy people who have sinned against thee and all their transgressions wherein they have transgressed against thee, and give them compassion in the presence of those who carried them captive, that they may have compassion on them;

51 For they are thy people and thine inheritance, whom thou didst bring forth out of Egypt, from the midst of the furnace of iron;

52 That thine eyes may be open to the supplication of thy servants and to the supplication of thy people Israel, to hearken to them in all that they call for unto thee.

53 For thou didst separate them from among all the people of the earth, to be thine inheritance, as thou didst speak through Moses thy servant, when thou didst bring our fathers out of Egypt, O LORD God.

54 And it came to pass, when Solomon had finished praying all this prayer and supplication unto the LORD God, he arose from before the altar of the LORD, from kneeling with his hands spread up to heaven.

55 And he stood and blessed all the congregation of Israel with a loud voice, saying,

56 Blessed be the LORD God, who has given rest to his people Israel, according to all that he promised; there has not failed one word of all his good promises which he promised by the hand of Moses his servant.

57 The LORD our God be with us, as he was with our fathers; let him not leave us nor forsake us;

58 That he may incline our heart unto him, to walk in all his ways and to keep his commandments and his statutes and his judgments, which he commanded our fathers.

59 And let these my words wherewith I have made supplication before the LORD be near to the LORD our God day and night, that he maintain the cause of his servant and the cause of his people Israel day by day;

60 That all the people of the earth may know that the LORD is God and that there is none else.

61 Let your heart therefore be perfect with the LORD our God, to walk in his ways and to keep his commandments, his covenant, his judgments, and his laws, as at this day.

62 ¶And the king and all Israel with

him offered sacrifice before the LORD.

63 And Solomon offered a sacrifice of peace offerings before the LORD, twenty-two thousand oxen and a hundred and twenty thousand sheep. So the king and all the children of Israel dedicated the house of the LORD.

64 The same day the king consecrated the interior of the court that was before the house of the LORD; for there he offered burnt offerings and meal offerings and the fat of the peace offerings; because the bronze altar that was before the LORD was too little to receive the burnt offerings and the meal offerings and the fat of the peace offerings.

65 And Solomon made a feast on that day, and all Israel with him, a great congregation, from the entrance of Hamath to the entrance of the river of Egypt, before the LORD our God, seven days and seven days, even fourteen days.

66 On the eighth day the people sent a delegation and blessed the king, and went to their tents joyful and glad of heart for all the goodness that the LORD had done for David his servant and for Israel his people.

CHAPTER 9

AND when Solomon had finished the building of the house of the LORD and the king's house and all Solomon's desire which he was pleased to do,

2 Then the LORD appeared to him the second time, as he had appeared to him at Gibeon.

3 And the LORD said to him, I have heard your prayer and your supplication that you have made before me; and I have hallowed for me this house which you have built to put my name there for ever; and my eyes and my heart shall be there perpetually.

4 And as for you, if you will walk before me, as David your father walked in integrity of heart and in uprightness, to do according to all that I have commanded you, and will keep my statutes and my judgments;

5 Then I will establish the throne of your kingdom over Israel for ever, as I promised to David your father, saying, There shall not fail you a man upon the throne of Israel.

6 But if you shall indeed turn from following me, you or your children, and will not keep my commandments and my statutes which I have set before you, but go and serve other gods and worship them;

7 Then I will destroy Israel from the face of the land which I have given them; and this house which I have hallowed for my name will I cast out of my sight; and Israel shall be a proverb and a byword among all peoples;

8 And this house shall be in ruins; every one that passes by it shall be astonished and shall hiss; and they shall say, Why has the LORD done thus to this land and to this house?

9 And they shall answer, Because they forsook the LORD their God, who brought forth their fathers out of the land of Egypt, and have taken hold upon other gods, and have worshipped them and served them; therefore the LORD has brought upon them all this evil.

10 ¶And it came to pass at the end of twenty years, when Solomon had built the two houses, the house of the LORD and the king's house

11 (Now Hiram the king of Tyre had furnished Solomon with cedar trees and fir trees and gold, according to all his desire), that then King Solomon gave Hiram twenty towns in the land of Galilee.

12 And Hiram came out from Tyre to see the cities which Solomon had given him; and they did not please him.

13 And he said, What kind of cities are these which you have given me, my brother? And he called them the land of Cabuli to this day.

14 And King Hiram sent to King Solomon one hundred and twenty talents of gold.

15 ¶And this is the portion of tribute which King Solomon levied to build the house of the LORD and his

own house. And he also built the wall of Jerusalem and Millo and Hazor and Megiddo and Gezer.

16 For Pharaoh king of Egypt had gone up and conquered Gezer and burned it with fire and slain the Canaanites who dwelt in the city and given it as a present to his daughter, Solomon's wife.

17 And Solomon built Gezer and Beth-hauran the lower

18 And Baalath and Tadmor in the land of the wilderness

19 And all the cities for storage that Solomon had, and the cities for the chariots and cities for the horsemen and whatsoever Solomon desired to build in Jerusalem and in Lebanon and in all the land of his dominion.

20 And all the people who were left of the Amorites, the Hittites, the Perizzites, the Hivites, and the Jebusites, who were not of the children of Israel,

21 Their children who were left after them in the land, whom the children of Israel were not able to destroy utterly, Solomon made slaves and tributaries to this day.

22 But of the children of Israel Solomon made no slaves; because they were his men of war and his servants and his princes and his mighty men and commanders of his chariots and his horsemen.

23 These were the superintendents who were over Solomon's work, five hundred and fifty, who had charge of the people and who supervised the work.

24 ¶But Pharaoh's daughter came up out of the city of David to the house which Solomon had built for her; then he built Millo.

25 ¶And three times in a year did Solomon offer burnt offerings and peace offerings upon the altar, and he burned incense upon it before the LORD. So he finished the house of the LORD.

26 ¶And King Solomon built a ship in Ezion-geber, which is beside Eloth, on the shore of the Red Sea, in the land of Arwad.

27 And Hiram sent his servants in the ship, seamen who had knowledge of the sea, with the servants of Solomon.

28 And they came to Ophir and took from there gold, four hundred and twenty talents, and brought it to King Solomon.

CHAPTER 10

AND when the queen of Sheba heard of the fame of Solomon and the name of the LORD, she came to try him out with proverbs.

2 And she came to Jerusalem with a very great train, with camels bearing spices and very much gold and precious stones; and when she was come to Solomon, she tested him with all that was in her heart.

3 And Solomon answered all her questions; there was nothing hidden from the king which he did not tell her.

4 And when the queen of Sheba had seen all Solomon's wisdom and the house that he had built

5 And the food of his table and the order in which his servants sat and the attendance of his ministers and their apparel, and his cupbearers and their clothing and his burnt offerings which he offered in the house of the LORD, she was greatly overcome.

6 And she said to the king, It was a true report that I heard in my own land of your sayings and of your wisdom.

7 Howbeit I did not believe the words until I came, and my own eyes had seen it; and, behold, the half was not told me; your wisdom and prosperity exceed the report which I heard.

8 Happy are your wives, happy are these your servants, who stand continually before you and hear your wisdom.

9 Blessed be the LORD your God, who has delighted in you and has set you upon the throne of Israel; because the LORD loved Israel for ever, therefore he has made you king, to do judgment and justice.

10 And she gave King Solomon one hundred and twenty talents of gold and a very great amount of spices and precious stones; and there came

no more such abundance of spices as these which the queen of Sheba gave to King Solomon.

11 And the ships also of Hiram, that brought gold from Ophir, brought in from Ophir a great amount of sandalwood and precious stones.

12 And the king made of the sandalwood ornaments for the house of the LORD and for the king's house, harps also and psalteries for singers; never before nor since came such sandalwood to this day.

13 And King Solomon gave to the queen of Sheba all that she desired, and whatsover she asked for, besides that which he gave her of his royal bounty. So she turned and went to her own land, she and her servants.

14 ¶Now the weight of gold that came to Solomon in one year was six hundred and sixty-six talents,

15 Besides that which came from the craftsmen and from the traffic of merchants and from all the kings of the Arabs and from the governors of the land.

16 ¶And King Solomon made two hundred shields of pure gold; six hundred minas of gold went into each shield;

17 And three hundred round shields of pure gold; and three hundred minas went into each shield; and the king put them in the house of the forest of Lebanon.

18 ¶Moreover the king made a great throne of ivory, and overlaid it with gold from Ophir.

19 The throne had six steps, and the top of the throne was round behind; and there were arm rests on either side at the place of the seat, and two lions stood on either side of the seat.

20 And twelve lions stood there on the one side and on the other upon the six steps; there was not the like in any kingdom.

21 ¶And all King Solomon's drinking vessels were of gold, and all the vessels of the house of the forest of Lebanon were of pure gold; silver was counted as nothing in the days of Solomon.

22 For the king had at sea a navy of ships of Tarshish with the navy of Hiram; once every three years came the navy from Tarshish, bringing silver and gold, ivory, apes and peacocks.

23 So King Solomon exceeded all the kings of the earth in riches and in wisdom.

24 ¶And all the kings of the earth sought to see the face of Solomon and to hear the wisdom which God had put in his heart.

25 And they brought every man his present, vessels of gold and vessels of silver, garments, armor, spices, horses, fancy chariots, and mules, year by year.

26 ¶And Solomon gathered together chariots and horsemen; and he had a thousand and four hundred chariots and twelve thousand horsemen, and he left some of the chariots in the cities and kept others with the king in Jerusalem.

27 And King Solomon made silver to be as plentiful in Jerusalem as stones, and he made cedar as abundant as sycamore trees that are on the plain.

28 ¶And Solomon had horses brought out of Egypt, and the king's merchants received a commission on the goods they bought.

29 And a chariot was delivered from Egypt for six hundred shekels of silver, and a horse for a hundred and fifty; and so for all the kings of the Hittites and for the kings of Aram, they brought many gifts with their own hands.

CHAPTER 11

BUT King Solomon loved many foreign women, as well as the daughter of Pharaoh, women of the Ammonites, Moabites, Edomites, Zidonians, and Hittites;

2 Of the nations concerning which the LORD had said to the children of Israel, You shall not mix with them, neither shall they mix with you, lest they turn away your heart after their gods; Solomon clung to these in love.

3 And he had seven hundred wives, princesses, and three hundred concu-

bines; and his wives turned away his heart.

4 For it came to pass, when Solomon was old, that his wives turned away his heart after other gods; and his heart was not perfect with the LORD his God, as was the heart of David his father.

5 For Solomon went after Ashtaroth the goddess of the Zidonians, and after Chemosh the god of the Moabites, and after Malcom the god of the Ammonites.

6 And Solomon did evil in the sight of the LORD, and went not fully after the LORD, as did David his father.

7 Then Solomon built a high place for Chemosh the god of Moab, on the mountain that is before Jerusalem, and for Malcom the god of the Ammonites.

8 And likewise did he for all his foreign wives, who burned incense and sacrificed to their gods.

9 ¶And the LORD was angry with Solomon, because his heart was turned from the LORD God of Israel, who had appeared to him twice,

10 And had commanded him concerning this thing, that he should not go after other gods; but he kept not that which the LORD commanded him.

11 Therefore the LORD said to Solomon, Forasmuch as you have done this, and you have not kept my covenant and my statutes and my commandments, which I have commanded you, I will surely rend the kingdom from you and will give it to your servant.

12 Nevertheless, in your days I will not do it for David my servant's sake; but I will rend it out of the hand of your son.

13 However I will not rend away all the kingdom; but will give one tribe to your son for David my servant's sake and for Jerusalem's sake, the city which I have chosen.

14 ¶And the LORD stirred up an adversary against Solomon, Hadad the Edomite; he was of the royal family in Edom.

15 For when David destroyed Edom, and Joab the commander of the army went up to bury the slain, he slew every male in Edom

16 (For Joab and all Israel with him remained there six months, until he had slain every male in Edom);

17 But Hadad fled, he and certain Edomites from among his father's servants into Egypt, Hadad being yet a little boy.

18 They set out from Midian and came to Paran; and they took men with them out of Paran and went into Egypt, to Pharaoh king of Egypt, who gave him a house and food, and said to him, Dwell with me; and gave him land.

19 And Hadad found great favor in the sight of Pharaoh, so that he gave him to wife the sister of his own wife, the sister of Tahpenes the queen.

20 And the sister of Tahpenes bore him Genubath his son, whom Tahpenes weaned in Pharaoh's house; and Genubath was in Pharaoh's household among the sons of Pharaoh.

21 And when Hadad heard in Egypt that David slept with his fathers and that Joab the commander of the army was dead, Hadad said to Pharaoh, Let me depart that I may go to my own country.

22 But Pharaoh said to him, What have you lacked with me that, behold, you seek to go to your own country? And he answered, Nothing; but do let me go.

23 ¶God also stirred up against Solomon another adversary, Hidron the son of Eliadah, who had fled from his lord Hadarezer king of Zobah;

24 And he gathered men to him, and became captain over a band, when David slew the people of Zobah; and they went to Damascus and dwelt in it, and Hadad reigned in Damascus.

25 And he was an adversary to Israel all the days of Solomon, because of the evil which he did; and Hadad oppressed the children of Israel and reigned over Aram [1] (Syria).

26 ¶And Jeroboam the son of Nebat, an Ephrathite of Zedda, Solomon's servant, whose mother's name

[1] At this time the King of Aram was an Edomite.

was Zoriah, a widow, even he lifted up his hand against King Solomon.

27 And this was the reason why he lifted up his hand against King Solomon. When Solomon built Millo and repaired the breaches of the city of David,

28 The man Jeroboam was a mighty man of valour; and Solomon, seeing that the young man was valiant, made him ruler over all the charge of the house of Joseph.

29 And it came to pass at the time when Jeroboam went out of Jerusalem that the prophet Ahijah the Shilonite encountered him on the road; and Ahijah had clad himself with a new garment; and the two of them were alone in a field;

30 And Ahijah caught the new garment that was on him, and tore it into twelve pieces;

31 And he said to Jeroboam, Take for yourself ten pieces; for thus says the LORD God of Israel, Behold, I will rend the kingdom out of the hand of Solomon, and will give ten tribes to you

32 (But he shall have one tribe for my servant David's sake and for Jerusalem's sake, the city which I have chosen out of all the tribes of Israel);

33 Because he has forsaken me and has worshipped Ashtaroth the goddess of the Zidonians, and Chemosh the god of the Moabites, and Malcom the god of the Ammonites, and has not walked in my ways and has not done that which is right in my eyes and has not kept my statutes and my judgments, as did David his father.

34 Nevertheless I will not take the whole kingdom out of his hand; but I will make him a ruler all the days of his life for David my servant's sake, whom I chose because he kept my commandments and my statutes;

35 But I will take the kingdom out of his son's hand and will give it to you, ten tribes.

36 And to his son I will give one tribe, that David my servant may have an heir always before me in Jerusalem, the city which I have chosen for myself to put my name there.

37 And I will give it to you, and you shall reign according to all that your soul desires, and you shall be king over Israel.

38 And if you shall hearken to all that I command you and will walk in my ways and do what is right in my sight and keep my statutes and my commandments, as David my servant did, I will be with you, and build you a sure house, as I built for David my servant, and will give Israel to you.

39 And for this I will afflict the descendants of David, but not for ever.

40 Solomon sought therefore to kill Jeroboam. And Jeroboam arose and fled to Egypt, to Shishak king of Egypt, and was in Egypt until the death of Solomon.

41 ¶And the rest of the acts of Solomon and all that he did and his wisdom, behold, they are written in the Book of the Acts of Solomon.

42 And the time that Solomon reigned in Jerusalem over all Israel was forty years.

43 And Solomon slept with his fathers and was buried in the city of David his father; and Rehoboam his son reigned in his stead.

CHAPTER 12

AND Rehoboam went to Shechem; for all Israel were come to Shechem to make him king.

2 And when Jeroboam the son of Nebat, who was yet in Egypt, heard of it (for he had fled from the presence of King Solomon, and Jeroboam dwelt in Egypt)

3 Then they sent and called him. And Jeroboam and all the people of Israel came, and spoke to Rehoboam, saying,

4 Your father made our yoke harsh; now therefore lighten some of the grievous service of your father, and his heavy yoke which he put upon us, and we will serve you.

5 And he said to them, Depart yet for three days, then come again to me. So all the people departed.

6 ¶And King Rehoboam consulted

with the old men who had stood before his father while he was still alive, and said to them, How do you advise that I may answer the people?

7 And they said to him, If you will be a servant to this people this day and will serve them and answer them and speak good words to them, then they will be your servants for ever.

8 But he forsook the counsel which the old men had given him and consulted with the young men who were grown up with him and who stood before him;

9 And he said to them, What counsel do you give, that we may answer the people who have spoken to me, saying, Make the yoke which your father did put upon us lighter?

10 And the young men who were grown up with him spoke to him, saying, Thus shall you speak to the people who have said to you, Your father made our yoke heavy, but make you it lighter for us; thus shall you say to them, My little finger is thicker than my father's thumb.

11 And now whereas my father laid a heavy yoke upon you, I will add to your yoke; my father has chastised you with whips, but I will chastise you with knouts.

12 ¶So Jeroboam and all the people came to Rehoboam the third day, as the king had commanded them, saying, Come to me again the third day.

13 And the king answered the people harshly, and forsook the old men's counsel that they gave him;

14 And spoke to them according to the counsel of the young men, saying, My father made your yoke heavy, but I will add to your yoke; my father also chastised you with whips, but I will chastise you with knouts.

15 Wherefore the king did not listen to the people; for the stirring of strife was from the LORD, that the LORD might perform his saying which he spoke by his servant Ahijah the prophet, the Shilonite, unto Jeroboam the son of Nebat.

16 ¶So when all Israel saw that the king did not listen to them, the people answered the king, saying, We have no portion in David, neither have we inheritance in the son of Jesse; to your tents, O Israel; now see to your own house, David. So Israel departed unto their tents.

17 And the children of Israel dwelt in their cities; but Judah made Rehoboam the son of Solomon king over them.

18 Then King Rehoboam sent Adoniram, who was over the tribute; and all Israel stoned him with stones. and he died. Therefore King Rehoboam made haste to ride in his chariot to flee to Jerusalem.

19 So Israel has rebelled against the house of David to this day.

20 And when all Israel heard that Jeroboam had returned, they sent and called him to the congregation and made him king over all Israel; there was none that followed the house of David but the tribe of Judah only.

21 ¶And when Rehoboam was come to Jerusalem, he assembled all the house of Judah and the tribe of Benjamin a hundred and eighty thousand chosen men of war to fight against the house of Israel, to bring the kingdom again to Rehoboam the son of Solomon.

22 But the word of the LORD came to Shemaiah the prophet of God, saying,

23 Speak to Rehoboam, the son of Solomon, king of Judah, and to all the house of Judah and Benjamin, and to the remnant of the people, saying,

24 Thus says the LORD: You shall not go up, nor fight against your brethren the children of Israel; return every man to his house; for this thing is from me. They hearkened therefore to the word of the LORD, and returned according to the word of the LORD.

25 ¶Then Jeroboam built Shechem in mount Ephraim and dwelt therein; and went out from thence, and built Penuel.

26 And Jeroboam said in his heart, Now the kingdom will return to the house of David;

27 If this people go up to do sacri-

fices at the house of the LORD in Jerusalem, then shall the heart of this people turn again to their lord, even to Rehoboam king of Judah, and they shall kill me and return to Rehoboam king of Judah.

28 So the king took counsel, and made two calves of gold, and said to all Israel, It is too much for you to go up to Jerusalem; behold your gods, O Israel, who brought you up out of the land of Egypt!

29 And he set the one in Beth-el, and the other he put in Dan.

30 And this thing became a sin; for the people went to worship before the one, even unto Dan.

31 And he made a temple of idols, and made priests from among the people who were not of the sons of Levi.

32 And Jeroboam made a feast in the eighth month, on the fifteenth day of the month, like the feast that is in Judah, and he went up to the altar to offer sacrifices. So did he in Beth-el, sacrificing to the calves that he had made; and he appointed in Beth-el priests for the temples of idols which he had made.

33 And he went to the altar which he had made in Beth-el, on the fifteenth day of the eighth month, even in the month which he had devised of his own heart; and made a feast to the children of Israel; and he went up to the altar to burn incense.

CHAPTER 13

AND, behold, there came a prophet out of Judah by the word of the LORD to Beth-el; and Jeroboam was standing by the altar to burn incense on the fifteenth day of the month, according to the feast which was in Judah. And he burned incense on the altar.

2 And the prophet cried against the altar by the word of the LORD, and said, O altar, altar, hear the word of the LORD, thus says the LORD: Behold, a son shall be born to the house of David, Josiah by name; and upon you he shall offer the priests of the temples of idols who burn incense upon you, and men's bones shall be burnt upon you.

3 And he gave a sign the same day, saying, This is the sign which the LORD has sent me: Behold, the altar shall be rent, and the ashes that are upon it shall be poured out.

4 And when the king heard the saying of the prophet of God which he had cried against the altar in Beth-el, the king, standing at the altar, put forth his hand, saying, Lay hold on him. And his hand which he put forth against him, dried up, so that he could not draw it back again to him.

5 The altar also was broken, and the ashes which were upon it poured out, according to the sign which the prophet of God had given by the word of the LORD.

6 And the king answered and said to the prophet of God, Pray for me before the LORD your God, and entreat for me that my hand may be restored to me. And the prophet of God prayed before the LORD, and the king's hand was restored to him, and it became as it was before.

7 And the king said to the prophet of God, Come home with me to eat and I will give you presents.

8 And the prophet of God said to him, If you give me half your house, I will not go home with you, neither will I eat bread nor drink water in this place.

9 For so it was charged me by the word of the LORD, saying, Eat no bread, and drink no water, nor return again by the way that you came.

10 So he went by another way, and did not return by the way that he came to Beth-el.

11 ¶Now there dwelt an old prophet in Beth-el; and his sons came and told him all the works that the prophet of God had done that day in Beth-el; and the words which he had spoken to the king, them they told also to their father.

12 And their father said to them, Which way did he go? And his sons showed him the way by which the prophet of God went, who came from Judah.

13 And he said to his sons, Saddle

me the ass. So they saddled him the ass; and he rode on it,

14 And went after the prophet of God, and found him sitting under an oak; and he said to him, Are you the prophet of God who came from Judah? And he said, I am.

15 Then he said to him, Come home with me and eat bread.

16 And he answered, I cannot return with you nor go to your house; neither will I eat bread with you, nor drink water in this place;

17 For so it was said to me by the word of the LORD, You shall not eat bread nor drink water there, nor return again by the same way that you came.

18 He said to him, I am a prophet also as are you; and an angel spoke to me by the word of the LORD, saying, Bring him back with you into your house, that he may eat bread and drink water. But he lied to him.

19 So he went back with him, and did eat bread in his house and drank water.

20 ¶And as they sat at the table, the word of the LORD came to the prophet who brought him back;

21 And he cried to the prophet of God who came from Judah and said to him, Thus says the LORD, Because you have disobeyed the word of the LORD and have not kept the commandment which the LORD your God commanded you,

22 But have come back and have eaten bread and drunk water in the place of which the LORD said to you, You shall not eat bread, nor drink water; therefore your corpse shall not come into the sepulchre of your fathers.

23 ¶And after the two prophets had eaten bread and had drunk, they saddled the ass for the prophet of God.

24 And when he was gone, a lion met him by the way and slew him; and his corpse was cast in the way, and the ass stood beside, and the lion also stood by the corpse.

25 And, behold, men passed by and saw the corpse cast in the way and the ass standing beside it, and the lion also standing beside the corpse; and

they came and told it in the city where the old prophet dwelt.

26 And when the prophet who brought him back from the way heard of it, he said, It is the prophet of God who disobeyed the word of the LORD; therefore the LORD has delivered him to the lion, which has torn him and slain him, according to the word of the LORD, which he spoke to him.

27 And he said to his sons, Saddle me the ass, and they saddled it.

28 And he went and found the corpse cast in the way, and the ass and the lion standing beside the corpse; the lion had not eaten the corpse nor torn the ass.

29 And the prophet took up the corpse of the prophet of God, and laid it upon the ass and brought it back to the city where the old prophet dwelt, to mourn over him and to bury him.

30 And he laid his corpse in the grave; and he mourned over him, saying, Alas, my brother! Alas, my brother!

31 And after he had buried him, he said to his sons, When I die, bury me in the sepulchre wherein the prophet of God is buried; lay my bones beside his bones;

32 For the saying which he cried out by the word of the LORD against the altar in Beth-el and against all the temples of idols which are in the cities of Samaria shall surely come to pass.

33 ¶After this thing Jeroboam did not turn from his evil way, but made again from among the people priests for the temples of idols; whosoever would become a priest, he offered an offering and thus became the priest of the temple of idols.

34 And this thing became a sin to the house of Jeroboam, even to cut it off, and to destroy it from off the face of the earth.

CHAPTER 14

AT that time Abijah the son of Jeroboam fell sick.

2 And Jeroboam said to his wife,

Arise and disguise yourself, that people may not know that you are the wife of Jeroboam; and go to Shiloh; behold, Ahijah the prophet is there, who told me that I should be king over this people.

3 And take with you ten loaves of bread and dried fruits and a pot of honey, and go to him; he shall tell you what shall become of the child.

4 And Jeroboam's wife did so, and arose and went to Shiloh, and came to the house of Ahijah. But Ahijah could not see; for his eyes were dim because of his age.

5 ¶And the LORD said to Ahijah, Behold, the wife of Jeroboam is coming to you, to ask word of you concerning her son, for he is sick; thus and thus shall you say to her; for it shall be, when she comes in, behold, she has disguised herself.

6 And when Ahijah heard the sound of her feet, as she came in at the door, he said, Come in, wife of Jeroboam; why do you disguise yourself? For I am sent to you with heavy tidings.

7 Go, tell Jeroboam, Thus says the LORD God of Israel: Forasmuch as I exalted you from among the people and made you ruler over my people Israel,

8 And tore the kingdom away from the house of David and gave it to you; and yet you have not been like my servant David, who kept my commandments and followed me with all his heart, to do that only which was right in my sight;

9 But you have done more evil than all who were before you; for you have gone and made for yourself molten gods, to provoke me to anger, and have cast me behind your back;

10 Therefore, behold, I will bring evil upon the house of Jeroboam, and will cut off from Jeroboam every male and him that possesses authority in Israel, and I will glean after the house of Jeroboam as they glean the vines of the vineyard when the gathering of the grapes is over.

11 Him that dies of Jeroboam in the city shall the dogs eat; and him that dies in the field shall the fowls of the air eat; for the LORD has spoken it.

12 Arise therefore, go to your own house; and when your feet enter into the city, the child shall die.

13 And all Israel shall mourn for him and bury him; for he only of Jeroboam shall come to the grave, because in him there is found some good thing in the sight of the LORD God of Israel in the house of Jeroboam.

14 Moreover the LORD shall raise up for himself a king over Israel who shall cut off the house of Jeroboam from that day.

15 And henceforth the LORD shall smite Israel as a reed is shaken by the wind, and he shall uproot Israel out of this good land which he gave to their fathers, and shall scatter them beyond the river (Euphrates), because they have made for themselves idols and have provoked the LORD to anger.

16 And he shall deliver Israel up because of the sins of Jeroboam, who did sin and caused Israel to sin.

17 ¶Then Jeroboam's wife arose and departed and came to Tirzah; and when she came to the threshold of her house, the child died;

18 And all Israel mourned over him, and buried him, according to the word of the LORD which he spoke by his servant Ahijah the prophet, the Shilonite.

19 And the rest of the acts of Jeroboam, how he warred and how he reigned, behold, they are written in the Book of the Chronicles of the Kings of Israel.

20 And the days which Jeroboam reigned over Israel were twenty-two years; and Jeroboam slept with his fathers, and Nadab his son reigned in his stead.

21 ¶And Rehoboam the son of Solomon reigned over Judah. Rehoboam was forty-one years old when he began to reign, and he reigned seventeen years in Jerusalem, the city which the LORD did choose out of all the tribes of Israel, to put his name there. And his mother's name was Naamah, an Ammonitess.

22 And Judah did evil in the sight of the LORD, and they provoked him to indignation in everything that their fathers had done and in their sins which they had committed.

23 For they also built for themselves high places and statues and idols on every high hill and under every green tree.

24 And there were also Sodomites in the land; and they did according to all the abominations of the nations which the LORD had destroyed before the children of Israel.

25 ¶And it came to pass in the fifth year of King Rehoboam, Shishak king of Egypt came up against Jerusalem;

26 And he took away the treasures of the house of the LORD and the treasures of the king's house; he even took away all the shields of gold which Solomon had made.

27 And King Rehoboam made in their stead shields of brass, and committed them into the hands of the chiefs of the guard who kept the door of the king's house.

28 And it was so, when the king went into the house of the LORD, the guards bore them and brought them back into the guard chamber.

29 ¶Now the rest of the acts of Rehoboam and all that he did, behold, they are written in the Book of the Chronicles of the Kings of Judah.

30 And there was war between Rehoboam and Jeroboam all their days.

31 And Rehoboam slept with his fathers and was buried in the city of David. And Abijah his son reigned in his stead.

CHAPTER 15

NOW in the eighteenth year of King Jeroboam the son of Nebat, Abijah reigned over Judah.

2 He reigned for three years in Jerusalem. And his mother's name was Maacah, the daughter of Abedshalom.

3 And he walked in all the sins of his father, which he had committed before him; and his heart was not perfect with the LORD his God, like the heart of David his father.

4 Nevertheless for David's sake did the LORD God give him an heir in Jerusalem, to set up his son after him and to establish him in Jerusalem;

5 Because David did that which was right in the sight of the LORD his God and did not turn aside from anything that he commanded him all the days of his life, except in the matter of Uriah the Hittite.

6 And there was war between Abijah the son of Rehoboam and Jeroboam all the days of their lives.

7 Now the rest of the acts of Abijah and all that he did, behold, they are written in the Book of the Chronicles of the Kings of Judah.

8 And Abijah slept with his fathers; and they buried him in the city of David; and Asa his son reigned in his stead.

9 ¶And in the twentieth year of Jeroboam king of Israel, Asa reigned over Judah.

10 And he reigned forty-one years in Jerusalem, and his mother's name was Maacah, the daughter of Abedshalom.

11 And Asa did that which was right in the sight of the LORD, as did David his father.

12 And he put the Sodomites out of the land and removed all the idols that his fathers had made.

13 Moreover he removed Maacah his mother from being queen, because she used to make a feast to her idol, and Asa destroyed her idol and burned it at the brook Kidron.

14 But the high places he did not remove; nevertheless Asa's heart was perfect with the LORD his God all his days.

15 And he brought the things which his fathers had dedicated and the things which he himself had dedicated into the house of the LORD, silver and gold and vessels.

16 ¶And there was war between Asa and Baasha king of Israel all their days.

17 And Baasha king of Israel went up against Judah and built Ramtha, and did not permit any to go out or come in to Asa king of Judah.

18 Then Asa took all the silver and

27

the gold that were left in the treasures of the house of the LORD, and the treasures of the king's house, and delivered them into the hand of his servants; and Asa king of Judah sent them to Bar-hadad, the son of Tabrimon, the son of Hezion, king of Aram, who dwelt in Damascus, saying,

19 There is a league between me and you and between my father and your father; behold, I have sent to you a present of silver and gold; come and break your league with Baasha king of Israel, that he may withdraw from me.

20 So when Bar-hadad heard from Asa, he sent the commanders of his armies against the cities of Israel and destroyed Ijon and Dan and Abel-beth-maacah and all the towns that are in all the land of Naphtali.

21 And when Baasha heard of it, he left off building Ramtha and dwelt in Tirzah.

22 Then King Asa made a proclamation throughout all Judah; none was exempted; and they carried away the stones of Ramtha and its timber with which Baasha had built it; and King Asa built with them Geba of Benjamin, and Mizpeh.

23 The rest of the acts of Asa and all his might and all that he did and the cities which he built, behold, they are written in the Book of the Chronicles of the Kings of Judah. But in the time of his old age he was diseased in his feet.

24 And Asa slept with his fathers and was buried with his fathers in the city of David his father; and Jehoshaphat his son reigned in his stead.

25 ¶And Nadab the son of Jeroboam began to reign over Israel in the second year of Asa king of Judah, and he reigned over Israel two years.

26 And he did evil in the sight of the LORD, and walked in the way of his father and in his sins wherewith he made Israel to sin.

27 ¶And Baasha the son of Ahijah, of the house of Issachar, conspired against him and slew him in Gath, which belonged to the Philistines; for Nadab and all Israel laid siege to Gath.

28 So Baasha slew him in the third year of Asa king of Judah, and reigned in his stead.

29 And when he reigned, he smote all the house of Jeroboam; he left not to Jeroboam any that breathed, until he had destroyed him, according to the saying of the LORD which he spoke by his servant Ahijah the prophet, the Shilonite;

30 Because of the sins of Jeroboam the son of Nebat which he sinned and which he made Israel sin, by his great provocation with which he provoked the LORD God of Israel to anger.

31 ¶Now the rest of the acts of Nadab and all that he did, behold, they are written in the Book of the Chronicles of the Kings of Israel.

32 And there was war between Baasha and Asa the king of Judah all their days.

33 In the third year of Asa king of Judah, Baasha the son of Ahijah began to reign over all Israel in Tirzah, twenty-four years.

34 And he did evil in the sight of the LORD, and walked in the ways of Jeroboam, the son of Nebat, and in his sins wherewith he made Israel to sin.

CHAPTER 16

THEN the word of the LORD came to Jehu the son of Hanan against Baasha, saying,

2 Thus says the LORD: Forasmuch as I have exalted you out of the dust and made you a ruler over my people Israel and you have walked in the ways of Jeroboam and have made my people Israel to sin to provoke me to anger with the evil work of their hands;

3 Behold, I will pluck out one by one the posterity of Baasha and the posterity of his house, and I will make his house like the house of Jeroboam the son of Nebat.

4 Him that dies of Baasha in the city shall the dogs eat; and him that dies in the fields shall the fowls of the air eat.

5 Now the rest of the acts of Baasha, and all that he did and all his might, behold, they are written in the Book of the Chronicles of the Kings of Israel.

6 So Baasha slept with his fathers and was buried in Tirzah; and Elah his son reigned in his stead.

7 And also by the prophet Jehu the son of Hanan the word of the LORD came against Baasha and against all his house, because of all the evil that he had done before the LORD, in provoking him to anger with the works of his hands, in being like the house of Jeroboam, and because he killed him.

8 ¶In the twenty-sixth year of Asa king of Judah, Elah the son of Baasha began to reign over Israel in Tirzah, two years.

9 And his servant Zimri, commander of the half of the horsemen, conspired against him as he was in Tirzah, drinking old wine in the house of cedar which he had built in Tirzah.

10 And Zimri went in and smote him and killed him, in the twenty-seventh year of Asa king of Judah, and reigned in his stead.

11 ¶And when he began to reign, as soon as he sat on his throne, he slew all the house of Baasha; he left him not one male child, neither of his kinsfolks nor of his friends.

12 Thus Zimri destroyed all the house of Baasha, according to the word of the LORD which he spoke against Baasha by Jehu the prophet

13 For all the sins of Baasha and the sins of Elah his son which they committed and made Israel to sin in provoking the LORD God of Israel to anger with their idols.

14 Now the rest of the acts of Elah and all that he did, behold, they are written in the Book of the Chronicles of the Kings of Israel.

15 ¶In the twenty-seventh year of Asa king of Judah, Zimri reigned seven days in Tirzah. And the people were encamped against Gath, which belonged to the Philistines.

16 And the people who were encamped heard the news that Zimri had conspired, and had also slain the king; wherefore all Israel made Omri, the commander of the army, king over Israel that day in the camp.

17 And Omri went up from Gath, and all Israel with him, and they besieged Tirzah.

18 And when Zimri saw that the city was taken, he went into the shrine of the king's house and burned the king's house over him with fire, and died,

19 Because of the sins which he committed in doing evil in the sight of the LORD, in walking in the ways of Jeroboam the son of Nebat, and the sins which he did to make Israel sin.

20 Now the rest of the acts of Zimri and the treason that he wrought, behold, they are written in the Book of the Chronicles of the Kings of Israel.

21 ¶Then the people of Israel were divided into two parts: half of the people followed Tibni the son of Ginath to make him king, and half followed Omri.

22 But the people who followed Omri prevailed against the people who followed Tibni; so Tibni died and Omri reigned.

23 ¶In the thirty-first year of Asa king of Judah, Omri began to reign over Israel, and reigned for twelve years; six years he reigned in Tirzah.

24 And he bought the hill of Samaria from Shemer for one talent of silver, and he built on the hill, and called the name of the city which he built after the name of Shemer, the owner of the hill of Samaria.

25 ¶But Omri did evil in the sight of the LORD, and did worse than all the kings who were before him.

26 And he walked in all the ways of Jeroboam the son of Nebat and in his sins wherewith he made Israel to sin, to provoke the LORD God of Israel to anger with their idols.

27 Now the rest of the acts of Omri, and all that he did and all his might, behold, they are written in the Book of the Chronicles of the Kings of Israel.

28 So Omri slept with his fathers

and was buried in Samaria; and Ahab his son reigned in his stead.

29 ¶And in the thirty-eighth year of Asa king of Judah, Ahab the son of Omri began to reign over Israel; and Ahab the son of Omri reigned over Israel in Samaria twenty-two years.

30 And Ahab the son of Omri did evil in the sight of the LORD above all who were before him.

31 And as though it had been a light thing for him to walk in the sins of Jeroboam the son of Nebat, he went and took to wife Jezebel the daughter of Ethbaal king of the Zidonians, and went and served Baal and worshipped him.

32 And he erected an altar for Baal in the house of Baal which he had built in Samaria.

33 And Ahab served idols; and Ahab did more to provoke the LORD God of Israel to anger than all the kings of Israel who were before him.

34 ¶In his days did Ahab build the accursed place, Jericho; he finished it with the death of Abiram, his firstborn, and set up its gates with the death of his younger son Shacob, according to the word of the LORD, which he spoke by Joshua the son of Nun.

CHAPTER 17

AND Elijah the Tishbite, who was of the inhabitants of Gilead, said to Ahab, As the LORD God of Israel lives, before whom I stand, there shall not be dew nor rain these years but according to my word.

2 And the word of the LORD came to him, saying,

3 Depart from here and turn eastward and hide yourself by the brook of Cherith that is before the Jordan.

4 And you shall drink from the brook; and I have commanded the ravens to feed you there.

5 So he went and did according to the word of the LORD; for he went and dwelt by the brook of Cherith that is before the Jordan.

6 And the ravens brought him bread and meat in the morning, and bread and meat in the evening; and he drank from the brook.

7 But after a while the brook dried up because there had been no rain in the land.

8 ¶And the word of the LORD came to him, saying,

9 Arise, go to Zarephath, which belongs to Zidon, and dwell there; behold, I have commanded a widow there to feed you.

10 So he arose and went to Zarephath. And when he came to the gate of the city, behold, the widow was there gathering sticks; and he called to her and said, Bring me a little water in a vessel, that I may drink.

11 And as she was going to fetch it, he called to her and said, Bring me a morsel of bread in your hand.

12 And she said, As the LORD your God lives, I have nothing but a handful of flour in a pot and a little oil in a cruse; and, behold, I am gathering a few sticks, that I may go in and bake it for me and my son, that we may eat it and die.

13 And Elijah said to her, Fear not; go and do as you have said; but first make a little cake and bring it to me, and afterward make for yourself and your son.

14 For thus says the LORD God of Israel, The pot of flour shall not be spent, and the cruse of oil shall not diminish, until the day that the LORD sends rain upon the earth.

15 And she went and did according to the saying of Elijah; and she and he and her household did eat many days.

16 And the pot of flour was not spent, neither did the cruse of oil diminish, according to the word of the LORD, which he spoke by Elijah.

17 ¶And it came to pass after these things that the son of the woman, the mistress of the house, fell sick; and his sickness was so sore that there was no breath left in him.

18 And she said to Elijah, What have I done to you, O prophet of God? Are you come to me to call my trespasses to remembrance and to slay my son?

19 And Elijah said to her, Give me

your son. And he took him from her bosom, and carried him up into the upper chamber where he abode, and laid him upon his own bed.

20 And he cried to the LORD and said, O LORD God, why hast thou also brought misfortune upon this widow with whom I sojourn, by slaying her son?

21 Then he stretched himself upon the boy three times and cried to the LORD and said, O LORD my God, let this boy's soul return to him again.

22 And the LORD heard the voice of Elijah; and the soul of the boy returned into him again, and he revived.

23 And Elijah took the boy and brought him down from the upper chamber into the house, and delivered him to his mother; and Elijah said to her, See, your son lives.

24 ¶And the woman said to Elijah, Now I know that you are a prophet of God and that the word of the LORD in your mouth is truth.

CHAPTER 18

AND it came to pass after many days, that the word of the LORD came to Elijah in the third year, saying, Go, show yourself to Ahab; and I will send rain upon the earth.

2 And Elijah went to show himself to Ahab. And there was a severe famine in Samaria.

3 And Ahab called Obadiah, who was the steward of his household. (Now Obadiah revered the LORD greatly;

4 For when Jezebel slew the prophets of God, Obadiah took a hundred prophets, and hid them by fifty in a cave, and fed them with bread and water.)

5 And Ahab said to Obadiah, Go through the land, to all fountains of water and to all brooks; perhaps we may find grass to save the horses and mules alive, that we may not lose all the beasts.

6 So they divided the land between them to pass throughout it; Ahab went one way by himself, and Obadiah went another way by himself.

7 ¶And as Obadiah was on the way, behold, Elijah met him; and he recognized him, and fell on his face and said, Is that you, my lord Elijah?

8 And he answered him, It is I; then he said to him, Go, tell your lord, Behold, Elijah is here.

9 And Obadiah said, What sin have I committed, that you would deliver your servant into the hand of Ahab, to slay me?

10 As the LORD your God lives, there is no nation or kingdom whither my lord has not sent to seek you; and when they said, He is not here, he took an oath of the kingdoms and nations, that they had not found you.

11 And now you say to me, Go, tell your lord, Behold, Elijah is here.

12 And as soon as I am gone from you, the Spirit of the LORD will take you up and carry you whither I know not; and so when I come and tell Ahab, and he cannot find you, he shall slay me; but I your servant have revered the LORD from my youth.

13 Has it not been told my lord what I did when Jezebel slew the prophets of God, how I took a hundred of the prophets of the LORD and hid them by fifty in a cave and fed them with bread and water?

14 And now you say to me, Go, tell your lord, Behold, Elijah is here; and he shall slay me.

15 And Elijah said, As the LORD of hosts lives, before whom I stand, I will surely show myself to him today.

16 So Obadiah went to meet Ahab, and told Ahab; and Ahab went to meet Elijah.

17 ¶And when Ahab saw Elijah, Ahab said to him, Are you he who troubles Israel?

18 And Elijah said to him, I have not troubled Israel; but it is you and your father's house, in that you have forsaken the commandments of the LORD and have followed Baal.

19 Now therefore send and gather to me all Israel at mount Carmel and the prophets of Baal four hundred and fifty and the prophets of the idols four hundred and fifty who eat at Jezebel's table.

20 So Ahab sent to all the children of Israel, and gathered the prophets together to mount Carmel.

21 Then Elijah came near to all the people, and said, How long will you halt between two opinions? If the LORD is God, follow him, but if Baal is god, then follow him. And the people answered him not a word.

22 Then Elijah said, I, even I only, remain a prophet of the LORD; but Baal's prophets are four hundred and fifty men.

23 Let them therefore give us two bullocks; and let them choose one bullock for themselves, and cut it in pieces and lay it on wood and put no fire under; and I will prepare the other bullock and cut it in pieces and lay it on wood and put no fire under it;

24 And you call on the name of your gods, and I will call on the name of the LORD my God; and the God who answers by fire, he is God. And all the people answered and said, You have spoken well.

25 Then Elijah said to the prophets of Baal, Choose for yourselves one bullock, and prepare it first; for you are many;

26 And they took the bullock which was given them and prepared it and called on the name of Baal from morning even until noon, saying, O Baal, answer us. But there was no voice nor any that answered. And they cut themselves [1] upon the altar which they had made.

27 And when it was noon, Elijah mocked them and said, Cry with a loud voice; for he is a god; perhaps he is meditating or he is busy or he is on a journey, or perhaps he is asleep and must be awakened.

28 And they cried with a loud voice and they cut themselves after their custom with daggers and lances, until their blood gushed out upon them.

29 And when midday was past, they prophesied until the time of the offering of the evening sacrifice, but there was no voice nor any to answer nor any to listen. Then Elijah said to the prophets of the idols, Now you can move, so that I may prepare my burnt offerings. And they moved aside.

30 And Elijah said to all the people, Come near to me. And all the people came near to him. And he repaired the altar of the LORD that was broken down.

31 And Elijah took twelve stones, according to the number of the tribes of the sons of Jacob, to whom the word of the LORD came, saying, Israel shall be your name;

32 And with the stones he built an altar in the name of the LORD; and he made a trench about the altar, as great as would contain two measures of seed.

33 And he put the wood in order and cut the bullock in pieces and laid it on the wood and said, Fill four jars with water and pour it on the burnt offering and on the wood.

34 And he said, Do it the second time. And they did it the second time. And he said, Do it the third time. And they did it the third time.

35 And the water ran round about the altar; and they filled the trench also with water.

36 And at the time of the offering of the evening sacrifice, Elijah the prophet came near and said, O LORD God of Abraham, of Isaac, and of Israel, let it be known this day that thou art God in Israel and that I am thy servant and that I have done all these things at thy word.

37 Answer me, O LORD, answer me, that all this people may know that thou art the LORD God and that thou hast turned their perverse heart back again.

38 Then the fire of the LORD fell, and consumed the burnt offering and the wood and the stones and the dust, and licked up the water that was in the trench.

39 And when all the people saw it, they fell on their faces; and they said, The LORD, he is God; the LORD, he is God.

40 And Elijah said to them, Seize the prophets of Baal, and let not one of them escape. And they seized them;

---

[1] Pagan priests inflicted injuries to their bodies when they prayed vehemently.

and Elijah brought them down to the brook Kishon and slew them there.

41 ¶And Elijah said to Ahab, Go up, eat and drink; for there is a rushing sound of heavy rain.

42 So Ahab went up to eat and to drink. And Elijah went up to the top of Carmel; and he bent himself down upon the earth, and put his face between his knees;

43 And said to his servant, Go up now, and look toward the sea. And he went up and looked, and said, There is nothing. And Elijah said to him, Go again seven times.

44 And at the seventh time, he said, Behold, there is a little cloud like a man's hand rising out of the sea. And he said to him, Go up, say to Ahab, Mount your horse, and get down before the rain stops you.

45 And while he busied himself here and there, the heavens were black with clouds and wind, and there was a great rain. And Ahab rode, and went to Jezreel.

46 And the hand of the LORD was on Elijah; and he girded up his loins and ran before Ahab till he entered Jezreel.

CHAPTER 19

AND Ahab told Jezebel all that Elijah had done, and how he had slain all the prophets of Baal and the prophets of the shrines with the sword.

2 Then Jezebel sent a messenger to Elijah, saying, So let the gods do to me, and more also, if I do not make your life as the life of one of them by tomorrow about this time.

3 And Elijah was afraid, and he arose and fled for his life, and came to Beer-sheba, which belongs to Judah, and left his disciple there.

4 ¶But he himself went a day's journey into the wilderness, and came and sat down under an oak tree; and he requested for himself that he might die, and said, It is enough for me; now, O LORD, take away my life; for I am not better than my fathers.

5 Then he lay down and slept soundly under the oak tree; and, be-

hold, an angel touched him and said to him, Arise and eat.

6 And he looked, and, behold, there was at his head a cake baked on the coals and a cruse of water. And he did eat and drink, and lay down again.

7 And the angel of the LORD came again the second time and touched him and said, Arise, eat and drink; because the journey is too great for you.

8 And he arose, and did eat and drink, and went in the strength of that food forty days and forty nights as far as Horeb the mount of God.

9 ¶And he entered into a cave and lodged there; and, behold, the word of the LORD came to him, and he said to him, What are you doing here, Elijah?

10 And he said, I have been very zealous for the LORD God of hosts; for the children of Israel have forsaken thy covenant, thrown down thine altars, and slain thy prophets with the sword; and I, even I only, am left; and they seek my life, to take it away.

11 And he said, Go forth and stand upon the mount before the LORD. And, behold, the LORD passed by, and a great and strong wind rent the mountains and broke in pieces the rocks before the LORD; but the LORD was not in the wind; and after the wind an earthquake; but the LORD was not in the earthquake:

12 And after the earthquake a fire; but the LORD was not in the fire; and after the fire a still small voice.

13 And when Elijah heard it, he wrapped his face in his mantle and went out and stood at the entrance of the cave. And, behold, there came a voice to him, and said to him, What are you doing here, Elijah?

14 And he said, I have been very zealous for the LORD God of hosts, because the children of Israel have forsaken thy covenant, thrown down thine altars, and slain thy prophets with the sword; and I, even I only, am left; and they seek my life, to take it away.

15 And the LORD said to him, Go,

return on your way to the wilderness of Damascus; then go and anoint Hazael to be king over Aram; [1]

16 And Jehu the son of Jamshi you shall anoint to be king over Israel; and Elisha the son of Shaphat of Abel-meholah you shall anoint to be prophet in your place.

17 And it shall come to pass, that him who escapes from the sword of Hazael shall Jehu slay; and him who escapes from the sword of Jehu shall Elisha slay.

18 Yet I have left me seven thousand in Israel, all the knees which have not bowed to Baal, and every mouth that has not kissed him.

19 ¶So he departed thence and found Elisha the son of Shaphat, who was plowing, and twelve ploughs were ahead of him, and he was one of the twelve; and Elijah came up to him and cast his mantle upon him.

20 And he left the plough and the oxen and went after Elijah and said to him, Let me kiss my father and my mother, and then I will follow you. And he said to him, Go back again; for what have I done to you?

21 And he returned back from him, and took a yoke of oxen and slew them and boiled their meat with wood from the yokes of the oxen and gave it to the people, and they ate. Then he arose and went after Elijah and ministered to him.

CHAPTER 20

AND Bar-hadad the king of Edom [2] gathered all his army together; and there were thirty-two kings with him, and horses and chariots; and he went up and besieged Samaria and fought against it.

2 And he sent messengers to Ahab king of Israel, and said to him, Thus says Bar-hadad,

3 Your silver and your gold are mine; and the most attractive of your wives and your children are mine also.

4 And the king of Israel answered and said, According to your word,

my lord, O king, I am yours, and all that I have.

5 And the messengers came again, and said, Thus says Bar-hadad, Although I sent to you at first, saying, You shall deliver to me your silver and your gold and your wives and your children;

6 Yet I will send my servants to you tomorrow at about this time, and they shall search your house and the houses of your servants; and whatsoever pleases them, they shall take in their hands and bring back.

7 Then the king of Israel called all the elders of the land and said to them, Know, and see how this man seeks mischief; for he sent to me for my wives and for my children and for my silver and for my gold; and I denied him not.

8 And all the elders and all the people said to him, Do not hearken to him, nor consent.

9 Wherefore he said to the messengers of Bar-hadad, Tell my lord the king, All that you did send for to your servant at the first I will do; but this thing I cannot do. And the messengers departed and brought him word again.

10 And Bar-hadad sent to him and said, The gods do so to me, and more also, if the dust of Samaria in handfuls shall suffice for all the people who are with me.

11 And the king of Israel answered and said, Let him talk; nevertheless, the one who ties a knot is not more able than the one who can untie it.

12 And when Bar-hadad heard this message as he was drinking, he and the kings in the pavilions, he said to his servants, Set yourselves in array against the city.

13 ¶And, behold, a prophet drew near to Ahab king of Israel and said to him, Thus says the LORD, Have you seen all this great army? Behold, I will deliver it into your hands this day; and you shall know that I am the LORD.

14 And Ahab said, By whom? And he said to him, By the young men and

---

[1] Syria was a name later given by the Greeks; derived from Sur (Tyre).
[2] King James, *Syria.* Apparently Syria and Edom were united at this time.

by the princes of the city. Then he said, Who shall begin the battle? And he answered, You.

15 Then he numbered the young men and the princes of the city, and they were two hundred and thirty-two; and after them he numbered all the people, even all the children of Israel, being seven thousand.

16 And they went out at noon, but Bar-hadad was drinking old wine in the pavilions, he and the kings, the thirty-two kings who were come to help him.

17 And the young men and the princes of the city went out first; and Bar-hadad sent out men, and they told him, saying, There are men come out of Samaria.

18 And he said, Whether they have come out for peace, take them alive; or whether they have come out for war, take them alive.

19 So these young men and these princes came out of the city, and the army followed them.

20 And they slew every one his man; and the Arameans fled; and Israel pursued them; and Bar-hadad the king of Aram escaped in chariots with horsemen.

21 And the king of Israel went out and destroyed the horses and chariots, and slew the Arameans with a great slaughter.

22 ¶And, behold, the prophet of God came near to Ahab king of Israel, and said to him, Go, strengthen yourself, and know, and see what you have to do; for at the beginning of the year[1] the king of Aram will come up against you.

23 And the servants of the king of Aram said to him, Their god is a god of the mountains; this is why they triumphed over us; but let us fight against them in the plain, and surely we shall triumph over them.

24 And do this thing: Remove the kings, every one from his command, and put officers in their places;

25 And number for yourself an army like the army that you have lost, horse for horse and chariot for chariot; and we will fight against them in the plain, and surely we shall be stronger than they. And he hearkened to their voice, and did so.

26 And it came to pass at the beginning of the year, that Bar-hadad gave orders to the Arameans, and went up to Aphek to fight against Israel.

27 And the children of Israel were mustered and set in array against them, like two little flocks of goats; but the Arameans filled the country.

28 ¶And a prophet of God drew near to Ahab the king of Israel, and said to him, Thus says the LORD, Because the Arameans have said, The LORD is a god of the mountains, but he is not a god of the valleys, therefore I will deliver all this great army into your hands, and you shall know that I am the LORD.

29 So they encamped, one over against the other, seven days. And on the seventh day the battle was joined; and the children of Israel slew of the Arameans a hundred thousand footmen in one day.

30 But the rest fled to Aphek, into the city; and there a wall fell upon twenty-seven thousand men that were left. And Bar-hadad fled and came into the city into an inner chamber.

31 ¶And his servants came near and said to him, Behold now, we have heard that the kings of Israel are merciful kings; let us put sackcloth upon our heads and gird ropes on our loins and go out to the king of Israel; perhaps he will spare our lives.

32 So they put sackcloth on their heads and girded ropes on their loins, and went to the king of Israel and said to him, Your servant Bar-hadad says, Let me live. And the king said, Is he still alive? He is my brother.

33 Now Bar-hadad was a soothsayer, and the men surmised and quickly caught his meaning, and they said, Behold your brother, Bar-hadad. Then he said, Go, bring him. Then Bar-hadad came forth to him; and Ahab caused him to sit with him in the chariot.

34 And Bar-hadad said to him, The cities which my father took from your father, I will restore; and I will

[1] Spring.

make a market place for you in Damascus, as my father made in Samaria. Then Ahab said, I will send you away with a covenant. So he made a covenant with him and sent him away.

35 ¶And a certain man of the sons of the prophets said to his neighbor according to the word of the LORD, Strike me. But the man refused to strike him.

36 Then he said to him, Because you have not obeyed the voice of the LORD your God, behold, as soon as you are departed from me, a lion shall slay you. And as soon as he departed from him, a lion found him and slew him.

37 Then he found another man and said to him, Strike me. And the man struck him, and wounded him.

38 So the prophet departed and waited for the king by the way, and disguised his face with ashes.

39 And, behold, as the king was passing by, he cried to the king and said, Your servant went out into the midst of the battle; and, behold, a man turned aside, and brought a soldier to me, and said, Keep this man; if by any means he be missing, then shall your life be for his life, or else you shall pay a talent of silver.

40 And as your servant was busy here and there, he was gone. And the king of Israel said to him, So shall your judgment be; you yourself have decided it.

41 And he hasted and wiped off the ashes from his face; and the king of Israel realized that he was of the prophets.

42 And he said to him, Thus says the LORD, Because you have let go out of your hand a man whom I appointed to utter destruction, therefore your life shall go for his life and your people for his people.

43 Then the king of Israel went to his house sad and displeased, and came to Samaria.

CHAPTER 21

AND it came to pass after these things that Naboth the Jezreelite had a vineyard in Jezreel, beside the palace of Ahab king of Samaria.

2 And Ahab spoke to Naboth, saying, Give me your vineyard that I may have it for a vegetable garden, because it is near to my house; and I will give you for it a better vineyard than it; or, if it seem good to you, I will give you its worth in money.

3 And Naboth said to Ahab, The LORD forbid that I should give you the inheritance of my fathers.

4 And Ahab went to his house sad and displeased because of the word which Naboth the Jezreelite had spoken to him; for he had said, I will not give you the inheritance of my fathers. And he laid him down on his bed and turned away his face and would eat no food.

5 ¶But Jezebel his wife came to him and said to him, Why is your spirit so sad, that you refuse to eat food?

6 And he said to her, Because I spoke to Naboth the Jezreelite, and said to him, Give me your vineyard for money; or else, if it please you, I will give you another vineyard for it, better than it; but he answered, I will not give you my vineyard.

7 And Jezebel his wife said to him, Are you really king over Israel? Arise, and eat bread, and let your heart be merry; I will give you the vineyard of Naboth the Jezreelite.

8 So she wrote a letter in Ahab's name and sealed it with his ring, and sent the letter to the elders and to the nobles who dwelt in the city with Naboth.

9 And she wrote in the letter, saying, Proclaim a fast and set Naboth on high among the people;

10 Then bring two wicked men and set them opposite him, and let them testify against him, saying, Naboth has reviled God and the king. And then take him out, and stone him, that he may die.

11 And the men of his city, even the elders and the nobles who dwelt in the city with Naboth, did as Jezebel had sent to them and as it was written in the letter which she had sent to them.

12 They proclaimed a fast and set Naboth on high among the people.

13 And they brought two wicked men, and seated them opposite him; and the wicked men witnessed against Naboth, saying, Naboth reviled God and the king. Then they took him outside the city and stoned him, so that he died.

14 Then they sent to Jezebel, saying, Naboth has been stoned, and he is dead.

15 ¶And when Jezebel heard that Naboth was dead, Jezebel said to Ahab, Arise, take possession of the vineyard of Naboth the Jezreelite, which he refused to give you for money; for Naboth is not alive but dead.

16 And when Ahab heard that Naboth was dead, Ahab rose up to go down to the vineyard of Naboth the Jezreelite, to take possession of it.

17 ¶And the word of the LORD came to Elijah the Tishbite, saying,

18 Arise, go down to meet Ahab king of Israel, who is in Samaria; behold, he is in the vineyard of Naboth the Jezreelite, for he has gone there to possess it.

19 And you shall say to him, Thus says the LORD: Behold, you have killed, and, behold, you have also taken possession; thus says the LORD, In the place where dogs licked the blood of Naboth shall dogs lick your blood, even yours.

20 And Ahab said to Elijah, Have you found me, O my enemy? And he answered, I have found you because you have exalted yourself to do evil in the sight of the LORD.

21 Behold, I will bring evil upon you, and will pluck one by one your posterity, and will cut off from Ahab every male child and every one who has authority in governing Israel,

22 And I will make your house like the house of Jeroboam the son of Nebat and like the house of Baasha the son of Ahijah for the provocation wherewith you have provoked me to anger and made Israel to sin.

23 And of Jezebel also the LORD spoke, saying, The dogs shall eat Jezebel in the inheritance which is in Jezreel.

24 Anyone belonging to Ahab who dies in the city shall the dogs eat; and anyone who dies in the field shall the fowls of the air eat.

25 ¶But there was none like Ahab, who thought to do evil in the sight of the LORD, whom Jezebel his wife incited.

26 And he did very abominably in following idols, just as the Amorites had done, whom the LORD destroyed before the children of Israel.

27 And when Ahab heard these words, he tore his clothes and put sackcloth upon his body and fasted and lay in sackcloth and walked barefooted.

28 And the word of the LORD came to Elijah the Tishbite, saying,

29 Have you seen how Ahab has humbled himself before me? Because he has humbled himself before me, I will not bring the evil in his days; but in his son's days will I bring the evil upon his house.

CHAPTER 22

AND three years passed without war between Aram and Israel.

2 And it came to pass in the third year, that Jehoshaphat the king of Judah came down to Ahab the king of Israel.

3 And the king of Israel said to his servants, Do you know that Ramath-gilead belongs to us, and how long shall we keep still and not take it out of the hand of the king of Aram?

4 And he said to Jehoshaphat, Will you go with me to battle to Ramath-gilead? And Jehoshaphat said, I will go as you go, my people as your people and my horses as your horses.

5 And Jehoshaphat said to the king of Israel, Enquire, I pray, for the word of the LORD this day.

6 Then the king of Israel gathered the prophets together, about four hundred men, and said to them, Shall I go to Ramath-gilead to battle or shall I forbear? And they said, Go up; for the LORD will deliver the Arameans into the hand of the king.

7 And Jehoshaphat said, Is there not here a prophet of the LORD that we might enquire of him?

8 And the king of Israel said to

Jehoshaphat, There is yet one man by whom we may enquire of the LORD; his name is Micah the son of Imlah; but I hate him, for he does not prophesy good concerning me, but evil. And Jehoshaphat said, Let not the king say so.

9 Then the king of Israel called a eunuch and said, Make haste and bring here Micah the son of Imlah.

10 And the king of Israel and Jehoshaphat the king of Judah were seated each on his throne, clothed with robes of different colors, at the entrance of the gate of Samaria; and all the prophets were prophesying before them.

11 And Zedekiah the son of a Canaanitish woman made for himself horns of iron; and he said, Thus says the LORD: With these you shall pierce the Arameans, until you have destroyed them.

12 And all the prophets prophesied so, saying, Go up to Ramath-gilead and you will triumph; for the LORD shall deliver them into your hands, O king.

13 And the messenger who went to call Micah spoke to him, saying, Behold now the words of the false prophets with one accord have predicted favorably concerning the king; let your word be like the word of one of them, and you also predict favorably.

14 And Micah said, As the LORD lives, whatsoever the LORD says to me, that will I speak.

15 ¶So he came to the king. And the king said to him, Micah, shall we go to Ramath-gilead to battle or shall we forbear? And he answered him, Go up and be victorious; for the LORD shall deliver them into your hand, O king.

16 And the king said to him, How many times shall I adjure you that you tell me nothing but that which is true in the name of the LORD?

17 And Micah said, I saw Israel scattered upon the mountains like sheep that have no shepherd; and the LORD said, These have no master; let them return every man to his own house in peace.

18 And the king of Israel said to Jehoshaphat, Did I not tell you that he would not prophesy good concerning me, but evil?

19 And Micah said, Hear therefore the word of the LORD; I saw the LORD sitting on his throne, and all the host of heaven standing by him on his right hand and on his left.

20 And the LORD said, Who shall persuade Ahab that he may go up and fall at Ramath-gilead? And one said in this manner and another said in that manner.

21 And there came forth a spirit, and stood before the LORD, and said, I will persuade him.

22 And the LORD said to him, By what means? And he said, I will go forth, and will be a lying spirit in the mouth of all his prophets. And he said to him, You shall persuade him and prevail also; go forth and do so.

23 Now therefore, behold, the LORD has put a lying spirit in the mouth of all these your prophets, and the LORD has spoken evil concerning you.

24 But Zedekiah the son of the Canaanitish woman went near and struck Micah on his cheek and said to him, Which way has the Spirit of the LORD departed from me and spoken to you?

25 And Micah said to him, Behold, you shall see in that day, when you shall go into an inner chamber to hide yourself.

26 Then the king of Israel said, Take Micah and deliver him to Amon the governor of the city and to Joash the king's son;

27 And say, Thus says the king: Put this fellow in the prison and feed him with bread of affliction and with water of affliction until I come in peace.

28 And Micah said, If you return in peace, then the LORD has not spoken by me. And he said, Hear, all you people.

29 So the king of Israel and Jehoshaphat the king of Judah went up to Ramath-gilead.

30 And the king of Israel said to

Jehoshaphat, I will disguise myself and enter into the battle; but you put on your robes. And the king of Israel disguised himself and went into the battle.

31 But the king of Aram commanded the thirty-two captains of his chariots, saying, Fight neither with small nor great, save only with the king of Israel.

32 And when the captains of the chariots saw Jehoshaphat, they thought he was the king of Israel. And they turned aside to fight against him; and Jehoshaphat cried out.

33 And when the captains of the chariots saw that he was not the king of Israel, they turned back from pursuing him.

34 And a certain man drew his bow toward him at a venture and smote the king of Israel between the joints of the breastplate; wherefore the king said to the driver of his chariot, Turn around and carry me out of the army; for the pangs of death have come upon me.

35 And the battle grew fiercer that day; and the king was standing in the chariot facing the Arameans, and died that evening; and the blood ran out of his wound into the hollow of his chariot.

36 And at sunset a herald proclaimed throughout the army, saying, Go, every man to his city and every man to his own country.

37 ¶So the king died and was brought to Samaria; and they buried him in Samaria.

38 And they washed the chariot on the hill of Samaria; and they washed his armor; and the dogs licked up his blood, according to the word of the LORD which he spoke.

39 Now the rest of the acts of Ahab and all that he did and the ivory house which he built and all the cities that he built, behold, they are written in the Book of the Chronicles of the Kings of Israel.

40 So Ahab slept with his fathers; and Ahaziah his son reigned in his stead.

41 ¶And Jehoshaphat the son of Asa began to reign over Judah in the fourth year of Ahab king of Israel.

42 Jehoshaphat was thirty-five years old when he began to reign; and he reigned twenty-five years in Jerusalem. And his mother's name was Arubah the daughter of Shilhi.

43 And he walked in all the ways of Asa his father; he did not turn aside from doing that which was right in the sight of the LORD; nevertheless he did not remove the temples of idols; for the people still offered sacrifices and burned incense on the high places.

44 And Jehoshaphat made peace with the kings of Israel.

45 Now the rest of the acts of Jehoshaphat and all the might that he showed and how he warred, behold, they are written in the Book of the Chronicles of the Kings of Judah.

46 And the remnant of the Sodomites, which remained in the days of his father Asa, he removed from the land.

47 There was then no king who reigned in Edom.

48 Jehoshaphat built ships at Tarshish to go to Ophir for gold; but they did not go; for the ships were broken at Ezion-geber.

49 Then Ahaziah the son of Ahab said to Jehoshaphat, Let my servants go with your servants in the ships. But Jehoshaphat would not consent.

50 ¶And Jehoshaphat slept with his fathers, and was buried with his fathers in the city of David his father; and Joran his son reigned in his stead.

51 ¶Ahaziah the son of Ahab began to reign over Israel in Samaria in the seventeenth year of Jehoshaphat king of Judah, and he reigned two years over Israel.

52 And he did evil in the sight of the LORD, and walked in the ways of his father and in the ways of his mother and in the ways of Jeroboam the son of Nebat who made Israel sin;

53 For he served Baal and worshipped him and provoked to anger the LORD God of Israel, according to all that his father had done.

THE SECOND BOOK OF THE

KINGS

commonly called

THE FOURTH BOOK OF THE KINGS

CHAPTER 1

THEN Moab rebelled against Israel after the death of Ahab.

2 And Ahaziah fell down from the balcony of his upper chamber in Samaria, and was injured; so he sent messengers and said to them, Go, inquire of Baal-zebub the god of Ekron whether I shall recover from this injury.

3 But the angel of the LORD said to Elijah the Tishbite, Arise, go up to meet the messengers of the king of Samaria and say to them, Is it because there is no God in Israel that you are going to inquire of Baal-zebub the god of Ekron?

4 Now therefore thus says the LORD: You shall not come down from the bed on which you are lying, but you shall surely die. And Elijah departed.

5 ¶And when the messengers returned to Ahaziah, he said to them, Why have you turned back?

6 And they said to him, A man came up to meet us and said to us, Go, turn again to the man who sent you and say to him, Is it because there is no God in Israel that you are sending to inquire of Baal-zebub the god of Ekron? Therefore thus says the LORD: You shall not come down from the bed on which you are lying, but you shall surely die.

7 And he said to them, What manner of man was he who came up to meet you and told you these words?

8 And they answered him, He was a hairy man and girt with a girdle of leather about his loins. And he said to them, It is Elijah the Tishbite.

9 Then he sent to him a captain of fifty with his fifty. And he went up to him; and he was sitting on top of a mountain. And he said to him, O prophet of God, the king says, Come down.

10 And Elijah answered and said to the captain of fifty, If I am a prophet of God, then let fire come down from heaven and consume you and your fifty. And there came down fire from heaven and consumed him and his fifty.

11 Again he sent to him another captain of fifty with his fifty. And he spoke to him, saying, O prophet of God, thus says the king, Come down quickly.

12 And Elijah answered and said to him, If I am a prophet of God, then let fire come down from heaven and consume you and your fifty. And the fire of God came down from heaven and consumed him and his fifty.

13 ¶And he sent again to him the third time a captain of fifty with his fifty. And the captain of fifty went up and fell on his knees before Elijah and besought him and said to him, O prophet of God, let my life and the lives of these fifty servants of yours who are standing before you be precious in your sight.

14 For behold, there came fire down from heaven and consumed the two captains of the former fifties with their fifties; therefore let now my life be precious in your sight.

15 And the angel of the LORD said to Elijah, Go down with him; be not afraid of him. And he arose and went down with him to the king.

16 And he said to him, Thus says the LORD: Because you have sent messengers to inquire of Baal-zebub the god of Ekron, is it because there is no God in Israel to inquire for his word? Therefore you shall not come down from the bed on which you are lying, but you shall surely die.

17 ¶So he died according to the word of the LORD which Elijah had spoken. And Joram, his brother, reigned in his stead in the second year of Joram the son of Jehoshaphat king of Judah, because he had no son.

18 Now the rest of the acts of Ahaziah and all which he did, behold, they are written in the Book of the Chronicles of the Kings of Israel.

CHAPTER 2

AND it came to pass, when the LORD was about to take Elijah up to heaven by a whirlwind, Elijah and Elisha had departed from Gilgal.

2 And Elijah said to Elisha, Wait for me here, for the LORD has sent me to Beth-el. And Elisha said, As the LORD lives, and as your soul lives, I will not leave you. So they went down to Beth-el.

3 And the sons of the prophets who were at Beth-el came forth to Elisha and said to him, Do you know that today the LORD will take away your master from over you? And he said, Yes, I also know it; hold your peace.

4 And Elijah said to Elisha, Wait for me here; for the LORD has sent me to Jericho. And he said, As the LORD lives, and as your soul lives, I will not leave you. So they came to Jericho.

5 And the sons of the prophets who were in Jericho drew near to Elisha and said to him, Do you know that today the LORD will take away your master from over you? And he answered, Yes, I also know it; hold your peace.

6 And Elijah said to Elisha, Wait for me here; for the LORD has sent me to the Jordan. And he said, As the LORD lives, and as your soul lives, I will not leave you. And they two went on.

7 And fifty men of the sons of the prophets went and stood to watch from afar; and they two stood by the Jordan.

8 Then Elijah took his mantle and wrapped it together and struck the waters of the Jordan, and they were divided half hither and half thither, so that they two crossed on dry ground.

9 ¶And when they had crossed, Elijah said to Elisha, Ask what I shall do for you before I am taken away from you. And Elisha said, Let a double portion of your spirit be upon me.

10 And he said, You have asked too much; nevertheless, if you see me when I am taken from you, it shall be so to you; but if not, it shall not be so.

11 And it came to pass, as they still went on and talked, behold, there appeared a chariot of fire and horses of fire, and separated the two; and Elijah went up by a whirlwind into heaven.

12 ¶And Elisha saw it and he cried, saying, My father, my father, the chariot of Israel and the horsemen thereof. And he saw him no more; and he took hold of his own clothes and tore them in two pieces.

13 Then he took up the mantle of Elijah that had fallen from him, and went back and stood by the bank of the Jordan;

14 And he took the mantle of Elijah that had fallen from him, and struck the waters and said, O LORD, the God of my lord Elijah! And when he also had struck the waters of the Jordan, they parted half hither and half thither; and Elisha went over.

15 And when the sons of the prophets who came to watch at Jericho saw him, they said, The spirit of Elijah rests on Elisha. And they came to meet him, and bowed themselves to the ground before him.

16 ¶And they said to him, Behold now, there are with your servants fifty strong men; let them go and seek your master, lest peradventure the Spirit of the LORD has taken him up and cast him upon one of the

mountains or into one of the valleys. And he said, You shall not send.

17 And when they urged him till he was embarrassed, he said, Send. So they sent therefore fifty men; and they sought him for three days, but found him not.

18 And when they came back to him (while he tarried at Jericho), he said to them, Did I not say to you, Do not go?

19 ¶And the men of the city said to Elisha, Behold, the situation of the city is pleasant, as our lord sees; but the water is bad and the ground is barren.

20 And he said, Bring me a new cruse and put salt in it. And they brought it to him.

21 And he went forth to the spring of water and cast the salt in there, and said, Thus says the LORD: I have healed these waters; there shall not be from thence any more death or barren land.

22 So the waters were healed to this day, according to the saying of Elisha which he spoke.

23 ¶And he went up from thence to Beth-el; and as he was going up along the way, there came forth little boys out of the city and mocked him, saying, Go up, you bald head, go up, you bald head.

24 And he turned back and saw them and cursed them in the name of the LORD. And there came forth two she-bears out of the forest, and tore forty-two of the boys.

25 And he went from thence to mount Carmel, and from there he returned to Samaria.

CHAPTER 3

NOW Joram the son of Ahab began to reign over Israel in Samaria in the eighteenth year of Jehoshaphat king of Judah, and he reigned twelve years.

2 And he did evil in the sight of the LORD; but not like his father and like his mother; for he put away the statue of Baal which his father had made.

3 Nevertheless he clung to the sins of Jeroboam the son of Nebat, who made Israel sin; he did not turn aside from them.

4 ¶Now Mesha king of Moab was a sheepmaster, and he used to bring up to the king of Israel a hundred thousand fat lambs and a hundred thousand rams, with their wool.

5 But it came to pass, when Ahab was dead, the king of Moab rebelled against the king of Israel.

6 ¶And King Joram went out of Samaria at the same time and numbered all Israel.

7 Then he went on and sent to Jehoshaphat king of Judah, saying, The king of Moab has rebelled against me; come with me, let us go to war against Moab. And Jehoshaphat said, I will go up as you go, my people as your people and my horses as your horses.

8 And he said to him, Which way shall we go up? And he answered, By the way of the wilderness of Edom.

9 So the king of Israel went with the king of Judah and the king of Edom, and traveled seven days' journey; and there was no water for the army and for the people who were with them.

10 And the king of Israel said, Alas! truly for this the LORD has called these three kings together, to deliver them into the hand of Moab!

11 But Jehoshaphat said, Is there not here a prophet of the LORD, that we may inquire of the LORD by him? And one of the king of Israel's servants answered and said, Here is Elisha the son of Shaphat, who used to pour water on the hands of Elijah.

12 And Jehoshaphat said, The word of the LORD is with him. So the king of Israel and Jehoshaphat and the king of Edom went down to him.

13 And Elisha said to the king of Israel, What have I to do with you? Go to the prophets of your father and to the prophets of your mother. And the king of Israel said to him, Truly for this the LORD has called these three kings together, to deliver them into the hand of Moab.

14 And Elisha said, As the LORD of hosts lives, before whom I stand, were it not that I regard the presence of

Jehoshaphat the king of Judah, I would not look toward you nor see you.

15 But now bring me a minstrel. And it came to pass, when the minstrel played, the hand of the LORD came upon him.

16 And he said, Thus says the LORD: Let this valley be made full of cisterns.

17 For thus says the LORD: You shall not see wind, neither shall you see rain; yet this valley shall be filled with water, that you may drink, both you and your cattle and your beasts.

18 And this is but a small thing in the sight of the LORD; he will deliver the Moabites also into your hands.

19 And you shall destroy every fortified city and every choice city, and shall fell every good tree and pollute all the springs of water and mar every good piece of land with stones.

20 And it came to pass in the morning, when the sacrifice was offered, that, behold, there came water by the way of Edom, and the land was covered with water.

21 ¶And when all the Moabites saw that the kings were come up to fight against them, they called out all that were able to gird themselves with the sword and stood on the border.

22 And they rose up early in the morning, and the sun shone upon the water, and the Moabites saw the water on the other side as red as blood;

23 And they said, This is blood; the kings are surely slain, and they have killed one another; now therefore, Moab, to the spoil.

24 And when they came to the camp of Israel, the Israelites rose up and smote the Moabites, so that they fled before them; but they continued attacking them, and they devastated Moab.

25 And they destroyed the cities, and on every good piece of land cast every man his stone and filled it; and they polluted every spring of water and felled all the good trees, till the stones in the walls of the capital city were left demolished; and the slingers surrounded it and destroyed it.

26 ¶And when the king of Moab saw that the battle was too sore for him, he took with him seven hundred men who drew swords, to break through to the king of Edom; but he could not.

27 Then he took his eldest son who was to reign in his stead and offered him as a burnt offering upon the wall. And there was great indignation against Israel; and kings departed from Moab and returned to their own country.

CHAPTER 4

NOW a certain woman of the wives of the sons of the prophets cried to Elisha, saying, Your servant my husband is dead; and you know that your servant did fear the LORD; and the creditor has come to take my two sons to be his bondmen.

2 And Elisha said to her, What shall I do for you? Tell me, what have you in the house? And she said, Your handmaid has nothing in the house except a pot of oil.

3 Then he said to her, Go, borrow for yourself vessels from the houses of all your neighbors, even empty vessels; borrow not a few.

4 And then go in, and shut the door upon you and upon your sons, and pour out into all these vessels; and the vessel which is full bring up to me.

5 So she went from him, and entered her house and shut the door upon herself and upon her sons who brought the vessels to her; and she poured out.

6 And when the vessels were full, she said to her son, Bring me more vessels. But her son said to her, There are no more vessels. And the oil stopped.

7 Then she came and told the prophet of God. And he said, Go, sell the oil, and pay your debt, and live, you and your sons, on what is left over.

8 ¶And it came to pass on the morrow, Elisha went and came to Shiloh, where was a wealthy woman; and she constrained him to eat food. So that

whenever he passed by, he turned in there to eat food.

9 And she said to her husband, Behold now, I perceive that the prophet of God is a holy man who passes by us continually.

10 Let us make for him a little upper room, and let us set for him there a bed and a table and a chair and a candlestick, so that when he comes to us, he shall turn in there.

11 And it happened on a certain day, he came there, and he turned in to the upper room and lay there.

12 And he said to Gehazi his servant, Call this Shilomite woman. And when he had called her, she stood before him.

13 And he said to her, Behold, you have shown us all this respect; what is to be done for you? Is there anything to be spoken on your behalf to the king or to the commander of the army? And she answered, I dwell among my own people quite well.

14 Then he said, What shall I do for her? And Gehazi said to him, Verily she has no son and her husband is old.

15 And he said, Call her. And when he had called her, she stood in the door.

16 And he said to her, About this season, you will be with child, and shall embrace a son. And she said, No, my lord, O prophet of God, do not lie to your handmaid.

17 And the woman conceived and bore a son; at the season that Elisha had said to her, she was with child.

18 ¶Now when the child had grown, he went out on a certain day to his father who was with the reapers.

19 And he said to his father, Oh, my head, my head! And his father said to a servant, Take him up and carry him to his mother.

20 And when he had taken him and brought him to his mother, he sat on her knees till noon and then died.

21 And she went up and laid him on the bed of the prophet of God, and shut the door upon him and went out.

22 Then she called to her husband and said, Send me one of the servants and one of the asses, that I may go hastily to the prophet of God.

23 And he said to her, Why will you go to him today? It is neither new moon nor sabbath. But the Shilomite gave orders;

24 And they saddled an ass for her, and she said to the servant, Drive fast; do not stop to dismount me unless I tell you.

25 So she went to the prophet of God at mount Carmel. And when the prophet of God saw her afar off, he said to Gehazi his disciple, Behold, there is the Shilomite:

26 Run now to meet her, and say to her, Is it well with you? Is it well with your husband? Is it well with the child? And she answered, It is well.

27 And when she came to the prophet of God to the mountain, she caught hold of his feet; but Gehazi came near to remove her. And the prophet of God said to him, Let her alone; for her soul is in bitter anguish; and the LORD has hidden it from me and has not told me.

28 Then she said, Did I ask a son of my lord? Did I not say to you, Do not ask a son for me?

29 Then he said to Gehazi, Gird up your loins and take my staff in your hand and go. If you meet any man, do not salute him; and if any man salutes you, do not answer him; and lay my staff upon the face of the child.

30 And the mother of the child said, As the LORD lives and as your soul lives, I will not leave you. And he arose and followed her.

31 And Gehazi went on before them and laid the staff upon the face of the child; but there was neither voice nor hearing. Therefore he returned to meet Elisha, and told him, saying, The child is not awake.

32 And when Elisha was come into the house, behold, the child was dead and lying upon his bed.

33 He went in therefore and shut the door upon the two of them, and prayed unto the LORD.

34 And he went up and lay upon the child and put his mouth upon his mouth, and his eyes upon his eyes,

and his hands upon his hands; and he stretched himself upon him, and the flesh of the child became warm.

35 Then he returned, and walked to and fro in the house; and went up and stretched himself upon him; and the child sneezed seven times, and the child opened his eyes.

36 And Elisha called Gehazi and said to him, Call this Shilomite. So he called her. And when she was come to him, he said to her, Take up your son.

37 Then she went in and fell at his feet and bowed herself to the ground and took up her son and went out.

38 ¶And Elisha returned to Gilgal; and there was a famine in the land; and the sons of the prophets were sitting before him; and he said to his disciple, Set on the great pot, and cook pottage for the sons of the prophets.

39 And one of them went out into the field to gather herbs and found a wild vine in the field and gathered from it his lap full of wild gourds, and came and put them into the pot of pottage; for he did not know what they were.

40 So he poured out for the men to eat. And as they were eating of the pottage, they cried out and said, O prophet of God, there is death in the pot. And they could not eat of it.

41 But he said, Take meal and cast it into the pot; and he said, Pour out for the people, that they may eat. And there was no harm in the pot.

42 ¶And there came a certain man from the city of giants, and brought the prophet of God bread of the first fruits, twenty loaves of barley and new wheat rubbed from the ears in a cloth. And he said, Give to the people, that they may eat.

43 And his servant said, What, should I set this before a hundred men? And Elisha said to him again, Give them to the people, that they may eat; for thus says the LORD, They shall eat and shall leave some.

44 So he set it before them, and they did eat and left some, according to the word of the LORD.

CHAPTER 5

NOW Naaman, general of the army of the king of Aram, was a great man with his master, and honorable, because by him the LORD had given deliverance to Aram; and Naaman was a valiant man, but he was a leper.

2 And the Arameans had gone out raiding, and had brought away captive out of the land of Israel a little maid; and she waited on Naaman's wife.

3 And she said to her mistress, Blessed would be my lord if he would go to the prophet who is in Samaria! for he would immediately cure him of his leprosy.

4 And they went in and told her lord, saying, Thus and thus said the maid who is from the land of Israel.

5 And the king of Aram said to him, Come, go, I will send a letter to the king of Israel. And he departed and took with him ten talents of silver and six thousand pieces of gold and ten changes of garments.

6 And he brought the letter to the king of Israel, and this was written in it: In the hour when this letter reaches you, behold, I have sent to you Naaman my servant that you may heal him of his leprosy.

7 And when the king of Israel had read the letter, he tore his clothes and said, Am I God, to kill and to make alive, that this man sends me a man to heal him of his leprosy? Wherefore consider, and see how he is seeking to pick a quarrel with me.

8 ¶And when Elisha the prophet of God had heard that the king of Israel had torn his clothes, he sent to the king, saying, Why have you torn your clothes? Let him come now to me, and he shall know that there is a prophet in Israel.

9 So Naaman came with his horses and with his chariots, and stood at the door of the house of Elisha.

10 And Elisha sent a messenger to him, saying, Go and wash in the Jordan seven times, and your flesh shall come again to you and you shall be clean.

11 But Naaman was angry, and went away and said, Behold, I thought, He will surely come out to me and stand and call on the name of the LORD his God and wave his hand over the place, and I will recover from the leprosy.

12 Are not Amnan and Pharpar, rivers of Damascus, better than all the waters of Israel? I will go and wash in them and be clean. So he turned and went away in a rage.

13 And his servants came near and spoke to him and said, Our lord, if the prophet had told you to do some great thing, you would have done it; but behold, he has told you to do a small thing. Go and wash, and be clean. And he listened to them and did so.

14 And he went down and washed seven times in the Jordan, according to the saying of the prophet of God; and his flesh came again like the flesh of a little child, and he was clean.

15 ¶And he returned to the prophet of God, he and all his company, and came and stood before him, and said to him, Behold, now I know that there is no God in all the earth but in Israel; now therefore, take this blessing from your servant.

16 But Elisha said, As the LORD lives, before whom I stand, I will receive none. And he urged him to take it; but he refused.

17 And Naaman said, Shall there not then be given to your servant two mules' burden of earth? For your servant will henceforth offer neither burnt offerings nor sacrifices to any other god but to the LORD.

18 In this matter may the LORD forgive your servant, when my master goes into the house of Rimmon to worship there; I am the king's aide and I worship also in the house of Rimmon; and when I worship in the house of Rimmon, the LORD pardon your servant in this matter.

19 And he said to him, Go in peace. So he departed from him a little way.

20 ¶Then Gehazi the disciple of Elisha the prophet of God, said, Behold, my lord has spared Naaman the Aramean, in not accepting from him that which he brought; but, as the LORD lives, I will run after him, and take something from him.

21 So Gehazi ran after Naaman. And when Naaman saw him running after him, he alighted from his chariot to meet him and said to him, Is all well?

22 And he said, All is well. My master has sent me, saying, There have just now come to me from mount Ephraim two men of the sons of the prophets; give them a talent of silver and two changes of garments.

23 And Naaman said, I am willing; take two talents. And he urged him and bound two talents of silver in two pieces of cloth, with two changes of garments, and he gave them to two of his servants; and they carried them before him.

24 And when they came to a secret place, he took them from their hand and put them in the house; and he sent the men away and they departed.

25 But he went in and stood before his master. And Elisha said to him, Where have you been, Gehazi? And he said, Your servant went nowhere.

26 And he said to him, My heart told me when the man alighted from his chariot to meet you. Is it a time to gain money and to gain garments and oliveyards and vineyards and sheep and oxen and menservants and maidservants?

27 The leprosy therefore of Naaman shall cleave to you and to your descendants for ever. And he went out from his presence a leper as white as snow.

CHAPTER 6

AND the sons of the prophets said to Elisha, Behold now, this place wherein we dwell with you is too small for us.

2 Let us go to the Jordan and cut from there every man a beam, and let us make a place for us to dwell there. And he said, Go.

3 And one of them answered and said, If you please, go with your servants. And he answered, I will go.

4 So he went with them. And when

they came to the Jordan, they cut down trees.

5 But as one of them was felling a beam, the axehead fell into the water; and he cried and said, I beseech you, my lord! it was borrowed by your servant.

6 And the prophet of God said to him, Where did it fall? And he showed him the place. And he cut off a stick and thrust it in there; and it stuck in the hole of the axehead.

7 And he said, Take it up to you. And he put out his hand and took it.

8 ¶Then the king of Aram warred against Israel, and took counsel with his servants, saying, In such and such a place shall we lie in wait.

9 And the prophet of God sent to the king of Israel, saying, Beware that you do not pass this place; for the Arameans are lying in wait.

10 And the king of Israel sent to the place of which the prophet of God told him and warned him about it, not once nor twice.

11 Therefore the heart of the king of Aram was sore troubled because of this thing; and he called his servants and said to them, Will you not show me who of us is for the king of Israel?

12 And one of his servants answered, and said, None of us, my lord O king; but Elisha, the prophet who is in Israel, tells the king of Israel the thing that you plan in your bedchamber.

13 ¶And he said, Go and see where he is, that I may send and take him. And it was told him, saying, Behold, he is in Dothan.

14 Therefore he sent there horsemen and chariots and a great army; and they came by night and surrounded the city.

15 And when the servant of the prophet of God arose early and went out, behold, an army surrounded the city both with horses and chariots. And his servant said to him, Alas, my master! what shall we do?

16 And he said to him, Fear not; for those who are with us are more than those who are with them.

17 And Elisha prayed to the LORD and said, O LORD, open his eyes that he may see. And the LORD opened the eyes of the young man; and he saw; and, behold, the mountain was full of horses and chariots of fire round about Elisha.

18 And when they came down to him, Elisha prayed to the LORD and said, Smite this people with dimness of vision. And he smote them with dimness according to the word of Elisha.

19 ¶And Elisha said to them, This is not the way, neither is this the city; follow me, and I will bring you to the man whom you seek. But he led them to Samaria.

20 And when they were come into Samaria, Elisha said, O LORD, open the eyes of these men, that they may see. And the LORD opened their eyes, and they saw; and, behold, they were in the midst of Samaria.

21 And the king of Israel said to Elisha when he saw them, My father, shall I slay them? Shall I slay them?

22 And he answered, You shall not slay them; would you slay those whom you have taken captive with your sword and with your bow? Set bread and water before them, that they may eat and drink and go to their master.

23 So he prepared for them a great banquet; and when they had eaten and drunk, they went to their master. So the raiders of Aram came no more across the border of Israel.

24 ¶And it came to pass after this, that Bar-hadad king of Aram gathered all his army, and went up and besieged Samaria and fought against it.

25 And there was a great famine in Samaria, as they besieged it, until an ass's head was sold for eighty pieces of silver and the fourth part of a cab [1] of dove's dung for five pieces of silver.

26 And as the king of Israel was passing by upon the wall, there cried a woman to him, saying, Help me, my lord, O king.

27 And he said to her, Let the

[1] About a pint, dry measure.

LORD help you; whence shall I help you? Out of the threshing floor or out of the wine press?

28 And the king said to her, What troubles you? And she said to him, This woman said to me, Give your son, that we may eat him today, and we will eat my son tomorrow.

29 So we cooked my son and ate him; and I said to her on the next day, Give your son, that we may eat him; but she had hidden her son.

30 ¶And when the king heard the words of the woman, he tore his clothes as he walked upon the wall, and the people looked, and behold, he was wearing sackcloth within upon his flesh.

31 Then he said, May God do so and more also to me, if the head of Elisha the son of Shaphat shall remain on him this day.

32 But Elisha was sitting in his house and the elders were sitting with him; and the king sent a messenger; but before the messenger came to him, he said to the elders, Do you see how this son of a murderer has sent to take away my head? Look, when the messenger comes, shut the door and push him outside, because the sound of his master's feet is behind him.

33 And while he was still speaking with them, the messenger came to him; and he said, Behold, this evil is from the LORD; why should I pray to the LORD any longer?

CHAPTER 7

THEN Elisha said, Hear the word of the LORD; thus says the LORD: Tomorrow about this time a measure of fine flour shall be sold for a shekel and two measures of barley for a shekel in the gate of Samaria.

2 Then the king's aide answered and said, If the LORD should make windows in heaven, could this thing be? And Elisha said to him, Behold, you will see it with your eyes, but you shall not eat of it.

3 ¶Now there were four leprous men sitting at the entrance of the gate; and they said to one another, Why do we sit here until we die?

4 If we say, We will enter into the city, the famine is severe in the city, and we shall die there; and if we still sit here, we die also. Now therefore come and let us go to the camp of Aram; if they save us alive, we shall live; and if they put us to death, we shall but die.

5 So they rose up early in the twilight to go to the camp of Aram; and when they were come to the uttermost part of the camp, behold, there was no man there;

6 For the LORD had made the army of Aram hear the noise of horses and the noise of chariots and the noise of a great army; and they said to one another, Lo, the king of Israel has hired against us the king of the Egyptians and the king of the Hittites to come upon us.

7 Wherefore they arose and fled in the twilight, and left their tents, their horses, and their asses, even their camp as it was, and they fled for their lives.

8 And when these lepers came to the uttermost part of the camp, they went into a tent and ate and drank and took from there silver and gold and clothing, and went and hid it; then they came again and entered into another tent and carried booty from there also and went and hid it.

9 Then they said one to another, We are not doing right; this day is a day of good tidings, and how long shall we remain silent? If we wait until the morning light, some mischief will come upon us; now therefore come, let us go and tell the king's household.

10 So they came and called to the doorkeepers of the city; and they told them, saying, We went to the camp of Aram, and behold, there was no man there, neither voice of man, but horses tied and asses tied and tents as they were.

11 And the doorkeepers called out and told it to the king's household within.

12 ¶And the king arose in the night and said to his servants, I will now tell you what the Arameans have done to us. They know that we are hungry;

therefore they have gone out of the camp to hide themselves in the field, saying, When they come out of the city, we shall capture them alive and then get into the city.

13 And one of his servants answered and said, Let some horsemen take five of the horses that remain; if they are captured, let them be considered a loss like all the army of Israel that has perished; therefore let us send and see.

14 So two couples of horsemen mounted, and the king sent them after the army of Aram, saying, Go and see.

15 And they went after them as far as the Jordan; and, lo, all the road was full of garments and vessels which the Arameans had left behind in their haste. And the messengers returned and told the king.

16 And the people went out and plundered the camp of Aram. So a measure of fine flour was sold for a shekel and two measures of barley for a shekel, according to the word of the LORD.

17 ¶And the king placed his aide in charge of the gate; and the people trod upon him at the gate and he died, as the prophet of God had said when he came down as a messenger to him.

18 And it came to pass as the prophet of God had foretold to the king, saying, A measure of fine flour for a shekel and two measures of barley for a shekel shall be sold tomorrow at this time in the gate of Samaria.

19 But that mighty man had answered the prophet of God and said, If the LORD should make windows in heaven, could this thing be? And the prophet had said, Behold, you shall see it with your eyes, but you shall not eat of it.

20 And so it happened to him; for the people trod upon him in the gate and he died.

CHAPTER 8

THEN Elisha said to the woman whose son he had restored to life, Arise and go, you and your household, and sojourn wherever you can; for the LORD has called for a famine; and it shall come upon the land for seven years.

2 So the woman arose and did according to the word of the prophet of God; and she went with her household and sojourned in the land of the Philistines seven years.

3 And at the end of the seven years, when the woman returned from the land of the Philistines, she went forth to cry to the king for her house and for her field.

4 And the king talked with Gehazi the servant of the prophet of God, saying, Tell me all the great things that Elisha has done.

5 And while he was telling the king how Elisha had restored a dead body to life, behold, the woman whose son he had restored to life cried to the king for her house and for her field. And Gehazi said, My lord, O king, this is the woman and this is her son whom Elisha restored to life.

6 And when the king asked the woman, she told him. So the king appointed to her a certain officer and said to him, Restore all that was hers and all the produce of her field from the day that she left the land even until now.

7 ¶And Elisha came to Damascus; and Bar-hadad the king of Aram was sick; and it was told him, saying, The prophet of God has come here.

8 And the king said to Hazael, Take a present with you and go to meet the prophet of God, and inquire of the LORD by him, saying, Shall I recover of this disease?

9 So Hazael went to meet him and took a present with him, even of every good thing of Damascus, forty camels' burden, and came and stood before him and said to him, Your son Barhadad king of Aram has sent me to you, saying, Shall I recover of this disease?

10 And Elisha said to him, Go, say to him, You shall surely recover; but the LORD has shown me that he shall surely die.

11 Then the prophet of God wept.

12 And Hazael said, Why does my

lord weep? And Elisha said to him, Because I know the evil that you will do to the children of Israel: their strongholds you will set on fire, their young men you will slay with the sword, and you will dash their children against the ground and rip up their women with child.

13 And Hazael said, But what, is your servant a dog, that he should do this terrible thing? And Elisha answered, The LORD has shown me that you shall be king over Aram.

14 So Hazael departed from Elisha and came to his master; and his master said to him, What did Elisha say to you? And he answered, Thus he said to me: You shall surely recover.

15 And on the morrow, Hazael took a thick cloth and dipped it in water and spread it on the king's face, so that he died; and Hazael reigned in his stead.

16 ¶And in the fifth year of Joram the son of Ahab king of Israel, Joram the son of Jehoshaphat, king of Judah, began to reign.

17 He was thirty-two years old when he began to reign; and he reigned eight years in Jerusalem.

18 And he walked in the way of the kings of Israel, as did the house of Ahab; for the sister of Ahab was his wife; and he did evil in the sight of the LORD.

19 Yet the LORD would not destroy Judah for David his servant's sake, as he promised to him that he would give an heir to his children all the days.

20 ¶In his days Edom revolted from under the hand of Judah and set up a king over themselves.

21 So Joram went over to Zair, and all the chariots with him; and he rose by night to smite the Edomites who had surrounded him and his commanders with chariots; but the people fled to their tents.

22 So Edom revolted from under the hand of Judah even to this day. Then Libnah revolted at the same time.

23 And the rest of the acts of Joram and all that he did, behold, they are written in the Book of the Chronicles of the Kings of Judah.

24 And Joram slept with his fathers and was buried with his fathers in the city of David; and Ahaziah his son reigned in his stead.

25 ¶In the eleventh year of Joram the son of Ahab king of Israel, Ahaziah the son of Joram king of Judah began to reign.

26 Ahaziah was twenty-two years old when he began to reign; and he reigned one year in Jerusalem. And his mother's name was Athaliah, the daughter of Omri king of Israel.

27 And he walked in the way of the house of Ahab, and did evil in the sight of the LORD, as did the house of Ahab; for he was the son-in-law of the house of Ahab.

28 ¶And he went with Joram the son of Ahab to war against Hazael the king of Aram at Ramath-gilead; and the Arameans wounded Joram.

29 And Joram the son of Ahab went back to be healed in Jezreel of the wounds which the Arameans had inflicted on him at Ramath, when he fought against Hazael king of Aram. And Ahaziah the son of Joram king of Judah went down to see Joram the son of Ahab in Jezreel, because he was sick.

CHAPTER 9

THEN Elisha the prophet called one of the sons of the prophets and said to him, Gird up your loins and take this flask of oil in your hand and go to Ramath-gilead;

2 And when you get there, look for Jehu the son of Jimshi, and go in and make him arise up from among his brethren, and bring him into an inner chamber;

3 Then take the flask of oil and pour it on his head, and say to him, Thus says the LORD, I have anointed you king over my people Israel. Then open the door and flee, and do not tarry.

4 ¶So the young prophet went to Ramath-gilead.

5 And when he came in, behold, the commanders of the army were sitting; and he said, I have an errand to you,

O commander. And Jehu said, To which of us? And he said to him, To you, O commander.

6 And he arose and went into an inner chamber; and he poured the oil on his head, and said to him, Thus says the LORD God of Israel, I have anointed you king over the people of the LORD, even over Israel.

7 And you shall smite the house of Ahab your master, that I may avenge the blood of my servants the prophets and the blood of all the servants of the LORD, at the hand of Jezebel.

8 For I will destroy the whole house of Ahab, and I will cut off from Ahab every male and every one in authority in Israel;

9 And I will make the house of Ahab like the house of Jeroboam the son of Nebat and like the house of Baasha the son of Ahijah;

10 And the dogs shall eat Jezebel in the inheritance of Naboth in Jezreel, and there shall be none to bury her. And he opened the door and fled.

11 ¶Then Jehu came forth to the servants of his lord; and they said to him, Is all well? Why did this mad fellow come to you? And he said to them, You know the man, and his folly.

12 And they said to him, You are lying; tell us now. And he said to them, Thus and thus he spoke to me, saying, Thus says the LORD: I have anointed you king over Israel.

13 Then they hastened and took every man his garment and put it under him on the top of the stairs and blew with trumpets, saying, Jehu is king.

14 So Jehu the son of Jimshi conspired against Joram. (Now Joram was holding Ramath-gilead, he and all Israel with him because of Hazael king of Aram.

15 But King Joram had returned to be healed in Jezreel of the wounds which the Arameans had inflicted on him when he fought against Hazael king of Aram.) And Jehu said, If it please you, let no one go forth nor escape out of the city to tell it in Jezreel.

16 So Jehu rode in a chariot and went to Jezreel; for Joram lay there. And Ahaziah king of Judah had come down to see Joram the son of Ahab who was sick in Jezreel.

17 And the watchman was standing on the tower of Jezreel, and he saw the chariot of Jehu as it was coming, and the watchman said, I see chariots. And Joram said, Take a chariot and send it to meet them, and let him say, Is it peace?

18 So there went a horseman to meet him and said to him, Thus says the king: Is it peace? And Jehu said, What have you to do with peace? Turn behind me. And the watchman told, saying, The messenger came to them, but he did not return.

19 Then he sent out a second horseman, who came to them and said, Thus says the king, Is it peace? And Jehu answered, What have you to do with peace? Turn behind me.

20 And the watchman told, saying, The messenger came to them, but he did not return; and the driving is like the driving of Jehu the son of Jimshi; for he drives furiously.

21 And Joram said, Make ready. And they made ready chariots. And Joram king of Israel and Ahaziah king of Judah went out, each in his chariot, and they went to meet Jehu and they met him in the field of Naboth the Jezreelite.

22 And when Joram saw Jehu, he said, Is it peace, Jehu? And Jehu answered, What peace, so long as the whoredoms of your mother Jezebel and her witchcrafts are so many?

23 Then Joram turned back and fled, and said to Ahaziah, There is treachery, O Ahaziah!

24 And Jehu drew a bow with his full strength, and smote Joram in his back, and the arrow went out at his heart, and he sank down in his chariot.

25 Then Jehu said to Bar-dekar his mighty man, Take him up, and cast him into the field of Naboth the Jezreelite; for I remember how when you and I were driving together after Ahab his father, and the LORD said this thing against him;

26 Surely I have seen yesterday the

blood of Naboth and the blood of his sons, says the LORD; and I will requite you in this field, says the LORD. Now therefore take him up and cast him into the field, according to the word of the LORD. So they cast him into the field of Naboth the Jezreelite.

27 ¶But when Ahaziah the king of Judah saw this, he fled by the way of the garden house. And Jehu pursued him, and said, Slay him also, and they slew him in his chariot at the ascent of the mound, which is by Nebleam. And he fled to Megiddo, and died there.

28 And his servants took him and carried him (in a chariot) to Jerusalem, and buried him in his sepulchre with his fathers in the city of David.

29 And in the eleventh year of Joram the son of Ahab, Ahaziah began to reign over Judah.

30 ¶And when Jehu was come to Jezreel, Jezebel heard of it; and she painted her eyelids with kohl, and adorned her head, and looked out a window.

31 And as Jehu entered in at the gate, she said, Is it peace, you Zimri, murderer of his master?

32 And he lifted up his face to the window, and said, Who is on my side? And there looked out at him two or three eunuchs.

33 And he said, Throw her down. So they threw her down; and some of her blood was sprinkled on the wall, and the horses entered and trod her under foot.

34 Then he went in to eat and drink, and he said, See now to this cursed woman, and bury her; for she is a king's daughter.

35 And they went to bury her; but they found no more of her than her skull and her feet and the palms of her hands.

36 And when they returned, they told him, and he said, This is the word of the LORD which he spoke by his servant Elijah the Tishbite, saying, In the field of Jezreel shall dogs eat the flesh of Jezebel;

37 And the corpse of Jezebel shall be as refuse upon the face of the field of Jezreel; and there will be none to bury her, so that they shall not say, This is Jezebel.

CHAPTER 10

AND Ahab had seventy sons in Samaria. And they were brought up by the nobles of the city. And Jehu wrote a letter and sent it to Samaria, to the princes of Jezreel, to the elders, and to those who brought up Ahab's children, saying,

2 Now as soon as this letter reaches you, seeing your master's sons are with you and there are with you chariots and horses, fortified cities also, and weapons;

3 Whichever seems to you good and best of your master's sons, set him on his father's throne and fight for your master's house.

4 But when they heard the letter, they were exceedingly afraid and said, Behold, two kings could not stand before Jehu; how then shall we stand before him?

5 So the overseer of the royal household, the governor of the city, the elders, and those who brought up the children, sent to Jehu, saying, We are your servants and will do all that you shall bid us; we will not make any man king over us; do whatever is good in your eyes.

6 Then he wrote to them a second letter, saying, If you are mine, and if you will hearken to my voice, then take the heads of your master's sons and bring them to me to Jezreel by this time tomorrow. Now the king's sons were seventy persons, and the nobles of the city brought them up.

7 And as soon as the letter reached them, they took the king's sons and slew them, seventy persons, and put their heads in baskets and sent them to him in Jezreel.

8 ¶And there came a messenger, and told him, saying, They have brought the heads of the king's sons. And he said, Lay them in two heaps at the entrance of the gate until morning.

9 And in the morning, he went out and said to all the people, You are righteous; I conspired against my

master and slew him; but who slew all these?

10 Know now that there shall fall to the earth nothing of the word of the LORD, of all which the LORD spoke concerning the house of Ahab; for the LORD has done that which he spoke by his servant Elijah.

11 So Jehu slew all that remained of the house of Ahab in Jezreel, and all his great men and his kinsfolks and his priests, until he left him none remaining.

12 ¶And he arose and departed and came to Samaria. And on the way he destroyed the houses of idols.

13 Then Jehu met with the brothers of Ahaziah king of Judah and said to them, Who are you? And they answered, We are the brothers of Ahaziah; and we have come down to salute the sons of the king and the sons of the queen.

14 And he said, Take them alive. And they took them alive and slew them and threw them into the pit of Beth-akar, forty-two persons; and he left none of them.

15 ¶And when he was departed from there, he found Jonadab the son of Rechab coming to meet him; and he blessed him, and said to him, Is your heart right, as my heart is with your heart? And Jonadab answered, It is, it is. And he said to him, Give me your hand. And he gave him his hand; and he took him up with him into the chariot.

16 And he said to him, Come with me and see my zeal for the LORD. So he made him ride in his chariot.

17 And when he came to Samaria, he slew all that remained to the house of Ahab in Samaria, till he had destroyed them, according to the saying of the LORD which he spoke to Elijah.

18 ¶Then Jehu gathered all the people together and said to them, Ahab served Baal a little; but Jehu shall serve him much.

19 Now therefore invite to come to me all the prophets of Baal, all his priests, and all who serve him; let none be missing; for I have a great sacrifice to make to Baal; whoever is missing, he shall not live. But Jehu did it deceitfully, with the intent to destroy the worshippers of Baal.

20 And Jehu said, Invite all the assembly to come to Baal. And they invited them.

21 And Jehu sent through all Israel; and all the worshippers of Baal came, so that there was not a man left who did not come. And they came into the house of Baal; and the house of Baal was full from one end to the other.

22 And he said to him who was over the vestry, Bring out vestments for all the worshippers of Baal. And he brought them forth vestments.

23 Then Jehu and Jonadab, the son of Rechab, went into the house of Baal and said to the worshippers of Baal, Search, and see that there be here with you none of the servants of the LORD, but the worshippers of Baal only.

24 And when they went in to offer sacrifices and burnt offerings, Jehu had posted three hundred and eighty men outside by the door, and said, If any of the men whom I have delivered into your hands escape, his life shall be for the life of him.

25 And as soon as he had made an end of offering the burnt offerings, Jehu said to the guards and to the mighty men, Go in and slay them; let none of them come forth. And they smote them with the edge of the sword; and the guards and the mighty men cast them out, and went to the city of the house of Baal.

26 And they brought forth the statue of Baal out of the house of Baal and burned it with fire.

27 And they broke down the image of Baal and demolished the house of Baal and made it a public toilet-room to this day.

28 Thus Jehu destroyed Baal out of Israel.

29 ¶But as for the sins of Jeroboam the son of Nebat, who made Israel to sin, Jehu did not depart from them, especially the worship of the golden calves that were in Beth-el and in Dan.

30 And the LORD said to Jehu, Because you have done well in my

sight, and have done to the house of Ahab according to all that was in my heart, your sons even to the fourth generation shall sit on the throne of Israel.

31 But Jehu did not try to walk in the law of the LORD God of Israel with all his heart; and he did not depart from the sins of Jeroboam the son of Nebat, who made Israel sin.

32 ¶In those days the LORD began to bring distress in Israel; and Hazael smote them in all the territory of Israel,

33 From the Jordan eastward, all the land of Gilead and of Gad and of Reuben and of Manasseh, from Adoer, which is by the river Arnon, even Gilead and Mathnin.

34 Now the rest of the acts of Jehu and all that he did and all his might, behold, they are written in the Book of the Chronicles of the Kings of Israel.

35 And Jehu slept with his fathers; and they buried him in Samaria. And Jehoahaz his son reigned in his stead.

36 And the time that Jehu reigned over Israel in Samaria was twenty-eight years.

CHAPTER 11

AND when Athaliah the mother of Ahaziah saw that her son was dead, she arose and destroyed all the royal heirs.

2 But Jehosheba, the daughter of King Joram, sister of Ahaziah, took Joash the son of Ahaziah and stole him from among the king's sons who were slain; and she hid him and his nurse in her bedchamber; thus she hid him from Athaliah, so that he was not slain.

3 And he was hidden with her in the house of the LORD six years. And Athaliah reigned over the land.

4 ¶And in the seventh year Jehoiada the priest sent and brought the captains of hundreds and the guards and the runners, and had them come to him into the house of the LORD and stationed them there, and made a covenant with them and took an oath of them and showed them the king's son.

5 And he commanded them, saying, This is the thing that you shall do: a third part of you who enter in on the sabbath shall keep guard of the king's house;

6 And a third part shall be at the gate of Kersa; and a third part at the gate of the house of the guards; so shall you keep the watch of the house, that it be in perfect order.

7 And two parts of all you that go off duty on the sabbath, even they shall keep the watch of the house of the LORD together with the king's house;

8 And you shall surround the king, every man with his weapons in his hand; and whosoever comes within range, let him be slain; and you be with the king as he goes out and as he comes in.

9 And the captains of the hundreds did according to all that Jehoiada the priest commanded them; and they took every man his men who were to be on duty on the sabbath, with those who were to be off duty on the sabbath, and came to Jehoiada the priest.

10 And the priest gave to the captains of hundreds King David's spears and shields, which were in the house of the LORD.

11 And the guards stood, every man with his weapons in his hand, from the right side of the temple to the left side of the temple and they surrounded the altar and the king's house.

12 And they brought forth the king's son and put the royal crown upon his head, and they anointed him and made him king; and they clapped their hands and said, Long live the king!

13 ¶And when Athaliah heard the noise of the uproar of the people as they rejoiced, she came to the people into the temple of the LORD.

14 And when she looked, behold, the king stood by the pillar, as was the custom of the kings, and the princes and the trumpeters were standing before the king, and all the people of the land were rejoicing, and blowing with trumpets; and

Athaliah tore her clothes and cried, Treason! Treason!

15 But Jehoiada the priest commanded the captains of hundreds and the officers of the army, and said to them, Take her forth outside the ranks; and whosoever follows her shall be slain with the sword. For the priest had said, Let her not be slain in the house of the LORD.

16 So they made room for her; and she went by the way of the horses' entrance to the king's house; and there she was slain.

17 ¶And Jehoiada the priest made a covenant between the LORD and the king and the people, that they should be the LORD's people; between the king also and the people.

18 And all the people of the land went into the house of Baal and demolished his altars and broke his images in pieces and slew Mattan the priest of Baal before the altar. And the priest appointed officers over the house of the LORD.

19 And he took the captains of the hundreds and the guards and the runners and all the people of the land; and they brought down the king from the house of the LORD, and came by the way of the gate of the guard to the king's house. And he sat on the throne of the kings.

20 And all the people of the land rejoiced, and the city was quiet; and they slew Athaliah with the sword in the king's house.

21 Joash was seven years old when he began to reign.

CHAPTER 12

IN the seventh year of Jehu Joash began to reign; and he reigned forty years in Jerusalem. And his mother's name was Zobah of Beer-sheba.

2 And Joash did that which was right in the sight of the LORD all his days wherein Jehoiada the priest instructed him.

3 But the temples of idols were not taken away; the people still sacrificed and burned incense on the high places.

4 ¶And Joash said to the priests, All the money of the dedicated things which is brought into the house of the LORD, even the money which every man gives for the salvation of his soul, the money which every man thinks in his heart to bring into the house of the LORD,

5 Let the priests receive it, every man from him who has decided to give; and let them spend it for the repairing of the house, wherever a breach to be repaired shall be found in it.

6 But it was so, that even in the twenty-third year of King Joash the priests had not repaired the breaches of the house.

7 Then King Joash called for Jehoiada the priest and the other priests, and said to them, Why have you not repaired the breaches of the house? Now therefore you shall not receive money from those who give it to you, but deliver it for the repair of the house.

8 So the priests agreed not to receive any more money from the people, nor to repair the breaches of the house.

9 But Jehoiada the priest took a chest and bored a hole in the lid of it and set it beside the altar, on the right side as one comes into the house of the LORD; and the priests who kept the door put therein all the money that was brought into the house of the LORD.

10 And when they saw that there was much money in the chest, the king's scribe and the high priest came up, and they counted and bound in bags the money that was found in the house of the LORD.

11 And they gave the money tied in bags to those who did the work, who had the oversight of the house of the LORD; and they gave it to the carpenters and to the builders who worked upon the house of the LORD,

12 And to the masons and the stonecutters, and to buy timber and hewed stones for the repair of the breaches of the house of the LORD, and for all that was spent to repair the house.

13 But there were not made for the house of the LORD bowls of silver,

snuffers, braziers for incense, trumpets or any vessels of gold or vessels of silver, of the money that was brought into the house of the LORD;

14 But they gave that to the workmen, and repaired with it the house of the LORD.

15 Moreover they did not ask an accounting from the men to whom they delivered the money to give it to the workmen; for they dealt faithfully in paying out the repair money.

16 The money from the trespass offerings and the money from the sin offerings was not brought into the house of the LORD; it was the priests'.

17 ¶Then Hazael king of Aram went up and fought against Gath and took it; and Hazael set his face to go up to Jerusalem.

18 And Joash king of Judah took all the hallowed things that Jehoshaphat and Joram and Ahaziah, his fathers, kings of Judah, had dedicated, and his own hallowed things and all the gold that was found in the treasures of the house of the LORD and in the king's house, and sent it to Hazael king of Aram; and he went away from Jerusalem.

19 ¶And the rest of the acts of Joash and all that he did, behold, they are written in the Book of the Chronicles of the Kings of Judah.

20 And the servants of Joash arose and made a conspiracy and slew Joash in the house of Millo, as he was going down to Silla.

21 It was Jozachar the son of Shimeath and Jehozabar the son of Shomer, his servants, who smote him so that he died; and they buried him with his fathers in the city of David; and Amaziah his son reigned in his stead.

CHAPTER 13

IN the twenty-third year of Joash the son of Ahaziah king of Judah, Jehoahaz the son of Jehu began to reign over Israel in Samaria, and he reigned seventeen years.

2 And he did that which was evil in the sight of the LORD and followed in the sins of Jeroboam the son of Nebat, who made Israel sin; he did not turn aside from them.

3 ¶And the anger of the LORD kindled against Israel, and he delivered them into the hand of Hazael king of Aram and into the hand of Bar-hadad the son of Hazael, all their days.

4 And Jehoahaz prayed before the LORD, and the LORD hearkened to him; for he saw the suffering of Israel, because the king of Aram oppressed them.

5 (And the LORD gave Israel a saviour, so that they went out from under the hand of Aram; and the children of Israel dwelt securely in their tents as beforetime.

6 Nevertheless they did not depart from the sins of Jeroboam the son of Nebat, who made Israel sin, but walked in them; and also the idol worship remained in Samaria.)

7 There was not left much of an army to Jehoahaz but fifty horsemen and ten chariots and ten thousand footmen; for the king of Aram had destroyed them and had made them like the dust under his feet.

8 ¶Now the rest of the acts of Jehoahaz and all that he did and his might, behold, they are written in the Book of the Chronicles of the Kings of Israel.

9 And Jehoahaz slept with his fathers; and they buried him in Samaria; and Jehoash his son reigned in his stead.

10 ¶In the thirty-seventh year of Joash king of Judah, Jehoash the son of Jehoahaz began to reign over Israel in Samaria and he reigned thirteen years.

11 And he did that which was evil in the sight of the LORD; he did not turn aside from the sins of Jeroboam the son of Nebat, who made Israel sin; but he walked therein.

12 And the rest of the acts of Jehoash and all that he did and his might and how he fought against Amaziah king of Judah, behold, they are written in the Book of the Chronicles of the Kings of Israel.

13 And Jehoash slept with his fathers; and Jeroboam his son sat

upon his throne; and Jehoash was buried in Samaria with the kings of Israel.

14 ¶Now Elisha was fallen ill of the sickness of which he was to die. And Jehoash the king of Israel came down to him and wept in his presence and said, O my father, my father, the chariots of Israel and the horsemen thereof!

15 And Elisha said to him, Take a bow and arrows. And he took a bow and arrows.

16 And he said to the king of Israel, Put your hand upon the bow. And he put his hand upon it; and Elisha put his hands upon the king's hands.

17 And he said, Open the window to the east. And he opened it. Then Elisha said, Shoot. And he shot. And he said, The arrow of the LORD's deliverance and the arrow of the deliverance from Aram; for you shall smite the Arameans in Aphek till you have consumed them.

18 And he said to him, Take an arrow. And he took it. And he said, Strike upon the ground. And he struck three times and stopped.

19 And the prophet of God was angry with him and said, You should have struck five or six times; then you would have smitten the Arameans till you would have consumed them; whereas now you shall smite Aram but three times.

20 ¶And Elisha died and they buried him. And bands of the Moabites invaded the land that very year.

21 And it came to pass as they were burying a man, behold, a band of raiders was seen; and they cast the man into the sepulchre of Elisha; and when the man was let down and touched the bones of Elisha, he revived and stood up on his feet.

22 ¶But Hazael king of Aram oppressed Israel all the days of Jehoahaz.

23 And the LORD was gracious to them and had compassion on them, and returned to them, because of his covenant with Abraham, Isaac, and Jacob, and would not destroy them, neither did he cast them from his presence as yet.

24 So Hazael king of Aram died; and Bar-hadad his son reigned in his stead.

25 Then Jehoash the son of Jehoahaz took again from Bar-hadad the son of Hazael the cities which he had taken from Jehoahaz his father by war. Three times did Jehoash defeat him, and restored the cities to Israel.

CHAPTER 14

IN the second year of Jehoash the son of Jehoahaz king of Israel, Amaziah the son of Joash king of Judah, began to reign.

2 He was twenty-five years old when he began to reign, and he reigned twenty-nine years in Jerusalem. And his mother's name was Jehoaddan of Jerusalem.

3 And he did that which was right in the sight of the LORD, yet not like David his father; he did according to all things that Joash his father did.

4 But the temples of idols he did not remove, and the people still were sacrificing and burning incense on the altars on the high places.

5 ¶And it came to pass, as soon as the kingdom was firmly in his hand, he slew his servants who had slain King Joash his father.

6 But the children of the murderers he did not kill, according to that which is written in the Book of the Law of Moses, wherein the LORD commanded, saying, The fathers shall not be put to death for the children, nor the children be put to death for the fathers; but every man shall be put to death for his own sin.

7 He slew of Edom in the valley of Salt twenty thousand, and destroyed Selah by war, and called the name of it Nakthael, which is its name to this day.

8 ¶Then Amaziah king of Judah sent messengers to Jehoash, the son of Jehoahaz son of Jehu, king of Israel, saying, Come let us look one another in the face.[1]

9 And Jehoash the king of Israel sent to Amaziah king of Judah, saying, The thistle that was in Lebanon sent to the cedar that was in Lebanon,

---

[1] Let us settle our troubles by war.

saying, Give your daughter to my son to wife; and there passed by a wild beast that was in Lebanon and trod down the thistle.

10 You have indeed smitten Edom, and your heart has lifted you up; glory in this, and tarry at your house; for why should you stir up trouble, so that you should fall, even you, and Judah with you?

11 But Amaziah would not listen to him. So Jehoash king of Israel and Amaziah king of Judah went up and they faced each other at Beth-she-mesh, which belongs to Judah.

12 And Judah was defeated before Israel; and they fled every man to his tent.

13 And Jehoash king of Israel captured Amaziah king of Judah at Beth-shemesh, and he entered Jerusalem and broke down the wall of Jerusalem from the gate of Ephraim to the corner gate, four hundred cubits.

14 And he took all the gold and silver and all the vessels that were found in the house of the LORD and in the treasures of the king's house, and hostages, and returned to Samaria.

15 ¶Now the rest of the acts of Jehoash and all that he did and his might and how he fought with Amaziah king of Judah, behold, they are written in the Book of the Chronicles of the Kings of Israel.

16 And Jehoash slept with his fathers and was buried in Samaria with the kings of Israel; and Jeroboam his son reigned in his stead.

17 ¶And Amaziah the son of Joash king of Judah lived after the death of Jehoash son of Jehoahaz king of Israel fifteen years.

18 And the rest of the acts of Amaziah, behold, they are written in the Book of the Chronicles of the Kings of Judah.

19 Now they made a conspiracy against him in Jerusalem; and he fled to Lachish; but they sent after him to Lachish and slew him there.

20 And they brought him on horses; and he was buried in Jerusalem with his fathers in the city of David.

21 ¶Then all the people of Judah took Uzziah, who was sixteen years old, and made him king instead of his father Amaziah.

22 He built Elath and restored it to Judah, and after that the king slept with his fathers.

23 ¶In the fifteenth year of Amaziah the son of Joash king of Judah, Jeroboam the son of Jehoash, the son of Jehoahaz king of Israel, began to reign in Samaria, and he reigned forty-one years.

24 And he did that which was evil in the sight of the LORD; he did not turn aside from all the sins of Jeroboam the son of Nebat, who made Israel sin, and he walked in them.

25 He restored the frontier of Israel from the entrance of Hamath as far as the sea of the plain, according to the word of the LORD God of Israel which he spoke by his servant Jonah, the son of Matai, the prophet, who was of Gath-hepher.

26 For the LORD saw the affliction of Israel, that it was very bitter; for there was no one in power, and there was no one to help Israel.

27 And the LORD did not say that he would blot out the name of Israel from under heaven; but he saved them by the hand of Jeroboam the son of Jehoash, the son of Jehoahaz.

28 ¶Now the rest of the acts of Jeroboam and all that he did and his might, how he warred, and how he recovered Damascus and Hamath to Israel, behold, they are written in the Book of the Chronicles of the Kings of Israel.

29 And Jeroboam slept with his fathers, and was buried with his fathers, with the kings of Israel; and Zachariah his son reigned in his stead.

CHAPTER 15

IN the twenty-seventh year of Jeroboam king of Israel, Uzziah the son of Amaziah king of Judah, began to reign.

2 He was sixteen years old when he began to reign, and he reigned fifty-two years in Jerusalem. And his mother's name was Jechoaniah of Jerusalem.

3 And he did that which was right in the sight of the LORD, according

to all that his father Amaziah had done;

4 But the temple of idols he did not remove; the people still sacrificed and burned incense on the high places.

5 ¶And the LORD smote the king, so that he was a leper to the day of his death, and he dwelt in a house in seclusion. And Jotham the king's son was over the house, judging the people of the land.

6 Now the rest of the acts of Uzziah and all that he did, behold, they are written in the book of the Chronicles of the Kings of Judah.

7 So Uzziah slept with his fathers; and they buried him with his fathers in the city of David; and Jotham his son reigned in his stead.

8 ¶In the thirty-eighth year of Uzziah king of Judah, Zachariah the son of Jeroboam reigned over Israel in Samaria six months.

9 And he did that which was evil in the sight of the LORD, as his father had done; he did not turn aside from the sins of Jeroboam the son of Nebat, who made Israel sin.

10 And Shallum the son of Jabesh conspired against him and smote him before the people and killed him, and reigned in his stead.

11 And the rest of the acts of Zachariah, behold, they are written in the Book of the Chronicles of the Kings of Israel.

12 Thus was fulfilled the word of the LORD which he spoke to Jehu, saying, Your sons shall sit on the throne of Israel to the fourth generation. And so it came to pass.

13 ¶Shallum the son of Jabesh began to reign in the thirty-ninth year of Uzziah king of Judah; and he reigned a full month in Samaria.

14 For Menahem the son of Gadi went up from Tirzah and came to Samaria and smote Shallum the son of Jabesh in Samaria, and slew him and reigned in his stead.

15 Now the rest of the acts of Shallum and the conspiracy which he made, behold, they are written in the Book of the Chronicles of the Kings of Israel.

16 ¶Then Menahem smote Tiphsah and all who were in it and the territory thereof from Tirzah; because they did not open the gate to him, therefore he smote it; and he ripped up all the women in it that were with child.

17 In the thirty-ninth year of Uzziah king of Judah, Menahem the son of Gadi began to reign over Israel and he reigned ten years in Samaria.

18 And he did that which was evil in the sight of the LORD; he did not turn aside all his days from all the sins of Jeroboam the son of Nebat, who made Israel sin.

19 And Pul the king of Assyria came against the land; and Menahem gave Pul a thousand talents of silver to help him and to confirm the kingdom in his hand.

20 And Menahem levied taxes upon Israel, even on all wealthy men of the land, each man fifty shekels of silver, to give to the king of Assyria. So the king of Assyria turned back and stayed not there in the land.

21 ¶And the rest of the acts of Menahem and all that he did, behold, they are written in the Book of the Chronicles of the Kings of Israel.

22 And Menahem slept with his fathers; and Pekahiah his son reigned in his stead.

23 ¶In the fiftieth year of Uzziah king of Judah, Pekahiah the son of Menahem began to reign over Israel in Samaria, and he reigned two years.

24 And he did that which was evil in the sight of the LORD; he did not turn aside from the sins of Jeroboam the son of Nebat, who made Israel sin.

25 But Pekah the son of Romaliah, his mighty man, conspired against him and slew him in Samaria in the palace of the king's house; he took with him Argob and Lani and fifty men of the Gileadites, and he killed him and reigned in his stead.

26 And the rest of the acts of Pekahiah and all that he did, behold, they are written in the Book of the Chronicles of the Kings of Israel.

27 ¶In the fifty-second year of Uzziah king of Judah, Pekah the son of

Romaliah began to reign over Israel in Samaria, and he reigned twenty years.

28 And he did that which was evil in the sight of the LORD; he did not turn aside from the sins of Jeroboam the son of Nebat, who made Israel sin.

29 In the days of Pekah king of Israel, Tiglath-pileser king of Assyria came and took Ijon, Abel, Mehola, and all Beth-maachah, and Niah, Kedesh, Hazor, Gilead, and Galilee, and all the land of Naphtali, and carried the people captive to Assyria.

30 And Hoshea the son of Elah made a conspiracy against Pekah the son of Romaliah, and smote him and slew him and reigned in his stead in the second year of Jotham the son of Uzziah.

31 And the rest of the acts of Pekah and all that he did, behold, they are written in the Book of the Chronicles of the Kings of Israel.

32 ¶In the second year of Pekah the son of Romaliah king of Israel, Jotham the son of Uzziah king of Judah, began to reign.

33 He was twenty-five years old when he began to reign, and he reigned sixteen years in Jerusalem. And his mother's name was Jerusha, the daughter of Zadok.

34 And he did that which was right in the sight of the LORD, according to all that his father Uzziah had done.

35 ¶But the temple of idols he did not remove; the people sacrificed and burned incense still on the high places. He built the upper gate of the house of the LORD.

36 ¶Now the rest of the acts of Jotham and all that he did, behold, they are written in the Book of the Chronicles of the Kings of Judah.

37 In those days the LORD began to provoke against Judah Rezin the king of Aram [1] and Pekah the son of Romaliah.

38 And Jotham slept with his fathers, and was buried with his fathers in the city of David; and Ahaz his son reigned in his stead.

[1] The modern name is Syria.

CHAPTER 16

IN the eighteenth year of Pekah the son of Romaliah, Ahaz the son of Jotham king of Judah began to reign.

2 Ahaz was twenty years old when he began to reign, and he reigned sixteen years in Jerusalem, and he did not do that which was right in the sight of the LORD his God, and thus was unlike David his father.

3 But he walked in the way of the kings of Israel, and also made his son to pass through the fire, according to the custom of the Gentiles whom the LORD had destroyed from before the children of Israel.

4 And he sacrificed and burned incense on the high places and on the hills and under every green tree.

5 ¶Then Rezin king of Aram, and Pekah the son of Romaliah king of Israel came up to Jerusalem to war against it; but they could not fight against it.

6 At that time Rezin king of Aram recovered Elath for Aram, and drove Judah from Elath; and the Arameans came to Elath and dwell there to this day.

7 So Ahaz sent messengers to Tiglath-pileser king of Assyria, saying, I am your servant and your son; come up and save me from the hands of the king of Aram and from the hands of the king of Israel, who are risen up against me.

8 And Ahaz took the silver and gold that was found in the house of the LORD and in the treasures of the king's house, and sent it as a present to the king of Assyria.

9 And the king of Assyria listened to him; so the king of Assyria went up against Damascus and took it and carried its people captive to Kir, and he slew Rezin.

10 ¶And when King Ahaz went to Damascus to meet Tiglath-pileser king of Assyria, he saw an altar that was in Damascus; and King Ahaz sent to Urijah the priest the fashion of the altar and the pattern of it, according to all the workmanship thereof.

11 So Urijah the priest built an altar according to all that King Ahaz had sent from Damascus; and Urijah the priest made it before King Ahaz came from Damascus.

12 And when the king was come from Damascus, King Ahaz saw the altar; and the king drew near to the altar and went up to it,

13 And burned his burnt offerings and his meal offerings, and poured his drink offerings and sprinkled the blood of his peace offerings upon the altar.

14 And the altar of brass, which was before the LORD, he removed from the forefront of the house, from between the altar and the house of the LORD, and put it on the north side of the altar.

15 And King Ahaz commanded Urijah the priest, saying, Upon the great altar burn the morning burnt offering and the evening meal offering and the king's burnt offering and his meal offering, with the burnt offerings of all the people of the land and their meal offerings and their drink offerings; and sprinkle upon it all the blood of the burnt offerings and all the blood of the sacrifices; and the bronze altar shall be for me to inquire of the LORD.

16 Thus did Urijah the priest, according to all that King Ahaz commanded him.

17 ¶And King Ahaz cut off the borders of the bases and removed the lavers from off them; and took down the sea from off the bronze oxen that were under it and put it upon a pavement of stones.

18 And the shelter for the sabbath which they had built in the house of the LORD and in the entrance of the outer gate, he turned round the house of the LORD because of the fear of the king of Assyria.

19 ¶Now the rest of the acts of Ahaz and all that he did, behold, they are written in the Book of the Chronicles of the Kings of Judah.

20 And Ahaz slept with his fathers and was buried with his fathers in the city of David; and Hezekiah his son reigned in his stead.

CHAPTER 17

IN the twelfth year of Ahaz king of Judah, Hoshea the son of Elah began to reign in Samaria over Israel, and reigned nine years.

2 And he did that which was evil in the sight of the LORD, but not as the kings of Israel who were before him.

3 ¶Against him came up Shalmaneser king of Assyria; and Hoshea became his servant and brought him tribute.

4 And the king of Assyria found conspiracy in Hoshea; for he had sent messengers to So king of Egypt, and did not bring up tribute to the king of Assyria, as he had been doing year by year; therefore the king of Assyria shut him up and bound him in prison.

5 ¶Then the king of Assyria came up against the whole land, and went up to Samaria and besieged it three years.

6 ¶In the ninth year of Hoshea, the king of Assyria took Samaria, and carried Israel away to Assyria and placed them in Halah and in Habor by the river of Gozan, the cities of Media.

7 For so it was, that the children of Israel had sinned against the LORD their God, who had brought them up out of the land of Egypt from under the hand of Pharaoh king of Egypt and had worshipped other gods,

8 And walked in the statutes of the nations whom the LORD had destroyed from before the children of Israel,

9 And the children of Israel had spoken words that were not right against the LORD their God, both they and their kings; and they built them temples of idols in all their cities, from the tower of the watchmen to the fortified city.

10 And they set up for themselves statues and idols on every high hill and under every green tree;

11 And there they burned incense on all the high places, as did the nations whom the LORD destroyed from before them; and wrought wicked things to provoke the LORD to anger:

12 For they served idols, of which the LORD had said to them, You shall not do this thing.

13 Yet the LORD testified against Israel and against Judah by all his servants the prophets and by all the seers, saying, Repent from your evil ways and keep my commandments and my statutes, according to all the law which I commanded your fathers and according to that which I sent to them by my servants the prophets.

14 But they would not hearken, but were stubborn more than were their fathers who did not believe in the LORD their God.

15 And they rejected my covenants, and my statutes which I commanded to their fathers and the testimonies which I testified against them; and they followed vanity and gained nothing, and they followed the nations concerning whom the LORD had commanded them that they should not do like them.

16 And they left all the commandments of the LORD their God and made for themselves molten images, even two calves, and they sacrificed to the idols and worshipped all the stars and served Baal.

17 And they caused their sons and their daughters to pass through the fire and used divinations and sorcery, and they purposed to do all manner of evil in the sight of the LORD to provoke him to anger.

18 Therefore the LORD was very angry with Israel, and removed them out of his sight; there was none left but the tribe of Judah only.

19 Also the children of Judah did not keep the commandments of the LORD their God, but walked in the statutes of Israel who had done that which is evil in the sight of the LORD and provoked him to anger all the days.

20 And the LORD rejected all the descendants of Israel and despised them, and delivered them into the hand of spoilers, until he had cast them out of his sight.

21 For the house of Israel had seceded from the house of David; and they made Jeroboam the son of Nebat king over themselves; and Jeroboam caused Israel to go astray from following the LORD, and made them sin great sins.

22 For the children of Israel walked in all the sins of Jeroboam which he did; they departed not from them

23 Until the LORD removed Israel out of his sight, as he had declared by all his servants the prophets. So was Israel carried away out of their land to Assyria, where they are to this day.

24 ¶And the king of Assyria brought people from Babylon and from Cuth and from Ava and from Hamath and from Sepharvim, and settled them in the cities of Samaria instead of the children of Israel; and they possessed Samaria, and dwelt in the cities thereof.

25 And at the beginning of their dwelling there, they did not reverence the LORD; therefore the LORD sent lions against them, which slew some of them.

26 Therefore they told the king of Assyria, saying, The nations which you have carried captive and placed in the cities of Samaria do not know the religion of the god of the land; therefore he has sent lions against them, and, behold, they slay them because they do not know the religion of the god of the land.

27 Then the king of Assyria commanded, saying, Take there one of the priests whom you have carried away from there; and let him go and dwell there, and let him teach them the religion of the god of the land.

28 Then one of the priests whom they had carried away from Samaria came and dwelt in Beth-el, and taught them how they should worship the LORD.

29 Nevertheless every nation served gods of their own, and put them in the houses of idols which had been made in Samaria, every nation in their cities wherein they dwelt.

30 And the men of Babylon served Succoth-benoth and the men of Cuth served Nergal and the men of Hamath served Ashima,

31 And the Avites served Jibzah and

Tartak, and the Sepharvites burned their children in fire to Ardammeleck and Amalek, the gods of Sepharvim.

32 So they worshipped the LORD, and made for themselves of their own people priests of the high places, who served for them in the houses of idols on the high places.

33 They worshipped the LORD and served their own gods after the manner of the nations. So the children of Israel were carried away out of their land

34 To this day, because they forsook the LORD and did according to the manner of the nations; they do not revere the LORD, neither do they according to the covenant or according to the ordinance or according to the law and commandment which the LORD commanded the children of Jacob, whom he named Israel;

35 With whom the LORD had made a covenant, and charged them, saying, You shall not revere other gods nor worship them nor serve them nor sacrifice to them;

36 But you must serve the LORD, who brought you up out of the land of Egypt with great power and with an outstretched arm, him shall you serve and him shall you worship and to him shall you sacrifice.

37 And the covenants and the ordinances and the laws and the commandments which he wrote for you, you shall observe to do for evermore; and you shall not revere other gods.

38 And the covenant that I have made with you, you shall not forget; neither shall you worship the gods of the Gentiles.

39 But the LORD your God you shall worship; and he shall deliver you out of the hand of all your enemies.

40 However they did not hearken, but they did according to their former customs.

41 So these nations also who dwelt in Samaria worshipped the LORD and served their graven images, also their children and their children's children; as did their fathers, so do they to this day.

CHAPTER 18

NOW in the third year of Hoshea son of Elah king of Israel, Hezekiah the son of Ahaz king of Judah began to reign.

2 He was twenty-five years old when he began to reign; and he reigned twenty-nine years in Jerusalem. His mother's name was Ahi, the daughter of Zechariah.

3 And he did that which was right in the sight of the LORD, according to all that David his father had done.

4 ¶He removed the high places and broke the images and cut down the idols and broke in pieces the bronze serpent that Moses had made; for the children of Israel had gone astray after it, and until those days they did burn incense to it; and they called it Nehushtan.

5 He trusted in the LORD God of Israel, so that after him there was none like him among all the kings of Judah nor among those who were before him.

6 For he held fast to the LORD and turned not aside from following him, but kept his commandments, according to all that the LORD commanded Moses.

7 And the LORD was with him; and wherever he went forth he conquered; and he rebelled against the king of Assyria and served him not.

8 He smote the Philistines as far as Gaza and the borders thereof, from the tower of the watchmen to the fortified city.

9 ¶In the fourth year of King Hezekiah, which was the seventh year of Hoshea son of Elah king of Israel, Shalmaneser king of Assyria came up against Samaria and besieged it.

10 And at the end of three years he took it, even in the sixth year of Hezekiah; that is, in the ninth year of Hoshea king of Israel, Samaria was taken.

11 And the king of Assyria carried away Israel to Assyria and put them in Halah and in Habor by the river of Gozan, the cities of Media,

12 Because they did not obey the voice of the LORD their God, but

transgressed his covenant and all that Moses the servant of the LORD commanded them, and would not hearken nor do them.

13 ¶Now in the fourteenth year of King Hezekiah, Sennacherib king of Assyria came up against all the fortified cities of Judah, and took them.

14 And Hezekiah king of Judah sent to the king of Assyria at Lachish, saying, I have offended; return from attacking me; and whatever tribute you lay on me I will bear. And the king of Assyria imposed upon Hezekiah king of Judah three hundred talents of silver and thirty talents of gold.

15 And Hezekiah gave him all the silver that was found in the house of the LORD and in the treasures of the king's house.

16 At that time Hezekiah stripped off the gold from the doors of the temple of the LORD and from the pillars which Hezekiah king of Judah had overlaid, and gave it to the king of Assyria.

17 ¶Then the king of Assyria sent Tartan and the Rab-shakeh [1] and Rab-sisak from Lachish to King Hezekiah with a great army to Jerusalem. And they came up against Jerusalem, and when they were come up they stood by the ascent of the conduit of the upper pool, which is in the highway of the palace's field.

18 And when they had called to the king, there came out to them Eliakim the son of Hilkiah, who was the steward of the household, and Shebna the scribe and Joah the son of Asaph the recorder.

19 Then the Rab-shakeh said to them, Speak now to Hezekiah, Thus says the great king, the king of Assyria: What confidence is this in which you trust?

20 You have said that you are a good speaker and that you have counsel and strength for war. Now on whom do you trust, that you have rebelled against me?

21 Now, behold, you have trusted upon the staff of the broken reed, even on Egypt, on which if a man leans, it will go into his hand and pierce it; so is Pharaoh king of Egypt to all who trust in him.

22 But if you say to me, We trust in the LORD our God; is it not he whose high places and whose altars Hezekiah has removed, and has said to Judah and Jerusalem, You shall worship before a single altar in Jerusalem?

23 Now therefore, make an alliance with my lord the king of Assyria, and I will give you two thousand horses, if you have riders to set upon them.

24 How then will you refuse the request of one of the least nobles of my master's servants and put your trust in the Egyptian to give you chariots and horsemen?

25 And now perhaps you think that I have come up without the LORD against this land to destroy it? The LORD said to me, Go up against this land and destroy it.

26 Then said Eliakim, the son of Hilkiah, and Shebna and Joah to Rab-shakeh, Speak to your servants in the Aramaic; for we understand it; and do not speak to us in the Jews' language [2] in the presence of the people who are on the wall.

27 But the Rab-shakeh said to them, It was not to you and to your master that my master has sent me to speak these words, but to the men who are sitting on the wall, that they may not eat their own dung and drink their own urine with you.

28 Then the Rab-shakeh stood and cried with a loud voice in the Jews' language, and spoke, saying, Hear the word of the great king, the king of Assyria;

29 Thus says the king: Let not Hezekiah deceive you; for he shall not be able to deliver you out of my hands;

30 Neither let Hezekiah make you trust in the LORD, saying, The LORD will surely deliver us, and this city shall not be delivered into the hand of the king of Assyria.

31 Do not hearken to Hezekiah; for thus says the king of Assyria: Make an agreement with me by a present,

---

[1] Aramaic, an army general.

[2] The literary language was Aramaic.

and come out to me, and then eat every one of you of his own vine and of his own fig tree and drink every one the waters of his own cistern,

32 Until I come and take you away to a land like your own land, a land of many kinds of fruit trees, a land of grain and vineyards, a land of olive trees and of fatness and of honey, that you may live and not die; and do not listen to Hezekiah, and let not Hezekiah deceive you, saying, The LORD will deliver us.

33 Has any of the gods of the nations been able to deliver his land out of the hand of the king of Assyria?

34 Where are the gods of Hamath and of Arpad? Where are the gods of Sepharvim, Dena, and Ivah? Have they delivered Samaria out of my hands?

35 Who are there among all the gods of these nations that have delivered their country out of my hands, that the LORD should deliver Jerusalem out of my hands?

36 But the people held their peace, and answered him not a word; for the king had commanded, saying, Do not answer him.

37 Then came Eliakim the son of Hilkiah, the steward of the household, and Shebna the scribe and Joah the son of Asaph the recorder to Hezekiah with their clothes torn and told him the words of the Rab-shakeh.

CHAPTER 19

AND when King Hezekiah heard it, he tore his clothes and covered himself with sackcloth and went into the house of the LORD.

2 And he sent Eliakim, the steward of the household, and Shebna the scribe and the elders of the priests, covered with sackcloth, to Isaiah the prophet the son of Amoz.

3 And they said to him, Thus says Hezekiah: This day is a day of distress and of rebuke and of anger; for the children have come to the birth, and there is no strength in the mother to bring forth.

¹ Aramaic, a spirit; a deadly wind.

4 It may be the LORD your God will hear the words of the Rab-shakeh, whom his master, the Assyrian king has sent to reproach the living God; and will rebuke him for the words which the LORD your God has heard; therefore beseech and pray for the remnant that is left.

5 So the servants of King Hezekiah came to Isaiah the prophet.

6 ¶And Isaiah said to them, Thus shall you say to your master: Thus says the LORD, Do not be afraid of the words that you have heard, with which the ambassadors of the king of Assyria have blasphemed me.

7 Behold, I will send a blast ¹ upon him, and he shall hear a rumor and shall return to his own land; and I will cause him to fall by the sword in his own land.

8 ¶So the Rabshakeh returned and found the king of Assyria warring against Libnah; for he had heard that he had departed from Lachish.

9 And when he heard it said concerning Tarhak king of Ethiopia, Behold, he is come out to fight against you, he sent messengers again to Hezekiah, saying,

10 Thus shall you say to Hezekiah king of Judah: Do not let your God in whom you trust deceive you, saying, Jerusalem shall not be delivered into the hands of the king of Assyria.

11 Behold, you have heard what the kings of Assyria have done to all lands by destroying them utterly; and shall you be delivered?

12 Have the gods of the nations delivered them which my fathers have destroyed, such as Gozan, Haran, and Rezeph, and the inhabitants of Eden who were in Thelasar?

13 Where is the king of Hamath, and the king of Arpad, and the king of Sepharvim, and of Dena, and Ivah?

14 ¶And Hezekiah received the letters from the hand of the messengers, and read them; and Hezekiah went up into the house of the LORD and spread them before the LORD.

15 And Hezekiah prayed before the LORD and said, O LORD God of Israel,

who sits upon the cherubim, thou art the God, even thou alone, over all the kingdoms of the earth; thou hast made the heaven and the earth.

16 O LORD, incline thine ear and hear; open thine eyes, O LORD, and see; and hear all the words of Sennacherib, who hath sent messages to reproach the living God.

17 Of a truth, O LORD, the kings of Assyria have destroyed the nations and their lands,

18 And have burned their gods in fire; for they were no gods, but the works of men's hands, wood and stone; therefore they have burned them.

19 Now therefore, O LORD our God, save us from his hands, that all the kingdoms of the earth may know that thou art the LORD God, even thou alone.

20 ¶Then Isaiah the son of Amoz sent to Hezekiah, saying, Thus says the LORD God of Israel: That which you have prayed to me concerning Sennacherib king of Assyria I have heard.

21 This is the word that the LORD has spoken concerning him: The virgin the daughter of Zion despises you and laughs you to scorn; the daughter of Jerusalem shakes her head behind you.

22 Whom have you reproached and blasphemed? And against whom have you raised your voices and lifted up your eyes on high? Even against the Holy One of Israel.

23 By your messengers you have reproached the LORD and have said, With the multitude of my chariots I will go up to the height of the mountains, to the sides of Lebanon, and will cut down the tall cedar trees thereof and the choice fir trees thereof; and I will enter into the extreme limits of the forest of Carmel.

24 I will dig and drink strange waters, and with the hoofs of my horses I will dry up all the great rivers.

25 Have you not heard long ago how I have done it, and of the days of old how I prepared it? And now I have brought it to pass, that you

lay waste fortified cities into ruinous heaps;

26 Therefore their inhabitants became weak, they were defeated and confounded, and became like the grass of the field and like the green herb, like the grass on the housetops, and like tender grass blasted before it is grown up.

27 But I know your dwelling place and your coming in and your going out and your rage against me.

28 Because you have dared and raged against me, and your blasphemy has come to my ears, therefore I will put a hook in your nose and a bit in your lips, and I will turn you back by the way by which you came.

29 And this shall be a sign to you: you shall eat this year that which grows of itself, and in the second year that which springs of the same; and in the third year sow and reap and plant vineyards and eat the fruits thereof.

30 And the remnant that is left of the house of Judah shall increase, they shall again take root downward and bear fruit upward.

31 For out of Jerusalem shall go forth a remnant, and they that escape out of the mount of Zion; the zeal of the LORD of hosts shall do this.

32 Therefore thus says the LORD concerning the king of Assyria: He shall not enter this city nor shoot an arrow there nor come before it with shields nor lay an ambush against it.

33 But by the way that he came, by the same shall he return, and shall not enter this city, says the LORD.

34 For I will abide in this city and save it for my own sake and for my servant David's sake.

35 ¶And it came to pass that night, the angel of the LORD went out and slew in the camp of the Assyrians a hundred and eighty-five thousand; and when the survivors arose early in the morning, they looked, and behold, their comrades were all dead.

36 So Sennacherib king of Assyria departed, and went and returned and dwelt at Nineveh.

37 And as he worshipped in the house of Nisroch his god, Adram-

meleck and Sharezer his sons slew him with the sword; and they escaped into the land of Armenia. And Sarhaddom his son reigned in his stead.

CHAPTER 20

IN those days Hezekiah became sick to death. And Isaiah the prophet the son of Amoz came to him and said to him, Thus says the LORD: Set your house in order; for you shall die, you shall not live.

2 Then Hezekiah turned his face to the wall and prayed to the LORD, saying,

3 I beseech thee, O LORD, remember now how I walked before thee in truth and with a perfect heart, and have done that which is good in thy sight. And Hezekiah wept bitterly.

4 And before Isaiah was gone out into the middle court, the word of the LORD came to him, saying,

5 Turn again and tell Hezekiah the ruler of my people, Thus says the LORD, the God of David your father: I have heard your prayer, I have seen your tears; behold, I will heal you; on the third day you shall go up to the house of the LORD.

6 And I will add to your days fifteen years; and I will deliver you and this city out of the hands of the king of Assyria; and I will defend this city and deliver it for my own sake and for my servant David's sake.

7 And Isaiah said, Let them take a cake of figs and lay it on the boil and he shall recover.

8 ¶And Hezekiah said to Isaiah, What shall be the sign that the LORD will heal me, and that I shall go up into the house of the LORD the third day?

9 And Isaiah said, This is the sign that you shall have from the LORD, that the LORD will do the thing that he has spoken: shall the shadow go forward ten degrees or backward ten degrees?

10 And Hezekiah answered, It is an easy thing for the shadow to go down ten degrees; not so, but let the shadow turn backward ten degrees.

11 And Isaiah the prophet cried to the LORD, and he brought the shadow ten degrees backward, by which it had gone down on the dial of Ahaz.

12 ¶At that time Merodach-baladan, the son of Baladan, king of Babylon, sent letters and presents to Hezekiah; for he had heard that Hezekiah had been sick and was healed.

13 And Hezekiah rejoiced with them, and showed them all his treasure house, the silver, the gold, the spices, the precious ointments, and all the house of his armor, and all that was found in his treasures; there was nothing in his house nor in all his dominion that Hezekiah did not show them.

14 ¶Then came Isaiah the prophet to King Hezekiah and said to him, What did these men say to you? And from whence did they come to you? And Hezekiah said, They have come to me from a far country, even from Babylon.

15 And he said, What have they seen in your house? And Hezekiah answered, They have seen all the things that are in my house; I left nothing in my treasure house that I did not show them.

16 Then Isaiah said to Hezekiah, Hear the word of the LORD.

17 Behold, the days are coming when all that is in your house and that which your fathers have laid up in treasure to this day shall be carried to Babylon; nothing shall be left for you, says the LORD.

18 And of your sons that shall issue from you, whom you shall beget, shall they take away; and they shall be eunuchs in the palace of the king of Babylon.

19 Then Hezekiah said to Isaiah, Good is the word of the LORD which you have spoken. But would that peace and justice shall be in my day!

20 ¶And the rest of the acts of Hezekiah and all his might and how he made a pool and a conduit and brought water into the city, behold. they are written in the Book of the Chronicles of the Kings of Judah.

21 And Hezekiah slept with his fathers; and Manasseh his son reigned in his stead.

CHAPTER 21

MANASSEH was twelve years old when he began to reign, and he reigned fifty-five years in Jerusalem. And his mother's name was Hephzibah.

2 And he did that which was evil in the sight of the LORD, according to the abominations of the nations which the LORD destroyed from before the children of Israel.

3 For he built up again the high places which Hezekiah his father had destroyed; and he erected altars for Baal and made idols, as Ahab king of Israel had done; and worshipped all the host of heaven and served them.

4 And he built an altar in the house of the LORD, of which the LORD had said, In Jerusalem will I put my name.

5 And he built altars for all the host of heaven in the two courts of the house of the LORD.

6 And he caused his son to pass through the fire, and used divinations and practiced augury and appointed men with familiar spirits and wizards; he wrought much which was evil in the sight of the LORD, to provoke him to anger.

7 And he set up the image and the idol that he had made in the house of the LORD, in the house of which the LORD said to David and to Solomon his son, In this house and in Jerusalem, which I have chosen out of all the tribes of Israel, will I put my name for ever;

8 Neither will I make the feet of Israel move any more out of the land which I gave to their fathers, only if they will observe to do everything that I have commanded them and all the laws that my servant Moses commanded them.

9 But they did not hearken; and Manasseh seduced them, and they did more evil than did the nations whom the LORD destroyed before the children of Israel.

10 ¶And the LORD spoke by his servants the prophets, saying,

11 Because Manasseh, the son of Hezekiah, king of Judah has done these abominations and has done more wickedly than all that the Amorites did, who were before him, and has made Judah also sin with his idols;

12 Therefore thus says the LORD God of Israel: Behold, I am bringing such evil upon Judah and upon Jerusalem that whoever hears of it, both his ears shall tingle.

13 And I will stretch over Jerusalem the line of Samaria and the plummet of the house of Ahab; and I will smite Jerusalem and destroy it because of all the abominations which Manasseh had done in Judah.

14 And I will forsake the remnant of my inheritance and deliver them into the hand of their enemies; and they shall become a prey and be trampled under the feet of all their enemies,

15 Because they have done that which was evil in my sight and have provoked me to anger since the day their fathers came forth out of Egypt, even to this day.

16 Moreover Manasseh shed very much innocent blood, till he had filled Jerusalem from one end to another, besides his sins wherewith he made Judah sin, in doing that which was evil in the sight of the LORD.

17 ¶Now the rest of the acts of Manasseh and all that he did and the sins that he sinned, behold, they are written in the Book of the Chronicles of the Kings of Judah.

18 And Manasseh slept with his fathers and was buried in the garden of his own house, in the garden of the treasury; and Amon his son reigned in his stead.

19 ¶Amon was twenty-two years old when he began to reign, and he reigned two years in Jerusalem. And his mother's name was Meshullemeth, the daughter of Haduz of Jotbath.

20 And he did that which was evil in the sight of the LORD, as his father Manasseh had done.

21 And he walked in all the ways that his father walked and served the idols that his father served and worshipped them;

22 And he forsook the LORD God

of his fathers, and walked not in the way of the LORD.

23 ¶And the servants of Amon conspired against him and slew him in his own house.

24 And the people of the land slew all those that had conspired against King Amon; and the people of the land made Josiah his son king in his stead.

25 Now the rest of the acts of Amon and all that he did, behold, they are written in the Book of the Chronicles of the Kings of Judah.

26 And they buried him in his sepulchre in the garden of the treasury; and Josiah his son reigned in his stead.

CHAPTER 22

JOSIAH was eight years old when he began to reign, and he reigned thirty-one years in Jerusalem. And his mother's name was Jedidah, the daughter of Azariah of Boscath.

2 And he did that which was right in the sight of the LORD, and walked in all the way of David his father, and did not turn aside to the right hand or to the left.

3 ¶Now in the eighteenth year of King Josiah, the king sent Shaphan the son of Alaziah, the son of Meshullam, the scribe, to the house of the LORD, saying,

4 Go up to Hilkiah the high priest that he may deliver the silver which has been brought into the house of the LORD, which the keepers of the door have collected from the people;

5 And let them deliver it into the hand of the workmen who have the oversight of the house of the LORD: and let them give it to the doers of the work which is in the house of the LORD, to repair the breaches of the house,

6 To the carpenters and to the builders and masons, and to buy timber and hewn stone to repair the house of the LORD.

7 However there was no accounting made with them of the money that was delivered into their hands, because they dealt faithfully.

1 See 2 Ch. 34:22.

8 ¶And Hilkiah the high priest said to Shaphan the scribe, I have found the book of the law in the house of the LORD. And Hilkiah gave the book of the law to Shaphan the scribe and he read it.

9 And Shaphan the scribe came to the king, and brought the king word again, saying, Your servants have delivered the money that was found in the house, and have delivered it into the hand of the workmen who have the oversight of the house of the LORD.

10 And Shaphan the scribe spoke to the king, saying, Hilkiah the priest has given me a book. And Shaphan read it before the king.

11 And when the king had heard the words of the book of the law, he tore his clothes.

12 And the king commanded Hilkiah the priest and Ahikam the son of Shaphan and Achbor the son of Micah and Shaphan the scribe and Ashaiah a servant of the king, saying,

13 Go, inquire of the LORD for me and for all the people and for all Judah concerning the words of this book that has been found; for great is the wrath of the LORD that is kindled against us, because our fathers have not hearkened to the words of this book, to do according to all that which is written in it.

14 So Hilkiah the priest and Ahikam and Achbor and Shaphan and Ashaiah went to Huldi the prophetess, the wife of Shallum the son of Tikvah, the son of Hadhas, the keeper of the weapons (now she dwelt in Jerusalem studying the Law 1), and they talked with her.

15 ¶And she said to them, Thus says the LORD God of Israel: Tell the man who sent you to me,

16 Thus says the LORD: Behold, I will bring evil upon this country and upon its inhabitants, even all the words of the book which the king of Judah has read,

17 Because they have forsaken me and have burned incense to other gods and have provoked me to anger with all the works of their hands;

therefore my wrath shall be kindled against this place and I shall destroy you, says the LORD.

18 But to the king of Judah who sent you to inquire of the LORD, thus shall you say to him: Thus says the LORD God of Israel concerning the words which you have heard:

19 Because your heart was sad and you trembled before the LORD when you heard what I spoke against this country and against its inhabitants, that they should become a desolation and a curse, and have torn your clothes and wept before me; I also have heard you, says the LORD.

20 Behold, therefore, I will gather you to your fathers, and you shall be gathered into your grave in peace; and your eyes shall not see all the evil which I will bring upon this country. And they brought the king word again.

CHAPTER 23

AND the king sent and they gathered to him all the elders of Judah and of Jerusalem.

2 And the king went up to the house of the LORD, and all the men of Judah and all the inhabitants of Jerusalem with him, and the priests and the prophets and all the people, both small and great; and he read before them all the words of the book of the covenant which was found in the house of the LORD.

3 ¶And the king stood by a pillar and made a covenant before the LORD, to walk after the LORD and to keep his commandments and his testimonies and his statutes with all their heart and all their soul, to perform the words of this covenant that were written in this book. And all the people agreed to the covenant.

4 Then the king commanded Hilkiah the high priest and the priests of the second order and the keepers of the doors to bring forth out of the temple of the LORD all the vessels that were made for Baal and for the idols and for all the host of heaven; and he burned them outside Jerusalem in the fields of Kidron, and carried their ashes to Beth-el.

5 And he slew the priests whom the kings of Judah had ordained to burn incense on the high places in the cities of Judah and in the places round about Jerusalem, and those also who burned incense to Baal, to the sun and to the moon and to the planets and to all the host of heaven.

6 And he brought out the idol from the house of the LORD, outside Jerusalem, to the brook Kidron and burned it at the brook Kidron, and ground it to dust and cast the dust of it upon the graves of the common people.

7 And he destroyed the houses of the Sodomites which were in the house of the LORD, and the houses of the women who wove hangings for the idols.

8 And he brought all the priests out of the cities of Judah and defiled the high places where the priests had burned incense in them, from Dan to Beer-sheba, and destroyed the shrine which was at the entrance of the gate of Salvation which was on a man's left hand at the gate of the city.

9 Nevertheless the priests of the high places did not come up to the altar of the LORD in Jerusalem, but they did eat of the unleavened bread with their brethren.

10 And he destroyed the high places which the kings of Judah had made in Taphath, which is in the valley of Bar-hannom, that no man might make his son or his daughter to pass through the fire to Amlech.

11 And he slew the horses which the kings of Judah had given to the sun, at the entrance of the house of the LORD, by the chamber of Nathan the king's eunuch, which was in the suburbs, and burned the chariot of the sun with fire.

12 And the altar that was on the top of the upper chamber of Ahaz, which the kings of Judah had made, and the altars which Manasseh had made in the two courts of the house of the LORD, did the king beat down, and broke them down from thence and cast the dust of them into the brook Kidron.

13 And the high places that were before Jerusalem, which were on the right hand of the mount of Corruption, which Solomon the king of Israel had built for Ashtoreth, the goddess of the Zidonians, and for Chemosh, the idol of Moab, and for Malcom, the idol of the children of Ammon, did King Josiah destroy.

14 And he broke in pieces the images and cut down the idols and filled their places with the bones of men.

15 ¶Moreover the altar that was at Beth-el and the high places which Jeroboam the son of Nebat, who made Israel sin, had made, both that altar and the high place he demolished, and burned the high place and ground it to dust and burned the idols.

16 And as Josiah returned, he saw the sepulchres that were there on the mount, and he sent and took the bones out of the sepulchres and burned them upon the altar and defiled it, according to the word of the LORD which the prophet of God proclaimed, who predicted these things.

17 Then the king said, What monument is that which I see? And the men of the city said to him, It is the sepulchre of the prophet of God, who came from Judah and proclaimed these things that you have done against the altar of Beth-el.

18 And he said, Let him alone; let no man touch his sepulchre, and let no man move his bones, so the bones of the prophet of God spared the bones of the prophet who came from Samaria from being burned.

19 And all the temples also of idols that were in the cities of Samaria, which the kings of Israel had made to provoke the LORD to anger, Josiah removed, and did to them according to all the acts that he had done in Beth-el.

20 And he slew all the priests of the high places, who burned incense upon the altars and burned men's bones upon them, and he returned to Jerusalem.

21 ¶And the king commanded all the people, saying, Keep the passover to the LORD your God, as it is written in the book of this covenant.

22 Surely no such a passover had been kept from the days of the judges who judged Israel nor in all the days of the kings of Israel nor of the kings of Judah,

23 Like that in the eighteenth year of King Josiah, when this passover was kept to the LORD in Jerusalem.

24 ¶Moreover the men with familiar spirits and the wizards and the images and the idols and all the abominations that were seen in the land of Judah and in the streets of Jerusalem did Josiah put away, that he might perform the words of the law which were written in the book that Hilkiah the priest found in the house of the LORD.

25 And like unto him was there no king before him, who turned to the LORD with all his heart and with all his soul and with all his might, according to all that which is written in the law of Moses; neither after him arose there any like him.

26 ¶Nevertheless the LORD did not turn from the fierceness of his great wrath wherewith his anger was kindled against Judah because of all the provocations with which Manasseh had provoked him.

27 And the LORD said, I will remove Judah also out of my sight, as I have removed Israel, and I will cast off this city Jerusalem which I have chosen, and the house of which I said, My name shall be there.

28 Now the rest of the acts of Josiah and all that he did, behold, they are written in the Book of the Chronicles of the Kings of Judah.

29 ¶In his days Pharaoh the Lame, king of Egypt went up against Mabog which is by the river Euphrates; and King Josiah went to meet him, to fight against him; and Pharaoh said to him, I have not come against you, turn aside from me; but Josiah did not listen to him; so Pharaoh smote him at Megiddo, when he saw him there.

30 And his servants carried him in a chariot dead from Megiddo, and brought him to Jerusalem and buried him there in his own sepulchre. And the people of the land took Jehoahaz the son of Josiah and anointed him

and made him king in his father's stead.

31 ¶Jehoahaz was twenty-three years old when he began to reign; and he reigned three months in Jerusalem. And his mother's name was Hamutal, the daughter of Jeremiah of Libnah.

32 And he did that which was evil in the sight of the LORD, just as Manasseh had done.

33 And Pharaoh the Lame, king of Egypt put him in bands at Diblath in the land of Hamath, when Pharaoh took over Jerusalem; and levied on the land a tribute of one hundred talents of silver and ten talents of gold.

34 And Pharaoh the Lame made Eliakim the son of Josiah king in the place of Josiah his father, and changed his name to Jehoiakim, and he took Jehoahaz away, and brought him to Egypt and he died there.

35 And Jehoiakim gave the silver and gold to Pharaoh; but he taxed the land to give the money as he was commanded by Pharaoh; he exacted silver and gold from the people of the land, of every one according to his means, to give it to Pharaoh the Lame.

36 ¶Jehoiakim was twenty-five years old when he began to reign; and he reigned eleven years in Jerusalem. And his mother's name was Zebudah, the daughter of Peraiah of Ramtha.

37 And he did that which was evil in the sight of the LORD, according to all that his fathers had done.

CHAPTER 24

IN his days Nebuchadnezzar king of Babylon came up against Jerusalem, and Jehoiakim became his servant three years; then he turned and rebelled against him.

2 And the LORD stirred up against him bands of the Chaldeans and bands of Edomites and bands of Moabites and bands of the children of Ammon, and sent them against Judah to destroy it, according to the word of the LORD which he spoke by his servants the prophets from the mouth of the LORD.

3 And there came a fierce wrath against Judah, to remove them out of his sight on account of the sins of Manasseh and all that he had done,

4 And also for the innocent blood that he had shed; for he filled Jerusalem with innocent blood, which the LORD would not pardon.

5 ¶Now the rest of the acts of Jehoiakim and all that he did, behold, they are written in the Book of the Chronicles of the Kings of Judah.

6 So Jehoiakim slept with his fathers; and Jehoiachin his son reigned in his stead.

7 And the king of Egypt did not again come out of his land; for the king of Babylon had taken all that had belonged to the king of Egypt, from the river of Egypt to the river Euphrates.

8 ¶Jehoiachin was eighteen years old when he began to reign, and he reigned three months in Jerusalem. And his mother's name was Nehushta, the daughter of Eliathan of Jerusalem.

9 And he did that which was evil in the sight of the LORD, according to all that his father had done.

10 ¶At that time Nebuchadnezzar king of Babylon came up against Jerusalem and the city was besieged.

11 And Nebuchadnezzar king of Babylon came against the city, and his servants were besieging it.

12 And Jehoiachin the king of Judah went out to the king of Babylon, he and his mother and his servants and his princes and his eunuchs; and the king of Babylon took him with him in the eighth year of his reign.

13 And he carried out from there all the treasures of the house of the LORD and the treasures of the king's house, and he cut in pieces all the vessels of gold which Solomon king of Israel had made for the temple of the LORD, as the LORD had said.

14 And he carried away all Jerusalem and all the princes and all the mighty men of valour, even ten thousand captives, and all the guardsmen and all the guard; and he left none except the poorest people of the land.

15 And he carried away Jehoiachin to Babylon and the king's mother and

the king's wives and his eunuchs and the princes of the land he carried into captivity from Jerusalem to Babylon.

16 And all the men of might, even seven thousand, and guardsmen and the guard of a thousand and all the men who were trained for war, even them the king of Babylon brought captive to Babylon.

17 ¶Then the king of Babylon made Mattaniah the king's uncle king in his stead and changed his name to Zedekiah.

18 Zedekiah was twenty-one years old when he began to reign and he reigned eleven years in Jerusalem. And his mother's name was Hamutal, the daughter of Jeremiah of Libnah.

19 And he did that which was evil in the sight of the LORD, according to all that Jehoiakim had done.

20 So the anger of the LORD was against Judah and against Jerusalem, until he cast them out from his presence, and Zedekiah rebelled against the king of Babylon.

CHAPTER 25

AND in the ninth year of his reign, in the tenth month, on the tenth day of the month, Nebuchadnezzar king of Babylon came, he and all his army against Jerusalem, and pitched against it and built forts against it round about.

2 And the city was besieged till the eleventh year of King Zedekiah.

3 And in the eleventh year of King Zedekiah, on the ninth day of the fifth month, the famine was severe in the city and there was no bread for the people of the land.

4 ¶And the city was breached, and all the men of war fled by night by the way of the gate between the two walls, which is by the king's garden (now the Chaldeans were round about the city), and they went by the way of the plain.

5 And the army of the Chaldeans pursued the king and overtook him in the plains of Jericho; and all his army was scattered from him.

6 So they took the king and brought him up to the king of Babylon at Diblath; and he pronounced judgment against him.

7 And the king of Babylon slew the sons of King Zedekiah before his eyes, and put out the eyes of Zedekiah, and bound him with fetters and carried him to Babylon.

8 ¶In the fifth month, on the seventh day of the month, which is the nineteenth year of Nebuchadnezzar king of Babylon, came Nebuzara-dan, the commander of the guard, a servant of the king of Babylon, to Jerusalem;

9 And he burned the house of the LORD and the king's house; and all the houses of Jerusalem and all the houses of the princes he burned with fire.

10 And all the army of the Chaldeans who were with the commander of the guard broke down the walls of Jerusalem round about.

11 Now the rest of the people who were left in the city and the deserters who had gone over to the king of Babylon, with the remnant of the multitude, Nebuzara-dan, the commander of the guard, carried away to Babylon.

12 But Nebuzara-dan, the commander of the guard, left some of the poor of the land to be vinedressers and husbandmen.

13 And the pillars of brass that were in the house of the LORD and the bases and the bronze sea that was in the house of the LORD the Chaldeans broke in pieces, and took all the brass and carried it to Babylon.

14 And the pots and the cauldrons and the large hanging pots and the snuffers and the spoons and all the vessels of brass with which they ministered, they took away.

15 And the censers and the bowls, which were of gold and silver, and the cups, the commander of the guard took away.

16 The two pillars, one sea, and the bases which King Solomon had made for the house of the LORD; the weight of the brass of all these vessels was beyond calculation.

17 The height of one pillar was eighteen cubits, and the capital upon it was of brass; and the height of the

capital was three cubits; and the carved ornaments and pomegranates upon the capital round about, all of brass; and the second pillar was likewise with carved ornaments, all of brass.

18 ¶And the commander of the guard took Sheriah the chief priest and Zephaniah the second priest and the three keepers of the door;

19 And out of the city he took an officer who was in charge of the men of war and five men of those who were in the king's presence, who were found in the city, and the scribe and the commander of the army who mustered the people of the land, and sixty men of the people of the land who were still in the city;

20 And Nebuzara-dan, the commander of the guard, took these, and brought them to the king of Babylon at Diblath;

21 And the king of Babylon smote them, and slew them at Diblath in the land of Hamath. So Judah was carried away captive out of their land.

22 ¶And as for the people who remained in the land of Judah, whom Nebuchadnezzar king of Babylon had left, he appointed over them Gedaliah the son of Ahikam, the son of Shaphan, ruler.

23 And when all the commanders of the armies, they and their men, heard that the king of Babylon had made Gedaliah ruler, they came to Gedaliah at Mizpah, even Ishmael the son of Nethaniah and Johanan the son of Korah and Sheriah the son of Tanhumeth and Tobia and Jaazaniah the son of Maachat, they and their men.

24 And Gedaliah swore to them and to their men, and said to them, Fear not the Chaldeans; dwell in the land and serve the king of Babylon; and it shall be well with you.

25 But in the seventh month, Ishmael the son of Nethaniah, the son of Ishmael of the royal seed came, and ten men with him, and smote Gedaliah, that he died, and also the Jews and the Chaldeans that were with him at Mizpeh.

26 And all the people of the land, both small and great, and all the commanders of the armies, arose and went to Egypt; for they were afraid of the Chaldeans.

27 ¶And in the thirty-seventh year of the captivity of Jehoiachin king of Judah, in the twelfth month, on the twenty-seventh day of the month, Aolmerodach king of Babylon in the first year that he began to reign honored Jehoiachin king of Judah and brought him out of the prison;

28 And he spoke kindly to him, and set his throne above the thrones of the kings who were with him in Babylon;

29 And changed his prison garments; and he did eat bread continually before him all the days of his life.

30 And his allowance was a continual allowance given him by the king of Babylon, a portion for every day, all the days of his life.

THE FIRST BOOK OF THE

CHRONICLES

CHAPTER 1

ADAM, Sheth, Enosh,
2 Kenan, Mahalalael, Jered,
3 Enoch, Methuselah, Lamech,

4 Noah, Shem, Ham, and Japheth.
5 ¶The sons of Japheth: Gomer, Mongolia, Madai, Javan, Tubal, Meshech, and Tiras.

6 And the sons of Gomer: Ashchenaz, Diphar, and Togarmah.

7 And the sons of Javan: Elishah, Tarshish, Kittim, and Doranim.

8 ¶The sons of Ham: Cush, Mizraim, Put, and Canaan.

9 And the sons of Cush: Seba, Havilah, Sabta, Raamah, and Sabachtha. And the sons of Raamah: Sheba and Daran.

10 And Cush begat Nimrod; and he began to be a mighty man in the earth.

11 And Mizraim begat Ludim, Jaabim, Lehabim, Naphtuhim,

12 Pathrusim, and Casluhim (of whom came the Philistines and Capedocians).

13 And Canaan begat Zidon his first-born and Heth and

14 The Jesubites and the Amorites and the Girgasites

15 And the Hivites and the Arkites and the Sinites

16 And the Arvadites and the Zemarites and the Hamathites.

17 ¶The sons of Shem: Elam, Asshur, Arphahshar, Lud, Aram, Uz, Hul, Gather, and Meshech.

18 And Arphahshar begat Shelah, and Shelah begat Eber.

19 And to Eber were born two sons; the name of the one was Peleg, because in his days the earth was divided, and his brother's name was Joktan.

20 And Joktan begat Almodad, Sheleph, Hazarmoth, and Jerah,

21 Hadoram, Uzal, Diklah,

22 Ebal, Abimael, Sheba,

23 Ophir, Havilah, and Jobab. All these were the sons of Joktan.

24 ¶Shem, Arphahshar, Shelah,

25 Eber, Peleg, Reu,

26 Serug, Nahor, and Terah;

27 Abram; the same is Abraham.

28 The sons of Abraham: Isaac and Ishmael.

29 ¶These are their generations: The first-born of Ishmael, Nebaioth; then Kadar, Arbal, and Mibsam,

30 Mishma, Romah, Massa, Hadad, Temna,

31 Nator, Naphish, and Kedemah. These are the sons of Ishmael.

32 ¶The sons of Kenturah, Abraham's concubine: she bore Zimran, Jokshan, Maran, Midian, Ishbak, and Shuah. And the sons of Jokshan: Sheba and Daran.

33 And the sons of Midian: Ephah, Epher, Henoch, Abida, and Eldaah. All these were the sons of Kenturah.

34 And Abraham begat Isaac. The sons of Isaac: Esau and Israel.

35 ¶The sons of Esau: Eliphaz, Reuel, Jeush, Elam, and Korah.

36 The sons of Eliphaz: Teman, Omar, Zoph, Gatham, Kenaz, Timna, and Amalek.

37 The sons of Reuel: Nahath, Zerah, Shammah, and Mizzah.

38 And the sons of Seir: Lotan, Shobal, Zibeon, Anah, Doshan, Ezar, and Dishan.

39 And the sons of Lotan: Horar and Homam; and Timna was Lotan's sister.

40 The sons of Shobal: Anon, Manahath, Ebal, Shaphar, and Onam. And the sons of Zibeon: Ana, and Annah.

41 The son of Annah: Dishon. And the sons of Dishon: Hamran, Ashkan, Ithran, and Cheran.

42 The sons of Ezer: Calhan, Zimran, and Jakan. The sons of Dishon: Uz, and Aram.

43 ¶Now these are the kings that reigned in the land of Edom before any king reigned over the children of Israel: Bela the son of Beor, and the name of his city was Dihab.

44 And when Bela died, Jobab the son of Zerah of Bozrah reigned in his stead.

45 And after him Husham of the land of Teman reigned in his stead.

46 And when Husham died, Hadad the son of Bedad, who defeated the Edomites in the fields of Moab, reigned in his stead; and the name of his city was Gewith.

47 And when Hadad died, Samlah of Masrekah reigned in his stead.

48 And when Samlah died, Shaul of Rehoboth by the river reigned in his stead.

49 And when Shaul died, Baal-hanan the son of Abcor reigned in his stead.

50 And when Baal-hanan died, He-

dad reigned in his stead; and the name of his city was Pao; and his wife's name was Mehetabel, the daughter of Matred, the daughter of Mezahab.

51 ¶Hadad died also. And the princes of Edom were prince Timnah, prince Anwa, prince Jetheth,

52 Prince Aholibamah, prince Elah, prince Pinon,

53 Prince Kenaz, prince Teman, prince Mibzar,

54 Prince Magdiel, prince Giram. These are the princes of Edom.

CHAPTER 2

THESE are the sons of Israel: Reuben, Simeon, Levi, Judah, Issachar, Zebulun,

2 Dan, Joseph, Benjamin, Naphtali, Gad, and Asher.

3 ¶The sons of Judah: Er, Onan, and Shelah; these three were born to him of Bathshua the Canaanitess. And Er, the first-born of Judah, was wicked in the sight of the Lord; and he slew him.

4 And Tamar his daughter-in-law bore him Pharez and Zerah. All the sons of Judah were five.

5 The sons of Pharez: Hezron and Hamul.

6 And the sons of Zerah: Zimri, Ethan, Haman, Calcol, Darda; five of them in all.

7 And the son of Carmi: Achar, the troubler of Israel, who transgressed in the thing dedicated.

8 And the son of Ethan: Azariah.

9 The sons of Hezron that were born to him: Rahmael, Ram, and Salbai.

10 And Ram begat Amminadab; and Amminadab begat Nahshon, prince of the children of Judah;

11 And Nahshon begat Salma; and Salma begat Boaz;

12 And Boaz begat Obed; and Obed begat Jesse;

13 ¶And Jesse begat his first-born Eliab, and Abinadab the second, and Shimma the third,

14 Nathanael the fourth, Darai the fifth,

15 Ozem the sixth, Eliho the seventh, and David the eighth,

16 Whose sisters were Zuriah and Abigail. And the sons of Zuriah: Abishai, Joab, and Ashail, three.

17 And Abigail bore Amasa; and the father of Amasa was Jether.

18 ¶And Caleb the son of Hezron begat Jedioth of Arubah his wife, and these were her sons: Asher, Jobab, and Adon.

19 And when Arubah died, Caleb took to him Ephrath, who bore him Hur.

20 And Hur begat Uri, and Uri begat Bezaliel.

21 ¶And afterward Hezron went in to the daughter of Machir the father of Gilead, whom he married when he was sixty years old; and she bore him Segub.

22 And Segub begat Jair, who had twenty-three towns in the land of Gilead.

23 And after that Hezron was dead in Caleb's land, Ephrath, then his wife, bore him Eshtawir the father of Tekoa.

24 And the sons of Jerahmeel the first-born of Hezron were Aram the first-born and Banah, Aran, and Azam their sister.

25 ¶Jerahmeel had also another wife, whose name was Atarah; she was the mother of Onam.

26 And the sons of Aram the first-born of Jerahmeel were Maaz, Nabin, and Aotar.

27 And the sons of Onam were Sabai, and Jada. And the sons of Sabai: Nadab and Abishur.

28 And the name of the wife of Abishur was Abihail, and she bore him Ahban and Molid.

29 And the sons of Nadab: Seled and Pelarim; but Seled died without children.

30 And the son of Pelarim was Isaiah. And the son of Isaiah: Shushan; and the son of Shushan: Ahlai.

31 And the sons of Jehoiada the brother of Sabai: Jether and Jonathan; and Jether died without children.

32 And the sons of Jonathan: Lapath and Aoza. These were the sons of Jerahmeel.

33 ¶Now Shushan had no sons, but daughters. And Shushan had a son-

in-law from Mizra, whose name was Jardaha.

34 And Shushan had given him his daughter to wife; and she bore him Attai.

35 And Attai begat Nathan, and Nathan begat Dabir,

36 And Dabir begat Ephil, and Ephil begat Jobab,

37 And Jobab begat Jehu, and Jehu begat Azariah,

38 And Azariah begat Helez, and Helez begat Eleasah,

39 And Eleasah begat Samsai, and Samsai begat Shallum,

40 And Shallum begat Elkamiah, and Elkamiah begat Elishama.

41 ¶Now the sons of Caleb the brother of Jerahmeel were Elishmai his first-born, who was the father of Ziph;

42 And the sons of Mareshah the father of Hebron were Korah, Tappuah, Rakim, and Shema.

43 And Shema begat Raham, the father of Jorkoam; and Jorkoam begat Samai.

44 And Auphnah, Caleb's concubine, bore Horan,

45 And Horan begat Gozan.[1]

46 And the son of Shammai was Maon; and Maon was the father of Bethzur.

47 And the sons of Jahdai: Regem and Jotham and Gesham and Pelet and Ephah and Shaaph.

48 Maachah, Caleb's concubine, bore Sheber and Tirhanah.

49 She bore also Shaaph the father of Madmannah, Sheva the father of Machbenah, and the father of Gibea; and the daughter of Caleb was Achsa.

50 ¶These were the sons of Caleb the son of Hur, the first-born of Ephratah: Shobal, who was born in Kirjath-narin;

51 Samla, who was born in Bethlehem; and Abi, who was born in Gader.

52 And sons were born to Shobal in Kirjath-narin; namely, Atroth, Jobal, Hazri,

53 Sepharvim, Netophath, Samla, Shemothim, Shechab, and Hama;

54 All these sons were born to Shobal in Kirjath-narin.

55 And the families of the scribes which dwelt at Jabez: the Tirathites, the Shimeathites, and Suchathites. These are the Kenites that came of Hemath, the father of the house of Rechab.

CHAPTER 3

NOW these were the sons of David that were born to him in Hebron: the first-born Hamnon, by Ahinoam the Jesreelitess; the second Caleb, by Abigail the Carmelitess;

2 The third Absalom, the son of Maachah the daughter of Talmai king of Geshur; the fourth Adonijah, the son of Haggith;

3 The fifth Shephatiah, the son of Abital; the sixth Ithream, by Eglah his wife.

4 These six sons were born to him in Hebron, where he reigned for seven years and six months; and in Jerusalem he reigned thirty-three years.

5 Now these are the names of the sons that were born to him in Jerusalem: Shimea, Shecob, Nathan, and Solomon,

6 Ibhar, Elishama, Eliadah,.

7 Eliphelet, Nogah, Nepheg,

8 Nephig, and Elishama.

9 These were all the sons of David, and Tamar was their sister.

10 ¶And Solomon's son was Rehoboam, Abijah was his son, Asa his son, Jehoshaphat his son,

11 Joram his son, Ahaziah his son, Joash his son,

12 Amaziah his son, Uzziah his son, Jotham his son,

13 Ahaz his son, Hezekiah his son, Manasseh his son,

14 Amon his son, Josiah his son.

15 And the sons of Josiah were: his first-born Johanan, the second Jehoiakim, the third Zedekiah, the fourth Shallum.

16 And the sons of Jehoiakim: Jeconiah his son, Zedekiah his son.

17 ¶And the sons of Jeconiah: Ashrashtiel his son,

[1] Some of the verses missing in the Eastern text of Chronicles are supplied from the King James version.

18 Malcom his son, Peraiah his son, Shaazar his son, Nekamiah his son, Shimei and Shaua his sons, and Nedabiah his son.

19 And the sons of Nedabiah were Zerubbabel and Shemei; and the sons of Zerubbabel: Meshullam and Hananiah, and Selkath was their sister;

20 And Hashubah, Jehoael, Beria, and Hasadiah.

21 And the sons of Hananiah: Pelatiah and Jesaiah; Arphaiah his son, Arnon his son, and Aobiah the son of Jesaiah.

22 And the son of Shechaniah: Shemaiah; and the sons of Shemaiah: Hattush, Negael, Azariah, and Hezekiah;

23 And the sons of Neariah: Elioenai, Hezekiah, and Azrikam, three.

24 Also Hodaiah, Eliashib, Pelaiah, Jacob, Johanan, Delaiah, and Anan.

CHAPTER 4

THESE are the sons of Judah: Pharez, Hezron, Carmi, Hur, and Shobal.

2 And Lana the son of Shobal begat Nahath; and Nahath begat Ahumai and Lahad. These are the families of Rehoboam.

3 And these are the sons of Aminadab: Ahizareel, Neshmah, and Dibash.

4 Pegoael and Hoshiah, these are the sons of Hur, the first-born of Ephratah, whose father was of Bethlehem.

5 ¶And Ashur the father of Tekoa had two wives.

6 And one of them bore Ahiram, Ephaor, Teman, and Hereshtar. These were the sons of one of them.

7 And the sons of Helah were, Zereth and Jezoar and Ethnan.

8 And Coz begat Anub and Zobebah and the families of Aharhel the son of Harum.

9 ¶And one of them was dear to his father and to his mother, so they called his name Our Eyes.

10 And they said to him, The LORD shall surely bless you and enlarge your territory, and his hand shall be with you and shall deliver you from evil, that it may not have power over you, and he shall grant you that which you request of him.

11 ¶And Caleb the brother of Ahijah begat Mehir, who was the father of Eshton.

12 And Eshton begat Tehiah, and Ropha begat Paseah, and Paseah begat Tehiah, and Tehiah begat Jazir.

13 These were the sons of Caleb the son of Jophaniah. The name of his first-born was Elah, and the name of the second was Naam, and the name of the third was Kenaz, and the name of the fourth was Ashiph, and the name of the fifth was Jamoael, and the name of the sixth was Jahrob.

14 These are the sons of Caleb the son of Jophaniah.

15 And the sons of Ezra were Jether, and Mered and Epher and Jalon; and she bore Miriam and Shammai and Ishbah the father of Eshtomoa.

16 And his wife Jehudijah bore Jered the father of Gedor and Heber the father of Socho and Jekuthiel the father of Zanoah. And these are the sons of Bithiah the daughter of Pharoah, which Mered took.

17 And the sons of his wife Hodiah the sister of Nahom, the father of Keilah the Garmite, and Eshtemoa the Maahathite.

18 And the sons of Shimon were, Annon and Rinnah, Benhanan, and Tilon. And the sons of Ishi were Zoheth and Benzoheth.

19 The sons of Shelah the son of Judah were Er, the father of Lecah, and Laadah the father of Mareshah, and the families of the house of them that wrought fine linen, of the house of Ashbea.

20 And the sons of Uriah's wife, the sister of Nahom the father of Keilah, were Zemri, Eshtemoa, Maachat, Eshtma, and Ashimon.

21 And the sons of Ashimon were Ammon, Domiah, Zerah, and Shelah.

22 These are the sons of Judah: Jemoael, Jamin, Ahar, Jachin, Zahar, Jarib, Zerah, and Saul.

23 These are the sons of Shelah.

24 The sons of Simeon were Mibsam his son, Mishma his son,

25 Shemati his son, Hamuel his son,

26 Zaccai his son, Shimei his son.
27 And Shimei had sixteen sons and six daughters; but his brothers had not many children, neither did all their family multiply until the children of Judah came to dwell with them.
28 And they dwelt with them in the towns of Beersheba, in Moladah, and in Darath-Shuah.
29 And in Bilhah, Ezem, and Tolad,
30 Bansel, Hirmah, Hazar-gadah, Heshmon, Hethpelet, and Zinglag,
31 And in Marmeranah and Samsalah. These were their cities until the reign of David.
32 And their villages were Akim, Ekin, Rimmon, Athchen, and Ashan, five cities;
33 And all the villages that were round about the same cities of Arkites.
34 These were the cities of their habitations, and they became very famous
35 And were situated in beautiful locations, and peace and tranquillity reigned round about them.
36 These were the names of the princes who were there in their families and in the house of their fathers.
37 And they came to the entrance of Geder, as far as the east side of the valley, to seek pasture for their flocks.
38 And they found good and rich pasture, and the land was wide and good, and tranquillity and peace there reigned;
39 For they who dwelt in it were the first settlers.
40 And these written by name came in the days of Hezekiah king of Judah, and destroyed their tents utterly
41 And polluted all the springs of water which were there to this day and dwelt in their places, because there was good pasture for their flocks.
42 And some of them and some of the sons of Simeon, five hundred men, went to mount Gebel. These are the names of the men who went as their leaders: Pelatiah, Metitha, Rephaiah, and Uzziel, the four sons of Ishi.
43 And they smote the rest of the Amalekites that escaped, and have dwelt in their place to this day.

[1] Genesis 49:10.

CHAPTER 5

NOW the sons of Reuben the first-born of Israel (for he was the first-born of his father; but, because he defiled his father's bed, his birthright was given to the sons of Joseph his brother, the son of Israel; and upon his two sons came the blessings more than all the tribes of Israel.
2 For from Judah shall come forth Messiah the King,[1] but the blessings shall be given to Joseph),
3 The sons of Reuben, the first-born of Israel were Hanoch, Pallu, Hezron, and Carmi.
4 The sons of Carmi: Shemaiah his son, Doag his son, Shimei his son,
5 Micah his son, Uriah his son, Balah his son,
6 Abdaiah his son, whom Tiglath-pileser king of Assyria carried away captive; he was the prince of the tribe of Reubenites.
7 And his brethren by their families, when the genealogy of their generations was reckoned: Azrael, their chief, and Zechariah, second in rank,
8 And Bela and the son of Uzai, the son of Shema, the son of Joel, who dwelt in Adoer and as far as Nebo and the plain of Meon,
9 And eastward he inhabited as far as the border of the desert from the river Euphrates, because their cattle were multiplied in the land of Gilead.
10 And in the days of Saul they made war against the Arabians, the inhabitants of Sekah, and were delivered into their hands; and they dwelt in their tents throughout all the east land of Gilead.
11 ¶And the children of Gad dwelt opposite them, in the land of Mathnin as far as the border of Siba and Salcah.
12 Joel was their chief, and he judged them and taught them good scriptures.
13 These are the sons of Abihail, the son of Khuri, the son of Zerah, the son of Gilead, the son of Machir,
14 The son of Abdael, the son of Eli, chiefs of the house of their fathers.

15 And they dwelt in Mathnin and its villages.

16 All these were reckoned by genealogies in the days of Jotham king of Judah, and in the days of Jeroboam king of Israel.

17 ¶The Reubenites, the Gadites, and the half tribe of Manasseh, valiant men, able to bear sword and shield and to shoot with bow, and skilled in war, were forty-four thousand six hundred and sixty-six.

18 All of these went out to war and fought against the inhabitants of Sekah.

19 And they were delivered into their hands, for they prayed to the LORD in the battle, and he heard their voice because they put their trust in him.

20 And they carried away abundant goods and cattle: fifty thousand camels, two hundred and fifty thousand sheep, two thousand asses, and a hundred thousand persons.

21 For many fell slain in the battle of those who dwelt in tents. And the remnant stayed in their tents.

22 And the children of the half tribe of Manasseh dwelt in the land of Mathnin, as far as the plain of mount Hermon and as far as Har, and there they multiplied and became great.

23 ¶These were the heads of the house of their fathers: Apha, Shob, Eldaa, Azriel, Adomiah, Uriah, and Hezaiel,

24 All mighty men of valour, famous men, and heads of the house of their families.

25 ¶And they transgressed against the God of their fathers, and went astray after the gods of the people of the land, whom God destroyed before them.

26 And the God of Israel stirred up the spirit of Tiglath-pileser king of Assyria, and he carried them away, even the tribe of Reuben and the tribe of Gad and the half tribe of Manasseh, and brought them to Halah and Habor, and to the river Gozan, cities of Media. And they still dwell there to this day.

CHAPTER 6

THE sons of Levi: Gershon, Kohath, and Merari.

2 And the sons of Kohath: Amram, Izhar, Hebron, and Uzziel.

3 And the children of Amram: Moses, Aaron, and Miriam. And the sons of Aaron: Nadab, Abihu, Eleazar, and Ithamar.

4 ¶Eleazar begat Phinehas, Phinehas begat Abishua,

5 And Abishua begat Abikar, and Abikar begat Uzzi,

6 And Uzzi begat Zerahiah, and Zerahiah begat Maro,

7 And Maro begat Amariah, and Amariah begat Ahitub,

8 And Ahitub begat Zadok, and Zadok begat Ahimaaz,

9 And Ahimaaz begat Azariah, and Azariah begat Johanan,

10 And Johanan begat Azariah (it was he who ministered in the priestly office in the temple that Solomon built in Jerusalem),

11 And Azariah begat Amariah, and Amariah begat Ahitub,

12 And Ahitub begat Zadok, and Zadok begat Shallum,

13 And Shallum begat Hilkiah, and Hilkiah begat Azariah,

14 And Azariah begat Seraiah, and Seraiah begat Zadok,

15 And Zadok was carried away captive when the LORD carried away Judah and Jerusalem by the hand of Nebuchadnezzar.

16 ¶The sons of Levi: Gershon, Kohath, and Merari.

17 And these are the names of the sons of Gershon: Libni and Shimei.

18 And the sons of Kohath were Amram, Izhar, Hebron, and Uzziel.

19 The sons of Merari: Mahli and Moshi. And these are the families of the Levites according to their fathers.

20 Of Gershon: Libni his son, Nahath his son, Zimmah his son,

21 Joah his son, Iddo his son, Jathor his son.

22 The sons of Kohath: Amminadab his son, Korah his son, Assir his son,

23 Hilkanah his son, Akinsaph his son,

24 Tahath his son, Uriel his son, Uzziah his son, and Shaul his son.

25 And the sons of Hilkanah: Amasai and Ahimoth.

26 As for Hilkanah, the sons of Hilkanah: Zoph his son, Nahath his son, Zerah his son, Shamla his son, Mari his son,

27 Eliab his son, Gadhiel his son, Hilkanah his son.

28 And the sons of Samuel: Joel his first-born, and the name of his second son Abijah.

29 The sons of Merari: Mahli, Libni his son, Shimei his son, Uzza his son,

30 Shimea his son, Ashaiah his son.

31 These are all of those whom David appointed to minister in the house of the LORD at the place where the ark stood.

32 And they ministered before the LORD in the tabernacle of the congregation with great singing, until Solomon built the house of the LORD in Jerusalem; and then he appointed them to their office according to their order.

33 And these are the ministers and their sons: of the sons of the Kohathites, of the family of the Levites, Haman, and Joel the son of Samuel,

34 The son of Hilkanah, the son of Jeroham, the son of Eliel, the son of Taho,

35 The son of Zuph, the son of Hilkanah, the son of Hamath, the son of Moshi,

36 The son of Hilkanah, the son of Joel, the son of Azariah, the son of Zephaniah,

37 The son of Tahath, the son of Assir, the son of Akhsiph, the son of Korah,

38 The son of Izhar, the son of Kohath, the son of Levi, the son of Israel.

39 And his brother Asaph, who stood on the right hand of Asaph the son of Berachiah, the son of Shimea,

40 The son of Michael, the son of Measiah, the son of Malchiah,

41 The son of Ethi, the son of Zerah, the son of Ariah,

42 The son of Ethan, the son of Zimmah, the son of Shimei,

43 The son of Joha, the son of Gershon, the son of Levi.

44 And their brethren the sons of Merari stood on the left hand: Ethan, the son of Kishi, the son of Amar, the son of Malluch,

45 The son of Hashabiah, the son of Amaziah,

46 The son of Hilkiah, the son of Nator,

47 The son of Mahli, the son of Moshi, the son of Merari, the son of Levi.

48 Their brethren also the Levites were appointed to all manner of service of the tabernacle of the house of the LORD.

49 ¶But Aaron and his sons offered upon the altar of burnt offerings and upon the altar of incense, and were appointed for all the work of the Holy of Holies, and to make an atonement for Israel, according to all that Moses the servant of God had commanded.

50 And these are the sons of Aaron: Eleazar his son, Phinehas his son, Abishua his son,

51 Bakki his son, Uzzi his son, Zerahiah his son,

52 Maro his son, Amariah his son, Ahitub his son,

53 Zadok his son, Ahimaaz his son.

54 ¶Now these are the names of the cities which they were assigned for the families throughout their boundaries, to the sons of Aaron, of the family of the Kohathites; for theirs was the first lot.

55 And they gave them Hebron in the land of Judah, and its suburbs round about it;

56 But all the fields of the city, and those which were round about it, they gave to Caleb the son of Jophaniah.

57 And to the sons of Aaron they gave all the cities of refuge, and to the priests, Hebron with its suburbs, Libnah with its suburbs, Jattir with its suburbs, Lehem with its suburbs, Eshtemoa with its suburbs,

58 Debir with its suburbs, Ashan with its suburbs,

59 Atrah with its suburbs, and Bethshemesh with its suburbs;

60 And out of the tribe of Benjamin,

Geba with its suburbs, Alemeth with its suburbs, and Anathoth with its suburbs. All their cities throughout their families were thirteen cities.

61 And to the sons of Kohath, who inherited out of the tribe of Manasseh, were given ten cities in number;

62 And to the sons of Gershon according to their families out of the tribe of Issachar and out of the tribe of Asher and out of the tribe of Manasseh and out of the tribe of Nahptali in Mathnin, thirteen cities.

63 To the sons of Merari were given by lot, according to their families, out of the tribe of Reuben and out of the tribe of Dan and out of the tribe of Zebulun, twelve cities.

64 And the children of Israel gave to the Levites these cities with their suburbs.

65 And they gave by lot out of the tribe of the children of Judah and out of the tribe of the children of Simeon and out of the tribe of the children of Benjamin, these cities, which are called by the name of the families of the Kohathites.

66 Moreover they had other cities and their territory out of the tribe of Ephraim.

67 And they gave to them, of the cities of refuge, Shechem with its suburbs in mount Ephraim and Gezer with its suburbs,

68 Beth-horon with its suburbs,

69 Aijalon with its suburbs, and Gath-rimmon with its suburbs;

70 And out of the half tribe of Manasseh: Anath with its suburbs, Jablin with its suburbs, for the inheritance of the families of the sons of Kohath;

71 And to the sons of Gershon were given out of the half tribe of Manasseh, Golan in Mathnin with its suburbs and Ashtor with its suburbs;

72 And out of the tribe of Issachar: Rakim with its suburbs, Deberath with its suburbs,

73 Elam with its suburbs;

74 And out of the tribe of Asher: Mashal with its suburbs and Abron with its suburbs

75 And Akik with its suburbs and Dahab with its suburbs;

76 And out of the tribe of Naphtali: Rakim in Galilee with its suburbs and Hammon with its suburbs and Koriathaim with its suburbs.

77 To the family of Merari, who inherited out of the tribe of Zebulun, were given Armoni with its suburbs, Tabor with its suburbs;

78 And on the other side of the Jordan by Jericho, on the east side of the Jordan, were given them out of the tribe of Reuben: Bozer in the wilderness with its suburbs, Mepophat with its suburbs, Jahaz with its suburbs.

79 Kedemoth with its suburbs, Mephaath with its suburbs,

80 Ramoth with its suburbs, Mahlam with its suburbs,

81 Jazer with its suburbs, and Heshbon with its suburbs.

CHAPTER 7

NOW the sons of Issachar were Tola, Puah, Shob, and Shimron, four.

2 The sons of Tola: Uzzi, Rephaiah, Joel, Lahmai, Jibsam, and Samuel, heads of their father's house; these were the sons of Tola. They were valiant men of might in their families and their generations, whose number was in the days of David twenty-two thousand and six hundred.

3 And the son of Uzzi: Izarhan; and the sons of Izarhan: Malchael, Obadiah, Joel, and Ishoa, four, all of them chief men.

4 And with them by their generations, according to their father's house, were valiant men of war, thirty-six thousand men; for they had many wives and sons.

5 And their brethren, all the families of Issachar, were valiant men of might, reckoned in all by their genealogy, eighty-seven thousand.

6 ¶These are the names of the sons of Benjamin: Bela, Akbar, Ashbel, Gera, Naaman, Ahai, Arosh, Maphai, Hitim, and Adar.

7 And the sons of Bela: Ezbon, Uzzi, Uzzaiel, Jermoth, and Azri, five; heads of the house of their fathers, valiant men of valour; and were reckoned by their genealogy, twenty-two-thousand and thirty-four.

8 And the sons of Akbar: Zemora, Joash, Eliezer, Elioenai, Omri, Jermoth, Abijah, Anathoth, and Alamoth. All these were the sons of Akbar.

9 And their number, according to their genealogy by their generations, heads of the house of their fathers, valiant men, was twenty-two thousand and two hundred.

10 And the son of Ashcol: Bilhan; and the sons of Bilhan: Joash, Benjamin, Ehud, Chenanah, Zethan, Tarshish, and Ahishahar.

11 All these were the sons of Ashcol, according to the heads of their fathers, mighty men of valour, seventeen thousand and two hundred soldiers, fit to go out in the army for battle;

12 Shaphan, also, and Huphis, the sons of Aod, of the children of Hoshah.

13 ¶The sons of Naphtali: Jahziel, Guni, Jezer, and Shallum, the sons of Bilhah.

14 ¶The sons of Manasseh: Asarchiel, whom his concubine bore him; she also bore Machir the father of Gilead;

15 And Machir took to wife the daughter of a prince, whose sister's name was Maachah; and the name of his eldest brother was Zelophehad; and Zelophehad had no sons but daughters.

16 And Maachah also the mother of Machir bore a son, and she called his name Peresh; and the name of his brother was Sheresh;

17 And the son of Ulam: Rakim, and the son of Rakim, Baran. These were the sons of Gilead, the son of Machir, the son of Manasseh.

18 And his sister Maachah bore Ashhor and Abiezer,

19 And Shemirah, Elenon, Shem, and Etham.

20 ¶And the sons of Ephraim: Shuthelah, Bachar his son, Tahath his son, Eladah his son, and Ahath his son,

21 ¶And Zabor his son, Shuthelah his son and Lazar his son, whom the men of Gath who were born in the land slew because they came down to take away their wealth.

22 And Ephraim their father mourned many days, and his brethren came to comfort him.

23 ¶And he went in to his wife, and she conceived and bore a son, and she called his name Beriah, because misfortune had befallen his house.

24 (And her daughter escaped in lower and upper Beth-horon.)

25 And all those who escaped were healed by her daughter; for she was a woman physician, and she healed the sick.

26 And she also healed Edan the son of Ammihud,

27 Of the sons of Nun, the father of Hosea.[1]

28 ¶And their possessions and habitations were: Beth-el and its towns and Shechem and its towns and Anath and its towns;

29 And by the borders of the children of Manasseh, Beth-sechem and its towns, Taanach and its towns, Megiddo and its towns, and Dor and its towns. In these cities dwelt the children of Joseph the son of Israel.

30 ¶The sons of Asher were Imnah, Ishuah, Ishuai, Beriah, and their sister Sarah.

31 And the sons of Beriah: Hepher and Malchiel, who is the father of Birzavith.

32 And Hepher begat Phelet, Shomer, Hotham, and Shua their sister.

33 And the sons of Phelet: Pasach, Bimhal, and Ashvath. These are the sons of Phelet: Arah, and Hananaiel.

34 And the sons of Shamer: Ahi, Rohgah, Jehubbah, and Aram.

35 And the sons of his brother Helem: Zophah and Imna and Shelesh and Amal.

36 The sons of Zophah: Suah and Harnepher and Shual and Beri and Imrah,

37 Bezer and Hod and Shamma and Shilshah and Ithran and Beera.

38 And the sons of Jether: Jophaniah, and Pispah and Ara.

39 And the sons of Ulla: Arah and Haniel and Rezia.

[1] Or Joshua.

40 These were the sons of Asher, heads of their father's house, according to their generations, valiant men, chiefs of the princes. Their number was reckoned in the army for battle, twenty-six thousand men.

CHAPTER 8

NOW Benjamin begat Bela his first-born, Akbar the second, Ashcol the third,

2 Gera the fourth, Naaman the fifth,

3 Ahai the sixth, Arosh the seventh,

4 Mathim the eighth, Hasim the ninth,

5 And Adar the tenth.

6 And the sons of Bela were Abdo, Gerah and Abihud,

7 Abishua, Naaman, and Ahiah,

8 And Saphim, Hupham, and Ahiram.

9 And these are the sons of Abihud;

10 These are the heads of their fathers by their families, and they were carried captive to the plain of Naaman.

11 And he begat of his wife Harash, Hobab,

12 Zebiah, and Malcom, and Manasseh, Seriah, Jarmanah, and Zebaz;

13 These were his sons, heads of the fathers.

14 And Mahshim begat Hobat and Elipaleg.

15 The sons of Elipaleg: Eber, Mishlam, and Shamer,

16 Who built Eio and Lod, with the hamlets thereof;

17 And he became the chief of the fathers over the inhabitants of Gath;

18 And Shishak and Jeremoth,

19 And Zebadiah, Azor, and Adai,

20 And Mancel, Anshephi, Ebron, and Zabdai,

21 And Henani, Henaniah, Aulam, Anatoth, Peraiah,

22 Phael, and the children of Shishak, and Shimirah.

23 These were the heads of the fathers, by their generations; these were the men who dwelt in Jerusalem at first.

24 And in Gibeon dwelt the father of Gibeon, whose wife's name was Maachah,

25 And his first-born son Abron, also Kish, Bela, and Nadab,

26 And Good, Ahib, Ezabar, and Mikloth.

27 And Mikloth begat Maa.

28 And these also dwelt with their brethren in Jerusalem, opposite them.

29 And Mir begat Kish, and Kish begat Saul, and Saul begat Jonathan, Malchishua, Jashui, and Ashbashul.

30 And the son of Jonathan was crippled in his feet, and Jashui had a son whose name was Merib-baal, and Merib-baal begat Micah.

31 And the sons of Micah were Pithon, Melech, Tarea, Ahor, and Aran.

32 And Ahor begat Jehoiadah; and Jehoiadah begat Alemoth, Azmaveth, and Zimri; and Zimri begat Moza,

33 And Moza begat Canaaniah, and Canaaniah begat Zopa, Elasah his son, and Azel his son.

34 And Azel had six sons, whose names are these: Azri his first-born, Kim his second, Ishmael his third,

35 And Sheadiah, Obadiah, and Hanan. All these were the sons of Azel.

36 And the sons of Eshek his brother were Ulam the first-born, Jehush the second, and Eliphelet the third.

37 And the sons of Ulam were mighty men of valour, archers,

38 And they instructed their sons and their sons' sons,

39 One hundred and fifty.

40 All these are of the tribe of the sons of Benjamin.

CHAPTER 9

SO all Israel and Judah were considered wicked, for they were carried captive to Babylon because of their wickedness.

2 ¶Now the first inhabitants who dwelt in their possessions in their cities were the Israelites, the priests, the Levites, and the proselytes.

3 And in Jerusalem dwelt some of the children of Judah and of the children of Benjamin and of the children of Ephraim and of Manasseh:

4 Zori the son of Ammihud, the son of Omri, the son of Imri, the son of

Benjamin, of the descendants of Pharez the son of Judah.

5 And of the land of the Shilonites: Asaiah the first-born, and Bezaiah his brother.

6 And of the descendants of Zerah: Jeuel, and their brethren, six hundred and ninety.

7 And of the descendants of Benjamin: Sallu the son of Meshullam, the son of Hodiah, the son of Jahbanah,

8 And Jocaniah the son of Jeroham. These were the descendants of Uzzi the son of Machir and Meshullam the son of Reuel, the son of Jocaniah;

9 And their brethren, according to their generations, nine hundred and ninety-nine. All these were valiant men, captains over hundreds according to their fathers' houses.

10 ¶And of the priests: Jonadab, Jodaiah, and Zachim,

11 And Azariah the son of Hilkiah, the son of Meshullam, the son of Zadok, the son of Maro, the son of Ahitub, whose house was situated opposite the house of the LORD.

12 And Azariah the son of Jeroham, the son of Pashur, the son of Malchijah, and Mansai the son of Adiel, the son of Johanan, the son of Meshullam, the son of Meshraoth, the son of Immer;

13 And their brethren, heads of the house of their fathers, one thousand seven hundred and sixty; very able men for the work of the service of the house of the LORD.

14 And of the Levites: Shemaiah the son of Hashum, the son of Azrikam, the son of Hashabiah,

15 Of the descendants of Merari: Jarhum the son of Hadush, the son of Alal, and Mattaniah the son of Micah, the son of Zabdai, the son of Asaph;

16 And Obadiah the son of Shemaiah, the son of Cala, the son of Jerithun; and Berechiah the son of Asaph, the son of Hilkanah, who dwelt in Ramtha.[1]

17 And the porters were Shallum, Jacob, Talan, Hamnon, Ahihom, and Shallum,

[1] Or Rama.

18 Who hitherto waited in the king's gate eastward; they were the porters in the companies of the descendants of Levi.

19 And Shallum the son of Kora, the son of Akhsiph, the son of Korah, and his brethren and the members of his father's house were over the work and over the keepers of the gates of the tabernacle; and their fathers, who were over the host, were the keepers of the exit and of the entrance.

20 And Phinehas the son of Eleazar was ruler over them in time past, and the LORD was with him.

21 And Zechariah the son of Meshallum was porter of the door of the tabernacle of the congregation.

22 All those who were chosen to be porters in the gates were two hundred and twelve. These were reckoned by their genealogy, whom David and Samuel the prophet appointed to their set office.

23 For they appointed them and their sons to keep the gates of the house of the LORD and the house of the tabernacle of the congregation, as guards.

24 The gates were open toward the four directions, toward the east, west, north, and south.

25 And their brethren who kept the watch in their generation did not enter into the temple except once every seven days from time to time,

26 For these Levites were in their set office, and were in charge of the four gates in the four directions; and stood on guard, and were over the work and over the treasuries of the house of the LORD.

27 ¶And they lodged round about the house of the LORD, because upon them was the duty of guarding the gates.

28 And certain of them had charge of inspecting all the vessels of service, which were counted every morning when they were brought in and when they were taken out.

29 And some of the Levites were appointed over the vessels and over all the instruments of the sanctuary,

over the altar and the vessels, the wine, the oil, the frankincense, and the pure spices.

30 And some of the sons of the priests prepared the incense for the censers, and the gifts were given by the Levites.

31 And Mattithiah, one of the Levites, who was the first-born of Shallum, was intrusted with the office of the mysterious rites.

32 And also some of the descendants of Kohath were over their brethren and over the shewbread, to prepare the meal every sabbath.

33 And these are the ministers, chiefs of the fathers of the Levites, who kept the watch in the chambers round about the temple, because they were over the work day and night.

34 These were chiefs of the fathers of the Levites, according to their generations; and these dwelt in Jerusalem.

35 ¶And in Gibeon dwelt the father of Gibeon, and the name of his first-born son was Joel, and the name of his wife was Maachah;

36 And his second son was Abron; then Zur, Kishon, Baal, Ner, and Nadab,

37 And Gedor, Ahiah, Zechariah, and Mikloth.

38 And Mikloth begat Shimaez. And they also dwelt with their brethren in Jerusalem, opposite their brethren.

39 And Ner begat Kish; and Kish begat Saul; and Saul begat Jonathan and Malchishua and Jeshui and Ashbashul.

40 And Jeshui had a son, whose name was Merib-baal: and Merib-baal begat Micah.

41 And the sons of Micah were Pithon, Melech, and Ahaz.

42 And Ahaz begat Jezaniah; and Jezaniah begat Alemoth; and Alemoth begat Zimri; and Zimri begat Moza;

43 And Moza begat Canaaniah; and Rephaiah his son, Azel his son, and Eleasah his son.

44 And Azel had six sons, whose names are these: Uzzi his first-born, Kim his second, Ashmah, Shadiah,

Obadiah, and Hanan. These were the sons of Azel.

CHAPTER 10

NOW the Philistines fought against Israel; and the men of Israel fled from before the Philistines, and many fell slain on mount Gilboa.

2 And the Philistines overtook Saul and his sons; and the Philistines slew Jonathan and Jeshui and Malchishua, the sons of Saul.

3 And the battle went sore against Saul, and the archers who were skilled in shooting with bows found him; and when Saul saw them, he was sore afraid of them.

4 Then Saul said to his armourbearer, Draw your sword, and thrust me through with it, before these uncircumcised come and slay me and torment me. But his armourbearer would not; for he was sore afraid. So Saul took his own sword and fell on it.

5 And when his armorbearer saw that Saul was dead, he fell likewise on his sword, and died with him.

6 So Saul died and his three sons and his armourbearer, and all his mighty men died on that day together.

7 And when all the men of Israel who were on the other side of the valley and on the other side of the Jordan saw that Israel had fled and that Saul and his sons were slain, they forsook the cities and fled; and the Philistines came and dwelt in them.

8 ¶And it came to pass on the morrow, when the Philistines came to strip the slain, they found Saul and his three sons fallen on mount Gilboa.

9 And they cut off their heads, stripped them of their armour, and sent them to the land of the Philistines, throughout the towns and cities and provinces, to carry the good tidings to their idols and to their people;

10 And they put their garments and their armour in the house of their idols, and hanged their bodies by the wall of Beth-jashan.

11 ¶Now when the inhabitants of

Jabesh-gilead heard all that the Philistines had done to Saul,

12 They arose, all the valiant men, and went all the night, and took away the body of Saul and the bodies of his sons from the wall of Beth-jashan, and brought them to Jabesh and burned them there; then they took their bones and buried them under the oak in Jabesh, and fasted seven days.

13 ¶So Saul died because of the transgression which he committed against the LORD, and because of the command of the LORD, which he kept not,

14 And also because he consulted men who had familiar spirits, and did not inquire of the LORD his God. Therefore his kingdom was given to David the son of Jesse.

CHAPTER 11

THEN all Israel gathered themselves to David to Hebron, saying, Behold, we are your blood and your flesh always;

2 And moreover in times past, even when Saul was king over us, it was you that led out and brought in Israel; and the LORD your God said to you, You shall feed my people Israel, and you shall be ruler over all the tribes of Israel.

3 Wherefore all the elders of Israel came to the king to Hebron; and King David made a covenant with them in Hebron before the LORD; and they appointed David king over Israel. Thus the words of Samuel the prophet were confirmed, which he spoke in the name of the LORD.

4 ¶Then David and all Israel went to Jerusalem (which was formerly called Jebus) where the Jebusites were, the inhabitants of the land.

5 And the inhabitants of Jebus said to David, You shall not come in here. Nevertheless David gathered all the people together and took the city of Zion, which is called the city of David.

6 And David said, Whoever smites a Jebusite person first shall be chief and commander of the army. So Joab the son of Zeruiah went up first, and King David appointed him chief and commander of the army.

7 And David dwelt in the city of Zion; therefore they called it the city of David.

8 And David built the city round about, even from Millo, which is outside; and David gave the east side of the city to the rest of the people who were in the villages.

9 So David became greater and greater; and the LORD of hosts was with him.

10 ¶These are the chiefs of David's mighty men, who strengthened themselves with him in his kingdom and helped him to be made king over all Israel, according to the word of the LORD which he spoke concerning Israel.

11 And this is the number of the mighty men whom David had: seated in the first rank, chief of thirty men, Gedho, a valiant man; he lifted up his spear and slew three hundred men in one hour.

12 And after him was Eleazar his uncle's son, of the city of Dakhokh, who was over three hundred men.

13 He was with David at Pasi-demaya, when the Philistines were fighting there, where there was a field of barley; and the people fled from before the Philistines.

14 And they set themselves in the midst of the field, and delivered it and slew the Philistines; and the LORD wrought a great victory.

15 ¶Now three of the thirty chieftains went down to David, into the cave of Arlam; and the host of the Philistines was encamped in the valley of Gabarey.[1]

16 And David dwelt then in the tent, and the garrison of the Philistines was then at Bethlehem.

17 And David longed, and said, Oh that one would give me a drink of water from the great cistern of Bethlehem that is at the gate of the city!

18 And as soon as three men heard it, they broke through the camp of the Philistines, and went and drew

[1] Giants.

water out of the cistern of Bethlehem that was by the gate of the city, and took it and brought it to David; but David would not drink of it, but poured it out in the presence of the LORD,

19 And said, The LORD forbid that I should do this thing in the presence of my God; for these men went forth with the jeopardy of their lives. Therefore he would not drink it. These things did these three valiant men.

20 ¶And Abishai the brother of Joab was chief of thirty; for he lifted up his spear against three hundred and slew them, and he was highly honored, promoted to be over thirty men.

21 He was more honorable than the thirty men, and he became their chief and fought like thirty men.

22 Benaiah the son of Jehoiada, a valiant man of the province of Kabzeel who had done good deeds; he slew the two mighty men of Moab; also he went down and slew a lion in the midst of a forest on a snowy day.

23 And he slew an Egyptian, a man of great stature, five cubits high; and in the Egyptian's hand was a spear like a weaver's beam; and he went down against him with a staff, and took the spear out of the Egyptian's hand and slew him with his own spear.

24 These things did Benaiah the son of Jehoiada, and was more renowned than the three valiant men.

25 And he was honorable among the three valiant men, for he fought like three mighty men; and David set him over his bodyguard and over the chiefs of the army;

26 ¶Also the valiant men of the army were: Ashail the brother of Joab, Elhanan his uncle's son of Bethlehem,

27 Shammoth of the mount, King Helez the Pelonite,

28 Ira the son of Ikkes of Tekoa, Abiezer of Anathoth,

29 Sabbai the Hushathite, Ilai the Ahohite,

30 Maharai the Netophathite, Heled the son of Baanah the Netophathite,

31 Ithai the son of Ribai of Gibeah, of the Benjamites, Benaiah the Pirathonite,

32 Hadai of the brooks of Gaash, Abiel the Arbathite,

33 Uzban the Marhomite, Elipha the Shaalbonite,

34 The sons of Shem the Gizonite, Jonathan the son of Shage of mount Carmel,

35 Ahiram the son of Sacim of mount Beta, Elipon the son of Ur of Begarthon,

36 Hepher the Mecherathite, Ahijah the Hasarite,

37 Hezro the Carmelite, Lazar the Aobite,

38 Joel the brother of Nathan, Machad the Gaddite,

39 Zelek the Ammonite, Mahrai the Berothite, the armorbearer of Joab the son of Zuriah,

40 Ira the Ithrite, Garab the Ithrite,

41 Uriah the Hittite, Zabad the son of Ahlai,

42 Adina the son of Shara the Reubenite, of the house of Reubenites, and he was a captain over thirty men,

43 Hanan the son of Maachah, and Azrai the Anathotite,

44 Jehoshaphat the Ashterathite, Shama and Emael the sons of Hotham the Aroerite,

45 Jediael the son of Shimri, and Joha his brother,

46 Amozoth and Anael, Moham, Mozel, Ribai and his son Ashua; Ahmael and Jathmah the Moabites,

47 Eliel, Jathmah, Ober, Lasiel, and Ashkir.

CHAPTER 12

NOW these are all the mighty men of David, who stood by him in the battle, and they came with David to the city of Zinklag, when he fled from Saul the son of Kish; and they were among the mighty men who stood before David. If David had wished, they would have slain Saul the son of Kish, for they were mighty men of war, but David would not permit them to slay Saul.

2 They held the bows with their left hand and the swords with their right, and their bows were filled with

arrows, but David was unwilling to slay Saul, because he was the chief, the prince of the tribe of Benjamin.

3 These are the names of the mighty men who were with David: Ahiezer and his son Joash; Joel of Macsite; Shemaiah the Gibeathite; Pelet and Berachiah, the sons of Arboth; and Jehu the Anatothite;

4 And Shemaiah the Gibeonite, who was captain over thirty men, and fought equal to all of them; and Jeremiah, Nahaziel, Zabor, Azar,

5 Gadai, Jermoth, Bealiah, Shemariah, Shephatiah, Habar,

6 Elkanah, Jesiah, Azariel, Shebnah, Asaph,

7 Joah and Zechariah, the sons of Jeroham of Gadar.

8 And those of the tribe of the Gadites separated themselves to David to go out with him to the stronghold in the wilderness; mighty men and men of stature and fit for battle, who could handle sword and shield, whose faces were like the faces of lions, and who were swift for war upon the mountains:

9 Ezra the chief of the mighty men, Obadiah the second, Eliab the third,

10 Ashur the fourth, Jeremiah the fifth,

11 Athar the sixth, Eliel the seventh,

12 Johanan the eighth, Elzabad the ninth,

13 Jeremiah the tenth, Shepatiah the eleventh.

14 These were of the descendants of Gad, commanders of the army; one of them was captain over a hundred, and the others were over a thousand.

15 These are they who crossed the Jordan in the month of Nisan,[1] when it had overflowed all its banks; and they put to flight all the army that was encamped in the valley, both toward the east and toward the west. And these are the numbers of the commanders of the army who gathered together and came to David to Hebron to give him the kingdom of Saul, so that the word of Samuel the prophet might be fulfilled, who spoke by the command of the LORD.

[1] April, the first month.

16 And there came some of the children of Benjamin and Judah to the camp to David.

17 And David went out to meet them and blessed them, and said to them, If you have come peaceably to me to help us, then may the LORD grant you a double portion of that which you have in your heart; but if you have come to betray me and to deliver me to my adversaries, seeing that I have not sinned against you and there is no wrong in my hands, the God of my fathers knows it, and he will rebuke whoever is wrong among us.

18 Then the spirit of might came upon Amasa, the son of Jatar, chief of the thirty, and he answered and said to David, Come on, David, come on, O son of Jesse! I am also with you, peace be to you, be not afraid, and peace will be given to you from your helpers; for your God is your helper in every hour. Then David received them, and made them captains of the army.

19 And some of the men of the tribe of Manasseh went over to David when he went to war with the Philistines against Saul to battle; but they would not go with Saul to war to help him, because they hated him, for they had gone and made a secret treaty with the princes of the Philistines, saying, Let us go first and fall on Saul our master;

20 And as he goes to Zinklag, we will besiege him and capture him alive. These are their names: Ada, Zabor, Jediael, Michael, Elihu, and Jozabad, commanders of thousands of the house of Manasseh.

21 And they helped David when he went against the band of raiders; for they were all mighty men of valor and commanders over all the army, and they did as they pleased through him.

22 For every day they went into the presence of David to eat food before him, for he loved them exceedingly.

23 ¶And of the children of Judah who bore sword and spear were six

thousand and eight hundred mighty men of war.

24 And of the children of Simeon, mighty men of valor for the war, eight thousand and seven hundred.

25 And of the children of Levi, four thousand and six hundred.

26 And Jehoiada was the leader of the family of the Aaronites, and with him were three thousand and seven hundred;

27 And Zadok, a young man mighty of valour, and of his father's house and his brothers, twenty-two officers.

28 And of the children of Benjamin, the kindred of Saul, three thousand; for until the day in which Saul was slain, they guarded the house of Saul.

29 And of the children of Ephraim, twenty thousand and eight hundred, mighty men of valour, famous throughout the house of their fathers.

30 And of the half tribe of Manasseh, eighteen thousand, who were renowned, and they came first to make David king.

31 And of the children of Issachar, men who had understanding in their times, who did good and upright deeds before the LORD; their chiefs were two hundred; and all their brethren did whatever they were commanded.

32 And of the tribe of Zebulun, such as went forth to battle, expert in war, with all weapons of war, fifty thousand, who were ready to fight against those whose loyalty was doubtful concerning the kingdom of David.

33 And of the children of Naphtali, a thousand officers; and with them were thirty-seven thousand men with shield and spear.

34 And of the Danites, expert in war, twenty-eight thousand and six hundred.

35 And of Asher, such as went forth to battle, valiant men of war, forty thousand.

36 And of the other side of the Jordan, of the Reubenites and of the Gadites and of the half tribe of Manasseh, armed with all manner of weapons of war, one hundred and twenty thousand.

37 All these mighty men of war went to battle with a perfect heart, and came to Hebron to make David king over all Israel; and also all the rest of the chiefs of Israel came with a sincere heart to make David king over Israel.

38 And they were there with David for three days, eating and drinking; for their brethren had prepared for them.

39 Now these were the names of the tribes who supplied them with food, who were near them:

40 The tribes of Issachar and Zebulun and Naphtali brought bread on asses and on camels and on mules, also flour and raisins and baskets of grapes and wine and oil and sheep and oxen in abundance; for there was great joy in Israel.

CHAPTER 13

AND David consulted with the commanders of thousands and of hundreds, and with all the leaders and governors of Israel.

2 And David said to all the assemblies of Israel, If it seems good to you, let us beseech the LORD our God to repair the breaches of our brethren who reside in all towns of Israel, and settle with them priests and Levites in their cities and suburbs;

3 So that they may gather themselves and come to us, and pray before the LORD our God and beseech him because of our sins; for we did not pray before him in the days of Saul.

4 And all the assemblies said that they would do so.

5 So David gathered all Israel together, from the river of Egypt even to the entrance of Hamath,[1] to bring the ark of the LORD from Koriath-narin.

6 And David went up, and all Israel, to Koriath-narin, which belongs to the tribe of Judah, to bring up from there the ark of the LORD God who dwells upon the high cherubim, which are known by his name.

7 And they placed the ark of the LORD in a new cart, and carried it out

1 Antioch.

of the house of Abinadab; and Uzza and his brothers drove the cart.

8 And David and all Israel played before the Lord with all their might, and with singing and with harps and with psalteries and with cymbals and with timbrels.

9 ¶And when they came to the threshing floor of Remin, Uzza put forth his hand to hold the ark; for the oxen ran toward the threshing floor.

10 And the anger of the Lord was kindled against Uzza, and he smote him there because he put forth his hand to the ark; and he died there before the ark.

11 And David was displeased because the Lord had smote Uzza; wherefore that place is called Toretha-di-Uzza to this day.

12 And David was afraid of the Lord that day, saying, How can I bring the ark of God home to me?

13 So David was unwilling to bring the ark home to the city of David. And David commanded it be carried to the house of Ober-edom the Gittite.

14 And the ark of the Lord remained in the house of Ober-edom the Gittite three months. And the Lord blessed the house of Ober-edom the Gittite and all that he had.

CHAPTER 14

NOW Hiram king of Tyre [1] sent messengers to David, and timber of cedars, with masons and carpenters, to build a house for him.

2 And David perceived that the Lord had chosen him to be king over Israel, for his kingdom was exalted because of his people Israel.

3 ¶And David took more wives in Jerusalem, after he had come from Hebron, and there were born to him more sons and daughters.

4 Now these are the names of the children who were born to him in Jerusalem: Shammua, Shocob, Nathan, and Solomon,

5 Ibhar, Elisha, Eliphalet,

6 Nogah, Nepheg, and Naphia,

[1] Sur.

7 And Elishama, Eliada, and Eliphalet.

8 ¶And when the Philistines heard that David was anointed king over all Israel, all the Philistines went up to seek David. And David heard of it, and went out against them.

9 And the Philistines came and encamped in the valley of giants.

10 And David inquired of the Lord, saying, Shall I go up against the Philistines? And wilt thou deliver them into my hands? And the Lord said to him, Go up; for I will deliver them into your hands.

11 So they came up to the valley of Toretha, and David smote them there. Then David said, The Lord has broken in upon my enemies before me like the breaking forth of waters; therefore they called the name of that place the valley of Toretha.

12 And when they had left their idols there, David gave a commandment to his mighty men, saying, Burn them with fire and scatter their ashes to the wind.

13 And the Philistines came up again and encamped in the valley of giants.

14 Therefore David inquired again of God; and God said to him, You shall not go up after them; but turn away from them, and go attack them from the front.

15 And it shall be, when you hear the sound of howling in the top of the mountain, then you shall go out to battle; for the Lord has gone forth before you to smite the army of the Philistines.

16 And David therefore did as the Lord commanded him; and they smote the army of the Philistines from Gibeon even to Gadar.

17 And the fame of David went out into all lands; and the Lord brought the fear of him upon all the nations.

CHAPTER 15

AND David built citadels for himself in the city of David, and also built a place for the ark of the Lord and for the instruments of the tabernacle.

2 Then David commanded the Levites to carry the ark of the LORD and the instruments of the tabernacle; for the Levites the LORD had chosen to minister and to carry the ark of the LORD, and to look after it for ever.

3 And David gathered all Israel together to Jerusalem, to bring up the ark of the LORD to the place which he had built for it.

4 And David assembled the descendants of Aaron and the Levites:

5 Of the sons of Kohath, Uriel the elder and his brethren, a hundred and twenty;

6 Of the sons of Merari, Ashiel the elder and his brethren, two hundred and twenty;

7 Of the sons of Gershon, Joel the elder and his brethren, a hundred and thirty;

8 Of the sons of Elizaphan, Shemaiah the elder and his brethren, two hundred;

9 Of the sons of Hebron, Eliab the elder and his brethren, eighty;

10 Of the sons of Uzziel, Amminadab the elder and his brethren, a hundred and twelve.

11 Then David called for Zadok the priest and Abiathar, and for the Levites, for Uriel, Amsah, Joel, Asaiah, Shemaiah, Uriel, and Amminadab,

12 And said to them, You are the chiefs of the fathers of the Levites; sanctify yourselves, both you and your brethren, that you may bring up the ark of the LORD God of Israel to the place which has been built for it before,

13 So that the LORD our God may not smite us because we did not seek him after the due order.

14 So the priests and the Levites sanctified themselves to bring up the ark of the LORD God of Israel.

15 And the Levites carried the ark of the LORD upon their shoulders with the poles thereon, as Moses had commanded according to the word of the LORD.

16 And David spoke to the elders of the Levites to appoint their brethren to be singers with instruments of music, psalteries and harps and cymbals, sounding by raising up their voices in joy.

17 So the Levites appointed Heman the son of Joel; and of his brethren, Asaph the son of Berechiah; and of the sons of Merari their brethren, Ethan the son of Kushaiah;

18 And with them their brethren of the second order, Zechariah the son of Neaiel, Jehiel, Eliab, Benaiah, Asa, Mattitha, Elipheleu, Mikiaho, Oberedom, and Jeiel.

19 Now these were all those who stood by the gates and sang: Heman, Asaph, and Ethan.

20 These were all who played with the instruments of brass to minister in the service: Azariah, Aziel, Jehiel, Unni, Eliab, Maasiah, and Benaiah;

21 And those who sang songs: Mattitha, Mikiaho, Ober-edom, Uzzael, and Uzzanaiah; these played with harps every day at three o'clock and at nine o'clock.

22 And Benaiah, chief of the Levites, played every day in the booth, for they had prepared a place for him.

23 And Berechiah and Hilkanah looked after the ark, providing for it what was needed.

24 And Shebaniah, Jehoshaphat, Nathanael, Amasai, Zechariah, Benaiah, and Eliezer, the priests, did blow with the trumpets before the ark of the LORD; and Ober-edom and Ahiah looked after the ark.

25 ¶So David and the elders of Israel and the commanders of thousands went to bring up the ark of the covenant of the LORD from the house of Ober-edom to the city of David with great joy.

26 And it came to pass when the LORD helped the Levites who carried the ark in which was the covenant of the LORD that they sacrificed seven bullocks and seven rams.

27 And David was clothed with robes of fine linen, and all the Levites who bore the ark were also clothed with robes of fine linen; and David wore upon his linen garments an ephod of fine linen.

28 Thus David and all Israel brought up the ark in which was the covenant of the LORD, with songs and with sound of straight trumpets and curved trumpets and shouting.

29 ¶And it came to pass as the ark in which was the covenant of the LORD reached the city of David, Michal the daughter of Saul looked out a window and saw David dancing and playing, and she despised him in her heart.

CHAPTER 16

SO they brought the ark of the LORD and set it in its place in the tent that David had pitched for it; and they offered burnt offerings and peace offerings before the ark of the LORD.

2 And when David had finished offering the burnt offerings and the peace offerings, he blessed the people of Israel in the name of the LORD of hosts.

3 And he distributed to all the people of Israel, both men and women and young men and the little ones, to every one a loaf of bread, a portion of meat, and a fine white loaf. Then all the people went away, every one to his own house.

4 ¶And he appointed certain of the Levites to minister before the ark of the LORD and to invoke and to thank and to praise the LORD God of Israel:

5 Asaph the chief, and second to him Zechariah, also Jeiel, Jehiel, Mattitha, Eliab, Benaiah, Asaph, Amminadab, Asaph, Nahaziel, and Asaph.

6 These were all the priests who sounded with trumpets continually before the ark of the LORD.

7 ¶Then on that day David delivered this psalm, both he and the chiefs of all the priests and the Levites to praise the LORD, in the company of Asaph and his brethren. These are the headings of the songs which David sang on that day before the ark of the LORD:

8 Give thanks to the LORD, call upon his name, make known his deeds among the peoples.

9 Sing to him, give thanks to him, tell of all his wondrous works.

10 Glory in his holy name; let the heart of those who seek the LORD rejoice.

11 Seek the LORD and his strength, pray before him continually.

12 Remember his marvellous works that he has done, his wonders and the judgments of his mouth,

13 O you descendants of Abraham his servant, children of Jacob, his chosen ones.

14 He is the LORD our God; his laws are in all the earth.

15 Be mindful of his covenant for ever, the word which he commanded to a thousand generations,

16 Even his oath to Abraham and the covenant which he made with the sons of Isaac;

17 And he has confirmed the same to Jacob for a law, and to Israel for an everlasting covenant,

18 Saying, To you I will give the land of Canaan, the lot of your inheritance;

19 When you were but few, even a few in numbers and strangers in it.

20 And when you were carried away captive from nation to nation and from kingdom to another kingdom,

21 He permitted not the rulers to harm you, yea, he chastened kings for your sakes,

22 Saying, Touch not my anointed ones and do my prophets no harm.

23 Sing to the LORD, all the earth; show forth from day to day his salvation.

24 Declare his glory among the nations;

25 For great is the LORD, and greatly to be praised; and he is to be revered above all kings.

26 For all the gods of the Gentiles are images; but the LORD made the heavens.

27 Glory and majesty are in his presence; strength and greatness are in his sanctuary.

28 Give thanks to the LORD, O families of the peoples, give thanks before the LORD due to his glory and strength.

29 Give thanks to the LORD with the honor due to his name; bring offer-

ings, and give thanks before him with the prayer of your mouth; worship the LORD with holy songs.

30 Tremble before him all the earth; the world also shall be stable, that it be not moved.

31 Let the heavens be glad, and let the earth rejoice; and let men say among the nations, The LORD reigns.

32 Let the sea roar and the fulness thereof; let the fields rejoice, and all that is therein.

33 Then shall the trees of the forest sing praises at the presence of the LORD because he comes to judge the earth. He shall judge the world with justice, and reprove the peoples in faithfulness;

34 Say also, O give thanks to the LORD; for he is good; for his mercy endures for ever.

35 Save us, O LORD, save us and gather us together, and bring us back from among the nations, that we may give thanks to thy holy name, and glory in thy praises.

36 Blessed be the LORD God of Israel for ever and ever. Then all the people shall say, Amen; and with a pleasant and pure mouth, let them praise their God.

37 ¶So he left there before the ark of the covenant of the LORD, Asaph and his brethren, to minister before the LORD continually, each man working in his appointed day;

38 And Ober-edom with his brethren, sixty-eight; Ober-edom the junior, the son of Jotham, and Haso. All of these were keepers of the outer gates;

39 And Zadok the priest, and his brethren the priests, these were all priests who ministered before the tabernacle of the LORD with a great joy in the town of Gibeon,

40 To offer burnt offerings to the LORD upon the altar of the burnt offering continually morning and evening, and to do according to all that is written in the law of the LORD, which he gave by the hand of Moses to teach to the children of Israel;

41 And these are the names of the men who stood up singing praises: Haman, Ariton, and the rest of the righteous men whose names were not expressed by name, to give thanks to the LORD because his mercy endures for ever;

42 And these righteous men gave thanks not with the instruments of singing, neither with the tambourines nor with the timbrels nor with the curved trumpets nor with the straight trumpets nor with the cymbals, but with a pleasant mouth and with pure and perfect prayer and with righteousness and with purity to the LORD God of hosts, the God of Israel.

43 Then David dismissed the people, and they went every man to his own house; and David returned to bless his household.

CHAPTER 17

NOW it came to pass when David dwelt in his house, David said to Nathan the prophet, Behold, I dwell in a house which is covered with the beams of cedars, but the ark of the covenant of the LORD is resting in the midst of the tent of hair of goats.

2 Then Nathan said to David, Go and do all that is in your heart.

3 ¶And it came to pass that same night, the word of the LORD came to Nathan the prophet, saying,

4 Go and thus say to my servant David, You shall not build me a house to dwell in;

5 For I have not dwelt in a house since the day that I brought up Israel out of Egypt to this day; but I moved from tent to tent.

6 Behold, wherever I have walked with all Israel, did I speak a word to any of the judges of Israel whom I commanded to judge my people Israel, saying, Why have you not built me a house which is covered with cedars?

7 Now therefore thus shall you say to my servant David, Thus says the LORD of hosts: I took you from the sheepfold, even from following the sheep, that you should be king over my people Israel;

8 And I have been with you wheresoever you went and have destroyed your enemies from before

you, and I have made you a great name, like the name of the great men who are on the earth.

9 I will also appoint a place for my people Israel and will cause them to settle, and they shall dwell in their place and shall be moved no more; neither shall the wicked men carry them captive any more, as formerly.

10 And since the day that I made you a judge over my people Israel, I have given you rest from all your enemies. Moreover the LORD has declared to you that the kingdom is established for ever.

11 ¶And it shall come to pass when your days are fulfilled that you shall go to be gathered with your fathers, I will raise up your offspring after you, who shall come out of your loins, and I will establish him in your kingdom.

12 He shall build a house to my name, and I will establish the throne of his kingdom for ever.

13 I will be his father and he shall be my son; and I will not take my mercy away from him, as I took it from Saul, who was before you.

14 But I will make him a ruler in my house and in my kingdom for ever; and his throne shall be established for evermore.

15 According to all these words and according to all this vision, so did Nathan speak to David.

16 ¶And King David came and sat before the LORD and said, Who am I in thy presence, O LORD God, and what is my house, that thou hast brought me to this eminence?

17 And yet this was a small thing in thine eyes, O LORD God; for thou hast also spoken of thy servant's house for a great while to come; for all the men who worship thee with all their heart, thou bringest out of the darkness into the light, O LORD God.

18 What more can David boast to speak before thee? For the works of thy servant are known, O LORD God.

19 For thou knowest that which is in the heart of thy servant, that thou hast done for him all this greatness in making great thy servant.

20 Therefore I know, O LORD God, there is none like thee and there is no God besides thee, according to all that we have heard with our ears.

21 And what other nation on earth is united like thy people Israel? For thou didst reveal thyself from heaven and saved them, and for their sakes thou didst perform great and terrible wonders and brought severe plagues upon the Egyptians until thou didst bring them out from among them.

22 For thy people Israel thou didst make thine own people for ever; and thou, O LORD, didst become their God.

23 Therefore now, O LORD, let the word that thou hast spoken concerning thy servant and concerning his house be established for ever, and do as thou hast said.

24 And let thy works be established for ever, and thy name be magnified in the world for ever, so that the people shall say, The LORD of hosts is the God of Israel; and let the house of David thy servant be established before thee for ever.

25 For thou, O my God, hast revealed the secret to thy servant, and hast said to him, Build for yourself a house; therefore thy servant has set in his heart to pray before thee this prayer.

26 And now, O LORD, thou art God, and all thy words are true, with which thou hast promised this goodness to thy servant;

27 Now therefore reveal thyself to bless the house of thy servant, that it may be before thee for ever; for thou, O LORD God, hast spoken, and of thy blessing shall all the houses of righteous men be blessed for ever.

CHAPTER 18

AND after these things it came to pass that David smote the Philistines and destroyed them, and took the power from the hand of the Philistines, and took Gath and the small villages that were round about it out of the hand of the Philistines.

2 And he smote Moab; and the Moabites became David's servants and brought tribute.

3 ¶Then David slew Hadarezer the king of Nisibin, as he went to establish his dominion by the river Euphrates.

4 And David took from him a thousand chariots and seven thousand horsemen, and David hamstrung all the chariot horses, but reserved of them a hundred chariots.

5 And when the Edomites and the Arameans of Damascus came to help Hadarezer king of Nisibin, David slew of the Edomites twenty-two thousand men.

6 Then David appointed governors in Damascus, and the Arameans became David's servants and brought tribute. Thus the LORD preserved David wheresoever he went.

7 And David took the shields of gold that were hanging on the horses of the servants of Hadarezer, and brought them to Jerusalem.

8 Likewise from Tibhath and from Berothi, cities of Hadarezer, David took very much brass, wherewith Solomon made the bronze sea and the pillars of brass and the oxen of brass and the vessels of brass in abundance.

9 ¶Now Pul, king of Hamath, heard that David had smitten the whole army of Hadarezer, king of Nisibin;

10 And he sent Jehoram his son to David to inquire of his welfare and to congratulate him because he had fought against Hadarezer and killed him (for Hadarezer was a valiant warrior) and Jehoram had with him all manner of vessels of gold and silver and brass.

11 ¶Some of these also King David dedicated to the LORD, together with the silver and the gold that he had captured from all the nations which he had subdued: from the Edomites, from the Moabites, from the children of Ammon, from the Philistines, and from the Amalekites.

12 Moreover Abishai the son of Zuriah brother of Joab slew the Edomites in the valley of salt, eighteen thousand men.

13 ¶And David appointed governors over the Edomites, and all the Edomites became David's servants.

Thus the LORD preserved David wherever he went.

14 ¶So David reigned over all Israel and executed justice and righteousness to all the people.

15 And Joab the son of Zuriah was over all the army; and Jehoshaphat the son of Ahilud was recorder.

16 And Zadok the son of Ahitub and Ahimelek the son of Abiathar were the priests; and Seriah was scribe;

17 And Benaiah the son of Jehoiadah was over the archers and the slingers; and the sons of David were princes of the realm.

CHAPTER 19

NOW it came to pass after this that Nahash the king of the children of Ammon died, and his son Hanun reigned in his stead.

2 And David said, I will show kindness to Hanun the son of Nahash, just as his father showed kindness to me. So David sent messengers to comfort him concerning his father. So David's servants came into the land of the children of Ammon to Hanun to comfort him.

3 But the princes of the children of Ammon said to Hanun their lord, Do you think that David really did honor your father when he was alive and that he has truly sent comforters to you? It is for the purpose of spying the city and knowing the entrances and the exits that David has sent his servants to us.

4 So Hanun took David's servants and shaved half of their beards and half of their heads and cut off their garments in the midst as far as their buttocks, and sent them away.

5 And when they had told David, he sent men to meet them, for the men were greatly ashamed. And the king said to them, Remain at Jericho until your beards have grown, and then return.

6 ¶And when the children of Ammon saw that they had made themselves odious to David's servants, Hanun and the children of Ammon sent a thousand talents of silver to hire for themselves chariots and

horsemen from Aram-nahrin,[1] from Haran, from Nisibin, and from Edom.

7 So they hired thirty-two thousand horsemen, and the king of Haran, the king of Edom, the king of Aram-nahrin, and the king of Nisibin, and all their armies; who came and encamped before Medeba. And the children of Ammon gathered themselves together from their cities and came to battle.

8 And when David heard of it, he sent Joab and all the army of the mighty men.

9 And the children of Ammon came out and set the battle in array before the gate of the city; and the kings who had come to them and their armies were encamping by themselves in the fields.

10 Now when Joab saw that the battle was fierce against him in front and in the rear, he chose some of all the valiant men of Israel and arrayed them against the Arameans.

11 And the rest of the people he placed under the command of Abishai his brother, and they pitched battle against the children of Ammon.

12 And he said to him, If the Arameans are too strong for me, then you shall come to my help; but if the children of Ammon are too strong for you, then I will come to help you.

13 Be of good courage, and let us be strong for the sake of our people and for the sake of the cities of our God; and let the LORD do that which is good in his sight.

14 So Joab and the people who were with him drew near against the Arameans to battle, and they fled before him.

15 And when the children of Ammon saw that the Arameans had fled, they likewise fled before Abishai his brother, and entered into the city. Then Joab returned to Jerusalem.

16 ¶And when the Arameans saw that they had been defeated before Israel, they sent messengers and brought out the Arameans who were beyond the river; and they came to Hilam, and Shobach the commander

of the army of Hadarezer went before them.

17 And it was told David; and he gathered all Israel and came against them, and set the battle in array against the Arameans and fought with them.

18 And the Arameans fled before Israel; and David slew of the Arameans seven thousand men who fought in chariots and four thousand footmen, and killed there Shobach the commander of the army of Hadarezer.

19 And when the servants of Hadarezer saw that they had been defeated before Israel, they made peace with David and served him; and the Arameans were not willing to help the children of Ammon any more.

CHAPTER 20

AND it came to pass that in the next year, at the time when kings go out to battle, Joab mobilized the armed forces and came and encamped against the land of the children of Ammon and took some of the towns, and came and besieged Rabbath their capital city. But David remained at Jerusalem. And Joab captured Rabbath and destroyed it.

2 And David took the crown of their king from off his head, and he weighed it and found it to weigh a talent of gold, and there were precious stones in it; and David set it upon his head; and he brought also much spoil out of the city.

3 And he brought out the people who were in it, and bound them with chains, iron bands, locks and fetters. And thus David did bind all of them, and did likewise to all men who were found in the cities of the children of Ammon; but he did not kill any one of them; and he brought them and settled them in the villages of the land of Israel. Then David and all the people returned to Jerusalem.

4 ¶And it came to pass after this that there arose war at Gaza with the Philistines; then Sibbechai the Hushathite slew Sippai, who was one of the descendants of the giants.

5 And there was war again with the

[1] Mesopotamia.

Philistines; and Elhanan the son of Jair slew Lahmi of the descendants of the giants, who was the brother of Goliath the mighty man of Gath, whose spear staff was like a weaver's beam.

6 And there was again war at Gath, where there was a man of great stature, who had six fingers on each hand and six toes on each foot, twenty-four in number; he also was the son of a giant.

7 But when he defied Israel, Jonathan the son of Shimea David's brother slew him.

8 These four were born to the giants in Gath; and they fell by the hand of David and by the hand of his servants.

CHAPTER 21

THEN Satan stood up against Israel and provoked David to number Israel.

2 So David said to Joab the son of Zuriah and to the princes of the people, Go, number the people of Israel from Beersheba even to Dan, and come back to me, that I may know the number of the people.

3 And Joab said to King David, May the LORD make his people a hundred times so many more as they are, and let the eyes of my lord the king see it, for they are all his servants; why then should our lord the king require this thing?

4 Nevertheless the king's word prevailed against Joab. Wherefore Joab departed and went throughout all Israel and came back to Jerusalem.

5 ¶And Joab gave the sum of the number of the people to David. And the total number of the children of Israel was one million and one hundred thousand footmen who drew the sword; and the tribe of Judah was four hundred and seventy thousand men who drew the sword.

6 But the Levites, the priests, and the tribe of Benjamin were not counted among them; for the king's word was abominable to Joab, and Joab was unwilling to number them.

7 And the LORD was displeased with this thing, because David had numbered Israel.

8 And David said to the LORD, I have sinned greatly in that I have done this thing; but now, take away the iniquity of thy servant; for I have done very foolishly.

9 ¶And David arose early in the morning, and the word of the LORD came to Gad, the prophet, saying,

10 Go and tell David, saying, Thus says the LORD: I offer you three disasters; choose one of them, that I may do it to you.

11 So Gad the prophet came to David and said to him, Thus says the LORD: Choose for yourself

12 Either three years of famine in the land or three months to be defeated before your enemies while they shall pursue you and rule over you or else three days the sword of the LORD in Israel. Now therefore advise what answer you will give to him who sent me to you.

13 And David said to Gad, I am in a great distress; let me be delivered into the hands of the LORD; for his mercies are very great; but let me not be delivered into the hand of men.

14 ¶So the LORD sent pestilence upon Israel; and there fell of Israel seventy thousand men.

15 And the LORD sent an angel to Jerusalem to destroy it; and as he was destroying it, the LORD saw and considered it and averted the disaster, and said to the angel that destroyed, You have destroyed a great many, stay now your hand. And the angel of the LORD stood by the threshing floor of Aran the Jebusite.

16 And David lifted up his eyes and saw the angel of the LORD standing between heaven and earth, having a drawn sword in his hand stretched out over Jerusalem. Then David and the elders of Israel, who were with him clothed in sackcloth, fell upon their faces.

17 And David said to the LORD, Is it not I who commanded the people to be numbered? Even I it is who have sinned, and the folly which I have committed is great; but as for these innocent sheep, what have they done? Let thy hand, O LORD my God, be against me and against my father's

house; but let the plague cease from the people.

18 ¶Then the angel of the LORD said to Gad the prophet, Go and say to David that David should go up and build an altar to the LORD in the threshing floor of Aran the Jebusite.

19 And David went up at the saying of Gad which he spoke in the name of the LORD.

20 And David saw the angel who was destroying the people, that he had stayed his hand and was destroying no more.

21 And as David came to Aran, Aran turned and saw David and went out of his threshing floor, and bowed himself to David with his face to the ground.

22 Then David said to Aran, Give me the place of this threshing floor, that I may build on it an altar to the LORD; you shall give it to me for money at a good price, that the plague may be stayed from the people.

23 And Aran said to David, Take it to you, and let my lord the king do that which is good in his eyes; and I will give you oxen also for burnt offering and the threshing instrument for wood and the wheat for the meal offering; everything which is needed I shall give it all.

24 But King David said to Aran, Far be it, but I will surely buy it with money for the full price; for I will not take that which is yours and offer a burnt offering to the LORD without cost.

25 So David bought from Aran that place of the threshing floor for fifty shekels.

26 And David built there an altar to the LORD, and offered burnt offerings and peace offerings of lambs, and prayed before the LORD and he answered him, and fire came down from heaven and consumed the burnt offerings that were upon the altar.

27 And the LORD commanded the angel; and he put back his sword again into its sheath.

28 ¶At that time when David saw that the LORD had answered him in the threshing floor of Aran the Jebu-site, then he offered there many sacrifices.

29 And he pitched there before the LORD the tabernacle which Moses had made in the wilderness when the children of Israel went forth out of Egypt.

30 At that time David was exceedingly afraid, and could not go to pray before the LORD for he was afraid because of the sword of the angel of the LORD.

CHAPTER 22

THEN David said, This is the house of the LORD God and this is the altar of the burnt offerings for Israel.

2 And David commanded to gather together all the proselytes who were in the land of Israel, to make some of them stonecutters to hew stones for the house of the LORD;

3 And to make some of them blacksmiths to forge iron to make axes and hatchets for hewing stones. And David prepared bars of iron, and brass in abundance without weight;

4 Also cedar trees in abundance; for the Tyrians and the Sidonians brought much cedar wood to David.

5 And David said, Solomon my son is still a small boy, and concerning him it is said in the book that he will build a house to the LORD which will be exceedingly magnificent, of fame and of glory throughout all countries; I will therefore prepare everything necessary for it while I am living. So David prepared everything that was needed for the house, and lacked nothing.

6 ¶Then he called for Solomon his son and said to him,

7 You shall build a house for the LORD God of Israel;

8 For he has sent to me by a prophet, saying, You have shed blood abundantly and have made great wars; you shall not build a house to my name because you have shed much blood upon the earth in my sight.

9 Behold, a son shall be born to you who shall be a man of peace; and I will give him rest from all his enemies round about; for his name

shall be Solomon, and there shall be peace and quietness to Israel in his days.

10 He shall build a house for my name; and he shall be to me like a son, and I will be to him like a father; and I will establish the throne of his kingdom over Israel for ever.

11 Now, my son, the Lord be with you, so that you may prosper, and build the house of the Lord your God, as he has said to me.

12 Only may the Lord give you wisdom and understanding, and give you charge concerning Israel, that you may keep the law of the Lord your God, just as he has commanded you.

13 Then you shall prosper if you take heed to observe these commandments and the statutes and judgments just as the Lord charged Moses to teach Israel, then you will be strong and of good courage; fear not, nor be dismayed.

14 Now, behold, I have prepared for you everything necessary for the building of the house of the Lord. I have prepared for you a hundred thousand talents of gold, a million talents of silver; and brass and iron without weight; no man knows its weight, for it is in abundance; timber also and stones I have prepared; and you may add thereto.

15 Moreover there are workers with you in abundance, stonecutters, masons, and carpenters,

16 Cunning men for every manner of work; of gold, silver, brass, and iron in abundance. Be strong therefore and be doing, and the Lord will help you.

17 ¶David also commanded all the elders of Israel, saying, You must help Solomon my son.

18 For behold, the Lord your God is with you; and he will help you and relieve you on every side. Behold he has delivered all the inhabitants of the land into your hand, and the land is subdued before the Lord and before his people.

19 Now set your heart and your soul to pray before the Lord your God; arise therefore, and build the sanctuary of the Lord God, and bring there the ark in which is the covenant of the Lord our God, and the holy vessels of the Lord our God; and build the house because of his great name by which we are known.

CHAPTER 23

WHEN David was old and full of days, he made Solomon his son king over Israel.

2 ¶And he gathered together all the elders of the priests and the Levites.

3 Now the Levites were numbered from the age of thirty years and upward; and their number by their polls, man by man, was thirty-eight thousand.

4 Of them David appointed overseers over the work of the house of the Lord, twenty-four men over every thousand workers; and judges and scribes, six men over each hundred workers

5 To look after the building, to carry on their work, to oversee the resources and the work, and to give an accounting of wealth and the alms which they had distributed to the poor.

6 And David appointed administrators and managers over the poor and needy, to provide and distribute to the poor; one person over each ten, and they lacked nothing. And David appointed them all in their courses according to the sons of Levi; namely, Gershon, Kohath, and Merari.

7 ¶Of the Gershonites were Laadan and Shimei.

8 The sons of Ladan: his first-born was Nahliel, and then Jotham and Joel, three.

9 And the sons of Shimei: Shelomoth, Haziel, and Aran, three. These were the chiefs of the fathers of Shimei.

10 And the sons of Shimei were, Nahat, Zabda, Jeush, and Beriah. These were the four sons of Shimei.

11 And Nahat was his first-born, Zabda the second; but Jeush and Beriah did not have many sons; therefore they were included in their father's family as one.

12 The sons of Kohath: Amram, Izhar, Hebron, and Uzziel, four.

13 The sons of Amram: Aaron and Moses; and Aaron was chosen to minister in the Holy of Holies, he and his sons for ever, to burn incense before the LORD, to minister to him, and to bless in his name for ever.

14 Now as for Moses the prophet of God, his sons were named among the tribe of Levi.

15 The sons of Moses were Gershon and Eliezer.

16 The son of Gershon was Samuel his first-born.

17 And the son of Eliezer was Arhimah his first-born. And Eliezer had no other sons; but the son of Arhimah was Ribbi his first-born.

18 And the son of Izhar was Shelomith his first-born.

19 The sons of Hebron: Joda his first-born, Amariah the second, Nahzaiel the third, and Nakmaiel the fourth.

20 The sons of Uzziel: Micah his first-born and Shoh the second.

21 ¶The sons of Merari: Mahli and Mushi. The sons of Mahli: Eleazar and Kish.

22 And Eleazar died, and had no sons, but daughters; and the sons of their uncle Kish took them for wives in marriage.

23 The sons of Mushi: Mahli, Eder, and Jeremoth, three.

24 ¶These were the sons of Levi after the house of their fathers, even the chiefs of the fathers, as they were counted by number of names by their polls, who were overseers over the work for the service of the house of the LORD, from the age of twenty years and upward.

25 For David said, The LORD God of Israel has given rest to his people, and he dwells in Jerusalem for ever;

26 And he also said to the Levites that they should carry the tabernacle and all the vessels for the service thereof.

27 For by the last words of David the Levites were numbered from twenty years old and upward,

28 Because he appointed them to the office to help the sons of Aaron to be overseers in the house of the LORD, over those who sound with straight and curved trumpets, and over the chambers in which the holy vessels of the LORD were stored;

29 And over the shewbread and the fine flour for meal offering and the unleavened cakes and over all those who sing and offer thanks,

30 And that they might arise every morning to thank and praise the LORD, and likewise at evening,

31 And to offer burnt offerings to the LORD on the sabbaths, in the new moons, and on the days of set feasts, by number, according to the order commanded to them, continually before the LORD,

32 And that they should have charge of the vessels of the tabernacle of the congregation and charge of the vessels of the sanctuary and charge of the sons of Aaron their brethren when they were needed to minister in the house of the LORD.

CHAPTER 24

NOW these are the divisions of the sons of Aaron. The sons of Aaron were Nadab and Abihu, Eleazar and Ithamar.

2 But Nadab and Abihu died during the lifetime of their father Aaron, and had no children; therefore Eleazar and Ithamar executed the priest's office.

3 And David divided them, both Zadok of the sons of Eleazar and Ahimelech of the sons of Ithamar, according to their offices in their service.

4 And there were more chief men found of the sons of Eleazar than of the sons of Ithamar; and thus he divided them. Among the sons of Eleazar there were sixteen chief men of the house of their fathers and eight of the sons of Ithamar, according to the house of their fathers.

5 Thus he divided them by lot, both families alike; for they were chief priests of the sanctuary and authorities over the priests, both of the sons of Eleazar and of the sons of Ithamar.

6 And Shemaiah the son of Nethaniel the scribe, one of the Levites, recorded them before King David and

the elders of Israel and Zadok the priest and Ahimelech the son of Abiathar and before the chiefs of the fathers of the priests and of the Levites, one principal family being taken for Eleazar and one taken for Ithamar.

7 Now the first lot fell to Jehoiadah, the second to Jedaiah,

8 The third to Haram, the fourth to Seorim,

9 The fifth to Malchijah, the sixth to Mijamin,

10 The seventh to Akkoz, the eighth to Abijah,

11 The ninth to Elishah, the tenth to Shecaniah,

12 The eleventh to Eliashib, the twelfth to Elikrab,

13 The thirteenth to Huppah, the fourteenth to Ahaziah,

14 The fifteenth to Baglah, the sixteenth to Immer,

15 The seventeenth to Ahaziah, the eighteenth to Pazin,

16 The nineteenth to Pethahiah, the twentieth to Ezekiel,

17 The twenty-first to Jachin, the twenty-second to Gamul,

18 The twenty-third to Delaiah, and the twenty-fourth to Maadiah.

19 These are their numbers according to their service, to come into the house of the LORD, according to their ordinances, as prescribed for them by the counsel of Aaron their father, as the LORD God of Israel had commanded him.

20 ¶And the rest of the sons of Levi were these: of the sons of Amram, Shubael; of the sons of Shubael, Jehdeiah and Rehabiah.

21 Of the sons of Rehabiah: his first-born was Jeshua, then

22 Zahor and Salmoth. Of the sons of Salmoth: Nahath,

23 Jeremiah, Hezaiel, and Neshamim.

24 Of the sons of Uzziel: Michah; of the sons of Michah: Shamir and Jeshua.

25 Of the sons of Jeshua: Zechariah.

26 The sons of Merari were Mahli and Mushi; the son of Jaaziah, Beno.

27 ¶The sons of Merari by Jaaziah: Beno and Shoham and Zaccur and Ibri.

28 Of Mahli came Eleazar, who had no sons.

29 Of Kish: the son of Kish was Jerahmeel.

30 The sons also of Mushi: Mahli and Eder and Jerimoth. These were the sons of the Levites, after the house of their fathers.

31 These likewise cast lots over against their brethren the sons of Aaron in the presence of David the king, and Zadok and Ahimelech, and the chief of the fathers of the priests and Levites, even the principal fathers, over against their younger brethren.

CHAPTER 25

MOREOVER David and the princes of the tribes set aside for the service of the sons of Asaph, Haman and Jeruthun, the sons of Azram his son. These are the Levites according to the families of their fathers. These likewise cast lots over their brethren the sons of Aaron in the presence of David the king and Zadok and Ahimelech and the chiefs of the fathers of the priests and Levites. The younger and the elder brother were reckoned alike in numbering; and the number of the workmen according to their service was,

2 Of the sons of Asaph: Zaccuri, Joseph, Nethaniah, and Israel. And the sons of Asaph whom the king placed under the direction of Jeruthun as singers.

3 Of the sons of Jeruthun: Azariah, Isaiah, Hashabiah, Mattithiah, and Jeruthun, six, under the direction of their father Jeruthun, who sang with harps and gave thanks to the LORD.

4 Of Heman: the sons of Heman, Bukkiah, Mattaniah, Uzziel, Shebuel, and Jerimoth, Hananiah, Hanani, Eliathah, Giddalti, and Romamtiezer, Joshbekashah, Mallothi, Hothir, and Mahazioth.

5 All these were the sons of Heman the king's seer in the words of God, to lift up the horn. And God gave to Heman fourteen sons and three daughters.

6 All these were under the hands of their father for song in the house of the LORD, with cymbals, psalteries,

and harps for the service of the house of God, according to the king's order to Asaph, Jeruthun, and Heman.

7 So the number of them, with their brethren who were instructed in the songs of the LORD, was two hundred and eighty-eight.

8 ¶And they cast lots for their courses, as well the younger as the elder, the pupil as the teacher.

9 Now the first lot fell for Asaph to Joseph; the second to Gedaliah, who with his brethren and his sons were twelve;

10 The third to Zori, he, his sons, and his brethren were twelve;

11 The fourth to Nazri, he, his sons, and his brethren were twelve;

12 The fifth to Nethaniah, he, his sons, and his brethren were twelve;

13 The sixth to Bukkiah, he his sons, and his brethren were twelve;

14 The seventh to Lasrael, he, his sons, and his brethren were twelve;

15 The eighth to Isaiah, he, his sons, and his brethren were twelve;

16 The ninth to Mattaniah, he, his sons, and his brethren were twelve;

17 The tenth to Shimei, he, his sons, and his brethren were twelve;

18 The eleventh to Azaiel, he, his sons, and his brethren were twelve;

19 The twelfth to Hashabiah, he, his sons, and his brethren were twelve;

20 The thirteenth to Shubael, he, his sons, and his brethren were twelve;

21 The fourteenth to Mattithiah, he, his sons, and his brethren were twelve;

22 The fifteenth to Jeremoth, he, his sons, and his brethren were twelve;

23 The sixteenth to Hananiah, he, his sons, and his brethren were twelve;

24 The seventeenth to Elishab, he, his sons and his brethren were twelve;

25 The eighteenth to Hanani, he, his sons, and his brethren were twelve;

26 The nineteenth to Malloth, he, his sons, and his brethren were twelve;

27 The twentieth to Eliab, he, his sons, and his brethren were twelve;

28 The twenty-first to Jattir, he, his sons, and his brethren were twelve;

29 The twenty-second to Rabbi, he, his sons, and his brethren were twelve;

30 The twenty-third to Mahazioth, he, his sons, and his brethren were twelve;

31 The twenty-fourth to Roman, he, his sons, and his brethren were twelve;

CHAPTER 26

CONCERNING the divisions of the porters whom David the king appointed as guards: Meshelemiah of the sons of Joseph.

2 And Meshelemiah had seven male children: namely, Zechariah his first-born, Jediael the second, Zechariah the third, Nathanael the fourth,

3 Elam the fifth, Johanan the sixth, Jadie the seventh.

4 Moreover, the sons of Ober-edom were Shemaiah his first-born, Jehozabad the second, Joah the third, Shabar the fourth, and Matlal the fifth,

5 Gemaiel the sixth, Issachar the seventh, Pali the eighth; for the LORD blessed him.

6 Also to Shemaiah his son were sons born, who ruled over the house of their fathers; for they were mighty men of valour.

7 The sons of Shemaiah: Gathael, Cadhael, Obedael, and Zechariah, the mighty man, and Elijah and Semachiah.

8 All these were of the sons of Ober-edom, they and their sons and their brethren, able men with strength for the service of the sanctuary, sixty-two sons of Ober-edom.

9 And Meshelemiah's eldest son had sons, mighty men, eighteen.

10 Also Hasah, of the children of Merari, had sons, mighty men; his eldest son died, and his father made the second the chief, but he did not call him by the name of the eldest.

11 Hilkiah the second, Tebaliah the third, Zechariah the fourth; all the sons and brethren of Hasah were thirteen.

12 Among these were the divisions of the porters, even among the chief

men, having watch one opposite another, to minister in the house of the LORD.

13 ¶And they cast lots, the least as well as the great, according to the house of their fathers, for every gate.

14 And the lot eastward fell to Shelemiah. Then for Zechariah his son, a wise counsellor, they cast lots; and his lot came out northward.

15 To Ober-edom southward; and to his sons the porches.

16 To Shuppim and Hasah the lot fell westward, as far as the gate which is made in the road that goes up, watch opposite watch.

17 Eastward were six Levites, northward four a day, southward four a day, and for the porches two by two.

18 At Parbar westward, four at the road and two at Parbar.

19 These are the divisions of the porters among the sons of Korah and among the sons of Merari.

20 And of the Levites, Ahijah was over the storehouses of the house of God and over the storehouses of the dedicated things.

21 The sons of Laadan: of the descendants of Gershon, Laadan, chiefs of the fathers, even of Laadan the Gershonite, was Nahli.

22 The sons of Nahli: Zetham and Joel his brother who were over the storehouses of the house of the LORD.

23 Of the Amramites and the Izharites, the Hebronites and the Uzzielites,

24 Samuel the son of Gershon, the son of Moses, was chief in charge of the storehouses.

25 And his brother Eliezer, Rehabiah his son and Isaiah his son and Joram his son and Zichri his son and Shelomith his son.

26 This Shelomith and his brothers were in charge of all storehouses of the dedicated things, which David the king, the chiefs of the fathers, the commanders of the thousands and the hundreds, and the commanders of the army had dedicated.

27 From spoils won in battles they dedicated some to maintain the house of the LORD.

28 And all that Samuel the seer and Saul the son of Kish and Abner the son of Ner and Joab the son of Zuriah had dedicated; and whoever had dedicated anything, it was under the charge of Shelomith and of his brothers.

29 ¶Of the Izharites: Chenaniah and his sons were for the secular business of Israel, as scribes and judges.

30 And of the Hebronites: Hashabiah and his brethren, men of valour, one thousand and seven hundred, were officers over the Israelites on this side of Jordan westward, in charge of all the business of the LORD and in the service of the king.

31 Among the Hebronites was Neriah the chief, even among the Hebronites, according to the generations of their fathers. In the fortieth year of the reign of David they were sought for, and there were found among them mighty men of valour at Jazer of Gilead.

32 And his brethren, men of valour, were two thousand and seven hundred chiefs of the fathers, whom King David made chiefs over the Reubenites, the Gadites, and the half tribe of Manasseh, for every matter pertaining to God and the affairs of the king.

CHAPTER 27

NOW the children of Israel after their number, the chiefs of the fathers and the commanders of thousands and of hundreds, and their governors who served the king in all matters of the divisions, those who came in and went out month by month throughout all the months of the year under every division were twenty-four thousand.

2 Over the first division for the first month was Shaabam the son of Zabdiel; and in his division were twenty-four thousand.

3 He was of the descendants of Perez; he was the chief of all the commanders of the army for the first month.

4 And over the division of the second month was David the Ahohite, and of his division was Mikloth also

the governor; in his division were twenty-four thousand.

5 The third commander of the army for the third month was Benaiah the son of Jehoiada, the chief priest; and in his division were twenty-four thousand.

6 This is the Benaiah, who was mighty among the thirty, and in command of the thirty officers; and in his division was Mizbar his son.

7 The fourth commander for the fourth month was Ashael the brother of Joab, and Zebadaiel his son after him; and in his division were twenty-four thousand.

8 The fifth commander for the fifth month was Shamhuth the Nezrahite; and in his division were twenty-four thousand.

9 The sixth commander for the sixth month was Ira the son of Ikkesh the Tekoite; and in his division were twenty-four thousand.

10 The seventh commander for the seventh month was Helez the Pelonite, of the descendants of Ephraim; and in his division were twenty-four thousand.

11 The eighth commander for the eighth month was Sibbecai the Hushathite, of the Zarites; and in his division were twenty-four thousand.

12 The ninth commander for the ninth month was Abiezer the Anatothite, of the Benjamites; and in his division were twenty-four thousand.

13 The tenth commander for the tenth month was Maharai the Netophathite, of the Zarhites; and in his division were twenty-four thousand.

14 The eleventh commander for the eleventh month was Benaiah the Pirathonite, of the descendants of Ephraim; and in his division were twenty-four thousand.

15 The twelfth commander for the twelfth month was Heldai the Netophathite, of Othniel; and in his division were twenty-four thousand.

16 ¶Furthermore over the tribes of Israel were these: the prince of the Reubenites was Eliezer the son of Zichri; of the Simeonites, Shephatiah the son of Maachah;

17 Of the Levites, Hashabiah the son of Kemuel; of the Aaronites, Zadok;

18 Of Judah, Elihu, one of the brothers of David; of Issachar, Omri the son of Michael;

19 Of Zebulun, Ishmaiah the son of Obadiah; of Naphtali, Jerimoth the son of Azriel;

20 Of the Ephraimites, Hoshea the son of Azariah; of the half tribe of Manasseh, Joel the son of Peraiah;

21 Of the half tribe of Manasseh in Gilead, Iddo the son of Zechariah; of Benjamin, Jaasiel the son of Abner;

22 Of Dan, Azariel the son of Jeroham. These were the princes of the tribes of Israel.

23 ¶But David did not number those twenty years old and under because the LORD had said he would increase Israel like the stars of the heavens.

24 Joab the son of Zuriah began to number, but he did not finish because there came wrath upon Israel for this, neither was the number put in the account of the chronicles of David.

25 ¶And over the king's treasures was Azmaveth the son of Gediel; and over the storehouses in the fields, in the cities, and in the villages, and in the castles was Jonathan the son of Uzziah;

26 And over those who did the work of the field for tilling of the ground was Ezri the son of Chelub;

27 And over the vineyards was Shimei the Ramathite; over the increase of the vineyards for the wine cellars was Zabdi the Shiphmite;

28 And over the olive trees and the sycamore trees that were in the low plains was Baalhanan the Gederite; and over the stores of oil was Joash;

29 And over the herds that fed in Sharon was Shitrai the Sharonite; and over the herds that were in the valleys was Shaphat the son of Adlai;

30 Over the camels was Abel the Ishmaelite; and over the asses was Judah the Meronothite;

31 And over the flocks was Jaziz the Hagerite. All these were overseers

of the substance which was King David's.

32 Also Jonathan David's beloved friend was a counsellor, a man of understanding, and a scribe; and Hananiel the son of Hachmoni was with the king's sons;

33 And Ahithophel was the king's counsellor; and Hushai the Archite was the king's friend;

34 And after Ahithophel was Jehoiada the son of Benaiah, and Abiathar; and Joab was the general of the king's army.

CHAPTER 28

AND David assembled all the princes of Israel, the princes of the tribes and the commanders of the divisions that ministered to the king and the commanders of the thousands and the captains of hundreds and the stewards of all the substance and herds of the king and of his sons, with the officers and with the mighty men of valour; and they all came to Jerusalem.

2 Then he said to them, Hear me, my brethren and my people: I had it in my heart to build a house of rest for the ark of the covenant of the LORD and for a dwelling place of our God, and I had made ready everything for the building of the house;

3 But the LORD said to me, You shall not build a house for my name because you are a man of war and have shed much blood.

4 However the LORD God of Israel chose me from all my father's house to be king over Israel for ever; for he has chosen out of the house of Judah to be the king; and of the tribe of Judah, the house of my father; and among the sons of my father he chose me to be king over Israel;

5 And of all my sons (for the LORD has given me many sons), he has chosen Solomon my son to sit upon the throne of the kingdom of the LORD over Israel.

6 And he said to me, Solomon your son, he shall build my house and my courts; for I have chosen him to be my son, and I will be a father to him.

7 Moreover I will establish the throne of his kingdom for ever if he continues to keep my commandments and my judgments as at this day.

8 Now therefore in the sight of all Israel the people of the LORD and in the presence of the LORD our God, keep and seek for all his commandments; and you shall possess this land for ever and leave it for an inheritance for your children after you for ever, and it shall not be destroyed.

9 ¶And you, Solomon my son, know everything that the LORD our God has commanded us, and serve him with a perfect heart and with a willing mind; for the LORD knows everything that is in the heart and understands all the imaginations of the thoughts of men; if you seek him, he will be found by you; but if you forsake him, he will cast you off for ever.

10 Know now and take heed; for the LORD has chosen you to build a house for the sanctuary of the name of the LORD; be strong, be valiant, and do it.

11 ¶Then David gave to Solomon his son the pattern of the porch and the measurements of the house and of its treasuries and of the upper chambers thereof and of the inner porticos thereof and of the outer porticos thereof and of the upper porticos thereof and of the lower porticos thereof;

12 And the pattern of the treasury and of the chambers for the service of the house of the LORD and the chambers of the cooks and the chambers of the butlers and the chamber of those in charge of the lamps;

13 Also for the divisions of the priests and the Levites, and for all the work of the service of the house of the LORD, and for all the vessels of service in the house of the LORD.

14 He gave of gold by weight for things of gold, for all vessels of all manner of service; silver also for all instruments of silver by weight, for all instruments of every kind of service;

15 And the place for the candlestick of gold and for their lamps of gold and the wicks thereof and the ornaments thereof and the vessels of

oil thereof. David recorded everything, and gave it to Solomon his son;

16 And tables of silver and tables of gold; dishes of silver and dishes of gold;

17 Also large spoons, flesh hooks, and bowls of silver; the gold of these vessels could not be weighed;

18 And for the altar of incense refined gold by weight; and gold for the pattern of the chariot of the cherubim that spread out their wings and covered the ark of the covenant of the LORD.

19 All this, said David, the LORD made me understand in writing by his hand upon me, even all the works of this pattern.

20 Then David said to Solomon his son, Be strong and of good courage, and do it; fear not, nor be dismayed; for the LORD God is with you; he will not fail you, nor forsake you, until you have finished all the work for the service of the house of the LORD.

21 And, behold, the divisions of the priests and of the Levites, I have given them authority over all the service of the house of the LORD; and they are with you, and shall be in charge of all the service; and they will do the work with skill, all the workmanship which is necessary for the service of the house of the LORD. And, behold, I have appointed over them authorities and overseers, so that they may seek and render all manner of service which is necessary.

CHAPTER 29

MOREOVER David the king said to all the assemblies of Israel, This Solomon my son is still a small boy, and yet the LORD has chosen him out of all my sons, because he is wise and has understanding, and this work which is given to him is not small, but it is great; for such a task has never been given to any man; now therefore be strong and of good courage, because the work belongs to the LORD our God.

2 Now I have provided with all my might and with all my wealth everything which is necessary for the house of the LORD my God: the gold for things to be made of gold, the silver for things of silver, the brass for things of brass, the iron for things of iron, and wood for things of wood; and cedars for things of cedar; precious stones and pearls.

3 Moreover, everything which is necessary for the house I have provided of my own sacrifices; I have also provided money for the expenses of the house of my God of my own sacrifices;

4 One million talents of gold, of fine gold, and two million talents of silver, to overlay the walls of the house:

5 The gold for things of gold, and the silver for things of silver, and for all manner of work to be made by craftsmen, so that the work may be completed in its month, and that no work should be left undone, but be finished in its due time, according to the expenses thereof.

6 ¶Then the chiefs of the fathers and the princes of the tribes of Israel and the commanders of thousands and of hundreds and the overseers of the king's work gathered together

7 And gave for the service of the house of the LORD five thousand gold talents and fine tin for the pipes two hundred thousand talents and silver twenty thousand talents and of Corinthian brass seventy thousand talents and one hundred thousand talents of iron.

8 Moreover they gave silver and gold, offering them willingly to the treasury of the house of the LORD by the hand of Gershon the treasurer.

9 Then all the people of Israel rejoiced in all these gifts because David offered them with perfect heart willingly before the LORD; and David also rejoiced with great joy. Therefore David sang great praises to the LORD.

10 ¶Wherefore David blessed the LORD before all the assemblies of Israel; and David said, Blessed be thou, O LORD God of Israel our father, for ever and ever.

11 For thine, O LORD, is the greatness and the power and the glory and

the beauty and the majesty and the honor; for thou art the ruler over all that is in the heaven and on the earth; thine is the kingdom, O LORD, and the wisdom and the might and the knowledge.

12 Both riches and honor come of thee, and thou rulest over all; and in thy hand is power and might; and in thy hand is to make great and to give strength to all creations which thou hast created.

13 Even now, O LORD our God, we thank thee and praise thy glorious name.

14 But who am I and what is my people, because all my teachers have taught me that thy way of life has helped us, and thou art our hope, O LORD our God.

15 For we are like the proverb of vapor and of the potter,[1] and we are sojourners before thee and a small people in the world, but thou didst rule over our fathers of old, and thou didst command them by which way they should walk and live.

16 And to thee we offer praise, O LORD our God, that thou mightest save us from all those who harm us, for the nations reproach us, saying, Where is your God, whom you serve?

17 I know also, my God, that thou triest the heart, and hast pleasure in uprightness. As for me, in the uprightness of my heart I have sung all these praises; and now I have seen that thy people who are present here praise thee with a great joy, saying,

18 O LORD God of Abraham, Isaac, and of Israel, our fathers kept all these things which thou hast promised us for ever, and now turn away our heart from evil, that we may not sin before thee, and prepare our hearts to worship thee.

19 And I David answered and said thus: O LORD my God, give to Solomon my son a perfect heart, to keep thy commandments, thy testimonies, and thy statutes, and to do all these things which I have commanded, and to build the temple for which I have made provision; for thy great name will be hallowed and praised in the world which thou hast created, in the presence of those who worship thee.

20 ¶Then David said to all the people of Israel, Now bless the LORD your God. And all the people blessed the LORD God of their fathers, and bowed down and worshipped the LORD, and they also blessed King David.

21 And they offered sacrifices to the LORD and offered burnt offerings to the LORD, and on the next day they sacrificed a thousand bullocks and a thousand rams and a thousand lambs, with their drink offerings, and sacrificed in abundance for all Israel;

22 And they did eat and drink before the LORD on that day with great gladness. And they made Solomon the son of David king, and appointed Zadok to be the priest.

23 Then Solomon sat on the throne of the kingdom of the LORD as king instead of David his father, and prospered; and all Israel obeyed him.

24 And all the mighty men and all the sons of King David submitted themselves to Solomon his son.

25 And the LORD magnified Solomon exceedingly in the sight of all Israel, and bestowed upon him such royal majesty as had not been on any king of Israel who had been before him.

26 ¶Thus David the son of Jesse made Solomon his son king over all Israel.

27 Now the time that David reigned over all Israel was forty years; he reigned seven years in Hebron and thirty-three years he reigned in Jerusalem, over all Israel and Judah.

28 And David the son of Jesse died in a good old age, full of days and great in worldly riches and honor; and Solomon his son reigned in his stead.

29 Now the acts of David the king from first to last, behold, they are written in the book of Samuel the prophet and in the book of Nathan the prophet and in the book of Gad the prophet,

---

[1] Vapor appears and disappears, and a potter breaks his vessels and remakes them.

30 With all his reign and his might and the times that passed over him and over Israel and over all the kingdoms of the countries. David did that which was good in the presence of the LORD, and he transgressed not against anything that he commanded him all the days of his life.

THE SECOND BOOK OF THE

CHRONICLES

CHAPTER 1

AND Solomon the son of David was strengthened in his kingdom, and the LORD his God was with him and exalted him exceedingly above all the kings of the earth.

2 Then Solomon spoke to all Israel, to the commanders of thousands and of hundreds, and to the judges, and to all the princes, the chiefs of the fathers.

3 So Solomon and all the people who were with him went to a great banquet that was at the town of Gibeon; for there was the tabernacle of the congregation of the LORD, which Moses the servant of the LORD had made in the wilderness.

4 But David had brought up the ark of the LORD from Koriath-kaproney to the place which David had prepared for it; for he had pitched a tent for it in Jerusalem.

5 Moreover the bronze altar that Bezaliel the son of Uri, the son of Hur, had made was placed before the tabernacle of the LORD; and Solomon and the whole congregation of Israel went to it.

6 And Solomon went up there to the bronze altar before the LORD, which was at the tabernacle of the congregation, and offered a thousand burnt offerings upon it.

7 ¶That night the LORD appeared to Solomon in a vision and said to him, Ask what I shall give you.

8 And Solomon said to the LORD, Thou hast shown great mercy to David my father, and hast made me to reign in his stead.

9 Now, O LORD my God, let thy promise to David my father be established; for thou hast made me king over this people, like the dust of the earth in multitude.

10 Give me now wisdom and knowledge, that I may go out and come in before this people; for who can judge this thy people that is so great?

11 And the LORD said to Solomon, Because this was in your mind, and you have not asked riches, honor, nor the life of your enemies, neither have you asked for long life; but have asked wisdom and knowledge for yourself that you may judge my people over whom I have made you king;

12 Also the things for which you have not asked will I grant to you. And I will give you wisdom and knowledge, wealth, riches, and honor, such as none of the kings have had that have been before you, neither shall there any after you have the like.

13 ¶Then Solomon came from his journey to the great banquet that was at the town of Gibeon, east of Jerusalem, from before the tabernacle of the congregation, and reigned over all Israel.

14 And Solomon gathered chariots and horsemen; and he had a thousand and four hundred chariots and twelve thousand horsemen, which he placed in the chariot cities, and some of them with the king in Jerusalem.

15 And the king made silver in Jerusalem as plenteous as stones, and he made cedar as the sand that is by the sea for abundance.

16 And the king's merchants purchased horses for Solomon from Egypt and from the city of the Apelites for a price.

17 And they went up and bought a chariot from Egypt for six hundred shekels of silver, and a horse for a hundred and fifty; and so through the king's merchants they brought horses for all the kings of the Hittites and for the kings of Aram.

CHAPTER 2

AND Solomon commanded to build a temple for the name of the LORD and a house for his kingdom.

2 And Solomon appointed seventy thousand men to bear burdens and eighty thousand stone cutters in the mountain and three thousand and six hundred to oversee them.

3 ¶And Solomon sent to Hiram king of Tyre, saying, As you showed great kindness to David my father, and sent him cedars to build him a house to dwell in,

4 Behold, I am building a house to the name of the LORD my God, to dedicate it to him and to burn before him sweet incense and to light a lamp continually and to offer burnt offerings morning and evening, on the sabbaths and on the new moons and on the solemn feasts of the LORD our God. This is an ordinance for ever to Israel.

5 And the house which I am about to build is very great, for our God is greater than all kings.

6 But who is able to build him a house, seeing the heaven and heaven of heavens cannot contain him? Who am I then, that I should build him a house or burn sweet incense before him?

7 Now therefore, send me a man skilled to work in gold and in silver and in brass and in iron and in purple and in fine linen and in crimson and in blue, and who has the skill to engrave with the skilled men who are with me in Judah and in Jerusalem, whom David my father did provide.

8 Send me also cedar trees, fir trees, and algum [1] timber out of Lebanon; for I know that your servants know how to cut cedar timber in Lebanon; and, behold, my servants shall be with your servants

9 And shall bring me timber in abundance; for the house which I am about to build will be very great and wonderful.

10 And I will provide carpenters who are skilled in woodwork, and will give provisions to your servants, twenty thousand measures of wheat and twenty thousand measures of barley and twenty thousand baths of wine and twenty thousand baths of oil.

11 ¶Then Hiram the king of Tyre answered in writing which he sent to Solomon, saying, Because the LORD has loved his people, he has made you king over them.

12 Hiram said moreover, Blessed be the LORD God of Israel, who created heaven and earth, who has given to David a wise son, endued with prudence and understanding, who has set his mind to build a house for the LORD and a house for his kingdom.

13 And now I have sent to you a skilful man, endued with understanding, even Hiram,

14 Who is the son of a widow of the house of Dan, and his father was a skilful man; he knows how to work in gold and in silver, in brass, in iron, in stones, in timber, in purple, in blue, in fine linen, in crimson and other red materials, also how to make any manner of keys for the doors, and to devise every kind of craft which shall be assigned to him from the LORD, with your craftsmen and with the craftsmen of our lord David your father.

15 Now therefore the wheat and the barley, the oil and the wine which my lord has promised to his servants, let him send them;

16 And we will cut cedar trees out of Lebanon, as many as you wish; and we will bring them to you in floats by

[1] Probably sandalwood.

sea to Joppa; and you shall carry them up to Jerusalem.

17 ¶Then Solomon gathered together all the proselytes who were in the land of Israel, after the numbering of them which David his father had done; and there were found a hundred and fifty-three thousand and six hundred.

18 And King Solomon set seventy thousand of them to be bearers of burdens and eighty thousand to be stonecutters in the mountain and three thousand and six hundred overseers to make the people work.

CHAPTER 3

THEN Solomon began to build the house of the LORD in Jerusalem on mount Moriah, in the place which David his father had prepared in the threshing floor which he had bought from Aran the Jebusite.

2 And he began to build the temple in the second month of the fourth year of his reign.

3 ¶Now these are the measurements which Solomon measured for the building of the house of the LORD: The length of the house by the measure of the sanctuary was sixty cubits, and its height thirty cubits, and its breadth twenty cubits.

4 And he made a porch in the front thereof; the length of it was the same as the breadth of the house, twenty cubits, and its height twenty cubits; and he overlaid it within with pure gold.

5 And the greater house he ceiled with cypress wood, which he overlaid with fine gold, and he carved on it the likeness of palm trees and flowers.

6 And he adorned the house with precious stones for beauty; and he overlaid all of it with fine gold.

7 He overlaid also the house, from the front of the porch and its walls and its door posts, with fine gold, and he carved on it the likeness of palm trees and flowers.

8 And he made the sanctuary of the holy of holies; its length was the same as the breadth of the house, twenty cubits, and its breadth twenty cubits; and he overlaid it with fine gold, amounting to six hundred talents.

9 And he also overlaid the altar with fine gold.

10 In the most holy house he made two cherubim of solid material, and overlaid them with gold.

11 ¶And the wings of the cherubim were twenty cubits long; one wing of the one cherub was five cubits, reaching to the wall of the house; and the other wing was likewise five cubits, reaching to the wing of the other cherub.

12 And one wing of the other cherub was five cubits, reaching to the wall of the house; and the other wing was five cubits also, joining to the wing of the other cherub.

13 The wings of these cherubim were spread forth twenty cubits; they stood on their feet and their faces were inward.

14 ¶And he made the veil of blue and purple and crimson and fine linen, and wrought cherubim on it, and placed the ark in it.

15 Also he made in front of the great house two pillars, eighteen cubits long, and the capitals that were on the top of each of them were five cubits high.

16 And he made chains, fifty cubits long, and put them on the tops of the pillars; and made a hundred pomegranates, and put them on the chains.

17 And he set up the two pillars in front of the temple, one on the right hand and the other on the left; and he called the name of that which he set on the right hand, Jachin, and the name of that on the left, Boaz.

CHAPTER 4

MOREOVER he made an altar of brass, twenty cubits its length and twenty cubits its breadth and ten cubits its height.

2 ¶And he made a molten sea of ten cubits from brim to brim, round in shape, and five cubits its height and thirty cubits its circumference.

3 And it stood upon twelve oxen, three facing north, three facing south, three facing west, and three facing east; and the sea was set above them, and their hinder parts were inward.

4 And the thickness of it was a handbreadth, and its brim was round like the brim of a cup, very beautiful.

5 And he made also ten poles, and put five on the right hand and five on the left, to carry with them the altar of burnt offering.

6 ¶And he made ten lavers of brass, and put five on the right hand and five on the left, so that the priests might wash their hands and their feet in them.

7 And he made ten candlesticks of gold according to their specifications, and set them in the temple, five on the right hand and five on the left.

8 He made also ten tables, and placed them in the temple, five on the right side and five on the left. And he made a hundred basins of fine gold.

9 ¶Furthermore he made a large court for the priests and for the Levites, and overlaid the doors and the bars with brass.

10 And he set the sea on the right side of the north end, over against the south.

11 And Hiram made the pots, and the shovels, and the basins. And Hiram finished the work that he was to make for King Solomon for the house of God;

12 To wit, the two pillars and the knobs and the capitals which were on the top of the two pillars, and the two wreaths to cover the two knobs of the capitals which were on the top of the pillars;

13 And four hundred pomegranates on the two wreaths; two rows of pomegranates on each wreath, to cover the two knobs of the capitals which were upon the pillars.

14 He made also bases, and lavers made he upon the bases;

15 One sea, and twelve oxen under it.

16 The pots also and the shovels and the fleshhooks and all their instruments did Hiram make for King Solomon, for the house of the LORD, of bright brass.

17 In the plain of Jordan did the king cast them, in the clay ground between Succoth and Zeredathah.

18 Thus Solomon made all these vessels in great abundance; for the weight of these vessels of brass that Solomon made could not be found out.

19 ¶And Solomon made all the vessels that were for the house of God, the golden altar also, and the tables whereon the shewbread was set;

20 Moreover the candlesticks with their lamps,[1] that they should burn after the manner before the oracle, of pure gold;

21 And the flowers and the lamps and the tongs made he of gold, and that perfect gold;

22 And the snuffers and the basins and the spoons and the censers, of pure gold; and the entry of the house, the inner doors thereof for the most holy place, and the doors of the house of the temple, were of gold.

CHAPTER 5

THUS all the work that Solomon made for the house of the LORD was finished; and Solomon brought in all the things which David his father had dedicated; and the silver and the gold and all the vessels he put in the treasures of the house of the LORD.

2 ¶Then Solomon assembled at Jerusalem all the elders of Israel and all the heads of the tribes, the chiefs of the fathers of the children of Israel, to bring up the ark of the covenant of the LORD from the city of David, which is Zion.[2]

3 Wherefore all the men of Israel assembled themselves to King Solomon at Jerusalem in the feast of tabernacles, which is in the seventh month.[3]

4 And all the elders of Israel came; and the priests took up the ark.

5 And they brought up the ark of the LORD and the tabernacle of the congregation and all the holy vessels that were in the tabernacle, these did the priests and the Levites bring up.

---

[1] According to ordinance.   [2] From the old city to the temple.   [3] August.

6 And King Solomon and all the people of Israel that were assembled to him before the ark sacrificed sheep and oxen which could not be counted nor numbered for multitude.

7 Then the priests brought in the ark of the covenant of the LORD, and put it in its place, into the most holy place under the wings of the cherubim:

8 For the cherubim spread forth their wings over the place of the ark, and the cherubim covered the ark and the poles thereof above.

9 And the poles were so long that the ends of the poles were seen from underneath the ark within the house, but they were not seen from the outside. And there they remain to this day.

10 There was nothing in the ark except the two stone tablets which Moses had put there, which he brought from mount Sinai. This is the same covenant which the LORD made with the children of Israel when they came out of the land of Egypt.

11 ¶And it came to pass, when the priests were come out of the holy place (for all the priests who were present there entered into the holy place;

12 Also the Levites, who were the singers, all of them of Asaph, of Heman, of Jeruthun, with their sons and their brethren, being arrayed in white linen, having cymbals and psalteries and harps, stood at the east end of the altar, and with them an hundred and twenty priests sounding with trumpets):

13 That the trumpeters and singers were as one, to make one sound to be heard in praising and thanking the LORD; and when they lifted up their voice with the trumpets and cymbals and instruments of music, and praised the LORD, saying, For he is good; for his mercy endures for ever; that then the house was filled with a cloud, even the house of the LORD,

14 So that the priests could not stand to minister because of the cloud; for the house of the LORD was filled with the brightness of his glory.

CHAPTER 6

THEN Solomon said, O LORD, thou hast declared that thou wouldst dwell in the thick darkness.

2 But I have built a house of habitation for thee, and a place for thy dwelling for ever.

3 Then the king turned his face and blessed the whole congregation of Israel; and all the congregation of Israel stood.

4 And he said, Blessed be the LORD God of Israel, who spoke with his own mouth to David my father, and with his word has fulfilled that which he had promised, saying,

5 Since the day that I brought forth my people out of the land of Egypt, I chose no city among all the tribes of Israel to build a house in, that my name might be there;

6 But I have chosen Jerusalem that my name might be there; and I have chosen David to be king over my people Israel.

7 Now it was in the heart of David my father to build a house for the name of the LORD God of Israel.

8 But the LORD said to David my father, Forasmuch as it was in your heart to build a house for my name, you did well in that it was in your heart;

9 Nevertheless you shall not build the house for my name, but your son who shall come forth out of your loins, he shall build the house for my name.

10 The LORD therefore has performed his word that he has spoken; for I have risen up in the place of David my father, and I sit on the throne of Israel, as the LORD promised, and I have built the house for the name of the LORD God of Israel.

11 And I have prepared a place for the ark, wherein is the covenant of the LORD that he made with our fathers when he brought them forth out of the land of Egypt.

12 ¶And Solomon stood up before the altar of the LORD in the presence of all the congregation of Israel, and spread forth his hands toward heaven;

13 For Solomon had made a bronze

platform, five cubits long, five cubits wide, and two cubits high, and had set it in the midst of the court; and he went up and stood upon it, and knelt down upon his knees in the presence of all the people of Israel and spread forth his hands in prayer toward heaven,

14 And prayed and said, O LORD God of Israel, there is no one like thee; thou art the LORD who dwellest in heaven above, and thy will is carried out upon the earth below; who keepest covenant and showest mercy to thy servants who walk before thee uprightly with all their hearts;

15 Thou who hast kept with thy servant David my father that which thou hast promised him; and thou didst speak with thy mouth, and hast fulfilled it with thy will, as it is this day.

16 Now therefore, O LORD God of Israel, keep with thy servant David my father the promise which thou hast made to him, saying, There shall not fail you a son in my sight to sit upon the throne of Israel; if only your children take heed to their way to walk in my law, as you have walked before me.

17 Now then, O LORD God of Israel, let thy words be confirmed which thou hast spoken to thy servant David.

18 For in truth the LORD has made his dwelling place with his people Israel on the earth. Behold, heaven and the heaven of heavens cannot contain thee; how much less this house which I have built!

19 Have regard therefore to the prayer of thy servant and to his supplications, O LORD my God, to hearken to the prayer and the supplication which thy servant prayeth before thee this day;

20 That this house may remain in thy presence, that thou mayest hearken to the prayer of whosoever may come to pray before thee in this house day and night, the place of which thou hast said that thou wouldst put thy habitation there.

21 Hearken therefore to the prayer of thy servant, and of thy people Israel, which they shall pray before thee in this place; hear thou from thy dwelling place, even from heaven; and when thou hearest, forgive.

22 ¶If a man should offend his neighbor, and it is decreed upon him that he should take an oath, and he should come and swear before thy altar in this house;

23 Then hear thou his prayer, even from heaven, and do, and judge thy servants, by requiting the wicked, by bringing his guilt upon his own head; and by justifying the righteous, by rewarding him according to his righteousness.

24 ¶And if thy people Israel are defeated before the enemy because they have sinned against thee, and shall return to thee and confess thy great name, and pray and make supplication before thee in this house;

25 Then hear thou from the heavens and forgive the sins of thy people Israel and bring them again to the land which thou gavest to them and to their fathers.

26 ¶And when the heaven is shut up and there is no rain, because they have sinned against thee; yet if they pray before thee in this place, and confess thy great name and turn from their sins when thou dost afflict them;

27 Then hear thou from heaven their prayer, and forgive the sins of thy servants and of thy people Israel when thou hast taught them the good way in which they should walk; and send rain of blessing upon the land which thou hast given to thy people for an inheritance.

28 ¶If there is famine in the land, if there is pestilence or blasting or mildew or locusts or caterpillars; if their enemies besiege them in the cities of their land; whatsoever trouble or whatsoever sickness there be;

29 Then what prayer or what supplication soever shall be made of any man or of all thy people Israel, when every one shall declare his own grief, and shall come and spread forth his hands in this house;

30 Then hear thou from heaven their prayer and forgive their sins, and render to every man according to all his ways, whose heart thou know-

est (for thou only knowest the hearts of all the children of men),

31 That they may revere thee, to walk before thee in thy ways so long as they live in the land which thou gavest to their fathers.

32 ¶Moreover concerning the stranger who is not of thy people Israel, but comes from a far country for thy great name's sake and thy mighty hand and thy stretched out arm; if they come and pray before thee on that day in this house;

33 Then hear thou from thy dwelling place, even from heaven, and do according to all that the stranger prays before thee, so that all the peoples of the earth may know thy name and worship before thee, as do thy people Israel, and that they may know that this house which I have built is called by thy name.

34 If thy people go out to war against their enemies by the way that thou shalt send them, and they pray to thee towards this land which thou hast given to their fathers, or towards this city which thou hast chosen for thyself, or towards the house which I have built for thy name;

35 Then hear thou from the heavens their prayer and their supplication, and plead their cause.

36 If they sin against thee (for there is no man who does not sin), and thou be angry with them and deliver them over to their enemies, and they carry them away captives to a land far off or near;

37 Yet if they pray before thee, and repent in the land to which they were carried captive, saying, We have sinned, we have provoked thee to anger and have dealt wickedly;

38 If they return to thee with all their heart and with all their soul in the land of their captivity to which they were carried captive, and pray toward their land which thou gavest to their fathers and toward the city which thou hast chosen for thyself and toward the house which I have built for thy name;

39 Then hear thou from the heavens, even from thy dwelling place, their prayer and their supplication,

and maintain their cause, and forgive thy people who have sinned against thee.

40 Now, O my God, let thy eyes be open and let thy ears be attentive to the prayer that is made in this place.

41 Now therefore arise, O LORD God, into thy resting place, thou and the ark of thy strength; let thy priests, O LORD God, be clothed with salvation, and let thy righteous men rejoice in thy goodness.

42 O LORD God, turn not away the face of thy anointed one; remember the mercies of David thy servant.

CHAPTER 7

NOW when Solomon had made an end of praying, the fire came down from heaven and consumed the burnt offerings and the wood; and the glory of the LORD filled the house.

2 And the priests could not enter into the house of the LORD because the glory of the LORD had filled the LORD's house.

3 And when all the children of Israel saw how the fire came down and the glory of the LORD filled the house, they bowed themselves with their faces to the ground upon the pavement and worshipped, and said to each other, Praise the LORD, for he is good; for his mercy endures for ever.

4 ¶Then the king and all the people offered sacrifices before the LORD.

5 And King Solomon offered a sacrifice of twenty-two thousand oxen and a hundred and twenty thousand sheep; so the king and all the people dedicated the house of the LORD.

6 And the priests waited on their offices; the Levites also with instruments of music praised the LORD, and this is what they said in their praises, in the songs of David, Give thanks to the LORD, for he is good; for his mercy endures for ever; and the priests sounded with curved and straight trumpets, and all the people of Israel stood.

7 Moreover Solomon consecrated the middle of the court that was before the house of the LORD; for there he offered burnt offerings and the fat of the peace offerings, because the

bronze altar which Solomon had made was too small to hold the burnt offerings and the meal offerings and the fat.

8 ¶Also at that time Solomon kept the feast seven days, and all Israel with him, a very great congregation, from Hamath to the river of Egypt the people were assembled before the LORD our God.

9 Seven days were given for the feast and seven days for the dedication of the house; the extent of both occasions was fourteen days.

10 And on the fifteenth day of the month of Tishrin the king dismissed the people; and the people blessed the king and departed to their towns, glad and merry in heart, and giving thanks and praises for all the goodness that the LORD had shown to David his servant and to Solomon his son and to Israel his people.

11 And it came to pass that King Solomon finished building the house of the LORD and the king's house; and all that Solomon had reasoned in his mind to make in the house of the LORD and in the king's house he successfully accomplished.

12 ¶And the LORD appeared to Solomon that night and said to him, I have heard your prayer and have chosen this place to myself for a house of sacrifice.

13 If I shut up the heavens so that there is no rain, or if I command the locusts to devour the land, or if I send pestilence among my people;

14 If my people who are called by my name shall humble themselves and pray and seek my face and turn from their wicked ways; then I will hear from heaven and will forgive their sins and will heal their land.

15 And even now my eyes shall be open and my ears attentive to the prayer that is made in this place.

16 For now I have chosen this house for myself, that my glory may be in it for ever, and that my good works and my will shall be done in the midst of it perpetually.

17 And as for you, if you will walk before me as David your father walked, with innocence of heart and uprightness, to do everything that I have commanded you and to observe my commandments and my statutes;

18 Then I will establish the throne of your kingdom for ever, as I have covenanted with David your father, saying, There shall not fail you a son in my presence to sit on the throne of Israel.

19 But if you turn away from my ways, both you and your children, and shall not keep my commandments and my statutes which I have set before you, and shall go and serve the idols of the nations and worship them;

20 Then I will scatter you out of this land which I have given you; and this house, which I have sanctified for my name, I will uproot out of my sight, and Israel shall be a proverb and a byword among all nations.

21 And this house shall be in ruins, and every one passing by shall stand and shake his head in amazement, and say, Why has the LORD done thus to this great city and to this house?

22 And they will say, Because they forsook the covenant of the LORD God of their fathers, who brought them forth out of the land of Egypt, and they went and revered the gods of the Gentiles and served them and worshipped them; therefore the LORD has brought all this evil upon them.

CHAPTER 8

AND it came to pass at the end of twenty years, wherein Solomon had built the house of the LORD and the royal palace,

2 That Solomon rebuilt the cities which Hiram had given to him, and caused the children of Israel to dwell in them.

3 And Solomon went to Hamath and besieged it, and destroyed it.

4 And he built Tadmor, which had been laid waste like the wilderness, and all the store-cities;

5 Also he built Beth-hauran the upper and Beth-hauran the lower;

6 And built all the store-cities that Solomon had and all the chariot cities and the cities for the horsemen and all that Solomon desired to build in

Jerusalem and in Lebanon and throughout all the land of his dominion.

7 ¶As for all the people who were left of the Amorites, the Hittites, the Perizzites, the Hivites, and the Jebusites, who were not of Israel,

8 But of their descendants, who were left after them in the land, whom the children of Israel could not destroy, these Solomon made servants for himself, and workers and tributaries to this day.

9 But of the children of Israel Solomon made no servants in his kingdom, for they were men of war and the commanders of his chariots and his horsemen.

10 And these were the governors and overseers of King Solomon, even two hundred and fifty, who exercised authority over the people, who did the work.

11 ¶And Solomon brought up the daughter of Pharaoh out of the city of David to the house which he had built for her; for he said, No wife shall dwell with me in the house of David king of Israel, because the place in which the ark of the LORD has come is holy.

12 ¶Then Solomon offered burnt offerings to the LORD, and peace offerings upon the altar of the LORD which he had built before the porch,

13 Even after a certain rate every day, offering according to the commandment of Moses, on the sabbaths and on the solemn feasts, three times in the year, in the feast of unleavened bread, and in the feast of the fasting, and in the feast of tabernacles.

14 ¶And he appointed, according to the order of David his father, the courses of the priests to their service, and the Levites to their charges, to praise and minister before the priests, as the duty of every day required; and the porters also by their courses, to guard the doors every day; for so had David the king of Israel, whom the LORD had made king, commanded.

15 And he did not depart from all that King David had commanded him concerning the priests and the Levites and concerning all the service of the house.

16 Thus all the work of Solomon was set in order from the day the foundations of the house of the LORD were laid until all its work was finished.

17 ¶Then Solomon went to Eziongeber, the town which is opposite Eloth, at the seaside in the land of Edom.

18 And Hiram sent his servants by ships, skilful mariners, who knew how to pilot ships in the sea, and they went with the servants of Solomon to the city of Ophir, and took from there four hundred talents of gold, and brought them to King Solomon.

CHAPTER 9

AND when the queen of Sheba heard of the fame of Solomon, she came to test Solomon with enigmas. And she came to Jerusalem with a very great company, and camels bearing spices and gold in abundance and precious stones; and when she was come to King Solomon, she told him all that was in her heart.

2 And King Solomon told her every secret that was in her heart; and there was nothing hidden from the king which he could not tell her.

3 And when the queen of Sheba had seen the wisdom of Solomon and the house that he had built

4 And the food of his table and the seating of his servants and the attendance of his ministers and their apparel, his cupbearers also and their apparel, and the sacrifices that he offered in the house of the LORD, there was no more spirit left in her to see more.

5 And she said to King Solomon, It was a true report which I heard in my own land of your acts and of your wisdom;

6 Howbeit I did not believe their words until I came and my eyes had seen it; and, behold, the half of the greatness of your wisdom was not told me; for you exceed the report which I heard.

7 Happy are these your servants,

who stand continually before you and hear your wisdom.

8 Blessed be the LORD your God, who has chosen you and set you on the throne of the kingdom of Israel; because the LORD loved Israel, he has made you king over them for ever, to do judgment and justice.

9 And she gave the king a hundred and twenty talents of gold, and of spices great abundance, and precious stones; there were no such spices in the world as those which the queen of Sheba gave to King Solomon.

10 And the servants also of Hiram and the servants of King Solomon brought gold from Ophir.

11 And they also brought algum wood for stools for the house of the LORD and for the house of King Solomon, and harps for singers, and there were none such seen before in the land of Judah.

12 And King Solomon gave to the queen of Sheba all that she asked, besides that which he had already given, and he told her all that was in her heart. So she turned and went away to her own land, she and her servants.

13 ¶Now the weight of gold that came to Solomon in one year was six hundred and sixty-six talents of gold,

14 Besides the taxes from the cities and the traffic which the merchants brought. And all the kings of Arabia and the governors of the land brought silver and gold to Solomon.

15 ¶And King Solomon made two hundred shields of fine gold; six hundred shekels of fine gold went into each shield.

16 And he made three hundred shields of fine gold; three hundred shekels of fine gold went to the handle of each shield. And the king put them in the House of the Forest of Lebanon.

17 Moreover the king made a great throne of ivory, and overlaid it with pure gold.

18 And there were six steps to the throne, and the rim of the throne encircled from behind it, with armrests on each side of the seat, and two lions standing behind the armrests.

19 And twelve lions stood there, on the one side and on the other side upon the six steps. There was not the like ever made in any kingdom.

20 ¶And all the vessels of the service of King Solomon were of gold, and all the vessels of the king's treasuries were of pure gold; silver was not accounted as anything in the days of Solomon.

21 For the king had ships that went to Tarshish with the servants of Hiram; once every three years the ships of Tarshish came loaded with silver and gold, elephants, apes, and peacocks.

22 Thus King Solomon excelled all the kings of the earth in riches and wisdom.

23 ¶And all the kings of the earth sought the presence of Solomon to hear the wisdom that the LORD had put into his heart.

24 And they brought every man his present, vessels of silver and vessels of gold and garments, myrrh and spices, horses and mules, a fixed amount year by year.

25 ¶And Solomon had four thousand stalls for horses and chariots, and twelve thousand horsemen, whom he placed in the chariot cities and with the king at Jerusalem.

26 ¶And Solomon ruled over all the kings from the river Euphrates to the land of the Philistines, and to the border of Egypt.

27 And King Solomon made silver as plentiful in Jerusalem as stones, and he made cedar trees as the sand that is by the sea in abundance.

28 And they brought to Solomon horses from Egypt and from all lands.

29 ¶Now the rest of the acts of Solomon, first and last, are they not written in the book of Nathan the prophet and in the prophecy of Ahijah the Shilonite and in the visions of Iddo the seer against Jeroboam the son of Nebat?

30 And Solomon reigned in Jerusalem forty years over all Israel.

31 And Solomon slept with his fathers, and they buried him in the city of David his father; and Rehoboam his son reigned in his stead.

CHAPTER 10

AND Rehoboam went to Shechem; for to Shechem were all Israel come to make him king.

2 And it came to pass, when Jeroboam and all Israel heard it,

3 They came and said to Rehoboam the son of Solomon,

4 Your father made our yoke grievous; now therefore lighten somewhat the harsh rule of your father and his heavy yoke that he put upon us, and we will serve you.

5 And he said to them, Go away and come again to me after three days. And the people departed.

6 ¶And King Rehoboam took counsel with the old men who had served Solomon his father while he was yet alive, saying, What counsel do you give me to return an answer to this people?

7 And they spoke to him, saying, If you will answer kindly to this people, and please them and speak good words to them, they will be your servants for ever.

8 But he forsook the counsel which the old men gave him, and took counsel with the young men who were brought up with him and stood before him.

9 And he said to them, What advice do you give me that we may return answer to this people who have spoken to me, saying, Lighten the yoke which your father did put upon us, and we will serve you?

10 And the young men who were brought up with him in the streets [1] spoke to him, saying, Thus shall you say to the people who have spoken to you, saying, Your father made our yoke heavy, but you make it somewhat lighter for us; thus shall you say to them, My little finger is thicker than my father's thumb.

11 And now, whereas my father put a heavy yoke upon you, I will add to your yoke; my father chastised you with whips, but I will chastise you with scorpions.

12 So Jeroboam and all the people came to Rehoboam on the third day,

[1] His former playmates.

as the king had bade them, saying, Come again to me on the third day.

13 And the king answered them with harsh words; and King Rehoboam forsook the counsel of the old men,

14 And spoke to them according to the advice of the young men, saying, My father made your yoke heavy, but I will add to your yoke; my father chastised you with whips, but I will chastise you with scorpions.

15 So the king did not listen to the people; for the decree had been made by God, that the LORD might perform the word of Ahijah the prophet the Shilonite concerning Jeroboam the son of Nebat.

16 ¶And when all Israel saw that the king would not listen to them, the people answered the king, saying, We have no portion in David, nor an inheritance in the son of Jesse; return every man to his house, O Israel; and now, David, see to your own house. So Israel went to their houses.

17 But as for the children of Israel who dwelt in the cities of Judah, Rehoboam reigned over them.

18 Then King Rehoboam sent Adoniram, who was in charge of tribute; and the children of Israel stoned him with stones, that he died. But King Rehoboam hastily got up into his chariot to flee to Jerusalem.

19 So Israel rebelled against the house of David to this day.

CHAPTER 11

AND when Rehoboam came to Jerusalem, he assembled of the house of Judah and Benjamin a hundred and eighty thousand chosen men who drew sword, and who were warriors, to fight against Israel to restore the kingdom to Rehoboam the son of Solomon.

2 But the word of the LORD came to Shemaiah, saying,

3 Speak to Rehoboam the son of Solomon, king of Judah, and to the house of Benjamin and to all Israel and to the rest of the people, saying,

4 Thus says the LORD: You shall not go up, nor fight; return every man

to his house, for this thing is done of me. And they obeyed the word of the LORD, and returned, to go every man to his house.

5 ¶And Jeroboam built Shechem on the mountain of the tribe of the house of Ephraim, and dwelt in it; and went out from there and built Penuel.

6 And Jeroboam said in his heart, Now shall the kingdom return to the house of David;

7 If this people go up to offer sacrifices in the house of the LORD in Jerusalem, then shall the heart of this people turn again to their LORD, and they shall kill me and restore the kingdom to Rehoboam the son of Solomon.

8 Therefore the king took counsel and made two calves of gold, and said to the people, It is too much for you to go up to Jerusalem, why should you go up to Jerusalem and come down? Then he said, These are your gods, O Israel, who brought you up out of the land of Egypt.

9 And he set the one in Beth-el, and the other he put in Dan.

10 And this thing became a sin; for the people went to worship before the calf, even to Dan. And this thing became a sin to all the house of Jeroboam, to be uprooted and destroyed from the earth.

11 At that time Abijah the son of Jeroboam fell sick; and Jeroboam said to his wife, Arise and disguise yourself, and be as a simple woman, that you may not be known to be the wife of Jeroboam; and go to Shiloh; behold, there is Ahijah the prophet, who told me that I should be king over this people.

12 Go to him; he shall tell you what shall become of this child.

13 And the LORD said to Ahijah, Behold, the wife of Jeroboam is coming to ask a thing of you concerning her son; for he is sick; thus and thus shall you say to her; for it shall be, when she comes in, that she will disguise herself.

14 And it came to pass, when Ahijah heard the sound of her feet as she came in at the door, he said to her, Come in, wife of Jeroboam; why have you disguised yourself? For I am sent to tell you harsh words.

15 Go, tell Jeroboam, Thus says the LORD God of Israel: I have exalted you from among the people and made you king over my people Israel,

16 And took the kingdom away from the house of David and gave it to you; and yet you have not been like my servant David, who kept my commandments and who walked in my statutes with all his heart to do that which was right in my presence;

17 But you have done evil above all kings who were before you; for you have gone and made for yourself idols of the nations, and images to blaspheme before me, and have cast my worship behind your back.

18 ¶And Rehoboam took to him Mahalath the daughter of Jerimoth, the son of David, to wife, and Abihail the daughter of Eliab the son of Jesse,[1]

19 Which bare him children; Jeush, and Shamariah and Zaham.

20 And after her he took Maachah the daughter of Absalom, which bore him Abijah and Attai and Ziza and Shelomith.

21 And Rehoboam loved Maachah the daughter of Absalom above all his wives and his concubines (for he took eighteen wives and sixty concubines; and begat twenty-eight sons, and sixty daughters).

22 And Rehoboam made Abijah the son of Maachah the crown prince, to be ruler among his brethren; for he thought to make him king.

23 And he dealt wisely, and dispersed all of his children throughout all the countries of Judah and Benjamin unto every fortified city; and he gave them food in abundance. And he desired many wives.

CHAPTER 12

AND it came to pass when Rehoboam had established the kingdom and had strengthened himself, he forsook the law of the LORD, and all Israel with him.

2 And it came to pass that in the

[1] Verses 18 to 23 are not in the Eastern text.

fifth year of King Rehoboam, Shishak king of Egypt came up against Jerusalem, because they had transgressed against the LORD,

3 With twelve hundred chariots and sixty thousand horsemen; and the people were without number that came with him out of Egypt; the Lubims, the Sukkiims and the Ethiopians.

4 And he took the fenced cities which pertained to Judah, and came to Jerusalem.

5 ¶Then came Shemaiah the prophet to Rehoboam and to the princes of Judah that were gathered together at Jerusalem because of Shishak, and said unto them, Thus says the LORD: You have forsaken me, and therefore have I also left you in the hand of Shishak.

6 Whereupon the princes of Israel and the king humbled themselves; and they said, The LORD is righteous.

7 And when the LORD saw that they humbled themselves, the word of the LORD came to Shemaiah, saying, They have humbled themselves; therefore I will not destroy them, but I will grant them some deliverance; and my wrath shall not be poured out upon Jerusalem by the hand of Shishak.

8 Nevertheless they shall be his servants, that they may know my service, and the service of the kingdoms of the countries.

9 So Shishak king of Egypt came up against Jerusalem, and took away the treasures of the house of the LORD and the treasures of the king's house; he took all; he carried away also the shields of gold which Solomon had made.

10 Instead of which King Rehoboam made shields of brass, and committed them to the hands of the chief of the guard that kept the entrance of the king's house.

11 And when the king entered into the house of the LORD, the guard came and fetched them, and brought them again into the guard chamber.

12 And when he humbled himself, the wrath of the LORD turned from him, that he would not destroy him

altogether; and also in Judah things went well.

13 ¶So King Rehoboam strengthened himself in Jerusalem, and reigned; for Rehoboam was forty-one years old when he began to reign, and he reigned seventeen years in Jerusalem, the city which the LORD had chosen out of all the tribes of Israel to put his name there. And his mother's name was Naamah an Ammonitess.

14 And he did evil before the LORD, for he did not prepare his heart to worship the LORD and to seek him with all his heart.

15 Now these are the acts of Rehoboam, first and last, to do evil before the LORD God of Israel. And there were wars between Rehoboam the son of Solomon and Jeroboam the son of Nebat continually.

16 And Rehoboam slept with his fathers, and was buried in the city of David; and Abijah his son reigned in his stead.

CHAPTER 13

IN the eighteenth year of King Jeroboam the son of Nebat Abijah began to reign over the tribe of Judah.

2 He reigned three years in Jerusalem. His mother's name was Maachah the daughter of Uriel of Ramtha.

3 And Abijah mobilized an army of valiant men of war, four hundred thousand young men, who took upon themselves to go and fight against Jeroboam the son of Nebat. And Jeroboam also had mobilized an army, and he came to fight against him with eight hundred thousand young men, being mighty men of valour.

4 ¶And Abijah stood up upon mount Zemaraim, which is in the border of mount Ephraim, and said, Hear me, O Jeroboam the son of Nebat, and all Israel;

5 Perhaps you know that the LORD God of Israel gave the kingdom over Israel to David for ever, even to him and to his sons by a covenant pertaining to the kingship.

6 Yet Jeroboam the son of Nebat,

the servant of Solomon the son of David, rose up and rebelled against his lord.

7 And he gathered to him certain wicked men, the children of iniquity, and he prevailed against Rehoboam the son of Solomon, when Rehoboam was young and not advanced in years and did not know what to say, and did not comfort the people concerning the heavy yoke which Solomon his father had laid upon them.

8 And even now what can you say? You went away and renounced the kingdom of the house of David and went and served dead gods. And I reign over a single tribe, but you over many tribes, and there are with you golden calves which Jeroboam the son of Nebat made for you.

9 And you have cast out the priests the sons of Aaron and the Levites, and have made priests for yourselves of the people of the land. And whosoever comes to offer an offering, you take from him a young bullock and seven rams, and he becomes a priest of them that are not gods.

10 But as for us, we have not forsaken the LORD our God, and the priests, who minister to the LORD, are the sons of Aaron, and the Levites serve as they should;

11 They offer to the LORD every morning and every evening burnt offering and sweet incense, and set the shewbread in order upon the pure table; and the candlestick of gold with its lamps, and a boy having charge of the lamps lights them every evening; thus we have charge of the ordinances of the LORD our God;

12 But you have forsaken him and have gone after dead gods, and you serve them and worship them; and have forsaken the LORD God of your fathers, therefore you shall not prosper in the world.

13 But Jeroboam caused an ambush to come about behind them; so they were before Judah, and the ambush was behind them.

14 And when Judah looked back, behold, the battle was before and behind; and they cried unto the LORD, and the priests sounded with the trumpets.

15 And it came to pass when the men of the house of Judah shouted, the LORD defeated Jeroboam the son of Nebat and all Israel before Judah and Abijah.

16 And the children of Israel fled before Judah;

17 And Abijah slew them with a great slaughter; so there fell slain of Israel five hundred thousand young men.

18 Thus the children of Israel were defeated at that time, and the children of Judah prevailed, because they said, We rely upon the LORD God of our fathers.

19 And Abijah pursued Jeroboam, and took some great cities from him, Beth-el with its pastures, Shelah with its pastures, and Ephron with its pastures.

20 Neither did Jereboam recover strength again in the days of Abijah; and the LORD struck Jeroboam, and he died.

21 ¶But Abijah became strong, and he married fourteen wives, and there were born to him twenty-two sons and sixteen daughters.

22 And the rest of the acts of Abijah and his ways, behold, are written in the poems of the prophet Iddo.

CHAPTER 14

SO Abijah slept with his fathers, and they buried him in the city of David; and Asa his son reigned in his stead. In his days the land was quiet for ten years.

2 And Asa did that which was good and right in the presence of the LORD his God;

3 For he demolished the altars of the strange gods and the shrines, and broke down the images and cut down the groves;

4 And he said to Judah, Come, let us pray before the LORD God of our fathers.

5 Also he uprooted out of all the cities of Judah the shrines on the high places and the idols; and his kingdom was quiet in his days, and he had no enemies on all his borders.

6 ¶And he built fenced cities in Judah; for the land had rest, and there was no one who made war against him in those years, because the LORD had given him rest.

7 Therefore he said to Judah, Come, let us build these cities, and surround them with walls and towers, gates, and bars, while the land is still quiet of wars; because we have sought the LORD our God, and he also has sought us and he has given us rest from all those who are round about us, and has comforted us and delivered us.

8 And Asa had an army of mighty men of valour that bore swords and spears out of the tribe of Judah, three hundred thousand, and out of Benjamin, that bore breastplate and drew bows, two hundred and eighty thousand; all these were mighty men of valour.

9 ¶And there came out against them Zerah the Ethiopian with a large army of a million men and thirty thousand chariots, and came to Mareshah.

10 Then Asa went out against him, and he fought against him in the valley of Mareshah.

11 And Asa prayed before the LORD his God and said, Thou art our LORD, thou art the help of thy people; and when thou dost deliver a great army in the hands of a small force, then all the inhabitants of the earth shall know that it is good to rely on thee; help us, O LORD our God, because in thy name we have come against this great army. O LORD our God, delay not thy might from us.

12 And when Asa had finished praying, the angel of the LORD routed the Ethiopians before Asa and before Judah; and the Ethiopians fled.

13 And Asa and the people that were with him pursued them as far as Gedar; and there fell of the Ethiopians so many that they could not be numbered; for they were defeated before the LORD and before his armies; and they took and carried away very much spoil.

14 And they smote all the cities round about Gedar, for the fear of the LORD came upon them; and they plundered all the cities; for there was exceeding much spoil in them.

15 They also carried away the tents of the Arabians and carried away sheep and camels in abundance, and brought them to Jerusalem.

CHAPTER 15

AND the Spirit of the LORD came upon Azariah the son of Azor;

2 And he went out to meet Asa and said to him, Hear me, Asa, and all Judah and Benjamin: The LORD is with you for ever and ever; and if you seek him, he will be found by you; but if you forsake him, he will forsake you.

3 Now for a long time Israel has not served their God in truth and has not accepted the teaching of their priests and would not obey their laws; therefore they were delivered into the hand of their enemies.

4 But when in their distress they prayed to the LORD God of Israel and sought him, he was found by them.

5 And in those early times when we did not worship our God, there was no peace to him that went out, nor to him that came in, because of great misfortune that came upon all the inhabitants of the land.

6 And we were scattered in every nation and people, and in towns and cities,

7 Because we had forsaken our God and would not listen to the voice of his servants, the prophets; so he rewarded us according to our works.

8 And when Asa heard these words of Azariah the son of Azor the prophet, he took courage and removed the idols from all the land of Judah and Benjamin and from the cities which he had taken in the land of Ephraim, and he repaired the altar of the LORD that was in the front of the porch of the LORD.

9 And he gathered all Judah and Benjamin and the proselytes with them out of Ephraim and Manasseh and out of Simeon; for they gathered together and came to him out of Is-

rael in abundance when they saw that the LORD his God was with him.

10 So they gathered themselves together at Jerusalem in the third month, in the fifteenth year of the reign of Asa.

11 And the same day they offered to the LORD of the spoil which they had brought, seven hundred oxen and six thousand sheep.

12 And they entered into a covenant to pray to the LORD God of their fathers with all their heart and with all their soul;

13 And that whosoever would not pray to the LORD God of Israel should be put to death, whether small or great, whether man or woman.

14 And they swore to the LORD with a loud voice, and with sounding of curved and straight trumpets.

15 And all Judah rejoiced at this report which they heard; for they sought him with all their heart and prayed to him with all their soul; and he was found by them, and he delivered them from all their enemies round about.

16 ¶And also Maachah the mother of Asa he removed from being queen mother, because she had a feast to her idols; and Asa cut down her idols and burned them at the brook Kidron.

17 But the altars on the high places were not taken away out of Israel; nevertheless the heart of Asa was perfect in the worship of the LORD his God all the days of his life.

18 ¶And he brought into the house of the LORD the things that his father had dedicated and that he himself had dedicated, silver and gold and vessels.

19 And there was no more war until the thirty-fifth year of the reign of Asa.

CHAPTER 16

IN the thirty-sixth year of the reign of Asa, Baasha king of Israel came up against Judah and built Ramtha, that he might let none go out or come in to Asa king of Judah.

2 Then Asa brought silver and gold out of the treasures of the house of the LORD and of the king's house, and sent them to Bar-hadad king of Aram, who dwelt in Damascus, saying,

3 There is a league between me and you, as there was between my father and your father; behold, I have sent you silver and gold; go, break your league with Baasha king of Israel, that he may withdraw from me.

4 And Bar-hadad hearkened to King Asa, and sent the commanders of his armies against the cities of Israel; and they came and encamped against the cities of Israel; and they took Ijon, Abel, and Beth-maacah, and all the store cities of Naphtali.

5 Then when Baasha heard of it, he stopped building Ramtha, and let his work cease.

6 Then Asa the king gathered together all Judah; and they carried away the stones of Ramtha and its timber with which Baasha was building; and King Asa built with them Ramtha of Benjamin and the town of Mizpah.

7 ¶And at that time Hanan the prophet came to Asa king of Judah and said to him, Because you have relied on the king of Aram and not relied on the LORD your God, therefore the army of Aram will flee.

8 And they will go and become strong, both they and the Ethiopians and the kings that are with them, and will become great armies with very many chariots and horsemen, but when you seek the LORD your God, he will deliver them into your hands.

9 For the eyes of the LORD run to and fro throughout the whole earth; therefore, be strong, and let your heart be perfect towards his worship, and understand all his wonders; for the LORD your God will fight for you.

10 Then Asa was wroth with the seer, and put him in prison because he reported things which he did not see and made the heart of the people tremble; therefore Asa kept himself aloof from the people at that time.

11 ¶And, behold, the acts of Asa, first and last, lo, they are written in the Book of the Kings of Judah and Israel.

12 And Asa was diseased in his feet

in the thirty-ninth year of his reign, and was laid in his house.

13 ¶And Asa slept with his fathers, and died in the forty-first year of his reign.

14 And they buried him in his own sepulchre in the city of David, and they laid him on a bier which was filled with many kinds of spices, and they made a very great burnt offering for him.

CHAPTER 17

AND Jehoshaphat his son reigned in his stead, and strengthened himself against Israel.

2 And he placed mighty men in all the fortified cities of Judah, and appointed governors in the land of Judah and in the cities of Ephraim which Asa his father had taken.

3 And the LORD was with Jehoshaphat because he walked in the first ways of his father David and did not pray to images;

4 But he prayed to the LORD God of his father and walked in his commandments and kept his statutes, and did not do according to the ways of Israel.

5 Therefore the LORD established the kingdom in his hand; and all Judah brought presents to Jehoshaphat and he had riches and honor in abundance.

6 And his heart was strengthened in the ways of the LORD; moreover he uprooted the altars and the high places which were within the territory of Judah.

7 ¶Also in the third year of his reign he sent and called his princes and the commanders of the armies, even to Obadiah, Zechariah, Nathanael, Melachiah, to teach in the cities of Judah.

8 And with them were the Levites, even Shemaiah, Nethaniah, Zechariah, Ashaiel, Natorah, Jonathan, Adonijah, and Tobiah. These were all Levites, and with them were Elishama and Jehoram, priests.

9 And they taught in all the land of Judah, having the book of the law of the LORD with them, and went about throughout all the cities of Judah and taught the people.

10 ¶And the fear of the LORD fell upon all the kingdoms of the lands that were round about Judah, so that they made no war against Jehoshaphat.

11 Also some of the cities of the Philistines brought Jehoshaphat presents, silver, and poll tax; and the Arabians brought him flocks, seven thousand and seven hundred rams, and seven thousand and seven hundred he-goats, yearly.

12 ¶And Jehoshaphat grew exceedingly rich; and he built in Judah castles and store cities.

13 And he had much business in the cities of Judah; and the men of war, mighty men of valour, were in Jerusalem.

14 And this is the number of them according to the house of their fathers. Of Judah, the commanders of thousands: Adino the chief, and with him mighty men of valour, three hundred thousand.

15 And next to him was Johanan the commander, and with him two hundred and eighty thousand valiant men.

16 And next to him was Shemai the son of Zerah, with whom the LORD was pleased, and with him two hundred thousand valiant men.

17 And of Benjamin: Eliada, a mighty man of valour, and with him, armed with bow and shield, two hundred thousand.

18 And next to him was Jehozabad, a mighty man, and with him a hundred and eighty thousand ready for the war.

19 These were all who served King Jehoshaphat, besides those whom the king put in the fortified cities throughout all the land of Judah.

CHAPTER 18

NOW Jehoshaphat had riches and honor in abundance, and he made an alliance with Ahab.

2 And after two years he went down to Ahab in Samaria. And Ahab killed sheep and oxen for him in abundance, and for the armed forces

that were with him, and advised him to go up to Ramath-gilead.

3 And Ahab king of Israel said to Jehoshaphat king of Judah, Will you go up with me to Ramath-gilead? And he answered him, I will go up as you do; and my people are as your people; and my horses as your horses, and we will go with you to war.

4 ¶And Jehoshaphat said to the king of Israel, Inquire, I pray, for the word of the LORD today.

5 Therefore the king of Israel gathered together of the prophets four hundred men, and said to them, Shall we go to Ramath-gilead to battle or shall I forbear? And they said to him, Go up; for the LORD will deliver your enemies into your hands.

6 But King Jehoshaphat said, Is there not here a true prophet of the LORD, that we may inquire of him?

7 And the king of Israel said to Jehoshaphat, There is yet one man by whom we may inquire of the LORD; but I hate him; for he never prophesies good concerning me, but always evil. His name is Micaiah the son of Imla. And Jehoshaphat said, Let not the king say so.

8 And the king of Israel called for one of the officers and said to him, Bring quickly Micaiah the son of Imla.

9 And the king of Israel and Jehoshaphat the king of Judah were sitting each man on his throne, clothed in their robes, and they sat at the entrance of the gate of Samaria; and all the false prophets were prophesying before them.

10 And Zedekiah the son of a Canaanitish woman had made for himself horns of iron,[1] and he said, Thus says the LORD: With these you shall pierce the Arameans until they are cut off and destroyed.

11 And all the prophets prophesied so, saying, Go up to Ramath-gilead, and triumph: for the LORD will deliver your enemies into your hands, O king.

12 And the messenger who went to call Micaiah spoke to him, saying, Behold, the words of the false prophets have declared good to the king with one accord; let your words, therefore, be pleasant like one of theirs, and you also prophesy good.

13 And Micaiah said, As the LORD God lives, what my God puts into my heart, that will I speak.

14 And when he was come to the king, the king said to him, Micaiah, shall we go to Ramath-gilead or shall I forbear? And he said to him, Go up and triumph, and they shall be delivered into your hands.

15 And the king said to him, How many times shall I adjure you that you say nothing but the truth to me in the name of the LORD?

16 Then he said, I saw all Israel scattered upon the mountains as sheep that have no shepherd; and the LORD said, These have no king; let them return therefore every man to his house in peace.

17 And the king of Israel said to Jehoshaphat, Did I not tell you that he would not prophesy good concerning me, but evil?

18 Then Micaiah said, Therefore hear the word of the LORD: I saw the LORD sitting upon his throne, and all the host of heaven standing on his right hand and on his left.

19 And the LORD said, Who shall entice Ahab king of Israel, that he may go up and be slain at Ramath-gilead? And one said, I will entice him after this manner, and another said, I will entice him after that manner.

20 Then there came out a spirit, and stood before the LORD and said, I will entice him, and the LORD said to him, With what?

21 And he said, I will go out, and be a lying spirit in the mouth of all his prophets. And the LORD said, You shall entice him, and you shall also prevail; go out, and do according to what you have said.

22 Now therefore, behold, the LORD has put a lying spirit in the mouth of these your prophets, and the LORD has decreed evil against you.

23 Then Zedekiah the son of the Canaanitish woman came near and struck Micaiah on his cheek, and said to him, Since when did the Spirit of

---

[1] A head-dress.

the LORD depart from me to speak to you?

24 And Micaiah said, Behold, you shall see on that day when you shall go into an inner chamber to hide yourself.

25 Then the king of Israel said, Take Micaiah, and carry him back and detain him in the house of Amon the governor of the city and in the house of Joash the king's son;

26 And say, Thus says the king: Put this fellow in the prison, and feed him with bread of affliction and with water of affliction until I return in peace.

27 And Micaiah said, If you certainly return in peace, then the LORD has not spoken by me. And he said, Hear, all you people.

28 So Jehoshaphat the king of Judah and Ahab the king of Israel went up to Ramath-gilead.

29 And the king of Israel said to Jehoshaphat, I will put on my armor, and go and stand in the battle array; and you put on your armor. So the king of Israel put on his armor, and went and stood in the battle array.

30 Now the king of Aram had commanded the captains of the chariots that were with him, thirty-two in number, saying, Fight not with small or great, but only with the king of Israel.

31 And it came to pass when the captains of the chariots saw Jehoshaphat, they said, It is the king of Israel. Therefore they came against him to fight him; but Jehoshaphat cried out and the LORD helped him; and he turned them away from him.

32 And it came to pass when the captains of the chariots saw that it was not the king of Israel, they turned back from pursuing him.

33 And a certain man shot an arrow unwittingly towards him, and smote the king of Israel between the joints of his breastplate; therefore he said to his chariot man, Turn your hand and carry me out of the host; for I am grievously wounded.

34 And the battle grew fiercer that day; but the king of Israel was seated in the chariot fighting against the Arameans until the evening, and at sunset he died.

CHAPTER 19

AND at the evening Jehoshaphat the king of Judah returned to his house in peace to Jerusalem.

2 And Jehu the son of Hanan the seer went out to meet him, and said to King Jehoshaphat, Should you go to help the ungodly, and love those who hate the LORD? Therefore the LORD is angry with you.

3 But I believe good reports have been heard about you, in that you have not shed innocent blood in the land and have prepared your heart to pray before the LORD in truth.

4 And Jehoshaphat dwelt at Jerusalem; and he went out again among the people from the city of Beersheba to mount Ephraim, and brought them back to worship the LORD God of their fathers.

5 ¶And he appointed judges in the land throughout all the fortified cities of Judah and the great cities.

6 And he said to the judges, Take heed what you do; for you judge not for man, but for the LORD our God.

7 Therefore be courageous and judge righteously, so that the LORD may be with you for ever; take heed and do it; for there is no iniquity with the LORD our God nor respect of persons nor taking of bribes.

8 ¶Moreover in Jerusalem also Jehoshaphat appointed men of the Levites and of the priests and of the chiefs of the fathers of the children of Israel for the judgment of the LORD; then he returned to Jerusalem.

9 And he charged them, saying, Thus shall you do in reverence of the LORD, in faithfulness and with a perfect heart.

10 And whatsoever case shall come to you of your brethren who dwell in your cities, between bloodshed and bloodshed, between law and commandment, between statutes and ordinances, you shall warn them so that they may not be guilty before the LORD, and thus he become angry with them and with their brethren; this do, and you shall not be guilty.

11 And, behold, I have appointed priests over you, that they may judge just and faithful judgments according to the commandment of the LORD. And Zechariah the son of Shemiah declared to all the people of Judah all the commandments of the king; he also declared to the scribes and the Levites, repeating everything before them, saying, Deal courageously, and the LORD will help you for ever.

CHAPTER 20

AND it came to pass after this, the children of Moab and the children of Ammon, with the mighty men of war, came against Jehoshaphat to battle.

2 Then there came messengers and told Jehoshaphat, saying, A great army has come against you from beyond the Red Sea; and, behold, they are encamping in Jericho, which is En-gad.

3 And Jehoshaphat feared, and he raised up his face to pray before the LORD and proclaimed a fast for all the inhabitants of Judah. And he said to them, Gather yourselves together and come let us beseech the LORD our God.

4 And all the inhabitants of Judah gathered themselves together, even from far off cities, and they came to beseech the LORD.

5 ¶And Jehoshaphat stood in the midst of the assembly of Judah in the house of the LORD, which is in Jerusalem, before the new court,

6 And he prayed and said, O LORD God of our fathers, thou art the God in heaven, and thou art ruler over all the kingdoms of the world, and thine is power and might, and now I stand before thee praying.

7 And thou art our God, who didst destroy the inhabitants of this land before thy people Israel and gavest it to the descendants of Abraham thy friend for ever.

8 And they have dwelt in it, and have built in it a sanctuary for thy name, saying,

9 Now, because there is a sanctuary among us, no evil shall come upon us, nor the sword nor judgment nor pestilence nor famine; and we shall come and stand before this house and before thee (for thy name has been invoked in this house), and we will pray before thee in this house, and thou wilt hear our prayer and save us.

10 And now, behold, the children of Ammon, of the mount of Gabel, and of Moab, with whom thou wouldst not let Israel mix when thou didst bring them out of the land of Egypt, and thou hadst removed the yoke of the Egyptians from them,

11 Behold, now they reward us; they are coming to drive us out of thy possession, which thou hast given us to inherit.

12 O our God, make thyself known and judge them, for we have no strength to stand before them; bring upon them the sword of thy judgment, for we do not know what to do; but our eyes are upon thee.

13 And all Judah stood before the LORD with their little ones, their wives, their sons, and their daughters.

14 ¶Then upon Hazaiel the son of Zechariah, the son of Benaiah, the son of Jehoiadah, the son of Mattaniah, a Levite of the sons of Asaph, came the spirit of might from before the LORD, and he was standing before the people of Israel;

15 And he said, Hearken, all Judah and inhabitants of Jerusalem and King Jehoshaphat, thus says the LORD your God: Be not afraid nor dismayed because of this great army; for the battle is not yours, but God's.

16 Hasten, go down against them; behold, they are coming up early in the morning; and you shall find them in the cliff of the valley, before the wilderness. They are coming up to fight against you.

17 And in that hour, stand still and see the salvation that the LORD will do for you, O Judah and the inhabitants of Jerusalem; fear not, nor be dismayed; tomorrow go out against them; for the LORD God will help you.

18 Then Jehoshaphat bowed his head with his face to the ground and worshipped; and all Judah and the

inhabitants of Jerusalem fell before the LORD, worshipping the LORD.

19 And the Levites of the descendants of the Kohathites and of the descendants of the Korhites stood up to praise the LORD God of Israel with a loud voice,

20 ¶And they rose early in the morning and went forth into the wilderness of Tekoa; and as they went forth, Jehoshaphat stood and said, Hear me, O Judah and inhabitants of Jerusalem: Believe in the LORD your God, so you shall be established; believe in his prophets, and you shall be delivered.

21 Then he stood in the midst of the people and said, Come, let us give thanks to the LORD, and give praise to the excellency of his holiness, as he is going forth before our armies to fight for us against our enemies. And they said, Give thanks to the LORD, for he is good; for his mercy endures for ever. Then the hills began to give praise and the mountains began to rejoice.

22 ¶And when they began to sing and to praise, the LORD set ambushments against the children of Ammon, Moab, and mount Seir, which were come against Judah; and they were smitten.

23 For the children of Ammon and Moab stood up against the inhabitants of mount Seir, utterly to slay and destroy them: and when they had made an end of the inhabitants of Seir, every one helped to destroy another.

24 And when Judah came toward the watchtower in the wilderness, they looked to the multitude, and, behold, they were dead bodies fallen to the earth, and none had escaped.

25 And when Jehoshaphat and the people of Israel came to take away the spoil from them, they found among them an abundance of booty: riches, bridles, horses, and precious jewels, and they took for themselves whatever they desired.

26 ¶And it came to pass after three days, when they were through taking the spoil, because it was so much,

they assembled themselves on the fourth day in the valley of Borktha; [1] for there they blessed the LORD God; therefore the name of that place was called the valley of Borktha to this day.

27 Then all the men of Judah returned to Jerusalem with Jehoshaphat at their head, for they were returning to Jerusalem rejoicing; for the LORD had made them rejoice over their enemies.

28 And they came to Jerusalem with songs, harps, lyres, and curved and straight trumpets, to the house of the LORD.

29 And the fear of the LORD fell on all the kingdoms of those countries when they heard that the LORD had fought against the enemies of Israel.

30 So the realm of Jehoshaphat was quiet; for the LORD gave him rest on all sides.

31 ¶And Jehoshaphat reigned over Judah; he was thirty-five years old when he began to reign, and he reigned twenty-five years in Jerusalem. And his mother's name was Arubah the daughter of Shilhi.

32 And he walked in all the ways of Asa his father, and did not turn aside from them, doing that which was right in the sight of the LORD.

33 However the shrines on the high places were not removed; for as yet the people had not prepared their hearts to the God of their fathers.

34 Now the rest of the acts of Jehoshaphat, first and last, behold, they are written in the sayings of Jehu the son of Hanan, which are written in the Book of the Kings of Israel.

35 ¶And after this Jehoshaphat king of Judah joined himself with Ahaziah king of Israel, who did very wickedly, more than all the kings of Israel.

36 And he joined himself with him to make ships to go to Tarshish; and they made the ships in Ezion-gaber.

37 Then Eliezer the son of Jehoshaphat's uncle prophesied in the city of Mareshah against Jehoshaphat, saying, Because of your partnership with Ahaziah, the LORD has confused all

1 Valley of Blessing.

your works. And the ships were damaged and were not able to go to Tarshish.

CHAPTER 21

NOW Jehoshaphat slept with his fathers, and was buried with his fathers in the city of David. And Jehoram his son reigned in his stead.

2 And he had brothers, the sons of Jehoshaphat, and these are their names: Azariah, Nahjaiel, Zechariah, Azariah, Malchael, and Shephatiah; all these were the sons of Jehoshaphat king of Judah.

3 And their father gave them great gifts of silver and of gold, and many other gifts, with fortified cities in Judah; but the kingdom gave he to Jehoram because he was his first-born.

4 Now when Jehoram was risen up to the kingdom of his father, he strengthened himself and slew all his brothers in the battle and also slew some of the elders of Israel.

5 ¶Jehoram was thirty-two years old when he began to reign, and he reigned eight years in Jerusalem.

6 And he walked in the ways of the kings of Israel, as did the house of Ahab; for Ahab's sister was his wife; and he did that which was evil in the presence of the LORD.

7 However the LORD would not destroy the house of David, because of the covenant that he had made with David and because he had promised to give an heir to him and to his sons for ever.

8 ¶In his days the Edomites revolted from under the dominion of Judah, and made themselves a king.

9 Then Jehoram crossed over the Jordan with his princes, and all his chariots with him; and he rose up by night and smote the Edomites who had surrounded him and the captains of the chariots.

10 So the Edomites revolted from the dominion of Judah to this day. At the same time also did the Edomites who dwelt in Libnah revolt from his rule, because Jehoram had forsaken the LORD God of his fathers.

11 Moreover he made shrines on high places in the mountains of Judah and caused the Nazarites of Jerusalem to drink wine and scattered the house of Judah.

12 ¶And there was brought to him a letter from Elijah the prophet, saying, Thus says the LORD God of David your father: Because you have not walked in the ways of Jehoshaphat your father nor in the ways of Asa king of Judah,

13 But have walked in the ways of the kings of Israel and have caused Judah and the inhabitants of Jerusalem to go astray with the whoredoms of the house of Ahab, and also have slain your brothers, your father's sons, who were better than yourself;

14 Behold, the LORD will smite you with a great plague, together with your people, your children, your wives, and all your goods;

15 And you yourself shall die with a severe sickness; and you shall be consumed with a great torment until your bowels fall out because of your sickness. And you shall be tormented for many years.

16 ¶Moreover the LORD stirred up against Jehoram the spirit of the Philistines and of the Arabians who dwelt near the Ethiopians;

17 And they came up against Judah and smote it, and carried away all the substance that was found in the king's house, and his sons also and his wives; so that no son was left to him except Ahaziah his youngest son.

18 ¶And after all this he was smitten in his bowels with an incurable disease.

19 And it came to pass that in the process of time, after the end of two years, the word of the prophet was fulfilled, his bowels fell out because of his sickness; so he died of sore disease. And his people did not honor him with a funeral according to the manner they had done for his fathers.

20 He was thirty-two years old when he began to reign, and he reigned eight years in Jerusalem, and his departure was not regretted. And he was buried in the city of David his father, but not in the sepulchres of the kings.

CHAPTER 22

THEN the inhabitants of Jerusalem made Ahaziah his youngest son king in his stead; for raiders had come to the camp and slain all the eldest. So Ahaziah the son of Jehoram king of Judah reigned.

2 Twenty-two years old was Ahaziah when he began to reign, and he reigned one year in Jerusalem. His mother's name was Athaliah the daughter of Omri.

3 And he walked in the ways of the house of Ahab, for he was the son of Ahab's sister.

4 He also committed many sins and did evil in the sight of the LORD like the house of Ahab; for they were his counsellors after the death of his father to his destruction,

5 ¶Because he walked after their counsel, and went with Joram the son of Ahab king of Israel to war against Hazael king of Aram at Ramath-gilead; and the Arameans smote Joram.

6 And he returned to be healed in Jezreel because of the wounds which he had received at Ramtha, when he fought with Hazael king of Aram. And Ahaziah went down to see Joram the son of Ahab in Jezreel because he was sick.

7 And the destruction of Ahaziah was determined by God, who decreed that he should go to Joram; for when he was come, he went out with Joram to meet Jehu the son of Jamshi, whom the LORD had anointed to destroy the house of Ahab.

8 And when Jehu was executing judgment upon the house of Ahab, he found the princes of Judah and the sons of the brothers of Ahaziah who ministered to Ahaziah and slew them.

9 And he sought Ahaziah and he caught him (for he was hiding in Samaria) and brought him to Jehu; and when they had slain him, they buried him; for they said, He is the son of Jehoshaphat, who sought the LORD with all his heart. So the house of Ahaziah had no one with power to rule over the kingdom.

10 ¶Now when Athaliah the mother of Ahaziah saw that her son was dead, she arose and destroyed all the king's sons of the house of Judah.

11 But Jehoshabeath, the daughter of the king, stole Joash the son of Ahaziah from among the king's sons who were about to be slain, and hid him and his nurse in her bedchamber. So Jehoshabeath, the daughter of King Jehoram, the wife of Jehoiadah the priest (for she was the sister of Ahaziah), hid him from Athaliah so that she did not slay him.

12 And he was hid with her in the house of the LORD six years; and Athaliah reigned over the land.

CHAPTER 23

AND in the seventh year Jehoiadah strengthened himself and took the captains of hundreds, Azariah the son of Jeruham and Ishmael the son of Johanan and Azariah the son of Obed and Shemiah the son of Ido and Elishaphat the son of Zichri, and they made a covenant together.

2 And they went about in Judah and gathered the Levites from all the cities of Judah and the chiefs of the fathers of Israel, and they came to Jerusalem.

3 And all the congregation made a covenant in the presence of the king in the house of the LORD. And Jehoiadah said to them, Behold, the king's son shall reign over you, as the LORD has spoken to David his servant.

4 This is the thing that you shall do: a third part of you who enter the temple on the sabbath, of the priests and of the Levites and of the porters shall be on guard;

5 And a third part shall be at the king's house; and a third part at the cook's gate; and all the people shall be on guard in the court of the house of the LORD.

6 But let no one enter the house of the LORD except the priests and the Levites; they shall enter, for they are holy; but all the people shall keep watch over the house of the LORD.

7 And the Levites shall surround the king, every man with his weapons in his hand; and whosoever else enters

the inner house shall be put to death; but you be with the king when he comes in and when he goes out.

8 So the Levites and all Judah did according to all that Jehoiadah the priest had commanded, and every man took his men who were to keep watch on the sabbath, with those who were to go out on the sabbath; for Jehoiadah the priest had dismissed them from their duties.

9 Moreover Jehoiadah the priest delivered spears and bucklers and shields to the captains of hundreds that had been King David's, which were in the house of the LORD.

10 And all the people stood up, every man having his weapon in his hand, from the right side of the temple to the left side of the temple, along by the altar and the temple, and by the king round about.

11 Then they brought out the king's son and put the crown on his head, and gave him the sceptre and made him king. And Jehoiadah and his sons anointed him and said, Long live the king!

12 ¶Now when Athaliah heard the noise of the people rejoicing and praising the LORD, she came to the king into the house of the LORD;

13 And she looked, and, behold, the king stood by the pillar according to the rite of the kings, and the people were sounding with curved and straight trumpets before the king; and all the people were rejoicing and blowing trumpets, and the singers accompanied with instruments of music. Then Athaliah tore her clothes and said, Treason! Treason!

14 Then Jehoiadah the priest commanded the captains of hundreds who were set over the army and said to them, Take her out of the ranks, and whosoever follows her, let him be slain with the sword. For the priest said, Do not slay her in the house of the LORD.

15 Then they made a passage for her, and she went into the entrance of the horse gate, and she was put to death there.

16 ¶And Jehoiadah made a covenant between himself and all the people, and between himself and the king, that they should be the LORD's people.

17 Then all the people went to the house of Baal and demolished it, and broke his altars and his images in pieces, and slew the priest of Baal before the altar.

18 Also Jehoiadah appointed officers in the house of the LORD, and the priests and the Levites, whom David had divided into groups, to be in charge of the house of the LORD, to offer burnt offerings to the LORD, as it is written in the law of Moses, with rejoicing and with singing, as it was ordained by David.

19 And he set the porters at the gates of the house of the LORD so that no one who was unclean in anything should enter in.

20 And he took the captains of hundreds and the governors of the people and all the people of the land, and they came through the high gate of the king's house and set the king upon the throne of the kingdom.

21 And all the people of the land rejoiced, sounding with trumpets, after they had slain Athaliah with the sword.

CHAPTER 24

JOASH was seven years old when he began to reign, and he reigned forty years in Jerusalem. His mother's name was Zibiah of the city of Beersheba.

2 And Joash did that which was right in the sight of the LORD all the days of Jehoiadah the priest.

3 And Jehoiadah the priest took for him two wives; and he begat sons and daughters.

4 ¶And it came to pass after this that Jehoiadah determined in his heart with Joash secretly to restore the house of the LORD and to repair everything that was needed in it.

5 And Jehoiadah the priest gathered together the priests and the Levites and said to them, Go out to the cities of Judah and gather from all the cities of Israel silver and gold to repair the house of your God from year to year, and see that you hasten the matter.

6 And the king called for Jehoiadah the chief priest and said to him, Why have you not required the Levites to go and bring in from Judah and from Jerusalem the gifts that were prescribed by Moses the servant of the LORD and summon the congregation of Israel for the feast of the tabernacle of the assembly?

7 For Athaliah taught wickedly, and had broken up the house of the LORD; and also given all the dedicated things that were in the house of the LORD for the worship of the idols.

8 And at the king's commandment, they made a chest, and set it outside the gate of the house of the LORD.

9 And they made a proclamation throughout Judah and Jerusalem to bring in to the LORD the portion that Moses the servant of the LORD laid upon Israel in the wilderness.

10 And all the princes and all the people rejoiced, and brought in gifts and took the chest and put it in its place and cast into it until it was full.

11 And when they saw that there was much money in the chest, then the king's scribe and the overseer of the high priest's house came and counted the money, and put it into bags.

12 And they gave it to those who did the work of the service of the house of the LORD, and hired masons and carpenters to repair the house of the LORD, and also workers in iron and brass to restore the house of the LORD.

13 So the workmen wrought, and the work was perfected by them, and they set the house of God in order and strengthened it.

14 And when they had finished it, they brought the rest of the money before the king and Jehoiadah, whereof were made vessels for the house of the LORD, even vessels to minister and to offer withal, and spoons, and vessels of gold and silver. And they offered burnt offerings in the house of the LORD continually all the days of Jehoiadah.

15 ¶But Jehoiadah grew old, and was full of days when he died; a hun-dred and thirty years old was he when he died.

16 And they buried him in the city of David among the kings, and they said, Such shall be rewarded to him who does good in Israel. And he also had contributed greatly to the house of the LORD.

17 Now after the death of Jehoiadah came the princes of Judah, and made obeisance to the king. Then the king listened to them.

18 And they left the house of the LORD God of their fathers, and went and served images and idols; and wrath came upon Judah and Jerusalem because they committed this sin.

19 Yet God sent prophets to them to bring them back from their ways, but they would not listen, so the prophets testified against them, but they would not give ear.

20 And the Spirit of the LORD came upon Zechariah the son of Jehoiadah the priest, and he went up and stood above the people and said to them, Thus says the LORD: Why do you transgress the commandments of the LORD, that you cannot prosper? Because you have forsaken my way, I will also forsake you.

21 And they conspired against him, and stoned him with stones at the commandment of the king in the court of the house of the LORD.

22 Thus Joash the king did not remember the kindness which Jehoiadah his father had done to him, but he slew his sons after him. And when his sons were about to be slain, they said, May the LORD see and avenge it.

23 ¶And it came to pass at the end of the year, the army of Aram came up against him; and they came to Judah and Jerusalem, and destroyed all the princes of the people, and sent all their spoil to the king of Damascus.

24 For the army of Aram came with a small company of men, and the LORD delivered a very great army into their hand because they had forsaken the LORD God of their fathers. So what Joash had done was condemned by the judges.

25 And when they were departed from him (for they left him in a state

of severe illness), his own servants conspired against him for the blood of the sons of Jehoiadah the priest, and slew him on his bed, and he died; and they buried him in the city of David his father, but they did not bury him in the sepulchres of the kings.

26 And these are the names of those who conspired against him: Zaccor the son of Shimeath an Ammonitess and Jehozabad the son of Netoroth a Moabitess.

27 ¶And his sons also and many other people conspired against him. And the rest of the sins which he committed in the house of the LORD, behold, they are written in the poems of the Book of the Kings. And Amaziah his son reigned in his stead.

CHAPTER 25

AMAZIAH was twenty-five years old when he began to reign, and he reigned twenty-nine years in Jerusalem. And his mother's name was Jehoaddan of Jerusalem.

2 And he did that which was right in the sight of the LORD, but not with a perfect heart.

3 ¶Now it came to pass when the kingdom was strengthened in his hand, he slew his servants who had killed the king his father.

4 But he did not slay the children of the murderers, because so it is written in the book of the law of Moses, where the LORD commanded, saying, The fathers shall not die for the children, neither shall the children die for the fathers, but every man shall die for his own sin.

5 ¶Then Amaziah gathered Judah together and appointed over them commanders of thousands and captains of hundreds, according to the houses of their fathers, throughout all Judah and Benjamin; and he numbered them from twenty years old and above, and found that they were three hundred thousand young men, able to go forth to war, that could draw sword and handle shield.

6 He hired also a hundred thousand mighty men of valour from Israel for a hundred talents of silver.

7 But there came a prophet of the LORD to him, saying, O king, let not all the army of Israel go with you; for the LORD is not with all Israel, neither with all the house of Ephraim.

8 You are to engage in a great battle, and the LORD will cause you to fall before your enemies because you have not praised the LORD, for he is the helper and one who exalts.

9 And Amaziah said to the prophet of the LORD, What folly have I committed in giving the hundred talents to the men of Israel? And the prophet of God said to him, The LORD your God is able to give you much more than this, double what you have given.

10 Then Amaziah separated the men that had come to him from Ephraim, to go home again; wherefore his anger was greatly kindled against Israel. And he sent them back home in his great anger.

11 ¶And Amaziah strengthened himself and led forth his people, and went to the valley of salt and slew ten thousand of the men of mount Gebal.

12 And another ten thousand left alive, the children of Judah captured and brought to the top of the rocks, and all of them came bound in chains.

13 ¶And the valiant men whom Amaziah had carried captive when he went to war, he set over the cities of Judah, and over Samaria, and over the towns of the Gentiles; and they smote three thousand men of the towns and took much spoil.

14 ¶Now it came to pass after Amaziah was come from slaughter of the Edomites, they brought to him the gods of the men of mount Gebal, and he set them up before him and worshipped before them and burned incense to them.

15 Therefore the anger of the LORD was kindled against Amaziah, and he sent to him a prophet, who said to him, Why have you prayed before the gods of the Gentiles, which could not deliver their own people out of your hands?

16 And it came to pass, as the prophet conversed with him, he said to him, The worship of wooden idols has been taken up by the kings.

Then the prophet withdrew from him, and said to him, Woe to you! for, behold, the LORD has determined to destroy you because you have done this and have not listened to my counsel.

17 ¶Then Amaziah king of Judah took counsel, and sent to Joash, the son of Jehoahaz, the son of Jehu, king of Israel, saying, Come, let us face each other in battle.

18 But Joash king of Israel sent to Amaziah king of Judah, saying, The thistle that is in Lebanon sent to the cedar that is in Lebanon, saying, Give your daughter to my son to wife; and there passed by a wild beast that was in Lebanon and trampled down the thistle.

19 Surely, because you have defeated the Edomites, your heart has lifted you up to boast; keep your dignity and stay at home; why should you stir up trouble, that you should fall, even you and all Judah with you?

20 But Amaziah would not listen; then Joash king of Israel and Amaziah king of Judah went up

21 And confronted each other in battle, at the town of Beth-shemesh, which is in the border of the land of Judah.

22 And Judah was defeated before Israel; and they fled every man to his tent.

23 And Joash the king of Israel captured Amaziah king of Judah in the town of Beth-shemesh, and brought him to Jerusalem, and broke down the wall of Jerusalem from the gate of Ephraim to the corner gate, four hundred cubits.

24 And he took all the silver and the gold and all the vessels that were found in the house of God, together with the vessels that were kept by Ober-edom, and the treasures of the king's house and the vessels of the king's house and the vessels of gold, and returned to Samaria.

25 ¶And Amaziah the son of Joash king of Judah lived after the death of Joash son of Jehoahaz king of Israel fifteen years.

26 Now the rest of the acts of Amaziah, first and last, behold, they are written in the Book of the Kings of Judah and Israel.

27 ¶Now from the time that Amaziah turned away from following the LORD, his servants made a conspiracy against him in Jerusalem; and he fled to Lachish; but they sent to Lachish after him, and slew him there.

28 And his servants brought him upon horses, and buried him with his fathers in the city of David.

CHAPTER 26

THEN all the people of Judah took Uzziah his son, who was sixteen years old, and made him king instead of his father Amaziah.

2 He built Eloth, and restored it to Judah after the king slept with his fathers.

3 Uzziah was sixteen years old when he began to reign, and he reigned fifty-two years in Jerusalem. His mother's name was Jeconiah of Jerusalem.

4 And he did that which was right in the sight of the LORD, according to all that his father David did.

5 And he prayed before the LORD in the days of Zechariah, who taught him in the worship of the LORD, and the LORD prospered all his ways.

6 And he went forth and made war against the Philistines, and broke down the wall of Gath and the wall of Gaza and the wall of Ashdod.

7 And God helped him against the Philistines and against the Arabians that dwelt in Gurbaal and the Mehunims.

8 And his fame spread as far as the land of Egypt; for he continued to fight.

9 Moreover Uzziah built towers in Jerusalem at the corner gate and at the western gate, and fortified them with iron bars.

10 He also built many towers in the cities which he had, and he built for himself many castles; for he had much wealth; and had farmers and workers both in the plains and on the mountains, because he had much cattle.

11 Moreover Uzziah had an army of mighty men that went out to war.

Their number was thirty-two thousand and six hundred.

12 And the others who dwelt in the open country were three hundred thousand; and the men who were girded with sword were seven thousand and five hundred,

13 Who stood up every day guarding the king.

14 And Uzziah prepared for them, throughout all the host, shields and spears and helmets and breastplates and bows and slings to cast stones.

15 And his fame spread throughout all the lands, until he became very rich.

16 ¶But when he became very rich, his pride was lifted up exceedingly, so he transgressed against the LORD his God and went into the temple of the LORD to burn incense upon the altar of incense.

17 And Azariah the priest went in after him and said to him,

18 It is not your place, O king, nor have you the right to burn incense upon the altar.

19 Then immediately King Uzziah's anger kindled against the priests, and he commanded to put them out of the sanctuary; and in that hour the leprosy went forth out of the sanctuary and fell on the forehead of King Uzziah as he entered to burn incense in the house of the LORD.

20 And Azariah the chief priest, and all the priests, turned toward him, and, behold, he hastened to go out because he knew that the LORD had smitten him.

21 And Uzziah the king was a leper to the day of his death, and dwelt in a house in solitude, being a leper; for he had blasphemed against the house of the LORD; and Jotham his son was over the king's house, judging the people of the land.

22 ¶Now the rest of the acts of Uzziah, first and last, behold, they are written by Isaiah the prophet, the son of Amoz.

23 So Uzziah slept with his fathers, and they buried him in the cemetery, not in the burial place which belonged to the kings; for they said, He is a leper; and Jotham his son reigned in his stead.

CHAPTER 27

JOTHAM was twenty-five years old when he began to reign, and he reigned sixteen years in Jerusalem. His mother's name was Jerushah, the daughter of Zadok.

2 And he did that which was right in the sight of the LORD, according to all that his father Uzziah had done; howbeit he neglected to enter into the temple of the LORD, and the people were still corrupt.

3 He built the upper gate of the house of the LORD, and completed the wall and improved it.

4 Moreover he built cities in the land of Judah, and in the forests he built castles and towers.

5 ¶He fought also with the Ammonites, and prevailed against them. And the Ammonites gave him that year a hundred talents of silver and ten thousand measures of wheat and ten thousand measures of barley. The Ammonites gave to him the same amount in the second year and in the third year.

6 So Jotham became mighty because he established his ways before the LORD his God.

7 ¶Now the rest of the acts of Jotham and all his wars and his ways, behold, they are written in the Book of the Kings of Israel and Judah.

8 He was twenty-five years old when he began to reign, and reigned sixteen years in Jerusalem.

9 ¶And Jotham slept with his fathers, and they buried him in the city of David; and Ahaz his son reigned in his stead.

CHAPTER 28

AHAZ was twenty-five years old when he began to reign, and he reigned sixteen years in Jerusalem; and he did not do that which was right in the sight of the LORD his God, like David his father;

2 But he walked in the ways of the kings of Israel, and also made altars for the idols.

3 Moreover he burned incense in great valleys, and passed his son through the fire, according to the cus-

tom of the nations whom the LORD had destroyed from before the children of Israel.

4 And he sacrificed also and burned incense upon the altars and on high places and under every beautiful tree.

5 Therefore the LORD God delivered him into the hand of the king of Aram; and he smote him with a great slaughter, and carried away a great multitude of people captive and brought them to Damascus. And he was also delivered into the hand of the king of Israel, who smote him with a great slaughter.

6 ¶For Pekah the son of Romaliah slew from the army of the king of Judah a hundred and twenty thousand in one day, all valiant men, because they had forsaken the LORD God of their fathers.

7 And Zichri, a mighty man of Ephraim slew Maasiah the king's son and Azrikai the governor of the palace and Elkanah who was next to the king.

8 And the children of Israel carried away captive of their brethren two hundred thousand and their sons and their daughters, and also took away much spoil from them, and brought the spoil to Samaria.

9 But a prophet of the LORD was there, whose name was Ado; and he went out before the army that came to Samaria, and said to them, Behold, because the LORD God of our fathers was angry with Judah, he has delivered them into your hands, and you have slain them and had no pity on them.

10 And now you purpose to make them menservants and maidservants to yourself, and even now you know that you have committed this sin in the presence of the LORD your God.

11 Now hear me, therefore, and send back those whom you have taken captive from your brethren, lest the fierce wrath of the LORD come upon you.

12 Then certain of the chiefs of the Ephraimites, Azariah the son of Johanan and Berechiah the son of Mekariah, stood up against them who came from the war,

13 And said to them, You shall not bring these captives here, that we may not sin again against the LORD our God; you intend to add more to our trespass and to our sins; for our sins are exceedingly great.

14 So they sent back all the captives to Jerusalem. But again they dealt deceitfully with the LORD.

15 And the men who were expressed by name [1] rose up, and took the captives, and with the spoil clothed all that were naked among them, and arrayed them and shod them, and gave them to eat and to drink, and anointed them, and carried all the feeble of them upon asses, and brought them to Jericho, the city of palm trees, to their brethren; then they returned to Samaria.

16 ¶At that time King Ahaz asked the king of Assyria to help him,

17 For until this time the Edomites came and smote Judah and carried away captives.

18 And the Philistines also had come and besieged the cities of the low country, and of the south of Judah, and had captured the town of Beth-shemesh and the town of Ajalon and the town of Azoroth and Shob with its villages and Timnah with its villages and Geram with its villages.

19 For the LORD brought Judah low because of the sins of Ahaz king of Judah; for he increased iniquity in Judah and transgressed grievously against the LORD.

20 And Tiglath-pilezer king of Assyria came against him, and encamped against him and distressed him greatly.

21 And King Ahaz took away the vessels that were in the house of the LORD and the vessels that were in the houses of former kings and in the houses of rich men, and gave them to the king of Assyria, that he might not harm him in the time of his distress.

22 ¶But they transgressed still more against the LORD: this same King Ahaz.

[1] The chiefs.

23 For he sacrificed to the gods of Damascus, saying, You are my gods and my lords; to you will I offer worship and to you will I make sacrifice; thus he was a stumbling block to Judah, he sinned and caused all the people of Judah to sin.

24 And Ahaz gathered together all the vessels of the house of the LORD, and cut in pieces the vessels that were in the house of the LORD, and shut up the inner and the outer doors of the house of the LORD, and he made for himself altars in every corner of Jerusalem.

25 And in every village and hamlet of Judah he made an altar to serve other gods.

26 ¶Now the rest of the acts of Ahaz and all his ways, first and last, behold, they are written in the Book of the Kings of Judah and Israel.

27 And Ahaz slept with his fathers, and they buried him in Jerusalem; for they did not bring him into the sepulchres of the kings of Judah; and Hezekiah his son reigned in his stead.

CHAPTER 29

HEZEKIAH began to reign when he was twenty-five years old, and he reigned twenty-nine years in Jerusalem. And his mother's name was Ani, the daughter of Zechariah.

2 And he did that which was right in the sight of the LORD, just as David his father had done.

3 ¶In the first year of his reign, in the first month, he opened the doors of the house of the LORD, and repaired them.

4 And he brought in the priests and the Levites, and gathered them together into the court of the sanctuary,

5 And said to them, Hear me, O Levites, sanctify now yourselves and sanctify the house of the LORD God of our fathers, and remove your evil works from your mind,

6 So that we may not do according to that which our fathers have done, for they did evil in the sight of the LORD our God, and have forsaken him and have turned away their faces from the habitation of the LORD, and turned their backs.

7 Also they have shut up the doors of the porches and put out the lamps, and have not burned incense nor offered burnt offerings upon the altar of the God of Israel.

8 Therefore the wrath of the LORD came upon Judah and Jerusalem, and he has delivered them to curse, to desolation, and to sword, as you see with your own eyes.

9 For, lo, our fathers have fallen by the sword, and our sons and our daughters and our wives are in captivity for this.

10 And even now, because we have gone astray from following the LORD our God and have forsaken the covenant which he gave to our fathers, therefore he also has forsaken us.

11 My sons, be not now negligent; for the LORD has chosen you to stand before him, to serve him and to minister unto him and burn incense.

12 ¶Then the Levites arose, Mahath the son of Amasai and Joel the son of Azariah, of the sons of the Kohathites; and of the sons of Merari, Kish the son of Abdi and Azariah the son of Jehalelel; and of the Gershonites, Joah the son of Zimmah and Eden the son of Joah;

13 And of the sons of Elzaphan, Shimri and Jeiel; and of the sons of Asaph, Zechariah and Mattaniah;

14 And of the sons of Heman, Jehiel and Shimei; and of the sons of Jeruthun, Shemaiah and Uzziel.

15 And they gathered their brethren, and sanctified themselves, and came, according to the commandment of the king by the words of the LORD to cleanse the house of the LORD.

16 And the priests went into the inner part of the house of the LORD, to cleanse it, and brought out all the uncleanness that they found in the temple of the LORD into the court of the house of the LORD. And the Levites took it to carry it out into the brook Kidron.

17 Now they began on the first day of the first month to sanctify, and on the eighth day of the month came they to the porch of the LORD; so

they sanctified the house of the LORD in eight days, and in the sixteenth day of the first month they made an end.

18 Then they went in to Hezekiah the king, and said, We have cleansed all the house of the LORD and the altar of burnt offering with all the vessels thereof, and the shewbread table with all the vessels thereof.

19 Moreover all the vessels which King Ahaz in his reign did cast away in his transgression have we prepared and sanctified, and, behold, they are before the altar of the LORD.

20 ¶Then Hezekiah the king rose early and gathered the elders of Jerusalem, and went up to the house of the LORD.

21 And they brought to him seven bullocks, seven rams, seven lambs, and seven he-goats for an atonement for the kingdom and for Judah and for the sanctuary. And he commanded the priests, the sons of Aaron, to offer them on the altar of the LORD

22 And to kill the bullocks, and commanded the priests to receive the blood and sprinkle it on the horns of the altar;

23 And to bring forth the he-goats before the LORD and before the king and before the congregation of Israel, and to lay hands upon them;

24 And that the priests should kill them and sprinkle their blood upon the horns of the altar to make an atonement for all Israel; for the king had commanded that all Israel should bring burnt offerings and sacrifices.

25 And he set the Levites in the house of the LORD with cymbals, with psalteries, and with the songs of David, and with the songs of Gad the prophet of King David and of Nathan the prophet of King David; for David used to sing the songs of the LORD his God as they were sung by the mouth of the prophets.

26 And the Levites stood singing the songs of David, and the priests sounded with curved and straight trumpets.

27 Then Hezekiah commanded to offer the burnt offerings upon the altar. And when the burnt offerings began, Hezekiah also began to sing the songs of the LORD, according to the songs of David king of Israel.

28 And all the congregation of Israel worshipped and sang songs and sounded with the curved and straight trumpets until the burnt offerings were finished.

29 And when they had made an end of offering, the king and all that were present with him knelt and worshipped.

30 Moreover Hezekiah the king and the princes commanded the Levites to sing praises to the LORD with the words of David and of Asaph the prophet. And they sang praises with gladness, and they bowed down and worshipped.

31 Then Hezekiah answered and said, Now you have consecrated yourselves to the way of the LORD; come near and bring sacrifices and thank offerings into the house of the LORD. And the people brought in sacrifices and thank offerings; everything which their hearts desired, they brought in.

32 And the number of the burnt offerings which the people brought was seventy bullocks, a hundred rams, and two hundred lambs; all these were for a burnt offering to the LORD.

33 And the consecrated things were six hundred oxen and three thousand sheep.

34 But the priests were too few, so that they could not slay all the burnt offerings; therefore their brethren, the Levites, helped them until the work was finished, and after this the priests sanctified themselves; for the Levites were meek in their hearts to sanctify themselves more than the priests.

35 And also the burnt offerings were in abundance, with the fat of the peace offerings and of the lambs for the burnt offerings. So the service of the house of the LORD was set in order.

36 And Hezekiah rejoiced, and all the people of Israel, because the service of the temple was accomplished; for the thing was done promptly.

CHAPTER 30

AND Hezekiah sent to all Israel and Judah, and wrote letters also to Ephraim and Manasseh, that they should come to the house of the LORD at Jerusalem to keep the passover to the LORD God of Israel.

2 For the king and his princes and all the congregation of Israel who were in Jerusalem had taken counsel to celebrate the passover to the LORD God of Israel in the second month.

3 For they could not keep it at the appointed time because the priests had not sanctified themselves, neither had the instructors of the people gathered themselves together to Jerusalem.

4 And the thing pleased the king and all the people of Israel.

5 So they confirmed a decree to carry it out; and they made a proclamation throughout all Israel from Beer-sheba even to Dan that they should come to celebrate the passover to the LORD God of Israel at Jerusalem; for they were exceedingly rich.

6 So the couriers went with the letters from the king and his princes throughout all Israel and Judah, and by the command of the king, saying, O you children of Israel, turn again to the LORD God of Abraham, Isaac, and Israel, and he will return to the remnant of you who have escaped from the hands of the king of Assyria.

7 And be not like your fathers and like your brethren who trespassed against the LORD God of our fathers so that he gave them up to desolation, as you see.

8 Now do not be stiffnecked as your fathers were, but enter into the sanctuary which he has sanctified for ever, and serve the LORD your God, that the fierceness of his wrath may turn away from you.

9 Because he has revealed himself to you, your children, and your brethren; and he shall grant you compassion before those who carry you captive, and shall bring you back to this land; for the LORD your God is gracious and merciful, and will not turn away his face from you when you return to him.

10 So the couriers of King Hezekiah passed from village to village throughout the land of Ephraim and Manasseh and as far as Zebulun;

11 But some of the wicked men, who were in the tribe of Asher, the tribe of Ephraim, the tribe of Manasseh, and the tribe of Zebulun, laughed them to scorn and mocked them.

12 Nevertheless the rest of the men of these tribes humbled themselves and came to Jerusalem with the tribe of Judah. And the hand of God was upon them to give them one heart to do the commandment of the king and of his princes, according to the word of the LORD.

13 ¶And there assembled at Jerusalem many people to celebrate the feast of unleavened bread in the second month, a very great congregation.

14 And they arose and demolished the altars that were in Jerusalem, and they destroyed all the shrines of idols and cast them into the brook Kidron.

15 Then they celebrated the passover on the fourteenth day of the second month; and the priests and the Levites sanctified themselves and brought in burnt offerings to the house of the LORD.

16 And they stood in their places after their manner, as it is written in the law of Moses the prophet of the LORD; the priests sprinkled the blood which they received from the hand of the Levites.

17 For there were many in the congregation of Israel who had not sanctified themselves; therefore the Levites had charge of the killing of the passover lambs, and they saw that every one was clean, to sanctify him to the LORD;

18 For there were a great many people in the assembly of Israel, from Ephraim, Manasseh, Issachar, and Zebulun, the four tribes, who had not cleansed themselves, yet they ate the passover unlawfully. But Hezekiah prayed for them, saying, May the good LORD pardon all the people of Israel,

19 For we have prepared our hearts to pray to the LORD God of our fathers, and sanctification would not purify us any more.

20 And the LORD hearkened to the voice of Hezekiah, and healed the people.

21 And the children of Israel that were present in Jerusalem kept the feast of unleavened bread seven days with great gladness; and the Levites and the priests praised the LORD day by day, singing songs of praise.

22 And Hezekiah spoke to all the Levites who were singing good songs before the LORD; and they ate throughout the feast seven days, offering peace offerings and making confession to the LORD God of their fathers.

23 And the whole assembly stayed over to celebrate another seven days; and they kept the other seven days with gladness.

24 For Hezekiah king of Judah gave to the assembly seven thousand of the choicest oxen, large and small, and also gave to the assembly of Israel a thousand of the choicest bullocks, and ten thousand sheep; and a great number of priests sanctified themselves.

25 And all the congregation of Judah, with the priests and the Levites, and all the congregation that came out of Israel, and the proselytes who came out of the land of Israel, and those who dwelt in Judah, rejoiced.

26 So there was great joy in Jerusalem; for since the time of Solomon the son of David king of Israel, there had been nothing like this in Jerusalem.

27 ¶Then the priests and the Levites arose and blessed the people of Israel; and the LORD heard their voice, and their prayer came up to his holy dwelling place, even to heaven.

CHAPTER 31

NOW when all this was finished, all Israel who were present went out to the cities of Judah, and broke the images in pieces and cut down the leopard statues and demolished the shrines and the altars that were in Judah and Benjamin and in Ephraim and Manasseh, until they had utterly destroyed them all. Then the Israelites returned, every man to his possession; and they entered in peace into their own cities.

2 ¶And Hezekiah appointed the times of serving of the priests and the Levites according to their divisions, every man according to his service, the priests and the Levites for burnt offerings and for peace offerings, to minister and to give thanks and to praise in the gates of the temple of the LORD.

3 And the king gave of his own substance oxen for the morning and evening burnt offerings, and the burnt offerings for the sabbaths and for the new moons and for the set feasts, as it is written in the law of the LORD.

4 Moreover he commanded the people who dwelt in Jerusalem to give the portion due to the priests and the Levites, that they might be encouraged in the law of the LORD.

5 ¶And as soon as the commandment was published in Israel, they brought the first fruits of grain, wine, oil, and of their cattle, and of the produce of the field; and the tithe of all things they brought in abundantly.

6 And the children of Israel and Judah who dwelt in the cities of Judah also brought in gifts and offered them to the LORD their God. And they brought in tithes upon tithes of grain, of wine, and of their cattle, and of the produce of the field. They brought the tithes and consecrated them to the LORD their God.

7 In the third month they began to lay the foundation of the tithe supplies, and in the seventh month Hezekiah took it and distributed it among the priests and the Levites.

8 And when Hezekiah and the princes saw that the tithe of the priests was so abundant, they blessed the LORD and prayed for Israel.

9 Then Hezekiah prayed for the priests and for the Levites concerning the abundance of the tithe.

10 And he called for Azariah the chief priest of the house of Zadok

and said to him, This tithe is ready for you, to be eaten, because it has been brought into the house of the LORD, now you can eat and be filled, and what is left of it, give it to the poor and to the fatherless, for the LORD has blessed his people and has given them this abundance. And what is left, give it to all the people of Israel.

11 ¶Then Hezekiah commanded that storehouses be prepared in the house of the LORD; and they prepared them,

12 And they brought in the tithes and the dedicated things faithfully; over them Cononiah the Levite was overseer and Shimei his brother was the next.

13 And Nehiel, Uzziah, Nahath, Ashail, Jerimoth, Jozabar, Eliel, Ismachiah, Matah, Benaiah, and Shemiah his brother were overseers under the hand of Cononiah, at the command of Hezekiah the king and Azariah the ruler of the house of the LORD.

14 And Kariah the son of Imnah the Levite, the porter of the east gate, was over the freewill offerings of the LORD and over the most holy things.

15 And next to him were Eden, Benjamin, Jeshua, Shemaiah, Amariah, and Shecaniah, in the cities of the priests, in their set office, to distribute portions to their brethren, to the great and small alike;

16 Besides that which is due to the males from three years old and upward, even to every one who entered into the house of the LORD, their daily portion for their service in their duties according to their divisions;

17 And oil and wine were given to the priests and the Levites according to the house of their fathers, from twenty years old and upward, in their charges by their divisions;

18 And oil was given for their lanterns, to their wives, their sons, and their daughters, and to all the congregation of Israel, for in their set office they sanctified themselves faithfully.

19 For the sons of Aaron the priest were holy, their flesh was holy, and they never touched women; and they went about in every village and suburb, men whose names were well known, to give portions to all the males among the priests and to all that were reckoned by the genealogies among the Levites.

20 ¶And thus did Hezekiah throughout all Judah, and he did that which was good and right, and walked in truth before the LORD.

21 And in every work that he began to do in the house of the LORD, and in the law and in the commandments, to seek his God, he did it with all his heart and prospered.

CHAPTER 32

AFTER these things and the faithful acts which Hezekiah did, Sennacherib king of Assyria came and invaded Judah and encamped against the fortified cities, and said to their inhabitants, Give me a pledge and come to me.

2 And when Hezekiah saw that Sennacherib king of Assyria and his armies had come to fight against Jerusalem,

3 He took counsel with his princes and his mighty men to conceal the waters of the fountains which were outside the city; and they did help him.

4 So there was gathered a great multitude of the people of Israel together, who concealed all the fountains and the great brooks that ran through the midst of the land, saying, Lest the king of Assyria come and find much water.

5 They also strengthened themselves and built up one wall opposite the other and polluted the canal which David had constructed. And Hezekiah made weapons, shields, and spears in abundance.

6 And he set captains of war over the people, each one over ten, and gathered them together to him in the market place of the city, and spoke to all of them, saying,

7 Be strong and courageous; do not be afraid nor dismayed in the pres-

ence of the king of Assyria, nor in the presence of all the armies that have come with him; for there is more with us than with him:

8 With him is an arm of flesh; with us is the LORD our God to help us and to fight our battles. And the people were encouraged with the words of Hezekiah king of Judah.

9 ¶After this Sennacherib king of Assyria sent Rab-shakey together with his servants, and they came to Jerusalem (but he himself was besieging Lachish, and all his commanders with him) to all the people of Judah that were in Jerusalem, saying,

10 Thus says Sennacherib king of Assyria: On whom are you trusting, that you remain in Jerusalem during the siege?

11 Hezekiah is deceiving you that he may give you over to die by famine and by thirst, and moreover he is misleading you, saying, The LORD our God shall deliver us out of the hands of the king of Assyria.

12 Has not the same Hezekiah removed his high places and altars, and commanded Judah and the inhabitants of Jerusalem, saying, You shall worship before one altar and burn incense upon it?

13 Perhaps you know what I and my fathers have done to all the people of other lands? And the gods of nations of those lands were not able to deliver their lands out of my hand.

14 Who is there among all the gods of those nations that my fathers utterly destroyed that was able to deliver his people out of my hand, that the LORD should be able to deliver you out of my hand?

15 Now therefore do not let Hezekiah deceive you nor make you to trust in this, and do not believe him; for your God will not be able to deliver you out of my hand; for all nations and kingdoms have not been able to deliver their cities out of my hand, and out of the hands of my fathers; your God also will not be able to deliver you out of my hand.

16 And his servants spoke these things before the LORD God of Israel

and in the presence of his servant Hezekiah.

17 And he wrote letters to revile the LORD God of Israel, and to speak to the people of Israel, saying, As the gods of the nations of these lands were unable to deliver their cities out of my hand, so shall not the God of Hezekiah be able to deliver his city out of my hand.

18 Then they cried with a loud voice in the Jewish language [1] to the people who were seated on the wall of Jerusalem, to frighten them and to trouble them, that they might capture the wall of the city.

19 And they spoke in the name of the gods of the people of the earth and also in the name of the God of Jerusalem, imploring him to reward them according to the work of their hands.

20 Then Hezekiah and Isaiah the son of Amoz, the prophet, prayed because of this, and the LORD heard the voice of their prayer.

21 ¶And the LORD sent an angel from before him, who smote all the mighty men of valour and the kings and the princes who were in the camp of the king of Assyria. So the king of Assyria returned in disgrace to his own land. And when he came into the house of his gods, his sons, who came forth of his own loins, slew him there with the sword.

22 Thus the LORD saved Hezekiah and the inhabitants of Jerusalem from the hands of Sennacherib the king of Assyria and from the hand of all of those who invaded their borders.

23 And many of the children of Israel brought gifts to the LORD to Jerusalem, and gave presents to Hezekiah king of Judah, so that he was exalted before all nations.

24 ¶In those days Hezekiah was sick to death, and he prayed before the LORD and said, Thou hast performed mighty miracles for me and thou hast rewarded me according to the works of my hands.

25 And the sickness of Hezekiah was due to the pride of his heart; therefore the wrath of the LORD came

[1] Aramaic or Hebrew dialect spoken by the Jews.

upon him and upon Judah and Jerusalem.

26 But Hezekiah humbled himself for the pride of his heart, both he and the inhabitants of Jerusalem, so that the wrath of the LORD did not come upon them in the days of Hezekiah.

27 ¶And Hezekiah had exceeding great wealth and honor; and he made for himself treasuries for silver and for gold and for precious stones and for spices and for shields and for all manner of pleasant vessels;

28 Storehouses also for the increase of grain and wine and oil; and stalls for all kinds of beasts;

29 And folds for herds and for flocks, and for oxen and other beasts; for the LORD had given him very much substance.

30 This same Hezekiah also buried the outlet for the waters of the upper spring and brought it straight down to the western cistern of the city of David. And Hezekiah prospered in all his works.

31 ¶And he sought the law of the LORD, as it was given in the land, and the LORD knew all that was in his heart.

32 ¶Now the rest of the acts of Hezekiah, and his goodness and his excellent ways, behold, they are written in the prophecy of Isaiah the prophet, the son of Amoz, and in the Book of the Kings of Judah and Israel.

33 And Hezekiah slept with his fathers, and they buried him in the city of David; and all Judah and the inhabitants of Jerusalem did him honor at his death, and they returned to Jerusalem. And Manasseh his son reigned in his stead.

CHAPTER 33

MANASSEH was twelve years old when he began to reign, and he reigned fifty-five years in Jerusalem;

2 And he did that which was evil in the sight of the LORD, according to the works of the nations which the LORD had destroyed before the children of Israel.

3 ¶For he built again the altars which Hezekiah his father had broken down, and he built shrines for the idols and made images of leopards, and worshipped them.

4 Moreover he worshipped all the host of heaven in the two courts of the house of the LORD.

5 And he built altars for all the host of heaven in the two courts of the house of the LORD.

6 And he also caused his son to pass through the fire in the great valley; and he practiced augury and soothsaying and sorcery, and inquired of the Chaldeans and of familiar spirits; and he did much evil in the sight of the LORD, to provoke him to anger.

7 And he set the image of the idol which had four faces, which he had made, in the house of the LORD, of which the LORD had said to David and to Solomon his son, In this house and in Jerusalem, which I have chosen for myself out of all the tribes of Israel, will I put my name for ever;

8 Neither will I any more remove the children of Israel from this land which I have given to their fathers; if only they will take heed to do all that I have commanded them, according to the whole law and my statutes and my ordinances which my servant Moses commanded them.

9 So Manasseh caused Judah and the inhabitants of Jerusalem to go astray and to do evil works like the nations which the LORD had destroyed before the children of Israel.

10 And the LORD spoke to Manasseh and to his people; but they would not hearken.

11 ¶Therefore the LORD brought against them the commanders of the army of the king of Assyria, who captured Manasseh alive and bound him with chains and carried him to Babylon.

12 But when he was in distress, he prayed before the LORD his God and reverenced greatly the LORD God of his fathers,

13 And he prayed before the LORD, and he heard his voice and heard his prayer, and brought him back to Jerusalem into his kingdom. Then Manasseh knew that the LORD was God.

14 Now after this he built an outer

wall to the city of David on the west side of the brook of Gihon to the entrance of the fish gate, and encircled the whole of Jerusalem with an outer wall and raised it up a very great height, and he appointed commanders of the army in all the fortified cities of Judah.

15 And he took away the strange gods and the idols out of the house of the LORD, and all the altars that he had built in the mount of the house of the LORD and in Jerusalem, and cast them out of the city.

16 And he built an altar to the LORD, and sacrificed upon it burnt offerings and peace offerings and thank offerings, and commanded Judah to keep the feast to the LORD God of Israel;

17 And not to sacrifice again to strange gods, nor to offer burnt offerings to them, but before the LORD their God only.

18 ¶Now the rest of the acts of Manasseh and his prayer to his God and the words of the prophets who prophesied concerning him in the name of the LORD God of Israel, behold, they are written in the Book of the Kings of Israel and Judah.

19 His prayer, also, and how the LORD heard his voice, and all his sins and his iniquity, and the places on which he built altars and appointed priests, and the shrines he built for the idols, behold, they are written among the sayings of Hanan the prophet.

20 ¶So Manasseh slept with his fathers, and they buried him in his own house, in the garden of the treasury; and Amon his son reigned in his stead.

21 ¶And Amon was twenty-two years old when he began to reign, and he reigned two years in Jerusalem.

22 And he did that which was evil in the sight of the LORD, as Manasseh his father had done; for Amon sacrificed to all the images and idols which Manasseh his father had made and worshipped them;

23 And he did not humble himself before the LORD his God, as Manas-seh humbled himself before the LORD his God; but Amon committed sins more and more.

24 And his servants conspired against him and slew him in his own house.

25 ¶But the people of the land slew all those who had conspired against King Amon; and the people of the land made Josiah his son king in his stead.

CHAPTER 34

JOSIAH was eight years old when he began to reign, and he reigned thirty-one years in Jerusalem.

2 And he did that which was right in the sight of the LORD, and walked in the ways of David his father, and he turned neither to the right hand nor to the left.

3 ¶For in the eighth year of his reign, while he was still a little boy, he began to pray to the LORD the God of David his father; and in the twelfth year he began to purge Judah and the inhabitants of Jerusalem. Moreover he began to demolish altars, idols, carved images, and idol temples,

4 And the decorations, necklaces, bells, and all the trees that were made for idols, he broke in pieces and ground them to dust and scattered their ashes upon the graves of those who had sacrificed to them.

5 And the bones of the priests who served them, he dug out of their graves and brought them and burned them, and cleansed Judah and Jerusalem.

6 And so did he in the cities of Manasseh and Ephraim and Simeon and Naphtali, in their streets round about.

7 And when he had broken down the altars and smashed in pieces the images, and ground them into dust and scattered it throughout all the land of Israel, he returned to Jerusalem.

8 ¶Now in the eighteenth year of his reign, when he had purged the land of Israel and his own house, he sent for Shaphan the son of Azaliah and Maasiah the scribe of the city,

and said to them, Go, repair the house of the LORD your God.

9 And when they came to Hilkiah the high priest, they delivered the money that was brought into the house of the LORD, which the Levites the keepers of the doors had collected from Manasseh and Ephraim and from all the remnant of Israel and from all Judah and Benjamin and from all the inhabitants of Jerusalem.

10 And they delivered it into the hands of the workmen who had the oversight of the house of the LORD, and they gave it to the workmen who did the work in the house of the LORD, to repair and to plaster the house;

11 And they gave it also to the carpenters and to the masons and to those who bought precious stones and timber for the repairing and for the plastering of the house which the kings of Judah had destroyed.

12 And the men did the work of the sanctuary faithfully; and the overseers over them were Nahat and Obadiah, the Levites, of the sons of Merari; and Zechariah and Shallum, of the sons of the Kohathites, and the singers and the Levites who played with the instruments of music,

13 And all those who did the work in any manner of service; and of the Levites there were scribes and officers and porters who acted as overseers.

14 ¶And when they carried out the money that had been brought into the house of the LORD, Hilkiah the priest found a book of the law of the LORD given by Moses.

15 And Hilkiah the priest said to Shaphan the scribe, I have found the book of the law in the house of the LORD. And Hilkiah the priest gave the book to Shaphan.

16 And Shaphan the scribe told the king what Hilkiah had told him, and brought him word, saying, All that you have committed to your servants, they do.

17 And they have spent the money for the repair of the house of the LORD, and have given account to the overseers and to the workmen.

18 Then Shaphan the scribe told the king, saying, Hilkiah the priest has given me a book. And Shaphan read it before the king.

19 And it came to pass when the king had heard the words of the law, he tore his clothes.

20 Then the king commanded Hilkiah and Ahikam the son of Shaphan and Abchor the son of Micah and Shaphan the scribe and Asaiah the steward of the king's household, saying,

21 Go, pray before the LORD for me and for the people of Israel and Judah concerning the words of this book that is found; for great is the wrath of the LORD that is poured out upon us, because our fathers have not hearkened to the words of the LORD to do after all that is written concerning us in this book.

22 So Hilkiah and those whom the king had appointed, went to Huldi the prophetess, the wife of Shallum the son of Tikvah, the son of Hisdah the keeper of the vessels (now she dwelt in Jerusalem in meditation) and they spoke to her according to the king's command.

23 ¶And she said to them, Thus says the LORD God of Israel: Tell the man who sent you to me,

24 Thus says the LORD: Behold, I will bring evil upon this place and upon its inhabitants, even all the curses that are written in the book which they have read before the king of Judah,

25 Because they have forsaken me and have worshipped other gods and have provoked me to anger with the works of their hands; therefore my wrath shall be poured out upon this place, and shall not be quenched.

26 And as for the king of Judah, who sent you to inquire of the LORD, so shall you say to him: Thus says the LORD God of Israel concerning the words which you have heard:

27 Because your heart was humbled, and you did tremble before the LORD when you heard these things which I will bring against this place and against its inhabitants, and have humbled yourself before me and have rent

your clothes and wept before me; I have heard you also, says the LORD.

28 Therefore, I will gather you to your fathers, and you shall be gathered to your grave in peace, and your eyes shall not see all the evil that I will bring upon this place and upon its inhabitants. So they brought back the word to the king.

29 ¶Then the king sent and gathered together all the elders of Judah and Jerusalem.

30 And the king went up into the house of the LORD, and all the men of Judah and the inhabitants of Jerusalem and the priests and the Levites and all the people, great and small; and he read before them all the words of the book of the covenant that was found in the house of the LORD.

31 And the king stood in his place and made a covenant before the LORD, to walk after the LORD and to keep his commandments and his statutes and his testimonies, with all his heart and with his whole soul, to perform the words of the covenant which are written in this book.

32 And he caused all who were present in Jerusalem and Benjamin to stand to it. And the inhabitants of Jerusalem did according to the covenant of the LORD God of their fathers.

33 And Josiah took away all the abominations which the LORD had destroyed before the children of Israel, and he made all the people who were found in Israel to serve the LORD their God. And they did not go astray from following the LORD God of their fathers.

CHAPTER 35

MOREOVER Josiah kept a passover to the LORD in Jerusalem; and he celebrated the feast on the fourteenth day of the first month.

2 And he set the priests in their charges, and appointed them over the service of the house of the LORD,

3 And he said to the Levites who dwelt in all Israel, Sanctify yourselves to the LORD, and put the holy ark in the house which Solomon the son of David king of Israel did build; for you have no longer to carry it upon your shoulders; serve now the LORD your God and his people Israel,

4 And prepare your hearts and the heart of your fathers, according to the writing of David, king of Israel, and according to the writing of Solomon his son,

5 And stand in the holy place according to the divisions of the families of your fathers and of your brethren the people, and after the divisions of the families of the Levites,

6 And kill the passover and sanctify yourselves and prepare the hearts of your brethren, that they may do according to the word of the LORD by the hand of Moses.

7 Then Josiah gave to the people sheep, lambs, and kids of the goats, all for the passover offerings, for all that were present, to the number of thirty thousand, and three thousand bullocks; these were of the king's substance.

8 And his princes gave willingly to the people and to the priests and to the Levites; Hilkiah and Zechariah and Nehiel, rulers of the house of the LORD, gave to the priests for the passover offerings two thousand and six hundred sheep and three hundred oxen.

9 Conaniah, also, and Shemaiah his nephew and Hashabiah and Jadiel gave to the Levites for passover offerings five thousand sheep and five hundred oxen.

10 So the service was prepared, and the priests stood in their places and the Levites in their courses,

11 And they killed the passover according to the king's command, and the priests sprinkled some of the blood,

12 And the Levites flayed the victims and gave the burnt offerings to the divisions of the families of the people, to offer to the LORD, as it is written in the law of Moses. And so they did every morning.

13 And they roasted the passover with fire according to the ordinance; but the other holy offerings they cooked in pots and in caldrons and in pans, and divided them speedily among all the people.

14 And afterward they prepared for themselves and for the priests, because the priests the sons of Aaron were busied in offering the burnt offerings and the fat until the Levites were through; then the Levites prepared for themselves and for the priests the sons of Aaron, who ministered.

15 And the singers the sons of Asaph were in their place, according to the commandment of David, and Haman and Jerithon, the king's seers; and the porters remained at every gate; they might not depart from their service; for their brethren the Levites served them.

16 So all the service of the LORD was prepared the same day, to keep the passover and to offer burnt offerings upon the altar of the LORD, according to the commandment of King Josiah.

17 And the children of Israel who were present kept the passover at that time, and the feast of the unleavened bread seven days.

18 And there was no passover like to that kept in Israel from the days of Samuel the prophet; neither did all the kings of Israel keep such a passover as Josiah kept, and the priests and the Levites and all Judah and Israel who were present in Jerusalem.

19 In the eighteenth year of the reign of Josiah was this passover kept.

20 ¶After all this, when Josiah had prepared the affairs of the temple, Pharaoh the lame king of Egypt came up to fight against Mabog [1] by Euphrates; and Josiah went out against him.

21 But he sent ambassadors to him, saying, What have I to do with you, O king of Judah? I am not coming against you this day, O king of Judah; for indeed I have not come to fight against you. The LORD has told you to frighten me; cease from meddling with God, who is with me, that he may not destroy you.

22 Nevertheless Josiah would not turn his face from him; for he had gone to fight with him. And he did

not listen to the words of Pharaoh the lame; for Josiah did not know that it was from the LORD, so he went forth to fight against him in the plain of Megiddo.

23 Then Pharaoh the lame shot two arrows at Josiah; and the king said to his servants, Take me away; for I am severely wounded.

24 So his servants took him out of the chariot, and put him into his own royal chariot; and they brought him to Jerusalem, and he died and was buried in the sepulchres of his fathers. And all Judah and Jerusalem mourned for Josiah.

25 ¶And Jeremiah lamented for Josiah, saying, All righteous men and righteous women, weep in your lamentations for Josiah. And he made them an ordinance in Israel, to this day; and, behold, these lamentations are written in the Book of Lamentations.

26 Now the rest of the acts of Josiah and his goodness, according to that which is written in the law of the LORD,

27 And his deeds, first and last, behold, they are written in the Book of the Kings of Israel and Judah.

CHAPTER 36

THEN the people of the land took Jehoahaz the son of Josiah, and made him king in his father's stead in Jerusalem.

2 And Jehoahaz was twenty-three years old when he began to reign, and he reigned three months in Jerusalem.

3 And the king of Egypt deposed him,

4 And he made Eliakim his brother king over Judah and Jerusalem, and changed his name to Jehoiakim. And Pharaoh the lame took Jehoahaz his brother and carried him to Egypt, and he died there.

5 ¶Jehoiakim was twenty-five years old when he began to reign, and he reigned eleven years in Jerusalem; and he did that which was evil in the sight of the LORD his God.

6 Against him came up Nebuchadnezzar king of Babylon, and bound

[1] Charchemish in Western texts. Perhaps the later name.

him in chains to carry him to Babylon.

7 Nebuchadnezzar also carried away some of the vessels of the house of the LORD to Babylon and put them in his temple in Babylon.

8 Now the rest of the acts of Jehoiakim and the abominations which he did, behold, they are written in the Book of the Kings of Israel and Judah; and Jehoiachin his son reigned in his stead.

9 ¶Jehoiachin was eighteen years old when he began to reign, and he reigned three months and ten days in Jerusalem; and he did that which was evil in the sight of the LORD.

10 And when the year was expired, Nebuchadnezzar king of Babylon sent a force against him and brought him to Babylon, both him and the precious vessels of the house of the LORD, and made Zedekiah his brother king over Judah and Jerusalem.

11 ¶Zedekiah was twenty-one years old when he began to reign, and he reigned eleven years in Jerusalem.

12 And he did that which was evil in the sight of the LORD his God, and did not humble himself before Jeremiah the prophet, who prophesied from the mouth of the LORD.

13 And he also rebelled against Nebuchadnezzar, who had made him swear by the name of the LORD; but he stiffened his neck and hardened his heart and would not pray before the LORD God of Israel.

14 ¶Moreover all the chiefs of the priests and of the Levites and of the people transgressed very much after all the abominations of the nations, and polluted the house of the LORD which he had hallowed in Jerusalem.

15 And the LORD God of their fathers sent to them by his messengers, giving useful advice in advance; because he had compassion on his people and on the flock that he had chosen;

16 But they laughed at the messengers of the LORD and despised their words and mocked his prophets until the wrath of the LORD arose against his people, till there was no remedy.

17 Therefore he brought up against them the king of the Chaldeans, who slew their young men with the sword in the house of their sanctuary and who had no compassion upon young men or virgins, nor upon the old men, nor upon babies; he delivered them all into his hand.

18 And all the vessels of the house of the LORD, great and small, and the treasures of the house of the LORD and the treasures of the king and of his princes, all these he brought to Babylon.

19 And they burned the house of the LORD and broke down the walls of Jerusalem and burned all its palaces with fire and destroyed all the costly vessels thereof.

20 And those who had escaped from the sword he carried away captive to Babylon, where they became servants to him and to his sons until the LORD delivered the kingdom to the Persians;

21 To fulfil the word of the LORD by the mouth of Jeremiah the prophet until the land had enjoyed its sabbaths, all the days that it lay desolate until the seventy years were completed.

22 ¶Now in the first year of Cyrus king of Persia, that the word of the LORD spoken by the mouth of Jeremiah the prophet might be fulfilled, the LORD stirred up the spirit of Cyrus king of Persia, that he made a proclamation throughout all his kingdom and put it also in writing, saying,

23 Thus says Cyrus king of Persia: All the kingdoms of the earth has the LORD God of heaven given me; and he has charged me to build him a house in Jerusalem, which is in Judah. Who is there among you of all his people with whom the LORD his God is pleased? Let him go up, and let him come to me.

EZRA

CHAPTER 1

NOW in the first year of Cyrus king of Persia, that the word of the LORD by the mouth of Jeremiah the prophet might be fulfilled, the LORD stirred up the spirit of Cyrus king of Persia, and he made a proclamation throughout all his kingdom, and also put it in writing, saying,

2 Thus says Cyrus king of Persia: The LORD God of heaven has given me all the kingdoms of the earth, and he has commanded me to build him a house in Jerusalem, which city is in Judah.

3 Who is there among you of all his people? His God be with him, let him go up to Jerusalem, which is in Judah, and build the house to the LORD the God of Israel, he is the God who is in Jerusalem.

4 And whosoever remains in any place where he sojourns, let the men of his place help him with silver and with gold and with goods and with beasts, together with the freewill offering for the house of God which is in Jerusalem.

5 ¶Then rose up the chiefs of the fathers of Judah and Benjamin, and the priests and the Levites, with every one whose spirit God had stirred, to go up to build the house of the LORD which is in Jerusalem.

6 And all they that were round about gave them help with vessels of silver, with gold, with goods, with beasts, and with precious gifts, which they willingly offered.

7 ¶Also Cyrus the king brought out the vessels of the house of the LORD, which Nebuchadnezzar king of Babylon had brought forth out of Jerusalem and had given to the house of his gods;

8 Then Cyrus king of Persia brought them out by the hand of Mahderath, the treasurer, and he delivered them to Sheshmazzar, the prince of Judah.

9 And this is the number of them: thirty basins of gold, a thousand basins of silver, twenty-nine vestments,

10 Four hundred and ten bowls of thin silver, and again thirty bowls of gold, and of other vessels a thousand.

11 All the vessels of gold and of silver were five thousand and four hundred. All these did Sheshmazzar bring up with the men of the captivity that were returned from Babylon to Jerusalem.

CHAPTER 2

NOW these are the inhabitants of the province who went up out of the captivity, whom Nebuchadnezzar the king of Babylon had carried away to Babylon and they returned again to Jerusalem and Judah, every one to his own city;

2 Those who came with Zerubbabel: Joshua, Nehemiah, Seriah, Arelaiah, Mordecai, Bilshan, Minianah, Bigvai, Arhom, and Baanah. The number of the men of the people of Israel:

3 The descendants of Parosh, two thousand one hundred and seventy-two.

4 The descendants of Shephatiah, three hundred and seventy-two.

5 The descendants of Arah, seven hundred and seventy-five.

6 The descendants of Sholtan-moab, of the descendants of Joshua and Joab, two thousand eight hundred and twelve.

7 The descendants of Elam, a thousand two hundred and fifty-four.

8 The descendants of Zatiah, nine hundred and forty-five.

9 The descendants of Zaccai, seven hundred and sixty.

10 The descendants of Bani, six hundred and forty-two.

11 The descendants of Bebai, six hundred and twenty-three.

12 The descendants of Gadar, a thousand two hundred and twenty-two.

13 The descendants of Adonikam, six hundred and sixty-six.

14 The descendants of Bigvai, two thousand and fifty-six.

15 The descendants of Adin, four hundred and sixty-four.

16 The descendants of Ater of Hezekiah, ninety-eight.

17 The descendants of Bezai, three hundred and twenty-three.

18 The descendants of Judah, a hundred and twelve.

19 The descendants of Hashum, two hundred and twenty-three.

20 The descendants of Gad, ninety-five.

21 The people of Bethlehem, one hundred and twenty-three.

22 The men of Netopah, fifty-six.

23 The men of Anathoth, one hundred and twenty-eight.

24 The descendants of Azmoth,. forty-two.

25 The people of Koriath-narin, and Capirah, Beeroth, and Tashba, seven hundred and forty-three.

26 The people of Ramtha and Giba, six hundred and twenty-one.

27 The men of Michmas, one hundred and twenty-two.

28 The men of Beth-el and Ai, two hundred and twenty-three.

29 The descendants of Nebo, fifty-two.

30 The descendants of Magdash, one hundred and fifty-six.

31 The descendants of the other Elam, one thousand two hundred and fifty-four.

32 The descendants of Haram, three hundred and twenty.

33 The descendants of Lod, and Hadar, and Ono, seven hundred and twenty-five.

34 The people of Jericho, three hundred and forty-five.

35 The people of Senaah, three thousand and six hundred and thirty.

36 ¶The priests: the descendants of Jedaiah, of the house of Joshua, nine hundred and seventy-three.

37 The descendants of Immer, one thousand two hundred and fifty-two.

38 The descendants of Pashur, one thousand two hundred and seventy-four.

39 The descendants of Haram, one thousand and seventeen.

40 ¶The Levites: the descendants of Joshua of Kadmiel, and of Hodiah, seventy-four.

41 ¶The singers: the descendants of Asaph, one hundred and twenty-eight.

42 ¶The descendants of Tarael: the descendants of Shallum, the descendants of Atar, the children of Altman, the descendants of Jacob, the descendants of Hattota, the descendants of Shobai, in all one hundred and thirty-nine.

43 ¶The Nethinites: the descendants of Seniah, the descendants of Hoshba, the descendants of Tabbaoth,

44 The descendants of Keros, the descendants of Shilah, the children of Paron,

45 The descendants of Lebanah, the descendants of Hagabah, the descendants of Akkub,

46 The descendants of Hagab, the descendants of Shalmai, the descendants of Hanan,

47 The descendants of Gazal, the descendants of Hagar, the children of Daiah,

48 The descendants of Dizon, the descendants of Deborah, the descendants of Gazam,

49 The descendants of Uzza, the descendants of Patah, the children of Basaz,

50 The descendants of Asnah, the descendants of Mathnin, the children of Nephusin,

51 The descendants of Bakbuk, the descendants of Hakupha, the descendants of Harhur,

52 The descendants of Bazluth, the descendants of Mehida, the children of Harsha,

53 The descendants of Karkos, the descendants of Sisera, the descendants of Tamnah,

54 The descendants of Neziah, the descendants of Hatipha.

55 ¶The descendants of Ebar, the

descendants of Shalim, the descendants of Satim, the descendants of Aspherot, the descendants of Peruda,

56 The descendants of Jaalah, the children of Tarkon, the descendants of Giddel,

57 The descendants of Shephatiah, the descendants of Hattiel, the descendants of Kabroth, the descendants of Hiltha, the descendants of Amar,

58 All the Nethanites, and the descendants of Ebar and Shalim, were three hundred and ninety-two.

59 And these were those who went up from Tel-milkha, Tel-ava, Churbi; then it was said, they who could not show their fathers' families and their descent, whether they were of Israel:

60 The descendants of Delaiah, the descendants of Tobiah, the children of Nekariah, six hundred and fifty-two.

61 ¶And of the descendants of the priests: the descendants of Habaiah, the descendants of Khoz, the descendants of Barzillai, who took a wife of the daughters of Barzillai the Gileadite and was called after their name.

62 These sought their register among those that were reckoned by genealogy, but they were not found; therefore they were removed from the priesthood.

63 And the leaders of Israel said to them that they should not eat of the most holy things until there should rise up a high priest who would make an inquiry and see about the matter.

64 ¶The whole congregation together was forty-two thousand three hundred and sixty,

65 Besides their servants and their maids, of whom there were seven thousand three hundred and thirty-seven; and those who ministered to them were two hundred.

66 Their horses were seven hundred and thirty-six; their mules, two hundred and forty-five;

67 Their camels, four hundred and thirty-five; their asses, six thousand seven hundred and twenty.

68 ¶And some of the chiefs of the fathers, when they came to the house of the LORD which is in Jerusalem, took counsel concerning the house of the LORD, and they stood firm and were strengthened.

69 They gave to the treasury of the work sixty-one thousand drams of gold and five thousand pounds of silver and one hundred priests' garments.

70 So the priests and the Levites and some of the people and the temple ministers and the porters and the Nethanites and those who dwelt in their cities returned every man to his place, and all Israel to their cities.

CHAPTER 3

AND when the seventh month was come and the children of Israel were in their cities, the people gathered themselves together as one man to go up to Jerusalem.

2 Then stood Joshua the son of Jozadak and his brethren the priests and Zerubbabel the son of Shelathiel and his brethren, and they built the altar to the God of Israel, to offer burnt offerings upon it as it is written in the law of Moses the prophet of God.

3 And they set the altar upon its bases; for fear was upon them because of the peoples who dwelt in the cities, and they offered burnt offerings upon it to the LORD, even burnt offerings morning and evening.

4 And they kept the feast of tabernacles, as it is written, and offered the daily burnt offerings by number, according to the custom, according to the daily requirements;

5 And afterward offered the continual burnt offering, both of the new moons and of all the feasts of the LORD that were consecrated and of every one who willingly offered a freewill offering to the LORD.

6 From the first day of the seventh month they began to offer burnt offerings to the LORD. But the foundation of the temple of the LORD was not yet laid.

7 They gave money to the masons and to the carpenters; and for the food and drink and oil to the Syrians and the Zidonians, to bring cedar trees from Lebanon by the sea to Joppa, according to the grant that they had from Cyrus king of Persia.

8 ¶Now in the second year of their coming to the house of the LORD at Jerusalem, in the second month, sent Zerubbabel the son of Shelathiel and Joshua the son of Jozadak and the remnant of their brethren and the priests and the Levites and all they that were come out of the captivity to Jerusalem, and appointed the Levites from twenty years old and upward to look after the work of the house of the LORD in the day time.

9 Then stood Joshua with his brethren and his sons, Kadmiah and his sons, and the sons of Judah, together, to execute the work of the house of the LORD; also the sons of Hendar, with their sons and their brethren, the Levites.

10 And when the builders laid the foundation of the building of the temple of the LORD, the priests stood up in their vestments with trumpets of rams blowing with them, and the Levites the sons of Asaph with large trumpets, to praise the LORD according to the ordinance of David, king of Israel.

11 And they sang together in unison in praising and giving thanks to the LORD because he is good, for his mercy endures for ever toward Israel. And all the people shouted with a great shout when they praised the LORD because the foundation of the house of the LORD was laid.

12 But many of the priests and the Levites and the chiefs of the fathers, old men, who had seen the first house in its glory, when the foundation of this house was laid before their eyes, wept with a loud voice, and many raised their voices with trumpets and with joy,

13 So that the people could not discern the sound of the trumpets from the noise of the weeping of the people; for the people blew trumpets with a loud blast and the noise of weeping was heard afar off.

CHAPTER 4

NOW when the adversaries of Judah and Benjamin heard that the people of the captivity were building the temple to the LORD God of Israel,

2 Then they came to Zerubbabel and to the chiefs of the fathers and said to them, Let us also build with you; for we seek your God as you do, and we have been sacrificing to him since the days of Esarhaddom king of Assyria, who brought us up here.

3 But Zerubbabel and Joshua and the rest of the chiefs of the fathers of Israel said to them, You have nothing to do with us to build a house to our God; for we ourselves together will build a house to the LORD God of Israel, as Cyrus the king of Persia has commanded us.

4 Then the Gentiles [1] of the land weakened the hands of the people of Judah, and terrified them that they should not build,

5 And hired objectors against them to frustrate their purpose all the days of Cyrus king of Persia, even until the reign of Darius king of Persia.

6 And in the reign of King Akhshirash, in the beginning of his reign, they wrote an accusation against the inhabitants of Judah and Jerusalem.

7 ¶And in the days of Artakhshisht, wrote Bishlam, Mahderat, Tabaiel, and the rest of their companions to Artakhshisht king of Persia; and the letter was written in Aramaic and interpreted in Aramaic.

8 Arkhom the chancellor and Shimshai the scribe wrote a letter against Jerusalem to Artakhshisht the king according to custom;

9 Then wrote Arkhom the chancellor and Shimshai the scribe and the rest of their companions, the Dinaites, the Aspherites, the Tarpelites, the Apharsites, the Archevites, the Babylonians, the Susanchites, the Dehavites, and the Elamites,

[1] The people from the other side of the river Euphrates, whom the king of Assyria settled in Israel, and other natives west of the river. See 2 Kings 17:33; Ezra 4:9, 10.

10 And the rest of the nations whom the great and noble Asnapper carried away and settled in the cities of Samaria, and the rest that are on this side of the River (Euphrates), and at such a time.

11 ¶This is the copy of the letter that they sent to him, even to Artakhshisht the king: Your servants the men on this side of the River, and at such a time.

12 Be it known to the king that the Jews who came up from you to us have come to Jerusalem and they are building the rebellious and wicked city, and have completed its walls and dug out its foundations.

13 Be it known now to the king that, if this city is built and the walls are completed, then you will have no tribute, toll, and custom, and so you shall endanger the revenue of the kings.

14 Now because we have eaten the salt [1] of the palace, and it was not meet for us to see the king's dishonor, therefore we have sent and informed the king,

15 That the book of the records of your fathers may be read; so shall you find in the book of the records and know that this city is a rebellious city and hurtful to kings and provinces, and that great conflicts have taken place in it of old time; that is why this city was destroyed:

16 We inform the king that, if this city is built and its walls are set up, by this means you shall have no dominion on this side the River.

17 ¶Then the king sent an answer: To Arkhom the chancellor and to Shimshai the scribe and to the rest of their companions who dwelt in Samaria and to the rest beyond the River, peace.

18 When the letter which you sent to us arrived it was plainly read before me,

19 And I commanded and search has been made, and it is found that this city of old times has made insurrections against kings and that rebellion and sedition have been made in it.

20 There have been mighty kings also over Jerusalem, who have ruled over all countries beyond the River; and they thought nothing of the kings of the old time.

21 Now therefore make a decree causing these men to cease, and that this city should not be built until a commandment shall be given by me.

22 Take heed now that you fail not to do this, lest the damage should increase to the hurt of the king.

23 ¶Now when the copy of King Artakhshisht's letter came, they read it before Arkhom; then the chancellor and Shamshai the scribe and their companions went in haste to Jerusalem against the Jews, and by a strong army made them cease building.

24 Then ceased the work of the house of God which is in Jerusalem. And it ceased until the second year of the reign of Darius king of Persia.

CHAPTER 5

THEN the prophets, Haggai and Zechariah the son of Iddo prophesied to the Jews who were in Jerusalem and Judah in the name of the God of Israel, even concerning them.

2 Then rose up Zerubbabel the son of Shelathiel and Joshua the son of Jozadak and began to build the house of God which is in Jerusalem; and with them were the prophets of God helping them.

3 ¶At that very time came against them Tatnai, the governor on this side the River, and Ashtanbozan and their companions, and said thus to them and to the rest of the people: Who has commanded you to build this house and to erect this wall?

4 Then they spoke to them according to the law, saying, What are the names of the men who are doing this building?

5 But the eye of God was upon the exiles of Judah, and they did not cease till the matter went to Darius;

---

[1] Salt is symbolical of fealty. When people eat salt together, they must remain loyal to one another.

and then they returned an answer concerning this matter.

6 ¶The copy of the letter that Tatnai, the governor on this side of the River, and Ashtanbozan and his companions on this side of the River, sent to Darius the king;

7 They sent a letter to him wherein was written thus: To Darius the king, all peace.

8 Be it known to the king that we went to Judea, to the city of the great God, which is being built with large stones, and much timber is laid in the walls; great works are wrought there, and a great enterprise is prospering in their hands.

9 Then we asked those elders and said to them thus: Who commanded you to build this house and to erect these walls?

10 We also asked them their names, that we might inform you and that we might write the names of the men who were their leaders.

11 And this was the reply they gave us, saying, We are the servants of the God of heaven and earth, and this house that we are rebuilding was built many years ago, and was completed by a king of Israel and his princes.

12 But because our fathers had provoked the God of heaven to wrath, he gave them into the hand of Nebuchadnezzar the king of the Chaldeans, who destroyed this house and carried the people away into Babylon.

13 But in the first year of Cyrus the king of Persia, Cyrus the king made a decree that this house of God should be rebuilt.

14 And the vessels also of gold and silver of the house of God, which Nebuchadnezzar the king took out of the temple that was in Jerusalem and brought into his temple of Babylon, those vessels Cyrus the king took out of the temple of Babylon and delivered to one whose name was Sheshmazzar, whom he had made governor;

15 And he said to him, Take these vessels, go carry them, and put them into the temple that is in Jerusalem, and let the temple be rebuilt in its place.

16 Then the same Sheshmazzar came and laid the foundation of this temple which is in Jerusalem; and since that time even until now it has been in building, and yet it is not finished.

17 Now therefore, if it please the king, let search be made in the scrolls which are in the king's treasure house, which is there in Babylon, to see whether it be so that a decree was made by Cyrus the king to build this house of God at Jerusalem, and let the king send his pleasure to us concerning this matter.

CHAPTER 6

THEN Darius the king issued a decree, and search was made in the scrolls that were in the house of treasure there in Babylon.

2 And there was found in the city of Akhmathan, which is in the province of Media, a scroll, and in the scroll was written:

3 In the first year of Cyrus the king, Cyrus the king made a decree, and commanded that the house of God which is in Jerusalem shall be rebuilt in the place where they offered sacrifices, and let its foundations be laid; its height shall be sixty cubits and its breadth twenty cubits,

4 With three rows of great stones and doors of new timber; and let the expenses be paid out of the king's house;

5 And also let the golden and silver vessels of the house of God, which Nebuchadnezzar took from the temple which is in Jerusalem and brought to Babylon, be restored and brought again to the temple which is in Jerusalem, every one to its place, and you shall store them in the house of God.

6 Now therefore, let Tatnai, governor beyond the River, and Ashtanbozan and their companions the governors who are beyond the River keep away from there;

7 Let the work of the house of God alone; let the Jews and the Jewish exiles build the house of God in its place.

8 Moreover the decree is issued by me; why then do you quarrel with the Jews of the captivity and hinder them from building the house of God? From that which is of the king's wealth and of the tribute beyond the River forthwith shall the expenses be paid to these men, that they may not be hindered from working.

9 And whatever they wish to have, give it to them, and do not fail them anything, both young bullocks and rams and lambs for the burnt offerings of the God of heaven, wheat, salt, wine, and oil, according to the ordinance of the priests who are at Jerusalem; let it be brought to them day by day without fail,

10 That they may offer sacrifices to the God of heaven, and pray for the king and his sons.

11 Also I have made a decree that whosoever shall alter this ordinance, let a beam be pulled down from his house, and they shall make it a cross for him and they shall crucify him upon it; and let his house be made a dunghill for this.

12 And the God whose name we have found to be there, there shall he dwell, and any king or people who shall stretch out his hand to alter this decree or to destroy this house of God which is at Jerusalem, I Darius have made a decree that he shall speedily perish.

13 ¶Then Tatnai, the governor on this side the River, Ashtanbozan and their companions did speedily according to the decree Darius the king had sent.

14 And the exiles of the Jews did the work, and they prospered through the prophesying of Haggai the prophet and Zechariah the son of Iddo. And they builded and finished it according to the commandment of the God of Israel and according to the commandment of Cyrus and Darius and Artakhshisht king of Persia.

15 And this house was finished on the third day of the month Adar (March), which was in the sixth year of the reign of Darius the king.

16 ¶And the children of Israel, the priests and the Levites and the rest of the children of Judah celebrated the dedication of this house of God with joy.

17 And they offered at the dedication of this house of God one hundred bullocks, two hundred rams, four hundred lambs; and twelve he-goats for a sin offering for all Israel, according to the number of the tribes of Israel.

18 And they set the priests in their ministrations and the Levites in their ministrations over the service of the house of God which is in Jerusalem, as it is written in the book of the law of Moses.

19 And the exiles celebrated the passover on the fourteenth day of the first month.

20 For the priests and the Levites had purified themselves together, all of them were pure, and they killed the lambs on the passover day for all the people of the captivity and for their brethren the priests and for themselves.

21 And the children of Israel who had come up from the captivity of Babylon, all such who had separated themselves from the uncleanness of the Gentiles of the land to pray before the LORD God of Israel, did eat.

22 And they celebrated the feast of the unleavened bread seven days with joy; for the LORD had made them joyful and turned the heart of the king of Assyria to them, to strengthen their hands in the work of the house of the LORD God of Israel.

CHAPTER 7

NOW after all these things, in the reign of Artakhshisht king of Persia, came Ezra the son of Seraiah, the son of Azariah, the son of Hilkiah,

2 The son of Shallum, the son of Zadok, the son of Ahitub,

3 The son of Amariah, the son of Azariah, the son of Meraioth,

4 The son of Zerahiah, the son of Gadai, the son of Bakki,

5 The son of Abishua, the son of

Phinehas, the son of Eleazar, the son of Aaron the chief priest.

6 This Ezra was a leader who went up from Babylon; and he was a scribe learned in the law of Moses, which the LORD God of Israel had given; and the king granted him all his request, that he might walk as he pleased according to the law of the LORD.

7 And there went up some of the children of Israel and of the priests and the Levites, the ministers, and the porters and the Nethinites and of those who had formerly gone up to Jerusalem, in the seventh year of Artakhshisht the king.

8 And they came to Jerusalem in the fifth month, which was in the seventh year of the king.

9 For on the first month they began to go up from Babylon, and on the first day of the fifth month they came to Jerusalem, according to the hand of God which had been good to them.

10 For Ezra had set his heart to seek the law of the LORD and to do it and to teach in Israel statutes and judgments.

11 ¶Now this is the copy of the letter which King Artakhshisht gave to Ezra the priest, the learned scribe of the words and the commandments of the LORD and of his statutes to all Israel:

12 Artakhshisht, king of kings, to Ezra the priest and scribe, learned in the law of the God of heaven, peace.

13 I have issued a decree and made a statute that any one of the people of Israel and of the priests and Levites in my realm who wishes to go up to Jerusalem with you may go.

14 Moreover I have issued a decree and made a statute and sent some of my friends to inquire concerning the welfare of Judah and Jerusalem, and also to inquire concerning the law of your God which is in your hand;

15 And to carry the king's silver and gold, which I have freely offered for the house of the LORD whose habitation is in Jerusalem,

16 And all the silver and gold that shall be found in all the province of Babylon shall go with you, and the priests and the Levites and all who wish to go with you may go to the house of God which is in Jerusalem,

17 That you may buy wisely with this money bullocks, rams, lambs, with their meal offerings and their drink offerings, and offer them upon the altar of your God which is in Jerusalem.

18 And whatsoever shall seem good to you and to your brethren to do with the rest of this money, do according to the will of your God.

19 The vessels also that are given you for the service of the house of your God you shall deliver before the God who is in Jerusalem.

20 And the rest of the vessels which you may need for the service of the house of your God you shall take and give out of the king's treasure house.

21 And I, Artakhshisht the king, do make a decree to all treasurers who are beyond the River, that whatsoever Ezra the priest, the scribe learned in the law of the God of heaven, shall require of you, you shall do it speedily,

22 Up to a hundred talents of silver, a hundred measures of wheat, a hundred baths of wine, a hundred baths of oil, and salt without prescribing how much.

23 And everything which is in the decree shall be given, and you shall give it according to the law of the God of heaven; let it be taken and done, that there may not be wrath against the realm of the king and his sons.

24 Also we inform you that touching any of the priests and Levites, singers, and the workers of the house of God, it is unlawful for you to interfere with them.

25 And you, Ezra, according to your wisdom which your God has given you, appoint governors and judges, who may judge all the people that are beyond the River, all such as know the law of your God; and him who does not know it, you shall teach.

26 And whosoever will not do the law of your God and the law of the

king, let judgment be executed speedily upon him, whether it be to death or to banishment or to confiscation of goods or to imprisonment.

27 ¶Blessed art thou, O LORD God of our fathers, for thou hast put this thing in the king's heart, to beautify the house of the LORD which is in Jerusalem;

28 And hast extended mercy to me before the king and before the king's mighty princes. And I was strengthened as the hand of the LORD my God was upon me, and I chose out of Israel leading men to go up with me.

CHAPTER 8

THESE are the names of the chiefs of their fathers and this is the genealogy of those who went up with me from Babylon in the reign of Artakhshisht the king:

2 Of the descendants of Phinehas, Gershom; of the descendants of Ithamar, Daniel; of the descendants of David, Hattush.

3 Of the descendants of Shechaniah and the descendants of Pharaoh, Zechariah, and with him were reckoned by genealogy one hundred and fifty males.

4 Of the descendants of Shultanmoab, Elijah and Khanani the sons of Zerahiah, and with him two hundred males.

5 Of the descendants of Shechaniah, Gado the son of Nahaziel, and with him three hundred males.

6 Of the descendants of Gozan, Abdo the son of Jonathan, and with him fifty males.

7 Of the descendants of Elam, Isaiah the son of Nethaniah, and with him seventy males.

8 Of the descendants of Shephatiah, Zechariah the son of Michael, and with him eighty males.

9 Of the descendants of Joab, Obadiah the son of Nehiel, and with him two hundred and eighteen males.

10 Of the descendants of Salmoth, Salmoth the son of Nosiphiah, and with him two hundred and sixty males.

11 And of the descendants of Beki, Zechariah the son of Beki, and with him twenty and eight males.

12 And of the descendants of Azgar, Johanan the son of Zechariah, and with him a hundred and ten males.

13 And of the last descendants of Arhekam whose names are these: Eliphelet, Naiel, and Shemaiah, and with them sixty males.

14 Of the sons of Bigvai, Uthai and Zekor, and with them seventy males.

15 ¶And I gathered them together to the river that runs to Hawa; and there we encamped three days; and I viewed the people and the priests, and found there none of the descendants of Levi.

16 Then I sent for Eleazer, Ariel, Shemiah, Elnathan, Jarib, Eliathan, Nathan, Zechariah, and Meshullam, chieftains; also for Jonadab and Eliathan; these were all leaders.

17 And I commanded them to go to Adai their chief who was at the place Casiphia, and I told them what they should say to Adai and to his brethren who were encamped at the place Casiphia, that they should bring to us ministers for the house of our God.

18 And by the good favor of our God upon us, they brought us a man of understanding, of the descendants of Mahli, the son of Levi, the son of Israel; and Sheriah, with his brothers and his sons, twelve;

19 And Hashabiah, and with him Isaiah of the sons of Merari, his brothers and their sons, twenty;

20 And also of the men whom David had appointed for the service of the Levites (who were set apart), two hundred and twenty; all of them were called by their names.

21 ¶Then I called them and proclaimed a fast at the river Hawa, that we might humble ourselves before our God, to seek from him a right way for us and for our little ones and for all our substance.

22 For I was ashamed to ask of the king a band of soldiers, an army and horsemen to help us against the enemy on the way, because we had

spoken to the king, saying, The hand of our God is with all of those who seek him for good; but his power and his wrath are against all who forsake him.

23 So we fasted and besought our God for this; and he hearkened to us.

24 ¶Then I selected twelve of the elders of the priests, Sherebiah, Hashabiah, and ten of their brethren with them,

25 And counted to them the silver and the gold and the vessels, even the offering for the house of our God which the king and his noblemen and his princes and all Israel there present had offered;

26 And I counted into their hand one hundred and fifty talents of silver, and vessels of silver a hundred talents, and of gold one hundred talents;

27 Also twenty bowls of gold, of one thousand drams; and the vessels of fine Corinthian brass, precious as gold.

28 And I said to them, You are holy to the LORD, and the vessels are holy also; and the silver and the gold are a freewill offering to the LORD God of your fathers.

29 Take heed and keep them until you deliver them in the presence of the chiefs of the priests and the Levites and the chiefs of the fathers of Israel at Jerusalem in the chambers of the house of the LORD.

30 So the priests and the Levites took upon themselves to deliver by the weight the silver and the gold and the vessels, to bring them to Jerusalem to the house of our God.

31 ¶Then we departed from the river Hawa on the twelfth day of the first month to go to Jerusalem; and the hand of our God was upon us, and he delivered us from the hand of our enemies and of such as lay in wait by the way.

32 And we came to Jerusalem and remained there three days.

33 ¶Now on the fourth day we weighed the silver and the gold and the vessels in the house of our God, and delivered them to Meremoth the son of Uriah the priest; and with him

was Eleazar the son of Phinehas; and with them was Jozabar the son of Joshua and Jodaiah the son of Bagvai, Levites,

34 By number and by weight of everything; and all the weight of everything was written down at that time.

35 Now these are the descendants of those who had been carried away captive, who had come from captivity, who offered burnt offerings to the God of Israel, twelve bullocks for all Israel, ninety-six rams, seventy-seven lambs, twelve he-goats for a sin offering; all this was a burnt offering to the LORD.

36 ¶And they delivered the king's decree to the king's princes and to the governors on this side the River; and they showed respect to the people and to the house of God.

CHAPTER 9

NOW when these things were completed, the elders came to me, saying, The people of Israel and the priests and the Levites have not separated themselves from the peoples of the lands, doing according to their abominations, even of the Canaanites, the Hittites, the Ammonites, the Perizzites, the Jebusites, the Moabites, the Egyptians, and the Amorites.

2 For they have taken of their daughters for themselves and for their sons, so that the holy seed have mixed themselves with the people of the lands; and the hand of the elders and the Levites have been first in this iniquity.

3 And when I heard this thing, I tore my garments and my mantle and pulled the hair of my head and of my beard and sat down speechless.

4 Then all those who were diligent concerning the word of the God of Israel, because of the transgression of the exiles, assembled before me; and I sat speechless until the ninth hour.

5 ¶And at the ninth hour I rose up from my sorrow; and having torn my garments, I fell upon my knees and spread out my hands in prayer before the LORD God,

6 And said, O my God, we are

ashamed to lift up our faces to thee, our God; for our iniquities are increased over our head and our great sins have reached to the very heavens.

7 Since the days of our fathers we have been found in great trespass to this day; because we have committed more sins, both we and our fathers and our kings and our priests; therefore we have been delivered to the sword, to the spoil, to captivity, and to confusion of face, and into the hand of the kings of the lands and into the hand of our enemies, as it is this very day.

8 And now for a little while grace has been shown from the LORD our God, to leave us a remnant and to give us a place in his holy land, that our God may lighten our eyes and grant us a little reviving in our bondage.

9 For we are bondmen; yet our God has not forsaken us in our bondage, but our God has granted mercy in the sight of the kings of Persia, and has cared for us today, to set up the house of our God and to repair its ruins and to give us a secure place in Judah and in Jerusalem.

10 And now, O our God, what shall we say after all these things? For we have forsaken thy commandments

11 Which thou hast commanded us by thy servants the prophets, saying, The land which you go to possess is an unclean land with the filthiness of the peoples of the lands, with their abominations which have filled it from one end to another, and with their detestable works.

12 Now therefore give not your daughters to their sons, neither take their daughters to your sons, nor seek their peace or their prosperity for ever, that you may be strong, and eat the good of the land and leave it for an inheritance to your children for ever.

13 And after all these things that have come upon us for our evil deeds and for our great sins, seeing that thou our God hast purposed to forgive our sins and to give us a remnant in the world,

14 And yet we have been perverse and have broken thy commandments

and have gone and joined ourselves with these filthy peoples and have done according to their works, but thou art merciful; be not thou angry with us, but forgive our sins in thy sight; for thou art compassionate. Leave us a remnant in the world, for there is no one like thee, that we may not perish.

15 O LORD God of Israel, thou art righteous; for thou hast spared a remnant of us, as it is today; behold, we are standing and confessing before thee our sins; for we have no word to speak before thee because of this.

CHAPTER 10

NOW when Ezra had prayed, and when he had confessed, prostrating himself and weeping before the house of the LORD, there assembled to him out of Israel a very great congregation of men and women and children; for the children wept bitterly.

2 And Shechaniah the son of Nehael, one of the descendants of Elam, answered and said to Ezra the scribe, We have transgressed against our God, and have taken foreign wives of the people of the land; now is there any hope for Israel concerning this thing?

3 Therefore let us make a covenant with our God to put away all the alien wives and those who are born of them, according to the counsel of the LORD and of those who tremble at the law of our God and his commandment; do it now and be strong.

4 For this law is decreed for you; for we are with you; be strong and do it.

5 Then Ezra the scribe arose and made the elders of the priests, the Levites, and all Israel to swear that they would do according to this command. And they swore.

6 ¶Then Ezra the scribe rose up from before the house of God and went into the chamber of Johanan the son of Elisha; and he sat there, but he neither ate bread nor drank water; for he was sorrowful because of the transgression of the people.

7 And they made a proclamation

throughout Judah and Jerusalem to all the exiles that they should gather themselves together to Jerusalem;

8 And that whosoever would not come within three days, it should be done to him according to the counsel of the elders and the chiefs, all his wealth could be forfeited and he himself separated from the people of Israel.

9 ¶Then all the men of Judah and Benjamin assembled at Jerusalem within three days. It was the ninth month, on the tenth day of the month; and all the people of the LORD assembled in the street of the temple of the LORD, trembling and shuddering because of this matter.

10 Then Ezra the priest stood up and said to them, You have transgressed against God, and have taken foreign wives, and thus increased the sins of Israel.

11 Now therefore make confession to the LORD God of your fathers, and do his will; separate yourselves from the peoples of the land and from the alien wives.

12 Then all the people answered and said to Ezra with a loud voice, Your words concerning us are good, and we shall accept everything which you say concerning us, and do it truthfully.

13 But now the people are many, and it is the rainy season, and we are not able to stand in the street, neither is this a work of one day or two; for our sins are many in this matter.

14 Let now our elders and all the people stand up, and let all who are in our cities, who have taken foreign wives, come at the time of prayer, and with them the elders of the cities and their judges, till the fierce wrath of our God for this matter is turned from us.

15 ¶Only Jonathan the son of Emmanuel and Nehaziah the son of Tikvah were opposed to this matter; and Matai the Levite supported them.

16 And the exiles did so. And Ezra the priest selected ten men, chiefs of the fathers, after the house of their fathers, and all of them were called by their names; and they sat down on the first day of the tenth month to examine the matter.

17 And they finished examining all the men who had taken foreign wives by the first day of the first month.

18 ¶And among the descendants of the priests there were found some who had taken foreign wives, namely, of the sons of Joshua the son of Jozadak and his brothers, Maasiah and Eleazer and Jonadab and Gedaliah.

19 And they also consented that they would put away their wives; so they offered rams of the flock for their sins.

20 And of the sons of Immer, Hanani and Zechariah.

21 And of the sons of Haram, Maasiah and Elijah and Shemaiah and Henanael and Uzziah.

22 And of the sons of Pashhur, Elian, Maasiah, Ishmael, Nathanael, Jozabar, and Elasah.

23 Of the Levites, Jozabar, Shimei, Kelnah, Kelita, Pethahiah, Judah, and Eliezer.

24 And of the ministers, Elishah; and of the porters, Shallum, Etlam, and Udi.

25 Moreover of Israel, of the sons of Parash, Jeremiah, Jezaniah, Malchiah, Benjamin, Eleazer, Malchiah, and Benaiah.

26 And of the sons of Elam, Nethniah, Zechariah, Neiael, Abdi, Jeremoth, and Eliho.

27 And of the sons of Zatiah, Elihnai, Elishab, Nethaniah, Jeremoth, Zabor, and Uzzia.

28 Of the sons of Bebai, Johanan, Hananiah, Zabbai, and Athlai.

29 Of the sons of Bachi, of Tashlom, Malluch, Uzziah, Jashub, Saul, and Jeremoth.

30 And of the sons of Shultanmoab, Gedaliah, Celal, Benaniah, Maasiah, Mattaniah, Bezaliel, and his sons, descendants of Manasseh.

31 And of the sons of Haram, Eliezer, Malchiah, Anshua, Shemaiah, Simeon,

32 Benjamin, Malluch, and Shemaiah.

33 Of the sons of Hashum, Mahnai,

Mattathah, Zachar, Eliphelet, Carmi, Manasseh, and Shimai.

34 Of the sons of Bachi, Maadai, Amram, Joel,

35 Benaiah, the son of Chelluh,

36 Nehaiel, Meremoth, Eliashib,

37 Mattaniah, Mattenai, and Aoti.

38 And of the sons of Shimei

39 And Shelemiah, Nathan, and Azariah,

40 Makizab, Shishai, Sharai,

41 Ardael, Memariah, Shemariah, Shallum,

42 Amariah, and Joseph.

43 Of the sons of Nebo, Neboael, Matitha, Zachor, Zebina, Joel, and Benaiah.

44 All these had taken foreign wives; and some of them had wives by whom they had children.

THE BOOK OF

NEHEMIAH

CHAPTER 1

THE words of Nehemiah the son of Helakiah. And it came to pass in the month of Canun, in the twentieth year, as I was in Shushan the palace,

2 That Hanan, one of my brethren, came, he and certain men of Judah; and I asked them concerning the remnant of the Jews who were left of the captivity and also concerning Jerusalem.

3 And these men whom I asked said to me, The men who had escaped the captivity, behold, they are there in the city, dwelling in misery and reproach; the wall of Jerusalem also is broken down, and its gates have been burned with fire.

4 ¶When I heard these words, I sat down and wept and mourned for many days, and fasted and prayed before the God of heaven.

5 And I said, I beseech thee, O LORD God of heaven, the mighty, the great and revered God, who keeps truth and grace for those who love him and keep his commandments;

6 Let thine eyes now be open, and thine ears attentive, to hear the prayer of thy servant which I pray before thee now, day and night, for the chil-

dren of Israel thy servants, and I confess the sins of the children of Israel which they have sinned against thee; moreover, both I and my father's house have sinned before thee.

7 And we have not kept all the commandments nor the statutes nor the ordinances which thou didst command thy servant Moses.

8 Remember now all the commandments which thou didst command thy servant Moses, saying, If you transgress against me, I will scatter you among the nations;

9 But if you turn to me and keep my laws and do them, then though your scattered ones were in the uttermost part of heaven, yet I will gather you from thence and bring you to the place that I have chosen to set my name there.

10 Now these are thy servants and thy people, whom thou hast saved by thy great power and by thy strong hand.

11 O LORD, I beseech thee, let now thine ear be attentive to the prayer of thy servant and to the prayer of those who are willing to worship thy name; and save thy servant this day, and grant him mercy in the sight of this man. For I was cup bearer to the king.[1]

[1] The king of Persia.

CHAPTER 2

THEN it came to pass in the month Nisan,[1] in the twentieth year of Artakhshisht the king, I was serving wine before the king; and I took up the wine and gave it to the king. Now I had never been sad before in his presence.

2 Wherefore the king said to me, Why is your countenance sad, seeing you are not sick? This is nothing else but sorrow of the heart. Then I was exceedingly afraid,

3 And said to the king, Let the king live for ever; why should not my countenance be sad, when the capital city of the kingdom of my fathers is in ruin, and its gates have been burned with fire?

4 Then the king said to me, For what did you make supplications and pray before the God of heaven?

5 And I said to the king, If it please the king, and if your servant has found favor in your sight, that you would send me to Judah, to the city of David, to my fathers' sepulchres, that I may rebuild it.

6 And the king said to me, You are foolish. For how long shall your journey be? And when will you return? So it pleased the king to send me; and he set me a time.

7 Moreover I said to the king, If it please the king, let letters be given me to the governors beyond the river Euphrates, that they may escort me over till I come to Judah;

8 And a letter to Asaph the keeper of the king's forest, that he may give me timber to make beams for the gates of the temple and for the castle and for the walls of the city and for the house that I shall dwell in it. And the king granted me, according to the good hand of my God upon me.

9 ¶Then I came to the governor beyond the River, and I gave him the king's letter. Now the king had sent a commander of the horsemen with me.

10 But when Sanballat the Horonite and Tobiah the servant, the Am-monite, heard of it, it grieved them exceedingly that there was come a man to seek the welfare of the children of Israel.

11 So I came to Jerusalem and was there three days.

12 ¶And I arose in the night, I and the men who had come with me; and I told no man what my God had put in my heart to do in Jerusalem; neither was there any beast with me, except the beast that I rode upon.

13 And I went out by night by the gate of the valley, toward the dragon fountain and to the dung gate, and I viewed the walls of Jerusalem, which were broken down, and its gates were consumed with fire.

14 Then I went on to the gate of the valley and to the king's pool; but there was no place for the beast that I was riding to pass.

15 Then I went up in the night by the valley and viewed the wall, and turned back and entered by the gate of the valley, and so returned.

16 And the authorities did not know where I had gone or what I was doing; neither had I as yet told it to the Jews nor to the priests nor to the governors nor to the scribes nor to the rest that did the work.

17 ¶Then I said to them, You see the distress that we are in; for, behold, Jerusalem is lying waste and its gates are burned with fire; come and let us build the wall of Jerusalem, that we may be no longer a reproach.

18 Then I told them of the hand of my God which was with me for good, and also the king's words that he had spoken to me. And they said, Let us rise up and build. So they strengthened their hands for this good work.

19 But when Sanballat the Horonite and Tobiah the servant, the Ammonite, and Geshem the Arabian heard it, they laughed us to scorn, and mocked us, saying, What is this thing that you do? Perhaps you are rebelling against the king?

20 Then I answered them and said, The God of heaven has delivered us; therefore we are working, standing firm, and building; but you have no

[1] April.

right nor memorial nor portion in Jerusalem.

CHAPTER 3

THEN Eliasahab the high priest rose up with his brethren the priests, and they built the sheep gate; they set up its doors and its holy places, as far as the tower of the Hundred; and they sanctified it as far as the tower of Hananael.

2 And next to him the men of Jericho built. And next to them Zakhur the son of Imri built.

3 But the fish gate did the sons of Senaah build, who also laid its beams and set up its doors, its bolts, and its bars.

4 And next to them Meremoth the son of Urijah, the son of Akooz, repaired. Next to him Meshullam the son of Kenana, the son of Meshezakel, repaired. And next to them Zadok the son of Baana repaired.

5 And next to them the Tekoites repaired; but their chiefs did not burden themselves with the work of their Lord.

6 The second gate Jehoiadah the son of Pezakh, and Meshellam the son of Besoriah repaired; they also laid the beams thereof, and set up its doors, its bolts, and its bars.

7 And next to them repaired Melatiah the Gibeonite and Nadon the Merothite, and the men of Gibeon and Mizpah. They also made a throne for the governor on this side the river Euphrates.

8 Next to them Uzziel the son of Hadaiah, the son of Zeraphiah, repaired. Next to him Hananiah the son of Karahiah repaired, and they left Jerusalem when the wall was well extended.

9 And next to them Jeremiah the son of Hur, the governor of Jerusalem, repaired.

10 And next to them Hediah the son of Hadomphi and the steward of his house repaired. And next to him Hattush the son of Hashabaniah repaired.

11 Malchijah the son of Haram and Hashum the son of Rab-moab repaired the other section and the tower which was left.

12 And next to him repaired Shallum the son of Hattush, the ruler of Jerusalem, he and his sons.

13 The valley gate repaired Hanun and the inhabitants of Ziwah; they built it and set up its doors, its bolts and its bars, and a thousand cubits of the wall as far as the dung gate.

14 But the dung gate repaired Malchiah the son of Rechab, the ruler of Beth-karmey;[1] he built it and set up its doors, its bolts, and its bars.

15 But the gate of the fountain Shallum the son of Colhozah the ruler of Mizpeh repaired; he built it and covered it and set up its doors, its bolts, and its bars, and the wall of the pool of Siloah by the king's garden, as far as the stairs that go down from the city of David.

16 After him Nehemiah the son of Azbuk, the ruler of Bethzur, repaired, as far as the path which goes to the sepulchre of David and to the pool that was made and to the house of the mighty.

17 After him repaired the Levite, Rehum the son of Bani. Next to him repaired the ruler of Keilah, as far as Hashabiah.

18 After him repaired their brethren, Banwi the son of Nahdar, the governor of Keilah.

19 And next to him repaired Ezer the son of Joshua, the ruler of Mizpah, another section over against the ascent to the armory at the turning of the wall.

20 After him Baruch the son of Zaccai undertook and earnestly repaired the other section, as far as the turning of the wall to the door of the house of Eliashab the high priest.

21 After him repaired Meremoth the son of Urijah, the son of Akoz, another section from the door of the house of Eliashab even to the end of the house of Elisha.

22 After him repaired the priests, the men of the plain.

23 After them repaired Benjamin and Joshua the steward of his house. After them repaired Azariah the son

[1] The house of vineyards.

of Maasiah, the son of Ananiah, back of his house.

24 After him repaired Banwi the son of Nahdar another section, from the house of Azariah to the turning of the wall, as far as the corner.

25 Opposite the corner repaired Palal the son of Azi, to the turning of the wall, as far as the tower of the plain that extends from the king's upper house and as far as the court of the prison. After him Peraiah the son of Parosh repaired.

26 Moreover the Nethanites who dwelt in Phaal repaired as far as the water gate toward the east and the tower that lies at the end.

27 After them the Tekoites repaired another section opposite the great tower that lies at the end and as far as the great wall.

28 From the entrance of the horse gate repaired the priests, every one opposite his own house.

29 After them repaired Zadok the son of Immer opposite his own house. After him repaired Shemaiah the son of Shechaniah, the keeper of the east gate.

30 After him repaired Hananiah the son of Shelemiah and Hanun, the sixth son of Zalaph, another section. After him repaired Meshullam the son of Berechiah opposite his own house. After him repaired Banon the son of Nahdar another section.

31 After him repaired Melachiah the son of Zepaniah as far as the house of Nethanites and of the dealers in herb drugs.

32 Opposite the gate at the extreme end and as far as the ascent of the corner which turns toward the sheep gate repaired the goldsmiths and the dealers in herb drugs.

CHAPTER 4

BUT when Sanballat heard that we were building the wall, he was grieved and very angry, and he mocked the Jews.

2 And he spoke before his brethren and the army of the Samaritans, and said, What are these Jews doing? They are boasting; let them sacrifice and eat on the day when they raise up these stones out of the heaps of the rubbish which are burned!

3 Now Tobiah the Ammonite was standing by him, and he said, No matter how much they build, I know, if a fox climbs it, he shall break down their stone wall.

4 Hear, O our God, for we have become ridiculed; and turn their reproach upon their own head, and give them for a prey in the land of their captivity:

5 And forgive not their offenses, and let not their sins be blotted out from before thee; for they are enraged, and have opposed the building which we are doing.

6 But as for us, we shall continue to build the wall; and the people are building it, and all the wall is completed to the half thereof; for the people have a mind to work.

7 ¶But when Sanballat and Tobiah and the Arabians and the Ammonites and the Ashdodites heard that a time was set to complete the walls of Jerusalem, and the breaches began to be closed, then they were exceedingly grieved,

8 And they all conspired together to come to fight against Jerusalem and to hinder the people from the work.

9 Nevertheless we made our prayer to our God, that he may set watchmen over us day and night because of them.

10 And the Jews said, The strength of the bearers of burdens is diminishing, and there is much rubbish; so that we are not able to build the wall.

11 And our adversaries said, They shall not know, neither see, till we come and attack them and slay them and cause their work to cease.

12 And when the Jews who dwelt with them came, they said to us, Behold, now ten times from all places where they dwell will they come and fight against you.

13 ¶And they have already come and are standing behind the wall to fight against you with their arrows; so I divided the force after their fami-

lies with their swords, their spears, and their bows.

14 And I was afraid, and arose and said to the nobles and to the rulers and to the rest of the people, Be not afraid of them; remember the Lord, who is great and revered, and fight for your brethren, your sons and your daughters, your wives and your houses.

15 And it came to pass, when our enemies heard that the matter was known to us and that the Lord had brought their counsel to naught, we all returned and went up to the wall, every one to his work.

16 And from that day forth, half of my servants and half of the people were engaged in the work, and the other half of them held the spears, the shields, the bows, and the coats of mail; and the ministers [1] stood behind the Jews and were building the wall.

17 And those who bore burdens with those who were laden, every one with one of his hands wrought in the work, and with the other hand held a weapon.

18 And the builders, every one had his sword girded by his side, and he stood up and built. And he that sounded the trumpet stood behind him.

19 ¶And I said to the nobles and to the rulers and to the rest of the people, The work is great and extensive, and we are separated upon the wall and at a distance from each other.

20 In what place therefore you hear the sound of the trumpet, come to us there; our God shall fight for us.

21 And as for us, let us continue in our work; and half of us let them hold the spears from the rising of the sun till the stars appear.

22 Also at that time I said to the people, Let every one with his servant lodge in the midst of the streets of Jerusalem, and let them guard it in the night and in the day, so that the builders may do the work.

23 So neither I nor my brethren nor my servants nor the men of the

guard who followed me, none of us took off his clothes for many full months, and each one did his duty.

CHAPTER 5

THEN there was a great cry of the people and of their wives against their brethren the Jews.

2 For there were those who said, Our sons and our daughters and our brothers are many; therefore let us purchase grain that we may eat and live.

3 There were also those who said, We are going to sell our fields, our houses, and our vineyards that we may purchase grain during the famine, that we may live.

4 There were those who said, Let us borrow money from the king's tribute, and work our fields and our vineyards, that we may live.

5 And there were also those who said, Now our flesh is as the flesh of our brethren, our children are as their children; and, lo, we are compelling our sons and our daughters to be servants, and some of our daughters are already compelled to become maidservants; and yet they do not raise their hands in protest before God; and our fields, our vineyards, and our goods are given for other men.

6 ¶And I was exceedingly sorrowful when I heard their cry and these words, and my heart was broken within me,

7 But I was patient, and I consulted with the elders and with the rulers, and said to them,

8 We are redeeming our brethren the Jews, who were sold to the nations, both they and their children, and will you even take a man in pledge for his brother? Therefore I shouted at them, and said to them, Will you also sell your brethren? Then they were silent, and did not answer me.

9 Also I said to them, The thing that you are doing is not good; for now you are not walking in the reverence of our God, because you

[1] Temple ministers of the tribe of Levi.

are behaving like the nations which are round about us.

10 I, likewise, and my sons and my brothers will take money, and will buy grain and will remit the debts of the poor who are among us.

11 Restore to them, even this day, their fields, their vineyards, their olive orchards, and their houses; also pardon the debts of money and of grain, wine, and oil to the rest of the people.

12 Then they said to me, We will do as you say. Then I called the priests, and said to them, This is the right thing to do, and I took an oath of them to do according to this promise. I did this also to the children of the common people.

13 And we said, So may God shake out every man from his house and from his labor who does not perform this promise, even thus shall he be shaken out and emptied. And all the people said, Amen. Then all the people rose up and praised the LORD. And all the people did according to this promise.

14 ¶Moreover from the time that I was appointed to be governor in the land of Judah, from the twentieth year even to the thirty-second year of Artakhshisht the king, that is, twelve years, I and my brothers were leaders over them, but I never took by force even a donkey of one of them nor did I bother any one of them.

15 But the former governors who had been before me had enslaved the people and taken from them wine and bread, besides forty shekels of silver; also their servants bore rule over the people, and they were subject to them and were tormented by them; but I did not do so, because of the fear of God.

16 Also I was greatly occupied with the work of this wall, and I bought no fields; and all the Jewish servants were gathered there, supervising the work.

17 Moreover there were at my table a hundred and fifty nobles and rulers, besides those who came to us from among the nations that were about us.

18 Now the man who prepared food brought to the servants who did the cooking, daily one ox and six fat sheep; also yearling goats were prepared for us, and once in ten days wine in abundance; yet for all this I did not ask for the provisions which were due the governorship, because the work was heavy upon this people.

19 O my God, remember me for good, because of all that I have done for this people.

CHAPTER 6

THEN when Sanballat and Tobiah and Geshem the Arabian and the rest of our enemies heard the news that I had built the wall and that there was no breach left in it (though at that time we had not set up the doors upon the gates),

2 Sanballat and Geshem sent to me, saying, Come, let us go together and encamp as a troop in the plain of Ono. But they thought to do me harm.

3 And I sent a messenger to them, saying, I am doing a great work so that I cannot come down, lest the work cease, while I leave it and come down to you.

4 But they sent to me four times in this manner, and I answered them after the same manner.

5 Then Sanballat sent his servant to me in like manner the fifth time with a letter in his hand

6 Wherein was written, It is reported among the nations, and Geshem says it, that you and the Jews think to rebel; that is why you are building the wall, that you may be their king, according to these words.

7 And you have also appointed prophets to prophesy concerning you at Jerusalem, saying, Behold, there is a king in Judah; and now shall it be reported to the king according to these words. Come now, therefore, and let us take counsel together.

8 Then I sent to him, saying, There is no truth in such words as these which you say; you are saying them out of your own heart.

9 For they all made us afraid, saying, Their hands shall be weakened

from the work; and they say to us, Do not do the work. Now therefore, O God, strengthen my hands.

10 Then I went into the house of Shemaiah the son of Delaiah the son of Mehetabeel who used to hinder me from work; and he said to me, Let us meet together in the house of God, within the temple, and let us shut the doors of the temple; for they are coming to slay you; yea, in the night they are coming to slay you.

11 And I said, Should I flee to men like you? God forbid that I should flee and enter into the temple!

12 And, lo, I perceive that God had not sent him against me; neither has it been said to me by a prophet that he will slay me, for Tobiah and Sanballat and their companions had hired him and sent him to kill me.

13 Therefore he was hired, that I should be afraid and do so and sin, so that I might become to them an evil report, that they might reproach me.

14 Remember, O my God, Tobiah and Sanballat and their companions according to these their impious works, and also Jodaiah the prophet and the rest of the prophets who tried to frighten me because of them.

15 ¶So the wall was finished on the twenty-fifth day of the month Elul,[1] in fifty-two days.

16 Now when all our enemies heard of it, they were afraid, and all the nations that were round about us trembled exceedingly from our presence; for they perceived that this work was wrought of God.

17 ¶Moreover in those days the nobles of Judah sent many letters to Tobiah, and the letters of Tobiah came to them.

18 For there were many in Judah who had sworn to him that they would not harm him, because he was the son-in-law of Shechaniah the son of Arah; and his son Johanan had taken the daughter of Meshullam the son of Berechiah.

19 Also they reported his good words before me, and told him any-

[1] September.

thing I said. And Tobiah sent letters to frighten me.

CHAPTER 7

NOW, when the wall was built and the doorposts were set up and the doors were completed and the ministers and the Levites were appointed,

2 I gave orders to my brother Hanani and Hananiah the governor of the palace and of Jerusalem, for he was an upright man and feared God and turned away from evil;

3 And I said to them, Let not the gates of Jerusalem be opened until the sun is high; and while the sun is still shining, let them shut the doors and bar them and appoint watches of the inhabitants of Jerusalem, every man in his watch, and every one to be opposite his own house.

4 Now the city was large and wide; but there were few people in it, and their houses were not built.

5 ¶And my God put it into my heart, and I gathered together the nobles and the rulers of the people according to their genealogy. And I found the book of the genealogy of those who came up at the first, and I found that the names were written therein,

6 These are the people of the province who went up out of the captivity, whom Nebuchadnezzar the king of Babylon had carried away and who returned to Jerusalem and to Judah, every one to his city;

7 Those who came up with Zerubbabel: Joshua, Nehemiah, Azariah, Raamiah, Nahamael, Mordecai, Belshan, Mespereth, Bigvai, Nahum, and Baanah. The number of men of the people of Israel was this:

8 The descendants of Parosh, two thousand one hundred and seventy-two.

9 The descendants of Shephatiah, three thousand and seventy-two.

10 The descendants of Arah, six hundred and fifty-two.

11 The descendants of Shultanmoab, of the descendants of Joshua

and Joab, two thousand eight hundred and eighteen.

12 The descendants of Elam, one thousand two hundred and fifty-four.

13 The descendants of Zattu, eight hundred and fifty-five.

14 The descendants of Zaccai, seven hundred and sixty.

15 The descendants of Bani, six hundred and forty-eight.

16 The descendants of Bachi, six hundred and twenty-eight.

17 The descendants of Azgar, two thousand three hundred and twenty-two.

18 The descendants of Arhikom, six hundred and sixty-seven.

19 The descendants of Bigvai, two thousand and sixty-seven.

20 The descendants of Adon, six hundred and fifty-five.

21 The descendants of Ater, of Hezekiah, ninety-eight.

22 The descendants of Hashum, three hundred and twenty-eight.

23 The descendants of Bezai, three hundred and twenty-four.

24 The descendants of Horam, one hundred and twelve.

25 The descendants of Gibeon, ninety-five.

26 The men of Bethlehem and Netophah, one hundred and eighty-eight.[1]

27 The men of Anathoth, one hundred and twenty-eight.

28 The men of Beth-ramoth, forty-two.

29 The men of Beth-naarin, Chephirah, and Beeroth, seven hundred and forty-three.

30 The men of Geba and Ramtha, seven hundred and twenty-one.

31 The men of Michmas, one hundred and twenty-two.

32 The men of Beth-el and Ai, one hundred and twenty-three.

33 The men of Nebo, fifty-two.

34 The descendants of the other Elam, one thousand two hundred and fifty-four.

35 The descendants of Haram, three hundred and twenty.

36 The descendants of Jericho, three hundred and forty-five.

37 The descendants of Lod, Hadir, and Ono, seven hundred and twenty-one.

38 The descendants of Senaah, three thousand nine hundred and thirty.

39 ¶The priests: the descendants of Jedaiah, of the house of Joshua, nine hundred and seventy-three.

40 The descendants of Immer, one thousand and fifty-two.

41 The descendants of Pashur, one thousand two hundred and forty-seven.

42 The descendants of Hadom, one thousand and seventeen.

43 ¶The Levites: the descendants of Joshua, of Kadmiel, and of the descendants of Hodiah, seventy-four.

44 ¶The singers: the descendants of Asaph, one hundred and forty-eight.

45 ¶The porters: the descendants of Shallum, the descendants of Ater, the descendants of Altman, the descendants of Akkub, the descendants of Hatita, the descendants of Shobai, one hundred and thirty-eight.

46 ¶The Nethanites: the descendants of Azha, the descendants of Hashupha, the descendants of Tabboath.

47 The descendants of Keros, the descendants of Sia, the descendants of Paron.

48 The descendants of Lebana, the descendants of Hagabah, the descendants of Shalmai.

49 The descendants of Hanan, the descendants of Ada, the descendants of Hagar.

50 The descendants of Ana, the descendants of Dizon, the descendants of Deborah.

51 The descendants of Gazzam, the descendants of Uzza, the descendants of Phaseah.

52 The descendants of Besai, the descendants of Methanim, the descendants of Nephusin.

53 The descendants of Bakbuk, the descendants of Hakupha, the descendants of Harhur.

54 The descendants of Bazlith, the

---

[1] There is another Bethlehem in the region of Netophah not far from Nazareth.

descendants of Mehadia, the descendants of Harsha.

55 The descendants of Bezuk, the descendants of Sisera, the descendants of Tamah.

56 The descendants of Neziah, the descendants of Hatopha.

57 ¶The descendants of Solomon's servants: the descendants of Sotai, the descendants of Sophereth, the descendants of Perida.

58 The descendants of Jaala, the descendants of Daron, the descendants of Giddel.

59 The descendants of Shephatiah, the descendants of Hattil, the descendants of Bachrut, the descendants of Zobin, the descendants of Amon.

60 All Nethanites and descendants of Solomon's servants were three hundred and ninety-two.

61 These were those who came up from Tel-milkha [1] to Tel-ava and Kerob, and they spoke, but they could not show their father's genealogy nor their descent, whether they were of Israel.

62 The descendants of Banai, the descendants of Delaiah, the descendants of Tobiah, the descendants of Zekora, six hundred and forty-two.

63 ¶And of the priests: the descendants of Hananiah, the descendants of Koz, the descendants of Barzillai, who took one of the daughters of Barzillai the Gileadite to wife and was called after their name.

64 These sought their register among those who were reckoned by genealogy, but it was not found; therefore they were barred from the priesthood.

65 And the elders of the priests said to them that they should not eat of the most holy things until there should rise a high priest who would make an inquiry and see about the matter.

66 ¶The whole congregation together was forty-two thousand four hundred and seventy.

67 Besides their menservants and their maidservants, of whom there were seven thousand three hundred and thirty-three; and they had two

hundred and forty-five attendants, male and female.

68 Their camels were four hundred and thirty-five;

69 Their asses six thousand seven hundred and twenty.

70 ¶And some of the chiefs of the fathers gave to the work of the temple. The elders among the priests gave to the treasury a thousand drams of gold, fifty bowls, five hundred and thirty priests' garments.

71 And some of the chiefs of the fathers gave to the treasury for the work twenty thousand drams of gold and two thousand and two hundred pounds of silver.

72 And that which the rest of the people gave was twenty thousand drams of gold and two thousand pounds of silver and sixty-seven priests' garments.

73 So the priests and the Levites and the porters and the attendants and some of the people and the Nethanites and all Israel returned to their own cities; and when the seventh month came, the children of Israel were in their cities.

CHAPTER 8

THEN all the people gathered themselves together as one man into the street which is before the water gate; and they spoke to Ezra the scribe to bring the book of the law of Moses which the LORD had commanded concerning Israel.

2 And Ezra the priest brought the book of the law before the congregation, both of men and women and all who could hear with understanding, on the first day of the seventh month.

3 And he read the book in the street that was in front of the water gate from the morning until midday, before the men and the women and before those who could hear; and the ears of the people were attentive to the book of the law.

4 And Ezra the scribe stood upon a wooden platform which they had made that he might speak upon it;

[1] The hill of salt.

and beside him stood Mattithiah, Shema, Hananiah, Urijah, Hilkiah, and Maasiah on his right hand; and on his left hand stood Periah, Mishael, Malchiah, Hashum, Hashabiah, Zechariah, and Meshullam.

5 And Ezra opened the book of the law in the sight of all the people (for he was above all the people), and when he opened it all the people stood up;

6 And Ezra blessed the LORD, the great God. And all the people answered, Amen, Amen, lifting up their hands; and they knelt down and worshipped before the LORD with their faces to the ground.

7 Also Jeshua and his sons and Serebiah, Jamin, Akkub, Shabbethai, Hodijah, Maasiah, Kelatiah, Azariah, Jozabad, Hanan, Penaiah, and the Levites ministered to the people, explaining the law; and the people stood in their place.

8 So they read in the book of the law of God distinctly, and gave the sense, so that they understood the reading thereof.

9 ¶And Nehemiah the high priest and Ezra the priest the scribe and the Levites who ministered to the people said to all the people, This day is holy to the LORD your God; do not mourn nor weep. For all the people wept when they heard the words of the law.

10 Then he said to them, Go your way, eat and drink and send portions to them for whom nothing is prepared; for this day is holy to the LORD; and do not be sad, for this is a day of joy of the LORD, and he will be your strength.

11 So the Levites stilled all the people, saying, Hold your peace, for the day is holy; and do not weep.

12 And all the people went their way to eat and to drink and to send portions and to rejoice because they had understood the words that were declared to them.

13 ¶And on the second day were gathered together the chiefs of the fathers of all the people, the priests, and the Levites, to Ezra the scribe to understand from him the word of the law.

14 And they found it written in the law which the LORD had commanded by Moses that the children of Israel should dwell in booths in the feast of the month of Tishrin [1]

15 And that they should hear everything which Moses wrote in the book of the law; and the heralds proclaimed throughout all towns and in Jerusalem, saying, Go up to the mountain and bring olive branches and walnut branches and palm branches and branches of citrons and branches of willow trees, and make booths, as it is written in the book of the law of Moses.

16 ¶So the people went forth and brought them, and made themselves booths, every one upon the roof of his house and in their courts and in the court of the house of the LORD and in the street of the water gate and in the street of the gate of Ephraim.

17 And all the people of those who had returned from the captivity made booths and dwelt in the booths; for since the days of Joshua the son of Nun to that day the children of Israel had not done so. And there was a very great gladness.

18 Also day by day, from the first day to the last day, they read in the book of the law of the LORD. And they celebrated the feast for seven days; and on the eighth day was a solemn assembly, according to that which is written.

CHAPTER 9

NOW on the twenty-fourth day of this month, the children of Israel were assembled with fasting and with sackcloth and ashes upon them.

2 And the descendants of Israel separated themselves from all the Gentiles, and stood and confessed their sins and the sins of their fathers.

3 And they stood up in their place and read in the book of the law of the LORD their God one fourth part of the day; and another fourth part

[1] October.

they confessed, and worshipped the LORD their God.

4 ¶Then the chiefs over the Levites, Joshua, Kadmiel, Bani, Heshabiah, Sherebiah, Hodiah, Shebaniah, and Pethahiah, stood up and prayed with a loud voice before the LORD their God.

5 Then the Levites, Joshua, Kadmiel, Bani, Heshabiah, Sherebiah, Hodiah, Shebaniah, and Pethahiah, said, Stand up and bless the LORD your God for ever and ever, and blessed be thy glorious name, which is exalted above all creations and praises.

6 Thou alone art the LORD; thou hast made heaven, the heaven of heavens, with all their host, the earth and all things that are therein, the waters and all that is therein, and thou preservest them all; and the host of heaven worships thee.

7 Thou art the LORD, the God who didst choose Abram and brought him forth out of Ur of the Chaldeans, and didst change his name to Abraham;

8 And didst find his heart pure before thee, and didst make a covenant with him to give him the land of the Canaanites, the Hittites, the Amorites, the Perizzites, the Hivites, the Jebusites, and the Girgashites, to give it to his descendants, and thou hast performed thy words with him, for thou art righteous;

9 And thou didst see the affliction of our fathers in Egypt and hear their cry by the Red Sea;

10 And didst show signs and wonders upon Pharaoh and upon all his servants and on all the people of his land; for thou knewest that they dealt wrongly with thy people. So didst thou get thee a name, as it is this day.

11 And thou didst open a passage in the sea before them, so that they went through the midst of the sea on the dry land; and their persecutors thou didst throw into the depths of the sea, as a stone that sinks in the mighty waters.

12 Moreover thou hast led them in the day by a cloudy pillar; and in the night by a pillar of fire, to give them light in the way in which they should go.

13 Thou didst come down also upon mount Sinai and speak with them from heaven, and didst give them right judgments and true laws, good statutes and commandments;

14 And thou didst make known to them thy holy sabbath and commandments and statutes and laws which thou commandedst by the hand of Moses thy servant;

15 And didst give them bread from heaven for their hunger, and brought forth water for them out of the rock for their thirst, and promised them that they should go in to possess the land which thy hand hadst sworn to give them.

16 But they and their fathers dealt wickedly and were stubborn and did not give ear to thy commandments,

17 And refused to obey, neither were mindful of thy wonders that thou didst among them; but turned their hearts to their evil works; yet thou art a God ready to pardon, gracious and merciful, slow to anger, and ready to hear petitions, and didst not forsake them.

18 Yea, when they had made for themselves a molten calf, and said, This is your God, O Israel, who brought you up out of the land of Egypt, and they wrought great wickedness;

19 Yet thou in thy manifold mercies didst not forsake them in the wilderness; the pillar of the cloud did not depart from them by day, to lead them on their journey; neither the pillar of fire by night, to lighten the way by which they should go.

20 Thou gavest also thy good spirit to instruct them, and didst not withhold manna from their mouths, and gavest them water for their thirst.

21 Yea, for forty years didst thou sustain them in the wilderness, and they lacked nothing; their clothes did not wear out, and their shoes had no holes in them.

22 Moreover thou gavest them the kingdoms of the Gentiles, and didst divide to them the land to every man;

so they possessed the land of Sihon and the land of the king of Heshbon and the land of Og king of Bashan.

23 Their children also thou didst multiply as the stars of heaven, and thou didst bring them into the land concerning which thou hadst promised to their fathers that they should go in to possess it.

24 So their children went in and possessed the land, and thou didst defeat before them the inhabitants of the land of the Canaanites, and didst deliver them into their hands with their kings and the people of the land, that they might do with them as they would.

25 And they captured fortified cities and a fertile land, and possessed houses full of all good things, wells digged, vineyards and olive orchards and fruit trees in abundance; so they did eat and were filled and became rich and delighted themselves in thy great goodness.

26 Nevertheless, they were disobedient and transgressed against thee and cast thy law out of their counsels and slew thy prophets, who warned them to turn to thee, and they committed great wickedness.

27 Therefore thou didst deliver them into the hand of their enemies, who distressed them; and in the time of their distress, when they prayed to thee, thou didst hear them from heaven; and according to thy manifold mercies thou gavest them a saviour, who saved them out of the hand of their enemies.

28 But after they had rest, they did evil again before thee; therefore thou didst leave them in the hand of their enemies, so that they had dominion over them; yet when they returned and prayed before thee, thou didst hear them from heaven; and many times didst thou save them according to thy great mercies.

29 And thou didst testify against them, that thou mightest bring them again to thy law; yet they dealt wrongfully and did not obey thy commandments, but sinned against thy judgments (which if a man ob-

serve them, he shall live in them); and they conspired and became stubborn and would not listen.

30 Yet many years didst thou admonish them, and didst testify against them by thy spirit through thy prophets; yet they would not obey; therefore thou didst deliver them into the hand of the Gentiles.

31 Nevertheless because of thy great mercy thou didst not utterly destroy them nor forsake them; for thou art a gracious and merciful God.

32 Now therefore, our God, the great, the mighty, and the holy God, who keepest covenant and truth, let there not be hidden from before thee all the hardship that has come upon us, upon our kings, upon our princes, upon our priests, and upon our prophets, and upon our fathers, and upon all the people, since the day of the kings of Assyria to this day.

33 Nevertheless thou art righteous in all that has come upon us; for thou hast done right, but we have done wickedly;

34 Neither have our kings, our princes, our priests, nor our fathers, kept thy law, nor given ear to thy commandments and thy testimonies, wherewith thou didst testify against them.

35 And they renounced thy kingdom and thy great blessing that thou gavest them and the good and fertile land that thou gavest them; neither did they serve thee nor did they turn away from their wicked works;

36 Therefore we are servants this day; and as for the land that thou gavest to our fathers to eat its fruit and its good things, behold, we are servants in it,

37 And its produce is taken by the kings whom thou hast set over us because of our sins; also they have dominion over our bodies and over our cattle at their pleasure, and we are living in a great distress.

38 And in view of all these things we make a sure covenant and bear witness over the seal, even our elders, Levites, and priests, and all those who have been spared of us.

CHAPTER 10

NOW those who took an oath and sealed it were: Nehemiah, the elder, the son of Hananiah, the high priest, and Zerahiah,

2 Seraiah, Azariah, Jeremiah,

3 Pashur, Amariah, Malchijah, Shepatiah,

4 Hattush, Shecaniah, Malluch,

5 Shakum, Azmoth, Ebariah,

6 Daniel, Gebiton, Baruch,

7 Meshullam, Abijah, Benjamin,

8 Maasiah, Bilgai, Shemaiah; these were the priests.

9 And the Levites: Joshua the son of Azaniah, Bani, Mabnai, Hadar, and Kadmiah;

10 And their brethren: Shecaniah, Urijah, Kelatiah, Pelatiah, Hanan,

11 Micha, Rehob, Hashabiah,

12 Zaccur, Sherebiah, Shecaniah,

13 Hodijah, the son of Bani.

14 The chiefs of the people: Parosh, Shalit-moab, Elam, the Zetites.

15 The sons of Azgar, the sons of Adonijah,

16 Bigvai and Adon,

17 Ater, Hezekiah, Azzur,

18 Urijah, Hashum, Bezai,

19 Hoziph, Anathoth, Nebai,

20 Mephgnish, Meshallum, Aziphi,

21 Meshezapael, Zadok, Jehoiadah,

22 Pelatiah, Hanan, Anaiah,

23 Hoshea, Hananiah, Joshua,

24 Hallosh, Pileha, Shobek,

25 Arhum, Hoshabiah, Maasiah,

26 And Ahijah, Hanan, Anan,

27 Malluch, Haram, Baanah.

28 ¶And the rest of the people, the priests, the Levites, the porters, the singers, the servants, and all those who had separated themselves from the people of the lands to return to the law of the LORD, both they and their wives, their sons and their daughters and every one having knowledge and understanding.

29 Strengthened their brethren, their neighbors, taking oaths and making a covenant to walk in the LORD's law which he gave by Moses the servant of God, and to observe and do all the commandments of the LORD our LORD and his judgments and his statutes;

30 And that we would not give our daughters to the people of the land nor take their daughters for our sons;

31 And if the people of the land should bring wares or provisions on the sabbath day to sell, we would not buy it of them, and whosoever should engage his animal in service on the sabbath day, he would not receive hire, nor should he carry a burden on the sabbath day because it is holy; and in the seventh year we would forego all debts due to us.

32 We also confirmed upon ourselves the ordinances, to give the third part of a shekel on the sabbath for the work of the house of our God;

33 For the shewbread and for the continual meal offering and for the continual burnt offering of the sabbaths, the new moons, the feasts, and the holy things, and for the sin offerings to make an atonement for Israel and for all the work of the house of our God.

34 And they cast lots among the priests, the Levites, and the people, for the wood offering, to bring it into the house of the LORD our God, as it is written in the book of law;

35 And to bring the first fruits of our ground and the first fruits of all fruit of the trees, year by year, to the house of the LORD;

36 Also the first-born of our sons and of our cattle, as it is written in the law of the LORD, and the firstlings of our herds and of our flocks, to bring to the house of our God, to the priests who minister in the house of our God;

37 And to give the first fruits of our dough, our threshing floors, and the fruit of all manner of trees, of wine and of oil, to the priests who minister before our God; and the tithes of our ground to the Levites, that the same Levites might take the tithes from all the country towns.

38 And the priest the son of Aaron shall be included with the Levites in the distribution of their tithes; and the Levites shall bring up the tithe

of the tithes to the house of our God, to the storehouses, into the treasure house.

39 For the children of Israel and the descendants of Levi shall bring the offerings of the grain, of the wine, and the oil to the storehouses where are the vessels of the sanctuary, and the priests, the Levites, the porters, and the guards shall not forsake the house of our God.

CHAPTER 11

LET the elders of the people dwell in Jerusalem; and the rest of the people shall cast lots to bring one out of ten to dwell in Jerusalem the holy city and the remaining nine-tenths to dwell in towns.

2 And the people blessed all the men who willingly offered themselves to dwell in Jerusalem.

3 ¶Now these are the chiefs of the province who dwelt in Jerusalem and in the towns of Judah (they dwelt every one in his own possession in their towns in Israel), along with the priests, the Levites, and some of the people, and also the descendants of Solomon's servants who dwelt in Jerusalem,

4 And in addition some of the children of Judah and of the children of Benjamin. And of the children of Judah: Nethaniah the son of Uzziah, the son of Zechariah, the son of Amariah, the son of Shephatiah, the son of Mahalalael. Of the descendants of Perez:

5 Maasiah the son of Baruch, the son of Colhozeh, the son of Neriah, the son of Azariah, the son of Jonadab, the son of Zechariah, the son of Shelah.

6 All the descendants of Perez who dwelt in Jerusalem were four hundred and sixty-eight valiant men.

7 And these are the descendants of Benjamin: Selah the son of Meshullam, the son of Joda, the son of Peraiah, the son of Kolaiah, the son of Maasiah, the son of Athnael, the son of Isaiah.

8 And after him were nine hundred and twenty-eight others.

9 And Joel the son of Zechariah was their overseer; and Judah the son of Senuah was second over the city.

10 Of the priests: Berachiah the son of Jehoiadah,

11 Seraiah the son of Hilkiah, the son of Meshullam, the son of Zadok, the son of Meraioth, the son of Ahitub, was the ruler over the house of the LORD.

12 And his brethren who did the work inside of the house were eight hundred and twenty-two; and Azariah the son of Jeroham, the son of Pelahiah, the son of Amzar, the son of Zechariah, the son of Pashur, the son of Malchiah,

13 And their brethren, chiefs of their fathers, two hundred and forty-two; and Amashai the son of Azarael, the son of Ahasai, the son of Meshillemoth, the son of Immer,

14 And their brethren, mighty men of valour, one hundred and twenty-eight; and their overseer was Zabdiel the son of one of the great men.

15 Also the Levites: Shemaiah the son of Joshua, the son of Azrikam, the son of Hashabiah, the son of Banni, the son of Shabbethai.

16 And Zozabar was in charge of outside work of the house of the LORD.

17 And of the chiefs of the Levites: Mattaniah, the son of Micha, the son of Zabdi, the son of Asaph, the principal among the Jews to begin the thanksgiving in prayer; and Bakbukah the second among his brethren, and Aira the son of Shammua, the son of Galal, the son of Jethron.

18 All the Levites in the holy city were two hundred and eighty-four.

19 Moreover the porters, Akkub and Altman, and their brethren who kept the gates, were one hundred and seventy-two.

20 ¶And the rest of Israel, of the priests and the Levites, were in all the cities of Judah, every one in his inheritance.

21 And their servants settled down every one in charge of his work and his plough.

22 The overseer of the Levites at Jerusalem was Abdai the son of Bani, the son of Hashabiah, the son of Mattaniah, the son of Micha, of the sons of Asaph, who ministered over the work of the house of the LORD.

23 For there was a commandment from the king concerning them and a decree concerning the singers daily.

24 And Pethahiah the son of Meshumael, of the descendants of Zerah, the son of Judah, was in charge of whatever the king had commanded concerning every man and over the numbering of the people

25 And over their overseers and over their villages and over their fields. Now some of the children of Judah dwelt in Koriath-arba and in its villages, and in Ribon and in its villages, and in Kebazeel and in its villages.

26 And in Hoshah and in Moladah and in Beth-phelet

27 And in Hazar-shua and in Beer-sheba and in the villages thereof

28 And in Zinklag and in Mekiah and in the villages thereof

29 And in En-rimmon and in Zadah and in Jarmuth,

30 Zanoah, Adullam, and in their villages, in Lachish and its villages, in Azekah and in its villages. And they dwelt from Beer-sheba as far as the valley of Hinnom.

31 The children of Benjamin also dwelt from Ramtha of Michmash, Ai, Beth-el, and in their villages,

32 And at Anothoth, Aojab, Ananiah,

33 Hazor, Ramtha, Gittaim,

34 Hadar, Zebaon, Neballat,

35 Lod and Ono, Niha and Harsha.

36 And of the Levites were divisions in Judah and in Benjamin.

CHAPTER 12

NOW these are the priests and the Levites who came up with Zerubbabel the son of Shealtiel and Joshua: Seraiah, Azma, Ezra,

2 Amariah, Malluch, Hattush,

3 Shechaniah, Rehum, Meremoth,

4 Ada, Azti, Abijah,

5 Benjamin, Meadriah, Belagiah,

6 Shemaiah, Nedo, Jedaiah,

7 Sallu, Amok, Hilkiah, Jedaiah. These were the chiefs of the priests and of their brethren in the days of Joshua.

8 Moreover the Levites: Joshua and his sons, Kadmiah, Sherebiah, Judah, and Mattaniah, who were in charge to begin the thanksgiving, he and his brethren.

9 Also Bakbukah and Unni; their brethren were opposite to them in the watches.

10 ¶And Joshua begat Joiakim, Joiakim begat Eliashib, and Eliashib begat Jehoiadah,

11 And Jehoiadah begat Jonathan, and Jonathan begat Jaddua.

12 And in the days of Joiakim were priests, the chiefs of the fathers; namely, Seraiah, Amariah, Jeremiah, Hananiah;

13 Azariah, Meshellum, Amariah, Johanan;

14 Malchiah, Jonathan, Shechaniah, Joseph;

15 Haram, Ariah, Meremoth, Lahmai;

16 Iddo, Zechariah, Gibton, Meshullam;

17 Abijah, Zichri, Benjamin, Moadiah, Polta;

18 Bilgah, Shammua, Shemaiah, Jonathan;

19 Jehoidah, Mathnai, Jedaiah, Uzzi;

20 Sallai, Kallai, Amok, Ebid;

21 Hilkiah, Hashabiah, Hodah, Nathanael.

22 The Levites in the days of Eliashib, Jehoiadah, Johanan, and Jaddua, were recorded chiefs of the fathers; also the priests, to the reign of Darius the Persian.

23 The descendants of Levi, the chiefs of the fathers, were written in the book of the chronicles, even until the days of Johanan the son of Eliashib.

24 And the chiefs of the Levites were Hashbiel, Sherebiah, Joshua the son of Kadmiel, with their brethren opposite them, to praise and to give thanks, according to the commandments of David the prophet of the LORD, watch opposite watch.

25 Mattaniah,   Bakai,   Obadiah,

Shallum, Atlam, and Akkub were porters keeping watch at the gates.

26 These were in the days of Joiakim the son of Joshua, the son of Jozadak, and in the days of Nehemiah the governor and of Ezra the priest and scribe.

27 ¶And when the wall of Jerusalem was finished, they gathered the Levites together in all their places, to bring them to Jerusalem to celebrate the dedication with gladness and rejoicing, with thanksgiving and with singing, with cymbals and with harps.

28 And the sons of the singers gathered themselves together from the plain country round about Jerusalem and from the villages of Netopha;

29 Also from Beth-gilgal and out of the valley of Gibeah and Armoth; for the singers had built for themselves villages round about Jerusalem.

30 And the priests and the Levites purified themselves and purified the people and the gates and the wall.

31 Then I brought up the chieftains of Judah upon the wall, and appointed two great companies; and they walked upon the wall toward the right of the great gate;

32 And with them went Hoshaiah and the half of the chieftains of Judah

33 And Azrael, Ezra, and Meshullam,

34 Judah and Benjamin and Shemaiah and Jeremiah

35 And certain of the priests' sons with trumpets; namely, Zechariah the son of Jonathan, the son of Shemaiah, the son of Mattaniah, the son of Malka, the son of Zaccur, the son of Asaph:

36 And his brethren, Shemaiah, Azrael, Melal, Gelal, Ater, Nathanael, Hanani, and Judah, with the musical instruments of David the prophet and servant of the LORD and Ezra the scribe went before them, above the fountain gate.

37 And opposite them, they went up by the stairs of the city of David, at the ascent of the wall, above the house of David, to the great gate eastward.

38 And they gave thanks and went up upon the wall, and I after them, and the half of the people went up upon the wall, and they stood upon the great tower and upon the high wall and upon the broad wall;

39 And from above the gate of Ephraim, as far as the old gate to the fish gate; and from the tower of Hananeel, as far as the great tower, even to the sheep gate; and they stood still in the great gate.

40 Then the two companies that gave thanks entered the house of the LORD, and I and the half of the chieftains who were with me;

41 And the priests: Eliakim, Maasiah, Malhin, Michaiah, Eliho, Ananai, Zechariah, and Hananiah;

42 And those with trumpets: Maasiah, Shemaiah, Eleazar, Uzzi, Johanan, Malchijah, Elam, Ezer, and Shamua, the singers, and Zerahiah the leader.

43 Also that day they offered great sacrifices and rejoiced; for the LORD had made them rejoice with great joy; the wives also and the children rejoiced; so that the joy of Jerusalem was heard even afar off.

44 ¶And on that day certain men were appointed over the chambers of the king's storehouses to gather into them the offerings, the first fruits, and the tithes of the towns, as it is written in the book of the law, for the priests and Levites, since the Jews were rejoicing because the priests and the Levites had stood up keeping watch in the house of their God.

45 And those who had charge of the ceremonial of purification, and the singers and the porters, served according to the commandment of David and of Solomon his son.

46 For Asaph was in charge in the day of David, and he stood up at the head of the singers and sang praises and gave thanks before the LORD God.

47 And all Israel in the days of Zerubbabel and in the days of Nehemiah gave gifts to the singers and to the porters, every day his portion; and they set aside holy things to the Levites; and the Levites set them aside for the descendants of Aaron.

CHAPTER 13

ON that day, when the book of the law of Moses was being read in the audience of the people, therein was found written that the Ammonites and the Moabites should never enter the congregation of the LORD for ever,

2 Because they did not meet the children of Israel with bread and water, but hired Baalam to curse them; but our God turned his curses into blessings.

3 Now when they had heard the words of the law, they separated from Israel all the mixed multitude.

4 ¶And before this, Eliashib the priest had come and built there for himself a large court,

5 Where they had formerly put the meal offerings, the frankincense, and the vessels containing the tithes of grain, the wine, and the oil, which were commanded to be given to the Levites and the singers and the porters, and the offerings for the priests.

6 But while these things took place I was not in Jerusalem; for in the thirty-second year of Artakhshist king of Babylon, I came to the king, and after certain days, I asked leave of the king;

7 And I came to Jerusalem, and understood the evil that Eliashib did for Tobiah in preparing for him a chamber in the court of the house of the LORD.

8 And it grieved me exceedingly; so I threw all the household stuff of Tobiah out into the street, outside the court.

9 Then I commanded, and they cleansed the court; and I brought back thither the vessels of the house of the LORD, with the meal offerings and the frankincense.

10 ¶And I learned that the portions of the Levites had not been given them and that the Levites and the singers and they that did the work had fled every one to his field.

11 Then I contended with the chiefs, and said to them, Why is the house of the LORD forsaken? And I gathered them together and set them in their place.

12 Then all the Jews brought the tithe of the grain and the wine and the oil to the storehouses.

13 And I appointed in charge of the storehouses, Shelemiah the priest and Zadok the scribe and of the Levites, Peraiah; and with them was Hanan the son of Zaccur, the son of Mattaniah; for they were counted faithful, and they were chosen by lot to be leaders over their brethren.

14 Remember me, O my God, concerning this, and do not wipe out my good deeds that I have done for the house of my God and for the rites thereof.

15 ¶In those days I saw in Judah highways filled with traffic on the sabbath, and men bringing burdens loaded on asses; and also wine, grapes, figs, and all manner of burdens which they brought into Jerusalem on the sabbath day; and I testified against them that they might not sell game.

16 And not to bring fish, neither to sell on the sabbath to the children of Judah and in Jerusalem.

17 Then I contended with the chiefs of Judah and said to them, Why are you doing this evil thing and profaning the sabbath day?

18 Your fathers did likewise, and God brought all this misfortune upon us and upon this city, yet you bring more wrath and anger upon Israel by profaning the sabbath.

19 Now when the gates of Jerusalem were opened before the sabbath, I commanded that the gates should be shut, and charged that they should not be opened till after the sabbath; and I set some of my servants at the gates, that there should be no burden brought in on the sabbath day.

20 So the merchants and the sellers of all kinds of merchandise lodged outside Jerusalem once or twice.

21 Then I testified against them and said to them, Why do you not enter by the gate of the wall while the sun is still high? Now if you refuse to obey this command, I will punish you. From that time forth

they did not enter on the sabbath.

22 And I commanded the Levites that they should cleanse themselves and that the guards and the porters should come and keep the gates to sanctify the sabbath day. O my God, remember me concerning this also, and spare me according to the abundance of thy mercy.

23 ¶In those days I also saw Jews who had married foreign wives of Ashdod, of Ammon, and of Moab;

24 And their children spoke half in the language of Ashdod and in the other half they could not intelligently speak in the Jewish language, but according to the language of each people.

25 And I contended with them and cursed them and smote some of them and buried them and made the others swear by God, saying, You shall not give your daughters to their sons, nor take of their daughters to your sons or for yourselves.

26 Solomon king of Israel sinned by these things. Yet among many nations there was no king like him, who was beloved by his God, and God made him king over all Israel; nevertheless even him did foreign women cause to sin.

27 And this thing was reported to you, and yet you committed this great evil, to transgress against our God in marrying foreign wives.

28 And one of the sons of Jehoiadah, the son of Eliashib the high priest, was son-in-law to Sanballat the Horonite; therefore I chased him from me.

29 Remember me, O my God, concerning the rest of the priesthood and concerning the rest of the priests and the Levites;

30 Thus I cleansed them from all the Gentiles and appointed them over their duties, both the priests and the Levites, every one in his work;

31 And for the gift offerings and the holy things in their appointed times, and for their feasts and for the first fruits. Remember me, O my God, for good.

THE BOOK OF

ESTHER

CHAPTER 1

NOW it came to pass in the days of Akhshirash,[1] who reigned from India even to Ethiopia, over one hundred and twenty-seven provinces,

2 In the days when King Akhshirash sat on the throne of his kingdom, which was in Shushan the palace,

3 In the third year of his reign, he made a great feast for all his princes and his servants, the mighty men of Persia and Media and the king's nobles and the governors of the provinces being before him.

4 Then he showed them the riches of his glorious kingdom and the honor of his excellent majesty many days, even a hundred and eighty days.

5 And when these days were completed, the king made a feast to all the people who were present in Shushan the palace, both great and small, seven days, in the court of the garden of the king's palace;

6 There were curtains of white cotton and wool, and hangings of violet, fastened with cords of fine linen and purple to silver rings and pillars of marble; the couches were of gold and

---

[1] Western versions, Ahasuerus.

silver, upon a pavement of marble, and the carpets were of fine white linen and silk.

7 And they gave the guests drink in vessels of gold (the vessels being different one from another), and royal wine was in abundance, according to the generosity of the king.

8 And the drinking was according to the law; none did compel; for so the king had commanded to all the stewards of his household, that they should do according to every man's pleasure.

9 Also Vashti the queen made a great feast for all the women in the royal house which belonged to King Akhshirash.

10 ¶On the seventh day, when the heart of the king was merry with wine, he commanded the eunuchs, Biztha, Rahbona, Bigtha, and Abagtha, Terash, Zethar, and Carcash, the seven eunuchs who served in the presence of Akhshirash the king,

11 To bring Vashti the queen before the king with the royal crown, to show the people and the princes her beauty; for she was fair to look upon.

12 But Queen Vashti refused to come at the king's command by the eunuchs; therefore the king was very wroth and his anger burned in him.

13 ¶Then the king spoke to the wise men who knew the times (for this was the king's custom, he discussed matters in the presence of all who knew law and judgment).

14 And those who were next to him were Barnashi, Shetar, Armoth, Remos, Tarshish, Mesriah, Meaucan, the seven princes of Persia and Media who sat in the presence of the king and were seen before him at the gate of the royal palace.

15 And he said, What shall we do to Queen Vashti, according to law, because she has not performed the command of King Akhshirash by the eunuchs?

16 And Meaucan said before the king and the princes, Vashti the queen has not done wrong to the king only, but also to all the princes, and to all the people that are in all the provinces of King Akhshirash.

17 For this deed of the queen shall reach all women, so that their husbands shall be despised in their eyes, and they shall say, King Akhshirash commanded Vashti the queen to be brought in before him, but she did not come.

18 Even this very day the princes of Persia and Media who have heard of the deed of the queen shall tell it to all the king's princes. Thus there shall be much contempt and wrath.

19 If it please the king, let there go forth a royal decree from him, and let it be written among the laws of Media and Persia, that it may not be altered, that Vashti the queen is to come no more before King Akhshirash; and let the king give her royal estate to another who is better than she.

20 And the king's decree shall be proclaimed and published throughout all his empire (for it is great), that all wives shall give honor to their husbands, both great and small.

21 And the saying pleased the king and the princes; and the king did according to the word of Meaucan;

22 And he sent letters to all the king's provinces, into every province according to the writing thereof and to every people according to its own language, that every man should bear rule in his own house and that it should be published according to the language of every people.

CHAPTER 2

AFTER these things, when the wrath of King Akhshirash was appeased, he remembered Vashti the queen and what she had done and what was decreed against her.

2 Then the king's servants and his ministers said to him, Let there be beautiful young virgins sought for the king;

3 And let the king appoint officers in all the provinces, that they may gather together all the beautiful young virgins to the house of the women, to the custody of Hegai the eunuch, keeper of women; and let

their things for purification be given them;

4 And let the maiden who pleases the king be queen instead of Vashti. And the thing pleased the king; and he did so.

5 ¶Now there was a certain Jew in Shushan the palace, whose name was Mordecai, the son of Jair, the son of Shimei, the son of Kish, a Benjamite;

6 Who had been carried away from Jerusalem with the captivity which had been carried away with Jeconiah king of Judah, whom Nebuchadnezzar the king of Babylon had carried away.

7 And he brought up Hadassah, that is Esther, his uncle's daughter; for she had neither father nor mother, and the maid was fair and beautiful; and when her father and mother died, Mordecai took her for his own daughter.

8 ¶So when the king's commandment and his decree were heard, and when many virgins were gathered together in Shushan the palace in the custody of Hegai, the eunuch, that Esther was brought also to the king's house to the custody of Hegai, the keeper of the women.

9 And the maiden pleased him, and she obtained favor of him; and he speedily gave her things for purification, such things which were her portion, and seven maidens who were worthy to be given her from the king's house; and he preferred her and her maidens much more than all the other women.

10 Esther had not made known her people nor her kindred; for Mordecai had charged her that she should not make it known.

11 And Mordecai walked every day before the court of the women's house to learn how Esther did and what should become of her.

12 ¶Now when the turn of each maiden was come to go in before King Akhshirash, after she had been twelve months, according to the manner of the women (for so were the days of their purification accomplished, every six days with oil of myrrh and every six days with spices and with other things for the purifying of the women);

13 Then thus came every maiden before the king; whatever she desired was given her to go with her out of the house of the women to the king's house.

14 In the evening she went in, and in the morning she returned to the house of the women to the custody of Shangashgeshir the king's eunuch, the keeper of the concubines; she did not come in to the king unless the king delighted in her and she was called by name.

15 ¶Now when the turn of Esther, the daughter of Abihail the uncle of Mordecai, who had taken her for his daughter, came to go in before the king, she asked for nothing but what Hegai the king's eunuch, the keeper of the women, appointed. And Esther obtained favor in the sight of all those who saw her.

16 So Esther entered before King Akhshirash into his royal house in the tenth month, that is, January, in the fourth year of his reign.

17 And the king loved Esther more than all the other women, and she obtained grace and favor in his sight more than all the other virgins; so that he set the royal crown upon her head and made her queen instead of Vashti.

18 Then the king made a great feast to all his princes, even Esther's feast; and he granted relief to the provinces and gave gifts, according to the generosity of the king.

19 And when the virgins were gathered together the second time, Mordecai was sitting in the king's gate.

20 But Esther had not yet made known her kindred nor her people, as Mordecai had charged her; for Esther obeyed the commandment of Mordecai, like as when she was faithfully brought up with him.

21 ¶In those days, while Mordecai was sitting at the king's gate, two of the king's eunuchs, Bigthan and Teresh, of those who kept the door, were wroth and sought to lay hands on King Akhshirash.

22 And the thing became known to Mordecai, who told it to Esther the queen; and Esther told the king in Mordecai's name.

23 And when the matter was investigated and found to be so, they were both nailed on crosses, and it was written in the book of chronicles before the king.

CHAPTER 3

AFTER these things King Akhshirash promoted Haman the son of Hammadatha the Agagite, and advanced him, and set his seat above all the princes who were with him.

2 And all the king's servants who were at the king's gate bowed down and did obeisance to Haman; for the king had so commanded concerning him. But Mordecai would not bow nor pay him reverence.

3 Then the king's servants who were at the king's gate said to Mordecai, Why do you transgress the king's commandment?

4 Now it came to pass when they spoke daily to him and he would not listen to them, they told Haman, to know whether Mordecai's words were the truth; for he had told them that he was a Jew.

5 And when Haman saw that Mordecai did not bow down nor do him obeisance, then Haman was full of wrath against Mordecai.

6 And he thought it nothing to lay hands on Mordecai alone; for they had revealed to him the people of Mordecai; wherefore Haman sought to destroy all the Jews who were throughout the whole kingdom of Akhshirash, even the people of Mordecai.

7 ¶In the first month, that is, the month of Nisan,[1] in the twelfth year of King Akhshirash, they cast lots before Haman from day to day and from month to month. Then in the twelfth month, that is, the month of Adar,[2]

8 ¶Haman said to King Akhshirash, There is a certain people scattered abroad and dispersed among the people in all the provinces of King Akhshirash; and their laws are different from those of all other people; and they do not keep the king's laws; therefore the king ought not to spare them.

9 If it please the king, let it be written that they may be destroyed; and I will weigh ten thousand talents of silver to the hands of those who have charge of the business, to bring it into the king's treasuries.

10 And the king took his ring from his hand and gave it to Haman the son of Hammadatha the Agagite, the enemy of the Jews.

11 And the king said to Haman, The silver is given to you, the people also, to do with them as it seems good to you.

12 Then the king's scribe was called on the thirteenth day of the first month, and there was written according to all that Haman had commanded to the king's commanders and to the governors that were over every province and to the princes of every people of every province according to the writing thereof and to every people according to their language; in the name of King Akhshirash it was written and sealed with the king's ring.

13 And the letters were sent by couriers to all the king's provinces, to destroy, to kill, and to cause to perish all Jews, both young and old, little children and women, in one day, even upon the thirteenth day of the twelfth month, which is the month Adar, and to take their wealth for a prey. In the same day on the thirteenth day of the month of Adar they were written.

14 The copy of the writing was given in every province, commanding all the people to be ready for that day.

15 The couriers went out, being hastened by the king's command, and the decree was given in Shushan the palace. And the king and Haman sat down to drink; but the city of Shushan was in an uproar.

---

[1] April.   [2] March.

CHAPTER 4

WHEN Mordecai learned all that was done, he tore his clothes and put on sackcloth and ashes, and went out into the midst of the city, howling with a loud and bitter lamentation;

2 And came even as far as the king's gate; for it was unlawful for any man to enter into the king's gate clothed with sackcloth.

3 And in every province, wherever the king's decree came, there was great mourning among the Jews, and fasting and weeping and wailing; and many lay in sackcloth and ashes.

4 ¶So when Esther's eunuchs and her maidens came in and told her, the queen was exceedingly disturbed; and she sent garments to clothe Mordecai and to take away his sackcloth from him; but he did not accept them.

5 Then Esther called for Hathan, one of the king's eunuchs, who had been appointed to attend her, and ordered him to go to Mordecai to know what this was and why it was.

6 So Hathan went forth to Mordecai to the streets of the city which were in front of the king's gate.

7 And Mordecai told him of all that had happened to him and of the sum of money that Haman had promised to pay to the king's treasuries for the Jews, to destroy them.

8 He also gave him a copy of the writing of the decree that was issued in Shushan the palace, to show it to Esther, and to charge her to go in to the king to make supplication to him and to make request before him for her people.

9 And Hathan came in and told Esther the words of Mordecai.

10 ¶Again Esther spoke to Hathan and commanded him to go to Mordecai, saying,

11 All the king's servants know that whosoever, whether man or woman, comes to the king into the inner court who is not called, for him there is but one law to put him to death, except the one to whom the king shall hold out the golden sceptre, that he may live; but I have not been called to come in to the king these three days.

12 And he told Mordecai Esther's words.

13 Then Mordecai told him to tell Esther, Think not in yourself that you shall escape because you are in the king's house, more than all the other Jews.

14 For if you altogether remain silent this time, then relief and salvation shall arise to the Jews from another place; but you and your father's house shall be destroyed; and who knows whether you have been called to come to the kingdom for such a time as this?

15 ¶Then Esther told him to return Mordecai this answer:

16 Go, gather together all the Jews who are present in Shushan the palace, and fast for me, and neither eat nor drink for three days, night or day; I also and my maidens will fast likewise; and then I will go in to the king, which is not according to the law; and if I perish, I perish.

17 So Mordecai went his way and did according to all that Esther had commanded him.

CHAPTER 5

NOW on the third day Esther put on her royal apparel and stood in the inner court of the king's house, opposite the king's house; and the king was sitting upon his royal throne opposite the gate of the house.

2 And when the king saw Esther the queen standing in the court, she obtained favor in his sight; and the king held out to Esther the golden sceptre that was in his hand. So Esther drew near and held the top of the golden sceptre.

3 Then the king said to her, What troubles you, Queen Esther? And what is your request? It shall be given you even to the half of the kingdom.

4 And Esther answered, If it please the king, let the king and Haman

come to the banquet that I have prepared for him.

5 Then the king said, Make haste to find Haman, that he may do as Esther has said. So the king and Haman came to the banquet that Esther had prepared.

6 ¶And the king said to Esther at the banquet of wine, What is your petition? And it shall be granted you; and what is your request? Even to the half of the kingdom it shall be given you.

7 Then Esther answered and said, My petition and my request is this:

8 If I have found favor in your sight, O king, and if it please the king to grant my petition and to perform my request, let the king and Haman come to the banquet that I shall prepare for them tomorrow, as the king has said.

9 ¶Then Haman went out that day joyful and glad in his heart; but when Haman saw Mordecai sitting in the king's gate, that he neither stood up nor moved for him, Haman was full of indignation against Mordecai.

10 Nevertheless Haman restrained himself; and when he went to his home, he sent and brought all his friends and Zeresh his wife.

11 And Haman told them of the glory of his riches and the multitude of his children, and how the king had promoted him and how he had advanced him above the princes and the servants of the king.

12 Haman said moreover, Even Esther the queen did let no man come in with the king to the banquet that she had prepared but me; and tomorrow I am invited by her together with the king.

13 Yet all this does not suffice me, so long as I see Mordecai the Jew sitting at the king's gate; for he does not move from before me.

14 ¶Then said Zeresh his wife and all his friends to him, Let a gallows be made fifty cubits high, and in the morning speak to the king that Mordecai may be hanged upon it; then go in merrily with the king to the banquet. And the thing pleased Haman exceedingly; and he had the gallows made.

CHAPTER 6

ON that night the king could not sleep, and he commanded to bring the book of the records of the chronicles; and they were read before the king.

2 And it was found written that Mordecai had told of Bigthan and Teresh, two of the king's eunuchs, the keepers of the door, who had sought to lay hands on King Akhshirash.

3 And the king said, What honor and dignity have been conferred upon Mordecai for this? Then the king's servants and his ministers said to him, There is nothing done for him.

4 ¶And the king said, Who is in the court? Now Haman was come into the outer court of the king's house to speak to the king to hang Mordecai on the gallows that he had prepared for him.

5 So the king's servants said to him, Behold, Haman is standing in the court. And the king said, Let him come in.

6 So Haman came in. And the king said to him, What shall be done to the man whom the king delights to honor? Now Haman thought in his heart, Whom would the king delight to honor more than myself?

7 And Haman answered the king, For the man whom the king delights to honor,

8 Let the royal apparel be brought which the king wears and the horse that the king rides, and let the royal crown be set upon his head:

9 And let the apparel and the horse be delivered to the hand of one of the king's most noble princes, and let him array the man whom the king delights to honor and mount him on the horse and take him round through the streets of the city and proclaim before him, Thus shall it be done to the man whom the king delights to honor.

10 Then the king said to Haman, Make haste and take the apparel and

the horse, as you have said, and do even so to Mordecai the Jew, who sits at the king's gate; let nothing fail of all that you have spoken.

11 Then Haman took the apparel and the horse, and arrayed Mordecai, and brought him on horseback through the streets of the city and proclaimed before him, Thus shall it be done to the man whom the king delights to honor.

12 ¶And Mordecai came again to the king's gate. But Haman went to his house mourning and having his head covered.

13 And Haman told Zeresh his wife everything that had befallen him. Then his friends and Zeresh his wife said to him, If Mordecai is of the Jewish race, before whom you have begun to fall, you shall not prevail against him, but will surely again be humbled before him.

14 And while he was still talking with them, the king's couriers arrived and hastened to bring Haman to the banquet that Esther had prepared.

CHAPTER 7

SO the king and Haman went in to the banquet which Esther the queen had prepared.

2 And the king said again to Esther on the second day of the banquet of wine, What is your petition and what is your request? It shall be granted you, even to the half of the kingdom.

3 Then Esther the queen answered and said, If I have found favor in your sight, O king, and if it please the king, let my life be given me at my petition, and my people at my request;

4 For we are sold, I and my people, to be slain, to be put to the sword, and to perish. But if we had been sold merely as bondmen and bondwomen, I would have held my tongue, but the enemy would not hesitate to cause damage to the king.

5 ¶Then King Akhshirash answered and said to Esther the queen, Who is he and where is he who dares to presume in his heart to do so?

6 And Esther said, The oppressor and enemy is this wicked Haman. Then Haman trembled before the king and the queen.

7 ¶And the king arose from the banquet of wine in his wrath and went into the palace garden; and Haman remained to beg for his life from Esther the queen; for he saw that there was evil determined against him by the king.

8 Then the king returned from the palace garden into the place of the banquet of wine; and Haman was prostrate upon the couch where Esther was seated. Then the king said, Will he disgrace the queen also before me in the house? As the word went out of the king's mouth, they covered Haman's face.

9 And Rahbona, one of his eunuchs, said before the king, Behold the gallows fifty cubits high, which Haman had made to hang Mordecai because he had spoken good concerning the king, stands in the house of Haman. Then the king said, **Hang him on it.**

10 So they hanged Haman on the gallows that he had prepared for Mordecai. Then was the king's wrath appeased.

CHAPTER 8

ON that day King Akhshirash gave the house of Haman the enemy of the Jews to Esther the queen. And Mordecai came before the king; for Esther had told what he was to her.

2 And the king took off the ring which he had taken away from Haman and gave it to Mordecai. And Esther set Mordecai over the house of Haman.

3 ¶And Esther came back and spoke again before the king, and fell down at his feet and besought him and entreated him earnestly to put away the mischief of Haman the Agagite and his device that he had devised against the Jews.

4 Then the king held out the golden sceptre toward Esther. So Esther touched it and stood before the king

5 And said, If it please the king and the thing seem right before the king

and if I have found favor in his eyes, let it be written to reverse the letters devised by Haman the Agagite which he wrote to destroy all the Jews who are in all the king's provinces;

6 For how can I endure to see the calamity that shall come to my people? Or how can I endure to see the destruction of my kindred?

7 ¶Then King Akhshirash said to Esther the queen, Behold, I have given you the house of Haman, and him they have hanged upon the gallows because he lifted up his hand against the Jews.

8 And write also concerning the Jews as it please you, in the king's name, and seal it with the king's ring; for the writing which is written in the king's name and sealed with the king's ring may not be reversed.

9 Then the king's scribes were called at that time in the third month, which is the month of Heziran,[1] on the twenty-third day thereof; and it was written according to all that Mordecai had written concerning the Jews, to the commanders of the armies and the governors and princes of the provinces from India to Ethiopia, a hundred and twenty-seven provinces, to every province according to its writing and to every people according to its own language and to the Jews according to their writing and according to their language.

10 And the letters were written in the name of King Akhshirash and sealed with the king's ring, and they were sent by runners and by riders of horses and by dromedaries.

11 In these letters the king permitted the Jews who were in every city to gather themselves together and to defend their lives, to destroy, to slay, and to cause to perish everyone that might oppress them, both little ones and women, and to take their goods for spoil.

12 Upon one day in all the provinces of King Akhshirash, namely, upon the thirteenth day of the twelfth month, which is the month Adar,

13 The copy of the writing was is-

[1] June.

sued in every province and it was decreed to all peoples that the Jews should be ready on that day to avenge themselves upon their enemies.

14 So the runners and the posts that rode on horseback went out, being hastened by the decree and the king's command which was given at Shushan the palace.

15 ¶Then Mordecai went out from the presence of the king in royal apparel of blue and fine white linen, and with a crown of gold and with a garment of fine white linen and purple; and the city of Shushan rejoiced and was glad.

16 The Jews had light and gladness and honor and joy.

17 And in every province and in every city whithersoever the king's decree and his commandment came the Jews had a great joy, a feast, and a good day. And many of the people of the land were alarmed; for the fear of the Jews fell upon them.

CHAPTER 9

NOW in the twelfth month, which is the month Adar, on the thirteenth day of the same, when the time drew near for the king's decree and his commandment to be put into execution, in the day when the enemies of the Jews hoped to overpower them (though the edict was turned to the contrary so that the Jews should have rule over those that hated them),

2 The Jews gathered themselves together in their cities throughout all the provinces of King Akhshirash to attack such as sought their hurt; and no man could withstand them; for the fear of them fell upon all people.

3 And all the princes of the provinces and the commanders of the armies and the governors and those who were employed in the king's work honored the Jews because the fear of the king fell upon them.

4 For Mordecai was great in the king's house, and his fame spread throughout all the provinces; for the man Mordecai grew greater and greater.

5 Thus the Jews smote all their enemies with the sword and slaughter and destruction, and did what they would to those who hated them.

6 And in Shushan the palace the Jews slew and destroyed five hundred men.

7 And they slew Shepiroth and Dalcon and Aspoth and

8 Parlat and Adalia and Derath

9 And Aprasmoth and Disai and Adri and Zoth,

10 The ten sons of Haman the son of Hammadatha, the enemy of the Jews; but they did not lay their hands on the plunder.

11 On that day the number of those that were slain in Shushan the palace was brought before the king.

12 ¶And the king said to Esther the queen, The Jews have slain and destroyed five hundred men in Shushan the palace and the ten sons of Haman; what have they done in the rest of the provinces? Now what is your petition? And it shall be granted you; and what is your request further? And it shall be done for you.

13 Then Esther said, Let it be granted to the Jews who are in Shushan to do tomorrow also according to this day's decree, and let Haman's ten sons be hanged on the gallows.

14 And the king commanded it so to be done; and the decree was given in Shushan, and the ten sons of Haman were hanged.

15 For the Jews who were in Shushan gathered themselves together on the fourteenth day also of the same month, and slew three hundred men in Shushan; but they did not lay their hands on the plunder.

16 And the rest of the Jews who were in the king's provinces gathered themselves together to defend their lives, and had rest from their enemies and slew of those who hated them seventy-five thousand, but they did not lay their hands on the plunder.

17 They began on the thirteenth day of the month Adar; and on the fourteenth day of the same they rested

18 And made it a day of feasting and gladness;

19 Therefore the Jews who are scattered, who dwell in widely separated towns, make the fourteenth day of the month Adar a day of gladness and feasting and a good day, and send portions one to another.

20 ¶And Mordecai wrote these things and sent letters to all the Jews who were in all the provinces of King Akhshirash, both near and far,

21 To agree among themselves that they should keep the fourteenth day of the month Adar and the fifteenth day of the same, yearly,

22 As the days on which the Jews rested from their enemies and the month which was turned for them from sorrow to joy and from mourning to a good day, that they should make them days of feasting and joy and of sending portions of food one to another and gifts to the poor.

23 And the Jews took upon themselves to do as they had begun and as Mordecai had written them;

24 Because Haman the son of Hammadatha, the Agagite, the enemy of all the Jews, had plotted against the Jews to destroy them, and had cast lots to consume them and to destroy them;

25 When Esther came before the king, the scribe would say, Let the wicked plots which were devised against the Jews return upon the head of him who had devised them, and let him and his sons be hanged on the gallows.

26 Therefore they called these days Porayey,[1] after the name Passover. Because of all the words of this letter and of that which they had seen concerning this matter and because of that which has befallen them,

27 The Jews ordained thus, and took upon themselves and upon their descendants and upon all such as joined themselves to them that it should not fail that they would keep these two days according to their writing and according to their appointed time every year,

28 And that these days should be

---

[1] Hebrew, *Purim.*

remembered and kept throughout every generation in every province and every city; and that these days of Porayey should not fail from among the Jews, nor the memorial of them perish from their descendants.

29 Then Esther the queen, the daughter of Abihail, and Mordecai the Jew wrote with all authority to confirm this letter of Porayey.

30 And they sent letters to all the Jews, to the hundred and twenty-seven provinces of the kingdom of Akhshirash the king, with words of truth and peace

31 To confirm these days of Porayey in their appointed times, according as Mordecai the Jew and Esther the queen had enjoined upon them and upon their children the decree of their fasting and their prayer.

32 And the decree of Esther confirmed these matters of Porayey which were written in the book.

CHAPTER 10

AND King Akhshirash laid a tribute upon the whole land and upon the Islands of the sea.

2 And all the acts of his power and of his might and the glory of the greatness of Mordecai unto which the king promoted him, behold, they are written in the book of the chronicles of the kings of Media and Persia.

3 For Mordecai the Jew was next to King Akhshirash and became the chief over the Jews, and he sought the good of his people and spoke on behalf of all his race.

THE BOOK OF

JOB

CHAPTER 1

THERE was a man in the land of Uz whose name was Job; and that man was innocent and upright, and one who revered God and turned away from evil.

2 And there were born to him seven sons and three daughters.

3 His substance was seven thousand sheep and three thousand camels and five hundred yoke of oxen and five hundred she-asses and a very great household; so that this man was the greatest of all the men of the East.

4 And his sons went and feasted in the house of each other on his appointed day; and they would send and invite their three sisters to eat and drink with them.

5 And it was so, when the days of their feasting were over, that Job sent and sanctified them, and rose up early in the morning, and offered burnt offerings according to the number of them all; for Job said, It may be that my sons have sinned, and cursed God in their hearts. Thus did Job continually.

6 ¶Now there was a day when the sons of God came to present themselves before the LORD, and Satan came also among them.

7 And the LORD said to Satan, Whence have you come? Then Satan answered the LORD, and said, From going to and fro in the earth, and from walking on it.

8 Then the LORD said to Satan, Have you considered my servant Job, that there is none like him in the earth, an innocent and upright man, one who reveres God, and turns away from evil?

9 Then Satan answered the LORD and said, Does Job revere God for nought?

10 Thou hast rested thy hand of protection upon him and upon his house and upon his children and upon everything that he has everywhere; thou hast blessed the work of his hands, and his substance is increased in the land.

11 But put forth thy hand now, and destroy all that he has, and he will curse thee to thy face.

12 And the LORD said to Satan, Behold, all that he has is in your power; only upon himself you shall not put forth your hand. So Satan went out from the presence of the LORD.

13 ¶And there was a day when Job's sons and his daughters were eating and drinking wine in their oldest brother's house;

14 And there came a messenger to Job, and said to him, The oxen were plowing, and the asses feeding beside them;

15 And robbers raided them, and carried them away, and they have slain the servants with the edge of the sword, and I only have escaped to inform you.

16 While he was yet speaking, there came another, and said to him, The fire of God is fallen from heaven, and has burned up the sheep and the shepherds, and consumed them; and I only have escaped to inform you.

17 While he was yet speaking, there came another, and said to him, The Chaldeans divided themselves into three bands, and raided the camels, and carried them away, and slew the servants with the edge of the sword; and I only have escaped to inform you.

18 While he was yet speaking, there came another, and said to him, Your sons and your daughters were eating and drinking wine in their oldest brother's house;

19 And, behold, there came a great wind from the wilderness, and smote the four corners of the house, and it fell upon the young men, and they are dead; and I only have escaped to inform you.

20 Then Job arose, and rent his mantle, and shaved his head, and fell down upon the ground, and worshipped,

21 And he said, Naked I came out of my mother's womb, and naked shall I return; the LORD gave, and the LORD has taken away; blessed be the name of the LORD.

22 In all these disasters, Job did not sin, nor did he blaspheme against the LORD.

CHAPTER 2

AGAIN there was a day when the sons of God came to present themselves before the LORD, and Satan came also among them to present himself before the LORD.

2 And the LORD said to Satan, Whence have you come? And Satan answered the LORD, and said, From going to and fro in the earth, and from walking on it.

3 And the LORD said to Satan, Have you considered my servant Job, that there is none like him in the earth, an innocent and upright man, one who reveres God, and turns away from evil? He still holds fast to his integrity, although you provoked me against him, to destroy him without cause.

4 And Satan answered the LORD, and said, Skin for skin, yea, all that a man has will he give for his life, to save it.

5 But put forth thy hand now, and touch his flesh or his bone, and he will curse thee to thy face.

6 And the LORD said to Satan, Behold, he is delivered into your hands; only spare his life.

7 ¶So Satan went forth from the presence of the LORD, and smote Job with cancer from the sole of his foot to his brain.

8 And he took a potsherd to scrape himself with it; and he sat down upon ashes.

9 ¶Then his wife said to him, Do you still hold fast your integrity? Curse God, and die.

10 But he said to her, You speak as one of the foolish women speaks. We have indeed received God's bless-

ings, now shall we not also receive his afflictions? In all these misfortunes Job did not sin, nor did he blaspheme against God with his lips.

11 ¶Now when Job's three friends heard of all this misfortune that had come upon him, they set a time of meeting, and came to him every one from his own place: Eliphaz the Temanite, Bildad the Shuhite, and Zophar the Naamathite; for they had made an appointment together to console and comfort him.

12 And when they lifted up their eyes from afar, they did not recognize him, and they lifted up their voices, and wept; and they rent every one his mantle, and threw dust upon their heads toward the heaven.

13 So they sat down with him upon the ground seven days and seven nights, and none spoke a word to him; for they saw that his affliction was very great.

CHAPTER 3

AFTER this Job opened his mouth, and cursed the day wherein he was born.

2 Then Job spoke and said,

3 Let the day perish wherein I was born, and the night in which it was said, A male child is conceived.

4 Let that day be darkness; let not God regard it from above, neither let the light shine upon it.

5 Let the darkness and the shadow of death cover it; let a cloud overshadow it; let those whose days are bitter be terrified by it.

6 As for that night, let thick darkness cover it; let that day not be reckoned in the number of the days of the year, let it not come into the number of the months.

7 Lo, let that night be desolate, let no voice of praise come therein.

8 Let them curse it who curse the day, who are ready to stir up Leviathan.[1]

9 Let the stars of twilight thereof be dark; let the people wait for light, but receive none; neither let them see the dawning of the day;

10 Because it did not shut the doors of my mother's womb, nor hide trouble from my eyes.

11 Why did I not die from the womb? Why did I come forth at birth?

12 Why was I reared at my mother's knee? Why did I suck the breasts?

13 For now I should have been laid in the grave and been quiet, I should have slept; then I should have been at rest,

14 With kings and governors of the earth who built desolate places for themselves;

15 Or with princes who had gold, who filled their houses with silver;

16 Or like a hidden untimely birth, as if I had not been; like infants that never saw the light.

17 There the wicked cease from troubling; and there the weary are at rest.

18 There the prisoners rest together; they hear not the voice of the oppressor.

19 The small and the great are there; and the servant is free from his master.

20 Why is light given to him who is in trouble, and life to the bitter in soul,

21 Who long for death, but it comes not, and seek it as one seeks a hidden treasure;

22 Who rejoice exceedingly, and are glad when they can find the grave?

23 Why is light given to a man whose way is hid, whom God has hedged in?

24 For my sighing comes before I eat, and my moanings are poured out like water.

25 For the thing which I greatly feared is come upon me, and that which I was afraid of has befallen me.

26 I am not at ease, neither am I calm, nor am I at rest; and yet misfortune came.

CHAPTER 4

THEN Eliphaz the Temanite answered and said,

2 If I venture to speak with you, will you be wearied? But who can

[1] A great evil.

restrain himself from speaking with you?

3 Behold, you have instructed many, and you have strengthened the weak hands.

4 Your words have upheld the weak, and you have strengthened the feeble knees.

5 But now because misfortune has come upon you, and you are weary; it touches you, and you are terrified.

6 Behold, your fear is to be blamed, and your trust in the integrity of your way.

7 Remember, I pray you, whoever perished, being innocent? Or where were the upright ever put to shame?

8 As I have seen, those who plow iniquity and sow trouble, reap the same.

9 By the breath of God they perish, and by the blast of his anger they are consumed.

10 The roaring of the lion, and the voice of the young lion are silenced, and the teeth of the lions are broken.

11 The lion perishes for the lack of prey, and the whelps of the lioness are scattered.

12 Now a thing was secretly brought to me, and my ear received a little of it.

13 In silence, in a night vision, when deep sleep falls on men,

14 Fear came upon me, and trembling, which made all my bones to shake.

15 Then a spirit passed before my face; the hair of my flesh stood up:

16 Then I arose, but I could not discern its meaning; there was no form before my eyes, but I heard a gentle voice, saying,

17 Shall mortal man be declared more righteous than God? Shall he be more pure than his Maker?

18 Behold, he put no trust in his servants; and his messengers he struck with amazement;

19 Even those who dwell in decorated houses of clay, whose foundation is in the dust, shall be humbled before the thick darkness.

20 They shall be afflicted from morning to evening, that they may not dwell for ever; yea, they shall perish.

21 Behold, their possessions are taken away from them; and the rest of them shall die without wisdom.

CHAPTER 5

CALL now, I pray you; is there any one to answer you? And to which of the holy ones will you turn?

2 For anger kills the foolish man, and enmity slays the silly one.

3 I have seen the wicked prosper; but his habitation is suddenly destroyed.

4 His children are far from salvation, and they are humiliated at the gate, and there is no one to deliver them.

5 His harvest the hungry eat up; and they shall pour out water to the thirsty, and the thirsty devour their substance.

6 For falsehood does not come forth from the dust, nor does iniquity spring out of the ground;

7 For man is born for trouble, as sure as the wild birds fly.

8 But as for me, I would seek God, and to God I would commit my cause,

9 Who has done great things without limit; and marvellous things without number.

10 Who gives rain upon the earth, and sends water upon the streets;

11 To set up on high those that are lowly; and the meek shall be exalted by salvation.

12 He frustrates the devices of the crafty, so that their hands cannot wisely perform their enterprise.

13 He takes the wise in their subtlety; and the counsel of the crafty is frustrated.

14 They handle things in the daytime as though they were in darkness, and grope in the noonday as in the night.

15 But he saves their lives from the sword, and the poor from the hand of the mighty.

16 So there shall be hope for the poor, but the wicked shall shut his mouth.

17 Behold, happy is the man whom God corrects; and he who does not

despise the chastening of the Almighty;

18 For it is he who wounds, and binds up; he smites, and his hands heal.

19 He shall deliver you in six troubles; yea, in seven there shall no evil touch you.

20 In famine he shall deliver you from death; and in war from the power of the sword.

21 You shall be protected from the scourge of the tongue; and you shall not be afraid of destruction when it comes.

22 At plunder and famine you shall laugh; and you shall not fear the wild beasts.

23 For you shall be in league with the stones of the field; and the wild beasts shall surrender to you.

24 You shall know that your tabernacle shall be in peace; and you shall return to your habitation, and shall not sin.

25 You shall know also that your descendants shall be many, and your offspring like the grass of the earth.

26 You shall come to your grave gently, like a shock of grain in its season.

27 Lo this thing we have searched, and it is so; we have heard it; and you know it for your good.

CHAPTER 6

THEN Job answered and said,
2 Oh that my grief were weighed, and my calamity laid in the balances against it!

3 For then it would be heavier than the sand of the seas; therefore my words are restrained.

4 For the arrows of the Almighty are in my flesh, and their poison drinks up my spirit; the terrors of God have frightened me.

5 Does the wild ass bray over grass? Or does the ox low over the fodder?

6 Or can that which is unsavory be eaten without salt? Or is there any taste in the white of an egg?

7 My soul is weary of its troubles, I lament like a drunken man in my affliction.

8 Oh that I might have my request;

and that God would grant me the thing that I long for!

9 So that God would hearken to cleanse me, and to spread out his hand and make me whole;

10 And to be again my comfort, so that I may be restored to my strength without measure; for I have not lied against the words of the Holy One.

11 What is my strength, that I should endure? And what is my end, that I should be patient?

12 Is my strength the strength of stones? Or is my flesh of brass?

13 Behold, his help is not in me, and his salvation is far off from me.

14 He who withholds peace from his friend, forsakes the worship of the Almighty.

15 My brethren have dealt deceitfully like dry brooks, like torrents which pass away.

16 Those who were afraid of ice, much snow has fallen upon them.

17 When the sun shines over them, they melt; when it is hot, they melt and disappear from their place.

18 The paths of their ways are winding; they go astray from their course and perish.

19 For they have looked toward the roads of the south, and have waited for the paths of Sheba.

20 They are ashamed in what they had hoped; they came there, and were confounded.

21 You also have become such to me; because before you saw terror, you were afraid.

22 Did I say, Bring me a present? Or from your wealth offer a bribe for my sake?

23 Or rescue me from my oppressor's hands; or deliver me from the hand of the mighty?

24 Teach me, and I will be silent; and cause me to understand wherein I have erred.

25 Why do you reject the words of truth? Who of you are able to rebuke and chastise?

26 Behold you are seeking to find words with which to reprove, and against my soul you are conjuring up words.

27 Behold, you overwhelm the

fatherless, and you grieve your friend.

28 Now therefore listen and take heed, and I will speak in your presence, and will not lie.

29 Repent, I pray you, and do not become like ungodly men; repent therefore and be justified.

30 Is there iniquity in my tongue? Or does not my mouth speak truth?

CHAPTER 7

BEHOLD there is an appointed time for man upon earth, and his days are like the days of a hireling.

2 As a servant who eagerly longs for eventide, and as a hireling who looks to complete his job;

3 So have I inherited months of vanity, and wearisome nights are meted out to me.

4 When I lie down, I say, When shall I arise? and the night seems long; when I go to rest, I toss about till the dawning of the day.

5 My flesh is covered with worms, and my body with dust; my skin is shrunk, and falls apart.

6 My days are swifter than a weaver's shuttle, and are spent without hope.

7 O remember that the spirit is still alive; even yet my eye shall again see good.

8 The eye of him who has seen me shall rejoice no more; thine eyes are upon me, and yet I am gone.

9 As the cloud fades away and disappears, so he who descends to Sheol shall not ascend any more.

10 He shall return no more to his house, neither shall he recognize his place any more.

11 Therefore I will not restrain my mouth; I will speak in the anguish of my spirit; I will complain in the bitterness of my soul.

12 Am I a sea, or a sea monster, that thou settest a watch over me?

13 For I said that thou shalt comfort me, and I will be relieved of the pain of my sickbed.

14 And, behold, thou dost scare me with dreams, and terrify me through visions;

15 Thou hast drawn my life out of destruction, and my bones out of death.

16 I am despondent; I would not live for ever; leave me alone, for my days are vanity.

17 What is man, that thou shouldst destroy him? And that thou shouldst think of him;

18 And that thou shouldst visit him every morning, and try him every moment?

19 How long wilt thou not depart from me, nor let me alone till I swallow my spittle?

20 If I have sinned; what have I done to thee, O thou Creator of men? Why hast thou caused me to encounter thee? Thou hast become a burden to me.

21 Until when wilt thou not forgive my transgressions and remove my iniquity? For now I shall lie in the dust; and thou shalt seek me, but I shall be no more.

CHAPTER 8

THEN answered Bildad the Shuhite, and said,

2 How long will you speak these things? And how long will your mouth utter proud words?

3 Does God pervert justice? Or does the Almighty pervert right?

4 If your children have sinned against him, he has sent them away in their transgressions.

5 If you would seek God and make supplication to the Almighty,

6 If you were innocent and upright, surely then he would be attentive to you, and would make the habitation of your righteousness prosperous,

7 So that though your beginning was small he would make your end very great.

8 For inquire, I pray you, of the former generations, and learn through the search of their fathers;

9 For we are but of yesterday, and know nothing, because our days upon earth are like a shadow;

10 And, behold, they shall teach you, and tell you, and utter words out of their heart.

11 Can papyrus grow in a thirsty

land? Can reeds grow where there is no water?

12 While they are yet in their greenness, and not cut down, they wither before any other herb.

13 So are the paths of all who forget God; and the hope of the heathen shall perish;

14 Whose confidence shall be cut off, and whose house is a spider's web.

15 The wicked shall put his trust in his house, but it shall not stand; he shall hold it fast, but it shall not endure.

16 He is like green vegetation before the sun, and his roots shall rest in a ground liable to be washed away.

17 He shall see his house a heap of stones.

18 If he is uprooted from his place, then he will deny him, saying, I have not seen thee.

19 Behold, it is he who examines all his ways, and out of the earth others shall sprout.

20 Behold, God will not reject the upright men, nor will he help the evildoers;

21 Until he fill your mouth with laughter, and your lips with a song.

22 Those who hate you shall be clothed with shame; and the tent of the wicked shall be destroyed.

CHAPTER 9

THEN Job answered and said,
2 Truly, I know that it is so; but how can a man be declared innocent before God?

3 If he should contend with him, he cannot answer him one out of a thousand.

4 He is wise in heart and mighty in strength; who has hardened himself against him, and had peace?

5 He who removes mountains and overthrows them with his anger, does he not know?

6 He shakes the earth out of its foundations, and its inhabitants tremble.

7 He commands the sun, and it does not rise; and seals up the stars.

8 He alone stretched out the heavens, and treads upon the mighty waves of the sea.

9 He made the Pleiades, Aldebaran, and Orion, and the chambers of the south.

10 He has done great things past finding out; yea, and wonders without number.

11 Lo, if he will pass by me, I will see him not; and if he will circle around me, I will not perceive him.

12 Behold, if he will destroy, who can resist him? Who can say to him, What doest thou?

13 God will not turn away his anger, the mighty shall be humiliated under him.

14 I will answer him also, and choose out my words in his presence.

15 If I am not justified I would not resist, but I would make supplication to my judge.

16 If I had called, and he had answered me, yet I would not believe that he had hearkened to my voice.

17 For he has crushed me with a tempest, and multiplied my wounds without cause.

18 He will not suffer me to take my breath, but fills me with bitterness.

19 If it is a matter of strength, lo, he is mighty; and if of judgment, who can summon him?

20 If I justify myself, my own mouth shall condemn me; though I say I am pure, he shall also prove me perverse.

21 Though I am pure, yet I would not know my soul; I would despise my life.

22 It is all the same; therefore I say, He destroys both the righteous and the wicked.

23 If his rod slays suddenly, he will laugh at the foolishness of the innocent.

24 The earth is handed over to the wicked; and the faces of the judges are covered; [1] if not, who can endure their wrath?

25 Now my days are swifter than a runner; they flee away, they see no good.

26 They are passed away like ships

---

[1] The judges are bribed.

of the enemy; like the eagle that swoops on the prey.

27 I have forgotten my bitterness; if my mind or my thought would leave me alone, then I would find rest.

28 Though I am at rest, I am afraid of every torment, because I know that thou wilt not declare me innocent.

29 Behold, if I am declared guilty, why then dost thou consume me in vain?

30 If I wash myself with snow why then dost thou consume me in my hands;

31 Yet thou shalt plunge me into the pit, and my own clothes shall be abhorrent to me.

32 For God is not a man as I am, that I might answer him, and that we should come together for trial.

33 O that there were a judge between us, that he might silence us both!

34 Let him take his rod away from me, and let not his fear terrify me;

35 Then I would speak, and I will not be afraid of him, for I have never been against him.

CHAPTER 10

MY soul is weary of my life; I have reasoned in my judgment; I will speak in the bitterness of my soul.

2 I will say to God, Do not condemn me; show me why thou dost contend with me.

3 Is it not enough to thee that thou shouldst oppress, that thou shouldst despise the work of thy hands, and regard the counsel of the wicked?

4 Hast thou eyes of flesh? Or seest thou as a man sees?

5 Are thy days as the days of men? Are thy years as man's days?

6 That thou enquirest after my iniquity, and searchest after my sins?

7 Thou knowest that I am innocent; and there is none that can deliver himself out of thy hands.

8 Thy hands have made me and fashioned me; and afterward thou wishest to condemn me, and to destroy me.

9 Remember that thou hast made me as clay; and wilt thou bring me into dust again?

10 Thou hast churned me as milk, and curdled me as cheese.

11 Thou hast clothed me with skin and flesh, and hast strengthened me with bones and sinews.

12 Thou hast granted me life and peace, and thy commandments have preserved my spirit.

13 And these things hast thou hid in thy heart; I know that this is in thy mind.

14 If I sin, then thou dost watch me, and thou dost not acquit me from my iniquity.

15 If I be wicked, woe is me! and if I be righteous, still I cannot lift up my head. I have enough of reproach; I have seen my affliction.

16 And if I exalt myself, thou dost hunt me like a lion, and then thou dost turn and show thyself gigantic over me.

17 Thou hast set thy armor against me, and increasest thy indignation toward me. Thou dost array one host after another against me.

18 Wherefore then hast thou brought me forth out of the womb? Would that I had died, and no eye had seen me!

19 I should have been as though I had not lived; I should have been carried from the womb to the grave.

20 The days of my life are few; let me alone, that I may be quiet and rest a little

21 Before I go from whence I shall not return, even to the land of darkness and the shadow of death,

22 A land of loneliness and deep darkness, and of the shadow of death, without any order or time; wearisome like a deep pit.

CHAPTER 11

THEN answered Zophar the Naamathite, and said,

2 The LORD does not answer because of the multitude of words, neither can a fluent speaker be justified by his discourse.

3 Behold, at your words, only the

dead can hold their peace; for when you speak, there is no one to stop you; and when you mock, there is no one to rebuke you.

4 For you say, I was led righteously, and I am pure in my sight.

5 But oh that God would speak, and open his lips against you;

6 And that he would show you the secrets of wisdom, for wisdom has inner chambers; then you would know that God would forgive your sins.

7 Can you understand the deep things of God? Or can you stand at the outer boundary of the Almighty?

8 Do you know the height of the heaven? Or the depth of Sheol? How can you know?

9 The measure thereof is longer than the earth, and broader than the sea.

10 If he should pass by, and besiege, or should cause men to die, who could hinder him?

11 For it is he who knows the beginning of time; and sees wickedness, and considers it.

12 For a pure man inspires courage, and a mighty man helps others.

13 If you make your heart right, and stretch out your hands toward him;

14 If iniquity should be in your hands, he would put it far away, and not let wickedness dwell in your tabernacle.

15 For then you will be courageous; yea, you will not be afraid of distress.

16 Because you shall forget your misery, and you shall be led like running water;

17 And the pit will be clearer than the noonday, and the thick darkness will be like the morning.

18 Then you will have confidence because there is hope; yea, you lie down and take your rest in safety:

19 Also you shall lie down, and none shall make you afraid; yea, many shall seek to see your face.

20 But the eyes of the wicked shall fail, and their strength shall vanish away together with the hope of their souls.

CHAPTER 12

AND Job answered and said,
2 Truly, you are the people, and wisdom shall die with you.

3 But I have understanding as well as you; I am not inferior to you; but to whom are such things as these not known?

4 And yet he who called upon God became ridiculous to his friends, and he answered him who is pleased with the righteous who are unblemished,

5 Who is ready to do away with contempt and iniquity, and to strengthen the slippery feet.

6 The tabernacle of robbers shall be removed, and the confidence of those who provoke God; for there is no God in their heart.

7 But ask now the beasts, and they shall teach you; and the fowls of the air, and they shall tell you;

8 Or speak to the earth, and it shall teach you; and the fishes of the sea shall declare to you.

9 Who does not know in all these that the hand of the LORD has made them?

10 Because in his hand are the souls of every living thing, and the breath of all mankind.

11 The ear hears the words, and the palate tastes food.

12 With the elders is wisdom; and in length of days, understanding.

13 With him is wisdom and might, he has counsel and understanding.

14 Behold, if he demolishes, who can build; and if he shuts up a man in prison, who can open?

15 If he withholds the waters, they dry up; if he releases them they ruin the land.

16 With him is strength and wisdom; with him is might and salvation.

17 He leads kings amazingly, and makes judges fools.

18 He brings kings down to beg at the gates, and girds their loins with girdles of power.

19 He leads priests with reverence, and overthrows the mighty.

20 He cancels the speech of trusty counsellors, and takes away the good judgment of elders.

21 He pours contempt upon princes, and weakens the strength of the mighty.

22 He uncovers deep things out of darkness, and brings the light out of the shadow of death.

23 He causes the nations to err, and destroys them; he strikes down the nations, and forsakes them.

24 He takes away the understanding of the chiefs of the people of the earth, and causes them to wander in a waste land where there is no way.

25 They search in darkness without light, and they grope in darkness without understanding; and he makes them stagger like a drunken man.

CHAPTER 13

LO, my eye has seen all this, my ear has heard and understood it.

2 What you know, I know also; I am not inferior to you.

3 But I would speak to the Almighty, and with my reproof would I reason with God.

4 But you are forgers of lies; you are all healers [1] of no value.

5 O that you would altogether keep silent! And it would serve you for wisdom.

6 Hear now my admonition, and hearken to the pleadings of my lips.

7 Will you speak wickedly against God? And talk deceitfully against him?

8 Will you respect his person? Will you contend with him?

9 Is it good for you that he should search you out? Or as you are judged by men, would you be judged by him?

10 He will surely reprove you, if you will show partiality.

11 His excellency shall seek vengeance of you, and his terror will fall upon you.

12 Remember that your power is from the earth, and your dwelling place is of clay.

13 Hold your peace, let me alone, that I may speak also, and tell everything that has come upon me.

14 Why am I so afflicted, and why is my life exposed to danger?

15 Though he slay me, yet will I look for him; because my ways are before him.

16 He also shall be my Saviour; for a hypocrite shall not come before him.

17 Listen diligently to my speech, and I will relate my declaration in your presence.

18 Behold now, I am also pleading my cause; and I know that I am innocent.

19 Who is he that will contend with me? For now I will keep silent and be at rest.

20 Only two things do not let depart from me; then I will not turn aside from thee:

21 Do not withdraw thy help from me; and let not thy dread terrify me.

22 Then call thou me, and I will answer; or let me speak, and answer thou me.

23 How many are my iniquities and sins? Make me to know my transgressions and my sins.

24 Wherefore dost thou hide thy face from me, and considerest me as thine enemy?

25 Wilt thou tread upon a fallen leaf? And wilt thou pursue the dry grass in the air?

26 For thou decreest chastisement against me, and makest me remember the iniquities of my youth;

27 Thou puttest my feet also in the stocks, and watchest all my ways; thou seest the imprints of my feet.

28 Yet a man is like a worn-out waterskin, and a garment that is moth-eaten.

CHAPTER 14

MAN that is born of a woman is of few days, and full of trouble.

2 He comes forth like a flower, and withers and fades away; he flees like a shadow, and continues not.

3 And dost thou open thine eyes upon such a one, and bring him into judgment with thee?

4 Who can bring a clean thing out of an unclean? No one.

5 Seeing his days are determined and the number of his months are decreed, thou hast appointed his bounds that he cannot trespass them;

[1] Physicians.

6 Turn thy face away from him, and his days will be spent like a hireling.

7 For there is hope for a tree, if it be cut down, that it will sprout again and its tender shoots will not cease.

8 Though its root wax old in the earth and its stock die in the ground,

9 Yet through the scent of water it will bud and bring forth leaves like a plant;

10 But man dies, and fades away; yea, man perishes, and he is no more.

11 As the waters fail from the sea, and a river becomes desolate and dries up;

12 So man who lies down does not rise again; until the heavens are no more, they shall not awake, nor be roused out of their sleep.

13 O that thou wouldst hide me in Sheol, that thou wouldst keep me in a secret place until thy wrath is spent, that thou wouldst appoint me a set time and remember me!

14 If a man die, shall he live again? All the days of his youth he waits till old age comes.

15 If thou wouldst call me, I would answer thee; thou wilt think of the work of thy hands.

16 For now thou numberest not my steps: and thou keepest not watch over my sins.

17 My transgressions are sealed up in a bag, and thou removest from me my sins.

18 Truly a great mountain falls, and a rock moves out of its place.

19 The waters wear away the stones and wash away the soil of the earth; so thou destroyest the hope of man.

20 Thou prevailest for ever against him, and he passes; thou castest him away with shame on his face.

21 If his sons multiply, he does not know it; if they decrease, he perceives it not of them.

22 But his flesh upon him shall have pain, and his soul within him shall mourn.

CHAPTER 15

THEN answered Eliphaz the Temanite, and said,

2 Should a spiritually minded man answer with knowledge and then become enraged?

3 Should he admonish with unprofitable talk, or with words that are worthless?

4 Yea, you also are discarding reverence, and talk too much in the presence of God.

5 For your mouth is accustomed to utter sinful things, and you choose the deceitful tongue of the crafty.

6 Your own mouth condemns you, and not I; yea, your own lips testify against you in my presence.

7 Are you the first man that was born? Or were you conceived before the hills?

8 Have you heard of the secrets of God? Has his wisdom been revealed to you?

9 Or what do you know that we do not know? Or what do you under-stand that we do not understand?

10 Behold, there are among us the gray-headed and the very aged men, much older in days than your father.

11 Now talk less of God's threats, and speak comfortingly to yourself.

12 Why does your heart boast? And what do your eyes wink at,

13 That you boast in the presence of God, and let such words go out of your mouth?

14 What is man, that he should be innocent? Or he that is born of a woman, that he should be righteous?

15 Behold, he puts no trust in his saints; yea, the heavens are not clean in his sight.

16 Even though man should be rejected and afflicted, yet he shall drink iniquity like water.

17 Hear me, I will show you; and that which I have seen I will repeat;

18 That which wise men have declared, and did not hide from their fathers;

19 To whom alone the land was given, and no stranger passed among them.

20 The wicked man magnifies himself all his days, and the number of the years of the violent man is hidden.

21 A dreadful sound is in his ears;

in prosperity the spoiler shall come upon him.

22 He does not believe that he shall be overthrown because of the darkness,[1] and that he shall see the sword.

23 He flees because of the threat of judgment; he does not know that the day of darkness is already at his hand,

24 Trouble and anguish shall overtake him, like a king ready for the battle,

25 Because he has stretched out his hand against God, and strengthened himself against the Almighty.

26 He runs against him proudly, and strangles him, with the multitudes of his shields;

27 Because he has deceived himself with his wealth, and he places Pleiades above Aldebaran.

28 And he dwells in desolate cities, which no man has inhabited; then he prepares for war.

29 He shall not continue, neither shall his strength endure, nor shall his words be established upon the earth.

30 He shall not depart out of darkness; the flame shall dry up his branches, and by the breath of his mouth shall he be rejected.

31 Let him not trust in deceptive vanity, for his growth is in vain.

32 He shall dry up before his time, and the work of his hands shall not be found.

33 He shall shake off his unripe grapes, as the vine, and shall cast off his flowers as the olive tree.

34 For the congregation of the godless shall be desolate, and fire shall consume the tabernacle of the wicked.

35 They conceive mischief and bring forth deceit, and their belly is full of guile.

CHAPTER 16

THEN Job answered and said,
2 I have heard many such things; wicked comforters are you all.

3 Do not grieve my spirit with words; even though you speak, I will not answer.

[1] Ignorance.

4 I also could speak as you do; I wish you were in my place, then I could try you out with words, and shake my head at you.

5 I would prove you with your own words, and the words of my lips would not spare you.

6 If I speak, my pain is not assuaged; and if I forbear, who can comfort me?

7 But now he has troubled me, and yet has preserved all of my testimony.

8 Thou didst appoint me and I became a witness, but my lies have testified against me; and I spoke in his presence.

9 He has torn me and broken me in his wrath; he gnashes upon me with his teeth; my enemy sharpens his eyes against me.

10 They have gaped upon me with their mouth reproachfully; they have smitten me upon my cheeks; they were filled with rage against me.

11 God has delivered me to the ungodly, and turned me over into the hands of the wicked.

12 I was at ease, but he has smitten me; he has also taken me by my neck, and shaken me to pieces, and set me up for his target.

13 His arrows are round about me, he shoots at my kidneys and does not spare; he pours out my gall on the ground.

14 He breaks me with breach upon breach; he runs against me like a giant.

15 I have girded sackcloth upon my skin, and I have covered my head with dust.

16 My face is troubled with weeping, and on my eyelids is the shadow of death;

17 But not for any iniquity in my hands; my prayer also is pure.

18 O earth, cover not my blood, and let my cry have no place!

19 And now, behold, my witness is in heaven, and my acquaintances are on high.

20 O my brethren and my neighbors! my eyes pour out tears to God!

21 O that one might plead for a

man with God, as a man pleads for his neighbor!

22 For the number of a man's years will come to an end; then he shall go the way from whence he shall not return.

CHAPTER 17

MY spirit is weary, my days are extinct; the grave is ready for me,

2 For there is no falsehood in me, and yet my spirit dwells in their bitterness.

3 Make me, I pray thee, a hostage with thee; then I will surrender myself.

4 For thou hast hid their heart from understanding; therefore they shall exalt themselves in their deception.

5 When a friend behaves insolently toward his friend, even the eyes of his children shall fail.

6 He has granted power to the nations; I shall be derided before them.

7 My eye is dim because of anger, and all my senses are like a shadow.

8 Upright men shall be amazed at this, and the innocent shall stir himself up against the guilty.

9 The righteous also shall hold to his way, and he that has clean hands shall be stronger and stronger.

10 But as for you all, you are hypocritical, and yet you return and come to me; but I cannot find a wise man among you.

11 O you time wasters! Dawdlers! Who think about nothing! O you destroyers of the hearts of the people!

12 You change the night into day; and you bring forth the light before the darkness is over.

13 If I wait, Sheol is my house; I have made my bed in the darkness.

14 I have said to corruption, You are my father; to the worm, You are my mother and my sister.

15 Where is now my hope and my trust? As for my hope, who shall find it?

16 They shall go down to the bottom of Sheol; they shall descend together into the dust.

CHAPTER 18

THEN Bildad, the Shuhite, answered and said,

2 How long will you resist words? Understand! and afterwards we will speak.

3 Wherefore are we counted as beasts, and have become abominable in your sight? O you who slays himself in his anger?

4 Shall the earth be forsaken for your sake? And shall the mountain be removed out of its place?

5 Yea, the lamp [1] of the wicked shall be put out, and the spark of his fire shall not shine.

6 The light shall be dark in his tent, and his lamp above him shall be extinguished.

7 He shall be deserted in his illness, and his own counsel shall cast him down.

8 For he has stretched out his feet into the net, and he walks upon a snare.

9 The trap seizes him by the heel, and thirst shall prevail against him.

10 A snare is laid for him on the ground, and a trap for him in his paths.

11 Terror shall make him afraid on every side, and shall drive him to his feet.

12 Let famine be his grief, let destruction be ready for his posterity.

13 Let force devour his towns, let his first-born die in violence.

14 His confidence shall be rooted out of his tent, and he shall be brought hastily by the king's executioner.

15 Others shall dwell in his tent, because there is no one in it; brimstone shall be scattered upon his habitation.

16 His roots shall be dried up beneath, and above shall his vintage be cut off.

17 His remembrance shall perish from the earth, and he shall have no name upon it.

18 He shall be driven from light into darkness, and chased out of the world.

---

[1] An Aramaic idiom which means *he shall have no heir.*

19 He shall neither have name nor remembrance among the people, nor any survivor in his dwelling place.

20 They that come after him shall be astonished at his day, as they that went before them were terrified.

21 Surely such is the dwelling of the wicked, and this is the place of him who knows not God.

CHAPTER 19

THEN Job answered and said,

2 How long will you grieve my soul, and make me sick with words?

3 For behold, these ten times you have rebuked me; and yet you are not ashamed that you make me sad.

4 If indeed I have erred, my error remains with myself.

5 If you have justly magnified yourselves against me, rebuked me, and reproached me,

6 Know then that God has condemned me, and spread his net over me.

7 If I howl, no one answers me; and if I complain, there is no one to avenge me.

8 He has fenced up my ways so that I cannot pass, and he has set darkness in my paths.

9 He has stripped me of my glory, and taken the crown from my head.

10 He has destroyed me on every side, and I am no more; and my hope has he removed like a piece of tree.

11 He has also kindled his wrath against me, and he counts me as his enemy.

12 His messengers have come together against me; they debated their ways against me, and encamped round about my tent.

13 My brothers are far off from me, and my acquaintances have deserted me.

14 My kinsfolk have failed me, and my familiar friends have forsaken me.

15 They that dwell in my house, and my maids, consider me as a stranger; I am an alien in their sight.

16 I called my servant, and he gave me no answer; I entreated him with my mouth and implored him.

17 I have become a stranger to my wife, and have implored the children of my own body.

18 Yea, even the wicked despise me; when I rise, they speak against me.

19 All my counselors abhor me; even my friends have turned against me.

20 My skin and my flesh cleave to my bones, and I am escaped with the skin of my teeth.

21 Have pity upon me, have pity upon me, O you my friends; for the hand of God has been against me.

22 Why do you also persecute me like God, and you are not satisfied with the hurt of my flesh?

23 Oh that my words were now written! Oh that they were inscribed in a scroll!

24 That they were engraved with an iron pen on lead or in the rock for ever!

25 For I know that my Saviour lives, and at the end he will reveal himself upon the earth;

26 Although devouring worms have covered my skin and my flesh,

27 Yet, if my eyes shall see God, then my heart also will see the light; but now my body is consumed.

28 For you will say, Why did we persecute him? For a good report will follow me and vindicate me.

29 Spare yourselves from the sword; for the wrath of sinners is a sword; for you shall yet know that there is judgment.

CHAPTER 20

THEN Zophar, the Naamathite, answered and said,

2 Therefore my discipline has caused me to discern, and for my help it has remained with me.

3 I will make you hear the instruction of my discipline, and the spirit of my understanding will cause me to answer.

4 This I know from of old, since man was created upon the earth,

5 That the triumphing of the wicked is short, and the joy of the godless but for a moment.

6 Though his excellency mount up

to the heavens and his head reach to the clouds,

7 Yet he shall perish for ever like a whirlwind; those who have seen him shall say, Where is he?

8 He shall fly away like a dream, and shall not be found; yea, he shall be chased away like a vision of the night.

9 The eye also which saw him shall see him no more; neither shall they see his place again.

10 His children shall be crushed with poverty, and he shall stretch out his hands toward them.

11 His bones are full of marrow, but they shall lie down with him in the dust.

12 Though his wickedness is sweet in his mouth, though he hide deceit under his tongue,

13 Though he spare it and forsake it not, but keep it still in his mouth;

14 Yet his food in his stomach is turned, it is the gall of asps within him.

15 The riches which he had swallowed down, he shall vomit up out of his belly; and God shall destroy him.

16 He shall suck the poison of asps; the tongue of an adder shall slay him.

17 He shall not see the rivers, the floods, the brooks of honey and butter.

18 That which he had labored for shall he restore, and shall not swallow it down; that which he had acquired by extortion he shall not enjoy;

19 Because he has thought to forsake the poor; because he has violently taken away a house which he did not build.

20 Because he knew no justice himself, he shall not be spared by his covetousness.

21 There shall none of his posterity be spared; therefore his good will not be remembered.

22 With the measure with which he had measured, he shall be recompensed; the hand of the wicked shall come upon him.

23 May his posterity go to destruction, may God cast the fury of his

wrath upon him, and deluge him while he wars against him.

24 For although he had escaped because of the breastplate of iron, the bow of brass shall pierce him through.

25 It is drawn, and it brings forth his inward parts; and the skin of his gall shall be pierced; terror shall be upon him continually.

26 All darkness is kept in store for his posterity; a blazing fire shall consume him; and the one who is left in his tent shall be destroyed.

27 The heaven shall reveal his sins; and the earth avenge itself upon him.

28 The foundations of his house shall be left bare and he shall be scourged in the day of his wrath.

29 This is the portion of a wicked man from God, and the heritage appointed to him from the Highest.

CHAPTER 21

THEN Job answered and said,

2 Listen diligently to my speech, and let this be your consolation.

3 Suffer me that I may speak; and after I have spoken, then mock on.

4 I will utter my complaint to men, why my spirit is distressed.

5 Return to me, and be astonished, and lay your hand upon your mouth.

6 Even when I think of it, I tremble, and terror takes hold of my flesh.

7 Why do the ungodly live, and why are the mighty in power full of years?

8 Their descendants are established in their sight with them, and their children before their eyes.

9 Their houses are safe from fear, neither is the rod of God upon them.

10 Their bull breeds, and fails not; their cow calves, and does not cast her calf.

11 Their children stand firm like a flock, and their boys dance.

12 They take the timbrels and harps, and rejoice at the sound of singing.

13 They spend their days in prosperity, and then suddenly go down to Sheol.

14 They say to God, Depart from us; for we do not desire to know thy ways.

15 Moreover, they say, Who is God, that we should serve him? And what would we gain, that we should pray to him?

16 Lo, they have no power over their prosperity; the counsel of the ungodly is far from me.

17 How often is it that the wicked are left without an heir! how often their destruction comes upon them! God distributes sorrows in his anger.

18 They are like straw before the wind, and like chaff that the storm carries away.

19 God reserves man's iniquity for his children; he pays it back to him, and he shall know it.

20 His eyes shall see his destruction, and he shall drink of the wrath of the Almighty.

21 For what pleasure has he in his house after him, when a portion of his years shall be reserved for his posterity?

22 Shall any teach God knowledge, seeing it is he who judges the proud?

23 One dies in his full strength, sound of body, being wholly confident, and at ease.

24 His body is full of fat, and his bones are filled with marrow.[1]

25 And another dies in the bitterness of his soul, never having tasted prosperity.

26 They shall lie down in the dust, and the worms shall cover them.

27 Behold, I know your thoughts, and the devices which you wrongfully imagine against me.

28 For you say, Where is the house of the righteous? And where is the place in which the wicked has pitched his tent?

29 Have you not asked those who pass by the way? And do you not recognize their tokens?

30 For the evil man is reserved for the day of destruction, he shall be remembered in the day of wrath.

31 Who can show him the way? And who shall repay him for what he has done?

32 Yet he shall be brought to the grave, he is reserved for misfortune.

33 The depths of the valley shall swallow him, and many shall be drawn in after him, even as there are innumerable ahead of him.

34 How then can you comfort me in vain, seeing that your abominable answers are multiplied before me?

CHAPTER 22

THEN Eliphaz, the Temanite, answered and said,

2 O man, can you converse with God; are you equal with him in wisdom?

3 What do you profit by trying to make it seem that your ways are perfect because you are afraid?

4 He will reprove you, and enter into judgment with you.

5 Behold, your wickedness is great, and there is no end to your sins.

6 For you have taken a pledge from your brothers for nothing, and stripped the naked of their clothing.

7 You have not given water to the weary to drink, and you have withheld bread from the hungry.

8 There is a man who sows a field for himself, and the mighty man seizes it from him by force.

9 You have sent widows away empty, and the arms of the fatherless you have broken.

10 Therefore snares are round about you, and sudden fear causes you to tremble;

11 Where is the darkness, that you cannot see; and the flood of water that covers you?

12 Behold, God is in the height of heaven, and sees the highest of the stars that are very high.

13 And yet you say, How does God know? Can he judge through the thick darkness?

14 Thick clouds are a covering to him, so that men cannot see him; and he walks upon the circle of the heaven.

15 Have you marked well the old way which wicked men have trodden long ago?

16 Those who were cut down before their time, who were stopped at the crossing place of the river of life,

[1] Prosperous.

and then did not remember who had laid down their pattern of living,

17 Who said to God, Depart from us; what can God do for us?

18 Yet he filled their houses with good things, and the counsel of the wicked kept away from them.

19 The righteous shall see it, and shall be glad; and the innocent shall laugh them to scorn.

20 If they are not prostrated because of their stubbornness, then their remnant shall be consumed with fire.

21 Make now an agreement with God, and offer to him of your good crops.

22 Receive the law from his mouth, and lay up his words in your heart.

23 If you shall repent before God, you shall be built up; if you shall put away iniquity from your dwelling place;

24 Then you shall lay up silver like dust, and the gold of Ophir as the sand of the valley.

25 Yea, God shall be your defense, and you shall have plenty of silver.

26 For then you shall lift up your face to God.

27 And you shall make your prayer to him, and he shall hear you, and you shall fulfill your vows.

28 You shall also decree a thing, and it shall be established for you; and the light shall shine upon your ways.

29 For it is said, He who humbles himself shall be exalted; and he who is meek shall be saved.

30 The innocent man shall be spared wherever he is, and he shall escape by the purity of his hands.

CHAPTER 23

THEN Job answered and said,

2 Even today is my complaint bitter; God's hand is heavier and increases my groaning.

3 Oh that I knew where I might find him, that I might come even to his seat!

4 I would lay my cause in order before him, and fill my mouth with arguments.

5 I would know what he would answer me, and understand what he would say to me.

6 Would he contend with me with his great power? If he would not, then he will put his fear into me.

7 There I might contend justly with him; and I might be justified and acquitted.

8 Behold, if he goes before me, I know not; or behind, I cannot perceive him.

9 I seek him on my left hand, but I cannot behold him; then I turn to my right hand, but I cannot see him.

10 But it is he who knows my way and my existence, and has tried me like gold, and I came forth pure.

11 My feet have held firm to his steps, and I have kept his ways.

12 I have not despised the commandments of his lips; neither have I departed from his will, and have kept the words of his mouth.

13 But in return for one of these, what has he granted me? What his soul desires, even that he does.

14 But he performs his covenant; and many such things are with him.

15 Therefore I am fearful at his presence; when I consider, I am afraid of him.

16 For God has troubled my heart, and my mind is confused:

17 Because I was not silenced before the darkness, and before the covering of the blackness.

CHAPTER 24

WHY are the wicked not hidden from the presence of God, and why do those who know him never enjoy their days?

2 The wicked remove the landmarks; they violently take away a flock.

3 They seize the ass of the fatherless, they take the widow's ox for a pledge.

4 The wicked hide themselves beside the road,[1] and the meek of the earth hide together.

5 Behold, like wild asses in the desert, they go forth early seeking food for their young ones.

[1] Bandits hide themselves beside the road to rob the poor and unarmed travelers.

6 They cut hay in a field which is not theirs; and they gather grapes from the vineyard of the wicked.

7 They cause the naked to lodge without clothing, and they have no covering in the cold.

8 They are wet with the showers of the mountains, and embrace the rock for want of shelter.

9 They take by force plunder of the fatherless, and they devour the poor.

10 They cause them to go naked without clothing, and they take away bread from the hungry,

11 Who are bent down under burdens during the reapers' banquets, and are hungry when they carry the large basket and the measure. At times they are hungry at the reapers' banquets; they tread the wine press, but they suffer thirst.

12 From the midst of the city the oppressed groan, and the souls of the wounded cry out; yet God does not accept their prayer.

13 They were in God's world; but they knew not his ways; nor did they walk in his paths.

14 The murderer arises at daylight, and kills the poor and needy, and in the night he is a thief.

15 The eyes also of the adulterer wait for the darkness, saying, No eye shall see me; and he disguises his face in the dark.

16 In darkness he breaks into houses which he has marked in the daytime. The wicked know not the light.[1]

17 Therefore they sought for themselves the shadow of death, and have found it: yea, they are in the terrors of the shadow of death.

18 They are swiftly carried away upon the face of the waters; their portion is cursed in the earth; they behold not the familiar way of the vineyards.

19 Drought and heat consume the snow waters; for they have sinned in Sheol.

20 They have gone astray from the womb; the worm shall suck them; after death they shall be remembered

no more; and the wicked shall be broken like a piece of wood.

21 An evil barren woman shall never bear; they do not good to the widow.

22 The wealth of a man of power is sustained by his own strength; he does not depend on divine guidance.

23 Though he be granted safety, wherein he has confidence, yet his eyes are upon his own evil ways.

24 Such men are exalted for a little while, but soon are no more; yea, all the provokers shall be brought low and destroyed; they wither and are shaken out like the heads of grain.

25 And if it is not because of his anger, then who will make me a liar, and make my speech worth nothing before God?

CHAPTER 25

THEN Bildad, the Shuhite, answered and said,

2 Dominion and reverence are with him, he has made peace in his heavens.

3 Is there any number to his armies? And upon whom does not his light shine?

4 How then can man be justified with God? Or how can he be declared blameless, he who is born of a woman?

5 Behold, even the moon cannot be justified; yea, the stars are not pure in his sight.

6 How much less man, who is dust, and the son of man, who is a worm!

CHAPTER 26

THEN Job answered and said,

2 Why do you try to help him who is powerless? Why do you try to save the arm that has no strength?

3 How have you counselled him who has no wisdom? And how have you expounded so many doctrines?

4 To whom have you uttered words? And whose soul has come forth from you?

5 Behold, the mighty men shall be slain, and they shall lie down quieter than still waters.

[1] Truth

6 Sheol is naked before him, and destruction has no covering.

7 He stretches out the north from the empty place, and hangs the earth upon nothing.

8 He binds up the waters in his thick clouds; and the cloud is not rent under them.

9 He holds fast the covering of the firmament, and spreads his cloud upon it.

10 He has circled the waters with bounds, until the day and night come to an end.

11 The pillars of heaven tremble and are astonished at his reproof.

12 He rebukes the sea with his power, and by his wisdom he saves many.

13 By his spirit he manages the heavens; his hand slew the fleeing serpent.[1]

14 Lo, these are merely parts of his ways; and what evil thing have we heard against him? And the greatness of his might who can understand?

CHAPTER 27

MOREOVER Job continued his parable, and said,

2 As God lives, who has wronged my judgment, and the Almighty, who has made my soul bitter;

3 As long as my soul is in me, and the spirit of God is in my nostrils;

4 My lips shall not speak wickedness, nor my tongue utter deceit.

5 God forbid that I should do evil, till I die I will not remove my innocence from me.

6 My righteousness I hold fast, and will not let it go; my heart shall not reproach me so long as I live.

7 Let my enemy be as the ungodly, and he that hates me as the wicked.

8 For though he has accumulated riches, what is the hope of the godless at the time when God takes away his life?

9 For God will not hear his prayer when trouble comes upon him.

10 But if he should trust in the Almighty, and always call upon God, God will hear him and answer him.

11 But as for you, I will deliver you into the hand of God; so that your works may not be hid from him.

12 Behold, all of you have seen it; why then do you boast in vain?

13 This is the portion of a wicked man with God, and the heritage of oppressors, which they shall receive from the Almighty.

14 If their children are multiplied, it is for the sword; and their offspring shall not be satisfied with bread.

15 Those who remain of them shall be buried in death; and their widows shall not weep over them.

16 Though they heap up silver like dust and accumulate clothes like clay,

17 They may pile them up, yet the righteous shall wear them, and shall also divide their silver.

18 For the wicked has built his house upon a spider's web, and like a booth he had made his shelter.

19 The rich man [2] shall lie down, but he shall not rise again; he opens his eyes, and he is gone.

20 Terrors overtake him like swift water, and like a tempest that rages.

21 The east wind shall carry him away in the night, and he is gone; and shall hurl him out of his place.

22 For God shall cast him out without pity, and he cannot escape out of his hand.

23 He shall smite him with his hand, and shall hiss against him from his dwelling place.

CHAPTER 28

SURELY there is a mine for silver, and a place where gold is refined.

2 Iron is taken out of the earth, and brass is smelted out of the stone.

3 God sets an end to darkness, and knows the end of everything, the deep and dark mine and the shadow of death.

4 They have inherited a ruined mine from an alien people; they are gone astray from the right path and

---

[1] The devil.

[2] Many rich men in the East acquired their wealth unjustly and by means of violence and confiscation.

their number has diminished from among men.

5 They lay open the earth, out of which comes sustenance; and from under it is turned up material as if it were burned with fire.

6 The stones of it are the place where sapphires are found, and it has dust of gold in its paths.

7 There is a path which no bird knows, and the vulture's eye has not seen;

8 Wild beasts have not trodden it, nor has the lion passed by it.

9 The miner puts forth his hand upon the hard rock to break it; he overturns the mountains from their foundations.

10 He divides the rivers by his might; and his eye sees every precious thing.

11 He binds up the rivers that they may not overflow; and the thing that is hid, he brings forth to light.

12 But where shall wisdom be found? And where is the place of understanding thereof?

13 No man knows the treasure thereof; neither is it found except in the land of the living.

14 The depth says, It is not in me, and the sea says, It is not with me.

15 It cannot be gotten for gold, neither shall silver be counted for its price.

16 It cannot be exchanged with the gold of Ophir, with precious onyx or sapphire.

17 The gold and the crystal cannot equal it; nor can precious pearls, jewels, and emeralds equal it.

18 For the price of wisdom is above that of precious stones. Nor can colored gems, emeralds, and diamonds equal it.

19 For the price of wisdom is above everything, and nothing can equal it. The pearls of Ethiopia and the topaz cannot equal it.

20 Whence then comes wisdom? And where is the place of understanding?

21 It is hid from the eyes of all living, and concealed from the fowls of the air.

22 Destruction and death say, We have heard the report of it with our ears.

23 Because only God understands the way of it, and he knows the place thereof.

24 For he looks to the ends of the earth, and sees under the whole heaven;

25 For he made a weight for the wind, and meted it out by the measure.

26 He made a decree for the rain, and a way for the lightning and the thunder.

27 Then he saw it, and declared it; he measured it, yea, and searched it out.

28 And to man he said, Behold, the reverence of God, that is wisdom; and to depart from evil is understanding.

CHAPTER 29

MOREOVER Job continued his parable, and said,

2 O that I were as in months past, as in the days when God took care of me;

3 When he put his worship high upon my head, when his lamp shone over me; and when by his light I walked through darkness.

4 O, that I were as in the days when I was in favor, when God abode in my tabernacle;

5 When the Almighty was yet round about me in my youth;

6 When I washed my steps with butter,[1] and the rock poured me out rivers of oil;

7 When I went out to the gate of the city and called on the people; and sat down like a poor man in the street,

8 The young men saw me and hid themselves; and the aged arose, and respected me.

9 The nobles held their peace, and laid their hands on their mouth.

10 The voice of the princes was restrained, and their tongues cleaved to the roof of their mouth.

11 For when the ear heard me, then

---

[1] When I was wealthy.

it praised me; and when the eye saw me, it gave testimony about me;

12 Because I delivered the poor out of distress, and the fatherless who had none to help him.

13 The blessing of him who was ready to perish came upon me; and I caused the widow's heart to rejoice.

14 I put on righteousness, and it clothed me like a robe and diadem of justice.

15 I was eyes to the blind, and feet was I to the lame.

16 I was a father to the poor; and the cause which I knew not I searched out.

17 And I broke the jaws of the wicked, and snatched the prey out of his teeth.

18 Then I said, I shall become straight like a reed, I shall deliver the poor and multiply my days like the sand of the seas.

19 My roots are planted by the waters, and the dew lies all night upon my boughs, and at the harvest season I shall be invited to the feast.

20 I shall take my bow with me, and renew it in my hand.

21 Men listened to me, and waited, and hearkened to my counsel.

22 And from my words they departed not, and my speech was pleasing to them.

23 They waited for me as for the rain; and they opened their mouths wide as for the spring rain.

24 If I ridiculed them, they did not take offense; and they did not turn from the light of my countenance.

25 I searched out their ways, and then returned and dwelt as a king in his army, like one who comforts the mourners.

CHAPTER 30

BUT now they laugh at me, those who are less than I,

2 Whose fathers I have disdained, and did not consider them equal to the dogs of my flocks.

3 Yea, the strength of their hands, of what use would it have been to me?

4 For they had lost their power completely.

5 They were forced by bare necessities, like a thief swept off his feet,

6 Fleeing to dwell in the cliffs of the valleys, in caves of the earth, in crevices,

7 In rocky places, and under bushes.

8 The children of fools shall be overthrown together with the children of the wicked; they shall be brought lower than the earth.

9 And now I am the subject of their mocking, yea, I have become a byword to them.

10 They abhor me, they flee far from me, and do not fail to spit in my face.

11 Because they began to deride me and humiliate me, they have also put their bridle in my mouth.[1]

12 They rise up against my right hand, they have tripped me up; they have perplexed me through the crookedness of their ways.

13 They mar my paths without a cause, they rejoice for what has befallen me; they shall have no helper.

14 They shall suffer a great ruin; they shall be broken by the hurricane.

15 For they have brought terror upon me; they have pursued my paths like the wind; and my help has passed away like a cloud.

16 And now my soul is weary; the days of affliction have taken hold upon me.

17 In the night my bones are in pain, and my body has no strength in it.

18 I have put on my garment; and girded up myself with my robe.

19 But they have cast me into the mire, and I am become like dust and ashes.

20 I cry to thee, and thou dost not answer me; I stand up and thou dost not consider me.

21 Thou hast treated me as an enemy to thee; with thy strong hand thou hast restrained me.

22 Thou liftest me up to the wind; thou causest me to ride upon it, and

---

[1] An Aramaic idiom which means *restricted, restrained,* or *dominated me.*

then thou afflictest me, and makest me wretched.

23 And yet I know that thou wilt bring me back from death to the meeting place for all living.

24 But he will not stretch out his hand against me, and when I cry to him he will save me.

25 I have wept for the poor in the daytime, and my soul was grieved for the fatherless.

26 But when I looked for good, evil came; and when I waited for light, there came darkness.

27 My heart was agitated, and did not rest; the days of affliction came upon me.

28 I walked mournfully without being resentful; I stood up and wept in the congregation.

29 I am become a brother to jackals, and a companion to ostriches.

30 My skin has shrunk upon me, and my bones are burned as with heat.

31 My harp is also turned to mourning, and my song to the voice of those who weep.

CHAPTER 31

I MADE a vow with my eyes that I would never lust after a virgin.

2 For what portion would I have then from God who is above, and what heritage from the Almighty who is on high?

3 For it is destruction to the wicked, and punishment to the workers of iniquity.

4 He sees my ways, and counts all my steps.

5 If I have walked with hypocrites, or if my foot hastened to deceit;

6 Let me be weighed in a just balance, that God may know my integrity.

7 I have not turned aside my steps from the way, and my heart has not followed after my eyes, and I have acquired nothing unjustly;

8 But when I sowed, then I ate, and when I planted, then I cultivated and gathered the crops.

9 And if my heart has been enticed by a strange woman, or if I have lain in wait at my neighbor's door;

10 Then let my wife grind for another, and let her bake bread at another man's place.[1]

11 For this is a heinous crime; yea, such an eye devises a crafty scheme.

12 For passion is a fire that consumes to destruction, and it would root out all my increase.

13 If I have rejected the cause of my manservant or my maidservant, when he contended with me,

14 Without saying, What then shall I do when God rises up in judgment, and when he inquires, what shall I answer him?

15 (For, behold, he who made me in the womb made him, and he created us in the same womb);

16 If I have withheld the poor from his desire, or have defrauded the widow,

17 Or have eaten my bread alone, and the orphans did not eat of it

18 (Because from my youth I was brought up in sorrows, and from my mother's womb with sighing);

19 If I have seen anyone perishing for want of clothing, or any poor without covering

20 (But they were reared upon my knees, and were warmed with the fleece of my sheep);

21 If I have lifted up my hand against the fatherless (when I saw him at the door I helped him);

22 Then let my arm fall from my shoulder blade, and let it be broken from the bone.

23 For the fear of God made me to tremble, and affliction from him came upon me, and because of terror I was unable to rise up.

24 If I have made gold my trust, or said about the precious stones, You are my confidence; or have said about fine gold, You are my hope;

25 If I have rejoiced because my wealth was great, and because my hand had gotten much;

26 If I have adored the sun when it shone, or the moon when in full brightness;

27 And if my heart has been se-

[1] Destitute people have no oven of their own.

cretly enticed, if I have consented to wrongdoings;

28 Then God has seen my crafty ways, and I have lied before him.

29 If I have rejoiced at the destruction of him who hated me, or exulted myself when misfortune befell him;

30 (But I have neither suffered my mouth to sin, nor has my soul wished for any of these things;

31 My friends said, Oh this man would give us even of his own flesh! but we are not satisfied,

32 And the stranger I did not let lodge in the street, and I opened my door to the guest);

33 If I have covered up my sins like some men, or if I have hid my guilt in secret places;

34 If I have trampled upon the rights of the others (but on the contrary, it is the multitude of families which has ruined me. Nor have I turned away anyone at the door; or engaged in gossip) let the provocations of God lay me low!

35 O that one would hear me! If God is present, let him answer me, and let him write the sentence in a book.

36 Surely I would take it upon my shoulder, and make it a crown to me.

37 I would declare to him the number of my steps; as a prince I would go near to him.

38 Let the earth lament over me, let its furrows weep together,

39 If I have eaten its fruits without money; or if I have grieved one whose life is bitter,

40 Then let thistles grow instead of wheat and thorns instead of barley. The words of Job are ended.

CHAPTER 32

SO these three men who wanted to condemn Job ceased answering him, because he was found righteous in their eyes.

2 Then Elihu the son of Barachel the Buzite, of the family of Ram, was angry; so his wrath against Job kindled, because he justified himself more than God.

3 His wrath also kindled against his three friends, because they had found no answer to Job so that they might condemn him.

4 Now Elihu had waited to correct Job with words, because the other men were older than he.

5 When Elihu saw that these three were unable to answer Job, then he was incensed.

6 And Elihu the son of Barachel the Buzite answered and said, Because I am younger than you in days and you are old, therefore I was afraid, and did not dare to show you my knowledge.

7 For I said, Days should speak, and the multitude of years should teach wisdom.

8 Truly, there is a spirit in men; and the breath of the Almighty gives them understanding.

9 It is not age that makes men wise; nor do the aged always understand judgment.

10 Therefore I say, Hearken to me; I also will show you my knowledge.

11 Behold, I kept silent while you spoke; I gave ear until you made an end of speaking, while you searched for words.

12 Yea, I understood your testimony, and, behold, there was none of you that could reprove Job, or that could answer his words,

13 So that you could not say, We have found wisdom. God has smitten him, not man.

14 Now Job has not directed his words against me; neither will I answer him with your speeches.

15 They were silent, they answered him no more; their words were all spent, so they held their peace;

16 They did not speak; they stood still, and answered him no more.

17 I will answer also on my part; I also will show my knowledge.

18 For I am full of words; the spirit within me constrains me.

19 Behold, I cannot restrain myself, nor can I find relief; I can no longer hold myself from talking.

20 I will speak so that I may find relief; I will open my lips and answer.

21 I will not be partial toward any person, neither will I be ashamed of the presence of any one.

22 For I do not know what shame is; else would my Almighty One soon take me away.

CHAPTER 33

WHEREFORE, hear my speech, O Job, and hearken to all my sayings.

2 Behold, now I have opened my mouth, my tongue speaks in my mouth.

3 The words of my mouth are upright, and the utterances of my lips are pure.

4 The Spirit of God has stirred me up, and the breath of the Almighty has given me life.

5 If you can answer me, then prepare yourself and stand up before me.

6 For I am also like you before God; I also am formed out of clay.

7 Therefore my admonishings will not make you to tremble, neither will my rebuke be heavy upon you.

8 Surely you have spoken in my hearing, and I have heard the voice of your words, saying,

9 I am blameless without transgressions, I am righteous; and there is no iniquity in me, and I am far removed from wickedness.

10 Behold, he finds occasions against me, he counts me as his enemy.

11 He puts my feet in the stocks, he watches all my paths.

12 Behold, in this you cannot justify yourself; I will answer you, that God is greater than man.

13 Why do you strive with him, seeing that he does not give an account of any of his matters?

14 For God speaks once; he does not speak a second time;

15 In a dream, in a vision of the night, when deep sleep falls upon men, while slumbering upon the bed;

16 Then he opens the ears of men, and humbles them according to their rebelliousness.

17 That he may cause man to depart from his evil-doings, and remove pride from him;

18 He spares his soul from corruption, and his life from perdition.

19 Man is chastened also with pain upon his bed, and the multitude of his bones with strong pain;

20 So that his flesh fails because of his fear, and his soul is not satisfied with bread, and covets food.

21 His flesh is wasted away because of his fear, so that a greater part of his bones can be seen.

22 Yea, his soul draws near to corruption, and his life to death.

23 If a man have an angel to whom one would listen once in a thousand times, the angel would show him the way of uprightness

24 And be gracious to him and say, Deliver this man lest he go down to corruption; he has found salvation;

25 Then his flesh will change to that of his childhood; and he shall return to the days of his youth;

26 And he shall pray to God, and he will hear him and be pleased with him, and God shall appear before him with glory; for he will render to men his righteousness.

27 Then the uprightness will bear witness concerning the man; and he shall say, I have truly sinned and I am at fault; and it profiteth me not;

28 Deliver my soul from perdition, and my life shall see the light.

29 Lo, all these things God does three times with a man,

30 To bring back his soul from corruption, to see the light of the living.

31 Incline your ear, O Job, hearken to me; be silent, and I will speak.

32 If you have anything to say, answer me; for I desire that you may be justified.

33 But if you will not listen, then be silent, and I shall teach you wisdom.

CHAPTER 34

MOREOVER Elihu continued and said,

2 Hear my words, O you wise men, and give ear to me, you that have knowledge.

3 For the ear tries words, and the palate tastes food.

4 Let us choose for us a judge; let him know among ourselves what is good.

5 For Job has said, I am righteous; and God has turned aside my judgment.

6 Who is the man who has perished without transgression?

7 What man is like Job, who drinks up scorning like water?

8 Who is a companion and friend of the workers of iniquity, and walks with wicked men?

9 For he has said that a man is not justified because he fears God.

10 Therefore hearken to me, O you men of understanding; far be it from God that he should do wickedness; and far be it from him that he should commit iniquity.

11 For he compensates a man according to his works, and causes every man to be rewarded according to his ways.

12 Truly, God does not commit iniquity, neither does God pervert justice.

13 Who has control over the earth? Or who has made all the world?

14 If he should turn his heart against man, man's spirit and his breath will be gathered to him.

15 Then all flesh would perish together, and man would return again to dust.

16 If now you have understanding, hear this; hearken to the voice of my words.

17 He who hates justice cannot be declared innocent, and he who is innocent will not be condemned justly;

18 He who says concerning the king that he is wicked, and yet he is a good ruler over princes and governors;

19 And not partial to princes, and does not discriminate against the poor (for they are all the work of his hands);

20 In a moment shall he die, and he shall be consumed at midnight, and pass away; he will be rendered powerless by the Almighty.

21 For his eyes are upon all the ways of man, and he sees all his goings.

22 There is no darkness, nor shadow of death, where the workers of iniquity may hide themselves.

23 For he has not set a time for a man that he should enter into judgment with God.

24 For he has brought misfortune to many men without number, and sets others in their places.

25 Therefore he knows them by their works, and he overturns them in the night.

26 Their works shall be crushed under the weight of their wickedness in a land of terror;

27 Because they turned aside from following him, and did not consider any of his ways.

28 The prayer of the poor comes to him, and he hears the cry of the afflicted.

29 When he forgives, who then can condemn? And when he turns his face away, who can forgive the people, or mankind altogether?

30 He sees to it that an impious and wicked man shall not reign over the people.

31 For God has said, I have forgiven, I will not destroy men who are without sin.

32 Inform me now, teach me, if you have committed iniquity;

33 I will not answer you any more, because you have sinned, for you have been examined, and not I; therefore speak out what you know.

34 Let men of understanding tell me, and let a wise man hearken to me.

35 Job has spoken without knowledge, and his words are without understanding.

36 Truly, Job has been tested to the end, and yet he is not counted among the wicked.

37 And if Job should add to his sins, then his transgression will affect us all, and he still will bring his complaint before God.

CHAPTER 35

AGAIN Elihu spoke, and said,

2 Do you think you were justified in saying, I have been found blameless by God?

3 If you have said it, what advantage will it be to you? And what

should I gain if I should condemn you?

4 I will answer you with words, you and your friends with you.

5 Look to the heavens, and observe the clouds which are higher than you.

6 If you sin, what difference does it make to him? And if your iniquities be multiplied, what does it matter to him?

7 If you are righteous, what do you give to him? Or what does he receive from your hand?

8 Your wickedness is to yourself; and your righteousness is to yourself.

9 Because of the multitude of oppressions men howl; and many cry out because of iniquity.

10 And none says, Where is God my Maker, who gives counsel in the night,

11 Who teaches us more than the beasts of the earth, and makes us wiser than the fowls of the air?

12 They cry, but he does not answer them,

13 Because God does not hear the empty pride of evildoers, nor does he praise it.

14 Although you have said, I will not praise him, plead before him and supplicate before him.

15 For now he does not punish with his anger; and he does not harm any soul.

16 Therefore Job has spoken in vain; he multiplies words without knowledge.

CHAPTER 36

THEN Elihu added, and said,
2 Bear with me a little, and I will show you; for there are yet words to speak on God's behalf.

3 I will fetch my knowledge from afar, and will ascribe righteousness to my Maker.

4 For truly my words are not deceitful, and my knowledge is blameless with you.

5 Behold, God is mighty, and does not despise him who is pure as milk.

6 He does not preserve the life of the wicked; but gives justice to the poor.

7 He does not withdraw his eyes from the righteous; he sets kings on the throne; yea, they are exalted for ever.

8 And if they be bound in chains, then they go down through destruction to poverty.

9 Then he shows them their works, and their transgression because they have exceeded their power.

10 He opens also their ears to discipline, and commands that they return from iniquity.

11 If they obey and serve him, they will spend their days in prosperity and their years in pleasures.

12 But if they do not obey, they shall perish by destruction, and they shall perish without knowledge.

13 But the hypocrites in heart shall be consumed, they shall not cry for help; yet they shall cry angrily when he binds them.

14 They shall die in youth, and their life is snatched by famine.

15 But the meek shall be delivered through his meekness, and he opens their way in time of oppression.

16 Even so he shall deliver you from the mouth of the mocker, and give you rest instead of distress; and he shall prepare a table with rich food.

17 But he shall judge the wicked to the limit: judgment and justice shall take hold on them.

18 He will not threaten you with a raging anger, nor will he cause you to be in need of a great ransom.

19 He shall join you, that he may deliver you; you shall not be distressed by any of those who are mighty in power.

20 He shall deliver you from those who drive you away in the night, and give peoples for your sake, and the nations for your life.

21 Take heed, that you may not return to iniquity: because for this you were tried by poverty.

22 Behold, God is mighty in power: who can teach like him?

23 Who has enjoined him his way?

Or who can say, Thou hast wrought iniquity?

24 Remember that his works are great, and all men have praised him.

25 All the peoples have seen it, and beheld it from afar.

26 Behold, God is great, and we know him not, the number of his years is unsearchable.

27 For if we should number the pillars of the heaven, and bind the drops of rain by themselves, which the skies do drop in their season;

28 And which the clouds pour down upon men, and cause them to be exceedingly glad;

29 Who can understand these things, or the spreading of the clouds out of the greatness of his tabernacle?

30 Behold, he spreads his light upon it, and covers the bottom of the sea.

31 For by these he judges the people; and he gives food to many.

32 He covers the light with the clouds, and then it shines upon them again that they may greet it.

33 He shows his possessions to his friends, and to the wicked also.

CHAPTER 37

AT this also man's heart trembles, and is moved out of its place.

2 Listen attentively to the raging of his voice, and the judgment that goes out of his mouth.

3 Under the whole of heaven the people shall praise him, and his light shines upon the ends of the earth.

4 In his own place, he thunders with the voice of his excellency; and he will not need to search them out when his voice is heard.

5 God thunders with his voice; great and marvellous things does he, which we cannot understand.

6 For he said to the snow, Fall on the earth; likewise to the gentle rain, and to the heavy rain;

7 He limits the power of every man, that all men may know his work.

8 Then the wild beasts go into their lurking places, and remain in their dens.

9 Out of the inner chambers comes the whirlwind; and cold out of the downpour.

10 By the breath of God ice is given; and he causes abundant water to pour down.

11 The clouds are stretched out greatly; he spreads the clouds by his light.

12 And they turn round about by his counsels, that they may do whatever he commands them upon the face of his habitable earth.

13 He causes it to rain, whether it be for the princes or for the land or for kindness to those who are found upon it.

14 Hearken to this, O Job: listen and consider the wondrous works of God.

15 Do you know what God has ordained for them, and what causes the light of his clouds to shine?

16 Do you know the balancing of the clouds, the wondrous works of him who is perfect in knowledge?

17 Do you know why your garments get hot when the earth changes its position after the equinox?

18 Were you with him when he spread out the great sky, helping him hold it up?

19 Teach us what we shall say to him, that we may not hide because of the darkness.

20 Relate to him that which he has said; and if a man speaks, surely he shall be consumed.

21 And now men cannot see the light which shines in the sky; but the wind passes and cleanses it.

22 Golden gleams come out of the north; and light shines from God.

23 As for the Almighty, he is excellent in power and in justice; the Prince of the righteous will not afflict his people.

24 Therefore men shall fear him, and all that are wise in heart shall tremble before him.

CHAPTER 38

THEN the Lord answered Job out of the whirlwind, and said,

2 Who is this that gives counsel by words without knowledge?

3 Gird up your loins now, like a valiant man; for I will question you, and you shall answer me.

4 Where were you when I laid the foundations of the earth? Declare, if you have understanding.

5 Who has laid its measures, if you know? Or who has stretched the line upon it?

6 Upon what are its limits resting? Or who laid the cornerstone thereof?

7 When did I create the morning stars, and all the angels shouted for joy?

8 Or who shut up the sea with gates, when it broke forth as if it had issued out of the womb?

9 When I made the cloud the garment of the earth, and thick darkness a swaddling band for it,

10 And prescribed limits for it, and set bars and doors,

11 And said, Thus far shall you come, but no farther; and here shall your proud waves be stayed?

12 Have you commanded the dawn since your days began; or do you know the place of the morning;

13 That it might take hold of the ends of the earth, that the wicked might be thrown out of it?

14 So that their bodies shall be turned into clay, and be thrown into a heap.

15 The light of sinners shall be withheld, and the arm of the arrogant shall be broken.

16 Have you entered into the depths of the sea? Or have you walked in the foundations of the deep?

17 Have the gates of death been revealed to you? Or have you seen the gates of the shadow of death?

18 Have you seen the whole breadth of the earth? Declare to me if you know it all.

19 Where is the dwelling place of light, and where is the place of darkness?

20 Do you know its borders and the path to its house?

21 Do you remember when you were born, and do you know if you will live many days?

22 Have you entered into the chambers of the snow? Or have you seen the storehouses of hail,

23 Which are reserved against the time of distress, against the day of battle and war?

24 Or in what manner is light distributed, and whence the wind comes forth upon the earth?

25 Who causes a flash of lightning and a clap of thunder?

26 Who causes it to rain on a land where no man is, in the wilderness where there is no inhabitant,

27 To saturate every thicket, and cause the tender grass to spring up?

28 Has the rain a father? Or- who has begotten the drops of dew?

29 Out of whose womb did the dew and ice come forth? And who begot the hoary frost of heaven?

30 The waters are hardened like a stone, and the face of the deep is frozen.

31 Can you stop the movement of the Pleiades, or have you seen the path of Orion?

32 Can you bring forth Mazzaroth in its season? Or can you stand in the paths of Aldebaran?

33 Do you know the laws of the heavens? Or do you make ordinances for the earth?

34 Can you lift up your voice to the clouds? Or can you cover them with abundance of waters?

35 Can you send forth the lightnings, that they may go, and say to you, Here we are?

36 Who has put wisdom in the inward parts? Or who has given vision to understanding?

37 Who has numbered the clouds by his wisdom? And who has raised the pillars of heaven?

38 Who has poured out soil upon the earth, and who has made the steep rocks?

39 Who has given prey for the lion? Or filled the appetite of the young lions?

40 Who has multiplied the beasts in the field? Or who has provided food for the raven?

41 For its young ones cry to God, and faint for lack of food.

CHAPTER 39

DO you know the time when wild goats bring forth in the steep rocks? Or can you watch the calving of hinds?

2 Can you number the months that they fulfill, and know the time when they bring forth?

3 And do you know when they kneel and bring forth their young ones?

4 They bring up their young ones, until they grow up and are weaned.

5 Who has left the wild ass to be free, and made him to escape the yoke?

6 For he has made the plain his house, and the salt land his dwelling place.

7 He scorns the multitude of cities, and is not afraid of the voice of rulers.

8 The tops of mountains are his pasture, and he treads over every green thing.

9 Will the unicorn be willing to serve you, or will he spend the night at your crib?

10 Can you bind the yoke on the neck of the unicorn? Or will he harrow in a rugged place?

11 Will you have confidence in him, because his strength is great? Or will you leave your labor to him?

12 Do you trust him, that he will winnow your threshing and gather your grain into the barn?

13 The ostrich rouses herself up haughtily; then she comes and makes her nest;

14 But she leaves her eggs in the earth to be warmed on the ground.

15 And because she has the feet of a bird, forgets that the wild beast may trample them.

16 She multiplies her young ones, though they do not stay with her; although her labor is in vain, she has no fear:

17 God has increased wisdom, but he has not given her a portion of it.

18 She raises herself high like a palm tree; she laughs at the horse and his rider.

19 Have you given the horse strength? Have you clothed his neck with armour?

20 Can you make him move like the locust? Or can you make him afraid?

21 He paws in the plain, and rejoices in the valley; he goes forth armed to the battle.

22 He laughs at a pit, and is not frightened; neither does he turn back from the sword.

23 The quiver rattles against him, the glittering spear and the lance.

24 He gallops with rage that makes the ground to tremble, nor does he fear the sound of the trumpet.

25 He makes the sound, Aha, aha; and he smells the battle from afar; he terrifies the officers with his neighing.

26 Is it by your wisdom that the hawk was created and wings his way toward the south?

27 Does the eagle soar at your command, and make his nest in steep rocks?

28 He dwells and lodges on the rock, upon the cliff of the precipice.

29 He is sustained by his prey, his eyes behold afar off.

30 His young ones suck up blood; and where the slain are, there is he.

CHAPTER 40

MOREOVER the LORD answered Job, and said,

2 Many are the counsels of God; he who reproves God must answer for it.

3 ¶Then Job answered the LORD, and said,

4 Behold, I am unworthy; what shall I answer thee? I will lay my hand upon my mouth.

5 Once I have spoken; but I will not answer; yea, twice, but I will proceed no further.

6 ¶Then the LORD answered Job out of the whirlwind, and said,

7 Gird up your loins now like a man; I will question you, and you shall declare to me.

8 Will you disannul my judgment? Will you even condemn me, that you may be justified?

9 Have you an arm like God? Or

can you thunder with a voice like him?

10 Deck yourself now with majesty and excellency; and array yourself with glory and beauty.

11 Cast away the rage of your wrath; and look upon everyone that is proud, and abase him;

12 And cast the sinners into their place.

13 Bury them in the earth together; cover their faces with fine dust.

14 Then will I also give you credit when your own right hand has saved you.

15 ¶Behold now the hippopotamus which I made for you; he eats grass like an ox.

16 Lo, his strength is in his loins, and his tail stands erect like a cedar tree.

17 The sinews of his thighs bulge out.

18 His bones are strong as pieces of brass; yea, they are like bars of iron.

19 He is the chief among God's creations; for he made him powerful to fight.

20 He roams about the mountains, and all the wild beasts of the field lie down under his protection.

21 He lurks in the covert of reeds, he couches as a lion.

22 The shady trees cover him with their shadow; the willows of the brook encircle him.

23 Behold, if he plunges into the river, he is not afraid; he is confident, though the Jordan reaches to his mouth.

24 Can one take him with a hook, or catch him with a net? Can one snare him in a trap, or can one bind his tongue with a rope?

CHAPTER 41

CAN you catch the Leviathan with a hook? Or draw him out with a cord in his mouth?

2 Can you put a bridle in his mouth? Or bore his jaw with a thorn?

3 Will he make many supplications to you? Or will he speak flattering words to you?

4 Will he make a covenant with you? Or will you count him as a servant for ever?

5 Will you play with him as with a bird? Or will you keep him as a pet for your children?

6 Shall fishermen gather over him? Shall they divide him among many people?

7 Can you fill his skin with meat? Or bake his head with fire?

8 Try to capture him; such a battle you will have! You will never forget it.

9 Behold, Job, you now are set free from your afflictions. So your God will also remove your bitterness.

10 One cannot go far off when Leviathan is stirred up; but who then is able to stand before me?

11 Who has pre-eminence over me, so that I should surrender?

12 Whatever is under the whole heaven is mine.

13 I will not keep silence because of his power, and the might of his sinews.

14 Who has removed his skin? Who can come near him when the net is lowered?

15 Who can open the doors of his mouth? His teeth are terrible round about.

16 His mouth is tied up, and closely shut, as with a seal.

17 His teeth are so close together that no air can come between them.

18 They are joined one to another, they stick together so that they cannot be separated.

19 His appearance is full of light, and his eyes are like rays of the dawn.

20 Out of his mouth go burning lamps, and sparks of fire leap out.

21 Out of his nostrils goes smoke, like a flame spreading round the sides of a pot.

22 His breath kindles coals, and a flame goes out of his mouth.

23 He has great strength in his neck, and fear is to him like dancing.

24 His meat is good and fat, and it is nourishing.

25 His heart is never made to quake for fear, but is firm like a stone; yea as hard as flint.

26 Because of the fear of him, the mighty are afraid;

27 And the strong are humbled.

28 The wound of the sword is of no effect; the lances of the mighty he removes.

29 He considers iron like straw, and brass like rotten wood.

30 The bow cannot make him flee; he treats slingstones as stubble.

31 He laughs at the spear; he is at home in the deep as if he were on the dry land.

32 With his strong body he walks upon the ground.

33 He brings to destruction whatever is proud.

34 He is a king over all things in the deep.

CHAPTER 42

THEN Job answered the LORD, and said,

2 I know that thou canst do all these things, and that no purpose can be hid from thee.

3 Who am I to think that I can give counsel without knowledge? Therefore thou hast declared to me that I have uttered that which I did not understand, things too wonderful for me which I did not know.

4 Hear me, I pray thee, and I will speak; I will ask thee, and declare thou to me;

5 I have heard of thee by the hearing of the ear, but now my eye sees thee.

6 Therefore, I will keep silent, and repent in dust and ashes.

7 ¶And it came to pass, after the LORD had spoken these words to Job, the LORD said to Eliphaz the Temanite, My wrath is kindled against you, and against your two friends; for you have not spoken in my presence that which is right, as my servant Job has.

8 Now therefore take for yourselves seven bullocks and seven rams, and go to my servant Job, and offer up for yourselves a burnt offering; and my servant Job shall pray for you; for him will I accept, lest I deal contemptuously with you, for you have not spoken in my presence the thing which is right, as my servant Job has done.

9 So Eliphaz the Temanite, and Bildad the Shuhite, and Zophar the Naamathite went, and did according as the Lord had told them; and the LORD favored Job.

10 And the LORD restored to Job all that he had lost, when he prayed for his friends; also the LORD gave Job twice as much as he had before.

11 Then came there to him all his brothers and all his sisters and all they that had been of his acquaintance before, and did eat bread with him in his house; for they had been in distress over him, and they comforted him for all the hardships that the LORD had brought upon him; and every man also gave him a ewe, and every one an earring of gold.

12 So the LORD blessed the latter end of Job more than his beginning; for he had fourteen thousand sheep and six thousand camels and a thousand yoke of oxen and a thousand she-asses.

13 He also had seven sons and three daughters.

14 And he named the first Jemima; and the name of the second was Kezia; and the name of the third, Karna-puch.

15 And in all the land were found no women as beautiful as the daughters of Job; and their father gave them an inheritance among their brothers.

16 After this Job lived one hundred and forty years, and saw his sons and his son's sons, even four generations.

17 So Job died, being old and contented and full of days.

THE BOOK OF

PSALMS

PSALM 1

BLESSED is the man who walks not in the way of the ungodly, nor abides by the counsel of sinners, nor sits in the company of mockers;

2 But his delight is in the law of the LORD, and on his law does he meditate day and night.

3 And he shall be like a tree planted by a stream of water, that brings forth its fruit in its season, whose leaves fall not off; and whatsoever he begins he accomplishes.

4 The ungodly are not so, but are like the chaff which the wind drives away.

5 Therefore the ungodly shall not be justified in the judgment, nor sinners in the congregation of the righteous;

6 For the LORD knows the way of the righteous; but the way of the ungodly shall perish.

PSALM 2

WHY do the Gentiles rage and the peoples imagine vain things?

2 The kings of the earth and the rulers have conspired and have taken counsel together against the LORD and against his anointed, saying,

3 Let us break their bands asunder, and let us cast away their yoke from us.

4 He that dwells in heaven shall laugh, and the LORD shall mock at them.

5 Then shall he speak to them in his anger, and terrify them in his wrath and say,

6 I have appointed my king over Zion, my holy mountain,

7 To declare my promise; the LORD has said to me, You are my Son; this day have I begotten you.

8 Ask of me, and I shall give you the heathen for your inheritance and the uttermost parts of the earth for your dominion.

9 You shall shepherd them with a rod of iron; you shall break them in pieces like a potter's vessel.

10 Be wise now, therefore, O kings; be instructed, O judges of the earth.

11 Serve the LORD with reverence, and uphold him with trembling.

12 Kiss the Son, lest he be angry, and you perish from his way while his wrath is kindled but a little. Blessed are all they that put their trust in him.

PSALM 3

O LORD, how my oppressors are increased! Many are they that rise up against me.

2 Many there are that say to my soul, You have no salvation in your God.

3 But thou, O LORD, art my help and my glory, and the lifter up of my head.

4 I have cried to the LORD with my voice, and he has answered me from his holy mountain.

5 I lay down and slept; and I awoke; for the LORD sustained me.

6 I will not be afraid of thousands of people that have surrounded me and set themselves against me.

7 Arise, O LORD my God, and save me; for thou hast smitten all my enemies upon their cheeks; thou hast broken the teeth of the ungodly.

8 For salvation belongs to the LORD; and thy blessing is upon thy people.

PSALM 4

WHEN I have called thee, thou hast answered me, O my God and Saviour of my righteousness; thou hast comforted me when I was in distress; have mercy upon me and hear my prayer.

2 Men, how long will you obscure my glory? how long will you love vanity? do you want deception forever?

3 But know that the LORD has set apart for himself him that is wonderful; the LORD will hear when I call to him.

4 Be angry and yet sin not; commune with your own heart and meditate upon your bed.

5 Offer the sacrifices of righteousness and put your trust in the LORD.

6 There are many that say, Who can show us a good man so that he may shine upon us the light of his countenance?

7 O LORD, thou hast put gladness in my heart more than in the time that their wheat and their wine and their oil increased.

8 In peace I will both lie down and sleep; for thou, O LORD, alone makest me dwell in safety.

PSALM 5

GIVE ear to my words, O LORD, and consider my meditation.

2 Hearken to the voice of my cry, my King and my God; for to thee do I pray.

3 My voice shalt thou hear in the morning, O LORD; and in the morning will I prepare myself and see thee.

4 For thou art not a God that hath pleasure in wickedness; neither shall evil dwell with thee.

5 The proud shall not stand in thy sight; thou hatest all workers of iniquity.

6 Thou shalt destroy them that speak falsehood; the LORD will reject the bloody and deceitful man.

7 But as for me, I will come into thy house in the multitude of thy mercy; and I will enter into thy house and worship in thy holy temple.

8 Lead me, O LORD, in thy reverence and righteousness; and because of mine enemies, make thy way straight before my face.

9 For there is no justice in their mouth; there is wickedness in them; their throat is an open sepulchre; they deceive with their tongues.

10 Condemn thou them, O God; let them fall by their own counsels; cast them out in the multitude of their wickedness, for they have provoked thee.

11 But let all those that put their trust in thee rejoice; they shall glorify thee forever, and thou shalt dwell among them; and all they that love thy name shall be strengthened by thee.

12 For thou wilt bless the righteous; O LORD, thou hast adorned me like a perfect shield.

PSALM 6

O LORD, rebuke me not in thine anger, neither chasten me in thy hot displeasure.

2 Have mercy upon me, O LORD; for I am weak; O LORD, heal me; for my bones are troubled.

3 My soul is also troubled exceedingly but thou, O LORD, how long?

4 Return, O LORD, and deliver my soul; save me for thy mercies' sake.

5 For in death there is no remembrance of thee; in Sheol who shall give thee thanks?

6 I am weary with my groaning; and every night I water my bed and wash my mattress with my tears.

7 Mine eye is weakened because of anger; and I am troubled by all my enemies.

8 Depart from me, all you workers of iniquity; for the LORD has heard the voice of my weeping.

9 The LORD has heard my supplication; the LORD has received my prayer.

10 Let all my enemies be ashamed and defeated; let them turn back and be destroyed suddenly.

PSALM 7

O LORD my God, in thee do I put my trust; save me; from all them that persecute me, deliver me,

2 Lest my soul be torn as by a lion, and there is no one to save me and to deliver me.

3 O LORD my God, if I have done this thing and if there be iniquity in my hands,

4 If I have been vengeful to him that has done me evil, and if I have oppressed my enemies without a cause;

5 Let the enemy pursue me and overtake me, yea, let him tread down my life upon the earth and lay my honor in the dust.

6 Arise, O LORD, in thine anger, lift up thyself over the neck of mine enemies; and make me alert in the judgment that thou hast commanded.

7 Let the congregation of the peoples circle thee about; and for their sakes therefore return thou on high.

8 The LORD shall judge the people; judge me, O LORD, according to my righteousness and according to the integrity that is in me.

9 Oh let the evil of the wicked come to an end; and establish thou the righteous, O thou searcher of hearts and souls.

10 O God who saveth the upright in heart, O righteous God, help me.

11 God is a righteous judge; yea he is not angry every day.

12 If he turn not from his anger, he will whet his sword and bend his bow and make it ready.

13 He has also prepared for himself the instruments of wrath; he pointed his arrows against the persecutor.

14 Because the wicked has become corrupt and has conceived mischief and brought forth falsehood,

15 He has made a well, and deepened it, and is fallen into the pit which he made.

16 His mischief shall return upon his own head, and his iniquity upon his own pate.

17 I will praise the LORD according to my righteousness; and I will sing praise to the name of the LORD most high.

PSALM 8

O LORD, our LORD, how excellent is thy name in all the earth! Thou hast set thy glory upon the heavens.

2 Out of the mouth of young men and infants hast thou established thy glory because of thine enemies, that thou mightest destroy the enemy and the avenger.

3 For thy heavens have seen the work of thy fingers, the moon and the stars, which thou hast ordained;

4 What is man, that thou art mindful of him? and the son of man, that thou visitest him?

5 For thou hast made him a little lower than the angels, and hast clothed him with glory and honor.

6 Thou madest him to have dominion over the works of thy hands; thou hast put all things under his feet,

7 All sheep and oxen, yea, and the beasts of the wilderness;

8 The fowl of the air and the fish of the sea which pass through the paths of the seas.

9 O LORD, our LORD, how excellent is thy name in all the earth!

PSALM 9

I WILL praise thee, O LORD, with my whole heart; I will show forth all thy marvelous works.

2 I will be glad and rejoice in thee and I will sing praise to thy name, O thou most High.

3 When mine enemies are beaten back, they shall stumble and perish before thy presence.

4 For thou hast maintained my right and my cause; thou hast sat on the throne, O thou righteous judge.

5 Thou hast rebuked the Gentiles and thou hast destroyed the wicked; thou hast blotted out their name for ever and ever.

6 My enemies have been annihilated by the sword for ever; and thou hast destroyed the villages and their very memory hath perished.

7 But the LORD shall endure for ever; he has prepared his throne for judgment.

8 And he shall judge the world in righteousness and the people in uprightness.

9 The LORD also will be a refuge for the poor, a refuge in times of trouble.

10 And they that know thy name will put their trust in thee; for thou hast not forsaken them that seek thee, O LORD.

11 Sing praises to the LORD, who dwells in Zion; declare among the people his skillful doings;

12 For he has remembered to avenge their blood; he forgets not the cry of the poor.

13 Have mercy upon me, O LORD, and consider my trouble which I suffer of them that hate me, O thou that removest me away from the gates of death,

14 That I may declare all thy praise in the gates of the daughter of Zion; I will rejoice in thy salvation.

15 The Gentiles are sunk down in the pit that they made; and their foot is caught in the net which they hid.

16 The LORD makes known the judgment which he executes; the wicked is snared in the work of his own hands.

17 The wicked shall be turned into Sheol, and all the peoples that forsake God.

18 For the poor shall not always be forgotten; and the hope of the poor shall not perish forever.

19 Arise, O LORD; let not man prevail; let the Gentiles be judged in thy sight.

20 Appoint for them a lawgiver, that the Gentiles may know themselves to be but men.

PSALM 10

WHY standest thou afar off, O LORD? and witholdest thy care in times of trouble?

2 The pride of the wicked maketh the poor to suffer; let them be taken in the devices that they have conceived.

3 For the ungodly boasts of his own desire, and the LORD is angry when the wicked is blessed.

4 The wicked in the pride of his countenance will not seek after God; and there is no God in all his thoughts.

5 His ways are always weak; thy judgments are far above out of his sight; as for all his enemies, he despises them.

6 He says in his heart, I shall not be moved from generation to generation; for he conceives evil.

7 His mouth is full of cursing and deceit and fraud; under his tongue is mischief and deceit.

8 He sits in the lurking place of a den; and in a secret place does he murder the innocent; his eyes spy on the destitute.

9 He lies in wait to snare the poor by drawing him into his net.

10 He shall be humbled and overthrown, and in his bones there shall be sickness and pain.

11 He says in his heart, God has forgotten; he has turned away his face; he will never see it.

12 Arise, O LORD; O my God, lift up thine hand; forget not the afflicted.

13 Why does the wicked provoke God? He says in his heart, God does not seek vengeance.

14 Thou hast seen it; for there is mischief and wrath, for thou beholdest that he hath surrendered himself unto thy hands; and the poor committeth himself unto thee; thou art the helper of the fatherless.

15 Break thou the arm of the wicked and the evil man; seek out his wickedness till thou find none.

16 The LORD is King for ever and ever; the Gentiles are perished out of his land.

17 LORD, thou hast heard the desire of the poor; thine ear hath heard the preparation of their heart;

18 Execute justice to the fatherless and to the afflicted, so that man may not be destroyed from the face of the earth.

PSALM 11

IN the LORD put I my trust; how say you to me, Flee as a bird to the mountains?

2 For, lo, the wicked bend their bow; they make ready their arrow

upon the string to shoot in the dark at the upright in heart.

3 For if they have destroyed the foundations which the LORD has prepared, what can the righteous do?

4 The LORD is in his holy temple, the LORD's throne is in heaven; his eyes behold, his eyelids examine, the children of men.

5 The LORD tries the righteous and the wicked; but his soul hates him that loves violence.

6 Snares have come down upon the wicked like rain; fire and brimstone and a destructive tempest shall be the portion of their cup.

7 For the LORD is righteous, and he loves righteousness; his countenance beholds the upright.

PSALM 12

SAVE, O LORD; for the godly man ceaseth; for faith hath disappeared from the earth.

2 Men speak vanity, every one with his neighbour; with flattering lips, and with a double heart do they speak.

3 The LORD shall destroy all flattering lips and tongues that speak proud things.

4 For they have said, With our tongue will we prevail; our lips are our own; who is lord over us?

5 Because of the oppression of the poor and the groans of the needy, now will I arise, says the LORD; and I will bring salvation openly.

6 The words of the LORD are pure words; as silver tried in a furnace on earth, they are purified seven times.

7 Thou shalt keep them, O LORD; thou shalt preserve me and save me from this generation for ever.

8 For the wicked walk everywhere with contemptible pride like the children of Edom.

PSALM 13

HOW long, O LORD, wilt thou forsake me? For ever? How long wilt thou turn away thy face from me?

2 How long shall I keep sorrow in my soul and misery in my heart daily? How long shall mine enemy be exalted over me?

3 Consider and hear me, O LORD my God; lighten mine eyes, lest I sleep in death,

4 Lest mine enemy say, I have prevailed against him, and those that trouble me rejoice when I am shaken.

5 But I have trusted in thy mercy; my heart shall rejoice in thy salvation.

6 I will sing unto the LORD, because he has saved me.

PSALM 14

THE fool has said in his heart, There is no God. They are corrupt, they have been defiled by their own devices; there is none that does good.

2 The LORD looked down from heaven upon the children of men to see if there were any that did understand and seek God.

3 They are all gone astray and have been rejected all together; there is none that does good; no, not one.

4 They recognized not the workers of iniquity, who devour my people as one eats bread; and they called not upon the LORD.

5 There were they in great fear; for God is in the generation of the righteous.

6 They have reproached the counsel of the poor, because he trusts on the LORD.

7 Who shall give out of Zion the salvation to Israel? When the LORD brings back the captivity of his people, Jacob shall rejoice and Israel shall be glad.

PSALM 15

LORD, who shall dwell in thy tabernacle? who shall inhabit thy holy mountain?

2 He that walks uprightly and works righteousness and speaks the truth in his heart.

3 He that deceives not with his tongue, nor does evil to his neighbor, nor accepts a bribe from his neighbor;

4 In whose eyes a detestable person is despised; but he honors them that

worship the LORD; he that swears to his neighbor and lies not;

5 He that lends not out his money with interest, nor takes a bribe against the innocent. He that does these things is upright and shall never be moved.

PSALM 16

PRESERVE me, O God; for in thee do I put my trust.

2 I have said unto the LORD, Thou art my LORD, and my goodness cometh from thee;

3 I said it also to the saints that are on the earth, and to the excellent, in whom is all my delight.

4 The sorrows of the wicked shall be multiplied in rapid succession that I may not pour out their libations of blood; nor will I mention their names with my lips.

5 The LORD is the portion of my inheritance and of my cup; thou shalt restore my inheritance.

6 My portion of the land fell to me in goodly places; yea, I have been pleased with my heritage.

7 I will bless the LORD, for he has given me counsel; my intuition also guides me during the night.

8 I have set the LORD always before me; because he is at my right hand, I shall not be moved.

9 Therefore my heart is glad and my glory rejoices; my flesh also shall rest in hope.

10 For thou hast left not my soul in Sheol; neither hast thou suffered thy Holy One to see corruption.

11 Thou wilt show me the path of life, and I shall be filled with the joy of thy countenance, with the pleasure of victory of thy right hand.

PSALM 17

HEAR, O Holy LORD, and consider my supplication; give ear unto my prayer that proceedeth not out of deceitful lips.

2 Let my judgment come forth from thy presence; let thine eyes behold the things that are just.

3 Thou hast proved my heart; thou hast visited me in the night; thou hast tried me, and thou hast not found iniquity in me; nothing hath come out of my mouth which is according to the deceitful works of men.

4 Through the conversation of my lips thou hast kept me from evil ways.

5 Thou hast strengthened my goings in thy paths, that my footsteps slip not.

6 I have called upon thee, for thou hast heard me. O God, incline thine ear unto me and hear my words.

7 Make thy Holy One a wonder and a Saviour to those who trust; but let him prevail against those that rise up against thy right hand.

8 Keep me as the apple of the eye; protect me under the shadow of thy wings,

9 From the sinners who plunder me, from the enemies of my soul who surround me.

10 Silence their mouth, for they have spoken vanity.

11 They have praised me, and now have surrounded me; they have determined to bury me in the ground.

12 They are like a lion that is eager to prey, and like a young lion lurking in secret places.

13 Arise, O LORD, humble them; cast them down; deliver my soul from the wicked and from the sword,

14 From the dead that die by thy hand, O LORD; and from the dead of the grave, divide their possessions among the living; fill their belly with thy treasure, so that their children are satisfied and have a portion remaining for their own children.

15 As for me, I will behold thy face in righteousness; I shall be satisfied when thy worship is revived.

PSALM 18

I WILL love thee, O LORD, my strength and my trust;

2 My refuge and my deliverer is the mighty God in whom I trust; he is my helper and the horn of my salvation and my glorious refuge.

3 I will call upon the LORD; so shall I be saved from mine enemies.

4 For the pains of death surrounded me, and the rush of ungodly men have confused me.

5 The travail of Sheol has taken hold of me: the snares of death preceded me.

6 In my distress I called upon the LORD, and cried to my God; he heard my voice out of his temple, and my cry came before him, even into his ears.

7 Then the earth shook and trembled; the foundations also of the mountains quaked and were shaken because he was angry.

8 There went up a smoke out of his wrath, and fire flamed from his face, and coals were kindled by it.

9 He bowed the heavens and came down; and thick darkness was under his feet.

10 And he rode upon cherubim and flew; yea, he soared upon the wings of the wind.

11 He made darkness his covert; his pavilion round about him was darkness of waters and thick clouds of the skies.

12 Out of the brightness of his shadow his clouds rained hailstones and coals of fire.

13 The LORD also thundered in the heavens, and the Highest gave his voice: hailstones and coals of fire.

14 Yea, he sent out his arrows and scattered them; and he multiplied his lightnings and confused them.

15 Then the brooks appeared, and the foundations of the world were laid open at thy rebuke, O LORD, at the blast of the breath of thine anger.

16 He sent from on high and quieted me; he received me out of great waters.

17 He delivered me from my strong enemies and from them which hated me; for they were too strong for me.

18 They confronted me in the day of my extremity, but the LORD was my deliverer.

19 He brought me forth into comfort; he delivered me because he delighted in me.

20 The LORD rewarded me according to my righteousness; according to the cleanness of my hands has he recompensed me.

21 For I have kept the ways of the LORD, and have not revolted against my God.

22 For all his judgments were before me, and his laws I did not put away from me.

23 I was also blameless before him, and I carefully kept myself from my sins.

24 Therefore has the LORD recompensed me according to my righteousness, according to the cleanness of my hands in his eyes.

25 With the pure thou shalt be pure; with an upright man thou shalt be upright.

26 With the clean thou shalt be clean; and from the crooked thou shalt turn aside.

27 For thou wilt save the afflicted people; but wilt humble the proud.

28 For thou wilt light my lamp; the LORD my God will enlighten my darkness.

29 For through thee I have pursued a band of robbers; and through my God have I leaped over a fence.

30 As for God, his way is perfect; the word of the LORD is pure: he is a help to all those that trust in him.

31 For there is no God save the LORD; and there is no one who is mighty like our God.

32 It is God that girds me with strength and makes my way perfect.

33 He makes my feet like hart's feet and sets me upon high places.

34 He trains my hands to war; and he strengthens my arms like a bow of brass.

35 Thou hast also given me the shield of thy salvation; and thy right hand hath held me up; and thy discipline hath made me great.

36 Thou hast steadied my legs under me, that my ankles may not be weakened.

37 I will pursue my enemies and overtake them; and I will not turn again till they are consumed.

38 I will smite them so that they shall not be able to stand; they shall fall under my feet.

39 For thou hast girded me with strength to the battle; thou hast subdued under me those that rose up against me.

40 Thou hast also defeated my enemies before me, that I might silence them that hate me.

41 They shall cry, but there will be none to save them; they shall beg the LORD, but he will not answer them.

42 Then I will beat them small as the dust before the wind; I will tread over them as the mire of the streets.

43 Thou wilt deliver me from the judgments of the people; and thou wilt make me the leader of the Gentiles; a people whom I have not known shall serve me.

44 As soon as they hear of me, they shall obey me; strangers shall submit themselves to me.

45 Strangers shall halt and shall be hindered from walking in their paths.

46 The LORD lives; blessed be the one who gives me strength; let my God and my Saviour be exalted.

47 It is God that avenges me and subdues the people under me.

48 He delivered me from my enemies; yea, thou liftest me up above those that rise up against me; thou hast delivered me from lawless man.

49 Therefore will I give thanks unto thee, O LORD, among the Gentiles, and sing praises unto thy name.

50 Great deliverance gives he to his king; and shows mercy to his anointed, to David and to his descendants for evermore.

PSALM 19

THE heavens declare the glory of God; and the firmament shows his handiwork.

2 Day after day utters speech, and night after night shows knowledge.

3 There is no speech nor language where their voice is not heard.

4 Their good news has gone out through all the earth, and their words to the end of the world. He has set his tabernacle in the sun among them.

5 And he is as a bridegroom coming out of his chamber, and rejoices as a strong man to run a race.

6 His going forth is from the end of the heaven, and his circuit unto the ends thereof; and there is nothing hid from the mist of his breath.

7 The law of the LORD is perfect, converting the soul; the testimony of the LORD is trustworthy, making wise the young men.

8 The statutes of the LORD are right, rejoicing the heart; the commandment of the LORD is pure, enlightening the eyes.

9 The reverence of the LORD is clean, enduring for ever; the judgments of the LORD are true and righteous altogether.

10 They are more to be coveted than gold; yea, than precious stones; sweeter also than honey and the honeycomb.

11 Moreover by them is thy servant warned; and if he keep them he shall be greatly rewarded.

12 Who can understand stumblings? Cleanse thou me from secret faults.

13 Spare thy servant also from presumptuous sins, lest the evil ones have dominion over me; then shall I be cleansed from my sins.

14 Let the words of my mouth and the meditation of my heart be acceptable in thy sight, O LORD, my helper and my Saviour.

PSALM 20

MAY the LORD answer you in the day of trouble; the name of the God of Jacob defend you;

2 Send you help from his sanctuary, and strengthen you out of Zion.

3 Let the LORD remember all your offerings, and make acceptable your burnt sacrifices.

4 May the LORD grant you according to your own heart, and fulfil all your counsel.

5 We will be glorified in your salvation, and in the name of our God we will be exalted; the LORD fulfil all your petitions.

6 Henceforth it is known that the LORD has saved his anointed; and has heard him from his holy heaven and saved with the strength of his right hand.

7 Some trust in chariots, and some in horses; but we will prevail through the name of the LORD our God.

8 They are bowed down and fallen; but we are risen and stand ready.

9 O LORD, save us, and let our King

answer us in the day when we call upon him.

PSALM 21

THE king shall rejoice in thy strength, O LORD; and in thy salvation how greatly shall he rejoice!

2 Thou hast given him his heart's desire, and hast not withheld the request of his lips.

3 For thou hast blessed him beforehand with the blessings of goodness; thou hast set a precious crown on his head.

4 He asked life of thee, and thou gavest it him, even length of days for ever and ever.

5 His glory is great in thy salvation; honor and majesty hast thou bestowed upon him.

6 For thou hast made him most blessed for ever; thou hast made him joyful in gladness with thy countenance.

7 For the king trusts in the LORD, and through the mercy of the most High he shall not be moved.

8 Your hand shall overcome all your enemies; your right hand shall overcome those that hate you.

9 You shall make them as a fiery oven in the time of your wrath; the LORD shall consume them in his wrath, and the fire shall devour them.

10 Their fruit shall you destroy from the earth, and their offspring from among the children of men.

11 For they have planned evil against you; they conceived a mischievous device, which they are not able to perform.

12 For you shall place a scar on them; and you shall make ready your array against their faces.

13 Be thou exalted, O LORD, in thine own strength; so will we sing and praise thy power.

PSALM 22

MY God, my God, why hast thou let me to live? and yet thou hast delayed my salvation from me, because of the words of my folly.

2 O my God, I call thee in the daytime but thou answerest me not;

and in the night season thou abidest not with me.

3 For thou art holy, and Israel dwells under thy glory.

4 Our fathers trusted in thee; they trusted, and thou didst deliver them.

5 They cried unto thee and were delivered; they trusted in thee and were not confounded.

6 But I am a worm, and not a man; a reproach of men, and despised of the people.

7 All they that saw me have laughed me to scorn; they shoot out with their lips, they shake their heads, saying,

8 He trusted in the LORD; let the LORD deliver him; let him save him, if he be delighted in him.

9 For thou art my trust since I came out of the womb, and my hope since I was upon my mother's breasts.

10 I was put under thy care from the womb; thou art my God from my mother's belly.

11 Be not far from me; for trouble is near; for there is none to help.

12 Many bulls [1] have surrounded me: strong bulls of Bashan have besieged me.

13 Their mouths snarl against me, as a ravening and roaring lion.

14 I am poured out like water and all my bones are out of joint; my heart is melted like wax, and my bowels are wasted in the midst of me.

15 My strength is dried up like a potsherd; and my tongue cleaves to my jaws; and thou hast thrown me into the dust of death.

16 For the vicious have surrounded me; the assembly of the wicked have inclosed me; they have pierced my hands and my feet.

17 My bones ached with pain; they looked and stared upon me.

18 They parted my garments among them, and cast lots upon my vesture.

19 But, O LORD, be not thou far from me; O God, O God, abide to help me.

20 Deliver my soul from the sword, my only one from the hand of the vicious.

[1] Oppressors.

21 Save me from the lion's mouth; save my meekness from the haughty,

22 That I may declare thy name to my brethren; in the midst of the congregation will I praise thee.

23 You that revere the LORD, praise him; all you the offspring of Jacob, glorify him; and fear him, all you descendants of Israel.

24 For he has not despised nor abhorred the affliction of the poor; neither has he turned away his face from him; but when he cried unto him, he heard him.

25 My praise shall be of thee in the great congregation; I will fulfil my vows before them that worship him.

26 The poor shall eat and be satisfied; they shall praise the LORD that seek him; their hearts shall live for ever.

27 All the ends of the world shall remember and turn to the LORD; and all the kindreds of the Gentiles shall worship before thee.

28 For the kingdom is the LORD's; he is the governor over the Gentiles.

29 All they that are hungry upon earth shall eat and worship before the LORD; all they that are buried shall kneel before him; my soul is alive to him.

30 An offspring shall serve him; the generations thereof shall proclaim the LORD.

31 They shall come and declare his righteousness to a people that shall be born, and tell that which the LORD has done.

PSALM 23

THE LORD is my shepherd; I shall not want.

2 He makes me to rest in green pastures; he leads me beside still waters.

3 He restores my soul. He leads me in the paths of righteousness for his name's sake.

4 Yea, though I walk through the valley of the shadow of death, I will fear no evil; for thou art with me; thy rod and thy staff they comfort me.

5 Thou preparest a table before me in the presence of mine enemies; thou anointest my head with oil; my cup runneth over.

6 Surely thy goodness and mercy shall follow me all the days of my life; and I shall dwell in the house of the LORD for ever.

PSALM 24

THE earth is the LORD's and the fulness thereof; the world and they that dwell therein.

2 For he has set the foundation thereof in the sea, and has furnished it with rivers.

3 Who shall ascend into the mountain of the LORD? or who shall stand in his holy place?

4 He who has clean hands and a pure heart; who has not sworn by his soul falsely, nor taken an oath deceitfully.

5 He shall receive the blessing from the LORD, and righteousness from God our Saviour.

6 This is the generation of them that seek thy face, that proclaim thy countenance, O thou God of Jacob.

7 Lift up your heads, O you gates; and be lifted up, O everlasting doors, that the King of glory may come in.

8 Who is this King of glory? The LORD, strong and mighty, the LORD mighty in battle.

9 Lift up your heads, O you gates; and be lifted up, O everlasting doors, that the King of glory may come in.

10 Who is this King of glory? The LORD of hosts, he is the King of glory forever.

PSALM 25

UNTO thee, O LORD, do I lift up my soul.

2 O my God, I trust in thee; let me not be ashamed, let not mine enemies triumph over me.

3 Yea, let none that trust in thee be ashamed; let the wicked be ashamed with their vanity.

4 Show me thy ways, O LORD; teach me thy paths.

5 Lead me in thy truth, and teach me; for thou art my God and my Saviour; on thee do I wait all the day.

6 Remember, O LORD, thy tender mercies and thy lovingkindnesses; for they are from the beginning of the world.

7 Remember not the foolishness of my youth, but according to thine abundant mercy remember thou me because of thy goodness' sake, O God.

8 Good and upright is the LORD; therefore will he direct sinners in the way.

9 He will guide the meek in judgment, and he will teach the poor his way.

10 All the paths of the LORD are mercy and truth unto such as keep his covenant and his testimonies.

11 For thy name's sake, O LORD, pardon mine iniquity; for it is great.

12 What man is he that fears the LORD? Him shall he teach in the way that he has chosen.

13 His soul shall abide with grace, and his offspring shall inherit the earth.

14 The LORD is mindful of them that worship him, and he will show them his covenant.

15 My eyes are ever toward the LORD; for he will release my feet out of the net.

16 Turn thou unto me, and have mercy upon me; for I am the only son and destitute.

17 The troubles of my heart are multiplied; O bring thou me out of my distresses.

18 Look upon my affliction and my labor; and forgive all my sins.

19 Consider my enemies; for they are many; and they hate me with an unjust hatred.

20 O keep my soul, and deliver me, because I have trusted in thee.

21 The innocent and the upright have followed me because I have trusted in thee.

22 God has saved Israel from all of his oppressors.

PSALM 26

JUDGE me, O LORD; for I have walked in my integrity; I have trusted also in the LORD; therefore I shall not waver.

2 Prove me, O LORD, and try me; examine my mind and my heart.

3 For thy lovingkindness is before my eyes, and I have walked in thy faith.

4 I have not sat with evil persons; neither have I associated with detestable persons.

5 I have hated the congregation of evildoers; and have not sat with the wicked.

6 I have washed my hands clean, and I have gone around thy altar, O LORD,

7 That I may hear the voice of thy praise and tell of all thy wondrous works.

8 LORD, I have loved the ritual of thy house and the place where thy glory dwelleth.

9 Destroy me not with sinners nor my life with bloody men,

10 In whose hands is mischief, and their right hand is full of bribes.

11 But as for me, I will walk in my integrity; save me and be merciful unto me.

12 My foot has stood in the straight way; in the congregation will I bless the LORD.

PSALM 27

THE LORD is my light and my salvation; whom shall I fear? The LORD is the strength of my life; of whom shall I be afraid?

2 When evildoers came upon me to devour me, even my enemies and those who hate me, they together stumbled and fell.

3 Though a host should encamp against me, my heart shall not fear; though war should rise against me, in this will I be confident.

4 One thing have I asked of the LORD, that will I seek after; that I may dwell in the house of the LORD all the days of my life, to behold the delight of the LORD, and to be in charge of his temple.

5 For in the day of trouble he shall hide me in his shelter; in the shadow of his tabernacle shall he hide me; he shall set me up upon a rock.

6 And now shall my head be lifted up above my enemies round about

me; therefore will I offer in his tabernacle sacrifices of joy; I will sing, yea, I will sing praises to the LORD.

7 Hear, O LORD, my voice when I call upon thee; have mercy also upon me and answer me.

8 My heart said unto thee, Let my face seek thy face.

9 Turn not away thy face from me, O LORD; trouble not thy servant in anger; thou hast been my help, O LORD; cast me not out, neither leave me, O my God and my Saviour.

10 Although my father and my mother have deserted me, the LORD has taken me up.

11 Teach me thy way, O LORD, and lead me in thy right paths.

12 Deliver me not over into the hands of my enemies; for false witnesses are risen up against me and have spoken cruelly.

13 But I have believed to see the goodness of the LORD in the land of the living.

14 Trust in the LORD, and be of good courage; yea, trust in the LORD.

PSALM 28

UNTO thee have I cried, O my God; be not silent to me, lest, if thou be silent to me, I become like them that go down into the pit.

2 Hear the voice of my supplications, when I cry unto thee, when I lift up my hands toward thy holy temple.

3 Count me not with the wicked and with the workers of iniquity, who speak peace with their neighbours, but mischief is in their hearts.

4 Reward them according to their deeds and according to their evil doings.

5 Because they have not understood the works of the LORD nor the operation of his hands, he shall destroy them and not build them up.

6 Blessed be the LORD, because he has heard the voice of my supplications.

7 The LORD is my helper and my protector; my heart trusted in him, and I am happy; I will praise him with glorious song.

8 The LORD is the strength of his people, and he is the protector of the salvation of his anointed.

9 Save thy people, O LORD, and bless thine inheritance; shepherd them also, and take care of them for ever.

PSALM 29

BRING unto the LORD the offspring of rams; bring unto the LORD glory and honour.

2 Give unto the LORD the glory due unto his name; worship the LORD in the court of his holy temple.

3 The voice of the LORD is upon the waters; the God of glory thunders; the LORD is upon many waters.

4 The voice of the LORD is powerful; the voice of the LORD is full of majesty.

5 The voice of the LORD breaks the cedars; yea, the LORD breaks the cedars of Lebanon.

6 He makes them also to skip like calves, Lebanon and Sirion like a young ox.

7 The voice of the LORD divides the flames of fire.

8 The voice of the LORD shakes the wilderness; the LORD shakes the wilderness of Kadesh.

9 The voice of the LORD makes the hinds to tremble, and uproots the forests; and in his temple every one speaks of his glory.

10 The LORD controls the flood; yea, the LORD sits King for ever.

11 The LORD will give strength to his people; the LORD will bless his people with peace.

PSALM 30

I WILL extol thee, O LORD; for thou hast lifted me up, and hast not made my foes to rejoice over me.

2 O LORD, my God, I have sought thee, and thou hast healed me.

3 Thou hast brought up my soul from Sheol; thou hast saved me that I should not join those who go down to the pit.

4 Sing unto the LORD, O ye saints of his, and give thanks at the remembrance of his holiness.

5 For there is rebuke in his anger and life in his good will; weeping

may last for a night, but joy comes in the morning.

6 In my security I said, I shall never be moved.

7 O God, by thy favor thou hast increased my glory; thou didst turn away thy face, and I was troubled.

8 I cried to thee, O LORD, and unto the LORD I made supplication.

9 What profit is there in shedding my blood, when I go down to corruption? The dust will not praise thee and it will not declare thy truth.

10 Hear, O God, and have mercy upon me; O LORD, be thou my helper.

11 Thou hast turned for me my mourning into joy; thou hast put off my sackcloth, and girded me with gladness;

12 Therefore, I will sing praise to thee, and not be silent. O LORD, my God, I will give thanks unto thee for ever.

PSALM 31

IN thee, O LORD, do I put my trust; let me never be ashamed; deliver me in thy righteousness.

2 Incline thine ear to me and answer me speedily; be thou unto me the God, the helper, and the house of refuge; and save me,

3 For thou art my strength and my refuge; therefore for thy name's sake comfort me and guide me.

4 Pull me out of the net that they have laid secretly for me; for thou art my protector.

5 Into thy hand I commit my spirit; thou hast redeemed me, O LORD God of truth.

6 I have hated them that observe false worship; but I trust in thee, O LORD.

7 I will be glad and rejoice in thy mercy; for thou hast seen my humility; thou hast known my soul in adversities;

8 And thou hast not surrendered me into the hand of my enemies; thou hast established my feet in tranquility.

9 Have mercy upon me, O LORD, for I am in distress; mine eye is troubled with wrath, yea, my soul and my body.

10 For my life is spent with grief, and my years with sighing; my strength is weakened because of poverty, and my bones are shaken because of my enemies.

11 I have become a reproach to my neighbors and a dread to my acquaintances: they that saw me on the street fled from me.

12 I am forgotten as a dead man out of mind; I am like something given up for lost.

13 For I have heard of the complicity of many persons; while they connived together against me, they schemed to take away my life.

14 But I trusted in thee, O LORD; I said, Thou art my God, O LORD.

15 The times are in thy hand; deliver me from the hand of mine enemies and from them that persecute me.

16 Make thy face to shine upon thy servant; save me through thy mercies.

17 Let me not be ashamed, O LORD; for I have called upon thee; let the wicked be ashamed, and let them be silent in the grave.

18 Let the lips of the wicked be silent; for they speak falsely and disdainfully against the righteous.

19 Oh how great is thy goodness, which thou hast laid up for them that worship thee, which thou hast wrought for them that trust in thee before the sons of men!

20 Hide them in the citadel of thy presence from the tumult of men; with thy shadow guard them from contention.

21 Blessed be the LORD, for he has elected for himself the chosen ones in a strong city.[1]

22 I said in my haste, I am lost from before thine eyes; nevertheless thou heardest the voice of my supplications when I cried unto thee.

23 O love the LORD, all you his righteous ones; for the LORD preserves the faithful, and rewards the wicked according to their works.

24 Be of good courage and he shall strengthen your heart, all you that trust in the LORD.

[1] Jerusalem.

PSALM 32

BLESSED is he whose transgression is forgiven and whose sin is blotted out.

2 Blessed is the man to whom the LORD has not reckoned his iniquity, and in whose heart there is no guile.

3 Because I suffered in silence all the day long, my bones waxed old during my deep slumber.

4 For day and night thy hand was heavy upon me; intense pain developed in my heart great enough to kill me.

5 I have acknowledged my sin unto thee, and mine iniquity have I not hid from thee. I said, I will confess my faults to the LORD; and thou forgavest all of my sins.

6 For this let every one that is chosen pray unto thee at an appointed time; surely even the floods of great waters shall not come near him.

7 Thou art my refuge; thou shalt protect me from mine enemies; thou wilt compass me about with glory and salvation.

8 I have made you to understand and have led you on the way which you shall take; I will follow you with my eyes.

9 Be not as the horse or as the mule, which have no understanding, which must be subdued with bit and bridle from their youth; no one goes near them.

10 The wicked has many sorrows; but he that trusts in the LORD, mercy shall surround him.

11 Be glad in the LORD and rejoice, you righteous; and praise him, all you that are upright in heart.

PSALM 33

REJOICE in the LORD, O you righteous; for praise is comely for the upright.

2 Praise the LORD with harp and guitar; sing praises to him with a harp of ten strings.

3 Sing to him a new song; play skilfully with a beautiful rhythm.

4 For the word of the LORD is right; and all his works are done in truth.

5 He loves righteousness and judgment; the earth is full of the goodness of the LORD.

6 By the word of the LORD were the heavens made; and all the host of them by the breath of his mouth.

7 The waters of the sea gathers he together as in a heap of waterskins; he lays up the depths in storehouses.

8 Let all the earth fear the LORD; let all the inhabitants of the world stand in awe of him.

9 For he spoke, and it was done; he commanded, and it stood fast.

10 The LORD brings the counsel of the Gentiles to nought; the LORD makes the devices of the people of no effect.

11 The counsel of the LORD stands for ever, the thoughts of his heart to all generations.

12 Blessed is the nation whose God is the LORD; and the people whom he has chosen for his own inheritance.

13 The LORD looks from heaven; he beholds all the sons of men.

14 From his throne he looks upon all the inhabitants of the earth.

15 He fashions their hearts alike; he considers all their works.

16 The king is not saved by the multitude of a host; neither a mighty man delivers by much strength.

17 A horse is a false thing for salvation; neither shall he deliver his rider by his great strength.

18 Behold, the eye of the LORD is upon the righteous, upon them that hope in his mercy

19 To deliver their soul from death and to keep them alive in famine.

20 Our soul waits for the LORD; he is our help and our shield.

21 For our hearts shall rejoice in him because we have trusted in his holy name.

22 Let thy mercy, O LORD, be upon us, according as we hope in thee.

PSALM 34

I WILL bless the LORD at all times; his praises shall continually be in my mouth.

2 My soul shall make its boast in the LORD; let the humble hear and be glad.

3 O magnify the LORD with me, and let us exalt his name together.

4 I sought the LORD, and he heard me and delivered me from all my troubles.

5 Look towards him and trust in him, and you shall not be disappointed.

6 This poor man called on him, and he heard him and saved him from all his troubles.

7 The host of angels of the LORD encamps round about them that worship him, and delivers them.

8 O taste and see that the LORD is good; blessed is the man that trusts in him.

9 The rich have become poor and suffer hunger;

10 They that seek the LORD shall not lack any good thing.

11 Come, you children, listen to me, and I will teach you reverence for the LORD.

12 Where is the man who desires not life and many days that he may see the good time to come?

13 Keep your tongue from evil and your lips from speaking guile.

14 Depart from evil and do good; seek peace and pursue it.

15 The eyes of the LORD are upon the righteous, and his ears are open to hear them.

16 The face of the LORD is against them that do evil, to cut off the remembrance of them from the earth.

17 The righteous cried, and the LORD hears, and delivers them out of all their troubles.

18 The LORD is near to them that are brokenhearted, and he saves those who are humble in spirit.[1]

19 Many are the afflictions of the righteous; but the LORD delivers him out of them all.

20 He keeps all his bones, not one of them is broken.

21 Evil shall slay the wicked, and they that hate the righteous shall be destroyed.

22 The LORD redeems the soul of his servants, and none of them that trust in him shall be condemned.

[1] Pride.

PSALM 35

PLEAD my cause, O LORD, with them that strive with me; fight against them that fight against me.

2 Take hold of shield and buckler, and stand up for my help.

3 Draw out the sword and flash it against them that persecute me; say unto my soul, I am your Saviour.

4 Let them be confounded and put to shame that seek after my soul; let them be turned back and brought to confusion that devise evil against me.

5 Let them be as chaff before the wind, and let the angel of the LORD chase them.

6 Let their way be dark and slippery, and let the angel of the LORD persecute them.

7 For they have dug pits for me and have spread a snare for my soul.

8 Let evil come upon them unawares; and let the net that they have hidden trap them; into that very pit which they have dug let them fall.

9 My soul shall be joyful in God; it shall rejoice in his salvation.

10 All my bones shall say, LORD, who is like unto thee, who deliverest the poor from his enemies, yea, the poor and the needy from him that seizes his property by force?

11 False witnesses rose up; they charged me with things that I knew not.

12 They rewarded me evil for good, and they destroyed my reputation among men.

13 But as for me, when they were sick, I wore sackcloth; I humbled my soul with fasting, and my prayer returned into my own bosom.

14 I behaved myself as though they had been my friends and brothers; I bowed down heavily, as one miserable in deep mourning.

15 During my misery they gathered together and rejoiced; yea, they gathered together against me for a long time, and I knew it not;

16 With their boasting and mocking, they gnashed at me with their teeth.

17 My LORD, I have suffered

enough; rescue my soul from their riot, my only one from the lions.

18 I will give thee thanks in the great congregation; I will praise thee among many people.

19 Let mine enemies not rejoice over me, nor the mockers who hate me for no reason; they wink with their eyes but they do not salute.

20 Against the meek of the earth, they devise mischievous things.

21 Yea, they opened their mouths wide against me, and said, Aha, aha, our eye has seen it.

22 This thou hast seen, O God; keep not silence; O my LORD, be not far from me.

23 Stir up thyself and awake to my judgment, see my suffering, my God and my LORD.

24 Judge me, O LORD my God, according to thy righteousness; and let them not rejoice over me.

25 Let them not say in their hearts, We have rid ourselves of him and we have buried him.

26 Let them be ashamed and brought to confusion who wish me evil; let them be clothed with shame and dishonour that magnify themselves against me.

27 Let them who are pleased with my victory shout for joy and be glad; yea, let them say continually, The LORD be magnified who has pleasure in the peace of his servant,

28 And my tongue shall speak of thy righteousness and of thy praise all the day long.

PSALM 36

THE unjust conceives wickedness within his heart, for there is no fear of God before his eyes.

2 He is unwilling to see his sins forgiven, or to hate them.

3 The words of his mouth are iniquity and deceit; he is unwilling to do good.

4 He devises mischief upon his bed; he walks in a way that is not good that he may do evil.

5 O LORD, thy mercy is in heaven; and thy faithfulness reacheth unto the universe.

6 Thy righteouess is like the moun-

tain of God; thy judgments are like a great deep; O LORD, thou preservest man and beast.

7 How abundant is thy lovingkindness, O God! therefore the children of men take refuge under the shadow of thy wings.

8 They shall flourish with the richness of thy house; and thou shalt give them to drink of the pleasant water of thy spring.

9 For with thee is the fountain of life; in thy light shall we see light.

10 O continue thy lovingkindness unto them that know thee, and thy righteousness to the upright in heart.

11 Let not the foot of pride come against me, and let not the hand of the wicked remove me.

12 For there the workers of iniquity will fall; they will be cast down, and will not be able to rise.

PSALM 37

FRET not because of evildoers, neither be envious of the workers of iniquity,

2 For they shall soon wither like grass, and fade away as the green herbs.

3 Trust in God, and do good; dwell in the land, and seek after faithfulness.

4 Trust in the LORD; and he shall give you the desires of your heart.

5 Commit your way to the LORD; trust also in him, and he shall bring it to pass.

6 He shall bring forth your righteousness as the light, and your judgment as the noonday.

7 Seek the LORD, and pray before him; envy not the man who does evil, and prospers in his way.

8 Cease from anger, and forsake wrath; fret not yourself in any wise to do evil.

9 For evildoers shall be cut off; but those who trust in the LORD shall inherit the earth.

10 For yet a little while, and the wicked shall be no more; yea, you shall look for his place, and you shall not find it.

11 But the meek shall inherit the

earth, and shall delight themselves in the abundance of peace.

12 The wicked plots against the just, and gnashes at him with his teeth.

13 The LORD shall laugh at him; for he sees that his day is coming.

14 The wicked have drawn out the sword and have bent their bow, to slay the poor and needy, and those who are upright in their way.

15 Their swords shall enter into their own hearts, and their bows shall be broken.

16 A little that a righteous man has is better than the great riches of the wicked.

17 For the arms of the wicked shall be broken; but the LORD upholds the righteous.

18 The LORD knows the days of the upright; and their inheritance shall be for ever.

19 They shall not be ashamed in the evil time; and in the days of famine they shall be satisfied.

20 For the wicked shall perish, and the rich who are enemies of the LORD shall be consumed; they shall vanish like smoke.

21 The wicked borrows, and pays not again; but the righteous shows mercy, and gives.

22 For the blessed of the LORD shall inherit the earth; and they that be cursed of him shall be wiped out.

23 The steps of a good man are established by the LORD; he sets his course.

24 Though he fall, he shall not be hurt; for the LORD upholds him with his hand.

25 I have been young, and now am old; yet I have not seen the righteous forsaken, nor his descendants begging bread.

26 But he is ever merciful and lends; and his offspring is blessed.

27 Depart from evil, and do good; and rest for evermore.

28 For the LORD loves justice, and he forsakes not his righteous ones; he keeps them for ever; but the seed of the wicked, he destroys.

29 The righteous shall inherit the land, and dwell therein for ever.

30 The mouth of the righteous speaks wisdom, and his tongue talks of justice.

31 The law of God is in his heart; none of his steps shall slide.

32 The wicked lies in wait for the righteous, and seeks to slay him.

33 The LORD will not leave him in his hand, nor condemn him when he is judged.

34 Trust in the LORD and keep his way, and he shall exalt you to inherit the land; when the wicked are cut off, you shall see it.

35 For I have seen the wicked boasting and spreading himself like stout forest trees;

36 Yet when I passed by, lo, he was not; yea, I sought him, but he could not be found.

37 Uphold the perfect and select the upright; for there is a good end for peaceful men.

38 But sinners shall be destroyed together; yea, the end of the wicked shall be destruction.

39 But the Saviour of the righteous is the LORD; he will help them in time of trouble.

40 And the LORD shall help them and deliver them; he shall deliver them from the wicked and save them, because they trust in him.

PSALM 38

O LORD, rebuke me not in thy wrath; neither chasten me in the heat of thine anger.

2 For thine arrows stick fast in me, and thy hand rests heavily upon me.

3 There is no peace in my flesh because of thine anger; neither is there any rest in my bones because of my sins.

4 For mine iniquities are gone over my head; as a great burden they are too heavy for me.

5 My wounds are loathsome and corrupt because of my foolishness.

6 I am greatly troubled; all the day long I walk sadly.

7 My loins are filled with trembling, and there is no peace in my body.

8 I am feeble and miserable; I have groaned because of the despair of my heart.

9 O LORD, all my desire is before

thee; and my groaning is not hidden from thee.

10 My heart is broken, my strength hath failed me; as for the light of mine eyes, it also is gone from me.

11 My neighbors and my friends stood aside from my grief; and my kinsmen stood off.

12 They also that seek after my life and wish me evil lay hold on me and speak mischievous things and imagine deceits all the day long.

13 But I, as a deaf man, heard not; and I was as a dumb man that opens not his mouth.

14 Thus I was as a man that hears not, and in whose mouth is no reproof.

15 For in thee, O Lord, do I hope; thou wilt answer me, O Lord my God.

16 Because I said, Hear me, lest they rejoice over me; they scoff at me when my feet waver.

17 I am prepared to suffer, and my sorrow is continually with me.

18 I will declare mine iniquity to thee; I will purify myself of my sins.

19 But mine enemies are strong and alert; and they that hate me wrongfully are multiplied.

20 They reward me evil for good; they reproach me because I seek after good things.

21 Forsake me not, O Lord; O my God, be not far from me.

22 Abide to help me and save me.

PSALM 39

I SAID, I will take heed to my ways that I sin not with my tongue; I will keep the words of my mouth under control while the wicked is before me.

2 I was dumb and sorrowful, I was wretched, I held myself aloof, even from good; and my sorrow was multiplied.

3 My heart was hot within me; and my body was on fire; then spoke I with my tongue,

4 Lord, show me mine end, and the measure of my days, what it is; that I may know my destiny.

5 Behold, thou hast given my days a limit; and mine age is as nothing

before thee; verily all men stand as a mere breath.

6 Because every man walks as an image, he disappears as a breath; he buries treasures and knows not who shall gather them.

7 Henceforth, what is my hope except in thee, O Lord?

8 Deliver thou me from all my transgressions; make me not the reproach of the unjust.

9 I was dumb, I opened not my mouth, because thou didst it.

10 Remove thy scourges from me; I am stricken by the blow of thy hand.

11 I am consumed by rebuke on account of my sins; thou dost chastise a man and dost remove his desires like stubble. Verily all men are like a breath.

12 Hear my prayer, O Lord; give ear unto my cry; hold not thy peace at my tears; for I am a dweller with thee and a sojourner, as all my fathers were.

13 O deliver me, that I may rest in peace before I pass away and be no more.

PSALM 40

I WAITED patiently for the Lord; and he turned towards me and heard my supplication.

2 He brought me up also out of a horrible pit, out of the mire of destruction, and set my feet upon a rock and established my goings.

3 And he has put a new song in my mouth, even praise unto our God, that many shall see it and rejoice and trust in the Lord.

4 Blessed is the man whose trust is in the name of the Lord, and who returns not to vanity; neither to lying conversation.

5 Many are thy works which thou hast done for us, O Lord our God, and thy wonderful care for us; I have declared that they are too many to be numbered; there is no one like unto thee.

6 Sacrifices and offerings thou didst not desire; but as for me, I now have understanding; burnt offering and sin offering hast thou not required.

7 Then said I, Lo, I come; in the beginning of the books, it is written of me,

8 I delight to do thy will, O my God; yea, thy law is within my heart.

9 I have preached thy righteousness in the great congregation; lo, I have not refrained my lips, O LORD, thou knowest.

10 I have not hid thy righteousness within my heart; I have declared thy faithfulness and thy salvation; I have not concealed thy lovingkindness and thy truth from the great congregation.

11 Withhold not thou thy tender mercies from me, O LORD; let thy lovingkindness and thy truth continually preserve me.

12 For innumerable evils have surrounded me; mine iniquities have overtaken me, so that I am not able to look up; they are more than the hairs of my head; and my heart fails me.

13 Be pleased, O LORD, to deliver me; O LORD, continue to help me.

14 Let them be ashamed and confounded who seek after my soul to destroy it; let them be driven backward and put to shame who wish me evil.

15 Let them be overthrown for their disgraceful conduct who say to me, Aha, aha!

16 Let all those that seek thee rejoice and be glad in thee; let such as love thy salvation say continually, The LORD be magnified.

17 But I am poor and needy; O my LORD, they have conspired against me; help me and deliver me; do not tarry, O my God.

PSALM 41

BLESSED is he who looks after the poor; the LORD will deliver him in time of trouble.

2 The LORD will preserve him and keep him alive, and he shall bless him upon the earth; he will not deliver him into the hands of his enemies.

3 The LORD will strengthen him upon his sick bed; he will wholly recover from his illness.

4 I have said, Thou art my LORD,

be merciful unto me and heal my soul, for I have sinned against thee.

5 Mine enemies speak evil of me: When shall he die, and his name perish?

6 When they come to see me, they speak falsely and their hearts devise evil; they go out into the street and gossip about me.

7 All that hate me whisper together about me; they devise evil against me.

8 They conceive unjust accusations against me; they say, Now that he lies sick in his bed, he shall rise up no more.

9 Yea, even the man who visits me, in whom I trust, who eats my bread and whom I trust, betrays me.

10 But thou, O LORD, be merciful unto me and heal me, that I may repay them.

11 By this I know that thou art pleased with me, because mine enemy doth not irk me.

12 And as for me, thou upholdest me in mine integrity, and settest me before thy face for ever.

13 Blessed is the LORD God of Israel from everlasting and to everlasting! Amen and Amen.

PSALM 42

AS the hart pants after the water brook so pants my soul after thee, O LORD.

2 My soul thirsts after thee, O living God; when shall I come to see thy face?

3 My tears have been my bread day and night, while they continually say unto me, Where is your God?

4 When I remember these things, my soul is agitated; therefore I will enter thy mighty citadel, even to the house of God, with the voice of joy and praise, with the many people who rejoice.

5 Why are you troubled, O my soul? and why are you bewildered? Trust in God; for I shall yet praise him, the Saviour of my honour and my God.

6 My soul is troubled within me; therefore will I remember thee from

the land of Jordan, from the mount of Hermon and from the hill.

7 Deep calls to deep at the sound of thy waterfalls: all thy waves and thy billows are gone over me.

8 Yet the LORD will command his lovingkindness in the daytime, and in the night his song shall be with me, and my prayer to the living God.

9 I will say to God, Why hast thou forsaken me? why go I mourning because of the oppression of my enemies?

10 When my bones are broken, mine enemies reproach me; while they say daily unto me, Where is your God?

11 Why are you disturbed, O my soul? and why are you bewildered? Hope in God; for I shall yet praise him, the Saviour of my honor and my God.

PSALM 43

JUDGE me, O God, and avenge my cause against a merciless people; O deliver me from the deceitful and unjust man.

2 For thou art the God of my strength; why has thou forsaken me? why go I mourning because of the oppression of the enemy?

3 O send out thy light and thy truth; let them comfort me; let them bring me unto thy holy mountain and to thy tabernacle.

4 Then will I go before the altar of God, to God who makes me joyful with the joy of youth; yea, upon the harp will I praise thee, O God, my God.

5 Why are you disturbed, O my soul? and why are you sad within me? Hope in God; for I shall yet praise him, who is the Saviour of my honor and my God.

PSALM 44

WE have heard with our ears, O God, our fathers have told us what work thou hast wrought in their days, in the times of old;

2 How thou didst destroy the Gentiles with thy hand, and established thy people; how thou didst vex the kingdoms, and strengthened thy people.

3 For they inherited not the land by their sword, neither did their own arm save them; but thy right hand and thine arm and the light of thy countenance, because thou wast pleased with them.

4 Thou art my King, O God; for thou commandest deliverances for Jacob.

5 Through thee will we pierce our enemies; through thy name will we tread them under that hate us.

6 For we trust not in our bows; neither on our armour to save us.

7 But thou hast saved us from those who hate us, and hast put to shame our enemies.

8 We glorify thee, O God, all the day long, and praise thy name for ever.

9 But now thou hast forsaken us and put us to shame, and goest not forth with our armies.

10 But thou makest us to be defeated; and our enemies have plundered us.

11 Thou hast sold us like sheep appointed for meat; and hast scattered us among the Gentiles.

12 Thou hast sold thy people as a bargain, and dost not profit by their exchange.

13 Thou makest us a reproach to our neighbours, a scorn and a derision to them that are round about us.

14 Thou makest us a byword among the Gentiles, a shaking of the head among the nations.

15 All the day long my disgrace is before me, and the shame of my face has covered me,

16 Because of the voice of him who reproaches and blasphemes; and because of the enemy that avenges.

17 All this is come upon us; yet have we not forgotten thee, neither have we dealt falsely in thy covenant.

18 We have not turned back, neither have we swerved our steps from thy way;

19 For thou hast humbled us a second time in the land, and covered us with the shadow of death.

20 And yet we have not forgotten the name of our God, or stretched out our hands to stranger gods;

21 God will look into this thing, for he knows the secrets of the heart.

22 Yea, for thy sake are we killed every day; we are counted as sheep for the slaughter.

23 Awake and sleep not, O LORD; remember us and forsake us not.

24 Turn not thy face from us, and forget not our humiliation and our oppression;

25 For our soul is humbled down to the dust; our body touches the earth.

26 Arise to help us; redeem us for thy mercies' sake.

PSALM 45

MY heart bubbles forth good news and I will tell my deeds to the king; my tongue is the pen of a ready writer.

2 You are fairer than the children of men; grace is poured into your lips; therefore God has blessed you for ever.

3 Gird your sword upon your thigh, O most mighty, with your glory and your majesty.

4 Your majesty is triumphant; ride upon the word of truth and meekness and righteousness; your law is upheld by reverence for your right hand.

5 Your arrows are sharp; let them pierce the heart of the king's enemies, and let the people fall under you.

6 Thy throne, O God, is for ever and ever; the sceptre of thy kingdom is a right sceptre.

7 You love righteousness and hate wickedness; therefore God, your God, has anointed you with the oil of gladness above your fellows.

8 All your garments smell of myrrh and aloes and cassia, out of the magnificent temple whereby they have made you glad.

9 The king's daughter stands in glory, the queen stands at your right hand in gold of Ophir.

10 Hearken, O my daughter, and consider and incline your ear; forget also your own people and your father's house.

11 So shall the king greatly desire your beauty; for he is your lord; make obeisance to him.

12 And the daughter of Tyre shall worship him; even the rich among the people shall seek your presence with gifts.

13 All the glory of the king's daughter is from within; her clothing is adorned with fine gold.

14 She shall be brought to the king with gifts; and her virgin companions shall follow in her train.

15 With gladness and rejoicing shall they be brought; they shall enter into the king's palace.

16 Instead of your fathers shall be your sons; you shall make them princes in all the earth,

17 I will make your name to be remembered in all generations; therefore shall the people praise you for ever and ever.

PSALM 46

GOD is our refuge and strength, a very present help in trouble.

2 Thou hast been with us always; therefore will we not fear when the earth quakes and mountains are shaken into the heart of the sea,

3 Though the waters thereof roar and be troubled, though the mountains shake with the force thereof.

4 There is a river, the streams whereof shall make glad the city of our God, The holy place of the most High.

5 God is in the midst of her; she shall not be moved; God shall help her in the early morning.

6 The heathen raged, the kingdoms trembled; he raised his voice, the earth quaked.

7 The LORD of hosts is with us; the God of Jacob is our refuge.

8 Come, behold the works of God, for he does wonders in the earth.

9 He makes wars to cease to the end of the earth; he breaks the bow and cuts the spear asunder; he burns the chariot in the fire.

10 Repent, and know that I am God; I am exalted among the heathen and I am exalted in the earth.

11 The LORD of hosts is with us; the God of Jacob is our refuge.

PSALM 47

O CLAP your hands, all people; shout to God with the voice of triumph.

2 For the LORD is most high and reverenced; he is a great King over all the earth.

3 For he has subdued the Gentiles under us, and the nations under our feet.

4 He has chosen us for the inheritance, and for the glory of Jacob whom he loved.

5 God is gone up with glory, the LORD with the sound of a trumpet.

6 Sing praises to God; sing praises to our King.

7 For God is the King of all the earth; sing praises unto him.

8 God reigns over the heathen; God sits upon his holy throne.

9 The rulers of the Gentiles have returned to the God of Abraham; for the dominions of the earth belong to God and he is greatly exalted.

PSALM 48

G REAT is our LORD, and exceedingly exalted in the city of our God and in his holy and glorious mountain.

2 Beautiful for situation, the joy of the whole earth, is mount Zion on the slopes of the north, the city of the great King.

3 God shows his might in her walled cities.

4 For, lo, the kings were prepared, and they passed by together.

5 They saw it, and so they marvelled; they were frustrated and hastened away.

6 Fear took hold of them, and pain, as of a woman in travail.

7 With a violent storm, the ships of Tarshish shall be broken.

8 As we have heard, so have we seen in the city of our God; God will establish it for ever.

9 We have trusted upon thy lovingkindness, O God, in the midst of thy temple.

10 As is thy name, O God, so is thy praise unto the ends of the earth; thy right hand is full of righteousness.

11 Let mount Zion rejoice, let the daughters of Judah be glad because of thy judgments, O LORD.

12 Circle Zion, and go round about her; count the towers thereof.

13 Mark well her strength and the depth of her bulwarks, that you may tell it to another generation.

14 For this God is our God for ever and ever; he will be our guide until death.

PSALM 49

H EAR this, all people; give ear, all inhabitants of the world,

2 Children of earth and sons of men, rich and poor together.

3 My mouth shall speak of wisdom; and the meditation of my heart shall be of understanding.

4 I will incline my ear to parables; I will chant my proverbs upon the harp.

5 I will fear not in days of evil, when the iniquity of my enemies shall surround me,

6 They who trust in their own strength and boast themselves in the multitude of their riches.

7 A brother cannot save a brother, nor can a man give to God a ransom for himself;

8 For the redemption of their souls is precious:

9 Do good for ever and you shall live for ever, and not see corruption.

10 But you will see wise men die; likewise the fool and the weak minded shall perish and leave their wealth to others.

11 Their graves shall be their only habitations for ever, and their dwelling places throughout generations; their marked graves will be their only remembrance on earth.

12 Nevertheless, such a man is not sustained by his honour; his end will be as the beasts, and he will perish.

13 This their way is their folly; in the end, demented, they will graze like cattle.

14 Like sheep they are consigned to the grave; death shall feed on them; and the upright shall have dominion over them in the morning;

the grave shall consume their beauty, and they shall be cast out from their glory.

15 But God will redeem my soul; from the power of the grave he will raise me up.

16 Be not afraid when one is made rich, when the glory of his house is increased;

17 For when he dies he shall carry nothing away; neither shall his glory descend after him.

18 For while he lived, he lived comfortably; he praised you when you favored him.

19 His end shall be as his father's was before him; they shall never see light.

20 Man cannot depend upon his honor for consolation, for if he does, he resembles the wild beasts.

PSALM 50

THE God of gods, the Lord, has spoken and called the earth from the rising of the sun to the going down thereof.

2 Out of Zion, the perfection of beauty, God has shined.

3 Our God shall come, and shall not keep silence; a fire shall consume before him, and it shall flame round about him greatly.

4 He shall call to the heavens from above and to the earth, that he may judge his people.

5 Gather unto him, O you, his saints, those that have made a covenant with him by sacrifice.

6 And the heavens shall declare his righteousness; for God himself is judge.

7 Hear, O my people, and I will speak to you; O Israel, I will testify to thee: I am God, even your God.

8 I reproved you not for your sacrifices or your burnt offerings; they are continually before me.

9 I will take no bullocks out of your house nor he-goats out of your folds.

10 For all the beasts of the forest are mine, and the cattle and the oxen upon the hills.

11 I know all the fowls of the air; and the wild beasts of the desert are mine.

12 If I were hungry, I should not tell you; for the world is mine and the fulness thereof.

13 I eat not the flesh of bulls, neither do I drink the blood of goats.

14 Offer to God the sacrifice of thanksgiving; and fulfil your vows to the most High.

15 Call upon me in the day of trouble; I will strengthen you, and you shall glorify me.

16 But to the sinner, God says, How have you followed the books of my law? You have observed my covenant lightly,

17 Seeing that you hate my instruction and cast my words behind you.

18 When you saw a thief, you joined with him, and you have been a partaker with adulterers.

19 You have given your mouth to evil and your tongue speaks deceit.

20 You sit and speak against your brother; you slander your own mother's son.

21 All of these things have you done, and I kept silence; you thought that I was wicked like you; but I will reprove you, and correct these sins before your eyes.

22 Now understand this, O you who forget God, lest you be crushed and there be none to deliver.

23 Whosoever offers the sacrifice of thanksgiving glorifies me; and to him will I show the way of the salvation of our God.

PSALM 51

HAVE mercy upon me, O God, according to thy lovingkindness; according to the multitude of thy tender mercies blot out my sins.

2 Wash me thoroughly from mine iniquity, and cleanse me from my sin;

3 For I acknowledge my transgressions, and my sin is ever before me.

4 Against thee, thee only, have I sinned, and done that which is evil in thy sight; for thou wilt be justified in thy reproof, triumphant in thy judgments.

5 For behold, I was formed in iniq-

uity; and in sin did my mother conceive me.

6 Behold, thou desirest truth, and the hidden things of thy wisdom thou hast made known to me.

7 Sprinkle me with hyssop, and I shall be clean; wash me, and I shall be whiter than snow.

8 Satisfy me with thy joy and gladness, that my broken spirit may rejoice.

9 Turn thy face away from my sins, and blot out all mine iniquities.

10 Create in me a clean heart, O God, and renew a right spirit within me.

11 Cast me not away from thy presence; and take not thy holy spirit from me.

12 Restore to me the joy of thy salvation; and uphold me with thy glorious spirit,

13 Then will I teach transgressors thy way, and sinners shall be converted unto thee.

14 Deliver me from bloodshedding, O God, thou God of my salvation, and my tongue shall sing aloud of thy righteousness.

15 O LORD, open thou my lips, and my mouth shall show forth thy praise;

16 For thou desirest not sacrifice; thou delightest not in burnt offerings.

17 The sacrifices of God are a broken spirit; a broken and a contrite heart, O God, thou wilt not despise.

18 Do good in thy good pleasure unto Zion; build the walls of Jerusalem.

19 Then shalt thou be pleased with the sacrifices of righteousness, with burnt offerings and whole burnt offerings; then shall they offer gifts upon thine altar.

PSALM 52

WHY do you boast of evil, O mighty man? Your tongue devises injustices against the innocent every day.

2 It is like a sharp razor, working deceitfully.

3 You love evil more than good, and lying rather than speaking righteousness.

4 You love all that speak evil and all deceitful tongues;

5 Therefore, God shall overthrow you, and he shall root you out of your dwelling place, and out of the land of the living.

6 Then shall the righteous see and rejoice, and shall trust in the LORD;

7 And they shall say, Lo, this is the man who trusted not in God; but trusted in the abundance of his riches, and boasted in his possessions.

8 But I am like a green olive tree in the house of God; I have trusted in the mercy of God for ever and ever.

9 I will praise thee for ever, because thou hast done it; and I will proclaim thy name before thy saints for generations.

PSALM 53

THE fool has said in his heart, There is no God. Corrupt are they, and abominable in their iniquities; and there is none that does good.

2 God looked down from heaven upon the children of men to see if there were any that did understand, that did seek God.

3 Every one of them has gone astray; they are altogether become filthy; there is none that does good, no, not one.

4 These people no longer recognize evil; they have consumed my people like bread; they have no respect for God.

5 There they feared where no fear was; for God has scattered the bones of hypocrites; they have been ashamed, because God has despised them.

6 Who out of Zion will give salvation to Israel? When God brings back the captivity of his people, Jacob shall rejoice and Israel shall be glad.

PSALM 54

SAVE me, O God, by thy name, and judge me by thy strength.

2 Hear my prayer, O God; give ear to the words of my mouth.

3 For strangers are risen up against me, and the mighty seek after my

life; they have disregarded thee, O God.

4 Behold, God is my helper; the LORD sustains my soul.

5 Bring disaster to mine enemies; silence them in thy truth.

6 I will freely sacrifice to thee; I will praise thy name, O LORD, for it is good;

7 For thou hast delivered me out of all troubles; and mine eye hath seen mine enemies defeated.

PSALM 55

GIVE ear to my prayer, O God; and reject not my supplication.

2 Hear me and answer me; return to my cry and incline to me,

3 Because of mine enemies, because of the oppression of the wicked; for they have devised iniquity against me, and reproached me.

4 My heart is greatly pained within me; and the terrors of death are fallen upon me.

5 Fearfulness and trembling are come upon me, and the shadow of death has overwhelmed me.

6 And I said, Oh that I had wings like a dove! Then would I fly away and be at rest.

7 Lo, then I would fly far off and dwell in the wilderness.

8 I would wait for him that will save me from the windy storm and the tempest.

9 Destroy, O LORD, and render useless their tongues; for I have seen violence and strife in the city.

10 Day and night they go about it, around its walls; injustice and mischief are in the midst of it.

11 Wickedness is in the midst of it; deceit and guile depart not from its streets.

12 For it was not mine enemy that reproached me; then I could have borne it; neither was it he that hated me that did magnify himself against me; then I would have hid myself from him;

13 But it was you, a man mine equal, my kinsman, and my friend.

14 We ate a meal together in the house of God, and we walked in harmony.

15 Bring death upon them; bury them alive in the grave, because there is evil among them.

16 As for me, I will call upon God; and God shall save me.

17 At evening and in the morning and at noon will I pray and cry aloud; and he shall hear my voice.

18 Deliver my soul from those who have been too wise for me, from those who have opposed me continuously.

19 God, even the Eternal one, shall hear and humble them. With them also there are no changes; therefore they fear not God.

20 They have put forth their hands against their neighbours, they have broken his covenant.

21 They were afraid because of the anger in his countenance and the wrath in his heart; his words were smoother than butter, yet were they sharp like the point of a spear.

22 Cast your worries upon the LORD and he will sustain you; he will never suffer the righteous to fear want.

23 But thou, O God, shalt bring them down into the pit of destruction; bloody and deceitful men shall not live out their days; but I will trust in thee.

PSALM 56

BE merciful to me, O God; for man has trodden me under foot; all the day long the fighting oppresses me.

2 Mine enemies have daily trodden me under foot; for many warriors have risen against me.

3 I fear not during the day, because I trust in thee.

4 In God I will be glorified, in God I have put my trust; I will not fear what man can do to me.

5 All the day long they conspired against me and they devised evil against me.

6 They will wait in hiding, they will watch my steps, inasmuch as they wish for my death.

7 He has no deliverer, they have said. Condemn them with the condemnation of the Gentiles.

8 O God, I have declared my faith unto thee; record thou my tears before thee in thy book.

9 Then shall mine enemies turn back; and I will know I have a God.

10 In God will I praise his word; in the LORD will I praise his word.

11 In God have I put my trust; I will not be afraid what man can do to me.

12 To thee shall I perform my vows, O God; I will offer them to thee with thank offering.

13 For thou hast delivered my soul from death and my feet from stumbling, that I may be pleasing in thy sight, O God, in the land of the living.

PSALM 57

BE merciful unto me, O God, be merciful unto me; for my soul trusts in thee; yea, in the shadow of thy wings will I make my refuge until these calamities be overpast.

2 I will cry to God most High, to God my Saviour.

3 For he has sent from heaven and delivered me; he has put mine enemies to shame. God shall send forth his mercy and his truth.

4 He has delivered my life from the vicious as I slept in fear, and from the sons of men, whose teeth are spears and arrows, and their tongues sharp swords.

5 Be thou exalted, O God, above the heavens; let thy glory be above all the earth.

6 They have prepared a net for my feet; they have digged a pit for my soul, into the midst of which they themselves have fallen.

7 My heart is made ready, O God, my heart is ready; I will sing and give praise in my glory.

8 Awake, my harp; awake, psaltery and harp; I myself will awake early.

9 I will praise thee, O LORD, among the people; I will sing unto thy name among the nations.

10 For thy mercy is exalted to the sky and thy faithfulness to the heavens.

11 Be thou exalted, O God, above the heavens; let thy glory be above all the earth.

PSALM 58

DO you indeed speak righteousness, O congregation? do you judge uprightly, O sons of men?

2 Behold you all speak evil on earth, and your hands are soiled with injustice.

3 The wicked are known from the womb; they go astray as soon as they are born, speaking lies.

4 Their poison is like the poison of a serpent; they are like the deaf adder that stops its ear,

5 And will not listen to the voice of the whisperer, neither to the charmer nor to the wise.

6 Break their teeth in their mouths, O God; pull out the fangs of the lions,[1] O LORD.

7 Let them be rejected as water which is contaminated; let God shoot his arrows until the wicked are destroyed.

8 Like the wax that melts, and drips before the fire, let them be destroyed; fire has fallen from heaven and they did not see; the light of truth has been given and they did not understand.

9 Let their thorns be increased, and fear of wrath shake them violently.

10 The righteous shall rejoice when he sees the vengeance; he shall wash his hands in the blood of the wicked,

11 So that a man shall say, Verily there is a reward for the righteous; verily there is a God that judges in the earth.

PSALM 59

DELIVER me from mine enemies, O God; defend me from them that rise up against me.

2 Deliver me from the workers of iniquity, and save me from bloody men.

3 For, lo, they lie in wait for my soul; evil have they multiplied against me; not because I have transgressed or because I have sinned, O LORD.

4 They run and prepare themselves

---

[1] Oppressors.

against me without considering whether I have been at fault;

5 Awake to help me, and behold, O thou LORD God of hosts, the God of Israel, awake to visit all the nations, and spare not any wicked transgressors.

6 They return at evening; they make a noise like dogs, and go round about the city.

7 Behold, they belch out with their mouths; swords are in their lips; for who, say they, does care?

8 But thou, O LORD, shalt laugh at them; thou shalt have all the nations in derision.

9 To thee shall I give praise, O God, for thou art my defense.

10 O God, thy lovingkindness has preceded me; God has let me live to see my enemies avenged.

11 Spare them for a living example, lest my people forget; but scatter them by thy power, and bring them down, O LORD my hope.

12 For the sin of their mouth and the words of their lips, let them even be taken in their pride; for it is cursing and lying that they speak.

13 Consume them in thy wrath, consume them, that they be no more, that they may know that God rules over Jacob and over the ends of the earth.

14 And at evening let them return; and let them make a noise like dogs, and go round about the city.

15 Let them be hungry and not be filled, neither let them find a lodging place.

16 But I will sing of thy power; yea, I will sing aloud of thy mercy in the morning; for thou hast been my defense and refuge in the day of my trouble.

17 Unto thee, O God, will I sing; for thou art God of my refuge and the God of my mercy.

PSALM 60

O GOD, thou hast forsaken us, thou hast scattered us, thou hast been displeased with us; O turn thyself to us again.

2 Thou hast made the earth to tremble; thou hast broken it; heal the breaches thereof, for it hath weakened.

3 Thou hast shown thy people hardships; thou hast made us to drink the dregs of wine.

4 Thou hast wrought a miracle to them that reverence thee, so that they need not flee from the bow.

5 That thy beloved may be prepared, save with thy right hand, and hear me.

6 God has spoken in his holiness: I will be strong, I will divide Shechem and mete out the valley of Succoth.

7 Gilead is mine and Manasseh is mine; Ephraim also is the strength of my head; Judah is my king.

8 Moab is my washpot; over Edom will I levy tribute; over Philistia will I triumph.

9 Who will lead me into Edom? Who will bring me into the strong city?

10 For behold, O God, thou hadst cast us off, and thou didst not go before us with our armies.

11 Give us strength against our enemies; for vain is the help of man.

12 Through God we shall do valiantly; for he it is who shall tread down our enemies.

PSALM 61

HEAR my cry, O God; attend to my prayer.

2 From the end of the earth will I cry unto thee, when my heart is overwhelmed; for thou hast led me upon a rock and hast comforted me.

3 For thou hast been a shelter for me, and a strong tower from my enemies,

4 I will abide in thy tabernacle for ever; I will make my refuge the shadow of thy wings.

5 For thou, O God, hast heard my vows; thou hast given an inheritance to them that revere thy name.

6 Thou hast added days to the days of the king, and his years as many generations.

7 He shall be established before God for ever; mercy and justice shall preserve him.

8 So will I sing praise unto thy

name for ever, when daily I fulfil my vows.

PSALM 62

MY soul waits upon God; from him comes my salvation.

2 He only is my God and my salvation; he is my great defense; I shall not be moved.

3 How long will you threaten a man so that you may kill him? Like a crumbling wall shall you be and as a tottering fence.

4 For you have thought to cast him down from his excellency; you delight in lies; you bless with your mouths, but curse with your hearts.

5 My soul, wait only upon God; for my salvation is from him.

6 He only is my God and my salvation; he is my defense; I shall not be moved.

7 In God is my salvation and my glory; God is my strength, my refuge, and my hope.

8 Trust in him at all times; you people, pour out your hearts before him; God is a refuge for us.

9 Surely all untrue men are like vapor; when they are placed in the balance, they are found wanting.

10 Trust not in oppression, and become not vain in robbery; if riches increase, let not your heart rejoice over them.

11 God has said this once; twice have I heard this; that power belongs unto God.

12 Also unto thee, O LORD, belongs mercy; for thou renderest to every man according to his work.

PSALM 63

O GOD, thou art my God; on thee I wait; my soul thirsteth for thee, my flesh longeth for thee as in a dry and thirsty land where no water is.

2 As, in purity, I have seen thee, so may I see thy power and thy glory.

3 Because thy lovingkindness is better than life, my lips shall praise thee.

4 Thus will I bless thee while I live; I will lift up my hands in thy name.

5 My soul shall be enriched as with cream and fatness; and my mouth shall praise thee with joyful lips.

6 I remember thee upon my bed and I meditate on thee in the night watches.

7 Because thou hast been my helper, therefore in the shadow of thy wings will I glory.

8 My soul follows hard after thee; thy right hand upholds me.

9 But those that seek my soul, to destroy it, shall go into the lower parts of the earth.

10 They shall fall by the sword; they shall be a portion for foxes.

11 But the king shall rejoice in God; every man that swears by him shall glory; but the mouths of those who speak lies shall be stopped.

PSALM 64

HEAR my voice, O God, as I pray to thee; preserve my life from fear of mine enemy.

2 Hide me from the wickedness of the evil one; from the corruption of the workers of iniquity,

3 Who whet their tongues like a sword, and charge their words with poison like an arrow,

4 That they may shoot in secret at the innocent; suddenly do they shoot at him, and fear not.

5 They encourage themselves with evil speech; they plan to hide snares; they say, Who shall see us?

6 They plan wickedness, but they are destroyed in order to consume evil from among men and from the depths of the heart.

7 But God is great; suddenly he shall shoot at them with an arrow;

8 So shall their tongues be silenced, and all that see them shall be frightened.

9 And all men shall fear, and shall declare the work of God; for they shall wisely consider the work of his hands.

10 The righteous shall be glad in the LORD, and shall trust in him; and all the upright in heart shall glorify him.

PSALM 65

PRAISE is befitting thee, O God, in Zion; and unto thee shall the vow be performed;

2 O hear my prayer; unto thee shall all flesh come.

3 The words of the wicked have prevailed against me; as for our transgressions, thou shalt purge them.

4 Blessed is the man in whom thou art pleased, he whom thou causest to approach unto thee, that he may dwell in thy courts and be satisfied with the goodness of thy house, even of thy holy temple.

5 From the majesty of thy righteousness answer us, O God of our salvation, who art the confidence of all the ends of the earth, and of the peoples who are afar off,

6 Who settest fast the mountains by his strength, and is mighty in his power;

7 He stills the tempest of the seas and the roar of their waves. The peoples shall be troubled.

8 The inhabitants of the earth shall tremble at thy wonders, from the coming of the morning to the evening.

9 With glory didst thou visit the earth and water it; thou hast blessed it with peace and hast greatly enriched it with the river of God, which is full of water; thou hast prepared food when thou hast established it.

10 Thou hast watered the fallowed ground thereof; to bring forth fruits, thou hast sprinkled its growth with showers and blessed it.

11 Thou crownest the year with thy goodness; and the calves have rich pasture.

12 They shall be filled with the pastures of the wilderness, and the hills shall be surrounded with glory.

13 The pastures shall be covered with fattening sheep, the valleys shall be clothed with wheat; they shall rejoice, yea, they shall sing.

PSALM 66

MAKE a joyful noise unto God, all lands.

2 Sing the honor of his name; sing the honor of his majesty.

3 Say unto God, How wonderful are thy works! Through the greatness of thy power shall thine enemies submit themselves unto thee.

4 All the earth shall worship thee, and shall sing unto thy name; they shall glorify thy name forever.

5 They shall say, Come and see the works of God; for his wonders are great toward the children of men.

6 He turns the sea into dry land; they crossed through the river on foot; there did we rejoice in him.

7 He rules by his power for ever; his eyes behold the nations; let not the rebellious exalt themselves.

8 O bless our God, you people, and make the voice of his praise to be heard,

9 Who holds our soul in life, and suffers not our feet to be moved.

10 For thou, O God, hast proved us; thou hast tried us as silver is tried.

11 Thou didst bring us into the net; thou didst lay affliction upon our loins.

12 Thou hast caused us to be in servitude; we went through fire and through water; finally thou didst bring us out into a comfortable place.

13 I will go into thy house with gifts; I will pay thee my vows,

14 Which my lips have uttered and my mouth has spoken when I was in trouble.

15 I will offer unto thee burnt sacrifices of fatlings, with the savour of rams; I will offer bullocks with goats.

16 Come and hear, all you servants of God, and I will declare what he has done for my soul.

17 I cried to him with my mouth, and he has answered me; I extolled him with my tongue.

18 If thou behold iniquity in my heart, O LORD, deliver me not.

19 But verily God has heard me; he has attended to the voice of my prayer.

20 Blessed be God, who has not rejected my prayer nor turned his mercy from me.

PSALM 67

GOD be merciful unto us and bless us; and cause his face to shine upon us,

2 That thy ways may be known upon earth, thy saving health among all nations.

3 Let the people praise thee, O God; let all the people praise thee.

4 O let the nations be glad and sing for joy; for thou shalt judge the people righteously, and govern the nations upon earth.

5 Let the people praise thee, O God; let all the people praise thee.

6 Then shall the earth yield her increase; and God, even our own God, shall bless us.

7 God shall bless us; and all the ends of the earth shall fear him.

PSALM 68

LET God arise, let his enemies be scattered; let them also that hate him flee before him.

2 As smoke is driven away, so let them vanish; as wax melts before the fire, so let the wicked perish at the presence of God.

3 But let the righteous be glad; let them be valiant in the sight of God; yea, let them rejoice in his pleasure.

4 Sing unto God, sing praises to his name; extol him who rides upon the heavens; the LORD is his name, rejoice before him.

5 A father of the fatherless and a judge of widows is God in his holy habitation.

6 God sets the solitary child in families; he triumphantly releases those who are bound with chains; but the rebellious dwell in waste places.

7 O God, when thou didst go forth before thy people, when thou didst march through the wilderness,

8 The earth shook, the heavens also lowered at the presence of God; even Sinai itself was moved at the presence of God, the God of Israel.

9 Thou, O God, didst send a plentiful rain whereby thou didst confirm thine inheritance when it was weary.

10 Thy living creatures have dwelt therein; thou O God, hast provided of thy goodness for the poor.

11 The LORD shall give good tidings with great power.

12 Then the kings of armies shall be defeated; and the household of God shall divide the spoil.

13 Though you sleep among thorns, yet shall you be protected as the wings of a dove covered with silver, and her feathers with yellow gold.

14 When God appointed a king over Zion, it became white like snow

15 Over Salmon, the mountain of God, over the mountains of Bashan and over the mountain ridges.

16 What do you want, O you mountains of Bashan? This is the ridge which God desires to dwell in; yea, the LORD will dwell in it for ever.

17 God rides with the host of angels; the LORD is among them, as in Sinai, in his holy place.

18 Thou hast ascended on high, thou hast carried away captives; thou hast blessed men with gifts; but rebellious men shall not dwell before the presence of God.

19 Blessed be the LORD, for he has chosen us as his heritage, even the God of our salvation.

20 He that is our God is the God of salvation, the LORD God who has the power of life and death.

21 But God shall sever the head of his enemies, and the hairy scalp of the head of those who persist in their sins.

22 The LORD said, I will rescue my people from the cliffs, I will bring my people from the depths of the sea;

23 That thy foot shall be dipped in the blood of thine enemies, and the tongue of thy dogs in the same.

24 They have seen thy goings, O God, even the goings of my God and my holy King.

25 The princes went before, the singers followed after; among them were the damsels playing with timbrels.

26 Bless God in the congregations, even the LORD, you that are of the fountain of Israel.

27 There is little Benjamin with

their ruler, the princes of Judah and their governors, the princes of Zebulun, and the princes of Naphtali.

28 Command, O God, thy strength; strengthen, O God, that which thou hast wrought for us.

29 Out of thy temple at Jerusalem shall kings bring presents unto thee.

30 Rebuke the wild beasts [1] of the marshes, the multitude of the wild bulls, the idols of the Gentiles which are covered with silver; scatter the people who delight in war.

31 Ambassadors shall come out of Egypt; Ethiopia shall soon stretch out her hands to God.

32 Sing to God, you kingdoms of the earth; O sing praises to the Lord.

33 To him who rides upon the heavens of heavens; out of the east he gives his voice, and that a mighty voice.

34 Ascribe glory unto God; his excellency is over Israel and his strength is in the heavens.

35 O God, thou art honoured out of thy holy place; the God of Israel is he that gives strength and power to his people. Blessed be God.

PSALM 69

SAVE me, O God; for the waters are come near to engulf me.

2 I sink in deep mire where there is no footing; I am come into deep waters, where the floods overflow me.

3 I am weary of my crying; my throat is dry; mine eyes fail while I wait for God.

4 They that hate me without a cause are more than the hairs of my head; they that would destroy me, being mine enemies wrongfully, are mighty; then I restored that which I took lawfully.

5 O God, thou knowest my foolishness; and my sins are not hid from thee.

6 Let not them that trust in thee be ashamed through me, O Lord God of hosts; let not those that seek thee be dishonored through me, O God of Israel.

7 Because for thy sake I have borne reproach; shame has covered my face.

8 I am become a stranger to my brethren and an alien to my mother's children.

9 For the zeal of thy house has made me courageous; and the reproaches of them that reproached thee are fallen upon me.

10 When I humbled and chastened my soul with fasting, that was to my reproach.

11 I made sackcloth also my garment and I became a proverb to them.

12 They that sit in the gate speak against me; and I was the song of the drunkards.

13 But as for me, my prayer is unto thee, O Lord, in an acceptable time; O God, in the multitude of thy mercy answer me, in the abundance of thy salvation.

14 Deliver me out of the mire, and let me not sink; let me be delivered from them that hate me, and out of the deep waters.

15 Let not the waterflood overflow me, neither let the deep swallow me up, and let not the well shut its mouth upon me.

16 Answer me, O Lord; for thy lovingkindness is good; turn to me according to the multitude of thy tender mercies.

17 And hide not thy face from thy servant; for I am in trouble; answer me speedily.

18 Draw near to my soul, and redeem it; deliver me because of mine enemies.

19 Thou knowest my reproach and my shame, and my dishonour is spread before all mine adversaries.

20 O thou, heal my broken heart and bind it; I looked for some to take pity, but there was none; and for comforters, but I found none.

21 They gave me bitter herbs for my food; and in my thirst they gave me vinegar to drink.

22 Let their table become a snare before them; and that which should have been for their reward, let it become a trap.

[1] Oppressors.

23 Let their eyes be darkened, that they see not; and make their backs continually to bend.

24 Pour out thine indignation upon them, and let thy wrathful anger take hold of them.

25 Let their habitation be desolate; and let none dwell in their tents.

26 The one which thou hast smitten, they have persecuted; they have added to the grief of him who is wounded.

27 Add punishment of iniquity to their iniquity, that they may enter not into thy righteousness.

28 Let them be blotted out of thy book of the living, and not be written with the righteous.

29 But I am poor and sorrowful; let thy salvation help me, O God.

30 I will praise the name of God with a song, and will magnify him with thanksgiving.

31 This shall please the LORD better than an ox or bullock that has horns and hoofs.

32 The humble shall see this and be glad; and your heart shall live that seek God.

33 For the LORD hears the poor, and despises not his prisoners.

34 Let heaven and earth praise him, the seas, and every thing that moves therein.

35 For God will save Zion, and will build the cities of Judah;

36 His servants shall dwell in it and shall inherit it; they that love his name shall dwell therein.

PSALM 70

MAKE haste, O God, to deliver me; make haste to help me, O LORD.

2 Let them be ashamed and confounded that seek after my soul; let them be turned backward and put to confusion that desire my hurt.

3 Let them be confounded by their recurring shame that say to me, Aha, aha!

4 Let all those that seek thee rejoice and be glad in thee; and let such as love thy salvation say continually, Let God be magnified.

5 But I am poor and needy; make haste unto me, O God; thou art my help and my deliverer; O LORD, tarry not.

PSALM 71

IN thee, O LORD, do I put my trust; let me never be confounded.

2 Deliver me in thy righteousness and rescue me; incline thine ear to me and save me.

3 Be thou to me a sheltering rock whereunto I may continually resort; give thou commandment to save me; for thou art my rock and my fortress.

4 Deliver me, O God, out of the hand of the wicked, out of the hand of the unrighteous and cruel man.

5 For thou art my hope, O LORD; thou art my trust from my youth, O God.

6 By thee have I been sustained from the womb; thou art my hope since I was in my mother's body; my praise is continually of thee.

7 I am as a wonder to many; but thou art my strong refuge.

8 Let my mouth be filled with thy praise and with thy honor all the day.

9 Cast me not off in the time of old age; forsake me not when my strength fails.

10 For mine enemies speak against me; and they that lie in wait for my soul take counsel together,

11 Saying, God has forsaken him; pursue and take him; for there is none to deliver him.

12 O God, be not far from me; O my God, make haste for my help.

13 Let them be ashamed and embarrassed who envy my soul; let them be covered with shame that seek my hurt.

14 But I will pray continually, and will praise thee yet more and more.

15 My mouth shall show forth thy righteousness and thy salvation all the day, for I cannot read.

16 I will go in the strength of the LORD; I will make mention of thy righteousness even of thine only.

17 O God, thou hast taught me from my youth, so that I might declare thy wondrous works.

18 Now also to old age and gray hairs, O God, forsake me not; until

I have shown thy strength and thy might to the generation that is to come.

19 Thy righteousness also, O God, has reached to the highest; thou hast done great things; O God, who is like unto thee!

20 Thou who hast shown me great and sore troubles, shalt quicken me again, and shalt bring me up again from the depths of the earth.

21 Thou hast increased my greatness, and hast returned to comfort me.

22 I will also praise thee with the psaltery, I will sing to thy truth, O my God; unto thee will I sing with the harp, O thou Holy One of Israel.

23 My lips shall greatly rejoice when I sing unto thee; and my soul, which thou hast redeemed.

24 My tongue also shall talk of thy righteousness all the day long; for they are confounded, for they are brought to shame that seek my hurt.

PSALM 72

GIVE the king thy judgments, O God, and thy righteousness to the king's son,

2 That he may judge thy people with righteousness and thy poor with justice.

3 The mountains shall bring peace to thy people, and the hills thy righteousness.

4 He shall judge the poor of the people; he shall save the children of the needy; and he shall crush the oppressor.

5 They shall revere thee as long as the sun and moon endure, throughout all generations.

6 He shall come down like rain upon the mown grass, as showers that water the earth.

7 In his days shall the righteous flourish, and abundance of peace so long as the moon endures.

8 He shall have dominion also from sea to sea, and from the river [1] to the ends of the earth.

9 They that dwell on the islands

[1] Euphrates.

shall bow before him; and his enemies shall lick the dust.

10 The kings of Tarshish and of the islands shall bring presents; the kings of Sheba and Seba shall offer gifts.

11 Yea, all kings shall worship him, all nations shall serve him;

12 For he shall deliver the needy from the mighty, the poor also, who has no helper.

13 He shall spare the poor and needy, and shall save the souls of the needy.

14 He shall redeem their souls from deceit and violence; precious shall their blood be in his sight.

15 And he shall live, and to him shall be given of the gold of Sheba; prayer also shall be made to him continually, and daily shall he be praised.

16 He shall multiply like wheat upon the earth; his seed shall spring up on the mountain tops, as on Lebanon; and they of the city shall flourish like grass of the earth.

17 His name shall endure for ever; his name shall be continued as long as the sun; and men shall be blessed in him; all nations shall call him blessed.

18 Blessed be the LORD God, the God of Israel, who alone does wondrous things.

19 And blessed be his glorious name for ever; and let the whole earth be filled with his glory. Amen and Amen.

PSALM 73

TRULY God is good to Israel, and to those who are pure in heart.

2 But as for me, my feet were almost gone; my steps had well nigh slipped.

3 For I was envious of the wicked when I saw the prosperity of the ungodly.

4 For there is no end to their death, and their folly is great.

5 They share not in the toil of men; neither are they scourged like other men.

6 Therefore pride holds them fast;

they have concealed their wickedness and ungodliness.

7 Their iniquity comes through like grease; they do according to the evil dictates of the heart.

8 They imagine and speak evil things; they talk unjustly against the most High.

9 They have set their mouths in the sky, but their tongues drag in the dirt;

10 Therefore will my people return hither, and they shall have everything in abundance.

11 They shall say, How does God know? and is there knowledge in the most High?

12 Behold, these are the ungodly, who prosper in the world; they are strong in power.

13 As for me, I have cleansed my heart, and washed my hands in innocence.

14 All the day long have I been plagued, and chastened every morning.

15 If I say, I shall do as they do, this is sinful for me.

16 When I thought to know this, it was too painful for me.

17 Until I went into the sanctuary of God; then understood I their end.

18 Thou didst appoint their portion according to their deceitfulness; thou didst cast them down when they exalted themselves.

19 How are they brought into desolation, as in a moment! They are utterly consumed with terrors.

20 As one who awakes from a dream, so, O LORD, thou shalt despise their idolatry.

21 Thus my heart was grieved, and my conscience troubled me.

22 So foolish was I, and ignorant; I was as a beast before thee.

23 Thou shalt comfort me with thy counsel, and lead me according to thy honour.

24 Whom have I in heaven but thee? and whom have I desired upon earth besides thee?

25 Nevertheless I am continually with thee; thou hast held me by my right hand.

26 My flesh and my heart fail; but God is the strength of my heart and my portion for ever.

27 For lo, they that are far from thee shall perish; thou hast destroyed all them that go astray from thee.

28 I was pleased to draw near to God; I have put my trust in the LORD God, that I may declare all thy works.

PSALM 74

O GOD, why hast thou cast us off for ever? Why hath thine anger become inflamed against the sheep of thy flock?

2 Remember thy congregation which thou hast possessed of old; the tribe of thine inheritance, which thou hast redeemed; this mount Zion, wherein thou hast dwelt.

3 Exalt thy servants over those who are carried away by power; all those who oppress are enemies of thy sanctuary.

4 Thine enemies exalted themselves in the midst of thy feasts; they set up their banners for signs.

5 Thou knowest this as the exalted one who sits on high; they have hewn down the doors with axes as they would cut the trees of the forest.

6 They have destroyed everything with axes and hammers.

7 They have set fire to and burned thy sanctuary; they have defiled the dwelling place of thy name on earth.

8 They said in their hearts, Let us destroy them together; let us abolish all the feast days of God from the land.

9 They did not see the wonders thereof; for there is no more any prophet, neither is there among us any wise man.

10 O God, how long shall the adversary reproach? Shall the enemy blaspheme thy name for ever?

11 Why withdrawest thou thy hand, even thy strength from the midst of thy congregation?

12 For God is our King, who of old has commanded the salvation of Jacob.

13 Thou didst divide the sea by thy strength; thou didst break the heads of the dragons in the waters.

14 Thou didst break the heads of Leviathan in pieces, and thou gavest him as food to a strong people.

15 Thou didst open the fountains in the valleys; thou didst dry up mighty rivers.

16 The day is thine, the night also is thine; thou hast prepared the light and the sun.

17 Thou hast set all the borders of the earth; thou hast made summer and winter.

18 Remember this, that the enemy has reproached, O LORD, and that the foolish people have blasphemed thy name.

19 O deliver not to destruction the soul that confesses to thee; forget not the souls of thy poor for ever.

20 Respect thy covenant, O LORD; for the habitations of the earth are full of ignorance and cruelty.

21 O let not the oppressed return ashamed; let the poor and needy praise thy name.

22 Arise, O God, plead thine own cause; remember how the foolish man reproacheth thee daily.

23 Forget not the voice of thine enemies; the tumult of those that rise up against thee ascendeth continually.

PSALM 75

UNTO thee, O God, do we give thanks, unto thee do we give thanks and call upon thy name.

2 We will declare all thy wondrous works; then the time will come when I will judge uprightly.

3 Then the earth and all the inhabitants thereof shall be humbled; thou hast ordained the people thereof.

4 Thou saidst to the fools, Deal not foolishly, and to the wicked, Lift not up the horn;

5 Lift not up your horn on high; speak not with a stiff neck.

6 For defence comes neither from the west nor from the east nor from the desert mountains.

7 But God is the judge; he puts down one, and sets up another.

8 For in the hand of the LORD there is a cup, full of a mixture of the dregs of wine; and he passes it from one to another; surely all the wicked of the earth shall drink the dregs thereof.

9 But I will live for ever; I will sing praises to the God of Jacob.

10 All the horns of the wicked also will I cut off; but the horns of the righteous shall be exalted.

PSALM 76

IN Judah is God known; his name is great in Israel.

2 In Salem also is his tabernacle, and his dwelling place in Zion.

3 There broke he the arms of the bow, the shield, and the sword, in the battle.

4 Thou art all glorious and excellent from thy mighty mountain.

5 All the foolish of heart were dismayed; the mighty men of valor slept their last sleep.

6 Their hands prevailed not because of thy rebuke, O God of Jacob; the horsemen are cast into a dead sleep.

7 Thou, even thou, art to be feared; who may stand in thy sight when once thou art angry?

8 Thou didst cause judgment to be heard from heaven; the earth saw it and trembled

9 When God arose to judgment, to save all the meek of the earth.

10 For the wisdom of man shall praise thee; the remainder of his wrath shalt thou restrain.

11 Vow and fulfil thy vows to the LORD thy God; let all that be round about him bring presents to him who is to be revered.

12 He shall humble the pride of the rulers; he is dreaded by the kings of the earth.

PSALM 77

I CRIED to God with my voice, and he heard me; I have lifted up my voice to him, and he answered me.

2 In the day of my trouble I sought the LORD; my torment continued through the night, and ceased not; there was no comforter for my soul.

3 When I remembered, O God, I

was troubled; I meditated, and my spirit was overwhelmed.

4 My eyes are dazed; I am dumb so that I cannot speak.

5 I have considered the days of old; I am mindful of the years of ancient times.

6 I meditated far into the night; I communed with mine own heart; I have examined my soul and said,

7 Has the LORD forsaken me for ever? and will he be favorable no more?

8 Is his mercy gone for ever? does his promise fail for evermore?

9 Has God forgotten to be gracious? has he in anger shut up his tender mercies?

10 And I said, This is my infirmity; it is another visitation of the power of the most High.

11 I will remember the works of the LORD; surely I will remember thy wonders of old.

12 I will meditate also of all thy works, and think of thy skillful doings.

13 Thy way, O God, is holy; there is none so great as our God.

14 Thou art the God that doest wonders; thou hast declared thy strength among the people.

15 Thou hast with thine arm saved thy people, the sons of Jacob and Joseph.

16 The waters saw thee, O God, the waters saw thee; they were afraid; the depths also were troubled.

17 The clouds poured out water; the skies sent out a sound; thine arrows also flew around.

18 The voice of thy thunder was in the heavens; the lightnings lightened the world; the earth trembled and shook.

19 Thy way is in the sea, and thy path is in the great waters, but thy footsteps are not seen.

20 Thou didst lead thy people like a flock by the hand of Moses and Aaron.

PSALM 78

GIVE ear, O my people, to my law; incline your ears to the words of my mouth.

2 I will open my mouth in parables; I will utter proverbs of old.

3 That which we have heard and known, and which our fathers have told us,

4 We will not hide from their children, showing to the generation to come the praise of the LORD and his strength and the wonderful works that he has done.

5 For he established a testimony in Jacob and appointed a law in Israel, which he commanded our fathers that they should make known to their children,

6 That the generation to come might know them, even the children which should be born, who should arise and declare them to their children;

7 That they might set their hope in God, and not forget the works of God, but keep his commandments;

8 And might not be as their fathers, a stubborn and rebellious generation, a generation that set not their heart aright, and whose spirit was not steadfast with God.

9 The children of Ephraim, being armed and throwing forth bows, turned back in the day of battle.

10 For they kept not the covenant of God, and refused to walk in his law;

11 And forgot his works and his wonders that he had shown them in the sight of their fathers.

12 Marvellous things did he in the land of Egypt and in the fields of Zoan.

13 He divided the sea, and caused them to pass through; and he made the waters to stand as in skins.

14 In the daytime also he led them with a cloud, and all the night with a light of fire.

15 He cleaved the rocks in the wilderness, and gave them drink as out of great depths.

16 He brought forth streams also out of the rock, and caused waters to run down like rivers.

17 But the people continued to sin, and to murmur against the most High in their thirst for water.

18 And they tempted God in their

hearts by asking food to satisfy their desires.

19 Yea, they complained against God; they said, Can God furnish tables of food in the wilderness?

20 Behold, he smote the rock, that the waters gushed out and the streams overflowed; can he give bread also? can he provide food for his people?

21 Therefore the LORD heard this and was angered; so a fire was kindled against Jacob, and anger also came up against Israel,

22 Because they believed not in God and trusted not in his salvation:

23 Though he had commanded the clouds from above and opened the doors of heaven,

24 And had rained down manna for them to eat and had given them of the bread of heaven.

25 Man did eat angels' food; he sent them game in abundance.

26 He caused winds to blow in the skies; and by his power he brought in the south wind.

27 He rained flesh also upon them like dust, and feathered fowls like the sands of the sea:

28 And he let these fall in the midst of their camp, round about their tents.

29 So they did eat and were well filled; for he gave them their own desire.

30 They relinquished not their craving. But while their food was yet in their mouths,

31 The anger of God came upon them and slew the richest of them, and made to bow the chosen men of Israel.

32 Nevertheless they sinned still, and believed not in his wondrous works.

33 Wherefore their days were spent in emptiness, and their years in impatience.

34 When he slew them, then they sought him; and they returned and drew nearer to him.

35 And they remembered that God was their helper, and the high God their Saviour.

36 Nevertheless they loved him with their mouths, and they lied to him with their tongues.

37 For their hearts were not right with him, neither were they steadfast in his covenant.

38 He is merciful, the forgiver of sins, and destroys not; yea, many a time turned he his anger away and did not stir up all his wrath.

39 For he remembered that they were but flesh; a wind that passes away and comes not again.

40 How oft did they provoke him in the wilderness, and grieve him in the desert!

41 Yea, they turned back and tempted God, and defied the Holy One of Israel.

42 They remembered not his hand, nor the day when he delivered them from the oppressor,

43 How he had wrought his signs in Egypt and his wonders in the field of Zoan,

44 Nor how he had turned their rivers into blood and their brooks, that they could not drink.

45 He sent swarms of insects among them, which devoured them, and frogs, which destroyed them.

46 He gave also their crops to the locusts, and their labor to the caterpillars.

47 He destroyed their vines with hail and their fig trees with frost.

48 He gave up their cattle also to the hail and their flocks to destruction.

49 He cast upon them the fierceness of his anger, wrath, indignation, and trouble, by the hand of an evil angel.

50 He resorted to strong measures; he spared not their souls from death, and gave their cattle over to the pestilence;

51 And smote all the first-born in Egypt, the fairest of their sons in the tabernacles of Ham;

52 But he led forth his own people like sheep, and guided them in the wilderness like a flock.

53 And he led them on safely so that they feared not; but the sea overwhelmed their enemies.

54 And he brought them to the border of his sanctuary, even to this

mountain, which his right hand had possessed.

55 He cast out the Gentiles from before them, and allotted them an inheritance by measure, and made the tribes of Israel to dwell in their tents.

56 Yet they tempted and provoked the most High God, and kept not his testimonies;

57 But turned back and dealt deceitfully like their fathers; they were crooked like a twisted bow.

58 For they provoked him to anger by sacrificing on high places, and made him indignant with their graven images.

59 When God heard this, he was wroth, and greatly abhorred Israel,

60 So that he forsook the tabernacle of Shiloh, the tent which he placed among men;

61 And he delivered his people into captivity, and his glory into the oppressor's hand.

62 He delivered his people to the sword, and disregarded his inheritance.

63 The fire consumed their young men; and their maidens were violated.

64 Their priests fell by the sword; and their widows made no lamentation.

65 Then the Lord awaked as one out of sleep and like a mighty man who has shaken off the effects of wine.

66 And he caused his enemies to retreat; he put them to a perpetual reproach.

67 Moreover he refused the tabernacle of Joseph, and chose not the tribe of Ephraim;

68 But chose the tribe of Judah, mount Zion which he loved.

69 And he built his sanctuary on a high place, and he established it upon the earth for ever.

70 He chose David also his servant, and took him from the sheepfolds;

71 From following the ewes that give suck, he brought him to feed Jacob his people and Israel his inheritance.

72 So he shepherded them according to the integrity of his heart; and guided them by the skilfulness of his hands.

PSALM 79

O GOD, the heathen are come into thine inheritance; thy holy temple have they defiled; they have laid Jerusalem in heaps.

2 The dead bodies of thy servants have they given to be meat to the fowls of the heavens, the flesh of thy saints to the beasts of the earth.

3 Their blood have they shed like water round about Jerusalem; and there was none to bury them.

4 We are become a reproach to our neighbours, a scorn and derision to them that are round about us.

5 How long, O Lord? wilt thou be angry for ever? shall thy anger burn like fire?

6 Pour out thy wrath upon the heathen that have not known thee, and upon the kingdoms that have not called upon thy name.

7 For they have devoured Jacob, and laid waste his dwelling place.

8 O remember not against us our former sins; let thy tender mercies speedily overtake us; for we are brought very low.

9 Help us, O God of our salvation, for the glory of thy name; and deliver us and purge away our sins, for thy name's sake.

10 Wherefore should the heathen say, Where is their God? Let him be known among the heathen in our sight by the revenging of the blood of thy servants which is shed.

11 Let the sighing of the prisoner come before thee; according to the greatness of thy power, free thou those that are appointed to die.

12 And render to our neighbours sevenfold into their bosom their reproach, wherewith they have reproached thee, O Lord.

13 So we thy people and sheep of thy pasture will give thee thanks for ever; we will tell thy wonders to all generations.

PSALM 80

G IVE ear, O Shepherd of Israel, thou that leadest Joseph like a flock; thou that sittest upon the cherubim, shine forth.

2 Before Ephraim and Benjamin and Manasseh show forth thy strength and come and save us.

3 Guide us again, O mighty God, and cause thy face to shine; and we shall be saved.

4 O LORD God of hosts, how long wilt thou be angry against the prayer of thy people?

5 Thou feedest them with the bread of tears; and givest them tears to drink in great measure.

6 Thou hast made us a jest to our neighbors; and our enemies laugh among themselves.

7 Guide us again, O God of hosts, and cause thy face to shine; and we shall be saved.

8 Thou hast brought a vine out of Egypt; thou hast cast out the heathen and planted it.

9 Thou didst prepare the ground and caused it to take deep root, and it filled the land.

10 The mountains were covered with the shadow of it, and the vine-shoots thereof were upon the cedars of God.

11 It sent out its roots unto the sea, and its branches to the rivers.

12 Why hast thou then broken down its hedges, so that all they who pass by the way tread over it?

13 The boar of the forest devours it, and the wild beasts of the field feed upon it.

14 Return we beseech thee, O God of hosts; look down from heaven, and behold, and visit this vine

15 And the vineyard which thy right hand has planted and the branch that thou madest strong for thyself.

16 It is burned with fire; it is cut down; they perish at the rebuke of thy countenance.

17 Let thy right hand be upon the man and upon the son of man whom thou madest strong for thyself.

18 So will we not go back from thee; quicken us, and we will call upon thy name.

19 Guide us again, O LORD God of hosts, cause thy face to shine; and we shall be saved.

PSALM 81

SING aloud to God our strength; make a joyful noise to the God of Jacob.

2 Take a psalm and bring hither the timbrel, the pleasant harp with the psaltery.

3 Blow trumpets in the new moon in the time appointed, on our solemn feast days.

4 For this was a statute for Israel and a law of the God of Jacob.

5 This he ordained in Joseph for a testimony when he went out to the land of Egypt, where he heard a language that he understood not.

6 I removed the yoke from his shoulder, I released his hands from the bonds.

7 He called on me in trouble, and I delivered him; I sheltered him under my glorious cover; I tested him at the waters of dispute.

8 Hear, O my people, and I will speak; O Israel, I will testify about you. If you will listen to me;

9 There shall be no strange god in you; neither shall you worship any strange god.

10 I am the LORD your God, which brought you out of the land of Egypt; open your mouth wide, and I will fill it.

11 But my people would not listen to my voice; and Israel would have none of me.

12 So they walked according to the desires of their own hearts and according to their own counsels.

13 Oh that my people had listened to me, and Israel had walked in my ways!

14 I would soon have destroyed their enemies, and turned my hand against their adversaries.

15 The haters of the LORD have lied to him; but they shall tremble for ever.

16 He has fed them also with the finest of the wheat; and with honey out of the rock has he satisfied them.

PSALM 82

GOD stands in the congregation of angels; he judges among the angels.

2 How long will you judge unjustly, and be partial to the wicked?

3 Defend the poor and fatherless; do justice to the afflicted and needy.

4 Deliver the poor and needy out of the hand of the wicked.

5 They know not, neither will they understand; they walk on in darkness; all the foundations of the earth are shaken.

6 I have said, You are gods; all of you are children of the most High.

7 Henceforth you shall die like men, and fall like one of the princes.

8 Arise, O God, judge the earth: for thou shalt inherit all nations.

PSALM 83

O GOD, who is like unto thee? Hold not thy peace, and be not still, O God;

2 For, lo, thine enemies are raging and they that hate thee have lifted up the head against thy people.

3 They have taken crafty counsel, and consulted against thy chosen ones.

4 They have said, Come, let us destroy them from among the nations, that the name of Israel may be no more in remembrance.

5 For they have agreed with one heart; they have made alliance against thee:

6 The tabernacles of Edom and the Ishmaelites; of Moab and the Gadarenes;

7 The people of the region of Ammon and Amalek; the Philistines with the inhabitants of Tyre;

8 The Assyrians have also joined with them; they have helped the children of Lot.

9 Do to them as to the Midianites; as to Sisera, as to Jabin, at the valley of Kishon;

10 Which perished at Endor; they became as manure for the earth.

11 Destroy their nobles like Oreb and like Zeeb; yea, all their princes as Zebah and as Zalmunna;

12 For they said, Let us inherit for ourselves the city of God.

13 O God, make them like a turning wheel; and like stubble before the wind.

14 As the fire burns a forest and as the flame sets the mountains on fire;

15 So persecute them with thy tempest, and make them afraid with thy storm.

16 Fill their faces with shame, that they may seek thy name, O LORD.

17 Let them be confounded and troubled for ever; yea, let them be put to shame, and perish,

18 That men may know that thou, whose name alone is the LORD, art the most high over all the earth.

PSALM 84

HOW amiable are thy tabernacles, O LORD of hosts!

2 My soul longs, yea, even faints for the courts of the LORD; my heart and my flesh give praise for the living God.

3 Yea, even the sparrow has found a house, and the pigeon a nest for herself, where they have raised their young beside thine altars, O LORD of hosts, my King, and my God.

4 Blessed are they that dwell in thy house; they shall praise thee for ever.

5 Blessed is the man whose help is from thee; in whose heart are thy ways.

6 They have passed through the valley of weeping, and have made it a dwelling place; the Lawgiver shall cover it with blessings;

7 They shall go from strength to strength; the God of gods shall be seen in Zion.

8 O LORD God of hosts, hear my prayer; give ear, O God of Jacob.

9 Behold, O God our shield, and look upon the face of thine anointed.

10 For a day in thy courts is better than a thousand. I would choose rather to dwell in the house of my God than to dwell in the tents of the wicked.

11 For the LORD God is our supply and our helper; the LORD will give grace and glory; no good thing will he withhold from them that walk uprightly.

12 O Lord of hosts, blessed is the man who trusts in thee.

PSALM 85

LORD, thou hast been favorable to thy land; thou hast brought back the captivity of Jacob.

2 Thou hast forgiven the iniquity of thy people, thou hast covered all their sin.

3 Thou hast taken away all thy wrath; thou hast withdrawn the fierceness of thine anger.

4 Restore us, O God our Saviour, and cause thine anger toward us to cease.

5 Be not angry with us for ever; hold not thine anger against all generations.

6 Restore us and revive us, that thy people may rejoice in thee.

7 Show us thy mercy, O Lord, and grant us thy salvation.

8 We will hear what the Lord our God will speak; for he will speak peace to his people and to his saints, that they may not turn again to folly.

9 Surely his salvation is near them that reverence him; let his glory dwell in our land.

10 Mercy and truth are met together; righteousness and peace have kissed each other.

11 Truth shall spring out of the earth; and righteousness shall look down from heaven.

12 Yea, the Lord shall give his goodness; and the land shall yield its fruits.

13 And the righteous shall go before him; and he shall establish his ways upon the earth.

PSALM 86

INCLINE thine ear, O Lord; hear me, for I am poor and needy.

2 Preserve my soul, for thou art holy; O thou God, save thy servant who trusts in thee.

3 Be merciful to me, O Lord; for I cry unto thee daily.

4 Rejoice the soul of thy servant; for unto thee, O Lord, do I lift up my soul.

5 For thou, O Lord, art good; and thy lovingkindness is abundant to all who call upon thee.

6 Give ear, O Lord, to my prayer; and attend to the voice of my supplications.

7 In the day of my trouble I have called upon thee, and thou hast answered me.

8 There is none like thee, O Lord my God; neither are there any works like thy works.

9 All the nations whom thou hast made shall come and worship before thee, O Lord, and shall glorify thy name.

10 For thou art great, and doest wondrous things; thou art God alone.

11 Show me thy way, O Lord; I will walk in the truth; my heart will rejoice with them that worship thy name.

12 I will praise thee, O Lord my God, with all my heart; and I will glorify thy name for evermore.

13 For great is thy lovingkindness toward me; and thou hast delivered my soul from the depths of hell.

14 O God, the wicked are risen against me, and the assembly of violent men has sought after my soul; and they have not been mindful of thee.

15 But thou, O Lord God, art full of compassion and gracious, longsuffering and plenteous in mercy and truth.

16 O turn to me and have mercy upon me; give strength to thy servant, and save the son of thy handmaid.

17 Show me a token for good, that they which hate me may see it and be ashamed, because thou, Lord, hast helped me and comforted me.

PSALM 87

HER [1] foundations are on his holy mountain.

2 The Lord loves the gates of Zion more than all the dwellings of Jacob.

3 Glorious things are spoken of you, O city of our God.

4 I will make mention of Rahab and Babylon, for they know my power; behold the Philistines and Tyre and

1 Jerusalem.

the people of Ethiopia; it shall be said this man was born there.

5 And of Zion it shall be said, This mighty man was born in her; and the same shall establish her.

6 The LORD shall number his people in the book: This man was born there!

7 The princes who dwell in you shall rejoice, and all that are humbled in you.

PSALM 88

O LORD God of my salvation, I have cried day and night before thee;

2 Let my prayer come before thee; incline thine ear unto my supplication;

3 For my soul is full of troubles and my life draws near to Sheol.

4 I am counted with them that go down into the pit; I am like a man who has no strength;

5 Like a nobleman abandoned among the dead, like the slain that lie down in the grave, whom thou rememberest no more; they are lost to thee.

6 Thou hast laid me in the lowest pit, in darkness, in the shadow of death.

7 Thy wrath rests hard upon me, and thou hast afflicted me with all thy waves.

8 Thou hast put away mine acquaintances far from me; thou hast made me an abomination to them; I am shut up and I cannot come forth.

9 Mine eyes are weakened from weeping; LORD, I have called daily upon thee; I have stretched out my hands to thee.

10 Behold thou wilt show wonders to the dead; the mighty ones shall rise and praise thee.

11 They that are in the graves shall declare thy lovingkindness, and thy faithfulness in destruction.

12 Thy wonders shall be known in the dark, and thy righteousness in the land that has been forsaken.

13 But to thee have I cried, O LORD; and in the morning shall my prayer come early before thee.

14 O LORD, forsake not my soul, and turn not thy face from me.

15 I am poor and afflicted from my youth; I have been proud, but now I am humbled and crushed.

16 Thy fierce wrath goes over me; thy terrors have silenced me.

17 They came round about me daily like water; they set themselves in array against me.

18 Friends and neighbors thou hast put far from me, and mine acquaintances thou hast kept away from me.

PSALM 89

I WILL sing of the mercies of the LORD for ever; with my mouth will I make known thy faithfulness to all generations.

2 For I have said, The world shall be built up with mercy; thy faithfulness shalt thou establish in the very heavens.

3 I have made a covenant with my chosen, I have sworn to David my servant,

4 Thy offspring will I establish for ever, and build up thy throne to all generations.

5 And the heavens shall praise thy wonders, O LORD, thy faithfulness also in the congregation of the saints.

6 For who in heaven can be compared to the LORD? who among the angels can be likened to the LORD?

7 God stands forth in the assembly of the saints, great and revered above all that are about him.

8 O LORD God of hosts, who is mighty like thee? and thy faithfulness is round about thee.

9 Thou rulest the splendor of the sea; thou stillest the waves thereof.

10 Thou hast humbled the proud as those that are slain; thou hast scattered thine enemies with thy strong arm.

11 The heavens are thine, the earth also is thine; as for the world and the fulness thereof, thou hast founded them.

12 The north and the south, thou hast created them; Tabor and Hermon glorify thy name.

13 Thine is the arm, and thine is

the might; thy hand is strong and thy right hand shall be exalted.

14 Thy throne is built on righteousness and judgment; mercy and truth go before thy face.

15 Blessed is the people that understand thy glory; they shall walk, O LORD, in the light of thy countenance.

16 In thy name shall they rejoice all the day; and in thy righteousness shall they be exalted.

17 For thou art the glory of our strength; and in thy favor our horn shall be exalted.

18 For the LORD is our hope; and the Holy One of Israel is our King.

19 Then he spoke in visions to his righteous one, and he said, I have given help to a man; I have exalted one chosen out of the people.

20 I have found David my servant; with my holy oil have I anointed him.

21 My hand has helped him; mine arm also has strengthened him.

22 The enemy shall not prevail upon him, nor the sons of the wicked afflict him.

23 And I will destroy his foes before his face, and plague them that hate him.

24 But my faithfulness and my mercy shall be with him; and in my name shall his horn be exalted.

25 I will set his hand also in the sea, and his right hand in the rivers.

26 He shall cry to me, Thou art my father, my God, and my mighty Saviour.

27 Also I will make him my firstborn, and will exalt him over the kings of the earth.

28 My mercy will I keep for him for evermore, and my covenant shall stand fast with him.

29 His offspring also will I make to endure for ever, and his throne as the days of heaven.

30 If his children forsake my law and walk not in my judgments;

31 If they break my statutes and keep not my commandments;

32 Then will I visit their transgression with the rod, and their iniquity with stripes.

33 Nevertheless my lovingkindness will I not utterly take from him, nor suffer my faithfulness to fail.

34 Neither will I reject my covenant, nor alter the thing that is gone out of my lips.

35 Once have I sworn by my holiness to David, and I will not lie.

36 His offspring shall endure for ever, and his throne as the sun before me.

37 It shall be established for ever as the moon, and as a faithful witness in heaven.

38 But thou hast forsaken us and despised us, thou hast made thine anointed one to turn his face.

39 Thou hast rejected the covenant of thy servant; thou hast cast his crown to the ground.

40 Thou hast broken down all his hedges; thou hast brought his strongholds to ruin.

41 All that pass by have trampled upon him; he has become a reproach to his neighbours.

42 Thou hast set up the right hand of his adversaries; thou hast made all his enemies to rejoice.

43 Thou hast turned the edge of his sword, and hast not sustained him in the battle.

44 Thou hast made his glory to cease, and cast his throne down to the ground.

45 The days of his youth hast thou shortened; thou hast covered him with shame.

46 How long, LORD, wilt thou be angry? for ever? shall thy wrath burn like fire?

47 Remember me from the time I was created; for thou hast not created all men in vain.

48 Who is the man who lives and shall not see death? Shall he deliver his soul from the hand of Sheol?

49 LORD, where are thy former lovingkindnesses, which thou didst swear to David in thy truth?

50 Remember, LORD, the reproach of thy servants; for I have borne throughout my life the mockery of the Gentiles;

51 Wherewith thine enemies have reproached me, O LORD; wherewith

they have reproached the footsteps of thine anointed.

52 Blessed be the LORD for evermore. Amen and Amen.

PSALM 90

L ORD, thou hast been our dwelling place in all generations.

2 Before the mountains were brought forth, or ever thou hadst formed the earth and the world, even from everlasting to everlasting, thou art God.

3 Thou turnest man to destruction; and sayest, Return, ye children of men.

4 For a thousand years in thy sight are but as yesterday when it is past, and as a watch in the night.

5 The span of their life will be as a sleep; in the morning they are like grass which changes.

6 In the morning it flourishes and grows up; in the evening it is cut down and withers.

7 For we are consumed by thine anger, and by thy wrath are we troubled.

8 Thou hast set our iniquities before thee, the sins of our youth in the light of thy countenance.

9 For all our days are passed away in thy wrath; we spend our years in emptiness.

10 The years of our lives are threescore and ten; and if by reason of strength they be fourscore years, yet most of them are labor and sorrow; for life is soon cut off and we fly away.

11 Who knows the power of thine anger and the fear of thy wrath?

12 So teach us to number our days that we may apply our hearts to wisdom.

13 Return, O LORD. How long? Wouldst thou not comfort thy servants?

14 O satisfy us early with thy mercy, that we may rejoice and be glad all our days.

15 Make us glad because our wickedness is dead, and the years wherein we have seen affliction.

16 Let thy work appear to thy servants, and thy glory to their children.

17 And let the beauty of the LORD our God be upon us; for the work of his hands made us, yea, he made us by the work of his hands.

PSALM 91

H E who dwells in the protection of the most High shall abide under the shadow of the Almighty.

2 I will say of the LORD, He is my refuge and my fortress; my God; in him will I trust.

3 Surely he shall deliver you from the snare of the fowler, and from vain gossip.

4 He will cover you with his feathers, and under his wings you shall trust; his truth shall be your shield and buckler.

5 You shall not be afraid for the terror by night, nor for the arrow that flies by day,

6 Nor for the conspiracy that spreads in darkness; nor for the pestilence that wastes at noonday.

7 Thousands shall fall at your side, and ten thousand at your right hand; but it shall not come near you.

8 Only with your eyes shall you behold the reward of the wicked.

9 For thou, O LORD, art my trust; thou hast established thy habitation in the highest.

10 There shall no evil befall you, neither shall any plague come near your dwelling.

11 For he shall give his angels charge over you to keep you in all your ways.

12 They shall bear you up in their hands, lest you dash your foot against a stone.

13 You shall tread upon the viper and adder; you shall trample under foot the lion and the great serpent.

14 Because he has loved me, therefore will I deliver him; I will set him on high because he has known my name.

15 He shall call upon me, and I will answer him; I will be with him in trouble; I will deliver him and honor him.

16 With long life will I satisfy him, and show him my salvation.

PSALM 92

IT is a good thing to give thanks to the LORD, and to sing praises to thy name, O Most High,

2 To show forth thy lovingkindness in the morning, and thy faithfulness every night.

3 I will play upon an instrument of ten strings and upon the psaltery; upon the harp with a solemn sound.

4 For thou, O LORD, hast made me glad through thy work; I will triumph in the works of thy hands.

5 O LORD, how great are thy works! and thy thoughts are very deep.

6 A stupid man knows not; neither does a fool understand this.

7 When the wicked spring as the grass, and when all the workers of iniquity flourish; it is that they shall be destroyed for ever;

8 But thou, LORD, art most high for evermore.

9 For, lo, thine enemies, O LORD, for lo, thine enemies shall perish; all the workers of iniquity shall be scattered.

10 But my horn shalt thou exalt like the horn of a wild ox; I shall be anointed with fragrant oil.

11 Mine eyes also shall see my desire on mine enemies, and mine ears shall hear my desire against the wicked that rise up against me.

12 The righteous shall flourish like the palm tree; he shall grow like a cedar in Lebanon.

13 Those that are planted in the house of the LORD shall flourish in the courts of our God.

14 They shall still bring forth fruit in old age; they shall be fair and desirable,

15 To show that the LORD is upright; he is mighty, and there is no unrighteousness in him.

PSALM 93

THE LORD reigns; he is clothed with majesty; the LORD is clothed with strength, wherewith he has girded himself; the world also is established, that it cannot be moved.

2 Thy throne is established of old; thou art from everlasting.

3 The rivers are full flowing, O LORD; the rivers have lifted up their voice; the rivers are flowing with purity.

4 The LORD on high is mightier than the noise of many waters, yea, than the mighty waves of the sea.

5 Thy testimonies are very sure; holiness becomes thy house, O LORD, for ever.

PSALM 94

O LORD God, to whom vengeance belongs, O God, to whom vengeance belongs, show thyself.

2 Lift up thyself, thou judge of the earth; render a reward to the proud.

3 LORD, how long shall the wicked, how long shall the wicked boast?

4 They shall utter and speak unjust things; they shall speak all kinds of evil things.

5 For they have humbled thy people, O LORD, and subdued thine heritage.

6 They slay the widow and the innocent, and murder the fatherless.

7 Yet they say, The LORD does not see, neither does the God of Jacob regard it.

8 Understand, you stupid among the people and you fools, when will you be wise?

9 He who planted the ear, shall he not hear? He who formed the eye, shall he not see?

10 He who chastises the nations, shall not he rebuke? He who teaches man knowledge, shall he not know?

11 The LORD knows the thoughts of man; they are like a breath.

12 Blessed is the man whom thou dost chasten, O LORD, and teachest out of thy law;

13 That thou mayest give him rest from the days of adversity, until the pit be digged for the wicked.

14 For the LORD will not cast off his people, neither will he forsake his inheritance.

15 For judgment shall return to the righteous, and all the upright in heart shall follow it.

16 Who will rise up for me against the evildoers? or who will stand up against the workers of iniquity?

17 Unless the LORD had been my help, my soul would soon have been in trouble.

18 When I said, My foot slips, thy mercy, O LORD, held me up.

19 In the multitude of my sorrows, within my heart thy comforts delight my soul.

20 Evil rulers shall not have fellowship with thee, for they have framed mischief against thy law.

21 They lay snares to trap the soul of the righteous, and condemn the innocent blood.

22 But the LORD is my defense; and my God is the rock of my refuge.

23 And he shall bring upon them their own iniquity, and shall silence them in their own wickedness; yea, the LORD our God shall silence them.

PSALM 95

O COME, let us sing to the LORD; let us make a joyful noise to the God of our salvation.

2 Let us come before his presence with thanksgiving, and make a joyful noise to him with psalms.

3 For the LORD is a great God and a great King above all gods.

4 In his hand are the foundations of the earth; the strength of the hills is his also.

5 The sea is his, and he made it; and his hands formed the dry land.

6 O come, let us worship and bow down; let us kneel before the LORD our Maker.

7 For he is our God; and we are the people of his pasture and the sheep of his hand. Today if you will hear his voice,

8 Harden not your heart, as in the provocation and as in the day of temptation in the wilderness,

9 When your fathers tempted me, proved me, and saw my work.

10 Forty years long was I grieved with that generation, and said, It is a people that do err in their heart, and they have not known my ways,

11 Unto whom I swore in my wrath that they should not enter into my rest.

PSALM 96

O SING to the LORD a new song; sing to the LORD, all the earth.

2 Sing to the LORD, bless his name; show forth his salvation from day to day.

3 Declare his glory among the heathen, his wonders among all people.

4 For the LORD is great and greatly to be praised; he is to be revered above all gods.

5 For all the gods of the nations are idols; but the LORD made the heavens.

6 Honor and majesty are before him; strength and beauty are in his sanctuary.

7 Give to the LORD, O you kindred of the people, give to the LORD glory and honor.

8 Give to the LORD the glory due to his name; bring an offering and come into his courts.

9 O worship the LORD in the temple of holiness; tremble before him, all the earth.

10 Say among the Gentiles that the LORD reigns; the world also shall be established that it shall not be moved; he shall judge the people righteously.

11 Let the heavens rejoice, and let the earth be glad; let the sea roar and the fulness thereof.

12 Let the field be joyful, and all that is therein; then shall all the trees of the forest rejoice

13 Before the LORD; for he comes, for he comes to judge the earth; he shall judge the world with righteousness, and the people with his truth.

PSALM 97

THE LORD reigns; let the earth rejoice; let the multitude of isles be glad thereof.

2 Clouds and darkness are round about him; righteousness and judgment are the foundation of his throne.

3 Fire goes before him, and burns up his enemies round about.

4 His lightnings enlightened the world; the earth saw, and trembled.

5 The hills melted like wax at the presence of the LORD, at the presence of the LORD of the whole earth.

6 The heavens declare his righteousness, and all the people see his glory.

7 Confounded are all they that serve graven images, that boast themselves of idols; worship him, all his angels.

8 Zion heard and was glad; and the daughters of Judah rejoiced because of thy judgments, O LORD.

9 For thou, LORD, art high above all the earth; thou art exalted far above all gods.

10 You who love the LORD, hate evil; he preserves the souls of his saints; he delivers them out of the hand of the wicked.

11 Light shone for the righteous, and gladness for the upright in heart.

12 Rejoice in the LORD, you righteous; and give thanks at the remembrance of his holiness.

PSALM 98

O SING to the LORD a new song; for he has done marvellous things; his right hand and his holy arm have gotten him the victory.

2 The LORD has made known his salvation; his righteousness has he revealed in the sight of the heathen.

3 He has remembered his mercy and his truth toward the house of Israel; all the ends of the earth have seen the salvation of our God.

4 Praise the LORD, all the earth; make ye merry and sing and give praise.

5 Sing to the LORD with the harp, with the harp and the voice of a choir.

6 With the sound of trumpets give praise before the LORD, the King.

7 Let the sea roar and the fulness thereof, the world and they that dwell therein.

8 Let the rivers clap their hands; let the hills be joyful together

9 Before the LORD; for he comes to judge the earth; with righteousness shall he judge the world, and the people with equity.

PSALM 99

THE LORD reigns; let the people tremble; he sits upon the cherubim; let the earth be moved.

2 The LORD is great in Zion; he is high above all the people.

3 Let them praise thy great and honored name; for it is holy.

4 The king's might also loves judgment; thou dost establish equity, thou executest judgment and righteousness in Jacob.

5 Exalt the LORD our God, and worship at his footstool; for he is holy.

6 Moses and Aaron were among his priests, and Samuel among them that call upon his name; they called upon the LORD, and he answered them.

7 He spoke to them in the cloudy pillar; they kept his testimonies and the covenant that he gave them.

8 Thou didst answer them, O LORD our God; thou wast an avenger for them. O God, reward them according to their works.

9 Exalt the LORD our God, and worship at his holy mountain; for the LORD our God is holy.

PSALM 100

MAKE a joyful noise to the LORD, all you lands.

2 Serve the LORD with gladness; come before his presence with singing.

3 Know that he is the LORD our God; it is he who has made us, and not we ourselves; we are his people, and the sheep of his pasture.

4 Enter into his gates with thanksgiving, and into his courts with praise; be thankful to him and bless his name;

5 For the LORD is good; his mercy is everlasting; and his truth endures to all generations.

PSALM 101

I WILL sing of mercy and judgment; unto thee, O LORD, will I sing.

2 I will behave myself wisely in a perfect way. O when wilt thou come to me? I will walk within my house with a perfect heart.

3 I will set no wicked thing before mine eyes; I hate the doers of evil, they shall not come near to me.

4 A perverse heart shall depart from me; I will know not evil.

5 He who accuses his neighbor falsely will I destroy; with him who has a high look and a proud heart I will not eat.

6 Mine eyes shall be upon the faithful of the land, that they may dwell with me; he who walks in a perfect way shall serve me.

7 He who works deceit shall not dwell within my house; he who tells lies shall not tarry in my sight.

8 In the early morning I will silence all the wicked of the earth; and I will destroy all the doers of iniquity from the city of the LORD.

PSALM 102

HEAR my prayer, O LORD, and let my cry come unto thee.

2 Turn not thy face from me in the day when I am in trouble; incline thine ear unto me; in the day when I call, answer me speedily.

3 For my days are consumed like smoke, and my bones are whitened as if they were burned.

4 My heart is smitten and withered like grass, so that I forget to eat my bread.

5 Because of the voice of my groaning, my bones cleave to my skin.

6 I am like a pelican of the wilderness; I am like an owl of the desert.

7 I am shaken and alone like a sparrow upon the house tops.

8 Mine enemies reproach me all the day; those who once praised me are now sworn against me.

9 I have eaten ashes like bread, and mingled my drink with weeping,

10 Because of thine indignation and thy wrath; for thou hast lifted me up, and cast me down.

11 My days are like a shadow that declines; and I am withered like grass.

12 But thou, O LORD, shalt endure for ever, and thy remembrance to all generations.

13 Arise and have mercy upon Zion; for it is time to have mercy upon her.

14 For thy servants take pleasure in her stones, and favor the dust thereof.

15 So the heathen shall worship the name of the LORD, and all the kings of the earth thy glory.

16 When the LORD builds up Zion, he shall appear in his glory.

17 He will regard the prayer of the destitute, and not despise their prayer.

18 This shall be written for the generation to come; and the people who shall be created shall praise the LORD.

19 For he has looked down from the height of his sanctuary; from heaven did the LORD behold the earth,

20 To hear the groaning of the prisoner, to loose those that are appointed to death,

21 To declare the name of the LORD in Zion and his praises in Jerusalem,

22 When the peoples are gathered together, and the kingdoms, to serve the LORD.

23 For they have weakened my strength on earth; they warned me of the shortage of my days.

24 O my God, take me not away in the midst of my days; thy years are throughout all generations.

25 Of old hast thou laid the foundation of the earth; and the heavens are the work of thy hands.

26 They shall perish, but thou shalt endure; yea, all of them shall wax old like a garment; as a vesture, they shall fade.

27 But thou art the same, and thy years shall have no end.

28 The children of thy servants shall continue and their descendants shall be established before thee.

PSALM 103

BLESS the LORD, O my soul; and all that is within me, bless his holy name.

2 Bless the LORD, O my soul, and forget not all his benefits,

3 Who forgives all your iniquities, who heals all your diseases.

4 Who redeems your life from destruction, who crowns you with lovingkindness and tender mercies,

5 Who satisfies your mouth with good things, so that your youth is renewed like the eagle's.

6 The LORD executes righteousness

and judgment for all that are oppressed.

7 He made known his ways to Moses, his acts to the children of Israel.

8 The LORD is merciful and gracious, slow to anger and plenteous in mercy.

9 He will not always chide; neither will he retain his anger for ever.

10 He has not dealt with us after our sins, nor rewarded us according to our iniquities.

11 For as the heavens are high above the earth, so great is his mercy toward them that revere him.

12 As far as the east is from the west, so far has he removed our transgressions from us.

13 As a father pities his children, so the LORD pities those who worship him.

14 For he knows whereof we are made; he remembers that we are dust.

15 As for man, his days are as grass; as a flower of the field, so he flourishes.

16 For when the wind passes over it, it is gone; and the place thereof is known no more.

17 But the mercy of the LORD is from everlasting to everlasting upon them that reverence him, and his righteousness to children's children,

18 To such as keep his covenant, and to those that remember his commandments to do them.

19 The LORD has prepared his throne in the heavens, and his kingdom rules over all.

20 Bless the LORD, O you his angels, that excel in strength, that do his commandments, hearkening to the voice of his word.

21 Bless you the LORD, all you his hosts; you ministers of his that do his pleasure.

22 Bless the LORD, all his works, in all places of his dominion; bless the LORD, O my soul.

PSALM 104

BLESS the LORD, O my soul. O LORD my God, thou art very great; thou art clothed with honour and majesty.

2 Thou coverest thyself with light as with a garment; who stretcheth out the heavens like a curtain,

3 Who layest the beams of his chambers in the waters, who makest the clouds his chariot, who walkest upon the wings of the wind,

4 Who makest his angels spirits, his ministers a flaming fire,

5 Who laid the foundations of the earth, that it should not be removed for ever.

6 Thou coveredst it with the deep as with a garment; the waters stood above the mountains.

7 At thy rebuke they fled; at the voice of thy thunder they hastened away.

8 The mountains ascend, the valleys descend to the place which thou hast founded for them.

9 Thou hast set a bound that they may not pass over, to cover the earth.

10 Thou hast sent the springs to the valleys, which run among the hills.

11 They give drink to every beast of the field; the wild asses quench their thirst.

12 By them the fowls of the heaven have their habitation; from among the hills they sing.

13 He waters the hills from his chambers; the earth is satisfied with the fruit of thy works.

14 He causes the grass to grow for the cattle, and herbs for the service of man, that he may bring forth food out of the earth,

15 And wine that makes glad the heart of man, and oil to make his face to shine, and bread which strengthens man's heart.

16 The trees of the LORD are full of sap, the cedars of Lebanon, which he has planted;

17 There the birds make their nests; as for the stork, her house is in the cypress.

18 The high mountains are a refuge for the wild goats, and the rocks a refuge for the conies.

19 He appointed the moon for seasons; the sun knows his going down.

20 He makes darkness and it is night, wherein all the beasts of the forest creep forth.

21 The young lions roar after their prey, and seek their food from God.

22 The sun rises; they gather themselves together, and lay them down in their dens.

23 Man goes forth to his work and to his labour until the evening.

24 O Lord, how manifold are thy works! In wisdom hast thou made them all; the earth is full of thy riches.

25 Behold this great and wide sea, wherein are things creeping innumerable, creatures both small and great.

26 On it sail the ships; there is that Leviathan, whom thou hast made to play therein.

27 These wait all upon thee, that thou mayest give them their food in due season.

28 With what thou givest them they are filled; thou openest thine hand, they are satisfied.

29 Thou hidest thy face, they are troubled; thou takest away their breath, they die and return to their dust.

30 Thou sendest forth thy spirit, they are created, and thou renewest the face of the earth.

31 The glory of the Lord endures for ever; the Lord shall rejoice in his works.

32 He looks on the earth, and it trembles; he rebukes the hills, and they smoke.

33 I will sing to the Lord as long as I live; I will sing praise to my God while I have my being.

34 Let my praise be acceptable to him; I will be glad in the Lord.

35 Let sinners be consumed out of the earth, and let the wicked be no more. Bless the Lord, O my soul. Praise the Lord.

PSALM 105

O GIVE thanks to the Lord, call upon his name, make known his deeds among the people.

2 Sing to him, sing psalms to him, talk of all his wondrous works.

3 Glory in his holy name; let the heart of them rejoice that seek the Lord.

4 Seek the Lord, and be strong, seek his face evermore.

5 Remember his marvellous works that he has done, his wonders, and the judgments of his mouth,

6 O you descendants of Abraham his servant, you children of Jacob his chosen.

7 He is the Lord our God; his judgments are in all the earth.

8 He has remembered his covenant for ever, the word which he commanded to a thousand generations.

9 For he made his covenant with Abraham, and his oaths to Isaac;

10 And confirmed the same to Jacob for a law, and to Israel for an everlasting covenant,

11 Saying, To you will I give the land of Canaan, the lot of your inheritance,

12 When they were but a few men in number, yea, very few, and strangers in it.

13 When they went from one nation to another, from one kingdom to another people;

14 He suffered no man to do them wrong; yea, he reproved kings for their sakes,

15 That they might touch not his anointed, and do his prophets no harm.

16 Moreover he called for a famine upon the land; he broke the whole stalk of their wheat.

17 He sent a man before them, even Joseph, who was sold for a servant,

18 Whose feet they bound with fetters; he was laid in iron

19 Until the time that his word came; the word of the Lord tried him.

20 The king sent and released him, and made him a ruler over his people,

21 He made him lord of his house, and ruler over all his possessions,

22 To discipline the governors at his pleasure and to teach the elders wisdom.

23 Israel also came into Egypt; and Jacob sojourned in the land of Ham.

24 And he increased his people greatly, and made them stronger than their enemies.

25 He turned their hearts to hate

his people, to deal subtly with his servants.

26 He sent Moses his servant, and Aaron whom he had chosen.

27 They showed his signs among them and wonders in the land of Ham.

28 He sent darkness, and made it dark; and yet they rebelled against his word.

29 He turned their waters into blood, and slew their fish.

30 Their land swarmed with frogs, even in the inner chambers of their kings.

31 He spoke, and there came different sorts of flies and lice in all their borders.

32 He turned their rain into hail; and brought flaming fire into their land.

33 He smote their vines also and their fig trees; and broke the trees within their borders.

34 He spoke and the locusts came and caterpillars, and that without numbers throughout their land.

35 And they devoured all the herbs and the fruit of their lands.

36 He smote also all the first-born of Egypt, the first-born of all their boys.

37 He brought them forth also with silver and gold; and there was not one feeble person among their tribes.

38 Egypt was glad when they departed; for the fear of them fell upon them.

39 He spread a cloud to shade them, and fire to give light in the night.

40 The people asked, and he brought quails and satisfied them with the bread of heaven.

41 He opened the rock and the waters gushed out; and water flowed in the dry land.

42 For he remembered his holy promise which he had given to Abraham his servant.

43 And he brought forth his people with joy, and his young men with gladness,

44 And gave them the lands of the Gentiles; and they inherited the labor of the people.

45 That they might observe his statutes and keep his laws. Praise the LORD.

PSALM 106

PRAISE the Lord. O give thanks to the LORD, for he is good; for his mercy endures for ever.

2 Who can utter the mighty acts of the LORD? Who can show forth all his praise?

3 Blessed are they that keep his judgments, and they that do righteousness at all times.

4 Remember us, O LORD, with the favor that thou bearest to thy people; O visit us with thy salvation,

5 That we may see the good of thy chosen, that we may rejoice in thy joy, and be glorified with thine inheritance.

6 We have sinned with our fathers, we have committed iniquity, we have done wickedly.

7 Our fathers understood not thy wonders in Egypt; they remembered not the multitude of thy mercies; but provoked him at the sea, even at the Red Sea.

8 Nevertheless he saved them for his name's sake, that he might make his mighty power to be known.

9 He rebuked the Red Sea also, and it was dried up; so he led them through the depths, as through the wilderness.

10 And he saved them from the hand of the enemy and delivered them from the hand of the oppressor.

11 And the waters covered their enemies; there was not one of them left.

12 Then believed they his words; they sang his praise.

13 But they soon forgot God; they trusted not in his counsel,

14 But craved exceedingly in the wilderness, and tempted God in the desert.

15 And he gave them their request; and he supplied them with abundance.

16 They plotted against Moses also in the camp, and Aaron the saint of the LORD.

17 The earth opened and swallowed up Dathan, and covered the company of Abiram.

18 And a fire was kindled in their

company; the flame burned up the wicked.

19 They made a calf in Horeb, and worshipped the molten image.

20 Thus they changed their Glorious One into the likeness of an ox that eats grass.

21 They forgot God their Saviour, who had done great things in Egypt,

22 Wondrous works in the land of Ham, and terrible things by the Red Sea.

23 Therefore he said that he would destroy them, had not Moses his chosen stood before him in the breach, to turn away his wrath, lest he should destroy them.

24 Yea, they despised the desired land, they believed not his word,

25 But murmured in their tents, and hearkened not to the voice of the LORD.

26 Therefore he lifted up his hand against them, to scatter them among the Gentiles,

27 To scatter their descendants also among the nations, and to lose them in the lands.

28 They worshipped also the idols of Baal-peor, and ate sacrifices offered for the dead.

29 Thus they provoked him to anger with their acts; they made him angry with their images, and the plague came upon them suddenly.

30 Then Phinehas stood up and prayed, and so the plague was stopped.

31 And that was counted to him for a victory to all generations for evermore.

32 They angered him also at the waters of strife, so that it went ill with Moses for their sakes,

33 Because they provoked his spirit, so that he spoke unadvisedly with his lips.

34 And they did not destroy the nations, concerning whom the LORD commanded them;

35 But they were mingled among the Gentiles, and learned their works.

36 And they served their idols, which were a snare to them.

37 Yea, they sacrificed their sons and their daughters to demons,

38 And shed innocent blood, even the blood of their sons and of their daughters, whom they sacrificed to the idols of Canaan; and the land was polluted with blood.

39 Thus were they defiled with their own works, and went awhoring with their own inventions.

40 Therefore was the wrath of the LORD kindled against his people, insomuch that he abhorred his own inheritance.

41 And he gave them into the hand of the Gentiles; and they that hated them ruled over them.

42 Their enemies also subdued them, and they were brought into subjection under their hand.

43 Many times did he deliver them; but they provoked him with their counsel, and were humbled for their iniquity.

44 Nevertheless he regarded their affliction and heard their prayer.

45 And he remembered his covenant, and pitied them, and led them according to the multitude of his mercies.

46 He made them also to be pitied of all those that carried them captives.

47 Save us, O LORD our God, and gather us from among the nations, that we may give thanks to thy holy name, and be glorified in thine inheritance.

48 Blessed be the LORD God of Israel from everlasting to everlasting; and let all the people say, Amen and Amen. Praise the LORD.

PSALM 107

O GIVE thanks to the LORD, for he is good; for his mercy endures for ever.

2 Let the redeemed of the LORD say so, whom he has redeemed from the hand of the oppressor,

3 And gathered out of the lands, from the east and from the west, from the north and from the islands in the sea.

4 They were lost in the wilderness in a place without water; they found not the right way to an inhabited town.

5 Hungry and thirsty, their soul fainted in them.

6 Then they cried to the LORD in their trouble, and he delivered them out of their distresses,

7 And he led them forth by the right way, that they might go to inhabited villages.

8 Let the righteous of the LORD give thanks to him; for his mercies are upon the children of men!

9 For he satisfies the longing soul, and fills the hungry soul with goodness,

10 Such as sit in darkness and in the shadow of death, being bound in affliction and iron;

11 Because they murmured against the words of God, and scorned the counsel of the most High;

12 Therefore he brought down their hearts with labor; they became weak and there was none to help.

13 Then they prayed to the LORD in their trouble and he saved them out of their distresses.

14 He brought them out of darkness and the shadow of death, and broke their bands asunder.

15 Let the righteous of the LORD give thanks to him; for his mercies are upon the children of men.

16 For he has broken the gates of brass, and cut the bars of iron asunder.

17 He helped them out of the way of their sins, he relieved them of their afflictions.

18 Their soul abhorred all manner of food, and they drew near to the gates of death.

19 Then they cried to the LORD in their trouble, and he delivered them out of their distresses.

20 He sent his word, and healed them, and delivered them from destruction.

21 Let the righteous of the LORD give thanks to him, for his mercies are upon the children of men!

22 Sacrifice to him the sacrifices of praise, and glorify him, O you, his servants, for his wonders.

23 They that go down to the sea in ships, that do business in great waters,

24 These see the works of the LORD and his wonders in the deep.

25 For he commands and raises the stormy wind, which lifts up the waves thereof.

26 They mount up to the sky; then they go down again to the depths; their soul is troubled within them.

27 They reel to and fro, and stagger like a drunken man, and are at their wit's end.

28 Then they cry to the LORD in their trouble and he brings them out of their distresses.

29 He makes the storm a calm, so that the waves thereof are still.

30 Then are they glad because they be quiet; so he brings them to their desired haven.

31 Let the righteous of the LORD give thanks to him; for his mercies are upon the children of men.

32 Let them exalt him also in the congregation of the people, and praise him in the assembly of the elders.

33 He turns rivers into a wilderness and the water-springs into dry ground,

34 A fruitful land into barrenness, for the wickedness of them that dwell therein.

35 He turns the wilderness into pools of water and dry land into watersprings.

36 And there he makes the hungry to dwell, that they may build villages and settle,

37 And sow the fields and plant vineyards, and eat of the fruits thereof.

38 He blesses them also, so that they are multiplied greatly; and suffers not their cattle to decrease.

39 Again, they are diminished and humbled through oppression, affliction, and misery.

40 He pours contempt upon rulers, and causes them to wander in the wilderness where there is no way.

41 He strengthens the poor and he multiplies their families like a flock.

42 The righteous shall see it, and rejoice; and all the ungodly shall shut their mouths.

43 Whosoever is wise, and will observe these things, even they shall

understand the lovingkindness of the LORD.

PSALM 108

O GOD, my heart is ready, my heart is ready; I will sing and give praise, even with my glory.

2 Awake, my harp; awake, psaltery and harp; I myself will awake early.

3 I will praise thee, O LORD, among the people; and I will sing praises unto thee among the nations.

4 For thy mercy is great to the heavens; and thy truth reaches to the heaven of heavens.

5 Be thou exalted, O God, above the heavens, and thy glory above all the earth,

6 That thy beloved may be delivered; save me with thy right hand, and answer me.

7 God has spoken in his holiness: I will rejoice, I will divide Shechem and mete out the valley of Succoth.

8 Gilead is mine, Manasseh is mine, Ephraim also is the strength of my head; Judah is my king;

9 Moab is my washpot; Edom will loosen my shoe; over Philistia will I triumph.

10 Who will bring me into the strong city? Who will lead me into Edom?

11 Wilt not thou, O God, who cast us off? and wilt not thou, O God, go forth with our hosts?

12 Give us strength against our enemies; for vain is the help of man.

13 Through God we shall do valiantly; for he it is who shall tread down our enemies.

PSALM 109

HOLD not thy peace, O God of my praise;

2 For the mouth of the wicked and the mouth of the deceitful are opened against me;

3 They have spoken against me with a lying tongue and with a hateful voice, and have fought against me without a cause.

4 For my love they reproach me; but I have prayed for them.

5 And they have rewarded me evil for good, and hatred for my love.

6 Command thou vengeance against them; and let Satan stand at their right hand.

7 When they shall be judged, let them be condemned, and let their prayer become sin.

8 Let their days be few; and let others take what they have stored.

9 Let their children be fatherless and their wives widows.

10 Let their children be continually vagabonds, and beg; let them seek their bread also out of their desolate places.

11 Let the creditor take all that they have, and let the strangers make them to be weakened.

12 Let there be none to extend mercy unto them; neither let there be any to pity their fatherless children.

13 Let their end be destruction, and in the generation following let their name be blotted out.

14 Let the iniquity of their fathers be remembered; and let not the sin of their mothers be blotted out.

15 Let them be before the LORD continually, that he may cut off the memory of them from the earth,

16 Because they remembered not to show mercy, but persecuted the poor and needy, and him whose heart is sorrowful to death.

17 They loved cursing, and delighted not in blessings.

18 They clothed themselves with cursing like armor; it penetrated into them like water, like oil into their bones.

19 Let it be to them like a mantle which covers them, and like a girdle wherewith they are girded continually.

20 These are the deeds of those who reproach the LORD, and of those who speak evil against me.

21 But thou, O LORD, do good to me for thy name's sake; because thy mercy is good, deliver thou me.

22 For I am poor and needy, and my heart is troubled within me.

23 I am bent like the shadow when it declines; I am tossed up and down as the locust.

24 My knees are weak through fasting; and my flesh wastes away.

25 And I became also a reproach to them; when they looked upon me they shook their heads.

26 Help me, O LORD my God; O save me according to thy mercy,

27 That they may know that this is thy hand, that thou, LORD, hast done it.

28 Let them be cursed; but thou shalt be blessed, and let thou thy servant rejoice.

29 Let them that had a grudge against me be clothed with shame, and let them cover themselves with it as with a mantle.

30 I will greatly praise the LORD with my mouth; yea, I will praise him among the multitude.

31 He has stood at the right hand of the poor, to save his soul from judgment.

PSALM 110

THE LORD said unto my Lord, Sit thou at my right hand until I make thine enemies thy footstool.

2 The LORD will send forth the sceptre of his power out of Zion, and he will rule over thine enemies.

3 Thy people shall be glorious in the day of thy power; arrayed in the beauty of holiness from the womb, I have begotten thee as a child from the ages.

4 The LORD has sworn, and will not lie, You are a priest for ever after the order of Melchizedek.

5 The LORD at your right hand will defeat the kings in the day of his wrath.

6 He will judge among the nations, he will count the slain; he will cut off the heads of many on earth.

7 He will drink of the brook in the way; therefore he will lift up his head.

PSALM 111

PRAISE the LORD. I will praise the LORD with my whole heart, in the assembly of the upright, and in the congregation.

2 The works of the LORD are great, sought out of all them that have pleasure therein.

3 His works are great and glorious, and his righteousness endures for ever.

4 He has made his wonderful works to be remembered; the LORD is gracious and full of compassion.

5 He has given food to them that revere him; he will ever be mindful of his covenant.

6 He has shown his people the power of his works, that he may give them the heritage of the Gentiles.

7 The works of his hands are truth and justice, and they endure for ever and ever.

8 All his commandments are sure, and are done in righteousness and truth.

9 He has sent salvation to his people; his covenant shall be remembered for ever; holy and revered is his name.

10 The reverence of the LORD is the beginning of wisdom; a good understanding have all they that do his commandments; his praise endures for ever.

PSALM 112

PRAISE the LORD. Blessed is the man who fears the LORD, who is vigilant in his commandments.

2 His descendants shall be mighty upon earth; he shall be blessed in the generation of the upright.

3 Wealth and riches shall be in his house; and his righteousness endures for ever.

4 To the upright there shines a light in the darkness; he is gracious and full of compassion upon the righteous.

5 Blessed is the man who shows mercy and lends; he shall proclaim his words with judgment.

6 Surely he shall not be moved for ever; the righteous shall be in everlasting remembrance.

7 He shall not be afraid of evil tidings; his heart is fixed, trusting in the LORD.

8 His heart is strengthened; he shall not be afraid, until he sees his desire upon his enemies.

9 He has given generously, he has given to the poor; his righteousness

endures for ever and ever; his horn shall be exalted with honor.

10 The wicked shall see it, and be grieved; he shall gnash his teeth and be confounded; the desire of the wicked shall perish.

PSALM 113

PRAISE the LORD. Praise, O you servants of the LORD, praise the name of the LORD.

2 Blessed be the name of the LORD from this time forth and for evermore.

3 From the rising of the sun to the going down of the same the LORD's name is great.

4 The LORD is high above all nations, and his glory above the heavens.

5 Who is like to the LORD our God, who dwells on high,

6 Yet who beholds the things that are in the deep, in heaven, and in the earth!

7 He raises up the poor out of the dunghill,

8 That he may set him with the princes of the people.

9 He makes the barren woman to keep house, and to be a joyful mother of children. Praise the LORD.

PSALM 114

WHEN Israel went out of Egypt, the house of Jacob from a people of a foreign language,

2 Judah was his sanctuary and Israel his glory.

3 The sea saw it and fled; Jordan was driven back.

4 The mountains skipped like rams, and the hills like lambs of the flock.

5 What ails you, O you sea, that you fled? You Jordan, that you were driven back?

6 You mountains, that you skipped like rams; and you hills, like lambs of the flock?

7 Tremble, earth, at the presence of the LORD, at the presence of the God of Jacob,

8 Who turned the rock into pools of water, the flint into a fountain of waters.

PSALM 115

NOT unto us, O LORD, not unto us, but unto thy name give glory for thy mercy and for thy truth's sake.

2 Wherefore the Gentiles have no cause to say, Where is now their God?

3 But our God is in the heavens; he has done whatever he pleased.

4 The idols of the Gentiles are silver and gold, the work of men's hands.

5 They have mouths, but they speak not; eyes have they, but they see not;

6 They have ears, but they hear not; noses have they, but they smell not;

7 They have hands, but they feel not; feet have they, but they walk not; neither speak they through their throats.

8 Let them that make them become like them; and every one that trusts in them.

9 The house of Israel trusts in the LORD; he is their help and their shield.

10 The house of Aaron trusts in the LORD; he is their help and their shield.

11 You who reverence the LORD, trust in the LORD; he is their help and their shield.

12 The LORD has been mindful of us; he will bless us; he will bless the house of Israel; he will bless the house of Aaron.

13 The LORD will bless them that worship him, both small and great.

14 The LORD will increase you more and more, you and your children.

15 You are blessed of the LORD who made heaven and earth.

16 The heavens, even the heavens, are the LORD's; but the earth has he given to the children of men.

17 The dead praise not the LORD, neither any that go down into darkness.

18 But we will bless the LORD from this time forth and for evermore. Praise the LORD.

PSALM 116

I LOVE the LORD, because he will hear the voice of my supplication.

2 He will incline his ear to me in the day when I call upon him.

3 The pangs of death have encompassed me, and the pains of Sheol have found me; I found trouble and sorrow.

4 Then called I upon the name of the LORD; O LORD, deliver my soul.

5 Thou art merciful, O LORD, and righteous; O God, thou art merciful.

6 The LORD preserves the little ones; he humbled me and saved me.

7 Return to your rest, O my soul; for the LORD has dealt bountifully with you.

8 For he has delivered my soul from death, and my feet from falling.

9 I will be acceptable to thee, O LORD, in the land of the living.

10 I believed, therefore have I spoken; I have been humbled exceedingly:

11 I said in my stupidity, All men are liars.

12 What shall I render to the LORD for all his benefits toward me?

13 I will take the cup of salvation and call upon the name of the LORD.

14 I will pay my vows to the LORD now in the presence of all the people.

15 Precious in the sight of the LORD is the death of his saints.

16 O LORD, truly I am thy servant; I am thy servant, and the son of thy handmaid; thou hast loosed my bonds.

17 I will offer to thee the sacrifice of thanksgiving and will call upon the name of the LORD.

18 I will pay my vows to the LORD now in the presence of all the people,

19 In the courts of the LORD's house, in the midst of thee, O Jerusalem. Praise the LORD.

PSALM 117

O PRAISE the LORD, all you nations; praise him, all you people.

2 For his merciful kindness is great toward us; and the truth of the LORD endures for ever. Praise the LORD.

PSALM 118

O GIVE thanks to the LORD; for he is good and his mercy endures for ever.

2 Let Israel now say that his mercy endures for ever.

3 Let the house of Aaron now say that his mercy endures for ever.

4 Let them that worship the LORD say that his mercy endures for ever.

5 Out of my distress I called upon the LORD; the LORD answered me and relieved me.

6 The LORD is my help, I will not fear; what can man do to me?

7 The LORD is my helper; therefore shall I see my desire upon them that hate me.

8 It is better to trust in the LORD than to put confidence in man.

9 It is better to trust in the LORD than to put confidence in princes.

10 All nations surrounded me; but in the name of the LORD I will destroy them.

11 They surrounded me; yea, they surrounded me; but in the name of the LORD I will destroy them.

12 They surrounded me like hornets; they are quenched like the fire of stubble; for in the name of the LORD I will destroy them.

13 I have been repelled that I might be overthrown and fall; but the LORD helped me.

14 The LORD is my strength and song, and has become my salvation.

15 The voice of rejoicing and salvation is in the tabernacles of the righteous; the right hand of the LORD does valiantly.

16 The right hand of the LORD has exalted me; the right hand of the LORD does valiantly.

17 I shall not die, but live, and declare the works of the LORD.

18 The LORD has chastened me severely; but he has not given me over to death.

19 Open to me the gates of righteousness; I will go into them, and I will praise the LORD.

20 This is the gate of the LORD, into which the righteous shall enter.

21 I will give thanks to thee; for

thou hast heard me, and art become my salvation.

22 The stone which the builders rejected has become the headstone of the corner.

23 This is the LORD's doing; it is marvellous in our eyes.

24 This is the day which the LORD has made; we will rejoice and be glad in it.

25 Save me, O LORD; O LORD, deliver me.

26 Blessed be he that comes in the name of the LORD; we have blessed you out of the house of the LORD.

27 O LORD, our God, enlighten us; bind our festival processions as an unbroken chain, even to the horns of the altar.

28 Thou art my God, and I will give thanks to thee; thou art my God, I will exalt thee.

29 O give thanks to the LORD, for he is good; for his mercy endures for ever.

PSALM 119
ALEPH

B LESSED are the undefiled in the way, who walk in the law of the LORD.

2 Blessed are they who keep his testimonies, and seek him with the whole heart.

3 They also do no iniquity; they walk in his ways.

4 Thou hast commanded them to keep thy precepts diligently.

5 O that my ways were directed to keep thy statutes!

6 Then shall I not be ashamed, when I have observed all thy commandments.

7 I will praise thee with uprightness of heart, when I shall have learned thy righteous judgments.

8 I will keep thy statutes; O forsake me not utterly.

BETH

9 With what shall a young man cleanse his way in order that he may observe thy commandments?

10 With my whole heart have I sought thee; O let me not wander from thy commandments.

11 Thy words have I impressed on my heart, that I might not sin against thee.

12 Blessed art thou, O LORD; teach me thy statutes.

13 With my lips have I repeated all thy righteous judgments.

14 I have been delighted in the way of thy testimonies, more than in all riches.

15 I have meditated in thy commandments, and am familiar with thy ways.

16 I have meditated in thy law in order that I may not forget thy words.

GAMEL

17 Answer thy servant, that I may live and keep thy words.

18 Open thou mine eyes, that I may behold wondrous things out of thy law.

19 I am a sojourner with thee; hide not thy commandments from me.

20 My soul is pleased and desires thy judgments at all times.

21 Thou hast rebuked the Gentiles, and cursed are those who go astray from thy commandments.

22 Remove from me reproach and contempt; for I have kept thy testimonies.

23 The ungodly sat and plotted against me; but I meditated in thy statutes.

24 I have meditated also in thy testimonies and in thy good counsel.

DALETH

25 My soul cleaves to the dust; quicken me according to thy word.

26 I have declared my ways and thou heardest me; teach me thy law.

27 Make me to understand the way of thy precepts; so shall I meditate on thy wondrous works.

28 My soul is vexed from meditation; quicken me according to thy word.

29 Remove from me the practices of the wicked, and teach me thy law.

30 I have chosen the way of thy truth: thy judgments have delighted me.

31 I have stuck unto thy testi-

monies: O Lᴏʀᴅ, put me not to shame.

32 I have walked in the way of thy commandments, because thou hast made me joyful.

HE

33 Teach me, O Lᴏʀᴅ, the way of thy commandments; and I shall keep them unto the end.

34 Give me understanding and I shall keep thy law; yea, I shall observe it with my whole heart.

35 Make me to go in the path of thy commandments; for therein do I delight.

36 Incline my heart unto thy testimonies, and not to fables.

37 Turn away mine eyes that they may not behold falsehood; and quicken thou me in thy way.

38 Strengthen thy word unto thy servant, who is devoted to thee.

39 Turn away my reproach: because thy judgments are good.

40 Behold, I have delighted in thy precepts: quicken me in thy righteousness.

VAU

41 Let thy mercies come also to me, O Lᴏʀᴅ, even thy salvation, according to thy word.

42 So shall I have wherewith to answer him who reproaches me; for I trust in thy word.

43 Let not the word of truth depart from my mouth; for I have hoped in thy judgments.

44 So shall I keep thy law continually for ever and ever.

45 And I will walk at liberty because I have been delighted in thy commandments.

46 I will speak truthfully before kings, and will not be ashamed.

47 And I will meditate on thy commandments, which I have loved.

48 My hands also will I lift up to thy commandments, which I have loved; and I will meditate in thy commandments, and I will be glorified in thy faith.[1]

¹ Religion.

ZEN

49 Remember thy word to thy servant, upon which thou hast made me to hope.

50 In it have I been comforted in my humiliation; for thy word has quickened me.

51 The ungodly have oppressed me greatly; yet have I not swerved from thy law.

52 I have remembered thy judgments of old, O Lᴏʀᴅ, and have been comforted; they have become a guide to me.

53 Horror has taken hold of me because of the wicked who forsake thy law.

54 Thy statutes have been my songs in the house of my pilgrimage.

55 I have remembered thy name, O Lᴏʀᴅ, in the night, and have kept thy law.

56 I have been comforted because I kept thy commandments.

KHETH

57 On the Lᴏʀᴅ's business have I meditated, that I may keep thy commandments.

58 I entreated thy favor with my whole heart; save me according to thy word.

59 I thought on my ways, and turned my feet to thy paths.

60 I prepared myself and delayed not to keep thy commandments.

61 The bands of the wicked have beset me; but I have not strayed from thy law.

62 At midnight I rise to give thanks to thee because of thy righteous judgments.

63 I am a friend of all them that worship thee, and of them that keep thy commandments.

64 The earth, O Lᴏʀᴅ, is full of thy mercy; teach me thy statutes.

TETH

65 Thou hast dealt well with thy servant, O Lᴏʀᴅ, according to thy word.

66 Teach me good judgment, grace,

and knowledge; for I have believed thy commandments.

67 Even before I was humbled I believed; and I kept thy word.

68 Thou art good, O Lord, and doest good; teach me thy statutes.

69 The injustice of the proud has multiplied; but I keep thy commandments with my whole heart.

70 Their hearts are stubborn; but I keep thy law.

71 It is good for me that I have been humbled, that I might learn thy statutes.

72 The law of thy mouth is better to me than thousands of things of gold and silver.

YOTH

73 Thy hands have made me and fashioned me; teach me thy law,

74 So that those who revere thee may see and rejoice, because I have hoped in thy word.

75 I know, O Lord, that thy judgments are right, and that thou in thy faithfulness hast humbled me.

76 Let, I pray thee, thy merciful kindness be for my comfort, according to thy word to thy servant.

77 Let thy tender mercies come to me, that I may live; for I have been taught thy law.

78 Let the wicked be ashamed, for they have humbled me unjustly; but I have meditated in thy precepts.

79 Let those who reverence thee turn unto me, and those who have known thy testimonies.

80 Let my heart meditate in thy statutes, that I be not ashamed.

CAPH

81 My soul hath longed for thy salvation, and I hope in thy word.

82 Mine eyes wait for thy word, when thou wilt comfort me.

83 For I have suffered all disgrace; yet do I not forget thy statutes.

84 How many are the days of thy servant? When wilt thou execute judgment on them that persecute me?

85 The wicked have digged a pit for me, which is not in accord with thy law.

86 All thy commandments are trust-worthy; yet the wicked persecute me.

87 They had almost destroyed me upon earth; but I forsook not thy commandments.

88 Quicken me after thy loving-kindness; so shall I keep the testimony of thy mouth.

LAMED

89 For ever thou art, O Lord; thy word is established in heaven.

90 Thy faithfulness is to all generations; thou hast established the earth, and it abides.

91 They continue this day according to thine ordinances; for all are thy servants.

92 Unless thy law had been my meditation, I should then have perished in mine affliction.

93 I will never forget thy commandments, because they are my very life.

94 I am thine, deliver me; for I have kept thy commandments.

95 The wicked have waited for me to destroy me; but I understand thy testimonies.

96 I have seen the futility of all things; but thy commandment is exceeding broad.

MEM

97 O how love I thy law! It is my meditation all the day.

98 Make me wiser than mine enemies, because I have obeyed thy commandments.

99 Give me more understanding than all my teachers; for thy testimonies are my meditation.

100 I understand more than the elders, because I keep thy statutes.

101 I have refrained my feet from every evil way, that I might keep thy commandments.

102 I have not departed from thy judgments; for thou hast taught me.

103 How sweet are thy words to the taste! yea, sweeter than honey to the mouth!

104 I have meditated on thy commandments; therefore I hate the way of the wicked.

NUN

105 Thy word is a lamp to my feet and a light to my path.

106 I have sworn, and I will perform it, that I will keep thy righteous judgments.

107 I am afflicted very much; quicken me, O LORD, according to thy word.

108 With the words of my mouth be pleased, O LORD, and teach me thy judgments.

109 My soul is continually in thy hands; I do not forget thy law.

110 Sinners have laid a snare for me; yet I erred not from thy commandments.

111 Thy testimonies have I taken as a heritage for ever; for they are the rejoicing of my heart.

112 I have inclined my heart to perform thy statutes truly, even to the end.

SEMKETH

113 I hate the wicked; but thy law do I love.

114 Thou art my shelter and my refuge; I hope in thy word.

115 Depart from me, O you evildoers, that I may keep the commandments of my God.

116 Uphold me according to thy word, and I shall live; and let me not be ashamed of my hope.

117 Help me and I shall be safe, and I will be continually mindful of thy commandments.

118 Thou hast rejected all them that stray from thee; for their thought is ungodly.

119 Sustain me, and I shall be safe, and I will always meditate on thy commandments.

120 My flesh shrinks for fear of thee; and I am afraid of thy judgments.

AI

121 O thou that doeth judgment and justice, leave me not in the hand of mine oppressors.

122 Comfort thy servant with goodness; let not the proud slander me.

123 Mine eyes long for thy salvation, and for the word of thy righteousness.

124 Deal with thy servant according to thy mercies, and teach me thy law.

125 I am thy servant; give me understanding, that I may know thy testimonies.

126 It is time to serve the LORD; for they have nullified thy law.

127 Therefore I love thy commandments above gold, yea, above precious stones.

128 Therefore I love all thy commandments; and I hate every way of the wicked.

PE

129 Thy testimonies are wonderful; therefore doth my soul keep them.

130 Make plain thy word and enlighten and give understanding to the simple.

131 I opened my mouth, and panted; for I longed for thy commandments.

132 Look upon me, and be merciful to me, because I love thy name.

133 Direct my steps in thy path; let not the wicked have dominion over me.

134 Deliver me from the oppression of man; so will I keep thy statutes.

135 Make thy face to shine upon thy servant; and teach me thy law.

136 Rivers of waters run down mine eyes, because they keep not thy law.

ZADDI

137 Righteous art thou, O LORD, and upright are thy judgments.

138 Thou hast commanded thy testimony in righteousness and faithfulness.

139 Zeal hath consumed me because thine enemies have forgotten thy word.

140 Thy word is very pure; therefore thy servant loves it.

141 I am small and despised; yet I do not forget thy commandments.

142 Thy righteousness is an everlasting righteousness, and thy law is truth.

143 Trouble and anguish have

taken hold of me; yet I meditate on thy commandments.

144 The righteousness of thy testimonies is everlasting; give me understanding, and I shall live.

KOPH

145 I cried with my whole heart; hear me, O LORD; I will keep thy statutes.

146 I cried to thee; save me, and I shall keep thy testimonies.

147 I arose at the dawn of the morning, and cried; I hoped in thy word.

148 Mine eyes open before the night watches, that I might meditate in thy word.

149 Hear my voice according to thy lovingkindness, O LORD; quicken me according to thy judgment.

150 They draw near who follow after mischief; they are far from thy law.

151 Thou art near, O LORD; and all thy commandments are truth. Mine eyes open before the night watch to meditate on thy word.

152 Concerning thy testimonies, I have known of old that thou hast founded them for ever.

RESH

153 Consider mine affliction, and deliver me; for I do not forget thy law.

154 Judge my case, and deliver me; quicken me according to thy word.

155 Salvation is far from the wicked; for they seek not thy statutes.

156 Great are thy tender mercies, O LORD; quicken me according to thy judgments.

157 Many are my persecutors and mine enemies; yet do I not decline from thy testimonies.

158 I beheld the transgressors and I knew they had not kept thy word.

159 Consider how I love thy commandments; quicken me, O LORD, according to thy lovingkindness.

160 The foundation of thy word is truth; and every one of thy righteous judgments endures for ever.

SHEEN

161 Princes have persecuted me without a cause; but my heart stands in awe of thy word.

162 I rejoice at thy word, as one that finds great spoil.

163 I hate and despise evil; but thy law do I love.

164 Seven times a day do I praise thee because of thy righteous judgments.

165 Great peace have they which love thy law; and they shall have no infirmity.

166 LORD, I have hoped for thy salvation, and done thy commandments.

167 My soul has kept thy testimonies, and I love them exceedingly.

168 I have kept thy commandments and thy testimonies; for all my ways are before thee.

TAU

169 Let my cry come before thee, O LORD; save me according to thy word.

170 Let my supplication come before thee; deliver me according to thy word.

171 My tongue shall speak of thy word; for all thy commandments are righteous.

172 My lips shall speak of thy praise when thou hast taught me thy commandments.

173 Let thine hand help me; for I have delighted in thy statutes.

174 I have longed for thy salvation, O LORD; and I meditate on thy law.

175 Let my soul live, and it shall praise thee; and let thy judgments help me.

176 I have gone astray like a lost sheep; seek thy servant, for I do not forget thy commandments.

PSALM 120

IN my distress I cried to the LORD, and he heard me.

2 Deliver my soul, O LORD, from lips of the ungodly and from deceitful tongues.

3 What shall be given to you? or what shall be added to you, you deceitful tongues?

4 The arrows of the mighty are sharp; they are as hot coals of oak.

5 Woe is me, that my sojourn is prolonged, that I dwell in the tents of Kedar!

6 My soul has long dwelt with him that hates peace.

7 I am for peace; but when I speak they fight with me.

PSALM 121

I WILL lift up mine eyes to the mountain [1] from whence comes my help.

2 My help comes from the LORD, who made heaven and earth.

3 He will not allow your foot to be moved; he who keeps you will not slumber.

4 Behold, he who keeps Israel will neither slumber nor sleep.

5 The LORD is your keeper; the LORD will protect you with his right hand.

6 The sun shall not smite you by day, nor the moon by night.

7 The LORD will preserve you from all evil; he will preserve your soul.

8 The LORD will preserve your going out and your coming in from this time forth and even for evermore.

PSALM 122

I WAS glad when they said to me, Let us go to the house of the LORD.

2 My feet shall stand within your gates, O Jerusalem.

3 Jerusalem is built like a city that is surrounded by a wall,

4 Whither the tribes go up, the tribes of the LORD, to the testimony of Israel, to give thanks to the name of the LORD.

5 For there are thrones of judgment set, the thrones of the house of David.

6 Greet Jerusalem with peace; they shall prosper who love you.

7 Peace be within your walls and prosperity within your palaces.

8 For my brethren and companions' sakes, I will now say, Peace be within you.

[1] **Mount Zion.**

9 For the sake of the house of the LORD our God, I will seek your good.

PSALM 123

TO thee lift I up mine eyes, O thou that dwellest in the heaven.

2 Behold, as the eyes of servants look towards their masters, and as the eyes of a maiden look towards her mistress; so also our eyes look towards the LORD our God, until he shall have mercy upon us.

3 Have mercy upon us, O LORD, have mercy upon us; for we have heard a great deal of contempt.

4 Our soul has enough of the scorn of mockers, and enough of the contempt of the proud.

PSALM 124

IF it had not been the LORD who stood on our side, now may Israel say,

2 If it had not been the LORD who stood on our side when men rose up against us,

3 Then would they have swallowed us alive when their wrath was kindled against us,

4 Then would they have drowned us in the waters, the stream would have gone over us;

5 Then the great waters would have gone over us.

6 Blessed be the LORD, who has not given us as a prey to their teeth.

7 Our soul has escaped as a bird out of the snare of the fowlers; the snare is broken, and we are delivered.

8 Our help is in the name of the LORD, who made heaven and earth.

PSALM 125

THEY who trust in the LORD in the mount of Zion shall not be moved, but shall dwell there for ever.

2 As the mountains are round about Jerusalem, so the LORD is round about his people from henceforth even for ever.

3 For the rod of the wicked shall not rest upon the portion of the righteous; neither shall the righteous put forth their hands to iniquity.

4 Do good, O LORD, to those who

are good, and to them who are upright in their hearts.

5 But as for those who follow their crooked ways, the LORD will scatter them together with the workers of iniquity; but peace will be upon Israel.

PSALM 126

WHEN the LORD brought back the people of Zion from captivity, we were like those that rejoice.

2 Then was our mouth filled with laughter, and our tongue with singing; then said they among the heathen, The LORD has done great things for them.

3 The LORD has done great things for us, whereof we are joyful.

4 Turn again our captivity, O LORD, like the streams in the south.

5 They that sow in tears shall reap in joy.

6 He who goes forth and weeps, bearing precious seed, shall doubtless come again with rejoicing, bringing his sheaves with him.

PSALM 127

EXCEPT the LORD build the house, they labor in vain who build it; except the LORD keep the city, the watchmen stay awake in vain.

2 It is in vain for those who rise up early, who sit up late; they eat the bread of sorrows, for so he gives in sleep to his beloved.

3 Lo, children are a heritage of the LORD; and the fruit of the womb is a reward.

4 Like arrows in the hand of a mighty man; so are children of the youth.

5 Blessed is the man who has his quiver full of them; he shall not be ashamed, but shall speak with enemies in the gate.

PSALM 128

BLESSED is every one who fears the LORD, that walks in his ways.

2 For you shall eat the labour of your hands; happy shall you be, and it shall be well with you.

3 Your wife shall be as a fruitful vine by the sides of your house; your children like olive plants round about your table.

4 Behold, thus shall the man be blessed who fears the LORD.

5 The LORD will bless you out of Zion; and you shall see the good of Jerusalem all the days of your life.

6 Yea, you shall see your children's children, and peace upon Israel.

PSALM 129

MY oppressors have been many from my youth, may Israel now say;

2 My oppressors have been many from my youth, yet they have not prevailed against me.

3 They have scourged me upon my back; they have made long their oppression.

4 The LORD is righteous; he will cut asunder the cord of the wicked.

5 Let them all be confounded and turned back that hate Zion.

6 Let them be as the grass upon the house tops, which pulls out and withers when the wind strikes it,

7 Wherewith the reaper fills not his hand, nor he who binds sheaves his bosom.

8 Neither do they who pass by say, The blessing of the LORD be upon you; we bless you in the name of the LORD.

PSALM 130

OUT of the depths have I cried to thee, O LORD, and thou hast heard my voice.

2 Let thine ears be attentive to the voice of my supplications.

3 If thou, LORD, shouldest mark iniquities, O LORD, who shall stand?

4 Because forgiveness comes from thee, thou mayest be revered.

5 I trust in the LORD, my soul waits for his word.

6 I have waited for the LORD from the morning watch even until the night watch.

7 Let Israel hope in the LORD; from him comes mercy, and with him is plenteous redemption.

8 He shall redeem Israel from all his iniquities.

PSALM 131

LORD, my heart is not haughty, nor mine eyes lofty; neither do I deal in great matters, nor in things too high for me.

2 Surely I have humbled and quieted myself, as a child that is weaned of its mother; my soul is even as a weaned child.

3 Let Israel hope in the LORD from henceforth and for ever.

PSALM 132

LORD, remember David, and all his afflictions:

2 How he swore to the LORD, and vowed to the mighty God of Jacob;

3 Surely I will not come into the tabernacle of my house, nor go up into my bed;

4 Nor will I give sleep to mine eyes or slumber to mine eyelids

5 Until I find a place for the LORD, a habitation for the mighty God of Jacob.

6 Lo, we heard of it at Ephratah; we found it in the fields.

7 We will go into his tabernacles; we will worship at his footstool.

8 Arise, O LORD, enter into the place of thy rest, thou, and the ark of thy strength.

9 Let thy priests be clothed with righteousness, and thy saints with glory.

10 For thy servant David's sake turn not away the face of thine anointed.

11 The LORD has sworn in truth to David (he will not turn from it): Of the fruit of your body will I set up your throne.

12 If your children will keep my covenant and my testimony that I shall teach them, their children shall also sit upon your throne for ever-more.

13 For the LORD has been delighted with Zion; he has chosen it for his habitation.

14 This is my rest for ever; here will I dwell, for I have desired it.

15 I will abundantly bless her hunters; I will satisfy her poor with bread.

¹ Give him an heir.

16 I will also clothe her priests with salvation and her saints with glory.

17 There shall I make the horn of David to shine, and light a lamp for his anointed.¹

18 His enemies will I clothe with shame; but my holiness shall cover him.

PSALM 133

BEHOLD, how good and how pleasant it is for brethren to dwell together in unity!

2 It is like the precious ointment upon the head and upon the beard, even Aaron's beard, that went down to the collar of his robe;

3 Like the dew of Hermon that falls upon the mount of Zion; for there the LORD commanded the blessing, even life for evermore.

PSALM 134

BEHOLD, bless the LORD, all you servants of the LORD, who by night stand in the house of the LORD.

2 Lift up your hands towards the sanctuary, and bless the LORD.

3 The LORD bless you out of Zion, even he who made heaven and earth.

PSALM 135

PRAISE the LORD. Praise the name of the LORD; praise him, O servants of the LORD.

2 You who stand in the house of the LORD, in the courts of the house of our God,

3 Praise the LORD; for the LORD is good; sing praises to his name, for he is delightful.

4 For the LORD has chosen Jacob to himself, and Israel for his congregation.

5 For I know that the LORD is great, and that our LORD is above all gods.

6 Whatsoever the LORD pleases, that he does in heaven and in earth, in the seas and in all deep places.

7 He causes the clouds to ascend from the ends of the earth; he makes lightnings for the rain; he brings the wind out of his treasuries.

8 He smote the first-born of Egypt, both of man and beast,

9 Who sent forth his signs and wonders into the midst of you, O Egypt, upon Pharaoh and upon all his servants,

10 Who smote many nations and slew mighty kings;

11 Sihon king of the Amorites, and Og king of Bashan, and all the kingdoms of Canaan;

12 And gave their land for a heritage, a heritage to Israel his people.

13 Thy name, O LORD, endures for ever; and thy memorial, O LORD, throughout all generations.

14 For the LORD will judge his people, and he will delight in his servants.

15 The idols of the heathen are silver and gold, the work of men's hands.

16 They have mouths, but they speak not; eyes have they, but they see not;

17 They have ears, but they hear not; neither is there any breath in their mouths.

18 Let them that make them become like them, and every one who trusts in them.

19 Bless the LORD, O house of Israel; bless the LORD, O house of Aaron;

20 Bless the LORD, O house of Levi; you who fear the LORD, bless the LORD.

21 Blessed be the LORD out of Zion, who dwells at Jerusalem. Praise the LORD.

PSALM 136

O GIVE thanks to the LORD, for he is good; for his mercy endures for ever.

2 O give thanks to the God of gods; for his mercy endures for ever.

3 O give thanks to the LORD of lords; for his mercy endures for ever.

4 To him who alone does great wonders; for his mercy endures for ever.

5 To him who by wisdom made the heavens; for his mercy endures for ever.

6 To him who stretched out the earth above the waters; for his mercy endures for ever.

7 To him who made great lights; for his mercy endures for ever;

8 The sun to rule by day; for his mercy endures for ever;

9 The moon and stars to rule by night; for his mercy endures for ever.

10 To him who smote the first-born of Egypt; for his mercy endures for ever;

11 And brought out Israel from among them; for his mercy endures for ever;

12 With a strong hand, and with a stretched out arm; for his mercy endures for ever.

13 To him who divided the Red sea into parts; for his mercy endures for ever;

14 And Israel to pass through the midst of it; for his mercy endures for ever;

15 But overthrew Pharaoh and his host in the Red sea; for his mercy endures for ever.

16 To him who led his people through the wilderness; for his mercy endures for ever.

17 To him who smote great kings; for his mercy endures for ever;

18 And slew mighty kings; for his mercy endures for ever;

19 Sihon king of the Amorites; for his mercy endures for ever;

20 And Og the king of Bashan; for his mercy endures for ever;

21 And gave their land for a heritage; for his mercy endures for ever;

22 Even a heritage to Israel his servant; for his mercy endures for ever.

23 Who remembered us during our affliction; for his mercy endures for ever;

24 And has saved us from our enemies; for his mercy endures for ever.

25 Who gives food to all flesh; for his mercy endures for ever.

26 O give thanks to the God who is in heaven; for his mercy endures for ever.

PSALM 137

B Y the rivers of Babylon, there we sat down, yea, we wept, when we remembered Zion.

2 We hanged our harps upon the willows in the midst thereof.

3 For there they that carried us away captive required of us a song; and our captors said to us, Sing us one of the songs of Zion.

4 How shall we sing the LORD's song in a strange land?

5 If I forget you, O Jerusalem, let my right hand forget me.

6 If I do not remember you, let my tongue cleave to my palate, if I prefer not Jerusalem above my chief joy.

7 Remember, O LORD, the children of Edom in the day of Jerusalem, who said, Raze it, raze it, even to the foundation thereof.

8 O daughter of Babylon, taker of spoils, blessed shall he be who rewards you as you have served us.

9 Blessed shall he be who takes and dashes your little ones against the stones.

PSALM 138

I WILL praise thee with my whole heart; before the kings will I sing praise to thee.

2 I will worship in thy holy temple, and praise thy name for thy lovingkindness and for thy truth; for thou hast magnified thy word above every name.

3 In the day when I cried to thee, thou didst answer me, and didst increase the strength of my soul.

4 All the kings of the earth shall praise thee, O LORD, for they have heard the words of thy mouth.

5 Yea, they shall praise the ways of the LORD; for great is the glory of the LORD.

6 Though the LORD be high, yet can he see those who have been brought low; but the proud he knows from afar.

7 Though I walk in the midst of trouble, thou wilt save me; thou shalt stretch forth thy hand against the wrath of mine enemies, and thy right hand shall save me.

8 O LORD, rest thy right hand upon me; thy mercy, O LORD, endures for ever; forsake not the works of thine own hands.

PSALM 139

O LORD, thou hast searched me and known me.

2 Thou knowest my downsitting and mine uprising, thou understandest my thoughts from above.

3 Thou knowest my way and my paths, and art acquainted with all my ways.

4 For if there is deception in my tongue, lo, O LORD, thou knowest it altogether.

5 From the beginning to the end, thou knowest me, O LORD, for thou hast formed and laid thy hand upon me.

6 Such knowledge is too wonderful for me; it is high, I cannot attain unto it.

7 Whither shall I go from thy Spirit? or whither shall I flee from thy presence?

8 If I ascend into heaven, thou art there; if I descend into Sheol, behold, thou art there also.

9 If I lift up my wings like those of an eagle, and dwell in the uttermost parts of the sea,

10 Even there also shall thy hand lead me, and thy right hand shall hold me.

11 If I say, Surely the darkness shall be as light upon me; even the night shall be light before my face.

12 The darkness shall not be dark to thee; but the night shines as the day; the darkness and the light are both alike to thee.

13 For thou hast made my heart; thou hast accepted me from my mother's womb.

14 I will praise thee, because of the wonders which thou hast done; marvellous are thy works; and that my soul knows right well.

15 My substance was not hid from thee, when I was made in secret, and marvellously wrought in the lowest parts of the earth.

16 Thine eyes did see my substance, yet being imperfect; and upon thy books all these things were written, even before day was and man was brought into existence.

17 How precious also are thy mer-

cies to me, O God! How great is the sum of them?

18 If I should count the best of them, they are more in number than the grains of sand; when I awake I am still with thee.

19 Surely thou wilt slay the wicked, O God; depart from me therefore, you bloody men.

20 For they speak against thee, and have taken thy city without cause.

21 I hate them, O LORD, who hate thee; and I am grieved with those who rise up against thee.

22 I hate them with perfect hatred; I count them mine enemies.

23 Search me, O God, and know my heart; try me, and know my ways,

24 And see if there be any wicked way in me, and lead me in the way everlasting.

PSALM 140

DELIVER me, O LORD, from the evil man; preserve me from violent men,

2 Who devise mischiefs in their heart; continually do they stir up contention.

3 They have sharpened their tongues like a serpent; adders' poison is under their lips.

4 Keep me, O LORD, from the hands of the wicked; preserve me from violent men, who have purposed to prevent my goings.

5 The proud have hid a snare for me; the cords of their net have they spread over my paths; they have set a trap for me.

6 I said to the LORD, Thou art my God; hear the voice of my supplications, O LORD.

7 O LORD, my mighty Saviour, thou art the shield of my head in the day of battle.

8 Grant not, O LORD, the desires of the wicked; further not their wicked devices; let them not accomplish their purpose.

9 Let the mischief of their own lips cover them.

10 Let burning coals fall upon them; let them fall into the fire, that they rise not up again.

11 Let not an evil speaker be estab-lished in the earth; evil shall hunt the violent man to destroy him.

12 I know that the LORD will defend the cause of the afflicted and the right of the poor.

13 Surely the righteous shall give thanks to thy name; the upright shall dwell in thy presence.

PSALM 141

LORD, I cry to thee; make haste to answer me; give ear to my words and accept them.

2 Let my prayer be set forth before thee as incense, and the gift of my hands as the evening sacrifice.

3 Set a watch, O LORD, before my mouth; keep the door of my lips,

4 So that my heart may not incline to evil things, and practise wicked works with men who work iniquity; let me not eat salt with them.

5 Let the righteous teach me and reprove me; let the oil of the wicked not anoint my head since my prayer has been against their evils.

6 When their judges are stopped by a strong hand, they shall hear my words; for they are sweet.

7 Like the ploughshare that scatters the earth, let their bones be scattered at the mouth of the grave.

8 I have lifted up mine eyes to thee, O LORD; I have trusted in thee; do not reject my soul.

9 Keep me from the hand of the proud, for they have set traps for me.

10 Let the wicked together fall into their own nets, whilst I shall pass over.

PSALM 142

I CRIED to the LORD with my voice; with my voice to the LORD did I make my supplication.

2 I poured out my complaint before him; I showed before him my trouble.

3 When my spirit was overwhelmed within me, then thou knewest my path. In the way wherein I walked have they secretly laid a snare for me.

4 I looked on my right hand, and there was no one to advise me; refuge failed me; no man cared for my soul.

5 I cried to thee, O LORD; I said,

Thou art my hope and my portion, O Lord, in the land of the living.

6 Attend to my cry; for I am brought very low; deliver me from my persecutors, for they are stronger than I.

7 Bring my soul out of prison, that I may praise thy name; thy righteous shall wait for me until thou shalt reward me.

PSALM 143

HEAR my prayer, O Lord, give ear to my supplications; in thine own words answer me, and in thy righteousness.

2 And do not let thy servant be brought to judgment; for in thy sight shall no man living be justified.

3 For the enemy has persecuted my soul; he has smitten my life down to the ground; he has made me to dwell in darkness, like those who have been long dead.

4 Therefore is my spirit overwhelmed within me; my heart within me is troubled.

5 I remember thee, O Lord, from days of old; I meditate on all thy works; I muse on the work of thy hands.

6 I stretch forth my hands to thee; my soul thirsts after thee, as a thirsty land.

7 Answer me speedily, O Lord; my spirit fails; hide not thy face from me, lest I be like them who go down into the pit.

8 Cause me to hear of thy lovingkindness in the morning; for in thee do I trust; cause me to know the way wherein I should walk, for I lift up my soul to thee.

9 Deliver me, O Lord, from mine enemies, and teach me to do thy will.

10 Because thou art my God, thy gentle spirit shall lead me into the way of life.

11 Comfort me, O Lord, for thy name's sake; for thy righteousness' sake bring my soul out of trouble.

12 And by thy mercy silence those who hate me, and destroy all the enemies of my soul; for I am thy servant.

PSALM 144

BLESSED be the Lord, my strength, who teaches my hands to war and my fingers to fight;

2 My refuge and my deliverer; my shield and my helper, upon whom I trust, who subdues nations under me.

3 Lord, what is man, that thou takest knowledge of him? or the son of man, that thou art mindful of him?

4 Man is like vapour; his days are as a shadow that passes away.

5 Bow thy heavens, O Lord, and come down; rebuke the mountains, and they shall smoke.

6 Cast forth lightning, and scatter them; shoot out thine arrows, and destroy them.

7 Stretch forth thy hand from above; deliver me out of great waters, from the hand of the ungodly,

8 Whose mouths speak vanity, and their right hand is a right hand of falsehood.

9 I will sing a new song to thee, O God; upon a psaltery and an instrument of ten strings will I sing praises to thee.

10 It is he who gives salvation to kings; who delivers David his servant from the hurtful sword.

11 Deliver me from the hand of the wicked, whose mouths speak vanity, and their right hand is a right hand of falsehood,

12 That our sons may be as plants grown up in their youth; that our daughters may be as brides richly adorned after the fashion of temples;

13 That our storehouses may be full to overflowing; that our sheep may multiply abundantly in our streets;

14 That our cattle may be strong and there be none barren among them; that there be no stealing, and that there be no mourning in our streets.

15 Happy is the people who have all these things; yea, happy is the people, whose God is the Lord.

PSALM 145

I WILL extol thee, O my Lord, the King; and I will bless thy name for ever and ever.

2 Every day will I bless thee; and I will praise thy name for ever and ever.

3 Great is our LORD, and greatly to be praised; and his greatness is unsearchable.

4 One generation shall tell thy works to another, and shall declare thy mighty acts.

5 I will speak of the glorious honor of thy majesty, and of thy wondrous works.

6 And men shall speak of the might of thy wonderful acts; and I will declare thy greatness.

7 They shall abundantly utter the memory of thy great goodness, thy righteous shall seek and shall find it.

8 The LORD is gracious and full of compassion, slow to anger and of great mercy.

9 The LORD is good to all, and his tender mercies are over all his servants.

10 All thy servants shall give thee thanks, O LORD, and thy saints shall praise thee.

11 They shall speak of the glory of thy kingdom, and talk of thy power,

12 To make known to the sons of men thy might and the glorious majesty of thy kingdom.

13 Thy kingdom is an everlasting kingdom, and thy dominion endures throughout all generations. The LORD is faithful in his words and righteous in all his works.

14 The LORD upholds all who fall, and raises up all who are bowed down.

15 The eyes of all wait upon thee; and thou givest them their food in due season.

16 Thou openest thy hand and satisfiest the desire of every living thing.

17 The LORD is righteous in all his ways and merciful in all his works.

18 The LORD is near to all who call upon him, to all who call upon him in truth.

19 He will fulfil the desire of those who worship him; he also will hear their cry and will save them.

20 The LORD preserves all who love him; but all the wicked he will destroy.

21 My mouth shall speak the praise of the LORD; let all flesh bless his holy name for ever and ever.

PSALM 146

PRAISE the LORD. Praise the LORD, O my soul.

2 While I live will I praise the LORD; I will sing praises to my God as long as I live.

3 Put not your trust in princes, nor in the son of man, in whom there is no help.

4 His breath goes forth, he returns to his earth; in that very day his thoughts perish.

5 Happy is he who has the God of Jacob for his help, whose hope is in the LORD his God,

6 Who made heaven and earth, the sea and all that therein is; who keeps truth for ever;

7 Who executes justice for the oppressed; who gives food to the hungry. The LORD releases the prisoners;

8 The LORD opens the eyes of the blind; the LORD raises those who are bowed down; the LORD loves the righteous;

9 The LORD takes care of the poor; he feeds the fatherless and widows; but the way of the wicked he turns upside down.

10 The LORD shall reign for ever, even your God, O Zion, to all generations. Praise the LORD.

PSALM 147

PRAISE the LORD; for it is good to sing praises to our God; for it is pleasant, and praise is comely.

2 The LORD builds up Jerusalem; he gathers together the scattered of Israel.

3 He heals the broken of heart, and binds up their wounds.

4 He counts the number of the stars; he calls them all by their names.

5 Great is our LORD, and great is his power; his understanding is infinite.

6 The LORD lifts up the meek; he humbles the wicked down to the ground.

7 Sing to the LORD with thanksgiving; sing praise upon the harp to our God,

8 Who covers the heavens with clouds, who gives rain upon the earth, who makes grass to grow upon the mountains.

9 He gives to the cattle their food, and to the young ravens which cry.

10 He delights not in the strength of the horse; he takes no pleasure in the legs of a mighty man.

11 The LORD takes pleasure in those who revere him, in those who hope in his mercy.

12 Praise the LORD, O Jerusalem; praise your God, O Zion.

13 For he has strengthened the bars of your gates; he has blessed your children within you.

14 He makes peace in your borders, and fills you with the finest of the wheat.

15 He sends forth his commandment upon earth; his word runs very swiftly.

16 He gives snow like wool; he scatters the hoarfrost like ashes.

17 He casts forth his ice like morsels; who can stand before his cold?

18 He sends out his word and melts them; he causes his wind to blow, and the waters flow.

19 He declares his word to Jacob, his statutes and his judgments to Israel.

20 He has not dealt so with all nations; and his judgments he has not made known to them. Praise the LORD.

PSALM 148

PRAISE the LORD. Praise the LORD from the heavens; praise him in the heights.

2 Praise him, all his angels; praise him, all his hosts.

3 Praise him, sun and moon; praise him, all stars and light.

4 Praise him, heavens of heavens, and waters that are above the heavens.

5 Let them praise the name of the LORD; for he spoke and they were made, he commanded and they were created.

6 He has also established them for ever and ever; he has made a decree which shall not pass.

7 Praise the LORD from the earth, you great serpents and all deeps;

8 Fire and hail, snow and ice, stormy wind fulfilling his word,

9 Mountains and all hills, fruitful trees and all cedars,

10 Wild beasts and all cattle, creeping things and flying fowl,

11 Kings of the earth and all people, princes and all judges of the earth,

12 Both boys and maidens, old men and young men, let them praise the name of the LORD;

13 For his name alone is excellent; his glory is on earth and in heaven.

14 He also exalts the horn of his people, the praise of all his saints; even of the children of Israel, a people near to him. Praise the LORD.

PSALM 149

PRAISE the LORD. Sing to the LORD a new song, and his praise in the congregation of saints.

2 Let Israel rejoice in him that made him; let the children of Zion be joyful in their King.

3 Let them praise his name with the timbrel and psaltery; let them sing praises to him with the harps.

4 For the LORD takes pleasure in his people; he has given salvation to the poor.

5 Let the righteous become mighty in glory; let them glorify him upon their beds.

6 Let them exalt God with their throats, and with a two-edged sword in their hand,

7 To execute vengeance upon the heathen, and punishments upon the peoples,

8 To bind their kings with fetters and their nobles with chains of iron.

9 To execute upon them the judgment that is written; and give glory to all his saints. Praise the LORD.

PSALM 150

PRAISE the LORD. Praise God in his sanctuary; praise him in the firmament of his power.

2 Praise him for his mighty acts;

praise him according to his excellent greatness.

3 Praise him with the sound of the trumpet; praise him with psaltery and harp.

4 Praise him with timbrel and pipe;

praise him with sweet stringed instruments.

5 Praise him upon loud cymbals; praise him with a mighty song.

6 Let every thing that has breath praise the Lord. Praise the Lord.

THE PROVERBS

CHAPTER 1

THE proverbs of Solomon the son of David, king of Israel:

2 To know wisdom and instruction; to perceive the words of understanding;

3 To receive discipline, reverence, righteousness, and justice, and equity;

4 To give subtlety to the simple, to the young men knowledge and discretion.

5 A wise man will listen and will increase learning; and a man of understanding shall attain to leadership;

6 To understand proverbs and figures of speech; the words of the wise and their dark sayings.

7 ¶The reverence of the Lord is the beginning of knowledge; but fools despise knowledge and instruction.

8 Hear, my son, the ordinance of your father, and forsake not the law of your mother;

9 For they shall be an ornament of grace for your head and a necklace about your neck.

10 ¶My son, if sinners entice you, consent not.

11 If they say to you, Come with us, let us lie in wait to shed blood, let us lie in wait for the innocent, wrongfully;

12 Let us swallow them up alive, as Sheol swallows the living, and whole as those who go down into the pit;

13 We shall find all his wealth and

precious things, we shall fill our houses with spoil;

14 Cast in your lot with us; let us all have one purse;

15 My son, do not walk in the way with them; but refrain your foot from their path;

16 For their feet run to evil, they make haste to shed blood.

17 Surely in deceit is the net spread in the sight of any bird.

18 And they lie in wait, they hide themselves to shed blood.

19 Such are the ways of all who practice iniquity, who take away the life of their owners.

20 ¶Wisdom is glorified in the market places; she raises her voice in the streets;

21 She preaches in the chief places of the concourse; in the openings of the gates of the city, she utters her words, saying,

22 How long, you simple ones, will you love childishness? And the scorners delight in their scorning, and fools hate knowledge?

23 If you will turn to my reproof, behold, I will pour out my spirit upon you; I will make known my words to you.

24 ¶For I have called, and you refused; I have stretched out my hand, and you did not listen;

25 But you have despised all my counsels, and you were not pleased with my reproof.

26 I also will laugh at your calamity; I will rejoice when terror and

sudden destruction come upon you;

27 When your destruction comes as a whirlwind; when distress and anguish come upon you,

28 Then they shall call upon me, but I will not answer them; they shall seek me early, but they shall not find me;

29 Because they hated knowledge, and did not choose the worship of the LORD.

30 They were not pleased with my counsels; they rejected all of my reproof.

31 Therefore they shall eat of the fruit of their own ways and be filled with their own devices.

32 For the turning away of the simple shall slay them, and the error of the weak-minded men shall destroy them.

33 But he who listens to me shall live in hope, and shall refrain from many evils.

CHAPTER 2

MY son, if you will receive my words and hide my commandments in your heart,

2 And incline your ear to wisdom and apply your heart to understanding,

3 Yea, if you cry after knowledge and lift up your voice to understanding,

4 If you seek it as silver, and search for it as for hidden treasure;

5 Then you will understand how to worship the LORD and find the knowledge of God.

6 For it is the LORD who gives wisdom; out of his mouth come knowledge and understanding.

7 He stores up hope for the upright; he helps those who walk without blemish.

8 He keeps the paths of justice, and preserves the ways of his saints.

9 Then you will understand righteousness and justice and the uprightness of all good ways.

10 ¶When wisdom enters into your heart and knowledge is pleasant to your soul,

11 Intelligence shall preserve you,

and the understanding of the pious men shall deliver you;

12 That you might be delivered from evil ways, from men who speak perverse things,

13 Who forsake the path of uprightness to walk in the way of darkness;

14 Who rejoice to do evil and delight in the perverseness of evil things;

15 Men whose ways are crooked and whose paths are perverse.

16 Wisdom shall deliver you from a strange woman who flatters with her words,

17 Who has forsaken the mother of her youth and forgotten the covenant of her God.

18 For she has forgotten the threshold of her house and the way of her paths.

19 None who go to her return again, neither do they remember the path of life.

20 Therefore you must walk in the way of good men and keep the path of the righteous.

21 For the upright shall dwell in the land, and those who are unblemished shall remain in it.

22 But the wicked shall be cut off from the earth and the ungodly shall be rooted out of it.

CHAPTER 3

MY son, do not forget my law; but let your heart keep my commandments;

2 For the length of days and long life will they add to you;

3 And peace, mercy, and truth will not forsake you; bind them about your neck; write them upon the tablets of your heart:

4 So you shall find favor, grace, and understanding in the sight of God and men.

5 ¶Trust in the LORD with all your heart, and rely not on your own wisdom.

6 In all your ways acknowledge him, and he shall direct your paths.

7 ¶Be not wise in your own eyes;

revere the LORD, and depart from evil.

8 It shall be healing to your flesh and marrow to your bones.

9 Honor the LORD with your substance and with the first fruits of all your crops;

10 So shall your barns be filled with plenty, and your wine presses shall burst out with new wine.

11 ¶My son, despise not the chastening of the LORD, neither be weary of his corrections.

12 For whom the LORD loves he corrects, even as a father corrects his son.

13 ¶Blessed is the man who finds wisdom, and the son of the man who finds understanding.

14 For the merchandise of it is better than the merchandise of silver, and its gains than fine gold.

15 She is more valuable than precious stones; and there is nothing to be compared to her.

16 Length of days is in her right hand; and in her left hand riches and honor.

17 Her ways are ways of pleasantness, and all her paths are peace.

18 She is a tree of life to those who lay hold of her; and blessed are those who wait for her.

19 The LORD by his wisdom has founded the earth; by his understanding he established the heavens.

20 By his knowledge the depths are broken up and the clouds drop down the dew.

21 ¶My son, let not my commandments depart from your eyes; keep my doctrine, and my counsels;

22 So shall they be life to your soul and grace to your neck.

23 Then you shall walk in your way with hope and your foot shall not stumble.

24 When you lie down, you shall not be afraid; yea, you shall lie down and your sleep shall be sweet.

25 You shall not fear sudden tumult, neither the violence of the wicked, when it comes.

26 For the LORD shall be with you and shall keep your foot that you may not be caught in the snare.

27 ¶Do not refuse to do that which is good, when it is in the power of your hand to do it.

28 When you have something, do not say to your neighbor, Go, and come again tomorrow, and I will give it to you.

29 Do not devise evil against your neighbor, seeing he dwells in peace beside you.

30 ¶Do not contend with a man without a cause, if he has done you no harm.

31 ¶Do not envy a wicked man, and choose none of his ways.

32 For the wicked man is an abomination in the presence of the LORD; but the secret of the LORD is with the upright.

33 ¶The curse of the LORD is in the house of the wicked; but he blesses the habitation of the righteous.

34 Surely he despises scorners; but he has compassion on the wise.

35 Wise men shall inherit glory; but fools shall receive disgrace.

CHAPTER 4

HEAR, O my children, the instruction of a father, and give ear to knowledge and understanding.

2 Because I give you good doctrine, do not forsake my law.

3 For I was also a son to my father, tender and the only begotten in the sight of my mother.

4 He taught me, and said to me, Let your heart hold fast my words; keep my commandments, and live; and let my law be as the pupil of the eye.

5 Get wisdom, get understanding; and turn not aside from the words of my mouth.

6 Do not forsake her, and she will preserve you; love her, and she will save you.

7 Wisdom is the principal thing; therefore get wisdom; and with all your substance get understanding.

8 Love her, and she shall exalt you; embrace her, and she shall honor you.

9 She shall put upon your head an ornament of grace; a crown of glory shall she bestow upon you.

10 Hear, O my son, and receive my

sayings; and the years of your life shall be many.

11 I have taught you the ways of wisdom; I have led you in right paths.

12 When you walk, your steps will not be unsteady; and when you run, you will not stumble.

13 Take fast hold of my instruction, and do not forsake her; keep her, for she is your life.

14 ¶Do not walk in the way of evil men, and do not envy the way of the wicked.

15 The place where they dwell, do not pass by it, turn away from it,

16 For they do not sleep until they have done mischief; and their sleep is taken away until their evil devices are carried out.

17 For they eat the bread of wickedness and drink the wine of violence.

18 But the path of the righteous is like the shining light that shines more and more unto the perfect day.

19 The way of the wicked is like darkness; they do not know at what they stumble.

20 ¶My son, attend to my words; incline your ear to my sayings.

21 Do not let them depart from your eyes; but keep them in the midst of your heart.

22 For they are life to him who finds them, and health to all his flesh.

23 ¶Keep your heart with all diligence, for out of it are the issues of life.

24 Put away from you a perverse mouth, and the counsel of deceit put far from your lips.

25 Let your eyes look straight forward, and let your eyelids look straight before you.

26 Keep your feet away from evil paths; then all your ways shall be firm.

27 Turn not to the right hand nor to the left; but remove your foot from evil.

CHAPTER 5

MY son, attend to my wisdom and incline your ear to my understanding,

2 That you may heed counsel and that your lips may keep knowledge.

3 ¶For the lips of a strange woman drop as a honeycomb, and her words are smoother than oil;

4 But the end of her life is bitter as wormwood, sharp as a two-edged sword.

5 Her feet cause men to go down to death; her steps take her to Sheol.

6 She does not tread upon the land of the living, her paths are devious, and are unknown.

7 Hear me now therefore, O you children, and do not depart from the words of my mouth.

8 Remove your way far from her, and do not come near the door of her house;

9 Lest you give your strength to others, and your years to the cruel;

10 Lest strangers be filled with your wealth, and your labors be in the house of strangers;

11 And you have remorse in your old age, when the flesh of your body is consumed,

12 And you say, Why did I hate instruction, and my heart despise reproof,

13 And why have I not obeyed the voice of my teacher, nor inclined my ear to them that instructed me?

14 I was in almost all kinds of evil in the midst of the congregation and assembly.

15 ¶Drink water out of your own well, and running water from your own spring.

16 Let your water overflow into your streets, let it be disbursed abroad.

17 Let it be for yourself alone, let not strangers be partners with you.

18 Let your fountain be blessed; and rejoice in the wife of your youth.

19 Let her be like a loving hind, and pleasant mountain roe; learn her ways always, and be mindful of her love.

20 My son, be not misled by a strange woman, neither embrace the bosom of a strange woman.

21 For the ways of man are before the eyes of the Lord, and all his paths lie open in his presence.

22 ¶The wicked shall be caught by his own iniquities, and he will be bound with the cords of his sins.

23 He shall die without instruction; and in the greatness of his folly he shall go astray.

CHAPTER 6

MY son, if you have become surety for your friend, if you have obligated yourself to a stranger,

2 Then you are snared with the words of your mouth, you are caught with the words of your lips.

3 Do this now, my son, and deliver yourself because, for the sake of your friend, you have fallen into the hands of your enemies; go, therefore, and stir up your friend for whom you have become surety to meet his obligation.

4 You shall not give sleep to your eyes nor slumber to your eyelids.

5 Deliver yourself like a gazelle from the snare, and like a bird from the hand of the fowler.

6 ¶Be like the ant, consider her ways, and be wise;

7 Though having no harvest and no ruler over her, neither any one to guide her,

8 She provides her bread in the summer and gathers her food in the harvest.

9 How long will you sleep, O sluggard? When will you arise from your sleep?

10 Yet a little sleep, a little slumber, a little folding of the hands on the chest;

11 And then poverty shall come upon you, and distress shall overtake you; become a successful man.

12 ¶A fool, a wicked man, is unscrupulous.

13 He winks with his eyes, he signals with his feet, he makes signs with his fingers;

14 He is perverse in his heart, he devises mischief continually; he sows discord.

15 Therefore his calamity shall come suddenly; suddenly will he be broken without remedy.

16 ¶There are six things which the LORD hates; yea, the seventh is an abomination to him:

17 Haughty eyes, a lying tongue, and hands that shed innocent blood,

18 A heart that devises wicked imaginations, feet that are swift in running to mischief,

19 A false witness who speaks lies, and he who sows discord among brothers.

20 ¶My son, keep your father's commandment and do not forsake the law of your mother;

21 Impress them firmly on your heart and tie them about your neck.

22 When you walk, let them follow you; let them be with you, keep them that they may keep you; and when you awake, meditate on them.

23 For the commandment is a lamp, and the law is a light, and the reproofs of instruction are the way of life,

24 To keep you from the evil woman, from the flattery of the tongue of a strange woman.

25 Do not lust after her beauty in your heart; neither let her snare you with her eyes, nor let her captivate you with her eyelids.

26 For the appearance of a harlot is tempting like a loaf of bread; and the adulteress hunts for the precious life.

27 Can a man take fire in his bosom, and his clothes not be burned?

28 Can one walk upon hot coals, and his feet not be burned?

29 So is he who goes in to his neighbor's wife and touches her; he shall not be innocent.

30 No one wonders at a thief when he is caught stealing, for he steals to satisfy himself when he is hungry;

31 But if he is caught, he shall pay sevenfold; he shall give all the goods of his house.

32 But he who commits adultery with a woman lacks understanding, and he destroys his own soul.

33 And he who does it brings dishonor upon himself; and his reproach shall not be wiped out.

34 For jealousy provokes a man's rage; therefore he will not spare in the day of vengeance.

35 He will not regard any ransom; nor will he listen, though you increase the bribe.

CHAPTER 7

MY son, keep my words and hide my commandments within you.

2 Keep my commandments and live, and my law as the pupil of your eye.

3 Bind them about your neck; write them upon the tablets of your heart.

4 Say to wisdom, You are my sister; and to understanding, You are my counselor

5 That they may keep you from the strange woman, from the stranger that flatters with her words.

6 ¶For from the window of her house and from the balcony she looked out,

7 And she beheld young men, she spied among the youths, and those who lacked understanding,

8 Passing through the street near the corner of her house,

9 In the twilight, in the evening, in the black and dark night;

10 And, behold, there came out a woman with the attire of a harlot to meet one of them, a woman who fluttered the hearts of young men.

11 She is rebellious and gluttonous; her feet do not abide in her house;

12 But she roams around outside, now in the streets, and now lying in wait at the corners.

13 So she caught him and kissed him, and, with an impudent face, said to him,

14 This day I have paid my vows, I have peace offerings with me;

15 Therefore I came out to meet you, for I have been waiting to see you, and now I have found you.

16 I have made my bed upon a carpet; I have covered it with fine linen of Egypt.

17 I have perfumed my bed with myrrh, aloes, and cinnamon.

18 Come, let us take our fill of love until the morning; let us embrace each other with passion.

19 For my husband is not at home, he has gone on a long journey;

20 He has taken a bag of money with him, and it will be a long time before he comes home.

21 With much fair speech she mis-led him, with the flattering of her lips she forced him.

22 He went after her as a little child, as an ox that goes to the slaughter, and as a dog to be muzzled;

23 And as a stag whose liver is pierced with an arrow, as a bird hastens to the snare, and does not know that he goes to his death.

24 ¶Now therefore, O my children, hearken to me, and attend to the words of my mouth.

25 Let not your heart incline to her ways, do not go astray in her paths.

26 For she has cast down many wounded; yea, many mighty men have been slain by her.

27 The ways to her house are the ways to Sheol, going down to the chambers of death.

CHAPTER 8

THEREFORE preach wisdom, and understanding will answer you.

2 For wisdom is on the top of high places, she stands between the ways and by the paths.

3 She cries at the gates, at the entrance of the city; she cries aloud, saying,

4 Unto you, O men, I call; and my voice is to the sons of men,

5 So that the simple ones may understand prudence and the fools understand in their heart.

6 Hear, for I will speak truth; and the opening of my mouth shall bring forth uprightness.

7 For my mouth shall speak truth, and lying lips are an abomination before me.

8 All the words of my mouth are in righteousness; there is nothing perverse or deceptive in them.

9 They are all plain to him who understands them, and right to those who are willing to find knowledge.

10 Receive discipline and not silver; and choose for yourself knowledge rather than fine gold.

11 For wisdom is much better than fine gold; yea, she is better than precious stones, and nothing can be compared to her.

12 I wisdom have created prudence,

and I possess knowledge and reason.

13 Reverence of the LORD despises evil; pride, arrogance, evil ways, and perverse speech do I hate.

14 Counsel and sound doctrine are mine; mine is understanding and might.

15 By me kings reign and princes decree justice.

16 By me princes and nobles rule, even all the righteous judges of the earth.

17 I love those who love me; and those who seek me shall find me.

18 Riches and honor are mine; yea, enduring riches and righteousness.

19 My fruit is better than fine gold, and my ingathering than choice silver.

20 I lead in the way of righteousness, in the midst of the paths of justice,

21 That I may cause those that love me to have hope; and I will fill their treasuries.

22 The LORD created me as the first of his creations, before all of his works.

23 I was established from everlasting, from the beginning, before he made the earth.

24 When there were no depths, I was brought forth; when there were no fountains abounding with water.

25 Before the mountains were settled, before the hills were formed was I conceived;

26 While as yet he had not made the earth nor the valleys nor the best soil of the world.

27 When he established the heavens, I was there; when he set a circle upon the face of the deep;

28 When he made firm the clouds above; when he strengthened the fountains of the deep;

29 When he gave to the sea its bounds, that the waters should not transgress his commandment; when he laid down the foundations of the earth:

30 I together with him was establishing them; and daily I was his delight, rejoicing always before him,

31 Rejoicing in his habitable earth; and my delights were with the sons of men.

32 Now therefore hearken to me, O you children; for blessed is he who keeps my ways.

33 Hear instruction and be wise and do not go astray.

34 Blessed is the man who heeds me, watching daily at my gates, waiting at my threshold.

35 For my objectives are the issues of life, they proclaim the will of the LORD.

36 Those who sin against me wrong their own soul; all those who hate me love death.

CHAPTER 9

WISDOM has built her house; she has set up in it seven pillars;

2 She has slaughtered her beasts; she has mingled her wine; she has also prepared her table.

3 She has sent forth her servants to cry out upon the highest places and say,

4 Whosoever is simple, let him come to me; as for him who lacks understanding, she said to him,

5 Come, eat of my bread and drink of the wine which I have mingled.

6 Forsake folly, and live; and go in the way of understanding.

7 Correction for a bad man brings disgrace; the wicked man is rebuked by his own blemish.

8 Reprove not a bad man, lest he hate you; rebuke a wise man, and he will love you.

9 Give an opportunity to a wise man, and he will be yet wiser; teach a just man, and he will increase in learning.

10 The reverence of the LORD is the beginning of wisdom; and the knowledge of the righteous is understanding.

11 For by her your days shall be multiplied, and the years of your life shall be increased.

12 My son, if you are wise, you are wise for yourself and for your friends; but if you are evil-minded, you alone shall bear your evils;

13 He who denies things falsely feeds on winds [1] and pursues fowl of the air; for he has forsaken the way to his vineyard and the paths of his labor, to journey in the wilderness without water; in the places that are trodden he travels thirsty and gains nothing.

14 A foolish woman is enticing; she does not know what shame is; she sits at the door of her home on a high seat,

15 She calls those who pass by, who go right on their ways;

16 She says, He who is simple, let him come to me; and as for him who lacks understanding, she says to him,

17 Stolen waters are sweet and bread eaten in secret is pleasant.

18 But he does not know that the mighty men perish with her and that her guests are in the depths of Sheol.

19 Now rise up, and do not abide in that place; do not cast your eye at her; thus pass by the waters of strangers; cross over a strange river, and turn away from the waters of strangers; you shall not drink of the waters of strangers. For in doing so a multitude of days and years of life shall be added to you.

CHAPTER 10

A WISE son makes his father glad, but a foolish son brings shame to his mother.

2 Treasures of wickedness profit nothing; but righteousness delivers from death.

3 The LORD will not suffer the soul of the righteous to famish; but he casts away the substance of the wicked.

4 Poverty humbles a man; but the hands of diligent men make rich.

5 He who works in summer is a wise man; but he who sleeps in harvest is a son that causes shame.

6 Blessings are upon the head of the righteous; but iniquity covers the mouth of the wicked.

7 The memory of the just is a blessing; but the heir of the wicked shall be extinct.

[1] He is weak-minded.

8 The wise in heart will receive commandments; but one whose lips are full of folly shall be caught.

9 He who walks uprightly walks in hope; but he who perverts his ways shall be known.

10 He who winks with his eyes deceitfully causes sorrow; but he who reproves openly makes peace.

11 The mouth of a righteous man is a fountain of life; but the mouth of the wicked is covered with iniquity.

12 Hatred stirs up strife; shame shall cover all the wicked.

13 He who brings forth wisdom out of his lips shall beat with a rod him that lacks understanding.

14 Wise men conceal knowledge; but a hasty mouth is near destruction.

15 The rich men's wealth is their strong cities; the destruction of the poor is their poverty.

16 The labor of the righteous tends to life; the harvest of the wicked to sin.

17 The true way of life brings discipline; but he who hates reproof is a fool.

18 The lips of the wicked are full of deceits, and he who utters a curse is a fool.

19 The wicked cannot be delivered by a multitude of words; but he who refrains his lips is wise.

20 The tongue of the righteous is like choice silver; the heart of the wicked is full of bitterness.

21 The lips of the righteous are full of mercy; but the fools die for want of wisdom.

22 The blessings of the LORD bring riches, and there shall be no sorrow in them.

23 It is sport to a fool to do mischief; but a man of understanding has wisdom.

24 The wicked shall be dragged to ruin; but the desire of the righteous shall be granted.

25 As the whirlwind passes suddenly, so wicked men shall perish and be no more; but the righteous are an everlasting foundation.

26 As unripe grapes are hurtful to the teeth, and as smoke to the eyes,

so does wickedness hurt those who indulge in it.

27 Reverence for the LORD prolongs life; but the years of the wicked shall be shortened.

28 The hope of the righteous shall be gladness; but the expectation of the wicked shall perish.

29 The way of the LORD is strength to the upright; but destruction shall be to the workers of iniquity.

30 The righteous shall never be removed; but the wicked shall not inhabit the earth.

31 The mouth of the righteous brings forth wisdom; but a perverse tongue shall be silenced.

32 The lips of the righteous know what is good; but the mouth of the wicked speaks perverse things.

CHAPTER 11

FALSE scales are an abomination to the LORD; but just weights are his delight.

2 Where baseness comes, then comes shame; but with the meek is wisdom.

3 The hope of the upright shall be granted; but the pride of the wicked shall be destroyed.

4 Riches profit not in the day of wrath; but righteousness delivers from death.

5 The righteousness of the upright shall direct his way; but the wicked shall fall by his own wickedness.

6 The righteousness of the upright shall deliver them; but the transgressors shall be caught in their own wickedness.

7 When a wicked man dies, his expectation perishes; and the hope of the evil doers perishes.

8 The righteous is delivered out of trouble, and the wicked comes in his stead.

9 With his mouth a wicked man destroys his neighbor; but through knowledge shall the righteous be strengthened.

10 When it goes well with the righteous, the city becomes powerful; and when the wicked perish, there is rejoicing.

11 By the blessings of the upright the city is exalted; but it is overthrown by the mouth of the wicked.

12 He who despises his neighbor lacks understanding; but a man of prudence lives in peace.

13 An adversary reveals secrets; but he who is faithful in his spirit conceals the matter.

14 A people who have no leader shall fall; but in the multitude of counsels there is deliverance.

15 The wicked oppresses the righteous when he meets him, because he hates those who wait and hope.

16 A gracious woman sustains the honor of her husband; a woman who hates the truth is the seat of dishonor. Lazy men are in want even when they are rich; and strong men retain knowledge.

17 A pious man does good to his soul; but he who is cruel destroys his own flesh.

18 The wicked man does a deceitful work; but he who sows righteousness has a true reward.

19 A son who is reared in righteousness lives long; but he who pursues evil pursues it to his own death.

20 Those who are perverse in heart are an abomination to the LORD; but those who are upright in their way are his delight.

21 He who stretches out his hand against his neighbor shall not go unpunished; but the offspring of the righteous shall be delivered.

22 Like a ring of gold in a swine's snout, so is a beautiful woman without discretion.

23 The desire of the righteous is only good; but the expectation of the wicked is wrath.

24 There is he who scatters his own seed abroad, and yet brings in plenty; and there is he who gathers that which is not his, and yet has less.

25 The liberal soul shall be enriched; and the accursed one shall be cursed more.

26 He who holds back grain in the day of distress shall fall into the hands of his enemies; but a blessing shall be upon the head of him who sells it.

27 He who diligently seeks good

procures favor; but he who seeks mischief, it shall come upon him.

28 He who trusts in his riches shall fall; but the righteous shall flourish like green leaves.

29 He who builds his house with deceit shall leave to his children sorrows; and he who fails to make his household tranquil shall bequeath the wind to his children; and the fool shall be servant to the wise.

30 The fruit of the righteous is a tree of life; but the souls of the wicked shall be driven out.

31 If the righteous lives in difficulty, how much more the wicked and the sinner!

CHAPTER 12

HE who loves discipline loves knowledge; but he who hates reproof is a fool.

2 A good man obtains favor of the LORD; but a wicked one will be condemned.

3 A man shall not be established by wickedness; but the root of the righteous shall flourish.

4 A virtuous wife is a crown to her husband; but a wife who does evil destroys her husband like a boring-worm, and like a termite.

5 The thoughts of the righteous are upright; but the counsels of the wicked are deceit.

6 The counsel of the wicked is to lie in wait for the shedding of the blood; but the mouth of the upright shall deliver them.

7 The wicked shall be overthrown, and shall not be found; but the house of the righteous shall stand.

8 A man is commended according to his wisdom; but he who lacks understanding shall be despised.

9 Better is a poor man who serves himself than one who is proud and yet lacks bread.

10 A righteous man regards the life of his beast; but the mercies of the wicked are suppressed.

11 He who tills his land shall be satisfied with bread; but he who follows vain pursuits lacks understanding.

12 The wicked desire to do evil; but the root of the righteous shall sprout.

13 The ungodly is caught by the wickedness of his lips; but the righteous shall come out of trouble.

14 A good man shall be satisfied with the fruits of his mouth; and the recompense of a man's hands shall be rendered to him.

15 The way of a fool is right in his own eyes; but he who listens to counsel is wise.

16 A fool's wrath is soon known, but a prudent man hides his shame.

17 A righteous man speaks truth as it is evident; but a false witness is deceptive.

18 There are those whose speech is like the piercing of a sword; but the tongue of the wise heals.

19 The lips of truth are forthright; but the tongue of a lying witness is wicked.

20 Deceit is in the heart of the wicked who plot evil; but those who give counsel of peace shall have joy.

21 A deceitful thing is not good in the eyes of the righteous; but the wicked are filled with mischief.

22 Lying lips are an abomination to the LORD; but those who deal truly are his delight.

23 A prudent man is the seat of knowledge; but the heart of fools proclaims evil.

24 The hand of the diligent shall bear rule; but the deceitful shall be under tribute.

25 A fearful word troubles a man's heart; but a good word makes it glad.

26 A righteous man gives good counsel to his neighbor; but the way of the wicked shall lead them astray.

27 The deceitful man shall not find his prey; but the substance of a diligent man is precious.

28 In the way of righteousness is life; but the way of animosity leads to death.

CHAPTER 13

A WISE son hears his father's instructions; but an evil son does not listen to rebuke.

2 A good man shall be satisfied with the fruit of his mouth; but the souls of the wicked shall perish.

3 He who guards his mouth keeps his life; he who speaks too much shall bring ruin upon himself.

4 A sluggard is always craving; but the soul of the diligent shall be enriched.

5 A righteous man hates lying; but a wicked man is loathsome, and shall be ashamed and confounded.

6 Righteousness keeps him that is upright in his way; but wickedness overthrows the sinner.

7. There are some who pretend to be rich, yet have nothing; there are others who pretend to be poor, yet have great riches.

8 The ransom of a man's life is his riches; but the poor ignores a rebuke.

9 The light of the righteous shall rejoice; but the lamp of the wicked shall be put out.[1]

10 A wicked man commits shameful things; but with the well-advised is wisdom.

11 Wealth acquired unjustly will diminish; but he who gathers justly shall increase his wealth.

12 Blessed is the man who is willing to help; more blessed is he than he who merely rests in hope, as a tree of life he bears fruit.

13 He who despises counsel shall be destroyed by it; but he who fears the commandment shall be spared. A deceitful man shall not benefit; but a wise man whose works are good shall prosper.

14 The law of the wise is a fountain of life to those who depart from the snares of death.

15 Good understanding brings mercy; but the way of transgressors leads to destruction.

16 Every prudent man deals wisely; but a fool speaks foolishness.

17 A wicked messenger falls into mischief; but a faithful ambassador is a healer.

18 Poverty and shame shall be to him who refuses instruction; but he who regards reproof shall be honored.

19 A noble desire is sweet to the soul; but the abomination of the wicked is far away from knowledge.

20 He who walks with wise men shall be wise; but a companion of fools shall suffer harm.

21 Evil pursues sinners; but to the righteous good shall be repaid.

22 A good man leaves an inheritance to his children's children; and the wealth of the sinner is laid up for the righteous.

23 Those who do not understand the manner of life are destroyed by riches; yea, many men are destroyed completely.

24 He who spares his rod hates his son; but he who loves his son disciplines him diligently.

25 The righteous man eats and is satisfied; but the belly of the wicked shall want.

CHAPTER 14

A WISE woman builds her house; but the foolish tears it down with her own hands.

2 He who walks in uprightness has reverence for the LORD; but he who is perverse in his ways despises him.

3 In the mouth of the foolish is provocation and disgrace; but the lips of wise men shall preserve them.

4 Where there are no oxen, the cribs are clean; but abundant crops come by the strength of the ox.

5 A faithful witness will not deceive; but a false witness will utter lies.

6 An evil man seeks wisdom, and finds it not; but knowledge is easy to a man of understanding.

7 Everything is a hindrance to a foolish man; but the lips of a wise man are like a weapon.

8 The wisdom of the prudent is to understand his way; but the way of fools is deceit.

9 Truly the households of the wicked need purifying; but the households of the righteous are acceptable.

10 Fools commit sins; but the children of the upright have good will.

11 A heart which has understanding knows its own bitterness; and a stranger does not share in its joy. The house of the wicked shall be destroyed; but the tabernacle of the upright shall flourish.

[1] Lamp means heir. The heir of the wicked will be extinct.

12 There is a way which seems right to a man, but the end thereof are the ways of death.

13 Even in laughter the heart is sorrowful; and the end of joy is grief.

14 The insolent in heart shall be filled with the fruit of his ways; and a good man shall be satisfied with the respect he receives.

15 The simple man believes every word; but the prudent discerns between good and evil.

16 A wise man is cautious, and departs from evil; but the fool tampers with it confidently.

17 A man hasty in whatever he does never seeks counsel; but a wise man is moderate.

18 Fools inherit folly; but the prudent dispense knowledge.

19 Evil men shall prostrate themselves before good men; and the wicked shall come to beg at the gates of the righteous.

20 The poor is hated even of his own neighbors; but the rich has many friends.

21 He who despises his neighbor sins; but he who has mercy on the poor, happy is he.

22 The wicked err when they devise evil; but compassionate and righteous men do all kinds of good. The workers of iniquity do not understand truth and mercy; kindness and truth are with the workers of good things.

23 In all your labor there is profit; but he who is young is carefree and at ease. The LORD heals every wound; but the talk of the lips of the wicked tends only to poverty.

24 The crown of the wise is their riches; but the perverseness of fools is their folly.

25 A true witness delivers lives; but a deceitful witness speaks falsehood.

26 In reverence for the LORD is strong confidence, and his children shall have a place of refuge.

27 Reverence for the LORD is a fountain of life to those who turn away from the snares of death.

28 In the abundance of population is the king's honor; but in the destruction of the people is the ruin of the king.

29 He who is slow to anger is of great understanding; but he who is hasty of temper is exceedingly foolish.

30 He who cools down his anger is a healer of his own heart; but wrath is the rottenness of the bones.

31 He who oppresses the poor provokes his Maker; but he who honors the LORD has mercy on the needy.

32 The wicked is overthrown through his wickedness; but he who is confident that he is without sin is a righteous man.

33 Wisdom shall rest in the heart of the righteous; but in the heart of fools it shall not be made known.

34 Righteousness exalts a nation; but sin is a reproach to any people.

35 The king's favor is toward a wise servant; but the wicked shall be overthrown by his own devices. He who is confident that he is without sin is righteous. Anger destroys even wise men.

CHAPTER 15

A SOFT word turns away wrath; but a harsh word stirs up anger.

2 The tongue of the wise uses knowledge aright; but the mouth of fools pours out curses.

3 The eyes of the LORD are in every place, beholding the good men and the bad.

4 A wholesome tongue is a tree of life, and he who eats of its fruit shall be filled with it.

5 A fool mocks his father's instruction; but he who regards reproof is prudent.

6 In the house of the righteous is much strength; but the crops of the wicked shall be destroyed.

7 The lips of the wise utter knowledge; but the hearts of fools are unjust.

8 The sacrifices of the wicked are an abomination to the LORD; but the prayer of the upright is his delight.

9 The way of the wicked is an abomination to the LORD; but he loves him who follows after righteousness.

10 The chastisement of those who

do not know evil is evident; but those who hate reproof shall die.

11 Sheol and destruction are before the LORD; how much more than the hearts of men?

12 An evil man does not love one who reproves him, neither will he walk with the wise.

13 A merry heart makes a cheerful countenance; but by sorrow of heart the spirit is broken.

14 The heart of the just seeks knowledge; but the mouth of the wicked utters evil.

15 All the days of the poor are filled with hardships; but those who are of merry heart have a continual tranquillity.

16 Better is a little with reverence for the LORD than the great treasures of the wicked.

17 Better is a dinner of vegetables where love is than fatted steer and hatred with it.

18 A wrathful man stirs up contention; but he who is slow to anger appeases strife.

19 The ways of the sluggard are full of thorns; but the paths of the upright are plain.

20 A wise son makes his father happy; but a foolish son is a disgrace to his mother.

21 A foolish man lacks understanding; but a man of understanding walks uprightly.

22 Those who have undue respect for the counsel fail to appreciate its purpose; but in the multitude of counsellors the counsel is established.

23 A man's joy is revealed by the word of his mouth; and he who speaks at the right time, how good is it to him!

24 The way of life leads upward for the wise, that he may depart from the depths of Sheol.

25 The LORD will destroy the house of the proud; but he will insure the possession of widows.

26 Evil thoughts are an abomination before the LORD; but pure words are pleasant to him.

27 He who accepts a bribe destroys his own soul; but he who hates a bribe shall live.

28 The heart of the righteous meditates in truth; but the mouth of the wicked pours out evil things.

29 The LORD is far from the wicked; but he hears the prayer of the righteous.

30 The light of the eyes rejoices the heart, and a good heart makes the bones fat.

31 The ear that hears the reproof of life abides among the wise.

32 He who refuses instruction despises his own soul; but he who listens to reproof gains wisdom.

33 Reverence for the LORD is the instruction of life; and the glory of the meek goes before him.

CHAPTER 16

THE reasoning of the mind is from man; but the answer of the tongue is from the LORD.

2 All the ways of a man are clean in his own eyes; but the LORD directs his way.

3 Commit your works to the LORD, and he will establish your thoughts.

4 All the works of the LORD are for those who will hearken to him; but the wicked are reserved for the day of calamity.

5 Every one who is proud in his heart is an abomination to the LORD; and he who stretches out his hand against his neighbor shall not be pardoned because of this evil.

6 By mercy and truth iniquity is purged; and reverence of the LORD causes men to depart from evil.

7 When a man's ways are according to the will of the LORD, even to his enemies he shall recompense.

8 Better is a little with righteousness than great ingathering acquired unjustly.

9 A man's heart devises his ways; but the LORD directs his steps.

10 Oracles are on the lips of the king; his mouth does not err in judgment.

11 The weight of a just balance is the LORD's judgment; all his works are just weights.

12 Kings who commit wickedness are an abomination; for a throne is established by righteousness.

13 The lips of a righteous man are the delight of a king; and he loves the word of the upright.

14 The wrath of a king is as messengers of death; but a wise man will pacify it.

15 In the light of the king's countenance is life; and his favor is like a cloud of the early rain.

16 To get wisdom is much better than gold; and to get understanding is better than silver.

17 The path of the upright causes one to turn away from evil; he who is careful of his soul safeguards his way.

18 Disgrace goes before destruction, and pride before misfortune.

19 It is better to be humble and lowly in pride than he who divides spoil with the mighty.

20 He who understands a command shall find good; who trusts in the LORD, happy is he!

21 The wise in heart is a man of discernment; and he whose speech is sweet increases learning.

22 Understanding is a spring of life to those who have it; but the instruction of the fools is folly.

23 The heart of the wise understands the speech of his mouth and adds learning to his lips.

24 The speech of a wise man is like honeycomb, sweet to his soul, and health to his bones.

25 There is a way that seems right in the eyes of men, but the paths thereof are the paths of death.

26 A sorrowful person grieves himself; from his own mouth comes his destruction.

27 An ungodly man devises evil; out of his mouth issues a burning fire.

28 A wicked man threatens justice and persecutes his neighbor without cause.

29 A wicked man entices his neighbor and leads him into the way that is not good.

30 He winks his eyes and devises corrupt things; he purposes with his lips and accomplishes mischief.

31 The hoary head is a crown of glory and is exalted in the way of righteousness.

32 He who is slow to anger is better than the mighty; and he who conquers himself than he who takes a city.

33 The evil of the vicious falls into his own bosom; and his judgment proceeds from before the LORD.

CHAPTER 17

BETTER is dry bread, and quietness with it, than a house full of feasting with strife.

2 A wise servant shall rule over a son who causes shame, and shall share the inheritance among the brothers.

3 The refining pot is for silver and the furnace for gold; but the LORD tries the heart.

4 A wicked man listens to perverse lips; but a righteous man does not heed the tongues of vicious men.

5 He who mocks the poor provokes his Maker; and he who is glad at calamity shall not be forgiven.

6 Children's children are the crowns of old men; and the glory of children is their fathers.

7 Excellent speech is unbecoming to a fool, and lying lips to a righteous man.

8 A precious stone is beautiful in the eyes of him who has it; wherever it turns it is admired.

9 He who forgets an offense seeks friendship; but he who hates to forget an offense estranges himself from a friend and neighbor.

10 A threat breaks the heart of a wise man; but the fool instead of a rebuke receives a scourging, and yet he is not conscious of it.

11 A quarrelsome man seeks mischief; therefore a cruel messenger shall be sent against him.

12 Meditation and reverence are suitable for a wise man; but a fool meditates in his folly.

13 He who rewards evil for good, evil shall not depart from his house.

14 He who sheds blood stirs up judgment before the ruler.

15 He who justifies the wicked and condemns the just is an abomination before the LORD.

16 What good is wealth in the pos-

session of a fool who has no desire to acquire wisdom?

17 A friend loves at all times; but a brother is born for adversity.

18 A foolish man pledges himself, for he becomes surety for his friend.

19 He who loves iniquity loves deceit and strife; and he who exalts himself seeks destruction.

20 He who slanders in heart will not find good; and he who has an evil tongue falls into mischief.

21 He who begets a fool does it to his own shame; his father will have no joy in him.

22 A merry heart makes the body healthy; but a broken spirit dries up the bones.

23 He who accepts a bribe is wicked; for he perverts the way of justice.

24 The face of a man of understanding is set toward wisdom; but the eyes of a fool are in the depths of the earth.

25 A foolish son provokes his father, and is bitterness to her who bore him.

26 To punish the just is not good, nor to scourge the righteous men who speak the truth.

27 He who spares his words has knowledge; and he who is patient is a wise man.

28 Even a fool when he holds his peace is considered wise; and he who shuts his lips is counted a man of understanding.

CHAPTER 18

WHEN a man is inactive he imagines lust and mocks at good instruction.

2 A fool has no delight in wisdom, because his mind devises folly.

3 When the wicked reaches the depths of evil, then folly comes upon him, inquity, disgrace, and shame.

4 The words of a man's mouth are like deep waters; and the fountain of wisdom is like a flowing brook.

5 It is not good to respect the person of the wicked, nor to pervert justice against the righteous.

6 A fool's lips enter into contention, and his mouth brings him to death.

7 A fool's mouth is his destruction, and his lips are the snare of his soul.

8 The words of a slothful man bring evil to him, and they cause him to go down into the inner chambers of Sheol.

9 He also that is slothful in his work is brother to him who is a destroyer.

10 The name of the LORD is a strong tower; the righteous and the mighty run into it.

11 The rich man's wealth is his strong city; and his dwelling place is fenced by a strong wall.

12 Before destruction the heart of a man is haughty; and before honor is humility.

13 He who gives answer before he hears is a fool and a reviler.

14 The spirit of a man will endure his suffering; but a distressing spirit, who can bear?

15 The heart of the prudent acquires wisdom; and the ear of the wise listens to knowledge.

16 A man's gifts make room for him and bring him before great men.

17 A man is deemed innocent in his lawsuit; but when his neighbor comes he examines him.

18 Casting lots causes contentions to cease and decides between mighty men.

19 A brother helped by a brother is like a city helped by its fortifications; and his helpers are like the bars of a castle.

20 A man's belly shall be satisfied with the fruits of his mouth; and with the fruits of his lips shall he be filled.

21 Death and life are in the power of the tongue; and those who love it shall eat the fruits thereof.

22 He who finds a good wife finds a good thing, and obtains favor from the LORD. And he who puts out a good wife, puts out good from his house.

23 The poor speak humbly; but the rich talk of great things.

24 There are friends who are merely friends; and there is a friend who sticks closer than a brother.

CHAPTER 19

BETTER is the poor man who walks in his integrity than the rich man who is perverse in his ways.

2 He who has no knowledge of his own soul, it is not good for him; and he who is hasty with his feet sins.[1]

3 The folly of a man perverts his ways; he frets in his heart against the LORD.

4 Wealth makes many friends; but a poor man is deserted by his friends.

5 A false witness shall not be unpunished, and he who speaks lies shall not escape.

6 Many serve in the presence of a prince; he gives gifts even to those who are bad.

7 All the brothers of the poor hate him; also his friends go far from him. He who makes mischief with his words is insincere.

8 He who gets wisdom loves his own soul; he who keeps faithfulness shall find good.

9 A false witness shall not be unpunished; and he who speaks lies shall perish.

10 To live in luxury is not fitting for a fool; much less is it seemly for a servant to rule over princes.

11 The discretion of a man is shown by his patience; he glories when his iniquity is removed.

12 The king's wrath is like the roaring of a lion; but his favor is like dew upon grass.

13 A foolish son is a disgrace to his father; and the contentions of a wife are like drippings.[2]

14 House and riches are the inheritance from fathers; but a wife is betrothed to a man from the LORD.

15 Slothfulness casts into a deep sleep; and a proud man shall suffer hunger.

16 He who keeps the law keeps his own soul; but he who despises right ways shall die.

17 He who has pity upon the poor is a companion of the LORD; and he shall be repaid according to his works.

18 Chasten your son while there is hope, and let not your soul share his dishonor.

19 A man of great wrath shall suffer harm; the more he is hostile the more he increases his burden.

20 Hear counsel and receive instruction that you may be wise in your ways.

21 There are many devices in a man's heart; nevertheless the counsel of the LORD shall stand firm.

22 The longing of a man is to do good; and a poor man is better than a rich man who lies.

23 Reverence for the LORD leads to life; and he who is satisfied with it shall abide; he shall not be visited with evil.

24 A sluggard hides his hands in his bosom and will not even try to bring them to his mouth again.

25 When an evil man is scourged, a wise man takes heed; and when a wise man is reproved, he will gain understanding.

26 He who plunders his father and grieves his mother is a son who causes shame and brings reproach.

27 Wait, my son, and hear the instruction, and do not forget the words of knowledge.

28 An ungodly witness scorns justice; and the mouth of the wicked devours him.

29 Grief is prepared for those who scoff at justice, and a scourge for foolish people.

CHAPTER 20

WINE is grievous, drunkenness is shameful; and whosoever drinks excessively is not wise.

2 The anger of the king is as the roaring of a lion; he who provokes him to anger sins against his own life.

3 It is an honor for a man to cease from strife; but every fool will delight in it.

4 The lazy man is reproached and he will not cease from talking; therefore he shall beg during harvest but will not receive even water.

---

[1] Hasty to do evil.

[2] In the East during the rainy season drops of water drip through the roof.

5 The counsel in a king's heart is deep; but a wise man will draw it out.

6 Many men are considered merciful; but a faithful man who can find?

7 The just man walks in his integrity; blessed are his children after him.

8 A king who sits on the throne of judgment scatters away all evil things from before him.

9 Who can say, I have made my heart clean, I am pure from my sins?

10 Diverse weights and diverse measures, both alike, are an abomination in the presence of the LORD.

11 Even a child is known by his doings, whether his works are pure and whether they are right.

12 The hearing ear and the seeing eye, the LORD has made even both of them.

13 Love not sleep lest you come to poverty; open your eyes and you shall be satisfied with bread.

14 A friend says to his friend, I have made a gain; then he boasts.

15 Again he says, Here is gold and a multitude of precious stones and precious vessels; but the lips of knowledge are precious jewels.

16 Take the garment of him who is surety for a stranger; and take his pledge for the sake of a stranger.

17 He who becomes surety for a man by means of deceitful gain will afterwards have his mouth filled with gravel.

18 A good purpose is established by counsel; but by provocation war is made.

19 He who reveals a secret causes slander; therefore do not meddle with him who is hasty with his lips.

20 He who curses his father or his mother, his lamp shall be extinguished.

21 An inheritance hastily acquired in the beginning, shall not be blessed in the end.

22 Do not say, I will recompense evil; but wait for the LORD that he may save you.

23 Diverse weights are an abomination in the presence of the LORD; and false scales are not good.

24 A man's steps are directed by the LORD; who is the man, then, who can direct his own way?

25 It is a snare for a man who vows to give something to a holy place, and regrets after he has vowed.

26 A wise king scatters the wicked and crushes them under the wheel.

27 The soul of a man is the lamp of the LORD, searching all the inward parts of the heart.

28 Mercy and truth preserve a king; and his throne is established by grace.

29 The glory of young men is their strength; and the beauty of old men is their grey hair.

30 Misery and torment befall the evil men; and wounds smite the inner parts of their body.

CHAPTER 21

LIKE streams of water, so is the king's heart in the hand of the LORD; he turns it wherever he will.

2 Every way of a man is right in his own eyes; but the LORD sets the heart in order.

3 He who does righteousness and justice is more acceptable to the LORD than he who offers a sacrifice.

4 Haughty eyes, a proud heart, and the posterity of the wicked are sinful.

5 The thoughts of the elect tend surely to plenteousness; but those of evil men cause want.

6 The getting of treasure by a lying tongue will bring destruction and death to those who seek it.

7 The destruction of the wicked shall come upon them because they refused to do justice.

8 He who perverts his own way acts strangely; but he who is pure, his works are right.

9 It is better to dwell alone in a corner of the housetop than to live with a quarrelsome woman in a large house.

10 The soul of a wicked man is hidden from his neighbor's eyes.

11 When a wicked man suffers harm, even the simple become wise; but a wise man receives knowledge through his own counsel.

12 The righteous man wisely understands the hearts of the wicked;

and he overthrows the wicked into mischief.

13 He who closes his ears at the cry of the poor, he also shall cry to God, but he shall not answer him.

14 A gift in secret pacifies anger; but he who is sparing with his gifts stirs wrath.

15 It is joy to the righteous to do justice, but destruction to the workers of iniquity.

16 The man who wanders from the way of understanding shall lie in the congregation of the dead.

17 He who lacks wealth and yet loves entertainment, wine, and pleasure shall not be rich.

18 The wicked shall be given as a ransom for the righteous, and the deceitful for the upright.

19 It is better to dwell in the wilderness than with a quarrelsome and an angry wife.

20 A coveted treasure and ointment are in a dwelling place; but the wisdom and understanding of men shall dispense it.

21 He who seeks after righteousness and mercy will find life, righteousness, and honor.

22 A wise man scales the defenses of the city of mighty men and conquers the stronghold in which they trusted.

23 He who keeps his mouth and his tongue keeps himself from trouble.

24 In his wrath a hasty and proud man commits iniquity.

25 The desire of the sluggard kills him; for his hands refuse to labor.

26 He covets greedily all the day long; but the righteous man gives and does not spare.

27 The sacrifice of the wicked is an abomination; because they bring it in an unjust way.

28 A false witness shall perish; but an obedient man speaks truth.

29 The face of a wicked man is shameless; but he who is upright amends his ways.

30 There is no wisdom nor understanding nor counsel like that of the LORD.

31 The horse may be prepared for the day of battle; but salvation is of the LORD.

CHAPTER 22

A GOOD name is better than great riches, and loving favor than silver and gold.

2 The rich and the poor meet together; the LORD is the maker of them both.

3 A prudent man sees an evil man scourged and is greatly instructed by it; but fools pass by and suffer loss.

4 The result of humility is reverence for the LORD, and riches and honor and life.

5 Snares and traps are found on a crooked way; he who keeps his soul shall be far from them.

6 Train up a child in the way he should go; and when he is old he will not depart from it.

7 The rich shall be ruled by the poor, and the servant shall loan to his former lender.

8 He who sows iniquity shall reap deceit; and the staff of his anger shall be broken.

9 He who has a bountiful eye shall be blessed; for he gives of his bread to the poor.

10 Destroy evil, cast out strife, do away with contention and reproach, lest they sit in the assembly and reproach all who are present.

11 The LORD loves him who is pure in heart and is gracious to the lips of the king's friends.

12 The eyes of the LORD preserve knowledge and destroy the words of deceit.

13 When he is sent on an errand, the sluggard says, There is a lion in the road! and, Behold, there is murder in the streets!

14 The mouth of a strange woman is a deep pit; he with whom the LORD is angry shall fall into it.

15 Foolishness moves the heart of a child; but the rod of correction shall drive it far from him.

16 He who oppresses the poor adds to his evil; and he who gives to the rich, shall suffer a loss.

17 Incline your ear, and hear the

words of the wise, and apply your heart to my knowledge.

18 For both of them are pleasant, keep them within you; let them together be made ready on your lips.

19 That your trust may be in the LORD, I have made these things known to you this day, even to you.

20 Behold, this is the third time that I have written them to you,

21 That I might make you know counsel and knowledge and peace and 'the words of truth; so that you could answer words of truth to him who might send to you.

22 Do not oppress the poor because he is poor; neither afflict the needy in the gate.

23 For the LORD will plead their cause and avenge the injustice which is done to them.

24 Make no friendship with wrathful man; and with a man given to anger you shall not go,

25 Lest you learn his ways and find a stumbling block to your soul.

26 Do not become a surety for a debt simply because you are ashamed to turn down those who ask you,

27 For if you have nothing to pay, they will take your bed from under you.

28 Remove not the ancient landmark which your fathers have set.

29 When you see that a man is diligent in his work, he shall stand before kings; he shall not stand before obscure men.

CHAPTER 23

WHEN you sit to eat with a ruler, consider diligently what is set before you,

2 That you may not put poison in your mouth. And if you are a man given to excessive appetite,

3 Be not desirous of his food; for his bread is bread of deceit.

4 Do not quarrel with a rich man; but keep away from him wisely.

5 For if you should fix your eye on him, you cannot see him; for he makes for himself wings like an eagle and flies away toward the sky.

6 Do not eat with a hypocrite, neither desire his food;

7 For he is like him that swallows pitch; in like manner you will eat and drink with him, but his heart is not with you.

8 The morsel which you have eaten you will vomit up, and you will lose your sweet words.

9 Do not speak in the presence of a fool; for he will despise the wisdom of your words.

10 Do not remove the old landmark; nor enter into the field of the fatherless;

11 For their saviour is mighty; he will plead their cause with you.

12 Apply your heart to instruction, and your ears to the words of knowledge.

13 Do not withhold chastisement from a child; for if you beat him, he will not die.

14 For when you beat him with the rod, you will deliver his soul from Sheol.

15 My son, if your heart be wise, my heart also will rejoice.

16 Yea, my heart shall rejoice, when your lips speak right things.

17 Let not your heart envy sinners; but revere the LORD all the day long.

18 For surely you will have a future; and your hope shall not be cut off.

19 Hear, my son, and be wise, and fasten my counsel in your heart.

20 Be not drunk with wine; and be not a gluttonous eater of meat:

21 For the drunkard and the gluttonous shall come to poverty; and drowsiness shall clothe a man with rags.

22 Listen to your father who begot you, and do not despise your mother when she is old.

23 Buy the truth, and do not sell wisdom; also buy understanding and instruction.

24 The father of a righteous man shall greatly rejoice; and he who begets a wise child shall be glad.

25 Your father and your mother shall rejoice in you; and the one who bore you shall be happy.

26 My son, give me your heart, and let your eyes observe my ways.

27 For a harlot is a deep pit; and a strange woman is a narrow well.

28 She destroys men suddenly, and increases iniquity among men.

29 Who has woe? Who has trouble? Who has contentions? Who has hardships? Who has wounds without cause? Who has redness of eyes?

30 Those who tarry long over the wine; and who search for a place of drinking. Be not drunken with wine, but converse with righteous men; walk and talk with them.

31 Do not look on the wine when it is red in the cup, but meditate on righteousness.

32 For at the last it bites like a serpent and stings like an adder.

33 When your eyes behold a strange woman, then your heart shall utter perverse things.

34 Yea, you shall be as he who lies down in the midst of the sea, or as a sailor in a tempest.

35 They have beaten me, you shall say, but I did not suffer, they have mocked me, but I did not know it; when I shall awake sober, I will go and seek it yet again.

CHAPTER 24

BE not envious of evil men, neither desire to be with them.

2 For their hearts devise evil and their lips talk of iniquity.

3 Through wisdom a house is built; and by understanding it is established;

4 And by knowledge the inner chambers are filled with all precious and pleasant riches.

5 A wise man is better than a strong man; yea, a man of knowledge than a mighty man.

6 For by provocation is war waged; and in a multitude of counsels there is salvation.

7 Wisdom crushes a fool; he opens not his mouth in the gate.

8 He who devises to do evil shall be called a mischievous person.

9 The thought of a fool is sin; and an abomination of men is evil.

10 The wicked shall be driven away by evil in the day of affliction.

11 Deliver those who are led away to death, and spare not to redeem those who are held to be slain.

12 If you say, Behold, I did not know it, then know that it is God who searches the thought of the heart; and he who keeps your soul knows it, and shall render to every man according to his works.

13 My son, eat honey because it is good, and the honeycomb, which is sweet to your taste.

14 Thus shall wisdom find your soul; and you will have good prospects, and your hope shall not be cut off.

15 Do not devise plots of iniquity in the dwelling of the righteous; do not spoil his resting place;

16 For a righteous man falls seven times and rises up again; but the wicked shall fall into mischief.

17 Do not rejoice when your enemy falls, and let not your heart be glad when he is overthrown,

18 Lest the LORD see it and it displease him and he turn away his anger from him.

19 Do not envy evildoers nor be jealous of the wicked;

20 For there shall be no future for evil men, and the lamp of the wicked shall be put out.

21 My son, fear the LORD and give good counsel; and meddle not with the fools;

22 For their calamity shall come suddenly; and who knows the end of their years?

23 These things I say to the wise: It is not good to show partiality in judgment,

24 Nor to say to a wicked man, You are righteous; him shall the people curse, and nations shall abhor him.

25 But to those who rebuke him shall be delight, and a good blessing shall come upon them.

26 The people shall kiss the lips [1] of those who give admonition.

27 Prepare your work out of doors, and make it ready in the field; and afterwards build your house.

28 Be not a false witness against

[1] An Aramaic idiom which means *shall approve the admonitions.*

your neighbor; and do not deceive him with your lips.

29 Say not, I will do so to him as he has done to me; I will render to him according to his works.

30 I passed by the field of a sluggard, and by the vineyard of the man void of understanding,

31 And, lo, it was all grown over with thorns, and nettles had covered the face thereof, and its stone wall was broken down.

32 Then I looked upon it, and considered it well, and I received instruction:

33 Yet a little sleep, a little slumber, a little folding of the hands upon your chest;

34 So shall poverty come upon you, and want shall overtake you suddenly like a runner.

CHAPTER 25

THESE are also profound proverbs of Solomon which the friends of Hezekiah king of Judah wrote.

2 It is the glory of God to keep secret a matter; but the glory of the king is to search it out.

3 The heaven for height, and the earth for depth, and the heart of the king is unsearchable.

4 Purge dross from silver that it may come forth a pure vessel.

5 Let wicked men be driven from the presence of the king, and his throne shall be established in righteousness.

6 Do not glorify yourself in the presence of the king, and do not stand in the place of great men;

7 For it is better that it be said to you, Come up higher, than that you should be put lower. In the presence of the ruler report what your eyes have seen.

8 Do not go forth hastily to bring a suit, lest when you plead your cause, at the end your neighbor shall reproach you.

9 Debate your cause with your neighbor himself; and do not disclose the secret to another,

10 Lest he who hears it reproach you and many people mock you.

11 A word fitly spoken is like apples of gold in a setting of silver.

12 Like an earring of gold, and a precious sardius, so is the reproof of the wise men to a listening ear.

13 Like the cold of snow in the time of harvest, which cools the air, so is a faithful messenger to those who send him; for he refreshes the soul of his masters.

14 Like clouds and wind without rain, so is the man who boasts of false gifts.

15 By long forbearing, a ruler is persuaded; and a soft tongue breaks the bones.

16 When you find honey, eat as much as is sufficient for you, lest you be filled with it and vomit it.

17 Do not visit your neighbor's house too frequently, lest he become weary of you and so hate you.

18 A man who bears false witness against his neighbor is like an iron bar, a sword, and a sharp arrow.

19 Like a sore tooth and a foot out of joint, such is the confidence in an unfaithful man in time of trouble.

20 As he who takes away a garment from his neighbor in cold weather, as one who drops sand on the string of a musical instrument, as he who afflicts a broken heart, as a moth on a garment, and as a boring-worm on a tree: such is the effect of sorrow on a man's heart.

21 If your enemy be hungry, give him bread to eat; and if he be thirsty, give him water to drink;

22 For when you shall do these things for him, you will heap coals of fire upon his head, and the LORD will reward you.

23 Like the north wind which brings forth rain, so are an evil countenance and a backbiting tongue.

24 It is better to dwell in a corner of the housetop than with a quarrelsome wife and a house divided against itself.

25 Like cold water to a thirsty soul, so is good news from a far country.

26 Like a stopped fountain or a polluted spring is a righteous man when he falls down before the wicked.

27 It is not good to eat much honey,

nor to search for high praises for oneself.

28 Like a breached city that has no wall, so is a man who is impatient.

CHAPTER 26

LIKE snow in summer and like rain in harvest, so honor is not seemly for a fool.

2 Like sparrows wandering and like birds flying in the air, so the curse that is causeless shall be driven away.

3 A whip for the horse, a goad for the ass, and a rod for the back of a fool.

4 Answer not a fool according to his folly, lest you be also like him.

5 But answer a fool according to your wisdom, lest he think in himself that he is wise.

6 He who sends a message by the hand of a fool drinks iniquity from under his own feet.[1]

7 As a lame man who cannot walk, so is a parable in the mouth of a fool.

8 Like a stone in a sling, so is he who gives honor to a fool.

9 Thorns spring up in the hand of a drunkard, and folly in the mouth of a fool.

10 The body of a fool is greatly afflicted, and a drunkard thinks that he can cross a sea.

11 As a dog that returns to his vomit, so is a fool that misbehaves in his folly.

12 If you should see a man wise in his own eyes, a fool is much better than he.

13 The sluggard says, when he is sent out, There is a lion in the way; a lion is in the streets.

14 As a door turns upon its hinges, so does the slothful turn on his bed.

15 The slothful hides his hands in his bosom; it grieves him to bring them again to his mouth.

16 The sluggard is wiser in his own eyes than seven men with good reasoning.

17 He who meddles with a quarrel not his own is like one who takes a dog by the ears.

18 Like haughty men who utter words sharp and deadly as arrows,

19 So is the man who deceives his neighbor; when he is caught, he says, I was merely jesting.

20 When there is no wood, the fire goes out; and where there is no troublesome person, the strife ceases.

21 As coals are to burning coals, and wood to fire; so is a malicious person to kindle strife.

22 The words of the malicious stir up trouble; they go down into the innermost parts of the heart.

23 Like silver dross which sticks to an earthen pot, so are enraged lips and an evil heart.

24 He who hates is known by his own speech; in his heart he entertains deceit;

25 Though he speaks in a gentle tone, believe him not; for there are seven abominations in his heart.

26 He who conceals hatred in his heart, his wickedness shall be revealed in the congregation.

27 He who digs a pit shall fall into it; and he who rolls a stone, it will return upon him.

28 A lying tongue hates the truth; and a troublesome mouth stirs up a quarrel.

CHAPTER 27

BOAST not for tomorrow; for you know not what a day may bring forth.

2 Let a stranger praise you, and not your own mouth; another, and not your own lips.

3 A stone is heavy and sand is weighty; but a fool's wrath is heavier than both.

4 Wrath is cruel and anger is outrageous; but who can stand before envy?

5 Open rebuke is better than deceitful friendship.

6 Better are the wounds of a friend than the kisses of an enemy.

7 A person who is full loathes a honeycomb; but to a hungry person even a bitter thing is sweet.

8 Like a bird that wanders from its nest, so is a man who is moved from his place.

9 As oil and perfume rejoice the

---

[1] An idiom which means *he damages his own cause.*

heart, so does the sweetness of a man's friend by hearty counsel.

10 Your own friend and your father's friend forsake not; neither go into your brother's house in the day of your calamity; for better is a neighbor who is near than a brother far off.

11 My son, be wise, and make my heart glad, and remove from me the reproach of those who reproach me.

12 A prudent man foresees the evil and hides himself; but the fools pass on and suffer loss.

13 He who is surety for a stranger, his cloak will be taken away from him and held in pledge for the stranger.

14 He who blesses his friend with a flattering loud voice is not different from him who curses.

15 Like a continual dripping on a rainy day, so is a quarrelsome woman.

16 The north wind is severe, but it is called the right wind.

17 Iron sharpens iron; so a man enlightens the face of his friend.

18 He who guards his fig tree shall eat its fruit; and he who is careful of his master shall be honored.

19 As faces do not resemble faces, so hearts do not resemble hearts.

20 Sheol and destruction are never full; so the eyes of man are never satisfied.

21 As the refining pot is for silver, and the furnace for gold, so is a man tested by the mouth of those who praise him. The heart of the wicked desires evil, and the heart of the pious desires knowledge.

22 Though you should beat a fool in the midst of an assembly, you will not do him any good, nor will you cause his foolishness to depart from him.

23 When you are feeding the sheep, know their faces and set your mind on the flock.

24 Possessions are not for ever; nor can riches be handed down from one generation to another.

25 The grass springs up, the tender growth shows itself, and the herbs of the mountains are gathered.

26 The lambs are for your clothing and the kids are for your sustenance;

27 And the goats' milk is for your food and for the food of your household.

CHAPTER 28

THE wicked flee when no man pursues them; but the righteous are confident as a lion.

2 Because of the transgression of a land many are the princes thereof; but by righteous men who know justice the stability thereof shall be prolonged.

3 A poor man who oppresses the poor is like a sweeping rain which is of no benefit.

4 Those who forsake the law glory in wickedness; but those who keep the law receive strength.

5 Evil men do not understand justice; but those who seek the LORD understand all good things.

6 Better is the poor man walking in his uprightness than a rich man whose ways are perverse.

7 He who keeps the law is a wise son; but he who is engaged in vanity shames his father.

8 He who increases his wealth by usury and unjust means shall leave it for him who is kind to the poor.

9 He who closes his ears from hearing the law, even his prayer is an abomination.

10 He who causes the righteous to go astray in an evil path shall fall himself into the pit; but the upright shall inherit good things.

11 The rich man is wise in his own eyes; but a poor man of understanding will reprove him.

12 When righteous men are strong, there is a great glory; but when the wicked rise to power, the glory diminishes.

13 He who hides his transgression shall not prosper; but he who confesses his sins and forsakes them, God will have mercy upon him.

14 Blessed is the man who is reverent always; but he who hardens his heart shall fall into mischief.

15 As a roaring lion and a raging bear, so is a wicked ruler over the poor.

16 A ruler who lacks understanding is also a great oppressor; but he who hates deceit shall prolong his life.

17 A man who is engaged in shedding of blood shall flee even to the jailer, and no one shall help him.

18 He who walks uprightly shall be saved; but he who is perverse in his ways shall fall into a pit.

19 He who tills the land shall have abundance of bread; but he who follows after vain pursuits shall have plenty of poverty.

20 A faithful man shall abound with blessings; but an evil man shall not be innocent.

21 A man who shows partiality is not good; for a piece of bread a man will become a traitor.

22 He who hastens to be rich has an evil eye and considers not that poverty shall come upon him.

23 He who rebukes a man shall find more favor afterwards than he who flatters with his tongue.

24 He who robs his father or his mother and says, It is no transgression, the same is the companion of a wicked man.

25 A greedy man stirs up strife; but he who puts his trust in the LORD shall be enriched.

26 He who trusts in his own heart is a fool; but he who walks with integrity will be delivered.

27 He who gives to the poor shall not lack; but he who turns his eyes away from the needy shall have many a curse.

28 When the wicked rise, men hide themselves; but when they perish, the righteous increase.

CHAPTER 29

HE who refuses reproof and stiffens his neck shall suddenly be destroyed, and that without remedy.

2 When the righteous are many, the people increase; but when the wicked are in authority, the people groan.

3 He who loves wisdom rejoices his father; but he who keeps company with harlots shall lose his substance.

4 The king by justice enriches the land; but a wicked man causes it to be in want.

5 A man who flatters his neighbor spreads a net for his feet.

6 An evil man shall be ensnared in his wickedness; but the righteous shall sing and rejoice.

7 A righteous man considers the cause of the poor; but the wicked has no understanding to regard it.

8 Scornful men set cities on fire; but wise men turn away wrath.

9 A wise man contends with a fool, and when he is angry, he laughs and does not scoff.

10 Bloodthirsty men hate the innocent; but the righteous have compassion upon them.

11 A fool utters all his wrath; but a wise man uses his mind.

12 If a ruler listens to lies, all his servants are wicked.

13 The poor man and the oppressor meet together, and the LORD lightens the eyes of both.

14 The king who faithfully judges the people, his throne shall be established for ever.

15 The rod and reproof give wisdom; but a child who lacks discipline brings shame upon his mother.

16 When the wicked are multiplied, transgression increases; but the righteous shall rejoice in their fall.

17 Correct your son, and he shall give you rest; yea, he shall give delight to your soul.

18 When the wicked men multiply, the people are ruined; but he who keeps the law, blessed is he.

19 A servant will not be corrected by words; for he knows then that he will not be beaten.

20 When you see a man who is hasty in his words, know that a fool is better than he.

21 He who is given to pleasures from his youth will be a servant, and in the end will groan.

22 An angry man stirs up strife, and a furious man abounds in transgression.

23 A man's pride shall bring him low; but his meekness shall add to his honor.

24 He who is a partner with a thief hates his own soul; they put him under oaths, but he does not confess.

25 The iniquity of a man becomes a stumblingblock to him; but he who puts his trust in the LORD shall become strong.

26 Many seek the ruler's favor; but a man's judgment comes from the LORD.

27 An unjust man is an abomination to the just; and a right way is an abomination to the wicked.

CHAPTER 30

THESE are the words of Agur the son of Jakeh, who prophesied and received power. He said to Ithliel,

2 Surely, I am weak minded, and have not the understanding of men.

3 I know not wisdom, nor have I learned the knowledge of the holy men.

4 Tell me, Who has ascended up into heaven and come down? Who has gathered the wind in his fists? Who has bound the waters in a handkerchief? Who has established all the borders of the earth? What is his name, and what is his son's name, if you can tell?

5 Every word of God is pure; he is a shield to those who put their trust in him.

6 Do not add to his words; lest he reprove you, and you be found a liar.

7 Two things have I asked of thee; deny them not to me before I die:

8 Remove far from me vanity and lies; give me neither poverty nor riches; give me life sufficient

9 Lest I be full, and lie, and say, Who is the LORD? Or lest I be poor and steal, and take the name of my God in vain.

10 Do not deliver a slave to his master, lest he curse you, and you be found guilty.

11 There is a generation that curses their fathers, and does not bless their mothers.

12 There is a generation that is pure in their own eyes, and yet is not washed from their filthiness.

13 There is a generation, O how lofty are their eyes! and their eyelids are lifted up.

14 There is a generation, whose teeth are like swords, and their jaw teeth like knives, to devour the poor from off the earth and the needy from among men.

15 A gluttonous man has three beloved daughters. There are three things that are never satisfied; yea, a fourth that never says, It is enough:

16 Sheol; and the barren womb; the earth that is not filled with water; and the fire that never says, It is enough.

17 The eye that mocks at his father and despises the old age of his mother, the ravens of the valley shall pick it out and the young vultures shall eat it.

18 There are three things that are hidden from me, yea, four which I do not know:

19 The way of an eagle in the air; the way of a serpent upon a rock; the way of a ship in the midst of the sea; and the way of a man in his youth.

20 Such is the way of an adulterous woman; she eats, and wipes her mouth, and says, I have done no evil.

21 Under three things the earth quakes, and under four it cannot endure:

22 Under a servant when he reigns; and under a fool when he is filled with bread;

23 Under an odious woman when she is married; and under a maidservant who ousts her mistress.

24 There are four things that are small upon the earth, but they are wiser than wise men:

25 The ants which have no strength, yet they provide their food in the summer;

26 The conies who lack strength, and yet they make their houses in the rocks;

27 The locusts who have no king, and yet they all gather together.

28 The chameleon which takes hold with her hands, but is found in kings' palaces.

29 There are three things that go well, yea, four are graceful in their going:

30 The lion which is mightiest among beasts, and neither fears nor turns back before any of the beasts:

31 The cock that walks proudly among the chickens; the he-goat that goes before the flock; and a king who speaks among the people.

32 Covet not that you may not be reproached; do not feed yourself by things acquired wrongfully.

33 Out of the richness of the milk comes forth butter; and if you press your hand on a raw grain of wheat, it will bring forth juices; thus out of the strife goes forth judgment.

CHAPTER 31

THE words of Moael, a king and prophet, which his mother taught him, saying,

2 Oh my son! Oh the son of my womb! Oh the son of my vows!

3 Give not your strength to women, nor your ways to the extravagance of kings.

4 Of kings, O Moael, be careful of kings who drink wine; and of princes who drink strong drink,

5 Lest you drink and forget the law and forsake the judgment of the afflicted.

6 Let strong drink be given to those who mourn, and wine to those who are of heavy heart,

7 That they may drink, and forget their sorrows, and remember their miseries no more.

8 Open your mouth with words of truth, and judge all the sons of the wicked.

9 Open your mouth, judge righteously, and plead the cause of the poor and needy.

10 ¶Who can find a diligent woman? For her price is far above rubies.

11 The heart of her husband safely trusts in her, and her food supplies never diminish.

12 She does him good and not evil all the days of her life.

13 She seeks wool and linen, and works willingly with her hands.

14 She is like the merchant's ship, she brings her merchandise from afar.

15 She rises also while it is yet night, and gives food to her household and work to her maids.

16 She considers a field, and buys it; with the fruit of her hands she plants a vineyard.

17 She girds her loins with strength, and strengthens her arms.

18 She perceives that her merchandise is good; her lamp does not go out all night.

19 She stretches out her arms diligently, and puts her hands to the spindle.

20 She stretches out her hands to the poor; yea, she stretches forth her arms to the needy.

21 The members of her household are not afraid of snow; for all of them are clothed with scarlet.

22 She makes herself a covering of tapestry; her clothing is silk and purple.

23 Her husband is known in cities, when he sits among the elders of the land.

24 She makes fine linen, and sells it; and delivers girdles to the merchants.

25 Strength and honor are her clothing; and she shall rejoice in time to come.

26 She opens her mouth with wisdom; and upon her tongue is the law of kindness.

27 The ways of her household are above reproach, and she does not eat the bread of idleness.

28 Her children rise up and call her blessed; and her husband also praises her.

29 Many daughters have become rich, but you have excelled them all.

30 Comeliness is deceitful and beauty is vain; but a woman who reverences the LORD shall be praised.

31 Give her of the fruit of her hands, and let her own works praise her in the gate.

ECCLESIASTES

OR, THE PREACHER

CHAPTER 1

THE words of Kohlat,[1] the son of David, king in Jerusalem.

2 Vanity of vanities, says the Preacher, vanity of vanities; all is vanity.

3 What profit has a man of all his labor at which he toils under the sun?

4 One generation passes away and another generation comes; but the earth abides for ever.

5 The sun rises and the sun goes down and hastens to the place where it rose that from thence it may rise again.

6 The wind blows toward the south, and turns about to the north; it whirls continually, and returns again according to its circuits.

7 All the rivers run into the sea, yet the sea is not full; to the place from whence the rivers flow, thither they return to flow again.

8 All things are wearisome: a man is not satisfied with utterance, his eye is not satisfied with seeing, nor his ear satisfied with hearing.

9 The thing that has been is that which shall be; and that which has been done is that which shall be done; and there is nothing new under the sun.

10 Whosoever speaks and says, Look, this is new, should know that it already has been in the ages which were before us.

11 There is no remembrance of former generations; neither shall there be any remembrance of generations that are to come with those that will come after.

12 ¶I the Preacher have been king over Israel in Jerusalem.

13 And I gave my heart to seek and to search out by wisdom concerning all things that are done under heaven; to be engaged in it is a difficult task that God has given to the sons of men.

14 I have seen all the works that are done under the sun; and, behold, all is vanity and vexation of spirit.

15 The chaotic cannot be made orderly; and he who is lacking knowledge cannot be supplied with it.

16 I have communed with my own heart, saying, Lo, I have become great, and have gotten more wisdom than all they who were before me in Jerusalem; yea, my heart has had great experience of wisdom and knowledge.

17 And I gave my heart to know wisdom and proverbs and understanding; but I have perceived that this also is vexation of spirit

18 Because in much wisdom there is much grief, and he who increases knowledge increases sorrow.

CHAPTER 2

I SAID to my heart, Come now, I will prove you with joy; therefore enjoy good things; and, behold, this also is vanity.

2 I said of laughter, What pleasure is there in it? and of mirth, What do you accomplish?

3 I thought in my heart to give myself to wine, but my heart reasoned with wisdom; and I laid hold upon understanding, till I might see what was good for the sons of men, which they should do under the sun all the days of their lives.

4 I multiplied my servants; I built myself houses; I planted vineyards for myself:

5 I made myself gardens and parks,

[1] The Preacher.

686

and planted in them trees of all kinds of fruit;

6 I made myself pools of water, to irrigate the nursery that produces trees.

7 I got for myself menservants and maidservants, and had a great household; also I had great possessions of cattle and flocks, above all who were before me in Jerusalem.

8 I gathered for myself silver and gold and the possessions of kings and cities; I got me men singers and women singers and the delights of the sons of men, and I appointed for myself butlers and waitresses.

9 So I became great, and my wealth increased more than all who were before me in Jerusalem; my wisdom also remained with me.

10 And whatsoever my eyes desired I did not keep from them; I withheld not my heart from any joy; for my heart rejoiced in all my labor; and this was my portion of all my labor.

11 Then I looked on all the works that my hands had wrought and on the labor that I had labored to do; and, behold, all was vanity and vexation of spirit, and there was no profit under the sun.

12 ¶So I looked around to behold wisdom and transgression and folly; for who is the man who can enter into judgment with the king? Especially with him who had created him.

13 Then I saw that wisdom excels folly, just as light excels darkness.

14 The wise man's eyes are in his head; but the fool walks in darkness; and I myself perceived also that one misfortune happens to them all.

15 Then I said in my heart, The misfortune of the fool will happen to me also; and why was I then more wise? Then I said in my heart, This also is vanity.

16 The fool speaks superficially, but there is no remembrance of the wise man more than of the fool for ever; seeing that which now is, in the days to come shall be forgotten. And just as the wise man dies, so the fool.

17 Therefore I hated life; because the work that is wrought under the sun is grievous to me; for all is vanity and vexation of spirit.

18 ¶Yea, I hated all my labor with which I had labored under the sun because I must leave it to the man who shall come after me.

19 And who knows whether he shall be a wise man or a fool? Yet he will have rule over all my labor wherein I have labored, and wherein I have shown myself wise under the sun. This also is vanity.

20 Therefore I changed my view concerning all the toil in which I had labored under the sun.

21 There is a man who labors with wisdom and knowledge and success; and yet he leaves his portion to a man who has not labored for it. This also is vanity and a great misfortune.

22 For what profit shall a man have of all his labor and of the desire of his heart wherein he has labored under the sun?

23 For all his days are full of sorrows, and his travail is grief; yea, even in the night his heart takes no rest. This also is vanity.

24 ¶There is nothing better for a man than that he should eat and drink, and that he should make his soul enjoy good in his labor. This also I saw, that it is from the hand of the LORD.

25 For who can eat or who can drink except he?

26 For, to a man who is good in his presence, God gives wisdom and knowledge and joy; but to the sinner he gives toil, to gather and to heap up, that he may give to him who is good in the presence of the LORD. This also is vanity and vexation of spirit.

CHAPTER 3

TO everything there is a season, and a time for every purpose under the sun:

2 A time to be born and a time to die; a time to plant and a time to pluck up that which is planted;

3 A time to kill and a time to heal; a time to tear down and a time to build up;

4 A time to weep and a time to laugh; a time to mourn and a time to dance;

5 A time to cast away stones and a time to gather stones together; a time to embrace and a time to refrain from embracing;

6 A time to lose and a time to seek; a time to tie up and a time to untie;

7 A time to rend and a time to sew; a time to keep silent and a time to speak;

8 A time to love and a time to hate; a time for war and a time for peace.

9 What profit has the worker in his labor?

10 I have seen the toil which the LORD has given to the sons of men to be engaged therewith.

11 He has made everything beautiful in its time; also he has made the world dear to man's heart, so that no man can find out the works which the LORD has done from the beginning to the end.

12 I know that there is no good in worldly things, but for men to rejoice and to do good in their lives.

13 And also that every man should eat and drink and enjoy the good of all his labor; it is the gift of the LORD.

14 I know that whatsoever the LORD does, it shall be for ever; nothing can be added to it and nothing taken from it; and the LORD has so made it that men should reverence him.

15 That which is now, already has been; and that which is to be, has already been; and God will avenge him who has been persecuted.

16 ¶And moreover, I saw under the sun the place of judgment, that wickedness was there; and in the place of righteousness, that iniquity was there.

17 I said in my heart, God shall judge the righteous and the wicked; for there is a time for every purpose and for every work.

18 I meditated in my heart concerning the estate of the sons of men whom God had created, and saw that they are like beasts.

19 For the same misfortune which befalls the sons of men befalls beasts; even one misfortune befalls them: as the one dies, so dies the other; yea, they have all one breath; so that man has no preeminence over the beast; for all is vanity.

20 All go to one place; all are of the dust, and all turn to dust again.

21 Who knows whether the spirit of men goes upward and the spirit of the beasts goes downward under the earth?

22 Wherefore I saw that there is nothing better in them but that man should rejoice in his works; for that is his portion; for who shall bring him to see what shall be after him?

CHAPTER 4

SO I turned and considered all the oppressions that are done under the sun; and behold, the tears of the oppressed, and they had no comforter to deliver them from the hand of their oppressors, having neither strength nor helper.

2 Wherefore I praised the dead who are already dead more than the living who are still alive.

3 But, better is he who has not yet been born than both of them, because he has not seen the evil work that is done under the sun.

4 ¶Then I saw that all the labor and all the work is successful because a man is more zealous than his neighbor. This is also vanity and vexation of spirit.

5 The fool folds his hands together and suffers hunger.

6 Better is a handful with quietness than both hands full with toil and vexation of spirit.

7 ¶Then I turned, and I saw vanity under the sun.

8 When there is but one man, and not a second, and he has neither son nor brother, there is no end to all his labor. Neither are his eyes satisfied with riches; neither does he say, For whom am I laboring and deny-

ing myself good things? This is also vanity, and a grievous vexation.

9 ¶Two are better than one, because they have a good reward for their labor;

10 For if they fall, the one will lift up his fellow; but woe to him who is alone when he falls; for there is none to lift him up.

11 Again, if two sleep together, they will be warm; but how can one be warm alone?

12 And if one is too strong for him, two shall withstand him; and a threefold cord is not quickly broken.

13 ¶Better is a youth who is poor and wise than a king who is old and foolish, and does not know how to receive admonition.

14 Out of prison he has come to reign, because also in his own kingdom he had been born miserable.

15 I considered all the living who walk under the sun, with the young men, who shall rise up in their place.

16 There is no end of all the people, even of all who have been before them; and those also who come after shall not rejoice in them. This also is vanity and vexation of spirit.

CHAPTER 5

LET your conduct be seemly when you go to the house of God; and to draw near to hear is better than the gift offerings of fools; for they know not to do that which is good.

2 Be not rash with your mouth, and let not your heart be hasty to utter a word before God; for God is in heaven, and you upon earth; therefore let your words be few.

3 For a dream comes because of the multitude of business; and a fool's voice is known by a multitude of words.

4 When you vow a vow to God, do not delay in fulfilling it; for he has no pleasure in fools; but as for you, pay that which you have vowed.

5 It is much better that you should not vow than that you should vow and not fulfill it.

6 Suffer not your mouth to cause your flesh to sin; neither say before God that it was an error, lest God be angry at your voice and destroy the work of your hands.

7 For in the multitude of dreams and vain things and many words is false worship; but you should worship God.

8 ¶If you see the oppression of the poor and violent perversion of judgment and justice in a city, do not marvel at the matter; for he who is higher than the highest is watching; and he who is higher is over them.

9 ¶Moreover the riches of the earth are for all; the king, himself, is served by cultivating his own field.

10 He who loves money shall not be satisfied with money; and he who loves wealth shall not retain it. This is also vanity.

11 When goods increase, they also are increased who eat them; and what profit is there to their owners, except the beholding of them with their eyes?

12 Sweet is the sleep of a laboring man, whether he eat little or much; but the abundance of the rich will not let him sleep.

13 There is also another grievous evil which I have seen under the sun, riches kept by the owner thereof to his own hurt.

14 And those riches are lost in a bad venture; for when he begets a son, there is nothing in his hand.

15 As he came forth from his mother's womb, naked shall he return to the earth to go as he came, and shall take nothing of his labor, which he may carry away in his hand.

16 And this also is a grievous evil; for just as he came, so shall he go; and what profit has he that has labored for the wind?

17 All his days also he eats in darkness, in much anger and wrath, in mourning and in sickness.

18 ¶This is what I, the Preacher, have seen: it is good and comely for one to eat and drink and to enjoy the good of all his labor for which

he toils under the sun all the days of his life, which the LORD has given him; for this is his portion.

19 To every man also the LORD has given riches and wealth, and has given power to eat thereof and to take his portion and to rejoice in his labor; this is the gift of God.

20 For he shall remember no more the days of his life; because God will keep him busy with the joy of his heart.

CHAPTER 6

THERE is an evil which I have seen under the sun, and it is common among men;

2 There is a man to whom God has given riches, wealth, and honor, so that he lacks nothing for his soul of all that he desires, yet God does not give him power to eat of them; but a stranger eats it. This is vanity, and it is an evil disease.

3 ¶If a man beget a hundred children and live a multitude of years so that the days of his years are many, and his soul is not filled with good things, and also that he have no burial, I say that an untimely birth is better than he.

4 For he comes in with vanity, and shall go into darkness, and his name shall be covered with darkness.

5 Moreover he has not seen the sun, [1] nor known anything, yet this one has more rest than the other.

6 ¶Yea, though he live a thousand years twice told, yet he has seen no good; do not all go to one place?

7 All the labor of a man is for his mouth, and yet his appetite is not filled.

8 The wise man has an advantage over the fool. What! Does the poor man know how to go through life?

9 ¶Better is the sight of the eyes than the wandering of the desire; this is also vanity and vexation of spirit.

10 That which has been before has already been named, and the nature of man is known, and he cannot contend in judgment with him that is stronger than himself.

11 ¶Seeing there are many things

---

[1] Light of truth.

---

that increase vanity, what advantage has man?

12 For who knows what is good for man in his life, all the days of his vain life which he spends like a shadow? For who can tell a man what shall be after him under the sun?

CHAPTER 7

A GOOD name is better than a precious ointment; and the day of one's death than the day of his birth.

2 ¶It is better to go to the house of mourning than to the house of feasting; for this is the end of all men; and the living will lay it to his heart.

3 Sorrow is better than laughter; for by the sadness of the countenance the heart is made better.

4 The heart of the wise is in the house of mourning; but the heart of fools is in the house of mirth.

5 It is better for a man to hear the rebuke of the wise than to hear the song of fools.

6 For as the crackling of thorns burning under a pot, so is the laughter of fools; this is also vanity.

7 ¶Surely slander destroys a wise man; and a bribe destroys the heart.

8 Better is the end of a thing than its beginning; and the patient man in humbleness is better than the proud in spirit.

9 Be not hastily angry, for anger rests in the bosom of the fools.

10 Say not, What is the cause that the former days were better than these? For you do not enquire wisely concerning this.

11 ¶Wisdom is better than weapons; yea, it is better for those who see the light of the truth.

12 For the protection of wisdom is like the protection of money; and the advantage of knowledge is that wisdom gives life to him who possesses it.

13 Consider the work of God; for who can straighten him who is crooked?

14 In the day of prosperity be joyful, but look after yourself in the day of adversity. God also has made one

thing opposite to another, to the end that man should know nothing after he is gone.

15 All things have I seen in the days of my vanity; there is a righteous man who perishes in his righteousness, and there is a wicked man who prolongs his life in his wickedness.

16 Be not overrighteous; neither make yourself overwise; lest you should become stupid.

17 Be not excessively wicked, lest you be hated much; neither be foolish, lest you die before your time.

18 It is good that you should take hold of this; yea, also from this withdraw not your hand; for he who reverences God shall follow all these things.

19 Wisdom strengthens the wise more than ten princes that are in the city.

20 For there is no just man upon the earth, that does good, and sins not.

21 Also take no heed of all words that are spoken by the wicked; neither listen to your servant when he curses you;

22 For your heart knows that you yourself have oftentimes cursed others.

23 ¶I have tried all these things by wisdom; I said, I will be wise; but wisdom was far from me.

24 Yea, wisdom was far off; it also had depth beyond depth; who can find it out?

25 I went around and applied my heart to know and to visit and to search for wisdom and reason and to know the wickedness of the fool, even folly and transgression.

26 And I find more bitter than death the woman whose heart is snares and nets, and whose hands bind him who is good; he who is good in the presence of God shall escape from her; but he who sins shall be caught by her.

27 Behold, I have found this, says the Preacher, weighing one thing against another to find out the purposes,

28 And again my soul sought but I found not: one man among a thousand have I found; but a woman among all these I have not found.

29 But behold, this thing I have found, that God has made men upright; but they have sought out many devices.

CHAPTER 8

WHO is like the wise man? And who knows the interpretation of a thing? A man's wisdom makes his face to shine, but he who is impudent shall be hated.

2 Keep the king's command, and in regard of the oath of God be not hasty.

3 Go from his presence; and do not stand firm in an evil matter; for he does whatsoever pleases him.

4 In what manner the king speaks is lawful; and who can say to him, What are you doing?

5 He who keeps a command shall know no evil thing; and a wise man's heart discerns both time and judgment.

6 ¶Because to every purpose there is time and judgment, because the misery of man is great upon him.

7 For there is no one who knows that which has been; and who can tell him what will be after him?

8 There is no man who has power over the wind to withhold the wind; neither has he power over the day of death; and there is no escape from duty in the day of battle; neither shall wickedness deliver those who are given to it.

9 All this have I seen, and applied my heart to every work that is done under the sun; there is a time wherein one man rules over another to hurt him.

10 And so I saw the wicked buried, who had come and gone from the holy place, and they were forgotten in the city where they had done such evil things; this also is vanity.

11 Because vengeance against the evil-doers is not executed speedily, therefore the heart of the sons of men is fully set in them to do evil.

12 ¶He who sins does evil a hundred times, and his days are prolonged, yet surely I know that it shall

be well with the worshippers of the Lord, that they may fear before him;

13 But it shall not be well with the wicked, neither shall he prolong his days, which are like a shadow; because he does not fear before God.

14 There is a vanity which is done upon the earth; there are just men, to whom it happens according to the work of the wicked; and there are wicked men, to whom it happens according to the deeds of the righteous; I said that this also is vanity.

15 Then I commended mirth, because there is nothing better for a man under the sun than to eat and to drink and to be merry; for that shall accompany him in his labor all the days of his life, which God gives him under the sun.

16 ¶Therefore I applied my heart to know wisdom, and to see the business which is done upon the earth; for there are those whose eyes see no sleep either day or night.

17 Then I saw all the work of God, that man cannot find out the work which is done under the sun; all that a man may labor to seek out, yet he will not find it; and whosoever says that he is wise yet will not be able to find it.

CHAPTER 9

FOR all the essence of these things have I considered in my heart, and my heart perceived all of this, that the righteous and the wise and their works are in the hand of God; no man knows either love or hatred; for everything which is before him is vanity.

2 All things happen alike to all; there is one chance for the righteous and for the wicked; to the good and to the bad, to the clean and to the unclean; to him who sacrifices and to him who does not sacrifice; as is the good man, so is the sinner; and he who swears is as he who fears an oath.

3 This is an evil among all things that are done under the sun, for there is one chance to all; yea, also the heart of the sons of men is full of evil, and grievous error is in their heart while they live, and after that they go to the dead.

4 ¶For him who is joined with all the living there is hope; for a living dog is better than a dead lion.

5 For the living know that they shall die; but the dead know not anything, neither have they any more a reward; for the memory of them is forgotten.

6 Also their love and their hatred and their envy have already perished; neither have they any more a portion for ever in anything that is done under the sun.

7 ¶Come now, eat your bread with joy and drink your wine with a merry heart; for God is pleased with your works.

8 Let your garments be always white; [1] and let your head lack no ointment.

9 Live joyfully with the wife whom you love all the days of your vain life, because she is your portion in life, and in your labor which you labor under the sun.

10 Whatsoever your hand is able to do, do it with your might; for there is no work nor device nor knowledge nor wisdom in Sheol whither you are going.

11 ¶I turned and saw under the sun that the race is not to the swift nor the battle to the strong nor bread to the wise nor riches to the men of understanding nor glory to the learned men; because time and chance happen to them all.

12 For man knows not his time; but as fish that are taken in a treacherous net and as birds that are caught in the snares, so are the sons of men snared in an evil time when it falls suddenly upon them.

13 ¶This wisdom I have seen also under the sun, and it seemed great to me:

14 There was a little city and few men in it; and there came a great king against it and beseiged it and built bulwarks against it;

15 Now there was found in it a poor wise man, and he by his wis-

[1] White is the symbol of purity and holiness.

dom delivered the city; yet no man remembered that same poor man.

16 Then said I, Wisdom is better than might; nevertheless the poor man's wisdom is despised and his words are not heeded.

17 The words of the wise men are heard in quiet more than the cry of a ruler who is a fool.

18 Wisdom is better than weapons of war; but one sin destroys much good.

CHAPTER 10

LIKE dead flies which make the container of precious ointment stink, so does a great folly outweigh wisdom and honor.

2 A wise man's heart thinks rightly; but a fool's heart thinks wrongly.

3 Yea also, when the fool walks by the way, he lacks wisdom, and whatever he reasons is folly.

4 If the temper of the ruler rises against you, do not leave your country; because healing forgives many sins.

5 There is an evil which I have seen under the sun, like an error which proceeds from before a ruler:

6 The fool is set in high and powerful places, and the rich shall sit in a low place.

7 I have seen servants riding upon horses, and princes walking like servants on the ground.

8 He who digs a pit shall fall into it; and he who breaks a hedge will be bitten by a serpent.

9 He who removes landmarks shall suffer pain by them; and he who cuts trees shall be wounded by them.

10 Just as the edge of a weapon may be blunt, and not sharpened, and yet may cause many to be slain, so wisdom is more advantageous to those who are diligent.

11 If the serpent bites without being charmed; then in vain is a charmer.

12 The words of a wise man's mouth are gracious; but the lips of a fool will ruin him.

13 The beginning of the words of his mouth is foolishness; and the end of his talk is mischievous madness.

14 A fool multiplies words; a man cannot tell what has been; and what shall be after him, who can tell him?

15 The labor of fools wears them out because they do not know how to buy and sell in the city.

16 ¶Woe to you, O land, when your king is a child, and your princes eat in the morning! [1]

17 Blessed are you, O land, when your king is the son of a noble and your princes eat in due time, for strength and not for drunkenness!

18 ¶By slothfulness a roof shall be brought down; and through idleness of hands water drips through.

19 ¶Bread and wine are made for joy, and oil makes life merry; but money brings one low and causes him to go astray in all things.

20 ¶Do not curse the king, no not even in your thought; and do not curse the rich in your bedchamber; for a bird of the air shall carry your voice, and that which has wings shall tell the matter.

CHAPTER 11

CAST your bread upon the waters; for you shall find it after many days.

2 Give a portion to seven, and also to eight; for you know not what misfortune shall come upon the earth.

3 If the clouds be full of rain, they empty themselves upon the earth; and if a tree fall toward the south or toward the north, in the place where the tree falls, there it shall be.

4 He who observes the wind shall not sow; and he who regards the clouds shall not reap.

5 As you do not know the path of the wind, and the manner of a woman who is with child; even so you do not know the works of the LORD who makes all.

6 In the morning sow your seed, and in the evening withhold not your hands: for you know not which shall prosper, either this or that, or whether they both alike shall be good.

---

[1] In the East people seldom eat in the morning, nor do they drink wine before the noon meal. But princes, nobles, and the rich eat in the morning and drink wine and strong drink.

7 ¶Truly light is sweet, and it is a pleasant thing for the eyes; but much more to those who see the sun.[1]

8 If a man live many years, and rejoice in them all; yet let him remember the days of darkness; for they shall be many. All that comes is vanity.

9 ¶Rejoice, O young man, in your youth; and it shall be well with you; and walk in the ways of your heart, and in the sight of your eyes; but know that for all these things the LORD will bring you into judgment.

10 Therefore remove anger from your heart, and put away evil from your flesh; for youth and ignorance are vanity.

CHAPTER 12

REMEMBER now your Creator in the days of your youth, before the evil days come and the years draw nigh when you shall say, I have no pleasure in them;

2 Before life ebbs, beauty fades, fortune fails, and poverty returns after prosperity;

3 In the day when the legs tremble and the arms weaken, and the teeth chew no more because they are few, and the eyes are dimmed,

4 And the ears shall be so dulled that the sound of women grinding at the mill is low, and a man shall rise up at the song of birds; and the sound of women singing shall be low;

5 He shall be afraid of that which is high, and shall tremble in his ways, and sleeplessness shall come upon him; the almond tree shall blossom, and the locust shall be multiplied, and fragrance shall scatter, and trouble shall cease; because man goes to the house of his reward and the mourners walk about the streets.

6 Remember him before the silver cord is cut off and the golden bowl is broken and the pitcher is broken at the fountain or the wheel is broken at the cistern,

7 Then the dust shall return to the earth as it was; and the spirit shall return to God who gave it.

8 ¶Vanity of vanities, says the Preacher, all is vanity.

9 And moreover, because the Preacher was wise, he still taught the people knowledge; yea, he gave good heed and sought out and composed many proverbs.

10 The Preacher sought to find agreeable words; and he wrote uprightly the words of truth.

11 The words of the wise are as goads, and as nails deeply fastened, which are arranged by workmen and given from one master builder.

12 Furthermore, my son, take heed; of writing many books there is no end; and much study is a weariness of the flesh.

13 ¶Let us hear the conclusion of the whole matter: Fear the LORD and keep his commandments; this is given by one Master to every man.

14 For the LORD shall bring every work into judgment, concerning everything which is hidden and known, whether it be good or whether it be evil.

---

[1] Sun is often used symbolically meaning the truth. Light is symbolical of enlightenment and understanding. God is often spoken of as sun.

THE

SONG OF SOLOMON

CHAPTER 1

THE song of songs, which is Solomon's, the son of David king of Israel.

2 Let him kiss me with the kisses of his mouth; for your love is better than wine.

3 Because of the fragrance of your good ointments your name is like ointment of myrrh, therefore do the virgins love you.

4 Draw me after you, let us run; the king has brought me into his chambers; we will be glad and rejoice in you, we will remember your love more than wine, and your affections more than the upright.

5 I have dark skin, but I am comely, O daughters of Jerusalem, like the tents of Kedar, like the curtains of Solomon.

6 Do not look at me because I have dark skin, because the sun has tanned me; my mother's sons contended with me; they made me the keeper of the vineyards; but my own vineyard I have not kept.

7 Tell me, O you whom my soul loves, where did I feed, where did I make my flock to rest at noon? Lest I become like a sheep which has gone astray from your flocks.

8 ¶If you do not know, O you most beautiful among women, come, follow in the footprints of the flock, and feed your kids beside the shepherds' tents.

9 I have compared you, O my beloved, to a mare in Pharaoh's chariot.

10 Your cheeks are comely with braided hair, and your neck with necklaces.

11 We will make for you golden chains with studs of silver.

12 ¶While you are seated with the king upon his cushion, spikenard sends forth its fragrance.

13 A bundle of myrrh is my beloved to me; he shall lie all night between my breasts.

14 My beloved is to me like a cluster of henna flowers in a vineyard of Engad.

15 Behold, you are beautiful, O my beloved; behold, you are fair; you have dove's eyes.

16 Behold, you are beautiful, my beloved, yea, pleasant; also our bed is spacious.

17 The beams of our house are of cedar, and our rafters of cypress.

CHAPTER 2

I AM like the rose of Sharon and the lily of the valley.

2 Like the lilies among thorns, so is my beloved among the daughters.

3 Like an apple tree among the trees of the forest, so is my beloved among the young men. I sat down under his shadow with great delight, and his fruit was sweet to my taste.

4 He brought me to the banqueting house, and assigned as my portion love.

5 Sustain me with delicacies, surround me with apples; for I am sick for love.

6 His left hand is under my head, and his right hand embraces me.

7 I adjure you, O daughters of Jerusalem, by the gazelles, or by young roes of the field, that you stir not up, nor awake my love until it please.

8 ¶The voice of my beloved! behold, he comes leaping upon the mountains, skipping upon the hills.

9 My beloved is like a gazelle or a young roe; behold, he stands behind

our wall, he looks through the windows, bending himself over the lattice.

10 My beloved spoke and said to me, Rise up, my love, my beautiful one, and come away.

11 For, lo, the winter is past, the rain is over and gone;

12 The flowers appear on the earth; the time of pruning has come, and the voice of the turtle dove is heard in our land;

13 The fig tree puts forth its green figs, and the vines with tender shoots give fragrance. Arise, my beloved, my beautiful one, and come away.

14 ¶O my dove, who nests in the clefts of the rock and in the secret places of the hedge, let me see your countenance, let me hear your voice; for sweet is your voice, and your countenance is comely.

15 Let us catch the foxes, the little foxes that spoil the vineyards, for our vines have tender shoots.

16 ¶My beloved is mine, and I am his; he feeds among the lilies.

17 Until the day cools and the shadows flee away, turn my beloved and be like a gazelle or a young hart upon the fragrant mountains.

CHAPTER 3

UPON my bed by night I sought him whom my soul loves; I sought him but found him not.

2 I will rise now and go about the city in the streets, and in the broad ways I will seek him whom my soul loves; I sought him but I found him not.

3 The watchmen that go about the city found me; I asked them, Have you seen him whom my soul loves?

4 Scarcely had I passed by them, when I found him whom my soul loves; I held him, and would not let him go until I had brought him into my mother's house and into the chamber of her that bore me.

5 I charge you, O daughters of Jerusalem, by the gazelles or by the young roes of the field, that you stir not up nor awake my love till it please.

6 ¶Who is this that comes up from the wilderness like pillars of smoke, perfumed with myrrh and frankincense, compounded from all kinds of powdered sweet spices?

7 Behold, the litter of Solomon is surrounded by sixty mighty men of the valiant of Israel.

8 They all hold swords, being expert in war; every man has his sword upon his thigh because of fear in the night.

9 King Solomon made himself a palace of wood of Lebanon.

10 He made its pillars of silver, the floor thereof of gold, the covering of it of purple, the inside thereof being paved with a love gift from the daughters of Jerusalem.

11 Go forth, O you daughters of Zion, and behold King Solomon with the crown with which his mother crowned him in the day of his wedding and in the day of the joy of his heart.

CHAPTER 4

BEHOLD, you are beautiful, my beloved; behold, you are beautiful; your eyes are doves' eyes behind your veil; your hair is like a flock of goats, which come up from mount Gilead.

2 Your teeth are like a flock of sheep that are shorn, which come up from the washing; every one of them bears twins, and none is bereft among them.

3 Your lips are like a thread of scarlet, and your speech is comely like the first flowers of the pomegranate.

4 Your neck beneath your veil is like the tower of David, built for an armory, whereon there hang a thousand bucklers, all quivers of valiant men.

5 Your two breasts are like two young roes, twins of a gazelle, which feed among the lilies.

6 Until the day is cool and the evening shadows decline, I will go to the mountains of myrrh and to the hills of frankincense.

7 You are all beautiful, my love; there is not even a spot in you.

8 ¶Come with me from Lebanon, O my sister, my bride! come with me

from Lebanon; you shall pass over the top of Amana, from the top of Shenir and Hermon, from the lions' dens, from the mountains of leopards.

9 You have encouraged me, O my sister, my bride; you have stolen my heart with a look of one of your eyes, with one necklace of your neck.

10 How beautiful are your breasts, O my sister, my bride! how much better are your breasts than wine! and the fragrance of your ointments than all spices!

11 Your lips drop as the honeycomb; honey and milk are under your tongue; and the fragrance of your garments is like the perfume of Lebanon.

12 A garden enclosed is my sister, my bride; yea, a garden guarded, a fountain sealed.

13 Your shoots are an orchard of pomegranates, with pleasant fruits; henna-flower with spikenard.

14 Spikenard and saffron; sweet cane and cinnamon, with all trees of frankincense; myrrh and aloes, with all the chief spices;

15 They are a fountain of gardens, a well of living waters, flowing from Lebanon.

16 ¶Awake, O north wind, and come, O you south wind; blow upon my garden that the perfume may flow out. Let my beloved come into his garden and eat his pleasant fruit.

CHAPTER 5

I AM come into my garden, my sister, my bride; I have gathered my myrrh with my spices, I have eaten my honeycomb with my honey, I have drunk my wine with my milk. Eat, O my friends; drink, yea, drink abundantly, O my beloved.

2 ¶I slept, but my heart was awake; it is the voice of my beloved who is knocking, saying, Open to me, my sister, my beloved, my harmless dove; for my head is filled with dew, and my locks with the drops of the night.

3 I have put off my coat; how shall I put it on? I have washed my feet; how shall I defile them?

4 My beloved put in his hand by the opening of the door, and my heart was moved for him.

5 I rose up to open to my beloved; and my hands dropped myrrh, yea, and my fingers dropped myrrh upon the handles of the lock.

6 I opened to my beloved; but my beloved had withdrawn himself, and was gone; my soul failed when he spoke; then I sought him but I could not find him; I called him but he did not answer me.

7 The watchmen that went about the city found me; they smote me, they wounded me; the keepers of the walls took away my veil from me.

8 I adjure you, O daughters of Jerusalem, if you should find my beloved, tell him that I am sick for love.

9 ¶What is your beloved more than another beloved, O you beautiful among women? What is your beloved more than another beloved, that you so adjure us?

10 My beloved is white and ruddy, the chiefest among ten thousand.

11 His head is like the finest gold, his locks straight and black as a raven.

12 His eyes are like the eyes of doves by brooks of water, washed with milk and fitly set.

13 His cheeks are like beds of spices, like sweet flowers; his lips like lilies, dropping myrrh and spikenard.

14 His hands are like golden girdles studded with precious stones; his belly is like a work of ivory overlaid with sapphires.

15 His legs are like pillars of marble set upon bases of gold; his chest is like Lebanon, excellent as the cedars.

16 His mouth is like sweet honeycombs; his garments are lovely. This is my beloved, and this is my friend, O daughters of Jerusalem.

CHAPTER 6

WHERE has your beloved gone, O you most beautiful among women? Where has your beloved turned aside, that we may seek him with you?

2 My beloved has gone down into his garden, to the beds of spices, to

feed in the gardens and to gather lilies.

3 I am my beloved's, and my beloved is mine; he feeds among the lilies.

4 ¶You are beautiful and desirable, O my beloved, comely as Jerusalem, and esteemed as one chosen among beauties.

5 Turn away your eyes from me, for they have overcome me; your hair is like a flock of goats which come up from the mount of Gilead.

6 Your teeth are like a flock of sheep which go up from washing; every one of them bears twins, and none is bereft among them.

7 Your cheeks, behind your veil, are like two pieces of pomegranate.

8 There are sixty queens and eighty concubines and virgins without number.

9 My perfect dove is but one; she is the only one of her mother; she is the choice one of her that bore her. The daughters saw her and praised her; yea, the queens and the concubines also praised her.

10 ¶Who is she that looks forth like the morning, fair as the moon, clear as the sun, and revered as a princess?

11 I went down into the garden of walnut trees to see the fruit of the valley and to see whether the vine had blossomed and whether the pomegranates had budded.

12 And being unfamiliar with the place, I sat in the public chariot which was ready.

13 Return, return, O Shulamite; return, return, that we may look upon you. What will you see in the Shulamite, who comes down joyfully, like the rejoicing of a host?

CHAPTER 7

HOW beautiful are your feet in sandals, O prince's daughter! The form of your thighs is like cut precious stones, the work of the hands of a skilled workman.

2 Your navel is like a round goblet in which mingled wine is never lacking; your belly is like a heap of wheat set about with lilies.

3 Your two breasts are like two young roes, twins of gazelles, that feed among lilies.

4 Your neck is like a tower of ivory; your eyes are like the pools in Heshbon by the gate of a princess; your nose is like the tower of Lebanon which looks toward Damascus.

5 Your head upon you is like Carmel, and the braiding of your hair is like royal purple bound with rows of stitching.

6 How beautiful you are, and how desirable, O beloved one, delightful daughter!

7 Your stature is like a palm tree, and your breasts are clusters of grapes.

8 I said, I will climb the palm tree, I will take hold of its boughs; and your breasts shall be like clusters of the vine, and the fragrance of your face like apples;

9 And your palate is like the best wine for my beloved, that goes down in the mouth of my beloved and makes me move my lips and my teeth.

10 ¶I am my beloved's, and his desire is toward me.

11 Come, my beloved, let us go forth into the field; let us lodge in the village.

12 Let us get up early to the vineyard; let us see if the vine has budded, whether the tender shoots appear, and the pomegranates are in bloom; there will I give you my breasts.

13 The mandrakes give forth fragrance, and at our gates are all manner of pleasant fruits, new and old, which I have kept for you, O my beloved.

CHAPTER 8

WHO shall give you to me for my brother that sucked the breasts of my mother? When I should find you in the street, I would kiss you; yea, I should not be despised.

2 I would lead you and bring you into my mother's house, into the chamber of her that bore me; I would give you a drink of my delicious wine, and of the sweet juice of my pomegranates.

3 His left arm is under my head, and his right hand embraces me.

4 I adjure you, O daughters of Jerusalem, that you stir not up nor awake love until he please.

5 Who is this that comes up from the wilderness, leaning upon her beloved? I awakened you under the apple tree; there your mother brought you forth; there she that bore you was in travail.

6 ¶Set me as a seal upon your heart, as a seal upon your arm; for love is strong as death; desire is cruel as Sheol; its flashes are flashes of fire and flame.

7 Many waters cannot quench love, neither can the rivers carry it away; and yet, if a man would give all the substance of his house for love, people would mock him.

8 ¶We have a little sister whose breasts have not developed; what shall we do for our sister in the day when they shall seek her hand?

9 If she be a wall, we will build upon her an upper chamber of silver; and if she be a door, we will enclose her with boards of cedar.

10 I am a wall, and my breasts are like towers; then I was in his eyes as one who has found favor.

11 Solomon had a vineyard, and its fruits were abundant; he let out the vineyard to keepers; a man offered for its fruits a thousand pieces of silver.

12 My vineyard which is mine is before me; a thousand pieces of silver are yours, O Solomon, and two hundred for the keepers of the fruit.

13 Those who sit in the gardens and listen to your voice, have reported your words to me.

14 ¶Make haste, my beloved, and be like a gazelle or a young hart upon the mountains of spices.

THE BOOK OF THE

PROPHET ISAIAH

CHAPTER 1

THE vision of Isaiah the son of Amoz, which he saw concerning Judah and Jerusalem in the days of Uzziah, Jotham, Ahaz, and Hezekiah, kings of Judah:

2 Hear, O heavens, and give ear, O earth; for the LORD has spoken, I have reared and brought up children, and they have rebelled against me.

3 The ox knows its owner, and the ass its master's crib; but Israel does not know, my people do not understand.

4 Ah sinful nation, a people laden with iniquity, an offspring of evildoers, children that are corrupt; you have forsaken the LORD, you have provoked the Holy One of Israel to anger, you have gone away backward.

5 ¶Why should you be stricken any more, and be chastised? The whole head is sick, and the whole heart faint.

6 From the sole of the foot even to the head there is no soundness in it; but wounds and bruises, and swelling sores; they have not been closed, neither bound up, nor softened with oil.

7 Your country is desolate, your cities are burned with fire; your land, strangers devour in your presence, and it is desolate, as overthrown by strangers.

8 And the daughter of Zion is left as a booth in a vineyard, and as a lodge in a garden of cucumbers, as a besieged city.

9 Except the Lord of hosts had left to us a few survivors, we should have been like Sodom, and we should have been like Gomorrah.

10 ¶Hear the word of the Lord, you rulers of Sodom; give ear to the law of our God, you people of Gomorrah.

11 Of what purpose is the multitude of your sacrifices to me? says the Lord; I am full of the burnt offerings of rams, and the fat of fed beasts; and I do not delight in the blood of bullocks, or of lambs, or of he-goats.

12 When you come to appear before me, who has required this at your hand, to tread my courts?

13 Bring no more vain offerings to me; their savour is an abomination to me; in the new moons and sabbaths, you call an assembly; I do not eat that which is obtained wrongfully, and taken by force.

14 Your new moons and your appointed feasts my soul hates; they are a burden to me; I am weary to bear them.

15 And when you spread forth your hands, I will hide my eyes from you; even though you make many prayers, I will not hear; your hands are full of blood.

16 ¶Wash yourselves, make yourselves clean; put away the evil of your doings from before my eyes; cease to do evil;

17 Learn to do good; seek justice, do good to the oppressed, plead for the fatherless, plead for the widows.

18 Come now, and let us reason together, says the Lord: though your sins be as scarlet, they shall be as white as snow; though they be red like crimson, they shall be like wool.

19 If you are willing and obedient, you shall eat the good of the land;

20 But if you refuse and rebel, you shall be devoured with the sword; for the mouth of the Lord has spoken it.

21 ¶How is the faithful city become a harlot! For once it was full of justice; and righteousness lodged in it, but now murderers.

22 Your silver has become dross, your wine mixed with water.

23 Your princes are rebellious and companions of thieves; every one of them loves a bribe and runs after rewards; they plead not the cause of the fatherless, neither does the cause of the widow come before them.

24 Therefore thus says the Lord of hosts, the Mighty One of Israel: Ah, I will avenge myself of my adversaries, I will take vengeance upon my enemies;

25 ¶And I will turn my hand against you, and purge away your rebellious men, and remove all your iniquities;

26 And I will restore your judges as at the first, and your counsellors as at the beginning; afterward you shall be called the city of righteousness, the faithful city.

27 Zion shall be redeemed with justice, and her captivity with righteousness.

28 ¶And the destruction of the transgressors and of the sinners shall be together, and those who have forsaken the Lord shall perish.

29 For they shall be ashamed of the idols which they have desired, and they shall be confounded by the witchcraft which they have chosen.

30 For they shall be like an oak whose leaves have fallen, and like a garden that has no water.

31 And their strength shall be like cotton, and their works like a spark, and they shall both burn together, and there shall be none to quench them.

CHAPTER 2

THE word that Isaiah the son of Amoz saw concerning Judah and Jerusalem:

2 And it shall come to pass in the last days, that the mountain of the Lord's house shall be established above the mountains, and shall be exalted above the hills; and all nations shall look to it.

3 And many people shall go and say, Come, let us go up to the mountain of the Lord, to the house of the God of Jacob; and he will teach us of his ways, and we will walk in his paths: for out of Zion shall go forth the law, and the word of the Lord from Jerusalem.

4 And he shall judge among the nations, and shall rebuke many peoples who are far off; and they shall beat their swords into plowshares, and their spears into sickles: nation shall not lift up sword against nation, neither shall they learn war any more.

5 O house of Jacob, come, and let us walk in the light of the LORD.

6 ¶For thou hast forsaken thy people the house of Jacob, because they are self-satisfied as in the olden days, and they practice augury like the Philistines, and they have reared many alien children.

7 Their land also is filled with silver and gold, and there is no end to their treasures; their land also is filled with horses, and there is no end to their chariots;

8 Their land also is filled with idols; they worship the work of their own hands, that which their own fingers have made:

9 And the common man is humbled, and the mighty man is brought low; therefore forgive them not.

10 ¶Enter into the rocks, and hide in the dust, for fear of the LORD, and for the glory of his majesty.

11 The lofty looks of man shall be humbled, and the haughtiness of man shall be brought low, and the LORD alone shall be exalted in that day.

12 For the day of the LORD shall be against every one that is proud and lofty, and against every one that is lifted up, that he shall be brought low;

13 And against all the cedars of Lebanon, that are high and lifted up, and against all the oaks of Bashan,

14 And against all the high mountains, and against all the hills that are lifted up,

15 And against every high tower, and against every fenced wall,

16 And against all the ships of Tarshish, and against all the pleasant sights.

17 And the loftiness of man shall be humbled, and the haughtiness of man shall be brought low; and the LORD alone shall be exalted in that day.

18 And the idols shall utterly pass away.

19 And the people shall go into the holes of the rocks, and into the caves of the earth, for fear of the LORD, and for the glory of his majesty, when he arises to conquer the earth.

20 In that day a man shall cast away to the moles and to the bats his idols of gold and his idols of silver, which they made each one for themselves to worship,

21 To go into the caves of the rocks, and into the clefts of the ragged rocks, for fear of the LORD, and for the glory of his majesty, when he arises to conquer the earth.

22 Shun the man who is hasty for of what account is he?

CHAPTER 3

FOR, behold, the LORD of hosts does take away from Jerusalem and from Judah the stay and the staff, the whole stay of bread, and the whole stay of water,

2 The mighty man and the man of war, the judge and the prophet and the diviner and the elder,

3 The captain of fifty and the honorable man and the counsellor and the skilful carpenter and the expert counsellor.

4 And I will appoint young men to be their princes, and mockers shall rule over them.

5 And the people shall oppress one another, every one his neighbor; and the young men shall provoke the elders, and the base men the honorable.

6 When a man shall take hold of his brother in the house of his father, and say to him, You have clothing, be our ruler, and govern this ruin;

7 In that day he shall answer, and say, I will not be a leader; for in my house is neither bread nor clothing; make me not a ruler over the people.

8 For Jerusalem has stumbled, and Judah has fallen; because their tongue and their doings are against the LORD, provoking God in the majesty of his glory.

9 ¶Their hypocrisy witnesses against

them; and they declare their sins like Sodom, they do not hide them. Woe to their soul! for they have wrought evil to themselves.

10 Say to the righteous that it shall be well with them; for they shall eat the fruit of their doings.

11 Woe to the wicked! it shall be ill with him, for the reward of his hands shall be given him.

12 ¶The princes shall pluck my people out, and women shall rule over them. O my people, your leaders have caused you to err, and disturbed the way of your paths.

13 The LORD stands up to plead, and stands to judge his people.

14 The LORD will enter into judgment with the elders of his people, and the princes thereof: for you have burned the vineyard; the spoil of the poor is in your houses.

15 Why did you sting my people, and shame the faces of the poor? says the LORD of hosts.

16 ¶Because the daughters of Zion have become haughty, and walk with stretched forth necks, and wanton eyes, making a tinkling with their feet, and thus provoking the LORD;

17 Therefore the LORD will bring low the heads of the daughters of Zion, and the LORD shall lay bare their secret parts.

18 In that day the LORD will take away the beauty of their apparel;

19 And their adornments and their necklaces and the braids of their hair and their chains and their bonnets and their veils,

20 The paint of their faces, their earrings and their strings of beads

21 And the ornaments of their legs and their bracelets and nose rings,

22 The garments of varied colors and the mantles and the fine linens, the purple garments,

23 The long outer garments, the purple robes, the scarlet robes, the wardrobe of all their adornments.

24 And it shall come to pass, that instead of a sweet smell there shall be a stink; and instead of an ornamental girdle, a worker's apron; and instead of curled hair, baldness; and instead

¹ Jerusalem's.

of purple robes, a girding of sackcloth; for their beauty shall be destroyed.

25 Your mighty men shall fall by the sword, and your valiant men in the battle.

26 And her gates ¹ shall lament and mourn; and her victory shall turn to defeat.

CHAPTER 4

AND in that day seven women shall take hold of one man, saying, We will eat our own bread, and wear our own apparel; only let us be called by your name, to take away our reproach.

2 In that day shall the glory and honor of the LORD shine forth, and the fruit of the earth shall be excellent and comely for the remnant of Israel.

3 And it shall come to pass, that he who is left in Zion, and he who remains in Jerusalem, shall be called holy, even every one who is written among the living in Jerusalem,

4 When the LORD shall have washed away the filth of the daughters of Zion, and shall have purged the bloodshed from the midst of Jerusalem, by the spirit of judgment, and by the spirit of purging.

5 And the LORD will create upon every dwelling place of mount Zion, round about, a cloud by day, and the smoke and shining of a flaming fire by night; for the glory of the LORD shall be a shelter over all.

6 And there shall be a shelter for a shade in the day time from the heat, and for a place of refuge, and for a shelter from the storm and from the rain.

CHAPTER 5

NOW I will sing to my well-beloved a song of my beloved concerning his vineyard. My well-beloved had a vineyard on the corner of a fertile land;

2 He cultivated it and fenced it and planted it with the choicest vines, and built a watchtower in the midst of it, and also made a winepress in it; and he expected that it should bring forth

grapes, but it brought forth wild grapes.

3 And now, O men of Judah, and inhabitants of Jerusalem, judge between me and my vineyard.

4 What more could have been done to my vineyard, that I have not done in it? Wherefore, when I expected that it should bring forth grapes, it brought forth wild grapes.

5 And now I will tell you what I will do to my vineyard; I will demolish its tower, and it shall be for spoil; and break down its fence, and it shall be trodden down;

6 And I will lay it waste; it shall not be pruned, nor digged; but there shall spring up in it briers and thorns; I will also command the clouds that they rain no rain upon it.

7 For the vineyard of the LORD of hosts is the house of Israel, and the men of Judah his pleasant plant; and I looked for justice, but behold oppression; for righteousness, but behold a cry.

8 ¶Woe to those who trespass the boundaries between houses, who remove the landmarks between the fields, to steal the land, that they may dwell alone in the midst of the earth!

9 In my ears said the LORD of hosts, Of a truth, it has been heard, that many houses shall be desolate, because there will be no one to dwell in them.

10 For ten acres of vineyard shall yield but one bath, and a homer of seed shall yield but an ephah.

11 ¶Woe to them who rise up early in the morning, and run after strong drink; that continue drinking until night, till wine inflames them!

12 They drink wine while listening to the harps, timbrels, tambourines, and flutes; but they do not regard the works of the LORD, neither consider the deeds of his hands.

13 ¶Therefore my people are gone into captivity, because they have no knowledge: and their dead are multiplied because of the famine, and have been overcome with thirst.

14 Therefore Sheol has enlarged itself, and opened its mouth without measure: and the glorious men, the honorable men, and the mighty men shall descend into it.

15 And the mean man shall be humbled, and the mighty man shall be brought down, and the eyes of the lofty shall be humbled:

16 But the LORD of hosts shall be exalted in judgment, and the Holy God shall be sanctified in righteousness.

17 Then shall the lambs feed there in their usual fashion, and the waste places that shall be rebuilt shall be the property of the rightful owners.

18 Woe to them that spin out their iniquities like a long rope, and their sins are like a bridle on the neck of a heifer;

19 Who say, Let the LORD make speed, and hasten his works, that we may see them; and let the counsel of the Holy One of Israel draw near, and let it come, that we may know it!

20 ¶Woe to them who call evil good, and good evil; who put darkness for light, and light for darkness; who put bitter for sweet, and sweet for bitter!

21 Woe to those who are wise in their own eyes and prudent in their own sight!

22 Woe to those who are mighty to drink wine, and strong men who mix strong drink;

23 Who justify the guilty because of his bribe, and take away justice from the righteous!

24 Therefore as the fire devours the stubble and the flame consumes the chaff, so they shall be consumed by the flame, and their root shall be as dust; and their blossom shall go up like chaff, because they have rejected the law of the LORD of hosts and despised the command of the Holy One of Israel.

25 Therefore is the anger of the LORD kindled against his people, and he has stretched forth his hand against them, and has smitten them: and the mountains trembled; and their carcasses were like mud in the streets. For all this his anger has not turned away, and his hand is stretched out still.

26 ¶And he will lift up an ensign to the nations from afar and will whistle

to them from the end of the earth; and, behold, they shall come swiftly with speed.

27 They shall not be weary nor stumble, they shall not slumber nor sleep, neither shall the girdle of their loins be loosed, nor the lace of their shoes be broken;

28 Their arrows are sharp and their bows are bent, their horses' hoofs shall be counted like flint, and their wheels like a whirlwind.

29 Their roaring shall be like a lion, and like the young lions that roar, and take hold on the prey and carry it off; and none shall deliver it.

30 And in that day he shall roar against them like the roaring of the sea; and if they look to the land, behold, there shall be darkness and distress, and the light shall be darkened with thick darkness.

CHAPTER 6

IN the year that King Uzziah died I saw the LORD sitting upon a throne, high and lifted up, and his train filled his temple.

2 And above him stood the seraphim; each one had six wings; with two he covered his face, and with two he covered his feet, and with two he did fly.

3 And one called to another, and said, Holy, holy, holy, is the LORD of hosts; the whole earth is full of his glory.

4 And the posts of the door shook at the voice of him who called, and the house was filled with smoke.

5 ¶Then I said, Woe is me, I am dismayed; for I am a man of unclean lips, and I dwell among a people of unclean lips; for my eyes have seen the King, the LORD of hosts.

6 Then one of the seraphim flew to me, having a live coal in his hand, which he had taken with the tongs from off the altar;

7 And he touched my mouth and said to me, Lo, this has touched your lips; your iniquity is taken away, and your sins are forgiven.

8 And I heard the voice of the LORD, saying, Whom shall I send, and who will go for us? Then said I, Here am I; send me.

9 ¶And he said to me, Go, and tell this people, You can hear indeed, but understand not; and you can see indeed, but do not perceive.

10 For the heart of this people is darkened and their ears are heavy and their eyes closed, so that they may not see with their eyes and hear with their ears and understand with their heart and be converted and be forgiven.

11 Then I said, How long, O LORD? And he said, Until the cities lie waste without inhabitants and the houses without men and the land be utterly desolate

12 And the LORD shall have cast off men far away and there shall be a great forsaking in the midst of the land.

13 ¶And they that remain in it shall be a tenth, and again they shall be burned and shall be made like the terebinth or like an oak which is fallen from its stump. The holy seed is the source thereof.

CHAPTER 7

AND it came to pass in the days of Ahaz the son of Jothan, the son of Uzziah, king of Judah, that Rezin the king of Aram,[1] and Pekah the son of Romaliah, king of Israel, went up to Jerusalem to war against it, but could not prevail against it.

2 And it was told the house of David, saying, Aram is confederate with Ephraim. And his heart and the heart of his people were moved, as the trees of the forest are moved with the wind.

3 Then the LORD said to Isaiah, Go forth now to meet Ahaz, you and Shear-Jashub your son, at the end of the conduit of the upper pool which is in the highway of the palace's field;

4 And say to him, Take heed and be quiet; fear not, neither be frightened by these two weakening troublemakers, by the fierce anger of Rezin, and by the son of Romaliah

1 Syria.

5 Because Aram, Ephraim, and the son of Romaliah have taken evil counsel against you, saying,

6 Let us go up against Judah and destroy it, and let us make a breach in it and set a king in the midst of it, even the son of Tabeal;

7 Thus says the LORD God: It shall not stand, neither shall it come to pass.

8 For the head of Aram is Damascus, and the head of Damascus is Rezin; and after sixty-five years Ephraim shall be broken, so that it will no longer be a people.

9 And the head of Ephraim is Samaria, and the head of Samaria is Romaliah's son. If you do not believe, surely you shall not understand.

10 ¶Moreover the LORD spoke again to Ahaz, saying,

11 Ask for yourself a sign of the LORD your God; ask something in the depth, or in the height above.

12 But Ahaz said, I will not ask, neither will I tempt the LORD my God.

13 And he said, Hear now, O house of David; it is a small thing for you to weary men, but will you weary my God also?

14 Therefore the LORD himself shall give you a sign; Behold, a virgin shall conceive and bear a son, and shall call his name Immanuel.

15 Butter and honey shall he eat, that he may know how to refuse the evil and choose the good.

16 For before the child shall know to refuse the evil and choose the good, the land before whose two kings you are harassed shall be forsaken.

17 ¶The LORD shall bring upon you and upon your people and upon your father's house days that have not come from the day when the king of Assyria parted Ephraim from Judah.

18 And it shall come to pass on that day that the LORD shall whistle for the flies that are in the uttermost part of the rivers of Egypt and for the bees that are in the land of Assyria.

19 And they shall come and shall rest all of them in the valley of Jathoth and in the holes of the rocks and in all the dens.

20 On that day shall the LORD shave [1] with a sharp razor the region that is beyond the river, by the king of Assyria, the head and the hair of the feet; and he shall also shave off the beard.

21 And it shall come to pass in that day that a man shall rear a young cow and two sheep;

22 And it shall come to pass because of the abundance of milk that they shall give he shall eat butter; for butter and honey shall every one eat that is left in the land.

23 And it shall come to pass in that day that every place where there were a thousand vines, worth a thousand silver pieces, shall become briers and thorns.

24 With arrows and with bows shall men come there, because all the land shall be filled with briers and thorns.

25 And on all the hills that once were ploughed with a plough, you shall not go for fear of briers and thorns; but it shall become pasture for cattle and for the treading of sheep.

CHAPTER 8

MOREOVER the LORD said to me, Take a large scroll and write on it plainly, To hasten the captivity, and to record the spoil.

2 And I took to me faithful witnesses to record, Uriah the priest and Zechariah the son of Berechiah.

3 Then I went to the prophetess; and she conceived and bore a son. Then the LORD said to me, Call his name Mesarhib-shabey-otakib-baz, Hasten to take away captives; speed to take away the spoil.

4 For before the child shall know how to cry, My father and my mother. the riches of Damascus and the spoil of Samaria shall be taken away before the king of Assyria.

5 ¶The LORD spoke to me again, saying,

6 Forasmuch as this people have refused the waters of Shiloah, that flow

---

[1] Humiliate by defeats.

softly, and rejoice in **Rezin** and the son of Romaliah;

7 Now therefore, behold, the LORD brings up against them the waters of the river (Euphrates), many and strong, even the king of Assyria and all his glory; and he shall come up over all their brooks, and walk over all their fortified walls;

8 And he shall pass through Judah and shall sweep on and go over; he shall reach even to the neck; and the stretching out of his wings shall fill the breadth of your land, O Immanuel.

9 ¶Tremble, O you people, and you shall be broken in pieces; and give ear, all you of far countries; gird yourselves, and you shall be defeated.

10 Take counsel together, and it shall come to nought; speak the word, and it shall not stand; for God is with us.

11 ¶For the LORD spoke thus to me, as he held me and led me aside that I should not walk in the way of this people, saying,

12 Do not say, A conspiracy, as this people has said conspiracy, neither shall you worship their idols nor be afraid of them.

13 Sanctify the LORD of hosts himself; he is your God and he is your helper.

14 And he shall be for a sanctuary; and for a stone of offense and for a rock of stumbling to both the houses of Israel, for a trap and a snare to the inhabitants of Jerusalem.

15 And many of them shall stumble by them; they shall fall and be broken and be snared and be taken.

16 Bind up the testimony, seal the law,

17 And in my teaching I will wait for the LORD, who has turned away his face from the house of Jacob, and I will look for him.

18 Behold, I and the children whom the LORD has given me are for a sign and for a wonder in Israel from the LORD of hosts, who dwells on mount Zion.

19 ¶And when they shall say to you, Inquire of men who have familiar spirits and of wise men who chirp and mutter, these men are not God's people, who inquire of the dead concerning the living.

20 As for the law and the testimony, if they do not speak according to this word, it is because they do not receive a bribe for it.

21 And they shall pass through the land sorely beset and hungry; and it shall come to pass, that when they shall be hungry, they shall be angry and will curse their king, and their God, and be haughty.

22 And they shall look to the earth; and behold trouble and darkness, tribulation and dimness shall scatter them; but he shall not afflict him who is in distress as in the former time.

CHAPTER 9

THE land of Zebulun and the land of Naphtali have rejoiced; the mighty dominion, the way by the sea, the country beyond the river Jordan, and Galilee of the Gentiles have rejoiced.

2 The people who walked in darkness have seen a great light; those who dwelt in the land of the shadow of death, upon them has the light shined.

3 Thou hast multiplied the people, and thou hast increased its joy; they joy before thee as those who rejoice in the harvest, and as men rejoice when they divide the spoil.

4 For thou hast broken the yoke of his burden and the staff of his shoulder and the rod of his oppressor, as in the days of Midian.

5 For every voice which is heard brings terror and garments rolled in blood; but this shall be for burning and fuel for fire.

6 For to us a child is born, to us a son is given; and the government will be upon his shoulder: and his name is called Wonderful Counsellor, The Mighty One, The Everlasting God, The Prince of Peace.

7 Of the increase of his government and of his peace there shall be no end, upon the throne of David and upon his kingdom, to establish it and to sustain it with justice and with righteousness from henceforth even

for ever. The zeal of the LORD of hosts will perform this.

8 ¶The LORD has sent a word to Jacob, and it has lighted upon Israel.

9 And all the people shall know, even Ephraim and the inhabitants of Samaria, who say in pride and haughtiness of heart,

10 We shall lay bricks and hew stones; the sycamores are cut down, but we will change them into cedars.

11 Therefore the LORD shall cause the adversaries of Rezin to prevail against him, and incite his enemies,

12 The Edomites from the east and the Philistines from the west; and they shall devour Israel with open mouth. For all this his anger is not turned away, but his hand is stretched out still.

13 ¶For the people did not turn to him till they were devoured, neither did they seek the LORD of hosts.

14 Therefore the LORD will cut off from Israel head and tail, tail and head, in one day.

15 The elder and honorable, he is the head; and the prophet who teaches lies, he is the tail.

16 For the leaders of this people shall cause them to err and cause them to sink low.

17 Therefore the LORD shall have no joy in their young men, neither shall he have mercy on their orphans and widows; for all of them are hypocrites and evildoers, and every mouth speaks folly. For all this his anger is not turned away, but his hand is stretched out still.

18 ¶For wickedness burns like the fire; it shall devour the briers and thorns, and shall kindle in the thickets of the forest, and the chosen ones shall roll up like the lifting up of smoke.

19 Through the rebuke of the LORD of hosts the land trembles, and the people shall be as the fuel of the fire; no man shall spare his brother.

20 And he shall snatch on the right hand, and be hungry; and he shall eat on the left hand, and shall not be satisfied; they shall eat every man the flesh of his own kinsmen;

21 Manasseh, Ephraim; and Eph-raim, Manasseh; and they together shall devour Judah. For all this his anger is not turned away, but his hand is stretched out still.

CHAPTER 10

WOE to those who decree unrighteous decrees, and who write unjust decrees;

2 To turn aside the needy from justice and to take away the right from the poor of my people, that they may plunder the widows and that they may rob the fatherless!

3 And what will you do on the day of recompense and in the storm which shall come from afar? To whom will you flee for help? And where will you leave your glory?

4 Without me you shall bow down under the prisoners, and you shall fall under the slain. For all this his anger is not turned away, but his hand is stretched out still.

5 ¶Ho, Assyrian! the rod of my anger, and the staff in their hand is my indignation.

6 I will send him against a hypocritical nation, and against a wrathful people will I give him a charge, to take captives and to take spoil and to tread them down like the mire of the streets.

7 But he does not look so, neither does his heart think so; but it is in his heart to destroy and annihilate nations not a few.

8 For he says, Are not my princes altogether kings?

9 Is not Calno like Carchemish? Is not Hamath like Arpad? Is not Samaria like Damascus?

10 As my hand has found the kingdoms of the idols, and whose graven images did excel those of Jerusalem and of Samaria;

11 And as I have done to Samaria and her idols, so will I do to Jerusalem and her idols.

12 Therefore it shall come to pass, that when the LORD has performed his whole work on mount Zion, and on Jerusalem, I will punish the fruit of the proud heart of the king of Assyria, and the glory of his pride.

13 For he has said, By the strength of my hand I have done it, and by my wisdom; for I am prudent, and I have removed the boundaries of the nations, and I have plundered their wealth, and subjugated the inhabited cities;

14 And my hand has found like a nest the riches of the peoples; and as one gathers eggs that have been forsaken, I have gathered all the earth; and there was none that moved a wing or opened the mouth or chirped.

15 Shall the ax boast itself over him who hews with it? Or shall the saw magnify itself over him who saws with it? Or shall a rod exalt itself over him who lifts it up?

16 Therefore shall the Lord God of hosts send destruction upon his rich ones; and instead of his glory he shall kindle a burning like the burning of a fire.

17 And the light of Israel shall be for a fire, and his Holy One for a flame; and it shall burn and devour his thorns and his briers in one day;

18 And it shall consume the glory of his forest and of his fruitful fields, both soul and body shall perish; and they shall be as if they never had been.

19 And the rest of the trees of his forest shall be so few that a child may write them down.

20 ¶And it shall come to pass in that day that the remnant of Israel, and those who are escaped of the house of Jacob, shall no more again trust upon him that smote them; but they shall trust in the Lord, the Holy One of Israel, in truth.

21 The remnant shall return, even the remnant of Jacob, to the mighty God.

22 For though your people Israel be as the sand of the sea, yet a remnant of them shall return; their number decreased, cut off, but flooded with righteousness.

23 For the Lord God of hosts shall bring destruction and make decrees throughout all the earth.

24 ¶Therefore thus says the Lord of hosts: O my people that dwell in Zion, be not afraid of the Assyrian, who shall smite you with his rod, and shall lift up his staff against you after the manner of Egypt.

25 For yet a very little while, and my indignation shall be accomplished, and my anger because of their destruction.

26 And the Lord of hosts shall stir up a scourge against them according to the slaughter of Midian at mount Horeb; and as his staff was upon the sea, so shall he lift it up after the manner of Egypt.

27 And it shall come to pass in that day that his burden shall be taken away from off your shoulder and his yoke from off your neck, and the yoke shall be destroyed from your neck because of your strength.

28 He has come to Anath, he has passed Megiddo; at Michmash he has laid up his supplies;

29 They have gone over the passage of Gibeah to Beth-bethan; Ramath is afraid; Gibeah of Saul has fled.

30 Lift up your voice, O daughter of Gallim; give ear, O Laish; answer me, O Anathoth.

31 Marmanah has been removed; the inhabitants of Gobin are resisting.

32 As yet he shall remain at Nob that day; he shall shake his hand against the mount of the daughter of Zion and against the hill of Jerusalem.

33 Behold, the Lord God of hosts shall overthrow the glorious ones with might; and the high ones of stature shall be humbled, and the haughty shall be brought down.

34 And he shall cut down the thickets of the forest with iron, and Lebanon with its glory shall fall.

CHAPTER 11

AND there shall come forth a shoot out of the stem of Jesse, and a branch shall grow out of his roots;

2 And he shall be at peace, and the Spirit of the Lord shall rest upon him, the spirit of wisdom and understanding, the spirit of counsel and might, the spirit of knowledge and of the reverence of the Lord;

3 And shall shine forth in the reverence of the Lord; and he shall not judge after that which his eyes see,

neither reprove after that which his ears hear;

4 But with justice shall he judge the poor, and reprove with uprightness for the meek of the earth; and he shall smite the earth with the rod of his mouth, and with the breath of his lips shall he slay the wicked.

5 Righteousness shall be the girdle of his loins, and faithfulness the girdle of his waist.

6 The wolf shall dwell with the lamb, and the leopard shall lie down with the kid; and the calf and the young lion and the ox shall feed together; and a little child shall lead them.

7 And the cow and the bear shall feed together; and their young ones shall grow up together; and the lion shall eat straw like the ox.

8 And the suckling child shall play with the serpent, and the weaned child shall put his hand into the hole of the asp.

9 They shall not hurt nor destroy in all my holy mountain; for the earth shall be full of the knowledge of the LORD as the waters cover the sea.

10 ¶And on that day there shall be a root [1] of Jesse, which shall stand as an ensign to the peoples; to him shall the Gentiles seek; and his rest shall be glorious.

11 And it shall come to pass in that day that the LORD shall set his hand again the second time to recover the remnant of his people which are left from Assyria and from Egypt and from Pathros and from Ethiopia and from Elam and from Seir and from Hamath and from the islands of the sea.

12 And he shall set up an ensign for the nations, and shall assemble the outcasts of Israel, and gather together the dispersed of Judah from the four corners of the earth.

13 The envy also of Ephraim shall depart, and the adversaries of Judah shall be destroyed; Ephraim shall not envy Judah, and Judah shall not oppress Ephraim.

14 But they shall fly upon the shoulder of the Philistines on the sea; [2]

they shall plunder them of the east together; they shall stretch out their hands against Edom and Moab; and the children of Ammon shall obey them.

15 And the LORD shall utterly dry up the sea of Egypt; and with his mighty wind he shall stretch his hand over the river, and shall smite it into seven streams, so that men may cross through it dryshod.

16 And there shall be a highway for the remnant of his people which shall be left from Assyria; as it was in the day that Israel came up from the land of Egypt.

CHAPTER 12

AND you shall say in that day, O LORD, I will praise thee; though thou wast angry with me, thine anger is turned away, and thou hast comforted me.

2 Behold, in God my Saviour I will trust, and will not be afraid; for the LORD is my strength and my song; and he has become my salvation.

3 Therefore with joy shall you draw water out of the spring of salvation.

4 And you shall say in that day, Praise the LORD, call upon his name, declare his doings among the Gentiles, make mention that his name is exalted.

5 Sing to the LORD; for he has done excellent things; this is known in all the earth.

6 Rejoice and give praise, O inhabitant of Zion; for great is he that is in your midst, the Holy One of Israel.

CHAPTER 13

THE prophecy concerning the fall of Babylon, which Isaiah the son of Amoz saw.

2 Lift up a banner on high mountains, raise the voice to them, wave the hand, that they may enter the gates of the princes.

3 I have commanded my sanctified ones, I have called the mighty ones in my anger, even them that became strong with my excellency.

4 The noise of tumult on the mountains, like as of many peoples; a tu-

---

[1] An heir.   [2] Rowing boats with Philistine galley slaves.

multuous noise of the kingdoms of nations gathered together; the LORD of hosts is performing wonders.

5 Warriors are coming from afar, and from the end of heaven, even the LORD and the weapons of his indignation, to destroy the whole land.

6 ¶Howl; for the day of the LORD is at hand; it shall come as a plunder which is made suddenly.

7 Therefore shall all hands be faint, and every man's heart shall melt;

8 And they shall be afraid; terror and pangs shall take hold of them; they shall be in pain as a woman in travail; they shall be amazed one at another; their faces shall be as flames.

9 Behold, the day of the LORD comes, which has no remedy, cruel both with wrath and fierce anger, to make the earth a desolation; and he shall destroy the sinners thereof out of it.

10 For the stars of heaven and their constellations shall not give their light; the sun shall be darkened in its rising, and the moon shall not cause its light to shine.

11 And I will punish the world for its evil, and the wicked for their iniquity; and I will cause the arrogancy of the proud to cease, and will bring low the haughtiness of the mighty.

12 I will make a man more precious than gold; even a man than the gold of Ophir.

13 Therefore I will shake the heavens, and the earth shall be moved out of its place, in the rebuke of the LORD of hosts, in the day of his fierce anger.

14 And they shall be like gazelles when they flee, and like sheep that have no one to gather them; every man shall turn to his own people, and every one flee to his own land.

15 Every one that is found shall be thrust through; and every one that escapes shall fall by the sword.

16 Their children shall be dashed to pieces before their eyes; their houses shall be spoiled and their wives ravished.

17 Behold, I will stir up the Medes against them, who have no regard for silver, and have no delight in gold.

18 The bows of young men shall be broken in pieces; and they shall have no pity on the fruit of the womb; their eyes shall not spare children.

19 ¶And Babylon, the glory of the kingdoms, the beauty of the Chaldean's excellency, shall be as when God overthrew Sodom and Gomorrah.

20 It shall never be inhabited, neither shall it be dwelt in from generation to generation; neither shall the Arabians encamp there; neither shall the shepherds make their folds there.

21 But wild beasts shall lie there; and their houses shall be full of doleful creatures; and ostriches shall dwell there, and satyrs shall dance there.

22 And the screech-owls shall cry in their palaces, and jackals in their pleasant temples; its time is soon to come, and its days shall not be prolonged.

CHAPTER 14

FOR the LORD will have mercy on Jacob, and will yet choose Israel, and will set them in their own land; and strangers shall accompany them, and they shall add to the house of Jacob.

2 And the Gentiles shall take them and bring them to their place; and the house of Israel shall possess them in the land of the LORD for menservants and women-servants; and they shall take them captive, whose captives they were; and they shall rule over their oppressors.

3 And it shall come to pass in the day that the LORD shall give you rest from your sorrow and from your anger and from the hard bondage wherein you were made to serve.

4 ¶You shall take up this proverb against the king of Babylon, and say, How has the ruler ceased! the zealous one ceased!

5 The LORD has broken the staff of the wicked and the sceptre of the rulers.

6 He who smote the peoples in wrath, smiting without instruction, who chastised the peoples in anger and persecuted them without pity.

7 The whole earth is at rest and is quiet; they break forth into singing.

8 Yea, the fir trees rejoice over you, and the cedars of Lebanon, saying, Since you are felled, no hewer is come up to cut us down.

9 Sheol beneath is murmuring at your coming; it stirs up against you all the mighty men, even all the rulers of the earth whom you overthrew from their thrones.

10 All the kings of the nations shall answer and say to you, Are you also become weak as we? Are you become like us?

11 Your pomp is brought down to Sheol, the noise of your harps is dead; the dust is spread under you, and the worms cover you.

12 How are you fallen from heaven! howl in the morning! for you have fallen down to the ground, O reviler of the nations.

13 For you have said in your heart, I will ascend into heaven, I will exalt my throne above the stars of God; I will dwell also upon the high mountains in the outer regions of the north.

14 I will ascend above the heights of the clouds; I will be like the most High.

15 From henceforth you shall be brought down to Sheol, to the bottom of the pit.

16 Those who see you shall stare at you and consider you, saying, Is this the man who made the earth to tremble, who shook kingdoms;

17 Who made the world as a wilderness and destroyed its cities; who did not free his prisoners?

18 All the kings of the nations, even all of them, lie in glory, every one in his own house.[1]

19 But you are cast out of your grave like an abominable person, and as the raiment of those that are slain, thrust through by the sword, that go down to the stones of the pit; as corpses trodden under foot.

20 You shall not rejoice with them in the grave, because you have destroyed your land and slain your people; the offspring of the evildoer shall never rise again.

21 Prepare slaughter for his children for the iniquity of their fathers; that they do not rise, nor possess the land, nor fill the face of the world with war.

22 For I will rise up against them, says the LORD of hosts, and will cut off from Babylon the name, its offspring, the family, and its generation, says the LORD.

23 I will also make it a possession for owls, and pools of water; and I will sweep it with the broom of destruction, says the LORD of hosts.

24 ¶The LORD of hosts has sworn, saying, Surely as I have thought, so shall it come to pass; and as I have purposed, so shall it stand;

25 I will break the Assyrian in my land, and upon my mountains tread him under foot; then his yoke shall depart from off them, and his burden depart from off their shoulders.

26 This is the end that is purposed against all the earth; and this is the land that is stretched out against all the nations.

27 For the LORD of hosts has purposed, and who can disannul it? And his hand is stretched out, and who shall turn it back?

28 The conquest of Philistia. In the year that King Ahaz died, came this burden.

29 ¶Rejoice not, whole Philistia, because the rod of him that smote you is broken; for out of the serpent's root shall come forth a viper, and its offspring shall be a fiery flying serpent.

30 And the first-born of the poor shall feed, and the needy shall lie down in safety; and I will kill your root with famine, and your remnant I shall slay.

31 Howl, O city; cry, O city; whole Philistia is in confusion; for there shall come from the north a smoke,[2] and none shall be left in their feasts.

32 What shall one then answer the messengers of the nations? That the LORD has founded Zion, and the poor of his people shall take refuge in it.

CHAPTER 15

THE prophecy concerning the fall of Moab. Because in the night the

---

[1] Sepulcher.   [2] Aramaic idiom, *a disaster*.

city of Moab is plundered and brought to silence; because in the night the defenses of Moab are despoiled and brought to silence;

2 They have gone up to the house of Ribon, to the high places, to weep; Moab shall howl over Nebo and over Medeba; on all their heads shall be baldness, and every beard cut off.

3 In their streets they shall gird themselves with sackcloth; on the housetops and in their streets every one shall howl, weeping vehemently.

4 Heshbon shall cry, and Elealeh; their voice shall be heard as far as Jazoth; therefore the armed soldiers of Moab shall cry out; his soul shall howl for him.

5 My heart shall cry out for Moab; they shall howl as they flee to Zoar; Moab was strong like a three year old heifer; for by the ascent of Luhith they shall go up with weeping; and in the way of Horonaim they shall raise up a cry of destruction.

6 For the waters of Nimrim shall be desolate; for the vegetation is withered away, and the green grass is dried up, there is no green thing.

7 Therefore what was left is gone, and that which they have stored shall they carry away over the brook of willows.

8 For the cry is gone round about the borders of Moab; the howling thereof as far as Eglaim, and the howling thereof to Beer-elim.

9 For the waters of Ribon are full of blood; and I will bring more upon Ribon, and I will plot against those who escape of Moab, and against the remnant of the land.

CHAPTER 16

THE prophecy concerning the rest of the land. I will send the son of the ruler of the land from the rock city [1] of the wilderness, to the mount of the daughter of Zion.

2 And he shall be like a bird that changes its nest, so the daughters of Moab shall be deserted at the fords of Arnon.

3 Take counsel, execute judgment; make your shadow as the night in the midst of the noonday; hide the outcasts; betray not him that wanders.

4 Let the outcasts of Moab dwell with you; be a shelter to them from the face of the spoiler; for the destroyer is at an end, and the spoiler ceases, the oppressors are consumed out of the land.

5 In mercy shall a throne be established, and he shall sit upon it, in truth in the tabernacle of David, a judge who seeks justice and hastens righteousness.

6 ¶We have heard of the majesty of Moab; he is very proud, even of his haughtiness and his wrath; his augurers so predict concerning him.

7 Therefore shall Moab howl; every one shall howl for Moab, for the foundations of the walls are destroyed; surely they groan like the sick.

8 For the fields of Heshbon languish, and the vine of Sibmah; the mighty men of the nations have broken down the branches thereof, they are come as far as Jazer, they wandered through the wilderness; its shoots spread out, they are gone over the sea.

9 ¶Therefore I will cause you to weep with the weeping of Jazer for the vine of Sibmah; I will water you with your tears, O Heshbon, and Elealeh; for an oppressor has come against your harvest and the gathering of your grapes.

10 And gladness and joy are taken away out of the plentiful field; and in the vineyards there shall be no rejoicing, neither shall there be shouting: nor shall they tread out wine in the press; nor shall men tread out wine with their feet; for I have made the vine treaders to cease.

11 Therefore my heart shall lament like a harp for Moab, and my soul for the fortified walls which will be destroyed.

12 ¶And it shall come to pass, when it is seen that Moab is weary on the high places, that he shall come to the sanctuary to pray; but he shall not prevail.

13 This is the word that the LORD

---

[1] Petra, rock city.

has spoken concerning Moab since that time.

14 But now the LORD has spoken, saying, Within three years, as the years of a hireling, the glory of Moab shall be despised, with all that great multitude of his people; and the remnant shall be very small and feeble.

CHAPTER 17

THE prophecy concerning the fall of Damascus. Behold, Damascus shall cease to be a city, and it shall be a ruinous heap.

2 The cities of Adoer shall be forsaken; they shall be for flocks which shall lie down in them, and none shall harm them.

3 The might also shall cease from Ephraim, and the kingdom from Damascus, and the remnant of Ephraim will be like the glory of the children of Israel, says the LORD of hosts.

4 And in that day it shall come to pass that the glory of Jacob shall wane, and the fatness of his flesh shall wax lean.

5 And it shall be as when the reaper harvests standing sheaves, and gathers the ears in his arms; and it shall be as he that gathers ears in the valley of Rephaim.

6 ¶Yet gleaning shall be left in it, as the shaking of an olive tree, two or three berries in the top of the uppermost bough, four or five on the outermost branches thereof, says the LORD God of Israel.

7 In that day a man shall trust in his Maker, and his eyes will look to the Holy One of Israel.

8 And he shall not trust in the altars, the work of his hands and the work which his fingers have made, neither shall he look at the idols or the images.

9 ¶In that day shall his strong cities be like a desolate well, and like an emirate [1] which was left destitute before the children of Israel; so you will become a desolation.

10 Because you have forgotten the God your Saviour, and have not been mindful of the rock of your strength; therefore you shall plant pleasant plants and shall graft them with strange branches;

11 On the day that you plant them, they shall put forth blossoms, and in the morning your seed shall flourish, but the harvest shall be a ruin in the day of grief and of desperate sorrow.

12 ¶Woe to the armies of many people, which make a noise like the roaring of the seas! And to the rushing of nations, that rush like the rushing of mighty waters!

13 He shall rebuke them, and they shall flee far off and shall be chased like the chaff of the mountains before the wind, and like dry grass before the whirlwind.

14 And behold at eveningtide violence; and before the morning they are no more. This is the portion of our oppressor, and the lot of those who plunder us.

CHAPTER 18

WOE to the land of shadowing wings which is beyond the rivers of Ethiopia;

2 That sends ambassadors by the sea, even in vessels of papyrus upon the waters, saying, Go, you swift messengers, to a nation who will be plundered and uprooted, to a nation whose strength was within it hitherto; to a people who will be dishonored and trodden down, whose land the rivers have ruined!

3 All you inhabitants of the world, and dwellers on the earth, you shall see when the ensign shall be lifted up upon the mountains; and when he blows a trumpet, you shall hear.

4 For thus the LORD said to me: I will rest, and I will look from my dwelling place as midday heat upon the river and as a cloud of dew in the day of harvest.

5 For before the harvest, when the bud has perished and the grape is ripening in the flower, he shall both cut off the lean shoots with pruning hooks and take away and shake off the branches.

6 They shall be left together to the fowls of the mountains and to the beasts of the earth; and the birds shall

---

[1] A principality or a sheikdom.

gather upon them, and all the wild beasts of the earth, shall devour them.

7 ¶At that time presents shall be brought to the LORD of hosts from a people plundered and uprooted, whose strength was within him hitherto; from a people dishonored and trodden under foot, whose land the rivers have spoiled, to the place of the name of the LORD of hosts, even to mount Zion.

CHAPTER 19

THE prophecy concerning the fall of Egypt. Behold, the LORD is riding upon swift clouds, and comes into Egypt; and the idols of Egypt shall be moved at his presence, and the heart of the Egyptians shall melt in the midst of it.

2 And I will stir up Egyptian against Egyptian; and they shall fight every one against his brother, and every one against his neighbor; city against city, and kingdom against kingdom.

3 And the spirit of the Egyptian shall fail in the midst thereof; and I will blot out their counsel; and they shall inquire of idols and of the sorcerers and of those who have familiar spirits and of wizards.

4 And I will deliver the Egyptians into the hands of the cruel Medes; and a fierce king shall rule over them, says the LORD of hosts.

5 And they shall cut off the water from the sea, and the river [1] shall be wasted and dried up.

6 And they shall divert the waters of the rivers, and shall diminish the great rivers; the reeds and rushes and papyrus shall wither.

7 The rushes by the river, and by the mouth of the river, and everything sown by the river shall wither, be driven away, and be no more.

8 The fishermen also shall lament, and all who cast hooks into the river shall mourn, and those who spread nets upon the water shall languish.

9 Moreover those who work in cotton, and those who comb cotton and weave with joy, shall be confounded.

10 And all those who make strong

drink for the drinking of the people shall be humiliated.

11 ¶Surely the princes of Zoan have become fools, the wise counsellors of King Pharaoh give foolish counsel; how can you say to Pharaoh, We are wise men, the sons of the ancient kings?

12 Where are your wise men? Let them tell you now, and let them know what the LORD of hosts has purposed against Egypt.

13 The princes of Zoan have become fools, the princes of Memphis have become haughty and have deceived Egypt, even the foundation of her families.

14 The LORD has mingled a spirit of deceit within her; and it has caused the Egyptian to err in all his works, as a drunken man staggers in his vomit.

15 Neither shall there be any leader for the Egyptians who can make head or tail of it, or tail or head.

16 On that day the Egyptian shall be like a woman, and he shall be afraid and tremble because of the shaking of the hand of the LORD of hosts, which he shakes against him.

17 And the land of Judah shall be a terror to the Egyptian; every one who makes mention of it shall be filled with dread because of the counsel of the LORD of hosts which he has determined against the Egyptian.

18 ¶In that day there shall be five cities in the land of Egypt which speak the language of Canaan and swear by the LORD of hosts; one of them shall be called Haris, the city of destruction.

19 On that day there shall be an altar to the LORD in the midst of the land of Egypt, and a pillar at its border to the LORD.

20 And it shall be for a sign and for a witness to the LORD of hosts in the land of Egypt; for they shall cry to the LORD because of the oppressors, and he shall send them a saviour and a judge, and he shall deliver them.

21 And the LORD shall be known

---

[1] Nile.

to the Egyptians, and the Egyptians shall know the LORD in that day, and shall offer sacrifices and oblations; yea, they shall vow a vow to the LORD and perform it.

22 And the LORD shall smite the Egyptians; he shall smite and heal them; and they shall return to the LORD, and he shall answer them and shall heal them.

23 ¶In that day there shall be a highway from Egypt to Assyria and from Assyria to Egypt, and the Assyrian shall come into Egypt and the Egyptian into Assyria, and the Egyptians shall serve the Assyrians.

24 In that day Israel shall be the third with Egyptians and with Assyrians, even a blessing in the midst of the land,

25 Whom the LORD of hosts shall bless, saying, Blessed be Egypt my people and Assyria the work of my hands and Israel my heritage.

CHAPTER 20

IN the year that Tartan came to Ashdod (when Sargon the king of Assyria sent him) and fought against Ashdod and took it,

2 At that time the LORD spoke by Isaiah the son of Amoz, saying, Go and loose the sackcloth from off your loins and put off your shoes from your feet. And he did so, walking naked and barefoot.

3 And the Lord said, As my servant Isaiah has walked naked and barefoot, so shall there be signs and wonders for three years upon Egypt and upon Ethiopia;

4 So shall the king of Assyria lead away the Egyptians prisoners, and the Ethiopians captives, young and old, naked and barefoot, with their buttocks uncovered, to the shame of Egypt.

5 And they shall be defeated and ashamed of Ethiopia their trust, and of Egypt their glory.

6 And the inhabitants of this isle shall say on that day, Behold, here is our trust, to whom we fled for help to be delivered from the king of Assyria; and how shall we escape?

CHAPTER 21

THE prophecy concerning the desert of the sea. As a whirlwind from the south, sweeping through from the wilderness; so it comes from a far off land.

2 A grievous vision is declared to me: the oppressor oppresses, and the plunderer plunders. Go up, O Elam, and the mountains of Media; all the sighing thereof I have made to cease.

3 Therefore my loins are filled with pain; pangs have taken hold upon me, as the pangs of a woman in travail; I was dismayed so that I could not hear, I was terrified so that I could not see.

4 My heart failed, pangs made me quake; the beauty of my pleasures has been turned into terror to me.

5 Prepare the tables, watch in the watchtowers, eat, drink; arise, O princes, and anoint the shields.

6 For thus has the LORD said to me: Go, set a watchman, that he may declare what he sees.

7 And he saw a chariot with a couple of horsemen, a rider on an ass and a rider on a camel; and he hearkened diligently with much heed;

8 Then the watchman cried into my ears, saying, I the LORD stand continually in the daytime, and I stand upon my watchtower every night.

9 And, behold, there came a man from the pair of horsemen. And he answered and said, Babylon is fallen, is fallen; and all the graven images of her gods are broken to the ground.

10 There is no one to reap and no one to thresh; that which I have heard of the LORD God of Israel, I have declared to you.

11 ¶The prophecy concerning Dumah. He called to me from Seir, Watchman, what of the night? Watchman, what of the night?

12 The watchman says, The morning comes, and also the night; if you will inquire, inquire; you will come back again.

13 ¶The prophecy concerning Arabia. In the evening you shall lodge in the forest, in the highway of Dornim.

14 Meet the thirsty, bring water, O

you inhabitants of the land of the south! Meet those who are fleeing with your bread.

15 For they have fled from the swords, from the drawn sword and from the bent bow and from the grievousness of war.

16 For thus has the LORD said to me: Within a year, according to the years of a hireling, all the glory of Kedar shall fail;

17 And the residue of the number of archers, the mighty men of the children of Kedar, shall be diminished; for the LORD God of Israel has spoken it.

CHAPTER 22

THE prophecy concerning the valley of vision. What do you see here, that you are all gone up to the housetops?

2 The city is full of tumult, the mighty city is full of noise; your slain men are not slain with the sword nor dead in battle.

3 All your princes are fled together, they are surrounded by the archers; all that were found in you are bound together; they have fled to far off places.

4 Therefore said I, Leave me alone, I will weep bitterly; trouble not yourself to comfort me, because of the destruction of the daughter of my people.

5 For it is a day of trouble and of treading down and of weeping before the LORD God of hosts in the valley of vision; they have surveyed the walls, and shouted upon the mountains.

6 And Elam bore the quiver with the chariots of men and horsemen, and the shields were seen on the wall.

7 And it shall come to pass that your choicest valleys shall be full of chariots, and the horsemen shall set themselves in array at the gates.

8 ¶And the defenses of Judah shall be laid bare, and you shall see on that day the armour of the house of the forest.

9 You have seen also the breaches of the city of David, that they are many; and you have gathered to-gether the waters of the lower pool.

10 And you have supplied the houses of Jerusalem with water, and you have broken down the houses to fortify the walls.

11 And you made ditches between the two walls for the water of the old pool; but you have not looked to the maker thereof, neither had respect to him who fashioned it long ago.

12 And in that day the LORD God of hosts called to weeping and to mourning and to baldness and to girding with sackcloth;

13 And behold joy and gladness, slaughtering oxen and killing sheep, eating meat and drinking wine; let us eat and drink, for tomorrow we shall die.

14 And it was revealed in my ears by the LORD of hosts, saying, Surely this iniquity shall not be purged from you till you die, says the LORD God of hosts.

15 ¶Thus says the LORD God of hosts: Go, get to this treasurer, even to Shebna, who is over the household, and say to him,

16 What do you here? And what have you here, that you have hewn a tomb for yourself, as he who hews for himself a tomb on high and carves a habitation for himself in a rock?

17 Behold, O man, the LORD will surely cast you away, and will surely forsake you.

18 And he shall afflict you like the affliction of a company of soldiers besieged in a fortress from which there is no escape; there shall you die, and there the chariots of your glory shall be the shame of your master's house.

19 And I will take away your glory, and will cast you down from your position.

20 ¶And it shall come to pass in that day, says the LORD, I will call my servant Eliakim the son of Hilkiah;

21 And I will clothe him with your robe and will gird him with your girdle, and I will commit your government into his hand; and he shall be a father to the inhabitants of Je-

rusalem and to the house of Judah.

22 And I will place upon his shoulder the keys of the house of David; so he shall open and none shall shut, and he shall shut and none shall open.

23 And I will fasten him as a nail in a sure place; and he shall be for a glorious throne to his father's house.

24 And they shall hang upon him all the glory of his father's house, both the honorable men and the glorious men, and all small vessels, from instruments of music to the harp.

25 In that day, says the LORD of hosts, shall the nail that is fastened in a sure place be removed and be overthrown and fall; and the burden that was upon it shall be destroyed; for the LORD has spoken it.

CHAPTER 23

THE prophecy concerning the fall of Tyre. Howl, O ships of Tarshish! for he who brings merchandise is plundered; from the land of China the news has been revealed to us.

2 Be still, O inhabitants of the islands, the merchants of Zidon that passed over the sea.

3 Your commerce is on many waters, O offspring of merchants; the harvest of the river is her revenue, and she is a mart of nations.

4 Be ashamed, O Zidon; for the sea has spoken, even the strength of the sea, saying, I have neither been in travail nor have I given birth to children, neither have I reared young men nor brought up virgins.

5 When the news reaches Egypt, they will be in pain over the report of Tyre.

6 Pass over to Tarshish; howl, O you inhabitants of the islands.

7 Is this your mighty city, whose antiquity is of ancient days? Her own feet shall carry her afar off to sojourn.

8 Who has taken this counsel against Tyre, the crowning city, whose merchants are princes, whose traders are the honorable of the earth?

9 The LORD of hosts has purposed it, to bring to an end the glory of every mighty man and to bring into dishonor all the honorable men of the earth.

10 Pass through your land like a river, O daughter of Tarshish; there is no one to drive you away.

11 He stretched out his hand over the sea, he shook the kingdoms; the LORD has given a commandment against Canaan to destroy its mighty men.

12 And he said, You shall no more become mighty, O you oppressed virgin, daughter of Zidon; arise, pass over to China; there also you shall have no rest.

13 Behold the land of the Chaldeans; this is the people, and not the Assyrians, who destroyed it; they appointed spies who spied on her palaces, and they brought it to ruin.

14 Howl, O ships of Tarshish; for your stronghold is plundered.

15 And it shall come to pass in that day that Tyre shall be forgotten for seventy years, according to the days of one king; after the end of seventy years they shall sing to Tyre a harlot's song.

16 Take a harp, go about the city, O you harlot that has been forgotten; play sweet melodies, sing many songs, that you may be remembered.

17 ¶And it shall come to pass at the end of seventy years that the LORD will visit Tyre, and she shall turn to her traffic and commit fornications with all the kingdoms that are upon the face of the earth.

18 And her merchandise and her hire shall be sanctified to the LORD; it shall not be treasured nor laid up; for her merchandise shall be for them that dwell before the LORD, to eat abundantly, and replace their old garments with new ones.

CHAPTER 24

BEHOLD, the LORD shall destroy the earth and lay it waste and turn it upside down and scatter its inhabitants.

2 And it shall be, as with the people, so with the priest; as with the servant, so with his master; as with the maid, so with her mistress; as with the

buyer, so with the seller; as with the lender, so with the borrower; as with the creditor, so with the debtor.

3 The land shall be utterly destroyed and utterly spoiled; for the LORD has spoken this word.

4 The earth howls and sits in mourning, the world wails and sits in mourning, the haughty people of the earth lament.

5 The earth also is defiled like its inhabitants, because they have transgressed the law, changed the ordinance, and nullified the everlasting covenant.

6 Therefore the earth shall sit in mourning, and all its inhabitants shall be condemned; therefore all the inhabitants of the earth shall be destroyed, and a few men shall be left.

7 The grain mourns, the vine languishes, all the merry-hearted sigh.

8 The mirth of the timbrels has ceased, the noise of those that rejoice has ended, the joy of the harp is over.

9 They shall not drink wine with a song; strong drink shall be bitter to those who drink it.

10 The city is plundered, every wine cellar is shut up, so that no one may come in.

11 There is a crying for wine in the streets; all joy has ended, the mirth of the land is gone.

12 The city is left in desolation, and its gates are broken with destruction.

13 ¶For thus it shall be in the midst of the land among the peoples, it shall be as the shaking of an olive tree and as the gleaning of grapes when the vintage is done.

14 They shall lift up their voice, they shall sing for the majesty of the LORD, they shall cry aloud from the sea.

15 Therefore glorify the LORD with a song, even the name of the LORD God of Israel in the islands of the sea.

16 ¶From the uttermost parts of the earth we have heard songs, even the glory of the righteous, saying, It is a mystery to me, it is a mystery to me, woe to me, the wicked have dealt

¹ Floods.

treacherously, yea, the wicked have dealt very treacherously.

17 Fear and the pit and the snare are upon you, O inhabitants of the earth.

18 And it shall come to pass that he who flees from the noise of the fear shall fall into the pit; and he who comes up out of the midst of the pit shall be caught in the snare; for the fountains ¹ from on high are open, and the foundations of the earth do shake.

19 The earth is utterly broken down, the earth is utterly moved, the earth is staggering exceedingly.

20 The earth shall reel to and fro like a drunkard and shall be shaken like a booth, and its transgression shall be heavy upon it; and it shall fall and not rise again.

21 And it shall come to pass in that day that the LORD shall punish the host of the lofty ones that are on high, and the kings of the earth upon the earth.

22 And they shall be gathered together as prisoners are gathered in the pit, and shall be shut up in the prison, and after many days they shall be saved.

23 Then the moon shall be confounded and the sun ashamed, for the LORD of hosts shall reign on mount Zion and in Jerusalem, and will be glorified in the presence of his saints.

CHAPTER 25

O LORD, thou art my God; I will praise thy name; for thou hast done wonderful things, and given faithful counsel from afar, amen.

2 For thou hast reduced a city to a heap, the fortified city to a ruin; the palace of the strangers and the city are never to be built again.

3 Therefore many peoples shall praise thee, the city of the mighty nations shall worship thee.

4 For thou hast been a strength to the poor, a helper to the needy in his distress, a refuge from the storm, a shade from the heat; for the blast of

the mighty ones is as a storm against the wall.

5 Thou shalt blot out the pride of aliens as the shadow at noonday, and as the heat is blotted out by the shade of a cloud; thus the branch [1] of the mighty ones shall be humbled.

6 ¶And on this mountain shall the LORD of hosts make for all peoples a lavish feast, a feast of old and rich wines, from the things that belong to our heavenly Saviour and the Mighty One.

7 And he will destroy on this mountain the prestige of the ruler who ruled over all the peoples, because of the slaughter which was made among all the peoples.

8 He will swallow up death in victory for ever; and the LORD God of hosts will wipe away the tears from off all faces; and the reproach of his people he shall take away from off all the earth; for the LORD has spoken it.

9 ¶And it shall be said on that day, Lo, this is the LORD our God; we have waited for him, and he shall save us; this is the LORD our God, we have waited for him, we will be glad and rejoice in his salvation.

10 For on this mountain shall the hand of the LORD rest, and Moab shall be trodden down under him, even as straw is trodden down with the threshing sled.

11 And he shall spread forth his hands in the midst of them, as a swimmer spreads forth his hands to swim; and he shall bring down their pride together with the spoils of their hands.

12 And the fortress of treason of your rebellious men and your strong walls he shall tear down, lay low, and bring to the ground, even to the dust.

CHAPTER 26

IN that day shall this song be sung in the land of Judah: O city whose salvation has prevailed, build the walls and the bulwarks;

2 Open the gates, that the righteous peoples who keep faith and that the truth may enter in.

3 Thou wilt keep us in perfect peace, for in thee we have trusted, O LORD, for ever and ever.

4 For the LORD God is an everlasting strength;

5 ¶He brings down those that dwell on high; the lofty city, he shall lay it low, even to the ground; he brings it even to the dust.

6 The foot shall tread it down, even the feet of the poor and the steps of the needy.

7 The way of the humble is straight; the path of the righteous is straight and level.

8 Yea, in the way of thy judgments, O LORD, have we waited for thee; the desire of our soul is for thy name, and to remembrance of thee.

9 My soul has desired thee in the night; yea, with my spirit within me will I seek thee early; for when thy judgments are in the earth, the inhabitants of the world will learn righteousness.

10 The wicked has gone far off that he may not learn righteousness; chastisement in the land brings correction; the wicked shall not behold the majesty of the LORD.

11 O LORD, when thy hand is lifted up, they will not see; but they shall see and be ashamed for the zeal of the people; yea, let the fire of the oven devour thine enemies.

12 ¶O LORD, thou wilt give us peace; for thou also hast wrought all our works for us.

13 O LORD our God, other lords besides thee have had dominion over us; but thy name alone will we mention;

14 For they do not raise the dead, they do not raise the mighty men; therefore thou hast visited and destroyed them, and made all their memory to perish.

15 Thou hast increased the nation, O LORD, thou hast increased the nation; thou hast removed it afar and scattered it to all the ends of the earth.

16 O LORD, in distress have they sought thee, and in siege they muttered the incantation invoking thy discipline.

17 Like a woman with child, who

[1] Heir.

draws near the time of her delivery, and is in pain, and cries out in her pangs; so have we been in thy sight, O Lord.

18 We have been with child, we have been in pain like those who brought forth wind; save us lest we perish in the earth, lest the inhabitants of the world come to an end.

19 Thy dead men shall live, their dead bodies shall arise. Those who dwell in the dust shall awake and sing, for thy dew is a dew of light, and the land of the giants thou shalt overthrow.

20 ¶Come, my people, enter into your chambers and shut your doors behind you; hide yourselves as it were for a little time, until my indignation has passed away.

21 For, behold, the Lord is coming out of his place to punish the inhabitants of the earth for their iniquity; and the earth also shall disclose her blood, and shall no more cover her slain.

CHAPTER 27

IN that day the Lord with his hard and great and strong sword shall punish Leviathan, the piercing serpent, even Leviathan that crooked serpent; and he shall slay the dragon that is in the sea.

2 In that day sing to Israel of a vineyard of wine.

3 I the Lord do keep it; I will water it continually; I will visit it and keep it night and day.

4 You have no hedge; who then did set in you the briers and the thorns? I will blow at the vineyard from near and will burn it together.

5 Or let Israel take hold of my strength, and I will make peace for him, peace will I give him.

6 He shall cause those that come of Jacob to take root; Israel shall blossom and bud and fill the face of the world with fruit.

7 ¶Has the Lord smitten the oppressor as he smote those who smote him? Or is he slain according to the slaughter of those who are slain by him?

8 In measure by which he has measured, will you judge him; in that which he has devised, in fierce anger on a day of blasting heat.

9 By this, therefore, shall the iniquity of Jacob be forgiven; and with all this fruit his sin will be taken away; when he makes all the stones of the altar as chalk-stones that are broken in pieces; likewise, the images and idols shall not stand up.

10 For the strong city shall be forlorn and deserted and forsaken and left desolate like a wilderness; there shall the calf feed, and there shall he lie down and consume its grass.

11 When its boughs are withered, they shall be broken off; the women come and set them on fire; for it is a people of no understanding; therefore he who made them will not have mercy on them, and he who formed them will show them no favor.

12 ¶And it shall come to pass in that day that the Lord shall stir up the people from the channel of the river Euphrates to the river of Egypt, and you shall be gathered one to another, O children of Israel!

13 And it shall come to pass in that day, the great trumpet shall be blown, and those who were lost in the land of Egypt and those who were scattered in the land of Assyria shall come in and worship the Lord in the land of the Lord, even on his holy mountain in Jerusalem.

CHAPTER 28

WOE to the crown of pride, to the drunkards of Ephraim, and woe to the shameful diadem of the strength of his glory, which dominates at the entrance of the fertile valley of those that are overcome with wine!

2 Behold, the strength and the might of the Lord are like a storm of hail and like a destroying whirlwind, and as a flood of mighty waters overflowing; I will give rest to this land by your hands:

3 The crown of the proud and of the drunkards of Ephraim shall be trodden under foot;

4 And the shameful garland of the strength of his glory, which dominates at the entrance of the fertile val-

ley, shall be as the firstfruits before the summer, which he who sees it picks up at once and devours.

5 ¶In that day shall the LORD of hosts be for a crown of glory and for a diadem of beauty to the remnant of his people,

6 And for a spirit of justice to him that sits in judgment, and for strength to those who turn away the battle from the gate.

7 ¶But these also have erred with wine, and with strong drink are gone astray; the priests and the prophets have erred with strong drink, they are overcome with wine, they stagger with strong drink, they err in judgment with drunkenness, they eat immoderately.

8 For all tables are full of vomit and filthiness, so that there is no place clean.

9 ¶To whom shall he teach knowledge? And whom shall he make to understand the report? Those who are weaned from the milk and drawn from the breasts.

10 For filth is upon filth, filth upon filth; vomit upon vomit, vomit upon vomit; a little here, a little there;

11 For with a difficult speech and with an alien tongue will he speak to this people.

12 For I have said to them, This is the place of my rest, wherewith I may cause the weary to rest; and this is the place of tranquillity; but they would not listen.

13 So the word of the LORD was to them filth upon filth, filth upon filth, vomit upon vomit, vomit upon vomit; a little here, a little there; that they might return and fall backward and be broken and snared and taken.

14 ¶Therefore hear the word of the LORD, O you scornful men, who rule this people that is in Jerusalem:

15 Because you have said, We have made a covenant with death, and with Sheol we have made an agreement; when the overflowing scourge shall pass through, it shall not come to us; for we have placed our hope in lies, and under falsehood we have hid ourselves;

16 ¶Therefore thus says the LORD

God: Behold, I lay in Zion a foundation, a stone, a tried stone, a precious corner stone, a sure foundation; he who believes shall not be afraid.

17 And I will make justice to the measuring line, and righteousness to the plummet; and the hail shall sweep away the refuge of lies, and the waters shall overflow the hiding place.

18 ¶And your covenant with death shall be disannulled, and your agreement with Sheol shall not stand; when the overflowing scourge shall pass through, then you shall be trodden down by it.

19 From the time that it passes through, it shall take you; for morning by morning shall it pass over, by day and by night; and it shall be a terror only to understand the report.

20 For the cloth is too short, and the warp grows weak and is insufficient for a garment.

21 For the LORD shall rise up as in a mountain pass, he shall be wroth as in the valley of Gibeon, that he may do his works, his strange works, and bring to pass his acts, his strange acts.

22 Now therefore do not mock, lest your chastisement be severe; for I have heard from the LORD of hosts that he will bring destruction and judgment upon the whole earth.

23 ¶Give ear and hear my voice; hearken and hear my speech.

24 Does the plowman plow all day to sow? Does he open and harrow his ground?

25 Does he not, after he has leveled its surface, scatter the dill and sow cummin, and put in wheat and barley, and rye in its borders?

26 For his God does instruct him to discretion, and does teach him.

27 For dill is not threshed under the feet of oxen, nor is a threshing instrument turned about upon cummin, but dill is beaten out with a staff, and cummin with a rod.

28 Grain is threshed for our sakes because man would not otherwise be threshing it, nor break it with many wheels of his threshing instruments, nor crush it under the feet of his oxen.

29 This also comes forth from the

LORD of hosts, who is wonderful in counsel and excellent in instruction.

CHAPTER 29

WOE to Ariel, to Ariel, the city where David dwelt! Add year to year; let them keep festivals.

2 Yet I will distress Ariel, and there shall be heaviness and lamentations; and it shall be to me as Ariel.

3 And I will encamp against you round about, and I will lay a siege against you with ramparts, and I will raise forts against you.

4 And you shall be brought down, and shall speak from the earth, and your words shall be low out of the dust, and your voice shall be heard from the ground like that of a diviner, and your speech shall whisper out of the dust.

5 Moreover the multitude of your oppressors shall be like fine dust, and the multitude of the terrible ones shall be as the chaff that passes away; yea, it shall be in an instant, suddenly.

6 You shall be visited by the LORD of hosts with earthquakes, thunder, and great noise, with storm and tempest and the flame of devouring fire.

7 ¶And the multitude of all the nations that fight against Zion, even all the armies and multitudes that distress her, shall be as a vision in the night.

8 And it shall even be as when a hungry man dreams that he is eating, and when he awakes he is weary and famished; or as when a thirsty man dreams that he is drinking, but when he awakes, he is faint, with his thirst not quenched; so shall the multitude of all the nations be that fight against mount Zion.

9 ¶They are dumbfounded and amazed; they are troubled and stagger; they are drunken, but not with wine; they stagger, but not with strong drink.

10 For the LORD has poured out upon them a spirit of deep sleep, and it has closed their eyes, and also the eyes of the prophets and rulers, and the seers, who see the hidden things.

11 And the vision of all is become to them as the words of a book that is sealed, which men deliver to one who is learned, saying, Read this, and he says, I cannot; for it is sealed:

12 And the book is given to him who is not learned, saying, Read this, and he says, I am not learned.

13 ¶Therefore the LORD said, Forasmuch as this people draw near me with their mouth, and with their lips do honor me, but have removed their heart far from me, and their reverence toward me is taught by the precepts and doctrine of men;

14 Therefore, behold, I will proceed to set apart this people by a great wonder, and in a marvelous manner, and the wisdom of their wise men shall perish, and the understanding of their prudent men shall be taken away.

15 Woe to them who act perversely to hide their counsel from the LORD; and their works are in the dark, and they say, Who sees us? And, Who knows what we do corruptly?

16 Surely you are esteemed as the potter's clay; for shall the work say of him that made it, He made me not? Or shall the thing formed say of him that formed it, He has not fashioned me wisely?

17 Behold, a little while, and Lebanon shall be turned into a fruitful field, and the fruitful field shall be reared as a forest.

18 ¶And in that day shall the deaf hear the words of the book, and the eyes of the blind shall see out of darkness and obscurity.

19 The meek also shall increase their joy in the LORD, and the needy shall rejoice in the Holy One of Israel.

20 For the oppressor is brought to nought, and the scorner is consumed, and all that incite to iniquity are cut off,

21 Those who cause men to sin by the word, and lay a snare for him that reproves, and turn aside the righteous into darkness.

22 Therefore thus says the LORD, who saved Abraham, concerning the house of Jacob, Jacob shall not now be ashamed, neither shall his face now grow pale.

23 But when his children see the

work of my hands in the midst of him, they shall sanctify my name and sanctify the Holy One of Jacob and shall glorify the God of Israel.

24 The foolish ones also whose spirit erred shall come to understanding, and fools shall learn to be obedient.

CHAPTER 30

WOE to the rebellious children, says the LORD, who take counsel, but not of me; and who offer wine offerings, but not of my spirit, that they may add sin to sin;

2 Who start to go down to Egypt, and have not asked at my mouth, to strengthen themselves by the strength of Pharaoh, and to take shelter in the shadow of Egypt!

3 Therefore shall the strength of Pharaoh be to your shame, and the shelter of the shadow of Egypt to your confusion.

4 For while Pharaoh is in Zoan, his princes and ambassadors shall act deceitfully.

5 They go fo a people that cannot profit them, neither be a help nor a profit, but shame and reproach.

6 The prophecy concerning the oppressors of the south: Into a land of trouble and anguish, from whence come the lion and the young lion, the viper and the fiery flying serpent, they will carry their riches upon the backs of young asses, and their treasures upon the humps of camels, to a people that shall not profit them.

7 For the Egyptians shall help in vain and in falsehood; therefore I have warned them, for this their trust is in vain.

8 ¶Now come, write it on these tablets and on the book of their covenant, that it may be for the time to come, for a testimony for ever and ever;

9 For this is a rebellious people, lying children, children who will not hear the law of the LORD;

10 Who have said to the seers, See not; and to the prophets, Prophesy not to us reproof; speak to us deception, prophesy lies;

11 Get you out of the way, turn aside out of the path, cause the Holy One of Israel to cease from before us.

12 Therefore thus says the LORD, the Holy One of Israel: Because you have despised this word and trusted in oppression and have complained and yet trusted in it;

13 Therefore this iniquity shall be to you as a breach ready to fall and as a high wall whose breaking comes suddenly at an instant.

14 And its breaking is as the breaking of the potter's vessel that is broken in pieces, without pity; so that there shall not be found in its fragments a shard to take fire from the hearth or to take water with it out of the cistern.

15 Therefore thus says the LORD, the Holy One of Israel: When you will repent and rest you will be saved; in quietness and in hope shall be your strength; but you would not listen.

16 But you said, Not so, for we will ride upon horses, and will flee upon swift ones; therefore you shall flee, and your pursuers shall be swift.

17 A thousand shall flee at the rebuke of one; at the rebuke of five shall you flee till you are left as a beacon on the top of a mountain and as an ensign on a hill.

18 ¶Therefore the LORD will begin to be gracious to you, and therefore he will be exalted that he may have mercy upon you; for the LORD is a God of judgment; blessed are all those who wait for him.

19 For the people shall dwell in Zion at Jerusalem; you shall weep no more; he will be very gracious to you at the voice of your cry; when he shall hear it, he will answer you.

20 And though the LORD give you the bread of adversity and the water of affliction, yet he will not gather any more those who have caused you to err, and your eyes shall see the misfortune of those who have caused you to err;

21 And your ears shall hear a word behind you, saying, This is the way, walk in it, and do not turn aside, either to the right hand or to the left.

22 And you shall defile the silver which is overlaid on your idols, and

the ornament of your molten images of gold; you shall cast them away like unclean water of a menstrous woman; and you shall take them outside like rubbish.

23 Then he shall give rain to your seed, with which you shall sow the ground; and grain of the increase of the earth, and it shall be fertile and plentiful; on that day shall your cattle graze in rich pastures.

24 The oxen and the young bullocks that till the ground shall eat clean provender which has been winnowed with the shovel and with the fan.

25 And there shall be upon every high mountain and upon every high hill, flowing streams of waters in the day of the great slaughter when the towers fall.

26 Moreover the light of the moon shall be as the light of the sun, and the light of the sun shall be sevenfold, as the light of seven days, in the day that the LORD binds up the breach of his people and heals the pain of their wound.

27 ¶Behold, the name of the LORD comes from afar, his wrath burns and his train is glorious; his lips are full of indignation and his tongue as a devouring fire;

28 And his breath as an overflowing torrent shall reach up to the neck to confuse the nations because of their erring vanity, and because of the bridle which is in the jaws of the nations, which causes them to err.

29 You shall have a song, even a garland which is sanctified in the night when a holy solemnity is kept; and gladness of heart, as when one walks rejoicing to come to the mountain of the LORD, to the mighty One of Israel.

30 And the LORD shall cause his glorious voice to be heard, and shall show the striking of his arm with the indignation of his anger and with the flame of a devouring fire, with the rainstorm and tempest and hailstones.

31 For from before the excellency of the LORD shall the Assyrian be defeated and smitten with a rod.

32 And in all his works, the staff of affliction which the LORD shall lay upon him shall be with tabrets and harps; and with a fierce battle he shall fight against him.

33 For he has prepared his punishment of old; yea, it is prepared to be executed; he has made it deep and large in his dwelling place; the wood and the fire are plentiful; the breath of the LORD, like a stream of brimstone, does kindle it.

CHAPTER 31

WOE to those who go down to Egypt for help and trust in horses and rely on chariots because they are many, and in horsemen, because they are very strong; but they do not trust in the Holy One of Israel, neither seek the LORD!

2 Yet in his wisdom, he will bring a calamity, and will not alter his words; but will arise against the house of evildoers and against the help of those who work iniquity.

3 Now the Egyptians are men and not God; and their horses are flesh and not spirit. When the LORD shall stretch out his hand, both the helper shall be overthrown, and he that is helped shall fall down, and they all shall be annihilated together.

4 For thus has the LORD spoken to me: As the lion, even the young lion, roars over his prey when a multitude of shepherds shout against him, is not afraid of their voice nor terrified by their multitude; so shall the LORD of hosts come down to fight for mount Zion and for the hill thereof.

5 As birds flying, so will the LORD of hosts alight on Jerusalem; he shall alight to deliver, rescue, and help.

6 ¶Repent, O children of Israel, for you have made your punishment severe.

7 For in that day every man shall despise the idols of gold and the idols of silver which your own hands have made for yourselves for a sin.

8 ¶Then shall the Assyrian fall with the sword, not with the sword of men; neither the sword of mighty men shall devour him; but he shall flee from the sword, and his young men shall be discomfited.

9 And he shall dwell in his rocky

habitation, and his princes shall be defeated from before the standard, says the LORD, whose fire is in Zion and his furnace in Jerusalem.

CHAPTER 32

BEHOLD, a king shall reign in righteousness, and princes shall rule in justice.

2 And a man shall be as a hiding place from the wind and as a shelter from the tempest; as streams of waters in a dry place, as the shadow of a great rock in a weary land.

3 And the eyes of those who see shall not be dim, and the ears of those who hear shall hearken.

4 The heart of the imprudent shall understand knowledge, and the tongue of stammerers shall hasten to speak plainly.

5 The fool shall be no more called ruler, nor shall the vain man be called a saviour.

6 For the fool will speak folly, and his heart will work iniquity, to practice hypocrisy and to utter error, to make empty the soul of the hungry and to deprive the thirsty of drink.

7 The instruments of the vain person are evil; he devises wicked devices to destroy the poor with lying words, even when the testimony of the needy is right.

8 But a great person devises great things, and on his greatness shall he stand.

9 ¶Rise up, O you rich women; hear my voice, O you daughters that publish glad tidings, give ear to my speech.

10 The days of the year shall be angry against those who publish glad tidings, for the vintage shall fail, the gathering shall not come.

11 Tremble, O you rich women; be troubled, O you who publish glad tidings; strip, and make yourselves bare and gird sackcloth upon your loins.

12 Mourn and beat upon your breasts, for the pleasant fields, for the fruitful vine.

13 Upon the land of my people shall grow up thorns and briers; yea, upon all the houses of mirth in the mighty city;

14 Because the palace is forsaken; the multitude of the city is deserted; and the beautiful houses have become dens for ever, thorns, and a joy of wild asses, a pasture of flocks;

15 Until the spirit be poured upon us from on high, and the wilderness become a fruitful field, and the fruitful field be counted for a forest.

16 Then justice shall dwell in the wilderness, and righteousness remain in the fruitful field.

17 And the work of righteousness shall be peace; and the effect of righteousness, quietness and assurance for ever.

18 And my people shall dwell in a peaceful habitation and in sure tabernacles and in a resting place of hope.

19 And hail shall come down on the forest, and the city shall be made low like a plain.

20 Blessed are you who sow beside all waters, the place which is trodden under the feet of the ox and the ass.

CHAPTER 33

WOE to you that plunder, but you shall not plunder, and let no one deal treacherously among you; for when you seek to plunder, they will plunder you; and when you seek to deal treacherously, they shall deal treacherously with you.

2 O LORD, be gracious to us; for in thee is our trust; be thou our helper every morning, our salvation also in the time of distress.

3 At the noise of thy tumult the people fled; at the lifting up of thyself the nations were scattered.

4 Henceforth your spoil shall be gathered like the gathering of the caterpillar; as a swarm of locusts when it is gathered together.

5 The LORD is exalted, for he dwells on high; he has filled Zion with justice and righteousness.

6 And faith shall be the stability of your times, and your salvation in a place of refuge; wisdom and knowledge and the reverence of the LORD is his treasure.

7 If he should be seen by them they shall howl violently; the ambassadors of peace shall weep bitterly.

8 The highways lie waste, the wayfaring man ceases, and the covenant is broken; the cities are despised, and there is no regard for man.

9 The earth mourns and languishes; Lebanon is ashamed and confounded; Sharon has become like a desert plain; and Bashan and Carmel are desolate.

10 Now I will arise, says the LORD; now I will be exalted; now I will lift up myself.

11 You shall conceive thorns, you shall bring forth stubble; your breath, as fire, shall devour you.

12 And the peoples shall be as the burning of lime; as thorns that are gathered together shall they be burned in the fire.

13 ¶Hear, you who are far off, what I have done; and you who are near, acknowledge my might.

14 The sinners in Zion are afraid; trembling has seized the heathen. Who among us shall dwell with devouring fire? Who among us shall dwell with everlasting burnings?

15 He who walks righteously and speaks uprightly; he who despises treachery and oppression, who refuses to accept a bribe, who stops his ears that he may not hear of bloodshed, and shuts his eyes that he may not see evil.

16 He shall dwell on high; his place of defense shall be the precipice of rocks; his bread shall be given him; his water shall be sure.

17 Your eyes shall see the king in his beauty; they shall behold the lands that are far off.

18 Your heart shall learn reverence. Where is the scribe? Where is the weigher? Where is he who counted towers for a mighty people?

19 You shall not see a fierce people, a people of a deeper speech, of a stammering tongue, so that he cannot be understood.

20 Look upon Zion, the city of our solemnities; your eyes shall see Jerusalem a rich habitation, a tabernacle that shall not be shaken to and fro; whose pegs shall never be removed,

neither shall any of its cords be broken.

21 For there the name of the LORD is glorious to us; he will be for us a place of light, an enlightenment, and an open space made by the hand; wherein the authority of a prince shall not reign, neither shall the mighty one be able to invade it.

22 For the LORD is our judge, the LORD is our lawgiver, the LORD is our king; and he is our Saviour.

23 Your riggings are loosed; they could not well hold straight their mast, they could not spread the sail; until they have divided the prey, a multitude of lame shall take it.

24 And the inhabitant shall not say, I am sick; the people who dwell therein shall be forgiven their iniquity.

CHAPTER 34

COME near, O you peoples, to hear; and hearken, O you nations; let the earth hear, and all that is therein; the world, and all that dwell in it.

2 For the indignation of the LORD is against all the nations, and his fury against all their armies, that he may destroy them and deliver them to the slaughter.

3 Their slain also shall be cast out, and the stink of their corpses shall come up, and the mountains shall be drenched with their blood.

4 And all the host of heaven shall be dissolved, and the heavens shall be rolled together as a scroll; and all their host shall fall down, as the leaf falls from off the vine and as a falling of premature figs from the fig tree.

5 For my sword shall be sharpened in heaven; behold, it shall come down upon the Edomites and upon a people that is condemned in judgment.

6 The sword of the LORD is filled with blood, it is made fat with the blood, and with the fatness of lambs and goats, with the fat of the kidneys of rams; for the LORD has a sacrifice in Bozrah and a great slaughter in the land of Edom.

7 And unicorns shall fall with them, and bullocks with the bulls; and the

land shall be soaked with their blood, and the soil enriched with their fatness.

8 For it is the day of the LORD's vengeance and the year of recompense for the cause of Zion.

9 And its streams shall be turned into pitch and its soil into brimstone, and its land shall become burning pitch.

10 It shall not be quenched night nor day; its smoke shall go up for ever; and it shall lie waste from generation to generation; none shall pass through it for ever and ever.

11 ¶But pelicans and owls shall possess it; ravens and ostriches shall dwell in it; and he shall stretch out upon it the measuring line of the sword,[1] and there shall be no joy in it.

12 They shall no more call it a kingdom there, and all her princes shall perish.

13 And thorns shall sprout up in her palaces, nettles and thistles in the fortresses thereof; and it shall be a habitation of dragons and a pasture for ostriches.

14 And insane men shall meet in it, and demoniacs shall cry out one to another; there has the screech owl perched and found for herself a place of rest.

15 There shall the great owl make her nest, and lay and hatch and gather under her shadow; there shall vultures also be gathered, every one with her mate.

16 ¶Seek out the book of the LORD, and read; no one of these shall fail, none sought for her mate; but he with his own mouth has commanded, and his spirit it has gathered them.

17 And he has cast the lot for them, and his hand has divided it to them by the measuring line; they shall possess it for ever; from generation to generation they shall dwell in it.

CHAPTER 35

THE parched wilderness shall be glad, and the desert shall rejoice and blossom like the crocus.

2 It shall rejoice like a mountain goat; the glory and honor of Lebanon shall be given to it, the excellency of Carmel and Sharon; they shall see the glory of the LORD and the excellency of our God, an admonition and comfort for the weak, for a Saviour is coming to save them.

3 ¶Strengthen the weak hands and make firm the feeble knees.

4 Say to those who are of a fearful heart, Be strong, fear not; behold, your God the avenger is coming, even God the Saviour is coming to save you.

5 Then the eyes of the blind shall be opened and the ears of the deaf shall be unstopped.

6 Then shall the lame man leap as a hart and the tongue of the dumb shall be loosed; for waters are bursting forth in the wilderness, and streams in the desert.

7 And the desolate land shall become a pool, and the thirsty land springs of water; in the habitation of dragons shall grow grass with reeds and rushes.

8 And a highway shall be there, and it shall be called the way of holiness; the unclean shall not pass over it; and there shall be no road beside it; fools shall not err therein.

9 No lion shall be there, nor shall any ravenous beast go up on it; they shall not be found there; but the redeemed shall walk therein;

10 And the ransomed of the LORD shall return and come to Zion with songs and everlasting joy upon their heads; they shall obtain joy and gladness, and sorrow and sighing shall flee away.

CHAPTER 36

NOW it came to pass in the fourteenth year of King Hezekiah, that Sennacherib king of Assyria came up against all the fortified cities of Judah and took them.

2 Then the king of Assyria sent the Rab-shakeh [2] from Lachish to Jerusalem to King Hezekiah with a great army. And he stood by the ascent of the conduit of the upper pool in the highway of the palace's field.

---

[1] Prisoners lined up for slaughter.

[2] The General of the army.

3 And there went out to him Eliakim, the son of Hilkiah, who was steward of the household, and Shebna the scribe, and Joah, the son of Asaph, the recorder.

4 ¶And the Rab-shakeh said to them, Say now to Hezekiah, Thus says the great king, the king of Assyria: What source of confidence is this wherein you trust?

5 Saying, I am an eloquent speaker, and have counsel and strength for war; now on whom do you trust, that you have rebelled against me?

6 Behold, you trust in the staff of this broken reed, in the Egyptian; on which, when a man lean, it will go into his hand and pierce it; so is Pharaoh, king of Egypt, to all who trust in him.

7 But if you say to me, We trust in the LORD our God; what has Hezekiah gained, in removing the shrines on the high places, and the altars, and in saying to Judah and to Jerusalem, You shall worship before one altar?

8 Now therefore make an alliance with my lord, king of Assyria, and I will give you two thousand horses, if you have riders to set upon them.

9 How then can you turn away the face of one of the least of my master's servants, and put your trust in the Egyptian to give you chariots and horsemen?

10 And am I now come up without the LORD against this land to destroy it? The LORD said to me, Go up against this land and destroy it.

11 ¶Then Eliakim, Shebna, and Joah said to the Rab-shakeh, Speak to your servants in the Aramaic language; for we understand it; and do not speak to us in the Jews' language,[1] in the presence of the people who are standing on the wall.

12 ¶But the Rab-shakeh said to them, My master has not sent me to you and to your master to speak these words, but to the men who sit on the wall, that they may not eat their own dung and drink their own urine with you.

13 Then the Rab-shakeh stood and

[1] The dialect of Aramaic spoken in Judah.

cried with a loud voice in the Jews' language and said, Hear the words of the great king, the king of Assyria.

14 Thus says the king: Do not let Hezekiah deceive you; for he shall not be able to deliver you.

15 Neither let Hezekiah make you trust in the LORD, saying, The LORD will surely deliver us; this city shall not be delivered into the hands of the king of Assyria.

16 Do not listen to Hezekiah; for thus says the king of Assyria: Do me a favor, and come out to me; and eat every one of his vines and every one of his fig tree and drink every one the waters of his own cistern;

17 Until I come and take you away to a land like your own land, a land of grain and oil, a land of olive orchards and vineyards.

18 Do not let Hezekiah deceive you, saying, The LORD will deliver us. Has any of the gods of the nations delivered his land out of the hand of the king of Assyria?

19 Where are the gods of Hamath and Arphad? Where are the gods of Sepharvim? And have they delivered Samaria out of my hands?

20 Who is he among all the gods of these lands that has delivered his land out of my hand, that the LORD should deliver Jerusalem out of my hand?

21 But they held their peace and answered him not a word; for the king had commanded, saying, Do not answer him.

22 ¶Then Eliakim, the son of Hilkiah, who was steward of the household, and Shebna the scribe, and Joah, the son of Asaph, the recorder, came to Hezekiah with their clothes torn, and told him the words of the Rab-shakeh.

CHAPTER 37

AND it came to pass, when King Hezekiah heard it, he tore his clothes and covered himself with sackcloth and went into the house of the LORD.

2 And he sent Eliakim, who was steward of the household, and Shebna

the scribe, and the elders of the priests, covered with sackcloth, to Isaiah, the prophet, the son of Amoz.

3 And they said to him, Thus says Hezekiah: This is a day of distress and of rebuke and of anger; for the children have come to the birth, and there is not strength to bring forth.

4 It may be the LORD your God will hear the words of the Rab-shakeh, whom the king of Assyria his master has sent to reproach the living God, and will reprove him on account of the words which the LORD your God has heard; wherefore beseech and pray for the remnant that is left.

5 So the servants of King Hezekiah came to Isaiah.

6 ¶And Isaiah said to them, Thus shall you say to your master: Thus says the LORD: Be not afraid of the words that you have heard, wherewith the messengers of the king of Assyria have blasphemed in my presence.

7 Behold, I will send a blast against him, and he shall hear a rumor and return to his own land; and I will cause him to fall by the sword in his own land.

8 ¶So the Rab-shakeh returned and found the king of Assyria warring against Libnah; for he had heard that he was departed from Lachish.

9 And he heard say concerning Tirhakah king of Ethiopia, He has come forth to fight with you. And when he heard it, he sent messengers to Hezekiah, saying,

10 Thus shall you speak to Hezekiah king of Judah, saying, Do not let your God, in whom you trust, deceive you, saying, Jerusalem will not be delivered into the hands of the king of Assyria.

11 Behold, you have heard what the kings of Assyria have done to all lands by destroying them utterly; and shall you be delivered?

12 Have the gods of the nations delivered them which my fathers have destroyed, even Gozan, Haran, Rezeph, the inhabitants of Eden, and them of Bedlassar?

13 Where is the king of Hamath and the king of Arphad and the king of the city of Sepharvim and of Dena and of Aka?

14 ¶And Hezekiah received the letters from the hand of the messengers and read them; and Hezekiah went up to the house of the LORD and spread them before the LORD.

15 And Hezekiah prayed before the LORD, saying,

16 O LORD of hosts, God of Israel, who sittest above the cherubim, thou art the God, even thou alone, of all the kingdoms of the earth; thou hast made heaven and earth.

17 Incline thine ear, O LORD, and hear; open thine eyes, O LORD, and see; and hear the words of Sennacherib, which he hath sent to reproach the living God.

18 Of a truth, O LORD, the kings of Assyria have laid waste all the nations and their lands;

19 And have burned their lands and their gods with fire; for they were no gods, but the work of men's hands, of wood, of silver, and of stone; therefore they have destroyed them.

20 Now therefore, O LORD our God, save us from his hands, that all the kingdoms of the earth may know that thou art the God, even thou only.

21 ¶Then Isaiah, the prophet, the son of Amoz sent to Hezekiah, saying, Thus says the LORD of hosts, the God of Israel: All that you have prayed before me concerning Sennacherib king of Assyria have I heard;

22 This is the word which the LORD has spoken concerning him: The virgin, the daughter of Zion, has despised you and laughs you to scorn; the daughter of Jerusalem wags her head at you.

23 Whom have you reproached and blasphemed? And against whom have you raised your voice and lifted up your eyes on high? Against the Holy One of Israel!

24 By the hand of your messengers you have reproached the LORD, and you have said, By the multitude of my chariots I am come up to the height of the mountains, to the sides of Lebanon; and I will cut down the tall cedars thereof, and the choice fir trees

thereof; and I will enter into the height of its border, to the forest of Carmel.

25 I will dig, and drink water; and with the hoofs of my horses will I dry up all the great rivers.

26 Have you not heard long ago, how I have done it; and of the days of old, that I have prepared it? Now I have brought it to pass, that you should be laid waste and desolate as when fortified cities are in ruin,

27 Whose inhabitants were weak, and were defeated and confounded, and became like the grass of the field and the green herb, as the grass on the housetops, as tender blades of wheat blasted before it is grown up.

28 I know your conduct and your going out and your coming in and your daring threat in my presence.

29 Because you have dared in my presence and your blasphemous words have come up into my ears, therefore I will put a hook in your nose and a bit between your lips, and I will cause you to return by the way by which you came.

30 And this shall be a sign for you: You shall eat this year such as grows of itself; and the second year that which springs of the same; and in the third year you shall sow and reap and plant vineyards and eat their fruit.

31 And the remnant that survives of the house of Judah shall again return, and shall again take root downward and bear fruit upward;

32 For out of Jerusalem shall go forth a remnant, and they that escape out of mount Zion; the zeal of the LORD of hosts shall do this.

33 Therefore thus says the LORD concerning the king of Assyria: He shall not enter this city nor shoot an arrow there nor come before it with shields nor cast siege-works against it.

34 But by the way that he came, by the same shall he return, and he shall not enter this city, says the LORD.

35 For I will defend this city and save it for my own sake and for my servant David's sake.

¹ Armenia.

36 Then the angel of the LORD went forth and smote in the camp of the Assyrians one hundred and eighty-five thousand: and when the soldiers arose early in the morning, behold, their comrades were all dead.

37 ¶So Sennacherib departed and went and returned and dwelt at Nineveh.

38 And it came to pass as he was worshipping in the house of Nisroch his god that Adrammeleck and Sharezar, his sons, slew him with the sword; and they escaped to the land of Kardo,¹ and Esar-haddon his son reigned in his stead.

CHAPTER 38

IN those days Hezekiah became deathly sick, and Isaiah, the prophet, the son of Amoz came to him and said to him, Thus says the LORD: Set your house in order; for you shall die, and not live.

2 Then Hezekiah turned his face toward the wall and prayed to the LORD, saying,

3 Remember now, O LORD, I beseech thee, how I have walked before thee in truth and with a perfect heart, and have done that which is good in thy sight. And Hezekiah wept bitterly.

4 ¶Then the word of the LORD came to Isaiah, saying,

5 Go and say to Hezekiah, king of Judah, Thus says the LORD, the God of David your father: I have heard your prayer, I have seen your tears; behold, I will add fifteen years to your days.

6 And I will deliver you and this city out of the hand of the king of Assyria, and I will defend this city.

7 And this shall be a sign to you from the LORD that the LORD will do this thing that he has spoken:

8 Behold, I will bring again the shadow of the degrees, which is gone down on the sundial of Ahaz your father, ten degrees backward. So the shadow of the sun returned the ten degrees by which it had gone down.

9 ¶The writing of Hezekiah king of

Judah, when he had been sick and was recovered of his sickness:

10 I said, In the midst of my days I shall die, at the gates of Sheol I am deprived of the rest of my years.

11 I said, I shall not see the LORD in the land of the living; I shall behold man no more among the inhabitants of the world.

12 My age is departed and removed from me as a shepherd's tent; my life has shrunk like a shoelace and as a weaver's web which is nearly ready to be cut off; from morning even to night thou hast delivered me to my fate.

13 Like a swallow twittering, so did I chatter; I did mourn like a dove; I have lifted my eyes on high; O LORD, deliver me and comfort me.

14 What shall I say? He has both spoken to me, and himself has done it, and has caused my sleep to flee because of the bitterness of my soul;

15 When the LORD is against men, shall they live? But because of the life of my spirit, heal me and make me to live.

16 Behold, it was for peace that I had great bitterness; but thou hast been pleased with my soul, that it may not waste in corruption; for thou hast cast all my sins behind thy back.

17 For Sheol cannot thank thee, death cannot praise thee; those that go down into the pit cannot hope for thy truth.

18 But the living shall give thanks to thee, as I do this day; the father to the children shall make known thy truth.

19 The LORD shall save us; therefore we will sing his songs all the days of our life in the house of the LORD.

20 And Hezekiah said, What is the sign that I shall go up to the house of the LORD?

21 And Isaiah said, Let them take a lump of figs, and lay it as a plaster upon the boil and he shall recover.

CHAPTER 39

AT that time Merodach-baladan, the son of Baladan, king of Babylon, sent letters and presents to Hezekiah;

for he had heard that he had been sick and was healed.

2 And Hezekiah was glad to receive them, and showed them his treasure house, the silver and the gold and the spices and the precious ointment and all the house of his armor and all that was found in his treasures; there was nothing in his house nor in all his dominion that Hezekiah did not show them.

3 ¶Then Isaiah the prophet came to King Hezekiah and said to him, What did these men say to you? And from whence did they come to you? And Hezekiah said, They have come from a far country to me, even from Babylon.

4 Then said he, What have they seen in your house? And Hezekiah answered, They have seen all the things that are in my house; I have left nothing in my house that I have not showed them.

5 Then Isaiah said to Hezekiah, Hear the word of the LORD of hosts:

6 Behold, the days are coming, when all that is in your house, and that which your fathers have laid up in store until this day, shall be carried to Babylon; nothing shall be left, says the LORD.

7 And some of your sons that shall issue from you, whom you shall beget, they shall take away; and they shall be eunuchs in the palace of the king of Babylon.

8 Then Hezekiah said to Isaiah, Good is the word of the LORD which you have spoken. For there shall be peace and truth in my days.

CHAPTER 40

COMFORT ye, comfort ye my people, says your God.

2 Speak comfortably to Jerusalem, and cry to her, for she was filled with violence and delighted in sin; and she has received from the LORD's hand double punishment for all her sins.

3 ¶The voice of him that cries in the wilderness, Prepare the way of the LORD, make straight in the desert a highway for our God.

4 Every valley shall be filled up,

and every mountain and hill shall be made low; and the steep place shall be made straight, and the rough places smooth;

5 And the glory of the LORD shall be revealed, and all flesh shall see it together; for the mouth of the LORD has spoken it.

6 The voice says, Cry. And he said, What shall I cry? All flesh is grass, and all its beauty is like the flower of the field;

7 The grass withers, the flower fades, because the breath of the LORD blows upon it; surely this people is like the grass.

8 The grass withers, the flower fades; but the word of our God shall stand for ever.

9 ¶O Zion, that brings good tidings, get you up upon the high mountain; O Jerusalem, that brings good tidings, lift up your voice with strength; lift it up, be not afraid; say to the cities of Judah, Behold your God!

10 Behold, the LORD God will come with might, and his arm with strength; behold, his reward is with him, and his work before him.

11 He shall feed his flock like a shepherd; he shall gather the lambs with his arm and carry them in his bosom, and shall feed again those who give suck.

12 ¶Who has measured the waters in the hollow of his hand and meted out heaven with a span and gathered the dust of the earth in a measure and weighed the mountains in scales and the hills in a balance?

13 Who has directed the Spirit of the LORD or who has been to him a counsellor?

14 With whom took he counsel, and who instructed him and made him to understand the path of justice and taught him knowledge and showed him the way of understanding?

15 Behold, the nations are like a drop out of a bucket, and are counted as the dipping of the balance; behold, the isles shall be cast away like fine dust.

16 And Lebanon is not sufficient for the fuel, nor the beasts thereof sufficient for a burnt offering.

17 All nations before him are as nothing; and they are counted to him for destruction and the sword.

18 ¶To whom then will you liken God? Or to what likeness will you compare him?

19 Is he an image which the carpenter has made and the goldsmith has overlaid with gold and fastened with silver chains?

20 He selects wood that is not worm-eaten; then chooses a carpenter, who fashions it with his skill, to make an image that will not be moved.

21 Have you not heard? Have you not known? Has it not been told you from the beginning? Have you not understood from the foundations of the earth?

22 It is he who sits upon the circle of the earth, and its inhabitants are like grasshoppers; who stretches out the heavens as a curtain and spreads them as a tent to dwell in;

23 Who brings princes to nought; and makes the judges of the earth as if they were nothing.

24 Yea, they shall not be planted; yea, they shall not be sown; yea, their stock shall not take root in the earth; and he shall blow upon them and they shall wither, and the whirlwind shall take them away as stubble.

25 To whom then will you liken me, or to whom shall I be equal? says the Holy One.

26 Lift up your eyes on high, and behold: who has created these things? Who brings out their host by number; he called them all by name, by the greatness of his glory and the strength of his power; not one is missing.

27 Why do you say, O Jacob, and say, O Israel, My way is hidden from the LORD and justice is not rendered by my God?

28 ¶Have you not known, have you not heard, that God is the LORD for ever, who has created the ends of the earth? that he does not faint, neither is weary? and that there is no searching of his understanding?

29 He gives power to the weary, and to them that are stricken with disease he increases strength.

30 Even the youths shall faint and

be weary, and the young men shall helplessly stumble;

31 But they who wait for the LORD shall renew their strength; they shall grow wings as a dove; they shall run and not be weary; and they shall walk and not faint.

CHAPTER 41

KEEP silence, O you islands; and let the people renew their strength; let them come near; then let them speak; let them come near together to judgment.

2 Who has stirred up the righteous one from the east, and hastened him on? The nations shall surrender before him, and kings shall be confounded. He gave them as the dust to his sword and as driven stubble to his bow.

3 He shall pursue them, then make peace; and he shall not pass that way on foot.

4 Who has prepared and done it, calling the generations from the beginning? I the LORD, the first and the last; I am he.

5 The islands saw it, and were afraid; and the ends of the earth were afraid, and they drew near and came.

6 They helped every one his neighbor; and every one said to his brother, Be of good courage.

7 The carpenter encourages the goldsmith, and he who smooths with the hammer him who strikes the anvil, saying, It is ready for the soldering; and they fasten it with nails, that it should not be moved.

8 But now, Israel, you are my servant, Jacob whom I have chosen, the descendants of Abraham my friend, whom I have strengthened.

9 I have called you from the ends of the earth and from among the prophets, and said to you, You are my servant; I have chosen you, and have not rejected you;

10 ¶Fear not, for I am with you; be not dismayed, for I am your God; I have strengthened you, and have also helped you, yea, I will also uphold you with the right hand of my righteousness.

11 All those that reproach you shall be ashamed and confounded; they shall be as nothing; and those who strive with you shall perish.

12 You shall seek them that strive with you, but you shall not find them; they that war against you shall be as if they were nothing.

13 For I am the LORD your God, the strengthener of your right hand. I have said to you, Fear not; I am your helper.

14 Fear not, O you helpless men of Jacob, O you remnant of Israel! I am your helper, says the LORD, and your Saviour, the Holy One of Israel.

15 Behold, I have made you as a new threshing instrument having teeth; a thing which tears and crushes to pieces; you shall thresh the mountains and beat them small, and shall make the hills as chaff.

16 You shall winnow them, and the wind shall carry them away, and the whirlwind shall scatter them; and you shall rejoice in the LORD and shall glory in the Holy One of Israel.

17 When the poor and needy seek water, and there is none, and their tongue is dried with thirst, I the LORD will answer them, I the God of Israel will not forsake them.

18 I will open rivers in the mountains and fountains in the midst of the valleys; I will make the wilderness pools of water, and the dry land springs of water.

19 I will plant in the wilderness the cedars, the acacia tree, the myrtle, and the olive tree; I will set in the desert the cypress and the pine and the box tree together;

20 That they may see and know and consider and understand that the hand of the LORD has done this and the Holy One of Israel has created it.

21 Bring near your cause, says the LORD; bring near your counsels, says the King of Jacob.

22 Let them come near and show us the things that are to come; show us the former things, that we may consider them, and know the latter end of them; or declare to us the things that are to come.

23 Show us the wonders that are to come hereafter, that we may know that you are gods; yea, do good, or

do evil, that we may relate it and behold it together.

24 Behold, you are nothing, and your works are corrupt; choosing you is an abomination.

25 I have stirred up one from the north, and he shall come from the rising of the sun, and shall call on my name; and the princes shall come, and shall be trodden down like mortar, and as the potter treads clay.

26 Who has declared it from the beginning, that we may know? And beforetime, that we may say, He is righteous? Yea, there is none that shows, yea, there is none that declares, yea, there is none that hears your words.

27 These things are the chief concern of Zion; behold, I will give to Jerusalem one that brings good tidings.

28 For I beheld, and there was no man who could meditate about these things, that I might ask him, and that he might give me an answer.

29 Behold, they are all nothing; their works are vanity; their images are wind and vanity.

CHAPTER 42

BEHOLD, my servant, whom I uphold, my elect in whom my soul delights; I have put my spirit upon him; he shall bring forth justice to the Gentiles.

2 He shall not cry, nor make a sound, nor cause his voice to be heard in the street.

3 A bruised reed shall he not break, and a flickering lamp he shall not extinguish; he shall truly bring forth judgment.

4 He shall not fail nor be discouraged till he has set justice in the earth; and the islands shall wait for his law.

5 ¶Thus says the LORD God, he who created the heavens and stretched them out, he who spread forth the earth and all that is in it, he who gives breath to the people upon it, and spirit to those who walk therein;

6 I the LORD have called you in righteousness and have held your hand and have strengthened you and have given you for a covenant to the people and for a light to the Gentiles;

7 That you may open the eyes of the blind, to release prisoners from bondage, and bring out of the prison house those who sit in darkness.

8 I am the LORD; that is my name; and my glory will I not give to another, neither my praise to graven images.

9 Behold, the former things have come to pass, and new things do I declare; before they spring forth I tell you of them.

10 Sing to the LORD a new song, and his praise from the ends of the earth, you that go down to the sea and all that is therein; the islands and those who dwell in them.

11 Let the wilderness and its towns rejoice; let Kedar be meadows; let the inhabitants of the steep rocks sing, let them shout from the top of the mountains.

12 Let them give glory to the LORD and declare his praise in the islands.

13 The LORD shall go forth as a mighty man, he shall stir up zealousness like a man of war; he shall shout and become valiant; he shall slay his enemies.

14 I have for a long time held my peace; I have kept silent, I have been patient like a woman in travail; I have remained speechless and completely confounded.

15 I will lay waste mountains and hills, and dry up all their herbs; and I will make the rivers islands, and I will dry up the pools.

16 And I will lead the blind by a way that they know not; and in the paths that they have not known I will make them walk; I will make darkness light before them, and crooked places straight. These things have I done to them and have not forsaken them.

17 ¶They shall be turned back, they shall be greatly ashamed, who trust in graven images, who say to molten images, You are our gods.

18 Hear, O you deaf! And understand and see, O you blind!

19 Who is blind but my servant? Who is deaf as my messenger whom

I send? Who is blind as the ruler? and blind as the LORD's servant?

20 I gave you counsel, but you observed it not; I opened your ears, but you heard not.

21 The LORD is well pleased for his righteousness' sake; he will magnify the law and make it honorable.

22 But this is a people robbed and downtrodden; all the young men are snared, and they are hid in prison houses; they have become a prey, and there is none to deliver; and trampled upon, and there is none to restore.

23 Who among you will give ear to this? Who will hearken to the other counsel?

24 Who gave Jacob to be trod under foot and Israel for a spoil? Was it not the LORD, because we have sinned against him? For we would not walk in his ways, neither were we obedient to his law.

25 Therefore he has poured upon them the fury of his anger and the fierceness of battle; and it has set them on fire round about, yet they knew it not; and it burned them, yet they laid it not to heart.

CHAPTER 43

BUT now thus says the LORD, who created you, O Jacob, and he who formed you, O Israel: Fear not; for I have saved you, I have called you by your name because you are mine.

2 When you shall pass through the sea, I will be with you; and through the rivers, they shall not overwhelm you; when you walk through the fire, you shall not be burned; neither shall the flame kindle upon you.

3 For I am the LORD your God, the Holy One of Israel, your Saviour; I gave Egypt for your sake, and Ethiopia and Sheba for you.

4 Because you are precious in my sight, you have been honorable and I have loved you; therefore I have given men for your sake and nations for your life.

5 Fear not; for I am with you; I will bring your descendants from the east, and gather you from the west;

6 I will say to the north, Give up; and to the south, Keep not back; bring my sons from afar, and my daughters from the ends of the earth;

7 Even every one who is called by my name; for I have created him for my glory, I have formed him and I have made him.

8 ¶Bring forth the blind people who have eyes, and the deaf who have ears.

9 Let all the peoples be gathered together and let all the nations be assembled; who among you can declare this and show us the former things? Let them bring forth their witnesses that they may be justified; or let them hear and say, It is truth.

10 You are my witnesses, says the LORD, and my servants whom I have chosen; that you may know and believe me and understand that I am he; before me there was no God created, neither shall there be after me.

11 I, even I, am the LORD; and besides me there is no lord.

12 I have declared that I have saved, and I have proclaimed that there is no strange god among you; therefore you are my witnesses, says the LORD, that I am God.

13 Yea, from the first day I am he; and there is none that can deliver out of my hands; what I will do, who can stop it?

14 ¶Thus says the LORD, your Saviour, the Holy One of Israel: For your sake I have sent to Babylon and have brought back all the fugitives and the Chaldeans who glory in their ships.

15 I am the LORD, your Holy One, the Creator of Israel, your King.

16 Thus says the LORD, who has made a way in the sea and a path in the mighty waters;

17 Who brings forth the chariots and horses and a mighty army; they shall lie down together, they shall not rise, they are extinguished like a flickering lamp:

18 ¶Remember not the former things, neither consider the things of old.

19 Behold, I will do a new thing; now it shall spring forth and you shall know it. I will even make a way in the wilderness and rivers in the desert.

20 The beasts of the field shall glorify me, the jackals and the ostriches, because I give waters in the wilderness and rivers in the desert to provide drink to my people, my chosen.

21 This people whom I have chosen for myself, they shall drink.

22 ¶But you have not called me, O Jacob; for I have called you, O Israel.

23 You have not brought me lambs of your burnt offerings; neither have you honored me with your sacrifices. I have not burdened you with request offerings, nor wearied you with demands for incense.

24 You have bought me no sweet cane with money, neither have you filled me with the fat of your sacrifices; but you have burdened me with your sins, you have wearied me with your iniquities.

25 I, even I, am he who blots out your transgressions for my own sake and will not remember your sins any more.

26 Put me in remembrance; let us plead together; that you may be justified.

27 Your first father has sinned, and your rulers have transgressed against me.

28 Your princes have profaned the sanctuary; therefore I have given Jacob to the curse and Israel to reproaches.

CHAPTER 44

NOW hearken to me, O Jacob, my servant, and Israel, whom I have chosen;

2 Thus says the LORD that made you and formed you from the womb and helped you: Fear not, O Jacob, my servant; and you, Israel, whom I have chosen.

3 For I will give water in a parched ground and streams on the dry land; I will pour my spirit upon your descendants and my blessings upon your offspring;

4 And they shall spring up as among the grass, as willows by the running streams.

5 One shall say, I am the LORD's; and another shall call himself by the name of Jacob; and another shall

subscribe with his hand to the LORD and surname himself by the name of Israel.

6 Thus says the LORD the King of Israel, and his Saviour, the LORD of hosts: I am the first and I am the last; and besides me there is no God.

7 And who is like me? Let him announce it and set it in order and declare it, since I placed the people on the earth for ever. And let them show the wonders that are coming.

8 Fear not, neither be alarmed; have not I announced to you from former time, and have declared it? You are my witnesses, that there is no God besides me, and no mighty one whom I do not know.

9 ¶The makers of images are all of them vanity; and there is no profit in the works which they desire to make; the craftsmen who make them are witnesses, for they see not, nor hear, nor know.

10 Therefore let them be ashamed, those who make gods or graven and molten images that are profitable for nothing.

11 Behold, all their craftsmen are dumb men; let them all be gathered together, let them stand up; they shall be ashamed and confounded together;

12 The carpenter sharpens an iron instrument, he shapes the image with a plane and fashions it with a chisel and works it with the strength of his arm; yea, he becomes hungry and also thirsty, he drinks no water and is faint.

13 The carpenter selects a piece of wood, and stretches out his rule; he marks it out with a line; he fashions it with planes and makes it into the likeness of a man, according to the beauty of a man;

14 Then he makes it to stand in the house, a piece of wood which was cut down out of the forest, something which the rain has nourished.

15 A thing for men to use as fuel; they take some of it and heat the oven and bake bread; yea, they also make a god of it and worship it; yea, they make it a graven image and worship it.

16 Half of it they burn in the fire;

and on its coals they roast meat, and they eat and are satisfied; they also warm themselves and say, Aha, I am warm, I have seen the fire;

17 And of the rest they make a god, even a graven image; and they worship it and pray to it and say, Deliver us; for thou art our god.

18 They have not known nor understood; for the vision of their eyes is shut that they cannot see, and the understanding of their hearts, so that they cannot understand.

19 And they considered not in their heart, neither did they know nor did they reason, saying, Half of it we burned in the fire; yea, also we have baked bread on its coals; we have roasted meat and eaten it; and from the rest of it we have made for ourselves an idol of wood and worshipped it.

20 Their imagination is dull; they are surely gone astray, and cannot deliver themselves, nor say, Our right hand has wrought falsehood.

21 ¶Remember these things, O Jacob and Israel, for you are my servant; I have formed you; you are my servant; O Israel, from henceforth forget me not.

22 I have blotted out your iniquities as a thick mist, and your sins as a cloud; return to me, for I have saved you.

23 Sing, O you heavens; for the LORD has done it; shout, O you foundations of the earth; break forth into singing, O mountains, O forest, and every tree therein! For the LORD has saved Jacob and glorified himself in Israel.

24 Thus says the LORD, who saved you and who formed you from the womb and helped you: I am the LORD who made all things; who stretched out the heavens alone; who spread out the earth by myself;

25 Who makes void the signs of the diviners and despises their divinations; who turns wise men backward and makes their knowledge foolish;

26 Who confirms the word of his servant and performs the counsel of his messengers; who said to Jerusalem, You shall be inhabited, and to the cities of Judah, You shall be built and I will raise up the ruins thereof;

27 Who said to the deep, Be dry, and who dried up the rivers;

28 Who said of Cyrus, He is my shepherd and shall perform all my pleasure; even saying to Jerusalem, You shall be built; and to the temple, Your foundations shall be laid.

CHAPTER 45

THUS says the LORD to his anointed, to Cyrus, whose right hand I have upheld, to subdue nations before him: I will loose the loins of kings, to open the doors before him, and the gates shall not be shut;

2 I will go before you, and make the crooked places straight; I will break in pieces the gates of brass and cut asunder the bars of iron;

3 And I will give you the treasures that are hidden in darkness and the buried riches of the secret places that you may know that I, the LORD, who call you by your name, am the God of Israel.

4 For the sake of my servant Jacob, and Israel my elect, I have even called you by your name; I have surnamed you, though you have not known me.

5 ¶I am the LORD, and there is none else; there is no God besides me; I have girded you, though you have not known me,

6 That they may know from the rising of the sun and from the west that there is none besides me; I am the LORD, and there is none else.

7 I form light and create darkness; I make peace and create hardship; I the LORD do all these things.

8 Drop down, O heavens, from above, and let the clouds pour down righteousness; let the earth open and let salvation be multiplied and let righteousness spring up; I the LORD have created these things.

9 Woe to him who strives with his Maker! An earthen vessel that strives with him who made it from the earth! Does the clay say to the potter, What are you making? Or am I not the work of your hands?

10 Woe to him who says to his

father, What are you begetting? Or to his mother, What have you conceived?

11 Thus says the LORD, the Holy One of Israel, and his Maker, the LORD of hosts is his name: Ask me of things to come concerning my children; and concerning the work of my hands, command me.

12 I have made the earth and created man upon it; I, even my hands, have stretched out the heavens, and all their host have I commanded.

13 I have stirred man up in righteousness, and I will make smooth all his ways; he shall build my city and shall send my exiles back, not for a price nor for a bribe, says the LORD of hosts.

14 Thus says the LORD: The labor of Egypt and the merchants of Ethiopia and of Sheba, men of stature, shall come over to you and shall be yours; they shall come after you; in chains shall they come over, and they shall fall down before you, and shall make supplication to you, saying, Surely God is in you, and there is no other God.

15 Truly thou art a shelter, O God, the God of Israel, and his Saviour.

16 They who walk in confusion and make idols are all ashamed and confounded together;

17 But the salvation of Israel is by the LORD, the Saviour of the world; you shall not be ashamed nor confounded for ever and ever.

18 For thus says the LORD who created the heavens (he is the God who formed the earth and made it; he has established it; he did not create it in vain, but that his creation might dwell in it): I am the LORD; and there is none else.

19 I have not spoken in secret, in a dark place of the earth; I said not to the descendants of Jacob, Seek me in vain; I the LORD speak righteousness; I declare things that are right.

20 ¶Assemble yourselves and come; draw near together, you who are delivered of the nations; they have no knowledge who carry a graven image of wood and pray to a god that cannot save.

21 Tell and draw near and consult together; who has declared this from ancient time? Was it not I, the LORD from the beginning? And there is no other God besides me; a just God and Saviour; there is none besides me.

22 Draw near to me and be saved, all the ends of the earth; for I am the LORD, and there is none else.

23 I have sworn by myself, the word is gone out of my mouth in righteousness and shall not return, that to me every knee shall bow, every tongue shall swear.

24 And they shall say, In the LORD is righteousness; even to him shall mighty men come; and all who reproach thee shall be ashamed.

25 In the LORD shall all the descendants of Israel be justified and shall glory.

CHAPTER 46

BEL has fallen down, Nebo is overthrown; their idols were loaded as burdens upon beasts, yea, upon weary beasts and cattle.

2 They were overthrown, they have fallen down together; they could not rescue those who carried them, but they themselves are gone into captivity.

3 ¶Hearken to me, O house of Jacob, and all the remnant of the house of Israel, even those who are borne in the belly and who still are carried in the womb:

4 Even to your old age I am he; and even to gray hairs I will endure. I have made and I will sustain; even I will carry and will deliver.

5 ¶To whom will you liken me and make me equal and compare me, that we may be alike?

6 To those who go astray, who pour out gold from their bags and weigh silver in the balance and hire a goldsmith; and they make it a god; they worship it, and they also pray to it?

7 They bear it upon their shoulders, they carry it and set it in its place, and it cannot rise up from its place; they also pray to it, but it does not answer them nor save them from their troubles.

8 Remember these things and dis-

cern; bring it again to your mind, O you transgressors!

9 Remember the former things of old; for I am God, and there is no other god; and there is none like me,

10 Declaring the end from the beginning and from ancient times the things that are not yet done, saying, My counsel shall stand, and I will do all my pleasure,

11 Calling a ruler swift as a bird from the east, the man who executes my counsel from a far land; yea, I have spoken it, I will also bring it to pass; I have purposed it, I will also do it.

12 ¶Hearken to me, O you stubborn of heart, that are far from righteousness;

13 My righteousness is near; it shall not be far off, my salvation shall not tarry; and I will give salvation in Zion and for Israel my glory.

CHAPTER 47

COME down and sit in the dust, O virgin daughter of Babylon, sit on the ground; there is no throne, O daughter of the Chaldeans; for you shall no more be called tender and delicate.

2 Take the millstone and grind flour; remove your veil, cut off your white hair, uncover your legs, pass through the rivers.

3 Your nakedness shall be uncovered, yea, your shame shall be seen; I will execute vengeance upon you, and I will not meet you as a man.

4 As for our Saviour, the LORD of hosts is his name, the Holy One of Israel.

5 Sit silent and go into darkness, O daughter of the Chaldeans; for you shall no more be called, The mightiest of kingdoms.

6 ¶I was angry with my people, for they have polluted my inheritance, so I delivered them into your hands; you showed them no mercy; upon the elders have you very heavily laid your yoke.

7 ¶And you said, I shall be a mighty one for ever; so that you did not lay these things to your heart, neither did remember the end thereof.

8 Now therefore let her hear these things, she who is given to pleasures, who dwells in tranquillity, who says in her heart, I am, and there is none else besides me; I shall not sit as a widow, neither shall I know the loss of children;

9 But these two plagues shall come upon you in a moment, in one day: the loss of children and widowhood; they shall come upon you suddenly, for the multitude of your sorceries, and for the multitude of your magicians.

10 ¶For you have trusted in your wickedness; you have said, None sees me. Your wisdom and your knowledge have misled you; and you have said in your heart, I am, and there is none else besides me.

11 ¶Therefore evil shall come upon you in the early morning, and you shall not know from whence it rises; and mischief shall fall upon you and you shall not be able to put it off; and desolation shall come upon you suddenly, which you shall not know.

12 Stand now with your magicians and with the multitude of your sorceries in which you have labored from your youth; perhaps you may be able to profit, perhaps you may strengthen yourself.

13 You are wearied in the multitude of your thoughts. Let now the Chaldeans stand up and save you, those who gaze into the heavens and at the stars; let them foretell by the moon the things that shall come upon you.

14 Behold, they have become as stubble which is consumed by the fire; they shall not deliver themselves from the power of the flame; there are no coals to warm them, nor fire to sit before.

15 Thus have become to you your merchants with whom you have labored from your youth: they have wandered every one to his quarter, and there is none to save you.

CHAPTER 48

HEAR these things, O house of Jacob, who are called by the name of Israel and are come forth from the loins of Judah, who swear by the name of the LORD and make mention of the God of Israel, but not in truth nor in righteousness.

2 For they are called out of the holy city and they rely upon the God of Israel; the LORD of hosts is his name.

3 I have declared the former things from the beginning; and they went forth out of my mouth, and I showed them to you; I did them suddenly, and they came to pass.

4 Because I knew that you are obstinate and your neck is an iron sinew and your brow brass;

5 I have made them known to you from of old; before they came to pass I declared them to you, lest you should say, My idols did them; and my graven images and my molten images have saved me.

6 I have heard and seen all these things; and will you not declare them? I have proclaimed to you new things from this time, even hidden things, and you did not know them.

7 They are created now, and not of old; even before the day when you did not hear of them, lest you should say, Behold, I knew them.

8 Yea, you have neither heard nor known of them; nor were your ears opened of old; for I knew that you surely would lie and that you were called a wicked one from the womb.

9 ¶For my name's sake will I defer my anger, and for my praise will I keep you, and I will not destroy you.

10 Behold, I have refined you, but not with silver; I have purified you in the furnace of affliction.

11 For my own sake, will I do it, that my name may not be polluted and that I may not give my glory to another.

12 ¶Hearken to me, O Jacob and Israel, whom I called; I am he; I am the first, I also am the last.

13 My hand has laid the foundations of the earth, and my right hand has stretched out the heavens; when I call to them, they stand up together.

14 Assemble, all of you, and listen; who is there among you who can declare these things? The LORD has loved him, that he may do his will on Babylon and on the land of the Chaldeans.

15 I, even I, have spoken; yea, I have also called him; I have brought him and I have made his way prosperous.

16 ¶Come near to me, listen to this; I have not spoken in secret from the beginning; from the creation, there am I; and now the LORD God, and his Spirit, has sent me.

17 Thus says the LORD, your Saviour, the Holy One of Israel: I am the LORD your God who teaches you not to do wrong, who leads you by the way that you should go.

18 O that you had hearkened to my commandments! Then your peace would have been as a river, and your righteousness as the waves of the sea;

19 Your descendants also would have been as the sand, and the offspring of your loins like the gravel thereof; their name would not perish nor be destroyed from before me.

20 ¶Go forth from Babylon, flee from the Chaldeans; with a voice of singing declare this, proclaim it, and publish it even to the ends of the earth; say, The LORD has saved his servant Jacob.

21 They thirsted not when he led them through the deserts; he caused the waters to flow out of the rock for them; he bored through the rock, and the waters gushed out.

22 There is no peace to the wicked, says the LORD.

CHAPTER 49

LISTEN to me, O isles; hearken to me, O you nations, the LORD has called me from afar; from the womb, and from the body of my mother has he made mention of my name.

2 He has made my mouth like a sharp sword; in the shadow of his hand has he hid me and made me a chosen arrow; in his quiver has he hid me,

3 And said to me, You are my servant, O Israel, in whom I will be glorified.

4 I have not said to the descendants of Jacob that I have labored in vain, nor that I have spent my strength for

nought. Surely my judgment is before the LORD, and my work before my God.

5 ¶Now, thus says the LORD, who formed me from the womb to be his servant, to bring Jacob back to him and gather Israel together; I am glorified in the eyes of the LORD, and my God has become my strength.

6 And he said: It is a small thing that you should be my servant to raise up the tribes of Jacob and to restore the scions of Israel; I have given you to be a light to the Gentiles, that you might be my salvation to the ends of the earth.

7 Thus says the LORD, the Holy One of Israel and his Saviour, to him whose soul is despised, to him who is abhorred by the people and by the servants of the rulers: Kings shall see and arise, princes also shall worship him, because of the LORD who is faithful, and the Holy One of Israel who has chosen you.

8 Thus says the LORD: In an acceptable time I have answered you, and in a day of salvation I have helped you; and I have formed you and have given you for a covenant to the people and a light to the Gentiles, to establish the earth, to cause you to possess the desolate heritages;

9 That you may say to the prisoners, Go forth; to those who are shut up, Show yourselves. Come out. They shall feed in the paths and their pastures shall be in all highways.

10 They shall not hunger nor thirst; neither shall the sultry heat nor the sun smite them; for he who is merciful to them shall lead them, and by the springs of water shall he bring them.

11 And I will make all mountains to be highways, and the highways shall be exalted.

12 Behold, these shall come from afar, and lo, these from the north and from the islands of the sea, and these from the coast of Sinim.

13 ¶Sing, O heavens, and be joyful, O earth, and break forth into singing, O mountains; for the LORD has comforted his people and will have mercy upon his afflicted.

14 But Zion said, The LORD has forsaken me and the LORD has forgotten me.

15 Can a woman forget her sucking child, that she should not have compassion on the son of her womb? Yea, they may forget, but I will not forget you.

16 Behold, I have inscribed you upon the palms of my hands; your fortified walls are continually before me.

17 Your sons who caused your destruction and those who laid you waste shall make haste to go forth from you.

18 ¶Lift up your eyes round about and behold; they all gather themselves together and come to you. As I live, says the LORD, you shall surely clothe yourself with them all as with an ornament, and you shall be adorned like a bride.

19 For your waste and your desolate places and the land of your destruction shall even now be too narrow by reason of the inhabitants, and those who swallowed you up shall flee away.

20 The children which you shall have during the time of your bereavement shall say again in your ears, The place is too narrow for us; make room for us to dwell.

21 Then you shall say in your heart, Who has borne me these? For, behold, I have been bereaved and barren, a captive, and wandering to and fro. And who has brought up these? Behold, I was left alone; and these children, where have they been?

22 Thus says the LORD God: Behold, I will lift up my hand to the Gentiles and set up my standard to the nations; and they shall bring your sons in their arms, and your daughters shall be carried upon their shoulders.

23 And kings shall be your foster fathers, and their queens your nursing mothers; they shall bow down to you with their faces to the ground and shall lick the dust off your feet; and you shall know that I am the LORD; for they who wait for me shall not be ashamed.

24 ¶Can the prey be taken away from the mighty, or a giant's captives be delivered?

25 For thus says the LORD: Even the prey of the mighty shall be taken away, and the captives of the mighty shall be delivered; and I will contend with him who contends with you, and I will save your children.

26 And I will cause your oppressors to eat their own flesh; [1] and they shall be drunken with their own blood as with new wine; and all men shall know that I the LORD am your Saviour and your Helper, the Mighty One of Jacob.

CHAPTER 50

THUS says the LORD: Where is the bill of the divorcement of your mother, whom I have put away? Or which of my creditors is it to whom I have sold you? Behold, for your iniquities were you sold, and for your transgressions is your mother put away.

2 Why, when I came, was there no man? When I called was there none to answer? Is my hand shortened at all, that it cannot save? Or have I no power to deliver? Behold, at my rebuke I dry up the sea, I make the rivers a wilderness; their fish stink because there is no water, and they die of thirst.

3 I clothe the heavens with darkness and make sackcloth their covering.

4 The LORD God has given me the tongue of the learned, that I should know how to speak and declare a word to the weary; he wakens me in the morning; in the morning he causes my ears to hear the teaching.

5 ¶The LORD God has opened my ears, and I have not turned back to the evil way, neither have I been rebellious.

6 I gave my back to the smiters and my cheeks to those who slap on the face; I turned not my face from shame and spitting.

7 ¶For the LORD God has helped me; therefore I am not confounded; therefore I have hardened my face like a flint, and I know that I shall not be ashamed.

8 For he who justifies me is near. Who will contend with me? Let us stand together. Who is my adversary? Let him come near to me.

9 Behold, the LORD God will help me; who is he that shall condemn me? Lo, they all shall wear out as a garment; the moth shall eat them up.

10 ¶Who is among you who reveres the LORD? Let him listen to the voice of his servant. He who walks in darkness and has no light, let him trust in the name of the LORD and be saved by his God.

11 Behold, all of you are like kindling wood and the sparks of the kindling. Walk in the light of your fire and in the sparks that you have kindled. This shall you have of my hands: you shall lie down in sorrow.

CHAPTER 51

LISTEN to me, you who follow after righteousness, you who seek the LORD; look to the mountain from which you were hewn, and to the hole of the pit from which you were digged.

2 Look to Abraham your father, and to Sarah who conceived you; for he was alone, and I called him and blessed him and multiplied him.

3 For the LORD will build Zion; he will build all her waste places; he will make her wilderness like Eden, and her desert like the garden of the LORD; joy and gladness shall be heard in the midst of her, thanksgiving and the voice of singing.

4 ¶Hearken to me, O people; and give ear to me, O nations; for a law shall go forth from me, and my justice is a light to the Gentiles.

5 My righteousness is near; my salvation is gone forth and my arms shall judge the peoples; the islands shall wait for me and on my arm shall they trust.

6 Lift up your eyes to the heavens, and look also upon the earth beneath; for the heavens shall vanish away like smoke, and the earth shall wear out like a garment, and they who dwell in

---

[1] An Eastern idiom which means *will endure hardships.*

it shall perish in like manner; but my salvation shall be for ever, and my righteousness shall not pass away.

7 ¶Hearken to me, you who know righteousness, the people in whose heart is my law; fear not the reproach of men, neither be afraid of their revilings.

8 For the moth shall eat them up like wool and like a garment; but my righteousness shall be for ever and my salvation from generation to generation.

9 ¶Awake, awake, put on strength, O arm of the LORD; awake as in the ancient days, as in the generations of old. Surely it was thou that didst decree a severe sentence that didst slay the dragon.

10 It was thou that didst dry the sea, the waters of the great deep; that didst make the depths of the sea a way for the redeemed to pass over.

11 Therefore the redeemed of the LORD shall return, and come with singing to Zion; and everlasting joy shall be upon their heads; they shall obtain gladness and joy; and sorrow and sighing shall flee away.

12 I, even I, am he that comforts you, says the LORD; who are you, that you should be afraid of a man that shall die, and of the son of man that dries up like grass;

13 And you have forgotten the LORD, your Maker, who stretched forth the heavens and laid the foundations of the earth; and have been afraid continually every day because of the fury of the oppressor, who was ready to destroy? And now where is the fury of the oppressor?

14 The oppressor hastened to destroy the mighty ones, but they shall not die or be destroyed, neither shall their bread fail.

15 For I am the LORD your God who rebukes the sea, and its waves are calm; the LORD of hosts is his name.

16 And I have put my words in your mouth, and I have covered you in the shadow of my hand, because I stretched forth the heavens and laid the foundations of the earth and said to Zion, You are my people.

17 ¶Awake, awake, stand up, O Jerusalem, because you have drunk at the hand of the LORD the cup of his fury; you have drunk to the dregs of the cup of trembling, and drained it.

18 There is none to comfort her among all the sons whom she has borne; neither is there any of all the sons that she has brought up that takes her by the hand.

19 These two things are come to you; who shall be sorry for you? You shall have plunder, destruction, famine, and sword; who shall comfort you?

20 Your sons have fainted, they lie at every street corner, they are faded like a wilted beet; they are full of the fury of the LORD, the rebuke of your God.

21 ¶Therefore hear now this, O you afflicted and drunken, but not with wine;

22 Thus says your LORD, the LORD, and your God, who pleads the cause of his people: Behold, I have taken out of your hand the cup of trembling, and you shall drink no more of the cup of my fury;

23 But I will put it into the hand of those who afflict you, who have said to your soul, Bow down that we may go over you; and you have made your people like the ground and like the street to them that passed by.

CHAPTER 52

AWAKE, awake, O Zion; put on your beautiful garments, O Jerusalem, the holy city; for henceforth there shall no more come into you the uncircumcised and the unclean.

2 Shake yourself from the dust; arise, and sit down, O Jerusalem; loose the bands from your neck, O captive daughter of Zion.

3 For thus says the LORD: You were sold for nought; and you shall be redeemed without money.

4 For thus says the LORD God: My people went down at the first into Egypt to sojourn there; and the Assyrian carried them away with violence.

5 Now therefore, what have I here, says the LORD, that my people have been carried away for nought? Their rulers make them to wail, says the LORD; and my name continually all the day is blasphemed.

6 Therefore my people shall know my name in that day; for it is I who spoke; behold, it is I.

7 ¶How beautiful upon the mountains are the feet of him who brings glad tidings of peace; who publishes good tidings of good, and who declares salvation; who says to Zion, Your God reigns!

8 Your watchmen shall lift up their voices; with the voice together shall they sing; for they shall see eye to eye, when the LORD shall bring again Zion.

9 ¶Break forth into joy, sing together, you waste places of Jerusalem; for the LORD has comforted his people, he has redeemed Jerusalem.

10 The LORD has made bare his holy arm in the eyes of all the nations; and all the ends of the earth shall see the salvation of our God.

11 ¶Depart, depart, go out from thence, touch no unclean thing; go out of the midst of her; purge yourselves, you who bear the vessels of the LORD.

12 For you shall not go out with haste nor go by flight; for the LORD will go before you; and the God of Israel will gather you together.

13 ¶Behold, my servant shall understand, he shall be exalted and extolled, and be very high.

14 Many were amazed at him; for his appearance was marred more than that of any man, and his form more than that of the sons of men;

15 So shall he purify many nations; kings shall shut their mouths because of him; for that which had not been told them shall they see; and that which they had not heard shall they understand.

CHAPTER 53

WHO has believed our report? And to whom is the arm of the LORD revealed?

2 For he grew up before him like an infant and like a root out of the dry ground; he had no form nor comeliness; and when we saw that he had no beauty, we denied him.

3 He is despised and humbled of men; a man of sorrows and acquainted with grief; and we turned our faces away from him; we despised him and we esteemed him not.

4 ¶Surely he has borne our sorrows and carried our griefs; but we considered him stricken, smitten of God, and afflicted.

5 But he was slain for our sins, he was afflicted for our iniquities; the chastisement of our peace was upon him, and with his wounds we are healed.

6 All we like sheep have strayed; we have turned every one to his own way; and the LORD has laid on him the sins of us all.

7 He drew near and he was afflicted, yet he opened not his mouth; he was led as a lamb to the slaughter; and as an ewe before her shearers is dumb, so he opened not his mouth.

8 He was taken from prison and from judgment; and who can describe his anguish? For he was cut off out of the land of the living; and some of the evil men of my people struck him.

9 He made his grave with the wicked, and with the rich in his death, although he had done no iniquity, neither was there any deceit in his mouth.

10 ¶Yet it pleased the LORD to afflict him; he has put him to grief; he laid down his life as an offering for sin, that posterity may see, and his days shall be prolonged, and the pleasure of the LORD shall prosper in his hand.

11 He shall see the reward of the travail of his soul, and be satisfied with the knowledge; he shall justify the righteous; for he is a servant of many, and he shall bear their sins.

12 Therefore I will divide him a portion with the great, and he shall divide the spoil with the strong, because he has poured out his life to death; and he was numbered with the transgressors; and he bore the sins

of many, and died the death of transgressors.

CHAPTER 54

GIVE praise, O barren, you who did not bear; break forth into singing and rejoice, you who have not travailed with child; for more are the children of the barren than the children of her that is beloved by her husband, says the LORD.

2 Enlarge the place of your tents, and stretch forth the curtains of your habitations; spare not, lengthen your cords and strengthen your tent pegs;

3 For you shall expand on the right hand and on the left; and your descendants shall inherit the Gentiles and make the desolate cities to be inhabited.

4 Fear not, for you shall not be ashamed; neither shall you be rebuked, for you shall not be put to shame; you shall forget the shame of your youth and shall not remember the reproach of your widowhood any more.

5 For your LORD shall do thus to you; the LORD of hosts is his name, and your Saviour the Holy One of Israel; the God of the whole earth shall he be called.

6 For the LORD has called you as a woman forsaken and grieved in spirit, and as a wife forsaken from her youth, says your God.

7 For in a little anger I have forsaken you; but with my great mercies I will gather you.

8 In a raging wrath I hid my face from you; but with my everlasting kindness I will have mercy on you, says the LORD, your Saviour.

9 This is like the days of Noah to me; for as I have sworn that the waters of Noah should no more go over the earth, so have I sworn that I would not be angry with you nor rebuke you.

10 For the mountains shall be brought low and the hills bent downward; but my kindness shall not depart from you, neither shall the covenant of your peace be removed, says the LORD, the Merciful One.

11 ¶O you afflicted one, tempest-tossed and not comforted, behold, I will set your stones in beryl, and lay your foundations with sapphires.

12 And I will make your walls of jasper and your gates of crystal and your borders of precious stones.

13 And all your children shall learn of me; and great shall be the peace of your children.

14 In righteousness shall you be established; you shall be far from oppression, for you shall not fear; and from ruin, for destruction shall not come near you.

15 All those who are brought back by my hand shall enter into you; and they shall be as a place of refuge to your inhabitants.

16 Behold, I have created the smith who blows the coals in the fire and brings forth an instrument for his work; and I have created the ravager to destroy.

17 ¶No weapon that is fashioned against you shall prosper; and every tongue that shall rise against you in judgment, you shall condemn. This is the heritage of the servants of the LORD, and their righteousness is of me, says the LORD.

CHAPTER 55

HO, every one that thirsts, come to the waters; and he who has no money, come, buy and eat; yea, come, buy wine and milk without money and without price.

2 Wherefore do you spend money for that which is not bread? And your labor for that which does not satisfy? Listen diligently to me, and you shall eat that which is good, and your soul shall be delighted in delicacies.

3 Incline your ear, and come to me; listen to me, and your soul shall live; and I will make an everlasting covenant with you, even the sure mercies of David.

4 Behold, I have given you for a witness to the Gentiles, a ruler and leader to the nations.

5 For you shall call nations that you know not, and nations that knew you not shall run to you because of the LORD your God, and because of

the Holy One of Israel; for he has glorified you.

6 ¶Seek the LORD; and when you find him, call upon him while he is near;

7 Let the sinner forsake his way, and the wicked man his thoughts; and let him return to the LORD, and he will have mercy upon him; and to our God, for he will abundantly pardon.

8 ¶For my thoughts are not like your thoughts, neither are my ways like your ways, says the LORD.

9 For as the heavens are higher than the earth, so are my ways higher than your ways, and my thoughts than your thoughts.

10 For as the rain and the snow come down from heaven, and returns not thither, but waters the earth and makes it bring forth and sprout and gives seed to the sower and bread to the eater;

11 So shall my word be that goes forth out of my mouth; it shall not return to me void, but it shall do what I please and it shall accomplish that for which I sent it.

12 For you shall go out with joy, and be led forth with peace; the mountains and the hills shall break forth before you into singing and all the trees of the field shall clap their hands.

13 Instead of the thorn shall come up the fir tree, and instead of the brier shall come up the myrtle; and it shall be to the LORD for a name, for an everlasting sign that shall not be cut off.

CHAPTER 56

THUS says the LORD: Keep judgment, and do justice; for my salvation will come soon and my righteousness will be revealed.

2 Blessed is the man who does this, and the son of man who lays hold on it; he who also keeps the sabbath that he may not profane it, and guards his hands from doing any evil.

3 ¶Do not let the son of the stranger who follows the LORD speak, saying, The LORD has utterly separated me from his people; neither let

the eunuch say, Behold, I am a dry tree.

4 For thus says the LORD: To the eunuchs who keep my sabbaths and choose the things that please me and take hold of my covenant,

5 I will give to them in my house and within my walls a place and a name better than sons and daughters; I will give them an everlasting name that shall not be cut off.

6 Also to the sons of the strangers who follow the LORD, to serve him and to love the name of the LORD, to be his servants, every one who keeps from profaning the sabbath and takes hold of my covenant,

7 Even them I will bring to my holy mountain and make them joyful in my house of prayer; their burnt offerings and their sacrifices shall be accepted upon my altar; for my house shall be called a house of prayer for all peoples.

8 Thus says the LORD God, who gathers the outcasts of Israel: Yet I will gather others to him, besides those who were gathered to him.

9 ¶All the beasts of the field, come to devour, yea, all you beasts in the forest.

10 All that are blind can see, but they know not; they are all dumb dogs, they cannot bark; they see, but they lie down and slumber.

11 Yea, they are greedy dogs that can never have enough, they are so wicked that they cannot understand; they all have turned aside to their own way, every one for his own gain and his own advantage.

12 Come, they say, let us get wine, and let us fill ourselves with strong drink; and tomorrow shall be as this day, and much more will be left over for us.

CHAPTER 57

BEHOLD, the righteous man has perished, and no one lays it to heart; and pious men are taken away, none considering that the righteous man is taken away from the evil to come.

2 And when peace comes, they shall relax, and make progress.

3 ¶But you draw near hither, you sons of the afflicted one, the offspring of the adulterer and the whore.

4 Against whom do you sport yourselves? Against whom do you open your mouth wide and draw out the tongue? [1] Are you not children of iniquity, an offspring of falsehood,

5 Comforting yourselves with idols under every green tree, slaying children as sacrifices in the valleys under the cliffs of the rocks?

6 Your portion and your heritage is in the parts of the valleys; even upon them you have poured a drink offering, you have offered meal offerings. Should I receive comfort in these things?

7 Upon high and lofty mountains you have set your bed; even thither you went up to offer sacrifices.

8 Behind the doors also and on the posts you have inscribed your remembrance; for you are carried away from me, and you are gone up, and you have enlarged your bed, and you have become one of them; you have loved their bed where you saw their nakedness.

9 And you did praise the kings with frankincense, and did increase your perfumes, and you did send your messengers far off, and you have brought yourself low, even down to Sheol.

10 You are wearied in the multitude of your corrupt ways; yet you did not say, I will cease; you have wasted away yourself with the guilt of your hands, therefore you did not make supplication.

11 And of whom have you been in dread and fear, that you have lied against me and have not remembered me nor laid it to your heart? Behold, I am the Holy One of old, and you did not revere me.

12 I will declare my righteousness, and your works shall not profit you.

13 ¶When you cry, let those who gather around you deliver you; but the wind shall carry them all away, and the whirlwind shall take them; but those who put their trust in me shall inherit the land and shall possess my holy mountain;

14 And shall say, Clear up, clear up, prepare the way, take up the stumblingblocks out of the path of my people.

15 For thus says the high and lofty One who inhabits eternity, whose name is Holy, whose abode is high and holy, to the meek and the distressed in spirit, to revive the spirit of the humble, and to revive the heart of those who are in pain:

16 I will not contend for ever, neither will I be always wroth; for the spirit proceeds from before me, and the breath, I have made it.

17 Because of the iniquity of her [2] treachery I was wroth and smote her; but she backslid and was wroth, and went away groaning in her heart.

18 I have seen her ways, and I have healed her and have comforted her, and I have given comfort to her and to her mourners.

19 I create the speech of the lips; peace, peace to those who are afar off and to those who are near, says the LORD; and I will heal them.

20 But the wicked are like the troubled sea, for it cannot rest, its waters cast up creeping things and mire.

21 There is no peace to the wicked, says my God.

CHAPTER 58

CRY aloud, spare not, lift up your voice like a trumpet and show my people their transgressions, and the house of Jacob their sins.

2 Yet they seek me daily and wish to know my ways, as a nation that did righteousness, and forsook not the ordinance of their God; they ask of me the ordinances of justice; they take delight in drawing near to God.

3 ¶Why have we fasted, and thou seest it not? Why have we afflicted ourselves, and thou takest no notice? Behold, in the day of your fast you do what you wish, and you present offerings to all of your idols.

4 Behold, you fast for strife and quarreling, and to strike violently

---

[1] Idiom meaning *talk too much and answer back.*   [2] Jerusalem.

with the fist of wickedness; you shall not fast as you do this day, to make your voice to be heard on high.

5 Is it such a fast that I have chosen? A day for a man to afflict his soul, to bow down his head like a bulrush, and to spread sackcloth and ashes under him? Will you call this a fast, and an acceptable day to the LORD?

6 This is the fast that I have chosen: to loose the bonds of wickedness, to cut off the bands of treachery, to let the oppressed go free, and to break every yoke;

7 To share your bread with the hungry, and to bring the stranger to your house; when you see the naked, to cover him; and to refuse not one of your own flesh.

8 ¶Then shall your light break forth as the morning and your right-eousness shall spring forth speedily; and your righteousness shall go before you; the glory of the LORD shall be your reward.

9 Then you shall call, and the LORD shall answer you; you shall cry, and he shall say, Here am I. If you remove deceit from your midst and re-lease the prisoners and cease speaking falsehood;

10 And give your bread to the hungry, and satisfy the afflicted soul; then shall your light shine in dark-ness, and your darkness be as the noonday;

11 And the LORD shall guide you continually and satisfy your soul with rich food; and strengthen your bones; and you shall be like a watered gar-den, and like a spring whose water fails not.

12 And some of you shall build the old waste places; you shall raise up the foundations of many genera-tions; and you shall be called the re-pairer of the breaches, the restorer of paths to dwell in.

13 ¶If you turn away your foot from the sabbath, from doing your pleasures on my holy day; and call the sabbath a delight, the holy of the LORD, honorable; and shall honor it, not doing on it your own ways, nor

doing on it your own pleasure, nor speaking idle words;

14 Then you shall put your trust in the LORD; and I will cause you to ride upon the high places of the earth and feed you with the heritage of Jacob your father; for the mouth of the LORD has spoken it.

CHAPTER 59

BEHOLD, the LORD's hand is not so short,[1] that it cannot save; neither is his ear dull that it cannot hear;

2 But it is your iniquities that have separated you and your God; and your sins have hid his face from you, that he will not hear.

3 For your hands are defiled with blood, and your fingers with iniquity; your lips have spoken lies, your tongue mutters wickedness.

4 There is no one who calls for jus-tice, neither is there any one who judges faithfully; they trust in vanity and speak lies; they conceive iniquity and bring forth grief.

5 They hatch adder's eggs, and weave a spider's web; he who eats of their eggs shall die, and those which hatch out will be found to be vipers.

6 Their webs shall not become gar-ments, neither shall they cover them-selves with their works; their works are works of iniquity, and acts of violence are in their hands.

7 Their feet run to evil, and they make haste to shed innocent blood; their thoughts are thoughts of in-iquity; plunder and destruction are in their paths.

8 The way of peace they know not; and there is no justice in their ways; they have made their paths crooked; whosoever walks in them shall not know peace.

9 ¶Therefore justice is far from us, and righteousness does not overtake us; we wait for light, but behold ob-scurity; for brightness, but we walk in darkness.

10 We grope for the wall like the blind, and we grope like men who have no eyes; we stumble at noonday

---

[1] An idiom which means *he is not helpless.*

as in the night; we groan as those who are near death.

11 We all roar like bears, and mourn sore like doves; we look for justice, but there is none; for salvation, but it is far off from us.

12 For our transgressions are multiplied before thee, and our sins testify against us; our iniquities are with us, and our sins are well known:

13 Transgressing and lying against the LORD, turning away from following our God, speaking oppression and revolt, conceiving and devising in our heart words of falsehood.

14 Judgment is turned backward, and righteousness stands afar off; for truth is fallen in the street, and equity cannot enter.

15 Yea, truth is hid, and understanding has departed from our mind; the LORD saw that there was no justice, and he was displeased.

16 ¶And he saw that there was no man, and wondered that there was no one to help; therefore his arm brought salvation to him, and his righteousness sustained him.[1]

17 For he put on righteousness as a breastplate, and a helmet of salvation upon his head; and he put on the garments of vengeance for clothing,

18 That he may seek vengeance upon those who hate him, and retribution to his adversaries, and to the islands he will render recompense.

19 So shall they revere the name of the LORD from the west, and his glory from the rising of the sun. For the oppressor shall come in like a flood, and the Spirit of the LORD shall humble him.

20 ¶And a Saviour shall come to Zion, and to those who turn from transgression in Jacob, says the LORD.

21 As for me, this is my covenant with you, says the LORD: my spirit that is upon you, and my words which I have put in your mouth, shall not depart out of your mouth, nor out of the mouth of your descendants, nor out of the mouth of your descendant's descendants, says the LORD, from henceforth and for ever.

[1] Israel.

CHAPTER 60

ARISE, shine; for your light is come, and the glory of the LORD shall rise upon you.

2 Behold, darkness will cover the earth, and thick darkness the nations; but the LORD shall shine upon you, and his glory shall be seen upon you.

3 And the Gentiles shall come to your light, and kings to the brightness of your rising.

4 Lift up your eyes round about and see; they all gather themselves together, they come to you; your sons shall come from afar, and your daughters shall be nursed in cradles.

5 Then you shall see, and your face shall brighten, and you shall rejoice; and your heart shall be at ease; because the riches of the sea shall be turned to you, the strength of the Gentiles shall come to you.

6 A multitude of camels shall cover you, the dromedaries of Midian and Ephah; all those from Sheba shall come; they shall bring gold and frankincense, and shall publish abroad the praises of the LORD.

7 All the flocks of Kedar shall be gathered together to you, the rams of Nebaioth shall minister to you; they shall come up with acceptance on my altar, and I will glorify the house of my beauty.

8 Who are these that fly like clouds and like the doves to their windows?

9 For the islands shall wait for me, and the ships of Tarshish as in former days, to bring your sons from afar, their silver and their gold with them, to the name of the LORD your God, and the Holy One of Israel, because he has glorified you.

10 And the sons of foreigners shall build up your walls, and their kings shall minister to you; for in my anger I smote you, but in my favor I have had mercy on you.

11 Therefore your gates shall be open continually; they shall not be shut day nor night, that men may bring to you the armies of the Gentiles, and their kings led captive.

12 For the nation and the kingdom that will not serve you shall perish; yea, those nations shall be utterly destroyed by the sword.

13 The glory of Lebanon shall come to you, the fir tree, the pine, and the cypress together, to beautify the place of my sanctuary; and I will make the place of my feet glorious.

14 The sons also of those who oppressed you shall come bowing down to you; and all those who provoked you shall make obeisance at the soles of your feet; and they shall call you, the City of the LORD, the Zion of the Holy One of Israel.

15 Whereas you have been forsaken and hated so that no man passed through you, I will make you an eternal excellency, a joy of many generations.

16 You shall also gain the wealth of the Gentiles, and shall obtain the wealth of kings; and you shall know that I the LORD am your Saviour and your Redeemer, the Mighty One of Jacob.

17 Instead of brass I will bring gold, and instead of iron I will bring silver, and instead of wood, brass, and instead of stones, iron; I will also make your officers peace and your rulers righteousness.

18 Violence shall no more be heard in your land, nor spoil and destruction within your borders; and they shall call your walls Salvation and your gates Praise.

19 The sun shall be no more your light by day; neither for brightness shall the moon give light to you; for the LORD shall be to you an everlasting light, and the days of your mourning shall be ended.

20 All of your righteous people shall inherit the land for ever; the branch of my planting, the work of my hands shall be glorified.[1]

21 The smallest one shall become thousands, and the least one a strong nation; I the LORD will hasten it in its time.

CHAPTER 61

THE Spirit of the LORD is upon me, because the LORD has anointed me and sent me to preach good tidings to the meek; to bind up the brokenhearted, to proclaim liberty to captives and release to prisoners;

2 To proclaim the acceptable year of the LORD, and the day of the salvation of our God; to comfort all that mourn;

3 To give to the mourners of Zion beauty instead of ashes, perfume instead of mourning, a cloak of beauty instead of the spirit of heaviness; they shall be called men of righteousness, the planting of the LORD, which is glorious.

4 ¶And they shall build the old ruins, they shall raise up the former desolations, and they shall repair the waste cities, the desolations of many generations.

5 And strangers shall stand and feed your flocks, and the sons of the alien shall be your plowmen and your vinedressers.

6 But you shall be named the priests of the LORD; men shall call you the ministers of our God; you shall eat the riches of the Gentiles, and in their glory shall you boast yourselves.

7 ¶Instead of your shame and your confusion, you shall have a double inheritance in their lands, and you shall rejoice in their portion; everlasting joy shall be yours.

8 For I the LORD love justice, and I hate robbery and iniquity; I will direct your work in truth and I will make an everlasting covenant with you.

9 Your offspring shall be known among the Gentiles, and your descendants among the nations; all who see you shall recognize you, that you are the offspring that the LORD has blessed.

10 I will greatly rejoice in the LORD and my soul shall be joyful in my God; for he has clothed me with the

---

[1] Verse 20 is seemingly a repetition of verse 19 in the King James Version. Western translators evidently had made two translations of the same verse and had forgotten to omit one of them.

garments of salvation, he has covered me with the robe of righteousness, as a bridegroom decks himself in splendor and as a bride adorns herself with jewels.

11 For as the earth brings forth its bud, and as the garden causes the seed which is sown in it to spring forth, so the LORD God will cause righteousness and praise to spring forth before all the nations.

CHAPTER 62

FOR Zion's sake I will not hold my peace, and for Jerusalem's sake I will not rest until her righteousness shall go forth as light and her salvation as a lamp that burns.

2 And the Gentiles shall see your righteousness, and all kings your glory; and you shall be called by a new name which the mouth of the LORD shall bestow upon you.

3 You shall also be a crown of glory in the hand of the LORD and a royal diadem in the hand of your God.

4 You shall no more be called Forsaken; neither shall your land any more be termed Desolate; but you shall be called My Delight, and your land shall be cultivated; for the Lord delights in you, and your land shall have husbandmen.

5 ¶For as a young man husbands a virgin, so shall your sons husband you; and as the bridegroom rejoices over the bride, so shall your God rejoice over you.

6 I have set watchmen upon your walls, O Jerusalem, every day, who shall not hold their peace day or night continually; so that those who make mention of the LORD may not keep silence, nor be still,

7 And give you no rest, until I, the Lord, establish you and until I make Jerusalem a praise in the earth.

8 The LORD has sworn by his right hand and by his strong arm, I will no more give your grain to be food for your enemies; neither shall the sons of strangers drink your wine for which you have labored;

9 But those who have gathered it shall eat it and praise the LORD; and those who have brought it together shall drink it in the courts of my holiness.

10 ¶Go through, go through the gates; prepare the way of the people; make the highway smooth, gather out the stones; lift up a standard for the people.

11 Behold, the LORD has proclaimed to the ends of the earth, Say to the daughter of Zion, Behold, your Saviour comes; behold, his reward is with him and his work before him.

12 And they shall call them The holy people, The redeemed of the LORD; and you shall be called, Avenged, Sought out, A city not forsaken.

CHAPTER 63

WHO is this that comes from Edom with crimson garments from Bozrah? And who is glorious in his apparel and mighty in the greatness of his strength? I that speak in righteousness, mighty to save.

2 Why is your apparel red and why are your garments like those of him who treads in the winepress?

3 I have trodden the winepress alone, and of the people there was none with me; I have trodden them in my anger and trampled them in my fury; and their blood is splashed upon my garments, and I have stained all my raiment.

4 For the day of vengeance is in my heart, and the year of my salvation is come.

5 And I looked, and there was none to help; and I wondered, and there was none to uphold; therefore my own arm saved me and my fury upheld me.

6 And I have trodden down the peoples in my anger, and made them drunk in my fury, and I have brought down their strength to the earth.

7 ¶I will mention the lovingkindnesses of the LORD and the praises of the LORD for all the things that the LORD has bestowed on us and the great goodness toward the house of Israel, which he has bestowed on us according to his mercies and accord-

ing to the multitude of his loving-kindnesses.

8 For he said, Surely they are my people, children that will not lie; so he became their Saviour.

9 In all their troubles he did not afflict them, and the angel of his presence saved them; in his love and in his pity he saved them and he lifted them up and carried them all the days of old.

10 ¶But they rebelled and grieved his holy Spirit; therefore he turned to be their enemy and he fought against them.

11 Then he remembered the days of old, of Moses his servant. Just as when he brought up out of the sea the shepherd of his flock, and as he put his holy Spirit within Moses,

12 Who led them by his right hand and by his glorious arm, dividing the waters before them and making for them an everlasting name

13 And leading them through the deep, as a horse is led in the wilderness, and they stumbled not,

14 And like cattle that go down into the valley, the Spirit of the LORD leading them; so didst thou lead thy people and make for thyself a glorious name.

15 ¶ Look down from heaven and behold from thy holy and glorious habitation. Where is thy zeal and thy strength? Turn thy tender mercies and compassion toward us. Are they restrained?

16 For thou art our Father, though Abraham knew us not and Israel did not acknowledge us; thou, O LORD, art our Father, and our Saviour; thy name is from everlasting.

17 ¶O LORD, why hast thou made us to err from thy way and hardened our heart so as not to reverence thee? Return, for thy servants' sake, the tribes of thy heritage.

18 The people of thy holiness have possessed the land but a little while; our oppressors have trodden down thy sanctuary.

19 We are thine from of old before thou didst rule over them; [1] they were not called by thy name.

[1] The Gentiles.

CHAPTER 64

OH that thou wouldst rend the heavens and that thou wouldst come down, that the mountains might flee at thy presence;

2 That they might melt as wax melts before the fire, and that fire might devour thy enemies, that thy name might be made known to thy enemies, so that the nations might tremble at thy presence!

3 When thou didst wondrous things which we looked not for, thou camest down, the mountains fled at thy presence.

4 For since the beginning of the world men have not heard nor perceived by the ear, neither has the eye seen, O God, any besides thee, because of what thou doest for those that wait for thee.

5 Thou meetest with joy him that works righteousness, those that remember thee in thy ways; behold, thou art wroth; for we have transgressed against thy ways, and yet we shall be saved.

6 For we have all become like an unclean thing, and all our righteousness is like filthy rags; we all fall off like leaves; and our iniquities, like the whirlwind, have taken us away.

7 There is none that calls upon thy name, that remembers to take hold of thee; for thou hast turned away thy face from us, and hast delivered us into the power of our sins.

8 But now, O LORD, thou art our Father; we are the clay, and thou our potter; and we are all the work of thy hand.

9 ¶Be not very angry, O LORD, neither remember our sins for ever; behold, see, we are all thy people.

10 Thy holy cities have become a wilderness, Zion is a wilderness, Jerusalem a desolation.

11 Our holy and beautiful temple, where our fathers praised thee, is consumed with fire; and all our pleasant possessions are laid waste.

12 Because of these things thou hast restrained thyself, O LORD, and held thy peace, and afflicted us very sore.

CHAPTER 65

I AM sought of those who did not ask for me; I am found of those who sought me not; I said, Here am I, here am I, to a nation that has never called my name.

2 I have spread out my hands all the day to a rebellious people, who walk in a way that is not good, after their own thoughts,

3 A people who provoke me to anger continually, who sacrifice in the gardens and burn incense upon altars of bricks;

4 Who sit in tombs and lodge in caves, who eat swine's flesh and pollute their vessels with unclean carcasses; to break the law and to defile the holy covenant, that they may provoke the LORD.

5 Who say, Keep away, do not come near me; for I am sanctified. These men are a smoke in my anger, a fire that burns all the day.

6 Behold, it is written before me: I will not keep silence until I recompense them a double portion into their bosom.

7 Their sins and the sins of their fathers are well known, says the LORD, for they have burned incense upon the mountains and reproached me upon the hills; therefore I will measure their former works into their bosom.

8 ¶Thus says the LORD: As the new wine is found in the cluster, and one says to another, Destroy it not, for a blessing is in it; so will I do for my servant's sake, and I will not destroy them all.

9 And I will bring forth an offspring out of Jacob, and out of Judah an inheritor of my mountains; my elect shall inherit it and my servants shall dwell there.

10 And Sharon shall be a fold for flocks, and the valley of Achor a place for the herds to lie down in for my people who have sought me.

11 ¶But as for you who have forsaken the LORD and have forgotten his holy mountain, who prepare tables for fortune tellers and have poured out wine into bowls for them,

12 I will deliver you up to the sword, and all of you shall bow down to the slaughter, because when I called, you did not answer; when I spoke, you did not listen; and you did evil in my presence, and did choose the thing wherein I do not delight.

13 Therefore thus says the LORD God: Behold, my servants shall eat, but you shall be hungry; behold, my servants shall drink, but you shall be thirsty; behold, my servants shall rejoice, but you shall weep;

14 Behold my servants shall sing for joy of heart, but you shall complain for sorrow of heart and for vexation of spirit.

15 And you shall leave your name for a curse to my chosen ones; for the LORD God shall slay you, and call his servants by another name;

16 So that he who blesses himself in the earth shall bless himself in the God of truth; and he who swears in the earth shall swear by the God of truth; because the former troubles are forgotten, and because they are hid from my presence.

17 ¶For, behold, I create new heavens and a new earth; and the former things shall not be remembered nor come into mind.

18 But my people shall be glad and rejoice for ever because I am creating; for, behold, I create Jerusalem a rejoicing, and I will rejoice in it.

19 And I will rejoice in Jerusalem, and joy in my people; and the voice of weeping shall be no more heard in her, nor the voice of wailing.

20 There shall be no more in her a child who dies in infancy nor an old man who has not filled his days; for the child shall die a hundred years old; but a sinner being a hundred years old shall be accursed.

21 They shall build houses and inhabit them; and they shall plant vineyards and eat their fruit.

22 They shall not build and others inhabit; they shall not plant and others eat; for like the days of trees are the days of my people, and my chosen ones shall eat the work of their hands.

23 They shall not labor in vain nor bring forth children for a curse; for they are the seed of the blessed of the LORD, both they and their children with them.

24 And it shall come to pass that before they call I will answer them; and before they speak I will hear them.

25 The wolf and the lamb shall feed together and the lion shall eat straw like the ox, and dust shall be the serpents' food. They shall not hurt nor destroy in all my holy mountain, says the LORD.

CHAPTER 66

THUS says the LORD: Heaven is my throne and the earth my footstool; what is the house that you build for me? And what is the place of my rest?

2 For all those things has my own hand made, and all those things belong to me, says the LORD; and to whom shall I look, and where shall I dwell? But to him who is calm and humble, and trembles at my word.

3 He who kills an ox is like him who slays a man; he who sacrifices a lamb is like him who kills a dog; he who offers a meal offering is like him who offers swine's blood; he who burns incense is like him who blesses an idol. Yea, they have chosen their own ways, and their soul delights in their idols.

4 I also will allow them to be humiliated and will recompense them according to their works; because when I called, none did answer; when I spoke, they did not listen; but they did evil in my sight, and chose the things in which I delighted not.

5 ¶Hear the word of the LORD, you who tremble at his word; say to your brethren who hate you and who despise you for my name's sake, Let the LORD be glorified, and rejoice in your joy, and they shall be ashamed.

6 A voice of tumult comes from the city, a voice from the temple, the voice of the LORD who renders recompense to his enemies!

7 Before she travailed, she gave birth; before her pain came, she was delivered of a male child.

8 Who has heard such a thing? Who has seen such things? Shall the earth be made to bring forth in one day? Or shall a nation be born in an hour? For as soon as Zion travailed, she brought forth her children.

9 Shall I bring to the birth, and not cause to bring forth? says the LORD; perhaps it is not I who causes to bring forth and who shuts the womb? says the LORD your God.

10 Rejoice with Jerusalem and be glad with her, all you who love her; rejoice in joy with her, all you who mourn over her,

11 That you may suck and be satisfied with the comfort of her breast; that you may milk out and be delighted with the abundance of her glory.

12 For thus says the LORD: Behold, I will extend peace to her like a river, like an overflowing torrent; and you shall suck the glory of the Gentiles; and you shall be carried on the litters and be dandled upon the knees;

13 As one whom his mother comforts, so will I comfort you; and you shall be comforted in Jerusalem.

14 And when you shall see this, your heart shall rejoice and your bones shall flourish like tender grass; and the hand of the LORD shall be stretched out toward his servants, and he shall destroy his enemies.

15 For, behold, the LORD will come with fire and with his chariot like a whirlwind, to pour out his anger with fury and his rebuke with flames of fire.

16 For by fire will the LORD judge, and by it will he test all flesh; and the slain of the LORD shall be many.

17 Those who sanctify themselves and purify themselves in the gardens, following one after another in the midst, eating swine's flesh and creeping things and mice, shall be consumed together, says the LORD.

18 For I know their works and their thoughts; when I come to gather all nations and tongues, they shall come and see my glory.

19 I will set a sign among them, and those who escape I will send among the nations, to Tarshish, Pul, and Lud, who draw the bow, to Tubal, and Javan, and to the islands afar off that have not heard my fame, neither have they seen my glory; and they shall declare my glory among the Gentiles.

20 And upon horses and in chariots and in litters they shall bring all your brethren for an offering to the Lord out of all nations to my holy mountain Jerusalem, says the Lord, as the children of Israel bring a meal offering in a clean vessel into the house of the Lord.

21 And I will also take some of them for priests and for Levites, says the Lord.

22 For as the new heavens and the new earth which I will make shall remain before me, says the Lord, so shall your descendants and your name remain.

23 And it shall come to pass that from one new moon to another and from one sabbath to another all flesh shall come to worship before me, says the Lord.

24 And they shall go forth and look on the dead bodies of the men that have transgressed against me; for their coals shall not die, neither shall their fire be quenched; and they shall be an abhorrence to all flesh.

THE BOOK OF THE

PROPHET JEREMIAH

CHAPTER 1

THE words of Jeremiah the son of Hilkiah, of the priests who were in Anathoth in the land of Benjamin,

2 To whom the word of the Lord came in the days of Josiah the son of Amon king of Judah, in the thirteenth year of his reign.

3 It came also in the days of Jehoiakim the son of Josiah king of Judah, until the end of the eleventh year of Zedekiah the son of Josiah king of Judah, until the inhabitants of Jerusalem were carried captive in the fifth month.

4 Then the word of the Lord came to me, saying,

5 Before I formed you in the belly I knew you; and before you came out of the womb I sanctified you and ordained you a prophet to the nations.

6 Then I said, I beseech thee, O Lord God! Behold, I cannot speak, for I am but a child.

7 ¶And the Lord said to me, Do not say, I am a child; for you shall go to all that I shall send you, and whatever I command you you shall speak.

8 Be not afraid of their presence; for I am with you to deliver you, says the Lord.

9 Then the Lord put forth his hand and touched my mouth. And the Lord said to me, Behold, I have put my words in your mouth.

10 See, I have this day set you over the nations and over the kingdoms, to root out and to pull down, and to overthrow and to destroy, to build and to plant.

11 ¶Moreover the word of the Lord came to me, saying, Jeremiah, what do you see? And I said, I see a rod of an almond tree.

12 Then the Lord said to me, You have well seen; for I will hasten my word to perform it.

13 And the word of the Lord came to me the second time, saying, What

do you see? And I said, I see a boiling caldron; and its face is toward the north.

14 Then the LORD said unto me, Out of the north an evil shall break forth upon all the inhabitants of the land.

15 For, lo, I will send and I will call all the tribes of the kingdoms of the north, says the LORD; and they shall come, and they shall set every one his throne at the entering of the gates of Jerusalem and against all its walls round about and against all the cities of Judah.

16 And I will utter my judgments against them, because of all their wickedness, for they have forsaken me, and have burned incense to other gods and worshipped the works of their own hands.

17 ¶Therefore gird up your loins, and arise and speak to all that I command you; be not afraid of them, lest I confound you before them.

18 For, behold, I have made you this day like a fortified city and like an iron pillar and like a brass fence against the whole land, against the kings of Judah, against their princes, against their priests, against their prophets, and against all the people of the land.

19 And they shall fight with you; but they shall not prevail against you; for I am with you to deliver you, says the LORD.

CHAPTER 2

MOREOVER the word of the LORD came upon me, saying,

2 Go and proclaim in the ears of the people of Jerusalem, and say, Thus says the LORD: I remember you, the kindness of your youth, the love of your long-suffering; for you walked after me in the wilderness, in the land that was not sown.

3 Israel has sanctified to the LORD the first fruits of his crops; all those who embezzle them shall be condemned; evil shall come upon them, says the LORD.

4 Hear the word of the LORD, O house of Jacob, and all the families of the house of Israel:

5 ¶Thus says the LORD: What iniquity have your fathers found in me, that they are gone far from me and have walked after vanity and have profited nothing?

6 Neither did they say, Where is the LORD who brought us up out of the land of Egypt, who led us through the wilderness, through a waste and depressed land, through a desolate land and a land of the shadow of death, a land that no man passed through, and where no man dwells?

7 And I brought you into a land of plenty, to eat its fruit and its goodness; but when you came in, you defiled my land and made my heritage an abomination.

8 The priests did not say, Where is the LORD? And those who handle the law did not know me; the leaders also transgressed against me, and the prophets prophesied by Baal, and went after things that do not profit.

9 ¶Therefore I will yet contend with you, says the LORD; and with your children's children I will contend.

10 For cross over to the islands of China and see; and send to Kedar, and understand diligently, and see if there ever has been such a thing as this.

11 Have the Gentiles changed their gods, which are not gods? But my people have changed their glory for that which does not profit.

12 Be astonished, O heavens, at this, and tremble and be exceedingly afraid, says the LORD.

13 For my people have committed two evils: they have forsaken me, the fountain of living waters, and they went and dug for themselves broken cisterns that can hold no water.

14 ¶Is Israel a servant? If he is a homeborn heir, why then is he plundered?

15 The lions have roared against him, and growled, and they made his land waste; his villages have become desolate without inhabitants.

16 Also certain rulers of the inhabitants of Memphis and Tahapanes shall rule over you.

17 Behold, such shall be done unto

you, because you have forsaken the LORD your God, at a time when he led you in his way.

18 And now, why is it that you go in the way of Egypt,[1] to drink the waters of Sihor? And why is it that you go in the way of Assyria, to drink the waters of the river (Euphrates)?

19 Your own evil shall chastise you, and your repentance shall reprove you; know therefore and see that it is an evil thing and bitter, for you have forsaken the LORD your God, and you have not revered me, says the LORD God of hosts.

20 ¶For of old time I have broken your yoke and cut your bands; and you said, I shall never serve another god again; and behold, now upon every high hill and under every green tree you wander, playing the harlot.

21 Yet I had planted you a good vine, wholly a right seed; why then have you turned against me and have become degenerate like a plant of a strange vine?

22 For though you wash yourself with nitre and use much sulphur, yet your sins within you are marked before me, says the LORD God.

23 How can you say, I am not polluted, I have not gone after Baal? See your ways in the valleys, and know what you have done: you have lifted up your voice, O you perverse in her ways;

24 You are like a wild ass which is untrained in the wilderness and follows her own will; you have snuffed up the wind, who can bring you back? Whoever seeks her shall weary himself, he shall find her only by means of her footprints.

25 Your feet are weary because they are unshod, and your throat is dry from thirst; but you said, I have become strong, I am unwilling to repent because I have loved strangers, and after them I will go.

26 As the thief is ashamed when he is found, so the children of Israel are ashamed; they, their kings, their princes, and their priests, and their prophets,

27 Who say to a piece of wood, You are our father; and to a stone, You have brought us forth; for they have turned their backs upon me and not their faces; but in the time of their trouble, they say, Arise and save us.

28 But where are your gods that you have made for yourself? Let them arise and save you in the time of your trouble; for according to the number of your cities are your gods, O Judah.

29 Why then do you contend with me? You all have transgressed against me, says the LORD.

30 In vain have I smitten your children; they have received no discipline; the sword has devoured your prophets like a destroying lion.

31 ¶As for you, O generation, hear the word of the LORD. Have I been like a wilderness to Israel? Or a waste land? Wherefore then say my people, We are humiliated; we will come no more to you?

32 Can a maid forget her ornaments or a bride her attire? Yet my people have forgotten me days without number.

33 Why do you deck yourself to induce love? For behold you have also learned evil by means of your conduct.

34 Also on your hands is found the blood of the souls of the poor innocents; I have not found it by hard search, for it is under every tree.

35 Yet you say, Because I am innocent, therefore he will turn his anger from me. Behold, I will contend with you, because you have said, I have not sinned.

36 Why do you gad about so much to change your ways? You shall also be ashamed of Egypt, even as you were ashamed of Assyria.

37 Yea, you shall go forth from him humiliated; for the LORD is angry against those upon whom you have put your trust, and you shall not prosper with them.

CHAPTER 3

IF a man put away his wife, and she go from him and become an-

---

[1] Why do you make alliances with Egypt and Assyria, and adopt their policy?

other man's wife, and he return to her again, behold, the land shall be defiled. But you have committed adultery with many rulers; return again to me, says the LORD.

2 Lift up your eyes to the highways, and see if there is a place where you have not defiled yourself. In the roads you have sat waiting for them, like an ostrich in the wilderness; and you have polluted the land with your whoredom.

3 And because of your wickedness the showers have been withheld, and there has been no latter rain; and you have become shameless like a whore, you have refused to be reproved.

4 Behold, now you say to me, My father, and thou art foster mother of my childhood.

5 Will God reserve his anger for ever? Or will he keep it to the end? Behold, you have spoken, and have done evil things beyond measure.

6 ¶The LORD said to me in the days of King Josiah, Have you seen the thing which she who dwells in Israel has done? She has gone up upon every high mountain and under every green tree, and there has played the harlot.

7 And I said after she had done all these things, Return to me, but she did not return. And her perverseness was seen by her sister Judah.

8 And she saw all Israel's evil-doings. And because the inhabitants of Israel committed adultery, I had put her away and given a bill of divorce; yet her perverse sister Judah did not fear, but went and played the harlot also.

9 And her whoredom was so excessive that she defiled the land and committed adultery with idols of stone and wood,

10 And yet, for all this her treacherous sister Judah has not returned to me with her whole heart, but only with falsehood, says the LORD.

11 And the LORD said to me, The inhabitant of Israel has justified herself more than her perverse sister Judah.

12 ¶Go proclaim these words toward the north, and say, Repent, O you inhabitant of Israel, says the LORD; and I will not be severe against you; for I am good, says the LORD, and I will not keep anger for ever.

13 Only acknowledge your iniquity, for you have sinned against the LORD your God, and have scattered your evil practices to the strangers under every green tree, and you have not obeyed my voice, says the LORD.

14 Repent, O backsliding children, says the LORD; for I was pleased with you; and took one person of you from every town and two from every family, and I brought you to Zion.

15 And I will give you rulers according to my own heart, who will govern you with knowledge and understanding.

16 And it shall come to pass when you have multiplied and increased in the land in those days, says the LORD, they shall say no more, The ark of the covenant of the LORD; neither shall it come to mind, nor shall they remember it, nor shall they visit it, nor shall that ritual be performed any more.

17 At that time they shall call Jerusalem the throne of the LORD; and all the nations shall look up to the name of the LORD; neither shall they walk any more after the imagination of their evil heart.

18 In those days the house of Judah shall walk with the house of Israel, and they shall come together out of the land of the north to the land that I have given as an inheritance to their fathers.

19 And I said, I will consider you as children, and give you a pleasant land, a goodly heritage of the hosts of nations; and I said, You shall call me, My father, and shall not turn away from me.

20 ¶Surely as a wife lies about her lover, so has the house of Israel lied against me, says the LORD.

21 A voice was heard on the highways, the weeping and supplications of the children of Israel; for they have perverted their ways, and they have forsaken the LORD their God.

22 Repent, O you backsliding children, and I will heal your backslid-

ings; and say, Behold, we are yours; for thou art the LORD our God.

23 Truly, in vain is salvation hoped for from the hills and from fortified mountains; truly, in the LORD our God is the salvation of Israel.

24 For shame has devoured the labor of our fathers from their childhood, their flocks and their herds, their sons and their daughters.

25 Let us lie down in our shame, and let our confusion cover us; for we have sinned against the LORD our God, we and our fathers, from our youth even to this day, and have not obeyed the voice of the LORD our God.

CHAPTER 4

IF you will repent, O Israel, says the LORD, return to me; and if you will put away your abominations from my presence, then you shall not be carried away.

2 And you shall swear, The LORD liveth in truth, in judgment, and in righteousness; and the Gentiles shall bless themselves in him, and in him shall they glory.

3 ¶For thus says the LORD to the men of Judah and to the inhabitants of Jerusalem, Light your lamp; and sow not among thorns.

4 Circumcise yourselves to the LORD, and take away the foreskins of your heart, you men of Judah and inhabitants of Jerusalem; lest my wrath come forth like fire, and burn so that no one can quench it, because of the evil of your doings.

5 Declare in Judah and publish in Jerusalem, and say, Blow the trumpet in the land; cry with a loud voice and say, Assemble yourselves, and let us enter into the fortified cities.

6 Set up the standard toward Zion; be strong, stay not; for I will bring evil from the north, and a great destruction.

7 A powerful king is come up like a lion from his thicket, and the destroyer of the Gentiles is on his way; he has gone forth from his country to make your land desolate; and your cities shall be laid waste without an inhabitant.

8 For this gird yourself with sackcloth, mourn and lament; for the fierce anger of the LORD is not turned back from you.

9 And it shall come to pass at that day, says the LORD, that the hearts of kings shall fail, and the hearts of princes; and the priests shall be astonished and the prophets shall wonder.

10 Then I said, I beseech thee, O LORD God, surely I have greatly deceived this people and Jerusalem; for I have said, You shall have peace; and behold, the sword reaches into the soul.

11 At that time it shall be said to this people and to Jerusalem, As a changing wind in the paths of the wilderness is the way of the daughter of my people, useful neither to fan, nor to cleanse,

12 But a strong wind from those places shall come to me; now also I will pronounce judgment against them.

13 Behold, he shall come up as clouds, and his chariots shall be as a whirlwind; his horses are swifter than eagles. Woe to us! for we are plundered.

14 O Jerusalem, wash your heart from wickedness that you may be saved. How long shall your evil thoughts remain in you?

15 For a voice declares from Dan and proclaims affliction from mount Ephraim.

16 Make mention to the nations and publish to Jerusalem, Behold, multitudes of Gentiles are coming from a far country, and they shall shout against the cities of Judah.

17 As keepers of the fields are they against her around about, because she has been rebellious against me, says the LORD.

18 Your ways and your doings have brought these things upon you; this is your wickedness; it is bitter, it has reached to your heart.

19 ¶I am in pain! I am in pain! I suffer in my heart; my heart throbs within me, and does not cease, because my soul has heard the sound of the trumpet and the shouting of war.

20 Destruction shall come upon destruction; for the whole land is plundered; suddenly are my tents spoiled, and my curtains are fallen down.

21 How long shall I see fugitives and hear the sound of the trumpet?

22 For my people are foolish; they have not known me; they are stupid children, and they have no understanding; they are wise to do evil, but to do good they have no knowledge.

23 I looked on the earth, and, lo, it was without form and void; and on the heavens, and they had no light.

24 And I looked on the mountains, and, lo, they trembled and all the hills were shattered.

25 I looked, and, behold, there was no man, and all the birds of the air had fled.

26 I looked, and, lo, the fruitful place was a wilderness, and all its towns were destroyed at the presence of the LORD and before his fierce anger.

27 For thus says the LORD God, The whole land shall be desolate; yet I will not make a full end.

28 For this the earth shall mourn and the heavens above shall be darkened; because of everything that I have spoken; I have purposed it and will not repent, neither will I turn back from it.

29 Because of the noise of the horsemen and bowmen, the whole city has fled; enter into the forests and climb up upon the rocks; all towns are deserted and no man dwells therein:

30 And you that are plundered, what will you do? Though you clothe yourself with crimson, though you deck yourself with ornaments of gold, though you paint your eyes with kohl, in vain shall you make yourself fair; your lovers have left you and they seek your life.

31 For I have heard a voice as of a sick woman, and the anguish as of a woman who is in travail to bring forth her child, the voice of the daughter of Zion, who is wearied and who spreads her hands, saying, Woe is me! for my soul faints because of my men who are slain.

CHAPTER 5

RUN to and fro through the streets of Jerusalem, and see now and know, and search in its broad places, if you can find a man, if there is any that executes justice, that seeks truth; and I will pardon them.

2 And though they say, The LORD lives; truly they swear falsely.

3 O LORD, thine eyes are upon the truth; thou hast stricken them, but they have not grieved; thou hast consumed them, but they have refused to receive correction; they have made their faces harder than a rock; they have refused to repent.

4 Therefore I said, It is because they are poor; they have gone astray, for they do not know the way of the LORD, nor the judgment of their God.

5 I will go to the princes and will speak to them; for they have known the way of the LORD and the judgment of their God; but truly they have altogether broken the yoke; they have burst the bonds.

6 Therefore a lion out of the forest shall slay them and hungry wolves of the evening shall tear them in pieces; a leopard shall lie in wait over their cities; every one that goes out thence shall be torn in pieces, because their transgressions are multiplied and become so strong that they will not repent.

7 ¶How shall I pardon you? Your children have forsaken me and sworn by those that are no gods; when I had fed them until they were satisfied, they then committed adultery, and they fought one another in the harlots' houses.

8 They were wanton like stallions, every one lusting after his neighbor's wife.

9 Shall I not punish them for these things? says the LORD; and shall I not avenge myself on such a people as this?

10 ¶Go up upon her walls and destroy; but make not a full end; spare her foundations, for they belong to the LORD.

11 For the house of Israel and the house of Judah have dealt very

treacherously against me, says the LORD.

12 They have lied against the LORD and said, It is not he; neither shall evil come upon us; neither shall we see sword nor famine:

13 And the prophets shall become a whirlwind [1] and will have nothing to say; thus shall it be done to them.

14 Therefore thus says the LORD God of hosts, Because you speak this word, behold, I will make my words fire in your mouth, and this people wood, and it shall devour them.

15 Lo, I will bring a nation against you, a people from afar, O house of Israel, says the LORD; it is a mighty nation, it is an ancient nation, a people whose language you do not know; neither can you understand what they say.

16 Their quiver is like an open sepulchre, they are all mighty men.

17 And they shall eat up your harvest and your bread, which your sons and your daughters should eat; they shall eat up your flocks and your herds; they shall eat up your vines and your fig trees; they shall impoverish with the sword your fortified cities in which you trust.

18 Nevertheless in those days, says the LORD, I will not make a full end of you.

19 ¶And it shall come to pass, when you shall say, Why does the LORD our God do all these things to us? Then you shall say to them, Thus says the LORD, Because you have forsaken me and served strange gods in your land, so you shall serve strangers in a land that is not yours.

20 Declare this in the house of Jacob and publish it in Judah, saying,

21 Hear now this, O foolish people who have no understanding, who have eyes and see not, who have ears and hear not:

22 Do you not revere me? says the LORD, and will you not tremble at my presence? I have placed the sand for the bound of the sea by a perpetual ordinance, that it cannot overflow;

though the waves roar, yet they cannot prevail; and though they toss, yet they cannot pass over it.

23 But this people has a contentious and rebellious heart; they have revolted and gone astray.

24 Neither do they say in their heart, Let us now worship the LORD our God, who gives rain, both the former and the latter,[2] in its season, who preserves for us the summer crops for the winter.

25 ¶Your iniquities have turned away these things, and your sins have withheld good things from you.

26 For among my people are found wicked men; they have laid snares like hedges that they may catch men with them.

27 As a cage is full of birds, so are their houses full of deceit;

28 Therefore they have become great and rich and have perverted judgment; they do not execute justice, and they do not judge aright the cause of the orphan; and the cause of the needy they did not judge.

29 Shall I not punish for these things? says the LORD; shall I not avenge myself on such a people as this?

30 ¶An astonishing and horrible thing is committed in the land:

31 The prophets prophesy falsely and the priests have supported them; and my people love to have it so; and what will you do at the end?

CHAPTER 6

O CHILDREN of Benjamin, flee out of the midst of Jerusalem! Blow the trumpet and set up a standard in Beth-keram; for I am bringing a calamity out of the north, and great destruction.

2 I have likened the daughter of Zion to a comely and delicate woman.

3 The shepherds [3] with their flocks shall come to her; they shall pitch their tents against her round about; they shall feed every one in his place.

4 Prepare war against her; and say, Arise, let us go up at noon. Woe to us! for the day is spent, and the

---

[1] Confused.   [2] *Former* means rain in the fall of the year; *latter*, when crops are ripening.
[3] Rulers.

shadows of the evening are lengthened.

5 Arise, and let us go up against her by night, and let us destroy her palaces.

6 ¶For thus says the LORD of hosts, Hew down her trees and cast a mound against Jerusalem; this is the city to be visited with destruction; all of her calumnies are in the midst of her.

7 As a cistern that gathers its water, so has she gathered her wickedness; violence and plunder are heard in her; before me continually are grief and wounds.

8 Be chastised, O Jerusalem, lest my soul abhor you; lest I make you desolate like an uninhabited land.

9 ¶Thus says the LORD of hosts, They shall thoroughly glean the remnant of Israel as a vine; turn back your hand as a grape gatherer when he gleans the grapes.

10 To whom shall I speak and give warning, that they may hear? Behold, their ears are dull and they cannot hear; behold, the word of the LORD is to them a reproach; they have no delight in it.

11 Therefore you are full of the fury of the LORD, and you are weary; I will measure and then I will pour it out upon the children in the streets and upon the assembly of young men together; for even the husbands and wives shall be taken, the old men with the infants.

12 Their houses shall be given to others, with their fields and wives together; for I will stretch out my hand against the inhabitants of the land, says the LORD.

13 For from the least of them even to the greatest of them every one commits treachery; and from the false prophets even to the priests every one of them deals falsely.

14 And yet they try to heal the wound of the daughter of my people mockingly, saying, Peace, peace, when there is no peace.

15 Now they are ashamed because they had committed abomination, but the impudent are not ashamed at all, neither do they know what chastisement is; therefore they shall fall among them that fall; at the time that I visit them with punishment they shall be overthrown, says the LORD.

16 Thus says the LORD, Stand in the ways and see, and ask for the old paths and see where is the good way, and walk in it and find rest for your souls. But you said, We will not walk therein.

17 Also I set watchmen over you, so that you might hearken to the sound of the trumpet. But you said, We will not hearken.

18 ¶Therefore hear, O nations, and know, O congregation, the deceit that is among them.

19 Hear, O earth! Behold, I will bring evil upon this people according to the fruits of their imaginations, because they have not hearkened to my words, and my law they have rejected.

20 To what purpose do you bring to me incense from Sheba and the cane of sweet incense from a far country? Your burnt offerings are not acceptable to me, nor do your sacrifices please me.

21 Therefore thus says the LORD, Behold, I will lay stumblingblocks before this people, and the fathers and the sons together shall fall upon them; and the neighbor and his friend shall perish.

22 Thus said the LORD, Behold, a people is coming from the north country, and a great nation shall be raised from the ends of the earth.

23 They shall be armed with bows and spears; they are cruel and have no mercy; their voices roar like the sea; and they ride upon horses set in array as men for war against you, O daughter of Zion.

24 We have heard the report of them; our hands wax feeble; anguish has taken hold of us, and pain as of a woman in travail.

25 Go not forth into the field, nor walk by the way; for the sword of the enemies is on every side.

26 ¶O daughter of my people, gird yourself with sackcloth and wallow in ashes; make for yourself mourning, as for an only son, most bitter lamentation; for the plunderers shall suddenly come upon you.

27 I have set you as a seer among my great people, that you may know and understand their ways.

28 Their rulers are all rebellious, walking treacherously; like brass and iron, they are corruptible.

29 The bellows are burned, the lead is consumed by their fire; the refiner purges in vain; for their evil does not come out.

30 Rejected silver, they are called, because the LORD has rejected them.

CHAPTER 7

THE word that came to Jeremiah from the LORD, saying,

2 Stand in the gate of the LORD's house and proclaim there this word, and say, Hear the word of the LORD, all the house of Judah who enter in these gates to worship the LORD.

3 Thus says the LORD of hosts, the God of Israel: Amend your ways and your doings, and I will cause you to dwell in this place.

4 Do not trust in the lying words of those who say to you, The temple of the LORD, the temple of the LORD.

5 For if you amend your ways and your doings, you are the temple of the LORD; if you execute justice between a man and his neighbor;

6 If you do not defraud and oppress the strangers, the fatherless, and the widows, and do not shed innocent blood in this country, neither walk after other gods to your hurt;

7 Then I will cause you to dwell in this country, in the land that I gave to your fathers for ever and ever.

8 ¶Behold, you trust in lying words that cannot profit.

9 Indeed you are thieves, you are murderers, and you commit adultery and swear falsely and burn incense to Baal and walk after other gods whom you know not;

10 And then you come and stand before me in this house, which is called by my name, and say, Deliver us; and yet you do all these evils.

11 Is this house which is called by my name become a den of robbers in your eyes? Behold, even I have seen it, says the LORD.

12 Therefore go now to my place which was in Shiloh, where I set my name at the first, and see what I did to it for the wickedness of my people Israel.

13 And now, because you have done all these works, says the LORD, and I warned you in advance and spoke to you, but you did not listen; and I called you, but you did not answer;

14 Therefore I will do to this house which is called by my name, in which you trust, and to this city which I gave to you and to your fathers, as I have done to Shiloh.

15 And I will cast you out of my sight, as I have cast out all your brethren, even all the descendants of Ephraim.

16 Therefore do not pray for this people, neither supplicate for them nor make intercession to me; for I will not hear you.

17 ¶Do you not see what they do in the cities of Judah and in the streets of Jerusalem?

18 The children gather wood and the fathers kindle the fire and the women knead dough to make cakes to the queen of heaven and they pour out drink offerings to other gods, that they may provoke me to anger.

19 It is not I that they provoke, says the LORD, but they provoke themselves so that they may be ashamed.

20 Therefore thus says the LORD God, Behold, my anger and my wrath shall be poured out upon this country, upon men and upon beasts and upon the trees of the field and upon the fruit of the ground; and it shall burn and shall not be quenched.

21 ¶Thus says the LORD of hosts, the God of Israel: Add your burnt offerings to your sacrifices and eat meat which I did not command your fathers to eat.

22 Neither did I command them concerning either burnt offerings or sacrifices in the day when I brought them out of the land of Egypt;

23 But this thing I commanded them, saying, Obey my voice, and I will be your God and you shall be my people; and walk in all the ways

that I have commanded you, that it may be well with you.

24 But they did not listen nor incline their ear to hear, but they walked in their own counsels and in the imagination of their evil heart, and went backward and not forward.

25 From the day that your fathers came forth out of the land of Egypt to this day I have sent to them all my servants the prophets, daily.

26 I sent them in advance to warn them; but they did not listen nor incline their ear toward me, but hardened their necks more than their fathers.

27 Therefore you shall speak all these words to them; but they will not hearken to you; you shall also call to them; but they will not answer you.

28 Truth is perished and is cut off from their mouth.

29 ¶Cut off your hair,[1] O Jerusalem, and cast it away, and take up a lamentation on high ways; for the LORD is angry and has forsaken this passing generation.

30 For the children of Judah have done evil in my sight, says the LORD; they have set their abomination in the house which is called by my name and they have polluted it.

31 And they have built altars by the Taphat (stream) which is in the valley of the son of Hinnom, to burn their sons and their daughters in the fire; which I commanded them not, neither did I think of it.

32 ¶Therefore, behold, the days come, says the LORD, that it shall no more be called Taphat, nor the valley of the son of Hinnom, but the valley of slaughter; for they shall bury in the stream for the lack of ground.

33 And the corpses of this people shall be meat for the fowls of the air and for the beasts of the earth; and there will be no deliverer.

34 Then I shall cause to cease from the cities of Judah and from the streets of Jerusalem, the voice of mirth and the voice of gladness, the voice of the bridegroom and the voice of the bride; for all the land shall become desolate.

CHAPTER 8

AT that time, says the LORD, they shall bring out of their graves the bones of the kings of Judah and the bones of their princes and the bones of their priests, and the bones of their prophets and the bones of the inhabitants of Jerusalem;

2 And they shall spread them before the sun and the moon and all the host of heaven, which they have loved and which they have served, and after which they have walked, and which they have sought and which they have worshipped; they shall not be gathered nor be buried; but they shall be like rubbish upon the face of the ground.

3 And they shall choose death rather than life, all the remnant of them that remain of this evil family, in all countries where I have driven them, says the LORD of hosts.

4 ¶Moreover you shall say to them, Thus says the LORD: They shall fall and not arise; and even if they would try to repent, they will not do so.

5 Why then is this people of Jerusalem perpetually backsliding? They hold fast to deceit, they refuse to repent.

6 I have given ear and heard, but they did not speak aright; no one repented of his evil, saying, What have I done? All of them walk according to their own will, as a horse that rushes into the battle.

7 Yea, the stork in the sky knows her appointed times; and the turtledove and the crane and the swallow observe the time of their coming; but my people know not the judgment of the LORD.

8 How do you say, We are wise, and the law of the LORD is with us? Lo, surely the lying pen of the scribes has made it for falsehood.[2]

9 The wise men are ashamed, they are defeated and caught because they have rejected the word of the LORD, and there is no wisdom in them.

10 Therefore I will give their wives to others and their fields as a spoil; for every one from the least even to

---

[1] In mourning.   [2] The scribes have interpreted it falsely, and written wrong comments on it.

the greatest deals treachery, from the prophet even unto the priest every one deals falsehood.

11 And they try to heal the wound of the daughter of my people mockingly, saying, Peace, peace, when there is no peace.

12 Now they are ashamed because they have committed abomination, but the impudent are not at all ashamed, neither do they know what chastisement is. Therefore they fall among the fallen; in the time of their punishment they shall be overthrown, says the LORD.

13 ¶I will surely consume them, says the LORD; there are no grapes on the vine nor figs on the fig tree, and the leaves are fallen down; and the things that I have given them are passed away from them.

14 And they shall say, Why do we dwell here? Let us gather together and let us enter into the fortified cities and let us be silent there; for the LORD our God has silenced us and has given us bitter water to drink because we have sinned against the LORD.

15 We looked for peace, but no good came; and for a time of healing, and behold distress has befallen us!

16 The snorting of his horses[1] was heard from Dan; the whole land trembled at the sound of the cry of his mighty men; for they are come and have devoured the land and all that is in it, the city, and those who dwell in it.

17 For, behold, I will send ferocious serpents[2] among you, which cannot be charmed, and they shall bite you, says the LORD.

18 ¶I am weary with sorrow, my heart is faint in me.

19 Behold the voice of the cry of the daughter of my people who dwell in a far land; for they say, Is not the LORD in Zion? Is not her king in her? For they have provoked me to anger with their graven images and with strange idols.

20 The harvest is past, the grapes are gathered, and we are not saved.

21 For the hurt of the daughter of my people I am sorrowful, and astonishment has seized me.

22 Is there no balm in Gilead; is there no healer[3] there? Why then is not the health of the daughter of my people restored?

CHAPTER 9

OH that my head were waters and my eyes a fountain of tears, that I might weep day and night for the slain of the daughter of my people!

2 Oh that I had in the wilderness a lodging place of wayfaring men, that I might leave my people and go away from them! For they are all adulterers, an assembly of liars.

3 And they bend their tongues like their bow; in falsehood and not in truth they are valiant upon the earth; for they proceed from evil to evil, and they do not know me, says the LORD.

4 Take heed every one of his neighbor and do not trust in any brother; for every brother henceforth will defraud and every neighbor will walk deceitfully.

5 And every man will lie against his neighbor and will not speak the truth; they have taught their tongues to speak lies, they are weary and worn out.

6 Your habitation is in the midst of deceit; through their deceit they refuse to know me, says the LORD.

7 Therefore thus says the LORD of hosts, Behold, I will refine them and try them; for what else shall I do because of the daughter of my people?

8 Their tongue is a sharp pointed arrow; it speaks deceit; one speaks peacefully to his neighbor with his mouth, but in his heart he lies in wait for him.

9 ¶Shall I not punish them for these things? says the LORD; shall I not avenge myself on a people such as this?

10 Take up weeping and wailing for the mountains and a lamentation for the camps of the shepherds in the wilderness, because they are desolate so that none can pass through them; neither can any one hear the voice

[1] Chaldean horses.   [2] Vicious enemies.   [3] Doctor.

of the cattle; both the fowl of the air and the beast have fled and they are gone.

11 And I will make Jerusalem heaps and a den of jackals; and I will make the cities of Judah desolate without an inhabitant.

12 ¶Who is the wise man that may understand this? And who is he to whom the mouth of the LORD has spoken, that he may declare it, why is the land perished and become desolate like a wilderness so that no one passes through it?

13 And the LORD says, Because they have forsaken my law which I gave to them and to their fathers, and have not obeyed my voice, neither walked according to my warnings;

14 But have followed after the imagination of their own evil heart and after the idols which their fathers taught them;

15 Therefore thus says the LORD of hosts, the God of Israel: Behold, I will feed them, even this people, with wormwood and give them bitter water to drink.

16 I will scatter them also among the Gentiles, whom neither they nor their fathers have known; and I will send a sword after them till I have consumed them.

17 ¶Thus says the LORD of hosts, Call for the mourning women that they may come; and send for women versed in lamentations that they may come;

18 And let them make haste and take up lamentations for us, so that our eyes may run down with tears, and our eyelids gush out with waters.

19 For a voice of wailing is heard out of Zion, saying, How are we plundered! We are greatly ashamed, because we have left the land, because our tents are dismantled.

20 Therefore hear the word of the LORD, O women, and let your ears receive the word of his mouth, and teach your daughters lamentations, and every one to her neighbor a melody.

21 For death is come up into our windows and is entered into our palaces, to cut off the children from the streets and the young men from the broad ways.

22 For thus says the LORD, The carcasses of men shall fall as rubbish upon the open field and as the grass after the reaper, and none shall gather them.

23 ¶Thus says the LORD, Let not the wise man glory in his wisdom, neither let the mighty man glory in his might, and let not the rich man glory in his riches;

24 But let him who glories glory in this: that he understands and knows me, that I am the LORD who executes lovingkindness, justice and righteousness in the earth; for in these things I delight, says the LORD.

25 ¶Behold, the days come, says the LORD, that I will punish all those who are circumcised together with the uncircumcised;

26 Egyptians and Jews and Edomites, and the children of Ammon and Moab, and all those who cut their beards, who dwell in the wilderness; for all these nations are uncircumcised in their flesh, and all the house of Israel is uncircumcised in heart.

CHAPTER 10

HEAR the word which the LORD speaks to you, O house of Israel:

2 Thus says the LORD, Learn not the way [1] of the Gentiles and be not afraid of the signs of heaven; for the Gentiles are dismayed at them.

3 For the gods of the Gentiles are nothing; they are cut from a tree in the forest, the work of the hands of a carpenter, things made with a plane.

4 They are decked with silver and with gold; men fasten them with hammers and nails, so that they may not fall apart.

5 They are set up straight as palm trees, but they do not speak; they must be carried, for they cannot walk. Be not afraid of them; for they cannot do evil, neither can they do good.

6 There is no one like unto thee, O LORD; thou art great, and thy name is great in might.

1 Religion.

7 Who would not revere thee, O King of nations? For to thee belongs the kingdom; for among all the wise men of the nations and in all their kingdoms there is none like thee.

8 But altogether the vain doctrines of wooden image worship shall be utterly destroyed and consumed.

9 Fine silver is brought from Tarshish and gold from Ophir; they are the work of the carpenter and of the hands of the silversmith; blue and purple is their clothing; they are woven by cunning men.

10 But the LORD is the true God; he is the living God and the everlasting King; at his anger the earth trembles, and the nations shall not be able to endure his indignation.

11 Thus shall you say to them: The gods that have not made the heavens and the earth, even they shall perish from the earth and from under these heavens.

12 The LORD has made the earth by his power; he has established the world by his wisdom, and has stretched out the heavens by his intelligence.

13 He causes the sound of roaring of waters that are in the heavens, and he causes the clouds to ascend from the ends of the earth; he makes lightnings for the rain, and brings forth the wind out of his treasure house.

14 Every man has acted foolishly because of lack of knowledge; all those who work in gold are ashamed because of the graven images which they made; for molten images are falsehood, and there is no breath in them.

15 They are vanity, and the work of vain folly; in the time when they are visited with punishment, they shall perish.

16 The portion of Jacob is not like them; for he who has created all things is their portion; and Israel is the tribe of his inheritance; The LORD of hosts is his name.

17 ¶Gather up your disgrace from the land, O inhabitant who dwells in distress.

18 For thus says the LORD, Behold, I will perplex the inhabitants of this land at this very time, so that they may seek me and find me.

19 ¶Woe to me for my hurt! my wound is grievous; but I said, Truly this is my grief and I must bear it.

20 My tabernacle is plundered and all its cords are cut off; my children have left me, and they are not; there is no one to pitch my tent again and to set up my curtains.

21 For the shepherds have misbehaved, and have not sought the LORD; and because they did not prosper, all of their flocks have been scattered.

22 Behold, the noise of the report is come, and a great commotion out of the north country, to make the cities of Judah desolate and a den of jackals.

23 ¶I know that the ways of the LORD are not like the ways of men; he does not walk as a man directing his steps.

24 O LORD, correct me justly, and not in thy anger, lest thou bring me to nothing.

25 Pour out thy wrath upon the nations who do not know thee and upon the families that call not on thy name; for they have devoured Jacob, yea, they have devoured him and consumed him and have made his habitation desolate.

CHAPTER 11

THE word that came to Jeremiah from the LORD, saying,

2 Hear the words of this covenant, and speak to the men of Judah and to the inhabitants of Jerusalem;

3 And you shall say to them, Thus says the LORD God of Israel: Cursed be the man who does not obey the words of this covenant

4 Which I commanded your fathers in the day that I brought them forth out of the land of Egypt, from the iron furnace,[1] saying, Hearken to my voice and do all that I command you; so shall you be my people, and I will be your God;

5 That I may perform the oaths which I have sworn to your fathers to give them a land flowing with milk

¹ Oppression.

and honey, as it is this day. Then I answered and said, So be it, O LORD.

6 Then the LORD said to me, Proclaim all these words in the cities of Judah and in the streets of Jerusalem, saying, Hear the words of this covenant and do them.

7 For I have solemnly testified against your fathers in the day that I brought them up out of the land of Egypt, even to this day; I sent messengers in advance, warning them, saying, Obey my voice.

8 But they neither obeyed nor inclined their ear, but walked every one in the imagination of his evil heart; therefore I brought upon them all the words of this covenant, which I commanded them to obey, but they did not.

9 And the LORD said to me, A conspiracy is found among the men of Judah and among the inhabitants of Jerusalem.

10 They are turned back to the iniquities of their fathers and have refused to hear my words; and they went after other gods to serve them; the house of Israel and the house of Judah have nullified my covenant which I made with their fathers.

11 ¶Therefore thus says the LORD of hosts, the God of Israel, Behold, I will bring evil upon them which they shall not be able to escape; and though they shall cry to me, I will not hearken to them.

12 Then shall the cities of Judah and the inhabitants of Jerusalem go and cry to the gods to whom they had offered incense; but they shall not save them at all in the time of their misfortune.

13 For according to the number of your cities were your gods, O Judah; and according to the number of the streets of Jerusalem you have set up altars to that shameful thing, even altars to burn incense to Baal.

14 Therefore pray not for this people, neither offer a supplication or prayer for them; for I will not hearken to them in the time that they call to me, in the time of their misfortune.

15 Why has my beloved wrought so much lewdness in my temple? Therefore the holy meat shall pass away from you, for your evil is exceedingly increased.

16 The LORD called your name, A green olive tree, fair, and of goodly fruit; but now with the noise of a great condemnation he has kindled fire upon it, and its branches are destroyed.

17 For the LORD of hosts, who planted you, has pronounced evil against you, for the evil of the house of Israel and of the house of Judah, which they have done against themselves to provoke me to anger in offering incense to Baal.

18 ¶The LORD has revealed it to me, and I know it; truly thou hast shown me their works.

19 But I was like an innocent lamb that is brought to the slaughter; and I did not know that they had conspired against me, saying, Let us destroy the tree with its fruit, and let us cut him off from the land of the living, so that his name may not be remembered.

20 But, O LORD of hosts, who judges righteously, who knows what is in the heart and mind, let me see thy vengeance on them; for to thee have I revealed my cause.

21 Therefore thus says the LORD concerning the men of Anathoth who seek your life, saying, Do not prophesy in the name of the LORD, that you may not die by our hands:

22 Therefore thus says the LORD of hosts, Behold, I will punish them; their young men shall die by the sword; their sons and their daughters shall die by famine:

23 And there shall be no remnant of them; for I will bring evil upon the men of Anathoth, even the year of their punishment.

CHAPTER 12

RIGHTEOUS art thou, O LORD, when I plead with thee; yet let me talk of justice before thee. Why does the way of the wicked prosper? Why are all the treacherous men rich?

2 Thou hast planted them; yea,

their roots have become strong; they grow, they bring forth fruit; thou art near in their mouth, and far from their hearts.

3 But thou, O LORD, knowest me; thou hast seen me and tried my heart before thee; prepare them like sheep for the slaughter, and invite them for the day of destruction.

4 How long shall the land mourn and all herbs of the field wither for the wickedness of those who dwell therein? The cattle and the birds are consumed because wicked men have said, We shall not see an end.

5 ¶If you have run with footmen, and they have wearied you, then how can you run with horses? And if on the level land, where you have confidence, they have wearied you, then how will you cross the raging Jordan?

6 For since your brethren and the house of your father, even they have dealt treacherously against you; yea, they also have gossiped about you; believe them not when they speak well of you.

7 ¶I have forsaken my house, I have left my heritage; I have given the dearly beloved of my soul into the hand of her enemies.

8 My heritage has become to me as a lion in the forest; it cries out against me; therefore I have hated it.

9 My heritage has become to me as a speckled bird, the birds round about are against her; go, assemble all the wild beasts of the field, bring them to devour her.

10 Many shepherds have destroyed my vineyard, they have trodden my portion under foot, they have made my pleasant portion as a desolate wilderness.

11 They have made it desolate and destroyed it, and now being desolate, it cries out to me; the whole land is made desolate, because no man lays the law to heart.

12 The robbers are come upon all highways in the wilderness; for the sword of the LORD devours from one end of the land even to the other: no flesh shall have peace.

13 They have sown wheat, but they shall reap thorns; they have labored hard, but they shall not profit; and they shall be ashamed of their crops because of the fierce anger of the LORD.

14 ¶Thus says the LORD: Against all neighboring shepherds,[1] who touch the inheritance which I have given to my people Israel to possess; behold, I will remove them out of their land, and pluck out the house of Judah from among them.

15 And after I have plucked them out I will return, and have compassion on them, and will bring them again, every man to his heritage and every man to his land.

16 And it shall come to pass, if they will diligently teach my ways to my people, to swear by my name, As the LORD lives (as they taught them to swear by the name of Baal), then they shall dwell in the midst of my people.

17 But if they will not obey, then I will utterly pluck up and destroy this people, says the LORD.

CHAPTER 13

THUS says the LORD unto me, Go and buy for yourself a linen girdle, and put it on your loins, and do not put it in water.

2 So I bought a girdle according to the word of the LORD and put it on my loins.

3 And the word of the LORD came to me the second time, saying,

4 Take the girdle which you have bought, and which is upon your loins, and arise, go to the Euphrates and bury it there in a hole of the rock.

5 So I went and buried it by the Euphrates, as the LORD commanded me.

6 And it came to pass after many days that the LORD said to me, Arise, go to the Euphrates and take from thence the girdle which I commanded you to bury there.

7 Then I went to the Euphrates and dug and took the girdle from the place where I had buried it; and, be-

[1] Rulers.

hold, the girdle was rotted and was good for nothing.

8 Then the word of the LORD came to me, saying,

9 Thus says the LORD of hosts, the God of Israel: In this manner will I destroy the proud men of Judah and the proud men of Jerusalem that are many.

10 This evil people, who refuse to hear my words, who walk in the imagination of their heart, and have gone after other gods to serve them and to worship them, shall be even as this girdle which is good for nothing.

11 For as the girdle cleaves to the loins of a man, so I have caused to cleave to me the whole house of Israel and the whole house of Judah, says the LORD; that they might be to me for a people and for a name and for a praise and for a glory; but they would not hearken.

12 ¶Therefore you shall speak to them this word: Thus says the LORD of hosts, the God of Israel, Every wineskin shall be filled with wine; and they shall say to you, Do we not know that every wineskin shall be filled with wine?

13 Then you shall say to them, Thus says the LORD: Behold, I will fill all the inhabitants of this land, even the kings that sit upon David's throne and the priests and the prophets and all the inhabitants of Jerusalem, with drunkenness.

14 And I will scatter them and separate them every man from his brother, even fathers and their children together, says the LORD; I will not pity, nor have mercy, nor spare, but destroy them.

15 ¶Hear and give ear; be not proud, for the LORD has spoken.

16 Give glory to the LORD your God before it becomes dark, and before your feet are injured upon the mountains in the darkness, and, while you look for light, he turns it into darkness and the shadows of death.

17 But if you will not hearken to him, then my soul shall weep in secret because of distress; and I will weep bitterly, and tears shall run down from my eyes because the LORD's flock is carried away captive.

18 Say to the king and to the princes, Humble yourselves and repent, for the crown of your glory has fallen from your heads.

19 The cities of the south are shut up, and there is no one to open them; Judah is carried away captive, yea, is wholly carried away captive.

20 Lift up your eyes and see those that come from the north. Where is the flock that was given to you, your beautiful flock?

21 What will you say when he shall punish you? For you have taught the people a doctrine which has caused them to be trodden under foot; behold, you shall be seized with pain as a woman in travail.

22 ¶And if you say in your heart, Why have these things come upon me? For the greatness of your iniquity are your skirts uncovered and your heels made bare.

23 Just as a Hindu cannot change his skin or a leopard his spots, you also cannot do good because you are accustomed to do evil.

24 Therefore I will scatter them like the stubble driven by the wind in the wilderness.

25 This is your lot, the portion of your inheritance from me, says the LORD; because you have forgotten me and trusted in falsehood.

26 Therefore I also will cause your skirts to be uncovered and lifted over your face, and your shame shall be seen.

27 I have seen your adulteries and your lusts, the lewdness of your whoredom and your abominations on the hills in the wilderness. Woe to you, O Jerusalem! for you are unwilling to be cleansed. How long will it be till you repent?

CHAPTER 14

THE word of the LORD that came to Jeremiah concerning the drought.

2 Judah mourns and her gates are

desolate; they are fallen on the ground, and the painful cry of Jerusalem is gone up.

3 And their nobles have sent their least ones for water; they came to the cistern, and found no water; they returned with their vessels empty; they were ashamed and confounded, and covered their heads.

4 Because of the evil deeds of the land, the ground is parched, no rain has fallen upon it; the farmers are ashamed, they covered their heads.

5 Yea, the hinds also gave birth in the field, and forsook their young ones because there was no grass.

6 And the wild asses stood in the paths, they snuffed up the wind like jackals; their eyes did fail because there was no grass.

7 ¶Though our sins testify against us, O LORD have mercy upon us for thy name's sake; for thy lovingkindness is great; we have sinned against thee.

8 O the hope of Israel, the saviour thereof in the time of trouble, be thou not as a stranger in the land and as a wayfarer who turns aside to tarry for a night.

9 Be thou not as a weak man, as a man who cannot save; yet thou, O LORD, art in the midst of us, and we are called by thy name; leave us not.

10 ¶Thus says the LORD to this people: They have loved to be unreliable, they have not restrained their feet from going after evil; therefore the LORD is not pleased with them; he will now remember their iniquity and punish their sins.

11 Then the LORD said to me, Do not pray for this people for their good.

12 For if they fast, I will not hear their prayer; and if they offer burnt offerings and an oblation, I will not accept them; but I will consume them by the sword and by famine and by pestilence.

13 ¶Then I said, Hear me, I beseech thee, O LORD God! Behold, the prophets say to the people, You shall not see the sword, neither shall you have famine, but I will give you assured peace and justice in this country.

14 Then the LORD said to me, The prophets prophesy lies in my name; for I did not send them, neither have I commanded them nor spoken to them; they prophesy to you false visions, oracles and divinations and the deceit of their hearts;

15 Therefore thus says the LORD concerning the prophets who prophesy in my name, and I did not send them; yet they say, Sword and famine shall not be in this land: By sword and famine shall those prophets be consumed.

16 And the people to whom they prophesy shall be cast out in the streets of Jerusalem because of sword and famine and pestilence; and they shall have none to bury them, neither their wives nor their sons nor their daughters; for I will pour out their wickedness upon them.

17 ¶Therefore you shall say this word to them: Let my eyes run down with tears night and day and let them not cease, for the virgin daughter of my people has suffered a terrible defeat; she is smitten with a very grievous wound.

18 If I go forth into the desert, then behold, the slain with the sword! And if I enter into the city, then behold, those who are suffering with famine! For also both the prophets and the priests are begging in the land unrecognized.

19 Hast thou utterly rejected Judah? Hast thy soul loathed Zion? Why hast thou smitten us, and there is no healing for us? We looked for peace, and there is no good; and for the time of healing, and behold fear!

20 We acknowledge, O LORD, our sins and the sins of our fathers; for we have sinned against thee.

21 Do not be angry, for thy name's sake, do not disgrace the throne of thy glory; remember, do not nullify thy covenant with us.

22 For the gods of the Gentiles cannot bring rain nor cause the heavens to give showers, but thou art our God;

therefore we will wait for thee; for thou hast made all these things.

CHAPTER 15

THEN the LORD said to me, Though Moses and Samuel stood before me pleading, yet my soul would not be pleased with this people; but I will cast them out of my sight and let them go.

2 And it shall come to pass, if they say to you, Where shall we go? Then you shall tell them, Thus says the LORD: Those numbered for death, to death; and those numbered for the sword, to the sword; and those numbered for famine, to famine; and those numbered for captivity, to captivity.

3 And I will decree against them four kinds of afflictions, says the LORD: The sword to slay, the dogs to tear, and the fowls of the air and the wild beasts of the earth to devour and destroy.

4 And I will cause them to be a horror in all the kingdoms of the earth, because of the transgressions of Manasseh the son of Hezekiah king of Judah, for that which he did in Jerusalem.

5 For who shall have pity upon you, O Jerusalem? or who shall bemoan you? or who shall go aside to inquire about your peace?

6 You have forsaken me, says the LORD, you are gone backward; therefore I will stretch out my hand against you and destroy you; and I shall not spare you again.

7 And I will fan them with a fan in the cities of the earth; I have bereaved them of their children, I have destroyed my people, and yet they did not return from their ways.

8 Their widows are increased in number more than the sand of the sea; I have brought against them, both against the mother and against the young men, robbers at noonday; I have caused terror and trembling to fall upon them suddenly.

9 She who has borne seven children languishes; her pride is gone; her sun [1] has gone down while it was yet day;

she has been ashamed and confounded; and the rest of them I will deliver to the sword before their enemies, says the LORD.

10 ¶Woe is me, my mother, that you have borne me a judge, a rebuker to the whole earth. I am neither a debtor, nor a creditor; yet all of them curse me.

11 The LORD said, Verily I shall not leave you at ease, but I will cause an enemy from the north to encounter you in the time of tribulation and in the time of evil;

12 For he is hard as iron and as brass.

13 Your riches, your treasures, and all your borders, I will give to the spoil, because of your sins.

14 And I shall cause you to be enslaved to your enemies in a land which you do not know; for a fire is kindled in my anger, which shall burn upon you.

15 ¶O LORD, thou knowest; remember me and save me and avenge me of my persecutors; take me not away in thy longsuffering; know that for thy sake I have suffered reproach.

16 Thy commandments have I kept and carried out, thy word was to me a delight and the joy of my heart; for I am called by thy name.

17 O LORD God of hosts, I did not sit in the assembly of the mockers, but I was afraid because of thy hand, and I sat alone; for thou hast filled me with indignation.

18 Why is my pain so grievous and my wound so severe that it refuses to be healed? Wilt thou be to me as a mirage that cannot be believed?

19 ¶Therefore thus says the LORD, If you repent, then I will bring you back again, and you shall stand before me; and if you bring forth the precious words and not the vile, you shall be as my mouth, says the LORD; the people shall turn to you; but you shall not turn to them.

20 I have made you to this people as a fortified wall of brass; and they shall fight against you, but they shall not prevail; for I am with you to save you and to deliver you, says the LORD.

[1] Glory, pride.

21 And I will deliver you out of the hand of the wicked, and I will save you from the hand of the mighty.

CHAPTER 16

THE word of the LORD came to me, saying,

2 You shall not take a wife for yourself, neither shall you have sons or daughters in this place.

3 For thus says the LORD concerning the sons and concerning the daughters that are born in this place, and concerning their mothers who bore them, and their fathers who begat them in this land;

4 They shall die the death of those who are ravaged by famine; they shall not be lamented, neither shall they be buried; but they shall be as refuse upon the face of the earth; and they shall be consumed by the sword and by famine, and their corpses shall be food for the fowls of the air and for the beasts of the earth.

5 For thus says the LORD, Do not enter into the house of mourning, neither go to lament nor bemoan them; for I have taken away my peace from the people, says the LORD, even lovingkindness and mercies.

6 Both the great and the small shall die in this land; they shall not be buried, neither shall any one mourn for them or lament for them, or shave his head for them;

7 Neither shall men tear themselves for them in mourning to comfort them for the dead; neither shall men give them the cup of consolation to drink for their fathers or for their mothers.

8 You shall not go into the house of feasting to sit with them to eat and to drink.

9 For thus says the LORD of hosts, the God of Israel: Behold, I will cause to cease out of this place, before your eyes and in your days, the voice of mirth and the voice of gladness, the voice of the bridegroom and the voice of the bride.

10 ¶And it shall come to pass, when you tell this people all these words, and they shall say to you, Why has the LORD pronounced all this great evil against us? or what is our iniquity, or what is our sin that we have sinned against the LORD our God?

11 That you shall say to them, Because your fathers have forsaken me, says the LORD, and have walked after other gods and have served them and have worshipped them, and have forsaken me and have not kept my law,

12 And you have done worse than your fathers; for, behold, you walk away every one after the imagination of his evil heart, that you may not hearken to me;

13 Therefore I will cast you out of this land into a land which you do not know, neither you nor your fathers; there you shall serve other gods day and night; and I will have no compassion upon you.

14 ¶Now, behold, the days are coming, says the LORD, when it shall no more be said, The LORD lives who brought up the children of Israel out of the land of Egypt;

15 But, the LORD lives who brought up the children of Israel from the land of the north and from all the lands where I had driven them; and I will bring them again into their land which I gave to their fathers.

16 ¶Behold, I will send for many fishers, says the LORD, and they shall fish them from islands; and afterward I will send for many hunters, and they shall hunt them from every mountain and from every hill and out of the holes of the rocks.

17 For my eyes are upon all their ways; they are not hid from my face, neither is their iniquity hid from my eyes.

18 And first I will doubly recompense them for their iniquities and their sins; because they have defiled my land with burnt offerings of their idols and have filled my inheritance with their abominations.

19 O LORD, my strength and my helper and my refuge in the day of affliction, the Gentiles shall come to thee from the ends of the earth, and shall say, Surely the idols of falsehood which our fathers have inherited

are nothing, and there is no profit in them.

20 Behold, men make gods to themselves, and they are no gods.

21 Therefore, behold, I will show them, and at this time I will make known to them my hand and my might; and they shall know that my name is the LORD.

CHAPTER 17

THE sin of Judah is written with a pen of iron and with the point of a diamond; it is engraved upon the tablets of their heart and upon the horns of their altars;

2 And their idols are under every green tree and upon every high hill and upon the mountains and in the open country.

3 I will give all your riches, all your treasures to the spoil, and that which is throughout your territory, because of your sins.

4 And I will cause you to lose the inheritance which I have given you; and I will cause you to serve your enemies in the land which you do not know; for you have kindled a fire in my anger, which shall burn for ever.

5 ¶Thus says the LORD, Cursed is the man who trusts in man and makes the son of the flesh his arm, and whose heart departs from the LORD.

6 For he shall be like a plant in the desert, and shall not see when good comes; but shall inhabit the parched places in the wilderness in a salt land not inhabited.

7 Blessed is the man who trusts in the LORD, and whose hope is in him.

8 For he shall be like a tree planted by the waters, that spreads out its roots by the stream, and it shall not be afraid when heat comes, but its leaves shall be green; and shall not be afraid in the year of drought, neither shall cease from yielding fruit.

9 ¶The heart is stubborn above all things; who can understand it?

10 I the LORD search the heart and try the reins, and give every man according to his ways and according to the fruits of his doings.

11 Like the partridge that calls to the eggs which she has not hatched, so is he who gets riches and not by right; he shall leave them in the midst of his days, and at his end he shall be in disgrace.

12 ¶A glorious high throne from the beginning is the place of our sanctuary.

13 The LORD is the hope of Israel; all who forsake thee shall be ashamed, and those who revolt against thee shall have their names written in the dust, because they have forsaken the LORD, the fountain of living waters.

14 Heal me, O LORD, and I shall be healed; save me, and I shall be saved; for thou art my praise.

15 ¶Behold, they say to me, Where is the word of the LORD? Let it come now.

16 As for me, I have not urged thee to bring evil; nor have I desired any man's woeful day; thou knowest; that which came out of my lips was before thy face.

17 Be not a terror to me; but abide with me in the day of trouble.

18 Let them be put to shame who persecute me, but let me not be put to shame; let them be defeated, but let me not be defeated; bring upon them the day of evil, and defeat them with double defeat.

19 ¶Thus said the LORD to me: Go and stand at the public gate by which the kings of Judah enter and by which they go out, and in all the gates of Jerusalem;

20 And say to them, Hear the word of the LORD, you kings of Judah and all the house of Judah and all the inhabitants of Jerusalem who enter by these gates.

21 Thus says the LORD: Take heed to yourselves, and bear no burden on the sabbath day nor bring it in through the gates of Jerusalem;

22 Neither carry a burden out of your houses on the sabbath day, nor do any work; but hallow the sabbath day as I commanded your fathers.

23 But they did not obey, neither inclined their ear, but hardened their neck that they might not hear nor receive instruction.

24 And it shall come to pass if you diligently listen to me, says the LORD, to bring in no burden through the gates of this city on the sabbath day, but hallow the sabbath day and do no work on it;

25 Then there shall enter through the gates of this city kings and princes who sit on the throne of David, riding in chariots and on horses, they and their princes, the men of Judah and the inhabitants of Jerusalem; and this city shall remain for ever.

26 And the people shall come from the cities of Judah and from the places round about Jerusalem and from the land of Benjamin and from the plain and from the mountains and from the south, bringing burnt offerings and sacrifices and incense, and bringing thank offerings to the house of the LORD.

27 But if you do not listen to me to hallow the sabbath day and do not refrain from carrying a burden through the gates of Jerusalem on the sabbath day, then I will kindle a fire in its gates, and it shall devour the palaces of Jerusalem, and it shall not be quenched.

CHAPTER 18

THE word that came to Jeremiah from the LORD, saying,

2 Arise and go down to the potter's house, and there I will cause you to hear my words.

3 Then I went down to the potter's house, according to the word of the LORD, and, behold, he was doing work on the wheel.

4 And the vessel which he was making of clay was spoiled in the hand of the potter; so he mixed the clay and made it into another vessel, as seemed good to him.

5 Then the word of the LORD came to me, saying,

6 O house of Israel, cannot I do with you as this potter? says the LORD, Behold, as the clay is in the potter's hand, so are you in my hand, O house of Israel.

7 If suddenly I should speak concerning a people and concerning a kingdom, to pluck up and to pull down and to destroy it;

8 And if that nation repent from its evil, I will turn away from it the evil which I thought to do to it.

9 And if at another instant I should speak concerning a people and concerning a kingdom, to build and to plant it;

10 And if it does evil in my sight and does not obey my voice, then I will turn away from it the good which I said I would do to it.

11 ¶Now therefore, speak to the men of Judah and to the inhabitants of Jerusalem, saying, Thus says the LORD: Behold, I am bringing evil against you and I am devising a device against you; repent you now, and return every one from his evil way and make your ways and your doings good.

12 But they said, We shall become strong and we will walk after our own devices and we will every man do the imagination of his evil heart.

13 Therefore thus says the LORD: Ask among the Gentiles, Who has done such things as these? The virgin of Israel has done a very horrible thing.

14 Does the green grass vanish from the mountain or the snow leave Lebanon? Does the cold water that gushes out and runs down cease from flowing?

15 Yet my people have forsaken me and have burned incense to vanity and have stumbled in their ways, and have departed from the ancient paths to walk in a way which was not trodden.

16 They have made their land desolate and a perpetual hissing; every one who passes through it shall be astonished and shake his head.

17 I will scatter them as with an east wind before the enemy; I will show them my back and not my face, in the day of their calamity.

18 ¶Then they said, Come and let us devise plots against Jeremiah; so that the law shall not perish from the priests nor counsel from the wise nor the word from the prophets. Come and let us smite him in his tongue,

and let us not listen to any of his words.

19 Give heed to me, O Lord, and hearken to the cry of my oppression.

20 Evil has been recompensed for good, for they have digged a pit for my soul. Remember that I stood before thee and spoke good for them to turn away thy wrath from them.

21 Therefore give their children to famine and deliver them to the sword; and let their wives be bereaved of their children, and become widows; and let their men be put to death and their young men be slain by the sword in battle.

22 Let wailing be heard from their houses, when thou shalt bring a band of raiders suddenly upon them; for they have digged a pit to take me and hid snares for my feet.

23 Yet, O Lord, thou knowest all their counsel against me to slay me; forgive not their iniquity, neither blot out their sins from thy sight, but let them be overthrown before thee; deal thus with them in the time of thine anger.

CHAPTER 19

THUS said the Lord to me, Go and buy a potter's earthen jug, and take with you some of the elders of the people and some of the elderly priests;

2 And go out to the valley of the son of Hinnom which is by the entrance of the east gate, and proclaim there the words that I shall tell you,

3 And say, Hear the word of the Lord, O kings of Judah and inhabitants of Jerusalem; Thus says the Lord of hosts, the God of Israel: Behold, I will bring evil upon this place, such that whosoever hears of it his ears shall tingle.

4 Because they have forsaken me and have polluted this place and have burned incense in it to other gods whom neither they nor their fathers nor the kings of Judah have known; and have filled this place with the blood of the innocents;

5 They have built also the high places of Baal to burn their sons with fire as burnt offerings to Baal, which

I did not command; nor did I speak of it, neither came it into my mind;

6 Therefore, behold, the days are coming, says the Lord, when this place shall no more be called Taphat, nor the valley of the son of Hinnom, but the valley of slaughter.

7 And I will make void the counsel of Judah and Jerusalem in this place; and I will cause them to fall by the sword before their enemies and by the hand of those who seek their lives; and their corpses will I give as food for the fowls of the air and for the wild beasts of the earth.

8 And I will make this city desolate and a hissing; so that every one who passes by it shall be horrified and hiss because of all its catastrophes.

9 And I will cause them to eat the flesh of their sons and the flesh of their daughters, and they shall eat every one the flesh of his neighbors in the siege and in the affliction with which their enemies and those who seek their lives shall inflict upon them.

10 Then you shall break a pot in the sight of the men who go with you,

11 And say to them, Thus says the Lord of hosts: Even so will I break this people and this city, as this potter's vessel is broken, so that it cannot be mended again; and they shall bury the dead in Taphat because of the lack of burial space.

12 Thus will I do to this place and to its inhabitants, says the Lord, and even make this city like Taphat;

13 And the houses of Jerusalem and the houses of the kings of Judah shall be defiled like the place of Taphat; and likewise all the houses upon whose roofs they have burned incense to all the host of heaven and have poured out drink offerings to other gods.

14 Then Jeremiah came from Taphat, where the Lord had sent him to prophesy; and he stood in the court of the Lord's house, and said to all the people,

15 Thus says the Lord of hosts, the God of Israel: Behold, I will bring upon this city and upon all its towns

all the evil that I have pronounced against it, because they have hardened their necks that they might not hear my words.

CHAPTER 20

NOW Pashur the son of Amariah the priest, who was governor in charge of the house of the LORD, heard Jeremiah the prophet prophesying these things.

2 Then Pashur smote Jeremiah the prophet, and put him in the stocks that were in the upper gate of Benjamin, which was by the house of the LORD.

3 And it came to pass on the morrow that Pashur brought forth Jeremiah out of the stocks. Then said Jeremiah to him, The LORD has not called your name Pashur, but a stranger and a beggar.

4 For thus says the LORD: Behold, I will make you a sojourner, you and your friends; and the people shall fall by the sword of their enemies, and your eyes shall see it; and I shall deliver all Judah into the hand of the king of Babylon, and he shall carry them captive into Babylon, and shall slay them with the sword.

5 Moreover I will deliver all the fortified places of this city and all the labor thereof; and all its precious things and all the treasures of the king of Judah will I deliver into the hand of their enemies, who shall plunder them and take them and carry them to Babylon.

6 And as for you, Pashur, you and all the members of your household shall go into captivity; and you shall go to Babylon, and there you shall die, and there you shall be buried, you, and all your friends, to whom you have prophesied lies.

7 ¶O LORD, thou hast comforted me, and I am comforted; thou art stronger than I, and hast prevailed; I have become a laughing-stock daily, every one mocks me.

8 For at the time when I spoke and cried out, I spoke against the extortioners and against the robbers; because the word of the LORD has become for me a reproach and derision daily.

9 Then I said, I will not make mention of him, nor speak any more in his name. But his word became in my heart like a burning fire kindling in my bones; and I sought to be patient, but I could not endure it.

10 ¶For I heard the evil intentions of many, who were gathering from every side inquiring of my peace with their mouth, but hating me in their heart, saying, Point him out to us; we will stand against him; perhaps we can win him over and we shall take our revenge on him.

11 But the LORD is with me as a mighty warrior; therefore all my persecutors shall be ashamed, and they shall not prevail; they have been greatly ashamed because they did not understand; their everlasting shame shall never be forgotten.

12 But, O LORD of hosts, who observest the right cause and seest the reins and the heart, let me see thy vengeance on them; for to thee have I revealed my cause.

13 Sing to the LORD; praise the LORD; for he has delivered the life of the poor from the hand of evildoers.

14 ¶Cursed be the day on which I was born; let not the day on which my mother bore me be blessed.

15 Cursed be the man who brought tidings to my father, saying, A son is born to you, making him very glad.

16 Let that man be like the cities which the LORD overthrew, and he was never reconciled towards them; and let him hear the cry in the morning and the howling at noon.

17 Because he did not slay me in the womb, so that my mother might have been my grave, and my conception would have remained in the womb for ever.

18 Why did I come forth out of the womb to see toil and sorrow? My days are spent in shame.

CHAPTER 21

THE word which came to Jeremiah from the LORD, when King Zedekiah sent to him Pashur the son of

Melchiah and Zephaniah the son of Maasiah, the priests, saying,

2 Enquire of the LORD for us; for Nebuchadnezzar king of Babylon is making war against us; perhaps the LORD will deal with us according to all his wondrous works, and cause the enemy to withdraw from us.

3 ¶Then said Jeremiah to them, Thus shall you say to Zedekiah:

4 Thus says the LORD God of Israel: Behold, I will destroy the weapons of war which are in your hands, with which you fight against the king of Babylon and against the Chaldeans who are besieging you outside the city, and I will assemble them into the midst of this city.

5 And I myself will fight against you with a strong hand and with an outstretched arm, even in anger and in great wrath.

6 And in great wrath will I smite the inhabitants of this city, both men and beasts; they shall die of a great pestilence.

7 And afterward, says the LORD, I will deliver Zedekiah king of Judah, and his servants and the people that are left in this city, from the sword and from the pestilence and from the famine into the hand of Nebuchadnezzar king of Babylon, and into the hand of their enemies, and into the hand of those who seek their lives; and he shall smite them with the edge of the sword; and he shall not spare them, neither have pity nor have mercy upon them.

8 ¶And to this people you shall say, Thus says the LORD: Behold, I set before you the way of life and the way of death.

9 He who abides in this city shall die by the sword and by famine and by pestilence; but he who surrenders to the Chaldeans who are besieging you, he shall live, and he shall save his life.

10 For I have set my face against this city for evil and not for good, says the LORD; it shall be delivered into the hand of the king of Babylon, and he shall burn it with fire.

11 ¶And concerning the house of the king of Judah, say, Hear the word of the LORD, O house of David; thus says the LORD:

12 Execute justice in the morning, and deliver him who is oppressed from the hand of the oppressor, lest my fury go out like fire and burn so that none can quench it, because of the evil of your doings.

13 Behold, I am against you, O inhabitant of the valley, O you who are hidden below the plain, says the LORD, who say, Who shall come down against us? or who shall enter into our habitations?

14 But I will punish you according to the fruit of your doings, says the LORD, and I will kindle a fire in its villages, and it shall devour all things round about it.

CHAPTER 22

THUS says the LORD: Go down to the house of the king of Judah and speak there this word, and say,

2 Hear the word of the LORD, O king of Judah, who sits on the throne of David, you and your servants and your people who enter by these gates;

3 Thus says the LORD: Execute justice and righteousness, and deliver the oppressed from the hand of the oppressor; and do no wrong, do no violence to the strangers, the fatherless, and the widows, nor shed innocent blood in this place.

4 For if you will do this thing indeed, then shall there enter in by the gates of this house kings who sit on the throne of David and princes who ride in chariots and on horses, a king and his servants and his people.

5 But if you will not listen to these words, I swear by myself, says the LORD, that this house shall become a desolation.

6 For thus says the LORD concerning the house of the king of Judah: You are like Gilead, like the head of Lebanon; but I will surely make you a desert, like an uninhabited city.

7 And I will prepare destroyers against you, every one with his axe in his hand; and they shall cut down your choicest cedars and cast them into the fire.

8 And many people shall pass by

this city, and they shall say every man to his neighbor, Wherefore has the LORD done such a thing to this great city?

9 Then they shall answer, Because they have forsaken the covenant of the LORD their God and worshipped other gods and served them.

10 ¶Weep not for the dead, nor bemoan him; but weep bitterly for him that goes away; for he shall return no more, nor see his native land.

11 For thus says the LORD concerning Shallum the son of Josiah king of Judah, who reigned instead of Josiah his father and who went away from this country: He shall not return here any more;

12 But he shall die in the country where they have carried him captive, and shall see this land no more.

13 ¶Woe to him who builds his house by unrighteousness and his upper rooms by injustice; who makes his neighbor work for him without wages, and does not give him his hire;

14 Who says, I will build for myself wide houses with spacious upper rooms; and cuts out windows for them and covers them with cedar and paints them with vermilion.

15 Shall you reign and rejoice by living in palaces built with cedar? Indeed, your father did eat and drink, but he also did justice and righteousness, therefore I did good to him.

16 He did justice to the cause of the poor and needy; and he did well; he who does these things, knows me, says the LORD.

17 But your eyes and your hearts are set for nothing else but for your wealth and for the shedding of innocent blood, and for oppression and for violence, to do it.

18 Therefore thus says the LORD concerning Jehoiakim the son of Josiah king of Judah: They shall not mourn for him, nor shall they say, Ah my brother! Ah my brother! They shall not lament for him, saying, Ah lord! Ah lord!

19 He shall be buried with the burial of an ass, dragged and cast forth beyond the gates of Jerusalem.

20 ¶Go up to Lebanon and cry; and lift up your voice in Mathnin [1] and cry from the other side of the sea; for all your lovers [2] are defeated.

21 I spoke to you in your prosperity; but you said, I will not listen. This has been your way from your youth, you did not obey my voice.

22 All of your shepherds shall be smitten by the east wind, and your lovers shall go into captivity; surely then you shall be ashamed and confounded for all your wickedness.

23 O inhabitant of Lebanon, who makes her nest in the cedars, how you shall groan when pangs come upon you and the pain as of a woman in travail!

24 As I live, says the LORD God, though Jecaniah the son of Jehoiakim king of Judah were the signet on my right hand, yet I would pull you off;

25 And I will deliver you into the hand of the men who seek your life, and into the hand of those whose presence you fear, even into the hand of Nebuchadnezzar king of Babylon, and into the hand of the Chaldeans.

26 And I will cast you out, and your mother who bore you, into another land, where you were not born; and there shall you die.

27 But to the land to which you hope to return, thither you shall not come back.

28 This Jecaniah is a little man and a fool, he is like a useless vessel; this is why he is carried away, he and his children, and cast into a land which he knows not.

29 O earth, earth, earth, hear the word of the LORD!

30 Thus says the LORD: Write this man down despised and childless, for none of his offspring shall prosper in his days, sitting upon the throne of David and ruling any more in Judah.

CHAPTER 23

WOE to the shepherds who destroy and scatter the sheep of my pasture! says the LORD.

2 Therefore thus speaks the LORD God of Israel against the shepherds who feed my people: You have scat-

---

[1] Bashan.   [2] Allies.

tered my flock, and have caused them to go astray, and have not visited them; behold, I will punish you according to your evil doings, says the LORD.

3 And I will gather the remnant of my flock out of all the countries where I have driven them, and I will bring them again to their folds; and they shall be fruitful and increase.

4 And I will set shepherds over them who shall feed them; and they shall fear no more, nor be scattered nor shall they go astray, says the LORD.

5 ¶Behold, the days are coming, says the LORD, when I will raise up for David a righteous Heir, and he shall reign over the kingdom with understanding, and shall execute justice and righteousness in the land.

6 In his days Judah shall be saved and Israel shall dwell securely; and this is the name whereby he shall be called, THE LORD OUR RIGHTEOUSNESS.

7 Therefore, the days are coming, says the LORD, when it shall never be said again, The LORD lives, who brought up the children of Israel out of the land of Egypt;

8 But, The LORD lives, who brought up and led the house of Israel out of the north country and from all the countries where they had been scattered; and they shall dwell in their own land.

9 ¶My heart is broken within me because of the prophets; all my bones shake; I am like a drunken man and like a man who is overcome by wine, because of the presence of the LORD and because of the words of his holiness.

10 For the land is full of adulterers and robbers; because of these men the land mourns and the pastures of the shepherds in the wilderness are dried up, and their yield has been poor, and they did not flourish.

11 For both prophets and priests have become pagans; yea, even in my house have I found their wickedness, says the LORD.

12 Therefore their ways shall be to them as slippery ways in the dark-

ness; they shall be driven on, and fall in them; for I will bring evil upon them, even the year of their punishment, says the LORD.

13 And I have seen falsehood in the prophets of Samaria; they prophesied by Baal and caused my people Israel to err.

14 I have seen also in the prophets of Jerusalem folly; they commit adultery and walk in lies; they strengthen also the hands of their friends, so that no one turns from his evil way; they are all of them to me like Sodom, and its inhabitants like Gomorrah.

15 Therefore thus says the LORD of hosts concerning the prophets: Behold, I will feed them with wormwood, and make them drink bitter water; for from the prophets of Jerusalem paganism has gone forth throughout all the land.

16 Thus says the LORD of hosts: Do not hearken to the words of the false prophets who prophesy to you and mislead you; they tell a vision of the imagination of their own hearts, and not from the mouth of the LORD.

17 They say still to those who provoke me, The LORD has said, You shall have peace; and they say to every one who walks after the imagination of his own heart, No evil shall come upon you.

18 For who has stood in the counsel of the LORD and has seen him and heard his word? or who has given ear to his word and heard him?

19 Behold, the punishment of the LORD is gone forth in fury, and the punishment will kindle; it shall fall upon the head of the wicked.

20 The wrathful indignation of the LORD shall not turn back until he has executed his devices, and till he has performed the thoughts of his mind; in the latter days you shall discern it perfectly.

21 I have not sent these prophets, yet they have gone forth; I have not spoken to them, yet they prophesied.

22 But if they had stood in my counsel and had caused my people to hear my words, then they would have turned them from their evil ways

and from the evil of their doings.

23 I am the God who is near, says the LORD God, and not a God afar off.

24 If any man should hide himself in secret places, I will see him, says the LORD; behold, heaven and earth are filled with me, says the LORD of hosts.

25 I have heard what the prophets have said, who prophesy lies in my name, saying, I have dreamed a dream.

26 How long shall there be in the mouth of the false prophets, prophecies of lies? prophecies of the deceit of their own heart?

27 Who think to cause my people to forget my name by their dreams which they tell every man to his neighbor, as their fathers forgot my name and served Baal.

28 The prophet who sees a dream, let him tell a dream; but he who has my words, let him speak my words faithfully. Why do you mix chaff [1] with the wheat? says the LORD.

29 Behold, my words issue like a fire, says the LORD, and like a hammer which breaks the rock in pieces.

30 Therefore, behold, I am against the prophets, says the LORD, who steal my words, every one from his neighbor.

31 Behold, I am against the prophets, says the LORD, who pervert their tongues, and say, Thus says the LORD.

32 Behold, I am against the prophets who see false dreams, says the LORD, and tell them, and lead my people astray by their lies and their wantonness; yet I did not command them nor send them; so they do not profit this people at all.

33 ¶And when this people, or a prophet or a priest, shall ask you, and say to you, What is the word of the LORD? you shall say to them, This is the word of the LORD: I will utterly uproot you, says the LORD.

34 And as for the prophet or the priest or the people who shall speak the word of the LORD, I will punish that man and his house.

[1] *Chaff* means *lies.*

35 Thus shall you say every one to his neighbor, and every one to his brother: What has the LORD answered? and, What has the LORD spoken?

36 And the words of the LORD you shall mention no more; for every man's word shall be to him his prophecy, for you pervert the words of the living God, the LORD of hosts, our God.

37 Thus shall you say to that person: What has the LORD answered you? and, What has the LORD spoken?

38 But if you speak the word of the LORD, therefore, thus says the LORD: Because you have said this word, The words of the LORD, and I have sent you, saying, You shall not say, The words of the LORD;

39 Therefore, behold, I will surely remove you, and I will cast you away, both you and the city that I gave to you and your fathers;

40 And I will bring an everlasting reproach upon you, and a perpetual shame which shall not be forgotten.

CHAPTER 24

AFTER Nebuchadnezzar king of Babylon had carried away captive Jeconiah the son of Jehoiakim king of Judah, with the craftsmen and the soldiers, from Jerusalem, and had brought them to Babylon, the LORD showed me, and, behold two baskets of figs were set before the temple of the LORD.

2 One basket had very good figs, like the figs that are first ripe; and the other basket had very bad figs, so that they could not be eaten, because they were so bad.

3 Then the LORD said to me, What do you see, Jeremiah? And I said, Figs; the good figs, very good; and the bad figs, very bad, so that they cannot be eaten because they are so bad.

4 ¶Again the word of the LORD came to me, saying,

5 Thus says the LORD, the God of Israel: Like these good figs, so will I acknowledge the exiles of Judah, whom I have sent out of this place

to the land of the Chaldeans for their good.

6 For I will set my eyes upon them for good and not for evil, says the LORD, and I will bring them again to this land; and I will build them and not overthrow them; and I will plant them and not pluck them up.

7 And I will give them a heart to know me, that I am the LORD; and they shall be my people, and I will be their God when they shall return to me with their whole heart.

8 ¶And like the bad figs which cannot be eaten because they are so bad; thus says the LORD, So will I deliver Zedekiah the king of Judah and his princes and the remnant of the people who are left in this city together with those who dwell in the land of Egypt;

9 And I will make them a horror, an abomination and an evil thing, a reproach in all the kingdoms of the earth, to be a reproach, a proverb, a taunt, and a curse in all the lands where I have driven them.

10 And I will send after them the sword, famine, and pestilence, till I shall destroy them off the land which I gave to them and to their fathers.

CHAPTER 25

THE word that came to Jeremiah concerning all the people of Judah in the fourth year of Jehoiakim the son of Josiah king of Judah, that was the first year of the reign of Nebuchadnezzar king of Babylon;

2 The year in which Jeremiah the prophet spoke to all the people of Judah and to all the inhabitants of Jerusalem, saying,

3 From the thirteenth year of Josiah the son of Amon king of Judah, even to this day, that is twenty-three years, the word of the LORD has come to me and I have spoken to you, warning you in advance daily; but you did not listen.

4 And the LORD has sent to you all his servants the prophets, sending them in advance to warn you; but you did not listen, nor incline your ear to hear.

5 They said, Repent every man from his evil way, and from the evil of his doings, and dwell in the land which the LORD has given to you and to your fathers for ever and ever;

6 And do not go after other gods to serve them and to worship them, and do not provoke me to anger with the works of your hands; that I may not hurt you.

7 Yet you have not hearkened to me, says the LORD; but you have provoked me to anger with the works of your hands to your own harm.

8 ¶Therefore thus says the LORD of hosts: Because you have not listened to my words,

9 Behold, I will send and take all the tribes of the kingdoms of the north, says the LORD, and Nebuchadnezzar the king of Babylon, my servant, and will bring them against this land and against its inhabitants and against all these nations round about, and I will utterly destroy them and make them an astonishment and a hissing, and an everlasting desolation.

10 Moreover I will take from them the voice of mirth and the voice of gladness, the voice of the bridegroom and the voice of the bride, the sound of the millstones and the light of the lamp.

11 And this whole land shall be a desolation and an astonishment; and these nations shall serve the king of Babylon seventy years.

12 ¶And it shall come to pass when seventy years are completed, I will punish the king of Babylon and his people for their iniquities, says the LORD; and also the land of the Chaldeans, I will make it a perpetual desolation.

13 And I will bring upon that land all words which I have pronounced against it, even all that is written in this book, which Jeremiah has prophesied against all the nations.

14 For many nations and great kings shall enslave them also; and I will recompense them according to their deeds and according to the work of their own hands.

15 ¶For thus says the LORD of hosts, the God of Israel to me: Take the wine cup of this fury from my

hand, and make all the nations to whom I send you drink it.

16 And they shall drink, and be dazed and be troubled because of the sword which I am sending among them.

17 Then I took the cup from the LORD's hand, and made all the nations to whom the LORD had sent me drink it:

18 Even to Jerusalem and the cities of Judah, its kings and its princes, to make them a desolation, an astonishment, a hissing, as it is this day;

19 And to Pharaoh king of Egypt and to all his servants and his princes and all his people

20 And all his borders and all the kings of the land of Uz and all the kings of the land of the Philistines and Ashkelon and Gaza [1] and Ekron and the remnant of Ashdod

21 Edom and Moab and the children of Ammon

22 And all the kings of Tyre and all the kings of Zidon and the kings of the islands which are beyond the sea

23 Deran and Tema and Buz and all of those who cut their beards

24 And all the kings whose boundaries are close to each other and all the kings of Arabia who dwell in the desert

25 And all the kings of Zimran and all the kings of Elam and all the kings of the Medes

26 And all the kings of the north, far and near, one with another, and all the kingdoms of the world which are upon the face of the earth; and the king of the Parthians shall drink after them.

27 Therefore you shall say to them, Thus says the LORD of hosts, the God of Israel: Drink and be drunken and stagger and fall and rise no more, because of the sword which I will send among you.

28 And if they refuse to take the cup from your hand to drink, then you shall say to them, Thus says the LORD of hosts: You shall certainly drink.

29 For behold, I begin to bring evil on this city which is called by my name, and you shall not be left unpunished, you shall not be blameless; for I am calling for a sword upon all the inhabitants of the earth, says the LORD of hosts.

30 Therefore you shall prophesy against them all these words, and say to them, The LORD shall roar from on high and utter his voice from his holy habitation; he shall mightily roar against his fold; he shall shout, Hurrah, hurrah, like those who tread the grapes, against all the inhabitants of the earth.

31 The noise shall reach even to the ends of the earth; for the LORD will contend against the nations; he will judge all flesh, and the wicked he shall deliver to the sword, says the LORD.

32 Thus says the LORD of hosts, the God of Israel, Behold, evil shall go forth from nation to nation, and a great whirlwind shall be raised up from the ends of the earth.

33 And those who are slain by the LORD shall be on that day from one end of the earth to the other end of the earth; they shall not be lamented, neither mourned nor wept over nor gathered nor buried; but they shall be like refuse upon the face of the ground.

34 ¶Howl, you shepherds, and cry; wallow in the ashes, you who have great flocks; for the days of your slaughter are at hand, and you shall be broken, and fall like choice vessels.

35 And the shepherds shall not find the way to flee, nor shall the rams of the flock escape.

36 A voice of the cry of shepherds, and the bleating of the rams of the flock shall be heard; for the LORD has plundered their flocks.

37 And the peaceful folds are destroyed because of the fierce anger of the LORD.

38 For they have deserted his fold like a lion that has forsaken his covert; for their land is desolate because of the anger of the LORD and because of the presence of his fierce anger.

---

[1] Aramaic, *Azzah.*

CHAPTER 26

IN the beginning of the reign of Jehoiakim the son of Josiah king of Judah, this word came to Jeremiah from the LORD, saying,

2 Thus says the LORD: Stand in the court of the LORD's house and speak to all the cities of Judah which come to worship in the house of the LORD all the words that I commanded you to speak to them; omit not a word:

3 Perhaps they will listen and turn every man from his evil way, so that I may cease from the harm which I purpose to do to them because of their evil doings.

4 And you shall say to them, Thus says the LORD: If you will not listen to me, to walk in my law which I have set before you

5 And to hearken to the words of my servants the prophets whom I have sent to you, warning you in advance, but you have not hearkened;

6 Then I will make this house like Shiloh and will make this city a curse to all the nations of the earth.

7 So the priests and the false prophets and all the people heard Jeremiah speaking these words in the house of the LORD.

8 ¶Now it came to pass when Jeremiah had finished speaking all that the LORD had commanded him to speak to all the people, then the priests and the false prophets and all the people seized him, saying,

9 He shall surely be put to death, for he has prophesied in the name of the LORD, saying, This house shall be like Shiloh, and this city shall be desolate without an inhabitant. And all the people were gathered against Jeremiah in the house of the LORD.

10 ¶When the princes of Judah heard these things, they came up from the king's house to the house of the LORD and sat down in the entry of the new gate of the LORD's house.

11 Then the priests and the false prophets spoke to the princes and to all the people, saying, This man is guilty of death; for he has prophesied against this city and against its inhabitants, as you have heard with your ears.

12 ¶Then Jeremiah spoke to all the princes and to all the people, saying, The LORD sent me to prophesy against this house and against this city all the words that you have heard.

13 Therefore now amend your ways and your doings, and obey the voice of the LORD your God; and the LORD will cease from the evil which he has pronounced against you.

14 As for me, behold, I am in your hands; do with me as it seems right and proper to you.

15 But you must know for certain that if you put me to death, you shall surely bring innocent blood upon yourselves and upon this city and upon its inhabitants; for of a truth the LORD has sent me to you to speak all these words in your ears.

16 ¶Then the princes and all the people said to the priests and to the false prophets, This man is not guilty of death; for he has spoken to us in the name of the LORD our God.

17 Then rose up certain of the elders of the land, and spoke to all the assembly of the people, saying,

18 Micah the Morashite prophesied in the days of Hezekiah king of Judah, and said to all the people of Judah, Thus says the LORD of hosts, the God of Israel: Zion shall be plowed like a field, and Jerusalem shall become heaps, and the mountain of the temple like a forest.

19 Did Hezekiah king of Judah and all Judah put him to death? No, but they feared the LORD and prayed before him, and the LORD refrained from the evil which he had pronounced against them. And now, we wish to bring great evil upon ourselves.

20 And there was also another man who prophesied in the name of the LORD, Uriah the son of Shemaiah from Koriath-narin, who prophesied against this city and against this land according to all the words of Jeremiah;

21 And when Jehoiakim the king, with all his servants and all the princes, heard his words, the king

sought to put him to death; but when Uriah heard of it, he was afraid; so he fled and went to Egypt;

22 And King Jehoiakim sent a certain Egyptian, namely, Eliathan the son of Achbor, and certain other men with him to Egypt.

23 And they fetched Uriah from Egypt, and brought him to King Jehoiakim; who slew him with the sword, and cast his dead body into the burial place of the common people.

24 Nevertheless the hand of Ahikam the son of Shaphan was with Jeremiah, so that they might not deliver him into the hand of the people to put him to death.

CHAPTER 27

IN the beginning of the reign of Zedekiah the son of Josiah king of Judah came this word to Jeremiah from the LORD, saying,

2 Thus says the LORD to me: Make yourself yokes and bands, and put them on your neck,

3 And send them to the king of Edom, the king of Moab, the king of the Ammonites, the king of Tyre, and the king of Zidon by the hand of the messengers who come to Jerusalem to Zedekiah king of Judah;

4 And command them to say to their masters, Thus says the LORD of hosts, the God of Israel: Thus shall you say to your masters:

5 I have made the earth and the men and the beasts that are upon the ground by my great power and by my outstretched arm, and I have given it to whom it seemed good in my sight.

6 And now I have given all these lands to serve Nebuchadnezzar the king of Babylon, my servant; and I have given him also the beasts of the field to serve him.

7 And all nations shall serve him and his son and his son's son, until the very time of his land shall come; many nations and great kings shall serve him.

8 And the nation and kingdom which will not serve the same Nebu-

chadnezzar the king of Babylon and that will not put its neck under the yoke of the king of Babylon, I will punish that nation with the sword and with famine, and with pestilence, says the LORD, until I have delivered them into his hand.

9 Therefore do not listen to your false prophets nor to your diviners nor to your dreamers nor to your enchanters nor to your magicians, who say to you, You shall not serve the king of Babylon;

10 For it is a lie which they are prophesying to you, that I may drive you out from your land, and that I should drive you out, and you should perish.

11 But the nation that brings its neck under the yoke of the king of Babylon and serves him, I will leave on its own land, says the LORD; and they shall till it and dwell in it.

12 ¶ I spoke also to Zedekiah king of Judah according to all these words, saying, Bring your necks under the yoke of the king of Babylon, and serve him and his people and live;

13 So that you may not die, you and your people, by the sword, by famine, and by pestilence, according to that which the LORD has spoken against the nation that will not serve the king of Babylon.

14 Therefore do not listen to the words of the false prophets who speak to you, saying, You shall not serve the king of Babylon; for they prophesy a lie to you.

15 For I have not sent them, says the LORD; yet they prophesy a lie in my name; that I might drive you out, and that you might perish, you and the prophets who prophesy to you.

16 I spoke also to the priests and to all this people, saying, Thus says the LORD: Do not hearken to the words of your prophets who prophesy to you, saying, Behold, the vessels of the LORD's house shall now shortly be brought back from Babylon; for they prophesy a lie to you.

17 Do not listen to them, says the LORD, but serve the king of Babylon and live, that this city might not become a desolation.

18 But if they are prophets and the word of the LORD is with them, then let them beseech the LORD of hosts that the vessels which are left in the house of the LORD and in the house of the king of Judah and in Jerusalem be not taken to Babylon.

19 ¶For thus says the LORD of hosts, the God of Israel, concerning the pillars and concerning the sea and concerning the bases and concerning the rest of the vessels that are left in this city,

20 Which Nebuchadnezzar king of Babylon did not take away, when he carried away captive Jeconiah the son of Jehoiakim king of Judah from Jerusalem to Babylon and all the princes of Judah and Jerusalem;

21 Thus says the LORD of hosts, the God of Israel, concerning the vessels that are left in the house of the LORD and in the house of the king of Judah and in Jerusalem:

22 They shall be carried to Babylon, and there shall they remain until the day when I visit them, says the LORD; then I will bring them up and restore them to this place.

CHAPTER 28

AND it came to pass that same year, in the beginning of the reign of Zedekiah king of Judah, in the fourth year, in the fifth month, Hananiah the son of Azur the false prophet, who was from Gibeon, spoke to me in the house of the LORD in the presence of the priests and in the presence of all the people, saying,

2 Thus says the LORD of hosts, the God of Israel: I have broken the yoke of the king of Babylon.

3 Within two years I will bring back to this place all the vessels of the LORD's house, which Nebuchadnezzar king of Babylon took away from this place and carried to Babylon.

4 And I will bring back to this place Jeconiah the son of Jehoiakim king of Judah, with all the captives of Judah who went to Babylon, says the LORD; for I will break the yoke of the king of Babylon.

5 ¶Then the prophet Jeremiah spoke to the false prophet Hananiah in the presence of the priests and in the presence of all the people who stood in the house of the LORD.

6 And Jeremiah said, Amen! may the LORD do so; the LORD perform the words which you have prophesied, to bring back the vessels of the LORD's house and all the captives from Babylon to this place.

7 Nevertheless, hear now this word which I speak before you and before all the people;

8 The prophets who have been before me and before you of old prophesied both against many countries and against great kingdoms, of war and of evil and of pestilence.

9 If a prophet prophesies of peace, then when the word of that prophet shall come to pass, he shall be known as the one whom the LORD has truly sent.

10 ¶Then Hananiah the false prophet took the bands of the yoke from off the neck of Jeremiah the prophet, and broke them.

11 And Hananiah spoke in the presence of all the people, saying, Thus says the LORD: Even so will I break the yoke of Nebuchadnezzar king of Babylon from the neck of all the nations within two full years. And the prophet Jeremiah went his way.

12 ¶Then the word of the LORD came to Jeremiah the prophet, after Hananiah the false prophet had broken the yoke bands from the neck of the prophet Jeremiah, saying,

13 Go and tell Hananiah the false prophet, Thus says the LORD: You have broken the yoke of wood; but you shall make in their place a yoke of iron.

14 For thus says the LORD of hosts, the God of Israel: I have put a yoke of iron upon the neck of all these nations, that they may serve Nebuchadnezzar king of Babylon; and they shall serve him; and I have given him the beasts of the field also.

15 ¶Then said the prophet Jeremiah to Hananiah the false prophet, Hear now, Hananiah, the LORD has not sent you; but you make this people to trust in a lie.

16 Therefore, thus says the LORD: Behold, I will cast you from off the face of the earth; this very year you shall die, for you have spoken iniquity in the presence of the LORD.

17 So Hananiah the false prophet died the same year in the seventh month.

CHAPTER 29

NOW these are the words of the letter which Jeremiah the prophet sent from Jerusalem to Babylon, to the rest of the elders who were in exile and to the priests and to the false prophets and to all the people whom Nebuchadnezzar king of Babylon had carried captive from Jerusalem to Babylon

2 (After Jeconiah the king and the queen and the eunuchs, the princes of Judah and Jerusalem, and the craftsmen and the guard had departed from Jerusalem),

3 By the hand of Elasah the son of Shaphan, and Gemariah the son of Hilkiah, whom Zedekiah king of Judah sent to Nebuchadnezzar king of Babylon, saying,

4 Thus says the LORD of hosts, the God of Israel, to all who are carried away captives, from Jerusalem to Babylon:

5 Build houses and live in them; and plant gardens and eat the fruit of them;

6 Take wives and beget sons and daughters; and take wives for your sons and give your daughters to husbands that they may bear sons and daughters; and multiply there, and not decrease.

7 And seek the peace of the city where I have caused you to be carried away captives, and pray to the LORD for it; for in the peace thereof shall you have peace.

8 ¶For thus says the LORD of hosts, the God of Israel: Do not let your prophets and your diviners who are among you deceive you, neither listen to your dreams which you dream.

9 For they prophesy falsely to you in my name; I have not sent them, says the LORD.

10 ¶For thus says the LORD: After seventy years are completed at Babylon I will deliver you and perform my good word toward you in bringing you back to this country.

11 For I know the thoughts that I think towards you, says the LORD, thoughts of peace and not of evil, to give you a good hope at the end.

12 Then you shall call upon me and pray to me.

13 And when you shall seek me with all your heart, you shall find me, says the LORD.

14 And I will bring back your exiles, and I will gather you from all the nations and from all the lands where I have driven you, says the LORD, and I will bring you back to the place from which I caused you to be carried away captive.

15 ¶Because you have said, The LORD has raised us up prophets in Babylon;

16 Therefore, thus says the LORD concerning the king who sits on the throne of David and concerning all the people who dwell in this city and your brethren who did not go out with you into captivity;

17 Thus says the LORD of hosts: Behold, I will send upon them the sword, famine, and pestilence, and I will make them like bad figs which are so bad that they cannot be eaten.

18 And I will pursue them with the sword, with famine, and with pestilence, and I will make them a horror to all the kingdoms of the earth, to be an astonishment, a curse, a reproach, and a hissing among all the nations where I have driven them,

19 Because they did not hearken to my words, and I sent to them all my servants the prophets, warning them in advance, but they did not listen to them, says the LORD.

20 ¶Hear therefore the word of the LORD, all you exiles who were carried away captive from Jerusalem to Babylon;

21 Thus says the LORD of hosts, the God of Israel, concerning Ahab, the son of Kolaiah, and concerning Zedekiah the son of Maasiah, who prophesy lies to you: Behold, I will deliver

them into the hand of Nebuchadnezzar king of Babylon; and he shall slay them before your eyes;

22 And of them shall be taken up a curse by all the exiles who are in Babylon; they shall say, The LORD make you like Zedekiah and like Ahab, whom the king of Babylon roasted in the fire;

23 Because they have done wickedness in Israel and have committed adultery with their neighbors' wives and have spoken lying words in my name, which I have not commanded them; even I know and I am a witness, says the LORD.

24 ¶And to Shemaiah the Nehelamite, you shall say,

25 Thus says the LORD of hosts, the God of Israel: Because you have sent a letter in his name to all the people who are in Jerusalem and to Zephaniah the son of Maasiah the priest and to all the priests, saying,

26 The LORD has made you priest instead of Jehoiadah the priest, to be an officer in the house of the LORD over every man who acts foolishly and prophesies falsehood, to put him in prison and in the stocks.

27 Now, therefore, why have you not rebuked Jeremiah of Anathoth, who prophesies to you?

28 For he has sent to us in Babylon, saying, You shall remain there for a long time; therefore, build houses and dwell in them; and plant gardens and eat the fruit of them.

29 And Zephaniah the priest read this letter in the ears of Jeremiah the prophet.

30 ¶Then the word of the LORD came to Jeremiah, saying,

31 Send to all of them who are in captivity, saying, Thus says the LORD concerning Shemaiah the Nehelamite: Because Shemaiah has prophesied to you the thing which I did not send him to prophesy and has caused you to trust in a lie;

32 Therefore, thus says the LORD: Behold, I will punish Shemaiah the Nehelamite and his posterity; he shall not have a man to dwell among this people; neither shall he see the good which I will do for my people, says the LORD, because he has spoken iniquity against the LORD.

CHAPTER 30

THE word that came to Jeremiah from the LORD, saying,

2 Thus says the LORD God of Israel: Write all the words that I have spoken to you in a book.

3 For behold, the days are coming, says the LORD, when I will bring back the captives of my people Israel and Judah, says the LORD; and I will bring them back to the land which I gave to their fathers and they shall possess it.

4 ¶And these are the words that the LORD spoke concerning Israel and concerning Judah.

5 Thus says the LORD: We have heard a sound of trembling and of fear; and there is no peace.

6 Ask now and see: Can a male bear a child? Wherefore do I observe every man with his hands on his loins, like a woman in travail, and all faces turned into paleness?

7 Alas! for that day is great, so that none is like it; it is a time of distress for Jacob; but he shall be saved out of it.

8 For it shall come to pass in that day, says the LORD of hosts, that I will break the yoke of the king of Babylon from off your neck, and I will cut off your bonds, and strangers shall no more enslave them;

9 But they shall serve the LORD their God and David their king whom I will raise up for them.

10 ¶Therefore fear not, O my servant Jacob, says the LORD; neither be dismayed, O Israel; for, lo, I will save you from afar and your offspring from the land of their captivity; and Jacob shall return, and shall be in rest, and be quiet, and none shall hurt him.

11 Fear not, O my servant Jacob, says the LORD, for I am with you to save you, says the LORD; for I will make a full end of all nations whither I have scattered you, yet I will not make a full end of you; but I will correct you justly, and will not declare you innocent.

12 For thus says the LORD: Your wound is grievous, and your affliction is severe.

13 There is none to plead your cause or to succor you and heal you.

14 All your friends have forgotten you; they seek your life; for I have smitten you with the wound of an enemy, with a severe chastisement because of the multitude of your iniquities, and because your sins were increased and you would not repent.

15 Why do you lament over your wound? Your wound is painful because of the multitude of your iniquities; and because your sins were increased, I have done these things to you.

16 Therefore, all who devour you shall be devoured; and all your enemies, every one of them, shall go into captivity; and those who trample over you shall be trampled over, and all those who plunder you I will give for a prey.

17 For I will restore health to you, and I will heal you of your wounds, says the LORD; because they have called you an outcast, saying, This is Zion who had no avenger.

18 ¶Thus says the LORD: Behold, I will bring again the captivity of Jacob's tents, and I will do to him as of old, and have mercy on his dwelling places; the city shall be built upon its own hill, and the temple shall be established after the former manner thereof.

19 And out of them shall proceed thanksgiving and the voice of those who sing; and I will multiply them, and they shall not decrease; I will also make them mighty, and they shall not be weak.

20 Their children also shall be as of old, and their congregation shall be established before me, and I will punish all who oppress them.

21 And their king shall be one of themselves, and their governors shall come forth from among themselves; and I will cause him to draw near, and he shall approach to me; for I will turn his heart towards me, says the LORD.

22 And you shall be my people, and I will be your God.

23 Behold, the whirlwind of the LORD goes forth with fury, a tornado; it shall rest upon the head of the wicked.

24 The fierce anger of the LORD will not turn back until he has executed his orders and until he has performed the intents of his heart; in the latter days you shall understand this.

CHAPTER 31

AT that time, says the LORD, I will be the God of all the families of Israel, and they shall be my people.

2 Thus says the LORD: The people who escaped from the sword found compassion in the wilderness when Israel went into exile.

3 The LORD has appeared to me from afar, saying, Yea, I have loved you with an everlasting love; therefore with lovingkindness have I drawn you.

4 Again I will build you, and you shall be built, O virgin of Israel; you shall again be adorned with your ornaments, and shall go forth in the assembly of those who make merry.

5 You shall again plant vineyards on the mountain of Samaria. Yea, you will plant vines and sing.

6 For the day is coming when the watchmen on mount Ephraim shall cry, saying, Arise, and let us go up to Zion to the LORD our God.

7 For thus says the LORD: Sing with gladness, O house of Jacob, and rejoice among the chief of the nations; publish, give praise, and say, O LORD, save thy people, the remnant of Israel.

8 Behold, I will bring them from the north land, and gather them from the uttermost parts of the earth, and also the lame and the blind who are among them, the woman with child and her that is in travail together; a great company shall they return here.

9 They shall go with weeping, but they shall return with fervent prayer; I will lead them by the paths that have water, in straight ways in which they shall not stumble; for I am a

father to Israel, and Ephraim is my first-born.

10 ¶Hear the word of the LORD, O you his people, and declare it in the isles afar off, and say, He who scattered Israel will gather him, and shall keep him as a shepherd keeps his flock.

11 For the LORD has saved his servant Jacob, and delivered him from the hand of him who was stronger than he.

12 Therefore they shall come and sing on the height of Zion, and they shall be happy because of the goodness of the LORD, for the wheat, for the wine, and for the oil, and for the young of the flock and of the herd; and their soul shall be like a watered garden; and they shall not lack any more.

13 Then shall the virgin rejoice and be glad, both young men and the old together; for I will turn their mourning into joy, and will comfort them and make them rejoice from their sorrow.

14 And I will satisfy the soul of the priests with fatness, and my people shall be satisfied with my goodness, says the LORD.

15 ¶Thus says the LORD: A voice was heard in Ramtha, lamentation and bitter weeping; Rachel is weeping for her children, and she refuses to be comforted because they are not.

16 Thus says the LORD: Restrain your voice from weeping and your eyes from tears; for there is a reward for your tears, says the LORD; and the people shall return from the land of the enemy.

17 And there is hope in your future, says the LORD, and the children shall come back to their own land.

18 ¶I have surely heard Ephraim bemoaning and saying, O LORD, thou hast chastised me, and I was chastened; I had become like a bullock which cannot be subdued; bring me back, and I will repent; for thou art the LORD my God.

19 Surely after I had repented, I have been comforted; and after I was instructed, I have found rest; I was ashamed, yea even reproved, because I did bear the reproach of my youth.

20 Ephraim is my dear son, and a beloved child; for when I speak of him, I do earnestly remember him still; therefore I have my mercy upon him, I will surely have compassion on him, says the LORD.

21 Set up a standard for yourself, and dwell in the wilderness; set your heart towards the straight highway; repent, O virgin of Israel, says the LORD, and dwell in these your cities.

22 ¶How long will you hesitate, O backsliding daughter? For the LORD has created a new thing on the earth, a woman shall love her husband.

23 Thus says the LORD God of hosts, the God of Israel: From henceforth they shall use this saying in the land of Judah and in its cities, when I shall bring them back from their captivity: The LORD bless you, O habitation of righteousness, O holy mountain.

24 And there shall dwell in Judah itself and in all its cities together, farmers and shepherds of flocks.

25 For I have satisfied the thirsty soul and I have replenished every hungry soul.

26 This is why I awoke and beheld; and my sleep was sweet to me.

27 ¶Behold the days are coming, says the LORD, when I will sow the house of Israel and the house of Judah with the seed of man and with the seed of beast.

28 And it shall come to pass that as I purposed against them, to uproot them and to break them down and to overthrow them and to destroy and to afflict; so will I be mindful of them, to build and to plant, says the LORD.

29 In those days they shall say no more, The fathers have eaten sour grapes, and the children's teeth are set on edge.

30 But every one shall die for his own sins; every man who eats the sour grapes, his teeth shall be set on edge.

31 ¶Behold, the days are coming, says the LORD, when I will make a

new covenant with the house of Israel and with the house of Judah;

32 Not like the covenant which I made with their fathers in the day that I took them by the hand and brought them out of the land of Egypt; and because they nullified my covenant, so I also despised them, says the LORD;

33 But this is the covenant which I will make with the house of Israel, after those days, says the LORD: I will put my law in the midst of them, and I will write it upon their hearts; and I will be their God, and they shall be my people.

34 And they shall teach no more every man his brother and every man his neighbor, saying, Know the LORD; for they shall all know me, from the youngest of them to the eldest of them, says the LORD; for I will forgive their iniquity and I will remember their sins no more.

35 ¶Thus says the LORD, who has ordained the sun for a light by day and the moon and the stars for a light by night, who rebukes the sea and stills its waves; the LORD of hosts is his name;

36 If those ordinances depart from before me, says the LORD, then the descendants of Israel also shall cease from being a nation before me for ever.

37 Thus says the LORD: If the heavens above can be measured and the foundations of the earth below explored, then I will also reject all the descendants of Israel for all that they have done, says the LORD.

38 ¶Behold, the days are coming, says the LORD, when the city shall be built to the LORD from the tower of Hananael to the gate of the corner.

39 And the measuring line shall go forth straight upon the hill Gareb, and shall curve about to Goath.

40 And the whole valley in which they dump refuse and ashes, as far as the brook Kidron and as far as the corner of the horse gate towards the east, shall be holy to the LORD; it shall not be uprooted nor demolished any more for ever.

CHAPTER 32

THE word that came to Jeremiah from the LORD in the tenth year of Zedekiah king of Judah, which was the eighteenth year of Nebuchadnezzar.

2 For then the army of the king of Babylon was besieging Jerusalem; and Jeremiah the prophet was shut up in the court of the guard, which was in the king of Judah's house.

3 For Zedekiah king of Judah had shut him up, saying, Why do you prophesy and say, Thus says the LORD: Behold, I will deliver this city into the hand of the king of Babylon, and he shall take it;

4 And Zedekiah king of Judah shall not escape out of the hand of the Chaldeans, but shall surely be delivered into the hand of the king of Babylon, and shall speak with him face to face, and they shall see each other eye to eye;

5 And he shall take Zedekiah to Babylon, and there shall he be until I visit him, says the LORD; though you fight with the Chaldeans, you shall not win.

6 ¶And the word of the LORD came to Jeremiah, saying,

7 Behold, Nahmael the son of Shallum your uncle is coming to you, saying, Buy my field which is at Anathoth, which is in the land of Benjamin; for the right of redemption is yours to buy it.

8 So Nahmael my uncle's son came to me in the court of the guard according to the word of the LORD, and said to me, Buy my field which is at Anathoth, which is in the land of Benjamin; for the right of inheritance is yours, and the redemption is yours; buy it for yourself. Then I knew that this was the word of the LORD.

9 And I bought the field of Nahmael my uncle's son, which was in Anathoth, and weighed him the money, even seventeen shekels of silver.

10 And I wrote the deed, and sealed it and called witnesses, and weighed him the money in the scales.

11 Then I took the deed of purchase, both that which was duly sealed according to law and a copy which was not sealed;

12 And I gave the deed of the purchase to Baruch the son of Neriah, the son of Maasiah, in the sight of Nahmael my uncle's son and in the presence of the witnesses whose names were written on the deed of purchase and in the presence of all the Jews who were seated in the court of the guard.

13 ¶And I charged Baruch in their presence, saying,

14 Thus says the LORD of hosts, the God of Israel: Take these deeds, both this deed of purchase which is sealed and this deed which is not sealed; and put them in an earthen vessel, so that they may be preserved for a long time.

15 For thus says the LORD of hosts, the God of Israel: Houses and fields and vineyards shall be bought again in this land.

16 ¶Now after I had given the deeds of purchase to Baruch the son of Neriah, I prayed to the LORD, saying,

17 Ah, LORD God! behold, thou hast made the heaven and the earth by thy great power and by thy stretched out arm, and there is nothing hidden from thee;

18 Thou showest lovingkindness to thousands of generations, and recompensest the iniquity of the fathers to the bosom of their children after them; thou art the Great God, the Mighty and Revered, the LORD of hosts is his name,

19 Great in counsel and mighty in work, whose eyes are open upon all the ways of the sons of men, to give every one according to his ways and according to the fruit of his doings.

20 For thou didst perform great signs and wonders in the land of Egypt, even to this day and in Israel and among other men; and hast made thee a name, as at this day;

21 And hast brought forth thy people Israel out of the land of Egypt with signs and with wonders and with a strong hand and with a stretched out arm and with a great spectacle;

22 And hast given them this land, which thou didst swear to their fathers to give them, a land flowing with milk and honey;

23 And they came in and possessed it; but they did not obey thy voice, neither walked in thy law; they did nothing of all that thou didst command them to do; therefore all this evil has come upon them.

24 Behold the siege ramparts are come against this city to take it; and because of sword and of famine and of pestilence the city is delivered into the hand of the Chaldeans, who are fighting against it; and what thou hast spoken is come to pass; and, behold, I see it.

25 And thou, O LORD God, hast said to me, Buy the field for money, and call witnesses; and, behold the city is given into the hand of the Chaldeans.

26 ¶Then came the word of the LORD to Jeremiah, saying,

27 I am the LORD, the God of all flesh; is there anything hidden from me?

28 Therefore thus says the LORD: Behold, I will deliver this city into the hand of the Chaldeans and into the hand of Nebuchadnezzar king of Babylon, and he shall take it;

29 And the Chaldeans shall come and fight against this city, and shall uproot this city and set fire to it, together with the houses upon whose roofs the people have offered incense to Baal and poured out drink offerings to other gods to provoke me to anger.

30 For the children of Israel and the children of Judah have done only that which is evil before me from their youth; for the children of Israel have always provoked me to anger with the work of their hands, says the LORD.

31 And because of them my anger and fury have come upon this city from the day that they built it even to this day; so that I may remove it from before my face,

32 Because of all the evil of the children of Israel and of the children of

Judah, which they have done to provoke me to anger, they, their kings, their princes, their priests and their prophets and the men of Judah and the inhabitants of Jerusalem.

33 And they have turned to me their backs and not their faces; though I have taught them, warning them in advance, yet they would not listen to receive instruction.

34 But they set their abominations in the house which is called by my name, to defile it.

35 And they built the high places of Baal in Taphat, which is in the valley of Hinnom, to burn their sons and their daughters as offerings to Molech; which I did not command them, nor did it come into my mind that they should do this abomination to cause Judah to sin.

36 ¶And now therefore thus says the LORD, the God of Israel, concerning this city, of which you say, It shall be delivered into the hand of the king of Babylon by sword and by famine and by pestilence;

37 Behold, I will gather them from all the lands to which I have driven them in my anger and in my fury and great wrath; and I will bring them back to this country, and I will cause them to dwell in safety;

38 And they shall be my people, and I will be their God;

39 And I will give them a new heart and a new spirit, that they may worship before me for ever; and it shall be good to them and to their children after them:

40 And I will make an everlasting covenant with them, that I will not turn away from them to do them good; and I will put my reverence in their hearts, that they may not go astray from me.

41 Yea, I will cause them to rejoice, and good shall come to them, and I will plant them in this land in truth, with my whole heart and with my whole soul.

42 For thus says the LORD: Just as I have brought all this great evil upon this people, so will I bring them all the good that I promise them.

43 And fields shall be bought in this land, of which you say, It is desolate, without man and beast; and it is delivered into the hand of the Chaldeans.

44 Men shall buy fields for money, and write deeds and seal them and call witnesses in the land of Benjamin and in the places about Jerusalem and in the cities of Judah and in the cities of the mountains and in the cities of the valleys and in the cities of the south; for I will bring them back from their captivity, says the LORD.

CHAPTER 33

MOREOVER, the word of the LORD came to Jeremiah the second time, while he was yet shut up in the court of the guard, saying,

2 Thus says the LORD who made you and formed you and established you: the LORD is his name:

3 Call to me and I will answer you and show you great and mighty things which you know not.

4 For thus says the LORD, the God of Israel, concerning the houses of this city and concerning the houses of the kings of Judah, which the robbers have uprooted by the sword:

5 They come to fight with the Chaldeans, but it is to fill the streets with the dead bodies of men whom I have slain in my anger and in my wrath; for I have turned my face from this city because of the evil which they did before me.

6 Behold, I will bring to it a long period of healing, and I will heal them and will reveal to them the paths of peace and truth.

7 And I will bring back the captivity of Judah and the captivity of Israel, and I will build them as at first.

8 And I will cleanse them from their iniquity whereby they have committed evil against me; and I will pardon all their trespasses whereby they have sinned against me, and whereby they have transgressed against me.

9 ¶And Israel shall be to me for a name and for a delight, and for rejoicing and for glory before all the nations of the earth, who shall hear of all the good that I do to them; and they shall fear and be angry because

of all the goodness and all the peace that I bring to them.

10 Thus says the LORD: Again there shall be heard in this country which you say is a waste without man and without beast, even in the cities of Judah and in the streets of Jerusalem, which are desolate, without man and without inhabitant and without beast,

11 The voice of joy and the voice of gladness, the voice of the bridegroom and the voice of the bride, the voice of those who say, Praise the LORD of hosts; for the LORD is good and pleasant, and his mercy endures for ever; even of those who bring a sacrifice of praise into the house of the LORD. For I will bring back the captivity of the land, as at the first, says the LORD of hosts.

12 Thus says the LORD of hosts: From henceforth in this place which is waste, without men and without beast, and in all its cities there shall be habitations of shepherds and folds of the flocks.

13 In the cities of the mountains, in the cities of the plain and in the cities of the south and in the land of Benjamin and in the places about Jerusalem and in the cities of Judah. flocks shall again pass under the hands of those who count them, says the LORD.

14 Behold, the days are coming, says the LORD, when I will perform the good things which I have spoken concerning the house of Israel and concerning the house of Judah, says the LORD.

15 ¶In those days and at that time I will cause an heir of righteousness to rise up to David; and he shall rule over the kingdom and shall have understanding and shall execute justice and righteousness in the land.

16 In those days Judah shall be saved and Jerusalem shall dwell safely; and this is the name by which they shall call him: The LORD our righteousness.

17 ¶For thus says the LORD, David shall never lack an heir to sit on the throne of the house of Israel;

18 Neither shall the priests and the Levites lack a man before me to offer burnt offerings and to burn meat offerings and to do sacrifice and to burn incense continually.

19 ¶And the word of the LORD came to Jeremiah, saying,

20 Thus says the LORD: if they can break my ordinances of the day, and my ordinances of the night, so that there should not be day and night in their appointed time;

21 Then may also my covenant which I made with David my servant be broken, so that he should not have an heir to reign upon his throne; and my covenant with the priests and the Levites, my ministers.

22 As the host of heaven cannot be numbered, neither the sand of the sea measured; so will I multiply the descendants of David my servant and of the Levites who minister to me.

23 Moreover the word of the LORD came to Jeremiah, saying,

24 Have you not considered what this people are saying, The two families which the LORD has chosen, he has rejected? Thus they have provoked my people to anger, that they should be no more a nation before me.

25 Thus says the LORD: If my covenant be not in effect with day and night, and if I have not appointed the ordinances of heaven and earth;

26 Then I will reject the descendants of Jacob and of David my servant so that I will not take any of his descendants to be rulers over the house of Abraham, Isaac, and Jacob; for I will bring them back from their exile and will have mercy upon them.

CHAPTER 34

THE word which came to Jeremiah from the LORD, when Nebuchadnezzar, king of Babylon, and all his army and all the kingdoms of the earth that were under his dominion and all the peoples who were fighting against Jerusalem and against all of its cities, saying,

2 Thus says the LORD, the God of Israel: Go and speak to Zedekiah king of Judah and tell him, Thus says the LORD: Behold, I will deliver this city into the hand of the king of

Babylon and he shall burn it with fire;

3 And you shall not escape from his hand, but shall surely be seized and delivered into his hand, and your eyes shall see the eyes of the king of Babylon, and you shall speak with him mouth to mouth, and you shall go to Babylon.

4 Yet hear the word of the LORD, O Zedekiah king of Judah; thus says the LORD concerning you, You shall not die by the sword; but you shall die in peace;

5 And as they mourned over your fathers, the former kings who were before you, so shall they mourn over you; and they shall lament for you, saying, Ah lord! for I have spoken this word, says the LORD.

6 Then Jeremiah the prophet spoke all these words to Zedekiah king of Judah in Jerusalem

7 When the king of Babylon's army was fighting against Jerusalem and against all the cities of Judah that were left, against Lachish and against Azekah; for these were the only fortified cities that remained of the cities of Judah.

8 ¶This is the word that came to Jeremiah from the LORD, after king Zedekiah had made a covenant with all the people that were in Jerusalem: Proclaim liberty to them;

9 That every man should set free his Hebrew manservant and maidservant, so that no man may enslave a Jew, his brother.

10 And all the princes and all the people obeyed, and took upon themselves to let every one his manservant and his maidservant go free, that they should not make them to serve them any more; so they let them go free.

11 But afterward they changed their minds, and caused to return both the male and female servants whom they had let go free, and brought them into subjection for servants and for handmaids.

12 ¶Therefore the word of the LORD came to Jeremiah, saying,

13 Thus says the LORD, the God of Israel: I made a covenant with your fathers in the day that I brought them forth out of the land of Egypt, out of the house of bondage, saying,

14 At the end of seven years you shall set free every man his brother, a Hebrew, who has been sold to you; and when he has served you six years, you shall let him go free from you; but your fathers did not hearken to me nor incline their ear.

15 And you now had turned, and had done that which is right in my sight, in proclaiming liberty every man to his neighbor, and you had made a covenant before me in the house which is called by my name;

16 But then you turned again and profaned my name, and caused every man his servant and every man his handmaid, whom he had set at liberty at their pleasure, to return and to be brought again into subjection, to be to you for servants and for handmaids.

17 Therefore thus says the LORD, the God of Israel: You have not hearkened to me in proclaiming liberty every one to his neighbor; behold, I proclaim for you liberty to sword, to famine, and to pestilence, says the LORD; and I will make you a horror to all the kingdoms of the earth.

18 And I will deliver up the men who have transgressed my covenant, who have not confirmed the words of the covenant which they had made before me, when they cut the calf in two and passed between the parts thereof,

19 The princes of Judah and the princes of Jerusalem, the eunuchs and the priests and all the people of the land, who passed between the parts of the calf;

20 And I will deliver them into the hand of their enemies and into the hand of those who seek their lives; and their dead bodies shall be food for the fowls of the air and for the beasts of the earth.

21 And Zedekiah king of Judah and his princes I will deliver into the hand of their enemies and into the hand of those who seek their lives and into the hand of the king of Babylon's

army, who are coming back against them.

22 Behold, I will command, says the LORD, and cause them to return to this city; and they shall fight against it and take it and burn it with fire; and I will make the cities of Judah a desolation without an inhabitant.

CHAPTER 35

THE word which came to Jeremiah from the LORD in the days of Jehoiakim the son of Josiah king of Judah, saying,

2 Go to the house of the Rechabites and speak to them, and bring them into the house of the LORD, into one of the chambers, and give them wine to drink.

3 Then I took Jaazaniah the son of Amariah, the son of Habaziniah, and his brothers and all his sons and the whole house of the Rechabites;

4 And I brought them into the house of the LORD, into the chamber of the sons of Hanan, the son of Gedaliah, a prophet of God, whose house was near the chamber of the princes, who dwell above the house of Maasiah the son of Shallum, the keeper of the door;

5 And I set before the sons of the house of the Rechabites vessels full of wine, and cups, and I said to them, Drink wine;

6 But they said, We will drink no wine; for Jonadab the son of Rechab our father commanded us, saying, You shall drink no wine, neither you nor your sons for ever;

7 Neither shall you build houses for yourselves nor sow seed nor plant vineyards nor have any; but you shall dwell in tents all your days; for you shall live many days in the land where you sojourn.

8 Thus we have obeyed the command of Jonadab the son of Rechab our father in all that he has charged us, to drink no wine all our days, neither we nor our wives nor our sons nor our daughters;

9 Nor to build houses for ourselves to dwell in; neither to have vineyards nor fields nor seed;

10 But we have dwelt in tents, and have obeyed and done according to all that Jonadab our father commanded us.

11 But it came to pass when Nebuchadnezzar king of Babylon came up against the land, we said, Come and let us go to Jerusalem for fear of the army of the Chaldeans and for fear of the army of Edom; so we dwell in Jerusalem.

12 ¶Then the word of the LORD came to the prophet Jeremiah, saying,

13 Thus says the LORD of hosts, the God of Israel: Go and tell the men of Judah and the inhabitants of Jerusalem, Will you not receive instruction to hearken to my words? says the LORD.

14 The words of Jonadab the son of Rechab, who commanded his sons not to drink wine, are performed; for to this day they drink none, for they have obeyed their father's commandment; yet I have spoken to you and warned you in advance; but you have not listened to me.

15 I have sent also to you all my servants the prophets, sending them in advance, saying, Repent now every man from his evil way and amend your doings and do not go after other gods to serve them, and you shall dwell in the land which I have given to you and to your fathers; but you have not inclined your ear nor listened to me.

16 Behold, the sons of Jonadab have faithfully kept the commandment of their father, who commanded them, but this people has not hearkened to me;

17 Therefore thus says the LORD of hosts, the God of Israel: Behold, I will bring upon Judah and upon all the inhabitants of Jerusalem all the evil that I have pronounced against them; because I have warned them, but they have not listened; and I have called to them, but they have not answered me.

18 ¶And Jeremiah said to the house of the Rechabites, Thus says the LORD of hosts, the God of Israel: Because you have obeyed the commandment

of Jonadab your father, and kept all his precepts and done according to all that he has commanded you;

19 Therefore thus says the LORD of hosts, the God of Israel: Jonadab the son of Rechab shall not lack an heir to stand before me for ever.

CHAPTER 36

AND it came to pass in the fourth year of Jehoiakim the son of Josiah king of Judah that this word came to Jeremiah from the LORD, saying,

2 Take a scroll of a book and write on it all the words that I have spoken to you against Israel and against Judah and against all the nations from the day I spoke to you, from the days of Josiah even to this day.

3 It may be that the house of Judah will hear all the evil which I purpose to do to them; that they may turn every man from his evil way; that I may forgive their trespasses and their sins.

4 Then Jeremiah called Baruch the son of Neriah; and Baruch wrote from the mouth of Jeremiah all the words of the LORD which he had spoken to him, upon a scroll of a book.

5 And Jeremiah commanded Baruch, saying, I am shut up; I cannot enter into the house of the LORD;

6 Therefore go and read the scroll which you have written from my mouth, the words of the LORD, in the presence of the people in the LORD's house on a fast day; and also you shall read them in the presence of all the people of Judah who come out of their cities.

7 It may be they will present their supplication before the LORD, and every one will turn from his evil way; so that the LORD may cease from the evil which he has pronounced against them; for great is the anger and the fury that he has pronounced against this people.

8 And Baruch the son of Neriah did according to all that Jeremiah the prophet commanded him, reading in the scroll the words of the LORD in the LORD's house.

9 And it came to pass in the fifth year of Jehoiakim the son of Josiah king of Judah, in the ninth month, when all the people in Jerusalem had proclaimed a fast before the LORD, Baruch read before all the people who came from the cities of Judah to Jerusalem.

10 Then Baruch the scribe read the words of the LORD which Jeremiah the prophet had spoken in the house of the LORD in the chamber of Gemariah the son of Shaphan the scribe in the upper court at the entry of the new gate of the LORD's house before all the people.

11 ¶When Michaiah the son of Gemariah, the son of Shaphan, heard all the words of the LORD from the book,

12 He went down from the king's house to the scribes' chamber; and he saw all the princes seated there: Elishama the scribe, and Belaiah the son of Shemaiah and Eliathan the son of Achbor and Gemariah the son of Shaphan and Zedekiah the son of Hananiah and all the princes.

13 Then Michaiah told them all the words that he had heard when Baruch the scribe read the scroll in the presence of the people.

14 Then all the princes sent Jehudi the son of Nethaniah, the son of Shelemiah, the son of Cushi, to Baruch, saying, Take in your hand the scroll which you have read before the people, and come. So Baruch the son of Neriah took the scroll in his hand and came to them.

15 And the princes said to him, Sit down now and read it in our presence; so Baruch read it in their presence.

16 Now it came to pass when they had heard all the words that they were alarmed, looking one to another, and they said to Baruch, We will surely tell the king of all these words.

17 And they asked Baruch, saying, Tell us now, how did you write all these words at his mouth?

18 Then Baruch answered them, Jeremiah dictated all these words to me and I wrote them with ink in the book.

19 Then the princes said to Baruch,

Go hide, you and Jeremiah; and let no man know where you are.

20 ¶Then the princes went to the king in the courtyard, but they placed the scroll in the chamber of Elishama the scribe, and told all the words in the presence of the king.

21 So the king sent Jehudi to bring the scroll; and he took it from the chamber of Elishama the scribe, and Jehudi read it before the king and before all the princes who stood before the king.

22 Now the king was sitting in the winter house in the ninth month; and there was a fire burning on the brazier before him.

23 And it came to pass that when Jehudi had read three or four pages, the king cut it with the scribe's penknife and threw it into the coals of fire; and the whole scroll was consumed in the fire that was on the brazier.

24 Yet neither the king nor any of his servants were afraid, nor did they tear their garments when they heard all these words.

25 Nevertheless Eliathan and Belaiah and Gemariah had entreated the king not to burn the scroll; but he would not listen to them.

26 And the king commanded Jerahmael the king's son and Seraiah the son of Azriel and Shelemiah the son of Abdael to seize Jeremiah the prophet and Baruch the scribe; but the LORD hid them.

27 ¶Then the word of the LORD came to Jeremiah after the king had burned the scroll and the words which Baruch wrote at the mouth of Jeremiah, saying,

28 Return from hiding and take another scroll and write on it all the former words that were on the first scroll, which Jehoiakim king of Judah has burned.

29 And you shall say to Jehoiakim king of Judah, Thus says the LORD: You have burned this scroll, saying, Why have you written in it and said, The king of Babylon shall certainly come and destroy this land and exterminate from it both man and beast?

30 Therefore, thus says the LORD concerning Jehoiakim king of Judah, He shall have not an heir to sit upon the throne of David; and his dead body shall be cast out in the day to the heat and in the night to the frost.

31 And I will punish him and his offspring and his servants for their iniquity; and I will bring upon them and upon all the inhabitants of Jerusalem and upon the men of Judah all the evil things that I have pronounced against them; because they did not hearken to my voice.

32 ¶Then Jeremiah took another scroll and gave it to Baruch the scribe, the son of Neriah, who wrote on it as Jeremiah dictated all the words which were written in the book which Jehoiakim king of Judah had burned in the fire; and he added to them many similar words.

CHAPTER 37

AND King Zedekiah the son of Josiah reigned instead of Coniah the son of Jehoiakim, whom Nebuchadnezzar king of Babylon made king in the land of Judah.

2 But neither he nor his servants nor the people of the land listened to the words of the LORD, which he spoke through Jeremiah the prophet.

3 And Zedekiah the king sent Jehucal the son of Shelemiah and Zephaniah the son of Maasiah the priest to Jeremiah the prophet, saying, Pray now for us before the LORD your God.

4 Now Jeremiah was free, going out and coming in among the people; for they had not yet put him in prison.

5 Then Pharaoh's army came forth out of Egypt; and when the Chaldeans who were besieging Jerusalem heard the report, they departed from Jerusalem.

6 ¶Then the word of the LORD came to Jeremiah the prophet, saying,

7 Thus says the LORD, the God of Israel: Thus shall you say to the king of Judah, who sent you to me to inquire of me: Behold, Pharaoh's army, which has come forth to help you, shall return to Egypt into their own land.

8 And the Chaldeans shall return

again and fight against this city, and they shall take it and burn it with fire.

9 Thus says the LORD: Do not think within yourselves, saying, The Chaldeans shall surely withdraw from us; for they shall not withdraw.

10 For even if you should destroy the whole army of Chaldeans that is fighting against you and there remained but wounded men among them, yet they would rise up every man from his tent and burn this city with fire.

11 ¶And it came to pass that when the Chaldean army had departed from Jerusalem for fear of Pharaoh's army,

12 Then Jeremiah went forth out of Jerusalem to go to the land of Benjamin to divide a portion of property there with the people.

13 And as he stood in the gate of Benjamin, an officer was there whose name was Neriah, the son of Shelemiah, the son of Hananiah; and he seized Jeremiah the prophet and said to him, You are escaping to the Chaldeans.

14 Then Jeremiah said, You lie; I am not escaping to the Chaldeans. But he would not listen to him; so Neriah seized Jeremiah and brought him to the princes.

15 And the princes were angry with Jeremiah; so they scourged him and put him in prison in the house of Jonathan the scribe; for he was appointed warden over the prisoners.

16 ¶And they lowered Jeremiah from the opening of the well into its depths, and Jeremiah remained there many days;

17 Then King Zedekiah sent and brought him up; and the king conferred with him secretly in the palace and said to him, Is there any word from the LORD? And Jeremiah said, There is. And the king said, What is it? Then Jeremiah said, You shall be delivered into the hand of the king of Babylon.

18 Moreover Jeremiah said to King Zedekiah, What offence have I done against you or against your servants or against this people, that you have put me into prison?

19 Where are now your prophets who prophesied to you, saying, The king of Babylon shall not come against you nor against this land?

20 Therefore now listen to me, O my lord the king; let my supplication be acceptable before you, that you may not cause me to return to the house of Jonathan the scribe, lest I die there.

21 Then King Zedekiah gave an order, and they allowed Jeremiah to stay in the court of the prison, and they gave him a loaf of bread daily from the bakers' street until all the bread in the city was gone. Thus Jeremiah remained in the court of the prison.

CHAPTER 38

THEN Shephatiah the son of Mattan, and Gedaliah the son of Pashur, and Jucal the son of Shelemiah, and Pashur the son of Malchiah heard the words that Jeremiah had spoken to all the people, saying,

2 Thus says the LORD: He who remains in this city shall die by sword, by famine, and by pestilence; but he who goes forth to the Chaldeans shall live; and shall save his life.

3 Thus says the LORD, This city shall surely be delivered into the hands of the army of the king of Babylon, which shall take it.

4 Then the princes said to the king, Let this man be put to death; for it is he who is weakening the hands of the men of war who remain in this city and the hands of all the people in speaking such words to them; for this man is not seeking the welfare of this people, but the hurt.

5 Then King Zedekiah said, Behold, he is in your hands; for the king cannot say anything to you.

6 Then they took Jeremiah and cast him into the well of Malchiah the son of the king, which was in the court of the prison; and they let down Jeremiah with ropes. And there was no water in the well, but only mire; so Jeremiah sank in the mire.

7 ¶Now when Ebed-melech the Ethiopian, a eunuch who was in the king's house, heard that they had put

Jeremiah in the well, the king then sitting in the gate of Benjamin;

8 So Ebed-melech went forth out of the king's house and spoke to the king, saying,

9 My Lord, these men have done evil in all that they have done to Jeremiah the prophet, for they have cast him into the well; and, behold, he will die of hunger, for there is no more bread in the city.

10 Then the king commanded Ebed-melech the Ethiopian, saying, Take from here thirty men with you, and go and draw up Jeremiah out of the well before he dies.

11 So Ebed-melech the Ethiopian took the men with him from the king's house, and went into the treasury which is below the palace and took from there some worn out towels and rags, and lowered them down by a rope into the well to Jeremiah.

12 And Ebed-melech the Ethiopian said to Jeremiah, Put these old towels and rags under your armpits under the rope. And Jeremiah did so.

13 So they drew up Jeremiah with the rope, and took him up out of the well; and Jeremiah remained in the court of the prison.

14 ¶Then King Zedekiah sent and took Jeremiah the prophet to him into the third entry that is in the house of the Lord; and the king said to Jeremiah, I will ask you a question, hide not a word from me.

15 Then Jeremiah said to Zedekiah, If I tell you, behold, you will surely put me to death; and if I give you counsel, you will not listen to me.

16 So King Zedekiah swore secretly to Jeremiah in the palace, saying, As the Lord lives, who created soul in us, I will not put you to death, neither will I deliver you into the hand of these men who seek your life.

17 Then Jeremiah said to Zedekiah, Thus says the Lord of hosts, the God of Israel: If you will go forth to the king of Babylon's princes, then you will spare your life, and this city shall not be burned with fire; and you and your household shall live;

18 But if you do not go forth to the king of Babylon's princes, then

this city shall be delivered into the hand of the Chaldeans, and they shall burn it with fire, and you shall not escape from their hands.

19 And King Zedekiah said to Jeremiah, I am afraid, because of the Jews, to go forth to the Chaldeans, lest they deliver me into their hands and they mock me.

20 But Jeremiah said, They will not deliver you. Obey the word of the Lord, which I speak to you; so it shall be well with you, and your life shall be saved.

21 But if you refuse to go forth, this is the word that the Lord has shown me:

22 Behold, all the women who are left in the king of Judah's house shall go forth to the king of Babylon's princes, and those women shall say, Your friends have deceived you and have prevailed against you; yea, they have caused your feet to sink in the mire, and they have turned away from you.

23 So they shall bring out all your wives and your children to the Chaldeans; and you yourself shall not escape from their hands, but shall be delivered into the hands of the king of Babylon; and this city shall be burned with fire.

24 ¶Then Zedekiah said to Jeremiah, Let no man know of these words and you shall not die.

25 But if the princes hear that I have talked with you, and they come to you and say to you, Declare to us now what you said to the king and what the king said to you, hide nothing from us and we will not put you to death;

26 Then you shall say to them, I was beseeching the king that he would not cause me to return to Jonathan's house to die there.

27 Then came all the princes to Jeremiah and asked him; and he told them according to all these words that the king had commanded him. So they ceased conversing with him because the matter was not made known.

28 So Jeremiah abode in the court of the prison house until the day that Jerusalem was taken.

CHAPTER 39

IN the ninth year of Zedekiah king of Judah, in the tenth month, came Nebuchadnezzar king of Babylon and all his army against Jerusalem and besieged it.

2 And in the eleventh year of King Zedekiah, in the fifth month, on the ninth day of the month, the city was breached.

3 And all the princes of the king of Babylon came in and sat in the middle gate, even Nergal-sharezar, Samgar-nebo, Sarsechim chief of eunuchs, Nergal-sharezar, Rab-mag,[1] with all of the princes of the king of Babylon.

4 ¶And it came to pass, when Zedekiah the king of Judah and all the men of war saw them, they fled and went out of the city by night by the way of the king's garden by the gate between the two walls; and they went out by the way of the plain.

5 But the Chaldean's army pursued them and overtook Zedekiah in the plains of Jericho; and all his army was scattered from him; and they took him and brought him up to Nebuchadnezzar king of Babylon to Diblath in the land of Hamath, where he pronounced judgment upon him.

6 Then the king of Babylon slew the sons of Zedekiah in Diblath before his eyes; also the king of Babylon slew all the princes of Judah.

7 Moreover, he put out Zedekiah's eyes and bound him in chains, to carry him to Babylon.

8 ¶And the Chaldeans burned the king's house and the houses of the people with fire, and broke down the entire wall of Jerusalem round about.

9 Then Nebuzaradan the general of the guard carried away captive into Babylon the remnant of the people who were left in the city and those who had deserted to him, with the rest of the people that remained.

10 But Nebuzaradan the general of the guard left in the land of Judah some of the poor people, who had nothing, and gave them vineyards and work at the same time.

---

[1] Chief of the soothsayers.

11 ¶Now Nebuchadnezzar king of Babylon gave orders concerning Jeremiah to Nebuzaradan the general of the guard, saying,

12 Take Jeremiah and treat him well and do him no harm; but do to him anything that he shall say to you.

13 So Nebuzaradan the general of the guard, Nebushazban the chief of the eunuchs, Nergal-sharezar, Rabmag, and all the princes of the king of Babylon

14 Sent and took Jeremiah out of the court of the prison and committed him to Gedaliah the son of Ahikam the son of Shaphan, that he should have him sent back to his home; so he dwelt among the people.

15 ¶Now the word of the LORD came to Jeremiah while he was shut up in the court of the guard, saying,

16 Go and say to Ebed-melech the Ethiopian, Thus says the LORD of hosts, the God of Israel: Behold, I will bring my words upon this city for evil and not for good; and they shall be accomplished in that day before you.

17 But I will deliver you in that day, says the LORD; and you shall not be delivered into the hand of men of whom you are afraid.

18 For I will surely deliver you, and you shall not fall by the sword, but your life shall be spared because you have put your trust in me, says the LORD.

CHAPTER 40

THE word that came to Jeremiah from the LORD, after Nebuzaradan the general of the guard sent him away from Ramtha, when he had taken him bound in chains among all the captives of Jerusalem and Judah who were carried away captive to Babylon.

2 And the general of the guard took Jeremiah, and said to him, The LORD your God has pronounced this evil upon this place.

3 Now the LORD has brought it and done according as he has said, because you have sinned against the

LORD and did not obey his voice, therefore this thing has come upon you.

4 And now, behold, I release you this day from the chains which are upon your hands. If you wish to come with me to Babylon, come, and I will take good care of you; but if you do not wish to come with me to Babylon, remain here. Behold, all the land is before you; wherever it seems good and convenient for you to go, thither go.

5 Then he said to him again, If you remain, dwell among the people with Gedaliah the son of Ahikam, the son of Shaphan, whom the king of Babylon has made governor over the cities of Judah; or go wherever it seems good to you to go. Then Nebuzaradan, the general of the guard gave him presents after the custom [1] and let him go.

6 Then Jeremiah went to Gedaliah the son of Ahikam, the son of Shaphan, to Mizpah, and dwelt with him among the people who were left in the land.

7 ¶Now when all the captains of the forces who were in the villages and their men heard that the king of Babylon had made Gedaliah the son of Ahikam governor in the land and had committed to him men and women and children and some of the poor of the land who had not been carried away captive to Babylon,

8 Then they came to Gedaliah at Mizpah, even Ishmael the son of Nethaniah, and Johanan and Jonathan the sons of Kareah, and Seraiah the son of Tanhumeth, and the sons of Ephai the Netophathite and Jezaniah the son of Maacath, they and their men.

9 And Gedaliah the son of Ahikam the son of Shaphan swore to them and to their men, saying, Fear not to serve the Chaldeans; dwell in the land and serve the king of Babylon, and it shall be well with you.

10 As for me, behold, I will dwell in Mizpah, to stand before the Chaldeans who will come to us; but you gather wheat, wine, oil, and summer fruits, and put them in your vessels, and dwell in the cities that you have taken.

11 Likewise when all the Jews who were in Edom, Moab, and among the Ammonites, and in all other countries heard that the king of Babylon had left a remnant of Judah and that he had appointed over them Gedaliah the son of Ahikam, the son of Shaphan;

12 Then all the Jews returned from all the places to which they had been driven and came to the land of Judah, to Gedaliah, to Mizpah, and gathered wine and summer fruits very much.

13 ¶Moreover, Johanan the son of Kareah and all the commanders of the forces who were in the villages came to Gedaliah to Mizpah,

14 And said to him, Do you not know that Baalis the king of the Ammonites has sent Ishmael the son of Nethaniah to slay you? But Gedaliah the son of Ahikam did not believe them.

15 Then Johanan the son of Kareah spoke secretly to Gedaliah at Mizpah, saying, Let me go and slay Ishmael the son of Nethaniah, and no man shall know it; lest he slay you, and all the Jews who are gathered to you should be scattered, and the remnant of the Jews should perish.

16 But Gedaliah the son of Ahikam said to Johanan the son of Kareah, You shall not do this thing; for you are speaking falsely of Ishmael.

CHAPTER 41

NOW it came to pass in the seventh month that Ishmael the son of Nethaniah the son of Elishama, of the seed royal, and the princes of the king, and twenty men with him came to Gedaliah the son of Ahikam to Mizpah; and there they did eat bread together in Mizpah.

2 Then Ishmael the son of Nethaniah and the twenty men who were with him rose up and smote Gedaliah the son of Ahikam the son of Shaphan with the sword, and slew him whom the king of Babylon had ap-

[1] After the manner of a king or as a king would give.

pointed governor over the land of Judah.

3 Ishmael also slew all the Jews who were with Gedaliah at Mizpah and the Chaldeans who were found there and the men of war.

4 And it came to pass the second day after Gedaliah had been slain, and no man had heard of it,

5 That there came certain men from Shechem, from Shiloh, and from Samaria, eighty men, agitated, having their beards shaven and their clothes torn, carrying offerings and incense to bring them to the house of the LORD.

6 And Ishmael the son of Nethaniah went forth from Mizpah to meet them, weeping all along as he went; and as he met them, he said to them, Come to Gedaliah the son of Ahikam.

7 And when they came into the çity, Ishmael the son of Nethaniah and the men who were with him slew them and cast them into a pit.

8 But ten men were found among them who said to Ishmael, Do not kill us; for we have in the field stores of wheat and of barley and of oil and honey. So he spared their lives, and did not slay them with their brethren.

9 Now the pit into which Ishmael cast all dead bodies of the men whom he had slain with Gedaliah was the same pit which Asa the king of Judah had made for fear of Baasha king of Israel; that same pit Ishmael the son of Nethaniah filled with the slain.

10 Then Ishmael carried away captive all the rest of the people that were in Mizpah, whom Nebuzaradan the general of the guard had entrusted to Gedaliah the son of Ahikam; Ishmael the son of Nethaniah carried them away captive and departed to cross over to the Ammonites.

11 ¶But when Johanan the son of Kareah and all the generals of the forces who were with him heard of all the booty that Ishmael the son of Nethaniah had carried away,

12 They took all the men and went to fight with Ishmael the son of Nethaniah, and found him by the great waters that are in Gibeon.

13 Now it came to pass when all the people who were with Ishmael saw Johanan the son of Kareah and all the commanders of the forces that were with him, then they rejoiced.

14 So all the people whom Ishmael had carried away captive from Mizpah turned back and came to Johanan the son of Kareah.

15 But Ishmael the son of Nethaniah escaped from Johanan with eight men and went to the Ammonites.

16 Then Johanan the son of Kareah and all the commanders of the forces that were with him took all the remnant of the people whom he had recovered from Ishmael the son of Nethaniah, from Mizpah, after he had slain Gedaliah the son of Ahikam, and carried away the men of war, the women and the children and the eunuchs whom he had brought back from Gibeon;

17 And they departed and dwelt at the threshing floors of Bimham, which is by the side of Bethlehem, to go into Egypt

18 Because of the Chaldeans; for they were afraid of them because Ishmael the son of Nethaniah had slain Gedaliah the son of Ahikam, whom the king of Babylon had made governor over the land.

CHAPTER 42

THEN all the officers of the forces and Johanan the son of Kareah and Jezaniah the son of Hoshaiah and all the people from the young to the old came near.

2 And said to Jeremiah, We beseech you, pray for us before the LORD your God, for we are left but a few of many, as your eyes see us;

3 That the LORD our God may show us the way by which we may go and the thing that we may do.

4 Then Jeremiah the prophet said to them, I have heard you; behold, I will pray before the LORD your God according to your words; and it shall come to pass that whatever the LORD shall answer you, I will declare it to you; I will hide nothing from you.

5 Then they said to Jeremiah, May the LORD be a true and faithful witness between us if we do not do according to the word with which the

LORD your God shall send you to us.

6 Whether it be good or whether it be bad, we will obey the voice of the LORD our God to whom we send you; that it may be well with us when we obey the voice of the LORD our God.

7 ¶And it came to pass after ten days that the word of the LORD came to Jeremiah the prophet.

8 Then he called Johanan the son of Kareah and all the officers of the forces that were with him and all the people from the young to the old,

9 And said to them, Thus says the LORD, the God of Israel, to whom you sent me to present your supplication before him:

10 If you will dwell in this land, then I will build you and not pull you down, and I will plant you and not pluck you up; for I will cease from the harm that I have done to you.

11 Be not afraid of the king of Babylon, of whom you are afraid; be not afraid of him, says the LORD, for I am with you to save you, says the LORD; and to deliver you from his hands.

12 And I will show mercy to you, that he may have mercy upon you and cause you to be settled in your own land.

13 ¶But if you say, We will not dwell in this land, because you would not obey the voice of the LORD your God,

14 Saying, Not so; but we will go into the land of Egypt that we may not see war nor hear the sound of the trumpet nor have hunger for bread; and there will we dwell;

15 And now therefore hear the word of the LORD, O remnant of Judah; thus says the LORD of hosts, the God of Israel: If you set your faces to enter into Egypt, and go to live there;

16 Then it shall come to pass that the sword which you fear shall overtake you there in the land of Egypt, and the famine of which you are afraid shall follow close after you there in Egypt; and there you shall die.

17 So shall it be with all the men who set their faces to enter into Egypt to live there; they shall die by sword, by famine, and by pestilence; and none of them shall remain or escape from the evil that I will bring upon them.

18 For thus says the LORD of hosts, the God of Israel: As my anger and my fury have been poured out upon the inhabitants of Jerusalem; so shall my fury be poured out upon you, when you shall enter into Egypt; and you shall be an execration and an astonishment and a curse and a reproach; and you shall see this place no more.

19 ¶The LORD has said concerning you, O remnant of Judah: Do not go to Egypt; know certainly that I have warned you this very day.

20 For you have deceived yourselves when you sent me to the LORD your God, saying, Pray for us before the LORD our God, and whatever the LORD our God shall say to you declare to us and we will do it.

21 And this day I have declared to you; but you have not obeyed the voice of the LORD your God; anything for which he has sent me to you, you have not done.

22 Now therefore know certainly that you shall die by sword, by famine, and by pestilence in the place where you desire to go to live.

CHAPTER 43

AND it came to pass when Jeremiah had finished speaking to all the people all the words of the LORD their God, for which the LORD their God had sent him to them to speak to them all these words,

2 Then Jezaniah the son of Hoshaiah, and Johanan the son of Kareah, and all the wicked men said to Jeremiah, You speak falsely; the LORD our God has not sent you to say to us, You shall not go into Egypt to sojourn there;

3 But Baruch the son of Neriah stirred you up against us to deliver us into the hand of the Chaldeans that they might kill us or carry us away captives into Babylon.

4 So Johanan the son of Kareah and all the officers of the forces and all the people did not obey the voice

of the LORD their God, to dwell in the land of Judah.

5 But Johanan the son of Kareah took all the officers of the forces and all the remnant of the people who were left from the house of Judah,

6 Men and women and children and the king's household and every person whom Nebuzaradan the general of the guard had left with Gedeliah the son of Ahikam the son of Shaphan, and Jeremiah the prophet and Baruch the son of Neriah.

7 So they came into the land of Egypt; for they did not obey the voice of the LORD; thus they came as far as Tahpanhes.[1]

8 ¶Then the word of the LORD came to Jeremiah in Tahpanhes, saying,

9 Take large stones in your hands and hide them in the mortar in the brickkiln which is at the entrance of Pharaoh's house in Tahpanhes, in the sight of the men of Judah;

10 And say to them, Thus says the LORD of hosts, the God of Israel: Behold, I will send and take Nebuchadnezzar the king of Babylon, my servant, and will set his throne above these stones that I have hid; and he shall spread his royal pavilion over them.

11 And he shall come and smite the land of Egypt, and he shall deliver those who are for death to death and those who are for captivity to captivity and those who are for the sword to the sword.

12 And he shall kindle a fire in the house of the gods of Egypt; and he shall burn them and carry them away captives; and he shall conquer the land of Egypt as easily as a shepherd puts on his woolen cloak; and he shall go away from thence peacefully.

13 He shall break also in pieces the image of Beth-shemesh which is in the land of Egypt; and the temples of the gods of the Egyptians he shall burn with fire.

CHAPTER 44

THE word that came to Jeremiah from the LORD to prophesy concerning all the Jews who dwell in the land of Egypt: those who dwell at Migdol and at Tahpanhes and at Memphis and in the land of Pathros, saying,

2 Thus says the LORD of hosts, the God of Israel: You have seen all the calamity that I have brought upon Jerusalem and upon all the cities of Judah; and behold, this day they are desolate, and no man dwells in them

3 Because of the wickedness which they have committed to provoke me to anger, in that they went and burned incense to other gods, whom they knew not, neither they nor their fathers.

4 And I sent to them all my servants the prophets, in advance, saying, Oh, do not do this abominable thing that I hate.

5 But they did not hearken nor incline their ear to turn from their wickedness, to burn no incense to other gods.

6 Therefore my fury and my anger were poured forth and a fire was kindled in the cities of Judah and in the streets of Jerusalem; and they became a desolation and an astonishment, as they are today.

7 And now thus says the LORD of hosts, the God of Israel: Why do you commit this great evil against yourselves, to cut off from you man and woman, the young and the little one out of Judah, to leave you none to remain;

8 And thus have provoked me to anger with the works of your hands, and have burned incense to other gods in the land of Egypt, where you have come to dwell, so that I may destroy you, and you shall become a curse and a reproach among all the nations of the earth?

9 Have you forgotten the wickedness of your fathers and the wickedness of the kings of Judah and the wickedness of their wives which they committed in the land of Judah and in the streets of Jerusalem?

10 They have not cleansed themselves even to this day, neither have they feared nor have they served me nor walked in my law nor in my stat-

[1] Aramaic, *Takhpis.*

utes which I set before them and before their fathers.

11 ¶Therefore thus says the LORD of hosts, the God of Israel: Behold, I will set my face against you for evil to destroy the whole house of Judah.

12 And I will crush the remnant of Judah who have set their faces to enter into the land of Egypt to live there, and they shall all be consumed in the land of Egypt; they shall die by sword and by famine and by pestilence; and they shall be an execration and an astonishment and a curse and a reproach.

13 For I will punish those who dwell in the land of Egypt, as I have punished Jerusalem, by sword, by famine, and by pestilence;

14 So that none of the remnant of Judah, who are gone into the land of Egypt to live there shall escape or remain that they may return to the land of Judah to which they hope to return to dwell there; and only a few shall return.

15 ¶Then all the men who knew that their wives were burning incense to other gods and all the women who stood by, a great multitude, and all the people who dwelt in the land of Egypt and in Pathros answered Jeremiah, saying,

16 As for the word that you have spoken to us in the name of the LORD, we will not listen to you.

17 But we will certainly do every word that has gone forth out of our own mouth, to burn incense to the queen of heaven and to pour out drink offerings to her, as we have done, we and our fathers, our kings and our princes in the cities of Judah and in the streets of Jerusalem; for then we had plenty of food and were well and saw no evil.

18 But since we left off burning incense to the queen of heaven and pouring out drink offerings to her we have lacked everything and have been consumed by sword and by famine.

19 And all the women said, When we burned incense to the queen of heaven and poured out drink offerings to her, it was not without our husbands' consent; nor without their knowledge did we make cakes for her and pour out drink offerings to her.

20 ¶Then Jeremiah said to all the people, to the men and to the women and to all the people who had given him that answer, saying,

21 The incense that you burned in the cities of Judah and in the streets of Jerusalem, you and your fathers, your kings and your princes and the people of the land, it was that incense that the LORD has remembered, and it has come into his mind.

22 So that the LORD could no longer forgive you because of your evil doings and because of the abomination which you have committed; therefore your land has become an astonishment and a curse and a desolation without an inhabitant, as it is this day.

23 It is because you have burned incense and because you have sinned against the LORD and have not obeyed the voice of the LORD nor walked in his law nor in his statutes nor in his testimonies; therefore this evil has overtaken you, as it is this day.

24 Moreover Jeremiah said to all the people, to men and women, Hear the word of the LORD, all you people of Judah who are in the land of Egypt;

25 Thus says the LORD of hosts, the God of Israel: You and your wives have both spoken with your mouths and fulfilled with your hands, saying, We will surely perform our vows that we have vowed, to burn incense to the queen of heaven and to pour out drink offerings to her; you have surely confirmed your oaths and performed your vows.

26 Therefore hear the word of the LORD, all you people of Judah who dwell in the land of Egypt: Behold, I have sworn by my great name, says the LORD, that my name shall no more be named in the mouth of any men of Judah in all the land of Egypt, nor shall they say, The LORD God lives.

27 For I will hasten to bring evil upon them, says the LORD; and all the men of Judah who are in the

land of Egypt shall be consumed by sword and by famine and by pestilence until I annihilate them.

28 And of those who escape the sword a few shall return from the land of Egypt to the land of Judah, and all the remnant of Judah who are gone to the land of Egypt to dwell there shall know whose words shall stand, mine or theirs.

29 ¶And this shall be a sign to you, says the LORD, that I will punish you in this place, that you may know that my words shall surely stand against you for evil.

30 Thus says the LORD: Behold, I will deliver Pharaoh the Lame,[1] the king of Egypt, into the hand of his enemies and into the hand of those who seek his life, as I delivered Zedekiah king of Judah into the hand of Nebuchadnezzar king of Babylon, his enemy, who sought his life.

CHAPTER 45

THE word that Jeremiah the prophet spoke to Baruch the son of Neriah; when he wrote these words on a scroll as Jeremiah dictated, in the fourth year of Jehoiakim the son of Josiah king of Judah, saying,

2 Thus says the LORD of hosts, the God of Israel, concerning you, O Baruch:

3 You said, Woe is me! for the LORD has added grief to my sorrow; I am weary in my sighing and I find no rest.

4 ¶Thus shall you say to him: Thus says the LORD: Behold that which you have built I will break down, and that which you have planted I will pluck up. I am laying waste the whole land.

5 And as for you who once sought great things for yourself, seek nothing that is of great value: for, behold, I will bring evil upon all flesh, says the LORD, but I will let you save your life in all countries where you go.

CHAPTER 46

THE word of the LORD which came to Jeremiah the prophet to prophesy concerning the Gentiles:

2 Concerning Egypt, concerning the army of Pharaoh the Lame, king of Egypt, which was encamped by the river Euphrates at Carchemish, whom Nebuchadnezzar king of Babylon slew in the fourth year of Jehoiakim the son of Josiah king of Judah, saying,

3 Thus says the LORD of hosts, the God of Israel: Take up the buckler and shield and draw near to battle.

4 Harness the horses and mount, O you horsemen; put on your helmets; polish the spears and wear the breastplates.

5 Because I have seen them defeated and retreating, and their mighty men are beaten down and are fled apace, and they look not back: for they were surrounded, says the LORD.

6 The swift cannot flee away, nor the mighty man escape; they have all stumbled and fallen by the river Euphrates.

7 Who is this that comes up like a river, and like rivers whose waters are raging?

8 The king of Egypt is rising up like a river, and his waters surge like the rivers; and he says, I will go up, and I will cover the earth; I will destroy the city and the inhabitants thereof.

9 Mount the horses, O you horsemen; sing, O you riders in the chariots; and let the mighty men come forth; the Ethiopians and the Putians, that handle the shield; and the Lydians, who are skilled in handling and bending the bow.

10 And let that day be the day of the LORD of hosts, a day of vengeance, that he may avenge himself of his enemies; and the sword shall devour, and it shall be satiated and made drunk with their blood: for the LORD of hosts shall bring slaughter in the north country by the river Euphrates.

11 Go up to Gilead and take balm, O virgin, the daughter of Egypt! In vain you shall use many medicines; for you shall not be healed.

12 The nations have heard of your

---

[1] Pharaoh-necho.

shame, and your wailing has filled the land; for soldier has stumbled against soldier, and they are fallen both together by the sword.

13 ¶The word that the LORD spoke to Jeremiah the prophet concerning the coming of Nebuchadnezzar king of Babylon to smite the land of Egypt.

14 Declare it in Egypt and publish it in Migdol and announce it in Memphis and in Tahpanhes. Say, Make ready and prepare yourselves; for the sword shall devour round about you.

15 Why are your valiant men defeated? They fell down and rose up no more because the LORD has overthrown them.

16 Multitudes of them are fallen; yea, one fell upon another and said, Arise, and let us go back to our own people and to the land of our nativity, from the oppressing sword.

17 They did invoke there the name of Pharaoh the Lame, king of Egypt, the troublemaker and passer of time.

18 As I live, says the LORD, whose name is the King of hosts, surely Pharaoh shall fall like a mountain slide, and like Carmel when it slides into the sea.

19 Furnish yourself with the clothes for exile, O virgin daughter of Egypt; for Memphis shall become waste and desolate without an inhabitant.

20 Egypt is like a very fair and pampered heifer, but an army from the north has come against her.

21 Also her hired men in the midst of her are like fatted bullocks; for they have turned back and fled together; they did not stand, because the day of their defeat was come upon them and the time of their punishment.

22 The sound of the army is like that of a serpent when it creeps; for they shall march with an army and come against her with axes, like hewers of trees.

23 Cut down her forests, says the LORD, for they are limitless; they are more than the locusts, and are innumerable.

24 The daughter of Egypt has been put to shame; she is delivered into the hand of the people of the north.

25 The LORD of hosts, the God of Israel, says, Behold, I will punish Amon of the waters of Thebes and Pharaoh and Egypt and her gods and her army and her kings, and even Pharaoh and all those who trust in him;

26 And I will deliver them into the hand of their enemies and into the hand of those who seek their lives and into the hand of Nebuchadnezzar king of Babylon and into the hand of his servants; and afterward Egypt shall regain her freedom, as in the days of old, says the LORD.

27 ¶But fear not, O my servant Jacob, and be not dismayed, O Israel; for, behold, I will save you from afar off, and your descendants from the land of their captivity; and Jacob shall return and be in rest and at ease, and none shall harm him.

28 Fear not, O Jacob my servant, says the LORD, for I am with you; for I will make a full end of all the nations whither I have driven you; but I will not make a full end of you, for I will correct you justly; but I will not wholly declare you blameless.

CHAPTER 47

THE word of the LORD that came to Jeremiah the prophet concerning the Philistines, before Pharaoh smote Gaza.

2 Thus says the LORD: Behold, I am bringing young soldiers from the north, and they shall become like an overflowing flood, and they shall overflow [1] the land and all that is in it, the city and those who dwell in it; then the men shall cry for help, and all the inhabitants of the land shall wail.

3 Because of the noise of the stamping of the hoofs of the horses of his mighty men and the rushing of his chariots and the rumbling of his wheels, the fathers shall not look back to their children for the feebleness of their hands;

4 Behold, the day has come to plun-

1 Plunder.

der all the Philistines and to destroy Tyre and Sidon and every helper that remains; for the LORD will smite the Philistines, the remnant of the islands of Caphtor.

5 Slaughter has reached to Gaza, Ashkalon is destroyed, and all that is left of their habitation is taken.

6 O, sword of the LORD, how long will it be till you be quiet and cease from destruction? put up yourself into your scabbard, rest and be still.

7 How can it be quiet, when the LORD has given it a charge against Ashkalon and against the coastal cities? For against these places he has decreed punishment.

CHAPTER 48

CONCERNING Moab, thus says the LORD of hosts, the God of Israel: Woe to Nebo! for it is spoiled; Koriathaim is ashamed and confounded; its defenders are confused and scattered.

2 The glory of Moab is no more; in Heshbon they have devised evil against her, saying, Come let us cut her off from being a nation. Though you shall keep your peace, the sword shall pursue you.

3 A sound of wailing is heard from Horonaim, plunder and great destruction.

4 Moab is destroyed; her poor people have published her lamentation.

5 For at the ascent of Luhith they shall go up weeping; and in the going down of Horonaim they shall raise a cry of tribulation and of destruction.

6 Hearken and flee, save your lives and be like a plant in the wilderness.

7 ¶For, because you have trusted in your fortifications and in your treasures, you shall also be taken; and Chemosh shall go forth into captivity together with his priests and his princes.

8 And the spoiler shall come upon all your cities, and no city shall escape; the valley also shall perish, and the plain shall be destroyed, as the LORD has spoken.

9 Give a garland to Moab, for she shall surely be destroyed, and all her cities shall become a desolation without any to dwell in them.

10 Cursed is he who does the work of the LORD deceitfully, and cursed is he who keeps back his sword from blood.

11 ¶The Moabites have been at ease from their youth, and they have settled on their lees, and have not been emptied from vessel to vessel,[1] nor have they gone into captivity; therefore their taste remains in them and their scent is not changed.

12 Therefore, Behold, the days are coming, says the LORD, when I will send robbers against them, and they shall plunder them and empty their vessels and destroy their wine containers.

13 And Moab shall be ashamed of Chemosh, as the house of Israel was ashamed of Beth-el their confidence.

14 ¶How can you say, We are mighty and valiant men of war?

15 Moab is plundered and his cities are burned and his chosen mighty men have been delivered to the slaughter, says the King, whose name is the LORD of hosts.

16 The calamity of Moab is soon to come, and his affliction hastens fast.

17 All who are round about him are troubled and shaken, and all who know his name, say, How is the strong staff broken, and the beautiful rod!

18 Come down from your glory and sit in disgrace, O inhabitant daughter of Ribon, for the spoiler of Moab has come up against you, and he has destroyed your strongholds.

19 Stand by the ways and look, O inhabitant of Adoer! Ask him who flees and him who escapes, and say, What has happened?

20 Moab is ashamed; for it is broken down; howl and cry in Arnon, for Moab is destroyed.

21 And judgment has come upon the land of Mashor, upon Holon and upon Jahazah and upon Mephaath

22 And upon Ribon and upon Nebo and upon Beth-diblathaim

---

[1] Moved from place to place.

23 And upon Koriathaim and upon Bet-gamul and upon Beth-moen

24 And upon Korioth and upon Bozrah and upon all the cities of the land of Moab, far and near.

25 The horn of Moab is cut off and his arm is broken, says the LORD.

26 ¶Make him to be a vagabond, for he magnified himself against the LORD; Moab also shall wallow in his filth and he shall be in derision.

27 Was not Israel a derision to you? He was found among thieves when you fought against him.

28 Leave the cities, and dwell in steep rocks, O you that dwell in Moab, and be like the dove that makes her nest in the sides of the mouth of a crag.

29 We have heard that the princes of Moab are exceedingly proud; their loftiness, their arrogance, and the haughtiness of their hearts I know well, says the LORD;

30 Their works were unjust, and yet their soothsayers did not predict such things against them.

31 Therefore wail for Moab; they cry out for all Moab from every place; for they shall devise evil against the men who dwell in his house.

32 With the weeping of Jazer I will weep for you, O vine of Sibmah; your branches are gone over the sea; they reach as far as the sea of Jazer, because the spoiler is fallen upon your summer fruits and upon your vintage.

33 Joy and gladness shall pass away from the fruitful field and from the land of Moab; and wine shall cease from the winepress; none shall tread with shouting; they shall not shout nor say Ho! Ho!

34 From the cry of Heshbon as far as Elealeh, and even to Jahaz, they have uttered their voice; from Zoar to Horonaim, to the city of Alis, they cried like a heifer of three years old; for the waters of Nimrim shall be desolate.

35 Moreover I will cause to cease in Moab, says the LORD, him that offers sacrifices in the high places and him that burns incense to his god.

36 Therefore, my heart shall sound for Moab like a harp because they have done evil and are perished.

37 For their heads are clipped and their beards shaved; upon all their hands are signs of mourning, and upon their loins sackcloth.

38 And upon all the housetops of Moab and in all the streets there is mourning, for I have broken Moab like a useless vessel, says the LORD.

39 How it is broken down! How Moab has turned his back and is put to shame! So shall Moab become a derision and a dismay to all that are round about him.

40 For thus says the LORD: Behold, he shall fly mightily as an eagle,[1] and shall spread his wings over Moab.

41 Kerioth is taken and the stronghold has been captured; the heart of the mighty men of Moab shall be in that day as the heart of a woman in her pangs.

42 And Moab shall be destroyed from being a people because he has magnified himself against the LORD.

43 Terror and the pit and the snare are upon you, O inhabitant of Moab, says the LORD.

44 He who flees from the terror shall fall into the pit; and he who gets up out of the pit shall be caught in the snare; for I will bring all these things upon Moab in the year of their punishment, says the LORD.

45 For a fire has gone forth out of Heshbon and a flame from the province of Sihon, and it shall devour the face of Moab and the crown of the head of the sons of Shaon.

46 Woe to you, O Moab! The people of Chemosh is perished; for your sons are driven away and your daughters are carried captives.

47 ¶Yet I will bring back the captivity of Moab in the latter days, says the LORD. Thus far is the judgment of Moab.

CHAPTER 49

CONCERNING the Ammonites, thus says the LORD: Has Israel no sons? Has he no heir? Why then

[1] Nebuchadnezzar.

has Malcolm inherited Gad, and why do his people dwell in its cities?

2 Therefore, behold, the days are coming, says the LORD, when I will cause an alarm of war to be heard against Rabbath of the Ammonites; and it shall become a desolate heap, and its little villages shall be burned with fire; then Israel shall be heir to those who were his heirs, says the LORD.

3 Howl, O Heshbon, for Ai is destroyed; call for help, O villages of Rabbath, gird you with sackcloth; mourn, be disquieted; for Malcolm [1] shall go into captivity, together with his priests and princes, says the LORD.

4 Why do you glory in your valleys and trust in your broad plains, O beloved daughter who trusts in her treasures, saying, Who shall come against me?

5 Behold, I will bring a terror upon you from all your borders, says the LORD of hosts; and I will drive the people in all directions; and none shall gather up the wanderers.

6 But afterward I will bring back the captivity of the children of Ammon, says the LORD.

7 ¶Concerning Edom, thus says the LORD of hosts: There is no more wisdom in Teman; the counsel is perished from the prudent; their wisdom is taken away.

8 Flee, turn back, dwell in deep crevices, O inhabitants of Deran! For I will bring the calamity of Esau upon him, the time of his punishment, says the LORD.

9 If grape-gatherers came to you, would they not leave gleaning grapes? If thieves came by night, they would destroy till they have enough.

10 But I have searched out Esau, I have uncovered his secret places, and he tried to hide himself but could not; his descendants are driven away, and his brethren and his neighbors are no more.

11 Leave your fatherless children; I will preserve them alive; and let your widows trust in me.

12 For thus says the LORD: Behold, those whose judgment was not to drink of the cup have assuredly drunken; and though you consider yourselves blameless, you shall not go unpunished; but you shall surely drink of the cup.

13 For I have sworn by myself, says the LORD, that Bozrah shall become an astonishment, a desolation, a reproach, and a curse; and all its cities shall become perpetual wastes.

14 I have heard a rumor from the LORD, and an ambassador is sent to the nations, saying, Arise, let us go up against her to the battle.

15 For, lo, I will make you small among the nations and despised among men.

16 Your wickedness has deceived you, and the pride of your heart, O you that dwell in the clefts of the rock, who hold the height of the hill; who say in your hearts, Who can bring us down to the ground? though you make your nest among the stars, and though you make your nest as high as the eagle's, I will bring you down from there, says the LORD.

17 And Edom shall become a desolation; every one who passes by it shall be astonished and shall hiss at all the plagues thereof.

18 It shall be overthrown just as God overthrew Sodom and Gomorrah, says the LORD, no man shall dwell there, neither shall any human being live in it.

19 Behold, he shall come up like a lion from the swelling of Jordan against the sheepfold of Atan; but I will suddenly make them run away from her; and I will charge young warriors against her; for who is like me? And who shall testify against me? And who is that leader who can prevail against me?

20 Therefore, hear the counsel that the LORD has devised against Edom, and his purposes that he has purposed against the inhabitants of Teman: Surely even the least of the flock they shall shear; and the enemy shall make their folds desolate over them.

21 The earth is moved at the sound of their fall, and the noise of their wailing is heard from the Red sea.

[1] God of Moab.

22 Behold, he shall come up and fly mightily like an eagle, and spread his wings over Bozrah; and the heart of the mighty men of Edom shall be in that day as the heart of a woman in her pangs.

23 ¶Concerning Damascus: Hamath and Arpad are put to shame, for they have heard evil tidings; they are dismayed, they are disturbed like the sea, they cannot find rest.

24 Damascus is weakened, and she turns to flee; trembling has seized her; anguish and pangs have taken her like a woman in travail.

25 How is the glorious city ruined, the city of joy!

26 Therefore her young men shall fall in her streets, and all the men of war shall be silenced, in that day, says the LORD of hosts.

27 And I will kindle a fire in the streets of Damascus, and it shall consume the palaces of Bar-hadad.

28 ¶Concerning Kedar and concerning the kingdoms of Hazor which Nebuchadnezzar king of Babylon smote; thus says the LORD: Arise, go up against Kedar and plunder the men of the east.

29 Their tents and their flocks shall the enemy take away; they shall carry away their curtains and all their vessels and their camels; and the oppressor shall shout against them on every side.

30 ¶Flee, get you far away, dwell in deep places, O inhabitants of Hazor, says the LORD; for Nebuchadnezzar king of Babylon has taken counsel against you and has conceived a purpose against you, saying,

31 Arise, get you up against a wealthy nation that dwells in tranquillity, says the LORD, that has neither gates nor bars, that dwells alone.

32 And their camels shall be booty, and the multitude of their cattle a spoil: and I will scatter to all the winds those whose beards are clipped; and I will bring their calamity from every side of them, says the LORD.

33 And Hazor shall be a dwelling place for jackals and a desolation for ever; there shall no one abide there, nor any human live in it.

34 ¶Concerning Elam, the word of the LORD that came to Jeremiah the prophet, that he might prophesy concerning Elam, in the beginning of the reign of Zedekiah king of Judah, saying,

35 Thus says the LORD of hosts: Behold, I will break the bow of Elam, the chief of their might.

36 And I will bring upon Elam the four winds from the four quarters of heaven, and will scatter the people to all these winds; and there shall be no nation whither the dispersed ones of Elam shall not come.

37 And I will cause Elam to be defeated before their enemies and before those who seek their lives; and I will bring evil upon them, even my fierce anger, says the LORD; and I will send the sword after them till I have consumed them;

38 I will set my throne in Elam, and I will destroy from thence the kings and the princes, says the LORD.

39 ¶But it shall come to pass in the latter days that I will bring back the captivity of Elam, says the LORD.

CHAPTER 50

CONCERNING Babylon, the word that the LORD spoke against Babylon and against the land of the Chaldeans by Jeremiah the prophet.

2 Declare among the nations and publish and raise an ensign; publish, and conceal not: say, Babylon is taken, Bel is fallen, Merodach is put to shame, her idols are confounded and her graven images are broken in pieces.

3 For out of the north there comes up a nation against her which shall make her land desolate, and none shall dwell in it; they shall flee, they shall depart, both man and beast.

4 ¶In those days and in that time, says the LORD, the children of Israel shall come, they and the children of Judah together, going and weeping and seeking the LORD their God.

5 They shall ask the way to Zion, with their faces towards it, saying,

Come, let us join ourselves to the LORD in an everlasting covenant which shall not be forgotten.

6 My people have been like lost sheep; their shepherds have caused them to go astray, they have scattered them on the mountains; they have gone from mountains to hills, they have forgotten their fold.

7 All who found them have devoured them; and their adversaries have said, We shall not spare them, because they have sinned against the LORD and against his righteous habitation; even the LORD, the hope of their families.

8 Flee from the midst of Babylon and go forth out of the land of the Chaldeans, and be as the he-goats before the flocks.

9 ¶For, behold, I will stir up and cause to come against Babylon a multitude of many nations from the north country; and they shall set themselves in array against her; from thence she shall be taken; their arrows shall be as those of an expert archer; none shall return empty.

10 And the land of the Chaldeans shall be a spoil; all that plunder her shall be satisfied, says the LORD.

11 Because you were glad, because you rejoiced over the destruction of my heritage, you leaped for joy like fat heifers and you danced like the rams of the flock;

12 Your mother is exceedingly ashamed; she who bore you is confounded; behold, the last of the nations shall become wilderness, waste, and desolation.

13 Because of the wrath of the LORD it shall not be inhabited, but it shall be wholly desolate; every one who passes by Babylon shall be astonished, and hiss at all her wounds.

14 Set yourselves in array against Babylon round about; all you that know how to bend the bow, shoot at her, spare no arrows; for she has sinned against the LORD.

15 Shout against her round about; she has surrendered, her foundations are fallen, her walls are demolished;

for it is the vengeance of the LORD. Take vengeance upon her; as she has done to others, do so to her.

16 Cut off from Babylon both the sower and him that handles the sickle in the time of harvest; because of the fear of the oppressing sword, they shall turn every one to his people, and they shall flee every one to his own land.

17 ¶Israel is a lost ewe; the lions have caused him to go astray; first the king of Assyria has devoured him; and at last this Nebuchadnezzar king of Babylon has inflicted a more grievous wound than the other.

18 Therefore, thus says the LORD of hosts, the God of Israel: Behold, I will punish the king of Babylon and his land, as I have punished the king of Assyria.

19 And I will bring Israel again to his habitation, and he shall feed on Carmel and on Mathnin and mount Ephraim and Gilead; and his soul shall be satisfied.

20 In those days and in that time, says the LORD, the iniquity of Israel shall be sought for, and there shall be none; and the sins of Judah, and they shall not be found; for I will pardon those whom I reserve as a remnant.

21 ¶Go up against the rebellious land, go up against it, and against its inhabitants; unsheath the sword and destroy them, says the LORD, and do according to all that I have commanded you.

22 A sound of battle is in the land, and of great destruction.

23 How is the mighty one of the whole earth defeated and taken! How has Babylon become an amazement among the nations!

24 Babylon has stumbled and she is taken; she did not know that she stood up against the LORD.

25 The LORD has opened his armory and brought forth weapons of his indignation; for this is the work of the LORD God of hosts in the land of the Chaldeans.

26 Come against her from round about her, open her gates; leave her as a naked woman and destroy her

utterly; let nothing be left of her.

27 Destroy her; and let all her offspring be delivered to the slaughter; woe to them! for their day is come, the time of their punishment.

28 The voice of those who flee and escape from the land of Babylon to declare in Zion the vengeance of the LORD our God, the vengeance of his temple.

29 Call together great armies against Babylon: all who know how to bend the bow shoot against her round about; let none be spared; recompense her according to her works; according to all that she had done, do to her; for she has ventured against the LORD, against the Holy One of Israel.

30 Therefore her young men shall fall in her streets, and all her men of war shall be silenced on that day.

31 Behold, I am against you, O boaster, says the LORD God of hosts; for your day has come, the time of your punishment.

32 And the boaster shall be overthrown and fall, and none shall raise him up; and I will kindle a fire in his cities, and it shall devour all round about him.

33 ¶Thus says the LORD of hosts: The children of Israel and the children of Judah are oppressed together; and all who took them captive have held them fast; they refused to let them go.

34 Their Saviour is strong; the LORD of hosts is his name; he shall thoroughly plead their cause, that he may give rest to the earth, and disquiet all the inhabitants of Babylon.

35 ¶A sword is upon the Chaldeans, says the LORD, and upon all the inhabitants of Babylon and upon her princes and upon her wise men.

36 A sword is upon her soothsayers, and they shall be dismayed; a sword is upon her mighty men, and they shall be defeated.

37 A sword is upon her horses and upon her chariots and upon all sojourners that are in the midst of her; and they shall become cowards; a sword is upon her treasures, and they shall be plundered.

38 A drought is upon her waters, and they shall be dried up; for she is the land of the makers of images, who boast in their idols.

39 Therefore screech-owls shall dwell in her, and ostriches shall inhabit her; and she shall be no more inhabited for ever; neither shall she be inhabited throughout generations.

40 She shall become like Sodom and Gomorrah when God destroyed them and their inhabitants; so no man shall dwell there, neither shall any son of man live there.

41 Behold, a people is coming from the north, a great nation, and many kings shall be stirred up from the uttermost parts of the earth.

42 They are armed with bows and lances; they are cruel and have no mercy; their voices are like the roaring of the sea, and they ride upon horses, arrayed as mighty men to the battle against you, O daughter of Babylon.

43 The king of Babylon has heard the report of them, and his hands weakened; anguish took hold of him, and pangs as of a woman in travail.

44 Behold, the enemy shall come up like a lion from the thickets of Jordan against the folds of Athan; and I will make the people suddenly run away from Babylon; and I will charge young warriors against her; for who is like me? Or who shall assail me? Or what leader is there who can prevail against me?

45 Therefore, hear the counsel of the LORD which he has taken against Babylon; and his purposes, that he has proposed against the land of the Chaldeans; for they shall shear even the least of the flock, and they shall make their folds a desolation upon them.

46 At the noise of the capture of Babylon the earth is moved and her wailing is heard among the nations.

CHAPTER 51

THUS says the LORD, the God of hosts: Behold, I will stir up against Babylon and against its inhabitants a man of cruel heart and like a destroying wind;

2 And I will send to Babylon destroyers, and they shall plunder her and tread her land under their feet; and they shall gather against her from every side in the day of trouble.

3 The archer shall not cease from bending his bow, and the warrior shall not put off his breastplate; spare not her young men; destroy utterly all her host.

4 Thus the slain shall fall in the land of the Chaldeans and the wounded lie in her streets.

5 For Israel and Judah have not been bereaved of their God, of the LORD of hosts their God; though their land was filled with wickedness before the Holy One of Israel.

6 Flee from the midst of Babylon, and let every man save his life; be not swallowed up in her iniquities; for this is the time of the LORD's vengeance; he will render to her according to her works.

7 Babylon has been a golden cup in the LORD's hand that made all the earth drunken of her wine; all the nations have drunk, and therefore the nations stagger with drunkenness.

8 Babylon is suddenly fallen and destroyed; wail for her, take balm for her wound; perhaps she may be healed.

9 We would have healed Babylon, but she is not healed; let us forsake her, and let us go every one to his own country; for her judgment has reached to heaven, and is lifted up even to the skies.

10 The LORD has made evident our innocence; come, let us declare in Zion the works of the LORD our God.

11 Gather the quivers; fill them with arrows; the LORD has stirred up the spirit of the king of the Medes; for his device is against Babylon, to destroy her; because it is the vengeance of the LORD, the vengeance of his temple.

12 Set up the ensign upon the walls of Babylon, set up a watch, drown her in waters; for the LORD has performed that which he had devised against the inhabitants of Babylon.

13 O you that dwell by many waters, abundant in treasures, your end has come and your wound is grievous.

14 The LORD of hosts has sworn by himself, saying, Surely I will fill you with men, numerous as locusts; and they shall lift up a shout against you, saying, It is done! It is done!

15 The LORD has made the earth by his power, he has established the world by his wisdom, and has stretched out heaven by his understanding.

16 When he utters his voice, he causes the rushing sound of waters in the heavens; and he causes the clouds to ascend from the ends of the earth; he makes lightnings for the rain, and brings forth the wind out of his storehouses.

17 Every man is brutish, lacking knowledge; all silversmiths are put to shame by the images they have made; for they have cast falsehood, and there is no breath in them.

18 They are worthless, the works of fools; in the time of punishment they shall perish.

19 The portion of Jacob is not the same; for he who has created everything, he is their portion and the sceptre of their inheritance; the LORD of hosts is his name.

20 Prepare weapons of war, for with you will I scatter the nations and with you will I destroy kingdoms;

21 And with you I will scatter horses and their riders, and with you I will scatter chariots and their riders,

22 With you will I scatter men and women, and with you will I scatter the old men and the youths, and with you will I scatter the young men and the maids,

23 And with you will I scatter the shepherd and his flock, and with you will I scatter the plowman and his yoke of oxen, and with you will I scatter rulers and governors.

24 And I will recompense to Babylon and to all the inhabitants of Chaldea, before your eyes, for all the evil that they have done in Zion, says the LORD.

25 Behold, I am against you, O destroying mountain, says the LORD, which destroys all the earth; I will stretch out my hand against you and

remove your foundation from the rock, and will make you a burnt mountain.

26 And they shall not take from you a stone for a corner nor a stone for foundations; but you shall be desolate for ever, says the LORD.

27 Set up a banner in the land, blow the trumpet among the nations; prepare the nations against her, call together against her the kingdoms of Ararat, Armenia, and Aschenaz; decree destruction against her; bring up horses like crawling locusts.

28 Prepare the nations for war against her, the king of the Medes and his princes and all his governors.

29 And the earth shall tremble and be confounded; for the purpose of the LORD against Babylon shall stand, to make the land of Babylon a desolation without an inhabitant.

30 The warriors of Babylon, together with those who man the strongholds, have ceased to fight; their strength has failed; they became cowards; they have dismantled her tents; her bars are broken.

31 One courier shall run to meet another, and one messenger to meet another, to tell the king of Babylon that his city is taken from every side,

32 And that the crossings are seized and the bastions are burned with fire and all the men of war are in confusion.

33 For thus says the LORD of hosts, the God of Israel: The daughter of Babylon is like a threshing floor, when wheat is ready to be threshed; yet a little while and the time of harvest shall come.

34 Jerusalem has said, Nebuchadnezzar the king of Babylon has devoured me, he has plundered me, he has made me like an empty vessel, he has swallowed me up like a dragon, he has filled his belly with my delicacies, and then he has caused me to go astray.

35 My spoil and my wealth are carried away to Babylon, my blood be upon the inhabitants of Chaldea, Jerusalem shall say.

36 Therefore thus says the LORD: Behold, I will plead your cause, and take vengeance for you; I will dry up the sea of Babylon, and make her springs dry.

37 And Babylon shall become heaps, a dwelling place for jackals, an astonishment and a hissing, without an inhabitant.

38 They shall roar together like lions; they shall growl like lions' whelps.

39 With venom I will prepare their drinks, and I will make them drunk, and they shall fall down and sleep a perpetual sleep, and not awake, says the LORD.

40 And I will deliver them like fatlings to be slain, like rams and he-goats to slaughter.

41 How is the royal city taken! the praise of the whole earth! How has Babylon become an astonishment among the nations!

42 The sea has come up upon Babylon; she is covered with the multitude of its waves.

43 Her cities have become a horror, like a dry land and a wilderness, a land in which no man shall dwell, neither shall any son of man live in it.

44 And I will punish Bel in Babylon, and I will bring forth out of his mouth that which he has swallowed up; and the nations shall not worship him anymore; yea, even the broad walls of Babylon shall fall.

45 My people, go out of the midst of her, and spare every man his life from the fierce anger of the LORD,

46 Lest your heart faint and be fearful at the rumors that shall be heard in the land; and a rumor shall come in one year, and the following year another rumor; and there shall be violence in the land, and ruler shall rise against ruler.

47 Therefore, behold, the days are coming, says the LORD, when I will break the graven images of Babylon; and her whole land shall be destroyed, and all her slain shall fall in the midst of her.

48 Then the heaven and the earth and all that is in them shall rejoice over Babylon; for the spoilers shall come to her from the north, says the LORD.

49 And also in Babylon there shall fall the slain of Israel, and the slain of Babylon shall fall all over the earth.

50 You that have escaped the sword, go away, stand not still; remember the LORD from afar off, and let Jerusalem come into your mind.

51 And the house of Israel shall say, We are exceedingly ashamed, because we have heard reproach; shame has covered our faces; for strangers have entered into the sanctuary of the LORD.

52 Therefore, behold, the days are coming, says the LORD, when I will bring punishment upon Babylon and destruction upon her graven images; and her slain shall fall throughout her land.

53 Though Babylon should mount up to heaven, and though she should set her fortifications in the heights, yet spoilers shall come from me upon her, says the LORD.

54 A sound of wailing comes from Babylon, and great destruction from the land of the Chaldeans

55 Because the LORD has spoiled Babylon and destroyed out of her both man and beast; the great sound of their voices goes up like the roaring of many waters.

56 The spoilers have come upon Babylon, and her mighty men are taken, and their bows are broken in pieces; for God is the LORD of recompense; he will surely requite them.

57 And I will make drunk her princes and her wise men, her noble men and her rulers and her mighty men; and they shall sleep a perpetual sleep, and not wake, says the King, whose name is the LORD of hosts.

58 Thus says the LORD of hosts: The broad walls of Babylon shall surely be utterly broken, and her high gates shall be burned with fire; and the people shall labor in vain, and the nations shall be weary with fire.

59 ¶The word which Jeremiah the prophet commanded Sheraiah the son of Neriah the son of Massaiah when he went with Zedekiah king of Judah to Babylon in the fourth year of his reign, and Sheraiah was commander of an army.

60 So Jeremiah wrote in a book all the evil that was to come upon Babylon, even all these words that are written concerning Babylon.

61 And Jeremiah said to Sheraiah, When you enter Babylon, see that you read all these words;

62 Then say, O LORD, thou hast spoken against this country, to destroy it, that none shall dwell in it, neither man nor beast, but that it shall be desolate for ever.

63 And when you have finished reading this scroll, then tie a stone to it and throw it into the Euphrates;

64 And say, Thus shall Babylon sink and shall not rise, because of the evil that I will bring upon her people; and they shall be weary. Thus far are the words of Jeremiah.

CHAPTER 52

ZEDEKIAH was twenty-one years old when he began to reign, and he reigned eleven years in Jerusalem. And his mother's name was Hamutal the daughter of Jeremiah of Libnah.

2 And he did that which was evil before the LORD, according to all that Jehoiakim had done.

3 Because of these evils the anger of the LORD came against Jerusalem and against Judah till he had cast them out from his presence, and King Zedekiah rebelled against Nebuchadnezzar king of Babylon.

4 ¶And it came to pass in the ninth year of his reign, in the tenth month, on the tenth day of the month, Nebuchadnezzar king of Babylon came, he and all his army, against Jerusalem and encamped against it and built forts against it round about.

5 So the city was besieged till the eleventh year of King Zedekiah.

6 And in the fifth month, on the ninth day of the month, the famine was severe in the city, so that there was no bread for the people of the land.

7 Then the city was breached, and all the men of war fled and went forth out of the city by night by the way of the gate between the two walls,

which was by the king's garden (now the Chaldeans were round about the city), and they went by the way of the plain.

8 ¶But the army of the Chaldeans pursued the king and overtook Zedekiah in the plain of Jericho; and all his army was scattered from him.

9 Then they took the king and brought him up to the king of Babylon to Diblath in the land of Hamath, where he gave judgment upon him.

10 And the king of Babylon slew the sons of Zedekiah before his eyes; he slew also all the princes of Judah in Diblath.

11 Then he put out the eyes of Zedekiah and bound him in chains, and the king of Babylon carried him to Babylon and put him in prison till the day of his death.

12 ¶Now in the fifth month, on the tenth day of the month, which was the nineteenth year of Nebuchadnezzar king of Babylon, Nebuzaradan, the general of the guard, came and stood before the king of Babylon to serve him in Jerusalem;

13 And he burned the house of the LORD and the house of the king of Judah and all the houses of Jerusalem and all the houses of the princes he burned with fire;

14 And all the army of the Chaldeans that were with the general of the guard broke down all the walls of Jerusalem round about.

15 Then Nebuzaradan, the general of the guard, carried away captive some of the poor of the people and the rest of the people who were left in the city and those who had fled to the king of Babylon and the rest of the people of the land.

16 But Nebuzaradan, the general of the guard, left some of the poor of the land for vine-dressers and for other work.

17 And the pillars of brass and the wine vessels and the bronze sea that were in the house of the LORD the Chaldeans broke in pieces, and they took all the brass of them and carried it to Babylon.

18 The pots, also, and the caldrons and the hanging pots and the sprinklers and the spoons and all the vessels of brass with which they ministered they took away.

19 And the braziers and the censers and the bowls and the pots and the candlesticks, and the spoons and the cups which were made of gold and of silver the general of the guard took away.

20 The two bronze pillars, one sea, the twelve bronze bulls which were under the sea, which King Solomon had made for the house of the LORD; the brass of all these vessels was without weight.

21 And as for the pillars, the height of one pillar was eighteen cubits, and a fillet of twelve cubits encircled it, and its thickness was four fingers, and it was hollow.

22 And a capital of brass was upon it; and the height of one chapiter was five cubits, with network and pomegranates upon the capitals round about, all of brass. The second pillar and the pomegranates were the same.

23 And there were ninety-six pomegranates on the side; all the pomegranates upon the network were one hundred round about.

24 ¶And the general of the guard took Sheraiah the chief priest and Zephaniah the second priest and the three keepers of the doors;

25 He took also from the city a eunuch who had been in charge of the men of war, and seven prominent men who had attended the king's person, who were found in the city, and the scribe the commander in chief of the army, who mustered the people of the land, and sixty men of the people of the land, who were found in the midst of the city.

26 So Nebuzaradan, the general of the guard, took them and brought them to the king of Babylon to Diblath.

27 And the king of Babylon smote them and put them to death in Diblath in the land of Hamath. Thus Judah was carried away captive out of his own land.

28 This is the number of people whom Nebuchadnezzar carried away

captive in the seventh year of his reign: three thousand and twenty-three Jews;

29 In the eighteenth year of the reign of Nebuchadnezzar king of Babylon he carried away captive from Jerusalem eight hundred and thirty-two persons;

30 In the twenty-third year of Nebuchadnezzar king of Babylon Nebuzaradan, the general of the guard, carried away captive of the Jews seven hundred and forty-five persons: all the persons were four thousand and six hundred.

31 ¶And it came to pass in the thirty-seventh year of the captivity of Jehoiakim king of Judah, in the twelfth month, in the twenty-fifth day of the month, Aol-merodach king of Babylon, in the first year of his reign, honored Jehoiakim king of Judah and brought him out of prison.

32 And he spoke kindly to him and set his throne above the thrones of the kings who were with him in Babylon,

33 And changed his prison garments; and he did continually eat bread before him all the days of his life.

34 And for his portion, there was a continual allowance given him of the king of Babylon, every day until the day of his death, all the days of his life.

THE LAMENTATIONS

OF JEREMIAH

CHAPTER 1

HOW does the city sit solitary that was full of people! How is she become like a widow! She that was so great among the nations, and she that was a princess of the cities has become a tributary!

2 She weeps bitterly in the night, and her tears run on her cheeks; among all her lovers [1] she has none to comfort her; all her friends have dealt treacherously with her, they have become her enemies.

3 Judah is gone into captivity because of affliction and because of great servitude; she dwells among the Gentiles, she finds no rest; all her pursuers overtook her in the midst of her affliction.

4 The ways of Zion mourn because none come to the solemn feasts; all her gates are desolate; her priests sigh, her virgins are humbled,[2] and she is in bitterness.

5 Her oppressors have become her rulers, and her adversaries have made an end of her; for the LORD has afflicted her for the multitude of her sins; her children are gone into captivity before the oppressor.

6 And from the daughter of Zion all her splendor is departed; her princes have become like harts that find no pasture, and they are gone without strength before the pursuer.

7 Jerusalem remembers in the days of her affliction and of her chastisement all her pleasant things that she had in the days of old. When her people fell into the hand of the oppressor and she had none to help her, her oppressors saw her, and mocked at her destruction.

8 Jerusalem has grievously sinned; therefore she has become an abom-

[1] Kings who had made a league with her.　　[2] Raped.

ination; all who honored her, despise her, because they see her nakedness; yea, she sighs and turns backward.

9 Her filthiness is in her skirts; she was not mindful of her end; therefore her glory is low; she has no comforter. O LORD, behold my affliction; for the enemy has magnified himself.

10 The oppressor has stretched out his hands upon all her pleasant things; for I have seen the Gentiles violate thy sanctuary, whom thou didst command that they should not enter into thy congregation.

11 All her people sigh, they seek bread; they have given their precious things for food to relieve their soul; see, O LORD, and consider; for I am despised.

12 ¶Is it nothing to you, all you that pass by? Understand, and see if there is any pain like my pain, which the LORD has dealt to me; for the LORD has afflicted me in the day of his fierce anger.

13 From above he sent fire into my bones, and it has brought me low; he has spread a net for my feet, he has turned me back; he has delivered me to the sword and I am miserable all the day.

14 My sins have wrought vengeance upon me; his yokes are bound by his hands upon my neck; my strength has failed; the LORD has delivered me into the hands of those before whom I cannot stand.

15 The LORD has brought into subjection all my mighty men in the midst of me; he has called an assembly against me to destroy my young men; the LORD has trodden as in a winepress the virgin daughter of Judah.

16 For these things I weep; my eyes run down with tears, because the comforter that should relieve my soul is far from me; my children are desolate, because the enemy has prevailed.

17 Zion stretches out her hands, and there is none to comfort her; the LORD has given commands against Jacob, and his oppressors are round about him; Jerusalem has become loathsome among them.

18 ¶The LORD is righteous; and I have rebelled against him; hear, all you peoples, and behold my grief; my virgins and my young men are gone into captivity.

19 I called for my lovers, but they deceived me; my priests and my elders perished in the city; they searched for food to relieve their souls, but they found it not.

20 Behold, O LORD, I am in distress; my soul is troubled, my heart is in pain; for I have grievously rebelled; outside the sword devours, and those who are in the house death consumes.

21 They have heard that I sigh; there is none to comfort me; all my enemies have heard of my trouble; they are glad that thou hast done it; hasten thou the day that thou hast announced, the enemy shall become like me.

22 Let all their wickedness come before thee; harass them, as thou hast harassed me for all my transgressions; for my sighs are many, and my heart is faint.

CHAPTER 2

HOW has the LORD in his anger covered the daughter of Zion with a thick cloud [1] and cast down from heaven to earth the glory of Israel, and has not remembered his footstool in the day of his wrath!

2 The LORD has drowned without pity all the habitations of Jacob, he has thrown down in his wrath the strongholds of the daughter of Judah; he has brought down to the ground her slain men, her kings, and her princes.

3 He has cut off in his fierce anger all the strength of Israel; he has drawn back his right hand from before the enemy and has kindled a fire in the land of Jacob, and the flaming fire has consumed mightily round about.

4 He has bent his bow like an oppressor; he has raised his hand like an enemy, and has slain all that were pleasant to the eye in the tabernacle

[1] Cloud in this instance is symbolic of mourning.

of the daughter of Zion; he has poured out his fury like fire.

5 The LORD has become as an enemy; he has drowned Israel, he has destroyed all her palaces; he has made havoc in all her provinces, and has increased in the daughter of Judah mourning and lamentation.

6 And he has thrown down his tabernacle like a shed in a garden; he has destroyed the places of his festivals; the LORD has caused the solemn feasts and the sabbath to be forgotten in Zion, and has rejected in the indignation of his anger kings and priests.

7 The LORD has forgotten his sanctuary, he has despised his altar, he has given up into the hand of the enemy the walls of her palaces; they have made a shout in the house of the LORD, as on a day of a solemn feast.

8 The LORD has purposed to destroy the walls of the daughter of Zion; he has stretched out a line, he has not withdrawn his hand from destroying her; therefore he has caused her forces to sit in mourning; her walls have become completely desolate.

9 Her gates are sunk into the ground; he has destroyed and broken her bars; her kings and her princes are among the Gentiles; the law is no more; her prophets also find no visions from the LORD.

10 The elders of the daughter of Zion sit on the ground and keep silence; they have cast dust on their heads; they have girded themselves with sackcloth; the virgins of Jerusalem hang down their heads to the ground.[1]

11 My eyes are dimmed with tears, my soul is disturbed, my pride is low to the ground, because of the destruction of the daughter of my people, because the little children and the babes faint in the streets of the city.

12 They say to their mothers, Where is wheat and wine and butter? when they faint like the slain in the streets of the city, when their soul is poured out into their mother's bosom.

13 What thing shall I testify for you, and to whom shall I liken you, O daughter of Jerusalem? Whom can I liken to you, that I may comfort you, O virgin daughter of Zion? For your breach is great like the sea; who can stop it?

14 Your prophets have seen false and deceptive visions for you; and they have not revealed to you anything of your sins, that you might repent and I should bring you back from captivity; but have seen for you false and deceptive prophecies.

15 All who pass by the road clap their hands at you; they hiss and wag their heads at the daughter of Jerusalem, saying, Is this the city which men called The perfection of beauty, The joy of the whole earth?

16 The LORD has done that which he had devised; he has fulfilled his word as he had commanded in the days of old; he has thrown her down without pity, he has caused your enemies to rejoice over you, he has given might to your oppressors.

17 All your enemies speak evil against you; they hiss and gnash their teeth; they say, We have devoured her; certainly this is the day we looked for; we have found it, we have seen it.

18 The people's heart cried to the LORD of the walls of the daughter of Zion; let your tears run down like a stream day and night; give yourself no rest; let not the apple of your eye cease from shedding tears.

19 Arise, offer praise in the night at the beginning of the watches; pour out your heart like water before the presence of the LORD; lift up your hands toward him for the lives of your little children who faint for hunger at the head of every street.

20 ¶See, O LORD, and consider to whom thou hast done thus? Shall the women eat their offspring, and the children be prostrated by famine? Shall the priest and the prophet be slain in the sanctuary of the LORD?

21 The young and the old lie on the ground in the streets; my virgins and my young men have fallen by

[1] Have been humiliated.

the sword; thou hast slain them in the day of thine anger; thou hast slaughtered without pity.

22 Thou hast called as to a festival day my adversaries round about me, so that in the day of the LORD's anger none escaped or survived; those that I have carried on my arms and brought up, my enemies have consumed.

CHAPTER 3

O MIGHTY God, see my affliction; I am chastised by the rod of his wrath.

2 He has led me, but I walked in darkness and not in light.

3 But surely is he turned against me, he turns his hand against me all the day.

4 My flesh and my skin he has made old; he has broken my bones.

5 He has built ramparts against me, and compassed me with bitterness and travail.

6 He has made me to dwell in darkness, like a dead man for ever.

7 He has hedged me about, that I cannot escape; he has made my chains heavy.

8 Though I beseech and pray, he does not hearken to my prayer.

9 He has enclosed my ways with thorns, he has made my paths crooked.

10 He has been to me as a wolf lying in wait, and as a lion in secret places.

11 He has made my ways crooked, and cut me to pieces; he has made me desolate.

12 He has bent his bow, and set me up as a mark for the arrow.

13 Behold, he has caused his arrows to enter into my reins.

14 I have become the ridicule of all nations; and their scoffing song all the day.

15 He has filled me with bitterness, he has made me drunken with wormwood.

16 He has broken my teeth with a stone, he has covered me with ashes.

17 My soul has gone astray from peace, I have forgotten prosperity.

18 And I said, My fame and my hope are perished from the LORD.

19 Remember my affliction and my chastisement, the bitterness and the sorrow.

20 Remember and restore my life.

21 This I recall to mind; therefore I have hope in God.

22 ¶Surely the kindness of the LORD never ceases and his mercies never fail.

23 They are new every morning; great is thy faithfulness.

24 The LORD is my portion, says my soul; therefore I will hope in him.

25 The LORD is good to him who waits for him, to the soul that seeks him.

26 It is good for a man that he should hope for both the truth and the salvation of the LORD.

27 It is good for a man that he bear thy yoke in his youth.

28 Let him sit alone and keep silence, because he has laid thy yoke upon him.

29 Let him humble himself, for there is hope.

30 Let him turn his cheek to him that smites him; let him be filled with reproach.

31 For the LORD will not forget for ever.

32 But though he cause affliction, yet he will have compassion according to the multitude of his mercies.

33 For he does not afflict willingly, but he afflicts the children of the mighty men,

34 To subdue under his feet all the prisoners of the earth,

35 To turn aside the right of a man toward the face of the Most High.

36 To subvert a man in his cause, the LORD does not approve.

37 ¶Who is he that says, and it comes to pass, when the LORD has not commanded it?

38 Out of the mouth of the Most High evil and good do not come.

39 Therefore, why should a living man question concerning punishment for his sins?

40 Let us search and try our ways, and turn again to the LORD.

41 Let us lift up our hearts with our hands to God in heaven.

42 We have transgressed and rebelled; and thou hast not pardoned.

43 Thou hast covered us with thy anger and pursued us; thou hast slain, thou hast not pitied.

44 Thou hast covered thyself with thy cloud; thou hast let our prayer pass by.

45 Thou hast made us uprooted and despised among the peoples.

46 My eyes run down with tears and do not cease, because there is no comforter,

47 Till the LORD look down and behold from heaven.

48 My eyes are worn with tears because of the destruction of all the daughters of the cities of my people.

49 All our enemies speak evil against us.

50 Fear and trembling have come upon us, a snare and destruction.

51 I wept vehemently over the destruction of the daughter of my people.

52 My enemies have hunted me like a bird, without cause.

53 They have cut off my life in a pit; they cast stones at me.

54 Water flowed over my head; then I said, I am cast far off.

55 ¶I called upon thy name, O LORD, out of the depths of the pit.

56 Thou didst hear my voice; turn not thine ear to my cry; but relieve me and save me.

57 Thou didst draw near in the day when I called upon thee; thou didst say, Fear not.

58 O LORD, thou hast pleaded my cause; thou hast saved my life.

59 O LORD, thou hast seen my affliction; thou hast judged my cause.

60 Thou hast seen all their vengeance and all their imaginations against me.

61 Thou hast heard their reproach, O LORD, and their devices against me,

62 The lips of those who rose up against me and their devices against me all day long.

63 Behold their conduct and their behavior I do understand, because of their devices.

64 ¶Render to them a recompense, O LORD, according to the work of their hands.

65 Give them sorrow of heart; let thy affliction pursue them.

66 Destroy them in thine anger from under thy heavens, O LORD.

CHAPTER 4

HOW is the fine gold rejected! how is the lovely color faded! the stones of the sanctuary are thrown down at the head of every street.

2 The precious sons of Zion, who were better than precious stones, how are they esteemed as earthen pots, the work of the hands of the potter!

3 The women uncover their breasts like jackals, they give suck to their young ones; the daughters of my people have become like wounds that cannot be healed and like ostriches in the wilderness.

4 The tongue of the suckling child cleaves to the roof of his mouth for thirst; the children ask bread, but no one breaks the loaf and gives it to them.

5 Those that fed on delicacies are destitute in the streets; those who were reared in scarlet sleep in dunghills.

6 For the iniquity of the daughter of my people is greater than the sin of Sodom, that was overthrown as in a moment and no hands were weary in destroying it.

7 Her Nazarites were purer than snow, they were whiter than milk; their cheeks were more ruddy than rubies, and their form more beautiful than sapphires.

8 But now their visage is blacker than charcoal; they are not recognized in the streets; their skin is shriveled on their bones; it has dried up and it has become like a stick.

9 Those who were slain by the sword are better than those who are slain with hunger; for these pine away, like those who are wounded and thrown in the field.

10 The hands of compassionate women have cooked their own children; they were their food in the destruction of the daughter of my people.

11 The LORD has accomplished his fury; he has poured out his fierce anger and has kindled a fire in Zion, and it has devoured the foundations thereof.

12 The kings of the earth did not believe, nor all the inhabitants of the world, that the enemy and the oppressor could come and enter into the gates of Jerusalem.

13 ¶It happened for the sins of her prophets and the iniquities of her priests, who have shed in the midst of her the blood of the righteous.

14 Her princes wander in her streets, they wallow in blood, so that no one could touch their garments.

15 Separate yourselves from them, call them unclean; depart, depart, do not touch them; for they have caused provocations and are troubled; among the Gentiles the people said, They shall no more sojourn there.

16 Our eyes have become dull waiting for help; our watchmen have watched in vain for a nation that could not save.

17 The presence of the LORD has divided them; he will no more regard them; they did not respect the persons of priests, they did not have compassion on the elders.

18 They hunt for the little people and for those who walk in the streets; our end is near, our days are finished, for our time is come.

19 Our pursuers were swifter than the eagles of the air; they chased us upon the mountains, they laid in wait for us in the wilderness.

20 Our very spirit, the anointed of the LORD,[1] was taken in their pits, of whom we had said, Under his shadow we shall live among the Gentiles.

21 ¶Rejoice and be glad, O daughter of Edom that dwells in the land of Uz; the cup also shall pass to you; you shall become drunken and you shall be harassed.

22 ¶Your iniquities have come to an end, O daughter of Zion; God will no more carry you away into captivity; but your iniquities will be

[1] The heir of David.

punished, O daughter of Edom; your sins are well uncovered.

CHAPTER 5

REMEMBER, O LORD, what has come upon us; behold, and see our reproach.

2 Our inheritance has been turned over to strangers, our houses to aliens.

3 We have become orphans and fatherless, our mothers are as widows.

4 We have drunken our water for money; our wood is sold to us.

5 Our necks are under yokes; we labor, and have no rest.

6 The Egyptians gave a helping hand, and we looked to the Assyrians to provide bread.

7 Our fathers have sinned, and are no more; and we have borne their iniquities.

8 Servants rule over us; there is none to deliver us out of their hands.

9 We get our bread with the peril of our lives, because of the sword in the wilderness.

10 Our skin has shriveled as though burned in an oven because of the suffering of famine.

11 Women are ravished in Zion, and virgins in the cities of Judah.

12 Princes are hanged up by their hands; the faces of the elders are not honored.

13 The young men grind the mill, and the youths stumble under loads of wood.

14 The elders have ceased from the gate, the young men from their joy.

15 The joy of our heart is ceased; our dance is turned into mourning.

16 The crown has fallen from our head; woe to us, for we have sinned!

17 For this our heart is faint; for these things our eyes are dim.

18 Because mount Zion is desolate, the foxes walk upon it.

19 But thou, O LORD, dost endure for ever; thy throne from generation to generation.

20 Therefore do not forget us for ever, nor forsake us for so long a time.

21 Bring us back to thee, O LORD, and we shall be restored; renew our days as of old.

22 For thou hast utterly rejected us; thou hast been exceedingly angry against us.

THE BOOK OF THE

PROPHET EZEKIEL

CHAPTER 1

NOW it came to pass in the thirtieth year, in the fourth month, on the fifth day of the month, as I was among the captives by the river Chebar, that the heavens were opened and I saw visions of God.

2 On the fifth day of the month, in the fifth year of the captivity of Jehoiachin king of Judah,

3 The word of the LORD came to Ezekiel the priest, the son of Buzi, in the land of the Chaldeans by the river Chebar; and the hand of the LORD was there upon me.

4 ¶And I looked, and behold, a whirlwind was coming out of the north, a great cloud, and a flaming fire and a brightness was round about it, and out of the midst of it there came as it were a figure out of the midst of the fire.

5 Also out of the midst of it came the likeness of four living creatures. And this was their appearance: they had the likeness of a man.

6 And every one had four faces, and every one had four wings.

7 And their legs were straight; and the soles of their feet were like the soles of a calf's feet; and they sparkled like the color of burnished brass.

8 And they had human hands under their wings on their four sides; and their faces and their wings were on their four sides.

9 Their wings were joined one to another; and when they went, they went straight forward; they turned not when they went.

10 And as for the likeness of their faces, each of the four had the face of a man and the face of a lion on the right side; and each of the four had the face of an ox and the face of an eagle on the left side.

11 And their faces and their wings were stretched upward; two wings of each creature were joined one to another, and two covered their bodies.

12 And they went every one straight forward; wherever the spirit was to go, they went; and they turned not when they went.

13 As for the likeness of the living creatures, their appearance was like burning coals of fire, like the appearance of a lamp going to and fro among the living creatures; and the fire was bright, and out of the fire went forth lightning.

14 And the living creatures ran, but returned not, and their appearance was like a flash of lightning.

15 ¶Now as I beheld the living creatures, behold wheels were upon the earth by the side of each of the four living creatures.

16 The appearance of the wheels and their work was like the colour of a beryl; and they four had the one likeness; and their appearance and their work was as it were a wheel within a wheel.

17 When they went, they went upon four sides; and they turned not when they went; and wherever the first one

turned to go, the other went after it, and turned not.

18 As for their rims, they were high and they could see; for the rims were full of eyes round about them four.

19 And when the living creatures went, the wheels went with them; and when the living creatures were lifted up from the ground, the wheels were lifted up with them.

20 Wheresoever the spirit was to go, they went, and the wheels were lifted up with them; for there was a living spirit in the wheels.

21 When the living creatures went, the wheels went; and when the creatures stood, they stood also; and when they were lifted up from the earth, the wheels were lifted up with them; for there was a living spirit in the wheels.

22 And over the heads of the living creatures there was the likeness of a firmament, resembling pure crystal, stretched out over their heads above.

23 And under the firmament were their wings straight, the one toward the other; over and under; two of them covering their faces and two covering their bodies.

24 And when they went, I heard the noise of their wings like the noise of great waters, like the voice of God, like the sound of speech in a host; and when they stopped, they let down their wings.

25 And there was a voice from the firmament that was over their heads; and when they stopped, they let down their wings.

26 ¶And above the firmament that was over their heads was the likeness of a sapphire stone, as the likeness of a throne; and upon the likeness of the throne was the likeness as the appearance of a man above it.

27 And I saw as it were the appearance of God, and the appearance of fire within it round about from his loins and upward; and from his loins and downward, I saw as it were the appearance of fire shining round about.

---

¹ A dangerous people.

28 As the appearance of the rainbow when it is in the clouds in the day of rain, so was the appearance of the brightness round about him. Such was the vision of the likeness of the glory of the LORD. And when I saw it, I fell upon my face and I heard the voice of one who spoke.

CHAPTER 2

AND he said to me, Son of man, stand upon your feet and I will speak with you.

2 And the spirit entered into me when he spoke to me, and he set me upon my feet, and I heard him that spoke to me.

3 And he said to me, Son of man, I am sending you to the children of Israel, to a rebellious people who have risen up against me; they and their fathers have transgressed against me, even unto this very day.

4 And they to whom I am sending you are impudent and stubborn children; and you shall say to them, Thus says the LORD God of hosts.

5 Perhaps they will listen and tremble (for they are a rebellious house), and they shall know that you are a prophet among them.

6 ¶And you, Son of man, be not afraid of them, neither be dismayed by their words, for they will deny you and denounce you; for you dwell among scorpions; ¹ fear not their words, nor be dismayed at their looks, for they are a rebellious house.

7 And you shall speak my words to them; perhaps they will listen and tremble; for they are a rebellious house.

8 But you, Son of man, hear what I say to you; and be not rebellious like that rebellious house; but open your mouth and eat what I shall give you.

9 ¶And when I looked, behold, a hand was stretched out to me; and, lo, a scroll of a book was in it.

10 And he spread it before me; and it was written within and without; and there were written in it chants, woes, and lamentations.

CHAPTER 3

MOREOVER he said to me, Son of man, eat that which you find; eat this scroll, and go speak to the house of Israel.

2 So I opened my mouth, and he caused me to eat that scroll.

3 And he said to me, Son of man, fill your belly with this scroll that I give you. Then I ate it and it was in my mouth sweet as honey.

4 ¶And he said to me, Son of man, go to them of the captivity, to the children of Israel, and speak my words to them.

5 For you are not sent to a people of a strange speech and of a hard language, but to the house of Israel;

6 Nor to many peoples whose speech you do not understand. Surely, if I send you to them, they would listen to you.

7 But the house of Israel will not listen to you; for they will not hearken to me; for all the house of Israel are impudent and stubborn of heart.

8 Behold, I have made your face strong against their faces, and your forehead hard against their foreheads.

9 As an adamant harder than flint have I made your forehead; fear them not, neither be dismayed at their looks, for they are a rebellious house.

10 Moreover he said to me, Son of man, all my words that I shall speak to you receive in your heart and hear with your ears.

11 And go and get you to them of the captivity, to the children of your people, and speak to them and tell them, Thus says the LORD God; perhaps they will listen, and tremble.

12 Then the spirit took me up, and I heard behind me the sound of a great rushing, saying, Blessed be the glory of the LORD from his place.

13 I heard also the sound of the wings of the living creatures touching one another and the sound of the wheels beside them and a noise of a great rushing.

14 So the spirit lifted me up, and carried me away, and I went in the strength of my spirit; and the hand of the LORD was strong upon me.

15 ¶Then I came to the exiles at Tel-akib, who dwelt by the river Chebar, and I stayed there astonished among them seven days.

16 And it came to pass at the end of seven days that the word of the LORD came upon me, saying,

17 Son of man, I have made you a watchman to the house of Israel; therefore hear the words of my mouth and give them warning from me.

18 When I say to the sinner, You shall surely die; but you have not warned him, nor have you spoken to warn the sinner from his wicked way, to save his life; the same sinner shall die in his iniquity; and his blood will I require at your hand.

19 But if you warn the sinner, and he turn not from his sin nor from his evil way, he shall die in his sins; but you have delivered your soul.

20 Again, when a righteous man turns from his righteousness and commits iniquity, I will lay a stumbling block before him, and he shall die; because you have not given him warning, he shall die in his sins and his righteousness which he had done shall not be remembered; and his blood will I require at your hand.

21 Nevertheless, if you warn the righteous man, that he may not sin, and he does not sin, the righteous man shall surely live, because he is warned; and you have delivered your soul.

22 ¶And the hand of the LORD was there upon me; and he said to me, Arise, go forth into the plain, and I will talk to you there.

23 Then I arose and went forth into the plain: and, behold, the glory of the LORD stood there, as the glory which I saw by the river Chebar; and I fell on my face.

24 Then the spirit entered into me and set me upon my feet, and spoke with me and said to me, Go, shut yourself in your house.

25 And you, O Son of man, behold, they shall put chains upon you, and shall bind you with them, that you cannot go out among them.

26 And I will make your tongue cleave to your palate, and you shall

be dumb and shall not be to them a reprover; for they are a rebellious house.

27 But when I speak with you, I will open your mouth and you shall say to them, Thus says the LORD God: He that hears, let him hear; and he that trembles, let him tremble; for they are a rebellious house.

CHAPTER 4

YOU also, O Son of man, take a brick and lay it before you, and draw upon it the outline of the city of Jerusalem;

2 And lay siege against it, and build forts against it, and cast a mount against it; and set some camps also against it, and set battering rams against it round about.

3 Moreover take an iron pan, and set it for an iron wall between you and the city; and set your face against it, and it shall be besieged, and you shall lay siege against it. This is a sign to the house of Israel.

4 Then lie upon your left side, and lay the iniquity of the house of Israel upon that side; according to the number of days that you shall lie upon it, you shall bear their iniquity.

5 For I have given you two tasks of iniquities, according to the number of the days, three hundred and ninety days; so shall you bear the iniquity of the house of Israel.

6 And when you have completed them, you shall lie again on your right side, and you shall bear the iniquity of the house of Judah forty days; I have appointed you each day for a year.

7 Therefore you shall set your face towards the siege of Jerusalem, and your arm shall prevail, and you shall prophesy against it.

8 And behold, I have laid chains upon you, and you shall not turn from one side to another until you have completed the days of your siege.

9 ¶And take for yourself wheat and barley, beans and lentils, millet and rye, and put them in one vessel, and make for yourself bread of them; according to the number of days that you shall lie upon your side, three hundred and ninety days, you shall eat of it.

10 And your food which you shall eat shall be by weight, twenty shekels a day; from time to time you shall eat it.

11 And you shall drink water by measure, a sixth part of a hin; from time to time shall you drink.

12 And you shall eat it as if you ate barley cakes, having baked it in their sight with the dung that comes out of men.

13 And the LORD said, Thus shall the children of Israel eat their bread unclean among the Gentiles, whither I shall drive them.

14 Then said I, Ah LORD God! behold, I have never defiled myself; and from my youth up even till now I have not eaten of that which dies of itself or is torn in pieces by wild beasts; neither has unclean meat entered into my mouth.

15 Then he said to me, Lo, I have given you oxen's dung instead of men's dung, that you shall bake your bread with it.

16 Moreover, he said to me, Son of man, behold, I will break the staff of bread in Jerusalem; and they shall eat bread by weight; and when thirsty, they shall drink water by measure;

17 And they shall lack bread and water, and they shall perish one with another, and shall be consumed in their iniquity.

CHAPTER 5

AND you, Son of man, take a sharp sword, like a barber's razor, and cause it to pass upon your head and upon your beard; then take scales to weigh it, and divide the hair into three parts.

2 A third part you shall burn with fire in the midst of the city, when the days of your siege are fulfilled; and you shall take a third part, and cut it with the sword, going round about the city; and a third part you shall scatter to the wind; and I will draw out a sword after Israel.

3 And you shall take from thence a few of the hairs and bind them in the skirt of your cloak.

4 Then take some of them again and cast them into the midst of the fire, and burn them in the fire; for from them shall come forth a fire into all the house of Israel.

5 ¶Thus says the LORD God: This is Jerusalem; I have set her in the midst of the nations, with all the cities round about her.

6 For she has exchanged my judgments for wickedness from the Gentiles, and my commandments for statutes from the cities that are round about her; for they have rejected my statutes and they have not walked in my commandments.

7 Therefore thus says the LORD God: Because you have regarded the statutes which you took from nations round about you, and have not walked in my statutes, neither have kept my judgments, but you have done according to the judgments of the nations that are round about you;

8 Therefore thus says the LORD God: Behold I, even I, am against you, and will execute judgments in your midst in the sight of the nations.

9 And I will do in you that which I have never done before, and the like of which I will never do again, because of all your abominations.

10 Therefore the parents shall eat their children in the midst of you, and the children shall eat their parents; and I will execute judgments in you, and the whole remnant of you I will scatter to all the winds.

11 Therefore, as I live, says the LORD God, Because you have defiled my sanctuary with all your detestable things and with all your abominations, therefore I will scatter you; neither shall my eye spare, neither will I have any pity.

12 ¶A third part of you shall die with the pestilence, and with famine shall they be consumed in the midst of you; and a third part shall fall by the sword round about you; and a third part I will scatter to all the winds, and I will draw out a sword after them.

13 Thus shall my anger be poured out, and I will cause my fury to rest upon them, and I will be comforted; and they shall know that I the LORD have spoken it in my zeal, when I have poured out my anger upon them.

14 Moreover I will make you waste, and a reproach among the nations that are round about you, in the sight of all that pass by.

15 So you shall be a reproach and a taunt, an example of punishment and a horror to the nations that are round about you, when I have executed judgments in you in anger and in fury and in furious rebukes. I the LORD have spoken it.

16 When I shall send upon you my grievous arrows of famine, which shall be for your destruction and which I will send to destroy you; I will increase the famine upon you, and will break the staff of your grain.

17 And I will send upon you famine and fierce beasts, and they shall devour you; and pestilence and blood shall pass through you; and I will bring the sword upon you. I the LORD have spoken it.

CHAPTER 6

AND the word of the LORD came to me, saying,

2 Son of man, set your face toward the mountains of Israel and prophesy against them,

3 And say, O mountains of Israel, hear the word of the LORD God; Thus says the LORD God to the mountains and to the hills, to the valleys and to the brooks: Behold, I am bringing a sword upon you, and I will destroy your high places.

4 Your altars shall be desolate, and your images shall be broken; and I will cast down your slain men before your idols.

5 And I will lay the dead bodies of the house of Israel before their idols; and I will scatter your bones round about your altars.

6 In all your dwelling places the cities shall be laid waste, and the high places shall be desolate, that your altars may be destroyed and made desolate, and your idols may be broken and made desolate, and your images may be cut down, and your works may cease.

7 And the slain shall fall in the midst of you, and you shall know that I am the Lord.

8 ¶Yet I will leave a remnant of you among the nations, those of you who shall escape the sword and are scattered through the cities.

9 And those who escape of you shall remember me among the nations whither they are carried captives; when I have destroyed their corrupt hearts, for they have departed from me, and with their eyes have gone astray after their idols; and they shall loath themselves for the evils which they have committed in all their abominations.

10 And they shall know that I am the Lord, and that I have not said in vain that I would do this evil to them.

11 ¶Thus says the Lord God, Strike with your hand, and stamp with your foot, and say, Alas for all the evil abominations of the house of Israel! for they shall fall by the sword, by famine, and by pestilence.

12 He that is far off shall die of pestilence; and he that is near shall fall by the sword; and he that remains and that escapes shall die by famine; thus will I accomplish my fury upon them.

13 Then they shall know that I am the Lord, when their slain shall be among their idols round about their altars upon every high hill and upon all the tops of the mountains and under every green tree and under every thick terebinth, the place where they did offer incense to all their idols.

14 So I will stretch out my hand against them and will make the land desolate and waste, more than the wilderness of Diblath, throughout all their habitations; and they shall know that I am the Lord.

CHAPTER 7

MOREOVER the word of the Lord came to me, saying,

2 Also, Son of man, thus says the Lord God to the land of Israel: The end is come upon the land of Israel, the end is come upon the four corners of the land.

3 Now the end is come upon you, and I will pour out my wrath upon you, and I will judge you according to your ways and will recompense you all your abominations.

4 And my eye shall not spare you, neither will I have pity; but I will recompense you according to your ways, and your abominations shall be in your midst; and you shall know that I am the Lord.

5 Thus says the Lord God: Behold, an evil is coming for every evil which you have committed.

6 An end is coming, and it shall afflict you.

7 The dawn of destruction is come upon you, O you inhabitant of the land; the time is come, the day of trouble is near.

8 Now I will shortly pour out my wrath upon you, and I will pour out my anger upon you; and I will judge you according to your ways, and will recompense you for all your abominations.

9 And my eye shall not spare you, neither will I have pity; but I will recompense you according to your ways; and your abominations shall remain in the midst of you; and you shall know that I am the Lord who has smitten you.

10 Behold the day is come, the dawn is gone forth; the staff [1] has blossomed, the shame has budded.

11 Violence has grown upon the staff of the wicked; none of them shall remain, neither their disturbances nor their works; nor shall I cease from punishing them.

12 The time is come, the day draws near; let not the buyer rejoice, nor the seller regret; for wrath is upon all their substance.

13 For the buyer shall not return to the seller, for they will not be living; for catastrophe shall not spare any of their possessions; neither shall a man spare his life by means of his corruptness.

14 They have blown the trumpet, and made all ready; but there is none

---

[1] The word staff is used symbolically, meaning oppression.

that goes to battle; for my wrath is upon all their substance.

15 The sword is in the streets, pestilence and famine in the houses; he that is in the field shall die by the sword; and he that is in the city, famine and pestilence shall devour.

16 ¶But those of them who escape shall escape on the mountains, and they shall take refuge like doves in the crags; all of them shall die every one in his own iniquity.

17 All hands shall be feeble and all knees shall be weak.

18 The people shall also gird themselves with sackcloth, and horror shall cover them; and shame shall be upon all faces, and baldness upon all heads.

19 They shall cast their silver into the streets, and their gold shall be despised; their silver and their gold shall not be able to deliver them in the day of the wrath of the LORD; they shall not satisfy their souls, neither fill their bellies; because this is their torment on account of their iniquity.

20 ¶And the beauty of their ornaments, which they made with excellency for the images and altars of their abominations, I have made, therefore, to be despised;

21 And I will give it into the hands of strangers for a prey and to the wicked of the earth for a spoil; and they shall pollute it.

22 And I will turn my face from them, and they shall pollute my sanctuary, and robbers shall enter into it and defile it.

23 ¶And they shall attack it with bricks; for the land is full of bloody crimes, and the city is full of iniquity.

24 Therefore I will bring shepherds of Gentiles, and they shall possess their houses; I will also make the excellency of the mighty ones to cease; and the Gentiles shall possess their sanctuary.

25 Indignation is coming; and they shall seek peace, and there shall be none.

26 Calamity shall come upon calamity, and rumor shall be upon rumor; then they shall seek a vision from the prophets; but the law shall perish from the priests, and counsel from the elders.

27 The king shall sit in mourning and the prince shall be clothed with desolation and the hands of the people of the land shall tremble; I will do to them according to their evil way, and according to their own judgments will I judge them; and they shall know that I am the LORD.

CHAPTER 8

AND it came to pass in the sixth year, in the sixth month, on the fifth day of the month, as I was sitting in my house, and the elders of Judah were sitting before me, that the hand of the LORD God fell there upon me.[1]

2 Then I beheld, and lo, a likeness as of the appearance of fire; from the loins and downward, fire; and from his loins and upward, brightness, as the appearance of God.

3 And he put forth the form of a hand, and caught me by a lock of my head; and the spirit lifted me up between the earth and the heaven, and brought me in a vision of God to Jerusalem, to the door of the inner gate that looks toward the north; where stood the image of lust, which provokes to lust.

4 And behold, the glory of the God of Israel was there, according to the vision which I saw in the plain.

5 ¶Then he said to me, Son of man, lift up your eyes now toward the way of the north. So I lifted up my eyes toward the way of the north, and behold, on the north side of the east gate stood the statue of lust in the entrance.

6 And he said to me, Son of man, do you see what they are doing, even the great abominations that the house of Israel are committing here, for they have gone far off from my sanctuary? But turn round again, and you shall see greater abominations which they are doing.

7 ¶And he brought me in to the door of the court; and I looked, and behold, there was a hole in the wall.

8 Then he said to me, Son of man,

[1] I prophesied.

dig in the wall; and when I had digged in the wall, behold, there I found a door.

9 And he said to me, Go in and see the abominations and wicked things that they do here.

10 So I went in and saw; and behold, every form of creeping things and abominable beasts and all the idols of the house of Israel portrayed upon the wall round about.

11 And there stood before them seventy men of the elders of the house of Israel, and in the midst of them stood Jaazaniah the son of Shaphan, and they were standing before him every man his censer in his hand; and the smoke of the cloud of incense went up.

12 Then he said to me, Son of man, do you see the thing which the elders of the house of Israel are doing in the dark, every man in his secret chamber? For they say, The LORD does not see us; because the LORD has forsaken the earth.

13 ¶He said also to me, Turn round again, and you shall see greater abominations that they are doing.

14 Then he brought me to the door of the gate of the LORD's house which was toward the north; and, behold, there sat women weeping for Tammuz.

15 ¶Then he said to me, Do you see this, O Son of man? Turn round again, and you shall see greater abominations than these.

16 And he brought me into the inner court of the LORD's house, and behold, at the door of the temple of the LORD, between the porch and the altar, there stood about twenty-five men, with their backs toward the temple of the LORD and their faces toward the east; and they worshipped the sun toward the east.

17 ¶Then he said to me, Do you see this, O Son of man? Is it a little thing to the house of Judah that they commit the abominations which they commit here? For they have filled the land with iniquity, and have returned to provoke me to anger; and they sneer at me.

18 Therefore I will also deal in my fury; my eye shall not spare, neither will I have pity; and though they cry in my ears with a loud voice, yet I will not listen to them.

CHAPTER 9

AND he cried in my ears with a loud voice, saying, Come near, O you avengers of the city, every man with his destroying weapons in his hand.

2 And behold, six men came from the way of the upper gate, which looks toward the north, and every man had his destroying weapons in his hand; and there was a man among them clothed with linen, and his loins were girded with girdles of sapphire; and they went in and stood beside the bronze altar.

3 And the glory of the God of Israel was gone up from the cherub which stood on the corner of the house. And he called to the man who was clothed with linen and whose loins were girded with girdles of sapphire;

4 And the LORD said to him, Go through the midst of the city, through the midst of Jerusalem, and set a mark upon the foreheads of the men who sigh and who are tormented on account of all the abominations and evil things that are done in the midst thereof.

5 ¶And to those who were with him he said in my sight, Go after him through the city and destroy; let not your eyes spare, nor have pity;

6 Slay utterly old and young, both virgins and little children and women; but touch not any man upon whom is the mark; and begin at my sanctuary. So they began with the elders who stood in front of the house.

7 And he said unto them, Defile the house, and fill the courts with the slain; then go forth and slay in the city.

8 ¶And it came to pass, when they had slain them, I was left; and I fell upon my face and cried with a loud voice mournfully, and said, Ah LORD God, wilt thou destroy all the residue of Israel? Wilt thou pour out thy fury upon Jerusalem?

9 Then he said to me, The iniquity

of the house of Israel and Judah is exceedingly great, the land is full of blood and the city full of treachery; for they said, The LORD has forsaken the earth and the LORD does not see us.

10 And as for me, I will have no mercy upon them, nor will I have pity; but I will recompense their evil ways upon their head.

11 And behold, the man clothed with linen answered, saying, I have done as thou hast commanded me.

CHAPTER 10

THEN I looked, and behold, in the firmament that was above the head of the cherubim there appeared over them something with the appearance of a sapphire stone, and the form of a throne.

2 And the voice spoke to the man clothed in linen, and said, Go in between the wheels, even under the cherubim; and fill your hand with the coals of fire from between the cherubim, and scatter them over the city. And he went in my sight.

3 Now the cherubim were standing on the right side of the house, when the man went in; and the cloud filled the inner court.

4 Then the glory of God went up from the cherub that stood over the threshhold of the house; and the house was filled with the cloud, and the court was full of the brightness of the LORD's glory.

5 And the sound of the wings of the cherubim was heard as far as the outer court, like the voice of God when he speaks.

6 And it came to pass, when he had commanded the man clothed with linen, saying, Take fire from between the wheels, from between the cherubim; he went in and stood beside the wheels.

7 Then one cherub stretched forth his hand from between the cherubim to the fire that was between the cherubim, and took thereof, and put it into the hands of the man who was clothed with linen, who took it and went out.

8 ¶And I looked, and behold, there appeared in the cherubim the form of a man's hand under their wings.

9 And I looked, and behold, there were four wheels beside the cherubim, one wheel beside each cherub, and the appearance of the wheels was like the color of beryl stone.

10 And as for their appearance and the form, the four of them were alike, as if a wheel were in the midst of a wheel.

11 When they went, they went upon four sides; they turned not as they went, but to the place whither the first one went they followed it, they turned not as they went.

12 And their whole body and their backs and their hands and their wings and the wheels were full of eyes when they turned on their sides.

13 And as for the wheels, he called them Rolling Wheels, in my presence.

14 And every one of them had four faces: the first face was the face of a cherub, and the second face was the face of a man, and the third the face of a lion, and the fourth the face of an eagle.

15 And the cherubim were lifted up. This is the same living creature that I saw by the river Chebar.

16 And when the cherubim went, the wheels also went beside them; and when the cherubim lifted up their wings to mount up from the earth, the wheels also turned not from beside them.

17 When they stood, these stood; and when they were lifted up, these were lifted up also; when the cherubim lifted their wings, the wheels also lifted up with them; for the spirit of life was in them.

18 Then the glory of the LORD departed from the corner of the temple, and stood over the cherubim.

19 And the cherubim lifted up their wings and mounted up from the earth in my sight; when they went out, the wheels also were beside them, and they stood at the door of the east gate of the LORD's house; and the glory of the God of Israel was over them.

20 These were the living creatures that I saw under the God of Israel by

the river Chebar; and I knew that they were the cherubim.

21 Each one had four faces, and each one four wings; and the likeness of a man's hand was under their wings.

22 And as for the likeness of their faces, they were like the same faces that I saw by the river Chebar, and their appearance was the same; they went every one straight forward.

CHAPTER 11

MOREOVER the spirit lifted me up and brought me to the east gate of the house of the LORD, which looks eastward; and I beheld at the entrance of the gate twenty-five men; and I saw among them Jaazaniah the son of Azur, and Pelatiah the son of Benaiah, princes of the people.

2 Then the LORD said to me, Son of man, these are the men who devise mischief and give wicked counsel in this city,

3 Saying, We have built houses in the midst of it; the city is the caldron, and we are the meat.[1]

4 ¶Therefore prophesy against them, prophesy, O Son of man.

5 And the Spirit of the LORD fell upon me, and he said to me, Speak, Thus says the LORD God: Thus have you desired, O house of Israel; for I know the inclination of your thought.

6 You have multiplied your slain in this city, and you have filled its streets with the slain.

7 Therefore thus says the LORD God: Your slain whom you have laid in the midst of it, they are the meat, and this city is the caldron; but I will bring you forth out of the midst of it.

8 You have feared the sword; and I will bring a sword upon you, says the LORD God.

9 And I will bring you out of the midst of it and deliver you into the hands of strangers, and I will execute judgments upon you.

10 You shall fall by the sword; I will judge you in the border of Israel; and you shall know that I am the LORD.

11 This city shall not be your cal-dron, neither shall you be the meat in the midst of it; but I will judge you in the border of Israel;

12 And you shall know that I am the LORD; for you have not walked in my statutes, neither executed my judgments, but have followed after the ordinances of the Gentiles that are round about you.

13 ¶And it came to pass, when I prophesied, that Palatiah the son of Benaiah died. Then I fell down upon my face, and cried with a loud voice, and said, Ah, LORD God! wilt thou make full end of the remnant of Israel?

14 And the word of the LORD came to me, saying,

15 Son of man, your brethren, your brethren, even your kindred, who are in your captivity, and all the house of Israel shall be annihilated, for the inhabitants of Jerusalem have said to them, Get you far from the LORD; to us is this land given for an inheritance.

16 Therefore say, Thus says the LORD God: I will cast them far off among the Gentiles, and I will scatter them among the countries, nevertheless I will be to them a little sanctuary in the countries where they have gone.

17 Therefore say, Thus says the LORD God: I will gather you from among the peoples and assemble you out of the countries where you have been scattered, and I will give you the land of Israel.

18 And they shall come thither, and shall remove from it all its idols and all its abominations.

19 And I will give them a new heart, and I will put a new spirit within them; and I will take the stony heart out of their flesh, and I will give them a heart of flesh,

20 That they may walk in my commandments and keep my ordinances and do them; and they shall be my people, and I will be their God.

21 But as for those whose heart followed after their images and abominations, I will recompense their evil ways upon their own heads, says the LORD God.

---

[1] An idiom which means *we belong to each other*.

22 ¶Then the cherubim lifted up their wings and the wheels beside them; and the glory of the God of Israel was above them.

23 And the glory of the LORD went up from the midst of the city, and stood upon the mountain which is on the east side of the city.

24 ¶Then the spirit lifted me up, and brought me in a vision by the Spirit of God into the land of Chaldea to those of the captivity. So the vision that I had seen departed from me.

25 Then I spoke to those of the captivity all the things that the LORD had shown me.

CHAPTER 12

THE word of the LORD came to me, saying,

2 Son of man, you live in the midst of a rebellious house, who have eyes to see and see not; who have ears to hear and hear not; for they are a rebellious house.

3 Therefore, Son of man, prepare for yourself the things which are necessary for captivity, and go into the captivity by day in their sight; go from your own place to another place, so that they may see, because they are a rebellious house.

4 Then bring out your belongings by day in their sight, as though they were the necessary things for captivity; and you shall go forth in the evening like those who go forth into captivity.

5 Make a breach through the wall in their sight and go forth through it.

6 Take the luggage on your shoulder and go forth in the dark; you shall cover your face, that you may not see the ground; for I have set you as a sign to the house of Israel.

7 And I did as he had commanded me: I brought forth my luggage by day as one who carries luggage into captivity, and in the evening I made a breach through the wall and went forth in the dark, carrying my luggage upon my shoulder in their sight.

8 ¶And the word of the LORD came upon me in the morning, saying,

9 Son of man, if the children of the rebellious house of Israel should say to you, What are you doing?

10 Say to them, Thus says the LORD God: Even so shall the prince carry such luggage in Jerusalem, and all the house of Israel with him.

11 Say to them, I am a sign to you; just as I have done, so shall it be done to you; you shall go into captivity.

12 And the leader who is among you shall carry his luggage upon his shoulder, and shall go forth in the dark, and shall make a breach through the wall and go out through it; he shall cover his face, that he may not see the ground.

13 And I will spread my net over him, and he shall be caught in it; and I will bring him to Babylon to the land of the Chaldeans; yet he shall not see the land, and there shall he die.

14 And I will scatter towards every wind all that are about him to help him and give him strength; and I will draw out the sword after them.

15 And they shall know that I am the LORD, when I shall scatter them among the nations and disperse them in the countries.

16 But I will spare a few men of them from the sword, from famine, and from pestilence, that they may declare all their abominations among the Gentiles whither they go; and they shall know that I am the LORD.

17 ¶Moreover the word of the LORD came to me, saying,

18 Son of man, eat your bread with quaking, and drink your water with trembling and with fear of scarcity;

19 And say to the people of the land, Thus says the LORD God concerning the inhabitants of Jerusalem, and concerning the land of Israel: They shall eat their bread with fear of lack, and drink their water with terror, for the land shall be desolate from all that is therein, because of the iniquity of all those who dwell in it.

20 And the cities that are inhabited shall be laid waste, and the land shall become desolate; and you shall know that I am the LORD.

21 ¶And the word of the LORD came unto me, saying,

22 Son of man, what is that proverb that you have in the land of Israel, saying, The days are prolonged, and every vision shall fail?

23 Tell them therefore, Thus says the LORD God: I will make this proverb to cease, and they shall no more use it as a proverb in Israel; but say to them, The days are at hand when every vision shall come true.

24 For there shall be no more any false vision nor doubtful divination among the children of Israel.

25 For I am the LORD; I have spoken, and the word which I speak I shall perform it; and I shall no more delay it; for in your days, O rebellious house, I will speak the word and will perform it, says the LORD God.

26 ¶Again the word of the LORD came upon me, saying,

27 Son of man, behold, the children of the house of Israel say, The vision that he sees is for the distant future, and he prophesies of the times that are far off.

28 Therefore say unto them, Thus says the LORD God: There shall none of my words be delayed any more, but the word which I have spoken I shall soon fulfil, says the LORD God.

CHAPTER 13

A ND the word of the LORD came unto me, saying,

2 Son of man, prophesy against the prophets of Israel who prophesy to the people, and say to them who prophesy out of their own heart, Hear the word of the LORD;

3 Thus says the LORD God: Woe to the foolish prophets, who follow their own pride, for they have not seen any vision!

4 O Israel, your prophets are like the foxes in the ruins.

5 You have not gone up to build the breaches, neither have you made up a hedge for the house of Israel to stand in the battle in the day of the LORD.

6 For they say, Thus says the LORD; and the LORD has not sent them; and they persist in confirming a false word.

7 Indeed you have seen a vain vision, and you have spoken a lying divination, and yet you say, The LORD said it; although I have not spoken.

8 Therefore thus says the LORD God: Because you have seen false visions and spoken lies; therefore, behold, I am against you, says the LORD God.

9 And my hand shall be against the prophets who see false visions and utter lying divinations; they shall not remain in the midst of my people, neither shall they be written in the book of the house of Israel, neither shall they return to the land of Israel; and you shall know that I am the LORD God.

10 ¶Because they have deceived my people, saying, Peace; and there was no peace; and when the people built up a wall, they daubed it with untempered mortar in such a manner that it shall fall.

11 Say to those who daubed it in such a manner that it shall fall, Behold, I will bring a violent rain which will sweep everything away, and hailstones shall fall, and a whirlwind;

12 And the wall shall be breached and shall fall; and it shall be said to you, Where is the mortar with which you daubed it?

13 Therefore thus says the LORD God: I will bring a whirlwind in my wrath; and there shall be a deluge of rain in my anger, and hailstones in my fury to consume it.

14 So I will demolish the wall that you have daubed and bring it down to the ground, so that its foundation shall be laid bare, and you shall be defeated and consumed in the midst of it; and you shall know that I am the LORD.

15 Thus will I accomplish my wrath upon the wall and upon those who have daubed it with untempered mortar so that it shall be said to you, Where is the wall? Where are those who daubed it?

16 Such are the prophets of Israel who prophesy concerning Jerusalem, and who see visions of peace for her, and there is no peace, says the LORD God.

17 ¶Likewise, you Son of man, set

your face against the daughters of your people, who prophesy out of their own heart; and prophesy against them, and say to them,

18 Thus says the LORD God: Woe to the women who embroider wristlets and make coverings for every head and for every type of person to snare the souls of men! Will you hunt the souls of my people, and will you save your own souls?

19 You have polluted my people for a handful of barley and a piece of bread, to kill persons who were not guilty of death, and to save the lives of those who should not live, and you have lied to a people who listen to lies.

20 Wherefore thus says the LORD God: Behold, I am against your embroidered garments with which you hunt the souls of the people, and I will tear them from your arms, and I will set free the souls of those that you hunt, and I will cause them to fly.

21 And I will tear your robes, and will deliver my people out of your hands, and they shall be no more delivered into your hands to be hunted; and you shall know that I am the LORD.

22 Because with lies you have made the heart of the righteous sad, whom I have not made sorrowful; and you have strengthened the hands of the wicked, so that they did not return from their wicked ways and live.

23 Therefore you shall no longer see false visions, nor work divinations any more; for I will deliver my people from your hands; and you shall know that I am the LORD.

CHAPTER 14

THEN came certain of the elders of Israel to me to inquire of the LORD, and sat before me.

2 And the word of the LORD came to me, saying,

3 Son of man, these men have set up their idols in their heart, and put the stumbling block of their iniquity before their faces; I will seek vengeance from them.

4 Therefore speak to them and say to them, Thus says the LORD God: Every man of the house of Israel who sets up his idols in his heart and puts the stumbling block of his iniquity before his face and comes to the prophet, I the LORD will be a witness against him because of the multitude of his idols,

5 That I may take the house of Israel in the imagination of their own hearts, because they have departed from me through all their idols.

6 ¶Therefore say to the house of Israel, Thus says the LORD God: Repent, and turn away from your idols; and turn away your faces from all your abominations.

7 For every one of the house of Israel, or of the proselytes who dwell in Israel, who departs from me and sets up idols in his heart and puts the stumbling block of his iniquity before his face and comes to a prophet to inquire of him, I the LORD will be a witness against him;

8 And I will pour out my anger against that man, and I will make him a sign and a proverb, and I will destroy him from the midst of my people; and you shall know that I am the LORD.

9 And when a prophet shall err and speak a word, I the LORD have deceived that prophet, and I will stretch out my hand against him, and I will destroy him from the midst of my people Israel.

10 And they shall both bear the punishment of their iniquity; the punishment of him who seeks to inquire shall be like the punishment of the prophet,

11 That the house of Israel may go no more astray from me, neither be polluted any more with all their transgressions; but that they may be my people and I may be their God, says the LORD God.

12 ¶The word of the LORD came to me, saying,

13 Son of man, if a land should sin against me and commit iniquity before me, then I will stretch out my hand against it, and will break the staff of its wheat; and I will send

famine upon it, and will destroy man and beast from it;

14 Though these three men, Noah, Daniel and Job were in the land, they would deliver but their own souls by their righteousness, says the LORD God.

15 ¶And if I should send vicious beasts against the land, and they destroy it so that it become desolate, so that no man could pass through because of the wild beasts;

16 Though these three men were in it, as I live, says the LORD God, they would deliver neither sons nor daughters; but they alone would be delivered and the land would be made desolate.

17 ¶Or if I should bring a sword upon that land, and say, Sword, go through that land, and I destroy man and beast from it;

18 Though these three men were in it, as I live, says the LORD God, they would deliver neither sons nor daughters, but they alone would be delivered.

19 ¶Or if I should send a pestilence into that land, and pour out my fury upon it in blood, and destroy from it man and beast;

20 Though Noah, Daniel and Job were in it, as I live, says the LORD God, they would deliver neither son nor daughter; but they would only deliver themselves by their righteousness.

21 For thus says the LORD God: How much more when I send four sore judgments upon Jerusalem: the sword and famine and vicious beasts and pestilence, to destroy from it man and beast.

22 ¶Yet there shall be left in it those who will be delivered, who will bring forth sons and daughters; and even they shall come forth to you, and you shall see their ways and their doings; and you shall be comforted concerning the evil that I have brought upon Jerusalem, even concerning all that I have brought upon it.

23 And they shall comfort you when you see their ways and their doings; and you shall know that I have not done without cause all that I have done in it, says the LORD God.

CHAPTER 15

AND the word of the LORD came unto me, saying,

2 Son of man, What shall happen to the wood of the vine more than to any wood, or to any branch of the trees which are among the trees of the forest?

3 Shall wood be taken from the vine to make anything from it? Or do men take a peg from it to hang vessels on it?

4 Behold, it is cast into the fire for fuel; and when the fire has consumed both ends of it and the middle of it is burned, is it good for any work?

5 Behold, when it was whole, it was not useful for implements; how much less shall it be useful when the fire has devoured it and it is destroyed?

6 ¶Therefore thus says the LORD God: As I have given the wood of the vine among all the trees of the forest to the fire for fuel, so I have given the inhabitants of Jerusalem.

7 And I will pour out my anger against them; they shall go out from one fire, and another fire shall consume them; and you shall know that I am the LORD, when I pour out my anger against them.

8 And I will make the land desolate and a horror because they have committed iniquity, says the LORD God.

CHAPTER 16

AGAIN the word of the LORD came unto me, saying,

2 Son of man, make known to Jerusalem her abominations,

3 And say, Thus says the LORD God to Jerusalem: Your root and your nativity is of the land of Canaan; your father was an Amorite and your mother a Hittite.

4 And as for the one who bore you, in the day you were born she did not cut your navel, neither did she wash you with water nor did she salt your body with salt nor wrap you in swaddling clothes at all.

5 Nor did her eye have pity upon you, to do any of these things to

you and to have compassion upon you; but you were cast out in the open field, to the loathing of your person on the day that you were born.

6 ¶And when I passed by you and saw you wallowing in your own blood, I said to you as you lay thus wallowing in your blood, Live,

7 And multiply like the grass of the field. And you have increased and grown great; then you went into the cities. Your breasts were formed and your hair had grown, but you were naked and bare.

8 Now when I passed by you and looked upon you, behold, you had reached the marriage age; and I spread my hand over you and covered your nakedness; yea, I swore to you and entered into a covenant with you, says the LORD God, and you became mine.

9 Then I bathed you with water, and I washed away your blood from you, and I anointed you with oil.

10 I clothed you also with embroidered clothes, and shod you with shoes; and I girded your loins with fine linen and clothed you with silk.

11 I decked you also with ornaments, and I put bracelets on your arms and a necklace on your neck.

12 And I put a jewel on your forehead and earrings in your ears and a beautiful crown on your head.

13 Thus you were decked with gold and gems, and you were clothed with fine linen and purple and embroidered cloth; and you ate fine flour and honey and oil; and you became exceedingly beautiful, and you grew prosperous among the kingdoms.

14 And your renown went forth among the Gentiles for your beauty, because of the beautiful crown of my glory which I put upon you, says the LORD God.

15 ¶But you trusted in your own beauty and played the harlot because of your renown, and poured out your fornications on every one who passed by;

16 And you took some of my garments and decorated the high places for yourself, and played the harlot upon them; they shall not be brought back, neither shall they be yours.

17 You have also taken your costly jewels of gold and silver which I had given you, and made to yourself images of men, and committed whoredom with them;

18 And you took your embroidered garments and covered them; and you have set my oil and my incense before them.

19 And the food which I gave you, the fine flour and oil and honey with which I fed you, you have set before them for a sweet savor; says the LORD God.

20 Moreover you have taken your sons and your daughters, whom you had borne to me, and these you have sacrificed to them for food. These things you did besides your whoredoms,

21 That you have slaughtered my children, and offered them to the idols after you had been ravished by them.

22 And in all your abominations and your whoredoms you have not remembered the days of your youth, when you were naked and bare and lay wallowing in blood.

23 And after all your wickedness, woe, woe to you! says the LORD God;

24 You have built yourself a house of idols, and made yourself altars in every street.

25 You have built yourself small temples for idol worship at every head of the way, and defiled your beauty and exposed yourself to every one that passed by, and multiplied your fornications.

26 You have also played the harlot with the Egyptians your neighbors, who have large male organs; and you have multiplied your fornications, to provoke me to anger.

27 Behold, therefore I have stretched out my hand against you and have abolished your ordinances and delivered you into the hand of those who hate you, the daughters of the Philistines, who rebuked you because of your ways of whoredom.

28 You have played the whore also

with the Assyrians, and yet you were not satisfied.

29 You have moreover multiplied your fornications in the land of Canaan and in Chaldea; and yet, even with them you were not satisfied.

30 How shall I judge you, O daughter,[1] says the LORD God, seeing that you did all these things, the works of a whore and a rebellious woman?

31 In that you built your notorious shrines at the head of every way, and set your altars in every street; and yet you were not as clever as a harlot who charges a price;

32 And even not as clever as a whorish wife who takes a price from strangers.

33 Men pay a price to all harlots; but instead you pay a price to all your lovers and bribe them with your whoredom, that they may come to you from every side round about you.

34 So you are different from other women in your whoredoms, in that you pay others a price, and no one pays a price to you.

35 ¶Therefore, O harlot, hear the word of the LORD;

36 Thus says the LORD God: Because you have practiced divination and exposed your nakedness through your whoredoms with your lovers, and because of all the idols of your abominations and the blood of your children which you offered to them;

37 Behold, therefore I will gather all your lovers with whom you have taken pleasure, and all those you have loved, with all those you have hated; I will even gather them against you from every side and will expose your nakedness in their presence, and they shall see all your nakedness.

38 And I will judge you with the judgment of an adulteress, and as those who shed blood are judged; and I will deliver you to slaughter and to fury and indignation.

39 And I will also deliver you into their hands, and shall demolish your brothels and tear down the houses of your idols; they shall strip you also of your clothes, and shall take your precious jewels and leave you naked and bare.

40 They shall also bring up multitudes of people against you, and they shall stone you with stones, and thrust you through with their swords.

41 And they shall burn you in the midst of fire, and execute judgments upon you in the sight of many women; and I will cause you to cease from playing the harlot, and you also shall give no hire to your lovers any more.

42 So will I make my wrath to rest upon you, and my indignation shall depart from you, and I will be quiet and will be no more angry.

43 Because you have not remembered the days of your youth, but have provoked me in all these things; behold, therefore I have also recompensed your evil ways upon your head, says the LORD God, because you have committed abomination and fornication.

44 ¶Behold, every one who uses a proverb shall use this proverb against you, saying, As is the mother, so is her daughter.

45 You are your mother's daughter, who deserted her husband and her children; and you are the sister of women who deserted their husbands and their children; your mother was a Hittite and your father an Amorite.

46 And your elder sister is Samaria, who dwells at your left hand with her daughters; and your younger sister, who dwells at your right hand, is Sodom with her daughters.

47 Yet you have not walked according to their ways, nor done according to their abominations; but in a very little time you became more corrupt than they in all your ways.

48 As I live, says the LORD God, Sodom your sister and her daughters have not done as you and your daughters have done.

49 Behold, this is the iniquity of Sodom your proud sister: she and her daughters had abundant food and lived in tranquillity, but she did not help the poor and needy.

50 And they were haughty and com-

---

[1] Israel. See verse 4.

mitted evil before me; therefore when I saw these things in them I overthrew them.

51 Neither has Samaria committed half of your sins; but you have multiplied your abominations more than they and have outdone your sisters in all your abominations which you have committed.

52 You also shall endure the shame because you have outdone your sisters in your sins, and have polluted yourself more than they; they are more righteous than you; you must be confounded also and bear your shame, for your sisters are more righteous than you.

53 I will bring back their captivity, the captivity of Sodom and her daughters and the captivity of Samaria and her daughters; then I will cause the captivity of your exiles to be carried among them,

54 That you may bear shame and be confounded in all that you have done to provoke my anger.

55 When your sister Sodom, with her daughters, shall be restored to their former state, and Samaria and her daughters shall be restored to their former state, then you and your daughters shall be restored to your former state.

56 For your sister Sodom was not a proverb in your mouth in the day of your pride,

57 Before your wickedness was exposed, as she was at the time of the reproach of the daughters of Edom, when all the daughters of the Philistines who were round about her used to despise her.

58 Now you bear your lewdness and your abominations, says the LORD God.

59 For thus says the LORD God: I will even deal with you as you have done, because you have despised my oaths and nullified my covenant.

60 ¶Nevertheless I will remember my covenant with you in the days of your youth, and I will establish with you an everlasting covenant.

61 Then you shall remember your evil ways and be ashamed, when I take your sisters, the elder and the younger, and give them to you for daughters, but not because of your covenant.

62 And I will establish my covenant with you; and you shall know that I am the LORD,

63 Because you shall remember and be ashamed, and never open your mouth any more because of your shame, for I have forgiven you for all that you have done, says the LORD God.

CHAPTER 17

AND the word of the LORD came to me, saying,

2 Son of man, put forth a riddle and speak a parable to the house of Israel,

3 And say, Thus says the LORD God: A great eagle with large wings and long pinions and fully developed claws, and thickly feathered, came to Lebanon and took the choicest branch of the cedar:

4 He cropped off the topmost of its tender twigs, and carried it to the land of Canaan; and he set it in a city of merchants.

5 He took also of the seed of the land, and planted it in uncultivated land; he placed it by many waters, and then set a watchman over it.

6 And it sprang up and grew into a spreading vine of low stature, so that its branches turned toward him and its roots were under him; so it became a vine, and brought forth branches and shot forth tendrils.

7 And, behold, there was also another great eagle with large wings and many claws: and, this vine bent its roots toward him, and shot forth its tendrils toward him, that he might water the soil where it was planted.

8 For it was planted in a good field, by many waters that it might bring forth branches and bear fruit and become a goodly vine.

9 Say now, Thus says the LORD God: It shall not prosper, but its roots shall be cut off, and its fruit shall dry up; and all the foliage which it has put forth shall wither; and it will not require a strong arm, nor many people to pluck it up by its roots.

10 Yea, behold, being planted, it shall not prosper; when the east wind strikes it, it shall wither in the soil where it grew.

11 ¶Moreover the word of the LORD came to me, saying,

12 Say now to the rebellious house, Do you know what these things mean? Tell them, Behold, the king of Babylon is coming to Jerusalem, and he shall take the king and the princes thereof and carry them with him to Babylon;

13 And he shall take one of the offspring of the royal family, and make a covenant with him and take an oath of him; and he shall carry away the rulers of the land, so that they may not boast again,

14 That the kingdom might be humbled, and that they might keep his covenant, and stand by him.

15 But he shall revolt against the king of Babylon, and shall send his ambassadors into Egypt, that they might give him horses and a large army. But he who does such things shall not prosper, nor shall he be delivered.

16 As I live, says the LORD God, surely in the very place where dwells the king of Babylon, who made him king and he despised my oath and nullified my covenant, even in the midst of Babylon, he shall die.

17 Neither shall Pharaoh fight against him with a great army nor with many horses, but by casting up mounds and building forts shall he destroy many lives.

18 Because he has despised the oaths and nullified the covenant, he shall surrender, but he shall not be delivered, because he has done all these things.

19 Therefore thus says the LORD God: As I live, because he has despised my oaths and nullified my covenant, I will punish him for it.

20 And I will spread my net upon him, and he shall be taken in it, and I will bring him to Babylon, the land of the Chaldeans, and judge him there for his trespass that he has trespassed against me.

21 And all his noble men and all his friends shall fall by the sword, and those that remain shall be scattered to all the winds; and you shall know that I the LORD have spoken it.

22 ¶Thus says the LORD God: I will also take one of the choicest branches of the highest cedar, and I will clip it; I will crop off from the top of its young twigs a tender one, and will plant it upon high and lofty mountains;

23 On the mountains of Israel will I plant it; and it shall bring forth boughs and bear fruit, and be a goodly cedar; and under it shall dwell all fowl of every wing; in the shadow of its branches shall they rest.

24 And all the trees of the field shall know that I the LORD have brought down the high tree, have exalted the low tree, have made dry the green tree, and have made the dry tree to flourish; I the LORD have spoken and have done it.

CHAPTER 18

THE word of the LORD came to me, saying,

2 Son of man, why do you use this proverb in the land of Israel, saying, The parents have eaten sour grapes, and the children's teeth are set on edge?

3 As I live, says the LORD God, this proverb shall never be used again in Israel.

4 Because all souls are mine; the soul of the father, so also the soul of the son is mine; the soul that sins, it shall die.

5 ¶But if a man be righteous and do justice and righteousness,

6 And has not eaten the meat sacrificed to idols on the mountains, neither has lifted up his eyes to the idols and the altars of the house of Israel, neither has defiled his neighbor's wife, nor has come near a menstruous woman,

7 And has not oppressed any man, and has not harmed any one, but has restored to the debtor his pledge; has given his bread to the hungry, and has covered the naked with a garment;

8 He has not lent money with usury, neither has loaned with a discount;

has withdrawn his hand from iniquity, and has executed true judgment between man and man;

9 Has walked in my commandments, and has kept my judgments, and has done justice; he who does so is a righteous man and shall surely live, says the LORD God.

10 ¶If he begets a son who is a wicked man, a shedder of blood, and he does any one of these evil things,

11 And eats the meat sacrificed to idols on the mountains, and defiles his neighbor's wife,

12 Oppresses the poor and needy, extorts from his neighbor, restores not the pledge to its owner, lifts up his eyes to the idols, commits abomination,

13 Lends money with usury, and takes a discount; shall he then live? He shall not live: because he has done all these evil things; he shall surely die; his blood shall be upon him.

14 ¶But if he begets a son, who sees all the sins that his father had committed, and shall not do likewise,

15 And who shall not eat meat sacrificed to the idols on the mountains, neither shall lift up his eyes to the idols of the house of Israel; shall defile not his neighbor's wife,

16 Oppresses no man, takes no pledge from any one, extorts no one, but shall give his bread to the hungry and cover the naked with a garment;

17 Who does not refuse to help the poor, who charges no usury or discount, executes my judgments, and walks in my commandments; he shall not die for the iniquity of his father, he shall surely live.

18 As for his father, because he cruelly oppressed and extorted from his brother and did nothing that is good among his people, lo, he is dead in his own sins.

19 ¶And if they should say, Why does not the son bear the sins of his father? say to them, Because the son has done that which is lawful and right and has kept all my commandments, he shall surely live.

20 The soul that sins, that soul shall die. The son shall not bear the sins of his father, neither shall the father bear the sins of his son; the righteousness of the righteous shall be upon him, and the wickedness of the wicked shall be upon him.

21 But if the wicked will turn from all his sins which he has committed, and keep all my commandments, and do that which is lawful and right, he shall surely live, he shall not die.

22 All his sins which he has committed, they shall not be remembered against him; but in the righteousness which he has done shall he live.

23 I have no pleasure in the death of a sinner, says the LORD God; but rather that he should return from his evil ways and live.

24 ¶But if the righteous man turns away from his righteousness and commits iniquity and abominations like those that the sinner has done, all the righteousness that he has done shall not be remembered to him, but in the iniquity which he has committed and in the sins that he has sinned, in them shall he die.

25 ¶Yet you say, The ways of the LORD are not fair. Hear now, O house of Israel; my ways are fair, but it is your ways that are not fair.

26 If a righteous man turns away from his righteousness and commits iniquity, in the iniquity that he has committed shall he die.

27 But if a wicked man turns away from the wickedness which he has committed and does that which is lawful and right, he shall save his soul alive.

28 And if he considers and turns away from all the sins that he has committed, he shall surely live, he shall not die.

29 Yet the house of Israel says, The ways of the LORD are not fair. O house of Israel, my ways are fair, but it is your ways that are not fair.

30 Therefore I will judge you, O house of Israel, every one according to his ways, says the LORD God. Repent and turn away from all your transgressions, so that your sins may not be your ruin.

31 ¶Cast away from you all the iniquities which you have committed; and make for yourselves a new heart

and a new spirit, so that you may not die, O house of Israel.

32 For I have no pleasure in the death of any one who dies, says the LORD God; wherefore repent and live.

CHAPTER 19

MOREOVER, you Son of man, take up a lamentation for the princes of Israel,

2 And say, What is your mother? O whelp of lions! she crouched among lions, she reared her whelps among young lions.

3 And one of her whelps grew up and became a young lion, and he learned to catch prey; and he devoured men.

4 The nations also heard of his fame; he was taken in their pit, and they brought him with a bridle to the land of Egypt.

5 Now when his mother saw that she had suffered and her hope was lost, then she took another of her whelps and made him a young lion.

6 And he went up and down among the lions; he became a young lion, and learned to catch the prey and devoured men.

7 Then he walked in his strength and ravaged cities and laid waste the land in its fulness by the noise of his roaring.

8 Then the nations gathered together against him from the provinces round about him, and spread their net over him; he was taken in their pit.

9 And they put him in a cage and brought him to the king of Babylon; and he threw him into prison, that his voice should no more be heard upon the mountains of Israel.

10 ¶Your mother is like a vine in your blood, planted by the waters; she was fruitful and full of branches by reason of many waters.

11 And she had strong rods for scepters of the rulers upon the great branches, and their stature rose up higher among its shoots, and their height was seen and the multitude of their tendrils.

12 But it was plucked **up in fury**

and was cast down to the ground, and the east wind dried up its fruit; its strong rods were broken and withered; the fire consumed it.

13 And now it is planted in the wilderness, in a thirsty and dry land.

14 And fire is gone out from its choice branches and has devoured its fruit, so that no strong rod was found in it, or a branch [1] to become a ruler's scepter. This is a lamentation, and shall be for a lamentation.

CHAPTER 20

AND it came to pass in the seventh year, in the fifth month, on the tenth day of the month, that certain of the elders of Israel came in to inquire of the LORD and sat down before me.

2 Then the word of the LORD came to me, saying,

3 Son of man, speak to the elders of Israel and say to them, Thus says the LORD God: Are you come to inquire of me? As I live, says the LORD God, I will not give you an answer.

4 You judge them, you judge them, O Son of man! and declare to them the abominations of their fathers;

5 ¶And say to them, Thus says the LORD God: In the day when I chose Israel and swore by lifting up my hand to the descendants of the house of Jacob and revealed myself to them in the land of Egypt, when I swore to them and said to them, I am the LORD your God;

6 On that day I swore to them to bring them forth out of the land of Egypt into a land that I had given to them, a land flowing with milk and honey, which is the glory of all lands;

7 And I said to them, Cast away every man his image from before his eyes, and do not defile yourselves with the idols of Egypt; I am the LORD your God.

8 But they rebelled against me and would not listen to me; they did not every man cast away the images from before their sight, nor did they forsake the idols of Egypt; then I said, I will pour out my fury upon them and accomplish my anger

---

[1] An heir to the ruler.

against them in the midst of the land of Egypt.

9 But I pitied them for my name's sake, that it should not be defiled among the Gentiles, in whose sight I revealed myself to them to bring them forth out of the land of Egypt.

10 ¶Wherefore I brought them forth out of the land of Egypt and brought them into the wilderness.

11 And I gave them my commandments and showed them my judgments, which if a man do he shall live by them.

12 Moreover also I gave them my sabbaths to be a sign between me and them, so that they might know that I am the LORD that sanctify them.

13 But the house of Israel rebelled against me in the wilderness; they did not walk in my commandments, and they despised my judgments, which if a man would do, he would live by them; and my sabbaths they greatly polluted; then I said, I will pour out my fury upon them in the wilderness and destroy them.

14 But I pitied them for my name's sake, that it should not be polluted in the sight of the Gentiles, in whose presence I brought them out.

15 So I swore to them in the wilderness that I would not bring them into the land which I had given them, flowing with milk and honey, which is the glory of all lands;

16 Because they despised my judgments and polluted my sabbaths exceedingly; for their hearts went after their idols.

17 Nevertheless my eye spared them and I did not destroy them, neither did I make an end of them in the wilderness.

18 But I said to their children in the wilderness, Walk not in the statutes of your fathers, neither observe their judgments nor defile yourselves with their idols;

19 I am the LORD your God; walk in my statutes and keep my judgments and do them;

20 And hallow my sabbaths; and they shall be a sign between me and you, that you may know that I am the LORD your God.

21 Notwithstanding the children of Israel rebelled against me; they did not walk in my commandments, neither did they keep my judgments to do them, which if a man shall do, he shall live by them; they polluted my sabbaths: then I said, I will pour out my fury upon them and accomplish my anger against them in the wilderness.

22 But I pitied them for my name's sake, that it should not be polluted in the sight of the Gentiles, in whose presence I brought them out.

23 But I swore to them in the wilderness, that I would scatter them among the Gentiles and disperse them through the countries;

24 Because they had not executed my judgments, but had despised my commandments and had polluted my sabbaths, and their eyes were after their fathers' idols.

25 Wherefore I gave them statutes that were not good and judgments whereby they could not live;

26 And I let them defile themselves through their own gifts, when they offered their first-born as sacrifices; that I might destroy them and that they might know that I am the LORD.

27 ¶Therefore, Son of man, speak to the house of Israel and say to them, Thus says the LORD God: Yet in this very manner your fathers have blasphemed before me in their iniquity which they dealt treacherously against me.

28 For when I had brought them into the land that I had sworn to give them, then they saw every high hill and every shady tree, and they offered there their sacrifices, and there they presented their offerings; there they also made their sweet savor and poured out there their drink offerings.

29 Then I said to them, What is the shrine to which you go? And its name is called Shrine of Idols to this day.

30 Wherefore say to the house of Israel, Thus says the LORD God: You have defiled yourselves after the manner of your fathers and you go astray after their idols;

31 And you offer your gift offerings and make your sons to pass through the fire; you have polluted yourselves with your idols, even to this day; and yet you wish to inquire of me, O house of Israel? As I live, says the LORD God, I will not give you an answer.

32 And that which is in your mind shall not come to pass at all, for you say, We will be like the Gentiles and like the families of the earth, to serve wood and stones.

33 ¶As I live, says the LORD God, surely with a strong hand and with a stretched out arm and with fury poured out will I rule over you.

34 And I will bring you out from the Gentiles, and will gather you out of the countries wherein you are scattered, with a mighty hand and with a stretched out arm and with a fury poured out.

35 And I will bring you into the wilderness of the Gentiles, and there will I judge you face to face.

36 Just as I pleaded with your fathers in the wilderness of the land of Egypt, so will I plead with you, says the LORD God.

37 And I will cause you to be subject to my scepter, and will bring you into the discipline of the covenant;

38 And I will purge out from among you the rebels and those who transgress against me; I will bring them forth out of the land where they sojourn, and they shall not enter into the land of Israel; and you shall know that I am the LORD.

39 As for you, O house of Israel, thus says the LORD God: If you will not hearken to me, go then and serve every one his own idols, but pollute not my holy name any more with your gift offerings and with your idols.

40 For on my holy mountain, even in the mountain height of Israel, says the LORD God, there shall all the house of Israel serve me perfectly; there will I be pleased with them, and there will I require their offerings and the first fruits of their harvest and the choicest of their gift offerings with all their holy things.

41 I will accept you with a sweet savor, when I bring you out from among the Gentiles and gather you out of the cities wherein you have been scattered; and I will be sanctified in you in the sight of the Gentiles.

42 And you shall know that I am the LORD, when I shall bring you into the land of Israel, into the country which I swore to give to your fathers.

43 And there you shall remember your ways and all your doings by which you have been defiled; and you shall loathe yourselves in your own sight for all the evils that you have committed.

44 And you shall know that I am the LORD who had pity upon you for my name's sake, not according to your evil ways nor according to your corrupt doings, O house of Israel, says the LORD God.

45 ¶Moreover the word of the LORD came unto me, saying,

46 Son of man, set your face toward the south, and look southward and prophesy against the forest which is in the south;

47 And say to the forest which is in the south, Hear the word of the LORD; Thus says the LORD God: Behold, I will kindle a fire in you, and it shall devour every green tree in you and every dry tree; the flaming fire shall not be quenched, and all faces from the south to the north shall be burned in it.

48 And all flesh shall see that I the LORD have kindled it; it shall not be quenched.

49 Then said I, Ah LORD God! Behold, they will say to me, You speak in parables.

CHAPTER 21

AND the word of the LORD came to me, saying,

2 Son of man, set your face toward Jerusalem and look at their holy places, and prophesy against the land of Israel.

3 And say to the land of Israel, Thus says the LORD God: Behold, I am against you; I will draw my sword

out of its sheath and will destroy from you the righteous and the sinner.

4 Seeing then that I will destroy from you the righteous and the sinner, therefore my sword shall go forth out of its sheath against all flesh from the south to the north,

5 That all flesh may know that I the LORD have drawn forth my sword out of its sheath; it shall not return any more.

6 And as for you, O Son of man, sigh with a broken heart, and with bitterness groan before their eyes.

7 And if they should say to you, Why do you sigh? you shall say to them, Because of news of disaster which is coming; and every heart shall melt and all hands shall be feeble and every spirit shall faint and all knees shall be weary; behold, it is coming and it shall be brought to pass, says the LORD God.

8 ¶Again the word of the LORD came to me, saying,

9 Son of man, prophesy, and say, Thus says the LORD God: A sword, a sword is sharpened;

10 It is sharpened to make a sore slaughter; it is burnished that it may glitter; and it is sharpened to cut off the family of my son; and to reject every other branch.

11 I have given it to be burnished, that it may be handled; the sword is sharpened and polished to deliver it into the hand of the slayer.

12 Cry and wail, Son of man; for it is against my people and against all the princes of Israel;

13 Clap your hands because this calamity is justified; if the royal family is rejected, it shall be no more, says the LORD God.

14 You therefore, Son of man, prophesy and clap your hands, and let the sword smite double, and the third stroke is the stroke of the slain; this is the sword for a great slaughter that causes them to tremble,

15 That their hearts may faint and the sufferers be multiplied in all their gates, for I have delivered them to the sword which is sharpened, glittering and drawn for the slaughter.

16 Take hold firmly my right hand, take hold firmly my left hand, wherever my face is turned;

17 I will also clap my hands, and I will cause my fury to rest; I the LORD have said it.

18 ¶The word of the LORD came to me, saying,

19 Also, Son of man, prepare for yourself two ways that the sword of the king of Babylon may come; both of them shall come forth out of the same land; and set a sign at the head of the highway to the choicest city.

20 And prepare a way, that the sword may come to Rabbath of the Ammonites, and to Judah and to Jerusalem, the mighty city.

21 For the king of Babylon stands at the parting of the way, at the head of the two ways, to use divination; he shoots an arrow, he inquires of his idol, he sees his triumph.

22 At his right hand was the divination against Jerusalem, saying to build mounds against her, to open his mouth threatening with all his strength, to lift up his voice with shouting, to set battering rams against the gates, to cast a mount, and to build siege forts.

23 And it shall be as a false divination to them; but he will call to remembrance their iniquity, that they may be captured.

24 Therefore thus says the LORD God: Because you have made your iniquity to be remembered clearly and your transgressions are uncovered so that in all your devices your sins are evident, therefore, with the hand shall you be caught.

25 ¶And as for you, filthy wicked prince of Israel, your day and the time of your iniquity and your end has come.

26 Thus says the LORD God: Remove the diadem and take off the crown; the low is exalted, and the proud is brought down.

27 Even this place I will cause to be a ruin; until he comes to whom it belongs by right, and I will deliver it to him.

28 ¶And you, Son of man, proph-

esy and say, Thus says the LORD God concerning the Ammonites and concerning their reproach: even say, The sword, the sword is drawn for the slaughter; it is sharpened and it glitters;

29 Because of your false vision and because of your false divination, to bring you upon the necks of the sinful and wicked men, whose day has come and the time of their iniquity and their end.

30 Return the sword to its sheath! for in the land wherein you were born, there will I judge you.

31 And I will pour out my indignation upon you; I will blow against you with the fire of my wrath, and I will deliver you into the hand of men brutish and skilful to destroy.

32 You shall be fuel for the fire; your blood shall be in the midst of the land; you shall be no more remembered; for I the LORD have spoken it.

CHAPTER 22

MOREOVER the word of the LORD came to me, saying,

2 Now, Son of man, judge the bloody city and declare to her all her abominations;

3 Then say, Thus says the LORD God: The city where blood is shed in the midst, her time has come, and the city that makes idols in the midst of her has defiled herself.

4 You have become guilty in the blood which you have shed, and have defiled yourself by the idols which you have made; now your days have drawn near, and the time of your years has come; therefore I have made you a reproach to the Gentiles and a derision to all cities.

5 Those that are near and those that are far from you shall mock you and shall say, O you filthy one, infamous and full of iniquity.

6 Behold, the princes of Israel, every one according to his own tribe, were in you to shed blood.

7 In you have they cursed father and mother; in the midst of you have they oppressed the proselytes; in you

have they wronged the fatherless and the widows.

8 You have despised my holy things and have profaned my sabbaths.

9 In you were merchants to shed blood, and in you have they eaten sacrifices upon the mountains; in the midst of you they committed lewdness.

10 In you have they uncovered the nakedness of their fathers' concubines; in you have they lain with menstruous women.

11 And one has committed abomination with his neighbor's wife; and another has lewdly defiled his daughter-in-law in committing adultery with her; and another in you has defiled his sister, his father's daughter.

12 In you have they taken bribes to shed blood; in you have they taken usury and exorbitant gains, and they have deceived their friends by extortion; and you have forgotten me, says the LORD God.

13 ¶Behold, therefore I will strike my hands together with anger because of the iniquity which you have done and because of the blood which has been shed in the midst of you.

14 Can your heart endure, or can your hands be strong, in the days that I deal with you? I the LORD have spoken it and will do it.

15 And I will scatter you among the Gentiles and disperse you in the countries.

16 And I will chastise you in the sight of the Gentiles, and you shall know that I am the LORD.

17 And the word of the LORD came to me, saying,

18 Son of man, the house of Israel is to me become dross; all they are like brass and like tin, and like iron and lead in the midst of the furnace when they are mixed with silver.

19 Therefore thus says the LORD God: Because you have all become mixed together, behold, therefore I will gather you in the midst of Jerusalem.

20 As they gather silver and brass and iron and tin and lead into the

midst of the furnace, and blow the fire upon it to melt it; so will I gather you in my anger, and in my fury will I melt you.

21 Yea, I will blow upon you the fire of my anger, and I will cause you to melt in the midst of it.

22 As silver is melted in the midst of the furnace, so shall you be melted in the midst of it; and you shall know that I the LORD have poured out my fury upon you.

23 ¶And the word of the LORD came to me, saying,

24 Son of man, say to her, You are the land that is not cleansed, and have refused to receive moisture, nor has rain come down upon you.

25 Her prophets in the midst of her have conspired; they are like a lion that roars and tears the prey; they have devoured lives with their might; they have taken the precious things of their palaces.

26 Her priests have violated my law and have profaned my holy things; they have put no difference between the holy and the profane, neither have they distinguished between the unclean and the clean, and have refused to keep my sabbaths, and I am profaned among them.

27 Her princes in the midst of her are like wolves tearing the prey, to shed blood and to destroy lives, to get dishonest gain.

28 And her prophets have daubed her walls with untempered mortar which will fall off, seeing for them visions of falsehood, and divining lies to them, saying, Thus says the LORD, when the LORD has not spoken.

29 They have oppressed the people of the land and humiliated them; and have extorted from the poor and needy; yea, they have oppressed wrongfully the proselyte.

30 And I sought for a man among them who would build up the fence and stand in the gap before me for the sake of the land, that I should not destroy it; but I found none.

31 Therefore have I poured out my indignation upon them; I have consumed them with the fire of my wrath; their own ways have I recompensed upon their heads, says the LORD God.

CHAPTER 23

THE word of the LORD came to me, saying,

2 Son of man, there were two women, the daughters of one mother;

3 And they committed whoredom in Egypt in their youth; there were their breasts fondled, there was their virginity broken.

4 And the name of the elder was Ahlah, and the name of the younger was Ahlibah; and they were mine, and they bore sons and daughters. Thus were their names: Samaria is Ahlah and Jerusalem is Ahlibah.

5 And Ahlah played the harlot when she was mine; and she doted on her lovers, on the Assyrians her neighbors,

6 Who were clothed with blue, lords and captains, desirable young men, all of them horsemen riding on horses.

7 Thus she committed her whoredoms with them, with all the chosen men of Assyria and with all on whom she doted; with all their idols she defiled herself.

8 Neither did she leave the whoredoms which she had committed in Egypt; for in her youth they defiled her and they broke her virginity and poured out their whoredom upon her.

9 Therefore I have delivered her into the hands of her lovers, into the hand of the Assyrians, upon whom she doted.

10 These uncovered her nakedness; they carried away her sons and daughters, and slew her with the sword; and she became a byword among women; for her paramours had executed judgment upon her.

11 And when her sister Ahlibah saw this, she was more corrupt in her excessive lust than she, and her whoredoms were more than the whoredoms of her sister.

12 She doted upon the Assyrians her neighbors, lords and captains clothed with blue, horsemen riding on horses, all of them desirable young men.

13 Then I saw that the ways of both of them were defiled.

14 And they added to their whoredoms; for when they saw men portrayed upon the wall, the images of the Chaldeans portrayed in vermilion,

15 Girded with girdles upon their loins and with turbans tied on their heads, all of them handsome men to look at, the likeness of the sons of Babylon and of the land of the Chaldeans, the land of their nativity;

16 As soon as she saw them with her eyes, she doted upon them, and sent messengers to them to the land of the Chaldeans,

17 And the Babylonians came to her into the bed of love, and they defiled her with their whoredom, and she was polluted by them; then her soul abhorred them.

18 So she exposed her fornications and uncovered her nakedness; then my soul abhorred her just as my soul abhorred her sister.

19 Yet she multiplied her whoredoms, remembering the days of her youth in which she played the harlot in the land of Egypt;

20 For she doted upon their servants, whose male organs are like those of asses, and whose privates are like those of horses.

21 Thus you have missed the wickedness of your youth, when your virginity was broken in Egypt, and the breasts of your youth were fondled.

22 ¶Therefore, O Ahlibah, thus says the LORD God: Behold, I will stir up your lovers against you, the lovers whom your soul has abhorred, and I will bring them against you.

23 And the Babylonians and the Chaldeans shall surround you, Pod Lod, and Koa, and all the Assyrians with them; all of them desirable young men, lords and captains, all renowned men, all of them riding on horses.

24 And they shall come against you well armed with chariots, wagons, and with a host of people, who shall set against you with spears, bucklers, shields, and helmets round about; and I will set judgment before them, and they shall judge you according to their judgments.

25 And I will set my indignation against you, and they shall crush your nose with fury and shall pluck out your ears; and your remnant shall fall by the sword; they shall carry away your sons and your daughters; and your residue shall be devoured by fire,

26 They shall also strip you of your clothes and take away your costly jewels.

27 Thus I will nullify your counsel and the whoredom which you brought from the land of Egypt, so that you shall not lift up your eyes to them, nor remember Egypt any more.

28 For thus says the LORD God: Behold, I will deliver you into the hands of those whom you hate, into the hands of the Assyrians whom your soul abhorred;

29 And they shall deal with you with hate, and shall take away all your labor, and shall leave you naked and bare, and the nakedness of your whoredoms and your iniquities shall be uncovered.

30 These things were done to you because of your whoredom, for you have played the harlot with the Gentiles and polluted yourself with their idols.

31 And because you have walked in the ways of your sister; therefore I will give her cup into your hands.

32 Thus says the LORD God: You shall drink your sister's cup deep and large; you shall become a laughingstock, and be ridiculed and scorned; for it contains much.

33 You shall be filled with drunkenness and sorrow, with the cup of horror and desolation, with the cup of your sister Samaria.

34 Then you shall even drink it and drain it out, and you shall cut off your hair and tear your breasts; for I have spoken it, says the LORD God.

35 Therefore thus says the LORD God: Because you have forgotten me and cast me off behind your idols,

therefore you also shall bear your lewdness and your whoredoms.

36 ¶The LORD said to me, Son of man, now you can judge Ahlah and Ahlibah, and declare to them their abominations;

37 For they have committed adultery, and blood is on their hands, and with their idols they have committed adultery and have also caused their sons, whom they bore to me, to be consumed in the fire.

38 Moreover this they have done to me: they have defiled my sanctuary in the same day and have profaned my sabbaths;

39 For when they had slain their children to their idols, they came the same day into my sanctuary and profaned it; and, lo, thus have they done in the midst of my house.

40 Also they sent for men who came from afar, to whom they had sent messengers; and, lo, as soon as they arrived, they bathed and painted their eyes, and adorned themselves with ornaments.

41 Then they sat on stately beds, and tables were prepared before them, and my oil and my incense were wasted on them.

42 And the sound of their merrymaking could be heard everywhere, and the voices of men who had come from Sheba and from the desert, who put bracelets upon their wrists, and beautiful crowns upon their heads.

43 Then I said, With these men have they played the harlot and committed the acts of harlots.

44 And they went in to them as to a woman who plays the harlot; so went they in to Ahlah and to Ahlibah, the harlots.

45 ¶And the righteous men shall judge them with the judgment of adulteresses and the judgment of those who shed blood, because they are adulteresses, and blood is on their hands.

46 For thus says the LORD God, I will bring up a multitude against them, and will give them over to terror and spoil.

47 And the multitude shall stone them with stones and thrust them

through with their swords; they shall slay their sons and their daughters and burn their houses with fire.

48 Thus will I put an end to lewdness from the land, that all women may be taught not to do after your whoredom.

49 And I will recompense your lewdness upon you, and you shall bear the sins of your idols; and you shall know that I am the LORD God.

CHAPTER 24

IN the ninth year, in the tenth month, on the tenth day of the month, the word of the LORD came to me, saying,

2 Son of man, write down the name of this day, for on this very day the king of Babylon has set himself against Jerusalem.

3 And devise a parable concerning the rebellious house, and say to them, Thus says the LORD God: Set a pot on the fire and pour water into it;

4 And put into it pieces of meat which are good and fat, a shoulder whose bone is broken from the choicest of the flock.

5 And burn also the bones under the pot, and make it boil well, and let the bones seethe in it.

6 ¶Therefore thus says the LORD God: Woe to the bloody city, in which the pot is set on the fire, and whose iniquity has not gone out of it! Cut her piece by piece, so destroyed that no one would divide her by lot.

7 For the blood is still in the midst of her; she splashed it upon the rock; she poured it not upon the ground to cover it with dust,

8 That it might cause my fury to come up, to take vengeance; I have set her blood on the top of a smooth rock, that it should not be covered.

9 Therefore, thus says the LORD God: Woe to the bloody city! I will even enlarge the fireplace and increase the fuel,

10 And I will kindle the fire, and the flesh shall be cooked and seethe, and the bones shall be burned.

11 Then set the pot empty upon the coals, that it may become hot and that its brass may melt and the filthi-

ness of it may be melted in it and that the scum of it may be consumed.

12 She has become like rotten figs, and her great iniquities have not gone out of her; her vengeance shall be in the fire.

13 Because you have polluted yourself with lewdness, and because I have cleansed you and you were not cleansed from your filthiness, you shall not be cleansed any more till I have caused my fury to rest upon you.

14 I the Lord have spoken it; it shall come to pass and I will do it; I will not have pity, neither will I spare nor will I have mercy; but I will judge you according to your ways; and according to your doings, shall I judge you, says the Lord God.

15 ¶And the word of the Lord came to me, saying,

16 Son of man, behold, I take away from you the desire of your eyes with a stroke; and you shall neither mourn nor weep, neither shall your tears run down.

17 Forbear to cry, make no mourning for the dead, put on your robe and put shoes on your feet; and do not cover your lips nor eat the bread provided for you.[1]

18 So I spoke of it to the people in the morning, and at evening my wife died; and in the morning of the next day I did as I had been commanded.

19 ¶And the people said to me, Will you not tell us the meaning of these strange things which you do?

20 Then I said to them, This is the word of the Lord which came to me, saying,

21 Speak to the house of Israel, Thus says the Lord God: Behold, I will allow my sanctuary to be profaned, the excellency of your strength, the desire of your eyes, the cleanser of your souls; and your sons and your daughters whom you leave behind shall fall by the sword.

22 And you shall do as I have done; you shall not cover your lips nor shall you eat the bread provided for mourners.

23 And your hair shall not be cut,

and your shoes shall be on your feet; you shall not mourn nor weep; but you shall pine away in your iniquities and shall try to comfort one another.

24 Thus Ezekiel shall be to you for a sign; according to all that he has done shall you do; and you shall know that I am the Lord God.

25 But you, O Son of man, on the day when I take away from them their strength, the joy of their glory, the desire of their eyes, and the cleanser of their souls, their sons and their daughters,

26 On that day a survivor shall come to you and cause you to hear it with your ears;

27 And on that day the survivor shall open your mouth, and you shall speak and be no more dumb; and you shall be a sign to them; and they shall know that I am the Lord.

CHAPTER 25

THE word of the Lord came to me, saying,

2 Son of man, set your face toward the Ammonites and prophesy against them;

3 And say to the Ammonites, Hear the word of the Lord God: Thus says the Lord God: Because you said, Aha, against my sanctuary when it was profaned, and against the land of Israel when it was laid waste, and over the house of Judah when they went into captivity;

4 Behold, therefore I will deliver you to the men of the east for a possession, and their army shall dwell in you and pitch their tents in you; they shall eat your fruit and they shall drink your milk.

5 And I will make Rabbath a stable for camels, and the Ammonites a fold for flocks, and you shall know that I am the Lord.

6 For thus says the Lord God: Because you have clapped your hands and stamped with your feet and rejoiced in yourself against the land of Israel;

7 Therefore, thus says the Lord God: I will stretch out my hand

---

[1] In the East mourners do not bake bread or cook. Food is brought to them by their sympathetic neighbors.

against you and will deliver you for a spoil to the nations; and I will cut you off from among the people, and I will destroy you out of the cities, and will make you desolate, and you shall know that I am the LORD.

8 ¶Thus says the LORD God: Because Moab and Seir have said, Behold, the house of Judah is dispersed among all the nations;

9 Therefore, behold, I will make a breach in Moab at the cities, at his royal city, at the towns round about him, the glory of the country of Beth-ashimon, Baal-meon, and Koriath-aim,

10 And I will give them, together with the Ammonites, to the men of the east as a possession, so that Rabbath of the Ammonites may not be remembered among the nations.

11 And I will execute judgment upon Moab; and they shall know that I am the LORD.

12 ¶Thus says the LORD God: Because Edom has dealt against the house of Judah by taking vengeance, and had ill-will toward them and envied them;

13 Therefore thus says the LORD God: Behold, I will stretch out my hand against Edom, and will destroy both man and beast from it; and I will make it desolate from Teman to Deran; and they shall fall by the sword.

14 And I will lay my vengeance upon Edom by the hand of my people Israel; and they shall avenge themselves from Edom according to my anger and my fury; and they shall know my vengeance, says the LORD God.

15 ¶Thus says the LORD God: Because the Philistines have taken vengeance, and have revenged themselves with satisfaction of their heart, thus destroying the friendship of old;

16 Therefore thus says the LORD God: Behold, I will stretch out my hand against the Philistines, and I will destroy Crete and lay waste the remnant of the seacoast.

17 And I will execute my great vengeance upon them with rebukes and anger; and they shall know that I am the LORD when I have executed my vengeance upon them.

CHAPTER 26

AND it came to pass in the eleventh year, on the first day of the month, the word of the LORD came to me, saying,

2 Son of man, because Tyre has said against Jerusalem, Aha, the gates of the people are broken; the people have turned to me; I shall be enriched, now that she is destroyed and is laid waste.

3 Therefore thus says the LORD God: Behold, I am against you, O Tyre, and will cause many nations to come up against you, as the sea causes its waves to come up.

4 And they shall destroy the walls of Tyre and demolish her towers, and remove the soil from her; and I will make her like a bare rock.

5 It shall be a drying place for nets in the midst of the sea, because I have spoken it, says the LORD God; and it shall become a spoil to the nations.

6 And her daughters who are in the field shall be slain by the sword; they shall know that I am the LORD.

7 ¶For thus says the LORD God: Behold, I will bring upon Tyre Nebuchadnezzar, king of Babylon, king of kings, from the north with horses and with chariots and with horsemen and a multitude and much people.

8 He shall slay with the sword your daughters who are in the field; and he shall set up forts against you and cast a mount against you and lift up the buckler against you.

9 And he shall strike the sharp points of his spears against your walls, and he shall destroy your towers with his swords.

10 By reason of the abundance of his horses, their dust shall cover you; your walls shall shake at the noise of his horsemen and of the wheels and of the chariots, when he shall enter your gates as men enter into a city in which is made a breach.

11 With the hoofs of his horses he shall tread down all your streets; he shall slay your people by the sword,

and your mighty altars shall he demolish to the ground.

12 And his army shall plunder your riches and make a prey of your merchandise; and they shall demolish your walls and destroy your pleasant houses; and they shall cast your stones and your timber and your wealth into the sea.

13 And I will cause the noise of the multitude of your songs to cease; and the sound of your harpers shall be heard no more.

14 And I will make you a bare rock, a drying place for nets; you shall be built no more: for I the LORD have spoken it, says the LORD God.

15 ¶Thus says the LORD God to Tyre: At the sound of your fall and of the torment of your slain and the slaughter which is made in the midst of you, the islands shall tremble.

16 Then all the princes of the sea shall come down from their thrones and lay away their robes and put off their embroidered garments; they shall clothe themselves with trembling; they shall sit upon the ground, and shall tremble and become restless, and be astonished at you.

17 And they shall take up lamentations over you, and say to you, How you are destroyed, O you inhabitant of the seas, O fortified city, which was strong in the sea, she and her inhabitants, who caused their terror to be on all the inhabitants thereof!

18 Now shall the isles tremble in the day of your fall; yea, the isles that are in the sea shall be troubled in the day of your fall.

19 For thus says the LORD God to Tyre: When I shall make you a desolate city, like the cities that are not inhabited; when I shall bring up the deep upon you, and great waters shall cover you;

20 When I shall bring you down with those who descend into the grave, with the people of old time, and shall set you in the lowest parts of the earth, in places desolate of old, with those that go down into the pit, that you be not inhabited; and I will not cause your resurrection in the land of the living:

21 I will give you to destruction, you will be sought for, yet you will not be found again for ever, says the LORD God.

CHAPTER 27

THE word of the LORD came to me, saying,

2 Now, Son of man, make a lamentation over Tyre;

3 And say to Tyre, O you that are situated at the entry of the sea, the trading center of the people and of many islands, Thus says the LORD God: O Tyre, you have said, I am the crown of beauty.

4 Your borders are in the midst of the seas, your builders have perfected your beauty.

5 They have brought you timber of fir trees from Senir for your ships; they have taken cedars from Lebanon to make masts for you.

6 Of the oaks of Bashan have they made your oars; they have made your benches of ivory brought from the isles of China.

7 Fine linen with embroidered work brought from Egypt was made for your sails; blue and purple they brought you from the islands of Alis for your covering.

8 The inhabitants of Zidon and Arwad were your mariners; your wise men, O Tyre, were your pilots.

9 The elders of Gebal and the wise men thereof were your caulkers; all the ships of the sea with their mariners were in your harbors.

10 The Persians, the Lydians, and the men of Put, all valiant men, were in your army; they hung the shields and the helmets in you; they were your glory.

11 The men of Arwad with your army manned your fortified walls and guarded your towers; they hung their shields upon your walls round about; they made your beauty perfect.

12 Tarshish was your market place by reason of the abundance and variety of your wealth: silver, iron, tin, and lead they brought in to you for sale.

13 Javan, Tubal, and Meshech were your merchants; they traded with you

in slaves and vessels of brass in your markets.

14 They of the house of Togarmah traded in your markets with horses and horsemen and mules.

15 The men of Deran were your merchants; many islands were the markets for the products of your hands; they brought you for presents horns of ivory for ointment, and frankincense.

16 Edom was your market place by reason of many of your products: your purple, fine linen, embroidered work, purple robes, bracelets, and agate.

17 Judah and the land of Israel, they were your merchants; they traded in your markets wheat, rice, millet, honey, oil, and balsam.

18 Damascus was your market place in the multitude of your products and your wealth; she traded with good wine and white wool.

19 Dan and Javan brought you merchandise to your markets from Usal, their iron ore, cassia, and cane.

20 Deran was your market place; her merchants brought you the choicest cattle.

21 They also brought you rams, lambs, and kids.

22 The merchants of Sheba and Raamah brought to your markets their best spices and precious stones and gold.

23 Haran and Canneh and Eden, the merchants of Sheba and Assyria, were your merchants.

24 These were your merchants, who brought you blue clothes and embroidered work and precious riches, which were wrapped up and bound with cords and laden in ships made of cedar.

25 The men of Tarshish who dwell west of you brought you loads of merchandise, and you were filled and became exceedingly strong.

26 ¶Your rowers have brought you into great waters; the east wind has broken you in the midst of the seas.

27 Your riches and your merchandise and your fairs, all your chosen warriors, your mariners and your pilots, your caulkers and the handlers of your merchandise and all your men of war and all the multitude of people who are in you shall fall in the midst of the seas in the day of your ruin.

28 Those who dwell round about you shall tremble at the sound of the wailing of your pilots.

29 And all that handle the oar, the mariners and all the pilots of the sea, shall come down from their ships, they shall stand on the shore,

30 And they shall lament over you a great and bitter lamentation and shall cast dust upon their heads and shall wallow in ashes:

31 And they shall shave their heads in mourning over you, and gird themselves with sackcloth, and they shall weep for you with bitterness of heart and bitter wailing.

32 And their sons shall take up lamentations for you and lament over you, saying, Who was like Tyre built in the midst of the sea?

33 When your wares went forth upon the seas, you filled many nations; you enriched the kings of the earth with the abundance of your riches and of your merchandise.

34 In the time when you shall be broken and sink in the depths of the sea, your merchandise and all your people in the midst of you shall fall.

35 All the inhabitants of the islands shall be astonished at you and their kings shall be sore afraid; tears shall run down their faces.

36 The merchants among the people shall hiss at you; you have become a ruin, and you never shall be any more.

CHAPTER 28

THE word of the LORD came to me, saying,

2 Son of man, say to the king of Tyre, Thus says the LORD God: Because your heart is lifted up and you have said, I am a god, I sit in the seat of God, in the heart of the seas; and yet you are a man, and not God, though you think of your heart as though it were the heart of God;

3 Perhaps you are wiser than Daniel,

or you have seen hidden things by your wisdom;

4 With your understanding you have become powerful, and have gotten silver and gold into your treasures;

5 By your great wisdom and by your trade you have increased your riches, and your heart is lifted up because of your riches;

6 Therefore thus says the Lord God: Because you think of your heart as though it were the heart of God;

7 Behold, therefore I will bring strangers upon you, the mightiest of the nations, and they shall draw their swords against the beauty of your wisdom, and they shall defile your glory.

8 They shall bring you down to ruin, and you shall die the death of those who are slain in the midst of the seas.

9 Perhaps you will still say before those who slay you, I am God. Yet you are but a man, and no God, in the hands of those who slay you.

10 You shall die by the hand of uncircumcised strangers; for I have spoken it, says the Lord God.

11 ¶Moreover the word of the Lord came to me, saying,

12 Son of man, take up a lamentation over the king of Tyre, and say to him, Thus says the Lord God: You were the seal of wisdom and the crown of beauty.

13 You have been in Eden, the garden of God; you were decked with every precious stone, the sardius, the topaz, and the emerald, the beryl, the onyx, and the jasper, the sapphire and pearls; and you have filled your treasuries with gold and your chests with precious stones; you had all of these things from the day you were created.

14 You were with the anointed cherub that shelters; and I have set you on the holy mountain of God; and you were safe in the midst of the stones of fire.

15 You were perfect in your ways, from the day that you were created till iniquity was found in you.

16 By the multitude of your merchandise you have filled your land with iniquity and you have sinned; therefore I will cast you from the mountain of God; and I will destroy you, O sheltering cherub, from the midst of the stones of fire.

17 Since your heart was lifted up because of your beauty, now your wisdom and your beauty are corrupted; I will cast you to the ground before kings, that you may be a spectacle before them.

18 By the multitude of your frauds, by the iniquity of your traffic, you have defiled your sanctuary; therefore I will bring forth a fire from the midst of you, and it shall devour you, and I will reduce you to ashes upon the earth in the sight of all those who see you.

19 All those who know you among the people shall be astonished at you; you shall be brought to destruction, and you never shall be any more.

20 ¶The word of the Lord came to me, saying,

21 Son of man, set your face against Zidon, and prophesy against it,

22 And say, Thus says the Lord God: Behold, I am against you, O Zidon; and I will be glorified in the midst of you; and the people shall know that I am the Lord, when I shall have executed judgments in her and shall be sanctified in her.

23 For I will send her pestilence and blood into her streets; and the wounded shall fall in the midst of her by the sword that is upon her on every side; and they shall know that I am the Lord.

24 ¶And there shall be no more a pricking brier to the house of Israel, nor a thorn [1] to cause them pain from all that are round about them, and that curse them; and they shall know that I am the Lord God.

25 Thus says the Lord God: When I have gathered the house of Israel from the peoples among whom they are scattered, and shall be sanctified by them in the sight of the nations, then shall they dwell in the land which I have given to my servant Jacob.

26 And they shall dwell in it safely, and shall build houses and plant vine-

[1] The enemies of Israel who were a thorn in their flesh.

yards; yea, they shall dwell with confidence after I have executed judgments on all those who hurt them round about them; and they shall know that I am the LORD their God.

CHAPTER 29

IN the tenth year, in the tenth month, on the twelfth day of the month, the word of the LORD came to me, saying,

2 Son of man, set your face against Pharaoh king of Egypt, and prophesy against him and against all Egypt;

3 Speak, and say, Thus says the LORD God: Behold, I am against you, Pharaoh king of Egypt, the great dragon that lies in the midst of the rivers, who says, The river is my own; I have made it for myself.

4 I will put hooks into your jaws, and I will cause the fish of your river to stick to your scales, and I will draw you up out of the midst of your river, and all the fish of your river shall stick to your scales.

5 And I will throw you into the wilderness, you and all the fish of your river; you shall fall upon the open fields; you shall not be gathered nor buried; I have given you for food to the wild beasts and to the fowls of the air.

6 And all the inhabitants of Egypt shall know that I am the LORD, because you have been a staff of reed [1] to the house of Israel.

7 When they held you with their hands, you pierced them; and when they leaned on you, you broke, and made all their loins to tremble.

8 ¶Therefore thus says the LORD God: Behold, I will bring a sword upon you and destroy from you man and beast.

9 And the land of Egypt shall be desolate and waste; and they shall know that I am the LORD, because you have said, The river is mine; I have made it.

10 Therefore I am against you and against your river, and I will make the land of Egypt utterly waste and desolate from the tower of Sona even to the border of Ethiopia.

11 No foot of man shall pass through it, neither foot of beast, nor shall it be inhabited forty years.

12 And I will make the land of Egypt desolate in the midst of the countries that are desolate, and her cities among the cities that are laid waste shall be desolate forty years; and I will scatter the Egyptians among the nations, and I will disperse them through the countries.

13 ¶Yet thus says the LORD God: At the end of forty years I will gather the Egyptians from the peoples among whom they were scattered:

14 And I will bring back the captivity of Egypt, and will cause them to dwell in the land of Pathros, into the land from which they were sold; and they shall be there a humble kingdom.

15 It shall be the humblest of the kingdoms; neither shall it exalt itself any more above the nations; for I will diminish them, that they shall no more rule over the nations.

16 And the Egyptians shall be no more the hope of the house of Israel, bringing their iniquity to remembrance, because they went after them; and Israel shall know that I am the LORD God.

17 ¶And it came to pass in the twenty-seventh year, in the first month, on the first day of the month, the word of the LORD came to me, saying,

18 Son of man, Nebuchadnezzar king of Babylon subjected all his army to many hardships against Tyre till every head was made bald and every shoulder weary; yet neither he nor his army received wages from Tyre for the service that he had performed against her;

19 Therefore, thus says the LORD God: Behold, I will give the land of Egypt to Nebuchadnezzar king of Babylon; and he shall take her wealth, carry away captives, and plunder her; and it shall be the wages for his army.

20 I have given him the land of Egypt for the labor with which he served against Tyre, says the LORD God.

[1] A weak ally.

21 ¶On that day I will cause the horn of the house of Israel to bud forth, and I will open your mouth among them; and they shall know that I am the LORD.

CHAPTER 30

THE word of the LORD came to me, saying,

2 Son of man, prophesy and say, Thus says the LORD God: Howl and cry, Oh, for the day!

3 For the day is near, even the day of the LORD is near; a cloudy day; a time of reckoning for the nations.

4 And the sword shall come upon Egypt, and great terror shall be in Ethiopia, when the slain shall fall in Egypt, and they shall take away her wealth, and her foundations shall be uprooted.

5 Ethiopians, Putians and Lybians and all Arabia and Chub and the men of the land that is in league with them shall fall with them by the sword.

6 Thus says the LORD God: Those also who help Egypt shall fall; and the strength of her greatness shall be broken; from the tower of Sona shall they fall in it by the sword, says the LORD God.

7 And they shall be desolate in the midst of the countries that are desolate, and her cities shall be in the midst of the cities that lie waste.

8 And they shall know that I am the LORD, when I have kindled a fire in Egypt and all her helpers are defeated.

9 On that day shall messengers go forth from me in haste to destroy Ethiopia which dwells in tranquillity, and there shall be confusion among them on the day of Egypt; for lo, it is coming.

10 Thus says the LORD God: I will also deliver the wealth of Egypt into the hand of Nebuchadnezzar king of Babylon.

11 Even to him and to the mighty men that are with him, who are coming to destroy the land; and they shall draw their swords against Egypt and fill the land with the slain.

12 And I will make the rivers dry, and deliver the land into the hand of the wicked; and I will lay the land waste, and all that is therein, by the hand of the strangers; I the LORD have spoken it.

13 Thus says the LORD God: I will also destroy the idols, and I will make an end to the images out of Memphis; and there shall be no more a prince in the land of Egypt.

14 And I will make Pathros desolate, and will set fire in Zoan, and will execute judgment in No.

15 And I will pour out my fury upon Seen, the strength of Egypt; and I will destroy the riches of No.

16 And I will set fire in Egypt; Seen shall be terrified, and No shall be breached, and Memphis shall fall.

17 The young men of Mapibest shall be weak, and they shall fall by the sword; and the remnant shall go into captivity.

18 And in Tahpanhes also the day shall be darkened, when I shall break there the sceptre of Egypt; and the pomp of her strength shall cease from her, a cloud shall cover her, and her daughters shall go into captivity.

19 Thus will I execute judgment in Egypt; and they shall know that I am the LORD.

20 ¶In the eleventh year, in the first month, on the seventh day of the month, the word of the LORD came to me, saying,

21 Son of man, I have broken the arm of Pharaoh king of Egypt; and, lo, it shall not be bound up to be healed, neither shall it be treated with ointment nor shall it be bound, and shall not heal so that he may hold the sword.

22 Therefore, thus says the LORD God: Behold, I am against Pharaoh king of Egypt, and I will break his strong arms, and I will cause the sword to fall from his hands.

23 And I will scatter the Egyptians among the nations and will disperse them through the countries.

24 And I will strengthen the arms of the king of Babylon and put my sword into his hands; and he shall cut off Pharaoh's arms, and Pharaoh

shall groan before him with the groanings of a mortally wounded man.

25 And I will strengthen the arms of the king of Babylon, and the arms of Pharaoh shall fall down; and they shall know that I am the LORD, when I shall put my sword into the hands of the king of Babylon, and he will draw it out against the land of Egypt.

26 And I will scatter the Egyptians among the nations and disperse them among the countries; and they shall know that I am the LORD.

CHAPTER 31

AND it came to pass in the eleventh year, in the third month, on the first day of the month, that the word of the LORD came to me, saying,

2 Son of man, speak to Pharaoh king of Egypt and to his armed forces: To whom do you liken yourself in your greatness?

3 ¶Behold, the Assyrian was like a cedar in Lebanon with fair branches giving a thick shade and of a high stature; and its top was among the thick boughs.

4 The waters made it grow, the deep made it to grow high, the rivers running round about its plants, and sent forth its branches over all the trees of the field.

5 Therefore its height was exalted above all the trees of the field, and its branches were multiplied, and its boughs became long because of many waters which caused it to grow.

6 All the fowls of the air made their nests in its boughs, and under its branches did all the beasts of the field bring forth their young, and under its shadow dwelt all great nations.

7 Thus was it beautiful in its greatness and in the multitude of its branches; for its roots were by the great waters.

8 The cedars in the garden of God could not surpass it; the fir trees did not equal its boughs; the plane trees were not like its branches; nor was any tree in the garden of God like to it in its beauty.

9 I made it beautiful by the multitude of its branches; so that all the trees of Eden that were in the garden of God envied it.

10 ¶Therefore thus says the LORD God: Because it has exalted itself and has shot up its top among the thick boughs and its heart is haughty because of its height,

11 I have therefore delivered it into the hand of the mighty one of the nations; he shall surely deal with it according to its sin; and he shall destroy it.

12 And foreigners, the most powerful of the nations shall destroy it, and leave it upon the mountains, and its branches shall fall in all the valleys, and its boughs shall be broken by all the rivers of the land; and all the people of the earth shall go down from its shadow, [1] and leave it alone.

13 And when it falls, all the fowls of the air shall alight upon it and all the beasts of the field shall be under its branches,

14 To the end that none of all the trees by the waters may exalt themselves for their height, neither shoot up their tops among the thick boughs, nor shall any of them stand up in their height like it, all that are planted by the water; for they are all delivered to death, to the nether parts of the earth, in the midst of the children of men who go down into the pit.

15 Thus says the LORD God: On the day when it went down to Sheol, I caused a mourning; I covered the deep for it and I restrained its rivers, and the great waters were stayed; and I caused Lebanon to mourn for it, and all the trees of the field trembled for it.

16 The earth trembled at the sound of its fall, when I brought it down to Sheol with those who go down into the pit; and all the trees of Eden, the choice and the best of Lebanon, all that drink water, were comforted in the nether parts of the earth.

17 They also went down to Sheol with it to those who are slain by the sword; and its posterity dwelt under its shadow among the nations.

18 ¶To whom are you thus like in glory and greatness among the trees

[1] Protection.

of Eden? Yet you were brought down with the trees of Eden to the nether parts of the earth; you shall lie among the uncircumcised with those that are slain by the sword. This is the fate of Pharaoh and all his army, says the Lord God.

CHAPTER 32

AND it came to pass in the eleventh year, in the twelfth month, on the first day of the month, that the word of the Lord came to me, saying,

2 Son of man, make a lamentation for Pharaoh king of Egypt and say to him, You are like a lion among the nations and you are like a sea monster; you come forth in your rivers, and trouble the waters with your feet and foul their rivers.

3 Thus says the Lord God: I will therefore spread out my net over you with a multitude of many people; and they shall bring you up in my net.

4 Then I will cast you out upon the land; I will cast you forth upon the open field, and will cause all the fowls of the air to alight upon you and will fill the wild beasts of the whole earth with you.

5 And I will scatter your flesh upon the mountains, and fill the valleys with your dust;

6 I will also drench the land of your seers with your blood, and the mountains and the valleys shall be filled with your flesh.

7 And when I shall put the light out of you, I will cover the heavens and make the stars thereof dark; the sun shall be covered with clouds, and the moon shall not give her light.

8 All the luminaries which give light in heaven will I make dark over you, and set darkness upon the land, says the Lord God.

9 I will also vex the hearts of many people when I bring the news of your destruction among the nations, into the cities which you have not known.

10 Yea, I will make many peoples aghast at you, and their kings shall be terrified because of you, when I brandish my sword in their presence; and they shall tremble and be alarmed, every man for his own life, on the day of your fall.

11 ¶For thus says the Lord God: The sword of Babylon shall come upon you.

12 By the sword of mighty men will I cause your might to fall, and with the sword of all the mighty men of the nations; and they shall spoil the strength of Egypt, and all its wealth shall be plundered.

13 I will also destroy its cattle from beside the great waters; neither shall the foot of man trouble them any more, nor the hoof of cattle trouble them.

14 Then I will make their waters clear, and cause their rivers to run smooth like oil, says the Lord God.

15 When I have made the land of Egypt desolate, the land shall be destitute in its fullness; when I shall smite all its inhabitants, they shall know that I am the Lord.

16 This is the lamentation with which they shall lament her; the daughters of the nations shall lament over Egypt; and over all her wealth shall they lament, says the Lord God.

17 ¶It came to pass in the eleventh year, in the fifteenth day of the month, that the Lord came to me, saying,

18 Son of man, make a lamentation over the army of Egypt, and cast down her people among the strong nations into the nether parts of the earth, with those who go down into the pit.

19 Come down from the sweet water, and go down to sleep with the uncircumcised.

20 They shall fall in the midst of those who are slain by the sword; they shall bring her to ruin, and all her strength.

21 The rulers of the nations shall speak to their young men out of the midst of Sheol; they shall go down, and the uncircumcised shall lie with those who are slain by the sword;

22 Assyria is there and all her people round about her grave; all of them are slain, fallen by the sword.

23 Those whose graves are set in

the sides of the pit and her people are round about her grave; all of them are slain, fallen by the sword, because they caused destruction in the land of the living.

24 Elam is there and all her army round about her grave, all of them slain, fallen by the sword, who went down uncircumcised into the nether parts of the earth, because they caused destruction in the land of the living; and they have borne their shame with those that go down into the pit.

25 They have set her a bed among the slain in the midst of her army; the graves of all the uncircumcised are round about her grave, all slain by the sword; because they caused destruction in the land of the living; they have borne their shame with those that go down into the pit, and they lie among the slain.

26 Meshech is there, and Tubal, and all her host around about their graves; all of them uncircumcised, slain by the sword, because they caused destruction in the land of the living.

27 And they shall lie with the valiant men who are fallen with the uncircumcised, who are gone down into Sheol with their weapons of war; and they have laid their swords under their heads, and their iniquities are upon their bones, because they caused destruction with their might in the land of the living.

28 You also shall sleep among the uncircumcised and shall lie among the slain by the sword.

29 Edom is there, her kings and all her princes, who with their might were laid with those who were slain by the sword; they shall lie with the uncircumcised and with those who go down to the pit.

30 There are princes of the north, all of them and all the Zidonians, who are gone down with those that are slain by the sword, ashamed and fallen from their might; and they lie uncircumcised with those that are slain by the sword, and have borne their shame with those who go down to the pit.

31 Pharaoh shall see them and shall be comforted over all his army slain by the sword, even Pharaoh and all his army, says the LORD God.

32 For I have caused his destruction in the land of the living, and caused him to be laid in the midst of the uncircumcised with those that are slain by the sword, even Pharaoh, he and all his army, says the LORD God.

CHAPTER 33

AND the word of the LORD came to me, saying,

2 Son of man, speak to your own people and say to them, When I bring the sword upon a land, let the people of the land take a man from among them and make him their watchman.

3 And when he sees the sword coming upon them, he shall blow the trumpet and warn the people;

4 Then whosoever hears the sound of the trumpet and does not heed the warning, if the sword should come and take his life away, his blood shall be upon his own head.

5 But if he should take heed, he shall deliver his life.

6 But when the watchman sees the sword coming and does not blow the trumpet and does not warn the people, and the sword comes and takes the life from among them, that life is taken away in his iniquity; but I will require his blood at the watchman's hand.

7 ¶So you, O Son of man, I have set you a watchman to the house of Israel; therefore you shall hear the word from my mouth, you shall warn them from me.

8 When I say to the wicked, O wicked man, you shall surely die; and you do not speak to the wicked man that he may take heed from his evil way, that wicked man shall die in his iniquity; but his blood I will require at your hands.

9 Nevertheless, if you warn the wicked that he may turn from his evil way; and if he does not turn from his evil way, he shall die in his iniquity; but you have delivered your soul.

10 You therefore, O Son of man, say to the house of Israel, Thus have you spoken, saying, Our iniquity and our sins be upon us, and we are pin-

ing away in them; how can we live?

11 Say to them, As I live, says the LORD God, I do not desire the death of the wicked; but that the wicked should turn from his evil way and live; therefore you must repent and turn from your evil ways, and you shall not die, O house of Israel.

12 Therefore, Son of man, say to your own people, The righteousness of the righteous shall not deliver him in the day that he sins; as for the iniquity of the wicked, he shall not fall by it in the day when he turns from his wickedness; neither shall the righteous be able to live because of his righteousness in the day that he sins.

13 When I shall say to the righteous that he shall surely live, and he trusts in his own righteousness and then commits iniquity, all his righteousness which he had done shall not be remembered to him; but for the iniquity which he has committed, he shall die.

14 Again, when I say to the wicked, You shall surely die, and he turns from his sins and does that which is just and right,

15 And he shall restore the pledge which he has taken and return what he has acquired unjustly and walk in the commandments of life, without committing iniquity; he shall surely live, he shall not die.

16 None of his sins which he has committed shall be remembered to him; but by the justice and righteousness which he has done, he shall surely live.

17 ¶Yet your people say, The way of the LORD is not fair; but it is their own ways that are not fair.

18 When a righteous man turns from his righteousness and commits iniquity, he shall die in his iniquity.

19 And when a wicked man turns from his wickedness and does that which is just and right, he shall live thereby.

20 ¶Yet you say, The way of the LORD is not fair; O house of Israel, I will judge every one of you according to his ways.

21 ¶And it came to pass in the eleventh year of our captivity, in the tenth month, on the fifth day of the month, that one who had escaped from Jerusalem came and said to me, The city has been destroyed.

22 Now the hand of the LORD had been upon me in the evening, before he who had escaped came; and had opened my mouth, until he came to me in the morning; and my mouth was opened and I was dumb no more.

23 Then the word of the LORD came to me, saying,

24 Son of man, those who inhabit these waste places of the land of Israel are saying, Abraham was only one man, and yet he inherited the land; but we are many; are we not going to inherit it?

25 Therefore say to them, Thus says the LORD God: Because you eat meat with the blood and lift up your eyes toward your idols and drink blood, do you expect to inherit the land?

26 You rely on your swords, you commit abomination, and you defile every one his neighbor's wife; and do you expect to inherit the land?

27 Say to them, Thus says the LORD God: As I live, all of those who dwell in the waste places shall fall by the sword; and he that is in the open field, I will give to the wild beasts to be devoured, and those who are in the forts and in the caves shall die of the pestilence.

28 For I will lay the land desolate and waste, and the pomp of her strength shall cease; and the mountains of Israel shall be desolate, that none shall pass through.

29 Then shall they know that I am the LORD, when I have laid the land desolate and waste because of their abominations which they have committed.

30 ¶And as for you, O Son of man, your people are gossiping about you by the walls and in the doors of the houses, and speak one to another, every one to his brother, saying, Come and hear what is the word that comes forth from the LORD.

31 And the people come to you and sit before you, and they hear your words, but they will not do them, because their mouths are full of false-

hood and they follow after the thoughts of their own hearts.

32 And, lo, you are to them like a song and like a pleasant voice and like the sweet sound of a harp; for they hear your words, but they do them not.

33 And when your words shall come to pass, then they shall know that you are a prophet among them.

CHAPTER 34

AND the word of the LORD came to me, saying,

2 Son of man, prophesy against the shepherds of Israel. Prophesy and say to them, O shepherds, thus says the LORD God: Woe to the shepherds of Israel who feed them! These shepherds do not feed the flock.

3 You eat the fat and clothe yourselves with the wool and sacrifice the fat ones; but you do not feed the flock.

4 The weak you have not strengthened, and that which was sick you have not healed, and that which was injured you have not bound up, and that which had gone astray you have not brought back, neither have you sought that which was lost; but with violence and with cruelty you have ruled them.

5 And my sheep were scattered because they had no shepherd; and they became food for all the wild beasts of the field.

6 My sheep wandered through all the mountains and upon every high hill; yea, my flock was scattered upon all the face of the earth, and there is no one to search after them nor is there any one to gather them.

7 ¶Therefore, you shepherds, hear the word of the LORD:

8 As I live, says the LORD God, because my flock became a prey and my sheep have become food for all the wild beasts of the field, because there was no shepherd; neither did the shepherds feed my flocks, but the shepherds fed themselves and have not fed my flock;

9 Therefore, O you shepherds, hear the word of the LORD:

10 Thus says the LORD God: Behold, I am against the shepherds; and I will require my flock at their hand, and cause them to cease from feeding my flock again; and I will deliver my sheep from their mouth, that they may not be food for them any more.

11 ¶For thus says the LORD God: Behold, I, even I, will search for my sheep and seek them out.

12 As the shepherd seeks out his flock on the day of violent rain with wind, so will I seek out my sheep, and will gather them from all countries where they have been scattered in the cloudy and dark day.

13 And I will bring them out from the nations and gather them from the countries, and will bring them to their own land; and I will feed them upon the mountains of Israel, in the valleys, and in all the inhabited places of the country.

14 I will feed them in a good pasture, and upon the high mountains of Israel shall be their fold; there shall they lie in a good fold, and on a fat pasture shall they feed upon the mountains of Israel.

15 I myself will feed my sheep and I will cause them to lie down, says the LORD God.

16 I will seek that which was lost and bring back that which was gone astray and bind up that which was injured and strengthen that which was sick; and I will protect the fat and the strong; and I will feed them with justice.

17 And as for you, O my flock, thus says the LORD God: Behold, I will judge between ewe and ewe, and between ram and ram.

18 Is it not enough for you, O shepherds, to feed on good pastures, but you must tread down under your feet the rest of your pasture? And to have drunk water, but you must foul with your feet that which is left?

19 And as for my flock, they feed on that which you have trodden; and they drink that which you have fouled.

20 ¶Therefore thus says the LORD God to them: Behold, I myself will judge between the fat ewe and the lean ewe.

21 Because they have thrust with their sides and shoulders, and pushed all the weak with their horns, till they have scattered them abroad;

22 Therefore I will save my flock, and they shall no more be a prey for them; and I will judge between ewe and ewe and between ram and ram.

23 And I will set up one shepherd over them, and he shall feed them, even my servant David; he shall feed them and shall be their shepherd.

24 And I the LORD will be their God, and my servant David shall be a prince among them;

25 And I will make with them a covenant of peace, and will cause evil beasts [1] to cease from the land; and they shall dwell safely in the desert and sleep in the forest.

26 And I will give them my blessing round about my hill; and I will send down the rain in its season; and it shall be a shower of blessing.

27 And the trees of the field shall yield their fruit, and the earth shall yield her increase, and they shall dwell securely in their land, and shall know that I am the LORD, when I have broken the bands of their yoke and delivered them out of the hand of those who had subjugated them.

28 And they shall no more be a prey to the nations, neither shall the wild beasts of the land devour them; but they shall dwell safely and none shall harm them.

29 And I will raise up for them a plantation of peace; and they shall be no more consumed with hunger in the land, neither bear the shame of the nations any more.

30 And they shall know that I am the LORD their God and that they, the house of Israel, are my people, says the LORD God.

31 And you are my sheep, the flock of my pasture; you are men, and I am your God, says the LORD.

CHAPTER 35

MOREOVER the word of the LORD came to me, saying,

2 Son of man, set your face against mount Seir and prophesy against it,

[1] Oppressors or vicious men.

3 And say to it, Thus says the LORD God: Behold, I am against you, O mount Seir, and I will stretch out my hand against you, and I will make you desolate and waste.

4 And I will lay your cities waste, and you shall be desolate, and you shall know that I am the LORD.

5 Because you have had a perpetual enmity and delivered the children of Israel over to the sword at the time of their calamity, at the time when their iniquity had come to an end,

6 Therefore, as I live, says the LORD God, I will deliver you to the slaughter, and blood shall pursue you; the blood which you have hated, that very blood shall pursue you.

7 I will make mount Seir waste and desolate, and destroy from it him that goes out and him that comes in.

8 And I will fill his mountains with his slain; on your crags and on your hills and in your valleys shall they fall that are slain with the sword.

9 I will make you a perpetual desolation, and your cities shall not be inhabited; and you shall know that I am the LORD.

10 Because you have said, These two nations and these two kingdoms are mine, and we will possess them, though the LORD was there;

11 Therefore, as I live, says the LORD God, I will do to you according to your own anger and according to your enmity which you showed toward them, and hatred to them; and I will make myself known among them when I have judged you.

12 And you shall know that I am the LORD and that I have heard all your blasphemies which you have spoken against the mountains of Israel, saying, They are laid desolate, they are given us to consume.

13 Thus you dared to speak against me with your mouth, and have multiplied your words against me; I heard them.

14 Thus says the LORD God to mount Seir which is situated at the happiest place on the earth: I will make you desolate.

15 As you rejoiced over the in-

heritance of the house of Israel because it was desolate, so will I do to you; you shall be desolate, O mount Seir, and all Edom, even all of it; and they shall know that I am the LORD.

CHAPTER 36

ALSO, you Son of man, prophesy concerning the mountains of Israel, and say to the mountains of Israel, Hear the word of the LORD;

2 Thus says the LORD God: Because the enemy has said against you, Aha, the ancient high places are ours for a possession;

3 Therefore prophesy and say, Thus says the LORD God: Because you have been reproached and made desolate and blasphemed from all those who are round about you; and you have become an inheritance to the rest of the nations, and you became the subject of gossip and of mocking among the nations;

4 Therefore, O mountains of Israel, hear the word of the LORD God: Thus says the LORD God to the mountains and to the hills and to the streams and to the valleys, to the desolate wastes and to the cities that are deserted, which became a prey and a mockery among the rest of the people round about;

5 Therefore, thus says the LORD God: Surely in the fire of my indignation have I spoken against the rest of the nations and against all Edom, because they partitioned my land to themselves for an inheritance; and with the joy of their heart they have reproached the people that they might carry them captive and plunder them.

6 Prophesy therefore concerning the land of Israel and say to the mountains and to the hills, to the streams and to the valleys, Thus says the LORD God: Behold, I have spoken in my indignation and in my fury, because you have borne the shame of the nations;

7 Therefore thus says the LORD God: I have lifted up my hand against the nations that are round about you, so that they may bear their shame.

8 ¶But you, O mountains of Israel, you shall shoot forth your grass and yield your fruit to my people Israel; for they are ready to come.

9 For, behold, I will turn to you, and you shall be tilled and sown;

10 And I will multiply men upon you, all the house of Israel, even all of it; and the cities shall be inhabited, and the ruined places shall be rebuilt.

11 And I will multiply upon you man and beast, and they shall be great and multiply; and I will settle you as in former days, and will do good to you as I did from the beginning; and you shall know that I am the LORD.

12 Yea, I will cause men to walk upon you, even my people Israel; and they shall possess you, and you shall be their inheritance, and you shall no longer bereave them of men.

13 Thus says the LORD God: Because they say to you, You are a land which devours her people and is bereaved of her inhabitants;

14 Therefore, from henceforth you shall devour men no more, neither shall you be bereaved of your people any more, says the LORD God.

15 Neither will I cause you to bear the shame of the nations any more, nor shall you bear the reproach of the people any more, nor shall you be bereaved of your people any more, says the LORD God.

16 ¶Moreover the word of the LORD came to me, saying,

17 Son of man, when the house of Israel dwelt in their own land, they defiled it by their evil ways and by their doings; their way was before me like the uncleanness of a menstruous woman.

18 Wherefore I poured out my fury upon them for the blood which they had shed in the land and for the idols with which they had polluted it,

19 And I scattered them among the nations and dispersed them through the countries; according to their ways and according to their evil doings I judged them.

20 And when they went to live among the Gentiles, wherever they went, they profaned my holy name; and the Gentiles said to them, These

are the people of the LORD, and now they are gone out of his land.

21 ¶But I had pity for my holy name, which the house of Israel had profaned among the Gentiles, whither they went.

22 Therefore say to the house of Israel, Thus says the LORD God: It is not for your sake, O house of Israel, that I am doing this; but for my holy name's sake, which you have profaned among the Gentiles, whither you went.

23 So that I may sanctify my great name, which has been profaned among the Gentiles, which you have caused to be profaned among them; and the Gentiles shall know that I am the LORD, says the LORD God, when my name shall be sanctified in you before their eyes.

24 For I will take you from among the nations and gather you out of all the countries and will bring you into your own land.

25 ¶Then I will sprinkle clean water upon you, and I shall purify you from all your filthiness and from all your idols.

26 A new heart will I give you, a new spirit will I put within you; and I will remove the heart of stone out of your flesh, and I will give you a heart of flesh.

27 And I will put my spirit within you and cause you to walk in my commandments, and you shall keep my judgments and do them.

28 And you shall dwell in the land which I gave to your fathers; and you shall be my people, and I will be your God.

29 I will also save you from all your uncleannesses; and I will call for the grain, and will increase it, and will not bring famine upon you.

30 And I will multiply the fruit of the trees and the produce of the field, that you may no more bear the reproach of famine among the nations.

31 Then you shall remember your own evil ways and your contemptible doings, and you shall loathe yourselves in your own sight for your iniquities and abominations.

32 But you must know, it is not for your sake that I am doing these things, says the LORD God; now be ashamed and refrain from your evil ways, that you may not die, O house of Israel.

33 Thus says the LORD God: On the day that I shall cleanse you from all your iniquities, I will also cause the cities to be inhabited and the ruined places rebuilt.

34 And the desolate land shall be tilled, that was a desolation in the sight of all that passed by.

35 And they shall say, This land that was desolate is become like the garden of Eden; and the ruined and demolished cities are now become fenced, and are inhabited.

36 Then the Gentiles that are left around about you shall know that I the LORD am rebuilding the ruined cities and planting that which was desolate; I the LORD have spoken it, and I will do it.

37 Thus says the LORD God: Moreover in this shall I avenge the house of Israel, to do these things for them; and I will increase them with men like a flock.

38 As the holy flock, as the flock comes into Jerusalem at the time of her solemn feasts, so shall the ruined cities be filled with flocks of men; and they shall know that I am the LORD.

CHAPTER 37

THE hand of the LORD was upon me, and he carried me out in the spirit of the LORD and set me down in a valley which was full of bones,

2 And he caused me to pass by them round about; and behold, there were very many in the valley; and lo, they were very dry.

3 And he said to me, Son of man, can these bones live? And I answered, O LORD God, thou knowest.

4 Again he said to me, Prophesy concerning these bones, and say to them, O dry bones, hear the word of the LORD.

5 Thus says the LORD God to these bones: Behold, I will cause breath to enter into you, and you shall live;

6 And I will lay sinews upon you

and bring flesh upon you and cover you with skin, and I will put breath in you, and you shall live; and you shall know that I am the LORD.

7 So I prophesied as he had commanded me; and as I prophesied, there was a noise, and behold a quake, and the bones came together, each bone to its joint.

8 And when I beheld, lo, sinews and the flesh came upon them and skin covered them; but there was no breath in them.

9 Then he said to me, Prophesy concerning the breath; prophesy, Son of man, and say to the breath, Thus says the LORD God: Come from the four winds, O breath, and breathe into these slain, that they may live.

10 So I prophesied as he had commanded me, and the breath came into them, and they lived and stood up upon their feet, an exceeding great army.

11 ¶Then he said to me, Son of man, all these bones are the bones of the children of Israel, who said, Our bones are dried and our hope is lost; we are completely gone.

12 Therefore prophesy and say to them, Thus says the LORD God: Behold, I will open your graves and bring you up out of them and bring you into the land of Israel.

13 And you shall know that I am the LORD, when I have opened your graves and brought you up out of them,

14 And I will put my spirit in you, and you shall live, and I shall place you in your own land; then you shall know that I am the LORD; I have spoken it, and I will do it, says the LORD God.

15 ¶The word of the LORD came again to me, saying,

16 Son of man, take a stick and write on it: For Judah and for the children of Israel his companions; then take another stick and write on it: For Joseph, on the stick of Ephraim, and for all the house of Israel his companions;

17 And join them one to another into one stick; and they shall become one stick in your hand.

18 ¶And if your people should say to you, Will you not show us what is the meaning of these sticks?

19 Say to them, Thus says the LORD God: Behold, I will take the stick of Joseph, which is in the hand of Ephraim, and the tribes of Israel his fellows, and will put them together with the stick of Judah, and make them one stick, and they shall be one in my hand.

20 ¶And the sticks on which you write, hold them in your hand before their eyes;

21 And say to them, Thus says the LORD God: Behold, I will take the children of Israel from among the nations whither they have gone, and will gather them together and bring them into their own land;

22 And I will make them one nation in the land upon the mountains of Israel; and one king shall be king over them all; and they shall be no more two nations, neither shall they be divided into two kingdoms any more.

23 Nor shall they defile themselves any more with their idols nor with their abominations nor with all their iniquity; but I will save them out of all their dwelling places, wherein they have sinned, and will cleanse them; so they shall be my people, and I will be their God.

24 And my servant David shall be king over them; and they all shall have one shepherd; they shall walk in my judgments and keep my commandments and do them.

25 And they shall dwell in the land that I gave to my servant Jacob, in which your fathers have dwelt; and they shall dwell in it, even they and their children and their children's children for ever; and my servant David shall be their prince for ever.

26 Moreover I will make a covenant of peace with them; it shall be an everlasting covenant with them; and I will multiply them and set my sanctuary among them for ever.

27 My dwelling place also shall be with them; yea, I will be their God, and they shall be my people.

28 And the Gentiles shall know that

I the LORD sanctify Israel, when my sanctuary shall be among them for evermore.

CHAPTER 38

AND the word of the LORD came to me, saying,

2 Son of man, set your face against China, and against the land of Mongolia, the chief prince of Meshech and Tubal, and prophesy against him and say,

3 Thus says the LORD God: Behold, I am against you, O China, the chief prince of Meshech and Tubal:

4 I will gather your people together and put a bridle in your jaws, and I will bring you forth out of your country, both you and all your army, horses and horsemen, all of them clothed in armor, a great host with spears and shields, all of them handling swords:

5 Persians, Ethiopians, and Lybians with them, all of them with shields and helmets.

6 Gomar and all her army, the house of Togarmah, and the uttermost parts of the north with all their hosts, and many other people who are with you.

7 Prepare yourself, you and all the people that are assembled with you, and be a protection to them.

8 ¶You have been commanded in former days, and in the later years you shall come against the mountains of Israel and against the land which is at peace and free from the sword, whose people were gathered from many nations, and now they all dwell safely in it.

9 And you shall come up like a storm and like a cloud which covers the land, you and all your army and many people who are with you.

10 Thus says the LORD God: It shall come to pass that in that very day thoughts shall come into your mind and you shall think an evil thought;

11 And you shall say, I will go up against a prosperous land, I will go against those who dwell in tranquility, without walls, and having neither bars nor gates,

12 To take captives and to take a spoil; to turn your hand against the desolate places that are now inhabited and against the people who were gathered together out of the nations, who have gotten cattle and goods, who dwell in the beauty of the land.

13 Sheba and Deran and the merchants of Tarshish and all its villages shall say to you, Are you come to carry off captives and to take a spoil? Have you mobilized your host to take silver and gold, to take away cattle and goods, and to take a great spoil?

14 ¶Therefore, Son of man, prophesy and say to China, Thus says the LORD God: On that day when my people Israel shall dwell in tranquillity, you shall know it.

15 And you shall come from your place out of the north parts, you, and many people with you, all of them riding on horses, a great host and a mighty army;

16 And you shall come up against my people Israel, like a cloud to cover the land; it shall be in the latter days, and I will bring you against my land, and the nations will know me, when I shall be sanctified through your defeat.

17 Thus says the LORD God: You are he of whom I have spoken in former days by my servants the prophets of Israel, who prophesied in those days and in those years that I would bring you against them.

18 And it shall come to pass at the same time when China shall come against the land of Israel, says the LORD God, that my anger shall be consumed in my fury and zeal.

19 For in the fire of my wrath have I spoken; surely in that day there shall be a great shaking in the land of Israel;

20 So that even the fish of the sea and the fowls of the air and the beasts of the field and all creeping things that creep upon the earth and all the men that are upon the face of the earth shall shake at my presence, and the mountains shall be thrown down and the towers shall fall and every wall shall tumble to the ground.

21 And I will call for a sword

against him throughout all my mountains, says the Lord God; every man's sword shall be against his brother.

22 And I will judge him with pestilence and with blood; and I will rain upon him and upon his princes and upon the many people that are with him, an overflowing rain, and great hailstones, fire, and brimstone.

23 Thus will I magnify myself and sanctify myself in the eyes of many nations, and they shall know that I am the Lord.

CHAPTER 39

AND you, O Son of man, prophesy against China and say, Thus says the Lord God: Behold, I am against you, O China, the ruler and the chief prince of Meshech and Tubal;

2 I will subdue you and gather you together, and I will cause you to come up from the north parts, and bring you upon the mountains of Israel;

3 And I will swerve your bow out of your left hand, and will cause your arrows to fall out of your right hand.

4 You shall fall upon the mountains of Israel, you and all your army and the many peoples that are with you; I have given you to the ravenous birds of the air and to the wild beasts of the field to be devoured.

5 You shall fall in the open field; for I have spoken it, says the Lord God.

6 And I will send a fire on Mongolia, and on the people who dwell peacefully in the islands[1]; and they shall know that I am the Lord.

7 So I will make my holy name known in the midst of my people Israel; and I will not let them profane my holy name any more; and the Gentiles shall know that I am the Lord, the Holy One of Israel.

8 ¶Behold, the day of which I have spoken is at hand, says the Lord God;

9 Then the inhabitants of the villages of Israel shall go forth, and shall set on fire and burn the weapons, both the shields and the spears, the bows and the arrows and the handstaves and the lances, and they shall burn them as fuel for seven years;

10 So that they shall not need wood for fuel out of the field or the forest; for they shall burn the weapons with fire, and they shall take captive those who had taken them captive and plunder those who had plundered them, says the Lord God.

11 ¶And it shall come to pass on that day that I will give to China a place there for burial in the land of Israel, the great valley which is east of the sea; and they shall close off the valley: and there they shall bury China and all his army; and it shall be called the valley of the annihilation of China.

12 And for seven months the house of Israel shall be busy burying them; and then the land shall be cleansed.

13 Yea, all the people of the land shall bury them; and it shall be to them a renowned day when I am glorified, says the Lord.

14 Even seven months after, there shall be men who will travel continually through the land burying those who are left lying on the face of the land, to cleanse it.

15 And every one who passes through the land, and sees a man's bone, then shall he set up a sign by it, till buriers have come and taken it and buried it in the valley of China.

16 And the name of the graveyard shall be, The Mighty City. Thus shall they cleanse the land.

17 ¶And you, Son of man, say to all the fowls of the air and to every beast of the field, Thus says the Lord God: Assemble yourselves and come; gather yourselves from every place to the great sacrifice that I perform for you upon the mountains of Israel, and you shall eat flesh and drink blood.

18 You shall eat the flesh of the mighty men and drink the blood of the princes of the earth, of rams, of fatlings, of he-goats, of bullocks, and of all the young bullocks of Bashan.

19 And you shall eat flesh till you are filled and drink blood till you are drunk at the great sacrificial feast which I am preparing for you.

20 Thus you shall be filled at my table with the flesh of horses and their riders, and with that of mighty men,

1 Japan.

and with that of all the men of war, says the LORD God.

21 And I will set my glory among the nations, and all the Gentiles shall see the judgment that I have executed, and the heavy punishment with which I have punished them.

22 So the house of Israel shall know that I am the LORD their God from that day and forward.

23 ¶And the Gentiles shall know that the house of Israel was carried into captivity for their iniquity; because they transgressed against me, therefore I turned away my face from them and delivered them into the hand of those who hate them, and they all fell by the sword.

24 According to their abominations and according to their iniquity have I rewarded them; and I turned away my face from them.

25 Therefore thus says the LORD God: Now I will bring back the captivity of Jacob, and have mercy upon all the house of Israel, and will be zealous for my holy name's sake;

26 After they have borne all their shame and their iniquity whereby they have transgressed against me; when they dwell securely in their own land, with no one to hurt them;

27 When I have gathered them from among the nations and brought them back from the cities of their enemies, and am sanctified by them in the sight of many nations;

28 Then shall they know that I am the LORD their God, who caused them to be carried captive among the nations, and that it is I who gathered them into their own land and have left none of them there any more.

29 Neither will I turn away my face from them; but I will pour out my spirit upon the house of Israel, says the LORD.

CHAPTER 40

IN the twenty-fifth year of our captivity, in the beginning of the year, on the tenth day of the month, in the fourteenth year after Jerusalem was destroyed, on that very day the hand of the LORD was upon me,

2 And he brought me into the land of Israel, in the visions of God, and set me upon a very high mountain, upon which was the plan of a city on the south.

3 And he brought me there, and behold, there was a man whose appearance was like the appearance of brass, with a line of flax and a measuring reed in his hand; and he was standing in the gate.

4 And the man said to me, Son of man, see with your eyes and hear with your ears, and set your heart upon all that I shall show you; for you were brought here that I might show you these things; and everything that you see, declare it to the house of Israel.

5 And behold, a wall round about the house, and in the man's hand a measuring reed six cubits and a hand breadth long; so he measured the breadth of the building, one reed; and the height, one reed.

6 ¶Then he came to the gate that looks toward the east, and climbed up the steps thereof and measured the threshold of the gate, which was one reed broad.

7 And every small room was one reed long and one reed broad; and between the small rooms were five cubits; and the threshold of the gate by the porch of the gate within was one reed.

8 He measured also the porch of the gate within, one reed.

9 Then he measured the porch of the gate eight cubits; and its posts from within two cubits.

10 And the small rooms of the gate eastward were three on this side and three on that side; the three were of the same measure; and the posts were of the same size on this side and on that side.

11 And he measured the breadth of the entrance of the gate, ten cubits; and the length of the gate, thirteen cubits.

12 The space also before the small rooms was one cubit on this side and one cubit on that side, and the small rooms were six cubits on this side and six cubits on that side.

13 He measured then the gate from

the roof of one small room to the roof of another; the breadth was twenty-five cubits from door to door.

14 He measured also the portico, sixty cubits; likewise to the portico of the court round about the gate, sixty cubits.

15 And from the face of the gate of the entrance to the face of the portico of the inner gate were fifty cubits.

16 And there were windows to the small rooms which were wide from within and narrow from without, and to their posts within the gate, and likewise to the arches; and windows were round about from within.

17 Then he brought me into the outer court, and lo, there were steps round about it; thirty were one upon the other.

18 And the steps by the side of the gates were opposite the stairway at the lower pavement.

19 Then he measured its breadth from the forefront of the gate of the court, one hundred cubits eastward and northward.

20 ¶And at the gate of the outer court that looks toward the north, he measured its length and its breadth.

21 And its small rooms were three on this side and three on that side; and its posts and its arches had the same measurements as those of the first gate; its length was fifty cubits, and its breadth twenty-five cubits.

22 And its windows and its porticoes had the same measurements as those of the gate that looks toward the east; and they went up to it by seven steps; and a portico was before them.

23 And the gates of the inner court were opposite the northeast gate; and he measured from gate to gate a hundred cubits.

24 ¶Then he brought me toward the south, and behold, a gate toward the south; and he measured its posts and its arches according to these measures.

25 And there were windows in it and in its arches round about, like the other windows; the length was fifty cubits, and the breadth twenty-five cubits.

26 And there were seven steps to go up to it, and there was a portico in front of it; and it had palm trees, one on this side and another on that side, upon its posts.

27 And there were gates in the inner court toward the south; and he measured from gate to gate toward the south a hundred cubits.

28 And he brought me to the inner court by the south gate; and he measured the south gate according to these measurements;

29 And its small rooms and its posts and its arches, according to these measurements; and there were windows in it and in its arches round about; it was fifty cubits long and twenty-five cubits broad.

30 And the arches round about it were twenty-five cubits long and five cubits broad.

31 And the arches of the outer court had palm trees upon them; and the stairway had eight steps.

32 ¶And he brought me into the inner court toward the east; and he measured the gate according to these measures.

33 And the small rooms thereof and its posts and its arches were according to these measurements; and there were windows in it and in its arches round about it; it was fifty cubits long and twenty-five cubits broad.

34 And its arches were toward the outer court; and palm trees were upon its posts, on this side and on that side; and the stairway had eight steps.

35 ¶And he brought me to the north gate, and measured it according to these measurements;

36 The small rooms thereof, its posts and its arches and the windows to it round about; the length was fifty cubits and the breadth twenty-five cubits.

37 And the porticoes thereof were toward the outer court; and palm trees were in its porticoes, on this side and on that side; and the stairway had eight steps.

38 And the rooms and the vestibules

thereof were by the porticoes of the gates, where they placed burnt offerings.

39 ¶And in the portico of the gate were two tables on this side and two tables on that side, to slay upon them the burnt offerings and the gift offerings and the sin offerings.

40 And at the side of the north gate, which is outside the place of the burnt offerings, were two tables; and on the other side, which was at the portico of the gate, were two tables.

41 Four tables were on this side and four tables on that side, by the side of the gate; eight tables in all, upon which they slaughtered their sacrifices.

42 And the four tables were of hewn stone for the burnt offerings, a cubit and a half long and a cubit and a half broad, upon which they laid the instruments with which they slaughtered the burnt offerings and the sacrifices.

43 And within were hooks, a hand broad, fastened round about; and upon the tables they placed the flesh of the offerings.

44 ¶Facing the inner court were the rooms of the princes, in the inner court, which was at the side of the north gate, which faces the south; one room was at the side of the east gate, facing the north.

45 And the man said to me, This room which faces toward the south is for the priests, the keepers who have charge of the house.

46 And the room that faces toward the north is for the priests, the keepers who have charge of the altar; these are the descendants of Zadok, who are among the descendants of Levi, who come near to the altar to minister to the LORD.

47 So he measured the court, a hundred cubits long and a hundred cubits broad, foursquare; and the altar that was before the house.

48 ¶And he brought me to the portico of the house, and measured each post of the portico, five cubits on this side and five cubits on that side; and the breadth of the gate was three cu-

bits on this side and three cubits on that side.

49 The length of the portico was twenty cubits, and the breadth eleven cubits; and by steps they went to it; and pillars stood by the posts, one on this side and another on that side.

CHAPTER 41

THEN he brought me into the temple, and measured the posts, six cubits broad on this side and six cubits broad on that side;

2 And the breadth of the door of the temple was ten cubits; and the sides of the door were five cubits on this side and five cubits on that side; and he measured its length, forty cubits; and the breadth, twenty cubits.

3 Then he went inside and measured the post of the door, two cubits; and the door, six cubits; and the breadth of the door, seven cubits.

4 And he measured the length of the sanctuary, twenty cubits; and the breadth, twenty cubits, before the nave; and he said to me, This is the Holy of Holies.

5 Then he measured the wall of the house, six cubits; and the breadth of every side chamber, four cubits, round about the house on every side.

6 And the side rooms were one over another, thirty-three in order; and they entered into the wall of the house for the side rooms round about, that they might hold fast, but they were separated from the wall.

7 And the side rooms rose higher, so that they encircled the house from above, thus enlarging the house from above; and from the lowest rooms they went up to the middle rooms, and from the middle rooms to the highest rooms.

8 I saw also the height of the house round about; and the side rooms were separated one from another a full measuring reed of six cubits.

9 The thickness of the outer wall which was for the side rooms was five cubits; and from within it was five cubits.

10 And between the rooms was the breadth of twenty cubits round about the house on every side.

11 And the doors of the side rooms were toward the place that was left open, one door toward the south, another door toward the north; and the breadth of the door that was left was five cubits round about.

12 Now the building that was in front of the separate place which is at the west gate was seventy cubits broad; and the wall of the building was five cubits thick round about, and its length ninety cubits.

13 So he measured the house, a hundred cubits long; and the separate place and the building, with its walls, a hundred cubits long;

14 Also the breadth opposite the house, and the separate place toward the east, a hundred cubits.

15 And he measured the length of the building in front of the separate place, and behind it, and its arches on the one side and on the other side, a hundred cubits, with the inner temple and the porticoes of the court;

16 And the door posts and the narrow windows and the arches round about on their three stories, over against the three gates that were ceiled with wood round about, and from the ground up to the windows;

17 And the windows which were covered above the door of the inner house, and the outside of all the walls round about, he measured from inside and from outside.

18 And it was made with cherubim and palm trees, so that a palm tree was between a cherub and a cherub; and every cherub had two faces;

19 So that the face of a man was toward the palm trees from this side and from that side; the house was made in this manner round about;

20 The space from the ground to above the doors was decorated with cherubim and palm trees.

21 And the wall of the temple was foursquare, and the face of the sanctuary as seen in the vision was like the appearance of a wooden altar;

22 It was three cubits high, two cubits long; and it had corners; and its sides and base were all made of wood; and he said to me, This is the table that is before the LORD.

23 And the temple and the sanctuary had two doors.

24 And the doors had two hinges apiece, two hinges for the one door and two hinges for the other.

25 And the doors of the temple were decorated with cherubim and palm trees, like those that were made on the walls; and there were thick planks upon the face of the portico without.

26 And there were narrow windows and palm trees on one side and on the other side; and the sides of the portico, and the side rooms of the temple were covered with wood boards.

CHAPTER 42

THEN he brought me forth into the outer court, to the way toward the north; and he brought me into the room opposite the separate place and opposite the building toward the north,

2 Towards the place where he measured a hundred cubits, which is at the north gate, and the breadth of it was fifty cubits.

3 Opposite the gate of the inner court, over against the pavement of the outer court, was gallery above gallery in three stories.

4 And before the rooms was a passage ten cubits broad, and its length a hundred cubits; and the door of the passage was toward the north.

5 Now the upper rooms were smaller because the stairway went through them.

6 For they were in three stories, but had no pillars like the pillars of the court; therefore the upper rooms were smaller than the lower rooms and the middle ones.

7 And the wall that was outside, which is opposite the rooms, was fifty cubits long.

8 For the length of the rooms that were in the outer court was fifty cubits; and those before the temple were a hundred cubits.

9 And the door of the room of the vestibule which goes into the outer court was on the east.

10 The rooms were in the breadth

of the wall of the court at the eastern gate opposite the separate place, and in front of the building where the rooms were.

11 And the passage in front of them was like the appearance of the rooms which were toward the north, and the rooms were of the same length and breadth; and all their exits, entrances, their appearance, and their doors were alike.

12 Like to the doors of the rooms that were toward the south was a door in the head of the way which was directly before the wall toward the place where the eastern valley starts.

13 ¶Then he said to me, The north rooms and the south rooms, which are in front of the separate place, they are rooms where the priests who make offerings to the LORD eat the most holy things; there they lay the most holy things, the meat offering, the sin offering, and the trespass offering; for the place is holy.

14 When the priests enter therein, they shall not go out of the holy place into the outer court, but there they shall lay their garments in which they minister; for they are holy; and they shall put on other garments; then they can make offerings on behalf of the people.

15 Now when he had finished measuring the inner house, he took me out toward the gate that looks toward the east, and he measured it round about.

16 He measured the east side, five hundred reeds with the measuring reed round about.

17 He measured the north side, five hundred reeds with the measuring reed round about.

18 He measured the south side, five hundred reeds with the measuring reed.

19 ¶He measured the west side, five hundred reeds with the measuring reed.

20 He measured it on the four sides; and the wall round about, five hundred reeds long and five hundred broad, making a separation between the sanctuary and the unconsecrated ground.

CHAPTER 43

AFTERWARD he brought me to the gate that looks toward the east.

2 And, behold, the glory of the God of Israel came from the direction of the east; and his voice was like the sound of many waters; and the earth shone with his glory.

3 And the vision I saw was like the vision which I had seen when I came to announce the destruction of the city, and like the vision which I had seen by the river Chebar; and I fell upon my face.

4 And the glory of the LORD came into the temple through the gate that looks toward the east.

5 And the spirit took me up and brought me into the inner court; and behold, the glory of the LORD filled the temple.

6 And I heard someone speaking to me out of the temple; and the man was standing by me.

7 ¶And he said to me, Son of man, this is the place of my throne and the place of the soles of my feet, where I dwell in the midst of the children of Israel for ever; and the house of Israel shall be no more defiled, and my holy name shall the house of Israel no more defile, neither they nor their kings, by their whoredom nor with the corpses of their kings and with their idols.

8 For they used to make their gates beside my gates, and their door posts beside my doorposts, and there was only a wall between me and them; they have even defiled my holy name by the iniquities which they have committed; therefore I have consumed them in my anger.

9 Now let them put away their whoredom, and the corpses of their kings from my presence, and I will dwell in the midst of them for ever.

10 ¶But you, Son of man, show to the house of Israel this temple, that they may be ashamed of their iniquities which they transgressed against me; and let them study the pattern thereof.

11 And if they be ashamed of all

that they have done, show them the form of the house, and its fashion and its entrances and its exits and all its forms and all its laws and ordinances, and draw the plans in their sight, that they may keep the whole design thereof, and all its form, and do them.

12 This is the vision of the house upon the top of the mountain; and all its borders round about are most holy.

13 ¶And these are the measurements of the altar by cubits (the cubit is a cubit and a hand breadth): even the base shall be a cubit, and the breadth a cubit, and its border to its edges round about shall be a span, and likewise on its sides.

14 And from the bottom on the ground to the lower seat shall be two cubits, and the breadth one cubit; and from the lower seat to the higher seat shall be four cubits, and the breadth, one cubit.

15 So the altar shall be four cubits; and from the altar and upward there shall be four horns.

16 And the altar shall be twelve cubits long, twelve broad, square on its four sides.

17 And the seat shall be fourteen cubits long and fourteen broad in its four squares; and the border about it shall be half a cubit; and the base of it shall be a cubit round about; and its steps shall look toward the east.

18 ¶And he said to me, Son of man, thus says the LORD God: These are the ordinances of the altar on the day when they shall make it, to offer burnt offerings upon it and to sprinkle blood upon it.

19 And you shall give to the priests and the Levites of the descendants of Zadok, who draw near to me to minister to me, says the LORD God, a young bullock for a sin offering.

20 And you shall take some of its blood, and sprinkle it on the four horns of the altar and on the four corners of the seat, and upon the border round about; thus shall you sprinkle blood on it, and it shall be cleansed.

21 You shall take the bullock also of the sin offering, and they shall take it to the side of the temple and burn it outside of the sanctuary.

22 And on the second day you shall offer a he-goat without blemish for a sin offering; and they shall cleanse the altar, as they cleansed it with the bullock.

23 When you have finished cleansing it, you shall offer a young bullock without blemish and a ram out of the flock without blemish.

24 And you shall offer them before the LORD, and the priests shall put salt on them, and they shall offer them up for a burnt offering to the LORD.

25 For seven days they shall offer daily a he-goat for the sin offering; they shall also offer a young bullock and a ram out of the flock without blemish.

26 For seven days they shall make offerings and shall cleanse the altar; and they shall consecrate themselves.

27 And when these days are expired, that is from the seventh day forward, then the priests shall make offerings upon the altar, both their burnt offerings and their peace offerings; and I will be pleased with them, says the LORD God.

CHAPTER 44

THEN he brought me back by way of the gate of the outer sanctuary which looks toward the east; and behold, it was shut.

2 Then the LORD said to me, This gate shall be shut; it shall not be opened, and no man shall enter in by it because the LORD, the God of Israel, will enter in by it; therefore it shall be shut.

3 Only the high priest shall sit in it to eat bread before the LORD; but he shall enter by way of the portico of the gate, and shall go out by the same way.

4 ¶Then he brought me by the way of the north gate before the house; and I looked, and behold, the glory of the LORD filled the house of the LORD; and I fell upon my face.

5 And the LORD said to me, Son of man, mark in your heart and see with your eyes and hear with your ears

all that I say to you concerning all the ordinances of the temple and all its patterns; and remember well the entrances of the house and the exits of the sanctuary.

6 Then say to the rebellious house of Israel, Thus says the LORD God: Have you not committed abominations enough, O house of Israel?

7 But you are also bringing strangers, who are uncircumcised in heart and uncircumcised in flesh, to be in my sanctuary, to pollute my house; when you offer my bread, the fat and the blood, and you nullified my covenant with all your abominations.

8 And you have not had charge of my sanctuary; but you have made the keepers of my sanctuary guards for yourselves.

9 ¶Thus says the LORD God: No foreigner, uncircumcised in his heart and uncircumcised in his flesh, shall enter into my sanctuary, nor any strangers who are among the children of Israel.

10 Neither shall the Levites who went away far from me when Israel went astray from me after their idols, and who have borne their iniquity.

11 For these Levites once served in my sanctuary and ministered at the gates of the temple; and they slaughtered burnt offerings and sacrifices for the people, and stood before the people and ministered to them.

12 But because they ministered to them before their idols and became a stumbling block of iniquity to the house of Israel; therefore I have lifted up my hand against them, says the LORD God, and they have borne their iniquity.

13 And they shall not come near to me, to minister to me, nor to come near to any of my holy things in the Holy of Holies; but they shall bear all their shame and all their abominations which they have committed.

14 And I will put them in charge of the temple, and make them laborers for all that shall be done in it.

15 ¶But the priests, the descendants of Zadok, and the Levites who had charge of my sanctuary when the children of Israel went astray from me, they shall come near to me to minister to me and they shall stand before me to offer to me the fat and blood, says the LORD God;

16 They shall enter into my sanctuary, and they shall come near to my table to minister to me, and they shall keep my charge:

17 ¶And when they enter the gate of the inner court, they shall be clothed with linen garments; they shall not wear any garments made of wool, while they minister at the gate of the inner court.

18 Also when they are within the inner court, they shall wear linen mitres upon their heads, and shall have linen breeches upon their loins.

19 And when they go out into the outer court to the people, they shall put off their garments in which they ministered and leave them in the holy chambers, and they shall put on other garments, that they may not sanctify the people with their garments.

20 Neither shall they shave their heads nor let their locks grow long; but they shall have their hair cut.

21 Neither shall the priests drink wine when they enter into the inner court.

22 Neither shall they marry a widow nor her that is put away; but they shall marry a virgin of the descendants of the house of Israel, or a widow who is the widow of a priest.

23 And they shall teach my people the difference between the holy and the unconsecrated, and cause them to discern between the unclean and the clean.

24 And in the case of lawsuits they shall be appointed as judges; and they shall judge according to my judgments; and they shall keep my laws and my statutes in all my appointed feasts; and they shall hallow my sabbaths.

25 And they shall not attend the funeral of a dead person, lest they defile themselves, except for father or for mother or for son or for daughter or for brother or for his

virgin sister who had never been married, otherwise they may become unclean.

26 And after a priest is unclean, he shall count for himself seven days, and then he shall be clean.

27 And on the day that he goes into the sanctuary, to the inner court to minister in the sanctuary, he shall offer his sin offering, says the LORD God.

28 And the sanctuary shall be to them for an inheritance; for I am their inheritance; and you shall give them no possession in Israel; for I am their possession.

29 They shall eat the meal offering and the meat of the sin offering, and every dedicated thing in Israel shall be theirs.

30 And the first of all the first-born of the sheep and cattle and of all things which you set aside for the LORD, shall be for the priests; and you shall also give the first of your dough to the priests, so that a blessing may rest in your houses.

31 The priests shall not eat of anything that is dead of itself, or torn, whether it be fowl or beast.

CHAPTER 45

MOREOVER, when you shall divide the land for an inheritance, you must set apart a portion for the LORD, and consecrate a portion of the land; its length shall be twenty-five thousand reeds, and the breadth ten thousand reeds. It shall be holy in all the borders thereof round about.

2 Of this there shall be for the sanctuary a space five hundred in length and five hundred in breadth, square round about with fifty cubits of open space round it.

3 And of this measure you shall measure the length of twenty-five thousand and the breadth of ten thousand cubits; and in it shall be the Holy of Holies.

4 The holy portion of the land shall be for the priests who minister in the sanctuary of the LORD, and who shall come near to minister to the LORD; and it shall be a place for their houses and a holy place for the sanctuary.

5 And there shall be a space of twenty-five thousand reeds long and ten thousand broad; and it shall be for a possession for the Levites who minister in the temple, twenty houses in all.

6 ¶And the portion for the city shall be five thousand broad and twenty-five thousand long, toward the portion of the sanctuary; it shall be for all the house of Israel.

7 ¶And a portion on the sides of the holy portion shall be for the ruler of the people and as a portion for the city, from the east side eastward and from the west side westward; and the length shall be like that of one of the portions from the east border to the west border.

8 The land shall be an inheritance to the children of Israel; and the rulers of my people shall no more oppress them; and the rest of the land they shall give to the children of Israel according to their tribes.

9 ¶Thus says the LORD God: It is enough, O princes of Israel; remove violence and plunder, and execute justice and righteousness, cease your oppression from my people, says the LORD God.

10 You shall have just balances and just weights and just measures.

11 You shall make a standard measure and a standard weight, so that you may receive tithes, one out of ten, evenly.

12 And the shekels shall be twenty gerahs; and each of the shekels shall be twenty-five minas; fifteen shekels shall be your mina.

13 This is the offering that you shall make: one sixth part of an ephah of a homer of wheat, and one sixth part of an ephah of a homer of barley;

14 And as for oil, you shall offer the tenth part of a bath out of the cor, which is a homer of ten baths, for ten baths are a homer;

15 And one ewe out of every two hundred sheep of the flocks of Israel for the meal offering and for the burnt offering and for the peace offering, that I may cleanse them, says the LORD God.

16 All the people of the land shall give this offering to the high priest of Israel.

17 And it shall be the high priest's part to provide burnt offerings, meal offerings, and the drink offerings, in the first day of the months, and sabbaths; and at all the feasts of the house of Israel, he shall offer the sin offering and the meal offering and the drink offering and the peace offerings, an offering to cleanse the children of Israel.

18 Thus says the LORD God: In the first month, on the first day of the month, you shall take a young bullock without blemish and cleanse the sanctuary;

19 And the priest shall take of the blood of the sin offering, and sprinkle it on the posts of the house and on the four corners of the seat of the altar and on the posts of the gate of the inner court.

20 And he shall do the same on the seventh day of the month for every one who had done wrong and had gone astray; so shall he cleanse the house.

21 In the first month, on the fourteenth day of the month, you shall celebrate the feast of the passover, and you shall eat unleavened bread for seven days.

22 And on that day the high priest shall offer on behalf of himself and on behalf of all the people of the land, a bullock for a sin offering.

23 And during the seven days of the feast he shall offer burnt offerings to the LORD, seven bullocks and seven rams without blemish daily for seven days, and a he-goat daily for a sin offering.

24 And he shall prepare a meal offering of an ephah for every bullock and an ephah for every ram and a hin of oil for each ephah.

25 In the seventh month, on the fifteenth day of the month, he shall celebrate the feast in the same manner for seven days, according to the sin offering, according to the burnt offering, according to the meal offering, and according to the oil.

CHAPTER 46

THUS says the LORD God: The gate of the inner court that looks toward the east shall be shut during the six working days; but on the sabbath day it shall be opened, and on the day of the new moon.

2 And the high priest shall enter by the way of the porch at the gate from without, and shall stand by the post of the gate, and the priests shall offer his burnt offerings and his peace offerings, and he shall worship at the threshold of the gate; then he shall go out; but the gate shall not be shut until evening.

3 Likewise the people of the land shall worship at the entrance of that gate before the LORD on the sabbaths and on the new moons.

4 And the burnt offerings that the high priest shall offer before the LORD on the sabbath day shall be six lambs without blemish and a ram without blemish.

5 And he shall offer a meal offering of an ephah for the bullock and an ephah for the ram; and for the lambs as much as he can afford, and add a hin of oil to an ephah.

6 And on the first day of the new moon it shall be a bullock without blemish and six lambs without blemish and a ram without blemish.

7 And he shall prepare the meal offering, an ephah for the bullock, and an ephah for the ram, and for the lambs as much as he can afford, and add a hin of oil to an ephah.

8 And when the high priest shall enter, he shall go in by the way of the portico of the gate, and he shall go out by the same way.

9 ¶But when the people of the land shall come before the LORD at the time of the solemn feasts, he who enters by the way of the north gate to worship shall go out by the way of the south gate; and he who enters by the way of the south gate shall go out by the way of the north gate; he shall not return by the way of the gate by which he came in, but shall go out straight ahead.

10 But the high priest who is among you, by the same gate that he enters by that gate shall he go out.

11 And at the time of the feasts and in the solemnities the meal offering shall be an ephah for a bullock, and an ephah for a ram, and for the lambs as much as he can afford, and a hin of oil shall be added to an ephah.

12 Now when the high priest shall offer burnt offerings or gift offerings to the LORD, the gate that looks toward the east shall be opened for him, and he shall offer his burnt offerings and his peace offerings, as he did on the sabbath day; then he shall go out, and after his going out the gate shall be shut.

13 He shall daily offer a burnt offering to the LORD, a lamb of the first year without blemish; he shall offer it every morning.

14 And he shall offer a meal offering for it every morning, the sixth part of an ephah and the third part of a hin of oil to be mixed with fine flour, a meal offering continually by a perpetual ordinance to the LORD.

15 Thus they shall offer lambs and the meal offering and the oil every morning for a continual burnt offering.

16 ¶Thus says the LORD God: If the high priest give a gift to any of his sons, the inheritance thereof shall be his sons; it shall be their possession by inheritance.

17 But if he give a gift of his inheritance to one of his servants, then it shall be his to the year of liberty; after that it shall return to the high priest; but what his sons inherit shall be theirs.

18 Moreover the high priest shall not take of the people's inheritance, nor shall he defraud them of their inheritance; but he shall give his sons inheritance out of his own possession; so that my people may not be driven away every man from his inheritance.

19 ¶Then he brought me through the vestibule, which was at the side of the gate, into the holy rooms of the priests, which look toward the north; and behold, there was a place at the end toward the west.

20 And he said to me, This is the place where the priests boil the sin offering, and where they bake the meal offering, that they may not go out into the outer court, to sanctify the people.

21 Then he brought me forth into the outer court, and caused me to pass by the four sides of the court; and behold, on every side of the court there was a court.

22 On the four sides of the court there were small courts forty cubits long and thirty broad.

23 And there was a row of rooms round about the four courts.

24 Then he said to me, This is the house of the cooks, where the ministers of the temple cook the sacrifice of the people.

CHAPTER 47

THEN he brought me again to the door of the temple; and, behold, water issued out from under the threshold of the house eastward; and the water was flowing down from under the side of the temple, at the south side of the altar.

2 And he brought me out by the way of the north gate, and led me about the way outside to the gate of the court that looks eastward; and, behold, water was running out from under the right side of the temple.

3 And a glorious man that had the measuring line in his hand went forth; he measured a thousand cubits and brought me through the water, and it was to the ankles.

4 Again he measured a thousand cubits and brought me through the water, and it was up to the knees. Again he measured a thousand cubits and brought me through the water, and it was up to the loins.

5 Afterward he measured a thousand cubits; and it was a torrent that no man could cross; for the waters were risen so high and the stream had become so turbulent that no one could cross it.

6 ¶And he said to me, Son of man,

do you see this stream? Then he brought me and made me to sit by the bank of the torrent.

7 Now when I was seated, I saw that at the bank of the stream were very many trees on the one side and on the other.

8 Then he said to me, These waters that are issuing out toward the east region and flowing down toward the north, shall go into the sea and mingle with the stagnant water, and make it fresh.

9 And it shall come to pass that every living creature that swarms wheresoever the torrent shall flow shall live; and there shall be many fish because of the waters that flow there and make the water fresh.

10 And it shall come to pass, that fishermen shall stand beside it from En-gad to En-eglain; it shall be a place to spread forth nets; and there shall be very many kinds of fish in it, as the fish of the great sea, exceedingly many.

11 But the water in its springs and mouths shall not be fresh, but it shall become salt.

12 And by the stream, on the banks thereof, on this side and on that side, shall grow all kinds of trees for food, their leaves shall not fall off, neither shall their fruit fail; but in the beginning of every month they shall bring forth new fruit, because the water with which they are irrigated flows from the sanctuary; and their fruit shall be for food and their leaves for healing.

13 ¶Thus says the LORD God: These are the borders by which you shall divide the land for the inheritance among the twelve tribes of Israel: Joseph shall have two portions.

14 And you shall inherit it, one as well as another, a land concerning which I swore by lifting up my hand to give it to your fathers; and this land shall be divided among you for an inheritance.

15 And this shall be the border of the land, on the north side, from the great sea, by the way of Hethron which goes to Zedad:

16 Hamath, Beroth, Sepharvim, which is between the border of Damascus and the border of Hamath; Hazar the central, which is on the border of Hauran.

17 And the border from the sea shall be Hazar-enan, which is within the border of Damascus, and Zipon which is toward the north within the border of Hamath. This is the north side.

18 And the east side border shall run to Beth-hauran from Damascus and from Gilead to the land of Israel; and Jordan shall be the boundary by the sea, east of Tamar. This is the east border.

19 And the south side shall be from Tamar as far as the waters of Maribath in Kadesh, then along the shores of the great sea. This is the south side.

20 And the border shall run as far as Nacakh which is at the entrance of Hammath. This is the west side.

21 So you shall divide this land among you according to the tribes of Israel.

22 ¶And it shall come to pass that when you divide it as an inheritance to you and to proselytes from among the aliens who dwell with you, who shall beget children among you; they shall be to you like the children of Israel; they shall have an inheritance with you among the tribes of Israel.

23 And whatever tribe which has the aliens who are proselytes, there you shall give him his inheritance, says the LORD God.

CHAPTER 48

NOW these are the boundaries of the tribes: From the north end, by the way of Hithron which is at the entrance of Hamath and of Khazar-enan, the border of Damascus northward to the border of Hamath; these are its sides east and west, a portion for Dan.

2 And by the border of Dan, from the east side to the west side, a portion for Asher.

3 And by the border of Asher, from the east side to the west side, a portion for Naphtali.

4 And by the border of Naphtali,

from the east side to the west side, a portion for Manasseh.

5 And by the border of Manasseh, from the east side to the west side, a portion for Reuben.

6 And by the border of Reuben, from the east side to the west side, a portion for Ephraim.

7 And by the border of Ephraim, from the east side to the west side, a portion for Judah.

8 ¶And by the border of Judah, from the east side to the west side, shall be the portion which you shall set apart, twenty-five thousand cubits in width, and in length the same as one of the other portions, from the east side to the west side; and the sanctuary shall be in the midst of it.

9 And the portion of the land which you shall set apart for the LORD shall be twenty-five thousand cubits in length and ten thousand in breadth.

10 And for the priests shall be the holy portion; toward the north twenty-five thousand cubits in length, and toward the west ten thousand cubits in breadth, and toward the east ten thousand cubits in breadth, and toward the south twenty-five thousand cubits in length; and the sanctuary of the LORD shall be in the midst of it.

11 It shall be for the priests that are consecrated of the descendants of Zadok; who have kept my charge, who did not go astray as the children of Israel went astray and as the Levites went astray.

12 And this portion shall be their portion out of the land which is set aside, the most holy by the border of the Levites.

13 And opposite the border of the priests the Levites shall have a portion twenty-five thousand cubits in length, and ten thousand in breadth: all their land shall be twenty-five thousand cubits in length and ten thousand cubits in breadth.

14 And they shall not sell any of it, neither exchange it, nor do away with the tithes of the land; for it is holy to the LORD.

15 ¶And the five thousand cubits that are left in the breadth over against the twenty-five thousand cu-

bits shall be common ground for the use of the city, for dwelling and for suburbs; and the city shall be in the midst of it.

16 And these shall be its dimensions: the north side four thousand and five hundred cubits, the east side four thousand and five hundred cubits, the south side four thousand and five hundred cubits, and the west side four thousand and five hundred cubits.

17 And the suburbs of the city shall be toward the north two hundred and fifty cubits and toward the south two hundred and fifty cubits and toward the east two hundred and fifty cubits and toward the west two hundred and fifty cubits.

18 And the remainder of the land opposite the holy portion shall be ten thousand eastward and ten thousand westward; and it shall be opposite the holy portion; and its produce shall be for food to those who work for the city.

19 And they that work for the city shall be recruited out of all the tribes of Israel.

20 The whole portion which is set aside shall be twenty-five thousand by twenty-five thousand; you shall separate the holy portion from the possession of the city.

21 ¶And the remainder shall be for the ruler of the city, on one side and on the other of the holy portion and of the possession of the city, opposite the twenty-five thousand cubits toward the east border, and westward twenty-five thousand cubits toward the west border, opposite the portion for the ruler; and it shall be the holy portion; and the sanctuary of the temple shall be in its midst.

22 Moreover part of the possession of the Levites and of the possession of the city shall be the portion of the ruler in the city, between the border of Judah and the border of Benjamin.

23 As for the rest of the tribes, from the east side to the west side, Benjamin shall have a portion.

24 And by the border of Benjamin, from the east side to the west side, Simeon shall have a portion.

25 And by the border of Simeon,

from the east side to the west side, Issachar a portion.

26 And by the border of Issachar, from the east side to the west side, Zebulun a portion.

27 And by the border of Zebulun, from the east side to the west side, Gad a portion.

28 And by the border of Gad, at the south side southward, the border shall be from Tamar to the waters of Maribath in Kadesh, and his possession shall extend as far as the great sea.

29 This is the land which you shall divide for a heritage to the tribes of Israel, and these are their portions, says the LORD God.

30 ¶And these shall be the limits of the city: on the north side, four thousand and five hundred measures.

31 And the gates of the city shall be after the names of the tribes of Israel: three gates on the north side; one gate for Reuben, one gate for Judah, one gate for Levi.

32 And at the east side four thousand and five hundred measures; and three gates: one gate for Joseph, one gate for Benjamin, one gate for Dan.

33 And at the south side four thousand and five hundred measures; and three gates: one gate for Simeon, one gate for Issachar, one gate for Zebulun.

34 At the west side four thousand and five hundred measures; and three gates: one gate for Gad, one gate for Asher, and one gate for Naphtali.

35 And the circumference of the city shall be eighteen thousand measures; and the name of the city [1] was given by the LORD from the day that it was built.

THE BOOK OF

DANIEL

CHAPTER 1

IN the third year of the reign of Jehoiakim king of Judah, Nebuchadnezzar king of Babylon came to Jerusalem, and besieged it.

2 And the LORD delivered it into his hand, together with Jehoiakim king of Judah and the vessels of the house of the LORD, which he carried away into the land of Sinar, to the house of his idol; and he brought the vessels into the treasure house of his idol.

3 ¶And the king spoke to Ashpaz the chief of the eunuchs, that he should bring some of the children of Israel, of the royal families, and of the Parthians;

4 Boys in whom was no blemish, who were handsome in their appearance and skillful in all wisdom and cunning in knowledge and understanding of science, those who were able to stand in the king's palace to minister to him, and whom they might teach the learning and the language of the Chaldeans.

5 And the king assigned them a daily portion of the king's delicacies and of the wine which he drank, to nourish them for three years, so that afterward they might stand before the king.

6 Now among these were of the children of Judah, Daniel, Hananiah, Mishael, and Azariah;

7 And the chief of the eunuchs gave them names; Daniel he named Belteshazzar; and Hananiah, Shadrach;

[1] Jerusalem, which means the city of peace.

and Mishael, Meshach; and Azariah, Abednego.

8 ¶But Daniel decided in his heart that he would not eat of the king's delicacies nor drink of the wine which he drank; therefore he requested of the chief of the eunuchs that he would not force him to eat.

9 Now God gave Daniel grace and mercy in the presence of the chief of the eunuchs.

10 And the chief of the eunuchs said to Daniel, I fear my lord the king, who has given orders concerning your food and concerning your drink; should he see your faces worse looking than the faces of the boys of your own age, then the king will have me beheaded.

11 Then Daniel said to Menezar, whom the chief of the eunuchs had appointed over Daniel, Hananiah, Mishael, and Azariah,

12 Test your servants for ten days; and let them give us vegetables to eat and water to drink.

13 Then let our appearance and the appearance of the boys who eat of the king's delicacies be examined; and as you see, deal with your servants.

14 So he consented to them in this matter and tested them for ten days.

15 And at the end of ten days he saw that their countenances were much fairer and fatter than those of all the boys who ate of the king's delicacies.

16 Thus Menezar took away the portion of their food and the wine that they should drink, and gave them vegetables to eat and water to drink.

17 ¶As for these four boys, God gave them knowledge and understanding in every book and wisdom; and Daniel had understanding in all visions and dreams.

18 Now when the days that the king had commanded were over, the chief of the eunuchs brought them in before King Nebuchadnezzar.

19 And the king spoke with them; and he found none among all of them like Daniel, Hananiah, Mishael, and Azariah; therefore they stood before the king.

20 And in all matters of wisdom and understanding that the king in-

quired of them he found them ten times better than all the magicians and astrologers that were in his whole realm.

21 And Daniel continued even to the first year of king Cyrus.

CHAPTER 2

AND in the second year of the reign of Nebuchadnezzar, Nebuchadnezzar dreamed a dream and his spirit was troubled and his sleep departed from him.

2 Then the king commanded to call the magicians and the astrologers and the sorcerers and the Chaldeans to show the king his dream. So they came and stood before the king.

3 And the king said to them, I have dreamed a dream, and my spirit is troubled to know the dream.

4 Then spoke the Chaldeans before the king in Aramaic, saying, O king, live for ever; tell your servants the dream, and we will show the interpretation.

5 The king answered and said to the Chaldeans, The word that I have spoken is true; if you do not make known to me the dream and its interpretation, you shall be cut in pieces and your houses shall be plundered.

6 But if you show me the dream and its interpretation, you shall receive from me gifts and wealth and great honor; only show me the dream and its interpretation.

7 They answered again and said, Let the king tell his servants the dream, and we will show its interpretation.

8 The king answered and said, Truly I know that what you want is time, because you see that my word is true.

9 But if you will not make known to me the dream, there is but one sentence for you; for you have prepared lying words and falsehoods to speak before me, to gain time; therefore tell me the dream, so that I shall know that you can show me its interpretation.

10 ¶The Chaldeans answered before the king and said, There is not a man upon the earth who can reveal what

the king asks; neither has any great king or ruler ever asked such a thing of any magician or astrologer or Chaldean.

11 For the thing that the king is asking is very difficult, and there is no man who can show it before the king except the gods, whose dwelling is not with men born of flesh.

12 Then the king was exceedingly furious, and he commanded angrily that all the wise men of Babylon should be destroyed.

13 And the decree went forth that the wise men should be slain; and guards sought Daniel and his companions to slay them.

14 ¶Then Daniel meditated and took counsel, and then said to Arioch the commander of the king's guardsmen, who had gone out to slay the wise men of Babylon,

15 Why is this decree from the king so urgent? Then Arioch made the thing known to Daniel.

16 Then Daniel desired of the king to give him time, and promised that he would show the king the interpretation.

17 Then Daniel went to his house and made the thing known to Hananiah, Mishael, and Azariah, his companions,

18 That they might ask mercy before the God of heaven concerning the mystery, so that Daniel and his companions might not perish with the rest of the wise men of Babylon.

19 ¶Then was the mystery revealed to Daniel in a night vision. And Daniel blessed the God of heaven.

20 Daniel answered and said, Blessed be the name of God for ever and ever; for wisdom and might belong to him;

21 And he changes seasons and times; he removes kings and sets up kings; he gives wisdom to the wise and knowledge to them who know understanding;

22 He reveals the deep and secret things; he knows what is in the darkness, and the light is with him.

23 To thee, O God of my fathers, I give thanks, and I praise thee, who hast given me wisdom and might,

and hast now made known to me what we desired of thee; for thou hast made known to us the king's matter.

24 ¶And in that very hour Daniel went to Arioch, whom the king had ordered to destroy the wise men of Babylon; he went and spoke thus to him: Destroy not the wise men of Babylon; but bring me in before the king and I will show the king the interpretation.

25 Then Arioch brought Daniel in before the king in haste, and spoke thus to him: I have found a man of the captives of Judah who will make known to the king the interpretation.

26 The king answered and said to Daniel, whose name was Belteshazzar, Are you able to make known to me the dream which I have seen, and its interpretation?

27 Daniel answered in the presence of the king, and said, The mystery which the king has demanded to know, can no wise men, sorcerers, nor the magicians, nor the astrologers reveal to the king;

28 But there is a God in heaven who reveals mysteries, who has made known to the King Nebuchadnezzar what shall be in the latter days. Your dream and the vision of your head upon your bed are these;

29 As for you, O king, your thoughts came into your mind concerning what shall come to pass hereafter; and he who reveals mysteries has made known to you what shall come to pass.

30 But as for me, this mystery is not revealed to me on account of any wisdom that I have more than any living person, but for the sake of the interpretation, that it might be known to the king and that you may know the thoughts of your heart.

31 ¶You, O king, were looking, and behold, a great image, whose brightness was excellent, stood before you; and its appearance was terrible.

32 This image's head was of fine gold, its breast and arms of silver, its belly and its thighs of brass,

33 Its legs of iron, its feet part of iron and part of clay.

34 Then you saw that a stone was

cut out without hands, which smote the image upon its feet that were of iron and clay, and broke them to pieces.

35 Then the iron, the brass, the clay, the silver, and the gold were all broken to pieces together, and became like the chaff of the summer threshing floors; and a strong wind carried them away so that no place was found for them; and the stone that struck the image became a great mountain and filled the whole earth.

36 ¶This is the dream; now I will tell its interpretation before the king.

37 You, O king, are a king of kings; for the God of heaven has given you a mighty kingdom and honor.

38 And every country in which men dwell, the fowls of the air and the beasts of the field, he has placed under your authority, and has made you ruler over them all. You are the head of gold.

39 And after you shall arise another kingdom inferior to you, and a third kingdom of brass, which shall rule over all the earth.

40 And the fourth kingdom shall be strong as iron; for just as iron hammers and breaks everything in pieces, so shall it break and conquer every kingdom.

41 And whereas you saw the feet and toes, part of potter's clay and part of iron, the kingdom shall be divided; but there shall be in it some of the strength of iron, just as you saw the iron mixed with miry clay.

42 And as for the toes of the feet which you saw, part of iron and part of clay, so some parts of the kingdom shall be strong and some parts weak.

43 And whereas you saw iron mixed with miry clay, so they shall mix themselves with one another in marriage; but they shall not cleave one to another, just as iron does not mix with clay.

44 And in the days of these kings shall the God of heaven set up an everlasting kingdom, which shall never be destroyed; and the kingdom shall not be left to other people, but it shall break in pieces and bring to an end all these kingdoms, and it shall stand for ever.

45 Forasmuch as you saw that the stone was cut out of the mountain without hands, and that it broke in pieces the iron, the brass, the clay, the silver, and the gold; the great God has made known to you what shall come to pass in the latter days. The dream is true, and its interpretation is sure.

46 ¶Then King Nebuchadnezzar fell upon his face and worshipped Daniel, and commanded that they should offer incense and sacrifices to him.

47 The king answered Daniel and said, Truly, your God is the God of gods and the LORD of kings and a revealer of mysteries, for you have been able to reveal this mystery.

48 Then the king advanced Daniel's rank and gave him a great many gifts and made him ruler over the whole province of Babylon and appointed him chief over all the generals of the armies and over all the wise men of Babylon.

49 Then Daniel requested of the king, and he appointed Shadrach, Meshach, and Abednego over the affairs of the province of Babylon; but Daniel himself remained in the king's gate.

CHAPTER 3

NEBUCHADNEZZAR the king made an image of gold, whose height was sixty cubits and its breadth six cubits; and he set it up in the plain of Dora, in the province of Babylon.

2 Then Nebuchadnezzar the king sent to gather together the generals of the armies, the lords, the governors, the judges, the treasurers, the counsellors, the sheriffs, and all the rulers of the provinces, to come to the dedication of the image which Nebuchadnezzar the king had set up.

3 Then all the generals of the armies, the lords, the governors, the judges, the treasurers, the counsellors, the sheriffs, and all the rulers of the provinces were gathered together to the dedication of the new image

which Nebuchadnezzar the king had set up; and they stood up before the image that King Nebuchadnezzar had set up.

4 Then a herald cried aloud, and said, To you it is commanded, O peoples, nations, and languages,

5 That at the hour when you hear the sound of the trumpet, flute, harp, sackbut, psaltery, and all kinds of music, you must fall down and worship the golden image which Nebuchadnezzar the king has set up;

6 And whosoever does not fall down and worship shall at the same hour be cast into the midst of a burning fiery furnace.

7 Therefore at the hour when the people heard the sound of the trumpet, the flute, the harp, the sackbut, the psaltery, and all kinds of music, all the peoples, the nations, and the languages fell down and worshipped the golden image which Nebuchadnezzar the king had set up.

8 ¶And at that very time certain Chaldeans came near and accused the Jews.

9 They said to King Nebuchadnezzar, O king, live for ever!

10 You, O king, have made a decree, that every man who shall hear the sound of the trumpet, the flute, the harp, the sackbut, the psaltery, and all kinds of music, shall fall down and worship the golden image which you have set up;

11 And whosoever does not fall down and worship shall be cast into the midst of a burning fiery furnace.

12 There are certain Jews whom you have appointed over the affairs of the province of Babylon: Shadrach, Meshach, and Abednego; these men, O king, have not regarded you; they do not serve your god, nor do they worship the golden image which you have set up.

13 ¶Then King Nebuchadnezzar in his rage and fury commanded to bring Shadrach, Meshach, and Abednego. And they brought them before the king.

14 Then Nebuchadnezzar the king spoke and said to them, Is it true, O Shadrach, Meshach, and Abednego,

that you do not serve my god nor worship the golden image which I have set up?

15 Now if you are ready, at the time you hear the sound of the trumpet, the flute, the harp, the sackbut, the psaltery, and all kinds of music, to fall down and worship the image which I have made, good; but if you do not worship, you shall at once be cast into the midst of a burning fiery furnace; and who is your god that shall deliver you out of my hands?

16 Shadrach, Meshach, and Abednego answered and said to King Nebuchadnezzar, There is no use to answer you concerning this matter;

17 For there is our God whom we serve, he is able to deliver us from the burning fiery furnace, and he will deliver us out of your hand, O king.

18 Then the king shall know that we will not serve your god nor worship the golden image which you have set up.

19 ¶Then Nebuchadnezzar the king was filled with fury, and the countenance of his face was changed against Shadrach, Meshach, and Abednego; and he commanded that the furnace should be heated seven times more than it was customarily heated.

20 And he commanded some of the mighty men in the army to bind Shadrach, Meshach, and Abednego, and to cast them into the burning fiery furnace.

21 Then the mighty men bound them in their trousers, their undergarments, their robes, and their hats, and cast them into the fiery furnace.

22 Because the king's command was hasty and the furnace was exceedingly hot, the flames of the fire killed those who had accused Shadrach, Meshach, and Abednego.

23 But the three men, Shadrach, Meshach, and Abednego, fell down bound into the midst of the burning fiery furnace. (And they rose up and walked bound in the midst of the flame, praising God and blessing the LORD.)

24 Then Nebuchadnezzar the king was alarmed and rose up in a great

fear, and spoke and said to his princes, Did we not cast three men bound into the midst of the fire? They answered and said to the king, True, O king.

25 The king answered and said, Behold I see men loose, walking in the midst of the fire, and they are not hurt; and the appearance of the fourth is like that of the Son of God.

26 ¶Then Nebuchadnezzar the king drew near to the mouth of the burning fiery furnace, and spoke and said, Shadrach, Meshach, and Abednego, servants of the most High God, come forth and come hither. Then Shadrach, Meshach, and Abednego, came out of the midst of the fiery furnace.

27 And all the people, generals of the armies, governors, lords, and the great men of the king, being gathered together, saw these men upon whose bodies the fire had no power nor was the hair of their head singed neither were their trousers burned nor had the smell of fire passed on them.

28 Then Nebuchadnezzar spoke and said, Blessed be the God of Shadrach, Meshach, and Abednego, who has sent his angel and delivered his servants that trusted in him, and have rejected the king's word and offered their bodies that they might not serve nor worship any god, except their own God.

29 Therefore I make this decree: Every people, nation, and language which speaks blasphemy against the God of Shadrach, Meshach, and Abednego, shall be cut in pieces, and their houses shall be plundered, because there is no other God that can deliver in this manner.

30 Then the king promoted Shadrach, Meshach, and Abednego, in the province of Babylon.

CHAPTER 4

THEN Nebuchadnezzar the king wrote to all peoples, nations and languages that dwelt in all the earth: Peace be multiplied to you.

2 I thought it good to publish the signs and wonders that the High God has wrought toward me.

3 How great are his signs! and how mighty are his wonders! His kingdom is an everlasting kingdom, and his dominion is from generation to generation.

4 ¶I, Nebuchadnezzar, was at rest in my house and at ease in my palace;

5 I saw a dream which made me afraid, and the visions of my head troubled me.

6 Therefore I made a decree to bring in all the wise men of Babylon before me, that they might make known to me the interpretation of the dream.

7 Then came in before me the magicians, the astrologers, the soothsayers, and the Chaldeans; and I told the dream before them; but they did not make known to me the interpretation thereof;

8 ¶Until Daniel came before me, whose name is Belteshazzar, according to the name of my god, and in whom is the spirit of the holy gods; and before him I told the dream, saying,

9 O Belteshazzar, master of the magicians, because I know that the spirit of the holy gods is in you and no mystery is hidden from you, this is the vision of my dream that I have seen; tell me the interpretation thereof.

10 These were the visions which I saw in my bed: I saw, and behold, a tree in the midst of the earth, and its height was great.

11 The tree grew high, and was strong, and its height reached to heaven and the view thereof to the end of all the earth.

12 Its leaves were beautiful and its fruit abundant; and in it was food for all; the beasts of the field dwelt under it, and the fowls of the air rested in its boughs, and all flesh was fed from it.

13 I saw in the visions of my head upon my bed, and behold, a holy angel came down from heaven,

14 And cried aloud and spoke thus: Hew down the tree and cut off its branches, shake off its leaves and scatter its fruit; let the beasts get away from under it and the fowls of the air from its branches;

15 Nevertheless leave the stump of its roots in the earth; but it shall be bound with a band of iron and brass in the green grass of the field; and let him be wet with the dew of heaven, and let his dwelling be with the beasts of the field in the grass of the earth;

16 Let his heart be changed from man's, and let a beast's heart be given to him; and let seven seasons change over him.

17 This decree is by the command of the angel at the request of the Holy One to the intent that the living may know that the Most High God rules in the kingdom of men and gives it to whomsoever he will, and appoints over it the lowest of men.

18 This dream I, King Nebuchadnezzar, have seen. Now you, O Belteshazzar, tell me the interpretation thereof, because all the wise men of my kingdom are not able to make known to me the interpretation; but you, Daniel, are able; for the spirit of the holy gods is in you.

19 ¶Then Daniel, whose name was Belteshazzar, was confused for an hour and his thoughts troubled him. The king spoke and said, Belteshazzar, let not the dream or the interpretation thereof trouble you. Daniel answered and said, My lord, may the dream be to those who hate you and the interpretation thereof to your enemies.

20 The tree which you saw, which grew and was strong, whose height reached to the heaven and the view thereof to all the earth;

21 Whose leaves were beautiful and its fruit abundant, and in it was food for all flesh; under which the beasts of the field dwelt, and upon whose branches the fowls of the air rested, and from it fed all flesh;

22 It is you, O king; for you have grown and become strong; you have grown high and reach to the heavens, and your dominion is to the end of the earth.

23 And whereas the king saw a holy angel coming down from heaven, crying aloud and saying, Hew down the tree and destroy it; but leave the stump and the roots thereof in the earth and let it be bound with a band of iron and brass in the green grass of the field; and let him be wet with the dew of heaven, and let his dwelling be with the beasts of the field in the grass of the earth; and let his heart be changed from man's, and let a beast's heart be given to him till seven seasons change over him.

24 This is the interpretation, O king: The decree of the Most High has come against my lord the king;

25 They shall drive you away from men, and your dwelling shall be with the beasts of the field, and they shall make you to eat grass like an ox, and you shall be wet with the dew of heaven, and seven seasons shall change over you, till you know that the Most High rules in the kingdom of men and gives it to whomsoever he will.

26 And whereas he commanded to spare the stump and the tree roots, your kingdom shall be sure to you after you have learned that authority is from heaven.

27 Wherefore, let my counsel be acceptable to you, and get rid of your sins by means of almsgiving, and your iniquities by showing mercy to the weak, till your transgressions are removed from you.

28 ¶All of these things came upon King Nebuchadnezzar.

29 At the end of twelve months King Nebuchadnezzar was walking on the roof of his royal palace which is in Babylon.

30 And he spoke and said, Is not this great Babylon that I have built for the seat of my kingdom and for my great dominion and my majesty?

31 While the word was in the king's mouth, there came a voice from heaven, saying, O King Nebuchadnezzar, to you it is spoken; for your kingdom is departed from you.

32 And they shall drive you from among men, and your dwelling shall be with the beasts of the field; they shall make you to eat grass like an ox, and you shall be wet with the dew of heaven; and seven seasons shall change over you, until you know that the Most High rules in the king-

dom of men and gives it to whomsoever he will, and he appoints the lowest of men over it.

33 The same hour the word was fulfilled upon King Nebuchadnezzar; and he was driven from among men, and did eat grass like an ox, and his body was wet with the dew of heaven, till his hair grew like eagles' feathers and his nails like bird's claws.

34 And when the days were fulfilled, I, Nebuchadnezzar, lifted up my eyes to heaven, and my sense was restored to me, and I blessed the Most High and I praised and glorified him who lives for ever, whose dominion is an everlasting dominion and whose kingdom is from generation to generation;

35 And all the inhabitants of the earth are reckoned as nothing in his presence; and he does as he pleases with the hosts of heaven and among the inhabitants of the earth; and none can resist his hand or say to him, What doest thou?

36 At the same time my sense returned to me, and my princes and my generals sought me; and I was established in my kingdom, and excellent majesty was added to me.

37 Now I, Nebuchadnezzar, praise and exalt and honor the King of heaven, for all his works are true and his ways just; and those who walk in pride he is able to humble.

CHAPTER 5

BELSHAZZAR the king made a great feast to a thousand of his princes, and drank wine in the presence of the thousand.

2 And Belshazzar, while he tasted the wine, commanded to bring the golden and silver vessels which his father Nebuchadnezzar had taken out of the temple which was in Jerusalem, that the king and his princes, his wives and his concubines might drink out of them.

3 Then they brought the golden vessels that were taken out of the temple of God which was at Jerusalem, and the king and his princes, his wives and his concubines drank out of them.

4 They drank wine and praised the gods of gold and of silver, of brass, of iron, of wood, and of stone.

5 ¶In that very hour there appeared the fingers of a man's hand, and wrote opposite the candlestick upon the plaster of the wall of the king's palace, and the king saw the palm of the man's hand that wrote.

6 Then the king's countenance was changed and his thoughts troubled him and the joints of his loins were loosed and his knees struck one against another.

7 Then the king cried aloud to bring in the astrologers, the Chaldeans, the soothsayers, and the wise men. And the king spoke and said to the wise men of Babylon, Whosoever shall read this writing and show me the interpretation thereof, shall be clothed with scarlet and have a chain of gold about his neck, and shall rule over a third of the kingdom.

8 Then came in all the king's wise men; but they could not read the writing nor make known to the king the interpretation thereof.

9 Then King Belshazzar was greatly troubled and his countenance changed and his princes were bewildered.

10 ¶Now the queen, because of the conversation of the king and his princes, came into the banquet house, and she spoke and said to the king, O king, live for ever; let not your thoughts trouble you nor let your countenance be changed;

11 There is a man in your kingdom in whom is the spirit of the holy gods; and in the days of your father light and understanding and wisdom like the wisdom of the gods were found in him; so that King Nebuchadnezzar your father appointed him master of the magicians, astrologers, soothsayers, and the Chaldeans

12 Because of his spiritual power, knowledge, and understanding which he possesses, to interpret the dreams, devise proverbs, and solve riddles, even Daniel, whom the king named Belteshazzar. Now let Daniel be called, and he will show the interpretation.

13 Then Daniel came in before the king. And the king spoke and said

to Daniel, Are you the Daniel of the exiles of Judah whom the king my father brought from Judea?

14 I have heard of you, that the spirit of the holy gods is in you and that light and understanding and excellent wisdom are found in you.

15 And now the magicians and the astrologers have been brought in before me, that they might read this writing and make known to me the interpretation thereof; but they could not show me the interpretation of the thing;

16 And I have heard of you, that you can make interpretations and solve riddles. Now if you can read this writing and make known to me the interpretation thereof, you shall be clothed with purple and have a chain of gold about your neck, and shall rule over a third of the kingdom.

17 ¶Then Daniel answered and said to the king, Let your gifts be to yourself, and give the honor of your house to others; but the writing I will read to the king, and make known to him the interpretation.

18 O king, the Most High God gave Nebuchadnezzar your father a kingdom and majesty and honor and glory.

19 And because of the greatness that he gave him, all peoples, nations, and languages trembled and feared before him; for whom he would he slew, and whom he would he kept alive, and whom he would he promoted, and whom he would he humbled.

20 But when his heart was lifted up and his pride increased, he was deposed from his kingly throne and his glory passed away from him;

21 And he was driven from among men; and his heart became like that of the beasts, and his dwelling was with the wild asses; they fed him with grass like an ox, and his body was wet with the dew of heaven, till his hair grew like eagles' feathers and his nails like birds' claws till he knew that the Most High God rules in the kingdom of men and that he gives it to whom he pleases and he appoints over it the weakest among men.

22 And you his son, O Belshazzar, have not humbled your heart, though you knew all these things;

23 But have lifted up yourself against the LORD of heaven; and they have brought the vessels of his house before you, and you and your princes, your wives and your concubines, have drunk wine out of them; and you have praised the gods of gold and silver, of brass, iron, wood, and stone, which neither see nor hear nor know; and the God in whose hands is your breath and all your ways, you have not glorified nor honored.

24 Then the palm of the hand was sent from his presence; and this writing was written.

25 ¶And this is the writing that was written: MENE, MENE, TEKEL, UPHARSIN.

26 This is the interpretation of the words: MENE, God has numbered your kingdom and brought it to an end.

27 TEKEL, You are weighed in the balances and found wanting.

28 PERES, Your kingdom is divided and given to the Medes and Persians.

29 Then commanded King Belshazzar, and they clothed Daniel with purple and put a chain of gold about his neck and made a proclamation concerning him that he should be a ruler over a third of the kingdom.

30 ¶In that night Belshazzar the Chaldean king was slain.

31 And Darius the Median took the kingdom, being about sixty-two years old.

CHAPTER 6

IT pleased Darius to appoint over the kingdom a hundred and twenty generals to be over his whole kingdom;

2 And over them three presidents, of whom Daniel was one, that the generals might give account to them, so that they might not trouble the king.

3 Then Daniel excelled above all the presidents and generals, because he was more spiritual; and the king thought to set him over his whole kingdom.

4 ¶Then the governors and generals sought to find occasion against Daniel concerning the affairs of the kingdom; but they could find no fault or occasion because he was faithful to his God, neither were they able to find any blame or charge against him.

5 Then these men said, We shall not find any occasion against this Daniel unless we find it against him in connection with the law of his God.

6 Then the governors and the generals came before the king, and said to him, King Darius, live for ever!

7 All the governors of the kingdom, the princes, the generals, and the lords have consulted together to establish a royal statute and to make a firm decree that whosoever shall ask a petition of any god or man for thirty days, except of you, O king, shall be cast into the den of lions.

8 Now, O king, establish this decree and let it be put in writing, that it be not changed, according to the law of the Medes and Persians, which cannot be altered.

9 Then King Darius signed the writing and issued the decree.

10 ¶Now when Daniel knew that the writing was signed, he went into his house, and the windows of his chamber were open toward Jerusalem; he knelt upon his knees three times a day, and prayed and gave thanks before his God, as he had done before.

11 Then these men spied, and found Daniel praying and making supplication before his God.

12 And they came near and said before the king, O king, live for ever! Did you not decree and sign, O king, that whosoever shall ask a petition of any god or man within thirty days, except of you, O king, shall be cast into the den of lions? The king answered and said, The decree is true, according to the law of the Medes and Persians, which cannot be altered.

13 Then they answered and said before the king, Daniel, who is of the exiles from Judea, has not regarded you, O king, nor the decree which you have made, but he makes his petition three times a day.

14 Then the king, when he heard these words, was very much grieved, and made up his mind to deliver Daniel; and he labored till the going down of the sun to deliver him.

15 But these men prevailed over the king, and said to him, Know, O king, that there is a law of the Medes and Persians that every edict and decree which the king establishes may not be changed.

16 Then the king commanded, and they brought Daniel and cast him into the den of lions. And the king spoke and said to Daniel, Your God whom you serve continually, he will deliver you.

17 And they brought a large stone and laid it upon the mouth of the den, and the king sealed it with his own signet and with the signet of his princes, so that the sentence might not be changed concerning Daniel.

18 ¶Then the king went to his palace and passed the night fasting; no food was brought before him, and his sleep departed from him.

19 Then the king arose in the morning early and went in haste to the den of lions.

20 And when he came to the den, he cried with a loud voice to Daniel, and the king spoke and said to Daniel, O Daniel, servant of the living God, has your God whom you serve continually been able to deliver you from the lions?

21 Then Daniel spoke to the king and said, O king, live for ever!

22 My God has sent his angel and has shut the lions' mouths, and they have not hurt me, because I was innocent before him; and also before you, O king, I have committed no offense.

23 Then the king was exceedingly glad for him, and commanded that they should take Daniel up out of the den. So Daniel was taken up out of the den, and no manner of hurt was found upon him, because he believed in his God.

24 ¶And the king commanded, and they brought those men who had ac-

cused Daniel, and they cast them into the den of lions, they, their wives, and their children; and before they reached the bottom of the den, the lions pounced upon them and broke all their bones in pieces.

25 ¶Then King Darius wrote to all the peoples, nations, and languages, that dwell in all the earth, Peace be multiplied to you.

26 I make a decree that in every dominion of my kingdom men tremble and fear before the God of Daniel; for he is the living God and endures for ever, and his kingdom shall not be destroyed and his dominion shall be even to the end.

27 He saves and rescues and delivers and performs signs and wonders in heaven and on earth, for he has rescued Daniel from the power of the lions.

28 So Daniel was promoted during the reign of Darius and during the reign of Cyrus the Persian.

CHAPTER 7

IN the first year of Belshazzar king of Babylon, Daniel saw a dream and the visions of his head as he lay upon his bed; then he wrote the dream and told the sum of the matter.

2 Daniel spoke and said, I saw in my vision by night, and behold, the four winds of heaven stirred up the great sea.

3 And four great beasts came up out of the sea, differing one from another.

4 The first was like a lion and had eagle's wings; I beheld till its wings were plucked off, and it rose up from the ground and stood upon its feet like a man, and a man's heart was given to it.

5 And the second beast was like a bear, and it stood up on one side, and it had three ribs in its mouth between its teeth; and they said thus to it: Arise, devour much flesh.

6 After these things I beheld, and lo, another beast, like a leopard, which had upon its sides four wings of a fowl; the beast had also four heads, and dominion was given to it.

7 After these things I saw in the night visions, and behold, a fourth beast, dreadful and mighty and exceedingly strong, and it had great iron teeth; it devoured and broke in pieces, and stamped the residue with its feet; and it was different from all the beasts that were before it, and it had ten horns.

8 And I considered the horns, and behold, there came up among them another little horn before which three of the first horns were plucked up from before it; and behold, in this horn were eyes like the eyes of man, and a mouth speaking great things.

9 ¶Then I beheld, and lo, thrones were placed, and the Ancient of days did sit; his garment was white as snow and the hair of his head like the pure wool; his throne was like a fiery flame, and its wheels were like burning fire.

10 A stream of fire issued and came forth from before him; a thousand thousands ministered to him, and ten thousand times ten thousand stood before him; the judge was seated and the books were opened.

11 I beheld, and lo, the beast was slain and its body destroyed and given to the burning flame.

12 As for the rest of the beasts, they had their dominion taken away, yet their lives were prolonged for a season and a time.

13 I saw in the night visions, and behold, one like the Son of man came upon the clouds of heaven, and came to the Ancient of days, and they brought him before him.

14 And there was given him dominion and glory and a kingdom, that all the peoples, nations, and languages should serve him; his dominion is an everlasting dominion, which shall not pass away, and his kingdom is one that shall not be destroyed.

15 ¶As for me, Daniel, my spirit was grieved in my bed and the visions of my head troubled me.

16 I came near to one of those who ministered and asked of him the truth concerning all these things. And he told me the truth and made me know the interpretation of these things.

17 Then he said to me, These four

great beasts which you saw are four kings which shall arise out of the earth.

18 But the saints of the Most High shall receive the kingdom and possess it for ever and ever.

19 Then I wanted to know the truth concerning the fourth beast, which was different from all the others, exceedingly dreadful, whose teeth were of iron and whose nails of brass, which devoured and broke in pieces and stamped the residue with its feet;

20 And concerning the ten horns that were on its head, and the other horn which came up between them, and before which three fell, the horn that had eyes and a mouth that spoke very great things, whose appearance was greater than its fellows.

21 I beheld, and the same horn made war with the saints and prevailed against them,

22 Until the Ancient of days came and gave judgment to the saints of the Most High; and the time came when the saints possessed the kingdom.

23 Thus he said to me: The fourth beast shall be the fourth kingdom upon the earth, which shall be greater than all the kingdoms and shall devour the whole earth, and shall tread it down and break it in pieces.

24 And as for the ten horns out of this kingdom, they are ten kings that shall arise and another king shall arise after them; and he shall be greater than the first, and he shall defeat three kings.

25 And he shall speak words against the Most High, and shall plot against the saints of the Most High, and think to change times and laws; and they shall be given into his hand for a time, times, and half a time.

26 But when the judge is seated in judgment, they shall take away his dominion, to consume and to destroy it to the end of his kingdom.

27 And the dominions and the greatness of the kingdom under the whole heaven shall be given to the holy people of the Most High, whose kingdom is an everlasting kingdom, and all dominions shall serve and obey him.

28 Hitherto is the end of the matter. As for me, Daniel, my thoughts troubled me greatly and my countenance changed in me; but I kept the matter in my heart.

CHAPTER 8

IN the third year of the reign of King Belshazzar a vision appeared to me, Daniel, after that which appeared to me at the first.

2 And I saw in my vision and it came to pass, I was at Shushan in the palace, which is in the province of Elam; and I saw in my dream that I was standing by the river Abol Ulai.

3 Then I lifted up my eyes and saw, and behold, there stood before the river Abol a ram which had two horns; and the two horns were high, but one was higher than the other, and the higher one came up last.

4 I saw the ram pushing westward and northward and southward; and no beasts could stand before him, and there was none that could deliver out of his hands; but he did according to his will, and became great.

5 And as I was considering it, behold, a he-goat came from the west on the face of the whole earth, without harming the ground, and the he-goat had a prominent horn between his eyes.

6 And he came to the ram that had two horns, which I had seen standing before the river Abol, and ran against him in the fury of his power.

7 And when he reached the ram, he was furious against him, and struck the ram and broke his two horns; and there was no power in the ram to stand before him, but he cast him down to the ground and stamped upon him; and there was none that could deliver the ram out of the hands of the he-goat.

8 Therefore the he-goat became exceedingly great; and when he was strong, his great horn was broken; and there came up four prominent ones under it towards the four winds of heaven.

9 And out of one of them came

forth a little horn, which grew exceedingly great, toward the south and toward the east;

10 And it waxed great, even to the host of heaven; and it cast down some of the host and of the stars to the ground and stamped upon them.

11 And it magnified itself even to the prince of the host, and it took away from him the continual sacrifice, and demolished the place of his sanctuary.

12 And a host was given to him against the continual sacrifice by reason of transgression, and the holy thing was cast down to the ground, and the horn went ahead and prospered.

13 ¶Then I heard a saint speaking, and another saint said to that certain saint who spoke, How long shall be the vision concerning the continual sacrifice, and how soon will the iniquity and corruption be over and the holy thing and host be trodden under foot?

14 And he said to him, For two thousand and three hundred days; then righteousness shall prevail.

15 ¶And it came to pass when I, Daniel, had seen this vision and sought to understand it, then behold, there stood before me as it were the appearance of a man.

16 And I heard a man's voice between the banks of Ulai, who called and said, Gabriel, make this man to understand the vision.

17 So he came near where I stood; and when he came, I was afraid and fell upon my face; but he said to me, Understand, O Son of man; for at the time of the end shall be the vision.

18 Now as he was speaking with me, I was in deep sleep on my face toward the ground; but he touched me and set me upright.

19 And he said to me, Behold, I will show you what shall be at the latter end of the indignation; for at the expiration of the time appointed the end shall be.

20 The ram which you saw with two horns represents the kings of Media and Persia.

21 And the he-goat is the king of Greece, and the great horn that is between his eyes is the first king.

22 And as for the horn that was broken, and there rose four others under it, four kings shall rise up out of the nation, but not by their own power.

23 And at the latter end of their kingdom, when the transgressions are come to an end, a king of fierce countenance who understands riddles shall arise.

24 And his power shall be mighty, but not by his own power; and he shall cause terrible destruction, and shall prosper and cross over and destroy the mighty and the holy people.

25 And through his craft and treachery his dominion shall prosper, and he shall magnify himself in his heart, and suddenly he shall destroy many; and he shall also rise up against the Prince of princes; but he shall be defeated easily.

26 And the vision of the morning and the evening which has been told is true; and as for you, Daniel, keep this vision a secret, for it shall not be for many days.

27 And I, Daniel, trembled and was troubled for some days; then I rose up and did the king's business; and I was astonished at the vision, but none understood it.

CHAPTER 9

IN the first year of Darius, the son of Ahasuerus, a descendant of the Medes who became king over the realm of the Chaldeans,

2 In the first year of his reign I, Daniel, understood by the scriptures the number of the years, seeing that the word of the LORD came to pass which the prophet Jeremiah said, that seventy years would elapse before the desolations of Jerusalem would come to an end.

3 ¶And I lifted up my face before the LORD God, to seek by prayer and supplications, with fasting and with sackcloth and with ashes;

4 And I prayed before the LORD my God and made my confession and said, I beseech thee, O LORD, the

great and revered God, who keepest the covenant and mercy to them that love him and to them that keep his commandments;

5 We have sinned and have committed iniquity and have done wickedly and have rebelled and have gone astray from thy commandments and thy judgments;

6 Neither have we listened to thy servants the prophets, who spoke in thy name to our kings, our princes and our fathers, and to all the people of the land.

7 O Lord, victory belongs to thee, but shame is ours, as at this day, to the men of Judah and to the inhabitants of Jerusalem and to all Israel that are near and that are far off, through all the countries whither thou hast driven them, because of their iniquity which they transgressed against thee.

8 O Lord, to us belongs shame of faces to our kings, to our princes, and to our fathers, because we have sinned against thee.

9 To the Lord God belong mercies and forgiveness of sins, for we have rebelled against him;

10 Neither have we obeyed the voice of the Lord our God, to walk according to his laws which he set before us by his servants the prophets.

11 Yea, all Israel have transgressed thy law and have gone astray and have not obeyed thy voice; therefore thou hast brought upon them the curses and the oaths that are written in the law of Moses the servant of God, because we have sinned in his presence.

12 And he has confirmed his words which he spoke against us and against our judges that judged us, by bringing upon us a great evil; for under the whole heaven has not been done as has been done upon Jerusalem.

13 As it is written in the law of Moses, all this evil has come upon us; yet we have not prayed before the Lord our God, that we might repent from our iniquities and understand thy truth.

14 Therefore the Lord has stirred up this evil and brought it upon us; for the Lord our God is righteous in all his works which he has done, and yet we have not obeyed his voice.

15 And now, O Lord our God, who didst bring thy people out of the land of Egypt with a mighty hand, and hast made thee a name, as at this day; we have sinned, we have done wickedly.

16 ¶O Lord, according to all thy righteousness which thou didst toward us, let thine anger and thy fury be turned away from thy city Jerusalem and from thy holy mountain, because for our sins, and for the iniquities of our fathers, thy people are scattered in every land, and Jerusalem has become a reproach to all peoples.

17 Now therefore, O God, hear the prayer of thy servant and his supplication, and cause thy face to shine upon thy sanctuary which is desolate, for thy name's sake, O Lord.

18 O my God, incline thine ear and hear; open thine eyes and behold our ruined and desolate places and the city which is called by thy name; for we do not present our supplications before thee for our righteousness, but for thy great mercies.

19 O Lord, hear; O Lord, forgive us; O Lord, hearken and do; delay not for thy own name's sake, O my God, because thy city and thy people are called by thy name.

20 ¶And while I was yet praying and confessing my offenses and the offenses of my people Israel and presenting my supplication before the Lord my God for the holy mountain of my God,

21 Yea, while I was speaking in prayer, the man Gabriel, whom I had seen in the vision before, came from heaven, flying swiftly, and drew near me at the time of the evening sacrifice.

22 And he came and talked to me and said to me, O Daniel, I am now come forth to instruct you, so that you might understand.

23 At the beginning of your prayer, the word came forth and I have come to make it known to you; for you are greatly beloved; therefore discern

the matter and understand the vision.

24 Seventy times seven weeks are determined upon your people and upon your holy city, to finish the transgressions and to make an end of sins and for the forgiveness of the iniquity and to bring in everlasting righteousness and to fulfill the vision of the prophets and to give the most holy to Messiah.

25 Know therefore and understand that from the going forth of the word to restore and build Jerusalem to the coming of the Messiah the king shall be seven times seven weeks, and sixty-two times seven weeks; the people shall return and build Jerusalem, its streets, and its broad ways at the end of the appointed times.

26 After sixty-two times seven weeks, Messiah shall be slain, and the city shall be without a ruler; and the holy city shall be destroyed together with the coming king; and the end thereof shall be a mass exile, and at the end of the war, desolations are determined.

27 And he shall confirm the covenant with many for seven weeks and half of seven weeks, then he shall cause the sacrifice and gift offerings to cease, and upon the horns of the altar the abomination of desolation; and the desolation shall continue until the end of the appointed time; the city shall remain desolate.

CHAPTER 10

IN the third year of Cyrus king of Persia a thing was revealed to Daniel, whose name was called Belteshazzar; and the thing was true, but the thing and the vision were discerned and understood with great difficulty.

2 In those days I, Daniel, was mourning three times seven weeks of days.

3 I ate no dainty food, neither meat nor wine entered into my mouth, neither did I anoint myself at all, till fully three times seven weeks of days were fulfilled.

4 On the twenty-fourth day of the first month, as I was by the side of the great river Euphrates.

5 I lifted up my eyes and looked, and behold, a certain man clothed in linen, whose loins were girded with glory and majesty.

6 His appearance was peculiar, and there is nothing like it; and his face as the appearance of lightning and his eyes as lamps of fire and his arms and his feet like the color of burnished brass and the sound of his words like the sound of many armies.

7 And I, Daniel, alone saw this vision; for the men who were with me did not see the vision; but a great fear fell upon them, so they fled because of the fear.

8 Wherefore I was left alone and saw this great vision, and there remained no strength in me; and my heart trembled, and there was no strength in me.

9 And when I heard the sound of his words, I fell down upon my face on the ground;

10 ¶And behold, a hand touched me and set me upon my knees and upon the palms of my hands.

11 And he said to me, Arise, O Daniel, O man greatly beloved; understand the words that I speak to you, and stand upright; for now I have been sent to you. And when he had spoken this word to me, I stood up trembling.

12 Then he said to me, Fear not, Daniel; for from the first day that you did set your heart to comprehend so that you might stand before your God, your words have been heard, and I have come in response to your words.

13 The ruler of the kingdom of Persia withstood me twenty-one days; but lo, Michael, one of the chief princes, came to help me; and I remained there against the wishes of the ruler of Persia.

14 Now I have come to let you know what shall befall your people in the latter days; for yet the vision is for the end of the days appointed.

15 And when he had spoken these words to me, I set my face towards the ground and was speechless.

16 And behold, one resembling a man touched my lips; then I opened

my mouth and spoke and said to him who stood before me, O my LORD, by the vision my heart trembled and I was unable to rise.

17 For how can the servant of my lord talk with this my lord? For, behold, there is no strength in me, neither is there breath left in me.

18 Then again the one whose appearance was like that of a man touched me and strengthened me,

19 And said, O man greatly beloved, fear not; peace be to you; have courage, be strong. And when he had spoken to me, I was strengthened and said, Let my lord speak; for I have been strengthened.

20 Then he said to me, Do you know why I have come to you? And now I will return to fight with the ruler of Persia; and when I went out, lo, the ruler of Greece came.

21 But I will show you that which is noted in the scripture of truth; and there is none to help me in these things but Michael your prince and myself.

CHAPTER 11

IN the first year of Darius the Mede, the angel stood up to encourage and strengthen me.

2 And he said, Now I will show you the truth. Behold, there shall arise yet three kings in Persia; and the fourth shall be far richer than all of them; and when he has become powerful in his own country, he shall stir up all the kingdoms of Greece.

3 And a mighty king shall arise, and he shall rule with great dominion, and do according to his will.

4 And when he has risen, his kingdom shall be broken and shall be scattered toward the four winds of heaven; but it will not extend to its former borders nor according to his dominion which he ruled; for his kingdom shall be uprooted, and there shall be no kingdoms beside the divisions of this kingdom.

5 ¶And the king of the south and his princes shall be strong, and the people shall follow him, and he shall rule over a great dominion.

6 And after some years they shall come to an agreement, and the daughter of the king of the south shall come to the king of the north to make peace between them; but she will be unable to achieve her purpose because of fear; and she shall surrender together with those who had brought her, her maids, and her allies at that time.

7 But an heir from his posterity shall rise over his land, and he shall come with an army and might against the king of the north, and he shall deal against them, and shall prevail.

8 And he shall also carry away captive into Egypt their idols, with their precious vessels of silver and of gold; and he shall rise up against the king of the north once or twice.

9 Then the king of the south shall invade the fortified cities of the king of the north, but he shall return to his own land.

10 But his sons shall be stirred up, and shall assemble a multitude of great forces; and they shall attack him and sweep through the land, and shall return destroying as far as his fortifications.

11 And the king of the south shall be enraged, and shall come forth to fight with the king of the north; and the king of the north shall raise a great army, but the army shall be given into his enemy's hand.

12 And when his enemy has destroyed the army, his heart shall be exalted; and he shall destroy many men, but he shall not prevail.

13 For the king of the north shall return and raise an army twice the size of the former, and shall come after certain years with a great army and with a strong cavalry.

14 And at that time many shall rise against the king of the north; also the wicked men of your own people shall exalt themselves to fulfil the vision; but they shall be overthrown.

15 So the king of the north shall come and set up ramparts and take the most strongly fortified cities; and the arms of the south shall not withstand, because they have no strength to withstand, and the chosen ones of the people shall rise up, but they can-

not resist because they have no strength to withstand.

16 But he who comes against him shall do according to his own will, and none shall stand before him; and he shall invade the land of Israel, and it shall be delivered into his hands.

17 Then he shall set his face to invade the fortified places of all kingdoms, and all the people who are with him shall advance; and a daughter of men shall be given to him so that she might destroy him, but it shall not prosper, nor shall he take her to himself.

18 After this he shall turn his face to the islands, and shall conquer many; and he shall do away with a ruler who had reproached him, and return his reproach to him.

19 Then he shall turn his face toward the fortified places of the earth; but he shall be overthrown and fall, and shall not be found.

20 Then shall rise up in his place a weak ruler and a vassal of the kingdoms; but within a short time he shall be destroyed, neither in anger nor in battle.

21 And in his place shall rise up a vile person, to whom they shall not bestow the royal honor; but he shall come suddenly and seize the kingdom by fraud.

22 And the fortified cities in the provinces shall be plundered, and shall scatter before him even the high priests of the covenant.

23 And some of those who will make a league with him shall work deceitfully against him.

24 And yet he shall become strong, and ally himself with a small people and with the rich cities; and he shall do that which his fathers have not done, nor his fathers' fathers; he shall carry away prey and spoil and riches; yea, and he shall devise plots against their provinces.

25 And for a time he shall stir up his power and his courage against the king of the south with a great and mighty army; and the king of the south shall be provoked to battle with a very great army; and he shall become exceedingly strong, but he shall

not stand; for they shall devise plots against him.

26 Yea, those who eat of his delicacies shall destroy him, and his army shall be scattered; and many shall fall down slain.

27 And both these kings' hearts shall be bent to do mischief, and they shall speak lies at one table; but they shall not prosper because the end shall come at the time appointed.

28 Then he shall return to his own land with a great army; and his heart shall be against the holy covenant;

29 And he shall do as at the former time, even so in the latter time.

30 ¶ For the hosts of China shall come against him; and they shall defeat him, and he shall return, and have indignation against the holy covenant; he shall have an understanding with those who had forsaken the holy covenant.

31 And their forces shall rise from among themselves, and they shall pollute the mighty sanctuary and shall do away with the daily sacrifice, and they shall place the abomination that makes desolate.

32 And those who act wickedly against the covenant shall he condemn; but the people who know their God shall be strong.

33 And the righteous men among the people shall teach many; yet they shall fall by the sword and by fire, by captivity and by spoil, for a thousand days.

34 Now when they fall, they shall receive a little help; but many other hardships shall be added to them by means of deception.

35 And some of the wise men shall fall, to test them and to discern, even to the time of the end; for there is a long period before the appointed time is to come.

36 And the king shall do according to his will; and he shall exalt himself and magnify himself above every god, and shall speak great vain things against the God of gods, and shall prosper till the indignation is accomplished; for that which is determined shall be done.

37 Neither shall he regard the God

of his fathers nor the desire of women, nor regard any god; for he shall magnify himself above all things.

38 But in his estate shall he honor the mighty God; and a god whom his fathers did not know he shall honor with gold and silver, and with precious stones and pleasant things.

39 He shall invade the strong provinces, fighting against strange gods, that he may see the victory and rule over many people, and he shall divide the land and sell it for a price.

40 And at the time of the end the king of the south shall fight against him; and the king of the north shall march against him with chariots and with horsemen and with many ships; and he shall invade the land.

41 He shall reach also the land of Israel, and many people shall be slain; but these shall be delivered out of his hands, even Edom and Moab and the remnant of the children of Ammon.

42 He shall stretch forth his hand also against other countries; and the land of Egypt shall not escape from his hands.

43 But he shall have power over the treasures of gold and silver, and over all the precious things of Egypt; and the Lybians and the Ethiopians shall be his allies.

44 But rumors from the east and from the north shall trouble him; therefore he shall go forth with great fury to destroy and to slay many.

45 And he shall pitch his royal tent in a plain between the sea and the mountain; and he shall guard the holy place; and the time of his end shall come, and none shall help him.

CHAPTER 12

AND at that time shall Michael arise, the great angel who has charge over your people; and there shall be a time of trouble such as never has been like it since the beginning of the world; and at that very time some of your people shall be delivered, every one whose name shall be found written in the book.

2 And many of those who sleep in the dust of the earth shall awake,

¹ Idol worship.

some to everlasting life and some to shame and everlasting contempt.

3 And those who have done good and the men of understanding shall shine as the brightness of the firmament; and those who have turned many to righteousness shall shine and stand like stars for ever and ever.

4 But you, O Daniel, seal these words and be silent, and seal this book even to the time of the end; many shall want to know the end, and knowledge shall be increased.

5 ¶Then I, Daniel, looked, and behold, two other angels stood one on this side of the bank of the river and the other on that side.

6 And they said to the man clothed in costly array who stood above the waters of the river, How long shall it be till the end of these things?

7 And I heard the man clothed in costly array who stood above the waters of the river. He held up his right hand and his left hand to heaven, and swore by him who lives for ever that it shall be for a time, times, and a half a time; and when holy people are delivered, all these things shall be fulfilled.

8 And I, Daniel, heard something, but I did not understand; then I said, O my lord, what shall come after these things?

9 And he said, Go your way, Daniel; for the words are closed up and sealed till the time of the end.

10 Many shall be chosen and made white and tried; but the sinners shall continue to sin; and none of the wicked shall understand; but those who have done good works shall understand.

11 And from the time that the daily sacrifice shall be abolished, and the abomination ¹ is given to destruction, there shall be a thousand two hundred and ninety days.

12 Blessed is he who waits and reaches to the thousand three hundred and thirty-five days.

13 But as for you, O Daniel, go your way and rest till the end; then you shall arise at your appointed time, at the end of the days.

HOSEA

CHAPTER 1

THE word of the LORD that came to Hosea, the son of Beeri, in the days of Uzziah, Jotham, Ahaz, and Hezekiah, kings of Judah, and in the days of Jereboam the son of Joash, king of Israel.

2 The beginning of the word of the LORD that came to Hosea: The LORD said to Hosea, Go, take to yourself a wife of whoredoms and children of whoredoms; for the land will commit great whoredom in departing from the LORD.

3 So he went and took Gomer the daughter of Diblaim; who conceived and bore him a son.

4 And the LORD said to him, Call his name Jezreel; for yet a little while, and I will avenge the blood of Jezreel upon the house of Jehu, and I will cause to cease the kingdom of the house of Israel.

5 And it shall come to pass on that day, I will break the bow of Israel in the valley of Jezreel.

6 ¶And she conceived again and bore a daughter. And the LORD said to him, Call her name La-ethrakhmath (not beloved); for I will no more have mercy upon the house of Israel; and I will utterly cause them to be carried away captive.

7 But I will have mercy on the house of Judah, and I will save them by the LORD their God, and will not save them by bow nor by sword nor by battle nor by horses nor by horsemen.

8 ¶Now when she had weaned La-ethrakhmath, she conceived again and bore a son.

9 Then the LORD said to me, Call his name La-ammi (not my people); for you are not my people and I will not be your God.

10 ¶Yet the number of the children of Israel shall be as the sand of the sea, which cannot be measured nor numbered; and it shall come to pass that in the place where it was said to them, You are not my people; there it shall be said to them, You are the sons of the living God.

11 Then shall the children of Judah and the children of Israel be gathered together, and they shall appoint themselves one head, and they shall come up out of the land; [1] for great is the day of Jezreel.

CHAPTER 2

SAY to your brethren, Ammi, my people; and to your sisters, Rek-himtha, beloved.

2 Plead with your mother, plead; for she is not my wife, neither am I her husband; let her therefore put away her whoredoms out of her sight and her adulteries from between her breasts,

3 Lest I strip her naked and leave her bare as in the day that she was born, and make her as a wilderness and as a dry land, and cause her to die with thirst.

4 And I will not have mercy upon her children; for they are the children of whoredoms.

5 For their mother has played the harlot; she that conceived them has done shamefully; for she said, I will go after my lovers who give me my bread and my water, my clothes and my linen, my oil and everything that I need.

6 ¶Therefore, behold, I will hedge up her way with thorns, and fence her paths so that she shall not find her paths.

7 And she shall follow after her lovers and shall not overtake them, and she shall seek them, but shall not find them; then shall she say, I will return and go to my first husband;

[1] Come up from captivity.

for it was better with me then than now.

8 For she did not know that it was I who gave her wheat and wine and oil, and multiplied her silver and gold, some of which they made for the images of Baal.

9 Therefore I will return and take away my wheat in its time and my wine in its season, and will take away my wool and my linen which I gave her to cover her nakedness.

10 And now I will uncover her nakedness in the presence of her lovers, and none shall deliver her out of my hands.

11 And I will cause all her mirth to cease, her feast days, her new moons, her sabbaths, and all her solemn feasts.

12 And I will destroy her vines and her fig trees, of which she said, These are presents which my lovers have given me; and I will make them a forest, and the beasts of the field shall eat them.

13 And I will punish her for the evils of the days of Baal, in which she burned incense to him and decked herself with her earrings and her pearls and went after her lovers and forgot me, says the LORD.

14 ¶Therefore, behold, I will comfort her, and bring her into the wilderness, and speak lovingly to her.

15 And I will give her vineyards from thence, and the valley of Achor that it may open her understanding; and she shall be humbled there, as in the days of her youth, and as in the day when she came up out of the land of Egypt.

16 And it shall be on that day, says the LORD, that you shall call me, my husband, and shall call me no more Baali.[1]

17 For I will take away the name of Baal out of her mouth, and they shall no more remember his name.

18 And on that day I will make a covenant for them with the beasts of the field and with the fowls of the air and with the creeping things of the ground; and I will do away with the bow and the sword and the battle out of the earth, and I will make them to dwell in safety.

19 And I will betroth you to me for ever; yea, I will betroth you to me in righteousness and in justice and in lovingkindness and in mercy.

20 So I will betroth you to me in faithfulness; and you shall know the LORD.

21 And it shall come to pass on that day, says the LORD, I will answer the heavens, and they shall answer the earth;

22 And the earth shall answer the grain and the wine and the oil; and they shall answer Jezreel.

23 And I will sow her for myself in the earth; and I will have mercy on La-ethrakhmath, not beloved, and I will call La-ammi, not my people, Ammi, my people, and they shall say, Thou art my God.

CHAPTER 3

THEN the LORD said to me, Go again, love a woman who is fond of doing evil things and an adulteress, as the LORD loves the children of Israel, though they have turned and have gone after other gods, and love raisin cakes.

2 So I bought[2] her for myself for fifteen pieces of silver and a homer and half of barley;

3 And I said to her, You shall dwell as my wife for many days; you shall not play the harlot, and you shall not be for other men; so will I also be for you.

4 For the children of Israel shall dwell many days without a king and without a ruler and without a sacrifice and without an altar, and without the one who wears an ephod and burns incense.

5 Afterward the children of Israel shall return and seek the LORD their God and David their king; and they shall know the LORD and his goodness in the latter days.

---

[1] *My Lord.*
[2] *Bought her for myself.* In the East the bridegroom pays a dowry to the father of the bride.

CHAPTER 4

HEAR the word of the LORD, O children of Israel; for the LORD has a controversy with the inhabitants of the land, because there is no justice or mercy or knowledge of God in the land;

2 But cursing, lying, murder, stealing, and committing adultery; they have increased and they mix blood with blood.

3 Therefore the land shall mourn, and all its inhabitants shall languish, even the beasts of the field and the fowls of the air; and the fish of the sea also shall perish.

4 Because none judges nor reproves another, for your people is engaged in controversy like a priest.

5 Therefore you shall stumble in the day, and the prophet of your people also shall stumble in the night, and yet your mother keeps silence.

6 ¶My people are silent for lack of knowledge; because you have rejected knowledge, I will also reject you from the priesthood; seeing you have forgotten the law of your God, I will also forget your children.

7 According to the multitude of them, so they have sinned against me; they changed their honor into shame.

8 They devoured my people unmercifully, and they have engulfed themselves in their iniquity.

9 The priest has become common like the people; and I will punish them for their ways and reward them for their deeds.

10 For they shall eat and not be satisfied; they shall commit whoredom, and shall not increase, because they have forsaken the LORD.

11 And they love whoredom, and wine and drunkenness take away their heart.

12 ¶My people ask counsel of their own imagination, and their staff declares to them the directions; [1] for the spirit of whoredom has caused them to go astray, so they have turned from their God.

13 They sacrifice upon the tops of the mountains and burn incense upon the hills, under oaks and poplars and terebinth, because their shadow is good; therefore your daughters shall commit whoredom and your brides shall commit adultery.

14 I will not punish your daughters when they commit whoredom nor your brides when they commit adultery; for they themselves are mingled with whores, and they sacrifice with shameless harlots; therefore a people that does not understand embraces the harlot.

15 ¶As for you, O Israel, you shall not condemn Judah; nor shall you go to Gilgal, neither come up to Beth-aon; nor shall you say, The LORD lives.

16 For as a heifer that slides back from the yoke, so Israel balks; now the LORD will feed them like lambs in a wide pasture.

17 Ephraim is joined to idols; let him alone.

18 They all commit whoredom, and they love shame and idolatry.

19 Let the wind rend asunder their robes; let them be ashamed of their altars.

CHAPTER 5

HEAR this, O priests; and give ear, O house of Israel; and listen, O house of the king; for the judgment is for you, because you have been a snare to prophets and a net spread upon Tabor.

2 And the hunters who hunt have laid hidden snares, but I will chastise them all.

3 I know Ephraim, and Israel is not hid from me; for now Ephraim has committed whoredom, and Israel is defiled.

4 Their evil devices will not permit them to turn to their God; for the spirit of whoredom is in the midst of them, and they have not known the LORD.

5 And the pride of Israel shall be humbled before his presence; and Israel and Ephraim shall fall in their iniquity; Judah also shall fall with them.

[1] Like a blind man who is guided by his staff.

6 They shall go with their flocks and with their herds to seek the LORD; but they shall not find him, because he has withdrawn himself from them.

7 They have dealt falsely with the LORD, for they have begotten alien children.

8 Blow the trumpet in Ramtha, blow the horn in Ramtha; cry aloud at Beth-aon; the enemy is after you, O Benjamin.

9 Ephraim shall be desolate in the day of rebuke; among the tribes of Israel I have made known that which shall surely be.

10 The princes of Judah were like those who remove a landmark; therefore I will pour out my wrath upon them like water.

11 Ephraim is oppressed and broken in judgment, because he willingly went after vain things.

12 Therefore I will be as a tempest to Ephraim, and to the house of Judah as a lion.

13 When Ephraim saw his sickness and Judah saw his wounds, then Ephraim went to Assyria, and sent to the great king; but he cannot heal you nor cure you of your wounds.

14 For I will be to Ephraim as a lion, and as a young lion to the house of Judah; I, even I, will tear and go away; I will take away, and none shall rescue.

15 ¶I will return and go to my place, till they acknowledge their guilt and seek my face; in their affliction they will seek me early.

CHAPTER 6

THEY shall say, Come, let us return and go to the LORD who has smitten us, and he will heal us; he has wounded us, and he will bind us up.

2 After two days he will revive us, and on the third day he will raise us up, and we shall live in his presence.

3 Then shall we know to follow after the knowledge of the LORD; his going forth is prepared as the dawn; and he shall come to us as the rain, as the spring rain which waters the earth.

4 ¶O Ephraim, what shall I do to you? O Judah, what shall I do to you? for your goodness is as a morning cloud, and as the early dew it goes away.

5 Therefore have I cut off the prophets, I have slain them by the words of my mouth; and my judgments shall go forth as the light.

6 For I desired mercy and not sacrifice; and the knowledge of God more than burnt offerings.

7 But they like men have transgressed my covenant; there have they dealt treacherously against me.

8 Gilead is a city of those who work iniquity, and wallows in blood. Your strength is as that of a robber.

9 The priests have joined them on the way, and they have destroyed Shechem, because they have committed iniquities.

10 I have seen a horrible thing in the house of Israel: there Ephraim committed whoredom, and Israel was defiled.

11 And you also, O Judah, set a day of harvest for yourself when I will bring back the captivity of my people.

CHAPTER 7

WHEN I would have healed Israel, then the iniquity of Ephraim was revealed and the wickedness of Samaria; for they committed falsehood in my presence; and the thief came in, and the robber robbed men in the streets.

2 And they never said in their hearts that I remember all their wickedness; now their own devices have beset them about; they were before my face.

3 They have made the kings glad with their wickedness, and the princes with their lies.

4 Their rulers are all adulterers, their passion is as an oven heated to bake bread, the baker who kneads the dough ceases from going to the city, and waits until it is leavened.

5 The day they start to give counsel, the princes begin to become inflamed with wine; they stretch out their hands with wicked men.

6 Because their heart is hot like an oven with their plots, all night their

anger is suppressed; and in the morning it burns as a flaming fire.

7 They are all hot as an oven, and have devoured their judges; all their kings have fallen; there is none among them who calls upon me.

8 Ephraim has mixed himself with Gentiles; Ephraim has become as a loaf of bread which is eaten before it is baked.

9 Thus strangers have devoured his strength, and he knows it not: yea, gray hairs have grown upon him, yet he knows it not.

10 And the pride of Israel has been humbled in his presence; and they do not return to the LORD their God, nor seek him for all this.

11 ¶Ephraim also is like a young dove without understanding; they have come to Egypt, they are gone to Assyria.

12 Wherever they shall go, I will spread my net upon them; I will bring them down as the fowls of the air; I will chastise them according to the testimony which is heard against them.

13 Woe to them! for they have fled from me; I will bring misfortune upon them because they have transgressed against me; though I have saved them, yet they have spoken lies against me.

14 And they have not cried unto me with their heart, but they howled upon their beds; they quarrel over wheat and wine, and they have rebelled against me.

15 Though I have disciplined and strengthened their arms, yet do they imagine mischief against me.

16 They have perverted themselves for nothing; they have become like a deceitful bow; their princes shall fall by the sword because of the boldness of their tongue; such shall be their entanglement in the land of Egypt.

CHAPTER 8

LET your mouth become like a trumpet. He [1] shall come as an eagle against the house of the LORD,

[1] The invader.

because they have transgressed my covenant and trespassed my law.

2 They have called to me, saying, O our God, we know thee.

3 Israel has forgotten the good; the enemy has pursued him.

4 They have set up kings, but not by me; they have made princes, but they did not let me know; of their silver and their gold they have made idols to themselves, that they may perish.

5 ¶They have been led astray by your calf, O Samaria; my anger is kindled against them; how long will it be before they can be declared innocent?

6 For the idol is the product of Israel; a carpenter made it, therefore it is not God; but your calf, O Samaria, was made for deception.

7 For they have sown the wind, and they have reaped the whirlwind; it has no stalk, nor an ear to yield meal; and if it were to yield, the strangers shall eat it.

8 Israel is swallowed up; now they are among the Gentiles as a vessel wherein is no use.

9 For they are gone up to Assyria, as a wild ass alone by himself; Ephraim has loved gifts.

10 Though they shall be delivered up to the Gentiles, I will gather them, and they shall rest a while from the burden of the kings and the princes.

11 Because Ephraim has made many altars to sin, altars have become to him for a great sin.

12 I have written to him many of my laws, but my words he considered as a strange thing.

13 They sacrifice the choicest of animals and eat the meat; but the LORD has no delight in them; now he will remember their iniquity and punish them for their sins; they shall return to Egypt.

14 For Israel has forgotten his Maker and built palaces; and Judah has multiplied fortified cities: but I will kindle a fire in his cities, and it shall devour the palaces thereof.

CHAPTER 9

REJOICE not, O Israel, leap not for joy, as others do; because you have gone astray from your God, you have loved gifts[1] from every threshing floor.

2 But the threshing floor and the winepress shall not satisfy them, and the oil shall fail them.

3 They shall not dwell in the LORD's land; but Ephraim shall return to Egypt, and they shall eat unclean things in Assyria.

4 They shall not offer wine offerings to the LORD, neither shall their sacrifices please him; their sacrifices shall be to them as the bread of affliction; all who eat of it shall be polluted; for their own bread shall not come into the house of the LORD.

5 What will you do on the solemn feast day, and on the day of the feast of the LORD?

6 For, lo, they are gone in the prey; Egypt shall gather them up, Memphis shall bury them; their valuable things of silver, strangers shall inherit them; thorns shall grow in their tents.

7 The days of vengeance have come, the days of recompense are near; then Israel shall know it; the prophet is a fool, a dull man possessed by a spirit of stupidity; because of the multitude of your iniquity, your lasciviousness has been increased.

8 The watchman of Ephraim was with my God; but the prophet is a snare and a stumbling block in all his ways, and wantonness in the house of God.

9 They have deeply corrupted themselves, as in the days of Ramtha; therefore he will remember their iniquity, and he will punish them for their sins.

10 I found Israel like grapes in the wilderness; I saw their fathers like the first fruit of the fig tree, but they went to Baal-peor, and separated themselves to that shameful thing, and became abominable like the things they loved.

11 As for Ephraim, their glory has flown away like a bird, they are cut off from the birth, from the womb, and from the conception.

12 Though they bring up their children, yet I will bereave them, that there shall not be a man left; yea, woe to them, for I will take vengeance upon them!

13 Ephraim's fate shall be like that of Tyre, as you have seen, though planted in a pleasant place with buildings; likewise Ephraim shall bring out his children to the slaughter.

14 Give them, O LORD: what wilt thou give? Give them a miscarrying womb and dry breasts.

15 All their wickedness is in Gilgal; for there I hated them; because of the wickedness of their doings, I will drive them out of my house, I will love them no more; all their princes are rebels.

16 Ephraim is smitten, their root is dried up, they shall bear no fruit; yea, though they bear children, I will cause them to die, even those who are tenderly beloved.

17 My God will reject them because they did not hearken to him; and they shall be wanderers among the nations.

CHAPTER 10

ISRAEL is a vine full of branches that brings forth its fruit; according to the multitude of his fruit he has increased the altars; according to the goodness of his land they have built shrines.

2 Their heart is wavering; and from now they shall be condemned; he shall demolish their altars; he shall plunder their shrines.

3 For from now they shall say, We have no king because we feared not the LORD; what then can a king do for us?

4 They have spoken words belonging to false altars; they have broken the covenant and paid the penalty; they are like briers in a barren field.

5 The inhabitants of Samaria shall sojourn to the shrine of the calf of Beth-aon; for they sat down mourning over it together with its priests; they shall rejoice over it, and over

[1] Grain taken as a bribe.

its glory because it is departed from it.

6 Even the idol itself shall be also carried to Assyria for a present to the great king; Ephraim shall receive shame, and Israel shall be ashamed of his own counsel.

7 Samaria has cast away her king like a chip on the face of the water.

8 The high places of the idol of Aon, the sin of Israel, shall be destroyed; thorns and thistles shall grow up on their altars; and they shall say to the mountains, Cover us; and to the hills, Fall on us.

9 O Israel, you have sinned from the days of Ramtha; there they shall remain, and the battle in Ramtha against the children of iniquity shall not overtake them.

10 In my rebuke I will chastise them; and the people shall be gathered against them when they shall be chastised for their two follies.

11 Ephraim is like a heifer that is trained, and loves to tread out the wheat; but I bent her neck under the yoke; I will make Ephraim to be ridden upon, I will cause Judah to tread wheat, and Jacob shall be plundered.

12 Sow for yourselves righteousness, and reap a harvest of mercy; light a lamp for yourselves; for it is time to seek the LORD, till he come and reveal his righteousness to you.

13 You have plowed sin and wickedness, you have reaped iniquity; you have eaten the fruit of lies. Because you have trusted in your ways, and in the multitude of your mighty men;

14 Therefore destruction shall come upon your people, and all your provinces shall be despoiled as plunder is divided when peace is concluded, even from Beth-el as far as the northern border; in the day of the battle the mother was dashed in pieces upon her children.

15 So they did to you, O Beth-el, because of your great wickedness; in a morning was the king of Israel confounded and ashamed.

CHAPTER 11

WHEN Israel was a child, then I loved him, and I called him, my son, out of Egypt.

2 Just as they were called, so they went away from my presence; they sacrificed to Baal and burned incense to idols.

3 It was I who cared for Ephraim and took them up in my arms; but they did not know that I healed them.

4 I drew them with cords of a man, with the bands of love; and I was to them as one who takes off the yoke from their neck, and I bent over them and fed them.

5 ¶They shall not return to the land of Egypt, but the Assyrian shall be their king, because they refused to repent.

6 The sword shall cause pain in their cities and consume their possessions, and they shall suffer because of their evil counsels.

7 And my people are inclined to backslide from me; though they shall call to God, they will take counsel together, and none at all would exalt him.

8 How shall I uphold you, O Ephraim? How shall I help you, O Israel? How shall I make you as Adamah? How shall I set you as Zeboim? My heart is turned within me, my tender mercies are moved.

9 I will not execute the fierceness of my anger, I will not return to destroy Ephraim; for I am God, and not man in the midst of you; I am the Holy One, and I will not come to attack the city.

10 They shall walk after the LORD; he shall roar like a lion; because he shall roar, some of the people shall tremble.

11 They shall come fast like a bird out of Egypt, and like a dove out of the land of Assyria; and I will bring them back to their dwelling place, says the LORD.

12 Ephraim has compassed me about with lies, and the house of Israel and Judah with deceit; until the people of God was humbled, a people once holy and faithful.

CHAPTER 12

EPHRAIM feeds on wind and follows after the tempest all the day long; they have multiplied lies and prey; they have made a covenant with the Assyrians, and oil is carried into Egypt.

2 The LORD has a controversy with Judah, and will punish Jacob according to his ways; and according to his devices will he recompense him.

3 ¶In the womb he deceived his brother, and by his might he became great in the presence of God;

4 Yea, he prevailed over the angel, he made supplication to him; he found him in Beth-el, and there he spoke with him.

5 Even the LORD the God of hosts has remembered him.

6 Therefore return to your God; keep mercy and justice, and wait for your God continually.

7 ¶The balances of deceit are in the hand of Canaan, he loves to oppress.

8 And Ephraim said, Yet I am become rich, I have found grief; but all my labors will not be enough to rid me of the sin which I have sinned.

9 I am the LORD your God who brought you up out of the land of Egypt. I will again make you to dwell in tents, as in the days of the solemn feasts.

10 I have spoken by the prophets, and I have multiplied visions and used similitudes by the ministry of the prophets.

11 In Gilead you suffered pain, and in Gilgal you sacrificed bullocks to falsehood; your altars are like dry stalks in a barren field.

12 Jacob fled to the land of Aram, and Israel served for a wife, and for a wife he kept sheep.

13 And by the prophets the LORD brought Israel out of Egypt, and by the prophets was he preserved.

14 Ephraim provoked him to anger most bitterly; therefore his blood shall come upon him, and his reproach shall his LORD return to him.

CHAPTER 13

WHEN Ephraim spoke, the people trembled; he became great in Israel; but when he was found guilty of Baal worship, he lost his power.

2 And even now they sin more and more, and have made to themselves molten images of their silver, and idols in their own likeness, the work of a carpenter; they said to the people, Let those men who sacrifice men kiss the image of the calf.

3 Therefore they shall be as the morning cloud and as the early dew that passes away, as the chaff that is driven with the wind out of the threshing floor and as the smoke out of the chimney.

4 Yet I am the LORD your God who brought you out of the land of Egypt, and you shall know no God but me; therefore there is no one who can save besides me.

5 ¶It was I who fed you in the wilderness, in a desolate land which is uninhabited.

6 I fed them, and they were filled; and their heart was exalted; therefore they have forgotten me.

7 Hence I will be to them like a lion; like a leopard by the way of Assyria.

8 I will meet them like a bear that tears its prey in pieces, and I will pierce the crust of their heart; and there a lion shall devour them; the wild beast shall tear them.

9 ¶O Israel, you have corrupted yourself; who can help you?

10 Where now is your king? Let him save you, and all your cities? And your judge of whom you said, Give me a king and a prince?

11 I gave you a king in my anger, and took him away in my wrath.

12 The iniquity of Ephraim is bound up; his sin is hid.

13 The pangs like those of a woman in travail shall come upon him because he is an unwise son; for now he shall not be in pain of childbirth.

14 I will save them from the power of Sheol; I will deliver them from death. O death, where is your victory? O Sheol, where is your sting? Consolation is hidden from my eyes.

15 ¶Because he shall be separated from his brothers, an east wind shall come, the wind of the LORD shall blow from the wilderness and dry up his fountains, and his springs shall

be dried up; it shall spoil the treasure of all valuable vessels.

16 Samaria shall be condemned because she has rebelled against her God; they shall fall by the sword; their infants shall be dashed in pieces, and their women with child shall be ripped up.

CHAPTER 14

O ISRAEL, return to the LORD your God; for you have fallen by your iniquity.

2 Pledge loyalty, and turn to the LORD your God; and pray to him, that he may forgive your iniquity and receive blessings; then he will recompense you for the prayer of your lips.

3 And say, Assyria shall not save us; we will not ride upon horses; neither will we call any more the work of our hands, gods; for thou wilt have mercy upon the fatherless.

4 ¶I will heal their backsliding, I will love their vows; and my anger shall turn away from them.

5 I will be as the dew to Israel; he shall spring up as the lily, and cast forth his roots as cedars of Lebanon.

6 His branches shall spread, and his beauty shall be like the olive tree, and his fragrance like that of Lebanon.

7 They shall return and dwell under his shadow; they shall flourish like grain, and grow as the vine; and their scent shall be like the wine of Lebanon.

8 Ephraim shall say, What have I to do any more with idols? I have humbled him, and I will glorify him; I am like a green fir tree. From me is your fruit found.

9 He who is wise shall understand these things; he who is prudent shall know them; for the ways of the LORD are right, and the righteous shall walk in them; but transgressors shall stumble therein.

JOEL

CHAPTER 1

THE word of the LORD that came to Joel the son of Bethuel:

2 Hear this, O you elders, and give ear, all you inhabitants of the land! Has such a calamity ever happened in your days, or in the days of your fathers?

3 Tell your children of it, and let your children tell their children, and their children to another generation.

4 What the palmerworm has left, the locust has eaten; and what the swarming locust has left, the crawling locust has eaten; and what the crawling locust has left, the cankerworm has eaten.

5 Awake, O you drunkards, and weep; and howl, all you drinkers of wine, because of the new wine; for it is cut off from your mouth.

6 A nation has come up against my land, strong, and without number; whose teeth are like the teeth of a lion, and his fangs as the fangs of a lion's whelp.

7 He has laid my vine waste, and has cut off my fig tree and thrown it away; the branches thereof are made white.

8 ¶Lament like a virgin girded with sackcloth for the husband of her youth.

9 The meal offering and the drink offering are cut off from the house of the LORD; the kings mourn, and the priests who minister to the LORD mourn.

10 The field is plundered, the land mourns; for the wheat is plundered, the new wine is dried up, the olive orchards are destroyed.

11 Be ashamed, O you husband-

men; howl, O you vinedressers, howl for the wheat and for the barley because the harvest of the fields is perished.

12 The vine is dried up, and the fig tree languishes; the pomegranate tree, the palm tree, and the apple tree, all the trees of the field are withered; joy is fled from the sons of men.

13 Gird yourselves with sackcloth and lament, O you priests; howl, O you ministers of the altar; go in, spend the night in sackcloth, O you ministers of my God, because the meal offering and the drink offering are withheld from the house of your God.

14 ¶Sanctify a fast, call a solemn assembly, gather the elders and all the inhabitants of the land into the house of the LORD your God, and cry to the LORD your God, and say,

15 Alas, alas for the day! for the day of the LORD is at hand, and as plunder from God shall it come.

16 And, behold, before our eyes the food is cut off from the house of our God, and gladness and joy have ceased.

17 The cows languish at their mangers, the granaries are laid waste, the winepresses are thrown down, and the grain is dried up.

18 How the beasts groan! the herds of cattle cry because they have no pasture; yea, the flocks of sheep also are perished.

19 O LORD, to thee will I cry; for the fire has devoured the camps of shepherds in the wilderness, and the flame has burned all the trees of the field.

20 Also the beasts of the field cry out to thee because the ponds of water are dried up, and the fire has devoured the camps of shepherds in the wilderness.

CHAPTER 2

BLOW the trumpet in Zion, and sound an alarm in my holy mountain; let all the inhabitants of the land tremble; for the day of the LORD is come;

2 And the day of darkness and gloom is near, a day of clouds and of thick darkness, like the morning spread upon the mountains; it shall come upon a great and strong people; there has not been ever the like from of old, neither shall be any more after it, even to the years of many generations.

3 A fire devours before them; and behind them a flame burns; the land is as the garden of Eden before them, and behind them a desolate wilderness; and nothing shall escape them.

4 The appearance of them is as the appearance of horses; and like horsemen so they run;

5 Like the noise of chariots that rumble on the tops of the mountains, like the noise of a flame of fire that devours the stubble, like a mighty people arrayed for war.

6 Before their presence the people shall tremble; all faces shall be dismayed and confounded.

7 They shall run like mighty men; they shall climb the walls like men of war; and they shall march in order every man on his way, and they shall not turn aside from their ranks;

8 Neither shall one push another; but they shall walk in order every one in his path; some of them shall fall down because of the weight of their armor, they shall not trample them.

9 They shall go up against the cities; they shall run upon the walls, they shall climb up upon the houses; they shall enter through the windows like thieves.

10 The earth quakes before them; the heavens tremble; the sun and the moon are darkened, and the stars have withdrawn their shining.

11 The LORD has shouted before his army; for his host is very great; mighty is the work executed by his word; for the day of the LORD is great and very terrible; who can endure it?

12 ¶Therefore now, says the LORD, return to me with all your heart, and with fasting and with weeping and with mourning;

13 And rend your hearts and not your garments, and turn to the LORD your God; for he is gracious and merciful, patient and of great kindness, and he averts disaster.

14 Who knows if he will return again and multiply us, and increase his blessing in his land, even a meal offering and a drink offering to the LORD your God?

15 ¶Blow the trumpet in Zion, sanctify a fast, call a solemn assembly;

16 Gather the people, sanctify the congregation, assemble the elders, gather the young men and those who suck the breasts; let the bridegroom leave his bedchamber, and the bride come out of her bridal chamber.

17 Let the priests, the ministers of the LORD, weep between the porch and the altar, and let them say, Spare thy people, O LORD, and give not thy heritage to reproach, that the Gentiles should rule over them, lest the Gentiles say, Where is their God?

18 ¶Then the LORD will be zealous for his land, and pity his people.

19 Yea, the LORD has answered and said to his people, Behold, I will send you grain and wine and oil, and you shall be satisfied; and I will no more make you a reproach of the nations.

20 But I will remove far off from you the northern army, and I will drive him into a dry and desolate land, with his face toward the last sea, and his rear toward the utmost sea, and his smell shall come up, and his stench shall arise because he has boasted to do great things.

21 ¶Fear not, O land; be glad and rejoice; for the LORD has exalted himself to do wonderful things.

22 Be not afraid, you beasts of the field; for grass has sprung up in the pastures of the wilderness; the tree bears its fruit, the vine and the fig tree have yielded their strength.

23 Be glad then, O children of Zion, and rejoice in the LORD your God; for he has given you food of righteousness, and he will cause to come down for you the rain, the early and the latter rain, as before.

24 And the threshing floors shall be full of grain, and the winepresses shall overflow with wine and oil.

25 And I will recompense you for the years that the locust has eaten, the crawling locust, the cankerworm, and the palmerworm, my great army which I sent against you.

26 And you shall eat in plenty and be satisfied, and praise the name of the LORD your God, who has dealt wondrously with you; and my people shall never be put to shame.

27 And you shall know that I am in the midst of Israel and that I am the LORD your God and there is none besides me; and my people shall never be ashamed.

28 ¶And it shall come to pass afterward that I will pour out my spirit upon all flesh; and your sons and your daughters shall prophesy, your old men shall dream dreams, your young men shall see visions;

29 And also upon the servants and upon the handmaids in those days will I pour out my spirit.

30 And I will show wonders in the heavens and on the earth, blood and fire and pillars of smoke.

31 The sun shall be turned into darkness and the moon into blood, before the great and the terrible day of the LORD comes.

32 And it shall come to pass that whosoever shall call on the name of the LORD shall be delivered; for in mount Zion and in Jerusalem shall be deliverance, as the LORD has said to the remnant whom the LORD has called.

CHAPTER 3

FOR behold, in those days and in that time, when I shall bring back the captivity of Judah and Jerusalem,

2 I will also gather all nations and will bring them down into the valley of Jehoshaphat, and I will enter into judgment with them there for the sake of my people and for the sake of my heritage Israel, whom they have scattered among the nations, and because they have divided up my land.

3 And they have cast lots for my people, and have given boys for the price of harlots, and sold the girls for wine, that they might drink.

4 What are you to me, O Tyre and Zidon and all the coasts of Palestine? Are you paying me a recompense?

and if you recompense me, swiftly and speedily will I return your recompense upon your own heads;

5 Because you have taken my silver and my gold, and have carried into your temples my beautiful vessels;

6 And the children of Judah and the children of Jerusalem you have sold to the Greeks, that you might remove them far from their own border.

7 Behold, I will stir them up from the place to which you have sold them, and will return your recompense upon your own heads;

8 And I will deliver your sons and your daughters into the hand of the children of Judah, and they shall sell them to the Sabeans, to a people far off; for the LORD had spoken it.

9 ¶Proclaim this among the Gentiles: Get ready for war, stir up the mighty men, let all the men of war draw near; let them come up.

10 Beat your plowshares into swords and your sickles into spears. Let the weak say, I am a mighty man.

11 Assemble yourselves, and come; all you nations round about, draw near; and there will the LORD break your might.

12 Let the nations be awakened, and come up to the valley of Jehoshaphat; for there I will sit to judge all the nations round about.

13 Put in the sickles, for the harvest is ripe; go in, tread down; for wheat pits are full, and the wine presses overflow; for their wickedness is great.

14 An uproar and tumult in the valley of decision; for the day of the LORD is near in the valley of decision.

15 The sun and the moon are darkened, and the stars have withdrawn their shining.

16 The LORD also shall roar out of Zion, and utter his voice from Jerusalem; and the heavens and the earth shall shake; but the LORD will have pity upon his people, and will strengthen the children of Israel.

17 Then you shall know that I am the LORD your God, dwelling in Zion, my holy mountain; then Jerusalem shall be holy, and there shall no foreigners sojourn in it any more.

18 ¶And it shall come to pass in that day that the mountains shall drip sweetness and the hills shall flow with milk, and all the brooks of Judah shall flow with water; and a fountain shall come forth from the house of the LORD, and shall water the valley of Shittim.

19 Egypt shall be a desolation, and Edom shall be a desolate wilderness, for the violence against the children of Judah, because they have shed innocent blood in their land.

20 But Judah shall dwell for ever and Jerusalem from generation to generation.

21 For I will avenge their blood, and I will not absolve the offenders; and the LORD will dwell in Zion.

AMOS

CHAPTER 1

THE words of Amos, who was among the herdsmen of Tekoa, which he saw concerning Israel in the days of Uzziah king of Judah, and in the days of Jeroboam the son of Joash king of Israel, two years before the earthquake.

2 And he said: The LORD will roar from Zion, and shout from Jerusalem; and the habitations of the shepherds shall mourn, and the top of Carmel shall wither.

3 Thus says the LORD: For three transgressions of Damascus, and for four, I will not turn away the punishment thereof, because they have

threshed Gilead with threshing instruments of iron;

4 But I will send a fire into the house of Hazael, which shall devour the palaces of Bar-hadad.

5 I will break also the bars of Damascus and cut off the inhabitants from the plain of Aon and him that holds the sceptre from the house of Eden; and the people of Aram shall go into captivity to Kir, says the LORD.

6 ¶Thus says the LORD: For three transgressions of Gaza, and for four, I will not turn away the punishment thereof, because they carried away captive the whole population to deliver them up to Edom;

7 But I will send a fire on the walls of Gaza, which shall devour the palaces thereof;

8 And I will cut off the inhabitants from Ashdod and him that holds the sceptre from Ashkelon, and I will turn my hand against Ekron; and the remnant of the Philistines shall perish, says the LORD God.

9 ¶Thus says the LORD: For three transgressions of Tyre, and for four, I will not turn away the punishment thereof, because they delivered up the whole population to Edom and remembered not the brotherly covenant.

10 But I will send a fire on the walls of Tyre, which shall devour the palaces thereof.

11 ¶Thus says the LORD: For three transgressions of Edom, and for four, I will not turn away the punishment thereof, because he did pursue his brother with the sword and did cast off all pity and he kept his anger perpetually and he kept his wrath for ever;

12 But I will send a fire upon Teman, which shall devour the palaces of Bozrah.

13 ¶Thus says the LORD: For three transgressions of the Ammonites, and for four, I will not turn away the punishment from them, because they have ripped up women with child in Gilead, that they might enlarge their border;

14 But I will kindle a fire in the streets of Rabbath, and it shall devour the palaces thereof, with shouting in the day of battle, with a tempest in the day of the whirlwind;

15 And Malcom shall go into captivity, he and his priests and his princes together, says the LORD.

CHAPTER 2

THUS says the LORD: For three transgressions of Moab, and for four, I will not turn away the punishment from the people thereof, because they burned the bones of the king of Edom into lime;

2 But I will send a fire upon Moab, and it shall devour the palaces of Kirioth; and Moab shall die with tumult, with shouting, and with the sound of the trumpet;

3 And I will cut off the judge from its midst, and will slay all its princes with him, says the LORD.

4 ¶Thus says the LORD: For three transgressions of Judah, and for four, I will not turn away the punishment from the people thereof because they have rejected the law of the LORD and have not kept his commandments, and the vain idols, after which their fathers have walked, have caused them to go astray.

5 But I will send a fire upon Judah, and it shall devour the palaces of Jerusalem.

6 ¶Thus says the LORD: For three transgressions of Israel, and for four, I will not turn away the punishment thereof, because they sold a righteous man for silver, and the poor for a pair of shoes, with which they tread the dust of the earth.

7 And they oppress the poor, and turn away justice from the fatherless; and a man and his father go in to the same woman, to profane my holy name.

8 And they laid themselves down in filthy clothes on the sides of every altar, and they drank old wine in the houses of their gods.

9 ¶Yet I destroyed the Amorite before them, whose height was like the height of a cedar, and he was strong as an oak; yet I destroyed his fruit

from above and his roots from beneath.

10 Also I brought you up from the land of Egypt, and led you forty years through the wilderness, and brought you here to possess the land of the Amorite.

11 And I raised up some of your sons for prophets, and some of your young men for Nazarites. Is it not even thus, O you children of Israel? says the LORD.

12 But you gave the Nazarites wine to drink; and commanded the prophets that they should not prophesy.

13 Behold, I am weary under your burdens, as a cart creaks that is full of sheaves.

14 Therefore the power to run shall perish from the swift, and the strong shall not possess his strength, neither shall the mighty deliver himself.

15 And he that handles the bow shall not stand; and he who is a fast runner shall not deliver himself; neither shall he who rides the horse deliver himself.

16 And he who is courageous like a mighty man shall flee away naked in that day, says the LORD.

CHAPTER 3

HEAR this word that the LORD has spoken against you, O children of Israel, against the whole family which I brought up from the land of Egypt, saying,

2 You only have I known of all the peoples and of all the families of the earth; therefore I will punish you for all your iniquities.

3 Will two men go on a journey together unless they have made an appointment?

4 Does a lion roar in the forest when he has no prey? Or does a lion cry out of his den if he has taken no prey?

5 Will a bird fall into a snare upon the earth without a hunter? Or can a trap spring up from the ground and catch the prey without being set?

6 Shall a trumpet be blown in the city, and the people be not afraid? Or shall there be misfortune in a city and the LORD has not done it?

7 Surely the LORD God does nothing without revealing his secret to his servants the prophets.

8 The lion has roared, who will not fear? The LORD God has spoken, who can but prophesy?

9 ¶Proclaim it in the palaces of Ashdod and in the palaces in the land of Egypt, and say, Assemble yourselves upon the mountain of Samaria, and see the great tumults in the midst thereof and the oppression which is in it.

10 For they do not know how to reprove, says the LORD, but they store up plunder and spoil in their palaces.

11 Therefore thus says the LORD: A calamity shall surround the land; and its strength shall be brought down, and its palaces shall be spoiled.

12 Thus says the LORD: As the shepherd takes out of the mouth of the lion two legs or a piece of an ear, so shall the children of Israel be delivered who dwell in Samaria, along with the people who dwell in Damascus, by a staff that strikes suddenly.

13 Hear, and testify in the house of Jacob, says the LORD God, the God of hosts of Israel,

14 That in the day that I punish the transgressions of Israel I will also punish the altars of Beth-el; and the horns of the altars shall be cut off and fall to the ground.

15 And I will destroy the winter house with the summer house; and the houses of ivory shall perish, and great houses shall be demolished, says the LORD.

CHAPTER 4

HEAR this word, O vicious men of Bashan, who are in the mountain of Samaria, who oppress the poor, who crush the needy, who say to their lords, Bring, and let us drink:

2 The LORD God has sworn by his holiness that, behold, the days are coming upon you when they shall take you away with weapons and the last of you shall be devoured.

3 And every woman shall run to the breach which is before her; and

they shall be cast away to the mountain of Armenia, says the LORD.

4 ¶Come to Beth-el and transgress; go to Gilgal and multiply transgressions; and bring your sacrifices every morning and your tithes every third day,

5 And offer a sacrifice of thanksgiving with leavened bread, and vow your vows and fulfill them; for thus you have loved to do, O children of Israel, says the LORD God.

6 ¶And I also have given you shortage of food in all your cities, and want of bread in all your places; yet you have not returned to me, says the LORD.

7 And I also have withheld the rain from you when there were yet three months to the harvest; and I caused it to rain upon one city, and caused it not to rain upon another city; one part was rained upon, and the other part on which it did not rain withered.

8 So the inhabitants of two or three cities gathered into one city to drink water; but they were not satisfied; yet you returned not to me, says the LORD.

9 I have smitten you with blight and mildew, and with hail stones; and many of your gardens and your vineyards and your fig trees and your olive trees were eaten by the creeping locust; and yet you did not return to me, says the LORD.

10 I have sent among you the pestilence after the manner of Egypt; I slew your young men with the sword, together with the spoil of your horses; and I made the stench of your camps to come up to your nostrils; yet you did not return to me, says the LORD.

11 I have overthrown you, as God overthrew Sodom and Gomorrah, and you have become like a firebrand which is plucked out of the burning; yet you did not return to me, says the LORD.

12 Therefore thus will I do to you, O Israel, at the end; and because I will do this to you, prepare, O Israel, that you might call to your God.

13 For lo, he who creates the wind and creates the mountains and declares to man what is his glory, who makes the morning darkness and walks upon the high places of the earth, The LORD, the God of hosts, is his name.

CHAPTER 5

HEAR this word which I take up concerning you, even a lamentation, O house of Israel:

2 The virgin of Israel is fallen, she shall no more rise; she is left lying on the ground, there is none to raise her up.

3 For thus says the LORD God: The city out of which went forth a thousand men, there shall be left in it a hundred men; and that out of which went forth a hundred men, there shall be left in it ten men to the house of Israel.

4 ¶For thus says the LORD to the house of Israel: Seek me and you shall live;

5 But do not seek Beth-el, nor enter into Gilgal, and pass not to Beer-sheba; for Gilgal shall surely go into captivity and Beth-el shall come to nought.

6 Seek the LORD and you shall live; lest he break out like fire in the house of Joseph and devour Beth-el, and there will be none to quench it.

7 You who turn justice into bitterness, and lower righteousness to the ground,

8 They have forsaken him who made Pleiades and Orion, and who turns the shadow of death into the morning, and makes the day dark into night; who calls the waters of the sea, and pours them out upon the face of the earth; the LORD is his name;

9 Who makes the weak to rule over the mighty, and exalts the meek over the proud.

10 They hate the poor at the gates, and they abhor him who speaks uprightly.

11 Therefore because you have beaten on the head of the poor and have taken from him the choicest gifts; the houses of hewn stone which you have built, you shall not dwell in; and from the pleasant vineyards

which you have planted, you shall not drink wine.

12 For I know your transgressions are many and your sins are great; you oppress the just, you take a bribe, and you turn aside the cause of the poor in the gate from their right.

13 Therefore the prudent shall keep silence in that time; for it is an evil time.

14 Seek good and not evil that you may live; and so the LORD, the God of hosts, shall be with you, as you have spoken.

15 Hate the evil and love the good, and establish justice in the gate; it may be that the LORD God of hosts will be gracious to the remnant of Joseph.

16 Therefore thus says the LORD, the God of hosts: In all streets there shall be wailing; and in all broad places they shall say, Alas! alas! and they shall call the farmers to mourning, and those who are skillful in lamentation to wailing.

17 And in all vineyards shall be wailing; for I will pass through the midst of you, says the LORD.

18 Woe to you who desire the day of the LORD! to what end is it for you? The day of the LORD? For it is a day of darkness and not light.

19 As when a man fled from a lion and a bear met him; or went into the house and leaned his hand on the wall and a serpent bit him.

20 Such is the day of the LORD; it is darkness and not light; yea, it is a day of thick darkness and no brightness is in it.

21 ¶I hate, I despise your feast days, and I will not smell the savor of your solemn assemblies.

22 Though you offer me your burnt offerings and your meal offerings, I will not accept them; neither will I regard the peace offerings of your fat beasts.

23 Take away from me the noise of your songs; for I will not hear the melody of your harps.

24 But let justice run down like waters, and righteousness as a mighty stream.

25 Did you offer to me sacrifices and offerings in the wilderness for forty years, O house of Israel?

26 But you carried the tabernacle of Malcom and Chiun your idol, the star which you made a god to yourselves.

27 Therefore I will cause you to go into captivity beyond Damascus, says the LORD whose name is the God of hosts.

CHAPTER 6

WOE to them who despise Zion and trust in the mountain of Samaria, who are chosen by the chiefs of the nations that have captivated the house of Israel!

2 Pass over to Caliah and see; and from thence go to Hamath the great; then go down to Gath of the Philistines. Are they better than these kingdoms? Or is their territory greater than your territory?

3 O you who wait for the evil day, and cause the sabbath [1] of violence to come near;

4 Who lie upon beds of ivory, and give themselves to pleasures upon their couches, and eat the fatlings from the flock and calves from the midst of the herd;

5 Who chant to the sound of the harp, and consider themselves skilled in the musical instruments like David;

6 Who drink pure wine, and anoint themselves with the finest perfumes; but they are not grieved for the affliction of Joseph.

7 ¶Therefore now they shall be carried captive with the first who go captive, and the joy shall be taken away from their rulers.

8 The LORD God has sworn by himself, says the LORD the God of hosts, I abhor the excellency of Jacob and hate his palaces; therefore I will deliver up the city with all that is in it.

9 And it shall come to pass, if there remain ten men in one house that they shall die.

10 And a man's uncle or one who is near to him shall carry the dead body out of the house; and he shall say

[1] The Hebrews were often attacked on the sabbath day.

to him who is in the house, Is there any one else in the house with you? And he shall say, There is no one, because they have perished; for they did not mention the name of the LORD.

11 For, behold, the LORD will go forth and he will smite the great house and cause it to quiver, and the little house will he make desolate.

12 ¶Do horses run upon rocks? Or does one plough with horses?[1] For you have turned justice into bitterness, and the fruit of righteousness into wormwood;

13 You who rejoice over nothing, who say, Have we not taken a city by our own strength?

14 Therefore, behold, I will raise up against you a nation, O house of Israel, says the LORD the God of hosts; and they shall drive you away from the entrance of Hamath to the valley of Arabah.

CHAPTER 7

THUS has the LORD God showed me: behold, a plague of locusts coming up in the beginning of springing up of the latter growth; and, lo, it was the latter growth after the king's mowings.

2 And it came to pass when they had finished eating the grass of the land, then I said, O LORD God, forgive. Who shall raise up Jacob? For he is small in numbers.

3 Then the LORD averted this calamity; it shall not be.

4 ¶Thus has the LORD God showed me: and, behold, the LORD God called the people to judge them by fire, and it devoured the great deep and did eat up a part.

5 Then I said, O LORD God, forgive. Who shall raise up Jacob? For he is small in numbers.

6 The LORD averted this calamity; this also shall not be.

7 ¶Thus he showed me: and, behold, the LORD was standing upon a wall made of adamant, and a plumbline was in his hand.

8 And the LORD said to me, Amos, what do you see? And I said, A

[1] Easterners plough with oxen.

plumbline. Then said the LORD, Behold, I will set a plumbline in the midst of my people Israel; I will not again pass by them any more:

9 And the absurd shrines of Israel shall be desolate, and the sanctuaries shall be laid waste; and I will rise against the house of Jeroboam with the sword.

10 ¶Then Amaziah the priest of Beth-el sent to Jeroboam king of Israel, saying, Amos has conspired against you in the midst of the house of Israel, and the land cannot bear all his words.

11 For thus Amos is saying: Jeroboam shall die by the sword, and Israel shall surely be carried away captive out of their own land.

12 Also Amaziah said to Amos, O you seer, go, flee away into the land of Judah, and there eat bread, and prophesy there;

13 But prophesy not again any more at Beth-el; for it is the king's sanctuary and it is the house of the kingdom.

14 ¶Then Amos answered and said to Amaziah, I am not a prophet, neither a prophet's son; but I was a shepherd and a gatherer of wild figs;

15 And the LORD took me as I followed the flock, and the LORD said to me, Go, prophesy against my people Israel.

16 ¶Now therefore hear the word of the LORD: You say, Do not prophesy against the house of Israel and do not teach against the house of Isaac.

17 Therefore thus says the LORD: Your wife shall play the harlot in your own city, and your sons and your daughters shall fall by the sword, and your land shall be divided by line; and you yourself shall die in a polluted land; and Israel shall surely be carried away captive from his land.

CHAPTER 8

THUS has the LORD God showed me: and behold, a sign of the end.

2 And the LORD said to me, Amos,

what do you see? And I said, A sign of the end. Then the LORD said to me, The end is come upon my people Israel; I will not again cause it to pass by them any more.

3 And the songs of the temple shall be howling in that day, says the LORD God; there shall be many dead bodies in every place; and they shall be cast away to destruction.

4 ¶Hear this, O you who wrong the poor, and cause the needy of the land to come to an end,

5 Saying, When will the month be over, that we may sell grain? When will the sabbath be over that we may open storehouses and make our measures small and enlarge weights and make deceitful balances?

6 That we may sell to the poor for silver, and pay the needy with the refuse of the wheat, and sell the refuse which is left on the floor of the storehouses.

7 The LORD, the Mighty One of Jacob, has sworn, Surely, I will never forget any of their works.

8 Shall not the land tremble for these things, and every one mourn who dwells in it? The end shall come up like a flooded river; and it shall cast things away, and then recede like the river of Egypt.

9 And it shall come to pass in that day, says the LORD, that I will cause the sun to go down at noon, and I will darken the earth in the daylight.

10 And I will turn your feasts into mourning and all your songs into lamentation; and I will put sackcloth upon all your loins and baldness upon every head; and I will make it as the mourning for an only son, and the end of it as a bitter day.

11 ¶Behold, the days are coming, says the LORD, when I will send a famine in the land; not a famine of bread, nor a thirst for water, but of hearing the word of the LORD;

12 And they shall gather together from sea to sea, and from the north even to the east; they shall run to and fro to seek the word of the LORD, and shall not find it.

13 In that day the beautiful virgins and the young men shall faint for thirst.

14 They that swore by the idols of Samaria, saying, As your god lives, O Dan, and, as the cult of Beer-sheba lives, even they shall fall and never rise again.

CHAPTER 9

I SAW the LORD standing over the altar; and he said, Smite the lintel of the door, that the thresholds may shake; and let their treachery be upon the heads of all of them, and I will slay those who are left of them with the sword; he that flees of them shall not escape, and he that is spared of them shall not be delivered.

2 Though they go down into Sheol, thence shall my hand bring them up; though they climb to heaven, thence will I bring them down;

3 And though they hide themselves in the top of Carmel, I will search and take them out from there; and though they be hid from my sight in the bottom of the sea, there I will command the serpent and it shall bite them;

4 And though they go into captivity before their enemies, there I will command the sword, and it shall slay them; and I will set my eyes upon them for evil and not for good;

5 Says the LORD God of hosts, who touches the earth and it quakes, and all who dwell in it mourn; and the end shall rise up like a river, and shall recede like the river of Egypt;

6 It is he who has built his stories in heaven, and has made his possessions in the earth; who calls for the waters of the sea, and pours them out upon the face of the earth; the LORD of hosts is his name.

7 Behold, you are like the Ethiopians to me, O children of Israel! says the LORD. Behold, I brought up Israel out of the land of Egypt and the Philistines from Capadocia and the Arameans from Kir.

8 Behold, the eyes of the LORD God are upon the sinful kingdom, and I will destroy it from off the face of the earth; but I will not utterly destroy the house of Jacob, says the LORD.

9 For behold, I will command, and I will scatter the house of Israel among all nations as they sift wheat in a sieve, but not even the smallest grain of it shall fall upon the ground.

10 All the sinners of my people shall die by the sword, who say, The evil shall not touch us nor overtake us.

11 ¶In that day I will raise up the tabernacle of David that is fallen and close up its breaches, and I will raise up its ruins and I will build it as in the days of old, and as in the years of many generations.

12 For they shall possess the remnant of Edom, and all the Gentiles who are called by my name, says the LORD who does these things.

13 Behold, the days are coming, says the LORD, when the threshing floor shall overtake the reaper, and the treader of grapes him that sows seed; and the mountains shall drop sweetness, and all the hills shall rejoice.

14 And I will bring back the captivity of my people Israel, and they shall build the ruined cities and inhabit them; and they shall plant vineyards and drink the wine thereof; they shall also plant gardens and eat the fruit of them.

15 And I will plant them upon their own land, and they shall no more be uprooted from the land which I have given them, says the LORD your God.

OBADIAH

THE vision of Obadiah: Thus says the LORD God concerning Edom: We have heard a rumor from the LORD, and an ambassador is sent among the nations, Arise, and let us rise up against her for battle.

2 Behold, I have made you the least among the nations; you are greatly despised.

3 ¶The pride of your heart has deceived you, you who dwell in the clefts of the rock, whose habitation is high; who says in his heart, Who shall bring me down to the ground?

4 Though you rise high like the eagle, and though your nest is set among the stars, thence I will bring you down, says the LORD.

5 If thieves come to you or robbers by night, how could you have remained silent till they had stolen enough? Or if grape gatherers came to you, would they not leave some gleanings?

6 How Esau is searched out! how are his hidden things sought out!

7 They have driven you to the border; all the men of your confederacy have deceived you and prevailed against you; the men who were at peace with you and who ate your bread have laid an ambush for you, because Esau has no understanding in him.

8 In that day, says the LORD, I will destroy the wise men out of Edom, and the men of understanding out of the mount of Esau.

9 And your mighty men, O Teman, shall be plundered, so that every man from mount Esau may perish.

10 ¶Because of the slaughter and because of the violence against your brother Jacob, shame shall cover you, and you shall be cut off for ever.

11 In the day that you stood against him, in the day that the strangers carried away captive his forces, and foreigners entered into his gates and cast lots upon Jerusalem, even you were as one of them.

12 But you should not have looked for the day of your brother's disaster, in the day when he was afflicted by strangers; neither should you have

rejoiced over the children of Judah in the day of their destruction; nor should you have spoken proudly in the day of distress.

13 You should not have entered into the gate of my people in the day of their calamity; yea, you should not have rejoiced over their misfortune in the day of their distress; nor should you have terrified his forces in the day of their calamity;

14 Neither should you have stood in the narrow pass to cut off his fugitives; neither should you have delivered up his survivors in the day of distress.

15 For the day of the LORD is near upon all nations; as you have done, it shall be done to you; your rewards shall return upon your own head.

16 For as you have drunk upon my holy mountain, so shall all the nations drink continually, yea, they shall drink, and they shall be confounded and troubled, and they shall be as though they had not been.

17 ¶But upon mount Zion shall be deliverance, and there shall be holiness; and the house of Jacob shall possess those who possessed them.

18 And the house of Jacob shall be a fire and the house of Joseph a flame and the house of Esau for stubble, and they shall kindle in them and devour them; and there shall be no fugitive remaining to the house of Esau; for the LORD has spoken it.

19 And those of the south shall possess mount Esau; and those of the plain, the Philistines; and they shall possess the fields of Ephraim and the fields of Samaria; and Benjamin shall possess Gilead.

20 The first exiles, that is, of the children of Israel, shall possess the lands from Canaan as far as Zarepath; and the exiles of Jerusalem who are in Spain shall possess the cities of the south.

21 And those who are saved shall come up to mount Zion to judge mount Esau; and the kingdom shall be the LORD's.

JONAH

CHAPTER 1

NOW the word of the LORD came to Jonah the son of Matai (Matthew), saying,

2 Arise, go to Nineveh, that great city, and preach against it; for their wickedness has come up before me.

3 But Jonah rose to flee to Tarshish from the presence of the LORD, and went down to Joppa; and he found a ship going to Tarshish; so he paid the fare and went on board to go with them to Tarshish to flee from the presence of the LORD.

4 ¶But the LORD sent out a great wind into the sea, and there was a mighty tempest in the sea, so that the ship was in danger of being broken.

5 Then the mariners were afraid and cried every man to his god, and they threw the wares that were in the ship into the sea to lighten it. But Jonah had gone down into the inner hold of the ship; and he lay and was fast asleep.

6 So the captain came to him and said to him, Why are you sleeping? Arise, call upon your God, perhaps God will deliver us, that we perish not.

7 And they said every one to his fellow, Come, let us cast lots, that we may know for whose cause this evil has come upon us. So they cast lots, and the lot fell upon Jonah.

8 Then they said to him, Tell us for what cause this evil has come upon us; what is your occupation?

And from what place do you come? What is your country? And of what people are you?

9 And Jonah said to them, I am a Hebrew; and I worship the LORD the God of heaven, who has made the sea and the dry land.

10 Then the men were exceedingly afraid and said to him, What have you done? For the men knew that he had fled from the presence of the LORD.

11 ¶And when he had told them everything, then they said to him, What shall we do to you that the sea may be calm for us? For behold, the sea continues to be more tempestuous against us.

12 Jonah said to them, Take me up and cast me into the sea, so that the sea may be calm to you; for I know that for my sake this great tempest is upon you.

13 Nevertheless the men rowed hard to bring the ship back to the land; but they could not; for the sea became more tempestuous against them.

14 Therefore they cried to the LORD and said, We beseech thee, O LORD, let us not perish for this man's life, and lay not upon us innocent blood; for thou art the LORD and hast done as it pleased thee.

15 So they took up Jonah and cast him forth into the sea; and the sea ceased from its raging.

16 And the men were greatly terrified from the presence of the LORD, and they offered sacrifices of righteousness to the LORD and made vows.

17 ¶Now the LORD had prepared a great fish, and it swallowed up Jonah. And Jonah was in the belly of the fish three days and three nights.

CHAPTER 2

THEN Jonah prayed before the LORD his God from the belly of the fish, saying,

2 I cried to the LORD in my distress and he answered me; out of the depths of Sheol cried I, and thou heardest my voice.

3 For thou hadst cast me into the deep, in the midst of the sea; and the flood compassed me about: all thy billows and thy waves have passed over me.

4 Then I said, I am cast afar out of thy sight; yet now I will see again thy holy temple.

5 The waters engulfed me, even to the soul; the depth closed me round about, my head lay at the bottom of the sea.

6 I went down to the bottoms oi the mountains; the earth shut up its bars against me for ever; yet thou hast brought up my life from corruption, O LORD my God.

7 When my soul fainted within me, I remembered the LORD; and my prayer came in to thee, into thy holy temple.

8 All those who revere false idols forsake thy mercy.

9 But I will sacrifice to thee with the voice of thanksgiving; I will pay the things that I have vowed, as a reward for the LORD.

10 ¶And the LORD commanded the fish, and it vomited out Jonah on the dry land.

CHAPTER 3

AND the word of the LORD came to Jonah the second time, saying,

2 Arise, go to Nineveh, that great city, and cry against it the proclamation which I tell you.

3 So Jonah arose and went to Nineveh, according to the word of the LORD. Now Nineveh was an exceeding great city in the presence of God, of three days journey.

4 And Jonah began to enter into the city a day's journey, and he cried and said, Yet forty days and Nineveh shall be overthrown.

5 ¶So the people of Nineveh believed in God and decreed a fast and put on sackcloth, from the greatest of them even to the least.

6 And when the news reached the king of Nineveh, he arose from his throne and took off his crown from his head and covered himself with sackcloth and sat in ashes.

7 And he caused it to be proclaimed and published through Nineveh by the decree of the king and his nobles,

saying, Let neither men nor beast, herd nor flock, taste anything; let them not feed nor drink water;

8 But let men and beasts be covered with sackcloth and cry to God with groaning; yea, let every man turn from his evil way and from the violence that is in his hands.

9 Who knows if God will return and have mercy upon us, and remove from us his fierce anger, that we may perish not?

10 ¶And God saw their works, that they turned from their evil ways; he turned away from them his fierce anger, and he did not destroy them.

CHAPTER 4

BUT it displeased Jonah exceedingly, and he was greatly grieved.

2 And he prayed to the LORD and said, I pray thee, O LORD, was not this what I said when I was yet in my country? That is why I fled before to Tarshish; for I knew that thou art a gracious and merciful God, patient and of great kindness, and thou art ready to turn away calamity.

3 Therefore now, O my LORD, take my life from me; for it is better for me to die than to live.

4 ¶Then the LORD said to him, Are you very sorrowful?

5 So Jonah went out of the city, and sat on the east side of the city, and there made a booth for himself,

and sat under it in the shade to see what would happen to the city.

6 And the LORD God commanded a tender shoot of gourd to spring up, and it sprang up and came over Jonah, and became a shade over his head, and comforted him of his grief. So Jonah was exceedingly glad because of the gourd.

7 But the next day at dawn, God commanded a worm, and it smote the gourd so that it withered.

8 And it came to pass when the sun arose, the LORD God commanded a sultry east wind; and it withered the gourd, and the sun beat upon the head of Jonah, that he was weary and wished that he might die, and said, O LORD, you can take my life from me, for I am not better than my fathers.

9 And the LORD God said to Jonah, Are you exceedingly grieved over the gourd? And Jonah said, I am exceedingly grieved, even unto death.

10 Then the LORD said to him, You have had pity on the gourd for the which you did not labor nor did you make it to grow; which sprung up in a night and withered in a night;

11 And should not I have pity upon Nineveh, that great city, in which are more than a hundred and twenty thousand persons that cannot discern between their right hand and their left hand,[1] and also much cattle?

MICAH

CHAPTER 1

THE word of the LORD that came to Micah the Morashite in the days of Jotham, Ahaz, and Hezekiah, kings of Judah, which he saw concerning Samaria and Jerusalem.

2 Hear, all you people; hearken, O earth and all that is in it; and let the LORD God be a witness among you,

even the LORD from his holy temple.

3 For behold, the LORD will come forth out of his place, and will come down and tread upon the high places of the earth.

4 And the mountains shall melt under him, and the valleys shall be rent asunder like wax before the fire, and like waters that run down a steep place.

---

[1] Who are too young to have understanding.

5 All this will happen because of the wickedness of Jacob and the sins of the house of Israel. What is the wickedness of Jacob? Is it not Samaria? And what is the sin of Judah? Is it not Jerusalem?

6 Therefore I will make Samaria as a ploughed field and a place for the planting of a vineyard; and I will pile her stones into a heap, and I will uncover the foundation thereof.

7 And all her graven images shall be broken to pieces and all her idols shall be burned with fire and all her shrines of worship I will lay desolate; for they were gathered of the hire of a harlot, and they shall return to the hire of a harlot.

8 Therefore I will mourn and howl, and walk bare footed and naked; I will make a wailing like the jackal and mourning like the owl.

9 For her wound is very painful; and disaster has reached Judah; it has come to the gate of my people, even to Jerusalem.

10 ¶Rejoice not in Gath, weep not at all; in the house of Aphrah roll yourselves in the dust.

11 Pass away, O you beautiful inhabitant; you came out naked and you are not shamed, O you inhabitant of Zanan; your wound will be like that of Beth-aozel.

12 For the rebellious inhabitant is sick of waiting for good; for disaster is come down from the LORD to the gate of Jerusalem.

13 You have harnessed horses to the chariots, O you inhabitants of Lachish; you were the beginning of sin to the daughter of Zion; for in you were found the transgressions of Israel.

14 Therefore you shall abandon the possessions of Gath; the shrines of falsehood have become a lie to the kings of Israel.

15 Yet will I bring an heir against you, O inhabitant of Mareshah; he shall exalt the glory of Israel for ever.

16 Make yourself bald, pull out your hair, for your delicate children; enlarge your baldness as the eagle; for they are carried into captivity from you.

CHAPTER 2

WOE to those who devise iniquity, and work evil upon their beds! They rise up early every morning and practice what they have devised; then they lift up their hands toward God to pray.

2 They covet fields and houses, and seize them by force; they oppress a man, taking away from him his possessions and his inheritance.

3 Therefore thus says the LORD God: Behold, against this people do I devise a disaster from which you shall not lift up your necks, neither shall you walk haughtily; for this is an evil time.

4 ¶In that day shall one take up a proverb against you, and lament with a wailing melody, and say, The robber has plundered us; the portion of my people he has divided with a measuring line; there is none to restore our fields with the measuring line.

5 Therefore you shall have none that shall measure by the measuring line and divide by casting the lots in the congregation of the LORD.

6 Shed not tears, and weep not over these things,

7 ¶That the shame which is spoken against the house of Jacob may not overtake you; for the spirit of the LORD is angry at these devices; behold, my words are good to him who walked uprightly.

8 My people stood up like a thief against his own peace; you strip the skin from the poor that they may lose their hope; you invite war.

9 The women of my people you have driven out from their pleasant houses; from their children you have taken away the glory for ever.

10 Arise and go away; for this is no place for your rest, because the pollution will bring destruction, and the destruction will be grievous.

11 When a man walks in the spirit of falsehood and deception, overwhelmed with wine and drunkenness,

he does so because of the anguish of this people.

12 ¶I will surely gather you, O Jacob, all of you; I will surely bring you together, O remnant of Israel; I will keep them like sheep when they are in danger, like a flock in the midst of their fold, which are protected from thieves.

13 The pathbreaker is come up before them; they have made a breach and have passed through the gate, and are gone out by it; and their king shall pass before them, and the LORD at the head of them.

CHAPTER 3

THEN the LORD said, Hear these things, O you chiefs of the house of Jacob and you princes of the house of Israel: Is it not meet for you to know justice?

2 O you haters of the good and lovers of evil, who strip the skin from off the people and the flesh from off their bones; [1]

3 Who oppress my people and flay their skin from off them and break their bones and chop them in pieces, as if they were to be put in the pot, like meat in a caldron.

4 Then shall they cry to the LORD, but he will not hear them; he will even turn away his face from them at that time, for they have behaved themselves ill in their doings.

5 ¶Thus says the LORD concerning the prophets who lead my people astray, who bite with their teeth and preach peace; and when one puts not bread into their mouths, they preach war against him.

6 Therefore it shall be night to you, that you shall not have a vision; and it shall be dark to you, that you shall not divine; and the sun shall go down upon the prophets, and the day shall be dark over them.

7 Then the seers shall be ashamed, and the diviners confounded; yea, they shall all cover their lips because God will not answer them.

8 ¶But truly I am full of power by the spirit of the LORD, and of justice and of might, to declare to Jacob his transgression and to Israel his sin.

9 Now hear this, O you chiefs of the house of Jacob and princes of the house of Israel, who abhor justice and pervert all equity;

10 Who build Zion with blood and Jerusalem with iniquity;

11 The chiefs thereof judge for a bribe, and its priests teach for hire, and its prophets divine for money; yet they rely upon the LORD, saying, The LORD is among us, no evil can come upon us;

12 Therefore, because of you, Zion shall be ploughed as a field, and Jerusalem shall become desolate, and the mountain of the house [2] like a forest.

CHAPTER 4

BUT it shall come to pass in the latter days that the mountain of the house of the LORD shall be established in the top of the mountains, and it shall be exalted above the hills; and all people shall gather to it.

2 And many nations shall come and say, Come, let us go up to the mountain of the LORD, and to the house of the God of Jacob; and he will teach us of his ways, and we will walk in his paths; for the law shall go forth out of Zion, and the word of the LORD from Jerusalem.

3 ¶And he shall judge between many people, and rebuke strong nations afar off; and they shall beat their swords into plowshares, and their spears into sickles; nation shall not lift up sword against nation, neither shall they learn war any more.

4 But they shall sit every man under his vine and under his fig tree; and there shall be none to harm them; for the mouth of the LORD of hosts has spoken it.

5 For all people will walk every one in the name of his god, and we will walk in the name of the LORD our God for ever and ever.

6 In that day, says the LORD, I will

---

[1] You who rob the people.   [2] Temple.

gather those who are afar off, and I will bring near those who have been driven out and those whom I have afflicted.

7 And I will make those who have been driven out a remnant, and those who are afar off a strong nation; and the LORD shall reign over them in mount Zion from henceforth, even for ever.

8 ¶And you, O gloomy ruler of the daughter of Zion, your time has come, and the former ruler of the kingdom of the daughter of Jerusalem is coming.

9 Now why do you commit iniquity? Is there no king in you? Or have your counsellors perished? For pangs have taken you like a woman in travail.

10 Be in pain, and labor to bring forth, O daughter of Zion, like a woman in travail; for now you shall go forth out of the city, and you shall dwell in the desert, and you shall go even to Babylon; there you shall be delivered; there the LORD shall save you from the hand of your enemies.

11 ¶Now many nations shall gather against you, who say, Let Zion be defiled, and let our eyes look upon it.

12 But they know not the thoughts of the LORD, neither do they understand his counsel; for he shall gather them as sheaves into the threshing floor.

13 Arise and thresh them, O daughter of Zion; for I will make your horns of iron, and your hoofs of brass; and you shall beat in pieces many peoples; and I will consecrate their possessions to the LORD, and their wealth to the LORD of the whole earth.

CHAPTER 5

NOW you shall go forth in a raid, O daughter of mighty raiders, for they have risen against us and have smitten the shepherd of Israel with a rod upon his cheek.

2 And you, Bethlehem Ephratah, though you are little among the thousands of towns of Judah, yet out of you shall come forth a ruler to govern Israel; whose goings forth have been predicted from of old, from eternity.

3 Henceforth he will deliver them, until the time when she who is in travail has brought forth; then the remnant of his brethren shall return to the children of Israel.

4 ¶And he shall arise and rule in the strength of the LORD, in the majesty of the name of the LORD his God; and the people shall return; for now his dominion shall extend to the ends of the earth.

5 And there shall be peace when the Assyrian shall come to invade our country, and shall tread in our palaces; then we will raise up against him seven rulers and eight princes of men.

6 And they shall waste the land of Assyria with the sword, and the land of Nimrod with their anger; thus shall he deliver us from the Assyrian, that he may not come to our land, and that he may not tread within our borders.

7 And the remnant of Jacob shall be in the midst of many nations like the dew from the LORD, like the showers upon the grass, which tarry not for man, nor wait for the sons of men.

8 ¶And the remnant of Jacob shall be among the Gentiles in the midst of many nations as a lion among the beasts of the forest, as a young lion among the flocks of sheep, who, when he selects his prey, cuts and tears in pieces, and there is none to deliver.

9 Your hand shall be lifted up against your adversaries, and all your enemies shall perish.

10 And it shall come to pass in that day, says the LORD, that I will destroy your horses from the midst of you, and will do away with your chariots;

11 And I will lay waste the towns of your land, and demolish all your strongholds.

12 And I will destroy the magicians from within your reach; and you shall have no more soothsayers;

13 And I will destroy your graven

images and your high places from the midst of you; and you shall no more worship the work of your hands.

14 And I will destroy your groves from the midst of you; and I will lay waste your cities.

15 And I will execute vengeance in anger and fury upon the nations that did not obey.

CHAPTER 6

HEAR now what the LORD says: Arise and judge upon the mountains, and let the hills hear your voice.

2 Hear, O you mountains, the judgment of the LORD, listen, O you deep foundations of the earth; for the LORD will contend with his people, and he will judge Israel;

3 O my people, what have I done to you? Or in what have I grieved you? Testify against me.

4 Have not I brought you up from the land of Egypt, and delivered you from the house of bondage? And I sent before you Moses, Aaron, and Miriam?

5 O my people, remember now what Balak king of Moab purposed against you, and what Balaam the son of Beor answered him from Shittim to Gilgal; for he knew the righteousness of the LORD.

6 ¶With what shall I come before the LORD, and how shall I be pleasing before the high God? Shall I come before him with burnt offerings, or with calves of a year old?

7 The LORD will not be pleased with thousands of rams, nor with ten thousands of heifers; if I should offer my first-born, it is an iniquity to myself, and the fruit of my body, it is a sin against my soul.

8 He has showed you, O man, what is good and what the LORD requires of you, that you shall do justice and love mercy and be ready to walk after the LORD your God.

9 The voice of the LORD cries upon the city, preaching doctrine to those who revere his name; hear, O tribe, him who testifies against you.

10 ¶For there is still fire in the house of the wicked and in the storehouses of iniquity and in the short measure of deceit.

11 How can they justify themselves with the wicked scales and with the bag of deceitful weights?

12 For the rich men of the land are full of deceit, and its inhabitants speak lies, and their tongue is treacherous in their mouth.

13 Therefore I will begin to smite you, and will make you desolate because of your sins.

14 You shall eat, but not be satisfied; and dysentery shall be in the midst of you; and you shall thresh wheat, but shall not keep it, and that which you retain, I will give up to the sword.

15 You shall sow, but you shall not reap; you shall tread the olives, but you shall not anoint yourselves with oil; you shall tread grapes but you shall not drink wine.

16 ¶For you have kept the statutes of Omri and all the works of the house of Ahab, and you have walked in their counsels; therefore I have made the land a desolation, and its inhabitants a hissing; thus you shall bear the reproach of my people.

CHAPTER 7

WOE is me! for I have become as when they have gathered the summer fruit, as the grape gleanings of the vintage; there is no cluster to eat; my soul craves the first ripe fruit.

2 The righteous man has perished from the earth, and there is none upright among men; they all lie in wait for blood; they hunt every man his brother for destruction.

3 ¶Their hands are ready to do evil, and they never do good; the governor asks for gold, and the judge says, Give me a bribe; and the prince speaks the desire of his soul.

4 They have rejected the best part of them, and have become like rags which are eaten by the moth; the day of your watchmen and your sal-

vation is come; but now it shall be their mourning.

5 ¶Trust not in your friends, put no confidence in your neighbors, guard the words of your mouth from your wife.

6 For the son curses his father, the daughter rises up against her mother, the daughter-in-law against her mother-in-law; a man's enemies are the members of his own household.

7 Therefore I will look to the LORD; I will wait for the God my Saviour; my God will hear me.

8 ¶Rejoice not over me, O my enemy, because I have fallen; I shall rise again; though I sit in darkness, the LORD shall be a light to me.

9 I will bear the affliction of the LORD, because I have sinned against him, until he pleads my cause and avenges me; he will bring me forth to the light, and I shall see his righteousness.

10 Then my enemy shall see it, and shame shall cover her [1] who said to me, Where is the LORD your God? My eyes shall behold her; now she shall be trodden down like the mire of the streets.

11 It is a day to build your walls; it is a day to be lifted up.

12 It is a day when the people shall come to you from Assyria and from the fortified cities and from Tyre even to the river and from sea to sea, as far as mount Hor.

13 Nevertheless the land shall be desolate to its inhabitants because of the fruit of their doings.

14 ¶Feed thy people with thy rod, the flock of thy heritage, who shall dwell alone like sheep in the midst of Carmel; let them feed in Mathnin and Gilead, as in the days of old.

15 As in the day when you came out of the land of Egypt will I again show them marvellous things.

16 ¶The nations shall see and be ashamed of all their might; they shall lay their hands upon their mouth, their ears shall be deaf.

17 They shall lick the dust like a serpent, they shall move out of their holes like worms of the earth; they shall tremble and be afraid of the LORD our God.

18 There is no God like thee, who pardons iniquity and removes the sins of the remnant of his inheritance; thou retainest not thy anger for ever, because thou delightest in mercy.

19 He will turn again and have mercy on us; he will sweep away our iniquity and cast all our sins into the depths of the sea.

20 Thou wilt grant truth to Jacob and mercy to Abraham, as thou hast sworn to our fathers from the days of old.

NAHUM

CHAPTER 1

THE wound of Nineveh, which is in the book of the visions of Nahum the Alkoshite.

2 God is zealous, and the LORD is avenging; the LORD is avenging and is furious; the LORD will take vengeance on his adversaries, and he reserves wrath for his enemies.

3 The LORD is slow to anger and great in power, and will not at all acquit the wicked; the LORD's way is in the whirlwind and in the tempest, and the clouds are the dust of his feet.

4 He rebukes the sea and makes it dry, and dries up all the rivers; Mathnin and Carmel languish, and the flower of Lebanon withers.

5 The mountains quake before him and the hills break loose; the earth

[1] Jerusalem.

trembles at his presence, yea, the world and all that dwell therein.

6 Who can stand before his indignation? Who can endure in the fierceness of his wrath? His fury burns like fire, and the mountains melt at his presence.

7 The LORD is good, a great help in the day of trouble; and he knows those who trust in him.

8 But with a rushing flood he will make an utter end of the place of his adversaries, and darkness shall pursue his enemies.

9 What do you imagine against the LORD? He will make an utter end; affliction shall not rise up the second time.

10 Because from the lowest among them up to their rulers they are rebellious, they stagger in their drunkenness; they have eaten and are filled with dry rubbish.

11 Out of you shall come forth one who imagines evil against the LORD and gives wicked counsel.

12 Thus says the LORD: Against the watersheds of many waters,[1] they have run down and vanished; though I have humbled you, I will humble you no more.[2]

13 For now I will break his yoke from off you, and will burst your bonds asunder.

14 And the LORD will give a commandment concerning you: Your name shall no more be propagated from the house of your god; I will destroy the graven images and the molten images; I will make your grave hastily.

15 Behold upon the mountains, the feet of him that brings good tidings, that publishes peace! O Judah, keep your solemn feasts and perform your vows; the wicked shall no longer transgress against you, for he is utterly destroyed.

CHAPTER 2

A RULER has come up against you who keeps a watch, guards the road, and girds loins; whose strength is exceedingly great.

2 For the LORD will restore the excellency of Jacob, as the excellency of Israel; for the oppressors have trampled upon them and destroyed their branches.

3 The shields of their mighty men are red, the valiant men parade with flaming torches and in chariots in the day of their preparation, and the horsemen are terrifying.

4 In the streets they sing praises and glory in their chariots, their appearance is like torches; they run like lightning.

5 The soldiers are obedient to their officers; they stumble as they march; they make haste to the wall, and the battlements are prepared.

6 The city gates are opened and the palace trembles.

7 And the queen summons her horsemen and flees northward; her maids are mourning in their hearts like doves.

8 And Nineveh is like a lake, and she is situated by the waters; her warriors flee away. Make a stand, make a stand, their officers cry; but none turns back.

9 Plunder the silver, plunder the gold; for there is no end to the precious ornaments, and abundance of every kind of precious vessels.

10 She is trampled upon, she is overthrown and breached; the heart faints and the knees tremble and pain is in all loins, and all of them are greatly ashamed.

11 Where is the lion's den and the feeding place of the young lions, where the lion went to enter there and the lion's whelp, and there was none to harm them?

12 The lion did tear in pieces enough to feed his whelps, and ripped apart for his lionesses, and filled his holes with prey and his dens with pieces of flesh.

13 Behold, I am against you, says the LORD of hosts, and I will burn up your multitudes in the smoke, and the sword shall devour your young lions; and I will cut off your prey from the earth, and the news of your deeds shall no more be heard.

[1] Assyria, the land of many, many waters.   [2] Jerusalem.

CHAPTER 3

WOE to the bloody city! it is all full of lies and iniquity; the plunder in it cannot be estimated.

2 The noise of the whip and the noise of rattling of the wheels and of the snorting of horses and of bounding chariots!

3 The horseman driving, with the flash of the sword and the glittering spear! And there is a multitude of slain, and a great number of corpses; there is no end to corpses; they stumble over their corpses.

4 Because of the multitude of the whoredoms of the harlot that was beautiful and mistress of witchcrafts, who brings up nations through her whoredoms and tribes through her witchcraft,

5 Behold, I am against you, says the LORD of hosts; and I will raise your skirts over your face and will show the nations your nakedness and the kingdoms your shame.

6 And I will cast filth upon you and disgrace you, and will make you a spectacle,

7 And it shall come to pass that all who look upon you shall abhor you and say, Nineveh is plundered; who will bemoan her? Whence shall I seek a comforter for you?

8 Are you better than Jawan of Ammon,[1] which is situated by the rivers, that had waters round about her, whose rampart was the sea, and water her wall?

9 Ethiopia and Egypt were her strength, and it was limitless; Put and the Libyans were her helpers;

10 Yet even she was carried away into captivity; her children were dashed in pieces at the head of all the streets; and they cast lots for her honorable men, and all her great men were bound in chains.

11 You also shall be grieved and you shall be despised; you also shall seek help because of your enemies.

12 All your strongholds shall be like fig trees with the first ripe figs; when they are ripe, they fall into the mouth of the eater.

13 Behold, your people in the midst of you are cowards; they will open the gates of your land to your enemies; the fire shall devour your bars.

14 Draw water for the siege, fortify your strongholds; mix the clay, tread the mortar, strengthen the foundations.

15 There shall the fire devour you, the sword shall cut you off; it shall devour you like the crawling locust because you have become many like the crawling locust and multiplied like the locust.

16 You have multiplied your merchants more than the stars of the heaven; the young locust swarms and flies away.

17 Your Nazarites are as the locusts, and your warriors as the swarms of locusts which settle on the hedges on a cold day, but when the sun arises they fly off, and it is not known where they are.

18 Your friends slumber, O king of Assyria; your allies have deserted; your people are scattered on the mountains, and they have none to gather them.

19 There is no one to grieve over your wound; your wound is painful; all who hear the news of you clap their hands over you; for your wickedness has gone forth against every man continually.

---

[1] Ammon in Thebes, Egypt.

HABAKKUK

CHAPTER 1

THE vision which Habakkuk the prophet saw:

2 O Lord, how long shall I cry, and thou wilt not hear? I cry to thee because of the plunderers, and thou wilt not deliver!

3 Why dost thou show me iniquity and deceit? For I see violence and evil; justice was on my side, but the judge accepted bribes.

4 Therefore the law is slacked, and justice never goes forth; for the wicked surely does evil to the righteous; thus justice goes forth perverted.

5 ¶Behold, O you presumptuous, see, wonder, and be amazed! for I will do a work in your days that you would not believe if a man should declare it to you.

6 For, behold, I raise up the Chaldeans, that hasty and bitter nation, who shall march through the breadth of the land to possess the dwelling places that are not theirs.

7 They are mighty and dreadful; their judgment and their notable doings proceed of themselves.

8 Their horses are swifter than eagles and more fierce than the evening wolves; and their horsemen shall swoop down and shall come from afar; they shall fly like an eagle that hastens to eat.

9 They all come for plunder; the appearance of their faces is fearful, and they shall gather booty as the sand.

10 They scoff at kings, and princes they mock; and they laugh at every stronghold; for they heap up earth and capture it.

11 Then shall his wind [1] change and pass away, and his army shall be found guilty before his god.

12 ¶Art thou not from everlasting, O Lord my God, my Holy One? Art thou without a law, O Lord? For thou hast ordained them for judgment, and thou hast created us for chastisement.

13 Thine eyes are too pure, they do not behold evil, and thou canst not look on wicked men; why dost thou look on presumptuous men, and art silent when the wicked devours the righteous man?

14 And thou didst make men as the fish of the sea, as the creeping things that have no ruler over them.

15 They take up all of them with the hook, they catch them in a net, and gather them in their drag; and when they gather them, they rejoice and are glad.

16 Therefore they sacrifice to their net and burn incense to their drag, because by them their portion is made rich, and their food dainty.

17 Therefore they cast their net continually, they slay peoples without pity.

CHAPTER 2

I WILL stand upon my place and set me upon the rock tower, and I will watch to see what he will say to me and what I shall answer because of my chastisement.

2 And the Lord answered me and said, Write the vision, and make it plain upon tablets, that he who reads it may understand it clearly.

3 For the vision will come to pass at its appointed time, and it shall be fulfilled at the end, it shall not lie; and if it should delay, do not be impatient, because it will surely come, it will not delay.

4 For his soul does not delight in iniquity, but the righteous man shall live by faith.

5 ¶The arrogant and greedy man is never satisfied, because he has enlarged his appetite like Sheol; and like death, he has never enough, but

[1] Luck.

gathers to him all peoples, and draws near to him all the nations.

6 Shall not all these take up a parable against him, and a taunting proverb against him, and say, Woe to him who gathers and increases that which is not his! How long will he load himself with earthly goods?

7 Behold, they shall rise up suddenly, those who shall bite you, and awake those who shall cause you trouble, and you shall be for spoil to them.

8 Because you have plundered many nations, so the remnant of the people shall plunder you; because of men's blood and the violence of the land, of the city, and of all that dwell therein.

9 ¶Woe to him who defrauds and heaps up evil for himself, who sets his nest on high that he may be delivered from evil!

10 You have devised shame to your house, you have plundered many peoples and caused your soul to sin.

11 For the stone shall cry out from the wall, and the nail in the wood shall answer it.

12 ¶Woe to him who builds a city with bloodshed and establishes a town by iniquity!

13 All these things are from the Lord of hosts that the people shall labor in fire, and the nations shall labor in vain.

14 For the earth shall be filled with the knowledge of the glory of the Lord, as the waters cover the sea.

15 ¶Woe to him who makes his neighbors drink the dregs of fury, and makes them drunk that he may look on their nakedness!

16 You are filled with dishonor instead of glory; drink yourself also and stagger, for the cup of the Lord's right hand shall come round to you, and shame shall cover your glory.

17 For the violence of Lebanon shall cover you, and the plundering of the beasts shall trouble you because of the blood of men, and for the violence of the land, of the city, and of all who dwell therein.

18 ¶What profit is a graven image

that its maker has fashioned? The molten image is a false doctrine, for the heart of its maker trusts in it, to fashion a dumb idol.

19 Woe to him who says to the wood, Awake! to the dumb stone, Arise! They are vain; even though they are overlaid with gold, there is no breath at all in them.

20 But the Lord is in his holy temple; let all the earth tremble before him.

CHAPTER 3

A PRAYER of Habakkuk the prophet:

2 O Lord, I have heard thy name and am afraid. O Lord, thy works are in the midst of the years of life, in the midst of years they shall be known; in wrath remember thy mercy.

3 God came from the south,[1] and the Holy One from mount Paran. The heavens were covered with the brightness of his glory, and the earth was full of his praise.

4 And his brightness was as the light; in the city which his hands had established shall he store his power.

5 Before him went pestilence, and birds [2] went forth before his feet.

6 He stood and measured the earth; he beheld and drove asunder the nations; and the everlasting mountains were scattered, the eternal hills were brought low; his ways are everlasting.

7 I saw the tents of Cushan in affliction; and the curtains of the tents of Midian did tremble.

8 Was the Lord angry against the rivers? Was thy anger against the rivers? Was thy rage against the sea, that thou didst ride upon thy horses and upon the chariots of thy salvation?

9 Thy bow was made ready, the arrows were abundant at the command of thy glorious word. Thou didst furrow the earth with rivers.

10 The mountains saw thee and they quaked; the downpour of the waters passed by; the deep uttered its voice and lifted up its hands on high.

[1] *Teman*, the south.   [2] Vultures.

11 The sun and moon stood still in their habitations; at the light of thine arrows they went, and at the shining of thy glittering spears.

12 Thou didst tread upon the earth in thy indignation, thou didst thresh the nations in thine anger.

13 Thou wentest forth to save thy people and to save thine anointed; thou didst cut off the head out of the house of the wicked, thou hast laid him bare from his foundations even to the neck for ever.

14 Thou didst break with his own staves the heads of his princes; for they trusted in their savagery to devour the poor secretly.

15 Thou didst tread upon the sea with thy horses, through the heap of great waters.

16 When I heard it, my body trembled, confusing the words of my mouth; fear entered into my bones and my knees trembled, for he searched me out and declared to me the day of trouble that comes upon the people.

17 ¶Though the fig tree has not blossomed and there are no leaves on the vine, though the produce of the olive tree has failed, the threshing-floors have not yielded grain, the sheep are cut off from the flocks, and there are no oxen in the herd;

18 Yet I will rejoice in the LORD, and I will joy in the God my Saviour.

19 The LORD God is my strength, for he has made my feet like hinds' feet, and made me stand on my high places that I may sing his praise.

ZEPHANIAH

CHAPTER 1

THE word of the LORD which came to Zephaniah the son of Cushi, the son of Gedaliah, the son of Amariah, the son of Helakiah, in the days of Josiah the son of Amon, king of Judah.

2 I will utterly remove all things from off the face of the earth, says the LORD.

3 I will remove man and beast; I will remove the fowls of the air and the fish of the sea; I will bring a stumbling block against the wicked; and I will destroy man from the face of the earth, says the LORD.

4 I will also stretch out my hand against Judah and against all the inhabitants of Jerusalem; and I will destroy the remnant of Baal from this place, and the name of the priests in charge, along with the priests;

5 And all of those who worship the host of heaven upon the housetops; and all who worship and swear by the LORD and also swear by Malcom;

6 And those who are turned back from the LORD; and those who have not sought the LORD, nor enquired for him.

7 Stand in awe at the presence of the LORD God; for the day of the LORD is at hand; yea, the LORD has prepared sacrifices, he has invited his guests.

8 And it shall come to pass in the day of the LORD's sacrifice that I will punish the princes and the king's children, and all such as are clothed in strange apparel.

9 In that day I will punish all those who do violence and those who plunder, who fill their storerooms with things acquired by means of extortion and deceit.

10 And it shall come to pass in that day, says the LORD, that there shall be the noise of a cry from the fish gate and a wailing from the second gate and a great crashing from the hills.

11 Wail, O inhabitants of Maktesh, for all the people of Canaan are confounded; all those who bear silver are cut off.

12 And it shall come to pass at that time that I will search Jerusalem with a lamp and punish the men who despise their watchmen, who say in their heart, The LORD will not do good, neither will he do evil.

13 Therefore their goods shall become a booty and their houses a desolation; they shall also build houses, but not inhabit them; and they shall plant vineyards, but not drink the wine thereof.

14 The great day of the LORD is near, it is very near, and hastens fast; even the voice of the day of the Lord; yea, it is bitter, harsh, and severe.

15 That day is a day of wrath, a day of trouble and distress, a day of confusion and desolation, a day of darkness and gloominess, a day of clouds and thick darkness,

16 A day of the trumpet and shouting against the fenced cities and against the high towers.

17 And I will bring distress upon men, that they shall walk like blind men, because they have sinned against the LORD; and their blood shall be poured out like dust, and their flesh like dung.

18 Neither their silver nor their gold shall be able to deliver them in the day of the LORD's wrath; but the whole land shall be consumed in the fire of his indignation; for he shall make a speedy destruction against all the inhabitants of the earth.

CHAPTER 2

GATHER yourselves, bind yourselves together, O people without discipline;

2 Before you become like the chaff which is driven away, before the fierce anger of the LORD comes upon you, before the day of the LORD's anger reaches you.

3 Seek the LORD, all you meek of the earth, execute justice; seek righteousness and meekness; perhaps you may find refuge in the day of the LORD's anger.

4 ¶For Gaza shall be deserted and Ashkelon a desolation; they shall carry captive Ashdod's people at the noon day, and Ekron shall be uprooted.

5 Woe to the inhabitants of the seacoast and the people of Crete! The word of the LORD is against you, O Canaan, the land of the Philistines; I will even destroy you, that there shall be no inhabitant.

6 And the seacoast shall become pastures for sheep, and Crete a pasture for flocks of sheep.

7 And the seacoast shall be for the remnant of the house of Judah; they shall feed thereupon; in the houses of Ashkelon they shall lie down in the evening; for the LORD their God shall visit them and bring back their captivity.

8 ¶I have heard the reproach of Moab and the blasphemies of the children of Ammon, whereby they have reproached my people and magnified themselves against their border.

9 Therefore as I live, says the LORD God of hosts, the God of Israel, surely Moab shall become as Sodom, and the children of Ammon as Gomorrah, for their plantations have been destroyed and their counsellors lost, and they have become a desolation for ever; the remnant of my people shall plunder them, and the survivors of my people shall possess them.

10 This disaster shall they have for their pride because they have reproached and magnified themselves against the people of the LORD of hosts, against Israel;

11 For the LORD has declared to them that he shall destroy all the kings of the earth; and men shall worship him, every one from his place, even all the isles of the seas.

12 ¶You Ethiopians also, you shall be slain by the sword.

13 And he will stretch out his hand against the north and destroy the Assyrian, and will make Nineveh a desolation and dry like a wilderness.

14 And flocks shall lie down in the midst of her, all kinds of beasts of the nations; both pelicans and the owls shall lodge in her houses; and wild beasts shall roar in the midst of her, and the sword shall be in

her gates; for her foundations are laid bare.

15 This is the mighty city that dwelt in security, that said in her heart, I am, and there is none like me; how is she become a desolation, a place for beasts to lie down in! Everyone that passes by her shall be amazed and hiss, and shake his hand, saying,

CHAPTER 3

OH, the famous city, the saved city; the city of Jonah!

2 She obeyed not the voice; she received not discipline; she trusted not in the LORD; she drew not near to her God.

3 Her princes within her are roaring like lions; her judges are like evening wolves; they wait not for the morning.

4 Her prophets are wanton and treacherous persons; her priests have polluted the sanctuary, they have done violence to the law.

5 But the just LORD is in her midst; he will not do iniquity; every morning he brings his justice to light, he is never late; but the wicked knows no shame.

6 I have destroyed the nations and removed the misery; I have made their streets waste, so that no one walks in them; their cities are desolate, without a man and without the inhabitants.

7 I said, Surely they will worship me, they will accept discipline from me; and she will not fail to see of all that I have decreed concerning her; but they hastened and corrupted all their doings.

8 ¶Therefore wait for me, says the LORD, until the day when I rise up to give testimony; for my judgment is at hand, to gather the nations and to bring the kingdoms near, to pour out my indignation upon them, even all my fierce anger; for in the fire of my zeal shall all the earth be devoured.

9 For then I will restore to the people a pure speech, that they may call upon the name of the LORD to serve him with one consent.

10 From beyond the rivers of Ethiopia they shall bring me sacrifices.

11 In that day you shall not be ashamed for all your doings wherein you have transgressed against me; for then I will remove from the midst of you the might of your pride, and you shall no more be haughty because of my holy mountain.

12 I will also leave in the midst of you an afflicted and humble people, and they shall trust in the name of the LORD.

13 The remnant of Israel shall not do iniquity, nor speak lies; neither shall a deceitful tongue be found in their mouth; for they shall feed and lie down, and none shall harm them.

14 ¶Sing, O daughter of Zion; sound a trumpet, O Israel; be glad and rejoice with all your heart, O daughter of Jerusalem.

15 The LORD has taken away your judgments, he has cast out your enemies; the King of Israel, even the LORD, is in the midst of you; you shall not see evil any more.

16 In that day it shall be said to Jerusalem, Fear not; and to Zion, Let not your hands be weak.

17 The LORD your God in the midst of you is a mighty Saviour; he will make you to rejoice with gladness; he will renew you with his love, he will make you joyful with a praise as in the day of a feast.

18 I will remove from you those who spoke reproach against you.

19 Behold, at that time I will humble all that are in the midst of you; and I will save her that has been subjugated, and gather her that was cast far off; and I will make them for fame and for praise in every land where they had been put to shame.

20 At that time I will bring you again, and at that very time I will gather you; for I will make you a name and a praise among all the people of the earth, when I bring back your captivity in the presence of your enemies, says the LORD.

HAGGAI

CHAPTER 1

IN the second year of Darius the king, in the sixth month, on the first day of the month, the word of the LORD came by Haggai the prophet to Zerubbabel, the son of Shealtiel, governor of Judah, and to Joshua, the son of Josedech, the high priest, saying,

2 Thus says the LORD of hosts: This people say the time has not yet come to build the house of the LORD.

3 Then came the word of the LORD by Haggai the prophet, saying,

4 Is it a time for you to dwell in your ceiled houses, and this house lie waste?

5 Now therefore thus says the LORD of hosts: Consider your ways.

6 You have sown much and stored little; you eat, but you never are satisfied; you drink, but you are not filled with drink; you clothe yourselves, but you are not warm; and he who trades among you, earns wages to put it into a bag with holes.

7 ¶Thus says the LORD of hosts: Consider your ways.

8 Go up to the mountain, and bring timber and build this house; and I will take pleasure in it and I will be glorified in it, says the LORD.

9 You looked for much, and, lo, it came to little; and when you brought it home, I blew it away. Why should these things happen? says the LORD. Because of my house that is waste, and you hasten every man to take care of his own house.

10 Therefore the heavens over you have stayed from dew and the earth has withheld its fruit.

11 And I have called for a drought upon the land and upon the mountains, and upon the grain and upon the wine and upon the oil and upon everything that the ground brings forth, and upon men and upon cattle and upon all the labor of their hands.

12 ¶Then Zerubbabel, the son of Shealtiel, and Joshua, the son of Josedech, the high priest, with all the remnant of the people, obeyed the voice of the LORD their God and the words of Haggai the prophet, whom the LORD their God had sent to them, and the people did fear before the LORD.

13 Then spoke Haggai the LORD's messenger according to the LORD's message to the people, saying, I am with you, says the LORD of hosts.

14 And the LORD stirred up the spirit of Zerubbabel, the son of Shealtiel, governor of Judah, and the spirit of Joshua, the son of Josedech, the high priest, and the spirit of all the remnant of the people; and they went and did work upon the house of the LORD of hosts, their God,

15 On the twenty-fourth day of the sixth month in the second year of Darius the king.

CHAPTER 2

IN the seventh month, on the twenty-first day of the month, the word of the LORD came by the prophet Haggai, saying,

2 Speak now to Zerubbabel, the son of Shealtiel, governor of Judah, and to Joshua, the son of Josedech, the high priest, and to all the rest of the people, saying,

3 Who is left among you that saw this house in its former glory? And how do you see it now? Is it not now in your sight considered as nothing?

4 Yet now be strong, O Zerubbabel. says the LORD; and be strong, O Joshua, son of Josedech, the high priest; and be strong, all you people of the land, says the LORD, and work; for I am with you, says the LORD of hosts.

5 According to the covenant which I made with you when you came out

of Egypt, so my spirit remains among you; fear not.

6 For thus says the Lord of hosts: Once more, in a little while, I will shake the heavens and the earth and the sea and the dry land;

7 And I will shake all nations, and they shall bring the precious things of all nations; and I will fill the house with glory, says the Lord of hosts.

8 The silver is mine and the gold is mine, says the Lord of hosts.

9 The glory of this latter house shall be greater than that of the former, says the Lord of hosts; and in this place will I give peace, says the Lord of hosts.

10 ¶On the twenty-fourth day of the ninth month, in the second year of Darius, came the word of the Lord by Haggai the prophet, saying,

11 Thus says the Lord of hosts: Ask now the priests concerning the law, saying,

12 If a man carries holy meat in the skirt of his cloak, and touches with his skirt bread or pottage or wine or oil or any kind of food, shall it be holy? And the priests answered and said, No.

13 Then said Haggai, If one who is unclean touches all these things, shall it be unclean? And the priests answered and said, It shall be unclean.

14 Then answered Haggai and said, So is this people and so is this generation before me, says the Lord; and so is every work of their hands; and what they offer there is unclean.

15 And now, consider in your hearts, from this day upward, before

a stone was laid upon a stone in the temple of the Lord;

16 When you came to a heap of grain of twenty measures, there were but ten; when you came to the wine press to draw out fifty vessels, there were but twenty.

17 I smote you with blight and with mildew and with hail in all the labor of your hands; yet you turned not to me, says the Lord.

18 Subdue your hearts from this day and upward, from the twenty-fourth day of the ninth month, even from the day that the foundation of the Lord's temple was laid, consider it.

19 Consider now in your hearts, for there is no grain for the seed in the threshing floor, and the vine, and as yet the fig tree and the pomegranate and the olive trees have not brought forth; from this day I will bless them, says the Lord.

20 ¶And again the word of the Lord came to Haggai, on the twenty-fourth day of the month, saying,

21 Speak to Zerubbabel, governor of Judah, saying, I will shake the heavens and the earth;

22 And I will overthrow the throne of the kingdoms, and I will destroy the strength of the kingdoms of the Gentiles; and I will upset the chariots over their riders; and the horses and the riders shall fall down, every one by the sword of his brother.

23 On that day, says the Lord of hosts, I will take you, O Zerubbabel, my servant, the son of Shealtiel, says the Lord, and I will make you as a signet; for I have chosen you, says the Lord of hosts.

ZECHARIAH

CHAPTER 1

IN the eighth month, on the first day of the month, in the second year of Darius, the word of the Lord came to Zechariah, the son of Berechiah, the son of Iddo the prophet, saying,

2 The Lord was very angry with your fathers.

3 Therefore say to them, Thus says the LORD of hosts: Return to me, says the LORD of hosts, and I will return to you, says the LORD of hosts.

4 Be not like your fathers, to whom the former prophets preached, saying, Thus says the LORD of hosts: Turn now from your evil ways and from your evil doings; but they did not listen, nor give ear to me, says the LORD.

5 Your fathers, where are they? And my prophets, do they live for ever?

6 But my words and my statutes which I commanded my servants the prophets, your fathers did remember them and thought of them, saying, As the LORD of hosts thought to deal with us, according to our ways and according to our devices, so has he dealt with us.

7 ¶On the twenty-fourth day of the eleventh month, which is the month of Shebat (February), in the second year of Darius, the word of the LORD came to Zechariah, the son of Berechiah, the son of Iddo the prophet, saying,

8 I saw by the night, and behold a man riding upon a red horse, and he stood among the myrtle trees which gave shade; and behind him were red horses, speckled, and white.

9 Then I said, O my LORD, what are these? And the angel that talked with me said to me, I will show you what they are.

10 And the man who stood among the myrtle trees answered and said to me, These are they whom the LORD has sent to walk to and fro through the earth.

11 And they answered and said to the angel of the LORD who stood among the myrtle trees, We have walked to and fro through the earth, and behold, all the earth sits still and is at rest.

12 ¶Then the angel of the LORD answered and said, O LORD of hosts, how long wilt thou not have mercy on Jerusalem and on the cities of Judah, against which thou hast had indignation these seventy years?

13 And the LORD answered the an-gel who talked with me with good words and comforting words.

14 So the angel who spoke with me said to me, Proclaim and say, Thus says the LORD of hosts: I am zealous for Jerusalem and for Zion with a great zeal.

15 And I am very angry with the nations who are raging; for while I was but a little angry, they helped to carry the disaster to the extreme.

16 Therefore thus says the LORD: I am returned to Jerusalem with mercies; my house shall be built in it, says the LORD of hosts, and a measuring line shall be stretched forth over Jerusalem.

17 Proclaim again, saying, Thus says the LORD of hosts: From henceforth the cities shall yet overflow with prosperity; and the LORD shall again build Zion and shall again choose Jerusalem.

18 ¶Then I lifted up my eyes and saw, and behold four horns.

19 And I said to the angel who talked with me, My lord, what are these? And he said to me, These are the horns which have scattered Judah, Israel, and Jerusalem.

20 And the LORD showed me four carpenters.

21 Then I said, What are these coming to do? And he said to me, These are the horns which have scattered Judah so that no man did lift up his head; but these are come to frighten and to uproot the horns of the Gentiles who lifted up their horn against the land of Judah to scatter it.

CHAPTER 2

I LIFTED up my eyes again and looked, and behold, a man with a measuring line in his hand.

2 And I said to him, Where are you going? And he said to me, To measure Jerusalem, to see what is its breadth and what is its length.

3 And behold, the angel who was talking with me went forth, and another angel came to meet him.

4 And he said to him, Run, speak to that young man, saying, Jerusalem shall be inhabited as towns without

walls for the multitude of men and cattle in it.

5 For I will be in the midst of her, says the LORD, as a wall of fire round about, and will be the glory in the midst of her.

6 ¶Ah! Ah! Flee from the land of the north, says the LORD; for I have scattered you abroad as the four winds of the heaven, says the LORD.

7 Deliver yourself, O Zion; deliver yourself, you who dwell with the daughter of Babylon.

8 For thus says the LORD of hosts: After the glory he has sent me against the nations who plundered you; for he who touches you touches the apple of his eye.

9 For, behold, I will stretch out my hand against them, and their works shall become plunder; and you shall know that the LORD of hosts has sent me.

10 ¶Sing and rejoice, O daughter of Zion; for, lo, I come, and I will dwell in the midst of you, says the LORD.

11 And many nations shall follow the LORD in that day, and shall be his people; and he shall dwell in the midst of you, and you shall know that the LORD of hosts has sent me to you.

12 And the LORD shall inherit Judah his portion in his holy land, and shall be pleased with Jerusalem again.

13 And all flesh shall be afraid of the LORD; for he is watchful from his high and holy habitation.

CHAPTER 3

THEN he showed me Joshua the high priest standing before the angel of the LORD, and Satan standing at his right hand to harm him.

2 And the angel of the LORD said to Satan, The LORD rebuke you, O Satan; even the LORD who has chosen Jerusalem rebuke you. Is not this a brand plucked out of the fire?

3 Now Joshua was clothed with filthy garments, and stood before the angel of the LORD.

4 And the angel answered and spoke to those who stood before him, saying, Take away the filthy garments from him. And to him he said, Behold, I have caused your iniquity

to pass from you, and I will clothe you with good raiment.

5 And he said, Let them put a clean mitre on his head and clothe him with good garments. And the angel of the LORD stood by.

6 And the angel of the LORD charged Joshua, saying,

7 Thus says the LORD of hosts: If you will walk in my ways and keep my commandments, then you shall also judge my house and keep my courts, and I will grant you to walk among these that stand by.

8 Hear now, O Joshua the high priest, you and your fellows who stand before you; for you are marvelous men: Behold, I will bring forth the rising of the sun upon my servant.

9 For behold the stone that I have laid before Joshua; upon one stone shall be seven facets; behold, I will open its gates, says the LORD of hosts, and I will remove the iniquity of that land in that day.

10 In that day, says the LORD of hosts, every man shall invite his neighbor under the vine and under the fig tree.

CHAPTER 4

AND the angel who talked with me came back and waked me, as a man is wakened out of his sleep,

2 And he said to me, What do you see? And I said, I have looked, and behold a candlestick all of gold, with a bowl on the top of it, and seven lamps on it, and seven mouths to the seven lamps which are on the top of it;

3 And two olive trees by it, one on the right side of the bowl and the other on its left side.

4 So I answered and spoke to the angel who talked with me, saying, What are these, my lord?

5 Then the angel who talked with me answered and said to me, Do you not know what these are? and I said, No, my lord, I do not know.

6 Then he said to me, This is the word of the LORD to Zerubbabel, saying, Not by power nor by might, but by my Spirit, says the LORD of hosts.

7 Who are you, O great mountain? Before Zerubbabel you shall become like a plain; and he shall bring forth the headstone of equity and of mercy.

8 Moreover the word of the LORD came to me, saying,

9 The hands of Zerubbabel have laid the foundations of this house; his hands shall also finish it; and you shall know that the LORD of hosts has sent me to you.

10 For who has despised the day of small things? For they shall look and shall see the plummet in the hands of Zerubbabel. These are the seven eyes of the LORD, which look over the whole earth.

11 ¶Then I answered and said to him, What are these two olive trees on the right side of the candlestick and on its left side?

12 And I answered the second time and said to him, What are these two olive branches which are beside the two golden pipes which pour the golden oil out of themselves?

13 And he said to me, Do you not know what these are? And I said, No, my lord.

14 Then said he, These are the two anointed ones who stand by the LORD of the whole earth.

CHAPTER 5

THEN I turned and lifted up my eyes and looked, and beheld a flying scroll.

2 And he said to me, What do you see? And I said, I see a flying scroll; its length is twenty cubits and its width ten cubits.

3 Then he said to me, This is the curse that goes forth over the face of the whole earth; for every one who steals shall be judged according to its contents; and every one who swears shall be judged according to it.

4 I will bring it forth, says the LORD of hosts, and it shall enter into the house of the thief and into the house of him who swears falsely by my name; and it shall remain in the midst of his house and shall consume it with the timber thereof and the stones thereof.

5 ¶Then the angel who talked with me went forth and said to me, Lift up your eyes and see what is this that goes forth.

6 And I said, What is it? And he said to me, This is an ephah that goes forth, and in it are the transgressions of the whole earth.

7 And behold, a talent of lead was lifted up, and a woman was sitting in the midst of the ephah.

8 And he said to me, This is wickedness. And he cast her into the midst of the ephah; and he cast the talent of lead upon its mouth.

9 Then I lifted up my eyes and looked, and behold, there came out two women, and the wind was in their wings; for they had wings like the wings of a stork; and they lifted up the ephah between earth and heaven.

10 Then I said to the angel who talked with me, Where are they carrying the ephah?

11 And he said to me, To build for it a house in the land of Babylon; and it shall be established and set there upon its own base.

CHAPTER 6

AND I turned and lifted up my eyes and looked, and behold, there came four chariots out from between two mountains; and the mountains were mountains of brass.

2 In the first chariot were red horses; in the second chariot black horses;

3 In the third chariot white horses; and in the fourth chariot grizzled horses.

4 Then I answered and said to the angel who talked with me, What are these, my lord?

5 And the angel answered and said to me, These are the four spirits of the heavens, who stand in the presence of the LORD of all the earth.

6 The chariot in which are black horses goes forth to the north country; and the white go forth after them; and the grizzled go forth to the south country,

7 And the red horses went forth, and sought to go that they might walk to and fro through the earth;

and he said to them, Go, walk to and fro through the earth. So they walked to and fro through the earth.

8 Then he cried and said to me, Behold, those who go toward the north country have quieted my spirit in the north country.

9 ¶And the word of the LORD came to me, saying,

10 Take of them of the captivity, even of Holdai and of Tobijah and of Jedaiah, and come the same day, and go into the house of Josiah the son of Zephaniah who has come from Babylon;

11 Then take his silver and his gold, and make a crown and set it upon the head of Joshua the son of Josedech, the high priest;

12 And say to him, Thus says the LORD of hosts: Behold, the man whose name is Denkha [1] shall rise up out of his place, and he shall build the temple of the LORD.

13 Even he shall build the temple of the LORD; and he shall bear the glory, and shall sit and rule upon his throne; and he shall be a priest upon his throne; and the counsel of peace shall be between them both.

14 And the crown shall be to Holdai and to Tobiah and to Jedaiah and to Josiah the son of Zephaniah, for a memorial in the temple of the LORD.

15 And those who are far off shall come and build in the temple of the LORD, and you shall know that the LORD of hosts has sent me to you. And this shall come to pass if you will diligently obey the voice of the LORD your God.

CHAPTER 7

AND it came to pass in the fourth year of King Darius, the word of the LORD came to Zechariah in the fourth day of the ninth month, which is Canun,

2 When they had sent to Beth-el, Sherezar and Rab-mag, and the king and his mighty men had sent word to pray for him before the LORD,

3 And to speak to the priests who were in the house of the LORD of hosts and to the prophets, saying, Should

[1] Sunrise.

I weep in the fifth month, separating myself, as I have done these so many years?

4 ¶Then the word of the LORD came to me, saying,

5 Speak to all the people of the land and to the priests, saying, When you fasted and mourned in the fifth and seventh months, for these seventy years, did you at all fast to me?

6 And when you did eat and when you did drink, did you not eat for yourselves and drink for yourselves?

7 These were the very words which the LORD proclaimed by the former prophets, when Jerusalem was inhabited and in prosperity, when her towns were round about her and when the mountains and plains were inhabited.

8 ¶And the word of the LORD came to Zechariah, saying,

9 Thus says the LORD of hosts: Execute true judgment, and show mercy and compassion every man to his brother;

10 And do not oppress the widow nor the orphan, the poor nor the proselyte; and let none of you imagine evil against his brother in his heart.

11 But they refused to hearken, they rebelled and stopped their ears, that they should not hear.

12 Yea, they made their hearts like adamant, lest they should hear the law, and the ordinances which the LORD of hosts has sent in his Spirit by the former prophets; therefore came a great wrath from the LORD of hosts.

13 Since I have called them and they would not hear, so they shall call me and I will not listen, says the LORD of hosts.

14 And I scattered them among all the nations whom they knew not. Thus the land was desolate after them, without any one to pass through it and without an inhabitant, because they made the pleasant land a desolation.

CHAPTER 8

AGAIN the word of the LORD came to me, saying,

2 Thus says the LORD of hosts: I

am moved for Zion with great zeal. I am moved for her with great indignation.

3 Thus says the LORD: I will be comforted in Zion and will dwell in the midst of Jerusalem; and Jerusalem shall be called the city of truth; and the mountain of the LORD of hosts, the holy mountain.

4 Thus says the LORD of hosts: From henceforth old men and old women shall sit in the streets of Jerusalem, every man with his staff in his hand because of his age.

5 And the streets of the city shall be full of boys and girls playing.

6 Thus says the LORD of hosts: If this thing is marvellous in the eyes of the remnant of this people in these days, should it also be marvellous in my sight? says the LORD of hosts.

7 Thus says the LORD of hosts: Behold, I will save my people from the east country and from the west country;

8 And I will bring them, and they shall dwell in Jerusalem; and they shall be my people, and I will be their God, in truth and in righteousness.

9 ¶Thus says the LORD of hosts: Let your hands be strong, all of you who hear in these days these words from the mouth of the prophets that were since the day that the foundation of the house of the LORD of hosts was laid, that the temple might be built.

10 For before those days and before that time there was no wage for man, nor any hire for beast; neither was there any peace to him who went out or came in because of the oppressor; for behold, I incited all men every one against his neighbor.

11 But now I will not be to the remnant of this people as in former days, says the LORD of hosts.

12 For the seed shall be prosperous; the vine shall give its fruit and the ground shall yield its increase and the heavens shall give their dew; and I will cause the remnant of this people to possess all these things.

13 And it shall come to pass that as you were a curse among the na-

tions, O house of Judah and house of Israel, so will I save you, and you shall be a blessing; so let your hands be strong, fear not.

14 For thus says the LORD of hosts: As I purposed to harm you, when your fathers provoked me to wrath, says the LORD of hosts, and I did not relent;

15 So again have I turned and thought in these days to do well to Jerusalem and to the house of Judah; fear not.

16 ¶These are the things that you shall do: Speak the truth every one to his neighbor; execute the truth, justice, and peace in your gates;

17 And let none of you devise evil in your heart against his neighbor; and love no false oaths; for all these are things that I hate, says the LORD of hosts.

18 ¶And the word of the LORD of hosts came to me, saying,

19 Thus says the LORD of hosts: The fast of the fourth month and the fast of the fifth and the fast of the seventh and the fast of the tenth shall be to the house of Judah joy and gladness and cheerful feasts; therefore love the truth and peace.

20 Thus says the LORD of hosts: Henceforth there shall yet come people and the inhabitants of many cities;

21 And the inhabitants of one city shall come to another, saying, Let us go and pray before the LORD and to seek the LORD of hosts; I will go also.

22 Yea, many people and strong nations shall come to seek the LORD of hosts in Jerusalem and to pray before the LORD.

23 Thus says the LORD of hosts: In those days ten men from the nations of every language shall take hold of the skirt [1] of a Jew, saying, We will go with you; for we have heard that God is with you.

CHAPTER 9

THE word of the LORD against the land of Hadrach and against Damascus, which shall be a gift to him; for to the LORD are revealed

---

[1] An Aramaic idiom which means *will beg.*

the ways of men and of all the tribes of Israel;

2 Against Hamath also which borders Damascus, and Tyre and Sidon, though they have become very wise.

3 Tyre has built herself a stronghold and heaped up silver like dust, and gold like the mire of the streets.

4 Therefore, the LORD will destroy her and cast her wealth into the sea; and she shall be devoured by fire.

5 Ashkelon shall see it and be afraid; Gaza also shall be very sorrowful, and Ekron; because her hope is confounded; and the king shall perish from Gaza, and Ashkelon shall not be inhabited.

6 And strangers shall dwell in Ashdod, and I will bring to an end the pride of the Philistines.

7 And I will take away their blood out of their mouths, and their abominations from between their teeth; and they also shall be a remnant for our God, and they shall be like the princes of Judah, and Ekron shall be as a Jebusite.

8 And I will cause to dwell over my house a governor because of him who passes by, and because of him who returns; and no oppressor shall come against them any more; for now I have seen with my own eyes.

9 ¶Rejoice greatly, O daughter of Zion! Shout, O daughter of Jerusalem! Behold, your King comes to you; he is righteous and a Saviour, lowly and riding upon an ass, upon a colt the foal of an ass.

10 And he will cut off the chariot from Ephraim and the horse from Jerusalem, and the bow shall be broken in the battle; and he shall speak peace to the nations; and his dominion shall be from sea even to sea, and from the river [1] even to the ends of the earth.

11 As for you also, by the blood of your covenant you have set free the captives out of the pit wherein is no water.

12 ¶Dwell in the stronghold, O you prisoners of the congregation; I will recompense you double for a day's work.

[1] Euphrates.

13 For I have bent my bow over Judah and filled my bow over Ephraim, and I have set your sons, O Zion, against your sons, O Greece, and made Jerusalem like the sword of a mighty man.

14 And the LORD shall be seen over the enemy, and his arrow shall go forth as the lightning; and the LORD God shall blow the trumpet, and shall go in the whirlwind to the south.

15 The LORD of hosts shall defend them; and they shall devour, and subdue with sling stones; and they shall drink trouble like wine; and they shall be filled like a bowl, and as the corners of the altar.

16 And the LORD their God shall save them in that day as the flock of his people; for they were holy stones cast upon his land.

17 How good and how excellent is wheat for the young men, and wine makes the maids cheerful.

CHAPTER 10

ASK from the LORD rain in the season of latter rain; and the LORD shall make gentle showers, and give you the early rain which causes the grass to grow in the field.

2 For the learned men have spoken iniquity, and the diviners have seen a lie and have told false dreams; they comfort in vain; therefore the people went their way like a flock, they were afflicted because they had no shepherd.

3 My anger is raging against the shepherds, and I will punish the flocks; for the LORD of hosts has visited his flock the house of Judah, and has made them as a splendid horse in the battle.

4 Out of them shall come forth the cornerstone, out of them the nail, out of them the battle bow, and out of them all their rulers together.

5 ¶And they shall be like mighty men who tread mire in the streets in the battle; they shall fight because the LORD is with them, and the riders on horses shall be confounded.

6 And I will strengthen the house of Judah, and I will save the house of

Joseph, and I will bring them back again; for I will have mercy upon them; and they shall be as though I had not forgotten them; for I am the LORD God and will answer them.

7 And they shall become like the mighty men of Ephraim, and their hearts shall rejoice as with wine; yea, their children shall see it and be glad; their hearts shall rejoice in the LORD.

8 I will whistle for them and gather them; for I will save them; and they shall increase as they were before increased.

9 And I will scatter them among the nations, yet they shall praise me in far countries; and they shall rear their children and return again.

10 And I will bring them back from the land of Egypt and gather them out of Assyria; and I will bring them back to the land of Gilead and Lebanon; and the lands shall not be enough for them.

11 And they shall pass through the sea of affliction, and he shall turn back the waves in the sea, and all the depths of the river shall dry up; and the pride of Assyria shall cease, and the government of Egypt shall pass away.

12 And I will strengthen them in the LORD; and they shall preach the good tidings of his name, says the LORD.

CHAPTER 11

OPEN your doors, O Lebanon, that the fire may devour your cedars.

2 Wail, O fir tree; for the cedar has fallen and the mighty are plundered! Wail, O oaks of Bashan; for the mighty forest has fallen!

3 ¶There is a voice of the howling of shepherds; for their glory is ruined; a voice of the roaring of the lions; because the forest of Jordan is spoiled.

4 Thus says the LORD my God: Feed the lean flock

5 Whose buyers slaughter them, and hold themselves not guilty; and those who sell them say, Blessed be the LORD; for he has enriched us; and their own shepherds have no pity on them.

6 For I will no more pity the inhabitants of the land, says the LORD: but, lo, I will deliver the men every one into his neighbor's hand and into the hand of his king; and they shall divide the land, and I will not deliver it from their hands.

7 So I fed the lean flock, for there were many sheep; and I took two staffs; the one I called Pleasant and the other I called Cord, and I fed the flock.

8 Three shepherds I did away with in one month; and my soul was wearied of them, and their soul also howled against me.

9 Then I said, I will not feed you; that which dies, let it die; and that which is to be lost, let it be lost; and let the rest eat every one the flesh of another.

10 ¶And I took my staff, even Pleasant, and I broke it, thus nullifying the covenant which I had with all the peoples.

11 And it was nullified in that very day; and so the meek of the flock who were watching me knew that it was the word of the LORD.

12 And I said to them, If it seems good in your sight, give me my wages; and if not, then you are doing me injustice. So they weighed for my wages thirty pieces of silver.

13 And the LORD said to me, Cast it into the treasury; a goodly price that I was prized at of them. And I took the thirty pieces of silver and cast them into the treasury in the house of the LORD.

14 Then I broke my other staff, even Measuring-line, that I might nullify the agreements between Judah and Israel.

15 ¶And the LORD said to me, Take to yourself the clothes of a foolish shepherd.

16 For, lo, I will raise up a shepherd in the land who shall not search for those that are lost, neither shall seek those that have gone astray nor bind those that are broken nor heal those that are sick nor feed those that stand still; but he shall eat the

flesh of the fat and break of their shanks.

17 Woe to you, O foolish shepherd, for you have left the flock neglected on your side and before your eyes! Let your right arm be withered and your right eye be blinded.

CHAPTER 12

THE vision of the words of the LORD concerning Israel. Thus says the LORD, who stretched out the heavens and laid the foundations of the earth and created the spirit of man within him:

2 Behold, I will make Jerusalem a fearful place to all the people round about her, also there shall be a siege both against Judah together with Jerusalem.

3 ¶And it shall come to pass in that day, I will make Jerusalem a stone for all the people to trample on; all who trample on it shall be cut in pieces, though all the people of the earth be gathered together against it.

4 On that day, says the LORD, I will smite all horses with stupor, and their riders with confusion; and I will open my eyes upon the house of Judah, and will smite every horse of the Gentiles with blindness.

5 And the princes of Judah shall say in their hearts, The inhabitants of Jerusalem are stronger than we through the LORD of hosts their God.

6 ¶On that day I will make the princes of Judah like a fiery coal in the midst of wood, and like a torch of fire in stubble; and they shall devour all the people round about, on the right hand and on the left; and Jerusalem shall be inhabited again in its own place, even in Jerusalem.

7 The LORD also shall visit the tents of Judah, as at first, that the glory of the house of David and the glory of the inhabitants of Jerusalem may not magnify itself over the house of Judah.

8 On that day the LORD shall defend the inhabitants of Jerusalem; so that he who is weak among them on that day shall be like David; and the house of David shall be like God, like the angel of the LORD who is before them.

9 ¶And it shall come to pass in that day that I will seek to destroy all the nations that come against Jerusalem.

10 And I will pour out upon the house of David and upon the inhabitants of Jerusalem the spirit of grace and of mercies; and they shall look upon me whom they have pierced, and they shall mourn for him as they mourn for an only son, and shall grieve for him as they grieve over the first-born.

11 On that day there shall be a great mourning in Jerusalem, like the mourning of Bar-amon in the plain of Megiddo.

12 And the land shall mourn, every family together; the family of the house of David together, and their wives together; the family of the house of Nathan together, and their wives together;

13 The family of the house of Levi together, and their wives together; and the family of the house of Simeon together, and their wives together;

14 All the families that are left shall mourn, each family together, and their wives together.

CHAPTER 13

ON that day there shall be a fountain opened for the house of David and for the inhabitants of Jerusalem for sprinkling and for cleansing.

2 ¶And it shall come to pass on that day, says the LORD of hosts, I will do away with the names of the idols from the land, and they shall no more be remembered; and also I will remove from the land the false prophets and the unclean spirits.

3 And it shall come to pass that if any man shall yet prophesy, his father and his mother shall say to him, You shall not live; for you speak lies in the name of the LORD; and his father and his mother who bore him shall cut him asunder when he prophesies.

4 And it shall come to pass in that

day that the false prophets shall be ashamed every man of the vision of his prophecy; neither shall they wear a hairy skin,[1] because they have lied.

5 But he shall say, I am no prophet, I am a farmer; and a man made me zealous to prophesy from my youth.

6 And they shall say to him, What are these wounds in your hands? And he shall say, These are wounds with which I was wounded in the house of my friends.

7 ¶Awake, O sword, against my shepherd and against the man who is my friend, says the LORD of hosts; smite the shepherd, and his sheep shall be scattered; and I will turn my hand against the great ones.

8 And it shall come to pass that in all the land, says the LORD, two parts therein shall perish and be destroyed; but the third shall be left therein.

9 And I will cause the third part to pass through the fire, and will refine them as they refine silver, and will try them as they try gold; they shall call on my name, and I will answer them; I will say, They are my people; and they shall say, The LORD is my God.

CHAPTER 14

BEHOLD, the day of the LORD is coming, and your spoil shall be divided in the midst of you.

2 For I will gather all nations against Jerusalem to battle; and the city shall be taken and the houses plundered and the women ravished; and half of the city shall go into captivity, but half of the people shall not perish from the city.

3 Then the LORD shall go forth and fight against those nations as when he fought in the day of battle.

4 ¶And his feet shall stand upon the mount of Olives, which is opposite Jerusalem on the east, and the mount of Olives shall split in two, half toward the east and the other half toward the west, and there shall be in it a great valley; and half of the mountain shall be left toward the north, and half of it toward the south.

5 And you shall flee to the valley of the mountains; for the valley of the mountains shall reach the place of disaster, and you shall flee as you fled from the earthquake in the days of Uzziah king of Judah; and the LORD my God shall come in, and all his saints with him.

6 And it shall come to pass in that day there shall be no light, but cold and ice.

7 It shall be a day which is known to the LORD; it shall be neither night nor day; and it shall come to pass that at evening time it shall be light.

8 And it shall be in that day that living waters shall go out from Jerusalem; half of them toward the eastern sea, and half of them toward the western sea; they shall continue to flow in summer and in winter.

9 And the LORD shall be king over all the earth; on that day shall there be one LORD, and his name one.

10 And he shall turn all the land into a plain from Geba to Rimmon south of Jerusalem; and Jerusalem shall be exalted and inhabited in its place, from the gate of Benjamin to the place of the first gate, as far as the corner gate, and from the tower of Hananeel to the king's wine press.

11 And the people shall dwell in it, and there shall be no more a curse; but Jerusalem shall dwell in safety.

12 ¶And this shall be the plague with which the LORD will smite all the people who have fought against Jerusalem: their flesh shall waste away while they stand upon their feet, and their eyes shall melt away in their sockets, and their tongues shall consume away in their mouths.

13 And it shall come to pass in that day that a great tumult from the LORD shall be among them; and they shall lay hold every one on the hand of his neighbor, and his hand shall cling warmly to the hand of his neighbor.

14 And Judah also shall fight at Jerusalem; and he shall gather together the wealth of all the nations round about it, gold and silver and garments in great abundance.

---

[1] Prophets wore hairy skins.

15 And so shall be the plague of the horse, of the mule, of the camel, of the ass, and of all the beasts that shall be in these camps; they shall face similar destruction.

16 ¶And it shall come to pass that every one that is left of all the nations that came against Jerusalem shall even go up from year to year to worship the King, the LORD of hosts, and to keep the feast of tabernacles.

17 And it shall be, whosoever will not come up of all the families of the earth to Jerusalem to worship the King, the LORD of hosts, there shall be no rain upon them.

18 And if the family of Egypt do not go up and do not come, then upon them also shall come the plague with which the LORD will smite the nations that do not come up to keep the feast of tabernacles.

19 This shall be the punishment of Egypt and the punishment of all nations that do not come up to keep the feast of tabernacles.

20 ¶On that day there shall be written upon the bridle of the horse, HOLY TO THE LORD; and the pots in the house of the LORD shall be as precious as the bowls before the altar.

21 Yea, every pot in Jerusalem and in Judah shall be holy to the LORD of hosts; and all they that sacrifice shall come and take of them and cook in them; and on that day there shall be no more the Canaanite in the house of the LORD of hosts.

MALACHI

CHAPTER 1

THE vision of the words of the LORD concerning Israel by Malachi.

2 I have loved you, says the LORD. But you say, In what way hast thou loved us? Was not Esau Jacob's brother? says the LORD; yet I have loved Jacob, and I have not favored Esau;

3 And I have made his mountains waste and his heritage for camps of shepherds in the wilderness.

4 And if the Edomites say, We are impoverished, but let us return and build the desolate places; thus says the LORD of hosts, They shall build, but I will demolish; and they shall call them, The border of wickedness and, The people against whom the LORD is angry for ever.

5 And your eyes shall see it, and you shall say, The LORD will be magnified beyond the border of Israel.

6 ¶A son honors his father, and a servant his master; if then I am a father, where is my honor? And if I am a master, where is my fear? says the LORD of hosts to you, O priests, who despise my name. And if you say, In what have we despised thy name?

7 In that you offer polluted bread upon my altar; and if you say, In what have we polluted it? In that you say, The table of the LORD is contemptible.

8 And when you offer a blind animal to the altar, is it not evil? And when you offer the lame and sick animals, is it not evil? Offer it now to your governor; will he be pleased with you or accept your person? says the LORD of hosts.

9 And now, pray before the LORD that he may be gracious to us: for this disaster has been brought by your means; I will not regard your persons, says the LORD of hosts.

10 Who is there among you who would guard my doors or offer on my altar for nothing? I have no pleasure in you, says the LORD of

hosts, neither will I accept an offering from your hand.

11 For from the rising of the sun even to its going down, my name is great among the Gentiles; and in every place they burn incense and offer to my name pure offerings; for my name is great among the Gentiles, says the LORD of hosts.

12 ¶But you are profaning it, in that you say, The table of the LORD is polluted and its food is contemptible.

13 And you say, This is because we are miserable; and I have sniffed at it, says the LORD of hosts; for you bring offerings that are taken by violence, the lame and the sick; I will not accept them from your hands, says the LORD.

14 Cursed be he who has in his flock a ram, and vows and sacrifices for the LORD that which is sick; for I am a great King, says the LORD of hosts, and my name is dreaded among the Gentiles.

CHAPTER 2

NOW therefore, O priests, this commandment is for you.

2 If you will not obey, and if you will not lay it to heart to give glory to my name, says the LORD of hosts, I will send curses upon you, and I will curse your blessings because you have not laid it to your heart.

3 Behold, I will rebuke the seed of the ground, and spread dung upon your faces, even dung upon your solemn feasts; and I will cause you to be taken away with it.

4 And you shall know that I have sent this commandment to you, that my covenant might be with Levi, says the LORD of hosts.

5 My covenant was with him, and I gave him life and peace; and as for fear, he feared me and trembled before my name.

6 The law of truth was in his mouth, and iniquity was not found in his lips; he walked with me in peace and uprightness, and he did turn many away from iniquity.

7 For the lips of a priest should keep knowledge, because men seek the law from his mouth; for he is the messenger of the LORD of hosts.

8 But you have turned aside from the way; you have caused many to stumble at the law; you have corrupted the covenant of Levi, says the LORD of hosts.

9 Therefore have I also made you contemptible and humiliated before all the people, because you have not kept the ordinances, but have been partial in the law.

10 Have we not all one father? Or has not one God created us? Why then do we deal treacherously every man against his brother by profaning the covenant of our fathers?

11 ¶Judah has dealt treacherously, and an abomination is committed in Israel and in Jerusalem; for Judah has defiled the sanctuary of the LORD of hosts and has loved and served foreign gods.

12 The LORD will destroy the man who does this, and also his son and his son's son out of the tabernacle of Jacob; and he shall have none to present the offering to the LORD of hosts.

13 And this is another thing that you have done: you have covered the altar of the LORD with tears, with weeping, and with groaning, because he does not regard your offering any more or accept it with good will at your hands.

14 ¶And if you say, For what reason? Because the LORD was witness between you and the wife of your youth, against whom you have dealt treacherously though she is your companion and the wife of your covenant.

15 Did not he make them one? And the rest of the spirits are his also. And therefore a man seeks one offspring from God. Therefore take heed to your spirit, and let none deal treacherously against the wife of his youth.

16 For the LORD, the God of Israel, says that no one should conceal the iniquity in his robe; therefore take heed to your spirit, and do not deal treacherously.

17 ¶You have wearied the LORD

with your words. And if you say, In what have we wearied him? In that you say, Every one who does evil is good in the sight of the LORD, and he delights in such; or, Where is the God who judges righteous judgments?

CHAPTER 3

BEHOLD, I will send my messenger and he shall prepare the way before me; and he for whom you are waiting shall suddenly come to the temple of the LORD, even the messenger of the covenant, in whom you delight; behold, he shall come, says the LORD of hosts.

2 But who can endure the day of his coming? And who can stand when he appears? For he is like a refiner's fire and like fullers' soap;

3 For he shall return to refine and purify the people like silver; and he shall cleanse the sons of Levi and purge them like gold and silver, that they may offer to the LORD an offering in righteousness.

4 Then shall the offering of Judah and Jerusalem be pleasant to the LORD, as in the days of old and as in former years.

5 And I will come near to you for judgment; and I will be a swift witness against the sorcerers and against the adulterers and against those who swear falsely and against those who defraud the laborer of his wages, the stranger, the orphan, and the widow; and those who turn aside him who turns to me, and do not fear me, says the LORD of hosts.

6 For I am the LORD, I change not; but you sons of Jacob have not departed from your iniquities.

7 ¶Even from the days of your fathers you have gone astray from my ordinances and have not obeyed them. Return to me and I will return to you, says the LORD of hosts. But you say, How shall we return?

8 ¶Will a man defraud God as you have defrauded me? But you say, How have we defrauded thee? In tithes and offerings.

9 You are cursed with curses, and yet you defraud me.

10 Bring all the tithes into my storehouse that there may be food in my house, and prove me now in this, says the LORD of hosts, and I will open the windows of heaven for you and pour out blessings for you until you shall say, It is enough.

11 And I will rebuke the devourer, so that it shall not destroy the fruits of the land; neither shall your vine cast its fruit before the time in the field, says the LORD of hosts.

12 And all nations shall praise you, when you shall be a land of my delight, says the LORD of hosts.

13 ¶Your words have been grievous against me, says the LORD. And you say, What have we spoken against thee?

14 You have said, We have served God in vain; what have we profited that we have kept his ordinances and that we have walked meekly before the LORD of hosts?

15 And henceforth we call the wicked blessed; yea, they that work wickedness are well established; they tempt God, and yet they are delivered.

16 ¶These were the things which those who revered the LORD spoke often one to another; and the LORD gave ear and heard it, and he wrote it in a book of remembrance before him for those who revere him and for those who praise his name.

17 And they shall be mine, says the LORD of hosts, on that day when I will assemble the people; and I will have pity on them as a man pities his own son who serves him.

18 Then shall you return and see the difference between the righteous and the wicked, between those who served God and those who served him not.

CHAPTER 4

FOR behold, the days are coming when my anger shall burn as an oven; and all the wicked and all who do iniquity shall be stubble; and the day that comes shall burn them up, says the LORD of hosts, that it shall leave them neither root nor branch.

2 ¶But for you who revere my

name shall the Sun of righteousness arise with healing upon his lips; and you shall go forth and leap for joy like the calves of the herd.

3 And you shall tread down the wicked; for they shall be ashes under the soles of your feet in the day that I shall do this, says the LORD of hosts.

4 ¶Remember the law of Moses my servant, which I commanded to him in Horeb for all Israel, with the statutes and judgments.

5 ¶Behold, I will send you Elijah the prophet before the coming of the great and dreadful day of the LORD;

6 And he shall turn the heart of the fathers to the children and the heart of the children to their fathers before I come and smite the earth to ruin.

THE END OF THE OLD TESTAMENT

THE
New Testament

THE BOOKS OF THE NEW TESTAMENT

THE GOSPEL ACCORDING TO

SAINT MATTHEW

CHAPTER 1

THE book of the genealogy of Jesus Christ, the son of David, the son of Abraham.

2 Abraham begot Isaac; Isaac begot Jacob; Jacob begot Judah and his brothers;

3 Judah begot Perez and Zerah of his wife Tamar; Perez begot Hezron; Hezron begot Aram;

4 Aram begot Aminadab; Aminadab begot Nahshon; Nahshon begot Salmon;

5 Salmon begot Boaz of his wife Rahab; Boaz begot Obed of his wife Ruth; Obed begot Jesse;

6 Jesse begot David the king; David the king begot Solomon of the wife of Uriah;

7 Solomon begot Rehoboam; Rehoboam begot Abijah; Abijah begot Asa;

8 Asa begot Jehoshaphat; Jehoshaphat begot Joram; Joram begot Uzziah;

9 Uzziah begot Jotham; Jotham begot Ahaz; Ahaz begot Hezekiah;

10 Hezekiah begot Manasseh; Manasseh begot Amon; Amon begot Josiah;

11 Josiah begot Jechoniah and his brothers, about the time of the captivity of Babylon.

12 And after the captivity of Babylon, Jechoniah begot Shelatiel; Shelatiel begot Zerubbabel;

13 Zerubbabel begot Abihud; Abihud begot Eliakim; Eliakim begot Azor;

14 Azor begot Sadok; Sadok begot Achim; Achim begot Eliud;

15 Eliud begot Eleazar; Eleazar begot Matthan; Matthan begot Jacob;

16 Jacob begot Joseph the husband of Mary, of whom was born Jesus, who is called Christ.

17 ¶Therefore all the generations from Abraham to David are fourteen generations; and from David to the Babylonian captivity fourteen generations; and from the Babylonian captivity to Christ fourteen generations.

18 ¶The birth of Jesus Christ was in this manner. While Mary his mother was acquired for a price for Joseph, before they came together, she was found with child of the Holy Spirit.

19 But Joseph her husband was a pious man, and did not wish to make it public; so he was thinking of divorcing her secretly.

20 While he was considering this, the angel of the Lord appeared to him in a dream, and said to him, O, Joseph, son of David, do not be afraid to take your wife Mary, because he that is to be born of her is of the Holy Spirit.

21 She will give birth to a son, and you will call his name Jesus; for he shall save his people from their sins.

22 ¶All this happened, that what was spoken from the Lord by the prophet might be fulfilled,

23 Behold, a virgin will conceive and give birth to a son, and they shall call his name Immanuel, which is interpreted, Our God is with us.

24 When Joseph rose up from his sleep, he did just as the angel of the Lord commanded him, and he took his wife.

25 And he did not know her until she gave birth to her first-born son; and she called his name Jesus.

CHAPTER 2

WHEN Jesus was born in Bethlehem of Judah, in the days of Herod the king, there came Magi from the East to Jerusalem.

2 And they were saying, Where is the King of the Jews who has been born? For we have seen his star in the East, and we have come to worship him.

3 But when Herod the king heard it, he trembled, and all Jerusalem with him.

4 So he gathered together all the high priests and the scribes of the people, and he kept asking them where the Christ would be born.

5 And they said, In Bethlehem of Judah,[1] for thus it is written in the book of the prophet:

6 Even you, Bethlehem of Judah, you are not insignificant in the eyes of the kings of Judah, for from you shall come out a king, who will shepherd my people Israel.

7 Then Herod called the Magi secretly, and he learned from them at what time the star appeared to them.

8 And he sent them to Bethlehem, and said to them, Go and inquire very carefully concerning the boy, and when you have found him, come back and let me know, so that I also may go and worship him.

9 When they had heard from the king, they went away; and behold, the same star that they had seen in the east was going before them, until it came and stood just above the place where the infant boy was.

10 When they saw the star, they rejoiced exceedingly.

11 And they entered the house and saw the infant boy with Mary, his mother; and they threw themselves down and worshipped him; and they opened their treasures and offered to him gifts, gold and frankincense and myrrh.

12 And they were told in a dream not to return to Herod, so they departed to their own country by another way.

13 When they had gone, the angel of the Lord appeared to Joseph in a dream, and said to him, Arise, take the infant boy and his mother, and flee to Egypt, and stay there until I tell you; for Herod is ready to de-

mand the child in order to destroy him.

14 Then Joseph rose up, took the infant boy and his mother in the night, and escaped to Egypt.

15 And he remained there until the death of Herod, so that what was said from the Lord by the prophet might be fulfilled: Out of Egypt have I called my son.

16 ¶When Herod saw that he was mocked by the Magi, he was greatly enraged, so he sent forth and had all the infant boys in Bethlehem and in its suburbs killed, from two years old and under, according to the time that he had inquired from the Magi.

17 Then was fulfilled what was said by the prophet Jeremiah who said,

18 A voice was heard in Ramah, weeping and wailing exceedingly, Rachel weeping for her sons, and she would not be comforted, because they could not be brought back.

19 ¶When King Herod died, the angel of the Lord appeared in a dream to Joseph in Egypt.

20 And he said to him, Arise, take the boy and his mother, and go to the land of Israel, for those who were seeking the boy's life are dead.

21 So Joseph rose up, took the boy and his mother, and came to the land of Israel.

22 But when he heard that Archelaus had become king over Judea,[2] in the place of his father Herod, he was afraid to go there; and it was revealed to him in a dream to go to the land of Galilee.

23 And he came and dwelt in a city called Nazareth, so that what was said by the prophet might be fulfilled, He shall be called a Nazarene.

CHAPTER 3

IN those days came John the Baptist; and he was preaching in the wilderness of Judea,

[1] There is also Bethlehem of Galilee, near Nazareth.
[2] The name for Judah used during the Roman occupation.

2 Saying, Repent, for the kingdom of heaven is near.

3 For it was he of whom it was said by the prophet Isaiah, The voice which cries in the wilderness, Prepare the way of the Lord, and straighten his highways.

4 Now this John's clothes were made of camel's hair, and he had leather belts around his waist, and his food was locusts and wild honey.

5 Then went out to him Jerusalem and all of Judea and the whole country around Jordan.

6 And they were baptized by him in the river Jordan, as they confessed their sins.

7 But when he saw a great many of the Pharisees and Sadducees who were coming to be baptized, he said to them, O offspring of scorpions, who has warned you to escape from the anger which is to come?

8 Bring forth therefore fruits which are worthy of repentance;

9 And do not think and say within yourselves, We have Abraham as our father; for I say to you that God can raise up children to Abraham from these stones.

10 Behold, the axe is already placed at the root of the trees; therefore, every tree which bears not good fruits shall be cut down and cast into the fire.

11 I am only baptizing you with water for repentance; but he who is coming after me is greater than I, one whose shoes I am not worthy to remove; he will baptize you with the Holy Spirit and with fire.

12 His shovel is in his hand, and he purifies his threshings; the wheat he gathers into his barns, and the straw he will burn in the unquenchable fire.

13 ¶Then Jesus came from Galilee to the Jordan to John, to be baptized by him.

14 But John tried to stop him, saying, I need to be baptized by you, and yet have you come to me?

15 But Jesus answered and said to him, Permit it now, for this is necessary for us so that all righteousness may be fulfilled; and then he permitted him.

16 ¶When Jesus was baptized, he immediately went up out of the water; and the heavens were opened to him, and he saw the Spirit of God descending like a dove, and coming upon him;

17 And behold, a voice from heaven which said, This is my beloved Son, with whom I am pleased.

CHAPTER 4

THEN Jesus was carried away by the Holy Spirit into the wilderness to be tempted by the devil.

2 So he fasted forty days and forty nights; but at last he was hungry.

3 And the tempter drew near and said to him, If you are the Son of God, command these stones to become bread.

4 But he answered, saying, It is written that it is not by bread alone that man can live, but by every word which proceeds from the mouth of God.

5 Then the adversary took him to the holy city, and he made him to stand on the pinnacle of the temple.

6 And he said to him, If you are the Son of God, throw yourself down; for it is written that he will command his angels concerning you, and they will bear you up on their hands so that even your foot may not strike a stone.

7 Jesus said to him, Again it is written that you shall not tempt the Lord your God.

8 Again the adversary took him to a very high mountain, and he showed him all the kingdoms of the world and their glory.

9 And he said to him, All of these I will give to you, if you will fall down and worship me.

10 Then Jesus said to him, Get away, Satan, for it is written, You shall worship the Lord your God, and him only shall you serve.

11 Then the adversary left him alone; and behold, angels drew near and ministered to him.

12 ¶Now when Jesus heard that John was delivered and imprisoned, he departed to Galilee.

13 And he left Nazareth, and came and settled in Capernaum, by the seaside, within the borders of Zebulun and of Napthali,

14 So that it might be fulfilled which was spoken by the prophet Isaiah, saying,

15 O land of Zebulun, O land of Napthali, the way to the sea, across the Jordan, Galilee of the Gentiles!

16 The people who dwelt in darkness saw a great light, and upon those who dwelt in the country and in the midst of the shadows of death, light shone.

17 ¶From that time Jesus began to preach and to say, Repent, for the kingdom of heaven is coming near.

18 ¶And while he was walking by the sea of Galilee, he saw two brothers, Simon who was called Peter and his brother Andrew, who were casting nets into the sea, for they were fishermen.

19 And Jesus said to them, Follow after me and I will make you become fishers of men.

20 So they immediately left their nets and followed him.

21 And when he departed he saw two other brothers, James the son of Zebedee and his brother John, in a ship with Zebedee their father, repairing their nets; and Jesus called them.

22 So they immediately left the ship and their father, and followed him.

23 ¶And Jesus travelled throughout Galilee, teaching in their synagogues and preaching the good news of the kingdom, and healing every kind of disease and sickness among the people.

24 And his fame was heard throughout Syria; so they brought to him all who were badly afflicted with different diseases, and those who were tormented with pains, and the insane and epileptics and cripples; and he healed them.

25 And great crowds followed him from Galilee and from the ten cities and from Jerusalem and from Judea and from across the Jordan.

CHAPTER 5

WHEN Jesus saw the crowds, he went up to the mountain; and as he sat down, his disciples drew near to him.

2 And he opened his mouth and taught them, saying,

3 Blessed are the humble,¹ for theirs is the kingdom of heaven.

4 Blessed are they who mourn, for they shall be comforted.

5 Blessed are the meek, for they shall inherit the earth.

6 Blessed are those who hunger and thirst for justice, for they shall be well satisfied.

7 Blessed are the merciful, for they shall have mercy.

8 Blessed are the pure in heart, for they shall see God.

9 Blessed are the peacemakers, for they shall be called sons of God.

10 Blessed are those who are persecuted for the sake of justice, for theirs is the kingdom of heaven.

11 ¶Blessed are you when men reproach you and persecute you and speak against you every kind of evil, falsely, for my sake,

12 Then be glad and rejoice, for your reward is increased in heaven; for in this very manner they persecuted the prophets who were before you.

13 ¶You are indeed the salt of the earth; but if the salt should lose its savor, with what could it be salted? It would not be worth anything but to be thrown outside and to be trodden down by men.

14 You are indeed the light of the world; a city that is built upon a mountain cannot be hidden.

15 Nor do they light a lamp and put it under a basket, but on a lamp stand, so that it gives light to all who are in the house.

16 Let your light so shine before men that they may see your good works and glorify your Father in heaven.

17 ¶Do not suppose that I have come to weaken the law or the prophets; I have not come to weaken, but to fulfil.

¹ Aramaic, *poor in pride; unassuming.*

18 For truly I say to you, Until heaven and earth pass away, not even a yoth [1] or a dash shall pass away from the law until all of it is fulfilled.

19 Whoever therefore tries to weaken even one of the least of these commandments, and teaches men so, he shall be called the least in the kingdom of heaven; but anyone who observes and teaches them shall be called great in the kingdom of heaven.

20 For I say to you that unless your righteousness exceeds that of the scribes and Pharisees, you shall not enter the kingdom of heaven.

21 ¶You have heard that it was said to those who were before you, You shall not kill, and whoever kills is guilty before the court.

22 But I say to you that whoever becomes angry with his brother for no reason is guilty before the court; and whoever should say to his brother, Raca (which means, I spit on you) is guilty before the congregation; and whoever says to his brother, you are effeminate,[2] is condemned to hell fire.

23 If it should happen therefore that while you are presenting your offering upon the altar, and right there you remember that your brother has any grievance against you,

24 Leave your offering there upon the altar, and first go and make peace with your brother, and then come back and present your offering.

25 Try to get reconciled with your accuser promptly, while you are going on the road with him; for your accuser might surrender you to the judge, and the judge would commit you to the jailer, and you would be cast into prison.

26 Truly I say to you that you would never come out thence until you had paid the last cent.

27 ¶You have heard that it is said, You shall not commit adultery.

28 But I say to you that whoever looks at a woman with lust, has al-ready committed adultery with her in his heart.

29 If your right eye should cause you to stumble, pluck it out and throw it away from you; [3] for it is better for you to lose one of your members, and not have all your body fall into hell.

30 And if your right hand should cause you to stumble, cut it off and throw it away from you; [4] for it is better for you to lose one of your members, and not have all your body fall into hell.

31 It has been said that whoever divorces his wife, must give her the divorce papers.

32 But I say to you that whoever divorces his wife, except for fornication, causes her to commit adultery; and whoever marries a woman who is separated but not divorced, commits adultery.

33 ¶Again you have heard that it was said to them who were before you, that you shall not lie in your oaths, but entrust your oaths to the Lord.

34 But I say to you, never swear; neither by heaven, because it is God's throne;

35 Nor by the earth, for it is a stool under his feet; nor by Jerusalem, for it is the city of a great king.

36 Neither shall you swear by your own head, because you cannot create in it a single black or white hair.

37 But let your words be yes, yes, and no, no; for anything which adds to these is a deception.

38 ¶You have heard that it is said, An eye for an eye, and a tooth for a tooth.

39 But I say to you that you should not resist evil; but whoever strikes you on your right cheek, turn to him the other also.[5]

40 And if anyone wishes to sue you at the court and take away your shirt, let him have your robe also.

41 Whoever compels you to carry a burden for a mile, go with him two.

42 Whoever asks from you, give

---

[1] Yoth is the smallest letter in Aramaic and Hebrew.   [2] Aramaic, *brutish; abnormal.*
[3] Aramaic idiom: *stop envying.*   [4] An Aramaic idiom, meaning *stop stealing.*
[5] "Turn your cheek" is an Aramaic idiom meaning, "Do not start a quarrel or a fight."

him; and whoever wishes to borrow from you, do not refuse him.

43 ¶You have heard that it is said, Be kind to your friend, and hate your enemy.

44 But I say to you, Love your enemies, bless anyone who curses you, do good to anyone who hates you, and pray for those who carry you away by force and persecute you,

45 So that you may become sons of your Father who is in heaven, who causes his sun to shine upon the good and the bad, and who pours down his rain upon the just and the unjust.

46 For if you love only those who love you, what reward will you have? Do not even the tax collectors[1] do the same thing?

47 And if you salute only your brothers, what is it more that you do? Do not even the tax collectors do the same thing?

48 Therefore become perfect, just as your Father in heaven is perfect.

CHAPTER 6

BE careful concerning your alms, not to do them in the presence of men, merely that they may see them; otherwise you have no reward with your Father in heaven.

2 Therefore when you give alms, do not blow a trumpet before you, just as the hypocrites do in the synagogues and in the market places, so that they may be glorified by men. Truly I say to you that they have already received their reward.

3 But when you give alms, let not your left hand know what your right hand is doing,

4 So that your alms may be done secretly, and your Father who sees in secret, shall himself reward you openly.

5 ¶And when you pray, do not be like the hypocrites, who like to pray, standing in the synagogues and at the street corners, so that they may be seen by men. Truly I say to you that they have already received their reward.

6 But as for you, when you pray, enter into your inner chamber and lock your door, and pray to your Father who is in secret, and your Father who sees in secret shall himself reward you openly.

7 And when you pray, do not repeat your words like the pagans, for they think that because of much talking they will be heard.

8 Do not be like them, for your Father knows what you need, before you ask him;

9 Therefore pray in this manner: Our Father in heaven, hallowed be thy name.

10 Thy kingdom come. Thy will be done, as in heaven so on earth.

11 Give us bread for our needs from day to day.

12 And forgive us our offences, as we have forgiven our offenders.

13 And do not let us enter into temptation, but deliver us from evil.[2] For thine is the kingdom and the power and the glory for ever and ever. Amen.

14 For if you forgive men their faults, your Father in heaven will also forgive you.

15 But if you do not forgive men, neither will your Father forgive even your faults.

16 ¶When you fast, do not look sad like the hypocrites; for they disfigure their faces, so that it may appear to men that they are fasting. Truly I say to you, that they have already received their reward.

17 But as for you, when you fast, wash your face and anoint your head,

18 So that it may not appear to men that you are fasting, but to your Father who is in secret; and your Father who sees in secret will reward you.

19 ¶Do not lay up for yourselves treasures buried in the ground, a place where rust and moth destroy and where thieves break through and steal.

20 But lay up for yourselves a treasure in heaven, where neither rust nor moth destroys and where thieves do not break through and steal.

---

[1] Synonym: *customs officers.*   [2] Wrong, wickedness, error.

21 For where your treasure is, there also is your heart.

22 The eye is the lamp of the body; if therefore your eye be bright, your whole body is also lighted.

23 But if your eye is diseased, your whole body will be dark. If therefore the light that is in you is darkness, how much greater will be your darkness.

24 ¶No man can serve two masters; for either he will hate the one and like the other; or he will honor one and despise the other. You cannot serve God and mammon (wealth).

25 For this reason, I say to you, Do not worry for your life, what you will eat and what you will drink, nor for your body, what you will wear. Behold, is not life much more important than food, and the body than clothing?

26 Observe the birds of the sky, for they do not sow, neither do they harvest nor gather into barns, and yet your Father in heaven feeds them. Are you not much more important than they?

27 Who is among you who by worrying can add one cubit to his stature?

28 Why do you worry about clothing? Observe the wild flowers, how they grow; they do not get tired out, nor do they spin.

29 But I say to you that not even Solomon with all of his glory was arrayed like one of them.

30 Now if God clothes in such fashion the grass of the field, which today is and tomorrow falls into the fireplace, is he not much more mindful of you, O you of little faith?

31 Therefore do not worry or say, What will we eat, or what will we drink, or with what will we be clothed?

32 For worldly people seek after all these things. Your Father in heaven knows that all of these things are also necessary for you.

33 But seek first the kingdom of God and his righteousness, and all these things shall be added to you.

34 Therefore do not worry about

tomorrow; for tomorrow will look after itself. Sufficient for each day is its own trouble.

CHAPTER 7

JUDGE not, that you may not be judged.

2 For with the same judgment that you judge, you will be judged, and with the same measure with which you measure, it will be measured to you.

3 Why do you see the splinter which is in your brother's eye, and do not feel the beam which is in your own eye?

4 Or how can you say to your brother, Let me take out the splinter from your eye, and behold there is a beam in your own eye?

5 O hypocrites, first take out the beam from your own eye, and then you will see clearly to get out the splinter from your brother's eye.

6 ¶Do not give holy things to the dogs; and do not throw your pearls [1] before swine, for they might tread them with their feet, and then turn and rend you.

7 ¶Ask, and it shall be given to you; seek, and you shall find; knock and it shall be opened to you.

8 For whoever asks, receives; and he who seeks, finds; and to him who knocks, the door is opened.

9 Or who is the man among you, who when his son asks him for bread, will hand him a stone?

10 Or if he should ask him for fish, will he hand him a snake?

11 If therefore you who err, know how to give good gifts to your sons, how much more will your Father in heaven give good things to those who ask him?

12 Whatever you wish men to do for you, do likewise also for them; for this is the law and the prophets.

13 ¶Enter in through the narrow door, for wide is the door and broad is the road which leads to destruction, and many are those who travel on it.

---

[1] *Do not speak words of wisdom to fools.*

14 O how narrow is the door and how difficult is the road which leads to life, and few are those who are found on it.

15 ¶Be careful of false prophets who come to you in lamb's clothing, but within they are ravening wolves.

16 You will know them by their fruits. Do they gather grapes from thorns or figs from thistles?

17 So every good tree bears good fruit; but a bad tree bears bad fruit.

18 A good tree cannot bear bad fruit, neither can a bad tree bear good fruit.

19 Every tree which does not bear good fruit will be cut down and cast into the fire.

20 Thus by their fruit you will know them.

21 ¶It is not everyone who merely says to me, My Lord, my Lord, who will enter into the kingdom of heaven, but he who does the will of my Father in heaven.

22 A great many will say to me in that day, My Lord, my Lord, did we not prophesy in your name and in your name cast out devils and in your name do many wonders?

23 Then I will declare to them, I have never known you; keep away from me, O you that work iniquity.

24 ¶Therefore whoever hears these words of mine, and does them, he is like a wise man who built his house upon a rock.

25 And the rain fell and the rivers overflowed and the winds blew and beat upon that house; but it did not fall, because its foundations were laid upon a rock.

26 And whoever hears these words of mine, and does them not, is like a foolish man who built his house upon sand.

27 And the rain fell and the rivers overflowed and the winds blew and beat upon that house; and it fell, and its fall was great.

28 ¶And when Jesus finished these words, the crowds were stunned at his teaching,

29 For he taught them as one who had power, and not as their own scribes and Pharisees.

CHAPTER 8

WHEN he came down from the mountain, large crowds followed him.

2 And behold, a leper came and worshipped him, and said, My Lord, if you wish, you can cleanse me.

3 And Jesus stretched out his hand and touched him, and he said, I do wish it, be cleansed. And in that hour his leprosy was cleansed.

4 Jesus then said to him, Look, why are you telling it to men? Go first and show yourself to the priests, and present an offering as Moses has commanded, for a testimonial to them.

5 ¶When Jesus entered Capernaum, a centurion approached him and appealed to him,

6 Saying, My Lord, my boy is lying in the house, paralyzed and suffering greatly.

7 Jesus said to him, I will come and heal him.

8 The centurion then answered, saying, My Lord, I am not good enough for you to enter under the shadow of my roof; but just say a word, and my boy will be healed;

9 For I am also a man under authority, and there are soldiers under my command; and I say to this one, Go, and he goes; and to the other, Come, and he comes; and to my servant, Do this, and he does it.

10 When Jesus heard it, he was amazed, and he said to those who accompanied him, Truly I say to you that not even in Israel have I found such faith as this.

11 And I say to you that a great many will come from the east and from the west, and sit down with Abraham and Isaac and Jacob in the kingdom of heaven.

12 But the sons of the kingdom will be put out into outer darkness; there shall be weeping and gnashing of teeth.

13 So Jesus said to the centurion, Go, let it be done to you according to your belief. And his boy was healed in that very hour.

14 ¶And Jesus came to the house

of Simon, and he saw his mother-in-law lying sick with fever.

15 And he touched her hand, and the fever left her, and she got up and waited on them.

16 ¶Now when evening came, they brought to him a great many lunatics, and he cured them just by a word; and he healed all who were badly afflicted.

17 So that what was spoken by the prophet Isaiah, might be fulfilled, saying, He will take our afflictions and bear our sickness.

18 ¶When Jesus saw large crowds surrounding him, he gave orders to go to the crossing place.

19 And a scribe drew near and said to him, O my teacher, I will follow you wherever you go.

20 Jesus said to him, The foxes have holes, and the birds of the air a resting place, but the Son of man has nowhere even to lay his head.

21 Another of his disciples said to him, My Lord, permit me first to go and bury my father.[1]

22 But Jesus said to him, Come after me, and let the dead bury their dead.

23 ¶And when Jesus went up into the boat, his disciples went with him.

24 And behold, the sea became very rough, so that the boat was almost covered by the waves; but Jesus was asleep.

25 And his disciples drew near and woke him, and said to him, Our Lord, save us, we are perishing.

26 Jesus said to them, Why are you fearful, O you of little faith? Then he got up and rebuked the wind and the sea, and there was a great calm.

27 But the men were astonished, saying, Who is this man, that even the winds and the sea obey him?

28 ¶And when Jesus came to the port on the other side, to the country of the Gadarenes, he was met by two lunatics,[2] who were just coming out of the cemetery. They were exceedingly vicious so that no man would dare to travel that road.

29 And they cried aloud saying, What business have we together, Jesus, son of God? Have you come here to torment us before the time?

30 Now there was near by them a large herd of swine feeding.

31 And the lunatics kept asking him, saying, If you are going to heal us, permit us to attack the herd of swine.

32 Jesus said to them, Go. And immediately they left and attacked the swine, and the whole herd went straight over the cliff and fell into the sea and were drowned in the water.

33 And they who fed them ran away and went to the city, and reported everything that happened, and told about the lunatics.

34 So all the city went out to meet Jesus; and when they saw him, they urged him to depart from their borders.

CHAPTER 9

SO he went up into the boat, and crossed over and came to his own city.

2 And they brought to him a paralytic, lying on a quilt;[3] and Jesus saw their faith, and he said to the paralytic, Have courage, my son; your sins have been forgiven.

3 Some of the scribes said among themselves, This man blasphemes.

4 But Jesus knew their thoughts; so he said to them, Why do you think evil in your hearts?

5 For which is easier to say, Your sins have been forgiven, or to say, Arise and walk?

6 But that you might know that the Son of man has authority on earth to forgive sins, then he said to the paralytic, Arise, take up your quilt and go to your home.

7 And he rose up and went to his home.

8 But when the crowds saw it, they were frightened, and they glorified God, because he had given such power as this to men.

9 ¶And as Jesus passed from that

---

[1] Aramaic idiom: *take care of my father.*
[2] Aramaic *devana* means lunatic or insane; those suffering from mental diseases were supposed to be possessed of devils or evil spirits.　　[3] Used as a bed.

place, he saw a man whose name was Matthew, sitting in the custom house, and he said to him, Follow me; and he got up and went after him.

10 ¶And while they were guests in the house, a great many tax collectors and sinners came, and they sat as guests with Jesus and with his disciples.

11 And when the Pharisees saw it, they said to his disciples, Why does your master eat with taxgatherers and sinners?

12 But when Jesus heard it, he said to them, Those who are well need no doctor, but those who are seriously sick.

13 Go and learn what this means, I want mercy and not sacrifice; for I came not to invite righteous men, but sinners.

14 ¶Then the disciples of John came up to him, and said, Why do we and the Pharisees fast a great deal, and your disciples never fast?

15 Jesus said to them, Is it possible for those at the wedding feast to fast as long as the bridegroom is with them? But the days are coming when the bridegroom will be taken from them, and then they will fast.

16 No man puts a new patch on an old garment, so as not to weaken that garment and make the hole larger.

17 Neither do they pour new wine into worn-out skins so as to rend the skins and spill the wine, and the wine runs out and the skins are ruined; but they pour new wine into new skins, and both of them are well preserved.

18 ¶While he was speaking these things with them, a leader of the synagogue came near and worshipped him; and he said, My daughter has just died, but come and put your hand on her and she will live.

19 And Jesus and his disciples rose up and went with him.

20 ¶And behold, a woman who had had a hemorrhage for twelve years, came up from behind him, and she touched the edge of his cloak;

21 For she was saying to herself,

1 Professional mourners.

If I can only touch his garment, I will be healed.

22 And Jesus turned around and saw her and said to her, Have courage, my daughter, your faith has healed you; and the woman was healed in that very hour.

23 ¶So Jesus arrived at the house of the synagogue leader, and saw the singers [1] and the excited crowds,

24 And he said to them, That is enough; for the little girl is not dead, but she is asleep; and they laughed at him.

25 But when he had put the people out, he went in and held her by her hand, and the little girl got up.

26 And this news spread all over that country.

27 ¶And as Jesus passed from there, he was delayed by two blind men, who were crying out and saying, Have mercy on us, O son of David.

28 And when he came into the house, the same blind men came up to him. Jesus said to them, Do you believe that I can do this? They said to him, Yes, our Lord.

29 Then he touched their eyes and said, Let it be to you according to your faith.

30 And immediately their eyes were opened; and Jesus charged them and said, See that no one knows it.

31 But they went out and spread the news all over that country.

32 ¶And when Jesus went out, they brought to him a dumb man who was demented.

33 And as soon as he was restored, the dumb man spoke, and the people were amazed and said, Such a thing has never been seen in Israel.

34 But the Pharisees said, He is casting out devils by the help of the prince of devils.

35 And Jesus travelled in all the cities and villages, teaching in their synagogues and preaching the gospel of the kingdom, and healing every kind of sickness and disease.

36 ¶When Jesus saw the multitudes, he had compassion on them, because they were tired and scattered, like sheep which have no shepherd.

37 So he said to his disciples, The harvest is great and the laborers are few;

38 Therefore urge the owner of the harvest to bring more laborers to his harvest.

CHAPTER 10

AND he called his twelve disciples, and gave them power over unclean spirits, to cast them out and to heal every kind of disease and sickness.

2 The names of the twelve apostles are these: The first of them Simon, who is called Peter, and Andrew his brother; James the son of Zebedee and John his brother;

3 Philip and Bartholomew, Thomas and Matthew the tax collector, James the son of Alphaeus and Lebbaeus surnamed Thaddaeus;

4 Simon the Zealot and Judas of Iscariot, who betrayed him.

5 These twelve Jesus sent out, and charged them and said, Keep away from pagan practices, and do not enter a Samaritan city;

6 But above all, go to the sheep which are lost from the house of Israel.

7 And as you go, preach and say that the kingdom of heaven is near.

8 Heal the sick, cleanse the lepers, cast out demons; freely you have received, freely give.

9 Do not accumulate gold or silver or brass in your purses;

10 Nor carry a bag for the journey, nor two shirts and shoes, nor a staff; for a laborer is at least worthy of his food.

11 Whatever city or town you enter, ask who is trustworthy in it, and remain there until you leave.

12 And when you enter into the house, salute the family.

13 And if the family is trustworthy, your salutation of peace shall come upon it; but if it is not trustworthy, your salutation shall return to you.

14 Whoever will not welcome you and will not listen to your words, when you leave the house or the village, shake off the sand from your feet.

15 Truly I say to you that it will be easier for the land of Sodom and Gomorrah on the day of judgment than for that city.

16 ¶Behold, I am sending you like lambs among wolves; therefore be wise as serpents and pure as doves.

17 But be careful of men; for they will deliver you up to the courts, and they will scourge you in their synagogues;

18 And they will bring you before the presence of governors and kings for my sake, as a testimony to them and to the Gentiles.

19 But when they deliver you up, do not worry as to how or what you will speak; for it will be given to you in that very hour what you are to speak.

20 For it is not you who speak, but the Spirit of your Father, which speaks through you.

21 Brother will deliver up his own brother to death, and father his son; and children will rise up against their parents and put them to death.

22 And you will be hated by everybody because of my name; but he who endures until the end shall live.

23 When they persecute you in one city, flee to another; for truly I say to you that you shall not finish converting all the cities of the house of Israel, until the Son of man returns.

24 No disciple is more important than his teacher, and no servant than his master.

25 It is enough for a disciple to be like his teacher, and for a servant to be like his master. If then, they have called the master of the house Beelzebub, how much more those of his household.

26 Therefore do not be afraid of them; for there is nothing covered that will not be uncovered, and hidden that will not be known.

27 What I tell you in the dark, tell it in the daylight; and what you hear in your ears, preach on the house tops.

28 Do not be afraid of those who kill the body, but who cannot kill the soul; but above all, be afraid of him who can destroy both the soul and the body in hell.

29 Are not two sparrows sold for a penny? And yet not one of them will fall on the ground without your Father's will.

30 But so far as you are concerned, even the hairs of your head are all numbered.

31 Therefore fear not; you are much more important than many sparrows.

32 Everyone therefore who will acknowledge me before men, I will also acknowledge him before my Father in heaven.

33 But whoever will deny me before men, I will also deny him before my Father in heaven.

34 ¶Do not suppose that I have come to bring peace on earth; I have not come to bring peace but a sword.[1]

35 For I have come to set a man against his father and a daughter against her mother and a daughter-in-law against her mother-in-law.

36 And a man's enemies will be the members of his own household.

37 Whoever loves father or mother more than me is not worthy of me; and whoever loves son or daughter more than me is not worthy of me.

38 And whoever does not take up his cross and follow me is not worthy of me.

39 He who is concerned about his life shall lose it; and he who loses his life for my sake shall find it.

40 Whoever receives you, receives me; and whoever receives me, receives him who sent me.

41 He who receives a prophet in the name of a prophet shall receive a prophet's reward; and whoever receives a righteous man in the name of a righteous man shall receive a righteous man's reward.

42 Whoever gives a drink to one of these little ones, if only a cup of cold water, in the name of a disciple, truly I say to you, he shall never lose his reward.

CHAPTER 11

WHEN Jesus had finished commanding his twelve disciples, he departed from that place to teach and to preach in their cities.

2 But when John heard in prison of the works of Christ, he sent by his disciples,

3 And said to him, Are you the one who is to come, or are we to expect another?

4 Jesus answered, saying, Go and describe to John the things which you see and hear.

5 The blind see and the lame walk and lepers are cleansed and the deaf hear and the dead rise up and the poor are given hope.

6 And blessed is he who does not stumble on account of me.

7 ¶When they went away, Jesus began to speak to the people concerning John, What did you go out to the wilderness to see? A reed which is shaken by the wind?

8 If not so, what did you go out to see? A man dressed in fine clothes? Behold, those who wear fine clothes are in kings' houses.

9 And if not so, what then did you go out to see? A prophet? Yes, I tell you, and much more than a prophet.

10 For this is he of whom it is written, Behold, I send my messenger before your face to prepare the way before you.

11 ¶Truly I say to you that among those who are born of women there has never risen one greater than John the Baptist; and yet even the least person in the kingdom of heaven is greater than he.

12 From the days of John the Baptist until now the kingdom of heaven has been administered by force, and only those in power control it.

13 For all the prophets and the law prophesied until John.

14 And if you wish to accept it, he is Elijah who was to come.

15 He who has ears to hear, let him hear.

16 ¶But to whom shall I liken this generation? It is like boys who sit in the street and call to their friends,

17 And say, We have sung to you, but you did not dance; and we have wailed to you, but you did not mourn.

18 For John came neither eating nor drinking, and they said, He is crazy.

[1] An Aramaic idiom meaning, "division."

19 The Son of man came eating and drinking, and they said, Behold, a glutton and a wine-bibber, and a friend of tax collectors and sinners. And yet wisdom is justified by its works.

20 ¶Then Jesus began to reproach the cities in which his many works were done, and which did not repent. And he said,

21 Woe to you, Chorazin! woe to you, Bethsaida! for if in Tyre and Sidon had been done the works which were done in you, they might have repented in sackcloth and ashes.

22 But I say to you, It will be easier for Tyre and Sidon in the day of judgment than for you.

23 And you, Capernaum, which have exalted yourself up to heaven, shall be brought down to Sheol; for if in Sodom had been done the works which were done in you, it would be standing to this day.

24 But I say to you, It will be easier for the land of Sodom in the judgment day than for you.

25 ¶At that time Jesus answered, saying, I thank thee, O my Father, Lord of heaven and earth, because thou hast hidden these things from the wise and the men of understanding, and hast revealed them to children.

26 O yes, my Father, for such was thy will.

27 Everything has been delivered to me by my Father, and no man knows the Son except the Father, nor does any man know the Father but the Son and he to whom the Son wishes to reveal him.

28 ¶Come to me, all you who labour and carry burdens, and I will give you rest.

29 Take my yoke upon you, and learn from me, for I am gentle and meek in my heart, and you will find rest for your souls.

30 For my yoke is pleasant and my burden is light.

CHAPTER 12

AT that time, Jesus walked on the sabbath through the wheat fields; and his disciples became hungry, and they began to pluck ears of grain and to eat.

2 But when the Pharisees saw them, they said to him, Behold, your disciples are doing what is unlawful to do on the sabbath.

3 But he said to them, Have you not read what David did when he and those who were with him were hungry?

4 How he entered into the house of God and did eat bread that was on the table of the Lord, that which was not lawful for him to eat, nor for those who were with him, but only for the priests?

5 Or, have you not read in the book of law that the priests in the temple disregard the sabbath and yet are blameless?

6 But I say to you that there is one here who is greater than the temple.

7 But if you only knew what it means, I want mercy and not sacrifice, you would not condemn those who are blameless.

8 For the Son of man is Lord of the sabbath.

9 ¶And Jesus departed from thence and came to their synagogue.

10 And there was a man there whose hand was withered. And they questioned him, saying, Is it lawful to heal on the sabbath? that they might accuse him.

11 He said to them, Who is the man among you who has only one sheep, and if it should fall into a pit on the sabbath, would he not take hold of it and lift it up?

12 How much more important is a man than a sheep? It is therefore lawful to do good on the sabbath.

13 Then he said to the man, Stretch out your hand. And he stretched out his hand, and it was restored like the other.

14 ¶And the Pharisees went out and took counsel against him, so as to do away with him.

15 But Jesus knew of it, and departed from thence; and a great many people followed him, and he healed them all.

16 And he charged them not to say where he was,

17 So that what was said by the prophet Isaiah might be fulfilled, namely,

18 Behold my servant with whom I am pleased, my beloved one, in whom my soul rejoices; I will put my Spirit upon him, and he will preach justice to the peoples.

19 He will not argue, nor will he cry aloud; and no man will hear his voice in the street.

20 He will not break even a bruised reed, and he will not extinguish a flickering lamp, until he brings justice to victory; [1]

21 And in his name will the Gentiles find hope.

22 ¶Then they brought near to him a lunatic, who was also dumb and blind; and he healed him, so that the dumb and blind man could speak and see.

23 All the people were amazed and said, Perhaps this man is the son of David?

24 But when the Pharisees heard of it, they said, This man does not cast out demons, except by Beelzebub, the prince of demons.

25 But Jesus knew their thoughts, and said to them, Every kingdom which is divided against itself will be destroyed; and every house or city that is divided against itself will not stand.

26 And if Satan cast out Satan, he is divided against himself; how then will his kingdom stand?

27 So if I cast out demons by Beelzebub, by what do your sons cast them out? For this reason they will be your judges.

28 And if I cast out devils by the Spirit of God, then the kingdom of God has come near to you.

29 Or, how can a man enter into a strong man's house and plunder his goods, except he first binds the strong man, and then plunders his house?

30 ¶They who are not with me are against me; and they who do not gather with me shall be dispersed.

31 Therefore I say to you that all sins and blasphemies will be for-

given to men; but the blasphemy against the Spirit shall not be forgiven to men.

32 And whoever speaks a word against the Son of man will be forgiven; but whoever speaks against the Holy Spirit shall not be forgiven, neither in this world nor in the world to come.

33 Either produce like a good tree with good fruits, or produce like a bad tree with bad fruits; for a tree is known by its fruits.

34 O generation of scorpions, how can you speak good things when you are bad? For the mouth speaks from the fullness of the heart.

35 A good man brings out good things from good treasures, and a bad man brings out bad things from bad treasures.

36 For I say to you that for every foolish word which men speak, they will have to answer for it on the day of judgment.

37 For by your words you shall be justified, and by your words you shall be found guilty.

38 ¶Then some of the men of the scribes and Pharisees answered, saying to him, Teacher, we would like to see a sign from you.

39 But he answered, saying to them, An evil and adulterous generation wants a sign; and no sign will be given to it, except the sign of the prophet Jonah.

40 For as Jonah was in the whale's belly three days and three nights, so the Son of man will be in the heart of the earth three days and three nights.

41 Even the men of Nineveh will rise up in judgment with this generation, and find it guilty; for they repented through the preaching of Jonah, and behold, a greater than Jonah is here.

42 The queen of the south will rise up in judgment with this generation and find it guilty; for she came from the far ends of the earth that she might hear Solomon's wisdom, and behold, a greater than Solomon is here.

[1] Or *until justice is triumphant.*

43 When an unclean spirit goes out of a man, it travels in places where there is no water and seeks rest, and does not find it.

44 Then it says, I will return to my own house from whence I came; so it comes back and finds it empty, warm, and well furnished.

45 Then it goes away and brings with it seven other spirits worse than itself, and they enter and live in him; and the end of that man becomes worse than at first. Such will happen to this evil generation.

46 ¶While he was speaking to the people, his mother and his brothers came and stood outside, and wanted to speak with him.

47 Then a man said to him, Behold, your mother and your brothers are standing outside, and they want to speak with you.

48 But he answered, saying to him who told him, Who is my mother and who are my brothers?

49 And he pointed his hand to his disciples and said, Behold my mother, and behold my brothers.

50 For whoever does the will of my Father in heaven is my brother and my sister and my mother.

CHAPTER 13

THAT same day Jesus went out of the house, and sat by the seaside.

2 And many people gathered around him, so that he had to go up and sit in a boat, and all the people stood on the seashore.

3 And he spoke many things to them in parables and said, Behold, a sower went out to sow;

4 And when he had sown, some seed fell on the roadside, and the fowls came and ate it.

5 Other seed fell upon the rock, where there was not sufficient soil; and it sprang up earlier because the ground was not deep enough;

6 But when the sun shone, it was scorched, and because it had no root, it dried up;

7 And other seed fell among thistles, and the thistles sprang up and choked it.

8 And other seed fell in good soil and bore fruit, some one hundredfold and some sixty and some thirty.

9 He who has ears to hear, let him hear.

10 ¶Then his disciples drew near to him and said, Why do you speak to them in parables?

11 He answered, saying to them, Because to you it is granted to know the mystery of the kingdom of heaven, but it is not granted to them.

12 For to him who has shall be given and it shall increase to him; but to him who has not, even that which he has shall be taken away from him.

13 This is the reason I speak to them in figures, because they see and yet cannot perceive; and they hear and yet do not listen, nor do they understand.

14 And in them is fulfilled the prophecy of Isaiah who said, Hearing you will hear, but you will not understand; and seeing you will see, but you will not know.

15 For the heart of this people has become hardened, and they hear with difficulty, and their eyes are dull; so that they cannot see with their eyes and hear with their ears and understand with their hearts; let them return, and I will heal them.

16 But as for you, blessed are your eyes, for they see; and your ears, for they hear.

17 For truly I say to you, a great many prophets and righteous men have longed to see what you see, and did not see it; and to hear what you hear, and did not hear it.

18 ¶Now listen to the parable of the seed.

19 Whoever hears the word of the kingdom and does not understand it, the evil one comes and snatches away the word which has been sown in his heart. This is that which was sown on the roadside.

20 That which was sown upon the rock, this is he who hears the word, and immediately accepts it with joy;

21 But it has no root in him, except for a while; and when trouble or

persecution comes because of the word, he immediately stumbles.

22 That which was sown among thistles, this is he who hears the word, but worldly thoughts and the deception caused by riches choke the word, and it becomes fruitless.

23 That which was sown upon good soil, this is he who hears my word and understands it, so he bears fruit and produces some one hundredfold and some sixty and some thirty.

24 ¶He related another parable to them, saying, The kingdom of heaven is like a man who sowed good seed in his field.

25 And when men slept, his enemy came and sowed tares among the wheat, and went away.

26 But when the blade sprang up and bore fruit, then the tares also appeared.

27 So the servants of the landowner came and said to him, Our lord, behold, did you not sow good seed in your field; whence did the tares come into it?

28 He said to them, An enemy did this. His servants then said to him, Do you want us to go and pull them out?

29 But he said to them, It might happen that while you were pulling out the tares, you might uproot with them also the wheat.

30 Let them both grow together until the harvest; and at the harvest season, I will say to the reapers, Pick out first the tares, and bind them into bundles to be burned; but gather the wheat into my barns.

31 ¶He related another parable to them, saying, The kingdom of heaven is like a grain of mustard seed, which a man took and sowed in his field.

32 It is the smallest of all seeds; but when it is grown, it is larger than all of the herbs; and it becomes a tree, so that the birds of the air come and nest in its branches.

33 ¶He told them another parable. The kingdom of heaven is like the leaven, which a woman took and buried in three measures of flour, until it was all leavened.

34 ¶Jesus spoke all these things to the people in parables; and without parables he did not speak to them.

35 So that it might be fulfilled which was said by the prophet, namely, I will open my mouth in parables and I will bring out secrets hidden before the foundation of the world.

36 Then Jesus left the multitudes and went into the house; and his disciples came up to him and said, Explain to us the parable of the tares and the field.

37 He answered, saying to them, He who sowed good seed is the Son of man.

38 The field is the world; the good seed are the sons of the kingdom; but the tares are the sons of evil.

39 The enemy who sowed them is Satan; the harvest is the end of the world; and the reapers are the angels.

40 Therefore, just as the tares are picked out and burned in the fire, so shall it be at the end of the world.

41 The Son of man will send his angels, and they will pick out from his kingdom all things which cause stumbling and all workers of iniquity.

42 And they will throw them into the furnace of fire; there shall be weeping and gnashing of teeth.

43 Then the righteous ones shall shine as the sun in the kingdom of their Father. He who has ears to hear, let him hear.

44 ¶Again, the kingdom of heaven is like a treasure which is hidden in the field, which a man discovered and hid, and because of his joy, he went and sold everything he had, and bought that field.

45 ¶Again, the kingdom of heaven is like a merchant who was seeking good pearls.

46 And when he had found one costly pearl, he went and sold everything he had, and bought it.

47 ¶Again, the kingdom of heaven is like a net which was thrown into the sea, and it gathered fish of every kind.

48 When it was filled, they drew it to the shore, and sat down and sorted

them; the good ones they put into bags, and the bad they threw away.

49 So will it be at the end of the world; the angels will go out and separate the bad from among the righteous,

50 And they will throw them into the furnace of fire; there shall be weeping and gnashing of teeth.

51 ¶Jesus said to them, Have you understood all of these things? They said to him, Yes, our Lord.

52 He said to them, Therefore every scribe who is converted to the kingdom of heaven is like a man who is a householder, who brings out new and old things from his treasures.

53 ¶When Jesus had finished these parables, he departed thence.

54 And he came to his own city; and he taught them in their synagogues in such a way that they were amazed and said, Where did he get this wisdom and these wonders?

55 Is he not the carpenter's son? Is not his mother called Mary? and his brothers, James and Joses and Simon and Judah?

56 Are not all his sisters with us? Where did he get all these things?

57 And they were perplexed about him. But Jesus said to them, No prophet is mocked, except in his own city and in his own house.

58 And he did not perform many miracles there because of their unbelief.

CHAPTER 14

AT that time Herod the tetrarch heard the news about Jesus.

2 And he said to his servants, This man is John the Baptist; he has risen from the dead; this is why great miracles are wrought by him.

3 ¶For Herod had arrested John and bound him, and put him in prison, because of Herodias, his brother Philip's wife.

4 For John had said to him, It is unlawful to have her as your wife.

5 So Herod wanted to kill him, but he was afraid of the people, because they accepted him as a prophet.

6 When Herod's birthday came, the daughter of Herodias danced before the guests, and it pleased Herod.

7 He therefore swore to her with oaths that he would give her anything that she would ask.

8 And she, because she was instructed by her mother, said, Give me right here on a tray the head of John the Baptist.

9 And the king was very sorry; but because of the oaths and the guests, he commanded that it be given to her.

10 So he sent and had John beheaded in the prison.

11 And his head was brought in on a tray, and given to the girl; and she took it to her mother.

12 Then his disciples came and took up his body and buried it, and they came and informed Jesus.

13 ¶When Jesus heard of it, he departed thence by boat, alone to a desert place; and when the people heard of it, they followed him by land from the cities.

14 And Jesus went out and saw large crowds, and he had pity for them and healed their sick.

15 ¶When it was evening, his disciples came to him and said, This is a lonely place, and it is getting late; dismiss the people so that the men may go to the villages and buy food for themselves.

16 But he said to them, It is not necessary for them to go; give them something to eat.

17 They said to him, We have nothing here, except five loaves of bread and two fish.

18 Jesus said to them, Bring them here to me.

19 And he ordered the people to sit down on the ground, and he took the five loaves of bread and the two fish, and he looked up to heaven and blessed them, and he broke them and gave them to his disciples, and the disciples placed them before the people.

20 So they all ate, and were satisfied; and they took up the fragments which were left over, twelve full baskets.

21 And the men who ate were five thousand, not counting the women and children.

22 ¶And immediately he urged his disciples to get into the boat, in advance of him, to the crossing place, while he dismissed the people.

23 And when he had dismissed the people, he went up to the mountain alone to pray; and when darkness fell he was still there alone.

24 But the boat was many miles away from the land, tossed by the waves, for the wind was against it.

25 And in the fourth watch of the night, Jesus came to them, walking on the water.

26 And his disciples saw him walking on the water, and they were frightened, and they said, It is a false vision; and they cried out because of their fear.

27 But Jesus spoke to them at once and said, Have courage; it is I; do not be afraid.

28 And Peter answered, saying, My Lord, if it is you, command me to come to you on the water.

29 Jesus said to him, Come. So Peter went down from the boat and walked on the water, to come to Jesus.

30 But when he saw that the wind was strong, he was afraid, and began to sink, and he raised his voice and said, My Lord, save me.

31 And our Lord immediately stretched out his hand and grasped him; and he said to him, O you of little faith, why did you doubt?

32 And when they got into the boat, the wind quieted down.

33 And they who were in the boat came and worshipped him; and they said, Truly you are the Son of God.

34 ¶And they rowed and came to the land of Gennesaret.

35 And the men of that country recognized him, and they sent word to all the villages around them; so they brought to him all who were seriously sick.

36 And they besought him that they

1 My offering to God.

might touch even the hem of his robe; and those who touched it were healed.

CHAPTER 15

THEN Pharisees and scribes from Jerusalem came up to Jesus, saying,

2 Why do your disciples disregard the tradition of the elders, and they do not wash their hands when they eat?

3 Jesus answered, saying to them, Why do you also disregard the commandment of God on account of your tradition;

4 For God said, Honor your father and your mother, and whoever curses his father or his mother, let him be put to death.

5 But you say, Whoever says to a father or to a mother, Whatever you may be benefited from me is Corban; 1 he need not honor his father or his mother.

6 So you have rendered useless the word of God for the sake of your tradition.

7 O you hypocrites, the prophet Isaiah well prophesied concerning you, saying,

8 This people honor me with their lips, but their heart is far away from me.

9 And they worship me in vain when they teach the doctrines of the commandments of men.

10 ¶Then he called the people and said to them, Listen and understand.

11 It is not what enters into the mouth which defiles a man; but what comes out of the mouth, that is what defiles a man.

12 Then his disciples came up and said to him, Do you know that the Pharisees who heard this saying were offended?

13 But he answered, saying to them, Every plant that my heavenly Father did not plant shall be uprooted.

14 Leave them alone; they are blind guides of the blind. And if the blind lead around the blind, both will fall into a pit.

15 And Simon Peter answered, say-

ing to him, My Lord, explain this parable to us.

16 And he said to them, Even yet do you not understand?

17 Do you not know that what enters into the mouth goes into the stomach, and thence, through the intestines, is cast out?

18 But what comes out of the mouth comes out from the heart; and that is what defiles man.

19 For from the heart come out evil thoughts, such as fornication, murder, adultery, theft, false witness, blasphemy.

20 It is these that defile a man; but if a man should eat when his hands are unwashed, he will not be defiled.

21 ¶And Jesus went out from thence, and he came to the border of Tyre and Sidon.

22 And behold, a Canaanite woman from these borders came out crying aloud, and saying, Have mercy on me, O my Lord, son of David; my daughter is seriously afflicted with insanity.

23 But he did not answer her. And his disciples came up to him and urged him, saying, Dismiss her, for she keeps crying aloud after us.

24 And he answered, saying to them, I am not sent, except to the sheep which went astray from the house of Israel.

25 But she came and worshipped him, saying, My Lord, help me.

26 Jesus said to her, It is not right to take the children's bread and throw it to the dogs.

27 But she said, Yes, my Lord, even the dogs eat of the crumbs which fall from their master's table, and they live.

28 Then Jesus said to her, O woman, your faith is great; let it be to you as you wish; and her daughter was healed from that very hour.

29 ¶And Jesus departed from thence, and he came toward the sea of Galilee; and he went up to a mountain and sat down there.

30 And a great many people came to him who had with them the lame, blind, dumb, maimed, and many others; and they laid them down at the feet of Jesus, and he healed them.

31 So that the people wondered to see the dumb speaking and the maimed healed and the lame walking and the blind seeing; and they praised the God of Israel.

32 ¶Jesus then called his disciples and said to them, I have compassion on this people, for they have remained with me three days, and they have nothing to eat; and if I dismiss them fasting, they might faint on the way; but this I do not wish to do.

33 His disciples said to him, Where can we get bread in this desolate place to feed all this people?

34 Jesus said to them, How many loaves of bread have you? They said to him, Seven, and a few small fish.

35 So he ordered the people to sit on the ground.

36 Then he took the seven loaves of bread and the fish, and gave thanks, and he broke them and gave to his disciples, and the disciples gave them to the people.

37 And all of them did eat and were satisfied; and they took up of the fragments that were left over, seven full baskets.

38 And those who did eat were four thousand men, besides women and children.

39 And when he had dismissed the people, he went in the boat and came to the border of Magadan.

CHAPTER 16

AND the Pharisees and Sadducees came to him to tempt him; and they asked him to show them a sign from heaven.

2 But he answered, saying to them, When it is evening, you say, It is clear, for the sky is red.

3 And in the morning you say, It is a winter day, for the sky is red and cloudy. O hypocrites, you know how to observe the face of the sky, but the signs of the present time you are not able to distinguish.

4 A wicked and adulterous generation wants a sign; and no sign shall be given to it, except the sign of the prophet Jonah. And he left them and went away.

5 When his disciples came to the crossing place, they had forgotten to take bread with them.

6 ¶He said to them, Watch and beware of the leaven of the Pharisees and of the Sadducees.

7 And they were reasoning among themselves and saying, It is because we have not brought bread.

8 But Jesus knew it and said to them, What are you thinking among yourselves, O you of little faith; is it because you have not brought bread?

9 Do you not yet understand? Do you not remember the five loaves of bread of the five thousand, and how many baskets you took up?

10 Neither the seven loaves of bread of the four thousand, and how many baskets you took up?

11 How is it that you did not understand that I was not talking to you about the bread, but to beware of the leaven of the Pharisees and of the Sadducees?

12 Then they understood, that he did not say that they should beware of the leaven of the bread, but of the teaching of the Pharisees and the Sadducees.

13 ¶When Jesus came into the country of Caesarea Philippi, he asked his disciples saying, What do men say concerning me, that I am merely a son of man?

14 They said, There are some who say John the Baptist, others Elijah, and still others Jeremiah, or one of the prophets.

15 He said to them, Who do you say that I am?

16 Simon Peter answered, saying, You are the Christ, the Son of the living God.

17 Jesus answered, saying to him, Blessed are you, Simon son of Jonah, for flesh and blood did not reveal it to you, but my Father in heaven.

18 I tell you also that you are the stone, and upon this stone I will build my church; and the doors of Sheol shall not shut upon it.

19 I will give you the keys of the kingdom of heaven; and whatever you bind on earth shall be bound in heaven, and whatever you loose on earth shall be loosed in heaven.

20 Then he charged his disciples not to tell any man that he was the Christ.

21 ¶From that time Jesus began to make known to his disciples that he would shortly have to go to Jerusalem and suffer a great deal from the elders and the high priests and scribes, and be killed, and rise up on the third day.

22 So Peter took him aside and began to rebuke him, saying, Far be it from you, my Lord, that this should happen to you.

23 But he turned and said to Peter, Get behind me, Satan; you are a stumbling block to me; for you are not thinking of the things of God, but of men.

24 ¶Then Jesus said to his disciples, He who wishes to follow me, let him deny himself, and take up his cross and follow me.

25 For whoever wishes to save his life shall lose it; and whoever loses his life for my sake shall find it.

26 For how would a man be benefited, if he should gain the whole world and lose his own soul? Or what shall a man give in exchange for his soul?

27 For the Son of man will come in the glory of his Father with his holy angels; and then he will reward each man according to his works.

28 Truly I say to you, There are men who stand here who will not taste death, until they see the Son of man coming in his kingdom.

CHAPTER 17

AND after six days Jesus took Peter and James and his brother John, and brought them up to a high mountain alone.

2 And Jesus was transfigured before them, and his face shone like the sun, and his clothes turned white like light.

3 And there appeared to them Moses and Elijah, as they were talking with him.

4 Then Peter answered, saying to Jesus, My Lord, it is better for us to

remain here; and if you wish, we will make three shelters here, one for you and one for Moses and one for Elijah.

5 And while he was speaking, behold, a bright cloud overshadowed them, and a voice came out of the cloud saying, This is my beloved Son, with him I am pleased; hear him.

6 When the disciples heard it, they threw themselves on their faces, and they were greatly frightened.

7 And Jesus came near them and touched them, and said, Arise, do not be afraid.

8 And they lifted up their eyes, and saw no man except Jesus alone.

9 And as they were going down from the mountain, Jesus commanded them, saying, Do not speak of this vision in the presence of anyone until the Son of man rises from the dead.

10 And his disciples asked him, Why then do the scribes say that Elijah must come first?

11 Jesus answered, saying to them, Elijah will come first, so that everything might be fulfilled.

12 But I say to you, Elijah has already come, and they did not know him, and they did to him whatever they pleased. Thus also the Son of man is bound to suffer from them.

13 Then the disciples understood that what he had told them was about John the Baptist.

14 ¶And when they came to the people, a man approached him and fell on his knees, and said to him,

15 My Lord, have mercy on me; my son is an epileptic and has become worse; he often falls into the fire, and often into the water.

16 And I brought him to your disciples, but they were not able to heal him.

17 Jesus answered, saying, O faithless and crooked generation, how long shall I be with you? and how long shall I preach to you? Bring him here to me.

18 And Jesus rebuked him, and the demon went out of him; and the boy was healed from that very hour.

19 Then the disciples came up to Jesus when he was alone and said to him, Why could we not heal him?

20 Jesus said to them, Because of your unbelief; for truly I say to you, If there is faith in you even as a grain of mustard seed, you will say to this mountain, move away from here, and it will move away; and nothing would prevail over you.

21 Nevertheless this kind does not come out except by fasting and prayer.

22 ¶While they were traveling through Galilee, Jesus said to them, The Son of man will shortly be delivered into the hands of men;

23 And they will kill him, and on the third day he will rise up. And they were very much grieved.

24 ¶And when they came to Capernaum, those who collect two coins of silver as head tax came to Peter and said to him, Would not your master give his two coins?

25 He said to them, Yes. And when Peter entered the house, Jesus anticipated and said to him, What do you think, Simon? From whom do the kings of the earth collect custom duties and head tax? from their sons, or from strangers?

26 Simon said to him, From strangers. Jesus said to him, Then the sons are free.

27 But so as not to offend them, go to the sea, and throw out a hook, and the first fish which comes up, open its mouth and you will find a coin; take it and give it for me and for you.

CHAPTER 18

AT that very hour the disciples came up to Jesus and said, Who is greatest in the kingdom of heaven?

2 So Jesus called a little child, and made him stand up in the midst of them,

3 And he said, Truly I say to you, Unless you change and become like little children, you shall not enter into the kingdom of heaven.

4 Whoever therefore will humble himself like this little child, shall be great in the kingdom of heaven.

5 And he who will welcome one

like this little child, in my name, welcomes me.

6 And whoever misleads one of these little ones who believe in me, it would be better for him that an ass' millstone were hanged on his neck and he were sunk in the depths of the sea.

7 ¶Woe to the world because of offences! Offences are bound to come; but woe to the man by whose hand the offences come!

8 If your hand or your foot offends you, cut it off and cast it away from you; [1] for it is much better for you to go through life lame or maimed, rather than having two hands or two feet, and fall into the everlasting fire.

9 And if your eye offends you, remove it and cast it away from you; it is better for you to go through life with one eye, rather than to have two eyes and fall into the Gehenna [2] of fire.

10 See to it that you do not despise one of these little ones; for I say to you, their angels always see the face of my Father in heaven.

11 For the Son of man has come to save what was lost.

12 What do you think? If a man should have a hundred sheep, and one of them is lost, would he not leave the ninety and nine on the mountain and go in search of the one which is lost?

13 And if he should find it, truly I say to you, he rejoices over it more than over the ninety and nine which were not lost.

14 Even so, your Father in heaven does not want one of these little ones to be lost.

15 ¶Now then, if your brother is at fault with you, go and rebuke him alone; if he listens to you, then you have won your brother.

16 But if he will not listen to you, take one or two with you, because at the mouth of two or three witnesses every word is established.

17 And if he will not listen to them, tell the congregation; and if he will not listen to the congregation, then regard him as a tax collector and a heathen.

18 Truly I say to you, Whatever you bind on earth will be bound in heaven, and whatever you release on earth will be released in heaven.

19 Again I say to you that if two of you are worthy on earth, anything that they would ask will be done for them by my Father in heaven.

20 For wherever two or three are gathered in my name, I am there among them.

21 ¶Then Peter came up and said to him, My Lord, if my brother is at fault with me, how many times should I forgive him? up to seven times?

22 Jesus said to him, I do not say to you up to seven times, but up to seventy times seventy-seven.

23 ¶Therefore the kingdom of heaven is likened to a king who wanted to take an accounting from his servants.

24 And when he began to take the accounting, they brought to him one who owed ten thousand talents.

25 And as he could not pay, his lord commanded him to be sold, together with his wife and children and all that he had, so that he could pay.

26 The servant then fell down, worshipped him, and said, My lord, have patience with me and I will pay you everything.

27 Then the master of that servant had pity, so he released him and cancelled his debt.

28 But that servant went out, and found one of his fellow servants, who owed him a hundred pennies; and he seized him and tried to choke him, saying to him, Give me what you owe me.

29 So his fellow servant fell down at his feet, and begged him, saying, Have patience with me and I will pay you.

30 But he was not willing; and he went and had him put into prison until he should pay him what he owed him.

31 When their fellow servants saw

---

[1] Aramaic idioms: foot offends, *stop trespassing;* cast it away, *stop it.*
[2] Figuratively, hell.

what had happened, they were sorry, and came and informed their master of everything that had happened.

32 Then his master called him and said to him, O wicked servant, I cancelled all your debt because you begged me.

33 Was it not right for you to have mercy on your fellow servant, just as I had mercy on you?

34 So his master was angry, and delivered him to the scourgers until he should pay everything he owed him.

35 So will my Father in heaven do to you, if you do not forgive each man his brother's fault from your hearts.

CHAPTER 19

WHEN Jesus had finished these sayings, he departed from Galilee, and came to the border of Judea, at the crossing of the Jordan.

2 And a great many people followed him, and he healed them there.

3 ¶And the Pharisees came up to him and were tempting him, saying, Is it lawful for a man to divorce his wife for any cause?

4 But he answered, saying to them, Have you not read, that he who made from the beginning made them male and female?

5 And he said, Because of this, a man shall leave his father and his mother, and shall be joined to his wife, and the two shall be one flesh.

6 Henceforth they are not two, but one body; therefore what God has joined together, let not man separate.

7 They said to him, Why then did Moses command to give a letter of separation and then to divorce her?

8 He said to them, Moses, considering the hardness of your heart, gave you permission to divorce your wives; but from the beginning it was not so.

9 But I say to you, Whoever leaves his wife without a charge of adultery and marries another commits adultery; and he who marries a woman thus separated commits adultery.

10 ¶His disciples said to him, If there is so much difficulty between man and woman, it is not worthwhile to marry.

11 He said to them, This saying does not apply to every man, but to whom it is given.

12 For there are eunuchs who were born so from their mother's womb; and there are eunuchs who were made eunuchs by men; and there are eunuchs who made themselves eunuchs for the sake of the kingdom of heaven. To him who can comprehend, this is enough.

13 ¶Then they brought little children to him, that he might lay his hand on them and pray; and his disciples rebuked them.

14 But Jesus said to them, Allow the little children to come to me, and do not stop them; for the kingdom of heaven is for such as these.

15 And he laid his hand on them, and went away from thence.

16 ¶Then a man drew near and said to him, O good Teacher, what is the best thing that I should do to have life eternal?

17 He said to him, Why do you call me good? There is no one who is good except the one God; but if you want to enter into life, obey the commandments.

18 He said to him, Which ones? And Jesus said to him, You shall not kill; You shall not commit adultery; You shall not steal; You shall not bear false witness;

19 Honor your father and your mother; and, Love your neighbor as yourself.

20 The young man said to him, I have obeyed all these from my boyhood; what do I lack?

21 Jesus said to him, If you wish to be perfect, go and sell your possessions and give them to the poor, and you will have a treasure in heaven; then follow me.

22 When the young man heard this word, he went away sad, for he had great possessions.

23 ¶Jesus then said to his disciples, Truly I say to you, It is difficult for a rich man to enter into the kingdom of heaven.

24 Again I say to you, It is easier

for a rope [1] to go through the eye of a needle, than for a rich man to enter into the kingdom of God.

25 When the disciples heard it, they were exceedingly astonished, saying, Who then can be saved?

26 Jesus looked at them and said, For men this is impossible, but for God everything is possible.

27 ¶Then Peter answered, saying to him, Behold, we have left everything and followed you; what will we have?

28 Jesus said to them, Truly I say to you that in the new world when the Son of man shall sit on the throne of his glory, you who have followed me shall also sit on twelve seats,[2] and you shall judge the twelve tribes of Israel.

29 And every man who leaves houses or brothers or sisters or father or mother or wife or children or fields, for my name's sake, shall receive a hundredfold, and shall inherit everlasting life.

30 But many who are first shall be last, and the last first.

CHAPTER 20

FOR the kingdom of heaven is like a man who is a householder who went out early in the morning to hire laborers for his vineyard.

2 He bargained with the laborers for a penny a day, and sent them to his vineyard.

3 And he went out at the third hour, and saw others standing idle in the market place.

4 And he said to them, You also go to the vineyard, and I will give you what is right. And they went.

5 And he went out again at the sixth and at the ninth hour, and did the same.

6 And towards the eleventh hour he went out and found others standing idle, and he said to them, Why do you stand all the day idle?

7 They said to him, Because no man has hired us. He said to them, You also go to the vineyard, and you will receive what is right.

8 When evening came, the owner of the vineyard said to his steward, Call the laborers and pay them their wages; and begin from the last ones to the first.

9 When those hired at the eleventh hour came, they each received a penny.

10 But when the first ones came, they expected to receive more; but they also got each one a penny.

11 And when they received it, they murmured against the householder,

12 Saying, These last ones have worked only one hour, and you have made them equal with us who have borne the burden of the day and its heat.

13 He answered, saying to one of them, My friend, I am not doing you an injustice; did you not bargain with me for a penny?

14 Take what is yours and go away; I wish to give to this last one the same as to you.

15 Have I no right to do what I wish with mine own? Or are you jealous because I am generous?

16 Even so the last shall be first, and the first last; for many are called, but few are chosen.

17 ¶Now Jesus was ready to go up to Jerusalem; and he took his twelve disciples apart on the road, and he said to them,

18 Behold, we are going up to Jerusalem, and the Son of man will be delivered to the high priests and the scribes, and they will condemn him to death.

19 And they will deliver him to the Gentiles and they will mock him and scourge him and crucify him; and on the third day he will rise up.

20 ¶Then the mother of the sons of Zebedee came up to him, together with her sons; and she worshipped him, and requested something of him.

21 He said to her, What do you wish? She said to him, Command that these two sons of mine may sit, one at your right and one at your left, in your kingdom.

22 Jesus answered, saying, You do not know what you are asking. Can you drink the cup that I am ready to

[1] The Aramaic word *gamla* means *rope* and *camel*.   [2] Smaller thrones used by princes.

drink, or be baptized with the baptism with which I am to be baptized? They said to him, We can.

23 He said to them, Indeed my cup you shall drink, and the baptism with which I am to be baptized, you too shall be baptized with; but to sit at my right hand and at my left, that is not mine to give, but it is for those for whom it is prepared by my Father.

24 When the ten heard it, they were angry at the two brothers.

25 And Jesus called them and said, You know that the princes of the Gentiles are also their lords; and their officials rule over them.

26 Let not this be so among you; but whoever wishes to be great among you, let him be a minister to you;

27 And whoever wishes to be first among you, let him be a servant to you;

28 Just as the Son of man did not come to be ministered to, but to minister and to give his life as a salvation for the sake of many.

29 And when Jesus went out of Jericho a large crowd followed him.

30 ¶And behold, two blind men were sitting by the roadside, and when they heard that Jesus was passing by, they cried aloud, saying, Have mercy upon us, O Lord, son of David.

31 But the people rebuked them, telling them to keep quiet; but they cried louder, saying, Our Lord, have mercy upon us, son of David.

32 And Jesus stopped and called them, and he said, What do you wish me to do for you?

33 They said to him, Our Lord, that our eyes may be opened.

34 And Jesus had mercy upon them; so he touched their eyes, and immediately their eyes were opened, and they followed him.

CHAPTER 21

WHEN he drew near to Jerusalem, he came to Bethphage on the side of the mount of Olives. Jesus then sent two of his disciples,

2 And he said to them, Go to that village which is in front of you, and straightway you will find an ass which is tied up, and a colt with her; untie them and bring them to me.

3 And if any man should say anything to you, tell him, Our Lord needs them; and he will immediately send them here.

4 All this happened, so that what was said by the prophet, might be fulfilled, saying,

5 Tell the daughter of Zion, Behold your king is coming to you, meek, and riding upon an ass, upon a colt, the foal of an ass.

6 And the disciples went and did as Jesus had commanded them.

7 And they brought the ass and the colt, and they put their garments on the colt, and Jesus rode on it.

8 And a great many people spread their garments on the road; and others cut down branches from the trees and spread them on the road.

9 And the people who were going before him and coming after him, were shouting and saying, Hosanna to the son of David; Blessed is he who comes in the name of the Lord; Hosanna in the highest.

10 When he entered Jerusalem, the whole city was stirred up, and they were saying, Who is this man?

11 And the people were saying, This is the prophet, Jesus, from Nazareth in Galilee.

12 ¶And Jesus entered into the temple of God, and drove out all who were buying and selling in the temple, and he overturned the trays of the moneychangers and the stands of those who sold doves.

13 And he said to them, It is written, My house shall be called the house of prayer; but you have made it a bandits' cave.

14 And in the temple they brought to him the blind and the lame, and he healed them.

15 But when the high priests and the Pharisees saw the wonders that he did, and the boys crying aloud in the temple and saying, Hosanna to the son of David, they were displeased.

16 And they said to him, Do you hear what they are saying? Jesus said to them, Yes; have you never read, From the mouths of infants and little

children you have composed a song?
17 ¶And he left them, and went outside of the city to Bethany and lodged there.

18 In the morning, as he returned to the city, he became hungry.

19 And he saw a fig tree on the roadside, and he came to it and found nothing on it except leaves; and he said to it, Let there be no fruit on you again for ever. And shortly the fig tree withered.

20 When the disciples saw it, they were amazed and said, How is it that the fig tree has withered so soon?

21 Jesus answered, saying to them, Truly I say to you, If you have faith and do not doubt, you will perform a deed not only like this of the fig tree, but should you say even to this mountain, Be removed and fall into the sea, it shall be done.

22 And everything that you will ask in prayer believing, you shall receive.

23 ¶When Jesus came to the temple, the high priests and the elders of the people came up to him, while he was teaching, and said to him, By what authority do you do these things? and who gave you this authority?

24 Jesus answered, saying to them, I will also ask you a question, and if you answer me, I will then tell you by what authority I do these things.

25 Whence is the baptism of John? Is it from heaven, or from men? And they reasoned with themselves, saying, If we should say from heaven, he will say to us, Why then did you not believe him?

26 And if we should say, From men, we are afraid of the people, for all of them regard John as a prophet.

27 So they answered, saying to him, We do not know. Jesus said to them, Neither will I tell you by what authority I do these things.

28 ¶What do you think? A man had two sons, and he came to the first one and said to him, My son, go and work today in the vineyard.

29 He answered, saying, I do not want to, but later he regretted and went.

30 And he came to the other one and spoke to him likewise. And he answered, saying, Here am I, my lord, and yet he did not go.

31 Which of these two did the will of his father? They said to him, The first one. Jesus said to them, Truly I say to you that even the tax collectors and harlots will precede you into the kingdom of God.

32 For John came to you in the way of righteousness, and you did not believe him; but the tax collectors and harlots believed him; but you, even though you saw it, did not repent, so that later you may believe him.

33 ¶Hear another parable. There was a man who was a householder, and he planted a vineyard and fenced it, and he dug in it a winepress and built a tower, and then he leased it to laborers and went away on a journey.

34 And when the fruit season was at hand, he sent his servants to the laborers, that they might send him some of the fruits of his vineyard.

35 And the laborers seized his servants, and some were beaten and some were stoned and some were killed.

36 Again he sent other servants, many more than the first; and they did likewise to them.

37 At last he sent his son to them, saying, They might feel ashamed before my son.

38 But when the laborers saw the son, they said among themselves, This is the heir; come, let us kill him and retain his inheritance.

39 So they seized him, and took him out of the vineyard and killed him.

40 When therefore the owner of the vineyard comes, what will he do to those laborers?

41 They said to him, He will destroy them savagely, and lease his vineyard to other laborers, who will give him fruits in their seasons.

42 Jesus said to them, Have you never read in the scripture, The stone which the builders rejected, the same

became the cornerstone; this was from the Lord, and it is a marvel in our eyes?

43 Therefore I say to you that the kingdom of God will be taken away from you, and will be given to a people who bear fruits.

44 And whoever falls on this stone will be broken, and whomever it falls upon, it will destroy.

45 When the high priests and Pharisees heard his parables, they understood that he was speaking against them.

46 So they wanted to arrest him, but they were afraid of the people, because they regarded him as a prophet.

CHAPTER 22

AND Jesus answered again by parables, and said,

2 The kingdom of heaven is like a king who gave a marriage feast for his son.

3 And he sent his servants to call those who were invited to the marriage feast, but they would not come.

4 Again he sent other servants and said, Tell those who are invited, Behold my supper is ready, and my oxen and fatlings are killed, and everything is prepared; come to the marriage feast.

5 But they sneered at it, and went away, one to his field, another to his business;

6 And the rest seized his servants and mocked them and killed them.

7 When the king heard it he was angry; and he sent out his armies and destroyed those murderers and burned their city.

8 Then he said to his servants, Now the marriage feast is ready, and those who were invited were unworthy.

9 Go, therefore, to the main roads, and whomever you may find, invite them to the marriage feast.

10 So the servants went out to the roads and gathered together every one they could find, bad and good; and the banqueting house was filled with guests.

11 When the king entered to see the guests, he saw there a man who was not wearing wedding garments.

12 And he said to him, My friend, how did you enter here, when you do not have wedding garments? And he was speechless.

13 Then the king said to the servants, Bind his hands and his feet and take him out into darkness; there shall be weeping and gnashing of teeth.

14 For many are called, and few are chosen.

15 ¶Then the Pharisees went away and took counsel how to trap him by a question.

16 So they sent to him their disciples together with the Herodians, and they said to him, Teacher, we know that you are true, and you teach the way of God justly; and you do not favor any man, for you do not discriminate between men.

17 Tell us, therefore, what do you think? Is it lawful to pay head tax to Caesar or not?

18 But Jesus knew their evil, and said, Why do you tempt me, O hypocrites?

19 Show me the head tax penny. And they brought to him a penny.

20 And Jesus said to them, Whose is this image and inscription?

21 They said, Caesar's. He said to them, Give therefore to Caesar what is Caesar's, and to God what is God's.

22 And when they heard it, they were amazed; and they left him and went away.

23 ¶That same day the Sadducees came and said to him, There is no resurrection of the dead; and they spoke to him,

24 And said, Teacher, Moses has told us, If a man die without sons, let his brother take his wife and raise up an offspring for his brother.

25 Now there were with us seven brothers; the first married and died, and because he had no sons, he left his wife to his brother.

26 Likewise the second, also the third, up to the seventh.

27 And after them all the woman also died.

28 Therefore at the resurrection, to

which of these seven will she be a wife? for they all married her.

29 Jesus answered, saying to them, You err, because you do not understand the scriptures nor the power of God.

30 For at the resurrection of the dead, men neither marry women, nor are women given to men in marriage, but they are like the angels of God in heaven.

31 But concerning the resurrection of the dead, have you not read what was told you by God, saying,

32 I am the God of Abraham, the God of Isaac, the God of Jacob? And yet God is not the God of the dead, but of the living.

33 And when the people heard it, they were amazed at his teaching.

34 ¶But when the Pharisees heard that he had silenced the Sadducees, they gathered together.

35 And one of them who knew the law, asked him, testing him,

36 Teacher, which is the greatest commandment in the law?

37 Jesus said to him, Love the Lord your God with all your heart and with all your soul and with all your might and with all your mind.

38 This is the greatest and the first commandment.

39 And the second is like to it, Love your neighbor as yourself.

40 On these two commandments hang the law and the prophets.

41 ¶While the Pharisees were gathered together, Jesus asked them,

42 Saying, What do you say concerning the Christ? Whose son is he? They said to him, The son of David.

43 He said to them, How is it then that David through the spirit calls him Lord? For he said,

44 The Lord said to my Lord, Sit at my right hand, until I put your enemies under your feet.

45 If David then calls him Lord, how can he be his son?

46 And no man was able to answer him, and from that day no man dared to question him.

CHAPTER 23

THEN Jesus spoke to the people and to his disciples,

2 Saying to them, The scribes and the Pharisees sit on the chair of Moses;

3 Therefore whatever they tell you to obey, obey and do it, but do not do according to their works; for they say and do not.

4 And they bind heavy burdens, and put them on men's shoulders, but they themselves are not willing to touch them, even with their finger.

5 And all their works they do, just to be seen by men; for they widen the fringes of their garments and they lengthen the ends of their robes,

6 And they like the chief places at feasts and the front seats in the synagogues,

7 And the greetings in the streets and to be called by men, Rabbi.

8 But you should not be called Rabbi; for one is your Master, and all you are brethren.

9 And call no one on earth, father, for one is your Father in heaven.

10 Nor be called leaders, for one is your leader, the Christ.

11 But he who is greatest among you, let him be your servant.

12 For whoever exalts himself shall be humbled; and whoever humbles himself shall be exalted.

13 ¶Woe to you, scribes and Pharisees, hypocrites! for you embezzle the property of widows, with the pretense that you make long prayers; because of this you shall receive a greater judgment.[1]

14 Woe to you, scribes and Pharisees, hypocrites! for you have shut off the kingdom of heaven against men; for you do not enter into it yourselves, and do not permit those who would to enter.

15 Woe to you, scribes and Pharisees, hypocrites! for you traverse sea and land to make one proselyte; and when he becomes one, you make him the son of hell twice more than yourselves.

---

[1] The order of verses 13 and 14 is reversed in the Eastern Text as compared with King James.

16 Woe to you, blind guides; for you say, Whoever swears by the temple, it is nothing; but whoever swears by the gold which is in the temple, he is guilty!

17 O you fools and blind! for which is greater, the gold or the temple that sanctifies the gold?

18 And whoever swears by the altar, it is nothing; but whoever swears by the offering that is upon it, he is guilty.

19 O you fools and blind! for which is greater, the offering, or the altar that sanctifies the offering?

20 Therefore he who swears by the altar, he swears by it and by everything that is on it.

21 And whoever swears by the temple, swears by it and by him who dwells in it.

22 And he who swears by heaven, swears by the throne of God and by him who sits on it.

23 Woe to you, scribes and Pharisees, hypocrites! for you take tithes of mint, dill, and cummin, and you have overlooked the more important matters of the law, such as justice, mercy, and trustworthiness. These were necessary for you to have done, and these very things by no means to have left undone.

24 O blind guides, who strain at gnats and swallow camels!

25 ¶Woe to you, scribes and Pharisees, hypocrites! you clean the outside of the cup and of the plate, but inside they are full of extortion and iniquity.

26 Blind Pharisees! clean first the inside of the cup and of the plate, so that their outside may also be clean.

27 Woe to you, scribes and Pharisees, hypocrites! for you are like tombs painted white, which look beautiful from the outside, but inside are full of dead bones and all kinds of corruption.

28 Even so, from the outside you appear to men to be righteous, but from within you are full of iniquity and hypocrisy.

29 Woe to you, scribes and Pharisees, hypocrites! for you build the tombs of the prophets, and you decorate the graves of the righteous;

30 And you say, If we had been living in the days of our forefathers, we would not have been partakers with them in the blood of the prophets.

31 Now you testify concerning yourselves, that you are the children of those who killed the prophets.

32 You also fill up the measure of your fathers.

33 O you serpents and offspring of scorpions! how can you flee from the judgment of hell?

34 ¶Because of this, I am sending to you prophets and wise men and scribes; some of them you will kill and crucify; and some you will scourge in your synagogues and pursue from city to city;

35 So that all the blood of the righteous shed on the ground may come upon you, from the blood of Abel the righteous down to the blood of Zachariah, son of Barachiah, whom you killed between the temple and the altar.

36 Truly I say to you, All of these things shall come upon this generation.

37 O Jerusalem, Jerusalem, murderess of the prophets and stoner of those who are sent to her! how often I wanted to gather your children, just as a hen gathers her chickens under her wings, and yet you would not!

38 Behold, your house will be left to you desolate.

39 For I say to you, from now you will not see me until you say, Blessed is he who comes in the name of the Lord.

CHAPTER 24

AND Jesus went out of the temple to go away; and his disciples came up to him, and were showing him the building of the temple.

2 But he said to them, Behold, do you not see all of these? Truly I say to you, Not a stone shall be left here upon another stone, which will not be torn down.

3 ¶While Jesus sat on the mount

of Olives, his disciples came up talking among themselves, and they said to him, Tell us when these things will happen and what is the sign of your coming and of the end of the world?

4 Jesus answered, saying to them, Be careful that no man deceives you.

5 For many will come in my name, and say, I am the Christ, and they will deceive many.

6 You are bound to hear of revolutions and rumors of wars; watch out and do not be disturbed; for all of these things must come to pass, but the end is not yet.

7 For nation will rise against nation, and kingdom against kingdom; and there will be famines and plagues and earthquakes in different places.

8 But all these things are just the beginning of travail.

9 Then they will deliver you over to be oppressed, and they will kill you; and you will be hated by all nations for my name's sake.

10 Then many will stumble, and they will hate one another and betray one another.

11 And many false prophets will rise and will mislead a great many.

12 And because of the growth of iniquity, the love of many will become cold.

13 But he who has patience to the end will be saved.

14 And this gospel of the kingdom shall be preached throughout the world as a testimony to all the nations; then the end will come.

15 When you see the sign of uncleanness and desolation, as spoken by the prophet Daniel, accumulating in the holy place (whoever reads will understand [1]),

16 Then let those who are in Judea flee to the mountain,

17 And he who is on the roof, let him not come down to take things out of his house.

18 And he who is in the field, let him not turn back to take his clothes.

19 But woe to those who are with child and to those who give suck in those days!

20 Pray that your flight may not be in winter, nor on the sabbath.

21 For then there will be great suffering such as has never happened from the beginning of the world until now, and never will be again.

22 And if those days were not shortened, no flesh would live; but for the sake of the chosen ones those days will be shortened.

23 Then if any man should say to you, Behold, here is the Christ, or there; do not believe it.

24 For there will rise false Christs and lying prophets, and they will show signs and great wonders, so as to mislead, if possible, even the chosen ones.

25 Behold, I have told you in advance.

26 Therefore, if they should say to you, Behold, he is in the desert, do not go out; or, Behold, he is in the chamber, do not believe it.

27 For just as the lightning comes out from the east, and is seen even in the west, so will be the coming of the Son of man.

28 For wherever the carcass is, there will the vultures gather.

29 ¶Immediately after the suffering of those days the sun will be darkened and the moon will not give its light and the stars will fall from the sky and the powers of the universe will be shaken.

30 Then the sign of the Son of man will appear in the sky; and all the generations of the earth will mourn, and they will see the Son of man coming on the clouds of the sky with power and great glory.

31 And he will send his angels with a large trumpet, and they will gather his chosen ones from the four winds, from one end of the heaven to the other.

32 From the fig tree learn a parable. As soon as its branches become tender and bring forth leaves, you know that summer is coming.

33 So even you, when you see all these things, know that it has arrived at the door.

34 Truly I say to you that this race

---

[1] Enemies desecrated the temple by pollution. Dan. 11:31.

will not pass away until all these things happen.

35 Even heaven and earth will pass away, but my words shall not pass away.

36 ¶But concerning that day and that hour, no man knows, not even the angels of heaven, but the Father alone.

37 Just as in the days of Noah, so will be the coming of the Son of man.

38 For as the people before the flood were eating and drinking, marrying and giving in marriage, until the day Noah entered into the ark,

39 And they knew nothing until the flood came and carried them all away; such will be the coming of the Son of man.

40 Then two men will be in the field; one will be taken away and the other left.

41 Two women will be grinding at the hand mill; one will be taken and the other left.

42 ¶Be alert, therefore, for you do not know at what hour your Lord will come.

43 But know this much, that if the master of the house knew at what watch of the night the thief would come, he would keep awake and would not let his house be plundered.

44 For this reason, you also should be ready, for the Son of man will come at an hour when you do not expect him.

45 Who then is the faithful and wise servant, whom his lord has appointed over his household, to give them food in due time?

46 Blessed is that servant, when his lord comes and finds him so doing.

47 Truly I say to you, he will appoint him over all that he has.

48 But if a bad servant should say in his heart, My lord will delay his coming,

49 And should begin to beat his fellow servants, and to eat and drink with drunkards,

50 The lord of that servant will come on a day when he does not expect him, and at an hour that he does not know.

51 And he will severely scourge him, and give him a portion like that of the hypocrites; there will be weeping and gnashing of teeth.

CHAPTER 25

THEN the kingdom of heaven will be like ten virgins, who took their lamps and went out to greet the bridegroom and the bride.

2 Five of them were wise, and five were foolish.

3 And the foolish ones took their lamps, but took no oil with them.

4 But the wise ones took oil in the vessels with their lamps.

5 As the bridegroom was delayed, they all slumbered and slept.

6 And at midnight there was a cry, Behold, the bridegroom is coming; go out to greet him!

7 Then all the virgins got up and prepared their lamps.

8 And the foolish ones said to the wise ones, Give us some of your oil, for our lamps are going out.

9 Then the wise ones answered, saying, Why, there would not be enough for us and for you; go to those who sell and buy for yourselves.

10 And while they went to buy, the bridegroom came; and those who were ready entered with him into the banqueting house, and the door was locked.

11 Afterward the other virgins also came and said, Our lord, our lord, open to us.

12 But he answered and said to them, Truly I say to you, I do not know you.

13 Be alert, therefore, for you do not know the day nor the hour.

14 ¶It is just like a man who went on a journey, who called his servants and put his wealth in their charge.

15 To one he gave five talents, to another two, to another one; to each one according to his ability; and immediately he went on a journey.

16 The one who received five talents then went and traded with them, and he earned five more.

17 Likewise the second one by trading gained two others.

18 But he who received one went

and dug in the ground and hid his lord's money.

19 After a long time the lord of those servants returned and took an accounting from them.

20 Then the one who received five talents came up and offered five others, and he said, My lord, you gave me five talents; behold, I have added five others to them.

21 His lord said to him, Well done, good and reliable servant; you have been faithful over a little, I will appoint you over much; enter into your master's joy.

22 Then the one with the two talents came and said, My lord, you gave me two talents, behold I have added two others to them.

23 His lord said to him, Well done, good and reliable servant, you have been faithful over a little, I will appoint you over much; enter into your master's joy.

24 Then the one who received one talent also came up, and he said, My lord, I knew that you are a hard man, and you reap where you did not sow and gather where you did not scatter.

25 So I was afraid, and I went and hid your talent in the ground; here is the very one you gave me.

26 His lord answered, saying, O wicked and lazy servant, you knew me that I reap where I did not sow and gather where I did not scatter.

27 You should then have put my money in the exchange, and when I returned I would have demanded my own with interest.

28 Therefore take away the talent from him, and give it to the one who has ten talents.

29 For to him who has, it shall be given, and it shall increase to him; but he who has not, even that which he has shall be taken away from him.

30 And the idle servant they threw into the outer darkness; there will be weeping and gnashing of teeth.

31 ¶When the Son of man comes in his glory, and all his holy angels with him, then he will sit upon the throne of his glory.

32 And all nations will gather before him; and he will separate them one from another, just as a shepherd separates the sheep from the goats;

33 And he will set the sheep at his right, and the goats at his left.

34 Then the King will say to those at his right, Come, you blessed of my Father, inherit the kingdom which has been prepared for you from the foundation of the world.

35 For I was hungry, and you gave me food; I was thirsty, and you gave me drink; I was a stranger and you took me in;

36 I was naked, and you clothed me; I was sick, and you visited me; I was in prison, and you came to me.

37 Then the righteous will say to him, Our Lord, when did we see you hungry, and feed you? or thirsty and gave you drink?

38 And when did we see you a stranger, and took you in? Or that you were naked and clothed you?

39 And when did we see you sick or in the prison, and came to you?

40 The king then will answer, saying to them, Truly I tell you, Inasmuch as you have done it to one of the least of these my brethren, you did it to me.

41 Then he will also say to those at his left, Go away from me, you cursed, to the everlasting fire which is prepared for the adversary and his angels.

42 For I was hungry and you did not give me food; I was thirsty and you did not give me drink;

43 I was a stranger and you did not take me in; I was naked and you did not clothe me; I was sick and in prison and you did not visit me.

44 Then they also will answer and say, Our lord, when did we see thee hungry or thirsty or a stranger or naked or sick or in the prison, and did not minister to thee?

45 Then he will answer and say to them, Truly I say to you, Inasmuch as you did not do it to one of these least ones, you also did not do it to me.

46 And these shall go into everlasting torment, and the righteous into eternal life.

CHAPTER 26

WHEN Jesus had finished all these sayings, he said to his disciples,

2 You know that after two days the passover will come, and the Son of man will be betrayed to be crucified.

3 Then the high priests and the scribes and the elders of the people assembled in the courtyard of the high priest, who is called Caiaphas.

4 And they took counsel concerning Jesus, to arrest him by treachery and kill him.

5 And they said, Not on the feast day, lest it cause a riot among the people.

6 ¶And when Jesus was at Bethany in the house of Simon the leper,

7 A woman came to him with an alabaster vessel of precious perfume, and she poured it upon the head of Jesus, while he was reclining.

8 When his disciples saw it, they were displeased, and said, Why this waste?

9 For it could have been sold for a great sum, and given to the poor.

10 But Jesus understood it and said to them, Why are you troubling the woman? She has done a good work to me.

11 For you always have the poor with you, but you will not have me always.

12 But this one who poured the perfume on my body did it as for my burial.

13 And truly I say to you, Wherever this my gospel is preached throughout the world, what she has done will also be told as a memorial to her.

14 ¶Then one of the twelve, called Judah of Iscariot, went to the high priests;

15 And he said to them, What are you willing to give me, if I deliver him to you? And they promised him thirty pieces of silver.

16 And from that time he sought an opportunity to betray him.

17 ¶On the first day of unleavened bread, the disciples came up to Jesus and said to him, Where do you wish us to prepare the passover for you to eat?

18 And he said to them, Go into the city to a certain man, and say to him, Our Master says, My time has come, I will observe the passover with my disciples at your house.

19 And his disciples did as Jesus had commanded them; and they prepared the passover.

20 And when it was evening, he was reclining with his twelve disciples.

21 And while they were eating he said, Truly I say to you that one of you will betray me.

22 And they felt very sad, and began to say to him one by one, Is it I, my Lord?

23 And he answered, saying, He who dips his hand with me in the dish will betray me.

24 The Son of man is going just as it is written concerning him; but woe to the man by whose hand the Son of man is betrayed! It would have been far better for that man never to have been born.

25 Then Judah the traitor answered, saying, Master, perhaps it is I? Jesus said to him, You say that.

26 ¶While they were eating, Jesus took bread and blessed it and broke it, and gave it to his disciples, and said, Take, eat; this is my body.

27 Then he took the cup and gave thanks, and gave it to them, saying, Take, drink of it, all of you.

28 This is my blood of the new testament which is shed for many for the remission of sins.

29 But I say to you, henceforth I shall not drink from this fruit of the vine until the day when I drink it anew with you in the kingdom of God.

30 And they offered praise, and went out to the mount of Olives.

31 ¶Then Jesus said to them, All of you will deny me this night; for it is written, I will smite the shepherd, and the sheep of his flock will be scattered.

32 But after I am risen, I will be in Galilee before you.

33 Peter answered, saying to him,

Even if every man should deny you, I will never deny you.

34 Jesus said to him, Truly I say to you that in this very night, before the cock crows, you will deny me three times.

35 Peter said to him, Even if I must die with you, I will never deny you. All the disciples said likewise.

36 ¶Then Jesus came with them to a place which is called Gethsemane, and he said to his disciples, Sit down here while I go to pray.

37 And he took Peter and the two sons of Zebedee, and began to be sorrowful and depressed.

38 He said to them, My soul is sorrowful even to death; wait for me here and watch with me.

39 And he went a little further and fell on his face and prayed, saying, O my Father, if it be possible, let this cup pass from me; but let it be, not as I will, but as thou wilt.

40 Then he came to his disciples and found them sleeping, and he said to Peter, So, you were not able to watch with me even for one hour?

41 Awake and pray, that you may not enter into temptation; the spirit indeed is ready, but the body is weak.

42 He went away again the second time and prayed and said, O my Father, if this cup cannot pass, and if I must drink it, let it be according to thy will.

43 He came again and found them sleeping, for their eyes were heavy.

44 And he left them and went away again and prayed the third time, and said the same words.

45 Then he came to his disciples and said to them, Sleep from now on and get your rest; behold, the hour has come, and the Son of man will be delivered into the hands of sinners.

46 Arise, let us go; behold, he who is to betray me has arrived.

47 ¶While he was speaking, behold, Judah the traitor, one of the twelve, came and with him a large crowd with swords and staves, from the high priests and the elders of the people.

48 Now Judah the traitor had given them a sign, saying, He whom I kiss is he; arrest him.

49 And immediately he came up to Jesus and said, Peace, Master; and he kissed him.

50 Jesus said to him, Is it for this that you have come, my friend? Then they came near and laid hands on Jesus, and arrested him.

51 And behold, one of those who were with Jesus stretched out his hand and drew a sword, and struck it at the servant of the high priest, and cut off his ear.

52 Then Jesus said to him, Return the sword to its place; for all who take swords will die by swords.

53 Or do you think that I cannot ask of my Father, and he will now raise up for me more than twelve legions of angels?

54 How then could the scriptures be fulfilled, that it must be so?

55 At that very hour Jesus said to the people, Have you come out with swords and staves to arrest me like a bandit? I sat with you every day, teaching in the temple, and you did not arrest me.

56 But this has happened so that the scriptures of the prophets might be fulfilled. Then all the disciples left him, and fled.

57 ¶And those who had arrested Jesus took him to Caiaphas the high priest, where the scribes and the elders had assembled.

58 But Simon Peter followed him at a distance, up to the courtyard of the high priest, and he went inside and sat with the soldiers to see the end.

59 Now the high priests and the elders and the whole council were seeking witnesses against Jesus so that they might put him to death.

60 But they could not find any; then there came a great many false witnesses; but at the end two came forward

61 And said, This man says, I can tear down the temple of God and build it in three days.

62 And the high priest stood up and said to him, You are not answering

anything. What is it that these men testify against you?

63 But Jesus was silent. Then the high priest answered, saying to him, I adjure you by the living God, to tell us if you are the Christ, the Son of God?

64 Jesus said to him, You say that. But I say to you that from henceforth you will see the Son of man sitting at the right hand of power and coming upon the clouds of the sky.

65 The high priest then tore his clothes and said, Behold, he is blaspheming; why therefore do we need witnesses? Behold, you have now heard his blasphemy.

66 What else do you want? They answered, saying, He is guilty of death.

67 Then they spat in his face, and struck him on his head, and others beat him,

68 Saying, O Christ, prophesy to us; who struck you?

69 ¶Now Peter sat outside in the courtyard; and a maidservant came up to him and said, You also were with Jesus the Nazarene.

70 But he denied it before all of them, saying, I do not understand what you are saying.

71 And as he was going to the porch, another one saw him and she said to them, This man was also there with Jesus the Nazarene.

72 Again he denied it with oaths, saying, I do not know the man.

73 After a while, those who were standing came up and said to Peter, Truly you also are one of them, for even your speech proves it.

74 Then he began to curse and to swear, saying, I do not know the man. At that very hour the cock crowed.

75 And Peter remembered the word which Jesus had said to him, Before the cock crows, you will deny me three times. And he went outside and wept bitterly.

CHAPTER 27

WHEN it was morning, the high priests and the elders of the people took counsel concerning Jesus, how to put him to death.

2 So they bound him and took him and delivered him to Pilate the governor.

3 ¶Then Judah the traitor, when he saw that Jesus was convicted, repented, and went away and brought back the same thirty pieces of silver to the high priests and the elders.

4 And he said, I have sinned, because I have betrayed innocent blood. But they said to him, What is that to us? That is your problem.

5 Then he threw the silver into the temple and departed; and he went and hanged himself.

6 The high priests took the silver and said, It is not lawful to put it into the house of offerings, because it is the price of blood.

7 And they took counsel, and bought with it the potter's field for a cemetery for strangers.

8 On this account that field is called The Field of Blood, to this day.

9 ¶Then what was spoken by the prophet was fulfilled, namely, I took the thirty pieces of silver, the costly price which was bargained with the children of Israel,

10 And I gave them for the potter's field, as the Lord commanded me.

11 And Jesus stood before the governor; and the governor asked him, saying, Are you the King of the Jews? Jesus said to him, That is what you say.

12 And while the chief priests and elders were accusing him, he gave no answer.

13 Then Pilate said to him, Do you not hear how much they testify against you?

14 But he did not answer him, not even a word; and because of this Pilate marvelled greatly.

15 Now on every feast day it was the custom of the governor to release one prisoner to the people, anyone whom they wanted.

16 They had a well-known prisoner, called Bar-Abba, who was bound.

17 When they were gathered together, Pilate said to them, Whom do you want me to release to you? Bar-Abba or Jesus who is called the Christ?

18 For Pilate knew that because of envy they had delivered him.

19 ¶When the governor was sitting on his judgment seat, his wife sent to him and said to him, Have nothing to do with that righteous man; for today I have suffered a great deal in my dream because of him.

20 But the high priests and the elders urged the people to ask for Bar-Abba, and to destroy Jesus.

21 And the governor answered, saying to them, Which of these two do you want me to release to you? They said, Bar-Abba.

22 Pilate said to them, What shall I then do with Jesus who is called the Christ? They all said, Let him be crucified.

23 Pilate said to them, What evil has he done? But they cried out the more and said, Let him be crucified.

24 ¶Now when Pilate saw that he was gaining nothing, but that instead confusion was increasing, he took water and washed his hands before the people, and said, I am innocent of the blood of this righteous man; do as you please.

25 All the people then answered, saying, Let his blood be on us and on our children.

26 ¶Then he released to them Bar-Abba, and had Jesus scourged with whips and delivered to be crucified.

27 Then the soldiers of the governor took Jesus into the Praetorium, and the whole company gathered around him.

28 And they removed his clothes and put on him a scarlet robe.

29 And they wove a crown of thorns and put it on his head, and a reed in his right hand; and they fell on their knees before him, and were mocking him and saying, Hail, King of the Jews!

30 And they spat in his face, and took the reed and struck him on his head.

31 And when they had mocked him, they took off the robe from him and put on him his own clothes and took him away to be crucified.

32 And as they were going out, they found a man of Cyrene, whose name was Simon, whom they compelled to carry his cross.

33 ¶And they came to a place which is called Golgotha, which is interpreted The Skull.

34 And they gave him to drink vinegar mixed with gall; and he tasted it, but he would not drink.

35 ¶And when they had crucified him, they divided his clothes by casting lots.

36 And they were sitting there and watching him.

37 And they placed above his head in writing the reason for his death: THIS IS JESUS THE KING OF THE JEWS.

38 ¶And there were crucified with him two bandits, one on his right and one on his left.

39 And those who passed by blasphemed against him, nodding their heads,

40 And saying, O you who can tear down the temple and build it in three days, deliver yourself, if you are the Son of God, and come down from the cross.

41 The high priests likewise were mocking, together with the scribes, the elders, and the Pharisees.

42 And they were saying, He saved others, but he cannot save himself. If he is the King of Israel, let him now come down from the cross, so that we may see and believe in him.

43 He trusted in God; let him save him now, if he is pleased with him; for he said, I am God's Son.

44 The bandits who were crucified with him were also reproaching him.

45 ¶Now from the sixth hour there was darkness over all the land until the ninth hour.

46 And about the ninth hour, Jesus cried out with a loud voice and said, Eli, Eli, lemana shabakthani! My God, my God, for this I was spared! [1]

47 Some of the men who were standing by, when they heard it, said, This man has called for Elijah.

48 And immediately one of them ran and took a sponge and filled it

[1] This was my destiny.

with vinegar, and put it on a reed and gave him to drink.

49 But the rest said, Wait, let us see if Elijah will come to save him.

50 ¶But Jesus again cried out with a loud voice and gave up his spirit.

51 And immediately the curtains at the door of the temple were torn in two, from the top to the bottom; and the earth quaked and rocks split;

52 And tombs were opened; and the bodies of a great many saints who were sleeping in death rose up

53 And went out; and after his resurrection, they entered into the holy city and appeared to a great many.

54 ¶When the centurion and those who were with him watching Jesus, saw the earthquake and all that had happened, they were frightened, and they said, Truly this man was the Son of God.

55 There were also many women there, who were looking from afar, those who had followed Jesus from Galilee, and who used to minister to him.

56 One of them was Mary of Magdala; and others were Mary the mother of James and Joses, and the mother of the sons of Zebedee.

57 ¶When it was evening, there came a rich man of Ramtha,[1] whose name was Joseph who was also a disciple of Jesus.

58 He went to Pilate and asked for the body of Jesus. And Pilate commanded that the body should be given to him.

59 So Joseph took the body, and wrapped it in a shroud of fine linen,

60 And laid it in his own new tomb which was hewn in a rock; and they rolled a large stone, and placed it against the door of the tomb and went away.

61 And there were there Mary of Magdala and the other Mary, who were sitting opposite the tomb.

62 ¶The next day, which is after Friday, the high priests and the Pharisees together came to Pilate,

63 And they said to him, Our lord, we have just remembered that that deceiver used to say when he was

___
[1] Arimathaea in Western versions.

alive, After three days I will rise again.

64 Now, therefore, command that precautions be taken at the tomb for three days. It is probable that his disciples may come and steal him at night, and then say to the people, He has risen from the dead; and the last deception will be worse than the first.

65 Pilate said to them, You have guards; go and take precautions as best you know.

66 So they went and kept a watch at the tomb, and together with the guards they sealed the stone.

CHAPTER 28

IN the evening of the sabbath, when the first day of the week began to dawn, there came Mary of Magdala and the other Mary to see the tomb.

2 And behold, a great earthquake took place; for the angel of the Lord came down from heaven, and went up and rolled away the stone from the door, and sat on it.

3 His appearance was like lightning, and his garments were white as snow.

4 And for fear of him the guards who were watching trembled and became as if they were dead.

5 But the angel answered, saying to the women, You need not be afraid; for I know that you are seeking Jesus who was crucified.

6 He is not here, for he has risen, just as he had said. Come, see the place where our Lord was laid.

7 And go quickly and tell his disciples that he has risen from the dead; and behold, he will go before you to Galilee; there you will see him; lo, I have told you.

8 And they went away hurriedly from the tomb with fear and with great joy, running to tell his disciples.

9 And behold, Jesus met them and said to them, Peace be to you. And they came up and laid hold of his feet and worshipped him.

10 Then Jesus said to them, Do not be afraid; but go and tell my brethren to go to Galilee, and there they shall see me.

11 ¶While they were going, some of the guards came into the city and told the high priests everything that had happened.

12 So they gathered with the elders and took counsel; and they gave money, not a small sum, to the guards,

13 Telling them, Say that his disciples came by night and stole him while we were sleeping.

14 And if this should be heard by the governor, we will appeal to him and declare that you are blameless.

15 So they took the money and did as they were instructed; and this word has gone out among the Jews even to this day.

16 ¶The eleven disciples then went to Galilee to a mountain where Jesus had promised to meet them.

17 And when they saw him, they worshipped him; but some of them were doubtful.

18 And Jesus came up and spoke with them, and said to them, All power in heaven and on earth has been given to me. Just as my Father has sent me I am also sending you.

19 Go, therefore, and convert all nations; and baptize them in the name of the Father and of the Son and of the Holy Spirit;

20 And teach them to obey everything that I have commanded you; and, lo, I am with you always, to the end of the world. Amen.

THE GOSPEL ACCORDING TO

SAINT MARK

CHAPTER 1

THE beginning of the gospel of Jesus Christ, the Son of God.

2 As it is written in Isaiah the prophet, Behold I send my messenger before your face, that he may prepare your way,

3 The voice that cries in the wilderness: Make ready the way of the Lord and straighten his highways.

4 John was in the wilderness, baptizing and preaching the baptism of repentance for the forgiveness of sins,

5 And the whole province of Judea went out to him, and all the people of Jerusalem; and he baptized them in the river Jordan, when they confessed their sins.

6 ¶John wore a dress of camel's hair, with a girdle of leather fastened around his loins; and his food was locusts and wild honey.

7 And he preached, saying, Behold, there is coming after me one who is mightier than I am, even the strings of whose shoes I am not good enough to bend down and untie.

8 I have baptized you with water; but he will baptize you with the Holy Spirit.

9 ¶And it came to pass in those days, that Jesus came from Nazareth of Galilee, and was baptized in the Jordan by John.

10 And immediately, as he came up out of the water, he saw the sky was wide open, and the Spirit like a dove came down upon him.

11 And a voice came from heaven, You are my beloved Son, I am pleased with you.

12 And immediately the Spirit drove him out into the wilderness.

13 And he was there in the wilderness forty days, being tested by Satan; and he was with the wild beasts; and the angels ministered to him.

14 ¶But after John was delivered up, Jesus came to Galilee, preaching the gospel of the kingdom of God,

15 Saying, The time has come to an end, and the kingdom of God is at hand; repent and believe in the gospel.

16 As he walked beside the sea of Galilee, he saw Simon and Andrew his brother throwing their nets into the sea; for they were fishermen.

17 And Jesus said to them, Follow me and I will make you fishers of men.

18 And straightway they left their nets and followed him.

19 And when he went a little further, he saw James the son of Zebedee and his brother John; they also were in a boat mending their nets.

20 And he called them; and immediately they left their father Zebedee with the hired men, and followed him.

21 When they entered into Capernaum, straightway he taught in their synagogues on the sabbaths.

22 And they were amazed at his teaching; for he taught them as one with authority, and not as their scribes.

23 ¶And there was in their synagogue a man who had in him an unclean spirit; and he cried out,

24 Saying, Jesus of Nazareth, what have we in common? Have you come to destroy us? I know who you are, Holy One of God.

25 And Jesus rebuked him, saying, Be silent and come out of him.

26 And the unclean spirit threw him down and cried out in a loud voice and left him.

27 And they were all astonished, and kept asking one another, saying, What does this mean? and what is this new teaching, that with such a power he commands even unclean spirits and they obey him?

28 ¶And his fame immediately spread throughout the country of Galilee.

29 Then they went out of the synagogue and came to the house of Simon and Andrew, together with James and John.

30 And Simon's mother-in-law was lying sick with fever; and they spoke to him about her.

31 And he went and held her hand, and lifted her up; and immediately the fever left her, and she ministered to them.

32 In the evening towards sunset, they brought to him all who were seriously sick, and the insane.

33 And the whole city was gathered at the door.

34 And he healed many who were seriously sick with various diseases, and he restored many who were insane; and he did not allow the insane to speak because some of them were his acquaintances.

35 And in the morning he rose up very early and went away to a lonely place, and there prayed.

36 And Simon and those who were with him were looking for him.

37 And when they found him, they said to him, Everyone is seeking you.

38 He said to them, Let us walk to the neighboring towns and cities, so that I may preach there also, because I came for this.

39 And he preached in all their synagogues throughout Galilee, and cast out demons.

40 And there came to him a leper, who fell down at his feet and begged him, saying, If you will, you can make me clean.

41 And Jesus had mercy on him, and stretched out his hand and touched him, and said, I am willing; be clean.

42 And in that hour his leprosy disappeared from him, and he became clean.

43 And Jesus rebuked him and put him out,

44 And said to him, Look, why are you telling it to the people? But go away, show yourself to the priests and present an offering for the sake of your cleansing, according to that which Moses commanded, as their testimonial.

45 But when he went out, he began to publish it still more, and to spread the word, so that Jesus was no longer able to enter the city openly, but he

remained outside in a lonely place; and yet they came to him from everywhere.

CHAPTER 2

AND Jesus entered again into Capernaum for a few days; and when they heard that he was in a certain house,

2 A great many gathered together so that it was impossible to hold them, not even in front of the entrance; so he spoke a few words to them.

3 And they came to him, and brought a paralyzed man, carried by four men.

4 But as they were unable to come near him because of the crowd, they went up to the roof and uncovered it over the place where Jesus was; and they lowered the quilt in which the paralyzed man lay.

5 When Jesus saw their faith, he said to the paralytic, My son, your sins are forgiven.

6 Now some of the scribes and Pharisees were sitting there, and they reasoned in their hearts,

7 Why does this man speak blasphemy? Who can forgive sins except God only?

8 But Jesus perceived in his spirit that they were reasoning among themselves, and he said to them, Why do you reason these things in your heart?

9 Which is the easier, to say to the paralytic, Your sins are forgiven; or to say, Rise, take up your quilt and walk?

10 But that you may know that the Son of man has power on earth to forgive sins, he said to the paralytic,

11 I tell you, Rise, take up your quilt, and go to your house.

12 And immediately he rose, and took up his quilt and went out before the eyes of them all; and they were all amazed, and gave glory to God, saying, We have never seen anything like it.

13 ¶And he went out again by the seaside, and all the people kept coming to him, and he taught them.

14 And as he passed by, he saw Levi the son of Alphaeus,[1] sitting at the custom house, and he said to him, Follow me; and he got up and followed him.

15 And it came to pass that while he was a guest at his house, a great many revenue officers [2] and sinners were also guests with Jesus and his disciples; for there were many, and they followed him.

16 And when the scribes and the Pharisees saw him eating with the revenue officers and sinners, they said to his disciples, Why does he eat and drink with revenue officers and sinners?

17 When Jesus heard it, he said to them, Those who are healthy need no doctor, but those who are seriously sick; I came not to call the righteous, but sinners.

18 The disciples of John and of the Pharisees were fasting; and they came and said to him, Why do the disciples of John and of the Pharisees fast, and your own disciples do not fast?

19 Jesus said to them, Can the sons of the wedding feast fast as long as the bridegroom is with them? No!

20 But the days will come when the bridegroom is taken away from them; then in that day they will fast.

21 No man takes a new patch and sews it on a worn out garment, so that the new patch may not weaken the old, and the hole become larger.

22 And no man pours new wine into old wineskins, so that the wine may not rend the skins and the skins be ruined and the wine run out; but they pour new wine into new wineskins.

23 ¶And it came to pass that while Jesus was going through the wheat fields on the sabbath, his disciples walked and pulled off the heads of wheat.

24 And the Pharisees said to him, Look what they are doing on the sabbath! that which is unlawful.

25 Jesus said to them, Have you not read what David did when he was in need and hungry, he and those who were with him?

26 How he entered into the house of God when Abiathar was the chief

---

[1] Aramaic, *Khalpi*.   [2] Or publicans.

priest, and ate the bread which was on the table of the Lord, which was not lawful to be eaten except by the priests, and he gave it also to those who were with him?

27 And he said to them, The sabbath was made for the sake of man, and not man for the sake of the sabbath.

28 The Son of man therefore is the Lord also of the sabbath.

CHAPTER 3

JESUS entered again into the synagogue, and there was a man there whose hand was withered.

2 And they watched him to see if he would heal him on the sabbath, that they might accuse him.

3 And he said to the man whose hand was withered, Stand up in the center.

4 Then he said to them also, Is it lawful to do good or evil on the sabbath, to save a life or to destroy it? But they were silent.

5 And he looked at them with anger, sad because of the hardness of their hearts; and he said to the man, Stretch out your hand, and he stretched it out; and his hand was restored.

6 ¶And the Pharisees immediately went out with the Herodians, and they took counsel concerning him how to do away with him.

7 So Jesus went to the sea with his disciples; and a great many people from Galilee followed him, and from Judea

8 And from Jerusalem and from Idumea and from around the Jordan and from Tyre and from Sidon; large crowds, who had heard all that he was doing, came to him.

9 And he told his disciples to bring a boat to him, because of the crowds, so that they might not press on him,

10 For he was healing so many that others pushed toward him so as to touch him.

11 And those who were afflicted with unclean spirits,[1] when they saw him, fell down before him and cried,

saying, You are indeed the Son of God.

12 And he cautioned them earnestly not to make him known.

13 ¶And he went up to the mountain, and called those he wanted; and they came to him.

14 And he chose twelve to be with him, that he might send them to preach,

15 And to have power to heal the sick and cast out devils;

16 Namely Simon surnamed Peter

17 And James the son of Zebedee and John the brother of James, surnamed B'nai Rakhshi, which means sons of thunder,

18 And Andrew and Philip and Bartholomew and Matthew and Thomas and James the son of Alphaeus and Thaddaeus and Simon the Zealot

19 And Judah of Iscariot, who betrayed him. And they came into a certain house.

20 And the crowd gathered again, so that they could not eat bread.

21 And his relatives heard of it, and went out to seize him, for they said, He has lost his mind.

22 ¶And the scribes who had come down from Jerusalem said, Beelzebub is with him, and, By the prince of demons he is casting out demons.

23 And Jesus called them, and said to them in parables, How can Satan cast out Satan?

24 If a kingdom is divided against itself, that kingdom cannot stand.

25 And if a household is divided against itself, that household cannot stand.

26 And if Satan rises up against himself and is divided, he cannot stand, but that is his end.

27 No man can enter into a strong man's house and plunder his goods, unless he first bind the strong man; and then he plunders his house.

28 Truly I say to you that all sins and blasphemies which men are guilty of shall be forgiven to them.

29 But he who blasphemes against the Holy Spirit shall never be forgiven, but is guilty before the everlasting judgment;

[1] Insane.

30 For they had said, He has an unclean spirit.[1]

31 ¶Then there came his mother and his brothers and stood outside, and they sent in to call him.

32 But the people were sitting around him; and they said to him, Behold, your mother and your brothers are outside, asking for you.

33 And he answered, saying to them, Who is my mother and who are my brothers?

34 And he looked at those who sat near him and said, Behold my mother and behold my brothers.

35 For whoever does the will of God is my brother and my sister and my mother.

CHAPTER 4

AGAIN he began to teach by the seaside; and many people gathered to him, so that he went up and sat in a boat on the sea; and all the people stood on the land by the sea.

2 And he taught them many things by parables, and in his teaching he said,

3 Listen: Behold, a sower went out to sow.

4 And when he had sown, some seed fell on the roadside, and the birds came and ate it.

5 Other seed fell upon the rock, where there was not sufficient soil; and it sprang up sooner because the ground was not deep enough;

6 But when the sun shone, it was scorched, and because it had no root, it dried up.

7 And other seed fell among thistles, and the thistles sprang up and choked it, and it bore no fruit.

8 But other seed fell in good soil, and it sprang up and grew and bore fruit, some thirty, and some sixty, and some a hundredfold.

9 And he said, He who has ears to hear, let him hear.

10 When they were alone, those who were with him together with the twelve asked him about that parable.

11 And Jesus said to them, To you is given to know the mystery of the

kingdom of God, but to outsiders everything has to be explained by parables.

12 For seeing they see, and yet do not perceive; and hearing they hear, and yet do not understand; if they should return, their sins would be forgiven.

13 And he said to them, Do you not understand this parable? How then will you understand all the parables?

14 ¶The sower who sowed, sowed the word.

15 Those on the roadside are those in whom the word is sown; and when they have heard it, Satan comes immediately and takes away the word which is sown in their hearts.

16 And those which were sown upon the rock are those who when they have heard the word, immediately receive it with joy;

17 And they have no root in themselves, but last for a while; and when trouble or persecution comes because of the word, they soon stumble.

18 And those which were sown among thistles are those who have heard the word,

19 And the thoughts of this world and the deception of wealth and the lusts of other things enter in and choke the word and bear no fruit.

20 And those which were sown in good soil are those who hear the word and receive it and bear fruit, one thirty, and one sixty, and one a hundredfold.

21 ¶And he said to them, Is a lamp brought and put under a basket or under a bed? Is it not put on a lamp stand?

22 For there is nothing hidden which will not be uncovered; and nothing done in secret which will not be revealed.

23 If any man has ears to hear, let him hear.

24 ¶And he said to them, Take heed what you hear; with what measure you measure it will be measured to you again and will increase, especially to them who hear.

25 For to him who has will be given; and from him who has not,

---

[1] He is crazy.

even that which he has will be taken away.

26 ¶And he said, Such is the kingdom of God as a man who casts seed into the ground.

27 And he sleeps and rises up night and day, and the seed springs up and grows while he is not aware of it.

28 For the earth causes it to yield fruit; and yet first it becomes a blade of grass, then an ear, and at last a full grain in the ear.

29 But when the fruit is ripe, then immediately comes the sickle, because the harvest is ready.

30 ¶And he said, To what shall we compare the kingdom of God? and with what parable shall we picture it?

31 It is just like a grain of mustard seed, which, when it is sown in the earth, is the smallest of all the seeds on earth.

32 But when it is sown, it springs up and becomes greater than all the herbs, and puts forth large branches, so that the birds can settle under their shadow.

33 ¶Jesus talked to them with parables like these, such parables as they were able to hear.

34 And without parables he did not speak to them; but to his disciples, among themselves, he explained everything.

35 On that day at evening, he said to them, Let us cross over to the landing place.

36 And they left the people, and took him away while he was in the boat. And there were other boats with them.

37 And there arose a heavy storm and wind, and the waves kept beating into the boat, so that the boat was nearly filled.

38 But Jesus was sleeping on a blanket in the stern of the boat; and they came and roused him and said to him, Teacher, do you not care that we are perishing?

39 So he got up and rebuked the wind, and said to the sea, Peace, be still. And the wind quieted down, and there was a great calm.

40 And he said to them, Why are you so fearful? and why do you have no faith? And they were exceedingly afraid, and said to each other, Oh, who is this, that even the wind and the sea obey him?

CHAPTER 5

AND they reached the port on the other side of the sea in the country of the Gadarenes.

2 And as he went out of the boat, he was met by a man from the cemetery, who had an unclean spirit.

3 He lived in the cemetery, and no man could bind him in chains,

4 Because whenever he was bound with fetters and chains, he broke the chains and cut the fetters, and no man could control him.

5 And always, night and day, he was in the cemetery and in the mountains, crying aloud and cutting himself with stones.

6 When he saw Jesus from afar, he ran and worshipped him,

7 And he cried with a loud voice, saying, What have we in common, Jesus, Son of the most high God? I adjure you by God, not to torment me.

8 For he said to him, Get out of the man, O you unclean spirit.

9 And Jesus asked him, What is your name? And he said to him, Our name is Legion, because we are many.

10 And he begged him eagerly that he would not send him out of the country.

11 Now there was near the mountain a large herd of swine feeding.

12 And the lunatics begged him saying, Send us to the swine, that we may attack [1] them.

13 And he permitted them. And the lunatics went out and attacked the swine; and the herd ran to the steep rocks, and fell into the sea; they were about two thousand, and they were drowned in the water.

14 And those who fed them, fled, and told it in the city and also in the villages. So they went out to see what had happened.

[1] The Aramaic word used in the manuscript means *to attack*. Had it meant *to enter into*, as in some other versions, it would read differently.

15 And they came to Jesus, and saw the lunatic,[1] clothed and well behaved, and sitting down quietly, even the one who once had the legion within him; and they were afraid.

16 And those who saw it told them just what happened to the lunatic and also to the swine.

17 So they began to urge him to leave their border.

18 As he went up to the boat, the lunatic begged him to remain with him.

19 And he would not permit him, but said to him, Go to your home, to your own people, and tell them what the Lord has done for you, and that he has had mercy on you.

20 And he went away, and began to preach in the ten cities about what Jesus had done for him; and they were all astonished.

21 ¶When Jesus crossed in the boat to the other side, large crowds again gathered around him while he was by the sea.

22 And there came one of the leaders of the synagogue, whose name was Jairus; and when he saw him, he fell at his feet,

23 And he besought him earnestly and said to him, My daughter is very seriously ill; come and lay your hand on her, and she will be healed, and live.

24 So Jesus went with him; and a large multitude followed him, and they pressed about him.

25 And there was a woman who had had a hemorrhage for twelve years,

26 Who had suffered much at the hands of many doctors, and had spent everything she had and was not helped at all, but rather became worse.

27 When she heard about Jesus, she came through the dense crowd from behind him, and touched his cloak;

28 For she said, If I can only touch his cloak, I shall live.

29 And immediately the hemorrhage was dried up; and she felt in her body that she was healed of her disease.

30 Jesus instantly knew that some power had gone out of him; so he turned around to the people and said, Who touched my garments?

31 His disciples said to him, You see the people pressing against you, and yet you say, Who touched me?

32 And he was looking round to see who had done this.

33 But the woman, frightened and trembling, because she knew what had happened to her, came and fell before him and told him the whole truth.

34 He said to her, My daughter, your faith has healed you; go in peace and be healed of your disease.

35 While he was still talking, some men came from the house of the leader of the synagogue, saying, Your daughter is dead; why do you trouble the Teacher?

36 Jesus heard the word which they spoke, and he said to the leader of the synagogue, Fear not, only believe.

37 And he did not permit any man to go with him, except Simon Peter and James and John the brother of James.

38 And they came to the house of the leader of the synagogue, and Jesus saw them in a tumult, weeping and wailing.

39 So he entered and said to them, Why are you excited and crying? The little girl is not dead, but she is asleep.

40 And they laughed at him. But Jesus put them all out, and took the little girl's father and mother and those who were with him, and he entered where the little girl was laid.

41 And he took the little girl by her hand, and said to her, Talitha, koomi, Little girl, rise up.

42 And immediately the little girl got up and walked; for she was twelve years old. And they were astonished with great amazement.

43 But he commanded them that no man should know this; and he told them to give her something to eat.

[1] Mark here refers to one lunatic who conversed with Jesus and then he mentions lunatics in ver. 12. There were doubtless many. Cf. Matt. 8:28.

CHAPTER 6

AND Jesus went out from thence and came to his own city; and his disciples followed him.

2 When the sabbath came, he began to teach in the synagogue, and many who heard him were astonished, and said, Whence did he receive all this? and what wisdom is this which is given to him, that wonders like these are wrought by his hands?

3 Is he not the carpenter, the son of Mary, and the brother of James and Joses and Judas and Simon? and behold, are not his sisters here with us? And they denounced him.

4 And Jesus said to them, There is no prophet who is belittled, except in his own city and among his own brothers and in his own house.

5 And he could not perform even a single miracle there, except that he laid his hand on a few sick people and healed them.

6 And he wondered at their lack of faith. And he travelled in the villages teaching.

7 ¶Then he called his twelve, and began to send them two by two; and he gave them power over unclean spirits, to cast them out.

8 And he commanded them not to take anything for the journey, except a staff only; no bag, no bread, no copper money in their purses;

9 But to wear sandals, and not to wear two shirts.

10 And he said to them, Whatever house you enter, stay there until you leave that place.

11 And whoever will not receive you nor hear you, when you leave that place, shake off the sand under your feet as a testimony against them. Truly I say to you, It will be easier for Sodom and Gomorrah in the day of judgment than for that city.

12 ¶And they went out and preached that they should repent.

13 And they cast out many demons, and anointed with oil many who were sick, and they were healed.

14 ¶And Herod the king heard about Jesus, for his name was known to him; and he said, John the Baptist has risen from the dead; this is why miracles are performed by him.

15 Others said, He is Elijah. And yet others, He is a prophet, just like one of the prophets.

16 But when Herod heard it, he said, It is John, whom I beheaded; it is he who has risen from the dead.

17 ¶For this same Herod had sent out and arrested John and cast him into prison, because of Herodias, wife of his brother Philip, whom he had married.

18 For John had said to Herod, It is not lawful for you to marry your brother's wife.

19 But Herodias was bitter towards him, and wanted to kill him; but she could not.

20 For Herod was afraid of John, because he knew that he was a righteous and holy man, and he guarded him; and he heard that he was doing a great many things, and he heard him gladly.

21 Then came a state occasion, when Herod on his birthday gave a banquet to his officials and captains and the leading men of Galilee.

22 And the daughter of Herodias entered and danced, and she pleased Herod and the guests who were with him; and the king said to the little girl, Ask me whatever you wish, and I will give it to you.

23 And he swore to her, Whatever you ask me, I will give you, as much as half of my kingdom.

24 She went out and said to her mother, What shall I ask him? She said to her, The head of John the Baptist.

25 And immediately she entered hesitantly to the king, and said to him, I do wish in this very hour that you might give me on a tray the head of John the Baptist.

26 And the king was exceedingly sorry; but because of the oaths and because of the guests, he did not wish to refuse her.

27 So the king immediately sent the executioner and commanded to bring the head of John. And he went and beheaded John in the prison,

28 And brought the head on a tray

and gave it to the girl; and the girl gave it to her mother.

29 And when his disciples heard of it, they came and took up his body and buried it in a grave.

30 ¶And the apostles gathered together to Jesus, and told him everything they had done and what they had taught.

31 And he said to them, Come, let us go to the wilderness all alone and rest awhile; for there were many coming and going, and they had no chance even to eat.

32 So they went away in a boat to a desert place by themselves.

33 And many people saw them when they were leaving and they knew them, and from all the cities they hurried by land and reached the place ahead of him.

34 And when Jesus went out he saw large crowds, and he had compassion on them because they were like sheep without a shepherd; and he began to teach them a great many things.

35 ¶And when it was getting late, his disciples came up to him and said to him, This is a desert place, and it is getting late;

36 Dismiss them so that they may go away to the farms and villages around us and buy bread for themselves; for they have nothing to eat.

37 He said to them, You give them to eat. They said to him, Shall we go and buy two hundred penny's worth of bread and give it to them to eat?

38 He said to them, Go and see how many loaves of bread you have here. And when they found out, they said to him, Five loaves of bread and two fish.

39 And he commanded them to make everyone sit down in groups on the grass.

40 So they sat down in groups, by hundreds and by fifties.

41 Then he took the five loaves of bread and the two fish, and he looked up to heaven and blessed and broke the loaves of bread, and gave them to his disciples to place before them;

and they divided the two fish among them all.

42 And they all ate and were satisfied.

43 And they took up the fragments of bread, twelve full baskets, and also of the fish.

44 And those who ate the bread were five thousand men.

45 ¶And immediately he urged his disciples to go up into the boat, and go in advance of him to the port at Bethsaida, while he dismissed the people.

46 And when he had dismissed them, he went up to the mountain to pray.

47 When evening came, the boat was in the midst of the sea and he was alone on the land.

48 And he saw them struggling as they were rowing, for the wind was against them; and in the fourth watch of the night, Jesus came to them, walking on the water, and he wanted to pass by them.

49 But when they saw him walking on the water, they thought it was a false vision, and they cried out;

50 For they all saw him and were frightened. And immediately he spoke to them, saying, Have courage, it is I, do not be afraid.

51 And he got into the boat with them and the wind quieted down; and they marvelled exceedingly, and were astonished.

52 Neither did they understand the miracle of the loaves of bread, because their hearts were confused.

53 ¶And when they had crossed to the port, they came to the land of Gennesaret.

54 And when they got out of the boat, the people of that place immediately knew him.

55 And they came running throughout that land; and began to bring those who were seriously sick, carrying them in quilts to places where they heard he was.

56 And wherever he entered into villages and cities, they laid the sick in the streets, and begged him that they might even touch the edge of his

robe; and all who touched him were healed.

CHAPTER 7

THEN there gathered to him Pharisees and scribes who had come from Jerusalem.

2 And they saw some of his disciples eating bread with their hands unwashed, and they reproached them.

3 For all the Jews, even the Pharisees, unless their hands were washed carefully, would not eat, because they strictly observed the tradition of the elders.

4 Even the things from the market, if they were not washed, they would not eat. And there are a great many other things which they have accepted to obey, such as the washing of cups and pots and copper utensils and the bedding of dead men.

5 And the scribes and Pharisees asked him, Why do your disciples not walk according to the tradition of the elders, but eat bread with their hands unwashed?

6 He said to them, The prophet Isaiah well prophesied about you, O hypocrites, as it is written, This people honor me with their lips, but their heart is far away from me.

7 And they worship me in vain when they teach the doctrines of the commandments of men.

8 For you have ignored the commandment of God, and you observe the tradition of men, such as the washing of cups and pots and a great many other things like these.

9 He said to them, You certainly do injustice to the commandment of God so as to sustain your own tradition.

10 For Moses said, Honor your father and your mother; and he who curses father or mother, let him be put to death.

11 But you say, A man may say to his father or his mother, What is left over is Corban (my offering);

12 And yet you do not let him do anything for his father or mother.

13 So you dishonor the word of God for the sake of the tradition which you have established; and you do a great many other things like these.

14 ¶Then Jesus called all the people and said to them, Hear me, all of you, and understand.

15 There is nothing outside of a man, if it should enter into him, which can defile him; but what goes out of him, that defiles the man.

16 Who has ears to hear, let him hear.

17 When Jesus entered into the house because of the people, his disciples asked him concerning that parable.

18 And he said to them, So even you find it hard to understand? Do you not know that whatever enters into a man from outside cannot defile him?

19 Because it does not enter into his heart, but into his stomach, and then is thrown out through the intestines, thereby purifying the food.

20 It is what goes out of man which defiles the man.

21 For from within, from the hearts of men come evil thoughts, such as fornication, adultery, theft, murder,

22 Extortion, wickedness, deceit, lust, an evil eye, blasphemy, pride, foolishness;

23 All these evils come from within, and they defile the man.

24 ¶Jesus moved away from thence, and came to the borders of Tyre and Sidon, and he entered into a house, and did not want any one to know about him. And yet he could not hide himself.

25 For immediately a woman heard about him, whose daughter had an unclean spirit; and she came and fell at his feet.

26 But the woman was a heathen, from Phoenicia in Syria; and she besought him to cast out the demon from her daughter.

27 And Jesus said to her, Let the children be first filled; for it is not right to take the children's bread and throw it to the dogs.

28 But she answered, saying to him, Yes, my Lord; even the dogs eat the

children's crumbs under the tables.

29 Jesus said to her, Go your way; just because of this word, the demon has gone out of your daughter.

30 So she went to her house and found her daughter lying in bed, and the demon gone out of her.

31 ¶Again Jesus went out from the border of Tyre and Sidon, and came to the sea of Galilee, to the border of the ten cities.

32 And they brought to him a deaf and dumb man; and they asked him to lay his hand on him.

33 So he drew him aside from the people, and put his fingers into his ears; then he spat, and touched his tongue;

34 And he looked up to heaven and sighed, and he said to him, Ethpatakh, which means, Be opened.

35 And in that very hour his ears were opened, and his tongue was loosened, and he spoke plainly.

36 And he warned them not to tell this to any man; but the more he warned them, so much the more they published it.

37 And they were greatly astonished, saying, He does everything so well. He makes the deaf hear and the dumb to speak.

CHAPTER 8

IN those days, when there was a large multitude, and they had nothing to eat, he called his disciples and said to them,

2 I have pity on this people, for they have remained with me three days, and they have nothing to eat;

3 And if I dismiss them to their homes while they are hungry, they will faint on the way, for some of them have come from a distance.

4 His disciples said to him, How can any man here in this lonely place feed all of these people with bread?

5 And he asked them, How many loaves have you? They said to him, Seven.

6 So he commanded the people to sit on the ground; and he took the seven loaves of bread, and he blessed them and broke them and gave them to his disciples to set before them;

and they set them before the people.

7 And there were a few fish; and he blessed them also and commanded to set them before the people.

8 So they ate and were satisfied, and they took up seven baskets of fragments which were left over.

9 The men who ate were about four thousand; and he dismissed them.

10 ¶And immediately he went into the boat with his disciples, and he came to the country of Dalmanutha.

11 And the Pharisees came out and began to question him, and they asked him for a sign from heaven, so as to test him.

12 And he sighed in his spirit and said, Why does this generation want a sign? Truly I say to you, No sign will be given to this generation.

13 And he left them, and went up into the boat, and departed from that port.

14 ¶And they had forgotten to take bread; except one loaf they had none with them in the boat.

15 And he commanded them and said to them, Watch out, and beware of the leaven of the Pharisees and of the leaven of Herod.

16 They were reasoning among themselves and saying, It is because we have no bread.

17 But Jesus knew it and said to them, What are you thinking, because you have no bread? Do you not even yet know, and do you not understand? Is your heart still hard?

18 You have eyes, and yet do you not see? You have ears, and yet do you not hear? And do you not remember?

19 When I broke the five loaves of bread for the five thousand, how many full baskets of fragments did you take up? They said to him, Twelve.

20 He said to them, And when the seven for the four thousand, how many baskets full of fragments did you take up? They said, Seven.

21 He said to them, How is it then that even yet you cannot understand?

22 ¶And he came to Bethsaida; and they brought to him a blind man, and they besought him to touch him.

23 And he took the blind man by the hand and brought him outside the town; and he spat on his eyes and put his hands on him and asked him what he saw.

24 And he looked and said, I see men like trees walking.

25 Again he put his hands over his eyes and he was restored and saw everything clearly.

26 And he sent him to his house, saying, Do not even enter into the town, nor tell it to anyone in the town.

27 ¶And Jesus went out, and his disciples, to the towns of Caesarea of Philippi; and on the road he asked his disciples, saying to them, Who do men say that I am?

28 They said, John the Baptist; and others, Elijah; and yet others, One of the prophets.

29 Jesus said to them, But you, who do you say I am? Simon Peter answered, saying to him, You are the Christ, the Son of the living God.

30 And he warned them not to tell any man about him.

31 ¶Then he began to teach them that the Son of man would have to suffer a great deal and be rejected by the elders and the high priests and the scribes, and be killed, and rise again on the third day.

32 And he spoke that word openly. So Peter took him aside and began to rebuke him.

33 But he turned around and looked on his disciples, and he rebuked Simon, saying, Get behind me, Satan; for you are not thinking the things of God, but of men.

34 And Jesus called the people together with his disciples, and said to them, He who wishes to come after me, let him deny himself and take up his cross and follow me.

35 For whoever wishes to save his life will lose it; and whoever loses his life for my sake and the sake of my gospel will save it.

36 For how could a man be benefited if he should gain the whole world and lose his life?

37 Or what could a man give in exchange for his life?

38 Whoever, therefore, is ashamed of me and of my words in this sinful and adulterous generation, the Son of man will also be ashamed of him when he comes in the glory of his Father with his holy angels.

CHAPTER 9

AND he said to them, Truly I say to you that there are men standing here who shall not taste death till they see that the kingdom of God has come with power.

2 ¶And six days after, Jesus took Peter and James and John, and brought them up to a high mountain alone; and he was transfigured before their eyes.

3 His clothes shone and became white like snow in such a manner that men on earth cannot make white.

4 And there appeared to them Moses and Elijah, talking with Jesus.

5 And Peter said to him, Teacher, it is better for us to remain here; and let us make three shelters, one for you and one for Moses and one for Elijah.

6 For he did not know what he was saying, for they were afraid.

7 And there was a cloud overshadowing them, and a voice out of the cloud said, This is my beloved Son; hear him.

8 And suddenly, when the disciples looked around, they saw no man except Jesus alone with them.

9 And as they came down from the mountain, he commanded them not to tell any man what they had seen until the Son of man had risen from the dead.

10 So they kept that saying to themselves, and they wanted to know what risen from the dead meant.

11 ¶And they asked him, saying, Why then do the scribes say that Elijah must first come?

12 He said to them, Elijah does come first to prepare everything; and as it is written concerning the Son of man that he will suffer much and be rejected.

13 But I say to you that Elijah has come, and they did with him what-

ever they pleased, as it is written of him.

14 ¶And when he came to his disciples, he saw a large crowd with them and the scribes debating with them.

15 And immediately all the people saw him and were greatly surprised, and they ran to greet him.

16 And he asked the scribes, What do you debate with them?

17 One of the multitude answered, saying, Teacher, I brought my son to you, for he has a spirit of dumbness.

18 And whenever it seizes him, it troubles him; and he foams and gnashes his teeth and faints. And I asked your disciples to cast it out, but they could not.

19 Jesus answered and said to him, O faithless generation, how long shall I be with you? and how long shall I preach to you? Bring him to me.

20 And they brought the boy to Jesus; and when the spirit seized him, it immediately troubled him; and he fell on the ground, gasping and foaming.

21 So Jesus asked his father, How long has he been like this? He said to him, From his childhood.

22 And many times it has thrown him into the fire and into the water to destroy him; but whatever you can do, help me and have mercy on me.

23 Jesus said to him, If you can believe, everything is possible to him who believes.

24 And immediately the father of the boy cried out weeping and said, I do believe, help my little faith.

25 When Jesus saw that people were running and gathering about him, he rebuked the unclean spirit and said to it, O deaf and dumb spirit, I command you, come out of him and do not enter him again.

26 And the epileptic cried out violently and was tortured, and the spirit went out; then the boy became as if dead, so that many said, He is dead.

27 Then Jesus took him by the hand and lifted him up.

28 When Jesus entered the house, his disciples asked him privately, Why could we not cast it out?

29 He said to them, This kind cannot be cast out by anything except by fasting and prayer.

30 And when they went out from thence, they passed through Galilee; and he did not want any man to know about him.

31 For he taught his disciples, and said to them, The Son of man will be delivered into the hands of men, and they will kill him; and after he is killed, he will rise on the third day.

32 But they did not understand the saying, and they were afraid to ask him.

33 ¶And they came to Capernaum; and when they entered the house, he asked them, What were you reasoning among yourselves on the road?

34 But they kept silent, for on the road they had argued with one another as to who was the greatest of them.

35 And Jesus sat down and called the twelve and said to them, He who wishes to be first, let him be the last of men, and the servant of every man.

36 And he took a little child and made him to stand in the midst; then he took him in his arms, and said to them,

37 Whoever receives a child like this in my name, he receives me; and he who receives me, does not receive me, but him who has sent me.

38 ¶John said to him, Teacher, we saw a man casting out demons in your name; and we forbade him because he did not follow us.

39 Jesus said to them, Do not forbid him; for there is no man who performs miracles in my name who will hastily speak evil of me.

40 Therefore, he who is not against you is for you.

41 For whoever gives you to drink even a cup of water only because you represent the name of Christ, truly I say to you that his reward shall not be lost.

42 And whoever shall cause one of these little ones who believe in me

to stumble, it were better for him that an ass' millstone were hanged on his neck and that he were thrown into the sea.

43 If your hand offends you, cut it off; it is much better for you to go through life maimed than to have two hands and go to Gehenna,

44 Where the embers do not die and the fire does not go out.

45 And if your foot offends you, cut it off; it is much better for you to go through life lame, than to have two feet, and fall into Gehenna,

46 Where the embers do not die, and the fire does not go out.

47 And if your eye offends you, remove it; it is better for you to enter the kingdom of God with one eye than to have two eyes and fall into the Gehenna of fire,

48 Where the embers do not die, and the fire does not go out.

49 For everything will be salted on the fire, and every sacrifice will be salted with salt.

50 O how good is salt; but if the salt should lose its savor, with what could it be salted? Let there be salt in you, and be at peace with one another.

CHAPTER 10

AND he departed from thence, and came to the border of Judea at the crossing of the Jordan; and a great many people went to him there, and he taught them again as he was accustomed to do.

2 ¶And the Pharisees came to him, tempting him and asking, Is it lawful for a man to leave his wife?

3 He said to them, What did Moses command you?

4 They said, Moses gave us permission to write a letter of separation, and then to divorce.

5 Jesus answered, saying to them, It was because of the hardness of your heart that he wrote for you this particular law.

6 But from the very beginning God made them male and female.

7 For this reason a man shall leave his father and his mother and cleave to his wife.

8 And both shall be one flesh; henceforth they are not two, but one flesh.

9 What therefore God has joined, let no man separate.

10 ¶And his disciples again asked him about this in the house.

11 And he said to them, Whoever divorces his wife and marries another commits adultery.

12 And if a woman divorces her husband and marries another, she commits adultery.

13 ¶And they brought little children to him, that he might touch them; but his disciples rebuked those who brought them.

14 But when Jesus saw it, he was displeased, and he said to them, Allow the little children to come to me, and do not forbid them; for the kingdom of God is for such as these.

15 Truly I say to you, Whoever does not receive the kingdom of God like a little child shall not enter it.

16 Then he took them in his arms, and put his hand on them and blessed them.

17 ¶While he was on the way, a man came running and fell on his knees and asked him, saying, O good Teacher, what shall I do to inherit life eternal?

18 Jesus said to him, Why do you call me good? There is no one who is good except the one God.

19 You know the commandments? Do not commit adultery, Do not steal, Do not murder, Do not bear false witness, Do not oppress, Honor your father and mother.

20 But he answered and said to him, Teacher, all of these I have obeyed from my boyhood.

21 Then Jesus looked at him and loved him, and he said to him, You lack one thing; go, sell everything you have and give it to the poor, and you shall have a treasure in heaven; and take up your cross and follow me.

22 But he felt sad because of this saying, and he went away depressed; for he had great wealth.

23 Then Jesus looked at his disciples and said to them, How hard

it is for those who have wealth to enter into the kingdom of God!

24 But the disciples were surprised at his words. And Jesus answered again, saying to them, My sons, how hard it is for those who trust in their wealth to enter into the kingdom of God!

25 It is easier for a rope to pass through the eye of a needle than for a rich man to enter into the kingdom of God.

26 But they were the more astonished, saying among themselves, Who then can be saved?

27 Jesus looked at them and said to them, With men this is impossible, but not with God; for everything is possible with God.

28 Then Peter began to say, Behold, we have left everything and followed you.

29 Jesus answered and said, Truly I say to you, There is no man who leaves houses or brothers or sisters or father or mother or wife or children or fields for my sake and for the sake of my gospel,

30 Who shall not receive now, in this time a hundredfold, houses and brothers and sisters and maidservants and children and fields and other worldly things, and in the world to come life everlasting.

31 Many who are first shall be last, and the last first.

32 ¶While they were going up on their way to Jerusalem, Jesus was ahead of them; and they were amazed; and they followed him with fear. And he took his twelve aside, and began to tell them what was surely to happen to him, saying,

33 Behold, we are going up to Jerusalem, and the Son of man will be delivered to the high priests and the scribes, and they will condemn him to death and deliver him to the Gentiles.

34 And they will mock him and scourge him and spit in his face and kill him; and on the third day he will rise up.

35 ¶And James and John, the sons of Zebedee, came up to him and said to him, Teacher, we wish you would do for us whatever we ask.

36 He said to them, What do you wish me to do for you?

37 They said to him, Grant us to sit, one at your right and one at your left, in your glory.

38 He said to them, You do not know what you are asking; can you drink the cup which I drink and be baptized with the baptism with which I am to be baptized?

39 They said to him, We can. Jesus said to them, The cup which I shall drink, you too will drink; and with the baptism with which I am baptized, you will be baptized also;

40 But to sit at my right and at my left is not mine to give; except to those for whom it is prepared.

41 When the ten heard it, they began to murmur at James and John.

42 Jesus called them and said to them, You know that those who consider themselves princes of the people are also their lords; and their officials rule over them.

43 Let not this be so among you; but he who wishes to be great among you, let him minister to you.

44 And anyone of you who wishes to be first, let him be a servant to all.

45 For the Son of man also did not come to be ministered to, but to minister, and to give his life as a salvation for the sake of many.

46 ¶And they came to Jericho; and when Jesus went out of Jericho with his disciples and a large crowd, a blind man, Timaeus, the son of Timaeus, sat by the roadside begging.

47 When he heard that it was Jesus of Nazareth, he began to cry aloud and say, O son of David, have mercy on me.

48 And many rebuked him and told him to keep quiet, but he cried out the more, saying, O son of David, have mercy on me.

49 Then Jesus stopped and commanded to call him. So they called the blind man, and said to him, Have courage, rise; he is calling you.

50 And the blind man threw off his robe and got up and went to Jesus.

51 Jesus said to him, What do you wish me to do for you? The blind

man said to him, Master, that I may see.

52 And Jesus said to him, See; your faith has healed you. And immediately he saw, and went on his way.

CHAPTER 11

WHEN he came near to Jerusalem, towards Bethphage and Bethany at the mount of Olives, he sent two of his disciples,

2 And he said to them, Go to the village ahead of us; and as soon as you enter it, you will find a colt tied up, on which no man of the sons of men has ever ridden; untie it and bring it.

3 And if any man should say to you, Why are you doing this? say to him, Our Lord needs it; and immediately he will send it here.

4 So they went and found the colt tied by the door, outside in the street. And as they were untying it,

5 Some of the men who stood there said to them, What are you doing, are you untying the colt?

6 And they answered them as Jesus had instructed them; and they consented.

7 And they brought the colt to Jesus, and they put their garments on it, and Jesus rode on it.

8 And many spread their garments on the road; and others cut down branches from the trees, and spread them on the road.

9 And those who were in front of him and those who were behind him were crying and saying, Hosanna! Blessed is he who comes in the name of the Lord;

10 And blessed is the kingdom of our father David, which is coming; Hosanna in the highest!

11 ¶And Jesus entered Jerusalem, and went into the temple; and he looked upon everything, and when evening came, he went out to Bethany with the twelve.

12 ¶And the next day, when they went out of Bethany, he became hungry.

13 And he saw a fig tree in the distance which had leaves on it. So he came to it to see if he could find anything on it; and when he came he found nothing on it except leaves; for it was not yet time for the figs.

14 And he said to it, From now and forever let no man eat of your fruit. And his disciples heard it.

15 ¶And they came to Jerusalem; and Jesus entered into the temple of God, and began to cast out those who were buying and selling in the temple; and he overturned the trays of the moneychangers and the stands of those who sold doves;

16 And he would not allow any man to bring goods into the temple.

17 And he taught them, saying, Is it not written, My house shall be called the house of prayer for all the peoples? But you have made it a bandits' cave.

18 And the high priests and the scribes heard it, and they sought how to do away with him; for they were afraid of him, because all the people were amazed at his teaching.

19 And when evening came, they went outside of the city.

20 ¶And in the morning, as they were passing, they saw the fig tree withered from its roots.

21 And Simon remembered and said to him, Master, behold, the fig tree which you cursed has withered.

22 Jesus answered, saying to them, If you have faith in God,

23 Truly I say to you, Whoever should say to this mountain, Be moved and fall into the sea, and does not doubt in his heart, but believes that what he says will be done, it will be done to him.

24 Therefore I say to you, Anything you pray for and ask, believe that you will receive it, and it will be done for you.

25 And when you stand up to pray, forgive whatever you have against any man, so that your Father in heaven will forgive you your trespasses.

26 But if you will not forgive, even your Father in heaven will not forgive you your trespasses.

27 ¶And they came again to Jerusalem; and while he was walking in the temple, the high priests and the

scribes and the elders came to him.

28 And they said to him, By what authority do you do these things? and who gave you this authority to do these things?

29 Jesus said to them, I will also ask you a word to tell me, and then I will tell you by what authority I do these things.

30 Whence is the baptism of John, from heaven or from men? Tell me.

31 And they reasoned among themselves and said, If we should say to him, From heaven, he will say to us, Why then did you not believe him?

32 And if we should say, From men, there is the fear of the people, for all of them regard John as a true prophet.

33 So they answered, saying to Jesus, We do not know. He said to them, I will also not tell you by what authority I do these things.

CHAPTER 12

AND he began to speak to them in parables. A man planted a vineyard and fenced it all around, and he dug in it a wine press, and built a tower in it, and then he leased it to laborers and went on a journey.

2 And in due season he sent his servant to the laborers to receive some of the fruits of the vineyard.

3 But they beat him and sent him away empty.

4 And again when he sent to them another servant, they stoned him also and wounded him and sent him away in disgrace.

5 And again he sent another, but they killed him; and he sent many other servants, some of them they beat and some they killed.

6 But finally, he had a very beloved son, and he sent him to them last of all, for he said, They might feel ashamed before my son.

7 But the laborers said among themselves, This is the heir; come, let us kill him, and the inheritance will be ours.

8 And they took and killed him, and threw him outside of the vineyard.

9 What then will the owner of the vineyard do? He will come and destroy those laborers, and give the vineyard to others.

10 Have you not read this scripture: The stone which the builders rejected, the same became the cornerstone?

11 This was from the Lord, and it is a wonder in our eyes.

12 ¶They wanted to seize him, but they were afraid of the people; for they knew that he spoke this parable against them; and they left him and went away.

13 ¶And they sent to him some men of the scribes and of the Herodians, that they might trap him by a word.

14 They came and asked him, Master, we know that you are true and you do not favor any man; for you are impartial, and you teach the way of God in truth. Is it lawful to give head tax to Caesar or not?

15 Shall we give or shall we not give? But he knew their scheme, and said to them, Why do you tempt me? Bring me a penny, that I may see it.

16 And they brought it to him. He said to them, Whose is this image and inscription? They said, Caesar's.

17 Jesus said to them, Give to Caesar what is Caesar's and to God what is God's. And they were amazed at him.

18 ¶Then the Sadducees came to him, those who say there is no resurrection; and they asked him, saying,

19 Teacher, Moses wrote to us that if a man's brother die and leave a wife and leave no children, his brother should take his wife and raise up offspring for his brother.

20 Now there were seven brothers; the first one took a wife and died, and left no offspring.

21 Then the second married her, and he died; he also left no offspring; and likewise the third one.

22 So all seven of them married her, and left no offspring. And after them all, the woman also died.

23 Therefore at the resurrection, whose wife will she be? for all seven had married her.

24 Jesus said to them, Is it not that you err because you do not understand the scriptures nor the power of God?

25 For when they rise from the dead, men neither marry women, nor are women given in marriage to men; but they are like the angels in heaven.

26 Now concerning the rising of the dead, have you not read in the book of Moses, how God said to him from the bush, I am the God of Abraham and the God of Isaac and the God of Jacob?

27 And yet he was not the God of the dead, but of the living. You therefore greatly err.

28 ¶And one of the scribes came near and heard them debating, and he saw that he gave them a good answer. So he asked him, Which is the first commandment of all?

29 Jesus said to him, The first of all commandments is, Hear, O Israel, the Lord our God is one Lord;

30 And you must love the Lord your God with all your heart and with all your soul and with all your mind and with all your might; this is the first commandment.

31 And the second is like to it, You must love your neighbor as yourself. There is no other commandment greater than these.

32 The scribe said to him, Well, Teacher, you have said the truth, that he is One, and there is no other besides him;

33 And that a man should love him with all the heart and with all the mind and with all the soul and with all the might, and love his neighbor as himself; this is far more important than all burnt offerings and sacrifices.

34 When Jesus saw that he replied wisely, he answering, saying to him, You are not far from the kingdom of God. And no man dared again to question him.

35 ¶And Jesus answered, saying as he taught in the temple, How do the scribes say that Christ is the son of David?

36 For David himself said through the Holy Spirit, The Lord said to my Lord, Sit on my right hand until I put your enemies as a stool under your feet.

37 Now therefore David himself calls him my Lord, and how can he be his son? And all the people heard him with pleasure.

38 ¶And in his teaching he said to them, Beware of the scribes, who like to walk in long robes and love to be saluted in the streets,

39 And take the front seats in the synagogues and the head places at banquets;

40 Those who embezzle the property of widows, under pretense of making long prayers.[1] They shall receive greater judgment.

41 ¶And when Jesus sat in front of the treasury, he watched how the people cast their alms into the treasury; and many rich men were casting in a great deal.

42 And there came a poor widow, and she cast in two coins, which are a few pennies.

43 And Jesus called his disciples and said to them, Truly I say to you that this poor widow has cast into the treasury more than all the men who are casting;

44 For all of them cast in of their abundance; but she of her poverty cast everything she had, even all of her possessions.

CHAPTER 13

WHEN JESUS went out of the temple, one of his disciples said to him, Teacher, behold, look at those stones and those buildings.

2 Jesus said to him, Do you see these great buildings? Not a stone shall be left here upon another stone, which shall not be torn down.

3 ¶While Jesus sat on the mount of Olives, towards the temple, Peter and James and John and Andrew asked him privately,

4 Tell us when these things will happen, and what is the sign when all these things are about to be fulfilled?

[1] Widows entrust their property to pious men.

5 Then Jesus began to tell them, Be careful that no man deceive you;

6 For many will come in my name and say, I am he; and they will deceive many.

7 And when you hear of wars and rumors of revolutions, do not be afraid; for this is bound to happen, but the end is not yet.

8 For nation will rise against nation, and kingdom against kingdom; and there will be earthquakes in different places, and there will be famines and uprisings. These things are just the beginning of travail.

9 Look out for yourselves; for they will deliver you to the judges, and they will scourge you in their synagogues; and you will stand before kings and governors for my sake, and as a testimony to them.

10 But my gospel must first be preached among all nations.

11 When they bring you to deliver you up, do not worry beforehand what you will speak; and do not think of anything except what is given you in that very hour; speak that; for it is not you who speak, but the Holy Spirit.

12 A brother will deliver his brother to death, and a father his son; and the children will rise up against their parents and put them to death.

13 And you will be hated by all men because of my name; but he who has patience to the end will be saved.

14 But when you see the sign of uncleanness and desolation, as spoken by the prophet Daniel, accumulating where it should not be (let him who reads understand), then let those who are in Judea flee to the mountain,

15 And let him who is on the roof not come down, and not enter to take anything out of his house,

16 And let him who is in the field not turn back to take his clothes.

17 But woe to those who are with child and to those who give suck in those days!

18 Pray that your flight may not be in winter.

19 For in those days there will be suffering such as has never been from the beginning of the creation which God made until now, and never will be again.

20 And if the Lord had not shortened those days, no flesh would live; but for the sake of the elect ones, which he chose, he shortened those days.

21 Then if any man should say to you, Behold, here is the Christ; or, behold, there; do not believe it.

22 For there will rise false Christs and lying prophets, and they will show signs and wonders, and mislead, if possible, even the chosen ones.

23 But be careful; behold, I have told you everything in advance.

24 ¶In those days, after that suffering, the sun will be darkened and the moon will not give its light,

25 And the stars will fall from the sky, and the powers of the universe will be shaken.

26 Then they will see the Son of man coming in the clouds, with a great army and with glory.

27 Then he will send his angels, and gather his chosen ones from the four winds, from the utmost part of the earth to the utmost part of heaven.

28 From the fig tree learn a parable. When its branches become tender and bring forth leaves, you know that summer is coming.

29 So even you, when you see all these things happen, understand that it is near, even at the door.

30 Truly I say to you that this nation will not pass away until all these things happen.

31 Heaven and earth will pass away, but my words will not pass away.

32 But concerning that day and that hour, no man knows, not even the angels of heaven, neither the Son, except the Father.

33 Watch, be alert, and pray; for you do not know when the time is.

34 It is just like a man who went on a journey, and left his house and gave authority to his servants and to each man his work, and he commanded the porter to keep awake.

35 Be alert therefore, for you do

not know when the owner of the house will come, in the evening or at midnight or at the cock-crow or in the morning.

36 He might come suddenly and find you asleep.

37 What I say to you I say to all of you: Be alert.

CHAPTER 14

AFTER two days, the passover of unleavened bread was to come; and the high priests and the scribes were seeking how to seize him by craft and kill him.

2 And they said, Not during the feast, for it may cause a riot among the people.

3 ¶When he was in Bethany, in the house of Simon the leper, while he reclined, there came a woman who had with her an alabaster vessel of perfume of pure nard, of good quality and very expensive; and she opened it and poured it upon the head of Jesus.

4 But there were some men of the disciples who were displeased within themselves, and said, Why was this perfume wasted?

5 For it could have been sold for more than three hundred pennies and given to the poor. So they were indignant at her.

6 Jesus said, Let her alone; why do you trouble her? She has done a good deed to me.

7 For you always have the poor with you, and when you wish, you can do good to them; but I am not always with you.

8 But this one has done it with what she had; she anointed my body in advance as for the burial.

9 And truly I say to you, Wherever this my gospel is preached throughout the world, what she has done will also be told as a memorial to her.

10 ¶Then Judah of Iscariot, one of the twelve went to the high priests to deliver Jesus to them.

11 When they heard it, they were glad, and promised to give him money. So he sought an opportunity to deliver him.

12 ¶On the first day of unleavened bread, on which the Jews sacrifice the passover, his disciples said to him, Where do you wish that we go and prepare the passover for you to eat?

13 And he sent two of his disciples, and said to them, Go to the city, and behold you will meet a man carrying a vessel of water; follow him.

14 And wherever he enters, say to the owner of the house, Our master says, Where is the guestchamber where I may eat the passover with my disciples?

15 And he will show you a large upper room furnished and prepared; there make ready for us.

16 And his disciples went out and came to the city, and they found just as he had told them; and they prepared the passover.

17 ¶And when it was evening, he came with his twelve.

18 And when they were reclining and eating, Jesus said, Truly I say to you, One of you who eats with me will betray me.

19 They began to feel troubled, and said to him one by one, What! is it I?

20 But he said to them, It is one of the twelve who dips with me in the dish.

21 The Son of man will go, as it is written of him; but woe to the man by whose hand the Son of man is betrayed! It would have been far better for that man never to have been born.

22 ¶While they were eating, Jesus took bread and blessed it, and he broke it and gave it to them, and he said to them, Take it; this is my body.

23 And he took the cup and gave thanks, and he blessed it and gave it to them, and they all drank of it.

24 And he said to them, This is my blood of the new covenant which is shed for the sake of many.

25 Truly I say to you, I shall not drink again of the fruit of the vine until that day in which I drink it new in the kingdom of God.

26 ¶And they offered praise, and went out to the mount of Olives.

27 Then Jesus said to them, All of

you will deny me this night; for it is written, I will smite the shepherd, and his sheep will scatter.

28 But when I am risen, I will be in Galilee before you.

29 Peter said to him, Even if all of them should desert you, I would not.

30 Jesus said to him, Truly I say to you that you, today, in this night, before the cock crows twice, will deny me three times.

31 But he kept telling him still more, Even if I must die with you, I will never deny you, O my Lord. All the disciples said also the same.

32 ¶And they came to a place which is called Gethsemane; and he said to his disciples, Sit down here, while I pray.

33 And he took with him Peter and James and John, and he began to be sorrowful and depressed.

34 And he said to them, My soul is sorrowful even to death; wait for me and keep awake.

35 And he went aside a little and fell on the ground, and prayed that if it were possible, the hour might pass away from him.

36 And he said, Abba, Ave, O Father, my Father, thou canst do everything; make this cup pass away from me; but not according to my will, but thine.

37 And he came and found them sleeping, and he said to Peter, Simon, are you sleeping? Could you not keep awake even for one hour?

38 Wake and pray that you may not enter into temptation; the spirit indeed is willing and ready, but the body is weak.

39 He went away again and prayed, and he said the same words.

40 And he returned again, and found them sleeping, because their eyes were heavy; and they did not know what to say to him.

41 Then he came the third time, and said to them, From now on sleep and get rest; the end has arrived and the hour has come; and behold, the Son of man will be delivered into the hands of sinners.

42 Arise, let us go; behold, he who is to deliver me is near.

43 ¶While he was speaking, Judah of Iscariot, one of the twelve, and many other people, came with swords and staves, from the high priests and the scribes and the elders.

44 And the traitor who was to do the delivering gave them a sign, and he said, He whom I kiss is the one; seize him carefully, and take him away.

45 And immediately he drew near and said to him, My Teacher, my Teacher; and he kissed him.

46 And they laid hands on him and arrested him.

47 But one of those who stood by drew a sword and struck at the servant of the high priest, and cut off his ear.

48 And Jesus answered, saying to them, Have you come out against me as against a bandit, with swords and staves to arrest me?

49 I was with you every day teaching in the temple, and you did not arrest me; but this has happened so that the scriptures might be fulfilled.

50 Then his disciples left him and fled.

51 And a young man was following him, naked, with a linen cloth around him; and they seized him.

52 But he left the linen cloth, and fled naked.

53 ¶And they took Jesus to Caiaphas the high priest; and there gathered to him all the high priests and the scribes and the elders.

54 But Simon followed him afar off, up to the courtyard of the high priest; and he sat with the servants, warming himself before the fire.

55 The high priests and the whole council were seeking testimony against Jesus so that they might put him to death; but they could not find it.

56 For even though many testified against him, their testimony was not worthy.

57 Then some men who were false witnesses stood up against him and said,

58 We heard him say, I will tear

down this temple which is made with hands, and in three days I will build another which is not made with hands.

59 But even this testimony was not worthy.

60 Then the high priest stood up in the midst, and asked Jesus, saying, Do you not answer? What do these men testify against you?

61 But Jesus was silent, and made no answer. Again the high priest asked him, saying, Are you the Christ, the Son of the Blessed One?

62 Jesus said to him, I am; and you will see the Son of man sitting at the right hand of power and coming upon the clouds of the sky.

63 Then the high priest tore his robe, and said, Why therefore do we need witnesses?

64 Behold, you have heard blasphemy from his own mouth; what do you think? And they all decided that he was guilty of death.

65 Then some of the men began to spit in his face, and they covered his face and struck him on his head, saying, Prophesy; and the soldiers smote him on his cheeks.

66 ¶And when Simon was below in the courtyard, there came a young maidservant of the high priest;

67 And she saw him warming himself, and looked at him, and said to him, You also were with Jesus the Nazarene.

68 But he denied it and said, I do not understand what you are saying. Then he went out to the porch, and the cock crowed.

69 And the same young maid saw him, and began to say to those who stood by, This one also is one of them.

70 But he denied it again. And a little later, those who stood by said to Peter, Truly you are one of them, for you also are a Galilean, and even your speech is like theirs.

71 And he began to curse and to swear, saying, I do not know this man of whom you speak.

72 At that very hour the cock crowed the second time. And Simon remembered the words that Jesus had said to him, Before the cock crows twice you will deny me thrice. And then he began to weep.

CHAPTER 15

AND immediately in the morning the high priests took counsel together with the elders and the scribes and with the whole council; and they bound Jesus and took him away, and delivered him to Pilate the governor.

2 And Pilate asked him, Are you the King of the Jews? He answered, saying to him, That is what you say.

3 And the high priests accused him of many things.

4 Then Pilate asked again and said to him, Do you not answer? See how many are testifying against you.

5 But Jesus gave no answer, so that Pilate marvelled.

6 ¶Now it was the custom on every feast to release to them one prisoner whom they asked for.

7 There was one called Bar-Abba, who was bound with those who made insurrection and who had committed murder during that insurrection.

8 And the people cried out, and began to ask Pilate to do for them according to the custom.

9 Pilate answered, saying, Are you willing that I release to you the King of the Jews?

10 For Pilate knew that the high priests had delivered him because of envy.

11 But the high priests incited the people the more, that he should release Bar-Abba to them.

12 Pilate said to them, What then do you wish me to do to this man whom you call the King of the Jews?

13 And they cried out again, Crucify him!

14 Then Pilate said to them, What evil has he done? But they cried aloud the more, Crucify him!

15 Now Pilate wanted to do the will of the people; so he released Bar-Abba to them, and he delivered to them Jesus, scourged, to be crucified.

16 Then the soldiers took him to the inner courtyard, which is the Praetorium; and they called together the whole company.

17 And they dressed him in purple, and wove a crown of thorns and put it on him.

18 And they began to salute him, Hail, O King of the Jews.

19 And they struck him on his head with a reed, and spat in his face, and fell on their knees and worshipped him.

20 And when they had mocked him, they took off the purple and put on him his own clothes, and took him out to crucify him.

21 ¶And they compelled one who was passing by, Simon the Cyrenian, who was coming from the field, the father of Alexander and Rufus, to carry his cross.

22 And they brought him to Golgotha, a place which is interpreted The Skull.

23 And they gave him to drink wine mixed with myrrh; but he would not take it.

24 And when they had crucified him, they divided his clothes and cast lots on them, to see what each man should take.

25 It was the third hour when they crucified him.

26 And the reason for his death was inscribed in writing, THIS IS THE KING OF THE JEWS.

27 And they crucified with him two bandits, one on his right and one on his left.

28 And the scripture was fulfilled which said, He was reckoned with the wicked.

29 ¶Even those who passed by blasphemed against him, nodding their heads and saying, O destroyer of the temple and builder of it in three days,

30 Deliver yourself and come down from the cross.

31 The high priests likewise were laughing among themselves, with the scribes, and saying, He saved others; but he cannot save himself.

32 O Christ, you are the King of Israel! Let him now come down from the cross, so that we may see and believe in him. Even those who were crucified with him reproached him.

33 And when the sixth hour was come, there was darkness over all the land, which lasted until the ninth hour.

34 And at the ninth hour, Jesus cried out with a loud voice, saying Eli, Eli, lemana, shabakthani! which means,[1] My God, my God, for this I was spared!

35 Some of the men who were standing by, when they heard it, said, He called for Elijah.

36 And one ran and filled a sponge with vinegar, and tied it on a reed to give him a drink; and he said, Hush, let us see if Elijah will come to take him down.

37 But Jesus cried with a loud voice, and the end came.

38 And the curtains at the door of the temple were torn in two, from the top to the bottom.

39 ¶And when the centurion, who stood near him, saw that he cried out in this manner and died, he said, Truly this man was the Son of God.

40 There were also women who were looking from afar, Mary of Magdala, and Mary the mother of James the young and of Joses, and Salome;

41 Who had followed him, when he was in Galilee and ministered to him; and many other women who had come up with him to Jerusalem.

42 ¶And when it was Friday evening, which is before the sabbath,

43 There came Joseph of Ramtha, an honorable counsellor, who was also waiting for the kingdom of God; and he dared to go to Pilate, and asked for the body of Jesus.

44 But Pilate marvelled that he was already dead. So he called the centurion and asked him if he had already died.

45 And when he learned it, he gave the body to Joseph.

46 And Joseph bought linen, and took him down and wrapped him in it, and laid him in a tomb which was hewn in a rock; and he rolled a stone against the door of the tomb.

47 But Mary of Magdala and Mary the mother of Joses saw where he was laid.

---

1 "which means" used by Mark to explain translation from one Aramaic dialect to another.

CHAPTER 16

WHEN the sabbath had passed, Mary of Magdala, and Mary the mother of James, and Salome, bought spices, that they might come and anoint him.

2 Early in the morning, on the first day of the week, they came to the tomb as the sun was just rising.

3 And they said among themselves, Who will roll away the stone from the door of the tomb for us?

4 And they looked and saw that the stone was rolled away, for it was very large.

5 And they entered the tomb, and saw a young man, sitting on the right, covered with a white robe; and they were astonished.

6 But he said to them, Do not be afraid. You seek Jesus the Nazarene, who was crucified; he has risen; he is not here; behold the place where he was laid.

7 But go away and tell his disciples, and Peter, that he will be before you in Galilee; there you will see him, just as he has told you.

8 And when they heard it, they fled and went out of the tomb, for they were seized with amazement and trembling; and they said nothing to any man, for they were frightened.

9 ¶Now he rose early on the first day of the week, and appeared first to Mary of Magdala, from whom he had cast seven demons.

10 And she went and brought glad tidings to those who were with him, who now were mourning and weeping.

11 And when they heard them saying that he was alive, and had appeared to them, they did not believe them.

12 ¶After these things he appeared to two of them in another manner, as they were walking and going to a village.

13 And they went and told the rest; but they did not believe them also.

14 ¶At last he appeared to the eleven while they were reclining, and he upbraided them for their little faith and the dulness of their hearts, because they had not believed those who saw him risen.

15 ¶And he said to them, Go into all the world and preach my gospel to the whole creation.

16 He who believes and is baptized shall be saved; and he who does not believe shall be condemned.

17 And wonders will follow those who believe these things. In my name they will cast out demons; and they will speak with new tongues;

18 And they will handle snakes; [1] and if they should drink any poison of death, it will not harm them; and they will lay their hands on the sick, and they will be healed.

19 ¶Then our Lord Jesus, after he had spoken to them, ascended to heaven and sat on the right hand of God.

20 And they went out and preached in every place; and our Lord helped them and strengthened their words by the miracles which they performed.

[1] Aramaic idiom for *enemies*.

THE GOSPEL ACCORDING TO

SAINT LUKE

CHAPTER 1

SINCE many have desired to have in writing the story of those works with which we are familiar,

2 According to what was handed down to us by those who from the beginning were eyewitnesses and ministers of that very word,

3 And since these were seen by me also because I was near and considered them all very carefully; I will therefore write to you everything in its order, most honorable Theophilus,

4 So that you may know the truth of the words by which you were made a convert.

5 ¶There was in the days of Herod, king of Judea, a priest whose name was Zechariah, of the order of ministry of the house of Abijah; and his wife was of the daughters of Aaron, and her name was Elizabeth.

6 They were both righteous before God, and walked in all his commandments, and in the righteousness of the Lord without blame.

7 But they had no son, because Elizabeth was barren, and they were both well on in years.

8 And it came to pass while he was ministering in the order of his ministry before God,

9 According to the custom of the priesthood, his turn came to burn incense; so he entered the temple of the Lord.

10 And all the congregation of the people prayed outside, at the time of incense.

11 And the angel of the Lord appeared to Zechariah, standing on the right of the altar of incense.

12 And when Zechariah saw him, he became dumbfounded, and fear came upon him.

13 And the angel said to him, Fear not, Zechariah; for your prayer has been heard, and your wife Elizabeth will bear you a son, and you will call his name John.

14 And you will have joy and gladness; and a great many will rejoice at his birth.

15 For he will be great before the Lord, and he will not drink wine and strong drink; and he will be filled with the Holy Spirit, while he is still in the womb of his mother.

16 And many Israelites he will cause to turn to the Lord their God.

17 And he will go before them with the spirit and the power of Elijah, to turn the hearts of parents to their children, and those who are disobedient to the wisdom of the righteous; and he will prepare a true people for the Lord.

18 And Zechariah said to the angel, How will I understand this? for I am an old man, and my wife is well on in years.

19 And the angel answered, saying to him, I am Gabriel, who stand in the presence of God; and I am sent to speak to you, and to bring you these glad tidings.

20 From henceforth you will be dumb, and not able to speak till the day these things happen, because you did not believe these my words which are to be fulfilled in their time.

21 Now the people stood waiting for Zechariah, and wondered because he remained so long in the temple.

22 When Zechariah came out, he could not speak with them; and they understood that he had seen a vision in the temple; and he made signs to

them with his eyes, but remained dumb.

23 And when the days of his ministry were finished, he went to his house.

24 And it came to pass after those days, his wife Elizabeth conceived, and hid herself for five months; and she said,

25 The Lord has done these things to me in the days that he has been mindful of me, to remove my reproach among men.

26 ¶Now in the sixth month the angel Gabriel was sent from God to Galilee, to a city called Nazareth,

27 To a virgin who was acquired for a price [1] for a man named Joseph, of the house of David; and the name of the virgin was Mary.

28 And the angel went in and said to her, Peace be to you, O full of grace; our Lord is with you, O blessed one among women.

29 When she saw him, she was disturbed at his word, and wondered what kind of salutation this could be.

30 And the angel said to her, Fear not, Mary; for you have found grace with God.

31 For behold, you will conceive and give birth to a son, and you will call his name Jesus.

32 He will be great, and he will be called the Son of the Highest; and the Lord God will give him the throne of his father David.

33 And he will rule over the house of Jacob for ever; and there will be no limit to his kingdom.

34 Then Mary said to the angel, How can this be, for no man has known me.

35 The angel answered and said to her, The Holy Spirit will come, and the power of the Highest will rest upon you; therefore the one who is to be born of you is holy, and he will be called the Son of God.

36 And behold, Elizabeth your kinswoman has also conceived a son in her old age; and yet this is the sixth month with her, who is called barren.

37 For nothing is impossible for God.

38 Mary said, Here I am, a handmaid of the Lord; let it be to me according to your word. And the angel went away from her.

39 ¶In those days, Mary rose up, and went hurriedly to a mountain, to a city of Judea.

40 And she entered the house of Zechariah, and saluted Elizabeth.

41 And when Elizabeth heard the salutation of Mary, the babe leaped in her womb; and Elizabeth was filled with the Holy Spirit.

42 And she cried in a loud voice saying to Mary, Blessed are you among women, and blessed is the fruit of your womb.

43 How does it happen to me that the mother of my Lord should come to me?

44 For behold, when the voice of your salutation fell on my ears, the babe in my womb leaped with great joy.

45 And blessed is she who believed; for there will be a fulfillment of the things which were spoken to her from the Lord.

46 And Mary said, My soul magnifies the Lord

47 And my spirit rejoices in God my Saviour;

48 For he has regarded the meekness of his handmaid; for behold, from henceforth, all generations shall bless me.

49 For he who is mighty has done great things to me; holy is his name.

50 And his mercy is for centuries and generations, upon those who reverence him.

51 He has brought victory with his arm; he has scattered the proud in the imagination of their heart.

52 He has put down the mighty from their seats, and he has lifted up the meek.

53 He has filled the hungry with good things; and dismissed the rich empty.

54 He has helped his servant Israel, and has remembered his mercy,

55 Just as he spoke with our forefathers, with Abraham and with his descendants for ever.

[1] Dowry.

56 ¶Mary stayed with Elizabeth about three months, and then returned to her own home.

57 ¶Now the time came for Elizabeth to be delivered, and she gave birth to a son.

58 And when her neighbors and relatives heard that God had increased his mercy to her, they rejoiced with her.

59 ¶And it came to pass on the eighth day that they came to circumcise the boy; and they would have called him Zechariah, after the name of his father,

60 But his mother said to them, Not so; but he shall be called John.

61 And they said to her, There is no man in your family who is called by this name.

62 Then they made signs to his father, asking what he wanted to call him.

63 And he asked for a tablet and wrote, saying, John is his name. And every one was surprised.

64 And immediately his mouth and his tongue were opened, and he spoke and blessed God.

65 And fear came on all their neighbors; and these things were spoken throughout the mountain of Judea.

66 And all who heard it reasoned in their hearts, saying, What a boy he will be! And the hand of the Lord was with him.

67 ¶And his father Zechariah was filled with the Holy Spirit, and prophesied, saying,

68 Blessed is the Lord, the God of Israel; for he has visited his people and wrought a salvation for them.

69 And he has raised up a horn of salvation for us in the house of his servant David;

70 Just as he spoke by the mouth of his holy prophets who have been for ages,

71 That he would save us from our enemies and from the hand of all who hate us.

72 He has shown mercy to our fathers, and he has remembered his holy covenants

73 And the oaths which he swore to Abraham our father,

74 To grant to us that we may be saved from the hand of our enemies, and serve before him without fear

75 In justice and righteousness all our days.

76 And you, boy, will be called the prophet of the Highest; for you will go before the face of the Lord to prepare his way,

77 To give knowledge of life to his people by the forgiveness of their sins,

78 Through the mercy and kindness of our God; whereby we shall be visited by a ray from above,

79 To give light to those who sit in darkness and in the shadow of death, to guide our feet into the way of peace.

80 The boy grew and became strong in spirit; and he was in the desert until the day of his appearance to Israel.

CHAPTER 2

AND it happened in those days that there went out a decree from Caesar Augustus to take a census of all the people in his empire.

2 This first census took place during the governorship of Quirinius in Syria.

3 And every man went to be registered in his own city.

4 Joseph also went up from Nazareth, a city of Galilee, to Judea, to the city of David, which is called Bethlehem; because he was of the house and family of David;

5 With his purchased bride Mary, while she was with child, that they might be registered there.

6 And it came to pass while they were there that her days to be delivered were fulfilled.

7 And she gave birth to her firstborn son; and she wrapped him in swaddling clothes and laid him in a manger, because they had no room where they were lodging.

8 ¶Now there were shepherds in that region where they were staying, and they were watching their flocks at night.

9 And behold, the angel of God came to them, and the glory of the

Lord shone on them; and they were seized with a great fear.

10 And the angel said to them, Do not be afraid; for behold, I bring you glad tidings of great joy, which will be to all the world.

11 For this day is born to you in the city of David, a Saviour, who is Christ the Lord.

12 And this is a sign for you: You will find the babe wrapped in swaddling clothes and lying in a manger.

13 And suddenly there appeared with the angel a heavenly host, praising God and saying,

14 Glory to God in the highest, and on earth peace and good hope for men.

15 ¶And it came to pass when the angels departed from them and went to heaven, that the shepherds spoke to one another, saying, Let us go to Bethlehem and see this thing that has happened as the Lord has shown to us.

16 And they came hurriedly, and found Mary and Joseph, and the babe laid in the manger.

17 When they saw it, they made known the word which was spoken to them concerning the boy.

18 And all who heard it were amazed at the things which were spoken by the shepherds.

19 But Mary treasured all these things and pondered them in her heart.

20 And the shepherds returned, glorifying and praising God for all that they had seen and heard, as it was spoken to them.

21 ¶And when eight days were fulfilled to circumcise the child, his name was called Jesus; for he was named by the angel before he was conceived in the womb.

22 ¶And when the days for their purification were fulfilled, according to the law of Moses, they brought him up to Jerusalem to present him to the Lord,

23 As it is written in the law of the Lord, Every male that opens the womb shall be called holy to the Lord,

24 And to offer a sacrifice, as it is commanded in the law of the Lord, A pair of turtledoves or two young pigeons.

25 Now there was a man in Jerusalem, whose name was Simon; and this man was pious and righteous, waiting for the consolation of Israel; and the Holy Spirit was upon him.

26 And it was said to him by the Holy Spirit, that he would not see death, until he saw the Anointed of the Lord.

27 This man was led by the Spirit to the temple; and when the parents brought in the boy Jesus, to do for him according to what is commanded in the law,

28 He received him in his arms, and blessed God, and said,

29 Now dismiss thy servant, O my Lord, in peace, according to thy word;

30 For behold, mine eyes have already seen thy mercies,

31 Which thou hast prepared before the face of all peoples,

32 A light for a revelation to the Gentiles and a glory to thy people Israel.

33 ¶And Joseph and Jesus' mother marvelled about these things which were spoken concerning him.

34 And Simon blessed them, and said to Mary, his mother, Behold, this one is appointed for the fall and for the rise of many in Israel, and for a sign of dispute;

35 And a sword will pierce through your own soul, so that the thoughts of the hearts of many may be revealed.

36 And Hannah the prophetess, the daughter of Phanuel, of the tribe of Asher, was of a great age; and she had lived seven years with her husband from the days of her virginity.

37 Then she became a widow for about eighty-four years, and she never left the temple, and with fasting and prayer she worshipped day and night.

38 She also stood up at that hour and gave thanks to the Lord, and spoke concerning him to every man who was looking forward to the salvation of Jerusalem.

39 ¶And when they had done every-

thing according to the law of the Lord, they returned to Galilee to their own city Nazareth.

40 The boy grew and became strong in spirit, filled with wisdom; and the grace of God was upon him.

41 ¶And his people went every year to Jerusalem during the feast of the passover.

42 And when he was twelve years old, they went up to the feast as they were accustomed.

43 And when the feast days were over, they returned; but the boy Jesus remained in Jerusalem; and Joseph and his mother did not know it.

44 They thought that he was with the children of their party; and when they went a day's journey, they sought for him among their own people and those who knew them.

45 But they could not find him; so they returned again to Jerusalem, looking for him.

46 After three days, they found him in the temple, sitting in the midst of the teachers, listening to them and asking them questions.

47 And all those who heard him were amazed at his wisdom and his answers.

48 And when they saw him, they were astonished; and his mother said to him, My son, why have you done so to us? Behold, your father and I have been looking for you with much anxiety.

49 He said to them, Why were you looking for me? Did you not know that I would be in the house of my Father?

50 But they could not understand the words which he said to them.

51 So he went down with them and came to Nazareth; and he was subject to them. And his mother treasured all these words in her heart.

52 And Jesus grew in his stature and in his wisdom, and in favor with God and men.

CHAPTER 3

IN the fifteenth year of the reign of Tiberius Caesar, during the governorship of Pontius Pilate in Judea, when Herod was tetrarch of Galilee, and his brother Philip tetrarch of Ituraea and of the region of Trachonitis, and Lysanius tetrarch of Abilene,

2 During the high priesthood of Hanan and Caiaphas, the word of God came to John, son of Zechariah, in the wilderness.

3 And he went throughout the country around Jordan, preaching the baptism of repentance for the forgiveness of sins;

4 As it is written in the book of the words of Isaiah the prophet, The voice which calls in the wilderness, Prepare the way of the Lord, make the paths of our God straight in the plain.

5 Let all the valleys be filled up, and all the mountains and hills be levelled; let the crooked places be made straight, and the rough places like a plain;

6 And let all flesh see the salvation of God.

7 ¶And he said to the people who were coming to him to be baptized, O offspring of scorpions, who has warned you to escape from the anger which is coming?

8 Therefore bring forth fruits which are worthy of repentance; and do not begin to say within yourselves, We have Abraham as our father; for I say to you that God can raise up children for Abraham from these stones.

9 Behold, the axe is already placed at the root of the trees; therefore every tree which bears not good fruits will be cut down and cast into the fire.

10 And the people asked him, saying, What then shall we do?

11 He answered, saying to them, He who has two shirts, let him give to him who has none; and he who has food, let him do likewise.

12 And there came also tax collectors to be baptized, and they said to him, Teacher, what shall we do?

13 He said to them, Do not exact anything more than what is commanded you to exact.

14 And the soldiers also asked him saying, What shall we do? And he

said to them, Do not molest any man, and do not accuse any man; your own wages should be enough for you.

15 ¶While the people were placing their hope on John, and all of them were thinking in their hearts, Perhaps he is the Christ;

16 John answered, saying to them, Behold, I baptize you with water; but one is coming after me, who is greater than I, the strings of whose shoes I am not worthy to untie; he will baptize you with the Holy Spirit and with fire;

17 He holds a shovel in his hand, and purifies his threshing; the wheat he gathers into his barns, and the straw he burns in the unquenchable fire.

18 Many other things also, he taught and preached to the people.

19 ¶Now Herod the tetrarch, because he was rebuked by John concerning Herodias wife of Philip his brother, and for all the evil things that he was doing,

20 Added this also to them all, that he put John into prison.

21 ¶It came to pass when all the people were baptized, Jesus also was baptized, and while he prayed, heaven was opened,

22 And the Holy Spirit descended on him, like a dove, and a voice from heaven, saying, You are my beloved Son; with you I am pleased.

23 ¶Now Jesus was about thirty years old, and he was supposed to be the son of Joseph, the son of Heli,

24 The son of Matthat, the son of Levi, the son of Melchi, the son of Jannai, the son of Joseph,

25 The son of Matthat, the son of Amos, the son of Nahum, the son of Hasli, the son of Naggai,

26 The son of Maath, the son of Mattath, the son of Shemei, the son of Joseph, the son of Judah,

27 The son of John, the son of Rheasa, the son of Zerubbabel, the son of Shelahiel, the son of Neri,

28 The son of Melchi, the son of Addi, the son of Kosam, the son of Elmodad, the son of Er,

29 The son of Jose, the son of Elie-zer, the son of Joram, the son of Mattitha, the son of Levi,

30 The son of Simon, the son of Judah, the son of Joseph, the son of Jonam, the son of Eliakim,

31 The son of Melea, the son of Mani, the son of Mattha, the son of Nathan, the son of David,

32 The son of Jesse, the son of Obed, the son of Boaz, the son of Salmon, the son of Nahshon,

33 The son of Aminadab, the son of Aram, the son of Hezron, the son of Perez, the son of Judah,

34 The son of Jacob, the son of Isaac, the son of Abraham, the son of Terah, the son of Nahor,

35 The son of Serug, the son of Arau, the son of Peleg, the son of Eber, the son of Shalah,

36 The son of Cainan, the son of Arphaxar, the son of Shem, the son of Noah, the son of Lamech,

37 The son of Methuselah, the son of Enoch, the son of Jared, the son of Mahalalael, the son of Cainan,

38 The son of Enosh, the son of Seth, the son of Adam, who was of God.

CHAPTER 4

NOW Jesus, full of the Holy Spirit, returned from the Jordan, and the Spirit carried him away into the wilderness

2 Forty days, in order that he might be tempted by the adversary. And he did not eat anything in those days; and when they were over, at last he became hungry.

3 ¶And the adversary said to him, If you are the Son of God, command this stone to become bread.

4 Jesus answered, saying to him, It is written, It is not by bread alone that man can live, but by every word of God.

5 Then Satan took him up to a high mountain and showed him all the kingdoms of the earth in a short time.

6 And the adversary said to him, I will give you all this power and its glory, which are entrusted to me and I give it to whom I please;

7 If therefore you worship me, it will all be yours.

8 Jesus answered, saying to him, It is written, You shall worship the Lord your God, and him only you shall serve.

9 And he brought him to Jerusalem and made him to stand up on the pinnacle of the temple, and said to him, If you are the Son of God, throw yourself down from here;

10 For it is written, He will command his angels concerning you, to keep watch over you;

11 And they will take you up in their arms, so that even your foot may not strike a stone.

12 Jesus answered, saying to him, It is said, You shall not tempt the Lord your God.

13 When the adversary was through with all his temptations, he left him for a while.

14 ¶So Jesus returned in the power of the Spirit to Galilee; and the fame about him went out through all the country round about.

15 And he taught in their synagogues, and was praised by every man.

16 ¶And he came to Nazareth, where he had been brought up; and he entered the synagogue on the sabbath day, as was the custom, and stood up to read.

17 And the book of the prophet Isaiah was given to him. And Jesus opened the book and found the place where it is written,

18 The Spirit of the Lord is upon me; because of this he has anointed me to preach good tidings to the poor; and he has sent me to heal the brokenhearted, and to proclaim release to the captives and sight to the blind; to strengthen with forgiveness those who are bruised

19 And to preach the acceptable year of the Lord.

20 And he rolled up the scroll and gave it to the attendant, and went and sat down. And the eyes of all who were in the synagogue were fixed on him.

21 And he began to say to them, Today this scripture is fulfilled in your ears.

22 And all testified about him, and were amazed by the words of grace which came out of his mouth. And they said, Is not this man the son of Joseph?

23 Jesus said to them, You might probably tell me this proverb, Physician, heal yourself; and all that we heard you did in Capernaum, do also here in your own city.

24 Then he said, Truly I say to you, No prophet is acceptable in his own city.

25 For truly I say to you, There were many widows in Israel in the days of the prophet Elijah when heaven was closed for three years and six months and there was a great famine throughout the land;

26 Yet Elijah was not sent to one of them, but to Zarephath of Sidon, to a widow.

27 And there were many lepers in Israel in the days of the prophet Elisha, and yet not one of them was cleansed except Naaman the Aramean.

28 When those who were in the synagogue heard these things, they were all filled with anger.

29 And they rose up and took him outside the city, and brought him to the brow of the mountain on which their city was built, that they might throw him down from a cliff.

30 But he passed through the midst of them and went away.

31 ¶And he went down to Capernaum, a city of Galilee, and he taught them on the sabbaths.

32 And they were astonished at his teaching; because his word had power.

33 And there was in the synagogue a man who had an unclean, demonic spirit, and he cried in a loud voice,

34 Saying, Let me alone; what have we in common, O Jesus the Nazarene? Have you come to destroy us? I know who you are, Holy One of God!

35 And Jesus rebuked him, saying, Keep quiet, and come out of him.

The demon threw him in the midst, and went out of him, and did him no harm.

36 And every man was seized with amazement, and the people spoke among themselves, saying, What kind of word is this that he commands unclean spirits with authority and power, and they go out!

37 And the fame about him went out through all the country around them.

38 ¶And when Jesus left the synagogue, he entered the house of Simon. And Simon's mother-in-law was suffering with a severe fever; and they besought him for her.

39 And he stood by her and rebuked the fever, and it left her; and she rose up immediately and ministered to them.

40 ¶When the sun was setting, all who had sick people suffering from various diseases brought them to him; and he laid his hand on each one of them and healed them.

41 Demons also came out of many, who cried out saying, You are the Christ, the Son of God. And he rebuked them, and would not allow them to speak; that people might not know that he was the Christ.

42 And in the morning, he came out and went to a desert place; and the people were looking for him, and came where he was; and they held him so that he might not leave them.

43 But Jesus said to them, I must preach the kingdom of God in other cities also, because I was sent for this.

44 And he preached in the synagogues of Galilee.

CHAPTER 5

IT came to pass when the people gathered around him to hear the word of God, he stood on the shore of the lake of Gennesaret.

2 And he saw two boats standing by the lake; but the fishermen had gotten out of them and were washing their nets.

3 One of them belonged to Simon Peter; so Jesus went up and sat in it, and he asked to row it a little way from the shore to the water. And he sat and taught the people from the boat.

4 When he was through speaking, he said to Simon, Row out to the deep, and cast your net for a catch.

5 Simon answered, saying to him, Teacher, we have toiled all night and have caught nothing; but just because of your word, I will cast the net.

6 And when they had done this, they inclosed a great many fish; and their net was breaking.

7 So they signalled to their partners in the other boat, to come and help them. And when they came, they filled both the boats, till they were almost sinking.

8 When Simon Peter saw it, he fell at the feet of Jesus, and said to him, I beg you, my Lord, leave me alone, for I am a sinful man.

9 For he was amazed, and all who were with him, because of the catch of fish which they took.

10 So also was it with James and John, sons of Zebedee, who were partners with Simon. But Jesus said to Simon, Do not be afraid; from henceforth you will be catching men to save them.

11 And they brought the boats to land, and left everything and followed him.

12 ¶When Jesus was in one of the cities, there came a man who was covered with leprosy; and he saw Jesus and fell on his face, and besought him, saying, My Lord, if you will, you can cleanse me.

13 And Jesus stretched out his hand and touched him, and said to him, I will, be clean; and immediately his leprosy left him.

14 And he charged him not to tell any man; but go and show yourself to the priests, and make an offering for your cleansing, as Moses commanded, for a testimony to them.

15 ¶And the fame concerning him went out the more; and many people

gathered to hear him and to be healed of their diseases.

16 But he departed into the wilderness and prayed.

17 ¶It came to pass on one of the days when Jesus was teaching that the Pharisees and the teachers of the law were sitting, who had come from every town of Galilee and Judea and Jerusalem. And the power of God was present to heal them.

18 And some men brought a paralytic on a quilt; and they wanted to go in and lay him before him.

19 And when they found they were not able to carry him in because of the multitude, they went up on the roof and lowered him down on his quilt from the ceiling into the midst before Jesus.

20 When Jesus saw their faith, he said to the paralytic, Man, your sins are forgiven.

21 And the scribes and the Pharisees began to reason saying, Who is this man who talks blasphemy? Who can forgive sins except God only?

22 But Jesus knew their thoughts and answered, saying to them, What do you reason in your heart?

23 Which is easier to say, Your sins are forgiven, or just to say, Arise and walk?

24 But that you may know that the Son of man has authority on earth to forgive sins, he said to the paralytic, I tell you, Arise, take up your quilt and go to your home.

25 And immediately he rose up before their eyes and took his quilt and went to his house, praising God.

26 And every man was seized with amazement, and they praised God and were filled with fear, saying, Today we have seen wonders.

27 ¶After these things, Jesus went out and saw a revenue officer named Levi, sitting at the custom house; and he said to him, Follow me.

28 So he left everything and rose up and went after him.

29 And Levi gave him a great reception in his house; and there was a large gathering of tax officers and others, who were guests with them.

30 And the scribes and the Phari-

sees murmured and said to his disciples, Why do you eat and drink with tax collectors and sinners?

31 And Jesus answered and said to them, A physician is not needed for those who are well, but for those who are seriously sick.

32 I have not come to call the righteous, but sinners to repentance.

33 ¶They said to him, Why do the disciples of John always fast and pray, and also those of the Pharisees; but yours eat and drink?

34 He said to them, You cannot make the sons of the wedding feast fast so long as the bridegroom is with them.

35 But the days will come when the bridegroom is taken from them; then they will fast in those days.

36 And he told them a parable, No man cuts a piece of cloth from a new garment and puts it on a worn-out garment, so that he may not cut the new, and the new piece will not blend with the old.

37 No man pours new wine into worn-out skins; else the new wine will rend the skins, and the wine will run out and the skins will be ruined.

38 But they pour new wine into new skins, and both are well preserved.

39 And no man drinks old wine and immediately wants new wine; for he says, The old is delicious.

CHAPTER 6

IT came to pass on the sabbath, as Jesus walked through the wheat fields, his disciples plucked heads of wheat, and rubbed them in their hands and did eat.

2 But some of the men of the Pharisees said to them, Why are you doing what is unlawful to do on the sabbath?

3 Jesus answered, saying to them, Have you not read what David did when he and those who were with him were hungry?

4 He entered into the house of God, and took the bread that was on the table of the Lord and did eat it, and he gave it to those who were with

him, that which was unlawful to eat but only for the priests.

5 And he said to them, The Son of man is Lord of the sabbath.

6 ¶And it came to pass on another sabbath he entered into the synagogue and taught; and there was there a man whose right hand was withered.

7 And the scribes and the Pharisees watched him to see if he would heal on the sabbath, so that they might find an accusation against him.

8 But he knew their thoughts, and said to the man whose hand was withered, Rise up and come to the center of the synagogue. And when he came and stood up,

9 Jesus said to them, I will ask you, What is lawful to do on the sabbath, that which is good or that which is bad? to save a life or to destroy it?

10 And he looked at all of them, and said to him, Stretch out your hand. And he stretched it out; and his hand was restored like the other.

11 But they were filled with bitterness, and discussed with each other what to do with Jesus.

12 ¶It came to pass in those days Jesus went out to a mountain to pray, and he remained all night in prayer to God.

13 And at daybreak he called his disciples; and he chose twelve from them, whom he called apostles:

14 Simon who is called Peter, and Andrew his brother, and James and John, and Philip and Bartholomew,

15 And Matthew and Thomas, and James the son of Alphaeus and Simon who is called the Zealot,

16 And Judas the son of James, and Judah of Iscariot, who became the traitor.

17 ¶And Jesus went down with them and stood up in the plain; and a large group of his disciples and a large crowd of people from all over Judea and from Jerusalem and from the sea coast of Tyre and Sidon came to hear his word and to be healed of their diseases;

18 And those who were suffering from unclean spirits were healed.

19 And all the people wanted to touch him, because power proceeded from him, and he healed them all.

20 ¶And he lifted up his eyes on his disciples and said, Blessed are you poor, for the kingdom of God is yours.

21 Blessed are you who hunger now, for you shall be filled. Blessed are you who weep now, for you shall laugh.

22 Blessed are you when men hate you and discriminate against you and reproach you and publish your names as bad, for the sake of the Son of man.

23 Be glad and rejoice in that day, for your reward is increased in heaven; for their fathers did the same to the prophets.

24 But woe to you, rich men! for you have already received your comforts.

25 Woe to you who are full! for you will hunger. Woe to you who laugh now! for you will weep and mourn.

26 Woe to you when men speak well of you! for so did their fathers to the false prophets.

27 But I say to you who hear, Love your enemies and do good to those who hate you,

28 And bless those who curse you, and pray for those who compel you to carry burdens.

29 And to him who strikes you on the cheek, offer to him the other; and to him who takes away your robe, do not refuse your shirt also.

30 Give to every one who asks you; and from him who takes away what is yours, do not demand it back again.

31 Just as you want men to do to you, do to them likewise.

32 For if you love those who love you, what is your blessing? For even sinners love those who love them.

33 And if you do good only to those who do good to you, what is your blessing? For sinners also do the same.

34 And if you lend only to him from whom you expect to be paid back, what is your blessing? For sinners also lend to sinners, to be paid back likewise.

35 But love your enemies and do good to them, and lend and do not cut off any man's hope; so your reward will increase and you will become sons of the Highest; for he is gracious to the wicked and the cruel.

36 Be therefore merciful, as your Father also is merciful.

37 Judge not, and you will not be judged; condemn not, and you will not be condemned; forgive, and you will be forgiven.

38 Give, and it will be given to you; good measure shaken down and running over they will pour into your robe.[1] For with the measure that you measure, it will be measured to you.

39 And he told them a parable, Can a blind man guide a blind man? Will they not both fall into a pit?

40 There is no disciple who is more important than his teacher; for every man who is well developed will be like his teacher.

41 Why do you see the splinter in your brother's eye, and do not see the beam in your own eye?

42 Or how can you say to your brother, My brother, let me take out the splinter from your eye, when behold, you do not see the beam in your own eye? O hypocrites, first take out the beam from your own eye, and then you will see clearly to take out the splinter from your brother's eye.

43 There is no good tree that bears bad fruit, nor a bad tree that bears good fruit.

44 For every tree is known by its own fruit. For they do not pick figs from thistles nor gather grapes from a bramble bush.

45 A good man brings out good things from the good treasure of his heart; and a bad man from the bad treasure of his heart brings out bad things; for from the abundance of the heart the lips speak.

46 Why do you call me, My Lord, my Lord, and do not do what I say?

47 Every man who comes to me and hears my words and does them, I will show you what he is like.

48 He is like a man who built a house and dug deep, and laid its foundations upon the rock; and when the flood came, it beat upon that house and could not shake it; for its foundation was laid upon a rock.

49 And he who hears and does not is like a man who built his house on the earth without a foundation; and when the river beat against it, it fell immediately, and the fall of that house was great.

CHAPTER 7

WHEN he had finished all of these words in the hearing of the people, Jesus entered Capernaum.

2 Now the servant of a centurion was seriously sick, one who was very dear to him; and he was near death.

3 And when he heard about Jesus, he sent to him Jewish elders, and besought him to come and heal his servant.

4 When they came to Jesus, they begged him earnestly, saying, He is worthy to have this done for him;

5 For he loves our people, and has even built us a synagogue.

6 Jesus went with them. And when he was not far from the house, the centurion sent some of his friends to him, and said, My Lord, do not trouble yourself; for I am not worthy that you should enter under my roof;

7 That is why I was not worthy to come to you; but just say a word and my servant will be healed.

8 For I am also a man under authority, and there are soldiers under my command; and I say to this one, Go, and he goes; and to another, Come, and he comes; and to my servant, Do this, and he does it.

9 When Jesus heard these things, he was amazed at him, and he turned and said to the people who followed him, I say to you, not even in Israel have I found such faith as this.

10 So those who were sent returned to the house, and found the servant who was sick, healed.

11 ¶And it came to pass on the next day he was going to a city called

---

[1] Easterners carry wheat from house to house in the folds of their robes.

Nain; and his disciples were with him, and many people.

12 And when they came near the gate of the city, he saw a dead man being carried out, who was the only son of his mother, and his mother was a widow; and many people of the city were with her.

13 When Jesus saw her, he had compassion on her, and said to her, Weep not.

14 Then he went and touched the bier, and those who carried it stood still. And he said, Young man, I tell you, Arise.

15 And the dead man sat up and began to speak. And he gave him to his mother.

16 And all men were seized with fear; and they praised God, saying, A great prophet is risen among us; and, God has visited his people.

17 And this word about him went out through all Judea, and through the country around them.

18 ¶And John's disciples told him all these things.

19 So John called two of his disciples and sent them to Jesus, and said, Are you the one who is to come? or are we to expect another?

20 And they came to Jesus and said to him, John the Baptist has sent us to you, saying, Are you the one who is to come? or are we to expect another?

21 In that very hour he healed a great many people of their diseases and plagues, and of evil spirits; and he gave sight to many blind men.

22 So Jesus answered, saying to them, Go and tell John everything that you have seen and heard, that the blind see and the lame walk and lepers are cleansed and the deaf hear and the dead rise up and the poor are given hope.

23 And blessed is he who does not stumble on account of me.

24 ¶When John's disciples had gone, Jesus began to speak to the people concerning John, What did you go out to the wilderness to see? A reed which is shaken by the wind?

25 If not so, what did you go out to see? A man dressed in fine clothes?

Behold, those who wear fine clothes and live delicately are in kings' houses.

26 And if not so, what did you go out to see? A prophet? Yes, I say to you, and much more than a prophet.

27 This is he of whom it is written, Behold, I send my messenger before your face to prepare the way before you.

28 I say to you that there is no prophet among those who are born of women who is greater than John the Baptist; and yet even the least person in the kingdom of God is greater than he.

29 And all the people who heard it, even the tax collectors, justified themselves before God, for they were baptized with the baptism of John.

30 But the Pharisees and the scribes suppressed the will of God in themselves, because they were not baptized by him.

31 ¶To whom, therefore, shall I liken the men of this nation? and to what are they like?

32 They are like boys who sit in the street, and call to their friends and say, We have sung to you but you did not dance; and we have wailed to you and you did not weep.

33 For John the Baptist came, neither eating bread nor drinking wine; and you say, He is insane.

34 The Son of man came, eating and drinking; and you say, Behold, a glutton and a winebibber, and a friend of tax collectors and sinners!

35 And yet wisdom is justified by all its works.

36 ¶Then one of the Pharisees came and asked him to eat with him. And he entered the house of that Pharisee and reclined as a guest.

37 Now there was in that city a woman who was a sinner; and when she knew that he was a guest in the Pharisee's house, she took an alabaster cruse of perfume,

38 And stood behind him at his feet, weeping, and she began to wet his feet with her tears and to wipe them with the hair of her head, and she kissed his feet and anointed them with perfume.

39 When the Pharisee who had invited him saw it, he reasoned in himself and said, If this man were a prophet, he would have known who she is and her reputation; for the woman who has touched him is a sinner.

40 Jesus answered, saying to him, Simon, I have something to tell you. He said to him, Say it, Teacher. Jesus said to him,

41 There were two men who were debtors to a certain creditor; one of them owed him five hundred pence, and the other fifty pence.

42 And because they had nothing to pay, he forgave them both. Which one of them will love him more?

43 Simon answered, saying, I think the one to whom he forgave more. Jesus said to him, You have judged truly.

44 And he turned to the woman, and said to Simon, Do you see this woman? When I entered your house, you did not give me even water for my feet; but she has wet my feet with her tears and wiped them with her hair.

45 You did not kiss me; but she, since she entered, has not ceased to kiss my feet.

46 You did not anoint my head with oil; but she has anointed my feet with perfume.

47 For this reason, I say to you, Her many sins are forgiven because she loved much; but he to whom little is forgiven, loves little.

48 And he said to the woman, Your sins are forgiven.

49 Then the guests began to say within themselves, Who is this man who forgives even sins?

50 So Jesus said to the woman, Your faith has saved you; go in peace.

CHAPTER 8

AND it came to pass after these things Jesus was traveling in cities and villages, preaching and giving good news of the kingdom of God. And his twelve were with him,

2 And the women who were healed of diseases and unclean spirits, Mary who is called of Magdala, from whom seven demons went out,

3 And Joanna, the wife of Chuza the steward of Herod, and Susanna, and many others, who ministered to them of their wealth.

4 ¶And when many people had gathered and were coming to him from all the cities, he spoke in parables.

5 A sower went out to sow his seed. And when he had sown, some seed fell on the roadside; and it was trodden under foot, and the birds ate it.

6 Other seed fell upon the rock; and sprang up quickly, and because it had no moisture, it dried up.

7 And other seed fell among thistles; and the thistles sprang up with it and choked it.

8 And other seed fell in good and fertile ground; and sprang up and bore fruit a hundredfold. And when he said this, he cried out, He who has ears to hear, let him hear.

9 ¶And his disciples asked him, What is this parable?

10 He said to them, To you it is granted to know the mystery of the kingdom of God; but to the rest it has to be said in figures; for while they see, they do not perceive; and while they hear, they do not understand.

11 ¶This is the parable: The seed is the word of God.

12 Those on the roadside are those who hear the word, and the enemy comes and takes away the word from their hearts, so that they may not believe and be saved.

13 Those on the rock are those who when they have heard, receive the word with joy; and yet they have no root, but their belief is for a while, and in time of trial they stumble.

14 That which fell among the thistles are those who hear the word, and then choke themselves with worries and riches and worldly covetousness, and bear no fruit.

15 But that in good soil, these are those who hear the word with a pure and good heart, and keep it, and bear fruit with patience.

16 ¶No man lights a lamp and

covers it with a vessel, or puts it under the bed; but he puts it on the lamp stand, that whoever enters sees its light.

17 For there is nothing covered which will not be uncovered; and nothing hidden which will not be known and come to light.

18 Take heed how you hear; for he who has, to him shall be given; and from him who has not, even that which he thinks he has shall be taken away.

19 ¶And there came to him his mother and his brothers, and they were not able to speak to him because of the crowd.

20 And they said to him, Your mother and your brothers are standing outside, and they want to see you.

21 He answered, saying to them, These are my mother and my brothers, those who hear the word of God and do it.

22 ¶It came to pass on one of the days Jesus went up and sat in a boat with his disciples; and he said to them, Let us cross to the other side of the lake.

23 And while they were rowing, Jesus fell asleep; and there rose a storm of wind on the lake; and the boat was near sinking.

24 And they came up and awoke him and said to him, Our Teacher, our Teacher, we are perishing. He got up and rebuked the winds and the waves, and they quieted down and there was a calm.

25 And he said to them, Where is your faith? But as they were frightened, they wondered, saying one to another, O who is this man, who even commands the winds and the waves and the sea obey him?

26 And they rowed and came to the country of the Gadarenes, which is on the shore opposite Galilee.

27 And when he landed, he was met by a man from the city, who had had a demon in him for a long time, and he did not wear clothes and did not live in a house, but in the cemetery.

28 When he saw Jesus, he cried out and fell before him, and said in a loud voice, What have we in common, Jesus, Son of the Most High God? I beg you not to torment me.

29 For Jesus commanded the unclean spirit to go out of the man. For it was a long time since he was possessed and bound with chains and kept in fetters; but he would often break off his bonds and was driven into the desert by the demon.

30 Jesus asked him, What is your name? He said, Legion, because many demons had entered into him.

31 And they besought him not to command them to go down into the abyss.

32 Now there was there a herd of many swine feeding on the mountain; and they besought him to permit them to attack the swine. And he permitted them.

33 Then the demons went out of the man, and they attacked the swine; and that whole herd went straight to the cliff, and fell down into the lake and were drowned.

34 When the herdsmen saw what had happened, they fled and told it in the cities and in the villages.

35 And some men went out to see what had happened; and they came to Jesus and found the man from whom the demons had gone out, dressed and well behaved and sitting at the feet of Jesus; and they were afraid.

36 And those who had seen it told them how that lunatic was healed.

37 Then all the people of the Gadarenes besought him to leave them, because they were seized with a great fear; and Jesus went up into the boat and returned from thence.

38 But the man from whom the demons had gone out besought him to remain with him; but Jesus dismissed him and said to him,

39 Return to your own house, and declare what God has done for you. And he went away and preached throughout the city what Jesus had done for him.

40 ¶When Jesus returned, a large multitude welcomed him, for they were all expecting him.

41 And a man named Jairus, a

leader of the synagogue, fell at the feet of Jesus and besought him to enter into his house.

42 For he had an only daughter, about twelve years old, and she was near death. And as Jesus went with him, a large crowd pressed against him.

43 ¶Now a woman who had had a hemorrhage for twelve years, and had spent all her wealth for doctors, could not be healed by anybody.

44 She came near him from behind, and touched the edge of his cloak; and immediately her hemorrhage stopped.

45 And Jesus said, Who touched me? And when all of them denied it, Simon Peter and those who were with him said to him, Teacher, the crowds are troubling you and pressing on you, and yet you say, Who has touched me?

46 But he said, Some one has touched me, for I know that power has gone out of me.

47 When the woman saw that she could not deceive him, she came trembling, and fell down and worshipped him; and she said in the presence of all the people for what purpose she had touched him, and how she was healed immediately.

48 Jesus said to her, Have courage, my daughter; your faith has healed you; go in peace.

49 ¶While he was still talking, there came a man from the house of the leader of the synagogue, and said to him, Your daughter has died, do not trouble the teacher.

50 Jesus heard it and said to the father of the girl, Do not be afraid, but only believe, and she will be restored to life.

51 Jesus came into the house, and he did not allow anyone to enter with him except Simon and James and John and the father and mother of the girl.

52 And all of them were weeping and mourning over her; but Jesus said, Do not weep, for she is not dead but asleep.

53 And they laughed at him, for they knew that she was dead.

54 Then he put everybody out, and held her by her hand and called her and said, Little girl, arise.

55 And her spirit returned, and she got up immediately; and he commanded to give her something to eat.

56 And her parents were amazed; but he warned them not to tell any man what had happened.

CHAPTER 9

THEN Jesus called his twelve, and gave them power and authority over all the demons, and to cure diseases.

2 And he sent them out to preach the kingdom of God and to heal the sick.

3 And he said to them, Do not take anything for the journey, neither a staff nor a bag nor bread nor money, nor have two shirts.

4 And into whatever house you enter, remain there, and depart from thence.

5 And whoever will not welcome you, when you leave that city, shake off even the sand from your feet for a testimony against them.

6 And the apostles went out, and travelled in villages and cities, preaching the gospel and healing everywhere.

7 ¶Now Herod the tetrarch heard of all that was done by his hand; and he was amazed, because some men said that John has risen from the dead.

8 But others, that Elijah has appeared; and others, that one of the old prophets has risen.

9 So Herod said, I have beheaded John; but who is this one concerning whom I hear these things? And he wanted to see him.

10 ¶When the apostles returned, they told Jesus everything which they had done. And he took them all alone to a lonely place in Bethsaida.

11 When the people found it out, they went after him; and he received them, and spoke to them concerning the kingdom of God, and he healed those who were in need of healing.

12 ¶And when the day began to wane, his disciples came up and said

to him, Dismiss the people, that they may go to the villages around us and to the farms, to lodge there and find food for themselves, because we are in a lonely place.

13 Jesus said to them, You give them to eat. But they said, We do not have more than five loaves of bread and two fish, unless we go and buy food for all this people;

14 For there were about five thousand men. Jesus said to them, Make them sit down in groups, fifty men in each group.

15 The disciples did so, making them all sit down.

16 And Jesus took the five loaves of bread and the two fish, and looked up to heaven and blessed them, and broke and gave them to his disciples to set before the people.

17 And they all ate and were filled; and they took up fragments of what was left over, twelve baskets.

18 ¶As he prayed by himself, his disciples were with him; then he asked them and said, What do the people say concerning me that I am?

19 They answered and said to him, John the Baptist; and others, Elijah; and others that one of the old prophets has risen.

20 He said to them, But you, who do you say that I am? Simon answered and said, The Messiah (the anointed one of God).

21 But he cautioned them, and warned them not to say this to anyone.

22 And he said to them, The Son of man must suffer a great many things, and he will be rejected by the elders and the high priests and the scribes, and they will kill him, and on the third day he will rise.

23 ¶Then he said in the presence of everyone, He who wishes to come after me, let him deny himself and take up his cross every day and follow me.

24 For he who wishes to save his life shall lose it; but he who loses his life for my sake shall save it.

25 For how can a man be benefited, if he gain the whole world, but lose his own soul, or even weakens it?

26 For whoever is ashamed of me and of my words, the Son of man will be ashamed of him when he comes with the glory of his Father accompanied by his holy angels.

27 I tell you the truth, that there are men who stand here who will not taste death until they see the kingdom of God.

28 ¶And it came to pass about eight days after these words, Jesus took Simon and James and John, and went up into a mountain to pray.

29 And while he prayed, the appearance of his face was changed and his clothes became white and dazzling.

30 And behold, two men were speaking with him, Moses and Elijah,

31 Who appeared in glory and spoke concerning his departure which was to end at Jerusalem.

32 And Simon and those who were with him were heavy with sleep; and when they awoke they saw his glory and the two men who stood with him.

33 And when they began to leave him, Simon said to Jesus, Teacher, it is better for us to remain here; and let us make three shelters, one for you, one for Moses, and one for Elijah; but he did not know what he was saying.

34 And when he had said these things, there came a cloud and overshadowed them; and they were frightened when they saw Moses and Elijah enter into the cloud.

35 And there came a voice out of the cloud, saying, This is my beloved Son; hear him.

36 And when the voice was heard, they found Jesus alone. And they kept silent, and in those days they did not tell any man what they saw.

37 ¶And it came to pass the next day, as they came down from the mountain, they were met by many people.

38 And one of the men of that crowd cried out and said, O Teacher, I beg you to have mercy on me. I have an only son,

39 And a spirit seizes him and he suddenly cries out and gnashes his

teeth and foams; and it hardly leaves him when it has tormented him.

40 And I besought your disciples to cast it out; and they could not.

41 Jesus answered, saying, O crooked and faithless generation, how long will I be with you and preach to you? Bring your son here.

42 And as he brought him, the demon attacked him and convulsed him. And Jesus rebuked the unclean spirit and healed the boy and gave him to his father.

43 ¶And they were all amazed at the greatness of God. And while every man wondered at everything which Jesus did, he said to his disciples,

44 Treasure these words in your ears; for the Son of man will be delivered into the hands of men.

45 But they did not understand this word, because it was hidden from them so that they might not know it; and they were afraid to ask him concerning this word.

46 ¶Then a reasoning entered into their minds as to who was the greatest among them.

47 But Jesus knew the reasoning of their hearts, and he took a boy and made him stand by him.

48 And he said to them, Everyone who receives a little child like this one in my name, receives me; and he who receives me receives him who sent me; for whoever is least among you, let him be great.

49 And John answered, saying, Teacher, we saw a man casting out demons in your name; and we forbad him, because he did not come with us as your follower.

50 Jesus said to them, Do not forbid; for he who is not against you is for you.

51 ¶And it happened when the days to go up on his journey were fulfilled, he set his face to go to Jerusalem.

52 So he sent messengers ahead of him; and they went away and entered into a Samaritan village to prepare for him.

53 But they did not receive him, because his face was set to go straight to Jerusalem.

54 When his disciples James and John saw it, they said to him, Our Lord, would you be willing that we command fire to come down from heaven and consume them, just as Elijah did?

55 He turned and rebuked them, saying, You do not know of what spirit you are.

56 For the Son of man did not come to destroy lives, but to save. And they went to another village.

57 ¶And while they were on the journey, a man said to him, My Lord, I will follow you wherever you go.

58 Jesus said to him, Foxes have holes, and the birds of the air a shelter; but the Son of man has no place even to lay his head.

59 He said to another, Follow me; but he said to him, My Lord, permit me first to go and bury [1] my father.

60 Jesus said to him, Let the dead bury their own dead; but you go and preach the kingdom of God.

61 Another one said to him, I will follow you, my Lord; but permit me first to entrust my household to some one, and then come.

62 Jesus said to him, No man who puts his hand on the plough handle and looks back is fit for the kingdom of God.

CHAPTER 10

AFTER these things, Jesus selected from his disciples seventy others, and sent them two by two before him to every place and city to which he was to go.

2 And he said to them, The harvest is great and the laborers are few; ask therefore the owner of the harvest to bring out laborers to his harvest.

3 Go forth; behold, I send you as lambs among wolves.

4 Do not carry purses nor bags nor shoes; and do not salute any man on the road.

5 And to whatever house you enter, first say, Peace be to this house.

6 And if a man of peace is there,

[1] Aramaic idiom, meaning *take care of until death.*

let your peace rest upon him; and if not, your peace will return to you.

7 Remain in that house, eating and drinking of what they have; for a laborer is worthy of his wages. Do not keep moving from house to house.

8 And into whatever city you enter, and they receive you, eat whatever they set before you;

9 And heal those who are sick in it, and say to them, The kingdom of God is come near to you.

10 But into whatever city you enter, and they do not receive you, go out into the street and say,

11 Even the sand of your city which cleaves to our feet we shake off to you; but know this that the kingdom of God has come near to you.

12 I say to you that it will be much easier for Sodom in that day than for that city.

13 Woe to you, Chorazin! Woe to you, Bethsaida! If the mighty works which were done in you had been done in Tyre and Sidon, perhaps they might have repented in sackcloth and ashes.

14 But, it will be easier for Tyre and Sidon at the judgment day than for you.

15 And you, Capernaum, which have exalted yourself up to heaven, you will be brought down to Sheol.

16 He who hears you hears me; and he who oppresses you oppresses me; and he who oppresses me oppresses him who sent me.

17 ¶So the seventy whom he had sent returned with great joy, and they said to him, Our Lord, even the demons have submitted to us in your name.

18 He said to them, I saw Satan falling like lightning from heaven.

19 Behold, I give you power to tread on snakes and scorpions, and overcome the power of the enemy; and nothing shall harm you.

20 But do not rejoice in this that the demons submit to you; but rejoice because your names are written in heaven.

21 ¶At that very hour, Jesus rejoiced in the Holy Spirit and said, I thank thee, O my Father, Lord of heaven and earth, because thou didst hide these things from the wise and men of understanding, and revealed them to children; yes, my Father, for so it was well pleasing in thy presence.

22 And he turned to his disciples and said to them, Everything has been entrusted to me by my Father; and no man knows who is the Son except the Father; and who is the Father except the Son, and to whomever the Son wishes to reveal him.

23 Then he turned to his disciples alone and said, Blessed are the eyes which see what you see.

24 For I say to you that many prophets and kings desired to see what you see, and did not see it; and to hear what you hear, and did not hear it.

25 ¶And behold, a scribe stood up to test him, and he said, Teacher, what shall I do to inherit eternal life?

26 Jesus said to him, What is written in the law? How do you read it?

27 He answered, saying to him, You must love the Lord your God with all your heart and with all your soul and with all your strength and with all your mind; and your neighbor as yourself.

28 Jesus said to him, You spoke the truth; do this and you shall live.

29 But as he wanted to justify himself, he said to him, And who is my neighbor?

30 Jesus said to him, There was a man who went down from Jerusalem to Jericho, and bandits attacked him and robbed him and beat him and left him with little life remaining in him, and they went away.

31 And it chanced a priest was going down that road; and he saw him and passed on.

32 And likewise a Levite came and arrived at that place, and saw him and passed on.

33 But a Samaritan, as he journeyed, came where he was, and when he saw him, he had compassion on him.

34 And he came to him and bound up his wounds and poured on them wine and oil; and he put him on his own ass and brought him to the inn and took care of him.

35 And in the morning, he took out two pennies and gave them to the innkeeper, and said to him, Take care of him; and whatever you spend more, when I return, I will give it to you.

36 Who therefore of these three, as it appears to you, became neighbor to him who fell into the hands of the bandits?

37 He said, The one who had compassion on him. Jesus said to him, You go also, and do likewise.

38 ¶And it came to pass while they were journeying, he entered into a village; and a woman named Martha received him into her house.

39 And she had a sister whose name was Mary, and she came and sat at the feet of our Lord and listened to his words.

40 But Martha was busy with many household cares, and she came and said to him, My Lord, you do not seem to care that my sister has left me to serve alone? Tell her to help me.

41 Jesus answered and said to her, Martha, Martha, you are worried and excited about many things;

42 But one thing is more important; and Mary has chosen the good portion for herself, which shall not be taken away from her.

CHAPTER 11

AND it came to pass while he was praying in a certain place, when he finished, one of his disciples said to him, Our Lord, teach us to pray, just as John also taught his disciples.

2 Jesus said to them, When you pray, pray like this, Our Father in heaven, Hallowed be thy name. Thy kingdom come. Thy will be done, as in heaven, so on earth.

3 Give us bread for our needs every day.

4 And forgive us our sins, for we have also forgiven all who have offended us. And do not let us enter into temptation; but deliver us from error.[1]

5 And he said to them, Who is there among you who has a friend, and if he should go to him at midnight and say to him, My friend, lend me three loaves,

6 For a friend has come to me from a journey and I have nothing to set before him,

7 Would his friend from inside answer, saying to him, Do not trouble me; the door is already locked and my children are with me in bed; I cannot get up and give you bread?

8 I say to you that if because of friendship he will not give him, yet because of his persistence, he will rise and give him as much as he wants.

9 I say to you also, Ask, and it shall be given to you; seek, and you shall find; knock, and it shall be opened to you.

10 For everyone who asks, receives; and he who seeks, finds; and he who knocks, it is opened to him.

11 For who is among you, a father, if his son should ask him bread, what! would he hand him a stone? and if he should ask him a fish, what! would he hand him a snake instead of a fish?

12 And if he should ask him for an egg, what! would he hand him a scorpion?

13 So if you, who err, know how to give good gifts to your children, how much more will your Father give the Holy Spirit from heaven to those who ask him?

14 ¶And while he was casting out a demon from a dumb man, it came to pass when the demon went out, the dumb man spoke; and the people were amazed.

15 But some of the men among them said, This man casts out devils by Beelzebub, the prince of devils.

16 And others, tempting him, asked him for a sign from heaven.

17 But Jesus knew their thoughts, and said to them, Every kingdom which is divided against itself shall be

1 Anything contrary to the truth; evil.

destroyed; and a house which is divided against itself shall fall.

18 And if Satan is divided against himself, how can his kingdom survive? And yet you say I am casting out devils through Beelzebub.

19 If I cast out devils through Beelzebub, by what do your sons cast them out? Therefore they will be your judges.

20 But if I cast out devils by the finger of God, then the kingdom of God is come near you.

21 When a strong man is armed and keeps watch over his courtyard,[1] his property is safe;

22 But if there should come one who is stronger than he, he will conquer him and take away his armor in which he trusted and divide his spoil.

23 He who is not with me is against me; and he who does not gather with me will scatter.

24 ¶When an unclean spirit is gone out of a man, it goes away and travels in places where there is no water, to seek rest; and when it finds it not, it says, I will return to my own house from whence I came.

25 And if it should come and find it warm and well furnished,

26 Then it goes away and brings seven other spirits worse than itself; and they enter and dwell there; and the end of that man will become worse than the beginning.

27 ¶While he was saying these things, a woman out of the multitude lifted up her voice and said to him, Blessed is the womb which bore you and the breasts which gave you suck.

28 He said to her, Blessed are they who hear the word of God and keep it.

29 ¶And when the people were gathering, he began to say, This evil generation wants a sign; and no sign will be given to it except the sign of the prophet Jonah.

30 For as Jonah was a sign to the Ninevites, so also will the Son of man be to this generation.

31 The queen of the south will rise up in judgment with the men of this generation and condemn them; for she came from the far ends of the earth to hear the wisdom of Solomon; and behold, a greater than Solomon is here.

32 The men of Nineveh will rise up in judgment against this generation and condemn it; for they repented at the preaching of Jonah; and behold, a greater than Jonah is here.

33 ¶No man lights a lamp and puts it in a hidden place or under a basket, but on a lamp holder, so that those who enter may see its light.

34 The lamp of your body is your eye; when therefore your eye is bright, your whole body will also be lighted; but if it is diseased, your whole body will also be dark.

35 Take heed, therefore, lest the light which is in you be darkness.

36 If your whole body is lighted and there is no part in it dark, the whole of it will give light, just as a lamp gives you light with its shining.

37 ¶While he spoke, a Pharisee asked him to dine with him; and he entered and reclined.

38 When the Pharisee saw him, he was amazed because he did not first wash before dinner.

39 And Jesus said to him, Now you Pharisees clean the outside of the cup and the dish; but within you are full of extortion and iniquity.

40 O you shortsighted, did not he who made the outside also make the inside?

41 But give alms of what you have; and, behold, everything will be clean to you.

42 But woe to you Pharisees! who take tithes of mint and dill and every kind of vegetable, but overlook justice and the love of God. These were necessary for you to have done, the very ones by no means to have been left undone.

43 Woe to you Pharisees! for you love chief seats in the synagogues and salutations in the streets.

44 Woe to you, scribes and Pharisees, hypocrites! for you are like

---

[1] The courtyard is often used to house cattle and sheep, which is the main property of an Easterner.

graves that cannot be recognized, and men walk over them and know it not.

45 One of the scribes answered, saying to him, Teacher, when you say these things, you reproach us also.

46 But he said, Woe also to you, scribes! for you lay heavy burdens on men, and you yourselves do not touch these burdens even with one of your fingers.

47 Woe to you! for you build the tombs of prophets whom your fathers killed.

48 Therefore you are witnesses, and you approve the works of your fathers; for they killed them, and yet you build their tombs.

49 For this reason the wisdom of God also said, Behold, I will send them prophets and apostles, some of whom they will persecute and kill;

50 That the blood of all the prophets which was shed since the creation of the world may be avenged on this nation;

51 From the blood of Abel to the blood of Zechariah, who was killed between the temple and the altar; yes, I say to you, it will be avenged on this nation.

52 Woe to you, scribes! for you have taken away the keys of knowledge; you did not enter, and those who were entering you hindered.

53 When he had said these things to them, the scribes and the Pharisees were displeased and they were enraged and criticised his words.

54 And they plotted against him in many ways, seeking to catch something out of his mouth so that they might be able to accuse him.

CHAPTER 12

WHEN a large number of people had gathered together so that they trod on one another, Jesus began to say to his disciples first of all, Beware of the leaven of the Pharisees, which is hypocrisy.

2 For there is nothing that is covered that will not be uncovered; and hidden that will not be known.

3 For whatever you have said in darkness will be heard in the light; and what you have whispered in the ears in the inner chambers will be preached on the housetops.

4 I say to you, my friends, Do not be afraid of those who kill the body, and after that have nothing more they can do.

5 But I will show you of whom to be afraid; of him who after he has killed has the power to throw into hell; yes, I say to you, Fear him.

6 Are not five sparrows sold for two pennies? And yet not one of them is lost before God.

7 But so far as you are concerned, even the hairs of your head are all numbered; therefore fear not, because you are much more important than many sparrows.

8 I say to you, Whoever will acknowledge me before men, the Son of man will also acknowledge him before the angels of God.

9 But he who denies me before men I will deny before the angels of God.

10 And whoever says a word against the Son of man will be forgiven; but he who blasphemes against the Holy Spirit will not be forgiven.

11 When they bring you to the synagogues before the leaders and authorities, do not worry how you will answer or what you will say;

12 For the Holy Spirit will teach you at that very hour what you ought to say.

13 ¶And one of the men from the crowd said to him, Teacher, ask my brother to divide the inheritance with me.

14 Jesus said to him, Man, who appointed me a judge or a property divider over you?

15 And he said to his disciples, Beware of all covetousness, because life does not depend on abundance of wealth.

16 Then he told them a parable. The land of a rich man brought him a great many crops.

17 And he reasoned within himself, saying, What shall I do, for I have no place to gather my crops?

18 So he said, I will do this: I will

tear down my barns and rebuild them and enlarge them, and gather there all my wheat and my good things.

19 And I will say to myself, Soul, you have many good things stored up for many years; rest, eat, drink, and be happy.

20 But God said to him, O you shortsighted man, this very night your life will be demanded of you; and these things which you have prepared, to whom will they be left?

21 Such is he who lays up treasures for himself and is not rich in the things of God.

22 And he said to his disciples, Therefore I say to you, Do not worry for your life, what you will eat; nor for your body, what you will wear.

23 For life is much more important than food, and the body than clothing.

24 Observe the ravens; for they do not sow or reap, and they have no storerooms and barns; and yet God feeds them; how much more important are you than the birds?

25 Who among you by worrying can add to his stature one cubit?

26 So if you are not able to do the smaller thing, why do you worry about the rest?

27 Observe the flowers, how they grow; for they do not toil nor do they spin; but I say to you that not even Solomon in all his glory was arrayed like one of these.

28 And if God clothes in such fashion the grass of the field, which today is and tomorrow falls into the fireplace; how much more is he to you, O you of little faith?

29 So do not be anxious about what you will eat or what you will drink, and let not your mind be disturbed by these things.

30 For worldly people seek after all these things; and your Father knows that these things are also necessary for you.

31 But seek the kingdom of God, and all of these things shall be added to you.

32 Do not be afraid, O little flock; for your Father is pleased to give you the kingdom.

33 Sell your possessions and give them as alms; make for yourselves purses which do not wear out, and a treasure in heaven that does not run short, where the thief does not come near, and moth does not destroy.

34 For where your treasure is, there also will be your heart.

35 ¶Let your girdle be fastened on your loins, and your lamps lighted.

36 And be like men who expect their master when he will return from the wedding house; so that when he comes and knocks, they will immediately open the door for him.

37 Blessed are those servants, whom their master, when he comes, finds awake; truly I say to you that he will gird himself and make them sit down, and come in and serve them.

38 If he should come in the second or the third watch and find them so, blessed are those servants.

39 But know this, that if the master of the house knew at what watch the thief would come, he would have kept awake and not allowed his house to be plundered.

40 Therefore, you also be ready; for the Son of man will come in that very hour which you do not expect.

41 ¶Simon Peter said to him, Our Lord, do you speak this parable to us or also to all men?

42 Jesus said to him, Who is the faithful and wise steward, whom his master will appoint over his household to give supplies in due time?

43 Blessed is that servant, whom his master when he comes will find so doing.

44 Truly I say to you that he will appoint him over all his wealth.

45 But if that servant should say in his heart, My master has delayed his coming; and begins to beat the menservants and maidservants of his master, and then begins to eat and drink and get drunk;

46 The master of that servant will come in a day and at an hour that he does not expect or know; and he will severely punish him, and place him with those who are not trustworthy.

47 And the servant who knows the wishes of his master, and does not make ready according to his wishes, will receive a severe beating.

48 But he who does not know, and does what is worthy of punishment will receive less beating. For to whomever more is given, of him more will be required; and to whom much is entrusted, more will be required of his hand.

49 ¶I came to set the earth on fire; and I wish to do it, if it has not already been kindled.

50 I have a baptism to be baptized with; and I am oppressed until it is fulfilled.

51 Do you think that I have come to bring peace on earth? I say to you, No, but divisions;

52 For from henceforth there will be five in a house, who will be divided, three against two, and two against three.

53 For a father will be divided against his son, and a son against his father; a mother against her daughter, and a daughter against her mother; a mother-in-law against her daughter-in-law, and a daughter-in-law against her mother-in-law.

54 ¶And he said to the people, When you see a cloud rise from the west, you immediately say, It will rain; and so it is.

55 And when the wind blows from the south, you say, It will be hot; and it is so.

56 O you hypocrites, you know how to discern the face of the earth and of the sky; how then is it that you do not discern this time?

57 Why do you not of yourselves judge what is right?

58 ¶For when you go with your accuser to the ruler, while you are on the way give something and settle with him; otherwise he might take you to the judge, and the judge will deliver you to the prison warden, and the prison warden will throw you into prison.

59 Truly I say to you, you will not come out from thence until you pay the last penny.

CHAPTER 13

AT that time there came some men and told him about the Galileans whose blood Pilate had mingled with their sacrifices.

2 And Jesus answered, saying to them, Do you think that those Galileans were greater sinners than all the other Galileans, because this happened to them?

3 No; but I say to you that all of you also, if you do not repent, will perish in the same way.

4 Or those eighteen upon whom the tower in Shiloha fell, and it killed them; do you think that they were greater sinners than all the other men who live in Jerusalem?

5 No, but I say to you that unless you repent, all of you will perish like them.

6 ¶And he spoke this parable: A man had a fig tree planted in his vineyard; and he came and sought fruit on it, and he did not find any.

7 So he said to the laborer, Behold, for three years I have been coming and seeking fruit on this fig tree, and found none; cut it down; why should the ground be wasted?

8 The laborer said to him, My lord, let it remain this year also, until I work it and fertilize it.

9 It might bear fruit; and if not, then you can cut it down.

10 ¶While Jesus was teaching in one of the synagogues on the sabbath,

11 There was there a woman who had been afflicted with rheumatism for eighteen years, and was bent down and could never straighten herself at all.

12 Jesus saw her and called her and said to her, Woman, you are cured of your sickness.

13 And he laid his hand on her, and immediately she straightened up and praised God.

14 But the leader of the synagogue answered with anger, because Jesus healed on the sabbath; and he said to the people, There are six days in which men should work; in those

days you ought to come and be healed, and not on the sabbath day.

15 Jesus answered, saying to him, O hypocrites, does not each one of you loose his ox or his ass from the manger, and go with it to give it drink?

16 This one is a daughter of Abraham, and behold, the adversary has bound her for eighteen years; was it not necessary for her to be loosened from this bond on the sabbath day?

17 And when he said these things, all who opposed him were ashamed; and all the people rejoiced over all the wonders which were done by his hand.

18 ¶Jesus said, To what is the kingdom of God like? and to what shall I liken it?

19 It is like a grain of mustard seed which a man took and cast into his garden, and it grew and became a large tree, and the birds of the air nested on its branches.

20 ¶Again Jesus said, To what shall I liken the kingdom of God?

21 It is like the leaven which a woman took and buried in three measures of flour until it was all leavened.

22 ¶And he journeyed through the villages and cities, teaching, while going to Jerusalem.

23 A man asked him, Are there only a few who are to be saved? Jesus said to them,

24 Strive to enter in through the narrow door; for I say to you, that many will seek to enter in and will not be able.

25 From the hour when the master of the house rises up and locks the door, you will be standing outside and knocking at the door, and you will begin to say, Our Lord, our Lord, open for us; and he will answer, saying, I say to you, I do not know you or where you come from.

26 And you will begin to say, We have eaten and drunk in your presence, and you taught in our streets.

27 And he will say to you, I do not know you or where you come from;

depart from me, O you workers of iniquity.

28 There will be weeping and gnashing of teeth when you see Abraham and Isaac and Jacob and all the prophets in the kingdom of God, but you will be thrown outside.

29 And they will come from the east and from the west and from the south and from the north, and sit down in the kingdom of God.

30 And behold, there are some who are last who will be first, and there are some who are first who will be last.

31 ¶In that very day some of the men of the Pharisees drew near and said to him, Get out and go away from here; for Herod wants to kill you.

32 Jesus said to them, Go and tell that fox, Behold, I cast out demons and I heal today and tomorrow, and on the third day I will be finished.

33 But I must do my work today and tomorrow, and I will leave the next day, because it is impossible that a prophet should perish outside of Jerusalem.

34 O Jerusalem, Jerusalem, murderess of prophets and stoner of those who are sent to her! How many times I longed to gather your children together as a hen gathers her chickens under her wings, but you were not willing!

35 Behold, your house is left to you desolate; and I say to you that you will not see me until you say, Blessed is he who comes in the name of the Lord.

CHAPTER 14

AND it came to pass when he entered the house of one of the leaders of the Pharisees to eat bread on a sabbath day, they watched him.

2 And there was a man before him who had dropsy.

3 And Jesus answered, saying to the scribes and Pharisees, Is it lawful to heal on the sabbath?

4 But they kept silent. So he took him and healed him and let him go.

5 And he said to them, Which one

of you, if his son or his ox should fall into a pit on the sabbath day, would not immediately pull and bring him out?

6 And they could not answer him concerning this.

7 ¶And he spoke a parable to those who were invited there, because he saw them choosing places among the front seats.

8 When you are invited of a man to a banquet house, do not go and sit in the front seat; it might be that a more honorable man than you is invited there;

9 And then he who has invited you and him will come and say to you, Give the place to him; and you will be embarrassed when you get up and take a lower seat.

10 But when you are invited, go and sit at the lower end, so that when he who has invited you comes, he will say to you, My friend, go up and sit higher; and you will have glory before all who sit with you.

11 For whoever exalts himself will be humbled; and whoever humbles himself will be exalted.

12 He also said to him who had invited him, When you give a dinner or a supper, do not invite your friends nor your brothers nor your relatives nor your rich neighbors; lest they invite you, and you will be repaid for this.

13 But when you give a reception, invite the poor, the maimed, the lame, and the blind;

14 And you will be blessed; for they have nothing to repay you; for you will be repaid at the resurrection of the righteous.

15 When one of the guests heard these things, he said to him, Blessed is he who will eat bread in the kingdom of God.

16 Jesus said to him, A man gave a great supper, and invited many.

17 And he sent his servant at supper time to tell those who were invited, Behold, everything is made ready for you, come.

18 One and all, they began to make excuses. The first said to him, I have bought a field, and I am forced to go

and see it; I beg you to excuse me for being called away.

19 Another said, I have bought five yoke of oxen, and I am just going to examine them; I beg you, excuse me for being called away.

20 Another said, I have just taken a wife, and therefore I cannot come.

21 And the servant came and told his master these things. Then the master of the house was angry, and said to his servant, Go out quickly to the streets and lanes of the city, and bring in here the poor, the afflicted, the maimed, and the blind.

22 And the servant said, My Lord, it has been done as you commanded, and yet there is more room.

23 Then the master said to his servant, Go out to the highways and hedges, and urge them to come in so that my house may be filled.

24 For I say to you that not one of those men who were invited shall taste of my supper.

25 ¶And while many people were going with him, he turned and said to them,

26 He who comes to me and does not put aside his father and his mother and his brothers and his sisters and his wife and his children and even his own life cannot be a disciple to me.

27 And he who does not take up his cross and follow me cannot be a disciple to me.

28 For which of you who wishes to build a tower does not at first sit down and consider its cost, to see if he has enough to finish it?

29 Lest after he has laid the foundation, he is not able to finish it, and all who see it will mock him,

30 Saying, This man began to build, but he was not able to finish.

31 Or which king who goes to war to fight against a king equal to him would not at first reason whether he is able with ten thousand to meet the one who is coming against him with twenty thousand?

32 And if not, while he is far away from him, sends envoys and seeks peace.

33 So every man of you who would

not leave all his possessions cannot be a disciple to me.

34 Salt is good; but if the salt lose its savor, with what can it be salted?

35 It is good neither for the ground nor for fertilizing; but it is thrown out. He who has ears to hear let him hear.

CHAPTER 15

THEN the tax collectors and sinners drew near to him to hear him.

2 And the scribes and Pharisees murmured, saying, He receives even the sinners and eats with them.

3 ¶So Jesus told them this parable:

4 What man among you has a hundred sheep, and if one of them should get lost, would he not leave the ninety and nine in the open, and go in search of the one which is lost, until he finds it?

5 And when he finds it he rejoices and takes it on his shoulders.

6 And he comes to his house, and invites his friends and neighbors, and says to them, Rejoice with me, for I have found my sheep which was lost.

7 I say to you that such will be the joy in heaven over one sinner who repents, more than over ninety and nine righteous who need no repentance.

8 ¶Or what woman who has ten coins, and should lose one of them, would not light a lamp and sweep the house and search for it carefully until she finds it?

9 And when she finds it, she calls her women friends and neighbors, and says to them, Rejoice with me, for I have found my coin which was lost.

10 I say to you that such will be the joy before the angels of God over one sinner who repents.

11 ¶And Jesus said to them again, A man had two sons;

12 And his younger son said to him, My father, give me the portion which is coming to me from your house. And he divided to them his possessions.

13 And after a few days, his younger son gathered everything that was his share, and went to a far country,

and there he wasted his wealth in extravagant living.

14 And when all he had was gone, there was a severe famine in that country; and he began to be in need.

15 So he went and got acquainted with one of the citizens of that country; and he sent him to the field to feed the swine.

16 And he craved to fill his stomach with the husks that the swine were eating; and yet no man would give him.

17 And when he came to himself, he said, How many hired workers are now in my father's house who have plenty of bread, and I am here perishing with hunger!

18 I will rise and go to my father and say to him, My father, I have sinned before heaven and before you;

19 And I am no longer worthy to be called your son; just make me like one of your hired workers.

20 And he rose up and came to his father. And while he was yet at a distance, his father saw him and had compassion on him, and he ran and fell on his neck and kissed him.

21 And his son said to him, My father, I have sinned before heaven and before you, and I am not worthy to be called your son.

22 But his father said to his servants, Bring the best robe and put it on him and put a ring on his hand and shoes on his feet;

23 And bring and kill the fat ox, and let us eat and be merry;

24 For this my son was dead and has come to life; he was lost and is found. And they began to be merry.

25 But his elder son was in the field; and as he came near the house, he heard the voice of the singing of many.

26 And he called one of the boys, and asked him what it was all about.

27 He said to him, Your brother has come; and your father has killed the fat ox because he received him safe and well.

28 And he became angry and would not go in; so his father came out and besought him.

29 But he said to his father, Behold,

how many years I have served you, and I never disobeyed your commandment; and yet you never gave me even a kid that I might make merry with my friends.

30 But for this son of yours, after he had wasted your wealth with harlots and come back, you have killed the fat ox.

31 His father said to him, My son, you are always with me, and everything which is mine is yours.

32 It was right for us to make merry and rejoice; for this your brother was dead and has come to life; and was lost and is found.

CHAPTER 16

AND he spoke a parable to his disciples, saying, There was a rich man, who had a steward; and they accused him that he was wasting his wealth.

2 So his master called him and said to him, What is this that I hear concerning you? Give me an account of your stewardship; for no longer can you be a steward for me.

3 Then the steward said to himself, What will I do? For my lord will take away from me the stewardship. I cannot dig, and I am ashamed to beg.

4 Now I know what I will do so that when I leave the stewardship, they will receive me in their houses.

5 And he called his lord's debtors, one by one, and said to the first, How much do you owe my lord?

6 He said to him, A hundred measures of butter. He said to him, Take your note; sit down quickly, and write fifty pounds.

7 And he said to another, And you, what do you owe to my lord? He said to him, One hundred bushels of wheat. He said to him, Take your note, and sit down and write eighty bushels.

8 And the lord praised the unjust steward because he had done wisely; for the children of this world are wiser in their generation than the children of light.

9 And I also say to you, Use this earthly wealth, however acquired, to make friends so that when it is gone, they will receive you and you will have everlasting habitation.

10 He who is faithful with little is also faithful with much; and he who is dishonest with little is also dishonest with much.

11 If, therefore, you are not faithful with the wealth of iniquity, who will believe that there is any truth in you?

12 And if you are not found faithful with that which is not your own, who will give you that which is your own?

13 No servant can serve two masters; for either he will hate the one and like the other; or he will honor one and despise the other. You cannot serve God and mammon (wealth).

14 ¶When the Pharisees heard all these things, because they loved money, they ridiculed him.

15 But Jesus said to them, You are the ones who make yourselves righteous before men; but God knows your hearts. For what is highly esteemed among men is disgusting in the presence of God.

16 The law and prophets were until John; from that time the kingdom of God is preached, and everyone presses to enter into it.

17 It is easier for heaven and earth to pass away than for one letter of the law to pass away.

18 He who divorces his wife and marries another commits adultery; and he who marries the one who is illegally separated commits adultery.

19 ¶There was a rich man, who used to wear purple and fine linen, and every day he made merry very lavishly.

20 And there was a poor man named Lazarus, who was laid down at that rich man's door, afflicted with boils;

21 He longed to fill his stomach with the crumbs that fell from the rich man's table; the dogs also came and licked his boils.

22 Now it happened that the poor man died, and the angels carried him into Abraham's bosom; and the rich man also died and was buried.

23 And while he was tormented in

Sheol, he lifted up his eyes from a distance, and saw Abraham with Lazarus in his bosom.

24 And he called in a loud voice, saying, O my father Abraham, have mercy on me and send Lazarus to dip his finger in water and wet my tongue; for I am tormented in this flame.

25 Abraham said to him, My son, remember you received your pleasures when you were living, and Lazarus his hardships; and behold now he is comfortable here, and you are suffering.

26 Besides all these things, a great gulf is fixed between us and you; so that those who wish to cross over from here to you cannot, neither from there to cross over to us.

27 He said to him, If that is so, I beseech you, O my father, to send him to my father's house;

28 For I have five brothers; let him go and testify to them, so that they may not also come to this place of torment.

29 Abraham said to him, They have Moses and the prophets;[1] let them hear them.

30 But he said to him, No, my father Abraham; but if only a man from the dead go to them, they will repent.

31 Abraham said to him, If they will not hear Moses and the prophets, neither will they believe even if a man should rise from the dead.

CHAPTER 17

AND Jesus said to his disciples, It is impossible but that offences should come; but woe to him by whose hand they come!

2 It were better for him that an ass' millstone were hanged on his neck, and he were thrown into the sea, than to cause one of these little ones to stumble.

3 ¶Beware among yourselves. If your brother should sin, rebuke him; and if he repents, forgive him.

4 And if he should offend you seven times in a day, and seven times in a day turn to you and say, I repent; forgive him.

5 ¶And the apostles said to our Lord, Increase our faith.

6 He said to them, If you have faith even as a grain of mustard seed, you could say to this mulberry tree, Be uprooted and planted in the sea; and it would obey you.

7 ¶Now which of you has a servant who ploughs or feeds sheep, and if he should come from the field, would say to him, Enter in and sit down?

8 But he will rather say to him, Prepare something that I may have my supper, and gird yourself and serve me until I eat and drink; and then you also can eat and drink.

9 What! will that servant receive praise, because he did what he was commanded to do? I do not think so.

10 Even you also, when you have done all the things which are commanded you, say, We are idle servants; we have only done what was our duty to do.

11 ¶And it came to pass while Jesus was going to Jerusalem, he went through Samaritan territory which is towards Galilee.

12 And when he drew near to enter a village, he was met by ten lepers, and they stood afar off;

13 And they lifted their voices saying, O Jesus, our Master, have mercy on us.

14 And when he saw them he said to them, Go show yourselves to the priests; and while they were going, they were cleansed.

15 But one of them, when he saw that he was cleansed, turned back, and with a loud voice praised God.

16 And he fell on his face at the feet of Jesus, thanking him; and this one was a Samaritan.

17 Jesus answering said, Were there not ten who were cleansed? Where are the nine?

18 Why did they separate themselves so as not to come and give praise to God, except this man who is of a strange people?

19 And he said to him, Arise, go; your faith has healed you.

[1] That is, the books of Moses and the prophets.

20 ¶When some of the Pharisees asked Jesus when the kingdom of God would come, he answered, saying to them, The kingdom of God does not come by observation.

21 Neither will they say, Behold, it is here! or, behold, it is there! for behold, the kingdom of God is within you.

22 And he said to his disciples, The time will come when you will covet to see one of the days of the Son of man, and you will not see it.

23 And if they should say to you, Behold, he is here! and behold, he is there! do not go.

24 For just as the lightning flashes from the sky, and all under the sky is lighted, such will be the day of the Son of man.

25 But first he must suffer a great many things, and be rejected by this generation.

26 Just as it happened in the days of Noah, such will it be in the days of the Son of man.

27 For they were eating and drinking, and marrying and giving in marriage, until the day when Noah entered the ark, and the flood came and destroyed every man.

28 And again, just as it happened in the days of Lot; they were eating and drinking, and buying and selling, and planting and building;

29 But in the day when Lot went out of Sodom, the Lord sent down a rain of fire and sulphur from heaven, and destroyed them all.

30 Such will it be in the day when the Son of man appears.

31 In that day, he who is on the roof, with his clothes in the house, will not come down to take them; and he who is in the field will not turn back.

32 Just remember Lot's wife.

33 He who desires to save his life shall lose it; and he who loses his life shall save it.

34 I say to you that in that very night two will be in one bed; one will be taken and the other left.

35 And two women will be grinding together; one will be taken and the other left.

36 Two will be in the field; one will be taken and the other left.

37 They answered, saying to him, Our Lord, to what place? He said to them, Wherever the carcass is, there will the vultures gather.

CHAPTER 18

HE also spoke to them a parable, that they should pray always and not get weary.

2 There was a judge in a city, who neither feared God nor regarded men.

3 And there was a widow in that city who used to come to him, saying, Avenge me of my accuser.

4 And he would not for a long time; but afterwards he said within himself, Though I am not afraid of God and have no regard for men;

5 Yet because this widow troubles me, I will avenge her, so that she may not keep coming and annoying me.

6 Then our Lord said, Hear what the unjust judge said.

7 Would not God avenge his chosen ones much more, who call upon him day and night and he has patience with them?

8 I say to you, he will avenge them promptly. But when the Son of man comes, will he find faith on the earth?

9 ¶And he spoke this parable against the men who relied upon themselves, that they were righteous, and despised every other man:

10 Two men went up to the temple to pray, one a Pharisee, and the other a tax collector.

11 And the Pharisee stood by himself, and prayed thus: O God, I thank thee, that I am not like the rest of men, extortioners, grafters, adulterers, and not like this tax collector.

12 But I fast twice a week, and I give tithes on everything I earn.

13 But the tax collector stood afar off, and he would not even lift up his eyes to heaven, but smote his breast, saying, O God, be merciful to me a sinner.

14 I say to you that this man went down to his house more righteous than the Pharisee. For everyone who exalts himself will be humbled; and

everyone who humbles himself will be exalted.

15 ¶They brought to him also little children, that he might touch them; and his disciples saw them and rebuked them.

16 But Jesus called them, and said to them, Permit the children to come to me, and do not stop them; for the kingdom of heaven is for those who are like these.

17 Truly I say to you, He who will not receive the kingdom of God like a little child will never enter into it.

18 And one of the leaders asked him, saying, O good Teacher, what shall I do to inherit life everlasting?

19 Jesus said to him, Why do you call me good? There is no one good but one, that is God.

20 You know the commandments: You shall not kill; You shall not commit adultery; You shall not steal; You shall not bear false witness; Honor your father and your mother.

21 He said to him, All these I have obeyed from my boyhood.

22 When Jesus heard it, he said to him, You lack one thing; go, sell everything you have and give it to the poor, and you will have a treasure in heaven; and come and follow me.

23 But when he heard these things, he felt sad, because he was very rich.

24 And when Jesus saw that he felt sad, he said, How difficult it is for those who have wealth to enter into the kingdom of God!

25 It is easier for a rope to go through the eye of a needle than for a rich man to enter into the kingdom of God.

26 Those who heard it said to him, Who then can be saved?

27 But Jesus said, Things impossible to men are possible to God.

28 Simon Peter said to him, Behold, we have left everything and followed you.

29 Jesus said to him, Truly I say to you that there is no man who leaves houses or parents or brothers or wife or children for the sake of the kingdom of God,

30 Who will not receive many times more at this time and in the world to come life everlasting.

31 ¶Then Jesus took the twelve and said to them, Behold, we are going up to Jerusalem, and all things written by the prophets concerning the Son of man will be fulfilled.

32 For he will be delivered to the Gentiles, and they will mock him and spit in his face.

33 And they will scourge him and curse him and kill him; and on the third day he will rise again.

34 But they understood not one of these things; and this saying was hidden from them, and they did not know these things which were spoken to them.

35 ¶And when he drew near Jericho, a blind man was sitting by the roadside and begging.

36 And he heard the voice of the people passing, and asked, Who is this?

37 They said to him, Jesus the Nazarene is passing.

38 And he cried, saying, O Jesus, son of David, have mercy on me!

39 And those who were going before Jesus rebuked him, telling him to keep quiet; but he cried the more, O son of David, have mercy on me!

40 So Jesus stood still, and commanded them to call him to him; and as he came near he asked him,

41 Saying, What do you wish me to do for you? He answered, My Lord, that I may see.

42 And Jesus said to him, See; your faith has healed you.

43 And he saw immediately, and followed him praising God; and all the people who saw it gave praise to God.

CHAPTER 19

AND when Jesus entered and passed through Jericho

2 There was a man named Zaccai, who was rich and chief of the tax collectors.

3 And he wanted to see who Jesus

was; but he could not because of the crowd, for Zaccai was small in stature.

4 So he ran ahead of Jesus, and climbed up into a leafless fig tree, that he might see him, because he was to pass that way.

5 When Jesus came to that place, he saw him and said to him, Make haste, come down, O Zaccai, for today I must stay at your house.

6 And he hastened and came down, and welcomed him with joy.

7 Now when they all saw it, they murmured, saying, He has entered to stay in the house of a sinner.

8 But Zaccai rose up and said to Jesus, Behold, my Lord, half of my wealth I will give to the poor; and I will pay fourfold to every man from whom I have extorted.

9 Jesus said to him, Today life has come to this house, because he also is a son of Abraham.

10 For the Son of man came to seek and save that which was lost.

11 ¶While they were listening to these things, he continued by speaking a parable, because he was near Jerusalem, and they were expecting that the kingdom of God would appear at that very hour;

12 And he said, A great man of a noble family went to a far country to receive for himself a kingdom and to return.

13 And he called his ten servants, and gave them ten pounds, and said to them, Transact business until I come back.

14 But the people of his city hated him, and sent messengers after him, saying, We do not want him to rule over us.

15 And when he received the kingdom and returned, he commanded to call his servants to whom he had given the money, that he might know what each one of them had gained in business.

16 The first one came and said, My lord, your pound has gained ten pounds.

17 He said to him, O good servant! Because you are found faithful in a little, you will have charge over ten talents.[1]

18 And the second came and said, My lord, your pound has gained five pounds.

19 He said to this one, You also will have charge over five talents.

20 But another one came and said, My lord, here is your pound which was with me, which I kept laid up in a purse.

21 For I was afraid of you, because you are a harsh man; you pick up what you have not laid down, and you reap what you have not sown.

22 He said to him, I will judge you from your own mouth, O wicked servant. You knew me that I am a harsh man, and pick up what I have not laid down, and reap what I have not sown.

23 Why then did you not give my money to the exchange, so that when I came I could demand it with its interest?

24 And he said to those who stood in his presence, Take away the pound from him and give it to him who has ten pounds.

25 They said to him, Our lord, he has already with him ten pounds.

26 He said to them, I say to you: To everyone who has shall be given; and from him who has not, even that which he has will be taken away from him.

27 But those my enemies, who were not willing that I should rule over them bring here, and kill them before me.

28 ¶And when Jesus had said these things, he went forward to go to Jerusalem.

29 And when he arrived at Bethphage and Bethany, on the side of the mountain which is called the Place of Olives, he sent two of his disciples,

30 Saying to them, Go to the village which is in front of us; and when you enter it you will find a colt tied, on

[1] The Aramaic word *Kakra*, talent, is similar to the word, *Karkha*, province or city, as in some other versions. A talent was the largest coin, equal to many pounds.

which no man has ever ridden; untie it and bring it.

31 And if any man should ask you, Why do you untie it? tell him this: Our Lord needs it.

32 And those who were sent went away and found just as he had told them.

33 And as they were untying the colt, its owners said to them, Why do you untie the colt?

34 And they said to them, Our Lord needs it.

35 And they brought it to Jesus; and they put their garments on the colt, and they set Jesus on it.

36 And as he went along, they spread their garments on the road.

37 And when he came near to the descent of the mount of the Place of Olives, the whole multitude of the disciples began to rejoice, praising God with a loud voice for all the miracles which they had seen,

38 Saying, Blessed is the king who comes in the name of the Lord; peace in heaven and glory in the highest.

39 But some of the Pharisees who were in the multitude said to him, Teacher, rebuke your disciples.

40 He said to them, I say to you that if these should keep silent, the stones would cry out.

41 ¶And when he drew near and saw the city, he wept over it;

42 And he said, If you had only known those who came for your peace, even in this your day! But now they are hidden from your eyes.

43 But the days will come when your enemies will surround you, and oppress you from every place,

44 And will overthrow you and your children within you; and they will not leave in you a stone upon a stone, because you did not know the time when you were to be visited.

45 ¶And when he entered the temple, he began to put out those who were buying and selling in it;

46 And he said to them, It is written, My house is the house of prayer; but you have made it a cave of bandits.

47 And he taught every day in the temple. But the high priests and the scribes and the elders of the people sought to get rid of him;

48 But they were not able to find what to do to him; for all the people gathered around him to hear him.

CHAPTER 20

AND it came to pass on one of the days, while he was teaching the people and preaching in the temple, the high priests and the scribes with the elders rose up against him.

2 And they said to him, Tell us by what authority you do these things, and who gave you this authority?

3 Jesus answered, saying to them, I will also ask you a question, and you tell me;

4 The baptism of John, was it from heaven or from men?

5 And they reasoned with themselves, saying, If we should say from heaven, he will say to us, why then did you not believe him?

6 And if we should say from men, all the people will stone us; for they regard John as a prophet.

7 So they said to him, We do not know whence it is.

8 Jesus said to them, Neither will I tell you by what authority I do these things.

9 ¶And he began to speak this parable to the people: A man planted a vineyard, and leased it to laborers, and went on a journey for a long time.

10 And at the season he sent his servant to the laborers to give him of the fruit of the vineyard; but the laborers beat him and sent him back empty.

11 And again he sent another of his servants; but they beat him also and treated him shamefully and sent him back empty.

12 And again he sent the third one; but they wounded him also and threw him outside.

13 Then the owner of the vineyard said, What shall I do? I will send my beloved son; perhaps they will see him and feel ashamed.

14 But when the laborers saw him,

they reasoned with themselves, saying, This is the heir; come, let us kill him, and the inheritance will be ours.

15 So they cast him out of the vineyard and killed him. What therefore will the owner of the vineyard do to them?

16 He will come and destroy those laborers, and give the vineyard to others. And when they heard it, they said, This will never happen.

17 But he looked at them and said, What is it that is written, The stone which the builders rejected, the same became the cornerstone?

18 Whoever falls on that stone will be broken; and whomever it falls upon, it will destroy.

19 The high priests and the scribes sought to lay hands on him that very hour; but they were afraid of the people; for they knew that he had spoken this parable against them.

20 ¶So they sent spies disguised as righteous men to ensnare him by a word, and to deliver him to the judge and then to the authority of the governor.

21 So they asked him, saying, Teacher, we know that you speak and teach truthfully, and you do not discriminate between men, but you teach the way of God justly.

22 Is it lawful for us to pay head tax [1] to Caesar or not?

23 But he understood their craftiness and said, Why do you tempt me?

24 Show me a penny. Whose image and inscription are on it? They said, Caesar's.

25 Jesus said to them, Give therefore to Caesar that which is Caesar's and to God what is God's.

26 And they were not able to get a word from him before the people; and they were amazed at his answer, and kept silence.

27 ¶Then came to him some of the men of the Sadducees, those who say there is no resurrection: and they asked him,

28 Teacher, Moses wrote to us that if a man's brother should die, and he has a wife without children, let his brother take his wife and raise up offspring for his brother.

29 Now there were seven brothers; the first married and died without children.

30 The second married his wife, and died without children.

31 And the third one married her again; and likewise the seven of them; and they died, leaving no children.

32 And at last the woman also died.

33 Therefore at the resurrection, to which one of them will she be a wife? For seven of them married her.

34 Jesus said to them, The sons of this world marry women, and women are given to men in marriage.

35 But those who are worthy of the other world and the resurrection from the dead, neither take women in marriage nor are women given in marriage to them.

36 For they cannot die again, because they are like angels; and they are sons of God, because they are sons of the resurrection.

37 Now concerning the resurrection of the dead, even Moses pointed it out (for he referred to it at the Bush) saying, The Lord God of Abraham and the God of Isaac and the God of Jacob.

38 God is not the God of the dead but of the living; for all live to him.

39 And some of the men of the scribes answered, saying to him, Teacher, you have well said.

40 And they did not dare again to question him concerning anything.

41 And he said to them, How can the scribes say concerning the Christ that he is son of David?

42 And yet David said in the book of Psalms, The Lord said to my Lord, Sit at my right hand,

43 Until I put down your enemies under your feet.

44 If, therefore David calls him my Lord, how then can he be his son?

45 ¶And while all the people were listening, he said to his disciples,

46 Beware of the scribes who like to walk in long robes, and love to be greeted in the streets, and take the

---

[1] This tax was levied on every male, and it is still resented in the East.

chief seats in the synagogues and the high places at the banquets,

47 Those who embezzle the property of widows with the pretense that they make long prayers; they will receive a greater judgment.

CHAPTER 21

JESUS then looked at the rich men who were casting their offerings into the treasury.

2 And he also saw a poor widow, who cast in two pennies.

3 And he said, Truly I say to you that this poor widow has cast in more than every man.

4 For all these cast into the house of the offerings of God of their abundance; but she out of her poverty has cast in everything she has earned.

5 ¶While some men were talking about the temple, that it was adorned with beautiful stones and gift offerings, Jesus said to them,

6 These things which you see will be destroyed; the days will come when not a stone will be left upon a stone, which will not be torn down.

7 And they asked him, saying, Teacher, when will these things happen? and what is the sign when these things are about to happen?

8 He said to them, Be careful that you may not be deceived; for many will come in my name, and say, I am the Christ; and the time is near; but do not follow them.

9 And when you hear of wars and revolutions, do not be afraid; for all these things must first come to pass; but the end is not yet.

10 For nation will rise against nation, and kingdom against kingdom.

11 And there will be great earthquakes in different places, and famines and plagues; and there will be alarming sights, and great signs will appear from heaven; and the winters will be severe.

12 But before all these things, they will lay hands on you and persecute you and deliver you to the synagogues and the prisons; and they will bring you before kings and governors for the sake of my name.

13 It will be to you for a testimony.

14 Treasure it in your hearts, and do not try to learn what to answer.

15 For I will give you a mouth and wisdom, which all your enemies will not be able to withstand.

16 You will be delivered up even by your parents and brothers, and your relatives and friends; and they will put some of you to death.

17 And you will be hated by every man because of my name.

18 And yet not a hair of your head will be lost.

19 By your patience you will gain your souls.

20 But when you see Jerusalem surrounded by an army, then know that its destruction is at hand.

21 Then let those who are in Judea flee to the mountain; and let those who are within it flee; and let those who are in the fields not enter into it.

22 For these are the days of vengeance, so that everything which is written must be fulfilled.

23 But woe to those who are with child, and to those who give suck in those days! For there will be great distress in the land, and wrath to this people.

24 And they will fall by the edge of the sword, and they will be taken captive to every country; and Jerusalem will be trodden under the feet of the Gentiles until the time of the Gentiles comes to an end.

25 ¶And there will be signs in sun and moon and stars; and on earth distress of the nations, and confusion because of the roaring of the sea;

26 And upheaval that takes life out of men, because of fear of what is to come on earth; and the powers of the universe will be shaken.

27 Then they will see the Son of man coming in the clouds with a large army and great glory.

28 But when these things begin to happen, have courage and lift up your heads, because your salvation is at hand.

29 And he spoke to them a parable, Look at the fig tree and all the trees;

30 When they put forth leaves, you immediately understand by them that summer is near.

31 Even so you also, when you see these things happen, know that the kingdom of God is near.

32 Truly I say to you, This generation will not pass away until all these things happen.

33 Heaven and earth will pass away, but my words will not pass away.

34 ¶But take heed to yourselves, that your hearts may not become heavy by extravagance and drunkenness and worries of this world, and that day come suddenly upon you.

35 For like a downpour it will entrap all those who dwell on the face of all the earth.

36 Therefore keep watch always and pray, that you may be worthy to escape all these things which are to happen, and that you may stand before the Son of man.

37 ¶During the day he taught in the temple; and at night he went out and lodged in the mountain which is called the Place of Olives.

38 And all the people came ahead of him to the temple, to hear him.

CHAPTER 22

NOW the feast of unleavened bread, which is called the passover, was at hand.

2 And the high priests and the scribes sought how to kill him; but they were afraid of the people.

3 ¶But Satan had taken possession of Judah called Iscariot, who was of the number of the twelve.

4 So he went away and spoke with the high priests and the scribes and officers of the temple about delivering him to them.

5 And they were glad and promised to give him money.

6 And he agreed with them, and sought an opportunity to deliver him to them in the absence of the people.

7 ¶Then the day of unleavened bread came, on which it was the custom to kill the passover lamb.

8 So Jesus sent Peter and John, and said to them, Go and prepare the passover for us to eat.

9 They said to him, Where do you wish us to prepare?

10 He said to them, Behold, when you enter the city, you will meet a man carrying a waterskin; follow him. And wherever he enters,

11 Say to the master of the house, Our Teacher says, Where is the guest room, where I may eat the passover with my disciples?

12 And behold, he will show you an upper room, large and furnished; there make ready.

13 And they went and found it just as he had said to them; and they prepared the passover.

14 ¶And when it was time, Jesus came and sat down, and the twelve apostles with him.

15 And he said to them, I have greatly desired to eat this passover with you before I suffer;

16 For I say to you that henceforth I will not eat it until it is fulfilled in the kingdom of God.

17 And he took the cup and gave thanks and said, Take this and divide it among yourselves.

18 For I say to you, I will not drink of the fruit of the vine until the kingdom of God comes.

19 ¶And he took bread and gave thanks and broke it, and gave it to them and said, This is my body, which is given for your sake; this do in remembrance of me.

20 And likewise also he took the cup, after they had eaten supper, and he said, This is the cup of the new covenant in my blood which is shed for you.

21 But behold, the hand of him who is to betray me is on the table.

22 And the Son of man will go, just as he has been destined; but woe to the man by whose hand he will be betrayed!

23 And they began to inquire among themselves which one of them was to do this act.

24 ¶There was also a dispute among them as to who was the greatest among them.

25 Jesus said to them, The kings of the Gentiles are also their lords, and those who rule over them are called benefactors;

26 But not so with you; let him who is great among you be the least, and

he who is a leader be like one who serves.

27 For who is greater, he who sits down or he who serves? Is it not he who sits down? But I am among you as one who serves.

28 You are those who have remained with me throughout my trials.

29 And I promise you, just as my Father has promised me, a kingdom,

30 That you may eat and drink at the table in my kingdom; and you will sit on seats and judge the twelve tribes of Israel.

31 ¶And Jesus said to Simon, Simon, behold, Satan wants to sift all of you like wheat;

32 But I have made supplication for you that your faith may not weaken; and even you in time will repent and strengthen your brethren.

33 Simon said to him, My Lord, I am ready with you, even for the prison and for death.

34 Jesus said to him, I say to you, Simon, the cock will not crow today until you have denied three times that you know me.

35 And he said to them, When I sent you out without purses and without bags and shoes, did you lack anything? They said to him, Not a thing.

36 He said to them, From now on he who has purses, let him take them, and the bag likewise; and he who has no sword, let him sell his robe and buy for himself a sword.

37 For I say to you that what is written must be fulfilled in me, He will be numbered among the wicked; for all the things concerning me will be fulfilled.

38 And they said to him, Our Lord, behold here are two swords. He said to them, That is enough.

39 ¶And he came out and went away, as it was his custom, to the mount of the Place of Olives; and his disciples also followed him.

40 And when he arrived at a certain place, he said to them, Pray that you may not enter into temptation.

41 And he withdrew from them, about the distance of a stone's throw, and he knelt down and prayed,

42 Saying, O Father, if thou wilt let this cup pass from me; but not as I will, but thy will be done.

43 And there appeared to him an angel from heaven, to strengthen him.

44 And he was in fear, and prayed earnestly; and his sweat became like drops of blood; and he fell down upon the ground.

45 Then he rose up from his prayer and came to his disciples and found them sleeping because of distress.

46 And he said to them, Why do you sleep? Rise and pray that you may not enter into temptation.

47 ¶While he was still speaking, behold, a multitude came and he who is called Judah, one of the twelve, coming before them; and he drew near to Jesus and kissed him. For this was the sign he had given them, He whom I kiss is the one.

48 Jesus said to him, Judah, do you betray the Son of man with a kiss?

49 When those who were with him saw what happened, they said to him, Our Lord, shall we smite them with swords?

50 And one of them struck the servant of the high priest, and cut off his right ear.

51 But Jesus answered, saying, It is enough for the present. And he touched the ear of him who was wounded, and healed it.

52 And Jesus said to the high priests and the elders and the officers of the temple who had come against him, Have you come out against me to arrest me with swords and staves, as if you were against a bandit?

53 I was with you every day in the temple, and you did not even point your hands at me; but this is your time, and the power of darkness.

54 ¶And they arrested him and brought him to the house of the high priest. And Simon followed him afar off.

55 And they kindled a fire in the midst of the courtyard, and sat around it; and Simon also sat among them.

56 And a young woman saw him sitting by the fire, and she looked at him and said, This man also was with him.

57 But he denied, saying, Woman, I do not know him.

58 And after a little while, another saw him and said to him, You also are one of them. But Peter said, I am not.

59 And after an hour, another one argued and said, Truly, this man also was with him; for he is also a Galilean.

60 Peter said, Man, I do not know what you are saying. And immediately while he was still speaking, the cock crowed.

61 And Jesus turned and looked at Peter. And Simon remembered the word of our Lord that was said to him, Before the cock crows you will deny me three times.

62 And Simon went outside and wept bitterly.

63 ¶And the men who held Jesus mocked him,

64 And they covered his head and smote him on his face, saying, Prophesy! Who has struck you?

65 And many other things they blasphemed and said against him.

66 ¶As soon as it was daybreak, the elders and the high priests and the scribes gathered together and brought him up to their council chamber.

67 And they said to him, If you are the Christ, tell us. He said to them, If I tell you, you will not believe me.

68 And if I ask you, you will not answer me nor release me.

69 From henceforth the Son of man will sit at the right hand of the power of God.

70 And they all said, Are you then the Son of God? Jesus said to them, You say that I am.

71 And they said, Why then do we need witnesses? For we have heard it from his own mouth.

CHAPTER 23

THEN the whole company of them rose up and brought him to Pilate;

2 And they began to accuse him, saying, We found this man misleading our people and forbidding to pay the head tax to Caesar; and he says concerning himself that he is a King, even the Christ.

3 Pilate asked him, saying, Are you the King of the Jews? He said to him, That is what you say.

4 Then Pilate said to the high priests and the people, I cannot find any fault against this man.

5 But they shouted and said, He has stirred up our people, teaching throughout Judea, and beginning from Galilee even to this place.

6 When Pilate heard the name Galilee, he asked if the man was a Galilean.

7 And when he knew that he was under the jurisdiction of Herod, he sent him to Herod, because he was in Jerusalem at that time.

8 ¶When Herod saw Jesus he was exceedingly glad, for he had wanted to see him for a long time, because he had heard many things concerning him, and he hoped to see some miracle by him.

9 And he asked him many questions; but Jesus gave him no answer.

10 Then the high priests and the scribes stood and accused him bitterly.

11 And Herod and his soldiers insulted him and mocked him, and dressed him in a scarlet robe and sent him to Pilate.

12 And that day Pilate and Herod became friends with each other; for there had been a long-standing enmity between them.

13 ¶Then Pilate called the high priests and the leaders of the people,

14 And he said to them, You brought me this man as if he were misleading your people; and behold, I have examined him before your own eyes, and I have found no fault in him concerning all that you accuse him.

15 Nor even has Herod; for I sent him to him; and behold, he has done nothing worthy of death.

16 I will therefore chastise him and release him.

17 For there was a custom to release to them one at the feast.

18 But all the people cried out say-

ing, Get rid of him and release to us Bar-Abba;

19 (Who because of sedition and murder which had happened in the city, was cast into prison.)

20 Again Pilate spoke to them, desiring to release Jesus.

21 But they cried out, saying, Crucify him, crucify him!

22 And he said to them the third time, What evil has he done? I have found nothing in him worthy of death; I will therefore chastise him and release him.

23 But they persisted with loud voices, and asked to crucify him. And their voices and that of the high priests prevailed.

24 Then Pilate commanded to have their request granted.

25 So he released to them the one who because of sedition and murder was cast into prison, whom they asked for; and he delivered Jesus to their will.

26 ¶And while they took him away, they laid hold of Simon, a Cyrenian, who was coming from a village, and they placed the end of the cross on him, to carry it with Jesus.

27 And many people followed him, and the women who were mourning and wailing over him.

28 But Jesus turned to them and said, O daughters of Jerusalem, do not weep over me; but weep over yourselves and over your own children.

29 For behold, the days are coming in which they will say, Blessed are the barren and the wombs that never gave birth and the breasts that never gave suck.

30 Then they will begin to say to the mountains, Fall on us; and to the hills, Cover us.

31 For if they do these things with the green wood, what will be done with dry wood?

32 ¶And there were coming with him two others, malefactors, to be put to death.

33 And when they came to a place which is called The Skull, they crucified him there, and the malefactors, one on his right and one on his left.

34 And Jesus said, O Father, forgive them, for they know not what they are doing. And they divided his garments and cast lots over them.

35 The people stood looking on. And even the leaders of the synagogue mocked him, and said, He saved others; let him save himself, if he is the Christ, the chosen one of God.

36 And the soldiers ridiculed him, as they came near him and offered him vinegar,

37 Saying to him, If you are the king of the Jews, save yourself.

38 There was also an inscription which was written over him, in Greek and Roman and Hebrew,[1] THIS IS THE KING OF THE JEWS.

39 ¶Now one of the malefactors who were crucified with him blasphemed against him, saying, If you are the Christ, save yourself and save us also.

40 But the other rebuked him and said to him, Do you not fear even God, for you are also in the same judgment?

41 And ours is just, for we are paid as we deserve and as we have done; but he has done nothing wrong.

42 And he said to Jesus, Remember me, my Lord, when you come in your kingdom.

43 Jesus said to him, Truly I say to you, Today [2] you will be with me in Paradise.

44 ¶Now it was about the sixth hour, and darkness fell upon the whole earth, and lasted until the ninth hour.

45 And the sun was darkened, and the curtains at the door of the temple were torn in the center.

46 Then Jesus cried with a loud voice, saying, O my Father, into thy hands I commit my spirit. He said this and it was finished

47 ¶When the centurion saw what had happened, he praised God and said, Truly this was a righteous man.

48 And all the people who were

---

[1] *Aramaic,* the language of the Jews.

[2] Ancient texts were not punctuated. The comma could come before or after *today.*

gathered together to see this sight, when they saw what had happened, returned, beating their breasts.

49 And all the acquaintances of Jesus stood afar off, and the women who had come with him from Galilee, and they were beholding these things.

50 ¶There was a man named Joseph the counsellor of Ramtha, a city of Judea, a good and righteous man.

51 He did not agree with their wishes and their actions; and he waited for the kingdom of God.

52 He went to Pilate and asked for the body of Jesus.

53 And he took it down and wrapped it in fine linen, and laid it in a hewn tomb in which no one was ever laid.

54 This was a Friday, and the sabbath was approaching.

55 ¶The women who had come with him from Galilee were near, and they saw the tomb and how his body was laid.

56 And they returned and prepared spices and perfumes. And on the sabbath they rested, as it is commanded.

CHAPTER 24

AND on the first day of the week, early in the morning, while it was yet dark, they came to the tomb and brought the spices which they had prepared; and there were with them other women.

2 And they found the stone rolled away from the tomb.

3 And they entered in, but they did not find the body of Jesus.

4 And it came to pass as they were confused about this, behold, two men stood above them, and their garments were shining;

5 And they were afraid and bowed their faces to the ground; and they said to them, Why do you seek the living among the dead?

6 He is not here, he has risen; remember that he spoke to you while he was in Galilee,

7 Saying that the Son of man had to be delivered into the hands of sinful men and be crucified and rise again on the third day.

8 And they remembered his words.

9 And they returned from the tomb, and told all these things to the eleven and to the rest.

10 They were Mary of Magdala, and Joanna, and Mary the mother of James, and the rest who were with them, who told these things to the apostles.

11 And these words appeared in their eyes as delusions; and they did not believe them.

12 But Simon rose up and ran to the tomb; and he looked in and saw the linen laid by itself, and he went away wondering in himself concerning what had happened.

13 ¶And behold two of them were going on that day to a village called Emmaus, about six miles from Jerusalem.

14 They were talking with each other concerning all these things that had happened.

15 And while they were speaking and asking each other, Jesus came and overtook them and walked with them.

16 But the sight of their eyes was blurred so that they could not recognize him.

17 And he said to them, What are these words that you are discussing with each other, as you walk and are sad?

18 One of them, named Cleopah, answered, saying to him, Are you alone a stranger from Jerusalem, that you do not know what has happened in it in these days?

19 He said to them, What things? They said to him, About Jesus of Nazareth, a man who was a prophet, mighty in word and deed before God and before all the people.

20 And the high priests and the elders delivered him up to the judgment of death, and they crucified him.

21 But we were hoping that he was the one to save Israel; and behold, it is three days since all these things happened.

22 And some of our women also

amazed us, for they went early to the tomb;

23 And when his body was not found, they came, and said to us, We saw angels there, and they said that he is alive.

24 And some of our men also went to the tomb, and they found it as the women had said; but they did not see him.

25 Then Jesus said to them, O dull-minded and heavy-hearted, slow to believe all that the prophets have spoken;

26 Did not Christ have to suffer all these things in order to enter into his glory?

27 And he began from Moses and from all the prophets, and interpreted to them from all the scriptures concerning himself.

28 And they drew near to the village to which they were going; and he made them think that he was going to a far place.

29 But they urged him and said, Remain with us; for the day is spent and it is near dark. So he entered to stay with them.

30 And it came to pass, as he sat at table with them, he took bread and blessed it and broke it and gave it to them.

31 And immediately their eyes were opened and they recognized him; and he was taken away from them.

32 And they said one to another, Were not our minds dull within us when he spoke with us on the road and interpreted the scriptures to us?

33¶ And they rose up that very hour and returned to Jerusalem; and they found the eleven gathered together, and those who were with them,

34 Saying, Truly our Lord has risen and has appeared to Simon.

35 And they also reported those things that happened on the road, and how they knew him as he broke bread.

36 ¶And while they were discussing these things, Jesus stood among them, and said to them, Peace be with you; it is I; do not be afraid.

37 And they were confused and frightened, for they thought they saw a spirit.

38 Jesus said to them, Why do you tremble? and why do thoughts arise in your hearts?

39 Look at my hands and my feet, that it is I; feel me and understand; for a spirit has no flesh and bones, as you see I have.

40 When he said these things, he showed them his hands and his feet.

41 And as they still did not believe because of their joy, and they were bewildered, he said to them, Have you anything here to eat?

42 They gave him a portion of a broiled fish and of a honeycomb.

43 And he took it and ate before their eyes.

44 And he said to them, These are the words which I spoke to you when I was with you, that everything must be fulfilled which is written in the law of Moses and in the prophets and in the psalms, concerning me.

45 Then he opened their mind to understand the scriptures.

46 And he said to them, Thus it is written, and it was right, that Christ should suffer and rise from the dead on the third day;

47 And that repentance should be preached in his name for the forgiveness of sins among all nations; and the beginning will be from Jerusalem.

48 You are witnesses of these things.

49 And I will send upon you the promise of my Father; but remain in the city of Jerusalem until you are clothed with power from on high.

50 ¶And he took them out as far as Bethany, and he lifted up his hands and blessed them.

51 And it came to pass, while he blessed them, he parted from them and went up to heaven.

52 And they worshipped him, and returned to Jerusalem with great joy;

53 And they were always in the temple, praising and blessing God. Amen.

THE GOSPEL ACCORDING TO

SAINT JOHN

CHAPTER 1

THE Word was in the beginning, and that very Word was with God, and God was that Word.

2 The same was in the beginning with God.

3 Everything came to be by his hand; and without him not even one thing that was created came to be.

4 The life was in him, and the life is the light of men.

5 And the same light shines in darkness, and the darkness does not overcome it.

6 ¶There was a man, sent from God, whose name was John.

7 He came as a witness to testify concerning the light, so that every man might believe by means of him.

8 He was not the light, but a witness to testify concerning the light.

9 He was the true light which lighted every man who came into the world.

10 He was in the world and the world was under his hand, and yet the world knew him not.

11 He came to his own, and his own did not receive him.

12 But those who received him, to them he gave power to become sons of God, especially to those who believed in his name,

13 Those who are not of blood nor of the will of the flesh nor of the will of man, but born of God.

14 And the Word became flesh and dwelt among us, and we saw his glory, a glory like that of the first-born of the Father, full of grace and truth.

15 ¶John witnessed concerning him and cried and said, This is the one of whom I said, He is coming after me, and yet he is ahead of me, because he was before me.

16 And of his fulness we have all received, grace for grace.

17 For the law was given by Moses; but truth and grace came into being by Jesus Christ.

18 No man has ever seen God; but the first-born of God, who is in the bosom of his Father, he has declared him.

19 ¶This is the testimony of John, when the Jews sent to him priests and Levites from Jerusalem to ask him, Who are you?

20 And he confessed and did not deny it; but he declared, I am not the Christ.

21 Then they asked him again, What then? Are you Elijah? And he said, I am not. Are you a prophet? And he said, No.

22 Then they said to him, Who are you? so that we may give an answer to those who sent us. What do you say concerning yourself?

23 He said, I am the voice of one crying in the wilderness, Straighten the highway of the Lord, as the prophet Isaiah said.

24 Those who were sent were from the Pharisees.

25 And they asked him, saying to him, Why then do you baptize, if you are not the Christ nor Elijah nor a prophet?

26 John answered, saying to them, I baptize with water; but among you stands one whom you do not know;

27 This is the one who comes after me and is ahead of me, the one even the strings of whose shoes I am not good enough to untie.

28 These things happened in Beth-

any at the Jordan crossing, where John was baptizing.

29 ¶The next day John saw Jesus coming to him, and he said, Behold the Lamb of God who takes away the sin of the world!

30 This is the one of whom I said, The man who comes after me is yet ahead of me, because he was before me.

31 And I did not know him; but that he might be made known to Israel, I came to baptize with water.

32 And John testified, saying, I saw the Spirit descending from heaven like a dove, and it rested upon him.

33 And yet I did not know him; but he who sent me to baptize with water said to me, The one upon whom you see the Spirit descending and resting, he is the one who will baptize with the Holy Spirit.

34 And I saw and testified that this is the Son of God.

35 ¶The next day John was standing with two of his disciples;

36 And he looked at Jesus while he walked, and said, Behold, the Lamb of God!

37 And when he said it, two of his disciples heard it; and they went after Jesus.

38 And Jesus turned around and saw them following him, and he said to them, What do you want? They said to him, Rabbi (Teacher), where do you live?

39 He said to them, Come, and you will see. And they came and saw where he stayed, and they remained with him that day; and it was about the tenth hour.

40 One of them who heard John and followed Jesus, was Andrew, the brother of Simon.

41 He saw his brother Simon first, and said to him, We have found the Christ.[1]

42 And he brought him to Jesus. And Jesus looked at him and said, You are Simon the son of Jonah; you are called Kepa (the Stone).

43 ¶The next day Jesus wanted to leave for Galilee, and he found Philip, and said to him, Follow me.

44 Now Philip was from Bethsaida, the city of Andrew and Simon.

45 Philip found Nathanael, and said to him, We have found that Jesus, the son of Joseph, of Nazareth, is the one concerning whom Moses wrote in the law and the prophets.

46 Nathanael said to him, Can anything good come out of Nazareth? Philip said to him, Come and you will see.

47 Jesus saw Nathanael coming to him and he said of him, Behold truly an Israelite, in whom there is no guile!

48 Nathanael said to him, Whence do you know me? Jesus said to him, Even before Philip called you, while you were under the fig tree, I saw you.

49 Nathanael answered, saying to him, Rabbi, you are the Son of God, you are the King of Israel.

50 Jesus said to him, Do you believe because I told you I saw you under the fig tree? You shall see greater things than these.

51 He said to him, Truly, truly, I say to all of you that from now on you will see heaven opened and the angels of God ascending and descending to the Son of man.

CHAPTER 2

ON the third day there was a marriage feast in Cana, a city of Galilee; and the mother of Jesus was there.

2 And Jesus and his disciples were also invited to the marriage feast.

3 And when the wine ran low, his mother said to Jesus, They have no wine.

4 Jesus said to her, What is it to me and to you, woman? My turn has not yet come.

5 His mother said to the helpers, Whatever he tells you, do it.

6 And there were six stone jars placed there for the purification of the Jews, which could hold several gallons each.

7 Jesus said to them, Fill the jars with water; and they filled them up to the brim.

[1] Aramaic, *Meshikha, Messiah.*

8 Then he said to them, Draw out now and bring it to the chief guest [1] of the feast. And they brought it.

9 And when the chief guest tasted the water that had become wine, he did not know whence it had come; but the helpers knew, who had drawn the water. Then the chief guest called the bridegroom

10 And said to him, Every man at first brings the best wine; and when they have drunk, then that which is weak; but you have kept the best wine until now.

11 This is the first miracle which Jesus performed in Cana of Galilee, and thus he showed his glory; and his disciples believed in him.

12 ¶After this he went down to Capernaum, he and his mother and his brothers and his disciples; and they remained there a few days.

13 ¶And the Jewish passover was nearing; so Jesus went up to Jerusalem.

14 And he found in the temple those who were buying oxen and sheep and doves, and the money changers sitting.

15 And he made a whip of cord, and drove them all out of the temple, even the sheep and the oxen and the money changers; and he threw out their exchange money and upset their trays;

16 And to those who sold doves he said, Take these away from here; do not make my Father's house a house of trading.

17 And his disciples remembered that it is written, The zeal for thy house has given me courage.

18 The Jews answered, saying to him, What sign do you show us, that you are doing these things?

19 Jesus answered, saying to them, Tear down this temple and in three days I will raise it up.

20 The Jews said to him, It took forty-six years to build this temple, and will you raise it up in three days?

21 But he spoke concerning the temple of his body.

22 When he rose from the dead, his disciples remembered that he had said this; and they believed the scriptures and the word which Jesus had said.

23 ¶Now when Jesus was in Jerusalem at the passover, during the feast, a great many believed in him, because they saw the miracles which he did.

24 But Jesus did not entrust himself to them, because he understood every man.

25 And he needed no man to testify to him concerning any man; for he knew well what was in man.

CHAPTER 3

THERE was at that place a man of the Pharisees, named Nicodemus, a leader of the Jews;

2 He came at night to Jesus and said to him, Rabbi, we know that you are a teacher sent from God; for no man can do these miracles that you are doing unless God is with him.

3 Jesus answered, saying to him, Truly, truly, I say to you, If a man is not born again,[2] he cannot see the kingdom of God.

4 Nicodemus said to him, How can an old man be born again? Can he enter again a second time into his mother's womb and be born?

5 Jesus answered, saying to him, Truly, truly, I say to you, If a man is not born of water and the Spirit, he cannot enter into the kingdom of God.

6 What is born of flesh is flesh; and what is born of the Spirit is spirit.

7 Do not be surprised because I have told you that you all must be born again.

8 The wind blows where it pleases, and you hear its sound; but you do not know whence it comes and whither it goes; such is every man who is born of the Spirit.

9 Nicodemus answered, saying to him, How can these things be?

---

[1] Master of ceremonies.

[2] *Born again* in Northern Aramaic means to change one's thoughts and habits. Nicodemus spoke Southern Aramaic and hence did not understand Jesus.

10 Jesus answered, You are a teacher of Israel, and yet you do not understand these things?

11 Truly, truly, I say to you, We speak only what we know, and we testify only to what we have seen; and yet you do not accept our testimony.

12 If I have told you about earthly things and you do not believe, how then will you believe me if I tell you about heavenly things?

13 No man has ascended to heaven except him who came down from heaven, even the Son of man who is in heaven.

14 ¶Just as Moses lifted up the serpent in the wilderness, so the Son of man is ready to be lifted up;

15 So that every man who believes in him should not perish, but have eternal life.

16 ¶For God so loved the world that he even gave his only begotten Son, so that whoever believes in him should not perish, but have eternal life.

17 For God did not send his Son into the world to condemn the world; but that the world should be saved by him.

18 He who believes in him will not be condemned; and he who does not believe has already been condemned for not believing in the name of the only begotten Son of God.

19 And this is the judgment, that light has come into the world and yet men have loved darkness more than light, because their works were evil.

20 For every one who does detestable things hates the light, and he does not come to the light, because his works cannot be covered.

21 But he who does truthful things comes to the light, so that his works may be known, that they are done through God.

22 ¶After these things, Jesus and his disciples came to the land of Judea, and he remained there with them and baptized.

23 ¶John also was baptizing at the spring of Aenon near to Shalim, because there was much water there; and they came and were baptized.

24 For John was not yet cast into prison.

25 ¶Now it happened that a dispute arose between one of John's disciples and a Jew about the ceremony of purifying.

26 So they came to John and told him, Teacher, he who was with you at the Jordan crossing, concerning whom you testified, behold, he also is baptizing and a great many are coming to him.

27 John answered, saying to them, No man can receive anything of his own will, except it is given to him from heaven.

28 You yourselves bear me witness that I said, I am not the Christ, but only a messenger to go before him.

29 He who has a bride is the bridegroom; and the best man of the bridegroom is he who stands up and listens to him, and rejoices greatly because of the bridegroom's voice; this my joy therefore is fulfilled.

30 He must become greater and I lesser.

31 For he who has come from above is above all; and he who is of the earth is of the earth, and he speaks of earthly things; but he who has come from heaven is above all.

32 And he testifies of what he has seen and heard, and yet no man accepts his testimony.

33 He who accepts his testimony has set his seal that God is true.

34 For he whom God has sent speaks the words of God; for God did not give the Spirit by measure.

35 The Father loves the Son, and has placed everything under his hand.

36 He who believes in the Son has eternal life; and he who does not obey the Son shall not see life, but the wrath of God shall remain on him.

CHAPTER 4

WHEN Jesus knew that the Pharisees had heard he made many disciples and was baptizing more people than John,

2 Though Jesus himself did not baptize, but his disciples;

3 He left Judea and came again to Galilee.

4 He had to go through Samaritan territory.

5 Then he came to a Samaritan city called Sychar, near the field which Jacob had given to his son Joseph.

6 Now Jacob's well was there; and Jesus was tired by the fatigue of the journey, and sat down by the well. It was about the sixth hour.

7 And there came a woman from Samaria to draw water; and Jesus said to her, Give me water to drink.

8 His disciples had entered into the city to buy food for themselves.

9 The Samaritan woman said to him, How is it? You are a Jew, and yet you ask me for a drink, who am a Samaritan woman? (For Jews have no social intercourse with Samaritans.)

10 Jesus answered, saying to her, If you only knew the gift of God and who is the man who said to you, Give me a drink, you would have asked him, and he would have given you living water.

11 The woman said to him, My lord, you have no leather bucket and no deep well; where do you get the living water?

12 What! are you greater than our father Jacob, who gave us this well, and he himself drank from it, and his sons and his sheep?

13 Jesus answered, saying to her, Everyone who drinks of this water will thirst again;

14 But whoever drinks of the water which I give him shall never thirst; but the same water which I give him shall become in him a well of water springing up to life everlasting.

15 The woman said to him, My lord, give me of this water, so that I may not thirst again and need not come and draw from here.

16 Jesus said to her, Go and call your husband, and come here.

17 She said to him, I have no husband. Jesus said to her, You said well, I have no husband;

18 For you have had five husbands; and the one you now have is not your husband; what you said is true.

19 Then the woman said to him, My lord, I see that you are a prophet.

20 Our forefathers worshipped on this mountain; and you say the place where men must worship is in Jerusalem.

21 Jesus said to her, Woman, believe me, the time is coming, when neither on this mountain nor in Jerusalem will they worship the Father.

22 You worship what you do not know; but we worship what we do know; for salvation is from the Jews.

23 But the time is coming, and it is here, when the true worshippers shall worship the Father in spirit and in truth; for the Father also desires worshippers such as these.

24 For God is Spirit; and those who worship him must worship him in spirit and in truth.

25 The woman said to him, I know that the Messiah (Christ) is coming; when he is come, he will teach us everything.

26 Jesus said to her, I am he who is speaking to you.

27 ¶While he was talking, his disciples came and were surprised that he was talking with a married woman; but no one said to him, What do you want? or, What are you talking with her?

28 The woman then left her water jar, and went to the city and said to the men,

29 Come and see a man who told me everything which I have done; What! is he the Christ?

30 And the men went out of the city, and came to him.

31 ¶During the interval his disciples begged him, saying, Teacher, eat.

32 But he said to them, I have food to eat of which you do not know.

33 The disciples said among themselves, What! did any man bring him something to eat?

34 Jesus said to them, My food is to do the will of him who sent me and to finish his work.

35 Do you not say that after four months comes the harvest? Behold,

I say to you, Lift up your eyes and look at the fields which have turned white and have long been ready for the harvest.

36 And he who reaps receives wages and gathers fruits to life everlasting, so that the sower and the reaper may rejoice together.

37 For in this case the saying is true, One sows and another reaps.

38 I sent you to reap that for which you did not labor; for others labored, and you have entered into their labor.

39 ¶A great many Samaritans of that city believed in him because of the word of that woman, who testified, He told me everything which I have done.

40 So when the Samaritans came to him, they begged him to stay with them; and he stayed with them two days.

41 And a great many believed in him because of his word;

42 And they were saying to the woman, Henceforth it is not because of your word that we believe in him; for we ourselves have heard and know that this is indeed the Christ, the Saviour of the world.

43 ¶Two days later, Jesus departed thence and went to Galilee.

44 For Jesus himself testified that a prophet is not honored in his own city.

45 When he came to Galilee, the Galileans welcomed him, for they had seen all the wonders he did at Jerusalem during the feast; for they also had come to the feast.

46 Then Jesus came again to Cana of Galilee, where he had made the water wine. And there was at Capernaum a servant of a king, whose son was sick.

47 This man heard that Jesus had come from Judea to Galilee; so he went to him and asked him to come down and heal his son; for he was near death.

48 Jesus said to him, Unless you see miracles and wonders, you will not believe.

49 The king's servant said to him, My Lord, come down before the boy is dead.

50 Jesus said to him, Go, your son is healed. And the man believed the word that Jesus said to him and went away.

51 And as he was going down, his servants met him and brought him good news, saying, Your son is healed.

52 And he asked them, At what time was he healed? They said to him, Yesterday at the seventh hour the fever left him.

53 And his father knew that it was at that very hour when Jesus told him, Your son is healed; so he himself believed and his whole household.

54 This is again the second miracle which Jesus did after he came from Judea to Galilee.

CHAPTER 5

AFTER these things there was a feast of the Jews; and Jesus went up to Jerusalem.

2 Now there was at Jerusalem a baptismal pool, which is called in Hebrew Bethesda, having five entrances.

3 And at these entrances a great many sick people were lying, the blind, the lame, and the crippled; and they were waiting for the water to be stirred up;

4 For an angel of God went down at a certain time to the baptismal pool and stirred up the water; and whoever went in first after the stirring of the water was healed of any disease he had.

5 A man was there who had been sick for thirty-eight years.

6 Jesus saw this man lying down, and he knew that he had been waiting for a long time; so he said to him, Do you wish to be healed?

7 The sick man answered, saying, Yes, my Lord; but I have no man, when the water is stirred up, to put me into the baptismal pool; but while I am coming, another one goes in before me.

8 Jesus said to him, Rise, take up your quilt and walk.

9 And the man was healed immediately, and he got up and took his

quilt and walked. And that day was the sabbath.

10 ¶So the Jews said to him who was healed, It is the sabbath; it is not lawful for you to carry your quilt.

11 He answered, saying to them, He who healed me told me, Take up your quilt and walk.

12 And they asked him, Who is this man who said to you, Take up your quilt and walk?

13 But he who was healed did not know who he was; for Jesus was pressed by a large crowd which was at that place.

14 After a while, Jesus found him in the temple, and said to him, Behold, you are healed; do not sin again, for something worse might happen to you than at first.

15 And the man went away and told the Jews that it was Jesus who had healed him.

16 ¶And for this reason the Jews persecuted Jesus and wanted to kill him, because he was doing these things on the sabbath.

17 ¶But Jesus said to them, My Father works even until now, so I also work.

18 And for this the Jews wanted the more to kill him, not only because he was weakening the sabbath, but also because he said concerning God that he was his Father, and he was making himself equal with God.

19 Jesus answered, saying to them, Truly, truly, I say to you that the Son can do nothing of his own accord, except what he sees the Father doing; for the things which the Father does, the same the Son does also.

20 For the Father loves his Son, and he shows him everything that he does; and he will show him greater works than these, so that you may marvel.

21 For just as the Father raises the dead and gives them life, even so the Son gives life to those whom he will.

22 For the Father does not judge any man, but he has entrusted all judgment to the Son;

23 So that every man should honor the Son, just as he honors the Father. He who does not honor the Son does not honor the Father who sent him.

24 Truly, truly, I say to you, He who hears my word and believes him who has sent me has everlasting life; and he does not come before the judgment, but he passes from death to life.

25 Truly, truly, I say to you, The time is coming, and it is now already here, when the dead will hear the voice of the Son of God; and those who hear it will live.

26 For as the Father has life in himself, even so he has given to the Son also to have life in himself.

27 And he has given him authority to execute judgment also, for he is the Son of man.

28 Do not wonder at this; for the time is coming, when all those who are in their graves will hear his voice,

29 And they will come out; those who have done good works to the resurrection of life; and those who have done evil works to the resurrection of judgment.

30 I can do nothing of myself; but as I hear I judge, and my judgment is just; for I do not seek my own will, but the will of him who sent me.

31 If I testify concerning myself, my testimony is not true.

32 ¶It is another one who testifies concerning me; and I know that the testimony which he testifies concerning me is true.

33 You sent to John, and he testified concerning the truth.

34 But I do not receive any testimony from men; but I tell you these things so that you may be saved.

35 He was a lamp which burns and gives light; and you were willing to delight in his light for a while.

36 ¶But I have a greater testimony than that of John; for the works which my Father has given me to finish, the same works which I do, testify concerning me, that the Father has sent me.

37 And the Father who sent me has testified concerning me. But you have never heard his voice nor seen his appearance.

38 And his word does not abide in you, because you do not believe in him whom he has sent.

39 ¶Examine the scriptures; in them you trust that you have eternal life; and even they testify concerning me.

40 Yet you will not come to me, that you might have life everlasting.

41 I do not receive any praise from men.

42 But I know you well, that the love of God is not in you.

43 I have come in the name of my Father, and you do not receive me; if another should come in his own name, you will receive him.

44 How can you believe, when you accept praise one from another, but the praise from God only, you do not want?

45 What! do you think that I will accuse you before the Father; there is one who will accuse you, even Moses, in whom you trust.

46 For if you had believed in Moses, you would also have believed in me; for Moses wrote concerning me.

47 If you do not believe his writings, how then can you believe my words?

CHAPTER 6

AFTER these things, Jesus went to the port of the sea of Galilee, at Tiberias.

2 And a great many people followed him, because they saw the miracles which he performed on sick people.

3 So Jesus went up to the mountain, and he sat there with his disciples.

4 And the feast of the passover of the Jews was at hand.

5 ¶And Jesus lifted up his eyes and saw a large crowd coming to him, and he said to Philip, Where can we buy bread that all these may eat?

6 He said this merely to test him; for he knew what he would do.

7 Philip said to him, Two hundred pennies worth of bread would not be sufficient for them, even if each one should take a little.

8 One of his disciples, Andrew the brother of Simon Peter, said to him,

9 There is a boy here who has with him five barley loaves and two fish; but what are these for all of them?

10 Jesus said to them, Make all the men sit down. There was much grass in that place. So the men sat down, five thousand in number.

11 And Jesus took the bread and blessed it, and distributed it to those who were sitting down; likewise the fish also, as much as they wanted.

12 When they were filled, he said to his disciples, Gather up the broken pieces which are left over, so that nothing is lost.

13 And they gathered them up, and filled twelve baskets with broken pieces which were left over by those who ate from five barley loaves.

14 Then the men who saw the miracle which Jesus performed said, Truly this is the prophet who is to come into the world.

15 ¶But Jesus knew that they were ready to come and seize him to make him a king, so he departed to the mountain alone.

16 And when evening came, his disciples went down to the sea

17 And entered into a boat, and were going to the port of Capernaum. And now it was dark, and Jesus had not yet come to them.

18 And the sea became rough, because a strong wind was blowing.

19 And they rowed about twenty-five or thirty furlongs, and they saw Jesus walking on [1] the sea; and as he drew towards their boat, they became afraid.

20 But Jesus said to them, It is I, do not be afraid.

21 So they wanted to receive him into the boat; but soon the boat reached the land to which they were going.

22 ¶The next day, the multitude which stood waiting at the seaport saw no other boat there, except the

---

[1] The Aramaic *al* means on or by. The disciples were going from Tiberias to Capernaum, both cities on the same side of the Sea of Galilee. The Church of the East believes that such miraculous appearances were by the Christ, God.

boat in which the disciples had entered, and that Jesus had not entered the boat with his disciples.

23 But other boats had come from Tiberias, near the place where they had eaten bread when Jesus blessed it.

24 And when the people saw that Jesus was not there, nor his disciples, they entered the boats and came to Capernaum, looking for Jesus.

25 And when they found him at the seaport, they said to him, Teacher, when did you come here?

26 Jesus answered, saying to them, Truly, truly, I say to you, You seek me, not because you saw the miracles, but just because you ate bread and were filled.

27 Do not labor for the food which perishes, but for the food which endures to life everlasting, which the Son of man will give you; for this one God the Father has sealed.

28 They said to him, What shall we do to work the works of God?

29 Jesus answered, saying to them, This is the work of God, that you should believe in him whom he has sent.

30 They said to him, What miracle do you perform that we may see and believe in you? What have you performed?

31 Our forefathers ate manna in the wilderness; as it is written, He gave them bread from heaven to eat.

32 Jesus said to them, Truly, truly, I say to you, It was not Moses who gave you bread from heaven; but my Father gives you the true bread from heaven.

33 For the bread of God is he who has come down from heaven, who gives life to the world.

34 They said to him, Our Lord, give us this bread always.

35 Jesus said to them, I am the bread of life; he who comes to me shall never hunger; and he who believes in me shall never thirst.

36 But I have said to you that you have seen me and yet you do not believe.

37 Everyone whom my Father has given me shall come to me; and he who comes to me I will not cast out.

38 For I came down from heaven, not merely to do my own will, but to do the will of him who sent me.

39 This is the will of him who sent me that I should lose nothing of all that he has given me, but should raise it up at the last day.

40 For this is the will of my Father, that whoever sees the Son and believes in him shall have life everlasting; and I will raise him up at the last day.

41 Now the Jews murmured against him, for he said, I am the bread which came down from heaven.

42 And they said, Is this not Jesus, the son of Joseph, whose father and mother we know? How can he say, I have come down from heaven?

43 Jesus answered, saying to them, Do not murmur one with another.

44 No man can come to me unless the Father who sent me draw him; and I will raise him up at the last day.

45 For it is written in the prophet, They shall all be taught by God. Everyone therefore who hears from the Father and learns from him will come to me.

46 No man can see the Father except him who is from God; he can see the Father.

47 Truly, truly, I say to you, He who believes in me has eternal life.

48 I am the bread of life.

49 Your forefathers ate manna in the wilderness, and yet they died.

50 This is the bread which came down from heaven, that a man may eat of it and not die.

51 I am the living bread because I came down from heaven; if any man eats of this bread, he shall live forever; and the bread which I will give is my body, which I am giving for the sake of the life of the world.

52 The Jews argued one with another, saying, How can this man give us his body to eat?

53 Jesus said to them, Truly, truly I say to you, Unless you eat the body of the Son of man and drink his blood, you have no life in yourselves.

54 He who eats of my body and

drinks of my blood has eternal life; and I will raise him at the last day.

55 For my body truly is the food, and my blood truly is the drink.

56 He who eats my body and drinks my blood will abide with me, and I with him.

57 Just as the living Father sent me, and I am living because of the Father, so whoever eats of me will also live because of me.

58 This is the bread which came down from heaven; it is not like that manna which your forefathers ate and died; he who eats of this bread shall live forever.

59 These things he said in the synagogue while he was teaching at Capernaum.

60 ¶Many of his disciples who heard it said, This is a hard saying; who can listen to it?

61 Jesus knew in himself that his disciples were murmuring about this; so he said to them, Does this cause you to stumble?

62 What then if you should see the Son of man ascending to the place where he was before?

63 It is the spirit that gives life; the body is of no account; the words which I have spoken to you are spirit and life.

64 But there are some of you who do not believe. For Jesus knew for a long while who were those who did not believe, and who was to betray him.

65 And he said to them, For this reason I have told you that no man can come to me unless it is given to him by my Father.

66 ¶Just because of this saying a great many of his disciples turned away and did not walk with him.

67 So Jesus said to his twelve, What! do you also want to go away?

68 Simon Peter answered, saying, My Lord, to whom shall we go? You have the words of eternal life.

69 And we have believed and known that you are the Christ, the Son of the living God.

70 Jesus said to them, Did not I choose you, the twelve, and yet one of you is Satan? [1]

71 He said it concerning Judah, the son of Simon Iscariot; for he was the one of the twelve who was going to betray him.

CHAPTER 7

AFTER these things Jesus travelled in Galilee; for he did not wish to travel in Judea because the Jews wanted to kill him.

2 Now the Jewish feast of the tabernacles was at hand.

3 And his brothers said to Jesus, Depart from here and go to Judea, so that your disciples may see the works that you do.

4 For there is no man who does anything in secret and yet wants it to become known. If you are doing these things, show yourself to the people.

5 For not even his own brothers believed in Jesus.

6 Jesus said to them, My time has not yet come; but your time is always here.

7 The world cannot hate you; but it hates me, because I testify against it, that its works are evil.

8 You go up to this feast; I am not going just now to this feast, for my time is not yet come.

9 He said these things, and remained in Galilee.

10 ¶But when his brothers had gone up to the feast, then he also went up, not openly, but as it were in secret.

11 The Jews were looking for him at the feast and said, Where is he?

12 And there was much murmuring among the people concerning him; for some said, He is good; and others said, No, but he just deceives the people.

13 But no man spoke openly about him, because of the fear of the Jews.

14 ¶Now about the middle period of the feast, Jesus went up to the temple and taught.

15 And the Jews marvelled, saying, How does this man know how to read when he has not been instructed?

16 Jesus answered, saying, My

---

[1] The Aramaic *satana* (Satan) is derived from *sta,* which means to slide, to slip, or to miss the mark, and applies to one who causes these results.

teaching is not mine, but his who sent me.

17 He who wills to do his will can understand if my teaching is from God or if I am just speaking of my own accord.

18 He who speaks of his own accord seeks glory for himself; but he who seeks the glory of him who sent him is true, and there is no deception in his heart.

19 Did not Moses give you the law? And yet no one of you obeys the law. Why do you want to kill me?

20 The people answered, saying, You are crazy; who wants to kill you?

21 Jesus answered, saying to them, I have done one work, and all of you marvel.

22 Moses gave you circumcision, not because it is from Moses, but because it is from the forefathers; and yet you circumcise a man on the sabbath.

23 So if a man is circumcised on the sabbath day, that the law of Moses may not be broken; yet you murmur at me, because I healed a whole man [1] on the sabbath day?

24 Do not judge by partiality, but judge a just judgment.

25 Then some of the men of Jerusalem were saying, Is not this the man whom they want to kill?

26 And yet he speaks openly, but they say nothing to him. Perhaps our elders have found out that he is the Christ?

27 Howbeit we know whence he comes; but when the Christ comes, no man will know whence he comes.

28 Jesus then lifted up his voice as he taught in the temple, saying, You know me, and you know whence I come; and yet I have not come of my own accord, but he who sent me is true, whom you do not know.

29 But I know him; because I am from him, and he sent me.

30 So they wanted to seize him; and no man laid hands on him, because his time had not yet come.

31 But a great many of the people believed in him and said, When the Christ comes, will he do greater wonders than this man does?

32 ¶The Pharisees heard the people talking about him; so they and the high priests sent soldiers to arrest him.

33 And Jesus said, I am with you just a short while, and I am going to him who sent me.

34 You will seek me, but you will not find me; and where I am you cannot come.

35 Then the Jews said among themselves, Where is he going, that we cannot find him? Is he planning to go to the countries of the Gentiles to teach the pagans?

36 What does this word mean which he said, You will seek me and you will not find me, and where I am you cannot come?

37 Now on the greatest day, which is the last day of the feast, Jesus stood and cried out, saying, If any man is thirsty, let him come to me and drink.

38 Whoever believes in me, just as the scriptures have said, the rivers of living water shall flow from within him.

39 He said this concerning the Spirit, which they who believe in him were to receive; for the Spirit was not yet given, because Jesus was not yet glorified.

40 ¶Many of the people who heard his words were saying, This man truly is a prophet.

41 Others were saying, He is the Christ; but others said, Is it possible that Christ should come from Galilee?

42 Does not the scripture say that Christ will come from the seed of David and from Bethlehem, the town of David?

43 So the people were divided because of him.

44 And there were some men among them who wanted to seize him; but no man laid hands on him.

45 ¶And the soldiers returned to the high priests and the Pharisees; and

[1] Circumcision affected only one part of the body. Jesus here healed the whole body; and so his work on the sabbath was more important than circumcision.

the priests said to them, Why did you not bring him?

46 The soldiers said to them, Never a man has spoken as this man speaks. 47 The Pharisees said to them, What! have you also been deceived?

48 Have any of the leaders or of the Pharisees believed in him,

49 Except this cursed people who do not know the law?

50 Nicodemus, one of them, who had come to Jesus at night, said to them,

51 Does our law convict a man unless it first hears from him and knows what he has done?

52 They answered, saying to him, What! are you also from Galilee? Search and see that no prophet will rise up from Galilee.[1]

53 So everyone went to his own house.

CHAPTER 8

THEN Jesus went to the mount of Olives.

2 And in the morning he came again to the temple, and all the people were coming to him; and he sat down and taught them.

3 Then the scribes and the Pharisees brought a woman who was caught in adultery;[2] and they made her to stand in the midst.

4 They said to him, Teacher, this woman was caught openly in the act of adultery.

5 Now in the law of Moses it is commanded that women such as these should be stoned; but what do you say?

6 They said this to tempt him, that they might have a cause to accuse him. While Jesus was bent down, he was writing on the ground.

7 When they were through questioning him, he straightened himself up and said to them, He who is among you without sin, let him first throw a stone at her.

8 And again as he bent down, he wrote on the ground.

9 And when they heard it, they left one by one, beginning with the elders; and the woman was left alone in the midst.

10 When Jesus straightened himself up, he said to the woman, Where are they? Did no man condemn you?

11 She said, No man, Lord. Then Jesus said, Neither do I condemn you; go away, and from henceforth, do not sin again.

12 ¶Again Jesus spoke to them, saying, I am the light of the world; he who follows me shall not walk in darkness, but he shall find for himself the light of life.

13 The Pharisees said to him, You testify concerning yourself; your testimony is not true.

14 Jesus answered, saying to them, Even though I testify concerning myself, my testimony is true, because I know whence I came and whither I go; but you do not know whence I came or whither I go.

15 You judge according to the flesh; but I judge no man.

16 And if I should judge, my judgment is true; because I am not doing it alone, but I and my Father who sent me.

17 And it is written in your own law that the testimony of two men is true.

18 I testify concerning myself, and my Father who sent me testifies concerning me.

19 They said to him, Where is your Father? Jesus answered, saying to them, You know neither me nor my Father; if you knew me, you would know my Father also.

20 These words he spoke in the treasury while he taught in the temple; and no man arrested him, for his time had not yet come.

21 ¶Jesus again said to them, I am going away, and you will seek me, and you will die in your sins; and where I am going you cannot come.

22 The Jews said, What! will he kill

[1] Galilee was the land of the Gentiles and of mixed races, the descendants of those who were transferred from Assyria during the captivity.
[2] The story of the woman taken in adultery is not found in the ancient Peshitta, but occurs in later Aramaic texts.

himself? For he says, Where I am going, you cannot come.

23 And he said to them, You are from below, and I am from above; you are of this world, but I am not of this world.

24 I told you that you will die in your sins; for unless you believe that I am he, you will die in your sins.

25 The Jews said, Who are you? Jesus said to them, Even though I should begin to speak to you,

26 I have many things to say and to judge concerning you; but he who sent me is true; and I speak in the world only those things which I have heard from him.

27 They did not understand that he spoke to them concerning the Father.

28 Again Jesus said to them, When you have lifted up the Son of man, then you will understand that I am he, and I do nothing of my own accord; but as my Father has taught me, so I speak just like him.

29 And he who sent me is with me; and my Father has never left me alone, because I always do what pleases him.

30 ¶While he was speaking these words, a great many believed in him.

31 Then Jesus said to the Jews who believed in him, If you abide by my word, you are truly my disciples.

32 And you will know the truth, and that very truth will make you free.

33 They said to him, We are the offspring of Abraham, and we have never been enslaved to any man; how do you say, You will be free people?

34 Jesus said to them, Truly, truly, I say to you, Whoever commits sin is a servant of sin.

35 And a servant does not remain in the house forever, but the son remains forever.

36 If therefore, the Son shall make you free, you shall be free indeed.

37 I know you are the descendants of Abraham; but still you want to kill me, because you have no room in you for my word.

38 I speak what I have seen with my Father; and you do what you have seen with your father.

39 They answered, saying to him, Our own father is Abraham. Jesus said to them, If you were the sons of Abraham, you would be doing the works of Abraham.

40 But behold, now you want to kill me, even a man who has told you the truth which I heard from God; this Abraham did not do.

41 But you do the works of your father. They said to him, We are not born of fornication; we have one Father, God.

42 Jesus said to them, If God were your Father, you would love me, for I proceeded and came from God; I did not come of my own accord, but he sent me.

43 Why therefore do you not understand my word? Because you cannot obey my word?

44 You are from the father of accusation, and you want to do the lusts of your father, he who is a murderer of men from the very beginning and who never stands by the truth, because there is no truth in him. When he speaks he speaks his own lie, because he is a liar, and the father of lies.

45 But because I speak the truth, you do not believe me.

46 Which one of you can rebuke me because of sin? If I speak the truth, why do you not believe me?

47 He who is of God, hears God's words; for this reason you do not hear, because you are not of God.

48 The Jews answered, saying to him, Did we not say well, that you are a Samaritan and that you are crazy?

49 Jesus said to them, I am not crazy; but I honor my Father, and you curse me.

50 I do not seek my glory; there is one who seeks and judges.

51 Truly, truly, I say to you, Whoever obeys my word shall never see death.

52 The Jews said to him, Now we are sure that you are insane. Abraham and the prophets have died; and yet you say, Whoever obeys my word shall never taste death.

53 What! are you greater than our

father Abraham who died, and the prophets who died? Whom do you make yourself?

54 Jesus said to them, If I honor myself, my honor is nothing; but it is my Father who honors me, the one of whom you say, He is our God.

55 Yet you have not known him, but I know him; and if I should say, I do not know him, I would be a liar like yourselves; but I do know him, and I obey his word.

56 Your father Abraham rejoiced to see my day; and he saw it and was glad.

57 The Jews said to him, You are not yet fifty years old, and yet have you seen Abraham?

58 Jesus said to them, Truly, truly, I say to you, Before Abraham was born, I was.

59 So they took up stones, to stone him; and Jesus hid himself and went out of the temple, and he passed through the midst of them and went away.

CHAPTER 9

AND as Jesus passed by, he saw a man who was blind from his mother's womb.

2 And his disciples asked him, saying, Teacher, who did sin, this man or his parents, that he was born blind?

3 Jesus said to them, Neither did he sin nor his parents. But that the works of God might be seen in him,

4 I must do the works of him who sent me, while it is day; the night comes when no man can work.

5 As long as I am in the world, I am the light of the world.

6 When he said these words, he spat on the ground and mixed clay with his saliva, and he placed it on the eyes of the blind man.

7 Then he said to him, Go and wash in the baptismal pool of Shiloha. He went and washed, and he came seeing.

8 His neighbors and those who had seen him before begging, said, Is not this he who used to sit down and beg?

9 Some said, It is he; and some said, No, but he resembles him; but he said, I am he.

10 Then they said to him, How were your eyes opened?

11 He answered, saying to them, A man whose name is Jesus made clay and placed it on my eyes, and he said to me, Go and wash in the water of Shiloha; and I went and washed, and I see.

12 They said to him, Where is he? He said to them, I do not know.

13 ¶So they brought to the Pharisees him who had been blind from his birth.

14 Now it was the sabbath when Jesus made the clay and opened his eyes.

15 Again the Pharisees asked him, How did you receive your sight? He said to them, He placed clay on my eyes, and I washed, and I see.

16 Then some of the Pharisees said, This man is not from God, because he does not observe the sabbath; others said, How can a man who is a sinner do these miracles? And there was a division among them.

17 They said to the blind man again, What do you say concerning him who opened your eyes? He said to them, I say he is a prophet.

18 But the Jews did not believe concerning him that he had been blind and had received his sight, until they called the parents of him who had received his sight.

19 And they asked them, Is this your son, who you say was born blind? How then does he now see?

20 His parents answered, saying, We know that he is our son and that he was born blind.

21 But how he sees now or who opened his eyes we do not know; he is of age, ask him, he will speak for himself.

22 His parents said these things because they were afraid of the Jews; for the Jews had decided already that if any man should confess that he is the Christ, they would put him out of the synagogue.

23 For this reason his parents said, He is of age, ask him.

24 So they called a second time

the man who had been blind, and said to him, Give praise to God, for we know that this man is a sinner.

25 He answered, saying to them, If he is a sinner I do not know; but I do know one thing, that I was blind and now behold, I see.

26 They said to him again, What did he do to you? How did he open your eyes?

27 He said to them, I have already told you, and you did not listen; why do you want to hear it again? What! do you also want to become his disciples?

28 Then they cursed him and said to him, You are his disciple, but we are disciples of Moses.

29 And we know that God spoke with Moses; but as for this man, we do not know whence he is.

30 The man answered, saying to them, This is surprising, that you do not know whence he is, and yet he opened my eyes.

31 We know that God does not hear the voice of sinners; but he hears the one who reveres him and does his will.

32 From ages it has never been heard that a man opened the eyes of one who was born blind.

33 If this man were not from God, he could not have done this.

34 They answered, saying to him, You were wholly born in sins, and yet do you teach us? And they cast him out.

35 ¶And Jesus heard that they had cast him out; and he found him and said to him, Do you believe in the Son of God?

36 He who was healed answered, saying, Who is he, my Lord, so that I may believe in him?

37 Jesus said to him, You have seen him, and he is the one who is speaking with you.

38 He said, I do believe, my Lord; and he fell down and worshipped him.

39 Then Jesus said to him, I have come for the judgment of this world, so that those who cannot see may see, and those who see may become blind.

40 ¶When some of the Pharisees who were with him heard these words, they said to him, What! are we also blind?

41 Jesus said to them, If you were blind, you would have no sin; but now you say, We see; because of this your sin remains.

CHAPTER 10

TRULY, truly, I say to you, He who does not enter by the door into the sheepfold, but climbs up from another place, is a thief and a bandit.

2 But he who enters by the door is the shepherd of the sheep.

3 To him the doorkeeper opens the door, and the sheep hear his voice, and he calls his own sheep by their names and brings them out.

4 And when he has brought out his sheep,[1] he goes before them; and his own sheep follow him, because they know his voice.

5 The sheep do not follow a stranger, but they run away from him, because they do not know the voice of a stranger.

6 Jesus spoke this parable to them; but they did not understand what he was telling them.

7 Jesus said to them again, Truly, truly, I say to you, I am the door of the sheep.

8 All who have come are thieves and bandits, if the sheep did not hear them.

9 I am the door; if any man enter by me, he shall live and he shall come in and go out and find pasture.

10 A thief does not come, except to steal and kill and destroy; I have come that they might have life, and have it abundantly.

11 I am the good shepherd; a good shepherd risks his life for the sake of his sheep.

12 But the hired person who is not the shepherd and who is not the owner of the sheep, when he sees the wolf coming, leaves the sheep and runs away; and the wolf comes and seizes and scatters the sheep.

13 The hired person runs away be-

[1] *His sheep* refers to the several flocks in the fold; *his own sheep* refers to his own flock.

cause he is hired and does not care for the sheep.

14 I am the good shepherd, and I know my own, and my own know me.

15 Just as my Father knows me, I also know my Father; and I lay down my life for the sake of the sheep.

16 I have other sheep also, which are not of this fold; them too I must bring, and they will hear my voice; and all the sheep will become one flock and one shepherd.

17 This is why my Father loves me, because I lay down my life so that I may take it up again.

18 No man takes it away from me, but I lay it down of my own will. Therefore I have the power to lay it down, and I have the power to take it up again. This command I received from my Father.

19 ¶There was again a division among the Jews because of these sayings.

20 And many of them said, He is insane and rambles; why do you listen to him?

21 Others said, These are not the words of a crazy man. Can a crazy man open the eyes of the blind?

22 ¶Then came the feast of dedication at Jerusalem, and it was winter.

23 And Jesus was walking in the temple in Solomon's porch.

24 Then the Jews surrounded him and said to him, How long do you vex our soul with uncertainty? If you are the Christ, tell us openly.

25 Jesus answered, saying to them, I have told you, but you do not believe; yet the works which I do in the name of my Father testify of me.

26 But you do not believe, because you are not of my sheep, just as I told you.

27 My own sheep hear my voice, and I know them and they follow me;

28 And I give to them eternal life; and they will never perish, and no man will snatch them from my hands.

29 For my Father who gave them to me is greater than all; and no man can snatch anything from my Father's hand.

30 I and my Father are of one accord.

31 Then the Jews again took up stones to stone him.

32 Jesus said to them, I have shown you many good works from my Father; for which one of them do you stone me?

33 The Jews said to him, It is not because of the good works we stone you, but because you blaspheme; for while you are only a man, you make yourself God.

34 Jesus said to them, Is it not so written in your law, I said, you are gods?

35 If he called them gods because the word of God was with them (and the scripture cannot be broken)

36 Why to the one whom the Father sanctified and sent to the world, do you say, You blaspheme, just because I said to you, I am the Son of God.

37 If I am not doing the works of my Father, do not believe me.

38 But if I am doing them, even though you do not believe in me, believe in the works, so that you may know and believe that my Father is with me and I am with my Father.

39 ¶And they wanted again to seize him; but he escaped from their hands.

40 And he went away to the Jordan crossing, to the place where John was, where he first baptized; and he remained there.

41 And many men came to him and said, John did not perform a single miracle; but everything which John said concerning this man is true.

42 And many believed in him.

CHAPTER 11

NOW there was a man who was sick, Lazar of the town of Bethany, the brother of Mary and Martha.

2 This is the Mary who anointed the feet of Jesus with perfume and wiped them with her hair. The Lazar who was sick was her brother.

3 His two sisters therefore sent to Jesus, saying, Our Lord, behold, the one whom you love is sick.

4 Jesus said, This is not a sickness of death, but for the sake of the glory

of God, that the Son of God may be glorified on his account.

5 Now Jesus loved Martha and Mary and Lazar.

6 When he heard he was sick, he remained two days in the place where he was.

7 After that he said to his disciples, Come, let us go again to Judea.

8 His disciples said to him, Teacher, not long ago the Jews wanted to stone you, and yet are you going there again?

9 Jesus said to them, Are there not twelve hours in the day? If a man walks by daytime, he will not stumble, because he sees the light of this world.

10 But if a man travels at nighttime, he will stumble, because there is no light in it.

11 Jesus said these things; and after that he said to them, Our friend Lazar is asleep; but I am going to awaken him.

12 His disciples said to him, Our Lord, if he is sleeping, he will get well.

13 But Jesus spoke of his death; and they thought that what he said was sleeping in bed.

14 Then Jesus said to them plainly, Lazar is dead;

15 And I am glad I was not there, for your sakes, so that you may believe; but let us walk there.

16 Then Thomas, who is called the Twin, said to his fellow disciples, Let us also go and die with him.

17 ¶So Jesus came to Bethany, and he found that Lazar had been four days in the tomb.

18 Now Bethany was towards Jerusalem, a distance of about two miles.

19 And many Jews kept coming to Martha and Mary to comfort their hearts concerning their brother.

20 When Martha heard that Jesus had come, she went out to meet him; but Mary sat in the house.

21 Then Martha said to Jesus, My Lord, if you had been here, my brother would not have died.

22 But even now I know that whatever you ask of God, he will give you.

23 Jesus said to her, Your brother will rise up.

24 Martha said to him, I know he will rise up in the resurrection at the last day.

25 Jesus said to her, I am the resurrection and the life; he who believes in me, even though he die, he shall live.

26 And whoever is alive and believes in me shall never die. Do you believe this?

27 She said to him, Yes, my Lord; I do believe that you are the Christ, the Son of God, who is to come to the world.

28 And when she had said these things, she went away and called her sister Mary secretly and said to her, Our teacher has come, and he is calling for you.

29 When Mary heard it, she rose up quickly and came to him.

30 Jesus had not yet come into the town, but he was still at the same place where Martha met him.

31 The Jews also who were with her in the house, comforting her, when they saw Mary rise up quickly and go out, followed her, for they thought she was going to the tomb to weep.

32 When Mary came where Jesus was and saw him, she threw herself at his feet and said to him, My Lord, if you had been here, my brother would not have died.

33 When Jesus saw her weeping and the Jews weeping, who had come with her, he was moved in his spirit and was greatly disturbed.

34 And he said, Where have you laid him? They said to him, Our Lord, come and see.

35 And Jesus was in tears.

36 The Jews then said, See how much he loved him!

37 Some of them said, Could not this man, who opened the eyes of that blind man, have also kept this man from dying?

38 As Jesus was disturbed in himself because of them, he came to the tomb. That tomb was a cave, and a stone was placed at the entrance.

39 Jesus said, Take away this stone.

Martha, the sister of the dead man, said to him, My Lord, already his body stinks, for he has been dead four days.

40 Jesus said to her, Did not I say to you that if you believe, you will see the glory of God?

41 So they took away the stone. And Jesus lifted his eyes upwards and said, O Father, I thank thee for thou hast heard me,

42 And I know that thou always hearest me; but I say these things just because of this people who stand around, so that they may believe that thou hast sent me.

43 And when he had said this, he cried with a loud voice, Lazar, come out.

44 And the dead man came out, his hands and feet bound with burial clothes, and his face bound with a burial napkin. Jesus said to them, Loose him and let him go.

45 ¶Many of the Jews who had come to Mary, when they saw what Jesus had done, believed in him.

46 And some of them went to the Pharisees and told them everything Jesus had done.

47 ¶So the high priests and the Pharisees gathered together and said, What shall we do? For this man does many miracles.

48 If we allow him to continue like this, all men will believe in him, and the Romans will come and take over both our country and our people.

49 But one of them, called Caiaphas, who was the high priest for that year, said to them, You know nothing;

50 Nor are you reasoning that it is much better for us that one man should die instead of the people, and not all the people perish.

51 He did not say this of himself; but because he was the high priest for that year, he prophesied that Jesus had to die for the sake of the people;

52 And not only for the sake of the people, but also to gather together the children of God who are scattered abroad.

53 And from that very day, they decided to kill him.

54 ¶Jesus therefore did not walk
69

openly among the Jews, but went away thence to a place which is close to the wilderness, in the province of Ephraim; and he remained there with his disciples.

55 Now the Jewish passover was at hand; and many went up from the towns to Jerusalem, before the feast, to purify themselves.

56 And they were looking for Jesus, and at the temple they kept saying to one another, What do you think, will he not come to the feast?

57 But the high priests and the Pharisees had already commanded that if any man should know where he was, he should let them know, so that they might seize him.

CHAPTER 12

SIX days before the passover, Jesus came to Bethany, where Lazar was, whom Jesus had raised from the dead.

2 And they gave him a banquet there; Martha served; but Lazar was one of the guests who were with him.

3 Then Mary took a cruse containing pure and expensive nard, and anointed the feet of Jesus, and wiped his feet with her hair; and the house was filled with the fragrance of the perfume.

4 And Judah of Iscariot, one of his disciples, who was about to betray him, said,

5 Why was not this oil sold for three hundred pennies, and given to the poor?

6 He said this, not because he cared for the poor, but because he was a thief, and the purse was with him, and he carried whatever was put into it.

7 Jesus then said, Let her alone; she has kept it for the day of my burial.

8 For you have the poor always with you, but me you have not always.

9 ¶Many people of the Jews heard that Jesus was there; so they came, not only on account of Jesus, but also to see Lazar, whom he had raised from the dead.

10 And the high priests were thinking of killing Lazar also;

11 Because on his account a great many Jews were leaving and believing in Jesus.

12 ¶On the next day, a large crowd which had come to the feast when they heard that Jesus was coming to Jerusalem,

13 Took branches of palm trees, and went out to greet him, and they cried out and said, Hosanna, Blessed is the king of Israel who comes in the name of the Lord.

14 And Jesus found an ass and sat on it; as it is written,

15 Fear not, O daughter of Zion; behold, your king comes to you, riding on the colt of an ass.

16 His disciples did not understand these things at that time; but when Jesus was glorified, then his disciples remembered that these things were written concerning him and that they had done these things to him.

17 The people who were with him testified that he had called Lazar from the tomb and raised him from the dead.

18 It was on this account that large crowds went out to meet him, for they heard that he had performed this miracle.

19 The Pharisees said one to another, Do you see that you have not been able to gain anything? Behold, all the people have gone after him.

20 ¶Now there were some Gentiles [1] among them who had come up to worship at the feast.

21 They came and approached Philip of Bethsaida of Galilee, and asked him, saying, My lord, we would like to see Jesus.

22 Philip came and told Andrew; then Andrew and Philip told Jesus.

23 Jesus answered, saying to them, The hour has come that the Son of man should be glorified.

24 Truly, truly, I say to you that unless a grain of wheat falls and dies in the ground, it will be left alone; but if it dies, it produces much fruit.

25 He who loves his life will lose it; and he who has no concern for his life in this world will keep it to life eternal.

26 If any man serve me, let him follow me; and where I am, there also will my servant be; he who serves me, him my Father will honor.

27 Now my soul is disturbed, and what shall I say? O my Father, deliver me from this hour; but for this cause I came to this very hour.

28 O Father, glorify thy name. Then a voice was heard from heaven, I am glorified, and I shall again be glorified.

29 And the people who stood by heard it and said, It was thunder; others said, An angel spoke to him.

30 Jesus answered, saying to them, This voice was not on my account, but for your sake.

31 Now is the judgment of this world; now the leader of this world will be cast out.

32 And I, when I am lifted up from the earth, will draw every man to me.

33 He said this to show by what kind of death he was to die.

34 The people said to him, We have heard from the law that the Christ shall remain forever; how do you say that the Son of man must be lifted up? Who is this Son of man?

35 Jesus said to them, The light is with you for a little while; walk while you have the light, so that the darkness may not overcome you; and he who walks in the darkness does not know where he goes.

36 While you have the light, believe in the light, so that you may become the sons of the light. Jesus spoke these things, and went away and hid himself from them.

37 ¶Even though he had performed all of these miracles before them, yet they did not believe in him,

38 So that the word of the prophet Isaiah might be fulfilled, who said, My Lord, who will believe our report, and to whom has the arm of the Lord been revealed?

39 For this reason, they could not believe, because Isaiah said again,

40 Their eyes have become blind

[1] The Aramaic *ammey* means *Gentiles*, that is, Syrians, Idumaeans, and other neighboring peoples. The word for Greeks is *yonaye*.

and their hearts darkened, so that they cannot see with their eyes and understand with their hearts; let them return and I will heal them.

41 Isaiah said these things when he saw his glory and spoke concerning him.

42 Many of the leading men also believed in him; but because of the Pharisees they did not confess it, so that they might not be cast out of the synagogue.

43 For they loved the honor of men more than the glory of God.

44 ¶Jesus cried out, saying, He who believes in me believes not in me but in him who sent me.

45 And he who sees me has already seen him who sent me.

46 I have come into the world as the light, so that whoever believes in me may not remain in the darkness.

47 And he who hears my words, and does not obey them, I will not judge him; for I have not come to judge the world, but to save the world.

48 He who oppresses me and does not receive my words, there is one who will judge him; the word which I have spoken, it will judge him at the last day.

49 For I did not speak of myself; but the Father who sent me, he commanded me what to say and what to speak.

50 And I know that his commandment is life everlasting; these things therefore which I speak, just as my Father told me, so I speak.

CHAPTER 13

NOW before the feast of the passover, Jesus knew the hour had come to depart from this world to his Father. He loved his own who were in this world, and he loved them to the end.

2 ¶During supper, Satan put into the heart of Judah, son of Simon of Iscariot, to deliver him.

3 But Jesus, because he knew that the Father had given everything into his hands and that he came from God and was going to God,

4 Rose from supper and laid aside his robe; and he took a cloth and tied it around his loins.

5 Then he poured water into a basin, and began to wash the feet of his disciples and to wipe them with the cloth which was tied around his loins.

6 When he came to Simon Peter, Simon said to him, Are you, my Lord, going to wash my feet?

7 Jesus answered, saying to him, What I am doing, you do not know now, but later you will understand.

8 Then Simon Peter said to him, You will never wash my feet. Jesus said to him, If I do not wash you, you have no part with me.

9 Simon Peter said to him, Then, my Lord, wash not only my feet but also my hands and my head.

10 Jesus said to him, He who has bathed does not need except to wash his feet only, for he is already all clean; so you are all clean, but not everyone of you.

11 For Jesus knew him who was to betray him; therefore he said, Not everyone of you is clean.

12 When he had washed their feet, he put on his robes and sat down; and he said to them, Do you know what I have done to you?

13 You call me Teacher and Lord; and what you say is well, for I am.

14 If I then, your Lord and Teacher, have washed your feet, how much more should you wash one another's feet?

15 For I have given you this as an example, so that just as I have done to you, you should also do.

16 Truly, truly, I say to you, There is no servant who is greater than his master; and no apostle who is greater than he who sent him.

17 If you know these things, blessed are you if you do them.

18 I do not say this concerning all of you, for I know those whom I have chosen; but that the scripture might be fulfilled, He who eats bread with me has lifted up his heel against me.

19 I tell you now before it happens, that when it happens, you may believe that I am he.[1]

20 Truly, truly, I say to you, He who

---

[1] The Messiah.

receives him whom I send receives me; and he who receives me receives him who sent me.

21 ¶Jesus said these things, and he was disturbed in spirit, and testified, saying, Truly, truly, I say to you, one of you will betray me.

22 The disciples then looked at each other, because they did not know concerning whom he spoke.

23 Now there was one of his disciples who was leaning on his bosom, the one whom Jesus loved.

24 Simon Peter beckoned to him, to ask him of whom he spoke.

25 So that disciple leaned himself on the breast of Jesus, and said to him, My Lord, who is he?

26 Jesus answered, saying, The one for whom I dip bread and give it to him. So Jesus dipped the bread, and gave it to Judah, the son of Simon of Iscariot.

27 And after the bread, Satan took possession of him. So Jesus said to him, What you are going to do, do it soon.

28 But no man of those who were sitting at the table understood what he said to him.

29 For some of them thought, because the purse was with Judah, that he ordered him to buy what was needed for the feast or to give something to the poor.

30 So Judah then received the bread and went outside immediately; and it was night when he went out.

31 ¶Jesus then said, Now the Son of man is glorified, and God is glorified by him.

32 If God is glorified by him, God will also glorify him by himself, and he will glorify him at once.

33 My sons, I am with you yet a little while, and you will seek me. And just as I said to the Jews, Where I go you cannot come; the same I now tell you also.

34 A new commandment I give you, that you love one another; just as I have loved you, that you also love one another.

35 By this every man shall know that you are my disciples, if you have love one for another.

36 Simon Peter said to him, Our Lord, where are you going? Jesus answered, saying to him, Where I go you cannot follow me now, but you will follow later.

37 Simon Peter said to him, My Lord, why can I not follow you now? I will even lay down my life for you.

38 Jesus said to him, Will you lay down your life for me? Truly, truly, I say to you, The cock shall not crow, until you have denied me three times.

CHAPTER 14

LET not your heart be troubled; believe in God, and believe in me also.

2 In my Father's house are many rooms; if it were not so, I would have told you. I go to prepare a place for you.

3 And if I go and prepare a place for you, I will come again and take you to me, so that where I am you may be also.

4 You know where I am going and you know the way.

5 Thomas said to him, Our Lord, we do not know where you are going; and how can we know the way?

6 Jesus said to him, I am the way and the truth and the life; no man comes to my Father except by me.

7 If you had known me, you would have known my Father also; from henceforth you know him and you have seen him.

8 Philip said to him, Our Lord, show us the Father, and that is enough for us.

9 Jesus said to him, All this time I have been with you, and yet you do not know me, Philip? He who sees me has seen the Father; and how do you say, Show us the Father?

10 Do you not believe that I am with my Father and my Father is with me? The words that I speak, I do not speak of myself; but my Father who abides with me does these works.

11 Believe that I am with my Father and my Father is with me; and if not, believe because of the works.

12 Truly, truly, I say to you, He who believes in me shall do the works

which I do; and even greater than these things he shall do, because I am going to my Father.

13 And whatever you ask in my name, I will do it for you, so that the Father may be glorified through his Son.

14 If you ask me in my own name, I will do it.

15 If you love me, keep my commandments.

16 And I will ask of my Father, and he will give you another Comforter, to be with you for ever,

17 Even the Spirit of truth, whom the world cannot receive, because it has not seen him and does not know him; but you know him because he abides with you and is in you.

18 I will not leave you bereaved, for I will come to you after a little while.

19 And the world will not see me, but you will see me; because I live, you shall live also.

20 In that day you will know that I am with my Father, and you are with me, and I am with you.

21 He who has my commandments with him and obeys them is the one who loves me; he who loves me will be loved by my Father, and I will love him and reveal myself to him.

22 Judah (not of Iscariot) said to him, My Lord, why is it that you will reveal yourself to us and not to the world?

23 Jesus answered, saying to him, He who loves me keeps my word; and my Father will love him, and we will come to him and make a place of abode with him.

24 But he who does not love me does not keep my word; and this word which you hear is not my own but the Father's who sent me.

25 I have spoken these things to you while I am with you.

26 But the Comforter, the Holy Spirit, whom my Father will send in my name will teach you everything, and remind you of everything which I tell you.

27 Peace I leave with you; my own peace I give you; not as the world gives, I give to you. Let not your heart be troubled and do not be afraid.

28 You heard that I told you, I am going away, and I will come to you. If you loved me, you would rejoice because I am going to my Father; for my Father is greater than I.

29 And now behold, I have told you before it happens, so that when it does happen, you may believe.

30 Hereafter I will not talk much with you; for the prince of this world comes; and yet he has nothing against me.

31 But that the world may know that I love my Father, and as my Father has commanded me, so I do. Arise, let us go away from here.

CHAPTER 15

I AM the true vine, and my Father is the laborer.

2 Every branch in me that does not bear fruit, he cuts off; and the one which bears fruit, he prunes so that it may bring forth more fruit.

3 You have already been pruned because of the word which I have spoken to you.

4 Remain with me and I with you. Just as a branch cannot give fruit by itself unless it remains in the vine, even so you cannot unless you remain with me.

5 I am the vine, you are the branches. He who remains with me, and I with him, will bear abundant fruit; for without me you can do nothing.

6 Unless a man remains with me, he will be cast outside like a branch which is withered, which they pick up and throw into the fire to be burned.

7 If you remain with me, and my words remain with you, whatever you ask shall be done for you.

8 In this the Father will be glorified, that you bear abundant fruit and be my disciples.

9 ¶Just as my Father has loved me, I also have loved you; abide in my love.

10 If you keep my commandments, you will abide in my love, even as I

have kept my Father's commandments and abide in his love.

11 I have spoken these things to you that my joy may be in you and that your joy may be full.

12 This is my commandment: That you love one another just as I have loved you.

13 There is no greater love than this, that a man lay down his life for the sake of his friends.

14 You are my friends if you do everything that I command you.

15 Henceforth I will not call you servants, because a servant does not know what his master does; but I have always called you my friends, because everything that I heard from my Father I have made known to you.

16 You did not choose me, but I chose you, and I have appointed you, that you also should go and produce fruit and that your fruit might remain, so that whatever you ask my Father in my name, he will give it to you.

17 I command these things to you so that you may love one another.

18 If the world hates you, know well that it has hated me before you.

19 If you were of the world, the world would love its own; but you are not of the world for I have chosen you out of the world; this is why the world hates you.

20 Remember the word which I said to you, that no servant is greater than his master. If they have persecuted me, they will also persecute you; if they kept my word, they will also keep yours.

21 But they will do all these things to you for the sake of my name, because they do not know him who sent me.

22 If I had not come and spoken to them, they would be without sin; but now they have no excuse for their sins.

23 He who hates me hates my Father also.

24 If I had not done works before their eyes, such as no other man has ever done, they would be without sin; but now they have seen and hated me and also my Father,

25 So that the word which is written in their law may be fulfilled, They hated me for no reason.

26 But when the Comforter comes, whom I will send to you from my Father, the Spirit of truth which proceeds from my Father, he will testify concerning me.

27 And you also will testify because you have been with me from the beginning.

CHAPTER 16

I HAVE spoken these things to you so that you may not stumble.

2 For they will put you out of their synagogues; and the hour will come that whoever kills you will think that he has offered an offering to God.

3 And these things they will do because they have not known my Father, nor me.

4 I have spoken these things to you that when their time does come, you may remember them, and that I told you. And these things I did not tell you before because I was with you.

5 ¶But now I am going to him who sent me, and yet no one of you asks me, Where are you going?

6 But because I told you these things, sorrow has come and filled your hearts.

7 But I tell you the truth, It is better for you that I should go away; for if I do not go away, the Comforter will not come to you; but if I should go, I will send him to you.

8 And when he is come, he will rebuke the world concerning sin, concerning righteousness, and concerning judgment;

9 Concerning sin, because they do not believe in me;

10 Concerning righteousness, because I go to my Father and you will not see me again;

11 Concerning judgment, because the leader of this world has been judged.

12 Again, I have many other things to tell you, but you cannot grasp them now.

13 But when the Spirit of truth is come, he will guide you into all the truth; for he will not speak from him-

self, but what he hears he will speak; and he will make known to you things which are to come in the future.

14 He will glorify me, because he will take of my own and show it to you.

15 Everything that my Father has is mine; this is the reason why I told you that he will take of my own and show it to you.

16 A little while, and you will not see me; and again a little while, and you will see me, because I am going to the Father.

17 Then his disciples said to one another, What is this that he said to us, A little while, and you will not see me; and again a little while, and you will see me; and, because I am going to my Father?

18 And they said, What is this that he said, A little while? We cannot understand what he talks about.

19 Jesus knew that they desired to ask him, and he said to them, Are you inquiring among yourselves concerning this that I told you, A little while, and you will not see me; and again a little while, and you will see me?

20 Truly, truly, I say to you that you will weep and wail, and yet the world will rejoice; and you will be sad, but your sadness will be changed into gladness.

21 When a woman is in travail, she is depressed because ʰʷˡ day has arrived; but when she has given birth to a son, she no longer remembers her troubles because of the joy that a male [1] child is born into the world.

22 So you also are depressed; but I will see you again, and your heart will rejoice, and your joy no man will take away from you.

23 In that day you will not ask me anything. Truly, truly, I say to you that whatever you ask my Father in my name, he will give it to you.

24 Hitherto you have asked nothing in my name; ask and you will receive, so that your joy may be full.

25 I have spoken these things in figures; but the time is coming when I will not speak to you in figures, but will plainly explain to you concerning the Father.

26 In that day you will ask in my name; and I will not say to you, I will ask the Father concerning you.

27 For the Father himself loves you because you have loved me and have believed that I came forth from the Father.

28 I came forth from the Father and I came into the world; again, I am leaving the world and I am going to the Father.

29 His disciples said to him, Behold, now you speak plainly and do not utter a single figure.

30 Now we understand that you know everything, and you need no man to ask you; by this we believe that you have come forth from God.

31 Jesus said to them, Believe;

32 For behold, the hour is coming, and it has now come, when you will be dispersed, every man to his own country, and you will leave me alone; and yet I am never alone because the Father is with me.

33 These things I have said to you that in me you may have peace. In the world you will have tribulation; but have courage, I have conquered the world.

CHAPTER 17

JESUS spoke these things, and then he lifted up his eyes to heaven and said, O my Father, the hour has come; glorify thy Son, so that thy Son may glorify thee,

2 Since thou hast given him power over all flesh, so that to all whom thou hast given him, he may give life eternal.

3 And this is life eternal, that they might know thee, that thou art the only true God, even the one who sent Jesus Christ.

4 I have already glorified thee on the earth; for the work which thou hadst given to me to do, I have finished.

5 So now, O my Father, glorify me with thee, with the same glory which

---

[1] When a girl is born in the East, the news is kept from the mother for a while if she is in danger. If a boy is born she is at once informed to cheer her up.

I had with thee before the world was made.

6 I have made thy name known to the men whom thou gavest me out of the world; they were thine and thou gavest them to me; and they have kept thy word.

7 Now they know that whatever thou hast given me is from thee.

8 For the words which thou gavest me I gave them; and they accepted them, and have known truly that I came forth from thee, and they have believed that thou hast sent me.

9 What I request is for them; I make no request for the world, but for those whom thou hast given to me; because they are thine.

10 And everything which is mine is thine; and what is thine is mine; and I am glorified by them.

11 Hereafter I am not in the world, but these are in the world; and I am coming to thee. O holy Father, protect them in thy name, which thou hast given me, that they may be one, even as we are.

12 While I was with them in the world, I protected them in thy name; those whom thou gavest me I protected, and not one of them is lost except the son of perdition, that the scripture might be fulfilled.

13 Now I am coming to thee; and these things I speak while I am in the world, that my joy may be complete in them.

14 I have given them thy word; and the world hated them, because they were not of the world, just as I am not of the world.

15 What I request is not that thou shouldst take them out of the world, but that thou shouldst protect them from evil.

16 For they are not of the world, just as I am not of the world.

17 O Father, sanctify them in thy truth, because thy word is truth.

18 Just as thou didst send me into the world, so I have sent them into the world.

19 And for their sakes, I am sanctifying myself, so that they also may be sanctified in the truth.

20 I am not making request for these alone, but also for the sake of those who believe in me through their word.

21 So that they all may be one; just as thou, my Father, art with me, and I am with thee, that they also may be one with us; so that the world may believe that thou didst send me.

22 And the glory which thou gavest me, I gave to them; so that they may be one just as we are one.

23 I with them and thou with me, that they may become perfected in one; so that the world may know that thou didst send me, and that thou didst love them just as thou didst love me.

24 O Father, I wish that those whom thou hast given me may also be with me where I am, so that they may see my glory which thou hast given me; for thou hast loved me before the foundation of the world.

25 O my righteous Father, the world did not know thee, but I have known thee; and these have known that thou hast sent me.

26 And I have made thy name known to them, and I am still making it known, so that the love with which thou hast loved me may be among them, and I be with them.

CHAPTER 18

JESUS said these things and went out with his disciples across the brook Kidron, to a place where there was a garden, where he and his disciples entered.

2 Judah the traitor also knew that place, for Jesus and his disciples frequently gathered there.

3 Judah, therefore, took a company of soldiers and also guards from the high priests and the Pharisees, and he came there with torches and lamps and weapons.

4 Jesus, knowing everything that was to happen, went out and said to them, Whom do you want?

5 They said to him, Jesus the Nazarene. Jesus said to them, I am he. Judah the traitor was also standing with them.

6 When Jesus said to them, I am he,

they drew back and fell to the ground.

7 Jesus again asked them, Whom do you want? They said, Jesus the Nazarene.

8 Jesus said to them, I have told you that I am he; if then you want me, let these men go away;

9 (That the word which he said might be fulfilled, Of those whom thou gavest me, I have lost not even one).

10 But Simon Peter had a sword, and he drew it and struck the high priest's servant, and cut off his right ear. The servant's name was Maleck.

11 And Jesus said to Peter, Put the sword into its sheath; shall I not drink the cup which my Father has given me?

12 ¶Then the soldiers and the captains and the Jewish guards seized Jesus and bound him.

13 And they brought him first to Hanan, because he was the father-in-law of Caiaphas, who was the high priest of that year.

14 Caiaphas was the one who had counselled the Jews that it was better for one man to die instead of the people.

15 Simon Peter and one of the other disciples followed Jesus. The high priest knew that disciple, so he entered with Jesus into the courtyard.

16 But Simon stood outside near the door. Then the other disciple, whom the high priest knew, went out and told the portress, and brought in Simon.

17 The young portress then said to Simon, Are you also one of the disciples of this man? He said to her, No.

18 And the servants and guards were standing and making a fire to warm themselves because it was cold; Simon also stood with them and warmed himself.

19 The high priest then questioned Jesus concerning his disciples and concerning his teaching.

20 Jesus said to him, I have spoken openly to the people, and I have always taught in the synagogue and in the temple where all Jews assemble; and I have spoken nothing secretly.

21 Why do you ask me? Ask those who heard what I have spoken to them; behold, they know everything which I said.

22 And as he said these things, one of the guards who stood by struck Jesus on his cheek and said to him, Is this how you answer the high priest?

23 Jesus answered, saying to him, If I have spoken any evil, testify to the evil; but if it is good, why did you strike me?

24 Hanan then sent Jesus bound to Caiaphas the high priest.

25 Now Simon Peter was standing and warming himself. They said to him, What! are you also one of his disciples? He denied and said, I am not.

26 Then one of the servants of the high priest, a kinsman of him whose ear Simon had cut off, said to him, Did I not see you with him in the garden?

27 Simon again denied it; and at that very hour the cock crowed.

28 ¶Then they brought Jesus from Caiaphas to the Praetorium; and it was morning; and they did not enter into the Praetorium, so that they might not be defiled before they ate the passover.

29 Pilate then went outside where they were, and said to them, What accusation do you have against this man?

30 They answered, saying to him, If he were not an evildoer, we would not have delivered him up to you.

31 Then said Pilate to them, Take him yourselves, and judge him according to your own law. The Jews said to him, We have no power to kill a man;

32 So that the word which Jesus had said might be fulfilled, when he signified by what kind of death he was to die.

33 Pilate then entered into the Praetorium, and called Jesus and said to him, Are you the King of the Jews?

34 Jesus said to him, Do you say this of yourself or have others told it to you concerning me?

35 Pilate said to him, Why, am I

a Jew? Your own people and the high priests have delivered you to me; what have you done?

36 Jesus said to him, My kingdom is not of this world; if my kingdom were of this world, my servants would have fought so that I should not be delivered to the Jews; but now my kingdom is not from here.

37 Pilate said to him, Then are you a king? Jesus said to him, You say that I am a king. For this I was born, and for this very thing I came to the world, that I may bear witness concerning the truth. Whoever is of the truth will hear my voice.

38 Pilate said to him, What is this truth? And as he said this, he went out again to the Jews and said to them, I am unable to find even one cause against him.

39 You have a custom that I should release to you one at the passover; do you wish, therefore, that I release to you this King of the Jews?

40 They all cried out saying, Not him, but Bar-Abba. Now this Bar-Abba was a bandit.

CHAPTER 19

THEN Pilate had Jesus scourged. 2 And the soldiers wove a crown of thorns and placed it on his head, and they covered him with purple robes;

3 And they said, Peace be to you, O King of the Jews! and they struck him on his cheeks.

4 Pilate again went outside and said to them, Behold, I bring him outside to you, so that you may know that I find not even one cause against him.

5 So Jesus went outside, wearing the crown of thorns and the purple robes. And Pilate said to them, Behold the man!

6 When the high priests and the guards saw him, they cried out, saying, Crucify him, crucify him! Pilate said to them, You take him and crucify him; for I find no cause in him.

7 The Jews said to him, We have a law, and according to our law he is guilty of death because he made himself the Son of God.

8 When Pilate heard this saying, he was the more afraid;

9 So he entered again into the Praetorium, and said to Jesus, Where do you come from? But Jesus gave him no answer.

10 Pilate said to him, Will you not speak even to me? Do you not know that I have the authority to release you, and I have the authority to crucify you?

11 Jesus said to him, You would have no authority whatever over me if it had not been given to you from above; for this reason the sin of him who delivered me to you is greater than yours.

12 And because of this Pilate wanted to release him; but the Jews cried out, If you release this man you are not a friend of Caesar; for whoever makes himself a king is against Caesar.

13 When Pilate heard this word, he brought Jesus outside; then he sat down on the judgment seat at a place which is called the Stone Pavement, but in Hebrew it is called Gabbatha.

14 It was Friday of the passover, and it was about six o'clock; and he said to the Jews, Behold your king!

15 But they cried out, Take him away, take him away, crucify him, crucify him! Pilate said to them, Shall I crucify your king? The high priests said to him, We have no king but Caesar.

16 Then he delivered him to them to crucify him. So they took Jesus and brought him forth,

17 Carrying his cross, to the place which is called The Skull, but in Hebrew it is called Golgotha,

18 Where they crucified him, and with him two others, one on either side, and Jesus between.

19 Pilate also wrote on a stone tablet, and placed it on his cross. And the writing was, THIS IS JESUS THE NAZARENE, THE KING OF THE JEWS.

20 And a great many Jews read this tablet, for the place where Jesus was

crucified was near the city; and it was written in Hebrew [1] and in Greek and in Roman.

21 The high priests then said to Pilate, Do not write that he is the King of the Jews; but that he said, I am the King of the Jews.

22 Pilate said, What I have written I have written.

23 ¶Now when the soldiers had crucified Jesus, they took his clothes and divided them into four parts, a part to each of the soldiers; but his robe was without seam, woven from the top throughout.

24 So they said one to another, Let us not tear it, but cast lots for it to see whose it shall be. And the scripture was fulfilled, which said, They divided my clothes among them, and for my robe they cast lots. These things the soldiers did.

25 ¶Now there were standing by the cross of Jesus his mother and his mother's sister and Mary of Cleopas and Mary of Magdala.

26 When Jesus saw his mother and the disciple whom he loved standing, he said to his mother, Woman, behold your son!

27 Then he said to the disciple, Behold your mother! And from that very hour the disciple took her with him.

28 After these things Jesus knew that everything was now accomplished; and that the scripture might be fulfilled, he said, I thirst.

29 Now there was a pitcher full of vinegar placed there; so they filled a sponge with vinegar and put it on the point of a reed and placed it on his mouth.

30 ¶When Jesus drank the vinegar, he said, It is fulfilled; and he bowed his head and gave up his spirit.

31 Now since it was Friday the Jews said, Let not these bodies remain on their crosses because the sabbath is dawning; for that sabbath was a great sabbath. So they besought Pilate to have the legs of those who were crucified broken, and to have the bodies lowered down.

32 So the soldiers came and broke the legs of the first, and of the other who was crucified with him.

33 But when they came to Jesus, they saw that he was dead already, so they did not break his legs.

34 But one of the soldiers pierced his side with a spear, and immediately blood and water came out.

35 And he who saw it testified, and his testimony is true; and he knows well that what he said is true, that you also may believe.

36 For these things happened that the scripture might be fulfilled, which said, Not even a bone shall be broken in him;

37 And again another scripture which said, They shall look on him whom they pierced.

38 ¶After these things Joseph of Ramtha, who was a disciple of Jesus, but secretly because of fear of the Jews, besought Pilate that he might take away the body of Jesus. And Pilate granted him permission. So he came and took away the body of Jesus.

39 And there came also Nicodemus, who at first had come to Jesus by night; and he brought with him a mixture of myrrh and aloes, about a hundred pints.

40 So they took away the body of Jesus and bound it in linen cloths with the spices, according to the custom of the Jews in burial.

41 Now there was a garden in the place where Jesus was crucified; and in the garden a new tomb, in which no man was yet laid.

42 So they laid Jesus there, because the sabbath was approaching and because the tomb was near.

CHAPTER 20

ON the first day of the week, early in the morning, while it was yet dark, Mary of Magdala came to the tomb; and she saw that the stone was removed from the tomb.

2 Then she ran and came to Simon Peter and to the other disciple whom Jesus loved, and she said to them, They have taken our Lord out of

[1] *Hebrew* here refers to nationality, but the language of the inscription was Aramaic.

that tomb, and I do not know where they have laid him.

3 So Simon and the other disciple went out and came to the tomb.

4 And they were both running together; but that disciple outran Simon and came first to the tomb.

5 And he looked in and saw the linen cloths lying; but he did not enter in.

6 Then Simon came after him and entered into the tomb; and he saw the linen cloths lying there,

7 And the burial napkin which was bound around his head was not with the linen cloths, but was wrapped up and put in a place by itself.

8 Then the other disciple who had come first to the tomb also entered in, and he saw and believed.

9 For they did yet not understand from the scripture that he had to rise from the dead.

10 So the disciples went away again to their lodging place.

11 ¶But Mary was standing near the tomb weeping; and as she wept, she looked into the tomb;

12 And she saw two angels in white sitting one at the head and the other at the feet, where the body of Jesus had lain.

13 And they said to her, Woman, why do you weep? She said to them, Because they have taken away my Lord, and I do not know where they have laid him.

14 She said this and turned around and saw Jesus standing, but she did not know that it was Jesus.

15 Jesus said to her, Woman, why do you weep? and whom do you want? She thought he was the gardener, so she said to him, My lord, if you are the one who has taken him away, tell me where you have laid him, and I will go and take him away.

16 Jesus said to her, Mary. She turned around and said to him in Hebrew, Rabbuli! which means, My Teacher!

17 Jesus said to her, Do not come near me; for I have not yet ascended to my Father; but go to my brethren and say to them, I am ascending to my Father and your Father, and my God and your God.

18 Then Mary of Magdala came and brought glad tidings to the disciples, that she had seen our Lord and that he had told her these things.

19 ¶When it was evening on that first day of the week, and the doors were shut where the disciples were staying for fear of the Jews, Jesus came, stood among them, and said to them, Peace be with you.

20 He said this, and then he showed them his hands and his side. The disciples rejoiced when they saw our Lord.

21 Then Jesus said to them again, Peace be with you; just as my Father has sent me, so I send you.

22 And when he had said these things, he encouraged them and said to them, Receive the Holy Spirit.

23 If you forgive a man his sins, they shall be forgiven to him; and if you withhold forgiveness of a man's sins, they are kept.

24 ¶But Thomas, one of the twelve, who is called the Twin, was not there with them when Jesus came.

25 And the disciples said to him, We have seen our Lord. He said to them, Unless I see in his hands the marks of the nails, and put my fingers in them, and put my hand into his side, I will not believe.

26 Eight days later, the disciples were again indoors, and Thomas with them. Jesus came, when the doors were locked, and stood in the midst, and said to them, Peace be with you.

27 Then he said to Thomas, Put your finger here, and see my hands; and reach out your hand and put it into my side; and be not faithless, but believing.

28 Thomas answered, saying to him, O my Lord and my God!

29 Jesus said to him, Now you believe because you have seen me? Blessed are those who have not seen me, and have believed.

30 ¶Many other miracles Jesus did in the presence of his disciples, which are not written in this book;

31 Even these are written, so that you may believe that Jesus is the

Christ, the Son of God; and when you believe you shall have life everlasting in his name.

CHAPTER 21

AFTER these things, Jesus showed himself again to his disciples by the sea of Tiberias; and he appeared in this way:

2 They were all together, Simon Peter and Thomas who is called the Twin and Nathanael of Cana of Galilee and the sons of Zebedee and two others of the disciples.

3 Simon Peter said to them, I am going to catch fish. They said to him, We also will come with you. So they went out and climbed up into the boat; and that night they caught nothing.

4 When morning came Jesus stood by the seaside; and the disciples did not know that it was Jesus.

5 So Jesus said to them, Boys, have you got anything to eat? They said to him, No.

6 He said to them, Throw your net on the right side of the boat, and you will find fish. So they threw it, and they were not able to draw the net because of the many fish which it had caught.

7 Then the disciple whom Jesus loved said to Peter, That is our Lord. When Simon heard that it was our Lord, he took his cloak and girded it around his waist, because he was naked; and he jumped into the sea to come to Jesus.

8 But the other disciples came by boat; for they were not very far from land, but about a hundred yards, and they were dragging the net of fish.

9 When they landed, they saw burning coals set, and a fish laid on them, and bread.

10 Jesus said to them, Bring some of the fish which you have now caught.

11 So Simon Peter went up and drew the net to land, full of large fishes, one hundred and fifty-three; and in spite of this weight, the net did not break.

12 Jesus said to them, Come, break your fast. But not one of the disciples dared to ask him who he was, for they knew he was our Lord.

13 Then Jesus drew near, and took bread and fish and gave to them.

14 This is the third time that Jesus appeared to his disciples after he rose up from the dead.

15 ¶When they had broken their fast, Jesus said to Simon Peter, Simon, son of Jonah, do you love me more than these things? He said to him, Yes, my Lord, you know that I love you. Jesus said to him, Feed my lambs.

16 He said to him again the second time, Simon, son of Jonah, do you love me? He said to him, Yes, my Lord, you know that I love you. Jesus said to him, Feed my sheep.

17 He said to him again the third time, Simon, son of Jonah, do you love me? It grieved Peter because he said to him the third time, Do you love me? So he said to him, My Lord, you understand well everything, you know that I love you. Jesus said to him, Feed my ewes.

18 Truly, truly, I say to you, when you were young, you tied up your girdle yourself, and walked wherever you pleased; but when you become old, you will stretch out your hands, and another will tie up for you your girdle and take you where you do not wish to go.

19 He said this to show by what death he would glorify God. And when he had said these things, he said to him, Follow me.

20 Simon Peter turned around and saw the disciple whom Jesus loved following him, the one who leaned on the breast of Jesus at the supper and said, My Lord, who will betray you?

21 When Peter saw him, he said to Jesus, My Lord, what about him?

22 Jesus said to him, If I wish him to remain until I come, what difference does that make to you? You follow me.

23 This word then went out among the brethren, that that disciple would not die. But what Jesus said was not that he would not die, but, If I wish that he should remain until I come

back, what difference does that make to you?

24 This is the disciple who testified concerning all of these things and who also wrote them; and we know that his testimony is true.

25 There are also a great many other things which Jesus did, which, if they were written one by one, not even this world, I believe, could contain the books that would be written.

THE

ACTS OF THE APOSTLES

CHAPTER 1

THE first book have I written, O Theophilus, concerning all the things which our Lord Jesus Christ began to do and teach

2 Until the day when he ascended, after he, through the Holy Spirit, had given commandments to the apostles whom he had chosen,

3 The very ones to whom he had also shown himself alive, after he had suffered, with many wonders during the forty days, while appearing to them and talking with them concerning the kingdom of God;

4 And as he ate bread with them, he commanded them not to depart from Jerusalem but to wait for the promise of the Father, the one of whom you have heard from me.

5 For, he said, John baptized with water; but you shall be baptized with the Holy Spirit not many days hence.

6 While they were assembled, they asked him, saying, Our Lord, will you at this time restore the kingdom to Israel?

7 He said to them, It is not for you to know the time or times which the Father has put under his own authority;

8 But when the Holy Spirit comes upon you, you shall receive power and you shall be witnesses to me both in Jerusalem and in all Judea also in the province of Samaria and to the uttermost part of the earth.

9 And when he had spoken these things, he ascended while they were looking at him; a cloud [1] received him and he was hidden from their sight.

10 And while they looked steadfastly toward heaven as he went up, behold two men stood by them in white robes;

11 And they said to them, Men of Galilee, why do you stand gazing up into heaven? This same Jesus who has ascended from you into heaven shall so come in like manner as you have seen him ascend into heaven.

12 ¶Then they returned to Jerusalem from the mount which is called Olivet, Place of Olives, which is near to Jerusalem, about a mile away.

13 And after they had entered into the city, they went into an upper room, where stayed Peter and John and James and Andrew, and also Philip and Thomas and Matthew and Bartholomew and James the son of Alphæus and Simon the Zealot and Judah the son of James.

14 These all continued together in prayer with one accord, also the women, and Mary the Mother of Jesus, and his brothers.

15 And in those days Simon Peter

[1] Until recent times Easterners believed that clouds were living creatures.

stood up in the midst of the disciples (there were there a number of men, about a hundred and twenty), and said,

16 Men and brethren, it was proper that the scripture should be fulfilled, that which the Holy Spirit foretold by the mouth of David concerning Judah, who was guide to them that seized Jesus.

17 For he was numbered with us and had a lot [1] in this ministry.

18 He is the one who earned for himself a field with the price of sin; and falling headlong, he burst open in the midst and all his bowels gushed out.

19 And this very thing is known to all who dwell in Jerusalem; so that the field is called in the language of the country, Khakal-Dema which is to say Koriath-dem, the field of blood.

20 For it is written in the book of Psalms, Let his habitation be desolate, and let no one dwell in it; and let his ministry be taken by another man.

21 It is necessary, therefore, that one of these men, who have been with us during all the time that our Lord Jesus went in and out among us,

22 Beginning from the baptism of John until the day he ascended from among us, become a partner with us as a witness of his resurrection.

23 So they appointed two: Joseph called Barshabas, who was surnamed Justus, and Matthias.

24 And as they prayed, they said, O Lord, thou knowest what is in the hearts of all men; show which of these two thou dost choose,

25 That he may receive the lot to the ministry and apostleship, from which Judah has been relieved to go his own way.

26 Then they cast lots, and the lot fell upon Matthias; and he was numbered with the eleven apostles.

CHAPTER 2

AND when the day of Pentecost was fulfilled, while they were assembled together,

2 Suddenly there came a sound from heaven as of a rushing mighty wind and it filled all the house where they were sitting.

3 And there appeared to them tongues which were divided like flames of fire; and they rested upon each of them.

4 And they were all filled with the Holy Spirit, and they began to speak in various languages, according to whatever the Spirit gave them to speak.

5 Now there dwelt at Jerusalem devout men and Jews from every nation under heaven.

6 And as the sound took place, all the people gathered together, and they were confused because every man heard them speak in his own language.

7 And they were all amazed and marvelled, saying one to another, Behold, are not all these who speak Galileans?

8 How is it that we hear every man in our own native language?

9 Parthians and Medes and Elamites and those who dwell in Mesopotamia, Jews and Cappadocians and those from Pontus and Asia Minor,

10 And those from the region of Phrygia and of Pamphylia and of Egypt, and of the regions of Lybia near Cyrene, and those who have come from Rome, both Jews and proselytes,

11 And those from Crete, and Arabians, behold we hear them speak in our own tongues of the wonderful works of God.

12 And they were all amazed and stunned, saying one to another, What does this mean?

13 Others mocking said, These men are full of new wine.

14 ¶And afterwards Simon Peter stood up together with the eleven disciples, and lifted up his voice and said to them, Men of Jewish race, and all that dwell at Jerusalem, let this be known to you, and harken to my words;

15 For these men are not drunken as you suppose, for behold it is but the third hour of the day.

[1] *Lot* means *vote.*

16 But this is that which was spoken by the prophet Joel:

17 It shall come to pass in the last days, said God, I will pour my spirit upon all flesh; and your sons and your daughters shall prophesy and your young men shall see visions and your old men shall dream dreams;

18 And upon my menservants and upon my maidservants will I pour out my Spirit in those days; and they shall prophesy;

19 And I will show wonders in heaven and signs on the earth: blood and fire and vapor of smoke:

20 The sun shall be changed into darkness and the moon into blood, before that great and fearful day of the Lord shall come.

21 And it shall come to pass that whoever shall call on the name of the Lord shall be saved.

22 Men of Israel, hear these words: Jesus of Nazareth, a man of God, who appeared among you by miracles and signs and wonders which God did by him among you, as you yourselves know,

23 The very one who was chosen for this purpose from the very beginning of knowledge and will of God, you have delivered into the hands of wicked men, and you have crucified and murdered him;

24 Whom God has raised up, having destroyed the pains of death, because it was not possible for Sheol to hold him.

25 For David said concerning him, I foresaw my Lord always, for he is on my right hand, so that I should not be shaken;

26 Therefore my heart is comforted and my glory is exalted; even my body shall rest in hope,

27 Because you will not leave my soul in Sheol, neither will you suffer your Holy One to see corruption.

28 You have revealed to me the way of life; you will fill me with joy with your presence.

29 Now men and brethren, permit me to speak to you openly concerning Patriarch David, who is dead and buried and whose sepulchre is with us to this day;

30 For he was a prophet, and he knew that God had sworn by an oath to him that of the fruit of his loins, according to the flesh, he would raise up one to sit on his throne.

31 So he foresaw and spoke concerning the resurrection of Christ, that his soul was not left in the grave, neither did his body see corruption.

32 This very Jesus, God has raised up, and we are all his witnesses.

33 It is he who is exalted by the right hand of God and has received from the Father the promise of the Holy Spirit, and has poured out gifts which you now see and hear.

34 For David did not ascend into heaven, because he himself said, The Lord said to my Lord, Sit thou on my right hand,

35 Until I make thy foes thy footstool.

36 Therefore let all the house of Israel know assuredly that God has made this very Jesus, whom you have crucified, both Lord and Christ.

37 ¶When they heard these things, their hearts were touched and they said to Simon and the rest of the apostles, Our brethren, what shall we do?

38 Then Simon said to them, Repent and be baptized, every one of you in the name of the Lord Jesus for the remission of sins, so that you may receive the gift of the Holy Spirit.

39 For the promise was made to you and to your children, and for all of those who are far off, even as many as the very God shall call.

40 And he testified to them with many other words and besought them, saying, Save yourselves from this sinful generation.

41 And those men among them who readily accepted his word and believed were baptized, and about three thousand souls were added in that day.

42 And they continued steadfastly in the teaching of the apostles and they took part in prayer and in the breaking of bread.

43 ¶And fear came upon every soul;

and many miracles and wonders were done by the apostles in Jerusalem.

44 And all believers were together and had all things in common;

45 And those who had possessions sold them and divided to each man according to his need.

46 And they went to the temple every day with one accord; and at home they broke bread and received food with joy and with a pure heart,

47 Praising God and finding favor with all the people. And our Lord daily increased the congregation of the church.

CHAPTER 3

IT came to pass as Simon Peter and John were going up together to the temple at the time of prayer, at the ninth hour,

2 Behold a certain man, lame from his mother's womb, was carried by men who were accustomed to bring him and lay him at the gate of the temple which is called Beautiful, so that he might ask alms from those who entered into the temple.

3 And when he saw Simon Peter and John entering the temple, he begged of them to give him alms.

4 And Simon Peter and John looked at him and said, Look at us.

5 And he looked at them, expecting to receive something from them.

6 Then Simon Peter said to him, Gold and silver have I none; but what I have I give to you. In the name of our Lord Jesus Christ of Nazareth rise up and walk.

7 And he took him by the right hand and lifted him up; and in that very hour his legs and his feet received strength.

8 And he, leaping up, stood and walked, and entered with them into the temple, walking and leaping and praising God.

9 And all the people saw him walking and praising God;

10 And they recognized that he was the beggar who had sat daily and asked alms at the gate which is called Beautiful; and they were filled with amazement and wonder at what had happened.

11 ¶And as he was assisted by Simon and John, all the people ran in astonishment towards them to the porch that is called Solomon's.

12 And when Simon Peter saw it, he said to them, Men of Israel, why are you wondering at this man or why are you looking at us as though by our own power or authority we had made this man to walk?

13 The God of Abraham and of Isaac and of Jacob, the God of our Fathers has glorified his Son Jesus whom you delivered up and denied in the presence of Pilate when he was determined to let him go.

14 But you denied the Holy One and the Righteous and asked a murderer to be given to you,

15 And killed the Prince of Life, whom God has raised from the dead; all of us are his witnesses.

16 Faith in his name has healed this man whom you see and know, and made him strong; it is the faith in him which has granted this healing before you all.

17 But now, my brethren, I know that you did this through ignorance just as your leaders did it.

18 But those things which God before had preached by the mouth of all the prophets that his Christ should suffer, he has so fulfilled.

19 Repent, therefore, and be converted, that your sins may be blotted out when the times of tranquillity shall come to you from before the presence of the Lord;

20 And he shall send to you One who has been prepared for you, even Jesus Christ,

21 Whom heaven must receive until all the things which God has spoken by the mouth of his holy prophets since the world began should be fulfilled.

22 For Moses said, The Lord shall raise up a prophet like me for you from among your brethren; listen to him in all that he shall say to you.

23 And it shall come to pass that every person who will not listen to that prophet shall be lost from his people.

24 Yea, and all the prophets from

Samuel and those that follow after, as many as have spoken and preached, have likewise foretold of these days.

25 You are the children of the prophets and of the covenant which God made with our fathers, saying to Abraham, By your seed shall all the kindred of the earth be blessed.

26 Now it was for you first, God appointed and sent his Son to bless you if you turn and repent from your evils.

CHAPTER 4

AND while they were speaking these words to the people, the priests and the Sadducees and the leaders of the temple rose up against them,

2 Being infuriated that they taught the people and preached through Jesus the resurrection from the dead.

3 And they arrested them and detained them until the next day, for it was now eventide.

4 Howbeit many of them who heard the word believed; and the number of the men was about five thousand.

5 ¶And the next day, the leaders and the elders and the scribes gathered together;

6 And also Annas the high priest, and Caiaphas and John and Alexander and those who were of the family of the high priest.

7 And when they had made them to stand in the midst, they asked, By what power or by what name have you done this?

8 Then Simon Peter, filled with the Holy Spirit, said to them, Leaders of the people and elders of the house of Israel, listen:

9 If we are convicted today by you, concerning the good which has been done to a sick man, on the ground of by what means he was healed;

10 Then let it be known to you and to all the people of Israel, By the name of Jesus Christ of Nazareth, whom you crucified, and whom God raised from the dead, behold this man stands before you, healed.

11 This is the stone which you builders have rejected, which is become the corner-stone.

12 There is no salvation by any other man; for there is no other name under heaven given among men whereby we must be saved.

13 Now when they had heard the speech of Simon Peter and John, which they had spoken boldly, and perceived that they were unlearned and ignorant men, they marvelled; and they recognized them that they had been with Jesus.

14 And because they saw the lame man who was healed standing with them they could say nothing against them.

15 But when they had commanded them to be taken aside out of the council, they conferred among themselves,

16 Saying, What shall we do to these men? For behold a miracle has openly been performed by them and it is known to all that dwell in Jerusalem; and we cannot deny it.

17 But, so that this news should not spread further among the people, let us threaten them, that they speak henceforth to no man in this name.

18 And they called them, and commanded them not to speak at all nor teach in the name of Jesus.

19 But Simon Peter and John answered, saying to them, Whether it be right before God to listen to you more than to God, you judge.

20 For we cannot stop speaking about the things which we have seen and heard.

21 So when they had further threatened them, they let them go; for they found no cause to punish them because of the people; for all men praised God for that which was done.

22 For the man on whom this miracle of healing had been wrought was more than forty years old.

23 ¶After they were released, they went to their brethren and told them all that the high priests and elders had said.

24 And when they heard this, they all together lifted up their voices to God and said, O Lord, thou art the God who hast made heaven and earth

and the seas and all that in them is;

25 Thou art the One who spoke through the Holy Spirit by the mouth of thy servant David when he said, Why do the people rage and the nations devise worthless things?

26 The kings and the rulers of the earth have revolted and have taken counsel together against the Lord and against his Anointed.

27 For truly, they assembled in this very city, together with both Herod and Pilate and with the Gentiles and with the people of Israel, against your holy Son Jesus,

28 To execute whatever thy hand and thy will had previously decreed to take place.

29 And even now, O Lord, look and see their threatenings; and grant to thy servants that they may freely preach thy word,

30 Just as thy hand is freely stretched out for healing and wonders and thy miracles which are done in the name of thy holy Son Jesus.

31 And when they had petitioned and made their supplications, the place in which they were assembled together was shaken, and they were all filled with the Holy Spirit and they spoke the word of God boldly.

32 ¶Now the congregation of the believers were of one soul and of one mind; not one of them spoke of the property he possessed as his own; but everything they had was in common.

33 And the apostles testified with great power concerning the resurrection of Jesus Christ; and they were all greatly favored.

34 There was not a man among them who was destitute; for those who possessed fields and houses sold them and brought the money for the things that were sold,

35 And placed them at the disposal of the disciples; and the proceeds were then given to every man according to his needs.

36 Now Joseph whom the apostles surnamed Barnabas (which is, interpreted, the son of consolation), a Levite of the country of Cyprus,

37 Had a field and he sold it and brought the money and placed it at the disposal of the apostles.

CHAPTER 5

BUT a certain man called Ananias, together with his wife named Shapphira, sold his field.

2 And he took some of the money and hid it, and his wife also knew of it, and he brought some of the money and placed it at the disposal of the apostles.

3 And Simon Peter said to him, Ananias, why has Satan so filled your heart that you should lie to the Holy Spirit and hide part of the money of the price of the field?

4 Was it not your own before you sold it? And after it was sold, had you not the sole authority over its money? What made you think to do this thing? You have not only lied to men but to God.

5 And when Ananias heard these words, he fell down and died; and great fear came upon all of those who heard these things.

6 The younger men among them arose and moved his body aside. Then they took him out and buried him.

7 Three hours later his wife also came in, not knowing what had happened.

8 Simon Peter said to her, Tell me if you sold the field for this price? She said, Yes, for this price.

9 Then Simon Peter said to her, Because you have been partners to tempt the Spirit of the Lord, behold the feet of the men who have buried your husband are at the door, and they shall carry you out also.

10 And in that very hour she fell down at their feet and died, and the young men came in and found her dead, and they picked her up and carried her away and buried her by the side of her husband.

11 And great fear came upon all the congregation and upon all who heard what had happened.

12 Many miracles and signs were wrought among the people by the apostles, and they were all gathered

together in the portico of Solomon.

13 And none of the unbelievers dared to interfere with them, but the people held them in respect.

14 And the number of those who believed in the Lord was greatly increased by multitudes both of men and women.

15 They even brought out the sick into the streets and laid them on quilts so that when Simon Peter should happen to pass by, his shadow might fall upon them.

16 Many came to them from other cities around Jerusalem, bringing the sick and mentally afflicted, and they were all healed.

17 ¶Then the high priest was filled with jealousy and all of those who were with him, for they were adherents to the teachings of the Sadducees,

18 So they laid hands on the apostles and arrested them and bound them in prison.

19 But during the night, the angel of the Lord opened the door of the prison and brought them forth and said to them,

20 Go, stand in the temple and speak to the people all these words of life.

21 Accordingly they went out early in the morning and entered into the temple and taught the people. But the high priest and those who were with him called their associates and the elders of Israel, and sent to the prison to bring the apostles.

22 And when those who were sent by them went and did not find them in the prison, they returned,

23 Saying, We found the prison carefully locked and also the guards standing at the doors; and we opened them but found no man there.

24 When the high priest and the leaders of the temple heard these words, they were astonished at them and they were reasoning how it could happen,

25 When a man came and informed them, Behold! The men whom you put in prison are standing in the temple and teaching the people.

26 Then the leaders went with the soldiers to bring them, not by force,

for they were afraid that the people might stone them.

27 And when they had brought them, they made them stand before the whole council, and the high priest proceeded,

28 Saying, Did we not strictly command you not to teach any man in this name? And behold, you have filled Jerusalem with your doctrine, and you intend to bring the blood of this man upon us.

29 Then Simon Peter with the rest of the apostles answered, saying to them, We must obey God rather than men.

30 The God of our fathers has raised up Jesus whom you murdered when you nailed him on the cross.

31 This very one God has appointed a Prince and a Saviour, and has lifted him up by his right hand so that he may grant repentance and forgiveness of sins to Israel.

32 And we are the witnesses of these words; so is also the Holy Spirit whom God has given to those who believe in him.

33 When they heard these words, they were enraged and thought to murder the apostles.

34 Then one of the Pharisees whose name was Gamaliel, a teacher of the law and honored by all the people, rose up and ordered them to take the apostles outside for a little while;

35 Then he said to them, Men of Israel, take heed to yourselves, and find out what is the best for you to do about these men.

36 For before these days, rose up Theudas, boasting himself to be a great man; and about four hundred men followed him; but he was slain; and those who followed him were scattered and nothing came of them.

37 After him rose up Judah, the Galilean, in the days when people were registering for the head tax, and he misled many people into following him. He died; and all of those who followed him were dispersed.

38 So now I tell you, Keep away from these men and let them alone; for if this thought and this work is of men, it will fail and pass away.

39 But if it be of God, you cannot suppress it, lest perchance you find yourself standing in opposition to God.

40 And they listened to him, and they called the apostles and scourged them, and commanded them not to speak in the name of Jesus, and let them go.

41 The apostles went out from the presence of the council, rejoicing that they had been worthy to suffer abuse for the sake of his name.

42 And they did not cease to teach daily in the temple and at home and to preach concerning our Lord Jesus Christ.

CHAPTER 6

AND in those days, when the number of disciples had increased, the Hellenist converts murmured against the Hebrew converts because their widows were discriminated against in the daily distribution.

2 So the twelve apostles called the whole multitude of the converts and said to them, It is not good that we should leave the word of God and serve food.

3 Wherefore, brethren, examine and select from among you seven men of good repute who are full of the Spirit of the Lord and of wisdom, so that we may appoint them to this task.

4 And we will give ourselves continually to prayer and to the ministry of the word.

5 This suggestion pleased the whole people, so they chose Stephen, a man full of faith and the Holy Spirit, and Philip and Prochorus and Nicanor and Timon and Parmenas and Nicolas, a proselyte of Antioch.

6 These men stood before the apostles, who, as they prayed, laid their hands on them.[1]

7 And the word of God spread; and the number of the converts in Jerusalem increased greatly; and many people of Jewish faith became converts.

8 ¶Now Stephen was full of grace

[1] Ordained them.

and power, and did great wonders and miracles among the people.

9 Then there arose certain men of the synagogue which is called the synagogue of the Libertines and Cyrenians and Alexandrians and Cilicians and some persons from Asia Minor, and they debated with Stephen.

10 But they were unable to stand up against the wisdom and the spirit by which he spoke.

11 Then they sent men and instructed them to say, We have heard him speak blasphemous words against Moses and against God.

12 And they stirred up the people and the elders and the scribes, and they rose up against him and seized him and brought him into the midst of the council.

13 And they appointed false witnesses who said, This man does not cease to speak against the law and against this holy place;

14 For we have heard him say that Jesus of Nazareth shall destroy this country and shall change the customs which Moses entrusted to you.

15 Then all who were seated at the council looked at him and saw that his face was like the face of an angel.

CHAPTER 7

THEN the high priest asked Stephen, Are these things so?

2 He said, Men, brethren and fathers, hearken: The God of glory appeared to our father Abraham when he was still in Mesopotamia before he came to dwell in Haran.

3 And he said to him, Get out of your land and from your relatives and come into the land which I shall show you.

4 Then Abraham left the land of the Chaldeans and came and settled in Haran and from thence, after his father's death, God removed him into this land in which you now live.

5 And he gave him no inheritance in it, no, not so much as to set his foot on; yet he promised that he would give it as an inheritance to him and to his posterity, when as yet he had no son.

6 God spoke to him and said, Your descendants will be settlers in a foreign land where they will be enslaved and mistreated for a period of four hundred years.

7 But the people to whom they will be enslaved I will condemn, said God, and after that, they shall go out and serve me in this land.

8 God gave Abraham the covenant of circumcision; and then Abraham begat Isaac, and circumcised him on the eighth day; and Isaac begat Jacob; and Jacob begat our twelve patriarchs.

9 And our forefathers were jealous of Joseph; so they sold him into Egypt; but God was with him,

10 And he saved him from all his oppressors and gave him favor and wisdom before Pharaoh, king of Egypt; and Pharaoh appointed Joseph to be overlord over Egypt and over all his house.

11 Now there came a famine which brought great distress throughout Egypt and the land of Canaan so that our forefathers found no sustenance.

12 But when Jacob heard that there was wheat in Egypt, he sent out our forefathers on their first venture.

13 When they went the second time, Joseph made himself known to his brothers; and Joseph's family was made known to Pharaoh.

14 Then Joseph sent and brought his father Jacob and all his family, seventy-five souls in number.

15 So Jacob went down to Egypt where he and our forefathers died.

16 And he was removed to Shechem and buried in the sepulchre which Abraham had bought for a sum of money from the sons of Hamor.

17 But when the time of the promise was at hand, which God had sworn to Abraham, the people had already increased and become strong in Egypt,

18 Till another king reigned over Egypt who knew not Joseph.

19 He dealt deceitfully with our kindred, illtreated our forefathers, and commanded that they cast out their male children to the end that they might not live.

20 During that very period Moses was born, and he was favored before God, so that for three months he was nourished in his father's house.

21 And when he was cast away by his mother, Pharaoh's daughter found him and reared him as a son for herself.

22 So Moses was trained in all the wisdom of the Egyptians and he was well versed in his words and also in his deeds.

23 And when he was forty years old, it came into his heart to visit his brethren, the children of Israel.

24 When he saw one of his own kindred mistreated, he avenged him and did justice to him, and killed the Egyptian who had mistreated him.

25 For he thought his brethren, the Israelites, would understand that God would grant them deliverance by his hand, but they understood not.

26 And the next day he found them quarreling one with another and he pleaded with them that they might be reconciled, saying, Men, you are brothers; why are you wronging one another?

27 But the one who was wronging his fellow thrust him aside and said to him, Who appointed you leader and judge over us?

28 Perhaps you want to kill me as you killed the Egyptian yesterday.

29 And because of this saying, Moses fled and took refuge in the land of Midian where two sons were born to him.

30 And when he had completed forty years, there appeared to him in the wilderness of mount Sinai an angel of the Lord in a flame of fire in a bush.

31 When Moses saw it, he wondered at the sight; and as he drew near to look at it, the Lord spoke to him in a loud voice,

32 Saying, I am the God of your fathers, the God of Abraham and of Isaac and of Jacob. And Moses trembled and dared not look at the sight.

33 Then the Lord said to him, Take off your shoes from your feet, for the ground on which you stand is holy.

34 Already I have seen the affliction of my people in Egypt, I have heard their groans, and I have come down to deliver them. And now come, I will send you into Egypt.

35 This Moses whom they had denied, saying, Who appointed you leader and judge over us? this very one God sent to be a leader and deliverer to them by the hand of the angel which had appeared to him in the bush.

36 It was he who brought them out after he had performed miracles, wonders, and signs in the land of Egypt and in the Red sea and in the wilderness for forty years.

37 This is the Moses who said to the children of Israel, The Lord your God will raise up for you a prophet like me from among your brethren; give heed to him.

38 It was he who was in the congregation in the wilderness with the angel who spoke to him and to our fathers in mount Sinai. He is the one who received the living words to give to us.

39 Yet our fathers would not listen to him, but they left him, and in their hearts turned towards Egypt.

40 They said to Aaron, Make us gods to go before us, for this very Moses who brought us out of the land of Egypt, we do not know what has become of him.

41 And they made a calf for themselves in those days and offered sacrifices to idols and were pleased with the work of their hands.

42 Then God turned and gave them up that they might worship the host of heaven as it is written in the book of the prophets, O Israelites, why have you offered me slain animals or sacrifices during the period of forty years in the wilderness?

43 Indeed you have borne the tabernacle of Malcom and the star of the god Derphan; and you have made images to worship them; therefore I will remove you beyond Babylon.

44 Behold the tabernacle of the testimony of our fathers was in the wilderness just as the Lord, who spoke to Moses, had commanded him to make it after the pattern which he had shown him.

45 And this very tabernacle, our fathers, together with Joshua, brought into the land which God took away from the peoples whom he drove out before them and gave it to them for an inheritance, and it was handed down until the days of David,

46 Who found favor before God and asked that he might find a dwelling place for the God of Jacob;

47 But Solomon built God a house.

48 Yet the Most High did not dwell in temples made with hands for as the prophet had said,

49 Heaven is my throne and earth is the footstool under my feet. What kind of house will you build me? says the Lord, or where is the place of my rest?

50 Behold, has not my hand made all these things?

51 O you stubborn and insincere in heart and hearing, you always resist the Holy Spirit; as your fathers did, so do you.

52 Which of the prophets have not your fathers persecuted and murdered? Especially have they slain those who foretold the coming of the Righteous One whom you betrayed and murdered.

53 You received the law by the disposition of angels, and have not kept it.

54 ¶When they heard these things, they were enraged, and gnashed their teeth at him.

55 But he, full of faith and Holy Spirit, looked up to heaven and saw the glory of God and Jesus standing at the right hand of God.

56 And he said, Behold I see the heavens opened and the Son of Man standing at the right hand of God.

57 Then they cried out with a loud voice and stopped their ears and with one accord shouted threats against Stephen.

58 And they seized him and took him outside the city and began to stone him. Those who testified against him placed their clothes under the care of a young man called Saul.

59 And they stoned Stephen as he

prayed, saying, **Our Lord Jesus,** accept my spirit.

60 And as he knelt down, he cried with a loud voice and said, Our Lord, do not hold this sin against them. When he had said this, he passed away.

CHAPTER 8

SAUL was pleased to have had a part in the murder of Stephen. At that very time there was severe persecution against the church at Jerusalem; and they were all, with the exception of the apostles, dispersed throughout the towns of Judea and Samaria.

2 And devout men took up Stephen and buried him, and they mourned over him in great sorrow.

3 As for Saul, he continued to persecute the church of God, entering into houses and dragging out men and women and delivering them to prison,

4 ¶So that they that were scattered abroad went everywhere preaching the word of God.

5 Then Philip went down to a Samaritan city and preached to them about Christ.

6 And when the people of that place heard his word, they gave heed and listened attentively to everything Philip said, because they saw the miracles which he did.

7 Many who were mentally afflicted cried with loud voices and were restored; and others who were paralytic and lame were healed.

8 And there was great joy in that city.

9 Now there was there a man called Semon, who had lived in that city a long time, and who had deceived the Samaritan people by his magic, boasting of himself and saying, I am the greatest one.

10 And both the noblest and the least followed him, saying, He is the greatest power of God.

11 All of them listened to him, because for a long time he had bewitched them with his sorceries.

12 But when they believed Philip, preaching the things concerning the kingdom of God in the name of our Lord Jesus Christ, they were baptized, both men and women.

13 Semon himself also believed and was baptized and attached himself to Philip, and as he saw the miracles and great signs performed by his hand, he marvelled greatly.

14 Now when the apostles at Jerusalem heard that the Samaritan people had accepted the word of God, they sent to them Simon Peter and John,

15 Who, when they went down, prayed over them that they might receive the Holy Spirit.

16 For as yet it had not come upon them although they had been baptized in the name of our Lord Jesus.

17 Then they laid their hands on them and they received the Holy Spirit.

18 And when Semon saw that the Holy Spirit was given by the laying on of the apostles' hands, he offered them money,

19 Saying, Give me also this authority so that on whomsoever I lay hands, he may receive the Holy Spirit.

20 Simon Peter said to him, Let your money perish with you because you have thought that the gift of God may be purchased with wealth.

21 You have no part nor lot in this faith because your heart is not right in the sight of God.

22 Repent, therefore, of this evil of yours, and beseech God that he may perhaps forgive you for the guile which is in your heart.

23 For I see your heart is as bitter as gall and you are in the bonds of iniquity.

24 Then Semon answered, saying, Pray God for me so that none of these things which you have spoken may come upon me.

25 Now when Simon Peter and John had testified and taught them the word of God, they returned to Jerusalem after they had preached in many Samaritan villages.

26 ¶And the angel of the Lord spoke to Philip, saying, Arise and go south by way of the desert that leads down from Jerusalem to Gaza;

27 So he arose and went; and he

was met by a eunuch, who had come from Ethiopia, an official of Candace, queen of the Ethiopians, who had the charge of all her treasure, and had come to worship at Jerusalem.

28 While he was returning, sitting in his chariot, he read the book of the prophet Isaiah.

29 And the Spirit said to Philip, Go near and keep close to the chariot.

30 And as Philip drew near and heard him reading from the book of the prophet Isaiah, he said to him, Do you understand what you are reading?

31 And the Ethiopian said, How can I understand unless some one teach me? and he invited Philip to come up and sit with him.

32 The portion of the scripture which he was reading was this: He was led like a lamb to the slaughter, and like a ewe lamb before the shearer, so he opened not his mouth.

33 In his humiliation, he suffered imprisonment and judgment; none can tell his struggle, for even his life is taken away from the earth.

34 And the eunuch said to Philip, I pray you, of whom does this prophet speak? of himself or of some other man?

35 Then Philip opened his mouth and began at that same scripture and preached to him concerning our Lord Jesus.

36 And as they went on their way, they came to a place where there was water; and the eunuch said, Behold here is water; what prevents me from being baptized?

37 And Philip said, If you believe with all your heart, you may. And he answered, saying, I believe that Jesus Christ is the Son of God.

38 And he commanded the chariot be stopped; and both went down into the water, and Philip baptized the eunuch.

39 And when they came up from the water, the Spirit of the Lord caught Philip away and the eunuch saw him no more; and he went on his way rejoicing.

40 Philip was found at Azotus; and from there he traveled around and preached in all the cities till he came to Cæsarea.

CHAPTER 9

NOW Saul was still filled with anger and with threats of murder against the disciples of our Lord,

2 And he asked the high priests to give him letters to the synagogues at Damascus, that if he should find anyone, man or woman, following this faith he might bring them bound to Jerusalem.

3 And as he journeyed, he came near Damascus; and suddenly a light from the sky shone round about him;

4 And he fell to the ground and heard a voice saying to him, Saul, Saul, why do you persecute me? You make it hard for yourself by kicking against the pricks.

5 Saul answered, saying, Who are you my Lord? And our Lord said, I am Jesus of Nazareth whom you persecute;

6 Arise and go into the city, and there you will be told what you must do.

7 And the men who journeyed with him stood speechless, hearing only a voice, but seeing no man.

8 And Saul arose from the ground, but he could not see even though his eyes were open; and they led him by the hand and brought him into Damascus.

9 And he was unable to see for three days, during which he neither ate nor drank.

10 ¶Now there was in Damascus a disciple named Ananias, and the Lord said to him in a vision, Ananias. And he said, Behold, I am here, my Lord.

11 And our Lord said to him, Arise, and go into the street which is called Straight and enquire at the house of Judah for Saul of the city of Tarsus; for behold, he is praying,

12 And he has seen in a vision a man named Ananias coming in and laying his hand on him to restore his sight.

13 Then Ananias said, My Lord, I have heard from many concerning this man, how much misery he has brought to your saints in Jerusalem.

14 And behold here also he has authority from the high priests to bind all who call on your name.

15 But the Lord said to him, Arise and go; he is the agent whom I have chosen for myself to carry my name to the Gentiles and kings and the children of Israel;

16 For I will show him how great things he must suffer for my name's sake.

17 Then Ananias went to him at the house, and laying his hands on him, said, Saul, my brother, our Lord Jesus, who appeared to you on the way when you were coming, has sent me that you may receive your sight and be filled with the Holy Spirit.

18 And in that hour, there fell from his eyes something like scales; and his eyesight was restored; and he arose and was baptized.

19 And when he had received food, he was strengthened, and he remained several days with the disciples in Damascus.

20 From that time on, he preached in the Jewish synagogues concerning Jesus, that he is the Son of God.

21 But all those who heard him were amazed and said, Is this not he who persecuted those who called on this name in Jerusalem, and behold, he was sent here for that very purpose that he might bring them bound to the high priests?

22 But Saul became more powerful, and he made the Jews who dwelt in Damascus tremble when he proved that Jesus is the Christ.

23 After he had been there many days, the Jews plotted against him to kill him.

24 But their conspiracy was made known to Saul, how they watched the gates of the city day and night to kill him.

25 Then the disciples placed him in a basket and let him down over the wall during the night.

26 Then Saul went to Jerusalem, and wanted to join the disciples, but they were all afraid of him, and could not believe that he was a convert.

27 But Barnabas took him and brought him to the apostles, and told them how he had seen the Lord on the way and how he had spoken to him and how in Damascus he had spoken openly in the name of Jesus.

28 So he went in and out with them at Jerusalem.

29 And he spoke openly in the name of Jesus, and debated with the Jews who understood Greek; but they wanted to kill him.

30 And when the brethren knew it, they brought him by night to Cæsarea, and from thence they sent him to Tarsus.

31 ¶Then the church throughout Judea and Galilee and Samaria was at peace, and strengthened itself and developed obedience and reverence to God, and by the consolation of the Holy Spirit it increased in numbers.

32 ¶And it came to pass while Simon Peter traveled to various cities, he came down also to the saints who dwelt at the city of Lydda.

33 And there he found a man named Æneas, who had been paralyzed and had lain in bed eight years.

34 And Simon Peter said to him, Æneas, Jesus Christ heals you. Arise, and make your bed. And he arose immediately.

35 And all who dwelt at Lydda and Sharon saw him and turned to God.

36 ¶Now there was in the city of Joppa a woman disciple called Tabitha, which means gazelle; she was rich in good works and in charitable acts.

37 And it came to pass in those days that she fell sick, and died; they bathed her body and laid it in an upper room.

38 And the disciples heard that Simon Peter was in the city of Lydda, which is beside Joppa; they sent to him two men, desiring him to come to them without delay.

39 Then Simon Peter arose and went with them. And when he had arrived, they took him to the upper room where all the widows were gathered around him weeping and they showed him shirts and cloaks which Tabitha had given them when she was alive.

40 But Simon Peter put all the people out and knelt down and

prayed; then he turned to the body and said, Tabitha, arise. And she opened her eyes, and when she saw Simon Peter, she sat up.

41 And he gave her his hand and lifted her up; then he called the saints and widows and presented her to them alive.

42 And this was known throughout the city and many believed in our Lord.

43 And he remained in Joppa many days, staying at the house of Simon, the tanner.

CHAPTER 10

THERE was in Cæsarea a man called Cornelius, a centurion of the regiment which is called the Italian,

2 A man righteous and God-fearing, as were all his household; who gave alms to the people abundantly, and always sought after God.

3 Very openly in a vision about three o'clock in the afternoon he saw an angel of God who came in to him, and said to him, Cornelius.

4 And he looked at the angel and was afraid, and he said, What is it, my Lord? And the angel said to him, Your prayers and your alms have come up for a memorial before God.

5 And now send men to the city of Joppa and bring here Simon who is called Peter:

6 Behold he is staying with Simon the tanner, whose house is by the seaside.

7 And when the angel who spoke to him had departed, Cornelius called two of his household and a soldier who believed in God and was obedient to him,

8 And he related to them everything that he had seen, and sent them to Joppa.

9 ¶The next day, while they were on their journey, drawing near to the city, Simon Peter went up upon the housetop to pray about noontime.

10 And he became hungry, and wanted to eat; but while they were preparing food for him, he fell into a trance.

11 And he saw the heaven open and something fastened at the four corners, resembling a large linen cloth, was let down from heaven to the earth;

12 And there were in it all kinds of fourfooted beasts and creeping things of the earth and birds of the air.

13 And there came a voice to him, saying, Simon Peter, rise; kill and eat.

14 But Simon Peter said, Far be it, my Lord; for I have never eaten anything which was unclean and defiled.

15 And again the voice came to him a second time, What God has cleansed, you should not call unclean.

16 This happened the third time; then the cloth was lifted up to the heaven.

17 Now while Simon Peter was bewildered, wondering in himself what the vision he had seen should mean, the men who were sent by Cornelius arrived, and enquired for the house in which Simon Peter had been staying, and they came and stood at the door of the courtyard.

18 And from there they called and asked if Simon who is called Peter stayed there.

19 While Simon Peter meditated about the vision, the Spirit said to him, Behold, three men seek you.

20 Arise, go down and go with them, without doubt in your mind; for I have sent them.

21 Then Simon Peter went down to the men and said, I am the man you seek. What is the purpose of your mission?

22 They said to him, A man called Cornelius, a righteous and God-fearing centurion of whom all the Jewish people speak well, was told in a vision by a holy angel to send and bring you to his house and to hear words from you.

23 So Simon Peter brought them into the place where he was staying and welcomed them. The next day he arose and went with them, and a few men from amongst the brethren of Joppa accompanied him.

24 ¶And the next day they entered Cæsarea. And Cornelius was waiting for them, and all his relatives and

also his dear friends were assembled with him.

25 And just as Simon Peter was entering, Cornelius met him and threw himself at his feet and worshipped him.

26 But Simon Peter raised him, saying, Stand up; I am but a man also.

27 And after he had talked with him, he went in and found a great many people had come there.

28 So he said to them, You know well that it is unlawful for a Jew to associate with a stranger who is not of his tribe; but God has showed me that I should not call any man common or unclean.

29 This is why I came at once when you sent for me; but now let me ask you, for what reason have you sent for me?

30 Then Cornelius said to him, Four days I have been fasting; and at three o'clock in the afternoon while I was praying in my house, a man dressed in white garments stood before me,

31 And said to me, Cornelius your prayer has been heard, and your alms are a memorial before God.

32 But send to the city of Joppa and bring Simon, who is called Peter; behold he is staying in the house of Simon the tanner, by the seaside; and he will come and talk with you.

33 At that very time I sent for you, and you have done well to come. Behold we are all here present before you, and we wish to hear everything commanded you from God.

34 ¶Then Simon Peter opened his mouth and said, Of a truth I perceive that God is no respecter of persons;

35 But among all people, he who fears him and works righteousness is accepted with him.

36 For God sent the word to the children of Israel, preaching peace and tranquility by Jesus Christ; he is the Lord of all.

37 And you also are familiar with the news which was published throughout Judea, which sprang from Galilee, after the baptism preached by John,

38 Concerning Jesus of Nazareth, whom God anointed with the Holy Spirit and with power, and who, because God was with him, went about doing good and healing all who were oppressed by the devil.

39 And we are witnesses of all things which he did throughout the land of Judea and in Jerusalem. This very one the Jews nailed on a cross and killed him;

40 Him God raised on the third day and made him seen openly;

41 Not to all the people, but to us who have been chosen by God to be his witnesses, for we did eat and drink with him after his resurrection from the dead.

42 And he commanded us to preach to the people and to testify that it is he who was ordained by God to be the judge of the living and of the dead.

43 Of him all the prophets testified that whosoever believes in his name shall receive remission of sins.

44 ¶While Simon Peter spoke these words, the Holy Spirit descended on all who heard the word.

45 And the Jewish converts who had come with him were seized with amazement because the gift of the Holy Spirit was poured out on the Gentiles also;

46 For they heard them speak with different tongues, and magnify God.

47 Then Simon Peter said to them, Can any man forbid water, that these people who have received the Holy Spirit, just as we have, should not be baptized?

48 And he commanded them to be baptized in the name of our Lord Jesus Christ. And they urged him to remain with them a few days.

CHAPTER 11

AND the apostles and the brethren who were in Judea heard that the Gentiles also had received the word of God.

2 And when Simon Peter had come up to Jerusalem, those who upheld the circumcision contended with him,

3 Saying he had entered into the houses of uncircumcised men and had eaten with them.

4 Then Simon began to recite the facts one after another, saying,

5 As I was praying in Joppa, I saw in a vision something like a linen cloth descending from heaven, and it was tied at its four corners; and it came even to me.

6 And as I looked at it, I saw that there were in it fourfooted beasts and creeping things of the earth, and birds of the air.

7 Then I heard a voice saying to me, Simon, arise, kill and eat.

8 And I said, Far be it, my Lord; for never has anything defiled and unclean entered my mouth.

9 But again the voice from heaven said to me, What God has cleansed do not call unclean.

10 This happened three times; then everything was lifted up into heaven.

11 And in that very hour, three men who were sent to me by Cornelius from Cæsarea came and stood at the gate of the courtyard where I was staying.

12 And the spirit said to me, Go with them, doubting nothing. And these six brethren accompanied me, and we entered the man's house.

13 And he related to us how he had seen an angel in his house, who stood and said to him, Send to the city of Joppa and bring Simon who is called Peter;

14 And he shall speak to you words by which you and all of your household shall be saved.

15 And as I began to speak, the Holy Spirit came on them, as on us at the beginning.

16 Then I remembered that word of our Lord, when he said, John indeed baptized with water; but you shall be baptized with the Holy Spirit.

17 Now, therefore, if God has equally given the gifts to the Gentiles who believe in our Lord Jesus Christ, just as he gave to us, who am I that I should dispute God?

18 When they heard these words, they held their peace and glorified God, saying, Perhaps God has also granted to the Gentiles repentance to life.

19 ¶Now those who had been dispersed by the persecution which occurred on account of Stephen traveled as far as Phœnicia and even to the land of Cyprus and to Antioch, preaching the word to none but to the Jews only.

20 But there were some men among them from Cyprus and from Cyrene; these men entered into Antioch and spoke to the Greeks and preached concerning our Lord Jesus.

21 And the hand of the Lord was with them; and a great number believed, and turned to the Lord.

22 ¶Then tidings of these things came to the attention of the members of the congregation at Jerusalem; and they sent Barnabas to Antioch.

23 When he came there and saw the grace of God, he was glad, and he pleaded with them that they should follow our Lord with all their hearts.

24 For he was a good man, and full of the Holy Spirit and of faith; and many people were added to our Lord.

25 Then Barnabas departed to Tarsus to seek for Saul.

26 And when he had found him, he brought him to Antioch. And for the whole year they assembled together in the church and taught a great many people. The disciples were called Christians first at Antioch and from that time on.

27 And in those days came prophets from Jerusalem to Antioch.

28 ¶And one of them named Agabus stood up and foretold by the spirit that a great famine was to come throughout the land, the famine which occurred in the days of Claudius Cæsar.

29 Then the disciples, each one according to his ability, determined to set something aside for relief to the brethren who dwelt in Judea.

30 This they did, and sent it there to the elders by the hands of Barnabas and Saul.

CHAPTER 12

NOW at that very time Herod the king surnamed Agrippa seized some of the people of the church to oppress them.

2 And he killed James the brother of John with the sword.

3 And when he saw that this pleased the Jews, he proceeded to arrest Simon Peter also. This happened during the days of unleavened bread.

4 So he seized him and put him in prison and delivered him to the care of sixteen soldiers to keep him, so that he might deliver him to the Jewish people after the passover.

5 And while Simon Peter was kept in the prison, continual prayer was offered for him to God by the church.

6 And on the very night before the morning that he was to be delivered up, while Simon Peter was sleeping between two soldiers, bound with two chains, and others were guarding the doors of the prison,

7 The angel of the Lord stood over him, and a light shone in all the prison; and the angel touched him on the side and woke him, and said to him, Rise up quickly. And the chains fell off from his hands.

8 And the angel said to him, Bind on your girdle and put on your sandals. And so he did. And again he said to him, Put on your robe and follow me.

9 And he went out and followed the angel, not knowing that what was done by the angel was true, but thought he saw a vision.

10 When they had passed the first and the second guard, they came to the iron gate and it opened to them of its own accord; and when they had gone out and had passed one street, the angel departed from him.

11 And when Simon Peter came to himself he said, Now I surely know that the Lord has sent his angel and has delivered me out of the hand of Herod, the king, and from all that the Jews were conspiring against me.

12 And when he understood, he went to the house of Mary the mother of John, whose surname was Mark, because many brethren were gathered there praying.

13 When he knocked at the door of the courtyard, a little girl named Rhoda came out to answer.

14 And when she recognized Simon's voice, because of her joy she did not open the door to him, but ran back and said, Behold, Simon Peter stands at the gate of the courtyard.

15 They said to her, You are excited. But she argued that it was so. Then said they, Perhaps it is his angel.

16 But Simon Peter continued knocking at the door; and they went out and saw him, and were astonished.

17 But he motioned to them with his hand to keep quiet; then he entered and related to them how the Lord had brought him out of the prison. And he said, Tell these things to James and to our brethren. And he went out and departed for another place.

18 Now when it was morning, there was great tumult among the soldiers as to what had become of Simon Peter.

19 When Herod had sought him and could not find him, he sentenced the guards and commanded that they should be put to death. And Simon Peter left Judea and stayed at Cæsarea.

20 ¶Herod was angry with the people of Tyre and Sidon, but they assembled together and came to him, and they appealed to Blastus, the king's chamberlain, and asked him that they might have peace, because their country was dependent upon the kingdom of Herod for food supplies.

21 Upon the set day Herod, arrayed in royal apparel, sat upon the throne and addressed the assembly.

22 And all the people shouted, saying, This sounds like the voice of God speaking and not that of a man.

23 And because he did not give the glory to God, in that very hour an angel of the Lord smote him, and he was eaten by disease and died.

24 But the gospel of God continued to be preached and to reach many.

25 ¶Barnabas and Saul, after they had fulfilled their ministry, returned from Jerusalem to Antioch, and took with them John whose surname was Mark.

CHAPTER 13

NOW there were in the church at Antioch prophets and teachers: Barnabas and Simon who was called Niger [1] and Lucius from the city of Cyrene and Manael, who was the son of the man who brought up Herod the tetrarch, and Saul.

2 As they fasted and prayed to God, the Holy Spirit said to them, Appoint for me Saul and Barnabas for the work to which I have called them.

3 So, after they had fasted and prayed and laid their hands on them, they sent them away.

4 ¶Thus these two were sent forth by the Holy Spirit, and they went down to Seleucia; and from there they sailed to Cyprus.

5 And when they had entered the city of Salamis, they preached the word of our Lord in the synagogues of the Jews; and John ministered to them.

6 And when they had traveled the whole island as far as the city of Paphos, they found a Jewish sorcerer, who was a false prophet and whose name was Bar-Shuma;

7 Who was a close friend to a wise man, the proconsul whose name was Sergius Paulus, who called for Saul and Barnabas and desired to hear from them the word of God.

8 But Bar-Shuma the sorcerer (whose name is interpreted Elymas) withstood them, seeking to turn away the proconsul from the faith.

9 Then Saul, who is called Paul, filled with the Holy Spirit, looked at him

10 And said, O man full of every kind of subtlety and of all evil things, son of the devil and enemy of all righteousness, will you not cease to pervert the right ways of the Lord?

11 And now the hand of the Lord is against you, and you shall be blind and shall not see the sun for a time. And in that very hour there fell on him a mist and darkness; and he went about seeking some one to lead him by the hand.

12 And when the proconsul saw what had happened, he was amazed and believed the teaching of the Lord.

13 ¶Then Paul and Barnabas sailed from the city of Paphos, and came to Perga, a city in Pamphylia; and John separated from them and went to Jerusalem.

14 But they left Perga and came to Antioch, a city in Pisidia, and on the sabbath day they went into the synagogue and sat down.

15 And after the reading of the law and the prophets, the elders of the synagogue sent to them, saying, O men and brethren, if you have a word of encouragement for the people, speak.

16 So Paul stood up, and lifting his hands said, O men of Israel and those of you who fear God, hear my words:

17 The God of this people of Israel chose our forefathers and exalted and multiplied them when they dwelt as strangers in the land of Egypt, and with a strong arm he brought them out of it.

18 And he fed them in the wilderness for forty years.

19 And he destroyed seven nations in the land of Canaan, and he gave them their land for an inheritance.

20 And for a period of four hundred and fifty years he gave them judges until the time of the prophet Samuel.

21 Then they asked for a king, and God gave them Saul the son of Kish, a man of the tribe of Benjamin, for a period of forty years.

22 And when in time God took Saul away he raised up to them David to be their king, concerning whom he testified, saying, I have found David, the son of Jesse, a man after my own heart, to do my will.

23 Of this man's offspring God has, according to his promise, raised to Israel a Saviour, Jesus,

24 Before whose coming, he had sent John to preach the baptism of repentance to all the people of Israel.

25 And as John fulfilled his ministry, he said, Who do you think I am? I am not he. But behold there comes one after me, the strings of

[1] Carpenter.

whose shoes I am not worthy to untie.

26 O men and brethren, descendants of the family of Abraham, and whosoever among you reverences God, to you is the word of salvation sent.

27 For inasmuch as the inhabitants of Jerusalem and their leaders did not understand him nor the books of the prophets which are read every sabbath day, they condemned him; but all the things which were written have been fulfilled.

28 And though they found no cause for his death, they asked Pilate that they might kill him.

29 And when they had fulfilled all that was written of him, they lowered him from the cross and laid him in a sepulchre.

30 But God raised him from the dead;

31 And for many days he was seen by them who had come up with him from Galilee to Jerusalem, and they are now his witnesses to the people.

32 And behold we also preach to you that that very promise which was made to our fathers,

33 Behold God has fulfilled it to us their children, for he has raised up Jesus, just as it is written in the second psalm, You are my son; this day I have begotten you.

34 And God raised him from the dead, no more to return to corruption, as he said, I will give you the sure mercies of David.

35 And again he said in another place, You shall not suffer your Holy One to see corruption.

36 ¶For David, after he had served his own generation according to the will of God, died; though he was a greater man than his fathers, yet he saw corruption.

37 But he whom God raised did not see corruption.

38 Be it known to you, therefore, brethren, that through this very one is preached to you the forgiveness of sins:

39 And by him all that believe are justified from all things, from which you could not be justified by the law of Moses.

40 Beware, therefore, lest that which is written in the prophets may come upon you.

41 Be careful, O you despisers, for you shall wonder and perish; for I will do a great work in your day which you will not believe even if a man tell it to you.

42 ¶And as Paul and Barnabas were leaving them, the people besought them to speak these things to them the next sabbath.

43 Now when the congregation was dismissed, a great many Jews, and also proselytes who feared God, followed Paul and Barnabas, who, speaking to them, persuaded them to continue in the grace of God.

44 And the next sabbath day the whole city gathered to hear the word of God.

45 But when the Jews saw the great crowd, they were filled with envy, and they bitterly opposed the words of Paul, and they blasphemed.

46 Then Paul and Barnabas said to them boldly, It was necessary that the word of God should first be spoken to you; but because you reject it, you have decided against yourselves and you are unworthy of everlasting life, so behold, we turn to the Gentiles.

47 For so has our Lord commanded us, as it is written, I have set you to be a light to the Gentiles, that you should be for salvation to the ends of the earth.

48 ¶And when the Gentiles heard this, they were glad and glorified God; and as many as were ordained to eternal life believed.

49 And the word of the Lord was published throughout all that region.

50 But the Jews incited the chief men of the city and the rich women who worshipped God with them, so that they stirred up a persecution against Paul and Barnabas and expelled them beyond their borders.

51 And as they went out, they shook off the dust of their feet upon them, and they came to the city of Iconium.

52 And the disciples were filled with joy and with the Holy Spirit.

CHAPTER 14

AND Paul and Barnabas entered into the Jewish synagogue and addressed the people in such manner that a great many of the Jews and of the Greeks believed.

2 But the Jews who would not listen stirred up the Gentiles to oppress the brethren.

3 So they remained there for a long time and spoke boldly concerning the Lord, and he gave them testimony to the word of his grace by means of signs and wonders which he performed by their hands.

4 But the people of the city were divided: part held with the Jews and part followed the apostles.

5 And they were menaced by both the Gentiles and the Jews and with their leaders who wanted to disgrace them and have them stoned.

6 And when they became aware of it, they departed and took refuge in Lystra and Derbe, cities of Lycaonia, and the villages near by.

7 And there they preached the gospel.

8 ¶And there dwelt in the city of Lystra a cripple who had been lame from his mother's womb, who never had walked.

9 He heard Paul speak; and when Paul saw him and perceived that there was faith in him to be healed,

10 He said to him with a loud voice, I say to you, in the name of our Lord Jesus Christ, stand upright on your feet. And he leaped and walked.

11 And when the people saw what Paul had done, they lifted their voices, saying in the language of the country, The gods have come down to us in the likeness of men.

12 So they called Barnabas the chief of the gods; and Paul they called Hermes, because he was the chief speaker.

13 Then the priest of Zeus, whose shrine was outside the city, brought oxen and garlands to the gate of the courtyard where they stayed, and he wanted to offer sacrifices to them.

14 When Barnabas and Paul heard of this, they tore their clothes and leaped to their feet and went out to the crowd, crying out

15 And saying, Men, what are you doing? We also are ordinary human beings like you, who preach to you that you should turn from these useless things to the living God who made heaven and earth and the sea and all things that are therein,

16 Who in generations past suffered all nations to walk in their own ways.

17 Nevertheless he did not leave himself without testimony, in that he bestowed good on them from heaven and gave them rain and caused the fruits to grow in their seasons and satisfied their hearts with food and gladness.

18 And even though they said these things, they had difficulty in restraining the people from offering sacrifice to them.

19 ¶But there came there Jews from Iconium and Antioch and stirred up the people against them, and they stoned Paul and dragged him out of the city, supposing him to be dead.

20 Howbeit, as the disciples gathered around him, he rose up and entered again into the city; and the next day he departed from there with Barnabas, and they came to the city of Derbe.

21 ¶And when they had preached the gospel to the people of that city and had converted many, then they returned to the city of Lystra and to Iconium and Antioch,

22 Strengthening the souls of the converts and exhorting them to continue in the faith, and telling them that only through much tribulation can we enter into the kingdom of God.

23 And when they had ordained them elders in every church and had prayed with them with fasting, they commended them to our Lord, on whom they believed.

24 And after they had traveled through the country of Pisidia, they came to Pamphylia.

25 And when they had preached the word of the Lord in the city of Perga, they went down to Attalia;

26 And thence they sailed and came

to Antioch, because from there they had been recommended to the grace of the Lord for the work which they fulfilled.

27 And as the whole congregation was gathered together, they related everything that God had done to them and how he had opened the door of faith to the Gentiles.

28 And there they remained a long time with the disciples.

CHAPTER 15

AND certain men who had come down from Judea taught the brethren, Unless you are circumcised in accordance with the custom of the law you cannot be saved.

2 And there was great dissension and controversy between them and Paul and Barnabas, and it reached such a point that it was necessary for Paul and Barnabas and others with them to go up to Jerusalem to the apostles and elders concerning this question.

3 They were given an escort and sent on their way by the church, and they traveled through all Phœnicia and the territory of the Samaritans, declaring the conversion of the Gentiles; and they caused great joy to all the brethren.

4 On their arrival at Jerusalem, they were received by the church, and by the apostles and elders; and they reported everything that God had done with them.

5 But some of the men who had been converted from the sect of the Pharisees rose up and said, You must circumcise them and command them to keep the law of Moses.

6 ¶Then the apostles and elders assembled to consider this matter.

7 And after much controversy, Simon Peter rose up and said to them, Men and brethren, you know that from the early days God chose that from my mouth the Gentiles should hear the word of the Gospel and believe.

8 And God, who knows what is in the heart, has testified concerning them and has given them the Holy Spirit just as he did to us.

9 And he did not discriminate between us and them, because he purified their hearts by faith.

10 Now therefore why do you tempt God by putting a yoke upon the necks of the disciples which neither our fathers nor we were able to bear?

11 But we believe that through the grace of the Lord Jesus Christ we shall be saved even as they.

12 Then the whole congregation was silent and listened to Paul and Barnabas, who were declaring the miracles and signs among the Gentiles and everything which God had wrought by their hands.

13 And when they had ceased speaking, James rose up and said, Men and brethren, hear me:

14 Simon Peter has told you how God from the beginning chose a people from the Gentiles for his name.

15 And with this the words of the prophets agree, as it is written,

16 After this I will return, and I will set up again the tabernacle of David which has fallen down; and I will repair what has fallen from it, and I will set it up,

17 So that the men who remain may seek after the Lord, and also all the Gentiles upon whom my name is called; so said the Lord who does all these things.

18 ¶The works of God are known from the very beginning.

19 Because of this I say, Do not trouble those who turn to God from among the Gentiles:

20 But let us send word to them that they abstain from defilement by sacrifices to idols and from fornication and from animals strangled and from blood.

21 For Moses, from the very early centuries, had preachers in the synagogues in every city to read his books on every sabbath day.

22 ¶Then the apostles and elders, with the whole church, chose men from among themselves and sent them to Antioch with Paul and Barnabas; namely, Judah who is called Barsabas and Silas, men who were leaders among the brethren;

23 And they wrote a letter and sent it by them after this manner: The apostles and elders and brethren to the brethren of the Gentiles in Antioch and Syria and Cilicia, greetings:

24 We have heard that certain men have gone out and disturbed you with words, thus upsetting your souls, saying, You must be circumcised and keep the law; concerning these things we have never commanded them.

25 Therefore, we have considered the matter while we are assembled, and we have chosen and sent men to you with our beloved Paul and Barnabas,

26 Men who have dedicated their lives for the name of our Lord Jesus Christ.

27 And we have sent with them Judah and Silas, so that they may tell you the same things by word of mouth.

28 For it is the will of the Holy Spirit and of us to lay upon you no additional burden than these necessary things:

29 That you abstain from sacrifices offered to idols and from blood and from animals strangled and from fornication; when you keep yourselves from these things, you will do well. Remain steadfast in our Lord.

30 ¶Now when those who were sent came to Antioch and when the whole people were gathered together, they delivered the epistle;

31 And when they had read it, the people rejoiced and were comforted.

32 And Judah and Silas, being prophets themselves also, confirmed the brethren with gracious words.

33 And after they had been there some time, the brethren let them go in peace to the apostles.

34 Notwithstanding it pleased Silas to abide there still.

35 Paul also and Barnabas remained in Antioch, teaching and preaching the word of God, with many others also.

36 ¶And some days after, Paul said to Barnabas, Let us return and visit the brethren in every city where we have preached the word of God and see how they do.

37 Now Barnabas wanted to take John who was also called Mark.

38 But Paul was unwilling to take him with them because he had left them when they were in Pamphylia and had not gone with them.

39 And because of this dispute, Paul and Barnabas separated from each other; and Barnabas took Mark, and they sailed to Cyprus,

40 But Paul chose Silas and departed, being commended by the brethren to the grace of God.

41 And he traveled through Syria and Cilicia, establishing churches.

CHAPTER 16

THEN he arrived at the city of Derbe and Lystra; there was there a disciple whose name was Timotheus, the son of a Jewess convert, but whose father was an Aramean.

2 And all the disciples of Lystra and Iconium gave good testimony concerning him.

3 Paul wanted to take this man with him, so he took him and circumcised him because of the Jews who were in that region; for they all knew that his father was an Aramean.

4 And as they went through the cities, they preached and taught the people to obey the decrees which the apostles and elders had written at Jerusalem.

5 And so the churches were established in the faith, and increased in number daily.

6 ¶Then they traveled through the countries of Phrygia and Galatia, and the Holy Spirit forbade them to speak the word of God in Asia Minor.

7 And when they came to the country of Mysia, they wanted to go from thence to Bithynia; but the spirit of Jesus permitted them not.

8 And when they had left Mysia, they came to the country of Troas.

9 And, in a vision of the night, there appeared to Paul a man resembling a Macedonian, standing and begging him, saying, Come over to Macedonia and help us.

10 And after Paul had seen this vision, we were desirous to leave for Macedonia at once, because we un-

derstood that our Lord had called us to preach the gospel to them.[1]

11 ¶When we sailed from Troas, we came in a direct course to Samothracia, and from thence on the following day, we came to the city Neapolis;

12 And from thence to Philippi, which is the capital of Macedonia, and is a colony; and we were in that city on certain holidays.

13 And on the sabbath day we went outside the city gate to the river side because a house of prayer was seen there, and when we were seated, we spoke to the women who had gathered there.

14 And a certain woman, named Lydia, a seller of purple of the city of Thyatira, feared God; her heart was so touched by our Lord that she listened to what Paul said.

15 And she was baptized together with her household, and she begged us, saying, If you are sincerely convinced that I believe in our Lord, come and stay in my house; and she urged us strongly.

16 ¶And it came to pass, as we went to the house of prayer, we were met by a young girl who was possessed of a spirit, and who brought her masters great gain by fortunetelling.

17 And she followed Paul and us, crying and saying, These men are the servants of the Most High God, and they preach to you the way of salvation.

18 And she did this for many days. So Paul was indignant and said to the spirit, I command you in the name of Jesus Christ to come out of her. And it left her the same hour.

19 And when her masters saw that the hope for their business was lost with her power, they seized Paul and Silas and beat them and brought them to the market place.

20 And they brought them before the soldiers and the city magistrates and said, These men are Jews, and they create disturbances in our city,

21 And they preach customs to us which are not lawful for us to accept and practice, because we are Romans.

22 And a large crowd gathered against them. Then the soldiers stripped them of their clothes and gave command to scourge them.

23 And when they had flogged them severely, they cast them into prison, charging the jailer to watch them carefully.

24 He, having received the charge, brought them in and put them into the inner chamber of the prison, and fastened their feet in the stocks.

25 ¶Now at midnight Paul and Silas prayed and glorified God; and the prisoners heard them.

26 And suddenly there was a great earthquake, so that the foundations of the prison were shaken, and immediately all the doors were opened and the bands of all were loosed.

27 When the keeper of the prison awoke and saw that the prison doors were open, he took a sword and would have killed himself, for he thought the prisoners had escaped.

28 But Paul cried with a loud voice, saying to him, Do not harm yourself, for we are all here.

29 Then he lighted a lamp and sprang in, trembling, and threw himself at the feet of Paul and Silas.

30 And he brought them out, and said, Sirs, what must I do to be saved?

31 And they said to him, Believe in our Lord Jesus Christ, and both you and your household will be saved.

32 And they spoke to him the word of the Lord and to all who were of his household.

33 And he took them at that hour of the night and washed their wounds; and then was baptized in that very hour, he and all his household.

34 And when he had brought them up into his house, he set food before them; and he and all the members of his household rejoiced, believing in God.

35 In the morning, the soldiers sent the lictors to tell the prison warden to release those men.

36 And when the keeper of the prison heard this, he went in and told Paul, saying, The soldiers have sent

---

[1] The author, Luke, used *they* and *them* in referring to Paul, Timothy and Silas when he was not with them. He used *we* and *us* when he was with them.

orders to release you; now therefore depart and go in peace.

37 But Paul said to him, Not having committed any offense, they flogged us, Roman citizens, in the presence of the people, and they cast us into prison; and now do they let us out secretly? No verily; let them come themselves and take us out.

38 And the lictors went and told the magistrates these words which were told to them; and when they heard that Paul and Silas were Roman citizens, they were afraid.

39 And they came to them and urged them to get out and depart from the city.

40 And they went out of the prison and entered into the house of Lydia where they saw the brethren and comforted them, and departed.

CHAPTER 17

THEN they passed by the cities of Amphipolis and Apollonia, and came to Thessalonica, where there was a synagogue of the Jews.

2 And Paul, as was his custom, went in to join them, and for three sabbaths he spoke to them from the scriptures,

3 Interpreting and proving that Christ had to suffer and rise again from the dead; and that he is the same Jesus Christ whom I preach to you.

4 And some of them believed and joined Paul and Silas; and many of them were Greeks who revered God, and many of them were well known women, a goodly number.

5 But the Jews, being jealous, secured a band of bad men from the streets of the city and formed a great mob, who caused disturbances in the city, and who came and assaulted the house of Jason and sought to bring them out from it and deliver them to the mob.

6 And when they failed to find them there, they dragged forth Jason and the brethren who were there and brought them before the authorities of the city, crying, These are the men who have created disturbances throughout the world, and behold, they have come here also,

7 And Jason has welcomed them; and all of them are against the decrees of Cæsar, saying that there is another king, Jesus.

8 The authorities of the city and all the people were alarmed when they heard these things.

9 So they took bail from Jason and some of the brethren and then let them go.

10 Then the brethren immediately sent away Paul and Silas by night to the city of Berea; and when they arrived there, they entered into the synagogue of the Jews.

11 For the Jews there were more liberal than the Jews who were in Thessalonica, in that they gladly heard the word daily and searched the scriptures to find out if these things were so.

12 And many of them believed; and of the Greeks there were many men and notable women.

13 But when the Jews of Thessalonica found out that the word of God was preached by Paul in the city of Berea, they came there also, and ceased not to stir up and alarm the people.

14 Then the brethren sent Paul away to go to the sea; but Silas and Timotheus remained in that city.

15 And those who escorted Paul went with him as far as the city of Athens; and when they were leaving him, they received from him an epistle to Silas and Timotheus, requesting them to come to him in haste.

16 ¶Now while Paul waited for them at Athens, he saw the whole city full of idols, and he murmured thereat in his spirit.

17 And he spoke in the synagogue to the Jews and to those who feared God, and in the market place daily with them who were there.

18 Philosophers, also, who were of the teaching of Epicurus, and others, who were called Stoics, argued with him. And some of them said, What does this babbler want? And others said, He preaches foreign gods, because he preached to them Jesus and his resurrection.

19 So they arrested him and brought him to the court house which is called Areopagus, and said to him, May we know what is this new doctrine which you preach?

20 For you proclaim strange words to our ears and we want to know what these things mean.

21 (For all the Athenians and the strangers who were there, were uninterested in anything except something new to tell or to hear.)

22 When Paul stood in the court at Areopagus, he said, Men of Athens, I see that above all things you are extravagant in the worship of idols.

23 For as I walked about, and viewed the house of your idols, I found an altar with this inscription: THIS IS THE ALTAR OF THE UNKNOWN GOD. He therefore, while you know him not but yet worship him, is the very one I am preaching to you.

24 For the God who made the world and all things therein, and who is the Lord of heaven and earth, does not dwell in temples made with hands;

25 Neither is he ministered to by human hands, nor is he in need of anything, for it is he who gave life and breath to all men.

26 And he has made of one blood all nations of men to dwell on all the face of the earth, and he has appointed seasons by his command, and has set limits to the age of men;

27 So that they should seek and search after God, and find him by means of his creations, because he is not far from any one of us;

28 For in him we live and move and have our being, as some of your own wise men have said, For we are his kindred.

29 ¶Now therefore, man, being of the family of God, is not bound to worship resemblances made of gold or silver or stone shapen by the skill and knowledge of man into resemblances of the Deity

30 For the times of ignorance God has made to pass, and at this time he has commanded all men, everywhere, to repent.

31 For he has appointed a day in which he will judge all the earth with righteousness by the man whom he has chosen, he who has turned every man towards his faith; on that account he has raised him from the dead.

32 ¶And when they heard of the resurrection of the dead, some mocked, and others said, We will hear you again on this matter.

33 So Paul left them.

34 Some of them, however, followed him and were converted; one of them was Dionysius, one of the judges of Areopagus, and another a woman named Damaris, and others with them.

CHAPTER 18

THEN Paul departed from Athens, and came to Corinth;

2 And there he found a Jew named Aquila, from the region of Pontus, who had just arrived from Italy with his wife Priscilla, because Claudius Cæsar had commanded all Jews to leave Rome; and Paul went to them.

3 And because he was of the same trade, he stayed with them and worked with them; for they were saddle makers by trade.

4 And he spoke in the synagogue every sabbath, and persuaded the Jews and the pagans.

5 And when Silas and Timotheus came from Macedonia, Paul felt he was not free to speak, because the Jews opposed him and blasphemed as he testified that Jesus is the Christ.

6 So he shook his garments and said to them, From henceforth I am not to be blamed for what I am about to do; I am going to the Gentiles.

7 And he departed thence and entered into the house of a certain man named Titus, a devout man whose household had joined the synagogue.

8 And Crispus, the chief of the synagogue, believed in our Lord, together with all his household; and many of the Corinthians hearing him believed in God and were baptized.

9 Then the Lord spoke to Paul in a vision, Be not afraid, but speak and be not silent.

10 For I am with you and no man

can harm you; and I have many people in this city.

11 For he had already been in Corinth a year and six months and had taught the word of God among them.

12 ¶And when Gallio was proconsul of Achaia, the Jews made insurrection with one accord against Paul; and they brought him to the judgment seat,

13 Saying, This fellow persuades men to worship God contrary to the law.

14 And as Paul was desirous to open his mouth and speak, Gallio said to the Jews, If your accusations were based on something criminal, fraudulent, or vicious, I would welcome you properly, O Jews;

15 But if they are a mere question of words and names and concerning your law, you can settle it better among yourselves; for I do not wish to be a judge of such matters.

16 And he drove them from his judgment seat.

17 Then the pagans seized Sosthenes, the elder of the synagogue, and beat him before the judgment seat. And Gallio disregarded these things.

18 And after Paul had remained there many days, he bade the brethen farewell and sailed for Syria, and with him Priscilla and Aquila, having shorn his head in Cenchrea because he had vowed a vow.

19 And they came to Ephesus, and Paul entered into the synagogue and spoke to the Jews.

20 When they wanted him to tarry a longer time with them, he consented not,

21 Saying, I must by all means celebrate the coming feast as is my custom at Jerusalem; but I will return to you again, God willing.

22 And he left Aquila and Priscilla at Ephesus and sailed and when he landed at Cæsarea, he went up and saluted the members of the church, and went on to Antioch.

23 ¶And after he had spent some special days there he departed and traveled all through the country of Phrygia and Galatia, increasing disciples in all of them.

24 And a certain Jew named Apollos, a native of Alexandria, an eloquent man and well versed in the scriptures, came to Ephesus.

25 He had been converted to the way of the Lord, and was fervent in the spirit; he spoke and taught very fully concerning Jesus, but he knew only the baptism of John.

26 And he began to speak boldly in the synagogue; and when Aquila and Priscilla heard him, they took him to their home and fully showed him the way of the Lord.

27 And when he was disposed to go to Achaia, the brethren gave him a warm reception and wrote to the disciples to welcome him; and when he had come, he greatly helped all believers by means of grace.

28 For he forcefully and publicly argued against the Jews, proving by the scriptures that Jesus is the Christ.

CHAPTER 19

AND it came to pass that while Apollos was at Corinth, Paul traveled through the northern countries and came to Ephesus, and inquired of the disciples whom he found there,

2 Have you received the Holy Spirit since you were converted? They answered, saying to him, We have not even heard that there is a Holy Spirit.

3 Then he said to them, By what baptism then were you baptized? They said, By the baptism of John.

4 Then said Paul, John verily baptized the people with the baptism of repentance, saying to them that they should believe on him who should come after him, that is, Jesus Christ.

5 When they heard these things, they were baptized in the name of our Lord Jesus Christ.

6 And when Paul laid his hands on them, the Holy Spirit came on them; and they spoke in different tongues, and prophesied.

7 And there were in all twelve persons.

8 Then Paul entered into the synagogue and spoke openly for a period

of three months, persuading the people concerning the kingdom of God.

9 But some of them were stubborn, and they disputed and cursed the way of God in the presence of the assembly. Then Paul withdrew and separated the disciples from them, and he spoke to them daily in the school of a man named Tyrannus.

10 And this continued for two years until all who dwelt in Asia Minor, both Jews and Arameans (Syrians), heard the word of God.

11 And God wrought great miracles by the hands of Paul,

12 So that even when from the clothes on his body, pieces of garments were brought and laid upon the sick, diseases were cured and even the insane were restored.

13 ¶Now certain Jews who went about exorcising evil spirits invoked the name of our Lord Jesus over those who were possessed, saying, We adjure you in the name of Jesus whom Paul preaches.

14 And there were seven sons of one Sceva, a Jew, and chief of the priests, who did this.

15 And the insane man answered, saying to them, Jesus I recognize and Paul I know; but who are you?

16 Then the insane man leaped on them and overpowered them and prevailed against them, so they fled out of that house naked and wounded.

17 And this became known to all the Jews and Arameans (Syrians) who dwelt at Ephesus; and fear fell on them all, and the name of our Lord Jesus Christ was magnified.

18 And many of them that believed came and told their faults and confessed what they had done.

19 Many magicians also gathered together their books and brought them and burned them before the presence of the people; and they counted the price of them, and it amounted to fifty thousand pieces of silver.

20 So mightily grew the faith of God and greatly increased in numbers.

21 ¶When these things had been accomplished, Paul made up his mind to travel through all of Macedonia and Achaia, and then to go to Jerusalem, saying, After I have been there, I must also see Rome.

22 So he sent to Macedonia two men of those who had ministered to him, Timotheus and Erastus; but he himself stayed in Asia Minor for a while.

23 And at that time there was a great uprising against those who followed in the way of God.

24 There was here a silversmith named Demetrius, who made silver shrines for Artemis, thus greatly enriching the craftsmen of his trade.

25 He called together all the craftsmen of his trade, with the workmen of like occupation, and said to them, Men, you know that all of our earnings are derived from this craft.

26 You also hear and see that not only the Ephesians, but almost throughout all Asia Minor, this Paul has persuaded and turned away many people simply by saying that gods made by the hands of men are not gods,

27 So that not only is this craft doomed, but also the temple of the great goddess Artemis will be disregarded, and the goddess of all Asia Minor, even she whom all peoples worship, will be despised.

28 And when they heard these things they were filled with wrath and cried out, saying, Great is Artemis of the Ephesians.

29 And the whole city was in tumult; and they rushed together to the theatre, and there seized and carried along with them Gaius and Aristarchus, Macedonians, members of Paul's escort.

30 And Paul wanted to go into the theatre, but the disciples stopped him.

31 And likewise some of the chiefs of Asia Minor, because they were his friends, sent to him, begging him not to risk his life by entering the theatre.

32 Now the multitude in the theatre was greatly confused; some cried one thing, and some another; and many of them did not know why they had assembled together.

33 And the Jews who were there appointed a Jew named Alexander.

And when he rose up, he gestured with his hand and would have addressed the people.

34 But when they knew he was a Jew, all of them cried out with one voice for about two hours, Great is Artemis of the Ephesians.

35 The mayor of the city finally quieted them, saying, Men of Ephesus, who among men does not know that the city of the Ephesians is the seat of great Artemis and her image that fell from heaven?

36 Since, therefore, no man can contradict this, you should keep quiet and do nothing hastily.

37 For you have brought these men here who have neither robbed temples nor have they reviled our goddess.

38 But if Demetrius and the men of his trade have a case against any man, behold there is a proconsul in the city; let the craftsmen come forward and settle with one another in the court.

39 But if you want something else, it must be determined in a lawful assembly.

40 For even now we are in danger of being charged with sedition, for we cannot give an answer concerning this day's meeting, because we have assembled for no reason, and have been tumultuous without a cause.

41 And when he had said these things, he dismissed the assembly.

CHAPTER 20

AND after the tumult had ceased, Paul called to him the disciples and comforted them and kissed them and then departed and went to Macedonia.

2 And when he had traveled through those countries and had comforted them with many words, he came to Greece.

3 There he remained three months. But the Jews laid a plot against him, just as he was about to sail for Syria; so he decided to return to Macedonia.

4 And there accompanied him as far as Asia Minor, Sopater of the city of Berea and Aristarchus and Secundus of Thessalonica and Gaius of the city of Derbe and Timotheus of Lystra, and from Asia Minor Tychicus and Trophimus.

5 These men went before us and waited for us at Troas.

6 But we departed from the Macedonian city of Philippi, after the days of unleavened bread, and sailed and arrived at Troas in five days, where we stayed seven days.

7 ¶And on the first day of the week, while the disciples were assembled to break bread, Paul preached to them, and because he was ready to leave the next day, he prolonged his speech until midnight.

8 Now there was a great glow of light from the torches in the upper chamber where we were gathered together.

9 And a young man named Eutychus was sitting at the window above and listening, and as Paul prolonged his speech, the youth fell into a deep sleep, and while asleep he fell down from the third loft, and was taken up as dead.

10 And Paul went down and bent over him and embraced him and said, Do not be excited for he still lives.

11 And when Paul was come up again, and had broken bread and eaten, he continued to speak till daybreak; then he departed to journey by land.

12 And they carried away the young man alive, and rejoiced over him exceedingly.

13 But we went on board the ship, and sailed to the port of Assos, where we were to take in Paul, as he had commanded us when he left to travel by land.

14 When we had welcomed him at Assos, we took him on board and came to Mitylene.

15 And we sailed thence the next day towards the island of Chios; and the following day we arrived at Samos, and tarried at Trogyllium; and the next day we came to Miletus.

16 For Paul had determined not to stop at Ephesus, fearing he might be delayed there, because he was hastening, if it were possible for him, to celebrate the day of Pentecost at Jerusalem.

17 ¶And from Miletus he sent and called the elders of the church of Ephesus.

18 And when they had come to him, he said to them, You know from the very first day that I entered Asia Minor, how I have been with you always,

19 Serving God with great humility and with tears and amid the trials which were brought upon me by conspiracies of the Jews.

20 And yet I did not neglect to preach to you about those things which were good for your souls, and I taught in the streets and from house to house,

21 Thus testifying both to the Jews and to the Arameans about repentance toward God and faith in our Lord Jesus Christ.

22 And now I am on my way to Jerusalem, bound in the spirit, not knowing what will happen to me there,

23 Save that in every city the Holy Spirit testifies to me, saying that bonds and afflictions await me.

24 But to me my life is nothing; I am not afraid. I desire only that I may finish my course with joy and the ministry which I have received from our Lord Jesus, to testify the gospel of the grace of God.

25 And now I know that you among whom I have traveled and preached the kingdom of God shall see my face no more.

26 Therefore, I testify to you this very day that I am innocent of the blood of all.

27 For I have never shunned to declare to you all the will of God.

28 Take heed therefore to yourselves and to all the flock over which the Holy Spirit has appointed you overseers, to feed the church of Christ which he has purchased with his blood.

29 For I know this, that after I have departed, fierce wolves will attack you, which will not spare the flock.

30 Also from among yourselves, men shall arise, speaking perverse things to draw away disciples after them.

31 Therefore watch and remember that for three years, night and day, I did not cease to teach every one of you with tears.

32 And now I commend you to God and to the word of his grace, which is able to build you up and to give you an inheritance among all the saints.

33 I have never coveted silver or gold or apparel.

34 Indeed you yourselves know that my own hands have provided for my needs and for those who have been with me.

35 I have showed you all things, how that one must work hard and be mindful of the weak and remember the words of our Lord Jesus, how he said, It is more blessed to give than to receive.

36 And when he had thus spoken, he knelt down and prayed with them all.

37 And they all wept bitterly, and they embraced him and kissed him;

38 But they were most distressed because of the words he spoke, that they would see his face no more. And they accompanied him to the ship.

CHAPTER 21

AND it came to pass after we separated from them, we sailed a straight course to the Island of Coos, and the following day we arrived at Rhodes, and from thence to Patara;

2 And we found there a ship sailing to Phoenicia, and we went on board and set forth.

3 Then we reached the Island of Cyprus, and passed it on the left hand, and sailed to Syria, and from thence we landed at Tyre, for there the ship was to unload her cargo.

4 And because we found disciples there, we stayed with them seven days; and every day they said to Paul through the Spirit that he should not go up to Jerusalem.

5 After these days, we departed on

our journey, and they all escorted us on our way with their wives and children till we were out of the city; then they knelt down by the seaside and prayed;

6 And when we had kissed one another good-bye, we took ship; and they returned to their homes.

7 We sailed from Tyre and arrived at the city of Akka (Ptolemais), and we saluted the brethren who were there, and tarried with them a day.

8 On the next day we departed and came to Cæsarea; and we went in and stayed at the house of Philip the evangelist, who was one of the seven.

9 He had four daughters, virgins, who prophesied.

10 And as we were there many days, there came down from Judea a prophet named Agabus.

11 And when he was come to us he took Paul's girdle and bound his own feet and hands, and said, Thus says the Holy Spirit: So shall the Jews at Jerusalem bind the man that owns this girdle and shall deliver him into the hands of the Gentiles.

12 And when we had heard these words, both we and the natives of the place besought him not to go up to Jerusalem.

13 Then Paul answered, saying, Why do you weep and break my heart? For I am ready not only to be bound but also to die at Jerusalem for the sake of the name of our Lord Jesus Christ.

14 And when he would not listen to us, we ceased, saying, Let the will of our Lord be done.

15 After those days we made our preparations and went up to Jerusalem.

16 And there came with us some of the disciples from Cæsarea, bringing with them a brother who was among the first converts, named Mnason, a native of Cyprus, who had before received us at his house.

17 ¶When we arrived at Jerusalem, the brethren welcomed us gladly.

18 And the next day when all the elders were present, we went in with Paul to James.

19 And when we had saluted them, Paul told them in successive order everything that God had done among the Gentiles by his ministry.

20 And when they heard it, they glorified God and said to Paul, Our brother, see how many thousands there are in Judea who are believers; and they are all zealous of the law:

21 But they have been informed about you, that you teach all the Jews who are among the Gentiles to forsake the law of Moses, stating that they ought not to circumcise their children, neither to follow after the customs of the law.

22 Now, therefore, they have heard that you have come here.

23 Do, therefore, what we tell you. We have four men who have vowed to purify themselves;

24 Take them and go purify yourself with them, and pay their expenses so that they may shave their heads; then every one will know that what has been said against you is false, and that you yourself have fulfilled the law and obey it.

25 As for the believers amongst the Gentiles, we have written that they should abstain from the things sacrificed to idols and from fornication and from what is strangled and from blood.

26 Then Paul took the men and on the next day he was purified with them and he entered into the temple, informing them how to complete the days of purification until the gift of every one of them was offered.

27 ¶And when the seventh day approached, and the Jews from Asia Minor saw him in the temple, they stirred up all the people against him and laid hands on him,

28 And cried out, saying, Men of Israel, help! This is the man who teaches everywhere against our people, against the law, and against this place; and further, he has brought Arameans into the temple and has defiled this holy place.

29 For they had previously seen Trophimus, the Ephesian, with him in the city, and they thought he had

entered into the temple with Paul.

30 So the whole city was in a tumult, and all the people ran together; they seized Paul and dragged him out of the temple; and the doors were immediately shut.

31 And as the mob sought to kill him, the news reached the captain of the company that all the city was in an uproar.

32 He immediately took a centurion and many soldiers, and ran down to them; and when they saw the chief captain and the soldiers, they ceased beating Paul.

33 Then the chief captain came near him and took him, and commanded him to be bound with two chains. Then he inquired, Who is he and what has he done?

34 And some of the mob cried against him one thing, some another; and because of their confusion he was unable to know what was true, so he commanded him to be taken to headquarters.

35 And when Paul reached the stairs, the soldiers carried him because of the violence of the people,

36 For a great many people followed after, crying and saying, Away with him.

37 And as Paul was about to be led into headquarters, he said to the chief captain, May I speak to you? The captain said, Can you speak Greek?

38 Are you not that Egyptian who some time ago created disturbances and led out into the desert four thousand malefactors?

39 But Paul said, I am a Jew of Tarsus in Cilicia, a citizen of a well-known city; I beg you, permit me to speak to the people.

40 ¶And when he had given him permission, Paul stood on the stairs and beckoned with his hand to them. And when they were quiet he spoke to them in the Hebrew (Aramaic) tongue and said to them,

CHAPTER 22

BRETHREN and fathers, hear my defense which I now make to you.

2 And when they heard him speak to them in the Hebrew tongue they were the more quiet. And he said,

3 I am a Jew, born in Tarsus of Cilicia, yet I was brought up in this city under the care and guidance of Gamaliel, and trained perfectly according to the law of our fathers, and was zealous toward God just as you are also.

4 And I persecuted this religion to the death, binding and delivering into prisons both men and women.

5 The high priest and all the elders can so testify about me, for it was from them that I received letters to go to the brethren at Damascus to bring those who were there bound to Jerusalem to be punished.

6 And it came to pass as I drew near to Damascus, at about noon, suddenly a great light from heaven shone round about me.

7 And I fell to the ground and heard a voice saying to me, Saul, Saul, why do you persecute me?

8 And I answered, saying, Who are you, my Lord? And he said to me, I am Jesus of Nazareth, whom you persecute.

9 And the men who were with me saw the light, but they did not) hear the voice that spoke to me.

10 And I said, What shall I do, my Lord? And our Lord said to me, Arise and go into Damascus; and there it shall be told to you all things which are appointed for you to do.

11 And when I could not see for the glory of that light, being led by the hand of them that were with me, I came into Damascus.

12 And a certain man, Ananias, righteous according to the law, as testified by all the Jews concerning him,

13 Came to me and said, My brother Saul, receive your sight. And instantly my eyes were opened and I looked upon him.

14 And he said to me, The God of our fathers has appointed you to know his will and to see the Righteous One and to hear the voice of his mouth.

15 And you shall be a witness for

him before all men of all that you have seen and heard.

16 And now why do you delay? Arise and be baptized and wash away your sins, calling on the name of the Lord.

17 And it came to pass that when I returned here to Jerusalem and was praying in the temple,

18 I saw a vision, saying to me, Make haste and get quickly out of Jerusalem; for they will not receive your testimony concerning me.

19 And I said, My Lord, they know that I imprisoned and beat in every synagogue those who believed in you;

20 And when the blood of your martyr Stephen was shed, I also was standing by and was in accord with his slayers, and was in charge of the garments of them who stoned him.

21 Then he said to me, Depart; for I will send you afar to preach to the Gentiles.

22 ¶They had given Paul audience up to this word, and then they lifted up their voices and cried out, Away with such a fellow from the earth; for it is not right that he should live.

23 And as they cried out and cast off their robes and threw dust into the air,

24 The chief captain commanded him to be brought into the castle, and ordered that he should be examined by scourging, that he might know for what cause they cried so against him.

25 And when they had bound him with thongs, Paul said to the centurion who stood over him, Is it lawful for you to scourge a Roman citizen who is uncondemned?

26 When the centurion heard that, he went to the chief captain and said, Be careful what you do; for this man is a Roman citizen.

27 Then the captain came and said to him, Tell me, are you a Roman? Paul said, Yes.

28 And the captain answered, saying, I obtained Roman citizenship with a great sum of money. Paul answered, But I was born to it.

29 Immediately those who were ready to scourge him left him alone, and the captain was afraid when he found out that he was a Roman citizen, because he had bound him.

30 ¶The next day, because he desired to know the truthfulness of the charges which the Jews had brought against Paul, he unbound him and commanded the high priests and all their council to appear before him, and he took Paul and brought him down and set him before them.

CHAPTER 23

AND as Paul beheld their assembly, he said, Men, my brethren, I have lived in all good conscience before God until this day.

2 ¶And the high priest Ananias commanded those who stood by his side to strike Paul on the mouth.

3 Then Paul said to him, God shall smite you, O you hypocrite; for you sit to judge me according to the law, yet you yourself transgress the law, when you command that I be smitten.

4 And those who stood by said to him, Do you even revile the high priest of God?

5 Then Paul said to them, Brothers, I did not know that he was a high priest; for it is written, You shall not revile the ruler of your people.

6 Now when Paul perceived that part of the people were Sadducees and the others were Pharisees, he cried out in the assembly, Men, my brethren, I am a Pharisee, the son of a Pharisee; and it is because of the hope of the resurrection of the dead that I am here to be judged.

7 And when he had said this, there arose a dissension between the Pharisees and the Sadducees; and the people were divided.

8 For the Sadducees say there is no resurrection, neither angels nor soul; but the Pharisees believe in them.

9 Then there arose a great cry; and the scribes that were of the party of the Pharisees rose up and argued, saying, We find no fault with this man; and if a spirit or an angel has spoken to him, there is nothing wrong in that.

10 ¶And because there was a great disturbance among them, the chief captain, fearing that they might tear Paul to pieces, sent Roman soldiers to go and seize him from among them and bring him into the castle.

11 During the night, our Lord appeared to Paul and said, Be strong, for as you have testified concerning me at Jerusalem, so also you are to testify at Rome.

12 And when it was morning, certain of the Jews banded together and bound themselves under oath that they would neither eat nor drink till they had killed Paul.

13 And those who had sworn to this conspiracy were more than forty persons.

14 And they went to the priests and elders and said, We have bound ourselves under an oath not to taste anything till we have killed Paul.

15 Now you and the leaders of the council ask the captain to bring him to you, as though you were desirous to have a thorough investigation of his acts, and we are ready to kill him before he shall arrive here.

16 When Paul's nephew heard this plot, he went into the castle and told Paul.

17 Then Paul sent for and called one of the centurions and said, Take this young man to the captain, for he has something to tell him.

18 So the centurion took the young man and brought him to the chief captain and said, Paul, the prisoner, called me and begged me to bring this young man to you, for he has something to tell you.

19 Then the captain took the young man by his hand, and drew him aside and asked him, What have you to tell me?

20 And the young man said to him, The Jews have decided to ask you to bring Paul down tomorrow to their council, as though they were desirous to learn something more from him.

21 You must not listen to them; for behold more than forty of them, who have bound themselves with an oath neither to eat nor to drink till they have killed him, are lying in wait for him; and behold they are ready and awaiting your reply.

22 Then the captain dismissed the young man and charged him, Let no man know that you have informed me of these things.

23 ¶And he called to him two centurions and said, Go and make ready two hundred Roman soldiers to go to Cæsarea and seventy horsemen and two hundred spearmen to leave at nine o'clock tonight.

24 And provide also an animal that they may set Paul on and carry him safe to Felix the governor.

25 And he wrote a letter after this manner and gave it to them:

26 Claudius Lysias to the most excellent governor Felix, greetings:

27 This man was seized by the Jews who intended to kill him; but I intervened with Roman soldiers and rescued him when I understood he was a Roman citizen.

28 And because I wanted to know the cause for which they accused him, I took him down to their council.

29 And I found that only concerning questions of their law was he accused, and that he had done nothing worthy of bonds or of death.

30 And when I was informed that the Jews had plotted secretly against him, I immediately sent him to you, and I have ordered his accusers to go and contend with him before you. Farewell.

31 ¶Then the Roman soldiers, as it was commanded them, took Paul and brought him by night to the city of Antipatris.

32 And the next day the horsemen dismissed the footmen so that they might return to the castle;

33 And they brought him to Cæsarea, and delivered the letter to the governor, and also presented Paul before him.

34 And when the governor had read the letter, he asked Paul of what province he was. And when he learned that he was of Cilicia,

35 He said to him, I will give you an audience when your accusers arrive. And he commanded him to be kept in the Prætorium of Herod.

CHAPTER 24

AND after five days Ananias the high priest went down with the elders, together with Tertullus, the orator, and they informed the governor against Paul.

2 And when he was called forth, Tertullus began to accuse him, saying, It is through you that we enjoy great tranquility, and owing to your care many excellent things have been done for this people.

3 And we all, everywhere, receive your favors, O most excellent Felix.

4 But while I desire not to weary you with lengthy discussions, nevertheless, I beg you to hear in brief our humble complaint.

5 We have found this man to be a pestilent fellow and a worker of sedition among the Jews throughout the world, for he is the ringleader of the sect of the Nazarenes.

6 He sought to defile our temple; therefore when we seized him, we would have judged him according to our law.

7 But the chief captain Lysias came, and by force took him away out of our hands and sent him to you;

8 Then he commanded his accusers to come to you. Now when you question him, you can learn for yourself concerning all these things of which we accuse him.

9 The Jews also witnessed against him, declaring that these things were true.

10 Then the governor beckoned to Paul to speak. Paul answered, saying, For inasmuch as I know that you have been a judge for many years to this people, therefore I do the more cheerfully answer in my own defense,

11 So that you may understand that it is not more than twelve days since I went up to Jerusalem to worship.

12 And they neither found me in the temple disputing with any man, nor have I had an assembly either in their synagogues or in the city;

13 Nor can they prove before you the things of which they accuse me.

14 But this I confess, that in that very teaching which they mention, I worship the God of my fathers, believing all the things which are written in the law and in the prophets;

15 And I have the same hope in God which they themselves hold, that there shall be a resurrection of the dead, both of the just and unjust.

16 For this reason, I labor to have always a clear conscience before God and before men.

17 Now after many years, I came to my own people to distribute alms and to present an offering.

18 So these men found me purifying myself in the temple, not in a crowd, nor in a riot, except the riot which was caused by the Jews who had come from Asia Minor,

19 Who ought to have been here with me before you to make whatever accusations they have against me.

20 Or else let these same people here say what fault they found in me when I stood before their council.

21 Except it be for this one saying which I cried, standing before them, It is for the resurrection of the dead that I am tried before you this day.

22 But because Felix was thoroughly familiar with this teaching, he deferred them, saying, When the chief captain comes down, I will give you a hearing.

23 And he commanded a centurion to keep Paul in comfort, and that none of his acquaintances should be prevented from looking after him.

24 ¶And after a few days, Felix with his wife Drusilla, who was a Jewess, sent for Paul and heard him concerning the Christian faith.

25 And as he spoke with them concerning righteousness, holiness, and the judgment to come, Felix was filled with fear and said, You may go, and when I have opportunity I will send for you.

26 Since he was expecting a bribe from Paul, he often sent for him to be brought and conversed with him.

27 And when Felix had completed two years, another governor succeeded him whose name was Porcius Festus; and Felix, to do the Jews a favor, left Paul a prisoner.

CHAPTER 25

NOW when Festus arrived at Cæsarea, after three days he went up to Jerusalem.

2 Then the high priests and Jewish leaders informed him against Paul.

3 They besought him as a favor to send for him and bring him to Jerusalem, for they were plotting to kill him on the way.

4 But Festus answered that Paul should be kept at Cæsarea, and that he himself was shortly going there.

5 Therefore, said he, let those who are able among you come down with us and accuse the man about any offense which can be found against him.

6 And when he had tarried in Jerusalem eight or ten days, he went down to Cæsarea, and the next day he sat on the judgment seat and commanded Paul to be brought.

7 And when he was come, the Jews who had come from Jerusalem surrounded him and brought against him many serious charges which they could not prove.

8 Then Paul answered, I have committed no offense against the Jewish law or against the temple or against Cæsar.

9 But Festus, because he was willing to do the Jews a favor, said to Paul, Would you be willing to go to Jerusalem and there be tried of these things before me?

10 Paul answered, saying, I stand before Cæsar's judgment seat, where I ought to be tried; I have done no wrong to the Jews, as you very well know.

11 If I had committed any crime or had done anything worthy of death, I should not refuse to die; but if there is no truth in the charges made against me, then no man may deliver me to them just to please them. I appeal to Cæsar.

12 Festus, when he had conferred with his counsellors, decreed, You have appealed to Cæsar. You will go to Cæsar.

13 ¶Some days later, King Agrippa and Bernice came down to Cæsarea to greet Festus.

14 And when they had been with him several days, Festus related Paul's case to the king, saying, There is a certain prisoner left by Felix;

15 And when I was in Jerusalem, the high priests and the elders of the Jews informed me about him, and asked to have judgment against him.

16 I told them, It is not the Roman custom to give up a man to be slain until his accusers come and accuse him face to face and give him a chance to defend himself against the charges.

17 So when I arrived here, the following day, without any delay, I sat on the judgment seat and commanded the man to be brought before me.

18 When his accusers stood up with him, they were unable to prove, as I had expected, any serious charges against him.

19 But they had certain grievances against him relative to their own worship and to one named Jesus, now dead, whom Paul affirmed to be alive.

20 And because I was not well acquainted with their controversy, I said to Paul, Would you be willing to go to Jerusalem and there be tried of these matters?

21 But he appealed to be kept as a prisoner for a trial before Cæsar. I accordingly commanded him to be kept in custody till I might send him to Cæsar.

22 Then Agrippa said to Festus, I would like to hear this man myself; and Festus replied, Tomorrow, you shall hear him.

23 ¶The next day Agrippa and Bernice came with great pomp, and entered into the court house, accompanied by the chief captains and principal men of the city. Festus commanded and Paul was brought in.

24 Then Festus said, King Agrippa and all men who are here present with us, against this man whom you see, all the Jewish people have complained to me both at Jerusalem and also here, crying that he ought not to live any longer.

25 But when I found he had done

nothing worthy of death, and because he himself had appealed to be kept in custody for a trial before Cæsar, I commanded to send him.

26 But I do not know what to write Cæsar concerning him, therefore I was pleased to bring him before you, and especially before you, O King Agrippa, so that when he is questioned, I may find something to write.

27 For it is not proper to send a prisoner, without writing down the charges against him.

CHAPTER 26

THEN Agrippa said to Paul, You have permission to speak in your own behalf. Whereupon Paul stretched forth his hand and answered, saying,

2 In view of all the things whereof I am accused by the Jews, I consider myself blessed, O King Agrippa, to defend myself today before you.

3 Especially because I know you are familiar with all the customs and questions and laws of the Jews; wherefore, I beg you to hear me patiently.

4 Even the Jews themselves, if they would be willing to testify, know well my manner of life from my childhood which started first among my own people at Jerusalem.

5 For they have been acquainted with me a long time, and know that I was brought up with the excellent doctrine of the Pharisees.

6 And now I stand and am on trial for the hope of the promise made by the God to our fathers.

7 It is to the fulfillment of this hope that our twelve tribes expect to arrive by means of earnest prayers day and night. And for this very hope's sake, I am accused by the Jews, O King Agrippa.

8 How can you judge? Is it improper to believe that God can raise the dead?

9 For at the very beginning I was determined that I ought to do many things contrary to the name of Jesus of Nazareth,

10 Which I also did at Jerusalem; I cast many of the saints into prison, having received authority from the chief priests; and when some were put to death, I took part with those who condemned them.

11 And I tortured them in every synagogue, thus compelling them to blaspheme the name of Jesus; and being exceedingly mad against them, I also went to other cities to persecute them.

12 I was on the way to Damascus for this purpose, with authority and commission from the chief priests, when,

13 At midday on the road, O king, I saw a light from heaven more powerful than that of the sun, shining round about me and upon those who journeyed with me.

14 When we all fell to the ground, then I heard a voice speaking to me, in the Hebrew tongue, Saul, Saul, why do you persecute me? It is hard for you to kick against the pricks.

15 And I said, My Lord, who are you? And our Lord said to me, I am Jesus of Nazareth whom you persecute.

16 Then he said to me, Rise and stand upon your feet; for I have appeared to you for this purpose, to appoint you a minister and a witness both of those things in which you have seen me and of those things in which you will also see me again.

17 And I will deliver you from the Jewish people and from the other peoples to whom I send you,

18 To open their eyes, that they may turn from darkness to light and from the power of Satan to God and receive forgiveness of sins and a portion with the saints who are of the faith in me.

19 Whereupon, O King Agrippa, I did not disobey the heavenly vision;

20 But I preached first to them of Damascus and at Jerusalem and throughout all the villages of Judea and then to the Gentiles, that they might repent and turn to God and do works worthy of repentance.

21 For these causes the Jews seized me in the temple and wanted to kill me.

22 But God has helped me to this

very day, and behold I stand and testify to the humble and to the great, saying nothing contrary to Moses and the prophets, but the very things which they said were to take place,

23 That Christ should suffer and that he should be the first to rise from the dead and that he should preach light to the people and to the Gentiles.

24 ¶And while Paul was pleading in this manner, Festus cried with a loud voice, Paul, you are overwrought. Much study has made you mad.

25 But Paul said to him, I am not mad, O most excellent Festus; but I speak the words of truth and soberness.

26 And King Agrippa is also familiar with these things, and this is why I am speaking openly before him, because I think not one of these words has been hidden from him; for they were not done in secret.

27 King Agrippa, do you believe the prophets? I know that you believe.

28 Then King Agrippa said to him, With little effort you almost persuade me to become a Christian.

29 And Paul said, I pray God that not only you, but also all of those who hear me today were as I am, except for these bonds.

30 ¶Then the king arose, and the governor and Bernice and they that sat with them;

31 And when they had departed, they talked between themselves, saying, This man has done nothing worthy of death or of imprisonment.

32 Then Agrippa said to Festus, This man could have been released had he not appealed to Cæsar.

CHAPTER 27

THEN Festus commanded him to be sent to Cæsar in Italy, and he delivered Paul together with other prisoners to a centurion of the company of Sebastian named Julius.

2 When we were ready to sail, we embarked in a ship of the city of Adramyttium, bound for Asia Minor, and there boarded the ship with us,

Aristarchus a Macedonian of the city of Thessalonica.

3 And the next day, we arrived at Sidon. And the centurion treated Paul with kindness, permitting him to visit his friends and to rest.

4 Then we sailed from there, and because the winds were contrary, we had to sail towards Cyprus.

5 And when we had sailed over the sea of Cilicia and Pamphylia, we arrived at Myra, a city of Lycia.

6 And there the centurion found a ship from Alexandria bound for Italy; and he put us on board.

7 And because for a number of days she sailed slowly, we arrived with difficulty towards the Island of Cnidus; and since the wind would not allow us to sail in a straight course, we had to sail around Crete towards the city of Salmone;

8 And after we had passed around it with difficulty, we arrived at a place which is called The Fair Havens; and nearby was the city of Lasea.

9 There we remained for a long time, even till the day of the Jewish fast was over and, since it had now become dangerous for any one to sail, Paul gave them advice,

10 Saying, Men, I see that this voyage will be beset with hardship and with great loss, not only of the cargo of our ship but also of our lives.

11 Nevertheless, the centurion listened to the master and owner of the ship more than to the words of Paul.

12 ¶And as the harbor was not commodious for wintering, many of us were desirous to sail from there, and if possible to reach and winter in a harbor at Crete which is called Phenice, which lies towards the south.

13 And when the south wind blew softly, they thought they could reach their destination as they had desired, and we sailed around Crete.

14 A short while after, there arose against us a hurricane called Typhonic Euroclydon.

15 And when the ship was caught and could not bear against the wind, we let her drive.

16 And as we passed under the lee of an island which is called Clauda,

we could hardly man the ship's boat.

17 And when we had launched it, we began undergirding and repairing the ship; and because we were afraid of grounding, we lowered the sail, and so we drifted.

18 And as the violent storm raged against us, the next day we threw our belongings into the sea.

19 And on the third day we cast overboard with our own hands the tackling of the ship.

20 And as the winter was so severe that for many days neither sun nor stars could be seen, all hope of surviving was given up.

21 Then as no man among them had eaten anything, Paul stood up in the midst of them, and said, Men, if you had listened to me, we would not have sailed from Crete, and we would have been spared this loss and suffering.

22 Now let me counsel you not to be depressed; for not a single life among you will be lost, but only the ship.

23 For there has appeared to me this night the angel of God to whom I belong and whom I serve,

24 And he said to me, Fear not, Paul; you must stand before Cæsar; and behold, God has granted you all of those who sail with you.

25 Therefore, men, be of good cheer; for I have confidence in God, that it shall be just as it was told me;

26 However, we will be cast upon an island.

27 And after fourteen days of being lost and weary in the sea of Adria, about midnight the sailors thought they were drawing near to land.

28 So they cast the sounding lead, and found twenty fathoms; and again, they sailed a little farther, and took soundings and found fifteen fathoms.

29 Then, fearing lest we find ourselves caught between the rocks, they cast four anchors from the stern of the ship, and prayed for the dawning of day.

30 The sailors sought to desert the ship; so they lowered the ship's boat into the sea, under pretense that they were going in it to make fast the ship to the land.

31 And when Paul found it out, he said to the centurion and to the soldiers, Unless these men remain on board the ship, you cannot be saved.

32 Then the soldiers cut off the ropes of the ship's boat from the ship and let her drift.

33 But Paul till the early morning kept begging them all to eat, saying to them, Today is the fourteenth day since you have tasted anything because of fear.

34 Wherefore, I pray you to take some food for the sustenance of your life; for not a hair shall be lost from the head of any of you.

35 And when he had thus spoken, he took bread and gave thanks to God in the presence of them all; and when he had broken it, they began to eat.

36 Then they were all cheerful, and received nourishment.

37 We were in all two hundred and seventy-six persons on board.

38 And when they had eaten enough, they lightened the ship by taking the wheat and throwing it into the sea.

39 When it was day, the sailors did not know what land it was; but they saw an inlet close to the shore, and thought if it were possible they would land the ship there.

40 So they cut off the anchors from the ship and threw them into the sea, and loosed the rudder ropes; then they hoisted the topsail to the wind and sailed toward shore.

41 But the ship struck on a shoal between two deep places in the sea and went aground; and the forward part rested upon the bottom and could not be moved, but the stern broke by the violence of the waves.

42 And the soldiers sought to kill the prisoners, lest some of them should swim away and so escape.

43 But the centurion stopped them from doing this, because he was willing to save Paul; so he commanded those who could swim to cast themselves first into the sea and get to land.

44 The others he made cross over on boards and on broken pieces of the ship. In this manner, all of them escaped and reached shore safely.

CHAPTER 28

AFTERWARDS they learned that the island was called Melita.

2 And the barbarians who inhabited it showed us much kindness; for they kindled a fire and called us all to warm ourselves, because of heavy rain and the cold.

3 And Paul picked up a bundle of sticks and laid them on the fire, and a viper, driven by the heat, came out and bit his hand.

4 And when the barbarians saw it hanging from his hand, they said, It may be that this man is a murderer, whom, though he has been rescued from the sea, yet justice does not permit him to live.

5 But Paul shook his hand and threw the viper into the fire and felt no harm.

6 However, the barbarians expected he would immediately swell up and fall to the ground dead; but after they had waited for a long while and saw he had not been harmed, they changed their talk and said that he was a god.

7 There were villages in that region, belonging to a man whose name was Publius, the chief man of the island; and he gladly received us at his house for three days.

8 But the father of Publius was sick with fever and dysentery; so Paul went in to where he was lying and prayed; then he laid his hand on him and healed him.

9 So when this was done, others also, sick in the island, came and were healed.

10 The inhabitants bestowed upon us great honors; and when we departed thence, they supplied us with provisions.

11 ¶After three months we left, sailing in an Alexandrian ship which had wintered in the island and which bore the sign of Castor and Pollux.

12 Landing at Syracuse, we remained there for three days.

13 From there we circled around and arrived at Rhegium. After a day the south wind blew in our favor, and in two days, we came to Puteoli, an Italian city,

14 Where we found brethren who invited us to stay; and we remained with them seven days; then we departed for Rome.

15 When the brethren there heard of our arrival, they came out to meet us as far as the street which is called Appiiforum and The Three Taverns. When Paul saw them, he thanked God and was greatly encouraged.

16 ¶Then we entered Rome; and the centurion gave permission to Paul to live wherever he pleased with a soldier to guard him.

17 And after three days, Paul sent and called the Jewish leaders; and when they were come together, he said to them, Men and my brethren, though I have done nothing against the people and the law of my fathers, yet I was delivered from Jerusalem in bonds into the hands of the Romans,

18 Who, when they had examined me, would have released me, because they found in me no cause worthy of death;

19 But as the Jews stood against me I was obliged to appeal to Cæsar, not that I had anything of which to accuse my own people.

20 This is the reason I begged you to come, for I wish to see you and to relate these things to you; because it is for the hope of Israel I am bound with this chain.

21 And they said to him, We have neither received a letter concerning you from Judea nor have any of the brethren who have come from Jerusalem made any evil report about you.

22 Nevertheless we desire to hear what you have to say; but if it is concerning this teaching, we know well that it is not acceptable to any one, and we do not want to hear about it.

23 So they appointed a day for him, and many gathered together and came to him where he was staying;

and he explained to them about the kingdom of God, thus testifying and persuading them concerning Jesus, both from the law of Moses and from the prophets, from morning till evening.

24 And some of them listened to his words, but others paid no attention.

25 And as they were dismissed, disagreeing among themselves, Paul said to them this saying, Well spoke the Holy Spirit by the mouth of the prophet Isaiah against your fathers,

26 Saying, Go to this people and say, Hearing you shall hear and shall not understand; and seeing you shall see and shall not perceive;

27 For the heart of this people is hardened and their ears are dull of hearing and their eyes have they closed; lest they should see with their eyes and hear with their ears and understand with their hearts, and repent before me, and I should forgive them.

28 ¶Let this be known to you therefore: this salvation of God is sent to the Gentiles, for they will listen to it.

29 And when he had said these words, the Jews departed, arguing much among themselves.

30 ¶And Paul hired a house for himself at his own expense and lived in it for two years; there he received all who came to him,

31 Preaching the kingdom of God and teaching openly about our Lord Jesus Christ without hindrance.

THE EPISTLE OF PAUL THE APOSTLE TO THE

ROMANS

CHAPTER 1

PAUL, a servant of Jesus Christ, called to be an apostle and chosen to proclaim the gospel of God

2 Which was promised from early days by his prophets in the holy scriptures,

3 Concerning his son who was born in the flesh of the seed of the house of David,

4 And who came to be known as the Son of God with power and with the Holy Spirit, because he arose from the dead, and he is Jesus Christ our Lord;

5 And by him we have received grace and apostleship among all the Gentiles, so that they may hear the faith which bears his name,

6 And you also are of them, and are called by the name of Jesus Christ;

7 To all who are in Rome, beloved of God, called and sanctified: Grace and peace to you from God our Father and from our Lord Jesus Christ.

8 ¶First, I thank my God through Jesus Christ for you all, that your faith has been heard of throughout the world.

9 For God, whom I serve in spirit in the gospel of his Son, is my witness that unceasingly I make mention of you in my prayers,

10 Beseeching that if the way is open to me by the will of God, I may come to you.

11 For I long to see you, and to impart to you the gift of the Spirit, in order that you may be strengthened by it,

12 And that we may be comforted together by our mutual faith.

13 Now I want you to know, my brethren, that often I have wanted to come to you, but I have been prevented thus far, that I might have

some fruit among you also, even as among other Gentiles,

14 Greeks and Barbarians, the wise and the unwise; for it is my duty to preach to everybody.

15 So I am eager to preach the gospel to you who are in Rome also.

16 ¶For I am not ashamed of the gospel of Christ; for it is the power of God to salvation to every one who believes, whether they are Jews first, or Arameans (Syrians).

17 For therein is the righteousness of God revealed from faith to faith; as it is written, The righteous shall live by faith.

18 ¶For the wrath of God is revealed from heaven against all the iniquity and wickedness of men who unjustly suppress the truth;

19 Because that which may be known of God is manifested to them, for God has revealed it to them.

20 For, from the very creation of the world, the invisible things of God have been clearly seen and understood by his creations, even his eternal power and Godhead; so that they are without excuse.

21 For they knew God and did not glorify him and give thanks to him as God, but became vain in their imaginations, and their hearts were darkened so that they could not understand.

22 And while they thought within themselves that they were wise, they became fools,

23 And they have changed the glory of the incorruptible God for an image made in the likeness of corruptible man, and in the likeness of birds and of four-footed beasts and of creeping things on the earth.

24 That is why God also gave them up to uncleanness through the lusts of their hearts, to dishonor their own bodies among themselves;

25 And they have changed the truth of God for lies, and worshipped and served the created things more than their Creator to whom belong glory and blessings for ever. Amen.

26 Therefore God has given them up to vile passions; for even their women have changed the natural use

of their sex into that which is unnatural;

27 And likewise also their men have left the natural use of the women and have run wild with lust toward one another, male with male committing shameful acts, and receiving in themselves the due recompense of their error.

28 And as they did not consent in themselves to know God, God has given them over to a weak mind, to do the things which should not be done; as,

29 Being filled with all manner of iniquity, fornication, bitterness, malice, extortion, envy, murder, strife, deceit, evil thoughts.

30 They are slanderers, backbiters, haters of God, revilers, proud boasters, inventors of evil things, weakminded, disobedient to their parents;

31 These have no respect for a covenant. They know neither love nor peace, nor is there mercy in them;

32 Knowing the judgment of God, that those who commit such things, he condemns to death, they not only do them, but also associate with those who practice them.

CHAPTER 2

THEREFORE you are inexcusable, O man, to judge your neighbor; for in judging your neighbor, you condemn yourself; for even you who judge practice the same things yourself.

2 But we know that the judgment of God is rightly against those who commit such things.

3 What do you think, O man? Do you think that you who judge those who practice such things, while you commit them yourself, will escape the judgment of God?

4 Do you stand against the riches of his goodness and forbearance, and the opportunity which he has given you, not knowing that the goodness of God leads you to repentance?

5 Because of the hardness and impenitence of your heart you are laying up for yourself a treasure of wrath for the day of wrath and the

revelation of the righteous judgment of God,

6 Who will render to every man according to his deeds:

7 To those who continue patiently in good works, seeking glory and honor and immortality, he will give eternal life;

8 But to those who are stubborn and do not obey the truth, but obey iniquity, he will render indignation and wrath;

9 He will render suffering and affliction, for every man who does evil, for the Jews first, and also for the Arameans;

10 But glory, honor and peace for every one who does good, to the Jews first, and also to the Arameans;

11 For there is no respect of persons with God.

12 For those who have sinned without law shall also perish without law; and those who have sinned in the law shall be judged by the law,

13 For it is not the hearers of the law who are righteous before God, but it is the doers of the law who shall be justified.

14 For if the Gentiles, who do not have the law, do by nature the things contained in the law, these having not the law are a law to themselves.

15 And they show the work of the law written on their hearts; and their conscience also bears them witness, when their thoughts either rebuke or defend one another,

16 In the day when God shall judge the secrets of men according to my gospel by Jesus Christ.

17 ¶Now if you who are called a Jew trust on the law and are proud of God,

18 And because you know his will and know the things which must be observed, which you have learned from the law,

19 And you have confidence in yourself that you are a guide of the blind and a light to them who are in darkness,

20 An instructor of the foolish, a teacher of children, you are the pattern of knowledge and of truth as embodied in the law.

21 Now, therefore, you teach others but fail to teach yourself. You preach that men should not steal, yet you steal.

22 You say, Men must not commit adultery, yet you commit adultery. You despise idols, yet you rob the sanctuary.

23 You are proud of the law but you dishonor God by breaking the law.

24 For the name of God is blasphemed among the Gentiles through you, as it is written.

25 ¶For circumcision is profitable only if you keep the law; but if you break the law, then circumcision becomes uncircumcision.

26 Therefore, if the uncircumcision keep the statutes of the law, behold would not the uncircumcision be counted for circumcision?

27 And the uncircumcision which fulfills the law naturally, will condemn you who, while in possession of the scripture and circumcision, transgress the law.

28 For it is not the one who is outwardly a Jew who is the real Jew; neither is circumcision that which is seen in the flesh.

29 But a real Jew is one who is inwardly so, and circumcision is of the heart, spiritually and not literally; whose praise is not from men but from God.

CHAPTER 3

WHAT then is the superiority of the Jew? or what is the importance of circumcision?

2 Much in every way; because the Jews were the first to believe in the words of God.

3 For what if some had not believed, could their unbelief nullify the faith of God?

4 Far be it; only God is true and no man is wholly perfect; as it is written, That you may be justified by your words, and triumph when you are judged.

5 Now if our iniquity serves to establish the righteousness of God, what then shall we say? Is God unjust

when he inflicts his anger? I speak as a man.

6 Far be it; for then how could God judge the world?

7 For if the truth of God is made abundant through my falsehood to his glory, why then am I to be judged as a sinner?

8 As for those who blaspheme against us, saying that we say, Let us do evil that good may come; their condemnation is reserved for eternal justice.

9 ¶What then do we uphold that is superior? We have already decided concerning both Jews and Arameans, for they are all under sin.

10 As it is written, There is none righteous, no, not one;

11 There is none who understands, there is none who seeks after God.

12 They are all gone astray and they have been rejected; there is none who does good, no, not one.

13 Their throats are like open sepulchres; their tongues are deceitful; the venom of asps is under their lips.

14 Their mouths are full of cursing and bitterness.

15 They are overquick to shed blood.

16 Destruction and misery are in their ways.

17 They have not known the path of peace.

18 There is no fear of God before their eyes.

19 Now we know that whatever the law says, it is said to those who are under the law, so that every mouth may be shut, and all the world may become guilty before God.

20 For by the deeds of the law, no flesh shall be justified before his presence; for by means of the law, sin is known.

21 ¶But now the righteousness of God without the law is manifested, and the very law and prophets testify to it;

22 But the righteousness of God is by the faith of Jesus Christ to every one, also to every man who believes in him, for there is no discrimination;

23 For all have sinned and are short of the glory of God;

24 For they are freely given righteousness by the grace of God through the salvation which is in Jesus Christ,

25 Whom God has foreordained to be a propitiation through faith in his blood for the remission of our sins that are past;

26 By the opportunity which God has given us through his forbearance, for the manifestation of his righteousness at the present time, that he might be declared righteous; and for the justification of righteousness to him who is in the faith of our Lord Jesus Christ.

27 Where is boasting then? It is worthless. By what law? of works? No; but by the law of faith.

28 Therefore we conclude that it is by faith a man is justified and not by the works of the law.

29 Why? Is God the God of the Jews only? Is he not also God of the Gentiles? Yes, he is God of the Gentiles also;

30 For it is one God, who justifies the circumcision by faith, and uncircumcision by the same faith.

31 What, then? Do we nullify the law through faith? Far be it; on the contrary, we uphold the law.

CHAPTER 4

WHAT then shall we say concerning Abraham, the chief of our forefathers, who lived according to the flesh before God called him?

2 For if Abraham was justified by works, he had reason to be proud; but not before God.

3 For what said the scripture? Abraham believed in God, and it was counted to him for righteousness.

4 But to him who works, wages are not considered as a favor but as that which is due to him.

5 And to him who works not, but only believes in him who justifies sinners, his faith is counted for righteousness.

6 Just as David also said about the blessedness of the man whom God declared righteous without works,

7 Saying, Blessed are they whose iniquities are forgiven, and whose sins are wiped away.

8 Blessed is the man whose sins God will not hold against him.

9 Now, therefore, is this blessedness on account of circumcision or on account of uncircumcision? For we say that Abraham's faith was accounted to him for righteousness.

10 How then was it given to him? by means of circumcision or in uncircumcision? It was not given in circumcision, but in uncircumcision.

11 For he received circumcision as a sign and a seal of the righteousness of his faith while he was uncircumcised, that he might become the father of all those who believe, though they be not circumcised, that righteousness might be reckoned also to them,

12 So that the father of circumcision is not only to those who are of circumcision, but also to those who walk in the steps of the faith of our father Abraham while he was yet uncircumcised.

13 For the promise to Abraham and his posterity that he should inherit the world was not made through the law, but through the righteousness of his faith.

14 For if they had become heirs by means of the law, then faith would have been empty and the promise made of no effect.

15 For the law causes provocation; for where there is no law, there is no transgression.

16 Therefore it is by faith that we will be justified by grace, so that the promise might be sure to all his posterity, not only to him who is of the law, but also to him who is of the faith of Abraham who is the father of us all;

17 As it is written, I have made you a father of many peoples, in the presence of the God in whom you have believed, who quickens the dead, and who invites those who are not yet in being, as though they were present.

18 For he who was hopeless trusted in hope, that he might become the father of many peoples; as it is written, So shall your descendants be.

19 His faith never weakened even when he examined his old body when he was a hundred years old, and the deadness of Sarah's womb.

20 He did not doubt the promise of God as one who lacks faith; but his faith strengthened him, and he gave glory to God.

21 He felt assured that what God had promised him, God was able to fulfill.

22 Therefore his faith was reckoned to him for righteousness.

23 ¶That his faith was reckoned for righteousness was not written for his sake alone,

24 But for us also; for he will number us also, who believe in him who raised our Lord Jesus Christ from the dead;

25 Who was delivered up for our offences and arose that he might justify us.

CHAPTER 5

THEREFORE, being justified by faith, let us have peace with God through our Lord Jesus Christ;

2 Through him we have been brought by faith into this grace wherein we stand, and are proud in the hope of the glory of God.

3 And not only so, but we also glory in our tribulations; knowing that tribulation perfects patience in us;

4 And patience, experience; and experience, hope;

5 And hope causes no one to be ashamed; because the love of God is poured into our hearts by the Holy Spirit which is given to us.

6 But Christ at this time, because of our weaknesses, died for the sake of the wicked.

7 Hardly would any man die for the sake of the wicked; but for the sake of the good, one might be willing to die.

8 God has here manifested his love toward us, in that, while we were yet sinners, Christ died for us.

9 Much more then, being justified by his blood, we shall be delivered from wrath through him.

10 For if when we were enemies, we were reconciled to God by the death

of his Son, much more, being reconciled, we shall be saved by his life.

11 And not only so, but we also glory in God through our Lord Jesus Christ, by whom we have now received the reconciliation.

12 ¶Just as sin entered into the world by one man, and death by means of sin, so death was imposed upon all men, inasmuch as they all have sinned;

13 For until the law was given, though sin was in the world, it was not considered sin, because there was no law.

14 Nevertheless, death reigned from Adam to Moses, even over them who had not sinned in the manner of the transgression of the law by Adam, who is the likeness of him that was to come.

15 But the measure of the gift of God was not the measure of the fall. If therefore, because of the fall of one, many died, how much more will the grace and gift of God, because of one man, Jesus Christ, be increased for many?

16 And the effect of the gift of God was greater than the effect of the offence of Adam; for while the judgment from one man's offence resulted in condemnation of many, the gift of God in forgiveness of sins resulted in righteousness to many more.

17 For if by one man's offence, death reigned, how much more those who receive abundance of grace and of the gift of righteousness shall reign in life by one, Jesus Christ.

18 In like manner as by one man's offence, condemnation came upon all men, even so by the righteousness of one man will the victory to life be to all men.

19 For as by one man's disobedience many were made sinners, so by the obedience of one man shall many be made righteous.

20 The introduction of the law caused sin to increase, and when sin had increased, grace became abundant.

21 Just as sin had reigned through death, so grace shall reign through righteousness to eternal life by our Lord Jesus Christ.

CHAPTER 6

WHAT shall we then say? Shall we continue in sin that grace may abound?

2 Far be it. How shall we who are dead to sin continue to live in it?

3 Do you not know that those of us who have been baptized into Jesus Christ have been baptized into his death?

4 Therefore, we are buried with him by baptism into death, so that as Jesus Christ rose from the dead by the glory of his Father, even so we also shall walk in a new life.

5 For if we have been planted together with him in the likeness of his death, so shall we be also in the likeness of his resurrection:

6 For we know that our old selves are crucified with him, so that the sinful body might be destroyed, that henceforth we should not serve sin.

7 For he who is dead is freed from sin.

8 Now if we are dead with Christ, let us believe that we shall also live with Christ.

9 We know that Christ rose from the dead, and dies no more; and that death has no more dominion over him.

10 For in dying he died once to sin; and in living he lives to God.

11 Likewise, you also must consider yourself as being dead to sin, but alive to God through Jesus Christ our Lord.

12 Let not sin therefore reign in your mortal body, that you should obey it in the lusts thereof.

13 Neither should you yield your members as instruments of iniquity to sin; but yield yourselves to God, just as if you were men who had risen from among the dead, and let your members be instruments of righteousness to God.

14 Sin shall not have dominion over you; for you are no longer under the law, but under grace.

15 ¶What then? Shall we sin because we are not under the law but under grace? Far be it.

16 Do you not know that to whom you yield yourselves servants to obey, his servants you are; for you obey

him, whether it be to sin or whether it be of obedience to righteousness?

17 But thank God that you, who were once the servants of sin, now obey from the heart that form of doctrine which has been delivered to you.

18 Now, being made free from sin, you become the servants of righteousness.

19 I speak after the manner of men because of the weakness of your flesh; for as you have yielded your members to the servitude of uncleanness and iniquity, so now yield your members to the servitude of righteousness and holiness.

20 For when you were the servants of sin, you were free from righteousness.

21 What kind of fruit did you have then in the things of which you are now ashamed? For the end thereof is death.

22 But now being made free from sin and become servants of God, your fruits are holy, and the end thereof is life everlasting.

23 For the wages of sin is death; but the gift of God is eternal life through our Lord Jesus Christ.

CHAPTER 7

DO you not know, my brethren, I speak to them who know the law, that the law has authority over a person as long as he lives?

2 Just as a woman is bound by the law to her husband as long as he lives; but if her husband should die, she is freed from the law of her husband.

3 Thus if, while her husband is alive, she should be attached to another man, she becomes an adulteress; but if her husband is dead, she is free from the law, so that she is not an adulteress though she becomes another man's wife.

4 Wherefore, my brethren, you also are become dead to the law by the body of Christ, that you might become another's, even to him who arose from the dead, so that you may bring forth fruit to God.

5 For when we were in the flesh, the pains of sin, which were by the law, worked in our members to bring forth fruits to death.

6 But now we are freed from the law, being dead to that which had hold upon us; and we should henceforth serve in newness of spirit and not in the oldness of the letter.

7 ¶What shall we say then? Is the law sin? Far be it. I would not have known the meaning of sin except by means of the law; for I would never have known the meaning of covetousness unless the law said, Thou shalt not covet.

8 So by means of this commandment, sin found an occasion and provoked in me every kind of desire. For without the law sin was dead.

9 Formerly I lived without the law; but when the commandment came, sin came to life and I died.

10 And the commandment which was ordained to life I found to be for death.

11 For sin, finding occasion by the commandment, misled me and by it killed me.

12 Wherefore the law is holy and the commandment holy and just and good.

13 ¶Has then that which is good become death to me? Far be it. But sin that is exposed as sin, and works death in me for that which is good, will be the more condemned by means of the law.

14 For we know that the law is spiritual; but I am of the flesh enslaved to sin.

15 For I do not know what I do; and I do not do the thing which I want, but I do the thing which I hate. That is exactly what I do.

16 So then if I do that which I do not wish to do, I can testify concerning the law that it is good.

17 Now then it is not I who do it, but sin which dominates me.

18 Yet I know that it does not fully dominate me (that is in my flesh); but as far as good is concerned, the choice is easy for me to make, but to do it is difficult for me.

19 For it is not the good that I wish to do, that I do; but it is the evil that I do not wish to do, that I do.

20 Now if I do that which I do not wish, then it is not I who do it, but the sin which dominates me.

21 I find therefore that the law agrees with my conscience when I wish to do good, but evil is always near, distracting me.

22 For I delight in the law of God after the inward man;

23 But I see another law in my members, warring against the law of my mind, and it makes me a captive to the law of sin which is in my members.

24 O wretched man that I am! Who shall deliver me from this mortal body?

25 I thank God for deliverance through our Lord Jesus Christ. Now therefore with my mind I am a servant of the law of God; but with my flesh I am a servant of the law of sin.

CHAPTER 8

THERE is therefore no condemnation to them who walk in the flesh after the Spirit of Jesus Christ.

2 For the law of the Spirit of life which is in Jesus Christ has made you free from the law of sin and death.

3 For the law was weak through the weakness of the flesh, so God sent his own Son in the likeness of sinful flesh, on account of sin, in order to condemn sin by means of his flesh,

4 That the righteousness of the law might be fulfilled in us; for we do not walk after the things of the flesh, but after the Spirit.

5 For they who are after the flesh mind the things of the flesh; but they who are after the Spirit mind the things of the Spirit.

6 To be carnally minded is death; but to be spiritually minded is life and peace,

7 Because the carnal mind is enmity against God; for it is not subject to the law of God, because it cannot be.

8 So then, they who are in the flesh cannot please God.

9 But you are not in the flesh but in the spirit, if the Spirit of God truly dwells within you. Now if any man does not have the Spirit of Christ, he does not belong to him.

10 And if Christ is within you, the body is dead because of sin; but the Spirit is life because of righteousness.

11 And if the Spirit of him who raised our Lord Jesus Christ from the dead dwells within you, so he who raised Jesus Christ from the dead will also quicken your mortal bodies by his Spirit that dwells within you.

12 ¶Therefore, my brethren, we are not indebted to the flesh to live after the flesh.

13 For if you live after the flesh, you will die; but if you, through the Spirit, subdue the deeds of the body, you shall live.

14 Those who are led by the Spirit of God are the sons of God.

15 For you have not received the spirit of bondage, to be in fear again; but you have received the Spirit of adoption, whereby we cry, Abba, Abon, Father, our Father.

16 And this Spirit bears witness to our spirit, that we are the children of God;

17 And if children, then heirs, heirs of God and joint heirs with Jesus Christ; so that if we suffer with him, we shall also be glorified with him.

18 ¶For I think that the sufferings of the present time are not worthy to be compared with the glory which shall be revealed in us.

19 For the earnest expectation of all mankind waits for the manifestation of the sons of God.

20 For man was made subject to vanity, not willingly, but by reason of him who gave him free will in the hope he would choose rightly,

21 Because man himself shall be delivered from the bondage of corruption into the glorious liberty of the children of God.

22 For we know that the whole creation groans and labors in pain to this day.

23 ¶And not only they, but ourselves also, who have the first fruits of the Spirit, even we groan within ourselves, waiting for the adoption, that is, the salvation of our bodies.

24 For we live in hope; but hope that is seen is not hope: for if we see it, why should we yet hope?

25 But if we hope for that which we do not see, then do we wait for it in patience.

26 Likewise the Spirit also helps our weaknesses; for we do not know what is right and proper for us to pray for; but the Spirit prays for us with that earnestness which cannot be described.

27 And he who searches the hearts knows what is the mind of the Spirit, for the Spirit prays for the saints according to the will of God.

28 ¶And we know that those who love God are helped by him in everything for good.

29 He knew them in advance and he marked them with the likeness of the image of his Son that he might be the first-born among many brethren.

30 Moreover, those whom he marked in advance, he has called, and those whom he has called, he has declared righteous, and those whom he has declared righteous, he has glorified.

31 What then shall we say concerning these things? If God be for us, who can be against us?

32 If he did not spare his own Son, but delivered him up for us all, why will he not freely give us all things with him?

33 Who is to complain against the chosen ones of God? It is God who justifies.

34 Who is he who condemns? It is Christ who died and rose again, and he is at the right hand of God making intercession for us.

35 What shall separate me from the love of Christ? Tribulation or imprisonment or persecution or famine or nakedness or peril or sword?

36 As it is written, For your sake we die every day, and we are accounted as lambs for the slaughter.

37 But in all these things we are more than conquerors through him who loved us.

38 For I am persuaded that neither death nor life nor angels nor empires nor armies nor things present nor things to come

39 Nor height nor depth nor any-

thing else created shall be able to separate me from the love of God which is in Jesus Christ our Lord.

CHAPTER 9

I TELL the truth through Christ, and I do not lie, my conscience also bears me witness through the Holy Spirit,

2 That I am exceedingly sorrowful, and the pain which is in my heart never ceases.

3 For I have prayed that I myself might be accursed because of Christ for the sake of my brethren and my kinsmen according to the flesh,

4 Who are Israelites; to whom belongs the adoption and the glory and the covenants and the law, and the rituals therein, and the promises,

5 And the fathers, from among whom Christ appeared in the flesh, who is God over all, to whom are due praises and thanksgiving, for ever and ever. Amen.

6 It is not as though the word of God had actually failed. For all those who belong to Israel are not Israelites;

7 Neither, because they are of the seed of Abraham are they all his children; for it was said, In Isaac shall your descendants be called.

8 That is, it is not the children of the flesh who are the children of God; but the children of the promise who are reckoned as descendants.

9 For this is the word of promise: I will come at this season, and Sarah shall have a son.

10 And not only this; but Rebecca also, even though she had intimacy with one only, our father Isaac;

11 Before her children were born or had done good or evil, the choice of God was made known in advance; that it might stand, not by means of works, but through him who made the choice.

12 For it was said, The elder shall be the servant of the younger.

13 As it is written, Jacob have I loved but Esau have I set aside.[1]

14 ¶What shall we say then? Is there injustice with God? Far be it.

15 For he said to Moses also, I will

[1] Not favored like Jacob.

have mercy on him whom I love, and I will have compassion on him whom I favor.

16 Therefore, it is not within reach of him who wishes, nor within the reach of him who strives, but it is within the reach of the merciful God.

17 For in the scripture, he said to Pharaoh, It was for this purpose that I have appointed you, that I might show my power in you, so that my name might be preached throughout all the earth.

18 Thus he has mercy on whom he pleases, and he hardens whom he pleases.

19 Perhaps you will say, Why then does he yet find fault? For who can resist his will?

20 However, O man, who are you to question God? Shall the thing formed say to him who formed it, Why have you made me like this?

21 Does not the potter have power over his clay, to make out of the same lump vessels, one for special occasions and the other for daily service?

22 Now then, if God wanted to show his anger and make his power known, would he not then, after the abundance of his patience, bring wrath upon the vessels of wrath which were ready for destruction?

23 But he poured his mercy upon the favored vessels, which were prepared for the glory of God;

24 Namely, ourselves, the called ones, not of the Jews only but also of the Gentiles.

25 As he said also in Hosea, I will call them my people, who were not my own people; and her beloved who was not beloved.

26 And it shall come to pass that in the place where it was said you are not my people, there shall they be called the children of the living God.

27 Isaiah also preached concerning the children of Israel, Though the number of children of Israel should be as the sand of the sea, only a remnant shall be saved.

28 For whatever the Lord has determined and decreed he shall bring to pass upon the earth.

29 Just as Isaiah had said before, If the Lord of Hosts had not increased the remnant, we should have been like Sodom, and should have resembled Gomorrah.

30 ¶What shall we say then? That the Gentiles who followed not after righteousness have attained to righteousness; that is, the righteousness which is the result of faith.

31 But Israel, who followed after the law of righteousness, has not attained to the law of righteousness.

32 Why? Because it was not sought by faith but by the works of the law. So they stumbled at that stumbling-stone.

33 As it is written, Behold, the prophet I give to Zion becomes a stumbling-stone, and rock of offence; but whoever believes in him shall not be ashamed.[1]

CHAPTER 10

MY brethren, my heart's desire and prayer to God for Israel is that they might be saved.

2 For I can testify for them that there is in them a zeal for God, but not according to the true knowledge.

3 For they know not the righteousness of God, but seek to establish their own righteousness, and because of this, they have not submitted themselves to the righteousness of God.

4 For Christ is the end of the law for righteousness to every one who believes.

5 ¶For Moses writes of the righteousness of the law thus: Whoever shall do these things shall live by them.

6 But the righteousness which is of faith, says thus: Do not say in your heart, Who has ascended to heaven and brought Christ down to earth?

7 And who has descended into the abyss of Sheol and brought up Christ from the dead?

8 But what does it say? The answer is near to you, even in your mouth and in your heart, that is, the word of faith which we preach;

9 So if you will confess with your mouth our Lord Jesus and will believe in your heart that God raised

---

[1] Jesus was the rock of offence which the builders rejected.

him from the dead, you shall be saved.

10 For the heart which believes in him shall be declared righteous, and the mouth that confesses him shall live.

11 For the scripture says, Whosoever believes in him shall not be ashamed.

12 And in this, it does not discriminate between the Jews and the Arameans; for the same Lord over all is rich to all who call upon him.

13 For whoever shall call on the name of the Lord shall be saved.

14 ¶How then can they call on him in whom they have not believed? Or how can they believe in him whom they have never heard? Or how can they hear without a preacher?

15 Or how can they preach if they are not sent forth? As it is written, How beautiful are the feet of those who preach peace, and of those who bring good tidings!

16 But all have not heard the preaching of the gospel. For Isaiah said, My Lord, who has believed the echoes of our voice?

17 So then faith comes by hearing, and hearing by the word of God.

18 But I say, Have they not heard? And behold the echoes of their voices have gone out over all the earth, and their words to the ends of the world.

19 But I say, Did not Israel know? First Moses spoke thus: I will provoke you to jealousy by a people that are not my people, and I will make you angry by a stubborn people.

20 Then Isaiah dared to say, I appeared to those who did not seek me, and was found by those who did not ask for me.

21 But to Israel he said, All the day long I have stretched out my hands to a quarrelsome and disobedient people.

CHAPTER 11

I SAY, then, has God rejected his people? Far be it. For I also am an Israelite, a descendant of Abraham, of the tribe of Benjamin.

2 God has not rejected his people whom he foreknew. Do you not know what the scripture says of Elijah? How he complained to God against Israel, saying,

3 My Lord, they have killed thy prophets and demolished thine altars; and I am left alone, and they seek my life.

4 And it was said to him in a vision, Behold I have reserved for myself seven thousand men who have not fallen on their knees to worship Baal.

5 Even so at the present time a remnant is preserved, elected by grace.

6 And if by grace, then it is not by works; otherwise grace is no more grace. But if by works, then it is not by grace; otherwise work is no more work.

7 What then? Israel has not obtained what it sought; but the elected ones have obtained it, and the rest were dulled in their minds.

8 As it is written, God has given them a stubborn spirit, eyes that cannot see, and ears that cannot hear, to this very day.

9 And David said, Let their table become a snare and a trap and a stumbling-block and a reward to them.

10 Let their eyes be darkened, that they may not see, and let their backs be bowed down always.

11 ¶I say then, Have they stumbled that they should fall? Far be it. But rather by their stumbling salvation has come to the Gentiles, in order to make them zealous.

12 Now if their stumbling has resulted in riches to the world, and their condemnation in riches to the Gentiles, how much more is their restoration?

13 It is to you Gentiles that I speak, inasmuch as I am the apostle to the Gentiles, and perhaps magnify my ministry;

14 But if I am able to make those who are my flesh zealous, I may thus save some of them.

15 And if their rejection has resulted in reconciliation of the world, how much more will their restoration be? Indeed it will be life from the dead.

16 For if the first fruit is holy, the rest of the lump is also holy; and if the root is holy, so are the branches.

17 And if some of the branches

were cut off, and you who are a branch of a wild olive tree have been grafted in their place, and you have become a partaker of the root and fatness of the olive tree,

18 Do not boast over the branches. For if you boast, it is not you who sustains the root, but the root sustains you.

19 Perhaps you may say, The branches were cut off that I might be grafted in their place.

20 Well, they were cut off because of their unbelief, but you exist by faith. Be not highminded, but reverence God.

21 For if God did not spare the natural branches, it may well be he will not spare you.

22 Consider therefore the goodness and severity of God: on those who fell, severity; but on you, goodness, if you continue in his goodness; otherwise you also will be cut off.

23 And even they, if they do not abide in their unbelief, will be grafted in; for God is able to graft them in again.

24 For if you who have been cut from the wild olive tree, which is natural to you, and grafted contrary to your nature to become a good olive tree; how much more fruitful would they be, if they were grafted into their natural olive tree?

25 I am desirous, my brethren, that you should know this mystery, so that you may not be wise in your own conceits; for blindness of heart has to some degree befallen Israel, until the end of the Gentiles shall come.

26 And then all Israel shall be saved; as it is written, A deliverer shall come out of Zion, and he shall remove ungodliness from Jacob;

27 And then they shall have the same covenant from me, when I have forgiven their sins.

28 ¶Now according to the gospel, they are enemies for your sake. But according to election, they are beloved for the patriarchs' sakes.

29 For God does not withdraw his gift and his call.

30 Just as you were formerly disobedient to God and have now obtained mercy because of their disobedience,

31 Likewise, they are also disobedient now to the mercy which is upon you, that there may be mercy upon them also.

32 For God has included all men in disobedience, that he might have mercy on every man.

33 ¶O the depth of the riches, the wisdom, and the knowledge of God! For no man has searched his judgment, and his ways are inscrutable.

34 For who has known the mind of the Lord or who has been his counsellor?

35 Or who has first given to him and then received from him?

36 For of him and through him and to him are all things. To him be glory and blessing for ever and ever. Amen.

CHAPTER 12

I BESEECH you therefore, brethren, by the mercies of God, that you present your bodies a living sacrifice, holy and acceptable to God, by means of reasonable service.

2 Do not imitate the way of this world, but be transformed by the renewing of your minds, that you may discern what is that good and acceptable and perfect will of God.

3 For I say, through the grace which is given to me, to all of you, not to think of yourselves beyond what you ought to think; but to think soberly, every man according to the measure of faith which God has distributed to him.

4 For as we have many members in one body, and all members have not the same function,

5 So we, being many, are one body in Christ, and every one members one of another.

6 Having then gifts differing according to the grace that is given to us, some have the gift of prophecy, according to the measure of faith,

7 Some have the gift of ministration, in their ministry; and some of teaching, in their doctrine.

8 Some of consolation, in consoling; he that gives, let him do it with sincerity; he that rules, with diligence; he

that shows mercy, with cheerfulness.

9 Let not your love be deceitful. Abhor that which is evil; hold fast to that which is good.

10 Be kindly affectioned one to another with brotherly love; in honor preferring one another;

11 Not slothful in business, fervent in spirit, serving the Lord;

12 Rejoicing in hope, patient in tribulation, continuing instant in prayer.

13 Distributing to the necessity of saints, given to hospitality.

14 Bless them who persecute you; bless, and curse not.

15 Rejoice with them who rejoice, and weep with them who weep.

16 Be of the same mind one toward another. Mind not vain glory, but associate with those who are humble. Be not wise in your own conceits.

17 Recompense to no man evil for evil. But be diligent to do good things before the presence of all men.

18 If it be possible, as much as lies in you, live peaceably with all men.

19 Dearly beloved, avenge not yourselves, but rather restrain your wrath; for it is written, Vengeance is mine; I will execute justice for you, said the Lord.

20 Therefore if your enemy hunger, feed him; if he thirst, give him drink; for in so doing, you shall heap coals of fire on his head.

21 Be not overcome by evil, but overcome evil with good.

CHAPTER 13

LET every soul be subject to the sovereign authorities. For there is no power which is not from God; and those who are in authority are ordained by God.

2 Whoever therefore resists the civil authority, resists the command of God; and they who resist shall receive judgment to themselves.

3 For judges are not a menace to good works, but to evil. Now if you wish not to be afraid of authority, then do good, and you will be praised for it.

4 For the ruler is the minister of God to you for good. But if you do

that which is wrong, be afraid; for he is not girded with the sword in vain; for he is the minister of God, and an avenger of wrath upon those who commit crime.

5 Wherefore, we must be obedient, not only in fear of wrath, but also for our conscience sake.

6 For, for this reason you pay head tax also; for they are ministers of God who are in charge of these things.

7 Render therefore, to every one as is due to him, head tax to him who is in charge of head tax, duty to him who is in charge of taxes; reverence to whom reverence is due, and honor to whom honor is due.

8 Owe no man anything, but love one another; for he who loves his neighbor has fulfilled the law,

9 Which says, Thou shalt not kill, Thou shalt not commit adultery, Thou shalt not steal, Thou shalt not covet; and if there is any other commandment, it is fulfilled in this saying, namely, Thou shalt love thy neighbor as thyself.

10 Love does not work evil to his neighbor, because love is the fulfillment of the law.

11 Know this also, that now is the time and the hour that we should awake from our sleep, for now our salvation is nearer than when we believed.

12 The night is far spent, the day is at hand; let us therefore cast off the works of darkness, and let us put on the armor of light.

13 Let us walk decently, as in the daylight; not in clamor and drunkenness, not in the practice of immorality, not in envy and strife.

14 But clothe yourselves with our Lord Jesus Christ, and disregard the lusts of the flesh.

CHAPTER 14

ASSIST him who is weak in the faith. And do not waver in your reasoning.

2 For one believes that he may eat all things; another who is weak eats vegetables.

3 Let not him who eats despise him

who eats not; and let not him who eats not judge him who eats; for God has received him also.

4 Who are you to judge another man's servant? For if he is a success, he is a success to his master; and if he is a failure, he is a failure to his master. As for his success, he will succeed for it is in the power of his master to make him succeed.

5 One person values one day above another; another values all days alike. Let every man be sure in his own mind.

6 He who is mindful concerning a day's duty is considerate of his master; and every one who is not mindful concerning a day's duty is inconsiderate of his master. And he who is wasteful is detrimental to his master even though he confesses it to God; and he who is not wasteful is not wasteful to his master, yet he likewise tells it to God.

7 For none of us lives to himself, and none of us dies to himself.

8 For whether we live, we live to our Lord; and whether we die, we die to our Lord; whether we live therefore, or die, we belong to our Lord.

9 For to this end even Christ both died and came back to life, and rose to be Lord both of the dead and living.

10 Why, then, do you judge your brother? or why do you despise your brother? For we must all stand before the judgment seat of Christ.

11 For it is written, As I live, said the Lord, every knee shall bow to me, and every tongue shall confess me.

12 So then every one of us shall answer for himself to God.

13 Let us not therefore judge one another any more; but rather be mindful of this, that you should never place a stumbling-block in the way of your brother.

14 For I know and have confidence in the Lord Jesus, that nothing unclean comes from him; but to him who believes a thing to be unclean, to him only is it unclean.

15 But now if you have caused your brother to grieve on account of meat, then you are not living in harmony.

Do not make food a cause to destroy a man for whose sake Christ died.

16 Let not our blessings be a reproach to any one;

17 For the kingdom of God is not meat and drink, but righteousness and peace and joy in the Holy Spirit.

18 For he who serves Christ in these things is acceptable to God and is approved by men.

19 Now let us strive after peace and help one another.

20 And let us not, because of food, destroy the work of God. All things indeed are pure; but it is wrong for the man who eats with offence.

21 It is better that we neither eat meat nor drink wine nor do any other thing whereby we cause our brother to stumble.

22 You who have a certain belief, keep it to yourself, in the presence of God. Blessed is he who does not condemn himself by doing those things which he has selected.

23 For he who is doubtful and eats, violates his beliefs; for whatever is not of faith is sin.

CHAPTER 15

WE then who are strong ought to bear the weaknesses of the weak, and not seek to please ourselves.

2 Let every one of us please his neighbor in good and constructive ways.

3 For even Christ pleased not himself; but as it is written, The reproaches of those who reproached you have fallen on me.

4 For whatever was written of old was written for our learning, that we through patience and comfort of the scriptures might have hope.

5 Now the God of patience and consolation grant you to regard one another to be equally worthy through the example of Jesus Christ,

6 That you may with one mind and one mouth glorify God, even the Father of our Lord Jesus Christ.

7 Therefore be friendly and bear one another's burdens, just as Christ also brought you close to the glory of God.

8 ¶Now I say that Jesus Christ was a minister of the circumcision, for the truth of God, to confirm the promises made to the fathers,

9 And that the Gentiles might glorify God for his mercies which were poured upon them; as it is written, Therefore I will praise you among the Gentiles and sing to your name.

10 And again he says, Rejoice, Gentiles, with his people.

11 And again, he says, Praise the Lord, all Gentiles; and praise him, all nations.

12 And again Isaiah said, There shall be a root of Jesse, and he that shall rise will be a prince to the Gentiles; and in him shall the Gentiles trust.

13 Now may the God of hope fill you with all joy and peace so that by faith you may abound in hope, through the power of the Holy Spirit.

14 ¶And I myself am persuaded concerning you, my brethren, that you also are filled with the same goodness, and made perfect with all knowledge, able also to admonish others.

15 Nevertheless, my brethren, I have written rather boldly to you, in order to remind you of the grace which is given to me by God,

16 That I may become a minister of Jesus Christ among the Gentiles, ministering the gospel of God, that the offering up of the Gentiles might be acceptable and sanctified by the Holy Spirit.

17 I am proud therefore to glory in Jesus Christ before God.

18 For I can scarcely speak of anything which Christ has not wrought by me for the obedience of the Gentiles, by word and deed,

19 Through mighty miracles and wonders, and by the power of the Spirit of God; so that from Jerusalem I went round about as far as Illyricum, and I have fully preached the gospel of Christ.

20 And I have so striven to preach the gospel, not at any place where Christ's name had already been preached, because I did not want to build on another's foundation;

21 But as it is written, Those to whom he was never mentioned shall see him; and those who have not heard of him shall be made obedient.

22 This is the reason why I have been many times prevented from coming to you.

23 But now since I have no place in these countries and I have been desirous for many years past to come to you,

24 When I leave for Spain, I hope to come to see you; and I hope that you will escort me thence after I have more or less fully enjoyed my visit.

25 But now I am going to Jerusalem to minister to the saints.

26 For the brethren in Macedonia and Achaia have been pleased to take part in helping the poor saints who are at Jerusalem.

27 They have been eager to do it, because they are indebted to them, for if the Gentiles have been made partakers with them of their spiritual things, they are indebted to minister to them in material things.

28 When, therefore, I have accomplished this and have finished distributing to them this kind of help, I will cross over toward you on my way to Spain.

29 I know that when I come to you, I shall come in the fulness of the blessing of the gospel of Christ.

30 Now, I beseech you, my brethren, by our Lord Jesus Christ and by the love of the Spirit, that you should strive together with me in your prayer to God for me,

31 That I may be delivered from those who are disobedient in Judea, and that the assistance which I carry to the saints in Jerusalem may be well accepted.

32 So that I may come to you with joy by the will of God and may with you be refreshed.

33 Now may the God of peace be with you all. Amen.

CHAPTER 16

I ENTRUST to your care Phebe, our sister, who is a deaconess of the church which is at Cenchrea,

2 That you may receive her in our

Lord with the respect which is due saints, and that you may assist her in whatever she may need of you; for she has been a help to many and to me also.

3 Salute Priscilla and Aquila, fellow workers with me in Jesus Christ,

4 Who have risked their necks for my sake. I am not the only one grateful to them, but also all the churches of the Gentiles.

5 Likewise salute the congregation that is in their house. Salute my well beloved Epænetus, who is the first-fruits of Achaia to Christ.

6 Greet Mary, who has labored hard among you.

7 Salute Andronicus and Junia, my kinsmen, who were prisoners with me, and well-known among the apostles, and who were believers in Christ before me.

8 Greet Amplias, my beloved in our Lord.

9 Salute Urbane, our fellow worker in Christ, and Stachys, my beloved.

10 Salute Apelles, chosen in our Lord. Salute the members of the household of Aristobulus.

11 Salute Herodion, my kinsman. Greet the members of the household of Narcissus, who are in our Lord.

12 Salute Tryphena and Tryphosa, who labor in the Lord. Salute the beloved Persis, who labored hard in our Lord.

13 Salute Rufus, chosen in our Lord, and his mother, who is also a mother to me.

14 Salute Asyncritus, Phlegon, Hermas, Patrobas, Hermes, and the brethren who are with them.

15 Salute Philologus and Julia, Nereus and his sister, and Olympas and all the saints who are with them.

16 Salute one another with a holy kiss. The churches of Christ salute you.

17 ¶Now I beseech you, my brethren, beware of those who cause divisions and offences contrary to the doctrine which you have been taught; keep away from them.

18 For those who are such do not serve our Lord Jesus Christ, but their own belly; and by smooth words and fair speeches deceive the hearts of the simple people.

19 But your obedience is known to every one. I rejoice therefore on your behalf, and I want you to be wise in regard to good things and pure concerning evil things.

20 The God of peace will soon crush Satan under your feet. The grace of our Lord Jesus Christ be with you.

21 ¶Timotheus, my fellow worker, and Lucius and Jason and Sosipater, my kinsmen, salute you.

22 I Tertius, who wrote this epistle, salute you in the Lord.

23 Gaius, my host and host of the whole church, salutes you. Erastus, the chamberlain of the city, salutes you; and Quartus, a brother.

24 Now I entrust you to God, who will confirm you in my gospel which is preached concerning Jesus Christ, in the revelation of the mystery which was hidden since the world began,

25 But now is made manifest by the scriptures of the prophets; and by the command of the eternal God, and is made known to all the peoples for the obedience of faith;

26 For God is the only wise one, and to him be glory through Jesus Christ for ever and ever. Amen.

27 The grace of our Lord Jesus Christ be with you all. Amen.

THE FIRST EPISTLE OF PAUL THE APOSTLE

to the

CORINTHIANS

CHAPTER 1

PAUL, called to be an apostle of Jesus Christ through the will of God, and brother Sosthenes,

2 To the church of God which is at Corinth, the invited and holy ones who are sanctified by Jesus Christ, and to all of them in every place who invoke the name of our Lord Jesus Christ, both theirs and ours:

3 Grace be to you and peace from God our Father and from our Lord Jesus Christ.

4 ¶I thank my God always on your behalf, for the grace of God that has been given to you by Jesus Christ;

5 For in everything you are enriched by him in all utterance and in all knowledge;

6 Because the testimony of Christ has been confirmed in you,

7 And you do not lack any of his gifts but wait for the manifestation of our Lord Jesus Christ,

8 Who will also strengthen you to the end, so that you may be blameless in the day of our Lord Jesus Christ.

9 God, by whom you have been called to the fellowship of his Son Jesus Christ our LORD, is trustworthy.

10 ¶Now I beseech you, my brethren, in the name of our Lord Jesus Christ, to be of one accord, and let there be no divisions among you but be perfectly united in one mind and in one thought.

11 For I have been informed about you, my brethren, by the household of Chloe that there are disputes among you.

12 Now this I say because there are some among you who say, I am a fol-lower of Paul; and some who say, I am a follower of Apollos; and some who say, I am a follower of Kepa; and some who say, I am a follower of Christ.

13 Why? Is Christ divided? or was Paul crucified for you? or were you baptized in the name of Paul?

14 I confess to my God that I have baptized none of you except Crispus and Gaius;

15 So no man can say that I have baptized in my own name.

16 And I baptized also the household of Stephanas. I do not know whether I have baptized any one else.

17 ¶For Christ did not send me to baptize but to preach the gospel; and not to rely on the wisdom of words, lest the cross of Christ should be in vain.

18 For the preaching of the cross to those who have gone astray is foolishness; but to us who are saved it is the power of God.

19 For it is written, I will destroy the wisdom of the wise, and I will do away with the understanding of the prudent.

20 Where is the wise? where is the scribe? where is the learned of this world? Has not God made foolish the wisdom of this world?

21 Because all the wisdom which God had given was not sufficient for the world to know God, it pleased God to save those who believe by the simple gospel.

22 For the Jews demand signs and the Arameans seek after wisdom;

23 But we preach Christ crucified, which is a stumbling block to the Jews and foolishness to the Arameans;

24 But for those who are called,

both Jews and Arameans, Christ is the power of God and the wisdom of God;

25 Because the foolishness of God is wiser than men, and the weakness of God is stronger than men.

26 For consider also your own calling, my brethren, not many among you are wise in terms of worldly things and not many among you are mighty and not many among you belong to the nobility.

27 But God has chosen the foolish ones of the world to put the wise to shame; and God has chosen the weak ones of the world to embarrass the mighty;

28 And he has chosen those of humble families in the world, and the lowly and those who are insignificant, in order to belittle those who consider themselves important,

29 So that no man should boast in his presence.

30 But you also belong to God through Jesus Christ who, from God, is wisdom and righteousness and sanctification and salvation to all of us.

31 As it is written, He who glories, let him glory in the Lord.

CHAPTER 2

AND I, my brethren, when I came to you, did not come with excellency of speech, nor did I preach to you with learning the mystery of God.

2 For I did not pretend to know anything among you except Jesus Christ, and even him crucified.

3 And I was with you with much reverence for God and in trembling.

4 And my speech and my preaching were not with enticing words of wisdom, but in demonstration of the Spirit and of power,

5 So that your faith might not rest in the wisdom of men, but in the power of God.

6 Howbeit we do discuss wisdom with those who have comprehension, yet not the wisdom of this world nor of the rulers of this world who pass away;

7 But we discuss the wisdom of God shown in a mysterious way, and it is hidden, but God ordained it before the world for our glory.

8 This none of the rulers of the world knew; for had they known it, they would not have crucified the Lord of glory.

9 But as it is written, The eye has not seen and the ear has not heard and the heart of man has not conceived the things which God has prepared for those who love him.

10 But God has revealed them to us by his Spirit; for the Spirit searches everything, even the depths of God.

11 For what man knows the mind of man, save the spirit of man which is in him? Even so, no one knows the mind of God except the Spirit of God.

12 Now we have received not the spirit of the world, but the spirit that is from God, that we may understand the gifts that are given to us by God.

13 For the things which we discuss are not dependent on the knowledge of words and man's wisdom, but on the teaching of the Spirit; thus explaining spiritual things to the spiritually minded.

14 For the material man rejects spiritual things; they are foolishness to him; neither can he know them, because they are spiritually discerned.

15 But the spiritual man discerns every thing, and yet no man can discern him.

16 For who knows the mind of the Lord that he may teach it? But we have the mind of Christ.

CHAPTER 3

SO I, my brethren, could not converse with you as with spiritual men, but as with worldly men and even as with little children in Christ.

2 I have fed you with milk, and not with meat; for hitherto you were unable to eat it, and even now you are not ready for it;

3 Because you are still worldly; for as long as there is among you envying and strife and divisions, are you not worldly and still following the material things?

4 For while one says, I am a follower of Paul; and another, I am a

follower of Apollos; are you not worldly?

5 ¶Who then is Paul and who is Apollos, but ministers through whom you were converted; each one is gifted according as the Lord gave to him.

6 I have planted, Apollos watered; but God gave the increase.

7 So then neither he who plants, nor he who waters deserves the credit; but God who gives the increase.

8 Thus the planter and the waterer are equal; and each one shall receive his own wages according to his own labor.

9 For we work together with God; you are God's work and God's building.

10 According to the grace of God which is given to me, as a wise masterbuilder, I have laid the foundation, and another builds upon it. But let every man be careful how he builds thereon.

11 For other foundation can no man lay than that which is already laid, which is Jesus Christ.

12 Now if any man build on this foundation gold, silver, precious stones, wood, hay, stubble;

13 Every man's work shall be plainly seen; for the light of day shall expose it, because it shall be revealed by fire; and the fire shall test every man's work and show of what sort it is.

14 And the builder whose work survives shall receive his reward.

15 And the one whose work shall be burned, he shall suffer loss; but he himself shall be rescued, even as one who has been saved from the fire.

16 Do you not know that you are the temple of God, and that the Spirit of God dwells in you?

17 And whoever defiles the temple of God, God will destroy; for the temple of God is holy, and that temple is you.

18 ¶Let no man deceive himself. Whoever among you thinks he is wise in this world, let him consider himself a fool so that he may become wise.

19 For the wisdom of this world is foolishness before God. For it is written, He catches the wise in their own craftiness.

20 And again, The Lord knows that the thoughts of the wise are vain.

21 Therefore, let no man boast about men. For all things are yours,

22 Whether Paul or Apollos or Kepa or the world or life or death or things present or things to come; all things are yours;

23 And you are Christ's and Christ is God's.

CHAPTER 4

THIS is the way you should consider us: as the servants of Christ and stewards of the mysteries of God.

2 Henceforth it is required of stewards that every one of them must be faithful.

3 But as for me, it is of little importance that I am judged by you or by any one else, because I do not judge myself.

4 For I know nothing of which I am guilty; yet I may not be right in this, for my judge is the Lord.

5 Therefore do not judge before the time, until the Lord comes and brings to light the hidden things of darkness and reveals the thoughts of the hearts; then shall every man have praise from God.

6 ¶These things, my brethren, concerning myself and Apollos I have pictured for your sakes, that in our example you may learn not to think beyond that which is written, and let no one exalt himself over his fellow man on account of any man.

7 For who has examined you? And what do you have which was not given to you? And if you did receive it, then why do you boast as if you had not received it?

8 ¶For a long time you have been full and enriched, and you have waxed strong without our counsel. And I would to God you were as kings, so that we also might reign with you.

9 For I think God has placed us, the apostles, last as if we were condemned to death; for we have be-

come a spectacle to the world and to angels and to men.

10 We are fools for Christ's sake, but you are wise in Christ; we are weak, but you are strong; you are praised, but we are despised.

11 Even to this very hour we both hunger and thirst, and are naked and mistreated and have no permanent home;

12 And labor, working with our own hands; being cursed we bless, being persecuted, we endure;

13 Being reviled, we intreat; we are looked upon as the refuse of the world, and we are the revilement of every man to this day.

14 I do not write these things to make you feel ashamed, but to advise you as beloved children.

15 For though you have ten thousand instructors in Christ, yet you will have not many fathers; for in Jesus Christ I have begotten you through the gospel.

16 I beseech you, therefore, to follow me.

17 This is why I have sent Timotheus to you, who is my beloved son and faithful in the Lord, who shall remind you of my manner of life in Christ, just as I teach in all the churches.

18 There are some among you who are puffed up, thinking I am unwilling to come to you.

19 But I will come to you very soon, if the Lord wills, and then I shall find out not the words of these men who exalt themselves, but their power.

20 For the kingdom of God is not in the word, but in power.

21 Now what do you desire? Shall I come to you with a rod or with love and in the spirit of meekness?

CHAPTER 5

IT is reported that immorality is common among you, and such immorality as is not known among pagans, that even a son should take his father's wife.

2 But instead of boasting as you have done, rather had you sat down mourning that he who has done this deed might have been removed from among you.

3 For while I am far away from you in body, yet I am near you in spirit, and I have already judged, as though I were present, him who has done this deed.

4 In the name of our Lord Jesus Christ gather together, and I will be with you in spirit and with the power of our Lord Jesus Christ,

5 So that you shall deliver this man to Satan for the destruction of his body, in order that the spirit may be saved in the day of our Lord Jesus Christ.

6 Your boasting is not good. Do you not know that a little leaven will leaven the whole lump?

7 Clean out therefore the old leaven, so that you may be a new lump, just as you are unleavened. For our passover is Christ, who was sacrificed for our sake.

8 Therefore let us celebrate the festival, not with the old leaven, neither with the leaven of evil and bitterness, but with the leaven of purity and sanctity.

9 I wrote to you in an epistle not to associate with immoral persons.

10 I do not mean that you should separate completely from all the immoral people of this world or from the fraudulent and extortioners or from idolaters; otherwise you would be obliged to leave this world.

11 Now what I have written to you is this: you are not to associate with any person who is known as a brother and yet is immoral or fraudulent or an idolater or a railer or a drunkard or an extortioner; with such a person you must not break bread.

12 For what business have I to judge those who are outside the church? But you may judge those who are within the church.

13 God will judge the outsiders. Therefore, put away from among yourselves those wicked persons.

CHAPTER 6

WOULD any of you, having a lawsuit against his brother, venture to go to trial before the wicked rather than before the saints?

2 Do you not know that the saints shall judge the world? And if the world is to be judged by you, are you not worthy to judge small affairs?

3 Do you not know that we are to judge angels? How much more then should we judge those who belong to this world?

4 You have worldly affairs to be settled, and yet you have put men of bad reputation in the church on the judgment seat.

5 I say this to you to make you feel ashamed. Is it so, that there is not a single wise man among you who could settle a dispute between brother and brother?

6 But brother goes to court against brother, and at that before unbelievers.

7 Now, therefore, you are already at fault because you go to court one with another. Why not rather suffer wrong? Why not rather let yourselves be defrauded?

8 No, you yourselves do wrong, and defraud even your brethren.

9 ¶Do you not know that the wicked shall not inherit the kingdom of God? Be not misled; neither the immoral nor idolaters nor adulterers nor the corrupt nor men who lie with males

10 Nor extortioners nor thieves nor drunkards nor railers nor defrauders shall inherit the kingdom of God.

11 And some of these evils were to be found in some of you, but you have been cleansed and have been sanctified and made righteous in the name of our Lord Jesus Christ and through the Spirit of our God.

12 All things are lawful for me, but all things are not advisable; indeed all things are lawful for me but I will not be brought under the power of any.

13 Food is for the stomach, and the stomach for food; but God will do away with both of them. Now the body is not meant for fornication, but for our Lord; and our Lord for the body.

14 ¶And as God has raised our Lord, so he will raise us also by his own power.

15 Do you not know that your bodies are the members of Christ? How then can one take a member of Christ and make it the member of a harlot? Far be it.

16 Or do you not know that he who joins his body to a harlot is one body with her? For it is said, The two shall become one body.

17 But he who unites himself with our Lord becomes one with him in spirit.

18 Keep away from fornication. Every sin that a man commits is outside his body; but he who commits adultery sins against his own body.

19 Or do you not know that your body is the temple of the Holy Spirit that dwells within you, which you have of God, and you are not your own?

20 For you have been bought with a price; therefore glorify God in your body and in your spirit, because they belong to God.

CHAPTER 7

NOW concerning the things which you wrote to me. It is proper for a husband not to have intimacy with his wife at times.

2 Nevertheless, because of the danger of immorality, let every man hold to his own wife, and let every woman hold to her own husband.

3 Let the husband give to his wife the love which he owes her; and likewise also the wife to her husband.

4 The wife has no authority over her own body, but her husband; and likewise also the husband has no authority over his own body, but his wife.

5 Therefore do not deprive one another except when both of you consent to do so, especially at the time when you devote yourselves to fasting and prayer; and then come together again, so that Satan may not tempt you because of your physical passion.

6 But I say this only to weak persons, for it is not part of the law.

7 For I would that all men were

like myself in purity. But every man has his proper gift from God, one after this manner and another after that.

8 I say this to those who have no wives and to widows: It is better for them to be as I am;

9 But if they cannot endure it, let them marry; for it is better to marry than to burn with passion.

10 But those who have wives, I command (yet not I but my Lord), Let not the wife be separated from her husband;

11 But if she separate, let her remain single, or be reconciled to her husband; and let not the husband desert his wife.

12 But to the rest, I say this, not my Lord: If any brother has a wife who is not a convert, and she wishes to live with him, let him not leave her.

13 And the woman who has a husband who is not a convert but is content to live with her, let her not leave him.

14 For the husband who is not a convert is sanctified through the wife who is a convert, and the wife who is not a convert is sanctified through the husband who is a convert; otherwise, their children would be impure, but in such cases they are pure.

15 But if the one who is not a convert wishes to separate, let him separate. In such cases, a convert man or woman is free; for God has called us to live in peace.

16 For how do you know, O wife, that you shall save your husband? Or how do you know, O husband, that you shall save your wife?

17 But every man, according as the Lord has distributed to him, and every man, as God has called him, so let him walk. And this I command also for all the churches.

18 ¶If a man was circumcised when he was called, let him not adhere to the party of uncircumcision. And if he was uncircumcised, when he was called, let him not be circumcised.

19 For circumcision is nothing, and uncircumcision is nothing, but the keeping of the Lord's commandments is everything.

20 Let every man remain in the station of life in which he is called.

21 If you were a slave when you were called, do not feel concerned about it; but even though you can be made free, choose rather to serve.

22 For he who is called by our Lord, being a slave, is God's free man; likewise he who is called, being a freeman is also Christ's servant.

23 You have been bought with a price; you must not therefore become slaves of men.

24 My brethren, let every man in whatever station of life he was called, remain therein, serving God.

25 ¶Now concerning virginity, I have no command from God; yet I give my advice as one who has been favored by God to be trustworthy.

26 And I suppose that this is good for the present necessity, therefore I say, It is better for a man to remain as he is.

27 If you are married, do not seek divorce. If you are divorced from a wife, do not seek a wife.

28 But if you marry, you do not sin; and if a virgin marry, she does not sin. Nevertheless such shall have trouble in the flesh; but I would spare you.

29 But this I do say, my brethren: The time is short; let those who have wives be as though they had none;

30 And those who weep, as though they had not wept; and those who rejoice, as though they had not rejoiced; and those who buy, as though they did not possess anything;

31 And those who make use of this world should not abuse it, for the fashion of this world is passing away.

32 Therefore I would that you were free from worldly cares. For he who is unmarried is concerned in the things of his Master, so as to please his Master.

33 And he who is married is concerned with worldly things, in order to please his wife.

34 So there is a difference between a married woman and a virgin. She who is unmarried is concerned about the welfare of her Lord, and to be pure both in body and spirit; but

she who is married is concerned with worldly things, in order to please her husband.

35 I am saying this for your own benefit; I am not trying to snare or put a yoke on you, but I exhort you to be perfect before the Lord, and faithful without distraction.

36 If any man thinks that he is shamed by the behavior of his virgin daughter because she has passed the marriage age and he has not given her in marriage and that he should give her, let him do what he will and he does not sin. Let her be married.

37 If he has sincerely decided and is not forced by circumstances, but has determined and decreed in his heart to keep his virgin daughter single, he does well.

38 So then he who gives his virgin daughter in marriage does well; and he who does not give his virgin daughter in marriage does even better.

39 ¶A wife is bound by the law as long as her husband lives; but if her husband dies, she is free to marry whom she pleases, but only in our Lord.[1]

40 But, in my opinion, she is happier to remain as she is. And I think also that I have the Spirit of God.

CHAPTER 8

NOW concerning sacrifices offered to idols: We know well that we all have knowledge; knowledge makes for pride, but love ennobles.

2 And if any man thinks that, of himself, he knows any thing, he knows nothing yet as he ought to know it.

3 But if any man loves God, the same is known of him.

4 As concerning the eating of food offered to idols, we know that an idol is nothing in the world, and that there is no other God but one.

5 For though there are those that are called gods, whether in heaven or earth, just as there are many gods and many lords,

6 To us there is one God, the Father, from whom comes every thing and by whom we live; and one

1 A Christian.

Lord Jesus Christ, by whom are all things, and we by him.

7 Howbeit there is not in every man that knowledge; for some with clear conscience eat that which has been offered idols as a sacrifice; and their conscience being weak is defiled.

8 But meat does not bring us closer to God; for neither, if we eat, are we the better; neither if we do not eat, are we the worse.

9 But be careful lest this liberty of yours become a stumbling block to the weak.

10 For if any one should see you, who has knowledge, at table in the temple of idols, shall not the conscience of him who is weak encourage him to eat that which is sacrificed to idols?

11 So the one who is weak and for whom Christ died will be lost through your indifference.

12 And if you offend your brothers, and so influence their weak conscience, you also offend Christ.

13 Therefore if meat causes my brother to stumble, I will eat no meat, so that I may not cause my brother to offend.

CHAPTER 9

AM I not a free man? Am I not an apostle? Have I not seen Jesus Christ our Lord? Are you not my work in my Lord?

2 If I am not an apostle to others, yet to you I am; for you are the seal of my apostleship.

3 So my answer to those who criticize me is this:

4 Have we not the right to eat and to drink?

5 And have we not the right to travel with a Christian wife, just as the rest of the apostles do, and as the brothers of our Lord, and as Kepa?

6 I and Barnabas, have not we the right to live without working?

7 What officer commands an army at his own expense? or who plants a vineyard and does not eat of its fruits? or who feeds sheep, and does not eat of the produce of his flock?

8 I say these things as a man. Behold the law says them also.

9 For it is written in the law of Moses, You shall not muzzle the ox that treads out the wheat. Why? Is God concerned only for the ox?

10 No. It is known that he said it for our sakes and it was written for our sakes because the ploughman must plough in hope, and he who threshes, threshes in hope of the crop.

11 Now if we have sown among you spiritual things, is it too much that we should reap material things from you?

12 If others have this authority over you, have we not the greater right? Nevertheless we have not used this authority; but we have endured all things so that we would not hinder the gospel of Christ.

13 Do you not know that those who work in the holy place are maintained out of the temple? And those who minister at the altar share the offerings with the altar?

14 Even so has our Lord commanded that those who preach his gospel should live by his gospel.

15 But I have used none of these privileges; neither have I written these things that it should be so done to me; for it were better for me to die, than that any man should declare my empty pride.

16 For though I preach the gospel, I have nothing to glory of; for I am under obligation; yea, woe to me if I preach not the gospel!

17 For if I do this thing willingly, I have my reward; but if against my will, it is like a stewardship intrusted to me.

18 What then is my wage? This is it. When I preach the gospel of Jesus Christ, I do it without thought of recompense, and I have not abused the power given to me in the gospel.

19 Because I am free from all these things, I have served all men that I may gain many.

20 So with the Jews I became as a Jew, that I might win the Jews; and with those who are under the law, I became as one who is under the law,

that I might win those who are under the law.

21 To those who are without law, I became like one who is without law, though I am not lawless before God because I am under the law of Christ, that I might win them who are without law.

22 With the weak I became as weak, that I might win the weak. I became everything to every man, that I might by all means save everyone.

23 And this I do for the gospel's sake, that I might be partaker of it.

24 Do you not know that the runners in a race all run, but only one is victorious? So you must run that you may obtain victory.

25 And every man who battles in the contest frees his mind from every thing else. And yet they run to win a garland which is perishable; but we to win one which is everlasting.

26 I therefore so run, not for something that is uncertain; and I so fight, not as one who beats the air;

27 But I conquer and subdue my body so that, by no chance, when I have preached to others, will I despise myself.

CHAPTER 10

MOREOVER, brethren, I want you to know that our fathers were all under the cloud and all passed through the sea;

2 And all were baptized by Moses, both in the cloud and in the sea;

3 And all ate the same spiritual food;

4 And all drank the same spiritual drink; for they drank of that spiritual Rock that followed them; and that Rock was Christ.

5 But with many of them God was not well pleased; for they were smitten in the wilderness.

6 But they became an example to us, so that we should not covet evil things as they did covet.

7 Neither should we become idolaters, as were some of them; as it is written, The people sat down to eat and drink, and rose up to quarrel.

8 Neither should we commit adultery, as some of them committed; for

in one day twenty-three thousand of them fell dead.

9 Neither should we tempt Christ, as some of them tempted; for they were destroyed by snakes.

10 Neither should you murmur, as some of them murmured; for they were destroyed by the hand of the destroyer.

11 Now all of these things which happened to them are an example for us; and they are written for our admonition, for the fulfillment of the ages has come in our time.

12 Therefore, let him who thinks he can stand, take heed so that he may not fall.

13 No other temptation has overtaken you but that which is common to man; but God is faithful; he will not suffer you to be tempted beyond your endurance; but will make a way for you to escape your temptation, so that you may be able to bear it.

14 Therefore, my beloved, keep away from idolatry.

15 I speak as to wise men; you are able to judge what I say.

16 The cup of thanskgiving which we bless, is it not the communion of the blood of Christ? The bread which we break, is it not the communion of the body of Christ?

17 For just as the loaf of bread is one, so we are all one body; for we are all partakers of that one bread.

18 Behold Israel whose observance is after the flesh; do not those who eat the sacrifices become partakers of the altar?

19 What do I say then? That the idol is anything, or that the sacrifice to idols is anything? No.

20 But what the pagans sacrifice, they sacrifice to devils and not to God; and I would not have you in fellowship with devils.

21 You cannot drink the cup of our Lord and the cup of devils; you cannot be partakers of the table of our Lord and of the table of devils.

22 Are we trying to provoke our Lord to anger? Are we stronger than he?

23 ¶Everything is lawful for me, but not everything is expedient; every-

thing is lawful for me, but everything does not edify.

24 But let no man seek for himself alone, but let every man seek for his neighbor also.

25 Anything for sale in the market place you can eat without question for conscience sake;

26 For the earth is the Lord's and the fulness thereof.

27 If any pagan man should invite you, and you wish to go, whatever is set before you eat without question for conscience sake.

28 But if any man say to you, This meat has been offered as a sacrifice, then do not eat it for the sake of him who told you and for conscience sake.

29 But the conscience of which I speak is not yours, but the conscience of him who told you; for why is my liberty judged by another man's conscience?

30 For if I by grace am made worthy, why should I be reproached for that for which I give thanks?

31 Whether therefore you eat or drink, or whatsoever you do, do all to the glory of God.

32 Give no offence, neither to the Jews nor to the Arameans nor to the church of God;

33 Just as I please all men in all things, not seeking my own good, but the good of many, that they may be saved.

CHAPTER 11

TAKE example by me, even as I also follow Christ.

2 Now I praise you, my brethren, that you remember me in all things and keep the ordinances as I delivered them to you.

3 But I would have you know that the head of every man is Christ; and the head of the wife is her husband; and the head of Christ is God.

4 Every man who prays or prophesies with his head covered dishonors his head.

5 And every woman who prays or prophesies with her head uncovered dishonors her head; for she is equal to her whose head is shaven.

6 For if a woman does not cover her head, let her also cut off her hair; but if it be a shame for a woman to be shorn or shaven, let her cover her head.

7 For a man indeed ought not cover his head, because he is the image and glory of God; but the woman is the glory of the man.

8 For the man was not created from the woman; but the woman was created from the man.

9 Neither was the man created for the woman; but the woman for the man.

10 For this reason the woman ought to be modest and cover her head as a mark of respect to the angels.

11 Nevertheless, in our Lord there is no preference between man and woman, neither between woman and man.

12 For as the woman is of the man, even so is the man also by the woman; but all things of God.

13 Judge for yourselves; is it comely for a woman to pray to God with uncovered head?

14 Does not even nature itself teach you that if a man have long hair, it is a disgrace to him?

15 But if a woman have long hair, it is a glory to her; for her hair is given her for a covering.

16 But if any man dispute these things, we have no precedent, neither has the church of God.

17 ¶Now I give you these commands, not to praise you, for you have not made progress but have become worse.

18 First of all, when you gather in the church, I hear that there are divisions among you; and I partly believe it.

19 For controversies are bound to be among you, that those who are approved may be made manifest among you.

20 When you gather together therefore, you do not eat and drink as is appropriate on the day of our Lord.

21 But some men eat their supper before others; and so it happens that one is hungry and another is drunken.

22 Why? Have you not houses to eat and drink in? Or do you not respect the church of God, and want to shame those who have nothing? What shall I say to you? Shall I praise you? No, for this, I cannot praise you.

23 For I myself received from our Lord that which I also delivered to you, That our Lord Jesus on that very night in which he was betrayed took bread;

24 And when he had given thanks, he broke it and said, Take, eat; this is my body, which is broken for you; this do in remembrance of me.

25 Likewise after supper, he gave also the cup and said, This cup is the new testament in my blood; do this, as often as you drink it, in remembrance of me.

26 For whenever you eat this bread and drink this cup, you commemorate our Lord's death until his coming.

27 Therefore whosoever shall eat of the Lord's bread and drink of his cup unworthily shall be guilty of the blood and body of the Lord.

28 For this reason, let a man examine himself and eat of this bread and drink of this cup.

29 For he who eats and drinks unworthily eats and drinks to his condemnation; for he does not discern the Lord's body.

30 This is the reason many are sick and weak among you, and many are dying.

31 For if we would judge ourselves, we would not be judged.

32 But when we are judged by our Lord, we are simply chastened, so that we may not be condemned with the world.

33 Hereafter, my brethren, when you come together to eat, wait for one another.

34 And if any man hunger, let him eat at home so that you may not come together unto condemnation. As to the rest of the things I will instruct you when I come.

CHAPTER 12

NOW concerning spiritual gifts, my brethren, I want to remind you

2 That once you were pagans, and without exception you were carried away by dumb idols.

3 Therefore I want you to understand that no man speaking by the Spirit of God calls Jesus accursed; and that no man can say that Jesus is the Lord but by the Holy Spirit.

4 Now there are diversities of gifts, but there is only one Spirit.

5 And there are diversities of ministries, but there is only one Lord.

6 And there are diversities of powers, but it is the one God who works all things in all men.

7 But the manifestation of the Spirit is given to every man as help to him.

8 For to one is given by the Spirit the word of wisdom; to another the word of knowledge by the same Spirit.

9 To another faith by the same Spirit; to another gifts of healing by the same Spirit;

10 To another the working of miracles; to another prophecy; to another the means to distinguish the true Spirit; to another different languages; to another the interpretation of languages.

11 But all of these gifts are wrought by that one and the same Spirit, dividing to every one severally as he will.

12 For as the body is one and has many members, and all the members of the body, even though many, are one body, so also is Christ.

13 For all of us are baptized by one Spirit into one body, whether Jews or Arameans, whether bond or free; and we have all received through the one Spirit.

14 The body is not one member, but many.

15 For if the foot should say, Because I am not the hand, I am not a part of the body; is it therefore not a member of the body?

16 And if the ear should say, Because I am not the eye, I am not a part of the body; is it therefore not a member of the body?

17 If the whole body were eyes, where would hearing be? And if the whole were hearing, where would smelling be?

18 But now God has set every member in the body, as it has pleased him.

19 If they were all one member, where would the body be?

20 But now they are many members, yet but one body.

21 The eye cannot say to the hand, I have no need of you; nor can the head say to the feet, I have no need of you.

22 But rather those members of the body which are considered to be delicate are necessary.

23 And on those members of the body which we think to be less honorable we bestow more abundant honor; and the parts that are uncomely we dress with greater care;

24 For our comely parts have no need for attention. But God has so tempered the body together, and has given greater honor to the member which is inferior,

25 That there may be no discord in the body, but that they may care one for another, all members should be equal.

26 So when one member is in pain, all the members suffer with it; and if one member is honored, all the members will glory with it.

27 Now you are the body of Christ and members in your respective places.

28 For God has set in his church, first apostles; after them, prophets; then teachers, then performers of miracles, then those who have the gift of healing, helpers, leaders, and speakers in diverse languages.

29 Are all apostles? Are all prophets? Are all teachers? Are all workers of miracles?

30 Have all the gifts of healing? Do all speak in diverse tongues? Or do all interpret?

31 ¶But if you are searching for the greater gifts, I will show you a more excellent way.

CHAPTER 13

THOUGH I speak with the tongues of men and of angels, and have not love in my heart, I am become as sounding brass or a tinkling cymbal.

2 And though I have the gift of prophecy, and understand all myster-

ies and all knowledge; and though I have all faith, so that I could remove mountains, and have not love in my heart, I am nothing.

3 And though I bestow all my goods to feed the poor, and though I give my body to be burned, and have not love in my heart, I gain nothing.

4 Love is long-suffering and kind; love does not envy; love does not make a vain display of itself, and does not boast,

5 Does not behave itself unseemly, seeks not its own, is not easily provoked, thinks no evil;

6 Rejoices not over iniquity, but rejoices in the truth;

7 Bears all things, believes all things, hopes all things, endures all things.

8 Love never fails; but whether there be prophecies, they shall fail; whether there be tongues, they shall cease; whether there be knowledge, it shall vanish away.

9 For we know in part and we prophesy in part.

10 But when that which is perfect is come, then that which is imperfect shall come to an end.

11 When I was a child, I spoke as a child, I understood as a child, I thought as a child; but when I became a man, I put away childish things.

12 For now we see through a mirror, darkly; but then face to face. Now I know in part; but then shall I know even as also I am known.

13 And now abide faith, hope, love, these three; but the greatest of these is love.

CHAPTER 14

FOLLOW after love, and desire spiritual gifts, above all that you may prophesy.

2 For he who speaks in an unknown tongue speaks not to men, but to God; for no man understands what he says; however through the Spirit he speaks mysteries.

3 But he who prophesies speaks to men for edification, encouragement, and comfort.

4 He who speaks in an unknown tongue edifies himself; but he who prophesies edifies the church.

5 I would that you all spoke various tongues, but I would rather that you prophesied; for he who prophesies is greater than he who speaks various tongues, unless he interprets; however, if he interprets, he edifies the church.

6 Now, my brethren, if I should come to you and speak in diverse tongues, what would I profit you, except I speak to you either by means of revelation or by knowledge or by prophesying or by teaching?

7 For even when things without life give sound, whether flute or harp, except they make a distinction between one tone and another, how shall it be known what is sung or played?

8 For if the trumpet give an uncertain sound, who will prepare himself for the battle?

9 Even so you, except you utter by the tongue words easy to be understood, how shall it be known what you say? You shall speak as into the air.

10 For, behold, there are many kinds of languages in the world, yet none of them without expression.

11 So if I do not understand the utterance, I shall be as a barbarian to the speaker, and the speaker shall be as a barbarian to me.

12 Likewise you, since you are zealous of spiritual gifts for the edification of the church, seek that you may excel in these gifts.

13 Thus he who speaks in an unknown tongue prays that he may interpret it.

14 For if I pray in an unknown tongue, my spirit prays, but my knowledge is fruitless.

15 What then shall I do? I will pray with my spirit and I will pray with my understanding also; I will sing with my spirit and I will sing with my understanding also.

16 Otherwise, if you say a blessing with the spirit, how can one who occupies the place of the unlearned say Amen to your thanksgiving, since he does not understand what you say?

17 For indeed you bless well, but your fellow man is not enlightened.

18 I thank God that I speak with tongues more than you all;

19 But in the church I had rather speak five words with my understanding, so that I might teach others also, than ten thousand words in an unknown tongue.

20 My brethren, be not like infants in your intelligence; only to evil things be like innocent children, but in your understanding be mature.

21 In the law it is written, With a foreign speech and in another tongue I will speak to this people; yet for all that, they will not listen to me, says the Lord.

22 Thus, the gift of languages is instituted as a sign, not for believers, but for unbelievers; but prophesying is meant, not for those who do not believe, but for those who believe.

23 If therefore the whole church assembles together and all speak in different tongues and there enter unlearned people or unbelievers, will they not say, They are fanatical?

24 But if all prophesy, and an unlearned man or an unbeliever enter, he will be convinced by all, and he will be set right by all.

25 Thus the secrets of his heart will be revealed, and then he will fall on his face, and he will worship God and say, Truly God is among you.

26 Therefore I say to you, my brethren, when you gather together, whoever among you has a psalm to sing, has a doctrine, has a revelation, has the gift of tongues, or the gift of interpretation, let everything be done for edification.

27 And if any man should speak in an unknown tongue, let two or at most three speak, and speak one by one; and let one interpret.

28 But if there is no one to interpret, let him who speaks in an unknown tongue keep silence in the church; and let him speak to himself and to God.

29 Let the prophets speak two or three in turn, and let the others discern what is said.

30 And if anything is revealed to another who is seated, let the first speaker hold his peace.

31 For you may all prophesy one by one, so that every one may learn and every one be comforted.

32 For the spirits of the prophets are subject to the prophets.

33 For God is not a God of confusion but of peace, and he is in all churches of the saints.

34 ¶Let your women keep silent in the church for they have no permission to speak; but they are to be under obedience as is said in the law.

35 And if they wish to learn anything, let them ask their husbands at home; for it is a shame for women to speak in the church.

36 What? Did the word of God come from you? Or did it come for you only?

37 If any one among you thinks he is a prophet or that he is inspired by the Spirit, let him acknowledge that these things that I write to you are the commandments of our Lord.

38 But if any man be ignorant, let him be ignorant.

39 Therefore, my brethren, desire earnestly to prophesy, and do not prohibit speaking in unknown tongues.

40 Let all things be done decently and in order.

CHAPTER 15

MOREOVER, my brethren, I declare to you the gospel which I preached to you and which you have accepted and for which you have stood firm,

2 By which also you are saved if you keep in remembrance that very word which I have preached to you, and if your conversion has not been in vain.

3 For I delivered to you first of all that which I had also received, that Christ died for our sins according to the scriptures;

4 And that he was buried, and that he rose again on the third day according to the scriptures;

5 And that he appeared to Kepa, then to the twelve;

6 After that, he appeared to more than five hundred brethren at once, of whom a great many are still living though some are dead.

7 And after that, he appeared to James; then to all the apostles.

8 And last of all he appeared to me also, ignorant and imperfectly trained as I was.[1]

9 For I am the least of the apostles, and I am not worthy to be called an apostle, because I persecuted the church of God.

10 But by the grace of God I am what I am; and his grace that is in me has not been in vain; for I labored more abundantly than them all, yet not I, but God's grace that is within me.

11 Therefore whether it were I or they, so we preached and so you believed.

12 Now if it is preached that Christ rose from the dead, how can some say among you that there is no resurrection of the dead?

13 And if there is no resurrection of the dead, then Christ also has not risen;

14 And if Christ is not risen, then is our preaching in vain and your faith is also in vain;

15 And we are also found false witnesses of God, because we have testified of God that he raised up Christ when he had not raised him.

16 For if the dead rise not, then neither did Christ rise;

17 And if Christ did not rise, your belief is in vain and you are yet in your sins.

18 And also, then those who have died in Christ have perished.

19 If in this life only we have hope in Christ, then we are of all men most miserable.

20 But now we know Christ is risen from the dead and become the firstfruits of those who have died.

21 For since by man came death, by man came also the resurrection of the dead.

22 For as in Adam all die, even so in Christ shall all be made alive.

23 But every man in his own order: Christ the first-fruits; afterward those who belong to Christ at his coming.

24 Then will come the end, when he shall have delivered up the kingdom to God, even the Father; when he shall have put down all rule and all authority and power.

25 For he must reign till he has put all enemies under his feet.

26 And the last enemy that shall be destroyed is death.

27 For he has put all things under his feet. But when he said all things are put under him, it is clear that he who put all things under him is excepted.

28 And when all things shall be subdued to him, then shall the Son also himself be subject to him who put all things under him, so that God may be all in all.

29 Else, what shall they do who are baptized for the dead, if the dead rise not at all? Why are they then baptized for the dead?

30 And why do we continue to stand in danger every hour?

31 I affirm by your pride, my brethren, which I have in our Lord Jesus Christ, I die daily.

32 If, after the manner of men, I were thrown to wild beasts at Ephesus, what good would come to me, if the dead rise not? If such is the case, let us eat and drink for tomorrow we die.

33 Do not be deceived: evil communications corrupt good manners.

34 Awake your hearts to righteousness and sin not; for some have not the knowledge of God. I say this to your shame.

35 ¶But some of you will say, How are the dead raised up? And with what body do they come?

36 O, you foolish man! The seed which you sow does not sprout unless it dies.

37 And what you sow is not the body that shall be, but the bare grain; it may chance to be of wheat or barley or some other seed.

38 But God gives it a body as it has pleased him, and to every seed, its own natural body.

39 All flesh is not the same flesh; but there is one kind of flesh of men, another flesh of beasts, another of birds, and another of fish.

[1] Paul had seen Jesus in a vision but had never known him in person.

40 There are also celestial bodies and bodies terrestrial; but the glory of the celestial is one, and the glory of the terrestrial is another.

41 There is one glory of the sun and another glory of the moon and another glory of the stars; for one star differs from another star in glory.

42 So also is the resurrection of the dead. It is sown in corruption; it is raised in incorruption:

43 It is sown in dishonor; it is raised in glory: it is sown in weakness; it is raised in power:

44 It is sown a natural body; it is raised a spiritual body. There is a natural body and there is a spiritual body.

45 And so it is written, The first man Adam was made a living soul; the last Adam was made a quickening spirit.

46 Howbeit, that was not first which is spiritual, but that which is natural; and afterward that which is spiritual.

47 The first man is of the earth, earthy; the second man is the Lord from heaven.

48 As is the earthy, such are they also that are earthy; and as is the heavenly, such are they also that are heavenly.

49 And as we have borne the image of the earthy, we shall also bear the image of the heavenly.

50 Now this I say, my brethren, that flesh and blood cannot inherit the kingdom of God; neither does corruption inherit incorruption.

51 Behold, I tell you a mystery: We shall not all die, but we shall all be changed,

52 In a moment, in the twinkling of an eye, at the last trumpet; for the trumpet shall sound and the dead shall be raised incorruptible and we shall be changed.

53 For this corruptible must put on incorruption and this mortal must put on immortality.

54 So when this corruptible shall have put on incorruption, and this mortal shall have put on immortality, then shall be brought to pass the saying that is written, Death is swallowed up in victory.

55 ¶O death, where is your sting? O Sheol, where is your victory?

56 The sting of death is sin; and the strength of sin is the law.

57 But thanks be to God, who has given us the victory through our Lord Jesus Christ.

58 Therefore, my beloved brethren, be steadfast, unmoveable, always abounding in the work of the Lord, for as much as you know that your labor is not in vain in the Lord.

CHAPTER 16

NOW concerning the collection for the saints: as I have given order to the churches of Galatia, likewise do you also.

2 On the first day of every week, let each of you put aside and keep in his house whatever he can afford, so that there may be no collections when I come.

3 And when I come, whomever you may select, I will send with a letter, to carry your gracious gift to Jerusalem.

4 And if it is right that I go also, they shall go with me.

5 I will come to you when I pass through Macedonia; for I do pass through Macedonia.

6 And perhaps I will remain some time with you or pass the winter with you, so that you may escort me wherever I go.

7 For I do not want to see you now just as a wayfarer; because I trust to tarry for a time with you, if my Lord permit me.

8 But I will tarry at Ephesus until Pentecost.

9 For a great door, full of opportunities, is opened to me, and adversaries are many.

10 ¶Now if Timotheus comes, see that he may be with you without fear; for he is engaged in the Lord's work, just as I am.

11 Let no man therefore despise him; but escort him in peace, that he may come to me; for I wait for him with the brethren.

12 My brethren, as for Apollos, I have often begged him to visit you with the brethren; probably it was not

intended that he should come to you; but he will come to you when he has an opportunity.

13 Watch, stand firm in the faith, be valiant, be strong.

14 Let all your deeds be done with love.

15 I beseech you, my brethren, concerning the household of Stephanas, for you know that they were the first converts from Achaia and that they have devoted themselves to the ministry of the saints,

16 That you may listen to all those who are as they are and to every one who labors with us and is of help.

17 I am glad of the coming of Stephanas and Fortunatus and Achaicus; for that which was lacking on your part, they have supplied.

18 For they have refreshed my spirit as well as yours; therefore recognize them who are similar.

19 ¶All the churches of Asia Minor salute you. Aquila and Priscilla salute you much in our Lord, with the congregation that meets in their house.

20 All the brethren greet you. Greet one another with a holy kiss.

21 ¶This salutation is from me, Paul, in my own handwriting.

22 Whoever does not love our Lord Jesus Christ, let him be accursed. Maranetha, that is to say our Lord has come.

23 The grace of our Lord Jesus Christ be with you.

24 My love be with you all in Christ Jesus. Amen.

THE SECOND EPISTLE OF PAUL THE APOSTLE

to the

CORINTHIANS

CHAPTER 1

PAUL, an apostle of Jesus Christ by the will of God, and Timotheus our brother, to the church of God which is at Corinth, with all the saints who are in all Achaia:

2 Grace be to you and peace from God our Father and from our Lord Jesus Christ.

3 ¶Blessed be God, even the Father of our Lord Jesus Christ, the Father of mercies and the God of all comfort,

4 Who comforts us in all our troubles, so that we also may be able to comfort those who are in any trouble, by the very comfort with which we ourselves are comforted by God.

5 For as the sufferings of Christ abound in us, so our consolation also abounds in Christ.

6 Even though we are oppressed, it is for the sake of your consolation and for the sake of your salvation that we are oppressed; and if we are comforted, it is so that you might be comforted also, to be strength in you that you may be able to bear these sufferings, the same which we also suffer.

7 And our hope concerning you is steadfast, for we know that if you are partakers of the sufferings, you are also partakers of the consolation.

8 For we would wish you to know, my brethren, about the trouble we had in Asia Minor, for we were greatly oppressed beyond our strength; insomuch that we despaired of our lives;

9 And we decided to die, not trusting in ourselves but in God who raises the dead,

10 Who delivered us from horrible deaths, and who will, we hope, again deliver us,

11 You also helping by your supplications for us, that for his gift bestowed upon us, by means of many persons, thanks may be given by many on our behalf.

12 ¶For our joy is this, the testimony of our conscience, in sincerity and in purity with the grace of God, we have conducted ourselves in this world, and not through the wisdom of the flesh; and above all, we have so dealt with you.

13 For we write nothing to you except those things which you know and understand, and I trust you will understand them to the end;

14 Just as you have understood in part that we are your pride and joy, even as you also are ours in the day of our Lord Jesus Christ.

15 ¶And in this confidence I wished to come to you before, that you might receive grace doubly;

16 And to pass by you on my way to Macedonia, and again to come back to you from Macedonia, so that you may accompany me on my way to Judea.

17 When I, therefore, was considering this, did I consider it lightly or are the things which I am considering wholly worldly? Because the answers should have been either yes yes, or no no.

18 But as God is true, our word to you was not yes and no.

19 For the Son of God, Jesus Christ, who was preached among you by us, even by me and Silvanus and Timotheus, was not yes and no, but with him always yes.

20 For all the promises of God were in Christ, yes; therefore by his hand, we are given Amen to the glory of God.

21 Now it is God who has confirmed us with you in Christ, and who has anointed us,

22 And who has sealed us, and pledged his Spirit in our hearts.

23 Moreover I testify to God concerning myself, that it was because I wanted to spare you that I did not come to Corinth.

24 Not that we are the masters of your faith, but we are helpers of your joy; for by faith you stand.

CHAPTER 2

BUT I determined this with myself, that I would not come again to you in sadness.

2 For if I make you sad, who can make me happy, but him whom I made sad?

3 And I wrote this same thing to you, so that when I come to you I may not be made sad by those who ought to make me joyful, having confidence in you all, that my joy is the joy of you all.

4 For out of great affliction and anguish of heart, I wrote you with many tears; not to make you feel distressed, but that you may know the abundant love I have for you.

5 ¶But if anyone has caused grief, he has not grieved me only, but to a certain degree all of you; therefore the news will not be a shock to you.

6 The rebuke of many persons is sufficient for such a man.

7 So that from henceforth you ought rather to forgive and comfort him, lest perhaps such a one will be overcome with excessive grief.

8 I beseech you therefore that you confirm your love toward him.

9 For that is why I wrote you, that I might know by your word whether you are obedient in all things.

10 To whom you forgive anything, I forgive also; for anything which I have forgiven, to whomever I forgave it, it is for your sakes I forgave it in the presence of Christ,

11 Lest Satan might take advantage of us; for we know his devices.

12 ¶Furthermore, when I came to Troas with the gospel of Christ, and a door was opened to me in the Lord,

13 I could not rest in my spirit, because I did not find Titus my brother; hence I took leave of them and left for Macedonia.

14 ¶Now thanks be to God, who has

made us in the pattern of Christ, and makes manifest the savour of his knowledge through us in every place.

15 For we are a sweet savour to God through Christ, in those who are saved and in those who perish;

16 To the one the savour of death to death; and to the other the savour of life to life. And who is worthy of these things?

17 For we are not like those who corrupt the word of God; but according to the truth, and as men of God we speak through Christ in the sight of God.

CHAPTER 3

DO we begin again to commend ourselves? Or do we need, as some others do, epistles of commendation concerning us written to you, or that you should write commending us?

2 You are our epistle written in our hearts, well-known and read by all men;

3 For you are known to be the epistle of Christ ministered by us, written not with ink, but with the Spirit of the living God; not on tablets of stone, but on tablets of the living heart.

4 Such is the trust that we have through Christ toward God.

5 Not that we are sufficient of ourselves to think anything as of ourselves; but our strength comes from God,

6 Who has made us worthy to be ministers of the new covenant; not of the letter, but of the Spirit; for the letter of the law punishes with death, but the Spirit gives life.

7 Now if the ministration of death, as contained in the letter of the law and engraved on stones, was so glorious that the children of Israel could not look at the face of Moses because of the glory of his countenance, which glory was not lasting,

8 Why then shall not the ministration of the Spirit be more glorious?

9 For if there be glory in the ministration of condemnation, much more will the ministration of righteousness exceed in glory.

10 Just as that which was not glorious became glorified; in comparison with that, this excels in glory.

11 For if that which was not lasting was glorious, much more glorious will that be which endures.

12 Seeing therefore that we have such hope, we conduct ourselves bravely;

13 And not as Moses who put a veil over his face, so that the children of Israel might not look upon the fulness of the glory which was not lasting;

14 But their minds were blinded; for to this day, when the Old Testament is read, the same veil rests over them, and it is not known to them that the veil has been removed through Christ.

15 But even to this day, whenever the books of Moses are read, the veil is upon their hearts.

16 Nevertheless whenever a man turns to the Lord, the veil is taken away.

17 Now the Lord is that very Spirit; and where the Spirit of the Lord is, there is liberty.

18 But we all, with open faces, see as in a mirror the glory of the Lord, and we shall be transformed into the same likeness, from one glory to another, just as the Spirit comes from the Lord.

CHAPTER 4

FOR this reason we are not weary of the ministry in which we are engaged, just as we are not weary of the mercies that have been upon us;

2 But we have renounced the hidden things of shame, and we do not practice cunning, nor do we handle the word of God deceitfully; but by manifestation of the truth we commend ourselves to every man's conscience before God.

3 If our gospel is hidden, it is hidden to those who are lost,

4 To those in this world whose minds have been blinded by God, because they did not believe, lest the light of the glorious gospel of Christ, who is the likeness of God, should shine on them.

5 For we do not preach about our-

selves, but about Christ Jesus our Lord; and as to ourselves, we are your servants for Jesus' sake.

6 For God, who said, Let light shine out of darkness, has shone in our hearts so that we may be enlightened with the knowledge of the glory of God in the person of Christ.

7 But we have this treasure in earthen vessels, that the excellency of power may be from God, and not from us.

8 We are distressed in every way, but not overwhelmed; we are harassed on all sides, but not conquered;

9 Persecuted, but not forsaken; cast down, but not destroyed;

10 For we always bear in our bodies the death of Jesus, that the life of Jesus might also be made manifest in our bodies.

11 For if we who live are delivered to death for Jesus' sake, so also will the life of Jesus be made manifest in our mortal bodies.

12 Thus death is close to us, but life is near to you.

13 We have the same spirit of faith; as it is written, I believed, and therefore have I spoken; we also believe, therefore we also speak,

14 Knowing that he who raised our Lord Jesus shall raise us also by Jesus and shall present us with you.

15 For all things are for your sakes that the abundant grace might, through the thanksgiving of many, redound to the glory of God.

16 ¶For this reason, we do not grow weary; for though our outward man perish, yet the inner man is renewed day by day.

17 For while the troubles of the present time are little and light, a great and limitless glory for ever and ever is prepared for us.

18 We do not rejoice in the things which are seen, but in the things which are not seen; for the things which are seen are temporal, but the things which are not seen are eternal.

CHAPTER 5

FOR we know that if our earthly house were destroyed, we still have a building made by God, a house not made with hands, eternal in heaven.

2 We also weary over this earthly house, earnestly longing to use our house which is in heaven.

3 If not so, even when we are clothed, we will still be naked.

4 While we are in this earthly house, we groan because of its weight; yet we are unwilling to leave it, but rather wish to add to it, so that death will be overcome by life.

5 Now he who has prepared us for this very thing is God, who also has given to us the pledge of his Spirit.

6 Therefore we know and are convinced that so long as we dwell in the body, we are absent from our Lord.

7 For we walk by faith, and not by sight.

8 This is why we are confident, and anxious to be absent from the body, and to be present with our Lord.

9 Wherefore we endeavor, that whether present or absent, we may be pleasing to him.

10 For we must all stand before the judgment seat of Christ, that every one may be rewarded according to that which he has done with his body, whether it be good or bad.

11 ¶Knowing therefore the fear of our Lord, we try in a persuasive way to win men; so we are very well understood by God; and I trust we are also understood by you.

12 We are not boasting of ourselves to you, but we give you occasion to be proud of us before those who glory as hypocrites but who are not sincere in heart.

13 For if we go wrong, we answer to God, and if we go right, it is for you.

14 For the love of Christ compels us to reason thus: that if one died for all, then were all dead;

15 And that he died for all, that those who live may not henceforth live for themselves, but for him who died and rose for them.

16 And now from henceforth we do not know any one in the body; even though once we had known Christ in the body, we no longer know him now.

17 Whoever from now on is a fol-

lower of Christ is a new creation; old things have passed away;

18 And all things have become new through God who has reconciled us to himself by Jesus Christ and has given to us the ministry of reconciliation;

19 For God was in Christ, who has reconciled the world with his majesty, not counting their sins against them; and has committed to us the word of reconciliation.

20 Now then we are ambassadors for Christ, as though God did beseech you by us; we beseech you for Christ, be reconciled to God.

21 For he who did not know sin, for your sakes made himself sin, that we may through him be made the righteousness of God.

CHAPTER 6

S O we beseech you, as helpers, that the grace of God which you have received may not be in vain among you.

2 For he said, I have answered you in an acceptable time, and I have helped you on the day of salvation; behold, now is the acceptable time; and behold now is the day of salvation.

3 Give no occasion for offence to any one in anything, so that there be no blemish in our ministry;

4 But in all things let us show ourselves to be the ministers of God in much patience, in tribulations, in necessities, in imprisonment,

5 In scourgings, in bonds, in tumults, in toilings, in vigils, in fastings;

6 By purity, by knowledge, by longsuffering, by kindness, by the Holy Spirit, by sincere love,

7 By the word of truth, by the power of God, by the armour of righteousness on the right hand and on the left,

8 By honour and dishonour, by praise and reproach, as deceivers, and yet true;

9 As unknown, and yet well known; as dying, and behold, we live; as chastened, and not dying;

10 As sorrowful, yet always rejoicing; as poor, yet enriching many;

as having nothing, and yet possessing all things.

11 O Corinthians, we have told you everything, and our heart is relieved.

12 You are not constrained by us, but are urged by your affections.

13 I speak as to my children, render me my reward which is with you, increase your love toward me.

14 ¶Do not unite in marriage with unbelievers, for what fellowship has righteousness with iniquity? Or what mingling has light with darkness?

15 Or what accord has Christ with Satan? Or what portion has a believer with an unbeliever?

16 Or what harmony has the temple of God with idols? For you are the temple of the living God; as it is said, I will dwell in them and walk in them; and I will be their God, and they shall be my people.

17 Wherefore come out from among them, and be separate, says the Lord, and touch not the unclean thing; and I will receive you,

18 And will be a Father to you, and you shall be my sons and daughters, said the Lord Almighty.

CHAPTER 7

H AVING therefore these promises, my beloved, let us cleanse ourselves from all filthiness of the flesh and spirit, and let us serve in holiness in the reverence of God.

2 ¶Be patient; my brethren, we have wronged no man, we have corrupted no man, we have defrauded no man.

3 I do not say this to condemn you; for I have said before that you are in our hearts, to die and live with you.

4 I am familiar enough to speak boldly with you, and I am very proud of you; I am filled with satisfaction, and I am overwhelmed with joy in all our troubles.

5 For ever since we came to Macedonia, our bodies have had no rest but have been troubled by everything, war without and fears within.

6 Nevertheless God, who comforts the meek, comforted us by the coming of Titus;

7 And not by his coming only, but also by the comfort with which he

was comforted in you, for he brought us the good news concerning your love toward us, your mourning and your zeal on our behalf; and when I heard it, I rejoiced exceedingly.

8 For even though I made you feel sorry with the epistle, I do not regret, even though it has caused sorrow; for I can see that though that very epistle has made you feel sorry, the sorrow was only for an hour.

9 But it has made me exceedingly happy, not that you were sorry, but that your sorrow led to repentance; for you were sorry over the things of God, so that you lack nothing from us.

10 For sorrow over the things of God causes enduring repentance of the soul, and brings one to life; but sorrow over the things of the world causes death.

11 For behold that very thing which distressed you on account of God has resulted much more in painstaking effort, in apology, anger, fear, love, zeal, and vengeance. In all things you have proved yourselves clear in this matter.

12 Be that as it may, though I wrote to you, I did not do it for the one who had done the wrong nor for the one who had suffered the wrong, but that your painstaking care for us might be known before God.

13 Therefore we were comforted and with our consolation we rejoiced exceedingly in the joy of Titus, for his spirit was refreshed by you all.

14 For I was not shamed in the things which I have boasted to him about you; but just as all the things about which we have spoken to you are true, even so our boasting to Titus is found to be true.

15 And his affections have increased more toward you, as he remembers the obedience of you all, how you received him in fear and trembling.

16 I rejoice therefore that I have confidence in you in all things.

CHAPTER 8

MOREOVER, our brethren, we want you to know that the grace of God has been bestowed on the churches of Macedonia;

2 How that in a great trial of affliction, the abundance of their joy and their deep-rooted poverty abounded to the riches of their liberality.

3 For to their power, I can testify, yes, and beyond their power they have shared of their own accord,

4 And besought us most earnestly that they might be partakers in the gift for the ministration to the saints.

5 And this they did, not only as we expected, but first they gave themselves to our Lord, and then to us by the will of God.

6 Insomuch as we desired Titus, that as he had begun, so he would also finish this same gift among you.

7 Therefore, as you abound in every thing, in faith, in the word of God, in knowledge, in all perseverance, and by our love toward you, you should likewise excel in this gracious favor also.

8 I am not making a demand on you, but I am prompted by the devotion of your fellow believers to test the sincerity of your love.

9 For you know the gracious gift of our Lord Jesus Christ, that though he was rich, yet for your sakes he became poor, so that you, through his poverty, might be rich.

10 Herein I give you my advice, that it may help you to go forward and accomplish what you, of your own accord, began to do last year.

11 Now therefore perform by works that which you wished to do; and as you were eager to promise it, so fulfil from that which you have.

12 For if there is a willingness to give, every man can give according to that which he has, and not according to that which he has not, and his gift will be acceptable.

13 This is not intended to relieve other men and add a burden to you;

14 But that there may be an equality at this particular time, that your abundance may be a supply for their want, that their abundance also may be a supply for your want, that there may be equality.

15 As it is written, He who had

gathered much had nothing over; and he who had gathered little had no lack.

16 But thanks be to God, who put the same vigorous care into the heart of Titus for you.

17 For indeed he has accepted our appeal; and because he was very desirous, he went to you of his own accord.

18 And we have also sent with him our brother, who has received praise throughout all the churches for his preaching of the gospel;

19 So that he also has been chosen by the churches to travel with us for this relief which is administered by us to the very glory of God and for our own encouragement;

20 But we are careful in this, lest any one should blame us in connection with this generous help which is administered by us.

21 For we are very careful to do the right thing, not only in the presence of God, but also in the presence of men.

22 And we have sent with them also our brother, who has often been proved by us in many things, that he is earnest, and now is more earnest because of the abundant trust he has in you.

23 And as to Titus, he is my partner and helper among you; and as to our other brethren, they are the apostles of the churches to the glory of Christ.

24 Henceforth you can show to them before all the churches the proof of your love and of our pride in you.

CHAPTER 9

CONCERNING the ministration to the saints, it is superfluous for me to write to you.

2 For I know that you have made up your minds, and that is why I boasted of you to the Macedonians, stating that Achaia was ready a year ago; and your zeal has stirred up a great many people.

3 Yet I have sent the brethren, so that our pride in you should not be in vain because of this question; for as I have said, you must be prepared,

4 Lest it happen that some Macedonians come with me and find you unprepared and we would be ashamed; for because of our pride in you, we would not say anything which would put the blame on you.

5 Therefore I thought it necessary to ask these, my brethren, to go before me to you, and make ready in advance the blessing of which you have long ago been notified, that you might have it ready as a blessing and not as though it were forced on you.

6 But remember this: He who sows sparingly shall reap also sparingly; and he who sows generously shall reap also generously.

7 So let every man give according to what he has decided in his mind, not grudgingly or of necessity; for God loves a cheerful giver.

8 God is able to make all goodness abound to you, and may you always have enough of everything for yourselves, and may you abound in every good work.

9 As it is written, He has distributed liberally, and given to the poor; and his righteousness endures for ever.

10 Now he who gives seed to the sower and bread for food will supply and multiply your seed and cause the fruits of your righteousness to grow,

11 That you may be enriched in everything, in all liberality; for such generosity enables us to perfect thanksgiving to God.

12 For the administration of this service not only supplies the wants of the saints, but it also is made abundant by many thanksgivings to God.

13 By this experiment of charitable service they glorify God in that you have subjected yourselves to the faith of the gospel of Christ, and through your generosity you have become partakers with them and with all men,

14 And they offer prayer on your behalf with greater love, because of the abundance of the grace of God which has been on you.

15 Thanks be to God for his incomparable gift.

CHAPTER 10

NOW I, Paul, beseech you by the gentleness and meekness of Christ; even though I am humble when present among you, I have the confidence when I am far away,

2 I beseech you not to be troubled, when I arrive, by the things which I hope to carry out; for it is my purpose to put to scorn those men who regard us as if we lived after the flesh.

3 For though we do live an earthly life, yet we do not serve worldly things.

4 For the weapons which we use are not earthly weapons, but of the might of God by which we conquer rebellious strongholds,

5 Casting down imaginations, and every false thing that exalts itself against the knowledge of God, and capturing every thought to the obedience of Christ;

6 And we are prepared to seek vengeance on those who are disobedient, when your obedience is fulfilled.

7 Do you judge by outward appearance? If any man thinks of himself that he belongs to Christ, let him know this of himself, that just as he belongs to Christ, so we also belong.

8 For if I should boast somewhat more of the authority which our Lord has given me, I should not be ashamed, for he has given it to us for your edification, and not for your destruction.

9 But I am hesitant, lest I seem as if I were trying to frighten you with my letter.

10 For there are men who say that his epistles are weighty and powerful; but his bodily appearance is weak, and his speech foolish.

11 But let him who supposes so consider this, that just as we express ourselves in our epistles when we are away, so are we also in deed when we are present.

12 For we dare not count or compare ourselves with those who are proud of themselves; for it is because they measure themselves by themselves that they do not understand.

13 We do not boast beyond our measure, but according to the measure of the rule which God has distributed to us, a measure to reach even to you.

14 It is not because we are unable to climb where you are; nor are trying to misrepresent ourselves; for we have climbed where we are through the gospel of Christ;

15 And we do not boast of things beyond our measure; that is, by other men's labor, but we have the hope, that when your faith grows, our pride shall be justified according to our measure.

16 And we shall become strengthened so that we may preach the gospel in the regions beyond you, and not boast of the things already done by others.

17 But he who boasts, let him glory in the Lord.

18 For it is not the one who praises himself who is approved, but the one whom the Lord commends.

CHAPTER 11

I WISH you to be patient with me for a while, so that I may speak plainly, and I am sure you will be.

2 For I am zealous for you with the zealousness of God, for I have espoused you to a husband, that I may present you as a pure virgin to Christ.

3 But I am afraid that just as the serpent through his deceitfulness misled Eve, so your minds should be corrupted from the sincerity that is in Christ.

4 For if he who has come to you preaches another Jesus, whom we have not preached, or if you have received another spirit, which you had not received, or another gospel, which you had not accepted, you might have listened to him.

5 For I think that I am not in the least inferior to the most distinguished apostles.

6 But though I am a poor speaker, I am not poor in knowledge; but we

have been thoroughly made manifest among you in all things.

7 Probably I have acted foolishly in humbling myself, that you might be exalted, because I preached to you the gospel of God freely.

8 I deprived other churches, taking supplies from them, in order to minister to you.

9 And when I came to you and was in need, I did not burden any of you for my wants were supplied by the brethren who came from Macedonia; I have taken care of myself in every way and I will so continue to keep myself that I will not be a burden to you.

10 As the truth of Christ is in me, no man shall stop me of this boasting in the regions of Achaia.

11 Why? Because I do not love you? God knows I do love you.

12 But what I do, I will continue to do, so as to give no occasion to those who seek an occasion; and that, in whatever they boast, they may not be found equal to us;

13 For they are false apostles and deceitful workers, posing as apostles of Christ.

14 There is no marvel in this; for if Satan disguises himself as the angel of light,

15 It is no great thing if his ministers also pose as the ministers of righteousness, whose end shall be according to their works.

16 I say again, let no man think me a fool; if otherwise, yet as a fool receive me, that I may boast myself a little.

17 What I now say, I speak not after our Lord, but as it were foolishly, on this occasion of boasting.

18 Because many boast on the things of the flesh, I boast also.

19 For you endure fools readily, knowing that you yourselves are wise.

20 For you endure the man who dominates you and the man who lives at your expense and the man who takes from you and the man who exalts himself over you and the man who smites you on the face.

21 I speak this as a reproach, as though we were weak. Now I speak foolishly; in whatsoever other men are bold, I venture also.

22 Now if they are Hebrews, so am I. If they are Israelites, so am I. If they are descendants of Abraham, so am I.

23 If they are ministers of Christ (I speak as a fool), I am greater than they; in labor more than they, in wounds more than they, in imprisonments more frequent than they, and in danger of death many times.

24 By the Jews I was scourged five times, each time forty stripes less one.

25 Three times I was beaten with rods, once I was stoned, three times I was in shipwreck, a day and a night I have been adrift in the sea in shipwreck.

26 On many journeys I have been in perils from rivers, in perils of robbers, in perils from my own kinsmen, in perils from the Gentiles, in perils in the city, in perils in the wilderness, in perils in the sea, in perils from false brethren;

27 In toil and weariness, in sleepless nights, in hunger and thirst, through much fasting, in cold and nakedness.

28 Besides other things and the many calling on me everyday, I have also the care of all the churches.

29 Who is sick that I do not feel the pain? Who stumbles that does not have my heartfelt sympathy?

30 If I must needs boast, I will boast of my sufferings.

31 The God and Father of our Lord Jesus Christ, who is blessed forever and ever, knows that I do not lie.

32 At Damascus the general of the army of King Aretas placed the city of the Damascenes under guard in order to seize me;

33 And I was lowered in a basket from a window over the city wall, and thus I escaped from his hands.

CHAPTER 12

BOASTING is proper, but there is no advantage in it, and I prefer to relate the visions and revelations of our Lord.

2 ¶I knew a man in Christ more than fourteen years ago, but whether I knew him in the body or out of the

body, I do not know; God knows; this very one was caught up to the third heaven.

3 And I still know this man, but whether in the body or whether out of the body, I cannot tell; God knows;

4 How that he was caught up to paradise and heard unspeakable words, which it is not lawful for a man to utter.

5 Of such a person, I will boast; but of myself, I will not boast, except in my weaknesses.

6 But even if I should desire to boast, I will not be a fool; for I will tell the truth; but now I refrain, lest any one should think more of me than what he sees me to be and what he hears from me.

7 And lest I should be exalted through the abundance of the revelations, there was delivered to me a thorn in my flesh, the angel of Satan to buffet me, lest I should be exalted.

8 Three times I besought my Lord concerning this thing, that it might depart from me.

9 And he said to me, My grace is sufficient for you; for my strength is made perfect in weakness. Most gladly therefore I would rather boast in my infirmities, that the power of Christ may rest upon me.

10 Therefore I am content with infirmities, insults, hardships, persecutions, and imprisonments for Christ's sake; for when I am physically weak, then I am spiritually strong.

11 Behold, I am foolish to boast but you have forced me; for you ought to have testified concerning me; for in no way am I less than those apostles who are highly honored, though I am nothing.

12 The miracles which the apostles have wrought I have wrought among you also in all patience, in signs, in wonders, and mighty deeds.

13 For what do you lack that other churches have, except it be that I myself was not burdensome to you? Forgive me this fault!

14 ¶Behold, this is the third time I am prepared to come to you; and I will not burden you; for I seek nothing from you but yourselves; for chil-

dren are not under obligation to lay up treasure for the parents, but the parents for the children.

15 I will gladly pay my expenses, and I will even give myself for the sake of your souls; though the more I love you, the less you love me.

16 ¶But be it so, I did not burden you; nevertheless as a shrewd man, I caught you with guile.

17 Why? Did I extort anything from you by any of the men whom I sent to you?

18 I requested Titus to visit you, and I sent brethren with him. Did Titus extort anything from you? Did we not walk in the same spirit, and did we not walk in the same steps?

19 ¶Why? Do you still think we are apologizing? No! We speak before God in Christ; and we do all these things, my beloved, for your edification.

20 For I fear, lest when I come to you, I shall not find you such as I wish to find you, and that you also will not find me as you wish to find me, lest there be controversies, envyings, angers, stubbornness, accusations, slanderings, boastings and disorders.

21 Perhaps when I come to you, my God will humble me, and I will mourn over many who have sinned and who have not repented of the impurity, immorality, and lasciviousness which they have committed.

CHAPTER 13

THIS is the third time I am ready to come to you, for by the mouth of two or three witnesses every charge is sustained.

2 I have told you before, and again I tell you in advance, just as I have told you on my two previous visits; and now even while I am far away I write to those who have sinned and to all others, that if I come again, I will not spare any one;

3 Since you seek a proof of Christ speaking in me, he has never been weak among you, but is mighty in you.

4 For though Jesus was crucified through weakness, yet he lives by the

power of God. As we are weak with him, so we are alive with him by the power of God who is within you.

5 Examine yourselves, whether you are in the same faith; heal your souls. Do you not realize that Jesus Christ is in you? If this is not so, then you are rejected.

6 But I trust that you shall know that we are not rejected.

7 And I pray to God that our testing will find nothing wrong with you; but that you may be found doing good things, even though we may appear as though we were rejected.

8 For we cannot do anything against the truth, but for the truth.

9 For we are glad when we are weak and you are strong; and this also we pray for, that you may be perfected.

10 Therefore I write these things while I am far away, so that when I come, I need not deal harshly with you, according to the authority which my Lord has given me, which is for your edification and not for your destruction.

11 ¶Henceforth, my brethren, rejoice, be perfect, be of good comfort, be of one mind, live in peace; and the God of love and peace shall be with you.

12 Greet one another with a holy kiss.

13 All the saints salute you.

14 The peace of our Lord Jesus Christ, the love of God, and the fellowship of the Holy Spirit, be with you all. Amen.

THE EPISTLE OF PAUL THE APOSTLE TO THE

GALATIANS

CHAPTER 1

PAUL, an apostle, not sent by men nor appointed by man, but by Jesus Christ and God the Father, who raised him from the dead,

2 And all the brethren who are with me, to the churches of Galatia:

3 Grace be to you and peace from God the Father and from our Lord Jesus Christ,

4 Who gave himself for our sins that he might deliver us from this present evil world, according to the will of God our Father;

5 To whom be glory for ever and ever. Amen.

6 ¶I am surprised how soon you have turned to another gospel, away from Christ who has called you by his grace,

7 A gospel which does not even exist; howbeit, there are men who have stirred you up and want to pervert the gospel of Christ.

8 But though we or an angel from heaven preach any other gospel to you than that which we have preached to you, let him be accursed.

9 As I have said before, so say I now again, If any man preaches any other gospel to you than that you have received, let him be accursed.

10 Do I now persuade men or God? Or do I seek to please men? For if I tried to please men, I should not be a servant of Christ.

11 ¶But I want you to know, my brethren, that the gospel which I preached was not from men.

12 For I did not receive it nor learn it from man, but through the revelation of Jesus Christ.

13 You have heard of the manner of my life in time past in the Jews' religion, how beyond measure I per-

secuted the church of God and tried to destroy it;

14 And how that I was far more advanced in the Jews' religion than many of my age among the people of my race; for above all, I was especially zealous for the doctrines of my forefathers.

15 But when it pleased God, who had chosen me from my birth and called me by his grace,

16 To reveal his Son to me, that I might preach him among the Gentiles, I did not immediately disclose it to any human being;

17 Neither did I go up to Jerusalem to them who had been apostles before me; but instead I went to Arabia and returned again to Damascus.

18 Then after three years I went up to Jerusalem to see Kepa, and stayed with him fifteen days.

19 But I did not see any one of the other apostles except James the brother of our Lord.

20 Now the things which I write to you, behold, I confess before God, I do not lie.

21 After that I went to the regions of Syria and Cilicia;

22 And I was unknown by face to the churches of Christ in Judea.

23 For they had heard only this much: that he who had persecuted us before now preached the faith which previously he tried to destroy.

24 And they praised God because of me.

CHAPTER 2

THEN, fourteen years later, I went up again to Jerusalem with Barnabas, and took Titus with me also.

2 And I went up because of a revelation, and I declared to them the gospel which I preached among the Gentiles, and I privately explained to those who were considered leaders among us, lest by any means I had labored or should labor in vain.

3 And Titus, also, who was with me, being Aramean, was not compelled to be circumcised,

4 But because of the false brethren who have come against us to spy out the freedom which we have in Jesus Christ, with the intention of enslaving us;

5 To those false brothers we did not submit, not even for an hour, that the truth of the gospel might remain with you.

6 Now those who were considered to be important (what they are makes no difference to me, for God does not discriminate among men), even these very persons, did not contribute additional knowledge to me.

7 But on the contrary, when they saw that the gospel of the uncircumcision was entrusted to me, as the gospel of the circumcision had been entrusted to Peter

8 (For he who made Kepa vigorous in the apostleship of the circumcision has also made me mighty in the apostleship of the Gentiles)

9 And when they knew that the grace had been given to me, then James, Kepa, and John, who were considered to be pillars, gave to me and Barnabas the right hand of fellowship, that we might labor among the Gentiles, and they, among the people of circumcision;

10 Only they would that we should remember the poor, and that I have endeavored to do.

11 But when Kepa came to Antioch, I reproved him to his face, because he was to be blamed.

12 For before certain men came from James, Kepa ate with the Gentiles; but after they came, he withdrew and separated himself because he was afraid of them who belonged to the circumcision.

13 And all the other Jewish converts cast their lot with him on this issue, insomuch that Barnabas also was carried away by their dissimulation.

14 But when I saw that they were not following uprightly according to the truth of the gospel, I said to Peter in the presence of them all, If you being a Jew live after the manner of Gentiles and not as do the Jews, why do you compel the Gentile converts to live as do the Jews?

15 For if we who are of Jewish origin and not sinners of the Gentiles

16 Know that a man is not justified by the works of the law but by the faith in Jesus Christ, even we have believed in Jesus Christ, that we might be justified by the faith in Christ and not by the works of the law; for by the works of the law shall no human being be justified.

17 But if, while we seek to be justified by Christ, we ourselves also are found sinners, is therefore our Lord Jesus Christ a minister of sin? Far be it.

18 For if I build again the things which I destroyed, I will prove myself to be a transgressor of the law.

19 For through the law I am dead to the law, that I might live to God.

20 I am crucified with Christ; henceforth it is not I who live, but Christ who lives in me; and the life which now I live in the flesh I live by the faith of the Son of God, who loved me and gave himself for me.

21 I do not frustrate the grace of God; for if righteousness comes by means of the law, then Christ died in vain.

CHAPTER 3

O FOOLISH Galatians, who has bewitched you from your faith after Jesus Christ, crucified, has been pictured before your eyes?

2 This only I want to know from you, Did you receive the Spirit through the works of the law or through obedience to faith?

3 Are you so foolish, after having begun with spiritual things, to end now with things of the flesh?

4 Have you believed all these things in vain? I hope that it is to no purpose.

5 Does he therefore who gives you the Spirit and works miracles among you do these things by the works of the law or by obedience to faith?

6 Just as Abraham believed God, and it was accounted to him for righteousness,

7 You must know therefore that those who trust in faith are the children of Abraham.

8 Because God knew in advance that the Gentiles would be declared righteous through faith, he first preached to Abraham, as it is said in the Holy Scripture, In you shall all the Gentiles be blessed.

9 So then, it is the believers who are blessed through Abraham the faithful.

10 For those who rely on the works of the law are still under the curse; for as it is written, Cursed is everyone who does not practice everything which is written in the book of the law.

11 But that no man is justified by the law before God, is evident; for, as it is written, The righteous shall live by faith.

12 Thus the law is not made by faith, but, Whosoever shall do the things which are written in it shall live in it.

13 Christ has redeemed us from the curse of the law by becoming accursed for our sakes (for it is written, Cursed is everyone who hangs on a cross),

14 That the blessing of Abraham might come on the Gentiles through Jesus Christ, that we might receive the promise of the Spirit through faith.

15 My brethren, I speak as I would to an assembly of men: Though it be but a man's covenant, yet if it be confirmed, no man can reject it or change anything in it.

16 Now the promises were made to Abraham and to his descendants as a covenant. He did not say, To your descendants, as of many, but, To your descendants, as one, that is Christ.

17 And this I say, that the covenant which was previously confirmed of God in Christ cannot be repudiated and the promise nullified by the law which came four hundred and thirty years later.

18 For if the inheritance is by the law, then it would not be as the fulfillment of promise; but God gave it to Abraham by promise.

19 ¶Then what is the use of the law? It was added because of transgression, till the coming of the heir

to whom the promise was made; and the law was given by angels by the hand of a mediator.

20 Now a mediator does not represent one alone, but God is one.

21 Is the law then against the promises of God? Far be it; for if a law had been given which could have wrought salvation, righteousness would truly have come as the result of the law.

22 But the scripture has included everything under sin, that the promise by the faith of Jesus Christ might be given to those who believe.

23 But before faith came, we were guided by the law, while we were waiting for the faith which was to be revealed.

24 The law then was our pathfinder to bring us to Christ, that we might be justified by faith.

25 But since faith has come, we no longer are in need of the pathfinder.

26 For you are all the children of God by faith in Jesus Christ.

27 For those who have been baptized in the name of Christ have been clothed with Christ.

28 There is neither Jew nor Aramean, there is neither slave nor free, there is neither male nor female; for you are all one in Jesus Christ.

29 So if you belong to Christ, then you are descendants of Abraham, and his heirs according to the promise.

CHAPTER 4

NOW this I say, That the heir as long as he is young cannot be distinguished from the servants, though he is the lord of them all.

2 But he is under guardians and stewards until the time appointed by his father.

3 Even so we, when we were young, were subject to the principles of this world;

4 But when the fulness of the time was come, God sent forth his Son who, born of a woman, became subject to the law,

5 To redeem them who were under the law, that we might receive the adoption of sons.

6 And because you are sons, God has sent forth the Spirit of his Son into your hearts crying, Abba, Abon, O Father, our Father.

7 From now on you are not servants but sons; and if sons, then heirs of God through Jesus Christ.

8 Howbeit then, when you did not know God, you served those things which from their nature were not gods.

9 But now after you have known God, and, above all, are known of God, you turn again to those weak and poor principles, and you wish again to come under their bondage.

10 You still observe days and months and times and years.

11 I am afraid that perhaps I have labored among you in vain.

12 ¶My brethren, I beseech you, put yourself in my place; just as once I put myself in your place. You have not offended me at all.

13 You know that I was weak in flesh when I preached the gospel to you at the first.

14 And yet you did not despise me nor reject me on account of my weakness; but you received me as an angel of God, even as Jesus Christ.

15 Where is then the blessedness you had? For I can testify concerning you that, if it had been possible, you would have plucked out your own eyes and have given them to me.

16 Am I therefore become your enemy because I tell you the truth?

17 These men do not envy you for good, but they would dominate you so that you might envy them.

18 But it is good that you should always envy after good things, and not only when I am present with you.

19 My little children, for whom I am in travail again until Christ be a reality in you,

20 I wish I could be with you now and could change the tone of my voice, because I am deeply concerned about you.

21 Tell me, you who desire to be under the law, do you not hear the law?

22 For it is written that Abraham

had two sons, one by a bondmaid and one by a freewoman.

23 But he who was born of the bondmaid was born after the flesh; but he who was born of the freewoman was born by promise.

24 Now these things are a symbol of the two covenants, the one from mount Sinai giving birth to bondage, which is Hagar.

25 For this Hagar is mount Sinai in Arabia, and surrenders to Jerusalem which now is, and is in bondage with her children.

26 But the Jerusalem which is above is free, and is the mother of us all.

27 For as it is written, Make merry, O you barren who bear not; rejoice and cry, O you who travail not; for the children of the one in disfavor are more numerous than the children of the one who is favored.

28 ¶Now we, my brethren, are the children of promise, as was Isaac.

29 But as then, he who was born after the flesh persecuted him who was born after the Spirit, even so it is now.

30 Nevertheless what does the scripture say? Cast out the bondmaid and her son; for the son of the maidservant shall not inherit with the son of the freewoman.

31 So then, my brethren, we are not children of the maidservant but children of the freewoman.

CHAPTER 5

STAND firm therefore in the liberty with which Christ has made us free, and be not harnessed again under the yoke of servitude.

2 Behold, I, Paul, tell you that if you are circumcised, then Christ is of no benefit to you.

3 For I testify again to every man who is circumcised, that he is under obligation to fulfill the whole law.

4 You have ceased to adhere to Christ, who seek justification by the law; you are fallen from grace.

5 For we through the Spirit wait for the hope of righteousness by faith.

6 For in Christ Jesus neither is circumcision anything nor uncircumcision, but faith which is accomplished by love.

7 You were progressing well; who confused you that you should not obey the truth?

8 Your persuasion comes from him who called you.

9 A little leaven leavens the whole lump.

10 ¶I have confidence in you through our Lord, that you will consider no other beliefs, that he who troubles you shall bear his judgment, whosoever he is.

11 And I, my brethren, if I still preach circumcision, why should I be persecuted? Why? Has the cross ceased to be a stumbling block?

12 I wish those who are troubling you would be expelled.

13 ¶For, my brethren, you have been called to liberty; only do not use your liberty for an occasion to the things of the flesh, but by love serve one another.

14 For the whole law is fulfilled in one saying, that is, You shall love your neighbor as yourself.

15 But if you harm and plunder one another, take heed lest you be consumed one by another.

16 This I say then: Lead a spiritual life, and you shall never commit the lust of the flesh.

17 For the flesh craves that which is harmful to the Spirit, and the Spirit opposes the things of the flesh; and the two are contrary to one another, so that you are unable to do whatever you please.

18 But if you are led by the Spirit, you are not under the law.

19 For the works of the flesh are well known, which are these: adultery, impurity, and lasciviousness,

20 Idolatry, witchcraft, enmity, strife, jealousy, anger, stubbornness, seditions, heresies,

21 Envyings, murders, drunkenness, revellings, and all such things; those who practice these things, as I have told you before and I say to you now, shall not inherit the kingdom of God.

22 But the fruits of the Spirit are love, joy, peace, patience, gentleness, goodness, faith,

23 Meekness, self-control; there is no law against these.

24 And those who belong to Christ have controlled their weaknesses and passions.

25 Let us therefore live in the Spirit, and surrender to the Spirit.

26 Let us not be desirous of vainglory, provoking one another, envying one another.

CHAPTER 6

MY brethren, if any one be found at fault, you who are spiritual, restore him in a spirit of meekness; and be careful lest you also be tempted.

2 Bear one another's burdens, and so fulfil the law of Christ.

3 For if man thinks himself to be something, when he is nothing, he deceives himself.

4 But let every man examine his own work, and then may he glory within himself alone and not among others.

5 For every man shall bear his own burden.

6 Let him who is taught the word become a partaker with him who teaches all good things.

7 Do not be deceived; God is not mocked; for whatever a man sows, that shall he also reap.

8 He who sows things of the flesh, from the flesh shall reap corruption; he who sows things of the Spirit, from the Spirit shall reap life everlasting.

9 Let us not be weary in welldoing; for in due season we shall reap, if we faint not.

10 Therefore, as we have opportunity, let us do good to all men, especially to those who belong to the household of faith.

11 ¶You can see how long a letter I have written to you with my own hand.

12 Those who desire to boast in the things of the flesh are the ones who compel you to be circumcised only lest they should suffer persecution for the cross of Christ.

13 For not even they who are circumcised obey the law; but they want you to be circumcised so that they may boast over your flesh.

14 But as for me, I have nothing on which to boast except the cross of our Lord Jesus Christ, by whom the world is crucified to me and I am crucified to the world.

15 For in Christ Jesus neither circumcision is anything, nor uncircumcision, but it is a new creation that counts.

16 And upon those who follow this path be peace and mercy; and upon the Israel of God be peace and mercy.

17 From henceforth let no man trouble me, for I bear in my body the marks of our Lord Jesus Christ.

18 My brethren, the grace of our Lord Jesus Christ be with your spirit. Amen.

THE EPISTLE OF PAUL THE APOSTLE TO THE

EPHESIANS

CHAPTER 1

PAUL, an apostle of Jesus Christ by the will of God, to those who are in Ephesus, saints and believers in Jesus Christ:

2 Peace be with you and grace from God our Father, and from our Lord Jesus Christ:

3 ¶Blessed be the God and Father of our Lord Jesus Christ, who has blessed us with all spiritual blessings in heaven through Christ;

4 Just as from the beginning he has

chosen us through him before the foundation of the world, that we may become holy and without blemish before him.

5 And he marked us with his love to be his from the beginning, and adopted us to be sons through Jesus Christ, as it pleased his will,

6 To the praise of the glory of his grace that he has poured upon us by his beloved one.

7 In him we have salvation, and in his blood, forgiveness of sins, according to the richness of his grace,

8 That that grace which has abounded in us, in all wisdom and spiritual understanding,

9 And made known to us the mystery of his will that he has ordained from the very beginning, to work through it;

10 As a dispensation of the fulness of times, that all things might be made new in heaven and on earth through Christ,

11 By whom we have been chosen, as he had marked us from the beginning so he wanted to carry out everything according to the good judgment of his will,

12 That we should become the first to trust in Christ, to his honor and his glory,

13 In whom, you also have heard the word of truth, which is the gospel for your salvation; in him you have believed, so you are sealed with the Holy Spirit that was promised,

14 Which is the pledge of our inheritance, for the salvation of those who are saved and for the glory of his honour.

15 ¶Wherefore I also, since I heard of your faith in our Lord Jesus Christ and your love toward all the saints,

16 Never cease to give thanks for your sakes and to mention you in my prayers,

17 So that the God of our Lord Jesus Christ, the Father of glory, may give you the spirit of wisdom and revelation in the knowledge of him,

18 And so that the eyes of your understanding may be enlightened, that you may know what is the hope of his calling and what are the glorious riches of his inheritance in the saints,

19 And what is the exceeding greatness of his power in us as the result of the things we believe, according to the skill of his mighty power,

20 Which he wrought through Christ when he raised him from the dead and set him at his own right hand in heaven,

21 Far above all angels and power and might and dominion and every name that is named, not only in this world but also in the world which is to come,

22 And has put all things under his feet, and made him, who is above all things, the head of the church,

23 Which is his body and confirmation of him who fulfills all things and every thing.

CHAPTER 2

AND he has quickened you also who were dead because of your sins and trespasses;

2 In which you previously walked according to the course of this world, and according to the will of the supreme ruler of the air, the spirit which is active in the children of disobedience.

3 In those very deeds in which we were also corrupted from the very beginning through the lusts of the flesh, fulfilling the wills of the flesh and of the mind, thereby we became completely the children of wrath, even as others.

4 But God, who is rich in mercy, for his great love with which he loved us,

5 Even when we were dead in our sins, has made us live together with Christ, by whose grace we are saved;

6 And he has raised us up with him, and seated us with him in heaven, through Jesus Christ.

7 In the ages to come he might show the exceeding riches of his grace in his kindness toward us through Jesus Christ.

8 For it is by grace that you are saved through faith; not of your doing; it is the gift of God:

9 Not of works, lest any man should boast.

10 For we are his creation, created through Jesus Christ ultimately for good works, and God has before ordained that we should live in them.

11 Wherefore remember that you were Gentiles in the flesh from the beginning, and you were called Uncircumcision, differing from that which is called Circumcision, which is the work of the hands in the flesh.

12 At that time you were without Christ, being aliens to the customs of Israel and strangers to the covenants of the promise, without hope and without God in the world.

13 But now, through Jesus Christ, you who sometimes were far off are brought near by the blood of Christ.

14 For he is our peace, who has made both one, and has broken down the wall of separation between them;

15 And he has abolished by his precious body the enmity between them, and he has abolished by his commandments the ordinances of the law, that he may create, in his person, from the two, a new man, thus making peace;

16 And he reconciled both in one body with God, and with his cross he destroyed the enmity;

17 And he came and preached peace to you who are far away and to those who are near.

18 Through him we both are able to draw near by one Spirit to the Father.

19 Thus from henceforth you are neither strangers nor foreigners, but fellow-citizens with the saints and children of the household of God;

20 And you are built upon the foundation of the apostles and prophets, Jesus Christ himself being the cornerstone of the building:

21 And through him the whole building is fashioned and grows into a holy temple through the help of the Lord;

22 You also are builded by him for a habitation of God through the Spirit.

CHAPTER 3

FOR this cause I, Paul, am a prisoner of Jesus Christ for the sake of you Gentiles.

2 Have you ever heard of the dispensation of the grace of God which was given to me for you?

3 For the mystery was made known to me by a revelation, as I have briefly written you before,

4 So that when you read it you can understand my knowledge of the mystery of Christ,

5 Which in ages past was not made known to the sons of men, as it is now revealed to his holy apostles and prophets by the Spirit,

6 That the Gentiles should be fellow heirs and partakers of his body and of the promise which is given through him by the gospel.

7 Of that very gospel, I have been a minister, according to the gift of the grace of God given to me by the effectual working of his power.

8 Even to me, who am less than the least of all the saints, this grace was given, that I should preach among the Gentiles the unsearchable riches of Christ,

9 And that I might enlighten all men that they may see what is the dispensation of the mystery which for ages had been hidden from the world by God who created all things;

10 To the intent that through the church the manifold wisdom of God may be made known to the angels and powers which are in heaven,

11 Which is the wisdom he prepared in ages past and has carried out in Jesus Christ our Lord;

12 In whom we have freedom of access with confidence in his faith.

13 Therefore I ask that I may not grow weary in my afflictions for your sakes, which is for your happiness.

14 For this cause I bow my knees to the Father of our Lord Jesus Christ,

15 For whom all fatherhood in heaven and in earth is named,

16 To grant you, according to the riches of his glory, to be strengthened with might by his Spirit,

17 That Christ may dwell in your

inner man by faith, and in your hearts by love, strengthening your understanding and your foundation,

18 So that you may be able to comprehend with all the saints what is the height and depth and length and breadth,

19 And to know the love of Christ which surpasses all knowledge, that you may be filled with all the fulness of God.

20 Now to him who is able by power to do for us more than anyone else, and to do for us more than we ask or think, according to his mighty power that works in us,

21 Unto him be glory in his church by Jesus Christ throughout all ages, world without end. Amen.

CHAPTER 4

I THEREFORE, a prisoner of our Lord, beseech you to live as is worthy of the rank to which you are called,

2 With all humility and gentleness and with patience, forbearing one another in love,

3 Endeavoring to preserve the harmony of the Spirit in the bond of peace,

4 That you may become one body and one Spirit, even as you are called in one hope of your calling;

5 There is one Lord, one faith, and one baptism;

6 One God and Father of all, who is above all and through all and in all of us.

7 But to every one of us is given grace according to the measure of the gift of Christ.

8 Wherefore it is said, He ascended on high, and took possession of heaven and gave good gifts to men.

9 Now that he ascended, what is it but that he also descended first into the inner parts of the earth?

10 So he that descended is the same also that ascended far above all heavens, that he might fulfil all things.

11 And he has assigned some as apostles and some as prophets and some as evangelists and some as pastors and some as teachers;

12 For the perfecting of the saints, for the work of the ministry, for the edifying of the body of Christ,

13 Until we all become one in faith and in the knowledge of the Son of God, and become a perfect man according to the measure of the stature of the fulness of Christ,

14 That we henceforth be not as children easily stirred and carried away by every wind of false doctrines of men, who through their craftiness are artful in deceiving the people;

15 But that we be sincere in our love, so that in everything we may progress through Christ who is the head.

16 It is through him that the whole body is closely and firmly united at all joints, according to the measure of the gift which is given to every member, for the guidance and control of the body, in order to complete the edifying of the body in love.

17 ¶This I say therefore and testify in the Lord, that you henceforth live not as other Gentiles, who live in the vanity of their mind,

18 And whose understanding is dark, and who are alienated from the life of God, because they have no knowledge, and because of the blindness of their hearts;

19 And who have given up their hope, and have surrendered themselves to wantonness and to the practice of all uncleanness in their covetousness.

20 But that is not what you have been taught about Christ;

21 If you have truly heard him and have been taught by him, as the truth is found in Jesus,

22 Lay aside all your former practices, that is to say, the old man, which is degenerated with deceitful lusts,

23 And be renewed in the spirit of your mind,

24 And put on the new man, who is created by God in righteousness and true holiness.

25 Therefore you must put away from you lying and speak the truth, every man with his neighbor; for we are members one of another.

26 Be angry, but sin not; and let

not the sun go down upon your anger:

27 And do not give the devil a chance.

28 From henceforth let him that stole steal no more; but rather let him labor with his hands and do good deeds, that he may have something to give to him who is in need.

29 Let no evil word proceed from your mouth, but words that are good and useful for edification, that they will impart blessing to those who hear them.

30 And do not grieve the Holy Spirit of God, whereby you are sealed to the day of salvation.

31 Let all bitterness and wrath and anger and clamoring and blasphemy be put away from you, together with all malice;

32 And be kind one to another and tenderhearted, forgiving one another, even as God has forgiven us through Christ.

CHAPTER 5

BE therefore Godlike, as beloved children.

2 And walk in love, as Christ also has loved us and has given himself for us, an offering and a sacrifice to God for a sweet savour.

3 ¶But let not immorality or any uncleanness or covetousness be heard of among you, as becomes saints;

4 Neither cursing nor foolish words nor insults nor words of flattery, none of which are necessary; but instead of these, let thanks be offered.

5 You should know this, that no one guilty of fornication, no unclean person, no covetous man who serves idols, has any inheritance in the kingdom of Christ and of God.

6 Let no man deceive you with vain words; for because of these things the anger of God comes on the children of disobedience.

7 Therefore do not be partakers with them.

8 For previously you were ignorant, but now you have been enlightened by our Lord, and should live therefore like children of light.

9 For the fruits of light are found in all goodness and righteousness and truth;

10 And so you must discern that which is acceptable before our Lord.

11 Have no part in the unfruitful works of darkness, but rather condemn them.

12 For it is a shame even to speak of the things that are done by them in secret.

13 For all things that are condemned are exposed by the light; and anything that is made manifest is light.

14 Therefore it is said, Awake, O sleeper and rise from the dead, and Christ shall give you light.

15 ¶Watch therefore, that you live a glorious life, not as foolish men but as wise,

16 Who take advantage of their opportunity; for these are difficult days.

17 Wherefore do not lack wisdom, but understand what the will of God is.

18 And do not become drunk with wine, wherein is intemperance; but be filled with the Spirit,

19 Speaking to your souls in psalms and hymns and spiritual songs, sing with your heart to the Lord,

20 Giving thanks always for all men to God the Father in the name of our Lord Jesus Christ.

21 ¶Submit yourselves one to another in the love of Christ.

22 Wives, submit yourselves to your husbands as to our Lord.

23 For the husband is the head of the wife, even as Christ is the head of the church, and he is the saviour of the body.

24 Therefore as the church is subject to Christ, so let the wives be to their own husbands in every thing.

25 Husbands, love your wives, even as Christ loved his church and gave himself for it,

26 That he might sanctify and cleanse it by the washing of water and by the word,

27 In order to build for himself a glorious church, without stain or wrinkle, or any such thing; but that

it should be holy and without blemish.

28 So should men love their wives as their own bodies. He who loves his wife loves himself.

29 For no man ever yet hated his own body, but nourishes it and cherishes it, even as Christ does for his church.

30 For we are members of his body, of his flesh, and of his bones.

31 For this reason shall a man leave his father and mother, and shall be joined to his wife, and they two shall be one flesh.

32 This is a great mystery; but I speak concerning Christ and his church.

33 Nevertheless, let every one of you so love his wife as himself, and the wife see that she reverence her husband.

CHAPTER 6

CHILDREN, obey your parents in our Lord, for this is right.

2 This is the first commandment with promise: Honor your father and your mother,

3 That it may be well with you and you may live long on the earth.

4 And parents, do not provoke your children to anger; but bring them up in the discipline and teaching of our Lord.

5 Servants, be obedient to your masters according to the flesh, with reverence and trembling and with a sincere heart, as to Christ;

6 Not with eyeservice, as hypocrites, but as the servants of Christ, doing the will of God from the heart.

7 And serve well with your whole soul, with love, as to our Lord, and not to men,

8 Knowing that whatever good thing any man does, the same shall he receive from our Lord, whether he be a slave or a freeman.

9 Also, masters, do the same things for your servants, forgiving their faults, because you also have your own Master in heaven; and there is no respect of persons with him.

10 ¶From henceforth, my brethren, be strong in our Lord and in the power of his might.

11 Put on the whole armor of God, that you may be able to stand against the wiles of the devil.

12 For your conflict is not only with flesh and blood, but also with the angels, and with powers, with the rulers of this world of darkness, and with the evil spirits under the heavens.

13 Therefore put on the whole armor of God, that you may be able to meet the evil one, and being prepared you shall prevail.

14 Arise, therefore, gird your loins with truth and put on the breastplate of righteousness;

15 And have your feet shod with the preparation of the gospel of peace;

16 Together with these, take for yourselves the shield of faith, for with it you shall be able to quench all the flaming darts of the wicked.

17 Put on the helmet of salvation and take the sword of the Spirit, which is the word of God;

18 And pray always, with all prayer and supplication in the Spirit; and in that prayer be watchful at all times, praying constantly and supplicating for all the saints,

19 And for me also, that words may be given to me as soon as I open my mouth, so that I may boldly preach the mystery of the gospel,

20 For which I am a messenger in chains, that I may speak openly about it, as I ought to speak.

21 ¶In order that you also may know my affairs and what I do, Tychicus, a beloved brother and a faithful minister in our Lord, shall make known to you all things;

22 Him I have sent to you for the same purpose, that you may know how I am and that he may comfort your hearts.

23 Peace be to our brethren, and love with faith, from God the Father and from our Lord Jesus Christ.

24 Grace be with all them that love our Lord Jesus Christ in sincerity. Amen.

THE EPISTLE OF PAUL THE APOSTLE TO THE

PHILIPPIANS

CHAPTER 1

PAUL and Timotheus, servants of Jesus Christ, to all the saints in Jesus Christ who are at Philippi, together with the elders and deacons:

2 Grace be to you and peace from God our Father and from our Lord Jesus Christ.

3 ¶I give thanks to my God for your steady remembrance of me.

4 In all my prayers for you, I make supplication with joy,

5 For your fellowship in the gospel from the very first day until now,

6 Being confident of this very thing, that he who has begun the good work among you, the same will continue it until the day of our Lord Jesus Christ;

7 And this is the right way for me to think of you all, for I have you in my heart because through all my imprisonment and my defense and confirmation of the truth of the gospel, you have been partakers with me of grace.

8 For God is my witness of how much I love you through the love of Jesus Christ.

9 And for this I pray, that your love may abound yet more and more in knowledge and in all spiritual understanding,

10 So that you may choose the things that are excellent and that you may be pure and without offence in the day of Christ,

11 And be filled with the fruits of righteousness which are by Jesus Christ, to the glory and the praise of God.

12 ¶Now I would have you know this, my brethren, that my work has been greatly furthered by the gospel;

13 And the reasons for my imprisonments have been made manifest by Christ to all Cæsar's court and to all men.

14 And many of the brethren in our Lord have grown confident by my imprisonment and, with increasing boldness, speak the word of God without fear.

15 While some of them preach only because of envy and strife, others preach Christ in good will and love;

16 For they know that I am appointed for the defense of the gospel;

17 But those who preach Christ out of contention, do it not sincerely, but do it expecting to increase the hardship of my imprisonment.

18 And I have rejoiced and still do rejoice in this, that in every way, whether in pretense or in truth, Christ is preached.

19 For I know that through your prayers and the gift of the Spirit of Jesus Christ, all these things will ultimately turn out for my salvation,

20 Just as it is my earnest hope and expectation that in nothing shall I be ashamed, but that openly as always, so also now will Christ be magnified through my body, whether in life or death.

21 For Christ is my life, and to die is gain.

22 Even if in this life of the flesh my labors bear fruits, I do not know what to choose.

23 For I am torn between two desires, the one to depart, that I may be with Christ, which is far better;

24 Nevertheless, for me to remain in the flesh is more needful for you.

25 And this I surely know, that I shall be spared and remain for your joy and for the furtherance of your faith,

26 So that when I come again to you, your rejoicing in Jesus Christ will abound through me.

27 ¶Only conduct yourselves as becomes the gospel of Christ, so that whether I come and see you or whether I am far away, I may hear of your good conduct, that you are standing firm in one spirit and in one soul, and triumphing together through the faith of the gospel,

28 And that in nothing are you terrified by our adversaries, whose conduct is the sign of their own destruction, but your salvation, and this is from God.

29 For it has been given to you not only to believe in Christ but also to suffer for his sake,

30 And that you may endure such trials as those which you have seen me in and such as you now hear that I am in.

CHAPTER 2

IF, therefore, you have found consolation in Christ or wholehearted love or fellowship of the Spirit or compassion and mercies,

2 Complete my joy by being in one accord and one love and one soul and one mind.

3 Do nothing through strife or vainglory; but in humility let each regard his neighbor better than himself.

4 Let no one be mindful only of his own things, but let every one be mindful of the things of his neighbor also.

5 Reason this within you which Jesus Christ also reasoned,

6 Who, being in the form of God, did not consider it robbery to be equal with God;

7 But made himself of no reputation and took upon himself the form of a servant and was in the likeness of men;

8 And, being found in the form of a man, he humbled himself and became obedient to death, even the death of the cross;

9 Therefore God also has highly exalted him and given him a name which is above every name,

10 That at the name of Jesus every knee should bow, of those in heaven, of those on earth, and those under the earth,

11 And every tongue shall confess that Jesus Christ is the Lord, to the glory of God his Father.

12 From now on, my beloved, just as you have always been obedient, not only in my presence, but much more in my absence, work out your own salvation with reverence and trembling.

13 For it is God who inspires you with the will to do the good things which you desire to do.

14 Do all things without disputing and doubting,

15 That you may be sincere and blameless, like the innocent children of God, in the midst of a crooked and perverse generation, among whom you shine as lights in the world;

16 For you are to them the light of life, for my pride and glory in the day of Christ; for I have not run in vain nor labored in vain.

17 Yes, even if my blood be offered upon the sacrifice and the service of your faith, I am happy and rejoice with you all.

18 Likewise you also must be happy and rejoice with me.

19 ¶But I trust in our Lord Jesus Christ to send Timotheus to you soon, that I also may be at ease when I learn of your well-being.

20 For I have no one here as interested as I am, who will sincerely care for your welfare;

21 For all seek their own, not the things which are Jesus Christ's.

22 But you know his record, that as a son with his father, he has served with me in the gospel.

23 I hope to send him to you presently, as soon as I see how it will go with me.

24 But I trust in my Lord that I also myself shall come shortly.

25 But right now I am forced through circumstances to send to you Epaphroditus, a brother, and assistant and co-worker with me, but he is also your apostle and one who ministers to my wants.

26 For he has been longing to see you all, and has been depressed because he knew you had heard that he had been sick.

27 For indeed he was sick to the point of death but God had mercy on him; and not on him only, but on me also, lest I should have sorrow upon sorrow.

28 Therefore I have sent him quickly, so that, when you see him again, you may rejoice and that I may be relieved from anxiety.

29 Welcome him, therefore, in the Lord with all joy; and honor those who are like him,

30 Because for the work of Christ he came near to death; and by his self-denial, he made good your lack of service to me.

CHAPTER 3

HENCEFORTH, my brethren, rejoice in our Lord. It does not bother me to write the same things to you, because they enlighten you.

2 Beware of vicious men, beware of evil workers, beware of circumcising.

3 For we are the true people of circumcision, who worship God in Spirit and glory in Jesus Christ, and yet do not rely on things of the flesh.

4 As for me, I once relied on things of the flesh. However, if a man thinks his hope is on things of the flesh, I have more hope than he has;

5 For I was circumcised when I was eight days old, being an Israelite by race, of the tribe of Benjamin, a Hebrew son of Hebrews, and according to the law a Pharisee;

6 And concerning zeal, I was a persecutor of the church; and according to the standards of righteousness of the law, I was blameless.

7 But these things which once were a gain to me, I counted a loss for the sake of Christ.

8 And I still count them all a loss for the sake of abundant knowledge of Jesus Christ my Lord, for whom I have lost everything, and I have considered all those things as refuse, so that I may abound in Christ

9 And be found in him, since I have no righteousness of my own gained from the law, but the righteousness which comes through the faith of Christ; that is, the righteousness which comes from God,

10 So that through this righteousness I may know Jesus and the power of his resurrection, and be a partaker of his sufferings, even to a death like his,

11 That I may by any means attain the resurrection from the dead.

12 Not as though I had already attained or were already perfect; but I am striving that I may reach that for which Jesus Christ appointed me.

13 My brethren, I do not consider that I have reached the goal; but this one thing I do know, forgetting those things which are behind, I strive for those things which are before me;

14 I press toward the goal to receive the prize of victory of God's highest calling through Jesus Christ.

15 Therefore let those of you who are perfect think about these things; and if you reason in any other way, God will reveal even that to you.

16 Nevertheless, whereto we have already attained, let us walk by the same path and with one accord.

17 My brethren, be followers like me, and observe those who walk such a path, and then you will be examples as we are.

18 For there are many who live otherwise, of whom I have often told you, and now I tell you with tears that they are the enemies of the cross of Christ,

19 Whose end is destruction, whose God is their belly, and whose glory is in their shame; whose thought is on earthly things.

20 But our labours are in heavenly things, from whence we look for our Saviour, our Lord Jesus Christ,

21 Who shall transform our poor body to the likeness of his glorious body, according to his mighty power, whereby he is able even to subdue all things to himself.

CHAPTER 4

HENCEFORTH, my dearly beloved brethren, my joy and crown, in this manner stand firm in our Lord, my beloved.

2 ¶I beseech Euodias and I beseech Syntyche to be of one accord in our Lord.

3 I beseech you also, my true yoke-fellow, help those women who laboured with me in the gospel, together with Clement, and with the rest of my fellow labourers, whose names are written in the book of life.

4 Rejoice in our Lord always; and again I say, Rejoice.

5 Let your humility be known to all men. Our Lord is at hand.

6 Do not worry over things, but always by prayer and supplication with thanksgiving let your requests be made known to God.

7 And the peace of God, which passes all understanding, shall keep your hearts and minds through Jesus Christ.

8 Finally, my brethren, whatever is true, whatever is honest, whatever is just, whatever is pure, whatever is lovely, whatever is of good report; if there is any virtue and if there is any praise, think about these things.

9 Those things which you have learned and received and heard and seen in me, do; and the God of peace shall be with you.

10 ¶But I rejoiced in our Lord greatly, that you have continued to care for me, just as you have always cared, even though you yourselves have not had sufficient.

11 Nor am I saying this simply because I am in want; for I have learned to make what I have sufficient to meet my needs.

12 I know what it is to be poor, and I know what it is to be rich; I have gone through many things and experienced many things, both to be full and to be hungry, both to have plenty and to be in want.

13 I can do all things through Christ who strengthens me.

14 But you have done well to share my difficulties.

15 Now you Philippians know also that in the beginning of the gospel, when I departed from Macedonia, no church shared with me as concerning giving and receiving, but you only.

16 For even at Thessalonica you sent more than once to meet my needs.

17 I do not say this because I want a gift, but because I want to see the fruits of the gospel increased to you.

18 I have received everything I need, and it is more than enough; I am satisfied, having received everything you sent me by Epaphroditus, and it was welcome as a fragrant perfume and a sacrifice acceptable and well pleasing to God.

19 But my God will supply all your needs according to his riches in the glory of Jesus Christ.

20 Now to God our Father be glory and honour for ever and ever. Amen.

21 ¶Salute every saint in Jesus Christ. The brethren who are with me greet you.

22 All the saints salute you, especially those who are of Cæsar's household.

23 The grace of our Lord Jesus Christ be with you all. Amen.

THE EPISTLE OF PAUL THE APOSTLE TO THE

COLOSSIANS

CHAPTER 1

PAUL, an apostle of Jesus Christ by the will of God, and Timotheus our brother,

2 To those who are at Colosse, holy brethren and believers in Jesus Christ: Peace be with you, and grace from God our Father and our Lord Jesus Christ.

3 ¶Always we give thanks to God, the Father of our Lord Jesus Christ, and always we pray for you,

4 Since we heard of your faith in Jesus Christ and of your love for all the saints,

5 For the hope which is preserved for you in heaven, of which you heard before in the true word of the gospel,

6 Which has been preached to you, just as it has been preached throughout the world, growing and bringing forth fruits, as it does also in you, since the day you heard of it and knew the grace of God in truth,

7 Just as you have learned it from Epaphras our beloved fellow servant, who is for your sakes a faithful minister of Christ,

8 And who has made known to us your love for spiritual things.

9 ¶For this cause we also, since the day we heard it, do not cease to pray for you and to ask that you might be filled with the knowledge of the will of God in all wisdom and in all spiritual understanding,

10 That you might live a righteous life, please God with all good works, and bring forth good fruits and grow in the knowledge of God;

11 And be strengthened with all might, according to the greatness of his glory, in all patience and longsuffering,

12 So that you may joyfully give thanks to God the Father, who has enlightened us and made us worthy partakers of the inheritance of the saints,

13 And has delivered us from the power of darkness and brought us to the kingdom of his beloved Son,

14 By whom we have obtained salvation and forgiveness of sins.

15 He is the image of the invisible God, and the first-born of every creature:

16 And through him were created all things that are in heaven and on earth, visible and invisible; whether imperial thrones or lordships or angelic orders or dominions, all things were in his hand and were created by him;

17 And he is before all things, and by him all things are sustained.

18 And he is the head of the body, the church; for he is the beginning, the firstfruits of the resurrection from the dead, that in all things he might be the first;

19 For it pleased God to complete all things in him;

20 And by his hand to reconcile everything to himself; and through his blood shed on the cross to make peace both for those who dwell on earth and for those who dwell in heaven.

21 ¶Even to you, who in times past were alienated and hostile in your minds because of your evil works, peace has now been given,

22 Through the sacrifice of his body and his death, so that he may raise you before him, holy and without reproach and blameless,

23 If you continue in your faith and your foundation is firm, and if you are not moved from the hope of the gospel which you have heard and which has been preached to every creature under heaven, and for which I, Paul, have become a minister;

24 And now rejoice in my sufferings for you, and make up that which is lacking of the sufferings of Christ in my flesh for his body's sake, which is the church;

25 For which I became a minister, according to the dispensation of God which has been given to me for you, fully to preach the word of God everywhere,

26 Even the mystery which has been hidden from ages and from generations, but now is revealed to his saints;

27 To whom God wanted to make known the riches of the glory of this mystery among the Gentiles; which is Christ in you, the hope of our glory.

28 Him we preach and teach and make known to every man in all wisdom, that we may cause every man to become perfect through Jesus Christ;

29 And to this end I labour and strive through the help of the power which is given to me.

CHAPTER 2

I WOULD that you knew how I struggled for your sakes and for the sake of those who are at Laodicea and for the rest who have not seen me personally,

2 That their hearts may be comforted, and that they may be brought near by love to all the riches of the full assurance of understanding of the knowledge of the mystery of God the Father and of Christ,

3 In whom are hidden all the treasures of wisdom and knowledge.

4 And I say this so that no man may beguile you with enticing words.

5 For though I am far away from you in the flesh, yet I am with you in spirit, and I rejoice to see your orderliness and the sincerity of your faith in Christ.

6 Just as you have therefore accepted Jesus Christ our Lord, so you must be led by him,

7 Rooted and built up in him, and established in the faith as you have been taught, abounding therein with thanksgiving.

8 Beware lest any man mislead you through philosophy and vain deceit, after the teaching of men, after the principles of the world, and not after Christ.

9 For in him is embodied all the fulness of the Godhead.

10 And it is through him that you also have been made complete, for he is the head of all angelic orders and powers,

11 In whom also you are circumcised with a circumcision made without hands, in putting off the sinful body by the circumcision of Christ;

12 And you were buried with him in baptism, and by him you were raised with him, for you believed in the power of God who raised him from the dead.

13 And you, who once were dead in your sins and the uncircumcision of your flesh, he has granted to live with him, and he has forgiven you all your sins;

14 And by his commandments he cancelled the written bond of our sins, which stood against us; and he took it out of the way, nailing it to his cross;

15 And by putting off his mortal body, he exposed the powers of evil, and through his person put them openly to shame.

16 Let no man therefore create a disturbance among you about eating and drinking, or about the division of the feast days, the beginning of the months and the day of the sabbath.

17 These are shadows of things to come; but the main objective is Christ.

18 Let no man, by pretense of sincerity, doom you so that you worship angels; for he is bold about the things he has not seen, and foolishly he is proud of his intellectual powers;

19 That very person does not uphold the Head by whom the whole body is constructed and stands with the joints and members, and grows through the discipline of God.

20 Therefore, if you have died with Christ and are apart from the principles of the world, why then should you be doomed as though living in the world?

21 Do not touch; do not taste; do not follow;

22 For these things are customs which are changeable and they are the commandments and doctrines of men.

23 And it appears there is some word of wisdom in these things when presented by the humble person in reverence for God, provided they disregard the things of the flesh, not those things which are honourable but only those things which satisfy the pleasure of the flesh.

CHAPTER 3

IF you then are risen with Christ, seek those things which are above, where Christ sits on the right hand of God.

2 Set your mind on things above, not on things on the earth,

3 For you are dead, and your life is hidden with Christ in God.

4 When Christ, who is our life, shall

appear, then shall you also appear with him in glory.

5 ¶Mortify therefore your earthly members: immorality, uncleanness, intemperate desires, evil lusts, and covetousness; for these are idolatry,

6 And it is because of these things that the wrath of God comes on the children of disobedience.

7 In the past you also lived among these things, and you were perverted by them.

8 But now put off from you all these: anger, wrath, malice, blasphemy, foul conversation.

9 Do not lie one to another, but put away the old life with all its practices;

10 And put on the new life which is renewed in knowledge after the pattern in which it was originally created,

11 Where there is neither Jew nor Aramean, circumcision nor uncircumcision, Greek nor barbarian, slave nor freeman; but Christ is all and in all men.

12 Therefore as the elect of God, holy and beloved, put on mercy, kindness, gentleness, humbleness of mind, meekness, patience;

13 Forbearing one another, and forgiving one another; and if any one has a complaint against his fellow man, just as Christ forgave you, so should you also forgive.

14 And with all these things have love, which is the bond of perfection.

15 And let the peace of Christ govern your hearts; for that end, you are called in one body; and be thankful to Christ;

16 And let his word dwell in you abundantly in all wisdom, teaching and admonishing one another in psalms, hymns, and spiritual songs, singing with grace in your hearts to God.

17 And whatever you do in word or deed, do it in the name of our Lord Jesus Christ, giving thanks through him to God the Father.

18 ¶Wives, submit yourselves to your own husbands, as it is appropriate in Christ.

19 Husbands, love your wives, and be not bitter toward them.

20 Children, obey your parents in all things, for this is well pleasing to our Lord.

21 Parents, do not provoke your children, that they may not be discouraged.

22 Servants, obey your human masters in all things, not with eyeservice, hypocrites; but with a sincere heart, in reverence for the Lord.

23 And whatever you do, do it with your whole soul, as to our Lord and not to men,

24 Knowing that from the Lord you shall receive the reward of the inheritance; for you serve the Lord Christ.

25 But the wrongdoer shall be rewarded according to the wrong which he has done; and there is no respect of persons.

CHAPTER 4

MASTERS, do to your servants that which is just and fair, knowing that you also have a Master in heaven.

2 ¶Continue in prayer, and watch in the same with thanksgiving;

3 And pray for us also, that God may open to us a door for preaching, to speak the mystery of Christ for whose sake I am a prisoner,

4 So that I may make it manifest and speak about it as I should.

5 Live wisely in peace with those who are outside the church, and avoid offending.

6 Let your conversation be gracious, seasoned with salt, and you should know how to answer every man.

7 ¶All things concerning me will be made known to you by Tychicus, who is a beloved brother and a faithful minister and fellow servant in the Lord,

8 Whom I send to you for this very purpose, that he may know the state of your affairs and comfort your hearts,

9 Together with Onesimus, a faithful and beloved brother, who is one of you. They shall make known to you all the things which have happened to us.

10 Aristarchus, my fellow prisoner, salutes you, together with Mark,

cousin to Barnabas, concerning whom you have been instructed; and if he comes, receive him,

11 And Jesus, who is called Justus. These are of the circumcision, and the only ones who have helped me toward the kingdom of God; and they have been a comfort to me.

12 Epaphras, who is one of you, a servant of Christ, salutes you, always labouring for you in prayer, that you may stand perfect and complete in all the will of God.

13 For I can testify concerning him that he has a great zeal for you and for those who are in Laodicea and Hierapolis.

14 Luke, the beloved physician and Demas greet you.

15 Salute the brethren in Laodicea, and salute Nymphas and his family and the congregation that meets at his house.

16 And when this epistle has been read to you, see that it is read also in the church of the Laodiceans; and likewise you read the epistle written from Laodicea.

17 And say to Archippus, Take heed to the ministry which you have received in our Lord and that you fulfill it.

18 This salutation is by the hand of me, Paul. Remember my imprisonment. Grace be with you. Amen.

THE FIRST EPISTLE OF PAUL THE APOSTLE

to the

THESSALONIANS

CHAPTER 1

PAUL and Silvanus and Timotheus, to the church of the Thessalonians which is in God the Father and in our Lord Jesus Christ: Grace be unto you and peace from God our Father and the Lord Jesus Christ.

2 ¶We give thanks to God always for you all, remembering you continually in our prayers,

3 Mentioning before God the Father the works of your faith and the labor of your love and the patience of your hope in our Lord Jesus Christ.

4 For we know that you are the elected ones, my brethren, and beloved of God.

5 For our preaching to you was not in words only, but also in power, and with the Holy Spirit and with sincere assurance; and you know also how

we lived among you for your sakes.

6 And you became followers of us and of our Lord, for you welcomed the word with much tribulation and with joy of the Holy Spirit;

7 Thus you have become examples to all the believers in Macedonia and Achaia.

8 Not only have you sounded out the word of our Lord in Macedonia and Achaia but also in every place your faith in God has been heard so that we need not speak anything about you.

9 For these people themselves relate how we entered first among you and how you turned to God from the worship of idols, to serve the living and true God,

10 To wait for his Son from heaven, even Jesus, whom he raised from the dead, for it is he who will deliver us from the wrath to come.

CHAPTER 2

SO you yourselves, my brethren, know that our entrance among you was not in vain,

2 But from the beginning we suffered and as you know were treated shamefully at Philippi; then with more struggle but with confidence in our God, we preached to you the gospel of Christ.

3 For our comfort did not spring from deception nor from uncleanness nor from enticing speech;

4 But just as we have been examined by God to be entrusted with his gospel, even so we speak, not to please men, but to please God who searches our hearts.

5 And we have never used flattering words, as you know, to conceal greed; God is witness:

6 And we have not sought support from men, neither from you nor from others, when we could have been burdensome on you for our maintenance, as the apostles of Christ should be.

7 But we were meek when we were among you, and like a foster mother who loves her children;

8 Likewise, we are affectionately desirous to give you not only the gospel of God but even our lives, because you were dear to us.

9 For you remember, brethren, that we labored hard, working night and day with our hands, so that we would not burden you.

10 You are witnesses, and God also, how we preached to you the gospel of God, purely and righteously, and we lived blamelessly among all the believers.

11 You know how we exhorted and encouraged and charged every one of you, as a father does his children,

12 And we bore the testimony to you, so that you may live a life worthy of God, who has called you to his kingdom and glory.

13 For this cause also we thank God continually, because, when you received the word of God which you heard from us you received it not as the word of men, but as it is in truth, the word of God, which works effectively in you who believe.

14 For you, my brethren, have taken the pattern of the churches of God in Judea which are in Christ Jesus; for you also have suffered from the people of your own tribe, even as they have suffered from the Jews,

15 Who both killed the Lord Jesus Christ and their own prophets, and have persecuted us; and they do not please God and are against all men,

16 Forbidding us to speak to the Gentiles that they might be saved, adding this to their sins always; but the wrath of God is upon them to the uttermost.

17 ¶But we, brethren, have been deprived of your affection for a little while, yet only in presence and not in heart, so we have with great love vigorously endeavored to see your faces.

18 And we have wanted to come to you; I, Paul, tried several times but Satan hindered me.

19 For what is our hope, our joy, or crown of our glorying? Is it not you in the presence of our Lord Jesus when he comes?

20 For you are our glory and our joy.

CHAPTER 3

AND because we could no longer withstand these obstacles, we decided to remain at Athens alone;

2 And send Timotheus, our brother, a minister of God and our helper in the gospel of Christ, to sustain you and comfort you concerning your faith,

3 So that no man among you might be disheartened by these tribulations; for you, yourselves, know that this is our destiny.

4 For verily when we were with you, we told you before that we should suffer tribulations, even as it has come to pass, and as you know.

5 For this reason also, when I could no longer wait, I sent to know your faith, lest by some means the tempter had tempted you and our labor was in vain.

6 But now since Timotheus has returned to us from you, and brought us good tidings of your faith and love, and that you have good remembrance of us always, longing to see us, just as we also long to see you;

7 Therefore, our brethren, we have been comforted by you, in the midst of all our distress and tribulations because of your faith;

8 Now we can live happily, if you stand firm in our Lord.

9 What thanks can we offer to God for you, for all the joy with which we rejoice for your sakes,

10 Except, before God to offer supplication abundantly night and day, to see your faces and to complete that which is lacking in your faith?

11 Now may God our Father and our Lord Jesus Christ direct our journey to you,

12 And may the Lord increase and enrich your love toward one another and toward all men, even as we love you;

13 And may he strengthen your hearts to be without blemish in holiness before God our Father at the coming of our Lord Jesus Christ with all his saints.

CHAPTER 4

FROM this time forth, my brethren, we beseech you and entreat you earnestly by our Lord Jesus that as you have been taught by us how you ought to live and to please God, so you will increase more and more.

2 For you know what commandments we gave you by our Lord Jesus.

3 For this is the will of God, even your sanctification, that you should abstain from fornication,

4 That every one of you should know how to keep his possessions in sanctification and honour;

5 And not through the passion of lust, even as the rest of the Gentiles who know not God;

6 And that no man overreach to transgress and defraud his brother in this matter, because our Lord is the avenger of all such, as we have also forewarned you and testified.

7 For God has not called you to uncleanness but to holiness.

8 Therefore, he who does an injustice does not wrong man but God who has also given to you his Holy Spirit.

9 ¶Now concerning brotherly love, you do not need me to write to you, for you yourselves are taught by God to love one another.

10 And indeed you show it toward all the brethren who are in Macedonia; but I beseech you, my brethren, that you increase your love more and more;

11 And that you endeavor to be quiet and to do your own business and to work with your own hands, as we commanded you,

12 That you may lead a life of good example toward outsiders, so that you depend on no man.

13 ¶Now I want you to know, my brethren, that you should not grieve over those who are dead, as those do who have no hope.

14 For if we believe that Jesus died and rose again, even so those who have died in Jesus, God will bring with him.

15 For this we say to you by the very word of our Lord, that we who are alive and remain until the coming of our Lord shall not overtake those who are dead.

16 For our Lord himself shall descend from heaven with a shout and the voice of the archangel and with the trumpet of God; and those who died in Christ will rise first.

17 Then we who are alive and remain shall be caught up together with them in the clouds to meet our Lord in the air; and so shall we ever be with our Lord.

18 Therefore comfort one another with these words.

CHAPTER 5

BUT of the times and seasons, my brethren, you have no need that I should write to you.

2 For you yourselves know perfectly well that the day of our Lord comes like a thief in the night.

3 For when they shall say, Peace

and tranquility; then sudden destruction will come upon them, as travail upon a woman with child; and they shall not escape.

4 But you, my brethren, are not in darkness that that day shall overtake you as a thief.

5 You are all the children of light and the children of the day; and you are not the children of the night nor the children of darkness.

6 Therefore let us not sleep, as do others, but let us watch and be sober.

7 For those who sleep, sleep in the night; and those who are drunken are drunken in the night.

8 But let us who are the children of the day be alert, putting on the breastplate of faith and love, and for a helmet put on the hope of salvation.

9 For God has not appointed us to wrath, but to obtain salvation through our Lord Jesus Christ,

10 Who died for us, that whether we wake or sleep, we shall live together with him.

11 Wherefore comfort one another and edify one another, even as also you do.

12 ¶We beseech you, my brethren, to respect those who labor among you and admonish you in our Lord and teach you,

13 That you esteem them very highly in love, and be at peace with them for their work's sake.

14 ¶Now we beseech you, my brethren, correct those who offend, comfort those who lack courage, bear the burdens of the weak, and be patient toward all men.

15 See that none of you render evil for evil; but always follow that which is good, both among yourselves and to all men.

16 Be joyful always.

17 Pray without ceasing.

18 In everything give thanks; for this is the will of God in Jesus Christ concerning you.

19 Do not quench the Spirit.

20 Do not reject prophecies.

21 Prove all things, uphold that which is good.

22 Abstain from every sort of evil.

23 May the very God of peace sanctify you wholly; and may your spirit and soul and body be preserved without blemish to the coming of our Lord Jesus Christ.

24 Faithful is he who has called you, and he will keep his word.

25 My brethren, pray for us.

26 Salute all our brethren with a holy kiss.

27 I adjure you by our Lord that this epistle be read to all the holy brethren.

28 The grace of our Lord Jesus Christ be with you. Amen.

THE SECOND EPISTLE OF PAUL THE APOSTLE

to the

THESSALONIANS

CHAPTER 1

PAUL and Silvanus and Timotheus, to the church of the Thessalonians in God our Father and our Lord Jesus Christ:

2 Grace be with you and peace from God our Father and from our Lord Jesus Christ.

3 ¶We are bound to give thanks to God always for you, my brethren, as it is appropriate to do, because

your faith grows exceedingly, and the love of all of you for one another increases,

4 So that even we ourselves boast of you in the churches of God over your faith and patience in all persecutions and tribulations that you endure;

5 This is an example of the righteous judgment of God, that you may be made worthy of his kingdom, for which you also suffer.

6 And if it seems a righteous thing before the presence of God, he will recompense tribulation to those who oppress you;

7 And to you who are oppressed he shall grant to be at peace with us when our Lord Jesus Christ shall be revealed from heaven with the host of his angels,

8 At which time he will avenge with flaming fire those who know not God and those who do not acknowledge the gospel of our Lord Jesus Christ;

9 For they, at the judgment day, shall be rewarded with everlasting destruction from the presence of our Lord and from the glory of his power,

10 When he comes to be glorified by his saints and to perform his wonders among his faithful ones, so that our testimony concerning you may be believed in that day.

11 Therefore we always pray for you, that God will vouchsafe you worthy of your calling and satisfy all your desires which are for goodness and the works of faith with power,

12 That the name of our Lord Jesus Christ may be glorified in you, and you in him, according to the grace of our God and our Lord Jesus Christ.

CHAPTER 2

NOW we beseech you, my brethren, concerning the coming of our Lord Jesus Christ and concerning our gathering together with him,

2 That you let not your minds be hastily excited or troubled, neither by word nor by prophecy of the spirit nor by an epistle supposedly from us, stating that the day of our Lord is at hand.

3 Let no man deceive you by any means; for that day shall not come unless it is preceded by a rebellion, and the man of sin be revealed as the son of perdition,

4 Who opposes and exalts himself above all that is called God or that is reverenced; so that even in the temple of God, he sits as a god, and shows himself, as though he were a god.

5 Do you not remember, that when I was with you I told you these things?

6 And now you know what has prevented him from being revealed in his time.

7 For the mystery of iniquity is already at work, until he who now is the obstacle is taken out of the way.

8 Then shall the Wicked One be exposed, that one whom our Lord Jesus shall consume with the spirit of his mouth and shall destroy with the revelation of his coming,

9 Even he whose coming is due to the working of Satan, with all power and signs and lying wonders,

10 And with all deceitfulness of unrighteousness in those who perish, because they received not the love of the truth, that they might be saved thereby.

11 For this reason God shall send them strong delusion that they should believe a lie,

12 That all who did not believe in the truth but preferred unrighteousness might be damned.

13 ¶But we are bound to give thanks always to God for you, my brethren beloved of our Lord, because God has from the beginning chosen you to salvation, through holiness of the Spirit and through a true faith;

14 And it is to these things that God called you by our preaching, to be the glory of our Lord Jesus Christ.

15 Henceforth, my brethren, stand fast and hold to the commandments which you have been taught, either by word or by our epistle.

16 Now our Lord Jesus Christ, himself, and God, even our Father, who has loved us and has given us ever-

lasting consolation and good hope through his grace,

17 Comfort your hearts and strengthen you in every good word and work.

CHAPTER 3

FINALLY, brethren, pray for us, that the word of our Lord may spread freely and be glorified in every place even as it is among you,

2 And that we may be delivered from evil and unreasonable men; for not every man has faith.

3 But the Lord is faithful; he will guide you and deliver you from evil.

4 We have confidence in you through our Lord, that the things we have commanded you to do, you have done and will continue to do.

5 And may our Lord direct your hearts into the love of God and into the patience of Christ.

6 Now we command you, my brethren, in the name of our Lord Jesus Christ, to shun every brother who leads an evil life and not in accord with the commandments which he received from us.

7 For you know well how you ought to imitate us; for our behaviour was not disorderly among you;

8 Neither did we eat bread for nothing from any of you, but worked with hard labor and toiled night and day so that we might not be a burden to any of you;

9 Not because we did not have the right, but to make ourselves an example to you to follow us.

10 For even when we were with you, we commanded this very thing to you, that whoever is unwilling to work should likewise not eat.

11 For we hear that there are some men among you who lead an evil life and do not work at all, but are busybodies.

12 Now it is these people that we command and exhort by our Lord Jesus Christ, that they work quietly and eat their own bread.

13 But you, brethren, be not weary in well doing.

14 And if any man does not obey our word in this epistle, note that man and do not associate with him, that he may be ashamed.

15 Yet do not consider him as an enemy, but admonish him as a brother.

16 Now the Lord of peace himself give you peace always in every thing you do. Our Lord be with you all.

17 ¶This salutation is in my own handwriting; I, Paul, wrote it, and it is the seal of all my epistles. This is the way I write.

18 The grace of our Lord Jesus Christ be with you all. Amen.

THE FIRST EPISTLE OF PAUL THE APOSTLE TO

TIMOTHY

CHAPTER 1

PAUL, an apostle of Jesus Christ by the commandment of God our Saviour and Christ Jesus our hope;

2 To Timotheus, a true son in the faith: Grace, mercy and peace from God our Father and Christ Jesus our Lord.

3 When I went to Macedonia, I besought you to remain at Ephesus, so that you might charge certain ones not to teach diverse doctrines,

4 And not to give heed to fables and stories of endless genealogies, which cause dispute rather than build up the faith of God.

5 Now the fulfillment of the com-

mandment is love out of a pure heart and of a good conscience and of a true faith,

6 From which some have gone astray and have turned aside to foolish words,

7 Desiring to be teachers of the law; not understanding what they speak, nor even whereof they argue.

8 But we know that the law is good, if a man use it lawfully;

9 Knowing this, that the law is not made for the righteous, but for the wicked and rebellious, for the ungodly and for sinners, for the profane and unholy, for those who abuse their fathers and ill-treat their mothers, for murderers,

10 For whoremongers, for those who defile themselves with males, for kidnappers of well-born sons, for liars, for perjurers, and for whatever is contrary to sound doctrine;

11 This is according to the glorious gospel of the blessed God, which was entrusted to me.

12 And I thank our Lord Jesus Christ who has given me strength and has counted me trustworthy and has appointed me to his ministry,

13 Who was before a blasphemer and a persecutor and a reviler; but I obtained mercy because I did it ignorantly in unbelief.

14 Now the grace of our Lord has become abundant in me, as well as my faith and love in Jesus Christ.

15 It is a trustworthy saying and worthy of all acceptation that Jesus Christ came into the world to save sinners, of whom I am chief.

16 Howbeit for this cause he had mercy on me, that in me first Jesus Christ may show forth all patience, for a pattern to those who should hereafter believe in him to life everlasting.

17 Now to the King eternal, immortal, invisible, the only God, be honor and glory for ever and ever. Amen.

18 This charge I commit to you, my son Timotheus, in accordance with the prophecies given before about you, that you might fight a good fight

19 In faith and good conscience; those who have rejected this charge have lost their faith;

20 Namely Hymenæus and Alexander, whom I have delivered to Satan to be disciplined so that they may no longer blaspheme.

CHAPTER 2

I BESEECH you, therefore, first of all to offer to God, petitions, prayers, supplications, and thanksgiving for all men,

2 For kings and for all in authority; that we may live a quiet and peaceable life, in all purity and Godliness.

3 For this is good and acceptable in the sight of God our Saviour,

4 Who desires all men to be saved and to return to the knowledge of the truth.

5 For there is one God, and one mediator between God and men, the man Jesus Christ,

6 Who gave himself a ransom for all, a testimony which came in due time.

7 For that testimony I was appointed a preacher and an apostle; I tell the truth and I lie not; and I became the teacher of the Gentiles in a true faith.

8 I wish, therefore, that men pray everywhere, lifting up their holy hands without anger and doubting thoughts.

9 In like manner also, let the apparel of women be simple and their adornment be modest and refined; not with braided hair or gold or pearls or costly array;

10 But let them be engaged in good works, as is becoming women who profess reverence for God.

11 Let the woman learn in silence with all subjection.

12 I do not think it seemly for a woman to debate publicly or otherwise usurp the authority of men, but she should be silent.

13 For Adam was formed first, then Eve.

14 And Adam was not deceived, but the woman was deceived and she transgressed the law.

15 Nevertheless, if her posterity continue in faith and have holiness

and chastity, she will live through them.

CHAPTER 3

THIS is a true saying: If a man desires the office of an elder, he aspires to a good work.

2 He who becomes an elder must be blameless, the husband of one wife, alert mentally, sober, of good behaviour, given to hospitality, and apt at teaching;

3 Not given to wine, not hasty to strike, not quarrelsome, but meek, not greedy of filthy lucre;

4 One who rules well his own household and keeps his children under submission to bring them up with all purity.

5 For if a man does not know how to rule well his own household, how shall he take care of the church of God?

6 He should not be a recent convert, lest he become proud and fall into the condemnation of the devil.

7 Moreover, he must have a good report from outsiders, lest he fall into reproach and the snares of the devil.

8 Likewise deacons must be pure, not double-tongued, not given to much wine, not greedy of filthy lucre;

9 But they must uphold the divine mystery of faith with a pure conscience.

10 Let these first be examined, and then let them minister after they have been found blameless.

11 Likewise their wives must be chaste, alert mentally, faithful in all things, and not slanderers.

12 Let the deacons be appointed from those who have not been polygamous, ruling their children and their own households well.

13 For those who minister well earn good recognition for themselves and grow more familiar with the faith of Jesus Christ.

14 ¶These things I write to you, although hoping to come to you shortly,

15 So that if I am delayed, you may know how you ought to conduct yourself in the house of God, which is the church of the living God, the pillar and foundation of the truth.

16 Truly great is this divine mystery of righteousness; it is revealed in the flesh, justified in the Spirit, seen by angels, preached to the Gentiles, believed on in the world, and received up into glory.

CHAPTER 4

NOW the Spirit says expressly that in the latter times some shall depart from the faith, following after misleading spirits and doctrines of devils,

2 Who with false appearance mislead and speak lies and are seared in their own conscience,

3 Who prohibit marriage, and demand abstinence from foods which God has created for use and thanksgiving of those who believe and know the truth.

4 For all things created by God are good; nothing is to be rejected if it is received with thanksgiving,

5 For it is sanctified by the word of God and prayer.

6 If you teach these things to the brethren, you will be a good minister of Jesus Christ, brought up by the words of faith and in the good doctrine which you have been taught.

7 Refuse foolish and old wives' fables, and train yourself in righteousness.

8 For physical training profits only for a little while; but righteousness is profitable in all things, having promise of the life that now is and of that which is to come.

9 This is a true saying and worthy to be accepted.

10 Because of this, we both toil and suffer reproach, because we trust in the living God, who is the Saviour of all men, especially of those who believe.

11 These things command and teach.

12 ¶Let no man despise your youth; but be an example to believers, in word, in behaviour, in love, in faith, and in purity.

13 And until I come, strive to study, and continue in prayer and teaching.

14 Do not neglect the gift that you have, which was given to you by

prophecy and by virtue of the laying on of the hands of the presbytery.

15 Meditate upon these things; give yourself wholly to them, so that it may be known to all that you are progressing.

16 Take heed to yourself and to your teachings; and be firm in them; for in doing this, you shall both save yourself and those who hear you.

CHAPTER 5

DO not rebuke an elder, but treat him as a father, and the younger men as your brothers;

2 And the elder women treat as mothers, and the younger as your sisters, with all purity.

3 Honor widows who are widows indeed.

4 And if any of the widows have children or grandchildren, let them know that aid should be first sought from those of their own household so that the children have the opportunity to repay their obligations to their parents; for this is acceptable before God.

5 Now she who is indeed a widow and destitute trusts in God and is constant in prayers and supplications both night and day.

6 But she who lives wholly for pleasure is dead while she lives.

7 Continually charge them with these things, so that they may be blameless.

8 But, if any man does not provide for his own, and especially for those who are of his own household who are of the faith, he has denied the faith and is worse than an unbeliever.

9 When you select a worthy widow to help, select therefore one who is not less than three score years, who has been the wife of one man only,

10 And is well spoken of for good works, if she has brought up children, if she has lodged strangers, if she has washed the feet of the saints, if she has comforted the distressed, if she has been diligent in every good work.

11 But refuse the younger widows; for when they have begun to wax wanton against Christ, they will marry.

12 Their judgment awaits them be-cause they have been untrue to their first faith.

13 And with it all, they learn to be idle, wandering about from house to house; and not only to be idle, but tattlers also and busybodies, speaking things which they ought not.

14 I would, therefore, that the younger widows marry, bear children, manage their own households, and give no occasion to the adversary for disdain.

15 For, as conditions are now, some have already strayed after Satan.

16 If any believers, either man or woman, have widows in their families, let them feed them, and do not let them be a burden on the congregation, so that the church may have enough for those who are widows indeed.

17 Let the elders who minister well be esteemed worthy of double honor, especially those who labor in the word and doctrine.

18 For the scripture says, You shall not muzzle the ox that threshes. And again, The laborer is worthy of his hire.

19 Do not accept an accusation against an elder unless it is supported by the testimony of two or three witnesses.

20 Those who sin, rebuke in the presence of all men, that others also may fear.

21 I adjure you before God and our Lord Jesus Christ and his elect angels that you observe these things without prejudice, doing nothing by partiality.

22 Do not lay hands hastily on any man, neither be a partaker of other men's sins; keep yourself pure.

23 Do not drink water in excess, but use a little wine for your stomach's sake and because of your frequent illnesses.

24 There are men whose crimes are well known and the notoriety of them precedes them to the house of judgment, and there are others, the notoriety of whose crimes follows after them;

25 Likewise also the fame of the good works of some is well known

beforehand; and if their acts are otherwise, they cannot be hidden either.

CHAPTER 6

LET all of those who are under the yoke of slavery honor and respect their masters in every way, so that the name of God and his doctrines may not be blasphemed.

2 Those who have masters who are believers, let them not despise them because they are brethren; but rather serve them more zealously because they are believers and beloved in whose service they find rest. These things teach and exhort.

3 ¶If there is any man who teaches a different doctrine and does not offer the wholesome words of our Lord Jesus Christ and the doctrine of reverence to God,

4 He is proud, knowing nothing, and dotes on an argument and quarrels on the use of a word and this is the cause of envy and controversy and blasphemy and evil premeditation

5 And strife among men whose minds are corrupt and who are cut off from the truth and who think worshipping God is for worldly gain; keep away from such people.

6 ¶But our gain is greater contentment, for it is the worship of God.

7 For we brought nothing into this world, and it is certain that we can carry nothing out.

8 Therefore, let us be satisfied with food and clothing;

9 For those who desire to be rich fall into temptation and snares, and into many foolish and hurtful lusts which drown men in degeneration and destruction.

10 For the love of money is the root of all evil; and there are some men who have coveted it and have thereby erred from the faith, and have brought to themselves many sorrows.

11 ¶But you, O man of God, flee these things; and follow after righteousness, piety, faith, love, patience, and meekness.

12 Fight the good fight of faith, lay hold upon eternal life to which you are called, having made a true profession before many witnesses.

13 I charge you in the presence of God, the giver of life to all, and before Jesus Christ, who gave a good testimony before Pontius Pilate,

14 That you obey this charge without spot and without stain until the appearing of our Lord Jesus Christ,

15 Who is to be revealed in his due time, blessed and almighty God, the King of kings and Lord of lords,

16 Who alone has immortality, dwelling in the light which no man can approach, and whom no man has seen, nor can see; to him be honor and dominion for ever and ever. Amen.

17 ¶Charge those who are rich in this world that they be not proud, nor trust in the uncertainty of riches, but in the living God who gives us all things so abundantly for our comfort,

18 That they do good works, and become rich in good deeds, and be ready to give and willing to share,

19 Laying up in store for themselves a good foundation against the time to come, that they may lay hold upon the true life.

20 O Timothy, be careful of that which is entrusted to you; flee from empty echoes and from the perversion of false science;

21 For those professing this have strayed from the faith. Grace be with you. Amen.

THE SECOND EPISTLE OF PAUL THE APOSTLE

to

TIMOTHY

CHAPTER 1

PAUL, an apostle of Jesus Christ by the will of God and by the promise of life which is in Jesus Christ,

2 To Timotheus, a dearly beloved son: Grace, mercy, and peace from God the Father and Jesus Christ our Lord.

3 ¶I thank God, whom I have served from boyhood with a pure conscience, that I have always remembered you in my prayers night and day.

4 I am anxious to see you and I still remember your tears; I am filled with joy,

5 Especially when I am reminded of your true faith, which dwelt first in your grandmother Lois and your mother Eunice, and I am sure now in you also.

6 For this reason, I remind you to stir up the gift of God which is in you by the laying on of my hand.

7 For God has not given us the spirit of fear but of power and of love and of good discipline.

8 Be not, therefore, ashamed of the testimony of our Lord, nor of me his prisoner; but bear the hardships that go along with the preaching of the gospel through the power of God,

9 Who has saved us and called us with a holy calling, not according to our works, but according to his own will and his grace, which was given us in Jesus Christ before the world began,

10 And is now made manifest by the appearing of our Saviour Jesus Christ, who has abolished death, and has revealed life and immortality through the gospel,

11 To which I am appointed a preacher, and an apostle, and a teacher of the Gentiles.

12 For this cause I suffer these things; nevertheless I am not ashamed; for I know whom I have trusted, and I am sure he will take care of me until that day.

13 Let this example of sound words which you have heard from me abide with you in the faith and love which is in Jesus Christ.

14 That good thing which was committed to you keep by the help of the Holy Spirit which dwells in us.

15 This you know, that all those in Asia Minor have turned away from me, of whom are Phygellus and Hermogenes.

16 Let our Lord grant mercy to the house of Onesiphorus; for he has often refreshed me, and he was not ashamed of the chains of my imprisonment;

17 But when he was in Rome, he searched for me diligently and found me.

18 Let our Lord grant to him that he may find mercy in heaven, where our Lord is, in that day; and of how he ministered to me at Ephesus, you know very well.

CHAPTER 2

YOU, therefore, my son, be strong in the grace that is in Jesus Christ.

2 And the things which you have heard from me by many witnesses, these entrust to faithful men, who shall be able to teach others also.

3 Therefore endure hardships as a good soldier of Jesus Christ.

4 No man can be a soldier and also entangle himself with the things of this life, if he would please him who has chosen him to be a soldier.

5 And if a man also strive for mastery in contest, he is not crowned except he compete lawfully.

6 The husbandman who labors should be the first to be sustained by the fruits.

7 Perceive these things: and may our Lord give you wisdom in all things.

8 Remember Jesus Christ who rose from the dead, he who was a descendant from David according to my gospel;

9 Because of him I suffer hardships, even to bonds like a malefactor; but the word of God is not restricted.

10 Therefore I endure all things for the sake of the elect, that they may also obtain the salvation which is in Jesus Christ, with eternal glory.

11 This is a true saying: For if we die with him, we shall also live with him:

12 If we suffer, we shall also reign with him; if we deny him, he also will deny us;

13 But if we believe not in him, yet he will still remain faithful; for he cannot deny himself.

14 You should keep these things in remembrance as a testimony before our Lord, that the faithful should not argue over words in which there is no profit but which are destruction to those who listen to them.

15 Strive to conduct yourself perfectly before God, as a soldier without reproach and one who preaches straightforwardly the word of truth.

16 Shun empty and worthless words, for they only increase the ungodliness of those who argue over them.

17 And their word will be like a canker eating in many; such are Hymenæus, and Philetus,

18 Who have strayed from the truth, saying that the resurrection of the dead is already passed, thus destroying the faith of some.

19 Nevertheless the foundation of God stands firm, having this seal: The Lord knows those who are his, and he will save from iniquity every one who calls upon the name of the Lord.

20 But in a great house there are not only vessels of gold and of silver, but also of wood and of earth; some for formal use on occasions of honor and others for service.

21 If therefore a man purifies himself from these things, he will become like a vessel pure for honor, worthy of the master's use, and ready for every good work.

22 Keep away from all the lusts of youth, and follow after righteousness, faith, love, peace, with those who call on our Lord with a pure heart.

23 Keep away from foolish disputes which do not educate; you know they cause strife.

24 A servant of our Lord must not quarrel, but be gentle to all men, apt at teaching and patient,

25 So that he may discipline gently those who argue against him; and perhaps God will grant them repentance and they will know the truth,

26 And come to themselves, and be saved from the trap of Satan, by whom they have been drawn to his will.

CHAPTER 3

KNOW this, that in the last days disastrous times will come.

2 And men shall be lovers of themselves and lovers of money, proud, conceited, blasphemers, disobedient to their own people, ungrateful, wicked,

3 False accusers, addicts to lust, brutal, haters of good things,

4 Traitors, hasty, boasters, lovers of pleasures more than lovers of God;

5 Having a form of godliness, but far from the power of God; from such turn away.

6 For of this sort are those who creep into houses and captivate women sunken in sin, led away with divers lusts,

7 Ever striving to learn, and never able to come to the knowledge of the truth.

8 Now just as Jannes and Jambres stood up against Moses, so do these also resist the truth, men of corrupt minds and far off from the faith.

9 But they shall not progress, for their folly is well known to every man, even as that of the others also was.

10 But you have been a follower of my teaching, manner of life, purpose, faith, patience, charity, love, steadfastness,

11 Persecution, and sorrows; you know the things which I endured at Antioch and at Iconium and at Lystra; how I was persecuted, and yet from all these my Lord delivered me.

12 Likewise, all those who wish to live a godly life in Jesus Christ shall suffer persecution.

13 But bad and deceptive men shall grow worse and worse, deceiving and being deceived.

14 But hold fast to the things which you have learned and have been assured of, knowing from whom you have learned them,

15 And knowing that you have learned from your childhood the holy scriptures which are able to make you wise to salvation through faith in Jesus Christ.

16 All scripture written by the inspiration of the Holy Spirit is profitable for doctrine, for reproof, for correction, and for instruction in righteousness;

17 So that God's people may become complete, thoroughly perfected for every good work.

CHAPTER 4

I SOLEMNLY charge you before God and our Lord Jesus Christ, who shall judge the quick and the dead when his kingdom is come,

2 Preach the word; and stand by it zealously in season and out of season; rebuke, reprove, through all patience and teaching.

3 For the time will come when men will not listen to sound doctrine; but they will add for themselves extra teachers according to their desires, being lured by enticing words;

4 And they will turn away their ears from the truth, and they will turn to fables.

5 But you must be awake to all things, endure hardships, do the work of a preacher, and fulfil your ministry.

6 From henceforth I am ready to die, and the time of my departure is at hand.

7 I have fought a good fight, I have finished my race, I have kept my faith:

8 Henceforth there is preserved for me a crown of righteousness, which my Lord, the righteous judge, will give me at that day; and not to me only but also to all those who have loved his appearing.

9 ¶Make every effort to come to me soon;

10 For Demas has forsaken me, having loved this world, and has gone to Thessalonica; Crespos to Galatia, Titus to Dalmatia.

11 Only Luke is with me. Take Mark and bring him with you; for he is useful to me for the ministry.

12 I have sent Tychicus to Ephesus.

13 The book-carrier [1] which I left at Troas with Carpus, bring it with you when you come, and the books, especially the parchment scrolls.

14 Alexander, the blacksmith, has done me much evil; our Lord reward him according to his works;

15 You beware of him also; for he has greatly opposed our words.

16 When I first wrote you, there was no one with me, for all had forsaken me; do not hold this against them.

17 Nevertheless, my Lord stood by me and strengthened me, that by me the preaching might be fulfilled and that all the Gentiles might hear; and I was delivered out of the mouth of the lion.

18 And my Lord shall deliver me from every evil work and will give me life in his heavenly kingdom. To him be glory for ever and ever. Amen.

19 ¶Salute Priscilla and Aquila and their household, and Onesiphorus.

20 Erastus has remained at Corinth; but I left Trophimus sick at the city of Miletus.

21 Make every effort to come before winter. Eubulus greets you, and Pudens and Linus and Claudia and all the brethren.

22 Our Lord Jesus Christ be with your spirit. Grace be with all of us. Amen.

---

[1] A bag made of leather or woolen cloth.

THE EPISTLE OF PAUL TO

TITUS

CHAPTER 1

PAUL, a servant of God and an apostle of Jesus Christ in the faith of God's elect and in the knowledge of true godliness;

2 In the hope of eternal life, which the true God promised ages ago;

3 And has in due time revealed his word by our preaching (which preaching has been intrusted to me by the command of God our Saviour);

4 To Titus, a true son in the common faith: Grace and peace from God the Father and our Lord Jesus Christ our Saviour.

5 ¶For this cause I left you in Crete, that you should set in order the things that are wanting and ordain elders in every city where there is a need as I had commanded you.

6 Appoint only an elder who is blameless and the husband of one wife, and one who has faithful children who do not swear and who are not intemperate.

7 For an elder must be blameless, as a steward of God; and he must not be self-willed, not quick tempered, not excessive in the use of wine, not too ready to strike with his hand, not a lover of filthy lucre;

8 But a lover of hospitality, a lover of good things, sober, just, pious, and temperate of worldly desires;

9 Holding fast the doctrine of faith, so that he may be able to comfort by his sound doctrine, and to rebuke those who are proud.

10 For there are many unruly and vain talkers and deceivers of the people, especially those who belong to the circumcision,

11 Whose mouths must be stopped, for they corrupt many families, teaching things which they ought not, for the sake of filthy lucre.

12 One of them, even a prophet of their own, said, The Cretians are always liars, vicious beasts with empty bellies.

13 This testimony is true. Therefore rebuke them sharply, that they may be sound in the faith,

14 And not give heed to Jewish fables and commandments of men who hate the truth.

15 To the pure, all things are pure; but nothing is pure to those who are defiled and faithless; even their mind and conscience is defiled.

16 They profess to know God, but in works they deny him, and they are abominable and disobedient, condemning every kind of good work.

CHAPTER 2

BUT you must preach the things which are proper to sound doctrine.

2 Teach the older men to be vigilant, sober, pure, sound in faith, in love, charity and patience.

3 Teach the older women likewise to behave as becomes the worship of God, not false accusers, not enslaved to much wine; but to become teachers of good things,

4 That they may teach the young women to be modest, to love their husbands and their children,

5 To be discreet, chaste, good homemakers, obedient to their own husbands, so that no one can reproach the word of God.

6 Likewise exhort the children to be modest.

7 In every thing show yourself an example in all good works, and in your teaching let your word be sound.

8 Choose sound words that are instructive so that no man can point the finger of scorn at us, and so that he who is against us may be shamed,

when he can find nothing evil to say about us.

9 Exhort servants to be obedient to their own masters and to please them well in all things; not contentious,

10 Not stealing but manifesting true sincerity that they may adorn the doctrine of God our Saviour in all things.

11 For the grace of God that brings salvation has been revealed to all men.

12 It teaches us to renounce ungodliness and worldly lusts, and to live in this world soberly, righteously, and in godliness,

13 Looking for that blessed hope and the glorious appearing of the great God and our Saviour Jesus Christ,

14 Who gave himself for us, that he might save us from all iniquity, and might purify us to be his own, a new people, zealous of good works.

15 These things speak, and exhort and rebuke with all authority. Let no man despise you.

CHAPTER 3

REMIND all to be obedient and submissive to princes and governors and to be ready for every good work,

2 And not to speak evil against any man, and not to be quarrelsome; but to be meek, in every respect showing gentleness to all men.

3 For we ourselves also were sometimes foolish, disobedient, misled, and serving various lusts and passions, living in malice and envy, hated and also hating one another.

4 But after the goodness and kindness of God our Saviour was manifested,

5 Not by works of righteousness which we have done, but according to his mercy, he saved us by the washing of regeneration and renewing of the Holy Spirit,

6 Which he shed on us abundantly, through Jesus Christ our Saviour,

7 That being justified by his grace, we should be made heirs to the hope of eternal life.

8 This is a true saying, and these things I want you to constantly affirm, so that those who believe in God may be careful to do good works continually. These things are good and profitable to men.

9 But avoid foolish questions and genealogies and contentions and the theological arguments of the scribes, for they are unprofitable and vain.

10 After you have admonished the heretic once or twice, shun him,

11 Knowing that he who is such is corrupt; he sins and condemns himself.

12 ¶When I send Artemas or Tychicus to you; endeavor to come to me at Nicopolis; for I have decided to winter there.

13 See that Zenas, the scribe, and Apollos are given a good farewell on their journey, that they lack nothing.

14 And let our people be taught to do good works in times of emergency, that they be not unfruitful.

15 All who are with me salute you. Greet those who love us in the faith. Grace be with you all. Amen.

THE EPISTLE OF PAUL TO

PHILEMON

PAUL, a prisoner of Jesus Christ, and brother Timotheus, to Philemon our dearly beloved and our fellow worker,

2 And to our beloved Apphia and Archippus our fellow labourer, and to the congregation in your house:

3 Grace be with you and peace from God our Father and our Lord Jesus Christ.

4 ¶I thank my God and always make mention of you in my prayers,

5 Since I have heard of your faith and love, which you have toward our Lord Jesus and toward all saints,

6 That the participation of your faith may bear fruits in works, and in knowledge of everything that is good which you have in Jesus Christ.

7 For we have great joy and consolation in your love, and the hearts of the saints are refreshed.

8 For this reason, I have great boldness in Christ, to command to you those things which are right,

9 And for love's sake I earnestly beseech you; even I, Paul, an old man as you know, and now also a prisoner for the sake of Jesus Christ.

10 I beseech you on behalf of my son Onesimus, whom I converted during my imprisonment:

11 But of whom in the past you could not make use, but now he is very useful both to you and to me.

12 I send him to you again; welcome him as my own child;

13 For I would have kept him with me to minister to me in your place during my imprisonment for the gospel;

14 But I did not wish to do anything without consulting you, that your good deeds might not be done as though by compulsion, but of your own desire.

15 Perhaps this was the reason why he left you for a while, that you can now have him for ever;

16 Henceforth not as a servant, but more than a servant, a brother beloved, specially to me, and much more to you, both in the flesh and in our Lord.

17 Now, therefore, if you still count me a partner, welcome him as you would me.

18 And if he has caused you any loss or if he owes you anything, put it on my account.

19 I, Paul, have written this with my own hand; I will repay it,[1] not reminding you that you owe to me even your own life.

20 Indeed, my brother, let me have comfort through you in our Lord; refresh my heart in Christ.

21 Because I have confidence in your obedience, I wrote to you knowing that you will also do more than I ask.

22 In addition to all this, prepare me a lodging; for I hope that through your prayers I shall be spared to come to you.

23 Epaphras, my fellow prisoner in Jesus Christ, salutes you;

24 So do Mark, Aristarchus, Demas, and Luke, my fellow workers.

25 The grace of our Lord Jesus Christ be with your spirit. Amen.

[1] This is an Aramaic idiom meaning *forget it*.

THE EPISTLE OF PAUL THE APOSTLE TO THE

HEBREWS

CHAPTER 1

FROM of old God spoke to our fathers by the prophets in every manner and in all ways; and in these latter days he has spoken to us by his Son,

2 Whom he has appointed heir of all things, and by whom also he made the worlds;

3 For he is the brightness of his glory and the express image of his being, upholding all things by the power of his word; and when he had through his person cleansed our sins, then he sat down on the right hand of the Majesty on high;

4 And he is altogether greater than the angels, just as the name he has inherited is a more excellent name than theirs.

5 For to which of the angels has God at any time said, You are my Son, this day have I begotten you? And again, I will be to him a Father, and he shall be to me a Son?

6 And again, when he brought the firstbegotten into the world, he said, Let all the angels of God worship him.

7 And of the angels he said thus: Who makes his angels spirits; his ministers a flaming fire.

8 But of the Son he said, Thy throne, O God, is for ever and ever; the scepter of thy kingdom is a righteous scepter.

9 Thou hast loved righteousness and hated iniquity; therefore, God, even thy God, has anointed thee with the oil of gladness more than thy fellows.

10 And from the very beginning thou hast laid the foundations of the earth; and the heavens are the works of thy hands;

11 They shall pass away; but thou shalt endure; and they all shall wear out like a garment;

12 And as a cloak thou shalt fold them up, and they shall be changed; but thou art the same, and thy years shall never end.

13 For to which of the angels has he at any time said, Sit thou at my right hand, until I make thine enemies the stool under thy feet?

14 Are they not all ministering spirits sent forth in the service for those who shall inherit life everlasting?

CHAPTER 2

THEREFORE we should give earnest heed to the things which we have heard, lest at any time they be lost.

2 For if the word spoken by angels has been affirmed, and every one who has heard it and transgressed it has received a just reward,

3 How shall we escape, if we neglect the very things which are our salvation and which were first spoken by our Lord and were proved to us by those who had heard him,

4 And to which God testified with signs and wonders and with various miracles, and with the gift of the Holy Spirit given according to his will?

5 ¶For he has not put into subjection to the angels the world to come, whereof we speak.

6 But as the scripture testifies, saying, What is man that thou art mindful of him? and the son of man, that thou visitest him?

7 For thou hast made him a little lower than the angels; and hast crowned him with glory and honor, and hast set him ruler over the works of thy hands;

8 Thou hast put all things in subjection under his feet. By putting all

things under his control, he left nothing that he did not put under subjection to him. But now we do not see yet that all things are in subjection to him.

9 We see that he is Jesus, who humbled himself to become a little lower than the angels through his suffering and his death, but now he is crowned with glory and honor; for he tasted death for the sake of every one but God.

10 ¶And it was meet and proper for him, in whose hand is everything and for whom are all things, to bring many sons to glory, so that from the very beginning of their salvation they are made perfect through sufferings.

11 For both he who sanctifies and those who are sanctified are all of one origin; for this reason he is not ashamed to call them brethren,

12 Saying, I will declare thy name to my brethren; in the midst of the congregation will I praise thee.

13 And again, I will put my trust in him. And again, Behold me and the children which God has given me.

14 Forasmuch then as the children are partakers of flesh and blood, he also likewise partook of the same; and by his death he has destroyed him who had the power of death, that is, the devil.

15 And has released them who through fear of death all their lives were subject to slavery.

16 For he did not take on him the likeness of angels; but he did take on him the offspring of Abraham.

17 Therefore, it was meet and proper that in every thing he should resemble his brethren, that he might be a merciful and faithful high priest in the things of God, to make reconciliation for the sins of the people.

18 For since he himself has suffered, being tempted, he is able to help others who are tempted.

CHAPTER 3

FROM henceforth, O my holy brethren, called by a call from heaven, look to this Apostle and High Priest of our faith, Jesus Christ,

2 Who was faithful to him who appointed him, as also Moses was faithful to all his house.

3 The glory of Jesus is much greater than that of Moses, just as the honor of the builder of the house is greater than the house itself.

4 For every house is built by some man; but he who builds all things is God.

5 And Moses as a servant was faithful to all his house, and was a testimony of those things which were to be spoken after;

6 But Christ as a son over his own house, whose house we are, if to the end we hold fast with confidence to the glory of his hope.

7 ¶Therefore, as the Holy Spirit said, Today if you will hear his voice,

8 Harden not your hearts to provoke him, as the murmurers did in the day of temptation in the wilderness.

9 Your fathers tempted me even though they examined and saw my works forty years;

10 Therefore I was not pleased with that generation, and said, These are a people whose hearts have been misled and they have not known my ways.

11 So I swore in my anger, They shall not enter into my rest.

12 ¶Take heed therefore, my brethren, lest perhaps there is a man among you who has an evil heart and is not a believer, and you will be cut off from the living God.

13 But search your hearts daily, until the day which is called The day, to the end that no man among you be hardened through the deceitfulness of sin.

14 For we are made partakers of Christ, if from the beginning to the very end we hold steadfast to this true covenant,

15 As it is said, Today, if you hear even the echoes of his voice, do not harden your hearts to anger him.

16 Who are those who have heard and provoked him? Were they not those who came out of Egypt under Moses, although not all of them?

17 But with whom was he displeased for forty years? Was it not especially

77

with those who had sinned and whose bones lay in the wilderness?

18 And against whom did he swear that they should not enter into his rest, except against those who did not listen?

19 So we see that they could not enter in because they did not believe.

CHAPTER 4

LET us therefore fear, while the promise of entering into his rest remains, lest some amongst you find they are prevented from entering.

2 For the gospel was preached to us as it was to them also, but the word they heard did not benefit them, because it was not mixed with faith in those who heard it.

3 But we who have believed will enter into rest, as he said, As I have sworn in my wrath, they shall not enter into my rest; for behold, the works of God were from the very foundation of the world.

4 For he said concerning the sabbath, God rested on the seventh day from all his works.

5 And here again he said, They shall not enter into my rest.

6 There was a chance for some to enter therein, but they to whom the gospel was first preached did not enter because they would not listen;

7 And again, after a long time he appointed another day, as it is written above; for David said, Today if you hear his voice, harden not your hearts.

8 For if Joshua the son of Nun had given them rest, he would not afterward have spoken of another day.

9 It is therefore the duty of the people of God to keep the sabbath.

10 For he who has entered into his rest also has ceased from his own works, as God did from his.

11 Let us strive therefore to enter into that rest, lest any man fall like those who were disobedient.

12 ¶For the word of God is living and powerful and sharper than any twoedged sword, piercing even to the point of division between soul and spirit, and between the joints and marrow and bones, and is a discerner of the thoughts and intents of the heart.

13 And there is no creature hidden from his sight; but all things are naked and open before the eyes of him to whom we are to answer.

14 ¶We have, therefore, a great high priest who has ascended into heaven, Jesus Christ, the Son of God; let us remain firm in his faith.

15 For we do not have a high priest who cannot share our infirmities, but we have one who was tempted with everything as we are, and yet without sin.

16 Let us, therefore, come openly to the throne of his grace, that we may obtain mercy and find grace to help in time of need.

CHAPTER 5

FOR every high priest chosen from among men is ordained on behalf of men about things pertaining to God, that he may offer both gifts and sacrifices for sins;

2 He is one who can humble himself and have compassion on those who are ignorant and go astray; for he himself also is subject to weaknesses.

3 Because of these, he is obliged, just as he offers sacrifices for the people, likewise to offer for himself on account of his own sins.

4 And no man takes this honor to himself, but only he who is called of God, as was Aaron.

5 So also Christ did not glorify himself by becoming a high priest, but he glorified him who said to him, Thou art my Son; today have I begotten thee.

6 And he said also in another place, Thou art a priest for ever after the order of Melchisedec.

7 Even when he was clothed in the flesh, he offered prayers and supplications, with vehement cries and tears, to him who was able to save him from death; and verily he was heard.

8 And though he was a good Son, because of fear and suffering which he endured, he learned obedience.

9 And he grew to be perfect and became the author of life everlasting to all who obey him;

10 So he was called by God a high priest after the order of Melchisedec.

11 ¶Now concerning this very Melchisedec we have much to say, but it is difficult to explain because you are dull of comprehension.

12 By now you should be teachers because you have been a long time in training; but even now you need to be taught the primary writings of the word of God; but you are still in need of milk, and not strong meat.

13 For every man whose food is milk is unfamiliar with the word of righteousness; for he is a babe.

14 But strong meat belongs to those who are of full age, even those who by reason of use have their senses exercised to discern both good and evil.

CHAPTER 6

THEREFORE, let us leave the elementary word of Christ, and let us go on to perfection. Why do you again lay another foundation for the repentance from past deeds and for faith in God?

2 And for the doctrine of baptisms and for the laying on of hands and for the resurrection of the dead and for eternal judgment?

3 If the Lord permits, this we will do.

4 But this is impossible for those who have once been baptized and have tasted the gift from heaven and have received the Holy Spirit

5 And have tasted the good word of God and the powers of the world to come,

6 For, for them to sin again and be renewed again by repentance, they crucify the Son of God a second time and put him to open shame.

7 For the earth, which drinks in the rain that falls abundantly on it, and brings forth herbs useful to those for whom it is cultivated, receives blessing from God;

8 But if it should produce thorns and briers it is rejected and not far from being condemned; and at the end this crop will be burned up.

9 But beloved brethren, we expect from you the things that are good and that pertain to salvation, even though we speak in this manner.

10 For God is not unjust to forget your works and your labor of love which you have made known in his name, for you have ministered to the saints and still do minister.

11 ¶We desire that every one of you show the same diligence toward the fulfillment of your hope, even to the end,

12 And that you be not slothful, but be followers of those who through faith and patience have become heirs of the promise.

13 For when God made a promise to Abraham, because there was none greater than himself by whom he could swear, he swore by himself,

14 Saying, Blessing, I will bless you, and multiplying, I will multiply you.

15 And so he was patient and obtained the promise.

16 For men swear by one who is greater than themselves; and in every dispute among them, the true settlement is by oaths.

17 Therefore, because God wanted more abundantly to show to the heirs of promise that his agreement was unchangeable, he sealed it by an oath.

18 Thus, by the promise and by the oath, both of which are unchangeable, and in neither of which could God lie, we find courage to hold fast to the hope that has been promised by him in whom we have taken refuge.

19 That promise is like an anchor to us; it upholds the soul so that it may not be shaken, and it penetrates beyond the veil of the temple;

20 Therein Jesus has previously entered into the temple for our sakes, and become the high priest for ever after the order of Melchisedec.

CHAPTER 7

FOR this Melchisedec was king of Salem, the priest of the most high God, who met Abraham returning from the slaughter of the kings and blessed him,

2 And to whom Abraham also set aside a tenth part from the choice things he had with him. His name is interpreted king of righteousness, and again, king of Salem, which means king of peace.

3 Neither his father nor his mother is recorded in the genealogies; and neither the beginning of his days nor the end of his life; but, like the Son of God, his priesthood abides for ever.

4 Now consider how great this man was, to whom even the patriarch Abraham gave tithes and paid head tax.

5 For those sons of Levi who received the office of the priesthood were authorized by law to take tithes from the people, even from their own brethren who also had come out of the loins of Abraham.

6 But this man who is not recorded in their genealogies took tithes even from Abraham and blessed him who had received the promises.

7 Beyond dispute, he who was less was blessed by him who was greater than himself.

8 And here mortal men receive tithes; but there he, of whom the scripture testifies that he lives, receives them.

9 Speaking as a man, through Abraham, even Levi, who received tithes, also gave tithes.

10 For he was yet in the loins of his forefather Abraham when Melchisedec met him.

11 If therefore perfection had been reached by the Levitical priesthood by which the law was enacted for the people, what further need was there that another priest should rise after the order of Melchisedec? Otherwise, the scriptures would have said that he would be after the order of Aaron.

12 Since there was a change in the priesthood, so also there was a change in the law.

13 For he concerning whom these things are spoken was born of another tribe, from which no man ever ministered at the altar.

14 For it is evident that our Lord sprang out of Judah, of which tribe Moses said nothing concerning the priesthood.

15 And yet it is far more evident because he said that another priest would rise after the order of Melchisedec,

16 One who was not appointed after the law of carnal commandments, but after the power of life which abides for ever.

17 For he testified concerning him, Thou art a priest for ever after the order of Melchisedec.

18 For the change which took place in the former law was made on account of its weaknesses and because it had become useless.

19 For the law made nothing perfect, but there has come in its place a better hope, by which we draw near to God.

20 And he confirmed it for us by oath.

21 For they were made priests without oaths; but this one was made a priest with an oath, as it was said concerning him by David, The Lord has sworn, and will not lie, Thou art a priest for ever after the order of Melchisedec.

22 All these things make a better covenant because Jesus is its surety.

23 And these priests were many, because they were mortal and they were not permitted to continue because of death;

24 But this one, because he is immortal, has a priesthood which remains for ever.

25 Therefore he is able to save forever those who come to God by him because he lives forever to make intercession for them.

26 ¶For this is the kind of high priest proper for us: pure, without evil, and undefiled, far away from sin, and made higher than the heavens;

27 And who needs not daily, as do those high priests, to offer up sacrifices, first for their own sins and then for the people's; for this he did once when he offered up himself.

28 For the law appoints imperfect men priests; but the word of the oath

which came after the law appoints the Son who is perfect for evermore.

CHAPTER 8

NOW above all we have a high priest who is seated at the right hand of the throne of the Majesty in heaven;

2 And he has become the minister of the sanctuary and of the true tabernacle which God pitched and not man.

3 For every high priest is appointed to offer gifts and sacrifices, therefore it is necessary that this man have something to offer also.

4 For if he were on earth, he would not be a priest, because there are priests who offer gifts according to the law,

5 Who serve the semblance and shadow of heavenly things, just as it was commanded to Moses when he was about to make the tabernacle: See that you make all things according to the pattern showed to you in the mount.

6 But now Jesus Christ has received a ministry which is greater than that; just as the covenant in which he was made a mediator is greater, so are the promises greater than those given in the old covenant.

7 ¶For if the first covenant had been faultless, then there would have been no need for the second.

8 For he found fault with them and said, Behold, the day is coming, says the Lord, when I will perfect a new covenant with the house of Israel and with the house of Judah;

9 Not according to the covenant that I made with their fathers in the day when I took them by the hand and led them out of the land of Egypt; and because they abode not in my covenant, I rejected them, says the Lord.

10 For this shall be the covenant that I will make with the house of Israel after those days, says the Lord: I will put my law into their minds and I will write it on their hearts; and I will be their God and they shall be my people.

11 And no man shall teach his neighbor, neither his brother, saying, Know the Lord; for all shall know me, from the youngest to the oldest.

12 And I will forgive their wickedness and I will no longer remember their sins;

13 For he has spoken of a new covenant; the first one has become old, and that which is old and obsolete is near destruction.

CHAPTER 9

THEN verily the first covenant had also ordinances of divine service and a worldly sanctuary.

2 For the first tabernacle which was made had in it the candlestick and the table and the shewbread; and it was called the sanctuary.

3 But the inner tabernacle, which is within the veil of the second door, was called the Holy of Holies.

4 And there was in it the golden censer and the ark of the covenant all overlaid with gold, and in it was the golden pot containing the manna, and Aaron's rod which budded and the tablets of the covenant;

5 And over it the cherubim of glory, overshadowing the mercy seat; now is not the time to describe how these things were made.

6 The priests always entered into the outer tabernacle and performed their service of worship;

7 But into the inner tabernacle, the high priest entered alone, once every year, with the blood which he offered for himself and for the faults of the people.

8 By this the Holy Spirit revealed that the way of the saints would not yet be made known so long as the old tabernacle remained.

9 Which was the symbol for that time, now past, in which were offered both gifts and sacrifices which could not make perfect the conscience of him who offered them,

10 But which served only for food and drink, and in various ablutions which are ordinances of the flesh and were imposed until the time of reformation.

11 But Christ, who had come, be-

came the high priest of the good things which he wrought; and he entered into a greater and more perfect tabernacle which was not made by hands and was not of this world;

12 And he did not enter with the blood of goats and calves, but by his own blood he entered in once into the holy place, and obtained for us everlasting salvation.

13 For if the blood of goats and calves and the ashes of a heifer sprinkled on those who were defiled sanctified them even to the cleansing of their flesh,

14 How much more will the blood of Christ, who through the eternal Spirit offered himself without blemish to God, purify our conscience from dead works so that we may serve the living God?

15 ¶For this cause he became the mediator of the new covenant and by his death he became salvation for those who transgressed the old covenant, that those who are called may receive the promise of eternal inheritance.

16 For where a will is presented, it shows the death of its maker.

17 For a will is of force only after men are dead, otherwise it is useless so long as its maker lives.

18 For this reason not even the first covenant was confirmed without blood.

19 For when Moses had given every precept to all the people according to the law, Moses took the blood of a heifer with water and scarlet wool and hyssop, and sprinkled it on the books and on all the people,

20 Saying, This is the blood of the covenant which has been ordained for you by God.

21 That very blood he also sprinkled on the tabernacle and on all the vessels used for worship,

22 Because nearly everything, according to the law, is purified with the blood; and without shedding of blood there is no forgiveness.

23 It is necessary, therefore, that the patterns of things which are heavenly should be purified with these; but the heavenly things themselves, with sacrifices better than these.

24 For Christ has not entered into the holy place made with hands, which is the symbol of the true one; but he entered into heaven itself to appear before the presence of God for our sakes.

25 Not so that he should offer himself many times, as does the high priest who enters into the holy place every year with blood which is not his own;

26 And if not so, then he would have been obliged to suffer many times from the very beginning of the world; but now at the end of the world, only once by his sacrifice did he offer himself to abolish sin.

27 And just as it is appointed for men to die once, and after their death, the judgment;

28 So Christ was once offered to bear the sins of many; so that at his second coming he shall appear without our sins for the salvation of those who look for him.

CHAPTER 10

FOR the law had in it a shadow of the good things to come, but was not the essence of the things themselves; hence although the same sacrifices were offered every year, they could not perfect those who offered them.

2 For if they had once been perfected, they would have ceased from their offerings; for, from henceforth their minds would not have driven them into the sins from which they had once been cleansed.

3 But in those sacrifices they remembered their sins every year.

4 For it is not possible that the blood of bulls and of goats could take away sins.

5 Therefore, when he entered into the world, he said, Sacrifices and offerings thou didst not desire, but a body thou hast prepared me;

6 Burnt offering and sin offering thou hast not required.

7 Then said I, Lo, I come; in the beginning of the books, it is written

of me, I delight to do thy will, O God.

8 Above when he said, Sacrifices and offerings and burnt offerings and offerings for sins, thou wouldst not have, the very ones which were offered according to the law;

9 And after that he said, Lo, I come to do thy will, O God. Thus he put an end to the first in order to establish the second.

10 By this very will we are sanctified through the offering of the body of Jesus Christ once for all.

11 For every high priest appointed ministered daily, offering the same sacrifices, which had never been able to cleanse sins;

12 But this one after he had offered one sacrifice for sins, sat down on the right hand of God for ever.

13 From henceforth there he will remain until his enemies are placed as a stool under his feet.

14 For by one offering he has perfected for ever those who are sanctified.

15 The Holy Spirit is also a witness to us; for he had said before,

16 This is the covenant that I will make with them after those days, says the Lord, I will put my law in their minds and write it on their hearts.

17 And their iniquities and sins will I remember no more.

18 For where there is forgiveness of sins, there is no need for offering for sins.

19 ¶Having therefore, my brethren, boldness to enter into the holiest by the blood of Jesus,

20 By a new and living way which he has made new for us through the veil, that is to say, his flesh,

21 And having a great high priest over the house of God,

22 Let us draw near with a true heart in full assurance of faith, having our hearts sprinkled and cleansed of evil thought and our bodies washed with pure water.

23 Let us remain firm in the profession of our faith without wavering, for he who has promised us is faithful.

24 And let us consider one another to arouse love and good works,

25 Not forsaking the assembling of ourselves together, as is customary for some; but exhorting one another, and so much the more when you see that day approaching.

26 For if any man sin wilfully after he has received the knowledge of the truth, then there is no more sacrifice to be offered for sins,

27 But he is ready for the fearful judgment and the fiery indignation which shall consume the adversaries.

28 He who transgressed the law of Moses, on the word of two or three witnesses, died without mercy:

29 How much more punishment do you think he will receive who has trodden underfoot the Son of God, and has considered the blood of his covenant, through which he had been sanctified, as ordinary blood and has blasphemed the Spirit of Grace?

30 For we know him who said, Vengeance is mine, I will repay, says the Lord. And again, The Lord shall judge his people.

31 It is a fearful thing to fall into the hands of the living God.

32 ¶Remember, therefore, the former days, in which, after you received baptism, you endured many tribulations.

33 By reproach and trouble you were made an object of ridicule; and you have also become companions of those men who have also endured these things.

34 And you had pity on those who were prisoners, and you took the seizure of your property cheerfully, for you know in yourselves that you have a better and a more enduring possession in heaven.

35 Do not lose, therefore, the confidence that you have, for it has a great reward.

36 For you have need of patience in order that you may do the will of God and receive the promise.

37 For the time is all too short, and he who is to come will come and will not delay.

38 But the righteous shall live by my faith; and if any draw back, my

soul shall have no pleasure in him.

39 But we do not belong to those who draw back to perdition, but to the faith which restores our souls.

CHAPTER 11

NOW faith is the substance of things hoped for, as it was the substance of things which have come to pass; and it is the evidence of things not seen,

2 And in this way it became a testimony concerning the elders.

3 For it is through faith we understand that the worlds were framed by the word of God, so that the things which are seen came to be from those which are not seen.

4 It was by faith Abel offered a more excellent sacrifice to God than Cain, and because of this, he received a testimony that he was righteous, and God testified to his offering; therefore, even though he is dead, he speaks.

5 By faith Enoch departed and did not taste death, and he was not found, because God took him; but before he took him away, there was a testimonial about him, that he pleased God.

6 Without faith man cannot please God; for he who comes near to God must believe that he is, and that he is a rewarder of those who seek him.

7 By faith Noah, when he was warned concerning the things not seen, became fearful and made an ark to save his household; and by it he condemned the world and became heir of righteousness which is by faith.

8 By faith Abraham, when he was called to depart for the land which he was to receive for an inheritance, obeyed; and he went out, not knowing where he was going.

9 By faith he became a sojourner in the land which was promised him as in a strange country, and he dwelt in tents with Isaac and Jacob, the heirs with him of the same promise;

10 For he looked for a city which has foundations, whose builder and maker is God.

11 Through faith also Sarah, who was barren, received strength to conceive an offspring, and was delivered of a child when she was past age, because she was sure that he who had promised her was faithful.

12 Therefore, there sprang from one who was as good as dead, as many as the stars of the sky in number and as the grains of sand which is on the sea shore, innumerable.

13 These all died in faith, not having received the promised land, but they saw it from afar, and rejoiced in it; and they acknowledged that they were strangers and pilgrims on earth.

14 For they who speak so declare plainly that they seek a country for themselves.

15 And if they had a desire for that very country from which they went out, they had time to return to it again.

16 But now it is evident that they desire a better city, that city which is in heaven; therefore God is not ashamed to be called their God; for he has prepared for them a city.

17 By faith Abraham, when he was tested, offered up Isaac; he lifted upon the altar his only begotten son, even that very one who had been received in the promise,

18 Of whom it was said, In Isaac shall your descendants be called;

19 And he reasoned in himself, It is possible for God even to raise the dead; and because of this, Isaac was given to him as a parable.

20 By faith in the things to come Isaac blessed Jacob and Esau.

21 By faith Jacob, when he was dying, blessed both of the sons of Joseph, and he worshipped, leaning upon the head of his staff.

22 By faith Joseph, when he died, made mention of the departure of the children of Israel and gave commandment concerning his bones.

23 By faith the parents of Moses hid him for three months after his birth, because they saw that the infant boy was fair; and they were not afraid of the king's commandment.

24 By faith Moses, when he came to manhood, refused to be called the son of Pharaoh's daughter,

25 Choosing rather to suffer affliction with the people of God than to enjoy the pleasures of sin for a short while.

26 And he reasoned that the reproach of Christ was greater riches than the treasures of Egypt; for he looked forward to receive a reward.

27 By faith he forsook Egypt, not fearing the wrath of the king; and he survived after he had seen God, who is invisible.

28 Through faith he instituted the passover and sprinkled the blood, lest he who destroyed the first-born should touch them.

29 By faith they passed through the Red sea as by dry land; but in it the Egyptians were drowned when they made the attempt.

30 By faith the walls of Jericho fell down after they had been encompassed seven days.

31 By faith Rahab the harlot did not perish with those who were disobedient, for she had received the spies in peace.

32 And what more shall I say? For time would fail me to tell of Gideon and of Barak and of Samson and of Jephthah and of David also and Samuel and of the rest of the prophets,

33 Who through faith conquered kingdoms, worked righteousness, obtained promises, stopped the mouths of lions,

34 Quenched the violence of fire, escaped the edge of the sword, out of weakness were made strong, became valiant in battle, routed the camps of enemies,

35 Restored to women their sons, raised people from the dead; while others died through tortures, not hoping for deliverance, that they might have a better resurrection;

36 Others endured mockings and scourgings; still others were delivered to bonds and imprisonment;

37 Some were stoned, some were sawn apart, some died by the edge of the sword; others wandered about, wearing sheepskins and goatskins, destitute, afflicted and tormented,

38 Of whom the world was not worthy; they were like those who are lost in the desert, and in mountains, and in dens and caves of the earth.

39 Thus these all, having obtained a testimonial through the faith, did not receive the promise,

40 Because God from the beginning provided for our help, lest without us they should not be made perfect.

CHAPTER 12

THEREFORE, seeing we also are surrounded with so great a cloud of witnesses, let us lay aside every weight and the sin which does so easily beset us, and let us run with patience the race that is set before us,

2 And let us look to Jesus, who was the author and the perfecter of our faith, and who, instead of the joy which he could have had, endured the cross, suffered shame, and is now seated at the right hand of the throne of God.

3 See, therefore, how much he has suffered from the hands of sinners, from those who were a contradiction to themselves, lest you become weary and faint in your soul.

4 ¶You have not yet come to the point of bloodshed in your striving against sin.

5 And you have forgotten the teaching which has been told to you as to children, My son, despise not the chastening of the Lord, not let your soul faint when you are rebuked of him,

6 For whom the Lord loves, he chastens, and he disciplines the son with whom he is pleased.

7 Now, therefore, endure discipline, because God acts toward you as toward sons; for where is the son whom the father does not discipline?

8 But if you are without discipline, that very discipline by which every man is trained, then you are strangers and not sons.

9 Furthermore if our fathers of the flesh corrected us and we respected them, how much more then should we willingly be under subjection to our Spiritual Father, and live?

10 For they only for a short while disciplined us as seemed good to them;

but God corrects us for our advantage, that we might become partakers of his holiness.

11 No discipline, at the time, is expected to be a thing of joy, but of sorrow; but in the end it produces the fruits of peace and righteousness to those who are trained by it.

12 ¶Therefore, be courageous and strong,

13 And make straight the paths for your feet, so that the member which is lame may not suffer but be healed.

14 Follow peace with all men, and holiness, without which no man shall see our Lord.

15 Take heed lest any man among you be found short of the grace of God, or lest any root of bitterness spring forth and harm you, and thereby many be defiled,

16 Or lest any man among you be found immoral and weak like Esau, who sold his birthright for a morsel of meat.

17 For you know that afterward when he wished to inherit the blessing, he was rejected, and he had no chance of recovery, even though he sought it with tears.

18 For you have yet neither come near the roaring fire nor the darkness nor the storm nor the tempest,

19 Nor to the sound of the trumpet and the voice of the word; which voice they heard but refused so that the word will not be spoken to them any more.

20 For they could not survive that which was commanded, for if even a beast drew near the mountain, it would be stoned.

21 And so terrible was the sight that Moses said, I fear and quake.

22 But you have come near to mount Zion and to the city of the living God, the heavenly Jerusalem, and to the innumerable multitude of angels

23 And to the congregation of the first converts who are enrolled in heaven and to God the Judge of all and to the spirits of pious men made perfect

24 And to Jesus, the mediator of the new covenant, and to the sprinkling of his blood, which speaks a better message than Abel did.

25 Beware, therefore, lest you refuse him who speaks to you. For if they were not delivered who refused him who spoke with them on earth, much more can we not escape if we refuse him who speaks to us from heaven.

26 He is the one whose voice shook the earth; but now he has promised, saying, Once more I will shake not only the earth, but also heaven.

27 And these words, Once more, signify the change of things which may be shaken, because they are made in order that the things which can not be shaken may remain.

28 Therefore, receiving a kingdom which cannot be shaken, let us hold fast that grace whereby we may serve and please God with reverence and godly fear;

29 For our God is a consuming fire.

CHAPTER 13

LET brotherly love remain in you. 2 And forget not hospitality toward strangers; for thereby some were worthy to entertain angels unawares.

3 Remember those who are in prison, as though you were a prisoner with them; remember those who suffer adversity, for you are human also.

4 Marriage is honourable in all, and the bed undefiled; but God will judge those who practice vice and adultery;

5 Do not be carried away by the love of money; but be content with what you have; for the Lord himself has said, I will never leave you nor forsake you.

6 So that we may boldly say, The Lord is my helper, and I will not fear what man may do to me.

7 Remember those who are your leaders, those who have spoken the word of God to you; mark the completeness of their works, and imitate their faith.

8 Jesus Christ is the same yesterday and today and for ever.

9 Do not be carried away by strange and different doctrines. For it is a

good thing to strengthen our hearts with grace; not with food because it did not help those who greatly sought after it.

10 We have an altar from which those who minister in the tabernacle have no right to eat.

11 For the flesh of the beasts whose blood is brought into the sanctuary by the high priest for sin is burned outside the camp.

12 Wherefore Jesus also, that he might sanctify his people with his own blood, suffered outside the city.

13 Let us go forth therefore to him outside the camp, bearing his reproach.

14 For here we have not a permanent city, but we seek one to come.

15 By him, therefore, let us always offer the sacrifice of praise to God, that is, the fruit of the lips giving thanks to his name.

16 And do not forget kindness and fellowship with the poor; for with such sacrifices God is well pleased.

17 Listen to your spiritual leaders and obey them; for they are watchful guardians of your souls, as one who must give account, that they may do it with joy and not with grief, for that is unprofitable for you.

18 Pray for us; for we trust we have a good conscience, being in all things willing to live honestly.

19 But above all, I beseech you to do this that I may return to you sooner.

20 ¶Now the God of peace who brought again from the dead our Lord Jesus, that great shepherd of the sheep, through the blood of the everlasting covenant,

21 Make you perfect in every good work to do his will, working in us that which is well pleasing in his sight, through Jesus Christ; to whom be glory for ever and ever. Amen.

22 ¶And I beseech you, my brethren, to be patient in the word of comfort; for I have written you very briefly.

23 You should know that our brother Timotheus has been set at liberty; and if he should come shortly, I will see you together with him.

24 Salute all your spiritual leaders and all the saints. All of the brethren of Italy salute you.

25 Grace be with you all. Amen.

THE GENERAL EPISTLE OF

JAMES

CHAPTER 1

JAMES, a servant of God and of our Lord Jesus Christ, to the twelve tribes which are scattered among the Gentiles: Greeting.

2 ¶My brethren, take it as a joy to you when you enter into many and varied temptations;

3 For you know that the trial of faith will increase your patience.

4 And let patience be a perfect work, that you may be perfect and entire, lacking nothing.

5 If any of you lack wisdom, let him ask of God, who gives to all men liberally and with grace, and it will be given him.

6 But let him ask in faith, not doubting. For he who doubts is like the waves of the sea driven by the wind and tossed.

7 Thus let not that man suppose that he will receive anything of the Lord.

8 A double-minded man is unstable in all his ways.

9 Let the brother who is humble rejoice because he is exalted.

10 Let the rich man rejoice in his

humbleness, because as the flower of the grass, so shall he pass away.

11 For as the sun rises with its burning heat and causes the grass to wither and the flower to fall and its beauty to perish, so also shall the rich man fade away in the course of his life.

12 Blessed is the man who endures temptations; for when he is tested, he shall receive the crown of life which God has promised to those who love him.

13 Let no man say when he is tempted, I am tempted of God; for God cannot be tempted with evil, neither does he tempt any man;

14 But every man is tempted by his own lust; he covets and is enticed.

15 Then when lust has conceived, it brings forth sin; and sin when it has matured, brings forth death.

16 Do not err, my beloved brethren.

17 Every good and perfect gift is from above, and comes down from the Father of lights, with whom there is no variableness nor shadow of change.

18 It is he who begot us of his own will with the word of truth, that we should be the first fruits of his creatures.

19 ¶Therefore, my beloved brethren, let every man be swift to hear and slow to speak and slow to anger;

20 For the wrath of man does not bring about the righteousness of God.

21 Therefore cast away all filthiness and all the multitude of evil things, and receive with meekness the engrafted word, which is able to save your souls.

22 ¶But be doers of the word, and not hearers only, deceiving your own selves.

23 For if any be a hearer of the word and not a doer, he is like a man who sees his face in a mirror;

24 For he sees himself and goes his way and forgets how he looked.

25 But whoever looks into the perfect law of liberty and abides in it is not merely a hearer of the word which can be forgotten but a doer of the work, and this man shall be blessed in his labor.

26 If any man thinks that he ministers to God, and does not control his tongue, he deceives his own heart, and this man's ministry is in vain.

27 For a pure and holy ministry before God the Father is this: To visit the fatherless and widows in their affliction, and to keep himself unspotted from the world.

CHAPTER 2

MY brethren, do not with hypocrisy uphold the glorious faith of our Lord Jesus Christ.

2 For if there should enter into your synagogue a man with gold rings and costly garments, and there should also enter a poor man in soiled clothing,

3 And you should attend to the one who wears the beautiful clothing and say to him, Sit here in a good place, and say to the poor man, Stand up there, or sit here before our footstool,

4 Are you not then showing partiality and thereby giving preference to evil thoughts?

5 Hear this, my beloved brethren: Has not God chosen the poor of the world who are rich in faith to be heirs of the kingdom which God has promised to those who love him?

6 But you have despised the poor. Do not rich men exalt themselves over you and drag you before the judgment seat?

7 Do not they blaspheme against that good name by which you are called?

8 If you fulfil the law of God by this, as it is written, You shall love your neighbor as yourself, you do well;

9 But if you discriminate among men, you commit sin and you will be condemned by the law as transgressors of the law.

10 For whoever shall keep the whole law, even though he fail in but one statute, he is guilty as to the whole law.

11 For he who said, You shall not commit adultery, said also, You shall not kill. Now if you do not commit adultery, but you kill, you have become a transgressor of the law.

12 So speak and so act as men who

are to be judged by the law of liberty.

13 For a judgment without mercy will be on him who does not show mercy; for you exalt yourselves by having mercy over judgment.

14 Though a man say he has faith, what profit is it, my brethren, if he does not have works? Can faith save him?

15 If a brother or sister be naked and lacking of daily food,

16 And one of you says to him, Depart in peace, be warmed and be filled; yet you do not give to him those things which are needed for the body, what does it profit?

17 Even so, by itself, faith without works is dead.

18 For a man may say, You have faith and I have works; show me your faith without your works, and I will show you my faith by my works.

19 You believe that there is one God; you do well. The devils also believe, and they tremble.

20 Would you know, O weak man, that faith without works is dead?

21 Was not our father Abraham justified by works, when he raised Isaac his son upon the altar?

22 You can see how his faith helped his works, and how by works his faith was made perfect.

23 And the scripture was fulfilled which said, Abraham believed God, and it was accounted to him for righteousness; and he was called the Friend of God.

24 You see then how a man by works becomes righteous, and not by faith only.

25 Likewise also was not Rahab the harlot justified by works when she welcomed the spies and sent them out another way?

26 For as the body without the spirit is dead, so also faith without works is dead.

CHAPTER 3

MY brethren, let not many teachers be among you; but know that we are under a great judgment.

2 For in many things we all stumble. Anyone who does not offend in word,

this one is a perfect man and able also to subdue his whole body.

3 Behold, we put bits into the mouths of horses, that they may obey us, and we turn about their whole body.

4 Behold also the ships; great as they are, when driven by severe winds, they are turned about with a very small rudder wherever the pilot wishes.

5 Even so the tongue is a little member and boasts great things. Likewise, a small fire sets ablaze large forests.

6 The tongue is a fire, and the sinful world a forest; that very tongue, while it is among our members, can defile our whole body and set on fire the course of our race which has rolled down from the beginning; and in the end it is consumed by fire.

7 For every kind of beasts and of birds and of creatures of the sea and of the land are under the subjugation of the will of man.

8 But the tongue no man can tame; it is an unruly evil, full of deadly poison.

9 By it we bless the Lord and the Father; and by it we curse men, who are made in the image of God;

10 Out of the same mouth proceed curses and blessings. My brethren, these things ought not so to be.

11 Can there spring forth from the same fountain both sweet water and bitter water?

12 Can the fig tree, my brethren, bear olives? Or the vine, figs? Likewise also salt water cannot be made sweet.

13 Who is wise among you and has training? Let him prove his words by his good deeds in the humbleness of wisdom.

14 But if you have bitter envying among you or strife in your hearts, do not boast and do not lie against the truth.

15 This wisdom does not come from above, but it is earthly, sensual, devilish.

16 For wherever envy and strife are, there is confusion and every sort of evil.

17 But the wisdom that is from above is first pure, then full of peace, and is gentle, obedient, full of mercy and good fruits, without partiality and without hypocrisy.

18 And the fruit of righteousness is sown in peace by the peacemakers.

CHAPTER 4

FROM whence come conflicts and quarrels among you? Is it not from the lusts that war in your members?

2 You covet and do not obtain; you kill and envy, but you cannot possess; you strive and fight, yet you have nothing, because you do not ask.

3 You ask and you do not receive because you do not ask sincerely, you ask that you may satisfy your lusts.

4 O you adulterers! Do you not know that the love for worldly things is enmity with God? Whoever, therefore, esteems worldly things is the enemy of God.

5 Or do you think that the scripture said in vain, The pride that dwells in us is provoked by jealousy?

6 But our Lord has given us abundant grace. Therefore he said, God humbles the proud, but gives grace to the humble.

7 Submit yourselves therefore to God. Resist Satan, and he will flee from you.

8 Draw near to God, and he will draw near to you. Cleanse your hands, O you sinners! And purify your hearts, O you of doubtful mind!

9 Humble yourselves and mourn; let your laughter be turned to weeping and your joy to sorrow.

10 Humble yourselves before the Lord and he will lift you up.

11 Do not speak against one another, my brethren, for he who speaks against his brother and judges his brother, speaks against the law and judges the law; but if you judge the law, you are not a doer of the law, but a judge of it.

12 For there is one lawgiver and judge, who is able to save and to destroy. Who are you to judge your neighbor?

13 ¶What then shall we say of those who say, Today or tomorrow we will go to a certain city and will work there a year and will trade and prosper?

14 They do not know what will happen tomorrow! For what is our life? It is but a vapour, which appears for a little while and then vanishes away.

15 Instead of that they should say, If the Lord will, we shall live and do this or that.

16 But now they are proud in their boasting; all such pride is evil.

17 Therefore he who knows to do good and does not do it, to him it is sin.

CHAPTER 5

O YOU rich men, weep and howl for the miseries which shall come upon you!

2 Your riches are destroyed and rotted, and your garments are motheaten.

3 Your gold and silver are tarnished, and the rust of them will be a testimony against you and will eat your flesh. The treasures which you have heaped together will be as fire to you for the last days.

4 Behold, the wage of the labourers who have reaped your fields, that which you have fraudulently kept back, cries; and the cry of the reapers has already entered into the ears of the Lord of sabaoth.

5 For you have had your luxuries on earth and have been greedy; you have fed your bodies as for the day of slaughter.

6 You have condemned and murdered the righteous; and yet he does not resist you.

7 ¶But my brethren, be patient until the coming of the Lord, just as the husbandman waits for the precious crop of his field, and has long patience for it, until he receives the early and the latter rain.

8 You be patient also; strengthen your hearts, for the coming of our Lord is at hand.

9 Complain not one against another, my brethren, lest you be con-

demned; for behold judgment is at hand.

10 My brethren, take the prophets who have spoken in the name of the Lord for an example of patience in your suffering.

11 Behold, we count them happy who endure. You have heard of the patience of Job, and you have seen what the Lord did for him at the end; for the Lord is very merciful and compassionate.

12 ¶But above all things, my brethren, do not swear, neither by heaven, neither by the earth, neither by any other oath; but let your words be yes, yes, and no, no, lest you fall under condemnation.

13 ¶If any among you be afflicted, let him pray. If any be merry, let him sing psalms.

14 ¶And if any be sick, let him call for the elders of the church, and let them pray over him, anointing him with oil in the name of our Lord:

15 And the prayer of faith shall heal the sick, and our Lord shall raise him up; and if he has committed sins, they shall be forgiven him.

16 ¶Confess your faults one to another, and pray one for another, that you may be healed. The effectual fervent prayer of a righteous man is powerful.

17 Even Elijah, who was a weak man like ourselves, prayed earnestly that it might not rain upon the land, and it did not rain for three years and six months.

18 And he prayed again, and the heaven gave rain and the earth brought forth her fruits.

19 My brethren, if any of you do err from the way of the truth, and some one converts him from his error,

20 Let him know that he who converts a sinner from the error of his way, shall save his soul from death and shall wipe out a multitude of sins.

THE FIRST EPISTLE GENERAL OF

PETER

CHAPTER 1

PETER, an apostle of Jesus Christ, to the chosen ones and pilgrims, scattered throughout Pontus, Galatia, Cappadocia, Asia Minor and Bithynia,

2 Who have been chosen by the foreknowledge of God the Father, through sanctification of the Spirit, to be obedient and to sprinkle the blood of our Lord Jesus Christ: Grace to you and peace be multiplied.

3 ¶Blessed be God, the Father of our Lord Jesus Christ, who by his abundant mercy has again renewed us spiritually to a lively hope by the resurrection of Jesus Christ from the dead,

4 To an inheritance incorruptible and undefiled, that does not fade away and is prepared in heaven for you,

5 While you are kept by the power of God through faith for the life eternal which is ready to be revealed at the last time.

6 Wherein you will rejoice for ever, though at present you are sorrowful for a while, through diverse trials which have come upon you,

7 So that the proof of your faith, being much more precious than refined gold which has been purified by fire, may be made manifest for the

glory and honour and praise at the appearing of Jesus Christ,

8 Whom you have not seen, but whom you yet love, and in whose faith you rejoice with exceeding joy that cannot be described;

9 And you will receive the reward for your faith, even the salvation of your souls.

10 For which very salvation the prophets searched diligently when they prophesied concerning the grace which was to be given to you.

11 They searched to find out at what time it would be revealed, and the Spirit of Christ which dwelt in them testified beforehand the sufferings of Christ and the glory that should follow.

12 And everything they were searching for was revealed to them because they did not seek for their own benefit, but they prophesied the things which concerned us, the things which now have been revealed to you by those who have preached the gospel to you through the Holy Spirit sent from heaven; which things the angels also desire to look into.

13 ¶Therefore gird up the loins of your mind, be wide awake and hope for the joy that is coming to you at the revelation of our Lord Jesus Christ;

14 Like obedient children, not partakers again in those sinful desires for which you once lusted in your ignorance;

15 But be you holy in all your conduct, as he who has called you is holy;

16 Because it is written, Be you holy, even as I am holy.

17 And if you call on the Father, who is impartial and who judges every man according to his works, conduct yourselves reverently during the time of your sojourning here,

18 Knowing that you have not been redeemed from your empty works which you have received from your fathers, by corruptible silver and gold,

19 But with the precious blood of the Lamb without blemish and without spot which is Christ,

20 Who verily was foreordained for this very purpose before the foundation of the world, and was manifest in these last times for your sakes,

21 Who by him you believe in God, who raised him up from the dead and gave him glory, that your faith and hope might rest on God.

22 Let your souls be sanctified by obedience to the truth, and be filled with sincere love, so that you may love one another with pure and perfect hearts,

23 Being born again, not of corruptible seed, but of incorruptible, by the word of God, which lives and abides for ever.

24 For all flesh is as grass, and all its glory is as the flower of the field. The grass withers and the flower fades away,

25 But the word of our God endures for ever. And this is the very word which has been preached to you.

CHAPTER 2

THEREFORE lay aside all malice and all guile and hypocrisies and envies and evil accusations,

2 And become like newborn babes, and long for the word as for pure and spiritual milk, that you may grow to salvation by it,

3 If you have tasted and found out that the Lord is good.

4 The one to whom you are coming is the living stone, whom men have rejected, and yet he is chosen and precious with God;

5 You also, as living stones, build up yourselves and become spiritual temples and holy priests to offer up spiritual sacrifices acceptable to God by Jesus Christ.

6 For as it is said in the scriptures, Behold, I lay in Zion, a chief cornerstone, approved, precious; and he who believes on him shall not be ashamed.

7 It is to you who believe, therefore, that this honour is given; but to those who are disobedient, he is a stumbling stone and a stone of trouble.

8 And they stumble over it because they are disobedient to the word for which they were appointed.

9 But you are a chosen people, ministers to the kingdom, a holy people, a congregation redeemed to proclaim the glories of him who has called you out of darkness to his marvelous light;

10 You, who in the past were not considered a people, but who are now the people of God, who had not obtained mercy, but who now have mercy poured out upon you.

11 ¶Dearly beloved, I beseech you as strangers and pilgrims, abstain from carnal desires, which war against the soul;

12 And let your conduct be good before all men, so that those who speak evil words against you may see your good works and glorify God at the day of trial.

13 Submit yourselves to all human authority for the sake of God, whether it be to kings because of their power,

14 Or to judges because from them officers are sent to punish offenders and to bestow honour on those who do good.

15 For such is the will of God that by your good works you may silence the mouths of foolish men who know not God.

16 Act as free men; not as men who use their liberty as a cloak for their maliciousness, but as the servants of God.

17 Honor all men. Love your brethren. Fear God. Honor the king.

18 ¶And as for the servants among you, let them be submissive to their masters with due respect, not only to those who are good and gentle, but also to those who are severe and difficult.

19 For such men have favor before God; because of a good conscience they endure sorrows which come upon them unjustly.

20 What praise have they who endure suffering because of their faults? But when you do good and are made to suffer and you take it patiently, then your glory is greater with God.

21 For to this purpose you were called, because Christ also died for us, leaving us an example, that we should follow in his steps.

22 He did no sin, neither was guile found in his mouth;

23 When he was reviled, he did not revile again; when he suffered he did not threaten, but committed his cause to him who judges righteously;

24 And he bore all our sins and lifted them with his body on the cross, that we, being dead to sin, should live through his righteousness; and by his wounds you were healed.

25 For you had gone astray like sheep, but you have now returned to the Shepherd and the Guardian of your souls.

CHAPTER 3

LIKEWISE, you wives, be submissive to your own husbands, so that those who obey not the word may be won without difficulty through your good example,

2 When they see that you conduct yourselves with respect and modesty.

3 And do not adorn yourselves with outward adornments such as the plaiting of your hair or the wearing of ornaments of gold or costly apparel;

4 But adorn yourselves by the spiritual man within you, with meek pride which is incorruptible and an ornament which is rich in the sight of God.

5 For so also in the past did the holy women who trusted in God adorn their lives and were submissive to their own husbands,

6 Even as Sara was submissive to Abraham and called him my lord; her daughters you are by reason of good works and so long as you are not confused by any kind of false value.

7 Likewise, you husbands, live with your wives with understanding, and hold them with tenderness like delicate vessels, because they also will inherit with you the gift of everlasting life; do this that you may not be hindered in your prayers.

8 ¶Finally, live in harmony, share the suffering of those who suffer, be affectionate one to another, and be kind and gentle;

9 Not rendering evil for evil, nor

railing for railing, but instead of these, render blessing; for to this end you have been called, that you may inherit a blessing.

10 Now, therefore, he who desires eternal life and wants to see good days, let him refrain his tongue from evil and his lips that they speak no guile:

11 Let him refrain from evil and do good; let him seek peace and pursue it.

12 For the eyes of the Lord are on the righteous, and his ears are open to their prayers, but the countenance of the Lord is against the wicked.

13 And who is he that can harm you if you are zealous followers of that which is good?

14 But if you suffer for righteousness' sake, you are blessed; and be not afraid of those who terrify you, neither be troubled.

15 But sanctify the Lord Christ in your hearts; and be ready to give an answer in meekness and reverence to everyone who seeks from you a word concerning the hope of your faith,

16 Having a good conscience, so that they who speak evil of you as of evildoers may be ashamed as men who belittle your good works in Christ.

17 For it is better, if it is the will of God, that you suffer for good deeds, rather than for evil doing.

18 For Christ also once suffered for our sins, a just man for sinners, that he might bring you to God, wherefore while he died in the flesh, he lives in the Spirit.

19 And he preached to the souls imprisoned in Sheol,

20 Those who in the past were disobedient; and in the days of Noah, when the Spirit of God had patience, he commanded an ark to be made in the hope of their repentance, but only eight souls entered into it, and were saved by its floating upon the water.

21 You also are saved in that very manner by baptism, not merely by washing the filth from the body, but by confessing God with a clean conscience and by the resurrection of Jesus Christ,

22 Who is taken up to heaven and is at the right hand of God, angels and authorities and powers being made subject to him.

CHAPTER 4

FORASMUCH then as Christ has suffered for you in the flesh, arm yourselves also with this very thought; he who subdues his body ceases from all sin,

2 That he should no longer live the rest of his time in the flesh to the lusts of men, but to the will of God.

3 For the time past sufficed to have wrought the will of the pagans when you lived in lasciviousness, drunkenness, revellings, indecent singing, and worship of idols.

4 And behold, they think it strange that you do not indulge with them in the past excesses, and they blaspheme against you.

5 And they shall answer to God, who is to judge the quick and the dead.

6 For, for this cause the gospel was preached also to those who are dead, that they might be judged according to men in the flesh, and live according to God in spirit.

7 But the end of all things is at hand; be devout therefore, and be mindful of prayer.

8 And above all things have fervent love toward one another, because love covers a multitude of sins.

9 Be hospitable to strangers without grudging.

10 So let everyone of you according to the gift he has received from God, minister the same to your fellowmen, like good stewards of the manifold grace of God.

11 If any man preach, let him preach the word of God; and if any man minister, let him do it according to the ability which God has given him, so that in everything you do, God may be glorified through Jesus Christ, to whom belongs glory and honour for ever and ever. Amen.

12 My beloved, do not think it strange at the trials that come upon you, as though some strange thing

happened to you, because these things are to prove you.

13 But rejoice, for you are partakers of Christ's sufferings; and when his glory shall be revealed you may be glad also with exceeding joy.

14 If you are reproached for the name of Christ, blessed are you, for the glorious Spirit of God rests upon you.

15 But let none of you suffer the fate of a murderer or a thief or a malefactor.

16 If any man suffers as a Christian, let him not be ashamed, but let him glorify God through that very name.

17 For the time is come that judgment must begin with the house of God; and if it first begins with us, what shall be the end of those who do not obey the gospel of God?

18 And if the righteous scarcely be saved, how shall the wicked and the sinner stand judgment?

19 Therefore let those who suffer according to the will of God commit their souls to him in well doing as to a faithful Creator.

CHAPTER 5

I EXHORT the ministers who are among you, for I also am a minister and a witness of the sufferings of Christ and a partaker of the glory that shall be revealed.

2 Feed the flock of God which is entrusted to your care and shepherd them spiritually, not by constraint, but willingly; not for filthy lucre, but with all your heart.

3 Live not as overlords over the flock, but as good examples to them.

4 And when the chief Shepherd shall appear, you shall receive a crown of glory that will not fade away.

5 And you too, young people, submit yourselves to your elders; and clothe yourselves with humility toward one another, for God resists the proud and gives grace to the humble.

6 Humble yourselves therefore under the mighty hand of God, that he may exalt you in due time,

7 Casting all your cares upon God, for he cares for you.

8 ¶Be vigilant and be cautious, because your adversary, the devil, like a roaring lion, walks about, seeking whom he may devour.

9 Rise up, therefore, against him, as you are steadfast in the faith, knowing that your brethren who are in the world also suffered these same afflictions.

10 But the God of all grace, who has called us to his eternal glory by Jesus Christ, whom God has given to us, will strengthen us to endure these little afflictions that we may be made steadfast and remain in him for ever.

11 To him be glory and dominion and honour for ever and ever. Amen.

12 ¶By Silvanus, a faithful brother, I have written you these things briefly according to my opinion, exhorting and testifying that this is the true grace of God wherein you stand.

13 The chosen church which is at Babylon and Mark, my son, salute you.

14 Greet one another with a holy kiss. Peace be with you all who are in Christ. Amen.

THE SECOND EPISTLE GENERAL OF

PETER

CHAPTER 1

SIMON Peter, a servant and apostle of Jesus Christ, to those who through the righteousness of our Lord and Saviour Jesus Christ have been made equal with us in the precious faith:

2 Grace and peace be multiplied to you through the knowledge of our Lord Jesus Christ,

3 Who has given us all things that pertain to the power of God, for life and worship of God, through the knowledge of him who has called us by his glory and excellence,

4 Whereby are given to us exceeding great and precious promises, that by these you might be partakers of the divine nature, having escaped the corruption that is in the world through lust.

5 And besides this, giving all diligence, add to your faith, virtue; and to virtue, knowledge;

6 And to knowledge, self-control; and to self-control, patience; and to patience, godliness;

7 And to godliness, brotherly kindness; and to brotherly kindness, love.

8 For when these things are found among you and abound, you are not empty nor unfruitful in the knowledge of our Lord Jesus Christ.

9 But he who lacks these things is blind and cannot see afar off, and has forgotten that he was cleansed from his former sins.

10 For this very reason, my brethren, be diligent; for through your good deeds, you make your calling and your election sure; and when you do these things, you shall never fall,

11 For by so doing, an entrance shall be given freely to you into the everlasting kingdom of our Lord and Saviour Jesus Christ.

12 ¶Wherefore I will not be negligent to put you always in remembrance of these things, though you know them well and you rely on this very truth.

13 Therefore I think it is right, as long as I am in this body, to stir you up by putting you in remembrance,

14 Knowing that shortly I must depart this life, even as our Lord Jesus Christ has shown me.

15 Be diligent always, that you may be able to keep these things in remembrance even after my departure.

16 For we have not followed cunningly devised fables when we made known to you the power and coming of our Lord Jesus Christ, for we were eyewitnesses of his majesty.

17 For he received from God the Father honor and glory when there came such a voice to him from the excellent and majestic glory, This is my beloved Son, in whom I am well pleased.

18 And this very voice which came from heaven we also heard when we were with him on the holy mountain.

19 We have also a true word of prophecy; you do well when you look to it for guidance, as you look to the lamp that shines in a dark place until the dawn of day, when the sun will shine in your hearts,

20 Knowing this first, that not every prophetic writing is made clear in its own book.

21 For the prophecy did not come by the will of man, but holy men of God spoke when they were inspired by the Holy Spirit.

CHAPTER 2

BUT there were false prophets also among the people, even as there will be false teachers among you, who shall bring in damnable heresies, even denying the Lord who has redeemed them, and thus bringing upon themselves swift destruction.

2 Many will follow their pernicious ways, by reason of whom evil will be spoken of the way of truth.

3 And through covetousness they will exploit you with feigned words, whose judgment from the very beginning has not ceased and their damnation is always active.

4 God did not spare the angels who sinned, but cast them down to hell and delivered them into chains of darkness to be reserved for tormenting judgment;

5 And he did not spare the old world, but saved Noah the preacher of righteousness, with his family, eight in all, when he brought the flood upon the wicked people,

6 And set afire the cities of Sodom and Gomorrah, and condemned them with an upheaval, making them an example to those who hereafter should live ungodly lives;

7 And delivered righteous Lot, mortified by the filthy conduct of the lawless;

8 For while that pious man dwelt among them, in seeing and hearing their unlawful deeds, his righteous soul was vexed from day to day.

9 The Lord knows how to deliver from distress those who revere him, and he will reserve the wicked to be punished at the judgment day.

10 And especially will he punish those who follow after filthy lusts of the flesh and have no respect for authority. Bold and self-willed are they who do not tremble when they blaspheme against the glory;

11 Whereas angels, who are greater in power and might, do not bring upon themselves the condemnation of blasphemy.

12 But these men, as natural brute beasts, made for slaughter and destruction, speak evil of the things which they do not understand; and shall utterly perish in their own corruption,

13 And shall receive the reward of iniquity as they consider it a delightful thing to revel in the daytime. Spots and blemishes have they, and sport themselves with their own pleasures as they feast in idleness,

14 And have eyes full of adultery and of sin that does not cease; beguiling, unstable souls are they, whose hearts are well versed in covetousness; accursed sons are they,

15 Who have forsaken the right path and are gone astray, following the way of Balaam, the son of Beor, who loved the wages of unrighteousness;

16 But who was rebuked for his iniquity; a dumb ass, speaking with man's voice, halted the folly of the prophet.

17 These men are springs without water, clouds that are carried with a tempest; the mist of darkness is reserved for them forever.

18 For when they speak great swelling words of vanity, they allure through the sensual lusts of the flesh; but there are those who flee at a word of warning from them who live in error.

19 They, while they promise liberty, themselves are the slaves of corruption; for a man is overcome by whatever it is that enslaves him.

20 For if after they have escaped the pollutions of the world through knowledge of our Lord and Saviour Jesus Christ, they are again entangled by these very things and overcome, the latter end is worse with them than the beginning.

21 Verily it would have been better for them not to have known the way of righteousness than, after they have known it, to turn from the holy commandment that was delivered to them.

22 It will come to pass with them according to the true proverb, The dog returns to his own vomit, and the sow that was washed to her wallowing in the mire.

CHAPTER 3

IT has been a long time since I have written you, my beloved, but now I write this second epistle; in both of them I have endeavored to stir up your pure minds by way of remembrance,

2 That you may be mindful of the words which were spoken before by the holy prophets, and of the commandment given through us, the apostles of our Lord and Saviour:

3 Knowing this first, that there shall come in the last days mockers who scoff, following after their own lusts

4 And saying, Where is the promise of his coming? For since our fathers died, all things continue as they were from the beginning of creation.

5 Of this they are willingly ignorant, that by the word of God the heavens were of old, and the earth standing out of water and in the water;

6 And those men, because of whose deeds the world of that time was overflowed with water, perished;

7 But the present heavens and earth are sustained by his word and are reserved for fire on the day of judgment, which is the day of destruction of ungodly men.

8 But, my beloved, do not forget this one thing, that one day is with the Lord as a thousand years, and a thousand years as one day.

9 The Lord is not negligent concerning his promises, as some men count negligence; but is longsuffering toward you, not wishing that any should perish, but that all should come to repentance.

10 But the day of the Lord will come as a thief in the night, when the heavens shall suddenly pass away and the elements shall separate as they burn, and the earth also and the works that are in it shall not be found.

11 Now since all these things are to be dissolved, what manner of persons ought you to be in your holy conduct and godliness,

12 Looking for and longing for the coming of the day of God, wherein the heavens being tested with fire shall be dissolved, and the elements shall melt with fervent heat?

13 Nevertheless we, according to his promise, look for new heavens and a new earth in which dwells righteousness.

14 ¶Therefore, my beloved, while you look for these things, be diligent that you may be found by him in peace, without spot and blameless.

15 And consider that the long suffering of the Lord is salvation; even as our beloved brother Paul also, according to the wisdom given to him, has written to you;

16 As also in all his epistles, he spoke concerning these matters, in which there are certain things so hard to be understood that those who are ignorant and unstable pervert their meaning, as they do also the other scriptures, to their own destruction.

17 You therefore, my beloved, seeing that you know these things beforehand, beware lest you follow the error of the lawless, and fall from your own steadfastness.

18 But grow in grace and in the knowledge of our Lord and Saviour Jesus Christ and of God the Father. To him be glory both now and for ever and through all eternity. Amen.

THE FIRST EPISTLE GENERAL OF

JOHN

CHAPTER 1

HE who was from the beginning, the one whom we have heard, and have seen with our eyes, have looked upon, and have touched with our hands, we declare to you is the Word of life.

2 For the life was manifested, and we have seen it and bear witness to it, and preach to you eternal life, which was with the Father and was revealed to us;

3 It is that which we have seen and heard that we declare to you, so that you also may have fellowship with us; and truly our fellowship is with the Father and with his Son Jesus Christ.

4 And these things we write to you that our joy in you may be complete.

5 ¶This then is the good news which we have heard from him and declare to you, that God is light and in him is no darkness at all.

6 If we say that we have fellowship with him and yet live in darkness, we lie and do not follow the truth;

7 But if we live in the light as he is in the light, we have fellowship with one another and the blood of Jesus his Son cleanses us from all sin.

8 If we say that we have no sin, we deceive ourselves and the truth is not in us.

9 If we confess our sins, he is faithful and just to forgive us our sins and to cleanse us from all our unrighteousness.

10 If we say that we have not sinned, we make him a liar and his word is not in us.

CHAPTER 2

MY little children, these things I write to you that you do not sin. And if any man sin, we have an advocate with the Father, Jesus Christ the righteous;

2 And he is the propitiation for our sins; and not for ours only but also for the sins of the whole world.

3 ¶And hereby we know that we know him, if we keep his commandments.

4 He who says I know him and does not keep his commandments is a liar, and the truth is not in him.

5 But whoever keeps his word, in him verily is the love of God perfected; hereby we know that we are in him.

6 He who says he abides in him ought himself also so to walk even as he walked.

7 ¶My beloved, I do not write a new commandment to you, but an old commandment which you had from the beginning. The old commandment is the word which you have already heard.

8 Again, a new commandment I do write to you, which thing is true in him and in you, because the darkness is past and the true light now shines.

9 He who says he is in the light but hates his brother is therefore in darkness even until now.

10 He who loves his brother abides in the light, and there is no cause for displeasure in him.

11 But he who hates his brother is in darkness and walks in darkness, and does not know where he is going, because that darkness has blinded his eyes.

12 I write to you, little children, because your sins are forgiven you for his name's sake.

13 I write to you, fathers, because you have known him who is from the beginning. I write to you, young men, because you have overcome the evil one. I write to you, little children,

because you have known the Father.

14 I have written to you, fathers, because you have known him that is from the beginning. I have written to you, young men, because you are strong and the word of God abides in you, and you have overcome the evil one.

15 Love not the world, neither the things that are in the world. He who loves the world, the love of the Father is not in him.

16 For all that is in the world is the lust of the body, the covetousness of the eyes, and the pride of material things; these things do not come from the Father but from the world.

17 And the world passes away, and the lust thereof; but he who does the will of God abides forever.

18 ¶My children, it is the last time; and as you have heard that a false christ shall come, even now there are many false christs, and from this we know that it is the last time.

19 They went out from among us, but they were not of us; for if they had been of us, they would have continued with us; but they left us, that it might be known they did not belong to us.

20 But you have been anointed by the Holy One, and you are enabled to distinguish between men.

21 I have written to you not because you do not know the truth, but because you know it, and are aware that no lie comes out of the truth.

22 Who is a liar but he who denies that Jesus is the Christ? He is a false christ, and whoever denies the Father, denies the Son also.

23 Whoever denies the Son, the same does not believe in the Father; but whoever acknowledges the Son, acknowledges the Father also.

24 As for you, let that, therefore, abide in you which you have heard from the very beginning. For if that which you have heard from the beginning shall remain in you, you also shall continue in the Father and in the Son.

25 And this is the promise that he has promised us, even eternal life.

26 These things I have written to you concerning those who seduce you.

27 And you also, if the anointing which you have received from him abides among you, need no one to teach you; that same anointing which is of God will teach you all things; it is the truth, and there is no lie in it; and even as I have taught you, abide in it.

28 And now, my children, abide in him, that when he shall appear, we may not be ashamed before him, but have pride at his coming.

29 If you know that he is righteous, you know also that every one who does righteousness is of him.

CHAPTER 3

SEE how abundant the love of the Father is toward us, for he has called us sons and made us; therefore the world does not know us because it did not know him.

2 My beloved, now we are the sons of God, and as yet it has not been revealed what we shall be; but we know that when he shall appear, we shall be in his likeness; for we shall see him as he is.

3 ¶Let every man who has this hope in him purify himself, even as he is pure.

4 Whoever commits sin commits evil; for all sin is evil.

5 And you know that he was manifested to take away our sins; and in him is no sin.

6 Whoever abides in him does not sin; and whoever sins has not seen him, neither known him.

7 My children, let no man deceive you; he who does righteousness is righteous, just as Christ is righteous.

8 He who commits sin is of the devil, because the devil has been a sinner from the beginning. For this purpose the Son of God appeared, that he might destroy the works of the devil.

9 Whoever is born of God does not commit sin because God's seed is in him and he cannot sin because he is born of God.

10 In this the children of God can

be distinguished from the children of the devil; whoever does not practice righteousness and does not love his brother does not belong to God.

11 ¶For this is the commandment that you have heard from the beginning, that you must love one another,

12 Not do as Cain did, who belonged to the wicked one and slew his brother. And why did he kill him? Because his own works were evil, and those of his brother were righteous.

13 So be not surprised, my brethren, if the world hates you.

14 We know that we have passed from death to life, because we love our brethren. He who does not love his brother abides in death.

15 Whosoever hates his brother is a murderer; and you know that no murderer has eternal life abiding in him.

16 By this we know his love for us, because he laid down his life for us; and we ought to lay down our lives for our brethren.

17 Whoever has worldly goods and sees his brother in need and shuts his mercy from him, how can the love of God dwell in him?

18 My children, let us not love one another in word and in tongue, but in deed and in truth.

19 ¶And by this we shall know that we are of the truth and shall assure our hearts before he comes.

20 For if our hearts condemn us, how much more, then, will God who is greater than our hearts and knows all things?

21 My beloved, if our hearts do not condemn us, then we have confidence before God.

22 And whatever we ask, we receive from him, because we keep his commandments and do those things that are pleasing to him.

23 And this is his commandment, That we should believe in the name of his Son Jesus Christ and love one another as he has commanded us.

24 Whosoever keeps his commandments will be guarded by him, and he will dwell in him. And by this we know that he abides in us, by the Spirit which he has given us.

CHAPTER 4

MY beloved, do not believe every prophecy, but examine the prophecies to find out if they are of God, because many false prophets have appeared in the world.

2 The Spirit of God is known by this: Every prophecy which declares that Jesus Christ is come in the flesh is from God.

3 And every prophecy which does not declare that Jesus Christ has come in the flesh is not from God, but it is the prophecy of the false christ, of whose coming you have heard and who is even now already in the world.

4 But you are of God, my children, and have overcome them, because he who is among you is greater than he who is in the world.

5 They are of the world; therefore they speak of the world, and the world hears them.

6 But we are of God; he who knows God hears us; he who is not of God does not hear us. By this we know the spirit of truth and the spirit of error.

7 ¶My beloved, let us love one another; for love is from God; and every one who loves is born of God and knows God.

8 He who does not love does not know God; for God is love.

9 By this was the love of God toward us made known, for God sent his only begotten Son into the world, that we might live through him.

10 Herein is love, not that we loved God, but that God loved us and sent his Son to be the propitiation for our sins.

11 My beloved, if God so loved us, we ought also to love one another.

12 No man has seen God at any time. If we love one another, God abides in us, and his love is perfected in us;

13 Hereby we know that we abide in him and he in us, because he has given us of his Spirit.

14 ¶And we have seen and do testify that the Father sent his Son to be the Saviour of the world.

15 Whoever shall confess that Jesus

is the Son of God, God abides in him and he in God.

16 And we have believed and have known the love that God has for us. God is love; and he who dwells in love abides in God.

17 Herein is his love made perfect in us, so that we may have boldness in the day of judgment; because as he is, so are we in this world.

18 There is no fear in love; but perfect love casts out fear, because fear is tormenting. He who fears is not made perfect in love.

19 We love God because he first loved us.

20 ¶If a man says, I love God, and yet hates his brother, he is a liar; for he who does not love his brother whom he has seen, how can he love God whom he has not seen?

21 And this commandment we have received from him, That he who loves God ought to love his brother also.

CHAPTER 5

WHOEVER believes that Jesus is the Christ is born of God; and everyone who loves him who begot, loves him also who is begotten of him.

2 And by this we know that we love the children of God, when we love God and keep his commandments.

3 For this is the love of God, that we keep his commandments; and his commandments are not difficult.

4 For whoever is born of God triumphs over the world; and this is the victory which conquers the world, even our faith.

5 Who is he who triumphs over the world but he who believes that Jesus is the Son of God?

6 ¶This is he who came by water and blood, even Jesus Christ, not by water only, but by water and blood.

7 And the Spirit testifies that that very Spirit is the truth.

8 And there are three to bear witness, the Spirit and the water and the blood; and these three are one.

9 If we accept the testimony of men, how much greater is the testimony of God; for this is the testimony of God which he has testified of his Son.

10 He who believes in the Son of God has this testimony in himself; he who does not believe God, has made him a liar; because he does not believe the testimony that God gave of his Son.

11 And this is the testimony, that God has given to us eternal life, and this life is in his Son.

12 He who believes in the Son has life; he who does not believe in the Son of God does not have life.

13 ¶These things I have written to you who believe in the name of the Son of God, that you may know that you have eternal life.

14 And this is the confidence that we have in him, that if we ask anything according to his will, he hears us;

15 For if we beseech him to hear us concerning the things that we ask of him, we are assured that we have already received from him those things that we desire.

16 ¶If any man sees his brother commit a sin which is not worthy of death, let him ask and life will be granted him, if he has not committed a sin worthy of death. There is a sin worthy of death; I do not say that anyone shall pray for it.

17 All unrighteousness is sin; but there is a sin which is not worthy of death.

18 ¶We know that everyone who is born of God does not sin; for he who is born of God guards himself, and the evil one does not come near him.

19 And we know that we are of God, and the whole world lies in wickedness.

20 And we know that the Son of God has come and has given us an understanding, that we may know him who is true; and we are in him who is true, even in his Son Jesus Christ. This is the true God and eternal life.

21 My children, keep yourselves from idols.

THE SECOND EPISTLE OF

JOHN

THE minister to the mother church and her children, those whom I love in the truth, and not I only, but also those who have known the truth,

2 For the sake of the truth which dwells in us and is with us for ever:

3 Grace be with us, mercy, and peace, from God the Father and from the Lord Jesus Christ, the Son of the Father, in truth and love.

4 ¶I rejoiced greatly that I found some of your children living in the truth, as we have received a commandment from the Father.

5 And now I beseech you, O mother church, not as though I wrote a new commandment to you, but that which we had from the beginning, that we love one another.

6 And this is love, that we walk according to his commandments. This is the commandment, that as you have heard from the beginning, you should follow it.

7 For many deceivers have appeared in the world, who do not acknowledge that Jesus Christ has come in the flesh. Such a person is a deceiver and an antichrist.

8 Look to yourselves, that you lose not those things which you have accomplished, but that you receive a full reward.

9 Whoever transgresses and does not abide in the teaching of Christ does not have God. He who abides in his doctrine has both the Father and the Son.

10 If anyone comes to you and does not bring this doctrine, do not welcome him to your house, neither bid him to eat;

11 For he who bids him to eat is partaker of his evil works.

12 ¶I have many things to say to you which I do not want to write with paper and ink; but I trust to come to you and speak face to face, that our joy may be full.

13 The children of your elect sister church greet you. Grace be with you. Amen.

THE THIRD EPISTLE OF

JOHN

THE elder to the well beloved Gaius, whom I love in the truth:

2 Our beloved, I pray above all things that you may prosper and be in good health, even as your soul prospers.

3 For I rejoiced greatly when the brethren came and testified concerning the truth that is in you, even as you live a true life.

4 I have no greater joy than to hear that my children follow the truth.

5 Our beloved, you do faithfully that which you do to the brethren, especially to those who are strangers.

6 Who have borne witness concern-

ing your love before the whole church for the good things which you have done for them by supplying their needs, as is pleasing to God,

7 Because they have gone forth for his name's sake, taking nothing from the Gentiles.

8 We, therefore, ought to welcome such, so that we may be fellow helpers to the truth.

9 ¶I wrote to the church that Diotrephes, who loves to have the preeminence among them, would not receive us.

10 Therefore, if I come, I will mention the things which he did, gossiping against us with malicious words; and not content with this, he not only did not receive the brethren, but also forbade those who would like to receive them, and cast them out of the church.

11 Our beloved, do not follow that which is evil, but that which is good. He who does good is of God; but he who does evil has not seen God.

12 Demetrius has been given a good report by all men and of the church, and of the truth itself; yea, we also testify for him, and we know that our testimony is true.

13 ¶I had many things to write, but I do not want to write them to you with ink and pen;

14 However I trust I shall shortly see you, and we shall speak face to face.

15 Peace be to you. Our friends salute you. Salute the friends every one by his name.

THE GENERAL EPISTLE OF

JUDE

JUDE, the servant of Jesus Christ and brother of James, to the Gentiles who have been called and are beloved by God the Father and are protected by Jesus Christ:

2 Mercy and peace, with love, be multiplied to you.

3 ¶My beloved, I write to you with all diligence concerning our common salvation, and it is needful that I should write and exhort you also to contend earnestly for the faith which was once delivered to the saints.

4 For certain men have falsely entered among you, and these were foreordained from the very beginning to this condemnation; they are ungodly men, turning the grace of God into lasciviousness, and denying the only Lord God and our Lord Jesus Christ.

5 ¶I will, therefore, remind you, though you once knew this, that God, having redeemed and saved the people out of the land of Egypt, afterward destroyed those who did not believe.

6 And the angels which did not keep their first estate but left their own habitation he has reserved in everlasting chains under darkness until the judgment of the great day,

7 Even as Sodom and Gomorrah and the neighbouring cities which in like manner gave themselves over to fornication, and followed after other carnal lusts, are condemned to judgment and placed under everlasting fire;

8 Likewise also, these filthy dreamers defile the flesh, despise authority, and blaspheme against the glory.

9 Yet Michael, the archangel, when contending with the devil about the body of Moses, did not dare to bring railing accusation against him, but said, The Lord rebuke you.

10 But these men blaspheme against those things about which they do not know; and what they know naturally as dumb beasts, in those things they corrupt themselves.

11 Woe to them! For they have gone in the way of Cain, and have run greedily after the error of Balaam for reward and have perished in the rebellion of Korah.

12 These people are those who lead a wasteful, feasting life and are blemished; they do not conduct themselves in reverence; they are clouds without rain, driven by winds; trees whose blossoms have withered without fruit, having died a second time, being pulled up by the roots;

13 Raging waves of the sea, foaming out their own shame; wandering stars, to whom is reserved the blackness of darkness for ever.

14 And Enoch also, the seventh from Adam, prophesied of these, saying, Behold, the Lord comes with ten thousands of his saints,

15 To execute judgment upon all, and to punish all who are ungodly for all their ungodly deeds which they have committed in an ungodly manner, and for all the harsh words which the ungodly sinners have spoken.

16 These are the ones who murmur and complain, following after their own lusts, and their mouths speak idle flattering words, praising people for the sake of gain.

17 But you, my beloved, remember the words which were spoken before by the apostles of our Lord Jesus Christ,

18 How they told you there will be mockers until the end of time, and they will always follow their own ungodly lusts.

19 These are those who prefer to associate with selfish people because they do not have the Spirit in them.

20 But you, my beloved, build up yourselves anew in the holy faith through the Holy Spirit, by means of prayer.

21 Let us keep ourselves in the love of God, looking for the mercy of our Lord Jesus Christ and for the life which is ours forever.

22 And on some of them whoever they may be, heap coals of fire;

23 And when they repent, have mercy on them with compassion; despise even a garment which is spotted with the things of the flesh.

24 ¶Now to him who is able to keep you from falling and to present you faultless before the presence of his glory with exceeding joy,

25 To the only God our Saviour, through Jesus Christ our Lord, be glory and majesty, dominion and power, both now and for ever. Amen.

THE REVELATION

OF SAINT JOHN THE DIVINE

CHAPTER 1

THE Revelation of Jesus Christ, which God gave to him to show to his servants those things which must soon come to pass; he sent and signified it by his angel to his servant John,

2 Who bore record of the word of God and of the testimony of Jesus Christ and of all things that he saw.

3 Blessed is he who reads and they who listen to the words of this prophecy and keep those things which are written in it; for the time is at hand.

4 ¶John to the seven churches which are in Asia: Grace be to you and peace from him who is and who was and who is to come; and from the seven Spirits which are before his throne;

5 And from Jesus Christ, who is the faithful witness, and the first to arise from the dead, and the prince of the kings of the earth. To him who loved us and washed us from our sins in his own blood,

6 And has made us a spiritual kingdom to God and his Father, to him be glory and dominion for ever and ever. Amen.

7 ¶Behold he will come with the clouds; and every eye shall see him, even the men who pierced him; and all the kindreds of the earth shall wail over him. Even so. Amen.

8 I am Aleph and Tau, the beginning and the ending says the Lord God, who is and who was and who is to come, the Almighty.

9 ¶I, John, your brother and companion in suffering and in the hope of Jesus Christ, was in the island which is called Patmos because of the word of God and because of the testimony of Jesus Christ.

10 The Spirit of prophecy came upon me on the Lord's day, and I heard behind me a great voice, as of a trumpet, saying,

11 What you see, write in a book and send it to the seven churches, to Ephesus and to Smyrna and to Pergamos and to Thyatira and to Sardis and to Philadelphia and to Laodicea.

12 And I turned to see the voice that spoke to me. And as I turned, I saw seven golden candlesticks,

13 And in the midst of the seven candlesticks one resembling the Son of man, wearing a long vestment and girded round his breast with a golden girdle.

14 His head and his hair were white as wool, as white as snow; and his eyes were as a flame of fire;

15 And his feet were like the fine brass of Lebanon, as though they were burned in a furnace; and his voice was as the sound of many waters.

16 And he had in his right hand seven stars; and out of his mouth came a sharp two-edged sword; and his countenance was like the sun shining in its strength.

17 And when I saw him, I fell at his feet as dead. And he laid his right hand upon me, saying, Fear not; I am the first and the last;

18 I am he who lives, and was dead; and, behold, I am alive for evermore. Amen. And I have the keys of death and of Sheol.

19 Write, therefore, the things which you have seen and the things which are and the things which shall be hereafter,

20 The mystery of the seven stars which you saw in my right hand, and the seven golden candlesticks. The seven stars are the angels of the seven churches and the seven candlesticks are the seven churches.

CHAPTER 2

TO the angel [1] of the church of Ephesus write: These things says the Omnipotent One who holds the seven stars in his right hand, who walks in the midst of the seven golden candlesticks.

2 I know your works and your labour and your patience and how you cannot endure those who are ungodly; you have tried those who say they are apostles and are not, and you have found them liars;

3 And you have patience, and have borne burdens for my name's sake, and have not wearied.

4 Nevertheless I have something against you, because you have left your first love.

5 Remember therefore from whence you have fallen and repent and do the first works; or else I will come to you very soon, and I will remove your candlestick from its place unless you repent.

6 But this you have in your favour, you hate the works of the Nicolaitanes, which I also hate.

7 He who has ears, let him hear what the Spirit says to the churches: To him who overcomes, I will give

---

[1] Angel in this case means the appointed head of the church.

to eat of the tree of life, which is in the midst of the paradise of my God.

8 ¶And to the angel of the church in Smyrna write: These things says the first and the last, which was dead and is alive:

9 I know your works and your suffering and poverty, but you are rich, and I know the blasphemy of those who say they are Jews and are not, but are of the synagogue of Satan.

10 Fear none of those things which you shall suffer; behold, the devil will cast some of you into prison, that you be tried; and you will be oppressed for ten days. Be faithful even to death, and I will give you a crown of life.

11 He who has ears, let him hear what the Spirit says to the churches: He who overcomes shall not be hurt by the second death.

12 ¶And to the angel of the church in Pergamos write: These things says he who has the sharp two-edged sword:

13 I know your works and where you dwell, even where Satan's seat is; and you uphold my name, and you did not deny my faith, even in those days when that witness of mine appeared, that faithful one of mine who was slain among you, where Satan dwells.

14 But I have a few things against you because you have there those who hold the teaching of Balaam, who taught Balak to cast a stumbling block before the children of Israel, to eat things sacrificed to idols and to commit adultery.

15 And also you have those among you who hold to the teaching of the Nicolaitanes.

16 Repent; or else I will come to you very soon and will fight against them with the sword of my mouth.

17 He who has ears, let him hear what the Spirit says to the churches: To him who overcomes, I will give to eat of the hidden manna, and I will give him a white stone, and on the stone a new name written, which no man knows except he who receives it.

18 ¶And to the angel of the church in Thyatira write: These things says the Son of God, who has eyes like a flame of fire, and whose feet are like fine brass from Lebanon;

19 I know your works and love and faith and service, and also your patience; and your last works are to be more abundant than the first.

20 Notwithstanding I have a few things against you because you allowed that woman of yours Jezebel, who calls herself a prophetess, to teach and to seduce my servants to commit fornication and to eat things sacrificed to idols.

21 And I gave her time to repent, but she did not repent from her fornication.

22 Behold I will cast her into a sick bed and those who commit adultery with her into great tribulation, unless they repent of their deeds.

23 And I will smite her children with death; and all the churches shall know that I am he who searches the minds and hearts; and I will give to everyone of you according to your works.

24 But I say to you, the rest of you in Thyatira, those who do not have this doctrine, and those who have not known, as they say, the depths of Satan, that I will not put upon you another burden.

25 But hold fast to that which you already have till I come.

26 And he who overcomes and keeps my works until the end, to him I will give authority over the nations;

27 And he shall shepherd them with a rod of iron; like the vessels of the potter, they shall be shattered, even as I was disciplined by my Father.

28 And I will give him the morning star.

29 He who has ears, let him hear what the Spirit says to the churches.

CHAPTER 3

AND to the angel of the church in Sardis write: These things says he who has the seven Spirits of God and the seven stars: I know your works; you have a name that you are alive and yet you are dead.

2 Awake, and hold fast to the things which remain but are ready to

die; for I have not found your works perfect before my God.

3 Remember, therefore, just as you have received and heard, so hold fast and repent. And if, therefore, you do not awake, I will come against you as a thief, and you shall not know at what hour I will come upon you.

4 But you have a few members at Sardis who have not defiled their names; and they shall walk with me in white, for they are worthy.

5 He who overcomes, the same shall be clothed in white robes; and I will not blot his name out of the book of life, but I will confess his name before my Father and before his angels.

6 He who has ears, let him hear what the Spirit says to the churches.

7 ¶And to the angel of the church in Philadelphia write: These things says he who is the holy one, he who is true, he who has the key of David, he who opens and no man shuts, and shuts, and no man opens;

8 I know your works and behold, I have set before you an open door which no man can lock, for you have but little strength and yet you have obeyed my word and have not denied my name.

9 Behold, I turn over those of the synagogue of Satan, who say that they are Jews and are not, but do lie; behold, I will make them to come and worship before your feet, and to know that I have loved you.

10 Because you have kept the word of my patience, I also will keep you from the hour of temptation which shall come upon all the world to try those who dwell upon earth.

11 Behold, I come quickly. Hold that fast which you have, so that no man take your crown.

12 He who overcomes I will make a pillar in the temple of my God, and he shall not go out again; and I will write upon him the name of my God and the name of the new Jerusalem which comes down out of heaven from my God; and I will write upon him my new name.

13 He who has ears, let him hear what the Spirit says to the churches.

14 ¶And to the angel of the church in Laodicea write: These things says the Amen, the faithful and true witness, the beginning of the creation of God;

15 I know your works, that you are neither cold nor hot; it is better to be either cold or hot.

16 So then because you are lukewarm, and neither cold nor hot, I will spue you out of my mouth.

17 You say, I am rich and my wealth has increased and I need nothing; and you do not know that you are miserable and a wanderer and poor and blind and naked.

18 I advise you to buy of me gold refined in the fire, that you may become rich; and white raiment, that you may be clothed, so that the shame of your nakedness may not be seen; and anoint your eyes with salve, that you may see.

19 I rebuke and chastise all those whom I love; be zealous, therefore, and repent.

20 Behold, I stand at the door and knock; if any man hear my voice and open the door, I will come in to him and will sup with him, and he with me.

21 To him who overcomes I will grant to sit with me on my throne, even as I also overcame and have sat down with my Father on his throne.

22 He who has ears, let him hear what the Spirit says to the churches.

CHAPTER 4

AFTER these things I looked and behold, a door was open in heaven; and the first voice which I heard was like a trumpet talking with me, which said, Come up here and I will show you things which must come to pass.

2 And immediately I was in the spirit; and behold, a throne was set in heaven, and one sat on the throne.

3 And he who sat resembled a stone of jasper and sardonyx, and round about the throne was a rainbow resembling emeralds.

4 Round about the throne were four and twenty seats; and upon the seats

I saw four and twenty elders sitting, clothed in white robes; and they had on their heads crowns of gold.

5 And out of the throne proceeded lightnings and thunderings and noises; and there were seven lamps of fire burning before the throne, which are the seven Spirits of God.

6 And before the throne was a sea of glass resembling crystal; and in the midst of the throne, and round about it and in front of it were four animals,[1] full of eyes before and behind.

7 And the first animal was like a lion and the second animal was like a calf and the third animal had a face of a man and the fourth animal was like a flying eagle.

8 And the four animals had each of them six wings; and they were full of eyes within; and they had no rest day and night saying, Holy, holy, holy, the Lord God Almighty who was and is and is to come.

9 And when those animals give glory and honor and thanks to him who sits on the throne, who lives for ever and ever,

10 The four and twenty elders fall down before him who sits on the throne, and worship him who lives for ever and ever, and cast their crowns before the throne, saying,

11 Thou art worthy, O our Holy Lord and God, to receive glory and honor and power, for thou hast created all things, and by thee they are, and by thy will they are and were created.

CHAPTER 5

AND I saw on the right hand of him who sat on the throne a book, written within and on the back and sealed with seven seals.

2 Then I saw a mighty angel proclaiming with a loud voice, Who is worthy to open the book and to loose the seals thereof?

3 And no man in heaven above nor on earth neither under the earth was able to open the book, neither to look on it.

4 And I wept exceedingly because no man was found worthy to open the book, neither to look on it.

5 And one of the elders said to me, Weep not; behold the Lion of the tribe of Judah, the Scion of David, has prevailed and he will open the book and the seven seals thereof.

6 And I beheld, and lo, in the midst of the elders, stood a Lamb as it had been slain, having seven horns and seven eyes, which are the seven Spirits of God sent forth into all the earth.

7 And he came and took the book from the right hand of him who sat upon the throne.

8 And as he took the book, the four animals and the four and twenty elders fell down before the Lamb, and everyone of them had a harp and a cup of gold full of incense, and these were the prayers of the saints.

9 And they sang new praise saying, Thou art worthy to take the book and to open the seals thereof; for thou wast slain and hast redeemed us to God by thy blood out of every tribe and tongue and people and nation;

10 And hast made them for our God kings and priests; and they shall reign on the earth.

11 And I looked, and I heard as it were the voice of many angels round about the throne and the animals and the elders; and their number was ten thousand times ten thousand, and thousands of thousands,

12 Saying with a loud voice, Worthy is the Lamb that was slain to receive power and riches and wisdom and might and honor and glory and blessing.

13 And every creature which is in heaven and on the earth and under the earth and all that are in the sea and all that are in them, I heard saying, To him who sits on the throne and to the Lamb be blessing and honor and glory and dominion for ever and ever.

14 And the four animals said, Amen. And the four and twenty elders fell down and worshipped him who lives for ever and ever.

---

[1] Or *creatures* or *beasts*.

CHAPTER 6

I SAW when the Lamb opened one of the seven seals, and I heard one of the four animals saying in a voice as of thunder, Come and see.

2 And I looked and beheld a white horse, and he who sat on him had a bow, and a crown was given to him; and he went forth conquering, and to conquer.

3 And when he opened the second seal, I heard the second animal say, Come and see.

4 And there went out another horse, and it was red, and to him who sat on it was given power to take away peace from the earth, that people should kill one another; and there was given to him a great sword.

5 And when he had opened the third seal, I heard the third animal say, Come and see. And behold, I saw a black horse; and he who sat on him had a pair of balances in his hand.

6 And I heard a voice in the midst of the four animals say, A measure of wheat for a penny, and three measures of barley for a penny; and see that you do not damage the oil and the wine.

7 And when he had opened the fourth seal, I heard the fourth animal saying, Come and see.

8 And I looked and beheld a green horse; and the name of him who sat on him was Death, and Sheol followed after him. And power was given him over the fourth part of the earth, to kill with sword and with famine and with death and with the wild beasts of the earth.

9 ¶And when he had opened the fifth seal, I saw under the altar the souls of those who had been slain for the sake of the word of God and for the testimony of the Lamb which they had;

10 And they cried with a loud voice saying, How long, O Lord, holy and true, dost thou not judge and avenge our blood on those who dwell on the earth?

11 And a white robe was given to every one of them; and it was said to them that they should rest yet for a little while, until the time should be fulfilled when their fellow servants and their brethren should be killed also as they had been.

12 ¶And I looked when he had opened the sixth seal, and behold, there was a great earthquake; and the sun became black as sackcloth of hair, and the moon became as blood;

13 And the stars of heaven fell to the earth, even as a fig tree casts its green figs when it is shaken by a mighty wind.

14 And the heavens separated, as a scroll when it is rolled separately; and every mountain and island shifted from its resting place.

15 And the kings of the earth and the great men and the commanders of thousands and the rich and the mighty men and every bondman and every freeman hid themselves in caves and in clefts of the mountain,

16 And said to the mountains and rocks, Fall on us, and hide us from the face of him who sits on the throne and from the wrath of the Lamb;

17 For the great day of his wrath is come, and who shall be able to stand?

CHAPTER 7

AND after these things, I saw four angels standing on the four corners of the earth, holding the four winds of the earth, that the wind should not blow on the earth nor on the sea nor on any tree.

2 And I saw another angel, and he ascended from the direction of the rising sun, having the seal of the living God; and he cried with a loud voice to the four angels to whom it was given to hurt the earth and the sea, saying,

3 Do not hurt the earth, neither the sea nor the trees, till we have sealed the servants of our God upon their brows.

4 And I heard the number of those who were sealed; and it was a hundred and forty and four thousand, of all the tribes of the children of Israel.

5 Of the tribe of Judah were sealed

twelve thousand; of the tribe of Reuben, twelve thousand; of the tribe of Gad, twelve thousand;

6 Of the tribe of Asher, twelve thousand; of the tribe of Naphtali, twelve thousand; of the tribe of Manasseh, twelve thousand;

7 Of the tribe of Simeon, twelve thousand; of the tribe of Levi, twelve thousand; of the tribe of Issachar, twelve thousand;

8 Of the tribe of Zebulun, twelve thousand; of the tribe of Joseph, twelve thousand; of the tribe of Benjamin, twelve thousand.

9 ¶After these things, I beheld, and lo, a great multitude which no man could number, of every nation and people and kindred and tongue stood before the throne and in the presence of the Lamb, clothed with white robes and with palms in their hands,

10 And cried with a loud voice, saying, Salvation to our God, who sits upon the throne, and to the Lamb.

11 And all the angels stood round about the throne and about the elders and the four animals, and fell before his throne on their faces, and worshipped God,

12 Saying, Amen! Blessing and glory and wisdom and thanksgiving and honor and power and might to our God for ever and ever. Amen.

13 And one of the elders answered, saying to me, Who are these who are arrayed in white robes? And from whence did they come?

14 And I said to him, My lord, you know. And he said to me, These are those who came out of great tribulation, and have washed their robes and made them white in the blood of the Lamb.

15 Therefore they are before the throne of God, and serve him day and night in his temple; and he who sits on the throne shall shelter them.

16 They shall hunger no more, neither thirst anymore; neither shall they be stricken by the sun nor by the heat.

17 For the Lamb who is in the midst of the throne shall shepherd them and shall lead them to fountains of living water. And God shall wipe away all tears from their eyes.

CHAPTER 8

AND when he opened the seventh seal, there was silence in heaven for about the space of half an hour.

2 ¶Then I saw the seven angels who stood before God, and seven trumpets were given to them.

3 And another angel came and stood at the altar, and he had a golden censer; and abundant incense was given to him, that he might offer it with the prayers of all saints upon the golden altar which was before the throne.

4 And the smoke of the incense which came with the prayers of the saints ascended up before God out of the angel's hand.

5 And the angel took the censer and filled it with fire of the altar and cast it upon the earth; and there were voices and thunderings and lightnings and an earthquake.

6 And the seven angels who had the seven trumpets prepared themselves to sound.

7 ¶The first angel sounded, and there followed hail and fire mingled with water, and they were poured upon the earth; and a third part of the earth was burnt up and a third part of the trees was burnt up and all green grass was burnt up.

8 ¶Then the second angel sounded, and as it were a great mountain aflame with fire was cast into the sea; and the third part of the sea became blood;

9 And the third part of the creatures which were in the sea, and had life, died; and the third part of the ships were destroyed.

10 ¶And the third angel sounded, and there fell a star from heaven, burning as though it were a lamp, and it fell upon the third part of the rivers and upon the fountains of waters;

11 And the name of the star is called Wormwood; and the third part of the waters became wormwood; and many men died of the waters, because they were made bitter.

12 ¶And the fourth angel sounded, and the third part of the sun was eclipsed and the third part of the moon and the third part of the stars, so that the third part of them was darkened, and the day was darkened for a third part of it, and the night likewise.

13 And I beheld, and heard an eagle, having a tail red as it were blood, flying through the midst of heaven, saying with a loud voice, Woe, woe, woe to those who dwell on the earth, by reason of the other sounds of the trumpets of the three angels which are yet to sound!

CHAPTER 9

AND the fifth angel sounded, and I saw a star fall from heaven upon the earth; and to him was given the key of the bottomless pit.

2 And he opened the bottomless pit; and there arose a smoke out of the pit like smoke belching from a great furnace; and the sun and the air were darkened by reason of the smoke of the pit.

3 And there came out of the smoke locusts upon the earth; and to them was given power as the scorpions of the earth have power.

4 And it was commanded them that they should not hurt the grass of the earth, neither any green thing, neither any tree; but only those men who do not have the seal of God on their brows.

5 And they were commanded that they should not kill them, but that they should be tormented five months; and their torment was as the torment of a scorpion when it strikes a man.

6 So in those days men shall seek death and shall not find it; and shall desire to die, and death shall flee from them.

7 And the shapes of the locusts were like horses prepared for battle; and on their heads were, as it were, crowns like gold, and their faces were like faces of men.

8 And they had hair like the hair of women, and their teeth were like the teeth of lions.

9 And they had breastplates as though they were breastplates of iron; and the sound of their wings was like the sound of chariots of many horses running to battle.

10 And they had tails like scorpions, and there were stings in their tails; and they had power to hurt men five months.

11 And they had a king over them, who was the angel of the bottomless pit, whose name in Hebrew is Abaddo, but in Greek his name is Apollyon.

12 The first woe is passed; and behold, two more woes follow after.

13 ¶And the sixth angel sounded, and I heard a voice from the horns of the golden altar which is before God,

14 Saying to the sixth angel which had the trumpet, Loose the four angels which are bound by the great river Euphrates.

15 And the four angels were loosed, those which were prepared for that hour and for that day and for that month and for that year, so that they might slay the third part of men.

16 And the number of the army of the horsemen was two hundred thousand thousand; I heard the number of them.

17 And thus I saw the horses in the vision and those who sat on them, and they had breastplates of fire and of jacinth and of brimstone; and the heads of the horses were like the heads of lions, and out of their mouths issued fire and smoke and brimstone.

18 And by these three plagues was the third part of men slain, by the fire and by the smoke and by the brimstone which issued out of their mouths.

19 For the power of the horses was in their mouths and in their tails; for their tails were like serpents and had heads, and with them they do harm.

20 And the rest of the men who were not killed by these plagues neither repented of the works of their hands, that is to say, the worship of devils and idols of gold and silver and brass and stone and of wood, which can neither see nor hear,

21 Nor repented of their murders nor of their witchcraft nor of their fornication nor of their thefts.

CHAPTER 10

AND I saw another mighty angel coming down from heaven, clothed with a cloud; and the rainbow of the cloud was upon his head, and his face was as though it were the sun, and his legs as pillars of fire;

2 And he had in his hand a little book open; and he set his right foot upon the sea, and his left foot on the land,

3 And cried with a loud voice as when a lion roars, and when he had cried, seven thunders sounded their voices.

4 And when the seven thunders had spoken, I was about to write; but I heard a voice from heaven saying, Seal up those things which the seven thunders uttered, and do not write them.

5 And the angel which I saw standing upon the sea and on the land raised his right hand to heaven, and

6 Swore by him who lives for ever and ever, who created heaven and the things which are therein, and the earth and the things which are therein, and the sea and the things which are therein, that there should be no more reckoning of time;

7 But in the days of the voice of the seventh angel, when he shall begin to sound, the mystery of God will be fulfilled, as he has proclaimed to his servants, the prophets.

8 ¶And the same voice which I had heard from heaven spoke to me again, saying, Go and take the little book which is open in the hand of the angel which stands on the sea and on the land.

9 And I went to the angel, and as I was about to say to him, Give me the little book, he said to me, Take it and eat it; and it shall make your belly bitter, but it shall be sweet as honey in your mouth.

10 So I took the little book out of the hand of the angel, and ate it; and it was sweet as honey in my mouth; but as soon as I had eaten it, my belly was bitter.

11 Then he said to me, You must prophesy again about many peoples and nations and the heads of nations and kings.

CHAPTER 11

AND there was given to me a reed like a rod; and the angel stood, saying, Arise and anoint the temple of God and the altar and those who worship therein.

2 But leave out the outer court of the temple, and do not anoint it; for it has been given to the Gentiles; and they shall tread the holy city under foot for forty and two months.

3 Then I will give power to my two witnesses, and they shall prophesy a thousand and two hundred and three score days, clothed in sackcloth.

4 These are the two olive trees and the two candlesticks standing before the Lord of the earth.

5 And if any man desires to harm them, fire will come out of their mouths and will consume their enemies; and if any man desires to harm them, he must in this manner be killed.

6 These have power to control the sky, so that it will not rain in those days; and have power over waters to turn them into blood, and to smite the earth with all plagues, as often as they will.

7 And when they have finished their testimony, the wild beast which ascends out of the bottomless pit shall make war against them and shall overcome them.

8 And their dead bodies shall be upon the street of the great city, which spiritually is called Sodom and Egypt, where also their Lord was crucified.

9 And their dead bodies will be seen by the peoples and kindred and nations and tongues for three days and a half, and it will not be permitted to bury their dead bodies in graves.

10 And those who dwell upon the earth shall rejoice over them and make merry, and shall send gifts

one to another, because these two prophets tormented those who dwelt on the earth.

11 And after three days and a half the spirit of life from God entered into them, and they stood upon their feet; and great fear fell on those who saw them.

12 And they heard a great voice from heaven saying to them, Come up here. And they went up to heaven in a cloud; and their enemies saw them.

13 And at the same hour there was a great earthquake, and the tenth part of the city fell, and the number of men killed in the earthquake was seven thousand; and the survivors were frightened, and they gave glory to God.

14 The second woe is passed; and behold, the third woe comes quickly.

15 ¶And the seventh angel sounded, and there were great rumblings of thunders, saying, The kingdoms of this world have become the kingdom of our Lord and of his Christ; and he shall reign for ever and ever.

16 And the four and twenty elders who sat before the throne of God on their seats fell upon their faces and worshipped God,

17 Saying, We give thanks to thee, O Lord God Almighty, who is and was, because thou hast taken to thyself thy great power and hast reigned.

18 And the nations were angry, and thy wrath has come, and the time of the dead, that they should be judged, and to reward thy servants, the prophets, and the saints and those who revere thy name, small and great; and to destroy those who corrupt the earth.

19 ¶And the temple of God was opened in heaven, and there was seen in his temple the ark of his covenant; and there were lightnings and thunderings and voices and an earthquake and a great hailstorm.

CHAPTER 12

AND a great sign was seen in heaven, a woman clothed with the sun, with the moon under her feet and upon her head a crown of twelve stars;

2 And she being with child cried, travailing in birth, and pained to be delivered.

3 ¶And there appeared another sign in heaven; and behold, there was a great fiery dragon, having seven heads and ten horns, and seven crowns upon his heads.

4 And his tail cut off a third of the stars of heaven and cast them to the earth; and the dragon stood before the woman who was ready to be delivered, so as to devour her child as soon as it was born.

5 And she brought forth a male child, who was to shepherd all the nations with a rod of iron; and her child was caught up to God, and to his throne.

6 And the woman fled into the wilderness, where she had a place prepared by God, that they should feed her there a thousand and two hundred and three score days.

7 ¶And there was war in heaven. Michael and his angels fought against the dragon; and the dragon and his angels fought

8 But did not prevail, neither was their place found any longer in heaven.

9 Thus the great dragon was cast out, that old serpent called the Devil and Satan, who deceives the whole world; he was cast out on the earth, and his angels were cast out with him.

10 And I heard a loud voice in heaven saying, Now the deliverance and the power and the kingdom of our God and the power of his Christ have been accomplished; for the accuser of our brethren, who accused them before God day and night, is cast down.

11 And they have conquered him by the blood of the Lamb and by the word of their testimony; and they did not spare themselves even to death.

12 Therefore rejoice, O heavens and you who dwell in them. Woe to the inhabitants of the earth and of the sea! For the Devil has come down to you; and his wrath is great, because he knows that his time is short.

13 ¶And when the dragon saw that he was cast down to the earth, he pursued the woman who had given birth to a son.

14 And to the woman were given two wings of a great eagle, that she might fly from the presence of the serpent to the wilderness, into her place, where she would be nourished for years and months and days.

15 Then the serpent sent a flood of water out of his mouth after the woman, so that he might cause her to be swept away by the flood.

16 But the earth helped the woman, and the earth opened its mouth and swallowed up the water which the dragon had spouted out of his mouth.

17 And the dragon was enraged at the woman, and he went to make war with the rest of her children, who keep the commandments of God and have the testimony of Jesus.

CHAPTER 13

AND as I stood on the sand of the shore, I saw a wild beast rise up out of the sea, having ten horns and seven heads, and upon his horns ten crowns, and upon his heads blasphemous words.

2 And the wild beast which I saw was like a leopard, and his feet were like the feet of a bear, and his mouth like the mouth of a lion; and the dragon gave him his power and his throne and great authority.

3 And one of his heads was as though mortally wounded; but his deadly wound was healed; and all the world wondered about the wild beast.

4 And they worshipped the dragon because he had given power to the wild beast, saying, Who can prevail against him to fight him?

5 And there was given to him a mouth, that he might utter boastful things and blasphemies; and power was given to him to make war for forty and two months.

6 And he opened his mouth in blasphemy against God, to blaspheme his name and his dwelling place and those who dwell in heaven.

7 And power was given to him over every tribe and kindred and tongue and nation, and it was given to him to make war with the saints and to overcome them.

8 And all who dwell upon the earth shall worship him, even those whose names are not written in the book of life of the Lamb slain from the foundation of the world.

9 If any man has ears, let him hear.

10 He who leads into captivity shall go into captivity; he who kills with the sword must be killed with the sword. Here is the patience and the faith of the saints.

11 ¶And I beheld another wild beast coming up out of the earth; and he had two horns like a lamb, and he spoke as a dragon.

12 And all the power of the first wild beast before him was exercised by him, and he caused the earth and those who dwell therein to worship the first beast, whose deadly wound was healed.

13 And he performed great wonders, to such an extent that he could even make fire come down from heaven on the earth in the sight of men,

14 Beguiling those who dwell on the earth to make an image to the wild beast who was wounded by the sword and yet lived.

15 And he had power to give life to the image of the wild beast, and to cause all those who would not worship the image of the wild beast to be killed.

16 And he compelled all, both small and great, rich and poor, freemen and slaves to receive a mark on their right hands or on their brows,

17 So that no man might buy or sell unless he who had the mark of the name of the beast or the code number of his name.

18 Here is wisdom: Let him who has understanding decipher the code number of the beast; for it is the code number of the name of a man; and his number is six hundred and sixty-six.[1]

[1] This number represents the Aramaic letters which spell *Nero Caesar*, namely 50, 200, 6, 50, 100, 60, 200.

CHAPTER 14

AND I looked, and, lo, the Lamb stood on mount Zion, and with him a hundred and forty-four thousand in number, having the name of his Father written on their brows.

2 Then I heard a voice from heaven, like the sound of many waters and like the sound of a great thunder; and the voice I heard was like the music of many harpists playing on their harps;

3 And they sang a new song before the throne and before the four animals and the elders; and no man was able to learn that song except the hundred and forty-four thousand who were redeemed from the earth.

4 These are those who were not defiled with women, for they are pure. These are those who follow the Lamb wherever he goes. These were redeemed by Jesus from among men to be the first fruits to God and to the Lamb.

5 And in their mouth was found no deceit; for they are without fault.

6 ¶And I saw another angel fly in the midst of heaven, having the everlasting gospel to preach to those who dwell on the earth, and to every nation and kindred and tongue and people,

7 Saying with a loud voice, Serve God and give glory to him; for the hour of his judgment has come; and worship him who made heaven and earth and the sea and the fountains of waters.

8 And another angel, a second, followed him, saying, Babylon has fallen, that great city which made all nations drink of the wine of the passion of her whoredom.

9 Then another angel, a third, followed them, saying with a loud voice, If any man worships the beast and his image and receives his mark on his brow or on his hand,

10 He also shall drink of the wine of the wrath of God, which is mixed with bitterness in the cup of his anger; and he shall be tormented with fire and brimstone in the presence of the holy angels and before the throne;

11 And the smoke of their torment will rise for ever and ever; and those who worship the beast and his image will have no rest day or night.

12 Here is the patience of the saints; here are they who keep the commandments of God and the faith of Jesus.

13 And I heard a voice from heaven saying, Write, Blessed are the dead who die in the Lord from henceforth. Yes, says the Spirit, that they may rest from their labours, for their works will follow them.

14 And I looked, and lo, I saw a white cloud, and upon the cloud sat one resembling the Son of man, having on his head a crown of gold and in his hand a sharp sickle.

15 ¶And another angel came out of the temple, and after he cried with a loud voice to him who sat on the cloud,

16 He thrust his sickle upon the earth, and the earth was harvested.

17 ¶And another angel came out of the temple which is in heaven; and he also had a sharp sickle.

18 Then out from the altar came another angel, who had power over fire, and cried with a loud voice to him who had the sharp sickle, saying, Thrust in your sharp sickle and gather the clusters of the vineyards of the earth, for her grapes are fully ripe.

19 And the angel thrust his sickle into the earth and gathered the vineyards of the earth, and cast the grapes into the winepress of the wrath of the great God.

20 And the winepress was trodden until the juice which came out reached even to the horse bridles, and the circumference of the winepress was a thousand and six hundred furlongs.

CHAPTER 15

AND I saw another sign in heaven, great and marvelous, seven angels having the seven last plagues; for in them is fulfilled the wrath of God.

2 And I saw what looked like a sea of glass mingled with fire; and those who were victorious over the wild

beast and over his image and over the number of his name were standing on the sea of glass and had the harps of God.

3 And they were singing the song of Moses, the servant of God, and the song of the Lamb, saying, Great and marvelous are thy works, Lord God Almighty; just and true are thy ways, O King of ages.

4 Who shall not revere thee, O Lord, and glorify thy name? For thou only art holy. All nations shall come and worship before thee; for thy righteousness hast been revealed.

5 And after these things, I looked and behold, the temple of the tabernacle of the testimony in heaven was opened;

6 And the seven angels having the seven plagues came out of the temple, clothed in pure and fine linen and having their breasts girded with golden girdles.

7 And one of the four animals gave to the seven angels seven golden bowls full of the wrath of God who lives for ever and ever.

8 And the temple was filled with smoke from the glory of God and from his power; and no man was able to enter into the temple, until the seven plagues of the seven angels were fulfilled.

CHAPTER 16

AND I heard a great voice saying to the seven angels, Go your ways and pour out the seven bowls of the wrath of God upon the earth.

2 And the first went and poured out his bowl upon the earth; and there came a severe and malignant sore upon the men who had the mark of the beast and upon those who worshipped his image.

3 ¶Then the second angel poured out his bowl upon the sea; and it became as the blood of a dead man, and every living soul died in the sea.

4 ¶And the third angel poured out his bowl upon the rivers and fountains of waters; and they became blood.

5 Then I heard the angel who has charge over waters say, Thou art

righteous, O Holy One, who is and wast, because thou hast condemned them.

6 For they have shed the blood of saints and prophets, and thou hast given them blood to drink; for they deserve it.

7 And I heard another out of the altar say, Yes, O Lord God Almighty, true and righteous are thy judgments.

8 ¶And the fourth angel poured out his bowl upon the sun; and power was given to him to scorch men with fire.

9 And men were scorched by intense heat, and they blasphemed the name of God, who has power over these plagues; and they did not repent to give him glory.

10 And the fifth angel poured out his bowl on the throne of the wild beast; and his kingdom was darkened; and men gnawed their tongues from pain

11 And blasphemed the God of heaven because of their wounds and sores, and did not repent of their deeds.

12 ¶Then the sixth angel poured out his bowl upon the great river Euphrates; and its waters dried up, that the way of the king of the East might be prepared.

13 And I saw three unclean spirits like frogs coming out of the mouth of the dragon and out of the mouth of the wild beast and out of the mouth of the false prophet.

14 For they are the spirits of devils, who work miracles which go forth to the kings of the whole world, to gather them to the battle of that great day of God Almighty.

15 And behold, I come as a thief. Blessed is he who watches and keeps his garments, lest he must walk naked and they see his shame.

16 And he gathered them together in a place which in the Hebrew tongue is called Armageddon.

17 ¶Then the seventh angel poured out his bowl into the air; and there came a great voice out of the temple from the throne, saying, It is done.

18 And there were voices, and thunders and lightnings; and there was

a great earthquake, the like of which had never happened since man was upon the earth, so mighty an earthquake, and so great.

19 And the great city was divided into three parts, and the cities of the nations fell; and great Babylon came in remembrance before God, to give to her the cup of the wine of the fierceness of his wrath.

20 And every island fled away, and the mountains could not be found.

21 And great hail, about the size of a talent, fell out of heaven upon men; and men blasphemed God because of the plague of the hail; for the destructive force of the hail was exceedingly great.

CHAPTER 17

THEN came one of the seven angels which had the seven bowls and talked with me, saying, Come, I will show you the condemnation of the great harlot who sits upon many waters,

2 With whom the kings of the earth have committed adultery, and the inhabitants of the earth have been made drunk with the wine of her adultery.

3 So he carried me away in the spirit into the wilderness; and I saw a woman sitting on a scarlet wild beast inscribed with many words of blasphemy and having seven heads and ten horns.

4 And the woman was arrayed in purple and scarlet, and adorned with gold and precious stones and pearls; and she had a golden cup in her hand full of abominations and filthiness of her adultery on earth.

5 And upon her forehead was a name written that not all could understand: BABYLON THE GREAT, THE MOTHER OF HARLOTS AND ABOMINATIONS OF THE EARTH.

6 And I saw that the woman was drunk with the blood of the saints and with the blood of the martyrs of Jesus; and when I saw her, I wondered with great amazement.

7 And the angel said to me, Why do you wonder? I will tell you the mystery of the woman and of the wild beast that carries her, which has the seven heads and the ten horns.

8 The wild beast that you saw was, and is not, and is ready to come up from the bottomless pit and go to be destroyed; and those who dwell on earth whose names were not written in the book of life from the foundation of the world shall wonder when they behold the beast that was, and is not, and now whose end has come.

9 Here is understanding for him who has wisdom: The seven heads are seven hills on which the woman sits.

10 And there are seven kings, of whom five have fallen and one is and the other has not yet come; and when he comes he shall continue only for a short time.

11 And the wild beast that was, and no longer is, even he is the eighth and is one of the seven destined to be destroyed.

12 And the ten horns which you saw are ten kings who have received no kingdom as yet, but receive authority as kings for one hour with the beast.

13 These are of one accord, and they shall give their strength and authority to the beast.

14 They will make war with the Lamb, and the Lamb will conquer them, for he is Lord of lords and King of kings; and those who are with him are called and chosen and faithful.

15 Then he said to me, The waters which you saw, where the harlot sits, are peoples and multitudes and nations and tongues.

16 And the ten horns and the wild beast which you saw shall hate the harlot, and shall make her desolate and naked, and shall eat her flesh and burn her with fire.

17 For God has put into their hearts to do his will and to be of one accord and to give their kingdom to the wild beast until the words of God shall be fulfilled.

18 And the woman whom you saw

is that great city which has dominion over the kings of the earth.

CHAPTER 18

AFTER these things I saw another angel come down from heaven, having great power; and the earth was lighted by his glory.

2 And he cried with a mighty voice, saying, Babylon the great is fallen and has become a habitation of those possessed with devils and the shelter of every foul spirit and the shelter of every unclean and detestable bird and the shelter of every unclean and loathsome wild beast.

3 Because all nations have drunk of the wine of her wrath and the kings of the earth have committed adultery with her and the merchants of the earth have become rich through the power of her trade.

4 ¶And I heard another voice from heaven, saying, Come out of her, O my people, so that you may not become partakers of her sins and lest you be smitten by her plagues.

5 For her sins have reached up to heaven, and God has remembered her iniquities.

6 Reward her even as she has rewarded you, and return to her a double portion according to her works; in the cup which she has mixed, mix for her double.

7 For as much as she has glorified herself and lived deliciously, give her so much torment and sorrow; for she says in her heart, I sit a queen, and am no widow and shall see no sorrow.

8 Therefore, her plagues shall come in one day, death and mourning and famine, and she shall be burned with fire; for mighty is the Lord God who judges her.

9 And the kings of the earth who committed adultery and lived deliciously with her will weep and mourn and wail over her when they see the smoke of her burning.

10 Standing afar off for the fear of her torment, saying, Woe, woe, that great city Babylon, that mighty city! For in one hour you have been condemned.

11 And the merchants of the earth shall weep and mourn over her; for no man buys their merchandise any more.

12 Never again will there be cargoes of gold and silver and precious stones, and pearls and fine linen and purple and silk and scarlet and every kind of aromatic wood, and all manner of vessels of ivory, and all manner of vessels of most precious wood, and of brass and iron and marble

13 And cinnamon and perfumes and spices and myrrh and frankincense and wine, and oil and fine flour and wheat and cattle and sheep, and horses and chariots and hides and slaves.

14 And the fruits which your soul lusted after are departed from you, and all things which were luxurious and goodly are lost to you, and you shall never find them any more at all.

15 The merchants of these things, who were made rich by her, shall stand afar off for the fear of her torment, and they shall weep and wail,

16 Saying, Woe, woe, that great city, which was clothed with fine linen and purple and scarlet, inlaid with gold, and precious stones and pearls! For in one hour these great riches are destroyed.

17 And every shipmaster and all the travelers in ships and sailors and all those who labor at sea stood afar off,

18 And cried when they saw the smoke of her burning, saying, What city is like to this great city!

19 And they threw dust on their heads and cried, weeping and wailing, saying, Woe, woe, that great city, where all who had ships on the sea were made rich by reason of her preciousness! For in one hour she is destroyed.

20 Rejoice over her, O heaven and angels, apostles and prophets, for God has avenged you on her.

21 And a mighty angel took up a stone like a great millstone and cast it into the sea, saying, So shall that great city Babylon be overthrown

with violence and shall be found no more at all.

22 And the sound of harpers and musicians and singers and trumpeters shall not be heard in you again; and no craftsman of whatever craft he be shall be found any more in you;

23 And the light of a lamp shall shine no more at all in you; and the voice of the bridegroom and of the bride shall be heard no more at all in you; for your merchants were the great men of the earth; for by your sorceries were all peoples deceived.

24 And in her was found the blood of prophets and of saints and of all who were slain upon the earth.

CHAPTER 19

AND after these things, I heard a great voice of a great multitude in heaven, saying, Halleluia! Salvation and power and glory and honor to our God,

2 For his judgments are true and righteous; for he has condemned the great harlot who has corrupted the earth with her adultery, and has avenged the blood of his servants at her hand.

3 And a second time, they said, Halleluia! And her smoke rose up for ever and ever.

4 And the four and twenty elders and the four animals fell down and worshipped God who sat on the throne, saying, Amen, Alleluia!

5 And a voice came out from the throne, saying, Praise our God, all you his servants and you who worship him, both small and great.

6 And I heard as it were the voice of a great multitude, like the voice of many waters and like the sound of mighty thunderings, saying, Halleluia! For our Lord God, omnipotent, reigns.

7 Let us be glad and rejoice and give glory to him, for the time of the marriage feast of the Lamb has come, and his bride has made herself ready.

8 And it was given to her that she should be arrayed in fine pure linen, clean and white; for fine linen is the righteousness of saints.

9 And he said to me, Write, Blessed are those who are invited to the wedding feast of the Lamb. Then he said to me, These words of mine are the true sayings of God.

10 And I fell at his feet to worship him. And he said to me, Do not do that; I am your fellow servant, and one of your brethren who have the testimony of Jesus; worship God, for the testimony of Jesus is the spirit of prophecy.

11 ¶And I saw heaven opened, and behold, I saw a white horse; and he who sat upon him was called Faithful and True, and in righteousness he judges and makes war.

12 His eyes were like a flame of fire, and on his head were many crowns; and he had names written thereon, and one of the names written, no man knew but he himself.

13 And he was clothed with a vesture dipped in blood; and he called his name, The Word of God.

14 And the armies which were in heaven followed him on white horses clothed in fine linen, pure and white.

15 And out of his mouth came a sharp two-edged sword, that with it he should smite the nations; and he will rule them with a rod of iron; and he will tread the winepress of the fierceness and wrath of Almighty God.

16 And he had a name written on his vesture and on his thigh, KING OF KINGS AND LORD OF LORDS.

17 ¶And I saw an angel standing in the sun; and he cried with a loud voice, saying to all the fowls that fly in the midst of heaven, Come and gather yourselves together for the great supper of God,

18 That you may eat the flesh of kings and the flesh of captains of thousands and the flesh of mighty men and the flesh of horses and of those who sit on them and the flesh of all men, both free and bond, both small and great.

19 Then I saw the wild beast and the kings of the earth and their armies gathered together to fight

against him who sat on the horse, and against his armies.

20 And the wild beast was taken and with him the false prophet who wrought miracles before him with which he deceived those who had received the mark of the wild beast and those who worshipped his image. These both were cast alive into a lake of fire burning with brimstone.

21 And the others were slain by the sword that came out from the mouth of him who sat upon the horse; and all the fowls were filled with their flesh.

CHAPTER 20

AND I saw an angel come down from heaven, having the key of the bottomless pit and a great chain in his hand.

2 And he seized the dragon, that old serpent, which is the Tempter and Satan, who deceived the whole world, and bound him a thousand years,

3 And cast him into the bottomless pit and shut him up and set a seal over him, that he should no more deceive the nations until the thousand years should be past; after that he will be loosed for a short time.

4 ¶And I saw thrones and those who sat upon them, and judgment was given to them; and the souls of those who were beheaded for the witness of Jesus and for the word of God and who had not worshipped the wild beast, neither his image, nor had received his mark upon their foreheads or on their hand, lived and reigned with their Christ these thousand years.

5 This is the first resurrection.

6 Blessed and holy is he who has part in the first resurrection; over such the second death has no power, but they shall be the priests of God and of his Christ, and they shall reign with him a thousand years.

7 And when the thousand years come to an end, Satan shall be loosed out of his prison,

8 And shall go out to deceive the nations which are in the four corners of the earth, even to China and Mongolia, to gather them together for war; the number of them is as the sand of the sea.

9 And they went up on a broad plain, and surrounded the camp of the saints and the beloved city; and fire came down from God out of heaven and consumed them.

10 And the devil who deceived them was cast into the lake of fire and brimstone, where also are the beast and the false prophet; and shall be tormented day and night for ever and ever.

11 ¶And I saw a great white throne and him who sat on it, from whose presence the earth and the heavens fled away; and there was no place found for them.

12 Then I saw the dead, small and great, stand before the throne; and the books were opened; and another book was opened, which is the book of life; and the dead were judged by those things which were written in the books, according to their works.

13 And the sea gave up the dead which were in it; and death and Sheol gave up the dead which were in them; and they were judged every man according to his works.

14 And death and Sheol were cast into the lake of fire. This is the second death, which is the lake of fire.

15 And whoever was not found written in the book of life was cast into the lake of fire.

CHAPTER 21

AND I saw a new heaven and a new earth; for the first heaven and the first earth had passed away; and the sea was no more.

2 And I saw the holy city, new Jerusalem, coming down from God, prepared as a bride adorned for her husband.

3 And I heard a great voice from heaven saying, Behold, the tabernacle of God is with men, and he will dwell with them, and they shall be his people, and the very God shall be with them and be their God;

4 And he shall wipe away all tears from their eyes; and there shall be no more death, neither sorrow nor

wailing, neither shall there be any more pain; for the former things have passed away.

5 And he who sat upon the throne said, Behold, I make all things new. Then he said to me, Write; for these are the trustworthy and true words of God.

6 And he said to me, I am Aleph and Tau, the beginning and the end. I will freely give of the fountain of living water to him who is thirsty.

7 He who overcomes shall inherit these things; and I will be his God, and he shall be my son.

8 But as for the fearful and the unbelieving and the sinful and the abominable and murderers and those who commit adultery and magicians and idolators and all liars, their portion shall be in the lake that burns with fire and brimstone, which is the second death.

9 And there came to me one of the seven angels who had the seven bowls full of the seven last plagues, and he talked with me, saying, Come, I will show you the bride, the wife of the Lamb.

10 And he carried me away in the spirit to a great and high mountain, and showed me that great city, the holy Jerusalem, descending out of heaven from God,

11 Having the glory of God, radiant as a brilliant light, resembling a very precious gem, like a jasper stone, clear as crystal.

12 It had a wall great and high and it had twelve gates, with names inscribed thereon, which are the names of the twelve tribes of the children of Israel.

13 On the east were three gates, on the north three gates, on the south three gates, and on the west three gates.

14 And the wall of the city had twelve foundations, and on them the twelve names of the twelve apostles of the Lamb.

15 And he who talked with me had a measuring rod of golden reed to measure the city and its gates and its wall.

16 And the city was laid foursquare, the length the same as the breadth; and he measured the city with the reed, twelve furlongs, twelve thousand paces. And the length and breadth and the height were equal.

17 And he measured the wall thereof, a hundred and forty and four cubits, according to the measure of a man, that is, of the angel.

18 And the wall was constructed of jasper; and the city itself was pure gold, resembling clear glass.

19 And the foundations of the wall of the city were adorned with all kinds of precious stones. The first foundation was jasper, the second sapphire, the third chalcedony, the fourth emerald,

20 The fifth sardonyx, the sixth sardius, the seventh chrysolyte, the eighth beryl, the ninth topaz, the tenth chrysoprasus, the eleventh jacinth, the twelfth amethyst.

21 And the twelve gates were adorned with twelve pearls, one for each of the gates, and each gate was made of a single pearl; and the great street of the city was of pure gold, as it were transparent glass.

22 But I saw no temple therein, for the Lord Almighty and the Lamb are the temple of it.

23 The city has no need of the sun, neither of the moon, to shine in it, for the glory of God brightens it and the Lamb is the lamp of it.

24 And the people who have been saved shall walk by that very light; and the kings of the earth shall bring their own glory and the honor of the peoples into it.

25 And the gates of it shall not be barred by day, for there is no night there.

26 And they shall bring the glory and the honor of the peoples into it.

27 And there shall not enter into it anything which defiles nor he who works abominations and lies; only those shall enter whose names are written in the Lamb's book of life.

CHAPTER 22

AND he showed me a pure river of water of life, clear as crystal, gushing out of the throne of God and of the Lamb.

2 In the midst of the great street of the city, and on either side of the river, was the tree of life, which bore twelve kinds of fruits, and each month it yielded one of its fruits; and the leaves of the tree were for the healing of the peoples.

3 And that which withers shall be no more, but the throne of God and of the Lamb shall be in it; and his servants shall serve him;

4 And they shall see his face, and his name shall be on their foreheads.

5 And there shall be no night there; and they shall neither need a candle nor the light of the sun; for the Lord God shines on them, and they shall reign for ever and ever.

6 ¶And he said to me, These sayings are faithful and true; and the Lord God who is the spirit of the prophets sent his angel to show to his servants the things which shortly must come to pass.

7 Behold, I am coming soon; blessed is he who keeps the sayings of the prophecy of this book.

8 ¶And I, John, heard and saw these things, and when I had heard and seen them, I fell down to worship before the feet of the angel who showed these things to me.

9 And he said to me, Do not do that; I am your fellow servant and of your brethren the prophets and of those who keep the words of this book. Worship God.

10 Then he said to me, Do not seal the words of the prophecy of this book, for the time is at hand.

11 He who is unjust will continue to be unjust, and he who is filthy will continue to be filthy, and he who is righteous will continue to do right-eousness, and he who is holy will continue to be holy.

12 Behold, I am coming soon and my reward is with me, to give every man according as his work shall be.

13 I am Aleph and Tau, the beginning and the end, the first and the last.

14 Blessed are those who do his commandments, that they may have the right to the tree of life, and may enter in through the gates into the city.

15 For without are the vicious and magicians and the immoral and murderers and idolaters and whoever loves to tell lies.

16 ¶I, Jesus, have sent my angel to testify to you these things in the churches. I am the root and the offspring of David, the bright morning star.

17 And the Spirit and the bride say, Come. And let him who hears say, Come. And he who is thirsty, let him come. And whosoever will, let him take of the living water freely.

18 ¶I testify to every man who hears the words of the prophecy of this book, If any man shall add to these things, God shall add to him the plagues that are written in this book;

19 And if any man shall take away from the words of the book of this prophecy, God shall take away his portion from the tree of life and from the holy city and from the things which are written in this book.

20 He who testifies these things says, Surely I am coming soon. Amen. Come, Lord Jesus.

21 ¶The grace of our Lord Jesus Christ be with you all, all you holy ones. Amen.

THE END OF THE NEW TESTAMENT

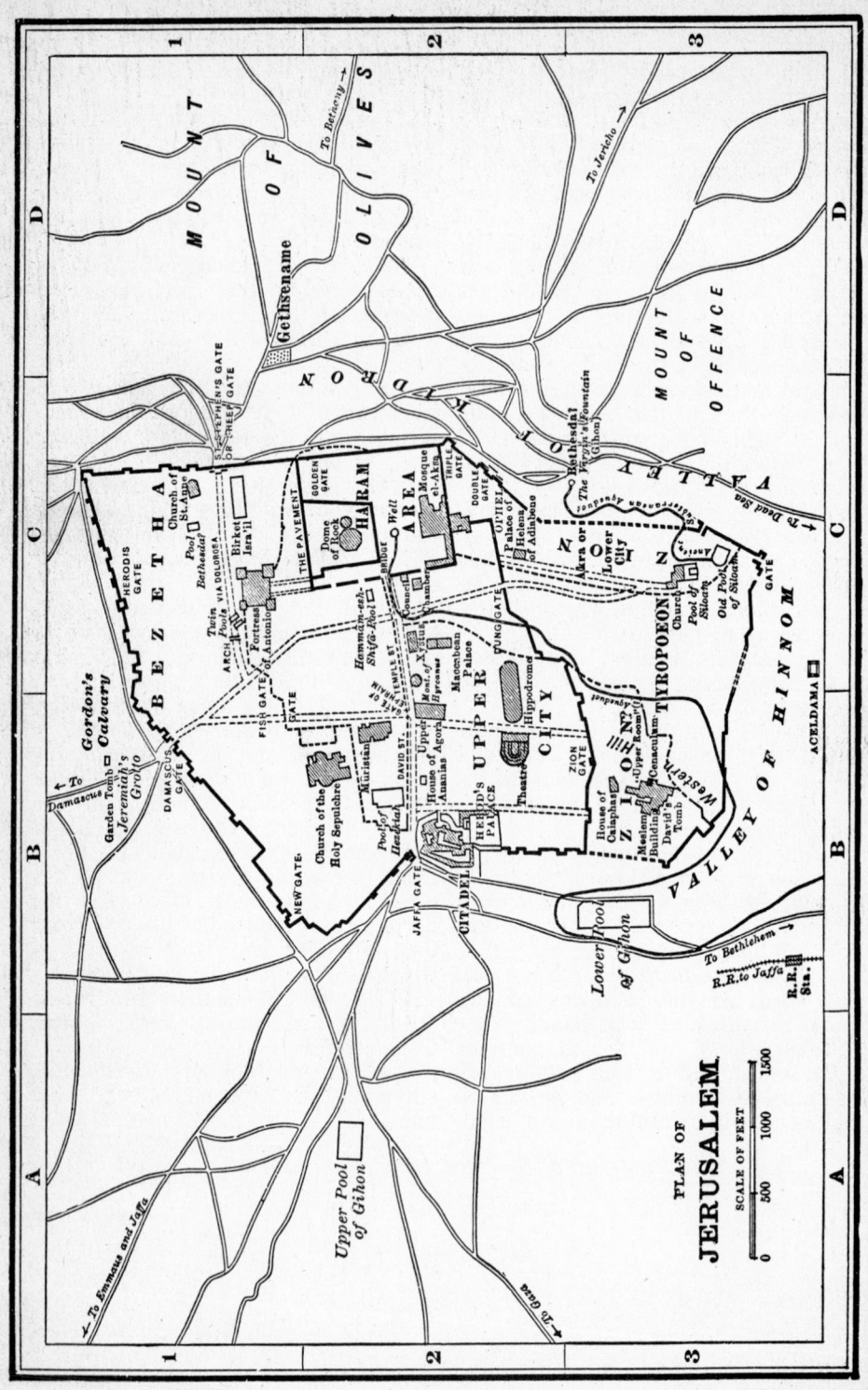

PLAN OF
JERUSALEM

SCALE OF FEET

0   500   1000   1500